WHO'S WHO
IN AMERICAN ART

WHO'S WHO
IN AMERICAN ART

16th EDITION

Edited by JAQUES CATTELL PRESS

R. R. BOWKER COMPANY
New York & London

Published by R. R. Bowker Co.
205 East Forty-second Street, New York, New York 10017

Copyright © 1984 by Xerox Corporation

International Standard Book Number: 0-8352-1878-3
International Standard Serial Number: 0000-0191
Library of Congress Catalog Card Number: 36-27014
Printed and bound in the United States of America

Contents

Preface

The 16th Edition of *Who's Who in American Art* profiles 10,700 contributors to the visual arts field in the United States, Canada and Mexico. There are representatives from all segments of the art world including artists, administrators, historians, educators, collectors, librarians, critics, curators, and dealers. The biographies are arranged alphabetically and also indexed by geographic location and professional classification. In addition, there is a necrology, cumulative from 1953.

Copy proofs were sent to all those listed in the 15th edition, and new information was provided by over 70% of the entrants. Listings for individuals who did not return a proof were discontinued unless current activity in art could be verified through public sources.

More than 1,000 entries appear for the first time. The names of the individuals listed for the first time were obtained from nominations provided by former entrants, art associations, galleries and museums, or from citations in professional publications. Each nominee received a questionnaire to complete, and selection for inclusion was made based on the information submitted. For artists, consideration was given to work in public collections, commissions, and exhibitions of an international, national and wide regional scope in noncommercial galleries and museums. Inclusion of entrants other than artists was based on position and experience in the art world. Among those represented are art administrators and curators with major museums, scholars and librarians with prominent institutions, and widely published art writers and critics.

Individual entries can be composed of many different elements depending on the activity and inclination of the entrant. These elements can include vital statistics, *professional classifications, education and training, *work in public collections, *commissions, *publications, positions held with schools, museums or organizations, *membership in art societies, *honors and awards, interest or research statement, media, dealer, and mailing address. Elements preceded by an asterisk are limited as to the number of items included. If the entrant exceeded these limitations the editors selected the most recent information.

Material submitted was included as completely as possible within limits set by format restrictions. While all precautions have been taken to avoid errors, the publishers do not assume and hereby disclaim any liability to any party for any loss or damage caused by errors or omissions, whether such errors or omissions result from negligence, accident or any other cause. In any event, the sole responsibility of the publisher will be the entry of corrected data in succeeding editions.

The editors would like to thank the many individuals and associations who sent information and nominations. The editors also thank the editorial assistants who worked so hard to make *Who's Who in American Art* a success.

As of June, 1984, the editorial offices of Jaques Cattell Press and R. R. Bowker will be combined. Please address any suggestions, comments, or questions to The Editors, *Who's Who in American Art*, R. R. Bowker Company, 205 East 42nd Street, New York, New York 10017.

Carol J. Borland, *Editor*
Renee Lautenbach, *Managing Editor*
Terence E. Basom, *General Manager*
JAQUES CATTELL PRESS

May, 1984

Abbreviations

abstr—abstract(s)
acad—academia, academic, academica, academie, academique, academy
accad—accademia
acoust—acoustic(s), acoustical
actg—acting
addn—addition, additional
adj—adjunct
Adm—Admiral
admin—administration, administrative
adminr—administrator
admis(s)—admission
adv—adviser(s), advisory
advan—advance(d), advancement
advert—advertisement, advertising
aesthet—aesthetics
affil—affiliate, affiliation
agr—agricultural, agriculture
akad—akedemi, akademia
Ala—Alabama
Atla—Alberta
Am—America, American
anal—analysis, analytic, analytical
analog—analogue
anat—anatomic, anatomical, anatomy
ann—annual
anthrop—anthropological, anthropology
antiq—antiquary, antiquities, antiquity
antiqn—antiquarian
app—appoint, appointed
appl—applied
approx—approximate, approximately
Apr—April
apt—apartment(s)
arch—archiv, archiva, achives, archivio, archivo
archeol—archeological, archeologie, archeologique, archeology
archit—architectural, architecture
Arg—Argentina
Ariz—Arizona
Ark—Arkansas
asn—association
asoc—asociacion
assoc(s)—associate(s), associated
asst(s)—assistant(s)
atty—attorney
Aug—August
auth—author
AV—audiovisual
Ave—Avenue

b—born
BC—British Columbia
bd—board
Belg—Belgian, Belgium

bibliog—bibliografia, bibliographic, bibliographical, bibliography(ies)
bibliot—biblioteca, bibliotek, bibliotheca, bibliothek, bibliotheque
biog—biographical, biography
bk(s)—book(s)
Bldg—Building(s)
Blvd—Boulevard
br—branch(es)
Brit—Britain, British
bull—bulletin
bur—bureau
bus—business
BWI—British West Indies

Calif—California
Can—Canada, Canadian, Canadien, Canadienne
Capt—Captain
Cath—Catholic
CBS—Columbia Broadcasting System
cent—central
Cent Am—Central America
cert—certificate(s), certification, certified
chap—chapter
chmn—chairman
c/o—care of
co—companies, company
Co—County
coauth—coauthor
co-dir—co-director
co-ed—co-editor
co-educ—co-educational
CofC—Chamber of Commerce
Col—Colonel
col(s)—college(s), collegiate
collab—collaboration, collaborative
collabr—collaborator
Colo—Colorado
com—commerce, commercial
comdr—commander
commun—communication(s)
comn(s)—commission(s), commissioned
comnr—commissioner
compos—composition
comt(s)—committee(s)
conf—conference
Cong—Congress, Congressional
Conn—Connecticut
conserv—conservacion, conservation, conservatiore, conservatory
construct—construction
consult—consult, consultant, consultantship, consultation, consulting
contemp—contemporary
contrib—contribute, contributing, contribution
contribr—contributor

conv—convention
coop—cooperating, cooperation, cooperative
coord—coordinate, coordinating, coordination
coordr—coordinator
corp—corporate, corporation
corresp—correspondent, corresponding
coun—council, counsel, counseling
counr—councilor, counselor
Ct—Court
ctr—center
cult—cultural, culture
cur—curator
curric—curriculum
Czech—Czechoslovakia

DC—District of Columbia
Dec—December
Del—Delaware
deleg—delegate, delegation
demonstr—demonstrator
dept—department, departmental
develop—development, developmental
dict—dictionaries, dictionary
dig—digest
dipl—diplom, diploma, diplomate, diplome
dir(s)—director(s), directory
dist—district
distribr—distributor
div—division, divisional, divorced
doc—document(s), documentary, documentation
Dom—Dominion
Dr—Doctor, Drive

E—East
econ—economic(s), economical, economist, economy
ed—edicion, edit, edited, editing, edition, editor(s), editorial, edizione
educ—educate, educated, educating, education, educational
elec—electric, electrical, electricity
elem—elementary
emer—emeritus, emeriti
encyl—encyclopedia
eng—engineering
Eng—England, English
environ—environment(s), environmental
equip—equipment
estab—established, establishment
estud—estudante, estudas, estudiante, estudio, estudo

Europ—European
exec(s)—executive(s)
exhib(s)—exhibit(s), exhibition
exped(s)—expedition(s)
explor—exploration(s), exploratory
expos—exposition
exten—extension

fac—faculty
Feb—February
fed—federal
fedn—federation
fel(s)—fellow(s), fellowship(s)
Fla—Florida
for—foreign
found—foundation
Fr—French
Ft—Fort
ft—feet, foot

Ga—Georgia
gen—general, generale
Ger—German, Germany
Ges—Gesellschaft
gov—governing, governor
govt—government, governmental
grad—graduate, graduated
Gt Brit—Great Britain
gym—gymnasium

handbk(s)—handbook(s)
hist—historia, historic, historica, historical,
 historique, historisch(e), history
HM—Her Majesty
hochsch—hochschule
hon(s)—honor(s), honorable, honorary
hosp(s)—hospital(s), hospitalization
hq—headquarters
Hwy—Highway

Ill—Illinois
illum—illuminating, illumination
illus—illustrate, illustrated, illustration
illusr—illustrator
Inc—Incorporated
incl—include, included, includes, including
Ind—Indiana
indust(s)—industrial, industries, industry
info—information
inst—institut, instituto
inst(s)—institute(s), institution(s)
instnl—institutional, institutionalized
instr(s)—instruct, instruction, instructors
instrnl—instructional
int—internacional, international, internazionale
introd—introduction
ist—istituto
Ital—Italia, Italian, Italiana, Italiano, Italica,
 Italien, Italienisch, Italienne(s)

J—Journal (title)
Jan—January
jour—journal (descriptive)
jr—junior
juv—juvenile(s)

Kans—Kansas
Ky—Kentucky

La—Louisiana
lab(s)—laboratories, laboratory
lang—language(s)

lect—lecture(s)
lectr—lecturer(s)
lett—letter(s)
lib—liberal
libr—libraries, library, librerio
librn—librarian
lit—literary, literaure, literatura, literature,
 littera, litterature
Lt—Lieutenant
ltd—limited

mag—magazine
maj—major
Man—Manitoba
Mar—March
Mass—Massachusetts
mat—material(s)
Md—Maryland
med—medical, medicine, medicinal
mem—member(s), membership(s), memoirs
Mem—Memorial
metrop—metropolitan
Mex—Mexican, Mexicano, Mexico
mgr—manager
mgt—management
Mich—Michigan
Minn—Minnesota
Miss—Mississippi
Mo—Missouri
mo—month
mod—modern, moderna, moderne, moderno
monogr—monograph
Mont—Montana
Mt—Mount
munic—municipal, municipalities
mus—musee, museo, museum(s)

N—North
nac—nacional
nat—nationaal, national, nationale, nationalis
naz—nazionale
NB—New Brunswick
NC—North Carolina
NDak—North Dakota
Nebr—Nebraska
Neth—Netherlands
Nev—Nevada
New Eng—New England
Nfld—Newfoundland
NH—New Hampshire
NJ—New Jersey
NMex—New Mexico
Norweg—Norwegian
Nov—November
NS—Nova Scotia
NSW—New South Wales
NY—New York
NZ—New Zealand

Oct—October
off—office, official
Okla—Oklahoma
Ont—Ontario
oper(s)—operation(s), operational, operative
Ore—Oregon
orgn—organization, organizational

Pa—Pennsylvania
Pac—Pacific
Pan-Am—Pan-American
partic—participant, participating
PEI—Prince Edward Island

philos—philosophic, philosophical,
 philosophy
photog—photographic, photography
photogr—photographer(s)
Pkwy—Parkway
Pl—Place
PO Box—Post Office Box
polytech—polytechnic, polytechnical
Port—Portugal, Portuguese
PQ—Province of Quebec
PR—Puerto Rico
prehist—prehistoric, prehistory
pres—president
Presby—Presbyterian
preserv—preservation
prof—profession, professional, professor
 professorial
prog(s)—program(s), programmed,
 programming
proj(s)—project(s), projection(s),
 projectional, projective
prom—promotion
prov—province, provincial
pub—public
publ—publication(s), published,
 publisher(s), publishing
pvt—private

Quart—Quarterly
Que—Quebec

Rd—Road
RD—Rural Delivery
rec—record(s), recording
regist—register, registered, registration
registr—registrar
relig—religion, religious
rep—represent, representative
Repub—Republic
res—research
rev—review, revised, revision
RFD—Rural Free Delivery
RI—Rhode Island
Rm—Room
RR—Rural Route
Rte—Route
Russ—Russian

S—South
S Africa—South Africa
S Am—South America, South American
Sask—Saskatchewan
SC—South Carolina
Scand—Scandinavia, Scandinavian
sch(s)—school(s)
scholar—scholarship
sci—science(s), scientific
SDak—South Dakota
sec—secondary
sect—section
secy—secretary
sem—seminar, seminary
Sen—Senator, Senatorial
Sept—September
ser—series
serv—service(s), serving
soc(s)—sociedad, societa, societas,
 societate, societe, societet, societies,
 society
Span—Spanish
spec—special
Sq—Square
sr—senior

St—Saint, Street
sta(s)—station(s)
Ste—Sainte
struct—structural, structure(s)
super—superieur, superior, superiore
suppl—supplement, supplemental,
    supplementary
supt—superintendent
supv—supervising, supervision
Swed—Swedish
Switz—Switzerland
symp—symposium(s)

tech—technical, technique
technol—technologic, technological, technology
tel—telegraph(y), telephone
Tenn—Tennessee
Terr—Terrace
Tex—Texas
transl—translation(s)
translr—translator
treas—treasurer, treasury

Twp—Township

UN—United Nations
undergrad—undergraduate
UNESCO—United Nations Educational,
    Scientific & Cultural Organization
univ(s)—universidad, universite, universities,
    university
US—United States
USA—United States Army
USAF—United States Air Force
USMC—United States Marine Corps
USN—United States Navy
USSR — Union of Soviet Socialist Republics

Va—Virginia
var—various
vchmn—vice chairman
Vet—Veteran(s)
VI—Virgin Islands
vis—visiting

vol(s)—volume(s)
vpres—vice president
Vt—Vermont

W—West
Wash—Washington
Wis—Wisconsin
wk—week
WVa—West Virginia
Wyo—Wyoming

yearbk—yearbook
YMCA—Young Men's Christian
    Association
YMHA—Young Men's Hebrew
    Association
yr(s)—year(s)
YWCA—Young Women's Christian
    Association
YWHA—Young Women's Hebrew
    Association

Who's Who in American Art

A

AACH, HERB
PAINTER, WRITER
b Cologne, Ger, Mar 24, 23; US citizen. *Study:* Art Acad Cologne, 36-37; Pratt Inst, 41-42; Stanford Univ, 43-44; Escuela di Pintura Y Escultura, Mex, 48-50; Brooklyn Mus Art Sch, 47-48 & 50-51. *Work:* Boston Mus, Mass; Everhart Mus, Scranton, Pa; Birla Acad, Calcutta, India; Chase Collection; William Penn Mem Mus, Harrisburg, Pa. *Exhib:* Color Forum/Austin, Univ Tex, 72; one-man shows, Martha Jackson Gallery, 74, Albright-Knox Mus, 75, Gramercy Fine Arts Gallery, NY, 77 & Allentown Art Mus, Pa, 78; Guild Hall, East Hampton, 83. *Teaching:* Brooklyn Mus, formerly; Skowhegan Sch Painting & Sculpture, 69 & 70; assoc prof art & painting, Queens Col, currently. *Bibliog:* L Finkelstein (auth), Color as system, Craft Horizons, 70. *Mem:* Founder Color Forum; Col Art Asn; Artists Workshop Club; Intersoc Color Coun; Exp in Art & Technol. *Res:* All phases of color, phenomenology, perception and fluorescence. *Publ:* Ed & translr, Goethe's Color Theory, Van Nostrand Reinhold, 71; contrib ed, J Color & Appearance, 72; auth, articles in Arts, Craft Horizons, Color Eng & many other magazines & journals. *Dealer:* Martha Jackson Gallery 28 E 69 St New York NY 10021; Aaron Berman Galleries 50 W 57th St New York NY 10019. *Mailing Add:* 523 E 14th St New York NY 10009

AALUND, SUZY
PAINTER, MINIATURIST
b Long Island, NY. *Study:* Extensive independent studies. *Exhib:* One-woman shows, Robert Brooks Gallery, Hyannis, Mass, 72 & 74 & Garden City Galleries, NY, 72 & 74; Am Soc Marine Artists Ann, 78, 79 & 80; Int Maritime Art Awards Show, 80-82; Contemp Am Marine Art, Peabody Mus, Salem, 81; Gallery 31, Greenwich, Conn, 83; and many others. *Awards:* Second Prize Oils, Long Beach Art Asn, 72; First Prize Oils, Nat Miniature Art Show, Miniature Art Soc NJ, 73. *Bibliog:* Article, La Rev Mod, 74. *Mem:* Charter mem Am Soc Marine Artists; Mystic Art Asn. *Media:* Watercolor, Oil. *Dealer:* Tradewinds Gallery 10 Water St Mystic CT 06355. *Mailing Add:* 1 Palmer St Stonington CT 06378

AARON, EVALYN (WILHELMINA)
PAINTER
b New York, NY. *Study:* Art Students League; pvt study with Mario Cooper, Motoi Oi, Prof Kawai & Betty Holiday. *Exhib:* Sumi-e Soc, Nippon Club, 72 & Japan House, 73, New York; Art Fac Show, Great Neck House, NY, 74; Great Neck Pub Libr, 75; one-person shows, Gallery 7 Soho Ltd, Great Neck, 75 & Mirage Gallery, New York, 78. *Teaching:* Instr sumi-e brush painting, Great Neck Continuing Educ, 64-74; pres & teacher painting, Workshop for Art, Port Washington, NY, 67-74; lectr & demonstrated, Int Platform Asn, 73, 74 & 77 & Art League Nassau Co, 78. *Awards:* Sumi-e Soc Award, Sumi-e Soc Am, 64 & Cup of Consul Gen of Japan, 66; Popular Award, Int Platform Asn, 74. *Bibliog:* Rhoda Amon (auth), article in Newsday, 11/74; Elizabeth Moore (auth), article in Talent, 5/75; Malcolm Preston (auth), review in Newsday, 8/75. *Mem:* Artists Equity; Art League of Nassau Co; Sumi-e Soc Am (secy, 62-67, pres, 72-74); Int Platform Asn (gov, 83-). *Media:* Watercolor, Acrylic. *Publ:* Auth & illusr, Sumi painting, Am Artist Mag, 9/78. *Dealer:* Caryl Shorin Long Island NY. *Mailing Add:* 270-03G Grand Central Parkway Floral Park NY 11005

AARONS, ANITA
GALLERY DIRECTOR, SCULPTOR
b Sydney, Australia; Australian & Can citizen. *Study:* Assoc Sydney Tech Col; East Sydney Tech Col; Nat Art Sch; Columbia Univ, New York, 64. *Work:* Charlottetown Nat Craft Collection, PEI; Nat Collection Can Craftsmen Guild, Toronto. *Comn:* Playground Sculpture, Phillip Park, Sydney, Australia. *Exhib:* 1st World Crafts Conf Exhib, Columbia Univ, 64; Nat Craft Exhib, Toronto, 68; 1st Outdoor Exhib, Sydney; Nat Sculpture Exhib, Melbourne, Victoria. *Pos:* Allied art ed, Architecture Canada, Toronto, 64-70; consult, Art Gallery Ont, 68-72; dir, Art Gallery Harbourfront, Toronto, 76-. *Teaching:* Sculptor in charge, East Sydney Tech, 48-49, Kindergarten Training Col, Melbourne, 50-54 & Caulfield Tech Training Col for Sec Arts & Crafts Sch, 54-64; teacher crafts, Central Tech, Toronto, 64. *Awards:* Can Coun Sr Grant, 71-72; Can Conf Arts Dipl d'hon, 83. *Bibliog:* Articles in Encycl Australian Art & Craft Horizons. *Media:* Silver, Bronze. *Mailing Add:* 641 Queen St E Toronto ON M5A 1T5 Canada

ABADI, FRITZIE
PAINTER, SCULPTOR
b Aleppo, Syria, US citizen. *Study:* Art Students League, New York; with Nahum Tschacbasov, New York. *Work:* Butler Inst Am Art, Youngstown, Ohio; Evansville Mus Arts & Sci, Ind; Slater Mem Mus, Norwich, Conn; Ga Mus Art, Athens. *Exhib:* Watercolor, Brooklyn Mus, NY; Ann Invitational, Whitney Mus Am Art, New York; Ann Invitational, Carnegie Inst, Pa; Ann Print Invitational, Libr Cong, DC; Acquisitional, Butler Inst Am Art, Youngstown, Ohio. *Awards:* Acrylic Painting Award, Nat Asn Women Artists, 74; Box Assemblage Award, Am Soc Contemp Artists, 78 & Oil Painting Award, 79. *Mem:* Nat Asn Women Artists (bd mem, 70); Am Soc Contemp Artists (pres, 70-72, vpres, 80-); New York Soc Women Artists (bd mem, 80); Women in the Arts. *Media:* Box Assemblage. *Publ:* Contribr, Collage and Small Environment, 74 & Assemblage and Construction, 75, Crown Inc. *Dealer:* Phoenix Gallery 30 W 57th St New York NY 10019. *Mailing Add:* 201 W 70th St New York NY 10023

ABANY, ALBERT CHARLES
PAINTER, PRINTMAKER
b Boston, Mass, Mar 30, 21. *Study:* Sch Mus Fine Arts, Boston, M O H Longstreth scholar, 42, dipl, 48; Tufts Univ, BS(educ), 49. *Exhib:* One-man shows, Carl Siembab Gallery, Boston, 56; Clark Univ, 63; Northeastern Univ, 67; Wessell Libr, Tufts Univ, 71; Art Inst Boston, 72. *Teaching:* Art teacher drawing & painting, Boston Ctr Adult Educ, 49-51; art teacher drawing, painting, printmaking & art hist, Art Inst Boston, 65-73; art teacher oil & acrylic painting, Brockton Art Mus, Mass, 75-77; art teacher drawing & painting, Danforth Mus Sch, Framingham, 75-77; teacher drawing, painting & hist art, Quincy Jr Col, 75-76. *Media:* Oil, Graphics, Mixed Media. *Mailing Add:* 42 MacArthur Rd Natick MA 01760

ABBE, ELFRIEDE MARTHA
SCULPTOR, ENGRAVER
b Washington, DC. *Study:* Col Archit, Cornell Univ, BFA, 40. *Work:* Rosenwald Collection, Nat Gallery Art; Mus Fine Arts, Boston; Houghton Libr, Harvard Univ; Sloniker Collection, Cincinnati Art Mus; Mus Fine Arts, Venice, Italy. *Comn:* The Hunter (large statue), New York World's Fair, 39; oak frieze, Mann Libr, Cornell Univ, 55 & bronze sculptures, Clive McCay Mem, 67; Napoleon (bronze head), McGill Univ Libr; The Illuminator (walnut carving), Sterling Mem Hunt Libr, Carnegie-Mellon Univ, 69. *Exhib:* Nat Acad Design, New York; San Diego Fine Arts Gallery, 60; Printing in the USA & United Kingdom, London Chappel Exhib, Eng, 63; Int Botanical Artists, Hunt Libr, Carnegie-Mellon Univ, 68; Nat Arts Club, New York, 69 & 70. *Awards:* Gold Medal, Nat Arts Club, 70 & Acad Artists Asn, Springfield, Mass, 76; Elliot Liskin Cash Award, Salmagundi Club, 79. *Bibliog:* Norman Kent (auth), The Book Art of Elfriede Abbe, Am Artist Mag, 60. *Mem:* Nat Arts Club; fel Nat Sculpture Soc; Nat Soc of Mural Painters. *Media:* Wood. *Publ:* Designed, illus & printed, Garden Spice & Wild Pot-Herbs, Cornell Univ, 55, The American Scholar, 56, Seven Irish Tales, 57 & Significance of the Frontier, 58. *Mailing Add:* Manchester Center VT 05255

ABBETT, ROBERT KENNEDY
PAINTER
b Hammond, Ind, Jan 5, 26. *Study:* Purdue Univ, BSc, 46; Univ Mo, BAArt, 48; Chicago Acad Fine Art, 48-50; Am Acad Art, Chicago, 49. *Work:* Cowboy Hall of Fame & Western Heritage Ctr, Oklahoma City; Diamond M Mus, Snyder, Tex; Genesee Country Mus, Rochester, NY. *Comn:* Mural, Univ Mo Student Union, 47; portrait of Mrs Roy Larsen, Audubon Soc, Fairfield, Conn, 73; portrait of Jimmy Stewart, Cowboy Hall of Fame, Oklahoma City, 75; portrait of Silver, comn by Ann Cox Chambers, US Embassy, Brussels, Belg, 77; and others. *Exhib:* Sporting Art, Brandywine River Mus, Chadds Ford, Pa, 73; Salmagundi Summer Exhib, New York, 73; Convocation Am Artists, Dallas, Tex, 73 & 74; Nat Acad Western Art, Cowboy Hall of Fame, 74 & 75; Soc Animal Artists Ann Exhib, New York, 78-81; Sportsman's Edge Ltd, New York, 81; Waterfowl Festival, Easton, Md, 81; and others. *Teaching:* Instr media, Silvermine Col, New Canaan, Conn, 59-61; instr drawing, Sisters of Notre Dame, Wilton, Conn, 70 & Washington Art Asn, Conn, 77. *Awards:* Outstanding Work, Artists & Books, Soc Illusr, 65; Citation of Merit, Soc Illusr Ann Exhib, 66; First Prize, Salmagundi Club, New York, 73. *Bibliog:* Nick Meglin (auth), Robert Abbett, Am Artist, 7/77; John Pierce (auth), About the artist, Yankee, 11/77 & Southwest Art, 12/79. *Mem:* Soc Illusr; Westport Artists (pres, 67); Soc

Animal Artists. *Media:* Oil. *Publ:* Illusr, Great Lives--Great Deeds, Reader's Digest Bks, 64; contribr, The Illustrator in America, Reinhold, 66; contribr, Great American Shooting Prints, Knopf, 72; contribr, Western Art Today, Watson-Guptill, 75; coauth, Outdoor Paintings of Robert K Abbett, Peacock/Bantam, 76. *Dealer:* Collectors Covey 15 Highland Park Village Dallas TX 75205; Dan May 172 Center St Jackson WY 83001. *Mailing Add:* Oakdale Farm Bridgewater CT 06752

ABDALLA, NICK
PAINTER, EDUCATOR
b Albuquerque, NMex, May 24, 39. *Study:* Eastern NMex Univ, 57-59; Univ Ill, Urbana-Champaign, 59-60; Univ NMex, BFA, 61, MA, 63. *Work:* El Paso Mus Art, Tex; Am Tel & Tel Permanent Collection, Ill Bell Tel System, Chicago; Fine Arts Mus, Santa Fe; Standard Oil Permanent Collection, Chicago; NC Nat Bank, Davidson; and others. *Exhib:* 16th Exhib Southwestern Prints & Drawings, Dallas Mus Fine Arts, Tex, 66; 13th, 14th & 18th Ann Sun Carnival Nat Art Exhib, Art Mus El Paso, 68, 69 & 74; 1st Graphics Ann, Miami Art Ctr, Fla, 73; Los Angeles Print Soc Exhib, Triad Gallery, 73; Nat Print & Drawing Exhib, Davidson Col, NC, 74. *Teaching:* Asst prof painting & drawing, Univ NMex, 71-81, assoc prof, 81-; guest artist, Tamarind Inst, Albuquerque, NMex. *Awards:* First Purchase Award, Nat Print & Drawing Exhib, McCray Gallery, Silver City, NMex, 69; Mus Purchase Award, NMex Biennial Exhib, Mus Fine Arts, Santa Fe, 73; Purchase Award, Nat Print & Drawing Exhib, Davidson Col, NC, 74. *Bibliog:* Camera Oscura/Camera Lucida: Abdalla and Wood, Artspace Mag, summer 77; New Mexico: open land and psychic elbow room, Art News, 12/77. *Media:* Acrylic, Pastel. *Dealer:* S Rudy Gallery 606 Paseo de La Loma Santa Fe NM 87501. *Mailing Add:* 515 11th St NW Albuquerque NM 87102

ABDELL, DOUGLAS
SCULPTOR, PAINTER
b Boston, Mass, Mar 16, 47. *Study:* Syracuse Univ, BFA(sculpture, hons), 70. *Work:* Corcoran Gallery Art, Washington, DC; H H Thyssen Bornemisza Collection, Lugano, Switz; Univ Notre Dame, Ind; Edwin Ulrich Mus Art, Wichita State Univ, Kans; Davenport Munic Art Gallery, Iowa; and many others. *Exhib:* One-man exhibs, Andrew Crispo Gallery, New York, 75, 78 & 79-82, Miami-Dade Community Col, 79-80, Sweet Briar Col, 80, Washington & Lee Univ, 80, Davenport Munic Art Gallery, Iowa, 80 & Dartmouth Col, NH, 80; and many others. *Awards:* Artists & Writers Revolving Fund, Nat Inst Arts & Lett, 71 & 72; Silvermine Award, New Canaan, Conn, 73; Artist Fel, Vt Coun on Arts, 73. *Bibliog:* John Canaday (auth), article, New York Times, 72; Grace Glueck (auth), article, New York Times, 77; Heinz Ohff (auth), rev, Der Tagesspeigel, Berlin, 81; and others. *Media:* Cast Bronze; Mixed. *Dealer:* LaPlaca 1155 Broadway New York NY 10001. *Mailing Add:* 458 Broadway 2nd Floor New York NY 10013

ABEL, RAY
ILLUSTRATOR, DESIGNER
b Chicago, Ill, Sept 19, 19. *Study:* Univ Chicago, AB; Art Inst Chicago; NY Univ, MA; Art Students League, with Kenneth Hayes Miller & George Grosz. *Comn:* Aviation (mural frieze), US Army Air Corps Cafeteria, Mitchel Field, NY, 44-45; bk illustrations, McKay, Prentice-Hall, Grolier, Lippincott, Viking & others, 50-; bk jackets, Harper & Row, Putnam, Dodd, Mead, Dutton & others, 50- *Exhib:* Artists of Chicago & Vicinity, Art Inst Chicago, 43; Nat Acad Design Ann Am Exhib, 42; Ann Exhib Am Art, Mint Mus, 44. *Pos:* Ed publ, Art Students League, 41-43; art dir, Ray Abel Assoc, 51- *Awards:* Hon Mention, Ill State Mus Ann Am Art, 41; Hon Mention, Mint Mus Ann Am Art Exhib, 73; Cert Excellence, Am Observed, Soc Illusr, New York, 72. *Mem:* Soc Illusr; Art Students League (mem bd control, 41-43 & 46-49). *Media:* Pen and Ink; Wash. *Publ:* Illusr, Mary C Jane (auth), Mystery of Nine-Mile Marsh, Lippincott, 67; illusr, Coal: Energy and Crisis, Harvey House, 74; illusr, Wylie Sypher (auth), The Turnabout Year, Atheneum, 76; illusr, Bret Hart (auth), The Outcasts of Poker Flat, Listening Libr, 77; co-illusr, The Complete Illustrated Shakespeare, Crown, 79. *Mailing Add:* 18 Vassar Pl Scarsdale NY 10583

ABELES, KIM VICTORIA
PAINTER, SCULPTOR
b Richmond Heights, Mo, Aug 28, 52. *Study:* Ohio Univ, BFA(painting), 74; Univ Calif, Irvine, MFA(studio art), 80. *Work:* Washington & Jefferson Col, Washington, Pa; Fashion Inst, Los Angeles, Calif. *Exhib:* Butler Inst Contemp Art, Youngstown, Ohio, 76 & 79; Los Angeles Inst Contemp Art, 81; Munic Art Gallery, Los Angeles, 81; Karl Bornstein Gallery, Los Angeles, Calif, 81, 82 & 83; Los Angeles City Hall, 82; Phyllis Kind Gallery, Chicago & New York, 83. *Awards:* Recognition Award, Southeastern Ohio Designer & Craftsman Show, 75; Merit Awards, Oglebay Inst, 76 & 77; US Steel Award, Assoc Artists Pittsburgh Mus Art/Carnegie Inst, 77. *Bibliog:* Ruth Weisburg (auth), Veiled Symmetries, Artweek, 11/14/81; Pamela Hammond (auth), articles, Images & Issues, spring 82; Charlotte Moser, Emerging artists flower, Sun-Times, 3/20/83. *Mem:* Los Angeles Contemp Exhibs; Artists Equity Asn; Int Sculpture Ctr. *Media:* Acrylic; Miscellaneous. *Publ:* Auth, Crafts, Cookery and Country Living, Van Nostrand Reinhold, 76; auth, Impressions, private publ, 79; contribr, Artery, William Patterson Col, 79; contribr, Compendium III, Univ Calif, Irvine, 79. *Mailing Add:* Fourth Floor 240 South Broadway Los Angeles CA 90012

ABELES, SIGMUND
PRINTMAKER, SCULPTOR
b New York, NY, Nov 6, 34. *Study:* Pratt Inst; Univ SC, BA, 55; Art Student League; Skowhegan Sch Painting & Sculpture; Brooklyn Mus Sch; Columbia Univ, MFA, 57. *Work:* Mus Mod Art, New York; Mus Arte, Ponce, PR;

Philadelphia Mus Art; Boston Mus Fine Arts; Brit Mus; and others. *Exhib:* Whitney Ann Sculpture & Prints, 67 & Human Concern & Personal Torment, 69, Whitney Mus Am Art, New York; 28 Am Printmakers, Rijksacademie, Amsterdam, Holland, 68; Am Contemp Prints--one, Inst Contemp Art, London, 70; Master Prints of the 20th Century, Boston Mus Fine Arts, 71; plus many other group and one-man shows. *Teaching:* Instr, Swain Sch Design, New Bedford, Mass, 61-64, Wellesley Col 64-69, Boston Univ, 69-70, Univ NH, 70-; Wellesley Col, 64-69; Boston Univ, 69-70; Univ NH, 70- *Awards:* Sabbatical Grant, Nat Coun Arts & Humanities, 66; Grant for Graphics, Louis Comfort Tiffany Found, 67; Hassam/Speicher Mus Purchase Prize, Nat Inst Arts & Letters, 83. *Mem:* Soc Am Graphic Artists; assoc Nat Acad of Design; Pastel Soc Am; NH Art Asn. *Publ:* Illusr, Maggie, a girl of the streets, Limited Ed Press, 75. *Dealer:* Assoc Am Artists Gallery 663 Fifth Ave New York NY 10022; Mary Ryan Gallery New York NY. *Mailing Add:* RFD 3 Huckins Rd Dover NH 03820

ABER, ITA
HISTORIAN, TAPESTRY ARTIST
b Montreal, Can, Mar 27, 32; US citizen. *Study:* Empire State Col, BA; Valentine Mus, hon cert, 82. *Work:* Jewish Mus, New York; Valentine Mus, Richmond, Va; Fashion Inst Technol, New York. *Comn:* Ark doors & scroll cover, SAR Acad, Riverdale, NY, 73 & 76; holy scroll covers, Conservative Synagogue, Riverdale, NY, 77 & 79; holy scroll covers, Moriah Congregation, Chicago, Ill, 81; holy scroll cover, Community Synagogue, French Hill, Jerusalem. *Exhib:* Nat Invitational, Soc Arts & Crafts, Boston, Mass, 79; Embroiderers Guild Am Biennial, New York, 80; Fabric of Jewish Life, Philadelphia Mus Judaica, Pa, 80; Tradition and Fantasy, Yeshiva Univ Mus, New York, 81-82; Continuing Legacy, Minneapolis, 83. *Pos:* Guest cur, Yeshiva Univ Mus, 76-77 & 81-82, textile conservator & consult, 78- *Teaching:* Instr judaic needlework, Jewish Mus, New York, 75-81; instr embroidery & textile conservation, Cooper Hewitt Mus, New York, 77-80. *Bibliog:* Russell Barber (auth), Religion Commentator, WNBC TV, 77; Ceil Stein (auth), article, Riverdale Press, 77-79; interview, WEVD Radio, 81. *Mem:* Nat Council Art Jewish Life (mem bd 77-); Pomegranate Guild Judaic Needlework (mem bd, 76-); Am Friends Israel Mus. *Media:* Needle, Thread; Paint, Found Objects. *Publ:* Auth, many articles for Antiques J, Embroidery Mag, Needle Arts, 75-81; auth, The Art of Judaic Needlework, Charles Scribner's Sons, NY, 79; auth, Embroidery section, Time-Life Encyclopedia of Collectibles, Time-Life Books, 79; auth, Tradition and Fantasy in Jewish Needlework, Yeshiva Univ Mus, 81. *Mailing Add:* One Fanshaw Ave Yonkers NY 10705

ABID, ANN B
LIBRARIAN
b St Louis, Mo, Mar 17, 42. *Pos:* Asst librn, St Louis Art Mus, 63-68, librn, 68- *Mem:* Mus, Arts, & Humanities Div, Spec Libr Asn; Art Libr Soc NAm; Mus Arch Task Force; Soc Am Archivists. *Publ:* Contribr, Museum column, Vol 7, No 4-5, 79 & Archives in art museums, Vol 8, No 2, 80, Art Libr Soc NAm Newsletter. *Mailing Add:* St Louis Art Mus Forest Park St Louis MO 63110

ABISH, CECILE
SCULPTOR, INSTRUCTOR
b New York, NY. *Study:* Brooklyn Col, BFA. *Comn:* Boxed Monuments-3, Multiples, Inc, 69; field quartering, Lakeview Ctr Arts, Peoria, Ill, 72; Renaissance Fix, Independent Curators, Inc, 79; Field quartering, Lakeview Ctr Arts, Peoria, Ill, 72; Atlanta Arts Festival, Piedmont Park, Georgia, 80; landmarks, Bard Col, 84. *Exhib:* Aldrich Mus Contemp Art, 71; Inst Contemp Art, Boston, 74; Mus Mod Art, New York, 77; Anderson Gallery, Richmond, Va, 81; Kunstgebaude, Stuttgart, Ger, 81; Fine Art Ctr, State Univ NY, Stony Brook, 82; Long Beach Mus, 83; Mus Mod Kunst, Viena, Austria, 84; and others. *Teaching:* Instr art, Queens Col, NY, Univ Mass, Amherst, Cooper Union, NY & Harvard Univ. *Awards:* CAPS Fel, 75; Nat Endowment for Arts Fel, 75 & 77. *Bibliog:* Lawrence Alloway (auth), article, Arts Mag, 2/77; Jeffrey Keefe (auth), article, Artforum, 10/78; Donald B Kuspit (auth), article, Art Am, 12/81; and others. *Publ:* Auth, Statements by sculptors, Art J, winter 75/76; auth, Situation esthetics, Artforum, 1/80; auth, Atlanta Art Papers, 5/80; and others. *Mailing Add:* PO Box 485 Cooper Station Cooper Station New York NY 10276

ABLOW, JOSEPH
PAINTER, WRITER
b Salem, Mass, Aug 16, 28. *Study:* Sch Mus Fine Arts, Boston, Paige traveling fel, dipl with highest hons, 51; Bennington Col, BA, 54; Harvard Univ, MA, 55; Fulbright grant, Paris, 58; advan study in painting with Oskar Kokoschka & in design with Gyorgy Kepes. *Work:* DeCordova Mus, Lincoln, Mass; Univ Mass, Boston; Amherst Col; Middlebury Col, Vt; Skowhegan Sch Collection, Maine. *Exhib:* 62nd Am Exhib, Art Inst Chicago, 57; retrospective exhib, Bard Col, 72; A Selection of American Art: The Skowhegan School, 1946-76, Inst Contemp Art, Boston; one-man shows, Princeton Gallery, 71, Mirski Gallery, 61, 66 & 69 & Pucker/Safrai Gallery, 79, 81 & 83; Retrospective Exhib, Simmons Col, 83; and others. *Teaching:* Instr, Middlebury Col, 55-58; asst prof, Bard Col, 59-61; asst prof, Wellesley Col, 62-63; chmn div art, Boston Univ, 64-67, prof art, 72-; vis artist, Mass Inst Technol, 73-; vis artist, Amherst Col, 75-76. *Media:* Multimedia. *Publ:* Auth, Hyman Bloom and the uses of the past, New Boston Rev, spring 76; auth, Two cheers for realism, New Boston Rev, 9/78; auth, Gombrich's art and/or illusion, Boston Univ J, Vol XXV/3, 78; auth, Boston expressionism, New Boston Rev, 2-3/79. *Dealer:* Pucker/Safrai Gallery 171 Newbury St Boston MA 02116. *Mailing Add:* 16 Monmouth Ct Brookline MA 02146

ABLOW, ROSELYN KAROL
PAINTER, PRINTMAKER
b Allentown, Pa. *Study:* Bennington Col, BA, 54; Boston Univ Sch Arts, with Walter Murch, 59-61; studied in Europe, 59-60 & 68-69. *Work:* Mobil Corp, Chemical Bank, New York; New England Mutual Life Insurance Co, Boston; Conn Gen Life, Hartford; Sears, Roebuck & Co, Chicago. *Exhib:* New American Monotypes, Smithsonian Inst Traveling Exhib, 78-80; Contemporary American Monotypes, Smith Anderson Gallery, Palo Alto, Calif, 79; solo exhibs, Impressions Gallery, Boston, 79 & Clark Gallery, Lincoln, Mass, 84; Nine Alumni, Boston Univ, 81; Monotypes, Philadelphia Print Club, 82. *Bibliog:* Elizabeth Oberg (auth), Rediscovering the monotype, Patriot Ledger, 3/31/77; Robert Taylor (auth), article, Boston Sunday Globe, 6/10/79; Kenneth Baker (auth), Lasting impressions, Boston Phoenix, 2/9/81. *Media:* Pastel; Monotype. *Dealer:* Victoria Munroe Gallery 56 W 57 St New York NY 10019. *Mailing Add:* 16 Monmouth Ct Brookline MA 02146

ABRAHAM, CAROL JEANNE
CERAMIST
b Philadelphia, Pa, 1949. *Study:* Tyler Sch Art, Philadelphia, 64-67; Boston Mus Sch Fine Arts, 67-71; Tufts Univ, Medford, Mass, BS, 67-71; Rochester Inst Technol, Sch Am Craftsmen, MFA, 73; Penland Sch Crafts, NC, 75. *Work:* Rochester Inst Technol, NY; Mus Ceramics, Bassano Del Grappa, Italy; Renwick Gallery, Smithsonian Inst, Washington, DC; Brigham Young Univ, Provo, Utah; Southern Utah State Col, Cedar City, Utah; and others. *Exhib:* Renwick Gallery, Smithsonian Inst, DC, 75; Tweed Mus Art, Duluth, Minn, 81; Celebration 81, Spokane, Wash; Interfaith Forum Relig, Art & Archit, 81; League NH Craftsmen, Manchester, 81; State Univ Mus Art, University Park, Pa, 81; Fletcher Brownbuilt Pottery Exhib, Auckland, NZ, 81; and many others. *Teaching:* Framingham Pub Schs, Mass, 70; Boston Pub Sch System Pilot Sch, 70; Boston State Col, 71; Rochester Inst Technol, Ceramics Dept, NY, 72-73; asst prof ceramics & sculpture, Southern Utah State Col, Cedar City, 75-77; El Camino Col, Torrance, Calif, 80-81. *Awards:* Third Prize, Long Beach Art Asn, Calif, 80; Grant, Burbank Fine Arts Fedn, 81; Purchase Award, Second Crossing Gallery, 81. *Bibliog:* Hildegard Storr-Britz (auth), article, Contemp Int Ceramics, 80; article in Tex Homes, 3/81; Jan Axel & Karen McCready (coauths), Porcelain: Traditions and New Visions, 81. *Mailing Add:* 917 McAndrew Rd Ojai CA 93023

ABRAMOWICZ, JANET
PAINTER
b New York, NY. *Study:* Art Students League, with Morris Kantor; Columbia Univ, BA; Accad delle Belle Arti, Bologna, Italy, with Giorgio Morandi, MFA. *Work:* Mus Mod Art, Kyoto; Dept of Prints, New York Pub Libr; Ohara Mus, Kurashiki; Contemporary Art, Mus d'Arte Mod, Bologna; Mus d'Arte Mod, La Spezia, Italy. *Exhib:* Twenty-third Nat Exhib Prints, Libr Cong-Nat Collection Fine Arts, 73; Works on Paper, Harvard Sch Design, 74; Abstract Art (sculpture), Boston City Hall, 75; solo exhib, Susan Caldwell Gallery, New York, 80, Nantenshi Gallery, Tokyo, 81 & Galleria del Milrong, Milano, Italy, 81. *Collections Arranged:* Giorgio Morandi (with catalog), Busch-Reisinger Mus, Harvard Univ, 68. *Pos:* Critic, Asahi Evening News, Tokyo & Print Collector's Newsletter. *Teaching:* Instr, Radcliffe Col, Worcester Art Mus, Accad delle Belle Arti & Univ Ill; lectr art hist, Div Educ, Boston Mus Fine Arts, 58-70; sr lectr printmaking & drawing, Fine Arts Dept, Fogg Art Mus, Harvard Univ, 71- *Awards:* MacDowell Colony Fel, 75 & 76; Sr Fulbright Fel, Japan, 78-79; Japan Found, 79-80. *Publ:* Auth, Vision and technique, the etchings of Giorgio Morandi, Print Collector's Newsletter, 9-10/82; auth, The liberation of the object, the art of Giorgio Morandi, Art in Am, 3/83; auth, A European sensibility: The photographs of Andre Kertesz, Print Collector's Newsletter, 9-10/83. *Dealer:* Tokyo Nanten Shi Gallery Kyo-Bashi Tokyo. *Mailing Add:* Fogg Art Mus 32 Quincy St Cambridge MA 02138

ABRAMS, EDITH LILLIAN
SCULPTOR
b New York, NY. *Study:* Brooklyn Col, BA, 74; Pratt Inst, MFA, 78. *Work:* Evansville Mus Arts & Science, Ind. *Exhib:* Int Sculpture Fair, Sheraton Hotel, New York, 79; 4th & 6th Ann Exhib Painting & Sculpture; Brooklyn Mus, 79 & 81; Catharine Lorillard Wolfe Art Club, Nat Arts Club, New York, 79-81; Audubon Artists 38th Ann Exhib, New York, 80; ArtExpo, New York Coliseum, New York, 80; Providence Art Club Centinnial Exhib Sculpture, RI, 80. *Teaching:* Instr sculpture & ceramics, Sephardic Community Ctr, New York, 82-83. *Awards:* Purchase Award, 1st Prize, Schulman Rehabilitation Inst, Brookdale Hosp, 76; Margaret Hirsch Levine Mem Prize, Audubon Artists 38th Ann, 80; Ann Hyatt Huntington Bronze Medal, Catharine Lorillard Wolfe Art Club 84th Ann, 80. *Mem:* Metrop Painters & Sculptors; New York Artists Equity Asn; Am Soc Contemp Artists (pres, 83-85); Nat Asn Women Artists; Catharine Lorillard Wolf Art Club. *Media:* Bronze, Polyester Resin. *Mailing Add:* 2820 Ave J Brooklyn NY 11210

ABRAMS, HERBERT E
PAINTER, LECTURER
b Greenfield, Mass, Mar 20, 21. *Study:* Norwich Art Sch, Conn; Pratt Inst, hon grad in illus; Art Student League, with Frank Vincent Du Mond. *Comn:* Portraits, Dr James McCord, Princeton Theol Sem, 70; Gen Anna Mae Hayes, Walter Reed Med Ctr, 71; Dr Phillip Bard, Johns Hopkins Univ, 72 & Dr Thomas B Turner, Turner Auditorium, 74; portraits, Anthony I Conrad & Edgar H Griffiths, RCA Corp, 77; and others. *Exhib:* Dallas Mus Fine Arts, 48; one-man shows, Grand Cent Art Galleries, New York, 60, 65, 68 & 79; Okla Mus Art, 69; West Point Libr, 73 & 74; Beaufort, SC Mus, 75. *Teaching:* TV lectr & demonstr, 67-80; guest lectr cadets, West Point Military Acad,

73-74. *Awards:* Best Still Life, Dr Byron Kenyon Award, Hudson Valley Art Asn, 68; Best Portrait, 70; Dines Carlsen Award, Hudson Valley Art Asn, 77. *Mem:* Hudson Valley Art Asn; Southern Vt Art Asn; Beaufort Art Asn; Art Students League. *Media:* Oil. *Mailing Add:* Heartwood Warren CT 06754

ABRAMS, JANE ELDORA
PRINTMAKER, PAINTER
b Eau Claire, Wis, Jan 2, 40. *Study:* Univ Wis-Stout, Menomonie, BS, 62, MS, 67; Ind Univ, Bloomington, with Pozzath & Lowe, MFA(with distinction), 71. *Work:* Ind Univ Mus Fine Arts; Univ Dallas, Tex; Tex Tech Univ; Tamarind Inst; Univ NMex. *Exhib:* Works on Paper Traveling Exhib, Univ Utah, Salt Lake City, Univ Tex, Houston & Los Angeles Co Mus of Art, Calif, 77; Works on Paper: Southwest 1978, Dallas Mus Fine Arts, 78; Art Inst Chicago, 81; Philadelphia Print Club, 81; Boston Art Inst, 81; Los Angeles Printmakers Soc, 81; and many others. *Teaching:* Instr art, Univ Wis-Stout, Menomonie, 67-69; from asst prof to assoc prof art, color, design & intaglio, Univ NMex, 71-; guest artist, Ind Univ, Bloomington, 76, Univ Tex, Austin, 83 & others. *Awards:* Purchase Award, Tex Tech Univ, 73; Univ NMex, 71-74, 76 & 79-80; Grant, Ford Found, 79; and others. *Mem:* Col Art Asn Am; Woman's Caucus on Art; Los Angeles Print Soc; Philadelphia Print Club. *Media:* Intaglio; Lithograph. *Publ:* Contribr, Colorprints, USA (slide series), 71-72. *Dealer:* Sebastian Moore Gallery Denver CO; Taylor Gallery PO Box LL Taos NM 87571. *Mailing Add:* 7811 Guadalupe Trail NW Albuquerque NM 87107

ABRAMS, RUTH (DAVIDSON)
PAINTER, CRITIC
b Brooklyn, NY. *Study:* Columbia Univ; Art Students League; New Sch Social Res; also workshops with Zorach, Archipenko & Harrison. *Work:* Carnegie Inst Technol; Neuberger Mus, Purchase, NY; Rose Art Mus, Brandeis Univ; NY Univ Art Collection; Corcoran Gallery Art, Washington, DC; also in pvt collections, US & SAm. *Exhib:* Dallas Mus Fine Arts, 63; one-man show, Mass Inst Technol, 64 & 69 & others; Women Art, 76 & Women Painters & Poets, 77 & 79, Visual Arts Coalition, Contemp Arts Gallery, NY Univ; Washington Int Art Show, Delson-Richter Gallery, Washington, DC, 76; 118 Artists, 77 & 10th St Artists at Landmark Gallery, New York, 77-78; Visual Artists Coalition, First Women's Bank, New York, 79; and others. *Pos:* Art dir, New Sch Social Res Asn, 65-66; auth & co-dir art film, Paradox of the Big; mem ed staff, Public Pictures on Exhibit: collectors guide to art shows. *Teaching:* Lectr, Parsons Sch Design, New York, 76, New York Univ Loeb, 77 & Ringling Sch Art, Sarasota, Fla, 79. *Publ:* Illusr, Ekistics, Athens, Greece & Arena Interbuild, London, Eng, 67. *Mailing Add:* 18 W Tenth St New York NY 10011

ABRAMS, VIVIEN (JOY)
PAINTER
b Cleveland, Ohio, July 26, 46. *Study:* Carnegie-Mellon Univ, BFA, 68; Inst Allende, San Miguel Allende, MFA, 71. *Work:* Cleveland Mus Art; Aldrich Mus Contemp Art; Columbus Mus Arts & Sci, Ga; Cleveland Art Asn; Nat City Bank Cleveland. *Comn:* Memory Structures (constructed painting), Am Tel & Tel Longlines. *Exhib:* Ohio Women Artists, Past & Present, Butler Inst Am Art, 76; one-artist show, 76 & Drawing as Process Travelling Show, 77, Akron Art Inst; Midyear Painting Show, Butler Inst Am Art, 77; New York Now, Phoenix Mus Art, 79; 60th & 62nd May Shows, Cleveland Mus Art, 79 & 82. *Teaching:* Vis artist, State Univ NY, Purchase, 83. *Awards:* MacDowell Colony Fels, 79 & 81; Yaddo Fels, 79 & 82; First Prize Painting, 62nd May Show, Cleveland Mus Art, 81. *Bibliog:* Helen Cullinan (auth), Art: A matter of math and logic, Sunday Plain Dealer Mag, 9/25/77; Stephen Westfall (auth), Arts reviews: Summer invitational, Arts Mag, 10/82. *Dealer:* Luise Ross 162 W 56 St #207 New York NY 10019. *Mailing Add:* 11 Worth St New York NY 10013

ABRIL, BEN (BENJAMIN)
PAINTER
b Los Angeles, Calif, Apr 11, 23. *Study:* Sch Allied Arts, 45-46; Glendale Col, 46-47; Los Angeles Co Mus Art, 47. *Work:* Los Angeles Co Mus Hist, Los Angeles; Charles & Emma Fry Art Mus, Seattle; US Navy Combat Art Collection, DC; Laguna Beach Art Mus, Calif; Glendale Fed Savings, Calif Art Collection. *Comn:* Rec Am Occupation in Japan, Secy Navy, Washington, DC, 65; Transportation of Water to Los Angeles, Dept Water & Power, Los Angeles, 65; Ann Los Angeles Times Christmas Cards, 76-79. *Exhib:* Calif Watercolor Soc, Mus Fine Arts, Richmond, Va, 57; Watercolor USA, Springfield Art Mus, Mo, 59; US Navy Collection, Frank Lloyd Wright-Barnsdal Park Mus, Los Angeles, 66; Calif Watercolor Soc, US Embassy Belles Art Mus, Mexico City, 68; Ben Abril's Bunker Hill, Los Angeles Co Mus Hist, Los Angeles, 69. *Pos:* Archit coordr, Los Angeles Co, 66-77. *Teaching:* Instr oil painting, Laguna Beach Art Sch, 66; instr oil painting, Glendale, Calif, 74. *Awards:* Dagmar-Haggstrom-Tribble, Am Watercolor Soc, New York, 59; First Prize, Calif Mus Sci, Los Angeles Trade Union, 76; Purchase Award, Santa Paula Calif Ann, 79. *Bibliog:* He Beat the Bulldozers, Los Angeles Examiner, 3/8/64; Stephany Edwards (auth), Ben Abril's Los Angeles, Ralph Story TV Prog, 68; William Pugsley (auth), Bunker Hill--Last of the Lofty Mansions, Trans-Anglo Bks, 77. *Mem:* Am Watercolor Soc; Nat Watercolor Soc; San Gabriel Art Asn; Glendale Art Asn. *Media:* Oil, Watercolor. *Publ:* Illusr, How Engines Talk, 61, Piggy Back, 62 & Shoofly, 62, Follet, Chicago. *Dealer:* Biltmore Galleries 515 S Olive Los Angeles CA 90013. *Mailing Add:* 2137 Via Venado La Canada CA 91011

ABULARACH, RODOLFO MARCO
PAINTER, PRINTMAKER
b Guatemala City, Guatemala, Jan 7, 33. *Study:* Nat Sch Plastic Arts, Guatemala City; Art Students League; Pratt Graphic Art Ctr, New York. *Work:* Mus Mod Art, New York; New York Public Libr; World Print Council, San Francisco; Metrop Mus Art, New York; Philadelphia Mus Art, Pa; and others. *Comn:* Print-engraving-etching, Hommage Aux Prix Nobel, Malmo, Sweden, 77; print edition, etching & engraving, World Print Coun, San Francisco, 80. *Exhib:* Mus Mod Art, New York, 60, 63, 64, 69 & 70; 100 Contemporary Graphics, Pratt Graphic Art Ctr at Jewish Mus, New York, 64; 17th Nat Exhib Graphics, Brooklyn Mus, New York, 70; 12 Latin-Am Artists, Ringling Mus, Fla, 71; Biennial Panamerican Graphic Arts, Mus Mod Art, La Tertulia, Columbia, 73; Biennial, Firence, Italy, 74; Biennal Prints, Mus Mod Art, Tokyo, Japan, 79; and others. *Teaching:* Instr graphic workshop, Univ Costa Rica, 76. *Awards:* First Prize in Drawing, Arte Actual, Spain, 63; First Prize in Drawing, Panamerican Exhib Graphic Arts, Columbia, 70; Special Ed Prize & Award of Merit, World Print Council, San Francisco, 80; and others. *Bibliog:* Stuart Preston (auth), 20th century sense & sensibility, New York Times, 5/7/61; John Canaday (auth), New talent in printmaking, New York Times, 5/27/67; Elisabeth Perez Luna (auth), The eyes of Abularach, Hombre Mag, 7/79. *Media:* Oil; Pen & Ink. *Publ:* Contribr, Art in America: New talent USA prints & drawings, Art Am, spring 60; contribr, Tamarind: Hommage to Lithography, Mus Mod Art, New York, 67; contribr, Rodolfo Abularach--Artista Testimonal, Ministerio de Education Guatemala, 74; contribr, Abularach E A Janela Do Ser, Arte Mag, Brazil, 78; contribr, Modern Masters: 33 Artists from 33 Lands, Galeria Borjeson, 79. *Mailing Add:* 14 West 17th Street New York NY 10011

ACCONCI, VITO
SCULPTOR
b New York, NY, Jan 24, 40. *Study:* Holy Cross Col, AB; Univ Iowa, MFA. *Work:* Mus Mod Art, Paris; Mus Mod Art, New York; Los Angeles Co Mus. *Exhib:* Information, Mus Mod Art, 70; Software, Jewish Mus, New York, 70; Prospect, Kunsthalle, Dusseldorf, Ger, 71; Sonnabend Gallery, New York, 72, 73, 75 & 76; Documenta 5, Kassel, 72; Eight Contemp Artists, Mus Mod Art, New York, 74; Venice Biennale, Italy, 76; Mus Fine Arts, Montreal, 80; Indianapolis Mus Art, 80; Young-Hoffman Gallery, Chicago, 81. *Teaching:* Lectr art theory, Sch Visual Arts, New York, 68-71; instr post-studio art, Calif Inst Art, 76. *Bibliog:* R Pincus-Witten (auth), Vito Acconci & the conceptual performance, Artforum, 4/72; Alan Sondheim (auth), Vito Acconci: Work 1973-4, Arts, 3/75; Mario Diacono (auth), Vito Acconci: Dal Testo-Azione Al Corpo Come Testo, Out-of-London Press, 76. *Publ:* Contribr, Conceptual Art, Dutton, 72; contribr, Vito Acconci Issue, Avalanche Mag, 72; auth, Pulse: from my mother, Multiplicata, 72; auth, Ten-Point Plan for Video, Video Art, Harcourt-Brace, 76; auth, Think/Leap/Rethink/Fall, Wright State Univ Press, 77. *Mailing Add:* c/o Sonnabend Gallery 420 W Broadway New York NY 10013

ACCURSO, ANTHONY SALVATORE
ILLUSTRATOR, PAINTER
b Brooklyn, NY, Apr 5, 40. *Study:* Brooklyn Mus Art Sch; Sch Art & Design, New York; Pratt Inst; Sch Visual Arts, New York. *Exhib:* Bronx Mus Art in coop with Metrop Mus Art, New York, 72; Contemp Courtroom Artists, traveling exhib, Univ Mus, Miss Law Sch, University & First State Capitol Bldg, Little Rock, Ark, 78; Galerie Vallombreuse, Biarritz, Paris, France, 77; Watergate: Am Court-trials, traveling exhib, Galerie Mouffe, Paris, France, 78; Atlantic Gallery, New York, 82; and others. *Pos:* Illusr/corresp, Good Morning America, ABC-TV News, 70-; art consult/actor, All My Children, ABC-TV, New York, 79 & 81; illusr/corresp, Nightline, ABC-TV News, 79, 20/20 News Mag, 79, MacNeil Lehrer Report, PBS-TV, 79, Closeup, 80, ABC-TV, New York; illusr/corresp & courtroom artist, Cable News Network, New York, 80, WNBC-TV News, New York, 82, WNET-TV, Newark, 83 & WPIX-TV News, New York, 83. *Awards:* Int Salon Award, Biarritz, France, 77; Gold Medal & Prize of Italy, Accademia Italia delle Arti del Lavoro, Parma, 80; and others. *Bibliog:* Harry Reasoner (interviewer), Trial Artists, Commentary, ABC-TV News, 74; Dick Cavett (interviewer), On UFO's, Dick Cavett Show, ABC-TV Wide World of Entertainment, 73; UFO's, Do You Believe?, NBC-TV News Documentary, 74. *Mem:* Graphic Artists Guild New York. *Media:* Multimedia. *Publ:* Illusr, King Robert of Sicily, KRON-TV, San Francisco, 81; Illusr (motion picture), Mysteries From Beyond Earth, Constantin Films, 75 & NBC-TV Doc, 77; illusr, Contemporary Courtroom Artists, The Today Show, NBC-TV, 76; illusr, close-circuit TV hosp-med instructional programming, NY & Calif, 76. *Dealer:* Harbor Gallery 43 Main St Cold Spring Harbor NY 11724. *Mailing Add:* 5309 Seventh Ave Brooklyn NY 11220

ACHEPOHL, KEITH ANDEN
PRINTMAKER, PAINTER
b Chicago, Ill, Apr 11, 34. *Study:* Knox Col, BA; Univ Iowa, MFA. *Work:* Nat Gallery Art & Pennell Collection, Libr Cong, Washington, DC; Los Angeles Co Mus, Los Angeles, Calif; Art Inst Chicago; Bibliot Nac, Madrid, Spain; and many others. *Exhib:* Nat Print Exhib, Libr Cong, 60, 61, 63 & 69; Brooklyn Mus, 68-74; Intaglio Invitational, Biella, Italy; 1st Int Print Exhib, Segovia, Spain; Des Moines Art Ctr, 79; Utah Mus Fine Arts, 80; Masters Am Watercolor, Mid Am Arts Alliance Travel Exhib, 80; Art Inst Chicago, 81; Nat Mus Am Art, Washington, DC, 82; Joslyn Mus, Omaha, Nebr, 83. *Teaching:* Instr printmaking, Univ Iowa, 64-67; vis artist printmaking, Univ Wash, summer 67; assoc prof, Pac Lutheran Univ, 69-72; vis artist printmaking, Univ Iowa, 72-73, assoc prof, 73-78, prof, 78- *Awards:* Tiffany Found Award, 66; Fulbright Sr Lectureship Award, Cairo, Egypt, 79-80; Gold Medal Printmaking, Mediterranean Biennale, Alexandria, Egypt, 82. *Dealer:* Assoc Am Artists Gallery Fifth Ave New York NY 10022; Roy Boyd Gallery 215 W Superior Chicago IL 60610. *Mailing Add:* 630 W Park Rd Iowa City IA 52240

ACKER, PERRY MILES
PAINTER, EDUCATOR
b Elk Rapids, Mich, Apr 6, 03. *Study:* With Fred Marshall, Eustace Ziegler & Harry Bonath. *Work:* Seattle Art Mus; Charles & Emma Frye Pub Art Mus. *Exhib:* Two Hundred Years of Watercolor Painting in America, Metrop Mus, 67; Am Watercolor Exhib, several times; Northwest Ann, Seattle Art Mus; Northwest Watercolor Exhib, several times. *Awards:* First Prize, Northwest Marine Exhib, 72; First Prize, Northwest Watercolor Soc, 74; Purchase Awards, Northwest Watercolor Exhib, 75, 77 & 78. *Mem:* Am Watercolor Soc; Northwest Watercolor Soc (pres, 60); Puget Sound Group Northwest Painters, Inc (pres, 59); West Coast Watercolor Soc. *Media:* Watercolor, Oil. *Publ:* Palette Talks, 81. *Dealer:* Gallery West 4836 Scholls Ferry Rd Portland OR 97225; Kirsten Gallery 5320 Roosevelt Way NE Seattle WA 98105. *Mailing Add:* 2291 NE 61st St Seattle WA 98115

ACKERMAN, FRANK EDWARD
PAINTER, DESIGNER
b Los Angeles, Calif, Jan 3, 33. *Study:* Sch Allied Arts, Glendale Col, Calif; Chouinard Art Inst. *Work:* Univ Utah, Logan; Hunt Collection Fine Art, Fullerton, Calif; Vincent Price Collection, Beverly Hills, Calif. *Comn:* Antartica Series, USN, Washington, DC, 67; Alaska, Alaskan CofC, 69; Vietnam War Mem, Co Los Angeles, Court of Flags, 73; Gen Omar Bradley, Patriotic Hall, Los Angeles, 75. *Exhib:* US Embassy Exhib, Acapulco, Mex, 60; US Naval World Tour, 70; Nat Acad Design, 73; one-man show, Brand Libr Fine Arts, Glendale, Calif, 73; Royal Watercolor Soc, London, 75. *Pos:* Illusr, Co of Los Angeles, 56-63, graphic artist, 66-68, head graphic artist, 68-70 & art dir, 70-80; chief exhib serv, Mus Natural Hist, 80- *Teaching:* Instr watercolor, Rex Brandt Sch Painting, Corona del Mar, Calif, 55-56; pvt classes, Los Angeles, 61-65 & instr painting & watercolor, Creative Arts Prog, Flintridge, Calif, 62-65. *Awards:* Painting of the Year Award, Ebell Club, Los Angeles, 63; Award of Merit, Home Savings & Loan, 64; Watercolor Award, Calif Nat Watercolor Soc, 71. *Mem:* West Coast Watercolor Soc; State Calif Artist Adv Bd; Calif Nat Watercolor Soc (first vpres & pres, 68-70); Soc of South Pole; Int Inst Arts & Lett, Switz. *Media:* Watercolor. *Publ:* Illusr, Earthquake Report on Los Angeles Co, 73; illusr, End of the Era, 75. *Mailing Add:* 1323 Columbia Dr Glendale CA 91205

ACKERMAN, GERALD MARTIN
HISTORIAN, EDUCATOR
b Alameda, Calif, Aug 21, 28. *Study:* Univ Calif, BA, 52; Munich Univ, 56-58, with Prof Sedlmayr; Princeton Univ, MFA, 60, PhD, 64, with Prof Lee & Panofsky. *Exhib:* San Francisco Mus Art; de Yound Mus Fine Art, San Francisco; Oakland Mus Art; Los Angeles Mus Art; Brooklyn Mus Art; San Diego Mus Art; Brandeis Univ, Mass; and others. *Collections Arranged:* Thiebaud Figures, Stanford Univ Mus, 65; Gerome, Dayton Art Inst, Minneapolis Art Inst, Walters Art Gallery, Baltimore, 72-73. *Teaching:* Instr art hist, Bryn Mawr Col, 60-64; asst prof, Stanford Univ, 65-70; assoc prof, Pomona Col, 71-76, prof, 76-, chmn art dept, 72-81. *Awards:* Fulbright Prof, Univ Leningrad, 80. *Mem:* Col Art Asn; Deutsche Verein fur Kunstwissenschaft; Societe Histoire Art Francaise. *Res:* 19th century realism in America and Europe, in particular academic realists such as Jean Leon Gerome and Thomas Eakins; art theory. *Publ:* Auth, Gerome and Manet, Gazette des Beaux-Arts, 70: 163-176; Lomazzo's treatise on painting, Art Bull, 59: 317-326; Gerome, the academic realist, Art News Ann, 33: 100-107; Thomas Eakins and His Parisian Masters, Gerome and Bonnat, Gazette des Beaux Arts, 72: 235-236; Gerome, exhib catalog, 72. *Mailing Add:* Art Dept Pomona Col Claremont CA 91711

ACKERMAN, JAMES S
HISTORIAN, EDUCATOR
b San Francisco, Calif, Nov 8, 19. *Study:* Yale Univ, BA, 41; NY Univ, MA, 47, PhD, 52; Kenyon Col, LHD, 61; Md Inst Art, Hon DFA, 72; Univ Md, Baltimore Co, LHD, 76. *Pos:* Ed in chief, Art Bulletin, 56-60. *Teaching:* Lectr, Yale Univ, 46 & 49; asst prof hist art & archit, Univ Calif, 52-56, assoc prof, 56-60; fel, Coun Humanities, Princeton Univ, 60-61; prof fine arts, Harvard Univ, 61-, chmn dept, 82-, Arthur Kinsley-Porter Prof, currently. *Mem:* Am Acad Arts & Sci; corresp Accademia Olimpica Vicenza; corresp Brit Acad; corresp, Royal Acad Uppsala. *Res:* History of architecture; critical and historical theory; interaction of art and science in the period of 1200-1700. *Publ:* Auth, The Architecture of Michelangelo, 2 vols, Zwemmer, London, Viking, 61 & Penguin, rev ed 71; coauth (with Rhys Carpenter), Art & Archaeology, Englewood Cliffs, NJ; auth, Palladio, Penguin, Eng, 66; coauth, Looking for Renaissance Rome (film), 77; auth, Palladio the Architect and his Influence in America, 80; and others. *Mailing Add:* Dept Fine Arts Fogg Art Museum Harvard Univ Cambridge MA 02138

ACKERMAN, RUDY SCHLEGEL
PAINTER, EDUCATOR
b Allentown, Pa, Mar 30, 33. *Study:* Kutztown State Col, BS(art educ), 58; Temple Univ, MS(educ), 63; Pa State Univ DEd, 67. *Work:* Allentown Art Mus, Pa; Pa State Col; Lehigh Univ; Moravian Col, Pa. *Comn:* 14ft metal sculpture, Pa Power & Light Co, Allentown, 67; tunnel mural, Allentown-Bethlehem-Easton Airport, Pa, 76; murals, The Marketplace, Bethlehem Mall, 78, Civic Ctr, Bethlehem, Pa, 84. *Exhib:* The Circle, Allentown Art Mus, 74; Works on Paper, Studio Proposte, Florence, Italy, 79; one-man show, Gallery Doshi, Harrisburg, 79, Lehigh Univ, 80 & Monotypes 81, Alain Bilham Gallery, New York, 81. *Pos:* Chmn art dept, Moravian Col, 63-; dir, Baum Sch Art, Allentown, 65- *Teaching:* Prof studio art & art hist, Moravian Col, 63- *Media:* Oil Paint. *Mailing Add:* 815 N Second St Emmaus PA 18049

ACOSTA, MANUEL GREGORIO
PAINTER, SCULPTOR
b Villa Aldama, Mex, May 9, 21; US citizen. *Study:* Univ Tex, El Paso; Chouinard Art Inst, Los Angeles; also with Urbici Soler, sculptor. *Work:* El Paso Mus, Tex; WTex Mus, Lubbock; Time, Inc Collection, New York; Harmsen's Western Collection, Colo; Nat Portrait Gallery, Washington, DC. *Comn:* Pioneer murals (with Peter Hurd), WTex Mus, 52; Southwest History (aluminum mural), Casa Blanca Motel, Logan, NMex, 56; fresco mural, First Nat Bank, Las Cruces, NMex, 57; aluminum fresco mural & hist panels, Bank of Tex, Houston. *Exhib:* Art USA, Mo, 58; Tex Watercolor Soc, Austin, 60; one-man show, Chase Gallery, New York, 62; Am Watercolor Soc, New York, 65. *Media:* Oil; Clay. *Publ:* Illusr, Cesar Chavez (cover), Time Mag, 69; illusr, Canto y Grito mi Liberacion, Doubleday, 72. *Dealer:* Baker Collector Gallery 1301 13th St Lubbock TX 79408. *Mailing Add:* 366 Buena Vista St El Paso TX 79905

ACTON, ARLO C
SCULPTOR
b Knoxville, Iowa, May 11, 33. *Study:* Wash State Univ, BA, 58; Calif Inst Arts, MFA, 59. *Work:* San Francisco Mus Art. *Exhib:* Some Points of View for '62, Stanford Univ, 62; The Artist's Environment: The West Coast, Ft Worth, Tex, 62; Fifty California Artists, Whitney Mus Am Art, New York, 62-63; California Sculpture, Kaiser Ctr, Oakland, Calif, 63; 3rd Paris Biennial, 63; and many others. *Teaching:* Univ Calif, Berkeley, 63. *Awards:* Edgar Walter Mem Prize, San Francisco Mus Art, 61; Second Prize, Richmond Art Asn Ann, 61; Award, San Francisco Art Asn, 64; plus others. *Bibliog:* Peter Selz (auth), Funk, Univ Calif, Berkeley, 67; Maurice Tuchman (auth), American Sculpture of the Sixties, Los Angeles Co Mus Art, 67. *Mailing Add:* PO Box 75 North San Juan CA 95960

ADAMS, ALICE
SCULPTOR
b New York, NY, Nov 16, 30. *Study:* Columbia Univ, BFA, 53; Fulbright travel grant, 53-54; French govt fel, 53-54; L'Ecole Nat d'Art Decoratif, Aubusson, France. *Work:* Univ Nebr, Lincoln; Hertz Corp, New York; Univ NC. *Exhib:* Contemp Am Sculpture, Whitney Mus Am Art, 70-71 & 73; Penthouse Gallery Exhib, Mus Mod Art, New York, 71; Am Women Artists, Kunsthaus, Hamburg, Ger, 72; 55 Mercer, NY, 70, 72, 73 & 75; Hal Bromm Gallery, 79; Neuberger Mus, Purchase, NY, 79-80. *Teaching:* Instr sculpture, Manhattanville Col, 61-; asst prof, Pratt Inst, 79-80. *Awards:* MacDowall Colony, MacDowall Found, 67; Nat Endowment Arts Grant, 79; Princeton Univ Fel, 80. *Bibliog:* Barbara Kafka (auth), The woven structures of Alice Adams, Craft Horizons, 3/67; Lucy Lippard (auth), The Abstract Realism of Alice Adams, Art Am, 9/79. *Mem:* Am Abstr Artists (secy, 67). *Media:* Wood, Metal. *Mailing Add:* 55 Walker St New York NY 10013

ADAMS, ANSEL EASTON
PHOTOGRAPHER
b San Francisco, Calif, Feb 20, 02. *Study:* Yale Univ, hon DFA, 73; Harvard Univ, hon DFA, 81. *Work:* Metrop Mus Art, New York; Mus Mod Art, New York; Victoria & Albert Mus, London, Eng; San Francisco Mus Art; Art Inst Chicago. *Exhib:* San Francisco Mus Art, 39; Photographs by Ansel Adams, Mus Mod Arts, New York, 44; Metrop Mus Art, 74 & Victoria & Albert Mus, 76; George Eastman House, Rochester, NY, 52; Ansel Adams & the West, Mus Mod Art, New York, 79; Ansel Adams, Nat Mus Art, Beijing, China. *Pos:* Vis mem art comt, Mass Inst Technol, 72-75. *Teaching:* Teaching photography at various workshops including, Mus Mod Art, New York, Los Angeles Art Ctr Sch, Ansel Adams Workshops, 40- *Awards:* Guggenheim Fels, 46, 48 & 58; John Muir Award, Dept Interior, 63; Presidential Medal Freedom, 80. *Bibliog:* Nancy Newhall (auth), The Eloquent Light, Sierra Club, 63; Ansel Adams (monogr), Morgan & Morgan, 72; Ansel Adams: Photographer (videotape & film), Filmamerica, 80. *Mem:* Friends of Photography (pres, 67-74, chmn, 74-). *Media:* Black and white photography. *Publ:* Contribr, This is the American Earth, 60; ed & illusr, Ansel Adams: Images 1923-1974, 74, 81; ed & illusr, Yosemite and the Range of Light, 79; The Portfolios of Ansel Adams, 78 & 81; The New Ansel Adams Photography Series, 80-; Examples: The Making of Forty Photographs, 83. *Mailing Add:* Rte 1 Box 181 Carmel CA 93923

ADAMS, BOBBI (BARBARA JEAN AUSTIN)
PAINTER
b Plainfield, NJ, July 30, 39. *Study:* Wheaton Col, Ill, BSc(high honors), 61; Art Students League, with R Brackman, R Philipp, M Cooper & V Vytlacil, 70-74; Nat Acad Design, New York, 73-74. *Work:* SC State Collection & Nat Bank SC, Columbia. *Exhib:* 43rd & 44th Ann Midyear, Butler Inst Am Art, Youngstown, Ohio, 79 & 80; Piccolo Spoleto, Dock Street Theater, Charleston, NJ, 79; Guild of SC Artists, Gibbes Gallery, Charleston, 80; Joint Guilds Exhib, Columbia Mus, SC, 81; Chautauqua Nat, 82; Guild SC Artists, Columbia Mus Art, 82. *Pos:* SC artist in res, 83-84. *Awards:* Purchase Award, State SC, 80; Westvaco Award, Gibbes Gallery, 80; Certificate Merit, Columbia Mus, 81. *Bibliog:* The Adams Papers, NJ Music/Arts, 75. *Mem:* Artists Equity Asn Inc; life mem Art Students League; assoc Allied Artists Am; Guild of SC Artists. *Media:* Oil, Pastel. *Mailing Add:* 215 S Heyward St Bishopville SC 29010

ADAMS, CELESTE MARIE
CURATOR, WRITER
b Cleveland, Ohio, July 4, 47. *Study:* Univ Mich, Ann Arbor, BA, 69; Univ Pa, Philadelphia, AM(art hist), 70; Harvard Univ, AM, 78. *Work:* Cleveland Mus Art, Ohio; Mus Fine Arts, Houston, Tex. *Collections Arranged:* In the Way of the Master: Chinese & Japanese Painting & Caligraphy (auth, catalog),

Mus Fine Arts, 81; Sunlight on Leaves: The Impressionist Tradition (auth, catalog), Mus Fine Arts, 81; The Diaghilev Heritage: Selections From Collection of Robert L B Tobin (auth, catalog), Mus Fine Arts, 81; Japanese Landscape and Figure Painting (auth, catalog), Mus Fine Arts, Houston, 83. *Pos:* Cur, Mus Fine Arts, Houston, Tex, 80- *Mailing Add:* c/o Mus Fine Arts 1001 Bissonnet at Main Houston TX 77005

ADAMS, CLINTON
LITHOGRAPHER, HISTORIAN
b Glendale, Calif, Dec 11, 18. *Study:* Univ Calif, Los Angeles, BEd, 40; MA, 42. *Work:* Mus Mod Art, New York; Chicago Art Inst, Ill; Amon Carter Mus Western Art, Ft Worth, Tex; Achenbach Found Graphic Arts, Calif; Grunwald Graphics Art Ctr, Univ Calif, Los Angeles. *Exhib:* Tamarind: Homage to Lithography, Mus Mod Art, New York, 69; 73rd Western Ann, Denver Art Mus, 71; Retrospective Exhibitions: Paintings, 61-71, Roswell Mus & Art Ctr, NMex, 72; Lithographs, Univ NMex Art Mus, 48-72; Here and Now, Albuquerque Mus, 80; and others. *Pos:* Assoc dir, Tamarind Lithography Workshop, Los Angeles, 60-61; dir, Tamarind Inst, Albuquerque, 70-; ed, Tamarind Papers, 73- *Teaching:* Asst prof painting & lithography, Univ Calif, Los Angeles, 46-54; chmn dept art, Univ Ky, 54-57; chmn dept art, Univ Fla, 57-60; dean col fine arts, Univ NMex, 61-76, prof art, 61- *Bibliog:* Van Deren Coke (auth), Clinton Adams, Univ NMex Art Mus, 73. *Publ:* Co-auth, Tamarind Book of Lithography: Art and Techniques, Abrams, 71; auth, Fritz Scholder: Lithographs, NY Graphic Soc, 75; auth, The Woodstock Ambience, Univ NMex Art Mus, 81; auth, American Lithographer, 1900-1960: The Artists and Their Printers, Univ NMex, 83; and others. *Mailing Add:* 1917 Morningside Dr NE Albuquerque NM 87110

ADAMS, HENRY
CURATOR, EDUCATOR
b Boston, Mass, May 12, 49. *Study:* Harvard Univ, BA, 71; Yale Univ, MA, 77, PhD, 80. *Pos:* Cur fine arts, Carnegie Inst Mus Art, Pittsburgh, Pa, 82- *Teaching:* Asst prof art hist, Univ Ill, 81-82; adj prof, Univ Pittsburgh, 83- *Publ:* Auth, A fish by John LaFarge, Art Bulletin, 80; auth, Mortal themes: Winslow Homer, Art Am, 83; auth, The development of William Morris Hunt's The Flight of Night, Am Art J, 83; auth, New books on Japonisme, 83 & A new interpretation of Bingham's Fur Traders Descending the Missouri, 83, Art Bulletin. *Mailing Add:* Carnegie Inst Mus Art 4400 Forbes Pittsburgh PA 15213

ADAMS, JAMES FREDERICK
COLLECTOR, PATRON
b Andong, Korea, Dec 27, 27; US citizen. *Study:* Univ Calif, Berkeley, BA, 50; Temple Univ, EdM, 51; Wash State Univ, PhD, 59. *Collection:* Colonial Spanish art from the 16th to the 19th century (Mexico, Central and South America). *Publ:* Auth, Collecting colonial Spanish art, The Clarion: America's Folk Art Mag, 78; auth, Colonial Spanish art: a collector's view, Americas, 7/79. *Mailing Add:* Grad Col Univ Nev Las Vegas NV 89154

ADAMS, JAY H
JEWELER, MEDALIST
b Clinton, Iowa, Sept 11, 37. *Study:* Lincoln Col, Ill, 58; Ill Wesleyan Univ, BFA, 62; Ill State Univ, MS, 68. *Work:* St Charles Art Ctr, Ill; Park Forest Art Ctr, Ill; Brooks Mem Art Gallery, Memphis, Tenn; Western Ill Univ Art Gallery. *Comn:* Candelabra, Lincoln Col, Ill, 71. *Exhib:* Goldsmith NAm Exhib, Renwick Gallery, Smithsonian Inst, Washington, DC, 74; Prof Jewelry Exhib, Univ Mo Fine Arts Gallery, Columbia, 76; NAm Goldsmith Exhib, Phoenix Art Mus, Ariz, 77; Am Goldsmiths Now, Washington Univ Gallery Art, St Louis, Mo, 78; Pewter Exhib, Tulsa Jr Col, Okla, 79; and others. *Teaching:* Instr jewelry/metals, Ill State Univ, 68-69; assoc prof jewelry/metals, Southwest Mo State Univ, 69- *Awards:* Best of Show, Mo Crafts Coun Ann Show, 76. *Bibliog:* Edgar A Albin (auth), The Arts, 11/28/71 & View Mag, 10/22/77, Springfield News-Leader & Jay Adams, Art Craft Mag, 12/79-1/80. *Mem:* Am Crafts Coun; Soc NAm Goldsmiths; Mo Crafts Coun. *Media:* Gold; Pewter. *Publ:* Auth, Goldsmiths J, Soc NAm Goldsmiths, 10/79. *Mailing Add:* 910 S Kickapoo St Springfield MO 65804

ADAMS, LOWELL G
MUSEUM DIRECTOR
b Davenport, Okla, May 9, 35. *Study:* Cent State Univ, Edmond, Okla, BA, 57; Wichita State Univ, Kans, MA, 67; Univ Kans, Lawrence. *Collections Arranged:* American Women: Twentieth Century (cataloged), 72; Manscape: 77 (cataloged), 77; Contemporary American Glass (cataloged), 78; Great American Storytellers (cataloged), 79; Living Masters of Latin America (cataloged), 80. *Pos:* Educ dir, Wichita Art Mus, Kans, 67-69; dir, Miss Art Asn, Jackson, 69-71; dir, Lakeview Ctr Arts/Sci, Peoria, Ill, 71-75; dir, Okla Art Ctr, Oklahoma City, 76- *Mem:* Am Asn Mus. *Mailing Add:* 3113 Pershing Blvd Oklahoma City OK 73107

ADAMS, MARK
TAPESTRY ARTIST, PAINTER
b Fort Plain, NY, Oct 27, 25. *Study:* Syracuse Univ; with Hans Hofmann & Jean Lurcat, France. *Work:* Dallas Mus Fine Arts; San Francisco Pub Libr; Santa Rosa-Sonoma Pub Libr, Calif; Hall Justice, San Francisco. *Comn:* Baptistry, All Saints' Episcopal Church, Carmel, Calif, 68; Man Flying (tapestry), Bank Calif, San Francisco, 68; tapestry, Weyerhaeuser Co, Tacoma, Wash, 71; stained glass, Temple Emanuel, 72 & St Thomas More Cath Church, San Francisco, 74. *Exhib:* Int Biennial of Tapestry, Lausanne, Switz, 62 & 65; Collector: Object/Environment, Mus Contemp Crafts, New York, 65; San Francisco Art Inst Ann, San Francisco Mus Art, 65; 400 Years of Tapestry, Norfolk Mus Arts & Sci, 66; one-man retrospective, Calif Palace Legion Honor, San Francisco, 70. *Media:* Watercolor, Stained Glass. *Mailing Add:* c/o John Berggruen Gallery 228 Grant Ave San Francisco CA 94114

ADAMS, PAT
PAINTER, INSTRUCTOR

b Stockton, Calif, July 8, 28. *Study:* Univ Calif, Berkeley, BA, 49; Brooklyn Mus Art Sch, with Max Beckmann & John Ferren; Fulbright fel, France, 56-57. *Work:* Whitney Mus; Joseph Hirshhorn Mus; Univ Calif, Berkeley; Yale Gallery Art; Brooklyn Mus. *Exhib:* Whitney Mus Painting Ann, 56, 61; Aquarellistes, Mus Mod Art traveling exhib in France, 57; New Acquisitions, Hirshhorn Mus, Washington, DC, 74-76; Aspects of the 70's: Painterly Abstraction, Berkshire Mus, 81; Craham Grand Collection: A Private Vision, Boston Mus Fine Arts, 82; Miro in America, Mus Fine Arts, Houston, 82; Art & Technology: Offset Prints, Lehigh Univ, 83; and many others. *Pos:* Vis critic painting, Yale Univ, 71-72. *Teaching:* Art fac painting, Bennington Col, 64-; vis critic painting, Yale Univ, 71-72; grad sem, Queens Col, fall 72; grad sem, RI Sch Design, fall, 81; instr, Grad Sch Art, Yale Univ, fall 83; vis artist, Univ Iowa, Univ NMex, Western Ky Univ, Columbia Univ & Kent State. *Awards:* Painting Award, Nat Coun Arts, 68; Nat Endowment Arts Grant, 76; Childe Hassam Purchase, Am Acad Arts & Letters, 80; and others. *Bibliog:* Martica Sawin (auth), So much to see: Pat Adams new paintings, Arts, 5/76, Richard Lorber (auth), Pat Adams' Modernity, Art Forum, summer 78; Robert Boyers (auth), Willingness and Reverence: Interview with Pat Adams, Bennington Rev, 9/78. *Media:* Oil/Isobutyl Methacrylate, Mixed. *Publ:* Auth, Art Now, 6/72; auth, On working, Quadrille, fall 77; auth, Subject and being, Art Journal, 82. *Dealer:* Virginia Zabriskie Gallery 29 W 57th St New York NY 10019. *Mailing Add:* Bennington Col Bennington VT 05201

ADAMS, ROBERT HICKMAN
PHOTOGRAPHER

b Orange, NJ, May 8, 37. *Work:* Mus Mod Art, New York; Mus Fine Arts, Houston; Metrop Mus Art, New York; Philadelphia Mus Art; Int Mus Photog, George Eastman House, Rochester, NY; and others. *Exhib:* Photographs by Robert Adams & Emmet Gowin, Mus Mod Art, 71-72; Landscape-Cityscape, Metrop Mus Art, 73-74; 14 American Photographers, Baltimore Mus Art, 75; New Topographics, Int Mus Photog, George Eastman House, 75; Castelli Graphics, New York, 76; Target Collection of ı m Photog, Mus Fine Arts, Houston, 77; The Great West, Univ Colo, Boulder, 77; Contemp Am Photographic Works, Mus of Fine Arts, Houston, 77; From the Missouri West, Castelli Graphics, New York, 79; Prairie, Museum of Mod Art, 79; American Images, Corcoran Gallery, DC, 79; The New West, Philadelphia Mus Art, 81; Robert Adams, Milwaukee Art Mus, 83. *Awards:* Nat Endowment Arts Fel Photog, 73 & 77; Guggenheim Found Fel Photog, 73 & 81. *Bibliog:* John Szarkowski (auth), Foreward to, The New West, 74. *Publ:* Auth & illusr, The New West: Landscapes Along the Colorado Front Range, Colo Assoc Univ, 74; auth & illusr, Denver: A Photographic Survey of the Metropolitan Area, Colo Assoc Univ Press, 77; auth & illusr, Prairie, Denver Art Mus, 78; auth & illusr, From the Missouri West, Aperture, 80; auth, Beauty in Photography, Aperture, 81. *Mailing Add:* 326 Lincoln St Longmont CO 80501

ADAMY, GEORGE E
EDUCATOR, SCULPTOR

b Manchester, Conn, Apr 19, 25. *Study:* Univ Conn, BS, 48; NY Univ, MBA, 54, PhD credits, 55; New Sch Social Res, with M Borne, 63; Mus Mod Art, with R Carpentier & S Weiner, 63-64; with F Dzubas & Knox Martin, 63-65. *Work:* Aldrich Mus of Contemp Art, Ridgefield, Conn; Vatican Art Collection, Vatican City; White Plains Hospital, NY; Mayo Clinic, Minn. *Comn:* Outdoor acrylic sculpture environment containing five 5ft laminated acrylic discs in an 800 sq ft area, 77 Water St, New York, 69-70. *Exhib:* Aldrich Mus of Contemp Art, 65; Neuberger Mus, State Univ of NY Col at Purchase, 75; Hudson River Mus, Yonkers, NY. *Pos:* Owner, GEA Co, 62-; plastics & mold-making consult to industs & artists; founder & pres, Life Reproductions Ltd, 81-; sr partner, Impressions, 81- *Teaching:* Instr pvt workshops, 68-; lectr plastics & mold-making, State Univ NY Col, Purchase, 73-; vis adj prof plastics & mold-making, Univ Bridgeport, Conn, 75; lectr plastics & mold-making, Elizabeth Seton Col, 74, Sarah Lawrence Col, 77. *Awards:* Numerous awards for sculpture & collage in plastics. *Bibliog:* Luisa Kriesberg & Kathie Beals (authors), articles in Westchester-Rockland newspapers, 63-; and others. *Mem:* Hudson River Contemp Artists. *Media:* Cement, Fabrics with Polymers. *Mailing Add:* c/o GEA Co 19 Elkan Rd Larchmont NY 10538

ADAN, SUZANNE RAE
PAINTER

b Woodland, Calif, Feb 12, 46. *Study:* Calif State Univ, Sacramento, BA, 69, MA, 71. *Work:* Crocker Art Mus, Sacramento. *Exhib:* San Francisco Art Institute Centennial Exhibition, San Francisco Mus Mod Art, 71; Extraordinary Realities, Whitney Mus Art, New York, 73-74; one-person exhib, Womanspace, Los Angeles, 74, Betsy Rosenfield Gallery, Chicago, 83 & Michael Himovitz Gallery, 84; three-person show, Richard Nelson Gallery, Univ Calif, Davis, 79; two-person show, Crocker Art Mus, Sacramento, 80 & Betsy Rosenfield Gallery, Chicago, 82; Welcome to the Candy Store, Crocker Art Mus, Sacramento, 81; and others. *Teaching:* Instr drawing, Am River Col, Sacramento, Calif, 75-76. *Awards:* Ayling Watercolor Award, 68 & Purchase Award, 73, Crocker Art Mus; Hardison, Komatsu, Ivelich & Tucker Award, Richmond Art Ctr, 80. *Mem:* Col Art Asn; Artists Equity Asn. *Media:* Oil painting on canvas. *Dealer:* Betsy Rosenfield Gallery Inc 212 W Superior St Chicago IL 60610; Michael Himovitz Gallery 15th & J Sts Sacramento CA 95814. *Mailing Add:* 3977 Rosemary Circle Sacramento CA 95821

ADDAMS, CHARLES SAMUEL
CARTOONIST

b Westfield, NJ, Jan 7, 12. *Study:* Colgate Univ, 29-30; Univ Pa, 30-31; Grand Cent Sch Art, New York, 31-32; Univ Pa, hon degree, 80; Southampton Col, hon degree, 83. *Exhib:* Fogg Art Mus; Original Drawings, Mus City New York, 56; Univ Pa, 57 & 79; Metrop Mus Art Print Exhib; Nicholls Gallery, New York, 74; and others. *Pos:* Freelance artist, New Yorker, 34- *Awards:* Humor Award, Yale Univ, 54. *Media:* India Ink, Watercolor. *Publ:* Auth, Black Maria, 60 & The Groaning Board, 64, Simon & Schuster; auth, The Charles Addams Mother Goose, Harper & Row, 67; auth, My Crowd, Simon & Schuster, 70; auth, Favorite Haunts, 76; auth, Creature Comforts, 81; and others. *Mailing Add:* c/o New Yorker Mag 25 W 43rd St New York NY 10036

ADDISON, BYRON KENT
PAINTER, EDUCATOR

b St Louis, Mo, July 12, 37. *Study:* Washington Univ, St Louis, Mo, BFA, 59; Univ Notre Dame, South Bend, Ind, MA, 60. *Work:* Univ Tulsa Libr, Okla; Maryville Col Libr, St Louis, Mo. *Comn:* Forest Park sculpture, St Louis Award Comt, Mo, 65; entrance wall sculpture, Continental Telephone Co, Wentzville, Mo, 67; wall sculpture, Westinghouse Electric Corp, Abington, Va, 71; fountain & sculpture, United Methodist Church, Sun City, Ariz, 74; religious sculpture, St Joseph Church, Manchester, Mo, 80. *Exhib:* Nat Watercolor Soc 62nd Ann, Laguna Beach Mus Art, Calif; Mid-Four Ann, Nelson-Atkins Mus Art, Kansas City, Mo, 83; Tri-State Exhib, Wichita Art Mus, Kans, 83; Rocky Mountain Nat Watermedia '83, Foothills Art Ctr, Golden, Colo, 83; Adirondacks Nat Exhib Am Watercolors 1983, Community Arts Ctr, Old Forge, NY, 83; and others. *Teaching:* Prof drawing & sculpture, Maryville Col, St Louis, Mo, 61-, chmn, Art Dept, 65-79. *Awards:* Southwest Nat Bank Tri-State Spec Cash Award, 82-; Alco Found Award, 83-; George Sponable Mem Award, 83. *Mem:* St Louis Artists' Guild; Southern Watercolor Soc; Midwest Watercolor Soc. *Media:* Welded Steel, Watercolor. *Mailing Add:* 616 Spring Meadows Dr Ballwin MO 63011

ADDISON, CHAUNCEY See Day, Chon

ADEL, JUDITH
DIRECTOR, DESIGNER

b New York, NY, Aug 8, 45. *Pos:* Art dir, Saturday Rev, 73-77; assoc art dir, Business Week, 76-79; advert & promotional mat for major corporations incl Teleprompter & CBS; art dir, Entermedia Theatre, 78; graphics dir, Unicorn Repertory Co, Inc; founder & creative dir, Savage Group, 79- *Teaching:* Guest lectr mag art direction, Parsons Sch Design, 81 & 82. *Awards:* Award Art Direction, Creativity, 73-79; Award of Merit, Soc Publ Designers, 75 & 78; Soc Illusr Los Angeles Award, 76; and others. *Publ:* Designer jacket & interior design, Great Male Dancers of the Ballet, Doubleday; jacket & interior design, The King's Ballet Master: A Biography of Denmark's August Bournonville, Dodd, Mead; jacket & interior design, Alicia Alonso and the Nacional Ballet de Cuba, Doubleday; interior design, How to Look at Dance, William Morrow; interior design, Twentieth-Century Theater, Facts on File; and others. *Mailing Add:* The Savage Group 142 E 16th St New York NY 10003

ADELMAN, BUNNY
SCULPTOR

b New York, NY, May 7, 35. *Study:* Mt Holyoke Col, Columbia Univ, BA, 56; Nat Acad Sch Fine Arts, with Stephen Csoka & Evangelos Frudakis, scholar, 76. *Comn:* Figure, comn by A Petaccio, Clifton, NJ, 77; B'Nai Brith Medal, comn by Roger Williams Mint, 78; presidential relief, M H Lamston Inc, New York, 78; Manager of Year Award, M H Lamston Inc, New York, 79; mem relief, W R Thomas Co, Warsaw, Ind, 80. *Exhib:* Allied Artists Am, Nat Acad Design, New York, 74-79 & 81; Nat Acad Ann, Nat Acad Design, New York, 76-78; Salmagundi Club Ann, New York, 78; one-woman show, Bergen Community Mus, Paramus, NJ, 79; Pen & Brush Soc, New York, 81. *Awards:* Gold Medal, Catharine Lorillard Wolfe Ann Show, 74; Coun Am Artists Soc Award, Nat Sculpture Soc, 75; Bronze Casting Award, Pen & Brush Ann, Joel Meisner Foundry, 81. *Mem:* Nat Sculpture Soc; Catharine Lorillard Wolfe Club; Sculptors Asn NJ (vpres, 79-81). *Media:* Bronze. *Mailing Add:* 68 Homestead Rd Tenafly NJ 07670

ADELMAN, DOROTHY (LEE) McCLINTOCK
PRINTMAKER, INSTRUCTOR

b Manhattan, NY. *Study:* Art Students League, with Roberto Delamonico & Michael Ponce de Leon; Westchester Art Workshop, White Plains, NY, with Ruth Bamberger; Silvermine Guild Artists, Inc, New Canaan, Conn. *Work:* Hudson River Mus; Westchester Art Workshop; Beneficial Life Insurance Co; Sears Roebuck; Int Bus Machines; and others. *Exhib:* Katonah Gallery, NY, 71-72 & 78-80; 2nd NH Int Graphic Ann; Greenwich Art Barn, Conn, 72 & 75; Nat Arts Club, New York; Manhattanville Col, Purchase, NY, 74; Lever House, New York; Knickerbocker Artist Juried Exhib, New York. *Teaching:* Instr painting, Am Red Cross, White Plains, 71; instr printing, Westchester Art Workshop, 71-82; instr, Elizabeth Seton Col, Yonkers, NY. *Awards:* Purchase Award, Westchester Art Workshop, 69 & Hudson River Mus, 71; First & Third Award, Mamaroneck Artist Guild, 72; First Award, Westchester Art Soc, 73 & 75. *Mem:* Art Students League; Mamaroneck Artists Guild; Abraxas. *Media:* Intaglio, Printing. *Dealer:* Sound Shore Gallery Inc Port Chester NY; Art Search New York Hastings-On-Hudson NY 10106. *Mailing Add:* 36-A E Hill Dr Somers NY 10589

ADICKES, DAVID (PRYOR)
PAINTER, SCULPTOR
b Huntsville, Tex, Jan 19, 27. *Study:* Kansas City Art Inst, 48; Sam Houston Univ, Huntsville, Tex, BS, 48; Atelier Fernand Leger, Paris, 48-50. *Work:* Houston Mus Fine Art, Tex; Pa Acad Fine Art, Philadelphia; James A Michener Found Mus, Univ Tex, Austin; Witte Mus Art, San Antonio; World Bank, New York. *Comn:* Permian Basin (tapestry), Petroleum Club, Houston, 61; Spring Trees (tapestry), Hyatt Regency Hotel, Houston, 69; Virtuoso (sculpture monument), Lyric Ctr Bldg, Houston, 83. *Exhib:* One-man shows, Mus Fine Art, Houston, 51; New Works, Witte Mus Art, San Antonio 57 & Laguna Gloria Art Mus, Austin, 57; retrospective, Ft Worth Art Ctr, 66. *Teaching:* Instr painting, Univ Tex, Austin, 55-57. *Awards:* First Purchase Prize, Houston Artists, Contemp Arts Asn, 54; First Purchase Prize, Houston Artists Ann, Mus Fine Arts, Houston, 55; Purchase Prize, Texas Art, D D Feldman, Dallas, 57. *Bibliog:* Campbell Geeslin (auth), Adickes (monograph), James Bute Co, 57; A Cantey (auth), Adickes (monograph), 62 & James A Michener (auth), Adickes, 68, Seix y Barral, Barcelona. *Media:* Oil, Bronze. *Publ:* Illusr, El Centauro, Seix Barral, 67 & illusr, Ingenioso Caballero Don Quixote de la Mancha: Cervantes, 68. *Dealer:* Beaux Arts Int 2001 Post Oak Blvd Houston TX 77056. *Mailing Add:* 2409 Kingston St Houston TX 77019

ADKISON, KATHLEEN (GEMBERLING)
PAINTER
b Beatrice, Nebr. *Study:* With Mark Tobey. *Work:* Seattle Art Mus; Seattle First Nat Bank; Bank Wash, Tacoma & Spokane; Butler Inst Am Art, Youngstown, Ohio; Cheney Cowles Mus, Spokane. *Exhib:* Butler Inst Am Art Ann, 61-69; World's Fair Northwest Artists, Seattle, 62 & 74; Pa Acad Fine Arts 159th Ann, 64; one-person shows, Univ Wash Mus Art, Pullman, 76, Univ Ore Mus Art, Eugene, 77 & Wash State Art Mus, Olympia, 77; Spokane World's Fair Expo 74 Northwest Art, Wash; and others. *Teaching:* Instr painting, Wash State Univ Exten, 55-67. *Awards:* Sun Carnival First Prize, El Paso Mus, 61; Dr Fuller Purchase Award, Northwest Ann, 61; Prize for Winter Retreat, Friends Am Art, 69. *Bibliog:* Twenty five years painting, Bellevue Art Mus, Wash, 81. *Media:* Oil. *Dealer:* Gordon Woodside Gallery 1101 Howell Seattle WA 98101. *Mailing Add:* 1203 Overbluff Blvd Spokane WA 99203

ADLER, ABE
DEALER
US citizen. *Study:* Univ Ariz, BFA, 55; Univ Calif, Los Angeles, MFA, 57. *Specialty:* 20th century modern & contemp art. *Mailing Add:* Adler Gallery 667 N La Cienega Blvd Los Angeles CA 90069

ADLER, LEE
PAINTER, PRINTMAKER
b New York, NY, May 22, 34. *Study:* Art Students League, 62-64; Brooklyn Mus Art Sch, 64-65; Pratt Graphics Ctr, New York, 69. *Work:* Metrop Mus Art, New York; Brit Mus, London; Whitney Mus Am Art, New York; Art Inst Chicago; Corcoran Gallery Art, Washington, DC. *Comn:* Graham Gallery, New York, 70; Book-of-the-Month Club, 73; New York Times/Quadrangle Books, 73; Hagley Mus, Wilmington, Del, 74. *Exhib:* Butler Inst Am Art, Youngstown, Ohio, 67, 68 & 77; Nat Acad Design, New York, 69; 17th Nat Print Biennial, Brooklyn Mus, 70; Print Acquisitions, Whitney Mus Am Art, 70; Mint Mus Art, Charlotte, NC, 78; Weatherspoon Art Gallery, Univ NC, Greensboro, 78; Aldrich Mus Contemporary Art, Ridgefield, Conn, 79; Edwin A Ulrich Mus Art, Wichita, Kans, 80; Nat Mus Art, New Delhi, 82; Mus Mod Art, Mexico City, 83; and others. *Awards:* Grumbacher Award, Jersey City Mus, 68; Purchase award, Childe Hassam Fund Competition, 69; Federico Castellon Purchase Award, Soc Am Graphic Artists, 79. *Bibliog:* Juan Acha (auth), Lee Adler, Mexico City Mus Mod Art, 76; Jeffrey Hoffeld (auth), Lee Adler, New York, 78; Carlus Dyer (auth), Lee Adler, Arts, 10/78. *Mem:* Soc Am Graphic Artists; Audubon Artists; Allied Artists Am; Painters & Sculptors Soc NJ. *Media:* Oil, Silk Screen Printing. *Dealer:* Allan Stone Gallery 48 E 86th St New York NY 10028. *Mailing Add:* 168 Clinton St Brooklyn NY 11201

ADLER, MYRIL
PRINTMAKER, PAINTER
b Vilebsk, USSR, Sept 22, 20; US citizen. *Study:* Brooklyn Mus Art Sch; Art Students League; Theatre Arts Workshop, NY, with Moi Solotaroff; Pratt Graphics Ctr; study with Seong Moy, Michael Ponce de Leon & Ansei Uchima. *Work:* New York Pub Libr, NY; Mus Mod Art, Caracas, Venezuela; Univ Calif, Berkeley; Univ RI, Providence; and others. *Exhib:* Salute to 1965, Mus Mod Art, Caracas, Venezuela, 65; Contemp Prints, Mus Mod Art, Warsaw, Poland, 66; one-person shows, Hudson River Mus, Yonkers, 72 & 74 & Katonah Gallery, NY, 72 & 76; Round Tower, Copenhagen, Denmark, 74; and others. *Awards:* First Prize Graphics & Watercolors, Westchester Art Soc, 64; First Prize Graphics & Sculpture, Artists of NWestchester, 68; Hudson River Mus Purchase Award, Yonkers Art Asn, 70. *Bibliog:* Norman Laliberte (auth), Collage, Montage, Assemblage, History and Contemporary Techniques, Van Nostrand Reinhold, 71; Norman Lalibert & Alex Mogelon (coauths), The Reinhold Book of Art Ideas, Van Nostrand Reinhold, 77. *Mem:* Artists Equity, New York; Am Crafts Coun; Nat Asn Women Artists; Yonkers Art Asn (bd dirs, 75-76, secy, 77). *Media:* Multimedia. *Publ:* Illusr, Dances of Palestine, B'Nai B'Rith Hillel Foundations, New York, 47. *Dealer:* Westlake Gallery Ltd 210 E Post Rd White Plains NY 10601; Katonah Gallery 28 Bedford Rd Katonah NY 10536. *Mailing Add:* 266 Dalmeny Rd Briarcliff Manor NY 10510

ADLER, ROBERT
PAINTER
b New York, NY, Jan 10, 30. *Study:* Syracuse Univ; Atelier 17, Paris, with Stanley Hayter. *Exhib:* Drawings, USA, 65; West Side Artists, Riverside Mus, New York, 66; 2nd Kent Show, Kent State Univ, Ohio, 68; A Sense of Place: The Artist & the American Land, Joslyn Art Mus, Omaha & Sheldon Mem Art Galleries, Lincoln, Univ Nebr. *Media:* Oil, Ink. *Dealer:* Poindexter Gallery 1160 Fifth Ave New York NY 10029. *Mailing Add:* 300 Central Park W New York NY 10024

ADLER, SEBASTIAN J
MUSEUM DIRECTOR
b Chicago, Ill, Sept 11, 32. *Study:* Winona State Col, BS; Univ Minn, Duluth. *Collections Arranged:* Robert Rauschenberg, 71; Roy Lichtenstein 1972; John McLaughlin 1973; Ronald Cooper 1973; Nancy Graves 1973; Innovations 1973; Robert Mangold 1974; Hilla and Bernd Becher 1974; Arman/Selected Works: 1958-1974; Donald Roller Wilson 1974; Jim Dine 1974; Marcia Hafif 1975; Stephen Rosenthal 1975; DeWain Valentine 1975; The Summers Collection, 1975, University Calif, Irvine 1965-1975, 1975, Kim MacConnel, 1975, Dennis O'Leary, 1976, Richard Anuszkiewicz, 1976, Patrick Ireland, 1977, The Modern Chair, 1977, Improbable Furniture, 1977, Four Californians, 1977, Eleanor Antin, 1977 & Richard Artschwager, 1980, La Jolla Mus Contemp Art, Calif. *Pos:* Founder-dir, Nobles Co Art Ctr, 58-60; dir, Sioux Falls Art Ctr, 60-62; asst dir, Wichita Art Mus, 63-64, dir, 64-65; dir, Contemp Arts Mus, Houston, 66-73; dir, La Jolla Mus Contemp Art, 73-83, San Diego Art Ctr, 83- *Mem:* Col Arts Asn; Am Asn Mus; Am Asn Art Mus Dir. *Mailing Add:* 1539 Nautilus 700 Prospect St La Jolla CA 92037

ADRIAN, BARBARA (MRS FRANKLIN TRAMUTOLA)
PAINTER, COLLECTOR
b New York, NY, July 25, 31. *Study:* Art Students League, with Reginald Marsh, 47-54; Hunter Col, 51; Columbia Univ, 52-54. *Work:* Butler Inst Am Art, Youngstown, Ohio; Univ Southern Ill, Carbondale; City Hall, San Juan, PR. *Exhib:* Butler Inst Am Art, 70; Gallery Mod Art, New York, 70; Suffolk Mus, Stony Brook, NY, 71; Whitney Mus, 75; Ranger Fund Exhib, Nat Acad Design, 81; Women in the Making of Art History, Art Students League New York, 82; Seventh Ann Nat Invitational Drawing Exhib, Norman Eprink Gallery, Emporia State Univ Univ, Kans. *Pos:* Art consult, R H Macy, New York, 60-61; Saks Fifth Ave, New York, 60; Doyle Dane & Bernbach, New York, 60. *Teaching:* Art instr painting & drawing, Art Student League, 68- *Awards:* Benjamin Altman Prize, Nat Acad Design, 68; Dorothy Haphman Ferriss Award, Pen & Brush, 83. *Bibliog:* Edmund Burk Feldman (auth), Art as image and idea, Prentice-Hall; Lucia Salemme (auth), Painting Techniques, Comprehensive Treatise, 81. *Mem:* Life mem Art Student League; Pen & Brush. *Media:* Oil. *Collection:* Reginald Marsh, John Sloan, Will Barnet, Henry Pearson, Rouault, Versalius, Goya, Martin Lewis. *Dealer:* Capricorn Galleries Washington DC 20014. *Mailing Add:* 420 E 64th St New York NY 10021

AEBI, ERNST WALTER
ILLUSTRATOR, PAINTER
b Zurich, Switz, Mar 25, 38; US citizen. *Study:* Zurich Univ, lic oec publ, 65. *Work:* Montclair Mus & Kasser Found, Montclair, NJ; Adriance Mus, Westchester, NY; Klimastation, Gais, Switz. *Comn:* Roosevelt Raceway (mural in lobby), NY Racing Comn, Long Island, 70; sculpture, Swiss Am Soc, New York, 70; sculpture, Sandoz Inc, Hanover NJ, 74. *Exhib:* New York Artists, Southampton Parrish Mus, 66; Community Art, Brooklyn Mus, 68; Contemporary Swiss Art, Prague State Mus, Czech, 69; Biennale Europeenne, Berheim-Jeune, Paris, 69; one-man show, NY Univ, 76. *Collections Arranged:* One Trillion People Falling Off the Edge of the Earth, James Yu, New York, 77. *Bibliog:* Henry J Seldis (auth), Phantasmagoria, Los Angeles Times, 66; Malcolm Preston (auth), The world of Ernst Aebi, Newsday, 70; Stuart Murray (auth), The restless artist, New York Times, 74. *Media:* Pen and Ink; Concrete. *Publ:* Illusr, New York Times & Harpers Mag, 76-79, Harvard Bus Rev & Time Mag, 77. *Dealer:* James Yu 393 W Broadway New York NY 10012. *Mailing Add:* 460 W Broadway New York NY 10012

AGAR, EUNICE JANE
EDUCATOR, PAINTER
b Great Barrington, Mass, May 14, 34. *Study:* Wellesley Col Mass, BA(art hist), 56; Art Student's League, 57-60 & 69, study under Jean Liberte, 57-63. *Exhib:* One-person show, Albany Inst Hist & Art, NY, 67. *Pos:* Asst ed, Am Artist, New York, 58-60, managing ed, 60-63, writer, 80-, contrib ed, 83- *Teaching:* Instr painting, drawing & printmaking, Simon's Rock Early Col, 69-78, chmn studio arts, 74-78, chmn arts div & studio arts, 75-78. *Bibliog:* Article, Am Artist, 2/84. *Media:* Oil, Casein. *Mailing Add:* RD 1 Box 18 Egremont Plain Rd Great Barrington MA 01230

AGEE, WILLIAM C
MUSEUM DIRECTOR, HISTORIAN
b New York, NY, Sept 26, 36. *Study:* Princeton Univ, AB, 60; Yale Univ, MA, 63. *Collections Arranged:* Synchromism and American Painting (auth, catalog), 65; Donald Judd (auth, catalog), 68; Modern American Painting: Toward a New Perspective (auth, catalog), 77; Patrick Henry Bruce (auth, catalog), 79; Morton Livingston Schamberg (auth, catalog), 82. *Pos:* Dir, Mus Fine Arts, Houston, 74-82; sr vis scholar, Arch Am Art, Smithsonian Inst, 83-85. *Mem:* Am Asn Mus. *Res:* Modern American and European art. *Publ:* Auth, Ralston Crawford, Twelve Trees Press, 83; auth, Herbert Ferber, Mus Fine Arts, Houston, 83. *Mailing Add:* 5 Dusenberry Rd Bronxville NY 10708

AGOOS, HERBERT M
COLLECTOR
b Boston, Mass, Dec 12, 15. *Study:* Harvard Col, AB; also fine arts mus course with Paul Sachs. *Collection:* 20th century modern art. *Mailing Add:* 21 Brown Cambridge MA 02138

AGOSTINI, PETER
SCULPTOR
b New York, NY, Feb 13, 13. *Study:* Leonardo da Vinci Sch Art, NY. *Work:* Mass Inst Technol; Univ Calif; Wadsworth Atheneum; Whitney Mus Am Art, Mus Mod Art, New York. *Exhib:* Whitney Mus Am Art, 64, 70 & 72; Sculpture of the 60's, Los Angeles, 67; Int Sculpture, Guggenheim Mus, 67 & Toronto, Ont, 68; Nat Inst Arts & Lett, 72; NY State Pavilion, World's Fair; and others. *Teaching:* Lectr & summer courses, Columbia Univ, 61-66; prof art, Univ NC, Greensboro, 66-; mem staff, Wagner Col, 68. *Awards:* Longview Found Purchase Awards, 60-62; Brandeis Univ Creative Arts Award, 64; Guggenheim Fel, 66. *Bibliog:* Article in Time Mag, 11/13/64. *Dealer:* Zabriskie Gallery 613 E 12th St New York NY 10009. *Mailing Add:* 151 Avenue B New York NY 10009

AHL, HENRY C
PAINTER, WRITER
b Springfield, Mass. *Study:* Harvard Col, with Arthur Pope & Martin Mower, AB; also with Henry Hammond Ahl. *Work:* Walker Gallery, Bowdoin Col; Farnsworth Mus, Rockland, Maine; Mus Art, Hickory, NC; Ga State Mus, Athens; Vanderpoel Art Collection, Beverly Hills-Chicago, Ill; plus others. *Pos:* Mem, Ctr for Study of Democratic Inst, Santa Barbara, Calif. *Mem:* Tommaso Camponella Int Acad Arts & Sci; NShore Arts Asn. *Media:* Oil. *Publ:* Auth & illusr, Dunes & Beaches of Essex County, Some Common Insects of Massachusetts, A Visit to Orchard House, A Visit to the Old Manse, Edgar Allan Poe; and others. *Mailing Add:* RFD Rowley MA 01969

AHLANDER, LESLIE JUDD
CRITIC, CURATOR
b New York, NY. *Study:* Acad Mod, Paris, with Fernand Leger; Pa Acad Fine Arts, with Henry MacCarter, dipl. *Collections Arranged:* Contemporary Religious Imagery (with catalog), 74; Syd Solomon (with catalog), 75; Continuing Surrealism (with catalog), 76; Latin Am Horizons (with catalog), 76; The Circus in Art (with catalog), 77. *Pos:* Asst to dir, Mus Mod Art, New York, 41-43; dir exhibs, US Off Educ, Washington, DC, 43-44; chief div visual arts, Pan Am Union, Washington, DC, 44-45; art critic, Washington Post, Washington, DC, 50-63; cur educ, Corcoran Gallery, Washington, DC, 69-70; From cur contemp art to dir educ, John & Mabel Ringling Mus Art, Sarasota, Fla, 71-82; art coordr, Dade Co, Miami, Fla, 76-83. *Awards:* Cresson Traveling Scholar, Pa Acad Fine Arts, Philadelphia, 38; Art Critics Award, Col Art Asn Am, 52. *Mem:* Am Asn Mus. *Publ:* Auth, Doris Leeper, 75. *Mailing Add:* 441 Cadagua Ave Coral Gables FL 33146

AHLGREN, ROY B
INSTRUCTOR, PRINTMAKER
b Erie, Pa. *Study:* Erie Tech Sch; Univ Pittsburgh, BS. *Work:* US Info Agency, Washington, DC; Minn Mus Art, St Paul; Seattle Art Mus, Wash; Tex Tech Univ Mus, Lubbock; Butler Art Inst, Youngstown, Ohio. *Comn:* Ed of serigraphs, Assoc Am Artists, New York, 70; edition serigraphs (54), WQLN, public TV station, 79; Int Art Guild, Santa Barbara, 74. *Exhib:* 21st Nat Exhib Prints, Libr Cong, Washington, DC, 69; Silvermine Guild of Artists Print Exhib, 76, 80 & 83; 8th Int Print Biennial, 80; Intergrafia, Katowice, Poland, 80; Int Exhib Graphic Art, Frechen, W Germany, 80; and others. *Pos:* Assoc, Galerie 8, Erie, 67-75; bd mem, Erie Art Ctr, 70-72. *Teaching:* Instr art, Tech Mem High Sch, Erie, 70-; asst prof printmaking, Edinboro State Col, 74. *Awards:* First Prize (graphics), 11th RI Arts Festival, Providence, 69; Purchase Award, Drawings, USA, Minn Mus Art, St Paul, 70 & 73; Merit Award, 4th Miami Int Graphic, Biennial, Miami, Fla, 80. *Bibliog:* Jane Abrams (auth), Educational slide collection, Univ NMex, 71; Lynwood Kreneck (auth), Colorprint USA filmstrip, Tex Tech Univ, 71; Joseph Cain (auth), Corpus Christi, Texas, Iman show, 73. *Mem:* Boston Printmakers; Philadelphia Print Club; Los Angeles Printmaking Soc; World Print Council, San Francisco, Calif; Northwest Pa Artists Asn; Erie Art Ctr. *Media:* Serigraphy. *Publ:* Contribr, Assoc Am Artists catalog, 71, Ferdinand-Roten catalog, 72. *Dealer:* Bentaman Gallerie Buffalo NY 14222; Peterson Fine Art Dallas TX 75225. *Mailing Add:* 1012 Boyer Rd Erie PA 16511

AHLSTROM, RONALD GUSTIN
COLLAGE ARTIST, PAINTER
b Chicago, Ill, Jan 17, 22. *Study:* Art Inst Chicago, BFA, with Paul Weighart; Univ Chicago; DePaul Univ. *Work:* Art Inst Chicago; Tacoma Art Mus, Wash; Philbrook Art Ctr, Tulsa; Blue Cross Collection, Chicago; Ill Bell Telephone. *Exhib:* 27th Corcoran Biennial, Washington, DC, 61; Chicago & Vicinity Exhib, Art Inst Chicago, 62; 12 Chicago Artists, McCormick Pl Gallery, 62; 50th Northwest Ann, Seattle Art Mus, 64; 6 American Artists, Touchstone Gallery, New York, 73; Zriny-Hayes Gallery, Chicago, 78. *Pos:* Asst Dir, McCormick Place Art Gallery, Chicago; dir, Tacoma Art Mus, Wash. *Awards:* Clyde Carr Prize, 55 & William H Bartels Prize, 58, Art Inst Chicago; Purchase Prize, 50th Northwest Ann, Ford Found, 64. *Bibliog:* Meilach & Ten Hoor (auth), Collage and found art, 64 & Collage, trends and technique, 73, Reinholt Publ; H Haydon (auth), article in Chicago Mag, New Chicago Found, 68; Gerald F Brommer (auth), The Art of Collage, Davis Publ, 78. *Media:* Collage & Acrylic (mixed media). *Dealer:* Zriny Galery 1963 N Halsted St Chicago IL 60614. *Mailing Add:* 121 W Park St Lombard IL 60148

AHN, DON C
PAINTER, DEALER
b Seoul, Korea, Jan 9, 37. *Study:* Art Students League; Miami Univ; Seoul Univ, BFA; Pratt Inst, MFA; NY Univ. *Work:* Mus Mod Art, New York; Dayton Mus Art, Ohio; Evansville Mus, Ind; C W Post Col, Long Island Univ. *Exhib:* Ohio Regional Show, Dayton, 63; one-man shows, Dayton Mus, 63 & Downey Mus, Los Angeles, 69; Int Print Biennale, Grenchen, Switz, 67 & Mus Mod Art, Tokyo, 71. *Pos:* Art dir, Korea Today, 61; dir, Ahn Tai Chi Studio, New York, 70-; adj instr, Dance Dept, Hunter Col, 74; dir, Lotus Gallery, New York, 74- *Teaching:* Instr print, C W Post Col, Long Island Univ, 64-68; asst prof painting, NY Inst Technol, 65-77; instr painting, Cooper Union, 66-71. *Awards:* First Prize for Painting, Ohio Regional Show, 63; McDowell Asn Fel, 64; First Prize for Print, E Coast Printer, Village Art Ctr, 64. *Bibliog:* John Canaday (auth), Drawings, New York Times, 12/11/71; Barbara Schwarts (auth), article, Art News, 12/71; Alvin Smith (auth), article, Art Int, 12/72. *Mem:* Col Art Asn Am. *Specialty:* Contemporary art done by minority Asian artists in the US. *Interests:* Promote arts which synthesize Western visual formality with Eastern spirituality. *Collection:* Indian; Far Eastern religious sculpture and painting; Chinese; Japanese; Korean; Tibetan; contemporary Asian artists in New York. *Mailing Add:* PO Box 301 Canal Sta New York NY 10013

AHRENDT, CHRISTINE
PAINTER
b Dayton, Ohio. *Study:* Fla State Univ; Ohio Univ; Provincetown Workshop, with Ben Shahn, Will Barnet, Victor Candell & Leo Manso. *Exhib:* Columbus Gallery Fine Arts, Ohio, 61-65, 69 & 70; Provincetown Art Asn Summer Shows, 62-72; Pa Acad Fine Arts, Philadelphia, 64; Butler Inst Am Art Midyear Show, Youngstown, Ohio, 65 & 74; one-man show, E Coast Gallery, Provincetown, 69; Salute the Women, Butler Inst Am Art, 75. *Awards:* Huntington Galleries Awards, WVa, 62-66; MacDowell Colony Fel, 65, 66 & 71; S M Levy Mem Award, Columbus Art League, 69. *Media:* Mixed. *Dealer:* Gallery 200 200 W Mound Columbus OH 43215. *Mailing Add:* 5 Old Peach Ridge Rd Athens OH 45701

AHRENS, KENT
MUSEUM DIRECTOR, HISTORIAN
b Martinsburg, WVa. *Study:* Dartmouth Col, AB, 61; Univ Md, MA, 66; Univ Del, PhD, 72. *Collections Arranged:* Watercolors and Drawings by Brevet Major General Truman Seymour, USMA 1846 (auth, catalog), US Military Acad, 74; Paintings from the Netherlands and German Speaking Countries, Wadsworth Atheneum, 78. *Pos:* Assoc cur paintings, Wadsworth Atheneum, 77-78; dir, Everhart Mus, 82- *Teaching:* Fac mem, Fla State Univ, 71-74 & Georgetown Univ, 79-82; fac mem & cur, Randolph-Macon Womans Col, 74-77. *Res:* American art. *Publ:* Auth, The portraits by Robert W Weir, 74 & ... Henry R Newman (1843-1917), 76, Am Art J; auth, Constantino Brumidi's Apotheosis of Washington ..., Rec Columbia Hist Soc, 76; auth, American paintings before 1900 at the Wadsworth Atheneum, Antiques, 78; auth, Jennie Brownscombe ..., Womans Art J, 81. *Mailing Add:* Everhart Mus Nay Aug Park Scranton PA 18510

AHVAKANA, ULAAQ (LAWRENCE REYNOLD)
SCULPTOR, GLASS BLOWER
b Fairbanks, Alaska, July 8, 46. *Study:* Inst Am Indian Arts, Santa Fe, sculpture with Allen Houser, 66-69; Cooper Union Sch Art, New York, 69-70; RI Sch Design, BFA(sculpture/glass). *Work:* Anchorage Hist & Fine Arts Mus; Port Authority Bldg, New York; Atlantic Richfield Corp, Anchorage; Visual Art Ctr Alaska. *Comn:* Wolf Dancer (welded steel sculpture), Inst Am Indian Arts, 69; Dancers (welded steel wall relief), Alaska State Ct Bldg, 74; Seal Smooth (welded steel sculpture), Calista Corp, Settlers Bay Lodge, Wassilla, Alaska, 76; dedication plaque, 77 & bronze sculpture, 80, NSlope Borouth, Barrow, Alaska. *Exhib:* Am Art Show, Brooklyn Mus, 71; Squash Blossom Gallery, Vail, Colo, 80; Sister-Brother Show, Artique, Anchorage, Alaska, 81; Sacred Circle Gallery Am Indian Arts, 81; Inst Am Indian Arts, NMex, 81; Santa Fe Festival Arts, Sweeny Convention Ctr, NMex, 81; and many others. *Collections Arranged:* Survival/Life & Art of the Alaskan Eskimo, Newark Mus, NJ, Am Fedn Arts, New York & Bowers Mus, Santa Ana, Calif. *Teaching:* Artist in residence/glass blowing & sculpture, Community of Barrow, 72-74; artist in residence/sculpture, Visual Art Ctr Alaska, 75-77; instr sculpture & glass, Inst Am Indian Arts, Santa Fe, NMex, 77-80; instr, Pratt Art Ctr, 80. *Awards:* Earth, Fire & Fiber Show Award in Glass, Anchorage Hist & Fine Arts Mus, 74; First in Wood, All-Alaska Juried Art Show, 76; First in Sculpture, Native Arts Invitational, Chevron Corp, 77. *Mem:* Visual Art Ctr Alaska; Raven's Bones Found (pres, 77-). *Media:* Multimedia. *Publ:* Illusr, New World J, Turtle Island Found, Vol 1, No 2 & 3, 77. *Dealer:* Von Grabill Gallery 6166 N Scottsdale Rd Scottsdale AZ. *Mailing Add:* Inst of Am Indian Arts 1300 Cerrillos Rd Santa Fe NM 87501

AHYSEN, HARRY JOSEPH
PAINTER, EDUCATOR
b Port Arthur, Tex, Sept 6, 28. *Study:* Tulane Univ; Univ Houston, BFA, 55; Univ Tex, Austin, MA, 62. *Work:* Gulf Oil Corp, Dallas; M Grumbacher, New York; Jacques Cousteau Mus, Monte Carlo, Monaco; Univ Houston; over 150 pvt collections. *Comn:* Painting, Sen Kent Caperton, Bryan-College Station, 82; three covers, Alumni Mag, Sam Houston State Univ, 83; design for mace, Sam Houston State Univ, 83; fifteen paintings & watercolors, Bankers' Land Co & MacArthur Found, West Palm Beach, Fla, 83; watercolor sketches, Bankers' Land Group & Frankel Group Boca Raton, Jupiter Island, Fla, 83. *Exhib:* First Nat Bank, Huntsville, 82; Odessa Oil Field Show, 82; All State Artists Show, Senate Chambers, Austin, 82; Tex Artists Mus Soc, Port Arthur, 82; Brazos Valley Art League Show, Bryan, 83; and

others. *Teaching:* From asst prof to prof oil painting, Sam Houston State Univ, 63- *Awards:* State Artist of Tex, State Legislature, 80-81; First Place Watercolor, 11th Int Show Brownsville Art League Mus, 82; Hon Mention, Brazos Valley Art Asn Show, Bryan, 83. *Media:* Oil, Watercolor. *Publ:* Auth, Sketch Workbook: Landscape and Seascape Devices, Kendall Hunt Publ, 78; auth, article, Palette Talk, No 52. *Mailing Add:* Dept of Art Sam Houston State Univ Huntsville TX 77340

AIDLIN, JEROME
SCULPTOR, INSTRUCTOR
b Cleveland, Ohio, Aug 6, 35. *Study:* Cleveland Inst Art, dipl indust design, BFA(sculpture); Carnegie-Mellon Univ; also with William McVey. *Work:* Cleveland Art Asn. *Comn:* Concrete wall relief, Methodist Hq Bldg, Honolulu, Hawaii; copper wall relief, Cafeteria Bldg, Univ Hawaii, Honolulu, 65; stainless steel relief, Sherwood Refractories, Inc, Cleveland, 68; forged steel sculpture, Ohio Nat Plaza Bldg, Columbus, 76. *Exhib:* Ceramics & Sculpture Ann, Butler Mus Am Art, Youngstown, Ohio, 62; Young American Craftsmen, Mus Contemp Crafts, NY, 63; Artists of Hawaii Ann, Honolulu Acad Art, 63-65; May Show Ann, Cleveland Mus Art, 62, 66, 67 & 72-74; one-man show, Cleveland Inst Art, 75; two-artist show, Sch Fine Arts, Willoughby, Ohio, 80. *Pos:* Staff indust designer, Peter Muller-Munk Assoc, Pittsburgh, 57-60. *Teaching:* Chmn sculpture dept, Univ Hawaii, 62-65; instr sculpture, Cleveland Inst Art, 65-, chmn dept, 71- *Awards:* Wishing Well Purchase, May Show, Cleveland Mus Art, 66. *Bibliog:* Helen Cullinan (auth), Poetic conclusions in metal, Cleveland Plain Dealer, 75; David Parkinson, Jr (auth), Aidlin's sculpture, Sun Press, 75. *Media:* Forged Steel, Copper; Cast Bronze, Aluminum. *Mailing Add:* 11141 East Blvd Cleveland OH 44106

AIGNER, LUCIEN
PHOTOGRAPHER, LECTURER
b Nove Zamky, Czech, Sept 14, 01; US citizen. *Study:* Univ Berlin, 20; Univ Budapest, 23; Sorbonne, 30; Columbia Univ, dipl, 45; Winona Sch Photog, cert, 56; NY Univ, dipl(movie making), 68; Prof Photogr Am, Hon MA(photog), 71. *Work:* Metrop Mus Art, New York; Int Mus Photog, Rochester, NY; Libr Cong; Bibliot Nat, Paris; Mus Mod Art, Stockholm. *Comn:* Einstein Mural, Smithsonian Inst, 79. *Exhib:* Forty Years of Candid Camera, Prof Photogr Am Convention, Denver, 79; Paris des annees 30s, Carnavalet, Paris, 81; Glimpses of History from Two Worlds, Addison Gallery Am Art, 82; Glimpses of History, Nagase Photo Salon, Tokyo, 82; solo exhib, Mus Mod Art, Stockholm, 82; retrospective, Nat Gallery, Budapest, 82; and many others. *Awards:* Leica Award, Third Ann Leica Show, 36; New York Art Directors Award, 41; First Prizes & Courts Hon, Prof Photog Asns New England & Conn, 58-76. *Bibliog:* Gene Thorton (auth), Remembrance of Paris past, New York Times, 80. *Mem:* Life mem Prof Photogr Am. *Publ:* Coauth, Are We to Disarm, Art Suisse, 32; illusr, What Prayers Can Do, Doubleday, 53; coauth, Windows of Heaven, Harper Brothers, 54. *Mailing Add:* 15 Desser Ave Great Barrington MA 01230

AIKEN, WILLIAM A
PAINTER
b Pittsburgh, Pa, May 26, 34. *Study:* Carnegie-Mellon Univ, BFA, 55. *Work:* City of San Francisco & Embarcadero Ctr, Calif; Carnegie Mellon Univ; Am Broadcasting Co, DC; Univ Santa Clara, Calif. *Comn:* Oil painting, Shaklee Corp, Emeryville, Calif, 74. *Exhib:* Paintings, USA, Mus Mod Art, New York, 61; Allied Artists Am, Nat Acad, New York, 74, 80 & 82, 39th Ann Midyear Show, Butler Inst Am Art, Youngstown, Ohio, 75; Sun Carnival Nat Art Exhib, El Paso Mus Art, Tex, 77; one-man show, San Francisco Art Comn Gallery, 78; The New Realists, Mongerson Gallery, Chicago, 82; Nature Interpreted, Cincinnati Mus Nat Hist, 82; and others. *Awards:* Purchase Awards, City of San Francisco, 61, 63 & 78 & Univ Santa Clara, 67; One-Man Show Award, San Francisco Art Comn, 78; Charles F Romans Award for Oil Painting, Allied Artists Am Ann Exhib, 80. *Bibliog:* Paul Perry (auth), View from the Rorshach Canvas, Southwest Art, 12/77. *Media:* Oil Paint; Oil Glaze. *Dealer:* Austin Gallery 7103 Main St Scottsdale AZ 85251; Galerie Bateau 5821 Collage Ave Oakland CA 94618. *Mailing Add:* 1587 35th Ave San Francisco CA 94122

AIRD, NEIL CARRICK
GOLDSMITH, DESIGNER
b Dumbarton, Scotland, Mar 13, 45; Can citizen. *Study:* Glasgow Sch Art, Scotland, DA(jewelry & silversmithing), 68. *Work:* Contemp Can Crafts Collection, Ont Crafts Coun. *Exhib:* Contemp Ont Crafts, Agnes Etherington Art Ctr, Queen's Univ, 76; Ont Crafts 77, Toronto-Dom Ctr, Toronto, Ont, 77; The Crafts Gallery, Toronto, 77; Can Nat Exhib, Toronto, Ont, 77; East Meets West, Vancouver, 81; Objets de Metaux Precieux, Montreal, 82; and others. *Collections Arranged:* Contemp Can Crafts, Ont Crafts Coun, 75-78; Contemp Ont Craftsmen, Agnes Etherington Art Ctr, Queen's Univ, 76-77; Artisan 78 Traveling Exhib, Can Crafts Coun, 78-80. *Pos:* Exec mem, Gallery Asn, Queen's Univ, 70-73; pvt dir crafts, Kingston Arts Coun, 72-74; exec, Crafts Collaborative, 81- *Teaching:* Master metal arts, St Lawrence Col, Kingston, Ont, 70- *Awards:* Diamonds Int Award, Int Exhib, De Beers, 67; Lipman Co Award, Medium is Metal Exhib, 76; Ont Crafts Coun Award, Ont Crafts 77 Exhib, 77. *Bibliog:* Himel & Lambert (auths), Handmade in Ontario, Van Nostrand Reinhold, 76; Anthony Ibbotson (auth), Profile--Neil Carrick Aird, Crafts Can, 2-3/77; Eva Douglas (auth), Humanism in a designer-goldsmith, Craftsman Mag, 6/79. *Mem:* Assoc mem Soc NAm Goldsmiths; Metal Arts Guild; Ont Crafts Coun; Can Crafts Coun; World Crafts Coun. *Media:* Miscellaneous. *Mailing Add:* 352 King St E Kingston ON K7L 3B6 Canada

AJAY, ABE
PAINTER, SCULPTOR
b Altoona, Pa, Mar 24, 19. *Study:* Art Student's League; Am Artists Sch. *Work:* Solomon R Guggenheim Mus, New York; Hirshhorn Mus, Washington, DC; Roy R Neuberger Mus, State Univ NY Col at Purchase; Pa Acad of the Fine Arts, Philadelphia; Johnson Mus of Art, Cornell Univ. *Comn:* Sculpture edition of 300, J Walter Thompson Co, New York, 68. *Exhib:* White on White, De Cordova Mus, Lincoln, Mass, 65; Pa Acad of Fine Arts Ann, Philadelphia, 68; Flint Inst of Art, 69; A Plastic Presence, Jewish Mus, New York, Milwaukee Art Ctr & San Francisco Mus of Art, 69; Storm King Art Ctr, Mountainville, NY, 72; Roy R Neuberger Mus, 74; Elaine Benson Gallery, Bridgehampton, NY, 78; and others. *Teaching:* Vis artist painting, Univ Minn, Duluth, 69-70; prof visual arts, State Univ NY, Purchase, 73- *Bibliog:* Irving Sandler (auth), The Poetic Constructivism of Abe Ajay, Arts Mag, 77; Burt Chernow (auth), Abe Ajay, Arts Mag, 12/78; Cathy Silver (auth), Abe Ajay, Arts Mag, 5/82. *Media:* Acrylic; Plaster, Wood. *Publ:* Auth, The prize, 71, Working for the WPA, 72 & Rev of the New Deal art projects & Art for the millions, by Francis V O'Connor, 72, Art Am. *Mailing Add:* Walnut Hill Rd Bethel CT 06801

AKAMU, NINA (NINA AKAMU SHEPPARD)
SCULPTOR
b Midwest City, Okla, July 11, 55. *Study:* Md Inst Col Art, BFA, 76. *Comn:* Bas relief (bronze), Soc Prevention of Cruelty to Animals, Washington DC, 80. *Exhib:* Game Conserv Int, San Antonio Conserv Ctr, Tex, 80; Ann Soc Animal Artists, New York, 81-83; Allied Artists Am, 82 & 83; Nat Acad, New York, 82; Nat Sculpture Soc Ann, New York, 82 & 83. *Awards:* Allied Artists Am Mem Award, 82; Joel Meisner Foundry Award, Pen & Brush, 83; Joyce & Elliot Liskin Purchase Award, Nat Sculpture Soc, 83. *Mem:* Soc Animal Artists; Nat Sculpture Soc. *Media:* Terra-cotta Clay, Bronze. *Dealer:* Grand Central Art Galleries 24 W 57th St New York NY 10019; Jerry Gildens Gallery Baltimore MD. *Mailing Add:* PO Box 276 Camden DE 19934

AKAWIE, THOMAS FRANK
EDUCATOR, PAINTER
b New York, NY, Feb 22, 35. *Study:* Los Angeles City Col, 53-56; Univ Calif, Berkeley, BA(art hist), 59, MA(painting), 63. *Work:* Milwaukee Art Ctr, Wis; Ithaca Col Art Mus, NY; Oakland Mus, Calif; Williams Col Mus, Williamstown, Mass. *Exhib:* One-man shows, La Jolla Mus Art, Calif, 67; Calif Palace Legion Hon, San Francisco, 72 & San Jose Mus Art, Calif, 77; Ann Exhib, Whitney Mus Am Art, New York, 69; Painting & Sculpture in Calif, San Francisco Mus Mod Art, 76 & Nat Collection Fine Arts, Smithsonian Inst, Washington, DC, 77; 4th Triennale-India 78 Inc, Thailand & Iran, 78; Calif Visionary Painting, Japan, 78; and others. *Teaching:* Asst prof painting & drawing, Univ Calif, Los Angeles, 65-66; instr spray-painting & drawing, San Francisco Art Inst, 66-; lectr painting & drawing, Univ Calif, Berkeley, 72-73. *Awards:* Los Angeles All-City Exhib Award, City of Los Angeles, Calif, 65; First Prize, Ann Downey Mus Invitational, Calif, 66; First Prize, Jack London Art Exhib, Oakland, Calif, 69. *Bibliog:* Charles Shere & John Coney (auths), Art of Tom Akawie, KQED-TV, 71. *Media:* Acrylic. *Publ:* Contribr, Visions, Pomegranate Publ, 77. *Dealer:* Gallery K 2032 P St NW Washington DC 20036. *Mailing Add:* 1740 University Ave Berkeley CA 94703

AKERS, GARY
PAINTER
b Pikeville, Ky, Feb 22, 51. *Study:* Morehead State Univ, BA, 72, MA, 74. *Work:* Boone Co Pub Libr & Art Gallery & Booth Hosp, Florence, Ky; Jenny Wiley State Park, Prestonsburg, Ky. *Comn:* Seltman Home, Florence, Ky, 78; Boone Co Exten Agent 4-H, Burlington, Ky, 80; Betsy Layne Boosters Club, Ky, 81; White Elephant Gallery, Flemingsburg, Ky, 82. *Exhib:* Ky Watercolor Soc, 78, 82 & 83; Southern Watercolor Soc, 79 & 83; Am Watercolor Soc, Nat Acad Galleries, New York, 79 & 82; Springfield Art Asn, Ill, 80; Allied Artists Am, Nat Arts Club, New York, 81 & 82. *Awards:* Friends Ky Watercolor Soc Award, 78; Dale Meyers Cooper Medal Honor, Southern Watercolor Soc Award, 83; Top Merit Award, Aqueous, Ky Watercolor Soc, 83. *Bibliog:* Jan Thompson (auth), Gary Akers: Artist, Channel 9 Cincinnati, 81; Bill R Booth (auth), Painting: Border brothers farm, Am Artist, 82 & Pages from a passing scene, Southwest Art, 82. *Mem:* Ky Watercolor Soc (regional dir, 80-); Southern Watercolor Soc. *Media:* Egg Tempera, Watercolor. *Publ:* Illusr, Hancock 29: Pictorial heritage of Hancock County, Ky Images, 78; illusr, The Liquitex Acrylic Color Chart and Mixing Guide, Binney & Smith, 82. *Dealer:* Gary-Lynn Galleries 8165 Mall Rd Florence KY 41042. *Mailing Add:* PO Box 100 Union KY 41091

AKSTON, JAMES
COLLECTOR, PATRON
b Warsaw, Poland; US citizen. *Study:* Sch Foreign Serv, Georgetown Univ. *Exhib:* One-man exhibs, Corcoran Gallery Art, Washington DC, 72, Bodley Gallery, New York, 76 & Kunst-Atelier 63, Klosters, Switzerland, 76; Monumental Bronzes & Tapestries, Norton Gallery & Sch Art, West Palm Beach, Fla, 82; Phantasmic Impulses, Boca Raton Ctr Arts, Fla, 82; and others. *Pos:* Pres, Arts Mag, New York; pres-founder, Art Voices, S Mag & Art Digest Newsletter, West Palm Beach, Fla; mem bd, Creative Arts Comn, Brandeis Univ, Waltham, Mass; exec chmn, Palm Beach Sponsors Comt, Fla; trustee, Mus of African Art, Washington, DC; mem bd dirs, Norton Gallery & Sch Art, West Palm Beach, Fla; regent, Georgetown Univ. *Awards:* Grant to Whitney Mus Art, Int Exhibs Found; Grant to Mus Modern Art, New York; and others. *Mem:* Life mem Metrop Mus of Art, New York; life mem Soc of the Four Arts, Palm Beach, Fla; life mem Henry Morrison Flagler Mus,

Palm Beach, Fla. *Collection:* Contemporary American, Italian and Spanish paintings, sculptures and tapestries; outdoor sculpture by international artists. *Publ:* Auth, Beginning of the Beginning, Harry Abrams Inc. *Mailing Add:* 444 N Lake Way Palm Beach FL 33480

ALAJALOV, CONSTANTIN
PAINTER, ILLUSTRATOR
b Russia, Nov 18, 1900; US citizen. *Study:* Univ Petrograd. *Work:* Brooklyn Mus; Philadelphia Mus Art; Mus Mod Art, New York; Mus City of New York; Dallas Mus Fine Arts, Tex; and others. *Comn:* Murals for SS America; The Hands of Leonard Bernstein, 67; sets for Michael Mordkin's Ballet & posters for many theatrical productions; portraits, Duke & Duchess Windsor, Mrs Vincent Astor, Countess Bismark and many others. *Exhib:* Many nat exhibs; one-man shows, Hollywood, Calif, New York, Dallas & Wichita, Kans. *Teaching:* Prof art, Phoenix Art Inst & Archipenko's Ecole Beaux-Arts. *Bibliog:* Janet Flanner (auth), Conversation Pieces, Esquire, 1/41 & Am Artist, 12/42. *Publ:* Illusr, George Gershwin's Song Book, Alice Duer Miller's Cinderella, Out Hearts Were Young & Gay, Nuts in May, Bottoms Up & others; contribr to many nat mag. *Mailing Add:* 140 W 57th St New York NY 10019

ALAUPOVIC, ALEXANDRA V
SCULPTOR, EDUCATOR
b Slatina, Yugoslavia, Dec 21, 21; US citizen. *Study:* Acad Visual Arts, Univ Zagreb, cert(sculpture & teaching), 48; Acad Visual Arts, Prague, 49; Univ Ill, Urbana-Champaign, 59-60; Univ Okla, MFA, 66. *Work:* Univ Okla Mus Art, Norman; Okla State Art Col; Continental Fed Savings & Loan, Okla Art Ctr, Oklahoma City. *Comn:* Sculptures, Oklahoma City Libr, 62, Okla Med Res Found, 64 & First Unitarian Church, Oklahoma City, 64; busts & pub sculpture, Mercy Health Ctr & Casady Sch, Oklahoma City, 74; sculpture, Okla Univ, Sam Viersen Gym Ctr, Norman, 82. *Exhib:* Exposition Asn Peintres, Graveurs et Sculpteurs de Croatie, Dubrovnik, Yugoslavia, 56; 35th Ann Springfield Art Mus, Mo, 65; On Music, Univ Okla Mus Art, 68; Salon des Nations, Paris, 83; Gallery II, Charlottesville, Va, 83; and others. *Teaching:* Instr drawing, basic form & sculpture, Univ Okla, 64-66; instr sculpture, Okla Sci & Arts Found, Oklahoma City, 69-75; assoc prof, Oklahoma City Univ, 72-77. *Awards:* Jacobson Award, Univ Okla, 64; First Sculpture Award, Seventh Ann Temple Emanuel Brother, Dallas, 69 & Philbrook Art Ctr, Tulsa, 70. *Mem:* Int Sculpture Ctr. *Media:* Marble, Metals. *Dealer:* Sales & Rental Gallery Oklahoma Art Ctr 3113 Pershing Blvd Oklahoma City OK 73107. *Mailing Add:* 11908 N Bryant Rte 1 Box 167A Oklahoma City OK 73111

ALBERGA, ALTA W
ETCHER, PAINTER
b Tuscaloosa, Ala. *Study:* Univ Wichita (Wichita State), Kans, AB, AM; Wash Univ, St Louis, BFA; Univ Ill, Urbana-Champaign, MFA; Art Students League, with Morris Kantor & Robert Beverly Hale. *Work:* Little Gallery, Wichita State Univ; Univ Ill, Champaign; SC Arts Commission. *Comn:* Print, Columbia Mus Art, SC, 73; painting, Daniel Int (Construct) Inc, Greenville, SC, 75; American Spinning, Greenville, SC, 78. *Exhib:* SC Artists Guild, Gibbs Gallery, Charleston, 73 & 79; Southeastern Ctr Contemp Art, Winston-Salem, SC, 75; Greenville Artists Guild, Greenville Mus Art, SC, 75, 79 & 81 & Falls Cottage Gallery, 80-81; Pickens Mus Art, 79; Interart, Washington, DC, 81. *Teaching:* Instr art hist & drawing, Wichita State Univ, 54-55; instr design, Webster Col, St Louis, 55-61; head visual arts, Presby Col, Clinton, SC, 69-75; lectr, Tri-county Tech Col, Pendleton, SC, 75-; instr, drawing & oil painting, Tempo Gallery & Greenville Co Mus Art, currently. *Awards:* Richard K Weil Award, City Mus of St Louis, 57; St Louis Artists' Ann Guild, 60; Purchase Prize, print, Columbia Mus, SC, 71. *Mem:* Artists Equity Asn (pres, St Louis Chap, 61); Art Students League; Southeastern Col Art Conf; Guild SC Artists; Greenville Artists Guild (pres, 84-85). *Media:* Oil, Acrylic; Intaglio. *Res:* Modern art history. *Publ:* Auth, Book reviews for Southeastern Col Art Conf publ, 73. *Dealer:* Garden Gallery Hwy 70 W Raleigh NC 27603; Second St Gallery Philadelphia PA. *Mailing Add:* 11 Overton Dr Greenville SC 29609

ALBERS, ANNI
DESIGNER, GRAPHIC ARTIST
b Berlin, Ger, June 12, 1899; US citizen. *Study:* Bauhaus, Weimar & Dessau, Ger, dipl; Md Col Art, Hon Dr, 72; York Univ, Toronto, Hon Dr, 73; Philadelphia Col Art, Hon Dr, 76; Univ Hartford, Hon Dr, 78. *Work:* Metrop Mus Art & Mus Mod Art, New York; Bauhaus Archives, Berlin; Art Inst Chicago; and others. *Comn:* Mem to Nazi victims, comn by List Family for Jewish Mus; Ark Curtain, Dallas & Woonsocket, RI. *Exhib:* Mus Mod Art, New York; Brooklyn Mus; Katonah Gallery, NY; Univ Hartford Art Sch; Queens Col Libr, NY; Monmouth Mus, NJ; Univ Calif, Riverside; and others. *Teaching:* Asst prof art, Black Mountain Col, 33-49; lectr, leading univs & mus. *Awards:* Citation, Philadelphia Col Art, 62; Tamarind Lithography Workshop Fel, Los Angeles, 64; Gold Medal, Am Craft Coun, 81. *Media:* Textile. *Publ:* Auth, Anni Albers: On Designing, Wesleyan Univ Press, 62 & 71; Anni Albers: On Weaving, Wesleyan Univ Press, 65 & 72; Anni Albers: Pre-Columbian Mexican Miniatures, Praeger, 70. *Mailing Add:* 808 Birchwood Dr Orange CT 06477

ALBERT, CALVIN
SCULPTOR, EDUCATOR
b Grand Rapids, Mich, Nov 19, 18. *Study:* Grand Rapids Art Gallery, with Otto Karl Bach; Art Inst Chicago; Inst Design, with Moholy-Nagy & Gyorgy Kepes; Archipenko Sch Sculpture. *Work:* Metrop Mus, Whitney Mus Am Art & Jewish Mus, New York; Art Inst Chicago; Detroit Inst Arts. *Comn:* Ark

Doors & Candelabra, Steinberg House, Park Ave Synagogue, New York, 54; Outdoor Candelabra, Temple Israel, Tulsa, Okla, 55; Crucifix, Tabernacle & Candlesticks, St Paul's Church, Peoria, Ill, 59; Facade Relief, Congregation Emanuel, Grand Rapids, 74. *Exhib:* Unknown Political Prisoner Prizewinners, Mus Mod Art, New York & Tate Gallery, London, 53; le Dessin Contemporains aux Etats Unis, Musee Nat d'Arte Moderne, Paris, 54; Whitney Ann Am Artists, 54-68; Univ Ill Contemp Painting & Sculpture, 57 & 65; 20th Century Masters of Drawing, Mus Mod Art, New York, 64; Phoenix Gallery, 82 & Ingber Gallery, 83; and others. *Teaching:* Instr sculpture & design, Inst Design, Chicago, 42-46; instr color & drawing, Brooklyn Col, 47-49; prof art & head grad sculpture prog, Pratt Inst, 49- *Awards:* Guggenheim Fel 66; Nat Inst Arts & Lett Award, 75; Award, Nat Acad Design, 81. *Media:* Bronze, Terra Cotta. *Publ:* Coauth, Figure drawing comes to life, 57. *Mailing Add:* 325 W 16th St New York NY 10011

ALBERTAZZI, MARIO
PAINTER, CRITIC
b Bologna, Italy, Dec 9, 20. *Study:* Instituto Tecnico, Bologna, Italy; Art Student League, New York. *Work:* Italian Consulate General & Casa Italiana, Columbia Univ, New York. *Exhib:* Galerie Internationale, 68; Ligoa Duncan Gallery, 69; New York Pub Libr, 69; Caravan House Galleries, 70; Pacem in Terris Gallery, New York, 71. *Pos:* Art ed, Il Progresso Italo-Americano, New York, 64-; corresp, Piccolo Trieste, Liberta, Piacenza, 70- *Awards:* First Prize Collage, Composers, Authors & Artists Am Nat Contest, 69. *Mem:* Composers Authors & Artists Am; Burr Artists. *Media:* Oil, Collage. *Mailing Add:* 545 W End Ave New York NY 10024

ALBIN, EDGAR A
EDUCATOR, CRITIC
b Columbus, Kans, Dec 17, 08. *Study:* Univ Tulsa, BA; State Univ Iowa, MA; Ariz State Univ; also with Grant Wood, Philip Guston, Donald Mattison & Mauricio Lasansky; Fulbright res grant, India, 54-55. *Work:* Little Rock Mus Fine Arts, Ark. *Exhib:* 14th Int Exhib of Northwest Printmakers, Seattle, 42; Mid-Western Artists, Nelson Galleries, Kansas City, 42; Southern Printmakers Circulating Exhib, 42; Tex State Art Asn Int, Elizabeth Ney Galleries, Austin, 43; one-man show, Thayer Mus, Univ Kans, 44. *Pos:* Pres, Mo Col Art Asn; mem sem Am insts & cult, Tata Inst, Bangalore, India, 55; auth weekly arts column, Leader & Press, Springfield, Mo, 71-; contrib ed, Art Forum, Kansas City Artists Coalition, 77-79. *Teaching:* Instr art & humanities, Tulsa Pub Schs, Okla, 31-39; assoc prof art hist & studio, Univ Tulsa, 39-47; prof art hist, Univ Ark, 47-62; vis prof, Stetson Univ, 50-52; prof & head dept art, Southwest Mo State Univ, 62-74, emer prof, 74- *Awards:* Drury Col Award for Excellence in The Arts, 79. *Mem:* Am Asn Univ Prof; hon Am Inst Architects; Delta Phi Delta. *Res:* Asian art and art of the 20th century. *Publ:* Auth, Al Allen, Painter, 5/79, Let's Paint Indian, 9/79 & Edward C Bernstein, 11/79, Art Voices/South; auth, Jayme Burchett and Roger K Thomason, Fibres, Artcraft, 12/79; and others. *Mailing Add:* 1332 S Rogers St Springfield MO 65804

ALBRECHT, MARY DICKSON
SCULPTOR, DESIGNER
b Dothan, Ala, June 4, 30. *Study:* Univ Houston; Tex Woman's Univ, BS(sculpture, with hons), 70. *Work:* Okla Art Ctr Mus, Oklahoma City; City Dallas Park & Recreation Dept, Tex. *Exhib:* 13th Nat Exhib Prints & Drawings, Okla Art Ctr, 71; 15th Tex Crafts Exhib, Dallas Mus Fine Arts, 71; Tex Fine Arts Asn State Citation Show, 72, 75 & 76 & 61st Ann Nat Exhib, 72, Laguna Gloria Mus, Austin; 14th Midwest Biennial, Joslyn Art Mus, Omaha, Nebr, 76; Tenth Nat Drawing & Small Sculpture Show, Del Mar Col, Corpus Christi, Tex, 76. *Teaching:* Sculpture classes, Dallas, Tex, currently. *Awards:* Juror's choice & circuit merit awards, Tex Fine Arts Asn State Citation Show, 71, 72 & 76; Purchase Award, Univ Tex, Arlington, 72. *Media:* Steel, Bronze. *Mailing Add:* PO Box 25026 Dallas TX 75225

ALBRIGHT, MALVIN MARR
PAINTER, SCULPTOR
b Chicago, Ill, Feb 20, 1897. *Study:* Univ Ill; Art Inst Chicago; Pa Acad Fine Arts. *Work:* Corcoran Gallery Art; Toledo Mus Art; Butler Inst Am Art; Libr Cong; Pa Acad Fine Arts; and others. *Exhib:* Nat Acad Design; Whitney Mus Am Art; Mus Mod Art; Pa Acad Fine Arts; Carnegie Inst; plus others. *Awards:* Altman Prize, Nat Acad Design, 42 & 62, Palmer Mem Prize; Corcoran Silver Medal, Washington, DC; Dana Medal, Pa Acad Fine Arts, 65; and others. *Mem:* Nat Acad Design; fel Royal Soc Arts; Int Inst Arts & Lett; Nat Sculpture Soc; fel Pa Acad Fine Arts; and others. *Mailing Add:* 1500 N Lake Shore Dr Chicago IL 60610

ALBRIGHT, THOMAS
CRITIC, WRITER
b Oakland, Calif, June 10, 35. *Study:* Univ Calif, Berkeley, BA. *Pos:* Art critic, San Francisco Chronicle, 66-; contrib ed, Visuals, Rolling Stone, San Francisco, 68-; San Francisco ed, Art Gallery, Ivoryton, Conn, 70-; San Francisco corresp, Art News, 74- *Publ:* Auth, San Francisco Rolling Renaissance (catalog), 68; auth, articles in New York Times, 69. *Mailing Add:* Art Gallery Main St Drawer B Ivoryton CT 06442

ALBUQUERQUE, LITA
PAINTER
b Santa Monica, Calif, Jan 3, 46. *Study:* Univ Calif, Los Angeles, BFA, 68; Otis Art Inst, 71. *Work:* Newport Harbor Art Mus, Newport Beach, Calif; Assoc Tel & Tel, Chicago; Los Angeles Co Mus Art, Security Pac Bank, Arco Corp, Los Angeles. *Exhib:* Mus Mod Art, New York, 76; Aesthetics of Graffiti, San Francisco Mus of Mod Art, 78; Change West, Los Angeles Co

Mus Art, 78; Marianne Jism Gallery, Chicago, Ill, 80; Diane Brown Gallery, Washington, DC, 80; Int Sculpture Conf, Washington, DC, 80; Directions, Hirshhorn Mus, Washington, DC, 81; Robin Cronin Inc, Houston, Tex, 82; and many other group & one-man shows. *Pos:* Gallery dir, Gallery 707, Los Angeles, Calif, 73-75; cur, Cedars-Sinai Med Ctr Exhib Comt, Los Angeles, 76-77. *Teaching:* Lectr painting & drawing, Calif State Univ, Los Angeles, 75-77; vis artist painting & drawing, Univ Calif, Santa Barbara, 77-78, Art Ctr Col Design, 79-80, Claremont Grad Sch, 80 & Univ Calif, Irvine, 80. *Awards:* Individual Artist Fel Grant, Nat Endowment Arts, 75. *Bibliog:* Carrie Rickey (auth), Curatorial conceptions, the Hirshhorn: Danger curves ahead, Artforum, 4/81; Grace Glueck (auth), How emerging artists really emerge: Putting the biennials together, Art News, 5/81; Jo Ann Lewis (auth), The new of the best, but the best of the new?, Art News, 5/81. *Dealer:* Janus Gallery 8000 Melrose Ave Los Angeles CA. *Mailing Add:* 1670 Sawtelle Blvd Los Angeles CA 90025

ALCALAY, ALBERT S
PAINTER, LECTURER
b Paris, France, Aug 11, 17; US citizen. *Study:* Studied in Paris, France & Rome, Italy. *Work:* Fogg Mus, Harvard Univ; De Cordova & Dana Mus; Mus Mod Art; Boston Mus Fine Arts; Rome Mus Mod Art; and others. *Exhib:* Mus Mod Art, 55; Whitney Mus Am Art, 56, 58 & 60; Inst Contemp Art, Boston, 60; Pa Acad Fine Arts, 60; 44 one-man shows, De Cordova Mus, Lincoln, Mass; Retrospective, Carpenter Ctr, Harvard Univ, 82; and others. *Teaching:* Lectr design, Carpenter Ctr, Harvard Univ, 59- *Awards:* Guggenheim Fel, 59-60; prize, Boston Art Festival, 60. *Media:* Gouche and Pen & Ink on Rice Paper; Oil, Plexiglas. *Mailing Add:* 66 Powell Brookline MA 02146

ALCOPLEY, L
PAINTER, GRAPHIC ARTIST
b Ger, June 19, 10; US citizen. *Study:* In Dresden, Ger. *Work:* Mus Mod Art, New York; Mus Mod Art, Tokyo; Stedelijk Mus, Amsterdam; Israel Mus, Jerusalem; Nat Gallery Iceland, Reykjavik; and many others. *Comn:* Mural, Univ Freiburg, Fed Repub Ger, 58. *Exhib:* One-man shows, Suermondt Mus, Aachen, WGer, 57 & Stedelijk Mus, 61; Byron Gallery, New York, 64; Israel Mus, 69-70; Retrospective 1944-1977, Kjarvalsstadir, Munic Art Gallery, Reykjavik, Iceland; also many others. *Pos:* Co-ed, Leonardo, Int J Contemp Artist, 68- *Bibliog:* Willem De Kooning & Franz Kline (auths), On Works of Mr Alcopley, 52; Michel Seuphor (auth), Ecritures-Dessins d'Alcopley, 54; Will Grohmann (auth), Alcopley-Voies et Traces, 61. *Mem:* Am Abstr Artists; Groupe Espace, Paris. *Media:* Oil, Acrylic; Watercolor, Ink. *Publ:* Auth, Einsichten, Drawings by Alcopley to Poems by S E Broese, 59; contribr, Art & Thinking, Bokubi Press, Kyoto, Japan, 63; coauth & illusr, Listening to Heidegger and Hisamatsu, 69; illusr, Herman Cherry's Poems of Pain--And Other Matters, Una Ed, New York, 76; illusr, Grete Wehmeyer's Edgard Varse, Gustav Bosse Verlag, Regensburg, Fed Repub Ger, 77; and many others. *Mailing Add:* 50 Central Park W New York NY 10023

ALDEN, GARY WADE
CONSERVATOR
b Somerville, NJ, May 18, 51. *Study:* Univ Chicago, BA, 73; Intermuseum Conserv Asn Training Prog, Oberlin Col, with Richard D Buck, cert(conserv), 76. *Pos:* Conservator, Intermuseum Conserv Asn Lab, Oberlin, 76-77; chief conservator, Balboa Art Conserv Ctr, San Diego, Calif, 77-78; dir, Balboa Art Conserv Ctr, San Diego, 78- *Mem:* Assoc mem Am Inst Conserv Hist & Artistic Works; Western Asn Art Conserv (secy/treas, 79-81); assoc mem Int Inst Conserv. *Interests:* Conservation of paintings and polychromed sculpture. *Mailing Add:* Balboa Art Conserv Ctr PO Box 3755 San Diego CA 92103

ALDEN, RICHARD
PAINTER
US citizen. *Study:* Pratt Inst, Brooklyn, BA(archit), 66, MA(archit), 68; Archit Asn, Fulbright Grant, 67. *Work:* Milford Fine Arts Coun, Conn; Trenton State Col, NJ. *Exhib:* Salmagundi Club 3rd Ann, New York, 80; Audubon Artists 38th Ann Exhib, New York, 80; Springfield Art League 115th Nat, Mass, 80; Nat Print Exhib, Holman Art Gallery, Trenton, NJ, 80; Mamaroneck Artists Guild, Larchmont, NY, 81; and others. *Teaching:* Asst prof design, Pa State Univ, 68- *Awards:* 3rd Prizes, 8th Ann, York Art Asn, 78 & Cent Pa Festival Arts, 78; 1st Prize, 21st Three Rivers Arts Festival, 80. *Media:* Colored Pencil. *Dealer:* Capricorn Gallery 4849 Rugby Ave Bethesda MD 20014. *Mailing Add:* 206 Eng Unit C University Park PA 16802

ALDRICH, LARRY
COLLECTOR
Pos: Chmn & founder, Larry Aldrich Mus Contemp Art, Ridgefield, Conn & founder & pres, SoHo Ctr for Visual Arts, New York, NY, currently. *Collection:* Contemporary painting and sculpture. *Mailing Add:* Larry Aldrich Assocs 40 Central Park S Rm 6 New York NY 10019

ALEXANDER, EDMUND BROOKE
DEALER
b Los Angeles, Calif, Apr 26, 37. *Study:* Yale Univ, BA, 60. *Pos:* Dir, Brooke Alexander Inc, currently. *Mem:* Art Dealers Asn Am. *Specialty:* Contemporary American prints; contemporary paintings, drawings and sculpture. *Publ:* Ed, Robert Motherwell/Selected Prints 1961-1974, 74, Jasper Johns/Screenprints, 77 & Sam Francis--The Litho Shop 1970-1979, 79, pvt publ. *Mailing Add:* 20 W 57th St New York NY 10019

ALEXANDER, JOHN E
PAINTER
b Beaumont, Tex, Oct 26, 45. *Study:* Lamar Univ, BA; Southern Methodist Univ, MFA. *Work:* Contemp Arts Mus, Houston; Mus Fine Art, Amarillo, Tex; Am Tel Collection, Chicago; Mus Fine Art, Beaumont; Southern Methodist Univ, Dallas. *Comn:* Poster (lithograph), Am Civil Liberties Union, 74; poster, comn by Dir James Harithas, Contemp Arts Mus, 75. *Exhib:* Drawings USA, Springfield, Ill, 70-71; Dallas Mus Art, 72; Artist of the Southwest, Atlanta, Ga, 72; one-man show, Contemp Arts Mus, Houston, 75. *Teaching:* Asst prof art, Univ Houston, 71- *Media:* Oil. *Mailing Add:* Dept Art Col Humanities & Fine Arts 4800 Calhoun Houston TX 77004

ALEXANDER, JUDITH
DEALER, COLLECTOR
b Atlanta, Ga, Mar 31, 32. *Study:* Univ NC, Chapel Hill, BA, 52; Acad Fine Art & Barnes Found, Philadelphia, 53-54; Hans Hoffman Sch Art, Provincetown, 55. *Pos:* Art dealer, New Arts Gallery, 57-65 & Alexander Gallery, 65- *Specialty:* Nationally known and local artists, specializing in abstract expressionism and Georgia folk art. *Mailing Add:* 3060 Pharr Ct North NW Atlanta GA 30305

ALEXANDER, JUDY
ADMINISTRATOR, CONCEPTUAL ARTIST
b Erie, Pa, Nov 22, 47. *Study:* Occidental Col, Los Angeles, 65-67; Ore Col Educ, Monmouth, BS, 76; Lone Mountain Col, San Francisco, MFA(fiberworks), 78. *Work:* Mus Fine Art, Univ Ore, Eugene; Arrowmont Sch Crafts, Gatlinburg, Tenn; Emanuel Hosp, Portland, Ore. *Comn:* Fiber wall reliefs, Cravinho Insurance Co, Salem, Ore, 76. *Exhib:* Celebration, Contemp Crafts, Portland, Ore, 77; Fac & Staff Exhib, Arrowmont Sch Crafts, Gatlinburg, Tenn, 77; Pieced Together, Ames Gallery, Berkeley, 78; Fiberworks, Marin Co Civic Ctr, San Rafael, 80. *Pos:* Asst dir symp on contemp textile art, Fiberworks, Ctr for Textile Arts, 78, dir spec studies, 79, exec dir, 79- *Awards:* Purchase Award, Ore State Fair, 75. *Mem:* Am Crafts Coun; Contemp Crafts Asn. *Media:* Mixed. *Publ:* Auth, Daniel Graffin: an interdisciplinary approach (exhib rev), Artweek, 79. *Mailing Add:* Fiberworks Ctr for Textile Arts 1940 Bonita Ave Berkeley CA 94704

ALEXANDER, KENNETH LEWIS
CARTOONIST
b Gridley, Calif, June 16, 24. *Study:* Univ Calif, Berkeley, 42-43; Rutgers Univ, 43-44; Calif Col Arts & Crafts, 46-47. *Pos:* Freelance com artist, 47-58; ed, Pictorial Living Mag, San Francisco Examnr, 58-63, Sunday art dir, 63-66, ed cartoonist, 66-; TV cd cartoonist, KGO-TV, 68-69. *Mem:* Soc Am Ed Cartoonist; Nat Cartoonists Soc; Am Newspaper Guild; Am Fedn TV Radio Artists. *Mailing Add:* c/o San Francisco Examiner 110 Fifth St San Francisco CA 94119

ALEXANDER, MARGARET AMES
HISTORIAN, EDUCATOR
b Sharon, Mass, May 21, 16. *Study:* Wheaton Col, AB, 38; Inst Fine Arts, NY Univ, MA, 41, PhD, 58. *Pos:* Co-dir, Corpus des Mosaiques de Tunisie, Tunis, 68- *Teaching:* Prof art, Univ Iowa, 62- *Mem:* Am Asn Univ Women; Archaeol Inst Am; Asn Int Study Antique Mosaics; Int Asn Classical Archaeol; Col Art Asn. *Res:* Roman and Early Christian mosaics. *Publ:* Auth of articles on NAfrica, Archaeol, 49-51 & Apollo, 83; coauth, Quelques Precisions a propos de la Chronologie des Mosaiques d'Utique, La Mosaique Greco-Romaine, Vol II; coauth, Utique et ses Environs, Fasc 1, 73 & Fasc 3, 76 & ed, Fasc 2, 74, Corpus des Mosaiques de Tunisie, Vol I; coauth, Thuburbo Majus, Fasc 1, 80. *Mailing Add:* 9 Forest Glen Iowa City IA 52240

ALEXANDER, PETER
SCULPTOR
b Los Angeles, Calif, Feb 27, 39. *Study:* Univ of Pa, University Park, 57-60; Univ of London, Eng, 60-62; Univ of Calif, Berkeley, 62-63; Univ of Southern Calif, Los Angeles, 63-64; Univ of Calif, Los Angeles, BA, 65, MFA, 68. *Work:* Walker Art Ctr, Minneapolis, Minn; Mus of Mod Art, New York; Minneapolis Inst of Art; Joslyn Art Mus, Omaha, Nebr; Los Angeles Co Mus of Art, Los Angeles. *Exhib:* West Coast Now, 68 & Am Art, 73, Seattle Art Mus; New Materials-New Methods, Mus of Mod Art, New York, 69; 14 Sculptors: The Indust Edge, Walker Art Ctr, 69; Whitney Mus of Am Art Ann, New York, 69; Highlights: 1968-1969, Larry Aldrich Mus of Contemp Art, Ridgefield, Conn, 69; Am Exhibs, Art Inst of Chicago, 69 & 72; Painting & Sculpture in Calif: The Modern Era, San Francisco Mus of Art, 76; solo exhibs, Calif State Univ, Long Beach, 76, Rico Mizuno, Los Angeles, 80 & James Corcoran, Los Angeles, 81; La Jolla Mus Contemp Art, 81; Art Ctr Col Design, Pasadena, 81; and others. *Pos:* Artist in Residence, Calif Inst of Technol, 70-71 & Calif State Col, Long Beach, 76. *Awards:* Nat Endowment Arts Fel, 80. *Bibliog:* Elizabeth Perlmutter (auth), Clear, cloudy, smoggy, 1/75 & Dizzy in the Ganzfeld, summer 76, Artnews; Nancy Marmer (auth), Sky Show, Artforum, 2/76; Henry Seldis (auth), article, Los Angeles Times, 8/7/77. *Mailing Add:* PO Box 1124 3233 Tuna Canyon Rd Topanga CA 90290

ALEXANDER, ROBERT SEYMOUR
EDUCATOR, DESIGNER
b Pittsburgh, Pa, Feb 1, 23. *Study:* Ad-Art Studio Sch, 41-42; Shrivenham Am Univ, Eng, 45; Carnegie Inst Technol, 47; Univ Ill, BFA, 51; Cranbrook Acad Art, MFA, 52. *Comn:* Indust designs for FMC Corp, Mich Dept Agr, Recordio Corp, Planet Corp & others. *Exhib:* Kresge Art Gallery, Mich State Univ, 73, 78, 82 & 84; 7th Photographic Art Competition, Saginaw Mus, Mich, 77; 14th Ann Painting, Lansing Art Gallery, Mich, 81 & 83; Partners

Gallery, Okemos, Mich, 83; and others. *Pos:* Artist-designer, James H Matthews Co, Pittsburgh, 46-47; training aids designer, USA, Ft Eustis, Va, 48; automotive designer, Ford Motor Co, Dearborn, Mich, 52-53; independent designer, 55-; group leader, design for educ proj, Princeton Univ, 66. *Teaching:* Prof art, Mich State Univ, 54- *Awards:* First Prize, Int furniture design competition, Nat Cotton Coun, 59; Second Prize, 7th Photographic Art Competition, Saginaw Mus, 77. *Bibliog:* J Fisher (auth), Education for design, Format Mag, 5/66. *Media:* Xerography. *Publ:* Auth, Industrial design, the alumni show, Kresge Art Ctr Bulletin, 4/75. *Mailing Add:* Dept of Art Mich State Univ East Lansing MI 48824

ALEXANDER-GREENE, GRACE GEORGE
EDUCATOR, ADMINISTRATOR

b Cleveland, Ohio, Sept 18, 18. *Study:* NJ State Teachers Col, with Sybil Browne, BS, 40; Hunter Col; NY Univ; Queens Col; Univ PR; Columbia Univ. *Pos:* TV producer-broadcaster art, New York City Bd Educ, 65-73; supervisor art, 73-77, dir art, 77-79; bd mem, Inst Study Art in Educ, 78 & 79; freelance TV producer art, 79- *Teaching:* Instr art educ, Queens Col, 71-72; instr visual literacy, Am Festival in Britain, 71; instr art educ, Sch Visual Arts, New York, 79- *Awards:* Ohio State Award, 63 & 73; Outstanding Alumni Award, Kean Col, 80. *Bibliog:* Barbara Y Newsom (auth), The Art Museum as Educator, Univ Calif, Press, 78; Potell Herbert (ed), Rationale for Art Education in the Eighties, High Points, 80. *Mem:* Nat Art Educ Asn; Univ Coun Art Educ; Am Women Radio & TV. *Publ:* Auth, Artists in New York, 66 & auth, The Moving Image, 70, New York City Bd Educ; auth, From the Teachers Corner, Am Educ US Dept Health Educ & Welfare, 78. *Mailing Add:* 12 West 72 St New York NY 10023

ALEXENBERG, (MELVIN) MENAHEM
CONCEPTUAL ARTIST, PAINTER

b New York, NY, Feb 24, 37. *Study:* Queens Col, BS; Yeshiva Univ, MS; Art Students League, with Will Barnet; NY Univ, EdD. *Work:* Int Sci & Technol Collection, NY. *Exhib:* One-man show, Adelphi Univ, Oakdale, NY, 67; Sky Art Exhib, BMW Mus, Munich, Ger, 83. *Teaching:* Asst prof visual arts & educ, Adelphi Univ, Oakdale, NY, 65-69; sr lectr, Tel Aviv Univ, Israel, formerly; assoc prof art, Bezalel Acad Arts & Design, Jerusalem, 70-71; sr lectr art, Haifa Univ, Israel, 70-72; assoc prof art, Columbia Univ, 73-77; assoc prof, Bar Ilan Univ, Israel, 77-; pres, Ramat Hanegev Col, Yeroham, Israel, 78-; fel, Mass Inst Technol Ctr Advan Visual Studies, 80. *Awards:* Blue Ribbon, Am Film Festival, 66; Founder's Day Award, NY Univ, 69. *Mem:* Int Soc Educ through Art; Israel Soc Painters & Sculptors. *Media:* Mixed; Encaustic. *Res:* Relationships between art and science; aesthetic components of creative processes; structural analysis of contemporary art forms; future art derived from the deep structure of Jewish consciousness. *Publ:* Auth, Toward an Integral Structure through Science & Art, 74; auth, Art Teachers as Designers of Alternative Environments for Learning, 75; auth, A Semiotic Taxonomy of Contemporary Art Forms, 75; auth, Aesthetic Experience in Creative Process, Bar-Ilan Univ Press, Israel, 81; coauth, Educating the Jewish Artist, 83. *Mailing Add:* 1015/4 Yeroham Israel

ALEXICK, DAVID FRANCIS
EDUCATOR, PAINTER

b Philadelphia, Pa, Jan 25, 42. *Study:* Richmond Prof Inst, BFA, 64; Va Commonwealth Univ, MFA, 66; Pa State Univ, PhD, 76. *Exhib:* Va Artists Biennial, Va Mus Fine Arts, Richmond, 64; one-man show, Robinson House, Va Mus Fine Arts, Richmond, 65; Longwood Col Fac Show, Bedford Gallery, Farmville, Va, 71-78; James River Show, Mariners Mus, Newport News, Va, 73. *Teaching:* Instr art, York Col Pa, 66-68; asst prof art, Longwood Col, Farmville, Va, 71-78; instr art educ, Col William & Mary, Williamsburg, Va, 79-80; asst prof art, Christopher Newport Col, Va, 79-82; assoc prof & dir art, Dept Arts & Communications, 82- *Awards:* Cert Distinction, Va Mus Fine Arts, 64; 1st Prize, SEastern Regional, Lynchburg Fine Arts Ctr, 67; Patron Arts Award, Lynchburg Art Festival, 78. *Mem:* Col Art Asn; Nat Art Educ Asn; Va Art Educ Asn. *Media:* Oil, Acrylic. *Res:* Programs of art and perceptual awareness for institutionalized retarded children. *Mailing Add:* 159 Highwood Circle Newport News VA 23602

ALF, MARTHA JOANNE
PAINTER, WRITER

b Berkeley, Calif, Aug 13, 30. *Study:* San Diego State Univ, with Everett Gee Jackson, BA, MA(painting), 63; Univ Calif, Los Angeles, with James Weeks, William Brice & Richard Diebenkorn, MFA(pictorial arts), 70. *Work:* Greenville Co Mus Art, SC; San Diego Mus Art; Santa Barbara Mus Art; Newport Harbor Art Mus, Newport Beach, Calif. *Exhib:* Whitney Biennial Contemp Art, Whitney Mus Am Art, 75; Black & White Are Colors, Lang Art Gallery, Scripps Col, 79; Italian Drawings & New Acquisitions, Los Angeles Co Mus Art, Calif, 79; Contemporary Drawings, Henry Gallery, Univ Wash, 80; Decade: Los Angeles Painting in the Seventies, Art Ctr Col Design, 81; Southern California Artists 1940-1980, Laguna Beach Mus Art, Calif, 81; solo shows, Pomona Col, Montgomery Art Gallery, Claremont, Calif, 81; and many other group & one-man shows. *Pos:* Guest cur, Painting: Color Form & Surface (17 Los Angeles Painters), Lang Art Gallery, Scripps Col, Claremont, Calif. *Teaching:* Instr drawing & painting, Los Angeles Harbor Col, Wilmington, Calif, 71-75; instr, Univ Calif Exten, Los Angeles, 71-78. *Awards:* First Prizes, Art Guild Exhib, San Diego Mus Art, 78; Nat Endowment Arts Grant, 79; Purchase Award, Los Angeles Co Mus Art, 79; and others. *Bibliog:* Henry Seldis (auth), Still lives precisely but poetically arranged, Los Angeles Times, 5/22/77; Suzanne Muchnic (auth), Martha Alf's illuminations, Artweek, 5/78; DaVid S Rubin (auth), Martha Alf, Arts Mag, 9/78. *Media:* Multimedia. *Publ:* Auth, My interest in women artists of the past, Womanspace J, Vol 1, No 2; auth, The psychological world of Joyce

Treiman, 3/76, auth, The structural language of Clair Falkenstein, 4/76 & auth, Women artists throughout history, 1/77, Artweek. *Dealer:* Newspace Gallery 5241 Melrose Ave Los Angeles CA 90038. *Mailing Add:* 5701 Waring Rd San Diego CA 92120

ALFORD, GLORIA K
SCULPTOR, CRAFTSMAN

b Chicago, Ill, Oct 3, 28. *Study:* Univ Calif, Berkeley, AB; Art Inst Chicago; Penland Sch Crafts, NC; Columbia Univ; Pratt Graphics Ctr. *Work:* Elvehjem Mus, Univ Wis-Madison; CUNA Art Collection, Madison, Wis; Prudential Art Collection, Monterey Mus Art, Calif. *Exhib:* Environ-Vision, Nat Competitive Exhib, Everson Mus, Syracuse, 72; In Her Own Image, Philadelphia Mus Art, 74; 19th Ann Print Exhib, Brooklyn Mus, 74; Wis Directions, Milwaukee Art Ctr, 75; Glass Backwards, Kohler Arts Ctr, Sheboygan, Wis, 79; solo shows, Monterey Peninsula Mus Art, 80 & Netherlands Inst Advan Study, Wassenar, 82; Placement/Displacement Sculpture Show, Cabrillo Col, 83. *Pos:* Vis artist, Cult Exchange Prog, France, 76. *Awards:* Top Honors, Univ Wis Art Show, Richland Ctr, 72. *Mailing Add:* 435 Meder St Santa Cruz CA 95060

ALHILALI, NEDA
ENVIRONMENTAL ARTIST, PAINTER

b Cheb, Czech, Nov 26, 38. *Study:* St Martin's Sch Art, London, Eng; Kunst Akademie, Munich, WGer; Univ Calif, Los Angeles, BA, 65, MA, 68. *Work:* Banff Art Ctr, Canada; Crocker Art Mus, Sacramento, Calif; Albright Col, Pa; ARAMCO, Houston; Central Mus Textiles, Lodz, Poland; and others. *Comn:* Blue Cross Hq, Los Angeles, 77; Hyatt Regency Hotels, Chicago, 77, also Los Angeles, Columbus, Maui & Palm Beach; Tishman Corp, Los Angeles, 78; Prince Kuhio Hotel, Hawaii, 80; Sheraton Hotel, Crystal City, Va; and others. *Exhib:* Mus of Contemp Art, Chicago, Pac Design Ctr, Los Angeles & Mus of Sci & Indust, Los Angeles, 76; Fiberworks, Cleveland Mus of Art, Ohio, 77; The Americas & Japan--Fiberworks, Nat Mus Mod Art, Tokyo & Kyoto, Japan, 77; one-woman shows, Allrich Gallery, San Francisco, Vanguard Gallery, Los Angeles, 77, Hunsaker Gallery, Los Angeles, Calif, 80 & 82 & Renwick Gallery, Washington, DC; Art Fabric: Mainstream, Am Fedn Arts: Mus Mod Art, San Francisco, Calif. *Collections Arranged:* Fiberworks (auth, catalog), Lang Art Gallery, Scripps Col, Claremont, Calif, 73; Inaugural Exhib, Mano Gallery, Chicago, 76; Paper Art (coauth, catalog), Galleries of the Claremont Cols, 77. *Teaching:* Asst prof art, Univ Calif, Los Angeles Exten, 70-77; from asst prof to assoc prof, Scripps Col & Claremont Grad Sch, 71-, chmn dept art, Scripps Col, 82- *Awards:* Nat Endowment for the Arts Grants, 74 & 79; First Scripps Col Fac Recognition Award, 81. *Bibliog:* Betty Pawk (auth), Interview with N Al-Hilali, Fiberarts Mag, 7/8/79; Scott Miller (auth), Cassiopeia's Court, Images & Issues, Vol 3, No 1; Nan Hackett (auth), Opposites, Seattle Post Intelligencer, 7/2/82. *Mem:* Artists Equity Asn; Am Crafts Coun; World Crafts Coun. *Media:* Mixed. *Res:* Historic textiles. *Dealer:* Allrich Gallery San Francisco CA; Joyce Hunsaker Gallery 812 N La Cienega Blvd Los Angeles CA 90069. *Mailing Add:* 2633 Sixth St Santa Monica CA 90405

ALICEA, JOSE
PRINTMAKER

b Ponce, PR, Jan 12, 28. *Study:* Acad Pov, Ponce; Inst PR Cult, with Lorenzo Homar. *Work:* Philadelphia Mus Art; Mus Mod Art, New York; Libr of Cong, Washington, DC; Boston Pub Libr; Mus Arte Ponce. *Comn:* Woodcut mural, Inst PR Cult for Guayanilla High Sch, 70. *Exhib:* 3rd Biennial Int Della Grafica, Florence, Italy, 72; 4th Int Exhib of Drawings, Yugoslavia; 10th & 11th Biennalle Int d'Art, Menton, France; 12th Bienal de Sao Paulo, Brazil; 2nd & 3rd Bienal Int de Grafica, Frechen, Ger; and others. *Pos:* Asst to dir, Inst PR Cult Workshop, 58-62, instr, currently; art dir, Revista del Cafe, Ponce. *Teaching:* Instr printmaking, Escuela Artes Plasticas, San Juan, 67- *Awards:* Prize for Graphic, Ateneo Puertorriqueno, 65; Mildred Boerike Prize, Print Club Philadelphia, 67; Travel Grant, Casa Del Arte, San Juan, 68. *Bibliog:* E Ruiz de la Mata (auth), The art of Jose R Alicea, San Juan Rev Mag, 7/66 & Graphics by Alicea, San Juan Star, 8/9/70; Gloria Borras (auth), El grabado en la vida de Jose R Alicea, El Mundo, 69. *Media:* Miscellaneous Media. *Publ:* Illusr, Trovas larenas, 68; auth, Rio grande de Loiza (portfolio of prints), 68; auth, Cancion de Baquine (portfolio of prints), 70; illusr, En las manos del pueblo, 72; illusr, Calambrenas. *Dealer:* Galeria Coabey Box 1744 San Juan PR 00903. *Mailing Add:* 911 Campo Rico Ave C Club Rio Piedras San Juan PR 00924

ALIKI (ALIKI LIACOURAS BRANDENBERG)
ILLUSTRATOR, WRITER

b Philadelphia, Pa. *Study:* Philadelphia Mus Col Art, grad. *Work:* Kerlan Collection, Walter Libr, Univ Minn, Minneapolis; de Grummond Collection, Univ Southern Miss, Hattiesburg; Seattle Pub Libr, Wash; Falvey Mem Libr, Villanova Univ, Pa; Rutgers Univ Children's Literature Collection, New Brunswick. *Exhib:* Children's Bk Coun Showcase Exhib; Biennale of Illus, Bratislava, Czech, 75; Soc Illusr Exhib, New York, NY; Am Inst Graphic Arts Bk Exhib. *Awards:* Boys Club of Am Jr Bk Award, 68; First Prize of NY Acad Science's Children's Bk Award, 76; Silveren Griffel Award, Netherlands, 81. *Bibliog:* Grace Hogarth (auth), Illustrators of Children's Books, Horn Bk Inc, 78; Monson & Sutherland (auths), Children & Books, Scott, Foresman, 81; Iris M Tiedt (auth), Exploring Books with Children, Houghton Mifflin, 79. *Media:* Gouache, Crayon, Pen and Ink. *Publ:* Auth & illusr, Mummies Made in Egypt, 79 & Digging Up Dinosaurs, 81, Crowell Publ; auth & illusr, The Two of Them, 79 & We Are Best Friends, 82, Greenwillow; auth & illusr, A Medieval Feast, T Y Crowell, 83. *Mailing Add:* 17 Regent's Park Terr London NW 1 7ED England United Kingdom

ALINDER, JAMES GILBERT
PHOTOGRAPHER, MUSEUM DIRECTOR
b Glendale, Calif, Mar 31, 41. *Study:* Macalester Col, BA, 62; Univ Minn, 62-64; Univ NMex, MFA, 68. *Work:* Mus Mod Art, New York; Bibliot Nat, Paris; Art Inst Chicago; Int Mus Photog, George Eastman House, Rochester, NY; Nat Gallery Can, Ottawa; and many others. *Exhib:* Light, Hayden Gallery, Mass Inst Technol, 68; solo exhibs, Sheldon Gallery, Univ Nebr, 69, Camerawork Gallery, San Francisco, 79 & Spiva Art Ctr, Joplin, Mo, 80; Be-Ing Without Clothes, Hayden Art Gallery, Mass Inst Technol, 70; The Great West: Real/Ideal, Univ Colo Art Mus & traveling, 77; The Extended Frame, Visual Studies Workshop, Rochester, New York, 77; 20th Century Photography, Centre Pompidou, Paris, 77; The Diana Show, Wynn Bullock Gallery, Carmel, Calif, 80; and many others. *Collections Arranged:* Wright Morris: Structures & Artifacts, Sheldon Mem Art Gallery, Lincoln, Nebr, 75; Crying for a Vision, 76; Twelve Photographers: A Mid-America Contemporary Document, 78; Jerome Liebling: Retrospective, 78; New Color Work: Divola, Fitch, North, Ollman & Pfahl, 78; Ruth Bernhard Retrospective (with catalog), 79; and others. *Pos:* Exec dir, Friends of Photog, Carmel, Calif, 77- *Teaching:* Assoc prof photog/photog hist, Univ Nebr, Lincoln, 68-77. *Awards:* Nat Endowment Arts Fel, 73 & 80; Woods Found Fel, 74. *Bibliog:* Article, Artforum, Vol 12, 75; N Geske (ed), Photographs, Univ Nebr Press, 77; J Enyeart (ed), Kansas Album, Kans Bankers Asn, 77. *Mem:* Soc Photog Educ (ed Exposure, 73-77, secy, 73-75, vchmn, 75-77, chmn, 77-79); Monterey Co Cult Coun (chmn, 81-82). *Media:* Photography. *Publ:* Auth, Ansel Adams: 50 Years of Portraits, 78; ed, Self-Portrayal, The Photographers Image, 78; ed, Carleton Watkins, Photographs of the Columbia River and Oregon, 79; auth, Robert Cumming, Photographs, 79; and many others. *Mailing Add:* c/o Friends of Photog PO Box 500 Carmel CA 93921

ALLAN, WILLIAM GEORGE
PAINTER, EDUCATOR
b Everett, Wash, Mar 28, 36. *Study:* San Francisco Art Inst, BFA. *Work:* Dallas Mus Fine Arts; San Francisco Mus Art; Philadelphia Mus Art; Whitney Mus Am Art, Mus Mod Art, New York. *Exhib:* Carnegie Int Exhib, Pittsburgh, 57; Continuing Surrealism, La Jolla Mus Art, Calif, 71; Whitney Painting Ann, New York, 72; 70th Am Exhib, Art Inst Chicago, 72; Indianapolis Mus Art Exhib, 72; Whitney Mus Am Art, New York, 73-74; Painting & Sculpture in California: The Mod Era, San Francisco Mus Mod Art, 76; Chicago Arts Club, 78. *Teaching:* Instr painting, Univ Calif, Davis, 65-67; instr painting, Univ Calif, Berkeley, 69; prof art, Calif State Univ, Sacramento, 68- *Media:* Acrylic, Watercolor. *Dealer:* Hansen-Fuller Gallery 228 Grant Ave San Francisco CA 94108 *Mailing Add:* Art Dept Calif State Univ 6000 J St Sacramento CA 95819

ALLARA, PAMELA EDWARDS
HISTORIAN, CRITIC
b Scarsdale, NY, Sept 11, 43. *Study:* Brown Univ, BA, 65; Johns Hopkins Univ, PhD, 71. *Teaching:* Asst prof art hist, Fine Arts Dept, Tufts Univ, 73-; Boston corresp, Art News, 78- *Res:* Contemporary art; modern art in Boston; photography; Robert Frank and A L Coburn. *Publ:* Coauth (with S Prokopoff), Christo's Urban Projects: A Survey, Inst Contemp Art, Boston, 79; auth, Nicholas Nixon's anonymous immortals, Art New England, 1/80; auth, The broad scope of Boston arts, Art News, 11/81; auth, A Boston School: Four Artists, Tufts Univ Gallery II, 82; auth, Herb Jackson: Drawings, Mint Mus Art, 83. *Mailing Add:* 48 Ledgemeadow Rd Wayland MA 01778

ALLEN, CLARENCE CANNING
PAINTER, CARTOONIST
b Cleveland, Ga, Nov 29, 1897. *Study:* Southeastern State Univ, with Dr Allen Berger & Ola Forbes; Art Student League, with George Bridgman & R P R Neilson; San Antonio Art Acad, Tex, with Jose Arpa', Xavier Gonzalez & Rolla Taylor; also with Molly Guion, Dimitri Romanovsky, Charles H Owens & Bettina Steinke. *Work:* Libr of Pres Truman, Eisenhower & Johnson; portraits: Sen Robert S Kerr, Heritage House, Oklahoma City, US Judges, Stephen Chandler & Luther Bohanon, Court House, 79; Will Rogers, Will Rogers Mem Hosp, Saranac Lake, NY; plus numerous pvt, hist & found collections. *Comn:* Early and Late Means of Disseminating News (murals), Newspaper Printing Corp, 53; Press Media Symbology, Tulsa Press Club, Okla, 57; Creek Tribe Council Tree (mural), Tulsa City Hall, 69. *Exhib:* Giornate Mediche Int, Verona, Italy, 63; La Caricature de Par le Monde, Troisieme Salon Int, Place Victoria, Montreal, 67; Witte Mus, San Antonio; Philbrook Mus, Tulsa; Lever House, NY; Metrop Mus, NY. *Pos:* Artist, Los Angeles Times/Mirror, 27; artist, art dir, ed & cartoonist, Tulsa World & Tulsa Tribune, 29-68, founder, Art Dept. *Teaching:* Instr graphic art, Cent High Sch, San Antonio, Tex, 24-27; instr fine art & oil painting, Tulsa. *Awards:* Five nat awards, Freedoms Found, 53, 55, 56, 58, 61 & top nat award, 54. *Bibliog:* John Chase (auth), Today's cartoon, Hauser Press, New Orleans, 62. *Mem:* Am Artists Prof League; Nat Soc Mural Painters; Soc Illus; Asn Am Ed Cartoonists; charter mem Nat Cartoonists Soc. *Media:* Oil. *Publ:* Auth, Sketching, 32; Biographical sketches of prominent Tulsans, 49; Originality, 50; Are you fed up with modern art?, 52; also articles in numerous nat & regional mag. *Mailing Add:* 1645 E 17th Pl Tulsa OK 74120

ALLEN, CONSTANCE OLLEEN WEBB
PAINTER, JEWELRY DESIGNER
b Camphill, Ala, June 10, 23. *Study:* George Washington Univ; Inst Allende, San Miguel de Allende, Mex; also with Richard Goetz, Oklahoma City. *Comn:* 20 Indian Portraits, A C Leftwich, Duncan, Okla, 72; Landscapes of Southwest Okla, comn by Susan Johnston, Oklahoma City, 78. *Exhib:* Int Art Show, Lawton, Okla, 71; Nat Miniature Art Show, Garden State Plaza, Paramus, NJ, 72; 1st Ann Western Art Roundup-Women Artists Am West,

Riverside, Calif, 73; 39th & 41st Ann Miniature Painters, Sculptors & Gravers Soc of Washington, DC, Art Club of Washington, 72 & 74. *Teaching:* Instr drawing & painting, Univ Sci & Arts of Okla, Chickasha, 74- *Awards:* First Place for Pastel, Chickasha Art Guild, Okla, 73; Merit Award Graphic, Fla Nat Miniature Art Show, 76; First Place Watercolor, Lawton Miniature Art Show, Okla, 78; and others. *Bibliog:* Dick Stoll (auth), Three artists for B Webb Family, 66, A C Leftwich (auth), Indian Hall of Fame, painted by Mrs Webb, 72 & Mrs N H Welch (auth), Mrs Webb has exhibit, 74, Chickasha Daily Express. *Mem:* Santa Rita Art League, Ariz (pres, 83-84); Artists Equity Asn. *Media:* Multimedia; Precious Metals, Gemstones. *Mailing Add:* 2811 S Camino Godoy Green Valley AZ 85614

ALLEN, EDDA LYNNE
PAINTER, DEALER
b Big Spring, Tex, July 29, 32. *Study:* With Randall Davey, Will Schuster & William Longley, 57-62; Southern Methodist Univ; Tex Tech Univ; Univ NMex; Col Santa Fe, BA(summa cum laude), 68. *Work:* Santa Fe Co Munic Ct, NMex State Capitol, Mayors Off, Santa Fe. *Exhib:* Joslyn Art Mus, Omaha, Nebr, 72; Artist Alpine Holiday, Ouray Arts Asn, Colo, 72; Arts Festival, NMex Art League, Albuquerque, 72-74; Roswell Mus & Art Ctr, NMex, 73; one-man show, NMex State Fair, 75. *Pos:* Owner-dealer, Edda Lynne Allen Studio-Gallery, 70- *Teaching:* Instr tech, Col of Santa Fe, 67-68; lectr alla prima tech, Univ NMex, 70-71. *Awards:* Award of Merit, Am Arthritis Found, 75; First in Show, Rio Grande Arts & Crafts, 77-78. *Mem:* Santa Fe Soc Art. *Media:* Oil, Watercolor. *Specialty:* Art of the American Southwest cultures, all media; regional works. *Mailing Add:* 1456 Diolinda St Santa Fe NM 87501

ALLEN, (HARVEY) HAROLD
PHOTOGRAPHER, HISTORIAN
b Portland, Ore, June 29, 12. *Study:* Art Inst Chicago, 37-41; Univ Chicago, 48-54; Art Inst Chicago, Hon DFA, 79. *Work:* Art Inst Chicago; Metrop Mus Art; Columbia Col, Chicago; Libr of Cong; Ill State Mus. *Exhib:* Architecture and Other Photographs, Univ Ill, Chicago Circle Ctr, 75; The Photographer and the City, Mus Contemp Art, Chicago, 77; Harold Allen's Egypt, Evanston Art Ctr, Ill, 77; Tut-Tut: A Survey of Egyptomania, Stanford Univ Mus Art, 79; Harold Allen--Photographs: 1949-1978, Ill State Mus, Springfield, 83; and others. *Teaching:* Instr photog, Art Inst Chicago, 48-60 & 66-77, Frederick Latimer Wells Prof, 71, retired, 77; instr beginning & documentary photog, Columbia Col, Chicago, 71 & 72. *Awards:* Chicago Art Awards, 78. *Mem:* Soc Photog Educ. *Res:* Egyptian Revival art and architecture in Europe and America. *Publ:* Auth & illusr, Egyptian influences in Wedgwood designs, Seventh Wedgwood Int Sem, 62; auth & illusr, Father Ravalli's Missions, The Good Lion, Art Inst Chicago, 72. *Mailing Add:* 1725 S Desplaines St Chicago IL 60616

ALLEN, JANE ADDAMS
EDITOR, CRITIC
b Chicago, Ill. *Study:* Univ Chicago, with Joshua Taylor and Harold Rosenberg, BA & MFA; San Francisco Sch Fine Arts, with Richard Diebenkorn. *Collections Arranged:* Chicago Like It Is and Was, Centennial Photog Exhib, Chicago State Univ, Chicago Civic Ctr, 69. *Pos:* Art & photog critic, Chicago Tribune, 71-73; ed, New Art Examiner, 73-82; art critic, Washington Times, 82- *Awards:* Critics Fel, Nat Endowment for Arts, 75 & 80. *Mem:* Chicago New Art Asn (pres, 70-); Col Art Asn. *Publ:* The declining power of review, New Art Examiner, 11/81; Metaphor: The mechanical obsession, New Art Examiner, 2/82; and others. *Mailing Add:* 2718 Ontario Rd NW Washington DC 20009

ALLEN, JERE HARDY
PAINTER, EDUCATOR
b Selma, Ala, Aug 15, 44. *Study:* Ringling Sch Art, Sarasota, Fla, four yr cert, 69, BFA, 70; Univ Tenn, Knoxville, MFA, 72. *Work:* Mobile Art Gallery, Ala; Coos Art Mus, Ore; Liberty Corp, Greenville, SC; R I Kahn Gallery, Houston. *Exhib:* Mainstreams 76, Marietta, Ohio, 76; American Drawings II, Portsmouth, Va; NDak Nat, Grand Forks, 77; West 79 and 80/The Law, Minn Mus Art, 79 & 80; one-artist shows, S/R Gallery, Beverly Hills, Calif, 77 & Nat Acad Sci, Washington, DC, 83; American Drawings II, Smithsonian Traveling Exhib, Portsmouth, Va, 78-81; and others. *Teaching:* Instr drawing, Carson-Newman Col, 71-72; assoc prof painting, Univ Miss, 72- *Awards:* Tenn Art League Purchase Award, The Parthenon, 74; Award of Distinction, Mainstreams of Marietta Col, 75; Award, Shreveport Nat, Barnwell Art Ctr, La, 75. *Mem:* Col Art Asn Am. *Media:* Oil, Mixed Media. *Mailing Add:* 1103 S 14th St Oxford MS 38655

ALLEN, JESSE
PRINTMAKER, PAINTER
b Nairobi, Kenya, Mar 11, 36. *US citizen. Study:* Oxford Univ; self-taught. *Work:* Stanford Univ Mus Art, Palo Alto, Calif; Ft Wayne Mus Art, Ind; Palm Springs Desert Mus, Calif; Mus Asn North Orange Co, Fullerton, Calif; Allen Mem Gallery, Oberlin, Ohio. *Exhib:* Fine Arts Mus, Calif Palace Legion of Honor, San Francisco, 70; San Francisco Mus Art, 71; Western Asn Art Mus Traveling Exhib, 74-75; one-man shows, Univ Wyo Mus Art, Laramie, 75, Lawrence Hall Sci, Univ Calif, Berkeley, 75, Mus North Orange Co, Fullerton, Calif, 77 & Taft Mus, Cleveland, 78; and many others. *Bibliog:* Muldoon Elder (producer), Bright Tempest: The Art of Jesse Allen (film); Thelma Newman (auth), Innovative Printmaking, Crown Publ, 77. *Media:* Acrylic; Graphics. *Dealer:* Vorpal Gallery New York NY & San Francisco CA. *Mailing Add:* c/o Vorpal Gallery 393 Grove St San Francisco CA 94102

ALLEN, KAOLA B
COLLAGE ARTIST, PRINTMAKER
b Cincinnati, Ohio, June 16, 52. *Study:* Univ NC, Chapel Hill, BA(art), 74. *Exhib:* Forty-eighth Southeastern Competition for Drawing, Photog & Printmaking, Southeastern Ctr Contemp Art, 80; Charlotte Juried Exhib, Spirit Sq Galleries, NC, 81; Ensemble: Collage & Assemblage, Green Hill Art Ctr, Greensboro, NC, 82; Southeastern Graphics, Mint Mus Art, 82; Collage: Southeast, Southeastern Ctr Contemp Art & traveling with Southern Arts Fedn, 82-83. *Awards:* Juror's Merit Award, Charlotte Exhib, 81; Best in Show Purchase Award, Southeastern Graphics Invitational, NC Nat Bank, 82. *Bibliog:* Allen, Irwin, Holsenbeck & Foster (producers), Birth Days: A Collaborative Room Installation (videotape), 82. *Mem:* Wash Women's Art Ctr. *Media:* Miscellaneous. *Mailing Add:* 838 Shady Lawn Rd Chapel Hill NC 27514

ALLEN, LORETTA B
PAINTER, DESIGNER
b Caney, Kans. *Study:* Fed Arts Schs, Minneapolis; Famous Artists Sch; also with Grace Chadwick & Marshall Lakey, Oklahoma City, Molly Guion & Dimitri Romanofsky, New York. *Exhib:* Oklahoma City Art Ctr; Tulsa Studio Group, 61 & 62; Osage Co Hist Mus, 69; plus others. *Pos:* Illusr, children's bks; fashion designer; fashion illusr, local publ. *Mem:* Am Artists Prof League. *Media:* Pen & Ink; Pastel, Acrylic. *Mailing Add:* 1645 E 17th Pl Tulsa OK 74120

ALLEN, MARGARET PROSSER
PAINTER, EDUCATOR
b Vancouver, BC, Jan 26, 13; US citizen. *Study:* Univ Wash, BA & MFA; also with Alexander Archipenko & Amadee Ozenfant. *Work:* Pastel, Del Art Mus; mixed media print & carbon pencil drawing, Univ Del Permanent Collection. *Exhib:* Six exhibs, Northwest Ann, 38-48; over ten exhibs, Del Ann, 42-64; Weyhe Gallery, New York, 47; The Carvings of Sanchi, photog exhib circulated by Smithsonian Inst, 68-72; Univ Del Fac Group Show, Del Art Mus, 72; plus regional & group shows, 65-79. *Teaching:* Instr design, Univ Del, 42-48; asst prof design, 49-72; assoc prof design, 72- *Awards:* Popular Prize, Northwest Ann, 48; First Prize, Wilmington Soc Fine Arts, 49; Univ Del Grant, 68. *Mailing Add:* 119 Briar Lane Newark DE 19711

ALLEN, MARGO (MRS HARRY SHAW)
SCULPTOR, PAINTER
b Lincoln, Mass. *Study:* Boston Mus Sch Fine Arts; Naum Los Sch Anat, Rome; Venturini Sch Encaustic Painting, Rome; marble carving at Gelli Studio, Querceta, Italy. *Work:* Dallas Mus Fine Arts, Tex; Mus Mod Art, Mexico City; Calif Palace Legion of Honor, San Francisco; Butler Mus Am Art, Youngstown, Ohio; Columbia Mus of Fine Arts, SC; Ringling Mus Art. *Comn:* 34 terra-cotta reliefs, First Nat Bank, Lafayette, La; bronze eagle, New Iberia Bank, La; USS Constitution (bronze Mem plaque), US Navy; garden fountains, Tex, Mass, Bermuda & others; many portrait commissions in bronze. *Exhib:* Nat Acad Design, New York; Pa Acad Fine Arts, Philadelphia; Boston Mus Fine Arts; New York Archit League; Addison Gallery Am Art, Andover, Mass. *Teaching:* Art League, SW La Inst, Bradenton; Art Ctr, Long Boat Key, Fla. *Mem:* Nat Sculpture Soc; Nat League Am Pen Women; Ringling Mus; New Eng Asn Contemp Sculpture; Sarasota Art Asn, Fla. *Media:* Bronze, Terra-Cotta. *Mailing Add:* 501 Sloop Lane Longboat Key FL 33548

ALLEN, RALPH
PAINTER, EDUCATOR
b Eng, 1926. *Study:* Sir John Cass Sch Art & Slade Sch Fine Arts, London. *Work:* Nat Gallery Can; Art Gallery Toronto; Queen's Univ, Ont; Queen's Park, Toronto; also in pvt collections. *Teaching:* Assoc prof art hist & dir, Agnes Etherington Art Ctr, Queen's Univ, Ont, formerly. *Awards:* Jessie Dow Award, Montreal, 59; Can Coun Scholar, 59 & Sr Fel, 68; Baxter Award, Toronto, 60. *Mem:* Ont Soc Artists; Royal Can Acad Arts. *Mailing Add:* 199 Albert St Kingston ON K7L 3V4 Canada

ALLEN, ROBERTA
CONCEPTUAL ARTIST, SCULPTOR
b New York, NY, Oct 6, 45. *Work:* Mus of Mod Art, New York; Worchester Art Mus, Mass; Cooper-Hewitt Mus, New York. *Exhib:* Solo exhibs, John Weber Gallery, New York, 74, 75, 77 & 79, Kunstforum, Städtische Gallerie im Lanbachhaus, Munich, 81; Galerie Walter Storms, Munich, 81 & Galeria Primo Piano, Rome, 81; Contemp Abstract Art: Works on Paper, Baltimore Mus of Art, 76; Abstract Drawings, Albright-Knox Art Gallery, Buffalo, NY, 76; MTL Galerie, Brussels, Belg, 78; and others. *Awards:* Creative Artist Pub Serv Grant, 78-79. *Bibliog:* Jeff Deitch (auth), Roberta Allen, Arts Mag, 6/77; Judith Lopez Cardozo (auth), Roberta Allen, Artforum, 2/78. *Media:* Drawing; photoworks. *Publ:* Auth, Partially Trapped Lines, Parasol Press, 75; auth, Pointless Arrows, pvt publ, 77; auth, Pointless Acts, The Collation Ctr, 77; auth, Possibilities, John Weber Gallery & Parasol Press, 77; auth, Everything in the World There is to Know is Known by Somebody, But Not by the Same Knower, Ottenhausen Verlag, Munich, 81. *Mailing Add:* 5 W 16th St New York NY 10011

ALLEN, TOM, JR
SCULPTOR, DESIGNER
b Havana, Cuba, Jan 23, 27; US citizen. *Study:* Univ Havana, cert(archit); Univ Madrid, cert(lit); Royal Acad Fine Arts San Fernando, Spain; Corcoran Sch Art; George Washington Univ, AA. *Work:* Am Numismatic Soc, New York; Carnegie Mus Natural Hist, Pittsburgh; Metrop Mus Art, New York; Muzeum Sztuki Medalierkiej, Crakow, Poland; World Heritage Mus,

Champaign, Ill. *Comn:* Heroic frieze, Poor Richard Club, Philadelphia, 52; statuary, John Wanamaker, Inc, Philadelphia, 53-55; insignia & medal, Dept Recreation, City Philadelphia, 58; monument, Zoological Garden Philadelphia, 74; plus many busts of numerous personalities. *Exhib:* Nat Sculpture Soc Ann Exhib, 57 & 72; Fidem Int Exhib; Cologne, Ger, 58; Artists Equity Exhib, Philadelphia Mus Art, Philadelphia Civic Ctr, 71 & 74; one-man show, Rutgers Univ, 72; Ten Crucial Days, NJ State Mus, Trenton, 76-77; and others. *Pos:* Scenic designer, Valley Forge Music Fair, Pa, 55; art dir, Burroughs Corp, Philadelphia, 56-57; dir advert & promotion, Johnson & Johnson Int, New Brunswick, NJ, 59-62. *Teaching:* Instr art, 20th Army Air Force, Guam, 46; instr arts & crafts, Moyamensing Prison, Philadelphia, 58-59; artisan-instr sculpture, Johnson Atelier, Princeton, 74-77; fac, Arts Inst, Rutgers Univ, summer 81 & 82. *Awards:* First Prize Drawing, Buenos Aires Herald, Arg, 39; Winner Nat Open Competition, Soc Medalists, 70. *Mem:* Artists Equity Asn (Philadelphia & NY chaps); prof assoc, Am Inst Archit. *Media:* Multimedia. *Publ:* Auth & contribr, numerous how-to articles. *Mailing Add:* Raleigh Ct Lymer Ave London SE19 1LS England 08873 United Kingdom

ALLEN, TOM R
SCULPTOR
b Corpus Christi, Tex, Aug 29, 47. *Study:* San Jacinto Col, Pasadena, Tex, AA, 74; San Houston State Univ, Huntsville, Tex, BA, 75, MFA, 77. *Work:* Sam Houston State Univ, Huntsville, Tex. *Comn:* Interior piece, F S Mutual, Houston, Tex, 81. *Exhib:* Mus Southwest Art Show, Midland Mus, Tex, 75; 22nd Ann Delta Art Exhib, Ark Art Ctr, Little Rock, 79; Tradition and Change, Univ Houston, Clear Lake City, Tex, 80; 80 Texans, Galveston Arts Ctr, Tex, 80; Third Tex Sculpture Symposium, Southwest Tex State Univ, San Marcos, 81. *Teaching:* Instr jewelry, Southwest Craft Ctr, San Antonio, Tex, 77-78; instr sculpture, San Antonio Art Inst, McNay Mus, Tex, 78; instr design, Southwest Tex State Univ, San Marcos, 78-80. *Awards:* First Place Contemp Sculpture, One Seguin Art Ctr, 78; Second Place Contemp Sculpture, Hill Country Art Found, 79; Cash Award, 13th Ann Drawing & Small Sculpture Show, 79. *Bibliog:* Fracine Carror (auth), Artist profile, Art Voices, 1/2/81. *Mem:* Tex Soc Sculptors; Tex Designer Craftsman; Tex Asn Sch Arts. *Media:* Mixed; Wood. *Publ:* Sandboxes, Houston Art Scene, 5-6/81. *Dealer:* S L Art Gallery 2133 Cedar Springs Rd Dallas TX 75201; Teni Jones Inc 1200 Bissonnet Houston TX 77005. *Mailing Add:* 100 Algarita San Marcos TX 78666

ALLEN, WILLIAM J
HISTORIAN, EDUCATOR
b Tuscaloosa, Ala, Nov 8, 45. *Study:* Univ Ala, BA, 68; Johns Hopkins Univ, MA, 73, PhD(Kress Fel, Am Res Inst Turkey Fel), 81. *Teaching:* Vis asst prof, Okla State Univ, 77-79; asst prof art hist, Ark State Univ, Jonesboro, 79-, chmn art dept, 83- *Mem:* Col Art Asn Am; Ark Col Art Asn (pres, 83-84). *Publ:* Auth, The spirit of fact in court: Southworth's testimony in Marcy vs Barnes, In: History of Photography, 82; auth, The Abdul Hamid II collection, In: History of Photography, 83. *Mailing Add:* PO Box 824 State University AR 72467

ALLENTUCK, MARCIA EPSTEIN
HISTORIAN, EDUCATOR
b Manhatten, NY, June 8, 28. *Study:* Washington Square Col, New York Univ, BA, 48; Columbia Univ, PhD, 64. *Teaching:* Prof hist art, Graduate Ctr, City Univ New York, 72- *Awards:* Sr res fel, Dumbarton Oaks, 72-73 & Nat Endowment Humanities, 73-74; res fel, British Acad, 80. *Mem:* Col Art Asn; Soc Architectural Historians of Great Britian; Soc Architectural Historians; Historians of Am Art; Asn Art Historians. *Res:* British, American & Canadian art & architectural history. *Publ:* Auth, Henry Fuseli: The Artist as Man of Letters & Critic, Univ Microfilm Am, 64; auth, Rosetti's Burd-Alane, Burlington Mag, 12/70; auth, John Graham's System & Dialectics of Art, Johns Hopkins Univ Press, 71; auth, Mark Gertler, Apollo, 10/74; auth, Furseli & Macklin, J of the Washbury & Courtauld Inst, 76. *Mailing Add:* 5 West 86th Street Apt 12B New York NY 10024

ALLGOOD, CHARLES HENRY
HISTORIAN, PAINTER
b Augusta, Ga, Apr 24, 23. *Study:* Univ Ga, with Lamar Dodd, Carl Holty, Yasuo Kunyoshi, BFA, MFA; Ecole du Louvre, Paris. *Exhib:* Painting of the Year, Atlanta, Ga, 63 & 65; Southeastern Art Exhib, Atlanta, 65; Miss Nat Exhib, Jackson, 66; Mid-South Exhib, Memphis, Tenn, 71. *Collections Arranged:* African Art & Artifacts, 74; Egyptian Art & Artifacts, 75. *Pos:* Dir, E H Little Gallery, Memphis State Univ. *Teaching:* Prof painting, Judson Col, Marion, Ala, 51-55; prof painting, Memphis State Univ, 55- *Media:* Oil, Transparent Watercolor. *Mailing Add:* 3886 Healy Rd Memphis TN 38111

ALLING, CLARENCE (EDGAR)
MUSEUM DIRECTOR, CERAMIST
b Dawson Co, Nebr, Jan 28, 33. *Study:* Washburn Univ, BFA; Ohio State Univ, with Edgar Littlefield; Univ Kans, with Sheldon Carey, MFA. *Work:* Excelsior Ins Co, New York. *Exhib:* One-man shows, Mulvane Art Ctr, Topeka, Kans, 63 & Sioux City Art Ctr, Iowa, 63; Area Artists, Sioux City, 63 & 65 & Des Moines, Iowa, 64; two-man show, L'Atelier, Cedar Falls, Iowa, 65; and others. *Pos:* Dir, Waterloo Munic Galleries, currently. *Awards:* Prizes, Designer-Craftsman Show, Lawrence, Kans, 59-61; Purchase award, Ceramic Nat, Everson Mus, Syracuse, NY, 60; Merit award, Sioux City, 65. *Mailing Add:* c/o Waterloo Munic Galleries 225 Cedar St Waterloo IA 50704

ALLMAN, MARGO
SCULPTOR, PAINTER
b New York, NY, Feb 23, 33. *Study:* Smith Col; Moore Col Art; Univ Pa; Univ Del; with Reginald Marsh & Hans Hofmann. *Work:* Del Art Mus, Wilmington; Philadelphia Mus Art. *Comn:* Travertine sculpture, comn by Mrs Werner Hutz & family, Kennett Square, Pa, 73; corten steel sculpture, comn by Richard Vanderbilt, Chadds Ford, Pa, 74; ferro-cement sculpture, Tidewater Publ Co, Centerville, Md, 75. *Exhib:* Del Art Mus, 56-81; Nat Woodcut & Wood Engraving Show, Print Club, Philadelphia, 56, 59 & 60; Univ Del, 65-72 & 76; one-person shows, Haas Gallery Art, Bloomsburg State Col, Pa, 76 & 77, Moore Col Art, 79 & Del State Art Coun, 81; and others. *Awards:* Mildred Boericke Prize, 32nd Ann Nat Exhib Woodcuts & Wood Engravings, Print Club Philadelphia, 58; Drawing Prize, 51st Ann Show, Del Art Mus, 65; Best Landscape Painted by Delaware Artist, Wilmington Trust Bank Prize, Del Art Mus, 69. *Mem:* Del Ctr Contemp Arts. *Media:* Wood, Stone; Acrylic, Ink. *Mailing Add:* 202 E State Rd West Grove PA 19390

ALLNER, WALTER H
PAINTER, DESIGNER
b Dessau, Ger, Jan 2, 09; US citizen. *Study:* Bauhaus-Dessau, with J Albers, V Kandinsky, Paul Klee. *Exhib:* Galeria Bonino, Soho, New York, 76; Bauhaus-Archiv, Berlin, Ger, 76; Toledo Art Mus, Ohio, 77; Kunstbibliothek, Staatliche Museen, Berlin, Ger, 80; Univ Del, Newark, 80; Lahti Art Mus, Finland, 81; Cooper-Hewitt Mus, New York, 81; and many others. *Pos:* Design consult, Johnson & Johnson, New Brunswick, NJ, 54-55; art dir, Fortune Mag, 63-74; design consult, RCA, 65-67; chmn jury, International Poster Exhib, Colorado State Univ, Fort Collins, 79 & 81. *Teaching:* Mem fac, Parsons Sch Design, New York, 74-; vis critic, Yale Univ Sch Art, 76, Ecole Superieure d'Art Graphique, Paris, 79; lectr, Swinburne Inst Technol, Melbourne, 83. *Awards:* Medal Bauhaus Dessau, Ger Acad Archit. *Mem:* Alliance Graphique Int (pres US Section, 72-74, int pres, 74-); Am Inst Graphic Arts. *Mailing Add:* 110 Riverside Dr New York NY 10024

ALLOWAY, LAWRENCE
EDUCATOR, CRITIC
b London, Eng, Sept 17, 26. *Collections Arranged:* Morris Louis Mem Exhib, 63, Francis Bacon, 63 & Int Award Exhib, Guggenheim Mus; William Baziotes Mem Exhib, 65; Barnett Newman: The Stations of the Cross, 66; Jean Dubuffet, 66. *Pos:* Cur, Solomon R Guggenheim Mus, 62-66; art ed, The Nation, 68-80; assoc ed, Artforum, 71-76. *Teaching:* Instr, Bennington Col, Vt, 61-62; prof art, State Univ NY, Stony Brook, 68-81, gallery dir, 77-81. *Awards:* Foreign Leader Grant, US State Dept, 68; award for distinction in art criticism, Frank Jewett Mather, 72. *Res:* 20th century American art and art criticism. *Publ:* Auth, The Venice Biennale 1895-1968, 68; auth, Violent America: The Movies 1946-1964, 71; auth, American Pop Art, 74; auth, Topics in American Art Since 1945, 75; auth, Roy Lichtenstein, 83; and others. *Mailing Add:* 330 W 20th St New York NY 10011

ALLRICH, M LOUISE BARCO
DEALER
b Ft Monroe, Va, Feb 16, 47. *Study:* Univ Calif, Davis, BA, 68; Univ Calif, Berkeley, post-grad work art hist & theory. *Pos:* Pres, Allrich Gallery, San Francisco, 71-; trustee, Fiberworks Ctr for Textile Arts, Berkeley, 72-81. *Teaching:* Lectr, Alta Col Art, 73, Wash State Univ, Pullman, 78, Los Angeles Co Mus, 79, Oakland Mus, 82, Art Inst Chicago, 82 & Portland Art Mus, 83. *Mem:* Soc Encouragement Contemp Art. *Specialty:* Contemporary textile art, painting and sculpture. *Publ:* Auth, Center for the Arts, pvt publ, 74; contribr, A look at fiber, Currant Mag, 76. *Mailing Add:* 251 Post St San Francisco CA 94108

ALLUMBAUGH, JAMES
SCULPTOR, EDUCATOR
b Dallas, Tex, Jan 27, 41. *Study:* ETex State Univ, BS & MS; NTex State Univ, EdD. *Work:* Richardson Pub Libr, Tex; Beaumont Art Mus, Tex; Houston Ctr 2, Tex; Tyler Art Mus, Tex; Seaman Collection, Corpus Christi, Tex. *Exhib:* Tex Painting & Sculpture, Dallas Mus of Fine Arts, 68 & 71; Tel Aviv Int, Israel, 78; James K Wilson Gallery, Dallas, Tex, 79; Int Shoebox Sculpture Exhib, Univ Hawaii, 82; solo show, Colo State Univ, 83; Ft Collins, Colo, 83; and others. *Pos:* Dir, Tex Col Sculpture Symposium, Dallas, 77- *Teaching:* Fel design, NTex State Univ, 66-68; assoc prof three-dimensional design, ETex State Univ, 68-81, prof, 81- *Bibliog:* Dennis Kowal & Donna Meilach (auth), Sculpture Casting, Crown, 72; Jan Butterfield (auth), The Young Texans, Arts Mag, 72. *Mem:* Artists Equity (vpres, Dallas chap, 77). *Media:* Sculpture. *Publ:* Illusr (cover illus), 16th Ann Invitational Exhib, Longview Arts Ctr, 74 & 45th Ann Exhib, Springfield Art Mus, 75; auth, Cubes Space and Light, Spiral Enterprises, 77. *Dealer:* Gallery One 4715 Camp Bowie Fort Worth TX. *Mailing Add:* 2009 St Francis Dallas TX 75228

ALLWELL, STEPHEN S
SCULPTOR
b Baltimore, Md, Oct 15, 06. *Study:* Md Inst, Baltimore. *Comn:* Folksinger, Mrs Robert Lindner, Baltimore, 69; copier, Alan Elkin, Baltimore, 70; Lacrosse, James F Welsh, Baltimore, 71. *Exhib:* Four shows, Miniature Painters, Sculptors & Gravers Soc, Washington, DC, 67-71; Acad Arts, Easton, Md, 67 & 71; Mariner's Mus Marine Art Exhib, Newport News, Va, 69; Washington Co Mus, Hagerstown, Md, 69; Peale Mus, Baltimore, 70. *Awards:* Grand Prize Outdoor Exhib, Baltimore Outdoor Art Show, 67; Purchase Award, Metromedia-WCBM, 67; Reese E McLeod Prize Sculpture, Miniature Painters, Sculptors & Gravers Soc, Washington, DC, 69. *Bibliog:* L'art a l'etranger, La Rev Mod, 7/68. *Mem:* Artists Equity Asn; fel Md Fedn Art; Baltimore Art Guild; Rehoboth Art League. *Mailing Add:* 803 Evesham Ave Baltimore MD 21212

ALMOND, PAUL
FILMMAKER, WRITER
b Montreal, Can, Apr 26, 31. *Study:* Bishop's Col Sch, 44-48; McGill Univ; Balliol Col, Oxford, BA & MA. *Pos:* Dir & producer, Can Broadcasting Corp, 63-65. *Awards:* Special Award of Merit for Documentary Film, Prague, 63; Canadian Film Awards, Best Motion Picture Director, 70; Best Television Drama Dir, 79. *Bibliog:* Janet Edsforth (auth), The Flame Within (a study of Paul Almond's Films), Can Film Inst, 71. *Mem:* Acad Can Cinema; Dir Guild Am; Dir Guild Can; Can Asn Motion Picture Producers. *Publ:* Auth, The Hill (TV play); co-auth, The Broken Sky (TV play); writer, producer & dir, Isabel (film), 68, Act of the Heart (film), 70 & Journey (film), 72; coauth, Ups & Downs (film), 82. *Mailing Add:* 1272 Redpath Crescent Montreal PQ H3G 2K1 Canada

ALMY, MAX (MARILYNN IRENE)
VIDEO ARTIST, DIRECTOR
b Omaha, Nebr, Sept 9, 48. *Study:* Univ Nebr, BFA, 70; Univ Minn, 71; Calif Col Arts & Crafts, MFA, 78. *Work:* Mus Mod Art, New York; Long Beach Mus Art; San Francisco Mus Mod Art; Va Mus Fine Arts; Stedilijk Mus, Amsterdam. *Comn:* Deadline (video installation), Mus Contemp Art, Chicago. *Exhib:* Electronic Art, Mus Contemp Art, Chicago, 80; Biennale Paris, Mus Art Mod, Paris, 80; California Video, Long Beach Mus Art, 80; Exchange Show, Arsenal, Berlin, 81; Performance Art, Mus Mod Art, New York, 82; Video Festivals, Ithaca, 82 & Athens, 83; Nat Video Festival, Am Film Inst, Los Angeles, 83; Video Art: A History Part II, Mus Mod Art, New York, 83. *Pos:* Mgr productions, One Pass Film & Video, 78-83; creative dir, Group One, 84- *Teaching:* Instr, Calif Col Arts & Crafts, 77-78; vis artist video, Art Inst Chicago, 84. *Awards:* Nat Endowment Arts Fel, 82; US Film & Video Festival Award, 82; Western States Regional Media Arts Fel, 83. *Bibliog:* Steve Seid (auth), Deadline for the future, Networks, 82; MOMA-TV: The push to artsify video, Village Voice, 83. *Mem:* Bay Area Video Coalition; Am Film Inst; Northern Calif Women Film & Video. *Media:* Video, Computer Animation. *Dealer:* Electronic Arts Intermix 84 Fifth Ave New York NY 10011. *Mailing Add:* 5855 Chabot Oakland CA 94618

ALONSO, MANUEL ZAVALA See Zavala, Manuel

ALONZO, JACK J
DEALER, COLLECTOR
b Brooklyn, NY, July 3, 27. *Study:* Brooklyn Col; NY Univ. *Pos:* Dir/pres, Alonzo Gallery, 65- *Specialty:* Contemporary paintings, photographs, drawings and others, predominately abstract. *Collection:* Catholic. *Publ:* Contribr, Arts Mag, 4/71. *Mailing Add:* 31 E 12th St New York NY 10003

ALPER, M VICTOR
EDUCATOR, WRITER
b Wilkes-Barre, Pa, Mar 23, 44. *Study:* Boston Univ, BA; NY Univ, MA & PhD; Harvard Univ; Rutgers Univ, MBA. *Pos:* Contrib ed, Arts Mag, New York, 70-74; res asst, Mod Lang Asn, New York, 72-73; dir, Am Hist Photo Arch, New York, 75-77; auth weekly radio series, WGBH, Boston, 76; asst to exec vpres, Rutgers Univ, 77-78; consult, Rutgers Univ Art Gallery, 77-78. *Teaching:* Instr humanities, NY Univ, 69-73; lectr, Mus City New York, 70-71; assoc prof humanities, Montclair State Col, 73-77; guest lectr, City Univ New York, 78; guest lectr, Univ Mass; dir commun & media & assoc prof, NY Univ, 78- *Mem:* Am Asn Univ Prof; Am Fedn Arts; NY State English Coun; Nat Acad TV Arts & Sci; Soc Am Historians. *Res:* Art and culture of the 18th & 19th centuries; interdisciplinary studies. *Publ:* Auth, America's Heritage Trail, 76 & America's Freedom Trail, 76, Macmillan; and others. *Mailing Add:* 145 W 79th St Apt 11-C New York NY 10024

ALPERT, BILL (WILLIAM H)
PAINTER, SCULPTOR
b Bronx, NY, Dec 21, 34. *Study:* Univ Calif Los Angeles, with Arthur Levine & John Paul Jones, BA, 63, MFA, 65. *Exhib:* Constructs Orgn Independent Artists, Bleecker Renaissance, New York, 78; Orgn Independent Artists Postcard Show, Bologna Art Fair, Italy, 78; Painting & Sculpture Today, Indianapolis Mus Art, 78; Albright-Knox Mus, 78 & 79; Current New York, Joe & Emily Lowe Art Gallery, Syracuse Univ, 80; Color on Structure, W Paterson Collection of NJ Wayne, 81; and others. *Collections Arranged:* Orgn of Independent Artists: Group Show, US Courthouse, 77 & Art in Public Places, 26 Fed Plaza, New York, 77. *Teaching:* Adj prof painting, Cooper Union Sch Art, New York, 79-82; adj instr drawing, Parsons Sch Design, New York, 81-82. *Awards:* Creative Artist Pub Serv Prog Finalist, 77-78, 80-81 & 81-82. *Bibliog:* Peter Frank (auth), New York Reviews, Art News, 11/77 & Ellen Lubell (auth), Arts Mag, 11/77; JoAnn Lewis (auth), Sculpture room, Washington Post, 5/27/78; Gregory Battcock (auth), Art Information, 5/81. *Mem:* NY Artists Equity Asn; Orgn Independent Artists (mem exhib comt, 77-78). *Media:* Acrylic, Oil; Wood, Constructions. *Publ:* Contribr, New York Art Yearbook, 75-76; contribr, Re-View, Vol I, Issue 1, Vered Lieb, 77; contribr, The Whitney Counterweight Catalog, 77; contribr, Sciences, New York Acad Sci, 3/78. *Mailing Add:* 64 Grand St New York NY 10013

ALPERT, GEORGE
PHOTOGRAPHER, GALLERY DIRECTOR
b New York, NY, Apr 3, 22. *Study:* NY Univ; NC State Col; Stanford Univ; Univ Calif, Berkeley; Inst Seven Arts, NY. *Work:* Il Diaframma, Milan, Italy; Miller-Plummer Collection, Philadelphia. *Exhib:* One-man shows, Alfred Stieglitz Gallery, New York, Neikrug Gallery, New York, Light Gallery, New York, Period Gallery West, Scottsdale, Ariz & Everson Mus. *Pos:* Chmn, pres & dir gallery, Sohophoto Found, 70- *Teaching:* Mem fac creative photog, New Sch Social Res, New York, 74-79. *Specialty:* Photography. *Publ:* Auth, The Queens, 75 & coauth, Second Chance to Live: The Suicide Syndrome, 75, Da Capo Press; auth, Taos Pueblo, Paradise House, 83. *Mailing Add:* 5702 N 55 Pl Paradise Valley AZ 85253

ALPS, GLEN EARL
EDUCATOR, PRINTMAKER

b Loveland, Colo, June 20, 14. *Study:* Univ Northern Colo, BA; Univ Wash, MFA; Univ Iowa, advanced study with Mauricio Lasansky. *Work:* Mus Mod Art, New York; Philadelphia Art Mus; Chicago Art Inst; Los Angeles Co Mus Art, Calif; Libr Cong, Washington, DC. *Comn:* Sculptural panel, Seattle Pub Libr, 60; fountain, Munic Bldg, City of Seattle, 61; wall sculpture, Magnolia Br, Seattle Pub Libr, 64; ed of prints, Washington State Arts Comn, 71; bronze fountain, First Christian Church, Greeley, Colo, 72. *Exhib:* 1st Editions traveling exhib, Ore & Wash Arts Comn, 78; The Collagraph: A New Print Medium, nat traveling exhib, Pratt Graphics, 78; Eight Pioneers in Collagraph Printmaking, Wenninger Gallery, Boston, 79; A Glen Alps Retrospective Exhib: The Collagraph Idea 1956-1980, Bellevue Art Mus, Wash, 79; Regional Photography & Printmaking traveling exhibition, works by 23 Northwest artists, Evergreen State Col, 79; and many others. *Pos:* Treas, Northwest Printmakers, 49-51, pres, 51-53 & 62-64. *Teaching:* Prof art, Univ Wash, 45-, chmn div printmaking, currently. *Awards:* Tamarind Fel, 60 & Tamarind Artist in Residence, 65, Ford Found; Gov Award, 72 & 78. *Bibliog:* Jules Heller (auth), Printmaking Today, Holt Rinehart & Winston, 72; The Complete Collagraph, 80; The Art of the Print, 80. *Mem:* World Print Coun; Soc Am Graphic Artists; Northwest Print Coun. *Dealer:* Francine Seders Gallery 6701 Greenwood Ave N Seattle WA 98103. *Mailing Add:* 6523 40th Ave NE Seattle WA 98115

ALQUILAR, MARIA
PAINTER, SCULPTOR

b Brooklyn, NY, May 25, 35. *Study:* Hunter Col, New York, AB(humanities), 55. *Work:* Chase Manhattan Bank, New York & Phoenix. *Exhib:* Animal Imagery, Renwick Gallery, Smithsonian Inst, 81; Animals: Celebration and Communion, San Jose Mus, Calif, 81; Inedible Renwick Birthday Cake, Smithsonian Inst, 82; Downey Mus Art, Calif, 82 & 83; Crocker Art Mus, Sacramento, Calif, 83 & 84; one-person exhib, Gorman Mus, Univ Calif, Davis, 83. *Pos:* Dir, Jennifer Pauls Gallery, Sacramento, Calif, 70- *Awards:* Crocker-Kingsley Award, 70, Camelia Invitational, 70 & Calif State Fair, 77, Crocker Art Mus. *Bibliog:* Marione Ashbourne (auth), Polarities, Suttertown News, 6/83; Ellen Schlesinger (auth), Sunday woman--artist in residence, Sacramento Bee, 8/83; Janice Edwards (auth), article, Ceramics Monthly, 12/83. *Media:* Clay; Acrylic, Pastel. *Specialty:* Narrative art. *Dealer:* John Pence Gallery 750 Post St San Francisco CA 94109. *Mailing Add:* 171 Donner Ave Roseville CA 95678

ALSDORF, JAMES W
PATRON, COLLECTOR

b Chicago, Ill, Aug 16, 13. *Study:* Wharton Sch Finance & Com, Univ Pa. *Pos:* Pres & dir, Alsdorf Found, Chicago, 49-; vpres, Art Inst Chicago, 65-72, vchmn, 72-75, chmn, 75-78, trustee, life gov, maj benefactor & mem of numerous comts; vchmn, contrib mem & mem trustee comt, Am Asn Mus, Washington, DC; founder, Old Masters Soc; mem nat comn, Univ Art Mus, Univ Calif, Berkeley; and many others. *Mem:* Gov life mem Chicago Hist Soc; assoc Arch Am Art; Asia Soc, New York; Renaissance Soc; life mem Antiquarian Soc, Chicago; and many others. *Collection:* Modern drawings, painting and sculpture; American nineteenth century trompe l'oeil school; Early Americana and folk art, archaic and classical art. *Mailing Add:* 301 Woodley Rd Winnetka IL 60093

ALTEN, JERRY
DIRECTOR, DESIGNER

b Philadelphia, Pa. *Study:* Philadelphia Col Art; Temple Univ, BA(fine arts). *Pos:* Owner, Shirt Sleeve Studio, Philadelphia, 59-62; sr designer, Container Corp Am, Oaks, Pa, 62-67; art dir, TV Guide Mag, 67-; mem staff, Triangle Publ Inc, Radnor, Pa, currently. *Teaching:* Lectr, cols in US & Europe. *Awards:* Awards of Excellence, NY Art Dirs Club, Soc Publ Designers & Soc Illusr; and others. *Mem:* Soc Publ Designers; Art Alliance Philadelphia; NY Art Dirs Club; Philadelphia Art Dirs; Philadelphia Col Art Alumni Asn. *Mailing Add:* 10 Wynnedale Circle Narberth PA 19072

ALTENBERND, RICHARD AUGUST
SCULPTOR

b Ames, Iowa, Nov 21, 42. *Study:* Univ Chicago, 60-61; Univ Iowa, BA(with honors), 64; Columbia Univ, 65-70. *Exhib:* Southwest Craft Bienial, Folk Art Mus, Santa Fe, NMex, 76; Craftsmen NMex, Mus Southwest, Midland, Tex, 77; Southwestern Crafts, Amarillo Mus, Tex, 78; Once a Tree, NMex Woodworker's, Santa Fe, 80 & 81. *Awards:* Artists of the Year, Santa Fean Mag, 80. *Bibliog:* M F Love (auth), Sculpture in wood, Santa Fean, 9/79; Tricia Hurst (auth), Artist profile, Art Voices, 1/81. *Media:* Wood. *Dealer:* The Artists Gallery 125 Palace Ave Santa Fe NM 87501. *Mailing Add:* Rt 2 Box 226 1/2 Santa Fe NM 87501

ALTERMAN, JOHNNY
PHOTOGRAPHER

b Miami, Fla, Aug 12, 42. *Study:* Univ Pa, BS, 64; Univ Miami, JD, 69; San Francisco State Univ, MA, 79. *Work:* Princeton Univ Art Mus, NJ; Chrysler Mus, Norfolk, Va; Ctr Creative Photog, Tucson, Ariz. *Exhib:* West-The Law, Minn Mus Art, Minneapolis & traveling, 79-80; Daughters, San Francisco Arts Comn Gallery, Calif, 79-80; Never Fail Imagery, Sch Mus Fine Arts, Boston, 80; Five Years/New American Nudes, Creative Photog Gallery, Mass Inst Technol, 81 & 82; Ooparts: The Uncategorical, BC Space Gallery, Laguna Beach, Calif, 83; Vertical Walkways, Bank Am World Hq, San Francisco, 83. *Teaching:* Asst photog, San Francisco State Univ, 78-79 & Ansel Adams Yosemite Workshop, Calif, summer 80. *Bibliog:* Colin Westerbeck (auth), Reviews: Falling women, Artforum, 4/82; Suzanne

Muchnic (auth), On photography, Los Angeles Times, 3/27/83. *Mem:* Soc Photog Educ. *Publ:* Contribr, New American Nudes, Morgan & Morgan, 81; auth, American photographer, G A Fisher, 3/82; contribr, Photographing Children, Life Libr Photog, Time-Life Bks, 83. *Mailing Add:* 847 N Point St San Francisco CA 94109

ALTERMANN, TONY
DEALER

b Dallas, Tex, Aug 10, 40. *Study:* NTex State Univ, BA & MS. *Pos:* Dir publicity & pub relations, MGM, Dallas, Tex, 70-72; vpres, Tex Art Gallery, Dallas, 72-78; owner & pres, Altermann Art Gallery, Dallas, 78- & Connally/Altermann Art Gallery, Houston, 83. *Specialty:* Western, wildlife and Americana subjects in all media. *Mailing Add:* c/o Altermann Art Gallery 2504 Cedar Springs Dallas TX 75201

ALTMAN, HAROLD
PRINTMAKER, EDUCATOR

b New York, NY, Apr 20, 24. *Study:* Art Students League, 41-42; Cooper Union, 41-47; New Sch Social Res, 47-49; Acad Grande Chaumiere, Paris, 49-52; Black Mountain Col, NC. *Work:* Mus Mod Art, Metrop Mus Art & Whitney Mus Art, New York; Art Inst Chicago; Nat Gallery Art, Washington, DC; and others. *Comn:* Entire print ed, Mus Mod Art, 60, Soc Am Graphic Artists, 62, Hilton Rockefeller Hotel, 63 & Jewish Mus, NY, 64. *Exhib:* One-man shows, Martha Jackson Gallery, New York, 58, Art Inst Chicago, 60, San Francisco Mus Art, 61, Sagot Le Garrec Gallery, Paris, 68 & 74 & State Gallery Fine Arts, Istanbul, Turkey, 75; and others. *Teaching:* Asst prof art, NY State Col Ceramics, Alfred Univ, 52-54, Univ NC, Greensboro, 54-56 & Univ Wis-Milwaukee, 56-62; prof art, Pa State Univ, 62-76. *Awards:* Two Guggenheim Fels, 60-62; Nat Inst Arts & Lett Award, 63; Fulbright Hays Sr Res Fel, 64-65. *Bibliog:* Articles, New York Times, Los Angeles Times, Vie Des Arts, and numerous others. *Publ:* Illusr, The Four Seasons, Pa State Univ, 65. *Dealer:* Assoc Am Artists 663 Fifth Ave New York NY 10022. *Mailing Add:* Box 57 Lemont PA 16851

ALTMANN, HENRY S
PAINTER, EDUCATOR

b Manhattan, NY, Dec 4, 46. *Study:* Pratt Inst, Brooklyn, BFA(art educ), 68; Queens Col, Flushing, NY, MFA(painting), 70; Fulbright fel painting, 70-71, Fine Arts Acad, Munich, Ger. *Work:* First Nat Bank New York; Skowhegan Sch Painting & Sculpture, New York; Shawmut Bank of Boston, Mass. *Comn:* Three stained glass windows & paintings for rear portal (with Maxine Ann Sorokin), Kehillath Jakob Synagogue, Newton, Mass, 73. *Exhib:* One-man shows, First St Gallery, New York & Meetinghouse Gallery, Boston, 73; Young Realist Show, Harbor Gallery, Cold Spring Harbor, Long Island, NY, 72; two-person exhib, Goethe Inst, Boston, 80; Jewish Community Ctr, Southern NJ Gallery, Cherry Hill, 80; plus many others. *Pos:* Exhib chmn, West Roxbury Art Asn, 77-; res comt arch, West Roxbury Hist Soc, 77-, dir visual arts, Jewish Community Ctr, Newton, Mass, 83- *Teaching:* Instr art, Boston Univ, 71-75; instr art, Art Inst Boston, 75-; Framingham State College, Mass. *Bibliog:* W Rox (auth), Boston Globe article, 5/81. *Mem:* Boston Vis Artists Union. *Media:* Oil, Pastel. *Dealer:* Crieger Art Assoc 801 Water St Framingham MA 01701; Boston Fine Arts Boylston St Boston MA. *Mailing Add:* 61 Perham St West Roxbury MA 02132

ALTMAYER, JAY P
COLLECTOR

b Mobile, Ala, Mar 1, 15. *Study:* Tulane Univ La, BA & LLB. *Pos:* Mem, Fine Arts Comt, State Dept. *Collection:* American paintings mostly dealing with plantation life and workers; paintings by William Aiken Walker, Sully, Rembrandt Peale, Gilbert Stuart, Severn Rosen, Jarvis and others; large collection of precious metal and jewelled historical American presentation swords. *Mailing Add:* 75 St Michael Mobile AL 36602

ALTSCHUL, ARTHUR G
COLLECTOR, PATRON

b New York, NY, Apr 6, 20. *Pos:* Mem gov bd, Yale Art Gallery, New Haven, Conn; drawing comt, Mus Mod Art; mem trustees coun, Nat Gallery Art, currently; mem nat bd, Smithsonian Assoc, Smithsonian Inst, currently. *Mem:* Fel perpetuity Metrop Mus Art, New York. *Collection:* American impressionists and The Eight; cubists and lesser known members of the neo-impressionist, Nabis and Pont-Aven schools. *Mailing Add:* 85 Broad St New York NY 10004

ALTVATER, CATHERINE THARP
PAINTER

b Little Rock, Ark, July 26, 07. *Study:* Grand Cent Sch Contemp Arts & Crafts; Art League Long Island, with F Spradling & E Whitney; Nat Acad Fine Arts, with Mario Cooper, Ogden Pleissner, Louis Bouche & Robert Phillips. *Work:* Museums in US, Europe, Japan & Can; also many pvt collections. *Exhib:* Nat Acad Design; Nat Arts Club; Audubon Artists, Metrop Mus Fine Arts; Elliott Mus, Stuart, Fla; Reading Mus, Pa; Mus Fine Arts, Mexico City; Royal Soc Watercolor Painters, London. *Pos:* Pres, Art League Long Island, secy, Hudson Valley Art Asn, treas (1st woman officer), Am Watercolor Soc & treas, Am Artists Prof League, all formerly; instr watercolor, Ark Art Ctr, Little Rock. *Teaching:* Workshops and demonstrations throughout the US. *Awards:* Over 70 awards including 20 first prizes. *Mem:* Am Watercolor Soc; Nat Art League; Allied Artists Am. *Media:* Watercolor. *Mailing Add:* 505 Douglas St New Smyrna Beach FL 32069

ALTWERGER, LIBBY
PAINTER, GRAPHIC ARTIST
b Toronto, Ont, July 13, 21. *Study:* Ont Col Art. *Exhib:* One-man shows, Pascall Gallery, Toronto, 64 & Sonneck Gallery, Kitchener, Ont, 68; London Art Gallery, Ont; Hamilton Art Gallery, Ont; and others. *Pos:* Can exchange artist with Am Watercolor Soc. *Teaching:* Former instr drawing, Ryerson Polytech Inst. *Awards:* Sterling Trust Award for Lithograph, 65; Royal Bank of Can Purchase Award, Ont Soc Artists Show, 79; Purchase Award, Watercolor Soc, 81. *Mem:* Can Soc Graphic Artists; Ont Soc Artists; Printing & Drawing Coun of Can; Can Soc Painters in Water Colour; Can Soc Painter-Etchers & Engravers. *Media:* Watercolor. *Mailing Add:* 526 Dovercourt Rd Toronto ON M6H 2W4 Canada

ALVAREZ-CERVELA, JOSE MARIA
EDUCATOR, HISTORIAN
b La Guardia, Spain, Sept 21, 22. *Study:* Univ Santiago, Spain, BA, 48, Lic en Derecho, 56, PhD(law & artistic works), 68; Middlebury Col, Vt, MA, 65. *Pos:* Dir, Fine Arts Mus, Univ PR, Mayaguez, 58-64. *Teaching:* Prof art & humanities, Univ PR, Mayaguez, 57- *Mem:* PR Acad Arts, Hist & Archaeol. *Res:* Woodcarving of saints in Puerto Rico; mural paintings on ceilings and vaults; funerary art in Puerto Rico. *Publ:* Auth, Signos y Firmas Reales, La Comercial, Santiago, Spain, 57; auth, A Pintura Mitologica e Alegorica nos Tectos e Abobodas do Escorial e do Palacio Real, Ed Imperio, Lisbon, 68; auth, Los Contratos de Obra Artistica de la Catedral de Santiago de Compostela en Siglo XVII, Industrias Graficas Noroeste, Spain, 68; auth, Woodcarving of saints in primitive style in Puerto Rico, Atenea, Univ PR, 73; auth, La Arguitectura Clasica Actual en Mayaguez, Antillian Col Press, Mayaguez, 83. *Mailing Add:* 79 Oviedo St (Belmonte) Mayaguez PR 00708

AMAROTICO, JOSEPH ANTHONY
PAINTER, CONSERVATOR
b Bronx, NY, Sept 3, 31. *Study:* Am Art Sch, New York, with Raphael Soyer; Pa Acad Fine Arts, Philadelphia, with Franklin Watkins, Walter Stuempfig, Hobson Pittman & Theodor Siegl. *Work:* George Washington Univ, Washington, DC; Glassboro Col, NJ; Washington, DC, District Court; Rutgers Univ Art Gallery, New Brunswick, NJ; Woodmore Art Ctr, Chestnut Hills, Pa; and others. *Comn:* Conserv of John Trumbull paintings in the Rotunda, US Capitol, Washington, DC. *Exhib:* Nat Exhib, Pa Acad Fine Arts, var times, 59-69; Nat Traveling Exhib, Am Fedn Arts, 64; 10th Mary Washington Exhib Mod Art, Fredricksburg, Va, 65; Art for Embassies, US Dept State, Jamaican Embassy, Kingston, 67; Ann Exhib, Butler Inst, Youngstown, Ohio, 69, 70 & 72. *Pos:* Conservator painting, Pa Acad Fine Arts, 68- *Teaching:* Instr painting, Pa Acad Fine Arts, 66- *Awards:* Mary Butler Award, Pa Acad Fine Arts Fel Exhib, 62; Painting Prize, Cheltenham Art Ctr, Philadelphia, 68; Endowment Fund Prize, Woodmere Art Ctr, Chestnut Hill, Pa, 72. *Mem:* Fel Am Inst for Conserv. *Media:* Acrylic, Oil. *Publ:* Auth, Thomas Cole in the Adirondacks, 78 & William James Stillman's Adirondack Sojourns, 83, Adirondack Life Mag. *Dealer:* Butcher More Galleries 1613 Walnut Street Philadelphia PA 19103; Mickelson Galleries 709 G St NW Washington DC 20001. *Mailing Add:* Broad and Cherry Streets Penn Acad Fine Arts Philadelphia PA 19102

AMASON, ALVIN ELI
PAINTER
b McKenny, Tex, Apr 6, 48. *Study:* Cent Wash Univ, BA, 73, MA, 74; Ariz State Univ, MFA, 76. *Work:* Nat Collection Fine Arts, Smithsonian Inst, Washington, DC; Nordjyllands Kunstmuseum, Aalborg, Denmark; Alaska State Mus, Juneau; Anchorage Hist & Fine Arts Mus, Alaska; Am Embassy, Brasilia, Brazil. *Comn:* Painting (with Robert Hudson, Sam Francis & Dan Flavin), Govt Serv Admin, Anchorage, 79. *Exhib:* Nat Collection Fine Arts, Washington, DC, 80. *Awards:* Jurors Award, Phoenix Mus Art, 75; Purchase Award, Alaska State Coun Arts, 80. *Bibliog:* Jamake Highwater (auth), The Sweet Grass Lives On, Harper & Row, 80; Sculpture out in the open, Newsweek, 8/18/80; Sandra B Betz (auth), Alvin Eli Amason, Arts & Cult N, 81. *Mem:* Alaska State Coun Arts (councilman, 79-80). *Media:* Oil, Mixed. *Dealer:* Suzanne Brown Gallery 7156 Main St Scottsdale AZ 85251. *Mailing Add:* 4701 San Leandro Oakland CA 94601

AMATEAU, MICHELE
PAINTER
b New York, NY, July 29, 45. *Study:* Boston Univ, BFA, 68; Univ Colo, Boulder, MFA, 73. *Work:* Chase Manhattan Bank, New York; Subaru Inc & Amoco Productions, Denver, Colo; Harte Hanks Inc Investments, San Antonia, Tex. *Exhib:* 1976 Bicentennial Painting & Sculpture Exhib, Indianapolis Mus Art, 76; Painting Invitational, 78 & Print Invitational, 82, Denver Art Mus; Cleveland Art Mus, 79; one person exhibs, Sheldon Art Mus, Univ Nebr, Lincoln, 79, Minneapolis Col Art & Design, Minn, 80 & Marianne Deson Gallery, Chicago, 82; Masks, 80 & New Work, 82, Laguna Gloria Art Mus, Austin, Tex. *Pos:* Interviewer & reviewer art & dance, Straight Creek J, Denver, 73-75 & Boulder Daily Camera, Colo, 76-77; cur exhib, Patrick Gallery, Austin, Tex, 80-81. *Teaching:* Grad painting & drawing dept head, Wichita State Univ, Kans, 77-78; vis artist, Minneapolis Col Art & Design, 79-80; vis prof, Univ Tex, San Antonio, 81-82. *Bibliog:* Allan Moore (auth), articles, Artforum, 75; Allan Ellenzweig (auth), articles, Arts Mag, 75 & 78; Peter Frank (auth), articles, Art News, 76 & 78. *Mem:* Nat Orgn Women Artists; Womens Caucus Art; founding mem Front Range Women, Colo. *Media:* All. *Dealer:* McIntosh/Drysdale Gallery 2008 Peden Houston TX 77019; Marianne Deson Gallery 340 W Huron Chicago IL 60610. *Mailing Add:* Star Rt 1A Box 77M Dripping Springs TX 78620

AMAYA, ARMANDO
SCULPTOR
b Puebla, Pue, Mex, Nov 29, 35. *Study:* Escuela Nac Pintura & Escultura La Esmeralda, with Francisco Zuniga. *Work:* Pasquale Iannetti Gallery, San Francisco & Carmel, Calif; Galleria Tere Hass, Galeria Misrachi, Mexico City; Galeria Tasende, Acapulco. *Comn:* Benito Juarez (bronze mask), Mex Govt, Santa Ursula, 69. *Teaching:* Prof art, Escuela Nac Pintura & Escultura La Esmeralda, 69- *Media:* Bronze. *Dealer:* Pasquale Iannetti 575 Sutter St San Francisco CA 94102. *Mailing Add:* Lopez 137 Depto 1 Mexico City 06070 CP Mexico

AMBROSE, CHARLES EDWARD
PAINTER, EDUCATOR
b Memphis, Tenn, Jan 6, 22. *Study:* Univ Ala, BFA, 49, MA, 50. *Work:* Univ Southern Miss; Carey Col; Biloxi Art Asn; First Nat Bank, Hattiesburg, Miss. *Comn:* Portrait reliefs, 58 & portraits, 60, Univ Southern Miss; Pat Harrison Waterways Bldg, 65; Carey Col; Miss Archives Bldg, 72. *Exhib:* Mid-Continent Exhib, Mo, 71; Watercolor USA, Springfield, Mo, 73; 1st Ann Bi-State, Meridian, Miss, 73; Central South, Nashville, Tenn, 75; 17th Dixie Ann, Montgomery, Ala, 75. *Teaching:* Assoc prof drawing & painting, Univ Southern Miss, 50-70; head art dept, Miss Univ for Women, 70-82. *Awards:* First Place Watercolor, Miss Art Asn, 68; First Place Drawing, Edgewater Ann, 70; Purchase Award/Drawing, 1st Ann Bi-State, 73. *Mem:* Southeastern Col Arts Conf; Nat Coun Art Adminr; Southern Asn Sculptors; Col Art Asn; Miss Art Asn. *Media:* Watercolor, Oil. *Mailing Add:* 1125 Seventh N Columbus MS 39701

AMEN, IRVING
PAINTER, PRINTMAKER
b New York, NY, July 25, 18. *Study:* Pratt Inst, scholar, 32-39; study in Paris, 50 & Italy, 53. *Work:* Mus Mod Art & Metrop Mus, New York; Butler Inst Am Art; Victoria & Albert Mus, London; Bibliot Nat, Paris; Albertina Mus, Vienna; and others. *Comn:* Peace Medal (commemorating end of Viet Nam War); Twelve Tribes of Israel (12 stained glass windows 16ft high), comn by Agudas Achim Synagogue, Columbus, Ohio. *Exhib:* Master Prints, Mus Mod Art, New York; Int Ausstellung Von Holzschnitten, Zurich, Switz; I Mednarodna Graficna Razstava, Ljubljana, Yugoslavia; L V Biannale di Pittura Americana, Bordighera, Italy; Dessins Americains Contemporains, US Info Serv. *Teaching:* Instr art, Pratt Inst & Univ Notre Dame. *Mem:* Int Inst Arts & Lett; Int Soc Wood Engravers; Accad Fiorentina delle Arti Disegno; Soc Am Graphic Artists; Am Color Print Soc; plus others. *Media:* Oil, Etching, Woodcut. *Publ:* Print ed, Irving Amen woodcuts 1948-1960, Irving Amen: 1964, Amen: 1964-1968 & Amen: 1968-1970; illusr, Gilgamesh, Ltd Ed Club. *Mailing Add:* 90 SW 12th Terrace Boca Raton FL 33432

AMEND, EUGENE MICHAEL
INSTRUCTOR, HISTORIAN
b Jefferson City, Mo, Oct 31, 50. *Study:* Univ Mo-Columbia, BA, 75, MA, 77; studied with Dr Saul Weinberg, Dr Edward Baumann & Dr Osmond Overby. *Collections Arranged:* Nathan Jones: Works on Paper, Univ Tex-Dallas, 79; Arie Van Selm: Recent Works, Tex Woman's Univ, Denton, 79; Charles Campbell: Retrospective, Longview Mus & Art Ctr, Tex, 79; Auguste Ravier, 1814-1895, Univ Tex, Dallas, 81. *Pos:* Cur & art historian, Stewart Gallery, Dallas, 78-; art adv & free lance cur, E M Amend & Assoc, Dallas, 80- *Teaching:* Instr art hist & humanities, Univ Mo-Columbia, 75-76; instr art hist, Richland Col, 80- *Mem:* Col Art Asn; Artist Coalition Tex (pres, 79-). *Res:* American artists and current art patrons and patronage in regional localities; Australian artist, Norman Lloyd (1895-1978). *Mailing Add:* 3130 Chatsworth Farmers Branch TX 75234

AMES, JEAN GOODWIN
DESIGNER, PAINTER
b Santa Ana, Calif, Nov 5, 03. *Study:* Pomona Col, hon DFA, 75; Art Inst Chicago, grad, 26; Univ Calif, Los Angeles, BE, 31; Univ Southern Calif, MFA, 37. *Work:* Mus Contemp Crafts, New York; Everson Mus, Syracuse, NY. *Comn:* Ceramic mural (with Arthur Ames), 56 & enamel mural, 58, Rose Hills Mem Park, Whittier, Calif; ceramic mural (with Arthur Ames), Guarantee Savings & Loan, Fresno, Calif, 58; tapestry designed for Garrison Theater, Claremont, Calif, 64; tapestry designed for Fed Plaza Bldg, Los Angeles, 68. *Exhib:* French & American Tapestries, Otis Art Inst, Los Angeles & La Jolla Art Ctr, Calif, 61; Mus Contemp Crafts Traveling Exhib, 67; Enamels, Everson Mus Fine Art, Syracuse, NY, 69; Scripps Col, 69-81. *Teaching:* Prof drawing & design, Scripps Col & Claremont Grad Sch, 40-69. *Awards:* First Award, Seventh Nat Decorative Arts & Ceramics, Wichita Art Asn, 52; award for distinguished archit decoration, Am Inst Architects, Southern Calif Br, 56 & 58; woman of the year in art, Los Angeles Times, 58. *Mem:* Am Crafts Coun. *Media:* Oil. *Mailing Add:* 4094 Olive Hill Dr Claremont CA 91711

AMES, LEE JUDAH
ILLUSTRATOR, WRITER
b New York, NY, Jan 8, 21. *Study:* Columbia Univ, with Carnahan. *Work:* Many pieces, layouts and finished illustrations in Univ Ore & Univ Southern Miss permanent collections. *Pos:* Art dir, Weber Assocs, New York, 47-52; pres, Ames Advert, New York, 53-54; artist-in-residence, Doubleday Publ Co, New York, 55-60; pres, Lee Ames & Zak Ltd, 75- *Teaching:* Instr comic art, Sch Visual Arts, New York, 48-49; lectr advert art, Dowling Col, 70- *Mem:* Nat Cartoonists Soc. *Media:* Mixed Media. *Publ:* Auth & illusr, Draw 50 Famous Cartoons, Draw 50 Famous Stars, Make 25 Crayon Drawings of the West, Make 25 Felt Tipped Drawings of the Circus & The Dot, Line and Shape Connection, Doubleday; plus illusr for over 100 addn bks. *Mailing Add:* 44 Lauren Ave Dix Hills NY 11746

AMFT, ROBERT
PAINTER, PHOTOGRAPHER
b Chicago, Ill, Dec 7, 16. *Study:* Art Inst Sch, grad; Oxbow Sch, Saugatuck, Mich. *Work:* Butler Inst Am Art, Youngstown, Ohio. *Exhib:* Pa Acad Ann, 58; Butler Inst Art, 58; Painting & Sculpture Today, Indianapolis, 78; one-man show, Art Inst Chicago Sales Gallery, 78, Hammer & Hammer Gallery, Chicago, 81, Joy Horwich Gallery, Chicago, 81 & Countryside Art Ctr, Arlington Heights, 82. *Awards:* First Prize Painting, 72 & Spec Award, 75, New Horizons; Renaissance Prize, 75th Artists of Chicago, 74. *Bibliog:* Great treasures from the Art Institute of Chicago, Chicago Mag, 4/77; Udo Kultermann (auth), Van Gogh in Contemporary Art, Art Voices South, 11-12/78; Alan Artner (auth), rev, Chicago Tribune, 7/24/81. *Mem:* Arts Club Chicago. *Publ:* Illusr, Photographs of sculptor Fred Smith, Life Mag, 11/69. *Dealer:* Joy Horwich 333 E Ontario Chicago IL 60611. *Mailing Add:* 7340 N Ridge Chicago IL 60645

AMINO, LEO
SCULPTOR, INSTRUCTOR
b Tokyo, Japan, June 26, 11; US citizen. *Study:* NY Univ; Am Artists Sch, New York. *Work:* Whitney Mus Am Art & Study Collection, Mus Mod Art, New York; Art, Andover, Mass; Grand Rapids Mus, Mich; Addison Gallery of Am Art, Mass; Massilon Mus. *Exhib:* Mus Mod Art, New York, 50; Metrop Mus Art, New York, 51; Whitney Mus Am Art, 56; Jewish Mus, New York, 70; San Francisco Mus Art, 70. *Teaching:* Instr sculpture, Black Mountain Col, 46 & 50 & Cooper Union Sch Art, 52-77. *Media:* Plastic. *Dealer:* Sculpture Ctr 167 E 69th St New York NY 10021. *Mailing Add:* 58 Watts St New York NY 10013

AMINOFF, JUDITH
WRITER, EDITOR
b San Diego, Calif, July 9, 47. *Study:* Univ Calif, Berkeley, BA, 70; McGill Univ, Montreal, 72-75. *Pos:* New York corresp, Flash Art, Milan, 79; contrib ed, Umbrella Mag, Calif, 79; ed, Cover Mag, 79- *Res:* Magazine of art presenting new works; artists in their own words and in dialogue with each other, critics, dealers. *Mailing Add:* 40 Harrison St Apt 25/D New York NY 10013

AMOSS, BERTHE
ILLUSTRATOR, PAINTER
b New Orleans, La, Sept 26, 20. *Study:* Newcomb Col, BA; Univ Hawaii; Kunsthalle Bremen, Ger, three yrs; Acad des Beaux Arts, Antwerp, Belg, one yr. *Work:* La State Libr; De Grummond Collection, Univ Southern Miss. *Teaching:* Instr writing & illus children's bks, Tulane Univ, 76-82. *Media:* Watercolor. *Publ:* Auth & illusr, The Marvelous Catch of Old Hannibal, 70, Old Hasdrubal and the Pirates, 71, Parents Publ; auth & illusr, Secret Lives, Atlantic/Little-Brown, 79; auth & illusr, The Loup Garou, Pelican, 79; and others. *Mailing Add:* 3723 Carondelet St New Orleans LA 70115

AMSDEN, FLOYD T
COLLECTOR, PATRON
b Wichita, Kans, May 25, 13. *Study:* Univ Kans, BS, 35; Wichita State Univ, post-grad studies in art hist, 73-75. *Interests:* University collections, Mus Art, Univ Kans & Ulrich Mus Art, Wichita State Univ. *Collection:* Bronzes, drawing and lithographs by Gerhard Marcks; figure drawings by P Pearlstein, R Diebenkorn, J Beal, W Theibaud, Theodore Roszak, Isabel Bishop, P Modersohn-Becker and others. *Mailing Add:* 158 N Quentin Wichita KS 67208

AMSTER, SALLY
PAINTER
b New York, NY. *Study:* Cornell Univ, BFA; Brooklyn Mus Art Sch; Columbia Univ, MFA. *Exhib:* Works on Paper, Brooklyn Mus, NY, 75; Olean Pub Libr, NY, 77; State Univ NY, Canton, 77; Richmond Col, City Univ New York, 78; 19th & 20th Century Women Artists, Allport Assoc Gallery, San Francisco, 79; one-person shows, Prince Street Gallery, New York, 73, 75, 77 & 79, Allport Assoc Gallery, 79 & Hull Gallery, DC, 80. *Teaching:* Lectr Am art, Soviet Union, 58, Women's art, 83. *Awards:* US Rep, First US-USSR Student Exchange, 58; Cornell Univ Fac Medal in Art, Cornell Univ, 59. *Bibliog:* In praise of women artists, article in Arts Mag, 6/77. *Mem:* Women's Caucus Art. *Media:* Oil, Watercolor. *Dealer:* Hull Gallery 3301 New Mexico Avenue NW Washington DC; Allport Gallery 126 Post St San Francisco CA 94108. *Mailing Add:* 470 West End Ave New York NY 10024

AMYX, LEON KIRKMAN
PAINTER, EDUCATOR
b Visalia, Calif, Dec 20, 08. *Study:* San Jose State Col, AB, 31; Claremont Grad Sch, MA, 42; Univ Calif, Berkeley; Mills Col; Calif Col Arts & Crafts, with McFee, Kroll, Sheets, Hinkle & Chapin. *Comn:* Textile designs, Seneca Textile Corp, New York, 54; paintings, Granite Construction Co, Watsonville, Calif, 73; paintings, Bud Antle Inc, Salinas, Calif, 79. *Exhib:* San Francisco Mus Art, 35; Golden Gate Expos, Treasure Island, San Francisco, 39; Am Watercolor Soc, Nat Acad Galleries, New York, 42; Traveling Exhib Through Latin Am, San Francisco Mus Art, 44; Nat Watercolor Soc, Riverside Mus, New York, 46; Calif Artists Invitational, San Jose State Univ, 58; and others. *Teaching:* Prof painting & hist art, Hartnell Col, Salinas, Calif, 36-72; prof painting, Sacramento State Univ, summers 49-52, San Jose State Univ, summers 55 & 56 & Univ Pac, Stockton, summer 59. *Awards:* Silver Medal, Oakland Calif Art Mus, 44; First Award, Monterey Calif Dist Fair, 49. *Bibliog:* Mary M Riddle (auth), Amyx's show demonstrates that it takes a complication of knowledge to be simple in art, Carmel Pine Cone, 11/19/48; Irene Lagorio (auth), Watercolors and oils by Leon Amyx, Monterey Peninsula Herald, 3/18/79. *Mem:* Nat Watercolor Soc; Carmel Art Asn (bd dirs, 48-49, 73-74, 80); hon mem Laguna Beach Art Asn; Assoc Am Watercolor Soc. *Media:* Watercolor, Oil, Acrylic. *Dealer:* Gallery Who's Who in Art Dolores & Fifth Carmel CA 93921. *Mailing Add:* 265 San Benancio Canyon Rd Salinas CA 93908

ANARGYROS, SPERO
SCULPTOR
b New York, NY, Jan 23, 15. *Study:* Study with William Zorack, New York, 34-35; asst to Mahonri Sharp Young, This is the Place Monument, Salt Lake City, Utah, 44-47. *Comn:* Four Heroic Groups (stone sculpture), State Capitol Restoration Proj, Sacramento, Calif, 83; Christ at Resurrection (12 ft bronze), Agana, Guam, 74; bronze portrait of Father Terry, pres, Santa Clara Univ, 77; Jubail commemorative plaque, Saudi Arabia, 77; bronze portrait of John Daley, pres, World Airways, 79; commemorative plaque, James Martin MacInnis Hastings Sch Law, San Francisco, 81; plus many others. *Exhib:* Nat Acad Design, 38-40, 53-56, 59 & 77; M H De Young Mem Mus, 53 & 62-63; one-man shows, Houston & Corpus Christi, Tex, 68, San Francisco, Calif, 69 & Egyptian Mus, San Jose, Calif, 69; Nat Sculpture Soc Ann, 77; plus many others. *Awards:* First Award Exhib, Tenth Ann Nat Exhib, Acad Artists Asn, 59; John Spring Art Founder Award, 42nd Ann Exhib, 75 & Coun Am Soc Award, 45th Ann Exhib, 78, Nat Sculpture Soc. *Bibliog:* Terence Busch (auth), Spero Anargyros and his 23 ton rock, San Francisco Mag, 11/65; Frederick Whitaker (auth), Spero Anargyros, sculptor, Am Artist, 2/67; Valerie Shields (auth), Man with a masterful thumb, Spectator, 2/57. *Mem:* Life mem Art Students League; fel Nat Sculpture Soc; fel Int Inst Arts & Lett; Nat Soc Lit & Arts. *Media:* Bronze, Marble. *Mailing Add:* PO Box 522 541A Tunnel Ave Brisbane CA 94005

ANASTASI, WILLIAM (JOSEPH)
PAINTER, SCULPTOR
b Philadelphia, Pa, Aug 11, 33. *Study:* Univ Pa, 53-58. *Work:* Metrop Mus Art, New York; Brooklyn Mus; Phoenix Mus Art, Ariz; Ga Mus Art, Athens; Univ NC, Greensboro. *Comn:* Viewing a Film of the Period (film), 78, Collapse (photo installation), 81 & Terminus II (photo installation), 81, Whitney Mus Am Art; Photo installation, Kunstmus, Dusseldorf, Ger, 79; Terminus I (photo installation), Hudson River Mus, New York, 79. *Exhib:* Open to New Ideas: Art for Jimmy Carter, Ga Mus, Athens, 76; Revisions, Perspectives and Proposals in Film and Video, Whitney Mus Am Art, 79; Coincidents, Kunstmus, Dusseldorf, WGer, 79; Für Augen und Ohren, Akad Kunste, West Berlin, Ger, 80; Ecouter par les Yeux, Mus D'Art de la Ville de Paris, France, 80; Coincidents, Whitney Mus Am Art, New York, 81; Ann Awards Exhib, Am Acad Arts & Lett, New York, 82. *Bibliog:* Gregory Battcock (auth), Minimal Art (Introduction), Dutton, 68; Lucy R Lippard (auth), Six Years: The De-materialization of the Art Object, Praeger, 73; Brian O'Doharty, Inside the white cube: Notes on the Gallery Space, Artforum, 3/76. *Dealer:* Galerie Max Hetzler Kamekestr 21 5000 Cologne WGer. *Mailing Add:* 640 Riverside Dr New York NY 10031

ANBINDER, PAUL
PUBLISHER, COLLECTOR
b Brooklyn, NY, Apr 19, 40. *Study:* Cornell Univ, AB, 60; Columbia Univ, grad work, 60-61. *Collections Arranged:* Cornell Collects (co-organizer), Hudson River Mus, Yonkers, NY, 76-77. *Pos:* Ed in chief, Shorewood Publ Inc, 64-69; exec ed & vpres, Harry N Abrams Inc, New York, NY, 69-74 & pres, 74-75; dir spec projs, Alfred A Knopf, Random House & ed/vpres, Ballantine Bks, New York, 75-78; pres, Hudson Hills Press, Inc, New York, 78- *Mem:* Col Art Asn; New York Friends of Johnson Mus, Cornell Univ (mem exec coun). *Collection:* Contemporary American prints and drawings. *Mailing Add:* c/o Hudson Hills Press Inc 220 Fifth Ave New York NY 10001

ANDERSEN, LEIF (WERNER)
PAINTER
b Baltimore, Md, Mar 6, 25. *Study:* Art Students League, with Reginald Marsh & Louis Bouche, 46-48. *Work:* Bordighera Mus, Italy. *Exhib:* Am Group Show, Venice, Italy, 52; Nat Acad Design Ann, New York, 57 & 62; Allied Artist Am Ann, Nat Acad Design, 58 & 61; and numerous one-man shows. *Awards:* S J Wallace Truman Award, Nat Acad Design Ann, 57; Margaret Cooper Prize, Allied Artist Am, Nat Acad Design, 61. *Media:* Oil, Acrylic. *Mailing Add:* 246 East 51st St New York NY 10022

ANDERSEN, WAYNE VESTI
HISTORIAN, EDUCATOR
b July 7, 28; US citizen. *Study:* Univ Calif, BA, 59; Columbia Univ, William Bayard Cutting fel, 61-62, MA, 61 & PhD, 66. *Pos:* Sr cur, Walker Art Ctr, Minneapolis, Minn, formerly; dir, Hayden Gallery, Mass Inst Technol, 65-77; pres, Vesti Corp, Boston, Mass, 78- *Teaching:* Prof art hist, Mass Inst Technol, 64-; vis prof, Yale Univ, New Haven, Conn, 69; prof visual studies, Harvard Univ, 77-79. *Awards:* Belg-Am Found CRB Fel, 62; Ford Found Grant Humanities, 62-63; Am Coun Learned Soc Fel. *Mem:* Col Art Asn Am. *Res:* Late nineteenth century painting; twentieth century art. *Publ:* Auth, Cezanne's portrait drawings, 69; auth, Gauguin's paradise lost, 71; auth, American sculpture in process, 75; and numerous articles in scholarly mags. *Mailing Add:* 137 Marlboro St Boston MA 02116

ANDERSON, ALEXANDRA C
CRITIC, WRITER
b Boston, Mass, May 14, 42. *Study:* Sarah Lawrence Col, BA, 61; Sorbonne, France, 63. *Pos:* Art ed, Paris Rev, 73-78; art ed, Village Voice, 74-77; sr ed, Portfolio Mag, 79- *Awards:* Nat Endowment Arts Critic Grant, 78. *Mem:* Int Asn Art Critics. *Res:* Contemporary art and artist's publications; 20th century art. *Publ:* Co-auth, Anderson and Archer's Soho: The Essential Guide to Art and Life in Lower Manhattan, Simon & Schuster, 79. *Mailing Add:* 333 E 68th St New York NY 10021

ANDERSON, BRAD J
CARTOONIST
b Jamestown, NY, May 14, 24. *Study:* Syracuse Univ, BFA, 51. *Work:* Albert T Reid Col; William Allen White Found, Univ Kans; Complete Collection Grandpa's Boy Original Comic Strips, Syracuse Univ Manuscripts Libr; Birchfield Mus, Buffalo, NY. *Exhib:* San Diego Fair Fine Arts & Cartoon Exhib; Punch, Brit-Am Exhib, 54; Cartoon Exhib, The Selected Cartoons of 14 Saturday Evening Post Cartoonists; Cartoon Americana, overseas exhib; Birchfield Mus, Buffalo, NY, 76; Albright-Knox Mus, Buffalo, NY, 76; San Francisco Mus Fine Arts, 77. *Pos:* Art dir, Graphic Art Dept, Syracuse Univ, 50-52; free-lance cartoonist, 50-; int syndicated cartoonist, Marmaduke, 54- & Grandpa's Boy, 54- *Mem:* Mag Cartoonist Guild; Newspaper Comics Coun. *Publ:* Illusr, Marmaduke Treasury, Sheed Andrews & McMeel, 78; illusr, Meet Marmaduke, Signet, 83; illusr, Marmaduke Mystery Puzzles, Scholastic, 83; illusr, Marmaduke Super Dog, Andrews & McMeel, 83; illusr, Marmaduke Large and Lovable, Tor, 83; and many others. *Mailing Add:* 422 Santa Marina Court Escondido CA 92025

ANDERSON, BRUCE JAMES
STAINED GLASS ARTIST, DEALER
b Denver, Colo, Nov 18, 40. *Study:* Ottawa Univ, Kans, BA, 63; Univ Manchester, Eng, 64; Univ Colo, Boulder, MA, 72. *Work:* Agate Community Church, Colo; Holy Mother God Byzantine Church, Denver; St Stephen Protomartyr Episcopal Church. *Comn:* Dutchman Restaurant, Denver, 73; Continental Broker, Denver, 76; six panels, Rik Fulcher, Denver, 79; Blackhawk Hotel, Davenport, Iowa, 79; Lunt Ave Marble Club, Scottsdale, Ariz, 79; and others. *Exhib:* Colo Glass Art, Boulder, 76-78. *Pos:* Owner, dir & designer, Wild Rose Studio & Gallery, 72- *Bibliog:* Joy Overbeck (auth), article, Leisure Living, fall 74; Marjorie Barrett (auth), Home living section, Rocky Mountain News, 10/23/76; Grant Tyson (auth), Gifts worth waiting for, Denver, 11/78. *Specialty:* Glass by Gary Feltner, Miles Thompson. *Mailing Add:* 1066 Pennsylvania Denver CO 80203

ANDERSON, DAVID C
SCULPTOR, PHOTOGRAPHER
b Jamestown, NY, Mar 10, 31. *Study:* Univ Tulsa, with Alexandre Hogue & Dwayne Hatchett, BA, 64. *Work:* Tulsa S Regional Libr; Univ Tulsa; Okla Educ TV Authority. *Comn:* Sculpture, Price Waterhouse & Co, Houston, 79; Univ Tulsa, 81, Western Nat Bank, Tulsa, 82, Excelsior Hotel, Tulsa, 82 & Royal Bank Can, Dallas, 83. *Exhib:* Oklahoma Sculpture Today, Okla Mus Art, 80; Sculpture in Wood, Wichita Art Mus, 81; Shidoni Ann, Santa Fe, 81 & 82; Art Ann IV, 83 & Okla Sculpture Exhib, 83, Okla Mus Art. *Teaching:* Private lessons sculpture, 78-; adj prof art, Univ Tulsa, 82. *Awards:* Best of Show & First Place Photog, Bartlesville, Okla, 79. *Bibliog:* Clive Cussler (auth), King Dave--from pinstriping to sculpture, Tulsa Mag, 6/78 & David Anderson--Oklahoma Art Gallery, Wall & Wall Publ, 80. *Mem:* Charter mem Okla Sculpture Soc; Int Sculpture Ctr. *Dealer:* 26 East Art Ctr Tulsa OK; Adelle M Fine Arts Dallas TX. *Mailing Add:* 4985 E 26th St Tulsa OK 74114

ANDERSON, DAVID K
DEALER, COLLECTOR
b Buffalo, NY, June 26, 35. *Pos:* Pres & owner, David Anderson Gallery Inc, New York, currently. *Mem:* Art Dealers Asn Am. *Specialty:* Art of 20th century since 1945. *Mailing Add:* 521 W 57th St New York NY 10019

ANDERSON, DAVID PAUL
SCULPTOR
b Los Angeles, Calif, Feb 3, 46. *Study:* San Francisco Art Inst; asst to Peter Voulkos, 72-73. *Exhib:* One-person shows, San Francisco Mus Art, 73; San Francisco Art Inst, 79, Braunstein Gallery, San Francisco, 83 & Linda Durham Gallery, Santa Fe, 83; Public Sculpture/Urban Environment, Oakland Mus, Calif, 74; 1975 Biennial Exhib Contemp Art, Whitney Mus, NY, 75; Fourth Tex Sculpture Symposium, Austin, 83; Phoenix Biennial, Phoenix Art Mus, 83. *Teaching:* Sculpture, San Francisco Art Inst, 76-79 & Calif Col Arts & Crafts, Oakland, 79. *Awards:* Grant, Soc for Encouragement of Contemp Art, San Francisco Mus, 73; Nat Endowment Arts Fel Grant, 74, 81. *Bibliog:* Artforum, 1/82; Artspace, 1/83. *Dealer:* Braunstein Gallery San Francisco; Linda Durham Gallery Santa Fe. *Mailing Add:* Rt 2 Box 204 Santa Fe NM 87501

ANDERSON, DENNIS RAY
DEALER, HISTORIAN
b Waynesboro, Va, Mar 8, 47. *Study:* Va Art Inst & Univ Va, Charlottesville; Greensboro Col, BA, 71; Univ NC, Greensboro, MFA, 72. *Collections Arranged:* The Gift of American Naive Paintings from the Collection of Edgar William and Bernice Chrysler Garbisch, 48 Masterpieces (auth, catalogue), 75, Chinese Export Porcelain (largest collection of export ever assembled; auth, catalogue), 75 & Three Hundred Years of American Art in the Chrysler Collection, A Catalogue of Selected Paintings (auth), 76, Chrysler Mus at Norfolk, Va; Ernest Lawson Retrospective (auth, catalogue), ACA Galleries, 76, Ernest Lawson and The Eight, American Flower Paintings (1850-1950) (auth catalogue & bk), 78. *Pos:* Dir, Anderson Fine Arts, New York. *Mailing Add:* PO Box 706 Gracie Station New York NY 10028

ANDERSON, DONALD MYERS
WRITER, CALLIGRAPHER
b Bridgewater, SDak. *Study:* Univ Iowa, MA, study with Phillip Guston & H W Janson; Mexico City Col, Mex. *Teaching:* Prof watercolor & calligraphy, Univ Wis, 58-82; retired. *Awards:* Typographical Excellence Award, Type Dir Club, New York, 71; Cert of Award, Chicago Bk Clinic, 73; Selected for Exhib, Am Inst Graphic Arts, 77. *Res:* History of writing. *Publ:* Auth & illusr, Elements of Design, 61 & The Art of Written Forms, 69, Holt, Rinehart & Winston, New York; auth & illusr, All, Calligraphy--Encyclopedia of Library and Information Science, Marcel Dekker, 70; auth & illusr, A Renaissance Alphabet, Univ Wis Press, 71; auth & illusr, Part, Calligraphy--Current Encyclopedia of Britain, W Benton, 74. *Mailing Add:* Rte 1 7822 Hwy 19 Dane WI 53529

ANDERSON, GUNNAR DONALD
PAINTER, ILLUSTRATOR
b Berkeley, Calif, Mar 3, 27. *Study:* Calif Sch Fine Arts, with Clyfford Still; Art Ctr Col Design, BFA, with Lorser Feitelson. *Work:* Brown-Forman Distillers, Louisville, Ky. *Comn:* Mrs Robert E Norcross, Tyronza, Ark, 68; Mr & Mrs Meredith Long, Houston, Tex, 71; Mr & Mrs George Weyerhauser, Tacoma, Wash, 72; Mr & Mrs Charlie Rich, Memphis, Tenn; Mr & Mrs Charles Schulz, Calif. *Exhib:* 5th Winter Invitational, Calif Palace of Legion of Honor, San Francisco, 64; M H de Young Mem Mus, San Francisco, 25th Ann, Soc of Western Artists, 68; Charles & Emma Frye Mus, Seattle, 71; Calif State Fair, Sacramento, 71; Grover M Hermann Fine Arts Ctr, Marietta Col, Ohio, 72. *Awards:* Best figure or portrait, 29th Ann, Soc Western Artists, 71; Third Prize, Calif State Fair, 71; best in fine art, Exhib One, Soc Art Ctr, Alumni, 72. *Bibliog:* Mrs Linda Hardwick (auth), Collage, educational TV, Memphis Community TV Found, 71-72; TV interview, Memphis, Tenn, 71; Don J Anderson (auth), Paintings of children, Chicago Today, 72. *Mem:* Soc Western Artists; Soc Art Ctr Alumni; Nat Soc Lit & Arts. *Media:* Oil. *Publ:* Illusr, Oscar Lincoln Busby Stokes, Harcourt, Brace & World Inc, 70. *Dealer:* Conacher Galleries San Francisco CA 94108; Bryant Gallery Jackson MS. *Mailing Add:* 4583 Belmont Ct Sonoma CA 95476

ANDERSON, GUY IRVING
PAINTER
b Edmonds, Wash, Nov 20, 06. *Study:* Pvt classes; Tiffany Found Fel. *Work:* Seattle Art Mus, Wash; Brooklyn Mus; Munson-Williams-Proctor Inst, Utica, NY; Metrop Mus Art, New York; Smithsonian Inst Nat Collection. *Comn:* Mural (oil on wood), Seattle Opera House, 62; cement & metal panels, Hilton Inn, Seattle; panel, workers, Edmonds Pub Libr; stone inlay, terrace, Seattle First Nat Bank; mural (oil on canvas), Bank of Calif, Seattle, 74. *Exhib:* Fine Arts Pavilion, Seattle World's Fair, 62; solo exhibs, Otto Seligman Gallery, Seattle, 63 & 65 & Francine Seders Gallery, Seatle, 71, 73, 75 & 77; A University Collects: Oregon, 67-68 & The Drawing Soc Nat Exhib, 70-72, Am Fedn Arts; 73rd Western Ann, Denver Art Mus, 72; Art of the Pacific NW, Smithsonian Inst Nat Collection; retrospective, Seattle Art Mus, Mod Pavilion, 77 & Henry Gallery, Univ Wash, 77. *Awards:* First Prize, Anacortes Art Festival, Wash, 64; Award Merit, Am Inst Archit, Seattle, 65; Guggenheim Fel, 75-76. *Bibliog:* Article, Holiday Mag, 59; article, Art in Am, 62; Guy Anderson, Gear Press, Seattle, 65. *Media:* Oil, Watercolor. *Mailing Add:* 415 E Caledonia La Conner WA 98257

ANDERSON, GWENDOLYN ORSINGER See Orsini

ANDERSON, HOWARD BENJAMIN
COLLAGE ARTIST, PHOTOGRAPHER
b Racine, Wis, June 26, 03. *Study:* Univ Wis-Madison, BA; Art Inst Chicago; Corcoran Gallery Art Sch, Washington, DC. *Exhib:* 150th Anniversary Exhib Lithography, Print Club Rochester, 48; Print Ann, Soc Am Graphic Artists, 50-59, 67-68 & 76; 69th Ann Exhib Chicago Artists & Vicinity, Art Inst of Chicago, 66; Am-Japanese Contemp Print Exhib, Tokyo, 67; Union League Art Show, Chicago, 72 & 76; one-man show, Ill Arts Coun Gallery, Chicago. *Mem:* Soc Am Graphic Artists; Chicago Soc Artists; Ft Dearborn Camera Club. *Mailing Add:* 2725 Devon Ave Chicago IL 60659

ANDERSON, IVAN DELOS
PAINTER, PRINTMAKER
b Yankton, SDak, Feb 13, 15. *Study:* Yankton Col, BA, with Frederic Taubes, Sergei Bongart, Rex Brandt & Hayward Veal. *Work:* Libr of Cong, Washington, DC; Los Angeles Co Mus, Los Angeles, Calif; Mus Mod Art, New York; William Cody Mus, Cody, Wyo; Roy Rogers' Mus, Victorville, Calif. *Comn:* Serigraph series, Ivan Anderson Children of the World (with Guy Maccoy), 75; portrait of William Boyd, comn by Grace Boyd for Hopalong Cassidy Poster, 76; Catalina Island Poster, Wrigley Catalina Island Hosp, 77; Laguna Beach Poster, City of Laguna Beach, Calif, 77. *Exhib:* Laguna Beach Mus, 70; Chaffey Mus, Cucamonga, Calif, 71; Laguna Beach Festival Arts, 73-74; Hunt-Wesson, 74; Art-A-Fair, Laguna Beach, 75-80. *Awards:* Best of Show, Catalina Festival of Arts, 67; Best Portrait of Year Award, Wilshire Ebell Club, 68; Purchase Award, Santa Paula Festival of Arts, 68. *Bibliog:* Phyllis Barton (auth), The difference between painting and pictures, SW Art, 12/76; George A Magnan (auth), Ivan Anderson's impressionistic serigraphs, Today's Art, 9/77; Ivan Anderson, Collectors Mart, 1/83. *Mem:* Art-a-Fair, Laguna Beach; Soc Am Impressionists. *Media:* Acrylic, Glaze. *Collection:* World's largest collection of Will Foster paintings. *Publ:* Auth, ed & illusr, Creative Hairshaping & Hairstyling, 47 & Hairstyles For You, 48, private publ. *Mailing Add:* 1060 Flamingo Rd Laguna Beach CA 92651

ANDERSON, JAMES P
SCULPTOR, EDUCATOR
b Tulsa, Okla, Mar 30, 29. *Study:* Eastern NMex Univ, BA, 54; Hardin-Simmons Univ, MA, 60; George Peabody Col, EdD, 64. *Work:* Franklin Co Hall of Justice, Columbus, Ohio. *Comn:* Sculpture (silver, plexiglas, wood), Morehead State Univ, 61; Urschlein XIV (bronze), Muskingum Col, 70; Benjamin Franklin (bronze), Columbus Found, Ohio, 72; Bone Form VI (bronze), Mus Arte Mod, Milan, Italy, 74; Benjamin Franklin (bronze),

Columbus, Ohio, 74. *Exhib:* X Mostro Int di Sculpture all Aperto, Mus Arte Mod, 74; Gallerie Pagani, Milan, Italy, 76; Ianuzzi Gallery, 78; Husberg Gallery, 78; Davenport Gallery of Art, 79. *Teaching:* Assoc prof art educ, Tex Tech Univ, 64-65; prof & chmn dept art, Muskingum Col, 66-74; prof & chmn dept art, Northern Ariz Univ, 74-78; prof art, St Ambrose Col, Davenport, Iowa, 79- *Bibliog:* M McGarey (auth), The shaping of a statue, Columbus Dispatch Mag, 5/74. *Publ:* Contribr, Franz Cizek, art education's man for all seasons, 10/69 & contribr, Humanism, art educational philosophy in transition, 10/75, Art Educ; contribr, Who shall teach children art, 11/69 & contribr, It's nice to be a pioneer, 12/70, Sch Arts. *Dealer:* Maxwell Gallery Ltd 551 Sutter St San Francisco CA 94102; Ianuzzi Gallery 7340 E Shoeman Lane Scottsdale AZ 85251. *Mailing Add:* 2335 Hillandale Rd Davenport IA 52804

ANDERSON, JOHN S
SCULPTOR
b Seattle, Wash, Apr 29, 28. *Study:* Los Angeles Art Ctr, Pratt Inst. *Work:* Mus Mod Art & Whitney Mus Am Art, New York. *Exhib:* Int Arts Festival, Providence, RI, 65; Albert A List Show, New Sch Social Res, 65; Cummer Gallery Art, Jacksonville, Fla, 66; eight one-man shows, Allan Stone Gallery, New York, 65-74, 77 & 81. *Teaching:* Instr sculpture, Pratt Inst, 59-62; instr sculpture, Sch Visual Arts, 68-70; instr sculpture, Cooper Union, 70-76; vis sculptor, Univ NMex, 69-70 & Univ Conn, 77-78. *Awards:* Guggenheim Found Grant, 65-66; Mini Grant, NJ State Coun Arts, 72. *Dealer:* Allan Stone Gallery 48 E 86th St New York NY 10028. *Mailing Add:* RD 2 Box 201 Asbury NJ 08802

ANDERSON, KENNETH EDMUND
SCULPTOR, EDUCATOR
b Alameda, Calif, Sept 22, 50. *Study:* Univ Nebr, Omaha, BGS, 77, BFA, 80; Univ Nebr, Lincoln, MFA, 83. *Work:* Sheldon Mem Art Gallery, Lincoln, Nebr. *Exhib:* Great Plains Sculpture Exhib, Sheldon Mem Art Gallery, Lincoln, Nebr, 81; First Int Shoebox Sculpture Exhib, Univ Hawaii, Honolulu, 82; two-person exhib, Joslyn Art Mus, Omaha, 82; 42nd Sioux City Exhib, Sioux City Art Mus, Iowa, 82; Fred Wells Show No 7, Elder Gallery, Lincoln, Nebr, 82. *Teaching:* Vis prof 3-D design & figure drawing, Univ Nebr, Omaha, 83-84. *Awards:* Second Place, Master's Touch Exhib, Col St Mary's, 80; Merit Award, Great Plains Sculpture Exhib, Nebr Arts Coun, 81. *Bibliog:* Dr Donald Doe (auth), article, Art Express, 9-10/81. *Mem:* Col Art Asn. *Media:* Steel, Wood. *Mailing Add:* 6840 Mason St Omaha NE 68106

ANDERSON, LENNART
PAINTER, INSTRUCTOR
b Detroit, Mich, Aug 22, 28. *Study:* Art Inst Chicago, BFA, 50; Cranbrook Acad Art, MFA, 52; Art Students League, 54. *Work:* Hirshhorn Mus; Whitney Mus Am Art; Brooklyn Mus, NY; Hirshhorn Mus, Washington, DC; Mus Fine Arts, Boston. *Exhib:* Carnegie Inst Mus Art, 64 & 67; Contemp Art USA, Norfolk, Va, 66; Whitney Mus Am Art Ann, 67; Vassar Col, 68; Ravinia Festival, High Park, Ill, 68; solo exhibs, Meredith Long & Co, Houston, 74 & Davis & Long Co, New York, 76; and others. *Teaching:* Instr, Chatham Col, 61-62; Pratt Inst, 62-64; Swain Sch, New Bedford, Mass, summer 63 & 64; Art Students League, Yale Univ, 67 & Skowhegan Sch, 68; prof painting & drawing, Brooklyn Col, 74- *Awards:* Raymond A Speiser Mem Prize, Pa Acad Fine Arts, 66; Nat Coun Arts Award, 66; Guggenheim Fel, 83. *Mem:* Nat Inst Arts & Lett. *Dealer:* Davis & Langdale 746 Madison Ave New York NY 10021. *Mailing Add:* 877 Union St Brooklyn NY 11215

ANDERSON, MARGARET POMEROY
COLLECTOR, CONSULTANT
b San Francisco, Calif, Mar 26, 43. *Study:* Univ Calif, Berkeley, BA, 65. *Pos:* Researcher, Pomeroy Galleries, San Francisco, 65-69; archivist, Hoover Gallery, San Francisco, 69-81, consult, 78-; owner, Am Soc Appraisers, 81- *Mem:* Arch Am Art; San Francisco Art Inst; West Coast Area Support Comt (chmn, 78-80). *Res:* Life of Marie Laurencin; nineteenth and twentieth century American and European provenance searches; Paul Manship. *Collection:* Original Marie Laurencin illustrated books, drawings, watercolors and oils. *Publ:* Contribr (catalogue), Dorothy Brown & Marie Laurencin, Univ Calif, Los Angeles. *Mailing Add:* PO Box 787 Southport CT 06490

ANDERSON, ROBERT RAYMOND
PAINTER, WRITER
b Orange, NJ, Nov 9, 45. *Study:* NJ Inst of Technol, 64-66; State Univ NY, Brockport, BS, 69; Pratt Inst, MFA, 72. *Work:* Univ Mass, Amherst; Public Serv Electric & Gas Co, NJ; Morris Mus of Arts & Sci, Morristown, NJ; State Univ NY, Brockport; Bloomfield Col, NJ; and others. *Comn:* Bicentennial painting of Nat Hist Site, 76; poster, Nat Coun Jewish Women. *Exhib:* Pratt Printers, Brooklyn Mus, 72; one-artist shows, Newark Mus, 75 & NJ State Mus, Trenton, 78; About Face, Squibb Gallery, 78; The Artist and the Airbrush, San Jose State Univ, 82; Biennial, New Jersey State Mus, 83; and others. *Collections Arranged:* Traveling exhib, NJ State Coun on the Arts, 71; 16 Contemp Artists, Hartwick Col, Oneonta, NY, 75; Presence & Absence in Realism, State Univ NY, Potsdam, 76; Viewpoint 76, Morris Mus of Arts & Sci, Morristown, NJ, 76; Contemp Portraits, E R Squibb Gallery, Princeton, NJ, 78; Super-Realism, Gallery 700, Wis, 78; Nat Graphics Exhib, Nat Arts Club, New York, 79. *Pos:* Treas, Artists Educ & Welfare Fund, 76- *Teaching:* Instr painting, Summit Art Ctr, NJ, 74-79 & Newark Mus, 76-79; asst prof art, County Col, Morris, NJ, 78-79. *Awards:* Grand Prize, New Eng Exhib, Silvermine Guild of Artists, 72; fel grant, NJ State Coun on the Arts, 76-77. *Bibliog:* Ruthann Williams (auth), Bob Anderson: An Artist Evolving, NJ Music & Arts Mag, 74; David Shirey (auth), Exhibit in Newark a Tribute to Jersey Artist, NY Times, 75, New Realism on View at the Morris Museum,

NY Times, 76 & At the Squibb-Anthology of Faces, 78; Robert Anderson (auth), article, Airbrush Mag, 83. *Mem:* Artists Equity Asn of NJ, Inc (treas, 76-79); Assoc Artists NJ; and others. *Media:* Acrylic. *Publ:* Coauth, Advanced Airbrush Techniques--The Art of the Dot, 84. *Mailing Add:* 37 Glenfield Rd Bloomfield NJ 07003

ANDERSON, ROSS CORNELIUS
MUSEUM DIRECTOR, HISTORIAN
b Washington, DC, May 2, 51. *Study:* Princeton Univ, AB, 73; Harvard Univ, MA, 77. *Pos:* Chief cur, Everson Mus Art, Syracuse, NY, 79-83; dir, Montgomery Mus Fine Arts, Ala, 83- *Teaching:* Instr, Syracuse Univ, 81, 82 & 83. *Res:* 19th and 20th century American painting and sculpture. *Publ:* Contribr, Grueby Pottery, 81, Abbott Handerson Thayer, 82 & American Clay Sculpture 1925-1950, 83, Everson Mus Art. *Mailing Add:* Mongomery Mus Fine Arts 440 S McDonough St Montgomery AL 36104

ANDERSON, SALLY J
PAINTER, PRINTMAKER
b Rockford, Ill, Feb 5, 42. *Study:* Inst Allende, San Miguel Allende, Mex, 62; Beloit Col, BA, 64; Univ Wis, 67. *Work:* Fed Bldg, Vickers Corp, Oklahoma City; Sunwest Bank, Albuquerque; Saks Fifth Ave, New York; Marriott Hotel Corp, Washington, DC. *Exhib:* Solo exhib, Roswell Art Mus, NMex, 70; Southwest Fine Arts Biennial, Mus NMex, Santa Fe, 75 & 79; Convergence 76, Carnegie Inst Mus Art, Pittsburgh, Pa, 76; Ariz Biennial, Phoenix Art Mus, 79; One Space, Three Visions, Albuquerque Mus, 80; and others. *Awards:* First Prize, NMex Crafts Biennial, Mus NMex, Santa Fe, 75; Nat Endowment Arts Grants, 76 & 77. *Bibliog:* Donald Locke (auth), article, Arts Mag, 9/83. *Media:* Acrylic, Oil; Lithography. *Dealer:* C G Rein Galleries, Edina, MN & Scottsdale AZ. *Mailing Add:* 7522 Bear Canyon NE Albuquerque NM 87109

ANDERSON, TROY
PAINTER
b Siloam Springs, Ark, Aug 23, 48. *Study:* WTex State Univ, Canyon, BS(art), 70. *Work:* Ark State Bank, Siloam Springs; Bur Indian Affairs, Washington, DC; Five Civilized Tribes Mus, Muskogee, Okla. *Exhib:* Denver Mus Natural Hist, 80; Am Indian & Cowboy Artists, San Dimas, Calif, 80-83; Five Civilized Tribes Mus, Muskogee, Okla, 81; and others. *Awards:* Best Indian Watercolor Gold Medal, Am Indian & Cowboy Artists, 81-83; Grand Award Master Artists, Five Civilized Tribes Mus, 82 & 83; First Place Painting, Cherokee Nat Hist Mus, Tahlequah, Okla, 83. *Mem:* Am Indian & Cowboy Artists. *Media:* Acrylic. *Dealer:* Troy Anderson Studio Route 1 Box 116H Siloan Springs AR 72761. *Mailing Add:* Rte 1 Box 116H Siloam Springs AR 72761

ANDERSON, WARREN HAROLD
EDUCATOR, PAINTER
b Moline, Ill, Sept 27, 25. *Study:* Western Ill Univ, BS, 50; Univ Iowa, MA, 51; Stanford Univ, PhD, 61. *Work:* Joseph H Hirshhorn Collection, Washington, DC; Phoenix Art Mus; Valley Nat Bank, Ariz. *Exhib:* Highway Drawings/Video, Phoenix Art Mus, Ariz, 79; US 80, Drawings, El Paso Mus Art, Tex, 79; one-man show, Vanishing Roadside America (prismacolor drawings), Ankrum Gallery, Los Angeles, 81, Tuscon Mus Art, 82 & Elaine Horwitch Galleries, Scottsdale, Ariz, 82. *Teaching:* Prof art, Univ Ariz, Tucson, 56- *Awards:* Several state and Southwest regional awards, 58-78; Creative Teaching Award in Art, Ariz Found, 82. *Bibliog:* John Perreault (auth), Impressions of Arizona, Art in Am, 4/81; Art on the Highway, Americana, 4/82. *Mem:* Nat Art Educ Asn; Ariz Art Educ Asn (pres 67-69). *Media:* Oil, Prismatic Pencil. *Res:* Environmental aesthetics; vernacular roadside art forms; Los Angeles as a visual metaphor; carsifacts--artifacts that exist because of cars. *Publ:* Auth, Art Learning Situations for Elementary Education, Wadsworth, 65; auth, Vanishing Roadside American, Univ Ariz Press, 81. *Dealer:* Ankrum Gallery 657 N La Cienega Los Angeles CA 90069; Elaine Horwitch Galleries 4211 N Marshall Way Scottsdale AZ. *Mailing Add:* 6802 N Longfellow Dr Tucson AZ 85718

ANDERSON, WILLIAM THOMAS
PRINTMAKER, PAINTER
b Minneapolis, Minn, Dec 13, 36. *Study:* Calif State Univ, Los Angeles, with Leonard Edmondson & Bob Fiedler; Chaffey Col; El Camino Col. *Exhib:* 18th Ann Nat Printmaking Show, Brooklyn Mus, NY, 73; World Print Competition, San Francisco Mus of Mod Art, 77; Invitational, Univ Puget Sound, 79; Stages/Four Printmakers, Mt St Mary's Col, Los Angeles, 79; Works on a Transparent Support, John Kohler Arts Ctr, Sheboygan, Wis, 79; American Indian Art in the 80's, Native Am Ctr Living Arts, Niagara Falls, 81; Invitational, C N Gorman Mus, Univ Calif, Davis, 81; and many others. *Teaching:* Prof art, Humboldt State Univ, 67- *Media:* Multimedia. *Mailing Add:* Dept Art Humboldt State Univ Arcata CA 95521

ANDERSON, WINSLOW
DESIGNER, PAINTER
b Plymouth, Mass, May 17, 17. *Study:* State Univ NY Col Ceramics, Alfred Univ, BFA; Plymouth Pottery, Mass; Hans Hofmann Sch Art, Provincetown, Mass; Pa Acad Fine Arts, Philadelphia; Pratt Graphics Ctr, New York. *Comn:* Triptych mural, Church of St Mary the Virgin Concert Hall, New York. *Exhib:* 5th & 11th Ceramic Exhibs, Syracuse Mus Fine Arts, NY, 40 & 46; Guggenheim Mus Ann, NY, 43-46; Kanawha Artists Asn, Charleston, WVa, 50. *Pos:* Glass designer, Blenko Glass Co, Milton, Va, 46-53; design dir, Lenox China Inc, Trenton, NJ, 53-64, dir dimensional design, 64-80. *Awards:* First Prize for African Mask (sculpture), Nat USA Contest, 44; First Prize for Fish (stained glass), Stained Glass Soc Washington, DC, 53. *Bibliog:* Don

Wallace (auth), Shaping America's Products, Reinhold Publ Co, 56. *Mem:* Am Crafts Coun. *Media:* Clay, Glass; Pastel, Oil. *Collection:* Haitian Primitives. *Publ:* Auth, Offhand design for offhand glass, Am Ceramic Soc J, 4/49. *Mailing Add:* 1245 Washington Ave Milton WV 25541

ANDRADE, EDNA WRIGHT
PAINTER
b Portsmouth, Va, Jan 25, 17. *Study:* Pa Acad Fine Arts, 33-38; Cresson European traveling scholar, Pa Acad Fine Arts, 36-37; Univ Pa Sch Fine Arts, BFA, 37. *Work:* Philadelphia Mus Art; Pa Acad Fine Arts, Philadelphia; Yale Art Gallery, New Haven; Montclair Art Mus, NJ; Marian Koogler McNay Art Inst, San Antonio, Tex. *Comn:* Mosiac mural, Columbia Br, Free Libr Philadelphia, 62; marble intarsia mural, Welsh Rd Br, Free Libr Philadelphia, 68; mobile sculpture, Roxborough Br, Free Libr Philadelphia, 69; granite paving, Salvation Army Div Hq, Philadelphia, 72; portfolio, etching, Print Club Philadelphia. *Exhib:* One-person shows, Pa Acad Fine Arts, Philadelphia, 67 & Marian Locks Gallery, Philadelphia, 71, 74, 77 & 83; two-person show, Rutgers Univ Art Gallery, New Brunswick, 71; Woman's Work, American Art 1974, Philadelphia Civic Ctr, 74; Philadelphia: 300 Yrs of Am Art, 76, Philadelphia Mus Art; In This Acad, Pa Acad of Fine Arts, 76; 20th Century Prints, Philadelphia Mus of Art, 77; Women's Caucus Art, Port Hist Mus, Philadelphia, 83; and others. *Teaching:* Prof art, Philadelphia Col Art, 57-72, 73-82, prof emer, 82; prof art, Temple Univ, 72-73; artist in residence, Ariz State Univ, 81. *Awards:* Mary Smith Prize, Pa Acad Fine Arts, 68; Gov Pa Hazlett Award, 80; Honor Award, Nat Women's Caucus Art, 83. *Mem:* Pa Acad Fellowship; Print Club (mem bd, 72); Artists Equity Asn; Col Art Asn. *Media:* Acrylic, Silkscreen. *Dealer:* Marian Locks Gallery 1524 Walnut St Philadelphia PA 19102. *Mailing Add:* 415 S Carlisle St Philadelphia PA 19146

ANDRE, CARL
SCULPTOR
b Quincy, Mass, Sept 16, 35. *Study:* With Patrick & Maud Morgan; Hollis Frampton; Michael Chapman; Frank Stella. *Work:* Nat Gallery Can, Ottawa; Tate Gallery, London; Mus Mod Art, New York; Albright-Knox Art Gallery, Buffalo; Art Inst Chicago; and others. *Exhib:* One-man shows, Stadtisches Mus, Monchengladbach, 68, Haags Gemeentemuseum, Den Haag, 69, Guggenheim Mus, 70, St Louis Art Mus, 71, Mus Mod Art, New York, 73 & Kunsthalle Bern, Switz, 75. *Publ:* 12 Dialogues 1962-1963, private publ & Hollis Frampton, New York Univ Press, 80. *Dealer:* Paula Cooper 155 Wooster St New York NY 10012. *Mailing Add:* PO Box 1001 Cooper Sta New York NY 10276

ANDREA, I (ANDREA HOFFMAN)
SCULPTOR, WRITER
b Los Angeles, Calif, Jan 3, 46. *Study:* Univ Calif, BA, 67; San Diego State Univ, MA, 74; Univ Southern Calif, 75-76; with Tommasi Foundry, Jacques Lipchitz & Robert Maclean. *Exhib:* Marble Biennale, Carrara, Italy, 72; 5th Ann Ai Frati, Camaiore, Italy, 72. *Pos:* Intern, Los Angeles Co Mus & J Paul Getty Mus, 75-76; freelance art writer, Art Week, Los Angeles Times & San Diego Mag, 78-; art critic, The Tribune, 79-82. *Teaching:* Instr art hist & writing, San Diego State Univ, 74-81. *Awards:* Visitor Grant, Archives of American Art, Smithsonian Inst, 75. *Bibliog:* M Cagetti (auth), Andrea Rovescia il mito D'Orfeo, La Nazione, 11/71; E Miller (auth), Andrea Hoffman, Sculptor, San Diego Mag, 1/83; J Dennehy (prod), The Discus Thrower (video), 6/83 *Mem:* San Diego Artists Guild; Artists Equity (vchmn); Calif Visual Artists Alliance (vchmn 75). *Media:* Marble, Bronze. *Publ:* Auth & cd, Issue on Stone Sculpture, Museum Registrars Report, 77; auth, The great Brezzo experiment, San Diego Mag, 81. *Mailing Add:* 2041 Del Mar Heights Rd Del Mar CA 92041

ANDREJEVIC, MILET
PAINTER
b Petrovgrad, Yugoslavia, Sept 25, 25; US citizen. *Study:* Sch Appl Arts, Belgrade, Yugoslavia, 41-44; Belgrade Acad Fine Arts, BFA, 50, MFA, 52. *Work:* Whitney Mus Am Art, New York; Hirshhorn Mus, Washington, DC; RI Sch Design, Providence; Mus, Univ Tex, Austin; Art Mus, Univ Va, Charlottesville; and others. *Comn:* Portrait, 72 & allegorical composition, 73, comn by Robert C Scull, New York. *Exhib:* Formalist Exhib, Washington Gallery Mod Art, 63; 28th Biennale, Corcoran Gallery Art, Washington, DC, 63; Green Gallery Revisited, Hofstra Univ, 72; Realism Now, New York Cult Ctr, NY, 72; 76 Jefferson St, Mus Mod Art, New York, 75; Figurative Art in New York--Artists Choice, I St Gallery, New York, NY, 77; Brooklyn Col Art Dept Past & Present, Davis & Long Gallery, New York, NY, 77; Artists Choice II, Frumkin Gallery, New York, 79; and others. *Teaching:* Instr art hist, NY Univ, 55-56, instr art hist & lib arts, Exten, 65-66; instr design, Brooklyn Col, 72-74, instr painting & drawing, 73-76. *Awards:* Nat Endowment Arts Grant, 76. *Bibliog:* Paul Katz (auth), Art now, New York, 12/69; Whee K Muller (auth), Iconography of past and present, Arts Mag, fall 72; Hilton Kramer (auth), articles in New York Times, 3/13/76 & 9/14/79. *Media:* Egg and Oil Tempera, Gouache. *Dealer:* Robert Schoelkopf 825 Madison Ave New York NY 10010. *Mailing Add:* 133 W 72nd St New York NY 10023

ANDRES, GLENN MERLE
HISTORIAN, EDUCATOR
b Chicago, Ill, July 15, 41. *Study:* Cornell Univ, BArch, 64; Princeton Univ, MFA, 67, PhD, 71; Am Acad Rome, fel, 67-69. *Collections Arranged:* Builders and Humanists,, Univ St Thomas, Houston, 66. *Pos:* Assoc dir, Johnson Gallery, Middlebury Col, 76-78. *Teaching:* Asst prof art hist, Middlebury Col, Vt, 70-78, assoc prof, 78-83, prof & chmn div arts &

humanities, 83- *Mem:* Sheldon Mus, Middlebury, Vt (trustee, 75- & vpres, 78-82). *Res:* 16th century Italian architecture; 19th century American architecture. *Publ:* Auth, A Walking History of Middlebury, Vermont, Addison Press, 75; auth, The Villa Medici in Rome, Garland Press, 76; contribr, New England Meeting House and Church: 1630-1850, Dublin Sem, 80. *Mailing Add:* Salisbury VT 05769

ANDRESON, LAURA F
CERAMIST, EDUCATOR
b San Bernardino, Calif, Oct 7, 02. *Study:* Univ Calif, Los Angeles, BA, 32; Columbia Univ, MA, 37. *Work:* Walker Art Ctr, Minneapolis; Baltimore Mus Art; Boston Mus Fine Arts; Acad Art, Honolulu. *Exhib:* One-man show, Calif Palace Legion Hon, 74; Calif Ceramics & Glass, Oakland Mus Art, 74; Everson Mus Art, 75; Craft Exhib, Philadelphia Mus Art, 77; Calif Ceramics 1898-1952, Oakland Mus Art, 78; A Century of Ceramics in US, Everson Mus Art, 79; A Century of Ceramics in US, 79 & Porcelain Exhib: 20 Ceramic Artists in USA, 80, Renwick Gallery, Smithsonian Inst. *Teaching:* Prof ceramics, Univ Calif, Los Angeles, 33-70, emer prof, 70- *Awards:* First Prize, Los Angeles Co Fair, Pomona; Purchase Prize, Oakland Mus Art, Calif; First Prize, Crocker Art Gallery, Sacramento, Calif. *Bibliog:* Elaine Levin (auth), Laura Andreson and Erwin and Mary Scheier, Ceramic Mo, 5/76; Hildegard Storr-Britz (auth), Ornaments and surfaces on ceramics, Kunst & Handwerk Verlagsanstalt, Dortmund, Ger, 77; Garth Clark & Margie Hughto (coauths), A Century of Ceramics, E P Dutton, 79. *Mem:* Am Ceramic Soc Southern Calif; fel Am Craft Coun; Calif Design; Southern Calif Designer Craftsmen (pres, 40-41); Contemp Craft Coun Los Angeles. *Media:* Porcelain. *Mailing Add:* 8400 De Longpre Ave Los Angeles CA 90028

ANDREW, DAVID NEVILLE
PAINTER, EDUCATOR
b Redruth, Eng, Apr 19, 34; Can citizen. *Study:* Falmouth Sch of Art, 54; Slade Sch of Fine Art, London, 58; influenced by Patrick Heron & Ben Nicholson. *Work:* Kettles Yard Mus, Cambridge Univ, Eng; Art Gallery of Ont, Toronto. *Exhib:* Imprint, Can Nat Exhib (touring), 76; Brit Int Print Biennale, 76 & 78; Premio Int Biella por Incisione, Italy, 76; Int Grafik Biennale, Grenchen, WGer, 76; 9th Burnaby Biennial Print Show, BC, 77; and others. *Pos:* External assessor, Croydon Col of Art, Eng, 73; dir, Falmouth Summer Sch, Cornwall, Eng, 74-77. *Teaching:* Vis artist painting, Portsmouth Col of Art, Eng, 61-70; vis artist painting & print, Bournemouth Col of Art, Eng, 62-69; assoc prof painting & printmaking, Queen's Univ, 71- *Awards:* Purchase Award, Can Cult Exchange to Hawaii, US Comn on Cult & Arts, 74; Horniansky Award, Imprint, Print & Drawing Coun of Can, 76; Purchase Award, 9th Burnaby Biennial Print Show, Burnaby Art Gallery, 77. *Mem:* Ont Soc Artists; Soc Can Artists; Print & Drawing Coun of Can. *Media:* Collage, Silkscreen. *Dealer:* Mira Godard Gallery 22 Hazleton Ave Toronto ON Can. *Mailing Add:* Dept of Art Queens Univ Kingston ON K7L 3N6 Canada

ANDREWS, BENNY
PAINTER, LECTURER
b Madison, Ga, Nov 13, 30. *Study:* Ft Valley State Col, 48-50; Univ Chicago, 56-58; Chicago Art Inst, BFA, 58. *Work:* Mus Mod Art, New York; Detroit Inst Art, Mich; Mus African Art, Washington, DC; High Mus, Atlanta; Butler Inst Am Art, Youngstown, Ohio. *Exhib:* Thirty Contemporary Black Americans, Minneapolis Inst Arts, Minn, 68; Martin Luther King Memorial, Mus Mod Art, 69; Afro-Americans: Boston and New York, Mus Fine Arts, Boston, 70; Symbols, Studio Mus Harlem, New York, 71; Artists as Adversary, Mus Mod Art, 71. *Pos:* Co-chmn, Black Emergency Cult Coalition, New York, 69- *Teaching:* Instr art, New Sch Social Res, 67-70; lectr art, Queens Col, 68-72; Dorne vis prof, Univ Bridgeport, 70. *Awards:* John Hay Whitney Fel, 65-66; NY State Creative Arts Prog Serv Grant, 71; Nat Endowment Arts Award, 74. *Bibliog:* Samella Lewis & Ruth Waddy (auth), Black artists on art, Contemp Crafts, 71; Elton Fax (auth), 17 Black Artists, Dodd, 71; Barry Schwartz (auth), The New Humanism, Praeger, 74. *Media:* Oil & Collage, Ink. *Publ:* Illusr, I Am the Darker Brother, Macmillan, 68; auth, On understanding black art, New York Times, 1/21/70; auth, The BECC (Black Emergency Cultural Coalition), Arts Mag, 4/70. *Mailing Add:* ACA Gallery 21 E 67th St New York NY 10021

ANDREWS, MICHAEL FRANK
EDUCATOR, SCULPTOR
b Cairnbrook, Pa, Mar 4, 16. *Study:* Univ Kans, BFA, MS; Ohio State Univ, PhD. *Work:* Wichita Mus Art, Kans; Univ Kans, Lawrence; Ohio State Univ; Univ Wis-Madison. *Exhib:* 3rd Int Sculpture Exhib, Philadelphia, 50; Finger Lakes Exhib, Rochester Mem Art Gallery, NY, 69; Sculptors Exhib, Elmira Col, 72; Everson Mus Art, Syracuse, NY, 72; William Rockhill Nelson Art Gallery, Kansas City, Mo, 73. *Pos:* Ed, Synaesthetic Educ, 71. *Teaching:* Instr sculpture, Univ Kans, Lawrence, 45-48; prof art educ, Univ Southern Calif, 50-52; prof sculpture, Univ Wis-Madison, 52-55; chmn dept synaesthetic educ, Syracuse Univ, 55-82, emer prof, 83- *Awards:* Wis Salon of Art Award, 54; Design for Hall of Educ Symbol, New York World's Fair, 62; award, NY State Art Teachers Asn, 78. *Bibliog:* James Schinneller (auth), Art, Search & Self-Discovery; Richard Lowe (auth), Problems in Paradise. *Mem:* Eastern Arts Asn (pres, 60-64); Nat Art Educ Asn (pres, Eastern Region, 60-64); Int Soc Educ Through Art; Creative Leadership Coun, Creative Educ Found. *Publ:* Auth, Creative Printmaking, 64 & Sculpture & Ideas, 65, Prentice-Hall; auth, Creative Education: The Liberation of Man, Syracuse Univ, 65; auth, Synaesthetic Education, 71, Sensory Learning at Syracuse Univ, 81, Syracuse Univ Press. *Mailing Add:* 69 Briarwood Rd Woodland Hills Asheville NC 28804

ANDREWS, SYBIL (SYBIL ANDREWS MORGAN)
PAINTER, PRINTMAKER

b Bury St Edmunds, Eng, 1898. *Study:* Heatherley Sch Fine Art, London, with Henry G Massey; also with Boris Heroys, London. *Work:* Victoria & Albert Mus, London; Nat Gallery South Australia; Dublin Mus, Ireland; Los Angeles Co Mus Art; Leeds Mus, Eng. *Exhib:* Sybil Andrews Exhib Colour Linocut Prints, Vancouver Art Gallery, 48; Primera Expos Arte Sacro Moderno, Buenos Aires, Arg, 54; Print Makers Soc Calif; Art Gallery of Greater Victoria, BC, 76; de Vooght Galleries, Vancouver, 78; and others. *Teaching:* Pvt classes. *Awards:* G A Reid Award, Soc Can Painter, Etchers & Engravers, 51. *Mem:* Soc Can Painter, Etchers & Engravers; Print & Drawing Coun Can. *Media:* Oil, Watercolor. *Mailing Add:* 2131 S Island Hwy Campbell River BC V9W 2G6 Canada

ANDRUS, JAMES ROMAN
PRINTMAKER, PAINTER

b St George, Utah, July 11, 07. *Study:* Otis Art Inst, Los Angeles; Colorado Springs Fine Arts Ctr; Art Students League; Brigham Young Univ, BA & MA; Columbia Univ; Univ Colo, EdD. *Work:* Utah State Capitol Collection, Salt Lake City; Brigham Young Univ; Dixie Col Collection, St George; Provo City Schs Collections; Granite Sch Dist Collection, Salt Lake City. *Comn:* Mural, St George Temple, Utah, 43; oil painting, Cent Utah Ment Health Ctr, 72; portraits of Charles E Maw, Joseph K Nicoles & Charles Redd, Brigham Young Univ; portrait of J C Moffitt, Provo Sch Dist. *Exhib:* Calif State Fair Exhib, 39; Utah State Inst Fine Arts Exhibs; Boston Mus Ann, Mass; Wichita Print Asn, Kans; Univ Utah Ann, Salt Lake City. *Pos:* Mem, Utah State Fair Art Comt, Salt Lake City; chmn visual arts div, Utah State Inst Fine Arts; mem, Utah State Bd Educ Elem Art Curric. *Teaching:* Spec instr painting, Brigham Young Univ, 40-43, asst prof painting & printmaking, 50-53, prof art, 58-74, emer prof art & educ, 75- *Awards:* Fac Award of Merit, Otis Art Inst, 38; Univ Colo Art Fel, 52; Purchase Prizes, Utah State Inst Fine Arts, 45, 50 & 54. *Mem:* Nat & Western Art Educ Asns; Utah Acad Sci, Arts & Lett; Cent Utah Art Bd. *Media:* Oil. *Mailing Add:* 1765 N 651 E Provo UT 84601

ANGEL, RIFKA
PAINTER

b Kalvaria, Russia, Sept 16, 1899; US citizen. *Study:* Art Student League, with Boardman Robinson; also with John Sloan, Alfred Maurer & Emil Ganso; Moscow Art Acad. *Work:* Honolulu Acad Fine Arts; Chicago Art Inst; Nelson Art Gallery & Mary Atkins Mus Fine Arts, Kansas City, Mo; Brandeis Univ; pvt collections of Laurence S Rockefeller & Bob Dylan. *Exhib:* Chicago Art Inst, 31, 33, 35 & 39; 16 Cities Exhib, Mus Mod Art, New York, 34; Brooklyn Mus, 37; one-man show & ann, Honolulu Acad, 40-41; one-man shows, Nelson Art Gallery & Mary Atkins Mus Fine Arts, 43; plus many other one-man shows in galleries. *Awards:* For originality in painting, Art Inst Chicago, 33; City Mus St Louis, 45; Design for Democratic Living, Am Fedn Arts, 48. *Bibliog:* C J Bulliet (auth), Apples and Madonnas, 30; Jacobson (auth), Art of Today, Chicago, Stein Publ, 33; F Pratt & B Fizzel (auth), Encaustic--Materials and Methods, Lear Publ, 49. *Mem:* Artists Equity Asn New York; fel Int Inst Arts & Lett; Nat Soc Lit & Arts. *Media:* Encaustic. *Mailing Add:* 79-81 MacDougal St New York NY 10012

ANGELINI, JOHN MICHAEL
PAINTER, WRITER

b New York, NY, Nov 18, 21. *Study:* Newark Sch Fine & Indust Art; spec studies in Europe, 61. *Work:* David L Yunich Collection, Bambergers, NJ; Bloomfield Col, NJ; Paterson Main Libr, NJ; Longlines Div, Am Tel & Tel; Morgan Guarantee Trust Co. *Exhib:* Audubon Artists Nat Ann, Nat Acad Design, New York, 63-81; Nat Arts Club Watercolor Ann, New York, 64; NJ Pavillion, New York World's Fair, 65; Watercolor USA, Nat Ann & Traveling Exhib, Springfield Mus, Mo, 66; NJ Watercolor Soc Ann, Newark, 74-80; plus many one-man shows in NY & NJ. *Pos:* Art dir, Berles Carton Co, Inc, Paterson, NJ, 50-79; adv bd, NJ Music & Arts, Chatham, 72-78; Int Exhib, Nabisco World Hq. *Awards:* Silver Medal for Watercolor, NJ Watercolor Soc, 63; Medal of Honor for Watercolor, Audubon Artists, Nat Acad, 63 & Nat Arts Club, 64; Artist of the Year, Hudson Artists, Inc, NJ, 74. *Bibliog:* L Pessolano (auth), John Angelini--a profile, 70 & R Williams (auth), John Angelini--A W S, 71, NJ Music & Arts; interview & watercolor demonstration, cable TV networks, NY & NJ. *Mem:* Am Watercolor Soc; Audubon Artists; Audubon Artists; Allied Artists Am. *Style & Technique:* Watercolors executed in the wet on wet technique, landscapes, cityscapes and seascapes described as romantic realism. *Media:* Watercolor, Pencil Rendering. *Publ:* Contribr, Prize winning watercolors, Book II, 66; contribr, NJ Music & Arts, 70-77; auth, articles, In: Am Artist, 72; auth, articles in Am Artist, 72. *Dealer:* Gallery Nine 9 Passaic Ave Chatham NJ 07928. *Mailing Add:* 7808 Pecan Tree Dr Hudson FL 33562

ANGELL, TONY
SCULPTOR, PAINTER

b Los Angeles, Calif, Nov 15, 40. *Study:* Univ Wash, BA, 62. *Work:* Rainier Bank, Safeco Plaza, Seattle; Tacoma Art Mus, Wash; Orbanco Northwest, Portland, Ore. *Comn:* Raven into Flight (sculpture) & Fishing Otters, Pac Northwest Bell, Seattle, 81; Family of Otters (sculpture), Olympia Pub Libr, Wash; Artic Visitor, Safeco Plaza Bldg, 82; Ascending Eagles, Bellevue, Wash. *Exhib:* Animals in Art, Royal Ont Mus, Toronto, 75-76; Birds in Am Art, Plantation of Sandwich Mus, Mass, 78; Birds in Art, Tacoma Art Mus, Wash, 79; Nat Acad Western Art, Oklahoma City, 81-83; Artists of Am Show, Denver, 81-83. *Collections Arranged:* Northwest Collection (with catalog), Rainier Bldg, Seattle, 78; Artists of America, Denver, 81. *Pos:* Comnr & chair, Visual Arts Comt, King Co Arts Comn, 78- *Teaching:* Guest lectr, City of Seattle, 83 & Artists of Am, Denver, 83. *Awards:* Wash State Gov Art Awards, 76 & 79. *Bibliog:* Rebecca Kelly (auth), PM Northwest: Tony Angell (film), TV Station KOMO, 80; Where all things belong (film), Essentia Productions, 76; Kim Patton (auth), article, Puget Soundings, 82. *Mem:* Asn Northwest Sculptors; Authors' Guild. *Media:* Marble, Bronze; Oils, Ink. *Publ:* Auth-illusr, Birds of Prey, Pac Search, 72; auth-illusr, Owls, 74 & Ravens, Crows, Magpies and Jays, 78, Univ Wash; co-auth-illusr, Marine Birds and Mammals of Puget Sound, Nat Oceanic & Atmospheric Admin, 82; illusr, Blackbirds of the Americas, Univ Wash Press, 84. *Dealer:* Foster/White Gallery 311 1/2 Occidental Ave Seattle WA 98104. *Mailing Add:* 18237 40th Ave NE Seattle WA 98155

ANGELO, EMIDIO
CARTOONIST, PAINTER

b Philadelphia, Pa, Dec 4, 03. *Study:* Philadelphia Mus Sch Indust Art; Pa Acad Fine Arts. *Exhib:* Pa Acad Fine Art Alliance. *Pos:* Ed cartoonist, (weekly), Main Line Times, 37-54 & 81- *Teaching:* Instr advan art class, Samuel S Fleisher Art Mem, Philadelphia. *Awards:* Charles K Smith Prize, Woodmere Art Gallery, 60; Gold Medal, Philadelphia Sketch Club, 69; Freedom Found Award, 83; and others. *Mem:* Da Vinci Art Alliance; fel Pa Acad Fine Arts; Nat Cartoonist Soc; Am Ed Cartoonists. *Publ:* Producer, short color film of Alighier's, The Inferno, 67; auth, Just be Patient, The Time of Your Life, Emily and Mabel; plus others. *Mailing Add:* 419 Redleaf Rd Wynnewood PA 19096

ANGELOCH, ROBERT (HENRY)
PAINTER, PRINTMAKER

b Richmond Hill, NY, Apr 8, 22. *Study:* Art Student League; Acad Fine Arts, Florence, Italy; also with Fiske Boyd. *Work:* Art Student League; Munson-Williams-Proctor Inst, Utica, NY; Russell Sage Col; Western Ky Univ. *Comn:* Murals, New York Bd Educ, Kellogg Corp, Brunswick, NJ & Queensboro Pub Libr. *Pos:* Artist-in-residence, Western Ky Univ, Bowling Green, 74; dir, Woodstock Sch Art Inc, 80- *Teaching:* Supvr, Woodstock Summer Sch, Art Student League, 60-68, instr, Art Student League, 64-79; instr, Woodstock Sch Art, 68-; instr, Russell Sage Col, 71-72. *Awards:* Purchase award, Woodstock Art Asn, 64; Jane Peterson Prize, Allied Artists Am, 64; First Prize, Springfield Mus Fine Arts, 68; plus others. *Bibliog:* S R Day (auth), Creative Woodstock, Mead Mt Press, 66. *Mem:* Art Student League; Woodstock Artists Asn. *Publ:* Auth & illusr, Rillet, 65 & Monhegan (bks drawings), 65; auth, Basic oil painting techniques, Pitman, 70; auth, Outdoor sketching, Am Artist Mag, 70; contribr, Angeloch: Color Prints, 80. *Dealer:* Paradox Gallery Woodstock NY 12498. *Mailing Add:* Box 95 Woodstock NY 12498

ANGLIN, BETTY LOCKHART
EDUCATOR, PAINTER

b Greenwood, SC, Apr 23, 37. *Study:* Univ Ga, 58, with Lamar Dodd; Col of William & Mary, Williamsburg, Va, BA, 72; additional study with Barclay Sheaks, Leone Cooper, Ferdinand Warren & Earnest Johnson. *Work:* Hampton Sch Syst, Va; Va Nat Bank Collection; Va Fair Collection; Ft Eustis Collection; Cecil Rawls Mus, Courtland, Va. *Comn:* Painting, Newport News Shipyard, 72; hist paintings, Hampton City Calendar, 77; four hist paintings, City of Stoney Creek, Va, 78. *Exhib:* Va Realists Show, Cecil Rawls Mus, 73-74; three-person show, Pa Arts Asn & Cecil Rawls Mus; Fac Exhib, Col of William and Mary & Peninsula Arts Asn, 81; Medley of Arts Invitational; Peninsula Arts Members Show, 81; and others. *Teaching:* Guest prof, Va Wesleyan Col, 72 & 74; art resource teacher, Trinity Lutheran Sch, 72-; art teacher, Cecil Rawls Mus, 73-; prof fine arts, Christopher Newport Col, 77- *Awards:* Best in Show, Va State Fair, 71; Award, Parthenon, Nashville, Tenn, 76; Life Bravissimo Award, Life Federal Savings and Loan Asn & WGH Radio, 80. *Mem:* Pa Art Asn; Va Beach Art Asn; Va Watercolor Asn. *Publ:* Auth, Painting with Acrylic from Start to Finish, 74 & Landscape Painting, 74, Davis Publ; illusr, Christmas Tugboat, 83. *Mailing Add:* 213 Parkway Dr Newport News VA 23606

ANGUIANO, RAUL
MURALIST, PAINTER

b Guadalajara, Mexico, Feb 26, 15. *Study:* Studies with prominent art teachers in Guadalajara; Art Students League. *Work:* Mus Mod Art, Mex; Mus Mod Art, New York; San Francisco Mus Art, Calif; Royal Mus Art & Hist, Brussels; Arch Monumental Art Mus, Lund, Sweden. *Comn:* Three murals, Centro Escolar Revolucion, Ministry of Educ, Mexico City, 37; Birth in the Jungle (mural), Laboratorios Hormona, Mexico City, 62; three murals, Mus Anthorp, Sect of Educ, Mexico City, 63; The Baptism of Christ (mural), Church of San Marcos, Jalisco, Mex, 65; mural, Nat Ballet of Jamaica, Olympia Hotel, Kingston, 70. *Exhib:* San Francisco Mus Mod Art, 53; Salon de la Plastica Mex, Mexico City, 69; one-man shows, Mus de Arte Mod, Mex, 71, Instituto-Italo-Latin-Americano, Rome, Italy, 75, Ctr Cult Mex, Paris, 80 & Palace Fine Arts, Mexico City, 82; and others. *Pos:* Gen secy, Art Teachers Union, Mexico City, 36-38; vpres, Mex Asn Plastic Arts, UNESCO Br, 70- *Teaching:* Art supvr adult educ, Esmeralda Art Sch, Mex, 42-64; teacher life drawing, Univ Mexico City, 42-69. *Awards:* Dipl Honor, Comt Int Exhib Bk Art, Leipzig, Ger, 60; Commendatore Decoration, Pres of Italy, 75; Diploma Honor, City Los Angeles, 82. *Bibliog:* Justino Fernandez (auth), Raul Anguiano, Ediciones de Arte, SAm, 48; Margarita Nelken (auth), Raul Anguiano, Editorial Estaciones, Mex, 58; Jorge Juan Crespo de la Serna (auth), En torno al arte y personalidad de Raul Anguiano, Cuadernos de Bellas Artes, 62. *Mem:* Soc Europeenne Cult; Acad Arts, Mex, 82. *Media:* Oil, Drawing. *Publ:* Auth, Expedicion a Bonampak, travel diary, Univ Mex, 59; auth, Adventura en Bonampak, Ediciones Novaro, Mex, 68; auth & illusr, Mawarirra, Ediciones Estaciones, Mex, 72. *Dealer:* Lodi Art Gallery 2557 Colorado Blvd Los Angeles CA 90041. *Mailing Add:* Francisco Sosa 114 Coyancan Mexico 21 DF Mexico

ANGULO, CHAPPIE
PAINTER, ILLUSTRATOR
b Mar 3, 28; US citizen. *Study:* Los Angeles City Col; Univ Calif, Los Angeles; Kahn Art Sch; Esmeralda, Inst Nac Bellas Artes, Mexico City; London Art Ctr. *Work:* Mus Cultures, Mexico City; Art Mus, Chilpantzingo Guerrero, Mex. *Comn:* Reproduction murals, Bonampak, 57, Chichen Itza & Tomb 7 Oaxaca, 58, Nat Mus Anthrop, Moneda; reproduction mural, Teotihuacan, Ballet Nac, Mex, 59. *Exhib:* One-man shows, Olympic Cult Prog, 69, Mus Fronterizo, Juarez, Mex, 71, Age Aquarius, Univ Las Americas, Cholula, 73, La Ciudadela, Monterrey, 74 & Gentes y Lugares Mus de las Cult, Mexico; retrospective, Museo Las Culturas, Mex, 76; La Mujer en la Plastica Bellas Artes, Mexico, Anglo Mexicano, 81. *Bibliog:* M Vazquez (auth), Museo de las Culturas, Inst Nat Antropologia, 65; A Pastrana (auth), El concreto, Arquitectura Arte & Urbanism Mag, 68. *Mem:* La Muerte-Unam. *Media:* Fiber, Paper; Acrylic, Oil. *Publ:* Illusr, Teotihuacan-un autoretrato cultural, 64; illusr, Tlalmanalli--encontrado en tlatelolco, 66; illusr, Relieves de Chalcatzingo; illusr, The Cuauhnahuac Museum-A Historic Recopilation; illusr, A Guide to Coatetelco; illusr, A Guide to Chalcatzingo, Arqueology Zunes. *Mailing Add:* A P Postal 1170 Cuernavaca Morelos 06200 Mexico

ANHALT, JACQUELINE RICHARDS
DEALER
b Kansas City, Mo, Jan 6, 25. *Study:* Col William & Mary. *Pos:* Owner/dir, Jacqueline Anhalt Gallery, Los Angeles. *Mem:* Art Dealers Asn Southern Calif (bd mem-treas, 70-79). *Specialty:* Contemporary paintings, sculpture and ceramic sculpture with emphasis on California artists. *Mailing Add:* Jaqueline Anhalt Gallery 748 1/2 N La Cienega Blvd Los Angeles CA 90069

ANKER, SUZANNE C
SCULPTOR
b Brooklyn, NY, Aug 6, 46. *Study:* Brooklyn Col, BA; Univ Colo, MFA. *Work:* St Louis Art Mus, Mo; Denver Art Mus, Colo; Williams Col Mus Art. *Exhib:* New Ways With Paper, Nat Collection Fine Arts, Smithsonian Inst, Washington, DC, 77 & Paper as Medium, 78; The Grid, Pace Editions, 79; The Great Big Drawing Show, PS I, Inst for Art & Urban Resources Show, 79; Walker Art Ctr, Minneapolis, 79; Richard Gray Gallery, Chicago, 79; and others. *Teaching:* Asst prof experimental printmaking, Washington Univ, St Louis, 76-78. *Mem:* Col Art Asn. *Media:* Paper, Stone. *Mailing Add:* 101 Wooster St New York NY 10012

ANKRUM, JOAN
DEALER
b Los Angeles, Calif. *Collections Arranged:* Of Time & the Image, Calif Artists, Phoenix Mus Art, Ariz, 64; People to People, exhib honoring People's Repub China, 72; The Art of African Peoples, private Black Collections, Ankrum Gallery, 73; Calif Artists Exhib, State Capitol Bldg, Sacramento, 75; Morris Broderson Retrospectives, Univ Ariz Mus Art, 75. *Pos:* Dir, Ankrum Gallery, Los Angeles. *Bibliog:* H Wurdeman (auth), Los Angeles Galleries, Art in Am, 62; Camilla Snyder (auth), A language without sound, Los Angeles Herald Examr, 5/10/70; Curtis (auth), A woman's place, New York Times, 11/26/71. *Mem:* Art Dealers Asn Southern Calif (bd mem, 70); Am Fedn Arts. *Specialty:* West Coast contemporary artists, primarily Californian, ethnic, including Black, Mexican-Indian (Huichol). *Publ:* Auth & ed, Drawings & Haiku, Janet Lessing, Commun Sci, 65. *Mailing Add:* Ankrum Gallery 657 N La Cienega ie Blvd Los Angeles CA 90069

ANNIS, NORMAN L
EDUCATOR, SCULPTOR
b Des Moines, Iowa, May 26, 31. *Study:* Univ Northern Iowa, BA, 53; Drake Univ; Univ Iowa, MFA, 59. *Work:* Central Col, Pella, Iowa; Corcoran Gallery Art, DC; Washington & Lee Univ, Lexington, Va. *Comn:* Life-size bronze figure, Gettysburg Col, Pa, 70; life-size welded steel figure, Frey Village, Middletown, 76; life-size cor-ten steel figure, Gettysburg Sr High Sch, 77. *Exhib:* Fourth Dulin Nat Prints, Dulin Gallery, Knoxville, 61; 4th Nat Drawing Exhib, Okla Art Ctr, Oklahoma City, 61; Drawings USA, St Paul Art Ctr, Minn, 61 & 63; 4th Nat Ultimate Concerns, Ohio Univ, Athens, 65; Washington Area Artists Series, Corcoran Gallery Art, DC, 65; Living Am Artists & Human Image, Pa State Univ Mus Art, State College, 74. *Teaching:* Instr sculpture, Univ Ill, Champaign, 59-60; prof sculpture, Gettysburg Col, 60-78; prof & head dept art, Southwest Mo State Univ, Springfield, 78- *Awards:* First Sculpture Award, Fifth Ann Pennational, 62; Purchase Award, St Paul Art Ctr, 63; Anna Hyatt Huntington Award, Corcoran Gallery Art, 63. *Media:* Bronze, Welded Steel. *Dealer:* Michelson Gallery 707 G St NE Washington DC 20002. *Mailing Add:* 940 S John Springfield MO 65802

ANNUS, JOHN AUGUSTUS
PAINTER
b Riga, Latvia, Oct 25, 35; US citizen. *Study:* Pratt Inst, with Richard Lindner & Enrico Catellon, BFA, 58; Nat Acad Design, with Louis Bouche, 58-59; Prix de Rome, Am Acad Rome, 59; Acad Belli Arti Liceo Artistico, Rome, 62-64. *Work:* The Baltimore Mus Fine Art, Md; Ohio Dominican Col, Columbus; Nat Acad Design, New York. *Exhib:* Am Acad Rome Ann, Italy, 61; Nat Acad Design Annuals, New York, 62, 64, 65, 67, 75, 77, 78 & 80; Omaggio Al Mare, Festival Int Cinematografico Del Mare, Fermo, Italy, 72; John Annus-Anna Annus Hagen, Univ Pa, Philadelphia, 76; Artists 77, Int Play Group, United Nations, New York, 77. *Awards:* H W Ranger Fund Purchase Prize, Nat Acad Ann, 65 & 75; S J Wallace Truman Prize, Nat Acad Design, New York, 67; Italian Govt Purchase Prize, Mostra Int de Arti Figurativi, 62. *Bibliog:* Carlo Battaglia (auth), Mostra del pittore John Annus, Giornale de Sicilia, 63; Giuseppe Sicaari (auth), Annus, un pittore lettone innamorato dell'Italia, Arte Sintesi, 64; Raffaele Carrieri (auth), Preferiscono il colosseo, Epoca, 68. *Mem:* Nat Acad Design; Soc Fel Am Acad in Rome; Nat Soc Mural Painters. *Media:* Oils, Multi-media. *Mailing Add:* Julia Black Inc Kit Carson Rd Taos NM 87571

ANSON, LESIA
SCULPTOR
b Kassel, Ger, Jan 14, 46; US citizen. *Study:* Westchester Community Col, AAS, 63; Art Students League, 75; sculpture with Cleo Hartwig. *Exhib:* Allied Artists, 78 & Audubon Artists, 79; Nat Acad Design, New York; Nat Asn Women Artists, Equitable Gallery, New York, 80; Wildlife, Pub Libr Mus Gallery, White Plains, NY, 81; Soc Animal Artists, Philadelphia Acad Sci, 81. *Awards:* Bronze Medal, Catharine Lorillard Wolfe Art Club, 77; Award of Merit for Sculpture, Soc Animal Artists, 80; Excalibur Award, Knickerbocker Artists, 80. *Mem:* Soc Animal Artists; Nat Asn Women Artists; Catharine Lorillard Wolfe Art Club; Artists Equity Asn, New York. *Media:* Stone, Marble. *Dealer:* Gallery Madison 90 1248 Madison Ave New York NY 10028. *Mailing Add:* 60 E 83rd St New York NY 10028

ANSPACH, ERNST
COLLECTOR
b Glogau, Ger, Feb 4, 13; US citizen. *Study:* Univ Munich; Breslau Univ, PhD. *Mem:* Fel in perpetuity Metrop Mus Art, New York; fel Univ Mus, Philadelphia. *Collection:* African tribal sculpture. *Mailing Add:* 118 W 79th St New York NY 10024

ANTHONISEN, GEORGE RIOCH
SCULPTOR, PAINTER
b Boston, Mass, July 31, 36. *Study:* Univ Vt, BA, 61; Nat Acad Design, 61-62; Art Students League, 62-64. *Work:* Carnegie Hall, New York; Chrysler Mus, Norfolk, Va; Atlanta Univ, Ga; Lindbergh Park, Philadelphia. *Comn:* Bush Hill United Presby Church, Hindman Mem Comt, Alexandria, Va, 74; Washington Sch Psychiat, Washington, DC, 75; Figure of late Sen Ernest Gruening (7ft bronze bronze), Hall of Columns, Capitol Bldg, Washington, DC, 77; sculpture, medallion, Presbyterian Home, Lynchburg, Va, 82; Henry Schoder Bank & Trust Co, New York, 82; and others. *Exhib:* One-man shows, Gentle Winds Gallery, Doylestown, Pa, 79, Bjorn Lindgren Gallery, 81 & 82; Allied Artist Am; Nat Sculpture Soc; Audubon Artists; and others. *Awards:* James Augustus Suydam Bronze Medal, Nat Acad Design, 68; Sculptor in Residence, Augustus St Gaudens Nat Hist Site, US Dept Interior, 71. *Bibliog:* Judy Tucker (auth), Artist gets wish for birthday, Philadelphia Sunday Bulletin, 10/2/77; Theo Morgan (auth), Architect of the Capitol, Art in the United States Capitol, Joint Comt on the Library, 78; Domenico Facci (auth), The medium and the method, Nat Sculpture Review, fall 82. *Mem:* Nat Sculpture Soc; Allied Art Am; Audubon Artists. *Media:* Bronze, Aluminum; Stainless Steel, Hydrostone. *Mailing Add:* Box 147 Solebury PA 18963

ANTHONY, LAWRENCE KENNETH
SCULPTOR, EDUCATOR
b Hartsville, SC, May 27, 34. *Study:* Washington & Lee Univ, BA; Univ Ga, MFA; study with Lamar Dodd & Howard Thomas. *Work:* Brooks Mem Art Gallery, Memphis, Tenn; Vanderbilt Univ Art Dept, Nashville, Tenn; Ark State Univ, Jonesboro; Gibbes Art Gallery, Charleston, SC; SC Art Comn, Columbia. *Comn:* Menorah form sculpture, Jewish Community Ctr, Memphis, 67; sculpture, Corinthian Broadcasting Co, New York, 71; wall sculpture, CBS-TV, Sacramento, Calif, 72; Audubon Park, Memphis; Vanderbilt Univ, Nashville. *Exhib:* One-man shows, Columbia Mus Art, 66, Brooks Mem Art Gallery, 68, Vanderbilt Univ, 72 & 74 & Terre Des Hommes, Pavilion, Montreal, 79. *Pos:* Dir, Clough Hanson Gallery, Southwestern at Memphis, currently. *Teaching:* Prof sculpture & drawing, Southwestern at Memphis, 61- *Media:* Metal, Wood. *Mailing Add:* 2082 Washington Memphis TN 38104

ANTHONY, WILLIAM GRAHAM
PAINTER, DRAFTSMAN
b Ft Monmouth, NJ, Sept 25, 34. *Study:* Yale Univ, BA, 58, with Josef Albers; San Francisco Art Inst, 59-60; Art Student League, 61; also with Theodoros Stamos. *Work:* Whitney Mus Am Art, New York; Wallraf-Richartz Mus, Cologne, Ger; Art Inst Chicago; Yale Univ Art Mus, New Haven; Corcoran Gallery Art, Washington, DC; plus others. *Exhib:* Allan Stone Gallery, New York, 61-64; one-man shows, Calif Palace Legion Hon, San Francisco, 62, Fischback Gallery, New York, 73, Razor Gallery, New York, 78 & Frank Marino Gallery, New York, 81. *Pos:* Dir, Spectrum Art Gallery, New York, 65-66. *Teaching:* Instr figure drawing, San Francisco Acad Art, 62-63. *Media:* Pencil, Oil. *Publ:* Auth, A new approach to figure drawing, Crown Publ, 65, Odhams, Ltd, Eng, 67 & Bonanza Publ; auth & illusr, Bible Stories, The Jargon Soc, 78. *Dealer:* Vibeile Levy Gallery 40 Great Jones St NY 10012. *Mailing Add:* H216 Westbeth 463 West St New York NY 10014

ANTIN, DAVID A
CRITIC, WRITER
b New York, NY, Feb 1, 32. *Study:* Col City New York, BA, 55; NY Univ, MA, 66. *Teaching:* Prof visual arts, Univ Calif, San Diego, 68-, chmn dept, 70-72, 80-81. *Awards:* Guggenheim Fel, 76-77; Nat Endowment Humanities Fel, 82-83. *Bibliog:* Spanos & Kroetsch (ed), Oral tradition & postmodernism, Boundary-2, State Univ NY Binghamton, spring 75; Barry Alpert (ed), Antin/Rothenberg, VORT 7, Eng Dept, Ind Univ, Bloomington, spring 75; Marjorie Perloff (auth), The Poetics of Indeterminacy, Princeton Univ Press, 81. *Mem:* Col Art Asn; Int Asn Art Critics. *Res:* Studies in modernism and post modernism; history of art criticism and theory; sociology of art; interpretation & meaning in cult & language. *Publ:* Auth, Television: Video's frightful parent, Artforum, 12/75; auth, Talking at the Boundaries, New Directions, 76; auth, Currency of the country, Discussion, London Press, 80; auth, The real thing, Art Am, 5/81; auth, Tuning, New Directions, 84. *Mailing Add:* PO Box 1147 Del Mar CA 92014

ANTIN, ELEANOR
PERFORMANCE ARTIST

b New York, NY, Feb 27, 35. *Study:* City Col of New York, BA; Tamara Daykarhanove Sch for the Stage. *Exhib:* One-woman exhibs, Mus Mod Art, New York, 73, Everson Mus, Syracuse, NY, 74, Clocktower, New York, 76, M L D'Arc Gallery, New York, 77, Ronald Feldman Fine Arts Gallery, New York, 77, 79, 80 & 83, Wadsworth Atheneum, Hartford, Conn, 77, Whitney Mus Am Art, New York, 78 & Long Beach Mus Art, Calif, 78. *Teaching:* Visual arts lectr, Univ Calif, Irvine, 74-75; asst prof visual arts, Univ Calif, San Diego, 75-77, assoc prof, 77-79, prof, 79- *Awards:* Nat Endowment Arts Grant, 79. *Bibliog:* Jonathan Crary (auth), Eleanor Antin: a Post-Modern Itinerary, Catalogue Essay, La Jolla Mus, 77; John R Clarke (auth), Life/Art/Life, Quentin Crisp & Eleanor Antin: Notes on Performance in the Seventies, Arts Mag, 2/79; Eleanor Munro (auth), Originals: American Women Artists, Simon & Schuster, 79. *Publ:* Auth, Autobiography of the artist as an autobiographer, J Los Angeles Inst Contemp Art, 10/74; auth, Some thoughts on autobiography & Olga Feodorova's story, winter 78-79 & A romantic interlude from: Recollections of My Life with Diaghiles, summer 80, Sun & Moon; High performance 13, Eleanora Antinova's J, spring 81; auth, Being Antinova, Astro Artz Press, 83. *Dealer:* Ronald Feldman Fine Arts New York NY. *Mailing Add:* PO Box 1147 Del Mar CA 92014

ANTONAKOS, STEPHEN
SCULPTOR

b Greece, Nov 1, 26; US citizen. *Work:* Whitney Mus Am Art & Mus Mod Art, New York; Milwaukee Art Ctr, Wis; LaJolla Mus, Calif; Guggenheim Mus, New York. *Exhib:* Neon, Fischbach Gallery, New York, 67-70 & 72; Contemp Am Sculpture Ann, Whitney Mus Am Art, 70; Works in Spaces, San Francisco Mus Art, 73; Ten Outdoor Neons, Ft Worth Art Mus, Tex, 74; John Weber Gallery, New York, 74 & 75; A Shade of Light, San Francisco Mus Art, Downtown Ctr, 78; Site Sculpture Proj, Joslyn Art Mus, Omaha, 78; Minimal Tradition, Aldrich Mus Contemp Art, Ridgefield, Conn, 79. *Teaching:* Vis artist, Yale Univ, fall 68; artist-in-residence, sculpture, Univ Wis-Madison, spring 71 & Fresno State Col, fall 71. *Awards:* NY State Creative Artists Pub Serv Prog Grant; Individual Artist's Grant, Nat Endowment Arts, 73. *Media:* Neon. *Mailing Add:* 435 W Broadway New York NY 10012

ANTONOVICI, CONSTANTIN
SCULPTOR, LECTURER

b Neamt, Romania, Feb 18, 11; US citizen. *Study:* Fine Arts Acad, Romania, MA; Fine Arts Acad, Vienna, Austria, with Prof Fritz Behn, 42-45; study with Constantin Brancusi, Paris, 47-51. *Work:* Le Salon des Artistes Independants, Paris; Vatican, Roma, Italy; Mus Fine Arts, Montreal. *Comn:* Monuments of St George, Fine Arts Comt, Vienna, 43 & St Joseph, 47; General De Gaulle, French Army Commandment, Tyrol, Austria, 46; Gen Dwight D Eisenhower, Pres Nixon Collection; Bishop Manning, Cathedral St John the Divine, 54; St Luke, St Luke's Hosp, New York, 55; Hacklei Art Mus, Muskegon, Mich, 76. *Exhib:* Asn Federative L'Art Libre, Paris, 51; General De Gaulle, French Army Commandment, Tyrol, Austria, 46; Can Artists Asn, 53; Art Alliance Gallery Am, Philadelphia, 62; NJ Mus Art Ann, 64; Nat Sculpture Soc Ann Exhib, New York, 71-81; Va Mus, Richmond, 77. *Awards:* Pro Mundi Beneficio medal & dipl, Brazilian Acad, 76; Mrs Louis Bennett Prize Sculpture, 50th Ann Exhib, Nat Sculpture Soc, 80. *Bibliog:* Ralph Fabri (auth), Sculpture, Today's Art, 3/70; Constantin Antonovici, Sculptor of Owls, Educ Res Coun Am, 75; Susan E Harrison (auth), article, Chronicle, Muskegon, Mich, 76; and others. *Mem:* Nat Soc Lit & Arts; fel Nat Sculpture Soc. *Media:* Marble, Bronze. *Mailing Add:* 310 W 106th St New York NY 10025

ANTREASIAN, GARO ZAREH
PAINTER, LITHOGRAPHER

b Indianapolis, Ind, Feb 16, 22. *Study:* Herron Sch Art, BFA; with Stanley William Hayter & Will Barnet; Purdue Univ, Indianapolis, Hon DFA, 72. *Work:* Metrop Mus Art, Mus Mod Art & Guggenheim Mus, New York; Art Inst Chicago; Los Angeles Co Mus Art, Calif. *Comn:* History of Indiana University, Bloomington, Ind, 54; Lincoln in Indiana (with Ralph Peck), Ind State Off Bldg, Indianapolis, 63. *Exhib:* Tamarind: Homage to Lithography, Mus Mod Art, New York, 69; Int Exhib Graphics, Montreal, Que, 71; Five Armenian Artists, Fresno Art Center, 83; Offset Prints, Lehigh Univ, 83; Wildine Gallery, Albequerque, 83; Solo Exhib, Iowa State Univ, 83; and others. *Pos:* Tech dir lithography, Tamarind Lithography Workshop, Inc, Los Angeles, 60-61; tech dir lithography, Tamarind Inst, Univ NMex, 70-72. *Teaching:* Instr art, Herron Sch Art, Indianapolis, 48-64; prof lithography & art, Univ NMex, 64-, chmn, Dept Art, 81- *Awards:* Purchase Awards, Nat Print Exhib, Northern Ill Univ, 68, State Univ NY Albany, 68 & 1st Hawaii Int, Honolulu Acad Arts, 71; Visual Artists Grant, Nat Endowment Arts, 82-83. *Mem:* Albuquerque Mus (bd dirs, currently)); World Print Coun, San Francisco (bd dirs, currently). *Publ:* Co-auth, The Tamarind Book of Lithography: Art & Techniques, 71. *Dealer:* Marjorie Kauffman Graphics The Galleria Houston TX 77056; Alice Simsar Gallery 301 N Main St Ann Arbor MI 48104. *Mailing Add:* 4909 Paseo del Rey NW Albuquerque NM 87120

ANUSZKIEWICZ, RICHARD JOSEPH
PAINTER

b Erie, Pa, May 23, 30. *Study:* Cleveland Inst Art, BFA, 53; Yale Univ, MFA, 55; Kent State Univ, BSEd, 56. *Work:* Corcoran Gallery Art, Washington, DC; Fogg Art Mus; Mus Mod Art & Whitney Mus Am Art, New York; Philadelphia Mus Art; and others. *Exhib:* The Structure of Color, Whitney Mus Am Art, New York, 70; Whitney Mus Am Art, New York, 71; Richard Anuszkiewicz-Recent Paintings, Andrew Crispo Gallery, New York, 74 & 75; Hirshhorn Mus, Washington, DC, 74; Corcoran Biennial, Washington, DC,

75; Two Decades of Printmaking, Mus Mod Art, New York, 79; one-man exhibs, Brooklyn Mus, 80, Carnegie Inst, 80, Univ Fine Arts Galleries, Tallahassee, 81 & Mus Fine Arts, St Petersburg, 81; and many others. *Teaching:* Artist in residence, Dartmouth Col, 67; instr, Univ Wis, 68, Cornell Univ, 68 & Kent State Univ, 68. *Awards:* Philosophers Stone Prize, 63 & First Prize, 64, Silvermine Guild. *Mailing Add:* 76 Chestnut St Englewood NJ 07631

ANZURES, RAFAEL
EDUCATOR, CRITIC

b Puebla, Mex, June 22, 17. *Study:* With Ruano Llopis, 36-40; also Gonzalez-Camarena, Mex, 42-55 & Justino Fernandez, Mex, 57; Nat Univ Mex, cert didactics, 74. *Comn:* Posters, Pemex, Mex, 40-58, mag covers, 46-58. *Pos:* Dir, Sch Design & Plastic Arts, Iberoamerican Univ, Mex, 59-61; secy, Nat Sch Plastic Arts, Nat Univ Mex, 63-66; secy, Mex Asn Art Critics, 64-70. *Teaching:* Instr drawing, Sch Design & Plastic Arts, Iberoamerican Univ, Mex, 58-61; prof mod & contemp art, Nat Sch Plastic Arts, Nat Univ Mex, 58-, prof hist visual commun, Dept of Graphic Commun, 74-, Pre-Hispanic & Colonial Art Mex, 80- *Awards:* Travel & Study Fel, Am Mus of Art & Design & Art Schs, US Govt, 62; Dipl for Educ Work, Nat Univ Mex, 66. *Mem:* Asn Int des Critiques d'Art, Sect Mex, Paris, France; Asoc Mex de Criticos de Arte. *Media:* Oil, Tempera. *Res:* Modern and contemporary art; Mexican painting and sculpture; history of visual communication. *Publ:* Auth, Critical & aesthetic essays on art in Cuadernos Medicos, 55 & 56; Artes de Mexico, 58 & 61, Mexico en la Cultura, 58 & Novedades, 64. *Mailing Add:* Privada Luis Mondragon 13 Coyoacan 04000 DF Mexico

APEL, BARBARA JEAN
PAINTER, EDUCATOR

b Falls City, Nebr, June 16, 35. *Study:* Kansas City Art Inst, BFA, 65; Univ Ill, MFA, 67; study with Lee Chesney. *Work:* Worcester Art Mus, Mass; Univ Wis, Fond-du-Lac; Dartmouth Col Mus; Univ Ill, Champaign-Urbana. *Exhib:* Boston Printmakers' Ann Exhib, 68 & 74; NW Printmaker's Int Exhib, Seattle Art Mus, Wash, 68; Nat Print Exhib, State Univ NY Col at Potsdam, 68; SAGA, Asn of Am Artists' Gallery, New York, 69; New Am Monotypes Traveling Exhib, Smithsonian Inst, Washington, DC, 78-80; Contemp Am Monotypes, Impressions Gallery, Boston, 81; Bridgewater Col Invitational, 81. *Teaching:* Art Inst Boston, 67- *Awards:* Print Prizes, Boston Printmakers, 68 & 74; MacDowell Fel, 79. *Publ:* Contribr, Women Artists in America II, Univ Tenn, 75; The Art of Responsive Drawing, 3rd ed, Prentice-Hall, 83. *Dealer:* Impressions Gallery 275 Dartmouth St at Newbury Boston MA 02116; Impressions Gallery 49 E 91st St New York NY. *Mailing Add:* 235 Rawson Rd Brookline MA 02146

APGAR, NICOLAS ADAM
PAINTER, EDUCATOR

b Gaillon, France, Dec 8, 18; US citizen. *Study:* Syracuse Univ, BFA, 58, MFA, 60; Univ Va, cert, 64; also with Louis Bouche, Fletcher Martin, Louis Bosa, Josef Albers & Jean Charlot. *Work:* Syracuse Univ, NY; Albany Inst Hist & Art, NY; Hyde Collection, Glens Falls, NY; Suksdorf Mem Collection, Hartwick Col, Oneonta, NY; also in private collections. *Exhib:* One-man shows, Skidmore Col, Saratoga Springs, 45, Albany Inst Hist & Art, NY, 50 & Randolph-Macon Woman's Col, Lynchburg, Va, 69; State Teachers Col, Albany, 58; Everson Mus Regional, Syracuse, 60. *Teaching:* Lectr anat, Syracuse Univ, 58-61; asst prof design & drawing, Richmond Prof Inst, 62-67; assoc prof design & drawing, Va Commonwealth Univ, 67-77, prof, 77- *Media:* Oil. *Publ:* Contribr, Interaction of color, 63; contribr, Search vs research, 71. *Mailing Add:* 2207 Buford Rd Richmond VA 23235

APP, TIMOTHY
PAINTER, EDUCATOR

b Akron, Ohio, July 5, 47. *Study:* Kent State Univ, BFA, 70; Tyler Sch Art, MFA, 74. *Work:* Univ NMex Art Mus, Albuquerque; Montgomery Gallery, Pomona Col; Kent State Univ. *Exhib:* Six Artists, Akron Art Inst, Ohio, 71; Abstract Painting From Southern California, Univ Akron, 77 & Univ SDak, Grand Forks, 78; Los Angeles Abstract Painting, Univ Calif, Riverside Mus, 79; Geometric Formalism in American Art, Univ NMex Art Mus, Albuquerque, 82; Phoenix Biennial, Phoenix Art Mus, 83. *Teaching:* Asst prof painting, Pomona Col, 74-78 & Univ NMex, Albuquerque, 78- *Awards:* Mellon Grant, Pomona Col, 78; Univ NMex Res Grant, 82-83. *Bibliog:* Constance Mallinson (auth), Timothy App's abstract classicism, Art Week, 79; Kathleen Shields (auth), Meditations on U, Artlines, 82; William Peterson (auth), Timothy App, Artspace, 82. *Media:* Acrylic, Oil. *Publ:* Auth, The gentle rigor of Patsy Krebs, 76 & Six approaches to formalist abstraction, 77, Artweek; auth, Karl Benjamin: Recent paintings, Tortue Gallery, 78; auth, Constance de Jong, 81 & Elen Feinberg, 83, Artspace. *Dealer:* Linda Durham Gallery 400 Canyon Rd Santa Fe NM 87501; Mattingly-Baker Gallery 3000 McKinney Ave Dallas TX 75204. *Mailing Add:* 2406 Silver Ave SE Albuquerque NM 87106

APPEL, ERIC A
SCULPTOR

b Brooklyn, NY, Dec 26, 45. *Study:* Pratt Inst, 63-67, BID, 67; Tyler Sch Art, Rome, 67-68; Tyler Sch Art, Temple Univ, Philadelphia, Pa, MFA(painting), 70. *Exhib:* St Peter's Col, NJ, 76; Don't Play With Your Food (performance), Avant-Garde Festival, Inst Contemp Art, Philadelphia, Pa, 77; Mus Contemp Crafts, New York, 78; Gardens of Delight, Cooper-Hewitt Mus, New York, 81; Spring Garden, Yves Arman Gallery, New York, 81; and others. *Bibliog:* Beth Fallow (auth), Make yourself at home in the mansion gardens, Daily News, 7/24/81; Robin Brentano & Mark Savitt (auth), 112 Workshop, 112 Green St, NY Univ Press, 81. *Media:* Mixed. *Dealer:* Yves Arman Gallery 817 Madison Ave New York NY 10021. *Mailing Add:* 102 Christopher St New York NY 10014

APPEL, KAREL
PAINTER, SCULPTOR
b Amsterdam, Holland, Apr 25, 21. *Study:* Royal Acad Fine Arts, Amsterdam, 40-43. *Work:* Tate Gallery, London, Eng; Mus Mod Art, New York, NY; Stedelijk Mus, Amsterdam; Mus Fine Arts, Boston, Mass; Mus Nat Art Mod, Paris. *Comn:* Questioning Children (mural), Cafeteria, City Hall, Amsterdam, 49; Garden Hall, Stedelijk Mus, 65; City People (mural), Univ Econ, Rotterdam, Holland, 65; Country People & City People (auth), New Cong House, The Hague, Holland, 67; polychrome statue, Rotterdam Trade Ctr, 73. *Exhib:* Works from the Peggy Guggenheim Foundation, Guggenheim Mus, New York, 69; Bonn Mus, WGer, 69; State Univ NY, Binghamton, 80; Bede Gallery, Jarrow, England, 80; FAME Gallery, Houston, Tex, 81; London Arts Gallery, Detroit, 81; also several retrospectives. *Awards:* UNESCO Prize, 27th Int Biennale, Venice, 54; Int Painting Prize, 5th Sao Paulo Biennale, 59; First Prize for Painting, Guggenheim Int Exhib, New York, 60. *Bibliog:* Sir Herbert Read, W Sandberg & Hugo Claus (auth), Karel Appel: Painter, Abrams, 62; Michel Tapie (auth), Karel Appel, Le Grandi Monografie, Fratelli Fabbri Editori, Milano, 68; Simon Vinkenoog (auth), Appel's Oogappels & Het Verhaal van Karel Appel, Brunz & Zoon, Altrecht/Antwerpen, 70. *Media:* Acrylic; Aluminum, Wood. *Publ:* Illusr, Appel: A Beast-Drawn Man, 62; auth, Karel Appel over Karel Appel, Triton Press, Amsterdam, 71. *Mailing Add:* c/o Martha Jackson Gallery 521 W 57th St New York NY 10019

APPEL, KEITH KENNETH
PAINTER, SCULPTOR
b Bricelyn, Minn, May 21, 34. *Study:* Mankato State Col, BA, BS & MS. *Comn:* Sculpture, Alaska Art in Public Places, 81; sculpture, Anchorage C of C, 81. *Exhib:* All Alaska Exhib, 64-80; Alaska Centennial, 67; one-man shows, 64, 65, 70, 74-81; Alaskan Smithsonian Exhib, 78. *Teaching:* Assoc prof art, Univ Alaska, Anchorage, 70-78, chmn art dept, 78- *Awards:* Alaska Centennial, 67; All Alaska Juried Exhibition Awards, var times, 67-77; Comn, $20,000 Sculpture Competition, Alaska State Art Coun. *Mem:* Alaska Artists Guild; Alaska State Arts Coun (mem bd); Nat Art Educ Asn. *Mailing Add:* 4705 Malibu Dr Anchorage AK 99503

APPEL, THELMA
PAINTER, INSTRUCTOR
b Tel Aviv, Israel, Jan 6, 40; US citizen. *Study:* St Martins Sch Art, London, dipl art & design, 61; Hornsey Col Art, London, art teacher's dipl, 62. *Work:* Milwaukee Arts Ctr, Wis; Am Tel & Tel Co, New York & Summit, NJ; Chase-Manhatten Bank & Metrop Life Co, New York; Vt State Legislature, Montpelier; Port Authority, NY. *Comn:* 5 paintings, Western Corp Bldg, Dallas, Tex, 80. *Exhib:* A Sense of Place, Robert Hull Fleming Mus, Burlington & Southern Vt Arts Ctr, Manchester, 76; one-man shows, Fischbach Gallery, New York, 79 & 82; New England Connections, Fed Reserve Plaza, Boston, 78. *Teaching:* Instr, Southern Vermont Col, 75-76; instr, Parsons Sch Art, 76-77; Summer Painting Workshop, Bennington Col, 76-80. *Awards:* Vt Coun Arts Award, 73; Yaddo Residency fel, 74; State of Vt Purchase Award, Vt Coun Arts & Nat Endowment Arts, 78. *Bibliog:* Gabrielle V Arnhem (auth), American Romantic Painting, Art Germany, 80; M Andre (auth), Art In America, 11/75; E Lubell (auth), Arts Mag, 75. *Mem:* Women's Caucus on the Arts; NY Artists Equity Asn. *Media:* Oil, Acrylic. *Mailing Add:* 136 W 24th St New York NY 10011

APPELHOF, RUTH A
CURATOR, HISTORIAN
b Washington, DC, Feb 14, 45. *Study:* Syracuse Univ, BFA(painting & art hist), 65, MFA(art hist), 74, grad studies humanities, PhD, 79. *Collections Arranged:* View from Upstate, AIR Gallery, New York, 82; Mark Sabin, PM & Stein Gallery, New York, 82; Outside New York City: From Drawing to Sculpture (auth, catalog), 82 & Margaret Bourke-White: The Humanitarian Vision (auth, catalog), 83, Syracuse Univ; and others. *Pos:* Lectr, Whitney Mus Am Art, 80-; cur exhib, Syracuse Univ, 81- *Teaching:* Assoc prof art, Cayuga Co Community Col, 74-79, gallery dir, 78-79; asst prof museology, Syracuse Univ, 81- *Mem:* Col Art Asn; Women's Caucus Art; Nat Women's Studies Asn; Women in the Arts; Asn Am Mus. *Res:* Contemporary women in art; iconography and historical context. *Publ:* Auth, Beth Ames Schwartz: Israel Revisted, Jewish Mus, 82; auth, Recent Developments in Landscape Painting, Whitney Mus, 81; auth, Nature as Image and Metaphor, Women's Caucus Arts, 82. *Mailing Add:* 25 E Lake St Skaneateles NY 13152

APPLE, JACKI (JACQUELINE B)
INTERMEDIA ARTIST, WRITER
b New York, NY. *Study:* Syracuse Univ, 59-60; Parsons Sch Design, 60-63. *Exhib:* Story Art: Recent American Narrative Traveling Exhib, Contemp Arts Mus, Houston, 77-78; Mus Mod Art, New York, 78; Schemes: A Decade of Installation Drawings Traveling Exhib, Elise Meyer Gallery, New York, 81-82; Sydney Biennale, Australia, 82; Live to Air, Tate Gallery, London, 82; Sonorita Prospettiche Traveling Exhib, Contemp Art Gallery, Rimini, Italy, 82-83; and others. *Collections Arranged:* Visual and Sculptural Bookworks, Montclair Mus, NJ & Seibu Mus, Tokly, 79; Artists Bookworks: Alterations and Transformations, Nelson Gallery, Kansas City, Mo, 80; Alternatives in Retrospect: An Historical Overview 1969-1975, New Mus, New York, 81; Art Lobby, Lower Manhattan Cult Coun, New York, 82. *Pos:* Cur exhibs & performances, Franklin Furnace, 77-80; guest cur, New Mus, New York, 81; producer/host, KPFK, Pacifica Radio, Los Angeles, 82-; freelance writer, 82; contrib ed, Artweek, 83-; Teaching: Instr, Concordia Univ, Montreal, fall 80, Calif State Univ, Long Beach, spring 83 & Art Ctr Col Design, Pasadena, summer & fall 83. *Awards:* Individual Artist Fel, Nat Endowment Arts, 79 & 81; NY State Coun Arts Grant, Creative Artists Pub Serv, 81. *Bibliog:*

Roselee Goldberg (auth), Performance, Live Art 1909-present, 79; Saibra Vickland (auth), article, Images & Issues, 9-10/82; Colin Gardner (auth), Tell me a story, sing me a song, Artweek, 8/13/83. *Mem:* Los Angeles Contemp Exhibs. *Media:* Multimedia. *Publ:* Coauth, Correspondence with Martha Wilson, 1973-74, Heresides Mag, 77; auth, Tracings, Tracks, 77; auth, Trunk Pieces, Visual Studies Workshop, Rochester, NY; The Mexican Tapes (110 records), 80; auth, The garden planet revisited, High Performance Mag, spring-summer 82. *Mailing Add:* 161 W 75th St New York NY 10023

APPLEBROOG, IDA
CONCEPTUAL ARTIST
b Bronx, NY. *Study:* NY State Inst Appl Arts & Sci, 50; Art Inst Chicago, 65-68. *Exhib:* Solo exhibs, Whitney Mus Am Art, New York, 78, Bowdoin Col Mus Art, Brunswick, Maine, 82, Nigel Greenwood Gallery, London, 82 & Ronald Feldman Gallery, New York, 82; Painting & Sculpture Today, Indianapolis Mus Art, Ind, 80; Directions '83, Hirshhorn Mus, Washington, DC, 83; 23 Nat Print Exhib, Brooklyn, 83; and others. *Teaching:* Asst painting, Art Inst Chicago, 62-66; instr painting & sculpture, Univ Calif, San Diego, 73-74. *Awards:* Nat Endowment Arts Grant, 80; Creative Artists Pub Serv Prog Fel, 83. *Bibliog:* Suzanne Muchnic (auth), article, Los Angeles Times, 2/5/83; Paula Dietz (auth), article, Harper's Bazaar, 4/83; John Ashbery (auth), article, Newsweek, 4/18/83. *Mem:* Col Art Asn. *Media:* Rhoplex on Vellum & Canvas. *Publ:* Auth, The I am Heathcliffe, says Catherine, syndrome: Women's humor, Heresies, 5/77. *Mailing Add:* 491 Broadway New York NY 10012

APPLEMAN, DAVID EARL
DESIGNER, PAINTER
b Mansfield, Ohio, May 9, 43. *Study:* Bob Jones Univ, BA & MA. *Work:* Bernhardt Industs; Westinghouse Corp; Pee Dee SC State Bank; SC State Art Comn Collection; Sunoco Oil Corp. *Comn:* Polymer painting, First Fed Bank, Greenville, SC, 73. *Exhib:* Massilon Mus Art, Ohio, 70; Hunter Mus Art Ann, Chattanooga, Tenn, 74; Guild SC Artists, Gibbes Gallery, Charleston, 74; State Col Ark, Conway, 75; Mid-S, Parthenon Mus, Nashville, Tenn, 75; Piedmont Painting & Sculpture Exhib, Mint Mus, Charlotte, NC, 77; Greenville Artists Guild, Greenville Mus, SC, 77. *Pos:* Art dir, Bob Jones Univ Media Mgt, 68- *Teaching:* Prof commun art, Bob Jones Univ, Greenville, SC, 68- *Awards:* Top Award, Mansfield Guild, Mansfield Mus, 69; Purchase Awards, 16th Guild of SC Artists, Gibbes, Greenville & Florence Mus, 72 & Appalachian Corridors, Charleston Gallery of Sunrise, 74. *Mem:* Guild SC Artists (mem bd adv, 75, treas, 81); Greenville Artists Guild; Greenville Art Asn. *Media:* Polymer; Collograph. *Mailing Add:* 111 Carmel St Greenville SC 29607

APT, CHARLES
PAINTER
b New York, NY, Dec 10, 33. *Study:* Pratt Inst, BFA, 56. *Work:* Chem Bank; Bowery Bank; Celanese Corp; Paine, Webber, Jackson & Curtis, New York. *Comn:* Painting, Am Stock Exchange, 68. *Exhib:* Allied Artists Am, New York, 64, 65, 67 & 69; Am Watercolor Soc, New York, 65, 66, 68 & 69; Nat Acad Design, New York, 65, 68, 73-81 & 83; Exposition Intercontinentale, Monaco, France, 66 & 68; Nat Mus Racing Ann, Saratoga, NY, 67. *Awards:* Best in Show, Saratoga Mus Racing, 67; 2nd Benjamin Altman Award, Nat Acad Design, 68; Le Prix Prince Souverain, Prince Rainier, Monaco, 68. *Bibliog:* Joan Hess Michael (auth), Charles Apt in Portugal, Am Artist Mag, 4/70; Leonard Kriegel (auth), Charles Apt, Arts Mag, 10/78. *Mem:* Nat Acad Design (academician-elect). *Media:* Oil, Pastel, Watercolor. *Dealer:* Talisman Gallery Bartlesville OK; Loring Gallery 661 Central Ave Cedarhurst NY 11516. *Mailing Add:* 27 W 67th St New York NY 10023

AQUINO, EDMUNDO
PAINTER, PRINTMAKER
b Zimatlan Oaxaca, Mex, June 30, 39. *Study:* Nat Sch Plastics Art, Nat Univ Mex, cert(teacher fine arts), 62; Ecole Nat Superieure Beaux-Arts, Paris, Fr Govt Scholar, 67-69; Slade Sch Fine Arts, London, Brit Coun Scholar, 69. *Work:* Nat Libr Paris; Univ Mass Collection; Mus Mod Art Latin Am, Washington, DC; Mus Mod Art, Mexico City, Mex; AGPA (Panamerican Graphic Art), Mus Fine Arts, Caracas, Venezuela; and others. *Exhib:* Mus Mod Art, Mexico City, 77-78; Biennial of Sao Paulo, Brazil, 79; Picasso Mus, Antibes, France, 80; Mex Mus, San Francisco, Calif, 80; Contemporary Latin American Art and Japan, Nat Mus Art, Osaka, 81; and others. *Teaching:* Instr drawing & painting & head plastic arts sect, Sch Fine Arts, Oaxaca, Mex, 63-67. *Awards:* First Prize Painting & Drawing, Hotel Monnaie, Paris, 69; Nat Prize, 6th Int Festival Painting, Cagnes-Sur-Mer, France, 74; Third Prize, First Iberoamerican Biennial of Painting, Mexico City, 78. *Media:* All. *Mailing Add:* Apartado Postal 21-031 Coyoacan 04000 Mexico DF Mexico

ARAKAWA (SHUSAKU)
PAINTER
b Japan, July 6, 36. *Work:* Mus Mod Art, New York; Basel Mus, Switz; Walker Art Ctr, Minneapolis; Japan Nat Mus, Tokyo; plus others. *Exhib:* One-person show, Mus Mod Art, New York, 74; Painting & Sculpture Today, Indianapolis Mus Art, Ind & Cincinnati Contemp Arts Ctr, Ohio, 74; Wallraf-Richartz Mus, Cologne, WGer, 74; Kennedy Ctr for Performing Arts, Washington, DC, 74; and others. *Awards:* DAAD Fel, WBerlin, 72. *Bibliog:* L Alloway (auth), Introduction to the mechanism of meaning, Bruckman Verlag, 71; N & E Calas (auth), Images & Icons, Dutton, 71. *Publ:* Auth, The Mechanism of Meaning, 71. *Mailing Add:* 124 W Houston St New York NY 10012

ARCHAMBAULT, LOUIS
SCULPTOR, EDUCATOR
b Montreal, Que, Apr 4, 15. *Study:* Univ Montreal, BA; Ecole des Beaux-Arts de Montreal, dipl ceramics. *Work:* Nat Gallery Can, Ottawa; Art Gallery Ont, Toronto; Mus Prov Quebec; Mus Int Della Ceramica, Faenza, Italy; Can Imperial Bank Com, Montreal. *Comn:* Mural sculpture, Place de Arts, Montreal, 63; aluminum sculpture, Toronto Airport, 64; 12 steel sculptures, Can Pavilion, Montreal's Expos, 67; bronze sculpture, Queens's Park, Toronto, 70; aluminum structural sculpture, Palais Justice Quebec, 83; and others. *Exhib:* 28th Venice Biennale, 56; Pittsburgh Int, 58; Int Exhib Contemp Sculpture, Expo 67, Montreal, 67; 11th Middelheim Biennale, 71; 10th Int Sculpture Conf, Toronto, 78; and others. *Teaching:* Prof sculpture, Univ Quebec, 69. *Awards:* Can Gov & Can Coun Fels, 53, 59, 62 & 69; Serv Medal, Order Can, 68; Awards, Ministere de l'Education, Que, 70-72. *Bibliog:* Bill Stephenson (auth), Louis Archambault's wonderful wall, MacLean's, Can, 1/18/58; Guy Robert (auth), Archambault, Vie des Arts, summer 72; Luc Epivent (auth), Vie Arts, Montreal, spring 81. *Mem:* Academician Royal Can Acad Arts. *Media:* Multimedia. *Mailing Add:* 278 Sanford Ave St Lambert PQ J4P 2X6 Canada

ARCHER, CYNTHIA
PRINTMAKER, PAINTER
b New Martinsville, WVa, Mar 28, 53. *Study:* Goucher Col, BA, 75; WVa Univ, MFA, 78. *Work:* Nat Art Gallery, Wellington, New Zealand; Portland Art Mus, Ore; Ill State Mus, Springfield; Mus Art & Archaeology, Univ Mo, Columbia. *Exhib:* Colby-Sawyer Col Print Invitational, NH, 81; American Printmakers, Ohio State Univ Gallery Fine Art, 82; Contemporary American Printmakers, US State Dept Traveling Exhib, Yugoslavia, 82; Benefit Exhib & Auction, Corcoran Gallery Art, 83; Contemporary Lithography in Chicago, Ill State Mus, Springfield, 83-85; Stone Metal Paper & Canvas, Fermi Lab Exhib Hall, Batavia, Ill, 84. *Pos:* Lithographer, Plucked Chicken Press, Chicago, 78-82; master lithographer, 82- *Awards:* Purchase Award, Huntington Art Galleries, Huntington, WVa, 77; Governor's Award, WVa Exhib, Charleston, 79; Merit Award, 6th Baer Art Competition, Beverly Art Ctr, Chicago, 82. *Media:* Acrylics; Lithography. *Dealer:* Fairweather Hardin Gallery 101 E Ontario Chicago IL 60611. *Mailing Add:* PO Box 5941 Chicago IL 60680

ARCHER, EDMUND
PAINTER
b Richmond, Va, Sept 28, 04. *Study:* With Nora Houston & Adele Clark, Richmond, Va; with Charles W Hawthorne, Provincetown, Mass; Univ Va; Art Students League, with Allen Tucker & Kenneth Hayes Miller; Acad Colarossi, Paris; independent study, Italy; with Jacques Maroger, New York. *Work:* Va Mus Fine Arts, Richmond; Mus Fine Arts, Boston; Whitney Mus Am Art; gift of Mrs John D Rockefeller, Jr, Fisk Univ; Corcoran Gallery Art. *Comn:* Mural, Pub Works Art Proj, Post Off, Hopewell, Va, 39; Gov John Garland Pollard (portrait), State of Va, State Capital, 42; Dean Radcliffe Heermance (portrait), Princeton Univ, 46; Dean Charles C Abbott (portrait), Grad Sch Bus Admin, Univ Va, 66; Fred M Carroll (portrait), IBM Corp, IBM Tech Hall of Fame, Yorktown Heights, NY, 68. *Exhib:* Exhib of Paintings & Sculpture, Century of Progress (Int Expos), Art Inst Chicago, 33-34; Golden Gate Int Expos, Dept Fine Arts, San Francisco, 39; Exhib Contemp Am Painting, New York World's Fair, 40; Am Watercolors, Drawings & Prints, Metrop Mus Art, 52; 131st Ann Exhib, Nat Acad Design, New York, 56. *Pos:* Mem bd control, Art Students League, 25; from asst to assoc cur, Whitney Mus Am Art, 30-40. *Teaching:* Drawing, painting & compos, Corcoran Sch Art, George Washington Univ, 44-68, emer teacher, 68- *Awards:* Corcoran Bronze Medal & Third W A Clarke Prize, Corcoran Gallery Art, 30; Purchase Award, Va Mus Fine Arts, 41; First Prize & Popular Prize, Norfolk Mus Arts & Sci, 50. *Mem:* Fel Int Inst Arts & Lett, Switz. *Mailing Add:* 13 S Foushee St Richmond VA 23220

ARCILESI, VINCENT J
PAINTER
b St Louis, Mo, May 5, 32. *Study:* Furman Univ, 49-50; Univ Okla, BFA(design), 53; Art Inst Chicago, BFA(painting), 56, MFA, 61. *Work:* Art Inst Chicago Mus; Ill State Mus, Springfield; Fashion Inst of Technol, New York; Hirshhorn Collection; Kemper Ins, Long Grove, Ill; plus pvt collections. *Exhib:* 70th Ann, Art Inst Chicago, 67; Visions/Painting & Sculpture, Distinguished Alumni 1945-Present, Art Inst Chicago Gallery, 76; one-man shows, Westbroadway Gallery, New York, 73-75 & 77; America 1976 Traveling Exhib, Corcoran Gallery, 76-78; Allan Frumkin Gallery, 80 & 82; Nat Acad Design, 80 & 82; Am Acad Inst Arts & Letters, New York, 81; Tibor De Nagy Gallery, New York, 83; and others. *Awards:* Creative Artists Pub Serv Prog Fel, 81-82; Nat Endowment Arts Grant, 82. *Bibliog:* Hilton Kramer (auth), Art: five gallery realist show, New York Times, 9/12/80; Frank H Goodyear Jr (auth), Contemporary American Realism Since 1960, New York Graphic Soc, 81; Pat Van Gelder (auth), Vincent Arcilesi, Am Artist, 10/83; and others. *Media:* Oil, Graphite. *Mailing Add:* 116 Duane St New York NY 10007

ARD, SARADELL (SARADELL ARD FREDERICK)
EDUCATOR, PAINTER
b Macon, Ga, Mar 22, 20. *Study:* Asbury Col, AB(art), 42; Univ Mich, MA, 43; Columbia Univ Teachers Col, DEd(art), 70. *Work:* Univ Ill, Edwardsville; Alaska State Mus, Juneau; Alaska Methodist Univ Collection Alaskan Artists, Univ Alaska & Anchorage Hist & Fine Arts Mus, Anchorage. *Exhib:* Solo exhibs, Teachers Col Galleries, Columbia Univ, New York, 68 & 70, Alaska State Mus, Juneau, 72 & Anchorage Hist & Fine Arts Mus, 76; Contemporary Alaskan Art, Smithsonian Inst, Washington, DC, 78; Univ

Alaska Campus Ctr Gallery, Anchorage, 78-83; Alaskaland Gallery, Fairbanks, 83; and others. *Collections Arranged:* 20th Century Alaska Eskimo Art, Smithsonian Inst, 82. *Pos:* Dir arts & crafts prog, European Theatre, US Army, 60-62; vchmn bd dirs, Visual Arts Ctr, Anchorage, 73-76; mem bd dirs, Mayor's Comt, Fine Arts Mus, Anchorage, 73-82. *Teaching:* Prof art, Alaska Methodist Univ, 62-73; prof art, Univ Alaska, Anchorage, 73-, actg dean, 76-77. *Awards:* Juror's Choice, Ann All Alaska Art Exhib, 66 & 1st Award Drawing, 67; Gov's Award, 80. *Mem:* Nat Art Educ Asn; Col Art Asn; Anchorage Fine Arts Mus Asn (pres, 81-82). *Media:* Oil, Acrylic. *Res:* Eskimo art of the Arctic Circle. *Publ:* Auth, Inuit Sculpture, summer 80 & Alaskan Eskimo Art Today, 72, Alaska J; auth, Native Alaskan Art Today, Am Illus, 76; auth, Roots in the past, Smithsonian Inst Press, 82; auth, Schitz-und graverkunst der Alaska-Eskimo in geschichte und gegenwart, In: Invitkunst, Linden Mus, Stuttgart, Ger, 83; and others. *Mailing Add:* c/o Univ Alaska Anchorage 3221 Providence Dr Anchorage AK 99507

ARGUELLES, JOSE A
WRITER, PAINTER
b Rochester, Minn, Jan 24, 39. *Study:* Univ Chicago, with John Rewald & Joshua Taylor, BA, 61, MA, 63, PhD, 69. *Comn:* Stairwell Mural, Psychology Dept, Univ Calif, Davis, 68; Dragon Stairwell Mural, Evergreen State Col, 72. *Exhib:* Transformations, Princeton Univ Art Mus, 68; Mandalas, Inner City Gallery, Los Angeles, 69; 25 Years on the Road: A Tribute to Jack Kerouac, Boulder Ctr Visual Arts, 82; Int Exhib, Univ Toronto, First Planetary Cong, 83. *Pos:* Prog coordr, Man & Arts Prog, Evergreen State Col, 71-73; Art critic, Boulder Camera, 78-81; prog coordr, Creative Arts, Union Grad Sch, Boulder, 83-; coordr, Planet Art Network, Boulder, 83- *Awards:* Samuel H Kress Found Sr Fel, 65-66; Outstanding Teacher of Year, Univ Colo, Denver, 82. *Bibliog:* George Medevoy (auth), Psychic artist, Sacramento Union, 1/24/71; Aida Ferrarone (auth), article, Imagen, 1/7/81; Carole Schlemmerint & Peter Selz (auths), The actual symposium, Arts Mag, 9/81. *Media:* Colored Pencil, Brush and Ink. *Publ:* Auth, Charles Henry and the Formation of a Psychophysical Aesthetic, Univ Chicago Press, 72; coauth, Mandala, 72, auth, The transformative vision, reflections on nature and history of human expression, 75, coauth, The feminine, spacious as the sky, 77 & auth, Earth ascending: Illustrated treatise on the law governing whole systems (in prep), Shambhala. *Mailing Add:* 262 Spruce St Boulder CO 80302

ARIAS-MISSON, ALAIN
VISUAL POET, GRAPHIC ARTIST
b Brussels, Belg, Dec 11, 36; US citizen. *Study:* Harvard Univ, BA(Greek lit; magna cum laude), 59. *Work:* Archief voor Visuele, Concrete en Experimentele Poezie, Dutch Lit Mus, Hague; Archive H Sohm, State Gallery, Stuttgart, Ger; Galleria Schwarz, Millan; Cabinet d'Estampes, Bibliotheque Nat, Paris; Dresden Mus; and others. *Exhib:* One-man shows, Art Fairs, Basle, Brussels & Dusseldorf, 74-75 & Studio 77, Brescia, 78; Mercato de Sale, Milan, 81; Arteder, Arte Grafico, Bilboa, 82; Graphik-Ausstellung 3, Liepzig, 82; and many others. *Teaching:* Creative writing, Columbia Univ, 81-82. *Bibliog:* S H Anderson (auth), When Reality becomes Superfiction, Int Herald Tribune, 5/75; M Dachy (auth), New York art, Critique, Paris, 81; M Dachy (auth), L'espace Amerique, Change, Paris; and others. *Publ:* Co-ed, 5 anthologies in Europe & America, 74; auth, Confessions of a Murderer, Bomber, Fascist, Rapist, Thief, Chicago Rev Press & Swallow, 75; co-ed, Poesia Visiva, Chicago Rev, 76; auth, The Public Poem Book, Arias-Misson, Factotum Press, Italy, 78-79; auth, Visual poetry, Paris Rev. *Dealer:* Sarenco-Galleria Factotum-Art Villa Colleoni 7-Illasi Verona 37031. *Mailing Add:* PO Box 24 Clarksburg NJ 08510

ARISS, HERBERT JOSHUA
PAINTER, ILLUSTRATOR
b Guelph, Ont, Sept 19, 18. *Study:* Ont Col Art. *Work:* Nat Gallery Can; Art Gallery Ont; Winnipeg Art Gallery; Vancouver Art Gallery; London Art Gallery, Ont. *Comn:* Casein, Huron & Erie Co, Chatham, 58; ceramic, John Labatt Brewery, London, 59; multimedia, Sir Adam Beck Sec Sch, London, 67; multimedia, Ont Govt Bldg, Toronto, 68; mural, Sch Med, Univ Western Ont, London. *Exhib:* 2nd & 3rd Can Biennial, Ottawa, 64-66; Can Soc Graphic Arts, 70; Can Printmakers, Nat Gallery, Can Int Show, 71; Can Soc Painters in Watercolour, London & New York, 72. *Pos:* Pres, Western Art League, 57-60; mem, London Art Gallery Bd, 68-71; dir, London Art Gallery Asn, 69-72; chmn acquisition comt, London Pub Libr & Art Mus, 70-71. *Teaching:* Instr drawing & painting, Doon Sch Fine Arts, 55-58; head dept art, H B Beal Art Sch, London, Ont, 65- *Awards:* Can Coun Sr Fel, 60-61; Dirs Purchase Award, Vancouver Art Gallery, 63; Honour Award, Can Soc Painters in Watercolour, 65. *Bibliog:* Bright lights of London, Time, 68; Barry Lord (auth), How Beal has made London an art centre, Toronto Star, 70; J Bryce (auth), Herb Ariss retrospective, Arts Can, 71. *Mem:* Ont Soc Artists; Can Soc Painters in Watercolour (vpres, 58-60); Can Soc Graphics Art; Can Group Painters; Royal Can Acad Arts. *Publ:* Illusr, Lectures variees, 58; illusr, La double mort de Frederic Belot, 58; illusr, Contes d'Aujour d'hui, 63; illusr, War, 71; auth, Encounters, London Regional Art Gallery, 82. *Mailing Add:* 770 Leroy Ave London ON N5Y 4G7 Canada

ARKUS, LEON A
CONSULTANT, MUSEUM DIRECTOR
b NJ, May 6, 15. *Study:* City Col New York, with Townsend Harris. *Collections Arranged:* 1970 Pittsburgh International, 70-71; Fresh Air Sch, 72; Art in Residence, 73; Twelve Years of Collecting, 74; Celebration, 74-75; Pittsburgh Corporations Collection, 75-76; Pittsburgh Int Series, Pierre Alechinsky, 77; Pittsburgh Int Series: Eduardo Chillida/Willem de Kooning, 79. *Pos:* Asst dir, Mus Art, Carnegie Inst, Pittsburgh, 54-62, assoc dir, 62-68, dir, 68-80, consult & dir emer, 80- *Awards:* Knight Cross of the Order of

Dannebrog, Queen Margrethe II of Denmark, 74; and others. *Mem:* Am Asn Mus; hon mem Assoc Artists Pittsburgh; Asn Art Mus Dirs; Pittsburgh Plan for Art (gov, 58-80); Century Club; and others. *Publ:* Auth, Three self-taught Pennsylvania artists: Hicks, Kane, Pippin, 66; Carl-Henning Pedersen: paintings, watercolors, drawings, 68; The art of Black Africa, 69; John Kane, painter (catalogue raisonne), Univ Pittsburgh Press, 71. *Mailing Add:* 303 S Craig Pittsburgh PA 15213

ARMAN
SCULPTOR
b Nice, France, 1928; US citizen. *Study:* Ecole Nat Art Decoratif, BPh; Ecole Louvre. *Work:* Hirshhorn Mus & Sculpture Garden, Washington, DC; Metrop Mus Art, New York; Mus Mod Art, New York; Mus Georges Pompidou, Paris; Nationale Gallery, Berlin. *Exhib:* Mus Mod Art, Paris, 75; Fort Worth Art Mus, Tex, 75; Des Moines Art Ctr, Iowa, 75; Albright Knox Art Gallery, Buffalo, 75; La Jolla Mus, Calif, 75; plus many others. *Teaching:* Instr, Univ Calif, Los Angeles, 67-68. *Awards:* Tokyo Biennel Second Prize, 64; Grand Marzotto Prize, 66. *Bibliog:* Otto Hahn (auth), Arman, Hatzan, 72; Henry Martin (auth), Arman, Abrams, 73; Arman Selected Activities, Gibson, 75; plus others. *Media:* Bronze, Metal. *Mailing Add:* 380 W Broadway New York NY 10012

ARMSTRONG, BILL HOWARD
PAINTER, EDUCATOR
b Horton, Kans, Dec 13, 26. *Study:* Bradley Univ, Peoria, Ill, BFA(cum laude), 49; Univ Ill, Urbana, MFA, 55, with Abraham Rattner. *Work:* Brooklyn Mus, NY; San Francisco Mus of Art, Calif; Springfield Art Mus, Mo; Albrecht Gallery, St Joseph, Mo; Art and the Law, West Publ Co, St Paul, Minn. *Comn:* Sci mural, Ken-Barr Resort, Paducah, Ky, 68; hist mural, Am Bank, Irving, Tex, 75. *Exhib:* Am Fedn Arts Int Traveling Exhib, 56; 20th & 24th Print Exhib, San Francisco Mus Art, 56 & 59; Butler Inst Am Art, Youngstown, Ohio, 56-67; Pa Acad Fine Art, Philadelphia, 56-67; 10th Ann Print Exhib, Brooklyn Mus, 59; Soc Am Graphic Artist Int Traveling Exhib, 60; Watercolor USA Nat Exhib, Springfield, Mo, 65-76; Calif Nat Watercolor Soc, La Angeles, 69-71; Art and the Law, 82-83. *Collections Arranged:* Watercolor USA Nat Invitational Exhib, 76. *Pos:* Art adv, Burma Transl Soc, Rangoon, Ford Found, 57-58. *Teaching:* Asst prof painting, Univ Wis, Madison, 56-63; prof watercolor & graphic design, Southwest Mo State Univ, 63- *Awards:* Purchase Award, 10th Ann Print Exhib, Brooklyn Mus, 59; Purchase Awards, Watercolor USA, 62-71 & Calif Nat Watercolor Soc, 69 & 70; and others. *Mailing Add:* RT 5 Box 6 Ozark MO 65721

ARMSTRONG, GEOFFREY
PAINTER, ARCHITECT
b Toronto, Ont, May 27, 28. *Study:* Univ Toronto, BArch, 52. *Work:* Art Gallery Windsor, Ont; Univ NB, Fredericton; City North Bay, Ont; Esso Resources, Calgary, Alta; Royal Bank, Toronto. *Exhib:* Art Gallery Hamilton; Montreal Mus Fine Arts; Art Gallery Ont; Trent Univ; Queens Univ, Kingston; Ont Soc Artists Traveling Exhib; Soc Can Artists Traveling Exhib. *Mem:* Royal Archit Inst Can; Prof Artists Can; Soc Can Artists; Ont Soc Artists (exec dir, 73-). *Media:* Acrylic on Canvas and Paper. *Publ:* Contribr, Art Mag, 68-70. *Dealer:* Roberts Gallery 641 Yonge St Toronto ON M4Y 1Z9; West End Gallery 12308 Jasper Ave Edmonton AB T5N 3K5. *Mailing Add:* 188 Davenport Rd Toronto ON M5R 1J2 Canada

ARMSTRONG, JANE BOTSFORD
SCULPTOR
b Buffalo, NY, Feb 17, 21. *Study:* Middlebury Col; Pratt Inst; Art Students League, with Jose De Creeft. *Work:* Eng Bldg, Mass Inst Technol; Columbus Gallery Fine Arts, Ohio; New Britain Mus Am Art, Conn; Rollins Col, Winter Park, Fla; Columbus Gallery Arts & Crafts, Ga. *Comn:* Flint Mich Art Mus; Eula and David Wintermann Libr, Eagle Lake, Tex; Tex Gulf Chemical Hq Bldg, Raleigh, NC; Wichita Art Mus, Kans; Rollins Col, Winter Park, Fla. *Exhib:* One-man shows, Columbia Mus Art, SC, 75, Spec Children's Exhib, Dallas Fine Arts Mus, Tex, 78, Wichita Art Mus, Kans, 78 & 82, Wadsworth Atheneum, Hartford, Conn, 79, Southeastern Ctr Contemp Art, 80, The Sculpture Ctr, New York, 81 & Sid Deutsch Gallery, New York, 83; Artists Am Exhib, Colo Heritage Galleries, Denver, 81-83. *Awards:* Gold Medals, Nat Arts Club, 68, 69, 72 & 77; Chaim Gross Found Award, 80; Maurice B Hexter Prize, 81. *Bibliog:* Nancy Tobin Willig (auth), JBA comes home to Buffalo, Courier Express Mag, Buffalo, NY, 1/19/75; Max Wyckes-Joyce (auth), Int Herald Tribune, London, 5/15/76; Diana Loercher (auth), Jane Armstrong--late blooming sculptor, Christian Sci Monitor, 12/19/77. *Mem:* Sculptors Guild; Nat Sculpture Soc; Allied Artists of Am; Audubon Artists; Nat Asn Women Artists. *Media:* Stone. *Publ:* Auth, Discovery in Stone, Eastwoods Press, 74; auth, From the mountains of Vermont, Nat Sculpture Rev, 74. *Dealer:* Sid Deutsch Gallery 20 West 57th St New York NY; Foster Harmon Galleries of American Art Sarasota FL. *Mailing Add:* 2909 S Ocean Blvd Highland Beach FL 33431

ARMSTRONG, MARTHA (ALLEN)
PAINTER, PHOTOGRAPHER
b Brunswick, Ga. *Study:* Converse Col, under August Cook, 53-56; Heatherly Sch Fine Art, London, Eng, advan painting, 67-69. *Work:* CBS Masterworks, Ltd, Can; C G Jung Educ Ctr, Rovi Tex Corp, Rapada Corp & White, Petrou & McHone, Houston, Tex; United Energy Resources, Houston, Tex. *Comn:* Poster & logo, Community Orchestra Soc, Houston, 79; cover, Performing Arts Mag, Houston, 81. *Exhib:* Houston Mus Fine Arts, Glassell Sch, 78; solo shows, La Gallery, Houston, 81, McMurtrey Gallery, Houston, 81 & 82 & Univ Houston, Clear Lake, 83; Jewish Community Ctr, Houston, 83; and others. *Collections Arranged:* 34 Houston

Artists Working in their Studios, 77. *Bibliog:* Mary Anne Piocentini (auth), interview, Houston Arts, spring 82; Pamela Rosinus (auth), Armstrong's Photographs, Inner View, 82; Patricia Johnson (auth), Martha Armstrong's photography is softly personal, Houston Chronicle, 82; and others. *Mem:* Cult Arts Coun Houston (bd dir 79-, vpres, 81, pres, 82, chmn bd, 83); Houston Ctr Photography (trustee, 83); Contemp Arts Mus (trustee, 78-80); Artists Equity. *Media:* Acrylic. *Dealer:* McMurtrey Gallery 1 Chelsea Pl Houston TX 77006; Graham Gallery 2811 Bartlett Houston TX 77098. *Mailing Add:* 2420 Brentwood Houston TX 77019

ARMSTRONG, ROGER JOSEPH
PAINTER, CARTOONIST
b Los Angeles, Calif, Oct 12, 17. *Study:* Pasadena City Col; Chouinard Art Inst; Sueo Serisawa Workshop. *Work:* City of Santa Fe Springs, Calif; City of Pico Rivera; Banking House of Rothschild, San Francisco; Laguna Beach Art Mus, Calif. *Exhib:* International Masters of Watercolor, Dalzell-Hatfield Galleries, Los Angeles, 67; one-man shows, Muckenthaler Cult Ctr, 69, Newport Beach Munic Gallery, 70 & Ettinger Gallery, Laguna Beach Sch of Art, 78; Griswold Gallery, Claremont, Calif, 74; Calif 100 Exhib, Laguna Beach Mus Art, 77; Dana Point Marine Inst, 81. *Collections Arranged:* Three-man exhib, Keith Finch, Edgar Ewing & Robert Frame, 63; West Coast Figurative, 64; First Ann West Coast Sculpture Exhib, 64; plus others. *Teaching:* Instr cartooning & watercolor painting, Laguna Beach Sch Art, 65-; instr watercolor, Pasadena City Col, 74-78; instr oil painting, Saddlebrook Community Col, Mission Viejo, 78; instr cartooning, Orange Coast Col, Costa Mesa, Calif, 81- *Awards:* Second Award for Watercolor, First Ann Orange Co Exhib, 63; First Purchase Award, First Ann Pio Pico Art Festival, 68; hon mention, East Meets West Exhib, Calif Nat Watercolor Soc, 72. *Bibliog:* Raymond Fisher & John Barnard (auths), Roger Armstrong, triple threat artist, World of Comic Art, winter 66-67. *Mem:* Nat Watercolor Soc; Laguna Beach Art Asn; Los Angeles Art Asn; Nat Cartoonists Soc; Comic Artists Professional Soc. *Media:* Watercolor, Ink. *Publ:* Coauth & illusr, Ella Cinders comic strip, United Features Syndicate, 50-61 & Napoleon & Uncle Elby, Los Angeles Times Syndicate, 50-60; auth & illusr, Flintstones, Little Lulu & others, Western Publ, 60-72; comic strip illusr, Scamp, Walt Disney Productions; and others. *Mailing Add:* Laguna Beach Sch Art 2222 Laguna Canyon Rd Laguna Beach CA 92651

ARMSTRONG, THOMAS NEWTON, III
MUSEUM DIRECTOR
b Portsmouth, Va, June 30, 32. *Study:* Art Students League, summer 53; Cornell Univ Col Archit, BFA(art & planning), 54; Inst Fine Arts, NY Univ, 65-67. *Pos:* From cur to assoc dir, Abby Aldrich Rockefeller Folk Art Col, Williamsburg, Va, 67-71; dir, Pa Acad Fine Arts, Philadelphia, 71-73; assoc dir, Whitney Mus Am Art, New York, 73-74, dir, 74- *Mem:* Am Fedn Arts (trustee); Int Exhib Fedn (trustee); Asn Art Mus Dir; Herbert F Johnson Mus Art, Cornell Univ (trustee & mem bd); Alumni Coun, Col Archit Art & Planning, Cornell Univ (comt Alumni Trustees Nominations). *Mailing Add:* c/o Whitney Mus Am Art 945 Madison Ave New York NY 10021

ARNASON, H HARVARD
HISTORIAN, WRITER
b Winnipeg, Man, Apr 24, 09; US citizen. *Study:* Univ Man; Northwestern Univ, BS & MA; Princeton Univ, MFA. *Pos:* Sr field rep, Off War Info, Iceland, 42-44, asst dep dir for Europe, Off War Info, 44-45; chief prog planning & eval unit, Off Int Info & Cult Affairs, Dept State, 46-47; US rep, Preparatory Comn, UNESCO, London & Paris, 46; tech adv to US deleg, First Gen Conf UNESCO, 46; dir, Walker Art Ctr, Minneapolis, 51-60; vpres art admin, Solomon R Guggenheim Found, 60-69. *Teaching:* Instr art, Northwestern Univ, 36-38; lectr, Frick Col, 38-42; vis assoc prof, Univ Chicago, 47; prof art & chmn dept, Univ Minn, 47-60; Carnegie vis prof, Univ Hawaii, 59. *Awards:* Chevalier, Ordre Arts et Lett, France; Knight, Order St Olav, Norway; Fulbright, Nat Endowment Humanities; and others. *Mem:* Solomon R Guggenehim Found (trustee); Joseph H Hirshhorn Mus, Washington, DC (trustee); Int Found Art Res (exec bd & chmn adv comt); and others; sculpture, 18th to 20th centuries. *Interests:* Modern painting, 19th and 20th centuries; sculpture, 18th to 20th centuries. *Publ:* Auth, History of Modern Art, Abrams, 68, rev ed, 76, textbook ed, Prentice-Hall, 69; co-auth, Alexander Calder, 69; co-auth, Jacques Lipchitz: My Life in Sculpture, 72; auth, The Sculptures of Houdon, Phaidon Press, & Oxford Univ Press, 75; auth, Robert Motherwell, Abrams, 76; and others. *Mailing Add:* 4 E 89th St New York NY 10028

ARNAUTOFF, JACOB VICTOR
SCULPTOR, PAINTER
b Coyoacan, Mex, Sept 11, 30; US citizen. *Study:* San Francisco City Col; Calif Col Arts & Crafts, BFA(indust design); San Francisco State Univ; Calif Inst Fine Arts. *Work:* Nat Arch, Washington, DC; Kodak Co, New York; Oakland Mus, Calif. *Comn:* Decorative permanent screen, Kaiser Hosp, Richmond, Calif, 74. *Exhib:* Kodak Int Color Competition, New York World's Fair, 64-65; Kingsley Art Club, Sacramento, Calif, 70; Fed Dept Housing & Urban Develop Competitive Exhib, 72. *Pos:* Dir arts & crafts, Piedmont Recreation Ctr, Calif, 59-63. *Awards:* Bronze Medallion Spec Award, Kodak Co, 64-65; Int Competition Award, Dept Housing & Urban Develop, 72. *Mem:* Artists Equity Asn (pres, Northern Calif Chap, 70-72, nat vpres, 72-75). *Media:* Oil; Polymer. *Res:* Development of art styles in post World War II era in relationship to socio-economic change. *Collection:* Japanese prints; pre-Columbian sculpture; contemporary prints. *Publ:* Auth catalog, Dept Housing & Urban Develop, 72. *Mailing Add:* 13902 W Lake Kathleen Dr SE Renton WA 98056

ARNESON, ROBERT
SCULPTOR, EDUCATOR

b Benicia, Calif, Sept 4, 30. *Study:* Calif Col Arts & Crafts, BA(educ), 54; Mills Col, MFA, 58. *Work:* Oakland Art Mus; Whitney Mus Am Art; Hirshhorn Mus; Nat Mus Mod Art, Kyoto, Japan; San Francisco Mus Mod Art. *Exhib:* Objects USA, Johnson Wax Collection touring US & Europe, 68-73; Human Concern/Personal Torment, Whitney Mus Am Art, 69 & Clay Works, 20 Americans, Mus Contemp Crafts, 71, New York; Contemporary Ceramic Art, Mus Mod Art, Kyoto & Tokyo, 71-72; retrospective, Mus Contemp Art, Chicago & San Francisco Mus Art, 74; West Coast Ceramics, Stedelijk Mus, Amsterdam, Holland, 79; Six Ceramic Artists, Whitney Mus Am Art, 81. *Teaching:* Instr design, Mills Col, 60-62; prof art, Univ Calif, Davis, 62- *Bibliog:* Dennis Adrian (auth), Robert Arneson's Feats of Clay, Art Am, 9/74; Alfred Frankenstein (auth), The Ceramic Sculpture of Robert Anderson, Art News, 1/76; Century of Ceramics in the United States, 1878-79, E P Dutton, 79. *Media:* Clay, Ceramic. *Dealer:* Fuller-Goldeen Gallery 228 Grant Ave San Francisco CA 94108; Allan Frumkin Gallery 50 W 57th St New York NY 10022. *Mailing Add:* Art Dept Univ Calif Davis CA 95616

ARNEST, BERNARD
PAINTER, EDUCATOR

b Denver, Colo, Feb 17, 17. *Study:* Colorado Springs Fine Arts Ctr. *Work:* Walker Art Ctr, Minneapolis; Minneapolis Inst Arts; Colorado Springs Fine Arts Ctr; Univ Nebr, Lincoln; Univ Ga, Atlanta. *Exhib:* Whitney Mus Ann Am Painting, New York; Carnegie Int, Pittsburgh; Corcoran Biennial, Washington, DC; Pa Acad, Philadelphia; Univ Ill Ann, Urbana-Champaign; Denver Art Mus; Kraushaar Galleries, New York; Retrospective, Colorado Springs Fine Arts Ctr. *Pos:* Chief war artist, European Theater Hq, US Army, 44-45; chmn advan placement in art comt, Col Entrance Exam Bd, 69-72. *Teaching:* Assoc prof drawing & painting, Univ Minn, 49-57; prof drawing & painting, Colo Col, 57- *Awards:* Guggenheim Fel, 40; int exchange prog, US Dept State, 60. *Media:* Oil, Acrylic. *Dealer:* Kraushaar Galleries 1055 Madison Ave New York NY 10028. *Mailing Add:* 1502 Wood Ave Colorado Springs CO 80907

ARNHEIM, RUDOLF
EDUCATOR, WRITER

b Berlin, Ger, July 15, 04; US citizen. *Study:* Univ Berlin, PhD, 28; Guggenheim fel, 42-43; RI Sch Design, Hon DFA, 76. *Teaching:* Mem fac psychol art, Sarah Lawrence Col, 43-68; prof, Harvard Univ, 68-74; vis prof, Univ Mich, 74- *Awards:* Distinguished Serv Award, Nat Art Educ Asn; Resident, Am Acad Rome, 78. *Mem:* Am Soc Aesthet (pres & trustee); Am Psychol Asn (pres, div arts, 70-72); Col Art Asn. *Publ:* Auth, Art and visual perception, Univ Calif Press, 54 & 74; auth, Visual thinking, 69, Entropy and art, 71, The dynamics of architectural form, 77 & The power of the center, 82. *Mailing Add:* Dept Art Hist Univ Mich Ann Arbor MI 48109

ARNHOLM, RONALD FISHER
DESIGNER, EDUCATOR

b Barre, Vt, Jan 4, 39. *Study:* RI Sch Design, BFA(graphic design), 61; Yale Univ, MFA(graphic design), 63. *Work:* Ga Comn Arts Traveling Exhib. *Comn:* Corp design prog (with Jack MacDonald), Am Tube & Controls, West Warwick, RI, 62; typeface: Jenson Roman, Mergenthaler Linotype Co, Plainview, NY, 64; wall mural, Mead Corp, Atlanta, Ga, 65; typefaces: Aquarius series, 70-74, Fovea series, 77-79, Visual Graphics Corp, Tamarac, Fla & Los Angeles Times, 80. *Exhib:* Composing Rm Award Typography Exhib, Gallery 303, New York, 63; one-man show, Ga Mus Art, Athens, 65; 45th Ann Art Dir Club New York Ann Exhib, 66; Southeastern Ann, High Mus Art, Atlanta, 67; Typomundus 20/2 Int Typography Exhib, Stuttgart, Ger, 70. *Pos:* Art dir, The Moderator Mag, New Haven, Conn, 62-63. *Teaching:* From instr to asst prof art, Univ Ga, 63-71; assoc prof, 71-82, prof, 82- *Awards:* Composing Room Award for Excellence in Typography, New York, 63; Award of Distinctive Merit, Art Dir Club, New York, 66; Cert of Merit, Typomundus 20/2, 70. *Bibliog:* Eugene Ettenberg (auth), The Word Paintings of Ronald Arnholm, Am Artist, 11/70; Edward M Gottschall (auth), The Word Paintings of Ronald Arnholm, Typographic, Vol 3, No 3. *Media:* Acrylic, Watercolor. *Res:* Aspects of visual perception. *Mailing Add:* Dept of Art Univ of Ga Athens GA 30602

ARNOLD, FLORENCE M
PAINTER

b Prescott, Ariz, Sept 16, 1900. *Study:* Mills Col, degree in music; Univ Southern Calif, BA; Claremont Grad Sch. *Work:* Long Beach Mus Art; Laguna Mus Art, Calif State Univ, Fullerton; Media Art Gallery, Santa Ana, Calif; Newport Harbor Art Mus, Mills Col Print Collection, City of Fullerton. *Exhib:* Gallerias Numero, Florence, Rome, Milan & Prato Venice, 63; Calif Hard-edge Painting, Newport Beach, 64; one-man shows, Long Beach Mus Art, 62-69 & Fresno Mus Art, 75; Retrospective, Muckenthaler Cult Ctr, 75; retrospective, North Orange County Mus honoring 80th birthday. *Awards:* First Prize, Muckenthaler Cult Ctr, 67 & 69; First Prize, Orange Co Art Asn, 68; La Mirada Festival Arts Purchase Award, 68. *Bibliog:* Monogr, Calif State Univ, Fullerton, 69; Nat Archives of Am Art, Smithsonian Inst, Washington, DC; Oral Hist Prog, Fullerton Col, interview published by college. *Mem:* Los Angeles Art Asn; Muckenthaler Cult Ctr (bd mem, 60-77); Fullerton Cult & Fine Arts Comn; Los Angeles Mus Art (charter mem). *Media:* Oil on Canvas. *Mailing Add:* 1136 Valencia Mesa Dr Fullerton CA 92633

ARNOLD, JACK
ART DEALER, PUBLISHER

b New York, NY. *Study:* Syracuse Univ, BS, 50. *Pos:* Pres, Collector's Workshop, New York, 76-78; vpres, Gallery Hawaii, Honolulu, 78-80; pres,

Falcon Fine Art, New York, 80-82; pres, Arnold Fine Arts, New York, 83- *Teaching:* Dir lithography, Shorewood Atelier, New York, 72-75. *Specialty:* Contemp paintings, drawings, watercolors & graphics. *Publ:* Contribr, The Contemporary Lithographic Workshop Around the World, Van Nostrand Reinhold Co, 74. *Mailing Add:* 5 East 67th St New York NY 10021

ARNOLD, PAUL BEAVER
EDUCATOR, PRINTMAKER

b Taiyuanfu, China, Nov 24, 18; US citizen. *Study:* Oberlin Col, AB, 40, MA, 41; Cleveland Inst Art; Univ Minn, MFA, 55. *Work:* Libr Cong, Washington, DC; Seattle Art Mus, Wash; Baltimore Mus, Md; Dayton Art Inst, Ohio. *Comn:* Pheasant (color intaglio), Int Graphic Arts Soc, New York, 56; White Peacock (color woodcut), Int Graphic Arts Soc, New York, 57; mural, Gilford Instrument Co, Oberlin, Ohio, 71. *Exhib:* May Show, Cleveland Mus, 61, 63, 66, 74 & 76; one-man shows, Jersey City State Col, NJ, 66 & 78, Miami Univ, Oxford, Ohio, 68, Univ Kans, Manhattan, 70; Contemporary Prints for Collectors, Columbus Gallery Art, Ohio, 75; two-man show, US Info Serv, US Embassy, Ankara, Turkey, 75. *Teaching:* From instr to prof art & chmn dept, Oberlin Col, 41-, Young-Hunter prof, 82-; guest prof, Tunghai Univ, Taiwan, 72 & Sarah Lawrence Col, Lacoste, France, 79 & 80. *Awards:* Ford Found Fac Fel Prog, 51-52; Audubon Artists Medal of Honor, 57; Great Lakes Cols Asn Res Grant, 65-66. *Mem:* Nat Asn Schs Art (bd dir, 70-81, vpres, 72-75, pres, 75-78); Col Art Asn (bd dir, 79-, secy, 82-); Mid-Am Col Art Asn. *Media:* Woodcut, Intaglio. *Publ:* Illusr, General chemistry & Laboratory experiments in general chemistry, Campbell & Steiner, 55; coauth, The Humanities at Oberlin, 57; auth, Printmaking today, 4/70 & Silkscreen printing, 12/74, Lalit Kala Contemp, New Delhi, India; contribr, Terra cotta army of Quin Shihuangdi, Ceramics Monthly, 11/80. *Mailing Add:* Dept Art Oberlin Col Oberlin OH 44074

ARNOLD, RALPH MOFFETT
PAINTER, EDUCATOR

b Chicago, Ill, Dec 5, 28. *Study:* Roosevelt Univ, BA; Art Inst Chicago, with Vera Berdich. *Work:* Whitney Mus Am Art, New York; Fisk Univ, Nashville, Tenn; Rockford Col, Ill; Commonwealth Pa; Ill Bell Tel Co, Chicago. *Comn:* Wall murals, James House, Arthur Rubloff Realty Co, 71. *Exhib:* Violence in American Art, Mus Contemp Art, Chicago, 69; American Prints Today, Mus Art, Utica, NY, 70; Afro-American Arts 1800-1969, Mus Philadelphia Civic Ctr, 70; Contemporary Black Artists in America, Whitney Mus Am Art, 71; Cornell Univ, 75. *Pos:* Adv bd, Arts & Sales & Rental Gallery, Art Inst Chicago; artist adv bd, Ill Arts Coun. *Teaching:* Instr painting, Rockford Col, 69-70; asst prof, Barat Col, Lake Forest, 70-; asst prof fine arts, Loyola Univ Chicago, 70-, chmn dept, currently. *Awards:* Artists-in-residence to help underprivileged children, Ill Art Coun, 69. *Mem:* Arts Club Chicago. *Dealer:* William Van Straaten 646 N Michigan Ave Chicago IL 60611. *Mailing Add:* 1858 N Sedgwick St Chicago IL 60614

ARNOLD, RICHARD R
DESIGNER, ADMINISTRATOR

b Detroit, Mich, July 14, 23. *Study:* Southwestern Univ; Wayne State Univ, BFA; Cranbrook Acad Art, MFA, with Zoltan Sepeshy; Tulane Univ; Univ Mich. *Work:* Cranbrook Mus Art; Northwestern Nat Life Ins Collection; Gen Mills Collections; Grey Found; Wayne State Univ. *Comn:* Mural, Essex Bldg, Minneapolis; designs, Chrysler Corp, Am Motors Corp, Gen Mills Co, Gen Elec Co & others. *Teaching:* Instr, Univ Wis, 48-51; asst prof, Cornell Univ, 53-56; asst prof, San Jose State Col, 58-60; assoc prof, Rochester Inst Technol, 60-64; prof & head design div, Minneapolis Sch Art, 64-71; vis prof, Univ Victoria, summer 68; prof & chmn art dept, State Univ NY Col Brockport, 71-77; prof art & dir, Sch Art, Univ Wash, 77- *Mem:* Nat Asn Art Adminr. *Mailing Add:* Sch of Art Univ of Wash Seattle WA 98195

ARNOLD, ROBERT LLOYD
PAINTER, EDUCATOR

b Buffalo, NY, June 28, 40. *Study:* NY State Univ Col, Buffalo, BS, 66; Fla State Univ, MS, 68; Ind Univ, EdD, 72. *Work:* NY Col Ceramics, Alfred; Nat Art Gallery NZ, Wellington; Fla State Univ, Tallahassee; Ind Univ. *Exhib:* Sign/Symbol, Nat Art Gallery NZ, 77; Artwords & Bookworks, Los Angeles Inst Contemp Art, 78; one-man shows, Ind Univ, Bloomington, 78, Ohio State Univ, 78, Ashland Col, Ohio, 79 & Bowling Green State Univ, 80. *Teaching:* Assoc prof contemp art, Ohio State Univ, 70- *Awards:* Mem Award, Lester C Bush, 74; Battelle Exhib Award, Dollar Savings, 76; Columbus Mus Award, 79. *Bibliog:* Gina Franz (auth), Six in Ohio, New Art Examiner, 78; Robert Pincus-Witten (auth) Six in Ohio, Ohio State Univ/Ohio Arts Coun, 78; Donald Kuspit (auth), Columbus, Art in Am, 79. *Mem:* Col Art Asn; Ohio Art Educ Asn; Nat Art Educ Asn; Columbus Art League (pres, 79 & 80); Ohio Found Arts. *Media:* Acrylic Paint; Canvas. *Res:* Contemporary art; art education. *Publ:* Auth, An analysis of selected teacher preparation programs: 1975, Art Educ, 76; auth, The spoken retrospective: Chris Burden at 30, Midwest Art, 76; auth, The development of a pluralistic avant-garde, Art Educ, 76; auth, An interview with Lawrence Alloway, Midwest Art, 77; auth, A new look at the teacher-critic, Ohio Art Educ Asn J, 78. *Dealer:* Van Straaten Gallery 646 N Michigan Ave Chicago IL 60611. *Mailing Add:* 383 Canyon Dr N Columbus OH 43214

ARNOLDI, CHARLES ARTHUR
SCULPTOR, PAINTER

b Dayton, Ohio, April 10, 46. *Study:* Chouinard, 68. *Work:* Los Angeles Co Mus Art; Mus Mod Art, New York; Chicago Art Inst; Mus Fine Arts, Menil Found. *Comn:* Wood relief paintings, Continental Nat Bank, Ft Worth, 81 & First Int Bank, Houston, 82. *Exhib:* Fifteen Los Angeles Artists, Pasadena Mus, 69; Permutations: Light & Color, Mus Contemporary Art,

Chicago, 70; Dokumenta 5, Kassel Mus, Ger, 72; solo exhib, Seattle Art Mus, 76; Painting & Sculpture in California Modern Era, San Francisco Mus Art, 76; Whitney Biennial, 81; America: The Landscape, Contemporary Arts Mus, Houston, 81; 38th Corcoran Biennale Exhib Am Painting, 83. *Awards:* Wittkowsky Award, Chicago Art Inst, 72; Fels, Nat Endowment Arts, 74 & 82 & Guggenheim Found, 75. *Bibliog:* Jane Livingstone (auth), Four Los Angeles artists, Art in Am, 9-10/70. *Media:* Wood, Bronze. *Dealer:* James Corcoran Gallery 8223 Santa Monica Blvd Los Angeles CA 90069. *Mailing Add:* 11A Brooks Ave Venice CA 90291

ARNOSKY, JAMES EDWARD
ILLUSTRATOR, WRITER
b New York, NY, Sept 1, 46. *Study:* Self taught. *Work:* Philadelphia Free Libr; Cambridge Pub Libr, Mass. *Exhib:* Cricket's Traveling Illustrator's Exhib 1 & 2. *Awards:* Outstanding Sci Bk for Possum Baby, Am Asn Sci Teachers, 78. *Bibliog:* Article in Jr Lit Guild, New York, 77. *Publ:* Auth & illusr, Animal Tracks & Wildlife Signs, G P Putnam's Sons, 79; auth & illusr, A Kettle of Hawks, Coward, McCann, 79; auth & illusr, Mudtime & More Nathaniel Stories, Addison-Wesley, 79; auth & illusr, Freshwater Fish and Fishing, Four Winds Press, 81; auth & illusr, Drawing from Nature, Lothrop, Lee & Shepard, 82. *Mailing Add:* South Ryegate VT 05069

ARONSON, CLIFF
DEALER
b Jan 16, 24; US citizen. *Pos:* Pres, Copenhagen Galleri, Solvang, Calif, 64-; pres, Christopher Galleries, Inc, Palm Springs, Calif, 74-76. *Specialty:* Contemporary American artists. *Mailing Add:* c/o Christopher Galleries 1618 Copenhagen Dr Solvang CA 93463

ARONSON, DAVID
PAINTER, SCULPTOR
b Shilova, Lithuania, Oct 28, 23; US citizen. *Study:* Boston Mus Fine Arts Sch, with Karl Zerbe, cert, 45; Nat Soc Arts & Lett grant, 58; Guggenheim fel, 60. *Work:* Smithsonian Inst, Washington, DC; Art Inst Chicago; Va Mus Fine Arts, Richmond; Boston Mus Fine Arts; Whitney Mus Am Art, New York. *Comn:* Great Ideas of Western Man, Container Corp Am, 63. *Exhib:* Fourteen Americans, Mus Mod Art, 45; Va Mus Fine Arts Biennial, 45; Nat Collection Fine Arts Opening Exhib, Smithsonian Inst, 65; retrospective exhibs, Brandeis Univ, 79, Jewish Mus, New York, 79 & Mus Am Jewish Hist, Philadelphia, 79; Bronfman Ctr, Montreal, 82; Southeastern Mass Univ, 83. *Teaching:* Instr painting, Boston Mus Fine Arts Sch, 43-54; chmn div art, Boston Univ, 54-63, prof art, 62- *Awards:* Grand Prize, Boston Arts Festival, 52-54; Nat Acad Design, 73, 74 & 75. *Bibliog:* Article in Time Mag, 11/63; Newman (auth), Wax as art form, 66 & Grossman (auth), Art & tradition, 67, Yosellof. *Mem:* Academician Nat Acad Design. *Media:* Encaustic, Bronze; Pastel. *Publ:* Auth, Encaustic, Artist Mag, 62; Real & Unreal: The Double Nature of Art, Boston Univ, 67. *Mailing Add:* c/o Puckner/Safrai Gallery 171-173 Newbury St Boston MA 02116

ARONSON, IRENE HILDE
PRINTMAKER, PAINTER
b Dresden, Ger, Mar 8, 18; US citizen. *Study:* Eastbourne Sch Art, Eng; Slade Sch Fine Arts, Univ London; Ruskin Sch Drawing, Oxford Univ; Columbia Univ, BFA, 60, MA, 62; Art Students League; Parsons Sch Design; also with Prof Schwabe, Polunin & William S Hayter. *Work:* Bibliot Nat Print Dept, Paris; Victoria & Albert Mus, London; Brit Mus Print Dept; Mus Mod Art Print Dept & Metrop Mus Art, New York. *Exhib:* Kunstmuseum, Bern, Switz, 57; Brooklyn Mus, NY & Boston Mus, Mass, 58; Int Print Show, Ljubljana, Yugoslavia, 59; one-woman show, Mus Arte Mod, Mexico City, 59 & Towner Art Gallery, Eastbourne, Eng, 61; Nat Asn of Women Artists, New York, 74-75; Acquisition of Two Linoleumcuts, Nat Collection Fine Arts, Washington, DC, 75. *Pos:* Asst costume designer, Barnum & Bailey Circus, Broadway, 44. *Teaching:* Instr art, continuing educ, Bryant Adult Ctr, 54-66; instr art (per diem), New York Jr High Sch, currently. *Awards:* Gold Medal, Slade Sch Fine Arts, 39; Medal of Honor, Nat Asn Women Artists, 57; plus others. *Mem:* Nat Asn Women Artists; Asn Univ Women. *Publ:* Auth, The printmaker, Design Mag, 55; contribr & illusr articles, In: Artist Mag, London sketches, 7/74 & How to make a linocut, 7/75; auth, Setting up a printmaking workshop, Graphic Processes; auth, How to make a lithograph, Am Artist; also illusr of var bks. *Mailing Add:* 63-20 Haring St Rego Park NY 11374

ARONSON, SANDA
SCULPTOR
b New York, NY, Feb 29, 40. *Study:* Oswego State Col, BS, 60; study with J De Creeft & Paul Pollaro at New Sch for Social Res, New York; Tulane Univ, New Orleans; Art Students League. *Exhib:* Exhib Women Artists, Manhattan Community Col, 75; Women Artists/Showing & Sharing, US Mil Acad, West Point, NY, 75; Works on Paper, Brooklyn Mus, NY, 75; Women in the Arts (travelling show), Chatham Col, Pittsburgh, Pa & State Univ NY Binghamton, 76; Four Artists, Women in the Arts Found, New York, 76; Nine/Plus or Minus, US Mil Acad, 77 & The Arsenal, New York, 78. *Teaching:* Artist-in-residence, NY Found for the Arts, 77-79. *Awards:* Hon Mention/Sculpture, Women Artists/Showing & Sharing, US Mil Acad, 76. *Bibliog:* J L Collins (ed), Women Artists in America, Vol II, Univ Tenn at Chattanooga Press, 75. *Mem:* Women in the Arts Found (bd mem-at-large, 75-76); NY Artists Equity Asn. *Media:* Collage. *Publ:* Contribr frontpiece, John Beecher (auth), Hear the Wind Blow, Int Press, 68. *Mailing Add:* 70 W 95th St New York NY 10025

ARTECHE (HECTOR ARTECHE MARTINEZ)
PAINTER, SCULPTOR
b Mex, DF, June 8, 34. *Study:* Univ Nac Autonoma Mex, MA, 52. *Work:* Inst Nac Bellas Artes, Mex, DF; Mus Arte Mod Contemp, Morelia, Michuacan; Tucson Mus Art; Mus Rennes, Bretagne; Ariz State Univ Collection. *Comn:* Fresco mural, Univ Sonora, Hermosillo, 64; sculpture, Banco Atlantico, Tijuana, Baja Calif, 77; mural painting & sculpture, Sonora State Govt, Hermosillo, 78; facade relief, Constructora Anza, Hermosillo, Sonora, 80; facade relief & sculpture, City Hall, Hermosillo, Sonora, 82. *Exhib:* Confrontacion 66, Mus Nac Arte Mod, Mex, DF, 66; solo exhib, La Vida del Seri, Art & Hist Mus, Chihuahua, 66 & Pinturas, Am Embassy, 13 countries, 70-72; Salon de Grabado 68, Inst Nac Bellas Artes, Mex, DF, 68; Spacial & Atmospheric, eight art ctrs, Colo, 70; and others. *Pos:* Jefe officer, Orgn Mus Cent Cult, Gobierno Estado Sonora, 75-77; restaurador CRN, Inst Nac Antropologia Hist, 78- *Teaching:* Prof drawing & painting, Inst Nac Bellas Artes, Mazatlan, 55-57 & Tula, Hidalgo, 57-59; prof art & dir artes plasticas, Univ Sonora, Hermosillo, 61-73. *Awards:* First Prize, Concurso Nac Pintura, Inst Nac Bellas Artes, 52; Premio Publico, Salon Pintura Contemp, Chihuahua, 64. *Bibliog:* Raguez Tibol (auth), Radiante correspondencia, Escuela Nac Artes Plasticas, 76 & Energia liberacion, News Week Proceso, 81; Robert Quinn (auth), Luz y espacio, Gobierno Estado Sonora, 81. *Media:* Fresco, Egg Tempera. *Publ:* Contribr, Oracle--Poems and Prints, Univ Ariz, 74. *Dealer:* Oonagh B Church 1157 S Swan Rd Tucson AZ 85711. *Mailing Add:* Apdo Postal A-043 Hermosillo Mexico

ARTEMIS, MARIA (MARIA ARTEMIS PAPAGEORGE SAWYER)
SCULPTOR, EDUCATOR
b Greensboro, NC, Apr, 21, 45. *Study:* Agnes Scott Col, Decatur, Ga, BA, 69; Univ Ga, Athens, MFA, 77. *Work:* NC Nat Bank, Charlotte; Lannon Found Contemp Art, Palm Beach, Fla; Univ Ga, Student Union, Athens. *Exhib:* Mostra, Cortona, Italy, 79; Avant-Garde/12 in Atlanta, High Mus Art, Ga, 79; Earth Art: Sand & Clay, SEastern Ctr Contemp Art, Winston-Salem, NC, 80; one-woman show, Nexus Inc 3rd Floor Gallery, Atlanta, Ga, 80; Atlanta Womens Art Collective, AIR Gallery, New York, 80. *Pos:* Vis artist slides, Univ Wis, Superior, 79; artist-in-residence, Cortona, Italy, 79; artist-in-residence, SEastern Ctr Contemp Art, Winston-Salem, NC, 80. *Teaching:* Fac mem sculpture foundation design, Atlanta Col Art, 79-81; vis lectr, Atlanta Col Art, spring 83. *Awards:* Merit Scholarship, Ford Found, 76-77; Merit Awards, Atlanta Arts Festival, 76 & 78; Exhib Grant, Nat Endowment Arts, 80. *Bibliog:* Dan Talley (auth), Conversation--An interview artist to artist, Art Papers, 4/78; article, Ceramic Monthly, 10/78; Jeff Kipnis (auth), article, Art Voices, 5-6/81. *Mem:* Int Sculpture Ctr; Atlanta Art Workers Coalition (bd mem 78-79); Atlanta Womens Art Collective . *Media:* Mixed Media. *Publ:* Andy Nasisse: Works off the Wall, Craft Horizon, 78. *Mailing Add:* 2854 North Hills Dr Atlanta GA 30305

ARTINIAN, ARTINE
COLLECTOR, PATRON
b Bulgaria, Dec 8, 07; US citizen. *Study:* Bowdoin Col, BA, 31; Harvard Univ, MA, 33; Columbia Univ, PhD, 41; Bowdoin Col, Hon LittD, 66. *Exhib:* Drawings by French Writers & Illustrators, var Am cols & univs, 68-74, Art Gallery, Auckland City, NZ, 77 & French Embassy-sponsored tour in US, 79-81; Music in Art, traveling, 71-73, Hats by French Artists, 80 & Florida Self-Portraits, 81, Henry Morrison Flagler Mus, Palm Beach, Fla; Artists' Letters with Drawings, Seton Hall Univ Libr, 78; and others. *Teaching:* Bard Col, 35-64; dir, Jr Yr in France, Sweet Briar Col, Va, 53-55 & US House, Cite Universitaire, Paris, summer 55, 56 & 58. *Awards:* Officier d'Academie, France, 48; Fulbright Res Scholar, France, 49-50; Am Philos Soc Res Grant, Paris, 60. *Mem:* Soc Four Arts, Palm Beach, Fla; Expressions, Paris (hon pres, 83-). *Collection:* Exhibited: Drawings and Paintings by French Writers; French Illustrators; The French Visage, A Century and a Half of French Portraits; Music in Art; Florida Self-portraits; Carolina Self-portraits; Miguel Covarubias Drawings of 1930. *Publ:* Auth numerous publ incl eight bks. *Mailing Add:* Winthrop House 100 Worth Ave, PH6 Palm Beach FL 33480

ARTSCHWAGER, RICHARD ERNST
PAINTER, SCULPTOR
b Washington, DC, Dec 26, 23. *Study:* Cornell Univ, AB; studio study with Amedee Ozenfant. *Work:* Whitney Mus Am Art; Tate Gallery; Chicago Art Inst; Mus Mod Art & Mus Am Art, NY. *Exhib:* Sonsbeek '71, Arnhem/ Utrecht, Holland, 71; Documenta, Kassel, Ger, 68 & 72; Venice Biennale, 76; Two Hundred Years of Am Sculpture, Whitney Mus Mod Art, 76; solo exhib, Kunstuerein, Hamburg, 78, Albright-Knox Art Gallery, Buffalo, Inst Contemp Art, Univ Pa, 79, La Jolla Mus Contemp Art, Calif, 80 & Contemp Mus, Houston, Tex, 80. *Awards:* Nat Endowment Arts, 71. *Bibliog:* E Baker (auth), Artschwager's mental furniture, Art News, 1/68; John Russell (auth), article, New York Times, 79; Roberta Smith (auth), article, Art in Am, 80. *Publ:* Auth, The hydraulic door check, Arts Mag, 11/67. *Dealer:* Leo Castelli Gallery 412 W Broadway New York NY 10012. *Mailing Add:* Box 99 Charlotteville NY 12036

ARUM, BARBARA
SCULPTOR
b Des Moines, Iowa, Oct 9, 37. *Study:* Studied with Raymond Rocklin, Vincent Leggiadro, Jane Colburn, Chaim Gross, Philip Listengart & Anthony Padavano. *Exhib:* Mus Hudson Highlands, 82; Hudson River Mus, 82; Pindar Gallery, 83; Northshore Sculpture Ctr, 83; Bergen Community Mus, 83; and others. *Pos:* Dir, Women & Arts, Now Westerchester, Scarsdale, NY, 80- *Awards:* First Prize, Scarsdale Art Asn, 79; Certificate of Merit, Salmagundi Club 3rd Ann Non-member Open, 80; First Prize, Beaux Arts Finale, Westchester, 81. *Bibliog:* Articles in Artspeak, 4/28/83, New York Times,

5/15/83 & Art World, 10/15/83. *Mem:* Nat Asn Women Artists; Contemp Artists Guild; Am Soc Contemp Artists; NY Artists Equity Asn; Mamaroneck Artists Guild; and others. *Media:* Wood, Steel. *Dealer:* Whichcraft Gallery South Orange NJ; Gallery Barnegat Light NJ. *Mailing Add:* 138 W 17th New York NY 10011

ARYE, LEONORA E
SCULPTOR
b New York, NY, May 22, 31. *Study:* Art Students League, 64-66; with Hana Geber, 65-70; with Lorrie Goulet, 70-72; Univ Mex. *Work:* Albany Inst Hist & Art, NY; Galeria Moderna, Mex; Mus Art, Bogota, Colombia. *Comn:* L'Chaim (stone), Jewish Community Ctr, Harrison, NY, 76; Justice (stone), Judge Jacob Fuchsberg, New York, 77. *Exhib:* Bridge Gallery, White Plains, NY, 79; Hudson River Mus, Yonkers, NY, 80; Silvermine Guild Artists, New Canaan, Conn, 80; Salmagundi Club, New York, 81; Nat Asn Women Artists, City Gallery, New York, 81; Bergen Mus, Paramus, NJ; and others. *Awards:* Am Soc Contemp Artists Award, Artists USA Publ, 80; Kellner Award, Nat Asn Women Artists, 80; Purchase Award, Sculpture Soc, 81. *Bibliog:* S Stanton (auth), Forms and faces, Lifestyles, 77; J Klausner (auth), Enjoying the arts/sculpture, Richard Rosen Press, 81. *Mem:* Nat Asn Women Artists (publ comt, 80-81); Am Soc Contemp Artists; Silvermine Guild Artists; Hudson River Contemp Artists; Mamaroneck Artists Guild. *Media:* Stone, Wood. *Dealer:* Mari Galleries East Prospect Mamaroneck NY 10543; Couturier Gallery 1814 Newfield Ave Stamford CT 06903. *Mailing Add:* 36 Crawford Rd Harrison NY 10528

ASAWA, RUTH (RUTH ASAWA LANIER)
SCULPTOR, PAINTER
b Norwalk, Calif, Jan 27, 26. *Study:* Milwaukee State Teachers Col, with Robert von Neumann; Black Mt Col, with Josef Albers. *Work:* Whitney Mus Am Art; Chase Manhattan Bank; City of San Francisco; Gov & Mrs Nelson Rockefeller. *Comn:* Two bronze wire sculpture in fountains, Phoenix Civic Plaza; bronze fountain, Ghirardelli Sq; bronze fountain, Hyatt Hotel, San Francisco Union Sq. *Exhib:* Whitney Mus Am Art, 55, 56 & 58; Mus Mod Art, 58; San Francisco Mus Art, 54, 63 & 73; one-man shows, de Young Mem Mus, San Francisco, 60 & Pasadena Mus Art, 65; US Info Agency Junk Art Travel Show, 72-73; plus others. *Pos:* Mem, San Francisco Art Comn, 68-76; co-founder, Alvarado Sch Art Workshop, San Francisco Unified Sch Dist, 68-; mem, Nat Endowment for the Arts Educ Panel, 74-78; mem, Calif Arts Coun, 76-78. *Awards:* Tamarind fel, 65; Purchase Award, San Francisco Art Festival, 66; Dymaxion Award, 66; plus others. *Mailing Add:* 1116 Castro St San Francisco CA 94114

ASCHENBACH, (WALTER) PAUL
SCULPTOR, EDUCATOR
b Poughkeepsie, NY, May 25, 21. *Study:* RI Sch Design, 40-41; with Randolph W Johnson, Deerfield, Mass, 42-45 & I Marshall, Philadelphia, 46-48. *Work:* Sculpture on the Highway, Vt Interstate Hwy; Sculpture Park, St Margarethen, Austria; De Cordova & Dana Mus, Lincoln, Mass; Mem Art Gallery, Univ Rochester, NY; Bundy Art Gallery, Waitsfield, Vt. *Comn:* Forged mild steel crucifix, Trinity Col, Burlington, Vt, 61; corten steel, Bundy Art Gallery, 66; fabricated bronze, Bailey Mem Libr, Univ Vt, Burlington, 63-64; forged steel, Mother Seton, St Josephs Col on the Ohio, Cincinnati, 65. *Collections Arranged:* Sculpture Park Symposium, Suwa, Japan, 78. *Pos:* Trustee, Vt Coun Arts, 65-68; coordr, Vt Int Sculpture Symp, 68-; coordr Mill 21, Sculpture Prog, Vt Marble Co, 69-70. *Teaching:* Assoc prof art, Univ Vt, 56- *Media:* Steel, Marble. *Mailing Add:* Charlotte VT 05445

ASCHER, MARY
PAINTER, PRINTMAKER
b Leeds, Eng; US citizen. *Study:* New York Sch Appl Design for Women; Hunter Col; Art Students League; also with Will Barnet, Vaclav Vytlacil & Morris Kantor. *Work:* Norfolk Art Mus, Va; Nat Mus Sports, New York; Bat Yam Mus & Ein Harod L'Osmanut, Israel; Nat Collection Fine Art, Smithsonian Inst, Washington, DC; Butler Inst Am Art, Youngstown, Ohio. *Comn:* Twelve Women of the Old Testament & Apocrypha, Wizo Bldg, Tel Aviv, Israel. *Exhib:* Exchange Exhib with Japanese Women Artists, 60; Exchange Exhib with Argentine Artists, USIA, 63; 18th New Eng Ann, Silvermine, 67; 30 Yr Retrospective, Nat Arts Club, New York, 73; Metrop Mus Art, New York, 79; and others. *Awards:* Huntington Hartford Found fel, 60; Int Women's Yr Award, 75-76; First Prize/Oil, Womanart Gallery, New York, 77; plus others. *Bibliog:* Interview, WNYC Radio, New York, 79. *Mem:* Fel Royal Soc Arts, London; Am Soc Contemp Artists (pres, 73-75); Nat Asn Women Artists; life mem Art Students League; Am Fedn Arts. *Media:* Oil, Watercolor. *Publ:* Auth, Poetry-painting, 58; contribr, Anthology of Readings for Use in Christian Education & Worship, Word Alive, 69 & News Extra, 71; auth, Twelve Women of the New Testament and Early Church, including 25 Portfolios. *Mailing Add:* 116 Central Park S Apt 10-N New York NY 10019

ASCIAN (JONATHAN GRANT MEADER)
PRINTMAKER, PAINTER
b Aug 29, 43; US citizen. *Work:* Whitney Mus Am Art, Metrop Mus Art, New York; Corcoran Gallery Art, Nat Collection Fine Art, Hirshhorn Mus, Washington, DC; and others. *Comn:* Serigraphs, Off Equal Employment Opportunity, 73; lithographs, Washington Printmakers' Workshop Proj, 74; serigraph, Washington Print Club, 75. *Exhib:* One-person shows, Corcoran Gallery Art, Dupont Ctr, 69, Green Panther Gallery, Frankfurt, Ger, 82, Fla Southern Col, 82 & others; Seven Young Artists, Corcoran Gallery Art, Washington, DC, 72; Baltimore Mus, 72; Illumination, San Francisco, Calif, 80; Sylvia Ullman Gallery, Cleveland, Ohio, 80; Zenith Gallery, Washington, DC, 80; and many others. *Awards:* Stern Family grant, 70; Washington

Printmaker's Proj, 74; Printmakers Grant, Nat Endowment Arts, 74. *Bibliog:* Dreamtime, The Washingtonian, 4/75; Paul Richard (auth), Making it as an artist, The Washington Post, 10/77. *Media:* Mixed. *Collection:* Fantasy and surrealism: Klinger, Milton, and others. *Publ:* Auth, The Unicorn, Viking Press, 80; illusr, The Unicorn Calendar, Pomegranite Press, 80 & 82. *Mailing Add:* PO Box 21146 Washington DC 20009

ASHBAUGH, DENNIS JOHN
PAINTER
b Red Oak, Iowa, Oct 25, 46. *Study:* Orange Coast Col, Costa Mesa, Calif, AA, 66; Calif State Col, Fullerton, BA, 68, MA, 69. *Work:* Rolls Royce Inc, New York; Miami Art Ctr, Fla; Toledo Art Mus, Ohio; Seattle Art Mus, Wash; Owens Corning Inc, New York. *Exhib:* One-man show, Whitney Mus Am Art, 75; Seattle Mus Art, Wash, 76; Brockton Art Ctr, 74; Whitney Mus Ann, 75; Rockefeller Arts Ctr, State Univ NY Col, Fredonia, 76; LeGrand Hornu, Le Mons, Belg, 76; Gallery Litho, Tehran, Iran, 76; Hall Walls, Buffalo, NY, 77; and other group & one-man shows. *Awards:* Creative Artists Pub Serv Grant, NY Coun Arts, 75; Guggenheim Found Fel, 76. *Bibliog:* Roberta Smith (auth), article, Artforum, 5/75; Bud Hopkins (auth), article, Artforum, 1/76. *Media:* Oil. *Mailing Add:* 30 West 13th St New York NY 10011

ASHBERY, JOHN LAWRENCE
ART CRITIC
b Rochester, NY, July 28, 27. *Study:* Harvard Col, BA(Eng lit), 49; Columbia Univ, MA(Eng lit), 51. *Pos:* Art critic Europ ed, New York Herald-Tribune, Paris, 60-65; Paris corresp, Art News, 64-65; art critic, Art Int, Lugano, Switz, 61-64; ed, Locus Solus, France, 60-62; ed, Art & Lit, Paris, 63-66; exec ed, Art News, 66-72; art critic, New York Mag, 78-80; poetry ed, Partisan Review, New York, 76-80; art critic, Newsweek, New York, 80- *Teaching:* Prof, Brooklyn Col, NY, 74-, distinguished prof, 80- *Bibliog:* David K Kermani (auth), John Ashbery: A Comprehensive Bibliography, Garland, 76. *Mem:* Am Acad & Inst Arts & Letters. *Publ:* Art criticism in anthologies & periodicals; texts for numerous exhib catalogs. *Mailing Add:* c/o Georges Borchardt Inc 136 E 57th St New York NY 10022

ASHBY, CARL
PAINTER, INSTRUCTOR
b San Rita, NMex, Mar 2, 14. *Study:* Univ Utah, BS; NY Univ, MA; Art Students League, NY; Grand Cent Sch Art, Atelier 17; also with Morris Kantor. *Work:* Purdue Univ. *Exhib:* Pa Ann; Corcoran Gallery, Washington, DC; Whitney Mus Ann, 47 & 49; Libr Cong Print Show; Tirca Karlis Gallery, 64-75; New Sch Social Res, 76, 77 & 79; Nat Acad Art Ann, 77, 79 & 80. *Pos:* Owner, Ashby Gallery, 45-48 & 80- *Teaching:* Instr painting, New Sch Social Res, 71- *Mem:* Artists Equity Asn; Art Students League (rec secy, Bd Control, 46). *Media:* Oil, Watercolor. *Mailing Add:* 18 Cornelia St New York NY 10014

ASHER, ELISE
PAINTER, WRITER
b Chicago, Ill. *Study:* Art Inst Chicago; Bradford Jr Col; Simmons Col, BS. *Work:* NY Univ Art Collection; Univ Calif Art Mus, Berkeley; Rose Art Mus. Brandeis Univ; John Michael Kohler Arts Ctr, Sheboygan, Wis; Corcoran Gallery, Washington, DC. *Comn:* Oil on Plexiglas window, comn by Dr John P Spiegel, Cambridge; cover for Poetry Northwest, autumn-winter 64-65; cover for The Chelsea, No 27, 70; jacket for Stanley Kunitz, The Testing-Tree (poems), Little, Brown, 71. *Exhib:* Lettering Traveling Show, Mus Mod Art, New York, 67; one-man shows, Bertha Schaefer Gallery, New York, 73, Univ Richmond, Va, 75 & Ingber Gallery, New York, 79, 81 & 83; Nat Collection Fine Arts, 76 & Nat Acad Sci, 83, Smithsonian Inst; Fine Arts Mus Long Island, 83. *Bibliog:* Brian O'Doherty (auth), articles, Art in Am & Art World, 79, 81 & 83; P Carlson (auth), Asher at the Ingber, Art In Am, 10/79; Elinor Munro (auth), Originals: American Women Artists, Simon & Schuster, 79 & Avon Press, 82. *Media:* Oil, Pencil & Ink. *Publ:* Illusr, This Book is a Movie, 71; contribr, Acrilic for Sculpture & Design, Van Nostrand, 72; contribr, Art: A Woman's Sensibility, Calif Inst Arts, 75. *Mailing Add:* 37 W 12th St New York NY 10011

ASHER, FREDERICK M
HISTORIAN, EDUCATOR
b Chicago, Ill, May 25, 41. *Study:* Dartmouth Col, BA; Univ Chicago, MA & PhD. *Pos:* Actg dir, Univ Gallery, Univ Minn, 71-72. *Teaching:* Instr art hist, Lake Forest Col, 67-70; assoc prof art hist, Univ Minn, Minneapolis, 70- *Mem:* Am Comt SAsian Art (treas, 72-74). *Res:* South Asian art. *Publ:* Various publications pertaining to the art of India. *Mailing Add:* 1776 James Ave S Minneapolis MN 55403

ASHER, LILA OLIVER
PRINTMAKER, PAINTER
b Philadelphia, Pa. *Study:* With Gonippo Raggi, Joseph Grossman & Frank B A Linton; Philadelphia Col Art, grad. *Work:* Corcoran Gallery Art, Georgetown Univ & Nat Mus Am Art, Washington, DC; Fisk Univ, Nashville; Univ Va, Charlottesville; and others. *Comn:* Oil paintings, two panels, Congregation Rodeph Shalom, Philadelphia, 40; murals, two rooms, Indian Spring Country Club, Glenmont, Md. *Exhib:* Thomson & Burr Galleries, New York; Green-Field Gallery, El Paso, Tex; Retrospective Exhib, Howard Univ, 78; one-woman shows in US, Japan, India, Iran & Pakistan, var times, 51-75. *Teaching:* Instr art, Howard Univ, 47-51; instr art, Wilson Teachers Col, 53-54; from lectr to prof art, Howard Univ, 61- *Awards:* Printmaker of the Year, High School Graphics Program, Nat Mus Am Art, 81. *Mem:* Am Asn Univ Prof; Soc Washington Artists; Soc Washington

Printmakers (rec secy, 68-75); Artist Equity Asn (treas, DC Chap, 71-74). *Media:* Wood & Linoleum Block, Oil. *Publ:* Contrib, American Prints from Wood, Smithsonian Inst. *Mailing Add:* 4100 Thornapple St Chevy Chase MD 20815

ASHER, MICHAEL
ENVIRONMENTAL ARTIST, SCULPTOR
b Los Angeles, Calif, July 15, 43. *Study:* Orange Coast Col, Costa Mesa, Calif, 61-63; Univ NMex, Albuquerque, 63-64; New York Studio Sch, 64-65; Univ Calif, Irvine, BA(fine arts), 66, 66-67. *Exhib:* I am Alive, Los Angeles Co Mus of Art, Calif, 67; Anti-Illusion: Procedures: Materials, Whitney Mus, New York, 69; solo exhibs, La Jolla Mus Art, 69 & Gladys K Montgomery Art Ctr, Pomona Col, Claremont, Calif, 70; 24 Young Los Angeles Artists, Los Angeles Co Mus Art, 71; Otis Art Inst Gallery, Los Angeles, 75; The Clocktower, New York, 75 & The Floating Mus, San Francisco, 76; and many others. *Teaching:* Asst instr sculpture, Univ Calif, Irvine, 66-67, painting instr, 67-68; instr industrial arts, Anaheim Union High Sch District & Garden Grove Sch District, Calif; vis artist, Univ Calif, 73, Calif Inst Arts, Valencia, 73 & 76, NS Col Art & Design, 74 & Otis Art Inst, Los Angeles, 75. *Awards:* Art Purchase Award, Contemp Art Coun, Los Angeles Co Mus, 67; John Simon Guggenheim Mem Fel, 74; Artist Fel Grant, Nat Endowment Arts, 75. *Bibliog:* Robert Morris (auth), The art of existence: Three extravisual artists, works in process, 1/71 & Peter Plagens (auth), Michael Asher: The thing of it is ..., 4/72, Artforum. *Mailing Add:* 826 1/2 Crestmon Pl Venice CA 90291

ASHTON, DORE
CRITIC, WRITER
b Newark, NJ. *Study:* Univ Wis, BA; Harvard Univ, MA; Moore Col Art, hon degree; Hamline Univ, hon degree. *Pos:* Assoc ed, Art Digest, New York, 52-54; art critic, New York Times, 55-60; contrib ed, Opus Int, Paris, 65-75 & Arts Mag, 74- *Teaching:* Prof art hist, Cooper Union, 69- *Awards:* Mather Award Art Criticism, Col Art Asn, 63; Guggenheim Fels, 64 & 69; Ford Found Award, 65; and others. *Mem:* Int Asn Art Critics (gov bd mem, 60-); Pen Club (mem exec bd); Col Art Asn. *Res:* Modern art. *Publ:* Auth, The New York School: A Cultural Reckoning, 72; auth, A Joseph Cornell Album, 74; auth, Yes, But..., A Critical Biography of Philip Guston, 76; auth, A Fable of Modern Art, 80; auth, About Rothko, 83. *Mailing Add:* 217 E 11th St New York NY 10003

ASKEVOLD, DAVID
CONCEPTUAL ARTIST, INSTRUCTOR
b Conrad, Mont, Mar 30, 40. *Study:* Univ Mont; Brooklyn Mus Sch Art, painting cert; Kansas City Art Inst, BFA(sculpture). *Work:* Stedelijk van Abbemuseum, Eindhoven, Holland; Mus Contemp Art, Houston, Tex. *Exhib:* Mus Mod Art, New York, 70 & 71; one-man shows, Found Art Resources, Los Angeles, 79 & Gancar/Kuhlenschmidt Gallery, 81; Text Visual, Commune di Milano, Italy, 79; Camerie Incantate, Milan, 80; Artist & Camera, Arts Coun Gt Brit, 80; 5 Wiener International Bienale, traveling exhib, 81; and many others. *Teaching:* Asst prof art, NS Col Art & Design, 68-73; vis lectr studio art, Univ Calif, Irvine, 76-77; spec appt photog & post studio art, Calif Inst Arts, Valencia, 77-78; lectr, Art Ctr, Col Design, Pasadena, Calif, 80-81; lectr, York Univ, Downsview, Ont, 81-82. *Awards:* Max Beckman Scholar Painting, Brooklyn Mus, 63; Can Coun Arts Bursary Award, 72 & 75. *Bibliog:* James Collins (auth), article, Artforum, 9/74; Alan Sondheim (auth), Individuals, Dutton, 77; Howard Singerman (auth), article, Artforum, 5/81; and others. *Media:* Film, Audio. *Publ:* Auth, Werner Lippert, ed, Extra, 75. *Dealer:* Enzo Cannaviello Piazza Beccaria 10 20122 Milan Italy; Paul Maenz 23 Lindenstrasse Koln D-500 WGer. *Mailing Add:* PO 898 Big Sky MT 59716

ASKEW, PAMELA
EDUCATOR, WRITER
b Poughkeepsie, NY. *Study:* Vassar Col, AB, 46; Inst Fine Arts, NY Univ, MA, 51; Courtauld Inst, Univ London, PhD, 54. *Teaching:* Instr art hist, Vassar Col, 56-57, asst prof, 57-62, assoc prof, 62-69, prof, 69-, chmn dept art, 71-74. *Awards:* Am Coun Learned Soc Fel Art Hist, 65-66; Fulbright Fel Art Hist, 65-66. *Mem:* Col Art Asn; Am Soc 18th Century Studies; Renaissance Soc; Friends of Vassar Art Gallery; Atwood Fund (trustee, 75-); Am Asn Univ Prof. *Res:* Fetti. *Publ:* Auth, The question of Fetti as fresco painter: A reattribution to Andreasi of Frescoes in the Cathedral and Sant 'Andrea at Mantua, Art Bulletin, 68; auth, The angelic consolation of St Francis of Assisi in post-tridentine Italian painting, J Warburg & Courtauld Insts, 69; auth, Domenico Fetti: Parable of the wicked husbandmen, Currier Gallery Art Bulletin, 73; auth, Domenico Fetti's portrait of an actor reconsidered, Burlington Mag, 2/78; auth, Ferdinando Gonzaga's patronage of the pictorial arts: The villa favorita, Art Bulletin, 6/78; plus others. *Mailing Add:* Dept of Art Vassar Col Poughkeepsie NY 12601

ASKIN, WALTER MILLER
PAINTER, PRINTMAKER
b Pasadena, Calif, Sept 12, 29. *Study:* Univ Calif, Berkeley, BA & MA; Ruskin Sch Drawing & Fine Art, Oxford Univ. *Work:* Mus Contemp Art, Chicago; Oxford Mus Mod Art, Eng; San Francisco Mus Art; Kunstlerhaus, Vienna; Albright-Knox Gallery, Buffalo. *Exhib:* One-man shows, La Jolla Mus Art, Calif, 67, Abraxas Gallery, Calif, 79, 80 & 81, Univ Southern Calif, 80 & Kunstlerhaus, Vienna, Austria, 81; Prints by Seven, Whitney Mus Am Art, 70; Int Biennial Graphic Art, Mus Mod Art, Ljubljana, Yugoslavia, 83. *Pos:* Bd trustees, Pasadena Art Mus, 63-68; bd dir, Los Angeles Inst of Contemp Art, Los Angeles, 77-81; bd gov, Baxter Art Gallery, Calif Inst Technol, 80-; artist rep, Graphic Arts Council, Los Angeles Co Mus Art, 80-; chmn visual arts panel, Nat Art Awards, 81-82. *Teaching:* Prof art, Calif State Univ, Los Angeles, 56-; vis prof art, Univ Calif, Berkeley, 68-69, Calif State Univ, Long Beach, 74-75 & Univ Hawaii, 83; vis artist, Kelpra Studio, London, 69 & 73, Tamarind Inst, Univ NMex, 72, Athens Sch Fine Arts, 73, Cranbrook Acad Art, 79, Ariz State Univ, 80 & 83, Ossabaw Island Found, Ga, 82 & Va Ctr Creative Arts, 83. *Awards:* Senator James Phelan Award, San Francisco Mus Art, 69; Artist Award, Pasadena Arts Coun, 70; Outstanding Prof Award, Calif State Univ, Los Angeles, 73. *Bibliog:* Violante (auth), American Printmakers '74, Graphics Group, 74; Newman (auth), Innovative Printmaking, Crown, 77; Walter Askin 1970-1980, Univ Southern Calif, 80. *Mem:* Col Art Asn Am; Los Angeles Inst Contemp Art; Los Angeles Printmaking Soc. *Media:* Oil, Acrylic; Mixed Media. *Mailing Add:* 846 Bank St South Pasadena CA 91030

ASKMAN, TOM K
PAINTER, EDUCATOR
b Leadville, Colo, Oct 27, 41. *Study:* Calif Col Arts & Crafts, BA(educ), BFA; Univ Colo, MFA. *Work:* City Seattle, Wash; Cheney Cowles Art Mus, Spokane, Wash; Ft Worth Art Mus, Tex; Mus Art, Univ Okla, Norman; Mus Art, Univ Colo, Boulder. *Comn:* Monument to Art Enigmas, with Lynn Gray, Gary Stoneman & Allegra Berrian Askman, Enigma Art Co, Goose Egg, Wyo, 71; State of Wash, 79. *Exhib:* New Orleans Mus Art, La, 71; Addison Gallery Am Art, Andover, Mass, 71; Minneapolis Art Inst, Minn, 71; Va Mus Fine Arts, Richmond, 72; Extraordinary Realities, Whitney Mus Am Art, New York, 73; Springfield Art Mus, Mo, 73-74; Contemp Arts Ctr, Cincinnati, Ohio, 74; Seattle Art Mus, Wash, 74; Private Views, Henry Gallery, Univ Wash, 80. *Teaching:* Instr, Univ Minn, Minneapolis, 68-70; assoc prof, Nicholls State Univ, Thibodaux, La, 70-72 & Eastern Wash Univ, Cheney, 72- *Awards:* Cheney Cowles Art Mus, Spokane, 74, 76, 80 & 81; Painting Award, 60th Ann NW Artists, Seattle Art Mus, Wash, 74; State Wash Commissions, 79. *Mailing Add:* W 524 13th Spokane WA 99204

ASMAR, ALICE
PAINTER, PRINTMAKER
b Flint, Mich. *Study:* Lewis & Clark Col, BA(magna cum laude); with Edward Melcarth & Archipenko, Univ Wash, MFA; Woolley fel, Ecole Nat Superieure des Beaux-Arts, Paris, with M Souverbie; Huntington Hartford Found residence fels, 61-64. *Work:* SW Mus, Los Angeles; Franklin Mint, Pa; Smithsonian Inst; Pub Int Mus, Gabrova, Bulgaria; Roswell Mus & Art Ctr, NMex; and others. *Comn:* Channel Island (mural), Joseph Magnin's, 64; California Triptich, Security Pac Int Bank, New York, 70; Calif State Bldg, Los Angeles, 78; lithographs, Artists Profusions, New York, 80; murals, Glendale Fed Savings, San Clemente, Calif, 81. *Exhib:* Seattle Art Mus, 52; Western Asn Art Mus Circulating Banner Exhib, 70-72; Drawings USA, Minn Mus Art Nat Travel Show, 71-73; West 79/The Law, Minn Mus Art, 79-80; Portland Art Mus, 79-80; one-woman shows, Sedona Art Ctr, Ariz, 79, Mus of Sci & Indust, Los Angeles, 81 & Sr Eye Art Gallery, Long Beach, 77 & 82; and others. *Pos:* Eng draftsman, Boeing Aircraft, 52-54; engraver, Nambe Mills, Santa Fe, NMex, 68- *Teaching:* Asst prof painting & drawing, Lewis & Clark Col, 55-58; instr painting, Lennox Adult Educ, Calif, 63-65. *Awards:* Menzione Onorevole, Biennale Delle Regione, 68-69; Purchase Award, Seattle Art Mus; First Prize, Southern Calif Expos. *Bibliog:* Articles in Seattle Times, 3/28/76, Los Angeles Times Home Mag, 3/78 & Southwest Art Mag, 11/78. *Mem:* Am Fedn Arts; Calif Arboretum Fedn; Artists Equity; League of the Americas. *Media:* Casein, Oil; India Ink, Lithographs. *Dealer:* Hatfield Dalzell Galleries Ambassador Hotel 3400 Wilshire Blvd Los Angeles CA 90010; Gallcry G Fine Arts Ltd 6611 E Central Wichita KS 67206. *Mailing Add:* c/o Asmar Studios PO Box 1963 Burbank CA 91507

ASOMA, TADASHI
PAINTER
b Iwatsuki, Japan, Apr 28, 23. *Study:* Saitama Teachers Col, Urawa, MS; Bijitsu Gakko, Tokyo, govt scholar; Grande Chaumiere, Paris, govt scholar; Art Students League. *Work:* Nelson Gallery, Kansas City; Am Express Co, New York; 3M Co, St Paul; Andrew Dickson White Mus, Ithaca, NY; San Diego Mus Art. *Exhib:* One-man shows, David Findlay Galleries, NY, biennially 65-81, Dubins Gallery, Los Angeles, 79, Foundry Sch Mus NY, 79 & Steckler/Haller Galleries, Scottsdale, Ariz; Tokyo Central Mus, 81. *Teaching:* Instr art educ, Iwatsuki Jr High Sch, 50-64. *Awards:* Second Prize, Saitama Bijitsu Ten, 55; Second Prize, Nat Exhib Prof Art, 68; People's Westchester Savings Bank Award Best in Show, 20th Ann Fine Art Show, Putnam Art Coun, Mahopac, NY, 82. *Bibliog:* Articles in Art News, New York Times & New York Post, 65, 67, 69, 79 & 81; and others. *Media:* Oil. *Dealer:* David Findlay Galleries 984 Madison Ave New York NY 10021. *Mailing Add:* Philipse Brook Rd Garrison NY 10524

ASTLEY-BELL, RITA DUIS See Duis, Rita

ASTMAN, BARBARA ANN
PHOTOGRAPHER, INSTRUCTOR
b Rochester, NY, July 12, 50. *Study:* Rochester Inst Technol, AA, 70; Ont Col Art, Toronto, Assoc, 73. *Work:* Victoria & Albert Mus, London, Eng; Art Gallery Ont, Toronto; Winnipeg Art Gallery; Nat Film Bd Can, Ottawa; Bibliot Nat, Paris, France. *Exhib:* Xerography, Art Gallery Ont, Toronto, 77; New Images, Nat Film Bd, Ottawa, 78; Contemp Can Photog Portrait, Edmonton Art Gallcry, Alta, 78; Winnepeg Perspectives, Winnipeg Art Gallery, 79; Alternative Imageing Systems, Everson Mus, Syracuse, NY, 79; Electroworks, George Eastman House, Rochester, NY, 79-80; one-woman show, Centre Culturel, Paris, France, 82. *Pos:* Coordr, Color Xerox Prog, Visual Arts Ont, 77- *Teaching:* Instr camera art, Ont Col Art, 75- *Awards:* Can Coun Arts Awards Grants, 76, 77, 80, 81 & 83; Prov Ont Coun Arts Grants, 74-82. *Bibliog:* Articles in Arts Can, 3/75, Arts Mag, 77 & Print Rev, No 7, Pratt Graphics Ctr, 77. *Dealer:* Sable Castelli Gallery Ltd 33 Hazelton Ave Toronto ON M5R 2E3 Can. *Mailing Add:* 2154 Dundas St W Toronto ON M6R 1X3 Canada

ASTON, MIRIAM
SCULPTOR, PAINTER
b New York, NY. *Study:* Soc Arts & Crafts, Detroit, with Sarkis Sarkisian, 54-58; Wayne State Univ, BA & MA; Univ Mich, with Gerald Damrowski; Claremont Grad Sch, Calif. *Exhib:* Detroit Inst Art Ann, 50-72; Calif Mus Science & Industry; Univ Ohio, Athens; Mich Acad Arts, Letters & Sci, Ann Arbor; Riverside Mus Art, New York. *Pos:* Dir develop, Mus Hist & Art, Ontario, Calif, currently. *Teaching:* Instr painting & sculpture, Univ Mich, Dearborn, 68-73; instr sculpture, Calif Polytech Univ, Pomona, 75-; instr drawing, Chaffey Col, Calif, currently. *Awards:* Gold Medal, Scarab Club, 65; Best Sculpture, Scarab Club; Best Painting, Mich Acad Arts, Lett & Sci. *Mem:* Artists Equity Asn; Womens Caucus Art. *Media:* Mixed Media. *Mailing Add:* PO Box 241 Claremont CA 91711

ATIRNOMIS (RITA SIMON)
PAINTER, PRINTMAKER
b New York, June 26, 38. *Study:* Cornell Univ Sch Archit, BFA; Acad Rome. *Work:* Joseph H Hirshhorn Mus Art, Washington, DC; Housatonic State Col Mus, Conn. *Comn:* Dalai Lama Portrait-Mural, The Tibet Ctr, New York, 77-78. *Exhib:* Inner Spaces-Outer Limits II, Lerner-Heller Gallery, New York, 72; Reality Plus, James Yu Gallery, New York, NY, 76; Manscapes, Okla Art Ctr, Oklahoma City, 77; Spacescapes, Sid Deutsch Gallery, New York, 77; Art Expo, New York, 79-82; Lanvin Galerie D'Art, Athens, Greece, 83; Trustees' Choice, Larry Aldrich Mus, 83. *Pos:* Rev ed, Arts Mag, New York, 67-70. *Bibliog:* First Person, Working Woman, 8/77; An American artist in Greece, Fantasia Mag, 83. *Media:* Oil; Pen & Ink. *Publ:* Auth, Robert Motherwell & Tamarind Workshop and June Wayne, Arts, 68; auth, Surrealism 1970, After Dark, 70. *Mailing Add:* 414 E 75th St New York NY 10021

ATKINS, GORDON LEE
DESIGNER, ARCHITECT
b Calgary, Alta, Mar 5, 37. *Study:* Col Archit & Urban Planning, Univ Wash, BArch. *Work:* Royal Can Acad Art; Nat Gallery Can; Massey Found. *Comn:* Studio, comn by Ed Drahanchuk, Bragg Creek, Alta, 68; Mayland Heights Sch, Calgary Pub Sch Bd, 68; Pinebrook Golf & Winter Club, comn by Wilbur Griffith, West of Calgary, 74-75; Stoney Indian Band Admin Bldg, comn by Chief John Snow. *Exhib:* Royal Can Acad Art, Ottawa; Environment '69 & '70, Edmonton & Calgary. *Teaching:* Archit technol, Southern Alta Inst Technol, 61-63; design, Dept Environmental Design, Univ Calgary, 63; interior design, Mount Royal Col, Calgary, 64-66. *Awards:* City Calgary Urban Design Award, 79 & 80; Practice Profile Award, Alberta Asn Architects 75th Anniv, 81; Gov Gen Medal, 82. *Bibliog:* Gordon Atkins/Architect, Cult Develop Br, Dept Prov Cult & South Alta, 70. *Mem:* Alta Asn Archit (pres Calgary chap, 64); Royal Archit Inst Can; academician Royal Can Acad Art. *Publ:* Contribr, Canadian Architecture 1960-1970, 70; auth, Plywood World, 70; auth, Investigation North, Arctic Housing Research for Fed Govt, 75. *Mailing Add:* 1909 17th Ave SW Calgary AB T2T 0E9 Canada

ATKINS, ROSALIE MARKS
PAINTER
b Charleston, WVa, July 21, 21. *Study:* Mason Col Music & Fine Arts, Charleston, WVa; Morris Harvey Col, Charleston; workshops with Leo Manso & Victor Candell, Provincetown, Mass; also with Bud Hopkins, Truro, Mass. *Work:* WVa Arts & Humanities Permanent Collection. *Exhib:* Nat League Am Pen Women Ann Show, Washington, DC, 72; Provincetown Art Asn Nat Show, Mass, 72-78; Am Drawing Show, Portsmouth, Va, 76; 39th Ann Exhib Contemp Am Paintings, Four Arts, Palm Beach, Fla, 77; Lighthouse Gallery, Tequesta, Fla, 78-79; and others. *Awards:* Selected for traveling show, Art in the Embassies Prog, 70 & Nat League Am Pen Women, 72 & 77; Purchase Awards, WVa Arts & Humanities, 72. *Bibliog:* Dorothy Seckler (auth), article in Provincetown Painters; article in Artists/USA, 79-80; article, Focus, 5/83. *Mem:* Allied Artists of WVa (vpres, 67); Am Pen Women (pres, Charleston Br, 73-74); Sunrise, Inc; Provincetown Art Asn. *Dealer:* Tequesta Galleries Tequesta FL; Gallery Eleven Charleston WV. *Mailing Add:* 1512 Quarrier St Charleston WV 25311

ATKINSON, TRACY
MUSEUM DIRECTOR
b Middletown, Ohio, Aug 10, 28. *Study:* Ohio State Univ, BFA(summa cum laude), 50; Mexico City Col, 50; Univ Pa, MA, 51; Bryn Mawr Col, 53. *Collections Arranged:* Antique Luster, Albright-Knox Art Gallery, Buffalo, 59; Contemporary American Painting & German Expressionism, Columbus Gallery Fine Arts, Ohio, 61-62; Pop Art and the American Tradition, 65, The Inner Circle, 66, Botero, 67, Options & The Bradley Collection, 68, Seymour Lipton & A Plastic Presence, 69, Aspects of a New Realism, 70, Portraits Exhibition, 71, Six Painters, 72 & The Urban River, 73, Milwaukee Art Ctr. *Pos:* Curatorial asst, Albright-Knox Art Gallery, 55-59; asst dir, Columbus Gallery Fine Arts, 59-61, actg dir, 61-62; dir, Milwaukee Art Ctr, 62-76; dir, Wadsworth Atheneum, 77- *Mem:* Midwest Mus Conf (vpres, Wis, 68-71, exec vpres, 70-71, pres, 71-72); Am Asn Mus; Asn Art Mus Dirs (trustee & 2nd vpres, 72-73); Int Coun Mus; Am Fedn Arts. *Publ:* Auth, German genre paintings from the Von Schleinitz collection, Antiques Mag, 11/69; auth introd, David Black, Recent Work, 71; also articles in prof journals, nat art news mags & newspapers. *Mailing Add:* c/o Wadsworth Atheneum 600 Main St Hartford CT 06103

ATKYNS, (WILLIE) LEE, JR
PAINTER, ADMINISTRATOR
b Washington, DC, Sept 13, 13. *Work:* Phillips Mem Gallery, Washington, DC; Talladega Col, Ala; Rockville Civic Ctr, Md; plus others. *Exhib:* Corcoran Gallery Art; Nat Collection Fine Arts; Baltimore Mus of Art; Butler Art Inst, Youngstown, Ohio; Nat Acad of Design, New York; Sweat Mem Mus, Portland, Maine; Hagerstown Mus, Md; Catholic Univ, Washington, DC; Dimmock Gallery, George Washington Univ, Washington, DC; and others. *Collections Arranged:* Music Themes in Painting, 70-71; Dynamic Liberated Lines, 72- *Pos:* Dir, Lee Atkyns Studio & Gallery of Art, Washington, DC, 50-75, Duncansville, Pa, 75- *Teaching:* Instr painting, Lee Atkyns Studio Sch Art, Washington, DC, 45-68 & summer classes, Puzzletown, Pa, 45-50. *Awards:* Landscape Club Washington, 54, 56, 60, 62, 68 & 71; Soc Washington Artists, 47-54; Am Artists Prof League, 61. *Mem:* Soc Washington Artists; Landscape Club of Washington; Artists Equity Asn; Washington Watercolor Club. *Media:* Acrylic; Oil; Watercolor. *Specialty:* Dynamic Liberated Lines series. *Mailing Add:* Lee Atkyns Puzzletown Art Studio Box 120 RD 2 Duncansville PA 16635

ATLAS, MARTIN & LIANE W
COLLECTORS
b New York, NY. *Pos:* Liane W Atlas, Mem bd, Washington Print Club, DC, 66-76, pres, 71-74. *Collection:* Prints from Goya to contemporaries; The Avant Garde in Theatre & Art: French Playbill of the 1890's, collected by us, was circulated by the Smithsonian Inst Traveling Exhib Serv for Exhib by Cleveland Mus Art, Clark Mus, Williamstown, Mass & others. *Mailing Add:* 2254 48th St NW Washington DC 20007

ATLEE, EMILIE DES
PAINTER, INSTRUCTOR
b Bethlehem, Pa, July 6, 15. *Study:* Spring Garden Inst, Philadelphia; also with Roswell Weidner & Joseph & Gertrude Capolino. *Work:* United Airlines, Philadelphia Airport; Palasaides High Sch, Bucks Co, Pa; La Salle Col & Franklin Inst, Philadelphia; Cult Arts Ctr Ocean City, NJ. *Comn:* Portraits, Libr Univ Del & Berks Co Ct House, Pa. *Exhib:* One-woman shows, Little Gallery, 63 & Newmans Gallery, Philadelphia, 70; Knickerbocker Artists Ann, New York, 64; Philadelphia Art Teachers Asn, 69-71; Harrisburg Mus, Pa, 71. *Teaching:* Instr, 53-69; instr, Main Line Ctr Arts, Bryn Mawr, Pa, 69-77. *Awards:* Hon mention, Nat, Ogunquit Art Ctr, 59 & Nat Benedictine Art Awards, 69; Gold Medal, Newtown Sq Arts Festival, 61. *Bibliog:* Dorothy Grafly (ed), The changing moods of art, Art in Focus, 71. *Mem:* Artists Equity Asn; Woodmere Art Gallery; Main Line Ctr Arts. *Media:* Oil, Pastel. *Dealer:* Newman Galleries 1624 Walnut St Philadelphia PA 19103. *Mailing Add:* 2117 Chestnut Ave Ardmore PA 19003

ATTIE, DOTTY
DRAFTSMAN
b Pennsauken, NJ, Mar 20, 38. *Study:* Philadelphia Col Art, BFA, 59; Brooklyn Mus Art Sch, Beckmann fel, 60; Art Students League, 67. *Work:* Allen Mem Art Mus; Univ Mass, Amherst; Fairleigh Dickinson Univ; Smith Col Art Mus; Spencer Art Mus; and others. *Exhib:* One-man shows, Air Gallery, New York, 76, O K Harris Gallery, New York, 77, Univ RI, 78, Contemporary Arts Mus, Tex, 79, Wadsworth Atheneum, Conn, 80, Pennsylvania Acad Fine Arts, Pa, 81; New Dimensions in Drawing, Aldrich Mus, Ridgefield, Conn, 81; Words as Images, Renaissance Soc, Chicago, 81; and others. *Teaching:* Adjunct prof, New York Univ & Manhattanville Col, 77. *Awards:* Creative Artists Pub Serv Grant, NY State Coun Arts, 76-77; Nat Endowment Arts Grants, 76-77 & 83-84. *Bibliog:* Corinne Robins (auth), Dotty Attie, Arts, 11/78; Susan Putterman (auth), Dotty Attie, Arts, 12/80; Maurice Berger (auth), The Empty Frame, Arts, 9/81; and others. *Media:* Pencil. *Dealer:* AIR Gallery 63 Crosby St New York NY 10012. *Mailing Add:* 334 E 22nd St New York NY 10010

ATWELL, ALLEN
EDUCATOR, PAINTER
b Pittsburgh, Pa, Oct 19, 25. *Study:* Cornell Univ, BA, 49 & MFA, 51. *Work:* Herbert F Johnson Mus Art, Cornell Univ, Ithaca, NY. *Exhib:* Everson Mus Art, Syracuse, NY, 74; Contemp Reflections, Aldrich Mus Contemp Art, Ridgefield, Conn, 75; Artists of Cent NY, Munson-Williams-Proctor Inst, Utica, NY, 74 & 75; The Abstract Tradition in Cent NY, 79; Herbert F Johnson Mus Art, Cornell Univ, Ithaca, NY, 74, 77 & 79; plus others. *Teaching:* From instr art to assoc prof art, 51-64, Cornell Univ, assoc prof art, New York Exten Prog, 64-65; lectr art, NY Univ, 65-66; Manhattan Community Col, 66 & Ithaca Col, NY, 71-77; teaching fel art, Inst Allende, Univ Guanajuato, Mex, 73. *Awards:* Ford Found Fel, India, 53-54; Fulbright Fel, India & Nepal, 61-62; Rockefeller Found Fel, Southeast Asia, Indonesia & Japan, 62-63. *Mem:* Col Art Asn. *Publ:* Auth & illusr, Kuo Hsi's Clearing Autumn Skies Over Mountains & Valleys and Indian Miniature Paintings & The Yama Tanka, 72, Aspen; auth & illusr, Indian art: From multiplicity to unity, Fulbright Newsletter, spring 74. *Mailing Add:* 432 N Tioga St Ithaca NY 14850

ATWOOD PINARDI, BRENDA
PAINTER, EDUCATOR
b Hyannis, Mass, Mar 14, 41. *Study:* Mass Col Art, BSE(art educ), 63; Acad Belle Arte, Rome, 63-64; RI Sch Design, MFA(painting), 67. *Work:* Coop Belle Arte, Verona, Italy. *Exhib:* New England Drawing Competition & Traveling Exhib, DeCordova Mus, Lincoln, Mass, 79; Third Ann Womens Art Exhib, Triangle Gallery, Washington, DC, 82; Nat Drawing Show & Tour, Laguna Gloria Mus, Austin, Tex, 82; Works on Paper, Stedman Gallery, Rutgers Univ, 83; Sixth Ann Small Painting Exhib, Mullaly-Matisse Gallery, Birmingham, Mich, 83. *Teaching:* Prof painting & drawing, Univ Lowell, Mass, 67-, coordr, Gallery 410, 75-80, chairperson art dept, 76-80. *Awards:* Best of Show, Northeast Art Competition, Univ Mass, Amherst, 81; Purchase Award, Appalachian Nat, Appalachian State Univ, 82. *Bibliog:* Figure

landscapes, New Haven Register, 82; Ann Schecter (auth), Artist's enigma, Lowell Sun, 83. *Mem:* Artists for Survival; Boston Visual Artists Union; Boston Humanist Artists & Writers (co-leader, 83-); Nat Drawing Soc. *Media:* Oil. *Dealer:* Kingston Gallery 129 Kingston St Boston MA 02111; Vorpal Gallery 465 W Broadway New York NY. *Mailing Add:* 87 Child St Hyde Park MA 02136

AUBIN, BARBARA
PAINTER, ASSEMBLAGE ARTIST
b Chicago, Ill, Jan 12, 28. *Study:* Carleton Col, BA, 49; Art Inst Chicago, BAE, 54, MAE, 55, George D Brown foreign travel fel, France & Italy, 55-56; Buenos Aires Conv Act grant, Haiti, 58-60. *Work:* Ill State Mus; Art Inst Chicago; Ball State Univ; Centre d'Art, Port-au-Prince, Haiti. *Exhib:* Mid-Year Shows, Butler Inst Am Art, Ohio, 61 & 62; Am Drawing Ann, Norfolk Mus Arts & Sci, 63; 10th Ann Nat Prints & Drawings Exhib, Okla Art Ctr, 68; Drawings USA, St Paul Art Ctr, Minn & traveling, 68; Fairweather-Hardin Gallery, Chicago, 75, 78 & 81. *Pos:* Reporter, Women Artists News, 77, 78 & 83; critic for var publ; curator, Send a Postcard to Barbara, Loyola Univ traveling, 79-80. *Teaching:* Asst prof painting, drawing & watercolor, Art Inst Chicago, 60-68; asst prof painting, drawing & design, Loyola Univ (Chicago), 68-71; lectr painting, drawing & design, St Joseph's Col, 71-74; assoc prof painting, drawing & visual fundamentals, Chicago State Univ, 71- *Awards:* Hon Mention for Dana Medal, Pa Acad Fine Arts, 53; Mich Watercolor Soc Award, 65 & 70; Ill Arts Coun Proj Completion grant, 77 & 78. *Mem:* Col Art Asn Am; Chicago Artists Coalition; Women's Caucus Art (vpres, midwest, 82 & 83). *Media:* Watercolor, Mixed Media. *Dealer:* Art Rental & Sales Gallery Art Inst of Chicago Michigan & Adams St Chicago IL 60603; Fairweather-Hardin Gallery 101 E Ontario St Chicago IL 60611. *Mailing Add:* 1500 W Henderson Chicago IL 60657

AUDETTE, ANNA HELD
PRINTMAKER, EDUCATOR
b New York, NY. *Study:* Smith Col, BA, 60; Sch Art, Yale Univ, BFA, 62 & MFA, 64. *Work:* Fitzwilliam Mus, Cambridge, England; Rijksprentenkabinett, Rijksmuseum, Amsterdam, Holland; Metrop Mus Art, New York; Nat Gallery Art & Nat Libr Sci, Washington, DC. *Comn:* Print ed, Barnard Col, New York, 79 & Barbara Gladstone Gallery, New York, 79, 80 & 83; Print Ed, Barbara Gladstone Gallery, New York, 79 & 80. *Exhib:* Silvermine Print Show, Silvermine Gallery, Conn, 66, 72 & 76; Nat Invitational Drawing, Okla Mus Art, Oklahoma City, 69; Mt Holyoke Col Mus, Mass, 76; solo show, Gallery Fikrun Wa Fann, Alexandria, Egypt, 77, Clark Art Inst, Williamstown, Mass, 78 & Wesleyan Univ, 82. *Collections Arranged:* In Their Own Image?, Southern Conn State Univ, New Haven, 75, 76 & 78. *Teaching:* Prof art, Southern Conn State Univ, 64- *Bibliog:* Article, Print Collectors Newslett, 7-8/79; article, Art News, 9/80. *Mem:* Artists Equity; Asn Yale Alumni; Col Art Asn. *Media:* Pastel, Photography. *Publ:* Auth & illusr, The Impress of Anatomy, Pratt Graphic Art Ctr, 65; illusr, Past & Present, The Continuity of Classical Myths, Hakkert, Ltd, Toronto, 72; illusr, Song in Stone, T Y Crowell, 83. *Dealer:* Barbara Gladstone 152 Wooster St New York NY 10019. *Mailing Add:* 24 Everit St New Haven CT 06511

AUER, JAMES MATTHEW
CRITIC, FILM MAKER
b Neenah, Wis, Dec 2, 28. *Study:* Writers Inst, Univ Wis-Madison, 49; Lawrence Col, BA, 50. *Comn:* Writer, dir & photogr, films, Operation Friendship, 59, Someone Who Cares, 64, It's Circus Day, 70, The Magic World of Patrick Farrell, 79 & The Bohrod Touch, 80. Wis Asn Ment Health. *Pos:* Asst Sunday ed & arts reviewer, The Post-Crescent, Appleton, Wis, 60-65, Sunday ed & arts reviewer, 65-72; art critic, Milwaukee Journal, 72- *Awards:* Award of Merit, State Hist Soc Wis; A Brush with History Award, 62; President's Award, Wis Heart Asn, 66. *Mem:* Am Asn Sunday & Feature Ed (pres, 71-72); Friends Bergstrom Art Ctr, Neenah (pres, 67-68); City Neenah Munic Found. *Publ:* The City of Light (play), 61 & Tell It to Angela (play), 70, Attic Theatre, Lawrence Univ; art reviews to various mags including Craft Horizons Antique World, Glass Mag & Wis Mag Hist. *Mailing Add:* Milwaukee Journal 333 W State St Milwaukee WI 53201

AULT, LEE ADDISON
COLLECTOR, DEALER
b Cincinnati, Ohio, Sept 30, 15. *Study:* Princeton Univ, 37. *Pos:* Publ, Art in Am, 57-69; trustee, Skowhegan Sch Painting & Sculpture, 68-78; adv coun, Princeton Univ Art Mus, 66-70, dir, 70-80; hon trustee, Inst Contemp Art, Boston; dir, Lee Ault & Co Gallery, currently. *Collection:* Twentieth century painting and sculpture; primitive art. *Mailing Add:* Lee Ault & Co Gallery 200 E 82nd St New York NY 10028

AUPING, MICHAEL GRAHAM
CURATOR, HISTORIAN
b Portland, Ore, Oct 17, 49. *Study:* Santa Ana Col, AA, 69; Calif State Univ, Fullerton, BA(art hist), 71; Calif State Univ, Long Beach, MA(art hist), 75. *Exhib:* Matrix: A Changing Exhib Contemp Art, Univ Art Mus, Berkeley, Calif, 78-80. *Pos:* Ed, Los Angeles Inst Contemp Art J, 76-78; assoc cur, Univ Art Mus, Berkeley, 78-80; cur 20th century art, John & Mable Ringling Mus Art, Sarasota, Fla, 80- *Teaching:* Instr art hist, San Francisco Art Inst & Univ Calif, Santa Barbara. *Res:* Contemporary art. *Publ:* Auth, Richard Serra: Drawings, 79 & Joseph Cornell: Works from the 30s, 79, Univ Art Mus, Berkeley; Florida Landscape: Fulton, Harrisons, Singer, Sonfist, 82; Tess: Paste-Ups 1951-1983, 83; John Chamberlain Wall Reliefs: 1960-1983, 83. *Mailing Add:* c/o Ringling Mus Art Box 1838 Sarasota FL 33578

AUSBY, ELLSWORTH AUGUSTUS
PAINTER, INSTRUCTOR
b Portsmouth, Va, Apr 5, 42. *Study:* Sch Visual Arts, BFA, 75; Pratt Inst. *Work:* Aldrich Mus Contemp Art, Ridgefield, Conn; Cinque Gallery, New York; Rice Univ, Houston; Atlanta Airport. *Comn:* Three pastel paintings, comn by Jean de Mevil, Houston, 71; Space Odyssey (enamel on steel), Howard Johnsons Co, New York, 79-80; Rock Paper Scissor (silkscreen), Path Train Station, New York; Space Odyssey (stainless steel sculpture), New York Technical Col, City Univ New York, 81. *Exhib:* New Black Artist, Brooklyn Mus Fine Arts, 69; Lamp Black, Boston Mus Fine Arts, 70; Black Artist, Whitney Mus Am Art, New York, 71; one-man show, Pa Acad Fine Arts, Philadelphia, 72; Millenium, Mus Philadelphia Civic Ctr, 73; Herbert F Johnson Mus Art, Cornell Univ, Ithaca, NY, 74; Contemp Reflections, Aldrich Mus Contemp Art, 75; Afro-American Abstractions, Public Sch 1, Long Island City, 80; Everson Mus, Syracuse, New York, 81. *Collections Arranged:* Some American History (auth, catalog), Rice Univ, 71; Contemporary Reflections (auth, catalog), Am Fedn Art, 75. *Teaching:* Instr painting, Sch Visual Arts, 75- *Awards:* Comprehensive Employment & Training Act artist grant, 78; Creative Artists Pub Serv Prog painting grant, NY State Coun Arts, 80. *Bibliog:* Barbara Rose (auth), Black artist, 9/70 & Henri Ghent (auth), Quo Vadis black art, 11/74, Art in Am; April Kingsley (auth), Ausby at the Soho Center, Soho Weekly News, 12/75. *Mem:* Cult Coun Found New York; Harlem Cult Coun Found. *Media:* Acrylic, Enamel. *Publ:* Illusr, Slavery (film), Silvermine Productions, 71; illusr, Tuesdays and Every Other Sunday Off, Doubleday, 72; illusr, Black Review Number Two, William Morrow & Co, 72; contribr, Encore Mag, 72; illusr, The Crossroads, Reed, Cannon, Johnson, 75. *Mailing Add:* PO Box 15 Brooklyn NY 11211

AUSTIN, BARBARA JEAN See Adams, Bobbi

AUSTIN, DARREL
PAINTER
b Raymond, Wash, June 25, 07. *Study:* Univ Notre Dame; Univ Ore; European Sch Art, with Emil Jaques. *Work:* Metrop Mus Art & Mus Mod Art, New York; Mus Fine Arts, Boston; Nelson Gallery Art, Kansas City, Mo; Phillips Mem Gallery, Washington, DC. *Comn:* Four oil panels, Med Col, Univ Ore, 36. *Exhib:* Whitney Mus, New York; Carnegie Inst, Pittsburgh; City Art Mus, St Louis; Contemp Painting in the US, toured in Latin Am countries; Inst Contemp Art, Boston; retrospective, McNay Art Inst, San Antonio, 82; and others. *Awards:* Lippincot Award for Figure Oil, Pa Acad Art, 53. *Bibliog:* Miller (auth), Americans 1942, Mus Mod Art, 42; Bird (auth), Darrel Austin, Art in Am, 43; Darrel Austin, Life Mag, 45. *Media:* Oil. *Dealer:* Perls Gallery 1016 Madison Ave New York NY 10021; Harmon Gallery Naples FL 33940. *Mailing Add:* RFD #3 Sawmill Hill Rd Fairfield CT 06812

AUSTIN, JO-ANNE JORDAN
DEALER, GALLERY DIRECTOR
b Springfield, Ohio, Nov 15, 25. *Study:* Western Reserve Univ & Cleveland Sch Art, BA(cum laude, Phi Beta Kappa); Chicago Acad Fine Art; San Diego State Col, MFA. *Pos:* Pub info officer, Fine Arts Gallery of San Diego, 56-57; dir & owner, Austin Gallery, Santa Barbara, Calif, 66-74 & Scottsdale, Ariz, 75- *Teaching:* Asst & teacher art for children, Fine Arts Gallery of San Diego Calif, 53-57; teacher art & English, La Cumbre Jr High, Santa Barbara, Cali, 58-60. *Awards:* Bronze Award for Reflections on Oil (film), Int Film & TV Festival of NY, 70; Chris Award, Columbus Film Festival, 70. *Specialty:* Paintings, original prints, and sculpture by living artists; diversity of styles. *Publ:* Der Brenz Entlang (catalog), 81. *Mailing Add:* 7103 Main St Scottsdale AZ 85251

AUSTIN, PAT
PRINTMAKER, EDUCATOR
b Detroit, Mich, Mar 17, 37. *Study:* Univ Mich, AB, 59; Univ Alaska with Alex Duffs Combs, Jr, 65, MFA, 76; Univ Wash, BFA(art), 71; Univ Alaska, Anchorage, MFA, 77. *Work:* Evergreen State Col, Olympia; Anchorage Hist & Fine Arts Mus, Alaska; Alaska State Coun Arts, Printmakers Alaska Permanent Collection, Anchorage; Anchorage Borough Sch Dist Permanent Print Collection; Visual Arts Ctr, Permanent Print Collection. *Exhib:* All Alaska Juried Exhib, Anchorage, 66-69 & 72-75; 50 Years of Alaskan Art, Alaska Methodist Univ Gallery, 67 & two person exhib, 69; 20 Printmakers Touring Invitational, Wash State Artmobile, 71-72; one-woman shows, Migrations of the Moon, 75 & Horizon Lines/Horizon Lies, 83, Anchorage Hist & Fine Arts Mus. *Teaching:* Instr art & Eng, Anchorage Borough Sch Dist, 65-69; instr printmaking & drawing, Univ Alaska, 71- *Awards:* Drawing Award, Alaska Purchase Centennial Exhib, State of Alaska, 67; Printmaking Award, All Alaska Juried Exhib, 69 & 74 & Mel Kohler Award Painting, 75. *Bibliog:* Connie Godwin (auth), Pat's art is exploring world, Anchorage Daily Times, 11/3/75; Virginia McKinney (auth), Pat Austin: Printmaker and more, Alaska J, winter 83. *Mem:* Anchorage Hist & Fine Arts Mus Asn; Anchorage Arts Coun; Visual Arts Ctr; Northwest Print Coun. *Media:* All; Drawing Collage, Watercolor. *Publ:* Auth, National Collection of Fine Arts (catalog), Washington, DC, 78; auth, Passing off reproductions as real art, Alaska J, winter 80. *Mailing Add:* 7030 Apollo Dr Anchorage AK 99504

AUSTIN, PHIL
PAINTER, LECTURER
b Waukegan, Ill, Jan 27, 10. *Study:* Univ Mich, AB, 33. *Work:* Ill State Libr, Lincoln Collection, Ill State Mus, Springfield; Wheaton Col Art Collection, Ill. *Exhib:* Five shows, Am Watercolor Soc Ann, New York, NY, 61-69; Watercolor USA, Springfield, Mo, 72 & 74; Mainstreams, Marietta, Ohio, 72 & 76; Am Artists Prof League Grand Nat, New York, 79 & 81; Ky Aqueous,

81; plus others. *Pos:* Mem staff, Kling Studios, Chicago, 45-50. *Teaching:* Guest instr watercolor, Wheaton Col, 63-70. *Awards:* Fox Purchase Award, Watercolor USA 74, Springfield, Mo, 74; President's Award, Am Artists Prof League, 79. *Bibliog:* Phil Austin, watercolorist, Am Artist, 10/71. *Mem:* Am Watercolor Soc; Nat Watercolor Soc; Midwest Watercolor Soc (pres emer, 81-); Am Artists Prof League. *Media:* Watercolor. *Dealer:* Jack Anderson Art Gallery Sister Bay WI 54234; Mongerson Gallery 620 N Michigan Chicago IL 60611. *Mailing Add:* Rte 1 Ellison Bay WI 54210

AUTH, ROBERT R
PAINTER, PRINTMAKER
b Bloomington, Ill, Oct 27, 26. *Study:* Ill Wesleyan Univ, BFA; Wash State Univ, MFA. *Work:* Salt Lake Art Ctr, Utah; Col Southern Idaho, Twin Falls; Ricks Col, Rexburg, Idaho; Boise Gallery Art, Idaho; Wash State Univ. *Exhib:* Intermountain Painting & Sculpture 4th Biennial, Salt Lake Art Ctr, 69; Fedn Rocky Mountain States Traveling Exhib, 71-72; Inaugural Exhib, Denver Art Mus, Colo, 71; 48th Ann Nat Apr Art Exhib, Springville Mus Art, Utah, 72; Realist Painting: 12 Viewpoints, Minneapolis, 72. *Pos:* Bd dir, Boise Gallery Art, 69- *Teaching:* Instr art, Burley High Sch, Idaho, 60-61; instr art & humanities, Boise High Sch, 61- *Awards:* Intermountain Painting & Sculpture 4th Biennial Award, 69; 36th Ann Exhib for Idaho Award, 72; Allied Arts Coun Artist of Year Award, 72. *Mem:* Idaho Art Asn (vpres, 70-72); Boise Art Asn (trustee, 69-). *Media:* Acrylic. *Dealer:* Gloria Brown c/o Brown's Gallery 711 S Latah St Boise ID 83705. *Mailing Add:* 530 Hillview Dr Boise ID 83702

AUTH, SUSAN HANDLER
CURATOR, EDUCATOR
b New York, NY, June 25, 39. *Study:* Swarthmore Col, BA; Univ London; Univ Mich, MA; Am Sch Classical Studies, Athens, Fulbright Scholar, 64-65; Bryn Mawr Col, PhD, 68. *Work:* Toledo Mus of Art, Ohio, 68; Newark Mus, NJ, 71. *Collections Arranged:* Myth & Gospel: Art of Coptic Egypt, Newark Mus, 77, Ancient Greece: Life and Art, 80; The Classical Collection, 81. *Pos:* Curatorial asst, Toledo Mus Art, Ohio, 67; cur classical collection, Newark Mus, 71- *Teaching:* Asst prof ancient art & archaeol, Dept Art, Rutgers Univ, Newark, 68-71. *Awards:* Am Numismatic Soc Summer Fel, 63; Res Travel Grants, Rutgers Univ, summer 69 & Smithsonian Inst, Washington, DC, summer 71. *Mem:* Archaeol Inst Am; Int Asn Hist Glass. *Res:* Ancient glass; Greek, Roman and Egyptian art and archaeology. *Publ:* Auth, Ancient Glass at the Newark Museum, from the Eugene Schaefer Collection of Ancient Glass, Newark Mus, 76; auth, var articles, Am J Archaeol, J Glass Studies, Archaeol & Annales Int d'Etude Hist du Verre. *Mailing Add:* Newark Mus 43-49 Washington St Newark NJ 07101

AUTH, TONY (WILLIAM ANTHONY), JR
EDITORIAL CARTOONIST
b Akron, Ohio, May 7, 42. *Study:* Univ Calif, Los Angeles, BA(biological illus). *Pos:* Syndicated ed cartoonist, Philadelphia Inquirer, 71- *Awards:* Sigma Delta Chi Award, Soc of Prof Journalists, 76; Pulitzer Prize, Columbia Univ Trustees, 76. *Bibliog:* Stephen Hess & Milton Kaplan (co-auth), The Ungentlemanly Art: A History of American Political Cartoons, MacMillan, 75. *Media:* Pen and ink. *Publ:* Auth, Behind the Lines, Houghton-Mifflin, 77. *Dealer:* Rosenfeld Gallery 113 Arch St Philadelphia PA 19104. *Mailing Add:* 400 N Broad St Philadelphia PA 19101

AUTIO, (A) RUDY
CERAMIST, EDUCATOR
b Butte, Mont, Oct 8, 26. *Study:* Mont State Univ, BS, 50; Wash State Univ, MFA, 52. *Work:* Henry Gallery, Seattle; Toledo Art Mus; Smithsonian Inst; Ore Univ Art Mus. *Comn:* Carved brick relief, First Methodist Church, Great Falls, Mont, 54; ceramic tile relief, Union Bank & Trust Co, Helena, 59-60 & Anthony's Cath Church, Missoula, Mont, 63; metal sculpture, Farm Credit Banks, Spokane, 70; mural, State Security Bank, Polson, Mont, 71. *Exhib:* One-man shows, Henry Gallery, Univ Wash, Seattle, 63 & Toledo Art Mus, 65; Everson Mus, Syracuse, 64; two-man show, Chicago Art Mus, 68; Am Studio Potters & Victoria & Albert Mus, London, 72; San Francisco Mus Mod Art, 72; Mus Contemp Crafts, New York, 74; Seattle Art Mus, 79. *Collections Arranged:* Objects USA, 69-71; One-Man Traveling Show, Ariz Comn Arts & Humanities, 76; Masters Show, Supermud 76, 76. *Pos:* Resident artist-dir, Archie Bray Found, 52-56; asst cur, Mont Mus Hist Soc, 56. *Teaching:* Prof ceramics & sculpture, Univ Mont, 57- *Awards:* Tiffany Found Award, 63; Purchase Award, Everson Mus, 64; Ceramic Art Award, Am Ceramic Soc, 78. *Bibliog:* Julie Hall (auth), Tradition and Change, 77 & Clark & Hughto (coauth), A Century of Ceramics in the United States, 79, E P Dutton; Lamar Harrington (auth), Ceramics in the Pacific Northwest: A History, Univ Wash Press, 79. *Mem:* Hon mem Nat Coun Educ Ceramic Arts; fel Am Craftsmen Coun; Archie Bray Found (trustee, 74). *Publ:* Coauth, Peter Voulkos, 54 & auth, Maxine Blackmer, 80, MIA Quart. *Dealer:* Alice Westphal c/o Exhibit A 233 E Ontario St Chicago IL 60611. *Mailing Add:* Dept of Art Univ of Mont Missoula MT 59812

AUTRY, CAROLYN (CAROLYN AUTRY ELLOIAN)
PRINTMAKER
b Dubuque, Iowa, Dec 12, 40. *Study:* Univ Iowa, Iowa City, BA, 63, MFA, 65; Yale-Norfolk Summer Sch, 62. *Work:* Libr of Cong, Washington, DC; Philadelphia Mus Art; Worcester Art Mus; Henderson Mus, Univ Colo, Boulder; Calif State Univ, San Diego; and others. *Exhib:* Solo exhib sponsored by US Info Serv, Am Ctr, Belgrade & museums in Yugoslavia; World Print Competition, San Francisco Mus Art, 73; Int Biennal of Graphic Art, Ljubljana, 75 & 81; A Tribute to the Print Club, Philadelphia Mus Art, 80; Mus Arts & Sciences, Macon, Ga, 83; 20 Printmakers 1981, Gruenwald

Found, Univ Southern Calif; Ten Printmakers, Univ Tenn, 83; Architecture in Prints, Pratt Manhattan Ctr, New York, 83; and others. *Teaching:* Instr art & art hist, Baldwin-Wallace Col, Berea, Ohio, 65-66; instr art hist, Toledo Mus Art & Univ Toledo Joint Degree Program, 66- *Awards:* Boston Printmakers, 71 & 81; Philadelphia Print Club, 72, 75 & 79; Wesleyan Col Int Award of Merit, 80; and other purchase awards; Ohio Arts Coun grant to individual artist, 80. *Mem:* Soc Am Graphic Artists; Calif Soc Printmakers; Boston Printmakers; Los Angeles Printmakers Soc; Women's Caucus for Art. *Mailing Add:* 3348 Indian Rd Toledo OH 43606

AUVIL, KENNETH WILLIAM
EDUCATOR, PRINTMAKER
b Ryderwood, Wash, Dec 18, 25. *Study:* Univ Wash, BA, 50, MFA, 53. *Work:* Achenbach Found, Palace Legion Honor, San Francisco; Seattle Art Mus, Wash; US Embassy, Bonn, Ger; Wichita Art Asn, Kans; Victoria & Albert Mus, London, Eng. *Comn:* Ed of 170 screen prints, Hilton Collection, New York, 62. *Exhib:* Northwest Printmakers Int Exhibs, Seattle Art Mus, 53-67 & 70; 4th Biennial di Pittura Americana, Bordighera, Italy, 57; Libr Cong Nat Exhibs, 59, 63 & 66; New Impressions for the Decade, Oakland Art Mus, Calif, 70; Int Print Exhib, Richmond Art Ctr, Calif, 72. *Teaching:* Prof art & printmaking, Calif State Univ, San Jose, 56- *Mem:* Northwest Printmakers (pres, 55-56); Calif Soc Printmakers. *Publ:* Auth, Serigraphy-Silk Screen Techniques for the Artist, Prentice-Hall, 65. *Mailing Add:* 605 Olson Rd Santa Cruz CA 95065

AVAKIAN, JOHN
PAINTER, INSTRUCTOR
b Worcester, Mass. *Study:* Yale Univ Sch Art & Archit, BFA & MFA; Boston Mus Sch, grad traveling scholar, dipl(hons) & cert. *Work:* Kans State Univ; Western Mich Univ; Bucknell Univ; Tulsa Civic Ctr, Okla; White, Weld & Co, Inc, Boston. *Exhib:* New Talent, New Eng, DeCordova Mus, Lincoln, Mass, 65; 20th Nat Exhib Prints, Libr Cong, Washington, DC, 66; 38th Int Printmakers Exhib, Seattle Art Mus, 67; one-man show, Higgins Wing, Worcester Art Mus, Mass, 71; 21st Ann Int Exhib, Beaumont Art Mus, Tex, 72. *Teaching:* Instr color & design, Worcester Art Mus Sch, Mass, 65- & Mt Ida Jr Col, 65-, chmn art dept, 66-71, dir art, 72- *Awards:* William E Brigham Prize, Providence Art Club, 68; Blanche E Colman Found Award, 70; Art Patrons League of Mobile Award, 72. *Mem:* Col Art Asn Am; Boston Visual Artist's Union. *Media:* Acrylic, Serigraph. *Dealer:* Assoc Am Artist 663 Fifth Ave New York NY 10022. *Mailing Add:* 43 Morse St Sharon MA 02067

AVEDISIAN, EDWARD
PAINTER
b Lowell, Mass, 1936. *Study:* Boston Mus Sch Art. *Work:* Guggenheim Mus, Whitney Mus Am Art & Metrop Mus Art, New York; Los Angeles Co Mus Art; Wadsworth Atheneum; and others. *Exhib:* John Powers Collection, Larry Aldrich Mus, 66; Robert Rowan Collection, San Francisco Mus Art, 67; Boston Inst Contemp Art, 67-68; Painters Under 40, Whitney Mus Am Art, 68; Six Painters, Albright-Knox Art Gallery, Buffalo, 71; solo exhibs, Gallery Moos, Toronto, 71; Janie C Lee Gallery, Houston, 74, Carriage House Gallery, Buffalo, 75; NY Univ, 77 & Nina Freudenheim Gallery, Buffalo, 78. *Teaching:* Artist in residence, Univ Kans, 69; instr, Sch Visual Arts, New York, 69-70, Univ Calif, Irvine, 72 & Univ La, 73. *Awards:* Guggenheim Found Fel, 67; Nat Coun Arts Award, 68. *Dealer:* Robert Elkon Gallery 1063 Madison Ave New York NY 10028. *Mailing Add:* 26 Warren Hudson NY 12534

AVEDON, BARRY
PAINTER, EDUCATOR
b Brooklyn, NY, Jan 2, 41. *Study:* Rochester Inst Technol Sch Art, BFA, 62, MFA, 64. *Work:* Eastern Mich Univ, Ypsilanti; Rochester Inst Technol, NY; Mich Ont 4 Comerica Gallery, Detroit. *Exhib:* Ann Exhib, Albright-Knox Mus Art, 64; Butler Inst Am Art Mid-Year Show, 66; Michigan Biennial, Detroit Inst Art, 71; Midland Ann, Midland Ctr Arts, Mich, 78; Ball State Nat Drawing Ann, Ball State Univ Gallery, 79; Mich Artists 80/81, Flint Inst Arts, Mich, 81; The Corporation Collects Art, Muskegon Mus Art, Mich, 83. *Teaching:* Prof painting & drawing, Eastern Mich Univ, 66- *Awards:* 26th Regional of Ossining Ann Award, Westchester Arts Coun, 61; Julius Hallgarten Award, Nat Acad Design Ann, 64; Purchase Award, Ethno-Art '81, Bank of Commerce, Hamtramck, Mich, 81. *Bibliog:* A Scaglione & B Parker (auth), Detroit Summer III, Park West Galleries, Inc, 82; Robert Iglehart (auth), article, Ann Arbor News, 83. *Mem:* Artists Equity Asn, Mich. *Media:* Oil; Pencil. *Mailing Add:* 806 Fifth St Ann Arbor MI 48103

AVEDON, RICHARD
PHOTOGRAPHER
b New York, NY, May 15, 23. *Study:* Columbia Univ. *Work:* Smithsonian Inst, Washington, DC; Metrop Mus Art, New York; Mus Mod Art, New York; Mus Fine Arts, Houston; Minneapolis Inst Arts, Minn; and others. *Exhib:* Family of Man, Mus Mod Art, New York, 55; Metrop Mus Art, 59, 60, 63 & 67; Musee Reattu, Arles, France, 65; NY World's Fair, 65-66; Fogg Art Mus, Cambridge, Mass, 67; Rhodes Nat Gallery, Salisbury, Rhodesia, 68; Expo 70, Osaka, Japan; one-man retrospective, Smithsonian Inst, 62, Minneapolis Inst Arts, 70 & Univ Art Mus, Berkeley, Calif, 80; one-man shows, Mus Mod Art, 74, Marlborough Gallery, 75 & Metrop Mus Art, 78, New York. *Pos:* Staff photogr, Harper's Bazaar, 45-65; photogr, French fashions, 47-; staff photogr, Vogue Mag, 66-; contribr photogr, Life, Look, Graphis Mag, US Camera Ann; visual consult, Paramount film Funny Face; television consult, dir & advert photogr. *Awards:* President's Fellow, RI Sch Design, 76; Chancellor's Citation, Univ Calif, Berkeley, 80; Hall of Fame, Art Dirs Club, 82. *Bibliog:* Roland Barthes (auth), Avedon, Photo, 1/77; Janet

Malcolm (auth), A series of proposals, The New Yorker, 10/23/78; Charles Michener (auth), The Avedon look, Newsweek, 10/16/78. *Mem:* Am Soc Mag Photogr. *Publ:* Ed, Diary of a Century, 70; photogrs, Alice in Wonderland: The forming of A Company, the Making of a Play, 73; photogrs, Bicentennial issue, Rolling Stone Mag, 76; auth & photogr, Portraits, 76; auth & photogrs, Avedon: Photographs 1947-1977, 78. *Dealer:* Norma Stevens 1075 Park Ave New York NY 10028. *Mailing Add:* 407 E 75th St New York NY 10021

AVISON, DAVID
PHOTOGRAPHER
b Harrisonburg, Va, July 13, 37. *Study:* Mass Inst Technol, ScB, 59; Brown Univ, PhD, 67; Inst Design, Ill Inst Technol, MS, 74. *Work:* Dallas Mus Fine Art; Int Mus Photog, George Eastman House, Rochester, NY; Mus Mod Art, New York; Mus Fine Arts, Boston, Mass; Art Inst Chicago; and others. *Exhib:* Panoramic Photog, Grey Gallery, New York Univ, 77; one-man shows, Recent Acquisitions, 78, American Photography in the 70's, 79 & Chicago Architecture, 83, Art Inst Chicago; 70's Wideview, Dittmar Mem Gallery, Northwestern Univ, Evanston, Ill, 78; The New Vision, Light Gallery, New York, 80; Panoramas Exhib, John Hansard Gallery, Univ Southampton, Eng; Northlight Gallery, Ariz State Univ, 81 & 82; and others. *Teaching:* Prof photog, Columbia Col, Chicago, 70- *Awards:* Nat Endowment Arts Photogr Award, 77. *Bibliog:* Gretchen Garner (auth), Organic landscapes, Afterimage, 4/75; David Elliott (auth), Wide view of Chicago, Chicago Daily News, 4/77; Lynne Warren (auth), David Avison, Midwest Art Quart, 4/77. *Mem:* Soc Photog Educ; Chicago Artists' Coalition; Soc Photog Sci & Engineers; Chicago Optical Soc. *Interests:* Designed and built 2 special panoramic cameras. *Dealer:* The Afterimage, Dallas, TX, 75201. *Mailing Add:* 399 Fullerton Parkway Chicago IL 60614

AXELROD, MIRIAM
SCULPTOR
b Russia; US citizen. *Study:* Art Students League, 35, studied with Yasuo Kunyoshi, Robert Cronbach & Jason Seeley; Pratt Inst, cert, 40; Brooklyn Mus Art Sch, 45. *Work:* C W Post Col; Brooklyn Col; Nassau Community Col, NY; Sun Oil Chemical Corp, New York; Int Bus Machines Corp, Long Island, NY. *Exhib:* Brooklyn Mus, NY, 45; Audubon Artists, New York, 63, 66 & 70; Fordham Univ, NY, 73; solo shows, C W Post Col, Long Island, NY, 76 & Adelphi Univ, Garden City, NY, 82; New York Inst Technol, Long Island, 76; and others. *Teaching:* Teacher sculpture, Mepham High Sch, 63-78; adult educ prog, Calhoun High Sch, 63-78. *Awards:* Intra-Am Award, Ceceile Gallery, New York, 62; First Prize, Emily Lowe Gallery Ann, 64. *Bibliog:* Jean Paris (auth), reviews, Long Island Press, 65, 66, 69 & 74; Malcolm Preston (auth), Art, Newsday, 69, 70, 74 & 76. *Media:* Mixed Media. *Mailing Add:* c/o Gallery 84 30 W 57th St New York NY 10019

AYASO, MANUEL
PAINTER, SCULPTOR
b Riveira, Spain, Jan 1, 34; US citizen. *Study:* Newark Sch Fine & Indust Arts, cert. *Work:* Whitney Mus Am Art, New York; Worcester Mus, Mass; Pa Acad Fine Arts, Philadelphia; NJ State Mus, Trenton; Newark Mus, NJ. *Exhib:* Drawings USA Circulating Exhib, 62 & 64-65; 22nd Int Watercolor Biennial, Brooklyn Mus, NY, 63; El Neo-Humanismo en el Dibujo de USA, Italia y Mexico, Univ Mex, 63; American Painting & Sculpture, Pa Acad Fine Arts, 67; Contemporary American Artists, Nat Inst Arts & Lett, 71; Contemp Am Spiritual Art, Mus Contemp Art, Vatican, Rome, 76. *Awards:* Tiffany Found Scholar in Painting, 62; Ford Found Purchase Award, 64; Childe Hassam Fund Purchase Award, 71. *Bibliog:* Brian O'Doherty (auth), NY Times, 5/31/61; John Canaday (auth), NY Times, 12/8/63; Barry Schwartz (auth), The New Humanism, Praeger Publ, 74. *Mem:* Am Fedn Arts. *Media:* Goldpoint, Mixed Media. *Dealer:* Jean Frank 25 E 83rd St New York NY 10021. *Mailing Add:* 12 Vincent Pl Verona NJ 07044

AYCOCK, ALICE
SCULPTOR
b Harrisburg, Pa, Nov 20, 46. *Study:* Douglass Col, New Brunswick, NJ, 64-68, BA; Hunter Col, New York, 68-71, MA, study with Robert Morris. *Work:* Mus of Mod Art, New York; Mus Ludwig, Koln, Germany; Guggenheim Mus; Kunstmuseum, Basel, Switzerland; and others. *Exhib:* Projects Room, Museum Mod Art, New York, 77; Whitney Biennial, Whitney Mus Am Art, 79; Mus Mod Art, New York, 79; one-person shows, Douglass Col, New Brunswick, NJ, 80-81, Plattsburgh Col, New York, 81 & John Weber Gallery, New York, 81; Machineworks, Inst Contemp Art, Univ Pa, Philadelphia, 81; Univ SFla, 81; Mus Contemp Art, Chicago, 83; Retrospective, Wurtt, Kunstrerein Sturrgart, Ger, 83; and many others. *Pos:* Vol asst, Conserv Dept, Guggenheim Mus, New York, 67; cur, Art Hist Slide Libr, Hunter Col, New York, 69-72. *Teaching:* Assoc prof, Hunter Col, 82-; artist-in-residence, Williams Col, 74; instr sculpture, Sch of Visual Arts, New York, 79-82. *Awards:* Nat Endowment Arts Grant, 75 & 80; Creative Artist Public Serv Grant, 76. *Bibliog:* Stuart Morgan (auth), Interview with Alice Aycock, Arts, 3/78; Donald Kuspit (auth), Aycock's dream houses, Art in Am, 9/80; Fourteen Americans: Directions of the 1970's, Blackwood film, 79; and many others. *Publ:* Auth, Five Semi-Architectural Projects, c 7500, Valencia, Calif, 73; auth, New York City Orientations, Triquarterly, Evanston, winter 75; auth, The Beginnings of a Complex...(1976-1977): Notes, Drawings, Photographs, Lapp Princess, Press Ltd, 77; auth, Work 1972-1974, In: Individuals: Post-Movement Art in America, E P Dutton & Co, Inc, New York, 76; and others. *Dealer:* John Weber Gallery 142 Greene St New York NY 10012; Protech McNeil 214 Lafayette St New York NY 10012. *Mailing Add:* 62 Greene St New York NY 10012

AYERS, CAROL LEE
PAINTER, GALLERY DIRECTOR
b Newark, NJ, Dec 25, 29. *Study:* Basically self-taught; Caldwell Col, studied with David Kwo & Allan Eldredge, 75-76. *Work:* Bicentennial Expos, Everson Mus, Syracuse, NY; Am Telephone & Telegraph Corp Hq, Bedminster, NJ; Westinghouse Corp, Bath, NY; Sterling Drug Corp, New York & Athens, Greece; Trenton Mus; and others. *Comn:* Mural, Windalume Corp, Kenvil, NJ, 64; acrylic wall panel, Archdiocese of Rochester, Geneva, NY, 70; mural, comn by B Burley, vpres Sterling Drug Corp, New York, 75. *Exhib:* Finger Lakes Wine Mus, Hammondsport, NY, 72; Silvermine Guild Artists, New Canaan, Conn, 75; Orange Co Watercolor Soc, Hall Fame Trotter, Goshen, NY, 81-83; Old Bergen Art Guild Traveling Show, 81-83; Sugarloaf Found Art Gallery, NY, 83. *Pos:* Dir, Esperanza Gallery, Yates Co, NY, 68-73; dir, Erincourt Gallery, Penn Yan, NY, 73-79; dir, Gallery-in-the-Gap, Delaware Water Gap, Pa, 80-83; dir, Sunflower Studio, 83- *Awards:* First Awards, Monroe Co Mus, 83, Chester Art Asn, 73 & Suburban Art League, 83. *Bibliog:* Article in NJ Music & Art Mag, Ridgewood, NJ, 6/77; T Noverro (auth), Save the gallery, Easton Publ Co, Pa, 9/81. *Mem:* Old Bergen Art Guild, Pa; Hunterdon Art Ctr; Orange Co Watercolor Soc. *Media:* Watercolor, Mixed Media. *Specialty:* Original contemporary paintings. *Mailing Add:* Sunflower Studio RD 1-Mt Hermon Rd Blairstown NJ 07825

AYLON, HELANE
PAINTER
b New York, NY. *Study:* Brooklyn Col, BA(cum laude); with Ad Reinhardt. *Work:* Whitney Mus Am Art, New York. *Comn:* Wall painting, Chapel, John F Kennedy Airport, NY, 66; lobby mural, NY Univ Med Ctr, New York, 67. *Exhib:* Lyrical Abstraction, Whitney Mus Am Art, Aldrich Mus Contemp Art & traveling, 69; one-woman shows, Max Hutchinson Gallery, New York, 70-72, Betty Parsons Gallery, New York, 75, Susan Caldwell Gallery, New York, 75, Grapestake Gallery, San Francisco, 76 & Mass Inst Technol, Cambridge, 76; Season's Highlights, Aldrich Mus Am Art, 71; Four Painters, Skidmore Col, Saratoga, NY, 71; and others. *Teaching:* Instr painting, Brooklyn Mus & Hunter Col, 72-73; instr, San Francisco State Univ, 73-75. *Awards:* MacDowell Col, 72; Nat Endowment Arts Fel, 73, 74 & 80. *Bibliog:* Grace Glueck (auth), Art: Highlights of downtown scene, New York Times, 12/11/70; Gregoire Muller (auth), Materiality and painterliness, Arts Mag, 9-10/71; Carter Ratcliff (auth), New York letter, Art Int, 6/73. *Mem:* Archit League NY. *Media:* Miscellaneous. *Mailing Add:* 463 West St 808A New York NY 10014

AYMAR, GORDON CHRISTIAN
PAINTER
b East Orange, NJ, July 24, 1893. *Study:* Yale Univ, AB, 14; Sch Mus Fine Arts, Boston, 15-17. *Work:* Yale Univ Art Gallery, New Haven; Addison Gallery Art, Phillips Acad, Mass; Nat Coun Churches, New York; New York Neurol Inst; Photographic Dept Permanent Study Collection, Mus Mod Art, New York. *Comn:* Portraits, Pres K Towe, Am Cyanamid, New York, 55; Pres W Wheeler, Jr, Pitney Bowes, Stamford, Conn, 58; Dr H S Coffin, Madison Ave Presby Church, New York, 61; Pres L W Wister, South Kent Sch, Conn, 69; Pres J Armstrong, Middlebury Col, Vt, 71. *Exhib:* Mus Art, Montreal, PQ, 60; Royal Soc Painters in Water Colour, London, Eng, 62; Charles & Emma Frye Art Mus, Seattle, Wash, 64; Nat Acad Design, New York, 68; Am Watercolor Soc, New York, 71. *Awards:* Awards, Darien Art Show, Conn, 63 & 64; Pomeraug Valley Art League, 75 & Housatonic Art League, 76 & 77. *Bibliog:* Salon des aquarellistes de New York, Rev Mod, Paris, 62; C R Cammel (auth), American masterpieces in watercolour, New Daily, London, 62; Dorothy Brazier (auth), Crowd enjoys charming picture, Seattle Times, 64. *Mem:* Am Watercolor Soc (vpres, 63); Washington Art Asn, Conn (trustee, 66); Kent Art Asn (bd dir, 77-81). *Publ:* Auth, The Art of Portrait Painting, Chilton Press, 67. *Mailing Add:* South Kent CT 06785

AYRES, LARRY MARSHALL
HISTORIAN
b Nov 15, 39. *Study:* Dartmouth Col, AB, 64; Univ Oxford, BLitt, 66; Harvard Univ, PhD, 70. *Pos:* Bd dirs, Int Ctr Medieval Art, 77- *Teaching:* Asst prof art hist, Univ Calif, Santa Barbara, 70-74, assoc prof, 74-79, chmn, 76-, prof, 79- *Awards:* Alexander von Humboldt Stiftung Res Fel, 79-80; Am Philos Soc Grants, 81 & 82; Prix Rome Res Fel, Am Acad Rome, 83-84. *Mem:* Col Art Asn Am; Mediaeval Acad Am; Southern Calif Art Historians. *Res:* Medieval art; history of the book. *Publ:* Auth, Sources of the lyre drawings, Speculum, 74; auth, English Painting and the Continent, Eleanor of Aquitaine: Patron and Politician, 76; auth, Salzburg affiliations of a bible fragment in Vienna, Zeitschrift Kunstgeschichte, 82; auth, Parisian Bibles in Berlin Staatsbibliothek, Pantheon, 82; auth, Romanesque Manuscript Illumination, Braziller (in prep). *Mailing Add:* Dept Art History Univ Calif Santa Barbara CA 93106

AZACETA, LUIS CRUZ
PAINTER, INSTRUCTOR
b Marianao, Cuba, Apr 5, 42; US citizen. *Study:* Sch of Visual Arts, New York, with Leon Golub, Frank Roth & Michael Loew, cert, 69. *Work:* Cintas Found, Inst of Int Educ, New York; Harlem Art Col, Harlem State Off Bldg, New York; Mus Del Barrio, New York. *Exhib:* Crimes of Compassion, The Chrysler Mus, Norfolk, Va, 81; Inside/Outself Beyond Likeness, Newport Harbor Art Mus, Calif, 81; IV Bienal De Arte De Medellin, Colombia, South Am, 81; one-man shows, Allan Frumkin Gallery, Chicago, Ill, 78 & New York, 80, 82 & 84; Richard Nelson Gallery, Univ Calif, Davis; and many others. *Teaching:* Vis artist, Univ Calif, Davis, La State Univ, Baton Rouge & Univ Calif, Berkeley. *Awards:* Grants, Cintas Found, 72-73 & 75-76, Nat Endowment Arts, 80-81 & Creative Artists Pub Serv, 81-82. *Bibliog:* John

Arthur (auth), Realist Drawings & Watercolors, Contemp Am Works on Paper; J Martin (auth), article, Arts Mag, 82; Ross Skoggard (auth), article, Art in Am, 82. *Media:* Acrylic, Watercolor. *Dealer:* Allan Frumkin Gallery 50 W 57th St New York NY 10019. *Mailing Add:* 1729 Greene Ave Ridgewood NY 11385

AZARA, NANCY J
SCULPTOR, PAINTER
b New York, NY, Oct 13, 39. *Study:* Finch Col, AAS, 59; Art Students League, sculpture with John Hovannes, painting & drawing with Edwin Dickinson, 64-67; Empire State Col, BS(sculpture), 74. *Work:* Sculptors, sound film strip, Harcourt, Brace, Jovanovich. *Comn:* About the Goddess KALI (wood sculpture), Pamela Oline, S France, 77. *Exhib:* Kathryn Markel Gallery, 81; Tenth Anniversary Retrospective Show-Women Artists Series, Douglass Col, New Brunswick, NJ & AIR Gallery, New York, 81; Artists Books: A Survey 1960-1981, William Patterson Col, 82; Artists Books: From the Traditional to the Avant Garde, Douglass Col, 82; and many others. *Teaching:* Lectr art, Sch Contemp Studies, Brooklyn Col, 73-75, lectr sculpture, 75-76; instr sculpture, Brooklyn Mus Sch, 74-77; instr, Col New Rochelle, NY, 79-82; instr, founding mem & mem bd dirs, New York Feminist Art Inst, currently. *Bibliog:* Miriam Brymer (auth), Organic image: women's image, Feminist Art J, 73; Women of the 80's, Ms Mag, 1/80; Eleanor Munro (auth), Originals American Women Artists, Simon & Schuster, 79; and others. *Mem:* Art Students League; Womens Causus Art (adv bd, 80-83). *Media:* Wood, Oil; Paper, Paint. *Publ:* Auth, Artists in their own image, MS Mag, 73; auth, The Group, Amandala, Heresies Mag, spring 79; and others. *Mailing Add:* 46 Great Jones St New York NY 10012

AZUMA, NORIO
SERIGRAPHER, PAINTER
b Kii-Nagashima-cho, Japan, Nov 23, 28. *Study:* Kanazawa Art Col, Japan, BFA; Chouinard Art Inst, Los Angeles; Art Students League. *Work:* Nat Collection Fine Arts, Smithsonian Inst, Washington, DC; Whitney Mus Am Art, New York; Philadelphia Mus Art; Brooklyn Mus Art; Art Inst Chicago. *Comn:* 1500 serigraph prints, IBM Corp, NY, 66. *Exhib:* Corcoran Biennial, Washington, DC, 63; 3rd Int Triennial Original Graphic, Grenchen, Switz, 64; Mus Mod Art, Tokyo Exhib, 65; Sculpture & Prints, Whitney Mus Am Art, 66; Silkscreen, History of a Medium, Philadelphia Mus Art, 72. *Awards:* Int Print Show, Seattle Mus Art, 60; Print Exhib, Soc Am Graphic Artists, 68; Print Exhib, Boston Printmakers, 70. *Mem:* Soc Am Color Prints; Print Club; Soc Am Graphic Artists; Print Coun Am. *Media:* Oil. *Dealer:* AAA Gallery 663 Fifth Ave New York NY 10022; Azuma Gallery 142 Greene St New York NY 10012. *Mailing Add:* 276 Riverside Dr New York NY 10025

B

BACH, DIRK
PAINTER, EDUCATOR
b Grand Rapids, Mich, Nov 27, 39. *Study:* Univ Denver, BFA(painting), 61, MA(painting), 62; Univ Mich, Ann Arbor, MA(Orient art hist), 64. *Work:* Denver Art Mus, Colo; Hopkins Ctr Art Galleries, Dartmouth Col, Hanover, NH; Lamont Gallery, Phillips Exeter Acad, NH; Loretto-Hilton Gallery, Webster Col, St Louis, Mo; Mus Art, RI Sch Design, Providence. *Comn:* Wall reliefs, Denver Art Mus, 62, NH Comn Arts for NH Voc Inst, Berlin, 68 & Grad & Music Schs, Univ NH, 68; St Gaudens Nat Hist Site, Cornish, NH, 72. *Exhib:* New Eng Drawing Exhib, Addison Gallery, Andover, Mass, 70; New England Drawing Competition, DeCordova Mus, Lincoln, Mass, 74; Phillips-Exeter Acad, 67, 74 & 79; Newport Art Asn, RI, 76, 77-81; RI Sch of Design Mus of Art, Providence, 69-83; Seasons Gallery, Den Haag, Netherlands, 80-81; and many others. *Collections Arranged:* One Hundred Years of American Art, 66 & The Rose Art Museum Collection at New Hampshire (with catalog), 69, Scudder Gallery, Durham, NH. *Pos:* Dir, Scudder Gallery, Univ NH, 65-69; adv & contribr, Newport Rev, 79-; coun mem, Art Asn Newport, 80-83. *Teaching:* Asst prof painting, Univ NH, 65-69; assoc prof art hist, RI Sch Design, 69-, chmn art hist dept, 78-; assoc & lectr, Asian Studies, Brown Univ, 70-; dir, RI Sch Design, European Honors Program, Rome, 74-75. *Awards:* Univ NH Cent Univ Res Grant Commemorative Stamp Paintings, 68; Nat Endowment Humanities Travel & Res Grant, Japan, 71. *Mem:* Col Art Asn Am; Artists Equity Asn; Newport Art Asn; NH Art Asn. *Media:* Oil, Masonite. *Res:* Development of Ch'an painting in China; production of cosmic diagrams in the Far East. *Publ:* Contribr, The Painting of Tao Chi, Univ Mich Mus Art, 67; auth, The stamp collection of Dirk Bach, Ramparts, 11/68; auth, Selections From the Oriental Collections, RI Sch Design, 72. *Mailing Add:* 15 Walnut St Newport RI 02840

BACH, LAURENCE
PHOTOGRAPHER, EDUCATOR
b Philadelphia, Pa, Jan 2, 47. *Study:* Philadephia Col Art, BFA, 68; Allgemeine Gewerbeschule, Basel, Switz, grad, 70. *Work:* Philadelphia Mus Art; Mus Fine Arts, St Petersburg, Fla. *Exhib:* Three Centuries Am Art, Philadelphia Mus Art, 76; solo exhibs, Modernism Gallery, San Francisco, 79, Robert Samuel Gallery, New York, 81, Photo Ctr Athens, Greece, 82 & Wesleyan Univ, Conn, 83; Group Photographs, Inst Contemp Art, Philadelphia, 80; and others. *Teaching:* Asst prof photog & design, Moore Col Art, 70-72, Philadelphia Col Art, 72-74 & State Univ NY, Purchase, 74- *Awards:* Photog Grant, Nat Endowment Arts, 80; Photog Study Grant,

Polaroid Corp, 81; NY State Coun Arts Grant, Visual Studies Workshop, 82. *Bibliog:* William Stapp (auth), Three Centuries of American Art (exhib catalog), Philadelphia Mus, 76; Don Ernst (auth), Laurence Bach: Paros shards, Aperture, No 82, 2/79; Owen Edwards (auth), Laurence Bach portfolio, Am Photog, 9/81. *Publ:* Auth, The Paros Dream Book, Visual Studies Workshop Press, 83. *Dealer:* Laurence Miller Gallery 38 E 57th St New York NY. *Mailing Add:* 1622 S Broad St Philadelphia PA 19145

BACH, OTTO KARL
MUSEUM DIRECTOR, WRITER
b Chicago, Ill, May 26, 09. *Study:* Dartmouth Col; Univ Paris; Univ Chicago, MA; Univ Denver, hon DH, 55. *Pos:* Dir, Grand Rapids Art Gallery, 33-44; dir, Denver Art Mus, Colo, 44-74; originator, Living Arts Ctr Pilot Educ Progs, 59- *Awards:* Am Creativity Award, 61; Chevalier Arts & Lett, 69. *Mem:* Am Asn Mus. *Publ:* Auth, A new way to Paul Klee, 45, American heritage, 49, Under every roof, 50, Pre Columbian gold, 51 & Life in America; plus others. *Mailing Add:* 140 Krameria St Denver CO 80220

BACHARDY, DON
PAINTER, DRAFTSMAN
b Los Angeles, Calif, May 18, 34. *Study:* Chouinard Art Inst, 56-60; Slade Sch Art, London Univ, 61. *Work:* Metrop Mus Art, New York; Nat Portrait Gallery England, London; Princeton Univ; Fogg Art Mus; Univ Tex, Austin. *Exhib:* Solo exhib, De Young Mem Mus, 64, Los Angeles Munic Art Gallery, 73 & 83 & New York Cult Ctr, 74; Inside-Out: Self Beyond Likeness, Newport Harbor Art Mus, 81; Portland Art Mus, 81; Joslyn Art Mus, 81; Decade: Los Angeles Painting in the 70's, Art Ctr, Col Design, Pasadena, Calif, 81. *Bibliog:* Christopher Isherwood (auth), October, Twelvetrees Press, 80; One Hundred Drawings, Twelvetrees Press, 83. *Media:* Ink, Acrylic. *Publ:* Illusr, Michigan Quart Rev, Univ Mich, winter 80; illusr, Paris Rev, Vol 23, No 79, 81; illusr, Paris Rev, Vol 25, No 89, 83. *Dealer:* Robert Miller Gallery 724 Fifth Ave New York NY 10019; James Corcoran Gallery 8223 Santa Monica Blvd Los Angeles CA 90046. *Mailing Add:* 145 Adelaide Dr Santa Monica CA 90402

BACHERT, HILDEGARD GINA
DEALER
b Mannheim, Ger, Apr 3, 21; US citizen. *Study:* Hunter Col, BA(summa cum laude), 54. *Collections Arranged:* Grandma Moses (contribr, catalog), Nat Gallery Art, Washington, DC, 81; Alfred Kubin, 83; Paula Modersohn-Becker, 83. *Pos:* Secy & asst, Nierendorf Gallery, New York, 39-40; exec secy, Galerie St Etienne, New York, 40-78, co-dir, 78- *Mem:* Art Dealers Asn Am. *Specialty:* Early 20th century Austrian and German art: Schiele, Klimt, Kokoschka, Kollwitz & Corinth; 19th and 20th century naive art. *Publ:* Contribr, Otto Kallir's Egon Schiele: Oeuvre Catalog of the Paintings, 66 & contribr, Otto Kallir's Egon Schiele: The Graphic Work, 70, Zsolnay, Vienna & Crown; contribr, Otto Kallir's Grandma Moses, Crown & Harry N Abrams, 73, Ger transl, DuMont, Cologne, Ger, 79. *Mailing Add:* 290 West End Ave New York NY 10023

BACHINSKI, WALTER JOSEPH
SCULPTOR, DRAFTSMAN
b Ottawa, Ont, Aug 6, 39; Can citizen. *Study:* Ont Col Art, AOCA, 65; printmaking with Frederick Hagen; Univ Iowa, with Mauricio Lasansky, MA(printmaking), 67. *Work:* Montreal Mus Fine Arts, Que; Offizi Gallery, Florence, Italy; Can Coun Art Bank, Ottawa, Ont; Civic Mus, Lugano, Switz; Kitchener-Waterloo Art Gallery, Kitchener, Ont. *Comn:* Three bas-reliefs on a humanitarian theme, Univ Waterloo, Ont, 75; Seated Woman with Child (bas-relief), Kitchener Ct House, Ont, 77; Squatting Mother and Child (bronze relief), Health Sci Ctr, Mohawk Col, Hamilton, 80. *Exhib:* 9th Bienniele of Prints & Drawings, Lugano, Switz, 72; one-man exhibs, Mount St Vincent Univ, 73, Walter Bachinski: Sculpture and drawing, Art Gallery, Hamilton, 81; 4th Int Bienniele of Graphic Arts, Florence, Italy, 74; Bachinski, A Decade (travelling exhib), Kitchener-Waterloo Art Gallery, 76-77; and others. *Teaching:* Assoc prof drawing & printmaking, Dept Fine Arts, Univ Guelph, 67- *Awards:* Merit Prize, 1st Los Angeles Printmaking Soc Ann Exhib, Calif, 73; Premio dell Instituto Bancario Si Paolo di Torino, 4th Int Biennal of Graphic Art, Florence, Italy, 74; Can Coun Materials Grant, 78-79; and others. *Bibliog:* Marshall Webb (auth), article, Gallery Moos, Art Mag, 2-3/80; Kay Kritzwiser (auth), article, Art Gallery Hamilton, Globe & Mail, 4/81; and others. *Dealer:* Gallery Moos 148 Yorkville Ave Toronto ON Can. *Mailing Add:* 65 Mont St Guelph ON N1H 2A5 Canada

BACIGALUPA, ANDREA
DESIGNER, PAINTER
b Baltimore, Md, May 26, 23. *Study:* Art Students League, painting with Arnold Blanch, summer 49; Md Inst Fine Arts, BFA, 50, painting with Jacques Maroger; Accad de Belli Arti, Florence, Italy, PG, painting with Ottone Rosai, 50-51. *Comn:* Designer & consult, St Laurence Cathedral, Amarillo, Tex, 75; San Lorenzo (bronze), St Lawrence Cathedral, Amarillo, Tex, 77; conceptual design, Bishop De Falco Retreat Ctr, Amarillo, Tex, 82. *Exhib:* One-man show, Mus of NMex, 59; Am House, New York, 60; US Church Archit Guild, Pittsburgh, 61; Gov's Gallery, Sante Fe, NMex, 78; Cooper-Hewitt Mus, New York, 81. *Awards:* Bronze Medallion Fine Arts, Md Inst, 50; 1st Prize, Santa Fe Competition, Art in Pub Places, 79. *Bibliog:* Maurice Lavanoux (auth), Liturgy & art, Liturgical Arts, 73; Clifford Stevens (auth), Sacred arts, Out Sunday Visitor, 74. *Media:* Oil; Ceramics. *Publ:* Auth, Santos & Saints Days, Sunstone Press, 72; auth, The coffeebreak journal (Sunday column), Santa Fe New Mexican, 72-75; auth, Journal of an itinerant artist, Our Sunday Visitor, 77; auth, A Good and Perfect Gift, OSV, 78; auth, The Song of Guadalupana, OSV, 79. *Mailing Add:* 626 Canyon Rd Santa Fe NM 87501

BACKUS, STANDISH, JR
PAINTER, MURALIST
b Detroit, Mich, Apr 5, 10. *Study:* Princeton Univ, AB; Univ Munich. *Work:* Santa Barbara Mus Art; Utah State Col; San Diego Fine Arts Soc; Nat Watercolor Soc; Los Angeles Mus Art. *Comn:* Mural, Beckman Instruments, Inc, 55; mosaic mural, Pac War Mem, Corregidor Island, Manila Bay, Philippines, 67-68. *Exhib:* Los Angeles Mus Art, 38-40; Art Inst Chicago, Ill, 40; Detroit Inst Art; Denver Art Mus; one-man show, Santa Barbara Mus Art; and others. *Pos:* Naval combat artist, Pac area & Japan, 45; off Navy artist, Byrd Exped to South Pole, 55-56. *Awards:* Prizes, Oakland Art Gallery, 39, Calif Watercolor Soc, 40 & Calif State Fair, 48 & 49. *Mem:* Nat Watercolor Soc; Am Fedn Arts; fel Int Inst Arts & Lett; Am Watercolor Soc; Los Angeles Art Asn; and others. *Mailing Add:* 2626 Sycamore Canyon Rd Montecito Santa Barbara CA 93108

BACON, PEGGY
PAINTER, WRITER
b Ridgefield, Conn, May 2, 1895. *Study:* NY Sch Fine & Appl Art; Art Students League. *Work:* Metrop Mus Art, Whitney Mus Am Art, Mus Mod Art, New York; Brooklyn Mus; and others. *Exhib:* One-man shows, Nasson Col, Maine, 71 & Mus of Art, Ogonquit, Maine, 73; retrospective exhib, Nat Collection Fine Arts, Smithsonian Inst, Washington, DC, 75; and others. *Awards:* Guggenheim Fel, 34; Nat Acad Arts & Lett Award, 44; Butler Inst Am Artists Prize, 55. *Mem:* Nat Acad Design; Soc Am Graphic Artists; Nat Inst Arts & Lett. *Publ:* Auth, The Inward Eye, 52; auth & illusr, Good American Witch, Hale, 57; auth, Ghost of Opalina, 57 & auth & illusr, Magic Touch, 68, Little; auth, Oddity, Pantheon, 62; also illusr over 60 bks. *Mailing Add:* c/o Kraushaar Galleries 724 Fifth Ave New York NY 10021

BACOT, HENRY PARROTT
HISTORIAN
b Shreveport, La, Dec 13, 41. *Study:* Baylor Univ, Waco, Tex, BA, 63; La State Univ, Baton Rouge, 64-65; Attingham Park Summer Sch Study Great English Country Houses, Shropshire, fel, 66; State Univ NY Cooperstown, MA(Scriven Found Fel, Cooperstown Grad Progs), 67. *Collections Arranged:* American Folk Art 1730-1968, 68; Southern Furniture & Silver: The Federal Period 1788-1830, 68; Louisiana Landscape 1800-1969, 69; Natchez-Made Silver of the 19th Century, 70; Sail & Steam in Louisiana Waters, 71; Louisiana Folk Art, 72; Crescent City Silver, 80. *Pos:* Dir, Anglo-Am Art Mus, Baton Rouge, 67-; hist interiors consult, Kings' Tavern, Natchez, Miss, 71-, Kent Plantation House, Alexandria, La, 71- & Magnolia Mound Plantation House, Baton Rouge, 72-; sponsor, Am Friends of Attingham Summer Sch, 77- *Teaching:* Asst prof art hist, La State Univ, 67-, asst prof hist of interior design, 73. *Mem:* Soc Archit Historians; Am Victorian Soc; Found Hist La (bd mem, 72-74). *Res:* Fine arts, architecture and decorative arts of the Deep South. *Publ:* Contribr, Antiques, 67-79; contribr, Antiques Monthly, 68-77; co-auth, Nineteenth century Natchez-made silver, Antiques, 71; contribr, Soc Archit Historians J, 74. *Mailing Add:* PO Box 20249 La State Univ Baton Rouge LA 70803

BACZEK, PETER GERARD
PRINTMAKER
b Webster, Mass, June 6, 45. *Study:* San Jose State Univ, BA(art), 70. *Work:* Achenbach Found Graphic Arts, Calif Palace Legion Hon, San Francisco; Brooklyn Mus; Philadelphia Mus Art; Metrop Mus Art Ctr, Coral Gables, Fla; Cooper-Hewitt Mus, New York. *Exhib:* 21st Nat Print Exhib, Brooklyn Mus, 79; Eighth Int Print Biennial, Crakow, Poland, 80; Boston Printmakers 33rd Nat Exhib, Boston Ctr Arts, 81; 25th Nat Exhib Am Art, Chautauqua Inst, NY, 82; Prints: USA, Pratt Graphics Ctr, New York, 82; Subjective Realities, Calif Palace Legion Hon, San Francisco, 82; Urban Documents: 20th Century American Prints, Cooper-Hewitt Mus, New York, 83; Rockford Int, Rockford Col, 83. *Awards:* Award of Merit, Miami Int Print Biennial, Metrop Mus, Coral Gables, Fla, 82; Patron Award, 57th Ann Int Competition, Print Club, Philadelphia, 82. *Bibliog:* Roberta Loach (auth), Book of Hours: A Portfolio of 21 Prints, Visual Dialog, 79; Julie van der Ryn (auth), Shadows and patterns in the everyday, City Arts Monthly Mag, 81; Robert Johnson (auth), Subjective Realities (catalog), Fine Arts Mus San Francisco, 82. *Mem:* Calif Soc Printmakers (vpres, 80, pres, 81); The Print Club; Los Angeles Printmaking Soc. *Media:* Etchings, Monotypes. *Dealer:* Assoc Am Artists 20 W 57th St New York NY 10019. *Mailing Add:* 2433 Scenic Ave Oakland CA 94602

BADALAMENTI, FRED
PAINTER, EDUCATOR
b Long Island, NY, June 25, 35. *Study:* Pratt Inst, 53-55; State Univ NY Col, New Paltz, BS, 60; Brooklyn Col, MFA(fel), 67; studied with Philip Pearlstein, Carl Holty & Burgoyne Diller. *Exhib:* One-person exhibs, Art Vane Ltd, Setauket, NY, 70; Islip Art Gallery, Suffolk Community Col, New York, 71 & First St Gallery, New York, 76 & 80; two-person exhib, First St Gallery, 73; Brooklyn College Art Department Past & Present, Robert Schoelkopf Gallery, NY, 77; Leopold Hoesch Mus, Duren, Ger, 80; and others. *Pos:* Dir, First St Gallery, 78. *Teaching:* Assoc prof drawing & painting, Brooklyn Col, 67-; dept chmn grad art, 72-; vis assoc prof drawing & painting, State Univ NY, Stony Brook, 77-78 & summers 80, 81 & 83. *Mem:* Col Art Asn; Am Asn Univ Prof; Am Asn Artist-Run Galleries. *Mailing Add:* 182 Lower Sheep Pasture Rd Setauket NY 11733

BADASH, SANDI BORR
PAINTER, FABRIC DESIGNER
b Hartford, Conn, Mar 2, 36. *Study:* Lesley Col, BS(educ); Southern Conn State Col, painting with Howard Fusner & Paul Tedeshi, MS(art educ); Paer

Sch Art, Yale Univ, with Dean Keller. *Exhib:* Denver Mus Art Summer Exhib, 70; Woburn Abbey Show, England, 70; one-man shows, Art Wagon Galleries, Scottsdale, Ariz, 74, William Sparrow Gallery, Montecito, Calif, 75 & 77, Lynn Kottler Gallery, New York, 78 & Rauschbach Gallery, Boca Raton, Fla, 84. *Teaching:* Drawing & crafts, Santa Barbara High Sch, 67-69; art supvr, Univ Calif, Santa Barbara, 73-74. *Mem:* Santa Barbara Art Asn (bd trustees, 71-72); Int Art Guild, Santa Barbara (art dir, 73-74). *Media:* Oil. *Dealer:* Rauschback Gallery Boca Raton FL; Ellie Page Cynelle Santa Barbara CA 93101. *Mailing Add:* 601 E Anapamo St Apt 325 Santa Barbara CA 93103

BADER, FRANZ
DEALER, PHOTOGRAPHER
b Vienna, Austria, Sept 19, 03; US citizen. *Study:* Univ Vienna. *Work:* Air & Space Mus, Washington, DC; Phillips Collection, Washington, DC; Cheekwood, Nashville, Tenn; Watkins Gallery, Am Univ, Washington, DC; Corcoran Gallery Art. *Exhib:* Corcoran Gallery Art, Washington, DC, 73; Nat Acad Sci, 75; one-man show, Phillips Collection, 77, Cheekwood, Nashville, Tenn, 80 & Watkins Gallery, Am Univ, Washington, DC, 81. *Pos:* Owner, Wallishaussersche Bookshop, Vienna, 39; vpres & gen mgr, Whyte Gallery, Washington, DC, 39-52; pres, Franz Bader Gallery, Washington, DC, 52- *Awards:* Goldene Ehrenzeichen Verdienste, Austria; Verdienstkreuz Erster Klasse, Germany; Mayor's Art Award, Washington, DC, 81. *Specialty:* Contemporary American art; Washington artists; original graphics; Can Eskimo art. *Collection:* Original graphics; contemporary artists and sculpture. *Mailing Add:* 2001 Eye St NW Washington DC 20006

BAEDER, JOHN
PAINTER
b South Bend, Ind, Dec 24, 38. *Study:* Auburn Univ, Ala, AB, 60. *Work:* Denver Art Mus; Whitney Mus of Am Art; Mus Mod Art Lending Serv; Cooper-Hewitt Mus; High Mus, Atlanta; and others. *Exhib:* Place, Product, Package, Cooper-Hewitt Mus, Smithsonian Inst, New York, 78; Kunstgewerbemuseum, Zurich, Switzerland, 79; Danforth Mus, Framington, Mass, 80; Philbrook Art Ctr, Tulsa, Okla, 80; Real, Really Real, Super Real, San Antonio Mus, 81; Contemp American Realism Since 1960, Pa Acad Fine Arts, 81; Painting New York, Mus City New York, 83-84; and others. *Bibliog:* Gregory Battcock (auth), Super Realism, Dutton, 75; D Filipacchi (auth), Les Hyper Realists Americans. *Media:* Lithography, Oil. *Publ:* Auth, Diners, Harry N Abrams, Inc, New York, 78; auth, Gas, Food and Lodging, Abbeville Press, 82. *Dealer:* O K Harris 383 W Broadway New York NY 10012. *Mailing Add:* 1025 Overton Lea Rd Nashville TN 37204

BAER, JO
PAINTER, WRITER
b Seattle, Wash, Aug 7, 29. *Study:* Univ Wash; Grad Fac, New Sch Social Res. *Work:* Mus Mod Art & Guggenheim Mus, New York; Kolnischer Kunstverein, Koln, WGer; Albright-Knox Art Gallery, Buffalo, NY; Nat Mus, Canberra, Australia. *Exhib:* Systematic Paintings, Guggenheim Mus, 66; Whitney Mus Am Art Biennial, New York, 67, 69, 73 & 75 & solo show, 75; Documenta IV, Mus Friedericianum, Kassel, Ger, 68; 31st Biennial, Corcoran Gallery Art, Washington, DC, 69; Options and Alternatives, Yale Univ, 73; one-person show, Mus Mod Art, Oxford, Eng, 77; Ft Worth Mus, Tex, 77; Indianapolis Mus, Ind, 77; Chicago Art Inst, 77. *Teaching:* Instr painting, Sch Visual Arts, New York, 69-70. *Awards:* Nat Coun Arts Award, 68 69. *Bibliog:* P Schjeldahl (auth), Jo Baer: Playing on the senses, New York Times, 5/14/72; C Ratcliff (auth), Jo Baer: Notes on 5 recent paintings, Artforum, 5/72; L R Lippard (auth), Color at the edge, Art News, 5/72. *Media:* Oil. *Publ:* Auth, Edward Kienholz: A sentimental journeyman, Art Int, 4/68; auth, Mach bands: Art & vision & Xerography & edge-effects (collateral essay), Aspen Mag, fall-winter 70; contribr, Symposium on art & politics, Artforum, 9/70; auth, Fluorescent light culture, Am Orchid Soc Bull, 9-10/71. *Dealer:* John Weber Gallery 420 W Broadway New York NY 10012. *Mailing Add:* Smarmore Castle Ardee Co Louth Ireland United Kingdom

BAER, MORLEY
PHOTOGRAPHER
b Toledo, Ohio, Apr 5, 16. *Study:* Univ Mich, MA, 37. *Work:* San Francisco Mus Art & DeYoung Mus, Calif; Amon Carter Mus, Ft Worth, Tex. *Teaching:* Photog, Ansel Adams June Workshop, Yosemite, 70- & Univ Calif Exten, 72- *Awards:* Medal Photog, Am Inst Architects, 65; Fel, Am Acad, Rome, Italy, 80. *Mem:* Friends of Photog, Carmel, Calif (trustee, 72-). *Dealer:* Photography West Box 4829 Carmel CA 93921. *Mailing Add:* PO Box 2228 Monterey CA 93940

BAER, NORBERT SEBASTIAN
EDUCATOR
b Brooklyn, NY, June 6, 38. *Study:* Brooklyn Col, BSc(chemistry), 59; Univ Wis, MSc(physical chemistry), 62; NY Univ, PhD(physical chemistry), 69. *Pos:* Ed adv & assoc ed, Studies in Conservation, J Int Inst for Conserv, 71-; co-chmn, Conserv Ctr, Inst Fine Arts, NY Univ, 75-83, actg dir admin, 78-79; assoc ed, Restaurator, 75-; US exec ed, Conservation in the Arts, Archaeology and Architecture, Butterworths, 79-; chmn, Advisory Comt on Preservation, Nat Archives & Records Service, 80-; chmn, Comt Conservation Historic Store Bldgs & Monuments, Nat Materials Advisory Bd, Nat Acad Sci, 80-82; mem, Vis Comt Dept Objects Conservation, Metrop Mus Art, 80- *Teaching:* Prof conserv, Inst Fine Arts, NY Univ, 69- *Awards:* Guggenheim Fel, 83-84. *Mem:* Fel Int Inst Conserv; fel Am Inst Conserv (bd dir, 73-76); fel Am Inst Chemists; Am Chemical Soc; Sigma Xi. *Res:* Application of physico-chemical techniques to the preservation and examination of artistic and historic works.

Publ: Coauth, Chemical Investigations on Ancient Near Eastern Archaeological Ivory Artifacts: III, Fluorine & Nitrogen Composition & Chemical Aspects of the Conservation of Archaelological Materials, Archaeological Chemistry II, Advances in Chemistry, 78; coauth, Synthetic Blue Pigments: IX-XVI Centuries, I, Literature, Studies in Conservation, 80; coauth, Mechanisms of air pollution-induced damage to stone, Sixth World Congress Air Quality, Paris, Vol 3, 83; and others. *Mailing Add:* One E 78th St New York NY 10021

BAGERIS, JOHN
PAINTER, INSTRUCTOR
b Fremont, Ohio, May 11, 24. *Study:* Art Inst Chicago, BFA, 50, MFA, 52. *Work:* Mus Mod Art & Whitney Mus Am Art, New York; Brooklyn Mus, NY; Wadsworth Atheneum, Hartford, Conn; Newark Art Mus, NJ. *Teaching:* Instr painting, Sch Visual Arts, New York, 61-72; instr painting, Art Inst Boston, Mass, 73-, chmn, Dept Fine Arts, 78- *Mailing Add:* 377 Walden St Cambridge MA 02138

BAGGETT, WILLIAM CARTER, JR
EDUCATOR, PAINTER
b Montgomery, Ala, Jan 12, 46. *Study:* Auburn Univ, BFA, 68, MFA, 73. *Work:* US Info Agency Embassy Collections, worldwide; Auburn Univ; Montgomery Mus Fine Arts, Ala; Univ Miss Mus, Oxford. *Comn:* Portrait William Faulkner, Univ Miss, Oxford, 77; multicolor lithographs, Vision Nouvelle, Paris, 80 & Nahan Ed, New Orleans, 81; portrait T K Mattingly & H M Hartsfield, Auburn Univ, 82. *Exhib:* New Orleans Biennial, New Orleans Mus Art, 73; 107th Ann Exhib Am Watercolor Soc, Nat Acad Design, New York, 74; Rocky Mountain Nat Watermedia Exhib, Foothills Art Ctr, Golden, Colo, 74. *Teaching:* Asst prof design, Univ Miss, 73-76; assoc prof visual communications, Auburn Univ, 76-83; prof & chmn dept art, Univ Southern Miss, 83- *Awards:* Jurors Best in Show, Tenth Dixie Ann Exhib, Montgomery Mus Art, 69. *Media:* Egg Tempera, Watercolor. *Dealer:* Kenneth Nahan 540 Royal St New Orleans LA 70130. *Mailing Add:* 605 Shady Lane Lake Serene Hattiesburg MS 39401

BAILEY, CLAYTON GEORGE
SCULPTOR, EDUCATOR
b Antigo, Wis, Mar 9, 39. *Study:* Univ Wis-Madison, BA, 61, MS, 62. *Work:* US Info Agency, Dept State; Mus Contemp Crafts, New York; Addison Gallery Am Art, Andover, Mass; Milwaukee Art Ctr; Hokkoku Shinbun, Korinbo, Japan. *Comn:* Exec Teapot, Kohler Co, Kohler, Wis, 79. *Exhib:* One-man shows, ceramics, Milwaukee Art Ctr, 61 & Mus Contemp Crafts, New York, 63; M H De Young Mus, San Francisco, 75; State Mus Alaska, Anchorage, 80; Triton Mus, Santa Clara, Calif, 81; and others. *Pos:* Cur Kaolithic Curiosities, Wonders World Mus, Port Costa, Calif, 71-76; artist-in-residence, Kohler Co, Sheboygan, Wis, 79. *Teaching:* Artist-in-residence ceramics, Wis State Univ, Whitewater, 64-67; prof ceramics, Calif State Univ, Hayward, 68-, chmn art dept, 79-81. *Awards:* Artists Grants, Louis Comfort Tiffany Found, 63, Am Craftsmen Coun, 63 & Nat Endowment Arts, 79; and others. *Bibliog:* With These Hands (film), Johnson Found, 70; Garth Clark (auth), A Century of American Ceramics, 79 & Julie Hall (auth), Tradition and Change, 79, Dutton; Jasin Reichardt (auth), Robots, Thames & Hudson, 79. *Mem:* Hon fel Nat Coun for Educ in Ceramic Arts (dir at large, 78-80). *Media:* Ceramic, Metal. *Publ:* Coauth, My father is a sculptor, Jack & Jill Mag, 70; auth, Wonders of the World Catalog of Kaolithic Curiosities, Artist, 75; auth, How to make a robot, Cinemagic Mag, 80; auth, Robot Builders Manual, Artist, 81. *Mailing Add:* Wonders of the World PO Box 69 Port Costa CA 94569

BAILEY, MARCIA MEAD
PAINTER
b Hartford, Conn, Jan 10, 47. *Study:* Self-taught. *Exhib:* Henry Ward Ranger Ann Exhib, Nat Acad Design, New York, 80; 39th-41st Ann, Audubon Artists, New York, 81-83; 68th-69th Ann, Allied Artists Am, New York, 81 & 82. *Awards:* S J Wallace Truman Prize, Nat Acad Design, New York, 80; Binney and Smith Liquitex Award, Audubon Artists, New York, 81; Gold Medal Honor, Allied Artists Am, 81. *Mem:* Audubon Artists; Allied Artists Am. *Media:* Oil. *Dealer:* Arts Exclusive Inc 6 Hartford Rd Simsbury CT 06070. *Mailing Add:* 189 Wickham Rd Glastonbury CT 06033

BAILEY, OSCAR
PHOTOGRAPHER, EDUCATOR
b Barnesville, Ohio, July 23, 25. *Study:* Wilmington Col, Ohio, BA; Ohio Univ, Athens, MFA. *Work:* Int Mus Photog, George Eastman House, Rochester, NY; Hist of Photog Collection, Smithsonian Inst, Washington, DC; New Orleans Mus Art, La; Mus Fine Arts, St Petersburg, Fla; Boston Mus Fine Arts. *Exhib:* The Sense of Abstraction in Contemp Photog, Mus Mod Art, New York, 60; Photog USA, De Cordova Mus, Lincoln, Mass & George Eastman House, Rochester, NY, 62; Photog in Fine Arts, Metrop Mus Art, New York, 63 & 76; Four Directions in Photog, Albright-Knox Art Gallery, Buffalo, NY, 64; Photog in the 20th Century, Nat Gallery of Can, Ottawa, 67; Wider View, Int Mus Photog, George Eastman House, 72; Light & Lens, Hudson River Mus, Yonkers, NY, 73; Time & Transformation, Lowe Art Mus, Univ Miami, Fla, 75; Photo/Synthesis, Cornell Univ, Ithaca, NY, 76; The Contemporary American South Traveling Exhib, US Info Agency, SE Asia & Europe, 77; Extended Frame Traveling Exhib, Visual Studies Workshop, Rochester, 78. *Pos:* Artist-in-residence, Artpark, Lewiston, NY, summer 77. *Teaching:* Prof photog, State Univ NY, Buffalo, 58-69 & Univ SFla, Tampa, 69- *Awards:* Photog Fel Grant, Nat Endowment Arts, 76. *Bibliog:* John Canaday (auth), New Talent--1960, Art in Am, 60; J Kirk T Varneodoe (ed), Modern Portraits--The Self & Others, Columbia Univ, 76.

Mem: Founding mem Soc Photog Educ. *Publ:* Coauth, Found Objects, State Univ NY, Buffalo, 65; ed, Silver Bullets, Dept Photog, Univ SFla, 72; contribr, Marcel DuChamp, Mus Mod Art, 73. *Mailing Add:* 2004 Clement Rd Lutz FL 33549

BAILEY, RICHARD H
SCULPTOR
b Dover, Del, June 24, 40. *Study:* Del Art Ctr, Wilmington; Art Students League; New Sch Social Res; study in Carrara, Italy; also with Jose DeCreeft, Lorrie Goulet, Leroy Smith & Oya Eraybar. *Work:* Am Mus Natural Hist, New York; Univ Del. *Exhib:* Silvermine Guild Artists, New Canaan, Conn; Int Exhib Sculpture, Carrara, Italy; Greer Gallery; one-man show, Del Art Mus, 74 & 84; Randall Galleries, New York, 75. *Awards:* Founders Award, Rehoboth Art League, Del, 71 & 75; Silvermine Guild Award Sculpture, 72 & 73. *Mailing Add:* RD 1 Box 51 Smyrna DE 19977

BAILEY, WALTER ALEXANDER
PAINTER, WRITER
b Wallula, Kans. *Study:* Kansas City Art Inst, Mo; Bus Col, Leavenworth, Kans; Fr Inst Lett, dipl; and with John Douglas Patrick, Anthony Angarola, Charles A Wilimovsky, Randall Davey, Ross Braught, Thomas Hart Benton & Leon Gaspard. *Work:* Springfield Pub Libr, Mass; Kansas City Pub Libr, Mo. *Comn:* Watercolor sketches, Univ Kans, Lawrence, 27 & Univ Tex, Austin, 28; two murals, William Rockhill Nelson Gallery Art, Kansas City, Mo, 35; four murals, Munic Auditorium Music Hall, Kansas City, 36. *Exhib:* Louis Comfort Tiffany Guild Exhibs, Anderson Galleries, New York, 26, 27 & 29; Midwestern Art Exhib Ann, Kansas City Art Inst; one-man show, Mexico City, 30; 13th Ann WCoast Paintings Exhib, Charles & Emma Frye Mus, Seattle, Wash, 67; All-City Outdoor Art Festival, Los Angeles, Calif, 68. *Pos:* Ed art dir, Kansas City Times, 17-27; contribr, Kansas City Star & Art Dig, 27-28; motion picture story-bd artist, educ films, Douglas Aircraft Co, Santa Monica, Calif, 41-42; scenic artist, motion picture studios, Hollywood, Calif, 43-44; contribr, Hearst Publ, 50-61; night art dir, Los Angeles Examiner, Calif, 50-61; art ed, Los Angeles Herald-Examiner, 62-67; writer, South Pasadena Rev, Calif, 72-79. *Teaching:* Instr, Master Class, Taos, NMex, 27-29, Master Class, Kansas City, Mo, 32-34 & Kansas City Art Inst, 38-39. *Awards:* Louis Comfort Tiffany Found Fel, 24; Am Inst Fine Arts Fel, 65; Jose Drudis Found Fel, 66. *Bibliog:* Sally Sooner (auth), article in Daily Sun Okla, Oklahoma City, 11/23/30; Allen Charles (auth), article in Art Dig, 36; Howard Burke (auth), article in Los Angeles Examr, 12/11/59. *Mem:* Am Inst Fine Arts (pres, 67-68); Calif Art Club (dir, 63 & 66-67); Valley Artists' Guild (vpres & dir, 62-64); Artists of the Southwest, Inc (dir, 68-78). *Media:* Oil, Acrylic. *Mailing Add:* 1417 12th Ave Los Angeles CA 90019

BAILEY, WILLIAM
PAINTER, EDUCATOR
b Council Bluffs, Iowa, Nov 17, 30. *Study:* Yale Univ, BFA(Alice Kimball English Traveling Fel), 55, MFA, 57; with Josef Albers. *Work:* St Louis Mus Art; Whitney Mus Am Art, New York; Pa Acad of Fine Arts, Philadelphia; Joseph Hirshhorn Mus; plus others. *Exhib:* One-man shows, Kansas City Art Inst, Mo, 67, Robert Schoelkopf Gallery, New York, 68, 71, 74 & 79 & Galerie Claude Bernard, Paris, 78; Twenty-two Realists, Whitney Mus Am Art, New York, 70; William Patterson Col, NJ, 78; Galleria Ilgabbiano, Rome, 80. *Teaching:* Prof fine arts, Ind Univ, 62-69; prof art, Yale Univ, 69-78, Kingman Brewster Prof, 78-, dean sch art, 74-75. *Awards:* First Prize Painting, Boston Arts Festival, 57; Guggenheim Found Fel Painting, 65; Isram Merrill Found Grant, 79-80. *Bibliog:* Jerrold Lanes (auth), Problems of representation--are we asking the right question?, Artforum, 1/72; Robert Hughes (auth), The realist as corn god, Time Mag, 1/31/72; John Groen (auth), William Bailey: Mastery and mystery, Art News, 11/79. *Media:* Oil. *Dealer:* Robert Schoelkopf 825 Madison Ave New York NY 10021. *Mailing Add:* 223 E Tenth St New York NY 10003

BAILIN, HELLA
PAINTER
b Dusseldorf, Ger, Oct 17, 15; US citizen. *Study:* Berlin Acad, 34, Reimann Sch, Berlin, 36, Newark Sch Fine & Indust Arts, 47 & 52-56. *Work:* Washington Sch Psychiatry, Washington, DC; Temple Beth Ahm, Springfield, NJ; and others. *Comn:* Painting & mural, Marshall Sch, South Orange, NJ, 63; murals, Mennen Prod, Morristown, NJ, 63 & Consol Gas Co, Metuchen, NJ, 63. *Exhib:* Nat Acad Design; Trenton Mus; Newark Mus; Jersey City Mus. *Pos:* Pvt instr & demonstr watercolor, portraits & figure painting. *Awards:* Ted Kautzky Award, Am Watercolor Soc, 70; David Wuject-Key Mem Prize, Allied Artists Am, 72; Marion de Sola Mendes Award, Nat Soc Painters in Casein & Acrylic, 73. *Mem:* Am & NJ Watercolor Socs; Allied Artists Am; Assoc Artists NJ; Portraits, Inc; and others. *Mailing Add:* 829 Bishop St Union NJ 07083

BAIRD, JOSEPH ARMSTRONG, JR
WRITER, DEALER
b Pittsburgh, Pa, Nov 22, 22. *Study:* Oberlin Col, BA(magna cum laude), 44; Harvard Univ, MA, 47, PhD, 51. *Collections Arranged:* Numerous exhib, Calif Hist Soc, San Francisco, 62-63, 67-70 & Univ Calif, Davis, 53- *Pos:* Cur, Calif Hist Soc, 62-63; art consult, 67-70; cataloguer, Robert B Honeyman, Jr Collection, Bancroft Libr, Univ Calif, Berkeley, 64-65; owner, North Point Gallery, San Francisco. *Teaching:* Instr art hist, Univ Toronto, 49-53; from instr to prof, Univ Calif, Davis, 53-68 & currently. *Awards:* Calif Hist Soc Merit Award, 62. *Mem:* Am Fedn Arts; Nat Trust Hist Preserv; Soc Archit Historians. *Res:* Latin American architecture; California architecture, painting and graphic arts. *Collection:* Urban art and life in the 19th and 20th centuries. *Publ:* Auth, Catalogue of the original paintings, drawings and water

colors in the Robert B Honeyman, Jr Collection, Bancroft Libr, Univ Calif, Berkeley, 66; California's pictorial letter sheets, David Magee, 67; Historic Lithographs of San Francisco, 72; The West Remembered, Calif Hist, 73; Wine and the Artist, Dover, 79. *Mailing Add:* 1830 Mountain View Dr Tiburon CA 94920

BAITSELL, WILMA WILLIAMSON
ADMINISTRATOR, CRAFTSMAN
b Palmyra, NY, July 5, 18. *Study:* State Univ NY Col Oswego, BSE & MSE; Syracuse Univ, art teaching cert; Western State Univ, Colo, with Josef Albers, Al Litchenson & Tom Seawell. *Work:* Sydney Teacher's Col, Newton, Australia; Yamaguchi Univ, Japan. *Pos:* Art supvr, Phoenix Cent Sch, Phoenix, NY, 60-71; art consult, NY State Dept Educ, summers, 68-70. *Teaching:* Asst prof, State Univ NY Col Oswego, 71-78, art supvr, Swetman Learning Ctr, 71-78. *Awards:* First Prize Acrylic Painting, Midstates Arts & Crafts Show. *Bibliog:* John Ritson & James Smith (auth), Creative Teaching of Art in the Elementary School, Allyn & Bacon, 75. *Mem:* Int Soc Educ Art; Nat Weaver's Asn; Nat Art Educ Asn; NY State Art Teacher's Asn; Oswego Art Guild. *Media:* Acrylic. *Publ:* Auth, Grow a tiny garden, Workbasket, 56; auth, Relationship of intelligence to art, 58 & auth, Relationship of intelligence to art, Brazil, 69, South Am Teachers; auth, Crafts for Campers, Maine Campers Asn, 73; auth, Mary's lamb comes to school, Search Mag, 76. *Mailing Add:* Rd 4 Box 330 Oswego NY 13126

BAKANOWSKY, LOUIS J
ENVIRONMENTAL ARTIST, ARCHITECT
b Norwich, Conn, Oct 8, 30. *Work:* Harvard Univ; Syracuse Univ; Trinity Col. *Comn:* Mem structure, Brunswick, Maine, 73. *Exhib:* View, 60 & Selection, 61, Inst Contemp Art, Boston, Mass; one-man show, Siembab Gallery, Boston, 60; Sculpture, DeCordova Mus, Lincoln, Mass, 64; New England Art Today, Boston, 65; Immanent Domains, Boston, New York & Philadelphia, 77. *Pos:* Archit, Cambridge Seven Assocs, Inc, 62- *Teaching:* Asst prof design, Cornell Univ, 61-62; prof design, Grad Sch Design, Harvard Univ, 63-81, prof & chmn, Dept Visual & Environ Studies, 72- *Awards:* Sculpture Prizes, Boston Arts Festival, 58 & Providence Art Festival, 59. *Bibliog:* Sculpture of Louis J Bakanowsky, Connection Mag, 61; article, Kenchiku Bunka Mag, 71. *Media:* Mixed. *Mailing Add:* 6 Parker St Lexington MA 02173

BAKATY, MIKE
PAINTER, SCULPTOR
b Trenton, NJ, Aug 19, 36. *Study:* Miami-Dade Jr Col, Fla, AA, 64; Fla Atlantic Univ, BA, 65; Univ Ore, MFA, 69. *Work:* Colo State Univ, Ft Collins; Miami-Dade Community Col. *Comn:* Outdoor monument, Colo State Univ, 75. *Exhib:* Mike Bakaty, Paley & Lowe Inc, New York, 71-72; Painting & Sculpture Today, 1972, Indianapolis Mus Art, 72; NY Artists, Baltimore Mus Art, Md, 72; Here Comes Tomorrow, Owen Corning Fiberglass Bldg, New York, 73; Mellon Art Ctr, Wallingford, Conn, 74; Am Inst Archit, 74 & Henri Gallery, 74, Washington, DC; and many others. *Teaching:* Adj asst prof art, NY Univ, 71-74; asst prof painting, Fla Int Univ, Miami, 73; adj lectr sculpture, Fiorello LaGuardia Community Col, City Univ New York, 73-78, asst prof, 78-82. *Awards:* State-wide Touring Exhib, State of Fla, 66; Award for Sculpture, Ft Lauderdale Mus Arts, 66. *Bibliog:* Julia Busch (auth), A Decade of Sculpture, Assoc Univ Press, 74; Thelma Newman (auth), Plastics as Sculpture, Chilton Bks, 74; Marcia Tucker (auth), Tatoo, state of the art, Artforum, 5/81. *Media:* Fiberglass; Graphite. *Mailing Add:* 295 Bowery New York NY 10003

BAKER, DINA GUSTIN
PAINTER
b Philadelphia, Pa, Nov 7, 24. *Study:* Philadelphia Col Mus Sch Fine Art; Barnes Found, Merion, Pa, with Dr Albert C Barnes & Violet DeMazia; Temple Univ Tyler Sch Fine Art, Philadelphia; Art Students League; Atelier 17, New York. *Work:* NY Univ; Barnes Found; Philadelphia Art Mus; Butler Mus Am Art, Youngstown, Ohio. *Exhib:* One-man shows, Roko Gallery, New York, 51 & 58, Angeleski Gallery, New York, 61, Southampton East Gallery, Long Island & New York, 65, Amerika House, Hamburg, Munich & Regensburg, Ger, 74 & Ingber Gallery, New York, 76 & 78; Nat Biennial, Pa Acad Fine Arts, Philadelphia; and many others. *Teaching:* Instr, Henry St Settlement, 54-55; dir pvt art classes, New York, 60-63. *Awards:* Barnes Found Award, 42-45; Art Students League Award, 46-47; Edward MacDowell Fel, 59. *Bibliog:* Allen Ellenzweig (auth), article, Arts Mag, 9/76. *Mem:* Women in the Arts. *Media:* Oil, Acrylic. *Dealer:* Ingber Gallery 3 E 78th St New York NY 11004. *Mailing Add:* 88 Eisenhower Dr Cresskill NJ 07626

BAKER, ELIZABETH C
EDITOR, CRITIC
b Boston, Mass. *Study:* Bryn Mawr Col, BA, 56; Radcliffe Col, MA, 58. *Pos:* From assoc ed to managing ed, Art News, 63-73; ed, Art in Am, 73- *Teaching:* Instr art hist, Boston Univ, 58-59; Wheaton Col, Norton, Mass, 60-61 & Sch of Visual Arts, New York, 68-74. *Mailing Add:* c/o Art in America 850 Third Ave New York NY 10022

BAKER, GEORGE
EDUCATOR, KINETIC ARTIST
b Corsicana, Tex, Jan 23, 31. *Study:* Col Wooster; Occidental Col, BA; Univ Southern Calif, MFA. *Work:* Mus Mod Art & Mus Am Art, New York; Mus 20th Century Art, Vienna, Austria; Forest of Sculptures, Hakone, Japan; San Diego State Col, Calif. *Comn:* Kinetic fountain, Int Sculptors Symposium, Osaka Worlds Fair, 70; kinetic hanging sculpture, comn by State Calif for San Diego State Col, 72; kinetic sculpture, Nebr Bicentennial Sculpture Proj;

kinetic wall sculpture, German Opera, WBerlin, comn by Am CofC for 75th Anniversary, 78. *Exhib:* Occidental Col, Los Angeles; Mus Mod Art, New York, 68; Whitney Mus Am Art, 68 & 70; Studio Marconi, Milan, Italy, 70; Springer Gallery, Berlin, 75. *Teaching:* Instr sculpture, Univ Southern Calif, 60-64; assoc prof sculpture, Occidental Col, 64-; artist in residence, WTex State Univ, 78. *Bibliog:* Articles in Art & Artists, London, 66, Art in Am, 66 & 67 & Leonardo, fall 75. *Mailing Add:* Occidental Col Dept Art 1600 Campus Rd Los Angeles CA 90041

BAKER, JILL (JILL BAKER HALVORSON)
PAINTER, ILLUSTRATOR
b Ilion, NY, Oct 12, 42. *Study:* Baylor Univ, BA, 64; Fla State Univ, with Karl Zerbe; Acad di Belle Arti, Florence, Italy, with Silvio Lofreddo; Pratt Inst, MFA, 81. *Work:* Merton Collection, Bellarmine Col, Louisville, Ky; Am Nat Bank, St Thomas Aquinas Chapel & Col Educ Collection, Western Ky Univ, Bowling Green; Goethe House, New York. *Exhib:* Hunter Mus Art, Chattanooga, Tenn, 76; US Info Serv, 77; Avery Fisher Hall, Lincoln Ctr, New York, 78 & 83; solo shows, Pratt Inst, Brooklyn, 80, Baylor Univ, Waco, Tex, 81 & Ward-Nasse Gallery, New York; Long Island Univ, Brooklyn, NY, 81; and many other group and solo shows. *Collections Arranged:* Target LA, Pasadena, Calif, 83. *Pos:* Mem bd dirs, Ward-Nasse Gallery, 76-81. *Teaching:* Instr, adult painting community educ prog, Bowling Green, Ky, 76-81; asst found prog, Pratt Inst, Brooklyn, 79-80. *Awards:* Achievement Award, Bank Am, State Calif, 60; Achievement Trophy, 60; scholar, Southern Women's Club, 63. *Bibliog:* Karen Wheeless (auth), Jill Baker, An artist who..., Baylor Line Quart, 12/75; article, Courier-J, Louisville, Ky, 8/17/80; article, Artspeak, New York, 2/4/82. *Mem:* Artists Equity Asn; founding mem Southern Ky Guild Artists & Craftsmen; Kappa Pi (Baylor chap vpres, 60-63); founding mem Northern Fla Guild Artists & Craftsmen; Women Arts. *Media:* All. *Publ:* Illusr, The More Things Change, Whippoorwill Press, 71; illusr, Songs of Bloody Harlan, Westburg Asn Press, 75; illusr, Spring of Violets, 76, Under the Sign of the Waterbearer, 76 & I Knew A Woman, 77, Love St Bks. *Mailing Add:* c/o Ward-Nasse Gallery 178 Prince St New York NY 10012

BAKER, RALPH BERNARD
PAINTER, EDUCATOR
b Salt Lake City, Utah, Aug 22, 32. *Study:* Univ Wash, BA & MFA. *Work:* Munic Collection, City of Seattle, Wash; Univ Alta, Mus Art; Univ Calgary Mus Art; Toronto Dominion Bank; Northwest Collection, Univ Ore Mus Art. *Exhib:* Northwest Ann, Seattle Art Mus, 59-61 & 71; Artists Alta, Edmonton Art Mus, 66; one-man shows, Univ Ore Mus Art, 72 & Cornish Inst, Seattle, Wash, 77; Artists of Ore, Portland Mus, 72; Lawrence Gallery, Portland, Ore, 82 & 83; Nat Drawing Invitational, Epink Mus, Emporia, Kans, 83; 2-D Nat Exhib, San Pedro, Calif. *Teaching:* Assoc prof paint & drawing, Univ Calgary, 64-70, asst dean fine arts, 68-70, gallery dir, 67-70; assoc prof paint & drawing, Univ Ore, 70- *Awards:* Gtr Seattle Purchase Award, Bus Orgns, 60; Mus & Art Found Award, 62; Prof Artists Ore Award, 76. *Bibliog:* Virgil Hammock (auth), Alberta through abstract eyes, Edmonton J, 4/69; David Thompson (auth), Prairie landscapes a force not a scene, Calgary Herald, 1/16/70; Mike Walsh (auth), Landscape abstracted into geometry, Artweek, 1/19/80. *Media:* Oil, Watercolor. *Mailing Add:* Dept of Art Univ of Ore Eugene OR 97403

BAKER, RICHARD BROWN
COLLECTOR
b Providence, RI, Nov 5, 12. *Study:* Yale Univ, BA, 35; Oxford Univ, BA & MA(Rhodes Scholar), 38; Art Students League; Hans Hofmann Sch Fine Arts; RI Sch Design, Hon DFA, 78. *Exhib:* Collection exhibited: RI Sch Design Mus Art, 59, 64 & 73; Eighty Works from the Richard Brown Baker Collection, Walker Art Ctr, Minneapolis, 61; Yale Univ Art Gallery, 63 & 75; Oakland Univ Art Gallery, Rochester, Mich, 67, 74 & 79; Mus Mod Art, Mexico City, 68; Univ Notre Dame, Ind, 69; Newark Mus, 74; Squibb Gallery, Princeton, NJ, 79; plus others. *Pos:* Mem comt on art gallery of univ coun, Yale Univ, 62-66 & 71-76, mem governing bd, 74-; acquisition comt, 79-; mem mus comt, RI Sch Design, 66-75, mem fine arts comt, 75-; mayoral app, Art Comn of New York, 77-80; mem drawings comt, Whitney Mus, 77- *Bibliog:* Kenneth B Sawyer (auth), Richard Brown Baker, US collector of modern art, Studio Int, London, 1/65; Paul Gardner (auth), Richard Baker's amazing mini-museum, Art News, 1/78; Nelson W Aldrich Jr (auth), Mr Baker takes a sabbatical, Art/World, 10/79. *Mem:* Mus Mod Art; life fel Metrop Mus Art; assoc Solomon R Guggenheim Mus; Whitney Circle, Whitney Mus Am Art; fel Pierpont Morgan Libr. *Collection:* Recent art in all media (earliest 1944); international in origin, although preponderantly by US artists. *Publ:* Auth, Notes on the formation of my collection, Art Int, 9/20/61. *Mailing Add:* 1185 Park Ave New York NY 10128

BAKKE, KAREN LEE
ASSEMBLAGE ARTIST, CALLIGRAPHER
b Everett, Wash, Nov 21, 42. *Study:* Univ Wash; Syracuse Univ, NY, BFA(design), 67, MFA(design), 69. *Work:* Everson Mus, Syracuse. *Comn:* Extensive calligraphy, Syracuse Univ. *Exhib:* Two-person show, Fabric Forms, Kirkland Art Ctr, Clinton, NY, 76; Rubberstamp Invitational, Lightworks Gallery, Syracuse, 81; Calligraphy & Rubberstamps, Everson Mus, 82; Clothing, The Put-On and the Poor Man's Art, Am Home Econ Asn NY State Convention, 82; Suspended in Media, You Are What You See, Cornell Univ, 82; International Calligraphy Today, Women in Design, 83. *Pos:* Asst cur, Syracuse Univ Art Collection, 67-69; vis artist soft sculpture, NY State Summer Sch of Arts, Fredonia & Chautauqua Inst. *Teaching:* Assoc prof & chairperson dept environ arts, Syracuse Univ, 69- *Awards:* Hancock Purchase Prize & One-Person Show Award, Cent NY Regional, Everson

Mus, 71. *Mem:* Am Crafts Coun; Soc Scribes; Handweavers Guild Am; Women in Design. *Media:* Fabric, Metal. *Publ:* Auth, Sewing Machine as a Creative Tool, Prentice-Hall, 76. *Mailing Add:* 1136 Cumberland Syracuse NY 13210

BAKKE, LARRY HUBERT
EDUCATOR, PAINTER
b Vancouver, BC, Jan 16, 32. *Study:* Univ Wash, BA & MFA; Syracuse Univ, PhD, art hist with Laurence Schmeckebier. *Exhib:* Figure Painting, Univ BC Fine Arts Gallery, Vancouver, 63; Nat Exhib Small Paintings, Purdue Univ Art Gallery, Ind, 54; The Painter & the Photograph, Univ NMex Art Gallery, Albuquerque, 64-65; 97th Ann, Am Watercolor Soc, New York, 64; Seven Syracuse Artists, Cortland Fine Arts Gallery, NY, 70; One-man shows, Rockefeller Art Ctr Gallery, State Univ NY, Fredonia, 82 & 83. *Pos:* Guest critic, RI Sch Design, 81; consult, Honeywell Inc, Edina, Minn, 81; guest artist, Alfred Univ, 83. *Teaching:* Vis prof, Univ Victoria, summers, 58-71; instr art hist, drawing & painting, Everett Col, 59-63; prof aesthetics, painting & art history, Syracuse Univ, 63-; vis prof, Villa Giglucci, Florence, Italy, summer 68; guest artist, NY Summer Sch Visual Arts, State Univ Col Fredonia & Chautauqua Inst, summers 76, 77, 79 & 81-83. *Awards:* First Prize, Northwest Watercolor, Seattle Art Mus, 62; Northwest Painters Award, Puget Sound Group Northwest Painters. 63; First Prize for Painting, Spokane-Northwest Painters, 63. *Bibliog:* Margaret Harold (auth), Prize-Winning Watercolors, Allied Publ, 63; Van Deren Coke (auth), Painter & the Photograph, Univ NMex; Laurence Schmeckebier (auth), Larry Bakke, Drawings & Paintings, 1957-1969, Syracuse Univ, 69. *Media:* Oil, Collage. *Publ:* Coauth, Synaesthetic Education, 71; auth, Interval, discontinuity, synaesthesia & their relation to the visual arts, Humanities J, 5/73. *Mailing Add:* 1136 Cumberland Ave Syracuse NY 13210

BAKKEN, HAAKON
ADMINISTRATOR, CRAFTSMAN
b Madison, Wis, Nov 28, 32. *Study:* Univ Wis, BSc, 58; Univ Oslo(Fulbright Fel), 59; Sch for Am Craftsmen, Rochester Inst Technol, MFA, 62. *Work:* Chalmers Collections, Ont Crafts Coun, Toronto; Sheridan Col Study Collection, Mississauga, Ont. *Comn:* Bronze door pull, Ont Crafts Coun, 76; sterling cigar box, Law Soc of Upper Can, Toronto, 74. *Pos:* Dir, Sch of Crafts & Design, Sheridan Col, 77-81; assoc dean, Sch of Visual Arts and Sch of Crafts & Design, Sheridan Col, 81- *Teaching:* Teaching master metal & jewelry, Sch of Crafts & Design, Sheridan Col, 67-77. *Mailing Add:* Sch of Crafts & Design Sheridan Col Trafalgar Rd Oakville ON L5H 1Z7 Canada

BALANCE, JERRALD CLARK
PAINTER
b Ogden, Utah, July 20, 44. *Study:* Univ Utah, Salt Lake City; mainly self-taught. *Work:* Chrysler Mus at Norfolk, Va; Atlantic City Fine Arts Ctr & Atlantic City Munic Bldg Collection, NJ; Coopers & Lybrand Corp, Washington, DC; US State Dept, Washington, DC; Sperry Corp, Reston, Va. *Exhib:* 19th Area Exhib, Corcoran Gallery Art, Washington, DC, 74; 14th Md Biennial, Baltimore Mus Art, 74; Five Am Abstract Painters, Northeastern Univ Gallery, Boston, 77; Best of NY--A Survey, Root Art Ctr, Hamilton Col, Clinton, 77; one-man shows, Genesis Gallery, New York, 78-79 & US State Dept, Washington, DC; Art in the Embassies Prog, Madrid, Spain & Bangkok, Thailand, 78-80. *Awards:* Nat Endowment Grant, Va Commission Arts & Humanities & Emerson Gallery, 76; Washington Cherry Blossom Festival Nat Art Competition Award in Sculpture, 72. *Bibliog:* Joe Mayer (producer), Beyond Abstract Expressionism: Balance & Chelimsky, Prince Georges Community Col. *Media:* Oil, Enamel; Plastic. *Publ:* Contribr, Washington artists, Artists Equity, 72. *Dealer:* Harriet Lebish Gallery 41 E 57th St New York NY 10022; Jane Hasley Gallery 406 Seventh St Washington DC. *Mailing Add:* 7800 Airpark Rd #9 Gaithersburg MD 20879

BALAY, FELICIE
DEALER
b New York, NY, June 14, 40. *Study:* New York Univ. *Pos:* Pres, Felicie Inc, New York, 65- & FKH Editions, New York, 74-75. *Specialty:* Works by Joseph Correale, Ralph Fasanella, Oliver Johnson and others. *Mailing Add:* 141 E 56th St New York NY 10022

BALAZS, GYONGYI
PAINTER
b Transylvania, Hungary, Mar 27, 26; US citizen. *Study:* Hungarian Royal Art Acad; Art Students League. *Exhib:* One-man shows, Bruce Mus, Greenwich, Conn, 73, Ward Nasse Gallery, 75, 77 & 79 & Ohana, London, 83; Audubon Artist Ann Exhib, 78; Knickerbocker Ann Art Exhib, 80; Lincoln Ctr, Avery Fisher Hall, New York, 81; Fran-Nell, Tokyo, 83. *Awards:* First Prize, Stampor Art Exhib, 77. *Media:* Oil, Gold Leafing. *Dealer:* Ward-Nasse Gallery 178 Prince St. *Mailing Add:* 22 Brookridge Dr Greenwich CT 06830

BALCIAR, GERALD GEORGE
SCULPTOR
b Medford, Wis, Aug 28, 42. *Work:* Wildlife World Art Mus, Monument, Colo. *Comn:* Challenge (bronze elk monument), Wildlife World Art Mus, Monument, Colo, 81. *Exhib:* Nat Acad Design, New York, 77; Nat Sculpture Soc, New York, 77-81; Nat Acad Western Art, Cowboy Hall Fame, Oklahoma City, 78; Allied Artists Am, New York, 77-80; North Am Sculpture, Golden, Colo, 81. *Awards:* Dr Maurice Hexter Prize, Nat Sculpture Soc, 78; Bronze Medal, Nat Sculpture Soc, 79; Chilmark Award, Nat Sculpture Soc, 83. *Mem:* Nat Sculpture Soc; Soc Animal Artists. *Media:* Marble, Bronze. *Mailing Add:* 5307 Jellison St Arvada CO 80002

BALDERACCHI, ARTHUR EUGENE
SCULPTOR, ADMINISTRATOR
b New York, NY, Mar 25, 37. *Study:* Duke Univ, BA, 60; Univ Ga, MFA, 65. *Work:* Duke Univ, Durham; St Lawrence Univ; State Univ NY Potsdam; Univ Ga, Athens. *Comn:* Seven ft high mem to Dr Martin Luther King, Roland Gibson Art Found, Potsdam, NY. *Pos:* Chmn dept arts, Univ NH, 74-80. *Teaching:* Assoc prof art, Univ NH, Durham, 65- *Mem:* Col Art Asn Am. *Media:* Welded Metals, Cast Metals; Drawing. *Mailing Add:* 18 Grand St Somersworth NH 03878

BALDESSARI, JOHN ANTHONY
CONCEPTUAL ARTIST
b National City, Calif, June 17, 31. *Study:* San Diego State Col, BA, 53, MA, 57; Univ Calif, Berkeley, 54-55; Univ Calif, Los Angeles, 55; Otis Art Inst, Los Angeles, 57-59. *Work:* Mus Mod Art, New York; Basel Mus, Switz; Los Angeles Co Mus Art. *Exhib:* Konzeption-Conception, Stadtischen Mus, Leverkusen, Ger, 69; Information, Mus Mod Art, New York, 70; Prosepect, Statischen Kunsthalle, Dusseldorf, Ger, 71; Documenta 5 & 7, Kassel, Ger, 72 & 83; Contemporanea, Rome, 73. *Teaching:* Asst prof art, Univ Calif, San Diego, 68-70; prof art, Calif Inst Arts, Valencia, 70- *Awards:* Nat Endowment Arts Grants, 73-75. *Bibliog:* James Collins (auth), John Baldessari, Artforum, 10/73. *Publ:* Auth, Ingres & Other Parables, 72; auth, Choosing: Green Beans, 72; auth, Throwing Three Balls in the Air to Get a Straight Line (Best of 36 Attempts), 73. *Dealer:* Sonnabend Gallery 420 W Broadway New York NY 10012. *Mailing Add:* 3552 Beethoven St Los Angeles CA 90066

BALDRIDGE, MARK S
GOLDSMITH, EDITOR
b Lyons, NY, Dec 7, 46. *Study:* State Univ NY Col, Buffalo, BS(art educ), 68; Cranbrook Acad Art, Bloomfield Hills, Mich, MFA(metalsmithing), 70. *Exhib:* 10th Piedmont Crafts Exhib, Mint Mus Art, Charlotte, NC, 73; Profiles in US Jewelry, 73, Lubbock, Tex, 73; Va Artists 1973, Va Mus Fine Arts, Richmond, 73; 11th Ann Southern Tier Art & Crafts Show, Corning Glass Ctr, NY, 74; Reprise, Cranbrook Acad of Art Mus, Bloomfield Hills, Mich, 75; Objects 75 Designer/Craftsman Show, Grand Junction, Colo, 75; Craft Art & Relig, Vatican Mus, Rome, 76; Marietta Col Crafts Nat, Ohio, 77; Va Craftsmen Biennial, Va Mus Fine Arts, Richmond, 80; SE Metalsmiths, Mint Mus Art; Metalsmith 81, Univ Kans, Lawrence, 81. *Pos:* Ed & creator, Goldsmiths J, 74-; co-ed, Metalsmith Mag, currently. *Teaching:* Instr metal/jewelry, Univ Evansville, 70-72; from asst to assoc prof metal/jewelry, Longwood Col, 72- *Awards:* First Prize/Metal, 40th Nat Cooperstown, NY, 75; First Prize, Lake Superior Int, 75; Merit Award, Goldsmiths 77, Soc NAm Goldsmiths, Phoenix Art Mus, 77. *Mem:* Va Crafts Coun (bd mem, 78-80); Soc NAm Goldsmiths (bd mem, 79-); SE Am Craft Coun (Va rep, 82-). *Media:* Sterling Silver, Gold. *Res:* American metalsmithing in the 1940's and 1950's. *Mailing Add:* 1600 Otterdale Midlothian VA 23113

BALDWIN, HAROLD FLETCHER
SCULPTOR, PAINTER
b Lebanon, NH, May 24, 23. *Study:* Self-taught. *Comn:* Carved map of Northeastern Seaboard, 200 Mormon Missionaries, Cambridge, Mass, 71; The Good Samaritan McKerley Med Care Ctr, Concord, NH, 76. *Exhib:* One-man shows, Concord Pub Libr, NH, 71 & Springfield Art & Hist Soc, Vt, 73; Burlington Mall, Mass, 73; NH Art Gallery, Concord; New Eng Woodcarvers' Asn, Concord Gallery, Mass, 73. *Awards:* Springfield Bicentennial Medallion, Springfield Pub Libr, Vt, 77-78. *Mailing Add:* Baldwin Studios 11 Woodland Dr Springfield VT 05156

BALDWIN, JOHN
EDUCATOR, SCULPTOR
b New York, NY, Jan 28, 22. *Study:* Pratt Inst, Brooklyn; Chouinard Art Sch, Los Angeles; Ohio Univ, BFA; Escuela Universitaria de Bellas Artes, Instituto Politecnico Nacional & Instituto Allende, Mex, MFA; study with Jean Charlot, David Alfaro Siqueiros, Jose Gutierrez & Rico LeBrun. *Work:* Butler Inst of Am Art, Youngstown, Zanesville Art Inst & Masselon Mus, Ohio; McAllen Int Mus, Tex. *Comn:* Bronze scroll, Manchester Col Libr, North Manchester, Ind, 64; Gorsuch Mem Fountain, Bethesda Hosp, Zanesville, 65; Anthony G Trisolini Mem Bronze, Trisolini Gallery, Ohio Univ, 74. *Exhib:* Ball State 22nd Ann Small Sculpture & Drawing Show, 76; McMallen Int Mus, Tex, 78; Zanesville Art Ctr, Ohio, 80; 25 Year Retrospective, Seigfred Gallery, Ohio Univ, 81; one-man show, Gallery 200, Columbus, Ohio, 81; and others. *Teaching:* Instr lithography, Escuela Universitaria de Bellas Artes, Mex, 48-49; instr painting, Instituto Allende, San Miguel Allende, Mex, 50-59; prof art sculpture, Ohio Univ, 59- *Awards:* Award for Excellence, Mainstreams USA, 74; Purchase Award, 25th Ann Ceramic & Sculpture Show, Butler Inst, 73. *Bibliog:* Thelma R Newman, Plastics as an Art Form, Chilton Publ Co, 64. *Media:* Cast Bronze, Fiberglass. *Publ:* Auth, Contemporary Sculpture Techniques: Welded Steel and Fiberglass, Reinhold, 67; auth, The Mexican Murals: A Revolution On the Walls, video tape, Ohio Univ Telecommunications Ctr, 77. *Mailing Add:* Sch of Art Ohio Univ Athens OH 45701

BALDWIN, RICHARD WOOD
ILLUSTRATOR, SCULPTOR
b Needham, Mass, June 8, 20. *Study:* Pa Acad Fine Arts, with George Harding; also with Harold Von Schmidt. *Work:* Smithsonian Inst, Washington, DC; Whitney Gallery Western Art. *Comn:* Murals, comn by USA, 42-45, now in Smithsonian Inst. *Pos:* Sr master sculptor, Franklin Mint, 70- *Awards:* Cresson Fel, Pa Acad Fine Arts, 41. *Media:* Oil, Watercolor; Clay, Plaster. *Publ:* Illus books & periodicals, 46-65. *Mailing Add:* RD 3 Dutton Mill Rd West Chester PA 19380

BALDWIN, RUSSELL W
EDUCATOR, GALLERY DIRECTOR
b San Diego, Calif, May 26, 33. *Study:* San Diego State Univ, BA, 58, MA, 63. *Work:* Joseph Hirshhorn Collection, Washington, DC; La Jolla Mus Contemp Art, Calif; Santa Barbara Mus Art; San Francisco Mus Mod Art; Newport Harbor Mus, Calif. *Exhib:* One-man shows, Santa Barbara Mus Art, 64, La Jolla Mus Contemp Art, 64, 73 & 81, Jewish Community Ctr, San Diego, 74 & Casat Gallery, La Jolla, 78; San Francisco Mus Mod Art, 81; Space Gallery, 82. *Collections Arranged:* Paintings by John Baldessari, 72; Robert Irwin (installation piece), 75; Photog as a Means, 76; James Collins, 77; Wayne Thiebaud, 78; William Wiley, 78; Masami Tenaoka, 80; Roland Reiss, 81. *Pos:* Dir, Dwight Boehm Gallery. *Teaching:* Assoc prof sculpture & printmaking, Palomar Col, San Marcos, Calif, 65- *Awards:* First Painting Award, La Jolla Mus Contemp Art, 60; Sculpture Award, Long Beach Mus Art, 63; First Award, Calif-Hawaii Regional, Fine Arts Mus San Diego, 74. *Mem:* La Jolla Mus Contemp Art. *Specialty:* Information art. *Mailing Add:* Art Dept Palomar Col San Marcos CA 92069

BALES, J (JEAN ELAINE)
PAINTER, SCULPTOR
b Pawnee, Okla, Dec 25, 46. *Study:* Okla Col Liberial Arts, BA(art), 69. *Work:* Southern Plains Indian Mus, Anadarko, Okla; Denver Mus Natural Hist, Colo; US Dept Interior, Washington, DC; Mus Northern Ariz, Flagstaff. *Exhib:* Nat Indian Exhib, Heard Mus, Phoenix, 73-79; Am Indian Art Ann, Okla Art Ctr, Oklahoma City, 79-81; Images 80, Denver Mus Natural Hist, Colo, 80; Trail of Tears, Cherokee Nat Mus, Talequah, Okla, 80; Native Am Invitational, Santa Fe Festival Arts, NMex, 81; and others. *Pos:* Bd dir, Indian Arts & Crafts Asn, 78-79. *Awards:* First in Watercolor, Indian Art Exhib, Heard Mus, 77 & 79; Div Award, Trail of Tears Show, Cherokee Nat Mus, 80; Mountain Bell Award, Gallup Int Tribal Ceremonial Exhib, Mountain Bell, 81. *Bibliog:* Tricia Hurst (auth), Nine major Indian artists, 80 & Crossing bridges, 81, Southwest Art. *Publ:* Illusr, Indian Cultures of Oklahoma, Okla State Dept Educ, 78. *Mailing Add:* J Bales Studio Box 274 Washita OK 73094

BALES, JEWEL
PAINTER
b Purcell, Okla, Aug 28, 11. *Study:* With William B Schimmel, Douglas Greenbowe & others. *Work:* Alhambra High Sch, Phoenix, Ariz; Mesa City Libr, Ariz; Baptist Hosp, Phoenix. *Exhib:* Am Watercolor Soc, Nat Acad Design Galleries, New York, 62; Tucson Regional, Art Ctr, Ariz, 63, 66 & 68; Ann, Ariz State Fair, Phoenix; Ann Traveling Exhib, Ariz Watercolor Asn; Open Watercolor Show, Phoenix Art Mus. *Awards:* First Award for Tree Study, Mesa Art League, 61; People's Choice for Winter Fun, Ariz State Fair, 69; Purchase Award for Winter Fun, Ariz Bank, 69. *Mem:* Ariz Watercolor Asn (pres, 69-71, treas, 72-78); Ariz Artist Guild (vpres, 64-66); Nat League Am Pen Women (treas, 73-76). *Media:* Watercolor. *Mailing Add:* 3030 W Altadena Phoenix AZ 85029

BALKIND, ALVIN LOUIS
CURATOR
b Baltimore, Md, Mar 28, 21; Can citizen. *Study:* Johns Hopkins Univ, BA; study at the Sorbonne. *Pos:* Dir fine arts gallery, Univ BC, 62-73; cur contemp art, Art Gallery Ont, 73-75; chief cur, Vancouver Art Gallery, 75-78; Can comnr, Biennale de Paris, 80. *Teaching:* Assoc prof, Univ BC, 62-73. *Bibliog:* Contribr, Visions, Douglas & McIntyre Publ, 83. *Mailing Add:* 4177 W 14th Ave Vancouver BC V6R 2X6 Canada

BALL, LYLE V
PAINTER, ILLUSTRATOR
b Reno, Nev, Dec 24, 09. *Study:* Am Watercolor Soc, with Edgar Whitney, New York & with Jack Pellow, Conn; Col of Pacific Union, St Helena, Calif, with Vernon Nye. *Work:* Nev Legis Bldgs, Carson City; Sparks Fire Dept, Nev; Reno City Hall; Las Vegas Art League; Senate Off Bldg, Washington, DC. *Comn:* Oil landscapes, comn by Security Nat Bank, Reno, Nev, 65; Settlemeyer Family, Gardnerville, 72, George Mason, 73 & Marvin Humphreys, Reno, 74; Watercolor wildlife, Edward LeBaron Las Vegas, 74. *Exhib:* Soc Western Artists Ann, DeYoung Mus, San Francisco, 67-70; Death Valley 49ers' Ann Encampment Show, 68-81; Artists Prof League, New York, 71- *Pos:* Gov Appt, Nev State Coun Arts, 71-76. *Awards:* Silver Medal/ Watercolor, Am Indian & Cowboy Artists Show, San Dimas, Calif, 77; First Prize/Mixed Media & Second Prize/Watercolor, Death Valley 49ers Show, 77; and others. *Mem:* Soc Western Artists, San Francisco; Am Indian & Cowboy Artists; Am Artists Prof League, New York; life mem Nev Art Gallery, Reno (dir, 70-71); charter mem Artists Co-op, Reno. *Publ:* Illusr, Ponderosa Country, Stanley W Paher, 72 & Int Turquoise Ann, Int Turquoise Asn, 75. *Mailing Add:* 181 Bret Harte Ave Reno NV 89509

BALL, WALTER N
PAINTER, EDUCATOR
b Pratt, Kans, Dec 14, 30. *Study:* Baker Univ, Baldwin City, Kans, BA, 55; Wichita State Univ, Kans, MFA, 57; Ohio State Univ, Columbus, PhD(painting), 68. *Work:* NE Mo State Univ, Kirksville; Univ Mont, Dillon; Wichita State Univ. *Exhib:* Mid-Am Exhib, Nelson-Atkins Gallery, Kansas City, Mo, 58 & 62; one-man shows, Oshkosh Pub Mus, Wis, 68 & NE Mo State Univ Art Gallery, 77; Centennial Exhib, Duerksen Fine Arts Ctr, Wichita, Kans, 70; Midwest Biennial, Joslyn Art Mus, Omaha, Nebr, 72; Mid-States Art Exhib, Evansville Mus Arts & Sci, Ind, 77; Artists of Chicago & Vicinity, Art Inst Chicago, 77; Mid-Am Nat Art Exhib, Owensboro Mus Fine Arts, Ky, 80-81; 42nd Ann Exhib Contemp Am Painting, Soc Four Arts, Palm Beach, Fla, 80; and many others. *Teaching:* Instr painting & drawing,

Sacramento State Col, 63-65; asst prof painting & drawing, Wis State Univ, Oshkosh, 65-68; prof painting & drawing, Northern Ill Univ, DeKalb, 68- *Awards:* Juror's First Award, Washington & Jefferson Col, Washington, Pa, 77; Mus Guild Purchase Award, Evansville Mus Arts & Sci, 77. *Mailing Add:* 821 Normal Rd De Kalb IL 60115

BALLANTYNE, CATHERINE TURK
PAINTER
b Wilmington, Del, Nov 2, 12. *Study:* Wilson Col, AB, 34; Columbia Univ, 35-36; studied under Herb Olsen & Diana Kan. *Exhib:* Nat Arts Club, New York, 76-81 & 83; Salmagundi Club, New York, 78-80; Am Inst Arts & Lett, New York, 80; Elliot Mus, Stuart, Fla, 81 & 83; solo exhib, Owensboro Mus, Ky, 83. *Awards:* Ralph Fabri Award, Allied Artists Am, 81; Kuhn Fine Paper Award, Sumie Soc, 82; Grumbacher Art Award, Pen & Brush, 82. *Mem:* Allied Artists Am (chmn pub relations); Am Artists Prof League; Salmagundi Club; Am Pen Women; Sumie Soc Am. *Media:* Watercolor. *Publ:* Contribr, Flowers in Watercolor--Ethel Todd George, Northlight, 80. *Dealer:* Orchard Knoll Gallery 825 LongTree Rd Elm Groves WI 53122. *Mailing Add:* 29 West Way Old Greenwich CT 06870

BALLARD, LOCKETT FORD, JR
MUSEUM DIRECTOR
b Cold Springs, NY, Aug 1, 46. *Study:* Hamilton Col, Clinton, NY, BA, 68; Cooperstown Grad Program, NY, MA, 79. *Collections Arranged:* Pewter in America (auth, catalog), 75; Lost Litchfield (auth, catalog), 81. *Pos:* Dir, Litchfield Hist Soc, Conn, 74-81; dir, Rosemount Victorian House Mus, Colo, 81- *Mem:* Am Asn Mus; Am Asn State & Local Hist; Colo Wyo Asn Mus; Mountain-Plains Mus Asn. *Collection:* 1893 Victorian House Museum; 1904 Civic Museum collection of world art & ethnographic materials. *Mailing Add:* PO Box 5259 419 West 14th St Pueblo CO 81002

BALLATORE-NELSON, SANDRA LEE
CRITIC, INSTRUCTOR
b Wausau, Wis, July 31, 41. *Study:* Southern Ill Univ, BA, 63; Pasadena City Col, 72-75; Univ Calif, San Diego, MFA(art hist/criticism), 81. *Collections Arranged:* Los Angeles 2001, 76; Four Solo Shows, Genn Hulick, Valledor & Scott (auth, catalog), Los Angeles Inst Contemp Art, Calif, 76; Miniature (auth, catalog), Calif State Univ Los Angeles, 77; The Intimate Object, Downtown Gallery, 81. *Pos:* Los Angeles ed, Artweek, 75-76; founder & dir, Fine Arts Commun Orgn. *Teaching:* Lectr contemp art, Univ Calif, Los Angeles; lectr, 19th century and modern Calif, Calif State Univ, Northridge; instr, North Orange Co Community Col, Calif, 74-77; instr & course planning, Univ Calif, Los Angeles Exten, 76-81. *Mem:* Assoc International des Critiques d'art; Century City Cult Comn; Santa Barbara Contemp Arts Forum. *Res:* Contemp art and alternatives in criticism. *Publ:* Auth, California Clay Rush, Art in Am, 76; auth weekly articles & reviews, Artweek, 74-76; auth reviews, Art Am, 76-80; auth, Lyn Hershman Solo Exhibition Catalog, Melbourne Univ Union Gallery, Parkville, Victoria, Australia, 77; auth, Spagnulo and Redl, Exhibition catalog, Newport Harbor Art Mus, Newport, Calif, 78; publ/ed, Images & Issues Mag, 80- *Mailing Add:* 1651B 18th St Santa Monica CA 90404

BALLINGER, JAMES K
MUSEUM DIRECTOR, HISTORIAN
b Kansas City, Mo, July 7, 49. *Study:* Univ Kans, BA, 72, MA(art hist), 74. *Collections Arranged:* Painter in Taos, Eiteljorg Collection, 80; Visitors to Arizona: 1846-80 (auth, catalog), Phoenix Art Mus, 80; Charles M Russell (auth, catalog), The Renner Collection, 81; Dale Eldred: Phoenix Project, 81; Beyond the Endless River Western Am Drawings & Watercolors (auth, catalog), Phoenix Art Mus, 79; Americans in Brittany and Normandy: 1810-1910, 82; Peter Hurd: Insight to a Painter (auth, catalog), 83. *Pos:* Registrar, Univ Kans Mus Art, Lawrence, 73-74; cur collections, Phoenix Art Mus, Ariz, 74-81; asst dir & chief cur, 81-82, dir, 82-; bd mem, Balboa Art Conservation Ctr, San Diego, 81- *Mem:* Western Asn Art Mus; Central Ariz Mus Asn; Western Regional Conference Am Asn Mus; Am Asn Mus; Am Art Mus Dirs. *Publ:* Auth, American Painting from the Whitney Mus, Phoenix Art Mus, 76; auth, Biennial 1979, Phoenix Art Mus, 79. *Mailing Add:* 1625 N Central Ave Phoenix AZ 85004

BALLOU, ANNE MACDOUGALL See MacDougall, Anne

BALMACEDA, MARGARITA S
EDUCATOR, WRITER
b Ponce, PR, Dec 30, 33; US citizen. *Study:* Manhattanville Col, Purchase, NY, BFA; Immaculate Heart Col, Hollywood, Calif, teaching cert; Cath Univ of PR, Ponce, MA. *Pos:* Asst dir, Ponce Art Mus, 67-74. *Teaching:* Prof art appreciation & art hist, Colegio Regional de Ponce, 73- *Res:* Expressionism; Puerto Rican art. *Publ:* Auth, poems, Tierra y Alma, Ed Ponce de Leon, Spain, 68; auth, El Uso del Museo de Arte de Ponce en la Ensenanza del Barroco, Ceiba, 77; auth, Grunewaold y Kokoschka: Dos expressionistas nordicos, Ceiba, 77; auth, Arte Bizantino, Prerrafaelista y Renacentista en el Museo de Arte de Ponce, 79; auth, Dos Misticos Espanoles, El Greco y Santa Teresa, Ceiba, 83. *Mailing Add:* Dept of Art Univ of PR Ponce Regional Col Ponce PR 00731

BALOG, MICHAEL
PAINTER, SCULPTOR
b San Francisco, Calif, Apr 30, 46. *Study:* Ventura Col, 66-67; Chouinard Art Sch, with Stephan Von Huene, grad(with hons), 59. *Work:* Herbert Distel Mus, Bern, Switz; Univ Iowa, Iowa City; Wichita Art Mus, Kans; Joslyn Art Mus, Omaha, Nebr. *Exhib:* One-man shows, Irving Blum Gallery, Los

Angeles, 70, Leo Castelli Gallery, New York, 72 & Jack Glenn Gallery, Newport Beach, Calif, 74; Documenta Five, Kasel, Ger, 72; Change Inc, Mus Mod Art, New York, 74. *Bibliog:* Article, Esquire, 11/74; Barbara Rose (auth), article, Vogue, 12/74; Melinda Wortz (auth), article, Art News, 1/75. *Media:* Multimedia. *Mailing Add:* c/o Leo Castelli Gallery 142 Greene St New York NY 10012

BALOSSI, JOHN
SCULPTOR, PAINTER
b Staten Island, NY, May 28, 31. *Study:* Columbia Univ, BFA & MA. *Work:* Mus Mod Art, Finch Col Mus, New York; Ponce Mus, PR; Univ PR Mus, Rio Piedras; Mus Art, Ft Lauderdale, Fla. *Comn:* Mural, Student Union Bldg, Univ PR, 69; aluminum wall relief, Inst Puerto Rican Cult, 71; mural, CRUV Pub Housing, Manati, PR, 72; mural, Pan Am Games, San Juan, 79. *Exhib:* Sculpture in Clay from Puerto Rico, Mus Fine Arts, Springfield, Mass, 80; Art Mus STex, Corpus Christi, 80; Newark Mus, 81; Bacardi Gallery, Miami, Fla, 81; 39th & 40th Int Competition of Artistic Ceramics, Faenza, Italy, 81 & 82. *Teaching:* Assoc prof fine arts, Univ PR, Rio Piedras. *Awards:* Ateneo Puertorriqueno Award, San Juan, 67; UNESCO Salon Award, San Juan, 74 & 79; R J Reynolds Tobacco Co Award, San Juan, 79. *Bibliog:* Maria Damoni (auth), Las nubes metalicas de John Balossi, Nuevo Dia, 3/4/72; Darcia Moretti (auth), Gente importante, John Balossi, Plus Ultra Educ Publ, 73; Myrna Rodriquez (auth), Balossi: A Selection of His Work from 1960 to 1982, 82. *Media:* Clay (fired); Acrylic on Canvas & Paper. *Dealer:* Studio B 865 49 St SE Reparto Metro Rio Piedras PR 00921. *Mailing Add:* 725 Cafeto Rio Piedras PR 00924

BALSLEY, JOHN GERALD
PAINTER, SCULPTOR
b Cleveland, Ohio, Apr 15, 44. *Study:* Univ Americas, 65; Ohio Northern Univ, BA, 67; Northern Ill Univ, MFA, 69. *Work:* St Louis Mus Art, Mo; Nelson-Atkins Gallery, Kansas City, Mo; Des Moines Art Ctr, Iowa; Joslyn Mus Art, Omaha, Nebr; Univ Iowa Art Mus, Iowa City. *Exhib:* Solo exhibs, Allan Stone Gallery, New York, 72-78, Minneapolis Col Art & Design, 75-76, Univ Wis, Stout, 75 & John Michael Kohler Arts Ctr, Sheboygan, Wis, 78; Painting & Sculpture Today, Indianapolis Mus Art, Ind, 76; Realisms, Ulrich Mus, Wichita State Univ, 76; Chicago Vicinity Show, Art Inst Chicago, 77; and others. *Teaching:* Asst prof sculpture, Univ Wis-Milwaukee, 76- *Awards:* Louis Comfort Tiffany Found Grant, 72; Nat Endowment Arts Grant, 73; Univ Wis-Milwaukee Grant, 78. *Bibliog:* Lou Dunkak (auth), Balsley sculptures explore man and machines, Arts, 12/76; Josh Kind (auth), Model art: The intimate enviroment, New Art Examr, 1/78; Betty Kaufman (auth), John Balsley at Allan Stone, Art World, 1/78. *Mem:* Col Art Asn Am. *Dealer:* Allan Stone Gallery 48 E 86th St New York NY 10028. *Mailing Add:* 3347 N Bartlett Milwaukee WI 50312

BALTZ, LEWIS
PHOTOGRAPHER
b Newport Beach, Calif, Sept 12, 45. *Study:* San Francisco Art Inst, BFA, 69; Claremont Grad Sch, MFA, 71. *Work:* Mus Mod Art, New York; Art Inst Chicago; Int Mus Photog, George Eastman House, Rochester, NY; Libr Cong, Washington, DC; Bibliotheque Nat, Paris, France. *Comn:* Eight Photographers View of the Nation's Capital in the Bicentennial Year, Corcoran Gallery Art, Washington, DC, 75. *Exhib:* One-man shows, Castelli Graphics, Leo Castelli Gallery, New York, 71, 73, 75, 77, 81 & 83, La Jolla Mus Contemp Art, Calif, Baltimore Mus Art, Md, Galerie December, Dusseldorf, Ger, 76; Sheldon Mem Art Gallery, Lincoln, Nebr & Univ Nebr, 77; Corcoran Gallery Art, 74-76; Philadelphia Col Art, 75; Mus Fine Arts, Houston, 76; San Francisco Mus Mod Art, 81; RI Sch Design, 83; Univ Art Mus, Univ Calif, Berkeley, 84. *Teaching:* Vis lectr, Univ Calif, Davis, fall, 81; regent's vis art, Univ Calif, Santa Cruz, spring, 82; vis artist, RI Sch Design, 83; vis prof, Univ Calif, Riverside, 84. *Awards:* Nat Endowment Arts Fel Grant Photog, 73 & individual fel, 76; Guggenheim Mem Found fel in photography; US-UK Bicentennial Exchange Fel, 80. *Bibliog:* Peter Plagens (auth), Los Angeles, Artforum, 10/71; A D Coleman (auth), Latent image, The Village Voice, 1/72. *Publ:* Auth, The New Industrial Parks Near Irvine, California, 75. *Dealer:* Castelli Graphics 4 E 77th St New York NY 10021. *Mailing Add:* PO Box 366 Sausalito CA 94965

BAMBAS, THOMAS REESE
METALSMITH
b Ann Arbor, Mich, Feb 2, 38. *Study:* Ferris State Col, AA, 60; Cranbrook Acad Art, BFA, 62 & MFA, 64. *Work:* Johnson Collection, Objects: USA, Smithsonian Inst. *Comn:* Altar lights, 70 & fount cover, 71, St Johns Episcopal Church, Mt Pleasant; chalis & paten, Grosse Pointe Woods Presby Church. *Exhib:* The Uncommon Smith, Kohler Arts Ctr, Cheboygan, Wis, 74; The Goldsmith, Renwick Gallery, Smithsonian Inst, 74; Reprise, Cranbrook Acad Art, 75; Forms in Metal, Mus Contemp Crafts, 75; 3rd Biennial Lake Superior Int Craft Exhib, 75; Remains to be Seen, 83. *Teaching:* Instr art, Interlochen Arts Acad, 64-66; asst prof art, Wichita State Univ, 65-69; prof art & metalsmithing, Cent Mich Univ, 69- *Awards:* Tiffany Grant, Louis Comfort Tiffany Found, 65; Cash Awards, Cent Mich Univ, 71, 75 & 82. *Bibliog:* Seitz & Finegold (auth), Silversmithing, Van Nostrand, 75; Thelma & Jay Newman (auth), The Container Book, Crown, 77; Jay & Lee Scott Newman (auth), The Mirror Book, Crown, 78. *Mem:* Soc NAm Goldsmiths. *Media:* Sterling Silver. *Res:* Exploration of raising and chasing in silver and gold. *Mailing Add:* 1008 S Arnold Mt Pleasant MI 48858

BANANA, ANNA LEE
PUBLISHER, CONCEPTUAL ARTIST
b Victoria, BC, Feb 24, 40. *Study:* Univ BC, Vancouver, BEd, 67. *Work:* Smithsonian Inst Libr, Nat Gallery of Art Serials Libr, Washington, DC; Mus Mod Art Libr, New York; G Pompidou Libr, Paris, France; Acad Fine Arts Libr, Rotterdam, Holland. *Exhib:* Can tour, 15 performances, 14 cities, 80; Univ Calif, Irvine, 80; San Diego State Univ, 80; Inter-Dada 80 Festival, Ukiah, Calif; Can/USA Tour, 15 performances in 15 cities, including Vancouver, Edmonton, Toronto, Montreal, Columbia, SC, Dallas, & San Jose, Calif; and many others, 82. *Pos:* Vis artist, Ont Col Art, Vancouver Sch Art, San Francisco Art Inst, San Francsico Art Acad, Sonoma State Univ & San Jose State Univ, 72-79; dir-ed-publ, Banana Productions, 76-79; vis artist & lectr, Can cols & univs, 80- *Awards:* Coord Coun of Lit Mag Assistance Awards, 75, 77 & 79; Can Coun Grants, 80-83. *Bibliog:* David Zack (auth), Discourse on mail-art, Art in Am, 1-2/73; Howardina Pindell (auth), Alternative space: Artists' periodicals, Print Collector's Newsletter, 9/77; Mary Stofflet (auth), La Mammelle Videozines, Art Forum, 3/80; and others. *Res:* Collection of information on a given topic via the mail-art network on an international basis; grass-roots level of art activity not represented in the art media or establishment; performance and organization of participatory public art events. *Interests:* Do-it-yourself mythmaking versus mass media. *Publ:* Contribr, The transformation of Anne Long, Maclean's Mag, Maclean Hunter Ltd, Toronto, 72; ed & publ, Vile Mag, No 1, 2, 3 & 5, 74-77, contrib & ed, No 4 & 6, 76-78, Banana Productions; contribr, The Rubber Stamp Album, Workman Publ, 78; ed & publ, About Vile, Vancouver, 83. *Mailing Add:* PO Box 3655 Vancouver BC V6B 3Y8 Canada

BANDA, PEDRO SALAZAR
PAINTER
Study: Sch Art & Sculpture, Esmeralda Nat Fine Arts Inst, MA(painting), 56. *Work:* Mus Mod Art, New York; Lultte Ctr, San Antonio, Tex; Polyforum Cult Siquieros, Mex Foreign Relations Dept, Nat Univ Mex, Mexico City. *Comn:* Mural, Mus Anthropology, Mexico City. *Exhib:* Contemp Mus Morelia, Michoacan, 68; Salon Ann Guadalajara, 69; Tortolitos Gallery, San Antonio, Tex, 70; Palacio Mineria, Mexico City, 72; Polyforum Siquieros, Mexico City, 81. *Awards:* Nat Landscape Award, Guadi Rojo, 64. *Mem:* Salon Plastica Mex; Soc Mex Artists. *Media:* Oil on Canvas, Watercolor. *Mailing Add:* Calle Langosta Lote 6 Manzana 121 Col Del Mar 13270 Mexico D F Mexico

BANDEL, LENNON RAYMOND
PAINTER
b Kansas City, Mo, Dec 10, 06. *Study:* Kansas City Art Inst, with Thomas H Benton & Ross Braught; Dayton Art Inst, with John King & Burroughs; John Huntington Polytech Inst, Cleveland, with Rolf Stoll & F Wilcox. *Work:* Luxemburg Mus, Europe. *Comn:* Six portraits of pres, Reorganized Church of Jesus Christ of Latter-Day Saints, 60; six portraits, Hillyard Chem Co, St Joseph, Mo, 70-71; portrait of Joseph Boley & Dr Frank Mantz, Univ Kans Med Ctr, 71; mural of River Jordan, First Christian Church, Iowa, Kans, 72; Trader's Nat Bank, Kansas City, Mo. *Exhib:* May Art Show, Cleveland Mus Art, 44-46; Plaza Art Fair, Kansas City, Mo, 56-74; Kansas City Art Inst Alumni Show, 73; Heritage Show, Kansas City Mus Natural Hist, 74. *Pos:* Designer-artist, Hallmark Cards Inc, Kansas City, 27-37; designer-artist, Stanley Mfg Co, Dayton, Ohio, 37-42; artist-art dir, Am Greeting Corp, Cleveland, 42-57. *Teaching:* Instr portrait, Kansas City Art Inst, 65-71; instr painting & drawing, Jewish Community Ctr, Kansas City, 65-71. *Awards:* Cleveland Mus Art Award, 44; Kansas City Mus Natural Hist Award, 61 & 64; Cowboy Hall of Fame. *Media:* Oil, Pastel. *Mailing Add:* 5327 Rosewood St Mission KS 66205

BANDY, GARY
PAINTER, EDUCATOR
b Pontiac, Mich, May 10, 44. *Study:* Oakland Univ, BA, 65; Columbia Univ, MFA, 68. *Work:* Norton Simon Inc & Muriel Siebert, New York; St Peter's Col, Jersey City, NJ. *Exhib:* Artists Market, Detroit, Mich, 64; Aldrich Mus Contemp Art, Ridgefield, Conn, 74; solo shows, Herbert H Lehman Col Gallery, Bronx, NY, 79 & F Marino Gallery, New York, 82; R van Buren's Tenth Ave Showplace, New York, 81; and others. *Teaching:* Adj instr art hist, St Peter's Col, Jersey City, NJ, 68-72; lectr & workshop instr, Mus Mod Art, New York, 77- *Bibliog:* Review, Art News, 9/74; Palmer Poroner (auth), review, Art Speak, 4/80; Susan Filen Yeh (auth), Gary Bandy, Arts Mag, 4/82. *Media:* Multimedia. *Mailing Add:* c/o Frank Marino Gallery 489 Broome St New York NY 10013

BANDY, MARY LEA
EDITOR, ADMINISTRATOR
b Evanston, Ill, June 16, 43. *Study:* Stanford Univ, BA, 65. *Pos:* Asst ed, Harry N Abrams, New York, 67-73; assoc coordr exhibs, Mus Mod Art, New York, 76-78; dir film dept, 80- *Publ:* Ed, Rediscovering French film (catalog), Mus Mod Art, 83; Michael Balcon (catalog), Mus Mod Art, 84. *Mailing Add:* 116 W 29th St New York NY 10001

BANDY, RON F
PAINTER, EDUCATOR
b Dayton, Ohio, Feb 18, 36. *Study:* Ohio Univ, Athens, BFA, 62; Univ Fla, Gainesville, MFA, 64; also with Hiram Williams & Enrique Montenegro. *Work:* Weatherhead Found; Ft Wayne Mus, Ind; Owens-Corning Corp, Toledo, Ohio; Hope Colgate Sloane, Bowling Green, Ohio. *Exhib:* Solo exhib, Ft Wayne Mus, Ind, 74; Owens-Corning Collection Show, 76 & Toledo May Show, 81; Toledo Mus, Ohio; Ft Wayne Mus Exhib, Ind, 82; Lady Poverty, Mem Mus, Lima, Ohio, 83. *Teaching:* Prof art, Bowling Green State Univ, 68- *Bibliog:* Lynn Stevenson (auth), Art from a can, Sunday Mag, Blade, 4/22/73. *Media:* Mixed. *Mailing Add:* 10271 Napoleon Rd Bowling Green OH 43402

BANE, (LUCY) MCDONALD
PAINTER, EDUCATOR
b Bland, Va, Mar 1, 28. *Study:* Va Polytech Inst & State Univ, BS, 49; Univ NC, Greensboro, with Gregory Ivy & John Opper, MFA, 59. *Work:* Mus Mod Art, New York; Weatherspoon Gallery, Greensboro, NC; Mint Mus Art, Charlotte, NC. *Exhib:* Okla Art Ctr, Oklahoma City, 70; Contemp Am Drawings V, Smithsonian Inst, traveling, 71-74; NC Mus Art, Raleigh, NC, 76; Univ Evansville, Ind, 76; solo exhibs, Southeastern Ctr Contemp Art, Winston-Salem, NC, 80 & Univ Ga Art Gallery, Athens, 81. *Pos:* Cur exhibs, Southeastern Ctr Contemp Art, Winston-Salem, NC, 77-80. *Teaching:* Asst prof, Calif State Univ, Fullerton, 66-68; instr, NC Sch Arts, Winston-Salem, 70-73; asst prof, Southern Ill Univ, Carbondale, 73-77; vis assoc prof, Va Polytech Inst & State Univ, 80. *Awards:* Best Show, Southeastern Ctr Contemp Art 39th Painting & Sculpture Competition, 73. *Media:* Oil. *Publ:* Ed, The Southeast Seven II, 78, Paper Making and Paper Using, 79, Art Patron Art, 79 & Southeast Seven III, 79 (catalogs), Southeastern Ctr Contemp Art, Winston-Salem, NC. *Dealer:* Gilliam & Peden Assocs 1322 New Hope Church Rd Raleigh NC 27609. *Mailing Add:* 156 West End Blvd Winston-Salem NC 27101

BANERJEE (BIMAL)
PAINTER, SCULPTOR
b Calcutta, India, Sept 4, 39; US citizen. *Study:* Indian Col Art, Calcutta, grad(first class hon), 55-60; Col Art, New Delhi, Indian Govt Nat Cult Scholar, 65-67; Atelier 17, Paris, with S W Hayter, Fr Govt Grant, 67-69; Ecole des Beaux Arts, Paris, Fr Govt Grant, 67-70; Pratt Inst Exten, New York, inst grants, 69 & 70-72; NY Univ, 76; Columbia Univ, EdM, 78, MA, 78, 83- *Work:* Mus Mod Art, Paris, France & Barcelona, Spain; Mus Fine Arts, Boston; Brooklyn Mus; Nat Gallery Mod Art, New Delhi; plus many others. *Comn:* Mural with five panels, comn by Mario Manto, Levanto, Italy, 68; mural with three panels, Proj Find Clinton Sr Citizens Ctr, New York, 79; Silk Screen Proj, NY & NJ Port Authority, CCF/CETA Artists Proj, New York, 79; plus others. *Exhib:* Paris Biennale, Mus Mod Art, Paris, 69; Mus Fine Arts, Montreal, 71; Honolulu Acad Arts, 71, 73, 79 & 81; Brooklyn Mus Biennial, 72-73 & 81; Tokyo Biennial, Nat Mus Mod Art, Tokyo & Kyoto, 72-73; Brit Biennale, Bradford City Art Galleries & Mus, Eng, 72, 76 & 82; Joan Miro Int Drawing Prize Contest, Barcelona, Spain, 74, 75 & 76; Rijeka Drawing Biennale, Mus Mod Art, Yugoslavia, 74, 76 & 80; World Print Competition, San Francisco Mus Mod Art, 77-79; and many others. *Pos:* Therapist, art & educ, St John's Episcopal Hosp, South Shore, Far Rockaway, NY, 81-83. *Teaching:* Vis asst teacher graphics, Nat Acad Fine Arts, New York, 69; guest lectr, Parsons Sch Design, New York, 79; lectr philos educ, Bloomfield Col, NJ, 80-81, Parsons Sch Design, NY, 83-; and many others. *Awards:* Nat Award, Nat Art Acad, New Delhi, 67 & 70; Centre Cult Int Award, City Univ, Paris, 68; Hawaii Biennial, 71, 73 & 81; and many others. *Bibliog:* Ajit K Dutta (auth), article, Nat Art Acad J, 9/74; Linda Bryant & Marcy Philips (auth), Contextures, JAM, New York, 78; John Digby (auth), Collage, Contemporary Method; Materials & Esthetics, Long Island Univ Press, 83; and others. *Mem:* Col Art Asn Am, New York; World Print Coun, San Francisco. *Media:* Carbon, Mascara; Eyeliner, Human & Horse Hair. *Publ:* Coauth, Mine, 64; contribr, Revolutionist Master-Artist Henri Matisse, 70; contribr, Painter Sonia Delaunay, 70; contribr, Metaphysical Master-Artist de Chirico, 72; auth, Picasso, 82; and many others. *Mailing Add:* Loft 2C 106 Ridge St New York NY 10002

BANEY, RALPH RAMOUTAR
SCULPTOR
b Trinidad, West Indies, Sept 22, 29. *Study:* Brighton Col Art, Eng, 57-62; Univ Md, MFA, 73, PhD, 80; also with Kenneth Campbell & Arthur J Ayres. *Work:* Nat Mus Art Gallery, Trinidad; Cent Bank, Trinidad; Trinidad & Tobago Embassy, London; Univ West Indies; Van Leer Found, Amsterdam, Holland. *Comn:* Relief sculpture, St Finbar's Church, Trinidad, 66; relief sculpture, Norweg Seamen's Mission, Trinidad, 69; nat coat of arms, Cent Bank Trinidad, 70; mosaic mural (with Vera Baney), Bishop's High Sch, Trinidad, 71; six portrait comns from various individuals. *Exhib:* Sussex Artists Ann, Eng, 59-61; Sao Paulo Biennial, Brazil, 67 & 69; one-man shows, Sculpture House Gallery, New York 73 & Pan Am Union, Washington, DC, 74; Sculptors Guild Mem Ann, Lever House, New York, 74-81. *Teaching:* Supvr art, Ministry Educ & Cult, Trinidad, 63-71; instr art, Univ Md, 72-75; instr art, Smithsonian Inst, 74-79; prof, Dundalk Community Col, 76- *Awards:* Gold Medal Merit, Govt Trinidad & Tobago, 73; First Prize Sculpture, Ten Md Juried Exhib, Easton Acad Md, 74; First Prize Sculpture, Spanish Am Art Exhib, 74. *Bibliog:* Rod Naylor (auth), Woodcarving Techniques, Batsford, 79; Nicholas Roukes (auth), Masters of Wood Sculpture, Watson Guptill, 80; Anthony Padovano (auth), Sculpture Processes, Doubleday, 81. *Mem:* Royal Soc Brit Sculptors; Sculptors Guild; Artists Equity Asn; Col Art Asn Am. *Media:* Wood, Ceramic. *Mailing Add:* 1112 Sulphur Spring Rd Baltimore MD 21227

BANEY, VERA
CERAMIST, PRINTMAKER
b Trinidad, West Indies, June 6, 30. *Study:* Brighton Col Art, Eng, 59-62; State Univ NY Col Ceramics, Alfred Univ, 68; Univ Md, BA, 80. *Work:* Nat Mus & Art Gallery, Trinidad; Cent Bank, Trinidad; Hilton Hotel, Trinidad; Naparima Col, Trinidad; Naparima Girls High Sch. *Comn:* Ceramic cross, Norweg Seamen's Mission, Trinidad, 69; ceramic relief, Alston's Ltd, Trinidad, 70; mosaic mural (with Ralph Baney), Bishop's High Sch, Trinidad, 71; ceramic lamp bases, Hilton Hotel; ceramic sculpture, Cent Bank Trinidad. *Exhib:* Expo 67, Montreal, 67; one-man shows, Trinidad, 67 & 69; Commonwealth Inst, London, 74; Sao Paulo Biennial, Brazil, 75; Contemp Crafts Americas, Colo State Univ, 75; 3 Artists from Trinidad, Pan Am Union,

Washington, DC, 76. *Teaching:* Instr ceramics, Dundalk Community Col, currently. *Awards:* Outstanding Young Potter, Creative Crafts Coun 11 Biennial, 74; First Place Ceramics, 2nd Int Art Exhib, Washington, DC, 74; Humming Bird Gold Medal Nat Award, Trinidad, 82. *Mem:* Artists Equity; Am Crafts Coun; Art League Northern Va. *Mailing Add:* 1112 Sulphur Spring Rd Baltimore MD 21227

BANKS, ANNE JOHNSON
SCULPTOR, EDUCATOR
b New London, Conn, Aug 10, 24. *Study:* Wellesley Col, BA, 46; Honolulu Sch Art, with Willson Stamper, 48-50; George Washington Univ, with Thomas Downing, MFA, 68. *Work:* Lyman Allyn Mus, New London; George Washington Univ. *Exhib:* Northern Va Fine Arts Asn Area Exhib, 72-74; one-person shows, Alexandria Art League, 73 & Foundry Gallery, Washington, DC, 78, 81 & 83; Hyatt Regency Competition, 81; Va Mus, Richmond, 83. *Teaching:* Lectr art, George Washington Univ, summer 68; instr art, George Mason Univ, 68-69; instr art, Northern Va Community Col, 71-72, asst prof & chmn dept, 73-80, assoc prof, 80. *Awards:* Six Merit Awards, Art League, Alexandria, Va, 71-74; Merit Award, Northern Va Fine Arts Asn, 72; Va Ctr Creative Arts Fel, Sweetbriar, 82. *Mem:* Womens Caucus Art; Alexandria Art League; Col Art Asn Am; Design Hist Soc. *Media:* Wood, Plastic. *Mailing Add:* 1104 Croton Dr Alexandria VA 22308

BANKS, VIRGINIA •
PAINTER
b Boston, Mass, Jan 12, 20. *Study:* Smith Col, BA; State Univ Iowa, MA. *Work:* Seattle Art Mus, Volunteer Park, Wash; IBM Collection, New York; San Francisco Mus Art; Univ Ill, Urbana-Champaign; Univ Ore Mus Art, Eugene. *Comn:* Portrait of Dr John Hogness, Univ Wash Sch Med, Seattle, 72; portrait of Dr Herbert S Ripley, Univ Wash Sch Med, Seattle, 75. *Exhib:* San Francisco Mus Art, 47 & 49; Dallas Mus Fine Arts, 47 & 52; 12 shows, Seattle Art Mus, 47-75; Butler Inst Am Art, Youngstown, Ohio, 48; Albright-Knox Art Gallery, Buffalo, NY, 48 & 50; Walker Art Ctr, Minneapolis, 49; 6 shows, Whitney Mus Am Art, New York, 48-59; Am Painting Today, Metrop Mus Art, New York, 50; Los Angeles Co Mus Art, Los Angeles, 50; Inst Contemp Art, Boston, 50; Corcoran Gallery, 50 & 56; Art Gallery of Greater Victoria, BC, 64 & 67; Kobe Munic Art Mus, Japan, 66; Andrew Dickson White Mus Art, Cornell Univ, 68; Duxbury Art Complex, Mass, 72; Univ Ore Art Mus, Haseltine Collection, 75; plus many one-man shows, 50-80. *Teaching:* Instr studio & art hist, State Univ Iowa, 42-47; instr studio & art hist, Univ Buffalo, Albright Art Sch & State Univ NY, 47-48; instr studio & art hist, Cornish Art Sch, Seattle, 51-52. *Awards:* Pepsi-Cola Competition, 48; Hallmark Int Art Award, 49. *Bibliog:* Lynch (auth), How to Make Collages, Viking, 61; Albe & Peck (auth), Artists of Puget Sound, Metrop Press, 62. *Media:* Watercolor. *Mailing Add:* 3879 51st Ave NE Seattle WA 98105

BANNARD, WALTER DARBY
PAINTER, WRITER
b New Haven, Conn, Sept 23, 34. *Study:* Phillips Exeter Acad; Princeton Univ. *Work:* Whitney Mus Am Art, New York; Mus Mod Art, New York; Guggenheim Mus; Metrop Mus Art, New York; Albright-Knox Art Gallery, Buffalo, NY; plus many others. *Exhib:* Six Painters, Albright-Knox Art Gallery, 71; Whitney Mus Ann, New York, 72; Abstract Painting in the 70's, Mus Fine Arts, Boston, 72; maj retrospective, Baltimore Mus Art, 73; The Great Decade of American Abstraction, Mus Fine Arts, Houston; Art in America after World War II, Guggenheim Mus, 79; plus many other group & one-man shows. *Pos:* Contrib ed, Artforum Mag, 73-74; deleg, Europ-Am Assembly Art Mus, England, 75; cur, Hans Hofmann, Hirshhorn Mus, Washington, DC, 76; mem, Int Exhib Comt, 78-79; co-chmn, Nat Endowment Arts Int Comt Visual Arts, 79- *Teaching:* Lectr at numerous universities; symposium & sem, Princeton Univ, New York Univ, Mus Fine Arts, Boston & others, 66- *Awards:* Nat Found Arts Award, 68-69; Guggenheim Fel, 68-69. *Bibliog:* New look for old tradition, Time Mag, 2/7/69; Canvases brimming with color, Life Mag, 9/24/71. *Publ:* Auth, Touch and scale, Artforum, 6/71; auth, The Art Museum and the Living Artist, Prentice-Hall, 75; auth, Hans Hofmann, Hirshhorn Mus, 76; auth, The emperor's old clothes, Arts Mag, 9/82; Painting of the 50s, Duke Univ, 83; and others. *Dealer:* Knoedler Gallery 19 W 70th St New York NY 10019. *Mailing Add:* Box 296 Rocky Hill NJ 08553

BANNING, JACK (JOHN PECK), JR
DEALER, LECTURER
b Mt Vernon, NY, June 12, 39. *Study:* Brown Univ, AB, 61. *Pos:* Owner, Poster Am, 74- *Specialty:* American and European poster art, 1890-1950. *Mailing Add:* c/o Poster America 174 Nineth Ave New York NY 10011

BANSEMER, ROGER LEWIS
PAINTER, PRINTMAKER
b Brockton, Mass, July 25, 48. *Study:* Ringling Sch Art, Sarasota, Fla, BA, 69. *Work:* Sperry Rand Corp & Pioneer Savings & Loan Asn, Fla; Clearwater Oaks Bank; Barnett Bank, Clearwater. *Comn:* Wall mural, Spyglass Hotel, Clearwater, 79; etching for Pres Carter, City of Clearwater, 79; mural, City Clearwater, 81; The Rocks (mural), Sydney, Australia, 82; painting for poster, City of Clearwater, 83. *Exhib:* Infinite Space & Kinetic Color, Adelphi Univ, 77; 15th Ann Maj Fla Artists, Harmon Gallery, Naples, Fla, 77; Pan-Am Bldg, DC, 79; Adelphi Univ, New York, 80; Byways Gallery, Sarasota, Fla, 81. *Pos:* Artist-in-residence, City of Clearwater, 78. *Bibliog:* Review by Jeanne Paris, Newsday, 77; Mixed Media (film), Channel 3, Tampa, 81; feature, Channel Eight, Tampa, 83. *Media:* Acrylics; Etching. *Publ:* Contribr, Southern Arts Mag, 77; contribr, cover & article, Curtain Call Mag, 78; contribr, feature article & cover, Bay Life Mag, 79. *Dealer:* Hodsell Gallery Sarasota FL; Joan Ling Gainesville FL. *Mailing Add:* 2352 Alligator Creek Road Clearwater FL 33575

BANZ, GEORGE
WRITER, ARCHITECT
b Lucerne, Switz, Dec 21, 28; Can citizen. *Study:* Swiss Fed Inst Technol, Zurich, with S Giedion, dipl archit; Okla State Univ, Stillwater, exchange fel, MS(archit eng). *Exhib:* Ontario Architecture: the Past, the Present, the Future, Art Gallery of Ont, Toronto, 63; Royal Can Acad of Arts Traveling Exhib, 68. *Pos:* Spec consult, Ministry State Urban Affairs, Ottawa, 72-74; delegate, RAIC Mission, China, 83. *Teaching:* Part-time fac mem, Dept of Archit, Univ of Toronto, 59-63 & 70-75; sessional lectr computers archit, 78-; sch archit, Univ Waterloo, 80; part-time fac mem, Dept Indust Des, Ontario Col Art, 80- *Awards:* Massey Award for Archit, V Massey Found & Can Govt, 61 & 67. *Mem:* Royal Archit Inst of Can; Royal Can Acad of Arts. *Res:* Systems aspects of form, particularly with regard to the applicability of computers in design. *Publ:* Auth, Elements of Urban Form, 70; auth, Computer Aids in Building Design, 83. *Mailing Add:* 498 St Clair Ave E Toronto ON M4T 1P7 Canada

BARANIK, RUDOLF
PAINTER
b Lithuania, Sept 10, 20; US citizen. *Study:* Art Inst Chicago, 46; Art Students League, 47; Acad Julian, Paris, France, 48; and with Fernand Leger, 49-50. *Work:* Whitney Mus Am Art & Mus Mod Art, New York; Nat Mus, Stockholm, Sweden; Hirshhorn Mus & Sculpture Garden; Everson Mus, Syracuse, NY; Brooklyn Mus, NY. *Exhib:* Whitney Mus Am Art Ann, 58 & 61; Am Collages, Mus of Ball State Univ, 71; Art of Conscience: The Last Decade Traveling Exhib, 81-82; War Games, Ronald Feldman Gallery, New York, 82; Four Manifestos, Lenner-Heller Gallery, New York, 82; The Monument Redefined, Gowanus Ann 11, New York, 82; The End of the World: Contemporary Visions of the Apocalypse, New Mus, New York, 83; and others. *Teaching:* Vis artist, Ball State Univ, 64; assoc prof, Pratt Inst, 66-76, adj prof art, 77-; instr painting, Art Students League, 68- *Awards:* Am Acad Arts & Lett Award in Art, 73; NY State Creative Artists Pub Serv Award in Painting, 75; Guggenheim Grant, 81. *Bibliog:* Edward Lucie-Smith (auth), Art in the Seventies, Phaidon Press Ltd, London, 80; Dane Ashton (auth), American Art Since 1945, Oxford Univ Press, 82; Lucy Lippard (auth), Get the Message?, Dutton, 84; and many others. *Mem:* Artists Equity (bd mem, 60-61); Artists Meeting for Cult Change. *Media:* Oil, Acrylic. *Publ:* Co-auth, The Attica Book, 72. *Dealer:* Lerner Heller Gallery 956 Madison Ave New York NY 10021. *Mailing Add:* 97 Wooster St New York NY 10012

BARAZANI, MORRIS
EDUCATOR, PAINTER
b Highland Park, Mich, June 24, 24. *Study:* Inst Design, Cranbrook Acad Art, Bloomfield Hills, Mich. *Work:* Gutenberg Mus, Ger; Blue Cross Blue Shield, Chicago, Ill; Gov's State Univ, Ill. *Exhib:* Art Inst Chicago, 59; Ill State Mus, 71; Pamlemousse, Chicago, 75; Chicago Gallery, Ill, 76; Zriny-Hayes Gallery, Chicago, 77 & 79-81; Gilman Galleries, 83. *Teaching:* Prof painting, Univ Ill, Chicago Circle, 69- *Media:* Oil, Collage. *Dealer:* Gilman Galleries 277 E Ontario St Chicago IL 60611. *Mailing Add:* c/o Sch Art & Design 601 S Morgan Chicago IL 60680

BARBAROSSA, THEODORE C
SCULPTOR
b Ludlow, Vt. *Study:* Yale Univ Sch Art & Archit, BFA; also with Cyrus Dallin, Heinz Warneke & Robert Eberhard; Susquehanna Univ, Hon DFA, 77. *Work:* Uncle Sam Monument, Arlington, Mass, 77; Susquehanna Univ, 77; Catholic Shrine, Washington, DC, 77. *Comn:* Many sculptures in stone, Cath Church Assumption, Baltimore, 57; five relief panels, Mus of Sci, Boston; two chapels & ten figures, Cath Shrine, Washington, DC, 62-65; sculptures in stone for St Thomas Episcopal Church, NY, 64 & Washington Cath & Episcopal Churches, 65-75; plus many others. *Exhib:* Whitney Mus, New York, 40; Nat Sculpture Soc; Nat Acad Design; Allied Artists; Audubon Artists. *Awards:* Lindsay Morris Mem Prize, Nat Sci Soc, 49; Gold Medal for Sculpture, Allied Artists, New York, 55; Henry Herring Citation for Sculpture, 61 & Hexter Prize, 77, Nat Sculpture Soc. *Mem:* Fel Nat Sculpture Soc; Audubon Artists; Allied Artists; Int Inst Arts & Lett; academician Nat Acad Design. *Mailing Add:* 12 Randolph St Belmont MA 02178

BARBEAU, MARCEL (CHRISTIAN)
PAINTER, SCULPTOR
b Montreal, Que, Feb 18, 25. *Study:* Ecole Meuble, dipl, 47; with Paul-Emile Borduas. *Work:* Nat Gallery Can; Stedelijk Mus, Amsterdam; Chrysler Mus, Norfolk, Va; Rose Art Mus, Brandeis Univ; Art Gallery Ont. *Comn:* Pipes' Dreams (tube sculptures), Confederation Ctr Art Gallery & Mus, Charlottetown, PEI, 74; aluminum sculpture, Lavallin, Boucherville, Que, 75; Don Quichotte (aluminum sculpture), Cojo, Montreal, Joliette, Que, 76. *Exhib:* Pen House Show, Mus Mod Art, New York, 65; The Deceived Eye, Ft Worth Art Ctr, 65; Op Art Seminar Show, Riverside Mus, New York, 65; Nine Canadians, Inst Contemp Art, Boston, 69; retrospective, Winnipeg Art Gallery & Mus Art Contemp, Montreal, 69; Borduas et les Automatistes, Grand Palais, Paris, 71; solo exhib, Mus Que & Mus Contemp, Montreal, 74-75 & Mus Beaux Arts Montreal, 77; Modern Painting in Canada, 78 & The Contemporary Art Society: Montreal 1939-1947, 80, Edmonton Art Gallery. *Teaching:* Artist in residence painting, Bishop Univ, Que, 78-80. *Awards:* Zacks Prize, Royal Can Acad, 64; Lynch-Staunton Award, Can Art Coun, 73. *Bibliog:* Don Thompson (producer), A Passionate Harmony (TV film), Vision Ser, TV Ont, 83. *Mem:* Conseil artistes peintres (vpres, 78-79); Fedn artistes arts visuels Que (pres, 78-79). *Publ:* Auth, Grande probite intellectuelle, Devoir, Que, 60; auth, L'artiste devant son oeuvre, Cahiers, Que, 79. *Dealer:* Galerie Samuel Lallouz 1620 Sherbrooke W Montreal PQ Can. *Mailing Add:* 1631 Amherst Montreal PQ H2L 3L4 Canada

BARBEE, ROB
PAINTER
b Memphis, Tenn, March 26, 40. *Study:* Covenant Col, BA, 63; Memphis State Univ, BS, 73. *Exhib:* Ky Watercolor Soc Nat Exhib, Louisville, 82; Am Watercolor Soc Ann, New York, 83; Allied Artists Am Ann, New York, 83; Nat Arts Club Ann Watercolor Exhib, New York, 83; Southern Watercolor Soc Ann, Asheville, NC, 83. *Awards:* Second Merit Award, Caroliniana Watercolor Exhib, 81; Fifth Merit Award, 81 & Ninth Merit Award, 83, SC Watercolor Soc Ann Exhib. *Mem:* Artists Guild, Greenville, SC; Guild SC Artists; Southern Watercolor Soc. *Media:* Watercolor. *Dealer:* Tempo Gallery 125 W Stone Ave Greenville SC 29602. *Mailing Add:* 6 Randy Ave Taylors SC 29687

BARBEE, ROBERT THOMAS
PAINTER, GRAPHIC ARTIST
b Detroit, Mich, Sept 25, 21. *Study:* Cranbrook Acad Art, BA & MFA; Centenary Col; also in Mex. *Work:* Butler Inst Am Art, Youngstown, Ohio; Cranbrook Acad Art, Bloomfield Hills, Mich. *Exhib:* Five shows, Va Mus Fine Arts, Richmond, 53-65 & Traveling Exhibs, 58 & 62; Birmingham Mus Art, 59; Norfolk Mus Art & Sci, 60; Mus Art of Ogunquit, Maine, 62 & 63; Am Fedn Arts, New York, 65; and others. *Teaching:* Instr painting & drawing, Univ Va, assoc prof art, 70- *Awards:* Prizes, Irene Leach Mem Exhib, Norfolk Mus Arts & Sci, 62 & 64 & Thalheimer's Exhib, Richmond, 63. *Mailing Add:* Dept of Art Univ of Va Charlottesville VA 22903

BARBER, RONALD
ADMINISTRATOR
Study: Union Col, Schenectady, NY; Goddard Col, Plainfield, Vt; Univ Without Walls, Skidmore Col, Saratoga, NY. *Collections Arranged:* Norman Rockwell Retrospective, 73; Pa Acad Fine Arts Fel Exhib, 74; Woman's Work, 74. *Pos:* Dir, Mus Philadelphia Civic Ctr, currently. *Teaching:* Adj fac painting & photog, Empire State Col, Albany, NY, 70-71. *Mailing Add:* Civic Ctr Mus Civic Ctr Blvd & 34th St Philadelphia PA 19104

BARBERA, JOE
CARTOONIST
b New York, NY. *Study:* Am Inst Banking. *Pos:* Freelance mag cartoonist; story man, MGM, 37; co-producer with Bill Hanna, Tom & Jerry Cartoon Series; partner, Hanna & Barbera Prod, New York, 57-, producers of Ruff & Reddy, Huckleberry Hound, Quick Draw McGraw, The Flintstones, Yogi Bear, The Jetsons & many others. *Awards:* Numerous awards for animated cartoons. *Mailing Add:* Hanna-Barbera Productions, Inc 3400 Cahuenga Blvd Hollywood CA 90068

BARBOUR, ARTHUR J
PAINTER, WRITER
b Paterson, NJ, Aug 23, 26. *Study:* Newark Sch Fine & Indust Art; and with Avery Johnson, Syd Brown & James Carlin. *Work:* US Navy Dept; Marietta Col; Norfolk Mus Arts & Sci; Prudential Life Ins Co; & many pvt collections. *Comn:* Watercolors, Woman's Day Mag, Ford Motor Co & Essex Chem Corp; mural, Am Artists Christmas Card Group. *Exhib:* Nat Acad Design, New York; Am Watercolor Soc, New York; Am Artists Prof League; one-man show, Beaumont Mus Art, Tex, 65; Wolf Gallery, Franklin, NJ, 73; Fritchman Galleries, Boise, Idaho, 74; and others. *Awards:* Plainfield Art Asn Awards, 64; Grumbacher Award, NJ Watercolor Soc & Silver Medal, 75; Allied Artists Am, 72. *Mem:* Am & NJ Watercolor Socs; Painters & Sculptors Soc NJ; Allied Artists; Nat Soc Painters Casein & Acrylic. *Media:* Watercolor. *Publ:* Auth, Painting Building in Watercolor 73, Painting the Seasons in Watercolor, 75 & Watercolor: The Wet Technique, Watson-Guptill; and others. *Mailing Add:* 29 Voorhis Pl Ringwood NJ 07456

BARCUS, DAVID L
ADMINISTRATOR, MUSEUM DIRECTOR
b Mt Vernon, Ohio, Sept 25, 49. *Study:* Northwestern Univ; Ohio State Univ, BA, 72; Bowling Green State Univ, MA, 74. *Pos:* Cult dir, Bicentennial Comn, Ft Wayne, Ind, 75-76; asst to dir, Ft Wayne Fine Arts Found, 77-78; bd dirs/secy, Artlink Galleries, Ft Wayne, 78-81; asst dir, Ft Wayne Mus Art, 79-81; dir development, Ore Mus Sci & Industry, 81- *Mem:* Ore Mus Asn; Western Mus Asn. *Publ:* Contribr, Discovery, FAF, 77; contribr, Buildings Reborn: New Uses, Old Places, Harper & Row, 78; contribr, City Limits, Delta Commun, 79. *Mailing Add:* 7315 SW Beaverton Hwy #206 Portland OR 97225

BARD, JOELLEN
PAINTER, SCULPTOR
b Brooklyn, NY, June 19, 42. *Study:* Syracuse Univ Art Sch, 59-62; Brooklyn Col, painting with Philip Pearlstein, MA, 67; Brooklyn Mus Art Sch, Max Beckman, scholar class, 70-73; Pratt Inst, Hon BFA. *Work:* Many pvt & corp collections. *Exhib:* Brooklyn Mus, 73 & 74; one-man shows, Brooklyn Mus Little Gallery, 73, Gallery 91, Brooklyn, 74-76 & Pleiades Gallery, New York, 75, 77, 79 & 82. *Collections Arranged:* Tenth St Days--The Co-ops of the 50s. *Pos:* Dir, Asn Artist Run Galleries, 77- *Teaching:* Art teacher, New York Bd Educ, 64-69 & 78-, Kingsborough Community Col, 79- *Bibliog:* Eileen Blair (auth), Mindscapes, 3/21/75, The Phoenix; David Shirey (auth), Artists forming sobro..., New York Times, 3/75; Helen Thomas (auth), article in Arts Mag, 3/79. *Mem:* Women in the Arts; Col Art Asn; Found for Community of Artists. *Media:* Acrylic; Plexiglas, Color Xerox. *Dealer:* Pleiades Gallery 164 Mercer St New York NY 10012. *Mailing Add:* 1430 E 24th St Brooklyn NY 11210

BARDAZZI, PETER
PAINTER
b New York, NY, Mar 5, 43. *Study:* Pratt Inst, BFA, 67; Yale Univ, MFA, 69; also study art & archit, Asia. *Work:* Mus Mod Art, New York; Purchase Mus, NY; Corcoran Gallery, Washington, DC; Rockefeller Univ. *Exhib:* One-man shows, Cordier & Ekstrom Gallery, 71, 72, 74, 76 & 78 & St Mary's Col, Md, 75; Whitney Mus Am Art Painting Ann, 72; Indianapolis Mus Art Painting & Sculpture Today, 72; Am Acad Arts & Lett, 73; Cordier & Ekstrom, 76; Corcoran Gallery, 76; Univ Tex, Austin, 76. *Pos:* Guest lectr & artist in residence, St Mary's Col, Md, 75. *Awards:* Fed Work Study Prog Award, 68; Painting Award, New Britain Mus, Conn, 69. *Bibliog:* Hilton Kramer (auth), 10/74 & Vivian Raynor (auth), 5/78, articles, New York Times; Peter Frank (auth), article, Art News Mag, 10/78; and others. *Mailing Add:* PO Box 60 Canal St Sta New York NY 10013

BARDIN, JESSE REDWIN
PAINTER
b Elloree, SC, Mar 26, 23. *Study:* Univ SC, AB & cert(painting); Art Students League, with Will Barnet & Harry Sternberg, Bernay Merit Scholar for advan study with Byron Browne & Vyclav Vytlaci. *Work:* Mint Mus, Charlotte, NC; Williams Col Art Mus, Williamstown, Mass; La State Univ, Baton Rouge, La; SC State Art Collection, Columbia Mus Art. *Comn:* Paintings in bus collections throughout the US. *Exhib:* 21 Americans, Berlin Acad Art, Ger; Pa Acad Fine Arts Ann, Philadelphia; Butler Inst Am Art, Youngstown, Ohio; 50 Artists-50 States, Am Fedn Arts, Burpee Mus, Ill & traveling; Contemp SC Artists Tricentennial Exhib, Greenville Co Art Mus, SC, 71; Art Patron Art, Southeastern Ctr Contemp Art, Winston-Salem, NC, 81; retrospective, Columbia Mus Art, 82 & Atlanta Arts Festival, 82; plus numerous other int, nat & regional exhibs. *Awards:* Ford Found Purchase Prize, NC State Mus, 60; First Purchase Prize, Hunter Ann, Hunter Gallery Art, 62; First Prize, Springs Mill Art Exhib for NC & SC, 3 consecutive years. *Bibliog:* Adger Brown (auth), South Carolina art, State Newspaper, 71. *Mem:* Life mem Art Students League; Southeastern Ctr Contemp Arts; Columbia Art Asn. *Media:* Oil, Mixed Media. *Res:* In museums in US, Europe and Central America. *Mailing Add:* 1723 Devine St Columbia SC 29201

BAREISS, PHILIP C
DEALER, COLLECTOR
b New York, NY, Oct 5, 49. *Study:* Yale Univ Grad Sch, MA, 73. *Collections Arranged:* Cowboys and Indians, Douglas Kent Hall Photog, Western Mus Tour. *Pos:* Dir, Maggie Kress Gallery, Taos, NMex, 79- *Collection:* Contemporary graphics, paintings and southwest art. *Mailing Add:* N Pueblo Rd Taos NM 87571

BAREISS, WALTER
COLLECTOR
b Tubingen, WGer, May 24, 19. *Study:* Yale Univ, BS; Columbia Law Sch. *Pos:* Mem gov bd, Art Gallery, Yale Univ; mem vis comt, Dept Greek & Roman Art, Metrop Mus, New York; mem purchasing comn 20th century art & chmn gallery asn, Bavarian State Mus, Munich, Ger. *Collection:* Twentieth century art; Greek vases, fifth and sixth centuries, BC. *Mailing Add:* 60 E 42nd St New York NY 10017

BARETSKI, CHARLES ALLAN
LIBRARIAN, HISTORIAN
b Mount Carmel, Pa, Nov 21, 18. *Study:* New York Univ, with Demetrios Tselos, Unified Study Curric scholarships, 35-37; Rutgers State Univ, BA(cum laude), 45; Columbia Univ, BSLS, 46, MSLS, 51; Am Univ, archival dipl, 51, advan archival admin dipl, 55; Univ Notre Dame, MA, 57, PhD, 58; Polish Arts Workshop, Univ Minn Exten, dipl, 60; New York Univ Grad Sch Arts & Sci, MA, 65, PhD, 69. *Collections Arranged:* International Folk & Handicrafts Exhibitions (series), 54-56; individual exhibs arts & crafts of Spain, Cuba, Port, Ukraine, Poland, PR, Lithuania, Italy, Greece, Iraq, Hungary, WCent Africa, Netherlands & others, 57- *Pos:* Prof librn, Newark Pub Libr, 38-44, sr art libr asst, 44-47, sr art librn, 48-54, br libr dir, 54-56 & 57-; founder & dir, Inst Polish Cult, Seton Hall Univ, South Orange, NJ, 53-54, res historian, 53-; fac mem, Rutgers State Univ--Newark Col, NJ, 65-66; historian, Polish Arts Club, 76-, pres, 80-; coordr & curric develop specialist, Slavic-Am Hist & Cult Studies, Sr Citizen Inst, Essex Co Col, NJ, 77-78. *Awards:* Distinguished Educator Am Award, 79; Nat Founder's Award for Distinguished Service, Polish Art Clubs, USA, 80; Outstanding Art Educator, US Achievement Acad, Lexington, Ky, 83. *Bibliog:* Dorothy Rowe (auth), Man of letters-the whole alphabet, NJ Music & Arts Mag, summer 53; Raymond F Wegrzynek (auth), Ironbound humanist extolled, Star-Ledger, 1/78; Dr Baretski is named distinguished educator, Vailsburg Leader, 3/79. *Mem:* Am Coun Polish Art Cult Clubs (nat archivist & historian, 54-). *Res:* Nineteenth century American painting; historical school of Polish painting in the nineteenth century; European folk art of nineteenth and twentieth centuries; history of Polish arts cultural clubs in the US. *Publ:* Auth, Reappraisal & reaffirmation, winter 53 & High horizons education program in New York City, 61, Art in Am; auth, History of the American Council of Polish Culture Clubs 1948-1973, 73; contrib auth, P S Arts--postscript on Polish art, 77. *Mailing Add:* 229 Montclair Ave Newark NJ 07104

BARKER, AL C
PAINTER, PRINTMAKER
b West Paterson, NJ, June 19, 41. *Study:* WVa Univ, BS, 64; Univ RI, MS, 67; Rutgers Univ, 69-70. *Work:* Sportman's Edge Ltd & Crossroads Sport, New York; Easton Waterfowl Mus, Md. *Comn:* NH Ducks Unlimited, Hooksett, 79 & 80; L A Frame Company, Green Brook, NJ, 80; American Hotel, Freehold, NJ, 81; 1st Nat State Bank, Newark NJ, 81; NJ State Ducks Unlimited, Monmouth, NJ, 81. *Exhib:* Easton Waterfowl Exhib, Tidewater Inn, Md, 70-81; Philadelphia Waterfowl Exposition, Mem Hall, Pa, 79-81; Safari Club Int, Am Fac Dallas-Ft Worth Airport, Tex, 80; Tulsa Wildlife Exposition, The Great Hall, Camelot Inn, Okla, 80 & 81; Southeastern Wildlife Exposition, Charleston, SC, 82. *Teaching:* Instr forestry, wildlife, Essec Agr Inst, Danvers, Mass, 67-69; instr, Univ RI, Kingston, 67; instr, NJ State Conservation Sch, Branchville, 69; instr biology, Hightstown High Sch, NJ, 71-78. *Awards:* Purchase Award, Graphic Excellance, Albany Print Club, 76; Arthur T Hill Award, Salmagundi Club, 78. *Mem:* Salmagundi Club, New York (bd dir 78-81); Somerset Art Alliance. *Media:* Watercolor, Oil; Graphics. *Mailing Add:* PO Box 703 214 Prince Street Bordentown NJ 08505

BARKER, WALTER WILLIAM
PAINTER, WRITER
b Coblenz, Ger, Aug 8, 21; US citizen. *Study:* Washington Univ, BFA, 48, with Phillip Guston & Max Beckmann; Iowa Univ, with Mauricio Lassansky; Univ Ind, with Alton Pickens & Henry Hope, MFA, 50. *Work:* Mus Mod Art & Brooklyn Mus, New York; Hirshhorn Collection, Washington, DC; Boston Mus Fine Arts; James Michener Collection, Univ Tex, Austin; and others. *Exhib:* Int Exhib Mod Graphic Art, Mus Mod Art, New York, 52; American Painting, Va Mus Fine Art, Richmond, 62; Painting & Sculpture Today, Herron Inst Art, Indianapolis, Ind, 67; Univ Tex, Austin; Weatherspoon Gallery; James A Michener Collection, Univ Tex, Austin, 75; Univ NC, Greensboro, 77; and others. *Pos:* Spec corresp, St Louis Post-Dispatch, 62-78. *Teaching:* Lectr art hist, Salem Col, 49-50; instr painting, Washington Univ, 50-62; instr basic found, Brooklyn Mus Sch, 63-66; assoc prof painting, Univ NC, 66- *Awards:* New Talent USA Award, 56; Spec Citation Art Rev, Col Art Asn, 66; Distinguished Alumnus, Washington Univ, 72. *Bibliog:* Ernest Smith (auth), Walter Barker, 1958-1968, Webster Col, 68; Joseph Pulitzer, Jr (auth), Walter Barker, Fogg Mus Art, Harvard Univ, 71; Patricia Krebs (auth), On the making of an artist, Greensboro Daily News, 77. *Mem:* Max Beckmann Gesellschaft, Munich, Ger; and others. *Res:* Max Beckmann's last years in the US. *Publ:* Auth introd, Max Beckmann in America (catalog), Viviano Gallery, 69; auth, Lucian Krokowski & Max Beckmann, Joseph Pulitzer Collection, Vol 3, 71; auth, Max Beckmann's advice to his students, Weatherspoon Gallery Asn Bulletin, Univ NC, 79; auth, Max Beckmann as a Teacher (exhib catalog), Prestel-Verlag, Munich, 84. *Dealer:* Betty Parsons Gallery 24 W 57th St New York NY 10019. *Mailing Add:* Dept of Art Univ of NC Greensboro NC 27412

BARKUS, MARIONA MARCIA
PAINTER, COLLAGE ARTIST
b Harvey, Ill, Mar 26, 48. *Study:* Art Inst Chicago, Ill, 66; Northwestern Univ, Evanston, Ill, BA, 70; Univ Calif, Los Angeles, 72; Pepperdine Univ, 74. *Work:* Freeport Art Mus, Ill; KFAC Radio, Los Angeles, Calif. *Exhib:* Solo exhib, Freeport Art Mus, Ill, 80; The American Dream Mediated, Los Angeles Contemp Exhibs, 82; Southern Exposure Gallery, San Francisco, 83; Conejo Valley Art Mus, 83; At Home, Long Beach Mus Art, 83; and others. *Pos:* Coordr, Open Wall Gallery, Woman's Bldg, Los Angeles, 79-80. *Bibliog:* Article, Feminist Studies, spring 82; Christopher Knight (auth), Eleven artists take on the media, Los Angeles Herald Examiner, 6/27/82. *Mem:* Los Angeles Inst Contemp Art; Womens Caucus Art; Woman's Bldg; Artists Equity. *Media:* Acrylic; Color Xerox, Collage. *Publ:* Auth, Illustrated History-1982, Litkus Press, 82. *Mailing Add:* PO Box 34785 Los Angeles CA 90034

BARNES, CAROLE D
PAINTER
b Bellefonte, Colo, Nov 12, 35. *Study:* Pa State Univ, BA(art ed), 57; also with Edward Betts, Glenn Bradshaw, Alex Nepote & Chen Chi. *Work:* Int Bus Machines, Austin, Tex; Utah State Univ, Logan; United Banks & Midland Savings, Colo. *Exhib:* Rocky Mountain Nat Watermedia Soc, Golden, Colo, 78-80 & 82-83; Am Watercolor Soc, New York, 75-78 & 83; Nat Acad Design Ann, New York, 76, 78 & 81-82; Allied Artists Ann, New York, 76-77 & 81-83; Nat Watercolor Soc, Los Angeles, 77-78 & 80-82. *Awards:* Ralph Fabri Medal Hon, Nat Soc Painters Casein & Acrylic, 80; Gold Medal, San Diego Nat, Calif, 82; Ford Times Award, Am Watercolor Soc, New York, 83. *Bibliog:* Gerald Brommer (auth), The Art of Collage; Barbara Nechis (auth), Watercolor: The Creative Experience; Fritz Henning (auth), article, Northlight Bk Club Mag, 1/83. *Mem:* Am Watercolor Soc; Allied Artists; Nat Watercolor Soc; Nat Soc Painters Casein & Acrylic; Rocky Mountain Nat Watermedia Soc. *Media:* Watercolor, Acrylic. *Dealer:* Rhoda Reiss 429 Acoma Denver CO 80204. *Mailing Add:* 3772 Lakebriar Dr Boulder CO 80302

BARNES, CARROLL
SCULPTOR
b Des Moines, Iowa, June 26, 06. *Study:* Wessington Springs Jr Col, SDak, 27-28; Corcoran Sch Art, Washington, DC, 38; Cranbrook Acad Art, Bloomfield Hills, Mich, scholar with Carl Milles, 40. *Work:* Duncan Phillips Gallery, Washington, DC; Ft Worth Art Mus, Tex; Los Angeles Co Mus; Fresno Arts Ctr, Calif; Cranbrook Acad Art Mus; and others. *Comn:* Paul Bunyan, giant redwood sculpture, Porterville Conv Ctr, Calif, 40; foyer sculpture in lignum vitae & stainless steel, Kern Co Pub Libr, 53; fountain of terrazo & aluminum, Fresno Co Courthouse Pk, 66; sculpture in corten steel, San Francisco Munic Transit Facil, 75; sculpture in mirror polished steel, North Calif Savings, Santa Rosa, Calif, 77; and others. *Exhib:* Mus Mod Art, Washington, DC, 39; Whitney Mus, New York, 40; San Francisco Mus Art, 42 & 49; Santa Barbara Mus Art, Calif, 50 & Palo Alto Cult Ctr, 73; and over 40 one-man shows since 1938. *Teaching:* Asst prof sculpture, Univ Tex, Austin, 47-48; instr, Santa Rosa Jr Col, 80. *Awards:* Cult Citation, Gov Earl

Warren, Calif, 48; Sculpture Prize, Sonoma Co Arts Coun, 73; Mayors Cult Award of Merit, Santa Rosa, 78. *Bibliog:* Arts: Big redwood carving, Time Mag, 42; Sculptor Carroll Barnes, film, Richard Simpson, PBS/NET of KVIE-TV, Sacramento, Calif; Nicholas Roukes (auth), Masters of Wood Sculpture, Univ Calgary. *Mem:* Sonoma Co Arts Coun (adv bd, 80-81). *Media:* Steel, Wood. *Dealer:* Source Gallery 1099 Folson St San Francisco CA 94103. *Mailing Add:* 1450 Tilton Rd Sebastopol CA 95472

BARNES, CLIFF (CLIFFORD V)
PAINTER, ILLUSTRATOR

b Bell, Calif, Mar 19, 40. *Study:* Art Ctr Sch Design, Los Angeles, BPA, 62. *Exhib:* Western Heritage, Arrapahoe Fairgrounds, Littleton, Colo, 80-83; American Indian & Cowboy Artists, San Dimas Mus, Calif, 80-83; Margaret Jamison Presents, Sweeney Convention Ctr, Santa Fe, 81; Three Men on the Mountain, San Bernardino Co Mus, Redlands, Calif, 84. *Awards:* Sid Burns Mem Award, Death Valley Invitational, 81-83; Gold Medal Oil & Drawing, Western Heritage, 82 & 83; Eagle Award & Gold Medal, Festival of Western Art, Am Indian & Cowboy Artists, 83. *Mem:* Am Indian & Cowboy Artists (pres, 81-82; bd mem, 82-84). *Media:* Oil, Watercolor; Charcoal. *Mailing Add:* PO Box 741 Lake Arrowhead CA 92352

BARNES, CURT (CURTIS EDWARD)
PAINTER, INSTRUCTOR

b Taft, Calif, Jan 17, 43. *Study:* Univ Calif, Berkeley, BA, 64; Pratt Inst, MFA, 66. *Work:* Mus Contemp Art, Bogota, Columbia; Prudential Insurance Corp Am, Newark, NJ; Franklin Furnace Arch, New York. *Exhib:* Red River Art Ann, Moorehead, Minn, 67; Chicago Ann, Art Inst of Chicago, 67; New Am Painting, Univ NMex, Albuquerque, 71; Salon Exhib, O K Harris Gallery, New York, 72 & 79; Contemporary Reflections, Aldrich Mus Contemp Art, Ridgefield, Conn, 75; one-man show, Allesandra Gallery, New York, 76; Hampshire Col Gallery, Amherst, Mass, 79. *Collections Arranged:* Six Artists, Paterson Col, Wayne, NJ, 75; Group Exhib, Allesandra Gallery, 75. *Teaching:* Instr painting & drawing, Univ Wis, Stevens Point, 66-67; instr drawing, Parsons Sch Design, New York, 67-71; assoc prof painting, drawing & 20th century art hist, Fordham Univ, 69-; vis assoc prof, Hampshire Col, 79-80; vis adj prof, Pratt Institute, 81. *Awards:* Yaddo Fel, summer 76. *Bibliog:* John Perreault (auth), Catching up, Soho Weekly News, 3/76; Nancy Grove (auth), Curt Barnes (rev), Arts Mag, 4/76; Joseph Wiltsee (auth), Investing in young artists, Bus Wk, 5/76. *Media:* Acrylic. *Mailing Add:* 114 W Houston St New York NY 10012

BARNES, EDWARD LARRABEE
ARCHITECT

b Chicago, Ill, Apr 22, 15. *Study:* Harvard Univ, BS(cum laude), 38; Harvard Grad Sch Design, MA(archit), 42. *Comn:* Walker Art Ctr, T B Walker Found, Minneapolis, 71; Sarah M Scaife Gallery, Carnegie Inst, Pittsburgh, 74; Asia House, Asia Soc, New York, 81; Dallas Mus Art, City of Dallas, Tex, 82. *Exhib:* Archit for Arts: State Univ NY Col, Purchase & Mus Mod Art, New York, 71; retrospective, Scaife Gallery, Carnegie Inst Mus Art, Pittsburgh, 74. *Pos:* Trustee, NY Studio Sch Painting & Sculpture, 70-, Mus Mod Art, 76- & Ft Lauderdale Art Mus, 82. *Teaching:* Vis critic archit design, Yale Univ, New Haven, Conn, 57-59; vis critic archit design, Harvard Grad Sch Design, 79-80. *Awards:* Hon Award, 72 & 77 & Firm Award, 80, Am Inst Archit; Louis Sullivan Award, Int Union Bricklayers & Allied Craftsmen & Am Inst Archit, 79. *Bibliog:* Hilton Kramer (auth), Grace, flexibility, esthetic tact, New York Times, 7/71; Peter Blake (auth), Brick on brick and white on white, Archit Plus, 7-8/74; Paul Goldberger (auth), What should a museum be?, Art News, 10/75. *Mem:* Academician Nat Acad Design; fel Am Acad Arts & Sci; Westchester Coun Arts (dir, 60, treas, 61). *Mailing Add:* 410 E 62nd St New York NY 10021

BARNES, KIT
PAINTER

b Wilson, NC, June 24, 46. *Study:* Univ NC, Chapel Hill, BFA, 73, MFA, 75. *Work:* Ackland Mus. *Exhib:* 37th Ann NC Artists Exhib, NC Mus Art, Raleigh, 74; Thesis Show, Ackland Mus, 75; Drawing Presentation of MFA Candidates, Corcoran Gallery, 75; The Glass Door: Artists Immigrant of Washington, Washington Proj Arts, 76; Biennial Exhib Piedmont Painting & Sculpture, Mint Mus, 79; solo exhib, PS1, Long Island City, NY, 79; Art on Paper, Weatherspoon Art Gallery, Greensboro, NC, 82; Chinese Chance 4th Ann Exhib, 1 Univ Pl, New York, 82-83. *Bibliog:* Valentin Tatransky (auth), Group show, Arts Mag, 3/83. *Media:* Oil on Canvas and Paper. *Mailing Add:* 45 W 28th St New York NY 10001

BARNES, LUCINDA ANN
HISTORIAN, GALLERY DIRECTOR

b Cincinnati, Ohio, May 16, 51. *Study:* NY Univ, with Robert Rosenblum, BA(art hist), 73; Williams Col, with George Heard Hamilton, Daniel Robbins, Franklin Robinson & Creighton Gilbert, MA(art hist), 78. *Collections Arranged:* Lines of Vision: Latin American Drawings (auth, catalog), Ctr Inter-Am Relations, 77; George Rickey: Drawings for Sculpture (auth, catalog), Williams Col Mus Art, 77; The Avant Garde in Russia (auth, catalog), Los Angeles Co Mus Art, 79. *Pos:* Cur & adminr, George Rickey Workshop, East Chatham, NY, 76-78; dir, Karl Bornstein Gallery, Santa Monica, Calif, 80- *Teaching:* Instr connoisseurship, Univ Calif, Los Angeles, 82-; instr art, Saddleback Col, 84. *Mem:* Col Art Asn. *Res:* Twentieth century European and American art. *Specialty:* Contemporary West Coast art. *Mailing Add:* 390 Ruby St Laguna Beach CA 92651

BARNES, MOLLY
DEALER, WRITER

b London, Eng, May 18, 36; US citizen. *Study:* Univ Calif, Berkeley, BA, 57. *Pos:* Art critic, KFWB Radio, Los Angeles, 74-78; owner & dir, Anhalt/Barnes Gallery, 74-79; asst, Frank Perls Gallery, 78; writer, Hollywood Reporter, 78-; owner & dir, Molly Barnes Gallery, 79- *Specialty:* Contemporary Californians, Robert Cottingham, Don Eddy, John Baldessari & Jack Reilly. *Mailing Add:* 750 N La Cienega Blvd Los Angeles CA 90069

BARNES, ROBERT M
PAINTER, EDUCATOR

b Washington, DC, Sept 24, 34. *Study:* Art Inst Chicago, BFA, 56; Univ Chicago, BFA, 56; Columbia Univ, 56; Hunter Col, 57-61; Univ London Slade Sch, Fulbright Grant, 61-63. *Work:* Mus Mod Art, Whitney Mus Am Art, New York; Art Inst Chicago; Pasadena Art Mus, Calif. *Comn:* Ed lithographs, New York Hilton Hotel, 62. *Exhib:* Mus Civico, Bologna, 65; Galerie Dragon, Paris, 67; Univ Ill, 67; Kansas City Art Inst, 72; Galeria Fanta Spade, Rome, 72; and others. *Teaching:* Instr grad painting, Ind Univ, 60-61; vis artist, Kansas City Art Inst, 63-64; asst prof painting & drawing, Ind Univ, Bloomington, 65-70, prof, Dept Fine Arts, 70- *Awards:* Copley Found Award, 61. *Dealer:* Allan Frumkin Gallery 620 N Michigan Ave Chicago IL 60603. *Mailing Add:* Dept of Fine Arts Ind Univ Bloomington IN 47401

BARNET, WILL
PAINTER, PRINTMAKER

b Beverly, Mass, May 25, 11. *Study:* Boston Mus Fine Arts Sch, with Phillip Hale, 27-30; Art Students League, with Charles Locke, 30-33. *Work:* Boston Mus Fine Arts; Whitney Mus Am Art; Metrop Mus Art; Guggenheim Mus; Cincinnati Art Mus; and others. *Exhib:* Inst Contemp Art, Boston; Mus Mod Art; Pa Acad Fine Arts, 70; retrospective, Assoc Am Artists, 72 & Portraits, Terry Dintenfass Gallery, New York, 82; one-man show, Hirschl & Adler Galleries Inc, 76 & 81; Will Barnet, 20 Years of Painting & Drawing, Neuberger Mus, Purchase, 79-80; Ringling Mus, Sarasota, Fla, 80; Wichita Art Mus, 83; and others. *Teaching:* Instr, Art Students League, 36-; instr, Cooper Union Art Sch, 45-65, prof, 65-; instr, Mont State Col, summer 51; vis critic, Yale Univ, 52 & 53; instr, Univ Ohio & Univ Minn, Duluth, 58 & Univ Wash, 63; instr, Des Moines Art Ctr, Iowa, 65; distinguished vis prof, Pa State Univ, 65-66; instr, Pa Acad Fine Arts, 67-; vis prof, Cornell Univ, 68-69. *Awards:* Walter Lippincott Prize, Pa Acad Fine Arts, 68; Benjamin Altman Prize, Nat Acad Design, 77; Childe Hassam Award, Arts & Letters, 82. *Bibliog:* James T Farrell (auth), Paintings of Will Barnet, Press Eight, New York, 50; Robert Beverly Hale (auth), Will Barnet--27 Paintings Completed 1960-1968, New York, 68. *Mem:* Am Abstr Artists; Nat Acad Design; Century Asn; Royal Soc Arts, London; Am Acad & Inst Arts & Lett. *Dealer:* Kennedy Galleries 40 W 57 St New York NY. *Mailing Add:* 15 Gramercy Park New York NY 10003

BARNETT, DAVID J
DEALER, COLLECTOR

b Milwaukee, Wis, Feb 22, 46. *Study:* Lincoln Col; Univ Wis-Milwaukee. *Pos:* Owner, David Barnett Gallery, currently. *Mem:* Milwaukee Art Ctr; Chicago Art Inst; Arch Am Art; Milwaukee Pub Mus; Appraisers Asn Am. *Specialty:* Nineteenth and twentieth century European and American masters. *Mailing Add:* David Barnett Gallery 2101 W Wisconsin Ave Milwaukee WI 53233

BARNETT, EARL D
DESIGNER, PAINTER

b Trenton, Tenn. *Study:* Cleveland Sch Art, with Henry G Keller, Viktor Schreckengost, Willard Combes, Kenneth Bates & Frank Wilcox. *Work:* Butler Inst Am Art; Grover M Hermann Fine Arts Ctr, Marietta, Ohio. *Comn:* Six past pres portraits, Bd Dir Room, Benefit Trust Life Ins Co, Chicago, Ill, 64-70; portrait, Hon Robert Downing, Glenview, Ill, 67; past pres portraits, Contracting Plasterers' & Lathers' Int Asn Union Hall, 67-82; portrait, Adm James Ross, Naval Armory, Chicago, 70. *Exhib:* Cooperstown Art Asn, NY, 62-72; Allied Artists, New York, 64-73; Butler Inst Am Art, 65-82; Union League Club Ann, Chicago, 67, 68 & 72; Mainstreams, Marietta, 72, 73, 76 & 78; Tex Fine Arts Asn Ann, 73 & 79. *Pos:* Art dir, W L Stensgaard & Assocs, Chicago, 45-47; asst art dir & designer, Kling Studios, Chicago, 48-61; vpres & creative dir, J M Callan Co, Chicago, 61-67; vpres & creative dir, Conway Displays, Inc, Niles, Ill, 67-74; merchandise mgr, NCM Int, Arlington Heights, Ill, 74-79; creative dir, Chicago Show Print, Morton Grove, Ill, 79- *Awards:* First Place W/C, Tex Fine Arts Asn Ann, 79; NMex Art League Ann, Albuquerque, 80; Spec Mention, Butler Inst Am Art, 82. *Media:* Oil, Watercolor. *Mailing Add:* 4150 Central Rd Glenview IL 60025

BARNETT, ED WILLIS
PHOTOGRAPHER, WRITER

b Birmingham, Ala, May 8, 1899. *Study:* With Adolf Fassbender, Arthur Underwood & Otto Litzel. *Work:* Metrop Mus Art & Mus Mod Art, New York; Birmingham Mus Art; Seattle Art Mus; Mariners Mus, Newport News, Va; and others. *Exhib:* One-man shows, Birmingham Mus Art, 75, McGuire Mem Mus, Richmond, Ind, 78, Vienna, Austria, 78 & many others; 2 of 50 Best All-Time US Color Prints, Royal Photog Soc, London & mus in Brit, also American Color Show, Kodak Gallery, Grand Cent Sta, New York, 62-63; Photo Europe, Juried, France, Switz & Belg, 65; Barcelona, 79; over 1500 hangings in some 800 exhibs around the world, 54- *Pos:* Dir, Ala Int Exhib Photog, 62, 73-75; pres, Ala Mus Photog, 74- *Awards:* Coupe de la Ville de Perigueux, Syndicat d'Initiative, Perigueux, France, 69; Litzel Gold Medal, 74; Two Silver Stars, Photog Soc Am J, 79; plus others. *Bibliog:* Tommy Black (auth), E W Barnett: Birmingham-World photo visionary, Birmingham News,

3/15/81. *Mem:* Fel Photog Soc Am; Fedn Int Art Photog; hon mem Fedn Nat Soc Photog France; hon mem Austrian Co Photogr; hon mem Cine-Photo Club Perigourdin; and others. *Publ:* Auth & illusr, Perigord--for Pleasure and Pictures, 67; auth, Samuel Chamberlain N A, an Appreciation, 70; auth, New Angles in Exhibitions, 74; auth & illusr, Man Ray in Retrospective, 77 & Shot with Luck, 78. *Mailing Add:* 4322 Glenwood Ave Birmingham AL 35222

BARNETT, JACK
PAINTER, INSTRUCTOR
b Ft Worth, Tex, Nov 18, 44. *Study:* Ft Worth Art Ctr, 68-70; Pa Acad Fine Arts, Cresson Mem Traveling Scholar, studied under Ben Kamihira, Louis Sloan & Julian Levi, 71-75. *Exhib:* Rutgers Univ, Camden, NJ, 76; Realist Show, Woodmere Art Gallery, 78 & New Generation Painters, Gross McCleaf Gallery, 81, Philadelphia; one-man shows, Philadelphia Art Alliance, 82 & Gross McCleaf Gallery, Philadelphia, 82; and others. *Teaching:* Instr, Pa Acad Fine Arts, Philadelphia, 79- *Awards:* S J Wallace Truman Prize, Nat Acad Design, 74 & 76; Purchase Prize, Butler Inst Am Art, 76. *Media:* Oil, Watercolor. *Dealer:* Gross McCleaf Gallery 1713 Walnut St Philadelphia PA 19103. *Mailing Add:* 805 S 8th St Philadelphia PA 19147

BARNETT, VIVIAN ENDICOTT
CURATOR
b Putnam, Conn, July 8, 44. *Study:* Vassar Col, AB, 65; Inst Fine Arts, NY Univ, MA, 71; Grad Ctr, City Univ New York. *Collections Arranged:* Kandinsky Watercolors from Solomon R Guggenheim Collection (auth, catalog), 81-82; Vasily Kandinsky (auth, catalog), Art Gallery New South Wales, 82; Kandinsky in Munich, 82 & Kandinsky: Russian and Bauhaus Years, 83, Guggenheim Mus. *Pos:* Res asst, Solomon R Guggenheim Mus, 73-77, curatorial asst, 78-79, assoc cur, 80-81, res cur, 81-82, cur, 82- *Mem:* Col Art Asn Am; Am Asn Mus; Int Coun Mus. *Res:* Kandinsky; Picasso; Beckmann. *Publ:* Auth, The Guggenheim Museum: Justin K Thannhauser Collection, 78; auth, Handbook: The Guggenheim Mus Collection 1900-1980, 80; auth, Kandinsky: From drawing and watercolor to oil, Drawing, 7/81; auth, Kandinsky at the Guggenheim, 83; auth, 100 Works by Modern Masters from the Guggenheim Mus, 84. *Mailing Add:* Solomon R Guggenheim Mus 1071 Fifth Ave New York NY 10128

BARNHART, C RAYMOND
ASSEMBLAGE ARTIST, SCULPTOR
b Ripley, WVa, June 28, 03. *Study:* Marshall Univ, AB, 32; Ohio State Univ, MFA, 36; Sch Design, Chicago, with Moholy-Nagy, 38; Black Mt Col, NC, with Josef Albers & Jean Charlot, 44; Inst Politech Nac, Mexico City, with Jose Gutierrez, 48-49, 53 & 55. *Exhib:* One-man shows, Caravan Gallery, New York, 55, Art Ctr, Louisville, Ky, 63-66, Cleveland Inst Art, 69, Richmond Art Ctr, Calif, 74, Berkeley Art Ctr, Calif, 72, plus over 50 one-man exhibs. *Teaching:* Prof drawing, design, painting & wood sculpture, Univ Ky, 36-68. *Awards:* Second Prize in Sculpture, Artrium Regional, Santa Rosa, Calif, 71-74 & Best of Show, 73. *Bibliog:* Rannells-Bayer (auth), The art of Raymond Barnhart, Univ Ky, 67; Meilach & Ten Hoor (auth), Collage and Assemblage, 73 & Box Art, 75, Crown. *Mailing Add:* 1947 Burnside Rd Sebastopol CA 95472

BARNWELL, JOHN L
PAINTER
b Los Angeles, Calif, Mar 17, 22. *Study:* Univ Calif, Berkeley, BA; Newark Sch Fine & Indust Art, NJ; Art Students League, with Frank Reilly; watercolor with Ed Whilney & Ferdinand Petrie. *Exhib:* Hunterdon Co Art Ctr State Show, 71; Am Artists Prof League Grand Nat Show, New York, 72-75; Benedictine Art Awards Finalist Show, New York, 72; Jersey City Mus, NJ, 77; Bergen Community Mus, NJ, 77; and others. *Awards:* Purchase Award, Hudson Artists State Show, 79; Best Watercolor, Miniature Art Soc, NJ, 83; Best Still Life, Am Artist Professional League, 83. *Mem:* Fel Am Artists Prof League; Miniature Art Soc NJ (pres, 75-); Art Students League. *Media:* Oil, Watercolor. *Dealer:* CAC Gallery Florham Park NJ; Artuenlure Gallery 202 Ridgewood Ave Ridgewood NJ 07450. *Mailing Add:* 3 Cosden Lane Wayne NJ 07470

BARON, HANNELORE
COLLAGE ARTIST
b Dillingen, Ger, June 8, 26; US citizen. *Study:* Self-taught. *Work:* Nat Collection Smithsonian Inst, Washington, DC; Ulster Co Community Col, Stoneridge, NY; Albright-Knox Art Gallery, Buffalo, NY. *Exhib:* One-person shows, Herbert E Feist Gallery, New York, 73, Hudson River Mus, 73; Katonah Gallery, 73, 76 & 77; Kathryn Markel Gallery, New York, 77 & 78; Gallery Schlesinger-Boisante, New York, 81. *Awards:* Nat Asn Women Artists Award, 68; Mus Purchase Award, Hudson River Mus, 72-77; Most Creative Aquarelle, Audubon Artists, 70, 72 & 73. *Mem:* Audubon Artists; Artists Equity Asn; Hudson River Contemp Artists; Nat Asn Women Artists. *Dealer:* Gallery Schlesinger-Boisante 822 Madison Ave New York NY 10021. *Mailing Add:* 5621 Delafield Ave Bronx NY 10471

BARONS, RICHARD IRWIN
MUSEUM DIRECTOR, HISTORIAN
b Bergen, NY, Apr 25, 46. *Study:* State Univ NY Col, New Paltz, BA, 70. *Collections Arranged:* Eighteenth and Nineteenth Century American Folk Pottery (auth, catalog), State Univ NY Col, New Paltz, 68; The American Cooking Hearth: Colonial and Post-Colonial Cooking Tools (auth, catalog), Broome Co Hist Soc, 76; The Folk Arts and Crafts of the Susquehanna and Chenango River Valleys, Roberson Ctr Arts & Sci, 78; Multiples: American Printmaking of the Last Ten Years, 79; Emil Holzhauer: Seventy-Five Years of an Artist's Life (auth, catalog), 80. *Pos:* Cur, Genesee Co Mus, 70-74; cur hist, Roberson Ctr Arts & Sci, 74-79; dir, Bement-Billings House, Newark Valley, NY, 83- *Teaching:* Instr art hist design, Broome Community Col, Binghamton, NY, 79- *Mem:* Am Asn Mus; Soc State & Local Hist; Soc Preserv Technol; Mus Am Folk Art. *Res:* Eighteenth and nineteenth century American arts and crafts. *Publ:* Coauth, Franck Taylor Bowers 1875-1932, 77 & auth, The Folk Tradition: The Early Arts and Crafts of the Susquehanna River Valley, 81, Roberson Ctr Arts & Sci. *Mailing Add:* Ransom House Maine NY 13802

BAROOSHIAN, MARTIN
PAINTER, PRINTMAKER
b Chelsea, Mass, Dec 10, 29. *Study:* Boston Mus Fine Arts Sch, full tuition scholars, dipls with highest hons, 52 & 55; Albert H Whitlin Traveling Fel, Europe, 52; Tufts Univ, BSEd, 53; Boston Univ, MA(art hist), 58; and with Gaston Dorfinant & S W Hayter, Paris;. *Work:* Mus Mod Art & Metrop Mus Art, New York; Libr Cong, Washington, DC; Mus Mod Art, Yerevan, USSR; Denver Art Mus; and others. *Exhib:* Boston Printmakers Traveling Exhibs; Soc Am Graphic Artists, New York; First Int Can Graphic Art Exhib, Montreal Mus Fine Art, 71; 1st & 2nd NH Int, 73 & 74; Retrospective, Art Complex Mus, Duxbury, Mass, 83; and others. *Teaching:* Instr printmaking workshops, Pratt Inst, New York, 60-69; chmn dept art, Burr's Lane Jr High Sch, Dix Hills, NY 65- *Awards:* Asian Studies Grant, US Dept Educ, 70; Print Prize, Nat Acad Design, 76; USSR Studies Grant, US Dept Educ, 79; and others. *Bibliog:* Helen Terzian (auth), Martin Barooshian, the changing face of art, Ararat, No 21, winter 65. *Mem:* Boston Printmakers; Soc Am Graphic Artists (pres, 72-74); Long Island Printmakers Soc; VAGA. *Dealer:* Martin Sumers Gallery 50 W 57th St New York NY 10019. *Mailing Add:* Eight Soundview Dr Northport NY 11768

BAROWITZ, ELLIOTT
PAINTER, INSTRUCTOR
b Westwood, NJ, Aug 22, 36. *Study:* Carnegie-Mellon Univ; RI Sch of Design, BFA; San Francisco Art Inst; Univ Cincinnati; Cincinnati Art Acad, MFA. *Work:* NJ State Mus, Trenton; Rose Mus, Brandeis Univ; Cincinnati Art Mus. *Exhib:* San Francisco Art Asn Mus, 61; Counterweight 3, 81, Blue Mountain Gallery, 83 & Ingber Gallery, 83, New York; Maine Coast Artists Gallery, 81; and others. *Pos:* Exec ed, Art & Artist News, 80- *Teaching:* Assoc prof painting & design, Drexel Univ, Philadelphia, 66-; instr painting & drawing, Portland Sch of Art, Maine, summers, 76- *Awards:* Grant, NY State Coun Arts. *Bibliog:* Articles, Arts Mag, 69 & Arts, 80. *Mem:* Artists Tenants Asn; Found for the Commun of Artists (pres bd dirs, 78-79). *Media:* Oil, Acrylic. *Publ:* Auth, The arts world: Who needs training, 79, auth & ed, The education of artists, 80, coauth, The critics' choice, 80 & auth, The polemics of realism, 82, Artworkers News; auth, The bear and the eagle, Art & Artist, 83. *Mailing Add:* 7 Washington Pl New York NY 10003

BARR, DAVID JOHN
SCULPTOR, PAINTER
b Detroit, Mich, Oct 10, 39. *Study:* Wayne State Univ, BFA & MA. *Work:* Detroit Inst Arts; Wayne State Univ Alumni Bldg; John Hancock Bldg; Portland Art Mus; AT&T; and others. *Comn:* Fairlane Ctr, Dearborn, Mich, 75; nine-part outdoor sculpture, Macomb Col, Warren, Mich, 76; five wall reliefs, Detroit Renaissance Ctr, 77; Sunset Cube, Oakland Univ, Rochester, Mich, 81; Lakeview Square, Battle Creek, Mich, 83. *Exhib:* Evanston Art Ctr, 69; Chicago Contemporary, Herron Mus, Atlanta High Mus & Cranbrook Art Mus, 69; one-man shows, San Jose Mus, Calif, 78 & Donald Morris Gallery, 79 & 81; and others. *Teaching:* Prof sculpture, Macomb Co Col, 64- *Awards:* Archit Awards, Louis Redstone Assocs, 65 & Albert Kahn Assocs, 65; Mich Found of the Arts Award, 77. *Bibliog:* Relief makers, Chicago Omnibus, 67; Chicago art, Art News, 68; Michael Greenwood (auth), article in Artscanada, winter 1976. *Media:* Masonite, Steel. *Publ:* Auth, Notes, 70; auth, Notes III, 72; auth, Structurist, 76; auth, Notes on Celebration, 80; auth, article, CoEvolution Quart, fall 81. *Dealer:* Richard Gray Gallery 620 N Michigan Ave Chicago IL 60611; Donald Morris Gallery Birmingham MI 48012. *Mailing Add:* 22600 Napier Northville MI 48167

BARR, NORMAN
PAINTER
b Melitopol, Russia, Mar 9, 08; US citizen. *Study:* Nat Acad Design. *Comn:* Portraits. *Exhib:* Pepsi-Cola Nat Traveling Exhib, US, 43; Conn Acad Fine Arts, 53; Tupperware Nat Traveling Exhib, US, 56; Eastern States Expos & Mus Fine Arts, Springfield, Mass, 57; Art: USA, New York, 58. *Pos:* Exec vpres NY chap, Artists Equity Asn, 46-50, mem nat exec comt, 48-50 & regional dir, 49-50; pres, New York Wash Proj for the Arts Artists, Inc, 77- *Awards:* Honorable Mention, ACA Gallery & Artists Cong, 42; Grumbacher Award, Am Soc Contemp Artists, 57; Bocour Award, Am Soc Contemp Artists, 64. *Mem:* Am Soc Centemp Artists. *Dealer:* Nancy Stein Gallery New York Ny; Ellen Sragow Gallery New York NY. *Mailing Add:* 775 Riverside Dr New York NY 10032

BARRELL, BILL
PAINTER, COLLECTOR
b London, England, Dec 4, 32. *Work:* Crysler Mus, Norfolk, Va; Walker Art Inst; Dayton Mus Fine Art; Housatonic Mus Fine Art, Conn; Columbia Univ. *Exhib:* One-man shows, Dorsky Gallery, New York; Castagno Gallery, New York; Aaron Berman Gallery, New York; Bienville Gallery, New Orleans; Jersey City Mus. *Pos:* Owner, Sun Gallery, Provincetown, 59-61. *Teaching:* Vis artist, La State Univ, fall 82. *Awards:* Harry Devlin Award, NJ State Coun Arts. *Bibliog:* Barry Barrell (dir), Fruits and Vegetables (film), Barrell Productions, 12/6/67; Peter Schjeldahl (auth), Bill Barrell hits the streets & George Preston (auth), The urbanscape as ideal still life, Potholes, 1/3/78.

Mem: Orgn Independent Artists. *Media:* Oil-Base Paints; Mixed Media. *Collection:* Red Groom's wood sculpture, Oldenburg's paper collage, Bob Beauchamp's drawings, Mimi Gross Groom's watercolors, Bob Thompson's paintings and drawings and Gandy Brody's gouache. *Publ:* Potholes, Custombook Inc, 78. *Dealer:* Down Under Gallery 140 Great Jones St New York NY. *Mailing Add:* 71 Sussex St Jersey City NJ 01302

BARRERES, DOMINGO
PAINTER, EDUCATOR
b Oliva, Valencia, Spain, Feb 23, 41; US citizen. *Study:* Sch Mus Fine Arts, Boston. *Work:* Worcester Mus, Mass; Addison Gallery Am Art, Andover, Mass; Minneapolis Inst Fine Arts, Minn; Brockton Mus, Mass. *Exhib:* Returned Traveling Scholars Exhib, Mus of Fine Arts, Boston, Mass, 68; Whitney Biennial, Whitney Mus Am Art, New York, 75; Boston Invitational, Brockton Mus, Mass, 75; For Collectors, Worcester Art Mus, Mass, 77. *Teaching:* Instr painting, Sch Mus Fine Arts, Boston, 67- *Awards:* Clarissa Barlett Traveling Grant, Sch of the Mus of Fine Arts, Boston, 65. *Media:* Oil, Acrylic. *Dealer:* Savage Sunne Gallery 123 N Washington Boston MA 02108. *Mailing Add:* 34 Farnsworth St Boston MA 02210

BARRETT, BILL
SCULPTOR
b Los Angeles, Calif, Dec 21, 34. *Study:* Univ Mich, Ann Arbor, BS(design), 58, MS(design), 59, MFA, 60. *Work:* Cleveland Mus Art, Ohio; Aldrich Mus Contemp Art; Norfolk Mus Art, Va; Lincoln Nat Life Insurance Found; Mercy Col, Dobbs Ferry, NY. *Comn:* Welded aluminum sculpture, Class of '42 for Univ Mich Dent Sch, 71; sculpture, Scottsdale Ctr for the Arts, Ariz, 79; sculpture, Pennington Recreational Park, Paterson, NJ, 79. *Exhib:* Nat Art Inst Show, San Francisco Mus Art, 64; Whitney Mus Am Art Sculpture Ann, New York, 70; Storm King Art Ctr, NY, 75; Shidoni, Santa Fe, NMex, 82-83; Outdoor Sculpture Exhib, Bronx Psychiatric Ctr, NY, 82-83; Phoenix Botanical Gardens, Ariz, 82-83; Sid Deutsch Gallery, New York, 83; one-man show, Sculpture Ctr, New York, 83. *Teaching:* Assoc prof sculpture, Eastern Mich Univ, 60-68; instr, Cleveland Art Inst, 63-64; asst prof, City Col New York, 69-76; lectr, Columbia Univ, 79- *Mem:* Sculptors Guild New York (pres, currently). *Media:* Aluminum, Bronze. *Mailing Add:* 11 Worth St New York NY 10013

BARRETT, LENI MANCUSO See Mancuso, Leni

BARRETT, ROBERT DUMAS
PAINTER
b Fulton, NY, Nov 23, 03. *Study:* Crouse Col Fine Arts, Syracuse Univ, BFA(painting), 25; Augusta Hazard Fel Grad Study Abroad, 25; study in Paris, 25-26. *Work:* El Paso Centennial Mus; Syracuse Univ; Brooklyn Col. *Exhib:* Syracuse Mus Fine Arts, 25; Oil Paintings, Hotel Barbizon, 43; Oil Paintings of the Southwest, El Paso Centennial Mus, 45; Watercolors, Thomas W Wood Art Gallery, 77; Am Watercolor Soc Ann, 64- & travelling shows; Allied Artists of Am. *Teaching:* Prof art, Brooklyn Col, City Univ New York, 32-67. *Awards:* Louis C Tiffany Found Summer Guest Artist, 27-28; Highest Award Figure Painting, Syracuse Mus Fine Arts Exhib, 25. *Mem:* Am Watercolor Soc (dir, 66); Allied Artists Am; Hudson Valley Art Asn; Artists Fel (pres, 57-62 & 64-67); Salmagundi Club. *Media:* Transparent Watercolor, Oil. *Mailing Add:* RD 1 Morrisville VT 05661

BARRETT, THOMAS R
PAINTER, INSTRUCTOR
b Woodhaven, NY, Feb 17, 27. *Study:* Wesleyan Univ, BA; Brooklyn Mus Art Sch; Univ NH, MA. *Work:* DeCordova & Dana Mus, Lincoln, Mass; Portland Art Mus, Maine; Phillips Exeter Acad, Exeter, NH; Farnsworth Mus, Rockland, Maine; Kresge Collection, Detroit. *Exhib:* Currier Gallery Art, 74-81; Art Ctr in Hargate, St Paul's Sch, 76, 78 & 81; Univ Maine, Orono, 77; Maine Coast Artists, Rockport, 78-79; Lamont Gallery, Exeter, NH, 79; Haystack Sch, Deer Island, Maine; and others. *Pos:* Pres, NH Visual Arts Coalition, 79-81; pres, Independent Sch Art Inst Asn, 77-80; adv bd visual arts, New England Found Arts, 82-; dir, Art Ctr-Hargate, St Pauls Sch, Concord, currently. *Teaching:* Instr painting & art hist & head art dept, St Paul's Sch, Concord, NH. *Awards:* Currier Gallery Art Award, 60 & 62; City Manchester Award, NH, 65; DeKalb Award, 72. *Mem:* NH Art Asn (pres, 68-69); Independent Sch Art Inst Asn (pres, 77-); Boston Visual Artists Union; Asn Am Mus; Col Art Asn Am; and others. *Media:* All Media. *Dealer:* Arnold Klein Gallery 4520 N Woodward Royal Oak MI 48072; Frost Gully Gallery 25 Forest Ave Portland Maine 04111. *Mailing Add:* St Paul's Sch Concord NH 03301

BARRIE, DENNIS RAY
MUSEUM DIRECTOR, HISTORIAN
b Cleveland, Ohio, July 9, 47. *Study:* Oberlin Col, MA, 70; Wayne State Univ, PhD, 83. *Collections Arranged:* Heritage and Horizon: The Words and Thoughts of American Artists (auth, catalog), 76 & John Singer Sargent (auth, catalog), 79, Detroit Inst Arts; Cranbrook USA: Painting and Sculpture (auth, catalog), Cranbrook Acad Art Mus, 82. *Pos:* Midwest regional dir & contrib ed Jour, Arch Am Art, Smithsonian Inst, Detroit, 72-83; dir, Contemp Arts Ctr, Cincinnati, 83- *Awards:* Silver Medal Best Doc Ser, Int Film & TV Festival New York, 83. *Res:* American 20th century art, especially regional artists. *Publ:* Auth, The school years 1926-1976, In: Arts and Crafts in Detroit 1906-1970, The Movement, The Society, The School, Detroit Inst Arts, 76; auth & producer TV docs, Artists in Residence--Portraits of Five Ohio Artists, 80, Artists in America--Portraits of Roger Brown, Richard Hunt, John Hegarty and Marshall Fredericks, 83 & Celebration: The Four Corners-- Project of David Barr, 83, Smithsonian Inst; auth, Artists in Michigan in the 20th Century, Wayne State Univ Press (in prep). *Mailing Add:* Contemp Arts Ctr 115 E Fifth St Cincinnati OH 45202

BARRIO, RAYMOND
WRITER, PRINTMAKER
b West Orange, NJ, 1921. *Study:* Univ Calif, Berkeley, BA, 47; Art Ctr Col Design, Calif, BPA, 52. *Work:* Boston Printmakers; Philadelphia Color Print Soc. *Comn:* Print ed, Collectors Am Art, New York, 59 & 60. *Exhib:* Oakland Art Mus, Calif, 55-60; Am Color Print Soc, Philadelphia, 56-60; San Francisco Mus Art, 56-58; Boston Printmakers, 56-60; Los Angeles Co Mus, 56, 57 & 60; plus over 60 nat exhibs. *Teaching:* Instr painting & drawing, var Calif cols, 61-75; instr art hist, Foothill Col, currently. *Awards:* Philadelphia Color Print Soc, 57; Boston Printmakers, 59; San Francisco Mus Art, 66. *Bibliog:* Zev Pressman (dir), Wet paint (film), 70; Graphics Group, Calif graphics-1974, Arcadia, Calif, 74. *Media:* Acrylic. *Publ:* Auth, Prism, 68, Art: Seen, 68, Selections from Walden, 69, Mexico's Art, 75 & Devil's Apple Corps, 76, Ventura Press. *Mailing Add:* Ventura Press PO Box 1076 Guerneville CA 95446

BARRIO-GARAY, JOSE LUIS
ADMINISTRATOR, HISTORIAN
b Zaragoza, Spain, Mar 17, 32. *Study:* Univ Madrid, Professorship(design); Columbia Univ, PhD(art hist); studied with Enrique Lafuente Ferrari, George Collins, Theodore Reff & Meyer Schapiro. *Pos:* Consult, Choice, 68-; foreign corresp in US & Can, Goya, Madrid, 72-; ed-in-chief, Newsletter, Am Soc Hispanic Art Hist Studies, 78-80, gen secy, 80- *Teaching:* Asst prof art hist & design, Univ Southern Miss, Hattiesburg, 62-65; preceptor art hist, Columbia Univ, 66-67; asst prof art hist, Univ Wis-Milwaukee, 67-73; dir & assoc prof art hist & criticism, Sch Art, Ohio Univ, Athens, 73-76; prof art hist & criticism & chmn, Dept Visual Arts, Univ Western Ont, London, 76- *Awards:* Var Fels & Grants. *Mem:* Col Art Asn Am; Univs Art Asn of Can; Nat Coun Art Admis; Am Asn Univ Prof; Can Asn of Univ Teachers. *Res:* Nineteenth and twentieth century European and American art history and criticism; history of Spanish art and architecture. *Publ:* Auth, Newton Harrison's fourth lagoon: Strategy against entrophy, Arts, 11/74; auth, Jose Gutierrez Solana: Paintings and Writings, 75; auth, George Segal: Environments, New Lugano Rev, No 10, 76; auth, Intention, object and signification in the work of Tapies, In: Antoni Tapies: Thirty-Three Years of His Work (exhib catalogue), Albright-Knox Art Gallery, 77. *Mailing Add:* Dept Visual Arts Univ Western Ont London ON N6H 4N5 Canada

BARRIOS, BENNY PEREZ
PAINTER, DEALER
b Bisbee, Ariz, Mar 20, 25. *Study:* Sacramento City Col, AA, 48; Chouinard Art Inst, 53; Calif State Univ, Sacramento, BA, 74. *Work:* Crocker Art Gallery, Sacramento; Oakland Art Mus, Calif; Smithsonian Inst, Washington, DC. *Exhib:* One-man shows, Los Angeles Co Mus, 52, San Francisco Mus, 52, De Young Mus, 52, Oakland Mus, 52 & Crocker Art Gallery, 53 & 63; 1st, 2nd & 3rd Invitational, Calif Palace Legion Hon, San Francisco, 56-58; Butler Inst Am Art, Youngstown, Ohio, 58; Gov Brown Invitational Chicano Art Exhib, Sacramento, 75. *Pos:* Owner, Barrios Gallery, Sacramento, 59- *Teaching:* Instr oils & acrylics, San Juan Unified Sch Dist, Sacramento, 62-77, Sacramento Unified Sch Dist, 68-77 & Sacramento City Col, 77-82. *Awards:* Second in Watercolor, Laguna Art Festival, 56; First in Oil, Northern Calif Arts, 58; Second in Oil, Auburn Art Festival, 62. *Bibliog:* Alfred Frankenstein (auth), Wetbacks, San Francisco Chronicle, 54; Charles Johnson (auth), Farm workers plight inspires artist, Sacramento Bee, 75; Peter Moore (auth), Lynton Kistler: The happy printer, Art News, 78. *Media:* Acrylic, Watercolor. *Specialty:* All medias; contemporary artists. *Mailing Add:* 4220 Watkins Dr Fair Oaks CA 95628

BARRON, ROS
PAINTER, VIDEO ARTIST
b Boston, Mass, July 4, 33. *Study:* Mass Col Art, BFA; and with Carl Nelson; Radcliffe Inst, Harvard Univ, fel, 66-68. *Work:* Addison Gallery Am Art, Andover, Mass; Worcester Art Mus; Dartmouth Col Collection; Harvard Univ; Boston Mus Fine Arts; and others. *Comn:* Seasons (wall painting), YMCA, Roxbury, Mass, 65; Rainbow, Rocket, Road (wall painting), Lawrence Sch, Brookline, Mass, 67; polarized light painting, comn by SDI, San Francisco, 69; ser wall paintings for Community Ctr, Wilmington, Del, 70; and others. *Exhib:* Whitney Ann Am Painting, Salon, 71-72; Surreal Image, De Cordova Mus; UNESCO Art in Architecture, Rotterdam, Holland; American Painting & Sculpture, US Info Agency Exhib, Europe; Montevideo Gallery, Holland, 78; Carnegie Inst, 78; Mus Mod Art, New York, 80; and many others. *Pos:* Dir, Zone, Visual Theater, currently. *Teaching:* Assoc prof, Univ Mass, Boston, formerly; vis artist, Univ Colo, Boulder, 83, and others. *Awards:* Rockefeller Found Grants, 77-79; Nat Endowment Arts Individual Fel, 75-76; Mass Coun Individual Art Fel in Video, 80-81; and others. *Bibliog:* Frames of reference: Ros Barron (film), co-produced by WGBH Educ Found, 80. *Mailing Add:* 30 Webster Pl Brookline MA 02146

BARROW, THOMAS FRANCIS
PHOTOGRAPHER, INSTRUCTOR
b Kansas City, Mo, Sept 24, 38. *Study:* Kansas City Art Inst, BFA(graphic design), 63; Northwestern Univ, film courses with Jack Ellis, 65; Inst Design, Ill Inst Technol, photog with Aaron Siskind, MS, 67. *Work:* Nat Gallery Can, Ottawa; Mus Mod Art, New York; San Francisco Mus Mod Art, Calif; Philadelphia Mus Fine Arts; Fogg Art Mus, Cambridge, Mass. *Exhib:* Sharp Focus Realism: A New Perspective, Pace Gallery, New York, 73; Light & Lens: Methods of Photography, Hudson River Mus, Yonkers, NY, 73; one-man show, Light Gallery, New York, 74, 76 & 79; The Extended Document, Int Mus Photog, Rochester, NY, 75; Am Photog: Past & Present, Seattle Art Mus, 76; Contemp American Photog Works, Mus Fine Arts, Houston, 77.

Collections Arranged: Light & Substance (with Van Deren Coke), 73 & Self as Subject, 83, Univ NMex Art Mus. *Pos:* Asst dir, George Eastman House, Rochester, NY, 71-72; assoc dir, Univ NMex Art Mus, 73-76. *Teaching:* Assoc prof, Univ NMex, 73-81, prof art, 81- *Awards:* Nat Endowment Arts Grant, 73 & 78. *Bibliog:* The Art of Photography, Time-Life Bks, 71; William Jenkins (auth), The Extended Document, Int Mus Photog, George Eastman House, 74. *Publ:* Auth, 600 faces by Benton, Aperture, Vol 15, No 2; auth, The camera fiend, Image, Vol 14, No 4; contribr, Britannica Encycl Am Art, 73; auth, Three photographers and their books, In: A Hundred Years of Photographic History: Essays in Honor of Beaumont Newhall, 75; ed, Reading Into Photography, Univ NMex Press, 82. *Dealer:* Light Gallery 724 Fifth Ave New York NY 10019. *Mailing Add:* Dept of Art Univ of NMex Albuquerque NM 87131

BARR-SHARRAR, BERYL
HISTORIAN, PAINTER
b Norfolk, Va. *Study:* Mt Holyoke Col, BA; Univ Calif, Berkeley, MA; Inst Fine Arts, NY Univ, MA, PhD. *Exhib:* Maisons Cult Amiens, Bourges, Mus Avignon, Besancon, Montpellier, Nancy & Ste-Etienne, 67; Mus Bourdeux, Menton & le Havre, 68; Sachs Gallery, 73, Livingstone-Learmonth Gallery, 75, New York & Art Galaxy Gallery, New York, 81. *Pos:* Co-founder, Col Art Study Abroad, Paris, 61, co-dir, 61-68. *Teaching:* Vis lectr painting, Mt Holyoke Col, 68-69; vis lectr art hist, Pratt Inst, 78; adj asst prof art hist, Fordham Univ, 81; vis prof art hist, Vassar Col, 82. *Awards:* Prix le France pour le jeune peinture, Paris, 64; Am Philos Soc Grants, 80 & 82; Am Coun Learned Socs Grants, 82. *Mem:* Am Inst Archaeology; Col Art Asn. *Publ:* Auth, Some aspects of early autobiographical imagery in Picasso's Suite 347, Art Bull, 12/72; auth, Dionysiac Frieze on the Derveni Krater, Bronzes Hellenistiques et Romains, Actes du Ve Colloque Int, 78; auth, Early Imperial Decorative Busts, Toreutik u figurliche Bronzes romischer Zeit, Berlin, 81; auth, Maccdonian Mctal Vascs, Studies in History of Art, Vol 12, 81; auth, Der veni, Krater, Archaeology 35, 6/82. *Mailing Add:* 30 West Ninth St New York NY 10011

BARRY, ANNE MEREDITH
PRINTMAKER, INSTRUCTOR
b Toronto, Ont, Aug 31, 32. *Study:* Ont Col of Art, 49-54, with Carl Schaefer & Eric Friefield; also printmaking with N Hornyansky, 63. *Work:* St Mary's Univ Art Gallery, Halifax, NS; Toronto Dominion Can Collection; Inco Can Collection, Toronto; Arts & Cult Centre, St John's, Nfld; Norcen Can Collection, Toronto; and many others. *Comn:* Ltd ed seriographs, Dow Chemical Co, Can Ltd, 72, Can Soc Crippled Children, 73 & Gallery Fore, Winnipeg, 75; ltd ed collagraphs, Arts Coun, Brantford Art Gallery, 74; Ont Assoc Art Galleries, 79; Ont Asn Art Galleries, 78; Toronto Dominion Bank, 82; and others. *Exhib:* One-person shows, Arts & Cult Centre, St John's, Nfld, 75 & 79, travelling exhibs; Int Miniature Print Exhib, Pratt Graphic Gallery, New York, 75 & 77; Biennial Am De Artes Graficas, Mus la Tertulia, Cali, SAm, 76; Japan-Can Print Exhib, Japanese Cult Centre, Toronto, 77; Printmaking Experience, traveling pub art galleries, 78-80 & Graphex VII, 79 & 80; Art Gallery Ont, 80, 82 & 83; and others. *Teaching:* Printmaking serigraphy, Mt St Vincent Univ, NS, 74 & 76; Instr workshops, Emily Carr Col Art & Design, 79-84. *Awards:* Merit Award, Art Gallery of Brant, 74. *Bibliog:* Barry and Henry Dunsmore (dirs), Shoreslines (film), 82; Kay Kritzwiser (auth), article, Arts Atlantic, spring 83; John Flood (auth), article, Northward J 28, 83. *Mem:* Print & Drawing Coun of Can; Visual Arts Ont (chmn bd, 79-80); Print & Drawing Coun Can (bd dirs, 79-80). *Media:* Woodcut, Collograph; Mixed Media. *Publ:* Auth, Dateline: Newfoundland, 72 & The Collage Print, Art Mag, 73; co-auth, An Introduction to the Collagraph Print, Ont Ministry of Cult & Recreation, 77; illusr, The Private Eye, pvt publ, 77. *Dealer:* Equinox Gallery 1525 W 8th Ave Vancouver BC Can V6J 1T5. *Mailing Add:* 81 Rameau Dr 7 Willowdale Toronto ON M2H 1T6 Canada

BARRY, FRANK (BARRY FRANCIS LEOPOLD)
PAINTER, EDUCATOR
b London, Eng, Apr 16, 13; Can citizen. *Study:* Ealing Art Sch, London, nat dipl in design (painting), 46-50; Hornsey Art Sch, London, art teachers dipl, 50-51; Sir George Williams Univ, Montreal, MA(art educ), 67-69. *Work:* McGill Univ; Sir George Williams Univ; Carlton Univ, Ottawa; Nat Gallery, Ottawa. *Exhib:* One-man show, Galerie Libre, Montreal, 69; L'Exposition des Createurs du Que, Mus d'Art Contemp, Montreal, 71; Soc d'Artistes Prof du Que, Galerie Claude Luce, 74; Intelstat Art Concours, Montreal, 75; Quebec Biannelle II, 79; RCA Exhib, Toronto, 81. *Teaching:* Art master art & craft, Grammar Sch, UK & High Sch, Montreal, 51-72; asst prof art & art educ, Sir George Williams Univ, 65- *Awards:* Brian Robertson Selection, Centennial Exhib Award, Art Inst Ont, 67; Quebec Art Competition Award, 70 & Createurs du Quebec Award, Quebec Ministry Cult Affairs. *Bibliog:* Slides, Frank Barry, Editions Yvan Boulerice, 74. *Mem:* Soc des Artistes en Arts Visuels du Quebec; Royal Can Acad Art. *Media:* Acrylic. *Publ:* Auth, School murals are not forever, Sch Arts, 73. *Mailing Add:* 201 Bedbrooke Ave Montreal PQ H4X 1S2 Canada

BARRY, ROBERT E
ILLUSTRATOR, EDUCATOR
b Newport, RI, Oct 7, 31. *Study:* Acad Fine Art, Munich, Ger; Kunstgewerbeschule, Zurich, Switz; RI Sch Design, BFA & MAT. *Work:* Kerlan Collection of Children's Literature & Illus, Univ Minn; Klingspor Mus, Frankfurt, Ger; Mus of the Book, San Juan, PR; Mus of the Virgin Islands, St Thomas. *Pos:* Dir, Art Gallery Southeastern Mass Univ, 77-78; originator & owner, Sportcards, 79- *Teaching:* Instr art, Averett Col, Danville, Va, 67-68; asst prof art, Tex Woman's Univ, Denton, 68-69; assoc prof art/

design, Southeastern Mass Univ, North Dartmouth, 69-81, prof, 81- *Awards:* Am Inst Graphic Arts 50 Books of the Year, 61; Award of Merit, NY Soc Illusrs, 65; New York Times Ten Best Illus Books of the Year, 65. *Publ:* Auth/illusr, Faint George, Houghton Mifflin Co, 63; auth/illusr, Mr Willowby's Christmas Tree, 68; The Musical Palm Tree, 71 & The Riddle of Castle Hill, 72, McGraw Hill; auth, Snowman's Secret, Macmillan, 75. *Mailing Add:* Driftwood Cliff Ave Newport RI 02840

BARRY, ROBERT THOMAS
CONCEPTUAL ARTIST
b New York, NY, Mar 9, 36. *Study:* Hunter Col, BFA, 57, MA, 63. *Work:* Stedelijk Mus, Amsterdam, Holland; Mus Mod Art, New York; Wadsworth Atheneum, Hartford, Conn; Wallraf-Richartz Mus, Cologne, Ger; Ctr George Pompidou, Paris; and others. *Exhib:* Informations, Mus Mod Art, New York, 70; solo shows, Van Abre Mus, Eindhoven, Holland, 77 & Folkwang Mus, Essen, WGer, 78; Documenta 6, Kassel, 77 & Cologne, 81, WGer; Joslyn Art Mus, 80; Documenta 7, Kassel, WGer, 82; Ulmer Mus, Ulm, WGer, 82; and others. *Pos:* Guest artist, Calif Inst of Art, 71 & 76, RI Sch of Design, Providence, 74 & Herron Sch Art, Indianapolis, 81. *Teaching:* Asst prof, Hunter Col, 69-77. *Awards:* Nat Endowment Arts Fel Grant, 76. *Bibliog:* Lucy Lippard (auth), Six Years: The De-Materialization of Art, Praeger, 73; Caolla Gottlieb (auth), Beyond Modern Art, Dutton, 76; Nikos Stangos (ed), Concepts of Modern Art, Harper & Row, 81. *Media:* Projections, Mixed Media. *Dealer:* Leo Castelli 420 W Broadway New York NY 10013. *Mailing Add:* 1091 Emerson Ave Teaneck NJ 07666

BARSANO, RON (RONALD JAMES)
PAINTER, PRINTMAKER
b Chicago, Ill, Jan 13, 45. *Study:* Am Acad Fine Art, William Mosby Scholar, 62-67. *Work:* Shenyang Nat Art Mus, China; US Army Headquarters, Washington, DC. *Exhib:* Allied Artists Am, New York, 72; Western Art Show, San Antonio, Tex, 73; The Taos 6, Philbrook Mus, Tulsa, Okla, 77; Western Art, Grand Central Art Galleries, New York, 78; Am Western Art, Beijing Exhib Palace, China, 81. *Bibliog:* Steve Parks (auth), articles, Profile Mag, 7/78 & Art Lines, 9/81; Brand Shelton (auth), article, SW Profile Mag, 10/83. *Media:* Oil, Conte Crayon; Serigraphy. *Publ:* Contribr, SW Art Mag, 10/74, NMex Mag, 2/82, Artists of the Rockies Mag, spring 82 & Am Artist, 6/82. *Dealer:* Linda Hill PO Box 2860 Taos NM 87571; Taos Art Gallery PO Box 1007 Taos NM 87571. *Mailing Add:* PO Box 2032 Taos NM 87571

BARSCH, WULF ERICH
PAINTER, PRINTMAKER
b Reudnitz, Ger, Aug 27, 43; US citizen. *Study:* Werkkunstschule, BFA, 68; Brigham Young Univ, MA, 70, MFA, 71. *Work:* Utah Mus of Fine Arts; Utah State Div of Fine Arts; San Francisco Mus of Art; Calif Col of Arts & Crafts, Oakland; States Senate, Hamburg, Ger. *Exhib:* Calif Col Arts & Crafts World Print Competition, San Francisco Mus, 73-76; Mus of Art, Monterey, Calif, 74; Davidson Nat Print & Drawing Competition, Cunningham Arts Ctr, Davidson, Calif, 74-76; Am Acad in Rome, Italy, 76; Smithsonian Inst Travelling Exhib, 77; Corcoran Biennial, 83. *Teaching:* Prof printmaking, Brigham Young Univ, 74- *Awards:* Calif Col Arts & Crafts World Print Competition, 73; Prix de Rome, Guerin fel, Am Acad in Rome, 75-76; Western States Art Found Fel, 80. *Media:* Lithography; Oil. *Mailing Add:* c/o Brigham Young Univ Provo UT 84602

BARSCHEL, HANS J
DESIGNER, PHOTOGRAPHER
b Berlin-Charlottenburg, Ger, Feb 22, 12; US citizen. *Study:* Munic Art Sch; Acad Fine & Appl Art, Berlin, MA, 35. *Work:* Mus Mod Art; NY Pub Libr; Libr Cong, Washington, DC. *Comn:* Graphic arts prog brochure, 54, photo art catalog of new campus art, 75, Rochester Inst Technol. *Exhib:* Am Inst Graphic Arts; Art Dir Club, 38, 39 & 50; A-D Gallery, 46; one-man shows, Bevier Gallery, Rochester Inst Technol, 54 & 65; Fac Art Exhibs, 57- *Pos:* Free-lance designer, Berlin, Ger & New York, 35-50; art dir, New York Health Dept, 50-52; exp designer for two printing co, Rochester, NY, 52-54. *Teaching:* Prof graphic commun & instr advan design for reproduction, Sch Art & Design, Rochester Inst Technol, 53-76, prof emer design, 75- *Awards:* Prize, Am Inst Graphic Arts, 38. *Media:* Graphics. *Publ:* Auth, A plea for substantialism & Personal reflections on my era, 64; Exploits into the Neo-Cosmos, a search for man's creative sources, 74; Personal recollections: Companion in Hell; Personal philosophy: Neo-Realism; article in Novum Mag, Munich, Ger, 2/76. *Mailing Add:* 37 Hartfeld Dr Rochester NY 14625

BART, ELIZABETH (ELIZABETH BART GERALD)
PAINTER, DESIGNER
b Cleveland, Ohio. *Study:* Cleveland Inst of Art; study with Hans Hoffmann, Andre Lhote & others. *Work:* Whitney Mus Am Art, New York; Brooklyn Mus Art; Mus Fine Arts, Houston; Cleveland Mus Art, Ohio; High Art Mus, Atlanta, Ga. *Exhib:* Carnegie Inst Int, 31-48; Mus Mod Art, 34; Whitney Mus Am Art Ann, 43 & 74; Corcoran Gallery Art Ann; Everson Mus of Art, Syracuse, NY, 71; one-person retrospective, Washington Art Gallery, Conn, 73; Albright-Knox Art Gallery, Buffalo, 74; Cranbrook Acad Art Mus, Bloomfield Hills, Mich & Canton Art Inst, Ohio, 74; one-person show, Collages at Cordier and Ekstrom, 77, Oil Paintings, 78, Meredith Long Gallery, Houston, Tex, 79. *Media:* Oil, acrylic. *Dealer:* Cordier & Ekstrom 417 E 75th New York NY 10021. *Mailing Add:* Roxbury CT 06783

BARTA, DOROTHY ELAINE
PAINTER, INSTRUCTOR
b Toledo, Ohio, June 23, 24. *Study:* Tex Women's Univ, Denton, 41; Dallas Mus Fine Arts, with Ed Bearden, Chapman Kelley, Stephen Wilder & Roger

Winter, 45-49; Art Students League, with Gustav Rehberger, Ray Goodbred, Thomas Fogarty, Ray Froman, Albert Handell, Ed Whitney, Joseph Magniani & Perry Nichols, Charles Reid & Jan Herring, 78-80. *Exhib:* Dallas Mus Fine Arts Co Ann, 56; Southwestern Watercolor Soc, 78, 82 & 83; Tex Fine Arts Citation, Dallas, 80 & 83; Pastel Soc Am, 80, 82 & 83; Pastel Soc Southwest, 81-83; Okla Art Ann, 82; and others. *Teaching:* Instr portrait painting, Richland and Brookhaven Col, Dallas, Tex, 70-80; instr life drawing & portrait painting, Artisan's Studio-Gallery, Dallas, Tex, 81- *Awards:* Merit Awards, Artists & Craftsmen Asn, Dallas, 80, 81 & 83; Southwestern Watercolor Soc, 82; Purchase Prize, Mus Show, El Paso Art Asn, 83. *Mem:* Pastel Soc Am, New York; Pastel Soc Southwest, Dallas (founder & pres, 79-83); Tex Fine Arts Asn, Dallas; Southwestern Watercolor Soc, Dallas; El Paso Art Asn; and others. *Media:* Miscellaneous. *Dealer:* Artisan's Studio-Gallery 1700 Routh St Dallas TX 75201. *Mailing Add:* 3151 Chapel Downs Dr Dallas TX 75229

BARTEK, TOM
PAINTER, PRINTMAKER
b Omaha, Nebr, July 25, 32. *Study:* Creighton Univ, Omaha, 50-53; Cooper Union Art Sch, New York, with Robert Gwathmey, 55-56; and studied with Arnold Blanch, 65 & 68. *Work:* Joslyn Art Mus, Omaha; Inst Mex-NAm Relaciones Cult, Mexico City; State Bldgs Iowa; Neville Pub Mus, Green Bay, Wis; Wichita Art Mus, Kans. *Comn:* World Insurance Co, Omaha; 10 murals, executed in glass mosaic by Scuola Mosaici, Murano, Italy. *Exhib:* Midwest Biennial, Joslyn Art Mus, Omaha, 62, 64, 66 & 70; one-man shows, Inst Mex-NAm Relaciones Cult, Mexico City, 65, Sheldon Gallery, Univ Nebr, Lincoln, 74 & Joslyn Art Mus, Omaha, 78; A Sense of Place, traveling, 73-74; Nebraska Seen, Sheldon Art Gallery, Univ Nebr, Lincoln & tour, 78; Mid-Four, William Rockhill Nelson Gallery Art, Atkins Mus Fine Arts, Kansas City, Mo, 78; one-man shows, Wesleyan Univ, Nebr, 81, Hastings Col, 82 & Kearney Col. *Pos:* Exhib mgr, Joslyn Art Mus, Omaha, 63-66. *Teaching:* Instr, Col St Mary, Omaha, 64-66; assoc prof, Creighton Univ, Omaha, 66-74. *Awards:* Honorable Mentions, Midwest Biennial, Joslyn Art Mus, 62, 64 & 66 & Mid-Four, Atkins Mus Fine Arts, Kansas City, Mo, 78. *Media:* Acrylic, Assemblage; Serigraph. *Dealer:* Ground Floor Gallery 1110 Douglas Omaha NE 68102. *Mailing Add:* 1110 Douglas St Omaha NE 68102

BARTH, CHARLES JOHN
EDUCATOR, PRINTMAKER
b Chicago, Ill, Nov 27, 42. *Study:* Chicago State Univ, BEduc; Inst Design, Ill Inst Technol, MS(art educ); Ill State Univ, EdD. *Work:* Art Inst Chicago; Philadelphia Mus Art; Okla Art Ctr, Oklahoma City; Cedar Rapids Mus Art, Iowa; Hunterdon Art Ctr, Clinton, NJ. *Comn:* Two prints & plates, Okla Christian Col, Oklahoma City, 71. *Exhib:* Ann Mid-Western Graphics Competition & Exhib, Tulsa City-County Libr, Okla, 74, 78 & 79; Biennial Open Exhib, The Print Club, Philadelphia, 79; Kans Nat Small Painting, Drawing & Print Exhib, Fort Hays State Univ, 80-83. *Teaching:* Instr art, Lincoln Univ, Jefferson City, Mo, 69-72; from assoc prof art to prof, Mt Mercy Col, Iowa, 72- *Awards:* Benton Spruance Mem Purchase Award, Black & White Exhib, The Print Club, Philadelphia, 69; Friends of Art Award, 15th Mid-Miss Valley Ann, Davenport Munic Gallery, Iowa, 77; Special Purchase Award, Wesleyan Int Exhib Prints & Drawings, Macon, Ga, 83; has received over 50 awards. *Mem:* The Print Club, Philadelphia; Am Color Print Soc, Philadelphia. *Media:* Etching, Collagraph. *Mailing Add:* 1307 Elmhurst Dr NE Cedar Rapids IA 52402

BARTH, FRANCES
PAINTER
b New York, NY, July 31, 46. *Study:* Hunter Col, BFA & MA. *Work:* Whitney Mus, New York; Mus Mod Art, New York; Albright-Knox Art Gallery, Buffalo; Metrop Mus Art. *Exhib:* Whitney Biennial Painting, New York, 72 & 73; Three NY Artists, Corcoran Gallery Art, Washington, DC, 73; Susan Caldwell Gallery, New York, 74-76, 78 & 79; American Painting of the 1970's, Albright-Knox Art Gallery, Buffalo; American Painting: The Eighties, Grey Art Gallery. *Teaching:* Sarah Lawrence Col. *Awards:* Nat Endowment Arts Grant, 74; Guggenheim Found Grant, 77; Nat Endowment Arts Grant, 82. *Bibliog:* C Robins (auth), article, 9-10/74 & Hayden Herrera (auth), article, 7-8/78, Art in Am. *Mailing Add:* 99 Van Dam St New York NY 10013

BARTH, JACK ALEXANDER
PAINTER
b Los Angeles, Calif, Sept 25, 46. *Study:* Calif State Univ, Northridge, BA, 69; Univ Calif, Irvine, MFA, 71. *Work:* Los Angeles Co Mus Art; San Francisco Mus Art; Oakland Mus Art, Calif; Brown Univ. *Exhib:* Calif Painting, Govett-Brewster Art Gallery, New Plymouth, NZ, 72; Los Angeles '72, Sidney Janis Gallery, New York, 72; Nine Artists, San Francisco Mus Art, 73; Fifteen Abstract Artists, Santa Barbara Mus Art, 74; 9th Biennale de Paris, Mus Mod Art, Paris, 75; New Selections, Los Angeles Co Mus Art, Los Angeles, 76. *Awards:* New Talent Purchase Award, Los Angeles Co Mus Art, 73. *Bibliog:* Barbara Rose (auth), California here it comes, New York Mag, 72; Peter Plagens (auth), Sunshine Muse, Praeger, 75; Howard Singerman (auth), Unstretched canvas, Los Angeles Inst Contemp Art J, 78. *Dealer:* Galerie Farideh Cadot 11 rue du Jura Paris France. *Mailing Add:* 472 Broome St New York NY 10023

BARTHE, RICHMOND
SCULPTOR
b Bay St Louis, Miss, Jan 28, 01. *Study:* Art Inst Chicago, studied with Charles Schroeder, 24-28; Xavier Univ, New Orleans, Hon MA, 34; St Francis Col, Brooklyn, Hon DFA, 47. *Work:* Theosophical Mus, Adyar, India; Metrop

Mus Art, Whitney Mus Am Art, New York; Pa Acad Mus, Philadelphia; and many others. *Comn:* Arthur Brisbane Monument, Friends of Brisbane, New York; Toussaint Loverture Monument & Gen Dessaline Monument, comn by Pres of Haiti, 49; Eagle, US Govt, Washington, DC, 36; Booker T Washington, Hall of Fame, New York, 76; and many others. *Exhib:* Ann exhibs, Whitney Mus, New York, 30; New York World's Fair, 39; Nat Portrait Gallery, Smithsonian Inst, Washington, DC; sculpture, Montclair Mus, NJ; Artists for Victory, Metrop Mus, New York, 42; Theatrical Personalities, Grand Central Galleries, New York, 46; Two Centuries of Black American Art, Los Angeles Co Mus, 76; Afro American Art, Mus Afro Am Art, Los Angeles, 81; and many others. *Awards:* Rosenwald Fel, 31 & 32; Guggenheim Fel, 41 & 42; Citation, League Allied Arts, Los Angeles, 81. *Bibliog:* A giant return home, Neworld Mag, No 6, 78; Ronald Moore (auth), For art's sake, Black Enterprise Mag, 2/81; Ronald Moore (ed), Twelve Black artists honored, Grapevine Mag, 6/81; and others. *Mem:* Nat Sculpture Soc. *Media:* Bronze, Marble. *Mailing Add:* 285 Barthe Dr Pasadena CA 91103

BARTHOLET, ELIZABETH IVES
DEALER, CONSULTANT
b New York, NY. *Study:* Bryn Mawr Col, BA; Grenoble Summer Sch, cert; Harvard Summer Sch, cert. *Pos:* Art columnist, Cambridge Tribune, Mass, 25-27 & Fortune, 29-31; owner/dir, Bartholet Gallery, New York, 57- *Mem:* Cosmopolitan Club, New York; Appraisers Asn Am, New York. *Specialty:* Nineteenth and twentieth century American paintings, with emphasis on impressionistic American paintings and The Eight. *Publ:* Auth, Solving the problems of art by x-ray, Am Art Mag, 26. *Mailing Add:* 55 E 76th St New York NY 10021

BARTLE, DOROTHY BUDD
CURATOR, LECTURER
b Caldwell, NJ, May 17, 24. *Study:* Randolph-Macon Women's Col, BA(art), 45; Columbia Univ, MA(fine arts), 50. *Pos:* Staff mem Newark Mus, 51-54, staff mem exhibs dept, 54-63, cur classical, crosses & coin collections, 63-71, cur coin collection, 71- *Teaching:* Instr art, Upsala Col, East Orange, NJ, 48-49; docent art hist, Newark Mus, 51- *Mem:* Am Asn Mus. *Publ:* Coauth, Crosses in the collection, 60, coauth, Fires & firefighters of Newark, 68 & auth, Black heroes in history, 71, Newark Mus Quart; ed, New Jersey's Money, Kenny Press, 76. *Mailing Add:* Newark Mus 49 Washington St Newark NJ 07101

BARTLETT, CHRISTOPHER E
GALLERY DIRECTOR, ILLUSTRATOR
b Stratford-on-Avon, Eng, Dec 11, 44. *Study:* St Pauls Col, Eng, cert educ, 70; Bristol Univ, hon BEd, 71; Syracuse Univ, with James McMullan, Robert Weaver, Tom Allen & Isadore Seltzer, MFA, 78. *Comn:* Illus & design, Van Sant Dugdale Advert, 79, General Electric, 80, Soc Security Admin, 81 & US Dept Health, 81. *Exhib:* Paper & Clay, Jewish Community Ctr Art Gallery, Baltimore, 76; Owl & the Pussycat, Nat Audubon Soc, DC, 77; Nat Paper & Clay, Memphis State Univ Art Mus, 78; Mus Am Illustration, New York, 81; American Clay, Baltimore, 81. *Collections Arranged:* Illustrators Invitational, Holtzman Gallery, Towson State Univ, 75, Technol Art Exhib, 76, New Directions in Fabric Design, 77, Function-non-Function, 79 & Low-Fire Clay Sculpture, 81. *Pos:* Dean, Md Col Art & Design, 72-74, pres, 73-74; dir, Holtzman Gallery, Towson State Univ, 74- *Teaching:* Assoc prof illus, Md Col Art & Design, 71-74; asst prof illus & ceramics, Towson State Univ, Baltimore, 74- *Awards:* Visual Design in Print Award, Brigham Young Univ, 81; Cert Distinction, Creativity, 82; Cert Merit, Soc Am Illusr, 82. *Bibliog:* Leon Nigrosh (auth), Claywork-Form and Idea in Ceramic Design, Davis, 75; Barbara Tipton (auth), article in Ceramics Mo, 77. *Mem:* Am Craft Coun; Artists Equity Asn; Md Craft Coun. *Media:* Pen & Ink, Watercolor. *Publ:* Illusr, Baltimore Mag; illusr, The Marvels of Animal Behaviour, Nat Geographic, 73; auth, Remains to be seen, Ceramics Monthly, 80; auth, article, Royal College of Art, 11/81; auth, Mixed Media, Graphics World, London, 2/83. *Dealer:* Eucalyptus Tree Studio 2220 N Charles St Baltimore MD 21218. *Mailing Add:* 6609 Grouse Circle Baltimore MD 21227

BARTLETT, DONALD LORING
SCULPTOR, EDUCATOR
b Quincy, Ill, Sept 20, 27. *Study:* Univ Tex, with Charles Umlauf, BFA; Cranbrook Acad Art, with Berthold Schiwetz, MFA; also with Bernard Frazier, summer 59. *Work:* Spiva Art Ctr, Joplin, Mo; Grover M Herman Fine Arts Ctr, Marietta, Ohio; Brooks Mem Art Gallery, Memphis, Tenn; Laguna Gloria Art Mus, Austin, Tex; Mo State Hist Soc, Columbia. *Comn:* Sculpture, Mo Pavilion, New York World's Fair, 64-65; Sculpture, Boone Co Nat Bank, Columbia, Mo, 71; sculpture, Journalism & Communication Bldg, Univ Fla. *Exhib:* Pa Acad of Fine Arts Ann, 60; Audubon Artists, New York, 60; Springfield, Mo, Ann, 61, 65-66 & 69; Ball State Drawing & Small Sculpture, Muncie, Ind, 70 & 74; Mid South Exhib, Memphis, Tenn, 72 & 75. *Teaching:* Prof sculpture, Univ Mo, 75- *Awards:* Fulbright Grant to France, 53-54. *Mem:* Tex Soc Sculptors. *Media:* Bronze; Epoxy Resin. *Mailing Add:* 1627 Wilson Ave Columbia MO 65201

BARTLETT, FRED STEWART
ADMINISTRATOR
b Brush, Colo, May 15, 05. *Study:* Univ Colo, AB, 28; Univ Denver, 32-35; Harvard Univ, Carnegie Fel, summer 37. *Collections Arranged:* New Accessions USA. *Pos:* Docent & actg dir, Denver Art Mus, 32-43; cur painting & asst dir, Colorado Springs Fine Arts Ctr, 43-55, dir, 55-71, dir emer, 71-, hon trustee, 75-; int chmn art dept, Colo Womens Col, 71-72; consult art dept, 72- *Awards:* Governor's Award Serv Arts & Humanities, 78. *Mem:* Colo Coun Arts & Humanities (bd mem, 71-77); hon mem Asn Art Mus Dirs; Am Asn Mus; US Air Force Acad Fine Arts Panel (chmn, 64-71). *Mailing Add:* 800 Washington St 801 Denver CO 80203

BARTLETT, JENNIFER LOSCH
PAINTER, WRITER
b Long Beach, Calif, Mar 14, 41. *Study:* Mills Col, BA, 63; Yale Univ, BFA, 64 & MFA, 65, with Jack Tworkov, James Rosenquist, Al Held & Jim Dine. *Work:* Walker Art Ctr, Minneapolis; Mus Mod Art, Metrop Mus Art, Whitney Mus Am Art, New York; Philadelphia Mus Art. *Comn:* 9-painting series, oil-painted canvas & baked enamel steel plates, Gen Serv Admin, 79. *Exhib:* Seven Walls, Mus Mod Art, New York, 71; Painting Ann, Whitney Mus Am Art, New York, 72; New York Now, Phoenix Art Mus, 79; solo exhibs, Albright-Knox Art Gallery, Buffalo, 80, Tate Gallery, London, 82, Heath Gallery, Atlanta, 83; Block Prints, Whitney Mus Am Art, New York, 82; Art in Our Times, Brooks Mem Art Gallery, Memphis, 82; American Prints: 1960-1980, Milwaukee Art Mus, Wis, 82; Recent American Woodcuts, Akron Art Mus, Ohio, 82; Valentines, Multiples, Marian Goodman Gallery, New York, 83; and numerous other group and solo exhibs. *Teaching:* Instr painting, Univ Conn, 68-72; vis artist, Chicago Art Inst, fall 72; instr painting, Sch Visual Arts, New York, 72- *Awards:* Lucas Vis Lect Award, Carleton Col, 79; Brandeis Univ Creative Arts Award, 83; Am Acad Arts & Letters Award, 83. *Bibliog:* Many articles & reviews in Am & Europ publ, incl Eric Gibson (auth), New York reviews, Rhapsody, Art Int, 3/79; Thomas B Hess (auth), Les nouvelle images de la peinture americane, Art Press Int, 5/79; Roberta Smith (auth), Bartlett's Summers, Art in Am, 11/79 and others. *Publ:* Auth, Cleopatra I-IV, Adventures in Poetry Press, 71. *Mailing Add:* c/o Paula Cooper Gallery 155 Wooster St New York NY 10012

BARTLETT, SCOTT
FILMMAKER
b Atlanta, Ga, Nov 4, 43. *Work:* Mus Mod Art, New York; Chicago Art Inst; Nederlands Filmmuseum, Amsterdam; Oesterriches Filmmuseum, Vienna; Smithsonian Inst, Washington, DC. *Exhib:* Oberhausen Film Festival, WGer, 69; Whitney Mus Am Art, New York, 69-73; Ann Arbor Film Festival, Mich & traveling, 69-73; Int Independent Filmmakers' Festival, London, 73; Cannes Film Festival, France, 74. *Pos:* Dir spec effects, Paramount & Columbia Studios, 80- *Teaching:* Film artist in residence, Columbia Univ, summer 72 & 73 & Dartmouth Col, summer 74; lectr film, San Francisco Art Inst, summer 75 & Univ Calif Los Angeles, 80. *Awards:* Guggenheim Fel, 70; Filmmaking Grant, Am Film Inst, 71 & Nat Endowment Arts, 72. *Bibliog:* Gene Youngblood (auth), Expanded Cinema, Dutton, 70; Amos Vogel (auth), Film as a Subversive Art, Random House, 74; Stephen Dwoskin (auth), Film Is, Studley Press, 75. *Mem:* Founder Film Arts Found; Canyon Cinema Coop (dir, 74). *Mailing Add:* 440 Davis Ct San Francisco CA 94111

BARTNICK, HARRY WILLIAM
PAINTER, EDUCATOR
b Newark, NJ, July 30, 50. *Study:* Tyler Sch Art, Temple Univ, BFA, 72; Syracuse Univ, MFA, 74. *Work:* Hyde Collection, Glens Falls, NY; DeCordova Mus, Lincoln, Mass. *Exhib:* New Directions in Realism, Danforth Mus, Framingham, Mass, 80; DeCordova Mus, Lincoln, Mass, 80; State Mus, Albany, NY 81; Fashion Inst of Tech, NY, 81; Univ Mass, Amherst, 82. *Collections Arranged:* Contemporary Drawing Invitational, Ctr for Music, Drama & Art, Lake Placid, NY, 76-77. *Teaching:* Instr painting & drawing, Lake Placid Sch Art, 74-78; New England Sch Art & Design, 78- *Awards:* Trustee's Prize, Everson Regional, 74; Creative Artists Pub Serv Grant, 77; Mass Artists Found Grant, 81. *Bibliog:* Article, Boston Globe, 10/16/80; The Boston art party, Art News, 11/80. *Mem:* Col Art Asn. *Media:* Oil, Acrylic on Canvas. *Dealer:* Helen Shlien Gallery Boston MA. *Mailing Add:* 5 Holly St Salem MA 01970

BARTON, AUGUST CHARLES
DESIGNER, PAINTER
b Szekesfehervar, Hungary, Nov 15, 1897; US citizen. *Study:* Ludovika Mil Acad, BS; Hungarian Tech Univ; Hungarian Acad Com Arts; Art Students League. *Exhib:* Am Watercolor Soc; Hudson Valley Art Asn; Silvermine Guild Artists. *Teaching:* Prof art, textile design, Moore Col Art, Philadelphia, Pa, 46-63; lectr, Silvermine Col Art, 62-65; lectr, Philadelphia Col Textiles & Sci, 63-79. *Mem:* Am Watercolor Soc; Silvermine Guild Art; Hudson Valley Art Asn; Textile Designers Guild Am. *Media:* Watercolor, Tempera. *Mailing Add:* 110 W 40th St New York NY 10018

BARTON, BRUCE WALTER
PAINTER, EDUCATOR
b Ottumwa, Iowa, Sept 2, 35. *Study:* San Francisco Art Inst, with Richard Diebenkorn, BFA; San Diego State Univ, MA. *Work:* San Francisco Art Inst; San Diego State Univ. *Exhib:* 73rd Ann, Denver Mus; San Francisco Art Inst Ann; Tucson Ann, Ariz; Spokane Ann, Wash; Va Commonwealth Univ; Univ Minn; Artist/Teacher USA, New York. *Pos:* Photogr, Convair/Astronautics, San Diego, 58-59; media specialist, Community Educ Resources, San Diego, 63-64; art dir, Boeing Co, Seattle, 64-65. *Teaching:* Lectr painting, Univ Man, Winnipeg, 66-67; prof art & chmn art dept, Ohio State Univ, Columbus, 67-69; prof art & chmn art dept, Univ Mont, Missoula, 69- *Awards:* Alfred J Wright Award, Ohio State Univ, 69; Educ Grant, Nat Endowment Humanities, US Off Educ & Bur Indian Affairs, 71 & 72. *Publ:* Auth, The Tree at the Center of the World, Ross-Erickson Publ. *Mailing Add:* 2966 Saddlewood Dr Bonita CA 92002

BARTON, GEORGIE READ
PAINTER, SCULPTOR
b Summerside, PEI; US citizen. *Study:* Mt Allison Sch Fine Arts, cert(fine arts), 24-27; Art Students League, with Frank Vincent Dumond, Edward McCartan & Arthur Lee, 29-34; Univ PEI, LLD, 83. *Work:* Art of the Western Hemisphere, IBM Corp Collection; Bruckner Mus, Albion, Mich; Confederation Art Gallery, Charlottetown, PEI. *Exhib:* Am Artists Prof League, New York; Hudson Valley Art Asn, White Plains, NY; Allied Artists Am, New York, 71-; Confederation Art Gallery, Charlottetown, PEI; Univ PEI, 83. *Teaching:* Art dir, Ottawa Ladies Col, Ont, 34-40; art dir, St Agnes Sch, Albany, NY, 40-44; pvt classes, 44- *Awards:* Gold Medal & Citation, Hudson Valley Art Asn, 72; Am Artists Prof League Award, 79; DuMond Award, Hudson Valley Art Asn, 81. *Bibliog:* Articles, Atlantic Advocate, 1/83 & Atlantic Insight, 12/83. *Mem:* Hudson Valley Art Asn (secy, 58-65, pres, 65-69, first vpres, 69-); Coun Am Artists Socs (dir bd, 66-); Salmagundi Club; fel Royal Soc of Arts; fel Am Artists Prof League (dir nat bd, 64-). *Media:* Oil. *Publ:* Contribr, Am Artists Prof League Bulletin, 71. *Mailing Add:* 3 Hillside Ave Summerside East PE C1N 4H3 Canada

BARTON, JOHN MURRAY
PAINTER, DEALER
b New York, NY, Feb 8, 21. *Study:* Art Students League; Tschacbasov Sch Art, New York. *Work:* Metrop Mus Art, New York; Mus Mod Art, Haifa, Israel; Butler Inst Am Art, Youngstown, Ohio; Philadelphia Mus Art, Pa; Bibliotheque Nationale, Paris; plus others. *Comn:* Murals (with Lumin Martin Winter), New York Bd Educ; History of Money (oil, with Louise August), SC State Bank, Columbia; oil & lacquer mural, Polyclinic Hosp, New York; acrylic on concrete (with Louise August), Gilbert's Hotel, Fallsburgh, NY. *Exhib:* Numerous nat & regional exhibs. *Pos:* Pres, John Barton Assocs, Inc, 65-; pres, J M B Publ Ltd, 68-; pres, Multiple Reproductions, Inc, 70-; secy-treas, Int Assoc Artists Ltd, 72- *Teaching:* Pvt classes at studio on creative expression, 60-65; lectr, creative expression, univ art depts, throughout the East Coast, 60-65. *Specialty:* Publisher of original fine art graphics; art shows at colleges, universities, galleries and others. *Publ:* Illusr, Space aeronautics, Print Mag & Printers Ink. *Mailing Add:* 45 Christopher New York NY 10014

BARTON, PHYLLIS SETTECASE
WRITER, CONSULTANT
b Dubuque, Iowa, Nov 5, 34. *Study:* Mount St Mary's Col, Los Angeles; Calif State Univ, Long Beach, BA(art hist), 78, MA(art hist), 82. *Pos:* Art ed & columnist, Santa Ana Register, Calif, 68-69; antique dealer & appraiser, Artistique, 68-; lectr, Am children's book illus. *Awards:* Award for Excellence, Monograph on Cecil C Bell, 1906-1970, 77 & Award for Excellence, Monograph, Alexander Dzigurski, 79, Printing Indust Asn Am. *Mem:* Nat League Am Pen Women; Am Soc Appraisers; Am Illusr Res Group. *Interests:* Development of 20th century American art; Oriental arts; American children's book illustration. *Collection:* Picasso, Roualt, Moti, Kuniyoshi, Dali, Kathe Kollwitz, Harold Frank, Marco Sassone, Cecil C Bell, Cecil Aldin, Ira Moskowitz, Peter Max, Will Foster & others. *Publ:* Auth, Cecil C Bell 1906-1970 (monograph), 77; auth, Harry Sternberg--A Visual Communicator, 4/77 & The Wyeths--N C, Andrew & Jamie--A Dynasty of Superstars, 5/77, Southwest Art Mag; auth, Monograph: Alexander Dzigurski--His Life and Work, McGrew Color Graphics, Kansas City, 78; auth, Jerry Crandall-Creative Credibility, Southwest Art, 10/80; and others. *Mailing Add:* 2601 E Victoria Apt 191 Dominguez Hills CA 90220

BARTZ, JAMES ROSS
PAINTER
b Bluffton, Ohio, Feb 20, 42. *Study:* Ohio State Univ, BS, 64, MA(art educ), 70. *Exhib:* Winter Art, Strecker Gallery, Manhattan, Kans, 83; Third Ann Small Oil Painting, Wichita Art Asn, 83; Mid-Four, Nelson-Atkins Mus Art, Kansas City, Mo, 83; Smoky Hill Art Exhib, Hays Libr, Kans, 83; Art Ann IV, Okla Art Ctr, Oklahoma City, 83; Fifth Salina Ann, Salina Art Ctr, Kans, 83; and others. *Teaching:* Asst prof art educ, Wichita State Univ, Kans, 70-78; painting instr figure, Wichita Art Asn, 80-83. *Awards:* Best Show, Second Ann Small Oil Painting, Wichita Art Asn, 82; Second Place, Third Ann Small Oil Painting, Wichita Art Asn, 83; Best Show, Fifth Salina Ann, Salina Art Ctr, Kans, 83. *Mem:* Artists Guild Wichita (pres, currently); Col Art Asn. *Media:* Acrylic, Oil. *Dealer:* Reuben Saunders Gallery 2906 E Central Wichita KS 67208; Kans Gallery Fine Arts 1527 Fairlawn Rd Topeka KS 60604. *Mailing Add:* 4802 Arlene Wichita KS 67220

BARUCH, JACQUES Z
DEALER, LECTURER
b Warsaw, Poland; US citizen. *Study:* Acad Fine Arts, Warsaw, fine arts; Polytechnica of Warsaw, architect. *Collections Arranged:* Contemporary Czechoslovakian Printmakers, Smithsonian Inst Traveling Exhib Serv, 79-; Jan Saudek, Photographs, Camden Arts Centre, London, England, 80; Images from Czechoslovakia: Jan Saudek and Josef Sudek, Univ Iowa Mus Art, Iowa City, 83; Czechoslovakian Printmakers, Gonzaga Univ AD Gallery, Spokane, 83; Jiri Anderle, Master Printmaker, Cincinnati Art Mus, 84. *Pos:* Partner & co-dir, Jacques Baruch Gallery, Chicago, 67- *Bibliog:* Nory Miller (auth), For Jacques and Anne Baruch home is where the art is, Chicago Daily News-Panorama, 74; Candida Finkel (auth), Separate but equal, New Art Examiner, 78; Barbara Varro (auth), Jacques Baruch, Chicago Sun Times-Chicago Style, 11/26/78. *Mem:* Chicago Art Dealers Asn; Asn Int Photog Art Dealers; Textile Soc & Print & Drawing Club, Art Inst Chicago. *Specialty:* Eastern European award winning graphics, internationally renowned tapestry and fiber artists from Europe and United States; photography, paintings and art nouveau. *Collection:* Outstanding prints, drawings, tapestries and photographs. *Publ:* Coauth, The World of Jan Saudek: Photographs, 79, Jiri Blacar--The Archives of an Artist, 79, The Figure in Fiber--Luba Krejci, Lilla Kulka and Izabella Marcjan, 80, Jiri Anderle, 80 & Vladimir Gazovic, 81, Jacques Baruch Gallery. *Mailing Add:* 900 N Michigan Ave Chicago IL 60611

BARZUN, JACQUES
WRITER, ART CRITIC
b Creteil, France, Nov 30, 07; US citizen. *Study:* Columbia Col, BA, 27; Columbia Univ, MA, 28 & PhD, 32. *Pos:* Lit consult, Charles Scribner's Sons, New York, currently. *Teaching:* Instr hist, Columbia Col, 29-38; asst prof hist, Columbia Univ, 38-42, assoc prof hist, 42-45, prof hist, 45-75, retired. *Res:* Intellectual history and culture. *Publ:* Auth, reviews and articles in Mag of Art, 43-53; auth, articles in Am Scholar, Art Digest & Harper's, 56-; auth, Art--by act of Congress, The Public Interest, fall 65; auth, Museum piece, 1967, Mus News, 4/68; auth, The arts to-day; consolidation or confrontation?, J of Royal Soc Arts, 3/72; auth, The Use & Abuse of Art, Mellon Lectures, Nat Gallery, 73 & Princeton Press, 74. *Mailing Add:* c/o Charles Scribner's Sons 597 Fifth Ave New York NY 10017

BASCOM, EARL W
SCULPTOR, PRINTMAKER
b Vernal, Utah, June 19, 06. *Study:* Brigham Young Univ, BS, 40, 65-66; Univ Calif, 69. *Work:* Whitney Mus Am Art; Dallas Mus Fine Arts; Denver Art Mus; Santa Barbara Mus Art; Utah Mus Fine Art. *Comn:* Equestrian bronze sculpture, Santa Anita Horse Show, Arcadia, Calif, 82, River Rd Ranch, Apple Valley, Calif, 82, Pitzer Ranch, Ericson, Nebr, 82 & Viking Ranch, Apple Valley, Calif, 83. *Exhib:* C M Russell Mus Mem, Great Falls, Mont, 80; Santa Anita Nat Horse Show, Arcadia, Calif, 82; Am-Can Classic, Billings, Mont, 82; Nat Salon, Springville Mus Art, Utah, 83; Governors Show, Old West Mus, Cheyenne, Wyo, 83. *Teaching:* Instr art, Barstow High Sch & J F Kennedy High Sch, Barstow, Calif, 66-67. *Bibliog:* Dick Dorwald (auth), Cowboy artist, Victor Valley Mag, 83; Lisa Johnson (auth), Wild west, Sentinel, 83; Jon Scott (dir), Midnights Last Ride--1933, KBTV, Denver, 83. *Mem:* High Desert Artists (pres, 64-65); Buckaroo Artists Am (pres, 78); Assoc Latter-Day Media Artists. *Media:* Bronze; Etching. *Publ:* Illusr, Memories I Could Do Without and Other Short Stories, Lyle Lybbert, 83. *Mailing Add:* Diamond B Ranch 15669 Stoddard Wells Rd Victorville CA 92392

BASHOR, JOHN W
EDUCATOR, PAINTER
b Newton, Kans, Mar 11, 26. *Study:* Washburn Univ, BA, 49; Univ Iowa, MFA, 53. *Work:* Nelson/Atkins Mus, Kansas City, Mo; Washburn Univ, Topeka, Kans; Springfield Art Mus, Mo; Sandzen Mem Mus, Lindsborg, Kans; Kans State Univ, Manhattan. *Comn:* Murals, Kaw Valley State Bank, Topeka, 64, Bethany Col, Lindsborg, 65 & First Nat Bank, Grand Island, Nebr, 65. *Exhib:* Mid-Am Ann, Nelson/Atkins Mus, 56; Nebr Invitational, Univ Nebr, Lincoln, 62; solo traveling exhib, State Pa, 62-63; Kansas' Artist, Nat Gov Traveling Exhib, 66; Fedn Rocky Mountain States Traveling Exhib, 68. *Teaching:* Assoc prof painting & prints, Bethany Col, 54-66; prof painting, Mont State Univ, 66-, dir sch art, 66-77. *Mem:* Mid-Am Col Art Asn; Col Art Asn Am; Mont Art Educ Asn. *Media:* Acrylic. *Mailing Add:* Sch of Art Mont State Univ Bozeman MT 59715

BASKERVILLE, CHARLES
PAINTER, MURALIST
b Raleigh, NC, Apr 16, 1896. *Study:* Cornell Univ; Art Students League; Acad Julien, Paris. *Work:* Nat Fine Arts Collection & Nat Portrait Gallery, Washington, DC; 65 off portraits for USAAF, Pentagon, Washington, DC; Metrop Mus Art, New York; Nat Mus Racing, Saratoga Springs, NY. *Comn:* Mural in relief lacquer, Main Lounge of SS America, 40; mural, Joint Comt Mil Affairs, US Capitol, Washington, DC, 47; Two Tigers (mural), Princeton Univ, 59; Mexican Pavilion (mural), comn by Cornelius Vanderbilt Whitney. *Exhib:* Carnegie Int, Pittsburgh, Pa, 40; Army Air Force Portraits, Nat Gallery Art, Washington, DC, 45 & Metrop Mus Art, New York, 47; Significant War Scenes, Chrysler Corp Collection, Corcoran Gallery Art, Washington, DC, 49; 17 one-man shows in New York & Palm Beach; retrospective 1918-1979, Johnson Mus, Cornell Univ, 79. *Bibliog:* Joe Singer (auth), Painting Women's Portraits & Painting Men's Portraits, Watson-Guptill, 77; Brendan Gill (auth), Here at the New Yorker, Random, 75; Janet Adams (auth), Decorative Folding Screens, Viking, 82. *Mem:* Nat Soc Mural Painters; Artists Equity, Century; Am Artists Prof League. *Media:* Oil, Acrylic; Watercolor, Lacquer. *Mailing Add:* 130 W 57th St New York NY 10019

BASKIN, LEONARD
SCULPTOR, GRAPHIC ARTIST
b New Brunswick, NJ, Aug 15, 22. *Study:* NY Univ, 39-41; Yale Sch Fine Arts, 41-43; New Sch Social Res, AB(Tiffany Found Fel), 49, DFA, 66; Acad Grande Chaumiere, 50; Acad Fine Arts, Florence, Italy, 51; Clark Univ, LHD, 66; Univ Mass, DFA, 68; Rutgers Univ; Univ Mass. *Work:* Mus Mod Art; Metrop Mus Art; Brooklyn Mus; Nat Gallery Art, Washington, DC; Fogg Mus Art; plus others. *Exhib:* Sao Paulo, Brazil; Mus Art Mod, Paris. *Teaching:* Prof sculpture & graphic arts, Smith Col, 53-74. *Awards:* Guggenheim Found Fel, 53; Medal, Am Inst Graphic Artists, 65; Medal of Merit Graphic Arts, Nat Inst Arts & Lett, 69. *Bibliog:* Raphael Soyer (auth), article, In: Homage to Thomas Eakins, etc, 65; Wayne Craven (auth), article, In: Sculpture in America, 68; Jaffe (auth), The Sculpture of Leonard Baskin, Viking Press, New York, 80; and others. *Mem:* Nat Inst Arts & Lett; Am Inst Graphic Artists. *Dealer:* Kennedy Galleries 40 W 57th St New York NY 10019. *Mailing Add:* Lurley Manor Lurley Nr Tiverton Devon England United Kingdom

BASQUIN, KIT (MARY SMYTH)
CRITIC, WRITER
b New York, NY, July 3, 41. *Study:* Goucher Col, BA, 63; Ind Univ, Bloomington, MA(art hist), 70; Bread Loaf Writers Conf, Middlebury Col, 83. *Pos:* Owner & dir, Washington Gallery, Frankfort, Ind, 72-77 & Indianapolis, 77-79 & Kit Basquin Gallery, Milwaukee, 81-; Wis ed, New Art Examiner, 80. *Teaching:* Instr art hist, Fine Arts Sch, Addis Ababa, Ethiopia, 67-68. *Bibliog:* Don Frick (interviewer), What is the Role of the Art Dealer?, WISH-TV, Indianapolis, 3/78; Holly Day (auth), Indianapolis, Cincinnati, Dayton, Art in Am, 7-8/79; Dean Jensen (auth), Basquin Gallery has different air, Milwaukee Sentinel, 10/2/81. *Mem:* Arts Club Chicago. *Res:* Contemporary art in the Midwest. *Publ:* Auth, Why an art gallery now?, Goucher Col Quart, summer 81; Indiana art in perspective, In: 68th Ind Artists Show, Indianapolis Mus Art, 81; Map imagery in contemporary art, In: Cartography Catalog, John Michael Kohler Arts Ctr, Wis, 81; Paintings and pushpins (short story), Format: Art and the World, fall 83. *Mailing Add:* 8064 N Beach Dr Milwaukee WI 53217

BASS, DAVID LOREN
PAINTER
b Conway, Ark, July 19, 43. *Study:* Univ NC, Greensboro, MFA; Univ NC, Chapel Hill; Aspen Sch of Contemp Art; Univ Cent Ark, BSE; study with Peter Agostini, Walter Barker, Andrew Martin & Larry Day. *Work:* Mint Mus, Charlotte, NC; Dillard Collection, Weatherspoon Art Gallery, Greensboro, NC; Fayetteville Mus Art, NC; Duke Univ, Durham, NC. *Exhib:* Biennial Exhib of Piedmont Painting and Sculpture, Mint Mus, Charlotte, 79 & 81; one-man show, Asheville Art Mus, 80; DuPont Art Gallery, W & L Univ, 80; High Point Exhib Ctr, 82; Four of North Carolina, Green Hill Gallery, Greensboro, 82; 5th North Carolina Artists Invitational, Salisbury, 82; and many others. *Collections Arranged:* Drawings & Sculpture by Peter Agostini, Du Pont Art Gallery, 76 & Prints, Dept of Fine Arts, 76, Du Pont Art Gallery, Washington & Lee Univ. *Teaching:* Instr painting, Washington & Lee Univ, Lexington, VA, 76. *Awards:* Yaddo Residency, Saratoga Springs, NY, 78, 81 & 84. *Bibliog:* Tom Dewey (auth), Southern realism, Miss Mus Art, 79. *Media:* Oil. *Mailing Add:* 1401 Roanoke Dr Greensboro NC 27408

BASS, JOEL
PAINTER
b Los Angeles, Calif, Dec 23, 42. *Study:* Art Ctr Col Design, 65-67. *Work:* Ft Worth Art Ctr; Mus Mod Art, Whitney Mus Am Art, New York; Albright-Knox Mus Art, Buffalo; San Francisco Mus Art. *Exhib:* The Structure of Color, Whitney Mus Am Art, New York, 71; Color & Scale: Eight Contemp Calif Painters, Oakland Mus, 71; The State of Calif Painting, Govett-Brewster Art Gallery, New Plymouth, NZ, 72-73; Southern Calif Attitudes, Pasadena Art Mus, Calif, 72; 1973 Biennial Exhib: Contemp Am Art, 73 & Recent Acquisitions Exhib, 73, Whitney Mus, New York; Printsequence, Mus Mod Art, New York, 75; Recent Am Etching, Davison Art Ctr, Wesleyan Univ, Middletown, Conn, 75; solo exhib, Kathryn Markel Fine Arts, New York, 77; and others. *Bibliog:* Jerome Tarshis (auth), article, Artforum, 4/71; Peter Plagens (auth), From school painting to a school of painting in Los Angeles, Art in Am, 3-4/73 & Just another rectangle painter, Artforum, 5/74. *Mailing Add:* 239 S Los Angeles St Los Angeles CA 90012

BASS, RUTH
EDUCATOR, PAINTER
b Boston, Mass, 38. *Study:* Radcliffe Col, BA(magna cum laude), 60; study with Irving Marantz, Victor Candell, Gabriel Laderman & Maurice Golubov, 60-64; Art Students League, 61-74; NY Univ, MA, 62, PhD, 78. *Exhib:* One-person show, Brata Gallery, New York, 73; NMex Int Art Show, Eastern NMex Univ, 75; Works on Paper--Women Artists, Brooklyn Mus, NY & Fairleigh Dickinson Univ, 75-76; Shreveport Parks & Recreation Dept Nat, Shreveport, La, 76; Artists Choice Traveling Exhib, 76-77. *Teaching:* Lectr, Univ Bridgeport, Conn, 63-64 & Queens Col, NY, 65-66; from instr to assoc prof art, Bronx Community Col, City Univ New York, 65-81, prof, 81-. *Awards:* State Univ NY Res Found Grant, 75-76; City Univ New York Fel, 82. *Bibliog:* Lawrence Campbell (auth), article, Art News, 3/73. *Mem:* Col Art Asn; Am Asn of Univ Prof; Artists Equity Asn of NY; Int Asn Art Critics; Art Students League. *Media:* Oil, Charcoal. *Res:* Contemporary American realist painting, including painterly realism; phenomenological criticism and aesthetics. *Publ:* Contribr, McGraw-Hill Dictionary of Art, 69 & auth, Josef Albers, In: Dictionary of 20th Century Art, 74, McGraw-Hill; contribr, Art News & Arts Mag, 79- *Mailing Add:* 125 E 87th St New York NY 10028

BASSET, GENE
POLITICAL CARTOONIST
b Brooklyn, NY, July 24, 27. *Study:* Univ Mo; Brooklyn Col, BA(design); Cooper Union; Art Students League; Pratt Inst. *Work:* Syracuse Univ Libr, NY; Wichita State Univ; Univ Mo; Univ Southern Miss. *Pos:* Polit cartoonist, Honolulu-Star Bull, 61-62, Scripps-Howard Newspapers, Washington, DC, 62- & United Features Syndicate, 72-; ed cartoonist, Atlanta J, 82- *Teaching:* Instr seminar, Gustavus Adolphus Col. *Awards:* Best Ed Cartoon, Population Inst, 74. *Mem:* Asn Am Ed Cartoonists (pres, 73-74); Nat Cartoonist Soc. *Media:* Ink. *Mailing Add:* 3210 Beechwood Dr Marietta GA 30067

BASSI (SOFIA CELORIO DE BASSI)
WRITER, PAINTER
b Ciudad Mendoza, Mex. *Study:* Self-taught. *Work:* Mus Mod Art, Mexico City; Smithsonian Inst, Washington, DC; NASA, Houston; Mus Mod Art, Tel Aviv, Israel; Selma Lagerloff Lyceum Mus, Estocolmo, Suecia. *Comn:* Mural, Univ State Guerrero, Acapulco, 69. *Exhib:* Mus Contemp Art, Morelia,

Michoacan, Mex, 74; Mus Cuidad, Mex, 78; Mus Carrillo Gil, Mex, 78; Mexican Graphic Works, Mus Bulgaria, 80; Polyforum Cult Siqueiros; and others. *Bibliog:* Hands that work, Mag Mex Red Cross, 73; Alfonso de Neuvillate (auth), Sofia Bassi, Mex Herald, 74; Raquel Tibol (auth), Sofia to the words, the words to Sofia, Kena Mag, Mex, 76. *Media:* Oil. *Mailing Add:* Sierra Leona 220 Mexico City 10 Mexico

BASSIN, JOAN
HISTORIAN, EDUCATOR
b St Louis, Mo, Oct 29, 38. *Study:* Swarthmore Col, BA; Ind Univ, MA & PhD; fel in residence for col teachers, Nat Endow for Humanities, 78-79; Andrew W Mellon sr fel in humanities, 81. *Pos:* Art columnist, City Mag, 78-79; partner & appraiser, Art Hist Res and Appraisals, 80-; art reviewer, Austin American-Statesman, 82-83. *Teaching:* Lectr mod archit, Dartmouth Col, Hanover, NH, 70; instr mod archit & mod sculpture, Kansas City Art Inst, 72-74; asst prof, 74-78; assoc prof, 78-. *Mem:* Midwest Art Hist Asn; Midwest Victorian Studies Asn; Kansas City Landmarks Comn (res priority adv selection comt); Women's Caucus Art (Kansas City pres, 75-77). *Res:* Eighteenth and nineteenth century English architecture and design; architectural competitions in nineteenth century England. *Publ:* Auth, The English landscape garden in the eighteenth century: The cultural importance of an English Institution, Albion, Spring 79; Auth, Architectural Competitions in 19th Century England, UMI Res Press, 84. *Mailing Add:* 25 Center Dr Roslyn NY 11576

BASTIAN, LINDA
PAINTER, EDUCATOR
b Ayer, Mass, Nov 7, 40. *Study:* Antioch Col, BA, 63; Tufts Univ, Boston Mus Sch, MEd, 65; New York Univ, PhD, 72. *Exhib:* Works on Paper, Brooklyn Mus, New York, 75 & Weathersbon Mus, Univ NC, Greensboro, 79; one-woman shows, Soho 20 Gallery, 78, 80 & 83; Salmagundi Third Ann, Drawing Prize, New York, 80; Animals in Art, Dept Cultural Affairs, New York, 81; Home Work, Women Make Art for the Home, Henry St, Syracuse Univ, 81; Translucency/Transparency, Fordham Univ & Col Art Asn, New York, 82. *Teaching:* Chairperson art educ, Sch Visual Arts, New York, 79- *Bibliog:* Articles in Arts Mag, 78, Diversion Mag, 82 & House Beautiful, 82. *Media:* Oil, Watercolor. *Dealer:* Soho 20 Gallery 99 Spring St New York NY 10012. *Mailing Add:* 325 Church St New York NY 10013

BATCHELOR, ANTHONY JOHN
PRINTMAKER, INSTRUCTOR
b Hull, Eng, Sept 3, 44. *Study:* Brighton Col Art, England, dipl(art & design), 67, 67-69; Brit Prix Rome, Italy, 72-74. *Work:* S London Gallery, Eng, Glasgow Art Gallery, Scotland; Bradford City Art Gallery, England; Ind State Univ; Cincinnati Art Mus, Ohio. *Comn:* Screen printed ceramic mural, Dept of Music, Ohio Univ, 71. *Exhib:* First & Third Brit Int Print Biennale, Bradford, 68 & 72; 8th Tyler Nat, Tyler Mus Art, Tex, 71; Mostra 73 & Mostra 74, Brit Acad, Rome, Italy, 73 & 74; one-man show, Cincinnati Art Mus, 75; Cincinnati Comn Arts Gallery, 83; and others. *Teaching:* Lectr, Sunderland Polytechnic, England, 69-70; vis asst prof printmaking & basic design, Ohio Univ, Athens, 70-72; instr printmaking & drawing, Art Acad Cincinnati, 75-, chmn found dept, 83- *Awards:* Purchase Award, Colorprint USA, Tex Fine Arts Comn & Tex Tech Univ, 71 & All-Ohio Graphics Biennale, Ohio Arts Coun, 71; Screen Printing Asn Int Grant, 83. *Bibliog:* Articles in Screen Printing Mag, 6/83 & 9/83. *Mem:* Col Art Asn; Screen Printing Asn Int. *Media:* Water-Based Screen Printing. *Dealer:* Janice Forberg Gallery Cincinnati OH. *Mailing Add:* 1159 Herschel Ave Cincinnati OH 45208

BATCHELOR, BETSY ANN
PAINTER, EDUCATOR
b Wilmington, Del, Dec 12, 52. *Study:* Philadelphia Col Art, BFA, 75; RI Sch Design, MFA, 77. *Work:* Continental Ill Bank & Trust, Chicago. *Exhib:* Marietta Col Nat, 78; Young Artists Show, Provincetown Art Asn & Mus, Mass, 80; Ann Exhib, Attleboro Mus, Mass, 80; Small Works, NY Univ, 80; Affect, Effect, Philadelphia, Col Art, 83. *Teaching:* Instr painting, drawing & design, RI Sch Design, 76-80 & Community Col RI, 77-80; asst prof painting & design, Millersville Univ, 83- *Awards:* Judges Awards, Providence Art Asn, 77, Marietta Col Nat, 78 & Attleboro Mus, Mass, 80. *Bibliog:* Ronald J Onorato (auth), Gallery, Art Express, 3/82; Sid Sachs (auth), Does Philadelphia have an imagist tradition too?, New Art Examiner, 2/83. *Mem:* Col Art Asn. *Dealer:* Jeffrey Fuller Fine Art 2108 Spruce St Philadelphia PA 19103. *Mailing Add:* 700 W Carpenter Lane Philadelphia PA 19119

BATEMAN, ROBERT MCLELLAN
PAINTER
b Toronto, Ont, Can, May 24, 30. *Study:* Univ of Toronto, BA(hon); pvt lessons at Toronto Arts & Lett Club from Gordon Payne; five yrs with Carl Schaeffer; Carlton Univ, Ottawa, DSc, 82; Brock Univ, St Catherines, LLD, 82; McMaster Univ, Hamilton, Ont, LHD. *Work:* Dominion Foundaries & Steel Corp Collection, Hamilton, Ont; Devonian Found, Calgary, Alta; Toronto Board of Trade; Prince of Wales; Am Artist Col, New York. *Comn:* Polar Bear (silver bowl commemorating endangered species), World Wildlife Fund, 76; Sugar Maple & Blue Jay, Toronto Bd Trade, 77; Endangered Species Stamps: Eastern Cougar, 77, Peregrine Falcon, 78, Bowhead Whale, 79 & Prairie Chicken, 80, Can Post Off. *Exhib:* Birds of Prey, Glenbow Inst, Calgary, Alta, 77; Bird Art Exhib, Leigh Yawkey Woodson Art Mus, Wausau, Wis, 77, 78 & 79; Queen Elizabeth Jubilee Show, Tryon Gallery, London, 77; one-man shows, Endangered Species Show, Tryon Gallery, 75 & 79 & Beckett Gallery, Hamilton, Ont, 78. *Pos:* Art consult, Halton Co Bd of Educ, 68-79. *Teaching:* Head dept art, Nelson High Sch, Burlington, 59-68 & Lord Elgin

High Sch, Burlington, 70-76. *Awards:* Merit Award, Soc Animal Artists, 79, 80 & 81; Merit Award, NW Rendezvous Show, 81; Master Artist, Leigh Yawkey Art Mus, Wausau, Wis, 82. *Bibliog:* Manuel Escott (auth), Creatures of the snow, Int Wildlife Mag, 3-4/78; Norman Lightfoot (auth), Images of the Wild, Nat Film Bd of Can, 78; Ramsay Derry (auth), The Art of Robert Baleman, Penguin-Viking Publ, Madison Press, 81. *Mem:* Soc Animal Artists; Royal Can Acad Arts; hon life mem Fedn Can Artists; hon life mem Fedn Ont Artists; Brit Soc Wildlife Artists; and others. *Media:* Acrylic and Oils. *Publ:* Illusr, The Nature of Birds, Natural Hist of Can Series, 74. *Dealer:* Mill Pond Press Inc 204 S Nassau St Venice FL 33595. *Mailing Add:* RR 2 Milton ON L9T 2X6 Canada

BATEMAN, RONALD C
PAINTER
b Caerphilly, Glamorgan, Wales, July 26, 47. *Study:* Cardiff Col of Art, predipl, study with Tom Hudson; Swansea Col of Art, study with William Price; Tyler Sch of Art, Temple Univ, study with David Pease & J Moore, MFA. *Work:* Philadelphia Mus of Art; Am Tel & Tel, Basking Ridge, NJ; Museo de Ayuntaimento De Pego, Alicante, Spain. *Comn:* Three murals, Wistar Inst, Univ of Pa, Philadelphia, 77; Creative Walls, Inc, Univ Pa. *Exhib:* Pego Ayuntamiento Mus Group Exhib, Alicante Province, Spain, 76; Ann Painting Exhib, Cheltenham Art Ctr, Pa, 76; Philadelphia: A Decade, Marian Locks Gallery, Philadelphia, 76; Contemp Artists in Philadelphia, 77; one-man show, Marian Locks Gallery, 77 & 82; About Face, Squibb Gallery, Princeton, NJ; What's Real, Marian Locks Gallery, 81. *Awards:* Elizabeth Greenshields Mem Found Grant, Can, 73; Primero Primio, Certimen de Pintura, Pascual Hermanos, Spain, 76; Mus Purchase, Cheltenham Art Ann, Philadelphia Mus of Art, 76. *Media:* Oil over Acrylic Underpainting on Canvas. *Dealer:* Marian Locks Gallery 1524 Walnut St Philadelphia PA 19102. *Mailing Add:* 2104 Delancey Pl Philadelphia PA 19103

BATES, BETSEY
DESIGNER, PAINTER
b Dobbs Ferry, NY, Nov 29, 24. *Study:* Beaver Col, BFA(magna cum laude); Barnes Found. *Work:* Butler Inst of Am Art, Youngstown, Ohio; Fed Reserve Bank, Philadelphia, Pa; Free Libr of Philadelphia; Smith-Kline, Philadelphia; McNeil Labs, Spring House, Pa. *Comn:* Commemorative screenprint, Graduate Hosp, Philadelphia, 79; ser collector's Christmas plates (farm & landscape scenes), 79- & porcelain plate ser, 79-87, World Book; postcard, Franklin Mint, 82; painting, Evans, Conger & Brown Insurance, Norristown, Pa, 82. *Exhib:* Butler Inst of Am Art, 70, 75 & 76; Woodmere Gallery, Chestnut Hill, Pa, 73-77, one-person show, 75; Mus of the Philadelphia Civic Ctr, 73, 75 & 78; Print Club, Philadelphia, 74 & 76; Del Art Mus, 75 & 76; Mickelson Gallery, Washington, DC, 76 & 77. *Pos:* Illusr, Jack & Jill Mag, Curtis Publ, 60-78 & Child Life, Rev Publ, 70-76; designer paper products, Contempo, 60- *Awards:* Golden Disc Award, Beaver Col, 75; Golden Plum, 77 & Award Cert, 78 & 79, Artists Guild Delaware Valley; Best of Show, Pa Coun Arts, Norristown, 80. *Mem:* Artist's Equity Asn, Philadelphia; Artist's Guild of Del Valley (bd mem, 77). *Media:* Designer's Tempera; Acrylic. *Publ:* Illusr, Needlework Book, Golden-Capitol, 61; illusr, many textbooks for Noble and Noble, Random House and others. *Mailing Add:* 1330 Valley Forge Rd RD 1 Norristown PA 19401

BATES, BILL
CARTOONIST
b Eastland, Tex, Jan 6, 30. *Study:* Tyler Jr Col, AA; Univ Tex. *Pos:* Cartoonist-illusr, San Francisco Examr, 60-64; ed-cartoonist, Fiji Times, Suva, Fiji Islands, 70-72; cartoonist, Serra's Place, Carmel Pine Cone, Calif, 72-75. *Awards:* Univ Tex Sr Advert Award, Dr Pepper, 51; First Place for Oil Painting, Air Training Command Art Award, USAF, 53. *Bibliog:* Robert Miskimon (auth), Perserving Fiji culture with pencil drawings, Carmel Pine Cone, 5/10/75. *Media:* Design Markers, Nikko Pen. *Publ:* Auth, Ping, 61-64; illusr, What If, 67; auth & illusr, The Funny Men, 67, The Golf Greats, 69 & Serra's Place, 74. *Mailing Add:* PO Box 4227 Carmel CA 93921

BATES, GLADYS EDGERLY
SCULPTOR
b Hopewell, NJ, July 15, 1896. *Study:* Corcoran Gallery Sch Art, Washington, DC, 10-16; Pa Acad Fine Arts, 16-21, Cresson European scholar, 20. *Work:* Pa Acad Fine Arts, Philadelphia, Pa; NJ State Mus, Trenton. *Exhib:* A Century of Progress, Art Inst Chicago, 34; Tex Centennial, Dallas, 36; Am Sculpture Exhib, Carnegie Inst, Pittsburgh, 38; Artists for Victory, Metrop Mus Art, New York, 42; Third Sculpture Int, Philadelphia Mus, 49. *Awards:* George D Widener Gold Medal, Pa Acad Fine Arts, 31; Third Purchase Prize, Artists for Victory, Metrop Mus Art, New York, 42; Nat Asn Women Artists Prize, 48. *Mem:* Fel Nat Sculpture Soc; Nat Asn Women Artists; Pen & Brush Club; Conn Acad Fine Arts; Mystic Art Asn. *Media:* Wood, Stone. *Dealer:* Stone Ledge Studio Art Galleries Noank CT 06340. *Mailing Add:* Stonecroft 15 Grove Ave Mystic CT 06355

BATES, KENNETH FRANCIS
ENAMELIST, CRAFTSMAN
b North Scituate, Mass, May 24, 04. *Study:* Mass Sch Art, BSEduc; also study abroad. *Work:* Cleveland Mus Art, Ohio; Butler Inst Am Art, Youngstown, Ohio; Arch Am Art, Smithsonian Inst. *Comn:* Murals, Campus Sweater Co, Cleveland & Lakewood Pub Libr; ecclesiastical enamels, Univ Notre Dame. *Exhib:* Cleveland Mus Art, 28-79; Smithsonian Inst Traveling Exhib; Nat Syracuse Traveling Exhib; one-man shows, Brooklyn Mus & Art Inst Chicago, 61; plus others. *Teaching:* Instr & lectr, Cleveland Inst Art, 27-71, emer instr, 71- *Awards:* Silver Medal, Cleveland Mus Art, 49, 57 & 66; Fine Arts Award of Cleveland, 63; Fac Grant Study Abroad, Cleveland Inst Art, 65. *Mem:* Fel

Int Inst Arts & Lett. *Publ:* Auth, Enameling, Principles & Practice, 51, Principles & Practice, 60, The Enamelist, 67 & Basic Design, 70, World Publ; auth, Salome's Heritage, Vantage, 77; auth, articles on enameling in Design Mag, Ceramics Mo, Encycl Arts and others. *Mailing Add:* 7 E 194th St Euclid OH 44119

BATES, LEO JAMES
PAINTER, FILMMAKER
b Pittsburgh, Pa, April 12, 44. *Study:* Yale Univ Summer Sch, 65; Carnegie Mellon Univ, BFA, 66. *Work:* Albright-Knox Art Gallery; Brooklyn Mus; Carnegie Mus Art, Pittsburgh; Columbia Mus Art, SC; NJ State Mus, Trenton. *Exhib:* One-person shows, Whitney Mus Art Resources Ctr, 73, 112 Greene St, New York, 73, Albright-Knox Art Gallery, 75, Picker Art Gallery, Dana Arts Ctr, Colgate Univ, 75 & Harriman Col, 78; All in Line, Joe & Emily Lowe Art Gallery, Syracuse Univ, 80 & Terry Dintenfass Inc, New York, 81; CAPS Grantees in Brooklyn, Brooklyn Mus, 81. *Awards:* Creative Artists Pub Serv Grant, 74. *Bibliog:* Rosemary Mayer (auth), article, Arts Mag, 11/73; Jean Reeves (auth), Bates pastel drawings visual challenge, Buffalo Evening News, 2/3/75; Robyn Brentano (auth), 112 Workshop, NY Univ Press, 81. *Media:* Casein and Rhoplex on Canvas; Film and Computer Animation. *Mailing Add:* 499 11th St Brooklyn NY 11215

BATHURST, DAVID C
GALLERY DIRECTOR
b London, Eng, Dec 15, 37. *Study:* Eton; Magdalen Col, Oxford Univ, Eng, grad. *Work:* Carnegie Inst, Pittsburgh. *Pos:* Mem staff, Carnegie Inst, Pittsburgh, 61; head, Mod Pictures Dept, Christie, Manson & Woods Int Inc, formerly, dir, 66-; pres, Christie's in Am, 78- *Specialty:* Impressionist and modern painting. *Mailing Add:* c/o Christies Fine Art Auctioneers 502 Park Ave New York NY 10022

BATT, MILES GIRARD
PAINTER, INSTRUCTOR
b Nazareth, Pa, Oct 12, 33. *Work:* Purdue Univ, Calumet, Ind; Ft Lauderdale Mus Arts; Home Savings & Loan Banking Group, Los Angeles; Southeast Banking Group (statewide), Miami, Fla; Art & the Law, West Publ, St Paul; plus others. *Comn:* Posters & stage settings, Theatre Wing, Nat Endowment for the Arts, Hollywood, Fla, 75; four paintings, Dade Co Art in Pub Bldg, Miami, Fla; two paintings, Fla State House of Rep, Tallahassee; and others. *Exhib:* Nat Exhib of Contemporary Painting, Soc of the Four Arts, Palm Beach, Fla, 67-82; Miami Metrop Mus Art Ann, 68-74; Watercolor USA, Springfield, Mo, 68-81; Abstract Real-Real Abstract, Louis K Meisel Gallery, NY, 74; A Change of View, Aldrich Mus, Conn, 75; '77 Photo Realists, Hollywood Cult Ctr, Fla & St Petersburg Mus Fine Arts, Fla, 78; plus others. *Teaching:* Instr watercolor, oil & acrylic, Ft Lauderdale Mus Arts, 69-78; instr watercolor, Norton Gallery & Sch Art, West Palm Beach, 70-73; instr watercolor, Miami Art Inst, 74-79; instr watercolor, Hewitt Int Painting Workshops, 79-84; instr, Broward Community Col, 80. *Awards:* Atwater Kent Award, Soc Four Arts Nat Exhib Contemp Am Painting, 73-81; Strathmore Award, Nat Watercolor Soc, 80; Cash & Purchase Award, Watercolor USA, Springfield Mus, 81; and many others. *Bibliog:* Jeanne Wolf (dir), Miles Batt, in Portrait (film), WPBT-2, Miami, 73; Howard Whitman (auth), Palm Beach has always had the cash-now it gets the culture, Art News, 2/74; Griffin Smith (auth), Why shouldn't a pro win four times in a row, Miami Herald Newspapers, 4/74. *Mem:* Nat Watercolor Soc (Los Angeles area rep, 71-79); Am Watercolor Soc; charter mem Fla Watercolor Soc; Rocky Mountain Nat Water Media Soc; Watercolor West, Redlands. *Media:* Acrylic; watercolor. *Publ:* Contribr, Transparent Watercolor, Davis Publ, 73; contribr, Ford Times Mag, 75-81; auth, Watercolor Workshop, slide-cassette, Exploring Watercolor, 78; contribr, Creative Seascape, Watson Guptil, 80; contribr, The Expressive Watercolor, Davis Publ, 81. *Dealer:* Miller Gallery 3112 Commodore Plaza Coconut Grove FL 33133. *Mailing Add:* 2120 Hammock Ln Ft Lauderdale FL 33312

BATTENBERG, JOHN
SCULPTOR, EDUCATOR
b Milwaukee, Wis, 31. *Study:* Univ Wis, 49; Minn State Col, BS, 54; Ruskin Sch of Fine Art & Drawing, Oxford, Eng; Mich State Univ, MA, 60; Calif Col of Art & Crafts. *Work:* San Francisco Mus of Mod Art; Tate Mus, London; Oakland Mus, San Jose Mus & Los Angeles Co Mus, Calif. *Exhib:* Am Fedn of Arts Travelling Exhib, 68; Mus of Mod Art, Belgrade, 69; Galleria d'Arte Moderna, Milano, 69; Denver Mus of Art, 71; Stanford Univ, 71; Los Angeles Munic Art Gallery, 73; San Francisco Mus of Mod Art, 76. *Collections Arranged:* 2nd Biennial Am Painting & Sculpture, Pa Acad Art, 60; Am Fedn of Arts Travelling Exhib, 68; Contemp Painting & Sculpture, Ind Mus of Art, 70; The Collectors Show, Crocker Gallery, Sacramento, 71; Sculpture of the Bay Area, James Willis Gallery, San Francisco, 76. *Teaching:* Instr sculpture, Contra Costa Col, Calif, 64-66; prof art, San Jose State Univ, Calif, 66-; casting instr sculpture, Calif Col of Arts & Crafts, 77- *Bibliog:* Aleta Watson (auth), One Step Beyond Printmaking, Marquee, 6/76; Gail Tagashira (auth), He Makes War Not Love, San Jose News, 9/76; Gay Weaver (auth), World Seen Through Sculptors Eyes, Palo Alto Times, 10/76. *Media:* Bronze. *Mailing Add:* 25567 Firhaven Lane Los Gatos CA 95030

BATTENFIELD, JACKIE (FRAZIER)
PAINTER, CURATOR
b Pittsburgh, Pa, May 13, 50. *Study:* Pa State Univ, BS, 71; Syracuse Univ, MFA, 78. *Exhib:* Artists of Central New York, Munson-Williams-Procter Inst Mus Art, Utica, 77; 42nd Ann Nat Art Competition & Exhib, Cooperstown Mus Art, NY, 77; Fiber Work, Del Mus Art, Wilmington, 78; solo exhib, Zoller Gallery, Pa State Univ Mus, 80; Selections from the Sasaki Collection,

Gallerie Saison, Tokyo, 82. *Pos:* Cur & dir, Rotunda Gallery, Brooklyn, 81- *Teaching:* Instr visual arts, Cushing Jr Col, 72-76; vis artist fiber arts, Syracuse Univ Col Visual & Performing Arts, 80; adj prof textile design, RI Sch Design, 80-81. *Awards:* First Prize, Arts Nine, Pa State Univ, 76; First Prize Sculpture, Cooperstown Arts Asn 42nd Nat Art Competition & Exhib, 77; Judges Award, Marietta Col Nat Exhib, 78. *Mem:* Am Asn Mus; Col Art Asn; Found Community Artists. *Publ:* Auth, Ikat Technique, Van Nostrand Reinhold, 78. *Dealer:* Schaeffer Ed 500 E 77th St New York NY. *Mailing Add:* 158 Franklin St New York NY 10013

BAUM, HANK
DEALER, LECTURER
b New York, NY. *Study:* Los Angeles City Col, AA; Univ Southern Calif, BA; New York Sch Printing, printing & related graphic arts degree; Univ Calif, Los Angeles, with Lester Longman & E Maurice Bloch; Calif State Col, Los Angeles, with H Glicksman. *Pos:* Assoc dir, Tamarind Lithography Workshop, Los Angeles, formerly; exec dir, Atelier Mourlot, New York, formerly; assoc dir, Collectors Press, San Francisco, currently; dir, Hank Baum Gallery, San Francisco, currently; ed, Calif Art Rev, currently; pres, Art Explorer's Tours, currently. *Teaching:* Lectr contemp graphics & art & artists, Univ Calif, Berkeley, triann & Univ Calif, Los Angeles, biann. *Mem:* Print Coun Am; Am & Calif Printmakers. *Specialty:* Contemporary art; painting, sculpture, drawings, fine original limited edition prints. *Collection:* Contemporary art. *Mailing Add:* Hank Baum Gallery 2140 Bush St Suite 6 San Francisco CA 94115

BAUM, JAYNE H
DEALER
b Newark, NJ, Dec 3, 54. *Study:* Clark Univ, Mass; NY Univ, BS(fine arts). *Pos:* Assoc & cur, Margo Feiden Galleries, New York, 75-77; dir & consult, Dan Greenblat Assoc, New York, 77-82; owner, Jayne Baum Gallery, New York, currently. *Specialty:* Fibreworks, handmade paper, monoprints, drawings, ceramics and contemporary fine arts limited editions, paintings and photography. *Publ:* Auth, Interior design, Whitney Comn Mag Div, 83; auth, Facilities Design and Management, Gralla Publ, 83. *Mailing Add:* 12 W 37th St New York NY 10018

BAUM, MARILYN RUTH
PAINTER, PRINTMAKER
b Pittsburgh, Pa, May 24, 39. *Study:* Univ Calif, Los Angeles, BFA, 62, 63-65. *Work:* Mus Mod Art, New York; Nat Mus Am Art; Achenbach Found Graphic Arts, Fine Arts Mus San Francisco; San Jose Mus, Calif; Jacksonville Art Mus, Fla. *Exhib:* Solo exhib, San Jose Mus, 81; California Artists, Oakland Mus, Calif, 81; Recent Acquisitions Part II, Achenbach Found, San Francisco, 83. *Bibliog:* Elise Miller (auth), Marilyn Baum--new paintings, Art Express, 3/82; Jeffrey Weiss (auth), article, Arts, 6/82; Frank Cebulski (auth), The selfish eye, Artweek, 1/83. *Dealer:* Allport Assoc Gallery 126 Post St San Francisco CA 94108. *Mailing Add:* 561 Summit Mill Valley CA 94941

BAUM, TIMOTHY
DEALER, HISTORIAN
b New York, NY, Aug 29, 38. *Study:* Trinity Col, Hartford, Conn, BA, 60. *Res:* All areas in the realms of art and literature related to the Dada and Surrealist movements, especially 1915-1945. *Specialty:* Paintings and drawings, original prints, photographs, illustrated books and related ephemera. *Collection:* Little magazines and documentary ephemera related to all avant-garde movements of 1915-1965. *Publ:* Ed & auth, The Surrealist Experience, Richard Gray Gallery, Chicago, 72; ed & auth, Art of the Dadaists, La Boetie, NY, 77; auth, Night Collages, Folker Skulima, Berlin, 81; coauth (with Gilbert E Kaplan), The Graphic Work of Rene Magritte, Institutional Investor Editions, 82. *Mailing Add:* 40 E 78th St New York NY 10021

BAUMBACH, HAROLD
PAINTER, PRINTMAKER
b New York, NY, 05. *Study:* Pratt Inst; Educ Alliance. *Work:* Hirschorn Mus, Washington, DC; Fleischer Art Mem; Chrysler Mus; NY Univ; Univ Ga Mus; Whitney Mus; and others. *Comn:* Five lithograph editions in color, Bank St Atelier, New York, 72. *Exhib:* Carnegie Int, 47; Ariz Mus Purchase Exhib, Metrop Mus Art, New York, 47; Second Ann Summer Show, Park-Bernet Galleries, New York, 64; one-man show, Univ Iowa Mus, 67; Free Form Exhib, Whitney Mus Am Art, 72; Am Acad Ann, Inst of Arts & Lett, 77. *Teaching:* Spec lectr art appreciation, Brooklyn Col, 60-66; adj asst prof art appreciation, Long Island Univ, 66-67; vis prof painting, Univ Iowa, summer 67, vis artist, 72-73. *Awards:* Hon Mention, Pepsi Cola Artists for Victory Competition, 46. *Mem:* Fedn Mod Painters & Sculptors. *Media:* Oil. *Dealer:* Gallery 99 1088 Kane Concourse Bay Harbor Island FL 33154. *Mailing Add:* 278 Henry St Brooklyn NY 11201

BAUR, JOHN I H
MUSEUM DIRECTOR, WRITER
b Woodbridge, Conn, Aug 9, 09. *Study:* Yale Univ, BA, 32, MA, 34. *Pos:* Supvr educ, Brooklyn Mus Art, NY, cur, 36-52; cur, Whitney Mus Am Art, New York, 52-58, assoc dir, 58-68, dir, 68-74, emer dir, 74-; consult dir, Terra Mus Am Art, Evanston, Ill, 79-; ed, Am Art J Books, 80- *Teaching:* Vis lectr Am art, Yale Univ, 51-52. *Publ:* Auth, Bernard Reder, 61; coauth, American Art of Our Century, 61; auth, Revolution & Tradition in Modern American Art, 51 & 67 & Joseph Stella, 71, Praeger; The Inlander: Charles Burchfield, Am Art J Books, 82; and others. *Mailing Add:* Mt Holly Rd Katonah NY 10536

BAVINGER, EUGENE ALLEN
PAINTER, EDUCATOR
b Sapulpa, Okla, Dec 21, 19. *Study:* Univ Okla, BFA; Inst Allende, Mex, MFA. *Work:* Addison Gallery Am Art, Andover, Mass; Nelson Gallery, Atkins Mus, Kansas City, Mo; Joslyn Art Mus, Omaha, Nebr; Masur Mus, Monroe, La; Mulvane Art Ctr, Topeka, Kans. *Exhib:* American Painting Today, Metrop Mus Art, New York, 50; 70th Western Ann Invitational-19 Artists, Denver Art Mus, Colo, 64; Fifty Artists from Fifty States, Am Fedn Arts Traveling Exhib, 66; one-man shows, Sheldon Art Gallery, Lincoln, Nebr, 67 & Joslyn Art Mus, Nebr, 69; Razor Gallery, New York, 78; Kauffman Gallery, Houston, 82. *Teaching:* Prof art, Univ Okla, 47-; retired. *Awards:* First Award, 22nd Ann Exhib, Ft Smith Art Ctr, Ark, 72; Purchase Award, 19th Ann, Ark Art Ctr, Little Rock, 76; Grand Award, Art Ann I, Tulsa, Okla, 80. *Mailing Add:* 730 NE 60 Norman OK 73071

BAXTER, BONNIE JEAN
PRINTMAKER, PAINTER
b Texarkana, Tex, July 30, 46. *Study:* Monticello Col, AS, 64-66; Kans Univ, 66-67; Cranbrook Art Acad, BFA, 67-69. *Work:* Mus Mod Art, Montreal; Monticello Col, Godfrey, Ill; Maison de la Cult, Montreal; Galleria Fenwick, Forano, Italy; Maison des Metiers, Rennes, France. *Comn:* Mural, Mich High Sch, Bloomfield Hills, 69; mural for tomb, comn by Gen Paciantiani, Forano, Italy, 73. *Exhib:* Que-Boston Exchange, Experimental Etching Studio, Boston, 82; 171 Artistes Quebecoise, Maison de la Cult, Montreal, 82; Quebec Artists, Maison des Metiers, Rennes, France, 83; Artists Book L'Ile, Mus Mod Art, Montreal, 83; l'Atelier de L'Ile, Delegation du Que, New York, 83; and others. *Pos:* Owner & dir, Le Scarabee Printing Studio, Val-David, Que, 82-; printer in residence, l'Atelier de L'Ile Asn, 80- *Teaching:* Instr wood-cut, Les Createurs Assoc, Que, 82-83. *Bibliog:* Jacques Gireldeau (dir), Etoile de Aurainegiea (film), Can Nat Film Bd, 78. *Mem:* Conseil Gravare Que; Am Graphics Soc; Les Createur Assoc Val-David (pres, 82-); Conseil Regional Cult Laurentides (exec dir, 83-). *Media:* All. *Publ:* Auth, Atelier d l'Ile a Boston, 81 & Atelier d l'Ile a New York, 82, Skis-Dite; illusr, L'Ile, Iconia Ed, 82; auth, Bonnie Baxter: Printmaker--fine arts director, Skis-Dite, 82; contribr, Quebec Artists 1970-1983, Iconia Ed, 83. *Mailing Add:* 3224 Ave du Pins CP 375 Val-David PQ J0T 2N0 Canada

BAXTER, DOUGLAS W
DEALER
b Ohio, Nov 8, 49. *Study:* Oberlin Col, with Ellen Johnson, BA(art hist), 72. *Pos:* Art dealer, Fischbach Gallery, 73-74; art dealer, Paula Cooper Gallery, New York, 74- *Specialty:* Contemporary art. *Mailing Add:* c/o Paula Cooper Gallery 155 Wooster New York NY 10012

BAXTER, PATRICIA HUY
DIRECTOR
b Washington, DC, Sept 18, 45. *Study:* Cornell Univ, Ithaca, NY, BA(art hist). *Collections Arranged:* Southern California Indian Rock Art (with catalog), Sonakinatography, by Channa Davis Horowitz & Joseph Raphael & Carlos Villa, 73; Books by Ed Ruscha, 74. *Pos:* Chief cur, art gallery, Univ Calif, San Diego in La Jolla, 75-; exec adminr & proj mgr, Edwin Schlossberg Inc, New York, formerly; asst vpres, Sotheby's, New York, currently. *Publ:* Auth, Polynesian Ornament, Dimensions of Polynesia, 74. *Mailing Add:* 19 West 96th St New York NY 10025

BAXTER, ROBERT JAMES
PAINTER
b Milwaukee, Wis, Nov 30, 33. *Study:* Univ Wis, BS(art), 56, MS(painting), 59 & MFA(painting), 60; with John Wilde. *Work:* Vatican Mus, Rome; Chase Manhattan Bank; San Diego Mus Art; Univ NC, Greensboro; Wichita Falls Mus, Tex; and others. *Exhib:* Conn Acad Fine Arts Ann, Wadsworth Atheneum, Hartford, 62-64; Smithsonian Inst, 63; Pa Acad Fine Arts, Philadelphia, 63 & 65; one-man show, San Francisco Mus Art, 70; San Diego Mus, Calif, 80 & 81; Gabinetto Nat Delle Stampe, La Farnesina, Rome, Italy, 81; Milwaukee Art Ctr, Wis, 81; Phoenix Mus Art, Ariz, 81-82; Gruenwald Col Graphic Arts, Univ Calif, Los Angeles, 81-82; San Francisco Mus Art, 81-82; and others. *Teaching:* Prof painting, San Diego State Univ, Calif, 62-75. *Awards:* Howard Penrose Prize, 52nd Conn Acad Fine Arts Exhib, Wadsworth Atheneum; Henry Clay Hofheimer Award, Am Drawing Ann XX, Norfolk Mus Arts & Sci, 63; Grant for Painting, Louis Comfort Tiffany Found, 72. *Bibliog:* Prof Daniel Mendelowitz (auth), Drawing, 66, A History of American Art, 70. *Media:* Egg Tempera. *Publ:* Contribr, Arts in Society, Univ Wis Exten Div, Vol 3, No 1. *Mailing Add:* Via Delle Mantelette 25-A Rome 00165 94022 Italy

BAYEFSKY, ABA
PAINTER, PRINTMAKER
b Toronto, Ont, Apr 7, 23. *Study:* Cent Tech Sch, Toronto. *Work:* Nat Gallery Can, Ottawa; Nat Gallery Victoria, Melbourne, Australia; Art Gallery Ont; Libr Cong, Washington, DC; Hebrew Univ, Jerusalem; and others. *Comn:* Mural, Northview Colliate, Toronto; tapestry, Synagogue Ont; mural, Ont Govt Bldg. *Exhib:* Major Can Art Soc Exhibs & 27 one-man shows. *Teaching:* Instr, Ont Col Art, formerly. *Awards:* Can Coun Grant to India, 58; Centennial Citation, Toronto, 67; Order of Canada, 79; and others. *Mem:* Academician Royal Can Acad Art; Can Soc Graphic Art; Can Soc Painters in Water Colour; Can Group Painters. *Media:* Graphics; Watercolor, Oil. *Mailing Add:* 7 Paperbirch Dr Don Mills ON M3C 2E6 Canada

BAYER, ARLYNE
PAINTER, PRINTMAKER
b Washington, DC, Jan 8, 49. *Study:* State Univ NY, Buffalo, BFA(fine arts), 70; Hunter Col, with Tony Smith & Rosalind Krauss, MA(fine arts), 75. *Work:* Herbert F Johnson Mus Art, Ithaca, NY; Chase Manhattan Bank, Citibank, New York; Prudential Insurance Co, Newark, NJ; Housatonic Mus Art, Bridgeport, Conn. *Exhib:* Contemporary Reflections, Aldrich Mus Contemporary Art, 75; Drawings, Jersey City Mus, NJ, 77; 15 New Talents, Aldrich Mus Contemporary Art, 79; Young Painters: 1980, Bronx Mus Art, 80; Coastal Currents, Corpus Christi State Univ, 81; One of a Kind: Prints and Paper, Bennington Col, 81; 55 Mercer Gallery Invitational, New York, 82. *Awards:* Creative Artists Pub Serv Grant, 76-77; MacDowell Colony Fel, 77. *Bibliog:* Jacqueline Moss (auth), article, Arts Mag, 2/80. *Dealer:* Robert L Kidd Gallery 107 Townsend St Birmingham MI 48011. *Mailing Add:* 50 Bond St New York NY 10012

BAYER, HERBERT
PAINTER, ARCHITECT
b Haag, Austria, Apr 5, 1900; US citizen. *Study:* Real-Gym, Linz, Austria; archit with G Schmidthammer, Linz, 19; with Emanuel Margold, Darmstadt, Ger, 20; wall paintings with Vassily Kandinsky, 21; Bauhaus, Weimar, 21-23; Univ Graz, Austria, Hon Dr; Philadelphia Col Art, Hon DFA; Art Ctr Col Design, Pasadena, Hon DFA. *Hon Degrees:* Univ Graz, Austria, Hon Dr; Philadelphia Col Art & Art Crt Col Design, Pasadena, DFA. *Work:* San Francisco Mus Art; Mus Mod Art; Guggenheim Mus; Bayer Arch Ctr Creative Photog, Tucson; Bayer Arch Bauhaus Arch, Berlin; plus many others in US & Europe. *Comn:* Murals, Mass & Aspen Inst Humanistic Studies, Aspen, Colo; designed articulated wall construction for 1968 Olympics, Mexico City; double ascension sculpture, Arco Plaza, Los Angeles; sculpture, Anaconda, Denver; flood water basin, Mill Creek Canyon Earthworks, Kent, Wash, 79. *Exhib:* San Francisco Art Mus, 49; Germanisches Nat Mus, Nuremberg; Hochsch Bildende Künste, Berlin, 57; Städtische Kunsthalle, Dusseldorf, 60; Marlborough Gallery, London, 68, New York, 71 & 79, Zurich, 74; Denver Art Mus, 80 & 82; Bauhaus Arch, Berlin, 82; Galerie Thomas, Munich, 83; and others. *Pos:* Master, Bauhaus, Dessau, 25-28; painter, photog, graphic designer & exhib architect, Berlin, 28-38; art dir, Vogue, Berlin, 29-30; dir, Dorland Studio, Berlin, 28-38; design consult & architect, Aspen Inst; chmn dept design, Container Corp Am, 56-67; art & design consult, Atlantic Richfield Co, 66- *Bibliog:* Hans M Wingler (auth), The Bauhaus; Alexander Dorner (auth), Way Beyond Art, Wittenborn & Schulz, 47; Ida Rodriguez Prampolini (auth), Un concepto total, Univ Mex, 75; plus others. *Mem:* Am Inst Architects; fel Aspen Inst Humanistic Studies; fel Am Acad Arts & Sci. *Publ:* Coauth, Bauhaus 1919-28, Mus Mod Art, 38; auth, World Geographic Atlas, Container Corp Am, 53; auth & designer, Herbert Bayer, Painter, Designer, Architect, Reinhold, 67; contribr, articles, In: Gebrauchsgraphik, Col Art J, Bauhaus Mag, Linea Grafica & Architecture Formes et Fonctions, Lausanne; plus others. *Dealer:* Marlborough Gallery 41 E 57th St New York NY 10022; Galerie Thomas Maximilianstrasse 25 Munich. *Mailing Add:* 184 Middle Rd Montecito CA 93108

BAYER, JEFFREY JOSHUA
EDUCATOR, SCULPTOR
b New York, NY, Aug 15, 42. *Study:* Univ NC, Chapel Hill, BA, 64, MFA, 67; NY Univ; post-grad courses in plastics technol, New York Univ, 70, 71 & 73. *Comn:* String Quartet (sculpture), Amen, Weisman & Butler Attorneys, New York, 62-65; sculpture collection, comn by Ms Marion McAdoo, Philadelphia, 64. *Exhib:* One-man shows, Univ SC Art Mus, 75, Vanderbilt Art Gallery, Vanderbilt Univ, Nashville, Tenn, 75, Brooks Mem Art Mus, Memphis, 75, Ark State Univ, 76, Univ WFla, 76 & James Madison Univ, Va, 77; plus many others. *Pos:* Mem acquisitions comt, City Huntsville Mus Art, 73-75; vpres, Hist Huntsville Found, 75-78; nat conf dir, Nat Sculpture Conf, 75 & 77; adv bd, Nat Sculpture Ctr, 75-77; adv bd, Int Sculpture Ctr, 77-79. *Teaching:* Prof sculpture & chmn dept art, Univ Ala, Huntsville, 67- *Mem:* Southeastern Col Art Conf (vpres, 79-); Southern Asn Sculptors (pres, 75-79); Chicago Archit Found; Friends Cast Iron Archit; Col Art Asn; and others. *Media:* Miscellaneous Media. *Publ:* Auth, Metallizing, Nat Handweaver J, 75; auth, Polymer chemistry for the artist, Sculptor J, 76; and others. *Mailing Add:* Univ Ala Dept Art PO Box 1247 Huntsville AL 35807

BAYLISS, GEORGE
PAINTER, ADMINISTRATOR
b Washington, DC, Oct 14, 31. *Study:* Univ Va; Univ Md, with Herman Maril, BA, 55; Cranbrook Acad Art, with Zoltan Sepeshy, MFA, 56; Corcoran Sch Art. *Work:* Akron Art Inst, Ohio; State Univ NY; Corcoran Gallery Art; Univ Mich; Ford Motor Co. *Comn:* Mural, Rural Elect Transmission, Mus Hist & Technol, Smithsonian Inst, 56-57. *Exhib:* Corcoran Biennial Contemp Am Painters, 55 & 59; New Accessions USA, Colorado Springs Fine Arts Ctr, 58; 12 Washington Painters, Univ Ky, 60; Four Washington Artists, Corcoran Gallery Art, 61; Drawings USA, circulated by Smithsonian Inst, 62. *Pos:* Dean, Parsons Sch Design, New York, 63-67. *Teaching:* Instr painting & drawing, Sch Akron Art Inst, Ohio, 57-59; instr painting & drawing, Flint Jr Col, Mich, 59-62; asst prof painting & drawing, State Univ NY Col Potsdam, 62-63; chmn dept art, State Univ NY Col, Fredonia, 67-72; chmn dept art, Univ Mich, 72-74, dean, Sch Art, 74- *Awards:* Principal Purchase Prize, Corcoran Gallery Art, 55; Award of Merit, South Bend Art Asn, Ind, 56; Bundy Co Prize, Bloomfield Hills Art Asn, 56. *Mem:* Nat Asn Schs Art & Design (bd dirs & pres). *Media:* Oil, Watercolor. *Dealer:* Zriny Gallery 1963 N Halsted Chicago IL 30614. *Mailing Add:* Sch Art Univ Mich Ann Arbor MI 48105

BAYNARD, ED
PAINTER
b Washington, DC, Sept 5, 40. *Work:* Chase Manhattan Bank, New York; Wadsworth Atheneum, Hartford, Conn; Whitney Mus, New York; Inst Contemp Art, Univ Pa, Philadelphia; Mus Mod Art, New York; and others. *Exhib:* New Am Painters, Munson-Williams-Proctor Inst, 71; Landscape, Mus Mod Art, New York, 72; Topography of Nature, Inst of Contemp Art, Philadelphia, 72; Am Drawing 1963-1973, Whitney Mus, New York, 73; Am Drawing, Fine Arts Gallery of San Diego, 77; Drawing Show, Cleveland Mus of Art, 78; A Collection of Contemporary Paintings and Sculpture, Nabisco, Inc World Hq, East Hanover, NJ, 79; Walker Art Ctr, Minneapolis, 80; American Still Life 1945-1983, Contemp Art Mus, Houston, 83; and others. *Bibliog:* Kenneth Wahl (auth), Ed Baynard, Arts Mag, 77. *Publ:* Illusr, Somewhere in Ho, Buffalo Press, 72; illusr (cover & frontispiece), Paris Rev, 74; illusr (cover), Miami, Donnes, 75; auth (interview), Arlene Slavin & Ed Baynard, NY Arts J, 76. *Mailing Add:* 290 Lafayette St New York NY 10012

BEACH, WARREN
PAINTER
b Minneapolis, Minn, May 21, 14. *Study:* Phillips Acad, Andover, Mass; Yale Univ, BFA, 39; Univ Iowa, MA, 40; Harvard Univ, MA, 47. *Exhib:* Art & Artists Along the Mississippi, 41; one-man shows, Minn State Fair, 41 & Grace Horne Gallery, Boston, Mass, 45; one-man retrospective, Telfair Acad Arts & Sci, Savannah, Ga, 75; Trend House Gallery, Tampa, Fla, 75. *Pos:* Dir exten serv, Walker Art Ctr, Minneapolis, 40-41; asst art mus, Addison Gallery Am Art, 46-47; asst dir, Columbus Gallery Fine Arts, 47-55; dir, Fine Arts Gallery San Diego, 55-69. *Teaching:* Dean, Columbus Art Sch, 47-49. *Mem:* Am Asn Mus; Fine Arts Soc San Diego. *Media:* Oil, Watercolor. *Mailing Add:* 3740 Pio Pico St San Diego CA 92106

BEADLESTON, WILLIAM L
DEALER
b 1938; US citizen. *Pos:* Dir, William L Beadleston Inc, currently. *Specialty:* European and American impressionist and 20th century masters. *Mailing Add:* 60 E 91st St New York NY 10028

BEAL, JACK
PAINTER
b Richmond, Va, June 25, 31. *Study:* Norfolk Div, Col William & Mary & Va Polytech Inst, 50-53; Art Inst Chicago, with Briggs Dyer, Isobel MacKinnon & Kathleen Blackshear, 53-56. *Work:* Whitney Mus Am Art, New York; Walker Art Ctr, Minneapolis; Art Inst Chicago; San Francisco Mus Fine Arts; Del Mus, Wilmington. *Comn:* Washington & Lee Univ, 74-75; US Dept Interior, 75-76; The Hist of Labor in Am (murals), US Labor Bldg, Washington, DC, 75-77. *Exhib:* Ann exhibs, Allan Frumkin Gallery, New York; Galerie Claude Bernard, Paris; Ten-Yr Retrospective, Boston Univ, Va Mus & Mus Contemp Art, Chicago, 73-74; Print Retrospective, Madison Art Ctr & Art Inst of Chicago, 77-78. *Teaching:* Visiting lecturer at over 60 schools and universities. *Awards:* Nat Endowment Arts Grant. *Bibliog:* Mark Strand (auth), Art of The Real. Potter, 83; John Arthur (auth), Nine Realists, Watson-Guptill, 83. *Mem:* NY Acad Art; Nat Acad Design. *Dealer:* Allan Frumkin Gallery 50 W 57th St New York NY 10019. *Mailing Add:* 67 Vestry St New York NY 10013

BEAL, MACK
SCULPTOR
b Boston, Mass, Apr 20, 24. *Study:* Harvard Univ, BS, 46; grad study, Dept of Art, Univ NH, Durham; apprentice to master blacksmith Joe Tucker, Milford, NH. *Work:* Addison Gallery Am Art, Phillips Acad, Andover, Mass; New Eng Ctr, Univ NH, Durham; Worcester Art Mus, Mass; Permanent Exhib, Symp Lindabruun, Bad Voslau, Austria. *Exhib:* Inst Contemp Art, Boston, Mass, 70-73; Addison Gallery Am Art, Phillips Acad, Andover, Mass, 74; Norfolk Art Ctr, Nebr, 79; Nat Ornamental Metal Mus, Memphis, 79; Rowe Gallery, Univ NC, 80; Int Conf Exhib, Hereford, Eng, 80; NH Comn Arts, 81; and many others. *Pos:* Dir, The Sculptors Workshop, Somerville, Mass, 70-80. *Mem:* NH Art Asn; NH League of Craftsmen; Boston Visual Artists Union; Ogunquit Art Asn; Artist Blacksmith Asn North Am (dir, 76-80). *Dealer:* NH Art Asn West Bridge St Manchester NH 03105. *Mailing Add:* Dundee Rd Jackson NH 03846

BEALE, ARTHUR C
CONSERVATOR
b Needham, Mass, Apr 12, 40. *Study:* Brandeis Univ, BA, 62; Boston Univ Sch Fine & Appl Arts, 62-64; Harvard Univ Fogg Art Mus, apprentice conservator, 66-68. *Pos:* Conservator, Joint Am Exped Idalion, Cyprus, 71; assoc conservator, Fogg Art Mus, Harvard Univ, 71-74; head conserv, Ctr Conserv & Tech Studies, 75-81, dir, 81-; conservator, Kress Collection Renaissance Bronzes & Medals, Nat Gallery Art, 72-75. *Teaching:* Asst appl arts, Boston Univ, 62-64; lectr fine arts, Harvard Univ, 74-78, sr lectr, 78-. *Mem:* Fel Int Inst Conserv; fel Am Inst Conserv; Nat Conserv Adv Coun; Nat Inst Conserv (pres, 81-82, chmn, 82-). *Publ:* Auth, Materials and Methods for the Packing and Handling of Ancient Metal Objects, Int Inst Conserv, 69; contribr, Daumier sculpture: a critical and comparative study, In: Materials and Techniques, 69 & Metamorphoses in Nineteenth Century Sculpture, 75, Fogg Art Mus, Harvard Univ; coauth (with Clifford Craine & Carol Forsythe), The conservation of plaster casts, Am Inst Conserv, 77; contribr, Sculpture By Antoine-Louis Barge in the Collection of the Fogg Art Museum, Vol 4, Fogg Art Mus Handbooks, 83. *Mailing Add:* Ctr for Conserv & Tech Studies 32 Quincy St Cambridge MA 02138

BEALL, DENNIS RAY
PRINTMAKER, EDUCATOR
b Chickasha, Okla, Mar 13, 29. *Study:* Oklahoma City Univ; San Francisco State Univ. *Work:* Achenbach Found for Graphic Arts, San Francisco; San Francisco Mus Art; Mus Mod Art, New York; Libr Cong, Washington, DC; Philadelphia Mus. *Comn:* Lone Star (ed 20, collagraph), C Troup Gallery-Codex Press, Inc, Dallas, 66; Emblem V (ed 75, relief & etching), Univ Calif, Berkeley Mus, 67; Emblem VI (ed 50, collagraph), San Francisco Mus Art, 67; Miz Am (ed 20, etching), Hansen-Fuller Gallery, 68; Ars Medicus (ed 20, etching & screen print), San Francisco Art Comn, 71. *Exhib:* San Francisco Mus Art, 60-65 & 67; 14th & 15th Nat, Brooklyn Mus, 64 & 65; Original Prints, Calif Palace of Legion of Honor, San Francisco, 64; Art in the Embassies Prog, US Dept State, Oakland Art Mus, Calif, 66; NY Ann, Whitney Mus Am Art, 66-67; one-man show, Achenbach Found Graphic Arts, 68-69; Cincinnati Art Mus, 73; 1st Bienal Int, Segovia, Spain, 73; 11th Biennial Graphic Art, Ljubljana, Yugoslavia, 75; and others. *Teaching:* Prof art, San Francisco State Univ, 65- *Awards:* Purchase Awards, Ultimate Concerns, Ohio Univ, Athens, 63, 25th & 26th San Francisco Art Festivals, 71 & 72 & 5th Ann Graphics Competition, De Anza Col, Cupertino, Calif, 76. *Bibliog:* Leonard Edmondson (auth), Etching, Van Nostrand, Reinhold, 73; Mimi Jacobs (auth), Arts--Interview, Pac Sun, 2/74. *Mem:* Calif Soc Printmakers (past chmn). *Media:* Intaglio, Screen Print. *Mailing Add:* 1 Appian Way 705-7 San Francisco CA 94080

BEALL, JOANNA
PAINTER, SCULPTOR
b Chicago, Ill, Aug 17, 35. *Study:* Yale Sch of Fine Art, with Josef Albers, 53-57; Sch of the Art Inst of Chicago, 57. *Comn:* Sculpture (wood), comn by B H Freidman, New York, 63. *Exhib:* Extraordinary Realities, Whitney Mus of Am Art, New York, 73; Wadsworth Atheneum Group Exhib, Hartford, Conn, 73; Univ Calif Riverside Group Exhib, 73; Visions, Art Inst of Chicago, 76; one-woman shows, James Corcoran Gallery, Los Angeles, Calif, 74 & Rebecca Cooper Gallery, Washington, DC, 75; Group Exhib, Reality of Illusion, Denver Art Mus, 79; Univ Southern Calif Art Galleries, 79 & Univ Art Mus, Austin, Tex, 80; plus others. *Pos:* Practicing prof artist. *Teaching:* Vis artist, Univ Colo, Boulder, 79 & 84. *Bibliog:* New Talent USA, Art in Am, New York, 64; Melinda Wortz (auth), The World of Joanna Beall, Art Week, Los Angeles, 74; Dennis Adrian (auth), Visions, Art Inst of Chicago, 76. *Mem:* Artists Equity. *Media:* Oil, Watercolor; Wood. *Dealer:* James Corcoran Gallery 8223 Santa Monica Blvd Los Angeles CA 90046. *Mailing Add:* Box 28 Brookfield Center CT 06805

BEALMER, WILLIAM
CONSULTANT, EDUCATOR
b Atlanta, Mo, Sept 9, 19. *Study:* Northeast Mo State Teachers Gol, BSc; Univ Colo, MFA; Chicago Inst Design; Des Moines Art Ctr; Univ Iowa. *Exhib:* Univ Colo Art Ctr; Des Moines Art Ctr; Sioux City Art Ctr; Joslyn Art Mus, Omaha, Nebr; Art Dept, Grinnell Col & Iowa State Col. *Pos:* Spec consult, many univs, schs, filmmakers, TV, art confs & other orgns & insts; asst supt & state supvr art educ, Springfield, Ill; dir educ, Springfield Art Asn, currently. *Teaching:* Assoc prof art, Northern Ill Univ, 70- *Awards:* Nat Art Educ Asn Distinguished Fel Award, 83. *Mem:* Nat Art Educ Asn (pres, 69-71); Int Soc Educ Through Art; Ill Educ Asn; Nat Educ Asn; Am Craftsmen's Coun; and others. *Publ:* Ed, The Arts: A basic component of general education, State Ill, 83. *Mailing Add:* 2106 Cardinal Dr Springfield IL 62704

BEAM, MARY TODD
PAINTER
b Dayton, Ohio, Feb 12, 31. *Study:* Cent State Univ, 61-65, Univ Dayton, 62-63; studied with Edward Betts, Maxine Masterfield, Homer Hacker, Edgar Whitney & John Pike. *Work:* Zanesville Art Ctr, Ohio; Bank One & Bank Ohio, Cambridge; Huntington Bank, Columbus; Dow Chemical Corp, Magna Oil Co, Houston. *Exhib:* San Diego Watercolor Soc Int Exhib, Bard Hall Gallery, 80, 81 & 83; Nat Soc Painters Casein & Acrylic, 81 & 83; Nat Watercolor Soc Ann, Desert Mus, Palm Springs, 81 & 83; Audubon Artists Ann, Nat Arts Club, 82; Rocky Mountain Nat, Foothills Art Ctr, Golden, Colo, 82 & 83; and many others. *Teaching:* Instr art, Zanesville Art Ctr, 79- *Awards:* Ralph Fabri Medal, Nat Soc Painters Casein & Acrylic, 80; Top Jurors Award, San Diego Watercolor Soc Int Exhib, 80; Lone Star Award, Burleson First Ann, 81. *Bibliog:* Jacqueline Hall (auth), Exuberant paintings show both versatility, dynamics, Columbus Dispatch, 10/81; People to watch in 1982, Columbus Monthly Mag, 1/82; Maxine Masterfield (auth), Painting the Spirit of Nature, Watson-Guptill, 84. *Mem:* Nat Watercolor Soc; Nat Soc Painters Casein & Acrylic; Audubon Artists; Soc Layerists Multi-Media; Ohio Watercolor Soc. *Media:* Watercolor, Acrylic. *Dealer:* Windon Gallery 1644 W Fifth St Columbus OH 43215. *Mailing Add:* 400 N Seventh St Cambridge OH 43725

BEAM, PHILIP CONWAY
ADMINISTRATOR, EDUCATOR
b Dallas, Tex, Oct 7, 10. *Study:* Harvard Col, AB, 33; Courtauld Inst, Univ London, cert, 36; Harvard Univ, MA, 43, PhD, 44. *Pos:* Dir, Bowdoin Col Mus Art, 39-64, cur, Winslow Homer Collection, 67-; consult, World of Winslow Homer, Time-Life Bks, 66, consult, World of John Singleton Copley, currently. *Teaching:* Asst prof art, Bowdoin Col, 39-46, assoc prof, 46-49, prof, 49-82, chmn dept, 49-82, Henry Johnson prof art & archaeol, 58-82, emer prof, 82-; vis prof Wesleyan Univ, summers 60 & 69; lectr, Shelburne Mus, summers 67 & 70; vis prof art, Univ Vt. *Mem:* Am Asn Univ Prof; Am Asn Mus; Maine Art Comn (chmn, 54-55); Col Art Asn Am. *Publ:* Auth, The Language of Art, Ronald, 58; auth, The Art of John Sloan, 62 & Winslow

Homer at Prouts Neck, 66, Little; contrib ed, A Dictionary of the Visual Arts, NY Graphic Soc, 73; auth, Winslow Homer, McGraw-Hill, 75; auth, Winslow Homer's Magazine Engravings, Harper, 79. *Mailing Add:* c/o Bowdoin Col Mus Art Walker Art Bldg Brunswick ME 04011

BEAMENT, HAROLD
PAINTER
b Ottawa, Ont, July 23, 1898. *Study:* Osgoode Hall Law Sch, Toronto, Barrister-at-law; Ont Col Art. *Work:* Nat Gallery Can, Ottawa; Beaverbrook Edmonton Gallery; Montreal Mus Fine Arts, PQ; Quebec Provincial Mus, PQ; Can War Mus, Ottawa; and others. *Comn:* Designed Canadian Eskimo ten-cent stamp, 55-67. *Exhib:* Brit Empire Exhib, Wembley, Eng, 24-25; Expos Art Can, Mus Jeu Paume, Paris, France, 27; Traveling, Southern Dominions of British Empire, 36; A Century of Canadian Art: Tate Gallery, London, Eng; Canadian War Art, Nat Gallery Eng, 44. *Pos:* Sr Naval War Artist, Royal Can Navy, 43-47. *Teaching:* Instr painting, Montreal Mus Fine Arts, 36-37 & NS Col Art, 62-63. *Awards:* Jessie Dow Prize, Montreal Mus Fine Arts, 36; Can Govt Medal, 67; Queen's Jubilee Medal, 77. *Mem:* Academician Royal Can Acad Arts (secy-treas, 60-61, vpres, 62-63, pres, 64-67). *Media:* Oil. *Mailing Add:* 1160 St Matthieu St 208 Montreal PQ H3H 2P4 Can

BEAMENT, TIB (THOMAS HAROLD)
PAINTER, LECTURER
b Montreal, PQ, Feb 17, 41. *Study:* Fettes Col, Edinburgh, Scotland, O level cert; Ecole Beaux-Arts, Montreal, dipl; Acad Belle Arti, Rome, Italian Govt grant; Ecole Beaux-Arts, Montreal, postgrad studies & teaching cert; Sir George Williams Univ, MA(art educ); also in graphic studios of Shirly Wales, France; Richard Lacroix, Albert Dumouchel & Atelier 838, Montreal. *Work:* Tate Gallery, London; Mus Mod Art, New York; Mus Rio de Janeiro; Nat Gallery Can, Ottawa; Art Inst Chicago. *Exhib:* 4th Biennial Paris, France, 65; Int Exhib Northwest Printmakers, Seattle, Wash, 65; 1st Biennial Graphics, Crakov, Poland, 66; Int Art Fair, Basel, Switz, 74; one-man show, Switzerland Union Bank, Zurich, 81. *Pos:* Mem, Executive Comt & Bd Dirs, Greenshields Foundation. *Teaching:* Dir art dept, Edgars & Cramps Sch, Montreal, 67-79; lectr drawing, McGill Univ, 74-82; lectr design & drawing, Concordia Univ, 76- *Awards:* Can Coun Grant, 66; Spec Mention, Price Fine Arts Awards, 70; Elizabeth T Greenshields Found Grant, 71 & 75. *Mem:* Royal Can Acad Arts; Print & Drawing Coun Can. *Media:* Pencil; Lithography. *Dealer:* Walter Klinkhoff Gallery 1200 Sherbrooke St W Montreal PQ Can; Roberts Gallery 641 Yonge St Toronto ON Can. *Mailing Add:* RR #1 Ayers Cliff PQ J0B 1C0 Canada

BEAN, JACOB
CURATOR
b Stillwater, Minn, Nov 22, 23. *Study:* Harvard Univ. *Pos:* Charge mission, Cabinet Dessins, Mus Louvre, Paris, France, 56-60; charge de mission honoraire, 60-; cur drawings, Metrop Mus Art, 61-; assoc ed, Master Drawings, 62- *Teaching:* Adj prof, Inst Fine Arts, NY Univ. *Publ:* Auth, Les Dessins Italiens de la Collection Bonnat, Bayonne, 60; auth, 100 European Drawings in the Metropolitan Museum of Art, 64; auth, Italian Drawings in the Art Museum, Princeton Univ, 66; auth, Dessins Francais du Metropolitan Museum, 73; auth, 17th Century Italian Drawings in the Metropolitan Museum of Art, 79. *Mailing Add:* Metrop Mus of Art Fifth Ave at 82nd St New York NY 10028

BEAR, MARCELLE L
PRINTMAKER, PAINTER
b Chicago, Ill, Jan 13, 17. *Study:* Chicago Acad & Am Acad, Chicago; Ecole des Arts Decoratifs, Paris, France; Art Inst Chicago, with Elliot O'Hara, John Caceres, Peterdi, W M Parker, M Ponce De Leon, A Daschaes, K Kerslake. *Work:* Jacksonville Art Mus, Fla; Wright State Univ, Dayton, Ohio; Ira Koger Corp Collection; Leonard Bocour Collection; Glidden Organics Corp Collection. *Comn:* Mural, comn by Mrs Ruth Ullrick, Mandarin, Fla, 56; painting, comn by Ben Jones, Universal Marion Corp, Jacksonville, 62; carved doors, Temple Ahavath Chesed, Jacksonville, 64 & 66; painting, comn by Duckett, Hubbard, Mason & Dow, 69; painting, comn by George Dickerson, Sutton Place, Jacksonville, 72. *Exhib:* Tenth Ann Drawing & Print, San Francisco Mus Art, 46; 14th New Yrs Show, Butler Art Inst, Youngstown, Ohio, 46; Mint Mus, Charlotte, NC, 64, 66 & 68; Hunterdon Co, Clinton, NJ, 63; Hunter Gallery, Charlotte, NC, 64 & 65; Metrop Mus & Art Ctr, Miami, Fla, 77; Nat, Panama City, Fla, 77, 78 & 79; Jacksonville Univ, 83; Jacksonville Art Mus, 83-84; and others. *Teaching:* Instr painting, Santa Maria Jr Col, Calif, 45; instr painting, Southside Womans Club, Jacksonville & Jacksonville Art Mus. *Awards:* Best in Show, 48-49 & First Painting, 61, 66 & 78, Jacksonville Art Mus; Seas Grand Award, 78. *Mem:* Fla Artists Group (treas, 75-80, vpres, 80-81). *Media:* Oil, Acrylic. *Mailing Add:* c/o Reddi-Arts Gallery 1037 Hendricks Ave Jacksonville FL 33207

BEARCE, JEANA DALE
PAINTER, PRINTMAKER
b St Louis, Mo, Oct 3, 29. *Study:* St Louis Sch Fine Arts, Washington Univ, with Fred Conway, Fred Becker, Paul Burlin & George Lockwood, BFA, 51; NMex Highlands Univ, MA, 54; Independent study, Italy, France, India. *Work:* St Louis City Art Mus, Mo; Brooklyn Mus Art; Sarasota Art Asn, Fla; Calif Col Arts & Crafts, Oakland; Cornell Unin; and others. *Comn:* Indian Sand Point (mural), NMex Highlands Univ, Las Vegas, 54; Seven Gifts (cross), Good Shepherd Church, Brunswick, Maine, 62; Search for Truth (mural), Bowdoin Col Libr, Brunswick, Maine, 65; 14 Stations to the Cross St Charles Borromeo, Brunswick, Maine, 75; Monumental Mary and Bartholomew, St Bartholomew's, Cape Elizabeth, Maine, 77; and others.

Exhib: One-man shows, Univ Maine, 57, 65 & 80; The Boston Show, Boston Mus Fine Arts, Mass, 57; Print Show, Philadelphia Print Club, 58; two-man show, St Peter's Church Gallery, New York, 74; Maine Art Gallery, 83; and others. *Teaching:* Instr drawing, painting & printmaking, Univ Maine, Portland, 65-66, asst prof, 66-70, assoc prof, 70-81; prof, Univ Southern Maine, 81- *Awards:* Putzell Purchase Prize, St Louis City Art Mus, Mo, 52; Purchase Prize, Sarasota Art Asn, 58; Eight Maine Artists, State of Maine, 64. *Media:* Oil, Encaustic; Intaglio. *Dealer:* Benbow Gallery 515 Thane St Newport RI. *Mailing Add:* 327 Maine Street Brunswick ME 04011

BEARD, MARION L PATTERSON
LECTURER, PAINTER
b Vincennes, Ind. *Study:* Ind State Univ, BS(art); Syracuse Univ, MFA. *Exhib:* Nat Asn Women Artists Ann, New York; Am Watercolor Soc, New York Watercolor Club; Hoosier Art Salon, Indianapolis; Nat Prof Exhib Ann, Ogunquit, Maine; one-man show, H Lieber Art Gallery, Indianapolis. *Teaching:* Art supvr, Vincennes City Schs, 36-; supvr art educ, Vincennes Community Schs Corp, 55-; art critic teacher, Ind State Univ, 57-; art critic teacher, Ind Univ, 61-62; prof painting, Adult Educ Art Dept, Vincennes Univ & Ind Univ, 51-; prof painting, Vincennes Univ Educ Ctr, 51- *Awards:* First Award, Margaret George Bridwell Mem Watercolor Award; First Award, William H Block Co Watercolor Award, Hoosier Art Salon; William E Tirey Mem Watercolor Award, Wabash Valley Artists; plus others. *Mem:* Nat Asn Women Artists; Ind Artists Club; Int Platform Asn; fel Int Biog Asn, Eng. *Mailing Add:* Rte 1 Vincennes IN 47591

BEARD, RICHARD ELLIOTT
PAINTER, EDUCATOR
b Kenosha, Wis, June 13, 28. *Study:* Univ Wis-Madison, BS & MA; Ohio State Univ, PhD. *Work:* Ohio State Univ; Univ Ky; Defiance Col; Kankakee Comm Col; Northern Ill Univ. *Exhib:* Purdue Univ, 74; Chicago Artists & Vicinity, Chicago Art Inst, 77; Beverly Art Ctr, Chicago, 78; New Horizons Show, Chicago, Ill, 80; West 80, Art and The Law, Minn Mus Art, St Paul, 80; and others. *Teaching:* Asst prof art, Maryville Col, 52-61; asst instr art, Ohio State Univ, 61-63; vis prof art, Univ Ky, 63-64; assoc prof art, Wis State Univ, Stevens Point, 64-66; prof art, Northern Ill Univ, 66- *Awards:* Catalog Prize, Cincinnati Artists & Vicinity Show, 63; Best Painting in Show, Kenosha Art Asn, 66; Rockefeller Residency Grant, Bellagio, Italy, 83. *Mem:* Col Art Asn; Mid Am Col Art Asn. *Media:* Oil, Acrylic, Chalk. *Dealer:* Am Print & Drawing De Kalb IL 60115; Neville-Sargent Gallery 509 Main St Evanston IL 60202. *Mailing Add:* 730 W Taylor De Kalb IL 60115

BEARDEN, ROMARE HOWARD
PAINTER
b Charlotte, NC, Sept 2, 14. *Study:* NY Univ, BS, 35; Art Students League, 36-37; Columbia Univ, 43; Sorbonne, cert, 51. *Work:* Mus Mod Art, Whitney Mus, New York; Brooklyn Mus; Albright Mus, Buffalo, NY; Boston Mus Fine Arts. *Exhib:* One-man shows, Corcoran Gallery, Washington, DC, 66, Mus State Univ NY, Albany, 68; Univ Calif Mus Art, Berkeley, Calif, 71; Cordier-Ekstrom Gallery, New York, 61-77; one-man retrospectives, Mus Mod Art, 71, Mint Mus Art, Charlotte, NC, 81; Albert Loeb Gallery, Paris, 75; Mus State Miss, 81; Baltimore Mus, 81; Mus State Virginia, 81; Brooklyn Mus, 81. *Pos:* Dir, Cinque Gallery, New York, 69- *Teaching:* Vis lectr African & Afro-American art & cult, Williams Col, 69; instr, Yale Col, 80. *Bibliog:* Dore Ashton (auth), Romare Bearden--projections, Quadrom 17, 65; Art of Romare Bearden, Abrams. *Mem:* Black Acad Art & Lett; Am Inst Arts & Lett. *Publ:* Coauth, Painters Mind, Crown, 69; coauth, Six Black Masters of American Art, Doubleday, 72. *Dealer:* Cordier & Ekstrom Inc 980 Madison Ave New York NY 10021. *Mailing Add:* 357 Canal St New York NY 10013

BEARDSLEY, BARBARA H
CONSERVATOR
b New York, NY, Mar 30, 45. *Study:* Elmira Col, BA; Europ Study Prog, Univ Wis, cert; Univ NMex; State Univ NY, Cooperstown, study with Kecks, MA(conserv), cert(advan standing); study with Louis Pomerantz; McCrone Res Inst. *Comn:* Cleveland Mus Art; I Tatti, Harvard Univ, Florence, Italy; Currier Gallery, Manchester, NH; William Hayes Fogg Art Mus, Cambridge, Mass. *Collections Arranged:* Mary Lester Field Collection of Santos, Albuquerque, NMex, 70; Harwood Collection, Span Colonial Art, Taos, NMex, 71. *Pos:* Conservator, Intermuseum Conserv Assoc Lab, Oberlin, Ohio, 73-75; conserv intern, Newberry Libr, Chicago, 74-75; guest lectr conserv methods, State Univ NY, Cooperstown, 75-77; conservator, New England Coun, Am Asn Mus, six locations, 75-76; chief conservator, Art Conserv Lab Inc, 75- *Bibliog:* K Schaal (auth), New life for old masters, NH Profiles, 10/77; J Dueland (auth), Barbara Beardsley's barn, Christian Sci Monitor, 1/78; S Goss (auth), The Art Conservation Laboratory, NH Times, 2/82. *Mem:* Int Coun Mus; fel Am Inst Conserv Hist & Artistic Works; Nat Conserv Adv Coun; Am Inst Conserv (dir, 76-79). *Res:* Polarizing pigment analysis, material studies, art history research, Spanish Colonial Santos. *Publ:* Auth, The field collection of Santos, Univ NMex Art Mus Bulletin, 70; auth, The adaptation of an examination microscope, Am Inst Conserv Bulletin, 72; auth, Basic Guide to a Healthy Collection, Art Conserv Lab, rev ed 76; auth, A Flexible Back for the Stabilization of a Botticelli Panel Painting, Oxford Wood Conference, Int Inst Conserv, 78. *Mailing Add:* Dudley Homestead Raymond NH 03077

BEARMAN, JANE RUTH
PAINTER, ILLUSTRATOR
b Minneapolis, Minn. *Study:* Univ Minn, BA(fine arts); Minneapolis Inst Arts; Walker Art Ctr, Minneapolis; Chicago Art Inst; Am Acad Art; Montclair Col, NJ. *Work:* Temple Beth Shalom, Livingston, NJ; Adath

Jeshuran Synagogue, Minneapolis; YMCA, Livingston, NJ; Christ Hospital, Jersey City, NJ. *Comn:* Painting, Congregation Beth Torah, Orange, NJ, 68; Sclavo Serum Inst, Siena, Italy, 69; painting, Wells Labs, Jersey City, NJ, 75; Torah cover (needlepoint design), Knesses Israel Congregation, Pittsfield, Mass, 77; paintings, Allied Commodities Corp, Minneapolis, 77. *Exhib:* 30 Artists in Watercolor & Casein, NJ State Mus, Trenton, 69; NJ Watercolor Soc, Morris Co Mus; Nat Asn Women Artists, Nat Acad, New York, 68-70; one-person show, Brandeis Univ, Hallmark Gallery, Kansas City; and others. *Pos:* Fashion illusr, Dayton Co, Minneapolis, 37-41; art dir, Dept Training, New York, 41-45; freelance illusr bks & mag, New York, 45-60. *Teaching:* Instr painting & life drawing, YM-YWHA of Metrop NJ-West Orange, 63-; instr art hist, Seton Hall Univ, 70-72. *Awards:* First in Graphics, Montclair Mus Ann, Russel T Mount, 61; Yelen Award Watercolor, Nat Asn Women Artists Ann Exhib, 70; Medal of Honor, Painters & Sculptors Soc, 73. *Bibliog:* Interview, First Estate--Religion in Review, Dr Russell Barber, NBC, 77. *Mem:* Nat Asn Women Artists; NJ Watercolor Soc; Assoc Artists NJ; Painters & Sculptors Soc NJ; Artists Equity. *Publ:* Auth & illusr, Jonathan, 65 & David, 65, Jonathan-David Co; contribr, T Newman's Contemporary Decoupage, 72 & Paper as Art & Craft, 73, Crown; auth & illusr, The Eight Nights, Union Am Hebrew Congregation, 78. *Mailing Add:* 30 Spier Dr Livingston NJ 07039

BEASLEY, BRUCE
SCULPTOR
b Los Angeles, Calif, May 20, 39. *Study:* Dartmouth Col; Univ Calif, Berkeley, BA. *Work:* Mus Mod Art & Solomon R Guggenheim Mus, New York; Los Angeles Co Mus Art, Los Angeles; Musee d'Art Moderne, Paris, France; Univ Art Mus, Berkeley. *Comn:* Apolymen (cast acrylic sculpture), State Calif, 70; cast acrylic sculptures, US Govt-GSA Art in Pub Places, San Diego, Calif, 76 & City of San Francisco, Calif, 77; metal sculptures, City of Eugene, Ore, 74, Miami Int Airport, Fla, 78 & San Francisco Int Airport, 79. *Exhib:* Art of Assemblage, Mus Mod Art, New York, 61; Painting and Sculpture Acquisitions, Mus Mod Art, New York, 66; Selected Acquisitions, Solomon R Guggenheim Mus, 66; one-man retrospective, M H DeYoung Mem Mus, San Francisco, 72; Salon de la Jeune Sculpture, Musee d'Art Mod, Paris, 73; Salon d'Mai, Luxembourge Gardens, Paris, 73; Oregon Int Sculpture Symposium, 74; Public Sculpture--Urban Environment, The Oakland Mus, Calif, 75; Forty Am Sculptors, XII Int Sculpture Conference, Washington DC, 80; and many others. *Awards:* Andre Malraux Purchase Award, Biennale de Paris, 63; Frank Lloyd Wright Mem Purchase Award, Marin Mus Asn, 65; Purchase Prize, San Francisco Arts Festival, 67. *Bibliog:* Bruce Beasley--Sculptor, Research & Architecture, 5/73; Bruce Beasley--sculptor of light, Art Week, 8/26/72; Thalacker (auth), The Place of Art in the World of Architecture, Chelsea Press, 80. *Media:* Acrylic Plastic, Metal. *Mailing Add:* 322 Lewis St Oakland CA 94607

BEASON, DONALD RAY
EDUCATOR, SCULPTOR
b Camden, Ark, Oct 22, 43. *Study:* Kilgore Col, 63; Stephen F Austin State Univ, BA, 65; Mich State Univ, MFA, 67. *Work:* Cult Exchange Between Italy & US, Rome; Centro Int Ceramica, Rome; Cameron Univ. *Exhib:* Drawing USA/71, Minn Mus Art, 71; solo exhib, San Antonio Sun Shine, San Antonio Art Inst, 82, Amarillo Sun Set, Amarillo Art Mus, 83 & Midnight Air, Tyler Mus Art, 83; East Texas Show, Tyler Mus Art, 82; Triennial 1983, New Orleans Mus, 83. *Teaching:* Prof art, Stephen F Austin State Univ, 67-; Regents prof, 83- *Awards:* Fulbright-Hays Fel, 72; Nat Endowment Arts Fel, 82. *Mailing Add:* Art Dept Box 13001 Stephen F Austin Univ Nacogdoches TX 75962

BEATTIE, GEORGE
PAINTER, ADMINISTRATOR
b Cleveland, Ohio, Aug 2, 19. *Study:* Cleveland Inst Art, 38-41. *Work:* Whitney Mus Am Art, New York; Montclair Mus, NJ; High Mus, Atlanta; Mead Corp; Larry Aldrich Collection, Conn. *Comn:* Murals, History of Agriculture in State of Georgia, State Agr Bldg, Atlanta, 56 & History of Middle Georgia, Fed Post Off Bldg, Macon, Ga, 68. *Exhib:* Mead Painting of the Year, 55 & 61; Int Drawing Ann, Uffizi Loggia, Florence, Italy, 57; Fulbright Exhib, Rome, Italy, 57; Smithsonian Traveling Exhib, 58-59; Art USA, 59. *Pos:* Artist, Link Archaeol Exped to Israel, 60 & Sicily, 62; exec dir, Ga Coun Arts, 67-75; dir pub serv in art, Ga State Univ, 75- *Teaching:* Head creative drawing, Ga Inst Technol Sch Archit, 57-67. *Awards:* Fulbright Grant to Italy, 56-57; Governor's Award Visual Arts, State Ga, 78. *Bibliog:* Nina Kaiden & Bartlett Hayes (auth), Artist & advocate, Renaissance Ed, 67. *Mem:* Atlanta Mem Arts Ctr, High Mus; hon life mem bd trustees Arts Festival Atlanta, Inc. *Media:* All. *Mailing Add:* 857 Woodley Dr NW Atlanta GA 30318

BEATTY, FRANCES FIELDING LEWIS
HISTORIAN, CRITIC
b New York, NY, Nov 23, 48. *Study:* Vassar Col, BA; Columbia Univ, with Meyer Schapiro & Theodore Reff, MA(art hist; Noble Found Fel), PhD(Vassar Col Fel, Grant). *Pos:* Sr ed, Art/World, 76-; vpres, Richard L Feigen & Co, currently. *Teaching:* Instr surrealism, Renaissance & 19th & 20th century art hist & lit, Ramapo Col, NJ, 74; instr art hist, Columbia Col, 74-76. *Res:* Work of Andre Masson in the 1920s and its relation to surrealist poetry and prose. *Publ:* Coauth, Louise Nevelson (catalog), Centre Nat d'Art Contemporain, Paris, 74; contribr, Andre Masson (catalog), Mus Mod Art, New York, 76. *Mailing Add:* 1235 Park Ave New York NY 10028

BEAUCHAMP, GEORGE
COLLAGE ARTIST, PAINTER
b Detroit, Mich, July 23, 33. *Study:* Univ Mich, Ann Arbor, BS(design), 56, MS(design), 58. *Exhib:* Pa Acad Fine Arts Ann Exhib Watercolors, Prints & Drawings, 63; Davidson Col Nat Print & Drawing Competition, 74; Butler Inst Ann Mid-Year Show, 78; Small Works, NY Univ, 80; Exhib Small Works, Key Gallery, New York, 81 & 83. *Media:* Collage. *Dealer:* Key Gallery 130 Greene New York NY 10012. *Mailing Add:* 151 Coles St Jersey City NJ 07302

BEAUCHAMP, ROBERT
INSTRUCTOR, PAINTER
b Denver, Colo, Nov 19, 23. *Study:* Colorado Springs Fine Arts Ctr; Cranbrook Acad of Art, Bloomfield Hills, Mich, BFA; Hans Hofmann Sch of Art. *Work:* Mus of Mod Art, New York; Whitney Mus of Am Art, New York; Carnegie Inst Int, Pittsburgh; Hirshhorn Mus & Sculpture Garden, Washington, DC; Denver Art Mus. *Exhib:* Walker Art Ctr, Minneapolis, 53; Carnegie Int, Carnegie Inst of Technol Mus of Art, Pittsburgh, 58 & 61; Whitney Mus of Am Art, 61-63, 65, 67 & 69; Mus of Mod Art, New York, 62; Artists Abroad, Inst of Int Educ, New York, 69; Ten Independents, Solomon R Guggenheim Mus, New York, 72. *Pos:* Prof, Lamar Dodd chair, Univ Ga, 81-84. *Teaching:* Instr painting, Brooklyn Col, 73 & Sch of Visual Arts, 74-76. *Awards:* Fulbright Grant, 59; Nat Found of Arts Grant, 66; Guggenheim Found Fel, 74. *Bibliog:* Scott Burton (auth), Paint the devil, Art News, 66. *Mem:* Artists Equity. *Media:* Oil, Graphite. *Mailing Add:* c/o Monique Knowlton 153 Mercer St New York NY 10012

BEAUDOIN, ANDRE EUGENE
PRESS MANUFACTURER, PHOTOGRAPHER
b Calais, France, Apr 11, 20; US citizen. *Study:* Ecole des Arts de Metiers, Paris, France, machine design & metallurgy; Brown Univ, photog. *Pos:* Owner, designer & constructor of etching & lithographic presses for artist printmakers, Am-French Tool Co, 69- *Mailing Add:* PO Box 227 Coventry RI 02816

BEAUMONT, MONA M
PAINTER, PRINTMAKER
b Paris, France; US citizen. *Study:* Univ Calif, Berkeley, BA & MA; grad study, Fogg Mus, Harvard Univ, Cambridge, Mass; spec study with Hans Hoffman, New York. *Work:* Oakland Mus Art, Calif; City & Co San Francisco; Hoover Found; Bulart Found, San Francisco. *Exhib:* Textile/Design Exhib, Mus Mod Art, New York, 45; San Francisco Art Inst, 58, 62-66 & 74, traveling exhib, 64 & 65; Calif Painters & Sculptors 35 & Under, Univ Calif, Los Angeles, 59; Regional Painters, de Young Mem Mus Art, San Francisco, 62; Regional Gallery Artists, Stanford Univ Art Mus, 66; Print & Drawing Ann, Richmond Art Ctr, Va, 68; Bell Tel Print/Drawing, Chicago, 69; one-person shows, Calif Palace of Legion of Honor, San Francisco, 64, San Francisco Mus Art, 68 & Palo Alto Cult Ctr, Calif, 77; Los Angeles Co Mus Art, 73; Honolulu Acad Art, Hawaii, 80; and others. *Awards:* Purchase Award, US Artists Tour of Asia, Grey Found, 63; Purchase & One-Person Show Awards, San Francisco Art Festival Ann, 66 & 75; Ackerman Award, San Francisco Woman Artists Ann, 68. *Bibliog:* Margarita Nelken (auth), Mona Beaumont at Proteo, Novedades, 9/60; Bernard Nebout (auth), Mona Beaumont & Art of the Pacific, Paris-Normandie, 2/66; Andrew De Shong (auth), Works on Paper--San Francisco Art Inst, Art Week Mag, 11/74. *Mem:* Arch Am Art; Soc Encouragement Contemp Art; Bay Area Graphic Arts Coun. *Media:* Acrylic, Mixed Media. *Publ:* Contribr, articles in Artforum, 5/64 & 12/64; contribr, Frankenstein, San Francisco Chronicle, 66 & 67. *Mailing Add:* 1087 Upper Happy Valley Rd Lafayette CA 94549

BECHTLE, C RONALD
PAINTER
b Philadelphia, Pa, Nov 14, 24. *Study:* ETenn Univ; Tyler Sch Fine Arts, Temple Univ; Fleisher Mem, Sch Indust Art; also with Benton Spruance, 52-53. *Work:* Munson-Williams-Proctor Inst, Utica, NY; Denver Art Mus, Colo; Santa Barbara Mus Art, Calif; Columbus Gallery Fine Art, Ohio; Nat Collection Fine Arts. *Exhib:* Pa Acad Fine Arts Regional, 65 & 69; one-man shows, Panoras Gallery, New York, 66, Santa Barbara Mus Art, 67, Miami Mus Mod Art, Fla, 68 & Philadelphia Art Alliance, 73, Storelli Gallery, 74 & E Tenn Univ, 77. *Pos:* Pres, Group 55, 56-57; pres, Philadelphia Abstract Artists, 57-63. *Mem:* Artists Equity; Am Fedn Arts; Col Art Asn Am. *Media:* Watercolor, Gouache. *Publ:* Auth, Information theory of art, Mensa J, 61. *Mailing Add:* Apt 12B 26 Strawberry Hill Ave Stamford CT 06902

BECHTLE, ROBERT ALAN
PAINTER
b San Francisco, Calif, May 14, 32. *Study:* Calif Col Arts & Crafts, BA & MFA; Univ Calif, Berkeley. *Work:* Whitney Mus Am Art, Mus Mod Art, Guggenheim Mus, New York; Univ Calif Art Mus, Berkeley; San Francisco Mus Art. *Exhib:* Image, Form & Color: Recent Paintings by 11 Americans, Toledo Mus of Art, Ohio, 75; Painting & Sculpture in Calif: The Mod Era, San Francisco Mus of Mod Art, 76; Am 1976, Corcoran Gallery of Art, Washington, DC, 76; Aspects of Realism/Du Realisme, Rothmans of Can Ltd, Montreal, 76-77; Illusion & Reality, Australian Gallery Dirs Coun, 77-78; Representations of Am, Pushkin Fine Arts Mus, Moscow, USSR, 78; Contemporary American realism since 1960, Pa Acad Fine Arts, Philadelphia, 81; Realism, Photorealism, Philbrook Art Ctr, Tulsa, Okla, 81; and many others. *Teaching:* Prof printmaking, Calif Col Arts & Crafts, 57-; guest artist, Univ Calif, Davis, 66-68; prof art, San Francisco State Univ, 68- *Awards:* James D Phelan Award in Painting, 65; Nat Endowment Arts Grant, 77 & 82. *Bibliog:* W Seitz (auth), The real and the artificial: painting of the

new environment, Art in Am, 11-12/72; G Battcock (auth), Super Realism, A Critical Anthology, Dutton, 75; C Lindey (auth), Superrealist Painting and Sculpture, William Morrow & Co, 80; and others. *Dealer:* O K Harris Gallery 383 W Broadway New York NY 10012. *Mailing Add:* 4250 Horton St Apartment #14 Emeryville CA 94608

BECK, DOREEN
WRITER, PRODUCER
b Medomsley, Durham, Eng, Mar 12, 35; US & UK citizen. *Study:* Leicester Univ Col, Univ London, BA(hons in French), 57; NY Univ, film prod; NY Sch Visual Arts, screen writing with Andrew Sarris. *Pos:* Writer & producer AV mat, UN; researcher & writer, MD Med Newsmag; research, ed & writing, BBC, World Bk Enc (int ed), The Observer, Thames & Hudson, Julian Press, Ved Mehta & New Yorker. *Publ:* Auth, Britain: An Enduring Heritage (script), 69; auth, Book of Bottle Collecting, 73; auth, Book of American Furniture, 73; auth, Country & Western Americana, 75; auth & producer UN exhib on Disarmament, Decolonization the Palestinians, Namibia, Apartheid, The Disabled, 75-81; plus var Fr transl including articles in Atlas Mag. *Mailing Add:* 100 W 57th St New York NY 10019

BECK, JAMES
HISTORIAN, CRITIC
b New Rochelle, NY, May 14, 30. *Study:* Oberlin Col, BA, 52; NY Univ, MA, 54; Columbia Univ, PhD, 63. *Teaching:* From asst prof to assoc prof, Columbia Univ, 64-72; prof art hist, 72- *Mem:* Col Art Asn; Renaissance Soc Am. *Publ:* Auth, Michelangelo: A Lesson in Anatomy, 75 & Leonardo's Rules of Painting, 79, Viking; auth, Raphael, Abrams, 76; coauth, Masaccio: the Documents, Augustin, 78; auth, Italian Renaissance Painting, Harper & Row, 81; and others. *Mailing Add:* Dept of Art Hist & Archaeol Columbia Univ New York NY 10027

BECK, LONNIE LEE
PAINTER, EDUCATOR
b Marion, Ind, Jan 6, 42. *Study:* Herron Sch Art, Ind Univ, BFA(advan design), 65, BFA(painting), 67; Miami Univ, MFA(painting), 69. *Work:* Herron Sch Art, Ind Univ, Indianapolis. *Exhib:* Indianapolis Mus Art, 68 & 69; Owensboro Mus Fine Arts, Ky, 80; Evansville Mus Art & Sci, Ind, 80; Appalachian State Univ, Boone, NC, 80; Okla Art Ctr, Oklahoma City, 81; Ball State Univ, Muncie, Ind, 82; and many others. *Collections Arranged:* Robert Berkshire Paintings, 75, Rockwell Kent (coauth, catalog), 79, Dean Howell Sculpture, 80, Terrance LaNoue, Jim Sullivan & Frank Owens Paintings, 81 & Dennis Puhalla Paintings, 82, Hiestand Gallery, Miami Univ. *Awards:* Best Show Painting, 500 Festival Arts Comn, 67; Purchase Award, Del Mar Col, 75; Purchase Award, Ball State Univ, 82. *Media:* Oil, Charcoal. *Mailing Add:* 125 East Central Ave Oxford OH 45056

BECK, MARGIT
PAINTER, EDUCATOR
b Tokay, Hungary. *Study:* Inst Fine Arts, Oradea Mare, Roumania; Art Students League; McDowell Resident Fels, 56, 57, 59, 60 & 75. *Work:* Whitney Mus Am Art, New York; J B Speed Mus, Louisville, Ky; Edwin A Ulrich Mus Art, Wichita, Kans; Lyman Allyn Mus, New London, Conn; Norfolk Mus Arts & Sci, Va; plus others. *Comn:* Traveling Drawing Exhib, Southern Mus. *Exhib:* Corcoran Gallery Art Biennial, 65; four shows, Pa Acad Fine Arts Ann, 57-68; Whitney Mus Am Art Ann, 58-61; four shows, Brooklyn Mus Int Watercolor Biennial, 59-67; Art Inst Chicago, 60-61; Childe Hassam Fund Exhib, Am Acad of Arts & Lett, 60, 62 & 66-71; Ann Exhib of Candidates for Grants, Nat Inst of Arts & Lett, New York, 60, 66-68; 22 one-woman exhibs. *Teaching:* Lectr art, Hofstra Univ, 66-67; adj asst prof art, New York Univ, 67-; adv & tutor art hist, Empire State Col, 74- *Awards:* Childe Hassam Purchase Award, Am Acad Arts & Lett, 68, 70 & 71; Medal of Hon, 68 & 72 & Stephen Hirsh Mem Award, Audubon Artists; plus others. *Bibliog:* Sharon Theobold (auth), Homes of distinguished Nassau artists, Mag Nassau, 6/74; John Gruen (auth), Margit Beck (monogr), Soho News, 3/3/75; Jeanne Paris (auth), Margit Beck (monogr), Long Island Press, 3/30/75; plus others. *Mem:* Artists Equity (exec bd mem, 65-70); Audubon Artists; academician, Nat Acad Design; Col Art Asn Am. *Media:* Oil, Ink. *Publ:* contribr, Women Artists: 25 Best Investments, Working Woman, 7/80. *Dealer:* ACA Gallery 21 E 67th St New York NY 10021. *Mailing Add:* 22 Florence St Great Neck NY 11023

BECK, MARTHA ANN
MUSEUM DIRECTOR, CURATOR
b Cleveland, Ohio, June 16, 38. *Study:* Vassar Col, BA, 60; NY Univ Inst Fine Arts, studied under Erwin Panofsky, 63-67. *Collections Arranged:* Works on Paper, Art Lending, Mus Mod Art, 74; Opening Exhib, 77, The Drawings of Antonio Gaudi, 77, The Travel Sketches of Louis I Kahn, 78, Musical Manuscripts, 78-79, Visionary Drawings of Architecture and Planning, 79 & Sculptors' Drawings over Six Centuries, 81, The Drawing Ctr. *Pos:* Curatorial asst, Mus Mod Art, New York, 68-75; dir, The Drawing Ctr, 75- *Publ:* New Drawing in America, The Drawing Ctr, 82. *Mailing Add:* The Drawing Ctr 137 Greene St New York NY 10012

BECK, ROSEMARIE (ROSEMARIE BECK PHELPS)
PAINTER, EDUCATOR
US citizen. *Study:* Oberlin Col; Columbia Univ; NY Univ. *Work:* Whitney Mus Am Art; Vassar Col Mus; State Univ NY Col New Paltz; Hirshhorn Collection; Nebr Art Mus. *Comn:* Mural painting, Rotron Mfg Co, 58. *Exhib:* Pa Acad Fine Arts; Nat Inst Arts & Lett; Whitney Mus Am Art; Art Inst Chicago; eleven one-man shows, Peridot Gallery; one-man show, Poindexter Gallery, New York. *Teaching:* Lectr painting, Vassar Col, 57-58, 61-62 &

63-64; lectr painting, Middlebury Col, 58-60 & 63; prof painting, Queens Col, 68- *Awards:* Ingram-Merrill Grant, 67 & 79. *Media:* Oil. *Dealer:* Ingber Art Gallery 3 E 78th New York NY 10021. *Mailing Add:* 6 E 12th St New York NY 10003

BECK, STEPHEN R
PAINTER, EDUCATOR
b Salt Lake City, Utah, Dec 28, 37. *Study:* Univ Utah, BFA; Cranbrook Acad Art, MFA. *Work:* Cranbrook Acad Art Galleries, Bloomfield Hills, Mich; Kingswood Sch-Cranbrook, Bloomfield Hills; Utah Mus Fine Arts, Salt Lake City; Univ Utah. *Exhib:* US Senate Bldg, Washington, DC, 65; Mich Ann, Detroit, 65; Western Regional Biennial, Salt Lake City, 71; Westminster Col Exhib, Salt Lake City, 71; 73rd Ann Western, Denver, Colo, 71. *Teaching:* Instr drawing & painting & admin asst, Univ Utah, 68-75; asst prof drawing & painting, Westminster Col, 75-77. *Awards:* Purchase Awards, Salt Lake Art Ctr, 70 & 72. *Media:* Acrylic Lacquer. *Mailing Add:* c/o Max Hutchinson Gallery 138-142 Greene St New York NY 10012

BECKER, BETTIE (BETTIE GERALDINE WATHALL)
PAINTER, GRAPHIC ARTIST
b Peoria, Ill, Sept 22, 18. *Study:* Univ Ill, BFA; Art Students League, with John Carroll; Art Inst Chicago, with Lewis Ritman; Inst Design, Ill Inst Technol, with Hans Weber. *Work:* Witte Mem Mus, San Antonio, Tex; Union League Club, Chicago, Ill; Bank Sturgeon Bay, Wis; Standard Oil Collection, Chicago; Cudahy Gallery Slide Collection; and others. *Comn:* Mural (with Frank Wiater), Talbot Materials Testing Lab, Univ Ill, Urbana, 40. *Exhib:* Drawings USA, St Paul, Minn, 66-68; one-woman show, Crossroad's Gallery, Art Inst Chicago, 73; Festival de Arte de las dos Banderas, US-Mexico, Douglas, Ariz, 72; Critic's Choice, Art Inst Chicago, 72; Union League Civic & Arts Found Exhibs, 67, 72 & 74; Print & Drawing Exhib, Artist's Guild, Chicago, 76; 36th NE Wis Art Ann, Neville Mus, Green Bay; Women in Art, Appleton Gallery Art, Wis, 82; Chicago Soc Artists Retro Exhib, Mus Sci & Industry, 83; and others. *Awards:* Newcomb Prize, Univ Ill Col Fine & Appl Arts, 40; First Prize for Print, Chicago Soc Artists, 67, 71 & 74; H Barry McCormick Purchase Prize, Union League Club, 74; plus others. *Bibliog:* Article, La Revue Moderne, Paris, 73; article, Door Co Advocate, 77 & 80. *Mem:* Chicago Soc Artists (rec secy, 68-77); Alumni Asn Art Inst Chicago; Northeastern Wis Arts Coun; Peninsula Arts Asn. *Media:* Collage, Acrylic. *Publ:* Auth, Life with Liberty, 43; illusr, Sat Rev Lit, 48, New York Times, 48, Chicago Tribune, 48 & 49 & Evanston Rev, 68; A child of autumn, Insight Mag, Milwaukee J, 79. *Mailing Add:* 3992 Juddville Rd Fish Creek WI 54212

BECKER, CAROLYN BERRY See Berry, Carolyn

BECKER, DAVID
PRINTMAKER, EDUCATOR
b Milwaukee, Wis, Aug 16, 37. *Study:* Univ Wis-Milwaukee, BS, 61; Univ Ill, Urbana, MFA, 65. *Work:* Libr of Cong, DC; Brooklyn Mus, NY; Mus de Arte Mod, Cali, Colombia; Portland Art Mus; Detroit Inst Arts, Mich; and others. *Comn:* Print, Detroit Inst Art Drawing & Print Club, 83. *Exhib:* 30 Yrs of Am Printmaking, Brooklyn Mus, NY, 76; Miami Int Print Biennial, Metrop Mus, Fla, 80; In Celebration of Prints, Philadelphia Art Alliance, 80; 13th Nat, Silvermine Guild Artists, New Canaan, Conn; 80; Ann Int Exhib, Philadelphia Print Club, 81; Intaglio, Univ Louisville, Ky, 81; and many others. *Teaching:* Prof art, Wayne State Univ, Detroit, Mich, 65-83; vis prof printmaking, Univ Wis-Madison, 78-79; vis artist, Utah State Univ, Logan, summer 81. *Awards:* Gold Medal, Mus de Arte Mod, 76; Vertha von Moschzisker Prize, Philadelphia Print Club, 79; Award, Silvermine Guild Artists, 80. *Mem:* Soc Am Graphic Artists; Philadelphia Print Club; Nat Acad Design. *Dealer:* Franz Bader Gallery 2001 I St NW Washington DC 20006. *Mailing Add:* 639 Neff Rd Grosse Pointe MI 48230

BECKER, HELMUT JULIUS
PRINTMAKER
b Castor, Alta, Can, Feb 24, 31. *Study:* Univ Sask, BA(with distinction), 54; Univ Wis, Madison, MA(art educ), 55; Acad Fine Arts, The Hague, with W J Rozendaal. *Work:* Burnaby Art Gallery, BC; Sask Arts Bd, Regina; Univ Calgary, Alta; Univ Regina, Sask; Banff Sch Fine Arts, Alta. *Exhib:* One-man show, Can Art Gallery, Calgary, 70; Burnaby Biennial, 73; Can Soc Graphic Art, 74; Calgary Graphics Exhib; two-man show, London Pub Libr & Mus, Ont. *Teaching:* Printmaking, NS Col Art & Design, Halifax, 64-65 & Univ Calgary, 66-71; asst prof printmaking, Univ Western Ont, London, 71- *Awards:* Can Govt Overseas Award Scholar, 55-56; Can Coun Grant, 70. *Bibliog:* Shirley Raphael (auth), Calgary workshop, Vie des Arts, 70; Electro-hydraulic printing press, Art Mag, 71. *Mem:* Can Soc Graphic Art (pres, 74-75); Univ Art Asn Can; Can Artists Representation. *Media:* Multimedia. *Res:* Designed and constructed large electro-hydraulic printing press for lithography, intaglio and relief; handmaking paper; experimental application of special handmade papers for painting, drawing and printmaking. *Mailing Add:* Dept Visual Art Univ Western Ont London ON N6A 5B8 Canada

BECKER, NATALIE ROSE
PAINTER
b Philadelphia, Pa. *Study:* Fleisher Art Mem, Philadelphia; Temple Univ, AA; Pa Acad Fine Arts; Art Students League, with Robert Phillip & Henry Gasser. *Work:* Fine Arts Galleries, Carnegie Inst; Bloomfield Col. *Exhib:* Allied Artists Am, Nat Acad Design, New York, 72, 73, 74, 78 & 79; Audubon Artists Am, 73-81; Nat Arts Club Invitational, 78; Bergen Mus Invitational, 80. *Teaching:* Instr drawing & painting, Union Col, Cranford, NJ. *Awards:* Grumbacher Award of Merit, Catharine Lorillard Wolfe Art Club, 72; Grumbacher Award, Nat Arts Club, 75; First Prize & Medal of Honor,

Audubon Artists Ann Exhib, 80. *Mem:* Audubon Artists; Allied Artist Am; Pen & Brush Club; Catharine Lorillard Wolfe Art Club; fel Am Artists Prof League (trustee, NJ chap, 75). *Media:* Oil, Pen & Ink. *Mailing Add:* 97 Barchester Way Westfield NJ 07090

BECKLEY, BILL
POST-CONCEPTUAL ARTIST
b Hamburg, Pa, Feb 11, 46. *Study:* Kutztown State Col, Pa, BFA; Tyler Sch Art, Temple Univ, with Steven Greene & Italo Scanga, MFA. *Work:* Mus Mod Art, New York. *Exhib:* Proj Pier 18, 71 & Seven, 73, Mus Mod Art, New York; San Francisco Art Mus, Calif, 76; New Art For Jimmy Carter, Ga Art Mus, Athens, 77; Art of the 70s, PS 1, New York, 77; one-man shows, Massina Valsecchi, Milan, Italy, 79, Hans Mayer, Dusseldorf, 79 & Daniel Templon, Paris, 80; and others. *Teaching:* Instr, Sch Visual Arts, 71- *Bibliog:* Barbara Radice (auth), article, Data, Milano, Italy, 4/76; Eric Cameron (auth), Bill Beckley's lies, Artforum, 2/77; Sam Hunter (auth), American Art, Abrams, 79. *Dealer:* Hans Mayer Grabbeplatz 2 4000 Dusseldorf WGer. *Mailing Add:* 155 Wooster St New York NY 10012

BECKMAN, ERICKA
FILMMAKER, SCULPTOR
b Hempstead, NY, July 7, 51. *Study:* Wash Univ, BFA, 74; Whitney Independent Study Prog, 75; Calif Inst Arts, MFA, 76. *Work:* Inst Contemp Art, London; Am Fedn Arts, New York. *Exhib:* Pictures Today, Padligione D'Artes Contemp, Milan, Italy, 80; Preview: Out of Hand, Kitchen, New York, 80; Super-8 Series, Bleeker St Cinema, New York, 81; Film as Play, WNET-Channel 13, New York, 83; You the Better, New York Film Festival & ICA, London, 83; Whitney Mus Biennial, 83. *Teaching:* Asst prof art, Fordham Univ, 80-83; asst prof film, New Sch Social Res, 80-83 & Mass Col Art, 83- *Awards:* Grants, NY State Coun Arts, 81, Jerome Found, 81 & Nat Endowment Arts, 83. *Bibliog:* J Hoberman (auth), article, 81 & Carrie Rickey (auth), article, 83, Art Forum; Sally Banes (auth), Films by Ericka Beckman, Millenium Film J, 83. *Publ:* Coauth, The spot syndrome, New Observations Mag, 83; auth, Chances territory, Effects Mag, 83; auth, The turn-about, Wedge Mag, 83. *Mailing Add:* 358 Broadway New York NY 10013

BECKMAN, WILLIAM GEORGE
PAINTER
b Montevideo, Minn, Oct 19, 42. *Study:* St Cloud Univ, BA, 66; Univ Iowa, MA, 68, MFA, 69. *Work:* Art Inst Chicago; Rose Art Mus, Brandeis Univ; Yale Art Gallery; Des Moines Art Ctr; Mus Mod Kunst, Vienna. *Exhib:* Direction, Hirshhorn Mus, 81-82; Real, Really Real, Super Real, San Antonio Mus, Indianapolis Mus & Carnegie Inst, 81-82; Contemporary American Realism Since 1960, Pa Acad Fine Arts, Va Mus & Oakland Mus, 81-82; Amerikanische Malerei 1930-1980, Haus Kunst, Munich, 81-82; Focus on the Figure, Whitney Mus Am Art, 82; Perspectives on Contemporary American Realism, Pa Acad Fine Arts & Art Inst Chicago, 83; Brave New Works Recent American Painting, Mus Fine Arts, Boston, 83; two-person retrospective, Rose Art Mus, Brandeis Univ & traveling, 84. *Media:* Oil, Pastels. *Dealer:* Allan Frumkin Gallery 50 W 57th St New York NY 10019. *Mailing Add:* N Tower Hill Rd Wassaic NY 12592

BECKMANN, ROBERT OWEN
PAINTER, MURALIST
b Philadelphia, Pa, Mar 20, 42. *Study:* Col Wooster, BA, 64; Univ Iowa, with Byron Burford, David Proctor, Herbert Katzman, MA & MFA, 67. *Work:* Denver Art Mus, Colo; Univ Iowa; Western Ill Univ; Idaho State Univ. *Comn:* Symbiosis, Friends of Contemp Art, Denver, 72; murals, Lynn Co Courthouse, Las Vegas & Clark Co, Nev, 76-80. *Exhib:* Ill Painters II, Ill Arts Coun, Traveling Exhib, 70-72; 73rd Ann Exhib, Artists Chicago & Vicinity, Art Inst Chicago, 71; Colorado-Nebraska Exchange 1973, Joslyn Mus, Omaha & Friends of Contemp Art, Denver, 73; one-man shows, Joseph Magnin Gallery, Denver, 74 & Boise Gallery of Art, Idaho, 76; Ten Artists (travelling exhib), Western Asn Art Mus, 77-78; and others. *Teaching:* Instr studio art, Univ Southern Ala, 67-68; instr life drawing, Northern Ill Univ, 68-71; instr art hist, Kendall Col, summer 69; instr art, Univ Nev, Las Vegas, 77-78. *Awards:* Laura Slobe Mem Prize, Art Inst Chicago, 71; Western States Arts Found Fel, 76. *Bibliog:* Patricia Raymer (auth), Climb aboard the Artrain, Am Educ, 12/73; Duncan Pollock (auth), rev in arts now, Rocky Mountain News, Denver, 9/22/74; Jean Morrison (auth), Project murals, Nevadan, 4/24/77. *Media:* Latex, Acrylic. *Mailing Add:* PO Box 4707 Las Vegas NV 89106

BEDNO, EDWARD
DESIGNER, EDUCATOR
b Chicago, Ill, Mar 8, 25. *Study:* Art Inst Chicago, BFA; Inst Design, Ill Inst Technol, MS. *Exhib:* Art Dirs Clubs, Chicago, New York, Detroit, Cincinnati, Indianapolis & Los Angeles; Soc Typographic Arts; Libr of Cong, Washington, DC; US Info Agency; Am Inst Graphic Arts; and others. *Pos:* Pres, Bedno Assocs, Chicago, Ill, 52-71; chmn dept exhib, Field Mus Natural Hist, 78-80; chief exhibs & presentations, Nat Air & Space Mus, 80-82; partner, Bedno/Bedno Inc, 82- *Teaching:* Instr, Northwestern Univ, Evanston, 51-52; instr, Inst Design, Ill Inst Technol, 57, lectr, 60-64, asst prof, 64-67, assoc prof, 67-71; assoc prof, Va Commonwealth Univ, 71-, dept chmn, 71-73. *Awards:* Midwest Film Festival, Art Dirs Club Chicago; Nat Endowment Arts. *Mem:* Am Inst Graphic Arts; Am Asn Mus; Soc Typographic Arts. *Publ:* Contribr, photog essay, Am Heritage Mag, 64; retrospective article, Commun Arts Mag, 70; contribr, two articles, Visible Language, 73; contribr, Print Mag, 76. *Mailing Add:* 3454 North Damen Ave Chicago IL 60657

BEEBE, MARY LIVINGSTONE
ADMINISTRATOR
b Portland, Ore, Nov 5, 40. *Study:* Bryn Mawr Col, Pa, BA, 62. *Pos:* Mus apprentice, Portland Art Mus, 63-64; asst to registr & secy, Mus Fine Arts, Boston, 65-66; secy & curatorial asst, Fogg Art Mus, Harvard Univ, 66-67; producer, Am Theater Co, Portland, 69-71; dir, Portland Ctr Visual Arts, 73-; bd mem, Henry Gallery, Univ Wash, Seattle; dir, Sculpture Garden, Univ Calif, San Diego, currently. *Awards:* Nat Endowment Arts Fel, 79. *Mem:* Western Asn Art Mus. *Mailing Add:* Portland Ctr for Visual Arts 117 NW Fifth Ave Portland OR 97209

BEELER, JOE (NEIL)
PAINTER, SCULPTOR
b Joplin, Mo, Dec 25, 31. *Study:* Univ Tulsa; Kans State Univ, BFA; Art Ctr Sch, Los Angeles. *Work:* Gilcrease Mus, Tulsa, Okla; Nat Cowboy Hall of Fame, Oklahoma City; Mont Hist Soc, Helena; Phoenix Art Mus; Five Civilized Tribes Mus, Muskogee, Okla. *Exhib:* One-man shows, Gilcrease Mus, 61 & 80, Nat Cowboy Hall of Fame, 63, Heard Mus, Phoenix, 68 & C M Russell Mus, Great Falls, Mont, 70; Cowboy Artist of Am Ann Show, 66-79; and others. *Awards:* Best of Sculpture, Cowboy Artist Show, 67, Silver Medal Sculpture, 69-74, Colt Award for Best Over All of Show, 71 & Silver Medal Drawing, 74. *Bibliog:* Jeff Dykes (auth), 50 Great Western Illustrators, Northland Press, 75; Don Hedgepeth (auth), The Joe Beeler Story, Northland Press, 78. *Mem:* Founding mem Cowboy Artist Am (pres, 70-71). *Media:* Oil, Watercolor; Bronze. *Publ:* Auth, Cowboys and Indians, Univ Okla, 67; illusr, Ben Green, Last Trail Drive through Downtown Dallas, 72; contribr, Abrams & Pat Broder, Bronzes of the American West, 74; auth, Joe Beeler Sketch Book, Northland Press, 75; illusr, Cowboy in Art, World Pub, 69. *Dealer:* Shriver Gallery Taos NM 87571; Trailside Galleries 7330 Scottsdale Mall Scottsdale AZ 85253. *Mailing Add:* Box 989 Sedona AZ 86336

BEELKE, RALPH G
EDUCATOR
b Buffalo, NY, Dec 16, 17. *Study:* Buffalo Sch Fine Arts, dipl; Columbia Univ, MA, 47, EdD, 52. *Pos:* Ed, Eastern Arts Asn Bulletin, 55-57; specialist educ in arts, Off Educ, Dept Health, Educ & Welfare, Washington, DC, 56-58; exec secy art educ, Nat Art Educ Asn, Washington, DC, 58-62; ed, Art Educ J & Western Arts Asn Bulletin, 58-62. *Teaching:* Instr art, pub schs & cols, 40-52; head dept arts, State Univ NY Col Fredonia, 51-56; head dept creative arts, Purdue Univ, 62-72 & 77-82, prof art & design, 72-76. *Awards:* Art Educator of Yr, Nat Art Educ Asn, 63. *Mem:* Col Art Asn Am; Nat Art Educ Asn (pres, 65-67); Am Soc Aesthet & Art Criticism. *Publ:* Contribr, Sch Arts Mag, 55-62; auth, Curriculum Development Art Education, 62; coauth, Spectrum of Music & Related Arts, 74. *Mailing Add:* 1728 Fernleaf Dr PO Box 2305 West Lafayette IN 47906

BEER, KENNETH JOHN
EDUCATOR, SCULPTOR
b Ferndale, Mich, May 4, 32. *Study:* Wayne State Univ, BA & MA. *Work:* Detroit Inst of Art; Thalhimers & First Merchants Bank, Richmond & Va Beach Art Ctr, Va. *Comn:* Campus libr relief, Eastern Mennonite Col, Harrisonburg, Va, 69; James Madison Mem (cast bronze), James Madison Univ, Harrisonburg, 77. *Exhib:* Ann Mich Artists, Detroit Inst of Art, 55-62; Va Artists Biennial, Va Mus, Richmond, 65, 67 & 73; Southern Sculpture, Mint Mus, Charlotte, NC, 65 & Birmingham Mus, Ala & Columbus Mus, Ga, 66; solo exhib, Columbia Mus, SC, 69 & Va Mus, 73; Drawing & Sculpture Ann, Ball State Univ Art Gallery, 74 & 76. *Teaching:* Assoc prof sculpture, James Madison Univ, Harrisonburg, 61- *Awards:* Whitcomb Prize, Mich Artists Ann, Detroit Inst of the Arts, 61; Best in Show, Thalhimers Invitational, 66; Distinction Award, Va Artists Biennial, Va Mus, 73. *Media:* Bronze, steel. *Publ:* Auth, Sanctum, The Emergence of a Form, Studies & Res Bull of Madison Col, 64. *Dealer:* Gallery II 218 W Main St Charlottesville VA 22901. *Mailing Add:* Rt 1 Box 343 Bridgewater VA 22812

BEERMAN, MIRAIM K (MIRIAM BEERMAN-JAFFE)
PAINTER
b Providence, RI. *Study:* RI Sch Design, BFA; Art Students League, with Yasuo Kuniyoshi; New Sch Social Res, with Adja Yunkers; Atelier 17, Paris, with Stanley Hayter. *Work:* Whitney Mus Am Art, New York; Brooklyn Mus; Andrew Dickson White Mus, Cornell Univ, Ithaca, NY; New Sch Social Res. *Exhib:* One-woman exhibs, Long Island Univ, Brooklyn, NY, 65 & 80, The Enduring Beast, Brooklyn Mus, NY, 71-72, Discovery Art Gallery, Clifton, NJ, 74 & 78, Montclair Art Mus, NJ, 74, Cathedral Mus at Cathedral of St John the Divine, 77, Montclair State Col, NJ, 78 & Camargo Found, Cassis, France; and numerous other group & solo shows. *Pos:* Guest artist, Burston Graphic Center, Jerusalem, Israel. *Teaching:* Adj asst prof, Queensborough Community Col, City Univ New York, 72-; instr, Jersey City State Col, 73-75; instr, Montclair Mus Art Sch, 74- *Awards:* Childe Hassam Purchase Award, Am Acad of Arts & Lett, 77; Award, Ossabaw Island Proj, 78; Camargo Found Grant, France. *Bibliog:* The new grotesques, Time Mag, 6/13/69; Barry Schwartz (auth), The New Humanism, Art in a Time of Change, Praeger, 74; Gert Schiff (auth), Images of Horror and Fantasy, Abrams, 79. *Media:* Intaglio, Lithography. *Publ:* Ed & illusr, The Enduring Beast, Doubleday, 72. *Dealer:* Graham Gallery 1014 Madison Ave New York NY 10021. *Mailing Add:* 6 Macopin Ave Upper Montclair NJ 07043

BEERY, ARTHUR O
PAINTER
b Marion, Ohio, Mar 4, 30. *Work:* Butler Inst Am Art, Youngstown, Ohio; Erie Art Ctr, Pa; Lessco Data, New York; J M Katz Collection, Pa. *Comn:* Murals of Athens, Greece, Monte Carlo, Stromboli, Rock of Gibralter &

Charleston, SC for US Navy Minecraft Base, Charleston, 54. *Exhib:* Pa Acad Fine Arts, Philadelphia, 68; Butler Inst Am Art, 68, 70, 72 & 73; Watercolor USA, Mo, 71 & 75; Tex Art Asn, 72 & 75; Contemp Am Art, Paris, France, 72; plus others. *Awards:* Butler Inst Am Art Award, 68 & 74; Richard P Stahl Award, Watercolor USA, 71; Columbus Ohio Art Festival Best of Show, 73; plus others. *Mem:* Mansfield Fine Arts Guild, Ohio; Columbus Art League, Ohio. *Media:* Oil, Acrylic. *Mailing Add:* c/o Cernuschi Galleries 210 E 86th St New York NY 10028

BEGGS, THOMAS MONTAGUE
CONSULTANT, PAINTER
b Brooklyn, NY, Apr 22, 1899. *Study:* Pratt Inst; Art Students League; Yale Univ, BFA; Ecole Am Beaux-Arts, Fontainebleu, France; Harvard Univ, Carnegie Scholar, 28-29. *Work:* Portrait of Jasper Newton Field, Redlands Univ. *Comn:* Club Room Overmantle, Miami Realty Bd, 26; Guild Hall Overmantle, Claremont Congregational Church, Calif, 28; Mem Court Bench, Pomona Col, 33. *Exhib:* Los Angeles Co Fair, 27; Ebell Club, Los Angeles, 37; Washington Watercolor Club, 48. *Collections Arranged:* Weather in Art, Pomona Col Art Gallery, 46; Pictorial Art of the American Indian, Nat Collection Fine Arts, 49; Art & Magic in Arnhem Land, 50 & Art & Archaeology of Vietnam, 59, Smithsonian Inst. *Pos:* Dir, Nat Collection Fine Arts, Smithsonian Inst, 48-64; spec asst to secy fine arts, 65. *Teaching:* Prof art & head dept, Pomona Col, 26-47. *Awards:* Fed Repub Ger Travel Grant, 54; Gold Medal for Advan Am Art, Am Artists Prof League, 63. *Mem:* Emer mem Cosmos Club, Washington, DC. *Media:* Oil, Tempera. *Publ:* Auth, Artist in residence, Parnassus, 12/40; auth, The golden brush of Kristian Krekovic, Am Mag Art; auth, Harriet Lane Johnston & the National Collection of Fine Arts, Smithsonian Report for 1954, 55. *Mailing Add:* 6540 Hitt Ave McLean VA 22101

BEGININ, IGOR
PAINTER, INSTRUCTOR
b Susak, Yugoslavia, Aug 31, 31; US citizen. *Study:* Wayne State Univ, AB, 63, MA, 66. *Work:* Fisher New Ctr, Chrysler Corp, Ford Motor Co, Detroit; Gen Motors, New York; Mich Educ Asn, East Lansing. *Exhib:* Doctor Collects, Detroit Inst Arts, 65; Nat Exhib Am Art, Chautauqua Gallery Art, NY, 67; Mid-Year Show, Butler Inst Am Art, 67-69; Illustrators Ten Show, Union Carbide Gallery, New York, 68; Nat Exhib Drawing & Small Sculpture, Ball State Univ Art Gallery, 68; Watercolor USA, Springfield Mus Art, Mo, 68 & 73; Nat Soc Painters Casein, Nat Arts Club, New York, 69; Winter Show, Anderson Fine Arts Center, Ind, 71, 78, 79, 81 & 82. *Teaching:* Asst prof watercolor & graphic design, Eastern Mich Univ, 70-77, assoc prof, 77-83, prof, 83- *Mem:* Mich Watercolor Soc (bd mem, 66-70 & 82-83, chmn, 74-77). *Media:* Transparent Watercolor, Gouache. *Publ:* Illusr, Eastern market, its exotic wares and people, 65; Gold inside the Goldern Tower, 66, Twelfth Street in perspective, 67; Who is that lady? Why Mrs Manzu of course, 69 & Expensive people, from a place called Fernwood, 69, Detroit Mag. *Dealer:* Gallery Renaissance Detroit MI. *Mailing Add:* 43524 Bannockburn Dr Canton MI 48187

BEGLEY, WAYNE E
HISTORIAN, PAINTER
b Kenvir, Ky, Dec 29, 37. *Study:* Univ Louisville, BA, 58; Univ Iowa, MFA, 62; Harvard Univ, 62-63; Univ Pa, PhD, 66. *Work:* Butler Inst Am Art, Ohio; Rose Art Mus, Mass; Albright-Knox Art Gallery, Buffalo, NY; Des Moines Art Ctr, Iowa. *Exhib:* Louisville Art Ctr Ann, J B Speed Art Mus, 56-63; one-man shows, Am Acad, Rome, 60, Louisville Art Ctr 61 & Univ Ky Art Gallery, Lexington, 62; Mid-Am Ann, William Rockhill Nelson Gallery Art, 62. *Collections Arranged:* Indian Buddhist Sculpture (auth, catalog), J B Speed Art Mus, 68; Pala Art (auth, catalog), Univ Iowa Mus Art, 69; The Hindu Pantheon (auth, catalog), Rice Mus, Houston, 75. *Teaching:* From asst prof to prof Indian & Islamic art, Univ Iowa, 66-; vis prof Indian & Islamic art, Univ Ill, Urbana, 67; A W Mellon prof Indian & Islamic art, Rice Univ, 74-75; Maude Kerns prof Indian & Islamic art, Univ Ore, 78. *Awards:* Rome Prize Fel, Am Acad in Rome, 59-61; Research Fel, Am Inst Indian Studies, 67-68 & 70-71; Guggenheim Fel, 75-76. *Bibliog:* In the abstract, Courier-Journal Mag, 10/61. *Res:* Indian and Islamic art. *Publ:* Auth, Indian Buddhist Sculpture in American Collections, J B Speed Art Mus, 68; auth, Identification of Ajanta Fragment in Boston Mus, Oriental Art, 68; auth, Visnu's Flaming Wheel: Iconography of Sudarsana-cakra, NY Univ Press, 73; auth, The myth of Taj Mahal and new theory of symbolic meaning, Art Bulletin, 79; auth, Amanat Khan and Calligraphy on Taj Mahal, Kunst des Orients, 80. *Mailing Add:* Sch Art Univ Iowa Iowa City IA 52242

BEHL, WOLFGANG
SCULPTOR, EDUCATOR
b Berlin, Ger, Apr 13, 18; US citizen. *Study:* Acad Fine Art, Berlin; RI Sch Design. *Work:* Pa Acad Fine Arts, Philadelphia; Addison Gallery Am Art; Conn Gen Ins Co; New Britain Mus Am Art; Cornell Univ. *Comn:* Welded menorah & eternal light, Temple Beth Sholom, Manchester, Conn, 64; bronze tabernacle & processional cross, Church of the Resurrection, Wallingford, Conn, 66; Reredos, Immanuel Lutheran Church, Attleboro, Mass, 69; woodcarving monument, Elemer Nagy Millard Auditorium, Univ Hartford, 75; welded sculpture, Town Bloomfield, Conn, 76; and others. *Exhib:* Plastics USA, Soviet Union, 60; Carnegie Inst Int, Pittsburgh, 64; Fogg Art Mus, Harvard Univ, Cambridge, 66; Hemisfair 68, San Antonio, Tex, 68; Retrospectives, New Britain Mus, 68; Sculpture Ctr, New York, 80; Univ Hartford, Bloomfield, Conn, 83; and others. *Teaching:* Asst prof sculpture & drawing, William & Mary Col, 45-53; prof sculpture, Univ Hartford, 55- *Awards:* Sculpture Awards, Conn Acad Fine Arts, 61, 63 & 64; Nat Inst Arts & Lett Grant, 63; Ford Found Purchase Award, 64. *Bibliog:* Eye to Eye (film),

WGBH TV, Boston, 71. *Mem:* Nat Sculpture Ctr (chmn adv bd, 68-); Sculptors Guild (dir, 72). *Media:* Wood, Bronze, Stone. *Publ:* Contribr, Masters of Wood Sculpture, 80; contribr, The Process of Sculpture, 81; contribr, Woodworking--The New Wave, 81; contribr, Adonis and Aphrodite, Viernheim Verlag, Ger, 61. *Dealer:* Arts Exclusive Gallery Simsbury CT; Rosenfeld Gallery 113 Arch St Philadelphia PA 19106. *Mailing Add:* 179 Kenyon St Hartford CT 06105

BEHNKE, LEIGH
PAINTER
b Hartford, Conn, Dec 22, 46. *Study:* Pratt Inst, BFA, 69; New York Univ, MA, 76. *Work:* H J Heinz Corp, Pittsburgh, Pa; Deloitte, Haskins, Sells, Marsh & McClennan Co & Xerox Corp, New York; Southeast Banking Corp, Miami, Fla; Currier Mus, Manchester, NH; and others. *Exhib:* Urban Landscape, Wave Hill, New York, 79; New Am Still Life, Westmaland Mus, Pa; On Paper, Inst Contemp Art, Va Mus, Richmond, 80; Real, Really Real, Super Real, San Antonio Mus, Tex, 81, Carnegie Inst, Pittsburgh, 81 & Indianapolis Mus, Ind, 81; Contemp Am Realist, Univ Art Gallery, Pittsburgh, Pa, 81; Lower Manhattan from Street to Sky, Whitney Mus, 82; and others. *Teaching:* Lectr fine art drawing and painting, Sch Visual Arts, New York, 79- *Bibliog:* Jon Friedman (auth), Leigh Behnke: Reviews Arts Mag, 1/80; Aladar Marburger (auth), New Faces/New Images, winter 80; New Editions: Leigh Behnke, Art News, 4/82. *Media:* Watercolor, Oil; Silkscreen. *Dealer:* Fischbach Gallery 29 W 57th St New York NY 10019. *Mailing Add:* 205 W 10th St New York NY 10014

BEHRENS, ROY R
ILLUSTRATOR, WRITER
b Independence, Iowa, June 27, 46. *Study:* Pond Farm Sch, with Bauhaus Potter Marguerite Wildenhain, 64; Univ Northern Iowa, BA, 68; RI Sch Design, MA(art educ), 72. *Exhib:* Paperworks, Waterloo Munic Galleries, Iowa, 73; 8th Ann Ed Design, New York, 73; Wisconsin Directions II, Milwaukee Art Ctr, 78. *Pos:* Design ed, NAm Rev, 72- *Teaching:* Assoc prof art design, Univ Northern Iowa, 72-77 & Univ Wis, Milwaukee, 77- *Awards:* Cert of Merit, Soc Publ Designers, 73; res grants, Univ Wis, Milwaukee, 78 & 80. *Res:* History and theory of camouflage; relation of visual arts to perceptual psychology, creativity and humor; fiction illustration. *Publ:* Illusr, The Painted Bird, Houghton Mifflin, 76; illusr, Christ preaching at the Henley Regatta, NAm Rev, 79; illusr, The life of fiction, Univ Ill Press, 77; auth, Art and camouflage: Concealment and deception in nature, art and war, NAm Rev, 81; auth, Design in the Visual Arts, Prentice-Hall, 84; and others. *Mailing Add:* Dept of Art Univ Wis-Milwaukee Milwaukee WI 53201

BEILIN, HOWARD
DEALER
Pos: Owner & dir, Howard Beilin Inc, currently. *Specialty:* Nineteenth and 20th century American art with a special emphasis on Norman Rockwell; European impressionists and post-impressionists. *Mailing Add:* 945 Fifth Ave New York NY 10021

BEITZ, LES
PAINTER, ILLUSTRATOR
b Buffalo, NY, May 11, 16. *Study:* Art Inst Buffalo; and with Charles S Bigelow. *Comn:* Murals, Officer's Club, Royal Air Force Sta, Fairford, Eng & Enlisted Men's Club, Schilling Air Force Base, Salina, Kans, 62; also recent oils, frontier subjects, comn by pvt collectors of Western art. *Pos:* Art dir & staff illusr, True West Mag, Frontier Times Mag & Old West Mag, currently; ed & assoc publ, Collector's World Mag & Bottles & Relics Mag, currently; collecting ed, Early Am Life Mag, currently; publ, Packsaddle Press, Austin, Tex. *Publ:* Auth, Overlooked Treasures, Barnes, 75; contribr & illusr, Tex Star & Spinning Wheel Mag. *Mailing Add:* 2407 Audubon Pl Austin TX 78741

BEKER, GISELA
PAINTER
b Zoppott, EGer; US citizen. *Study:* Kunstinstitut, Rostock, EGer, 48-50; with Rudolf Kroll (of Bauhaus Sch), Dusseldorf, WGer. *Work:* Everson Mus, Syracuse, NY; Palm Springs Mus, Calif; Arts & Sci Ctr, Baton Rouge, La; and others. *Exhib:* One-woman show, Arts & Sci Ctr, Baton Rouge, La, 75; Mus Mod Art, Paris, France, 74; NY Univ, 76; Chrysler Mus, Norfolk, Va; New Orleans Mus Art, La; Phoenix Art Mus, Ariz; and other group & one-woman shows. *Awards:* Gold Medal, Int Exhib Painters & Sculptors, Paris, 74; Silver Medal (watercolor), Grand Prix Humanitaire de France, Paris, 75; and others. *Bibliog:* The feminist movement in art, Southwest Art, 7/74; Gisela Beker art Arts & Science Center, Arts Mag, 2/75; Gregory Battcock (auth), Why Art, Dutton, 77. *Mailing Add:* 530 E 72nd St New York NY 10021

BELCHER, GEORGE
DEALER
b Raymondville, Tex, Oct 21, 41. *Study:* Pan Am Univ, Edinburg, Tex, BA, 64. *Pos:* Owner, George Belcher Gallery, San Francisco, currently. *Specialty:* Nineteenth and twentieth century Mexican and Latin American paintings. *Mailing Add:* 500 Suttet St San Francisco CA 94102

BELFIORE, GERARDO
PAINTER, INSTRUCTOR
b Italy, Jan 15, 14; US citizen. *Work:* Philadelphia Mus Art; Atwater Kent Mus, Philadelphia Art Alliance; Woodmere Art Gallery; Pa Hist Soc, Philadelphia. *Exhib:* Pa Acad Fine Arts, 40; Boston Mus Art, 41; Nat Acad Design, 44; Libr of Cong, 44; Philadelphia Mus Art, 73; Nat Exhib of Italian-Am Artists in US, Stone Park, Ill, 77; Distinguished Mid Atlantic Artists: Four Decades of Growth, Univ Del, 80. *Teaching:* Instr printmaking, Main

Line Ctr of the Arts, Philadelphia, 72-73; instr drawing & watercolor, Community Arts Ctr Wallingford, Pa, 74- *Awards:* The Woodmere Prize, Woodmere Art Gallery, 62; Watercolor Prize, Regional Watercolor Exhib, Philadelphia Art Alliance, 66; Gold Medal, Ann Exhib, Da Vinci Art Alliance, 71-73. *Mem:* Philadelphia Watercolor Club; Da Vinci Art Alliance; Community Arts Ctr of Wallingford. *Media:* Multimedia. *Publ:* Illusr, Pennsylvania Cavalcade, 42; contribr, Charette, 63. *Mailing Add:* 6234 Chelwynde Ave Philadelphia PA 19142

BELFORT-CHALAT, JACQUELINE
SCULPTOR, PAINTER
b Mt Vernon, NY, Feb 23, 30. *Study:* With Frederick V Guinzburg, 43, Ruth Nickerson, 44, Columbia Univ, sculpture with Oronzio Maldarelli & casting with Ettore Salvatore, 47; Art Students League, life drawing with Klonis, 48; Univ Chicago, AB, 48; Fashion Inst Technol, 48-50; Royal Acad Fine Arts, Copenhagen, Denmark, 60-62. *Comn:* Transfiguration, Monastery of the Transfiguration, Windor, NY, 81; plaque, St Patrick Cathedral, New York, 81; plaque, Bishop Francis J Mugavero, Brooklyn, 82; plaque, Dr Eugene J Fisher, Washington, DC, 83; Holy Family (terra cotta releif), St Michael's Church, NY, 83; and others. *Exhib:* Nat Collection of Fine Arts, Washington, DC, 63; Washington Gallery Art, 66; Everson Mus, Syracuse, NY, 72; one-man shows, Everson Mus, 79, City Hall, Syracuse, 81 & Wilson Gallery, Le-Moyne Col, 83; and others. *Teaching:* Prof & dir fine arts, LeMoyne Col, Syracuse, NY, 69- *Bibliog:* P Scala (auth), Begotten not made (film), ABC-TV, Syracuse, NY, 74. *Mem:* Nat Soc Am Pen Women; Theta Chi Beta; Am Aesthetic Soc; Soc for Art, Relig & Cult; Col Art Asn Am. *Media:* All Media. *Mailing Add:* 321 Hurlburt Rd Syracuse NY 13224

BELING, HELEN
SCULPTOR, INSTRUCTOR
b New York, NY, Jan 1, 14. *Study:* Nat Acad Design, with Paul Manship & Lee Lawrie, 30-37; Art Students League, with William Zorach, 44-45. *Work:* Butler Inst Am Art, Youngstown, Ohio; Hirshhorn Mus, Washington, DC; Norfolk Mus Arts & Sci, Va; St Lawrence Univ, Canton, NY; Syracuse Univ Mus; and others. *Comn:* Menorah (bronze), Temple Israel, Waterbury, Conn, 59; Eternal Light (bronze), Temple B'nai Jacob, Woodbridge, Conn, 61; Eternal Light (bronze), Temple Beth Am Shalom, White Plains; Candelabra Room (ceramic), Pleasant Valley Home, West Orange, NJ, 62; Exodus (wall relief), Temple Emanu-el, Yonkers, NY, 66. *Exhib:* Nine one-man shows, Pa Acad Fine Arts, 50-66; Metrop Mus Art Sculpture Exhib, 51; Sculptors Guild Ann, 54-83; St Louis Mus, Mo; Everson Mus, Syracuse, NY; Whitney Mus Am Art, 55; Univ Ill, 57; Am Acad & Inst Arts & Lett, 81; Sculpture Exhib, Sculpture Ctr, Pa Acad Fine Arts, 84. *Teaching:* Instr sculpture, Westchester Art Workshop, White Plains, 50-66 & 77-82, NY Univ, 61-62 & Col New Rochelle, 70-71. *Awards:* Medal Honor, Audubon Artists, 65; Medal Honor, Nat Asn Women Artists, 68; Medal Merit, Audubon Artists, 80. *Mem:* Nat Asn Women Artists; Sculptors Guild (pres, 72-74); Fine Arts Fedn (vpres, 74-83, dir, 78-79). *Media:* Reinforced Fiber Glass, Welded Stainless Steel. *Dealer:* Sculpture Ctr 167 E 69th St New York NY 10021. *Mailing Add:* 287 Weyman Ave New Rochelle NY 10805

BELKIN, ARNOLD
PAINTER, MURALIST
b Calgary, Alta, Dec 9, 30. *Study:* Vancouver Art Sch, 45-47; Nat Polytech Inst, Mex, 47-50; asst to David Alfaro Siqueiros, 51. *Work:* Mus Arte Mod, Mexico City; Phoenix Art Mus, Ariz; Betzalel Nat Mus, Jerusalem, Israel; Gen Motors Collection, Austin, Tex; Los Angeles Co Mus Art. *Comn:* Mural, Fed Penitentiary, Mexico City, 61; Gov Sch Handicapped Children, Mex, 63; Jewish Community Cult Ctr, Mex, 67; portable mural, Mex Pavillion, Expo'67, Montreal; mural, Humanities Bldg, Lock Haven State Col, 71. *Exhib:* Guggenheim Int Award Exhib, New York, 64; 2nd Latin Am Graphics Biennale, San Juan, PR, 72; 3rd Biennale, Medellin, Colombia, 72; solo exhibs, Lerner-Heller Gallery, New York, 72, Palace Fine Arts, Mexico City, 77 & Mus Bellas Artes, Caracas, Venezuela, 77. *Pos:* Founder, ed & co-publisher, Nueva Presencia--A Humanist Manifesto, 61-64. *Teaching:* Asst prof mural techniques, Univ Americas, Mexico City, 53-60; prof theatre design, Univ Motolinia, Mexico City, 54-60; vis instr painting, Pratt Inst, 67-71. *Awards:* Theatre Design Award, Mex Theater Critics, 61; Nat Purchase Prize Painting, Salon Plastica Mex, 63; Purchase Prize, 2nd Graphics Biennale, San Juan, 72. *Bibliog:* Henry Seldis (auth), article, Los Angeles Times, 67; Raquel Tibol (auth), Secuencia y consecuencia de A Belkin, Excelsior, Diorama Cult, 71. *Mem:* Salon Plastica Mex; Salon Los Independientes, Mex; Mus Latino Am, New York. *Media:* Acrylic. *Dealer:* Richard Nardin Galleries 25 E 73rd St New York NY 10021. *Mailing Add:* Parque Espana 49-2 Mexico 11 DF Mexico

BELL, ALISTAIR MACREADY
PRINTMAKER, PAINTER
b Darlington, Eng, Oct 21, 13; Can citizen. *Work:* Nat Gallery Can, Ottawa, Ont; Mus Mod Art, New York; Victoria & Albert Mus, London, Eng; Mus Ugo Carpi, Italy; Vancouver Art Gallery, BC. *Exhib:* First Int Biennial Graphics, Tokyo & Osaka, Japan, 57; 3rd Int Exhib Graphics, Lubljana, Yugoslavia, 59; 6th Bianco e Nero, Lugano, Switz, 60; Recent Prints, Canada, Mus Mod Art, 67; 1st Int Triennial of Contemp Xylography, Carpi, 69; and others. *Awards:* Can Coun Sr Arts Fel, 59, Sr Arts Award, 67. *Mem:* Royal Can Acad Art. *Media:* Woodcut, Watercolor. *Dealer:* Bau-Xi Gallery 3045 Granville St Vancouver BC V6H 3J9 Can. *Mailing Add:* 2566 Marine Dr West Vancouver BC V7V 1L4 Canada

BELL, CHARLES S
PAINTER
b Tulsa, Okla, Feb 2, 35. *Comn:* Spieser Collection, 74. *Exhib:* New Realism, Wadsworth Atheneum, 74; Butler Inst Am Art, 75; Sewall Gallery, Rice Univ, Houston, 77; Solomon R Guggenheim Mus, New York, 77; Tulane Univ, La, 78; Indianapolis Mus, 78; Phoenix Art Mus, 79. *Bibliog:* Articles, Illus London News, 1/75, Chicago Tribune, 76 & Jacksonville J, 2/77. *Media:* Oil. *Mailing Add:* c/o Louis K Meisel 141 Prince St New York NY 10012

BELL, COCA (MARY CATLETT)
PAINTER
b Weleetka, Okla, Sept 26, 24. *Study:* Univ Okla, BA(lang); painting with Milford Zornes, Edith & Richard Goetz & Charles Reid; drawing with Don Coen & Robert Kaupelis. *Comn:* Oil painting, Gov Mansion, Oklahoma City, 70; three comns, Kerr Conf Ctr, 83. *Exhib:* 14th Ann Eight State Exhib, Okla Art Ctr, 72; 18th Ann Eight State Exhib, 76, four-man show, 77 & two-man shows, 78, 79 & 81, Okla Art Ctr, Oklahoma City; Distinguished Artists of Okla Exhib, Midwestern Gov's Conf, 77; Living Women, Living Art, Gov Gallery, 81; Nat Gov Asn Conf, Okla, 82; Diamond Jubilee Arts Festival, Okla State Capitol, 82; and others. *Awards:* Fourth Award, 10th Ann Southwestern Watercolor Soc Regional Exhib, 73; Second Award Watercolor 74, Okla Watercolor Asn, 74. *Bibliog:* Interview, Okla Educ TV, 79. *Mem:* Philbrook Art Ctr; Okla Art Ctr; Okla Watercolor Asn. *Media:* Watercolor, Oil. *Mailing Add:* 2 Colony Lane Oklahoma City OK 73116

BELL, DONALD ALLEN
DEALER, CONSULTANT
b Chicago, Ill, Sept 1, 38. *Study:* Univ Colo, BFA, 59. *Mem:* Sr mem Am Soc Appraisers. *Specialty:* 19th and 20th century American painting. *Publ:* Contribr, American Art Antiques Mag, Billboard, 3/4/79. *Mailing Add:* 7100 Main St Scottsdale AZ 85281

BELL, JAMES M
ADMINISTRATOR
b 43. *Study:* NTex State Univ, BA; Stephen F Austin Univ, MA. *Pos:* All level art supvr, Pub Sch Syst, Texarkana, Ark, 66-68; asst educ cur, Wichita Art Mus, Kans, 68-70; dir, Abilene Fine Arts Mus, Tex, 70-73; dir, Tampa Bay Art Ctr, 73-78; dir, Ft Wayne Mus Art, Ind, 78-82; develop dir, Oklahoma Art Ctr, Oklahoma City, currently. *Mailing Add:* Okla Art Ctr 3113 Pershing Blvd Oklahoma City OK 73107

BELL, KATHRYN LEISE
CALLIGRAPHER, EDUCATOR
b Chicago Ill, Mar 9, 42. *Study:* Bob Jones Univ, BS, 65, MA, 67; with Peter Thornton & Michael Hughey, 81. *Work:* Lloyd J Reynolds Mem Collection Calligraphy, Portland Art Mus, Ore; Off of Congressman Carroll A Campbell, DC. *Comn:* Manuscripts, Hebrews 3:4, Northway Construct, Greenville, SC, 78 & Ezekiel 36: 34-36, Jack E Shaw Builders, Greenville, SC, 79. *Exhib:* Guild SC Artists' Ann, Columbia Art Mus, 77; Calligraphy--the Art of Letterforms, Presby Col, Clinton, SC & Silver Eye Studio, Greenville, SC; Greenville Artists Guild, Falls Cottage, 81; Pickens Co Art Mus, 81; Teasler Libr, Wafford Col, 82; and others. *Teaching:* Instr calligraphy & hist art, Bob Jones Univ, 67- *Bibliog:* Michael Ginsberg (auth), World of art thumbs nose at calligraphers, Greenville News, 9/77; Jim Barnhill (producer), Calligraphy, radio presentation, WEPR, 10/79. *Mem:* Greenville Co Art Asn; Greenville Artists' Guild; Carolina Lettering Arts Soc (vpres, 79-80); Soc Scribes. *Media:* Multimedia. *Publ:* Contribr, 1978 Calligrapher's Calendar, Soc of Scribes, 78; contribr, Soc Scribes Calendar, 81; contribr, Ligature, 83. *Mailing Add:* 102 Buena Vista Dr Greenville SC 29607

BELL, LARRY STUART
SCULPTOR
b Chicago, Ill, Dec 6, 39. *Study:* Chouinard Art Inst, Los Angeles, with Robert Irwin, Richards Ruben, Robert Chuey & Emerson Woelfer, 57-59. *Work:* Nat Collection Fine Arts; Mus Mod Art, New York; Whitney Mus Am Art, New York; Tate Gallery, London, Eng; Gallery New S Wales, Australia. *Exhib:* Southern Calif Painting & Sculpture Ann, Los Angeles Co Mus Art, Los Angeles, 59; Mus Mod Art, New York, 65; Contemp Am Sculpture & Prints Ann Exhib, Whitney Mus Am Art, 66; Guggenheim Mus, New York, 67; Walker Art Ctr, Minneapolis, 68; three-man show, Tate Gallery, London, 70; USA WCoast, Kunstverein, Hamburg, WGer, 72; Detroit Inst Arts, Mich, 73; Sculpture: Am Directions 1945-1975, Nat Collection Fine Arts, Smithsonian Inst, Washington, DC, 75; Painting & Sculpture in Calif: The Mod Era, San Francisco Mus Mod Art, 76 & Smithsonian Inst, 77; Fullerton Art Gallery, Calif State Univ, 80; Bronx Mus, NY, 80; Whitney Mus Am Art, 80; Fruitmarket Gallery, Edinburgh, Scotland, 80. *Teaching:* Instr sculpture, Univ SFla, Tampa, Univ Calif, Berkeley & Univ Calif, Irvine, 70-73. *Awards:* Copley Found, 62; Guggenheim Mus Fel, 70; Nat Endowment for the Arts Grant, 75. *Bibliog:* Barbara Rose (auth), American Art Since 1900, Thames & Hudson, London, 67; Peter Plagens (auth), Larry Bell reassessed, Artforum, 10/72; Henry J Seldis (auth), article, Los Angeles Times, 10/21/73. *Media:* Light. *Mailing Add:* PO Box 1778 Taos NM 87571

BELL, LILIAN A
SCULPTOR, ASSEMBLAGE ARTIST
b London, Eng, Nov 5, 43; US citizen. *Study:* William Morris Tech Sch, London; Linfield Col, McMinnville, Ore, 69-70. *Work:* Portland Art Mus; Visual Art Ctr, Beer Sheva, Israel. *Exhib:* Biennial of the Pacific, Metrop Mus Manila, Philippines, 80; Visual Arts Ctr, Beer Sheva, Israel, 81; Book Art Now, Elvehjem Mus Art, Madison, Wis, 83; Handmade Paper, Liberty Gallery, Louisville, Ky, 83; Gibbes Art Mus, Charleston, SC, 84; and others.

Pos: Guest lectr, US & abroad, 73-; guest cur, Univ Ore Traveling Exhib, 80-82; abstract writer, Art & Archaeology, NY Univ Conservation Ctr, 81- *Teaching:* Instr papermaking, Ore Sch Arts & Crafts, Portland, 76- *Awards:* Western States Arts Found Visual Arts Fel, 77. *Bibliog:* Mike E Walsh (auth), Symbolic images from four artists, Artweek, 4/29/78; How eight craftsmen won the west, Craft Horizons, 12/78; Textured objects, West Art, 7/24/81. *Mem:* Artists Equity Asn (bd mem Ore chap, 78-79); World Print Coun; Int Sculpture Ctr, Washington, DC. *Media:* Cast Paper Assemblage. *Publ:* Contribr, Collage and Assemblage, Crown, 73; contribr, Contemporary Crafts of the Americas, Henry Regnery, 75; auth, Plant Fibers for Papermaking by Lilian A Bell, Liliaceae Press, 81; contribr, The Art of Papermaking, Davis, 83; auth, Papyrus, Tapa, Amate & Rice Paper, Liliaceae Press, 83. *Dealer:* Augen Gallery 619 SW Tenth Ave Portland OR 97205; Galeria de Arte Ave Presidente Masaryk 379 Esq Seneca 11510 Mexico City Mexico. *Mailing Add:* 1970 S Davis St McMinnville OR 97128

BELL, MICHAEL STEVEN
CURATOR, ADMINISTRATOR
b Joplin, Mo, July 4, 46. *Study:* Calif Inst Arts, with Emmett Williams, BFA(scholar), 70; Univ Ky, with Wendell Berry, MFA, 72; Mus Mgt Inst, Univ Calif, Berkeley, cert(scholar), 79. *Collections Arranged:* William Hahn: Genre Painter, 76; Gordon Onslow-Ford Retrospective, 78 & George Inness: Signature Years, 79, Oakland Mus; 20 American Artists: 1982, San Francisco Mus Mod Art, 82. *Pos:* Registrar, Oakland Mus, 76-80; dir, Midland Art Coun, Mich, 80-81; curatorial asst, San Francisco Mus Mod Art, 82- *Awards:* Nat Endowment Arts Scholar, 80; G Murphy Award Promotional Lit, 83. *Mem:* Proj Sculpture, Pub Sites (treas, 83); Am Asn Mus. *Res:* American surrealism since 1960; 19th century American painting. *Publ:* Contribr, Arts in Society, Vol 7, No 1, 70; contribr, Points of Departure, Wiley & Sons, 71; contribr, Visual dialog, Roberta Loach, 76; contribr, Fine Arts Insurance Handbook, Asn Art Mus Dirs, 80; auth, CCAC: 75 Years, San Francisco Mus Mod Art, 83; contribr, Artweek, 83 & Leonardo, 84. *Mailing Add:* 763 45th Ave San Francisco CA 94121

BELL, PHILIP MICHAEL
ADMINISTRATOR, HISTORIAN
b Toronto, Ont, Dec 31, 42. *Study:* Univ Toronto, BA & MA(fine art). *Collections Arranged:* W H Coverdale Collection of Canadiana, 73, Western Odyssey, Drawings by S P Hall, 74, Ouebec and Its Environs, Drawings by J P Cockburn (with catalog), 75; Goodridge Roberts: Drawings, 76; William Sawyer: Portrait Painter, 79. *Pos:* Cur paintings, drawings & prints, Public Archives Can, Ottawa, Ont, 68-73; dir, Agnes Etherington Art Ctr, Queen's Univ, 73-78; visual arts officer, Ont Arts Coun, 78-79; asst dir, Public Programs, Nat Gallery Can, 79-81, actg dir, 81; dir & chief exec officer, McMichael Can Collection, 81- *Teaching:* Instr Can art hist, Queen's Univ, Kingston, Ont, 75-76. *Awards:* Governor-General's Award for Non-Fiction for Painters in a New Land, Can Coun, 74. *Mem:* Coun Can Mus Asn. *Res:* Nineteenth century Canadian art. *Publ:* Auth, Painters in a New Land, 73; ed, Braves and Buffalo, Paintings by A J Miller, 73; auth, William Goodridge Roberts 1904-1974: Drawings, 76; auth, The Last Lion . . . Rambles in Quebec with J P Cockburn, 78; auth, William Sawyer: Portrait Painter, 79. *Mailing Add:* McMichael Canadian Collection Kleinburg ON L0J 1C0 Canada

BELL, R MURRAY
COLLECTOR
Study: Univ Alta; Osgoode Hall Law Sch, Toronto. *Collection:* Chinese ceramics, with special interest in blue and white Chinese porcelain. *Mailing Add:* 134 Forest Hill Rd Toronto ON M4V 2L9 Canada

BELL, TREVOR
PAINTER, EDUCATOR
b Leeds, Eng, Oct 18, 30. *Study:* Leeds Col Art, NDD, 49, ATD, 50. *Work:* Tate Gallery, London; Victoria and Albert Mus, London; IBM, Atlanta; Rouse Company, Ohio. *Comn:* (painting) The Art of Fugue, Phillips Collection, Holland, 64; Southern Light (painting), Lewis State Bank, Fla, 75; Fla Queen (painting), Orlando Aviation Authority, Fla, 81; painting, Tallahassee Civic Ctr, Fla, 82. *Exhib:* Retrospective, Demarco, Edinburgh Arts Coun N Ireland, Sheffield, England, 70; New Work, Corcoran Gallery, Washington, DC, 73; Whitechapel Gallery, London, 73; Print Exhib, Tate Gallery, London, 77; Spoleto Festival, SC, 78; Artspace, Miami, 82; New Works, Nat Acad Sci, Washington, DC, 82; and others. *Pos:* Fla Fine Arts Coun Grants Review Panel, 79 & 80. *Teaching:* Head of painting, Winchester Col Art, United Kingdom, 66-70; chairperson art, Fanshawe Col, Ontario, 70-71; prof graduate painting, Fla State Univ, Tallahassee, 72- *Awards:* Int Painting Prize, Paris Biennale, 59; Gregory Fel, Univ Leeds, United Kingdom, 60-64; Fla Fine Arts Coun Individual Fel, State Fla, 81. *Bibliog:* Patrick Heron (auth), Two Cultures, Studio International, 70; John Elderfield (auth), Studio International, 70; Robert Martin (auth), Tampa Times, 77. *Media:* Acrylic. *Dealer:* Virginia Miller Galleries 169 Madeira Ave Coral Gables FL 33134. *Mailing Add:* 3920 Century Park Circle N Tallahassee FL 32304

BELLAMY, RICHARD
DEALER
Pos: Pres, HEGD Co; dealer, Oil & Steel Gallery Inc, currently. *Mailing Add:* 157 Chambers St New York NY 10007

BELLE, ANNA (ANNA BELLE BIRCKETT)
PAINTER
b Crescent, Okla. *Study:* Cent State Univ, Edmond, Okla; also with John Pike, Robert E Wood, Mel Crawford, Merlin Enabnit, John Pellew, Edgar Whitney, Gene Dougherty & Jack Vallee. *Exhib:* Eight Okla Mus Art Ann;

Southwestern Watercolor Soc, Dallas; one-man shows, Haven Collectable Gallery, Raton, NMex, 74; Ponca City, Okla, Owens Gallery & Wilson Gallery, Oklahoma City, 74 & 75; Seths' Canyon Rd Gallery, Santa Fe, NMex; 8th Ann Watercolor Okla. *Pos:* Dir, Okla Mus Art, 67-75. *Teaching:* Instr watercolor, Okla Mus Art, 73-74. *Awards:* Purchase Awards, Watercolor Okla. *Mem:* Okla Mus Art; Southwestern Watercolor Soc (vpres, 69, pres, 70); Watercolor Okla Soc (secy, 74-75). *Media:* Watercolor, oils. *Dealer:* Blue Door Gallery 4208 N Classen Oklahoma City OK 73118; House Gallery 5536 N Western Oklahoma City OK 73118. *Mailing Add:* 417 NW 41st Oklahoma City OK 73118

BELZ, CARL IRVIN
MUSEUM DIRECTOR
b Camden, NJ, Sept 13, 37. *Study:* Princeton Univ, BA, 59, MFA, 62, PhD, 63. *Pos:* Dir, Mills Col Art Gallery, 65-68; dir, Rose Art Mus, Brandeis Univ, 74- *Teaching:* Asst prof mod art, Mills Col, Oakland, Calif, 65-68; asst prof mod art, Brandeis Univ, 68-74, lectr mus studies, 74- *Publ:* Auth, Painted in Boston, Inst Contemp Art, Boston, 75; auth, Mitchell Siporin: A Retrospective, Brandeis Univ, 76; auth, Frank Stella: Metallic Reliefs, Brandeis Univ, 79; auth, Frankenthaler: The 1950s, Brandeis Univ, 81; auth, Charles Garabedian: Twenty Years of Work, Brandeis Univ, 83. *Mailing Add:* Rose Art Mus Brandeis Univ Waltham MA 02254

BENDELL, MARILYN
PAINTER, INSTRUCTOR
b Grand Ledge, Mich, Sept 19, 21. *Study:* Am Acad Art; and with Arnold E Turtle & Pierre Nuyttens. *Work:* Principia Col, St Louis; Saginaw Mus, Mich; Hadley Sch for Blind, Winnetka, Ill; Huntington Mus Fine Arts, WVa. *Comn:* Juggler of Notre Dame, comn by Sen Schuch, Saginaw Mus, 50; portrait of founder Principia Col, comn by William E Morgan, St Louis, 58; portrait of Helen Keller, Hadley Sch for Blind, 58; portrait of Mrs Paul Schulze, comn by Paul Schulze, Chicago, Ill, 60; David & Kim, Huntington Mus Fine Arts, 65. *Exhib:* Chicago Galleries, Ill, 55; Ill State Fair, Springfield, 58; 16th Ann Mem Exhib, Acad Artists Asn, Springfield, Mass, 64; Famous Florida Artists, Frank Oehlschlaeger Galleries, Sarasota, 64 & 65; Acad Artists Asn Nat Show, Springfield, 72. *Teaching:* Instr portrait, figure & still life, Longboat Key Art Ctr, Fla, 52-68; instr still life, Oak Park-River Forest Art League, Ill, 57-59; instr portrait, figure & still life, Cortez Art Sch, Fla, 68-74; pvt art classes, 74-; instr, Bendell Galleries & Art Sch, Fla, 74-82. *Awards:* Popular Award for Bus Stop, Ill State Fair, 61; First in Portrait for Jeri, 64 & First in Portrait & Figure, Portrait of a Young Woman, 70, Springfield Mus Fine Arts. *Bibliog:* Edith Weigle (auth), Wonderful world of art, Chicago Tribune 8/17/58; W C Burnett (auth), Two art shows reviewed, Sarasota Herald Tribune, 64; Charles Benbow (auth), She reflects her colorful oil paintings, St Petersburg Times, 11/13/71. *Mem:* Brown Co Art Gallery Asn; fel Royal Soc Arts; Am Artists Prof League; Acad Artists Asn, Springfield; Sarasota Art Asn. *Media:* Oil. *Dealer:* Lester Kierstead Henderson Galleries 712 Hawthorne Monterey CA 93940; Wadle Galleries Ltd 128 W Palace Santa Fe NM 87501. *Mailing Add:* Route 1 Box 92MN Santa Fe NM 87501

BENDER, BEVERLY STERL
SCULPTOR, ENVIRONMENTAL ARTIST
b Washington, DC, Jan 14, 18. *Study:* Knox Col, BA; Art Students League; Sculpture Ctr, New York; Mus Natural Hist, New York. *Work:* James Ford Bell Mus Natural Hist, Minneapolis; Schmid Gallery, New York. *Comn:* Mem, Disco, Mystic Seaport, Conn, 69. *Exhib:* Nat Arts Club, New York, 69-81; Smithsonian Inst, Washington, 70 & 71; one-man shows, Grist Mill Gallery, Chester, Vt, 74 & Southern Vt Art Ctr, Manchester, 75; Hiram Halle Mem Libr, Poundridge, NY, 79; Acad Natural Sci, Philadelphia, 81. *Pos:* Artist & designer, Johns-Manville, New York, 43-72. *Awards:* Award Merit, Soc Animal Artists, 81; Art Delux Reproduction Co Award, 83; Elliot Liskin Award, 83. *Mem:* Soc Animal Artists (bd dir, 74-); Southern Vt Art Ctr; Catharine Lorillard Wolfe Art Club (mem bd dirs, 76-80 & 83-84); Knickerbocker Artists; Am Artists Prof League. *Media:* Stone, Wood. *Mailing Add:* Rt 3 Box 13A Pound Ridge NY 10576

BENDER, BILL
PAINTER
b El Segundo, Calif, Jan 5, 20. *Work:* US Air Force Acad, Colorado Springs, Colo; US Navy, Pensacola, Fla; Pentagon, Washington, DC; Living Desert Asn, Palm Desert, Calif; Visitors Ctr, Death Valley, Calif. *Exhib:* Death Valley 49'er Art Exhib, 50-78; Mountain Oyster Contemp Western Art Show, Tucson, Ariz, 72-83; Tex Cowboy Reunion & Art Exhib, Stamford, 74-80; 14th Ann Round-up of Western Art, Saddleback Western Art Gallery, Santa Ana, Calif, 80; American Miniatures Exhibit, Settlers W Galleries, Tucson, Ariz, 84. *Awards:* Best of Show, 19th Ann Catalina Festival Art, 77; Second Place, 27th Ann Death Valley Exhib, 77; Gold Medal (oils), Am Indian & Cowboy Artists 2nd Ann Exhib. *Bibliog:* Ed Ainsworth (auth), Painters of the desert, Desert Mag, 60; Ed Ainsworth (auth), The Cowboy in Art, World Publ, 69; Peggy & Harold Samuels (auths), Contemporary Western Artists, 83. *Mem:* Am Artists Prof League, New York; life mem & fel Am Fine Arts; hon life mem, Mountain Oyster Club, Tucson; Death Valley 49ers Inc (dir). *Media:* Oil, Watercolor. *Publ:* Illusr, Christmas cards, stationery & calendars, Leanin' Tree Publ, 60-80; illusr, Beakoning Desert, Prentice-Hall, 62; auth & illusr, My Friend John, Los Angeles Westerners, 70; auth & illusr, Day I Clumb Down from the Horse, Brand Bk 3, San Diego Westerners, 73. *Mailing Add:* Star Rte Box 154 Oro Grande CA 92368

BENDIG, WILLIAM CHARLES
PAINTER, PUBLISHER
b Corry, Pa, Dec 1, 27. *Study:* Trinity Col; Chelsea Sch Art, Univ London, with Ceri Richards; pvt study in Greece & Italy. *Work:* Trinity Col, Hartford, Conn. *Exhib:* Various juried exhibitions since 1956. *Pos:* Publ & ed-in-chief, Art Gallery, 57- *Teaching:* Instr painting, drawing & art hist, Brunswick Sch, Greenwich, Conn & Cheshire Acad, Conn; lectr art hist, mediaeval art & archit, Trinity Col, 65, Chautauqua, 70, Bowling Green Univ, 75, Cranbrook Acad, 78 & Wichita Art Mus, 80. *Mem:* Essex Art Asn (vpres, 59-61); Mediaeval Acad Am. *Mailing Add:* Hollycroft Ivoryton CT 06442

BENEDICT-JONES, LINDA L
PHOTOGRAPHER, CURATOR
b Beloit, Wis, Oct 21, 47. *Study:* Univ Wis-LaCrosse, BS, 69, Univ Lisboa, Portugal, dipl, 72, Mass Inst Tech, MS(visual studies, Arts Coun Gr Brit Grant), 82. *Work:* Bibliotheque Nat, Paris; Mus Cantini, Marseilles, France; Mus Art Hist Fribourg, Switzerland; Dept Environ, London; Polaroid Collection, Cambridge, Mass. *Exhib:* Imagens de Portugal, Ctr Cult Am, Lisboa, Portugal, 73; solo exhib, Madison Art Gallery, Wis, 76; Serpentine Gallery, London, 78; Quiet Places, Graves Art Gallery, Sheffield, England, 79; Les Autoportraits, Ctr Georges Pompidou, Paris, 81; Contemporary Self Portraiture, Hayden Gallery, Mass Inst Technol, 83. *Pos:* Asst dir, Clarence Kennedy Gallery, Polaroid Corp, Cambridge, Mass, 82- *Teaching:* Lectr photog, London Col Printing, England, 77-79; instr, Mass Inst Technol Creative Photo Lab, 81, DeCordova Mus Sch, Lincoln, Mass, 82-83 & Northeastern Univ, Mass, 83. *Bibliog:* Au Coeur d'Elle Meme, Le Nouveau Photo-Cinema, Paris, 76; Roberto Salbitani (auth), Linda Benedict-Jones Progresso Fotografico, Milan, 78; Women on Women, Avrum Press, London, 78. *Publ:* Auth, biography, Print Letter 24, Switzerland, 79; auth, Minor White: Contributions & controversy, Positive, Mass Inst Technol, 81; auth, Lee Friedlander, Positive, Mass Inst Technol, 82; auth, Whither documentary? Ten contemporary British photographers, Positive, Mass Inst Technol, 82. *Dealer:* Galerie Fiolet Herengracht 86 Amsterdam Holland; Photogr Gallery 8-12 Gt Newport St London England. *Mailing Add:* 43 Royal Ave Cambridge MA 02138

BENEDIKT, MICHAEL
CONSULTANT, CRITIC
b New York, NY, May 26, 35. *Study:* NY Univ, BA; Columbia Univ, MA. *Pos:* New York corresp, Art Int Zurich, Switz, 65-67; ed assoc, Art News, New York, 63-72; consult mixed media, NY State Coun Arts, 77; mem, NY Art Critics Circle, 79-; designated panelist, Nat Endowment Humanities, 82- *Teaching:* Vis prof writing, Sarah Lawrence Col, Bronxville, NY, 69-74; assoc prof, Hampshire Col, Amherst, Mass, 73-75; vis prof writing, Vassar Col, 76-77 & Boston Univ, 77-79. *Awards:* Guggenheim Fel, 68; Nat Endowment Arts Fel, 79. *Res:* 19th century French painting; surrealist poetry-art relationships; realist tradition in American art, historical and contemporary. *Publ:* Auth, The minimum of melodrama: Fairfield Porter, Art News, 64; contribr, New York Letter on Sculpture as Architecture in Minimal Art (anthology), 68; The visionary French Symbolist painters in the Grand Eccentrics (anthology), 71; auth, Notes on Yoko Ono, Art & Artists, 72; ed, The Poetry of Surrealism (anthology), Little Brown, 75; Poetry & Videotape in New Artists Video, Dutton, 78; and others. *Mailing Add:* 315 West 98th St New York NY 10025

BENENSON, EDWARD HARTLEY
COLLECTOR, PATRON
b New York, NY, Mar 27, 14. *Study:* Duke Univ, BA, 34. *Mem:* Friends Duke Univ Mus Art. *Collection:* Highly diversified, quality pieces only, ranging from Courbet to present-day artists. *Mailing Add:* 510 Park Ave New York NY 10022

BENES, BARTON LIDICE
COLLAGE ARTIST, SCULPTOR
b NJ, Nov 16, 42. *Study:* Pratt Inst, painting with Walter Murch, 60-61; Beaux Arts, Avignon, France, graphics, 68; Atelier Jean D'Orcier, Le Barroux, France, batik, 68. *Work:* Univ Iowa Mus Art; Princeton Univ Rare Bks Collection; Bibliot Nat, Paris; Nat Gallery, Australia; Art Inst Chicago. *Comn:* Fed Reserve System, Washington, DC; Am Express; Paper Works, First Bank Minneapolis; International, New York; and others. *Exhib:* Artists Books, Albright/Knox Gallery, Buffalo, 77; The Object as Poet, Renwick Gallery, Nat Collection Fine Arts, 77; The Open and Closed Book, Victoria & Albert Mus, London, Eng, 79; Patterns Plus, Dayton Art Inst, Ohio, 79; Galleriet-Lund, Sweden; 7 Artists, 7 Visions, Queens Mus, NY; The State Mus, Albany, NY; and others. *Collections Arranged:* The Book as Art, Fendrick Gallery, 76; The Animal Image, Renwick Gallery, Nat Collection Fine Arts, Washington, DC; Remains to Be Seen, Kohler Arts Ctr, Sheboygan, Wis; Decorative Fabricators, Inst Contemp Art Va Mus, Richmond; Ikons/Logos, Word As Image, Alternative Mus, New York. *Awards:* Creative Artists Pub Serv Prog grant, 77; Ariana Found Arts Grant, 82; Grant for Graphics, Rutgers Univ, 83. *Bibliog:* Lowry Thompson & Joni Miller (auth), Prince of Rubberstamps, Workman Publ Co, 78; Jacqueline Brody (auth), On and off the wall with Benes, Print Collectors Newslett, 79; New editions, Art News, 83. *Media:* Rubberstamps; Mixed. *Publ:* Illusr, Excerpts from the Diaries of the Late God, Harper & Row, 68; auth, The Dog Bite, Plainwrapper Press, 70; auth, The Mugging (A Primer of Urban Living), Winterhouse Ltd, 70; auth, I Have Found a Cockroach in Your Product, Wedgepress & Cheese, 82; illusr, Money Matters, Solo Press, 83. *Dealer:* Kathryn Markel Fine Arts 50 W 57th St New York NY 10019; Fendrick Gallery 3059 M St NW Washington DC 20007. *Mailing Add:* 463 West St Apt 956H New York NY 10014

BENGLIS, LYNDA
SCULPTOR, PAINTER
b Lake Charles, La, Oct 25, 41. *Study:* Yale Norfolk Summer Fel, 63; Newcomb Col, Tulane Univ, with Ida Kohlmeyer, Pat Trivigno, Zolton Buki & Halrold Carney, BFA, 64; Brooklyn Mus Art Sch, with Rubin Tam, Max Beckman Scholar, 65. *Work:* Whitney Mus Am Art; Solomon R Guggenheim Mus; Mus Mod Art, New York; Hokkaido Mus Mod Art, Sapporo, Japan; Gihon Found, Dallas; and others. *Comn:* Adhesive products, Walker Art Ctr, Minneapolis, 71; Hartsfield Int Airport, Atlanta, 80; Leo W O'Brien Fed Bldg, Albany, 81; Fairmont Hotel, Denver, 82; Prudential Life Insurance Co, Parsippanny, NJ, 82. *Exhib:* Directions 3: 8 Artists, Milwaukee Art Ctr, 71; one-man shows, Hayden Gallery, Mass Inst Technol, Cambridge, 71, Univ SFla Tampa, 80 & Lowe Art Mus, Miami, Fla, 80; 32nd Ann Exhib, Soc for Contemp Art, Art Inst Chicago, 72; 1973 Biennial Exhib Am Painting & Sculpture, Whitney Mus Am Art, New York, 73 & Art at Work: Recent Art From Corporate Collections, 78; 14 Artists, Baltimore Mus Art, 75; Recent Acquisitions, Solomon R Guggenheim Mus, New York, 77; Pittura Ambiente, Palazzo Reale, Milan, 79; Developments in Recent Sculpture, Whitney Mus, Am Art, 81; Galerie Albert Baronian, Brussels, 81; Univ Ariz Mus Art, Tucson, 81; and many others. *Teaching:* Asst prof, Hunter Col, 72-73, prof, 80-81; vis prof, Calif Inst Arts, 74 & 76 & Princeton Univ, 75; vis artist, Kent State Univ, 77 & Skowhegan Sch Painting & Sculpture, 79; vis prof, Univ Ariz, 81; vis artist, Sch Visual Arts, New York, 82-83. *Awards:* Australian Art Coun Award, 76; Nat Endowment Arts Grant, 79. *Bibliog:* Robert Pincus-Witten (auth), The Frozen Gesture & Benglis, Video Medium to Media, In: Post Minimalism, 77; Doug Davis (auth), article, Art Cult, 77; Lynda Benglis (auth), interview in Ocular, summer 79. *Dealer:* Paula Cooper Gallery 155 Wooster St New York NY 10012. *Mailing Add:* 222 Bowery St New York NY 10012

BENGSTON, BILLY AL
PAINTER
b Dodge City, Kans, June 7, 34. *Work:* Mus Mod Art, New York; Art Inst Chicago; Los Angeles Co Mus Art; Whitney Mus Am Art, New York; Mus of Contemp Art, Houston, Tex; and others. *Exhib:* Chicago Biennial Painting Exhib, Art Inst Chicago, 63 & 72; Eighth Biennial, Sao Paulo, Brazil, also shown Smithsonian Inst, 65; Whitney Ann Painting Exhib, Whitney Mus Am Art, 67, 69 & 79; retrospective, Los Angeles Co Mus Art, 68; Kompas IV, Stekelijk van Abbemuseum, Eindhoven, Holland, 69; Billy Al Bengston Watercolors, Honolulu Acad Arts, Hawaii, 80; Billy Al Bengston Watercolors 1974-1980, Corcoran Gallery Art, Washington, DC, 80; A Decade of Billy Al Bengston: The Seventies, San Diego State Univ, Calif, 81. *Pos:* Founder, Artist Studio, Venice, Calif, 60; pres, Westside Strokers, Los Angeles, 78-79; pres, Pelican Club Publ, Ltd. *Awards:* Nat Found Arts Grant, 67; Tamarind Fel, Tamarind Lithography Workshop through Ford Found, 68 & 82; Guggenheim Found Fel, 75. *Bibliog:* Fidel Danieli (auth), Billy Al Bengston's Dentos, 5/67 & Peter Plagens (auth), Billy Al Bengston's new paintings, 3/75, Artforum. *Media:* Mixed. *Publ:* Coauth, Business cards, Heavy Indust Publ, 68; auth, Late fifties at the Ferus, Artforum, 1/69; auth, Los Angeles artists' studios, Art in Am 11-12/70. *Mailing Add:* Artist Studio 110 Mildred Ave Venice CA 90291

BENGTZ, TURE
MUSEUM DIRECTOR, PAINTER
Study: In Finland; Sch Mus Fine Arts, Boston, Mass, dipl; Slade Sch, London, Eng; Fontainebleau, Paris, France; Paige traveling scholar to Europe, summers 33-37; Tiffany Found fels, 40-41. *Work:* Mus Fine Arts, Boston; Addison Gallery, Andover, Mass; Libr Cong, Washington, DC; Seattle Art Mus, Wash; Cincinnati Art Mus, Ohio; and many other pub & pvt collections. *Comn:* Design of stained glass window, 12th century church, Finland, 68. *Exhib:* Nat Acad Design, New York; Brooklyn Mus, New York; Chicago Art Inst; Calif Palace Legion Hon, San Francisco; Am Fedn Arts Watercolor Traveling Show, Australia, India & Japan; and many other one-man shows, group exhibs & traveling exhibs. *Pos:* Tech illusr radar equip, Raytheon Corp, Waltham, Mass, 41-45; mus dir, Art Complex, Inc, Duxbury, Mass, 69-76. *Teaching:* Instr drawing & painting, Sch Mus Fine Arts, Boston, 34-38, instr artistic anat, 38-39, instr graphic arts, 39-41, head drawing & graphic arts dept, 41-69; demonstr & lectr drawing & anat, WGBH-TV, 57-60; lectrs & demonstrations drawing, composition, anat, painting & printmaking, US & abroad, currently. *Awards:* Palmer Mem Prize, Nat Acad Design, 44; Boston Mus Prize, Boston Printmakers, 65, Boston Printmakers Prize & Gendrot Prize, 69; and many others. *Bibliog:* The Lithographs of Ture Bengtz, Art Complex Mus, Duxbury Mass. *Media:* Oil, Watercolor. *Publ:* Illusr, White Squaw, Heath. *Mailing Add:* Art Complex Inc PO Box 1411 Duxbury MA 02332

BENHAM, PAMELA J
PAINTER
b Hollywood, Calif, Sep 25, 47. *Study:* Art Students League New York, with N B Hale & Bruce Dorfman, 68-71; Cooper Union, New York, with Leland Bell, Paul Resika & Cusamano, BFA, 72; Skowhegan Sch Painting & Sculpture, Maine, scholar, 73; Ecole des Beaux-Arts, Paris, Ateliere Caron, 73-75. *Exhib:* Chateau de Bois, France, 74; Mus Mod Art, Paris, 75; Place de la Bastille, Paris, 75; UNESCO, Paris, 75; Salon Grand Palais, Paris, 76; New York Coalition Women Artists, Broome St, New York, 79 & 80; and others. *Awards:* Grant, Ford Found, 69; Reginald Marsh Scholarship, 70. *Media:* Oil, Acrylic. *Dealer:* A B Condon Gallery 413 West Broadway New York NY 10012. *Mailing Add:* 2 Thompson St New York NY 10013

BENHAM, ROBERT CHARLES
PAINTER

b Gloucester, Mass, June 29, 13. *Study:* Bucksport Acad, Maine; also with Paul Strisik. *Exhib:* Allied Artist, Nat Acad, New York; Salmagundi Club, New York; Rockport Art Asn; Springfield Mus Fine Arts; Butler Mus, Ohio. *Teaching:* Instr in pvt classes. *Awards:* Curtis News Award, 69; Aldro Hibbard Award, 74; Harriet Preston Award, 74; and others. *Bibliog:* Herb Rugoff (auth), Some notions on oceans, 69, Painting fog, 75, Surf & rocks, 80, Palette Talk. *Mem:* Rockport Art Asn; North Shore Art Asn; Allied Artist of Am; Acad Artists, Springfield; Am Artists Prof League. *Media:* Oil. *Mailing Add:* 4 Harbor Rd Bass Rocks Gloucester MA 01930

BENINI
PAINTER, SCULPTOR

b Imola, Bologna, Italy, April, 17, 41. *Study:* Liceo Classico, Cento & Bologna, Italy, 54-57; Enalc, Assisi, Italy, 57-59; also with Morandi, 61-63. *Work:* Pensacola Art Ctr & Mus, Fla; Greenville Art Mus, SC; Brevard Art Ctr & Mus, Melbourne, Fla; Empire Am, Deland, Fla; Thomas Ctr Arts, Gainesville, Fla. *Exhib:* Solo exhib, Brevard Art Ctr & Mus, Melbourne, Fla, 82 & State Capitol Bldg, Tallahassee, 83-84; Baroque and Beyond, Ormond Beach Art Mus, Fla, 82; A Pilgrim's Garden, Thomas Ctr Arts, Gainesville, Fla, 82; Garden of Spatial Delights, Empire Am, Deland, Fla, 83. *Bibliog:* Sam Francis (auth), Benini: Brief Encounters, Orlando, 80; Lorraine Lind (auth), The rose: A celebration in nature and art, Evening Herald, 11/7/82. *Media:* Acrylics. *Mailing Add:* Rte 1 Box 290HA Oviedo FL 32765

BENJAMIN, KARL STANLEY
PAINTER, EDUCATOR

b Chicago, Ill, Dec 29, 25. *Study:* Northwestern Univ; Univ Redlands, BA, 49; Claremont Grad Sch, MA, 60. *Work:* Whitney Mus Am Art, New York; Los Angeles Co Mus Art; San Francisco Mus Art; Wadsworth Atheneum, Hartford, Conn; Nat Collection Fine Arts, Smithsonian Inst, Washington, DC. *Exhib:* Purist Painting, Am Fedn Arts Traveling Exhib, shown at Andrew Dickson White Mus, NY, Walker Art Ctr, Minneapolis, Minn, Speed Mus, Louisville, Ky & others, 60; Geometric Abstraction in America, Whitney Mus Am Art, 62; The Responsive Eye, Mus Mod Art, New York, 65; 30th & 35th Ann Exhib Am Painting, Corcoran Gallery, Washington, DC, 67 & 77; Pac Cities Painting, Auckland, New Zealand, 71; Painting & Sculpture in Calif: The Mod Era, San Francisco Mus of Mod Art & Nat Collection of Fine Arts, Smithsonian Inst, Washington, DC, 76-77; Los Angeles Hard Edge: The Fifties & the Seventies, Los Angeles Co Mus of Art, Los Angeles, 77; Am Art from Corp Collections, Corcoran Gallery, Washington, DC & Ala, Indianapolis & San Diego Mus, 79; Color in Contemporary Painting, Henry Gallery, Univ Wash, 82. *Teaching:* Prof art & artist-in-residence, Pomona Col. *Awards:* Nat Endow Arts Grant, 83-84. *Bibliog:* Archives Am Art (interview), Smithsonian, Calif Oral History Project. *Media:* Oil. *Dealer:* Modernism 236 8th St San Francisco CA 91403; Francine Seders Gallery 6701 Greenwood Ave N Seattle WA 98103. *Mailing Add:* 675 W Eighth St Claremont CA 91711

BENJAMIN, LLOYD WILLIAM, III
HISTORIAN, ADMINISTRATOR

b Painesville, Ohio, Sept 2, 44. *Study:* Emory Univ, BA, 66; Univ NC, Chapel Hill, PhD, 73. *Collections Arranged:* The Art of Designed Environments in the Netherlands (auth, catalog), 83-85. *Teaching:* Asst prof art hist, ECarolina Univ, 70-76, chmn dept, 74-76; from asst to assoc prof, Univ Ark, Little Rock, 76-82, chmn dept art, 80-, prof, 83-, dean, Col Fine Arts, 83- *Mem:* Am Endowment Humanities (bd mem & treas, 77-83); Southeastern Col Art Conf (bd mem, 78-83); Col Art Asn Am; Medieval Acad Am. *Res:* Twentieth century Dutch art and environmental design. *Publ:* Contribr, Rubens in Prints, Col William & Mary, 77; auth, The history of early Netherlandish painting, Studies in Iconography, 77; auth, Herbals and their illustrators, Herbarist, 81; auth, The art of designed environments in the Netherlands, Livability, 82 & Stichting Kunst Bedrijf, 83. *Mailing Add:* Dept Art Univ Ark Little Rock AR 72204

BENNETT, DON BEMCO
PAINTER, PRINTMAKER

b McGlaughlin, SDak, Jan 8, 16. *Study:* Univ Wash; Edison Voc Sch, Seattle; also with the late Eliot O'Hara. *Work:* Cheney-Cowles Fine Arts Mus, Spokane, Wash; Ford Motor Co Collection of Am Art, Dearborn, Mich. *Exhib:* Fourth Ann Art Exhib, Merchant Seamen UN, Corcoran Gallery, 46; US Info Agency Exhib Contemp Am Artists Worldwide Traveling Exhib, 60; Craftsman Competition, Pac Northwest Painters, Fry Mus, Seattle, 68; 15th Ann Exhib, Acad Artists Asn, Mus Fine Arts, Springfield, Mass, 64; Am Natural Hist Art Show, James Ford Bell Mus, Univ Minn, Minneapolis, 71. *Awards:* First Place in graphics, Acad Artists Asn, 64; Top Twenty Award, Craftsman Press, Seattle, 68; Second Place Award, Representational Watercolor, 28th Ann Exhib Idaho Artists, Boise Art Asn. *Mem:* Graphics Soc. *Media:* Watercolor, Oil; Lithography. *Publ:* Auth & illusr, Ford Times Mag, 58- *Mailing Add:* PO Box 105 Sun Valley ID 83353

BENNETT, HARRIET
PAINTER

b New York, NY. *Study:* Art Students League, with Robert Brackman & Byron Browne; Brooklyn Mus, with Minna Citron; New Sch Social Res; Pratt Graphic Art Ctr; YWCA Craft Ctr. *Work:* Five paintings, Inst High Fidelity, New York. *Exhib:* One-man shows, Cichi Gallery, Rome, Italy, 62, Galerie de L'Univ, Paris, France, 62 & Woodstock Gallery, London, Eng, 65; NY Artists Equity Asn, 78; Murray Hill Art Asn, New York, 79. *Awards:* Falmouth Artists Guild Award, 62; Int Women's Slide Exhib Award, 75-76.

Bibliog: Mario Federici (auth), Harriet Bennett's paintings, Brochure, Rome, 1/62; Enrico Centardi (auth), Harriet Bennett, Voce Del Sud, Rome, 2/3/62; Raymond Charmet (auth), Fusion in light, Arts, Lettres, Spectacles du, Paris, 9/6/62. *Mem:* Artist's Equity Asn of New York, Inc; Women's Interart Ctr, New York; Women in the Arts, New York. *Mailing Add:* PO Box 839 Grand Cent Sta New York NY 10017

BENNETT, JAMIE
ENAMELIST, SCULPTOR

b Philadelphia, Pa, Oct 6, 48. *Study:* Univ Ga, BBA & BFA; State Univ NY New Paltz, MFA. *Work:* Univ Ga; Ark Art Ctr. *Exhib:* Schumk-Tendenzen, Schumk Mus, Pforzheim, Ger, 77; Nat Metal Invitational, Humboldt State Univ, Arcata, Calif, 77; Am Metal, Schunk Mus, WGer, Victoria & Albert Mus, London & traveling, western Europe, 79-81; one-man shows, Belson-Brown Gallery, Ketchum Idaho, 80 & Eastern Ky Univ, 80; and others. *Collections Arranged:* Six at Univ Tex, Arlington, group exhib & symp, 77; Enamelists, Established & Emerging, Chastain Arts Ctr, 77. *Pos:* Artist-in-residence, Kohler Art Ctr, Sheboygan, Wis, 74; vis artist, Penland Sch Crafts, 74, 76, 77 & 80, Fla Int Univ, 77 & Colo Mountain Col, 77 & 78, Boston Univ, 79-80, Carnegie-Mellon Univ, 80 & Haystack, Deer Isle, Maine, 80. *Teaching:* Instr metal, Bradley Univ, Peoria, Ill, 74-76; asst prof metal & drawing, Memphis Acad Art, Tenn, 76- *Awards:* Nat Endowment for the Arts, Craftsmen's fel, 75 & 79; First Place, Nat Enamels Exhib, Alexandria, Va, 79; First Place, Nat Prints, Drawings & Crafts Exhib, Ark Art Ctr, Little Rock, 79. *Bibliog:* Sandy Ballatore (auth), Jewelers USA, 3/76 & Enamelists, 11/76, Art News; Lisa Hammel (auth), Enameling, New York Times, 12/76. *Mem:* Soc NAm Goldsmiths. *Media:* Precious Metals; Enamels. *Publ:* Contribr, Jewelry Making, Prentice Hall, 74; contribr, The Box Book & The Mirror Book, Crown, 76. *Mailing Add:* Memphis Art Academy Overton Park Memphis TN 38112

BENNETT, PHILOMENE
PAINTER, EDITOR

b Lincoln, Nebr, Jan 2, 35. *Study:* Univ Nebr, BFA, 56. *Work:* Albrecht Art Mus, St Joseph, Mo; Mushkin Art Mus, Atcheson, Kans; Atkins Mus Fine Arts, William Rockhill Nelson Gallery Art, Kansas City, Mo. *Comn:* Paintings, Crown Ctr Hotel, Kansas City, Mo, 74 & Rockhurst Col Libr, Kansas City, Mo, 75; stained glass windows, St Charles Church, North Kansas City, Mo, 74; 14 Stations of the Cross, Conway Chapel, Rockhurst Col, Kansas City, Mo, 75. *Exhib:* 7 Mo Painters, Mo State Coun on Arts Presentation, 71; Selected Painters' Invitational, Mulvane Mus, Topeka, Kans, 77; Biennial, Joslyn Art Mus, Omaha, Nebr, 78; Summer Show, Atkins Mus Fine Arts, William Rockhill Nelson Gallery Art, Kansas City, Mo, 79; Artists Choose Artists, Univ Mo-Kansas City, 79; Porcelains, Sheldon Gallery, Univ Nebr, 81. *Pos:* Mem prof bd, Mo Arts Coun, Kansas City, 79-82; art ed, Helicon Nine, 79-; mem bd, Kansas City Arts Council, 82-83. *Teaching:* Artist-in-residence painting, Rockhurst Col, 69-70, Kans City Art Inst, 83; pvt instr painting, Bennett-Marak Studio, Kansas City, Mo, 73-79. *Awards:* Purchase Award, William Rockhill Nelson Gallery Art, Kansas City, Mo, 62; Award Winner, Univ Mo-Kansas City Women's Caucus for Arts, 77; Eller Outdoor Advert & Kansas City Arts Comn Billboard Award, 79. *Bibliog:* Film-interview, Johnson Co Community Col, 74; Walter Brayman (auth), Philomene Bennett, interview, Forum, Kansas City Artists Coalition, 79; Patrick White (auth), article, New Art Examiner, 82. *Mem:* Kansas City Artists Coalition (co-founder, vpres, 75, pres, 76, prog chmn, 77); Women's Nat Caucus for Arts. *Media:* Acrylic, Oil. *Publ:* Missouri Historical Review, Mo State Hist Soc, 75; Artists at work, Artefact, summer 79. *Dealer:* Batz Gallery Kansas City MO; Jan Weiner Gallery Topeka KS. *Mailing Add:* 8900 Renner Rd Shawnee Mission KS 66219

BENNETT, RAINEY
PAINTER, ILLUSTRATOR

b Marion, Ind, July 26, 07. *Study:* Univ Chicago, PhB, 30; Art Inst Chicago; Am Acad Art; Art Students League; George Grosz-Maurice Sterne Sch. *Work:* Metrop Mus Art, Mus Mod Art; Cranbrook Mus; Art Inst Chicago; many pvt collections. *Comn:* Mural, Post Off, Dearborn, Mich, 37, Rushville, Ill, 38 & Naperville, Ill, 41; 13 panel mural, Neil House, Columbus, Ohio, 39; watercolors, comn by Nelson Rockefeller, Standard Oil Co, SAm, 39 & 41. *Exhib:* Downtown Gallery, New York; Art Inst Chicago; Cleveland Mus; Toledo Mus; Whitney Mus; Fairweather Hardin Gallery, Chicago. *Pos:* Supvr, Fed Art Proj, Chicago, 35-38. *Dealer:* Fairweather Hardin Gallery 101 E Ontario Chicago IL. *Mailing Add:* 5761 Dorchester Ave Chicago IL 60637

BENNEY, ROBERT
PAINTER, ILLUSTRATOR

b New York, NY. *Study:* Cooper Union; Nat Acad Design; Grand Cent Art Sch; Art Students League; also with Harry Wickey, Frank A Nankivell, Harry Sternberg & Harvey Dunn. *Work:* Corcoran Gallery Art, Washington, DC; USN, USA, USAF & USMC Art Collections, Washington, DC; de Young Mus Art, San Francisco; Mariners Mus Art, Newport News, Va; Chrysler Collection, Detroit Mus, Mich; and others. *Comn:* Paintings, Am Sugar Refining Co, New York, 52-55; paintings of hist events, Reader's Digest, 64-; Vietnam combat art, USMC, 68-70; and many portraits. *Exhib:* Nat Gallery Art, Washington, DC; Metrop Mus Art, New York; de Young Mus; Brooklyn Mus; Corcoran Gallery Art; Fine Arts Gallery, San Diego; Portland Art Mus, Ore; Norfolk Mus Arts & Sci; Dallas Mus Fine Arts, Tex; one-man shows, Mus City New York, Lincoln Ctr Libr/Mus, Architectural League, New York, New York Public Libr, Pratt Inst & Soc Illustrators; Carnegie Inst; Brooklyn Mus; Art Inst Chicago; and others. *Teaching:* Instr painting, drawing & compos, Sch Visual Arts; instr illus, Pratt Inst, 49-52; assoc prof fine & com art, Dutchess Co Col, 63-73. *Awards:* First Award, Philadelphia

Mus Art, Pa; Gold Medal, Chicago Art Dirs Club; Cert Commendation Fine Arts, USN, 74. *Mem:* Soc Illusr; Artists Equity Asn; life mem Art Students League; Artists & Writers Asn; Appraisers Asn Am. *Media:* Oil, Acrylic, Etching, Aquatint. *Publ:* Illusr, Reader's Digest, True, Argosy, Time, Life & Fortune; contribr, Life's Picture History of World War II, Our Flying Navy--James Jones' WWII, Men without Guns, Life of Joshua & others. *Mailing Add:* 50 W 96th St New York NY 10025

BENSON, ELAINE K G
DEALER, WRITER
b Philadelphia, Pa, Apr 30, 24. *Study:* Univ Pa, BA, 44. *Pos:* Dir pub rels, Philadelphia Col Art, 57-64; dir, Elaine Benson Gallery, 65-; co-dir summer art prog, Southampton Col, 67-69; ed, Hamptons Mag, 83- & Our Hampton Heritage, 83-84. *Teaching:* Coordr fashion fields, Philadelphia Col Art, 63-64. *Mem:* Am Fedn Art. *Specialty:* Contemporary European and American paintings, sculpture and fine crafts. *Publ:* Criticism and articles on art and artists in many publications. *Mailing Add:* PO Box AJ Bridgehampton NY 11932

BENSON, ELIZABETH POLK
HISTORIAN, WRITER
b Washington, DC, May 13, 24. *Study:* Wellesley Col, BA, 45; Catholic Univ Am, MA, 56. *Pos:* Cur & aide, Nat Gallery Art, Washington, DC, 47-61; cur, Dumbarton Oaks, Washington, DC, 62-79; dir, Ctr Pre-Columbian Studies, 71-78; res assoc, Inst Andean Studies, Berkeley, Calif, 80- *Teaching:* Lectr, Catholic Univ, Washington, DC, 68-69; adj prof, Columbia Univ, New York, 73. *Mem:* Arts Club Wash; Soc Women Geographers; Asn Latin Am Art; Soc Am Archaeology. *Res:* Pre-Columbian art of the Moche (Peru), Maya and Olmec. *Publ:* Auth, The Maya World, Thomas Y Crowell, 67, 72 & 77; auth, The Mochica: A Culture of Peru, Praeger Publ, 72; auth, A man and a feline in Mochica art, Dumbarton Oaks, 74; ed, The Olmec and their neighbors, Dumbarton Oaks, 81; coauth, Museums of the Andes, Newsweek Books, 81. *Mailing Add:* 8314 Seven Locks Rd Bethesda MD 20817

BENSON, GERTRUDE ACKERMAN
WRITER, CRITIC
b Rumania, Aug 6, 04. *Study:* Hunter Col, BA; NY Univ Inst Fine Arts, MA; Princeton Univ, Carnegie fels art & archaeol, 28-31. *Pos:* Feature writer & critic, New York Times, 31-57; Philadelphia Bull, 49-64, Philadelphia Inquirer, 50-57 & Drexel Univ, 64-70; art ed, Philadelphia Inquirer, 50-57. *Teaching:* Asst prof humanities, Philadelphia Col Art, 60-63. *Publ:* Auth, Greco-Roman influence on Utrecht Psalter, Art Bulletin, 31; Exploding the Van Gogh myth, Mag Art, 35; La tour & le Nain, Mag Art, 35; Lewis Carroll, New York Times Mag, 57; interviews with John Marin, Jacob Epstein, DeKooning, Stuart Davis, Lipchitz, Knaths, Rouault, Nolde, Calder, Watkins, Shahn & many others; also many articles & book reviews in nat mag & newspapers. *Mailing Add:* 201 W 74th St New York NY 10023

BENSON, MARTHA J
GALLERY DIRECTOR, SCULPTOR
b Kansas City, Mo, July 30, 28. *Study:* Univ Kansas City; Baker Univ, BA; spec study Kans Univ, Iowa State Univ & Utrecht, Holland. *Comn:* five wood-assemblage panels, St David's Episcopal Church, Ames, 75; six wood-assemblage panels, Chapel, Mary Greeley Hosp, Ames, 77. *Collections Arranged:* Lithuanian Book Plates, 70; Twelve Dutch Potters, 71; Three Chilean Printmakers, 73; Technol & the Artist-Craftsman-A Nat Crafts Exhib, 73-75; The Artists of San Miguel, 74-75; The Octagon Art Ctr, Ames; British Ceramics Today, US Tour, 79-81; and others. *Pos:* Dir, The Octagon Art Ctr, Ames, 68-; bd dirs, British Am Art Asn. *Teaching:* Prof oil painting, Iowa State Univ, 69, basic design, 72. *Awards:* Recognition Award: One of Five Outstanding Women Art Dirs, Iowa Women's Caucus, 76; Nat Endowment Arts Fel, 78-79. *Bibliog:* Annabelle Liu (auth), Martha Benson-A Profile, Craft Connection, 75. *Media:* Wood. *Mailing Add:* 928 Garfield Ames IA 50010

BENSON, ROBERT FRANKLIN
PAINTER, EDUCATOR
b Arcata, Calif, Apr 3, 48. *Study:* Humboldt Co Schs, Indust Arts Scholar, 65; Humboldt State Univ, Art Dept Scholar, 70 & BA, 71; Univ Ill, Creative & Performing Arts Fel, 72; Univ Ill, Champaign-Urbana, MFA, 73; also with Morris Graves, 73. *Exhib:* Six from Northwest Coast, Henry Galleries, Univ Wash, Seattle, 75; one-man show, Univ Southern Calif, Los Angeles, 76; Humboldt Artists, Ankrum Gallery, Los Angeles, 77; Ankrum Gallery, Los Angeles, 78, 79, 80 & 81; Foster White Gallery, Seattle, Wash, 80. *Teaching:* Instr studio courses, Col of the Redwoods, Eureka, Calif, 73- *Dealer:* Ankrum Art Gallery 657 N LaCienega Los Angeles CA 95501. *Mailing Add:* 541 First Ave Blue Lake CA 95525

BENTHAM, DOUGLAS WAYNE
SCULPTOR
b Rosetown, Sask, Apr 16, 47. *Study:* Univ Sask, BA & advan degree in fine arts. *Work:* Sask Arts Bd, Regina, Sask; Edmonton Art Gallery, Alta; Art Gallery Windsor, Ont; Univ Sask, Saskatoon; Univ Calgary, Alta. *Comn:* Outdoor sculpture (corten steel), Nat Sci Libr, Ottawa, comn by Govt Can Dept Pub Works. *Exhib:* Mendel Art Gallery, 69, 70 & 72; one-man shows, Regina Pub Libr Art Gallery, 70 & 73, Edmonton Art Gallery, 73; Saskatchewan-Art & Artists, Norman Mackenzie Art Gallery, Regina, 71; West 71, Edmonton Art Gallery; Kingston Spring Exhib, Ont, 72; Waddington Galleries, Montreal, 74; Saskatoon Pub Art Gallery, 74; Glenbow-Alta Art Gallery, 75; Art Gallery of York Univ, Toronto, 76; three-man exhib, Can Cult Ctr, Paris, 79. *Awards:* For work in sculpture, Sask Arts

Bd, 69; Can Coun Arts Bursaries, 70-71 & 72-73; Purchase Award for Sculpture, West '71, Edmonton Art Gallery, 71. *Bibliog:* Terrence Heath (auth), Bentham's recent sculpture, Winter 75-76 & David Burnett (auth), Three Toronto Reviews, Winter 76-77, Artscanada; Karen Wilkin (auth), Rugged individualists with no urge to roam, Art News, 2/79. *Mem:* Royal Can Acad Arts. *Mailing Add:* RR 2 Dundurn SK S0K 1K0 Canada

BENTLEY, CLAUDE
PAINTER, MURALIST
b New York, NY, June 9, 15. *Study:* Northwestern Univ; Art Inst Chicago. *Work:* Krannert Mus, Univ Ill; Denver Art Mus; Art Inst Chicago; Ill State Mus; plus others. *Comn:* Murals, 3600 Lake Shore Dr Bldg, Chicago, Ill; comn as design consult, Plaza del Lago Shopping Ctr, Winnetka, Ill. *Exhib:* Corcoran Gallery Art; San Francisco Mus Art; Whitney Mus Am Art; Art Inst Chicago; Denver Art Mus; plus others. *Awards:* John G Curtis Jr Award, 63; Old Orchard Art Fair Award, 63; Purchase Award, Ill State Mus, 63; and others. *Bibliog:* Literary Times, 4/65; Creating art from anything, Meilach, 68. *Media:* Multimedia, Collage. *Collection:* African, oceanic, pre-Columbian art & Spanish colonial art of Mex and NMex. *Dealer:* Little Plaza Gallery 125 E Palace Ave Sante Fe NM 87501. *Mailing Add:* 310 Otero St Santa Fe NM 87501

BENTON, FLETCHER
SCULPTOR
b Jackson, Ohio, Feb 25, 31. *Study:* Miami Univ, BFA. *Work:* Whitney Mus Am Art, New York; Hirshhorn Mus, Washington, DC; San Francisco Mus Mod Art, Calif; Univ Calif, Los Angeles; Rockefeller Collection, New York; and others. *Comn:* IBM Corp, Morgan Hill, Calif; Thruman Arnold Bldg, Washington, DC; Univ Calif, Los Angeles; Davies Symphony Hall, San Francisco; public sculpture, City of Offend Bach, WGermany; and others. *Exhib:* Art Inst Chicago 28th Ann, 68; Whitney Mus Am Art Sculpture Ann, 68 & 73; Am Sculpture of the 60's, Los Angeles Co Mus, Calif; The Arts Council Great Britain, Hayward Gallery, London; Albright-Knox Art Gallery, Buffalo, NY, 69 & 71; San Francisco Mus Art, 70 & 76; Int Mus Fine Arts, Osaka, Japan, 70; Stanford Univ Mus, Calif, 70 & 71; Hirshhorn Mus, Washington, DC; Univ Minn, Minneapolis, 76; John Berggruen Gallery, San Francisco, 77, 79 & 81; plus others. *Teaching:* Instr, Calif Col Arts & Crafts, 59 & San Francisco Art Inst, 64-68; prof art, San Jose State Univ, 68- *Awards:* Award in Sculpture for Work of Distinction, Am Acad & Inst Arts & Letters, 79; President's Scholar Award, San Jose State Univ, Calif; Award of Hon for Outstanding Achievement in Sculpture, San Francisco Art Comn, 82. *Bibliog:* Peter Selz (auth), article in Directions in Kinetic Sculpture, Univ Calif, Berkeley, 66; George Rickey (auth), Constructivist Tendencies, 71; J Butterfield (auth), Interview with Fletcher Benton, Art Int, 80. *Dealer:* John Berggruen Gallery 228 Grant Ave San Francisco CA 94108. *Mailing Add:* 250 Dore St San Francisco CA 94103

BENTON, SUZANNE E
SCULPTOR, ART WRITER
b New York, NY, Jan 21, 36. *Study:* Queens Col, New York, BA(fine arts), 56; studies in New York at Art Students League, Columbia Univ, NY Univ, Brooklyn Col, Brooklyn Mus Art Sch & Mus Mod Art; Silvermine Col Art, Conn. *Work:* Oakton Community Col, Ill; Nat Mus Mod Art, New Delhi, India; Birla Acad, Calcutta, India; Tokyo Sch Fine Arts, Japan; Deree Pierce Col, Athens, Greece; and others. *Comn:* Sculptured theatre sets, Viveca Lindfors I Am A Woman Theatre Co, 73; The Sun Queen, large-scale bronze sculpture & Throne of the Sun Queen, bronze & corten steel, Art Park, Lewiston, NY, 75. *Exhib:* Expo 74, Spokane, Wash, 74; Touching Ritual, Wadsworth Atheneum, Hartford, Conn, 75; one-person shows, Helenic Am Union, Athens, Greece, 76 & Korean Cult Ctr, New York, 83; Oklahoma City Univ, 81; Amerika Haus, Koln, WGer, 83; and others. *Pos:* Convener-coordr, Arts Festival-Metamorphosis I, New Haven, Conn, 69-70 & Conn Feminists in the Arts, 69-72; producer-dir, Four Chosen Women, New York, 72; art consult, Xerox, 73-76; art consult, Boeringer Ingelheim Ltd, 80- *Teaching:* Instr welded sculpture, Brookfield Craft Ctr, Brookfield, Conn, 72-73. *Awards:* Susan B Anthony Award, Eastern Regional Conf, Nat Orgn Women, 72; Sculpture Award Number One, Conn Artists, Stamford Mus, Conn, 76; Amelia Peabody Award, Nat Asn Artists, 80. *Bibliog:* Ivan Kostka, Masks that Bare a Woman's Soul, Statesman Ltd, India, 77; article, New York Times, 12/82. *Mem:* Artists Equity; Am Crafts Coun; Nat Orgn Women, Women Arts; hon mem Nat Korean Sculptress Asn; Nat Asn Women Artists. *Media:* Welded Metal, Monoprints. *Publ:* Contribr, Masks, Face Coverings and Headgear, Van Nostrand Reinhold, 73; contribr, Woman in the Year 2000, Arbor House, 74; auth, The Art of Welded Sculpture, Van Nostrand Reinhold, 75; illusr, Women Artists in America, Collins, 75; contribr, Survivor's Box, Possum Press, 77. *Mailing Add:* 22 Donnelly Dr Ridgefield CT 06877

BENTOV, MIRTALA
SCULPTOR
b Kharkov, USSR, Apr 29, 29; US citizen. *Study:* Boston Mus, Sch, cert; Grande Chaumiere, Paris, France, with Zadkine; Ecole Arts Decoratifs, Paris, with Couturier; Tufts Univ, BFA(magna cum laude), 65. *Work:* Park Synagogue Mus, Cleveland, Ohio; Art Complex Mus, Duxbury, Mass; Ford Motor Co, Detroit, Mich; Tufts Univ; Harvard Univ. *Comn:* Medal, Sixth Cong, Int Soc Hemat, 56; portraits, Missionary Order Maryknoll, NY, 62; portrait, Slavic Depts of Harvard Univ & Mass Inst Technol, 69; portrait of Pres Milton Grahm, Grahm Jr Col, Boston, 70; St Alan's Church, Troy, NY, 83. *Exhib:* One-person shows, Attleboro Mus, Mass, 78, Cayuga Mus, Auburn, NY, 81, Bentley Col, 81, Roerich Mus, NY, 83 & Univ Mass, Boston, 83; and others. *Awards:* Second Prize Sculpture, Boston Art Festival, 56;

Boston Mus Sch Albert Whitin Traveling Scholar, 57; Prize, Providence Art Club, 72. *Media:* Bronze. *Publ:* Auth (Mirtala Kardinalovska), Poems (in Russian), Madrid, 72 & Rainbow Bridge (in Ukrainian), New York, 76; auth, Thought-Forms, sculptures & poetry, Branden Press, Boston, 75; auth, Mandalas, sculptures & commentary, Boston, 80. *Dealer:* Pucker-Safrai Gallery 171 Newbury St Boston MA 02116. *Mailing Add:* 241 Glezen Lane Wayland MA 01778

BEN TRE, HOWARD
SCULPTOR, DRAFTSMAN
b Brooklyn, NY, May 13, 49. *Study:* Portland State Univ, BSA, 78; RI Sch Design, MFA, 80. *Work:* Metrop Mus Art, New York; Nat Mus Mod Art, Tokyo, Japan; Nat Mus Am Hist, Smithsonian Inst; Leigh Yawkey Woodson Art Mus, Wausau, Wis; Mus Art, RI Sch Design. *Comn:* Outdoor installation, Vernal House, Los Angeles, 83. *Exhib:* New Glass Touring Exhib, Corning Mus Glass, Metrop Mus Art & Renwick Gallery, Nat Collection Art, 78-82; Contemp Glass, Nat Mus Mod Art, Kyoto & Tokyo, Japan; Art Gallery Western Australia, Perth, 82; World Glass Now 82, Hokaido Mus Mod Art, Sapporo, Japan, 82; Four Sculptors, Jesse Besser Mus, Alpena, Mich, 82; Columns, Ornament & Sculpture, Cooper Hewitt Mus, New York, 82. *Awards:* Grant, RI State Coun Arts, 79; Nat Endowment Arts Fel, 80; Grant, Change Inc, 82. *Bibliog:* T Brewster (auth), Avant glass, Life Mag, 2/82; K Baker (auth), Howard Ben Tre--Columns, Arts Mag, 9/82; B Jepson (auth), This sculptor's world is made of glass, Wall St J, 11/9/83. *Media:* Cast Glass. *Dealer:* Habatat Galleries Lathrup Village MI & Bay Harbor Islands, FL. *Mailing Add:* 115 Elton St Providence RI 02906

BENTZ, HARRY DONALD
EDUCATOR, PAINTER
b Robesonia, Pa, Dec 2, 31. *Study:* Kutztown State Col, 53; Pa State Univ, with Hobson Pittman, 58; Lehigh Univ, 68; watercolor portraiture with Lester Stone. *Work:* Bank of Pa, Reading. *Comn:* Two murals, Spec Educ Ctr, Reading Sch Dist, 62; 15 display units, Daniel Boone Homestead, Birdsboro, Pa, 63. *Exhib:* Pa Art Educ Exhib, Millen Penn Mem Mus, 54; Washington Co Mus of Fine Arts Exhib, 65-67; Second Ann Watercolor Exhib, Millersville State Col, 76. *Teaching:* Art, Columbia High Sch, 55-60; art supervisor, Reading Sch Dist, 60-71; prof painting, Shippensburg State Col, 70-, chmn dept art, 71- *Awards:* Hayes Art Materials Award, 43rd Ann Cumberland Valley Exhib, 75; Purchase Award, 43rd Ann Cumberland Valley Exhib, Farmers & Merchants Bank, 75; First Prize, Huntingdon Co Arts Festival, Huntingdon Co Arts Coun, 76. *Mem:* Nat Art Educ Asn; Pa Art Educ Asn; Cumberland Valley Arts Coun; Pa Soc Watercolor Painters. *Media:* Watercolor, Oil. *Mailing Add:* RD 5 Shippensburg PA 17257

BENY, ROLOFF
PHOTOGRAPHER, WRITER
b Medicine Hat, Alta, Jan 7, 24. *Study:* Banff Sch Fine Arts, scholar, 39; Trinity Col, Univ Toronto, BA & BFA, 45; State Univ Iowa, with Mauricio Lasansky, MA & MFA(fel), 47; Columbia Univ; Inst Fine Art, NY Univ, scholar, 47-48; study & travel in Europe, 48-49 & 51-52; Univ Lethbridge, LLD, 72. *Work:* Nat Gallery Can, Ottawa, Ont; Art Gallery of Ont, Toronto; Mus Mod Art, New York; Milione Gallery, Milan, Italy; Redfern Gallery, London, Eng; plus many other pub & pvt collections. *Comn:* Photographic murals, Nesbitt-Thomson, Toronto-Dominion Bank Ctr, 67; Image Canada (38 photo-murals), comn for Fed Pavilion of Expo, Montreal, 67; The Renaissance (photo exhib), Ontario Music Educ Asn & Govt Ont Coun Arts, 68; Island-Ceylon (book with John Lindsay), Govt Ceylon, 71; Persia--Bridge of Turquoise, Empress of Iran, 75. *Exhib:* Ont Soc Artists Show, Art Gallery Toronto, 45; 32nd Nat Exhib, Soc Am Etchers, Gravers, Lithographers, New York, 47; Second Nat Print Ann Exhib, Brooklyn Mus, NY, 48; Exhib Current Am Prints, Dept Fine Arts, Carnegie Inst, 48; Nat Gallery Can, Ottawa; Palace of the Legion of Honor, San Francisco; San Francisco Mus; Libr of Cong, Washington, DC; Dallas Mus of Fine Art, Tex; plus many other group & one-man shows. *Awards:* Can Gold Medal, 67; Gold Medal, Int Bk Fair, 68; Can Coun Award, 68. *Bibliog:* Merle Shain (auth), Roloff Beny in Rome, Chatelaine, 5/7/70; Kay Kritzwiser (auth), Roloff Beny: Breathtaking odyssey, Toronto Globe & Mail, 5/1/71; Arnold Edinborough (auth), Superb camera art of Roloff Beny, Financial Post, 5/22/71. *Mem:* Life mem Royal Can Acad. *Publ:* Coauth, The Thrones of Earth & Heaven, 58, A Time of Gods, 62, Pleasure of Ruins, 64, To Every Thing There is a Season, 67, Japan in Colour, 67 & In Italy, 74; and others. *Mailing Add:* 432 13th St S Lethbridge AB T1J 2V9 Canada

BENZ, LEE R
PRINTMAKER, PAINTER
b Neponset, Ill. *Study:* Bradley Univ, BA & MA; Salzburg Col, Austria. *Exhib:* Aurora, 79; Western Ill Univ, Macomb, 79, 81 & 83; Ill Cent Col, East Peoria, 79 & 82; Colorprint USA, 79-81, Women & Art, Springfield, Ill, 79; Prints 1400-1979, Springfield Art Mus, 79. *Teaching:* Prof printmaking, design & drawing, Ill Cent Col, 69-83, retired. *Awards:* Printmaking Salon of 50 States Award, NY, 74; Rennick Award, Peoria, 74, 76, 77 & 83; Purchase Award/Printmaking, Quincy, Ill, 77; Ill Art League Show, 81-82. *Mem:* Peoria Art Guild; Lakeview Ctr; Nat Soc Lit & Arts; Int Soc Artists; Ill Art League; and others. *Media:* Intaglio, Woodcut; Watercolor. *Dealer:* Peoria Art Guild 1831 N Knoxville Peoria IL 61604; Lakeview Ctr 1125 Lake St Peoria IL 61604. *Mailing Add:* 1125 Fondulac Dr East Peoria IL 61611

BEN-ZION
PAINTER, SCULPTOR
b Ukraine, July 7, 1897; US citizen. *Work:* Mus Mod Art, Metrop Mus Art & Whitney Mus Am Art, New York; Art Inst Chicago; Jewish Mus, New York; plus others. *Exhib:* Advancing American Art, State Dept Traveling Show, 47; Bezalel Mus, Jerusalem, Israel, 57; A Retrospect, Jewish Mus, New York, 59; Whitney Mus Am Art Rev, 60-61; Collector's Choice, Denver Art Mus, Colo, 61; Retrospective, Mus of Haifa, 75 & 78. *Teaching:* Instr painting, Cooper Union, 43-50; instr painting, Ball State Univ, summer 56; instr painting, Univ Iowa, summer 59. *Bibliog:* Ralph Pearson (auth), The Modern Renaissance in American Art, Harper & Row, 54; Emery Grossman (auth), Art & Tradition, Thomas Yoseloff, 67. *Media:* Oil, Watercolor; Ironwork. *Publ:* Eight Portfolios of Etchings. *Mailing Add:* 329 W 20th St New York NY 10011

BERD, MORRIS
PAINTER, EDUCATOR
b Philadelphia, Pa, Mar 12, 14. *Study:* Philadelphia Col Art; Univ per Strangeri, Perugia, Italy, cert. *Work:* Philadelphia Mus Art; Pa Acad Fine Arts, Philadelphia; Philadelphia Col Art; Arco Collection, Los Angeles; Univ Pa Law Col; and others. *Comn:* History of Oil (mural), Sun Oil Co, Franklin Inst; History of Architecture (mural), Gimbel Bros, Philadelphia. *Exhib:* Many Pa Acad Fine Arts Ann & Philadelphia Mus Art Regionals; also over 15 one-man shows, including Wilcox Gallery, Swarthmore Col, 73 & The Four Season, Marian Locks Gallery, 80; Drawing Exhib, Beaver Col, 76; Sketch Bk Exhib, Philadelphia Col Art, 77-83. *Teaching:* Prof painting, Philadelphia Col Art, 36-76, co-chmn dept, 50-71, prof emer, 82. *Awards:* Silver Medal, YMHA Jubilee Show; Katzman Prize, Philadelphia Print Club, 62. *Media:* Mixed. *Publ:* Alan Gussow (auth), A Sense of Place, Vol II, 74; William Scott (auth), Four seasons, Am Artist, 2/80. *Mailing Add:* 350 Howarth Rd Media PA 19063

BEREN, STANLEY O
PATRON
b Parkersburg, WVa, Feb 1, 20. *Study:* Harvard Col, AB, 41, Harvard Univ, MBA, 43. *Pos:* Pres, Wichita Art Mus Mem Found Inc, 68, chmn bd, Wichita Art Mus, 70-72, mem bd, 72-; mem adv bd, JFK Ctr, 70- *Mem:* Am Asn Mus; Int Coun Mem. *Interests:* Special interest in raising funds for accessions for Wichita Art Mus. *Collection:* Modern painting and pre-Columbian artifacts. *Mailing Add:* 257 N Broadway Wichita KS 67202

BERG, SIRI
PAINTER, INSTRUCTOR
b Stockholm, Sweden; US citizen. *Study:* Inst Art & Archit, Univ Brussels; Pratt Graphics Ctr, New York. *Work:* Chase Manhattan Bank, New York; Carter Orgn, New York; Ted Bates Advert, Stockholm, Sweden; Herbert F Johnson Mus, Cornell Univ; Guggenheim Mus; and others. *Exhib:* One-person shows, US Cult Ctr, Jerusalem, 76, Hansen Galleries, 77, Björn Lindgreu Gallery, 81, and others; Contemp Reflections 76-77, Aldrich Mus, Ridgefield, Conn, 77; group shows, Unknown Universes, Pace Univ Gallery, 79, Sylvia Pizitz Collection, Birmingham Mus, 80; Am Scandinavian Found, New York, 81; and many others. *Pos:* Dir art prog, Riverdale Mental Health Clinic, Bronx, NY, 66- *Teaching:* Instr, Col New Rochelle, 74-82; color theory workshop, New Sch-Parsons Sch of Design, 77-82. *Awards:* NY State Coun Arts Grant, 78. *Bibliog:* David Shirley (auth), Art in public places, New York Times, 4/30/78; Helen Thomas (auth), article, Arts Mag, 1/79; Jerry Tallmer (auth), Yen for circles defined, New York Post, 3/17/79. *Mem:* Nat Asn Women Artists. *Publ:* Auth, Therapeutic art programs around the world; Uses of art in educational day treatment center, Am J Art Ther, 70. *Mailing Add:* 530 W 236th St Apt 6K Bronx NY 10463

BERG, TOM
PAINTER
b Cheyenne, Wyo, Feb 10, 43. *Study:* Univ Wyo, BA, 66, MA, 68, MFA, 72; Univ Ore, 69. *Work:* Amoco Corp, Denver; Standard Oil, Chicago; Champlin Oil, Denver; Getty Oil, Denver; Exeter Corp, Denver. *Comn:* Group mural with NY Correspondence Sch Vancouver, Nat Res Libr, Ottawa, Can, 73. *Exhib:* Twenty-third Nat Print & Drawing Show, Smithsonian Inst, Washington, DC, 73; Ten Artists, Western States Arts Found Touring Show, Mus in Idaho, NDak, NMex, Wis, Utah, Wash & Ariz, 77-79; one-person shows, Heydt Bair Gallery, Santa Fe, 80 & 81, Eason Gallery, Santa Fe, 82 & 83 & Davis-McClain Gallery, Houston, 84; Rosalind Constable Invites Santa Fe Art Festival, 81. *Collections Arranged:* US Mail (mail art), Univ Maine, Augusta, 73. *Pos:* Vis lectr, Univ Rochester, 71; artist-in-residence, Univ Maine, Augusta, 72-73; Wyo Artists in Schs Prog, 73-76 & Delta State Univ, Cleveland, Miss, 76. *Teaching:* Instr art, Point Park Col, Pittsburgh, Pa, 69-71; vis lectr painting, Univ Wyo, Laramie, summer, 77. *Awards:* Visual Arts Fel Wyo, Western States Arts Found, Denver, 76-77. *Media:* Oil. *Dealer:* Eason Gallery 338 E De Vargas Santa Fe NM 87501; Davis-McClain Galleries 2818 Kirby Dr Houston TX 77098. *Mailing Add:* Rt 1 Box 171A Santa Fe NM 87501

BERGE, DOROTHY ALPHENA
SCULPTOR, INSTRUCTOR
b Ottawa, Ill, May 8, 23. *Study:* St Olaf Col, Northfield, Minn, BA, 45; Minneapolis Sch Art, BFA, 50; Ga State Univ, Atlanta, MVA, 76. *Work:* Minneapolis Inst Art, Walker Art Ctr & Univ Minn Gallery, Minneapolis; High Mus Art, Atlanta, Ga. *Comn:* Copper wall sculpture, Mead Packaging Corp, Atlanta, Ga, 66; corten steel sculpture, Great Southwest Indust Park, Atlanta, 68 & 100 Colony Sq, 69; corten steel sculpture, St Olaf Col, comn by Mrs John Oslund, Northfield, Minn, 75; aluminum wall sculpture, Metrop Atlanta Rapid Transit Authority, 80. *Exhib:* Minn Biennial, Minneapolis Inst Art, 54; Recent Sculpture USA, New York, 57; 16 Younger Minn Artists, Walker Art Ctr, Minneapolis, 58; one-person shows, Walker Art Ctr, 59 & High Mus Art, Atlanta, 68; Ga Artists 1, 2 & 6, High Mus Art,

Atlanta, 71, 72 & 79. *Pos:* Registr, Walker Art Ctr, Minneapolis, 54-60; coordr circulating exhibs, Mus Mod Art, New York, 60-63. *Teaching:* Instr sculpture, drawing & ceramics, St Olaf Col, Northfield, Minn, 46-48; artist-in-residence sculpture, Nat Endowment Arts, Ga, 71-72. *Awards:* Purchase Award, Ford Found Prog Humanities & Arts, 60. *Media:* Welded Metal. *Dealer:* Heath Gallery 416 E Paces Ferry Rd NE Atlanta GA 30309. *Mailing Add:* 4586 Roswell Rd NW Apt Z3 Atlanta GA 30342

BERGE, HENRY
SCULPTOR
b Baltimore, Md, May 29, 08. *Study:* Md Inst Fine Arts; Rhinehart Sch Sculpture with J Maxwell Miller. *Work:* Hagerstown Mus Fine Arts; approx 300 portrait heads for figures in 12 waxworks mus in US & Can. *Comn:* Portrait relief, Joseph D Baker, Mem Tower, City Park, Frederick, Md, 41; large tympanum relief, Angel of Truth, First Unitarian Church, Baltimore, Md, 55; portrait reliefs, Henrietta & Jacob Blaustein, Oheb Shalom Temple, Baltimore, 63; and others. *Exhib:* Baltimore Mus Art, 40; Nat Acad Design, New York, NY; Pa Acad Fine Arts; Nat Sculpture Soc Ann, Lever House, New York, 68-75; Rhinehart Sch Sculpture 75th Anniversary, Baltimore, 71. *Mem:* Fel Nat Sculpture Soc; Charcoal Club, Baltimore. *Media:* Stone, Plastic. *Mailing Add:* 5 Merrymount Rd Baltimore MD 21210

BERGEN, D THOMAS
COLLECTOR
b Albert Lea, Minn, June 16, 30. *Study:* Harvard Col, AB, 52, Harvard Bus Sch, MBA, 54. *Collection:* Works on paper by late nineteenth to early twentieth century artists, notably focusing on Die Brucke; expressionism and Germanic art to circa 1930. *Mailing Add:* Harvard Club 27 W 44th St New York NY 10036

BERGEN, SIDNEY L
DEALER
b New York, NY, Sept 27, 22. *Study:* Alfred Univ. *Pos:* Owner & dir, ACA Galleries, New York, currently. *Mem:* Art Dealers Asn Am. *Specialty:* Early 20th century and contemporary American and European art. *Mailing Add:* ACA Galleries 21 E 67th St New York NY 10021

BERGER, GUSTAV A
CONSERVATOR
b Vienna, Austria, July 28, 20; US citizen. *Work:* Hirshhorn Mus & Sculpture Garden, DC; Metrop Mus Art, New York; Boyman-van Beuningen Mus, Rotterdam, Holland; High Mus Art, Atlanta, Ga; Nat Gallery Australia, Canberra. *Comn:* Paxson Murals, Bd Co Comnr, Missoula, Mont, 78-79; Atlanta Cyclorama, City of Atlanta, Ga, 79-81; Vanderlyn Panorama, Metrop Mus, New York, 82. *Awards:* Samuel H Kress Found Res Grants, 67, 68, 72 & 83; Nat Endowment Arts Res Grant, 73; Award of Excellence, Atlanta Urban Design Comn, 82. *Bibliog:* Adam Raft (auth), Beva 371, Ein neues Klebemittel fuer Restauratoren, Maltechnik/Restauro, 72; R B Renshaw-Beauchamp (auth), Another use of Beva 371, 74 & Pat Reeves (auth), Use of Beva in the conservation of a Nazca textile, 79, Bull of Am Inst Conserv. *Mem:* Fel Int Inst Conserv Hist & Artistic Works; fel Am Inst Conserv Hist & Artistic Works; Appraisers Asn Am; Int Coun on Mus. *Publ:* Auth, The Testing of Adhesives for the Consolidation of Paintings, Int Inst Conserv-Am Group, 70; auth, Formulating Adhesives for the Conservation of Painting In: Conservation & Restoration of Pictorial Art, Butterworth, London, 76; auth, Unconventional Treatments for Unconventional Paintings, Studies in Conserv, 76; auth, Preventive Conservation of Painted Objects, Int Coun on Mus, 78; coauth, The Behavoir of Canvas as a Structural Support for Painting, Int Inst Conserv, 82; and others. *Mailing Add:* 1014 Madison Ave New York NY 10021

BERGER, JASON
PAINTER, PRINTMAKER
b Malden, Mass, Jan 22, 24. *Study:* Boston Mus Fine Arts Sch, 42-43 & 46-49; Univ Ala, 43-44; Ossip Zadkine Sch Sculpture, Paris, 50-52. *Work:* Guggenheim Mus Art, Mus Mod Art, Chase Manhattan Bank, New York; Smith Col Mus Art; Brandeis Univ; and others. *Exhib:* Carnegie Inst Mus, 54 & 55; Recent Drawings USA, Mus Mod Art, New York, 56; Pa Acad Fine Arts, 62; Silvermine Guild; Providence Art Festival, RI, 69; and others. *Teaching:* Instr painting, Boston Mus Fine Arts Sch, 55-69; vis prof, State Univ NY, Buffalo, 69-70; instr painting, Art Inst Boston, 73- *Awards:* Grand Prize, 55 & First Prize, 61, Boston Art Festival; Boston Mus Fine Arts Sch Traveling Fel; Purchase Prize, Sheraton-Boston Hotel, 65; and others. *Media:* Oil, Watercolor; Woodcut. *Publ:* Illusr, Foundation Course in French, 56. *Mailing Add:* 40 University Rd Brookline MA 02146

BERGER, JERRY ALLEN
DIRECTOR, CURATOR
b Buffalo, Wyo, Oct 8, 43. *Study:* Univ Wyo, BA(psychology), 65, BA(art), 71, MA(art hist), 72. *Pos:* Cur collections, Univ Wyo Art Mus, Laramie, 72-, asst dir, 81- *Mailing Add:* Univ of Wyo Art Mus Box 3138 Univ Sta Laramie WY 82071

BERGER, MAURICE
CRITIC, EDUCATOR
b New York, NY, May 22, 56. *Study:* Hunter Col, City Univ New York, BA(Thomas Hunter Scholar), 78; City Univ New York Grad Ctr, Herman Muehlstein Found Res Fel, 78- *Pos:* Asst to dir exhibs, City Univ New York Grad Ctr, 81-; cur, Hunter Col Art Gallery, 83- *Teaching:* Adj lectr art hist, Hunter Col, New York, 80-; vis lectr, Queens Col, City Univ New York, 81- *Mem:* Int Asn Art Critics; Asn Historians Am Art. *Res:* History and theory of modernist painting, sculpture & architecture; history of performance art. *Publ:* Auth, Edward Burne-Jones' Perseus cycle: The vulnerable Medusa, 80, auth, Pictograph into burst: Adolph Gottlieb and the structure of myth, 81, auth, The empty frame: Dotty Attie's J and Armand tour the world, 81 & auth, The mythology of ritual: Reflections of Laurie Anderson, 83, Arts Mag; auth, Joel Shapiro: War games, In: Re.dact, Frank & Willis, 83. *Mailing Add:* 740 W End Ave New York NY 10025

BERGER, OSCAR
GRAPHIC ARTIST
b Presov, Eperjes, Czechoslovakia, May 12, 01; US citizen. *Work:* Libr of Cong & Nat Portrait Gallery, Washington, DC; Metrop Mus Art, New York; also pvt collections & mus. *Comn:* design, League of Nations, Geneva, 26; posters, Brit Transport & Gen Post Off, London, 38; curtain design, Palladium, London; mag pages (San Francisco Conf of UN), New York Times, London Daily Telegraph, King Features Syndicate, 45; logo design, United Nations World Assembly Aging, New York, 82. *Exhib:* One-man show, Gallery of Mod Art, New York Cult Ctr, 68. *Bibliog:* Geoffrey Holme (auth), Caricature of today, The Studio, London, 28; Oscar Berger, France Dimanche, Paris, 48; Norman Kent (auth), Famous faces by Oscar Berger, Am Artist, 63. *Mem:* Nat Press Club, Washington, DC; Nat Regist Indust Art Designers. London. *Media:* Pencil, Ink. *Publ:* auth, Aesop's Foibles, 49; auth, Famous Faces, 50; auth, My Victims, 52; auth, I Love You, 60; auth, The Presidents, 68. *Mailing Add:* 120 Central Park South New York NY 10019

BERGER, PAUL ERIC
PHOTOGRAPHER, EDUCATOR
b The Dalles, Ore, Jan 20, 48. *Study:* Art Ctr Col of Design, Los Angeles, with Tod Walker, 67-69; Univ of Calif, Los Angeles, with Robert Heinecken & Robert Fichter, BA, 69-70; Visual Studies Workshop, State Univ NY, Buffalo, with Nathan Lyons, MFA, 70-73. *Work:* Int Mus of Photog/George Eastman House, Rochester, NY; Bibliot Nationale, Paris, France; Art Inst Chicago; San Francisco Mus Mod Art; Art Mus Princeton Univ, NJ. *Exhib:* One-man show, Photographs, 72-79; Opened Bk, Art Inst Chicago, 75, Mathematics Series, Tyler Sch Art Gallery, Philadelphia, 79, Seattle Art Mus, 80, Seattle Subtext, Light Gallery, New York, 82 & BC Space, Los Angeles, 83; Am Photog in the 70's, Art Inst Chicago, 79. *Teaching:* Lectr photog, Univ Ill, Champaign, 74-78; from asst to assoc prof photog, Univ Wash, Seattle, 78- *Awards:* Young Photogr Award, Int Meeting Photog, Arles, France, 75; Nat Endowment for Arts photogr fel, 79. *Bibliog:* Paul Berger, mathematics series, Print Collector's Newslett, 77; Leroy Searle (auth), Paul Berger's mathematics photographs, Afterimage, Rochester, 78; Jim Burns (auth), From Old Images to New, Argus Publ, Seattle, Wash, 79. *Mem:* Soc for Photog Educ (bd dirs, 80-84). *Media:* Photography. *Dealer:* Light Gallery 724 Fifth Ave New York NY 10019. *Mailing Add:* 6712 Division NW Seattle WA 98117

BERGGRUEN, JOHN HENRY
DEALER
b San Francisco, Calif, June 18, 43. *Study:* San Francisco State Col, AB, 67. *Pos:* Pres & owner, John Berggruen Gallery, San Francisco, 70-; mem bd trustees, San Francisco Art Inst. *Mem:* Soc Encouragement Contemp Art; Art Dealers Asn Am. *Specialty:* Paintings, drawings and original prints of the 20th century. *Mailing Add:* 228 Grant Ave 3rd Floor San Francisco CA 94108

BERGHASH, MARK W
PHOTOGRAPHER, PAINTER
b Buffalo, NY, Mar 8, 35. *Study:* Univ Buffalo, 52-55; Univ Vienna, Austria, 55-56; Art Students League, with George Grosz, 57-60; with George Tice & Philippe Halsman, 76-78. *Work:* Metrop Mus Art, Jewish Mus & Franklin Furnace Archive, New York; Calif Mus Photography, Riverside; Daytona Art Inst, Dayton, Ohio. *Exhib:* The Portrait Extended, Mus Contemp Art, Chicago, Ill, 80; Counterparts and Affinities, Metrop Mus Art, New York, 82; Indelible Images, The Jewish Mus, New York, 82; Holocaust Survivors Remembered, Jewish Ctr, Buffalo, NY; one-man shows, Nudes in Parts, Gallery Photographic Art, Tel Aviv, 84 & Segmented Photographs, Marcuse Pfeifer Gallery, New York, 84; and others. *Mem:* Art Students League. *Media:* Silver Emulsion. *Mailing Add:* 1841 Broadway Rm 608 New York NY 10023

BERGLING, VIRGINIA CATHERINE (MRS STEPHEN KOZAZCKI)
BOOK DEALER, EDITOR
b Chicago, Ill, Nov 6, 08. *Mem:* Miami Art League. *Res:* All phases of technical art and design. *Interests:* Genealogy and heraldic arts; coats of arms. *Publ:* Ed, Art monograms & lettering, 20th ed, 64; ed, Ornamental designs & illustrations, 4th ed, 64; ed, Art alphabets & lettering, 9th ed, 67; ed, Heraldic designs & engravings, Illus Manual Rev, 66. *Mailing Add:* 1150 NE 110th St Miami FL 33161

BERGSTROM, EDITH HARROD
PAINTER, INSTRUCTOR
b Denver, Colo. *Study:* Pomona Col, Calif, BA, 63; Stanford Univ, Calif, MA, 64. *Work:* Palm Springs Desert Mus, Calif; San Jose Mus Art, Calif; Utah State Univ, Logan; Hallmark Cards, Inc, Kansas City, Mo; Claremont Graduate Sch, Calif; and others. *Exhib:* Am Watercolor Soc, 75, 76, 82 & 83; Rocky Mountain Nat Watermedia Exhib, 76, 77, 78, 81-83; Nat Watercolor Soc, 76, 79, 80, 81 & 83; Watercolor USA, 79-81 & 83; Butler Inst Am Art 45th Nat, Youngstown, Ohio, 81; one-woman show, Monterey Peninsula Mus Art, Calif, 83; and others. *Awards:* Century Award of Merit, Rocky Mountain Nat, 77 & 82; The Hunt Purchase Award, Nat Watercolor Soc, Hunt Manufacturing Co, 81; Carl Folke Sahlin Award, Am Watercolor Soc, 83.

Bibliog: Christopher Schink (auth), Mastering Color & Design in Watercolor, Watson-Guptill, 81; Mary Carhartt (auth), Watercolor: See for Yourself, Brumbacher, 84. *Mem:* Rocky Mountain Nat Watermedia Soc; Nat Watercolor Soc; Watercolor West; Am Watercolor Soc; W Coast Watercolor Soc. *Media:* Watercolor, Oil. *Publ:* Illusr, 81 & auth, Watercolor Page, 82, Am Artist Mag. *Dealer:* Louis Newman Galleries 322 N Beverly Dr Beverly Hills CA 90210; Van Doren Associates 3800 Washington St San Francisco CA 94133. *Mailing Add:* 670 Guinda St Palo Alto CA 94301

BERGUSON, ROBERT JENKINS
PAINTER, EDUCATOR
b Blossburg, Pa, Dec 6, 44. *Study:* Corning Community Col, NY, AA, 64; Univ Iowa, Iowa City, BA, 67, MA, 68, MFA, 70. *Work:* Norfolk Mus Arts & Sci, Va; Univ NDak Art Gallery, Grand Forks; Univ Iowa Sch Art Gallery, Iowa City; Hunter Mus Art, Bluff View, Chattanooga, Tenn; Miss Mus Art, Jackson. *Exhib:* XXIII Am Drawing Biennial, Smithsonian Traveling Exhib Serv, Norfolk Mus Arts & Sci, Va, 69; 11th Midwest Biennial, Josyln Mus Art, Omaha, Nebr, 70; Am Artist Biennial, New Orleans Mus Art, La, 71 & 73; All Media Art Exhib, Assistance League, Houston, Tex, 76; 19th & 25th Ann Delta Art Exhib, Little Rock Art Ctr, Ark, 76 & 83; 18th Dixie Ann, Works on Paper Exhib, Montgomery Mus Fine Arts, Ala, 77; 16th Hunter Ann Painting & Drawing Exhib, Hunter Mus Art, Bluff View, Tenn, 77; Washington Sq East Galleries, 80; 7th Ann Small Works Show, NY Univ, 83; and others. *Teaching:* Asst prof painting & drawing, La Tech Univ, Ruston, 70-76, assoc prof, 77-83, prof, 83- *Awards:* Purchase Award, XXIII Am Drawing Biennial, Norfolk Art Mus, 69 & 13th NDak Exhib Prints & Drawings, Univ NDak, 70; Merit Award, 16th Hunter Mus Art, Lincoln-Davies, Inc, Bluff View, Chattanooga, Tenn, 77. *Mem:* Col Art Asn. *Media:* Gouache. *Publ:* Auth, article, Art Voices/South, 7-8/79; illusr, Upper & lower case, Int J Typographics, 79. *Mailing Add:* 1211 Robinette Dr Ruston LA 71270

BERHANG, MATTIE
SCULPTOR, LECTURER
b New York, NY. *Study:* Tyler Sch Art, BFA; Art Students League, with R B Hale & J DeCreeft; New York Studio Sch, with G Spaventa, R Nakian & M Matter. *Work:* Lannan Found Mus, Lake Worth, Fla; Reich & Tang Inc, Leukemia Soc Am, New York; Sigal Construction Corp, Washington, DC; Imperial Silver Co, London. *Exhib:* Sculpture Tricentennial, Philadelphia Art Alliance, 82; The Suspended Object, Berkshire Mus, Pittsfield, Mass, 83; Varför New York?, Grafikhuset Futura, Stockholm, 83; Stockholm Int Art Exposition, Sollentuna Massan, 83; Sculpture: The Tradition in Steel, Nassau Co Mus Fine Art, Roslyn Harbor, NY, 83. *Teaching:* Guest lectr, Syracuse Univ, 81, New Sch Social Res, New York, 81 & Univ Wis, Eau Claire, 83. *Bibliog:* Lewis Chapin (auth), Sculptor Mattie Berhang, Christian Sci Monitor, 7/10/73; Malcolm Preston (auth), An even dozen from Queens, Newsday, 2/10/80; Ralph Herrmanns (auth), Varför New York?, Förlags AB Wiken, 82. *Media:* Mixed. *Dealer:* O K Harris Works Art 383 W Broadway New York NY 10012. *Mailing Add:* 2-24 51st Ave Long Island City NY 11101

BERKMAN, AARON
PAINTER, GALLERY DIRECTOR
b Hartford, Conn, May 23, 1900. *Study:* Hartford Art Sch; Mus Art Sch, Boston; Yaddo Found fel; Huntington Hartford Found fel. *Exhib:* Kaufman Art Gallery, New York, NY, 60 & 63; Bercone Galleries, New York, 70 & 75; one-man show, Audubon Artists, 71; Audubon Artists, 71-78. *Pos:* Art dir, 92nd St YMHA Art Ctr, 55-65; art dir, Bercone Studios, New York, 67- *Teaching:* Instr & lectr art, 92nd St YMHA Art Ctr, New York, 43-65. *Mem:* Artists Equity; Audubon Artists. *Media:* Acrylic, Oil, Watercolor. *Publ:* Auth, Art & Space, 49; auth, Amateur standing, monthly column in Art News, 55-61; auth, The Functional Line in Painting, 57. *Dealer:* Bercone Galleries 1305 Madison Ave New York NY 10028. *Mailing Add:* 230 E 88th St New York NY 10028

BERKMAN, LILLIAN
COLLECTOR
Pos: Pres, Rojtman Found Inc; fel, Morgan Libr; fel in perpetuity, Metrop Mus Art, New York; overseer, Univ Pa Mus; trustee, Telfair Mus, Savannah, Ga; mem bd adv, Inst Fine Arts, NY Univ. *Mem:* Drawing Soc. *Collection:* Paintings, prints, drawings. *Mailing Add:* 22 E 64th St New York NY 10021

BERKO, FERENC
PHOTOGRAPHER
b Nagyvarad, Hungary, Jan 28, 16; US citizen. *Study:* London Univ Exten, 38. *Work:* Mus Mod Art, Metrop Mus Art, New York; San Francisco Mus Art; Ctr Creative Photog, Tucson; Gernsheim Collection, Austin, Tex. *Exhib:* Bronzes of Southern India, Victoria & Albert Mus, 47; Photography USA, De Cordova Mus, Lincoln, Mass, 68; solo exhib, Amon Carter Mus, Ft Worth, 72 & New Gallery Contemp Photog, Cleveland, 81; Color Photography 30 Years Ago, Photokina, Köln, Ger, 78; two-person exhib, Ctr Creative Photog, Tucson, 80. *Teaching:* Instr film & photog, Inst Design, Chicago, 47-48. *Bibliog:* Karl Steinorth (auth), Ferenc Berko--a master of muted color, Format, Ger, 78; James Enyeart (auth), Ferenc Berko, Am Photogr, 80; Helmut Gernsheim (auth), Ferenc Berko, In: The World's Ten Greatest, Foto Mag, Ger, 83. *Publ:* Contrib, Creative Camera, Maco Corp, 60; contribr, The Aspen Idea, Univ Okla Press, 75; contribr, Camera, Switz, 10/76; contribr, Histoire Mondiale de la Photographie en Couleurs, Hachette, France, 81-82; contribr, Lexikon der Fotografen, Rowohlt, Ger, 81. *Mailing Add:* Box 360 Aspen CO 81612

BERKON, MARTIN
PAINTER
b Brooklyn, NY, Jan 30, 32. *Study:* Brooklyn Col, BA; New York Univ, MA; Pratt Inst. *Work:* Aldrich Mus Contemp Art. *Comn:* Painting, NASA, 84. *Exhib:* One-man shows, Brooklyn Mus, 58, Genesis Gallery, New York, 78 & Adelphi Univ, 83; Butler Inst Am Art Ann Midyear Show, 65, 67 & 69; Contemporary Reflections, Aldrich Mus Contemp Art, Ridgefield, Conn, 74, 75 & 82; New Brit Mus, Conn, 74; Flint Inst, 75; Oakland Univ, Rochester, Mich, 75; Am Fedn Arts Traveling Exhib, 75-76. *Teaching:* Instr elements of design, Fairleigh Dickinson Univ, 66-67; instr drawing & painting, City Col New York, 68-69; guest lectr, Middlebury Col, 77 & Nassau Community Col, 82. *Awards:* Patron's Prize, Nat Soc Painters in Casein, 65. *Bibliog:* Grace Glueck (auth), Art notes, New York Times, 12/1/74; Margaret Pomfret (auth), Review at Genesis, Arts, 10/78; Evalyn E Milman (auth), article, Bridgeport Sunday Post, 1/24/82. *Media:* Oil, Acrylic. *Mailing Add:* 51-25 Van Kleek St Elmhurst NY 11373

BERKOWITZ, HENRY
PAINTER, DESIGNER
b Brooklyn, NY, Feb 5, 33. *Study:* Brooklyn Mus Art Sch, with Sidney Simon; Workshop Sch Advert & Ed Art; Sch Visual Arts, New York. *Work:* Gutenberg Mus, Main, Ger. *Exhib:* Berkshire Mus, Pittsfield, Mass, 71; Galeries Raymond Duncan, Paris, 74; Art Festival Thours, France, 74; Parrish Art Mus, 75; Surindependants, Paris, 75; plus others. *Pos:* Art dir, Pyramid Publ, New York, 63-77. *Awards:* Award of Merit, New York Coliseum, 70; Am Vet Soc for Artists Award for an Abstract Work of Art, 72; Palmas de Oro, Int Art Festival, Paris, 74; plus others. *Mem:* Am Vet Soc Artists; Huntington Art League; Berkshire Art Asn; Awixa Pond Art Asn; Shore Arts Asn. *Publ:* Auth & illusr, Fish, Facts and Fancies, Banyan Books, 81. *Dealer:* Ligoa Duncan Gallery 1045 Madison Ave New York NY 10021. *Mailing Add:* 11701 NW 29th Manor Sunrise FL 33323

BERKOWITZ, LEON
PAINTER
b Philadelphia, Pa, 19. *Study:* Univ Pa, BFA; George Washington Univ, MA; Art Students League; Corcoran Gallery Art Sch; Mexico City Univ; Acad Grande Chaumiere, Paris, France; Acad Bella Arti, Florence, Italy. *Work:* Wadsworth Atheneum, Hartford, Conn; Mus Fine Arts, St Petersburg, Fla; Everson Mus Art, Syracuse, NY; Mus Mod Art, New York; Des Moines Art Ctr, Iowa. *Comn:* Murals, Harris Nat Trust, Chicago, 75. *Exhib:* Corcoran Mus, Washington, DC, 73; Everson Mus, Syracuse, 74; Chicago Arts Club, 77; Middendorf-Lane Gallery, Washington, DC, 77; Mus Fine Arts, St Petersburgh, Fla, 78; McKissick Mus, Columbia, SC, 80; traveling show, Los Angeles & Air & Space Mus, Washington, DC, 83; and others. *Pos:* Co-founder & dir, Workshop Ctr Arts, Washington, DC, 47-55. *Teaching:* Prof art, Corcoran Sch Art, 68- *Awards:* Purchase Prize, Second Flint Invitational, 70; Nat Found Arts & Humanities Grant, 71. *Media:* Oil. *Dealer:* Middendorf-Lane Gallery 2009 Columbia Rd NW Washington DC 20009. *Mailing Add:* 2003 Kalorama Rd NW Washington DC 20009

BERKOWITZ, ROGER M
CURATOR, MUSEOLOGIST
b Denver, Colo, May 30, 44. *Study:* Western Reserve Univ, AB, 66; Univ Mich, MMP, 70, PhD, 77. *Collections Arranged:* The Art of Louis Comfort Tiffany (auth, catalog), 77; El Greco of Toledo, 82; Reinstallation permanent collection Toledo Mus Art, 83. *Pos:* Chief cur & cur, Decorative Arts, Toledo Mus Art, 74- *Teaching:* Vis lectr art hist, Univ Mich, 73 & 79- *Awards:* Chester Dale Fel, Nat Gallery Art, 72-73. *Mem:* Decorative Arts Chap, Soc Archit Historians. *Res:* Eighteenth to nineteenth century English silver. *Publ:* Contribr, Toledo Mus Art: European Paintings, 76 & The Museum Collects: Treasures by Sculptors and Craftsmen, 80, Toledo Mus Art; auth, The patriotic fund vases, regency awards to the navy, Apollo, 81. *Mailing Add:* PO Box 1013 Toledo OH 43697

BERLANT, TONY
SCULPTOR
b New York, NY, Aug 7, 41. *Study:* Univ Calif, Los Angeles, MA(painting) & MFA(sculpture). *Work:* Whitney Mus Am Art, New York; Art Inst Chicago; Los Angeles Co Mus Art; Philadelphia Mus Art; Wichita Mus Art, Kans. *Exhib:* One-man show, Whitney Mus Am Art, New York, 74; Newport Harbor Art Mus, 78; Tex Gallery, Houston, 79; Xavier Fourcade, Inc, New York, 82; Los Angeles Louver, 82; John Berggruen Gallery, San Francisco, 83; and others. *Dealer:* Xavier Fourcade Inc 36 E 75th St New York NY 10021. *Mailing Add:* 2802 Second St Santa Monica CA 95060

BERLIN, BEATRICE WINN
PRINTMAKER, PAINTER
b Philadelphia, Pa, May 27, 22. *Study:* Fleisher Art Mem, Philadelphia; Moore Col Art; Philadelphia Col Art; printmaking with Sam Maitin & Victor Lasuchin. *Work:* Philadelphia Mus Art; Brooklyn Mus Art; Lessing J Rosenwald, Jenkintown, Pa; Grunwald Col, Univ Calif; New York Pub Libr Print Collection; plus others. *Exhib:* Nat Acad Design Ann, New York, 65 & 66; Pa Acad Fine Arts Ann (watercolor & prints), 65, 67 & 69; Libr of Cong 21st Nat Print Show, 69; Print Club Philadelphia Ann Int, 69, 73 & 75; one-woman show, Philadelphia Print Club, 70. *Awards:* First Prize, Cheltenham Art Ctr Print Show, 70; Purchase Prize, Lebanon Valley Col, 73; Best in Show, Ocean City Boardwalk, NJ, 73. *Bibliog:* Wenniger (auth), Collograph-Printmaking, Watson-Guptill, 75; Frym (auth), Second Stories, Chronicle Books, 79. *Mem:* Am Color Print Soc; Philadelphia Watercolor Soc; Artists Equity Asn; Calif Soc Printmakers; Philadelphia Print Club. *Dealer:* Assoc Am Artists 663 Fifth Ave New York NY 10022. *Mailing Add:* 927 Taylor Ave Alameda CA 94501

BERLIND, ROBERT
PAINTER, EDUCATOR
b New York, NY, Aug 20, 38. *Study:* Columbia Col, BA, 60; Sch Art & Archit, Yale Univ, BFA, 62, MFA, 63. *Exhib:* One-man shows, Maison de la Cult, L'Isle sur Sorgue, Vaucluse, France, 69, Green Mountain Gallery, New York, 72 & 78, Alexander Milliken Gallery, New York, 81; Anna Leonowens Gallery, Halifax, NS, 76; Minneapolis Inst Art Biennial, Minn, 70; Yale at Norfolk Summer Prog Show, Norfolk, Conn, 72; Younger Artists, Tibor de Nagy Gallery, New York; Artists' Choice Mus, 80; Views of Landscape, Univ Akron, Ohio, 81; Haber TheodoreGallery, New York, 81. *Teaching:* Asst prof, Minneapolis Sch Art, 64-66 & 69-70; asst prof art hist & humanities, Haarlem, Neth, 66-68; assoc prof & dir grad studies, NS Col Art & Design, 74-76; assoc prof, State Univ NY at Purchase, currently. *Bibliog:* Gerrit Henry (auth), Painterly realism & the modern landscape, Art in America, 9/81; John Yau (auth), Art in America, summer 81; Robert Yoskowitz (auth), Arts Magazine, 9/81. *Media:* Oil; Acrylic. *Mailing Add:* 215 W 20th St New York NY 10011

BERLYN, SHELDON
PAINTER, PRINTMAKER
b Worcester, Mass, Sept 6, 29. *Study:* Yale Norfolk Summer Art Sch, 49; Worcester Art Mus Sch, cert, 50; Art Acad Cincinnati with Herbert Barnett, 54-55. *Work:* Worcester Art Mus, Mass; E B Crocker Art Gallery, The Art Mus City Sacramento, Calif; Dayton Art Inst, Ohio; Albright-Knox Art Gallery, Buffalo, NY; State Univ NY Brockport Gallery Collection; and numerous pvt & corp collections. *Exhib:* One-man shows, Dana & Decordova Mus, Lincoln, Mass, 55 & Schuman Gallery, Rochester, NY, 65-66 & 70; Western NY Exhib, Albright-Knox Art Gallery, Buffalo, NY, 58-66 & 77 & one-man show, 76; Drawings Above the Pa Line, Roberson Ctr Arts, Binghamton, NY, 68; American Drawings, Moore Col Art, Philadelphia, 68; Begegnung-Mass Inst Technol, Auslands Inst, Dortmund, WGer, 76. *Teaching:* Assoc prof painting & drawing, State Univ NY Buffalo, 58- *Awards:* Stephen Wilder Traveling Fel, Cincinnati Mus Asn, 55-56; State Univ NY Res Found Fel, 66-68; Sattler Award Painting, Western NY Exhib, Albright-Knox Art Gallery, 60 & Reeb Award Drawing, 64. *Media:* Acrylic, Oil; Serigraph. *Dealer:* Oxford Gallery 267 Oxford St Rochester NY 14607. *Mailing Add:* 813 Richmond Ave Buffalo NY 14222

BERMAN, AARON
DEALER, GALLERY DIRECTOR
b New York, NY, Nov 21, 22. *Study:* Brooklyn Col, BA; Columbia Univ, MA; Bezalel Acad, Jerusalem, dipl painting & sculpture, with Itzhak Danziger. *Pos:* Art dir mod & contemp art, Spencer Enterprises, New York, 57- & Aaron Berman Gallery, 76-; art consult & appraiser, United Jewish Appeal, New York, 69- & Am Friends Haifa Univ, Israel, 73- *Teaching:* Lectr contemp art, New Sch for Social Res, New York, 76- *Bibliog:* Robin Landa (auth), Introduction to Design, Prentice Hall, 83. *Mem:* Am Fedn Arts; Brooklyn Mus Art Sch (bd trustee, 73). *Specialty:* Modern and contemporary art with emphasis on abstract expressionism; abstract figurative expressionism; abstract illusionism. *Collection:* Flemish period to modern and contemporary American and European art, 19th and 20th centuries. *Publ:* Auth, 13 Mini Retros-Pictures on Exhibit, 4/79; auth, Grace Knowlton, Arts, 9/81; auth, Women's Art-Miles Apart, Valencia Col, 2/82. *Mailing Add:* 50 W 57th St New York NY 10019

BERMAN, ARIANE R
PAINTER, PRINTMAKER
b Freeport, Danzig, Mar 27, 37; US citizen. *Study:* Hunter Col, BFA, 59; Yale Univ, MFA(scholar), 62; Ecole Beaux Artes, Am Asn Univ Women & Fondation Etats-Unis Grants, 62-63; and with Stanley William Hayter & Jacques Desjobert. *Work:* Metrop Mus Art; Philadelphia Mus Art, Pa; Philadelphia Art Alliance; Litton Indust; Hearst Corp. *Comn:* Painting, Seventeen Mag, 71; painting, Shipley Sch, Bryn Mawr, Pa, 71; painting, Charles E Ellis Col, Newtown Square, Pa, 71; plus others. *Exhib:* Butler Inst Am Art 36th Ann, 72; Ward-Nasse Gallery, New York, 75-84; Philadelphia Art Alliance, 80; one-man shows, Kornblee Gallery, 82 & many others; Fairleigh Dickinson Univ; Allentown Art Mus; and others. *Awards:* Catherine Lorillard Wolfe Arts Club Gold Medal, 73; D L Ferriss Award, Pen & Brush Inc; Award Excellence, Sheffield Art League. *Bibliog:* Cover story, Host Mag, 73. *Mem:* Am Color Print Soc; Nat Asn Women Artists; Silvermine Guild Artists; Philadelphia Art Alliance; Artists Equity Asn. *Media:* Acrylic, Serigraphs. *Dealer:* Assoc Am Artists 663 Fifth Ave New York NY 10022; Ward-Nasse Gallery 131 Prince St New York NY 10012. *Mailing Add:* 161 W 54th St New York NY 10019

BERMAN, BERNARD
COLLECTOR
b Pennsburg, Pa, Aug 28, 20. *Mem:* Am Asn Mus, Washington, DC (trustee); Allentown Art Mus, Pa (pres bd trustees, 71-). *Collection:* German Expressionist, Italian sculpture, American artists. *Mailing Add:* 2830 Gordon St Allentown PA 18104

BERMAN, FRED J
PAINTER, PHOTOGRAPHER
b Milwaukee, Wis, Nov 3, 26. *Study:* Milwaukee State Teachers Col, BS; Univ Wis-Madison, MS. *Work:* Norton Mus Art, Fla; Elvejhem Art Ctr, Madison, Wis; Ft Lauderdale Mus, Fla; Milwaukee Art Ctr. *Exhib:* Walker Art Ctr Biennials, Minneapolis, Minn, 47, 51, 54, 56 & 62; 6th Biennial Contemp Am Paintings, Va Mus of Fine Arts, Richmond, 48; Pa Acad Fine Arts Ann, Philadelphia, 51, 52 & 53; Am Watercolors, Drawings & Prints, Metrop Mus of Art, New York, 52; Corcoran Biennials, Corcoran Gallery Art,

Washington, DC, 53, 55 & 59; Am Exhib, Art Inst Chicago, 54 & 57; Whitney Ann, 59 & Young Am, 60, Whitney Mus Am Art, New York; San Francisco Mus Art Ann, 60 & 65; one-man exhibs, Collectors Gallery, Milwaukee, 81, Kresge Art Gallery, Mich State Univ, 82, Reading Univ, England, 83 & Camden Arts Centre, London, England, 83; two-man exhib, Bradley Galleries, Milwaukee, 83; and others. *Teaching:* Instr painting & printmaking, Layton Sch Art, Milwaukee, Wis, 49-60; prof design & drawing, Univ Wis-Milwaukee, 60- *Awards:* Milwaukee Art Inst Award, Milwaukee Art Ctr, 47, 52, 53, 54 & 56; Joseph Eisendrath Award, Chicago & vicinity, Art Inst Chicago, 50; Wis Union Top Purchase Award, Wis Salon Art, Univ Wis-Madison, 67. *Media:* Oil, Charcoal. *Dealer:* Posner Gallery 7641 N Port Washington Rd Milwaukee WI 53217; Bradley Galleries 2565 N Downer Ave Milwaukee WI 53211. *Mailing Add:* 3133 N Marietta Ave Milwaukee WI 53211

BERMAN, GRETA W
HISTORIAN, CURATOR
b New York, NY. *Study:* Antioch Univ, BA, 65; Univ Stockholm, MA, 68; Columbia Univ, with Theodore Reff & Barbara Novak, PhD, 75. *Collections Arranged:* Amerika: Traum und Depression 1920-1940 (contribr, catalog), West Berlin & Hamburg, 80-81; Realism & Realities: The Other Side of American Painting 1940-1960 (co-auth, catalog), Rutgers Univ, 82. *Teaching:* Instr art hist, State Univ NY, Stony Brook, 70-79; instr & lectr art hist, Juilliard Sch Music, 79-; instr & lectr art hist, Parsons Sch Design, 81. *Awards:* Dissertation Research Grant, Smithsonian Inst, 74; State Univ NY Fac Fel, 77; Chester Dale Fel, Metrop Mus Art, 79-80. *Mem:* Col Art Asn Am; Asn Historians Am Art. *Res:* 19th and 20th century American and European painting; especially American 1930's, 40's & 50's; French 19th century symbolism. *Publ:* Auth, The Paradox of Odilon Redon, Konsthistorisk Tidskrift, 70; auth, Strindberg, Painter, Critic, Modernist, Gazette des Beaux Arts, 75; auth, The Lost Years: Mural Painting in New York Under the WPA/FAP 1935-1943, Garland Press, 78. *Mailing Add:* 80 LaSalle St New York NY 10027

BERMAN, MURIEL MALLIN
COLLECTOR, PATRON
b Pittsburgh, Pa, June 21, 24. *Study:* Univ Pittsburgh; Carnegie-Mellon Univ; Pa Col Optom; Cedar Crest Col; Muhlenberg Col. *Pos:* Mem, Pa Coun Arts; hon chmn, Bucks Co Collectors Art Show, New Hope, Pa, 66; co-chmn, Episcopal Diocese Bicentennial Art Comn, 71; numerous other govt, civic & educ positions. *Teaching:* Lectr on African art and its origins, American, French, Picasso, Wyeth, fakes, forgeries and reproductions. *Mem:* Art Collectors Club Am; Am Fedn Arts; Friends Whitney Mus Am Art; Arch Am Art, Detroit; Mus Mod Art, New York; plus many others. *Interests:* Collection on loan, Art in the Embassies Programs founder and donor, Carnegie-Berman College Art Slide Library Exchange; Berman Circulating Art Exhibitions, in colleges and museums in the East. *Collection:* Early 20th century American modern, pop and op art; Eskimo, Japanese, Aboriginal Australian, French and African. *Mailing Add:* 20 Hundred Nottingham Rd Allentown PA 18103

BERMAN, PHILIP I
COLLECTOR, PATRON
b Pennsburg, Pa, June 28, 15. *Study:* Ursinus Col, LLD, 68; Lehigh Univ, LHD, 69. *Pos:* Pres, Philip & Muriel Berman Found; chmn vis comt, Fine & Creative Arts, Lehigh Univ, 66-; many other positions in bus, govt, educ, civic & art activities. *Mem:* Life fel Metrop Mus Art, New York; Aspen Ctr Contemp Art; Am Fedn Arts; Art Collectors Club Am; Arch Am Art; plus many other art mus & associations; many paintings on permanent loan to civic and educational institutions in Lehigh Valley area; participant in Art in the Embassies Program. *Interests:* Collections on traveling exhibitions and temporary loan in the US; many paintings on permanent loan to civic and educational institutions in Lehigh Valley area; participant in Art in the Embassies Program. *Collection:* American, French and Japanese art. *Mailing Add:* 20 Hundred Nottingham Rd Allentown PA 18103

BERMAN, STEVEN M
PAINTER, PRINTMAKER
b Chicago, Ill, Jan 18, 47. *Study:* Kansas City Art Inst, BFA, 70; Chicago Art Inst, MFA, 72. *Work:* House Cult, Moscow, USSR; Wichita Art Mus, Kans; Playboy Enterprises, Chicago; Western Ill Univ, Macomb; Kansas City Art Inst, Mo. *Exhib:* One-man shows, Phyllis Kind Gallery, Chicago & Chicago Art Inst, 72 & Rebecca Cooper Gallery, Washington, DC, 77; Extraordinary Realities, Whitney Mus Am Art, New York, 73-74; Mid Am Five, Nelson Mus Art, Kansas City, 74; The Small Scale in Contemporary Art, Chicago Art Inst, 75. *Teaching:* Instr painting & drawing, Wichita State Univ, 72-76, asst prof painting & drawing, 76-77. *Awards:* Ryerson Traveling Fel Grant, Chicago Art Inst, 72; Renaissance Prize for painting, 73; St Louis Art Mus Prize for painting, 74. *Bibliog:* Ivan Karp (auth), Olympics of Art, New York, 74; B J Smith (auth), Featured artist, Cimarron Review, Okla State Univ, 75. *Mem:* Wichita Fine Arts Coun (vchmn, 75-76); Wichita Artist Guild (bd mem, 75-76). *Media:* Acrylic; Lithography. *Publ:* Illusr, A sporting life, Playboy Mag, 1/76, Italian issue, 2/76. *Dealer:* Rebecca Cooper Gallery 2130 P St NW Washington DC 20037. *Mailing Add:* 9343 Oak Park Ave Morton Grove IL 60053

BERMAN, VIVIAN
PRINTMAKER
b New York, NY, Aug 28, 28. *Study:* Cooper Union, BFA; Art Students League; Brandeis Univ. *Work:* Wiggin Collection, Boston Pub Libr, Mass; Pa Acad Art; De Cordova Mus, Lincoln, Mass; Hopkins Art Ctr, Dartmouth Col;

United States Information Agency. *Exhib:* Boston Printmakers Ann, 68-83; Libr Cong Nat Print Exhib, 70; Davidson Nat Print & Drawing Competition, Davidson Col, 72-73; 18th Nat Print Exhib, Brooklyn Mus, 73; Nat Exhib Collagraphs, Pratt Graphic Ctr, New York, 75; British Biennale 1979, Bradford, England. *Teaching:* Instr, DeCordova Mus Sch, Lincoln, Mass. *Awards:* Purchase Award, Libr Cong Pennel Fund, 70 & Nat Print Show, Western NMex Univ, 71; MacDowell Colony Fel, 81; and others. *Bibliog:* Ross & Ramano (auth), The Complete Collagraph, Free Press, 80; Wenniger (auth), Collagraph Printmaking, Macmillan, 78. *Mem:* Cambridge Art Asn; Boston Visual Artists Union; Boston Printmakers; NH Art Asn; World Print Council. *Media:* Mixed. *Dealer:* Ainsworth Gallery 42 Bromfield St Boston MA 02108; Assoc Am Artists 663 Fifth Ave New York 10022. *Mailing Add:* 11 Barberry Rd Lexington MA 02173

BERMANT, DAVID W
COLLECTOR, DIRECTOR
b New York, NY, July 16, 19. *Study:* Yale Univ, BA, 40. *Pos:* Pres, Nat Shopping Ctr, Inc, 65-; Dir art for Public Space, Inc. *Mem:* Life fel Metrop Mus Art, New York; assoc Guggenheim Mus, New York; Whitney Mus (directors circle). *Collection:* Art based on technology and science plus its placement in the work-a-day world. *Mailing Add:* 150 Purchase St Rye NY 10580

BERMINGHAM, JOHN C
PAINTER
b Wharton, NJ, Jan 12, 20. *Study:* Univ Notre Dame, Ind, BFA, 42. *Exhib:* Audubon Artists Ann Exhib, Nat Acad Galleries, New York, 73-77 & 81; Allied Artists Ann Exhib, Nat Acad Galleries, New York, 73-79 & 81; Ann Exhib Am Watercolor Soc, Nat Acad Galleries, New York, 73, 74, 76, 77, 78 & 81; Am Watercolor Soc Traveling Exhib, 74, 78 & 81; Acad Artists Nat Exhib, Springfield Mus, Mass, 75-82; Ann Exhib Nat Acad Design, Nat Acad Galleries, New York, 76, 80 & 82. *Awards:* Edgar A Whitney Award, Am Watercolor Soc, 81; Cert of Merit, Nat Acad Design, 82; First Award, Grand State Watercolor, 82. *Mem:* Allied Artists Am; Am Watercolor Soc; NJ Watercolor Soc (pres, 77-78); Acad Artists; Hudson Valley Art Asn. *Media:* Watercolor. *Mailing Add:* 245 S Main St Wharton NJ 07885

BERMINGHAM, PETER
MUSEUM DIRECTOR, CURATOR
b Buffalo, NY, Nov 6, 37. *Study:* Univ Md, BA(Nat Endowment Humanities Mus Training Fel), 64, MA(art hist), 68; Univ Mich, PhD(Smithsonian Doctoral Fel), 72. *Collections Arranged:* Jasper Cropsey: Retrospective View of America's Painter of Autumn (auth, catalog), Univ Md, 68; American Art in the Barbizon Mood (auth, catalog), 74, The Art of Poetry (auth, catalog), 77 & Alan Sonfist/Trees (auth, catalog), 78, Nat Collection Fine Arts, Smithsonian Inst; New Deal in the Southwest: Arizona and New Mexico (auth, catalog), Univ Ariz Mus Art, 80. *Pos:* Cur educ, Nat Collection Fine Arts, Smithsonian Inst, 73-78; dir/chief cur, Univ Ariz Mus Art, 78-. *Teaching:* Asst prof art, Univ Cincinnati, 72-73. *Mem:* Western Asn Art Mus; Col Art Asn. *Res:* Primarily in 19th century American landscape painting; early 20th century American painting. *Publ:* Ed, Paintings and Sculpture in the University of Arizona Museum of Art (exhib catalog), Univ Ariz Mus Art, 83. *Mailing Add:* Univ Ariz Mus of Art Olive & Speedway Tucson AZ 85721

BERMUDEZ, EUGENIA M See Dignac, Geny

BERMUDEZ, JOSE YGNACIO
SCULPTOR, PAINTER
b Havana, Cuba, Aug 6, 22; US citizen. *Study:* With Roberto Diago, Havana, Cuba, 52-53; Bell Voc Sch, Washington, DC, 61. *Work:* Mus Mod Art, New York; Corcoran Gallery Art, Washington, DC; Phoenix Art Mus, Ariz; Philadelphia Mus Art; Mus Mod Art, Cali, Colombia. *Comn:* Metal Relief 1961, First Americana Ann Mural Competition, 61; Galaxy (mural), Module 3, Phoenix Airport, 79. *Exhib:* New Media-New Form I & II, Martha Jackson Gallery, New York, 60; Corcoran Gallery Art, Washington, DC, 61; Mus Bellas Artes, Caracas, 67; Sculptures & Drawings, Pyramid Galleries, Washington, DC, 70; 3rd Biennial Art Coltejer, Medellin, Colombia, 72; Fountain at Scottsdale Civic Ctr Mall, Ariz, 76. *Pos:* Asst visual arts, Cult Dept, Orgn Am States, Washington, DC, 53-58, chief graphic serv div, 58-71. *Teaching:* Instr, Univ Costa Rica, San Jose, 76, 81. *Awards:* Fourth Prize for Painting, 6th Ann Art Exhib, Havana, 53; Second Prize, 9th Festival Art, Cali, 69. *Bibliog:* L J Ahlander (auth), article in Washington Post, 7/29/62; T Alvarengo (auth), Imagen, Arte y Technologia, 71. *Media:* Metal. *Dealer:* ART Beasley 2802 Juan St San Diego CA. *Mailing Add:* 4109 E Via Estrella Phoenix AZ 85028

BERNAL, LUCRECIA ALEJANDRA
GALLERY DIRECTOR, CURATOR
b Santa Clara, Cuba, Jan 9, 50. *Study:* Mundelein Col, BFA, 72. *Exhib:* Seventy-sixth Chicago & Vicinity Art Exhib, Mus Chicago Art Inst, 77. *Pos:* Art dir, Bernal Gallery, 76- *Teaching:* Art, Chicago Bd Educ, 73-74. *Bibliog:* Wendy Hoffman (auth), L A Bernal in a group exhibition, New Art Examiner, 7/77; Alan G Artner (auth), L A Bernal solo exhibition, Chicago Tribune, 1/79. *Specialty:* Contemporary, Chicago area artists' works. *Mailing Add:* Bernal Gallery 612 N Michigan Ave Chicago IL 60611

BERNARD, DAVID EDWIN
PRINTMAKER, EDUCATOR
b Sandwich, Ill, Aug 8, 13. *Study:* Univ Ill, BFA; Univ Iowa, MFA; and with Mauricio Lasansky & Humbert Albrizio. *Work:* Wichita Art Mus, Kans; Otis Art Inst, Los Angeles, Calif; Free Pub Libr, Philadelphia, Pa; Joslyn Mus,

Omaha, Nebr. *Comn:* Mural (steel & wood), Duerksen Fine Art Ctr, Wichita State Univ, 57; free standing tree symbol (steel), Camp Fire Girls Orgn, Wichita Art Mus, Kans, 60; sculpture (steel, wood & brass), Irene Vickers Baker Children's Theatre, Wichita; pair of standing tree shapes, Art Asn Wichita, 71-72. *Exhib:* God and Man in Art, Am Fedn Arts Traveling Exhib, 57; First Ann, Otis Art Inst, 61; Univ Nebr Print Exhib, Sheldon Art Gallery, Lincoln, 67; one-man exhib prints, Philbrook Art Ctr, Tulsa, Okla, 67; retrospective, Wichita Art Mus, Kans, 83. *Teaching:* Instr art prog, Maryville Col, 46-48; prof printmaking, Wichita State Univ, 49-83, prof emer, 83. *Awards:* Purchase Award for Hombre y Toro (intaglio), Pennell Collection, Libr Cong, 53; Purchase Award for Calvary (colored intaglio), Mid-Am Ann, Nelson Gallery, 55; Kans Gov's Artist's Award, Kans Arts Comn, Topeka, 82. *Bibliog:* Howard E Wooden (auth), David Bernard: Prints and Sculpture, A Retrospective, 1947-1982, Wichita Art Mus, 83. *Mem:* Soc Am Graphic Artists; Artists Guild Wichita (pres); Wichita Art Mus Mem. *Media:* Intaglio, Collagraph. *Publ:* Auth, The collagraph print, Artists Proof, 62; illusr, A West Wind Rises, 62 & Sun City, 64, Univ Nebr Press. *Mailing Add:* 2243 N Yale Ave Wichita KS 67220

BERNAY, BETTI
PAINTER
b New York, NY. *Study:* Pratt Inst; Nat Acad Design, New York, with Louis Bouche; Art Students League, with Frank Mason; also with Robert Brackman. *Work:* Circulo Amistad, Cordoba, Spain; Columbus Mus Arts & Crafts, Ga; Columbia Mus Art, SC; Andre Weil Collection, Paris. *Comn:* Painting, pres of Renault, Madrid, Spain, 64; painting, Children Have No Barriers, IOS Found, Geneva, 69; paintings, Macaws, Seacost E Bldg, Miami Beach, Fla, 69 & mural, Sandy Cove, S Bldg, 70. *Exhib:* Mus of Mod Art, Paris, France, 63; Salon des Artistes Independants, Grand Palais, Paris, 63; Salon Populiste, Mus Mod Art, Paris, 63; Mus of Bella Artes, Malaga, Spain, 65; Bacardi Gallery, Miami, Fla, 67; Metrop Mus & Art Ctr, Miami, 75; Rosenbaum Gallery, Palm Beach, Fla, 77; and many other group & one-man shows. *Awards:* Artistic Merit Medal, City of New York, 42; Prix de Paris, 58; Medal of Honor, Mus Bellas Artes, Malaga, 65. *Mem:* Artists Equity Asn; Am Artists Prof League; Nat Asn Painters & Sculptors Spain; Soc Artistes Francais; Prof Artists Guild; and others. *Media:* Oil, Pastel. *Mailing Add:* 10155 Collins Ave Apt 1705 Bal Harbour FL 33154

BERNECHE, JERRY DOUGLAS
EDUCATOR, PAINTER
b Greentown, Ind, July 24, 32. *Study:* John Herron Art Sch, BFA, 56, studies painting and printmaking with Garo Antreasian; Ohio Univ, MFA, 59, study with Robert Friemark. *Work:* Butler Mus Am Art, Youngstown, Ohio; Springfield Art Mus, Mo; Canton Art Mus & Massillon Mus, Ohio; Mo State Hist Soc, Columbia. *Exhib:* Drawing USA Nat, Walker Art Mus, 62; Mid-Am Nat Exhib, Butler Mus Art, 62-64; Chautauqua Exhib Art, NY, 65-67; Springfield Regional Exhib, 66-75; Watercolor USA Nat, Springfield, 73-74. *Teaching:* Instr art, Cooper Art Sch, Cleveland, Ohio, 62-65 & Mont State Univ, Bozeman, 65-66; assoc prof drawing & painting, Univ Mo, Columbia, 66-81, prof, 81- *Awards:* Mrs E J Bellinger Award, Chautauqua Nat Exhib, 65 & 67; Watercolor Purchase Award, Watercolor USA, 73; Purchase Award, Mo State Fair, 83. *Media:* Acrylic, Watercolor. *Mailing Add:* 3708 Oakland Gravel Rd Columbia MO 65202

BERNHARD, RUTH
PHOTOGRAPHER
b Berlin, Ger, Oct 14, 05; US citizen. *Study:* Acad Art, Berlin, 25-27. *Work:* San Francisco Mus Mod Art; Mus Mod Art, New York; Ctr Creative Photog; Bibliot Nat, Paris; George Eastman House, Rochester. *Teaching:* Instr workshops, Univ Calif Exten, San Francisco, 66-74. *Awards:* Dorothea Lange Award, Oakland Mus, 76; Outstanding Achievement Visual Arts, Womens Caucus Art, 81; Honoree, Rencontres Int Photog, Arles, France, 83. *Bibliog:* Margaretta Mitchell (auth), Recollections: Ten Women of Photography, Viking Press, 79. *Mem:* Friends Photog, Carmel, Calif; Mus Soc, San Francisco. *Publ:* Auth, Growth of a photographer, Contact Mag, 64. *Mailing Add:* 2982 Clay St San Francisco CA 94010

BERNS, PAMELA KARI
PAINTER, ADMINISTRATOR
b Sturgeon Bay, Wis, Sept 4, 47. *Study:* Lawrence Univ, Appleton, Wis, BA, 69; Univ Wis, Madison, MFA(painting), 71. *Work:* Bergstrom Art Ctr, Neenah, Wis; Kemper Insurance Companies, Inc, Long Grove, Ill; Miller Art Ctr, Sturgeon Bay, Wis; Andersen Window Corp, Bayport, Minn. *Exhib:* One-person show, Bergstrom Art Ctr, Neenah, Wis, 70; Watercolor Wis, Wustum Mus Art, Racine, 72-79 & 81-82; New Horizons, Chicago, 75; Women in the Arts, West Bend Mus Art, Wis, 76; Art Inst Chicago, 83. *Pos:* Coordr educ programs, Chicago Artists' Coalition, 80-83. *Awards:* Second Prizes, Artists Guild Chicago, 76 & Watercolor Wis, 81; Best of Show in Painting, Idea Corp, 79. *Bibliog:* M Tourtelot (auth), Resume--A Selective Guide, The Studios, 75; R Dozer (auth), Recording Door County's singularity, Chicago Tribune, 75; Door County Creations, Strom Channel 10, 77. *Mem:* Chicago Artists' Coalition (int dir, 79); Wis Watercolor Soc; Wis Painters & Sculptors Asn; Peninsula Arts Asn, Fish Creek, Wis. *Media:* Watercolor, Acrylic. *Dealer:* Edgewood Orchard Gallery Peninsula Players Rd Fish Creek WI 54212; Van Straaten Gallery 361 W Superior Chicago IL 60610. *Mailing Add:* 447 Oakdale Chicago IL 60657

BERNSTEIN, BENJAMIN D
COLLECTOR
b New York, NY, June 24, 07. *Pos:* Patron, Whitney Mus; mem bd trustees, Pa Acad Fine Arts. *Mem:* Life mem Am Fedn Arts; Metrop Mus Art; fel

Philadelphia Mus Art; Mus Mod Art, New York; Buten Mus of Wedgewood; Philadelphia Art Alliance. *Collection:* Large collection of contemporary oils, gouache, drawings, prints and sculpture including a great many Cobra works; large collections of art from New Guinea, Africa, and American Indian art. *Mailing Add:* 1824 Delancey Pl Philadelphia PA 19103

BERNSTEIN, EDWARD I
COLLECTOR, PATRON
b Philadelphia, Pa, Nov 15, 17. *Work:* Located at Philadelphia Mus Art, Pa Acad Fine Arts, La Salle Col Art Gallery & Dept Art & Hist, Villanova Univ, Pa. *Mem:* Wilson Peale Soc; Pa Acad Fine Art; Haviland Soc. *Collection:* Contemporary art includes oils, gouche, drawings, prints and sculpture; African paintings and sculpture; Elizabeth Frink. *Mailing Add:* 1810 Rittenhouse Sq Philadelphia PA 19103

BERNSTEIN, GERALD
PAINTER, RESTORER
b Indianapolis, Ind, Aug 25, 17. *Study:* John Herron Art Inst; Art Students League, with George Bridgman & Yasuo Kuniyoshi; NY Univ, BA, Inst Fine Arts, MA. *Work:* Staten Island Inst Arts & Sci. *Exhib:* Staten Island Inst Arts & Sci Ann, 50-81; Pietrantonio Gallery, New York, 59-62; one-man show, Kade Gallery, Wagner Col, 73; Metrop Mus, 75; Avery Fisher Hall, Lincoln Ctr, 75; one-man exhib, West Indian Themes, La Galerie. *Collections Arranged:* Artist Look at Nature, Surveys of American Painting & one-man & group exhibs, Staten Island Mus, 50-56. *Pos:* Cur art, Staten Island Mus, 50-56; owner & dir, Island Art Ctr, Staten Island, 58- *Teaching:* Artist in residence, Staten Island Community Col, 70-71. *Awards:* Staten Island Savings Bank Award, 79; Islander Award, 82; NY Telephone Award, 83. *Media:* Oil, Watercolor. *Mailing Add:* 1639 Richmond Rd Staten Island NY 10304

BERNSTEIN, JUDITH
PAINTER, LECTURER
b Newark, NJ, Oct 14, 42. *Study:* Pa State Univ, BS & MS; Yale Univ Sch Art & Archit, BFA & MFA. *Work:* Mus Mod Art, New York; Univ Colo Mus, Boulder; Int Mus Erotic Art, San Francisco. *Comn:* Two wall pieces, William N Copley, 77. *Exhib:* Warren Benedek Gallery, New York, 73; Five Americans a Paris, Galerie Gerald Piltzer, Paris, 75; Year of the Women, Bronx Mus Arts, NY, 75; Contemp Women: Consciousness & Content, Brooklyn Mus, NY, 77; Venerezia-Revenice, Palazzo Grassi, Venice, Italy, 78; The Great Big Drawing Show, PS 1, New York, 79; Feministische Kunst Int, Haags Gemeentemuseun, Noordbrants Mus & Nijmeegs Mus, Holland, 79-81; and others. *Teaching:* Pratt Inst; Rutgers Univ; asst prof fine arts, State Univ NY Stony Brook, 74-78; asst prof fine arts, State Univ NY Purchase, 78- *Awards:* Elizabeth Canfield Hicks Mem Scholar, Yale Univ Sch Art & Archit, 64-67; Nat Endowment Arts Grant, 74-75. *Bibliog:* Jeremy Gilbert-Rolfe (auth), Judith Bernstein, Artforum, 6/74; Cindy Nemser, (auth), Four artists of sensuality-Antin, Benglis, Bernstein, Wilke, Arts Mag, 3/75; Thomas Lawson (auth), Judith Bernstein at Brooks Jackson Iolas, Art in Am, 1/79. *Mem:* Col Art Asn Am; Nat Soc Lit & Arts; Women's Caucus Art. *Publ:* Guggenheim Panel Discussion Drawings, Soho Weekly News, 3/12-18/80. *Mailing Add:* 45 E Broadway New York NY 10002

BERNSTEIN, SARALINDA
DEALER, HISTORIAN
b New York, NY, Jan 7, 51. *Study:* Ecole Pratique des Hautes Etudes, Sorbonne, Paris, 70-71; Swarthmore Col, Pa, BA(magna cum laude), 72; NY Univ Sch Arts, 72; New Sch Social Res, New York, 74. *Collections Arranged:* Edvard Munch: Paradox of Woman (auth, catalog), Aldis Browne Fine Arts, New York, 81; Prints about Prints, 81-82; Nineteenth and Twentieth Century Works on Paper (auth, catalog), 82 & Edgar Chahine: Images of Venice and The Belle Epoque (auth, catalog), 83, Aldis Browne Fine Arts. *Pos:* Asst to dir, Asn Am Artists, New York, 72-78; exec vpres & dir, Int Exhibs, Aldis Browne Fine Arts, New York, 78- *Teaching:* Lectr, Soc Ethical Cult, New York, 81. *Res:* Form and function of original prints in society; the concept and definition of form in visual arts, particularly in late 19th through early 20th century European works. *Publ:* Contribr, 10 Jahre Galerie Kühl, Galerie Kühl, 77. *Mailing Add:* 1018 Madison Ave New York NY 10021

BERNSTEIN, SYLVIA
PAINTER, SCULPTOR
b Brooklyn, NY, Apr 11, 18. *Study:* Nat Acad Design; and with Arthur Covey, Gifford Beal, Sidney Dickinson, Charles Hinton, Carl Anderson & Leon Kroll. *Work:* New Brit Mus Am Art, Conn; Corcoran Gallery of Art, Washington, DC; Adlai Stevenson Mem Inst, Chicago; Univ Maine, Orono; Norfolk Mus, Va; Va Mus Fine Arts, Richmond. *Exhib:* 21st Nat Watercolor Biennial, Brooklyn Mus, 61; Childe Hassam Fund Paintings Exhib, Am Acad Arts & Lett, 61; Contemporary American Drawings, Smithsonian Inst Traveling Exhib, 66-67; 200 Years of Watercolor Painting in America, Metrop Mus Art, New York, 66 & Philadelphia Art Alliance Watercolor Painting in America, 67; Philadelphia Art Alliance Watercolor Show, 71-72; Whitney Mus, Butler Inst Am Art, NY Univ, Munson-Williams-Proctor Inst, Wadsworth Atheneum, Kalamazoo Inst Arts, Minneapolis Inst Art, Pa Acad Fine Arts, Parrish Mus, Southhampton & Okla Mus Art; Hove Mus, England. *Awards:* Medal of Honor for Watercolor, 63 & Medal of Honor for Oils, 74, Nat Asn Women Artists; Medal of Honor for Watercolor, Nat Arts Club. *Mem:* Nat Asn Women Painters (chmn watercolor jury, bd dirs); Philadelphia Watercolor Soc; Am Watercolor Soc; Audubon Artists; NY Soc Women Artists. *Media:* Watercolor, Oil. *Mailing Add:* 8 Circle Rd Scarsdale NY 10583

BERNSTEIN, THERESA
PAINTER, PRINTMAKER
b Philadelphia, Pa. *Study:* Pa Acad Fine Arts; Art Students League. *Work:* Metrop Mus Art, New York; Brooklyn Mus; Harvard Univ; Phillips Art Gallery, Washington, DC; Nat Mus, Smithsonian Inst. *Comn:* First Orchestra in America, Treas Dept for Mannhein, Pa, 40; portrait of David Lyons, Harvard Univ Biblical Mus Fac, 54; portrait Robert Pheiffer, Harvard Univ, 56; portrait Henrietta Szold, Hadassan, 59. *Exhib:* Exhib Am Painters, Metrop Mus Art, New York, 50; Carnegie Inst, Pittsburgh; Biennial Am Art, Corcoran Gallery Art, Washington, DC; Nat Mus, Smithsonian Inst, Washington, DC, 56; New York Ann, Nat Acad Design; one-woman show, Summit Gallery, New York, 78; New York Hist Soc Exhib, 83. *Awards:* Jeanne d'Arc Medal, Fr Inst Arts & Lett, 29; John A Johnson Award, North Shore Arts Asn, 71; Matson Mem Award, Rockport Art Asn, 79. *Bibliog:* E A Jenell (auth), articles, New York Times, 45 & Menorah J, 48; article, Am Artist, 80. *Mem:* Nat Asn Women Artists; Audubon Artists; Soc Am Graphic Artists; Allied Artists Am; New York Soc Women Artists (dir, 28-). *Media:* Oil, Aquarelle; Graphics. *Res:* Graphic art; American art. *Publ:* Auth, William Meyerowitz, 58 & auth, History of Jewish Artists, 58, Zukenft; auth, History-American artists, Gloucester Times, 70; auth, History North Shore Arts Association, 72; auth, History New York Society of Women Artists, 72. *Mailing Add:* 54 W 74th St New York NY 10023

BERNSTEIN, WILLIAM JOSEPH
DESIGNER, GLASSBLOWER
b Newark, NJ, Dec 3, 45. *Study:* Philadelphia Col Art, BFA, 68; Penland Sch, NC, 68-70. *Work:* Mint Mus Art, Charlotte, NC; Nat Collection Fine Art, Washington, DC; Craft & Folk Art Mus, Los Angeles; R J Reynolds Collection, Winston-Salem, NC; and others. *Exhib:* Fun & Fantasy for Children, Xerox Corp, Fairtree Gallery, Xerox Hall, Rochester, NY, 73; Baroque '74, Mus Contemp Crafts, New York, 74; In Praise of Hands, 1st World Crafts Exhib, Toronto, Can, 74; Craft Multiples, Renwick Gallery, Smithsonian Inst, Washington, DC, 75; Philadelphia Mus of Art, 77; Am Crafts in the White House, White House, Washington, DC, 77; Victoria & Albert Mus, Eng; and others. *Awards:* Nat Endowment Arts Fel, 74; Louis Comfort Tiffany Found Grant, 75. *Bibliog:* R L Grover (auth), Contemporary Art Glass, Crown Publ, 75; F Kulasiewicz (auth), Glassblowing, Watson-Guptill, 75; Design in Modern Interiors, Studio Vista, 75. *Mailing Add:* Box 309 Rte 5 Burnsville NC 28714

BERRY, CAROLYN (CAROLYN BERRY BECKER)
PAINTER, WRITER
b Sweet Springs, Mo, June 27, 30. *Study:* Univ Mo, BA, 53; Humboldt State Col, 71. *Exhib:* ISCA, 82 & 83; Crackerjack's Halloween Show, 82; Woman's Caucus Art, New York, 82 & San Francisco, 83; Art/Life 83, San Francisco; Long Beach Mus Art, 83; plus others. *Pos:* Artist-in-residence, Calif Arts Coun, Pacific Grove, 79. *Awards:* First Graphic Award, Monterey Peninsula Mus Art, 74. *Mem:* Women's Caucus for Art; Nat & Northern Calif. *Media:* Acrylic, Watercolor. *Publ:* Contribr, Vinnie Ream, Portrait of a young sculptor, Feminist Art J, 77; contribr, Quill Art, Heresies, 79; contrib, Comenha, Frontiers, 82; contribr, Back to you Fred (Ginger Rogers), Salome, 83 & Zone, 83. *Dealer:* The Innerworks 122 Broadway Santa Monica CA 90401; Artworks 170 S La Brea Los Angeles CA 90036. *Mailing Add:* 78 Cuesta Vista Monterey CA 93940

BERRY, GLENN
PAINTER, EDUCATOR
b Glendale, Calif, Feb 27, 29. *Study:* Pomona Col, BA(magna cum laude); Art Inst Chicago, BFA & MFA. *Work:* Storm King Art Ctr, Mountainville, NY; Joseph H Hirshhorn Collection, Washington, DC; Kaiser Aluminum & Chem Corp, Oakland, Calif; Palm Springs Desert Mus, Calif; Calif State Univ, Humboldt. *Exhib:* Phelan Awards Exhib & Artists Behind Artists, Calif Palace Legion Hon, San Francisco, 67; one-man shows, Ankrum Gallery, Los Angeles, 70, Esther Bear Gallery, Santa Barbara, Calif, 71 & Humboldt State Univ, 75; Six Northern Calif Artists, Henry Gallery, Univ Wash, 75; two-man show, Humboldt Cult Ctr, Eureka, Calif, 77; and others. *Teaching:* Prof painting, Humboldt State Univ, 56-81, prof emer, 81- *Media:* Acrylic, Oil. *Dealer:* Ankrum Gallery 657 N La Cienega Blvd Los Angeles CA 90069. *Mailing Add:* Dept of Art Humboldt State Univ Arcata CA 95521

BERRY, WILLIAM AUGUSTUS
EDUCATOR, GRAPHIC ARTIST
b Jacksonville, Tex, Sept 29, 33. *Study:* Univ Tex, Austin, BFA(summa cum laude), 55; Circolo Artistico, Rome, 56; Univ Southern Calif, MFA, 57. *Exhib:* Tex Ann, Dallas Mus Fine Arts, 51 & 57; one-man show, US Info Agency Gallery, Athens, Greece, 59; Ann Nat Exhib, New York Soc Illusr Gallery, 65, 67 & 69; Works on Paper, Boston Univ Art Gallery, 74; plus many others. *Pos:* Free-lance illusr, The Reporter, Newsweek, Esquire, Opera News Mag, New York, 60-68; art dir & designer, Tex Mo Mag, 72-73. *Teaching:* Vis assoc prof, Grad Summer Sch Teachers, Wesleyan Univ, 67; asst prof art, Univ Tex, Austin, 68-74; assoc prof art & chmn graphic design area, Boston Univ, 74-78; prof art & head graphic design area, Univ Mo-Columbia, 78- *Awards:* Dorothy Thompson Traveling Fel, 65-66; Citations of Merit, New York Soc Illusr, 65, 67 & 70; Univ Mo Summer Res Fel, 79. *Bibliog:* Illustrators '65, '67 & '70, Ann Am Illus, New York; Susan E Meyer (auth), William A Berry, illustrator/painter, Am Artist, 3/70; Ruth Seidler (auth), Drawing the human form, Libr J, 11/01/77; plus others. *Mem:* Am Inst Graphic Art; Col Art Asn Am. *Media:* Multimedia. *Res:* Drawing, technique and theory; perspective drawing theory of Piero della Francesca. *Publ:* Coauth, Paper Construction for Children, Van Nostrand Reinhold, 66; illusr, Carter Wilson's On Firm Ice, Crowell, 69; auth, Visual puns, Print Mag, 9/71; auth, Drawing the Human Form, Van Nostrand Reinhold, 77; and many others. *Mailing Add:* 908 Edgewood Ave Columbia MO 65201

BERSHAD, DAVID L
HISTORIAN, EDUCATOR
b San Francisco, Calif, Mar 11, 42. *Study:* Stanford Univ, AB, 62; Univ Calif, Los Angeles, PhD(with distinction), 70. *Teaching:* Asst prof art hist, Ariz State Univ, 70-72; prof art hist, Univ Calgary, 75- *Mem:* Univ Art Asn Can. *Res:* Seventeenth and 18th century Italian painting and sculpture, with specific emphasis on Roman art. *Publ:* Auth, A series of papal busts by Domenico Guidi, 70, auth, Domenico Guidi and Nicolas Poussin, 71, auth The cardinal Marco Bragadino tomb in the church of San Marco in Rome, 77 & auth, New documents concerning Michelangelo's deposition in Florence, 78, Burlington Mag; auth, The tapestries of Raphael and their re-acquisition in 1808, Antologia di Belle Arte, 78. *Mailing Add:* 2105 90th Ave Apt 504 Calgary AB T2V 0X5 Canada

BERTHOT, JAKE
PAINTER
b Niagara Falls, NY, Mar 30, 39. *Study:* New Sch Social Res. *Work:* High Mus, Atlanta; Va Mus Fine Arts, Richmond; Whitney Mus Am Art, New York; Aldrich Mus Contemp Art, Ridgefield, Conn. *Exhib:* Ann, 69 & 73, Recent Acquisitions, 71 & Continuing Abstraction in Am Art, 74, Whitney Mus Am Art; Contemp Drawings, Chicago Art Inst, 71; Eight New York Painters, Univ Calif Art Mus, Berkeley, 72; Paris Biennale, France, 73; Recent Abstract Painting, Pratt Inst, Brooklyn, NY, 74; Corcoran Biennial, Corcoran Gallery, Washington, DC, 75; Fundamental Painting, Stedelijk Mus, Amsterdam, 75; Venice Biennale, US Pavilion, 76; From Women's Eyes, Rose Art Mus, Brandeis Univ, Mass, 77; New Acquisitions Show, Mus Mod Art, New York, 77; Eight Abstract Painters, Inst Contemp Art, Univ Pa, 78; New Painting--New York, Hayward Gallery, London, 79; one-man exhibs, Nigel Greenwood Gallery, London, 79 & Nina Nielsen Gallery, Boston, 79; L'Amerique aux Independents 1944-1980, Grand Palais, Paris, 80. *Bibliog:* Dore Ashton (auth), Peinture, peinture-o, painterly painting, Plural, 9/73 & article, Arts, 6/74; Peter Plagens (auth), Peter and the pressure cooker, Artforum, 6/74. *Dealer:* Daivd McKee Gallery 140 E 63rd St New York NY 10021. *Mailing Add:* 66 Grand St New York NY 10013

BERTONI, DANTE H
PAINTER, ILLUSTRATOR
b New York, NY, Nov 13, 26. *Study:* Parson's Sch Design, New York, Advert Design Cert, 51; Art Students League, with Bernard Klonis, 52-54; NY Univ, 60. *Work:* US Navy Combat Art Collection, Washington Naval Yard; Forbes Mag Collection, New York; Hotel DuPont Collection, Wilmington, Del; Mutual Benefit Life Ins Co Collection, New York; Cent Intel Agency off, White House, Washington, DC. *Comn:* Sea Mule (illus), Lederle Labs, Am Cyanamid Co, Wayne, NJ, 71; Atomic Submarine Base, New London, Conn, Rear Adm L R Geis, US Navy, 70, Exotic Dancer (exercise), Rear Adm William Thompson, 71, Oper Homecoming & Endsweep, Capt D M Cooney, 73; Proceedings (cover illus), US Naval Inst, Annapolis, Md, 72; Oper Cuba-Sealift, Adm John B Hayes Us Coast Guard, Washington, DC. *Exhib:* Am Watercolor Soc, NY, 55-; Nat Acad Fine Arts, 56-; Nat Arts Club, 60-; Salmagundi Sketch Club, 55-; US Navy Combat Art Exhibit Travel Show, Washington Navy Yard, 70- *Pos:* Asst art dir, J Walter Thompson, New York, 51-57; graphics designer, Lippencott & Margulies Co, 62-63; package designer, Reigel Paper Co, 64-66; artist, Equitable Bag Co, 72- *Awards:* NACAL Gold Medal, Louis E Seley, 72; Grand Prize Washington Sq Outdoor Art Exhib, Lufthansa Air Lines, 73; First US Coast Guard Art Program Medal, 83. *Bibliog:* Mary O'Flaherty (auth), Artist pictures way through Navy activity, New York News, 11/14/71. *Mem:* Am Watercolor Soc, New York; Salmagundi Sketch Club (vchmn NACAL, 70); US Naval Inst, Annapolis, Md; Long Beach Art Asn, NY. *Publ:* Auth, Painting in contrasts, Palette Talk, Vol 41, 80. *Dealer:* Chadd's Ford Gallery Inc Rte 1 & 100 Chadd's Ford PA 19317. *Mailing Add:* 52-02 Eighth Ave Brooklyn NY 11220

BESANT, DEREK MICHAEL
PAINTER, INSTRUCTOR
b Ft MacLeod, Alberta, Can, July 15, 50. *Study:* Univ Calgary, Alberta Can, BFA, 73. *Work:* DeCordova Mus, Boston, Mass; Metrop Mus, Miami, Fla; Can Coun Art Bank, Ottawa, Ont; Calif Col Arts & Crafts, Los Angeles; Glenbow-Alberta Mus, Calgary. *Comn:* Flatiron mural, A E LePage, Royal Insurance Lavalin Inc, Toronto, Ont, 80; Eau Claire Peel, Bourgeau Developments Sturgets Architects, Calgary, Alta, 82. *Exhib:* Boston Printmakers, Boston Ctr Arts, Mass, 78; 8th Int Triennial Color Prints, Grenchen Arts Mus, Switzerland, 79; Other Realities, Can House London England, Paris, France, 79; Royal Canadian Soc Arts, Mickle Arts Mus, Calgary, Alta, 80; Canadian Prints, Asn Print Workshops Great Britain, Edinborough, Scotland, 80; Ten Canadian Print Artists, Nat Mus Can Japanese Print Coun, Tour Japan Nat Mus, 80-81; and others. *Pos:* Exhibs designer, Glenbow Mus, Calgary, 73-77; Alta ed, Artmagazine, Toronto, 74-; drawing chmn, Alta Col Art, 77-; comt mem, Alta Legislature Art Acquisition Comt, 81-82. *Teaching:* Guest artist collaborations, Univ Arts Asn, Univ Alta, 76; guest artist printmaking, Mem Univ, Newfoundland, 77; lectr public art, Univ Regina, Sask, 81; lectr murals, Red Deer Col, 82. *Awards:* Canada Coun Grant, 77; Second Prize, Miami Biennale, Mus Mod Art, 77; Award Winner, Andrew Nelson Wheehead Co, 78. *Bibliog:* Ann Paine (auth), Derek Besant, Arts West, 78; John Bently Mays (auth), Flatiron Toronto's biggest hit, Globe & Mail, 80; Francis Welch (auth), Tronmpe l'Oeuil, Macleans, 82. *Mem:* Royal Can Acad Arts; Print & Drawing Coun Can (vchmn, 76-78); Can Artists Representation; Visual Arts Ont; World Print Coun. *Media:* Watercolor, Ink. *Res:* Contemporary Canadian. *Publ:* Illusr, The Back Room, Oberon, 80; A Culinary Palette, Merritt, 81; contribr, Artmagazine, 81; contribr, Artviews, Visual Arts Ont, 82; Macleans, Maclean Hunter, 82. *Mailing Add:* Box 520 Midnapore AB T0L 1J0 Canada

BESNER, J JACQUES
SCULPTOR, MURALIST
b Vaudreuil, Que, Can, Sept 28, 19. *Study:* Teachers' Col, Univ Montreal, Que, 42; study of archit, Int Corresp Sch, Chicago, Ill, three yrs. *Work:* Phoenix Art Mus, Ariz; Bhirla Mus, Calcutta, India; Mus d'Art Contemporain, Thomas More Inst, Montreal, Que; Winston Collection, Dearborn, Mich. *Comn:* Aluminum murals, Aluminum Co Jamaica-Kingston, 72, Aluminum Co Can Ltd, Montreal, 76, Chromasco-Timminsco Inc, Montreal, 76, Ottawa Civic Hosp & Am Airlines, Logan Airport, Boston. *Exhib:* Montreal Mus Fine Arts, Can, 64; Mus d'Art Contemporain, Montreal, Que, 65-68; Pagani Found, Milan, Italy, 68; Rose Fried Gallery, New York, 68; Nat Cult Ctr, Ottawa, Ont, 70; Que Pavilion, Expo 70, Osaka, Japan, 70; Int Arts Fair, Basel, Switz, 73; and others. *Collections Arranged:* Stratford Festival, Ont, Can, 76; Salon de l'Acier, Brussels, Belg, 68; Pagani Found, Milan, Italy, 68; 20 Years of Que Sculpture, Mus Rodin, Paris, 70. *Pos:* Dir visual arts (Man the Creator), Expo 67, Montreal, Que, 64-67; dir, Maison des Arts la Sauvegarde, Montreal, 67-69. *Teaching:* Part-time prof, Visual Arts Ctr, Montreal, 69-71 & Saydie Bronfman Ctr, Montreal, 71-73; prof sculpture, Dawson Col, Montreal, 73-75; chmn dept visual arts, Univ Que, Trois Rivieres, 75-; instr, Univ Que, Hull, 82- *Awards:* Rothman's Award, Rothman's of Pall Mall, Stratford, Ont, 65; Que Competition Award, Mus Art Contemporain, Montreal, Cult Affairs, Que, 66; Thomas More Award, Thomas More Inst, Montreal, 69. *Bibliog:* F Sigouin (auth), Critique, Le Figaro, Paris, 66; Paul Gladu (auth), Monograph, Que Sculptors' Asn, 68; L Levesque (auth), pictorial article, Vie des Arts Mag, Montreal, 71. *Mem:* Arts Club, Montreal; Prof Artists Asn Que. *Media:* Metal; Stained Glass. *Mailing Add:* 404 St Henri St Montreal PQ H3C 2P5 Canada

BESSEMER, AURIEL
MURALIST, DEALER
b Grand Rapids, Mich, Feb 27, 09. *Study:* Western Reserve Acad, scholar, 24-27; Columbia Univ, Columbia Univ Club Scholar, 27-30; Nat Acad Design, with Arthur Covey & Leon Kroll, 27-30; Master Inst United Arts, with Howard Giles, Roerich Mus Scholar, 31-33; Art Students League; State Univ NY, 49, George Washington Univ; Wilson Teacher's Col. *Comn:* Southern Tapestry (mural), Post Off, Winnsboro, SC, 38; Life in the Southern Cotton Belt (mural), Post Off, Hazlehurst, Miss, 39; six murals, Post Off, Arlington, Va, 39-40; six murals, Wabash Railroad parlor cars, 49; twelve murals, Pa Railroad parlor cars, Congressionals NY to Washington run, 51-52; and many other murals & portraits. *Exhib:* One-man shows at 16 art ctrs in the US incl Pub Libr, Washington, DC, City Hall, Asheville, NC, Art Ctr, Raleigh, NC, Currier Gallery, Manchester, NH & Bowdoin Col Mus Fine Arts, Brunswick, Maine, 35-43. *Pos:* Art gallery dir, Gallery Mod Masters, 36-42; spec asst to dir, Univ Sci & Philosophy, Waynesboro, Va, 62; dir, New Renaissance Gallery Art, Long Beach, 79- *Teaching:* Instr art, Nat Art Sch, Washington, DC, 45-46, Jean Morgan Art Sch, New York, 47-49, Roerich Acad Arts, 48-52, Pan Am Art Sch, 49-51, Catan-Rose Art Inst, Forest Hills, NY, 50 & Montclair Sch Art, NJ, 50; pvt art classes, 63-70; artist-illusr, Summit Lighthouse, Colorado Springs, 72- *Awards:* Maximillian Toch Prize, Nat Acad Design, 30; Chaloner Prize, 32; Dipl & Silver Medal, 70 & Gold Medal, 72, Tommaso Campanella Int Acad Rome; and others. *Bibliog:* Marian Slater (auth), Auriel Bessemer--artist, philosopher, poet, Voice Universal, 11/62. *Media:* Oil. *Publ:* Illusr, Climb the Highest Mountain, 72 & Light from Heavenly Lanterns, 73, Summit Lighthouse. *Mailing Add:* 1779 Locust Ave Long Beach CA 90806

BESSER, ARNE CHARLES
PAINTER
b Hinsdale, Ill, May 11, 35. *Study:* Univ NMex; Art Ctr Sch, Los Angeles, with John Audobon Tyler and Lorser Feidelsson. *Comn:* Portrait of Mr Aldrich, Chmn Bd, Chemical Bank, 68; painting, Stuart M Speiser, 73; painting, Gen Chas Spofford, 76; painting, Dr S Grossman, 77. *Exhib:* Lowe Art Mus, Coral Gables, Fla, 74; Pa State Mus Art, University Park, 74; Butler Inst Am Art, Youngstown, Ohio, 75; Louis K Meisel Gallery, New York, 75; Baltimore Mus Art, 75; Smihtsonian Inst, 81; Terra Mus Am Art, Evanston, Ill, 83. *Awards:* Butler Inst of Am Art Medal of Merit, Today's Art Mag, 75. *Media:* Oil on Canvas, Watercolor. *Mailing Add:* c/o Louis K Meisel Gallery 141 Prince St New York NY 10012

BETENSKY, ROSE HART
PAINTER, ADMINISTRATOR
b New York, NY. *Study:* Painting with Josef Presser. *Exhib:* Nat Acad Galleries, New York, 60-77; Royal Acad, Edinburgh, Scotland, 63; Norfolk Mus of Arts & Sci, Va, 64; Cult Inst of Tolsa, Guadalajara, Mex, 65; Palazzo Vecchio, Florence, Italy, 72. *Pos:* Pres, New York Soc of Women Artists, 69-70, Nat Asn of Women Artists, 70-72 & Am Soc of Contemp Artists, 77-79. *Awards:* Marion de Sola Mendel Award, Nat Asn Women Artists, 78; Award of Merit, Am Soc Comtemp Artists, 81; Dr Samuel Gelband Prize, Nat Asn Women Artists, 83. *Mem:* Audubon Artists; Nat Asn of Women Artists; New York Asn of Women Artists; Am Soc of Contemp Artists. *Media:* Acrylic. *Mailing Add:* 66 Hayloft Lane Roslyn Heights NY 11577

BETTERIDGE, LOIS ETHERINGTON
SILVER & GOLDSMITH, LECTURER
b Drummonville, Que, Nov 6, 28. *Study:* Ont Col Art, 47-48; Univ Kans, BFA, 51; Cranbrook Acad Art, MFA, 57. *Work:* Ont Craft Coun, Toronto; Nat Mus Natural Sci, Ottawa; Seagrams Mus, Kitchener; Cranbrook Acad Art, Mich; Scottish Mus, Edinburgh. *Comn:* Communion set, Christ Church Cathedral, Vancouver, 74; bronze sculptures, IBM Can, 75; desk sets, Can Pac Railways; bronze sculptures, Imperial Oil Can; McLuhan Teleglobe Can Award, Int Commun, UNESCO. *Exhib:* First Nat Fine Crafts Exhib, Nat

Gallery Can, Ottawa, 57; Jewellery 71, Art Gallery Ont, Toronto, 71; Reprise, A Retrospective, Cranbrook Acad Art, Mich, 75; Contemp Ont Crafts, Agnes Etherington Gallery, Kingston, Ont, 77; Metalsmiths, Soc NAm Goldsmiths, Phoenix Art Mus, Ariz, 77; Artisans Touring Exhib, Can, 78; Reflections in Silver and Gold Traveling Exhib (solo), Mus Natural Sci, Ottawa & seven others, 81-83; Remains To Be Seen, John Michael Kohler Arts Ctr, Sheboygan, Wis, 82; Silversmithing--Three and a Half Decades, Cranbrook Acad Art, Mich, 82; The Michigan Influence, Eastern Mich Univ, Ypsilanti, 82. *Teaching:* Lectr design, metal & weaving, Univ Guelph, Ont, 57-61; vis lectr & workshop leader, worldwide, 69-; vis prof, NS Col Art & Design, summer 81. *Awards:* Two Commendations, De Beers Int Diamond Ring Competition, London, 66; Citation Distinguished Prof Achievement, Univ Kans, 75; Saidye Bronfman Award for Excellence in Crafts, 78. *Mem:* Ont Crafts Coun (mem bd, 72-73); distinguished mem Soc NAm Goldsmiths; Can Crafts Coun; Visual Arts Ottawa Region (crafts chmn & vpres, 74-77); fel Royal Can Acad Arts. *Media:* Silver, Gold. *Publ:* Auth, The function of the artist in Canada, Ont Crafts Coun Rev, 58; auth, The techniques of chasing and repousse, Crafts Can, 75. *Mailing Add:* 62 Parc Champlain Mont St Hilaire PQ J3H 3R6 Canada

BETTINSON, BRENDA
EDUCATOR, PAINTER
b King's Lynn, Eng, Aug 17, 29; US citizen. *Study:* St Martins Sch Art, London, 46-48; Cent Sch Arts & Crafts, London, 48-50, Nat Dipl in Design, 50; Acad de la Grande Chaumiere, Paris, 51; Ecole Pratique des Hautes Etudes, Sorbonne, 51-53, Eleve Titulaire, 52. *Comn:* St Anselm's Abbey, Washington, DC; St Mary's Benedictine Abbey, Morristown, NJ; Dominican House of Studies, Washington, DC; Our Lady of Grace Monastery, New Guilford, Conn; murals, Chapel Calvary Hosp, Bronx, 78; and others. *Exhib:* Comn on Worship & Fine Arts, Bridgeport, Conn, 65; Int Exhib Relig Art, Nat Arts Club, New York, 66; Cranbrook Acad Art, Detroit, 69; Episcopal Ctr, Chicago, 71; murals, Calvary Hospital, Bronx, 78; plus numerous one-man shows. *Pos:* Art ed, Riverside Radio WRVR-FM, New York, 61-65; mem art comt, Contemporary Christian Art Gallery, New York, 63-79; consult, Soc for Renewal of Christian Art, 69- *Teaching:* Prof art & chairperson art & design, Pace Univ, Westchester, 63-; lectr art, Katonah Gallery, NY, 72-75. *Awards:* Gold Medal, Nat Arts Club, New York, 66. *Bibliog:* The Beginning (film), Columbia Univ Press, 62. *Mem:* Col Art Asn. *Media:* Oil, Acrylic. *Publ:* Auth, Patron of the Living Arts, America, 63; auth, Maurice Lavanoux, Crusador Extraordinary, Sign Mag, 75; illusr, Gates of Heaven & Gates of Joy, C Stern, 79. *Dealer:* Contemporary Christian Art Gallery 217 E 66 New York NY. *Mailing Add:* 255 W 75th St New York NY 10023

BETTMANN, OTTO LUDWIG
HISTORIAN
b Leipzig, Ger, Oct 15, 03; US citizen. *Study:* Univ Leipzig, PhD, 27, MSLS, 32; Fla Atlantic Univ, DHL, 79. *Exhib:* Bettmann Panopticon Exhib, New York, 63. *Pos:* Assoc ed, C F Peters Co, Leipzig, 27-28; ed, Axel Juncker Publ, Berlin, 28-30; cur rare bks, State Art Libr, Berlin, 30-33; founder, Bettmann Archive, Inc, 36-78. *Teaching:* Adj prof Am studies, Fla Atlantic Univ, 74- *Awards:* Award of Merit, Inst Graphic Arts, 67, 68 & 71; LHD, Fla Atlantic Univ, 79. *Bibliog:* John F Baker (auth), Living in the past with Dr Otto Bettmann, Publ Weekly, 11/25/74; Helen Markel (auth), The Bettmann behind the archives, New York Times, 10/81; article, From Freud to bicyling monks, Time Mag, 3/21/81. *Res:* Pictorial documentation of all aspects of cultural history. *Publ:* Auth, A pictorial history of medicine, 56; co-auth, Our literary heritage, 56; co-auth, Pictorial history of music, 60; auth, The good old days-they were terrible, 74; auth, The Bettmann Portable Archive, 67, A Word From the Wise, 77 & The Bettmann Archive Picture History of the World, 78. *Dealer:* 855 S Federal Highway, Boca Raton, FL 33432. *Mailing Add:* 2600 S Ocean Blvd Boca Raton FL 33432

BETTS, EDWARD HOWARD
PAINTER, EDUCATOR
b Yonkers, NY, Aug 4, 20. *Study:* Art Students League; Yale Univ, BA, 42; Univ Ill, MFA, 52. *Work:* Fogg Mus Art, Cambridge, Mass; Butler Inst Am Art, Youngstown, Ohio; Va Mus Fine Arts, Richmond, Va; Univ Rochster Mem Art Gallery, NY; Indianapolis Art Mus, Ind; and others. *Exhib:* Five Corcoran Biennials, Washington, DC, 47-59; American Painting Today-1950, Metrop Mus Art, New York, 50; Int Watercolor Exhibs, Brooklyn Mus, NY, 53, 55 & 61; Watercolor USA, Springfield Art Mus, Mo, 63-71 & 74-75; Am Watercolor Soc, NY, 50-80; Nat Acad of Design 53- *Teaching:* Prof painting, Univ Ill, Champaign, 49- *Awards:* First Altman Landscape Prize, Nat Acad Design, 57, 59 & 66; Purchase Award, Childe Hassam Purchase Fund Exhib, 66; M Cooper Award, Am Watercolor, Soc NY, 77; and others. *Bibliog:* A S Weller (auth), Edward Betts, Art in Am New Talent Issue, 2/55. *Mem:* Nat Acad Design; Am Watercolor Soc; life mem Art Students League. *Media:* Acrylic, Watercolor. *Publ:* Auth, Master Class in Watercolor and Acrylics, Watson-Guptill, 75; auth, Creative Landscape Painting, Watson-Guptill, 78; auth, Creative Seascape Painting, Watson-Guptill, 81. *Dealer:* Midtown Galleries 11 E 57th St New York NY 10022. *Mailing Add:* 804 Dodds Dr Champaign IL 61820

BEVERIDGE, KARL J
PHOTOGRAPHER, SCULPTOR
b Ottawa, Ont, Nov 7, 45. *Study:* Ont Col Art, 65-66; New Sch, Toronto, Ont, 66-67. *Work:* Nat Gallery Can & Can Coun Art Bank, Ottawa, Ont; Vancouver Art Gallery, BC; Owens Art Gallery, Sackville, NB. *Exhib:* New Trends, Galerie de France, Paris, 69; Third Int Pioneer Galleries Exhib, Mus Mod Art, Paris, 71; 3rd Biennial de Arte Coltejer Medellin, Colombia, 72; Carmen Lamanna at Owens Art Gallery,

Sackville, NB, 75; It's Still a Privileged Art, Art Gallery Ont, Toronto, 76; 76 Venice Biennale, Italy, 76; solo exhibit, Art Gallery Ont, 76 & Canada House, London, Eng, 76; Social Criticism & Art Practice, San Francisco Art Inst, Calif, 77. *Pos:* Ed, Fox Mag, New York, 76; ed, Red Herring Mag, New York, 77-78; ed, Centerfold/Fuse Mag, Toronto, 79-80. *Teaching:* Instr, Hartford Sch Art, Conn, 74; instr, NS Col Art & Design, Halifax, 75-76; instr, Univ Guelph, Ont, 78. *Awards:* Can Coun grants, 68-71, 76 & 79. *Bibliog:* It's still privileged art, Vie des Arts, fall 76; Art and politics, Art in Am, 9/77; Phillip Monk (auth), Reading and representation in political art, Parachute, 79. *Mem:* Can Artists Representation (chmn, 79-80). *Media:* Photography; Graphics. *Publ:* Auth, Words on Michael Snow, Artscanada, 71; auth, A forum on art forum, The Fox, 75; coauth, Maybe Wendy's Right, Toronto, 79; auth, The Canada Council on Bay Street, Parallel Rev, No 3, 80. *Mailing Add:* Carmen Lamanna Gallery 840 Yonge St Toronto ON M4W 2H1 Canada

BEVLIN, MARJORIE ELLIOTT
PAINTER, WRITER
b The Dalles, Ore, May 9, 17. *Study:* Univ Colo, BFA; Univ Wash, Col of Archit; NY Univ, MS; also with Jimmy Ernst, 56. *Comn:* Two murals, Otero Jr Col, La Junta, Colo, 55. *Exhib:* Brit Women's Exhib, Liverpool, 64; 8th Ann Prix de Deauville, France, 72; Prix de Rome, 72; one-man shows, Colorado, 75; Orcas Island, 81. *Pos:* Dir & founder, Ark Valley Sch Arts Festival, 56-75. *Teaching:* Founding chmn fine arts, Otero Jr Col, 55-75. *Awards:* Selectionee de Jury, Prix de Deauville, 72. *Mem:* Nat Asn Women Artists; Delta Phi Delta (vpres Rho Chap, 38). *Media:* Mixed Watercolor & Acrylic, Oil. *Res:* All areas of design and the application of natural elements and principles in the artist's work. *Publ:* Auth, Design Through Discovery, Holt, Rinehart & Winston, Inc, 63, brief ed, 80 & 4th ed, 83; contribr, Junior Col Journal, Colorado State Art Asn. *Mailing Add:* Star Rte 95 Eastsound WA 98245

BEYER, STEVEN J
SCULPTOR, LECTURER
b Minneapolis, Minn, Aug 27, 51. *Study:* Macalester Col, St Paul, Minn, BA, 73. *Work:* Whitney Mus Am Art, New York; Walker Art Ctr & Minneapolis Inst Art, Minn; Newport Harbor Art Mus, Newport Beach, Calif; Madison Art Ctr, Wis. *Comn:* Sculpture, Golden Valley High Sch, Minn, 75; sculpture, City St Paul, Park Bd, Minn, 75; sculpture, Spring Hill Conference Ctr, Wayzata, Minn, 77; sculpture, General Mills Corp, Minneapolis, Minn, 78; sculpture, Northern Ill Univ, DeKalb, Ill. *Exhib:* Spaces, Univ Notre Dame, Ind, 73; New Works by Twin Cities Artists, Landmark Ctr, Minn Mus Art, St Paul, 79; Recent Acquisitions, Walker Art Ctr, Minneapolis, Minn, 79; Beyer, Dumke & Larson, Minneapolis Inst Art, Minn, 79; Artists and Printer, Walker Art Ctr, Minneapolis, Minn, 80; Words as Images, Univ Chicago, Ill, 81. *Teaching:* Vis artist sculpture, Kansas City Art Inst, Mo, 79; vis assoc prof sculpture, Univ Iowa, Iowa City, 79-81; instr sculpture, Minneapolis Col Art & Design, 81-82. *Awards:* Guggenheim Fel, 78; Nat Endowment Arts Fel, 81; Bush Found Fel, 82. *Bibliog:* Articles, Midwest Art & Art Am, 79; Bob Arnold (dir), Family Systems (film), 81. *Mem:* Col Art Asn Am. *Mailing Add:* 610 Summit Ave #205 St Paul MN 55102

BHAVSAR, NATVAR PRAHLADJI
PAINTER
b Gothava, India, Apr 7, 34. *Study:* Bombay State Higher Art Exam, India, AM, 58, Govt Dipl Art, 59; Gujarat Univ, India, BA, 60; Univ Pa, MFA, 65. *Work:* Whitney Mus Am Art, New York; Mass Inst Technol, Cambridge; Metrop Mus Art, New York; Boston Mus Fine Arts, Mass; Australian Nat Gallery, Canberra; and others. *Exhib:* Whitney Mus Am Art Painting Ann, 70-71; Two Generations of Color Painting, Inst Contemp Art, Univ Pa, Philadelphia, 70; Beautiful Paintings & Sculpture, Jewish Mus, New York, 70; one-man shows, Max Hutchinson Gallery, New York, 71, 72, 77 & 78 & Gloria Luria Gallery, Miami, 78; and others. *Teaching:* Art instr, Univ RI, spring semesters 67-69. *Awards:* John D Rockefeller III Fund Fel, 65-66; Guggenheim Fel, 75-76. *Bibliog:* Christopher Andreae (auth), Painters philosophy, goal beyond objects, Christian Sci Monitor, 1/24/70; Carter Ratcliff (auth), article, Art Int, 10/72; Elwyn Linn (auth), article, Art Int, 4/77. *Media:* Dry Pigment, Acrylic. *Mailing Add:* 131 Greene St New York NY 10012

BIALA, JANICE
PAINTER
b Biala, Poland, Oct 18, 03; US citizen. *Study:* Nat Acad Art, New York; Art Students League. *Work:* Whitney Mus, New York; Centre Contemp Art, Paris, France; Duncan Phillips Collection, Washington, DC; Mus Cantonal de Lausanne, Switz; Corcoran Gallery; and others. *Exhib:* Bignou Gallery, New York, 42; Jeanne Bucher Gallery, Paris, 46; Stable Gallery, New York & Le Point Cardinale, Paris, 61; exposition, La Famille In Portrait, Mus Arts Decorative, Louvre Mus, 79. *Bibliog:* Biala paints a picture, Art News, 56; Chefs--d'oeuvre de l'art, Hachette, 65; Dora Vallier (auth), Biala, Pour l'Art, 60 & Repères la Peinture en France...1870-1970, Alfieri & Lacroix. *Mailing Add:* 8 Rue du General Bertrand Paris France

BIALOBRODA, ANNA
PAINTER
b Lodz, Poland. *Study:* Otis Art Inst, BFA, 71; MFA, 73; Whitney Mus Am Art Independent Study Prog, 73. *Work:* Albright-Knox Art Gallery; Chemical Bank, DeBevoise & Plimpton, New York; European Fine Art Found, Geneva; Galerie Fahlbusch, Ludwigshafen, Ger. *Exhib:* American Painting: The 80s, Grey Art Gallery, New York, 79, Mus Contemp Art, Houston, 79 & Ludwig Mus, Aachen, Ger, 80; On Paper, Inst Contemp Art, Va Mus Fine Art, 80;

Drawings, Castelli Gallery, New York, 80; Recent Paintings, Marilyn Pearl Gallery, New York, 80-82; Sommerausstellung, Galerie Fahlbusch, Ludwigshafen, Ger, 82; American Painting, Mira Godard Gallery, Toronto, 82. *Awards:* Nat Endowment Arts Grant, 75. *Bibliog:* John Yau (auth), article, Art in Am, 2/82; John Russell (auth), article, New York Times, 11/26/82; Barbara Rose (auth), article, Paris Vogue, 4/83. *Media:* Acrylic, Oil. *Mailing Add:* c/o Marilyn Pearl Gallery 38 E 57th St New York NY 10022

BIANCO, PAMELA RUBY
PAINTER
b London, Eng, Dec 31, 06; US citizen. *Study:* Guggenheim fel for creative painting abroad, 30. *Work:* Mus Mod Art & Chase Manhattan Bank, New York; Whitney Mus Am Art; New York Pub Libr; Hirshhorn Mus Art, Washington, DC. *Exhib:* One-woman exhibs, Leicester Galleries, London, 19-20, Anderson Galleries, New York, 21, Knoedler Galleries, New York, 24, Graham Gallery, New York, 69 & 76 & Santa Barbara Mus Art, 70. *Bibliog:* J B Manson (auth), Drawings of Pamela Bianco, Studio, 11/25/20; Louis Untermeyer (auth), Drawings of Pamela Bianco, Century Mag, 7/22; Joseph Stella (auth), Pamela Bianco, An appreciation, Playboy, 25. *Media:* Oil. *Publ:* Illusr, Flora, William Heinemann, London, 20; illusr, Natives of Rock, Francesco Bianco, 25; illusr, Skin Horse, George H Doran, 27; auth & illusr, Beginning with A, Oxford Univ, 47; auth & illusr, Valentine Party, Lippincott, 54. *Dealer:* Graham Gallery 1014 Madison Ave New York NY 10021. *Mailing Add:* 428 Lafayette St New York NY 10003

BIBERMAN, EDWARD
PAINTER, GRAPHIC ARTIST
b Philadelphia, Pa, Oct 23, 04. *Study:* Univ Pa, BS(econ); Pa Acad Fine Arts, Philadelphia. *Work:* Butler Inst Am Art, Youngstown, Ohio; Mus Pa Acad Fine Arts; Mus Fine Art, Houston, Tex; Brandeis Univ, Waltham, Mass; Los Angeles Co Mus, Los Angeles. *Comn:* Wall murals, Fed Bldg, Los Angeles, 37 & 40 & Venice, Calif, 39. *Exhib:* 46 Under 35, Mus Mod Art, New York, 30 & Mural Projs Exhib, 32; var ann exhibs, Whitney Mus Am Art, New York, 30-40, Los Angeles Co Mus Art, 36-65 & Los Angeles Munic Art Gallery, 71. *Teaching:* Instr drawing, Art Ctr Sch Design, 38-50; lectr art hist, Univ Calif, Los Angeles, Irvine & San Diego Campuses, 67- *Awards:* Lambert Fund Purchase Prize, Pa Acad Fine Arts, 30; Tupperware fel, Orlando, Fla, 57; Los Angeles City Ann Award, 68. *Mem:* Nat Soc Mural Painters. *Publ:* Auth, The Best Untold, Blue Heron Press, 54; Time & Circumstance, Ritchie, 68. *Dealer:* Gallery Z 1634 Tower Grove Dr Beverly Hills CA 90210. *Mailing Add:* 3332 Deronda Dr Los Angeles CA 90028

BICE, AMY MIDDLETON HAMOUDA See Hamouda, Amy

BICE, JACK (JOHN AVERY)
VIDEO ARTIST, PAINTER
b Longmont Colo, Nov 30, 23. *Study:* Univ Col, with Max Beckmann, Ben Shahn, Mark Rothko & Clyfford Still in painting, BFA, 49, MA, 55, MFA, 64. *Work:* Mus Holography, New York; Media Studies Inc, Buffalo, NY, WNED TV & State Univ NY Col, Buffalo. *Comn:* Ceramic mosaic mural & (with Amy Hamouda) Venetian glass mural, Colo State Univ, Ft Collins, 61. *Exhib:* one-man shows, Video Art, Univ Newcastle, Eng, 77 & Video Sketchbook, WNED TV, Buffalo, 80; Video, Albright-Knox Art Gallery, Buffalo, NY, 79; Beau Fleuve, Am Video Art, Ctr for Media Art, Paris, France, 79, Espace Lyonnais Action Cult, Lyon, France, 79 & Mus Cantini, Marseille, France, 79. *Teaching:* Prof fine arts, painting & drawing, State Univ NY Col at Buffalo, 63- *Awards:* Printmaking, Western NY Exhib, Albright-Knox Art Gallery, Liberty Nat Bank, 74. *Media:* Processed Video; Stereoptic (Three Dimensional) Tableaus. *Mailing Add:* 368 Voorhees Ave Buffalo NY 14216

BICKFORD, GEORGE PERCIVAL
COLLECTOR
b Berlin, NH, Nov 28, 01. *Study:* Harvard Col, AB, 22, Harvard Law Sch, LLB, 26. *Pos:* Trustee & vpres, Cleveland Inst Art, Ohio, 55-; trustee, Cleveland Mus Art, 57-; trustee, Am Comt S Asian art; vis comt, Dept Fine Arts, Harvard Univ. *Teaching:* Lectr Indian hist & cult, Cleveland Col, 48-50. *Mem:* Am Asn Mus; Am Oriental Soc; Am Asn Asian Studies. *Collection:* East Indian antiquities. *Mailing Add:* 2247 Chestnut Hills Dr Cleveland OH 44106

BICKLEY, GARY STEVEN
EDUCATOR, SCULPTOR
b Lebanon, Va, Apr 25, 53. *Study:* E Carolina Univ, BFA, 76; Univ Ga, MFA, 78. *Work:* Southeastern Ctr Contemp Art, Winston-Salem, NC; Portsmouth Community Arts Ctr, Va; City of Rockville, Md; First Nat Bank, Roanoke, Va. *Exhib:* Painting and Sculpture Today, Indianapolis Mus Art, 78; solo exhibs, Southeastern Ctr Contemp Art, Winston-Salem, NC, 78, 80 & 82; American Drawing III, Portsmouth Fac & Smithsonian Inst, traveling, 80; Rutgers Nat Works on Paper, Stedman Art Gallery, Camden, NJ, 81; Virginia Painting and Sculpture, Va Mus Fine Arts, Richmond, 81; Clayworks, New York; Exhib 280, Huntington Galleries, WVa; 20 Sculptors Outdoor Exhib, Va Mus Fine Arts. *Teaching:* Asst prof, Va Polytech Inst & State Univ, Blacksburg, 78-; vis prof, Univ Ga, Cortona, Italy, 81. *Awards:* Ford Found Scholar, Univ Ga, 77-78; Summer Stipend, Nat Endowment Humanities, Va Polytech Inst & State Univ, 81; Work Stipend for Clayworks Workshop, Nat Endowment Arts. *Media:* Welded & Cast Metals. *Mailing Add:* Rte 1 Box 232A Blacksburg VA 24060

BIDDLE, JAMES
ADMINISTRATOR, COLLECTOR
b Philadelphia, Pa, July 8, 29. *Study:* Princeton Univ, BA, 51. *Pos:* Cur, Am Wing, Metrop Mus Art, 63-67; pres, Nat Trust Hist Preservation, Washington, DC, 67-; trustee, Corcoran Gallery Art, formerly. *Mem:* Drawing Soc; Am Fedn Arts; White House Hist Asn. *Mailing Add:* State Rd Bensalem PA 19020

BIDDLE, LIVINGSTON LUDLOW, JR
ADMINISTRATOR
b Bryn Mawr, Pa, May 26, 18. *Study:* Princeton Univ, AB, 40; Mt St Mary Col, LHD, 78; Univ Cincinnati, Hon DFA, 79; Catholic Univ Am, Hon DL, 79; Long Island Univ, Hon DFA, 79; Providence Col, RI, Hon DFA, 80; Drexel Univ, Pa, Hon DLett, 80; Notre Dame Univ, Hon DFA, 80. *Pos:* Dep chmn, Nat Endowment Arts, 65-67, liaison dir, 74-76, chmn, 77-; chmn div arts, Liberal Arts Col, Fordham Univ, 67-70; dir, Subcommittee, Educ Arts & Humanities, US Senate, 76-77; co-chmn, Fed Coun Arts & Humanities, 77- *Awards:* Distinguished Service Award, Asn Am Univ Presses, 79; Bronze Medallion for Outstanding Public Service, The Chapel of Four Chaplains, 80; Medal of Achievement, Philadelphia Arts Alliance, 80. *Mem:* Int Coun Fine Arts Deans. *Publ:* Author of works of fiction & non-fiction. *Mailing Add:* 2914 P St NW Washington DC 20007

BIDNER, ROBERT D H
PAINTER, PRINTMAKER
b Youngstown, Ohio, Mar 14, 30. *Study:* Cleveland Inst Art, BFA, 53. *Work:* Nat Collection Fine Arts, Washington, DC; Columbus Mus Art, Ohio; Butler Inst Am Art, Youngstown; Nat Acad Design, New York; Kalamazoo Inst Art, Mich. *Comn:* Murals, Bd Educ, Cleveland, Ohio, 53, William A Stenson, Greenwich, Conn, 69 & Fordham Univ, New York, 70. *Exhib:* Mid-Year Shows, Butler Inst Am Art, 51-55, 72, 74-75, 77 & 81; 25th Biennial Exhib, Corcoran Gallery Art, Washington, DC, 57; Dark Mirror, Am Fedn Arts, New York, 64-65; Contemporary American Artists, Westmoreland Co Mus Art, Pa, 69; Art in Embassies Prog, US State Dept, Washington, DC, 69-81; Contemp Am Art, Indianapolis Mus, 76 & 78. *Pos:* Asst art dir, G M Basford Inc, New York, 57-58; art dir, Fuller Smith & Ross Inc, New York, 58-66; vpres & sr art dir, Ted Bates & Co Inc, New York, 66-81. *Awards:* Medal for a Creative Painting, Allied Artists Am, 66; Third Medal Purchase Award, Butler Inst Am Art, 74; Purchase Awards, Am Acad Arts & Letters, 76 & 78. *Bibliog:* Vivien Raynor (auth), article, New York Times, 11/77; Marilyn Pearl (auth), article, Art News Mag, 1/78; Donna Wilkinson (auth), article, Am Artist Mag, 1/79; and others. *Dealer:* Hammer Gallery 33 W 57th St New York NY 10019. *Mailing Add:* 559 First St Brooklyn NY 11215

BIEBER, ELINORE MARIA KOROW
PAINTER, DESIGNER
b Akron, Ohio, July 31, 34. *Study:* Cleveland Inst Art, with Rolf Stoll, Paul Riba & John Teyral; Sienna Heights Womens Col. *Work:* Hebrew Acad, Cleveland Heights, Ohio; Berkowicz Kumin Mem Chapel; Cleveland Play House Gallery. *Comn:* Portraits of Richard Oberlin, Dir, Play House Gallery Collection, Cleveland, Louis Triscaro, Pres of Teamsters Local 436, George Hilden, Pres of Osco Drugs, Chicago, Jerome Weinberger, Pres Gray Drugs, Charles Walgreen, Pres Walgreen Drugs and others. *Exhib:* Butler Inst Am Art, Youngstown, Ohio, 68-70; World Trade Ctr, Am Artists Prof League, New York, 80; one-woman show, Chagrin Valley Little Theatre, Ohio, 80; One Bratenahl Place, Bratenahl, Ohio, 80; Miniature Painting Show, Bath, Ohio, 81; Malcolm Brown Gallery, Shaker Heights, Ohio, 81; and many others. *Pos:* Staff artist & designer, Am Greetings Corp, Cleveland, 71-73. *Teaching:* Instr painting, drawing & portraiture, Metrop Campus, Cuyahoga Community Col, 79-; fac mem, Orange Arts Coun, currently. *Awards:* Award of Excellence, Jewish Community Ctr, 72; Jurors Spec Mention, Valley Art Ctr, 8th Ann Juried Exhib, Chagrin Falls, Ohio, 79; Merit Award, Int Platform Asn, Washington, DC, 80. *Mem:* Charter mem Ohio Watercolor Soc; Women's Art Club Cleveland; New Orgn Visual Arts. *Media:* Acrylic, Oil. *Dealer:* Strongs Gallery 33 Public Square Blvd Cleveland OH 44113. *Mailing Add:* 19201 Van Aken Blvd Apt 404 Shaker Heights OH 44122

BIEDERMAN, CHARLES (KAREL JOSEPH)
SCULPTOR
b Cleveland, Ohio, Aug 23, 06. *Study:* Art Inst Chicago, 26-29; Minneapolis Col Art & Design, Hon DFA, 73. *Work:* Tate Gallery, London; Albright-Knox Art Gallery, Buffalo; Dallas Mus Fine Arts, Tex; Metrop Mus Art, New York; Whitney Mus Art, New York; and others. *Comn:* Three constructionist pieces, Interstate Med Clin, Red Wing, Minn, 40; work in pub plaza, Nat Endowment Arts, Red Wing, 71. *Exhib:* One-man show, Gallery 12, Minneapolis, 71; retrospectives, Walker Art Ctr, Minneapolis, 65, Hayward Gallery, London, 69, Minneapolis Inst Arts, 76 & Grace Borgenicht Gallery, New York, 80 & 82; Abstract Painting and Sculpture in America 1927-1944, Mus Art, Carnegie Inst, Pittsburgh, 83. *Awards:* Ford Found Purchase Award, 64; Nat Coun Arts Grant, 66; Nat Endowment Arts Award, 73. *Bibliog:* Jan van der Marck (auth), Charles Biederman & the structurist direction in art, Feistbundel F vanderMeer, 66; Leif Sjoberg (auth), London ahead of New York?, Studies in the 20th Century, 71. *Media:* Aluminum. *Publ:* Auth, Letters on the New Art, 51; auth, The New Cezanne, 58; auth, Dialogue II, Creative or Conditioned Vision, Faber, 68; auth, A Note on New Arts, Studio Int, 70. *Dealer:* Grace Borgenicht Gallery 724 Fifth Ave New York NY. *Mailing Add:* Rte 2 Red Wing MN 55066

BIELER, ANDRE CHARLES
PAINTER, MURALIST
b Lausanne, Switz, Oct 8, 1896; Can citizen. *Study:* Art Students League, Woodstock, with Charles Rosen & Eugene Speicher; Acad Ranson, Paris, France, with Paul Serusier & Maurice Denis; also execution of frescoes with Ernest Bieler, Switz. *Work:* Nat Gallery Can, Ottawa; Mus Quebec, PQ; Montreal Mus Fine Art, PQ; Agnes Etherington Art Ctr, Queen's Univ, Kingston, Ont; Art Gallery Ont, Toronto. *Comn:* Saguenay: People & Hydro-Electric Development, Shipshaw (on aluminum panels), Aluminum Co Can, 48; Rehabilitation (oil), Vet Welfare Serv, Ottawa, 55; Scenes de Quebec (oil), Procter & Gamble, Pointe Claire, PQ, 57; aluminum foil, plaster & aluminum plates, comn by Aluminum Labs, Tokyo Aluminum Co, Japan. *Exhib:* A Century of Canadian Art, Tate Gallery, London, Eng, 38; Int Watercolour Exhib, Chicago, Ill, 39; Golden Gate Int Exhib Contemp Art, San Francisco, Calif, 39; one-man retrospective, Andre Bieler-50 Years 1920-1970, 11 cities, 70-71; Int Exhib Graphics, Montreal Mus Fine Arts & Traveling Exhib, 71- *Pos:* Dir, Agnes Etherington Art Ctr, 57-63. *Teaching:* Resident artist & prof art hist, appreciation & painting, Queen's Univ, 36-63. *Awards:* J W L Forster Award, Ont Soc Artists, 57; C W Jeffery Award, Can Soc Graphic Art, 64; Centennial Medal, Can Govt, 67. *Bibliog:* M Barbeau (auth), Painters of Quebec, Toronto Press, 46; Frances K Smith (auth), A Canadian artist in the market place, Can Collector, 2/71; Frances K Smith (auth), Andre Bieler: An Artists' Life and Times, Toronto, Merritt, 80. *Mem:* Academician Royal Can Acad Arts; Ont Soc Artists; Can Soc Graphic Art; Can Group Painters; Can Soc Painters in Watercolour. *Media:* Acrylic, Oil. *Collection:* French Canadian furniture and artifacts; Canadian and European paintings. *Publ:* Ed, Kingston Conf Proc, 41; contrib, Can Art, IX: 70-71; auth, Twelve Pines Press (monogr), Agnes Etherington Art Ctr, 72. *Dealer:* Walter Klinkhoff 1200 Sherbrooke W Montreal PQ Can; Wallack Galleries 202 Bank St Ottawa ON Can. *Mailing Add:* 185 Ontario, Apt 304 Kingston ON K7L 2Y7 Canada

BIELER, TED ANDRE
EDUCATOR, SCULPTOR
b Kingston, Ont, July 23, 38. *Study:* Sculpture with Ossip Zadkine, Paris, 53; tapestry with Jean Lurcat, St Cere, France, 54; Slade Sch Art, London, 54; Cranbrook Acad Art, BFA, 61. *Work:* Montreal Mus Fine Arts; Can Coun, Ottawa; Univ Toronto; Agnes Etherington Art Centre, Queen's Univ, Kingston; McMaster Univ; York Univ. *Comn:* Star-Cross'd (sculpture ballet set), comn by Brian MacDonald, Ottawa, 73; stainless steel sculpture, Forensic Sci Bldg, Govt Ont, 75; aluminum tetrahedra sculpture, Portsmouth Harbour, Kingston, Govt Can, 75; sculpture for Govt of Can Bldg, comn by Macy Dubois & Shore Tilbe Henschel Irwin, Architects, Toronto, 77; cast aluminum relief sculpture for Wilson Sta, comn by Spadina Subway Line, Toronto, 78; and others. *Exhib:* Signs & Symbols, Art Gallery Ont Traveling Show, 71; Rehearsal, Harbourfront Art Gallery, Toronto, 77; one-man shows, York Univ, 77 & Univ Rochester, 77; Performance, Harbourfront Art Gallery, Toronto, Ont, 78; Monumental Sculpture, Toronto Dominion Ctr, 78. *Teaching:* Assoc prof sculpture, York Univ, 70- *Awards:* Allied Arts Medal, Royal Archit Asn Can, 69. *Bibliog:* L Sabbath (auth), Sculpture in Canada, 62 & H McPherson (auth), Scope of Sculpture in '64, 64, Can Art; William Withrow (auth), Canadian Sculpture, Graph, Montreal, 67. *Mem:* Royal Can Acad Arts (mem coun, 75-77); Int Sculpture Ctr, Lawrence, Kans. *Mailing Add:* Visual Arts Dept York Univ 4700 Keele St ON M3J 2R1 Canada

BIER, JUSTUS
MUSEOLOGIST, HISTORIAN
b Nürnberg, Ger, May 31, 1899; US citizen. *Study:* Univs Munich, Erlangen, Jena & Bonn, 18-24; Univ Zurich, PhD, 24; Duke Univ, Hon DFA, 70; Louisville Univ, DHL, 72. *Pos:* Dir & cur, Kestner-Gesellschaft Art Inst, Hanover, Ger, 30-36; founder & dir, Mus Vorbildliche Serienprodukt, Hanover, 30-36; critic & art ed, Courier-J, Louisville, Ky, 44-53; dir, Allen R Hite Art Inst, 46-60; dir, NC Mus Art, Raleigh, 61-70, dir emer, 70-, cur res, 70-72, cur sculpture, 72-74, consult, 74- *Teaching:* Lectr, Tilmann Riemenschneider, Franconian & 20th century sculpture; docent & instr art hist, Munich Univ, Nürnberg, 25-30; asst prof art hist & actg head dept fine arts, Univ Louisville, 37-41, assoc prof, 41-46, prof, 46-60; vis prof, Free Univ Berlin, 56; vis prof, Univ Southern Calif, 59; Fulbright lectr & vis prof, Univ Wurzburg, 60-61; vis prof, Univ Tex, Austin & Univ Wis-Milwaukee, 75. *Awards:* Guggenheim Fel, 53-54 & 56-57; Fulbright Award, 60-61; Commander's Cross, Fed Ger Repub, 73. *Mem:* Col Art Asn Am; Am Soc Aesthet; assoc Int Asn Art Critics; Am Fedn Arts; Am Asn Univ Prof; and others. *Publ:* Auth, Tilmann Riemenschneider, 48, 73 & 78; contrib, Art Bulletin, Art in Am, Art Quart & Gazette Beaux-Arts; and others. *Mailing Add:* 201 Peartree Lane PO Box 14182 Raleigh NC 27610

BIERLY, EDWARD J
PAINTER, ILLUSTRATOR
b Buffalo, NY, Apr 23, 20. *Study:* Univ Buffalo, NY, BFA, 49. *Exhib:* Am Natural Hist Art Show, James Ford Bell Mus, Minneapolis, Minn, 71; one-man shows, Nat Zoo, 73 & Nat Wildlife Fedn, 74 & 83, Washington, DC; Animals in Art, Royal Ontario Mus, Toronto, Can, 75; Soc Animal Artists, Acad Natural Sciences, Philadelphia, 81. *Pos:* Free-lance illusr, 49-56; mus exhibs designer, Nat Park Service, Washington, DC, 56-70. *Awards:* Winner Migratory Waterfowl Hunting Stamp Competition, 56-57, 63-64 & 70-71. *Mem:* Soc Animal Artists; Springfield Va Art Guild. *Media:* Oil, Acrylic. *Publ:* Illusr, Mammals of the Southwest Mountains & Mesas, Southwest Monuments Asn, 61; illusr, Mammals Rhodesia, Zambia & Malawi, Collins, London, 66; illusr, Grzimeks Tierleben, Kindler, Munchen, 72; auth & illusr, Nat Wildlife & International Wildlife Mag, Nat Wildlife Fedn, 72-78; illusr, The History of Wildlife in America, Nat Wildlife Fedn, 75. *Mailing Add:* c/o EJB Editions 8833 Lake Hill Dr Lorton VA 22079

BIESER, NATALIE
PAINTER
b Grand Junction, Colo, Dec, 14, 48. *Study:* Chouinard Art Sch, Los Angeles; Calif Inst Arts, BFA, 70. *Work:* Va Mus Art, Richmond; Whitney Mus Am Art, New York. *Exhib:* Document V, 1972, Kassel, Ger, 72; one-woman show, Nancy Hoffman Gallery, New York, 72, 74, 75 & 77 & Baum-Silverman Gallery, Los Angeles, 77; Biennial Contemp Am Art, Whitney Mus Am Art, 73; Watercolors & Related Media by Contemp Californians, Baxter Art Gallery, Calif Inst of Technol; Both Kinds: Contemp Art from Los Angeles, Univ Art Mus, Berkeley, 75. *Media:* Multimedia. *Mailing Add:* Baum Gallery Los Angeles CA 90036

BIFERIE, DAN (DANIEL ANTHONY), JR
PHOTOGRAPHER, EDUCATOR
b Miami, Fla, Dec 17, 50. *Study:* Daytona Beach Community Col, AS(with honors), 71; Ohio Univ, BFA(summa cum laude), 72, MFA, 74. *Work:* High Mus; New Orleans Mus Art; Baltimore Mus Art; Santa Barbara Mus Art; Bibliotheque Nationale, Paris; and others. *Exhib:* Four Photographers, Mass Inst Technol, Boston, 76; one-man shows, Brevard Art Mus, Fla, 79 & Univ Central Fla, Orlando, 81; Fla Light Invitational, Loch Haven Art Ctr, Orlando, 79; Four Southeastern Photographers, Contemp Arts Ctr, New Orleans, La, 81. *Pos:* Dir, Gallery Fine Arts, Daytona Beach Community Col, Fla, 78- *Teaching:* Instr photog, Daytona Beach Community Col, Fla, 75- *Bibliog:* Photographic Artists, Dan Biferie--Photography, Tampa Press, Fla, 75. *Mem:* Soc Photog Educ (pres 77-84); Daytona Beach Community Col Photog Soc (founder & pres 79-81); Fla Art Mus Dirs Asn; Am Asn Mus; Art Gallery Asn Fla; and others. *Res:* History and criticism of photography, photographic aesthetics. *Publ:* Contrib, Photographic Annual, Middle Tenn State Univ, 75; contribr, Florida Light, Loch Haven Art Ctr, 79; contribr, Volusia Photographers, Volusia Photographic J, 80. *Dealer:* Light Images Gallery 216 Park Avenue South Suite 3 Winter Park FL 32789. *Mailing Add:* Daytona Beach Community College PO Box 1111 Daytona Beach FL 32015

BIGELOW, ROBERT CLAYTON
EDUCATOR, PAINTER
b Los Angeles, Calif, July 31, 40. *Study:* Chouinard Art Inst, BFA, 67. *Work:* Gruenwald Graphic Arts Found, Univ Calif, Los Angeles; Mus Mod Art, New York; Nat Gallery Can, Ottawa; Can Coun Art Bank, Ottawa; Bank of Montreal, Can. *Exhib:* Two-man show, Univ Calgary, Alta, 69; Contemp Am Prints, Krannert Art Mus, Univ Ill, 70; Contemp Prints & Drawings, Hartnell Col Art, Salinas, Calif, 71; Otis Art Inst Gallery, Los Angeles, 74; Prints & Drawings from The West Coast, traveling, Can, 75. *Pos:* Printer, Gemini Gel, Los Angeles, Calif, 66-67 & 74-75; asst mgr & printer, Tyler Workshop, 75-76; studio mgr, Robert Motherwell, Greenwich, Conn, 76-78. *Teaching:* Instr painting, Vancouver Sch Art, BC, 60-70; sr lectr lithography, Nottingham Col Art, UK, 72-73; MFA dir studio arts, Concordia Univ, 78 & 83. *Awards:* Tamarind Fel, Ford Found, 66; Canada Coun Grants, Can Govt, 69 & 70. *Media:* Oil, Acrylic; Lithography. *Publ:* Coauth, Reconciliation Elergy, Rizzoli Int Publ, 80; contribr, The Painter and the Printer, Am Fedn Art, 80. *Dealer:* Don Stewart Gallery 1460 Ouest Rue Sherbrooke Montreal PQ Canada H3G 1K4. *Mailing Add:* 2301 Wilson Ave Montreal PQ H4A 2T4 Canada

BIGGER, MICHAEL D
SCULPTOR
b Waukegan, Ill, Oct 10, 37. *Study:* Miami Univ, Oxford, Ohio, BA(archit), 66; RI Sch Design, MFA(sculpture), 68. *Work:* Oakland Mus Art, Calif; Evansville Mus Arts & Sci, Ind; Atlantic Richfield Collection, Los Angeles; Embarcadero Ctr, San Francisco; Vassar Col. *Comn:* Monumental sculpture, Provincial Govt Man, Thompson, 77; large-scale sculpture, First Nat Bank, Erie, Pa, 80; monumental sculpture, Cincinnati Zoological Soc. *Exhib:* Annual Contemporary Sculpture, Whitney Mus Am Art, 68; Structured Art, DeCordova Mus, Lincoln, Mass, 69; Sculpture on the Prairies, Winnipeg Art Gallery, Man, 77; 25th Ann, Longview Mus, Tex, 83; Int Art Expos, Navy Pier, Chicago, 83; Fourth Tex Sculpture Symp, Univ Tex, Austin, 83. *Teaching:* Instr three dimensional design, Atlanta Sch Art, 70-71; chmn sculpture dept, Univ Man, Winnipeg, 75-79; asst prof, Univ Tex, San Antonio, 81- *Awards:* Olivetti Award Sculpture, 23rd Ann New England Exhib, 72; Judge's Award, Drawing & Small Sculpture, Galveston Art Ctr, 81; First Prize, Expos Plaza Sculpture Competition, 4-M Properties, 81. *Media:* Steel. *Mailing Add:* PO Box 521 Boerne TX 78006

BIGGERS, JOHN THOMAS
EDUCATOR, PAINTER
b Gastonia, NC, Apr 13, 24. *Study:* Hampton Inst, 41-46; Pa State Univ, BS & MS(art educ), 48, DEduc, 54. *Work:* Houston Mus Fine Arts; Dallas Mus Fine Arts; Reader's Digest Collection; Tex Southern Univ; Golden State Mutual Life Ins Co. *Exhib:* Tex Contemp Artist, M Knoedler & Co, New York, 52; Regional & Nat Drawing Soc Exhib, Houston & New York, 65; one-man show, Houston Mus Fine Arts, 68; Tex Painting & Sculpture, the 20th century, six Tex mus & galleries, 71-72; Reflections: The Afro-Am Artist, Benton Conv Ctr, Winston-Salem, NC, 72. *Pos:* Mem, Houston Fine Arts Comn, 68-72 & Tex Fine Arts Comn, Houston, 70-73. *Teaching:* Distinguished prof painting, drawing & art hist, Tex Southern Univ, Houston, 49-, head art dept, currently. *Awards:* Art Fel in Africa, UNESCO, 57. *Bibliog:* Cedric Dover (auth), American Negro Art, New York Graphic Soc, 60; Ralph E Shikes (auth), The Indignant eye, Beacon Press, 69; Elton Fax (auth), 17 Black Artists, Dodd, Mead, 71. *Mem:* Fel Int Inst Arts & Lett; Tex Col Art Asn; Tex Fine Arts Soc; Nat Soc Mural Painters; Pa State Grad Club in Art Educ. *Media:* Conte Crayon; Oil & Tempera. *Res:* African art and culture. *Publ:* Auth, Ananse, Web of Life in Africa, 69; illusr, Good earth, Readers' Digest Series, 66; illusr, I Momolu, Crowell Co, 66; illusr, Cross timbers, Univ Tex, 66; contribr, Afro-American Art, Van Nostrand Reinhold Co, 72. *Mailing Add:* 3338 Prospect St Houston TX 77004

BILLECI, ANDRE GEORGE
SCULPTOR, EDUCATOR
b New York, NY, Dec 2, 33. *Study:* State Univ NY Col of Ceramics, Alfred, BFA(ceramics; cum laude), 60, MFA(ceramic art), 61. *Work:* Corning Mus of Glass, NY; Lannan Found, Palm Beach, Fla; Australian Nat Gallery, Canberra; Galleries Nat de Prague, Czech; Mus ü Kunsthandwerk, Frankfurt, Ger. *Exhib:* one-man shows, Mus of Contemp Crafts, New York, 70, Corning Mus of Glass, 72 & NY State Col Ceramics, Alfred Univ, 80; Reflections, Long Beach Mus of Art, Calif, 71; Int Glass Sculpture, Lowe Art Mus, Univ Miami, Coral Gables, Fla, 73; New Am Glass, Huntington Galleries, WVa, 76; Glassmaking & Purchase Exhib, Corning Mus of Glass, 76; and others. *Pos:* Mem bd dirs, NY State Craftsmen, Ithaca, 70-72; artist-in-residence, Blenko Art Glass Co, Milton, WVa, 71 & Steuben Glass Co, Corning, NY, 72; founding trustee, Naples Mill Sch of Arts & Crafts, NY, 72-74; consult, Corning Mus Glass, Egyptian Core Vessles, 79 & Mary McFadden Inc, New York, 80. *Teaching:* Assoc prof sculpture/glass, State Univ NY Col, Alfred, 61- & Summer Sch, Sheridan Col of Applied Arts & Technol, Toronto, Ont, 71; lectr, Cleveland Art Inst, 78, Carnegie-Mellon Univ, 78, Univ Ill, Champaign-Urbana, 79 & Univ Wis, 81. *Awards:* Purchase Award, Toledo Glass Nat II, Toledo Mus of Art, Ohio, 68; Corning Glass Found Grant, 76. *Mem:* Int Sculpture Ctr; Glass Art Soc. *Media:* Glass; mixed media. *Publ:* Auth, Electric Melting Unit for Covered Melting, Corning Mus of Glass, 76; auth, Annealing Glasses & Understanding Glass Calculations, Glass Studio Mag Publ Develop Corp, 78 & 79. *Mailing Add:* Thurston Studio RD 1 Box 408 Campbell NY 14821

BILLIAN, CATHEY R
SCULPTOR, INSTRUCTOR
b Chicago, Ill, Feb 24, 46. *Study:* Art Inst Chicago, 64; Art Students League, 67; Univ Ariz, BFA, 69; Pratt Inst, fel, MFA, 77. *Work:* Philadelphia Mus Art; New York Pub Libr Print Collection; Morris Mus; Norton Simon Inc & Chem Bank, New York; and others. *Comn:* Sculpture, Newark Airport, New York Port Authority, 81; sculpture, Creative Time, Battery Park, New York, 81; sculpture, Liberty State Park, 83; sculpture, Sun Valley Ctr Arts, 84; light, sculpture & dance environment, Whitney Mus, 84. *Exhib:* Aldrich Mus, 74; one-person shows, Elise Meyer Gallery, 80 & 82; Sculpture as Ornament, Sculpture Ctr, 83; Recent Trends in Light, Morris Mus, 83; Dept Cultural Affairs, NY, 83; Port Hist Mus, Philadelphia, 83; and others. *Pos:* Consult, Artpark, NY, currently, NJ State Coun Arts, 82-83; media interviewee, Feminism and Art, CBS News, 73. *Teaching:* Lectr current art topics, Columbia Univ, Brown Univ & Pratt Inst; Instr, Parsons Sch, 80, Pratt Inst Grad Dept, 80, Rutgers Univ, 80-82. *Awards:* National Park Service Utah Canyon Project, 76; Clayworks, New York Lava Projects, 78 & 79; Residency, Artists Environment Found, 75, 78 & 81. *Bibliog:* Helen Harrison (auth), New York Times, 79 & 81; Olejarz (auth), Arts Mag, 80; Grace Glueck (auth), New York Times, 81. *Mem:* Women's Caucus for Art. *Media:* Mixed Media, Sculpture & Light Environments. *Dealer:* Elise Meyer Gallery 410 W Broadway New York NY 10012. *Mailing Add:* 456 Broome St New York NY 10013

BILLINGS, HENRY
PAINTER, ILLUSTRATOR
b Bronxville, NY, July 13, 01. *Study:* Art Students League. *Work:* Whitney Mus Am Art; William Allen White Libr, Kans State Teachers Col. *Comn:* Painting, Ford Motor Co, New York World's Fair, 38; paintings comn by US Treas Dept Fine Arts Div for Saranac Post Off, NY, 37, Medford Post Off, Mass, 38, Wappinger Falls Post Off, NY & Columbia Court House, Tenn, 40. *Exhib:* Carnegie Inst, Pittsburgh, Pa, 47; Whitney Mus Ann, 32, 37 & 40. *Teaching:* Vis lectr painting, Bard Col, 35-53; instr painting, Art Students League, 40; instr painting, Art Students League Summer Sch, Woodstock, NY, 60-61. *Media:* Oil. *Publ:* Auth & illusr, Construction Ahead, 50, All Down the Valley, 52 & Bridges, 55, Viking Press. *Dealer:* Salander O'Reilly Galleries 22 E 80th St New York NY 10021. *Mailing Add:* RFD 3 North Haven Sag Harbor NY 11963

BILLMYER, JOHN EDWARD
DRAFTSMAN, EDUCATOR
b Denver, Colo, Aug 17, 12. *Study:* Univ Denver; Kirkland Sch Art; Case Western Reserve Univ, BA & MA; also study abroad. *Work:* Cleveland Mus Art; Denver Art Mus. *Exhib:* Cleveland Mus Art; Denver Art Mus, 47-68 & Metrop Show, 52-67; five shows, Syracuse Mus Fine Art, 48-56; Wichita Mus Art, 51, 55 & 57; Colorado Springs Fine Arts Ctr, 60; and others. *Mem:* Denver Art Mus (trustee, 62-71); Col Art Asn Am. *Mailing Add:* 7301 E Placita Sinaloa Tucson AZ 85710

BILOUS, PRISCILLA HALEY See Haley, Priscilla J

BIMROSE, ARTHUR SYLVANUS, JR
CARTOONIST
b Spokane, Wash, Mar 18, 12. *Study:* San Francisco Art Inst Col, 31; Univ Ore, 33. *Work:* State Hist Soc, Mo; Wayne State Univ; Libr Cong; Lyndon Johnson Libr; John F Kennedy Libr. *Pos:* Free-lance commercial artist, 34-37; staff artists, Oregonian, Portland, 37-39, ed cartoonist, 49-83; retired. *Awards:* Freedoms Found Award, 52, 61 & 65; Bronze Smokey Award, US Forest Serv, 81. *Mem:* Asn Am Ed Cartoonist. *Mailing Add:* 1632 SW Westwood Ct Portland OR 97201

BINAI, PAUL FREYE
PAINTER, CURATOR
b Lancaster, Pa, July 3, 32. *Study:* Indiana Univ, with Alton Pickens & Leo Steppat, AB & MFA; Yale Univ; John Herron Art Inst; Ecole Fontainebleau,

Paris, France, Walter Damrosch Fel for Study in Painting, 62. *Work:* Purdue Univ Art Ctr; Miami Mus Mod Art. *Exhib:* Palais Fontainebleau, France, 62; Am Fedn Arts, 64-65; Akron Art Inst, 64; one-man shows, Miami Mus Mod Art, Ligoa Duncan Gallery, New York & Raymond Duncan Gallery, Paris, 64; and many others. *Pos:* Asst cur graphic arts, Detroit Inst Art, 71-75, cur, Mus Art, Carnegie Inst, Pittsburgh, Pa, 73-80. *Teaching:* Instr art & design, Purdue Univ, 60-64; instr art, Akron Art Inst, 64-68. *Awards:* Purdue Univ Res Found Grant, 61. *Mem:* Col Art Asn Am; Am Asn Mus. *Mailing Add:* 1162 Murray Hill Ave Pittsburgh PA 15217

BINGHAM, ALICE
DEALER, CONSULTANT
b Memphis, Tenn, Dec 9, 36. *Study:* Bennett Col, AA, 56; Univ Florence, Italy; Memphis State Univ; Memphis Acad Arts. *Collections Arranged:* First Tennessee Heritage Collection Traveling Exhibit (auth, catalog), 83; Dulin Gallery Art, Knoxville, 83; Hunter Mus Art, Chattanooga, 83; Fine Arts Ctr-Cheekwood, Nashville, 83-84. *Pos:* Bd dirs, Dixon Gallery Arts & Gardens, Memphis, 78-; cur, First Tenn Bank Collection, 79-; pres, Alice Bingham Gallery, 79- *Mem:* Tennessee Arts Com. *Specialty:* Original works by regional artists; prints by regional and international artists. *Mailing Add:* 24 S Cooper St Memphis TN 38104

BINGHAM, LOIS A
ADMINISTRATOR, LECTURER
b Iowa Falls, Iowa, July 8, 13. *Study:* Oberlin Col, scholar, BA & MA; Sch Fine Arts, Yale Univ, scholar; Inst d'Art & Archeol, Univ Paris, Carnegie grant for grad study. *Collections Arranged:* More than 200 exhibs arranged & supervised incl Nation of Nations, to inaugurate Berlin Cong Hall, 54, Modern Painting & Sculpture, Moscow, 59 & biennial exhibs at Sao Paulo, Venice, Santiago, New Delhi & Paris, 61- *Pos:* Staff, Nat Gallery Art, 43-48, assoc cur educ, 48-54; chief fine arts div, exhib br, US Info Agency, 54-65; chief, Int Art Prog, Smithsonian Inst, Nat Mus Am Art, Washington, DC, 65-72, chief, Off of Exhibs Abroad, 72-76, chief, Off of Prog Support, 76-81; retired, 81. *Teaching:* Lects, Medici: Patrons of Art, Index of Am Design, Dutch Painting, Manuscripts of the Middle Ages & Duccio's Maestra, Nat Gallery Art. *Publ:* Auth, How to look at works of art, Care, NY; auth, Highlights of American painting, Care, NY; contribr, Favorite paintings from The National Gallery of Art. *Mailing Add:* 374 North St SW Washington DC 20024

BINKS, RONALD C
PHOTOGRAPHER, PAINTER
b Oak Park, Ill, Oct 20, 34. *Study:* George Eastman House, with Minor White, 54; RI Sch Design, BFA, 56; Berlin Art Acad, cert(Fulbright Award), 58; Yale Univ, MFA, 60. *Work:* Southwest Art Mus, Lubbock, Tex; San Antonio Mus Art, Tex. *Exhib:* Fulbright Aritsts, Whitney Mus Am Art, New York, 58; 20th Century Photog, George Eastman House, Rochester, 60; Abilene Mus Fine Arts, 83. *Pos:* Ed adv, Photographer's Forum, 79- *Teaching:* Assoc prof art, RI Sch Design, 62-76, chmn film dept, 68-72; prof & dir, Div Art & Design, Univ Tex, San Antonio, 76- *Awards:* Prix de Rome, Am Acad Rome, 60-62. *Bibliog:* Beaumont Newhall (auth), Young photographers, Art in Am, 60. *Mem:* Soc Photog Educ; Nat Asn Sch Art; Tex Asn Schs Art (bd dir, 80-82); Col Art Asn Am; Nat Coun Art Adminr (chmn, 82-). *Mailing Add:* PO Box 404 Helotes TX 78023

BINNING, ROBIN
PRINTMAKER, SCULPTOR
b Rosset, North Wales, Dec 16, 09. *Study:* Plymouth Sch Art, Eng; also with Leon Underwood. *Work:* Kungliets Kunstmuseet, Stockholm; Imp War Mus, London; Arthur M Sakler Collection, New York. *Comn:* Reliefs, Hilton Hotels, 67; Altars, lecterns & font, Church St Dominic, Barbados, 72. *Exhib:* Penwith Soc, St Ives, Corwall, 53 & 57; Neutida Englska Gafisk, Stockholm, 56; NW Printmakers Int, Seattle Wash, 56 & 57; one-man shows, Bristol Mus Art, RI, 71 & Clark Gallery, 78. *Teaching:* Teacher sculpture, workshop, Bowdoin Col, 71; prof sculpture, New Eng Sch Art, 72-78; guest lectr Putnam Sculptures, Princeton Univ, 75. *Awards:* Giles Mem Bequest Prize, 56. *Mem:* Fel MacDowell Colony. *Media:* Stone; Bronze and Sheet Aluminum. *Dealer:* Clark Gallery Lincoln MA. *Mailing Add:* 205 A Street Boston MA 02110

BIRCKETT, ANNE BELLE See Belle, Anna

BIRDSALL, BYRON
PAINTER
b Buckeye, Ariz, Dec 18, 37. *Study:* Seattle Pacific Col, BA; Stanford Univ, MA. *Work:* Anchorage Hist & Fine Arts Mus; Jean Haydon Territorial Mus, Pago Pago, Am Samoa. *Comn:* Painting, Alaska Bank of Com, Anchorage, 76; paintings, Alyeska Pipeline Co, Anchorage, 77; paintings, RCA, Anchorage, 77. *Exhib:* All Alaska Watercolor Exhib, Alaska Watercolor Soc, 75-77; Anchorage Hist & Fine Arts Mus, 76; All Alaska Exhib, Anchorage Hist & Fine Arts Mus, 78; also many one-man shows. *Teaching:* Instr, Makerere Univ, Kampala, Uganda, 66-70; feature prog, art dir, KVZK Television, Pago Pago, Am Samoa, 72-73 & Graphix West Advertising Agency, Anchorage, Alaska, 75-76. *Awards:* Alaska Arts & Crafts League First Prize in Watercolor; Alaska Watercolor Soc First Prize, 76 & Second Prize, 77, Alaska Watercolor Show; Third Prize, All Alaska Art Exhib, 82. *Bibliog:* Lana Johnson (auth), Watercolorist forsakes his palm trees, Anchorage Times,

11/77; Barbara Whipple (auth), Byron Birdsall paints Alaska, Am Artist, 4/81; Janet O'Hara (auth), Byron Birdsall, artist of the world, Wien Air Alaska Flight Time, 9/83. *Mem:* Alaska Watercolor Soc (pres, 76); Alaska Artists Guild. *Media:* Watercolor, Stone. *Publ:* Auth, Letters from Africa, Anchorage Times, 6/81. *Dealer:* Artique Gallery 314 G St Anchorage AK 99501; Kirsten Gallery 5320 Roosevelt Way NE Seattle WA 98105. *Mailing Add:* 4057 Brentwood Dr Anchorage AK 99502

BIRELINE, GEORGE LEE
PAINTER, EDUCATOR
b Peoria, Ill, Aug 12, 23. *Study:* Bradley Univ, BFA, 49; Univ NC, MACA, 52. *Work:* Everson Mus, Syracuse, NY; NC Mus Art, Raleigh; Mint Mus Art; Francis & Sydney Lewis Found Collection; Hirshhorn Mus & Sculpture Garden. *Comn:* Wall mural relief, Mecklenberg Co Off Complex, 61; decorative solar screen, bank bldg, SC, 63 & NCNB Bldg, Charlotte, 65; outdoor environ sculpture cast concrete, Mecklenburg Co Libr, Albemarle, 71. *Exhib:* Post Painterly Abstraction, Los Angeles Co Mus Art, 64; retrospective, NC Mus Art, Raleigh, 76; Late 20th Century Art, Francis & Sydney Lewis Found, 79; NC Artists, Squibb Int Hq Gallery, Princeton, NJ, 81; Realist Invitational, SECCA, Winston-Salem, 81; Painting in the South, Va Mus, Richmond, 83. *Teaching:* Vis lectr design & painting, Univ NC, Chapel Hill, 65-66; prof design, Sch Design, NC State Univ, 57- *Awards:* First Purchase Awards, NC Mus Art, Artists Ann, 56, 57 & 64; Nat Coun on Arts Grant, 67-68; Guggenheim Found Grant for painting, 68-69. *Bibliog:* L Lippard (auth), rev in Art Forum, 67; D Kuspit (auth), Southern Realism, rev in Art in Am, 12/80. *Media:* Oil, Watercolor. *Mailing Add:* 228 East Park Dr Raleigh NC 27605

BIRKIN, MORTON
PAINTER
b Philadelphia, Pa, Apr 27, 19. *Study:* Philadelphia Mus Col of Art, with Earl Horter, 36-40; Tyler Col Art, Temple Univ, with Franklin Watkins, Boris Blai, BFA, 45, MFA, 51; NY Univ, with Hale Woodruff, 55-58. *Work:* Wurlitzer Mus, Taos, NMex; Philadelphia Pub Schs; Philadelphia Mus Art; Bruce Payne Collection, Time Life Bldg, New York. *Comn:* Mural, Dept of Navy, Mexico City, 39; mural, Reptile Rm, Philadelphia Zool Gardens, 40; mural, Recreation Rm, Aberdeen Proving Grounds, Ft Meade, Md, 41. *Exhib:* Pa Acad Fine Arts, 47; Brooklyn Mus Nat Exhib, 51; Metrop Mus Art, New York, 52; Emily Lowe Award Competition Exhib, 52; NJ State Exhib, Ringwood State Park, 69; Nat Am Drawings, Portsmouth Mus, Va, 76; Smithsonian Inst Traveling Exhib, 77-79; 153rd Ann Exhib, Nat Acad Design, New York, 78. *Teaching:* Instr painting & drawing, Temple Univ, 42-48; instr painting & drawing, Philadelphia Mus Art, 43-49; instr painting, Mus Mod Art, Amagansett, NY, 62-63; instr painting & drawing, Rockland Community Col, Suffern, NY, 70- *Awards:* Wurlitzer Nat Fel Painting, Wurlitzer Found, 58 & 67; First Prize Oils, NJ State Exhib, 69. *Mem:* Nat Art Educ Asn. *Media:* Oil, Watercolor. *Mailing Add:* 13-34 Sunnyside Dr Fair Lawn NJ 07410

BIRMELIN, A ROBERT
PAINTER, DRAFTSMAN
b Newark, NJ, Nov 7, 33. *Study:* Cooper Union Art Sch; Yale Univ, BFA & MFA. *Work:* Mus Mod Art, New York; Hirshhorn Mus, Washington, DC; Whitney Mus Am Art; Metrop Mus Art, New York; Mus Contemp Art, Nagaoka, Japan; plus others. *Exhib:* Am Landscape Bicentennial Traveling Exhib, Corcoran Gallery & 12 other mus, 76-78; The Narrative Impulse, Hayden Gallery, Mass Inst Technol, 79; one-man show, Bowdoin Col Mus, Maine, 80; Artist Choice Mus, New York, 83. *Teaching:* Instr, Yale Summer Sch, 60; prof art, Queens Col, New York, 64-; instr, Columbia Univ, summers 65 & 66; instr, Skowhegan Sch Painting, 67. *Awards:* NJ Coun Arts Grant, 80; Childe Hassam Purchase Award, Nat Inst Arts & Lett, New York, 81; Nat Endowment for Arts, 82. *Dealer:* Odyssia Gallery FDR Station Box 1688 New York NY 10022. *Mailing Add:* 176 Highwood Ave Leonia NJ 07605

BIRNBAUM, MILDRED
PAINTER
b New York, NY. *Study:* NY Univ; Columbia Univ; Manhattanville Col; New York Sch Design; studies with Leo Manso, Anthony Toney & Marvin Horowitz. *Work:* Am Can Co, Armonk, NY; Court Gallery, Lincoln Ctr, New York; Hyatt Collection. *Exhib:* El Paso Mus, Tex, 71; Sarah Lawrence Col Mus, Bronxville, NY, 75; Hudson River Mus, Yonkers, NY, 76; The Nat Acad Design, New York, 76-77; Univ Conn, Stamford, 77; Branchville Soho Gallery, 82; Pindar Gallery, New York, 84; Silvermine Guild, 84; and others. *Pos:* Gallery dir, Greenwich Art Barn, Conn, 70-, vpres, 72- *Awards:* Best in Show, Westchester Art Soc, 72-73 & Greenwich Art Soc, 80; Purchase Award, Silvermine Guild Ctr Arts. *Mem:* Nat Asn Women Artists; Silvermine Artist Guild; Hudson River Contemp; Am Soc Contemp Painters; Greenwich Art Coun. *Mailing Add:* Burying Hill Rd Greenwich CT 06830

BIRNBERG, GERALD H
DEALER
b New York, NY, Oct 15, 31. *Study:* Syracuse Univ, NY, BA. *Collections Arranged:* One Hundred Years of American Drawings, Prince Arthur Galleries, Toronto, Ont, 77. *Pos:* Co-owner, Prince Arthur Galleries, 76- *Specialty:* Nineteenth and 20th century international art; concentration on 20th century figurative expressionism, including the work of Leonard Baskin, Will Barnet, Ben Shahn, Bruno Lucchesi, Francoise Gilot and Jack Levine. *Mailing Add:* Prince Arthur Galleries 33 Prince Arthur Ave Toronto ON M5R 1B2 Canada

BIRNBERG, RUTH CARREL
DEALER
b Buffalo, NY, Mar 8, 33. *Study:* Univ Buffalo, NY, BA. *Collections Arranged:* One Hundred Years of American Drawings, Prince Arthur Galleries, Toronto, Ont, Can, 77. *Pos:* Co-owner, Prince Arthur Galleries, 76- *Specialty:* Nineteenth and twentieth century international art; concentration on twentieth century figurative expressionism including the work of Leonard Baskin, Will Barnet, Ben Shahn, Bruno Lucchesi, Francoise Gilot and Jack Levine. *Mailing Add:* Prince Arthur Galleries 33 Prince Arthur Ave Toronto ON M5R 1B2 Canada

BISCHOFF, ELMER NELSON
PAINTER, EDUCATOR
b Berkeley, Calif, July 9, 16. *Study:* Univ Calif, Berkeley, BA, 38, MA, 39; Otis Art Inst Parsons Sch Design, Los Angeles, Hon DFA, 83. *Work:* Metrop Mus Art, Mus Mod Art, Whitney Mus Am Art, New York; Hirshhorn Mus, Nat Mus Am Art, Smithsonian Inst, Washington, DC; Metrop Mus Art, New York. *Exhib:* Whitney Mus Am Art Ann Exhib Contemp Am Painting, 59; Recent Painting USA: The Figure, Mus Mod Art, New York, 62; '54 to '64, Painting & Sculpture of a Decade, Tate Gallery, London, 64; American Painting of the 70's, Albright-Knox Art Gallery, Buffalo, NY, 78; one-man shows, Arts Club Chicago, 80, Contemp Arts Mus, Houston, 80 & John Berggruen Gallery, San Francisco, 83; and others. *Teaching:* Instr painting & drawing, San Francisco Art Inst, Calif, 46-52, 56-63; prof painting & drawing, Univ Calif, Berkeley, 63- *Awards:* Ford Found Grant, 59; Nat Inst Arts & Lett Grant, 63; Distinguished Teaching Award, Col Art Asn Am, 83. *Bibliog:* Jeff Perrone (auth), Elmer Bischoff: San Francisco Art Institute, Artforum, summer 75; Charles Shere (auth), Bischoff paintings make handsome museum show, Oakland Tribune, 10/19/75; Thomas Albright (auth), Elmer Bischoff: Bay Area figurative, Currant, 12/75-1/76. *Media:* Acrylic. *Dealer:* John Berggruen Gallery 228 Grant Ave 3rd Floor San Francisco CA; Hirschl & Adler Modern New York NY. *Mailing Add:* 2571 Shattuck Ave Berkeley CA 94704

BISGYER, BARBARA G (COHN)
SCULPTOR
b New York, NY, June 7, 33. *Study:* Sarah Lawrence Col; Sculptors & Ceramic Workshop, New York; also indust design with R R Kostellow. *Work:* US Consular Small Sculpture Collection, Smithsonian Inst; Larry Aldrich Mus Contemp Art; Savin Bus Machines Corp. *Exhib:* Union Carbide; Aldrich Mus; Avery Fisher Hall, Lincoln Ctr; Hudson River Mus; Pratt Sch Design; Sarah Lawrence Col; and others. *Awards:* Merit Award for Outstanding Design & Craftsmanship in Sculpture, Artist Craftsmen New York; President's Award, Mamaroneck Artists Guild, Westchester Art Soc. *Bibliog:* Articles in Art News & Today's Art. *Mem:* Artists Craftsmen, New York; Mamaroneck Artists Guild; Artists Equity Asn, NY; Am Soc Contemp Artists; Abraxas. *Media:* Miscellaneous. *Dealer:* Environment Gallery 405 E 54th St New York NY 10022; Courtyard Gallery Chappaqua NY 10514. *Mailing Add:* 50 Lake Rd Rye NY 10580

BISHOP, BARBARA LEE
EDUCATOR, PRINTMAKER
b Roanoke, Va, Sept 9, 38. *Study:* Longwood Col, BS(art educ), 60; Univ NC, Greensboro, MFA, 62; Am Ctr Students & Artists, study with Misch Kohn, 65; Teachers Col, Columbia Univ, advanced study, 68-74; Penland Sch Crafts, 76. *Work:* Phillip Morris, Inc & First & Merchants Bank, Richmond, Va; Gen Elec Co, Salem, Va & Charlotteville, Va; Hayes, Seay, Mattern & Mattern, Roanoke, Va. *Comn:* Varied Publ, Longwood Col, Farmville, Va, 65- *Exhib:* Eastern Regional Drawing Exhib, Philadelphia Mus Art, Pa, 65; The Print in Am/Nat Print Show, Peabody Col, Nashville, Tenn, 66; Soc Am Graphic Artists 50th Ann Exhib, New York, 69; Va Mus Fine Arts, Richmond, 71, 73, 75, 76, 79 & 80; Am Print & Drawing Exhib, Winston-Salem Gallery Contemp Art, 72; Va Artist, Int Women's Arts Festival, New York, 75; 25 one-woman shows, Va, NY, Alaska, NC & Pa, 62-81. *Collections Arranged:* Thomas Sully, 73; Thomas Sully and His Contemporaries, 78 & A View Am Painter from Va Collectors, 81, Bedford Gallery, Longwood Col. *Pos:* Adminr Dir, Longwood Fine Arts Ctr, Longwood Col, 72-; ed arts comn, Va Mus, Richmond, 74-; art ed & vpres, New Va Review, 79-81. *Teaching:* Prof drawing, printmaking & photog & chmn dept art, Longwood Col, Farmville, Va, 65- *Awards:* Certificate of Distinction, Va Photogrs, 71, Va Artists, 79 & Va Mus Fine Arts, Richmond. *Mem:* Nat Art Educ Asn; Va Art Educ Asn; Southeastern Col Art Asn; Richmond Artists Asn; and others. *Media:* Silk-screen, Papermaking. *Dealer:* Baldridge Gallery Sycamore Square Richmond VA. *Mailing Add:* Rte 3 Box 568-B Farmville VA 23901

BISHOP, BENJAMIN
PAINTER, EDUCATOR
b New York, NY, Feb 10, 23. *Study:* Art Students League, 45-47; Univ Nebr, BFA; NY Univ Inst Fine Arts, 50-51; Columbia Univ; Univ Calif, Berkeley, MA, 65. *Work:* Norfolk Mus Art & Sci, Va; State Univ NY Col Potsdam; Univ Mass, Amherst; Syracuse Univ Mus; State Univ NY Binghamton. *Exhib:* Alonzo Gallery, New York, 67-69; Mari Gallery, Woodstock, NY, 68; Monterey Peninsula Mus; First St Gallery, New York, 77; Monoprints, Vassar Col, 81. *Teaching:* Instr art, Memphis Acad Art, Tenn, 47-48, Vassar Col, 51, Univ Mo, Columbia, 52-54 & Santa Catalina Sch Girls, Monterey, Calif, 64-65; prof art, State Univ NY Col New Paltz, 65- *Awards:* Delta Pi Delta Award, Joslyn Art Mus, 48; First Prize for Drawing, Monterey Co Fair, Calif, 65; Childe Hassam Fund Purchase Award, Am Acad Arts & Lett, 68. *Media:* Oil. *Mailing Add:* Rte 1 Box 450B High Falls NY 12440

BISHOP, BUDD HARRIS
MUSEUM DIRECTOR
b Canton, Ga, Nov 1, 36. *Study:* Shorter Col, Ga, AB, 58; Univ Ga, MFA, 60, with Lamar Dodd & Howard Thomas; Arts Admin Inst, Harvard Univ, 70. *Collections Arranged:* Tenn State Collection of Sculpture; The Collection of Hunter Mus of Art; Sculpture Collection, Columbus, Mus; Ogilvy Collection Chinese & Japanese Art. *Pos:* Dir creative serv, Transit Advert Asn, New York, 64-66; dir, Hunter Mus Art, 66-76; dir, Columbus Mus Art, Ohio, 76- *Teaching:* Lectr art hist, Vanderbilt Univ, 61-62; art dir children's prog, Ensworth Sch, Nashville, Tenn, 61-64; lectr art, Univ Chattanooga, 67-68. *Awards:* Tenn Arts Comt Award, 71; Shorter Col Alumni Award, 79. *Mem:* Am Asn Mus; Midwest Mus Conf; Tenn Asn Mus (pres, 71-); Asn Art Mus Dirs; Ohio Mus Asn. *Res:* Early Tennessee artists; early Southern American painting; George Bellows. *Mailing Add:* 545 City Park Ave Columbus OH 43215

BISHOP, ISABEL (MRS HAROLD G WOLFF)
PAINTER, ETCHER
b Cincinnati, Ohio, Mar 3, 02. *Study:* Wicker Art Sch, Detroit, Mich; New York Sch Appl Design for Women; Art Students League; Moore Inst, Hon DFA. *Work:* Metrop Mus Art, Whitney Mus Am Art, New York; Boston Mus Fine Art, Mass; Phillips Mem Gallery, Washington, DC; Victoria & Albert Mus, London; and many others. *Comn:* Mural for post off in New Lexington, Ohio, US Govt Sect Fine Arts. *Exhib:* Venice Biennials; Pittsburgh Int; Nat Exhib Prints, Brooklyn Mus; one-man shows, Berkshire Mus, Pittsfield, Mass, Whitney Mus Am Art, New York, 74 & Midtown Galleries, New York, 79. *Teaching:* Instr figure painting & drawing, Art Students League, 35-37; instr art, Skowhegan Sch Painting & Sculpture, 56 & 58. *Mem:* Am Soc Graphic Artists (vpres, 69-72); Nat Arts Club; Audubon Artists; Royal Soc Arts, London; Nat Acad Design. *Dealer:* Midtown Galleries 11 E 57th St New York NY 10022. *Mailing Add:* 355 W 246th St New York NY 10471

BISHOP, JAMES
PAINTER
b Neosho, Mo, Oct 7, 27. *Study:* Syracuse Univ, New York, BA, 46-50; Wash Univ Sch Fine Arts, 51-54; Black Mountain Col, study with Esteban Vicente, 53; Columbia Univ, 55-56. *Work:* San Francisco Mus of Art. *Exhib:* Albright-Knox Art Gallery, Buffalo, NY, 67; Corcoran Gallery, Washington, DC, 67; Painting Ann, Whitney Mus of Am Art, New York, 67; San Francisco Mus Art, Calif, 68; Director's Choice, Dallas Mus of Fine Arts, Tex, 70; Mus of Mod Art, New York, 74; one-man shows, Annemarie Verna Gallery, Zurich, Switz, 76, Galerie Jean Fournier, Paris, France, 76 & Droll Kolbert Gallery, New York, 79; L'Art Moderne Dans les Musees Francaises, Grand Palais, Paris, 78; Dessin et Couleur, Beaubourg, Paris, 79; and others. *Pos:* Ed assoc, Art News, 69-72. *Teaching:* Instr, Cooper Union, 69-70, Univ Calif, Irvine, 70, Carnegie-Mellon Inst, 71 & Sch of Visual Arts, New York, 72. *Awards:* Guggenheim Found Fel, 70. *Bibliog:* Phyllis Derfner (auth), New York Letter, Art Int, 9/73; John Russell (auth), Review of James Bishop drawings at Rosa Esman, 4/20/74 & Inaugural Show, the Drawing Ctr, 1/21/77, New York Times; Joseph Dreiss (auth), article, Arts Mag, 6/74. *Mailing Add:* c/o Frank Kolbert Gallery 30 W 15th St New York NY 10011

BISHOP, JEFFREY BRITTON
PAINTER, EDUCATOR
b Berkeley, Calif, Feb 18, 49. *Study:* Boston Mus Sch, Dipl(with honors), 73; Tufts Univ, BFA, 74; Univ Wash, MFA, 77. *Work:* Seattle Art Mus, Wash. *Comn:* Large wall installation, City Seattle, Wash, 80. *Exhib:* New Ideas, Seattle Art Mus, Wash, 78; Wash Open, Seattle Art Mus, Wash, 79; one-man shows, Linda Farris Gallery, Seattle, Wash, 80 & 82, Mirage Gallery, Los Angeles, Calif, 81 & Seattle Art Mus, 83; Eight Seattle Artists: Installations, Los Angeles Inst Contemp Art, Calif, 80; Wash Year, Henry Gallery, Univ Wash, Seattle, 81; Collage & Assemblage, Miss Mus Art, Jackson & traveling, 81-83. *Teaching:* Lectr mod art, Univ Wash, Seattle, 78; program dir, Henry Gallery Lecture Series, Seattle, Wash, 78-82; lectr & instr mod art, drawing & painting, Cornish Inst, Seattle, Wash, 79-82. *Awards:* 66th James William Paige Traveling Fel, Boston Mus Fine Arts, 74; Betty Bowen Award, Seattle Art Mus, 82. *Bibliog:* Mathew Kangas (auth), Seattle, Artforum, 5/79 & Art in am, 81; Barbara Taylor (auth), Eight Seattle Artists, Los Angeles Inst Contemp Art, 80. *Mem:* Allied Arts of Seattle; founding mem Ctr Contemp Art. *Media:* Water Media, Charcoal. *Publ:* Auth, interview with Susan Sontag, Insight, 82. *Dealer:* Linda Farris Gallery 322 2nd Ave S Seattle WA 98104; Mirage Gallery 1662 12th St Santa Monica CA 90404. *Mailing Add:* 6032 31st St NE Seattle WA 98115

BISHOP, JEROLD
EDUCATOR, PAINTER
b Salt Lake City, Utah, Apr 14, 36. *Study:* Southern Utah State Col, Cedar City, AB, 56; Utah State Univ, Logan, BS, 60, MFA, 66. *Work:* Valley Nat Bank, Phoenix; Glendale Community Col, Ariz; Starr Commonwealth Boys, Albion, Mich; Court House Collection, Douglas, Ariz. *Exhib:* Mormon Festival Arts, Brigham Young Univ Art Ctr, Provo, Utah, 77-79; Watercolor USA, Springfield Art Mus, Mo, 77 & 80; Univ Ariz Fac Shows, Mus Art, Tucson, 77-81; Watercolor Biennial, Scottsdale Ctr Arts, Ariz, 80; and others. *Pos:* Art dir, Thiokol Chemical Corp, Brigham City, Utah, 63-64 & 66-67; production artist & art dir, Utah State Univ, Logan, 64-66. *Teaching:* Asst prof art, Univ Ariz, Tucson, 67-72, assoc prof, 72- *Awards:* Masters Meed Medallion, Tubac Festival Arts, Santa Cruz Valley Art Asn, 76; Special Award, 4th Ann Western Fedn Watercolor Socs Exhib, 79; Silver Medal, 57th Ann Nat, Springville Mus Art, Utah, 81. *Mem:* Western Fedn Watercolor Socs; Southern Ariz Watercolor Guild; Ariz Watercolor Asn; Midwest Watercolor Soc. *Media:* Watercolor, Mixed Media. *Mailing Add:* 9133 E Speedway Tucson AZ 85710

BISHOP, MARJORIE CUTLER
PAINTER
b Melrose, Mass. *Study:* Art Students League; New Sch Social Res; and with Guy Pene du Bois, Moses Soyer, Sol Wilson & Valero, Paris, France. *Work:* Walker Art Ctr, Minneapolis, Minn; Photo Researchers, Inc, New York. *Exhib:* Carnegie Inst, Pittsburgh, Pa, 45; Pa Acad Fine Arts, Philadelphia, 45; Audubon Artists, New York, 47, 52 & 54; Hecksher Mus, Huntington, NY & Guild Hall, Easthampton, NY, 65; State Univ NY Col, Stony Brook, 78; Gallery North, Setauket, NY, 80 & 83; and many one-man shows in New York & Long Island. *Pos:* Art Coun, Suffolk Mus, Stony Brook, NY, 61-65. *Teaching:* Instr creative painting & art hist, Bishop Art Studio, Oldfield, NY, 56- *Awards:* Purchase Prize, Walker Art Ctr, 45; Exhib Award, St Paul-de-Vence, France, 53. *Media:* Oil, Sand. *Publ:* Women Artists in America: 18th Century to the Present. *Dealer:* Gallery North North Country Rd Setauket NY 11733. *Mailing Add:* Flax Pond Woods Setauket NY 11733

BISHOP, ROBERT CHARLES
MUSEUM DIRECTOR, WRITER
b Readfield, Maine, Aug 25, 38. *Study:* Univ Mich, Ann Arbor, PhD(Am cult), 76. *Pos:* Cur furniture, Henry Ford Mus, Dearborn, Mich, 69-71; mus ed, 71-77; asst ed, Antique Monthly, 70-; dir, Mus Am Folk Art, New York, 77- *Teaching:* Lectr Am decorative arts, Univ Mich, Ann Arbor, 75-77; adj prof, Folk Art Studies, NY Univ, 79- *Awards:* Silver Medal, NY Film Festival, 76; Gold Medal, Int Cult Soc, 76. *Mem:* Am Asn Mus; Metrop Mus Art Connoisseur Club; Midwest Mus Conf; Victorian Soc; Impresario Cult Soc (pres, 75-76). *Publ:* Auth, Centuries and Styles of the American Chair, 1640-1970, 72, How to Know American Antique Furniture, 73, American Folk Sculpture, 74, New Discoveries in American Quilts, 75 & coauth, A Gallery of Amish Quilts, 76, Dutton. *Mailing Add:* c/o Mus Am Folk Arts 49 West 53rd New York NY 10019

BISONE, EDWARD GEORGE
PAINTER
b Buffalo, NY, Nov 19, 28. *Study:* Univ Buffalo, with Seymour Drumlevitch. *Exhib:* Ann Small Drawing & Sculpture Show, Ball State Univ, 71-81; 35th Ann Western NY Art Show, Albright Knox Art Gallery, 75; State of NY Images/Shapes, Clinton Co Govt Ctr, NY, 76; Watercolor Show, AAO Gallery, Buffalo, NY, 79 & 9th Ann Open Exhib, 79; Fifth Ann Drawing Show, Emporia State Univ, Kans, 81; Aqua Media Show, AAO Gallery, Buffalo, 83. *Awards:* First Prize Painting, Burnhams Gallery Sight & Sound, 63; Tony Sisti Award, Leisureland Show, 68; First Prize Drawing, 10th Ann Open, AAO Gallery, 80. *Bibliog:* Discussed in La Rev Mod, Paris, France, 67; Art Rev Mag, 68. *Media:* Mixed Media. *Publ:* Auth, Art Notebook, Vol 1, No 2; illusr, Tour the World of Cooking in 15 Minutes, 72. *Dealer:* Jerel Gallery & Framery Snyder NY 14226. *Mailing Add:* 79 Edgebrook Estates Apt 5 Cheektowaga NY 14227

BISSELL, CHARLES OVERMAN
CARTOONIST
b Nashville, Tenn, June 29, 08. *Pos:* Lithographic artist, 24-45; ed cartoonist & mem staff, Nashville Tennessean, 43-; art dir, Sunday Mag, 45-70. *Awards:* Cartoon Award, Nat Headliners Club, 63; Distinguished Serv Award, Sigma Delta Chi, 64; Pub Serv Award, Nat Safety Coun, 66. *Mem:* Asn Am Ed Cartoonists; Nat Cartoonist Soc. *Publ:* Creater cartoon feature Bissell's Brave New World, 62. *Mailing Add:* 4221 Farrar Ave Nashville TN 37215

BISSELL, PHIL
CARTOONIST, ILLUSTRATOR
b Worcester, Mass, Feb 1, 26. *Study:* Sch Practical Art, Boston, Mass; Art Instr Inc, Minneapolis, Minn, grad. *Work:* Baseball Hall Fame, Cooperstown, NY; Basketball Hall Fame, Springfield, Mass; Football Hall Fame, Canton, Ohio; Hockey Hall Fame, Toronto, Can; Swimming Hall of Fame, Ft Lauderdale, Fla; and others. *Comn:* New Eng Patriots (Nat Football League) insignia. *Exhib:* Southern Calif Expo, 64; Nat Cartoonists Soc, New York, 71 & Washington, DC, 72-79; Man & His World, 9th Int Salon Cartoons, Montreal, PQ, annually. *Pos:* Ed cartoonist, Lowell Sun, Mass. *Awards:* Best Ed Cartoons, 74-81, Scarlet Quill Award for Outstanding Coverage of Intercollegiate Athletics, 76. *Mem:* Asn Am Ed Cartoonists. *Media:* Ink, Tempera. *Publ:* The World Encyclopedia of Cartoons, Horn, Chelsea House, 80. *Mailing Add:* 47 Shetland Rd Rockport MA 01966

BISSETTE, SAMUEL DELK
PAINTER, PATRON
b Wilson, NC, Aug 10, 21. *Study:* Var studies at Ind Univ, Sorbonne in Paris & Worcester Col, Oxford, Eng; Univ NC, 72; also watercolor with John Pike, Woodstock, NY, 72-75. *Work:* Gov's Mansion, Raleigh, NC; Wilkes Mus, North Wilkesboro, NC; Fed Reserve Bank, Richmond, Va. *Comn:* Paintings, Planters Bank, Wilmington, NC & Rocky Mount, NC, 75; Portrait of North Carolina (paintings), Wachovia Bank, Winston-Salem, NC, 76; paintings, United Carolina Bank, Whiteville, NC, 78; murals, Belk Beery Co, Charlotte, NC, 78-79; Paintings, First Union Nat Bank, Charlotte, NC, 82. *Exhib:* Solo exhib, St John's Mus Art, Wilmington, NC, 74; Univ NC Weatherspoon Gallery, Greensboro, NC, 74 & 76; Asheville Mus Art, NC, 75; NC Mus Art, Raleigh, 77; 82nd US Open Watercolor Exhib, Nat Arts Club, New York, 82; and others. *Pos:* Pres, St John's Mus Art Inc, Wilmington, NC, 72-74; corp dir, NC Art Soc, Raleigh, 75-82; trustee, NC Mus Art, 80- *Awards:* First Place, NC Watercolor Soc, 75; Purchase Award, Hunt Manufacturing Co, Philadelphia, 75; and others. *Bibliog:* Dennis M Julian (auth), Sam Bissette captures the state's beauty for Wachovia, NC Citizens Asn, 6/77. *Mem:* Assoc Am Watercolor Soc New York; NC Watercolor Soc (vpres, 80). *Media:* Watercolor. *Publ:* Auth, Watercolor page, Am Artist, 3/84. *Dealer:* St John's Mus Art Inc 114 Orange St Wilmington NC 28401. *Mailing Add:* 1939 South Live Oak Parkway Wilmington NC 28403

BITTLEMAN, ARNOLD I
PAINTER, EDUCATOR
b New York, NY, July 4, 33. *Study:* Yale Univ, BFA, 56, Alice Kimball Eng traveling fel, 56-57, MFA, 58. *Work:* Mus Mod Art & Whitney Mus Am Art, New York; Boston Mus Fine Arts, Mass; Brooklyn Mus, NY; Fogg Mus, Harvard Univ, Cambridge, Mass; Rose Mus, Brandeis Univ; and others. *Exhib:* Yale Univ, Norfolk, Conn, 71-75; Albany Inst Hist & Art, NY, 76; Berkshire Mus, Pittsfield, Mass, 77; Mus Mod Art, New York, 78; US Embassy, Moscow, USSR, 79-81; US Embassy, Seoul, South Korea, 81-83. *Teaching:* Instr drawing, Yale Univ, 58-63 & summer art prog, 73-75; asst prof art, Skidmore Col, 64-66; vis lectr, Minneapolis Sch Art, 65; prof drawing & painting, Union Col, Schenectady, NY, 66- *Awards:* Prizes, Berkshire Mus, Pittsfield, Mass, 77 & 78; Art in Embassies Prog, US State Dept, Moscow, USSR, 80-82 & Seoul, 82-83. *Bibliog:* Bernard Chaet (auth), The Art of Drawing, Holt; Neysa McMein (auth), His recollection: Spain 1957-58: A Whitney Museum purchase award, In: American Art of Our Century, by Lloyd Goodrich & John I H Saur, Praeger. *Dealer:* Milliken Gallery 98 Prince St New York NY 10012. *Mailing Add:* RFD Eagle Bridge NY 12057

BITTLEMAN, DOLORES DEMBUS
WEAVER, CONSERVATOR
b New York, NY, Jan 3, 31. *Study:* Columbia Univ, BS(cum laude), 52; Fulbright Fel, Paris, 54-55; Univ Calcutta, 55-56. *Work:* Mus Mod Art & Columbia Univ, New York; Yale Univ, New Haven, Conn; Silvermine Col Art, New Canaan, Conn. *Exhib:* New Weavings to Look At, Silvermine Col Art, New Canaan, Conn, 67; Wall Hangings, Mus Mod Art, New York, 69, 70 & 72; Biennale Int de la Tapisserie, Mus des Beaux Arts, Lausanne, Switz, 71; Warszawskiej Ekspozycji V Miedzynarodowego Biennale Tkaniny Artystyczjej W Lozannie, Zacheta Gallery, Poland, 71; Artists & Craftsmen of Cent NY, Munson-Williams-Procter Inst, Utica, 73; Collaborations in Art, Science & Technology, Everson Mus Art, 75. *Collections Arranged:* Five Process Sculptors, Schenectady Mus, NY (auth, catalog), 76-77. *Pos:* Proprietor & founder, Cambridge Textiles, NY, 79- *Teaching:* Instr textile, Creative Arts Workshop, New Haven, Conn, 62; instr weaving, Troy Arts Workshop, NY, 66; instr art, Union Col, Schenectady, NY, 69-74. *Awards:* Purchase Prize, Columbia Univ, 52; Nat Endowment Arts Master Craftsman & Apprentice Grant, 75-76. *Bibliog:* Jack Lenor Larsen (auth), Two views of the fifth tapestry biennale, Craft Horizons Mag, 10/71. *Mem:* Centre Int D'Etude Textiles Anciens; Am Inst Conservation of Hist & Artistic Works; Am Soc Appraisers. *Media:* Silk, Natural Fibers. *Mailing Add:* RFD Eagle Bridge NY 12057

BITTNER, HANS OSKAR
PAINTER, ILLUSTRATOR
b Breslau, Ger, Jan 25, 05; US citizen. *Study:* Breslau Kunstschule; Munich Acad. *Work:* Crown Prince William of Ger; Breslau Kunst Mus; Breslau Art Galleries; also in pvt collections. *Exhib:* Ill Festival Art, Chicago, 64; Three Main Libr, Chicago; Chicago Chap Artists Equity Asn; Rockford Col, Kenosha Col & Univ Wis-Stevens Point; work also exhibited on ABC & NBC. *Pos:* Glass & display designer, Goldblatt Stores, Chicago, 30-35; commercial artist, Vogue Wright, 35-45; artist & designer, Wilding Picture Studio, 52-68. *Awards:* Several Second Place Awards, Palette & Chisel Acad & Munic Art League, Chicago; Col Frank Chesrow Gold Medal, Chicago, 72. *Mem:* Palette & Chisel Acad; Munic Art League; Artist Guild Chicago. *Mailing Add:* 10357 Loma Blanca Dr Sun City AZ 85351

BJORKLUND, LEE
PAINTER, EDUCATOR
b Wadena, Minn, June 20, 40. *Study:* Univ Minn, Minneapolis, BA, 69 & MFA, 73. *Work:* Walker Art Ctr, Minneapolis; Univ Gallery, Univ Minn; Fed Reserve Bank, Northwest Nat Bank & First Nat Bank, Minneapolis; Amerada Hess Corp, New York; Minneapolis Inst Art. *Exhib:* Introduction: Seven Young Artists, Walker Art Ctr, 72; Six Young Artists, Foster Gallery, Univ Wis, Eau Claire, 72; An Int Cyclopedia of Plans & Occurrences, Va Commonwealth Univ, 73; Walker Art Ctr, 75; Minneapolis Inst of Arts, 76 & 81; Russell-Cowles Gallery, Minneapolis, 78; Peter M David Gallery, Minneapolis, 80-82. *Pos:* Visual arts coordr, Minn State Arts Bd, Minneapolis, 74-75. *Teaching:* Instr studio art, Univ Minn, 70-72; instr studio art, Minn Mus Art Sch, St Paul, 72-73; asst prof studio art, Minneapolis Col Art & Design, 73-, chmn visual studies div, 75-78, assoc prof, 81- *Awards:* Minn State Arts Bd Grant, 72 & 79; Ford Found Grant, 77; Mellon Found Grant, 82 & 83; and others. *Bibliog:* Mike Steele (auth), Practitioners explore the modern art mystique, Minneapolis Tribune, 5/18/75; Eleanor Heartney (auth), article, New Art Examiner, summer 81; William Hegeman (auth), article, Art News, 11/81. *Mem:* Minneapolis Soc Fine Arts. *Media:* Mixed Media. *Mailing Add:* 2742 Bryant Ave S Minneapolis MN 55408

BLACK, DAVID EVANS
SCULPTOR, EDUCATOR
b Gloucester, Mass, May 29, 28. *Study:* Skowhegan Sch, Maine, summer 49; Wesleyan Univ, AB, 50; Ind Univ, Bloomington, MFA, 54. *Work:* Neue Nat Galerie, West Berlin, Ger; Addison Gallery Am Art, Mass; Dayton Art Inst; Springfield City Hall, Ohio; Ohio State Univ, Columbus; and others. *Comn:* Neue Nat Galerie Sculpture Ct, West Berlin, 72, Credit Life Insurance Co, Springfield, Ohio, 75, New City Bldg, Columbus, 79, Int Airport, Columbus, Ohio, 81 & Ohio State Univ, 82; and others. *Exhib:* One-man shows, Contemp Gallery, New York, 67, Amerika-Haus, West Berlin, 71; Nat Gallery, WBerlin, Ger, 77 & Lehmbruck Mus, Duisberg, Ger, 77; Plastics Presence, Jewish Mus, New York, Milwaukee Art Ctr, Wis & San Francisco Mus Art, 69-70; Alloway Selects, Columbus Mus Art, 77. *Pos:* Mem, DAAD Artists Prog, Berlin & WGer Govt, 70-72. *Teaching:* Prof sculpture, Ohio State Univ,

54- *Awards:* Nat Endowment Arts Award, 66; Ford Grant, 79; Ohioana Citation, 80; and others. *Bibliog:* Tracy Atkinson (auth), David Black, recent work & George Rickey (auth), David Black, Art Int, 12/72; Kuspit on Black, Dialogue, 9/82; and others. *Media:* All Media. *Publ:* Auth, Transparent sculpture, Ohio State Univ Arts, 2/72. *Mailing Add:* Dept of Art Ohio State Univ Columbus OH 43210

BLACK, FREDERICK (EDWARD)
PAINTER
b Providence, RI, May 24, 24. *Study:* Univ NMex, BS, BA & MA. *Work:* Univ NMex; Roswell Art Mus; Long Beach Mus Art. *Exhib:* Phoenix Art Mus, 63; Univ Ill Biennial Invitational; one-man shows, Calif Palace Legion Hon & Paul Rivas Gallery, Los Angeles, 65; Whitney Mus Am Art Invitational; and many others. *Pos:* Dir, State Art Mus, Santa Fe, NMex; dir, Tucson Art Ctr, Ariz; adv prof painting, Art Ctr Sch, Los Angeles; dir, Long Beach Mus Art, 61-66. *Teaching:* Vis prof art, Univ Colo, summers 60 & 61; prof art, Univ Ariz Exten, 60-61; vis prof art, Otis Art Inst, summers 65 & 66; vis prof art hist, Univ Calif, Los Angeles, 65; vis prof art hist, Calif State Col, Long Beach, summer 66; assoc prof art, Univ Albuquerque, 66-69. *Awards:* First Prize, Providence Art Club, 53. *Mem:* Western Mus League (past pres); Long Beach Arts Coun (pres); Artists Equity Asn; Am Asn Mus; Western Asn Art Mus. *Media:* Oil, Acrylic. *Publ:* Contribr, bk revs, NMex Quart, 53 & 64; contribr, Director's choice, Art in Am, 62; auth, Long & Evangel, Craft Horizons, 3-4/70. *Mailing Add:* 7300 Arroyo Del Oso Ave NE Albuquerque NM 87109

BLACK, LISA
PAINTER, GRAPHIC ARTIST
b Lansing, Mich, June 19, 34. *Study:* Univ Paris, Sorbonne, dipl, 55; Univ Mich, BA, 56. *Exhib:* New Haven Paint & Clay Club Art Exhib, Conn, 71, 72 & 83; Springfield Art League 53rd Nat Exhib, Mass, 72; 32nd Ann Art Exhib, Cedar City, Utah, 72; 15th Nat Exhib Am Art, Chautauqua, NY, 72; Milford Fine Arts Art Exhib, 83. *Teaching:* Children's art lessons, pvt studio, 79- *Awards:* Second Award Graphics, Springfield Art League Nat, 72; First Award Graphics, Easter Seal Salute to Arts, Westport, 74; First Award Graphics, Conn Painters, Sculptors & Printmakers Exhib, 75. *Mem:* Stamford Art Asn; New Haven Paint & Clay Club. *Media:* Acrylic, Ink. *Mailing Add:* 17 Brushy Hill Rd Darien CT 06820

BLACK, MARY CHILDS
CURATOR, WRITER
b Pittsfield, Mass. *Study:* Univ NC, Greensboro, BA; George Washington Univ, MA; Cath Univ Am. *Collections Arranged:* Edward Hicks, 60, Erastus Salisbury Field (with catalog), 63, & traveling & spec exhibs, 57-65, Abby Aldrich Rockefeller Folk Art Collection; Ammi Phillips (coauth, catalog), 68, Limners of the Upper Hudson, 69, & other major exhibs, Mus Am Folk Art; City of Promise, Jewish Life in New York, New York Hist Soc, 70; Audubon's Birds of America, 72; series of nine special bicentennial exhibitions, 76 & 77; and other major exhib. *Pos:* From registr to cur & dir, Abby Aldrich Rockefeller Folk Art Collection, Williamsburg, Va, 57-65; dir, Mus Am Folk Art, New York, 65-70; cur painting & sculpture, New York Hist Soc, 70- *Mem:* Am Asn Mus. *Res:* American folk art subjects 1640 to 1840. *Publ:* Coauth, American Folk Painting, 66; coauth, What's American in American Art, 71; coauth, Old New York in Early Photographs, 73; coauth, American Advertising Posters of the 19th Century, 76. *Mailing Add:* 149 W 94th St New York NY 10025

BLACK, MARY MCCUNE
CURATOR, PAINTER
b Broadwell, Ohio, Feb 14, 15. *Study:* Ohio Univ, BS(educ), 37, MFA, 58; Amagansett Sch Art, Sarasota, Fla; workshop study with Charles Burchfield, William Thon, Aaron Bohrod, Paul Sample, Elliot O'Hara & Hilton Leech. *Work:* FMC Corp; McJunkin Corp; Kanawha Co Pub Libr; Art in Embassies Prog; Lutheran Church, Parkersburg, WVa. *Comn:* Three murals for pediatric ward, Charleston Gen Hosp Auxiliary, WVa, 53. *Exhib:* Smithsonian Inst, 63; Nat League Am Pen Women, Tulsa, Okla, 68; Exhib WVa Artists, 77; Nat Exhib, Sacramento, 78; WVa Juried Exhib, 79 & 83; Allied Artists WVa, 82; and others. *Collections Arranged:* Permanent collection exhibition; Fiber & Fabrics; Collectors Exhibition of Kanawha Valley. *Pos:* Dir, Charleston Art Gallery Sunrise, 63-75, cur fine arts of Sunrise, 75-77; mem arts & humanities adv comt, WVa Col Grad Studies, 77-; art juror, Fine Arts Exhib at Art & Craft Fair, Cedar Lakes, WVa, 79 & 80; retired; mem adv bd, Fine Arts Dept, West State Col. *Teaching:* Instr art, Sandusky Jr High Sch, 37-39; instr painting, adult prog, Kanawha Co Bd Educ, 58-64; instr art, Valley Day Sch, 60-63; instr painting, YMCA & Charleston Art Gallery, 63-68. *Awards:* Honorable Mention Award, Nat League Am Pen Women, 78; Merit Award, Nat League Am Pen Women, 83. *Mem:* Assoc Am Watercolor Soc; Allied Artists WVa; Nat League Am Pen Women; Southern Watercolor Soc; Venice Area Art League, Fla. *Media:* Watercolor, Acrylic. *Mailing Add:* 954 Ridgemont Rd Charleston WV 25314

BLACK, RICHARD R
PRINTMAKER, EDUCATOR
b Farnhamville, Iowa, July 18, 32. *Study:* Drake Univ, BFA, 57; Univ Wis, Madison, 58. *Work:* Milwaukee Art Ctr, Wis; Springfield Art Mus, Mo; Indianapolis Mus Art; Wichita Art Mus, Kans. *Exhib:* Boston Printmakers Exhib, Mus Fine Arts, Boston, 70; Fifth Biennial Int Exhib, Dickinson State Col, ND, 74; Color Print USA, Tex Tech Univ, 79; Nat Print Invitational, Southeast Mo State, 81; Prints in Suites, Haggerty Art Ctr, Irving, Tex, 81; solo print exhib, Lakeside Studio, Mich, 82. *Pos:* Dir, David Strawn Art Gallery, Jacksonville, Ill, 59-60. *Teaching:* Instr art, Ill Col, Jacksonville, 59-60; prof, Drake Univ, 60- *Bibliog:* Douglas Warner (auth), Workshop/Lakeside Studio, Graphics Mag, 1-2/79; Charles Roberts (auth), The prints the thing, Iowan, 80. *Media:* Intaglio. *Mailing Add:* 1809 26th St Des Moines IA 50310

BLACKBURN, ED M
PAINTER

b Amarillo, Tex, June 15, 40. *Study:* Univ Tex, BFA, 62; Brooklyn Mus, Beckman Scholar, 63; Univ Calif, Berkeley, MA, 65. *Work:* Ft Worth Art Mus; Dallas Mus Fine Art. *Comn:* Mural on canvas, USAA, San Antonio, 75; Larger Canvas II (billboard), Houston Nat Bank, 78. *Exhib:* Off the Wall, San Antonio Mus Art, 81; solo exhib, Ft Worth Art Mus, 82; American Still Life 1945-1983, Contemp Arts Mus, Houston, 83; Texas Images and Vision, Univ Tex Huntington Gallery, Austin & Amarillo Art Ctr, 83; 38th Corcoran Biennial & Second Western States, 83-84. *Bibliog:* Ken Harrison (dir), Ed Blackburn (film), PBS, 75. *Media:* Acrylic, Oil. *Dealer:* Moody Gallery 2015 J West Gray Houston TX 77019. *Mailing Add:* 2237 Warner Ft Worth TX 76110

BLACKBURN, LENORA WHITMIRE
COLLECTOR

b Midland, Tex, Aug 21, 04. *Study:* Univ Tex, Austin, BA, 27; also grad study. *Mem:* Mobile Art Asn; Art Patrons League Mobile. *Interests:* Exhibiting collection for groups and giving lectures on artists. *Collection:* Old Masters including Titian, Ghirlandaio, Rubens, Van der Helst, Bol, Franz van Mieris, Van Dyck, Constable, Turner, Watteau, Ingres, John F Herring Sr, Daubigny, Theodore Rousseau, Gainsborough, Monet, Roualt and many others; Americans including Charles Wilson Peale, Inness, Sully, Easkins, William Marshall, Bierstadt, Blakelock, Robert Henri, Peter Hurd, John Sloan, Childe Hassam, Guy Wiggins, Thomas Moran, George Lukas, Potthast, John Carroll, Grandma Moses, Endre Szabo, Melvin Warren and many others. *Mailing Add:* 4505 N Sunset Dr Mobile AL 36608

BLACKBURN, LOREN HAYNER
PAINTER, ILLUSTRATOR

b South Glens Falls, NY, Mar 5, 29. *Study:* Self-taught. *Work:* Coopers Cave Collection Lake George; Summer Youth Theater Group, Lake George, NY; US Air Force Permanent Collection. *Exhib:* Solo exhibs, Crandall Libr Mus, Glens Falls, NY, 79, Saratoga Golf & Polo Club, NY, 81, Appleland Gallery, Burnt Hills, NY, 83 & Aqueduct Race Track, Jamaica, NY, 83; Fine Arts Pavilion, Worlds Fair, Knoxville, Tenn, 82. *Awards:* Blue Ribbon, 32nd Ann Glens Falls Regional Art Exhib, 79; Second Place & Artists Choice, 12th Ann Old Saratoga Hist Asn Exhib, 80; Best of Watercolors, Lower Adirondack Regional Art Coun Outdoor Show, 80. *Bibliog:* Jeffrey Wilkin (auth), Artist spotlights local themes, Glens Falls Post Star, 5/17/80; Tina Lincer (auth), A man of the Times, Sunday Album Times Union, 12/20/81; Peg Churchill Wright (auth), Area artist gets national attention, Schenectady Gazette, 2/23/83. *Mem:* Lower Adirondack Regional Art Coun (mem exec bd, 80-85, pres, 81-82). *Media:* Watercolor; Pastels, Oil. *Publ:* Auth, Watercolor page, Am Artist Mag, 3/83. *Mailing Add:* 525 Bay Rd Glens Falls NY 12801

BLACKETER, JAMES RICHARD
PAINTER, ART DEALER

b Laguna Beach, Calif, Sept 23, 31. *Study:* Santa Ana Col; also with Bennett Bradbury. *Exhib:* Laguna Beach Invitational Marine Show, Calif, 59; Los Angeles Co Fair Invitational Exhib, Pomona, Calif, 60; Hunt-Wesson Foods Show, Fullerton, Calif, 72. *Pos:* Art dir, Fed Sign & Signal Corp, Los Angeles, 58-60, Santa Ana, 60-72; owner, The Studio (art gallery), Laguna Beach. *Teaching:* Pvt classes oil painting, 60- *Awards:* Laguna Beach Art Asn Awards, 51, 58, 59 & 60; Festival of Arts Award, 58; Ebell Club Los Angeles Award, 60. *Mem:* Laguna Beach Art Asn (secy, 60); Am Inst Fine Arts; Laguna Beach Festival Arts, Showcase 21. *Media:* Oil. *Specialty:* Marine oil paintings. *Mailing Add:* c/o The Studio 1444 S Coast Hwy Laguna Beach CA 92651

BLACKEY, MARY MADLYN
PAINTER, PRINTMAKER

b Glen Cove, NY. *Study:* Albright Art Sch, NY, cert, 52; State Univ NY, Buffalo, BS(art educ), 53; Art Students League, 54-55 & 61-63; Ruth Leaf Etching Studio, 71-73; Donn Steward Etching Workshop, 77-79. *Work:* Columbia Broadcasting Studio, NY; Col Eastern Utah; Int Bus Machines; Conoco Oil; Nassau Community Col. *Exhib:* Am Watercolor Soc Travel Show, Butler Inst Am Art, 66; one-man shows, Nassau Co Ctr Fine Arts, NY, 75 & New Eng Ctr/Univ NH, 77; New Eng Ann Exhib Painting & Sculpture, Silvermine Guild Artists Gallery, 75; Watercolor West, Utah State Univ, 76 & 77; Nat Soc Painters in Casein & Acrylic Ann, Am Acad & Inst Arts & Lett, New York, 79; and others. *Teaching:* Instr watercolor, Jackson Heights Art Club, 71-72, Five Towns Music & Art Found, 77-79, Great Neck Adult Prog, 81-83 & Port Washington Adult Prog, 83- *Awards:* Edgar A Whitney Award, Am Watercolor Soc Ann, 76; Medal Honor, Bergen Mus, NJ, 81; Silver Award, Nassau Co Fine Arts Mus Competition, 83; and others. *Bibliog:* Barbara Nechis (auth), Watercolor--A Creative Experience, Reinhold Nostrand, 79. *Mem:* Am Watercolor Soc; Nat Soc Painters Casein & Acrylic (bd dir, 82-); Philadelphia Watercolor Club; Knickerbocker Artists; Audubon Artists (vpres watercolor, 82-83). *Media:* Watercolor, Acrylic; Etching. *Dealer:* Signatures Gallery Far Hills NJ 07931; Art Resource Consult Denver CO. *Mailing Add:* 2 Benjamin St Glen Head NY 11545

BLACKMAN, THOMAS PATRICK
DIRECTOR, PRINTMAKER

b Des Moines, Iowa, May 15, 51. *Study:* Univ Iowa, Iowa City, BFA, 76. *Collections Arranged:* Chicago Sculpture Int--Mile 1, 2, 3, 82-84. *Pos:* Sponger & shop asst, Landfall Press, Chicago, 78-80; intaglio printer, Metropress, Chicago, 80-81; dir, Chicago Int Art Exposition, 81- *Mailing Add:* 1957 S Halsted Chicago IL 60608

BLACKMUN, BARBARA WINSTON
EDUCATOR, HISTORIAN

b Merced, Calif, June 29, 28. *Study:* Univ Calif, Los Angeles, BA(fine arts; hons), 49; Ariz State Univ, MA(art hist), 71. *Pos:* Founding dir, Univ Arts Workshop, Malawi, Africa, 68-69; co-founder & chmn, Pub Arts Adv Coun, Co of San Diego, 76- *Teaching:* Lectr art hist & chmn art subject bd, Univ Malawi, Limbe, Malawi, Africa, 67-69; instr art hist, San Diego Mesa Col, Calif, 71-, chmn dept visual arts, 76- *Mem:* Col Art Asn; Archaeol Inst Am; San Diego Mus Art; Art Historians Southern Calif. *Res:* The Nyau masks of the Maravi and their significance in African art; the bronze and terracotta sculpture of Ife, Nigeria, a classification through style analysis. *Publ:* Coauth, Masks of Malawi, summer 72 & auth, Maravi Nchawa Mask, autumn 75, African Arts. *Mailing Add:* 9850 Ogram Dr La Mesa CA 92041

BLACKWELL, TOM (THOMAS LEO)
PAINTER

b Chicago, Ill, Mar 9, 38. *Work:* Guggenheim Mus, Mus Mod Art, New York; Elveh Jem Mus Art, Madison, Wis; Nat Air & Space Mus, Smithsonian Inst. *Exhib:* Human Concern-Personal Torment, Whitney Mus Am Art, New York, 69; Whitney Mus Am Art Painting Ann, 72; New Painting, Indianapolis Mus Art, Ind, 72; Hyperrealistes Americains, Galerie 4 Movements, Paris, 72; Jacksonville Art Mus, Fla, 77; Recklinghausen Mus, Ger, 77; Nat Air & Space Mus, Smithsonian Inst, Washington, DC, 77-78; Breaking the Picture Plane, Tomasulo Gallery, Union Col, Cranford, NJ, 78; and many others. *Bibliog:* John Russell (auth), Tom Blackwell, New York Times, 2/8/75; Carlo Lamagna (auth), Tom Blackwell's new paintings, Art Int, 12/76; William Zimmer (auth), article, Arts Mag, 3/77. *Media:* Oil. *Mailing Add:* c/o Louis K Meisel Gallery 131 Prince St New York NY 10012

BLACKWOOD, DAVID (LLOYD)
PAINTER, PRINTMAKER

b Wesleyville, Nfld, Nov 7, 41. *Study:* Ont Col Art, Toronto, 59-64. *Work:* Nat Gallery Can; Nat Gallery Australia; Art Gallery Ont; Montreal Mus Fine Arts; NB Mus. *Exhib:* Int Graphics, Montreal Mus Fine Arts, 71; 1st Norweg Biennial, Frederickstad, 72; Biennial de l'Estampe, Paris, France, 73. *Pos:* Artist-in-residence, Univ Toronto, 69-75. *Teaching:* Art master, Trinity Col Sch, Port Hope, Ont, 63-75. *Awards:* Ingres Medal, Govt France, 63; Purchase Award Can Biennial, Nat Gallery Can, 64; Hornansky Award Int Graphics, Montreal Mus Fine Arts, 71. *Bibliog:* Rex Bromfield (auth), David Blackwood (film), CBC, 72; Farley Mowat (auth), Survivor, Wake of the Great Sealers, McClelland & Little Brown, 73; Blackwood (film), NFB, 75. *Mem:* Royal Can Acad Art (vpres, 79). *Dealer:* Gallery Quan 112 Scollard St Toronto ON M5R 1G2 Can. *Mailing Add:* 22 King St Port Hope ON L1A 2R5 Canada

BLADEN, RONALD
SCULPTOR

b Vancouver, BC, July 13, 18. *Study:* Vancouver Art Sch; Calif Sch Fine Arts. *Work:* Mus Mod Art; Los Angeles Co Mus Art; Albright-Knox Gallery; La Jolla Mus, Calif; South Albany Mall, NY. *Exhib:* Whitney Mus Am Art, 66 & 68; Guggenheim Mus Art, 67; Corcoran Gallery Art, 67; Minimal Art, The Hague, 68; Documenta, Kassel, 68; Contemp Drawing, William Patterson Col, NJ, 75; Monumentalists in Mod Sculpture, Mus Contemp Art, Houston, 75; The Golden Door: Artist Immigrants of America 1876-1976, Hirshhorn Mus, 76; 200 Years of American Sculptue, Whitney Mus Am Art, 76; Project: New Urban Monuments, Akron Art Inst, Ohio, 77; and others. *Awards:* Guggenheim Found Fel, 70; and others. *Mailing Add:* c/o Max Hutchinson Gallery 138 Greene St New York NY 10012

BLAGDEN, ALLEN
PAINTER, PRINTMAKER

b New York, NY, Feb 21, 38. *Study:* Hotchkiss Sch; Yale Univ Summer Art Sch; Cornell Univ, BFA. *Work:* Berkshire Mus, Pittsfield, Mass; Garvan Collection, Peabody Mus, New Haven, Conn; New Britain Mus Am Art, Conn. *Comn:* Many pvt portrait comns. *Exhib:* Silvermine Guild Artists, Conn, 67; St Gaudens Mus, NH, 67; Wadsworth Atheneum, Hartford, Conn, 68; Albright-Knox Art Gallery, Buffalo, NY, 69; Denver Rotary Exhib; one-man shows, Rehn Gallery, New York. *Pos:* Illusr dept ornithology, Smithsonian Inst, Washington, DC, 62-63. *Teaching:* Instr painting, Hotchkiss Sch, 68-69; artist is residence, Cornell Univ, 82. *Awards:* Allied Artist Award, 63; Century Club Art Prize, 71. *Mem:* Century Asn, New York. *Media:* Watercolor, Oil; Etching, Lithography. *Dealer:* Kennedy Gallery 40 W 57th Ave New York NY 10021. *Mailing Add:* Salisbury CT 06068

BLAGDEN, THOMAS P
PAINTER

b Chester, Pa, Mar 29, 11. *Study:* Yale Univ, BA, 33; Pa Acad Fine Arts, 33-35; spec study with Henry Hensche & George Demetrios. *Work:* Addison Gallery Am Art, Andover, Mass; Wadsworth Atheneum, Hartford, Conn; Berkshire Mus, Pittsfield, Mass; New Britain Mus Am Art, New Britain, Conn. *Exhib:* Pa Acad Fine Arts, Philadelphia, 38; Corcoran Gallery Art, Washington, DC, 41; Metrop Mus Art, New York, 50; Am Acad Arts & Lett, NY, 61; Loeb Drama Ctr, Harvard Univ, Cambridge, Mass, 71; one-man show, Keene State Col, NH, 79 & 21 other one-man exhibs, incl nine in New York (Milch Galleries & others), St Gaudens Mus, New Britain Mus,

Americanart. *Teaching:* Instr art, Hotchkiss Sch, Lakeville, Conn, 35-56. *Awards:* Purchase Prize, Wadsworth Atheneum & Berkshire Mus. *Mem:* Century Club, New York; Conn Watercolor Soc. *Mailing Add:* Town Hill Rd Lakeville CT 06039

BLAHOVE, MARCOS
PAINTER

b Ukraine, Apr 22, 28; US citizen. *Study:* Acad Vicente Puig, Buenos Aires, Arg; Nat Acad Design, New York. *Work:* Nat Collection Fine Arts, Nat Portrait Gallery, Smithsonian Inst, Washington, DC; Duke Univ, NC; NC State Univ, Raleigh; Salmagundi Club, New York. *Comn:* Portrait of Aaron Copland, Mrs F Copland, New York, 72; portrait of Lt Barbara A Allen, Naval Art Coop & Liaison Comt, 74; portrait of Bill Koghlerr, Salmagundi Club, New York, 74; portrait of Senator Sam J Ervin, Jr, NC State Univ, Humanities Found, 81. *Exhib:* Fine Arts Festival, Parrish Art Mus, Southampton, NY, 71; Artists Exhib, Southampton Col, NY, 71; Art on Paper, Weatherspoon Art Gallery, Univ NC, Greensboro, 74; Contemporary Portraits by American Painters, Lowe Art Mus, Coral Gables, Fla, 74. *Awards:* Purchase Prize, Artists Exhib, Southampton Col, NY, 71; Eliot Liskin Award, Salmagundi Club, 72; Fine Arts Comn Purchase Award, Am Drawings 76, Portsmouth Mus, 76. *Bibliog:* Lois Miller (auth), Marcos Blahove at the heart of his subject, Am Artist, 7/73; Susan E Meyer (auth), 20 Figure Painters and How They Work, Watson-Guptill, 79. *Mem:* Salmagundi Club. *Publ:* Coauth, (with Joe Singer), Painting Children in Oil, Watson-Guptill, 78. *Dealer:* Art Gallery Originals 120 Reynolda Village Winston-Salem NC 27106. *Mailing Add:* 4908 Manning Dr Greensboro NC 27410

BLAI, BERTHA
CERAMIST, CRAFTSMAN

b Baltimore, Md. *Study:* Tyler Sch Art, Temple Univ, BFA; with Rudy Staffel, Raymond Gallucci, Toshieko Takieuzi & Karen Karns. *Exhib:* Philadelphia Civic Ctr, 70; Paley Libr, Temple Univ, 71; DuCret Sch Art, North Plainfield, NJ, 71; Widener Col, Chester, Pa, 72; Glassboro State Col, NJ, 74. *Teaching:* Instr, Ocean Co Col, 68-69; instr, DuCret Sch Art, 69-72; artist in residence ceramics, Glassboro State Col, 72- *Mem:* Hon mem Pa Guild Craftsmen; Am Craftsmen Asn; Artists Equity Asn; hon life mem Long Beach Island Found of Arts & Sci, NJ. *Media:* Pottery Clay, Glazes. *Mailing Add:* Fourth & High Aves Melrose Park PA 19126

BLAI, BORIS
SCULPTOR, EDUCATOR

b Russia, July 24, 1898; US citizen. *Study:* Imperial Acad Russia; Ecole Beaux-Arts, Paris, France; student of Rodin, France; Glassboro State Col, LLD, 75. *Work:* Rhythm of the Sea (bronze), Philadelphia Mus Art, Pa; busts of all five presidents & other portraits, Temple Univ, Philadelphia; busts of Frank Lloyd Wright & Pres Spivey, Fla Southern Col, Lakeland; also in many pvt collections. *Exhib:* First Open Air Show, Rittenhouse Sq, Philadelphia, 27; Chicago Art Inst, 32; Philadelphia Art Alliance, 37; Philadelphia Acad Ann, 40; retrospectives, Long Beach Island Found Arts & Sci, NJ, 68 & Harcum Jr Col, Bryn Mawr, Pa, 69. *Pos:* Founder & hon pres, Long Beach Island Found Arts & Sci, 49-; artist in residence, Glassboro State Col, 72- *Teaching:* Dir & instr art, Oak Lane Country Day Sch, 27-30; founder, prof art & dean, Tyler Sch Fine Arts, Temple Univ, 30-60, emer dean, 60-; dean, DuCret Sch Art, Plainfield, NJ, 69-72; founder, Blai Sch Fine Arts, Melrose Park, Pa, 72- *Awards:* Page One Award, Newspaper Guild Greater Philadelphia, 60; Philadelphia Art Alliance Medal, 60; Samuel S Fels Medal, Fels Jr High Sch, 62. *Bibliog:* Dr Millard E Gladfelter & Dr Herman S Gunderheimer (auth), The Stella Elkins Tyler School of Fine Arts of Temple University, 53; Louis A deFuria (auth), Boris Blai...sculptor, educator, NJ Music & Arts Mag, 10/70. *Media:* Bronze, Wood. *Publ:* Auth, The arts in education, Educ & the Exceptional Child, 35; auth, The future of art in America, Dept Art Educ Bulletin, 41; auth, Your happiness is in your hands, Am Mag, 40 & Reader's Dig, 40 & 62. *Mailing Add:* Fourth & High Ave Melrose Park Philadelphia PA 19126

BLAINE, NELL
PAINTER

b Richmond, Va, July 10, 22. *Study:* Richmond Prof Inst, 39-42; Hans Hofmann Sch Fine Arts, 42-43; Atelier 17, etching & engraving with William S Hayter, 45; New Sch Social Res, 52-53; Moore Col Art, Hon Dr, 80. *Work:* Mus Mod Art, Whitney Mus Am Art, Metrop Mus Art, New York; Brooklyn Mus, NY; Va Mus Fine Arts, Richmond; plus many others. *Comn:* Two murals, landscapes & cityscapes of Paris, Revlon, Inc, New York, 58. *Exhib:* Solo exhib, Watson-de Nagy Gallery, Houston, 77, Fischbach Gallery, New York, 79 & 81, Va Mus Fine Art, 79 & Hull Gallery, Washington, DC, 79; NAD Ann, 78; The New American Still Life, Westmoreland Co Mus Art, 78; Hans Hofmann as Teacher: Drawings by His Students, Mus Mod Art, 79. *Awards:* Guggenheim Fel, 75; Nat Endowment Arts Award, 76; Gov Award Art, Va, 79. *Bibliog:* Homage to Nell Blaine, Art News Mag, 12/59; James R Mellow (auth), The flowering summer of Nell Blaine, New York Times, 10/11/70; Eleanor Munro (auth), article, In: Originals: American Women Artists, Simon & Schuster, 79. *Mem:* Artists Equity Asn. *Media:* Oil, Watercolor. *Publ:* Coauth, Prints/Nell Blaine--Poems/Kenneth Koch, 53; illusr, In Memory of My Feelings, Mus Mod Art, 68; auth, Getting with Lester & Mondrian in the forties, Jazz & Painting, 72; contribr, A Sense of Place--the Artist & the American Landscape, 72; illusr, Loves Aspects, 75. *Dealer:* Fischbach Gallery 29 W 57th St New York NY 10019. *Mailing Add:* 210 Riverside Dr Apt 8A New York NY 10025

BLAIR, CARL RAYMOND
PAINTER, DEALER

b Atchison, Kans, Nov 28, 32. *Study:* Univ Kans, BFA, 56; Kansas City Art Inst; Sch Design, MFA, 57. *Work:* Mint Mus Art, Charlotte, NC; Greenville Co Mus Art, SC; Greenville Col, Ill; SC Arts Comn, Columbia, SC. *Exhib:* 33rd Butler Ann Painting Exhib, Youngstown, Ohio; Soc Four Arts, Palm Beach, Fla; Piedmont Painting & Sculpture Exhib, Charlotte, 65; Appalachian Corridors I, Charleston, WVa, 68; Int Platform Asn, Washington, DC, 71. *Pos:* Co-founder & pres, Hampton III Gallery, Taylors, SC. *Teaching:* Prof drawing & painting, Bob Jones Univ, 57-; summer sch, Kansas City Art Inst & Greenville Co Mus Art. *Awards:* Piedmont Painting & Sculpture Exhib, Mint Mus Art, 65; Appalachian Corridors I, SC Arts Comn, 68; Int Platform Asn, 68. *Bibliog:* La Revue Moderne, Paris, France, 65-68; Jack A Morris, Jr (auth), Contemporary artists of South Carolina, 70. *Mem:* SC Artists Guild (adv bd, 57-); Greenville Artists Guild (pres, 71-); SC Arts Comn (acquisitions comt, 69-). *Media:* Oil. *Dealer:* Hampton III Gallery Ltd Gallery Ctr Taylors SC 29687. *Mailing Add:* 1 Oakleaf Rd Greenville SC 29609

BLAIR, HELEN (HELEN BLAIR CROSBIE)
SCULPTOR, ILLUSTRATOR

b Hibbing, Minn, Dec 29, 10. *Study:* Mass Sch Art, with Cyrus Dallin; Boston Mus Sch; Archipenko Sch Art, with Archipenko. *Comn:* Plaques of Dr Waring, Colo Med Sch, 69 & of Dr Porter, Porter Mem Hosp, Denver, 70; plaque of Robert Ledbettor, Rome, Ga; bust of Peter Dominick, Colo State Capitol, Denver. *Exhib:* One-man shows, Ardan Studios, New York, 38, Portraits, Inc, New York, 41-42, Vose Galleries, Boston, 44, St Paul Art Ctr, Minn, 62 & Martin Gallery, Phoenix, 73-74; C G Rein Gallery, Palm Beach, 79. *Teaching:* Instr art educ, Boston Univ, 37-40. *Bibliog:* K S Thompson (auth), Figurines step into a new role, Boston Transcript, 34; Peter Barrett (auth), Moulder of youth, Am Mag, 46; Marjorie Barrett (auth), Helen Blair's little people, Denver Post, 70. *Mem:* Artists Equity Asn; Nat Arts & Lett Soc; Ariz Artists Guild. *Publ:* Illusr, Jeanne-Marie, 34, Great Day in the Morning, 46, Assorted Sisters, 47, House Under the Hill, 49 & Hetly & the Grand Deluxe, 51, Houghton Mifflin. *Dealer:* O'Meara Gallery 130 W Palace Santa Fe NM 87501; C G Rein Galleries Minneapolis MN and Scottsdale AZ. *Mailing Add:* 1919 E Claremont St Phoenix AZ 85016

BLAIR, LEE EVERETT
PAINTER, FILMMAKER

b Los Angeles, Calif, Oct 1, 11. *Study:* Chouinard Sch Art, Los Angeles, 33; Art Students League, New York, 47-50. *Work:* Calif Palace Legion Hon, San Francisco; Los Angeles Co Mus Art, Los Angeles; Am Watercolor Soc, William Church Osborn Collection, New York; Art Inst Chicago. *Exhib:* Int Olympic Art Competition, Los Angeles, 32 & Berlin, Ger, 36; Calif Watercolor Soc, Los Angeles Co Mus, Los Angeles, 35-49; Los Angeles Co Fair, Pomona, Calif, 35-58; Am Watercolor Soc, Nat Acad Art, New York, 35-; Soc Illusr, New York, 58-67; Santa Cruz Art League Statewide, Calif, 78-80. *Teaching:* Instr landscape painting, Chouinard Sch Art, Los Angeles, 38-42; instr film animation art, Cabrillo Col, Aptos, Calif, 75-79 & Univ Calif, Santa Cruz, 77- *Awards:* Silver Medal, 47 & William Church Osborn Purchase Award, 53, Am Watercolor Soc; Watercolors Award, Santa Cruz Art League, 79. *Bibliog:* Dale Pollock (auth), Animating fantasia, Santa Cruz Sentinel, 75. *Mem:* Calif Watercolor Soc (pres, 38-42); New York Film Producers Asn (pres, 68-70); life mem Am Watercolor Soc; exhib mem Soc Western Artists; Calif Inst Arts. *Media:* Watercolor, Oil. *Mailing Add:* 3465 Crestline Way Soquel CA 95073

BLAIR, ROBERT NOEL
PAINTER, SCULPTOR

b Buffalo, NY, Aug 12, 12. *Study:* Sch Mus Fine Arts, Boston, Mass. *Work:* Metrop Mus Art, New York; Butler Inst Am Art, Youngstown, Ohio; Munson-Williams-Proctor Inst, Utica, NY; Twain Mus Hist Art; Ford Motor Co Collection, Dearborn, Mich; and others. *Comn:* Sermon on the Mount (oil, tempera), US Army Chapel, Ft McClellan, Ala, 43; Open Hearth (oil), Bethlehem Steel Plant, Lackawanna, NY, 47; Olean in 1890's (two tempera panels), Olean House, NY, 61; Venetian Feast (oil panel), Lakeview Hotel, NY; fountain with three figures (fiberglass-epoxy sculpture), Dr & Mrs Hal Meisburger, Patchen, NY, 62-65. *Exhib:* Corcoran Biennial, Corcoran Gallery Art, Washington, DC, 47; Watercolor Int, Art Inst Chicago, Ill, 48; Pa Acad Fine Arts Nat, Philadelphia, 48; Butler Art Inst Nat & Metrop Mus Art Watercolor Nat, 53; one-man retrospective, Community Tribute Exhibition, State Univ NY Col Buffalo, 66; plus 30 one-man shows. *Pos:* Dir, Art Inst Buffalo, 46-49; illusr, Ford Times Mag, 58-61. *Teaching:* Instr painting, Art Inst Buffalo, 38-55, Albright Art Sch, 55 & State Univ NY Col Buffalo, 71. *Awards:* Guggenheim Fels, 46 & 51; Watowsky Prize, Art Inst Chicago, 48; First Watercolor Prize, Butler Inst Am Art, 53. *Mem:* Buffalo Soc Artists. *Media:* Watercolor, Oil. *Res:* Expansion of technical possibilities in painting. *Publ:* Illusr, St Lawrence Seaway, 57; illusr, Am Artist Mag, 66; illusr, Jeannie's world, 66; illusr & auth, Watercolorists at work, 71. *Mailing Add:* RD 1 Olean Rd Holland NY 14080

BLAKE, JOHN CLEMENS
ARTIST

b Providence, RI, Jan 11, 45. *Study:* Carnegie Inst of Technol, 63-67, BA, 67; Yale-Norfolk Sch, 66; Royal Col of Art, London, 67-69, MA, 69. *Work:* Victoria & Albert Mus, Eng; Nat Gallery of Australia, Canberra; Eastern Arts Asn, Eng; Art Coun Great Britain; British Coun. *Exhib:* Victoria & Albert Mus, London, 72; Cortps Garde, Groningen, Neth, 82; Apollohuis, Eindhoven, Neth, 82; De Vleeshal, Middleburg, Neth, 83; Cultureet, Centrum T'Hoogt, Utrecht, Neth, 83; Bonnefantenmuseum, Maastricht,

Neth, 83; and many others. *Teaching:* Vis lectr photog & fine arts at various colleges. *Awards:* Fulbright, New York, 68; Arts Coun Award for filmmaking, London, 74; Nat Endowment for the Arts Award, 76. *Mailing Add:* 103 B Earls Court Rd London W 8 England United Kingdom

BLAKE, PETER JOST
ARCHITECT, CRITIC
b Berlin, Ger, Sept 20, 20; US citizen. *Study:* Univ London, 38; Regent St Polytech, Sch Archit, London, 39; Univ Pa, 41; Sch of Archit, Pratt Inst, BArch, 49. *Pos:* Writer, Archit Forum, New York, 42-43, assoc ed, 50-54 & 58-61, managing ed, 61-64, ed, 64-72; cur archit & design, Mus Mod Art, New York, 48-50; partner, Peter Blake & Julian Neski, 58-61; partner, James Baker & Peter Blake, Architects, New York, 64-72; ed-in-chief, Archit Plus, New York, 72-75; chmn, Sch Archit, Boston Archit Ctr, Mass, 75-79; chmn dept archit & planning, Catholic Univ Am, Washington, DC, 79- *Teaching:* Vis critic/lectr, var US & foreign cols & univs. *Awards:* Citation for Design Am Archit Exhib Sent to Iron Curtain Countries, 58; Archit Critic's Medal, Am Inst Archit, 75; Hon Mention, Vietnam Veterans' Mem Competition, 81. *Mem:* Fel Am Inst Architects; Archit League New York (vpres archit, 66-68, mem scholar & awards comt, 68-69, pres, 71-72); Int Design Conf, Aspen, Colo (bd dirs, 65-70); Regional Plan Asn. *Publ:* Auth, Master Builders, Knopf, 60; auth, God's Own Junkyard, Holt, Rinehart & Winston, 64; auth, Form Follows Fiasco, Why Modern Architecture Hasn't Worked, Atlantic Monthly Press & Little, Brown & Co, 77; also contribr articles pop mags & newspapers. *Mailing Add:* Dept Archit Catholic Univ Am Washington DC 20064

BLAKE, WENDON See Holden, Donald

BLAKESLEE, SARAH (SARAH BLAKESLEE SPEIGHT)
PAINTER
b Evanston, Ill, Jan 13, 12. *Study:* Corcoran Sch Art; Pa Acad Fine Arts, Cresson Europ Traveling Scholar; Barnes Found; also with Catherine Critcher, Washington, DC. *Work:* Pa Acad Fine Arts; Nat Acad Design; NC Mus Art; Muskegon Mus, Mich; Greenville Mus Art, NC. *Comn:* Portraits, ECarolina Univ, Greenville & St Mary's Col, Raleigh. *Exhib:* Art Inst Chicago Ann, 39 & 40; Corcoran Gallery Art Biennial, 40; Pa Acad Fine Arts Ann, Philadelphia; Nat Acad Design Ann; NC Mus Art Collectors Exhib, 68; solo exhibs, Hines Gallery, Rocky Mt & Greenville Art Ctr. *Teaching:* Instr art, Lankenau Sch, Philadelphia, 52-61; instr art, var art ctrs, NC, 61- *Awards:* Mary Smith Prize, Pa Acad Fine Arts, 41; First Prize, Woodmere Art Gallery, Philadelphia, 56; First Prize & Gold Medal, Penn-Nat-Ligonier Pa, 61. *Media:* Oil. *Mailing Add:* 508 E Ninth St Greenville NC 27834

BLANC, (WILLIAM) PETER
SCULPTOR, PAINTER
b New York, NY, June 29, 12. *Study:* Harvard Univ, BA; St John's Univ, LLB; Corcoran Sch Art; Am Univ, MA. *Work:* Va Mus Fine Arts, Richmond; Ft Worth Art Ctr, Tex; NY Univ; Tweed Mus, Duluth, Minn; Guild Hall, Easthampton, NY. *Exhib:* Ashawagh Hall, Springs, NY, 71-77, 80, 82-83; Guild Hall Mus, East Hampton, NY, 81; Goat Alley Gallery, Sag Harbor, NY, 83; Baltimore Mus of Art, Md; Brooklyn Mus, NY; Corcoran Gallery, Washington, DC; Fogg Art Mus, Cambridge, Mass; Mus of Santa Fe, NMex; Nat Collection of Arts, Washington, DC; Va Mus of Fine Arts, Richmond, Va; Whitney Mus of Am Art, New York; and others. *Teaching:* Pvt classes in painting & drawing, 47-54; instr painting & drawing, Am Univ, 50-53. *Awards:* First Prize for Drawing, Corcoran Gallery Art, 49; Special Award, Washington Watercolor Club, 49 & 52; Hon Mention, Soc Washington Artists, 51 & 53. *Mem:* Artists Equity Asn New York (bd dir, 63-71); Am Soc Contemp Artists. *Media:* Wood. *Publ:* Auth, Artist & the atom, Mag of Art, 51. *Dealer:* Goat Alley Gallery Sag Harbor NY 11963. *Mailing Add:* 161 W 75th St New York NY 10023

BLANCHARD, CAROL
PAINTER, ILLUSTRATOR
b Springfield, Mass, Aug 29, 18. *Study:* Colby Jr Col; Art Students League; Painter's Workshop, Harvard Fogg Mus. *Work:* Albright Art Gallery, Buffalo; City Art Mus, St Louis; Kalamazoo Inst Art, Mich; Walker Art Ctr, Minneapolis; Grace-Horne Gallery; also in pvt collections. *Comn:* Murals in Paasangrahn, St Martin, BWI, Bay Roe, Jamaica, BWI & San Miguel Allende, Mexico. *Exhib:* Perls Galleries, New York, 43-47; Art Inst, Zanesville, Ohio, 50; Carnegie Inst, Pittsburgh, 51-59; Walker Art Ctr, Minneapolis, 60; Kalamazoo Inst Art, Mich; and others. *Awards:* Award, Carnegie Inst Art, 51-53 & 59 & Art Dirs Club, 55 & 56; Benedictine Art Award Creative Arts, 67 & 68; plus others. *Publ:* Illusr, Always Ask a Man; illusr, seven bks by Mary Stolz; illusr, Village Voice, Women's Wear Daily & other newspapers. *Mailing Add:* 375 Bleecker St New York NY 10014

BLANCHETTE, ANTOINE
DEALER, COLLECTOR
Can citizen. *Collections Arranged:* Man Eater and Pretty Ladies (contribr, catalog), Montreal Mus Fine Art, 71. *Pos:* Art dealer, Galerie Treize, currently. *Mem:* Art Curial, Paris; life mem Montreal Mus Fine Arts. *Specialty:* Works on paper by major Canadian artists including F Charron, D Demers, A Dumouchel, M Forger, D Juneau, R Lavoie, J F L'Homme, A Magrini, R Savoie, J P Seguin, F Simonin, P L Tetreault and R M Tremblay. *Collection:* Pre-Columbia Art, figurines and potteries from Las Bocas to Mayan civilizations. *Publ:* Auth, Les Plasticiens, Mus Contemp Art, 74; auth, Modern art 1905-1945, 79; auth, East Wing, National Gallery Art, Washington, DC, & Vie des Arts, 79. *Mailing Add:* c/o Galerie Treize 13 4015 Drolet St Montreal PQ H2L 2W3 Canada

BLANCO, SYLVIA
CERAMIST
b Santurce, PR, Nov 29, 43. *Study:* Univ PR, BBA, 64; Inst Cult Puertorriquena, 74; studied with John Balossi, 77; Liga Arte, 77. *Work:* Inst Cult Puertorriquena, San Juan; Ponce Art Mus, PR; Performing Arts Ctr, Ateneo Puertorriqueno, Santurce, PR; Mus Ceramica, Faenze, Italy. *Comn:* Sculptures (clay), Copan & Art Students League, Santurce, PR, 79. *Exhib:* Peter Valley Craftsmen, NJ, 76; Livingston Art Gallery, Rutgers Univ, 77; Concorso Int Ceramica, Faenza, Italy, 78-82; Sculpture in Clay From Puerto Rico, Mus Fine Arts, Springfield, Mass, Art Mus STex, Corpus Christi, Newark Mus & Bacardi Gallery, Miami, 80-81; Women Artists From Puerto Rico, Cayman Gallery, New York, 83. *Teaching:* Instr ceramics, Art Students League, 79-; prof, Interamerican Univ, 82- *Awards:* Purchase Prize, Concorso Ceramica, Faenza, Italy, 83; Purchase Prize & First Prize Sculpture, Ateneo Puertorriqueno, 83. *Media:* Ceramics. *Mailing Add:* c/o Galeria Botello Plaza Las Americas San Juan PR 00421

BLATTNER, ROBERT HENRY
PAINTER, ILLUSTRATOR
b Lynn, Mass, Dec 8, 06. *Study:* Mass Col Art, BS(educ). *Pos:* Illusr, Christian Sci Monitor, 34-42; art dir, Marschalk & Pratt Advert Agency, 43-45; art dir, Reader's Digest, 45-72, consult art dir, 77-78; retired 78. *Teaching:* Instr design, Boston Univ, 37-38; instr design, Col New Rochelle, 39-41. *Awards:* Soc Illustrators Award of Merit & Gold Medal, 71; Hon Mention & Gold Medal, Am Watercolor Soc; Silver Medal, Art Dirs Club. *Mem:* Soc Illustrators; Art Dirs Club (pres, 60-61); Am Inst Graphic Arts (dir, 58-59); hon mem Am Watercolor Soc; Dutch Treat Club, New York. *Media:* Watercolor. *Publ:* Illusr, Reader's Digest. *Mailing Add:* Loch Lane Port Chester NY 10573

BLAUSTEIN, AL
PAINTER, PRINTMAKER
b Bronx, NY, Jan 23, 24. *Study:* Cooper Union Art Sch, grad fine arts. *Work:* Whitney Mus Am Art, New York; Metrop Mus Art, New York; Chicago Art Inst; Libr Cong, Washington, DC; Pa Acad Fine Arts, Philadelphia. *Comn:* Drawing assignment, Life & Brit Overseas Food Corp, Tanzania, EAfrica, 48-49; fresco mural, S Solon Meeting House, Maine, 53; painting assignment, Fortune Mag, 70. *Exhib:* Four shows, Pa Acad Fine Arts, 51-67; Metrop Mus Art, 50 & 66; Whitney Mus Am Art Ann, 53 & 57; six shows, Brooklyn Mus Print Ann, 57-70; one-man shows, Nordness Gallery, New York, Terry Dintenfass Gallery, Philadelphia Art Alliance, Albany Art Inst & Laeubli Gallery, Zurich, Switz; and others. *Teaching:* Lectr fine arts, Yale Univ, 59-62; prof fine arts, Pratt Inst, 59-; instr printmaking, Pratt Graphic Ctr, 64-69. *Awards:* Prix de Rome Fel, 54-57; Am Acad Arts & Lett Grant, 58; Guggenheim Fel, 58 & 61. *Mailing Add:* 141 E 17th St New York NY 10003

BLAYTON, BETTY (BETTY BLAYTON-TAYLOR)
PAINTER, ADMINISTRATOR
b Williamsburg, Va, July 10, 37. *Study:* Syracuse Univ, BFA, 59; Art Students League, 61; studied with Arnold Prince & Munoru Niizuma. *Work:* Studio Mus Harlem, Metrop Mus Art, New York; Fisk Univ; Philip Morris Corp; Chase Manhattan Bank. *Exhib:* Thirty Contemporary Black Artists, Minneapolis & traveling, 68; Professional Artist for Young Artists, Metrop Mus Art, New York; Black American Contemporary Artist, Zamoia, Africa, 75; solo exhib, Caravan House Gallery, New York, 75 & Fisk Univ, 80; Eight Women, Harvard Univ Gallery, 76; San Francisco Mus Art; Boston Mus Art; High Mus Art; Minneapolis Inst Art; Everson Mus Art; Milwaukee Art Ctr. *Pos:* Supv artist graphics & plastics, Harlem Youth Unlimited, 64-67; pres & artistic dir, Children's Art Carnival, New York, 68- *Teaching:* Consult, New York City Bd Educ, 72-; prof art educ, City Col New York, 78- *Bibliog:* Fire (film), Silvermine Films, 72; Forever Free, Univ Ill Press, 81; Muriel Silverstein (auth), Doing Art Together, 81. *Mem:* Arts & Bus Coun (bd mem, 78-). *Media:* Oil Collage. *Publ:* Auth, People who make things happen, Art Gallery Guide, 69. *Mailing Add:* 140 Nassau St New York NY 10038

BLAZEJE, ZBIGNIEW
SCULPTOR, PAINTER
b Barnaul, USSR, June 2, 42; Can citizen. *Study:* Royal Conserv Music, Toronto; Ont Col Art. *Work:* Art Gallery Ont, Toronto; Norman McKenzie Art Gallery, Regina, Sask; Confedn Art Gallery, Charlettetown, PEI; Hart House, Univ Toronto; Sir George William Univ, Montreal, PQ. *Comn:* Structural sculpture, Libr-Ross Bldg, York Univ, 72; and others. *Exhib:* Canadian Art, Art Gallery Can Pavillion Expo 67, Montreal; Sculpture 67, City Hall Toronto; Electric Art, Univ Calif, Los Angeles Art Gallery & Phoenix, Ariz, 69; Sensory Perceptions Traveling Exhib, Art Gallery Ont, 70-71; Electronic Paintings, Cybernetic Environment, Hart House Art Gallery, Univ Toronto, 81; and others. *Pos:* Pres & dir, Arts Sake Inc, Inst Visual Art, 79- *Teaching:* Instr environ, Ont Col Art, 70-81; instr environ, New Sch Art, Toronto, 71-72. *Awards:* Can Coun Jr Grants, 66, 67 & 69; Ont Art Coun Grants, 79 & 81. *Bibliog:* H Malcomson (auth), Sculpture in Canada, Artforum, 10/67; G M Dault (auth), In the galleries Toronto, Artscanada, 6/71; Electric Gallery plus 3, McCurdy-Bursell Films, Toronto, 4/72. *Mem:* Royal Can Acad Arts. *Mailing Add:* 1254 Dundas W Toronto ON M6J 1X6 Canada

BLAZEY, LAWRENCE EDWIN
DESIGNER, PAINTER
b Cleveland, Ohio, Apr 6, 02. *Study:* Cleveland Inst Art, grad(scholar), 24; Slade Sch, Univ London, with Prof Tonks, 26; Cranbrook Acad, Bloomfield Hills, Mich, with Mia Grotell, 53. *Work:* Cleveland Mus Art; Butler Inst Am Art, Youngstown, Ohio; City of Cleveland Munic Art Collection. *Comn:* Big

Band Hall of Fame (mural), for composers showcase, Galt Ocean Mile Hotel, Ft Lauderdale, Fla. 75; Chapel Furniture, Lorain, Temple, Ohio. *Exhib:* Everson Mus Nat Ceramic, Syracuse, NY, 50-54; Int Art Benefit, Cleveland, 70; Ann Nat Watercolor Show, Butler Inst Am Art, 72-73; Ann Ceramic Show, Butler Inst; Bratenahl Ann Invited Exhib, 79-81. *Pos:* Vpres & dir design, Designers for Indust Inc, Cleveland, 42-52. *Teaching:* Instr ceramics, John Huntington Polytech Inst, Cleveland, 51-54; instr painting & advan art, Beck Ctr, Lakewood, Ohio, 78- *Awards:* Prizes in Painting, Cleveland Mus Art May Show, 37-45; Butler Inst Am Arts Ceramic Prizes, 69-70. *Mem:* Cleveland Soc Artists; Indust Designers Soc Am; Ohio Designer Craftsmen; Nat Orgns Visual Artists. *Media:* Ceramics, Graphics; All Media. *Dealer:* Bonfoey Gallery Cleveland OH. *Mailing Add:* 537 Juneway Dr Bay Village OH 44140

BLECKNER, ROSS
PAINTER
b New York, NY, 1949. *Study:* NY Univ, BA, 73; Calif Inst Arts, MFA, 76. *Work:* Joslyn Art Mus; J B Speed Art Mus. *Exhib:* Whitney Mus Art Biennial, 75; Contemporary Reflections, Aldrich Mus, 75; New Painting--New York, Haywork Gallery, London, 79; Four Artists, Hallwalls, Buffalo, 79; New Work in Black & White, Mus Mod Art, New York, 81. *Bibliog:* Roberta Smith (auth), article, Art in Am, 1/81; Peter Halley (auth), article, 5/82 & Robert Pincus-Witten (auth), Defenestrations, 11/82, Arts Mag. *Media:* Oil on Canvas. *Dealer:* Mary Boone Gallery 417 W Broadway New York NY 10012. *Mailing Add:* 77 White St New York NY 10013

BLEDSOE, JANE KATHRYN
HISTORIAN, ADMINISTRATOR
b Independence, Mo, Sept 9, 37. *Study:* Calif State Univ, Long Beach, BA, MA(art hist) & cert mus studies; Western Asn Art Mus, Mus Mgt Inst, 81. *Collections Arranged:* Maria Poveka, American Potter (with catalog), 74; Masterworks in Modern Sculpture from the Collection of Ben C Deane (with catalog), 75; Anna A Hills, American Impressionist, 76; Bruce Nauman, Monumental Sculpture Commission, 82. *Pos:* Admin dir, Art Mus & Galleries, Calif State Univ, Long Beach, 74- *Res:* Southwestern American Indian ceramics, 19th and 20th centuries. *Mailing Add:* 1071 N Gardner Dr Orange CA 92667

BLEIFELD, STANLEY
SCULPTOR, MEDALIST
b Brooklyn, NY, Aug 28, 24. *Study:* Albert C Barnes Found, Meryon, Pa, 42-43; Tyler Sch Art, Temple Univ, BFA, 49, BS(educ), 49, MFA, 50. *Work:* Temple Univ, Philadelphia, Pa; Tampa Bay Art Ctr, Fla; Pa State Mus, Philadelphia; New Brit Mus of Am Art, Conn; Univ Edinburgh, Great Britain. *Comn:* Vatican Pavilion, New York Worlds Fair, 64-65; Fr McGivney Memorial, Knights Columbus Plaza, NH, Conn, 82; US Navy Memorial, Washington, DC, 82. *Exhib:* Am Fedn Arts, 66-67; IFA Galleries, Washington, DC, 68 & 71; FAR Gallery, New York, 71, 73 & 77; New Britain Mus Am Art, 74; Reflections, Images of Am, US Info Agency Travelling Exhib, 76-77; and others. *Pos:* ed bd, Nat Sculpture Rev, 70. *Teaching:* Asst prof art, Southern Conn State Col & Western Conn State Col, 53-63; instr sculpture, Silvermine Guild, New Canaan, Conn, 63-66; dir sculpture, Bleifeld Studio, Westport, Conn, 66- *Awards:* Tiffany Found Fel, 65 & 67; Shikler Award, Nat Acad Design, 77; Proskauer Prize, 83. *Bibliog:* A sculptor hails the Bible, Life Mag, 6/28/63; article in, Am Artist Mag, 72; Artists of the Rockies, 81. *Mem:* Fel Nat Sculptor Soc. *Dealer:* Jones Gallery 1264 Prospect St La Jolla Ca 92037; Stremmel Gallery Reno NV. *Mailing Add:* 27 Spring Valley Rd Weston CT 06883

BLEVINS, JAMES RICHARD
ADMINISTRATOR, EDUCATOR
b Feb 1, 34; US citizen. *Study:* David Lipscomb Col, BA, 56; George Peabody Col, MA, 60, PhD, 70; Univ Calif, Los Angeles, 75. *Pos:* Chmn, Div Humanities, Ind State Univ, 69-; mem bd dirs, Evansville Mus, 70-, chmn, Fine Arts Comt, 76-; chmn, Ohio River Arts Festival, 72. *Mem:* Evansville Arts & Educ Coun (vpres, 73). *Mailing Add:* 801 SE Third St Evansville IN 47713

BLINDER, MARTIN S
DEALER, PUBLISHER
b Brooklyn, NY, Nov 18, 46. *Study:* Adelphi Univ, BBA, 68. *Work:* Hirshhorn Mus, DC; Chicago Inst Fine Art; Los Co Mus Art; Guggenheim Mus & Mus Mod Art, New York; Newport Art Mus; and others. *Pos:* Publ, Martin Lawrence Ltd Ed, 75; dir, Visual Artists Mgt Corp, 78- & Gallery Hawaii, 78-; monthly column, Eye on Art & Collectors Mart; project orgn, American Bicentennial Comt Manned Space Flight, 76. *Teaching:* Lectr, art & bus symposia. *Specialty:* Publisher of Limited Edition graphics by Victor Vasarely, Salvador Dali, Yaacov Agam, Joan Miro, Yankel Ginzburg, Aldo Luongs, Hiro Yamagata, Charles Bragg, Fritz Scholder and others. *Mailing Add:* Martin Lawrence Ltd Ed 7011 Hayvenhurst Ave Van Nuys CA 91406

BLINDERMAN, BARRY ROBERT
DEALER, CRITIC
b Bethlehem, Pa, June 11, 52. *Study:* Boston Univ, BA(art hist), 75; Univ Pa, MA(art hist), 78. *Collections Arranged:* That Obscure Object of Desire, Bard Col, 83. *Pos:* Free-lance writer, Arts Mag & Arts Exchange Mag, 78-82; dir, Semaphore Gallery, New York, 80- *Teaching:* Guest lectr, Tyler Sch Art, Univ Pa, Boston Mus Fine Art & NAME Gallery, 79- *Res:* Contemporary American painting. *Specialty:* Paintings and drawings of symbolic popular imagery by young American artists. *Publ:* Auth, Steve Reich's minimal music, Arts Exchange, 79; auth, Robert Longo's Men in the Cities: Quotes and

commentary, 81, Keith Haring's Subterranean Signatures, 81, Modern myths: An interview with Andy Warhol, 81 & Ed Paschke: Reflections and digressions on The Body Electric, 82, Arts Mag. *Mailing Add:* 151 Rivington Third Floor New York NY 10002

BLIZZARD, ALAN
PAINTER, EDUCATOR
b Boston, Mass, Mar 25, 39. *Study:* Mass Sch Art, Boston, with Lawrence Kupferman; Univ Ariz, with Andreas Andersen; Univ Iowa, with Stuart Edie, James Lechay & Byron Burford. *Work:* Brooklyn Mus, NY; Metrop Mus Art, New York; Art Inst Chicago; Denver Art Mus, Colo; La Jolla Mus Art, Calif. *Exhib:* Many exhibs in leading mus, col & univs. *Teaching:* Chmn & prof painting, Scripps Col & Claremont Grad Sch, currently; chmn art dept, Scripps Col. *Mailing Add:* Scripps Col Claremont CA 91711

BLOCH, E MAURICE
HISTORIAN, EDUCATOR
b New York, NY. *Study:* NY Univ Sch Archit, BFA; Harvard Univ; NY Univ Inst Fine Arts, MA & PhD; Nat Acad Design; Art Students League, with Brackman. *Pos:* Vpres & dir, Virginia Steele Scott Found, Pasadena, currently. *Teaching:* Lectr, Univ Mo, 43-44, NY Univ, 44-45 & Univ Minn, Minneapolis, 46-47; asst prof & cur, Cooper Union, 49-55; prof Am art, hist prints & hist drawings & dir, Grunwald Ctr Graphic Arts, Univ Calif, Los Angeles, 56- *Awards:* Belg-Am Educ Found Fel, 51; Founders Day Award of Achievement, NY Univ, 57; Western Heritage Ctr Award, 68. *Mem:* Print Coun Am; life mem Art Students League; Art Historians Southern Calif. *Res:* American art of the 18th and 19th centuries; history of European and American drawings and graphic arts. *Publ:* Auth, George Caleb Bingham: Evolution of an artist and a catalogue raisonne, Vols I & II, 67; auth, The Drawings of George Caleb Bingham: A Catalogue Raisonne; articles in, Gazette Beaux Arts, New York Hist Soc Quart, Connoisseur, Art in Am & others. *Mailing Add:* 2253 Veteran Ave Los Angeles CA 90064

BLOCH, MILTON JOSEPH
ADMINISTRATOR, MUSEUM DIRECTOR
b Bronx, NY, Apr 4, 37. *Study:* Pratt Inst, Brooklyn, NY, BID, 58; Univ Fla, Gainesville, MFA, 61. *Exhib:* Romaro Bearden 1920-1980, 80. *Collections Arranged:* Three Centuries of Art in New Jersey, 71; New Jersey Arts & Crafts; The Colonial Expression, 73; American Crafts, Nat Endowment Humanities, 75; Romare Bearden, 79; London Col Am Art, 80; Ed Budnagurio Paintings, 82; Herb Jackson Paintings, 83. *Pos:* Dir, Pensacola Art Ctr, Fla, 64-66; dir, Mus Sci & Natural Hist, Little Rock, Ark, 66-68; dir, Monmouth Mus, Lincroft, NJ, 69-76; dir, Mint Mus, 76- *Teaching:* Instr art & chmn dept, Lake Sumter Col, Fla, 61-63; instr art, Belmont Abbey Col, NC, 79-80. *Mem:* Am Asn Mus; Southeastern Mus Conf; NC Arts Coun; Asn of Art Mus Dirs. *Publ:* Series of six articles on improvised exhibiton design, Mus News, 66-68; Articles for Southeastern Mus Conf J, 80-81. *Mailing Add:* 501 Hempstead Pl Charlotte NC 28207

BLOCK, AMANDA ROTH
PAINTER, PRINTMAKER
b Louisville, Ky, Feb 20, 12. *Study:* Smith Col; Univ Cincinnati; Art Acad Cincinnati; Art Students League; Herron Sch Art, Ind Univ-Purdue Univ, Indianapolis, BFA; and with Garo Antreasian. *Work:* J B Speed Mus, Louisville, Ky; Cincinnati Art Mus, Ohio; Brooklyn Mus, NY; Tucson Mus of Art, Ariz; Philadelphia Mus Art, Pa. *Exhib:* American Sculpture Show, Chicago Art Inst, Ill, 41; Soc Am Graphic Artists Show, 67-; Philadelphia Print Club; Watercolor, Drawing & Print Biennial, Pa Acad Fine Arts, Philadelphia, 69; Butler Inst Am Art, Youngstown, Ohio; Bus & Corp Collect, Indianapolis Mus of Art, Ind, 77. *Teaching:* Lectr lithography & drawing, Herron Sch Art, 69-72; Indianapolis Art League, 72- *Awards:* Katherine Mattison Watercolor Award, Indianapolis Mus Art, 63; Watercolor Award, Indiana Artists Exhib, Sheldon Swope Art Gallery, 64; Ben & Beatrice Goldstein Award, Soc Am Graphic Artists Exhib, Kennedy Gallery, New York, 71. *Mem:* Soc Am Graphic Artists. *Media:* Acrylic, Oil; Serigraph, Lithograph. *Dealer:* Editions Limited Gallery 919 Westfield Blvd Indianapolis IN 46220; Editions Limited West San Francisco CA. *Mailing Add:* 6000 Spring Mill Rd Indianapolis IN 46208

BLOCK, DOROTHY
PAINTER
b Brooklyn, NY, Oct 31, 04. *Study:* Julliard Sch Music; Cooper Union, 20; Art Students League, with William von Schlegel; also with Louis Keilar. *Work:* Living Arts Found, New York; Eisenhower Col, Seneca Falls, NY; Archives Am Art, Smithsonian Inst; Corcoran Gallery Art. *Exhib:* Nat Competition, Am Soc Contemp Artists, New York, 52; Third Biennial Am Painting, Bordighera, Italy, 52; Art USA, Madison Square Garden, New York, 58; Artists Choice, Art Festival, Soho, NY, 78; Mont Mus; Brooklyn Mus, NY. *Mem:* Artists Equity Asn (bd dirs, 52); Figurative Alliance Artists; Am Soc Contemp Artists; life mem Art Students League. *Media:* Oil, Watercolor. *Dealer:* Marie Pellicone Gallery 47 Bond St New York NY. *Mailing Add:* 10 Downing St New York NY 10014

BLOCK, GAY (S)
PHOTOGRAPHER
b Houston, Tex, Mar 5, 42. *Study:* With Sophie Newcomb, 59-61; Univ Houston, 71-72 & 76; with Geoff Winningham, Garry Winogrand & Anne Tucker, 74-76. *Work:* Mus Fine Arts, Houston, Tex; Ft Worth Art Mus, Tex; Portland Mus Art, Maine; Ctr Creative Photog, Tucson, Ariz. *Exhib:* SECA, San Francisco Mus Mod Art, Calif, 80; Triennial, New Orleans Mus Art, La, 80; Tex Photo Sampler, Washington Project Arts, Washington, DC, 81;

Inside/Out: The Self Beyond Likeness, Newport Harbor Art Mus, Calif, 81; one-woman show, Contemp Arts Mus, Houston, Tex, 82; Houston Ctr Photog, 83. *Teaching:* Vis artist photog, Univ Houston, 79-80 & 82-83. *Awards:* Nat Endowment Arts Photographers Fel Grant, 78; Nat Endowment Arts Survey Grant to Women & Their Work, 81. *Bibliog:* Jon Holmes (auth), Deep in the heart of Texas, Camera Mag, 8/77; Susie Kalil (auth), Portrait of a community, Artweek, 6/16/79; Demetra Bowles (auth), Lone-star tapestry, Artweek, 11/7/81. *Mem:* Women's Caucus Art; Houston Arts Coun; Rice Design Alliance; Houston Ctr Photog. *Media:* Black & White, Color. *Publ:* Contribr, Self-Portrayal, Friends of Photog, 78; illusr, My Body is Something Special, Union Am Hebrew Congregations, 81. *Mailing Add:* 2341 Sunset Blvd Houston TX 77005

BLOCK, JOYCE
CALLIGRAPHER, PHOTOGRAPHER
b Chicago, Ill. *Study:* Univ Calif, Los Angeles, BA; Teachers Col, Columbia Univ, MA; Tenshin Calligraphy Res Inst, Tokyo, with Kakei Fujita. *Exhib:* Ann calligraphy exhib, Nihon Shodo Bijutsuin, Tokyo, 63-80, Yokohama Shodo Renmei, 68-75 & Gen Nichi Sho Ten, 70-76; Japanese Calligraphy of Joyce Block, Great Western Savings & Loan, Berkeley, 80; First Federal Savings & Loan of San Rafael, Oakland, 80 & 82. *Teaching:* Instr, Calif & Ariz, eight years, Dept Defense Overseas Dependents Schs, Italy, two years, Yokohama, Japan, 60-79. *Awards:* Seven awards, Nihon Shodo Bijutsuin, Tokyo; Awards, Yokohama Sho doRenmei. *Bibliog:* Mary Castagnozzi (auth), Joyce Block's calligraphy is on display in Berkeley, East/West, 8/6/80. *Mem:* Fiberworks; Nat Asn Retired Teachers; Am Asn Univ Women. *Media:* Sumi Ink, Dyes. *Mailing Add:* 360 Alcatraz Ave Oakland CA 94618

BLODGETT, ANNE WASHINGTON
PAINTER
b New York, NY, Apr 17, 40. *Study:* Smith Col, BA, 61; Boston Mus Sch Fine Arts, 61-62; Cambridge, Eng, Sch of Fine Arts, 64; also with George Demetrios, Boston, 63. *Work:* Berkshire Mus, Pittsfield, Mass; Fitzwilliam Col Collection, Cambridge; Wilson Co, Minneapolis; Charles River Partnership II, Boston; Quixote Co, Chicago; and others. *Comn:* Davis, Polk & Wardwell Co, New York, 81. *Exhib:* One-woman shows, Berkshire Mus, 71, Caravan House Gallery, New York, 71 & 74 & Medici Gallery, London, 73; New Grafton Gallery, London, 72; Bodley Gallery, New York, 80 & 82. *Media:* Oil, Collage. *Mailing Add:* 55 East 72nd St New York NY 10021

BLODGETT, PETER
SCULPTOR, EDUCATOR
b New York, NY, June 5, 35. *Study:* RI Sch Design, BFA(painting), 60; study with Conte Prof Carlo Alberto Petrucci, Rome, Italy, 61; Sch Mus Fine Arts, Boston, 67; RI Sch Design, MFA(sculpture), 73. *Exhib:* The Goldsmith, Renwick Gallery, Smithsonian Inst, Washington, DC, 74 & Minn Mus Art, 74; Brockton Art Ctr, Mass, 75; Visual Arts Gallery, Pensacola, Fla, 75; The Metalsmith, Phoenix Mus Art, 77; Blacksmiths, Bowling Green, Ohio, 77; Master Craftsmen, Mus Fine Arts, Boston, 78; and others. *Collections Arranged:* Amulets & Talismans, New York, 73. *Pos:* Mgr pavilion, Southern Vt Art Centre, Manchester, 62-64; head designer, Wuersch Assoc, Fall River, Mass, 64-67. *Teaching:* Artist-in-residence & head dept, Marlboro Col, Vt, 62-63; instr metals & form design, RI Sch Design, Providence, 72-74; instr metals workshop, Haystack Mt Sch, Deer Isle, Maine, 74; instr metals, Sch Mus Fine Arts, Boston, 74- *Awards:* Merit Award, Renwick Gallery, Smithsonian Inst, 74. *Bibliog:* M Chamberlain (auth), Jewelry Techniques, Watson-Guptill, 76; Ralph Turner (auth), Modern Jewelry, A Critical Assessment, Van Nostrand, 76. *Mem:* Am Crafts Coun; Soc NAm Goldsmiths. *Media:* Multimedia. *Dealer:* Helen Drutt Gallery 1625 Spruce St Philadelphia PA 19103; Mary Brenda Cortell Harckus Krakow Gallery 7 Newbury St Boston MA 02116. *Mailing Add:* 72 1/2 John St Providence RI 02906

BLOEDEL, JOAN (STUART) ROSS
PAINTER, PRINTMAKER
b Boston, Mass, Sept 21, 42. *Study:* Conn Col, with R Lukosius & W McCloy BA, 64; Yale Univ, with J Albers, G Peterdi & Stillman, 65; Univ Iowa, with M Lasansky & E Ludins, MA, 67, MFA, 68. *Work:* Rainier Collection & City Light Collection, Seattle; Ore Arts Found, Salem; Seattle Art Mus. *Comn:* Environ sculpture, Seattle Arts Comn & Nat Endowment Arts, Seattle, 76; five woodcut prints, King Co Arts Comn & three mixed-media paintings, 78-79; 7 mixed-media panals, King Co Architecture Division, 80. *Exhib:* Red River Ann Exhib, Fargo Art Ctr, 68; 6th Ann Exhib Paintings & Sculpture, Tacoma Art Mus, 75; Original Ed, traveling exhib, Ore Arts Found, 78; 31st Spokane Ann Exhib, Cheney-Cowles Mem Mus, 79; Rutgers Nat Drawing, Rutgers Univ Mus, 79; New Ideas IV, Seattle Art Mus, 81. *Collections Arranged:* Monoprint, Northwest Region, 78; Monoprint Workshop, Sr Artists Monotypes, 79. *Teaching:* Instr printmaking & drawing, Seattle Pac Univ, 70-73; instr printmaking, Factory Visual Art, 74-76; instr drawing, Green River Community Col, 78. *Awards:* Original Editions Award, Ore Arts Found, 78; Gaiser Award, Cheney-Cowles Mem Mus, 79; Betty Bowen Award, Seattle Art Mus, 81. *Bibliog:* Ruth Hayes (auth), Seattle Artists, film documentary, Seattle Arts Comn, 79; R Glowen (auth), Gesture and control, Artweek, 81. *Media:* Mixed-Media Painting; Mixed-Media Printmaking. *Publ:* Illusr, The Lamp in the Spine, Moore & Hampl, 71; illusr, Backbone: Seven Northwest Poets, Seal Press, 77; illusr, Talk and contact, Seal Press, 78. *Dealer:* Foster/White Gallery 311 1/2 Occidental S Seattle WA 98104; Karl Bornstein Gallery Los Angeles CA. *Mailing Add:* 2207 E Republican Seattle WA 98112

BLOOM, DONALD S
PAINTER
b Roxbury, Mass, Sept 3, 32. *Study:* Mass Col Art, BFA, 53; Art Students League, 53-55, with Barnet, Levi & Trafton; Inst Allende, San Miguel Allende, Mex, MFA, 57. *Work:* New Brunswick Pub Libr, NJ; NJ Food Coun; Fairleigh Dickinson Univ, Madison, NJ; Montclair State Col, NJ; Rutgers Univ. *Exhib:* Whitney Ann Am Painting, Whitney Mus Am Art, New York, 60; Silvermine Guild Ann, New Canaan, Conn, 63; Audubon Artists Ann, Nat Acad Galleries, New York, 63; NJ Pavilion, New York World's Fair, 65; Springfield Watercolor Asn Traveling Show, Mo, 65; NJ State Mus Ann, 66 & 73. *Pos:* Staff cartoonist, Sentinel (newspapers), 78- *Teaching:* Instr painting & collage, Morris Co Art Asn, NJ, 60-68; instr painting, Bloomfield Col, 65-66; dist chmn art dept, Piscataway Schs, NJ, 66-; instr watercolor, Summit Art Ctr, 74; instr art, Trenton State Col, 83- *Awards:* Guggenheim Fel Creative Painting, 61; Silvermine Guild Award, 63; Huntington Hartford Found Fel, 64. *Bibliog:* E Genauer (auth), rev in New York Herald Tribune, 9/61; J Beck (auth), rev in Art News, 10/61; V Raynor (auth), rev in Arts, 10/61. *Mem:* Assoc Artists NJ. *Media:* Oil, Watercolor; Pastel, Collage. *Publ:* Auth, We learned about color & design, Sch Arts Mag, 58; illusr, Seventeen Mag, 61; illusr, Country & Western Issue, Billboard Mag, 63; auth, Batik in the classroom & Woodcuts by children, 72 & Two for one, 75, Instructor. *Dealer:* Karlebach Gallery 11-18 Saddle River Rd Fair Lawn NJ 07410. *Mailing Add:* 31 Dexter Rd East Brunswick NJ 08816

BLOOM, EDITH SALVIN
DEALER, PAINTER
b Boston, Mass, April 26, 17. *Study:* Mass Col Art, 36-38; Boston Mus Sch Art, 39-45; DeCordova Mus Art Sch, 45-74; also with D Hall, Marian Steele, J Chetcuti & Emile Gruppe; Boston Univ Sch Fine & Applied Arts, Hon Degree. *Comn:* Wall murals (vitrified enamel), private comns, Mass & Maine, 65-75. *Exhib:* Islesboro Inn Exhib, Dark Harbor, Maine, 63-78; Camden Nat Bank, Maine, 63-83; Copley Soc Boston, 80; Shawmut Bank Boston, 81-83; Boston City Hall Exhib, 82. *Pos:* Art dir, Collector's Gallery, Camden, Maine, 63- *Teaching:* Instr vitrified enamel, privately, 65-75. *Awards:* First Prize Landscape, DeCordova Mus, 60; First Prize Watercolors, TI Group Exhibs, 68-75; Juror's Choice Photog, Copley Soc, 82. *Bibliog:* Ivy Dodd (auth), Art along the shore, Courier-Gazette, Rockland, Maine, 7/29/82; Photo essay at Camden bank, Camden Herald, 5/26/83; article, Bangor Daily News, 6/3/83. *Mem:* Copley Soc Boston (bd mem, 65-83). *Media:* Oil, Vitrified Enamel. *Specialty:* Paintings and photographs. *Mailing Add:* Box 155 Chestnut Hill MA 02167

BLOOM, HYMAN
PAINTER
b Riga, Latvia, Mar 29, 13. *Study:* West End Community Ctr, Boston, Mass, study with Harold Zimmerman; Harvard Univ, study with Denman W Ross. *Work:* Harvard Univ; Hirshhorn Mus & Sculpture Garden, Smithsonian Inst, Washington, DC; Kalamazoo Inst of Arts, Mich; Mus of Mod Art, New York; Whitney Mus of Am Art, New York. *Exhib:* Americans 1942, Mus of Mod Art, New York; Mus of Fine Arts, Boston; Whitney Mus of Am Art, New York; two-man show, Univ Calif Los Angeles; one-man shows, Stuart Gallery, Boston, 45, Inst of Contemp Art, Boston, Whitney Mus of Am Art, 68, Univ of Conn, 69 & Terry Dintenfass Inc, 72 & 75; Retrospective, Albright-Knox Art Gallery, Buffalo, NY, 54. *Teaching:* Instr, Wellesley Col, 49-51 & Harvard Univ, 51-53. *Dealer:* Kennedy Galleries 40 W 57th St New York NY 10019. *Mailing Add:* 80 Hills Ferry Rd Nashua NH 03060

BLOOMFIELD, LISA DIANE
PHOTOGRAPHER, CONCEPTUAL ARTIST
b Los Angeles, Calif, Aug 9, 51. *Study:* Univ Calif, Berkeley, BA, 73; Calif Inst Arts, MFA(art & design; scholar), 80. *Work:* J Paul Getty Mus, Malibu, Calif. *Exhib:* Solo exhib, San Jose Inst Contemp Art, 81 & Arco Ctr Visual Art, 83; Mem Show, Friends Photog, Carmel, Calif, 82; Phantasy, Santa Barbara Mus Art, 82; Archeological Constructs, Hampshire Col, Mass, 83. *Collections Arranged:* Photographs: Griffith Observatory: 1935-1978, Los Angeles, 78; The Theater of Gesture, Los Angeles Ctr Photog Studies, 83. *Teaching:* Instr photog, Chaffey Col, 81-, Orange Coast Col, 81- & Otis Art Inst, 82- *Awards:* Purchase Award, Six State Exhib, Univ NMex, Albuquerque, 82; Calif Arts Coun Grant, 83. *Bibliog:* J Hugunin (auth), Mocking objects, Afterimage, 12/80; D Berland (auth), On photography, Los Angeles Times, 5/15/83; J Brumfield (auth), Loaded implications, Art Week, 5/28/83. *Mem:* Friends Photog; Los Angeles Ctr Photog Studies; Soc Photog Educ. *Mailing Add:* 414 N Stanley Ave #5 Los Angeles CA 90036

BLOOMGARDEN, JUDITH MARY
LIBRARIAN
b Brooklyn, NY, Jan 29, 42. *Study:* Univ London, 61-62; Elmira Col, BA, 63; Boston Univ, 63-64; Columbia Univ, 64-66; Pratt Inst, MLS, 69. *Pos:* Libr asst, Elmira Col Libr, 62-63, Sch Educ Libr, Boston Univ, 64 & Fine Arts Libr, Columbia Univ, 65; sr cataloguer, Mus of Mod Art Libr, New York, 66-70; libr consult, NY State Coun Arts, 69-71; head of tech servs, Art & Archit Libr, Yale Univ, 71-; consult, Comt for the Preservation of Archit Records, NY, 77- *Mem:* Art Libr Soc NAm; Conn Archit Rec & Drawings Survey; Nat Arts Club; Nat Trust Hist Preserv; Soc Archit Historians. *Mailing Add:* c/o Yale Art & Archit Libr Box 1605A Yale Station New Haven CT 06520

BLOS, MAY (ELIZABETH)
ILLUSTRATOR, DESIGNER
b Sebastopol, Calif, May 1, 06. *Study:* Univ Calif, Berkeley, AB(cum laude), 26; also with Perham Nahl, Eugen Neuhaus, M Heymann & Hans Hoffman, Munich. *Work:* Hunt Botanical Libr, Carnegie Inst Technol. *Comn:* Murals,

Migration of Molluscs, 68 & displays, Paleobotany, Carboniferous & Echinoderms, 71, Paleontology Dept, Univ Calif, Berkeley (with help of staff); Mex Dancers & Musicians, DeAnza Hotel, Calexico, 50. *Exhib:* Hunt Botanical Libr, Carnegie Inst Technol, Pittsburgh, Pa, 63 & 77; Canessa Gallery, San Francisco, Calif, 70; Univ Calif, Berkeley, 71; Lawrence Hall Sci, Berkeley, 75; Exhib Sci Artists, Oakland Mus, 80. *Mem:* Oakland Mus Asn; Ethnic Guild, Oakland Mus; Guild Sci Illus. *Media:* Tempera, Acrylic; Pen & Ink, Crayon. *Publ:* Illusr, Cambrian Invertebrate Restorations, var publ, 67-78; illusr, display maps for seismology, Univ Calif, Berkeley, 70-71; illusr, Genus Nicotiana, Cactus & Succulents J, Pac Discovery. *Mailing Add:* 29 Live Oak Rd Berkeley CA 94705

BLOS, PETER W
PAINTER, INSTRUCTOR
b Munich, Ger, Oct 29, 03; US citizen. *Study:* State Acad Art, Munich, with Groeber & von Stuck; also French schs, Paris. *Work:* Oakland Art Mus, Calif; Alta Bates Community Hosp, Berkeley, Calif; Calif Farm Bur Fedn, Sacramento; Univ Calif, Berkeley; Univ Manila, Philippines; and others. *Comn:* 16 portraits of faculty members, Univ Calif, Berkeley, 62-75; portrait of Dr R Bahmer, former dir Nat Archives, Washington, DC, 77; portrait, Bertram C Crocheron, founder, Calif Farm Bur Fedn, Sacramento, 79 & Howard Peterson, Caterpillar, San Leandro, 79-80. *Exhib:* Oakland Mus Art; Soc Western Artists Ann, San Francisco, Calif, 55-81; Rosicrucian Art Gallery, San Jose, Calif, 63 & 77-78; Haggin Gallery, Pioneer Mus, Stockton, Calif, 67; Walnut Creek Civic Arts Ctr, 75; Marin Soc Artists, 81; and others. *Pos:* Adv, Am Indian Artists, Redwood City, 75- *Teaching:* Instr portraits & figures, Walnut Creek Civic Arts Ctr, 62- *Awards:* Klumpke Figure Painting Award, Soc Western Artists, 41 & 70; Gold Medal, Oakland Mus, 51; Second Prize for Oils, Springville Invitational, Utah, 69; and others. *Mem:* Oakland Mus Asn; Oakland Art Asn; East Bay Artists Asn; Soc Western Artists; Marin Soc Artists. *Media:* Oil, Acrylic. *Collection:* Navaho rugs, Indian baskets and paintings, Kodachromes. *Mailing Add:* 29 Live Oak Rd Berkeley CA 94705

BLUE, PATT
PHOTOGRAPHER, EDUCATOR
b Apr 27, 45; US citizen. *Study:* State Univ NY, Stony Brook, BA, 74. *Work:* City Mus New York; John F Kennedy Libr, Boston; Polaroid Corp, Cambridge, Mass. *Exhib:* Creative Artists Pub Serv Prog Winners, Nikon House, New York, 81 & Picker Art Gallery, Colgate Univ, 82; Other People, CEPA Gallery, Buffalo, NY, 83; Personal Expressionism, Valencia Col, 84; Ann Invitational, AIR Gallery, New York, 84. *Teaching:* Instr photog, Int Ctr Photog, 76- & NY Univ, 83-; asst prof, Moore Col Art, 84- *Awards:* Creative Artists Pub Serv Prog Grant, NY Coun Arts, 81; Medal of Excellence, Leica Corp, 82; MacDowell Fel, 83. *Publ:* Contribr, Family of women, Ridge Press, 77; contribr, Journal of Photography Annual, Henry Greenwood & Co, 81; contribr, Documentary Photography, Time-Life, 83; contribr, Close-up, Polaroid, 83; auth, Babies having babies, Life Mag, 83. *Mailing Add:* 201 W 77th St New York NY 10024

BLUHM, NORMAN
PAINTER
b Chicago, Ill, Mar 28, 20. *Study:* Ill Inst Technol; and with Mies Van der Rohe. *Work:* Dallas Mus Fine Arts, Tex; Dayton Art Inst, Ohio; Mus Mod Art, New York; Whitney Mus of Am Art, New York; Corcoran Gallery, Washington, DC; plus others. *Exhib:* Carnegie Inst, 58; Am Abstract Image, Guggenheim Mus, 61; Two Decades Am Painting, Mus Mod Art, 66; Large Scale Am Painting, Jewish Mus, 67; one-man shows, Leo Castelli Gallery, 57 & 60, Corcoran Gallery Art, 69 & 77, Martha Jackson Gallery, 70-74, Everson Mus, 73, Vassar Col, 74 & Contemp Arts Mus, Houston, Tex, 76. *Media:* Oil. *Mailing Add:* PO Box 1992 East Hampton NY 11937

BLUM, ANDREA
SCULPTOR
b New York, NY, Apr 6, 50. *Study:* Univ Denver; Boston Mus Sch Fine Arts, BFA, 73; Sch Art Inst Chicago, MFA, 76. *Work:* Art Inst Chicago; AT&T, Chicago; Marina Bank, Chicago; Univ Iowa Mus Art, Iowa City; Nat Collection Fine Arts, Washington, DC. *Exhib:* Boston Mus Sch, 73; Fel Exhib, Art Inst Chicago, 76, Drawings of '70's, 77 & Works on Paper, 78; 3 Sculptors, Northern Iowa Univ Gallery Art, Cedar Falls, 79; Art from Chicago, Koffler Found Collection, Nat Collection Fine Arts, Washington, DC; one-woman show, Marianne Deson Gallery, Chicago, 78 & 80; Beyond Object, Aspen Ctr for Visual Arts, Colo, 80; Creative Time, New York, 81; Installation, Hudson River Mus, New York, 81; DeCordova Mus, Mass, 81; and others. *Teaching:* Vis artist & lectr, Univ Iowa, Iowa City, 77, Kalamazoo Inst Art, Mich, 77, Univ Ill, Chicago Circle, 77, Univ Hartford, Conn, 78, Univ Northern Iowa, Cedar Falls, 79 & Univ Chicago, 79; vis artist, Art Inst Chicago, 81. *Awards:* Nat Endowment for Arts individual grants, 80. *Bibliog:* Franz Schulze (auth), Nothing but abstract, summer 76 & Kay Larson (auth), Rooms with a point of view, 10/77, Art News; C L Morrison (auth), rev in Artforum, 10/76. *Mem:* Col Art Asn Am. *Mailing Add:* 38 White St New York NY 10013

BLUM, HELAINE DOROTHY
SCULPTOR, PAINTER
b Cleveland, Ohio. *Study:* Cleveland Art Inst; Western Reserve Univ; Art Students League; Columbia Univ. *Work:* Detroit Inst Art; Israel Mus Art, Jerusalem; Skirball Mus, Los Angeles. *Comn:* Portrait Samuel Golter, City Hope Med Ctr, Duarte, Calif, 72; portrait Marcel Marceau, Friends Marcel Marceau, Paris, 76. *Exhib:* May Show, Cleveland Mus Art, 45-60s; American Sculpture, Metrop Mus Art, New York, 51; Max Weber Exhib, Jewish Mus, New York, 56; Jewish Art, Smithsonian Inst, 60s; Sculpture, Corcoran Mus,

65; Acad Med, New York, 68; American Art, Calif Palace Legion Hon, 68; Sculpture, O'Hara Gallery, London, 69. *Awards:* L'Esprit, Silvermine Guild Artists, 59 & 65; Nat Coun Jewish Women Award, 67-82; Nat Asn Women Artists Award, 68. *Bibliog:* Articles, New Yorker, 60, New York Times, 66 & Art News, 71. *Mem:* Artists Equity Asn; Nat Asn Women Artists; Silvermine Guild. *Media:* Bronze. *Mailing Add:* PO Box 93 Santa Monica CA 90406

BLUM, JUNE
PAINTER, CURATOR
b Maspeth, NY, Dec 10, 39. *Study:* Brooklyn Col, MA, 59; Brooklyn Mus Art Sch, with Reuben Tam & Tom Doyle, 59-67; New Sch, New York, with Laurie Goulet, 65. *Work:* Brooklyn Col, NY; Okla Art Ctr Mus; Cocoa Beach Libr, Fla. *Comn:* Light Environments (Time-Space), Suffolk Mus, Stony Brook, NY, 70, Okla Art Ctr Mus, Oklahoma City, 72, Hudson River Mus, Yonkers, NY, 73 & Nassau Co Mus Fine Arts, Roslyn, NY, 80. *Exhib:* Works on Paper/Women Artists, Brooklyn Mus, 75; Sons & Others, Queens Mus, Flushing, NY, 76; one-woman show, Paintings, Bronx Mus, NY, 76; 3 Contemp Am Women Realists, Miami-Dade Community Col, 78; The Opposite Sex, Univ Mo-Kansas City, 79; A Woman's Space, Nassau Co Mus Fine Arts, Roslyn, NY, 80; Art to Wear, Barbara Gillman Gallery, Miami, Fla, 81; and others. *Pos:* Cur contemp art, Suffolk Mus, Stony Brook, NY, 71-76; dir, Women for Art, 76- *Awards:* Anne Eisner Putnam Mem Prize, Nat Acad, Nat Asn Women Artists, 68; Hon Mention, White Mountain Festival Arts, Jefferson, NH, 77. *Bibliog:* Dolores Tarzan (auth), Blum paints Friedan, Seattle Times, 2/15/77; Judith A Hoffberg (auth), Letters, Umbrella Assocs, 9/78; Joan Gabriel (auth), Artists in the sunshine, Today, 2/81. *Mem:* Women's Caucus for Art (nat & NY chap); Col Art Asn Am; Artists' Equity Asn; Am Asn Mus. *Media:* Oil, Fabric. *Publ:* Auth, Metamorphosis of June Blum, 76, auth, Betty Friedan ser, 76, auth, Female connection, 78 & auth, A woman's space, 80, Women for Art; auth, Women's Art, Miles Apart (catalog intro), Valencia Community Col, Fla, 82. *Dealer:* Barbara Gillman Gallery Miami FL; NN Gallery Seattle WA. *Mailing Add:* 120 Boca Ciega Rd Cocoa Beach FL 32931

BLUM, SHIRLEY NEILSEN
HISTORIAN
b Petaluma, Calif, Oct 14, 32. *Study:* Stockton Col, AA; Univ Chicago, MA; Univ Calif, Los Angeles, PhD. *Pos:* Ed monogr ser, Col Art Asn. *Teaching:* Instr, Univ Calif, Riverside, 62-73; Dana Prof fine arts, Colgate Univ, 73-74; prof, State Univ NY Col Purchase, 76- *Awards:* Distinguished Teaching Award, Univ Calif, Riverside, 69; Nat Endowment Humanities Fel, 74. *Publ:* Coauth, Jawlensky & the Serial Image, 66, Cubist Circle, 70 & Early Netherlandish Triptychs: A Study in Patronage, 69, Univ Calif. *Mailing Add:* Div Humanities State Univ NY Purchase NY 10577

BLUMBERG, BARBARA GRIFFITHS
PAINTER, INSTRUCTOR
b Wheelersburg, Ohio, Dec 30, 20. *Study:* Stratford Col, Danville, Va; Marshall Univ; also with Fletcher Martin, Elliott O'Hara, Leo Manso & Victor Caudall. *Work:* Charleston Art Gallery, WVa; WVa Col Grad Studies; WVa State Capitol Bldg; FMC Corp, New York; Kanawaha Co Libr, Charleston. *Comn:* Mural, Marshall Univ, 57; tapestry, WVa State House, 70; painting, comn by Gov Hulette Smith, 71; tapestry, T F Goldthorpe Collection, Fla, 73. *Exhib:* Two Hundred Eighty, Huntington, WVa, 54-74; Int Fabric Exhib, Asher Gallery, London, Eng, 68; Fabric Structures (one-man nat touring exhib), 69; Appalachian Corridors, Fabric Sculpture, 70; Norfolk Biennial Drawing & Graphics, Va, 70- *Pos:* Guest artist, Maine, 68-69 & Bowling Green, Ohio, 70-71; consult, State WVa, 72-75. *Teaching:* Instr creative expression, WVa Col Grad Studies, Institute, WVa, formerly, art therapist in pediatrics, currently; instr painting & drawing, Charleston Art Gallery, 70-; instr painting & drawing, Univ Hawaii, Honolulu, 70-71. *Awards:* Purchase Award, Huntington, WVa, 70, Ala Moana Art Festival, Honolulu, 72 & Allied Artists WVa, 74-75. *Bibliog:* Bill Bellinger (auth), Art with a purpose, WVa Illus, 70; Connie Shearer (auth), Full page life style, Charleston Gazette, 71. *Mem:* Nat Asn Am Pen Women (pres, 69); Allied Artists WVa (vpres, 70); Provincetown Art Asn, Mass; East Coast Gallery, Mass. *Media:* Watercolor, Oil. *Res:* Art therapy; art for mentally retarded and physically handicapped. *Publ:* Auth, Creative approach to mental retardation, WVa Sch J, 61; illusr & contribr, Inklings, Nat Asn Am Pen Women, 72-; illusr & contribr, Art & Develop Disabilities J, 74. *Mailing Add:* 1422 Wilkie Dr Charleston WV 25314

BLUMBERG, RON
PAINTER, INSTRUCTOR
b Reading, Pa. *Study:* Nat Acad Design; Art Students League; Acad Grande Chaumiere, Paris, France. *Work:* Los Angeles Co Mus, Calif; Calif Executive Mansion, Sacramento; Bart Lytton Collection, Los Angeles; Hirshhorn Collection, Washington. *Exhib:* One-man shows, Esther Robles Gallery, Los Angeles, 58, Raymond Burr Galleries, Los Angeles, 62-63, Dallas North Galleries, Tex, 66, Cowie Galleries, Los Angeles, 70 & Rosequist Galleries, Tucson, Ariz, 71. *Pos:* Cult chmn, Westwood CofC, West Los Angeles, 69-73. *Teaching:* Pvt classes painting & drawing, 50- *Awards:* J Coun Prize & Purchase Award, Los Angeles Co Mus Art, 50; Calif Watercolor Soc Award, 63; award, Inland VI, San Bernardino, 71. *Mem:* Artists for Econ Action (pres, 74-75 & 80); Los Angeles Art Asn; Calif Confederation Arts (bd dir, 80-81). *Media:* Oil, Watercolor. *Mailing Add:* 974 Teakwood Rd Los Angeles CA 90049

BLUMBERG, SANDRA TROP See Trop-Blumberg, Sandra

BLUME, PETER
PAINTER
b Russia, Oct 27, 06; US citizen. *Study:* Educ Alliance Sch Art, 19-24; Art Students League; Beaux Arts Inst Design. *Work:* Boston Mus Fine Arts; Columbus Gallery Fine Arts; Mus Mod Art; Metrop Mus Art; Whitney Mus Am Art; plus others. *Comn:* Murals, US Post Off, Cannonsburg, Pa, Rome, Ga & Geneva, NY. *Exhib:* Boston Mus Fine Arts; Whitney Mus Am Art; Metrop Mus Art; Mus Mod Art; plus many others. *Pos:* Artist in residence, Am Acad Rome, 56-57, 61-62 & 73. *Awards:* Guggenheim Fel, 32 & 36; Prizes, Carnegie Inst, 34. *Bibliog:* Lloyd Goodrich & I H Baur (auth), American Art of Our Century, Whitney Mus Am Art, 61; George A Flanagan (auth), Understanding and Enjoying Modern Art, Crowell, 62; plus others. *Mem:* Assoc Nat Acad Design; Nat Inst Arts & Lett; Am Acad Arts & Lett. *Mailing Add:* Rte 1 Box 140 Church Rd Sherman CT 06784

BLUMENTHAL, FRITZ
PAINTER, PRINTMAKER
b Mainz, Ger, June 16, 13; US citizen. *Study:* Univ Wuerzburg, Frankfurt, Freiburg, Berne. *Work:* Metrop Mus Art, New York; Nat Gallery Art, Nat Mus Am Art, Smithsonian Inst, Washington, DC; Mus Fine Arts, Boston; Victoria & Albert Mus, London, Eng; and many others. *Comn:* Prog cover designs, Gtr Middletown Arts Coun, NY State Coun Arts in collection of Mus Performing Arts at Lincoln Ctr, New York Pub Libr. *Exhib:* One-man show, Kunstverein Ulm, 65; group shows, Herbert E Feist Gallery, New York, 72; Print Club, Philadelphia, 60 & 72; Traveling Exhib, Pratt Graphics Ctr, 74-76; Distinguished Mid-Atlantic Artists, Univ Del, 80; and others. *Awards:* First Prize Painting, Nantucket Artists Asn, 61. *Bibliog:* Dr Werner Spanner (auth), Fritz Blumenthal, Das Neue Mainz, 64 & Mainz, 83; La Liberte & Mogelon (coauths), The Art of Monoprint, Van Nostrand, 74; Dr D A W Koning (auth), article, De pharmacie en de Kunst, Vol IV, 76; and others. *Media:* Oil, Casein; Monoprints. *Mailing Add:* 422 Silver Lake Scotchtown Rd Middletown NY 10940

BLUMENTHAL, MARGARET M
DESIGNER
b Latvia, Sept 7, 05. *Study:* Berlin, Ger, with B Scherz & Bruno Paul. *Exhib:* Monza, Italy; Metrop Mus Art, New York; Pratt Inst Gallery. *Pos:* Indust & textile designer, 43-; freelance designer & stylist, Libbey-Owens Co, Fallani & Cohn Co, Drulane Co, Toscony Fabrics, Franco Mfg Co, Colortex Co & Astorloid Soc. *Media:* Textiles. *Mailing Add:* 689 Columbus Ave New York NY 10025

BLUMRICH, STEPHEN
DESIGNER, EDITOR
b Gotha, Germany, June 9, 41; US citizen. *Study:* Kunstgewerbeschule Dept Fabric Design, BFA, 58. *Work:* Nat Collection Fine Arts; Thomson Activities Coun, Thomson, Ga. *Exhib:* Ann Southern Tier Art Show, Corning Mus Glass, NY, 70-74; Lake Superior Int Craft Exhib, Tweed Art Mus, Duluth, Minn, 74; The New Fabric Surface, Renwick Gallery, 78; Surface Design Invitational, Purdue Univ, West Lafayette, Ind, 78; Games & Crafts, Philadelphia Art Alliance, 79; Show Biz, Fashion Inst Technol, New York, 80; Opening Exhib, Greenwood Gallery, 80. *Awards:* Craft/Art S, Thomson, Ga, 81; Golden Isles Art Festival, St Simons Island, Ga, 81. *Bibliog:* Dona Z Meilach (auth), The great Batik revival, Sphere Mag, 73; Mike O'Brien (auth), A special craftsman, Regist Guard, Eugene, Ore, 75. *Mem:* Am Crafts Coun; World Crafts Coun; Int Guild Craft Journalists, Auth & Photogr. *Dealer:* Greenwood Gallery 1025 Connecticut Ave NW Washington DC 20036; Norman Worrell Assoc 2328 Golf Club Ln Nashville TN 37215. *Mailing Add:* 311 E Washington Fayetteville TN 37334

BOAL, SARA METZNER
PAINTER, INSTRUCTOR
b Wheeling, WVa, Jan 10, 1896. *Study:* Wellesley Col, BA; Cornell Univ; Columbia Univ; and with M A Rasko, Richard Marwede, Dmitri Romanovsky & Carle Blenner. *Work:* Librs, Barnesville, Ohio & Wheeling, WVa; Starr Mus, Albion, Mich; Wellesley Col, Mass; Hammond Mus; Hispanic Mus. *Comn:* Many pvt commissions. *Exhib:* Academic Artists of Springfield, Mass, Springfield Mus Art, 55; Fifty American Artists, Schoneman Gallery Art, New York; Belgian Pavilion, New York World's Fair, 64-66; Catharine Lorillard Wolfe Art Club, Nat Acad Design, 69-71; Burr Artists, Metrop Mus Art, New York. *Teaching:* Pvt classes in art. *Awards:* Norbury Mem Prize, Catharine Lorillard Wolfe Art Club, 53; Kramer Montgomery Medal of Honor, Ogunquit Art Studio, 59; First Prize in Landscape, Ahde Arzt Gallery, Soc Composers, Authors & Artists, 69. *Mem:* Catharine Lorillard Wolfe Art Club (pres, 65-68); Composers, Authors & Artists Am (pres, NY Chap, 70-72); life fel Royal Soc Arts; Nat Arts Club New York; Salmagundi Club NY. *Media:* Oil. *Publ:* Auth, Sketches of the Alps, 60, Sketches of Greece, 63, Sketches of New York, 65, Sketches of Japan, 67 & Sketches of Segovia, 71. *Mailing Add:* 246 Corona Ave Pelham NY 10803

BOARDMAN, SEYMOUR
PAINTER
b Brooklyn, NY, Dec 29, 21. *Study:* City Col New York, BSS, 42; Art Students League; Ecole Beaux Arts, Paris, France; Acad Grande Chaumiere, Paris; Atelier Fernand Leger, Paris, 46-52. *Work:* Whitney Mus Am Art; Guggenheim Mus; Walker Art Ctr, Minneapolis, Minn; Santa Barbara Mus Art; New York Univ; plus others. *Exhib:* Whitney Mus Am Art, 55, 61 & 67; Kunsthalle, Basel, Switz, 64; Santa Barbara Art Mus, 64; Albright-Knox Gallery, Buffalo, NY, 67; Andrew Dickson White Mus of Art, Cornell Univ, 71; one-man shows, Galerie Mai, Paris, 51, Dorsky Gallery, New York, 72,

and more; plus others. *Teaching:* Instr painting & drawing, Wagner Col, Staten Island, NY, 57-58. *Awards:* Longview Found Award, 63; Guggenheim Fel, 72; Gottlieb Found Award, 79. *Media:* Acrylic, Oil. *Mailing Add:* 234 W 27th St New York NY 10001

BOBAK, BRUNO JOSEPH
PAINTER, PRINTMAKER
b Poland, Dec 28, 23; Can citizen. *Study:* Cent Tech Sch, Toronto, Ont, dipl, 42; City & Guilds Art Sch, London, 60. *Work:* Nat Gallery Can & Can Coun Art Bank, Ottawa, Ont; Oslo Kunstforening, Norway; S London Art Gallery, Eng; Seattle Art Gallery. *Comn:* Murals, Expo, Montreal, 67, Univ NB & Dept Pub Works, Fredericton, 70. *Exhib:* Int Woodcuts, Victoria & Albert Mus, London, 56; 1st Biennial Exhib, Mus Mod Art, Tokyo, 57; Brussels Int, Can Pavilion, Brussels, 58; 20th Biennial Int, Brooklyn Mus Art, 58; Contemp Can Art, Mex, 60; 19 Can Painters '62, Speed Mus, Louisville, 62; 4 Can Printmakers (traveling), Cent Wash State Col, 76; and others. *Pos:* Dir, Art Centre, Univ NB, 61- *Bibliog:* R H Hubbard (auth), Development of Can Art, Nat Gallery, Ottawa, 63; J R Harper (auth), Painting in Canada, Univ Toronto Press, 66; Jerrold Morris (auth), Nude in Canadian Painting, New Press, Toronto, 72. *Media:* Oil; Woodcuts. *Dealer:* Walter Klinkoff Gallery 1200 Quest Rue Sherbrooke Montreal PQ H3A 1H9 Can. *Mailing Add:* 72 Landsdowne Fredericton NB E3B 1T2 Canada

BOB & BOB (FRANCIS SHISHIM & PAUL VELICK)
ART TEAM
F Shishim, b Santa Monica, Calif, May 8, 53 & P Velick, b Detroit, Mich, Feb 8, 52. *Study:* P Velick, Art Ctr Col, Antioch Col, BFA, 75; F Shishim, Art Ctr Col, BFA, 75; both with Tom Wudl, Llyn Foulkes & Lorser Feitelson. *Work:* Ace Gallery, Toronto, Can. *Exhib:* Sex is Stupid, Los Angeles Inst Contemp Art, 79; Nature Is Perfect, Animals Are Perfect, What Are Humans?, Washington Hall Performance Gallery, Seattle, 80; Bob to Bob, Marianne Deson Gallery, Chicago, 82; The Least I Can Do (solo by Dark Bob), San Francisco Art Inst, 83; I Was Wondering About My New Pictures, I-V (solo by Light Bob), Walker Art Ctr, 83; Views From LA, MVC Inc traveling exhib, 83; and many other forms of performance. *Awards:* Golden Turkey Award, Young Turks, DTLA Administration. *Bibliog:* L F Burnham (auth), BOB & BOB: The First Five Years, Astro Artz, 80; Joan Hugo (auth), Bob & Bob again, Artweek Mag, 2/81; Alyson Pov (auth), Across america, Art Papers, 1/81. *Mem:* The Young Turks, Los Angeles. *Publ:* Contribr, High Performance/Public Spirit, Astro Arts, 79; contribr, Performance Anthology, Carl Loeffler, 80; Across America (record), MITB Records, Beverly Hills, 81; The Least I Can Do (record), MITB Records, Beverly Hills, 82; We Know You're Alone (record), Polydor Records, 83; and many other forms of technological reproduction. *Mailing Add:* PO Box 6461 Beverly Hills CA 90212

BOBICK, BRUCE
PAINTER, EDUCATOR
b Clymer, Pa, Oct 25, 41. *Study:* Indiana Univ Pa, BS, 63, MS, 67; Univ Notre Dame, MFA, 68. *Work:* Mt Mercy Col, Cedar Rapids, Iowa; Western Ill Univ, Macomb; Springfield Art Mus, Mo; Laura Musser Art Mus, Muscatine, Iowa. *Comn:* Portrait, Nat Instnl Food Distribr Assoc, Atlanta, 78; three fabric wall hangings, Hilton Inn, Columbus, Ga, 82; watercolor painting & stained glass windows, Grace Lutheran Church, Carrollton, Ga, 83; watercolor paintings, People's Bank, Carrollton, Ga, 83. *Exhib:* Nat Exhib Watercolor Soc of Ala, Birmingham Mus Art, 69 82; 164th Ann Am Watercolors, Prints & Drawings, Pa Acad Fine Arts, Philadelphia, 69; 145th & 146th Ann, Nat Acad Design, New York, 70 & 71; 12th & 14th Midwest Biennial Exhib, Joslyn Art Mus, Omaha, Nebr, 72 & 76; 17th Hunter Ann Exhib Paintings & Drawings, Hunter Mus Art, Chattanooga, Tenn, 78; 2nd Ann Exhib Southern Watercolor Soc, Columbus Mus Arts & Sci, Ga, 78; 1st Ann Ga Watercolor Soc Exhib, Mem Arts Ctr, Atlanta, 79; Mus Arts & Sci, Macon, Ga, 82. *Teaching:* Assoc prof art, Western Ill Univ, 68-76; from assoc prof to prof & chmn dept art, WGa Col, 76-; vis prof painting, Univ Ga Studies Abroad, Cortona, Italy, 80. *Awards:* Purchase Award, Ill State Mus, 71, Watercolor USA, 75 & New Horizons in Art, 76. *Mem:* Watercolor Soc, Nat, Pittsburgh, Ga, Midwest & Ala. *Media:* Watercolor. *Res:* Communication between artist and viewer. *Mailing Add:* 40 Forrest Dr Carrollton GA 30117

BOBROWICZ, YVONNE P
INSTRUCTOR, FIBER ARTIST
b Maplewood, NJ, Feb 17, 28. *Study:* Cranbrook Acad Art; study with Anni Albers; study with Paolo Soleri at Haystack Mountain. *Comn:* Woven wall, comn by Louis I Kahn, Kimball Mus, Ft Worth Tex, 72; woven wall hanging, Savings & Loan Bank, Pittsburgh, Pa, 77. *Exhib:* Detroit Art Mus, Mich, 50; Walker Art Ctr, Minneapolis, Minn, 53; Wichita Art Mus, Kans, 54; Mus of Contemp Crafts, New York, 60; Philadelphia Mus of Art, 63, 300 yrs of Philadelphia Art, 76; Civic Ctr Mus of Philadelphia, 67-73; Univ of Pa Mus, Philadelphia, 75; and others. *Teaching:* Lectr textiles & weaving, Drexel Univ, Philadelphia, 66-; instr weaving, Peters Valley, Leyton NY, summers 72 & 76. *Awards:* First Prize, Los Angeles County Fair, 51. *Mem:* Am Craft Coun; World Craft Coun; Philadelphia Guild Handweavers. *Media:* Thread (fiber or metal). *Publ:* Contribr, Rugmaking, Golden Bks, 72; contribr, Hooked and Rya Rugs, Van Nostrand Reinhold, 74; contribr, Am Rugs and Carpets, William Morrow, 78. *Dealer:* Helen Drutt 1625 Spruce St Philadelphia PA 19103. *Mailing Add:* 2312 Spruce St Philadelphia PA 19103

BOCCIA, EDWARD EUGENE
PAINTER
b Newark, NJ, June 22, 21. *Study:* Pratt Inst Art Sch, NY; Art Students League; Columbia Univ, BS & MA. *Work:* City Art Mus St Louis; Denver Art

Mus; Univ Mass; St Louis Univ; State Hist Soc Mo; and others. *Comn:* Stained glass, Clayton Inn, Mo; four wall paintings, First Nat Bank, St Louis; Stations of the Cross, Old Cathedral, St Louis; mural, Stations of the Cross & stained glass windows, Newman Chapel, Washington Univ, St Louis; religious drawings & 14 mural paintings, Temple Brith Sholom Kneseth Israel, St Louis; and others. *Exhib:* Italian Am Artists in USA, Stone Park, Ill, 77; St Louis Univ, 78; Washington Univ, 79; Univ Arkansas, 81; Dada Gallery, Athens, Greece, 81; retrospective, Mitchell Mus, Ill. *Teaching:* Dean, Columbus Art Sch, Ohio, 48-51; guest instr, Univ Sask, summer 60; guest instr, Webster Groves Col, summer 65; prof fine arts, Washington Univ, currently. *Awards:* Ital Govt Fel Award Res & Painting in Italy, 58-59; Bronze Medal, Temple Israel, St Louis, 62; Knighted to Cavaliere, Pres Ital Repub, 79. *Bibliog:* Interview, Newsbeat Program, KSD-TV, St Louis. *Publ:* Contribr, St Louis Post-Dispatch & Washington Univ Mags. *Mailing Add:* 600 Harper Ave Webster Groves MO 63119

BOCHNER, MEL
CONCEPTUAL ARTIST, WRITER
b Pittsburgh, Pa, 40. *Study:* Carnegie Inst Technol, Pittsburgh, BFA(painting), 62. *Work:* Los Angeles Co Mus Art, Calif; Mus Nat d'Art Mod, Paris, France; Whitney Mus Am Art. *Exhib:* Plans & Proj, Kunsthalle, Bern, Switz, 69; 057, 087, Seattle Art Mus, Wash, 69; Info, Mus Mod Art, New York, 70 & 71; one-man shows, 112 Greene St Gallery, New York, 71, Mus Mod Art, New York, 71, Sonnabend Gallery, New York, 71, 72 & 75 & Univ Calif, Berkeley, 75; Documenta 5, Kassel, WGer, 72; Am Drawings: 1963-1973, Whitney Mus Am Art, New York, 73; Art & Image in Recent Art, Art Inst Chicago, 74; one-man shows, 112 Greene St Gallery, New York, 71, Mus Mod Art, New York, 71, Sonnabend Gallery, New York, 71, 72 & 75 & Univ Calif, Berkeley, 75. *Teaching:* Instr, Sch Visual Arts, New York, 65. *Bibliog:* Lucy R Lippard (auth), Ultra-conceptual art, Art Int, 3/68; B Boice (auth), Axiom of indifference, Arts Mag, 4/73; R McDonald (auth), Mel Bochner, Artweek, 9/74. *Publ:* Auth, Background is not the margin, Art in Process, 69; auth, Ten Misunderstandings: A Theory of Photography, New York, 70; auth, No thought exists, Arts Mag, 4/70; auth, Excerpts from speculation, Artforum, 5/70; auth, Mental exercise: No 1 counting, Data, 2/72. *Dealer:* Sonnabend Gallery 924 Madison Ave New York NY 10021. *Mailing Add:* c/o School of Visual Arts 209 E 23rd St New York NY 10012

BOCK, WILLIAM SAUTS-NETAMUX'WE
ILLUSTRATOR, PAINTER
b Sellersville, Pa, Sept 18, 39. *Study:* Philadelphia Col of Art, BFA(illus), spec study with Robert Riggs; Lutheran Sem, Philadelphia, MA. *Comn:* Watercolor series of Am cities, comn by Marriott Corp for reproduction in many cities, 3-dimensional art (Indian Mexican) & murals, Marriott Camelback Inn, Phoenix, Ariz, 69-70; watercolor for Christmas card, Book of the Month Club, New York, 71 & 74; Olympic designs for Plexiglas etching, McDonalds, Willow Grove, Pa, 75. *Awards:* Honored by Exhib for Illustrations for Crusader King, Am Inst of Graphic Arts, New York, 74; Monthly Choice Award for Illustrations for Malcolm Yucca Seed, Philadelphia Children's Reading Round Table, 78. *Bibliog:* Mr & Mrs Philip Berman (interview), Berman Collection, Pub TV, Allentown, Pa, 69; B A Bergman (auth), The First Aristocrats, Sunday Bulletin, Philadelphia, 2/75; Gerry Wallerstein (auth), William Sauts-Netamux'we Bock, Record Keeper of the Lenape, Bucks Co Panorama Mag, 1/76. *Mem:* Philadelphia Children's Reading Round Table. *Media:* Pen & Ink; Watercolor, Acrylic. *Publ:* Illusr, Wolf Hunt, Little Brown, 70; illusr & auth, Coloring Book of the First Americans, Lenape Indian Drawings, Middle Atlantic Press, 74; illusr, Tom Sawyer, Field Enterprizes, World Bk, 75; illusr, Of Whales & Wolves, Lothrop, Lee, 78; illusr, White Fang (film strip), Spoken Arts, 78. *Mailing Add:* 252 E Summit St Souderton PA 18964

BODE, ROBERT WILLIAM
DESIGNER, PAINTER
b New York, NY, Nov 20, 12. *Study:* Sch Fine & Appl Arts, Pratt Inst; also with Ogden Pleissner. *Comn:* Designs for US postal stamps, Johnny Appleseed, Davy Crockett & Energy Conservation. *Pos:* Exec art dir, Kudner Agency, 51-57; creative art supvr, J Walter Thompson, 57-67. *Awards:* Art Dirs Awards; Am Watercolor Soc; Hudson River Valley Awards. *Mem:* Am Watercolor Soc; Soc Illusr; Art Dirs Club. *Mailing Add:* PO Box 917 South Harwich MA 02661

BODEM, DENNIS RICHARD
MUSEUM DIRECTOR
b Milwaukee, Wis, July 27, 37. *Study:* Wabash Col, BA, 59; Grad Sch, Univ Wis-Madison, 59-61. *Pos:* Dir, Jesse Besser Mus, 75- *Mem:* Thunder Bay Arts Coun; Mich Coun Arts; Mich Mus Asn. *Interests:* Representative works of outstanding US, Midwest and Michigan artists of the late 19th and 20th centuries for museum collection. *Mailing Add:* 121 E White Alpena MI 49707

BODIN, PAUL
PAINTER
b New York, NY, Oct 30, 10. *Study:* Nat Acad Design, 28; Art Students League, 29. *Work:* Albright Knox Art Gallery; Univ WVa. *Exhib:* Santa Barbara Mus, 49; Brooklyn Mus, 49 & 59; Metrop Mus, New York, 52; Springfield Mus, 52; one-man exhibs, New Gallery, New York, 52 & Betty Parsons Gallery, New York, 59 & 61; Hudson River Mus, 60; and others. *Awards:* Longview Found Award, 59. *Mem:* New York Artists Equity Asn. *Media:* Oil, Watercolor. *Dealer:* Mary Ryan Gallery 452 Columbus Ave New York NY 10024. *Mailing Add:* 207 W 86th St New York NY 10024

BODNAR, PETER
PAINTER, EDUCATOR
b Andrejova, Czech, Nov 27, 28; US citizen. *Study:* Flint Inst Arts, Mich, 41-44; Western Mich Univ, BS, 51; Mich State Univ, MA, 56. *Work:* Dallas Mus; Isaac Delgado Mus, New Orleans; Ft Worth Art Mus; Lakeview Ctr for Arts, Peoria, Ill; De Waters Art Ctr, Flint. *Exhib:* One-man retrospectives, Isaac Delgado Mus, 66, Ill Art Coun Galleries, Chicago, 71 & Newport Harbor Art Mus, Newport Beach, Calif, 74; Spirit of the Comics, Inst Contemp Art, Univ Pa, 69; one-man show, Lakeview Ctr for Arts, Peoria, 72. *Pos:* Vis artist, Bradley Univ, spring 70; vis artist, Southern Methodist Univ, Dallas, 72, artist in residence, summer workshop, Taos, NMex, 72; vis artist, Univ Southern Calif, 74. *Teaching:* Asst prof art, State Univ NY Col Plattsburgh, 56-58; asst prof art, Univ Fla, 60-62; prof painting, Univ Ill, Urbana-Champaign, 62- *Awards:* Tamarind Lithography Workshop Inc Grant, 64; Univ Ill Fel, Ctr for Advan Study, 67-68; Nat Endowment Arts Fel, 75- *Bibliog:* Hiram Williams (auth), Notes for a Young Painter, Prentice-Hall, 65; Franz Schulze (auth), article, Art Int, summer 67; Daniel Wells (auth), article, Chicago Tribune, summer 71. *Media:* Oil, Acrylic. *Publ:* Contribr, Strung Out with Elgar on a Hill, 70; contribr, Portrait: Converse, 75. *Mailing Add:* Dept Art Univ Ill Urbana IL 61801

BODO, SANDOR
CONSERVATOR, RESTORER
b Szamosszeg, Hungary, Feb 13, 20; US citizen. *Study:* Col Fine & Appl Art, Budapest, Hungary. *Comn:* Bronze reliefs, Hungarian Reformed Fedn Am, 65; portrait of Andrew Jackson, Royal Palace, Copenhagen, Denmark, 71. *Exhib:* Nat Housing Ctr, Washington, DC; Butler Inst Am Art, Youngstown, Ohio; Nat Acad Galleries, New York; Smithsonian Inst, Washington, DC; Brooks Mem Art Gallery, Memphis, Tenn. *Awards:* Gold Medal Honor Watercolor, Am Art Week Exhib, 61; Gold Medal Honor Sculpture, 63 & Gold Medal Honor Oil Painting, 66, Nat Arts Club, New York. *Mem:* Fel Am Artists Prof League; Nat Arts Club; Allied Artists Am. *Mailing Add:* Bodo's Art Studio 6513 Hwy 100 Nashville TN 37205

BOEDEKER, ARNOLD E (BOEDIE)
ILLUSTRATOR, PAINTER
b Sheboygan, Wis, June 5, 1893. *Study:* Art Inst Chicago; and with John Pike, Edgar Whitney, Jerry Farnsworth, Don Stone, Tom Nichols, Dong Kingman, Millard Sheets, Rex Brandt, Caude Croney, Robert E Wood, John Pellew, George Post & Franklin Jones. *Work:* Canton Art Inst; Massillon Art Mus; Akron Art Inst; Cuyahoga Valley Art Ctr; Drawing Room Gallery. *Exhib:* Mainstreams, Am Watercolor Soc, Marietta, Ohio, 72-73 & 75-76; Butler Inst Am Art; Wichita Centennial Exhib; Canton Art Inst; Massillon Art Mus; plus many others. *Pos:* Art dir, Goodyear Tire & Rubber Co, Akron, Ohio, 15-61. *Awards:* First Place Award, Cuyahuga Valley Art Ctr Ann, 75-79; Ohio Watercolor Soc, 80; Art Council Award for Individual Artist Visual, State of Ohio, 79; and others. *Mem:* Am Artists Prof League; Akron Soc Artists (pres, 66-68); Cuyahoga Valley Art Ctr (trustee, 61-81, pres, 62-63); Whiskey Painters Am; Ohio Watercolor Soc. *Media:* Watercolor, Oil. *Mailing Add:* 2965 Silver Lake Blvd Cuyahoga Falls OH 44224

BOESE, ALVIN WILLIAM
COLLECTOR
b St Paul, Minn, Mar 24, 10. *Pos:* Manager department devoted to research & development of improved surfaces for artists, 3M Co, St Paul. *Collection:* Mainly contemporary American art, all media except sculpture. *Mailing Add:* c/o 3M Co 3M Ctr St Paul MN 55101

BOEVE, EDGAR GENE
EDUCATOR, PAINTER
b Marshalltown, Iowa, Sept 27, 29. *Study:* J Franklin Sch of Prof Arts, Inc, New York, cert; Calvin Col, Grand Rapids, Mich, AB; Univ Mich, Ann Arbor, MSD. *Work:* Calvin Theological Seminary Grand Rapids, Mich; Dordt Col, Sioux Center, Iowa; Catholic Info Ctr, Lansing, Mich. *Comn:* Sculpture, Pine Rest Hosp, Cutlerville, Mich, 74 & 77; banners, Woodland Church, Grand Rapids, Mich, 75; mural, Holland Church, Mich, 76; sculpture, Faith, Prayer, Tract League, 83; logo, Fifth Reformed Church, 83; and others. *Exhib:* Detroit Art Inst, Mich, 65; Kresge Art Ctr, East Lansing, Mich, 68; Kalamazoo Art Ctr, Mich, 72; Grand Rapids Art Mus, Mich, 75. *Teaching:* Prof art hist, Calvin Col, Grand Rapids, Mich, 58- *Awards:* First Prize, 63 & 70 & Second Prize, 73 & 81, Christian Art Show, Peace Lutheran. *Mem:* Christians In the Visual Arts (pres, 79-83); Midwest Col Art Conf; Col Art Asn. *Media:* Oil. *Res:* Art education. *Publ:* Auth, Childrens Art and the Christian Teacher, Nat Union Christian Sch, Concordia, Mo, 67, 2nd ed, 77; illusr, Youth Hymnal, Eerdmans, 68; illusr, The Touch of His Hand, World Home Bible, 76; illusr, The Gifted Church, Home Mission, Can Relig Conf, 77. *Mailing Add:* 9468 Whispering Sands Dr West Olive MI 49460

BOGAEV, RONNI (RONNI BOGAEV GREENSTEIN)
LECTURER, PAINTER
b Philadelphia, Pa. *Study:* Hussian Sch Art; portrait painting with Lazar Raditz. *Work:* Ft Lauderdale Mus Arts, Fla; Le Moyne Art Found, Tallahassee; Temple Beth Am, Miami; Bleemer & Levine Art Found, Miami; Tallahassee State Bank. *Comn:* Six mag covers, Adult & Child, Didactic, Inc, Chicago, 69; portrait, comn by John McMullan, Knight Newspaper, 72; portrait, comn by Karl Katz, Cur, Metrop Mus Art, New York, 74. *Exhib:* Major Fla Artists Exhib, Harmon Gallery, Naples, Fla, 72; Piedmont Painting & Sculpture, Mint Mus, Charlotte, NC, 73; Contemporary Portraits by American Artists, Lowe Mus, Miami, 74; Miami Deals, Metrop Mus & Art Ctr, Fla, 74; New Talent, ACA Gallery, New York, 74; solo exhib, David Findlay Galleries, 79. *Awards:* Temple Beth Am First Prize Painting, 72;

Hilton Leech Mem Award, Fla Artist Group, 75; Best in Show Award, 15th Ann Maj Fla Artists Exhib, 78. *Bibliog:* Ted Krail (auth), Artist's mini memoir, Miami Beach Sun Mag, 68; Griffin Smith (auth), The artists of Miami, Tropic Mag, Miami Herald, 72; Mary Jo Hall (auth), Woman's Way, Channel 11 TV, 75. *Mem:* Fla Artists Group Inc. *Media:* Oil, Pencil. *Dealer:* David Findlay Galleries 984 Madison Ave New York NY 10029. *Mailing Add:* 3845 Park Ave Miami FL 33133

BOGARIN, RAFAEL
SERIGRAPHER, PAINTER
b El Tigre, Venezuela, Jan 20, 46. *Study:* Cristobal Rojas, Caracas, Venezuela, BA, 66; Pratt Graphics Ctr, New York, 70-71, study with Michael Ponce de Leon; Blackburn Workshop, New York, 71-73. *Work:* Mus of Fine Arts, Caracas; White House, Caracas; Corcoran Gallery of Art, Washington, DC; Chase Manhattan Bank, New York; Mus of Mod Art, New York. *Comn:* Three-floor-high mural, comn by Venezuelan Govt, Venezuelan Consulate, New York, 74. *Exhib:* Semana Cult, Miami Libr, Fla, 73; Young Artists, Union Carbide Bldg, New York, 74; one-man shows, Frank Fedele, Gallery, New York, 80, Galeria El Tunel, Guatemala City, 80, Galeria Garces Velasquez, Bogota, Colombia, 81; and many others. *Teaching:* Prof plastic arts, Sch of Plastic Arts, 67-70; prof plastic arts, Sch of Arts & Sci, Caracas, 69-70; asst etching & intaglio, Pratt Graphic Ctr, New York, 71-; instr serigraph workshop, Univ San Jose, Costa Rica. *Awards:* Roma Prize, Salon de Arte Venezoland, Italian Govt, 68. *Bibliog:* Calvin J Goodman (auth), Master Printers and Print Workshops, Am Artists, 10/76. *Mailing Add:* 14 W 17th St 5th Floor New York NY 10011

BOGART, GEORGE A
PAINTER
b Duluth, Minn, Oct 30, 33. *Study:* Univ Minn, Duluth, BA; Univ Wash, MFA; also with Fletcher Martin, Philip Evergood & Dong Kingman. *Work:* Delgado Mus Art, New Orleans, La; Ill State Univ; Washburn Univ, Topeka, Kans; Okla State Collection; Univ Okla. *Exhib:* Delgado Mus Art, 61 & 64; New York World's Fair, 64; Dallas Mus Fine Arts, 64 & 65; Okla Art Ctr, 75 & 78; Amarillo Art Mus, 75; and others. *Teaching:* Instr, Univ Wash, formerly; prof art, Univ Tex, Austin & Pa State Univ, State College, formerly; prof art, Univ artist, Univ Calif, Berkeley, 78-79; prof art, Univ Okla, 70- *Awards:* Prize, Washburn Univ, 71 & Amarillo Art Mus, 75; Visions '80-'81, Midwest Art Asn. *Publ:* Contribr, Southwestern Art; illusr, George Bogart drawings and paintings, 67. *Mailing Add:* 100 S Sherry Ave Norman OK 73069

BOGART, MICHELE HELENE
HISTORIAN, CURATOR
b New York, NY, Oct 5, 52. *Study:* Art Students League; Smith Col, BA, 79; Univ Chicago, MA, 75, PhD, 79. *Exhib:* The Seelye Years, Smith Col Mus Art, Northampton, Mass, 74; Am Art Quest for Unity, Detroit Inst Art, Mich, 82-83. *Pos:* Guest cur, Student Exhib, Smith Col Mus Art, 74; research asst, Smithsonian Art Index, Washington, DC, 78-79; asst to vis cur, Nat Mus Am Art, Washington, DC, 79; guest cur sculpture, Detroit Inst Art, Mich, 80- *Teaching:* Instr art, Am Sch, Chicago, Ill, 76-77; asst prof art hist, Univ Ga, Athens, 79- *Awards:* Fel, Smithsonian Inst, 77-78. *Mem:* Col Art Asn; Popular Culture Asn. *Res:* Nineteenth and twentieth century sculpture; architectural sculpture; reproductions and copies. *Publ:* Auth, In art the ends don't always justify the means, Smithsonian, 6/79; auth, Photosculpture, Art Hist, winter 80; auth, On women and art, Ga Review, winter 80; auth, Development of a popular market for sculptre, J Am Culture, spring 81; auth, Four sculpture sketches for the New York Public Library, Bulletin Ga Mus, winter, 82. *Mailing Add:* c/o Visual Arts Bldg Univ Ga Athens GA 30602

BOGART, RICHARD JEROME
PAINTER
b Highland Park, Mich, Oct 30, 29. *Study:* Art Inst Chicago, dipl, 52; Univ Ill, 54; Black Mountain Col, NC, 56. *Work:* Brooklyn Mus; Yellowstone Art Ctr, Billings, Mont. *Exhib:* The American Landscape, A Living Tradition, circulated by Am Fedn Arts, Peridot Gallery, New York, 68; Conn Painting, Drawing & Sculpture Exhib, 78; one-man shows, Poindexter Gallery, New York, 68-83; Meredith Long & Co, Houston, Tex, 77 & GMB Gallery Inc, Birmingham, MI, 82. *Bibliog:* Alan Gussow (auth), A sense of place--the artist & the American land, Sat Rev Press. *Media:* Oil, Pastel. *Dealer:* Poindexter Gallery 1160 Fifth Ave New York NY 10029. *Mailing Add:* 378 Judd Rd Easton CT 06612

BOGDANOVIC, BOGOMIR
PAINTER
b Senje, Yugoslavia, Aug 20, 23. *Study:* Belgrade Univ, with Prof S Strala, Prof A Samojlov. *Work:* Over 3,000 in private collections; Mus Anchorage, Alaska; Presidential Palace, Indonesia; New York Times. *Exhib:* One-man shows, Scarborough Gallery, New York & Quadrangle Gallery, Dallas, 67-80; Pa Acad Fine Arts, Philadelphia; Nat Acad Fine Art, New York; Am Watercolor Soc, New York; Kennedy Galleries, New York. *Pos:* Guest artist & demonstr for various art asns. *Awards:* Charles Dana Medal, Pa Acad Fine Arts, 63; Silver Medal, Am Watercolor Soc, 71; Gold Medal, Franklin Mint, 73. *Bibliog:* Article, Am Artist Mag, 12/71. *Mem:* The Dolphin Fel-Am Watercolor Soc; Audubon Artists; Allied Artists Am; Knickerbocker Artist; hon mem Southwestern Watercolor Soc. *Media:* Oil, Pastel Watercolor. *Mailing Add:* Old Ridge Rd RD 4 Box 152 Warwick NY 10990

BOGGS, FRANKLIN
MURALIST, SCULPTOR
b Warsaw, Ind, July 25, 14. *Study:* Ft Wayne Art Sch, Ind; Pa Acad Fine Arts. *Work:* Univ Wis, Madison; Tulane Univ, New Orleans, La; US War Dept, Washington, DC; Univ Wis, Milwaukee; Am Telephone and Telegraph, NJ; and others. *Comn:* Post office mural, Federal Works Agency, Washington, DC, 46; mural, New Mayo Clinic, Rochester, Minn, 53; mural, Crippled Children's Sch, Helsinki, Finland, 59; sculpture relief mem wall, Cumberland Gap, Tenn, US Dept Interior, 73; bronze relief wall, Beloit Corp, Wis, 81; and many others. *Exhib:* Pa Acad Fine Arts. *Pos:* Illusr, Tenn Valley Auth, 40-44. *Teaching:* Prof & artist in residence, Beloit Col, 45-82, chmn art dept, 55-78; lectr Am Indian Art, Finland & Sweden, 58-59. *Awards:* Gimbels Wis Exhib Prize, 52; Fulbright Res Grant to Finland, 58; Award of Merit for Precast Concrete Sculpture, 63. *Publ:* Army med paintings reproduced in art mags. *Mailing Add:* 2542 Hawthorne Dr Beloit WI 53511

BOGGS, JEAN SUTHERLAND
MUSEUM DIRECTOR, HISTORIAN
b Negritos, Peru, June 11, 22; Can citizen. *Pos:* Dir, Nat Gallery Can, 66-76; dir, Philadelphia Mus Art, currently. *Teaching:* Asst prof art, Skidmore Col, 48-49; asst prof art, Mt Holyoke Col, 49-52; assoc prof art, Univ Calif, 54-62; Steinberg prof hist art, Washington Univ, 64-66; prof fine arts, Harvard Univ, 76-79. *Awards:* Officer of the Order of Can. *Mem:* Am Asn Mus; Asn Art Mus Dirs; fel Royal Soc Can; Col Art Asn (bd mem, 78-); and others. *Publ:* Auth, Portraits by Degas, 62, Drawings by Degas, 66, The National Gallery of Canada, 71 & The Last Thirty Years, Picasso 1881-1973, 73. *Mailing Add:* Philadelphia Mus Art PO Box 7646 Philadelphia PA 19101

BOGGS, MAYO MAC
SCULPTOR, EDUCATOR
b Ashland, Ky, Mar 22, 42. *Study:* Univ Ky, with Mike Hall, BA(art); Univ NC, Chapel Hill, with Robert Howard, MFA(sculpture). *Work:* Gerald R Ford Library; NC Govs Mansion; SC Govs Mansion; Huntington Galleries, WVa; NC Nat Bank, Charlotte. *Comn:* Fountain sculpture, Charles Lea Ctr for Handicapped, Spartanburg, SC, 73; garden sculpture, Spartanburg Arts Coun, 75; Bronze tablets of state bird, tree & flower of all 50 states, 80. *Exhib:* Midstates Sculpture, Lexington, Ky, 69; 9 in 69, Peabody Mus, Nashville, Tenn, 69; 1969 Regional Fine Arts Biennial, J B Speed Mus, Louisville, 69; Southeastern How, Gallery Contemp Arts, Winston-Salem, NC, 70; SC Artists Ann, Gibbes Gallery, Charleston, SC, 71-72. *Teaching:* Assoc prof sculpture, Converse Col, Spartanburg, SC, 70-; guest artist, Penland Sch Crafts, NC. *Awards:* John W Oswald Res & Creativity Award, Univ Ky, 69; Kathryne Amelia Brown Fac Award, Converse Col, 72. *Mem:* Spartanburg Artists Guild; Am Asn Univ Profs. *Media:* Steel Construction, Bronze and Aluminum Casts. *Mailing Add:* 394 Forest Ave Spartanburg SC 29302

BOGHOSIAN, VARUJAN
SCULPTOR, EDUCATOR
b New Britain, Conn, June 26, 26. *Study:* Vesper George Sch Art, Boston; Yale Univ Sch Art & Archit, BFA & MFA. *Work:* Mus Mod Art & Whitney Mus Am Art, New York; Addison Gallery Am Art, Andover, Mass; Worcester Mus, Mass; Currier Gallery Art, Manchester, NH. *Exhib:* One-man shows, Stable Gallery, 63-66 & Cordier & Ekstrom, 69, 71, 73, 75 & 77-80, New York. *Teaching:* Prof sculpture, Dartmouth Col, 68- *Awards:* Fulbright Grant, 53; sculptor-in-residence, Am Acad Rome, 67; Nat Inst Arts & Lett Award, 72. *Bibliog:* Dore Ashton (auth), article, Studio Int, 4/65; article, Time Mag, 2/9/70; article, Art Int, 3/81. *Media:* Constructions, Collage. *Dealer:* Cordier & Ekstrom Inc 417 E 75th St New York NY 10021. *Mailing Add:* One Read Rd Hanover NH 03755

BOGORAD, ALAN DALE
ILLUSTRATOR
b Brooklyn, NY, July 29, 15. *Study:* Pratt Inst, AA, 34. *Work:* Pentagon, Washington, DC; Air Force Mus, Wright-Patterson Field, Dayton, Ohio. *Exhib:* Alwin Gallery, London; Diogenes Galleries, Athens; Col New Rochelle; Great Neck Libr, NY; Soc Illusr, New York. *Pos:* Designer, The First Ten Years--Martin D'Arcy Gallery of Art, Loyola Univ Chicago, 79. *Bibliog:* Mona Moffitt (auth), article, Athens Post, 73; article, People, Places & Parties, fall 77; also articles in Graphis & Art Direction Mag. *Mem:* Soc Illusr; Graphic Artists Guild; Artist's Fel. *Media:* Acrylic & Paper Collage. *Dealer:* Phyllis Lucas Gallery 981 Second Ave New York NY 10021. *Mailing Add:* 320 E 42nd St New York NY 10017

BOGOUNOFF, MOLLIE
PAINTER, COLLECTOR
b Bryn Mawr, Pa, Mar 23, 20. *Study:* Pa Acad Fine Arts; Philadelphia Mus Sch; Am Univ, DC; also with Gene Davis, DC. *Work:* Art in Embassies Prog, State Dept (work in 5 foreign embassies); Bank of Norfolk, Va; also represented in var pvt collections in US & Europe. *Exhib:* Group shows, Kuala Lumpur, Malaysia, 53, Singapore, 54, Va Commonwealth Univ, Richmond, Va, 73, Art Barn, DC, 73-74, Cornell Col, Iowa, 74, WPA, DC (drawings from DC artists), 75, Pleiades Gallery, New York, 76, DC Bicentennial, Mayor's Off, DC & Gallery 10, DC, 79; one-woman shows, Gallery Amsterdam, McLean, Va, 75 & Foundry Gallery, DC, 78. *Awards:* Purchase Award, James River Juried, Newport News, Va, 72; Gold Medal, Art League of Northern Va, Alexandria, 74. *Mem:* DC Women's Art Registry; Artists' Equity Asn. *Media:* Acrylic, Collage. *Collection:* Contemporary paintings, drawings and sculpture by Picasso, Braque, Kenzo Okada, Ed McGowin, Gene Davis and Fritz Scholder. *Mailing Add:* 3007 P St NW Washington DC 20007

BOGUCKI, (EDWIN ARNOLD)
SCULPTOR, PAINTER
b Racine, Wis, July 5, 32. *Study:* Wis Art Acad; also with Christopher Thompson, Baltimore, Md; Leon Pescheret, Whitewater, Wis & Alex Dzigurski, Chicago. *Comn:* Portraits, comn by Mrs Parker Poe, Harrodsburg, Ky, 64; bronze & painting, Mrs Guilbert Humphrey, Cleveland, 70, Daniel C Gainey, Owatonna, Minn, 71-75 & Phil Witter, Baton Rouge, La; Ga Rageyma (bronze), Arabian Horse Registry, Denver, 74; and others. *Dealer:* The May Gallery Scottsdale AZ & Jackson Hole WY. *Mailing Add:* 8110 Foley Rd Racine WI 53402

BOHLEN, NINA (CELESTINE EUSTIS BOHLEN)
PAINTER
b Boston, Mass, Mar 5, 31. *Study:* Radcliffe Col, drawing & painting with Hyman Bloom, BA, 53. *Work:* Fogg Mus Art; Boston Pub Libr; private collections. *Exhib:* Libr Boston Athenaeum, 71, 75 & 76; Am Acad Arts & Lett Awards Exhib, 77; FAR Gallery, New York, 78; Hassam Fund Exhib, Am Acad Arts & Lett, 78 & 82; Harvard Mus Comparative Zoology, 82. *Teaching:* Pvt instr drawing & painting, 73-77. *Awards:* Am Acad Arts & Lett Award in Art, 77. *Media:* All. *Mailing Add:* 55 Hagen Rd Newton MA 02159

BOHLER, JOSEPH STEPHEN
PAINTER
b Great Falls, Mont, June 12, 38. *Study:* With Robert Lougheed, Wilson Hurley, John Pike, Robert Wood, Bill Reese & others; Art Instruction Sch, Minneapolis, Minn, 60. *Work:* Wildlife World Mus, Monument, Colo; Coca Cola Bottling Company, Kansas City, Mo; Johnson Co Bank, Kansas City, Kans; Phoenix Bank & Trust, Ariz; Smithsonian Inst, Washington, DC. *Comn:* Indian Heritage (watercolor), comn by Rick Shannon, Monument Colo, 80; Western Scene (watercolor), comn by Warren Ahnell, Wash, 81; Mexico Balloon Man (watercolor), comn by John Crewes, Wash, 81; Mountain Man (oil), comn by Sandra Strandlund, Wash, 81; Great Falls City Scene, comn by Marlene Copenhauer, Mont, 81. *Exhib:* Watercolor USA, Springfield Art Mus, Mo, 71; one-man show, C M Russell Mus, Great Falls, Mont, 72; Pastel Soc Am, New York, 80; Am Watercolor Soc, New York, 81; Allied Artists Am, Nat Arts Club, New York, 81-82. *Pos:* Bd dirs, Stuart Anderson Black Angus Enterprises, 80-81. *Teaching:* Instr watercolor, Beartooth Watercolor Workshops, Shelby, Mont, 81 & 82. *Awards:* Best of Show, C M Russell Mus, 81; Nat Arts Club Award, Allied Artists Am, 81; Artists Choice Award, Northwest Rendezvous Group, 83. *Mem:* active mem Am Watercolor Soc; founding mem Northwest Rendezvous; Soc Animal Artists. *Media:* Mixed. *Publ:* Contribr, Western Painting Today, Watson-Guptill, 74; illusr, cover, Kansas City Mag, 74; illusr, cover, Readers Digest, 78; contribr, Art West, 80; contribr, Southwest Art Mag, 1/84. *Dealer:* Stu Johnson 6420 N Campbell Ave Tucson AZ 85719; Trailside Galleries Jackson WY 83001. *Mailing Add:* 1400 Deer Creek Rd Monument CO 80132

BOHNEN, BLYTHE
CONCEPTUAL ARTIST, PAINTER
b Evanston, Ill, July 26, 40. *Study:* Smith Col, BA; Boston Univ, BFA; Hunter Col, MA. *Work:* Dallas, Mus Fine Arts, Tex; McCrory Corp, New York; Whitney Mus Am Art, Mus Mod Art & Metrop Mus Art, New York. *Exhib:* Penthouse, Mus Mod Art, New York, 72; Painting and Sculpture Today, Indianapolis Mus Art, Ind, 72; New American Abstract Painting, Vassar Col Mus, 72; American Women Artists, Kunsthaus, Hamburg, Ger, 72; Wadsworth Atheneum, Hartford, Conn, 75; Documenta, Kassel, WGer, 77; Extraordinary Women, Mus Mod Art, New York, 77; Critique 1979, Palais de Beaux Arts, Brussels, 80. *Teaching:* Lectr, Metrop Mus Art, 67-72; instr, Parsons Sch Design, 77-80. *Bibliog:* Lawrence Alloway (auth), Blythe Bohnen, Art Forum, 11/76; A M Fischer (auth), Der Graphit-Stift in Verbindung mit dem fotoapparat, Kunstmagazin, 77; Judy Tannenbaum (auth), Blythe Bohnen, Arts Mag, 6/77. *Media:* Acrylic, Graphite. *Mailing Add:* New York NY

BOHNENKAMP, LESLIE GEORGE
SCULPTOR, INSTRUCTOR
b West Point, Iowa, Mar 28, 43. *Study:* St Ambrose Col, Davenport, Iowa, 64-66; Univ Iowa, Iowa City, BA, 66, MA, 71. *Work:* Portland Mus Art, Maine; Columbus Mus Fine Arts, Ohio; Univ Iowa, Iowa City. *Exhib:* New York: A Selection from the Last Ten Years, The Otis Inst Parsons Sch Design, Los Angeles, Calif, 79; Betty Parsons Gallery, New York, 79; Columbus Invitational, Columbus Mus Fine Arts, Ohio, 81; PS1, Richmond, Va, 82. *Pos:* Gallery asst, Betty Parsons Gallery, 78-80. *Teaching:* Vis artist sculpture, Worcester Art Mus Sch, 80- *Awards:* Individual Grant Sculpture, Nat Endowment Arts, 73; Fel, Fine Arts Work Ctr, Provincetown, Mass, 73-75; Individual Sculpture Grant, Nat Endowment Arts, 80. *Bibliog:* Michael Florescu (auth), Les Bohnenkamp, Arts Mag, 2/79; Lila Zeiger (auth), Les Bohnenkamp: Constructing Horizons, Arts Mag, 6/80. *Mailing Add:* 184 Second Ave New York NY 10003

BOHNERT, THOM (THOMAS ROBERT)
CERAMIST, EDUCATOR
b St Louis, Mo, Jan 3, 48. *Study:* Southern Ill Univ, Edwardsville, BA, 69; Cranbrook Acad Art, Bloomfield Hills, Mich, MFA, 71. *Work:* Flint Inst Art, Mich; Minneapolis Art Inst, Minn; Univ Iowa Mus, Iowa City; Cranbrook Acad Art, Bloomfield Hills, Mich; Boyman Mus, Rotterdam, Holland. *Exhib:* Young Americans/Clay Glass, Tucson Mus Art, Ariz, 78; Century Ceramics in the US 1878-1978, Everson Mus, Syracuse, NY, Renwick Gallery, Smithsonian Inst, Washington, DC & Cooper-Hewitt, New York, 79; one-person show, Exhibit A Gallery, Chicago, Ill, 79 & 81; A Response to Wedgewood, 2 Yr Traveling Exhib, Mus Philadelphia Civic Ctr, Pa, 80;

Basket-Works, John M Kohler Arts Ctr, Sheboygan, Wis, 81; Painting and Sculpture Today: 1982, Indianapolis Mus Art, 82; American Clay Artists: Philadelphia 83, Marian Locks Gallery East, 83. *Teaching:* Instr ceramic & drawing, Southern Ill Univ, 71; instr ceramics & drawing, C S Mott Community Col, 71-; vis artist ceramics, Univ Mich, 77-78. *Awards:* Award, Detroit Inst Art, 76; Nat Endowment Arts Craftsmen Fel, 78-79; Creative Artists Grant, Mich Coun Arts, 83-84. *Bibliog:* Helen Williams Drutt (auth), Contemporary Ceramics: A Response to Wedgewood, 81; Elaine Levin (auth), History of American Ceramics, Watson-Guptill, 84; Gottfried Borrmann (auth), Ceramics of the world, Kunst & Handwerk, Dusseldorf, WGer, 84. *Media:* Ceramic, Metal. *Dealer:* Alice Westphal Exhibit A Gallery 233 East Ontario St Chicago IL 60611. *Mailing Add:* 2430 Gold Flint MI 48503

BOHROD, AARON
PAINTER, EDUCATOR
b Chicago, Ill, Nov 21, 07. *Study:* Art Inst Chicago; Art Students League, with John Sloan. *Work:* Art Inst Chicago; Corcoran Gallery Art, Washington, DC; Metrop Mus Art, New York; Philippines Mus Art, Manila; Whitney Mus Am Art, New York. *Exhib:* Art Inst Chicago Int Watercolor Exhibs, 32-40; Guggenheim Found Exhib, 36-38; Carnegie Inst Int Exhib, 36-38 & 40; Artists for Victory Exhib, Metrop Mus Art, 42; Pa Acad Fine Arts, 42; Nat Acad Fine Arts Exhibs, 53-72; plus many others. *Pos:* Artist war corresp, US Corps Engr & Life Mag, 42-45. *Teaching:* Artist in residence, Southern Ill Univ, Carbondale, 41-42 & Univ Wis, Madison, 48-73. *Awards:* Clark Prize & Silver Medal, Corcoran Gallery Art; Artist for Victory Exhib Prize, Metrop Mus Art; First Logan Prizes, Art Inst Chicago, 37 & 45. *Bibliog:* Harry Salpeter (auth), Bohrod: Chicago's gift to art, Esquire Mag, 40; article in Life Mag, 41; plus others. *Publ:* Auth, A Pottery Sketch Book, 59 & A Decade of Sill Life, 66, Univ Wis Press; Wis Sketches, Stanton & Lee, 75. *Mailing Add:* 4811 Tonyawatha Trail Madison WI 53716

BOLAS, GERALD DOUGLAS
MUSEUM DIRECTOR, EDUCATOR
b Los Angeles, Calif, Nov 1, 49. *Study:* Univ Calif, Santa Barbara, BA, 72, MA(art hist), 75. *Collections Arranged:* Gyorgy Kepes, 78, Richard Hunt: Three Places, 79, Old and Modern Master Drawings, 80, Greek Vases and Roman Glass, 80 & Arthur Osver: The University Years, 81, Washington Univ Gallery Art. *Pos:* Asst to dir, Yale Univ Art Gallery, 75-77; dir, Washington Univ Gallery Art, 77- *Teaching:* Asst, Univ Calif, Santa Barbara, 73-74; adj asst prof, Washington Univ, 77- *Mem:* Asn Art Mus Dir; Col Art Asn; Am Asn Mus; Midwest Art Hist Soc; Asian Art Soc, Washington Univ. *Res:* Nineteenth century American art; history of taste, patronage and connoisseurship; medieval manuscript illumination. *Publ:* Auth, Illustrated Checklist of the Washington University Collection, 81. *Mailing Add:* Washington Univ Gallery Art Campus Box 1214 St Louis MO 63130

BOLEN, JOHN E
DEALER, COLLECTOR
b Ft Gordon, Ga, Aug 27, 53. *Study:* Univ Calif, Los Angeles, AB, 75. *Collections Arranged:* Painting into Bronze: The Polychromed Bronze of Harry Jackson, Southwest Mus, Highland Park, Calif, 79; The Cowboy, San Diego Mus Art, 81. *Pos:* Dir, Bolen Gallery Inc, Calif, 78- *Teaching:* Lectr art collecting, privately, 76-78. *Mem:* Art Dealers Asn Calif (bd dirs, 80-83, vpres, 82-83). *Specialty:* Nineteenth and twentieth century modern and western paintings, sculptures and original prints. *Publ:* Ed, Arthur Secunda Monograph, Bolen Gallery Inc, 80; Six Decades of American Prints 1900-1960, 82; Grant Wood, 83. *Mailing Add:* 2904 Main St Santa Monica CA 90405

BOLEN, LYNNE N
DEALER, COLLECTOR
b San Diego, Calif, Feb 19, 54. *Study:* Univ Calif, Los Angeles, BS, 76. *Pos:* Dir, Bolen Gallery, Santa Monica, Calif, 78-, Bolen Publ, Playa Del Rey, Calif, 79- & Bolen Gallery, Los Angeles, 81- *Bibliog:* Critical reviews in Santa Monica Evening Outlook, 78-; var issues, Art Voices, 80- *Mem:* Art Dealers Asn Calif (secy & mem bd dirs, 82-83). *Specialty:* Nineteenth and twentieth century modern and western paintings, sculptures and original prints. *Publ:* Six Decades of American Prints 1900-1960, 82; Grant Wood, 83. *Mailing Add:* 2904 Main St Santa Monica CA 90405

BOLINSKY, JOSEPH ABRAHAM
SCULPTOR, EDUCATOR
b New York, NY, Jan 17, 17. *Study:* Columbia Univ, MA; Stourbridge Col Art, Eng; Skowhegan Sch Painting & Sculpture, with Jose de Creeft; Iowa Univ, MFA. *Work:* Newark Mus Art, NJ; Tel Aviv Mus Art, Israel; State Univ NY Col Buffalo; Waterloo Recreation Ctr, Iowa; Kean Col, Union, NJ. *Comn:* Carved ark doors & welded menorah, Sons Jacob Synagogue, Waterloo, Iowa, 52; cast bronze group of six figures, Jewish Community Fedn Bldg, Cleveland, Ohio, 66; bronze screen, St Mary's Hosp, Rochester, NY, 70; carved ark doors, Temple Shaarey Zedek, Amhurst, NY, 71; two wood carvings, Holocaust, Temple Sinai, Amherst, NY, 76. *Exhib:* Western NY Regional, Albright-Knox Gallery, Buffalo, NY, 59; Art on Paper, Skowhegan Sch Painting & Sculpture, 69; Our Legacy of Art in Western New York, Charles Birchfield Ctr, 72; retrospective 1948-78, Brock Univ, Can, 78; Sensation Art through Feeling, Senses, and Perception Traveling Exhib, Burchfield Ctr, Buffalo, NY, 82. *Teaching:* Instr sculpture, Univ Northern Iowa, 49-53; prof sculpture, State Univ NY Col Buffalo, 54-; vis sculptor, Stanislaus State Univ, summer 71. *Awards:* First Prize for Stone Carving, Des Moines Art Ctr, 52; First Prize for Stone Carving, Albright-Knox Gallery, 59; Award for Bronze Casting, Rochester Festival of Religious Art, 70. *Mem:* Patteran Art Asn, Buffalo. *Media:* Bronze, Stone. *Publ:* Contribr, Jewish form symbolism, Ethos Mag, 58; demonstr, Carved Sculpture (film), US Info Serv, 68. *Mailing Add:* 10 Ames Ave Tonawanda NY 14150

BOLLINGER, WILLIAM
CONCEPTUAL ARTIST
b Brooklyn, NY, 39. *Study:* Brown Univ, Providence, RI, 57-61. *Exhib:* Cool Art, Aldrich Mus Contemp Art, Ridgefield, Conn, 68; Six Kuenstler, Galerie Ricke, Cologne, 69; Op Losse Schroeven/Square Tags in Round Holes, Stedelijk Mus, Amsterdam, Holland; Anti-Illusion: Procedures/Material, 69 & Ann, 69 & 73, Whitney Mus Am Art, New York; Info, Mus Mod Art, New York, 71; Drawings, Univ RI, 74; one-man shows, Bianchini Gallery, New York, 66, Bykert Gallery, New York, 67 & 69, Galerie Ricke, Cologne, 68, O K Harris Gallery, New York, 72 & 74, 10 Bleecker St Gallery, New York, 72 & Bard Col, 73; Retrospective, Bennington Col, 73; and many others. *Bibliog:* Rev in Arts, New York, 4/72 & Artforum, New York, 10/72; N Foote (auth), Rev in Art in Am, 75. *Mailing Add:* c/o O K Harris Works of Art 383 W Broadway New York NY 10013

BOLOMEY, ROGER HENRY
SCULPTOR
b Torrington, Conn, Oct 19, 18; US & Swiss citizen. *Study:* Acad Bella Arte, Florence, Italy, 47; Univ Lausanne, 47-48; Calif Col Arts & Crafts, Oakland, 48-50. *Work:* Mus Mod Art, Whitney Mus Am Art, New York; Univ Calif Mus Art, Berkeley; San Francisco Mus Mod Art, Calif; Stadtische Kunst, Mannheim, Ger. *Comn:* Aluminum sculpture, Southridge Mall, Milwaukee, Wis, 70; two reliefs, Mutual of NY, Syracuse, 71; two bronze sculptures, S Mall Proj, Albany, 71; cor-ten steel sculpture, Lehman High Sch, Bronx, 71-72; stainless steel sculpture, NY State Off Bldg, Hauppauge, 73. *Exhib:* Carnegie Inst Int, Pittsburgh, 64; Whitney Mus Am Art Sculpture Ann, 64; Quatriene Exposition Suisse Sculpture, Bienne, Switz, 66; Contemporary American Paintings & Sculpture, Univ Ill, Urbana, 67; American Sculpture, Univ Nebr, Lincoln, 70. *Collections Arranged:* Forgotten Dimension: A Survey of Small Sculpture in California Now Traveling Exhib, 82-84; *Teaching:* Assoc prof art, Herbert H Lehman Col, 68-75; prof & chmn dept art, Calif State Univ, Fresno, 75- *Awards:* First Prize & Purchase Award, Bundy Art Mus Sculpture Int, Waitsfield, Vt, 63; Sculpture Prize, San Francisco Art Inst 84th Ann, 65; Res Found Award, City Univ NY, 70. *Mem:* San Francisco Art Inst; Am Fedn Arts; hon fel Acad Fine Arts, The Hague, Netherlands. *Media:* Steel, Aluminum. *Mailing Add:* 4014 N Van Ness Blvd Fresno CA 93704

BOLSTER, ELLA S
DESIGNER, WEAVER
b Helena, Mont, Dec 8, 06. *Study:* Mont State Univ; art metalwork with Alexander Bick, Colo State Univ; handweaving with Mary Meigs Atwater, Univ Mont; handweaving gold brocades, Nat Col Arts & Crafts, Tehran, Iran; pottery with Pieter Grueneveld, The Hague, Neth; handweaving with Anni Albers, Haystack Mountain Sch Crafts, Maine. *Work:* Handwoven formal tablecloth, Wichita Art Mus, Kans. *Comn:* Handwoven altar hanging, pulpit antipendium, burse & veil, St Mary's Episcopal Church, Arlington, Va, 62; plus several individual handweaving & stitchery commissions. *Exhib:* Int Textile Exhib, Greensboro, NC, 54; Fiber, Clay, Metal, St Paul Gallery & Sch Art, Minn, 55; Decorative Arts & Ceramics Exhib, Wichita, 55-57; Contemp Handweaving, Univ Nebr Art Gallery, Lincoln, 61; Textiles by Outstanding Am Designer-Weavers, Univ Gallery Fine Art, Lafayette, La, 61; plus many others including one-man shows. *Teaching:* Instr art metalwork, Mont State Univ, summer 44; instr canvaswork & macrame, Univ Ariz, Tucson, summer 71 & 72; traveling lectr, Weavers' Guild, east & midwestern states & other orgns throughout the US; lectr sem, 40 Years in the Textile Arts, State Weavers' Conf, 79. *Awards:* Purchase Prize, Ann Nat Exhib, Wichita Art Asn, 55; First in Fiber, St Paul Gallery & Sch Art, 55; First in Textiles, Nat League Am Pen Women Biennial Exhib, Smithsonian Inst, Washington, DC, 64, Miami, 74; plus many others, 54- *Bibliog:* Mickey Gates Maker (auth), Her weaving is a creative art, Alpha Gamma Delta Quart, 58; Mary Alice Smith (auth), Ella Bolster, experiments in many techniques, Handweaver & Craftsman Mag, 61; Opal Johnston (auth), Weaver magna cum laude, Southwest Art Scene Mag, 68; plus many others. *Mem:* Hon life mem Designer Weavers of Washington; Am Craftsmen's Coun; Nat League Am Pen Women; Nat Art Bd. *Mailing Add:* 17610 Conestoga Dr Sun City AZ 85373

BOLT, RON
ENVIRONMENTAL ARTIST, PAINTER
b Toronto, Ont, Oct 13, 38. *Study:* Ont Art Col; Ryerson Polytechnic Sch. *Work:* Sir George Williams Univ, Montreal; Univ Guelph; Univ Western Ont; Xerox Corp; Shell Can Ltd. *Comn:* Stamp design, Can Post, 79; Newmarket Courthouse (mural), Govt Ont, 80; tapestry designs, Indo-Asian Tapestries Ltd, Toronto, 82. *Exhib:* Univ Guelph, 72; McMichael Can Collection, Ont, 76; Windsor Art Gallery, Ont, 77; The Inner Ocean Traveling Exhib, 79-80; Printmakers, Art Gallery Ont, 82; Can Printmakers Traveling Exhib, Bronx Mus, 82-84; Art Gallery Alcoma, Ont, 84. *Teaching:* Instr art, Northern Tech Sch, 71-74; Learning Resources Ctr, Toronto, 72-73 & Hibbs Cove Art & Music Ctr, Nfld, 72-73. *Awards:* Award Distinctive Merit, Graphica, Montreal, 70 & Hadassah, Montreal, 75; Purchase Award, Univ Guelph, Ont, 79. *Bibliog:* Barbara Young (dir, The Inner Ocean, CBC Nat News, 81. *Mem:* Visual Arts Ont (dir, 75-81); Can Artists Rep; Soc Can Artists (pres, 69-72). *Publ:* Contribr, Art Mag, 68-70; auth, High north, Beaver Mag, 81; auth, Acrylic Painting, Ministry Cult, Ont. *Dealer:* Gallery Moos 136 Yorkville Ave Toronto ON M5R 1C2; Miriam Perlman 505 N Lake Shore Dr Chicago Il 60611. *Mailing Add:* RR 1 Baltimore ON K0K 1C0 Canada

BOLT, SUSAN HAMILTON See Hamilton, Susan

BOLTON, MIMI DUBOIS
PAINTER
b Gravlot, France, Dec 12, 02; US citizen. *Study:* Marquette Univ, 22; Corcoran Sch Art, 34-40; Phillips Sch Art, with Karl Knaths, 40-41. *Work:* Corcoran Gallery Art, DC; Tyler Mus Art, Tex; San Antonio, Tex; Am Inst Architects; Fed Deposit Ins Corp. *Exhib:* New York City Ctr; Corcoran Gallery Art; Baltimore Mus Art; Boston Mus Fine Arts; Butler Art Inst; Nat Acad Design; retrospectives, La State Univ, 74, Anglo Am Mus, Baton Rouge, La, 82; Alexandria Mus & Visual Ctr, 83; and many others. *Teaching:* Pvt art classes, formerly. *Awards:* Winner of numerous awards. *Dealer:* DuBose Gallery Kirby Dr Houston TX 77019. *Mailing Add:* 1404 Twisted Oak Lane Oak Hills Baton Rouge LA 70810

BOLTON-SMITH, ROBIN LEE
CURATOR, HISTORIAN
b Washington, DC, Oct 30, 41. *Study:* Smith Col, Northampton, Mass, BA, 63; Inst Fine Arts, NY Univ, MA, 75. *Pos:* Cur res asst, Nat Collection Fine Arts, Smithsonian Inst, 63-67, asst cur, 71-76, assoc cur, 76-; cur res asst, Metrop Mus, New York, 67-69; asst cur, Nat Collection Fine Arts, Smithsonian Inst, 71-76, assoc cur, 76- *Res:* History of the American portrait miniature. *Publ:* Auth, Portrait Miniatures in Private Collections, Smithsonian Inst, 76; auth, The sentimental paintings of Lilly Martin Spencer, Antiques Mag, Vol CIV, Number 1, 7/73; auth, Five miniature collections, Col Art J, summer 79; auth, Fraser's place in the evolution of miniature portrait, In: Charles Fraser of Charleston (cxhib catalog), Gibbes Art Gallery, Charleston, SC, 83; auth, introd to Anson Dickinson, The Celebrated Miniature Painter 1779-1852 (exhib catalog), Conn Hist Soc, 83. *Mailing Add:* c/o Nat Mus Am Art 8th & G St NW Washington DC 20007

BOND, ORIEL EDMUND
ILLUSTRATOR, PAINTER
b Altus, Okla, July 18, 11. *Study:* Rockford Col, exten courses with Marquis E Reitzel, Einar Lundquist & Alice McCurry. *Work:* Works in private collections only. *Exhib:* Six shows, Rockford Art Asn, Ill, 56-63; Ill State Fair, Springfield, 59-61; Sovereign Exhibs Ltd, Winston-Salem, NC & Williamsburg, Va, 70; Am Artists Prof League, New York, 71 & 72. *Pos:* Chief artist, J L Clark Mfg Co, Rockford, 38-77. *Awards:* Popular Award, Ill State Fair, 59; First Place Display Award, Trading Post Days, Rockton, 72; First Place & Popular Award, Colonial Village Mall, 72. *Mem:* Fel Am Artists Prof League; Nat Soc Lit & Arts. *Media:* Oil and Polymer. *Mailing Add:* 7816 Bond Dr The Ledges Roscoe IL 61073

BOND, ROLAND S
COLLECTOR
b Van Alstyne, Tex, Dec 25, 1898. *Pos:* Trustee, Dallas Mus Fine Arts. *Collection:* Paintings by contemporary French and American artists. *Mailing Add:* 4600 Brookview Dr Dallas TX 75220

BONEVARDI, MARCELO
PAINTER, SCULPTOR
b Buenos Aires, Arg, May 13, 29. *Study:* Univ Cordoba, 48-51. *Work:* Mus Mod Art, United Nations, Guggenheim Mus, Brooklyn Mus, New York; Mus d'Art Contemporain de Montreal, Can. *Exhib:* One-man exhibs, Galeria Pecanins, Mexico City, 74, Galeria Ponce, Mex, 78, Galeria Sandiego, Bogota, Colombia, 79, Art Contact Gallery, 79 & Galeria del Retiro, Buenos Aires, 79. *Teaching:* Instr, Nat Univ Cordoba, 56. *Awards:* Int Award, 10th Bienal de Sao Paulo, Brazil, 69. *Media:* Mixed. *Mailing Add:* c/o Galeria Bonino Ltd 48 Great Jones St New York NY 10012

BONGART, SERGEI R
PAINTER, INSTRUCTOR
b Kiev, Russia. *Study:* Kiev Art Acad. *Work:* Mus Russian Art, State Mus Ukrainian Art, Theater Mus, Kiev, Russia; Nat Acad Design, New York; Tretyakov Gallery, Moscow. *Exhib:* Charles & Emma Frye Art Mus; Los Angeles Co Mus Art, Calif; Nat Acad Design & Metrop Mus Art, New York; M H De Young Mem Mus, San Francisco. *Teaching:* Instr drawing & painting, Sergei Bongart Sch Art, Santa Monica, Calif, 49- *Awards:* Grand Nat Gold Medal, Am Artists Prog League, New York, 59; Silver Medal of Honor, Am Watercolor Soc, 69; Winslow Homer Award, Watercolor USA, 74. *Bibliog:* Janice Lovoos (auth), The paintings of Sergei Bongart, Am Artist, 9/62; Nancy Kalis (auth), Sergei Bongart: Romantic realist with a Russian soul, Art Rev, 69; Wendon Blake (auth), Complete Guide to Acrylic Painting, Watson-Guptill, 71. *Mem:* Nat Acad Design; Nat Acad Western Art; Am Watercolor Soc; Royal Soc Arts; Soc Western Artists. *Media:* Oil, Acrylic. *Publ:* Contribr, Joe Singer's Painting Men's Portraits, Watson-Guptill, 77. *Mailing Add:* 533 West Rustic Rd Santa Monica CA 90402

BONGIORNO, LAURINE MACK
HISTORIAN
b Lima, Ohio, Apr 17, 03. *Study:* Oberlin Col, AB, 25; Radcliffe Col, PhD, 30. *Pos:* Ed, Allen Art Mus Bull, 50-67. *Teaching:* Asst prof art hist, Wellesley Col, 30-42, assoc prof art hist, 42-44; lectr art hist, Oberlin Col, 55-66. *Res:* Italian Renaissance sculpture; Giotto. *Publ:* Notes on the Art of Silvestro dell'Aquila, Art Bull, 42; A fifteenth century stucco & art of Verrochio, Allen Art Mus Bull, 62; The date of the Altar of the Madonna in Santa Maria Sorccoro, Aquila, Art Bull, 44; Theme of old and new law in Arena Chapel, Art Bull, 68; Umbrian statue of Saint Sebastian, Allen Art Mus Bull, 71; auth, Fruits of Idealism, Apollo, 76; auth, Benefactors of the Allen Memorial Art Museum, Allen Art Mus Bull, 76-77. *Mailing Add:* 19 N Park St Oberlin OH 44074

BONINO, FERNANDA
DEALER
b Torino, Italy, Jan 5, 27. *Pos:* Pres & dir, Galeria Bonino, Ltd, New York, 63-74; pres & dir, Galeria Bonino Ltd, Buenos Aires, Argentina, 74-81. *Mem:* Art Dealer Asn Am. *Specialty:* Contemporary paintings and sculptures; American; European; South American. *Mailing Add:* 48 Great Jones St New York NY 10012

BONSTROM, DANA ORLIN
DEALER, WRITER
b St Cloud, Minn, Nov 24, 54. *Study:* Harvard Col, AB, 77. *Pos:* Dir, Cleary Galleries, Boston, 77-79 & Daedalus Gallery, Minneapolis, 81- *Res:* Clement Haupers, 1900-1982. *Specialty:* American contemporary. *Publ:* Ed, Duncan Hannah, Daedalus Press, 82. *Mailing Add:* 430 First Ave N Minneapolis MN 55401

BONY, JEAN VICTOR
HISTORIAN, EDUCATOR
b Le Mans, France, Nov 1, 08. *Study:* Univ Paris, licence & agregation, 33; studied hist art with Henri Focillon, 29-33. *Teaching:* Lectr art hist, French Inst, London, 46-61; Slade Prof Fine Art, Cambridge Univ, Eng, 58-61; prof art hist, Univ Calif, Berkeley, 62-80, prof emer, 80-; Kress prof, Nat Gallery Art, Washington, DC, 82; vis Andrew W Mellon prof fine arts, Univ Pittsburght, fall 83; Algur H Meadows prof art hist, Southern Methodist Univ, Dallas, 84- *Awards:* John Simon Guggenheim Mem Fel, 81; Haskins Medal Medieval Acad Am, 83. *Mem:* Soc Francaise Archeol; Royal Archaeol Inst (vpres, 55-61); Col Art Asn; Soc Archit Historians; hon fel Soc Antiquaries, London. *Res:* Romanesque and Gothic architecture, particularly in France and England. *Publ:* Coauth, French Cathedrals, Thames & Hudson, 51; ed, H Focillon's The Art of the West in the Middle Ages, Phaidon Press, 63; auth, The English Decorated Style, Phaidon & Cornell Univ Press, 79; auth, French Gothic Architecture of the 12th & 13th Centuries, Univ Calif Press, 83. *Mailing Add:* Dept of Art Hist Univ of Calif Berkeley CA 94720

BOODMAN, H CITRON
PAINTER, PRINTMAKER
b Pittsburgh, Pa, July 17, 27. *Study:* Carnegie-Mellon Univ, BFA, 48; DeCordova Mus, Lincoln, Mass with Donald Stoltenberg. *Work:* Free Libr Philadelphia, Pa; Univ Wyo; DeCordova Mus, Lincoln, Mass; Atlantic Richfield Oil Company, New York; IBM Corporate Collection; and others. *Comn:* 50 prints, Cambridge Art Asn, Mass, 68. *Exhib:* Minot Print & Drawing Nat Exhib, NDak, 74; Okla Nat Print Exhib, 74 & 76; 8th & 10th Nat Print Exhib, Silvermine Guild Artists, Conn, 74 & 76; DeCordova Mus, Lincoln, Mass, 75, 78, 79 & 80; one-person show, Cummings Art Ctr, Conn Col, New London, 76; Mus Fine Arts, Boston, Mass, 76; In Celebration of Prints, Philadelphia Print Club Invitational, Pa, 80. *Pos:* Designer, Architectural Design Dept, Pittsburgh Plate Glass, Pa, 48-50; illustrative draftsman, State Dept, Washington, DC, 50-53. *Teaching:* Instr printmaking, pvt classes. *Awards:* First Prize, Corcoran Gallery, Washington, DC, 50; Purchase Prize, Strathmore Paper Company Award, Springfield, Mass, 76; Purchase Prize, 6th Ann Art Festival, NH, 76. *Bibliog:* C R Wasserman (auth), Ms Boodman Traces Stages of Printmakers' Art, Boston Globe, 72. *Mem:* Cambridge Art Asn; Boston Visual Artists' Union; Women Exhibiting Boston; Boston Printmakers (pres, 82-83). *Media:* Crayon, Pastels; Ink. *Dealer:* The Garret Galleries 340 Huron Ave Cambridge MA 02138. *Mailing Add:* 4 Linmoor Terrace Lexington MA 02173

BOOKATZ, SAMUEL
PAINTER, SCULPTOR
b Philadelphia, Pa, Oct 3, 10. *Study:* Cleveland Inst Art; Boston Mus Sch Art; Harvard Univ; Acad Grande Chaumiere & Colarossi, Paris; Am Acad Rome; also with Oskar Kokoschka Chaim Soutine & Ivan Mestrovic. *Work:* Corcoran Gallery Art, Phillips Gallery & Smithsonian Inst, Washington, DC; Cleveland Mus Art, Ohio; Norfolk Mus Art & Sci, Va. *Comn:* Portraits of Pres & Mrs F D Roosevelt, 41; murals, comn by US Govt, US Naval Hosp, Norfolk, Va & San Diego, Calif, 42-45; murals, Govt Turn Key Housing for Aged, Prince George's Co, Md & Della Ratta Off Bldg, Bethesda, Md, 71; portrait, Gov David L Lawrence, Pa, 65; portrait of Joseph H Hirshhorn, Hirshhorn Mus & Sculpture Garden, Washington, DC, 78. *Exhib:* One-man shows, Cleveland Mus Art, 40 & Corcoran Gallery Art, 46; Pa Acad Fine Arts, Philadelphia, 52; Va Mus Art, Richmond, 55; Baltimore Mus Art, Md, 60. *Pos:* Govt artist & White House artist, 41-43. *Teaching:* Dir art, Samuel Bookatz Sch Art, Washington, DC, 45- *Awards:* William Page Award & Prix de Rome Award in the Arts, Boston Mus, 37; Inst Allende Fel, 54; Ford Found Grant, 62. *Mailing Add:* 2700 Q St NW Washington DC 20007

BOOKBINDER, JACK
PAINTER, PRINTMAKER
b Odessa, Ukraine, Jan 15, 11; US citizen. *Study:* Univ Pa, BS; Pa Acad Fine Arts; Tyler Sch Art, Temple Univ, MFA; Moore Col Art, Philadelphia, Hon DFA, 76. *Work:* Frye Art Mus, Seattle; Pa Acad Fine Arts, Philadelphia; Philadelphia Mus Art; Libr Cong & Nat Gallery Art, Washington, DC. *Comn:* Mosaic mural (with Frederick Geasland), Church of the Redeemer, Bryn Mawr, Pa, 64; painting of Hahnemann Med Col, Squibb Pharmaceutical, 66; Sidney Zubrow (portrait), Pa Hosp, Philadelphia, 81; Dean Donald C Carroll (portrait), Wharton Sch, Univ Pa, 83. *Exhib:* One Hundred American Water Colorists Exhibition, Royal Acad Arts, London, 62; Two Hundred Years of American Watercolors, Metrop Mus Art, 66; Fifty American Watercolorists, Mexico City, 68; Retrospective, William Penn Mem Mus, Harrisburg, Pa, 74; one-man shows, Gross McLeaf Gallery, Philadelphia, 76; Distinguished Mid-Atlantic Artists: Four Decades of Growth, Univ Del, 80; and others. *Pos:*

Consult dept educ, Philadelphia Mus Art, 45-46; spec asst to dir art educ, Sch Dist Philadelphia, 46-59, dir art educ, 59-77. *Teaching:* Barnes Found, Merion, Pa, 36-44, Univ Pa, 47-59, Pa Acad Fine Arts, 49-61 & Pa State Univ, summer 50. *Awards:* William Church Osborn Mem Award, Am Watercolor Soc, 68; Juv Diabetes Found Super Achiever Award, 76; Grumbacher Award & Gold Medal, Allied Artists Am, 83. *Bibliog:* Henry Pitz (auth), Jack Bookbinder, painter and educator, Am Artists Mag, 3/61. *Mem:* Nat Acad Design; Audubon Artists; Am Watercolor Soc; Allied Artists Am; Philadelphia Art Alliance. *Media:* Oil, Casein; Lithography. *Publ:* Auth, History of sculpture & Art in the life of children, Compton's Encycl. *Dealer:* Newman Galleries 1625 Walnut St Philadelphia PA 19103; Associated American Artists Gallery 663 Fifth Ave New York NY 10022. *Mailing Add:* 323 S Smedley St Philadelphia PA 19103

BOONE, MARY
DEALER
b Pa, Oct 29, 51. *Collections Arranged:* New Work/New York, Los Angeles, Calif, 77; Painting 75/76/77, Sarah Lawrence Col, Bronxville, NY, 77; Painting, Hal Bromm Gallery, New York, 77. *Pos:* Asst dir, Bykert Gallery, formerly; dir, Mary Boone Gallery, 78- *Specialty:* Contemporary art. *Mailing Add:* 420 W Broadway New York NY 10012

BOOTH, BILL
EDUCATOR
b Wallins Creek, Ky, June 20, 35. *Study:* Cumberland Jr Col, Williamsburg, Ky, 55; Eastern Ky State Univ, Richmond, AB, 60; George Peabody Col, Nashville, Tenn, MA, 64, EdS, 65; Univ Ga, Athens, PhD, 70. *Teaching:* Instr art appreciation, George Peabody Col, 63-65; asst prof art hist, Wis State Univ, Oshkosh, 65-68; prof art hist & head dept, Morehead State Univ, Ky, 70- *Bibliog:* A friendship renewed, J Oomoto Found, 10-12/81. *Mem:* Col Art Asn; Am Fedn Arts. *Res:* Frank Duveneck, 1848-1919. *Publ:* Auth, Oriental motifs in 19th century European and American art, Asian Cult Quart, autumn 81 & Bulletin Nat Mus Hist, 12/81. *Mailing Add:* Big Perry Rd Morehead KY 40351

BOOTH, DOT
PAINTER, PRINTMAKER
b Chicago, Ill. *Study:* Univ Ala, Birmingham, 63-64; Univ South Fla, Tampa, 68-70. *Work:* Miss Mus Art, Jackson; Macon Mus Arts & Sci, Ga; City Miami, Fla; Columbus Mus, Ga; Pensacola Art Ctr, Fla. *Exhib:* Best of Fla, Pensacola Art Ctr, 70; Invitational, Mus Arts & Sci, Daytona Beach, Fla, 72; Selections from Permanent Collection, Miss Mus Art, Jackson, 78; Artists in Ga, High Mus Art, Atlanta, 78-79; 40th & 43rd Ann Contemp Am Paintings, Soc Four Arts, Palm Beach, Fla, 78 & 81; Loch Haven Art Ctr Show, Orlando, Fla, 83. *Pos:* Scenic artist, EPCOT, 82. *Awards:* Atwater Kent Award, 31st Ann Soc Four Arts, Palm Beach, Fla, 69; Purchase Award, Frontal Images, Jackson, Miss, 72; Best of Show, Gasparilla, Tampa, Fla, 78. *Bibliog:* Dot Booth--Hard Edge Realism, Orange Co Public TV, Fla, 73. *Media:* Oil, Acrylic; Serigraphy. *Dealer:* Galleries Int 517 N Virginia Winter Park FL 32789. *Mailing Add:* 1939 Taylor Ave Winter Park FL 32792

BOOTH, GEORGE WARREN
PAINTER, ILLUSTRATOR
b Omaha, Nebr, Jul 6, 17. *Study:* Ohio Univ, teaching fel, with L C Mitchell, AB, MA; Chouinard Sch Art, with Pruett Carter; John Huntington Polytech, with Rolf Stoll. *Exhib:* Nat Acad Design, Am Watercolor Soc & Allied Artists Am, New York; Calif Watercolor Soc, Los Angeles; San Francisco Mus Art. *Pos:* Art dir, J Walter Thompson Co, New York, 48-59. *Awards:* Gold Medal & Kerwin H Fulton Medal, Art Dirs Club New York, 54; Grand Award, 100 Best Posters of Yr, Outdoor Advert Asn Am, 54. *Bibliog:* Linette Albert (auth), George Warren Booth: The thoroughbred scene, Am Artist, 7/75; Alyse Lounsberry (auth), Art over easy, Ocala Star-Banner, 4/12/81 & Equine artist George Warren Booth, Fla Horse, 9/81. *Mem:* Art Dirs Club New York; Soc Illus; Artists Equity, New York. *Media:* Miscellaneous Media, Acrylic. *Dealer:* Sporting Gallery PO Box 146 Middleburg VA 22117; Gateway Art Gallery 333A Peruvian Ave Palm Beach FL 33480. *Mailing Add:* 1771 Southwest 55th Rd Ocala FL 32674

BOOTH, JUDITH GAYLE
ADMINISTRATOR, CURATOR
b Pawhuska, Okla, Nov 18, 42. *Study:* Cent State Univ, Edmund, Okla, BA; Univ Mo, Columbia; Univ NMex, Albuquerque, MA. *Pos:* Cur, Tamarind Inst, 71-72, asst dir & cur, 72-76, asst dir, 76-78; cur & adminr, Unified Arts, Albuquerque, currently. *Mailing Add:* Unified Arts 1212 Lovato Rd SW Albuquerque NM 87105

BOOTH, LAURENCE OGDEN
SCULPTOR, ARCHITECT
b Chicago, Ill, July 5, 36. *Study:* Stanford Univ, BA, 58; Mass Inst Technol, BArch, 60. *Work:* Art Inst Chicago. *Exhib:* Richard Gray Gallery, 76; Chicago 7 Architects, Walter Kelly Gallery & Richard Gray Gallery, 77; Frumkin Struve Gallery, Chicago, 80-81; New Chicago Architecture, Verone, Italy, 81; Harvard Grad Sch Design, 81; and many other group & one-man shows. *Pos:* Vis critic, Harvard Univ, 81-82; bd dirs, Mus Contemp Art, Chicago. *Teaching:* Instr archit, Univ Ill, Chicago Circle, 69-71; vis prof, Univ Ill, 82. *Bibliog:* Amy Goldin (auth), Vitality vs greasy kid stuff, Art Gallery Mag, 72; article, Chicago Archit J, 81; article, New Chicago Archit, 81; and others. *Media:* Multimedia. *Publ:* Auth, Spiritual content of order, Arc Mag, 68; auth, Review of Stanley Tigerman sculpture, Art Scene Mag, 69. *Mailing Add:* 553 W Fullerton Chicago IL 60614

BOOTH, ROBERT ALAN
SCULPTOR
Study: Art Inst Boston, 71-73; Mass Col Art, BFA, 76; Syracuse Univ, MFA, 78. *Work:* Lowe Art Gallery, Syracuse Univ. *Comn:* Site sculpture, comn by Ted Stetler, Syracuse, NY, 77; sculpture, TRW Bearings Corp, Jamestown, NY, 81; site sculpture, Artpark, Lewiston, NY, 83 & Chautauqua Co Asn Arts, Jamestown, NY, 83. *Exhib:* Artists of Central New York, Munson-Williams-Proctor Inst, Utica, NY, 77; Syracuse Show, Everson Mus Art, 78; solo exhib, Henri Gallery, Washington, DC, 81, Zaner Gallery, Rochester, NY, 82 & Bruce Gallery, Edinboro Univ, 83; Outside New York City: From Drawing to Sculpture, Lowe Art Gallery, Syracuse Univ, 82; In Western New York, Albright-Knox Art Gallery, 83. *Teaching:* Asst prof sculpture, State Univ NY Col, Fredonia, 78- *Awards:* State Univ NY Fac Res Fel, 82 & 83. *Media:* Wood, Steel. *Dealer:* Zaner Gallry 302 N Goodman Rochester NY 14607; Henri Gallery 1500 21 St NW Washington DC 20036. *Mailing Add:* 767 Main St Dunkirk NY 14040

BOOTHE, POWER ROBERT
PAINTER, INSTRUCTOR
b Mar 12, 45; US citizen. *Study:* Colo Col, BFA, 67; Whitney Mus, independent study prog, 67-68. *Work:* Guggenheim Mus; Hirshhorn Mus; Chase Manhattan Bank; New York Bank for Savings; Lehman Brothers. *Exhib:* Theodoron Award Show, 71, Art of this Decade, 74 & Recent Acquisitions, 75, Guggenheim Mus, New York; Painting Endures, Inst of Contemp Art, Boston, 75; one-man exhibs, A M Sachs Gallery, 73, 74, 76, 77 & 81, Pvt Images, Los Angeles Co Mus Art, Calif, 77, Painting Show, PS1 Gallery, Brooklyn, NY, 77 & Art and Dance, Inst Contemp Art, Boston, 82; Book-Objects by Contemporary Artists, Albright-Knox Art Gallery, Buffalo, NY, 77; Transitions: American Abstract Artists, Summit Art Ctr, NJ, 81. *Teaching:* Instr painting, Sch Visual Arts, New York. *Awards:* Nat Endowment Arts Grant, 75. *Bibliog:* Hal Foster (auth), Power Boothe, Artforum, 12/77; Dore Ashton (auth), Power Boothe's Gait, Arts Mag, 6/81; Dore Ashton (auth), American Art Since 1945, Oxford Univ Press, 82. *Mem:* Abstract Artists Asn. *Media:* Oil. *Mailing Add:* 49 Crosby St New York NY 10012

BOOTH-OWEN, M(ARY ANN)
PAINTER, PRINTMAKER
b Winston-Salem, NC, Sept 28, 42. *Study:* Univ Tenn, 66-67; Ga State Univ, 68-70. *Work:* Westinghouse Electric Corp Collection, Pittsburgh, Pa; Delta Airlines, Coca Cola & Arthur Andersen & Co, Atlanta, Ga; Shamrock-Hilton Collection, Houston, Tex; Hunt Inst Botanical Doc, Carnegie Mellon Univ, Pa. *Comn:* 4 art decorative murals, Noelles Restaurant, Atlanta, Ga, 78. *Exhib:* Winter Park Art Festival, Fla, 77-79 & 83; Southern Watercolor Soc, Columbia Mus Arts & Sci, SC, 80 & La Tech Univ, Reston, 81; Southern Watercolor Soc, La Tech Univ, Reston, 81; Botanical Mus & Gardens, Nashville, Tenn, 82 & 84; Arnold Arboretum, Harvard Univ, 84. *Awards:* Award of Merit, Winter Park Art Festival, 78 & 83; Best of Show, Fine Art Powers Crossroads, 78 & 83. *Mem:* Southern Watercolor Soc; Nat Mus Gallery Registration Asn, Washington, DC; Ga Watercolor Soc. *Media:* Watercolor. *Dealer:* Booth-Owens Arts 3961 Loch Highland Pass Roswell GA 30075. *Mailing Add:* 3961 Loch Highland Pass Roswell GA 30075

BOPP, EMERY
PAINTER, EDUCATOR
b Corry, Pa, May 13, 24. *Study:* Pratt Inst Art Sch, NY; Yale Sch Painting & Design, with Josef Albers & William de Kooning, BFA; NY Univ; Rochester Inst Technol, MFA. *Work:* Addison Gallery Am Art, Andover, Mass; Greenville Co Mus Art, SC; SC Arts Comn Collection. *Exhib:* Bob Jones Univ, 62-64; Butler Inst Am Art Exhib, 66; Birmingham Mus Art, 66; Southeastern Exhib, Atlanta, Ga, 67; Greenville Co Mus Art, 68; plus others. *Teaching:* Chmn div art, Bob Jones Univ, 55- *Awards:* Purchase Award, Hunter Gallery Art, Chattanooga, Tenn, 65; Merit Award, Southeastern Exhib, Atlanta, 67; Purchase Award, Greenville Co Mus Art, 68. *Mem:* Southeastern Col Art Conf; Guild SC Artists; Col Art Asn Am; Cooperstown Art Asn, NY. *Mailing Add:* Div of Art Bob Jones Univ Greenville SC 29614

BORCOMAN, JAMES
CURATOR
b Ontario, Can, Jan 17, 26. *Study:* Univ NB, BA; Univ BC, Vancouver; State Univ NY Buffalo, MFA; hist photog with Beaumont Newhall & Nathan Lyons. *Collections Arranged:* Goodridge Roberts Retrospective, 1969, 69, Four 19th Century Canadian Photographers, 70 & Photographs from the Collection, 75, Nat Gallery Can; The Photograph as Object Traveling Exhib (with catalog), 69; Nathan Lyons: Notations in Passing Traveling Exhib (with catalog), 72; Charles Negre (with catalog), Ottawa, 76; Brit Photographs from the Collection, 1844-1914, 76; Recent Acquisitions, 77; The Painter as Photogr: D O Hill, Charles Negre, Auguste Salzmann (with monograph), 78; The Magical Eye: Definitions of Photography, 80. *Pos:* Educ officer, Nat Gallery Can, 60-66, dir educ dept, 66-69 & cur photographs, 67-83. *Teaching:* Part time lectr hist photog & photog workshop, Univ Ottawa, Ont, 71-75. *Awards:* Prize for Distinguished Achievement in Photog Hist, Photog Hist Soc of NY; Seal of City of Arles, France; Bronze Medal, Leipzig Bk Fair. *Bibliog:* Peter Bunnell (auth), The National Gallery photographic collection, An inquiry into the aesthetics of photography (series), Artscanada, 75. *Mem:* Soc Photog Educ. *Res:* Canadian art; history of photography. *Publ:* Auth, Notes on the early use of combination printing, In: 100 Years of Photographic History, 75; auth, Eugene Atget: A brief life, In: Eugene Atget, Six Photographs, 79; auth, David Heath: A Dialogue with Solitude, Nat Gallery Can, 79. *Mailing Add:* 1 Marco Lane Ottawa ON K1S 5A1 Canada

BORDEAUX, JEAN LUC
HISTORIAN, CURATOR
b Laval, France, Feb 13, 38. *Study:* Univ Paris, Fac Sci, PCB, 60; Mus Nat d'Art Mod, Paris, study of museology with Jean Cassou, 58-60; Iowa State Univ, BS(journalism), 64; Ariz State Univ, MA(art hist), 66; Univ Calif, Los Angeles, PhD(art hist), 70. *Pos:* Art critic & writer, Connaissance des Arts, 55-; lectr, J Paul Getty Mus, Malibu, Calif, 67-68, asst cur paintings, 69-72; dir, Fine Arts Gallery, Calif State Univ, Northridge, 72-81; guest cur, Calif Palace of the Legion of Honor, San Francisco, 75; charge de mission, Musee du Louvre, France, 79; organized and curated numerous exhibitions since 1972. *Teaching:* Instr art hist, Univ Calif, Los Angeles, 69-72; prof art hist, Calif State Univ, Northridge, 69- *Awards:* Kress Fel, Louvre, Hermitage & Pushkin Mus (France & Soviet Union), 70-71; Calif Arts Coun Exhib Grants, 74-75. *Mem:* Fr Soc Hist Art; Col Art Asn; Art Hist from Southern Calif; Western Asn Am Mus. *Res:* French painting from 17th to early 19th centuries. *Interests:* Contemporary art; art since 1945 in the US. *Publ:* Auth, articles, Burlington Mag, Am Art Rev, Art Int, Art in Am, Jour J Paul Getty Mus & others. *Mailing Add:* 640 Kingman Ave Santa Monica CA 90402

BORDES, ADRIENNE
PAINTER, INSTRUCTOR
b New York, NY, Dec 20, 35. *Study:* NY Univ, with Philip Guston, BA, 57; Hunter Col, New York, with Tony Smith & Vincent Longo. *Exhib:* One-man shows, Capricorn Gallery, New York, 67 & 68 & Wilkes Col, Pa, 78; Six Artists, NY Univ, 65; Some New Beginnings, Brooklyn Mus, 68; Women in the Arts, Univ Wis, 72; Transitions, Wallace Gallery, State Univ NY, 79; Four Artists & A Writer, Fed Hall, New York, 82. *Teaching:* Adj instr painting, Hunter Col, New York, 78-80; adj instr painting, Adelphi Univ, 79-80; adj instr hist archit & interior design, Fashion Inst Technol, 80- *Awards:* Painting Grant, Millay Colony Arts, Austerlitz, NY, 75. *Media:* Acrylic. *Mailing Add:* 369 Seventh Ave New York NY 10001

BOREN, JAMES ERWIN
PAINTER
b Waxahachie, Tex, Sept 26, 21. *Study:* Kansas City Art Inst & Sch Design, BFA & MFA; Univ Kansas City. *Work:* Nat Cowboy Hall of Fame, Oklahoma City; Diamond M Found, Snyder, Tex; Read Mullin Mus, Phoenix, Ariz; Rockwell Mus, Corning, NY. *Exhib:* One-man show, Tex Art Gallery, Dallas, 69-81; Cowboy Artists of Am, Nat Cowboy Hall of Fame, 70-72 & Phoenix Mus, Ariz, 70-81; Whitney Gallery Western Art, Cody, Wyo, summer 73; Mont Hist Soc, Helena, 73; Western Heritage Sale, Houston, 73-83. *Pos:* Concept illusr, Martin-Marietta Co, Denver, Colo, 56-64; art dir, Nat Cowboy Hall of Fame, 65-69. *Teaching:* Art instr, St Mary Col, Kans, 51-53. *Awards:* Excellence Award, Soc Tech Writers & Publ, 64; nine gold & eight silver awards, Cowboy Artists of Am, 68-81. *Bibliog:* Joe M Dealey, Jr (auth), The treasured West of James Boren, Southwest Scene, Dallas Morning News, 9/17/72; feature article, Art West, 9-10/81. *Mem:* Cowboy Artists Am (secy-treas, 69-70, pres, 73-74 & 79-80, dir, 74-75 & 78-79). *Media:* Watercolor, Oil. *Publ:* Illusr, Harmsen's Western Americana, 71; illusr, Ariz Hwys, 12/73; illusr, How Come I Wrote a Book, 74; illusr, Royal B Hassrick's Western Painting Today, 75 & Mary Carroll Nelson's Masters of Western Art, 82, Watson-Guptill. *Mailing Add:* PO Box 533 Clifton TX 76634

BORETZ, NAOMI
PAINTER, EDUCATOR
b New York, NY. *Study:* Art Students League; Boston Mus Sch; Rutgers Univ; City Col New York, MA(fine arts), 71. *Work:* Joslyn Art Mus, Omaha, Nebr; Fordham Univ at Lincoln Ctr, New York; Hove Mus Art, Sussex, Eng; Glasgow Mus, Scotland; Western Elec Corp. *Exhib:* Awards Exhib, Brooklyn Mus Art, 72; solo exhib, Hudson River Mus, 75; Randolph-Macon Woman's Col, Va, 77; Katonah Gallery, NY, 78; Queens Col, New York, 78; Middlesex Co Mus, NJ, 81; and many others. *Teaching:* Instr, City Col New York, 68-71 & Princeton Art Asn, 72-73; asst prof art & dir art prog, Rider Col, Lawrenceville, NJ, 73-80; asst prof theater, Beaver Col, Pa, 80- *Awards:* Watercolor Award, Brooklyn Mus Art, 71; Va Ctr Creative Arts Fel, 73, 75 & 80; Ossabaw Arts Found Fel, 75. *Bibliog:* Ian Woodcock (auth), article, Arts Mag, 7/72; interview, Brit Broadcasting Co Radio, 72-73; article, New York Times, 3/81. *Media:* Acrylic, Watercolor. *Publ:* Auth, The reality underlying abstraction, In: Perception and Pictorial Representation, Praeger, 79; auth, Watercolours with acetate, Leonardo, 78. *Mailing Add:* Beaver Col Glenside PA 19038

BORGATTA, ISABEL CASE
SCULPTOR, EDUCATOR
b Madison, Wis, Nov 21, 21. *Study:* Smith Col, 39-40; Yale Univ Sch Fine Arts, BFA, 44; New Sch Social Res, 44-45; Studio of Jose de Creeft, 44-45; Art Students League, 46; Edward MacDowell Fels, 68, 73 & 74; Yaddo fel, 71 & 72. *Work:* Wadsworth Atheneum, Hartford, Conn; Yeshiva Univ, New York; Krannert Mus, Univ Ill, Champaign; Norfolk Mus, Va; Benton Mus, Univ Conn. *Comn:* Mem sculpture, New Rochelle, New York, 72; Grand Hyatt Hotel, New York; plus others. *Exhib:* Pa Acad Fine Arts Ann, Philadelphia, 49-55; Whitney Mus Am Art, 51-52; retrospective, Briarcliff Col Mus, 71; one-woman shows, Frank Rehn Gallery, 68, 71, 74 & 77; Brooklyn Mus, 75; Nardin Galleries, 78; Galerie Coach, Paris, 79; Sid Deutsch Gallery, 84; and others. *Teaching:* lectr sculpture, City Col New York, 60-71; assoc prof, Col New Rochelle, 73-78, prof, 78- *Awards:* Jacques Lipchitz Award, 61; plus others. *Bibliog:* Mark van Doren (auth), The sculptures of Isabel Case Borgatta, Galerie St Etienne, 54; William D Allen (auth), Borgatta's marbles, Arts Mag, 68; James R Mellow (auth), article in New York Times, 74. *Mem:* Col Art Asn; Womens Caucus for Art; Artists Equity; Sculptors Guild. *Media:* Stone, Wood. *Mailing Add:* 617 West End Ave New York NY 10024

BORGATTA, ROBERT EDWARD
PAINTER, SCULPTOR

b Havana, Cuba, Jan 11, 21; US citizen. *Study:* Nat Acad Design, 34-37; NY Univ, Sch Archit & Allied Arts, BFA, 40, Inst Fine Arts, 46-53; Yale Univ Sch Fine Arts, MFA, 42. *Work:* Norfolk Mus, Va; Ford Found. *Comn:* Mural & sculpture, Gutman Assocs, New York; stained glass design, Temple Emanu-el, Yonkers, NY, 60. *Exhib:* Audubon Artists Ann, 53-72; Whitney Mus Am Art Prizewinners Show, 54; Schettini Gallery, Milan, Italy, 57; Corcoran Gallery Art, 68; one-man shows, Babcock Galleries, 64 & 68 & Southern Vt Art Ctr, 77. *Teaching:* Prof painting & drawing, City Col New York, 47-80. *Awards:* Tiffany Fel, 42; Emily Lowe Found Award, 57; Newman Medal, Nat Soc Painters Casein, 69. *Bibliog:* American artists in Italian exhibit, Valligia Diplomatica, 10/57; An artist in his studio, House Beautiful, 3/60; John Canaday (auth), article, New York Times, 3/15/69. *Mem:* Audubon Artists; Am Watercolor Soc; Nat Soc Painters Casein. *Media:* Oil, Marble. *Dealer:* Babcock Galleries 20 East 67th St New York NY 10021 *Mailing Add:* 366 Broadway New York NY 10013

BORGENICHT, GRACE (GRACE BORGENICHT BRANDT)
DEALER, COLLECTOR

b New York, NY, Jan 25, 15. *Study:* Columbia Univ, MA, 37; also with Andre Lhote, Paris, 34. *Pos:* Dir & owner, Grace Borgenicht Gallery, 51- *Specialty:* Contemporary American painting and sculpture. *Collection:* Cezanne, Matisse, Picasso, de Kooning, Bonnard, Mondrian, Degas, Vuillard, Avery, Leger, de Rivera. *Mailing Add:* 724 Fifth Ave New York NY 10019

BORGLUM, JAMES LINCOLN DE LA MOTHE
SCULPTOR, PHOTOGRAPHER

b Stamford, Conn, Apr 9, 12. *Study:* With father 12 years and in Europe, 29-31. *Comn:* Statue, Our Lady of Loreto, La Bahia Mission, Goliad, Tex; statue of Gladys Porter, founder of Gladys Porter Zoo, Brownsville, Tex; statue of St Francis, Rockport, Tex; designed carving of world's largest-known ruby (22,000 karat), Ada Wilson, Corpus Christi, Tex. *Exhib:* Color photog exhib in salon at Milwaukee, Rochester, NY & New York. *Pos:* With, Mt Rushmore Nat Mem, Black Hills, SDak, 32-, in-chg of measurement and enlarging models, 34-38, appt supt, Mem Comn, 38, appt to complete Mem following father's death, 40, mem, Comn, 60-; tech adv, carving world's largest known sapphires in likeness of Washington, Jefferson & Eisenhower. *Mem:* Mt Rushmore Nat Mem Soc (trustee). *Publ:* Cover for This Week & Sat Eve Post; auth, My Father's Mountain, 65; coauth, with June Zeitner, Mt Rushmore, Borglums Unfinished Dream, North Plains Publ, 76; auth, Mt Rushmore, The Story Behind the Scenery, K C Publ, 77. *Mailing Add:* Box 908 La Feria TX 78559

BORGO, LUDOVICO
HISTORIAN

b Naples, Italy, Aug 30, 30; US citizen. *Study:* Washington Univ, BA; Harvard Univ, PhD. *Teaching:* Asst prof Renaissance art, Washington Univ, St Louis, Mo, 66-69; prof Renaissance art, Brandeis Univ, Waltham, 69- *Publ:* Auth, The problem of the Ferry Carondelet altarpiece, 71 & auth, Guiliano da Maiano's Santa Maria del Sasso, 72, Burlington Mag; auth, The Works of Mariotto Albertinelli, Garland, 76; auth, Fra Bartolommeo's beginnings--once more with Berenson, 77 & auth, New questions for Piero's Flagellation, 79, Burlington Mag. *Mailing Add:* 5 Solon St Wellesley MA 02181

BORIS, BESSIE
PAINTER

b Johnstown, Pa. *Study:* Art Students League, 40-42; study with George Grosz & Vaclav Vytlacil. *Work:* Smith Col Mus Art, Northhampton, Mass; New York Univ, New York; NJ Mus, Newark; Montclair Mus, NJ; Chase Manhattan Bank, New York. *Exhib:* Corcoran Gallery of Art, Washington, DC, 49; Pa Acad Fine Arts Ann Drawing Show, 63 & 69; Am Acad Arts & Lett, Childe Hassam Show, New York, 70-72 & 76; Babcock Gallery, New York, 70; Image Gallery Stockbridge, Mass, 71, 76, 77, 80 & 83; Touchstone Gallery, New York, 76. *Awards:* First Prize Purchase Award, Mo Valley Artists, Mulvane Mus, 48; Dana Watercolor Medal, Pa Acad Fine Arts, 61; Blanche Colman Award, 78. *Bibliog:* Articles in Chrysalis, 51 & The Insiders, Vol 4, La State Univ Press, 60. *Media:* Acrylic, Ink. *Mailing Add:* Box 187 Stockbridge MA 01262

BORN, JAMES E
SCULPTOR

b Toledo, Ohio, Nov 16, 34. *Study:* Toledo Mus Sch, cert; Univ Toledo, BA; Univ Iowa, Iowa City, MFA. *Work:* Univ Iowa, Iowa City. *Exhib:* 9th Biennial Michiana, S Bend Art Ctr, Ind, 76; Sculpture & Ceramics Exhib, Butler Inst Am Art, Youngstown, Ohio, 76; 19th Ann Mich Exhib, Midland Art Ctr, 78-81; 24th Drawing & Sculpture Show, Ball State Univ, 78; one-man shows, Cent Mich Univ, 69 & 77 & Muskegon Community Col, 79. *Teaching:* Asst prof sculpture, painting, design & drawing, Univ Calif at Humboldt, Arcata, 62-64 & Calif Western Univ, San Diego, 64-65; asst prof sculpture, design & painting, Univ Calif at Stanislaus, Turlock, 65-68; assoc prof sculpture, Cent Mich Univ, Mt Pleasant, 68-76, acting chmn, 72-74, prof sculpture, 76- *Awards:* Sculpture Award, 28th Ann Exhib, Ball State Univ, 82; Grand Purchase Award, 15th Nat Exhib, Pine Bluff Art Mus, Ark, 82; Excellence Award, Mich Fine Arts Competition, Birmingham-Bloomfield Art Ctr, 83. *Mem:* Col Art Asn; Mid-Am Art Asn. *Media:* Bronze. *Mailing Add:* 502 S University Mt Pleasant MI 48858

BORNE, MORTIMER
SCULPTOR, PAINTER

b Poland, 1902; US citizen. *Study:* Art Students League; Nat Acad Design; Ecole Beaux Arts. *Work:* Boston Mus; Fogg Art Mus; Nat Gallery Art & Libr Cong, Washington, DC; Metrop Mus Art, New York; Mus Mod Art, New York; and many others. *Exhib:* One-man shows, Spec Exhib of Drypoints, Corcoran Gallery Art, Washington, DC, 41, drypoints, Mus Fine Arts, Montreal, Can, 42, Color Drypoints--A New Medium, US Nat Mus, Smithsonian Inst, Washington, 44 & color drypoints, Currier Gallery, Manchester, NH; drypoints, Brit Mus, Victoria & Albert Mus & Detroit Inst Art; Philadelphia Mus; Mus Fine Arts, Houston; Wadsworth Atheneum; NY Hist Soc Mus. *Teaching:* Lectr art, New Sch, New York, 45-67. *Awards:* Talcott Prize, 39 & Noyes Prize, 43, Soc Am Etchers. *Bibliog:* Leila Mechlin (auth), The art world, Washington Sun Star, 12/10/44; H M (auth), Mortimer Borne and a note on color prints, New York Pub Libr Bull, 5/44; The chromatic wood sculpture of Mortimer Borne, Nat Hist, 11/70. *Publ:* Auth, Idiomatic specialization, 52; auth, Modern art goes below the surface, Rotarian, 10/60; auth, New art techniques, 69 & auth, Chromatic versus polychrome sculpture, 71 & Convex canvas painting, 74, Leonardo Mag. *Dealer:* Tappan Zee Art Ctr Nyack NY 10960. *Mailing Add:* 107 S Broadway Nyack NY 10960

BORNSTEIN, ELI
PAINTER, SCULPTOR

b Milwaukee, Wis, Dec 28, 22. *Study:* Univ Wis, BS, 45 & MS, 54; Art Inst Chicago; Univ Chicago, 43; Acad Montmartre of Fernand Leger, Paris, 51; Acad Julian, Paris, 52. *Work:* Walker Art Ctr, Minneapolis, Minn; Nat Gallery Can, Ottawa; Univ at Calgary, Alberta; Univ of Saskatchewan, Saskatoon; Saskatchewan Arts Board, Regina; and others. *Comn:* Aluminum construction, Sask Teacher's Fedn, Saskatoon, 56; structurist relief, Univ Sask, Saskatoon, 58; structurist relief, Int Air Terminal, Winnipeg, 62; structurist construction, Wascana Ctr Authority, Regina, 83. *Exhib:* Retrospectives, Mendel Art Gallery, Saskatoon, 64 & 83; Nat Gallery Can Biennial, Ottawa, 67; 2nd Int Biennial, Medellin, Colombia, 70; Can Cult Centre, Paris, France, 76; Glenbow-Alta Inst, Calgary, 76; York Univ Art Gallery, Toronto, 83; and others. *Pos:* Ed, The Structurist, 60- *Teaching:* Instr drawing, painting & sculpture, Milwaukee Art Inst, 43-47; instr design, Univ Wis, 49; prof art, Univ Sask, 50-, head dept art, 63-71. *Awards:* Hon mention, 2nd Int Biennial Exhib, Medellin, Colombia, 70; Gov Gen's Queen Elizabeth Silver Jubilee Medal, 77; Diploma of Nomination with Gold Medal, Academia Italia delle Arti e del Lavoro, Parma, Italy. *Publ:* Auth, The color molecule in art, 73-74, Art toward nature, 75-76, Four conversations on art and vision, 77-78, Mimesis and metaphor, 79-80 & Art, technology and nature: Toward new affinities, 81-82, Structurist. *Mailing Add:* Box 378 Univ of Sask Saskatoon SK S7N 0W0 Canada

BOROCHOFF, (IDA) SLOAN
PAINTER

US citizen. *Study:* High Mus Art, 39; Univ Ga, 39-40; Ga State Univ, 40; Chicago Sch Interior Decorating, dipl, 66; Atlanta Art Inst, 68. *Work:* Ga Inst Technol, Vet Admin & Lovett Sch, Atlanta; The Temple, Tucson, Ariz; Nat Acad Eng, Washington, DC. *Comn:* Noah's Ark (print), Atlanta Jewish Welfare Fedn, 71; painting, Am Art Campaign, Atlanta, 72. *Exhib:* One-woman shows, Dzikalas Gallery, 61, Ga Inst Technol Student Ctr & Lovett Sch Show, 71 & 75; 3rd Nat Art Competition, B'nai B'rith Woman, 65 & Int Platform Asn Art Exhib, 71, Washington, DC; Atlanta Merchandise Mart. *Pos:* Vpres, Designs Unlimited Inc, Atlanta, 64-; pres, Sloan Borochoff Gallery; auth & artist, Atlanta Playhouse Theatre Ltd, 75-, artistic dir, 79- *Teaching:* Lectr, schs & pvt, 70- *Awards:* Award for Three Boats, Sandy Springs Jr Woman's Club, 71; Award for Designs in Art, Scottdale Enterprises, Inc, 72; Leading Lady, Atlanta JC Singles, 76. *Mem:* Atlanta Col Arts; Atlanta Writers Club; Atlanta Press Club. *Media:* Oil. *Mailing Add:* 3450 Old Plantation Rd NW Atlanta GA 30327

BOROFSKY, JON
PAINTER

b Boston, Mass, 42. *Study:* Carnegie Mellon Univ, BFA, 64; Ecole de Fontainbleau, summer 64; Yale Sch Art & Archit, MFA, 66. *Exhib:* 10th Anniversary Group Show, Paula Cooper Gallery, New York, 78; Whitney Biennial, Whitney Mus of Am Art, New York, 79; Born in Boston, De Cordova Mus, Lincoln, Mass, 79; one-man shows, Wadsworth Atheneum, 76, Univ Calif, Irvine, 77, Protetch-McIntosh Gallery, Washington, DC, 78, Hayden Gallery, Mass Inst Technol, Cambridge, 80, Contemp Arts Mus, Houston, Tex, 81, Kunsthalle, Basel, Switzerland, 81 & Inst Contemp Art, London, 81; Int Austellung, Westkunst, Cologne, WGermany, 81; Baroques 81, Musee de la Ville de Paris, 81; and many others. *Teaching:* Instr, Sch Visual Arts, New York, 69-77; instr, Calif Inst Arts, Valencia, 77- *Bibliog:* Mark Rosenthal (auth), Jon Borofsky, Matrix 18, Wadsworth Atheneum, 4-5/76; Phillip Smith, Jon Borofsky, Arts Mag, 3/78; John Russell (auth), Art: transformations of Jonathan Borofsky, New York Times, 10/24/80. *Mailing Add:* c/o Paula Cooper Gallery 155 Wooster St New York NY 10012

BORSO, RICHARD GEORGE
PAINTER

b Ann Arbor, Mich, June 29, 46. *Study:* Am Acad Art, with Arvydas Algminas & Irving Shapiro, 73-80. *Work:* Standard Oil Ind, Bear, Stearns & Co, Chicago; Hollister Inc, Libertyville, Ill; Angus Chemical Co, Northbrook, Ill. *Exhib:* Watercolor Okla, Owens Gallery, Oklahoma City, 77; Midwest Watercolor Soc, Tweed Mus Art, 78 & Rahr-West Mus, Manitowoc, Wis, 79; Watercolor Ill, Paul Sargent Art Gallery, Eastern Ill Univ, 79; 58th Ann Nat April Salon, Springville Mus Art, Utah, 82; Ill State Fair Prof Art Exhib,

Springfield, 83. *Awards:* Purchase Award, Midwest Watercolor Soc, Tweed Mus Art, 78; John Lindstrom Award, Midwest Watercolor Soc, 78. *Bibliog:* Michael Hirsley (auth), Fulfillment as an art with growth, dividends, Chicago Tribune, 7/8/79. *Mem:* Chicago Artists Coalition. *Media:* Oil, Watercolor. *Dealer:* Neville-Sargent Gallery 511 Main St Evanston IL 60202; Driscol Gallery Fairmont Hotel Pavilion 555 17th St Suite 160 Denver CO 80202. *Mailing Add:* 1502 W Bryn Mawr Chicago IL 60660

BORSTEIN, ELENA
PAINTER, EDUCATOR
b Hartford, Conn, Feb 5, 46. *Study:* Skidmore Col, BS; Univ Pa, BFA & MFA. *Work:* Mus Mod Art; Mass Inst Technol; Everson Mus; Newark Mus; Phoenix Mus; and others. *Comn:* Ottawa Silica Corp, Ill; Whitco Chemical Co, New York. *Exhib:* Contemporary Reflections, Aldrich Mus Art, Ridgefield, Conn, 74; 14 Am Artists, Corcoran Gallery/Aarhus Kunstmuseum Traveling Exhib, 77; Gifts of Drawing, Mus Mod Art, New York, 79; Herbert Johnson Mus Art, Ithaca, NY, 81; Rochester Inst Technol, 81; Everson Mus, 81; Skidmore Col, Saratoga Springs, NY, 82; Kathryn Markel Gallery, New York, 83; and others. *Pos:* Art consult, Aarhus Kunstmuseum, Denmark, 74-75; vis artist, St Marys Col, Ind, Md Art Inst & Sch Visual Arts, 81. *Teaching:* Asst prof painting & photog, York Col, City Univ New York, 70- *Awards:* Childe Hassam Purchase Award, Am Acad Arts & Lett, 75; Nat Endowment Arts Grant, 80; Creative Artists Pub Serv Prog Grant, 80. *Bibliog:* David Shirey (auth), article, Arts Mag, 9/78; articles, Art Int, 1/80 & New York Times, 3/16/80. *Mem:* Col Art Asn (mem, Women's Caucus). *Mailing Add:* 451 Broome St New York NY 10013

BOSSE, JANET C
PAINTER, PRINTMAKER
b Detroit, Mich. *Study:* Coronado Sch Fine Art, Calif, 53-54; Univ Mich, 55-56; Pratt Graphic Art Ctr, 63-70. *Work:* US Info Serv; Pace Univ, Am Express Int, Int Bus Machines Corp & Chase Manhattan Bank, New York. *Exhib:* Soc Am Graphic Artists Ann, New York, 67; Brooklyn Mus, New York, 68; Int Miniature Print Exhib, New York, 68 & 77; Silvermine Guild Artists, New Canaan, Conn, 75 & 77; Bronx Mus Art, New York, 76; Sarah Inst, New York, 80. *Pos:* Pres & found mem, Noho Gallery, 75- *Teaching:* Instr, Hofstra Univ, 72-73. *Bibliog:* Leslie Plummer (auth), Gallery reviews, New York Arts J, 11/77; Barnaby Ruhe (auth), Janet Bosse, 2/80 & James T McCartin (auth), Janet Bosse, 5/81, Arts Mag. *Media:* Acrylic. *Dealer:* Barbara Ingber 460 West Broadway New York NY. *Mailing Add:* 40 Perry St New York NY 10014

BOSSON, JACK (JOHN EDWIN), JR
PAINTER, PRINTMAKER
b Charleroi, Pa, Sept 18, 37. *Study:* Cooper Union, with Victor Candell, Charles Cajori & John Kacere, cert(Fulbright fel), 63; Univ Paris, with Marcel Brion, 64; Cornell Univ, MFA, 66. *Work:* New York Port Authority Collection; Herbert F Johnson Mus Art, Ithaca, NY; Smithsonian Inst Space Mus Collection, DC; State Univ NY Albany. *Comn:* Painting of solar eclipse, Nat Aeronautics & Space Admin, Houston, 67. *Exhib:* Big Print Show, Original Art Gallery, State Univ NY Albany, 67; one-man show, Berkshire Mus, Pittsfield, Mass, 67; Arts & Univ/Trends in the Sixties, Albright-Knox Art Gallery, Buffalo, NY, 67; Five Printmakers, Ithaca Col Mus Art, NY, 69; Contemp Drawings Invitational, Lake Placid Art Ctr, NY, 77; Drawings & Prints--New York, Rush Rhees Gallery, Univ Rochester, NY, 78; 7th Ann Contemp Reflections, Aldrich Mus, Ridgefield, Conn, 78. *Collections Arranged:* The Ithaca Paintings, 1970-1976 (cataloged), Rathbone Gallery, Albany, NY, 77. *Pos:* Pres, 55 Mercer Gallery, New York, 79-80. *Teaching:* Asst prof drawing & painting, Cornell Univ, 69-75; assoc prof, Col New Rochelle, NY, 75- *Awards:* Purchase Award, Albright-Knox Art Gallery, NY State Univ Comt Arts, 67; Artists Fel, Nat Endowment Arts, 80; and others. *Bibliog:* Grace Glueck (auth), article, Art in Am, 11/72; Michael Florescu (auth), article, Arts Mag, 11/79; Fred Mangones & Philip Jones (auth), Tides (film), 72. *Media:* Acrylic, Oil; Silkscreen, Lithography. *Mailing Add:* 454 Broome St New York NY 10013

BOSTELLE, THOMAS (THEODORE)
PAINTER, SCULPTOR
b West Chester, Pa, Nov 16, 21. *Work:* Del Art Mus; West Chester Univ, Pa; Butler Inst Am Art, Youngstown, Ohio; Phillips Collection, Washington, DC; Nat Portrait Gallery, Washington, DC. *Exhib:* Over 50 one-man shows; retrospectives, George Washington Univ, 69, Del Art Mus, 73, Woodmere Art Gallery, Philadelphia, 77 & 80 & Shippensburg State Col, 81. *Pos:* Aesthetic adv, One world or none & Stuff for stuff (documentaries), Phillip Ragan Assocs, 47-49. *Teaching:* Instr drawing & painting, Fleisher Art Mem, 52-55; instr, Wilmington Soc Fine Arts, 56-77 & Chester Co Art Asn, West Chester, Pa, 77-80; pvt classes & lectures, 60- *Awards:* Four Christian Brinton First Prize Awards & three NC Wyeth First Prize Awards, 46-72. *Bibliog:* Jill Gollatz (auth), On Bostelle's Portrait of Horace Pippin, Daily Local News, 1/31/80; Edmund Morris (auth), A World of Suggestion, Quest, 6/81; Tania Boucher (auth), Bostelle: Seated Self, Aeolian Palace Press, 80. *Media:* Oil, Wood. *Publ:* Auth, Hob House, Aeolian Palace Press, 83. *Dealer:* Aeolian Palace Gallery Box 8 Pocopson PA 19366. *Mailing Add:* Box 8 Pocopson PA 19366

BOSTICK, WILLIAM ALLISON
PAINTER, CALLIGRAPHER
b Marengo, Ill, Feb 21, 13. *Study:* Carnegie Inst Technol, BS; Cranbrook Acad Art, with Zoltan Sepeshy; Detroit Soc Arts & Crafts, with John Foster; Wayne State Univ, MA(art hist). *Work:* Detroit Inst Arts, Mich; Evansville Mus Arts & Sci, Ind; Cranbrook Acad Art Mus, Detroit; Detroit Pub Libr; Wayne State Univ, Detroit. *Comn:* 32 calligraphic panels on wood, 11 calligraphic lecterns & 1 large calligraphic quotation (with Christopher Bostick), Cath Cemeteries of Chicago for Resurrection Mausoleum, Justice, Ill, 71. *Exhib:* Exhib Mich Artists, Detroit Inst Arts, 36-63; Pepsi-Cola Exhib, 45; Scarab Club Gold Medal Exhib, 47-81; Mich Water Color Soc, 48-81; one-man exhib, Arwin Galleries, 67 & 75. *Pos:* Typographer & graphic designer, Evans-Winter-Hebb, Detroit, 36-37; exec secy, Founders Soc, Detroit Inst Arts, 46-60; adminr & secy, Detroit Inst Arts, 46-76; ed, Midwest Mus Quart, 59-60. *Teaching:* Instr drawing, Wayne State Univ, 46-47; instr calligraphy, Detroit Soc Arts & Crafts Art Sch, 61-63; instr hist of the book, Wayne State Univ Grad Sch, 62-67; instr calligraphy & art hist, Grosse Pointe War Mem & Edison Inst, 73-82. *Awards:* Scarab Gold Medal, Scarab Club Detroit, 62, 68 & 79; Knight, Order of Ital Solidarity; Chevalier, French Order of Arts & Lett. *Mem:* Scarab Club Detroit; Midwest Mus Conf; Am Inst Graphic Arts; Am Asn Mus. *Media:* Watercolor, Acrylic. *Publ:* Illusr, Many a Watchful Night, 45; auth & illusr, England Under GI's Reign, 46; illusr, The Mysteries of Blair House, 48; auth, A Guide to the Guarding of Cultural Property, UNESCO, 77; auth & publ, A Manual on the Acquiring of a Beautiful and Legible Handwriting, La Stampa Calligrafica, 77, 2nd ed, 80. *Mailing Add:* 9340 W Outer Dr Detroit MI 48219

BOSZIN, ANDREW
PAINTER, SCULPTOR
b Pilis, Hungary, May 5, 23; Can & UK citizen. *Study:* House Creation, Independent Sch Art; Col Art. *Work:* Nat Gallery Art, Budapest, Hungary; Scottish Camp Asn, Edinburgh, Scotland; Sculptors Soc Can, Toronto; Pa State Univ, Fayette Campus, Uniontown; British Mus, London; and others. *Exhib:* One-man show, Old Nat Gallery, Budapest, Hungary, 48; Hungarian Graphics, Nat Mus Art, Stockholm, 48; London Group, British Royal Soc Art, London, 64; Hungarian Art Fedn, House Congress, Washington, DC, 70-75; Canadian Medal Exhib, Public Archive, Ottawa, 72. *Awards:* Grand Prix De Penture, Prix De Nat, 64; Honor Award, Spanish Medalist Asn, 68; Best Watercolor, Cosmopoliton Club, 81. *Bibliog:* Mikos Rajnai (auth), Endre Boszin, Woodstock Gallery, London, 59; Ian Ferguston (auth), Endre Boszin, Douglass Foulis, Edinburgh, 64; Tamas Tuz (auth), Endre Boszin, Kronika, Toronto, 79. *Mem:* Sculptors Soc Can (pres, 71-73, 79-83). *Media:* Cast Aluminum; Oil, Watercolor. *Mailing Add:* 39 Gilgorm Rd Toronto ON M5N 2M4 Canada

BOTERF, CHECK (CHESTER ARTHUR)
PAINTER, LECTURER
b Ft Scott, Kans, Apr 7, 34. *Study:* Univ Kans, BA, 59; Art Student League; Hunter Col, 63-64; Columbia Univ, MFA, 65. *Work:* Mus Mod Art, Chase Manhattan Bank, Columbia Univ, New York; Larry Aldrich Mus, Ridgefield, Conn; Des Moines Art Ctr, Iowa; and others. *Exhib:* Solo exhibs, Tibor De Nagy Gallery, New York, 67, 68 & 70, Rice Univ, 74 & John Bernard Myers Gallery, New York, 71, 73 & 74; Indianapolis Mus Art, Inc, 68-69; Finch Col, 71; Recent Acquisitions, Mus Mod Art, New York, 71. *Teaching:* Lectr design & drawing, Hunter Col, 65-71; Brooklyn Mus Art Sch, 73; vis assoc prof fine arts, Rice Univ, Houston, 73-75, assoc prof art, 76-, chmn art & art hist, 79-82. *Media:* Acrylic. *Mailing Add:* 46 MacDougal St New York NY 10012

BOTERO, FERNANDO
SCULPTOR
b Madelin, Colombia, 32. *Study:* Acad San Fernando, Spain, 53; Prado Mus, Madrid, 54; Univ Florence, Italy, art hist with Roberto Longhi. *Work:* Mus d'Arte del Vaticano, Rome; Mus de Arte Contemp, Madrid; Mus de Arte Mod, Bogota, Colombia; Mus Mod Art, New York; Guggenheim Mus, New York. *Exhib:* Recent Acquisitions, Mus Mod Art, New York, 61; Selection from the Carnegie, Hudson Gallery, Detroit, Mich, 65; The Emergency Decade, Guggenheim Mus, 66; 5th Biennale of Paris, France, 67; one-man shows, Malborough Gallery, New York, 72-74 & Overzichtstenroonstelling, Bogota, 73; Retrospective (touring WGer), Staatliche Kunsthalle, Baden-Baden, WGer, 70; and others. *Bibliog:* Fernando Botero at Marlborough, Artsmag, 4/72; Un falso ingenuo: Botero, Goya, Madrid, 1/73; G R Hocke (auth), Fernando Botero: a continent under the magnifying glass, Art Int, Lugano, 12/74. *Mailing Add:* c/o Marlborough Fine Arts 40 W 57th St New York NY 10019

BOTHMER, BERNARD V
HISTORIAN, INSTRUCTOR
b Ger, Oct 13, 12; US citizen. *Collections Arranged:* Egyptian Sculpture of the Late Period, 700 BC to AD 100, 60; Art from the Age of Akhenaten, 73; Africa in Antiquity: The Arts of Ancient Nubia and the Sudan, 74. *Pos:* From asst to asst cur, Dept Egyptian Art, Mus Fine Arts, Boston, 46-56; assoc cur ancient art, Brooklyn Mus, 56-64, cur ancient art, 64-72, cur Egyptian & class art, 73-77, chmn dept Egyptian & class art, 78-82. *Teaching:* Adj prof fine arts, Grad Sch Arts & Sci, NY Univ, 60-78; prof fine arts, Inst Fine Arts, 79-82; Lila Acheson Wallace Prof Egyptian Art, 82- *Mem:* Am Res Ctr in Egypt; Egypt Explor Soc; Archaeol Inst Am; Col Art Asn Am; Int Coun Mus. *Res:* Ancient Egyptian portraiture, Egyptian sculpture of the late period. *Publ:* Coauth, The Pomerance Collection of Ancient Art, 66; ed, Wilbour monographs, Vols I-VII, 68-74; coauth, Brief guide, Dept Ancient Art, Brooklyn Mus, 70 & 74; coauth, The Luxor Museum of Ancient Egyptian Art (catalog), 79, German ed 81. *Mailing Add:* c/o NY Univ Inst Fine Arts One E 78th St New York NY 10021

BOTHMER, DIETRICH FELIX VON
CURATOR, EDUCATOR
b Eisenach, Ger, Oct 26, 18; US citizen. *Study:* Friedrich Wilhelm Univ, Berlin, Ger; Oxford Univ, dipl(class archaeol); Univ Chicago; Univ Calif, PhD. *Pos:* Asst cur, Dept Greek & Roman Art, Metrop Mus Art, 46-51, assoc cur, 51-59, cur, 59-73, chmn, 73- *Teaching:* Adj prof Greek art, Inst Fine Arts, NY Univ, 65- *Awards:* Guggenheim Fel, 67. *Mem:* Archaeol Inst Am; Soc Promotion Hellenic Studies; Vereinigung der Freunde antiker Kunst; Deutsches Archaol Inst; Acad Inscriptions & Belle-Lettres. *Res:* Greek and Roman art and archaeology. *Publ:* Auth, Ancient Art from New York Private Collections, 60; coauth, An Inquiry into the Forgery of the Etruscan Terracotta Warriors, 61; auth, Corpus Vasorum Antiquorum USA, Fascicule 12, 63, Fascicule 16, 76; auth, Greek Vase Painting, 72; auth, Greek Art of the Aegean Islands, 79. *Mailing Add:* 373 Centre Island Rd Oyster Bay NY 11771

BOTHWELL, DORR
PAINTER, PRINTMAKER
b San Francisco, Calif, May 3, 02. *Study:* Calif Sch Fine Arts & Rudolph Schaeffer Sch Design, San Francisco; Univ Ore; Abraham Rosenberg Fel for art study abroad, 49-51. *Work:* Metrop Mus Art, Mus Mod Art, Whitney Mus Am Art, New York; Fogg Mus, Cambridge; All papers in Am Arch Art, De Young Mus, San Francisco. *Exhib:* 3rd Bienale, Sao Paulo, Brazil; Meltzer Gallery, New York, 58; one-man shows, De Young Mem Mus, 58 & 63 & Bolles Gallery, 72, San Francisco; Bali Seen, 76 & All Kinds of Cats, 77, Bay Window Gallery, Mendocino, Calif; Thirty Yrs of Am Printmaking, Brooklyn Mus, NY, 77; Falkirk Mus, San Rafael, Calif, 77; Praise of Things, Bay Window Gallery, 82. *Teaching:* Instr design, Calif Sch Fine Arts, 44-48 & 53-58, Parsons Sch Design, New York, 52, San Francisco Art Inst, 59-61 & Women's Guild, Kauai, Hawaii, 80; instr, Mendocino Art Ctr, 61- & Ansel Adams Photog Workshop, Yosemite Nat Park, Calif, 64-78; Summer in Mendocino, Univ Calif, Santa Cruz, 76-77; instr composition, Victor Sch, Colo, 79- *Awards:* Award for Visual Arts, Mayor of San Francisco, 79. *Mem:* Mendocino Art Ctr; Hi-Desert Play House Guild, Joshua Tree, Calif. *Media:* Oil, Acrylic, Serigraph. *Publ:* Coauth, Notan dark-light design, Van Nostrand Reinhold, 68, Danish transl, 77. *Mailing Add:* Star Rte 1 Box 1055 Joshua Tree CA 92252

BOTT, H J
ASSEMBLAGE ARTIST, PAINTER
b Greeley, Colo, Dec 28, 33. *Study:* Art Ctr Sch Los Angeles; Inst Fine Arts, NY Univ; Art Students League; Kunstakademie-Dusseldorf & Bamberg, Ger, MBK, 55. *Work:* Kunsthalle der Garten, Dusseldorf; Rice Univ; New Orleans Mus Art; San Antonio Art Mus; Denver Art Mus. *Exhib:* Pa Acad Fine Arts, 66; one-man shows, Amarillo Art Ctr, 77, Bienville Gallery, New Orleans, 77 & 79 & many others; Contemporary Art in Texas, Roots Art Ctr, Clinton, NY, 79; Fire, Contemp Arts Mus, Houston, 79; numerous multi-media DOV-Z ROBOTT performances, 79-; and many others. *Pos:* Artist in residence, Loft-on-Strand, Galveston, Tex, 69-78. *Awards:* Plastik Reisestipeduim, Museen der Stadt Koln, Ger, 56; Premier Les Plus Sculpture, Prix de Paris, France, 65; and many others. *Bibliog:* Robert M Murdock & Richard Van Buren (coauths), The Drawings & Sculpture of H J Bott, pvt publ, 2/77; Charlotte Mosher (auth), Squaring off, Art News, 4/77; Joe Cain (auth), H J Bott monochromes at Charlton, Art Voices, 12/78. *Publ:* Auth, ROBOTT Opera: A Time-warp Newscast, Univ St Thomas, Houston, 83. *Dealer:* Jan Cicero Gallery Chicago IL. *Mailing Add:* 5400 Memorial Dr #703 Houston TX 77007

BOTT, MARGARET DEATS See Deats, Margaret

BOTT, PATRICIA ALLEN
PAINTER, CRITIC
b Old Lyme, Conn. *Study:* With George Burr & Malcolm Fraser; Art Students League, with Ivan Olinsky & Harry Sternberg. *Work:* Greenville Mus Art, SC; Hickory Mus Art, NC; Bronx Zoo Galleries, New York; Riveredge Found, Calgary; EAfrican Wildlife Soc, Nairobi, Africa. *Exhib:* Soc Animal Artists Travel & Ann Shows, New York, 55-; Grand Cent Art Galleries, New York, 65-; one-man shows, African Wildlife, Hilton Galleries, Nairobi, 70 & others; EAfrican Wildlife Galleries, Nairobi, 71-72; Adler Fine Arts, Inc, New York, 78. *Pos:* Dir, Burr Galleries, New York, 50-61; art reviewer, Host, 56-, Villager, 56-70 & Pendulum, 59-; secy & sales, Salmagundi Club, 62-66; sales, Grand Cent Art Galleries, New York, 66-77; rep, Adler Fine Arts Inc, New York, currently. *Awards:* Am Vet Soc Artists Award; Best Show Medal, 69 & Medal, 70, Gotham Painters. *Bibliog:* Articles, The Standard, 71 & Christian Sci Monitor, 71. *Mem:* Hon mem Soc Animal Artists; Am Artists Prof League; Nat Asn Women Artists; Salmagundi Club; Catharine Lorillard Wolfe Club (bd, 79). *Media:* Oil, Watercolor. *Dealer:* Adler Gallery of Fine Arts 20 E 67th St New York NY 10021. *Mailing Add:* 151 Carroll St Bronx NY 10464

BOTTINI, DAVID M
SCULPTOR
b Santa Clara, Calif, June 1, 45. *Study:* Calif State Univ, San Jose, BA, 69, MA, 70. *Work:* De Saisset Mus, Univ Santa Clara; Oakland Mus; Calif State Univ, San Jose; San Jose City Col Permanent Collection. *Comn:* Sculpture, M & M Robert Bernard, Lafayette, Calif, 70; sculpture, Oakland Mus, 74. *Exhib:* One-man shows, Oakland Mus, 76, Reed Col Art Gallery, 77, Walnut Creek Civic Arts Ctr, 82, Fresno Art Ctr, 83, Triton Mus, 83 & Gallery Paule Anglim, 83; and others. *Teaching:* Instr, Cal State, San Jose, 77-78, Cal State, Fresno, 83. *Awards:* Contemp Art Comt Ann Artist Award, Oakland Mus, 75; KQED Channel 9 Special Art Award, 75; James Phelan Award for

Sculpture, San Francisco Found, 82; and others. *Bibliog:* Alfred Frankenstein (auth), San Francisco Chronicle, 77; Frank Cebulski (auth), Artweek, 81; Allan Temko (auth), San Francisco Chronicle, 82. *Media:* Steel, Stainless Steel. *Mailing Add:* c/o Gallery Paule Anglim 14 Geary St San Francisco CA 94111

BOTTO, RICHARD ALFRED
PAINTER, INSTRUCTOR
b Union City, NJ, May 5, 31. *Study:* Pratt Inst, with Walter Klett, Charles Mazoujian, Walter Murch, Stephen Peck & Edgar Whitney, cert 56, AS, 58; Art Students League, with Frank Reilly. *Comn:* Last Supper (mural), Immaculate Conception Sem, Darlington, NJ. *Exhib:* Nat Acad Design, 71, Allied Artists Am, 72 & Am Artists Prof League, 72, New York; Hudson Valley Art Asn, White Plains, NY, 72; State Exhib, NJ State Mus, Trenton, 72. *Pos:* Pres, Hudson Artist Inc, Jersey City, 66-68, chmn bd, 69-; pres, Reilly Sch Art, New York, 67-68; chmn dept fine arts, Jersey City Mus, 68-69; founder-dir, Renaissance Sch Art, NJ, 74. *Teaching:* Instr fine art, Frank Reilly Sch Art, New York, 64-68. *Awards:* Best-in-Show Medal, Jersey City Mus, 67; Gerald Lubeck Prize, Allied Artists Am, 71; Gold Medal, Grand Nat, Am Artists Prof League, 72. *Mem:* Allied Artists Am; Am Artists Prof League; Hudson Valley Art Asn; Painters & Sculptors Soc NJ; Hudson Artists. *Media:* Oil. *Mailing Add:* 138 Union Pl Ridgefield Park NJ 07660

BOTWINICK, MICHAEL
MUSEUM DIRECTOR
b New York, NY, Nov 14, 43. *Study:* Rutgers Col, BA, 64; Columbia Univ, MA, 67. *Collections Arranged:* Coordr exhib, The Year 1200, Metrop Art Mus, NY, 69-70 & Masterpieces of 50 Centuries, 71. *Pos:* Asst cur, Medieval Art & the Cloisters, Metrop Mus Art, New York, 69, assoc cur, 70, asst cur in chief, 70-71; asst dir art, Philadelphia Mus Art, 71-74; dir, Brooklyn Mus, 74-82; dir, Corcoran Gallery Art, 82- *Teaching:* Instr, Columbia Univ, New York, 68-69 & City Univ New York, 69. *Awards:* Order of Leopold II, Belgian Govt, 80. *Mem:* Am Asn Mus; Nat Conserv Adv Coun; Col Art Asn; Asn Art Mus Dirs. *Mailing Add:* Corcoran Gallery Art 17th St & New York Ave NW Washington DC 20006

BOUCHER, TANIA KUNSKY
PAINTER, DEALER
b Vilno, Lithuania, Feb 17, 27; US citizen. *Study:* City Col New York, BS; Univ Pa, MS; Univ Del, BA; also with Tom Bostelle. *Exhib:* one-woman shows, Westtown Friends Sch, 71 & Univ Del, 73; Carspecken Scott Art Gallery, Wilmington, Del, 74; Aeolian Palace Gallery, 78, 81; Woodmere, Philadephia, 80. *Pos:* Dir, Aeolian Palace Gallery, Pocopson, Pa, 74-; ed, Aeolian Palace Press, 76- *Teaching:* Instr, Westtown Friends Sch, Pa, 64-69; art teacher, West Chester Adult Night Sch, 70-72. *Awards:* First Drawing Award, Chester Co Art Asn, 67; First Painting Award, Del Art Mus, 68; Judges Award, Old York Rd Art Guild, 69. *Bibliog:* Warren Hope (auth), article in Wilmington News J, 4/23/78; Gordon Roehrs (auth), Daily Local News, Westchester, Pa, 4/29/78; Clint Collins (auth), biographical article, Delaware Today Mag, 9/81. *Media:* Oil, Pastel. *Specialty:* Contemporary painting & sculpture. *Mailing Add:* Box 188 Mendenhall PA 19357

BOUCKAERT, HARM J G
DEALER
b Maastricht, Neth, June 6, 34; US citizen. *Study:* Neth Col Representation Abroad, BBA, 53. *Pos:* Owner, Harm Bouckaert Gallery Corp, currently. *Bibliog:* Articles, Venture Mag, 12/82 & Art Economist 5/31/82. *Specialty:* Contemporary American art. *Mailing Add:* 100 Hudson St New York NY 10013

BOUGHTON, WILLIAM HARRISON
PAINTER, EDUCATOR
b Dubuque, Iowa, Feb 19, 15. *Study:* Univ Iowa, BA, 43; Univ Calif, Berkeley, MA, 45; James Phelan Fel (foreign travel & independent study), 45-47; Far East & Near East, 70-71; with Earl Loran, Fletcher Martin, Grant Wood, Emil Ganso, Lester Longman, Worth Ryder, Stephen Peper, H W Janson & Shaefer-Simmern. *Work:* New York Schs; Luxury Liners, SS Constitution & SS Independence; Am Embassy, Paris; Libr Cong, Washington, DC; Fla State Univ Gallery. *Comn:* Mural, Student Union, Lamar Univ, 55 & sculpture, Quadrangle, 57. *Exhib:* Serigraphies Americaines, Paris, 53; Dix Peintres Americaines, Paris, 54; L'aquarelles Contemporarines Aux Etats Unis, France, 55; Kunst Uit Amerika, Breda, Neth, 57; L'arte Grafica, Villa Giula, Rome, 57. *Teaching:* Asst prof art, Fla State Univ, 47-54; head art dept, Lamar Univ, 54-70, prof art, 54-77. *Awards:* Elected mem & Silver Medal, Int Acad Arts, Tommaso Campanella, Rome, 70. *Bibliog:* F Dugas (auth), Texas Professor has Shown his Work World Wide, Facets, Tex Fine Arts Soc, 71. *Mem:* Nat Serigraph Soc; Col Art Asn; Am Color Print Soc; Beaumont Art Asn. *Media:* Oil. *Publ:* Auth, Maskoid and the silk screen, Art Mat Trade News, 50; Maskoid stencil technique, Fla Newspaper News & Radio Dig, 50. *Dealer:* Meredith J Long Galleries 2323 San Felipe Rd Houston TX 77019. *Mailing Add:* PO Box 376 El Prado NM 87529

BOURDEAU, ROBERT CHARLES
PHOTOGRAPHER
b Kingston, Ont, Nov 14, 31. *Study:* Univ Toronto; Queens Univ, Kingston, Ont. *Work:* Nat Gallery Can; Nat Film Board Can, Pub Arch Can, Ottawa; Smithsonian Inst; Mus d'art Contemp, Montreal. *Exhib:* Light 7, Hayden Gallery, 68; two-man exhib, New England Sch Photog, Cambridge, Mass, 75; Nat Gallery Can, 75; one-man exhib, Int Ctr Photog, New York, 80, Vancouver Art Gallery, 80, Art Gallery Ont, 81 & Aferimage Gallery, Dallas, 83. *Teaching:* Instr large format photog, Univ Ottawa, Ont, 80- *Bibliog:* P Cousineau (auth), The Banff Purchase, John Wiley Publ, 79; monograph, Mintmark Press, 80. *Dealer:* Jane Corkin Gallery 144 Front St W Toronto ON. *Mailing Add:* 1462 Chomley Crescent Ottawa ON K1G 0V1 Canada

BOURDON, DAVID
CRITIC, EDITOR
b Glendale, Calif, Oct 15, 34. *Study:* Columbia Univ, BS. *Pos:* Art critic, Village Voice, New York, 64-66 & 74-77; asst ed, Life Mag, New York, 66-71; assoc ed, Smithsonian Mag, Washington, DC, 72-74 & Arts Mag, New York, 73-; art critic, Vogue, 78-, assoc features ed, 83- *Mem:* Am Sect Int Asn Art Critics (pres, 82-83). *Publ:* Auth, Christo, 72; auth, Carl Andre Sculpture 1959-1977, 78; consult ed, Christo: Running Fence, 79; auth, Calder: Mobilist, Ringmaster, Innovator, 80. *Mailing Add:* 30 Fifth Ave New York NY 10011

BOURDON, ROBERT SLAYTON
SCULPTOR, EDUCATOR
b West Chester, Pa, Nov 13, 47. *Study:* Dartmouth Col, AB, 70; Univ Calif, Berkeley, with Harold Paris, Peter Voulkos & Robert Hudson, MA, 72. *Work:* Carnegie Inst Mus, Pittsburgh, Pa; Del Art Mus, Wilmington; Weatherspoon Art Mus, Greensboro, NC; Dartmouth Col Art Mus, Hanover, NH; Ariz State Univ Art Mus, Tempe. *Exhib:* The Metal Experience, Oakland Mus, Calif, 71; Art Inst Centennial, M H DeYoung Mem Mus, San Francisco, Calif, 71; Collage and Assemblage, traveling USA, 81-84; Second Ann Wild West Show, Calgary, Alberta, Can, 83; Trompe L'oeuil and Illusion, Boise Art Gallery, Idaho & touring, 83-85; Sculpture on The Wall, San Antonio Inst Art, Tex, 83; one-man show, Allen Stone Gallery, New York, 84. *Collections Arranged:* Soul Series--Harold Paris, Dartmouth Col, 72; Drawings from New England Private Collections, Dartmouth Col, 73; Art of Caneroons, Dartmouth Col, 73; Wood Works (auth, catalog), touring exhib, 73-74. *Teaching:* Asst prof sculpture, Univ Ky, Lexington, 79-80; vis lectr sculpture & art hist, Univ Calif, Santa Barbara, 81-; asst prof, Univ Houston, 82-. *Awards:* The Eisner Prize, Univ Calif, Berkeley, 72; Wyo Council Arts Fel, State Wyo, 78; Nat Endowment Arts Fel, 79. *Bibliog:* John R Lane (auth), article, Arts, 6/80; Charles Stuckey (contrib auth), article, Art In Am, 9/80; Harold Oleijarz (auth), article, Arts, 9/80. *Mem:* Col Art Asn; Brooklyn Waterfront Artist Asn; Santa Barbara Arts Forum. *Media:* Wood. *Dealer:* Allan Stone Gallery New York NY. *Mailing Add:* 4402 Lillian Houston TX 77007

BOURGEOIS, LOUISE
SCULPTOR
b Paris, France, Dec 25, 11; US citizen. *Study:* Lycee Fenelon, Paris, Baccalaureate, 32; Sorbonne, 32-35; Ecole du Louvre, 36-37; Acad Beaux-Arts, 36-38; Acad Grande Chaumiere, 37-38; Atelier Fernand Leger, 38. *Work:* Mus Mod Art, Whitney Mus Am Art, New York; NY Univ; Mus RI Sch Design, Providence; Harvard Univ, Cambridge, Mass. *Exhib:* The New American Painting & Sculpture, The First Generation, Mus Mod Art, 69; Whitney Biennial, 73; one-man exhibs, Hamilton Gallery Contemp Art, New York, 78; Xavier Fourcade Inc, New York, 78-79 & Univ Calif, 79; Perspective 78, Albright Col, 78; Hidden Desires, State Univ NY, Purchase, 80; and others. *Teaching:* Instr sculpture, Pratt Inst, 64-65; instr sculpture, Brooklyn Col, 63 & 68; field fac sculpture, Goddard Col, 71; instr, Cooper Union, New York, 78-79. *Awards:* Hon DFA, Yale Univ, 77; Outstanding Achievement in Arts Award, Women's Caucus, 80. *Bibliog:* Daniel Robbins (auth), Sculpture by Louise Bourgeois, Art Int, 10/64; William Rubin (auth), Some reflections on the work of Louise Bourgeois, 4/69; J P Marandel (auth), Louise Bourgeois, 71. *Mem:* Am Abstract Artists. *Media:* Mixed. *Mailing Add:* c/o Robert Miller Gallery 724 Fifth Ave New York NY 10019

BOUTIS, TOM
PAINTER, COLLAGE ARTIST
b New York, NY, Aug 25, 22. *Study:* Cooper Union, New York, BFA, 48; Skowhegan Sch Painting & Sculpture, summer 51; Cooper Union, hon BS. *Work:* Art Inst Chicago; Cibi-Geigy Collection, Ardsley, NY; Canton Art Inst, Ohio; Colby Col. *Comn:* Drawings, New York Hilton Collection Am Art, 62. *Exhib:* One-man shows, Landmark Gallery, New York, 73, 75 & 77; Drawings Exhib, Uffizzi Mus, Florence, Italy, 57; Selected Painters of Soho, Lehigh Univ Mus, 74; Cibi-Geigy Collection, Summit Art Mus, NJ, 74; and others. *Teaching:* Artist in residence painting, Summer Art Prog, Cooper Union, 69. *Awards:* Mark Rothko Found, 76; Nat Endowment for the Arts, 76; Adolphe Esther Cuttleib Found Grant, 83. *Media:* Monoprints, Oils; Collage. *Dealer:* Landmark Gallery 469 Broome New York NY 10013. *Mailing Add:* 162 E 82nd St New York NY 10028

BOVA, JOE
SCULPTOR, CERAMIST
b Houston, Tex, June 1, 41. *Study:* Univ Houston, BFA, 67; Univ NMex, MA, 69. *Work:* Greenville Co Mus, SC; State of Tenn, Tenn Art Comn, Nashville; State of La, Old State Capitol Galleries, Baton Rouge; Miami Univ Gallerie, Oxford, Ohio; McAllen Mus, Tex. *Exhib:* Young Americans, 69 & The Great American Foot, 78, Mus of Contemp Crafts, New York; 7th-10th Ann Piedmont Crafts, Mint Mus, Charlotte, NC, 69-72; 12th Midwest Biennial, Joslyn Mus of Art, Omaha, 71; Artists of the Southeast & Tex, New Orleans Mus of Art, 72; 35 Artists of the Southeast, High Mus of Art, Atlanta, 77; Objects of Play, Pa State Univ, 78; 36th Ann Scripps Invitational, Claremont, Calif, 80. *Teaching:* Asst prof design & ceramics, Nicholls State Univ, Thibodaux, 69-71; assoc prof ceramics & sculpture, La State Univ, Baton Rouge, 71; instr ceramics, Penland Sch of Crafts, 74 & 77. *Bibliog:* Jacob Eleasari (auth), Clay artists, Eleasari & Hahn Films, Nashville, 75; Paul Donhauser (auth), History of American Ceramics, Kendall/Hunt, Dubuque, Iowa, 78. *Mem:* Am Crafts Coun; Nat Coun Educ Ceramic Arts; La Crafts Coun. *Dealer:* Bienville Gallery 1800 Hastings Pl New Orleans LA 70130. *Mailing Add:* 644 Camelia Baton Rouge LA 70806

BOVE, RICHARD
PAINTER, EDUCATOR
b Brooklyn, NY, Oct 21, 20. *Study:* Pratt Inst, BFA; Art Students League; Brera Acad, Milan, Italy. *Exhib:* Am Acad Design, New York; Philadelphia Mus Art; Corcoran Gallery Art, Washington, DC; Whitney Mus Art & Metrop Mus Art, New York. *Teaching:* Instr painting, Art Students League, 55-65; chmn dept painting, Pratt Inst, 70-74, prof painting, Grad Sch, 73- *Awards:* Nat Acad Design Award; Louis Comfort Tiffany Found Award; Fulbright Fel, Italy. *Media:* Concrete, Plastics. *Mailing Add:* 180 Emerson Pl Brooklyn NY 11205

BOWATER, MARIAN
DEALER, COLLECTOR
b Emmons, Minn, Sept 5, 24. *Study:* Gustavous Adolphus Col. *Pos:* Owner, Bowater Gallery. *Mem:* Art Dealers Asn of Southern Calif. *Specialty:* Late 19th & 20th century American paintings. *Collection:* American impressionists and English Old Masters. *Mailing Add:* 12300 Kenny Dr Granada Hills CA 91344

BOWER, GARY DAVID
PAINTER
b Dayton, Ohio, May 10, 40. *Study:* Ohio State Univ, BA(philos), 62 & MFA(painting), 65. *Work:* Whitney Mus Am Art, New York; Allen Art Mus, Oberlin, Ohio; Akron Art Inst; Dayton Art Inst; Walker Art Ctr, Minneapolis. *Exhib:* Four Painters, Leo Castelli Warehouse Gallery, New York, 69; Whitney Mus Ann, 70; one-man shows, O K Harris Gallery, New York, 69 & 72, Univ Ky, 71, Akron Art Inst, 72 & Edward Thorp Gallery, New York, 84. *Teaching:* Staff critic painting, Dept Educ, Whitney Mus Am Art, 68-74. *Awards:* James Broadus Award, Chicago Art Inst, 67; Achievement in Painting, Ohio State Fair, 70. *Bibliog:* Carter Ratcliff (auth), Gary Bower at the New Gallery, Art Am, 5-6/78; Robert Berlind (auth), Gary Bower at Max Protech, Art Am, 1/81; Michael Klein (auth), Gary Bower, Arts, 5/82; and others. *Media:* Oil & Acrylic on Canvas. *Mailing Add:* c/o Edward Thorp Gallery 103-105 Prince St Charlotteville NY 12036

BOWERS, CHERYL OLSEN
PAINTER, EDUCATOR
b Berkeley, Calif, Sept 11, 38. *Study:* San Francisco Art Inst, MFA(with honors); Univ Calif, Berkeley with Fred Martin, Bob Hudson, Harold Paris & Peter Plagens. *Work:* Univ Mus, Univ Calif, Berkeley; Arts Coun Gt Brit; Oakland Mus; San Francisco Mus Mod Art; Metrop Mus Art, New York. *Exhib:* Nat Drawing Exhib, Potsdam, NY, 73; Davidson Nat Print & Drawing, NC, 73; Women From Permanent Collection, Univ Mus, Berkeley, 73; Biennial, Whitney Mus Am Art, New York, 75; San Francisco Mus Art, 75; 18 Bay Area Artists, Los Angeles Inst Contemp Art, 76; New Work, Oakland Mus, 76; Hamilton Gallery Contemp Art, New York, 79; Ruth Schaffner Gallery, Los Angeles, 79; Ian Birksted, London; Fresh Paint--15 Calif Artists (auth, catalog), San Francisco Mus Mod Art, 82. *Teaching:* Lectr painting, Calif State Univ, Hayward, 75; vis lectr painting, Univ Calif, Berkeley, 75-79; assoc prof painting & drawing, Univ Calif, Santa Barbara, 79- *Awards:* Tamarind Lithographic Inst Fel, 72; SECA Award, Soc Creative Arts, San Francisco, 75; Louis Comfort Tiffany Award, 80. *Bibliog:* Mary Stofflet (auth), Three Bay Area Artists, UC Riverside; Charles Shere (auth), Cheryl Bowers (catalog), Kirk deGooyer Gallery, 83; Alfred Jan (auth), Images/Issues, 11-12/83. *Mem:* Santa Barbara Contemporary Art Forum, New Mus, New York. *Media:* Oil, Watercolor; Lithography, Etching. *Dealer:* Ivory Kimpton San Francisco CA; Kirk de Gooyer Los Angeles CA. *Mailing Add:* 1710 Calle Cerro Santa Barbara CA 93101

BOWES, BETTY MILLER
PAINTER, CONSULTANT
b Philadelphia, Pa. *Study:* Moore Col Art; Univ Pa; George W Elkins Europ Fel. *Work:* Philadelphia Mus Art, Pa Acad Fine Arts, Philadelphia; Reading Mus, Pa; Nat Acad Design, New York; Univ Southern Calif, Los Angeles. *Comn:* Maquette for tapestry, Sun Oil Co Inc, Radnor, Pa, 76 & comn by Mr & Mrs Harvey Stack, New York, 78. *Exhib:* Am Watercolor Soc, Nat Acad, New York, 58-79; Philadelphia Art Festival, Philadelphia Mus, 65; one-man shows, Reading Mus, Pa, 69 & Lehigh Mem Gallery, Bethlehem, 70; Nat Acad Art, New York, 70-; Del Mus Ann, Wilmington Soc Fine Arts, 71; Pa Acad Fine Arts Ann, Philadelphia. *Pos:* Art consult, Sun Oil Co Inc, Radnor, 75- *Awards:* Bronze Medal, 75 & 77 & Silver Medal, 79, Am Watercolor Soc. *Bibliog:* Norman Kent (auth), 100 Watercolor Techniques, 68, Wendon Blake (auth), Complete Guide to Acrylic Painting, 71 & Edward Betts (auth), Creative Landscape Painting, 78, Watson-Guptill. *Mem:* Am Watercolor Soc; Nat Acad Design; Philadelphia Art Alliance; Philadelphia Watercolor Club; Audubon Artists. *Media:* Acrylic. *Mailing Add:* 301 McClenaghan Mill Rd Wynnewood PA 19096

BOWIE, WILLIAM
SCULPTOR
b Youngstown, Ohio, Feb 15, 26. *Study:* Youngstown Univ; Bethany Col. *Work:* New York Bank Savings; Globe-Wernicke Showroom, New York; Hertz Skyctr Airport, Huntsville, Ala; Brown & Williamson Tobacco Corp, Louisville, Ky; Glass Container Div, Owens-Ill, Scarsdale, NY. *Comn:* Exec off, Am Brands, Inc, New York; Brooklyn Col Student Ctr; Honeywell, Inc, Framingham, Mass; Irving Trust Co, Caracas, Venezuela, Frankel Rare Book Room, Univ Houston Libr. *Exhib:* Meltzer Gallery; George Jensen's; Am House; Sculpture Exhib, Butler Inst Am Art, 65; For Your Home, Krannert Art Mus, Univ Ill; Symposium 66, Purdue Univ, 66; plus many others. *Pos:* Judge Sculpture Exhib, Butler Inst Am Art, 66. *Awards:* Purchase Award,

Sculpture Exhib, Butler Inst Am Art, 65; Good Design Award, Purdue Univ, 66; spec award outstanding merit in craftsmanship, Artist-Craftsmen New York. *Media:* Metal. *Mailing Add:* c/o Sculpture Studio Inc 441 Lafayette St at 8th St New York NY 10003

BOWLER, JOSEPH, JR
PAINTER, ILLUSTRATOR
b Forest Hills, NY, Sept 4, 28. *Study:* Charles E Cooper Studios, New York; Art Students League. *Work:* Sanford Low, Hartford Mus; Soc of Illusr; US Air Force. *Comn:* Portraits, Rose Kennedy, Rose Kennedy Wing, Albert Einstein Hosp, 71, Gen DeGaulle, Time cover, Julie & David Eisenhower, Sat Eve Post cover, Dr Peter LaMotte, Hilton Head Hosp, 75 & Mr & Mrs Frank E Fowler, Lookout Mountain, Tenn, 76 & 80. *Exhib:* Ann Exhib of Published Work for 1977, Soc Illusr, 78. *Teaching:* Instr painting, Parsons Sch Design, New York, 68-72; instr, MFA Independent Study Degree Prog, Syracuse Univ, 80-83. *Awards:* Artist of Yr, Artists' Guild New York, 67. *Bibliog:* Cory SerVaas (auth), Artist in the White House, Saturday Evening Post, summer 72; Joe Bowler--Artist Illustrator (film), SCETV; Artist Joe Bowler, Southern Accents, winter 82. *Mem:* Soc Illusr. *Media:* Oil. *Dealer:* Marilyn C Bowler 9 Baynard Cove Rd Hilton Head Island SC 29928. *Mailing Add:* 9 Baynard Cove Rd Hilton Head Island SC 29928

BOWLES, MARIANNE VON RECKLINGHAUSEN
PAINTER, SCULPTOR
b Munich, Ger, Jan 24, 29; US citizen. *Study:* Self taught. *Exhib:* One-woman shows, Hudson River Mus, Yonkers, NY, 63 & 84 & Katonah Gallery, NY, 82; 19th Area Exhib, Corcoran Gallery Art, Washington, DC, 74; The Animal Image, Renwick Gallery, Smithsonian Inst, Washington, DC, 81; Assemblage & Collage Traveling Exhib, Miss Mus Art, Jackson, 81-83; Germans in New England, Goethe House, Boston, 83; Catholic Univ Art Gallery, Washington, DC, 83. *Teaching:* Lectr, Kayonas Gallery, 82, Univ Lowell, Mass, 83. *Awards:* Painting Award, 16th Ann New England Exhib, Charles of the Ritz Found, New York, 65; Award, Ann Show, Westchester Art Soc, 65 & 66. *Bibliog:* Stephanie Brush (auth), Inner vision, VIVA Int Mag, 3/78; Vivien Raynor (auth), Portrait of artists as their models, New York Times, 12/14/80; Jo Ann Lewis (auth), Expressly German: Bowles' constructions at CU, Washington Post, 11/3/83. *Mem:* Artists Equity; Silvermine Guild. *Media:* Acrylic on Wood; Sequential Painted Contructions. *Mailing Add:* 5 Sage Ct White Plains NY 10605

BOWLING, FRANK
PAINTER
b Bartica, Guyana, Feb 29, 36; US & Guyanese citizen. *Study:* Slade Sch Fine Art, Univ London; ARCA. *Work:* Contemp Art Soc, Tate Gallery, London; NJ State Mus, Trenton; Mus Mod Art, Whitney Mus, New York; Mus Fine Arts, Boston; and others. *Exhib:* Whitney Ann, 69-72; Artist Immigrants to Am 1876-1976, Hirshhorn Mus, Washington, DC; solo exhibs, Whitney Mus Am Art, 71 & Tibor de Nagy Gallery, New York, 75, 76, 79, 80 & 82; Currier Gallery Art, Manchester, NH, 82; Art Ctr Hargate, St Pauls Sch, Concord, NH, 82; Heckscher Mus, Huntington, NY, 82; Kresge Art Ctr Gallery, Mich State Univ, 82. *Awards:* Guggenheim Fel, 67 & 73; Creative Artists Pub Serv Award, 75; Arts Coun Gt Brit Award, 77. *Media:* Acrylic, Oil. *Mailing Add:* c/o Tibor de Nagy Gallery 29 W 57th St New York NY 10019

BOWLT, JOHN
HISTORIAN, EDUCATOR
b London, Eng, Dec 6, 43. *Study:* Univ Birmingham, Eng, BA, 65 & MA, 66; Moscow Univ, USSR, 66-68; Univ St Andrews, Scotland, PhD, 71. *Pos:* Dir, Inst of Modern Russian Cult, 79- *Teaching:* Lectr Russian, Univ St Andrews, Scotland, 68-69; asst prof Russian, Univ Kans, Lawrence, 70-71; prof Russian art & lang, Univ Tex, Austin, 71- *Awards:* Brit Coun Scholar for Moscow Univ, USSR, 66-68; Woodrow Wilson Nat Fel, 71; Fel Nat Humanities Inst, Yale Univ, 77-78; Fulbright-Hays Award to France, 81. *Mem:* Am Asn Advan Slavic Studies. *Res:* Russian art and architecture of 18th, 19th and 20th centuries. *Publ:* Auth, The Russian Avant-garde, Theory & Criticism 1902-34, Viking, 76; translr, Benedikt Livshits: The One-and a Half-Eyed Archer, 77; auth, The Silver Age, 79; auth, Scenic Innovation-Russian Stage Design 1900-1930, 82; coauth, Pvel Filonov: A Hero and His Fate, 83. *Mailing Add:* Dept of Slavic Lang Univ Tex Box 7217 Austin TX 78712

BOWMAN, BRUCE
PAINTER, WRITER
b Dayton, Ohio, Nov 23, 38. *Study:* San Diego City Col, Calif, AA; Calif State Univ, Los Angeles, BA & MA; Univ Calif, Los Angeles. *Exhib:* Cypress Col, Calif, 77; Designs Recycled Gallery, Fullerton, Calif, 77; Pierce Col, Los Angeles, 78; Pepperdine Univ, Malibu, 78; Leopold/Gold Gallery, Santa Monica, 80-81. *Teaching:* Instr art, West Los Angeles Col, Culver City, 69-, chmn art dept, 75-76, 83; instr art, Cypress Col, 76-77. *Media:* Acrylic. *Res:* Contemporary art forms and techniques. *Publ:* Auth, articles in Arts & Activities Mag, Design Mag & Sch Arts Mag; auth, Shaped Canvas, 76 & Toothpick Sculpture & Ice Cream Stick Art, 76, Sterling. *Mailing Add:* 28322 Rey De Copas Malibu CA 90265

BOWMAN, DOROTHY (LOUISE)
PAINTER, PRINTMAKER
b Hollywood, Calif, Jan 20, 27. *Study:* Chouinard Art Inst, with Rico Lebrun & Jean Charlot; Jepson Art Inst, Los Angeles; Otis Co Art Inst, Los Angeles; Webster Col, St Louis, BA, 79. *Work:* Brooklyn Mus; Mus Mod Art; Libr Cong; Los Angeles Co Mus Art; De Cordova Mus. *Comn:* Ed serigraphs, Int Graphics Art Soc, New York, 58-69; Hilton Hotel, New York, 62. *Exhib:*

Brooklyn Mus Nat Print Show, 54-62; Boston Mus Print Ann, 60; Mus Arte Mod, Sao Paulo, Brasil, 61; 50 American Printmakers, Am Fedn Arts Traveling Show, Japan & Moscow, 64; Manila Hilton Art Ctr, Philippines, 71. *Teaching:* Pvt instr, 83- *Awards:* Many awards, Brooklyn Mus Print Shows, Libr Cong Nat Print Shows & Boston Mus Shows, 54-71. *Bibliog:* Enciclopedia internazionale degli artisti, 70; Bruce Cody (auth), Modern American Printmaking. *Mem:* Western Serigraphic Soc. *Dealer:* Oscar Salzer PO Box 36523 Los Angeles CA 90036. *Mailing Add:* Star Route 1 Ste Genevieve MO 63670

BOWMAN, JEFF RAY
EDUCATOR, ADMINISTRATOR
b Oneida, Ky, Sept 5, 43. *Study:* Eastern Ky Univ, AB, 65; Ball State Univ, MA, 69, EdD(art, admin, coun psychol), 71; Yale Univ, 77. *Teaching:* Art instr, Jackson Co Sch Syst, McKee, Ky, 65-66; asst & doctoral fel, Dept Art & Teachers Col, Ball State Univ, 68-71; prog chmn art educ, Univ Houston, 71-74; guest lectr, Art & Pub Sch Groups, Tex & Miss, 73-75; prof art, Univ Southern Miss, 74-, chmn dept, 74-82. *Awards:* Nat Endowment for Humanities Award, 77. *Mem:* Nat Art Educ Asn; Ky Guild Artists & Craftsmen; Hattiesburg Civic Asn; Tex Art Educ Asn; Miss Alliance for Arts Educ. *Publ:* Coauth, Parochial Education Within the Diocese of Fort Wayne-South Bend, Ind, Phase I, Educ Serv Assocs, Muncie, 70; auth, Meeting the needs, Art Teacher, fall 74; auth, The spirit of the mountains, Southern Quart, 1/78; plus many others. *Mailing Add:* 312 Third Ave Hattiesburg MS 39401

BOWMAN, KEN
PAINTER
b Denver, Colo, Mar 28, 37. *Study:* Univ Colo; Art Inst Chicago, BFA, 63. *Work:* Utah Mus Fine Arts, Salt Lake City; Univ Art Mus, Berkeley, Calif; Denver Art Mus. *Exhib:* One-man exhibs, Tibor de Nagy Gallery, Inc, New York, 70-71, 73 & 79; Art on Paper, Weatherspoon Gallery, Univ NC, 71; 3rd Biennial Art, Medellin, Colombia, SAm, 72; Painting and Sculpture Today 1972, Indianapolis Mus Art, Ind, 72; 100 Artists 100 Yrs, Art Inst Chicago, 80. *Teaching:* Instr painting, Black Hawk Sch Art, Colo, summers. *Media:* Acrylic Polymer, Collage. *Mailing Add:* 3115 W 25th Ave Denver CO 80211

BOWMAN, RICHARD
PAINTER
b Rockford, Ill, Mar 15, 18. *Study:* Art Inst Chicago, Ryerson Traveling Fel, 38-42; Univ Iowa, MFA, 49. *Work:* San Francisco Mus Art; Oakland Mus; Stanford Univ; Univ Tex Mus; Santa Barbara Art Mus; Recent Acquisitions, Mus Am Art, New Britain, Conn; plus others. *Exhib:* Retrospectives, Stanford Univ, 56 & San Francisco Mus Art, 61 & 72; Carnegie Int, 61 & 64; Whitney Mus Am Art, 62; solo exhib, San Francisco Mus Art, 70; Roswell Mus & Art Ctr, NMex, 72; Gerard Schriener Gallery, Basel, Switz, 79; and others. *Awards:* Prizes, Montreal, 52 & Winnipeg Art Gallery, 53; Artist in Residence Grant Painting, Roswell Mus & Art Ctr, 72; plus others. *Mailing Add:* 178 Springdale Way Redwood City CA 94062

BOWMAN, RUTH
CRITIC, MUSEOLOGIST
b Denver, Colo, June 14, 23. *Study:* Bryn Mawr Col, AB, 44; NY Univ Inst Fine Arts, MA, 71; Rockefeller Found Sr Fel, Metrop Mus Art, 76. *Collections Arranged:* The New York Painter, A Century of Teaching: From Morse to Hofmann, Marlborough-Gerson Gallery, 67; A University Collects (tour with Am Fedn Arts), 65-68; Twentieth Century Painting and Sculpture from the NY Univ Art Collection, Hudson River Mus, 71; Murals Without Wall (auth, catalog), Newark Airport Murals of Arshile Gorky, Newark Mus, 78-79; Am Fedn Arts tour six mus, 79-80. *Pos:* Asst cur, Jewish Mus, 62-63; cur & dir, NY Univ Art Collection, 63-74; dir educ, Los Angeles Co Mus Art, 74-75; consult, Metrop Mus Art, 77; mus educ consult, Nat Mus Can, 79 & Univ Mid-Am, Lincoln, Neb, 79-82; art commentator, KUSC/fm, Los Angeles, 79- *Teaching:* Adj asst prof art hist, Sch Continuing Educ, NY Univ, 65-70 & Sch Educ, 72-73; lectr art, Washington Sq Col, 72-73 (Sunrise Semester-CBS); mus training, art hist courses, lectrs radio & TV, New York & Los Angeles. *Awards:* Nat Endowment for Arts Grant, 75; Nat Endowment for Humanities, 78-80. *Mem:* Am Asn Mus (vpres, 76-79); Am Fedn Arts (mem exhib comt, 70-); Col Art Asn; Coun for Arts at Mass Inst Technol; Craft & Folk Art Mus, Los Angeles (vpres, 75-). *Res:* 19th and 20th century American and European art and architecture. *Publ:* Auth, catalog introd, Thirtieth anniversary exhibition, American Abstract Artists, 66; auth, Double exposure (catalog), Am Fedn Arts, 69; auth, Nature, the photograph and Thomas Anshutz, Col Art Asn J, fall 73; auth, The artist as model: portrait of David Wilson Jordan by Thomas Anshutz, Univ Kans Register, fall 73. *Mailing Add:* 1008 Amalfi Dr Pacific Palisades CA 90272

BOWNE, JAMES DEHART
MUSEUM DIRECTOR, HISTORIAN
b Philadelphia, Pa, Mar 5, 40. *Study:* George Washington Univ; Corcoran Sch Art; Sandhills Community Col, Southern Pines, NC, AA, 68; ECarolina Univ, Greenville, NC, AB, 70; Univ NC, Chapel Hill, MA, 72. *Collections Arranged:* Reflections of Our Heritage--The Art of the American Indian, 76, 20th Century German Expressionist Prints, 76, Collectors Choice Exhibition, 76 & Annual Wabash Valley Exhib, 77, Sheldon Swope Art Gallery, Terre Haute, Ind; and many others. *Pos:* Dir & cur, Lauren Rogers Libr & Mus Art, 73-75; dir, Sheldon Swope Art Gallery, 75-78; dir, Everhart Mus, 78-81; exec dir, Greenville Co Mus Art, 81- *Teaching:* Instr drawing/painting, Lauren Rogers Libr & Mus of Art, Laurel, Miss, 73-75. *Mem:* Am Asn Mus; Col Art Asn; Assoc Coun Arts; Southeast Mus Conf; SC Fedn Mus; and others. *Res:* Reception of German expressionism in America between the World Wars. *Publ:* Contribr, A Medieval Treasury From Southeastern Collections, Univ NC, Chapel Hill, 71. *Mailing Add:* c/o Greenville Co Mus Art 420 College St Greenville SC 29601

BOWRON, EDGAR PETERS
MUSEUM DIRECTOR
b Birmingham, Ala, May 27, 43. *Study:* Colgate Univ, AB, 65; Inst Fine Arts, NY Univ, AM, 69, PhD, 79; Metrop Mus Art, cert(mus training; Ford Found Fel), 69. *Collections Arranged:* Art in 18th Century Rome, 71 & cur in charge, J Paul Getty Collection Exhib (with catalog), 72, Minneapolis Inst Arts, Minn; Masters of Italian Painting 76 & Renaissance Bronzes in the Walters Art Gallery, 78, Baltimore, Md. *Pos:* Educ lectr, Metrop Mus Art, 69-70; registr, Minneapolis Inst Arts, 70-73; cur Renaissance & baroque art, Walters Art Gallery, 73-78; cur Renaissance & baroque art & admin asst to dir, Nelson Gallery-Atkins Mus, 78-81; dir, NC Mus Art, 81- *Awards:* Nat Endowment Arts Fel, 75-76; Am Acad Rome Fel Grant, 79-; and others. *Mem:* Col Art Asn Am; Am Eighteenth Century Soc. *Res:* Roman painting, 17th and 18th centuries. *Publ:* Articles in Minn Inst Arts Bulletin, Apollo & Mus News; ed, Anthony M Clark's Studies in 18th Century Roman Painting, 81; ed, Anthony M Clark's Catalogue raisonne of the paintings and drawing of Pompeo Batoni, 1708-1787, 83. *Mailing Add:* 525 Wade Ave Raleigh NC 27605

BOXER, STANLEY (ROBERT)
PAINTER, SCULPTOR
b New York, NY, June 26, 26. *Study:* Brooklyn Col; Art Student League. *Work:* Whitney Mus, Guggenheim Mus, Mus Mod Art, New York; Boston Mus Fine Arts; Corcoran Gallery Art. *Exhib:* One-man shows, Tibor de Nagy Gallery, New York, 71-75, 77, 80 & 82, Andre Emmerich Gallery, New York & Zurich, 75-, Pa Acad Fine Arts, Philadelphia, 76, Edmonton Art Gallery, Alberta, Can, 77, Mus Fine Arts, Boston, 77, Mint Mus Art, NC, 78, Thomas Segal Gallery, Boston, 78-82, Meredith Long & Co, Houston, 79- & Gallery One, Toronto, 80- *Awards:* John S Guggenheim Mem Found Fel, 75. *Bibliog:* Valentin Tatransky (auth), article, Arts Mag, 5/82; Grace Glueck (auth), article, New York Times, 6/4/82; Donald Kuspit (auth), article, Artforum Mag, 5/83. *Dealer:* Andre Emmerich Gallery Inc 41 E 57 St New York NY 10022. *Mailing Add:* 37 E 18th St New York NY 10002

BOYCE, GERALD G
EDUCATOR, PAINTER
b Embarrass, Wis, Dec 29, 25. *Study:* Wis State Col, BS; Milwaukee Art Inst; Am Guatemalan Inst, Guatemala City; Univ Iowa, MFA; Univ Ill; study & res, Brit Mus & Courtauld Inst, London, Worcester Col, Oxford Univ, Eng, 79. *Work:* Evansville Col; St John's Univ; Wabash Col; Minot Col; DePauw Univ. *Exhib:* Los Angeles Co Mus; San Francisco Mus Art; Art Inst Chicago, 54; Mus Mod Art, New York, 56; Corcoran Gallery Art, Washington, DC, 71; Mus Contemp Crafts, New York. *Pos:* Consult, Ind Bell Tel Co, 67-70; consult, US Post Off Dept, 72 & Smithsonian Inst. *Teaching:* Prof art hist & studio, Ind Cent Univ, 50-; lect art hist, DePauw Univ, 68- *Awards:* First Prizes, Ind Artists Club, St John's Univ Nat & Minot Col Show, 71. *Mem:* Nat Col Art Conf; Am Crafts Coun; Nat Conf Art Adminr. *Media:* Mixed Media. *Mailing Add:* RR1 Box 239A Morgantown IN 46160

BOYCE, WILLIAM G
MUSEUM DIRECTOR, EDUCATOR
b Fairmont, Minn, July 25, 21. *Study:* Univ Minn, Minneapolis, BS, 49, MEd, 52; Mills Col, 54-55. *Collections Arranged:* Cataloged the George P Tweed Memorial Art Collection; Dedicatory Exhibition Honoring Mrs Alice Tweed Tuohy; Tweed at Twenty Exhibition; A University Collects-Tweed Gallery Traveling Exhib; David Ericson Exhibition; and many others. *Pos:* Ed cur, Tweed Gallery, Univ Minn, Duluth, 57-65, assoc dir, 65-69, dir, Tweed Mus Art, Univ Minn, Duluth, 69- *Teaching:* Prof art, Univ Minn, Duluth, 70- *Mem:* Life mem Nat Educ Asn; Minn Art Educ Asn (pres, 63-65); Midwest Mus Conf (Minn vpres, 67-70); Am Asn Mus; Univ Ed Asn. *Publ:* Auth, David Erickson (monogr), Edgewater Press, 63; also many catalogs. *Mailing Add:* Tweed Mus Art Univ Minn Duluth MN 55802

BOYD, DONALD EDGAR
INTERMEDIA ARTIST, WRITER
b Sparta, Ohio, Feb 20, 34. *Study:* Ohio State Univ, BFA(cum laude), 56; Harvard Univ, with Mirko Basadella, MAT, 61; Univ Iowa, MFA, 66; with Elliot Offner & Robert Laurent; Hobart Welding Sch, with Richard Stankiewicz, 68; SC Educ TV, with Stan Vanderbeek & Jack Perlmutter, 74; also with Dick Higgins & Alison Knowles, 76. *Work:* Dayton Art Inst, Ohio. *Exhib:* Blossom Music Ctr Sculpture, Kent, Ohio, 71 & 73; Spring Mills Traveling Show, 74; SDak Biennial, 75; Venice Biennale, 76; Young Fluxus, Artist's Space, New York, 82; thirteen one-person shows. *Pos:* Dir, Community Cult Ctr, Brookings, SDak, 79-81. *Teaching:* Asst prof sculpture & drawing, Kenyon Col, 66-72; artist-in-residence, SC Arts Comn, 73-74; asst prof sculpture & design, SDak State Univ, 74-78, assoc prof, 79- *Awards:* Purchase Prize for sculpture, Dayton Art Inst, 69; Biddle Award, Mansfield, Ohio Art Ctr, 69; Purchase Prize Sculpture, Mem Art Ctr, SDak, 83. *Bibliog:* Ken Friedman (auth), Parallels between the lives and work of Joseph Beuys and Don Boyd, Nat Arts Guide, 3-4/80. *Mem:* Fluxus West (dir). *Media:* Intermedia Leather; Found Objects. *Publ:* Eclat, int art quart, 68-72; producer, Electronic Gallery, SC Educ TV & Nat Endowment for the Arts, 75; auth, 50 Characteristics of Fluxus, 76. *Mailing Add:* 723 Seventh Ave Brookings SD 57006

BOYD, JAMES HENDERSON
PRINTMAKER, SCULPTOR
b Ottawa, Ont, Dec 16, 28. *Study:* Art Students League, with Will Barnet; Nat Acad Design; Contemporaries Graphic Workshop, with M Ponce de Leon. *Work:* Nat Gallery Can, Ottawa; Mus Mod Art, New York; Victoria & Albert

Mus, London; Lugano Art Mus; Sorsbie Art Gallery, Nairobi, SAfrica. *Comn:* Carved doors, Centennial Libr, Campbellton, NB, 67 & 72; carved doors, Pub Serv Alliance Bldg, Ottawa, 69; entrance sculpture, Can Pavilion, Osaka World's Fair, 70; mural, MacDonald Bldg, Univ Ottawa, 73. *Exhib:* Cincinnati Biennial Prints, 62; 1st Biennial Prints, Santiago, Chile, 63; 8th Int Black & White Exhib, 64; Tokyo Biennial Prints, 64; Centennial Art Exhib, Toronto, 67. *Pos:* Hon cur, Univ Western Ont, 67-69; adv, Visual Arts Ottawa, 74- *Teaching:* Resident artist, Univ Western Ont, 67-69; prof printmaking, Ont Col Art, 71-, head dept, 70-71; prof painting, Munic Art Ctr, Ottawa, 70-72; prof visual arts dept, Univ Ottawa, 73- *Awards:* Purchase Award, 8th Int Black & White Exhib, 64; First Prize, 1st Nat Print Exhib, Burnaby, BC; Venezuela Prize, Best Foreign Artist, 2nd Biennial Prints, Santiago, Chile, 65. *Mem:* Fel & life mem Int Inst Arts & Lett; Can Graphic Art Soc. *Dealer:* Isaacs Gallery 832 Yonge St Toronto ON Can M4W 2H1. *Mailing Add:* PO Box 2400 Sta D Ottawa ON K1P 5W5 Canada

BOYD, JOHN DAVID
EDUCATOR, PRINTMAKER
b London, Ark, Jan 22, 39. *Study:* Calif State Univ, Long Beach, with Richard Swift, BA; Cranbrook Acad Art, with Lawrence Barker, MFA. *Work:* Tex Tech Univ; Ga State Univ; Univ NC, Chapel Hill; State Univ NY Col Potsdam; Springfield Art Mus, Mo. *Exhib:* 12th & 13th Ann Nat Print Exhib, Silvermine Guild, New Canaan, Conn, 78 & 80; 19th, 21st & 23rd Ann Nat Exhib Prints & Drawings, Okla Art Ctr, Oklahoma City, 77, 79 & 81; 2nd Nat Print Competition, Edinboro State Col, Pa, 81; Nat Print & Drawing Exhib, Northern Ill Univ, Dekalb, 81; Works on Paper, nat exhib, Visual Arts Ctr Alaska, Anchorage, 81; and many others. *Teaching:* Assoc prof printmaking & drawing, Wichita State Univ, 72- *Media:* Intaglio, Lithography. *Mailing Add:* 421 S Glenn Wichita KS 67213

BOYD, KAREN WHITE
EDUCATOR, FIBER ARTIST
b Akron, Ohio, Sept 8, 36. *Study:* Kent State Univ, BA(art educ), 58 & MA(studio art), 64; Tyler Sch Art, Temple Univ, MFA(weaving), 75. *Exhib:* Regional Craft Biennial, J B Speed Mus, Louisville, Ky, 70; Mid-States Craft Exhib, Evansville Mus, Ind, 73; Nat Fiber Design Show, Calif Polytech State Univ, San Luis Obispo, 75; 3rd Int Exhib Miniature Textiles, Brit Crafts Centre, London, 78. *Teaching:* Assoc prof weaving & textiles, Murray State Univ, 67-81, prof, 81- *Awards:* Juror's Award, Ted Hallman, Nat Fiber Design Show, 75; Honorable Mention, Southeast 80 Craft Exhib, Tallahassee, Fla. *Mem:* Ky Guild Artists & Craftsmen; Handweaver's Guild Am; Asn British Craftsmen. *Dealer:* Am Art Inc Atlanta GA. *Mailing Add:* 211 S 16th St Murray KY 42071

BOYD, LAKIN
EDUCATOR, PRINTMAKER
b Athens, Ala, Aug 27, 46. *Study:* Univ Ala, BFA, 68 & MA, 70; Pratt Graphic Ctr, 70-71, intaglio with Michael Ponce de Leon. *Work:* Oscar Wells Mem Mus, Birmingham, Ala; Univ Ala, Tuscaloosa; Ala Arts Comn; Univ South; Pratt Graphic Ctr Print Collection, New York. *Exhib:* Nat Student Printmakers Travel Exhib, 68; 13th Dixie Ann, 72; one-man shows, Univ Ala & Judson Col, 73; 14th Ann Reece Regional, 74. *Teaching:* Asst prof graphics & art inst, Ala A&M Univ, Huntsville, 71-82. *Awards:* Purchase Award, Birmingham Art Asn, 67; Fulbright Grant to Belg & Neth, 75. *Mem:* Southeastern Col Art Conf; Am Asn Univ Prof; Nat Art Educ Asn; Am Crafts Coun; Ala Art Educ Asn. *Media:* Intaglio, Lithography. *Mailing Add:* 426 Eustis Ave SE Huntsville AL 35801

BOYD, MICHAEL
PAINTER, GRAPHIC ARTIST
b Waterloo, Iowa, Nov 27, 36. *Study:* With Philip Evergood, 57; Univ Northern Iowa, BA, 59. *Work:* Baltimore Mus Art; Santa Barbara Mus Art; Phoenix Art Mus; Chrysler Mus Art, Norfolk, Va; Newark Mus, NJ. *Comn:* Mural, E F MacDonald Co, Dayton, 82. *Exhib:* Munson-Williams-Proctor Inst, Utica, NY, 70; Collection in Progress, Moore Col Art, 77; NY State Artists Ser, Johnson Mus Art, Cornell Univ, 77; Cornell Artists, Mem Art Gallery, Rochester, NY, 79; Art From New York, Mattingly-Baker Gallery, Dallas, 81; 101 Recent Acquisitions, Everson Mus Art, 81; Recent Acquisitions, Albright-Knox Art Gallery, 81; Recent Acquisitions, Baltimore Mus Art, 82. *Teaching:* Assoc prof design, Cornell Univ, 68- *Awards:* Purchase Award, Everson Mus Art, 71; Yaddo Fel, 74. *Bibliog:* Pat Sloan (auth), article, Arts Mag, 79; Valerie Natsios (auth), article, New York Arts J, 81; Barbara Flug Colin (auth), A profile, Art Now, 81. *Media:* Acrylic on Canvas and Paper. *Dealer:* Andre Zarre Gallery 41 E 57th St New York NY 10022. *Mailing Add:* 315 Pleasant St Ithaca NY 14850

BOYER, JACK K
MUSEUM DIRECTOR, CURATOR
b Van Houten, NMex, Sept 2, 11. *Pos:* Dir & cur, Kit Carson Home & Mus, Taos, NMex, 54- *Mem:* Am Asn Mus; Archaeol Soc NMex; NMex State Hist Soc; Clearing House Western Mus. *Mailing Add:* Kit Carson Mem Found Old Kit Carson Rd Taos NM 87571

BOYLAN, JOHN LEWIS
PAINTER, PRINTMAKER
b Cleveland, Ohio, Oct 8, 21. *Study:* Oberlin Col, 39-42; Cleveland Inst Art, 42; Univ NMex, BFA, 47; Art Students League, 47-50; study with Vaclav Vytlacil, Morris Kantor, Harry Sternberg & Will Barnet. *Work:* Metrop Mus Art, New York; New York Pub Libr; Roswell Mus, NMex; Univ Pa Art Mus. *Exhib:* Soc Am Graphic Artists, 50 & 71; Royal Soc Painter-Etchers & Engravers, London, 54 & 56; solo exhib, Roswell Mus, 59 & 66; Japan Print

Soc, Tokyo, 67. *Teaching:* Dir painting & design, Roswell Mus Art Sch, 50-51; instr painting & design, Inst Am Indian Art, Santa Fe, NMex, 66-, actg head fine arts, 74-75. *Awards:* Award of Merit, Am Asn State & Local Hist, 60. *Mem:* Soc Am Graphic Artists; Artists Co-op Gallery (co-dir, 75). *Media:* Oil, Acrylic; Woodcut, Metal Plate Lithograph. *Mailing Add:* 1218 Bishops Lodge Rd Santa Fe NM 87501

BOYLE, KEITH
PAINTER, EDUCATOR
b Defiance, Ohio, Feb 15, 30. *Study:* Ringling Sch Art, Sarasota, Fla; Univ Iowa, BFA. *Work:* San Francisco Mus Art & Stanford Univ Mus, Calif; Mead Paper Corp, Atlanta, Ga; Nat Fine Arts Collection, Washington, DC; Oakland Mus, Calif; Continental Bank, Chicago. *Exhib:* Current Bay Area Art, Stanford Univ Mus, 64; The Colorists, San Francisco Mus Art, 65; Drawings by 100 American Artists, Ann Arbor, Mich, 65; A Century of California Painting, 1870-1970, 70; Looking Westward, Joslyn Art Mus, Omaha, Nebr, 70; Retrospective Exhib of Paintings: 1965-1977, San Jose Mus Art, Calif, 78. *Teaching:* Prof painting & drawing, Stanford Univ, 62-, chmn grad studio prog, 83- *Awards:* National Endowment Arts Grant, 81-82. *Mailing Add:* 515 Newell Rd Palo Alto CA 94303

BOYLE, RICHARD J
HISTORIAN, WRITER
b New York, NY, June 3, 32. *Study:* Adelphi Univ, BA; Oxford Univ, with Edgar Wind & John Pope-Hennessy; Art Student League, with Will Barnet. *Collections Arranged:* John Twachtman Retrospective, 66, Laser Light: A New Visual Art, 69, The Early Work of Paul Gauguin, 71 & Robert S Duncanson: A Centennial Exhibition, 72, Cincinnati Art Mus; American Paintings from Newport, Wichita Art Mus, 69. *Pos:* Cur, Int Art Found, Newport, RI, summer 62; dir, Middletown Fine Arts Ctr, Ohio, 63-65; cur painting, Cincinnati Art Mus, 65-73; dir, Pa Acad Fine Arts, 73-82; art comn chmn, Redevelop Authority, Philadelphia. *Teaching:* Visiting scholar, Moore Col Art, Philadelphia, 83-84. *Awards:* Benjamin Franklin Fel, Royal Soc of Art, London, Eng. *Mem:* Nat Trust Hist Preservation. *Res:* Late nineteenth and twentieth century painting, especially late nineteenth century American painting. *Publ:* Co-auth, Rediscovery: Thomas Cole's voyage of life, Art in Am, 67; auth, From Hiram Powers to laser light, Apollo, 71; contribr, French impressionists influence American impressionists, Lowe Art Mus, Fla, 71; contribr, Genius of American painting, Weidenfeld & Nicolson, 73; John Twachtman, Watson-Guptill, 79. *Mailing Add:* 2121 Delancey Pl Philadelphia PA 19103

BOYLEN, MICHAEL EDWARD
CRAFTSMAN, WRITER
b Stoughton, Wis, Dec 12, 35. *Study:* Yale Univ, with Josef Albers, AB, 58; Sch Am Craftsmen, pottery with Frans Wildenhain; Univ Wis, with Harvey K Littleton, MS, MFA. *Work:* Corning Mus Glass, NY; Cleveland Mus Art, Ohio; Mus Kunst & Gewerbe, Hamburg, Ger; Victoria & Albert Mus, London; Chrysler Mus at Norfolk, Va. *Exhib:* New Am Glass, Dallas Mus Fine Arts, Tex, 67; Del Art Mus, Wilmington, 71 & 75; one-man shows, Fleming Mus, Univ Vt, Burlington, 75; Bergstrom Mus, Neenah, Wis, 76; Corning Mus Glass, NY; Mickelson Gallery, Washington, DC, 78; and others. *Teaching:* Instr ceramics, Cleveland Inst Art, Ohio, 66; lectr design & ceramics, Lyndon State Col, Lyndonville, Vt, 67-76; lectr ceramics, Marlboro Col, Vt, 80- *Awards:* L C Tiffany Found Grant, 65. *Bibliog:* Clemens Kalischer (auth), Glass--Michael Boylen, Vt Life Mag, 72; R & L Grover (auths), Contemporary Art Glass, Crown, 75; Paul Hollister (auth), Hollister on glass, Acquire, 12/76. *Mem:* Glass Art Soc; Vt Coun Arts (pres, 74-76). *Media:* Blown Glass; Clay. *Publ:* Auth, Studio glass in perspective, Studio Potter, 73 & In: 74 Crafts Annual, NY State Craftsmen, 74; auth, Glass of Joel Phillip Myers, Am Craft, 10-11/80; auth, Karen Karnes Workshop, Ceramics Monthly, 1/81. *Dealer:* Contemp Art Glass Group 806 Madison Ave New York NY 10021. *Mailing Add:* Marlboro Col Marlboro VT 05344

BOYNTON, JACK (JAMES) W
PAINTER, PRINTMAKER
b Ft Worth, Tex, Jan 12, 28. *Study:* Tex Christian Univ, BFA & MFA. *Work:* Mus Mod Art, Solomon R Guggenheim Mus & Whitney Mus, New York; Mus Fine Arts, Houston; Los Angeles Co Mus, Calif; and others. *Comn:* Go Freedom, 2nd Liberty Gala, Houston ACLU, Equal Justice, 6th Liberty Gala & Law and Order, 7th Liberty Gala, Tex; Amarillo Art Ctr; Houston Festival 79, City of Houston. *Exhib:* Whitney Mus Am Art, 57-58 & 67-68; Los Angeles Mus Art, 69; Collections of Mus of Southwest, Washington, DC, 78; Wood in Art, Mus Fine Arts, Houston, 79; one-man show, Univ Houston, Clear Lake City, Tex, 79; retrospective, Amarillo Art Ctr, 80; and others. *Teaching:* Instr, Univ NMex, summer 63; instr, Houston Mus Sch, 68-69; instr art, Mus Fine Arts, Houston, 68-69; instr art, Univ St Thomas, Houston, 69-; Univ St Thomas, Tex, 69-70. *Awards:* Tamarind Workshop Fel, 67. *Bibliog:* Douglas MacAgy (auth), James Boynton (monogr), Barone Gallery Inc, 59. *Media:* Mixed. *Mailing Add:* c/o Moody Gallery 2015-J W Gray Houston TX 77005

BOZ, ALEX (ALEX BOZICKOVIC)
PAINTER, LECTURER
b Sarajevo, Yugoslavia, July 8, 19; US citizen. *Study:* Univ Belgrade, BFA, 43; Belgrade Acad Fine Arts, 43-50; Belgrade, 48-50. *Work:* Contemp Mus Art, Rijeka, Yugoslavia; Contemp Mus Art, Novisad, Yugoslavia; City of Bremen, WGer; Bell Tel Co, Chicago; City Hosp, Bremen. *Comn:* Murals, Zopas Corp, Rome, Italy, 53 & City Planning Comn, Bremen, WGer, 55. *Exhib:* One-man shows, Los Angeles, Milwaukee, Chicago, New York, Toronto & Europe, 52-72; Kunsthall Exhib, Bremen, 55; Gallery Boheme, Copenhagen,

Denmark, 55; Old Orchard Festival, Chicago, 59-67; Art Inst Chicago, 60. *Teaching:* Prof art, Rijeka, Yugoslavia, 50-52; instr painting & printmaking, Americana Art Ctr, Northfield, Ill, 65-68. *Awards:* Awards from Gallery Boheme, Copenhagen, 55 & Old Orchard Festival, Chicago, 66. *Media:* Casein, Oil. *Mailing Add:* c/o Americana Galleries 271 Waukegan Rd Northfield IL 60093

BRACH, PAUL HENRY
PAINTER
b New York, NY, Mar 13, 24. *Study:* State Univ Iowa, BFA, 48, MFA, 49. *Work:* Mus Mod Art; Whitney Mus Am Art; St Louis Mus; Los Angeles Co Mus of Art, Los Angeles; Smith Col Mus; plus others. *Exhib:* Leo Castelli, NY, 57 & 59; Cordier, Ekstrom Gallery, NY, 62 & 64; Dwan Gallery, Los Angeles, 60; Yares Gallery, Scottsdale, Ariz, 80 & 81; Janus Gallery, Venice, Calif, 80; Bernice Steinbaum Gallery, New York, 83; and many others. *Pos:* Fel, Tamarind Lithog Workshop, Los Angeles, 64, Tamarina, NMex, 80; artist in residence, Am Fedn Arts, Albuquerque, 65. *Teaching:* Mem fac, Univ Mo, 49-51, New Sch Social Res, 52-55, NY Univ, 54-56, Parsons Sch Design, 56-67, Cooper Union, 60-62 & 78-80 & Cornell Univ, 65-67; prof art & chmn dept, Univ Calif, San Diego, 67-69; dean sch art, Calif Inst Art, 69-75; chmn div arts, Lincoln Ctr Campus, Fordham Univ, 75-79. *Publ:* Auth, John Mandel, Arts, 9/75; auth, rev in Artforum, 10/76 & Art in Am, 3-4/78. *Mailing Add:* 393 W Broadway New York NY 10012

BRADBURY, ELLEN A
CURATOR, ADMINISTRATOR
b Louisville, Ky, Feb 26, 40. *Study:* Yale Univ; Univ Vienna, Austria, 60; Univ NMex, BA & MA, 66. *Collections Arranged:* African Oceanic Art, American Indians, North and South; shows arranged: Black Kingdoms, Art of the Benin and Ashanti; catalogued: Meso American Collections, 20th century regional Am art, Collections Mus NMex. *Pos:* Res asst, Minneapolis Inst Art, 69-70, asst registrar, 70-72, registrar, 72-75 & cur primitive art, 75-79; dir, Mus Fine Arts, Mus NMex, 79; dir, Santa Fe Festival Arts, 82- *Mem:* Col Art Asn; Am Asn Mus; NMex Asn Mus. *Publ:* Co-auth, Moi Kavakava, Minneapolis Inst Arts Bull, LX:76-81; auth, Black Kingdoms, African Arts, 75; auth, I Wear the Morning Star (catalog), American Indian Ghost Dance, 79; auth, Art in Santa Fe and elsewhere, Artspace, fall, 83. *Mailing Add:* Santa Fe Festival of the Arts 227 E Palace Ave Santa Fe NM 87501

BRADFORD, HOWARD
PRINTMAKER, PAINTER
b Toronto, Ont, July 14, 19; US citizen. *Study:* Chouinard Art Inst, Los Angeles; Jepson Art Inst, Los Angeles; Calif Sch Fine Arts, San Francisco. *Work:* Philadelphia Mus Fine Arts; Boston Mus Fine Arts; Bibliotheque Nat France; Los Angeles Co Mus; New York Pub Libr. *Comn:* Print editions (100), Dallas Mus Fine Arts, 53, Hilton Hotel, New York, 64 & Assoc Am Artists, New York, 67-69; Brentanos: Print Editions 1977-78. *Exhib:* Libr Cong Nat Print & Drawing Exhib, 51; Brooklyn Mus Print Ann, 52; Dallas Mus Fine Arts Nat Print Exhib, 53; 60 American Printmakers, US Info Serv, Europe, 56; Carmel Art Asn, Calif, 72 & 76. *Awards:* Birds by Beach (serigraph), Libr Cong, 51 & Dallas Mus Fine Arts, 53; Guggenheim Fel Creative Printmaking, 60. *Mem:* Am Color Print Soc; Western Serigraph Inst, Los Angeles; Carmel Art Asn. *Media:* Silk Screen; Acrylic. *Dealer:* Oscar Salzer 448 N Detroit St Los Angeles CA 90036. *Mailing Add:* 684 Alice St Monterey CA 93940

BRADLEY, DAVID P(AUL)
PAINTER, SCULPTOR
b Eureka, Calif, Mar 8, 54. *Study:* Inst Am Indian Arts, AFA, 79; Col Santa Fe, BFA, 80. *Work:* Atlantic Richfield Corp, Tucson; Inst Am Indian Arts Mus, NMex Fine Arts Mus, Santa Fe; Albuquerque Mus; Ann Maytag Found, Tesuque, NMex. *Comn:* State Arch Bldg, Santa Fe, 80. *Exhib:* Univ Minn Mus, Minneapolis, 80; Heard Mus, Phoenix, 80; Nat Mus Inst Art Am Indians, Lima, Peru, 81; Univ Calif Mus, Davis, 81; Mus SW, Midland, Tex, 81; and others. *Pos:* Bd regents, Native Am Coun Regents Inst Am Indian Arts, Santa Fe, 78-79; guest artist, Artists in Schs Program, 81-82. *Awards:* Award Merit, Minn Chippewa Tribe, 79; Fel, Southwestern Asn Indian Affairs, 80; Artist of Yr, Santa Fean Mag, 82. *Bibliog:* Jim Lenfestey (auth), American Indian artists with roots in Minnesota, Minneapolis-St Paul Mag, 7/81; Don H Jones (auth), David Bradley, artist, 8/81 & Betty Bauer (auth), Artists of the year, 1/82, Santa Fean Mag. *Media:* Acrylic; Stone, Bronze. *Dealer:* Elaine Horwitch Galleries 129 West Palace Ave Santa Fe NM 87501. *Mailing Add:* PO Box 5692 Santa Fe NM 87502

BRADLEY, DOROTHY
DEALER, PAINTER
b Wild Rose, Wis, Oct 21, 20. *Study:* Milwaukee State Teachers Col; Oshkosh State Teachers Col, cert; Layton Art Sch, Milwaukee, with Gerrit Sinclair. *Work:* Milwaukee Pub Libr, Wis. *Exhib:* Wis Painters & Sculptors, Milwaukee, 65; one-woman shows, Rahr-West Mus, Manitowoc, Wis, 71, Allis Art Libr, Milwaukee, 71, Oshkosh Pub Mus, Wis, 72 & Wustum Mus, Racine, Wis, 72. *Pos:* Dir, Bradley Galleries, Milwaukee, 60- *Media:* Watercolor. *Specialty:* Wisconsin artists and art of Haiti. *Mailing Add:* c/o Bradley Galleries 2565 N Downer Ave Milwaukee WI 53211

BRADSHAW, DOVE
PAINTER, SCULPTOR
b New York, NY, Sept 24, 49. *Study:* Boston Mus Sch Fine Arts, BFA, 73. *Work:* Metrop Mus Art, New York; Philadelphia Mus Art; Brooklyn Mus Art; Muestra Int de Arte Grafico, Bilbao, Italy; Piccolo Mus Novoli, Italy. *Comn:* Break to Activate (wall piece), PS1, Inst Art & Urban Resources, New

York 77; Dazzle Camouflage Set Design, Time and Space Theatre, New York, 83. *Exhib:* Couples, 78 & Sound, 79, PS1, Inst Art & Urban Resources, New York; Arteder '82, Muestra Int de Arte Grafico, 82; Ann Awards Exhib, Am Acad Arts & Lett, New York, 82; Exhib in Honor of John Cage, Am Ctr Paris, France, 82. *Teaching:* Instr, Sch Visual Arts, 75-81. *Awards:* Sculpture Award, Nat Endowment Arts, 75. *Bibliog:* Stuart Little (auth), A piece of the Met, New York Mag, 79; Gene Moore (auth), Windows at Tiffany's: The Art of Gene Moore, Harry N Abrams, 80; Peter Frank (auth), New York reviews, Art News, 82. *Media:* All. *Mailing Add:* 640 Riverside Dr New York NY 10031

BRADSHAW, GLENN RAYMOND
PAINTER, EDUCATOR
b Peoria, Ill, Mar 3, 22. *Study:* Ill State Univ, BS, 47; Univ Ill, MFA, 50. *Work:* Butler Inst Am Art, Youngstown, Ohio; Springfield Art Mus, Mo; Lakeview Mus Arts & Sci, Peoria, Ill; El Paso Mus, Tex; San Diego Mus, Calif; and others. *Exhib:* 200 Years of Watercolor Painting in America, Metrop Mus Art, New York, 66-67; A View of Contemporary Watercolor, Cleveland Inst Art, Ohio, 68; Watermedia '70, Univ Colo, Boulder, 70; Watercolor USA Bicentennial, Springfield Art Mus, Mo, 76; Univ San Diego, 81; Univ Ill Fac Exhib, Nihon Univ, Tokyo, 83; and others. *Teaching:* Prof art, Univ Ill, 52- *Awards:* Ed Whitney Prize, Am Watercolor Soc, 74; First Prize, Nat Watercolor Soc, 77; Barse Miller Mem Prize, 83. *Bibliog:* Gerald Brommer (auth), The Art of Collage, Davis, 78; Edward Betts (auth), Creative Landscape Painting, Watson-Guptill, 78; Lawrence Goldsmith (auth), Watercolor Bold & Free, Watson-Guptill, 80; and others. *Mem:* Am Watercolor Soc; Nat Watercolor Soc; Nat Soc Painters in Casein & Acrylic; Rocky Mountain Nat Watermedia Soc. *Media:* Watercolor, Collage. *Dealer:* Neville-Sargent Gallery 509 Main St Evanston IL 60202. *Mailing Add:* 906 Sunnycrest St Urbana IL 61801

BRADSHAW, LAWRENCE JAMES
EDUCATOR, PAINTER
b St Paul, Kans, Sept 21, 45. *Study:* Pittsburg State Univ, Kans, BFA, with Reed Schmickle, Bert Keeney, Alex Barde, Robert Blunk, Robert Russell, MA; Ohio Univ, MFA with William Kortlander, Dana Loomis, Gary Pettigrew. *Work:* Sioux City Art Ctr, Iowa; Joslyn Art Mus, Omaha; Sheldon Art Mus, Univ Nebr, Lincoln; Bailey Lewis and Assocs, Lincoln, Nebr. *Comn:* Posters, Union Oil Co of Calif, Honolulu, Hawaii, 67; logo, Telesystems Inc, Omaha, 81; logo, Riverfront Forum, Assoc Artists Omaha, 77; logo, Metrop Arts Coun, Omaha, 76. *Exhib:* Appalachian Nat Traveling Exhib, NC Mus, 80-81; Two-Person Exhibition, Joslyn Art Mus, 81; Two-Person Exhibition, Esta Robinson Gallery, New York, 82; Invitational Group Exhibition, Sheldon Art Gallery, Lincoln, Nebr, 82; IV Permanent Exhibition, Museo Nazionale dell' Accademia Italia, Terme, Italy, 83; and many others. *Pos:* Production manager, Writers' Serv, Hollywood, 68-69; dir, Art Gallery, 74-76, Univ Nebr, Omaha. *Teaching:* Instr life-drawing, painting & silkscreen, Akron Art Inst, Ohio, summer 73; assoc prof drawing, design & painting, Univ Nebr at Omaha, 73- *Awards:* Best of Show, Col St Mary, Omaha, 78; Academic Italy with Gold Medal, Accademia Italia delle Arti e del Lavoro, Parma, 80. *Mem:* Visual Artists & Gallery Asn; Visual Individualists United, New York; Artists Equity. *Media:* Mixed. *Publ:* Auth, The Omaha Collectors Show, Abbatoir Press, 74; illusr, Painting with Acrylics, Van Nostrand-Reinhold, 74; illusr, Only You Can Unlock the Door, Am Cancer Soc, 75; illusr, Riverfront: The Humanist Speaks, Univ Nebr, 75; illusr, August Fires, Glover Davies, Abattoir Press, 78. *Mailing Add:* 5607 Howard Omaha NE 68106

BRADSHAW, ROBERT GEORGE
PAINTER, EDUCATOR
b Trenton, NJ, Mar 13, 15. *Study:* Princeton Univ, AB; Columbia Univ, MA. *Exhib:* NJ State Mus; Am Watercolor Soc; Boston Mus Fine Art; Cape Ann Soc Mod Art; New York World's Fair, 65; plus others. *Teaching:* Lectr art appreciation & hist; prof art, Douglass Col, Rutgers Univ, New Brunswick, 46-79, actg chmn dept art, 64-65, emer prof, 79- *Awards:* Prize, NJ Watercolor Soc, 59 & Montclair Art Mus, NJ, 63. *Mem:* NJ Watercolor Soc; Hunterdon Co Art Ctr. *Media:* Watercolor, Acrylic. *Mailing Add:* 48 Hilltop Blvd East Brunswick NJ 08816

BRADT, KETHLEEN WEIL-GARRIS
EDUCATOR, HISTORIAN
b Cheam, Surrey, Eng. *Study:* Vassar Col, AB, 56; Univ Bonn, 57; Harvard Univ, AM, 58, PhD, 65. *Pos:* Ed, Art Bull, 77-81; art historian in residence, Am Acad Rome, 75 & 81. *Teaching:* Prof Renaissance art, NY Univ, 65-, Harvard, 80-81. *Mem:* Col Art Asn. *Res:* Art of the 15th and 16th century in Italy. *Publ:* auth, Comments on the Medici Chapel Etc, Burlington Mag, 73; auth, Cloister, Court and City Square, Gesta, 74; auth, Leonardo and Central Italian Art, NY Univ Press, 74; auth, The Santa Casa di Loreto, Garland Press, 77; coauth (with j D'Amico), The Renaissance Cardinal's Ideal Palace, Elefante Press, Rome, 82. *Mailing Add:* One E 78th St New York NY 10021

BRADY, CHARLES MICHAEL
PAINTER
b New York, NY, July 27, 26. *Study:* Art Student League, 48-51, with John Groth & Morris Kantor. *Work:* Seven works in Irish Arts Coun Collection, Dublin; Northern Ireland Arts Coun; NW Trust; Northern Bank Finance Corp; Bank of Ireland Collection; and others. *Exhib:* Pa Acad Fine Arts, Philadelphia, 67; one-man show, Keys Gallery, Derry, Northern Ireland, 77; John Taylor Gallery, Dublin, 79 & 81; Delighted Eye, London, 80; Keys Gallery, Derry, Northern Ireland, 80; and others. *Teaching:* Artist-instr

graphics, dept archit, Col Technol, Dublin, 70-71; lectr, Nat Col Art, Dublin, 75-83. *Awards:* Douglas Hyde Gold Medal, Oireachtas Art Exhib, Dublin Univ, 73; P J Carroll Award, Living Art Exhib, Trinity Col, Dublin, 78; Appointment to the Institution of Honor for Creative Artists, Irish Arts Coun, 81. *Mem:* Life mem Art Student League; United Arts Club (hon chmn artist group, 71), Dublin. *Media:* Oil. *Dealer:* John Taylor Dawson St Dublin Ireland. *Mailing Add:* One Royal Terr W Dun Laoghaire Ireland United Kingdom

BRADY, LUTHER W
COLLECTOR, PATRON
b Rocky Mount, NC, Oct 20, 25. *Study:* George Washington Univ, Washington, DC, AB, 46, MD, 48. *Pos:* Chmn, Friends Philadelphia Mus Art, 67-70; bd dirs, Settlement Music Sch, Philadelphia, 75-; bd trustees, Philadelphia Mus Art, 75-; bd dirs, Art Alliance Philadelphia, 78-80; bd dirs, Santa Fe Opera, 79- *Collection:* American contemporary art; Asian and Far Eastern porcelains and stone carvings; English sculpture. *Mailing Add:* 230 N Broad St Philadelphia PA 19102

BRAGAR, PHILIP FRANK
PAINTER, PRINTMAKER
b New York, NY, May 10, 25. *Study:* Esmeralda Sch Painting & Sculpture, Mexico City, with Raul Angulano, Carlos Orozco Romero, Alfonso Ayala & Ignacio Aguirre, 54-59. *Work:* New York Pub Libr; Pasadena Art Mus, Calif; NJ State Mus, Trenton; Los Angeles Co Mus Art; Libr Cong, Washington, DC; and others. *Exhib:* One-man shows, Galeria Antonio Souza, Mexico City, 68, Galeria Pecanins, Mexico City, 69 & 73 & Lynn Kottler Gallery, New York, 81; Nineteen Years of Woodcut Prints, Galeria Pecanins, 78; Biennial of Graphics, Mus Fine Arts, Mexico City, 79; and many others. *Teaching:* Instr drawing, painting, design & printmaking & dir art dept, US Int Univ, 70-75. *Bibliog:* Duchamps (auth), Mexican landscape was made for painting, says Bragar, Excelsior, 5/16/73; Raquel Tibol (auth), Sixty woodcut prints by Philip Bragar, Proceso, 4/10/78; Graciela Kartofel (auth), Bragar and drawing, Excelsior, 4/28/83. *Media:* Oil. *Publ:* Illusr poem, In: Armando Zarate's El Corazon Cae Fuera del Camino, 63; illusr, Dr Oswaldo Schon's Americans Under Mexican Law, 71. *Dealer:* Galeria Pecanins Hamburgo 103 Mexico DF Mex; Libreria Hardy's Genova 2 Local J Bis Mexico 6 DF. *Mailing Add:* Corregedora 6 (antes Callede las Flores) Campestre-Tlacopac Deleg Villa Obregon Mexico DF 01040 Mexico

BRAIDEN, ROSE MARGARET J
PAINTER, ILLUSTRATOR
b Los Angeles, Calif, Nov 25, 23. *Study:* Study: Mt St Mary's Col, Los Angeles, BFA; Calif Col of Arts & Crafts, Oakland, MFA; Long Beach State, study printmaking with Dick Swift; Univ of Southern Calif; Univ Calif at Los Angeles. *Work:* Mt St Mary's Col, Libr & Gallery, Los Angeles. *Comn:* St Bernard's Church, stained glass windows, Glendale; Design for wall mural, St Lawrence Church, 65; stained glass work, Roger Darricarrere Studios, 69; portraits, Univ Calif, Northridge, 76; bk illus, comn by Steve Pouliot, Banner & Assoc, 78. *Exhib:* Etchings, Long Beach State Gallery, 68; Paintings & Icons, Faulkner Gallery, Santa Barbara, Calif, 77. *Teaching:* Prof art hist, Mt St Mary's Col, 68-70; prof, Santa Barbara City Col, 70- *Bibliog:* Ann Vail Van Horn (auth), Iconography & Icons of the Spirit, News & Rev, 78. *Mem:* Soc of Photographic Educators; Artist Mem of Religious Guild, Am Inst of Archit. *Media:* Ink, Pencil; Egg Tempera, Watercolor. *Dealer:* Yellow Dog Graphics Santa Barbara CA. *Mailing Add:* 2929 Paseo Tranquillo Santa Barbara CA 93105

BRAIG, BETTY LOU
PAINTER
b Naylor, Mo, Apr 21, 31. *Study:* Phoenix Col, AA, 64; Ariz State Univ, BA, 70, MA, 73. *Work:* Valley Nat Bank, United Bank, Empire Machinery, Am Express, Phoenix, Ariz; Glendale Star, Ariz. *Comn:* Free Hanging Cross, Am Evangelical Lutheran Church, Phoenix, 72; Maryvale High Sch, Phoenix, 83; Heavenly Valley Resort, Lake Tahoe, Calif, 83. *Exhib:* Nat Soc Painters Casein & Acrylic, New York, 80; Am Watercolor Soc Traveling Exhib, 80 & 82; Ariz Biennial, Tucson Mus Art, 82; San Diego Int Watercolor Exhib, San Diego Art Mus, 82; Nat Energy Art Exhib, Denver, 82. *Teaching:* Instr art, Maryvale High Sch, Phoenix, 70- *Awards:* Grumbacher Art Award, Ariz Watercolor Asn, 81; David Gayle Found Award, Western Fedn Watercolor, 82. *Mem:* Assoc mem Am Watercolor Soc; Ariz Watercolor Asn; Ariz Artist Guild; 22-30 Watercolorist Ariz. *Media:* Watercolor, Acrylic. *Dealer:* Westside Gallery 4411 N 19th Ave Phoenix AZ 85015. *Mailing Add:* 3020 W Marshall Phoenix AZ 85017

BRAINARD, JOE
GRAPHIC ARTIST, PAINTER
b Salem, Ark, Mar 11, 42. *Work:* Colorado Springs Fine Arts Ctr, Colo; Harvard Univ; Whitney Mus Am Art; Mus Mod Art, New York; Utah Mus Fine Arts, Salt Lake City. *Exhib:* In Memory of My Feelings: Frank O'Hara, Mus Mod Art, New York, 67; Va Mus Fine Arts, 68; White on White, Contemp Mus Art, Chicago, 72; Seven Young Artists, Corcoran, 72; solo exhibs, Suzette Schochett Gallery, Newport, RI, 76, Coventry Gallery, Paddington, NSW, 76, Hamilton Col, NY, 77, Benson Gallery, Bridgehampton, NY, 77 & Art 3 Assoc, Savannah, Ga, 78; and others. *Teaching:* Instr, Cooper Union, 67-68. *Awards:* Copley Found Grant. *Dealer:* Fischbach Gallery 29 W 57th St New York NY 10019. *Mailing Add:* 8 Greene St New York NY 10013

BRAINARD, OWEN
PAINTER, EDUCATOR

b Kingston, NY, Sept 6, 24. *Study:* Columbia Univ, 46, with Dong Kingman; Syracuse Univ, BFA, 48, with Stephen Peck; State Univ NY Albany, 51; Syracuse Univ, with Fred Haucke, MFA, 52. *Work:* Ford Collection Am Art; Chicago Pub Libr; Univ Ryukyus, Okinawa; Mich State Univ; Oldsmobile Collection. *Comn:* Mosaic wall mural, Everett High Sch, Lansing, Mich, 59. *Exhib:* Walker Art Ctr Biennial, Minneapolis, 53; Regional Art Today, Joslyn Mus, Omaha, 57; Art: USA, Madison Sq Garden, NY, 58; 16th Nat Print Exhib, Libr Cong, 58; 3rd Nat Print Exhib, New Canaan, Conn, 60; Drawing Exhib, Buenos Aires, Arg, 78; plus many others. *Teaching:* Asst prof design & painting, Drake Univ, 52-57; prof painting & serigraphy, Mich State Univ, 57- *Awards:* Western Mich Ann Award, Friends of Art, 60; Midland Art Asn Ann Award, 62; Lansing Arts Coun. *Mem:* Col Art Asn; Nat Soc Arts & Lit; Screen Printing Asn Int. *Media:* Acrylic. *Dealer:* Rubiner Gallery Royal Oak MI. *Mailing Add:* 321 Kresge Art Ctr Mich State Univ East Lansing MI 48824

BRAITSTEIN, MARCEL
SCULPTOR, EDUCATOR

b Charleroi, Belg, July 11, 35; Can citizen. *Study:* Ecole Beaux-Arts Montreal, dipl; Inst Allende, San Miguel Allende, Mex. *Work:* Montreal Mus Fine Arts, PQ; Art Gallery Ont, Toronto; Winnipeg Art Gallery, Man; Confederation Ctr, PEI. *Comn:* Sunscreen, Firemen's Bank, Montreal, 65; monument to Rt Hon A Meighen, Dept Pub Works, Can Govt, 69. *Exhib:* Quebec Prov Competition, Quebec, 59; Spring Show, Montreal Mus Fine Arts, 61; Vermont USA, Bundy Art Gallery, 66; Panorama of Quebec Sculpture, Mus Rodin, Paris, France, 70; First Int Biennial Small Sculpture, Budapest, Hungary, 71. *Teaching:* Prof sculpture, Ecole Beaux-Arts Montreal, 65-69; prof sculpture, Univ Quebec, Montreal, 69-73 & 75-; prof, Mt Allison Univ, 73-75. *Awards:* Sculpture Prizes, Quebec Govt, 59; Sculpture Prize, Montreal Mus Fine Arts, 61. *Bibliog:* Guy Robert (auth), Marcel Braitstein, Vie des Arts, Montreal, 62; E H Turner (auth), Sculpture in Canada, Can Art, 62; Jean Simard (auth), Marcel Braitstein, Sculpteur (Monogr), Quebec Sculptors Asn, 69. *Mem:* Quebec Sculptors Asn (vpres, 69-71); Royal Can Acad Arts. *Media:* Welded Steel, Bronze. *Mailing Add:* PO Box 385 Hudson Heights PQ J0P 1J0 Canada

BRAKHAGE, JAMES STANLEY
FILMMAKER, LECTURER

b Kansas City, Mo, Jan 14, 33. *Study:* San Francisco Art Inst, Hon Dr, 81. *Pos:* Lectr film, US & Europe, 55-; lectr film hist, Art Inst Chicago, 69-81. *Teaching:* prof, Univ Colo, Boulder, 81. *Awards:* Nat Endowment Arts Grants, 74, 75, 77, 80 & 83; Guggenheim Fel, 78; Telluride Film Festival Medallion, 81; and others. *Bibliog:* Eisenstein/Brakhage issue, Artforum Mag, 1/73; P Adams Sitney (auth), Visionary Film, Oxford Univ, 74; Parker Tyler (auth), Underground Film, Grove Press, 73. *Mem:* Film-Makers Co-op, New York; Canyon Cinema Co-op San Francisco; London Film-Makers Co-op; Cooperative Cinestes Independants, Montreal. *Publ:* Auth, Metaphors on Vision, 63; auth, A Moving Picture Giving & Taking Book, 71; auth, The Brakhage Lectures, 72; auth, Seen, 75; auth, Film Biographies, 77. *Mailing Add:* Box 170 Rollinsville CO 80474

BRAKKE, P(ERRY) MICHAEL
PAINTER, EDUCATOR

b Douglas, Ariz, Apr 16, 43. *Study:* Univ Minn, BA, 66; Yale Univ Sch Art & Archit, BFA, 68, MFA, 68. *Work:* Solomon R Guggenheim Mus, New York; Joslyn Art Mus, Omaha; Mus Contemp Art, Chicago; Indianapolis Mus Art. *Exhib:* Solo exhib, Joslyn Art Mus, Omaha, 80; Exxon Nat Exhib, Solomon R Guggenheim Mus, New York, 81; Art Inst Chicago, 81; Indianapolis Mus Art. *Teaching:* Assoc prof painting, Oakland Univ, Rochester, 68-76; assoc prof painting, Univ Ill, Chicago-Circle, 76-81; assoc prof painting, Univ Tenn, Knoxville, 81- *Awards:* Proj Completion Grant, 80 & Artists' Fel, 81, Ill Arts Coun. *Bibliog:* Jack Burnham (auth), Icons of the prairies: Mike Brakke's photo-paintings, New Art Examiner, Chicago, 80; Judith Russi Kirshner (auth), Michael Brakke, Artforum, summer 82. *Media:* Paint, Photographs. *Publ:* Co-ed, Artbook 2, 80 & auth, illusr, Anima Hostility, the Painting, Waiting, 80, NAME Gallery, Chicago & Nat Endowment Arts. *Dealer:* Marianne Deson Gallery 340 W Huron Chicago IL 60610. *Mailing Add:* 606 W 18th St 5 Chicago IL 60608

BRALEY, JEAN (J MCNEIL SARGENT)
PRINTMAKER, PAINTER

b Wilkesboro, NC. *Study:* Univ Calif, San Diego BA; Pratt Graphics Ctr, New York; Art Students League; La Reparata Graphic, Florence, Italy; Sch Prof Art, New York; Atelier 17, Paris; NY Univ. *Work:* Biblioteque Nat, Paris; Libr Cong, Washington, DC; NZ Embassy, Washington, DC; Imperial Savings & Loan, Westwood, Calif; Pratt Graphics Ctr, New York; and others. *Comn:* Wall paintings, Glendale Fed Bank, San Diego, 75; five color intaglio ed, Orr's Graphic Ctr, San Diego, 76-77; wall paintings, Calif First Bank, San Diego, 77. *Exhib:* Calif-Hawaii Biennial, San Diego, 76; Palace Fine Arts, Mexico City, 76; 50 Calif Printmakers Nat Tour, 76 & 77; Soc Am Graphic Artists, New York, 77; Yokohama Citizens Mus, Japan, 79; and many others. *Pos:* Prof illusr, publ & advert agencies, New York & Washington, DC, 50-68; vchmn, Docents, Fine Arts Gallery Mus, San Diego, 74-75. *Teaching:* Instr design & drawing, Luther Rice Col, Franconia, Va, 70-71; instr advan oil, San Diego Community Col, 71-78; instr, Mira Costa Col, 79-81. *Awards:* San Diego Top Woman Artist, 80; Purchase Awards, Southern Calif Expo, 81 & Pratt Graphics Ctr, 82; Awards, SW Ann Regional, Washington, DC, 68-70; and others. *Bibliog:* Printmaking Processes (film), Fine Arts Gallery, San Diego, 11/76; M Petersen (auth), On view, Jean Braley, Applause, 11/80; and

others. *Mem:* Artists Equity Asn San Diego (founder, 72, pres, 73 & 74); Calif Art Comn; Printmaker's Atelier (dir, 82-83); and others. *Media:* Intaglio, Oil. *Dealer:* Pat Kery Fine Arts 137 Sullivan New York NY 10012. *Mailing Add:* 519 Stratford Ct Del Mar CA 92014

BRAMHALL, KIB
PAINTER

b Morristown, NJ, June 12, 33. *Study:* Princeton Univ, AB(art & archeol), 55. *Work:* First Nat Bank of Boston, John Hancock Mutual Life Insurance Co & New England Life, Boston; Russell Reynolds Assoc, New York; Smart Fabrics, Ltd, Montreal. *Comn:* Painting for Cox Cancer Ctr, comn by Henry Guild, Boston, 75. *Exhib:* Fourteen one-man shows, New York, Boston, Santa Fe, Cincinnati, Palm Beach, New Haven, Martha's Vineyard, Cape Cod and Nantucket, 60-80; 24 New England Realists, Munson Gallery, Santa Fe, 78; 300 Years of Northeast Art, Copley Soc, Boston, 80; American Realists, Coe Kerr Gallery, New York, 82 & 83. *Mem:* Copley Soc of Boston. *Media:* Oil. *Dealer:* Coe Kerr Gallery 49 E 82nd St New York NY 10028. *Mailing Add:* Seven Gates Farm RFD Vineyard Haven MA 02568

BRAMLETT, BETTY JANE
ADMINISTRATOR, PAINTER

b Augusta, Ga. *Study:* Converse Col, Spartanburg, SC, BA; Univ NC, Chapel Hill; Columbia Univ, MA; Univ SC, Columbia, EdD, 83. *Work:* SC State Collection, Columbia; Spartanburg Arts Ctr Gallery, SC; Springs Mills Res & Develop Bldg, SC; C S Nat Bank Collection, Columbia, SC; Greenville City Hall Collection, SC. *Exhib:* Sixth Ann Piedmont Painting & Sculpture Exhib, Mint Mus of Art, Charlotte, NC, 65; one-woman show, The Gallery, Spartanburg, 70; three-woman show, Tryon Arts Ctr, NC, 70; El Paso's 17th Nat Sun Carnival Art Exhib, El Paso Art Mus, Tex, 72; 25th Ann SC Artists Exhib, Gibbes Art Gallery, Charleston, 72; 41st Ann Show, Greenville Mus of Art, SC, 77; and others. *Pos:* Art Supvr, Spartanburg Co Sch Dist 7, 59-; arts comnr, SC Arts Comn, 77-80. *Teaching:* Instr art hist & art educ, Univ SC, Columbia, 69-73. *Awards:* Cash Award/Painting, Appalachian Corridors Exhib 2, 70 & Spartanburg Bank & Trust Ann, 73; Best-in-Show & Cash Award/Painting, Spartanburg Art Asn, 76; Best in Show, Spartanburg Arts Festival, 83. *Bibliog:* Jack Bass (auth), Porgy Comes Home, World Publ, 70; Seth Vining (ed), article, Tryon Daily Bulletin, NC, 70; Bramlett's Art Goes on Display, Spartanburg Herald-J, 70. *Mem:* Greenville Artists Guild; SC Watercolor Soc; SC Artists Guild (pres-elect, 77); SC Art Educ Asn (pres-elect, 77); Nat Art Educ Asn (dir-elect, Southern Regional chap, currently). *Media:* Watercolor, Acrylic. *Publ:* Auth, Glass on Glass, Sch Arts, 4/63; auth, Spartanburg's Adventure in Art, 4/67 & A Federal Program Can Be Successful, spring 73, SC State Dept; auth, Elementary Art Media, 73 & co-auth, Elementary Art Aids, 73, Spartanburg Co Sch Dist 7. *Mailing Add:* 502 Perrin Dr Spartanburg SC 29302

BRAMS, JOAN
PAINTER, SCULPTOR

b Montreal, PQ. *Study:* Ont Col Art. *Comn:* Walter Heller Corp, NY; U P Corp Environ, Stockholm, Sweden; Russell, Gibson, Van D Ohlen, Inc, Conn; The Rowland Co, NY; Robert Lennox Asn, Minn; and others. *Exhib:* Columbia Mus Art, SC; Birmingham Mus Art, Ala; John Herron Mus Art, Indianapolis, Ind; Worcester Art Mus, Mass; Mountain View Col, Ind; Palm Beach Col, Fla; plus others. *Awards:* Award Merit, Ft Lauderdale Mus, Fla, 65 & 78; 2nd Prize, St Petersburg Art Ctr, Fla, 74; 1st Prize, Palm Beach Art Inst, Fla, 75; and others. *Bibliog:* Articles in La Revue Mod des Arts, France, 71, Art News, 74 & 1/78 & Arts Mag, 10/77. *Media:* Bronze; Acrylic with Aggregates on Wood or Fibre. *Dealer:* David Findlay Galleries 984 Madison Ave New York 10021; Gallery 99 1135 Kane Concourse Bal Harbour FL 33154. *Mailing Add:* 324 Eden Rd Palm Beach FL 33480

BRAMSON, PHYLLIS HALPERIN
PAINTER, INSTRUCTOR

b Madison, Wis, Feb 20, 41. *Study:* Yale Summer Art Sch, Norfolk, Conn, 62; Univ Ill, Champaign, BFA, 63; Univ Wis, Madison, MA(Vilas Fel), 64; Art Inst Chicago, MFA, 73. *Work:* Southern Ill Univ; Mus Contemp Art, Chicago; Art Inst Chicago; Ind State Univ; Ill State Mus. *Exhib:* Chicago & Vicinity Show, Art Inst Chicago, 74; Smithsonian Inst, Washington, DC, 76; one-person show, Monique Knowlton Gallery, New York, 77, 79, 81 & 82; Works on Paper, Art Inst Chicago, 78; Color in Sticks, Mus Contemp Art, Chicago, 79; Fariden Cadot, Paris, 80; Dart Gallery, 80 & 83; Marilyn Butler Gallery, 83. *Teaching:* Instr drawing & painting, Columbia Col, Chicago, 72-82; vis artist, Univ Ill, 75, Univ Iowa, 79, Univ Chicago, 80, Art Inst Chicago, 81, Ind State Univ, 81, Univ Wis, 83 & Northwestern Univ, 83. *Awards:* Nat Endowment Arts Craft Grant, 76; Louis Comfort Tiffany Grant, 80; Ill Arts Coun Fel, 81. *Bibliog:* In a Pictorial Framework, New Mus, New York, 79; John Russell (auth), article, New York Times, 3/12; Lisa Peters (auth), article, Arts Mag, 3/82. *Media:* Oil, Mixed Media. *Dealer:* Monique Knowlton Gallery 153 Mercer St New York NY 10012; Dart Gallery 212 W Superior St Chicago IL 60610. *Mailing Add:* 300 Flora Ave Glenview IL 60025

BRANDENBERG, ALIKI LIACOURAS See Aliki

BRANDT, FREDERICK ROBERT
PAINTER, CURATOR

b Paterson, NJ, June 7, 36. *Study:* Pa State Univ, BA, 60, MA, 63. *Work:* Chrysler Mus, Norfolk, Va; Va Polytech Inst & State Univ, Blacksburg, Va; Richmond Humanities Ctr, Va; St Mary's Hosp, Richmond; Stuart Circle Hospital, Richmond, Va. *Exhib:* 20th Irene Leache Biennial Exhib, Chrysler Mus, Norfolk, 70; Virginia Artists 1971, Va Mus Fine Arts, Richmond, 71; one-man show, Va Mus Fine Arts, Richmond, 72; Virginia Artists 1973, Va

Mus Fine Arts, Richmond, 72; 16th Dixie Ann, Montgomery Mus Fine Arts, Ala, 74; Irene Leache Mem Exhib, Chrysler Mus, Norfolk, Va, 80. *Collections Arranged:* William Hogarth, 67; Art Nouveau (contrib, catalog), 71; Francisco Goya: Portraits in Paintings, Prints and Drawings (contribr, catalog), 72; Nell Blaine (contribr, catalog), 73; Picasso: Paintings and Prints, 74; Jose Puig, 74; American Pewter, 76; American Marine Painting, 76; Allan D'Arcangelo, 79. *Pos:* Interpretation asst, gallery div, Va Mus Fine Arts, 60-61; teaching asst, Pa State Univ, 61-63; asst prog dir, Va Mus Fine Arts, 63-77, assoc cur, 77-79; cur, Sydney & Frances Lewis Collection, 72-; dir, Sydney & Frances Lewis Foundation, 80-; bd trustees, Valentine Mus, Richmond, Va. *Mem:* Victorian Soc Am. *Media:* Acrylics. *Publ:* Auth various articles in antique periodicals, 71-80; coauth (with Susan Butler), Late Twentieth Century Art: The Sydney and Frances Lewis Foundation Collection, 81. *Mailing Add:* 3207 Monument Ave Richmond VA 23221

BRANDT, GRACE BORGENICHT See Borgenicht, Grace

BRANDT, REX (REXFORD ELSON)
PAINTER, PRINTMAKER
b San Diego, Calif, Sept 12, 14. *Study:* Univ Calif, Berkeley, AB(art), 36; Stanford Univ, 38. *Work:* San Diego Fine Arts Gallery, San Francisco Mus Art & Los Angeles Co Mus Art, Calif; Currier Gallery Am Art, Andover, NH; Nat Acad Design Galleries, New York. *Comn:* Metropolitan Aqueduct, portfolio for Fortune Mag, 37; scraffiti tile murals, Corona del Mar State Beach Park, 65; San Diego County, Calif, portfolio for Copley Found, La Jolla, Calif, 68; carved wall relief, Irvine Coast Country Club, 68; murals, Southern Calif First Nat Bank, Newport, 69. *Exhib:* Int Watercolor Exhib, Chicago Art Inst, 36 & 37; one-man shows, Los Angeles Co Mus of Art, 39 & 41, Calif Palace of the Legion of Honor, San Francisco, Crocker Gallery of Art, Sacramento, 40 & 60, Santa Barbara Art Mus, Major Retrospective, Laguna Beach Art Mus, 67, San Diego Fine Arts Gallery, Faulkner Gallery of Art, Santa Barbara & Southern Methodist Univ, Dallas, Tex; Nat Gallcry Art, Washington, DC, 41; Royal Soc Painters in Watercolour, London, 62; Am Watercolor Soc Ann, 60-75; Nat Acad Design Ann, 62-75; plus many others. *Teaching:* Dir of Brandt Painting Workshops, Corona del Mar, Calif, also in Europe & Mex, 46- *Awards:* First Prize, Calif Watercolor Soc, 38 & 70; Samuel F B Morse Medal, Nat Acad Design Ann, 68 & 70; Bronze Medal, Am Watercolor Soc, 70. *Bibliog:* Norman Kent (auth), Seascapes and landscapes, Am Artist, 56; Ernest Watson (auth), Composition in Landscape and Still Life, Watson-Guptill, 59; Cynthia Lindsay (auth), The Natives Are Restless, New Am Libr, 60. *Mem:* Am Watercolor Soc; Nat Acad Design; plus many regional soc. *Media:* All Media. *Publ:* Auth, Watercolor landscape, 63, The artists' sketchbook and its uses, 66, San Diego, land of the sundown sea, 69, Watercolor Technique Methods, 77, West Coast Sketches, 78 & Seeing with a Painter's Eye, 81. *Mailing Add:* 405 Goldenrod Corona Del Mar CA 92625

BRANDT, WARREN
PAINTER
b Greensboro, NC, 18. *Study:* Pratt Inst, 35-38; Wash Univ, BFA(hons); with Philip Guston & Max Beckmann; John J Milliken traveling fel; Univ NC, Greensboro, MFA. *Work:* Metrop Mus Art, New York; Currier Gallery, NH; Nat Collection Fine Arts, Smithsonian Inst; Rochester Mus, NY; and many other public & pvt collections. *Exhib:* Metrop Mus Watercolor Exhib; Am Fedn Arts; Whitney Mus Am Art; Artists by Artists, New Sch Social Res, 67 & Drawings of the Sixties, 69; one-man retrospectives, Allentown Art Mus, 69 & Beaumont Tex, 76; and many others. *Teaching:* Head dept art, Salem Col, 49-50; instr art, Pratt Inst, 50-51; instr art, Guilford Col, Greensboro, 52-54; chmn dept art, Univ Miss, 57-59; chmn dept art, Southern Ill Univ, 59-61; dir, New York Studio Sch, 67- *Media:* Oil. *Publ:* Auth, Painting With Oils, Van Nostrand Reinhold, 71. *Mailing Add:* 870 United Nations Plaza New York NY 10017

BRANSBY, ERIC JAMES
MURALIST, EDUCATOR
b Auburn, NY, Oct 25, 16. *Study:* Kansas City Art Inst, Mo, with Thomas Hart Benton & Fletcher Martin, cert(painting & printmaking); Colorado Springs Fine Arts Ctr & Colo Col, with Boardman Robinson & Jean Charlot, BA & MA(mural painting); Yale Univ, with Josef Albers & Carol Meeks, MFA(painting). *Work:* Colorado Springs Fine Arts Ctr; Mo State Hist Soc Collection, Columbia; Brigham Young Univ Gallery; Nelson Gallery, Kansas City. *Comn:* Mural (polymer tempera), Western Ill Univ, 65, Rockhurst Col, 68 & Univ Mo, Kansas City, 75; twelve paneled mural, Munic Bldg, Sedalia, Mo, 83; mural, Munic Bldg, Liberty, Mo. *Exhib:* Nat Soc Mural Painters Traveling Exhib, New York Archit League & Moscow, Russia, 63; one-man show, Colorado Springs Fine Arts Ctr, 67; Joslyn Mus Biennial, Omaha, 72 & 78; Nat Ctr Fine Arts, Washington, DC, 73-75; Housing & Urban Develop Nat Community Art Competition; and many others. *Teaching:* Instr drawing, Univ Ill, Urbana, 50-52 & Colorado Springs Fine Arts Ctr, 58-63; asst prof drawing & painting, Western Ill Univ, 63-65; assoc prof drawing, painting & printmaking, Univ Mo-Kansas City, 65-70, prof, 70- *Awards:* Edwin Austen Abbey Found Fel for Mural Painting, 52; Kansas City Art Trusts & Founds, 70; Veatch Award, Univ Mo, 78. *Mem:* Col Art Asn; Am Asn Univ Prof; Nat Soc Mural Painters; and others. *Media:* Multimedia. *Res:* Design analysis of Piero della Francesca's mural cycle in the Church of San Francesco at Arezzo, Italy; development of lightweight portable presco panels. *Mailing Add:* Dept of Art Univ of Mo Kansas City MO 64110

BRASELMAN, LIN EMERY See Emery, Lin

BRASETH, JOHN E
DEALER, CONSULTANT
b Seattle, Wash, May 23, 59. *Study:* Seattle Cent Community Col; studied with Gordon W Woodside; St Martins Col. Hon Dr Humanities, *Pos:* Dir, Gordon Woodside-John Braseth Galleries. *Mem:* Seattle Art Mus; Portland Art Mus. *Specialty:* Northwest masters: Carl Morris, William Ivey, Mark Tobey, Paul Horiuchi, Hilda Morris; plus others. *Dealer:* Woodside Braseth Gallery 1101 Howell St Seattle WA 98101. *Mailing Add:* 1101 Howell St Seattle WA 98101

BRATCHER, DALE
PAINTER
b Rockport, Ky, Jan 10, 32. *Study:* Univ Louisville, BCE, MCE. *Work:* Citizens Bank, Evansville, Ind; Evansville Mus Arts & Sci, Ind; Morehead State Univ, Ky; Coca Cola Co, Elizabethtown, Ky; Household Int Corp, Prospect Heights, Ill; and others. *Comn:* Paintings, Lewisport Sch & Lewisport City Hall, Ky, 77; Pate House, Hancock Co, Ky, 77; 3 paintings, Hancock City, Ky; painting, Liberty Nat Bank & Trust, Louisville, Ky. *Exhib:* Watercolor USA, Springfield, Mo, 74 & 83; Midwest Watercolor Soc Ann, 78, 79 & 83; Rocky Mountain Nat Watermedia, Golden, Colo, 80-82; one-man shows, Grand Canyon Nat Park, Ariz, 81, Morehead State Univ, Ky, 83, and many others; Nat Arts Club Open Watercolor Exhib, New York, 81 & 82. *Awards:* First Place, Art Works Show, Frankfort, Ky, 81; Best of Show, Woman's Club Louisville, Ky, 82; Purchase Award, Reflections '83, Covington, Ky, 83. *Bibliog:* Article, North Light, 3/83. *Mem:* Watercolor Soc Ala; Ky Watercolor Soc; Tenn Art League; Southern Watercolor Soc; Midwest Watercolor Soc. *Media:* Multimedia. *Dealer:* Owensboro Mus Fine Art 901 Frederica St Owensboro KY 42301; Speed Mus Rental-Purchase Gallery 2035 S 3rd St Louisville KY 40208. *Mailing Add:* 655 Upland Rd Louisville KY 40206

BRAUDY, DOROTHY McGAHEE See McGahee, Dorothy

BRAUER, CONNIE ANN
DESIGNER, GOLDSMITH
b Denver, Colo, May 4, 49. *Study:* Colo State Univ, BFA, 71; Inst of Europ Studies, Vienna, Austria, 71; Rochester Inst of Technol, 72-73. *Exhib:* All-Colo Show, Denver Art Mus, 74; Flux, Fusion & Fireworks, Contemp Crafts Gallery, Portland, Ore, 80; Young Americans/Metal, New York, 81; Metalsmith 81, Univ Kans; Concepts Gallery, Carmel, 82; Hanson Gallery, Houston, 83; and others. *Teaching:* Instr jewelery, Metrop State Col, 83. *Awards:* Cash Award, Copper, Brass & Bronze Exhib, Univ Ariz, Tucson, 77; Cash Award, Colo Artist Craftsman Ann Show, 80; Cash Award, Inamori Jewelry Design Competition, 83. *Bibliog:* Fashion swirls into spring, 2/82, Fall fashion forecast, 8/83 & Fashion forecast, 8/83, Jewelers Circular Keystone. *Mem:* Am Craft Coun; Soc NAm Goldsmiths; and others. *Media:* Precious Metals, Enamel. *Publ:* Contribr cover photograph, Small Sculptures Nat Catalogue, Cypress Col, 76. *Mailing Add:* 3710 S Huron Englewood CO 80110

BRAUNSTEIN, H TERRY (MALIKIN)
PHOTOGRAPHER, EDUCATOR
b Washington, DC, Sept 18, 42. *Study:* Univ Mich, Ann Arbor, BFA, 64; Pratt Graphic Art Ctr, New York, 65; Md Inst Art, Baltimore, MFA, 68. *Work:* Mus Mod Art, New York; Corcoran Gallery Art Libr; Libr Congress; Bibliotheque Nationale, Paris; Univ Utah; and others. *Exhib:* Corcoran Gallery Art, 65 & 74; American Narrative/Story Art Traveling Exhib, Contemp Arts Mus, Houston, 78-80; Re: Pages Traveling Exhib, New Eng found Arts Vis Touring Program, 80-82; one-person exhibs, Fendrick Gallery, Washington, DC, 80, Artworks, Los Angeles, 82 & Washington Project Arts, 82; Repeated Exposure: Phographic Imagery in the Print Media, Nelson Gallery Art, 82; Evocations, Seven Photographers, Los Angeles Ctr Photogr Studies, 82; and others. *Pos:* Vis artist, Smithsonian Inst, 78; guest cur Bookworks, Washington Project Arts, Washington, DC, 80; vis guest artist, Univ Wis, Stevens Point, 81. *Teaching:* Instr, Prince Georges Community Col, Largo, Md, 71-74; instr, Washington Women's Art Ctr, 76- & Northern Va Community Col, Annandale, 76-78; instr printmaking, Corcoran Sch Art, DC, 78-79; assoc prof, 3rd & 4th yr Fine Arts prog, Corcoran Sch Art, 79- *Bibliog:* Dinah Berland (auth), Her work is an open bood, Los Angeles Times, 8/15/82; Robert St John (auth), Windows by H Terry Braunstein, Washington Review, 10-11/82; JoAnn Lewis (auth), Art through the pages, Washington Post, 10/7/82. *Mem:* Adhibit Comt, Washington, DC (mem bd dirs, currently); The List, Independent Curators Inc, New York; Washington Project Arts, Washington, DC (mem bd dirs, currently). *Publ:* Auth, Windows, Vis Studies Workshop Press, 82. *Dealer:* Fendrick Gallery 3059 M Street NW Washington DC. *Mailing Add:* 317 Fifth St SE Washington DC 20003

BRAUNSTEIN, RUTH
DEALER
b Minneapolis, Minn. *Collections Arranged:* California Era, Update, Huntsville Art Mus, Ala. *Pos:* Dir, Braunstein Gallery, San Francisco, 61- *Mem:* San Francisco Art Dealers Asn (pres, 75-77). *Specialty:* Contemporary art: sculpture, painting and drawing; ceramic sculpture, mostly California artists. *Mailing Add:* 254 Sutter St San Francisco CA 94108

BRAVMANN, RENE A
HISTORIAN, EDUCATOR
b Marseilles, France, Dec 10, 39; US citizen. *Study:* Cleveland Mus Art, 57-61; Western Reserve Univ, BA, 61; Univ Wis, 61-63; Ind Univ, MA(fine arts), 65, PhD, 71. *Teaching:* Asst prof art hist, Univ Wash, Seattle, 68-72, assoc

prof, 72-76, prof, 77 , chmn African studies, 69-75. *Awards:* Ford Found Fel, Am Coun Learned Socs, 66-68; Post-doctoral Res Grant, Soc Sci Res Coun, 72-73; Am Philos Soc Grant, 74. *Publ:* Auth, West African Sculpture, 70 & auth, Open Frontiers: The Dynamics of Art in Black Africa, 73, Univ Wash; auth, The diffusion of Ashanti political art, In: African Art & Leadership, 72; auth, Islam & Tribal Art in West Africa, Cambridge Univ, 74; auth, An urban way of death, African Arts, Vol 8, No 3. *Mailing Add:* Sch of Art Univ of Wash Seattle WA 98195

BRAWLEY, ROBERT JULIUS
PAINTER, DRAFTSMAN
b Brainerd, Minn, April 24, 37. *Study:* Cent Wash Univ, 56-57; Frye Art Mus Sch, 58-61; San Francisco Art Inst, BFA, MFA, 64. *Work:* Art Inst Chicago; San Francisco Art Inst; Moore Col Art; Hoyt Inst Fine Arts, Lancaster, Pa. *Exhib:* Beyond the Actual--California New Realism, Haggin Galleries, Pioneer Mus, Stockton, Calif, 71; San Francisco New Realism--Through the Photograph to Painting, San Francisco Mus Art, 71; The New Realists, Mongerson Galleries, Chicago, 82; Small Works, NY Univ, 82; Hoyt Nat Painting Show, Hoyt Inst Fine Arts, Lancaster, Pa, 82; Mid-Year Nat Exhib, Butler Inst Am Art, 82 & 83; Four American Realists, Mongerson Galleries, Chicago, 83. *Teaching:* Dir & instr drawing & painting, Acad Art Col, San Francisco, 69-71; assoc prof art hist & studio art, dir grad art studies & chmn art dept, Lone Mountain Col, 71-78; lectr, St Marys Col, Moraga, Calif, 81- *Awards:* Fulbright Fel, 66-67; Painting Awards, Mid-Year Painting Exhib, Butler Inst Am Art, 82 & Hoyt Nat Painting Show, Hoyt Inst Fine Arts, 82. *Bibliog:* Robin Longman (auth), article, Am Artist Mag, 8/83. *Media:* Alkyd; Graphite. *Dealer:* Mongerson Galleries 620 N Michigan Ave Chicago IL 60611; Capricorn Galleries 4849 Rugby Ave Bethesda MD. *Mailing Add:* 2118 Nottingham Dr Fairfield CA 94533

BRAYBROOKE, VALERIE V
MUSEUM DIRECTOR
b New York, NY. *Study:* Smith Col, with Mervin Jules, Leonard Baskin & Oliver Larkin, AB; George Washington Univ, MA; Smithsonian Inst; Mus Mgt Inst. *Collections Arranged:* Eight from California (coauth, catalog), 74-75; Images of an Era: The American Poster 1945-75 (coauth, catalog), 75; Three Stitchery Artists, 77; Three Sculptors from Mississippi, 78; The Eye of the Law (auth, catalog), 79. *Pos:* Curatorial asst, Nat Collection Fine Arts, Smithsonian Inst, 75; dir, Univ Miss Mus, 76-83; dir, Ft Wayne Mus Art, 83- *Mem:* Am Asn Mus; Southeastern Mus Conf (coun, 79-83); Miss Mus Asn (pres, 79-80); Yoknapatawpha Arts Coun (bd dir, 79-81). *Publ:* Coauth, Through the Maze: Guide to the Graduate Program In Art History at George Washington University, George Washington Univ, 72; auth, University Museums, Phase I-Cultural Center for the University of Mississippi, Univ Miss, 77; auth, Directory of Appraisers: Personal Property, Southeastern Mus Conf, 79. *Mailing Add:* Ft Wayne Museum of Art Ft Wayne IN 46802

BRCIN, JOHN DAVID
SCULPTOR
b Gracac, Yugoslavia, Aug 15, 1899; US citizen. *Study:* Art Inst Chicago, BFA(Byron Lathror Travel Fel), 22; Ohio State Univ, MA, 49. *Work:* Witte Mem Mus, San Antonio, Tex; Joslyn Mem Art Mus, Nebr; Mark Twain Mus, Hartford, Conn; Pioneer Mus Art, Stockton, Calif; Evansville Mus Art, Ill. *Comn:* Relief sculpture bldg, Joslyn Art Mus, Nebr, 29; Stephen Decatur Monument, USN Acad, Annapolis & City Decatur, Ill; Cyrus McCormick Monument, Washington & Lee Univ, Lexington, Va; Gov Henry Horner Monument, City Chicago, Ill. *Exhib:* Nat Acad Design; Pa Acad Fine Arts; Art Inst Chicago; Detroit Inst Art; Albright Art Gallery; Dayton Art Inst. *Awards:* Gold Medal, Wm R French Award, 26; Hickox Prize, Hoosier Salon, 36. *Mem:* Cliff Dwellers Club. *Mailing Add:* 350 Ponca Place Boulder CO 80303

BRECHT, GEORGE
CONCEPTUAL ARTIST, ASSEMBLAGE ARTIST
b New York, NY, 1926. *Study:* Philadelphia Col Pharmacy & Sci, Pa, BSc, 50; New Sch Social Res, New York, with John Cage, 58-59. *Work:* Mus Mod Art, New York; Stadtisches Mus, Monchengladbach, Ger, Arch Sohm, Margroningen; Musee Nat d'Art Moderne, Centr Georges Pompidou, Paris; Nat Gallerie, Berlin; Mus Moderner Kunst, Vienna. *Comn:* Music and sets, James Waring Dance Co, New York. *Exhib:* The Art of Assemblage, Mus Mod Art, New York, 61; Mixed-Media & Pop Art, Albright-Knox Art Gallery, Buffalo, NY, 63; Black, White & Gray, Wadsworth Atheneum, Hartford, Conn, 64; Eleven from the Reuben Gallery, Guggenheim Mus, New York, 65; Art by Tel, Mus Contemp Art, Chicago, 69; one-man shows, Toward Events, Reuben Gallery, New York, 59 & Los Angeles Co Mus Art, Calif, 69; and many more. *Teaching:* Res fel, Leeds Col Art, Eng, 68-69. *Bibliog:* Allan Kaprow (auth), Assemblage, Environments & Happenings, New York, 66; Jan van der Marck (auth), George Brecht: an art of multiple implications, art in Am, 7-8/74; Henry Martin (auth), An Introduction to George Brecht's book of the Tumbler on Fire, Multhipla Edizioni, Milan. *Publ:* Auth, Chance imagery, Collage, Palermo, Italy, 12/64; auth, Dances, events & other poems, Something, Vol 1, 65; coauth, Vicious Circles & Infinity, New York, 75; auth, Seng Ts'an, Hsin-hsin-ming, Editions Hossmann-Lebeer, Brussels, 80. *Dealer:* Arturo Schwarz via Gesu 17 Milan 20121 Italy. *Mailing Add:* Wildenburgstrasse 9 Cologne-Sulz Germany, Federal Republic of

BRECKENRIDGE, BRUCE M
CERAMIST, EDUCATOR
b Chicago, Ill, Oct 29, 29. *Study:* Wis State Col-Milwaukee, BS, 52; Cranbrook Acad Art, Bloomfield Hills, Mich, MFA, 53; Acad Grande

Chaumier, Paris, 56. *Work:* Elvehjem Art Ctr, Univ Wis-Madison; Westum Mus, Racine, Wis. *Exhib:* Objects as Objects, Mus Contemp Crafts, New York, 68 & Coffee Tea and Other Cups, 71; National Ceramics Invitational Exhibition, Nelson Gallery Atkins Mus, Kansas City, 69; National Ceramics Invitational, Scripps Col, 71; The Plastic Earth, John Michael Kohler Arts Ctr, Sheboygan, Wis, 73. *Collections Arranged:* Richmond Art Ctr, Calif, 59-61; Mus Contemp Crafts, New York, 65-66. *Pos:* Asst dir, Richmond Art Ctr, 59-61; installation asst, Mus Mod Art, New York, 64-65; asst dir, Mus Contemp Crafts, New York, 65-66. *Teaching:* Instr ceramics, Brooklyn Mus Art Sch, 65-68; prof art-ceramics, Univ Wis-Madison, 68- *Media:* Ceramics. *Publ:* Auth, New ceramic forms, 65, Wisconsin designer-craftsman, 69, Don Reitz exhibition, 70 & National invitational exhibition II, glass, 71, Craft Horizons. *Mailing Add:* 1715 Regent Madison WI 53705

BREDER, HANS DIETER
SCULPTOR, VIDEO ARTIST
b Herford, Ger, Oct 20, 35; US citizen. *Study:* Hochschule fuer Bildende Kunste, Hamburg, Ger, with Willem Grimm, asst to sculptor, George Rickey. *Work:* Cleveland Mus, Ohio; Joseph H Hirshhorn Collection, Washington, DC; Whitney Mus of Am Art, New York; Mus of Art, State Univ NY Col, Purchase; Mus of Art, Iowa City. *Comn:* Three outdoor sculptures, City of Hanover, Ger, 71. *Exhib:* La Jolla Mus of Art, Calif, 69; Gallery Marcel Liatowitsch, Basel, Switz, 72; Max Hutchinson Gallery, New York, 72; Int Cult Centrum, Antwerpen, Belg, 76; Signals, Mus of Mod Art, New York, 77; one-man shows, Wolfgang Foerster Galerie, 79 & Hachmeister & Schnake Galerie, Muenster, Germany, 81. *Pos:* Co-dir, Corroboree: Gallery of New Concepts, Univ Iowa, Iowa City, 77- *Teaching:* Prof multimedia, Univ Iowa, Iowa City, 77- *Bibliog:* George Rickey (auth), Constructivism--Origins & Evolutions, George Braziller, 68; R G Dienst (auth), Deutsche Kunst: Eine Neue Generation, Dumont Schauberg, Ger, 70; Michael Kirby (auth), Hybrids, Drama Rev, 73. *Publ:* Coauth, Speculum, Ctr for New Performing Arts, 73; coauth, Participatory Art and Body Sculpture with Mirrors, Leonardo: Art, Sci & Technol, 74. *Mailing Add:* Dept Art Univ Iowa Iowa City IA 52242

BREDLOW, TOM
DESIGNER, BLACKSMITH
b Pontiac, Mich, Oct 18, 38. *Study:* Tex A&M Col, BA(math). *Comn:* Grilles, door hardware, fireplace accessories, weathervanes, gates, railings, tables & chandeliers, pvt residences in US & Mex, 64-; gates, railings, candlestick & flower stands, Washington Cathedral, 68-; Barrio-Historico (grilles, gates, doors, railings, downspouts), comn by H Kelley Rollings, Tucson, 70-; hand rails, comn by Harriet Hubbell, Hubbell House (SW Span Craftsmen), Santa Fe, NMex, 71; Peopleplay (public sculpture), Steven Nanini, Tucson, 80; and others. *Exhib:* One-man show, Boyer Gallery, Tucson, 68 & 70; Ann Western Art Show, Mountain Oyster Club, Tucson, 72-; Iron-Solid Wrought, Mus Southern Ill Univ, Mus Contemp Crafts, New York & Smithsonian Inst, Washington, DC, 76-77. *Pos:* Owner & sole craftsman, Bredlow's Blacksmith Shop, Tucson, 64- *Teaching:* Guest lectr hist archaeol, Univ Ariz, speaker-demonstr, Ironworking Conv, . *Awards:* Biennial Prize, Quinnell Biennial, Surrey, England, 76. *Bibliog:* Ty Harrington (auth), Last Cathedral, Prentice-Hall, 79; R T Feller (auth), For Thy Great Glory, Community, 79. *Mem:* Hon artist Mountain Oyster Club, Tucson, 78. *Media:* Metals. *Publ:* Auth, Stagecoach, Frontier Times, summer 60; auth, Anvils and coal smoke, Old West, winter 66; auth, Crown Sculptural and Decorative Ironwork, Meilach, 77. *Mailing Add:* 1827 E Limberlost Tucson AZ 85719

BREED, CHARLES AYARS
SCULPTOR, EDUCATOR
b Paw Paw, Mich, Jan 31, 27. *Study:* Western Mich Univ, BS; Univ Wis, MA. *Work:* Midland Ctr Arts, Mich. *Comn:* Cross (glass & brass), Mem Presby Church, Midland, Mich, 57; Eternal Flame (Plexiglas), Temple Beth El, Spring Valley, NY, 66; Icon Screen (polyester), Hellenic Orthodox Church, Bloomfield Hills, Mich, 68; sculptural panels, Richard Howell, 81; sculpture, Alden D Dow Ctr Arts, Midland, 82; and others. *Exhib:* Craftsman USA 66, Mus Contemp Crafts, New York, 66, Plastic as Plastic Nat Invitational, 68; Made of Plastic Nat Invitational, Flint Inst Art, Mich, 68; Exhib 70, Columbus Art Gallery, Ohio, 70; First Biennial Int Small Sculpture Exhib, Budapest, Hungary, 71. *Pos:* Bd dirs, Awareness Inc, Lansing, Mich, 62-64; bd dirs, Midland Art Coun, Mich, 65-68; bd dirs, Midland Ctr Arts, 67-72; mem, Coun Arts, Lansing, 71-72. *Teaching:* Dir art, Nat Music Acad, 58-62; prof art & chmn dept, Delta Col, 62-83. *Awards:* Nat Merit Award, Mus Contemp Crafts, New York, 66; Outstanding Teacher Year, Bergstein Found, 67; Mich Coun Arts Artist Grant, 81. *Bibliog:* Jack Brickhouse (auth), Everything is Double in Paw Paw, Paramount Films, 48; Curtis Bessinger (auth), Where does the design of a house begin, House Beautiful, 1/62; Rite of Spring--Detroit (videotape), PM Mag, 81-83. *Mem:* Life mem Nat Educ Asn; Mich Art Educ (treas, 55, pres, 56); Am Craftsmen Coun; Mich Coun Ar. *Media:* Plastic. *Publ:* Auth, Plastic as a new art form, House Beautiful, 2/62; co-auth, Plastic-the visual arts in crafts, Crafts & Craftsmen, 67; auth, Unite equal opposites, Symposium, 80. *Dealer:* Lee Nordness Galleries 252 West 38th St New York NY 10018. *Mailing Add:* 4202 Sherwood Ct Midland MI 48640

BREEN, HARRY FREDERICK, JR
PAINTER, EDUCATOR
b Chicago, Ill, Mar 4, 30. *Study:* Art Inst Chicago, with John Rogers Cox & Paul Wiegarht, BA, 53; Univ Ill, Urbana-Champaign, MA, 59. *Work:* Ill State Mus, Springfield; Butler Mus Am Art, Youngstown, Ohio; Krannert Art Mus, Champaign, Ill; Union League Club, Chicago; Lakeview Ctr Arts & Sci, Peoria, Ill. *Comn:* Illinois Prairie (mural), 1st Trust & Savings Bank,

Taylorville, Ill, 77; Scott Memorial (sculpture), Krannert Ctr Performing Arts, Urbana, Ill, 79; Illinois Landscapes Series, Burnham Atheneum Law Off, Champaign, Ill, 81; Holy Family (mural), Mercy Hosp, Urbana, Ill, 82; chapel murals, Holy Cross Church, Champaign, Ill, 83. *Exhib:* Mid-Yr Ann, Butler Mus Am Art, Youngstown, Ohio, 62, 63 & 65; Pa Acad Fine Art, 63; Communication Through Art, Abby Gray Found, traveling in Europe, 64; Realism Revisited, Flint Art Inst, Mich, 66; 5th Biennial Relig Art, Cranbrook Acad, Detroit, Mich, 66; Ill Arts Coun Traveling Exhib, 67; retrospective, Lakeview Ctr Arts & Sci, Peoria, Ill, 77; Univ Ill Painting Fac, Univ Tokyo & Nat Hist Mus in Taipei, 81; and others. *Teaching:* Instr art, Pub Schs, Gary, Ind, 54-57; instr art, Univ High Sch, Univ Ill, 57-59; vis prof art, Univ Wis, Madison, 68-69; prof art, Sch Art & Design, Univ Ill, Champaign, 59- *Awards:* Second Purchase Prize, Fourth Union League Exhib, Chicago, 61; Fourth Purchase Prize Oils, Mid-Yr Ann, Butler Mus Am Art, 63; Second Prize Sculpture, Ann Exhib, Hoosier Salon, Indianapolis, 63. *Media:* Oil, Watercolor. *Dealer:* Neville-Sargent Gallery 509 Main St Evanston IL 60202. *Mailing Add:* 1107 W Church St Champaign IL 61820

BREER, ROBERT C
SCULPTOR, FILMMAKER
b Detroit, Mich, Sept 30, 26. *Study:* Stanford Univ, BA. *Work:* Mus Mod Art, New York; Mod Mus, Stockholm, Sweden; Anthology Film Archives, New York; Mod Art Mus, Krefeld, Ger; Centre Beaubourg, Paris, France. *Comn:* Design Pepsi Cola Pavilion, Expo '70, Japan; kinetic sculpture, IBM Plaza, Pittsburgh Arts Fete, 74; Mural, Film Forum, NY. *Exhib:* The Machine as Seen at the End of the Mechanical Age, Mus Mod Art, New York, 68; Albright-Knox Art Gallery, Buffalo, NY, 71; solo exhibs, Mus Mod Art, New York, Albright-Knox Art Gallery, 76, Collective Living Cinema, New York, 77, Walker Art Ctr, 79 & Millenium, New York, 79; retrospective, Whitney Mus Am Art, 77 & 80; Drawings for Animated Film, Drawing Ctr, New York, 78; Film as Film, Hayward Gallery, London, 79; New York Film Festival, 79; Whitney Biennial, 79; and others. *Pos:* Mem bd dirs, Filmmakers Coop, New York, 67-72 & 75- *Teaching:* Prof kinetics, Cooper Union, 71-; instr, Hampshire Col, 74-79 & NY Univ, 77. *Awards:* Nat Endowment Arts Grant, 76; Am Film Inst Grant, 77; Guggenheim Found Fel, 78-79. *Bibliog:* Adrienne Mancia & William Van Dyke (auth), Four artists as film makers, Art in Am, 1/67; Calvin Tompkins (auth), Onwards and upwards with the arts, New Yorker, 10/70; Lois Mendelson (auth), Robert Breer, UMI Res Press, 81. *Mailing Add:* 25 Shadyside Ave Nyack NY 10960

BREESKIN, ADELYN DOHME
ADMINISTRATOR, CONSULTANT
b Baltimore, Md, July 19, 1896. *Study:* Bryn Mawr Col; Radcliffe Col; Sch Fine Arts, Boston; Goucher Col, Hon LittD, 53; Washington Col, Hon DFA, 61, Wheaton Col, 63, Hood Col, 66, Morgan State Col, 66, Md Inst, 75. *Pos:* Cur prints & drawings, Baltimore Mus Art, 30-, gen cur, 38, actg dir, 42, dir, 47-62; first dir, Wash Gallery Mod Art, 62-64; art consult & cur contemp art, Nat Col Fine Arts, Smithsonian Inst, 64-74, consult, 74- *Teaching:* Instr art, McCoy Col, Johns Hopkins Univ, 37-50; lectr, US & abroad; also radio & TV appearances; Am specialist lect tour of Orient, State Dept, 64-65. *Awards:* Star of Solidarity for Promoting Intercultural Betterment, Ital Govt, 54. *Mem:* Am Asn Mus Dirs; Print Coun Am; Int Graphic Arts Soc; Am Fedn Arts (trustee, 60-74). *Publ:* Ed, Graphic Art of Mary Cassatt, H Bittner & Co, 48, & Smithsonian, 79; ed, Raisonne of the Paintings, Pastels, Watercolors & Drawings of Mary Cassatt, Smithsonian, 70. *Mailing Add:* Rm 256 Nat Collection Fine Arts Smithsonian Inst Washington DC 20560

BREIGER, ELAINE
PAINTER, PRINTMAKER
b Springfield, Mass. *Study:* Art Student League; Cooper Union, cert fine arts; spec master printing with Krishna Reddy. *Work:* Brooklyn Mus, NY; Libr Cong, Washington, DC; Honolulu Acad Art, Hawaii; Chase Manhattan Bank, New York; De Cordova Mus, Lincoln, Mass. *Comn:* Print, Container Corp Am, 70. *Exhib:* Glaser Gallery, La Jolla, Calif; Contemp Gallery, Dallas; Leslie Rankow Gallery, New York; Martha Jackson Gallery, New York, 74; Pace Gallery, New York, 76; Source Gallery, San Francisco, Calif, 77. *Pos:* Mgr, Printmaking Workshop, 68-70. *Teaching:* Instr techniques etching & intaglio printing, 92nd St YMHA, New York, 71-76, chmn dept art, 72-76; color etching, Sch of Visual Arts, New York, 77- *Awards:* Creative Arts Pub Serv Fel, 74; Nat Endowment Arts Grant, 75. *Bibliog:* Van Johnson (auth), American Prints & Printmakers, Doubleday, 80. *Mem:* VAGA. *Media:* Acrylic, Oil. *Mailing Add:* 112 Greene St New York NY 10012

BREININ, RAYMOND
PAINTER, SCULPTOR
b Vitebsk, Russia, Nov 30, 10. *Study:* Chicago Acad Fine Arts, Vitebsk Acad-Artist Uri Pen. *Work:* Metrop Mus Art; Mus Mod Art; Brooklyn Mus; Art Inst Chicago; Phillips Collection, Washington, DC; and others. *Comn:* Costumes & settings, Ballet Theatre's Undertow; murals, Winnetka High Sch, Ill, State Hosp, Elgin, Ill, US Post Off, Wilmette, Ill & Ambassador E Hotel, Chicago; and others. *Teaching:* Artist in residence, Univ Southern Ill; instr art, Univ Minn; instr, Breinin Sch Art, Chicago; instr painting & drawing, Art Students League; instr, Nat Acad Design, New York. *Awards:* Prizes, Art USA, 58, Art Inst Chicago (seven) & Pa Acad Fine Arts (two); plus others. *Bibliog:* Rosamond Frost (auth), included in: Contemporary Art: The March of Art from Cezanne Until Now, Crown, 42; Emily Genauer (auth), included in: Best of Art, Doubleday, 48; and others. *Mem:* Nat Acad Design; Artists Equity Asn New York. *Mailing Add:* 121 Inwood Rd Scarsdale NY 10583

BREITENBACH, WILLIAM JOHN
SCULPTOR, DRAFTSMAN
b Milwaukee, Wis, Jan 21, 36. *Study:* Univ Wis, Milwaukee, BS, 62 & MS, 65; Stephen F Austin State Univ, MFA, 71. *Work:* Brentwood Col, NY; Del Mar Col, Corpus Christi, Tex; Stephen F Austin State Univ, Tex; Houston Baptist Univ, Tex. *Comn:* Sculptural fountain, William Robert Murfin, Houston, 72; plywood wall sculpture, Performing Arts Ctr, Sam Houston State Univ, Huntsville, Tex, 76; Cent Tex Col, Killeen, 83. *Exhib:* Creative Collab, Rice Univ, Houston, 72; 9th Monroe Ann, Masur Mus Art, Monroe, La, 72; Southwest Graphics Invitational, Mex-Am Cult Exchange Inst, San Antonio, Tex, 72; Inst Visual Arts, Puebla, Mex, 81; Mus Anthropology, Tehuacan, Mex, 81; and others. *Pos:* Chmn, Houston Area Art Curric Develop Comt, 82-83. *Teaching:* Supvr elem art, South Door Co Sch Dist 1, Brussels, Wis, 62-65; assoc prof art educ & drawing, Sam Houston State Univ, 65- *Awards:* First Prize in sculpture, 5th Ann Exhib, Del Mar Col, 71; Merit Award for creative collab, Rice Univ, 71; Third Place Award, Assistance League Houston, 73. *Mem:* Tex Art Educ Asn; Nat Art Educ Asn. *Media:* Cast Aluminum, Fabricated Plywood; India Ink. *Publ:* Auth, Art education and the modern age, Tex Trends in Art Educ, 68. *Dealer:* Umbrella Arts 2615 Old Houston Rd Huntsville TX 77340. *Mailing Add:* Box 2023 Sam Houston State Univ Huntsville TX 77341

BREITHAUPT, ERWIN M
PAINTER, HISTORIAN
b Columbus, Ohio, Nov 12, 20. *Study:* Miami Univ, BFA; Ohio State Univ, MA & PhD; Oak Ridge Inst Nuclear Studies. *Exhib:* Design of the Future, Mus Mod Art, New York, 54 & Merchandise Mart, Chicago, 55. *Collections Arranged:* F L Wright Centennial Exhib, 66. *Teaching:* Assoc prof art hist & design, Univ Ga, 47-62; prof art & chmn dept art hist & design, Ripon Col, 62-82, prof emer, 82- *Awards:* Gen Educ Bd Fel, Rockefeller Found, 51; Severy Award, 65 & Uhrig Award, 69, Ripon Col. *Mem:* Col Art Asn. *Res:* Area of the art institution and creativity. *Publ:* Auth, A New Approach to Art Education, 56; auth, The Basic Art Course at Georgia, 57; coauth, An Institutional Approach to Aesthetics, 59; contribr, The Creative Life of Man, 70. *Mailing Add:* Dept Art Ripon Col Ripon WI 54971

BREJCHA, VERNON LEE
GLASSBLOWER, EDUCATOR
b Ellsworth, Kans, Jan 30, 42. *Study:* Ft Hays State Univ, BA & MS; Univ Wis-Madison, MFA with Harvey K Littleton. *Work:* Corning Mus of Glass, NY; Mus of Contemp Crafts, New York; Kunstmuseum, Dusseldorf, WGer; J & L Lobmerr, Vienna, Austria; Leigh Yawkey Woodson, Wausau, Wis; and others. *Exhib:* The Craftsman, St Louis Art Mus, Mo, 72; Lake Superior Nat, Tweed Mus Art, Duluth, Minn, 72 & 77; Glass Art Soc Exhib, Corning Mus of Glass, NY, 76; one-man show, Sheldon Mem Mus, Lincoln, 78; Wichita Art Mus, Kans, 78; Contemporary Glass in Am, Okla Art Ctr, Oklahoma City, 78; Am in Glass, Leigh Yawkey Woodson, 79; Glas Aus USA, Glasmus, Frauenau, WGer; Nat Glass Exhib, Habitat Gallery, 81; and others. *Teaching:* Asst prof glass, ceramics & sculpture, Tusculum Col, Greenville, Tenn, 72-76; asst prof design glass, Univ Kans, 77-81, assoc prof, 81- *Awards:* First Place Purchase, Ceramics Northwest, C M Russell Mus, Great Falls, Mont, 70; Cash Award, Miss River Show, Brooks Mem Art Gallery, Memphis, 75; Purchase Award, Tenn Bicentennial Art Exhib, State of Tenn, 76. *Bibliog:* Frank Kulasiewicz (auth), Glassblowing, Watson-Guptill, 74; Polly Rothenberg (auth), The Complete Book of Creative Glass Art, Crown, 74; Elizabeth Campbell (auth), Kansas-Theme of glass artist Vernon Brejcha, Neues Glas, Dusseldorf, 82. *Mem:* Am Crafts Coun; Nat Coun on Educ for the Ceramic Arts (glass panel chmn, 77); Glass Art Soc; Kans Artist-Craftsmen Asn. *Publ:* Auth, Throw the Lid First, Ceramics Monthly, 76; contribr, The Complete Book of Creative Glass Art, Crown, 74; contribr, Crafts & Craftsmen of the Tennessee Mountains, Summit Press; auth, British hot glass, Glass Studio, 82. *Mailing Add:* 308 Mississippi Lawrence KS 66044

BRENDEL, BETTINA
PAINTER, LECTURER
b Luneburg, Ger; US citizen. *Study:* Hamburg, Ger, BA, 40; Kunstschule Schmilinsky, Hamburg, 41-42; Landes Hochschule Bildende Künste, Hamburg, 45-47, with Erich Hartmann; Univ Southern Calif, 55-58; New Sch Social Res, 68-69. *Work:* Grunwald Graphic Arts Ctr, Univ Calif, Los Angeles, San Francisco Mus Art, Pasadena Art Mus, Long Beach Mus Art & La Jolla Art Mus, Calif. *Exhib:* Los Angeles Co Mus Ann, Los Angeles, 55, 57, 59 & 61; Intern Ctr, Torino, Italy, 64; 58th Ann, San Francisco Mus Art, 66; On Mass and Energy, Santa Barbara Mus Art, 66; Spectrum Gallery, New York, 67; A Study Exhibition, Downey Mus Art, 75; Women Artists, Santa Monica Col Art Gallery, Calif, 77; and others. *Teaching:* Instr, The Emergence of Mod Painting, Univ Calif, Los Angeles, 58-61, lectr art, Exten, spring 76; lectr, Thematic Option Prog, Univ Southern Calif, 80. *Awards:* Award, La Jolla Art Mus, 58 & 59; Long Beach Mus Art, 60; First Purchase Award, San Francisco Mus Art, 66. *Bibliog:* Michel Tapie (auth), Musee manifeste, Fratelli Pozzo Editori, Torino, 62; Constance Perkins (auth), article in Art Forum, 4/62; H Von Breton (auth), article in Santa Barbara News Press, 2/66. *Mem:* Artists for Econ Action. *Media:* Acrylic. *Res:* Theoretical physics and its relation to the arts. *Publ:* Auth, The painter and the new physics, Art J, fall 71; auth, The influence of atomic physics, Leonardo Mag, 73; auth, Whenever in the World, Stockton Press, 77. *Mailing Add:* 1061 N Kenter Ave Los Angeles CA 90049

BRENDER A BRANDIS, GERARD WILLIAM
PRINTMAKER, ILLUSTRATOR
b Maarn, Neth, May 13, 42; Can citizen. *Study:* McMaster Univ, BA(fine arts), 65; study with Norma Waters, Rosemary Kilbourn. *Work:* Nat Gallery,

Ottawa; Art Gallery of Hamilton; London Pub Libr & Art Mus, Ont; Art Gallery of Brant; Ont Inst Studies Educ. *Exhib:* Int Miniature Prints, Pratt Graphics Ctr, New York, 68; mini-traveling show, Art Gallery Ont, 77; The Date, 83; Victoria Col, Toronto, 83; Hunt Botanical Libr, Pittsburgh, 83; and others. *Bibliog:* Bookwright (film), Mobius Productions, France, 80; *Mem:* Canadian Bk Binders & Bk Artists Guild; Alcuin Soc, Vancouver, BC. *Publ:* Illusr, Flora, Brandstead Press, 80; illusr, Wood, Ink and Paper, Porcupine's Quill, 81; illusr, The Tinderbox, Porcupine's Quill, 82; illusr, More than Sand and Sea, Brandstead Press, 82; illusr, With Cheerful Heart, Brandstead Press, 83. *Dealer:* Alice Peck Gallery 2100 Lakeshore Burlington ON L7R 1A3 Can. *Mailing Add:* Carlisle ON L0R 1H0 Canada

BRENNAN, FRANCIS EDWIN
EDITORIAL CARTOONIST, DESIGNER
b Maywood, Ill, July 14, 10. *Study:* Univ Wis; Art Inst Chicago. *Pos:* Chief of graphics & exhib, OWI, 42-45; assoc art dir, Life Mag; art ed, Fortune Mag; picture ed, Life Picture Hist World War II; art adv to ed in chief, Time Inc; ed consultant & cartoonist syndicated by Newsweek Int Ed Serv, currently. *Awards:* Order Merite Commercial, France, 50; Legion Honor, France, 60. *Publ:* Designer & picture ed, Sara & Gerald, New York Times Bks, 82. *Mailing Add:* Hampton House 123-35 82nd Rd Kew Gardens NY 11415

BRENNER, SHORE HODGE
WEAVER, EDUCATOR
b Honolulu, Hawaii, July 29, 49. *Study:* Univ Hawaii, BA, 72, BFA, 76, MFA, 79. *Work:* State Found Cult & Arts, Contemp Art Ctr, Bank Hawaii, Hawaiian Tel Co, Honolulu; Int Savings, Waikiki. *Comn:* Woven hanging, King Kalakaua Clinic, Honolulu, 78; woven wall panels, Archit Hawaii, Kaanapali, Maui, 80; weaving, Gushman MacNaughton, Honolulu, 81; woven walls, LDS Archit, Aiea, Hawaii, 83. *Exhib:* Fiber Maquettes, Barnhart Gallery, Lexington, Ky, 79; Fiber As Art, Metrop Mus, Manila, Phillipines, 80; 15th Ann Drawing & Small Sculpture Show, Del Mar Col, Tex, 81; New Photographics, Sarah Spurgeon Gallery, Ellensburg, Wash, 82; Small Works Nat, Zaner Gallery, Rochester, NY, 82. *Pos:* Art reviewer, Honolulu Star Bulletin, 82- & Cult Climate, 82- *Teaching:* Asst prof fiber art, Univ Hawaii, Honolulu, 82- *Awards:* Jurors Award, Multi-Media Miniature Show, 81. *Bibliog:* Frank Stewart (auth), Progressions in weaving, Honolulu Str Bulletin, 10/21/79; Ronn Ronck (auth), Five artists, Honolulu Advertiser, 9/3/81. *Mem:* Am Crafts Coun; Handweavers Guild Am; Hawaii Artists League; Hawaii Craftsmen; Hawaii Alliance Arts Educ. *Media:* Fiber. *Mailing Add:* 41 A Dowsett Ave Honolulu HI 96817

BRESCHI, KAREN LEE
SCULPTOR
b Oakland, Calif, Oct 29, 41. *Study:* Calif Col Arts & Crafts, BFA, 63; Sacramento State Univ, 60-61; San Francisco State Univ, MA, 65; San Francisco Art Inst, 68-71. *Work:* Oakland Mus, Calif; Crocker Art Gallery, Sacramento; San Francisco Mus Art. *Exhib:* Fac Show Sculpture, 73 & Ceramic Sculpture, 74, San Francisco Art Inst; Clay, Whitney Mus, New York, 74; Exchange DFW/SFO, San Francisco Mus Art, 76; Illusionistic-Realism Defined in Contemp Ceramic Sculpture, Laguna Beach Mus, Calif, 77; The Great Am Foot, Mus Contemp Crafts, New York, 78; West Coast Sculptors, 78 & A Century of Clay, 79, Everson Mus; Clayworks, Univ Santa Barbara Mus, 79; A Century of Ceramics in the US 1878-1978, Renwick Gallery, Smithsonian Inst, 79-80; solo show, Braunstein/Quay Gallery, 81; and many others. *Teaching:* Instr sculpture, San Francisco Art Inst, 71-77; instr sculpture, San Francisco State Univ, 74-79; instr, Univ Calif, Davis, 80-81. *Awards:* First Place for Painted Flower, Oakland Art Mus, 62; Women's Archit League Award, Crocker Art Mus, 63; Award, Calif State Fair, 63. *Mem:* West/East Bag. *Media:* Clay, Mixed. *Mailing Add:* c/o Braunstein Gallery 254 Sutter St San Francisco CA 94102

BRESLIN, WYNN
PAINTER, SCULPTOR
b Hackensack, NJ, Nov 6, 32. *Study:* Syracuse Univ, 50; Ohio Wesleyan Univ, BFA, 54; Univ Del, MFA, 60. *Work:* Univ Del Fine Arts Collection, Newark; Syracuse Univ Fine Arts Collection; Maine Collection, Haystack Sch Art, Deer Isle; Del Trust Co, Wilmington; Fine Arts Collection, Del Blue Cross & Blue Shield; and others. *Comn:* Teacher & Child (sculpture), Immanuel Episcopal Church, Wilmington, Del, 70; landscape painting, First Fed Savings & Loan, Wilmington, 73. *Exhib:* Del Art Mus Regional Shows, 56-75; Benedictine Art Awards, Am Fedn Arts, 67; Woodmere Art Gallery, Philadelphia, 73-75; Philadelphia Art Alliance, 74; Catharine Lorillard Wolfe Art Club, Nat Arts Club, 74. *Teaching:* Art instr, Del Pub Schs, 54-63; art instr, Del Art Mus, 56-76; instr adult pvt classes, 63-; art instr, Tatnall Sch, 64; artist-in-the-schools, 83. *Awards:* First Prize Watercolor, Nat Orgn Women Art Exhib, Wilmington, 73; Ethel M Schnader Art Prize, Woodmere Art Gallery, Philadelphia, 74; 1st Prize, Chester Co Art Asn, Pa, 81; and others. *Bibliog:* From an artistic viewpoint, Univ News, Univ Del, 67. *Mem:* Nat League Am Pen Women (treas, Diamond State Br, 72-74); Wilmington Soc Fine Arts; Del Ctr Contemp Art; Rehoboth Art League; Chester Co Art Asn; and others. *Media:* Oil, Watercolor. *Mailing Add:* 470 RD 2 Terrapin Ln Newark DE 19711

BRESSI, BETTY
PAINTER, EDUCATOR
b Brooklyn, NY. *Study:* Calif Sch Fine Arts, San Francisco, with Clyfford Still & David Park, 48; Brooklyn Mus Art Sch, with Rueben Tam, 54-60; Columbia Univ, with Federico Castellon, MA, 65, EdD, 70. *Exhib:* Ann Exhib, Staten Island Mus, 72-76; Drawing & small sculpture, Ball State Univ, 74-75; Invitational, Hansen Galleries, New York, 77; group exhib, Bronx Mus Arts,

78; Fed of Staten Island Artists, New House Gallery, 79; Noho Gallery, 81. *Pos:* Ed, Glassworks Press, 75-78. *Teaching:* Instr fine arts, Queens Col, City Univ New York, 55-68, asst prof, Richmond Col, 68-74. *Awards:* First Award, Weissglas Fund, 72; Milnes-Dennen Award, 76. *Mem:* Univ Coun Art Educ (chmn exhib comt, 75-76). *Media:* Acrylic. *Publ:* Auth, article in Artview, Fed Staten Island Artists, Craftsmen, 77 & Women Artists News, 82. *Mailing Add:* 74 Claradon Lane Staten Island NY 10305

BRETTELL, RICHARD ROBSON
CURATOR
b Rochester, NY, Jan 17, 49. *Study:* Yale Univ, BA, MA, PhD, 76. *Collections Arranged:* Four Directions in Modern Photography (auth, catalog), Yale Art Gallery, 73; The Drawings of Camille Pissarro (coauth, catalog), Ashmolean Mus, Oxford, England, 79; Camille Pissarro, Mus Fine Arts, Boston, 80-81; Paper and Light: The Calotype in France & Great Britain (coauth, catalog), Mus Fine Arts, Houston. *Pos:* Cur, European Painting & Sculpture, Art Inst Chicago, 80- *Teaching:* Asst prof hist art, Univ Tex, Austin, 75-80. *Mem:* Col Art Asn; Soc Archit Hist. *Res:* French drawing, printmaking & painting, 1800-1914; American architecture of the 19th century; landscape painting; history of photography 1839-1900. *Publ:* Auth, Historic Denver, Architects & Architecture 1858-1893, Hist Denver, 74; coauth (with Carol B Brettell), Painters and Peasants in the 19th Century, Skira-Rizzoli, 83. *Mailing Add:* Art Inst Chicago S Michigan Ave & E Adams Chicago IL 60603

BREVERMAN, HARVEY
PAINTER, PRINTMAKER
b Pittsburgh, Pa, Jan 7, 34. *Study:* Carnegie Inst Technol, BFA; Ohio Univ, MFA. *Work:* Whitney Mus Am Art, New York; Albright-Knox Art Gallery, Buffalo; Baltimore Mus, Md; Philadelphia Mus, Pa; Mus of Mod Art, New York. *Exhib:* Corcoran Biennial, Washington, DC, 63; Brooklyn Mus Biennial, New York, 64; 35 Yrs in Retrospect, Butler Inst Am Art, Youngstown, Ohio, 71; Three Artists, Mod Mus Art, Oxford, England, 74; Honolulu Acad of Arts, 75; 8th Int Art Fair, Basel, Switz, 77; Arte Fiera 78, Int, Bologna, Italy, 78; Art Gallery Ont, Toronto, 79; Works on Paper: Recent Acquisitions, Albright-Knox Art Gallery, Buffalo, 79; Hassam Fund Exhib, Am Acad & Inst Arts & Letters, 80 & 81; Minn Mus Art, 81 & 82; Jewish Themes/Contemporary American Artists, Jewish Mus, New York, 82; Joanna Dean Galleries, New York, 83; and many others. *Teaching:* Prof art, State Univ NY Buffalo, 61-; artist-in-residence, State Acad Fine Arts, Amsterdam, Neth, 65-66; vis artist, Oxford Univ Ruskin Sch Fine Arts, Eng, summer 74 & 77. *Awards:* Tiffany Found Grant, 62; Creative Artists Pub Serv Grant, 72; Nat Endowment Arts Fels, 74-75 & 80-81. *Media:* Oil. *Dealer:* Gadatsy Gallery 45 Stephanie St Toronto ON M5T 1B2; Assoc Am Artists 663 Fifth Ave New York NY 10022. *Mailing Add:* 76 Smallwood Dr Buffalo NY 14226

BREWSTER, MICHAEL
SCULPTOR, EDUCATOR
b Eugene, Ore, Aug 15, 46. *Study:* Sao Paulo Grad Sch, Brazil, dipl, 64; Pomona Col, Claremont, Calif, with John Mason & David Gray, BA, 68; Claremont Grad Sch, with David Gray & Mowry Baden, MFA, 70. *Exhib:* Floating in Coincidence, Galleria del Cavallino, Venice, Italy, 79; Whistle Fill, Sound at Proj Studio One, New York, 79; Happenstance, Herron Gallery, Indianapolis, 80; Whitney Mus Am Art, 81; Los Angeles Co Mus Art, 81; Comune di Rimini, Italy, 82; and many others. *Teaching:* Instr sculpture, drawing & painting, Pomona Col, 71-73; asst prof, Dept Fine Arts, Claremont Grad Sch, 73-81, chmn dept, 75 & 79, assoc prof art, 81- *Awards:* Nat Endowment Arts Fel, 76 & 78. *Bibliog:* Hilton Kramer (auth), Strategy for viewing the Whitney Biennial, New York Times, 2/6/81; Kay Larson (auth), The problem with pantheons, New York Mag, 3/2/81; Suzanne Muchnic (auth), Hide and seek: Sixteen projects in sight and sound, Los Angeles Times, 8/25/81; and others. *Dealer:* Jean Milant Cirrus Gallery Ltd 542 S Alameda Los Angeles CA 90013. *Mailing Add:* 11 Navy St Venice CA 90291

BREZIK, HILARION
PAINTER, EDUCATOR
b Houston, Tex, Aug 5, 10. *Study:* Univ Notre Dame, BFA, MA & MFA. *Comn:* God Bless America (three walls), Recreation Rm, St Charles Boys Home, Milwaukee, Wis, 41; Winter Wonderland (painting), Dining Hall, Boysville of Mich, Clinton, 54; Signs of Zodiac (mural), Mary Moody Northern Theater, St Edward's Univ, Austin, Tex, 72. *Exhib:* Southwestern Univ, Georgetown, Tex; Reflections, St Edward's Univ, Austin, 81; Reflections (four verbal & visual sequences); Incarnate Word Col, San Antonio, 82; A New Mexican Portfolio, 83. *Collections Arranged:* Brothers of Holy Cross Nat Exhib Biennial, Austin, 61-69. *Pos:* Ed, South West Rev, Austin, 58-68; dir, St Edward's Univ Exhib Prog, 67-79. *Teaching:* Assoc prof watercolor & art hist, St Edward's Univ, 67-79. *Awards:* Hon mention, Wis Art Asn, 43. *Mem:* Am Fedn Arts; Tex Asn Schs Art. *Media:* Watercolor. *Publ:* Auth, A man from Texas sees a parade, Christian Art Quart, Vol II, No 3; auth, Art and the Catholic artist, Assoc St Joseph, Vol XXVI, No 4 & Vol XXVII, No 1; illusr, The happy heart, Dujarie Press. *Mailing Add:* Dept Art St Edward's Univ Austin TX 78704

BREZZO, STEVEN LOUIS
MUSEUM DIRECTOR
b Woodbury, NJ. *Study:* Clarion State Col, BA, 69; Univ Conn, MFA, 73. *Pos:* Chief cur, La Jolla Mus Contemp Art, 74-76; asst dir, San Diego Mus Art, 76-78, dir, 78- *Mailing Add:* 6190 Terryhill Dr La Jolla CA 92037

BRIANSKY, RITA PREZAMENT
PAINTER, PRINTMAKER
b Grajewa, Poland, July 25, 25; Can citizen. *Study:* Montreal Mus Fine Arts, with Jacques de Tonnancour; also with Alexandre Bercovitch & Anne Savage, Montreal; Ecole Beaux-Arts Montreal; Art Students League. *Work:* Vancouver Art Gallery, BC; Art Gallery Hamilton, Ont; London Art Mus, Ont; Can Dept External Affairs, Ottawa, Ont; Dofasco, Hamilton, Ont; and others. *Exhib:* Second Int Biennial Exhib of Prints, Tokyo & Osaka, Japan, 60-61; Salon Int Femme Vichy, France, 60-61; UNICEF Int, UN, New York, 65; La Soc des Artistes Prof du Que, Edinburgh, Scotland & London, Eng; 24 solo shows since 1957. *Teaching:* Instr, Ctr des Arts Visuels & Saidye Bronfman Ctr, Montreal, currently. *Awards:* Third Prize, 1st & 2nd Nat Exhib Prints, Burnaby, BC, 60 & 63; Can Coun Grant, 62 & Arts Award, 67; Purchase Award, Dawson Col, Montreal, 82. *Bibliog:* E Kilbourn (auth), 18 print-makers, Can Art, 61; and others. *Publ:* Illusr, Rubaboo Reader, 68; illusr, Grandmother Came From Dworitz, Tundra Bks, Montreal, 69; illusr, Ten Etchings from Wm Shakespeare's Sonnets, 72; illusr, On Stage Please, McClelland & Stewart, Toronto, 77 & Holt, Rinehart & Winston, New York, 79; illusr, Le Nu dams l'art au Quebec, Marcel-Broquet Publ, 82. *Dealer:* West End Art Gallery 1358 Greene Ave Montreal PQ Can; Wallack Art Galleries 201 Bank St Ottawa ON K2P 1W8. *Mailing Add:* 2284 Regent Ave Montreal PQ H4A 2R1 Canada

BRICE, WILLIAM
PAINTER, PRINTMAKER
b New York, NY, Apr 23, 21. *Study:* Chouinard Art Inst; Art Student League. *Work:* Metrop Mus Art; Whitney Mus Am Art; Mus Mod Art; Los Angeles Mus Art; Santa Barbara Mus Art. *Exhib:* Va Mus Fine Arts, 66; Des Moines, 67; one-man shows, Univ Calif, San Diego, Dallas Mus Fine Art & San Francisco Mus Art, 67; Los Angeles Inst Contemp Art, 78; and others. *Teaching:* Prof art, Univ Calif, Los Angeles, 53- *Awards:* Awards, Los Angeles, 47 & Los Angeles City Exhib, 51. *Bibliog:* Nathaniel Pousette-Dart (auth), Paintings, watercolors, lithographs, Clayton Spicer Press, 46. *Mem:* Artists Equity Asn. *Mailing Add:* 427 Beloit St Los Angeles CA 90049

BRIER, HELENE
PAINTER, EDUCATOR
b Bronx, NY, May 16, 24. *Study:* Art Students League with G Bridgeman & W Kantor, 42-45; Nat Acad Design, with Robert Philipp, 45-47; NY Univ, with Don Eddy, BS(fine art), 74. *Work:* Andrew Dickson White Mus Art, Cornell Univ, NY; Univ Notre Dame Art Gallery, Ind; NY Univ Art Collection; Housatonic Mus & Univ Bridgeport, Conn. *Exhib:* Silvermine Ann, 70-80; Carlson Gallery Fac Art, 75-79; Art Northeast USA, 83; Collection '83, Silvermine Ctr Arts, Richardson-Vicks Inc, Wilton, Conn, 83; solo exhibs, Silvermine Ctr Arts, 84, Slade Mem Mus, Norwich, Conn, 84 & Mattatuck Mus, Waterbury, Conn, 84. *Collections Arranged:* Mus Sci Art Ann Exhibs, 63-77; Window Series, Grand Central Moderns, 67; Artists of Today, Carlson Gallery, 69; Silvermine Ann, 70-80; Carlson Gallery Fac Art, 75-79. *Teaching:* Instr drawing & design, Univ Bridgeport, Conn, 75-79. *Awards:* First Prize, Lloyd Goodrich, 68; First Prize, Lawrence Alloway, 69; Silvermine Ann New England Exhib, Thomas Hess, 78. *Bibliog:* Gregory Battcock (auth), Window series, Arts Mag, 67; Burt Chernow (auth), Beach People, Westport News, 79; Virginia Mann (auth), Beach People, Brier Art Resources Conn, 4/78. *Mem:* Conn Acad Art; life mem Art Students League; New Haven Paint & Clay Club; Silvermine Ctr Arts. *Media:* Oil, Watercolor. *Publ:* Contribr, Gregory Battcock, Arts Mag, 67; ed, Judy Chapman, Fairfield Citizen News, 78; contribr, Mia Brech, Fair Press, 79; Eliz O'Neil, Fairfield Co Mag, 79; contribr, Martha Scott, Bridgeport Post, 79. *Mailing Add:* 58 Random Rd Fairfield CT 06432

BRIGADIER, ANNE
PAINTER, LECTURER
b New York, NY. *Study:* Art Student League, with Kimon Nicolaides & Morris Kantor; also with Rudolph Ray; study in France, Italy & Spain. *Work:* Syracuse Univ Mus, NY; NC Mus Art, Raleigh; Univ Md, Baltimore; Finch Col Mus, New York; Newark Mus Art, NJ; Norfolk & Chrysler Mus, Vermont; Wichita Mus, Kansas; plus others. *Exhib:* One-woman shows, ROKO Gallery, 61-66, Tirea Kallis Gallery, Provincetown, 75-76, Cottage Gallery, Provincetown, 79; Mus Mod Art Lending Serv, Libr, New York, 66-68; Philadelphia Mus Art Lending Serv, Pa, 70-72; Provincetown Artists, Everson Mus, Syracuse, NY, 77; Women in Am Art, Summit Gallery, New York, 77; plus others. *Teaching:* Pvt classes & lect demonstrations in collage. *Awards:* Oil Painting Award, November Woods, Cape Cod Art Asn, 57. *Bibliog:* F Crotty (auth), Why try to imitate the past says noted Provincetown artist, Worcester Sun Telegram, 11/9/58, Provincetown Advocate, 11/13/58 & Interior Design Mag, 10/58. *Mem:* Am Fedn Arts; Provincetown Art Asn (hon vpres, 65-70, trustee, 58-64 & 71-). *Media:* Oil, Acrylic, Collage, Encaustic. *Publ:* Auth & illusr, Collage, a complete guide for artists, Watson-Guptill, New York & London, 11/70. *Dealer:* Visual Images Gallery Wellfleet MA 02667. *Mailing Add:* 69 Fifth Ave New York NY 10003

BRIGGS, ERNEST
PAINTER, INSTRUCTOR
b San Diego, Calif, Dec 24, 23. *Study:* Rudolf Schaeffer Sch Design; Calif Sch Fine Art, 50. *Work:* San Francisco Mus Mod Art, Calif; Oakland Art Mus, Calif; Whitney Mus Am Art, New York; Brooklyn Mus Art, NY; Carnegie Inst, Pittsburgh. *Exhib:* San Francisco Art Asn Ann, San Francisco Mus Mod Art, Calif, 48, 49 & 53; New Directions, Stable Gallery, New York, 55; Whitney Ann, Whitney Mus Am Art, New York, 55, 56 & 61; 12 Americans, Mus Mod Art, New York, 56; Corcoran Biennial, Corcoran Gallery Art, Washington, DC, 61; Carnegie Int, Carnegie Inst, Pittsburgh, 61; San

Francisco 1945-50, Oakland Mus, Calif, 73; California Art, Nat Collection, Washington, DC, 77. *Teaching:* Instr painting, Univ Fla, 58; instr painting & drawing, Pratt Inst, Brooklyn, NY, 61; instr drawing, Yale Univ, Grad Sch Art, 67-68. *Awards:* Albert Bender Grant, 51; Anne Bremmer Mem Prize for Painting, 53; Creative Artists Public Serv Program, 75. *Bibliog:* Mary Fuller McChesney (auth), A Period of Exploration, Oakland Mus Art, 73; Peter Plagens (auth), Sunshine Muse, Praeger, 74; Irving Sandler (auth), New York School, Harper & Row, 78. *Media:* Oil. *Dealer:* Thomas Gruenebaum 38 East 57th St New York NY 10022. *Mailing Add:* 50 W 29th St New York NY 10001

BRIGHT, BARNEY
SCULPTOR
b Shelbyville, Ky, July 8, 27. *Study:* Davidson Col; Univ Louisville; Art Ctr, Louisville, Ky. *Work:* J B Speed Art Mus, Louisville; Milwaukee Art Ctr, Wis; Childrens Art Gallery, Louisville; Univ Ky, Lexington; Libr Bldg, Jeffersonville, Ind; represented in more than 500 pvt collections, more than 25 pub collections. *Comn:* Sculpture for Old Stag Distillery, Frankfort, Ky, 65; The Louisville Clock, Louisville, Ky; sculpture at WAVE Garden, WAVE Inc, Louisville; sculpture of Dean A C Russell, Univ Louisville Law Sch; plus many others. *Exhib:* Friendship Exhib, France, 58; Sculpture Today, John Herron Art Inst, Indianapolis, 61; Tri-State Exhib, Evansville Mus Arts & Sci, Ind, 62; Parrish Art Mus, South Hampton, NY, 70; Suffolk Co Mus, Stony Brook, NY, 71. *Media:* Metals, Marble. *Mailing Add:* 2031 Frankfort Ave Louisville KY 40206

BRIGHTWELL, WALTER
PAINTER
b Del Rio, Tex, July 14, 19. *Study:* Art Student League, with Frank Dumond. *Work:* US Navy Combat Art Collection, Washington, DC; Elliot Mus, Stuart, Fla. *Comn:* Mural, West Side Savings Bank, New York, 57. *Exhib:* Mus Marine, Paris, 63; Allied Artists Am, Nat Acad Design, 66, Coun Am Artists Soc, 66 & Am Watercolor Soc, 69; Ft Lauderdale Mus Arts, Fla, 69; Elliot Mus, Stuart, Fla, 82. *Awards:* George Burr Gold Medal, Nat Arts Club, New York, 59; Gwynne Lennon Award, Salmagundi Club, New York, 63; Purchase Award, Am Watercolor Soc, 66. *Mem:* Allied Artists Am; Am Watercolor Soc (dir, 69-71); Artists Fel (corresp secy, 63-69); Salmagundi Club (art chmn, 63-67); Grand Cent Art Galleries. *Media:* Acrylic, Watercolor. *Dealer:* Hobe Sound Galleries Hobe Sound FL 33455. *Mailing Add:* 946 Reef Lane Vero Beach FL 32960

BRILLIANT, RICHARD
EDUCATOR
b Boston, Mass, Nov 20, 29. *Study:* Yale Univ, BA, 51, MA, 56, PhD, 60; Harvard Univ, LLB, 54. *Teaching:* From asst prof to prof art hist, Univ Penn, 62-70; prof, Columbia Univ, 70-; vis Mellon Prof fine arts, Univ Pittsburgh, 71. *Mem:* Col Art Asn; Archaeol Inst Am; Ger Archaeol Inst. *Res:* Greek and Roman art and archaeology; theory and method in art history. *Publ:* Auth, Arch of Septimius Severus in Rome, Am Acad Rome, 67; auth, Arts of the Ancient Greeks, McGraw-Hill, 73; auth, Roman Art, Phaidon, 74; auth, Pompeii, AD 79: The Treasure of Rediscovery, Volair, 79; auth, Visual Narratives, Cornell, 84. *Mailing Add:* 10 Wayside Lane Scarsdale NY 10583

BRINKERHOFF, DERICKSEN MORGAN
HISTORIAN, EDUCATOR
b Philadelphia, Pa, Oct 4, 21. *Study:* Taft Sch, dipl, 39; Williams Col, BA(art), 43; Yale Univ, MA(art hist), 47; Univ Zurich, 48-49; Harvard Univ, PhD(fine arts), 58. *Teaching:* Instr art hist, Brown Univ, Providence, 52-55; from instr to assoc prof art hist, RI Sch Design, Providence, 52-59; assoc prof art hist, Pa State Univ, University Park, 61-62; assoc prof art hist, Tyler Sch Art, Temple Univ, 62-65; assoc prof art hist, Univ Calif, Riverside, 65-67, prof art hist, 67- *Awards:* Cash Prize, Am Numismatic Soc, New York, 52; Sr Fel Classical Studies, Am Acad Rome, 59-61. *Mem:* Col Art Asn Am; Riverside Art Asn (trustee, 68-72, mem exhib comt, 71-). *Publ:* Auth, New examples of the Hellenistic statue group, The Invitation to the Dance, and their significance, Am J Archaeol, 65; auth, A Collection of Sculpture in Classical & Early Christian Antioch, 70; contribr, Studies Presented to G M A Hanfmann, 71; auth, Hellenistic Statues of Aphrodite, Outstanding Dissertations in the Fine Arts, 78. *Mailing Add:* Dept of Art Hist Univ of Calif Riverside CA 92521

BRISTOW, WILLIAM ARTHUR
PAINTER, EDUCATOR
b San Antonio, Tex, Feb 1, 37. *Study:* Univ Tex, BFA, 58; Univ Fla, MFA, 60; also with Clinton Adams, Ernest Briggs & George Lockwood. *Work:* Dallas Mus Fine Art; Houston Mus Fine Art; San Antonio Art League; WTex Mus, Lubbock; Longview Jr League, Tex. *Comn:* Migration (aluminum fountain sculpture), US Govt, HemisFair, San Antonio, 68; steel sculpture fountain, Turbine Support Co, San Antonio, 69; two tapestry murals, La Mansion Hotels, San Antonio, 80 & 81; tapestry mural & tapestry, Frost Nat Bank, San Antonio. *Exhib:* Southwest Print & Drawing Soc, Dallas Mus Fine Art, 60, Tex Ann, 60-63; Painting in the Southwest, Okla Art Ctr, Oklahoma City, 62; Artist of the Year, San Antonio Art League, Witte Mus, 65; 14th Ann Prints & Drawings & 24th Ann Delta Competition, Ark Arts Ctr, Little Rock, 81. *Teaching:* Instr painting & drawing, Univ Fla, Gainesville, 58-60; assoc prof painting & drawing, Trinity Univ, San Antonio, 60-79, prof, 79-, chmn dept design & drawing, 65-78. *Awards:* Purchase Prize, Tex Ann, Houston Mus Fine Art, 62; First Prize Southwest Print & Drawing, Mrs Edwin B Hopkins Fund, Dallas Mus, 64; Mus STex Prize for Sculpture, Coca Cola Bottling Co, 66. *Mem:* Col Art Asn Am. *Media:* Oil, Acrylic. *Publ:* Illusr, Animal Tales of the West, 74. *Dealer:* Dorothy Katz Sol del Rio Gallery 1020 Townsend Ave San Antonio TX 78209. *Mailing Add:* 344 Wildrose Ave San Antonio TX 78209

BRITSKY, NICHOLAS
PAINTER, EDUCATOR
b Weldirz, Western Ukraine, Dec 11, 13; US citizen. *Study:* Yale Univ, BFA; Syracuse Univ; Cranbrook Acad Art. *Work:* Evansville Mus, Ind; Ford Motor Co Collection, Dearborn, Mich; Univ Ill, Chicago; Prudential Life Ins Co, New York; Springville Mus, Utah; and many others. *Comn:* Mosaic tile mural, Allen Park High Sch, Galesburg, Ill, 54; com mural, E B Evans Co, Philadelphia, 64; wood crucifix & mural decoration, St Boniface Church, Seymour, Ill, 78; fiberglass & stainless steel crucifix, St Patricks Church, Urbana, Ill, 80; plexiglas window, Chapel Mercy Hosp,, Urbana, Ill, 83. *Exhib:* Denver Mus, Colo, 51, 53 & 55; Butler Inst Am Art, Youngstown, Ohio, 52-54; Nat Acad Design, New York, 60; Evansville Mus, 61, 67 & 68; Mainstreams USA, Marietta Col, Ohio, 69-72. *Teaching:* Prof art, Univ Ill, formerly, prof emer, currently. *Awards:* First Prize Oil-Casein, Evansville Ind Mus Art, 61; First Prize, Springville Mus Art, Utah, 74; Gov Award Outstanding Contrib Arts, Ill, 81. *Mem:* Am Fedn Arts. *Media:* Multimedia. *Publ:* Contribr, Encycl Slavonica, Philos Press, 49; illusr, Ford Times Mag, 64. *Dealer:* Grand Central Galleries 40 Vanderbilt Ave New York NY 10017. *Mailing Add:* Dept Art Univ Ill Champaign IL 61820

BRITT, AL
PAINTER, EDUCATOR
b Cuthbert, Ga, Nov 16, 34. *Study:* Ala State Col, BA & BS, 59; Univ Mex, Mexico City, 64; Univ NMex, MFA, 65; Univ Ghana, Lagon, 70; Univ Nigeria, Lagos, 71; Fal State Univ, PhD, 74. *Work:* Atlanta Univ, Afro-Am Collection; Oakland Mus, Calif; Dusable Mus Afro-Am Hist, Chicago. *Comn:* Mixed media sculpture, Kiah Mus, Savannah, Ga, 71; Historical Wall, Savannah State Col, 72. *Exhib:* Nat Conf Artists Exhib, 50-75; Smith Mason Gallery, Washington, DC, 71; Expo 72, San Francisco; Expo 73, Chicago. *Collections Arranged:* Southern Univ, New Orleans; Savannah State Col; Itta Bena; Ala State Univ, Montgomery, *Pos:* Art demonstr, cols, univ, churches & art ctrs, 50-74. *Teaching:* Head art dept, Mo State Penitentiary, 65; prof & head dept, Savannah State Col, Ga, 69-75; prof & head dept art, Ala State Univ, Montgomery, 75- *Awards:* First Prize, Crystal Caves, Birmingham, Ala, 62. *Mem:* Nat Art Educ Asn; Nat Conf Artists (regional dir, 70-73); Col Arts Asn; Creative Artist Asn; Ga Art Educ Asn. *Media:* Junk. *Res:* Afro-Amerrican art; drawings by five-year olds. *Collection:* Afro-Am artists. *Publ:* Contribr, Black Artist on Art, 69; contribr, Black Dimensions in Contemporary Art, 71; contribr, An American History, Appleton, 72; contribr, Afro American Art, 73; contribr, Atlanta Univ Bulletin. *Mailing Add:* Dept of Art Ala State Univ Montgomery AL 36101

BRITT, NELSON CLARK
PAINTER, ADMINISTRATOR
b Rochester, NY, Nov 13, 44. *Study:* Yale Univ, 66; State Univ NY Col, Buffalo, BA, 67; RI Sch Design, MFA, 73. *Work:* RI Sch Design; Tishman Corp, Sperry Hutchinson Bldg, New York. *Exhib:* Newport Art Asn Nat, Newport, RI, 73; Silvermine Artist Guild, 75; one-man show, Winfisky Gallery, Salem State Col, 81; Springfield Art Asn Gallery, Ill, 82; 59th Ann, Burpee Art Mus, Rockford, Ill, 83; Midwest States Exhib, Evansville Mus Art & Sci, Ind, 83; Western NY Open, Albright-Knox Art Gallery. *Pos:* Coordr art educ, Peabody Pub Schs, Mass, 75-82. *Teaching:* Instr painting, Newport Art Asn, RI, 71-73; teaching fel, RI Sch Design, 71-73; adj prof art educ, Boston Univ, 72. *Awards:* First Prize Acrylic, Albright-Knox Art Gallery, 68; Best of Show, Westchester Open Competition, Pleasantville, NY, 70; Award Painting, Silvermine Artist Club, 75. *Mem:* Springfield Art Asn (exec dir, 82-). *Media:* Acrylic. *Mailing Add:* 3617 Timothy Rd Springfield IL 62707

BRITT, SAM GLENN
EDUCATOR, PAINTER
b Ruleville, Miss, Sept 26, 40. *Study:* Memphis Acad Art, BFA; Univ Miss, MFA; Cape Cod Sch Painting, Provincetown, Mass, with Henry Hensche; Frudakais Acad Sculpture, Philadelphia, with Angelous Frudakais. *Work:* Union Bldg, Delta State Univ, Munic Art Gallery, Jackson, Miss; Winterville Mounds, Greenville, Miss; First Nat Bank, Cleveland, Miss. *Comn:* Drawing depicting the life style of ancient Indians, Winterville Mounds Mus, Miss, 67. *Exhib:* One-man show, Gov's Mansion, Jackson, Miss; Bryant Galleries, Jackson, Miss & New Orleans, La, 83; Gallery Three, Roanoke, Va, 83; National Bank Commerce, Memphis, Tenn, 83; Symphony Ball, Peabody Hotel, Memphis, Tenn, 83; and others. *Teaching:* Instr drawing & painting, Delta State Univ, 66-73, asst prof, 73-78, assoc prof art, 78- pvt instr, Clarksdale, Miss, 73-; Painting workshops, Art Asn, Yazoo City, Miss, Northwest Jr Col, Senatobia, Miss & Booneville Art Asn, Miss. *Awards:* Second Prize, Nat Painting Exhib, 64; Most Outstanding Work, Nat Small Painting Exhib, Hadley, 74; Best in Show, Crosstie Festival, 79. *Bibliog:* Ed Phillips (auth), Finding God's beauty in a simple world, Delta Scene Mag, 75; Featured on Miss Educ TV as a Miss Artist, spring 80. *Media:* Oil, Pastel. *Mailing Add:* Box 3236 Delta State Univ Cleveland MS 38733

BRITTON, DANIEL ROBERT
PRINTMAKER, EDUCATOR
b Colorado Springs, Colo, Apr 1, 49. *Study:* Univ Colo, BFA, 74, MFA, 76. *Work:* Univ Colo, Boulder; Ariz State Univ, Tempe. *Exhib:* Stockton Nat, Pioneer Mus, Calif, 78; San Diego Nat, Univ Art Gallery, Calif, 80; Tenth Nat Print Competition, Univ Art Gallery, Minot, NDak, 81; DeKalb 81 Nat Print Competition, Swen Parsons Gallery, Ill, 81; Moravian Print Nat, Church Street Gallery, Bethlehem, Pa, 81; American Drawing IV, Portsmouth Mus, 83. *Pos:* Co-dir, Print Research Fac, Ariz State Univ, Tempe, 78- *Teaching:* Assoc prof printmaking, Ariz State Univ, 76- *Awards:* Purchase Award, 4th Univ Dallas Print Nat, 78; Am Art Heritage Award, Ariz Print Competition, 79; Award of Merit, DeKalb Print Nat, 81. *Bibliog:* Roberta Loach (auth),

Printmakers, Visual Dialogue Mag, 79; Art in the Sun Belt, Art News, 80; Carol Kotrozo (auth), Drawing and Printmaking, Art Week, 81. *Media:* Lithography, Oil. *Publ:* Tamarind Technical Papers, 79. *Mailing Add:* 1005 South Una Ave Tempe AZ 85281

BROADD, HARRY ANDREW
PAINTER, HISTORIAN
b Chicago, Ill, Feb 17, 10. *Study:* Univ Chicago, PhB, 30; Columbia Univ, AM, 31; Art Inst Chicago; Univ Mich, PhD, 46. *Exhib:* Int Exhib Watercolors, Art Inst Chicago, 32; Artists of Chicago & Vicinity Show, Art Inst Chicago, 33, 36 & 37; Mich Artists Exhib, Detroit Inst Arts, 46; one-man retrospective, 1931-1961, Philbrook Art Ctr, Tulsa, Okla, 61. *Teaching:* Asst prof art & art educ, Eastern Mich Univ, 37-47; prof art hist, Univ Tulsa, 47-67; prof art hist, Northeastern Ill Univ, 67-79, emer prof, 79-; vis prof art, Okmulgee State Tech, 81; adj prof art, Oral Roberts Univ, Tulsa, Okla, 82. *Media:* Oil, Acrylic. *Publ:* Auth, Music as a stimulus to design & literature as a stimulus to expression, Design, 35; auth, articles on graphic arts, block printing & others, In: World Bk Encycl, 62; auth, Sandpaper lithographs, 69 & Art appreciation and history/who needs it?, 70, Arts & Activities. *Mailing Add:* 153 W Jefferson Pl Broken Arrow OK 74012

BROADLEY, HUGH T
HISTORIAN, ADMINISTRATOR
b Sacramento, Calif, June 5, 22. *Study:* Park Col, AB; Yale Univ, AM; NY Univ, PhD. *Pos:* Mus cur, Nat Gallery Art, 54-61; cur art collections, Ariz State Univ, 65-67; dir, Phoenix Art Mus, 67-69. *Teaching:* Prof art hist, Bowling Green State Univ, 61-65; prof art hist, Ariz State Univ, 69- *Mem:* Western Asn Art Mus (pres, 68); Col Art Asn Am; Am Asn Mus; Friends Mex Art; Int Coun Mus. *Res:* Flemish painting of the fifteenth and sixteenth centuries. *Mailing Add:* 4102 N 50th Pl Phoenix AZ 85018

BROCK, ROBERT W
SCULPTOR, EDUCATOR
b Tacoma, Ohio, June 27, 36. *Study:* Sch of Dayton Art Inst, 54-60, dipl, with Robert C Koepnick; Univ Dayton, BFA, 60; Ohio Univ, MFA, 62, with David Hosteller. *Work:* Dayton Art Inst; State Univ NY Col, Fredonia. *Exhib:* Artists of Southern Ohio, Dayton Art Inst, 60 & 61; Ohio Sculpture & Ceramic Show, Butler Inst Am Art, Youngstown, 64; Western NY Show, Albright-Knox Art Gallery, Buffalo, 65-67, 69 & 75 & Outdoor Sculpture Exhib, 68; Unordinary Realities, Xerox Ctr, Rochester, 75. *Pos:* Mem adv comt, Burchfield Ctr, 70-; chmn fine arts dept, State Univ Col, Buffalo, 70-73 & 81-85; pres, Patteran Artists Inc, Buffalo, 77-78. *Teaching:* Prof sculpture, State Univ NY Col, Buffalo, 62- *Media:* Polyester Resin and Formica, Mixed Media. *Mailing Add:* 104 Fordham Dr Buffalo NY 14216

BROD, STANFORD
DESIGNER, EDUCATOR
b Cincinnati, Ohio, Sept 29, 32. *Study:* Col of Design, Archit & Art, Univ Cincinnati, BS(design), 55. *Work:* Nat Collection of Fine Arts, Washington, DC; Mus Mod Art, New York; Hebrew Union Col, Jewish Inst Relig Mus, Los Angeles; Contemp Art Ctr & Cincinnati Art Mus, Ohio. *Comn:* Urban Walls: Cincinnati (ten story bldg wall mural), Solway Gallery for Cincinnati Community, 72; Six Urban Banners, Contemp Art Ctr, 75. *Exhib:* Greetings, Mus Mod Art, New York, 66; Third Int Poster Exhib, Listowel, Ireland, 77; Int Calligraphy Today; Urban Banner Designs Cincinnati Downtown Commercial Districts, 81; Tel Aviv Mus, 82; Int Art Exhib DRUPA, Dusseldorf, Ger, 82. *Pos:* Designer, Rhoades Studio, Cincinnati, 55-62; designer, Lipson Assocs Inc, Cincinnati, 62- *Teaching:* Teacher exp typography, Art Acad Cincinnati, 60-75; adj prof graphic design, Col Design, Archit & Art, Univ Cincinnati, 69- *Awards:* Communication Arts Award, Commun Arts J, 59, 64, 66 & 70; Typomundus 20/2 Int Award, 70; Int Typographic Composition Award, 70-72 & 75. *Publ:* Illusr, How Would You Act, 62; contribr, Graphis Ann, 67-; contribr, Mod Publicity, 69-; contribr, HUD Nat Community Art, 73; auth, Packaging Design, 73. *Mailing Add:* 429 W Galbraith Rd Cincinnati OH 45215

BRODER, PATRICIA JANIS
HISTORIAN, WRITER
b New York, NY, Nov 22, 35. *Study:* Smith Col, 53-54; Barnard Col, Columbia Univ, BA, 57; Rutgers Univ Grad Sch, 62-63. *Pos:* Stock brokerage trainee, A M Kidder & Co, New York, 58; regist rep, Thomas & McKinnon, New York, 59-61; regist investment adv, 62-64; writer & lectr Am art hist, art appraisal & authentication and brokerage. *Awards:* Herbert Adams Mem Medal for serv to Am sculpture, Nat Sculpture Soc, New York, 75; Western Heritage Wrangler Award for best article on the Am West, Nat Cowboy Hall of Fame & Western Heritage Ctr, Oklahoma City, 76; Western Heritage Award for Best Book, Nat Cowboy Hall Fame, 81; and others. *Publ:* Auth, Dean Cornwell: Dean of Illustrators, Watson-Guptill, 78; auth, Hopi Painting: The World of the Hopis, Brandywine Press/E P Dutton, 78; Great Paintings of Old American West, 79 & American Indian Painting and Sculpture, 80, Abbeville Press/Crown; Toas: a Painter's Dream, New York Graphic Soc, 80; auth, The American West: The modern vision, New York Graphic Soc, 84. *Mailing Add:* 488 Long Hill Dr Short Hills NJ 07078

BRODERICK, HERBERT REGINALD, III
HISTORIAN
b Bethesda, Md, July 16, 45. *Study:* Columbia Col, AB, 67; Columbia Univ, MA, 68, MPhil, 75, PhD, 78. *Teaching:* Instr art hist, Columbia Univ, 74-77, asst prof, 78; asst prof, Herbert H Lehman Col, City Univ New York, 78- *Awards:* Mrs Giles Whiting Found Fel, 74-75; Nat Endowment Humanities Fel, 81-82. *Mem:* Col Art Asn Am; Int Ctr Medieval Art. *Res:* Iconography

of the Old Testament in medieval art; Anglo-Saxon manuscript illumination. *Publ:* Auth, Solomon and Sheba revisited, Gesta, Vol XVI, 77; auth, A note on Solomon and Bathsheba as Fürstenspiegel, Studies in Iconography, Vol VI, 80; auth, Some attitudes toward the frame in Anglo-Saxon manuscripts of the 10th and 11th centuries, Artibus & Historiae, Vol V, 82. *Mailing Add:* 530 West End Ave New York NY 10024

BRODERICK, JAMES ALLEN
ADMINISTRATOR, PHOTOGRAPHER
b Chicago, Ill, July 25, 39. *Study:* St Ambrose Col, BA, 62; Univ Iowa, MA, 66. *Exhib:* Engraving 1974, Albrecht Gallery & Mus, St Joseph, Mo, 74; Photog Exhib, Mus Art, Univ Iowa, 75; Works on Paper, Dallas Mus Fine Arts, Tex, 78; Nat Juried Photo Exhib, Ala Arts Alliance, Birmingham, 79; Carlsbad Fine Arts Mus, NMex, 80; Photo Spiva, Spiva Art Ctr, Joplin, Mo, 80; State of Texas, Ctr Visual Commun, Dallas, 81; and others. *Pos:* Gallery dir, Northwest Mo State Univ, 69-76. *Teaching:* Prof prints & photog, Northwest Mo State Univ, Maryville, 66-76, chmn, Dept Art, 71-76; prof & chairperson, Dept Art, Tex Tech Univ, Lubbock, 76- *Mem:* Tex Asn Schs Art; Nat Coun Art Adminr; Nat Asn Schs Art. *Mailing Add:* 2910 20th St Lubbock TX 79410

BRODERSON, MORRIS
PAINTER
b Los Angeles, Calif, Nov 4, 28. *Study:* Pasadena Mus, life drawing classes with De Erdeley; Univ Southern Calif, spec studies in art, four yrs. *Work:* Whitney Mus Am Art, New York; Mus Fine Arts, Houston; Joseph H Hirshhorn Collection & Nat Collection Fine Arts, Washington, DC; San Francisco Mus Art, Calif. *Exhib:* One-man shows, M H De Young Mem Mus, San Francisco, 61, Staempli Gallery, New York, 79, Gallaudet Col, Washington, DC, 81, San Diego Mus, 82 & Ankrum Gallery, Los Angeles, 83; Am Watercolors, Mitchell Mus, Mt Vernon, Ill, 79. *Awards:* New Talent, USA, Art in Am, 60; Excellence in Art, Art Dirs Club Philadelphia, 63; Great Ideas of Western Man, Container Corp Am, 63. *Bibliog:* John Canaday (auth), The special world of Broderson, New York Times, 11/13/71; Diane Hines (auth), Speaking thru his art, Am Artist, 5/10/80; Arden Neisser (auth), The Other Side of Silence, 83. *Mailing Add:* c/o Ankrum Gallery 657 N La Cienega Blvd Los Angeles CA 90069

BRODERSON, ROBERT
PAINTER
b West Haven, Conn, July 6, 20. *Study:* Duke Univ, AB, 50; State Univ Iowa, with Mauricio Lasansky, James Lechay & Stuart Edie, MFA, 52. *Work:* Nat Inst Arts & Lett, NY; Whitney Mus Am Art; Wadsworth Atheneum, Hartford, Conn; Colorado Springs Fine Arts Ctr; Princeton Univ Art Mus. *Exhib:* Four shows, Pa Acad Fine Arts, 51-67; Denver Art Mus, 63; Univ Ill, 63 & 65; Nebr Art Asn, 64; Carnegie Inst, 64; plus others. *Teaching:* Instr, Duke Univ, 57-64. *Awards:* Duke Univ Summer Res Fel, 63; Guggenheim Fel, 64; Childe Hassam Purchase Award, 68; plus others. *Dealer:* Terry Dintenfass Inc 18 E 67th St New York NY 10021. *Mailing Add:* PO Box 190 Raleigh NC 27602

BRODHEAD, QUITA
PAINTER
b Wilmington, Del. *Study:* Pa Acad Fine Arts; Grande Chaumiere & Julienne's, Paris; with Arthur Carles & Alexander Archipenko; Fel Pa Acad Fine Arts. *Work:* Westerdahl Collection, Spain; Widener Col Mus, Pa; Pa Acad Fine Arts. *Comn:* Mural, St Johns Episcopal Church, Bala-Cynwyd, Pa, 30; mural, comn by F Ennalls Berl, Wilmington, Del, 33; portrait, comn by Mrs Graham Cummin, Paoli, Pa, 53. *Exhib:* Motion in Space, 48 & Abstract, Pa Acad Fine Arts; Butler Art Inst; La Nuit et le Jour, Salon D'Automne, Paris, 50; and many one-man shows. *Pos:* Mem bd dirs, Fel Acad Fine Arts, Pa, 40-50. *Awards:* Gold Medal Award, 43 & Caroline Gibbons Granger Mem Award, 48; Second Prize, Ohio Col Art, 49. *Bibliog:* Edourdo Westerdahl (auth), The Painting of Quita Brodhead, El Dia, 61. *Mem:* Am Fedn Arts; Artists Equity; Philadelphia Art Alliance. *Media:* Oil, Acrylic. *Mailing Add:* 211 Atlee Rd Wayne PA 19087

BRODIE, AGNES HAHN
SCULPTOR, PAINTER
b Budapest, Hungary, Oct 26, 24; US citizen. *Study:* Acad Montmartre, Paris, BFA, 46; Cleveland Inst Art; Corcoran Sch Art, dipl(fine arts), 75. *Work:* Atkins Mus Fine Arts, Kansas City, Mo; Sidney Lewis Collection, Richmond, Va; Ariz State Univ; Mus Fine Arts, Budapest, Hungary; Del Art Mus, Wilmington. *Exhib:* Solo exhib, Athenaeum, Richmond Mus, Alexandria, Va, 80, Ariz State Univ, 82, Cath Univ Am, Washington, DC, 83 & Del Mus Art, Wilmington, 83; Hommage a La Terre Natale, Mus Fine Arts, Budapest, Hungary, 82. *Pos:* art dir, Sterling-Lindner, Cleveland, Ohio, 63-65, advert & sales promotion dir, 65-68. *Teaching:* Vis artist watercolor, Corcoran Gallery, 75; lectr studio arts, Northern Va Community Col, 76- *Awards:* Award, Jr CofC Ninth Ann, Cleveland, 63; First Prize & Judge's Choice, Drawing Show, Alexandria Art League, Va, 76. *Bibliog:* Helen Cullinan (auth), Arches and columns, Cleveland Plain Dealer, 11/6/77; Benjamin Forgey (auth), Surveying Agnes Brodie, Washington Star, 11/30/80. *Mem:* Artist Equity Asn, Washington, DC; Col Art Asn Am; Women's Caucus Art. *Media:* All. *Dealer:* Gallery K 2032 P St Washington DC 20036. *Mailing Add:* 1203 Corbin Ct McLean VA 22101

BRODIE, REGIS CONRAD
POTTER
b Pittsburgh, Pa, Nov 19, 42. *Study:* Ind Univ Pa, BSc(art educ) & MEd; Temple Univ, MFA. *Work:* Univ Utah Art Mus, Salt Lake City; Del Art Mus,

Wilmington; Everson Mus of Art, Syracuse, NY; Tyler Sch of Art, Temple Univ, Philadelphia; Schenectady Mus, NY. *Exhib:* Soup Tureens: 1976, Mus of Contemp Crafts, New York, 76; Nat Functional Ceramics: 1977, Wooster Mus, Col of Wooster, Ohio, 77; two-man show, Everson Mus of Art, Syracuse, 76; Incorporated Galleries, New York, 79; Thirteen Collection Exhib, Sotheby Parke Benet, New York, 79; Nat Invitational Exhib Currents 80, Murfreesboro, Tenn. *Teaching:* Prof studio art, Skidmore Col, 69-, dir, Six summer art prog, 72- *Awards:* Second Prize/Ceramics, Wichita Nat Crafts Show, 72; Purchase Prize, 17th Ann Exhib of Contemp Crafts, Del Art Mus, Wilmington, 73; First Prize/Ceramics, Ann Nat Art Exhib, Cooperstown, NY, 74, 77 & 82. *Mem:* Nat Coun on Educ for Ceramic Arts; Am Crafts Coun; World Craft Coun. *Media:* Clay, Porcelain; Stoneware, Raku. *Publ:* Auth, The Energy-Efficient Potter, Watson-Guptill Publ, 82; auth, Insulating existing kilns, Ceramics Monthly, 9/83. *Mailing Add:* Skidmore Col Saratoga Springs NY 12866

BRODSKY, HARRY
LITHOGRAPHY
b Newark, NJ, July 20, 08. *Study:* Philadelphia Col Art, 28-31; Univ Pa, 37-39. *Work:* Bazalel Mus, Jerusalem; Princeton Mus; Hirshhorn Mus & Sculpture Garden & Nat Mus Am Art, Washington, DC. *Exhib:* Paintings & Prints, Philadelphia Artists, Whitney Mus, 34; Ann Exhib, Pa Acad Fine Arts, Philadelphia, 39, 49 & 62; Nat Exhib Prints, Libr Cong, 45-; Soc Am Graphic Artists, Nat Acad, New York, 48-; First Nat Biennial Color Lithography, Cincinnati Mus, 50-52; American Watercolors, Drawings & Prints, Metropolitan Mus Art, 52; Les Peintres Gravers Actuels Aux Etats Unis, Bibliotheque Nat, Paris, 53; American Prints Around the World Travelling Exhib, S Am, US Info Agency, 63. *Pos:* Art dir & mgr, Wescutt & Thomson Gallery, Philadelphia, 56-58; art dir, Campbell Soup Co, 70-72. *Teaching:* Instr vocational art & design, Dobbins Vocational Sch, Philadelphia, 37-43 & Mastbaum Vocational Sch, Philadelphia, 50-52. *Awards:* Purchase Award, First Nat Print Show, Brooklyn Mus, 47; Prize, Ann Print Show, Philadelphia Print Club, 48. *Mem:* Audubon Artists; Artists Equity. *Media:* Lithography. *Mailing Add:* 6633 N Eighth St Philadelphia PA 19126

BRODSKY, JUDITH KAPSTEIN
PRINTMAKER, EDUCATOR
b Providence, RI, July 14, 33. *Study:* Radcliffe Col, BA(art hist); Tyler Sch Art, Temple Univ, MFA. *Work:* Libr Cong, Washington, DC; Fogg Art Mus, Cambridge; NJ State Mus, Trenton; Princeton Univ, NJ; Newark Mus. *Comn:* The Magic Muse, traveling art environ (with Ilse Johnson, M K Johnson & Jane Teller), Asn Arts NJ State Mus, 72; Bicentennial Portfolio, Princeton, NJ, 75. *Exhib:* One-person shows, Brown Univ, 73, NY State Mus, 75, Douglas Col, 78 & Assoc Artists, Philadelphia, 79; many group shows, US & abroad. *Pos:* Assoc dir, Princeton Graphic Workshop, Inc, 66-68; owner, Castle Howard Press; actg assoc provost, Rutgers Univ, 82- *Teaching:* Lectr art hist, Tyler Sch Art, 66-71; asst prof printmaking, Beaver Col, 72-77, assoc prof, 77, actg chmn art dept, 77; assoc prof & chmn art dept, Rutgers Univ, 78-81, assoc dean, 81-82. *Awards:* Purchase Prizes, NJ State Mus, 70 & 71 & Boston Printmakers, 71; Stella C Drabkin Mem Award, Am Color Print Soc, 77; and others. *Bibliog:* Miller & Swenson (auth), Lives and Works: Talks with Women Artists, Scarecrow Press, 81. *Mem:* Col Art Asn Am; Philadelphia Print Club; Calif Soc Printmakers; Boston Printmakers; Soc Am Graphic Artists; founding mem Coalition Women's Art Orgn. *Media:* Intaglio, Lithography. *Publ:* Auth, Some notes on women printmakers, Art J, summer 76; designed & publ, B J O Nordfeldt, Etchings, 77, Friends and Foes from A to Z, by Dorothea Greenbaum, 78 & Woman, A Portfolio, 78; auth, Rediscovering Women Printmakers: 1500-1850, Counterproof, spring 79; The Status of Women in Art, Feminist Collage, Columbia Teachers Col Press, 79. *Dealer:* Princeton Gallery of Fine Art Nassau St Princeton NJ 08540; Assoc Am Artists 1614 Latimer St Philadelphia PA 19103. *Mailing Add:* 59 Castle Howard Ct Princeton NJ 08540

BRODSKY, STAN
PAINTER, EDUCATOR
b Brooklyn, NY, Mar 23, 25. *Study:* Univ Mo, BJour; Univ Iowa, with Jim Lechay & Byron Burford, MFA; Columbia Univ, EdD. *Work:* NY Univ; Port Authority, World Trade Ctr, New York; Heckscher Mus, Huntington, NY; Newsday, Melville, NY; also pvt collection of Dr James Watson, Cold Springs Harbor, NY. *Comn:* Electronic Abstract Symbols (lobby mural), PRD Electronics, Syosset, NY, 70. *Exhib:* Mus Stony Brook, NY, 77; Benson Gallery, Bridgehampton, NY, 77; Roberson Arts Ctr, Binghamton, NY; NY State Mus, Albany, 79; Viewpoints, Long Island Contemp Artists, 80; Appalachian State Univ Drawing Ann, NC, 81; Abstract Landscape, Loft Gallery, 81. *Teaching:* Prof art, C W Post Col, LI Univ, 60- *Awards:* Second Prize, Huntington Twp Art League, 68; Second Prize, N Shore Community Art Ctr, Great Neck, NY, 71; MacDowell Colony Fel, 71. *Bibliog:* E Betts (auth), Creative Seascape Painting, Watson-Guptill, 81; Peter Scheer (auth), Infusion (film), 82; Poets & Painters, Street Press, spring 84. *Mem:* Univ Coun Art Educ. *Media:* Oil, Pastel, Casein, Charcoal, Ink, Watercolor. *Dealer:* Loonam Gallery Bridgehampton NY; Linden Gallery New York NY 10022. *Mailing Add:* 7 Glen-A-Little-Trail Huntington NY 11743

BRODY, ARTHUR WILLIAM
PRINTMAKER, PAINTER
b New York, NY, Mar 2, 43. *Study:* Harvey Mudd Col, BS, 65; Claremont Grad Sch & Univ Ctr, MFA, 67. *Work:* Southern Ill Univ, Carbondale, Ill, St Lawrence Univ, Canton, NY; Neville Mus, Green Bay, Wis; Art Bank, State of Alaska, Anchorage; Historical and Fine Arts Mus, Anchorage, Alaska; Univ Alaska, Fairbanks. *Exhib:* 1st & 3rd Los Angeles Printmaking Soc Print Exhib, 64 & 67; 14th & 15th Black & White Exhib, Print Club, Philadelphia,

66, 67 & 82; Albrecht Dürer Commemorative Competition, Univ Wis, Milwaukee, 72; Mainstreams 74, Marietta, Ohio; Potsdam Prints, State Univ NY, Potsdam, 74; Int Invitational Print Show, Calif, 83; Northwest Printmakers/LA Printmaking Soc Exchange, 83. *Teaching:* Asst prof, Ripon Col, Wis, 70-75; asst prof, Univ Alaska, 77-80, assoc prof, 80- *Awards:* Achievement Award, Riverside Art Asn, Riverside, Calif, 66; Merit Award, 71 & First Prize, 74, NE Wis Ann, Green Bay; Print Award, All Alaska Juried, 80. *Mem:* Col Art Asn; Print Club; World Print Coun; NW Printmakers. *Media:* Woodcut, Intaglio; Acrylic, Oil. *Publ:* Auth, Communications & Intent, Communications--Tyrant or Liberator?, Ripon Col, 74. *Dealer:* The Gathering 28 Creek St Ketchikan AK 99901. *Mailing Add:* Sr 10276 Fairbanks AK 99701

BRODY, BLANCHE
PAINTER, PRINTMAKER
b Brooklyn, NY. *Study:* Hunter Col, 41-44; Boston Univ, BS, 49, MEd, 51; San Francisco Art Inst, with Richard Diebenkorn, 57-59. *Work:* Itel, San Francisco, Calif; El Dorado Press, Berkeley, Calif. *Exhib:* San Francisco Women Artists, San Francisco Mus Art, Calif, 57, 58, 60, 62, 63, 66 & 67; Calif Painters Ann, Oakland Mus, 58, 62-64; Painted Flower Invitational, Oakland Mus, Calif, 59 & 64; Jack London Square, Oakland Mus, Calif, 59-67; Mid Year Ann, Butler Inst Am Art, Youngstown, Ohio; West Coast Oil Painting Ann, Frye Art Mus, Seattle, Wash, 62, 63, 66 & 66; Natural & Supernatural, San Francisco Art Inst, Calif, 64-66; The Contemp Landscape, San Francisco Art Inst, Calif, 68-69. *Awards:* Second Prize, Oakland Mus, Jack London Square, 61; Diplome D'Honneure, Biennale Int deVichy, France, 64; First Prize, San Francisco Women Artists, 66. *Bibliog:* James Normile (auth), The subject is children, Archit Dig, 11-12/73; Louis Chapin (auth), Looking west--to exuberance, Christian Sci Monitor, 10/25/78. *Mem:* Artists Equity (mem bd 60-63); Valley Art Ctr. *Media:* Oil, Watercolor; Monotypes. *Dealer:* Allan Stone Gallery 48 E 86th St New York NY 10028; Manolides Gallery 89 Yessler Way Seattle WA. *Mailing Add:* 19 Vista Del Orinda Orinda CA 94563

BRODY, JACOB JEROME
MUSEUM DIRECTOR, EDUCATOR
b Brooklyn, NY, Apr 24, 29. *Study:* Brooklyn Mus Art Sch, with Gross & Ferren, 46-50; Art Students League, with Groth, 47; Cooper Union, cert, 50; Brooklyn Col, 50-52; Univ NMex, BA, 56, MA, 64 & PhD, 71. *Collections Arranged:* Early Masters of Modern Art, Isaac Delgado Mus Art, New Orleans, La, 59; Indigo, Mus Int Folk Art, Santa Fe, NMex, 61; Myth, Metaphor & Mimbreno Art, Maxwell Mus Anthrop, Univ NMex, Albuquerque, 77; Between Traditions, Univ Iowa Mus, 76; The Chaco Phenomenon, Maxwell Mus Anthropol, 83; Mimbres Painted Pottery, Am Fedn Arts; Mimbres Pottery, Roswell Mus Fine Arts, 83; and others. *Pos:* Cur art, Everhart Mus, 57-58; cur collection, Isaac Delgado Mus Art, 58-60; cur collection, Mus Int Folk Art, 61-62; dir & cur, Maxwell Mus Anthrop, NMex, 62- *Teaching:* Prof museology, Univ NMex, 63-, prof Am Indian art, 65- *Awards:* Tom L Popejoy Dissertation Award, Univ NMex, 72; Art Book Award, Border-Regional Libr Asn, 78; Hist Preserv Award, NMex Hist Soc, 78; and others. *Res:* Native American art; Southwest Pueblo Indian prehistoric & historic painting. *Publ:* Auth, The creative consumer, In: Ethnic & Tourist Arts, 77; auth, Mimbres painting and the northern frontier, in: Across the Chichimec Sea, 78; contribr, Hopi Kachina: Spirit of Life, 79; coauth, Yazz-Navajo Painter, Northland Press, 83; coauth, Mimbres Pottery, AFA, 83. *Mailing Add:* Maxwell Mus Anthrop Univ NMex Albuquerque NM 87131

BRODY, JACQUELINE
EDITOR
b Utica, NY, Jan 23, 32. *Study:* Vassar Col, AB, 53; London Sch of Econ, 53-57. *Pos:* Ed, The Print Collector's Newsletter, 72- *Mailing Add:* c/o Print Collector's Newsletter 16 E 82nd St New York NY 10021

BRODY, MYRON ROY
SCULPTOR, ADMINISTRATOR
b New York, NY, Apr 5, 40. *Study:* Nat Inst Fine Arts, Mexico City; Philadelphia Col Art, BFA, 65; Grad Sch Fine Art, Univ Pa, MFA, 68; Ateneum, Helsinki, Finland, 68-69; Univ Va, 70-71; Harvard Univ, 75. *Work:* Philadelphia Col Art; Princeton Univ Art Mus, NJ; Univ Va Art Mus, Charlottesville; Mus Nac Bellas Artes, Rio de Janeiro. *Comn:* Polished bronze, N Patrol Sta, Kansas City Police Dept, Mo, 77; polished bronze, Prudential Insurance Co Am, Plymouth, Minn, 81. *Exhib:* Nelson Gallery-Atkins Mus, Kansas City, Mo, 77; Allan Stone Gallery, New York, 77; Wichita Art Mus, Kans, 77; Kansas City Art Inst, 79; Minneapolis Inst Arts, 81; and other group & one-man shows. *Pos:* Bd mem & pres, Mo USA/Para Brazil, Partners of the Americas, 79 & Kansas City Arts Coun, 79. *Teaching:* Asst prof sculpture & design, Va Western Community Col, 69-76, chmn dept art, 69-72; instr ceramics, art educ & sculpture, Univ Va Sch Continuing Educ, 70-76; lectr sculpture, Hollins Col, Va, 75-76; chmn art dept & prof, Avila Col, Kansas City, Mo, 76- *Awards:* Nat Community Art Competition, HUD, Washington, DC, 73; Fulbright-Hays Fels, US Govt, 68-69 & 73-74; Va Comn Arts & Humanities Award, 75. *Mem:* Col Art Asn; Kansas City Artists Coalition (vpres, 79); Arts & Bull Soc Kansas City (founder). *Media:* Multimedia. *Publ:* Contribr, Decorative Art in Modern Interiors, 73-74; contribr, New Designs in Ceramics, 70. *Mailing Add:* 1309 West 50th St Kansas City MO 64112

BRODY, RUTH
PAINTER, PRINTMAKER
b New York, NY, Aug 11, 17. *Study:* Hunter Col, BA, 38; Columbia Univ, MA, 40. *Exhib:* 9th Ann, Knickerbocker Artists, New York, 56; Nat Soc Painters Casein & Acrylics, New York, 63-65, 67, 69 & 73; 14th New Eng Ann, Silvermine Guild, Conn, 63; Bronx Ann, Bronx Mus, NY, 68, 69, 70, 75, 77 & 80; Graphics and Crafts Show, Hudson River Mus, Yonkers, NY, 70 & 71; Westchester/Putnam Art Teachers Exhib, Neuberger Mus, Purchase, NY, 77. *Teaching:* Instr art, Secondary Schs, New York, 40-53; chmn art dept, Roosevelt High Sch, Yonkers, NY, 67-79. *Awards:* Best in Show, Riverdale Neighborhood, 68; Second Prize, Bronx Coun Arts Paint Out, 75. *Bibliog:* An artist is inspired, Riverdale Press, NY, 11/6/80. *Mem:* New York Artists Equity Asn; Found Community Artists; Bronx Coun Arts; Am Soc Contemp Artists. *Media:* Watercolor, Pen & Ink; Intaglio, Monoprints. *Publ:* Auth, Using artwork in the school yearbook, Columbia Scholastic Press Asn Advisers Asn Bull, 71; auth, Chance and Choice: An art game for the creation of a mural, Nat Art Educ Asn, 75. *Dealer:* Gallery 84 30 West 57th St New York NY 10019. *Mailing Add:* 3338 Giles Pl Bronx NY 10463

BROEMEL, CARL WILLIAM
PAINTER, ILLUSTRATOR
b Cleveland, Ohio, Sept 5, 1891. *Study:* Cleveland Sch Art, 1906-10; Royal Sch Appl Arts, Munich, Ger, 13-15; Art Student League & Nat Acad, 17-18. *Work:* Cleveland Mus Art; New Brit Mus Am Art; Brooklyn Mus Art, NY; USAF Art Mus, Washington, DC. *Exhib:* American Paintings & Sculpture, Art Inst Chicago, 32-33; Exhib Am Paintings, Cleveland Mus Art, 37; Am Watercolor Soc, New York, 41; Nat Watercolor Competition, Springfield Art Mus, Mo, 68; Berkshire Art Mus, Pittsfield, Mass, 69. *Teaching:* Instr watercolor, pvt classes, 25-28. *Awards:* First Prizes Watercolor, May Show Cleveland Mus, 28 & 29; Third Prize Abstr, Berkshire Art Asn, Mass, 67. *Mem:* Life mem Am Watercolor Soc; Kent Art Soc; USAF Art Prog. *Media:* Watercolor, Oil. *Publ:* Auth, Specialty shops, Archit Forum, 24; auth, American watercolor series, Am Artist, 59; auth, article, North Light, 71. *Dealer:* Bonfoey Co 1710 Euclid Ave Cleveland OH 44115. *Mailing Add:* 805 Palm Grove Ct Daytona Beach FL 32019

BROER, ROGER L
PAINTER
b Omaha, Nebr, Nov 9, 45. *Study:* Eastern Mont Col, BA, 74; Cent Wash Univ, 74- *Work:* Mus Native Am Cult, Spokane, Wash; US Dept Interior, Browning, Mont; Eastern Mont Col, Billings; Safeco Insurance Co Am, Seattle; Seafirst Bank Collection, Seattle; and others. *Exhib:* Ball State Drawing Show, Ball State Univ, 75 & 78; Mus Native Am Cult, Spokane, 79; Indian Painters in Paris, Espace de Pierre Cardin, Paris, 79; Indian Market, Santa Fe, 82 & 83; Gallery Mack, Seattle, 83; and others. *Teaching:* Iowa State Arts Comn Workshop, 81; artist in schs, Arts Alaska Inc, 83-84. *Awards:* Gold Medal, Am Indian & Cowboy Artists Asn, 79, 81, 82 & 83; Best of Show, Rapid City Boys Club, 81 & 82; and others. *Bibliog:* Theo Nassar (auth), Western art has begun to take on some vast new meanings, Spokesman, 3/79; O J Parsons (auth), Western impressions, Spokesman, 6/79; and others. *Mem:* Puget Sound Group Northwest Painters; Am Indian & Cowboy Artists. *Mailing Add:* 10819 SE 231st Kent WA 98031

BROIDO, LUCY
WRITER, DEALER
b New York, NY, Jan 19, 24. *Study:* Cornell Univ, 41-44; Teacher's Col, Columbia Univ, BS, 45; Adelphi Col, Garden City, NY, 50-51. *Exhib:* French Opera Posters, Mus Performing Arts, Lincoln Ctr, New York, 74. *Pos:* Pres, Lucy Broido Graphics, Ltd, 72-; dir, Stairwell Gallery, Bryn Mawr, Pa, 72-; dir, Arts Exchange Mag, 77-79. *Teaching:* Fac mem, The New School, New York, 81. *Res:* Nineteenth century graphic arts. *Specialty:* Nineteenth and twentieth century posters and related prints. *Publ:* Auth, French Opera Posters, 1868-1930, 76 & auth, Jules Cheret: Catalogue Raisonne, 80, Dover Publ. *Mailing Add:* 908 Wootton Rd Bryn Mawr PA 19010

BROKAW, LUCILE
PAINTER
b New York, NY, Mar 12, 15. *Study:* Grand Cent Sch Art, 27-29; sculpture, Paris, France, 30-32; George Grosz Art Sch, New York, 33-34. *Work:* Many pvt collections. *Exhib:* San Francisco Mus Art Ann, 59; Theatre Collects American Art, Whitney Mus Am Art, New York, 61; Craftsmen USA, Los Angeles Co Mus, 66; California Stitchery, Calif Arts Comn Traveling Exhib, 69-70; People Figures, Smithsonian Traveling Exhib, 69-70; Pacific-Asia Mus, Pasadena, 81; and others. *Awards:* Nat Orange Show Award, San Bernardino, 55; 8th All City Outdoor Art Festival Award, 60; First Prize, Artist-Craftsman-Westside Jewish Community Ctr, 64. *Bibliog:* Bentley Schaad (auth), The Realm of Contemporary Still Life Painting, Reinhold, 62; Dona Meilach (auth), Contemporary Rugs and Wall Hangings, Abelard, 70; Meilach Snow (auth), Creative Stitchery, Reilly & Lee, 70. *Mem:* Artists for Econ Action; Am Crafts Coun; Los Angeles Art Asn. *Mailing Add:* 831 Paseo Miramar Pacific Palisades CA 90272

BROKER, KARIN
DRAFTSMAN, PRINTMAKER
b Pittsburgh, Pa, July 27, 50. *Study:* Univ Iowa, Iowa City, BFA, 72; Atelier 17, Paris, with Stanley Hayter, 73; Univ Wis, Madison, with Warrington Colescott & Jack Damer, MFA, 80. *Work:* Cabo Frio Bienal Collection, Brazil; US Info Serv, Middle East; Wilson Collection, Houston; CVAA Gallery, La Grange, Ga. *Comn:* Trophy (3-D drawing), InterFirst Bank & Houston Symphony, 83. *Exhib:* Printed by Women, Penns Landing Mus,

Philadelphia, 83; World Print Four, San Francisco Mus Mod Art, 83; Showdown, Alternative Mus, New York, 83; Sculpture on the Wall, San Antonio Art Inst, 83; Printmakers and the South Traveling Exhib, 83-84; New American Graphics 3, Cairo Mus & traveling, Middle East, 83-84. *Teaching:* Instr drawing, painting & design, Seton Hill Col, Pa, 76-78; teaching asst drawing, Univ Wis, Madison, 79-80; asst prof etching, lithography & drawing, Rice Univ, 80- *Awards:* Purchase Award, 23rd NDak Print Ann, 80; Purchase & Jury Awards, La Grange Nat VII, 82. *Bibliog:* Joachim Kusber (auth), Gedanken zur Ausstellungs-Efoeffnung: Karin Broker, Speiker, 82; Leslie leubbers (auth), Colorprint USA exhibit and symposium, Print News, 83; article, Print Collectors Newslett, 83. *Mem:* Tex Print Alliance (treas, 83-); Southern Graphics Coun (treas, 82-); Col Art Asn Am. *Media:* Etching. *Publ:* Auth, Mad Artist-Printmaker (catalog), Tex Tech Univ, 83. *Dealer:* Hadler-Rodriguez Galleries Houston TX & New York NY. *Mailing Add:* 6100 S Main St Houston TX 77005

BROMBERG, FAITH
PAINTER
b Los Angeles, Calif, Mar 8, 19. *Study:* Univ Southern Calif; Otis Art Inst; also with Wayne Thiebaud & June Wayne; Univ Calif, Northridge. *Exhib:* Butler Inst Art, Ohio, 68; Springfield Art Mus, Mo, 69; one-person shows, Jaqueline Anhalt Gallery, Los Angeles, 71-74, Roko Gallery, New York, 75 & 77 & Art Space, Los Angeles, 79; Univ Calif, Santa Barbara, 81; and many others. *Awards:* Purchase Award, Am Acad Arts & Lett, 75 & 76; Artist's Fel, Nat Endowment Arts, 80. *Mem:* Womanspace; Los Angeles Inst Contemp Art; Artists for Econ Action; Artists Equity Asn; Woman's Caucus Arts. *Media:* Oil, Spray Paint. *Publ:* Auth, Designers West, 75; contribr to Artweek, Feminist Art J, Arts Mag & Los Angeles Times. *Mailing Add:* PO Box 11853 Marina Del Rey CA 90295

BROMM, HAL
DEALER, INSTRUCTOR
b NJ, June 6, 47. *Study:* Pratt Inst, BA. *Pos:* Dir, Hal Bromm Gallery, New York. *Teaching:* Instr, Sch Visual Arts. *Mem:* Nat Trust; Victorian Soc; Am Friends Attingham. *Specialty:* Painting, sculpture, drawing, photography, video and film by contemporary American and European artists. *Publ:* Auth, Selections from Hal Bromm, Eaton/Shoen Gallery, 80-81; auth, Moving 77, Hal Bromm Gallery, New York, 78; auth, For love and money: Dealers choose, Pratt Inst, Brooklyn, 81; auth, Introduction, In: Agitated Figures: The New Emotionalism, Hallwalls, 82. *Mailing Add:* 90 W Broadway New York NY 10007

BROMMER, GERALD F
PAINTER, WRITER
b Berkeley, Calif, Jan 8, 27. *Study:* Concordia Teachers Col, BSc(educ); Univ Nebr, MA; Chouinard Art Inst; Otis Art Inst, Univ Southern Calif; Univ Calif, Los Angeles. *Work:* Howard Ahmanson Collection, Los Angeles; Hughes Laboratories, Malibu; Festival of the Arts Collection, Laguna Beach, Calif; State of Calif Collection, Sacramento; Utah State Univ. *Exhib:* Am Watercolor Soc, New York, 69, 72 & 73; Nat Acad Design, New York, 71; Watercolor USA, Springfield, Mo, 73, 75 & 76; Nat Watercolor Soc, Los Angeles, 74, 75 & 77-; Royal Watercolor Soc, London, 75; plus over 100 one-man shows. *Pos:* Chief designer, Daystar Designs, Inc, 63-73. *Teaching:* Chmn dept art, Lutheran High Sch, Los Angeles, 55-74. *Awards:* Landmark Purchase Award, Watercolor USA, 69; Crescent Cardboard Co Purchase Award, Nat Watercolor Soc, 72; Utah State Purchase Award, Watercolor West Invitational, 73. *Bibliog:* Article in SW Art Mag, 8/77; Virginia Timmons (auth), Painting: Ideas, Materials, Processes, Davis, 78; article, Am Artist, 2/84. *Mem:* Nat Watercolor Soc (treas, 63, vpres, 65-66, 80-81, pres, 67-68, 81-82); WCoast Watercolor Soc; Nat Art Educ Asn; Artists Equity; Rocky Mountain Nat Watermedia Soc. *Media:* Transparent Watercolor; Collage. *Publ:* Auth, Transparent Watercolor: Ideas and Techniques, 73; auth, Art in Your World, 77; auth, The Art of Collage, 78; Discovering Art History, 81; and many others. *Dealer:* Challis Galleries 1390 S Coast Hwy Laguna Beach CA 92652; Fireside Gallery PO Box 3374 Carmel CA 93921. *Mailing Add:* 11252 Valley Spring Ln North Hollywood CA 91602

BRONER, ROBERT
PRINTMAKER, PAINTER
b Detroit, Mich, Mar 10, 22. *Study:* Wayne State Univ, BFA, 44, MA, 46; Soc Arts & Crafts, Detroit, 42-45; painting with Stuart Davis, 49-50; Atelier 17, New York, with S W Hayter, 49-52. *Work:* Guggenheim Mus, Mus Mod Art, New York; Los Angeles Co Mus; Philadelphia Mus Art; Bibliot Nat, Paris; Nat Collections, Smithsonian Inst, Washington, DC; and others. *Comn:* Ed etchings, Detroit Inst Arts, 67 & London Arts Gallery, 67-69. *Exhib:* Eight shows, Brooklyn Mus Prints Nat, 51-76; Brit Int Print Biennale, 68, 70 & 72; Salon de Mai, Mus Art Mod, Paris, 69 & Belgrade, 70; Soc Am Graphic Artists, 69, 71, 76 & 77. *Teaching:* Prof art & art hist, Wayne State Univ, 64- *Awards:* Print Purchase Prize, Brooklyn Mus, 64; Purchase Prize, Soc Am Graphic Artists, 69; Detroit Inst Award, 61 & 66. *Mem:* Soc Am Graphic Artists; Philadelphia Print Club; Drawing & Print Club, Detroit Inst Arts (bd dirs, 66-76); Mich Asn of Printmakers (pres); Nat Print Asn (pres). *Mailing Add:* Dept Art Wayne State Univ Detroit MI 48202

BRONSON, A A (GENERAL IDEA)
POST-CONCEPTUAL ARTIST, WRITER
b Vancouver, BC, June 16, 46. *Work:* Can Coun Art Bank, Ottawa; Nat Gallery Can; Ctr Art Contemp, Geneva; Lucio Amelio Gallery, Naples; Mod Art Gallery, Vienna. *Comn:* Ursa Major and Taurus: Pavillion Fragments from the Starry Vault, Toronto Stock Exchange, 83. *Exhib:* 1971 Miss General Idea Pageant, Art Gallery Ont, 71, Videoscape, 74; Canada

Trajectoires, Mus Mod Art, Paris, 73; Paris Biennale, France, 77; Kunsthalle, Basel, Switz, 78; Lucio Amelio, Naples, 78; Stedlijk Mus, Amsterdam, 79; Venice Biennial, 80; Artistic Collaboration in the 20th Century, Hirshhorn Mus, 84; P is for Poodle, Nat Gallery Can, 84; and others. *Pos:* Ed, File Mag, Toronto, 72- *Awards:* Can Coun Arts Awards, 68-83; Ont Arts Coun Award Art Criticism, 74. *Bibliog:* Willoughby Sharp (auth), Gold-Diggers of '84, Avalanche, New York, 73; John Mays (auth), General Idea, Open Letter, Toronto, summer 74; Germano Celant (auth), General Idea in Canada, Domus, Milan, Italy, 10/74. *Publ:* Auth, Menage A Trois, Gen Idea, 78; co-ed, Performance by artists, Art Metropole, 79; auth, Getting Into the Spirits Cocktail Book, Gen Idea, 80; co-ed, Museums by artists, Art Metropole, 83. *Mailing Add:* Carmen Lamanna Gallery 840 Yonge St Toronto ON M4W 2H1 Canada

BRONSON, CLARK EVERICE
SCULPTOR
b Kamas, Utah, Mar 10, 39. *Study:* Art Instr Inst, 56-57; Univ Utah, 59. *Comn:* Hartford Stag (bronze), Hartford, Conn, 80; Chadwick Ram (bronze), Boone Crockett Buffalo Bill Hist Ctr, Cody, Wyo, 82. *Exhib:* Nat Acad Western Art, Nat Cowboy Hall Fame, 73, 74 & 75; Mzuri Safari Found Conf, Reno, Nev, 73 & 74; Mont Hist Soc, Helena, 78; C M Russell Art Show & Auction, Great Falls, Mont, 79-81; Nat Sculpture Soc, New York, 81. *Pos:* State of Utah Fish & Game Staff Artist, 60-63. *Awards:* First Prize, Nat Art Competition, Art Instr Inst, 57; Silver Medal (bronze sculpture), Nat Acad Western Art, 74, 75 & 77; Silver Medal (bronze sculpture), Nat Sculpture Soc, 81. *Bibliog:* Don Jardine (auth), The continuing success of Clark Bronson, Illustrator, 71; Scott Dial (auth), Symbols of freedom, Southwest Art, 1/80; Richard P Christenson (auth), Bronson's love of life is forever frozen in bronze, Deseret News, 9/81. *Mem:* Nat Acad Western Art; Nat Sculpture Soc; Soc Animal Artists; Wildlife Artists Int; Northwest Rendezvous Group. *Media:* Bronze sculpture and painting. *Publ:* Illusr, Nat Wildlife Mag, 63; High Uintahs--Hi, 64; illusr, Album of North American Animals, 66; illusr, Album of North American Birds, 67; illusr, Biography of a Grizzly, 69. *Mailing Add:* 17 Hitching Post Rd Bozeman MT 59715

BROOKE, DAVID STOPFORD
MUSEUM DIRECTOR
b Walton-on-Thames, Eng, Sept 18, 31. *Study:* Harvard Univ, AB, 58, AM, 63. *Pos:* Asst cur, Fogg Art Mus, Cambridge, Mass, 60-61; asst to dir, Smith Col Mus, Northampton, 63-65; chief cur, Art Gallery Ont, Toronto, 65-68; dir, Currier Gallery Art, Manchester, NH, 68-77; dir, Clark Art Inst, 77- *Mem:* Asn Am Art Mus Dirs. *Res:* British painting of the eighteenth and nineteenth centuries. *Publ:* Coauth, James Tissot (catalog), Art Gallery Ont, 68; auth, Mortimer at Eastbourne and Kenwood, Burlington Mag, 68; auth, James Tissot's amateur circus, Boston Mus Bulletin, 69; coauth, The Dunlaps of New Hampshire, Antiques, 70; auth, Raeburn's portrait of John Clerk of Eldin, Currier Gallery Bulletin, 71. *Mailing Add:* 63 Park St Williamstown MA 01267

BROOKE, PEGAN
PAINTER
b Orange, Calif, July 19, 50. *Study:* Univ Calif, San Diego, BA, 72; Drake Univ, BFA(painting), 76; Univ Iowa, Iowa City, MA(painting), 77; Stanford Univ, MFA(painting), 80. *Work:* Guggenheim Mus; Univ Nebr Art Mus, Omaha; Iowa State Capitol Bldg, Des Moines; Bank Am Int Hq, San Francisco. *Exhib:* The Chosen Object, Joslyn Art Mus, 77; Eight Painters, Univ Nebr Art Mus, Omaha, 78; Bay Area Paintings, Calif State Univ, Hayward, 81; solo exhib, Fuller Goldeen Gallery, San Francisco, 81 & 83 & Scottsdale Ctr Arts, Ariz, 83; Emerging Northern California Artists, Orange Co Ctr Contemp Arts, Santa Ana, 82; New Perspectives in American Art, Guggenheim Mus, 83. *Teaching:* Lectr, Univ Calif, Berkeley, 82, Davis, 83, Calif Col Arts & Crafts, 83 & Sonoma State Univ, 83. *Bibliog:* Andree Marechal-Workman (auth), A logic of conflict, Artweek, 83; Chuck Andresen (auth), From the bay to the valley, Phoenix New Times, 83; Alfred Jan (auth), Pegan Brooke at Fuller Goldeen, Images & Issues, 83. *Media:* Acrylic, Oil Pastel. *Dealer:* Fuller Goldeen Gallery 228 Grant Ave San Francisco CA 94108. *Mailing Add:* 2200 Adeline #200 Oakland CA 94607

BROOKINS, JACOB BODEN
CONSULTANT, SCULPTOR
b Princeton, Mo, Aug 28, 35. *Study:* Boise Jr Col, AA(painting); Univ Ore, BS(ceramics), MFA(metalsmithing & sculpture); also with Max Nixon, Jan Zach, Robert James & James Hanson. *Exhib:* Ariz Comn for Arts & Humanities Touring Exhib, 72-73; Southwestern Invitational, Yuma, Ariz, 72-73; Intermountain Crafts Exhib, Flagstaff, 73; Mus Northern Ariz, 77-79; Coconino Co Arts Ctr, 80-81; and others. *Collections Arranged:* Nat Coun Educ Ceramic Arts Conf '72 Exhib, 72; Intermountain Crafts Exhib, Ariz Designer Craftsmen, Flagstaff, 73. *Pos:* Dir, Mus Northern Ariz Art Inst, 75-79; founder, Cosnino Found, 79-; chmn, Coconino Co Arts Comn, 81- *Teaching:* Instr jewelry, Univ Ore, 67-68; instr sculpture, Northern Ariz Univ, 69-75; instr ceramics, Yavapai Col, 79-80. *Mem:* Nat Coun Educ Ceramic Arts; World Crafts Coun; Am Crafts Coun; Ariz Designer Craftsmen (mem bd dir, 70-75, state pres, 71-72); Nat Sculptors Conf; and others. *Media:* Metal, Ceramic. *Mailing Add:* Cosnino Found Res Ctr 431 Cosnino Rd Flagstaff AZ 86001

BROOKS, (JOHN) ALAN
PAINTER, INSTRUCTOR
b Burbank, Calif, Oct 11, 31. *Study:* City Col San Francisco; San Jose State Col, with Eric Oback, MA; San Francisco Art Inst, with William Morehouse. *Work:* City San Francisco. *Exhib:* Pioneer Mus & Haggan Galleries, Stockton,

Calif, 62; Phelan Awards Biennial, San Francisco, 65, 67 & 69; one-man show, St Marys Col Calif, 67; John Bolles Gallery, San Francisco, 68-71; Newman Ctr, Univ Calif, Berkeley, 69. *Teaching:* Instr painting, City Col San Francisco, 71- *Awards:* Second Award, Santa Clara Co Fair, 59; Purchase Award, Calif State Fair, 60. *Media:* Oil, Watercolor. *Publ:* Contribr, Sch Arts Mag, 71. *Dealer:* Van Doren Gallery 10 Gold St San Francisco CA 94133. *Mailing Add:* Dept of Art 50 Phelan Ave San Francisco CA 94112

BROOKS, BRUCE W
PAINTER, SCULPTOR
b New York, NY, July 10, 48. *Study:* Pratt Inst, BFA(art educ), 70, MFA(painting), 75. *Exhib:* 415 W Broadway, New York, 78; William Patterson Col, NJ, 81; Miss Mus Art, 81; one-man shows, O K Harris, New York, 81 & 83 & Ron Hunnings, New York, 81. *Teaching:* Vis instr painting & drawing, Pratt Inst, 72-, asst to chmn dept, 72-74; adj asst prof painting, sculpture, art hist, design, LaGuardia Community Col, 77- *Mem:* Japan Soc; Japanese Sword Soc; Col Art Asn. *Media:* Alkyd, Paper. *Mailing Add:* c/o O K Harris Gallery 383 W Broadway New York NY 10012

BROOKS, H(AROLD) ALLEN
HISTORIAN, LECTURER
b New Haven, Conn, Nov 6, 25. *Study:* Dartmouth Col, BA, 50; Yale Univ, MA, 55; Northwestern, PhD, 57. *Teaching:* Prof, Univ Toronto, Ont, 58-; Mellon chair, Vassar Col, 70-71; vis prof, Archit Asn Sch Archit, London, 77- *Awards:* Fels, Can Coun, 62, 75 & 78 & Guggenheim, 73; Alice Davis Hitchcock Book Award, Soc Archit Historians, 73. *Mem:* Soc Archit Historians (pres, 64-66, dir, 61-64, 67-70 & 71-74); Soc Archit Historians Gt Brit; Soc Study Archit Can; Int Comt Monuments & Sites. *Res:* Frank Lloyd Wright & LeCorbusier. *Publ:* Auth, The Prairie School: Frank Lloyd Wright and His Midwest Contemporaries, 72 & ed, Prairie School Architecture: Studies from the Western Architect, 75, Univ Toronto Press; ed & contribr, Writings on Wright: Selected Comment on Frank Lloyd Wright, MIT Press, 81; ed & contribr, The LeCorbusier Archive, 32 vols, Garland Publ, 82-; auth, Frank Lloyd Wright and the Prairie School, Braziller, 83. *Mailing Add:* Dept Fine Art Univ Toronto Toronto ON M5S 1A1 Canada

BROOKS, JAMES
PAINTER
b St Louis, Mo, Oct 18, 06. *Study:* Southern Methodist Univ, 23-25; Dallas Art Inst, with Martha Simkins, 25-26; Art Student League, with Kimon Nicolaides & Boardman Robinson. *Work:* Brooklyn Mus, Solomon R Guggenheim Mus, Mus Mod Art & Metrop Mus Art, New York; Tate Gallery, London; plus many others. *Comn:* Murals, Woodside Libr, NY, La Guardia Airport, New York, US Post Off, Little Falls, NY & Mobil Hq, Fairfax, Va. *Exhib:* San Francisco Mus Art, Calif, 63; retrospective, Whitney Mus Am Art, 63-64; Dunn Int, Tate Gallery, London, 64; one-man show, Philadelphia Art Alliance, Pa, 66; The New American Painting and Sculpture, Mus Mod Art, New York, 69; plus many other group & one-man exhibs. *Teaching:* Instr drawing, Columbia Univ, 46-48; instr lettering, Pratt Inst Art Sch, 48-59; vis critic, Yale Univ, 55-60; artist-in-residence, Am Acad Rome, 63; vis artist, New Col, Sarasota, Fla, 65-67; Miami Beach Art Ctr, Fla, 66; prof art, Queens Col, 66-67, 68-69. *Awards:* Norman Wait Harris Silver Medal & Prize, 61; Ford Found Purchase Award, 62; Guggenheim Found Fel, 67-68; plus others. *Bibliog:* George A Flanagan (auth), Understanding and Enjoying Modern Art, Thomas Y Crowell, 62; Sam Hunter (auth), James Brooks, Whitney Mus Am Art, 63; Sam Hunter (ed), New Art Around the World, Abrams, 66; plus many others. *Dealer:* Gruenebaum Gallery 38 E 57th St New York NY 10022. *Mailing Add:* 128 Neck Path The Springs East Hampton NY 11937

BROOKS, JOHN H
ADMINISTRATOR, EDUCATOR
b Cambridge, Mass, June 13, 35. *Study:* Princeton Univ, BA, 58; Columbia Univ, MA, 64. *Pos:* Staff lectr, Nat Gallery Art, Washington, DC, 64-68; assoc dir, Sterling & Francine Clark Art Inst, Williamstown, Mass, 68- *Teaching:* Lectr Am art, Univ Md Col, 67-68 & North Adams State Col, Mass, 71-75. *Awards:* Grace May Tilton Prize in Fine Arts, 58. *Mem:* Am Asn Mus; Int Coun Mus. *Publ:* Ed, Active connections: paintings and other arts, Prism, Mus Art, Carnegie Inst, 80; Highlights of the Sterling and Francine Clark Art Institute, Williamstown, Mass, 81. *Mailing Add:* 43B Gale Rd Williamstown MA 01267

BROOKS, LOIS ZIFF
TEXTILE ARTIST, EDUCATOR
b Chicago, Ill, May 6, 34. *Study:* Art Inst Chicago, 53; Univ Calif, Los Angeles, BA, 56, MFA, 69; Ctr for the Visual Arts, Harvard Univ, with Sekler, 64; Mass Inst Technol, with Filopowski, 65. *Comn:* Textile mural, Disneyland Hotel, Anaheim, Calif, 70; wall hanging, Arco Ctr Law Off, Los Angeles, 74; ark curtain, Temple Isaiah, Los Angeles, 76. *Exhib:* Fiber Art by Am Artists, Ball State Univ, Muncie Ind, 72; Southern Calif Designer-Crafts, Mus Art, Laguna Beach, 73; Focus on Crafts, Univ Minn, St Paul, 77; one-person shows, Gallery Batsheva de Rothchild, Tel Aviv, Israel, 73 & SW Craft Ctr Gallery, San Antonio, Tex, 76; and others. *Collections Arranged:* The Near East in UCLA Collections (auth, catalog), 69 & Ceramics, Form and Function (auth, catalog), 71, Univ Calif, Los Angeles. *Pos:* Res assoc, Mus Cult Hist, Univ Calif, Los Angeles; co-ordinator, Professional Designation in Textiles, Univ Calif, 75-76; designer, Filmways Inc, Los Angeles, 80. *Teaching:* Instr textile art, Univ Calif Exten, Los Angeles, 70- & Immaculate Heart Col, Los Angeles, 74-80; instr textile art, Immaculate Heart Col, Los Angeles, 74-80. *Bibliog:* Dona Meilach (auth), Contemp Batik & Tie-dye, Crown 73; Esther Dendel (auth), African Fabric Crafts, Taplinger Publ Co,

74; Robin Tucker (auth), Art & Artisan: Lois Ziff Brooks, Designers W Mag, 2/78. *Mem:* World Craft Coun (Am rep, 78); Am Craft Coun; Surface Design Asn; Southern Calif Designer Crafts; Col Art Asn. *Media:* Dye, Resist Media. *Publ:* Auth, Adire Eleko, Starch Resist Method of Textile Design, Craft Horizons, 71. *Mailing Add:* 2669 Stoner Ave Los Angeles CA 90064

BROOKS, LOUISE CHERRY
COLLECTOR, CERAMIST
b Phoenix City, Ala, Aug 28, 06. *Study:* With Kelly Fitzpatrick, Charles Shannon & Wright Putney. *Pos:* Mem bd trustees, Montgomery Mus Fine Arts, Alabama Art Guild & Alabama Historical Asn, currently. *Awards:* Ala Art League & Nat Soc Arts & Lett. *Collection:* Early English Staffordshire figures, especially ceramic bird groups. *Mailing Add:* 3604 Narrow Lane Rd Montgomery AL 36106

BROOKS, ROBERT
PAINTER
b Fall River, Mass, Oct 19, 22. *Study:* Swain Sch Design, New Bedford, Mass; Vesper George Sch Art, Boston, Mass, scholar. *Work:* Guild House, Barnstaple, Eng; First Nat Bank, Boston; Bass River Savings Bank, Hyannis; Gen Electric Corp, Framingham. *Comn:* Series of int scenes, Nationwide Insurance Co, Columbus, Ohio, 67-68; mural, Am Legion of Yarmouth, Mass, 77; series of paintings, comn by Arthur A Kaplan, Inc, New York, 77; mural, Cape Cod Synagogue, Hyannis, 78. *Exhib:* one-man shows, New Bedford Pub Libr, 46, Lincoln Savings Bank, New York, 75, Cape Cod Art Asn, Barnstable, 76 & Richards Gallery, Hyannis, Mass, 82 & 83; Acad Artists Asn, Springfield, Mass, 81. *Pos:* Illusr, Armed Forces, 43-46; designer, NE Stencil Engraving Co, New Bedford, 46-53; artist, Screencraft Prod, Yarmouth, 53-67; gallery dir, Robert Brooks Art Gallery, Hyannis, 69-80. *Teaching:* Art instr drawing, Swain Sch Design, 46-47; tutor design, Veteran's Admin, 47-49; instr painting, Cape Cod Community Col, summer 81-83. *Awards:* First Prize in Watercolor, All New Eng Show, Cape Cod Art Asn, 81; Grumbacher Gold Medal, Acad Artist's Nat Exhib, Springfield, Mass, 81; First Prize in Watercolor, Cape Cod Art Asn, 83. *Mem:* Cape Cod Art Asn; Soc Marine Painters; Acad Artist's Asn. *Media:* Watercolor. *Dealer:* Market Barn Gallery Falmouth MA; Richards Gallery, Hyannis, MA. *Mailing Add:* 236 Bearse's Way Hyannis MA 02601

BROOKS, WENDELL T
PRINTMAKER, EDUCATOR
b Aliceville, Ala, Sept 10, 39. *Study:* Ind Univ, BS(art educ), 62, MFA(printmaking); Martin Luther King Jr Fel, scholar, Southern Fel), 71; Woodstock Artist's Asn, scholar, summer 61; Pratt Graphic Art Asn, scholar, 62; Univ Md, 65-66; Howard Payne Col, 66-67. *Work:* Libr of Cong, Washington, DC; Nasson Col; Mount Union Col; Carleton Col; Bethel Col; plus others including pvt collections. *Exhib:* A Return to Humanism, Burpee Art Mus, Rockford, Ill, 71; Social Comment in Recent Art, Concordia Teachers Col, Seward, Nebr, 71; The Black Experience in Prints, Pratt Graphic Ctr, New York, 72; Black Artists of America, NJ State Mus, Trenton, 72; New Jersey, 1972, 7th Ann Exhib, Trenton, 72; A Very Spec Invitational Show, McCarter Theatre, Princeton, NJ, 79; Black Artists/South, 79. plus many other group & one-man shows. *Teaching:* Instr printmaking, Ala A&M Univ, 67-68; asst prof printmaking & artist in residence, Nassau Col, 70; asst prof printmaking, Trenton State Col, 71-; lectr art at var art groups, cols & univs, 69-72. *Bibliog:* Article in Negro Heritage, 10/68; article in Chalkboard, 11/68; article in Christian Sci Monitor, 6/22/70; plus many other newspapers. *Mem:* Philadelphia Print Club. *Mailing Add:* Dept of Art Trenton State Col Trenton NJ 08625

BROOME, RICK (RICHARD RAYMOND)
PAINTER
b Pueblo, Colo, Oct 13, 46. *Study:* Northrop Univ, 67-71; Northrop Inst Tech, 68. *Work:* USAF Acad, Colorado Springs, Colo; Naval Air Mus, Pensacola, Fla; Air Force Mus, Dayton, Ohio; San Diego Art & Space Mus, Calif; Northrop Univ, Inglewood, Calif. *Comn:* T-33/Colo Rocky Mountains, 74, F-105/Vietnam, 75, B-1/USAF Acad, 79, F-15/USAF Acad, 81 & T-Birds/ USAF Acad, 82, USAF Acad Cadets, Colorado Springs. *Exhib:* JOC Aviation Art Show, Craig Air Force Base, Selma, Ala, 76 & Scott Air Force Base, Ill, 77. *Awards:* Best Cover/Year, Rocky Mountain Collegiate Asn, 75. *Bibliog:* Will Robinson (dir), From Time to Time (film), KRDO TV, 80 & 81; Gary Olson (auth), Airplanes in art: Broome a master, Colo Springs Sun, 3/7/80. *Media:* Acrylic. *Res:* Created 1450 plus historically accurate aviation originals involving complete detailed research. *Publ:* Illusr, 12 covers of Frontier Mag, Inflight Publ, 74-82; illusr, 3 covers of Talon Mag, USAF Acad, 75-82; illusr, 2 covers of Check Points Mag, USAF Acad, 80; illusr, 3 covers of Aerospace Historian, Univ Kans, 79-82. *Dealer:* Kemper Galleries 1624 N Academy Blvd Colorado Springs CO 80915. *Mailing Add:* 2809 Old Broadmoor Rd Colorado Springs CO 80906

BROOMFIELD, ADOLPHUS GEORGE
PAINTER, DESIGNER
b Toronto, Ont, Aug 26, 06. *Study:* Ont Col Art, Toronto & Port Hope; studied with Lismer, MacDonald & Carmichael. *Work:* War Collection, Nat Gallery Can; Imperial War Col, Ottawa; Can Wire & Cable Co Collection, Toronto. *Exhib:* RCAF World Wide Exhib, Can & Eng, 45; Can Traveling Show, Montreal & Vancouver, 62; Royal Can Acad Arts, Montreal & Toronto, 65. *Bibliog:* L Schrag (auth), article, Broomfield, Globe & Mail, 64; Out of the wilderness, Can Crafts, 8/78; H Robertson (auth), A terrible beauty in Canada at War, James Lorimer Publ, 77. *Mem:* Royal Can Acad Arts. *Media:* Oil; Drypoint Etching, Heavy Textile Tapestry. *Mailing Add:* Brackenwood 232 Isabella Ave Mississauga ON Canada

BROSE, MORRIS
SCULPTOR
b Wyszkow, Poland, May 16, 14. *Study:* Detroit Inst Arts & Crafts; Wayne State Univ; Cranbrook Acad Art, Bloomfield Hills, Mich. *Work:* Detroit Inst Art; Grosse Pointe Libr, Mich; Chase Manhattan Bank Collection, New York; Zieger Osteop Hosp, Detroit; J L Hudson Eastland Ctr, Mich; plus others. *Exhib:* Mich Artists Ann, 54-; Mus Mod Art, 61; Spoleto Festival, Italy, 61; Westminster Sculpture Exhib, 69; Cranbrook Acad Art Alumni Exhib, 68; Retrospective, Art Gallery Windsor, Ont, 77; plus others. *Teaching:* Lectr contemp sculpture, Detroit Inst Art, Wayne State Univ, Montieth Col & others; instr sculpture, Cranbrook Acad Art & Soc Arts & Crafts; instr, Oakland Univ. *Awards:* Prize, Detroit Soc Women Painters & Sculptors, 59; Leon & Joseph Winkleman Found Prize, 59; Mich Artists Founders Prize, 62; plus others. *Mailing Add:* 65 McLean St Highland Park MI 48203

BROSK, JEFFREY OWEN
SCULPTOR
b New York, NY, Feb 15, 47. *Study:* Univ Pa, BA & BS, 70; Mass Inst Technol, MA(archit), 76. *Work:* Mercy Col, Dobbs Ferry, NY. *Exhib:* Aldrich Mus Contemp Art, Ridgefield, Conn, 78; PS1, Queens, NY, 78; Hudson River Mus, Yonkers, NY, 78; solo exhib, Hammarskjold Plaza Sculpture Garden, New York, 79; Albright-Knox Art Gallery, Buffalo, NY, 79; Construct Gallery, Chicago, 81; Galerie Alain Oudin, Paris, 81; and many others. *Bibliog:* Grace Glueck (auth), Art people, New York Times, 7/13/79; Patricia Ensworth (auth), Shaped spaces: New work by Jeffrey Owen Brosk, Arts Mag, 10/79; Hal Foster (auth), article, Artforum, 12/79. *Mem:* Artists Rep Environ Arts Inc, New York (bd dirs, 78-). *Dealer:* Max Hutchinson Gallery 138 Greene St New York NY 10012. *Mailing Add:* 135 Spring St New York NY 10012

BROSS, ALBERT L, JR
PAINTER
b Newark, NJ, June 29, 21. *Study:* Art Students League, with Messrs Dumond, Bridgeman & McNulty. *Work:* NJ State Mus, Trenton; Am Tel & Tel, New York; Roebling Collection; Springville Mus Art, Utah; Hanover Park High Sch. *Exhib:* Nat Arts Club Print Show, New York, 72; Hudson Valley Art Asn Regional Show, White Plains, NY, 72; Acad Artists Asn, Springfield, Mass, 72; Springville Mus Art, 72. *Awards:* Oil Award, Nat Show, Springville, 70; Award, Am Asn Univ Women, 72; Lt Melvin D Brewer Mem Award, 76. *Mem:* Life mem Art Students League; Hudson Valley Art Asn; Acad Artists Asn; Hunterdon Co Art Ctr, NJ; Summit Art Ctr, NJ. *Media:* Oil. *Mailing Add:* Village Rd New Vernon NJ 07976

BROTHERTON, NAOMI
PAINTER, INSTRUCTOR
b Galveston, Tex. *Study:* Baylor Univ, Waco, Tex, BA(fine arts); Art Students League, with Edgar A Whitney, Milford Zornes, Gerry Peirce, Robert E Wood, John Pike, Rex Brandt, John C Pellew & Charles Reid. *Work:* SArk Art Ctr, Eldorado; Baylor Univ Permanent Collection; Ft Worth Pub Sch Syst; Brownsville Art Asn Gallery; Republic Nat Bank, Dallas; and others. *Exhib:* Am Watercolor Soc, New York, 67; Southwestern Watercolor Soc, 64-81; Southwestern Watercolor Soc Regional Exhib, 69; Tex Fine Arts Asn, Austin, 73; Watercolor Okla, Oklahoma City, 75-76. *Teaching:* Instr adult watercolor painting, Artisan's Studio-Gallery, Dallas, 62-; instr, Sul Ross State Univ, Tex, 80 & 81, Eastern NMex Univ, Rosewell, 83. *Awards:* Merrit Awards, Artists & Craftsmen Asn, 82 & 83; Best of Show, Mt Pleasant Art Asn, 82; First in Watercolor, Coppini Acad Fine Arts, San Antonio, 83. *Mem:* Tex Fine Arts Asn; Tex Watercolor Soc; Southwestern Watercolor Soc (pres, 67-68); Artists & Craftsmen Assoc, Dallas. *Publ:* Illusr, Ford Times Mag, 63, 64 & 69; Spotlight on the artist, SWS Scene, Southwestern Watercolor Soc, 3/77; coauth, Variations in Watercolor, 77. *Mailing Add:* 4808 Oak Trail Dallas TX 75232

BROUDE, NORMA FREEDMAN
HISTORIAN, EDUCATOR
b New York, NY, May 1, 41. *Study:* Hunter Col, AB, 62; Columbia Univ, MA(Woodrow Wilson Found Fel), 64, PhD(Woodrow Wilson Dissertation Fel), 67. *Teaching:* Instr art hist, Conn Col, New London, 66-67; vis asst prof, Oberlin Col, Ohio, 69-70; asst prof art hist, Columbia Univ, New York, 72-73; vis asst prof, Vassar Col, Poughkeepsie, NY, 73-74; asst prof art hist, Am Univ, Washington, DC, 75-77, assoc prof art hist, 77-. *Awards:* Nat Endowment Humanities Fel, 81-82; Mina Shaughnessy Scholar, 82. *Mem:* Col Art Asn of Am; Women's Caucus Art. *Res:* Late 19th and early 20th century painting. *Publ:* Auth, The Macchiaioli: Effect and Expression in 19th century Italian Painting, 70 & New Light on Seurat's Dot, 74, Art Bulletin; auth, The Influence of Rembrandt Reproductions on Seurat's Drawing Style, Gazette Beaux-Arts, 76; auth, Degas' Misogyny, Art Bulletin, 77; ed, Seurat in Perspective, Prentice-Hall, 78; co-ed (with Mary D Garrand), Feminism and Art History: Questioning the Litany, Harper & Row, 82. *Mailing Add:* The Dept of Art Am Univ Washington DC 20016

BROUDO, JOSEPH DAVID
EDUCATOR, CERAMIST
b Baltimore, Md, Sept 11, 20. *Study:* Alfred Univ, BFA, 46; Boston Univ, MEd, 50. *Work:* Int Mus Ceramics, Faenza, Italy; Prieto Collection, Mills Col, Calif; Joan Mannheimer Collection. *Exhib:* Int Exhib, Ostend, Belg, 60; Ten Boston Area Craftsmen, New York World's Fair, 64-65. *Teaching:* Dept head & prof art, Endicott Col, 46-. *Awards:* Grand Prize, Int Exhib, Ostend, Belg, 60; Top Honors, Eastern States Expos & De Cordova Craftsmen Exhib; and others. *Mem:* Mass Asn Craftsmen (chmn, 55-56, dir, 72); Am Crafts Coun (exec coun, 71-72); Boston Soc Arts & Crafts (dir, 62-78). *Mailing Add:* c/o Endicott College Dept Art Beverly MA 01915

BROUGH, RICHARD BURRELL
EDUCATOR, DESIGNER
b Salmon, Idaho, May 31, 20. *Study:* Chouinard Art Inst, Los Angeles, dipl; Witte Mem Mus, San Antonio, Tex. *Work:* Montgomery Mus Fine Arts, Ala; Birmingham Art Mus, Ala; Ford Motor Co, Dearborn, Mich. *Comn:* 12 hist paintings, Gulf States Paper Corp, 60; 14 paintings, Vulcan Mat Corp, Birmingham, Ala. *Exhib:* American Painting Today, Metrop Mus Art, New York, 50; US Variety Show, US Info Agency, traveling exhib to Mid East, 66; Ford Exhib, New York World's Fair, 64; 21 paintings in Hyplar, Grumbacher US Traveling Collection, 69. *Teaching:* Prof graphics, Univ Ala, 48-. *Awards:* First Award, Loveman, Joseph & Loeb, 60; First Purchase Award, Bluff Park Asn, 70-74; Purchase Award, Ala Watercolor Soc, 74. *Bibliog:* Meet the artist, TV spec, Birmingham, Ala, 69. *Mem:* Birmingham Art Asn; Ala Watercolor Soc; Tex Watercolor Soc. *Media:* Watercolor, Acrylic. *Publ:* Illusr, 99 Fables, 65; illusr, Ford Times, 50-74. *Mailing Add:* Dept Art Univ Ala University AL 35486

BROUILLETTE, AL
PAINTER, INSTRUCTOR
b Holyoke, Mass, Jan 9, 24. *Study:* Ft Worth Art Ctr Sch, Tex. *Work:* Hermann Fine Arts Ctr, Marietta, Ohio; New York Transit Authority, Brooklyn; Univ Texas Sch Law, Arlington; Hallmark, Kansas City, Mo; NMex Watercolor Soc. *Exhib:* Southwestern Watercolor Soc, Dallas, 69-74; Tex Watercolor Soc, San Antonio, 69-75; Watercolor USA, Springfield, Mo, 74-75 & 77; Nat Acad Design, New York, 74-75; Am Watercolor Soc, New York, 75-80. *Pos:* Art dir, Dallas-Ft Worth Ad Agencies, 52-. *Teaching:* Instr acrylics, workshops. *Awards:* Antoinette Graves Goetz Award, 77; Windsor-Newton Award, 79; Emily Lowe Mem Award, 82. *Bibliog:* Judy Spargin (auth), Art Voices S, 9-10/79; Edward Betts (auth), Creative Seascape, 81; Christopher Schink (auth), Color and Design in Watercolor, 81; Pecos to the Rio Grande, Texas A&M Univ Press. *Mem:* Assoc Nat Acad Design; Southwestern Watercolor Soc (prof standards, 74-75); Allied Artists of Am; Am Watercolor Soc; Nat Watercolor Soc. *Media:* Acrylic, Watercolor, Masonite Panels. *Mailing Add:* 1300 Sunset Ct Arlington TX 76013

BROUN, ELIZABETH GIBSON
CURATOR, HISTORIAN
b Kansas City, Mo, Dec 15, 46. *Study:* Univ Kans, BA, 68, MA, 69, PhD 76. *Collections Arranged:* Prints of Anders Zorn (auth, catalog), 79, Forain at the Front (auth, catalog), 81, Kansas Printmakers (auth, catalog), 81, Engravings of Marcantonio Raimondi (auth, catalog), 81-82 & Prints and Drawings by Pat Steir (auth, catalog), 82, Spencer Mus Art, Lawrence, Kans. *Pos:* Cur prints & drawings, Spencer Mus Art, Univ Kans, Lawrence, 77-, actg dir, currently. *Teaching:* Asst prof, Univ Kans, 80- *Res:* History of American art and graphic arts. *Publ:* Ed, Reverse Paintings on Glass, 78 & coauth, Benton's Bentons, 80, Spencer Mus Art, Univ Kans, Lawrence. *Mailing Add:* c/o Spencer Mus Art Univ Kans Lawrence KS 66045

BROUSSARD, NORMAJ
COLLECTOR, PAINTER
b Lake Providence, La, Aug 28, 31. *Study:* Stephen F Austin State Univ; Univ Tex Corresp Workshops; Danish Sch Design, Paris; also with Jan Maters, Prof Harry Ahysen & Prof Jerry Newman. *Work:* Tex Artists Mus Soc, Port Arthur; Columbia Folk Art Mus. *Comn:* Louisiana Sunset, comn by C Arthur French, Lake Providence; Summer Memory, Gulf States Theatres. *Exhib:* Beaumont Art League, Tex; Sabine Area Art Show, Beaumont; Lone Star Conservative Art Guild State Conv; Cav-Oil-Cade Art Exhib; La Art & Folk Festival, Columbia. *Pos:* Columnist, Art Happenings, News, Port Arthur, 72-; pres & chmn bd, Travel Magic Corp & Broussard Enterprises Inc. *Awards:* First in Fedn, Gen Fedn Women's Clubs; Three First Place Awards, La Art & Folk Festival; Tex Artists of Year, 75. *Mem:* Tex Artists Mus Soc (pres, 72-75); Tex Fine Arts Asn; Southeast Tex Arts Coun (treas, 74-75); Tex Fedn Women's Clubs (fine arts chmn, Magnolia Dist); Beaumont Art Mus. *Media:* Oil, Acrylic. *Interests:* To promote a museum and art activities in Jefferson County to preserve works of Texas artists. *Collection:* Approximately 300 paintings, including those by Archile Gorky, Robert Woods, Edouard Cortes, A D Greer, Gisson, Fried Pal & Makk. *Publ:* Contribr, Sweet Seventies Anthology, 74. *Mailing Add:* 4801 Seventh St Apt 1 Port Arthur TX 77642

BROWN, ALAN M, JR
DEALER, CONSULTANT
b New Rochelle, NY. *Study:* Syracuse Univ, BS, 69. *Pos:* Dir, Alan Brown Gallery, Hartsdale, NY, 72- *Mem:* Coun Arts Westchester (trustee, currently). *Res:* Contemporary artists. *Collection:* Contemporary American art; folk art. *Mailing Add:* 210 E Hartsdale Ave Hartsdale NY 10530

BROWN, ALICE DALTON
PAINTER
b Danville, Pa, Apr 17, 39. *Study:* Acad Julian, Paris, 57; Cornell Univ, 58-60; Oberlin Col, Ohio, BA, 62. *Work:* FMC Corp, Chicago; Metrop Life Insurance Co & Western Electric Co, New York; Midland Nat Bank, Metro Park, NJ; 3-M Co, Minn; First Nat Bank & Trust Co, Chicago. *Exhib:* Large Works, A M Sachs Gallery, New York, 81; Collectors Choice, McNay Art Inst, San Antonio, Tex, 81; one-man shows, A M Sachs Gallery, New York, 82 & 83; Realist Painters, Women's Caucus Art, New York, 82; Architectural Images, Summit Art Ctr, NJ, 82; and others. *Bibliog:* James F Cooper (auth), article, New York Tribune, 6/13/83. *Mem:* Women's Caucus Art, New York. *Media:* Oil. *Mailing Add:* c/o A M Sachs Gallery 29 West 57th St New York NY 10019

BROWN, BETTY ANN
EDUCATOR, CRITIC
b Oklahoma City, Okla, June 6, 49. *Study:* Southern Methodist Univ, BFA, 71; Univ Tex, Austin, MA, 73; Univ NMex, Albuquerque, PhD, 77. *Collections Arranged:* Faces of Fiesta, San Diego State Univ, 82; Susan Kleinberg, Univ Southern Calif, Davidson Conf Ctr, 82; Sensuous Surfaces, Univ Southern Calif, 82; Generations, Conejo Valley Art Mus, 83; Caretas Mexicanas, Mexican mask exhib, Southwest Mus, 83. *Pos:* Dir visual arts prog, Col Continuing Educ, Univ Southern Calif, Los Angeles, 81-; art critic for weekly newspaper, Reader, 81-83; auth, monthly series of previews on Los Angeles art exhibs, Artscene, 82-; auth, monthly column, Arts Mag, 82- *Teaching:* Asst prof art hist, Ill State Univ, 77-79; asst prof, Calif State Univ, Northridge, 79-81; adj prof, Univ Southern Calif, 81- *Mem:* Art Table; Women's Caucus Art; Asn Latin Am Art (secy, 81-); Inst Hispanic Media & Cult (bd dirs, 82-). *Res:* Ancient and contemporary arts of Latin America. *Publ:* Auth, numerous articles on Pre-Columbian art history and contemporary folk arts of Latin America. *Mailing Add:* 405 Howland Canal Venice CA 90291

BROWN, BLANCHE RACHEL
HISTORIAN, EDUCATOR
b Boston, Mass, Apr 12, 15. *Study:* NY Univ, BFA, 36, MA, 38, PhD, 67. *Teaching:* Staff lectr, Metrop Mus Art, New York, 41-66; from assoc prof to prof art hist, NY Univ, 66- *Mem:* Col Art Asn; Archaeol Inst Am (pres, New York Soc, 70-72, bd dirs, currently); Ancient Civilization Group; assoc mem Columbia Univ Sem Classical Civilization. *Res:* History of the fourth century BC and the Hellenistic Period. *Publ:* Auth, Ptolemaic Paintings and Mosaics, Archaeol Inst Am, 57; auth, Five Cities: An Art Guide to Athens, Rome, Florence, Paris, London, Doubleday, 64; auth, Anticlassicism in Greek Sculpture of the 4th Century BC, Archaeol Inst Am, 73; auth, Questions about the late Hellenistic period, In: Art Studies, H N Abrams, 75; auth, Out of the ashes: Glowing treasures of Pompeii, New York Times Mag, 78. *Mailing Add:* 15 W 70th St New York NY 10023

BROWN, BRUCE ROBERT
PAINTER, SCULPTOR
b Philadelphia, Pa, July 25, 38. *Study:* Tyler Sch Art, Temple Univ, BFA(painting), 62, MFA(sculpture), 64. *Work:* Telfair Acad Arts & Sci, Savannah, Ga; Festival Arts Collection, Erie, Pa. *Exhib:* Carnegie Inst, 55-57; Nat Show, Pa Acad Fine Arts, Philadelphia, 62; Nat Show, Butler Inst Am Art, Youngstown, Ohio, 62 & 63; Am Acad Arts & Lett, New York, 68; 21st Ann Int Exhib, Beaumont, Tex, 72; and many others. *Teaching:* Instr, adult painting prog, Dept Recreation, Philadelphia, 61-64; instr ceramics & art, Philadelphia Pub Sch, 65-66; instr art, West Liberty State Col, 67-68; assoc prof art, Monroe Community Col, State Univ NY, 69- *Awards:* Award Painting, Appalachian Corridors: Exhibition I, Charleston, WVa, 68; Purchase Award, Arts & Humanities Coun WVa, 68; Purchase Award, Am Acad Arts & Lett, 68. *Mem:* Col Art Asn Am; Southern Sculptors Asn; Rochester Print Club; Artist's Equity Asn, New York. *Media:* Oil. *Mailing Add:* 17 Sedgewick Dr Honeoye NY 14771

BROWN, C W See Crow, Carol (Wilson)

BROWN, CATHARINE HOMAN
POTTER
b Washington, DC, May 23, 44. *Study:* Mills Col, Oakland, Calif, with Antonio Prieto, BA; Univ Mass, with Lyle N Perkins, MFA; Haystack Mountain Sch Crafts, Deer Isle, Maine, with Arline Fisch. *Work:* First & Merchant's Bank, Richmond, Va; Mills Col, Oakland; Hand Work Shop, Richmond. *Exhib:* Art of Organic Forms, Smithsonian Inst, Washington, DC, 68; Crafts Biennial, Va Mus Fine Arts, Richmond, 68-76; Ceramic & Glass Competition, Corning Mus, NY, 72; Object Makers & All Creatures, 20th Century Gallery, Williamsburg, Va, 74-77; Collector's Show, NC Mus, Raleigh, 76-77; Christmas Invitational, Crafts Concepts, Ridgewood, NJ, 76-77; New Faces Invitational, New York, 76-77; Baltimore Winter Market, 78. *Pos:* Art consult, Chesterfield Co Sch, Va, 69-70. *Teaching:* Instr crafts & design, Va Commonwealth Univ, Richmond, 68-69; teacher porcelain, Richmond, 70-76; instr, Bennington Col, Vt, 75. *Awards:* Ceramics Award, 65 & Sculpture Award, 66, Mills Col; Merit Award, Portsmith Nat Art Show, Va, 75. *Mem:* Am Crafts Coun; Va Crafts Coun; Piedmont Craftsmen Inc; Carolina Designer Craftsmen; Object Makers (pres, 76-77). *Mailing Add:* 6218 W Franklin St Richmond VA 23256

BROWN, DAVID ALAN
HISTORIAN, CURATOR
b Bellevue, Ohio, July 25, 42. *Study:* Harvard Col, BA(magna cum laude), 64; Cambridge Univ, Fulbright fel, 64-65; Yale Univ, MA, 67, PhD, 73. *Collections Arranged:* Berenson and the Connoisseurship of Italian Painting, 79, From Leonardo to Titian: Italian Renaissance Paintings from the Hermitage, 79, Raphael and America, 83 & Leonardo's Last Supper: Before and After, 84, Nat Gallery Art, Washington, DC. *Pos:* Cur Italian Renaissance painting, Nat Gallery Art, Washington, DC, currently. *Teaching:* Lectr art hist, Yale Univ, New Haven, Conn, 73-74 & Smithsonian Assoc Prog, Washington, DC, 75- *Awards:* Finley Fel, Nat Gallery Art, 68-71; Fel Villa I Tatti, Harvard Ctr for Renaissance Studies, Florence, 69-70. *Mem:* Renaissance Soc Am; Col Art Asn. *Res:* Italian Renaissance painting; Leonardo Da Vinci; Correggio. *Publ:* Auth, articles on Leonardo Da Vinci and on Correggio, Mitteilungen des Kunst Historischen Inst, Florence, 71, Mus Studies, 72, Master Drawings, 74 & 75. *Mailing Add:* Nat Gallery of Art Sixth St & Constitution Ave Washington DC 20565

BROWN, DIANE
DEALER
b Cleveland, Ohio, Nov 23, 47. *Study:* Univ Wis, Madison, BA, 69; Univ Md, College Park. *Pos:* Owner & dir, Diane Brown Galley & Diane Brown Sculpture Space, New York, currently. *Teaching:* Lectr, Smithsonian Inst, 80. *Bibliog:* Sculpture carves out audience in US, US News & World Report, 9/1/81; Lee Fleming (auth), Washington's very best galleries, The Washingtonian, 9/81; Washington comes of age, Newsweek, 9/14/81. *Mem:* Int Sculpture Conf; Washington Performing Arts Soc; Washington Art Dealers Asn. *Specialty:* Contemporary art. *Mailing Add:* 100 Greene St New York NY 10012

BROWN, GARY HUGH
PAINTER, EDUCATOR
b Evansville, Ind, Dec 19, 41. *Study:* DePauw Univ, Greencastle, Ind, BA, 63; Acad Belli de Arti, Rome & Florence, Italy, 63-64; Univ Wis-Madison, MFA, 66. *Work:* Elvehjem Art Ctr, Madison, Wis; Yale Univ, New Haven, Conn; Glenbow Art Mus, Alta, Can; Utah Mus of Fine Arts, Salt Lake City; Tyler Mus Art, Tex; and others. *Comn:* Ltd ed paper suite, Source Gallery, San Francisco, publ by Twinrocker, Ind, 76. *Exhib:* One-man shows, Fleischer-Anhalt Gallery, Los Angeles, Calif, 68, Mayan Journey, de Saisset Art Gallery, Univ Santa Clara & Santa Barbara Mus of Art, 71-72, Comsky Gallery, Beverly Hills, Calif, 75, United Arts Club, Dublin, Ireland, 75, Source Gallery, San Francisco, 76 & 78 & Art/Life Gallery, Santa Barbara, 82. *Pos:* Artist-in-residence, Int Inst for Experimental Papermaking, Pajaro Dunes, Calif, 74, New Harmony, Ind, 76, Atelier Haus Worpswede, WGer, 82. *Teaching:* Prof painting, papermaking & drawing, Univ Calif, Santa Barbara, 66- *Awards:* Greenshields Found Grant for Europ Travel/Study, 63. *Mem:* Col Art Asn. *Publ:* Illusr, Peter Whigham's The Blue Winged Bee, Anvil, 69; illusr, John Logan (auth), Poem in Progress, Dryad, 75; illusr, Morton Marcus (auth), The Santa Cruz Mountain Poems, Capra, 75; illusr, The Music of the Trobadours, Ross-Erikson, 79; illusr, Electroworks, George Eastman House & Chanticleer Press, 80. *Dealer:* Source Gallery 1099 Folsom St San Francisco CA 94103. *Mailing Add:* Art Studio Dept Univ of Calif Santa Barbara CA 93106

BROWN, GWYNETH KING
PAINTER
b Barry, Wales; US citizen. *Study:* Pa Acad Fine Arts, Philadelphia; also with Arthur B Carles & Dr R Tait McKenzie. *Work:* Libr Cong; Princeton Univ Graphics Collection; Calif State Libr; Smith Col; Free Libr Philadelphia. *Exhib:* Art Inst Chicago, 58; Carnegie Art Inst, 50; Nat Acad Design, New York, 51; Newark Mus, NJ, 51; Pa Acad Fine Arts, 64; Art Alliance Bicentennial Show, 76; Nam-Han Gallery, Fort Lee, NJ, 80. *Bibliog:* Articles, Free Asia Press, Manila Art News & New York Sunday Times. *Mem:* Philadelphia Artists Equity; Philadelphia Art Alliance, Pa. *Mailing Add:* 173 Nassau St Apt D Princeton NJ 08540

BROWN, HILTON
PAINTER, EDUCATOR
b Momence, Ill, Sept 22, 38. *Study:* Goodman Theatre & Sch Drama, Art Inst Chicago, 56-58; Univ Chicago, 59; Skowhegan Sch Painting & Sculpture, Maine, summers 60 & 61; Art Inst Chicago, dipl fine arts(George T & Isabelle Brown foreign travel fel), 62, BFA, 63, MFA, 64; Univ Ill, Chicago, 62-63. *Work:* Baltimore Mus Art; Ball State Univ Art Collection; Macomb Co Community Col, Detroit; Goucher Col; Univ Md, College Park. *Comn:* Exterior wall paintings, City of Baltimore, 73-75; mural, T Johnson Sch, Baltimore, 79-80. *Exhib:* Chicago & Vicinity Show, Art Inst Chicago, 60; Nat Print Exhib, Brooklyn Mus, 64; Twelve Chicago Painters, Walker Art Ctr, Minneapolis, 65; 20th Mo Show, City Art Mus, St Louis, 66; Md Regional Exhib, Baltimore Mus Art, 75; Kornblatt Gallery, Baltimore, Md, 79; Leslie Lohman Gallery, New York, 80; Baltimore Mus Art, 83. *Pos:* Mem contemp art accession comt, Baltimore Mus Art, 68-78; contrib ed, Am Artist Mag, 81- *Teaching:* Instr color, drawing & design, Art Inst Chicago, 62-65; asst prof drawing & compos, Sch Fine Arts, Washington Univ, 65-68; chmn art dept & prof drawing, painting & printmaking, Goucher Col, 68-78; vis prof artists mat & tech, Winterthur Prog Conserv Art, Univ Del, 74-78, assoc dir, 78-80; prof art, Univ Del, 78- *Awards:* Renfrow Art Award, City Art Mus, St Louis, 65; Berney Award Painting, Baltimore Mus Art, 70. *Bibliog:* Franz Schultz (auth), Chicago Art Inst, 3/67; John Brod Peters (auth), Art views: Hilton Brown: New directions, St Louis Globe Democrat, 8/12/67; Lincoln F Johnson (auth), Retrospective shows Brown growth, The Sun, Baltimore, 2/24/77. *Mem:* Col Art Asn Am; Am Inst Conserv; Artists Equity Asn; Am Soc Testing & Materials; Inter-Soc Color Coun. *Media:* Oil, Acrylic. *Publ:* Auth, Hilton Brown: The artist comes out, The Gay Paper, Baltimore, 9/80; auth, Looking at paintings: Joseph Stella and John Storrs silverpoint drawings, 5/81, Looking at paintings: Paul Cadmus' playground, 1/82, History of watercolor, 3/83 & History of landscape painting, 2/84, Am Artist Mag. *Mailing Add:* Winterthur Art Conserv Prog Univ of Del Newark DE 19711

BROWN, JAMES
PAINTER, GRAPHIC ARTIST
b Brooklyn, NY. *Study:* Long Island Univ, BA, 54; Brooklyn Col, MS, 55; NY Univ & Yeshiva Univ. *Work:* Corpus Christi Mus, Tex; New York City Pub Schs; Tuscan Dairies, NJ; Vanguard Fuel Oil Co, Brooklyn, NY; and others. *Comn:* Portraits, New York City Pub Schs, 79; illus, Nat Asn Advan Colored People, New York, 80; illus, Revlon, USV Lab, 80; Black Winners (illus), comn by Melvin Douglas, 84; and others. *Exhib:* Through Black Eyes, Queens Mus, Flushing, NY, 79; Cross Sect, Brooklyn Mus, NY, 79; West '79/The Law, Minn Mus Art, St Paul, 79 & Albrecht Art Mus, St Joseph, Mo, 80; Mus Afro-Am Life Cult, Dallas, Tex, 81; Passaic Co Col, Patterson, NJ, 83; and

others. *Pos:* Supervisor art, New York City Bd Educ, 74- *Teaching:* Critic, New Jersey State Col, 75; instr drawing, painting & printmaking, Intermediate Sch, New York, 76-78; guest artist, Corpus Christi Mus, 78; lectr bus of art, Col New Rochelle, NY, 79. *Awards:* Purchase Award & First Prize, CofC, Union, NJ, 79; Award, Greater Patterson Arts Coun NJ, 80; Best in Show, Festival on the Green, NJ, 81; and others. *Bibliog:* Laila Kain (critic), Brown's paintings teach, Daily News, Springfield, Mass, 3/9/78; M Gerard Pavoine (dir), The World of James Brown (film) Telecable de Que, Channel 9, 6/79; David L Shirey (auth), Realism stands out in show by Blacks, New York Times, 2/22/81; and others. *Mem:* Coalition Black Artists (dir, 78-); Long Island Black Artists Asn (pres, 83-); Asn Afro-Am & Carribbean Artists; and others. *Media:* Oil, Pastel; Carbon Pencil. *Publ:* Contrib, Interracial Books for Children, Coun on Interracial Bks for Children, New York, 79; illusr, Ten Little Niggers, St Albans Printing, New York, 81; illusr, Black Winners, Nat Asn Advan Colored People, 84. *Dealer:* Dorsey's Art Gallery 553 Rogers Ave Brooklyn NY 11225; Atelier-Galerie Fontaine Inc 56 rue Saint-Pierre PQ GIK 4A1 Can. *Mailing Add:* 117-54 219th St Cambria Heights NY 11411

BROWN, JAMES MONROE, III
MUSEUM DIRECTOR
b Brooklyn, NY, Oct 7, 17. *Study:* Amherst Col, BA, 39; Harvard Univ, MA, 46, Advan Mgt Prog, 58; Amherst Col, Hon MA, 54. *Pos:* Asst to dir, Inst Contemp Art, Boston, 41, asst dir, 46-48; asst to dir, Dumbarton Oaks Res Libr & Collection, Washington, DC, 46; dir, William A Farnsworth Art Mus, Rockland, Maine, 48-51; dir, Corning Glass Ctr, 51-63, dir pub affairs, 56-59, dir mgt develop, 59-61; pres, Corning Found, 61-63; pres, Corning Mus Glass, 61-63; dir, Oakland Mus, Calif, 64-67; dir, Norton Simon Inc Mus Art, 68-69; dir, Va Mus Fine Arts, Richmond, 69-76; dir, Soc Four Arts, Palm Beach, currently. *Mem:* Am Asn Mus (pres, 70-72); Asn Art Mus Dirs; Am Fedn Arts; Int Coun Mus; Int Exhibs Found. *Mailing Add:* Soc of the Four Arts Four Arts Plaza Palm Beach FL 33480

BROWN, JEANETTE H
COLLECTOR, ADMINISTRATOR
b Brooklyn, NY, Dec 20, 11. *Pos:* Dir, The Tyringham Inst, Jean Brown Archive, Mass. *Collection:* Dada, surrealism, fluxus, happenings, concrete poetry, lettrisme, conceptual art. *Mailing Add:* Shaker Seed House Tyringham MA 01264

BROWN, JEFFREY ROGERS
DEALER, COLLECTOR
b Rockville Centre, NY, Feb 7, 40. *Study:* Dartmouth Col, AB, 61; Univ Pa, AM, 68; Univ Md. *Collections Arranged:* Jewish Art (collection of Mr & Mrs Jacob Schulman), 65; George Ortman, 71; Alfred Thompson Bricher (with catalog), 73; Leonard Baskin in Massachusetts, 74; Three American Purists: Mason, Miles, von Wiegand, 75. *Pos:* Cur educ, Munson-Williams-Proctor Inst, Utica, NY, 64-67; cur collections, Indianapolis Mus Art, 69-73; dir, Mus Fine Arts, Springfield, Mass, 73-75. *Teaching:* Asst prof art, State Univ NY Cortland, 67-68. *Mem:* Am Asn Mus; Asn Art Mus Dir. *Res:* American painting of 19th century; James Peale & Alfred Bricher. *Publ:* Contribr, Recent Accessions--A Six Year Retrospective, Indianapolis, 72; auth, Alfred Thompson Bricher, Am Art Rev, Vol 1, 74 & Antiques, 76. *Mailing Add:* PO Box 537 North Amherst MA 01059

BROWN, JOHN CARTER
MUSEUM DIRECTOR
b Providence, RI, Oct 8, 34. *Study:* Harvard Univ, AB, 56, MBA, 58; Munich Univ, 58; with Bernard Berenson, Florence, Italy, 58-59; Neth Inst Art Hist, 60; NY Univ Inst Fine Arts, MA, 62; Brown Univ, Hon LLD, 70; Mt St Mary's Col, Hon LHD, 74; Georgetown Univ, Hon LHD, 75. *Pos:* Asst to dir, Nat Gallery Art, 61-63, asst dir, 64-68, dep dir, 68-69, dir, 69- *Awards:* Gold Medal of Honor, Nat Arts Club, 72. *Mem:* Asn Art Mus Dirs; Col Art Asn Am; Am Asn Mus; Soc Archit Historians; hon Am Inst Architects. *Res:* Seventeenth century Dutch art. *Publ:* Auth & dir, American Vision (film), 65. *Mailing Add:* c/o Nat Gallery Art 4th St & Constitution Washington DC 20565

BROWN, JOHN HALL
PAINTER, ARCHITECT
b Houston, Tex, June 6, 10. *Study:* Tex A&M Col, BA, 33, 35-36. *Work:* City Richardson Pub Libr, Tex; Art Soc Permanent Collection, Sherman, Tex. *Exhib:* Tex Fine Arts Soc Regional; Artists & Craftsmen Regional; Richardson Civic Art Soc Regional; Jefferson Arts Festival National, New Orleans, La; Tex Watercolor Soc Regional. *Awards:* Best Show, Richardson Civic Art Soc, 71; Second Prize, Nat Okla Watercolor, 77; 37 regional & local awards. *Mem:* Southwest Watercolor Soc (vpres, 70); Richardson Civic Art Soc (vpres, 72); Artists & Craftsmen; Tex Fine Arts Soc. *Media:* Watercolor. *Dealer:* Curl Gallery 4843 Massachusetts Ave NW Washington DC 20016. *Mailing Add:* 120 Westshore Dr Richardson TX 75080

BROWN, JONATHAN
HISTORIAN
b Springfield, Mass, July 15, 39. *Study:* Dartmouth Col, AB, 60; Princeton Univ, PhD, 64, Guggenheim Mem Fel, 81-82. *Pos:* Dir, Inst Fine Arts, NY Univ, 73-78; vis mem, Inst Advan Study, 78-79. *Teaching:* Asst prof art hist, Princeton Univ, 65-71, assoc prof, 71-73; assoc prof, Inst Fine Arts, NY Univ, 73-77, prof, 77-; Slade prof fine art, Oxford Univ, 81-82. *Awards:* Arthur Kingsley Porter Prize, Col Art Asn Am, 71; Nat Endowment Humanities Fel, 78-79. *Mem:* Metrop Mus Dept Europ Paintings, New York; Master Drawings, New York. *Res:* Spanish art 16th-19th centuries. *Publ:* Auth, Prints & Drawings by Jusepe de Ribera, Zurbaran, 73; auth, Murillo and His

Drawings, 76; auth, Images and Ideas in Seventeenth-Century Spanish Painting, 78; coauth (with J H Elliott), A Palace for a King: The Buen Retiro and the Court of Philip IV, 80; El Greco and Toledo, In: El Greco of Toledo, 82. *Mailing Add:* 1 E 78th St New York NY 10021

BROWN, JOSEPH
SCULPTOR, EDUCATOR
b Philadelphia, Pa, Mar 20, 09. *Study:* Temple Univ, BS(educ); apprentice & studio asst to R Tait McKenzie, 31-38. *Work:* Pa Acad Fine Arts, Philadelphia; RI Sch Design Mus Art, Providence; NC Art Mus, Raleigh; Univ Tex, Austin; Yale Univ, New Haven. *Comn:* Discus Thrower and Runner (bronzes), Johns Hopkins Univ, Baltimore, 65; Gymnasts (bronze), Temple Univ, Philadelphia, 69; four heroic athletic statues (bronze), City Philadelphia, Vet Stadium, 70; portrait bust, James Michener; portrait figure, John Curry. *Exhib:* Pa Acad Fine Arts Ann, Philadelphia, 32-; Nat Acad Design, New York, 33-; Art Exhib, Olympic Games, Berlin, 36; Int Sculpture Exhib, Philadelphia Mus Art, 49; Expo 67, Montreal, 67. *Pos:* Mem Philadelphia Art Comn. *Teaching:* Sculptor-in-residence, Princeton Univ, 39-68, emer, 68- *Awards:* First Prize Sculpture, Montclair Mus Art, NJ, 40; Barnett Prize, Nat Acad Design, 44; Distinguished Serv Citation, Am Asn Health, Phys Educ & Recreation, Nat Educ Asn, 67. *Bibliog:* Harry Olesker (auth), Shaping things and vice-versa (TV film), NBC-TV, 55. *Mem:* Fel Nat Sculpture Soc; Pa Acad Fine Arts; Artists Equity Asn. *Media:* Bronze. *Publ:* Auth, Unpredictability--margin for inspiration, Archit Rec, 9/55; auth, Dynamics of group interaction, viewpoint of an artist, Am J Psychiat, 3/66; auth, And you hear your name, Univ Mag, summer-fall 66; auth, Movement and figurative sculpture, Quest, 1/75. *Mailing Add:* 173 Nassau St Princeton NJ 08540

BROWN, JUDITH GWYN
ILLUSTRATOR, PAINTER
b New York, NY, Oct 15, 33. *Study:* New York Univ, with Philip Guston, BA, 56; Parsons Sch of Design, with Richard Lindner, 56-57. *Work:* Metrop Mus of Art, New York; Huntington Libr, San Marino, Calif; Kerlan Collection, Univ Minn, Minneapolis; Boston Pub Libr, Mass. *Mem:* Graphic Artist's Guild. *Media:* Pen & Ink, Conte Crayon; Watercolor, Oil. *Publ:* Illusr, Chad and the Elephant Engine, Atheneum, 75; auth & illusr, Alphabet Dreams, Prentice-Hall, 76; illusr, Jeminalee, McGraw-Hill, 77; illusr, Hilarion, Houghton Mifflin, 79; illusr, The Tie That Binds, Scribner's, 81; illusr, A New Treasury of Children's Poetry, Doubleday, 84; and others. *Mailing Add:* 522 E 85th St New York NY 10028

BROWN, JUNE GOTTLIEB
PAINTER
b Dunn, NC, June 21, 32. *Study:* With Leon Stacks, 64-70, Frederick Taubes, 73 & 75 & Robert F Calrow, 77 & 81. *Work:* DuPont & Co, Leland, NC; Dalton Collection, Charlotte, NC; Springs Mills, New York; United Carolina Bank, Southport, NC; Brunswick Co, Bolivia, NC. *Exhib:* North Carolina Realism, Mint Mus, 74; Ann Open Exhib, Catharine Lorillard Wolfe Show, New York, 80, 82 & 83; Hoyt Nat Painting Show, Hoyt Inst Fine Arts, New Castle, Pa, 82; Allied Artists Am Ann Exhib, New York, 82; Nat Mid-Year Exhib, Butler Inst Am Art, 82 & 83; Salmagundi CLub Open Competition, New York, 83; Henley Southeastern Spectrum, Galleries 214, Winston-Salem, NC, 83. *Teaching:* Instr art, Brunswick Community Col, 78- *Awards:* Mae Berlind Bach Award, Catharine Lorillard Wolfe Show, 82; Emily Morse Mem Award, Salmagundi Club, 83; Traveling Show Award, Henley's Southeastern Spectrum, 83. *Mem:* Assoc Artists Southport, NC (mem bd dirs, 70-, pres, 77-80); Assoc Artists Winston-Salem, NC; Artists Fel Inc; Am Artists Prof League; Salmagundi Club. *Media:* Acrylic. *Dealer:* Gilliam & Peden Assoc 1322 New Hope Church Rd Raleigh NC 27609. *Mailing Add:* 122 Caswell Beach Rd Southport NC 28461

BROWN, LARRY K
PAINTER
b New Brunswick, NJ, June 1, 42. *Study:* Wash State Univ, Pullman, BA, 67; Univ Ariz, MFA, 70. *Work:* Walker Art Ctr; Indianapolis Mus Art; Minn Mus Art; Portland Mus Art; St Lawrence Univ. *Exhib:* Drawing USA, Minn Mus Art, 71; Invitation: 74, Walker Art Ctr, 74; solo exhib, RI Sch Design, 74, Lamagna Gallery, New York, 75; O K Harris Works Art, 77, 79, 82 & 84 & Morgan Gallery, Kansas City, Mo, 78 & 80; Abstraction: Alive and Well, State Univ NY, Potsdam, 76; Painting & Sculpture Today, Indianapolis Mus Art, 78. *Teaching:* Vis artist painting, Mont State Univ, Bozeman, 78, Iowa State Univ, Ames, 82 & Ohio State Univ, Columbus, 82. *Awards:* Nat Endowment Arts Fel, 79-80. *Dealer:* O K Harris Works Art 383 W Broadway New York NY 10012; Morgan Gallery 1616 Westport Rd Kansas City MO 64111. *Mailing Add:* 54 Franklin St New York NY 10013

BROWN, LAWRIE
EDUCATOR, PHOTOGRAPHER
b San Jose, Calif, Mar 11, 49. *Study:* Univ Colo, Boulder; San Jose State Univ, Calif, BA, 72; Calif Col Arts & Crafts, Oakland; San Francisco State Univ, MA, 75. *Work:* Oakland Mus, Calif; San Francisco Mus Mod Art, Calif; Bibliotheque National, Cabinet Des Estampes, Paris, France; Ctr Creative Photography, Tucson; Stanford Univ Mus Art, Calif. *Exhib:* One-woman show, Everson Mus Art, Syracuse, NY, 77; Photog Works, San Francisco Mus Mod Art, Calif, 78; Arco Ctr Visual Art, Los Angeles, 79; Il Diaframma-Canon, Milan, 82; In Color, Oakland Mus, Calif, 83; Arranged Image Photography, Boise Gallery Art, Idaho, 83. *Teaching:* Lectr, Art Dept, San Jose State Univ, Calif, 76-82; dir, Photog Dept, Cabrillo Col, Calif, 79- *Awards:* Photographer's Fel, Nat Endowment Arts, 79. *Bibliog:* Peter Hunt Thompson (auth), Untitled 6, Quarterly Friends Photog, 73; Hal Fischer

(auth), Don Worth, Barbara Thompson, Lawrie Brown, Casey Williams, Art Week, 9/25/76; Leland Rice (auth), Contemporary California Photography, Camerawork Gallery, 78. *Mem:* Soc Photog Educ; Friends Photog; Visual Studies Workshop. *Publ:* Popular Photog Ann, 76; contrib, Out of State, San Francisco State Univ, 78; Il Diaframma, Fotofrafia Ital, No 256, 81; Color, Artweek, 7/2/83; Darkroom Photog, San Francisco, 9-10/83. *Dealer:* G Ray Hawkins Gallery 7224 Melrose Ave Los Angeles CA 90046; Focus Gallery 2146 Union St San Francisco CA 94123. *Mailing Add:* 1006 N Branciforte Ave Santa Cruz CA 95062

BROWN, MARION B
PAINTER, INSTRUCTOR

b Brooklyn, NY, Oct 15, 13. *Study:* Pratt Inst, Sch Fine & Appl Arts, cert teaching; also with Edgar A Whitney. *Work:* Dimes Savings Bank New York, Brooklyn; First Nat City Bank, Syosset, NY; Long Island Lighting Co. *Exhib:* Hudson Valley Art Asn, White Plains, NY, 61-82; Am Watercolor Soc, Nat Acad Design Galleries, New York, 62, 69, 71-74 & 76-78; Am Artists Prof League, New York, 66-82; Catharine Lorillard Wolfe Art Club, Nat Arts Club, New York, 67-81; Frye Mus, Seattle, Wash, 73, 76, 77 & 78; Columbia Mus Art, SC, 74 & 76; Mus Fine Arts, St Petersburg, Fla, 76; and others. *Teaching:* Watercolor workshops, Malverne, NY, 67-; instr watercolor, Garden City Community Club, NY, 67- *Awards:* Herb Olsen Award, Am Watercolor Soc, 71; Gold Medal, Hudson Valley Art Asn, 71; Gold Medal, Franklin Mint Gallery of Am Art, 73. *Mem:* Am Watercolor Soc; Hudson Valley Art Asn; Am Artists Prof League; Catharine Lorillard Wolfe Art Club; Nat Art League. *Media:* Watercolor. *Dealer:* Garden City Galleries Ltd 923 Franklin Ave Garden City NY 11530. *Mailing Add:* 18 Nassau Ave Freeport NY 11520

BROWN, MARVIN PRENTISS
PAINTER, SCULPTOR

b New York, NY, July 2, 43. *Study:* Brooklyn Mus Art Sch, 61-62; Yale Univ Summer Sch, Yale-Norfolk Fel, 64; Philadelphia Col Art, BFA, 65; Ind Univ, 65-66; Brooklyn Col, 67. *Work:* Minami Gallery, Tokyo, Japan; Eastern Mich Univ, Ypsilanti; Corp Design Ctr, Westinghouse Corp, Gateway Ctr, Pittsburgh; Health & Hosp Corp, New York; Moravian Col, Bethlehem, Pa. *Comn:* Wall sculpture, Howard Beach Br, Queensborough Pub Libr, Dept Gen Serv, New York, 71. *Exhib:* Ann Exhib Contemp Am Painting, 69 & 72, Ann Exhib Contemp Am Sculpture, 70, Whitney Mus Am Art; Afro-American Artists: New York and Boston, Mus Fine Arts, Boston, 70; Untitled I, Art Lending Serv, Mus Mod Art, New York, 71; American Drawings: The Last Decade, Katonah Gallery, NY, 71; Painting or Sculpture?, Newark Mus, NJ, 72; Oakland Mus, Calif, 79. *Teaching:* Lectr painting, Philadelphia Col Art, Pa, 70-71; adj lectr art, Hunter Col, 71-; lectr, Calif State Univ, Hayward, 72-73; asst prof, Brown Univ, 74-80. *Awards:* Corp Yaddo Residence Award, 68; John Simon Guggenheim Mem Found Fel, 73; Fulbright Sr Scholar Grant in Fine Arts, Australia, 77. *Bibliog:* Barbara Rose (auth), Black art in America, Art in Am, 9-10/70; Carter Ratcliff (auth), The Whitney Annual: Part I, Artforum, 4/72; Holloway (auth), Memory, Arts Melbourne, 77. *Media:* Mixed. *Dealer:* Gimpel & Weitzenhoffer Ltd 1040 Madison Ave New York NY 10021; Rutland Gallery 32A St George St Hanover Square London England. *Mailing Add:* Box 423 West Kingston RI 02892

BROWN, MARY RACHEL See Marais

BROWN, MILTON WOLF
HISTORIAN

b Newark, NJ, July 3, 11. *Study:* New York Univ, BA, 32, MA, 35, PhD, 49; Courtauld Inst, summer 34; Univ of Brussels, summer 37; Harvard Univ, 38-39. *Collections Arranged:* Jacob Lawrence Retrospective, Whitney Mus of Am Art, New York, 74; Modern Spirit, American Painting & Photography, Arts Coun of Great Brit, 77; Masterpieces of American Painting from Washington DC Public Collections, Inst Contemp Art, Mexico City, 80. *Teaching:* From instr to prof art hist, Brooklyn Col, NY, 46-70; prof art hist & exec off, PhD Prog in Art Hist, Grad Sch, City Univ New York, 71-79, resident prof, 79- *Awards:* Sachs Fel, 38-39 & Fogg Mus Fel, 40-41, Harvard Univ; Bollingen Found Fel, 59-60. *Mem:* Col Art Asn of Am; Soc of Archit Hist; Archives of Am Art (adv coun, 65-); Smithsonian Inst (coun, 76-); Victorian Soc in Am. *Res:* American art, especially early 20th century, art nouveau. *Publ:* Auth, American Painting from the Armory Show to the Depression, Princeton Univ Press, 55; co-auth, Encyclopedia of Painting, Crown, 55; auth, Story of the Armory Show, Hirshhorn Found, 63; auth, American Art to 1900, H N Abrams, 77; auth, 100 Masterpieces from Washington, DC, Public Collections, Smithsonian Press, 83. *Mailing Add:* 15 W 70th St New York NY 10023

BROWN, PAUL L
PAINTER, EDUCATOR

b June 25, 39. *Study:* Brandeis Univ, BA, 61; Yale Sch Art & Archit, BFA, 63; Skowhegan Sch Painting & Sculpture, 64. *Exhib:* Indianapolis Mus Art, 70; Inst Contemp Art, Boston, 70, 75 & 76; State House, Boston, 73; Fogg Art Mus, Cambridge, 74; one-man shows, Rose Art Mus, Brandeis Univ, Waltham, Mass, 74 & Harcus Krakow Gallery, Boston, 78; Brockton Art Ctr, 75; Inst Contemp Art, Boston, 75; Corcoran Gallery Art, Washington, DC, 77; Hayden Gallery, Mass Inst Technol, Cambridge, 79; and others. *Teaching:* Instr, Cooper Union, Queens Col, Pratt Inst & New York Inst Technol, 66-69; asst prof fine arts, Brandeis Univ, 69-82. *Awards:* Nat Endowment Arts Fel, 74. *Bibliog:* Carl Belz (auth), article, Art in Am, 1-2/74; Robert Taylor (auth), article, Boston Globe, 12/74; Bonny Saulnier (auth), Paul Brown's discovery, New Boston Review, 6-7/79. *Mailing Add:* 84 Forsyth St New York NY 10002

BROWN, PEGGY ANN
PAINTER

b Ft Wayne, Ind, Mar 15, 34. *Study:* Marquette Univ, BS(jour); Ft Wayne Art Inst. *Work:* Ind Univ, Bloomington; Columbus Art Ctr, Ohio; Ricks Col, Rexburg, Idaho; Cooperstown NY Art Asn; Menninger Found, Topeka, Kans. *Exhib:* Allied Artists Am, New York, 70-82; Nat Watercolor Soc, Los Angeles, 72-74, 76 & 79-82; Am Watercolor Soc, New York, 74, 76, 79 & 82; one-person shows, Ft Wayne Mus of Art, Ind, Burpee Mus, Ill, 82 & Purdue Univ, 82. *Awards:* Gold Medal Watercolor, Allied Artists Am, 78; Harrison Cady Award, Am Watercolor Soc, 79; Ranger Purchase Award, Nat Acad Design, 80. *Bibliog:* James Voirol (auth), Catalog, Ft Wayne Mus Art Publ, 75; Women in Design Compendium, 82. *Mem:* Nat Watercolor Soc; Allied Artists Am; Watercolor West; Am Watercolor Soc; Rocky Mountain Watermedia Soc. *Media:* Transparent Watercolor, Drawings. *Publ:* Auth, Watercolorist, Northlight Mag, 80. *Mailing Add:* 5209 Westbreeze Trail Ft Wayne IN 46804

BROWN, PETER C
SCULPTOR, EDUCATOR

b Port Chester, NY, Oct 10, 40. *Study:* Ohio Wesleyan Univ, BFA, 63; Cranbrook Acad of Art, MFA, 65. *Work:* Cranbrook Acad of Art, Bloomfield Hills, Mich; Miami Univ, Oxford, Ohio; Baldwin-Wallace Col, Berea, Ohio. *Exhib:* Butler Inst Am Art, Youngstown, Ohio, 66 & 67; Tweed Mus, Philadelphia Mus Art, 73; Contemp Reflections 1976, Aldrich Mus Contemp Art, Ridgefield, Conn, 76; solo exhib, Queens Mus, Flushing, NY, 82; Art Lending Gallery, Mus Mod Art, New York, 82; Green Space Gallery, New York, 83; 55 Mercer St Gallery, 83; State Univ NY, Purchase, 83; and others. *Teaching:* Asst prof fine art, Western Col, Oxford, Ohio, 65-70; instr painting, Philadelphia Art Mus, 71-72; assoc prof fine art & coordr art dept, La Guardia Col, City Univ New York, 73- *Awards:* Artists Assistance, 55 Mercer St Gallery, Comt Vis Arts, Artists Space, 80; Juror's Award, Small Works Show, NY Univ, 82; Sculpture Fel, Creative Artists Pub Serv Prog, NY State Coun Arts, 83-84. *Bibliog:* Joseph Masheck (auth), Constructive issues in relief, Artforum, 11/82; Grace Glueck (auth), article, New York Times, 12/31/82; Stephen Westfall (auth), article, Arts Mag, 3/83. *Media:* Wood, Plaster. *Dealer:* Harm Bouckaert Gallery 100 Hudson St New York NY 10013. *Mailing Add:* 40 White St New York NY 10013

BROWN, PETER THOMSON
PHOTOGRAPHER, EDUCATOR

b Northampton, Mass, June 5, 48. *Study:* Stanford Univ, BA, 71, MFA, 77. *Work:* Mus Fine Arts, Houston; Stanford Univ Mus Art; Piton Found, Denver, Colo; Santa Barbara Mus Art; Meril Collection, Houston. *Exhib:* New Photography, Stanford Mus, Calif, 79; Tony Cronin Mem Exhib, Mus Fine Arts, Houston, Tex, 79; Emerging Texas Photographers, Laguna Gloria Mus, Austin, 81; Color from the Collection, Mus Fine Arts, Houston, 82; Art from Houston, Stavanger Mus, Norway, 82. *Teaching:* Lectr photog, Stanford Univ, 76-77; lectr photog, Rice Univ, 78- *Awards:* National Prize, Bicentennial Traveling Show, Miled Photo, 76; Grad fel, Carnegie Found, 77. *Bibliog:* Elliot Klein (auth), article, Palo Alto Weekly, 11/81; Terry Byrne-Dodge (auth), Straight shooters, Houston Post, 7/4/82; Joan Murray (auth), Words and images, Artweek, 5/21/83. *Mem:* Col Art Asn; Soc Photog Educ. *Media:* Color, Black & White. *Publ:* Illusr, Learning to Die, Learning to Live, Fortress Press, 76; Popular Photography Annual, 76. *Dealer:* Harris Gallery 1100 Bissonnet Houston TX 77006; Smith-Andersen Gallery 200 Homer St Palo Alto Ca 94301. *Mailing Add:* 1113 Milford St Houston TX 77006

BROWN, REYNOLD
PAINTER, INSTRUCTOR

b Los Angeles, Calif, Oct 18, 17. *Study:* Otis Art Inst, Los Angeles; Chouinard Art Sch; also with Will Foster. *Work:* Alamo Mus, San Antonio, Tex; Home Savings & Loan Collection, Los Angeles. *Comn:* Portrait of VPres Eng, NAm Aviation, 45; Portrait of Col Dean Hess, US Air Force, 65; Portrait of First Pres, Sch Dentistry, Univ Calif, Los Angeles, 72, Portrait of Second Pres, 74. *Exhib:* Calif State Fair, 35; Laguna Beach Festival; Los Angeles All City Festival, 71; Buena Park All City Festival, 72; San Gabriel All City Festival, 72-76; Pasadena Arts Coun, Calif, 75-76; Ambassador Col, Pasadena, 77. *Pos:* Illusr, NAm Aviation, Los Angeles, 42-49; free lance advert illusr mag story & cover, New York, 49-55; illusr & art dir advert, all major motion picture co, 50-73. *Teaching:* Prof illus, Los Angeles Art Ctr Col Design, 50- *Awards:* Purchase Award, Los Angeles All City Festival, 72; Best of Show, Buena Park All City Festival, 72 & 75 & San Gabriel All City Festival, 72, 75 & 80. *Mem:* Master & fel Am Inst Fine Arts; Los Angeles Soc Illusr; San Gabriel Fine Art Asn. *Media:* Oil, Watercolor. *Dealer:* Trailside Gallery Jackson WY 83001 & Scottsdale AZ 85251; Peppertree Western Art Show Santa Inez CA. *Mailing Add:* Box 28 Crawford NE 69339

BROWN, RHETT DELFORD (HARRIETT GURNEY BROWN)
FIBER ARTIST, ILLUSTRATOR

b Atlanta, Ga, Nov 12, 24. *Study:* Duke Univ, BA; New Sch for Social Res; Sch of Visual Arts, cert; Valentine Mus, study in mixed media stitchery, study with Constance Howard & photography with Bob Hanson. *Work:* Smithsonian Inst; ICA, London; also in pvt collections. *Exhib:* One-person exhib, Great Building Crack-Up, 74; Union Carbide Invitational, 78; Yeshiva Mus, 81. *Pos:* Founder & dir, Cricket Theatre, New York, 59-63; dir, Great Building Crack-Up Gallery, New York, 70-76; founder & dir, Ctr Contemp Fabric Arts, New York, 78- *Teaching:* Instr fabric as art medium, New Sch Social Res, 77- *Bibliog:* Anne Beatts (auth), Double Your Pleasure Dots Double Your Fun, Oui Mag, Vol 3, No 5, 5/74; Merridee Merzer (auth), Homespun Hardcore, Penthouse Mag, 1/75. *Mem:* Women's Art Caucus. *Media:* Fabric; Threads. *Publ:* Contribr & illusr, Titters, Macmillan, 76; contribr & illusr, Hardcore Crafts, Ballantine, 76. *Mailing Add:* c/o Great Bldg Crack-Up 251 W 13th St New York NY 10011

BROWN, RICHARD MORGAN
ENVIRONMENTAL ARTIST, SCULPTOR
b Philadelphia, Pa, Nov 20, 48. *Study:* Univ Ga, Athens, BFA, 73; Washington Univ, St Louis, Mo, MFA, 75. *Work:* Nat Air & Space Mus, Smithsonian Inst, DC. *Exhib:* Mid-Am 5, Kansas City Mus, Mo, 74; Ann Exhib, Okla Art Mus, Oklahoma City, 74; Mid-S Biennial, Brooks Mem Art Gallery, Memphis, Tenn, 75; Mid-State Art Exhib, Evansville Mus Arts & Sci, Ind, 75; Drawing as Process, Akron Art Inst, Ohio, 78; Proj of the 70's, Sullivant Hall Gallery, Columbus, Ohio, 79; and others. *Teaching:* Instr sculpture, Univ Tex, Austin, 75-77; asst prof sculpture, Ohio State Univ, Columbus, 77-82. *Awards:* Best in Show, Brooks Mem Art Gallery, 75; Ohio Arts Coun aid to individual artists, 79; Ford Found grant, 80. *Media:* Mixed Media. *Mailing Add:* 1516 Wilton Dr Columbus OH 43227

BROWN, ROBERT (EARL)
PHOTOGRAPHER, EDUCATOR
b Gouverneur, NY, Jan 26, 37. *Study:* Rochester Inst Technol, NY, AAS, 57, with Minor White, BFA, 59; San Francisco State Univ, MA, 67; San Francisco Art Inst, MFA, 72. *Work:* Int Mus Photog, George Eastman House, Rochester, NY; Mass Inst Technol Creative Photo Lab, Cambridge, Mass; Oakland Mus, Calif. *Exhib:* Light 7, Hayden Art Gallery, Mass Inst Technol, Cambridge, Mass, 69; one-man shows, George Eastman House, Rochester, NY, 68 & 72; Los Angeles Inst Contemp Art, 81; Adventuresome Eye, San Francisco Art Mus, 69; Photog into Sculpture, Mus Mod Art, New York, 70; Object Illusion Reality, Calif State Univ, Fullerton, 79 & European Tour, US Int Commun Agency, 81-82; Object Illusion Reality, Calif State Univ, Fullerton, 79; and others. *Teaching:* Asst prof art, Calif State Univ, Northridge, 67-70; assoc prof art, Univ Nev, Las Vegas, 76- *Awards:* Calif State Univ, Northridge fac res grants, 68 & 69; Nat Endowment for Arts photog fel, 75; Fac Res Grant, Univ Nev, Las Vegas, 80-81. *Bibliog:* Thomas H Garver (auth), New Photography: San Francisco and the Bay Area, M H De Young Mus, San Francisco, 74; Van Deren Coke (auth), Light and Substance, Univ NMex, Albuquerque, 74; Dextra Frankel (auth), Object Illusion Reality, Calif State Univ, Fullerton, 79. *Mem:* Soc Photog Educ. *Publ:* Auth, Daisies Daisies Daisies Daisies, privately publ, 70; contribr, rev in Artforum, 10/75; contribr, Art Wk, 7/75; contribr, Art News, 9/75. *Mailing Add:* 13001 Las Vegas Blvd S Las Vegas NV 89124

BROWN, ROBERT DELFORD
CONCEPTUAL ARTIST
b Portland, Colo, Oct 25, 30. *Study:* Univ Calif, Los Angeles, BA, 52, with Howard Warshaw, 54-55, MA, 58. *Work:* Smithsonian Inst, Washington, DC; RCA Collection, New York; Archive, Sohm, Ger; Yale Univ; Polaroid Collection, Boston, Mass. *Comn:* Meat Show, Nathan Romanoff, New York, 64; London St Happening, Robert Frazier Gallery, London, 66. *Exhib:* Ann Exhib Painting, Los Angeles Co Art Mus, Los Angeles, 58; Graphics, Brooklyn Mus, NY, 63; Altered Photog, M H de Young Mem Mus, San Francisco, 75; Victory Over Dumbness Day, New York, 76; NC Mus Art, Raleigh, 77; 15 Yr Retrospective, 1963-1978, Iran-Am Ctr, Tehran, Iran, 78; Osuna Gallery, Washington, DC, 80; Phyllis Kind Gallery, New York, 81; and many others. *Pos:* Founder, First Nat Church of the Exquisite Panic, Inc, 64 & Great Bldg Crack-Up, 67. *Awards:* Strangest Artist in the World, Olympics of Art, Donald Collender, 72. *Bibliog:* Lil Picard (auth), The work of art, Das Kunstwerk, Ger, 12/64; Lette Eisenhauer (auth), Portrait Bob Delford Brown, Art & Artists, London, 7/73; Contemporary Artists, St James Press, London & St Martin's Press, New York, 77. *Media:* Sight, Sound. *Publ:* Auth, Hanging, 67, First Class Portraits, 73, Ulysses by Robert Delford Brown, An Altered Plagiarism, 75 & Ikonobiles & Maranathas, 78, First Nat Church of the Exquisite Panic Press; contribr, A D Coleman, ed, Grotesque Photography, Ridge Press, 77. *Mailing Add:* c/o Great Bldg Crack-Up 251 W 13th St New York NY 10011

BROWN, ROBERT K
DEALER
b Springfield, Mass, May 22, 42. *Study:* Boston Univ, BS; Annenberg Sch Commun, Univ Pa, MCommun Arts. *Pos:* Dir & co-owner, Reinhold-Brown Gallery, New York, currently. *Mem:* Antiquarian Booksellers Asn Am; Int League Booksellers. *Specialty:* Rare posters relating to the early avant-garde including constructivism, functionalism, art nouveau-deco, Vienna secession; rare books on 20th century art and architecture. *Publ:* Contribr, Art Deco Minneapolis Inst, 70; ed, Art in Design in Vienna, 72; auth, Art Deco Internationale, Quick Fox, 77. *Mailing Add:* 120 E 86th St New York NY 10028

BROWN, STEPHEN PAT
PAINTER, SCULPTOR
b Greeley, Colo, Aug 26, 50. *Study:* Colo State Univ, BFA, 72; Skowhegan Sch Painting & Sculpture, with Paul Georges, 72; Art Students League, with Gabriel Laderman; Brooklyn Col, with Philip Pearlstein, Allan D'Arcangelo, Lennart Anderson & Lois Dodd, MFA, 78. *Work:* Colo State Univ Gallery, Ft Collins. *Exhib:* New Realism, Terrain Gallery, New York, 80; Hobart & William Smith Colleges, Geneva, NY, 82; Cortlandt Univ Gallery, NY, 82; one-man show, Rosenberg Gallery, New York, 82; Bodies and Souls, Artists Choice Mus, New York, 83; and others. *Pos:* Studio asst, Alice Neel, New York, 74-75. *Teaching:* Guest artist studio art, Louisiana State Univ, 79; instr printmaking, Sch Art League, Brooklyn, NY, 79-80; guest lectr painting, Cortlandt Univ, NY, 82; artist in residence, Parsons Sch Design, 83. *Awards:* Charles Shaw Painting Scholarship, Brooklyn Col, 78; Yaddo Residency, NY State Coun Arts, 79; Millay Residency, Edna St Vincent Millay, 80. *Bibliog:* Harold Lujar (auth), Stephen Brown, Arts Mag, 11/78; John Perrault (auth), New talent in NY, Soho Weekly News, 79. *Media:* Oil. *Mailing Add:* 671 Westminster Rd 20 West 57th Brooklyn NY 11230

BROWN, SUZANNE GOLDMAN
GALLERY OWNER, COLLECTOR
b New York, NY, Sept 8, 29. *Study:* Radcliff Col, BA(cum laude; Am hist since 1785), 51; Harvard Law Sch, 51-52; Tufts Col, grad work in hist, 52-53; Ariz State Univ, 68-69. *Collections Arranged:* Numerous exhibs arranged through docent prog, Phoenix Art Mus, 60-63. *Pos:* Gallery owner, The Suzanne Brown Gallery & Art Images West, 68-; officer, Friends of Mex Art, Phoenix, 68-70; mem & docent, Phoenix Art Mus League, 69-73; pres, Main St Art Asn, 76-; mem bd, Ariz Theatre Co, 80-82. *Teaching:* Guest lectr, Ariz State Univ, Northern Ariz Univ, Phoenix Col, Scottsdale Ctr Arts & Art News Conf. *Awards:* Woman Yr Award, Ariz Women's Caucus Arts, 82. *Bibliog:* Articles in Ariz Republic, 80 & 81, Southwest Art Mag, 81 & Art Talk, 84. *Res:* Mexican art history with emphasis on Orozoco; in-depth study of history of Southwestern art from the 1830's; Aleschinsky; graphics. *Specialty:* Contemporary Southwestern art. *Publ:* Contribr, Southwestern Art, Craig Cornelius, 76. *Mailing Add:* The Suzanne Brown Gallery 7156 Main St Scottsdale AZ 85251

BROWN, THEODORE MOREY
HISTORIAN, WRITER
b Winthrop, Mass, Nov 11, 25. *Study:* Mass Inst Technol, BArch, 53; Harvard Univ, MA, 56; Univ Utrecht, Neth, PhD, 58. *Teaching:* From asst prof to assoc prof art hist, Univ Louisville, Ky, 58-67; from assoc prof to prof art hist, Cornell Univ, Ithaca, NY, 67- *Mem:* Col Art Asn; Soc Archit Historians; Am Studies Asn; Technol & Soc. *Res:* Nineteenth and twentieth century art, photography and architecture. *Publ:* Auth, The Work of G Rietveld, Architect, Bruna & Zoon, 58; auth, Introduction to Louisville Architecture, Louisville Free Pub Libr, 60; coauth, Old Louisville, Univ Louisville, 61; auth, Mondrian and Rietveld, In: Nederlands Kunsthistorisch Jaarboek, Utrecht, 68; auth, Margaret Bourke-White, Photojournalist, A D White Mus, Cornell Univ, 72. *Mailing Add:* Dept of Hist of Art Cornell Univ Ithaca NY 14850

BROWNE, ALDIS J, III
DEALER
b Chicago, Ill, Oct 23, 39. *Study:* Yale Univ; Univ Chicago, Grad Sch Business. *Collections Arranged:* 19th & 20th Century Prints (auth, catalog), Iran-Am Soc, 77; 500 Yrs of European Prints (auth, catalog), Wadsworth & Co, 77; Currier & Ives (auth, catalog), Esmark, Chicago, 77; Prints by European Masters (auth, catalog), Wadsworth & Co, 79; Prints & Selected Drawings (auth, catalog), Wadsworth & Co, 81; Edvard Munch--Paradox of Women, 81; Edvard Munch--Mirror of His Life, 83; M C Escher--Universe of Mind Play, Tokyo, 83. *Pos:* Pres, Aldis Browne Fine Arts, Ltd, 72- *Mem:* Art Dealers Asn Am, Inc; Associated Am Artists (vpres, 65-72). *Specialty:* 19th & 20th century works on paper. *Publ:* Auth & ed, M C Escher, 81 & co-auth & ed, Salvador Dali Retrospective, 82, Art Life Tokyo. *Mailing Add:* 1018 Madison Ave New York NY 10021

BROWNE, ROBERT M
COLLECTOR, PATRON
b Brooklyn, NY, Apr 12, 26. *Study:* Univ Rochester, NY, BA(with distinction), 46; Johns Hopkins Univ Sch Med, MD, 50. *Exhib:* Collection exhibited: Oceanic Arts, Honolulu Acad Arts, Hawaii, 67; Sculpture of Polynesia, Art Inst Chicago, 67 & Mus Primitive Art, New York, 68; Arts of Oceania, Dallas Mus Fine Arts, 70; Art of the Sepik River, Art Inst Chicago, 71; Art Collections in Hawaii, Univ Hawaii Art Gallery, 76; The Art of the Pacific Islands, Nat Gallery Art, 79-80. *Bibliog:* Terence Barrow (auth), The Art of Tahiti and the Neighbouring Societies, Austral and Cook Islands, Thames & Hudson, London, 79. *Mem:* Honolulu Acad Arts; Western Reciprocal Mus; Bishop Mus Asn; Contemp Art Ctr Hawaii; Arts Coun Hawaii. *Interests:* Primative and tribal arts; contemporary painting, sculpture and ceramics; Japanese Mingei folkcraft. *Collection:* Oceanic and Pre-Columbian art; Japanese Mingei folkcraft. *Mailing Add:* 3625 Anela Pl Honolulu HI 96822

BROWNE, SYD J
PAINTER
b Brooklyn, NY, Aug 21, 07. *Study:* Pratt Inst; Art Student League. *Work:* Libr Cong, Washington, DC; New Brit Inst, Conn; New York Pub Libr, NY; Staten Island Inst, NY; Fairleigh Dickinson Univ, NJ. *Awards:* Mischa Lempert Mem Purchase Prize, Salmagundi Club, 50; William Church Osborn Purchase Prize, Am Watercolor Soc, 50; Soc Am Artists Award, Salmagundi Club, 70. *Mem:* Nat Acad Design; Salmagundi Club. *Media:* Oil, Watercolor. *Dealer:* Grand Cent Galleries Hotel Biltmore New York NY 10017. *Mailing Add:* Winter Harbor ME 04693

BROWNE, VIVIAN E
PAINTER, ADMINISTRATOR
b Laurel, Fla, Apr 26, 29. *Study:* Hunter Col, BS, MFA; Art Students League; Pratt Graphics Ctr; New Sch Social Res. *Work:* City Chemical Bank, Bronx Hosp, Chase Manhattan Bank, Schomburg Collection Libr, New York; Southeast Ark Arts & Sci Ctr. *Exhib:* Mus Mod Art, New York, 68; Rutgers Fac Exhib, 79; Soho 20 Gallery, 80; Ill State Univ, 80-82; New Mus, New York, 81; Douglass Col, 83; Franklin Marshall Col, 83; and many others. *Teaching:* Asst prof painting, Rutgers Univ, Newark, 71-75, assoc prof painting, 75-, chmn, Dept Art, 75-78; vis prof, Univ Calif, Santa Cruz, 83- *Awards:* Huntington Hartford Found Painting Fel, 64; Rutgers Univ res grants, 73 & 75; fel, MacDowell Colony, 80. *Bibliog:* Archives of American Art, Smithsonian Inst, 69; Grace G Alexander (dir), Making more than one, WNYE TV Series on Printmaking, 71; Oakley N Holmes (dir), Black Artists (film), 75. *Mem:* Col Art Asn; Women's Caucus for Art; Nat Conf of Artists. *Media:* Oil, Acrylic; Intaglio, Lithography. *Publ:* Contribr, Eight by Ten Art

Portfolio, Elohim Raman, 71-73; auth, Afro-American Art: An Annotated Bibliography, New York City Bd Educ, 72; contribr, Graphics Portfolio, Printmaking Workshop, 72; contribr, Attica Book, Benny Andrews & Rudolf Baranik, (auth), 72; contrib ed, Heresies Mag, 82. *Dealer:* Soho 20 469 Broome St New York NY. *Mailing Add:* 451 W Broadway New York NY 10012

BROWNETT, THELMA DENYER
PAINTER, CONSERVATOR
b Jacksonville, Fla, Oct 26, 24. *Study:* Wesleyan Conserv, BFA(magna cum laude), 46, with Emile Holzhauer; Columbia Univ, 48, with Dr Edwin Ziegfield; Univ Ga, MFA, 52, with Lamar Dodd, James Johnson Sweeny & William Zorack. *Work:* Ga Mus Art, Athens; Gertrude Herbert Art Mus, Augusta, Ga; Atlanta Art Mus, Ga; Ringling Mus Art, Sarasota, Fla; also pvt collections in the US & abroad. *Comn:* Mural, Puppet Playhouse, Augusta, Ga, 51; hundreds of portraits, 56-; Reredos, St Peter's Church, Jacksonville, Fla, 58; Triptych, St Mark's Episcopal Church, Jacksonville, 63; mural, Off Bldg, San Jose Plaza, Jacksonville, 65. *Exhib:* High Mus Art, Atlanta; Ga Mus Art, Athens; Columbia Mus Art, SC; Beaumount Art Mus, Tex; Bradenton Art Mus, Fla; 1984 Retrospective Exhib, Kent Campus, Fla Jr Col, Jacksonville. *Pos:* Dir, Gertrude Herbert Art Inst, 51-55; art comnr, State of Ga, 54-57; chmn visual arts, Arts Festival Eleven, Jacksonville, 68-69; dir & owner, Oxford Gallery Ltd, Jacksonville, Fla, 75- *Teaching:* Chmn dept art, Augusta Col, 52-55; chmn dept art, Jacksonville Univ, 56-58; chmn dept art, Fla Jr Col, 65-70, prof art, 70-; restorer of paintings, pvt studio, 56- *Bibliog:* Articles in Mademoiselle, 6/53 & La Rev Mod, Paris, 55. *Mem:* Asn Ga Artists (pres, 53-55); Fla Artist Group (secy-treas, 74-); Fedn Fla Artists (bd dir, 57-59); Jackson Coun Arts (mem bd dirs, 69-). *Publ:* Auth, Painting, Student Handbook, 71 & 75; auth, Painting Studio Handbook, 78. *Mailing Add:* 4774 Apache Ave Jacksonville FL 32210

BROWNING, COLLEEN
PAINTER
b Fermoy, Co Cork, Ireland, May 18, 29; US citizen. *Study:* Slade Sch Art, London, Eng. *Work:* Detroit Art Inst; Columbia Mus, SC; Milwaukee Art Ctr; St Louis Art Mus, Mo; Wichita Art Mus, Kans. *Comn:* Olympic Editions 1976 (lithograph); Kent Bicentennial Portfolio (lithograph). *Exhib:* Five shows, Whitney Mus Am Art Contemp Ann, New York, 51-63; Art Inst Chicago, 54; ann shows, Nat Acad Design, New York, 57-78; Cleveland Mus, Ohio, 75; Indianapolis Mus, Ind, 76; solo exhibs, five at Kennedy Galleries, 68-82 & Towson State Col, Md, 78; Towson State Col, Md, 78. *Teaching:* Instr painting & drawing, City Col New York, 60-76; instr, Nat Acad Design, 79-81. *Awards:* Figure Composition Award, Stanford Univ, 56; Second Prize for oils, Butler Inst Am Art, 60 & 74; Adolph & Clara Obrig Prize, Nat Acad Design, 70. *Bibliog:* Jerry Tallmer (auth), NY Post, 76 & 79; Leonard Kriegel (auth), Arts Mag, 2/79; article, Am Artists, 9/81. *Mem:* Academician Nat Acad Design (corresp secy, 72-73); Audubon Artists. *Media:* Oil. *Publ:* Illusr, Portrait of a Lady, Ltd Ed Club, 67; illusr, The Poet's Eye, Prentice-Hall, 69; illusr, Every Man Heart Look Down, Crowell-Collier, 70; illusr, Downtown Is, McGraw-Hill, 72. *Mailing Add:* 100 LaSalle St New York NY 10027

BROWNING, DIXIE BURRUS
PAINTER, WRITER
b Elizabeth City, NC, Sept 9, 30. *Study:* Mary Washington Col; Richmond Prof Inst; and with Barclay Sheaks, Ray Prohaska & Ric Chin. *Work:* US Coast Guard Mus, New London, Conn; Statesville Mus Arts & Sci, NC; Duke Hospital Collection, Durham, NC; Wachovia Bank & Trust, Z Smith Reynolds Found, Winston-Salem. *Exhib:* Marine Exhib, James River Juried, Mariners Mus, Newport News, Va; Irene Leache Mem Biennial, Norfolk Mus Art, Va, 68; Regional Gallery Art, Boone, NC, 71 & 74; Manufacturers Hanover Trust Gallery, New York, 71; Southeastern Ctr for Contemp Art, Winston-Salem, 76. *Pos:* Founder & co-dir, Art Gallery Originals, Winston-Salem, 68-73; co-dir, Art V Gallery, Clemmons, NC, 74-75. *Teaching:* Teacher watercolor & acrylics, Arts & Crafts Asn Inc, Winston-Salem, 67-73; watercolor lectr & demonstr in schs & art orgns, NC, currently. *Awards:* Three First Prizes & one Second Prize, Southport Art Festival, 67, 68 & 71; Best in Show, Assoc Artists NC, 71; Third Prize, Watercolor Soc NC, 76. *Bibliog:* Ola Mae Foushee (auth), North Carolina Artists, Univ NC; Anthony Swider (auth), Going to the Gallery, Winston-Salem & Forsyth Co Sch Syst, 69; Ward Nicholls (auth), Artists & Craftsmen in North Carolina, Wilks Art Guild, 74. *Mem:* Int Soc Artists; Assoc Artists Winston-Salem (vpres, 68-69); Watercolor Soc NC (co-organizer & pres, 72-73); Winston-Salem Arts Coun; Arts & Crafts Asn, Inc. *Media:* Watercolor, Chinese Ink. *Publ:* Illusr, North Carolina Parade, Univ NC, 66; contribr, Drawing & Painting the Natural Environment, Davis, 74; auth introd, Artists/USA 79-80, Found Advan Artists; auth film, Acrylics, The Contemporary Colors, Hunt Mfg Co. *Dealer:* ERL Art Agency 1004 Englewood Winston-Salem NC 27106. *Mailing Add:* 5316 Robinhood Rd Winston-Salem NC 27106

BRUCKER, EDMUND
PAINTER, EDUCATOR
b Cleveland, Ohio, Nov 20, 12. *Study:* Cleveland Inst Art, dipl(painting), 34, 34-36; Wayman Adams Summer Sch, 44. *Work:* Cleveland Mus Art; Indianapolis Mus Art, Ind; Butler Inst Am Art, Youngstown, Ohio; Evansville Mus Arts & Sci, Ind; Dartmouth Col, Hanover, NH. *Comn:* Portrait of President, Ind State Univ, 75; Portrait of Chancellor, Taylor Univ, Ind, 80; Portraits of Mr & Mrs Anton Hulman, 500 Indianapolis Motor Speedway Hall Fame Mus, 82; Portrait of Former Coach, Depauw Univ, Ind, 82; Portrait of President, Purdue Univ, Ind, 83; and others. *Exhib:* Directions in American Painting, Carnegie Inst, Pittsburgh, Pa, 41; 145th Ann of Painting & Sculpture, Pa Acad Fine Arts, Philadelphia, 50; Metrop Mus Art, New York,

52; Cincinnati Mus Art, Ohio, 55; Herron Mus Art, Indianapolis, 63; La State Univ Int Drawing Invitational, Baton Rouge, 65; Contemp Ind Artists, Ind State Mus, Indianapolis, 75; 200 Yrs Ind Art, Indianapolis Mus Art, 76; 69th Ind Artists Show, Indianapolis Mus Art, 83. *Pos:* Portrait cover artist, Ind Bus & Indust Mag, Culver, 60-71. *Teaching:* Instr drawing, Cleveland Inst Art, 36-38; instr drawing & painting, John Herron Art Sch, Indianapolis, 38-67; prof drawing & painting, Herron Art Sch, Ind Univ, Indianapolis, 67-83, prof emer, 83- *Awards:* First Prize in Oils, Ill State Fair 12th Prof Art Exhib, 58; Millikin Award for Artistic Achievement, Art Asn Indianapolis, 63; Best Show, 58th Ann Hoosier Salon, Indianapolis, 82. *Bibliog:* Jacob Getlar Smith (auth), The drawings of Edmund Brucker, Am Artist Mag, 56; Medium of the ancients, Indianapolis Star Mag, 59. *Mem:* Ind Artists Club (first vpres, 70); Hoosier Salon Patrons Asn. *Media:* Oil. *Mailing Add:* 545 King Dr Indianapolis IN 46260

BRUDER, HAROLD JACOB
PAINTER, EDUCATOR
b Bronx, NY, Aug 31, 30. *Study:* Cooper Union, cert, 51; New Sch Social Res; Pratt Graphic Art Ctr. *Work:* NJ State Mus, Trenton; Sheldon Mem Gallery, Lincoln, Nebr; Hirshhorn Mus, Washington, DC; Univ NMex Mus. *Exhib:* Corcoran Gallery Biennale, Washington, DC, 63; Modern Realism & Surrealism, Am Fedn Arts Traveling Show, 64, The Realist Revival, 72-73; 22 Realists, Whitney Mus Am Art, New York, 70; Aspects of the Figure, Cleveland Mus Art, 74; Am Family Portraits, Philadelphia Mus Art, 76; and many others. *Pos:* Artist-in-residence, Aspen Sch Contemp Art, summer 67. *Teaching:* Assoc prof art, Kansas City Art Inst, 63-65; vis lectr, Pratt Inst, 65-66; prof art, Queens Col, 65-, chmn art dept, 82- *Awards:* Purchase Prize, Am Acad Arts Letters, 78; PSC-BHE Fac Res Award, 76 & 79. *Bibliog:* Ralph Pomeroy (auth), Harold Bruder and immediate family, Art & Artists, 10/68; Alan Gussow (interviewer), A sense of place, Saturday Rev Press, 72; Ralph Pomeroy (auth), Harold Bruder's Metaphors, Arts, 10/82. *Mem:* Col Art Asn. *Media:* Oil. *Publ:* Auth, Notes from the Prado, Art J, fall 72. *Dealer:* Armstrong Gallery New York NY. *Mailing Add:* 175 Madison Ave New York NY 10016

BRULC, DENNIS (MEL VAPOUR)
PRINTMAKER, PAINTER
b Milwaukee, Wis, Aug 30, 46. *Study:* Univ Wis, BFA, 69; Arts Tech Inst, MFA, 72. *Work:* Winston Collection, Detroit, Mich; Univ Wis, Milwaukee Art Ctr, Milwaukee; Univ Wis, Madison; Miller Brewing Co; and others. *Comn:* Pneumatic Matrice (with Richard Tupper & Orrel Thompson), Akron Art Inst, 69; Pneumatic Matrice II (with John Loyd Taylor), Milwaukee Art Ctr, 70; and others. *Exhib:* Printmakers Midwest, Walker Art Ctr, Minneapolis, 73; Nat Print Invitational, Calif State Univ, 74; New Paper Icons, Monterey Conf Gallery, Monterey Mus Art, Calif, 81; one-man show, Don't Take Art From Strangers, Electro Arts Gallery, San Francisco, Calif, 81; Wearable Art Collection, Ft Mason Ctr, San Francisco, 81; and others. *Awards:* 37th Madison Salon Art First Prize, Univ Wis-Madison, 71; Albrecht Durer Print & Drawing Show First Prize, Goethe House, 72. *Bibliog:* C Kohlmann (auth), Directions, Midwest Art, 3/75; Lisa deGarrido (auth), Images of the 80's, Calif Weekly, 81; Posners vs the artist Dennis Brulc, Artcar Mag, 81; and others. *Mem:* Arts Technol Found; Negative Movement (dir, 66-69); Artsupports, Inc (pres, 75); Artoffensive Artsquad; Artcar Motor Klub. *Publ:* Contribr, Fashions of Moving Times, 67; coauth, Pneumatic matrice (color movie), Milwaukee Art Ctr, 70; contribr, Expose on artdealer fraud, Artcar Mag, 81; and others. *Mailing Add:* 1442A Walnut St Suite 281 152 W Wisconsin Ave Berkeley CA 94709

BRULC, LILLIAN G
PAINTER, SCULPTOR
b Joliet, Ill. *Study:* Art Inst Chicago, with Louis Ritman, Robert Lifvendahl & Egon Weiner, MFA(George D Brown Foreign Travel Fel), 64; Univ Chicago, with Max Kahn & Joshua Taylor, MFA, 64; also with Franz Gorse, Austria & sculptor Mustafa Naguib. *Work:* Major works in permanent architectural environments, smaller works in private collections. *Comn:* Sculptures (assisted by Che Torres & Ruben Arboleda), Chapel & Garden, San Miguelito, 68-69; murals, Archdiocesan Latin Am Comt, Chicago, 71; life-size bronze, St Victor Church, Calumet City, Ill, 79; life-size bronze, mural, environ design, SVD Theologate, Chicago, 79-80; bronze relief, Iron Range Interpretative Ctr, Chisholm, Minn, 83. *Exhib:* Prints, Drawings & Watercolors 2nd Biennial by Ill Artists, Art Inst Chicago, 64; one-man show, Drawings & Lithographs, Casa de Escultura, Panama City, 69; Murals for People (slide of Chicago works), Mus Contemp Art, Chicago, 71. *Pos:* Artist in residence, Chicago Archdiocese Panama Mission, San Miguelito, 65-70, art adv & part-time resident, 73-79; artist in residence, Archdiocesan Latin Am Comt, Chicago, 71-72 & SVD Theologate, Chicago, 79-80. *Teaching:* Asst instr lithography, Art Inst Chicago, 61-64; lectr theol & art, Divine Word Sem, Techny, Ill, 66-68; instr design, mat, portrait & drawing, Chicago Acad Fine Arts, 72-78. *Bibliog:* Charlando (TV presentation), Univ Chicago WGN-9, 68; Jorge Amado (auth), Perfiles, Cuem en Marcha, Panama City, 70; Edward Gobeyz (auth), Lillian Brulc, Painter, Sculptor, Printmaker, Success Stories, SRCA, 79. *Mem:* Alumni Art Inst Chicago. *Media:* Acrylic, Oils; Bronze. *Publ:* Illusr & auth, Make me a people, Bible Today Mag, 74; illusr, Thirsting For the Lord, Alba House, 76; auth, Visit with Franz Gorse in Carinthia, Austria, SRCA Bull, 78; illusr, Dream Visions, SRCA Publ; illusr, Old Testament Message (23 vols), Michael Glazier Inc. *Mailing Add:* 909 Summit St Joliet IL 60435

BRUMBAUGH, THOMAS BRENDLE
HISTORIAN, WRITER
b Chambersburg, Pa, May 23, 21. *Study:* Indiana Univ Pa, BS; State Univ Iowa, MA; Ohio State Univ, PhD; Harvard Univ, East Asian Studies Fel, 59. *Teaching:* Instr, Ohio State Univ, 53-54; from asst prof to assoc prof, Emory Univ, 55-63; from assoc prof to prof, Vanderbilt Univ, 64- *Awards:* Fulbright Fel, India, 60. *Mem:* Archaeol Inst Am. *Res:* Nineteenth century American painting, sculpture and architecture; J A D Ingres. *Publ:* Ed, Middle Tenn Archit, 74; auth, articles on art and artists in Art News, Art Quart, Art J, Gazette Beaux-Arts & others. *Mailing Add:* Box 1648 Station B Nashville TN 37235

BRUMER, MIRIAM
PAINTER, EDUCATOR
b New York, NY, Oct 7, 39. *Study:* Univ of Miami, BA(art & eng); Boston Univ, MFA(painting). *Work:* Chase Manhattan Bank, New York; Citibank, New York; Boston Univ, Mass; and many pvt collections. *Comn:* Painting for office, New York Bank Savings, 73. *Exhib:* Tweed Gallery, Plainfield, NJ, 82; Tossan-Tossan Gallery, New York, 82, Three Artists, Hankook Gallery, 82 & 83, Eight, ESTA Robinson Gallery, 83, New York; one-person show, Hankook Gallery, New York, 82; and others. *Pos:* Writer & ed, Feminist Art J, New York, 72-74. *Teaching:* Asst prof studio art & art hist, NY Inst of Technol, Old Westbury, 69-75; lectr studio art & art hist, Marymount Manhattan Col, New York, 76-; instr, Hunter Col, 76-81; instr, NY Univ, 83- *Awards:* Ludwig Vogelstein Found Grant, 76-77; Comt Visual Arts Grants, 79 & 80. *Bibliog:* Kay Kenny (auth), Views by Women Artists, 82; Michele Kidwell (auth), Miriam Brumer, Arts Mag, (in prep); Diana Morris (auth), Eight, Women Artist Show, 83. *Media:* Acrylic; Pencil. *Dealer:* Hankook Gallery 50 W 57th St New York NY 10019. *Mailing Add:* 250 W 94th St New York NY 10025

BRUMER, SHULAMITH
SCULPTOR, INSTRUCTOR
b Russia, July 5, 24; US citizen. *Study:* Art Students League, with William Zorach; Columbia Univ, with Oronzio Malderelli. *Exhib:* One-man shows, Sculpture Ctr, New York, 65, 68, 73 & 79 & Union Am Hebrew Congregations, 81; Philbrook Mus, Tulsa, Okla; Nat Acad Design, New York; Riverside Mus, New York; Va Mus Fine Arts; Bergen Mus, NJ. *Teaching:* Instr stone & wood carving, Sculpture Ctr Art Sch, 71-80. *Awards:* Knickerbocker Prizes, 57, 76 & 80; Audubon Artists Awards, 58 & 62. *Mem:* Sculpture Ctr (coun, 71-); Nat Asn Women Artists; Salmagundi Club; Allied Artists; Knickerbocker Artists. *Media:* Stone. *Dealer:* Sculpture Ctr 167 E 69th St New York NY 10021. *Mailing Add:* 473 Franklin D Roosevelt Dr New York NY 10002

BRUMFIELD, JOHN RICHARD
PHOTOGRAPHER, WRITER
b Los Angeles, Calif, Apr 1, 34. *Study:* Los Angeles State Col, BA, 60, MA, 61; Univ Calif, Berkeley, MA, 70; Calif Inst Arts, MFA, 72. *Work:* Mus Mod Art, New York; Los Angeles Co Mus Art, Los Angeles; San Francisco Mus Mod Art; Santa Barbara Mus Art, Univ Calif Los Angeles; Minneapolis Inst Art. *Exhib:* One-man shows, de Saisset Mus, Santa Clara, Calif, 78, Washington Proj Arts, DC, 78 & Camerawork Gallery, San Francisco, 79; Attitudes of the 1970's, Santa Barbara Mus, Calif, 79; Southern Calif Invitational Retrospective, Univ Southern Calif, 79; Albright-Knox Mus, Buffalo, 81; G Ray Hawkins Gallery, Los Angeles, 81; and others. *Pos:* Contribr photog, J Los Angeles Inst Contemp Art, 80-; consult photog, San Joaquin Valley Hist Proj, Calif State Col, Bakersfield, 80-; guest ed, photog issue, The Dumb Ox, 80-; vis artist, Art Inst Chicago, 81. *Teaching:* Assoc dean sch art & design, chmn photog prog & instr art, Calif Inst Arts, 70-; instr, Art Ctr Col Design, Pasadena, Calif, 79-80; instr, Visual Studies Workshop, Rochester, NY, summer 80. *Awards:* Nat Endowment Arts Photog Grant, 80. *Bibliog:* Hal Fischer (auth), Portraits in Sequence, Art Week, 79; Jim Hugunin (auth), Hot Shots, Afterimage, 79; Michael Starenko (auth), Photography and Language, New Art Examiner, 79. *Mem:* Col Art Asn. *Media:* Photography. *Publ:* Auth, Beneath the plot it thickens, In: Lew Thomas, ed, Structuralism and Photography, 78; auth, Count Dracula in the olive grove, J Los Angeles Inst Contemp Art, 80; auth, (et ego in Arcadia) Hortense Always was High Strung, Obscura, 81; auth, The Americans and the Americans, Afterimage, 80; auth, Photography, world order and other fictions, The New Art Examiner, 80. *Mailing Add:* Star Rte Cuddy Valley Frazier Park CA 93225

BRUN, THOMAS
SCULPTOR, INSTRUCTOR
b London, Eng, Nov 1, 11; US citizen. *Study:* Soc Arts & Crafts, Detroit, with John Foster, Sarkis Sarkisian, Guy Palozolla, Jay Bursma & Lilly Saarimen. *Work:* Detroit Inst Arts; Edison Elec Co; also several pub schs in Detroit. *Comn:* Lansing Birdman, Forbes Cohen, Lansing, Mich, 70; Bronze Hippo & Bird Mobile (four wood figures), Kalamazoo, Mich, 71; Bronze Hippo & Bird in Flight, Jackson, Mich, 72. *Exhib:* Detroit Inst Arts, 50-70; regional exhibs, Ill, Mich, Minn & Wis, 53-57; Pa Acad Fine Arts, 64. *Teaching:* Instr clay modeling, Detroit Inst Arts, 60-65; instr clay modeling, Birmingham Art Asn, 65-67; instr wax modeling, Detroit Jewish Community Ctr, 67- *Awards:* Purchase Prize, Detroit Inst Arts, 59, Lawrence Fleischman Award, 53. *Bibliog:* Work reviewed by Broner, Detroit Times, M Driver, Detroit Free Press & H Shiff, Detroit News, 49-72. *Mailing Add:* 4811 Orion Rd Rochester MI 48063

BRUNDAGE, SUSAN LOUNSBURY
DEALER
b Orange, NJ, June 18, 49. *Study:* Smith Col, BA, 71. *Work:* Paine Webber Inc, New York. *Pos:* Treas, White Columns, New York, 78-; dir, Leo Castelli Gallery, New York, currently. *Specialty:* Contemporary American art. *Mailing Add:* 448 W 23 St New York NY 10011

BRUNEAU, KITTIE
PAINTER, PRINTMAKER
b Montreal, Que, Oct 12, 29. *Study:* Ecole Beaux Arts Montreal, EBA. *Work:* Mus d'Art Contemporain, Montreal; Mus Que; Univ Montreal Libr; Univ Que Libr, Montreal; Sir George William Univ. *Exhib:* Peintures Dessins, Mus d'Art Contemporain, Montreal, 66; Vancouver Print Int, 67; l'Expo Centenaire l'Ont, Toronto, 67; 2nd Biennale Gravure Cracovie, Pologne, 68; Foire Int Bale, Suisse, 72; and many other group & one-man shows. *Bibliog:* Guy Viau (auth), Kittie Bruneau-peintre et sculpteur, Cite Libre, Montreal, 62; J de Roussan (auth), Kittie Bruneau, Lidec, Montreal, 67. *Mem:* Conseil de la Gravure du Que; Guilde Graphique. *Media:* Acrylic, Graphics. *Mailing Add:* 911 Duluth E Montreal PQ H2L 1B7 Canada

BRUNELL, RICHARD HOWARD
EDUCATOR, DESIGNER
b Pawtucket, RI, May 26, 16. *Study:* Pratt Inst, with Tom Benrimo, dipl(design), 39; RI Sch Design, with John Howard Benson & John Frazier, BFA, 46; Black Mountain Col, with Joe Albers, 47; Brown Univ, BA, 49. *Work:* Centre Georges Pompidou, Centre de Creation Industrielle, Paris. *Comn:* Nat traveling exhib Trademarks, US Trademark Asn, DC, 56. *Exhib:* Southeastern Ann, High Mus Art, Atlanta, Ga. *Collections Arranged:* Design Process, Mus Dirs Nat Asn, RI Sch Design, 47; Profession of Art, High Mus Art, Atlanta, 56. *Pos:* Art dir, GM Basford Advert, New York, 39-42 & 50-53; dean, Atlanta Art Inst, 56-58; dean, Kansas City Art Inst & Sch Design, 58-60. *Teaching:* Prof design, Univ Ga, Atlanta, 53-55; prof art, Wash Univ, St Louis, Mo, 60-82, chmn dept design, 70-82. *Awards:* Special Commendation, Combat Illus, US Eighth Air Force, 45; Gold Medals, Art Dirs Atlanta, 57 & Art Dirs St Louis, 64. *Bibliog:* Edward Gottschall (auth), Profile/Dick Brunell, Typographic, Vol 2, No 2, 70. *Mem:* Int Cong Graphic Design Asns. *Mailing Add:* 1120 Weidman Rd Manchester MO 63011

BRUNER, LOUISE KATHERINE (MRS PAUL ORR)
CRITIC, WRITER
b Cleveland, Ohio, June 13, 10. *Study:* Denison Univ, BA; Bowling Green State Univ, MA. *Pos:* Art critic, Toledo Blade, 58-79; oral interviewer, Archives of Am Art, 73-; trustee, Univ Toledo Carlson Libr, 75- *Teaching:* Instr reviews & criticism, Univ Toledo, 72- *Awards:* Roy Neuberger Found Award, Am Fedn Arts Nat Coun Arts Criticism Workshop, 68; First Prize for Critical Writing, Ohio Newspaperwomen's Asn, 71; Alumni Citation, Denison Univ, 71. *Mem:* Toledo Artists Club; Toledo Mod Art Group; Arts Comn Greater Toledo; Presidents Coun Toledo Mus Art. *Publ:* Contribr, Arts Mag, 64-; contribr, Craft Horizons, 71; contribr, Am Artist, Art Gallery Mag & Antiques. *Mailing Add:* 560 E Sixth St Perrysburg OH 43551

BRUNI, UMBERTO
PAINTER, GRAPHIC ARTIST
b Montreal, Que, Nov 24, 14. *Study:* With Guido Mincheri, Montreal, 30-37; Ecole Beaux-Arts, Montreal, grad prof, 37. *Comn:* Bust of Brother Andre, St Joseph Shrine, Montreal, 39; religious scene at church (fresco), Montreal, 58; historical scene (oil), Rougier et Freres, Montreal, 59; Da Giovanni (mosaic mural), Montreal, 60; religious mosaic mural, Ste Elizabeth Church, Ville Emard, Que, 61. *Exhib:* Solo exhibs, Figuratif a L'Abstrait, Mus Beaux-Arts, Montreal, 61 & Giotto Art Gallery, Rome, Italy, 62; Can Artist in Paris, Maison Que, France, 62; Art Coun Can, O'Keefe Ctr, Toronto, 62. *Pos:* Cur, Univ Que, Montreal, 70-80, founder & dir, Gallery, 74-80. *Teaching:* Prof, Ecole Beaux-Arts, Montreal, 47-69; prof, Univ Que, Montreal, 70-80; retired. *Awards:* Fel to Rome & Paris, Art Coun Can, 61-62; Research Fel to Rome & Paris, Que Govt, 72. *Mem:* Royal Can Acad Arts; Acad Gentium Pro Pace, Rome; Int Inst Conserv Hist & Artistic Works. *Media:* All. *Interests:* Didactical presentation of exhibitions. *Publ:* Auth, Signatures, Marcel Broquet Ed, 81. *Mailing Add:* 1325 Blvd D'Auteuil Laval PQ H7E 3J4 Canada

BRUNKUS, RICHARD ALLEN
PRINTMAKER, CURATOR
b Cleveland, Ohio, Mar 31, 50. *Study:* Miami Univ, Oxford, Ohio, BFA(printmaking & painting) 72 & MFA(printmaking), 74. *Work:* Minot State Col, NDak; Univ Mich Mus, Ann Arbor. *Exhib:* Cincinnati Art Mus Print Invitational, Ohio, 74; 15th Nat Print Exhib, Bradley Univ Art Mus, 75; 17th Ann Nat Print & Drawing Exhib, Oklahoma City, Okla, 75; 3rd US Int Graphics Ann, Hollis, NH, 75; Colorprint US, Tex Tech Univ Art Mus, 76; 11th Dulin Nat Print and Drawing Competition, Knoxville, Tenn, 77; 4th Nat Hawaii Print Exhib, Honolulu Acad of Arts, 78; and others. *Collections Arranged:* Japanese Book Illustrations from the 18th and 19th centuries, 76; An American Image 1900-1950, 76; Architectural Prints of the 17th, 18th and 19th Centuries, 76; 20th Century Master French Prints, 77; Georges Rouault's Miserere Et Guerre, 77. *Pos:* Cur of print collection, Albion Col, 75-. *Teaching:* Asst prof, Albion Col, Mich, 74-83, assoc prof visual arts, 83- *Awards:* Purchase Award, Colorprint US, Tex Tech Univ, 74, 15th Nat Bradley Print Exhib, Bradley Univ, 75 & 3rd Nat Hawaii Print Exhib, Honolulu Acad Arts, 75. *Mem:* Graphics Soc, Hollis, NH. *Media:* Engraving, Color Intaglio. *Collection:* Early 18th and 19th century Japanese woodblock prints of courtesans; prints by Giovanni Battista Piranesi, 18th century printmaker. *Dealer:* Miriam Perlman Gallery Lakepoint Tower Chicago IL. *Mailing Add:* 28450 C-Dr N Albion MI 49224

BRUNO, PHILLIP A
DEALER, COLLECTOR
b Paris, France. *Study:* Columbia Col, BA(hist fine arts & archit); Inst Fine Arts, NY Univ. *Comn:* Restored 17th century house on Martha's Vineyard, Mass, 64. *Collections Arranged:* Ralph Rosenborg Retrospective,

Washington, DC, 52; Jose Luis Cuevas, Paris, 55; Elmer Livingston Macrae, Nashville, 63; Tschang-yeul Kim, 79 & Enrico Donati, 80, FIAC, Grand Palais, Paris; Tschang-yeul Kim/Wolfgang Kubach & Anna Marie Wilmsen, 81. *Pos:* Weyhe Gallery, New York, 50-51; co-founder & assoc dir, Grace Borgenicht Gallery, 51-55; dir, World House Gallery, New York, 56-60; dir, Am Exhibs for La Napoule Found, New York & France; dir, Staempfli Gallery, New York, 60-80, co-dir, 81-; adv bd mem, Ossabaw Found, Savannah, Ga, 78-; art consult, First Am Nat Bank, Nashville, 80-81. *Teaching:* Guest lectr, Foreign Ministry Finland, Helsinki, 78. *Mem:* Hon life mem St Paul Art Ctr; hon mem Tenn Fine Arts Ctr Cheekwood, Nashville; Dukes Co Hist Soc, Edgartown, Mass; Munic Art Soc; Nat Trust Hist Preservation. *Collection:* Mainly mid-twentieth century American watercolors and drawings, ranging from Marin to Kline, including Lachaise, Demuth, Tobey, Bravo, Lopez-Garcia, Wunderlich. Part of the collection has been exhibited at the Krannert Art Museum, Tennessee Fine Arts Center, Finch College Museum of Art and Minnestoa Museum. *Mailing Add:* 342 E 67th St New York NY 10021

BRUNO, VINCENT J
HISTORIAN, ADMINISTRATOR
b New York, NY, Feb 8, 26. *Study:* Bard Col, 46-48; Academie Julian, Paris, cert painting, 49; Kenyon Col, BA(philos art), 51; Columbia Univ, MA, 62, PhD, 69. *Teaching:* Instr art hist, Wellesley Col, 64-65; assoc prof, C W Post Col, Long Island Univ, 65-66; assoc prof, State Univ NY, Binghamton, 66-76, chairperson, 72-76; prof & chairperson dept art, Univ Tex, Arlington, 76- *Awards:* John Simon Guggenheim Mem Fel, 78-; Am Coun Learned Soc Grant-in-Aid, 80; Am Philos Soc Grant-in-Aid, 82. *Bibliog:* Martin Robertson (auth), The classical palette, Times Lit Suppl, London, 8/5/77. *Mem:* Col Art Asn Am; Archaeol Inst Am; Am Inst Nautical Archaeol. *Res:* Conducted excavations at Cosa under auspices of American Academy in Rome and State Univ of New York at Binghamton, 68-72; ancient painting techniques. *Publ:* Auth, The Parthenon, Norton Critical Studies in the History of Art, 74 & Form and Color in Greek Painting, 77, W W Norton & Co; articles in the Am J of Archaeol, Archaeol Mag; Princeton Encyclopedia of Classical Sites, Int J Nautical Archaeol, In Memoriam Otto J Brendel. *Mailing Add:* 800 Briarwood Blvd Arlington TX 76013

BRUSCA, JACK
PAINTER
b New York, NY, Nov 18, 39. *Study:* Univ NH; Sch Visual Arts, New York, with Alex Gottlieb, Alex Katz, Joe Tilson & Helen Frankenthaller. *Work:* Aldrich Mus Contemp Art, Ridgefield, Conn; Whitney Mus, New York; RI Sch Design; Albright-Knox Art Gallery, Buffalo, NY; Cleveland Mus Art, Ohio. *Exhib:* Plastic Presence, Jewish Mus, New York, 69; Flint Invitational, Mich, 70; Toledo Mus Art, Ohio, 70; Paintings & Sculptures of Today, Indianapolis Mus Art, Ind, 70; Highlights of the Season, Aldrich Mus Contemp Art, 70; Fischbach Gallery, New York, 78. *Teaching:* PUC Univ, Rio de Janeiro, Brazil. *Media:* Acrylic. *Dealer:* Bonino Gallery 48 Great Jones St New York NY 10001; Fischbach Gallery 29 W 57th St New York NY 10019. *Mailing Add:* 109 W 26th St New York NY 10001

BRUSH, GLORIA (ELIZABETH) DEFILIPPS
PHOTOGRAPHER, EDUCATOR
b Chicago, Ill, Mar 29, 47. *Study:* Sch Art Inst Chicago, BFA, 68, MFA, 72; and asst to Sonia Landy Sheridan. *Work:* Central Washington State Univ; Murray State Univ; Film in the Cities, St Paul, Minn; work in many private collections. *Exhib:* New Photographics, Sarah Spurgeon Gallery, Ellensburg, Wash, 81 & 83; solo exhib, Tweed Mus Art, Duluth, Minn, 81 & 83; Minn Mus Art, St Paul, 82; Silver Image Gallery, Seattle, Wash, 83; Project Art Ctr, Cambridge, Mass, 83; Midwest Photog Invitational II, Univ Wis, Green Bay, 83; Divergence II, G H Dalsheimer, Baltimore, 83; and many others. *Collections Arranged:* Minnesota Energy (auth, catalog), Tweed Mus Art, 80; Tweed Mus Upper Midwest Photog Exhio (with Peter Feldstein; auth, catalog), 83. *Pos:* Ed, Arrowhead Arts Quart, 77-81; arts policy adv, Charles K Blandin Found, 80-83; reviewer, New Art Examiner, 80-; bd mem ex-officio, Arrowhead Regional Arts Coun, 81-83. *Teaching:* Asst prof photog, Univ Minn, Duluth, 81- *Awards:* Minn State Arts Bd Grant, 82; Nat Endowment Arts Photogr Fel, 83; Bush Found Artist Fel, 84. *Bibliog:* Annette Jessup (auth), article, 1/81 & John Steffl (auth), article, 5/81, New Art Examiner; Ron Glowen (auth), article, Artweek, 2/5/83. *Mem:* Friends of Photog; Soc Photog Educ; Col Art Asn; Photo Coun; Minneapolis Inst Arts. *Mailing Add:* 2909 Jefferson St Duluth MN 55812

BRUSH, LEIF
SOUND SCULPTOR, INSTRUCTOR
b Bridgeport, Ill, Mar 28, 32. *Study:* Art Inst Chicago, dipl(fel), 70, MFA(fel), 72. *Work:* Mills Col Libr; Inst Recherche Coord Acoustique & Musique Libr; and others. *Exhib:* Minneapolis Inst Arts, 77 & 79; Walker Art Ctr, Minneapolis, 79 & 80; Neuberger Mus, Purchase, NY, 81; Suono/Ambiente/Musica, Milan, Italy, 82; Minneapolis Col Art & Design, 82; Hudson River Mus, New York, 82; Mail Music, Monza, Italy, 83; and others. *Pos:* Vis artist, Univ Victoria, 73, Univ Colo, 75, State Univ NY, Alfred, 76, Univ Md, Baltimore Co, 77, Wright State Univ, 78, Art Res Ctr, Kansas City, Univ NDak & ZBS Found, Fort Edward, NY, 79; res artist, Visual Studies Workshop, 84. *Teaching:* Instr audible constructs, Art Inst Chicago, 70-72; asst prof, Univ Iowa, Iowa City, 72-76; asst prof sculpture, Univ Minn, Duluth, 76-79, assoc prof, 79- *Awards:* Fels, McKnight Found, 81, Jerome Found, 82 & Nat Endowment Arts, 83; and others. *Bibliog:* Oscar Brand (auth), Voices in the Wind, Nat Pub Radio, 75; Jerome Downs & Stewart Turnquist (dir), Leif Brush: Inside the Hidden Landscape (videotape), Minneapolis Inst Arts, 78; KTCA, New Music (videotape), Minneapolis, 80.

Mem: Int Sculpture Ctr; Audio Independents. *Publ:* contribr, Fifth Assembling, New York, 75; contribr, Minnesota Energy, Tweed Mus Art, 80; contribr, New Music America, Walker Art Ctr, 80; contribr, Soundings, Neuberger Mus, 81; dir, The Terrain Instruments Soundworks (videotape), Univ Wis, Stevens Point, 83; and others. *Mailing Add:* 2909 Jefferson Ct Duluth MN 55812

BRUSSEL-SMITH, BERNARD
PRINTMAKER
b New York, NY, Mar 1, 14. *Study:* Pa Acad Fine Arts, 31-36. *Work:* Libr Cong; Brooklyn Mus; Philadelphia Mus; Carnegie Inst; J B Speed Mus; and others. *Pos:* Art dir, Geyer Publ, 39-42; head advert dept, Chance-Voight Aircraft Co, 42-44; art dir, Noyes & Sproul, 44-45; freelance wood engraver, 45- *Teaching:* Instr, Cooper Union, Brooklyn Mus, Philadelphia Mus Sch Art, Nat Acad Design & City Col New York. *Awards:* Samuel Morse Award; Cannon Award; John Taylor Arms Mem Prize, 70; and others. *Mem:* Art Dirs Club; Type Dirs Club; Nat Acad Design. *Mailing Add:* 328 Cherry St Bedford Hills NY 10507

BRUSTLEIN, DANIEL
PAINTER
b Mulhouse, France, Sept 11, 04; US citizen. *Study:* Ecole des Arts, Geneva, Switz, cert of capacity. *Work:* Centre Nat d'Art Contemp, Mus Pompidou, Paris, France; Ministere des Affaires Culturelles, Paris; Baltimore Mus. *Exhib:* Corcoran Gallery Ann, Washington, DC, 58; Nat Inst Arts & Lett, 67; Patricia Learmonth Gallery, New York, 77; Am Painters in the French Nat Collections, Centre Beaubourg, Paris, 77; A M Sachs Gallery, New York, 78 & 81; La Famille des Portraits, Mus des Arts Decoratifs with Mus du Louvre, Paris, 79-81; and others. *Awards:* Premiere Selection du Prix P L Weiller, Mus Marmottan, Paris, 71. *Bibliog:* Cover illus, Art News, 10/60; Jack Tworkov (auth), Religious art without God, Art News, 11/64. *Mailing Add:* 8 rue de General Bertrand Paris 75007 France

BRY, EDITH
ASSEMBLAGE ARTIST, COLLAGE ARTIST
b St Louis, Mo, Nov 30, 1898. *Study:* Ethical Cult Sch, 17; Art Students League, with lithographers, Charles Locke, G P Dubois, Winold Reiss, Archipenko & Abraham Rattner. *Work:* Mus City New York; NY Hist Soc; Lincoln Ctr Libr, New York; Wichita State Univ Art Mus, Kans. *Comn:* Carnegie Hall, Philadelphia; Metrop Mus Art, New York. *Exhib:* Fedn Mod Painters & Sculptors Ann; Am Soc Contemp Artists Ann; Pa Acad Fine Arts, Philadelphia; Whitney Mus Am Art, New York; Los Angeles Co Mus Art; Seattle Mus, Wash; Union Theological Sem; Butler Inst Am Art, Youngstown, Ohio. *Awards:* Nat Asn Women Artists Award; Am Soc Contemp Artists Award; Painters & Sculptors Soc NJ Award. *Bibliog:* American Archives, Smithsonian Inst, Washington, DC. *Mem:* Fedn Mod Painters & Sculptors; Am Soc Contemp Artists; Artist-Craftsmen, New York. *Media:* Oil, Fused Glass. *Mailing Add:* c/o 211 Central Park W New York NY 10024

BRYANS, JOHN ARMOND
INSTRUCTOR, PAINTER
b Marion, Ohio, July 21, 25. *Study:* Ringling Sch Art, Sarasota, Fla, 47-49; Burnsville Painting Classes, NC, 48-50; Jerry Farnsworth Studio, Sarasota, 50. *Work:* Columbus Mus, Ga; Abilene Mus & McMurray Col, Abilene, Tex; Muskingum Col, New Concord, Ohio. *Comn:* Murals, Foundry Methodist Church, DC, 72 & 78, Coral Gables Methodist Church, Fla, 83. *Exhib:* 7th, 9th, 10th & 12th Ann Area Exhib, Corcoran Gallery Art, 52, 55, 56 & 58; Md Regional, Baltimore Mus, 57; Regional Exhib, Baltimore Watercolor Club, Md, 78; 2nd Ann Southern Watercolor Soc, Columbus Mus, Ga, 78; Virginia Watercolor Soc Invitational, Hollins Col, Va, 81; Nat Soc Painters Casein & Acrylic, New York, 83; Acad Artists Nat, Springfield, Mass, 83. *Teaching:* Instr drawing & painting, Hill's Art Sch, Arlington, Va, 52-77; head dept art, McLean Arts Ctr, Va, 65-73 & 78-; co-dir, Painting in the Mountains, Burnsville, NC, 65-; instr watercolor, Md Col Art & Design, Silver Spring, 80-81. *Mem:* Southern Watercolor Soc; Potomac Valley Watercolorists; Va Watercolor Soc. *Media:* Watercolor, Acrylic. *Mailing Add:* 2264 N Vernon St Arlington VA 22207

BRYANT, EDWARD ALBERT
MUSEUM DIRECTOR, HISTORIAN
b Lenoir, NC, June 23, 28. *Study:* Univ NC, Chapel Hill, BA(art), 50, MA(art hist), 55; Univ Pisa, Fulbright Grant, 54-55; Univ Ravenna, cert(Byzantine art), 55; Brooklyn Mus Training Prog, fel, 57-58. *Work:* Munson-Williams-Proctor Inst, Utica, NY. *Exhib:* Drawings USA, St Paul Art Ctr, Minn, 64; Nat Graphic Arts & Drawing Exhib, Wichita Art Asn, 67; Drawing & Small Sculpture Ann, Ball State Univ, 67; Piedmont Graphics, Mint Mus Art, Charlotte, NC, 67; Artists of Cent NY Ann, Munson-Williams-Proctor Inst, 72, 76 & 77; and many one-man exhibs. *Collections Arranged:* Beaumont Newhall, 81, Williard Midgette, 81, Marion Faller, 82, Scott Hyde, 82, Geometric Formalism in American Art, 82, Ellen Carey, 82, Bart Parker, 82, Joan Lyons, 82, Bonnie Gordon, 82, Images from New Mexico, 82, Michael Bishop, 82, John Divola, 82, Concepts & Issues in Contemporary Art Series, 82-82, Univ Art Mus, Univ NMex; and many others. *Pos:* Gen cur, Wadsworth Atheneum, Hartford, Conn, 59-61; assoc cur, Whitney Mus Am Art, New York, 61-65; dir univ gallery, Univ Ky, 65-68; dir, Picker Gallery, Colgate Univ, 68-80; dir, Univ Art Mus, Univ NMex, 80- *Teaching:* Asst prof art hist & studio courses, Univ Ky, 65-68; assoc prof, Colgate Univ, 68-80, chairperson dept fine arts, 76-77; prof, Univ NMex, 80- *Awards:* Mus Prof Fel Grant, Nat Endowment Arts, 74. *Mem:* Gallery Asn NY; Col Art Asn. *Media:* Watercolor, Drawing Media. *Res:* 20th century artists, primarily Americans; 19th century sepulchral sculpture. *Publ:*

Coauth, Forty Under Forty, 62 & auth, Jack Tworkov, 64, Praeger; auth, Robert Broderson: 32 Drawings, Duke Univ, 64; contribr, Art in Educational Institutions in the United States, Scarecrow, 74; auth, Joseph Pennell's New York Etchings, Dover, 80; and many others. *Mailing Add:* 1400 Marron Circle NE Albuquerque NM 87112

BRYANT, LINDA GOODE
ART DEALER, GALLERY DIRECTOR
b Columbus, Ohio, July 21, 49. *Study:* Spelman Col, BA, 72; City Univ New York, MA candidate. *Pos:* Dir, Just Above Midtown Gallery, New York, 74-; dir educ, Studio Mus in Harlem, 74-75; panelist, NY State Coun on the Arts & DCA, 77- *Awards:* Grad Intern, Metrop Mus, 73, Rockefeller Fel, 73-74. *Bibliog:* Satterwhite (auth), Black Dealer/57th St, New York Post, 11/74; USA's Linda Bryant, African Woman, 76; Essence Woman, Essence Mag, 7/77. *Res:* American abstract art; theory on stylistic development in the 1970s termed contextures. *Specialty:* New and emerging artists working in contexturalist vein; utilizing materials not heretofore used as primary in art object (smoke, hair, clothes, nylon mesh). *Publ:* Co-auth, Contextures (American Abstract Art 1945-1978), Just Above Midtown, 78. *Mailing Add:* c/o LMCC Suite 808 32 Broadway New York NY 10004

BRYANT, OLEN L
SCULPTOR, EDUCATOR
b Cookeville, Tenn, May 4, 27. *Study:* Murray State Col, BS; Cranbrook Acad Art, MFA; Inst Allende, San Miguel, Mex; Cleveland Inst Art; Art Students League. *Work:* Tenn Fine Arts Ctr Collection, Nashville; Hunter Gallery, Chattanooga, Tenn; Carroll Reece Mus, Johnson City, Tenn. *Exhib:* One-man shows, Tenn Fine Arts Ctr, 68 & 82, Hunter Gallery, 69, Evansville Mus, Ind, 70, Haas Gallery Bloomsburg, Pa, 71, Morehead Univ, 71 & Vanderbuilt Gallery, Nashville, 83. *Teaching:* Instr art, Shaker Heights Schs, Ohio, 58-61; instr art, Union Univ, 62-65; prof art, Austin Peay Univ, 66- *Mem:* Nashville Artists Guild; Am Crafts Coun; World Crafts Coun. *Media:* Wood, Clay. *Mailing Add:* Dept of Art Austin Peay Univ Clarksville TN 37040

BRYANT, TAMARA THOMPSON See Thompson, Tamara

BRYCE, EILEEN ANN
PAINTER
b Tulsa, Okla, June 8, 53. *Study:* Inst European Studies, Vienna, Austria, 73; Southern Methodist Univ, BFA, 75; Univ Tulsa, MA, 78. *Work:* Chautauqua Art Mus, NY. *Exhib:* Chautauqua Nat Exhib of Am Art, Chautauqua Art Mus, NY, 81; Art Ann Two, Okla Art Ctr, Oklahoma City, 81; Tex Fine Arts Asn Nat Exhib, Laguna Gloria Mus, Austin, 82; Alexandria Mus Visual Arts, La, 82; First Ann, Provincetown Art Mus, Mass, 83; Nat Print & Drawing Exhib, Lee Hall Gallery, Clemson Univ, 83. *Awards:* Purchase Prize, Chautauqua Nat Exhib Am Art, NY, 80; Plaque of Distinction, Marietta Nat Exhib Am Art, 81; Painting Award, Alexandria Mus Vis Arts Invitational, 82. *Bibliog:* Articles, Art Voices, 9-10/81 & Tulsa Mag, 6/82; Arts Chronicle, Okla Educ TV Authority, 82. *Media:* Oils, Acrylic. *Dealer:* Leslie Levy Gallery 7141 Main St Scottsdale AZ 85251. *Mailing Add:* 1616 S Florence Pl Tulsa OK 74104

BRYCE, MARK ADAMS
PAINTER, PRINTMAKER
b San Francisco, Calif, July 4, 53. *Study:* Philadelphia Col Art, 69-71; Pa Acad Fine Arts, with Hobson Pitman, Morris Blockburn & Arthur DeCosta, 70-74. *Work:* Free Libr Philadelphia; Moore Col Art; FMC Corp. *Comn:* Portrait, comn by Marian Locks, Philadelphia, 76. *Exhib:* Earth Art, Philadelphia Civic Ctr Mus, 73; Int Competition, Philadelphia Print Club, 75; Currents, NJ State Mus, Trenton, 76; solo exhibs, Marian Locks Gallery, Philadelphia, 76 & 78 & Del Art Mus, Wilmington, 83; Philadelphia Painters, Southern Allegheny Mus Art, Pa, 82; Nat Mid-Year Show, Butler Inst Am Art, 82. *Teaching:* Instr drawing, Philadelphia Col Art, 80-82; lectr painting, Wilmington Soc Fine Arts, 83-84. *Awards:* Outstanding Painting, Earth Art, Philadelphia Civic Ctr Mus, 74; Charles Smith Endowment Prize, Woodmere Open, 76; Award Merit, Reading Art Mus, 83. *Mem:* Philadelphia Print Club. *Media:* Oil, Pencil; Lithography. *Mailing Add:* 128 W Gay St West Chester PA 19380

BRYCELEA, CLIFFORD
PAINTER, PRINTMAKER
b Shiprock, NMex, Sept 26, 53. *Study:* Ft Lewis Col, Colo, study with Mick Reber & Stan Englehart, BA(art), 75. *Work:* Los Angeles Athletic Club, Calif; Transcoe Co, Houston, Tex; Bank Durango & Jackson David Bottling Co, Durango, Colo; Albuquerque Federal Savings And Loan Asn, NMex; Tamarron Resort, Durango, Colo; and others. *Comn:* Mural, The Indian Ctr, Ft Lewis Col, Colo, 73; mural, Ft Lewis Administration, Colo, 74; mural, The Indian Ctr, Durango, Colo, 74; Dulce High Sch, 83. *Exhib:* Gallup Ceremonial, Red Rock Park, NMex, 76-81; Am Inst Contemp Art Ann, San Dimas Exhib Hall, Calif, 80-82; Navajo Show, Mus Northern Ariz, Flagstaff, 80-82; Death Valley 49'ers Show, Mus Death Valley, Calif, 81; Indian Shows, Navajo Tribal Mus, Window Rock, Ariz, 82. *Awards:* Purchase Awards, NMex Watercolor Soc II, 76 & NMex State Fair, 77; Gold Medal Winner, Am Indian & Cowboy Asn Show, 81. *Bibliog:* Carey Vicanti (auth), Clifford Brycela, Jicarilla Chiratin Newspaper, 6/81. *Mem:* Indian Arts & Crafts Asn; Am Indian & Cowboy Asn. *Media:* Acrylic, Watercolor; Stonelitho, Photoprint. *Publ:* Illusr, Am Way Mag, 77; contribr, Art Fever, Gallery West Inc, 81; contribr, Haunted Mesa, Bantam Books, 82; illusr, Pieces of White Shell, 84. *Dealer:* Tohatin Gallery 145 W Ninth St Durango CO 81301. *Mailing Add:* PO Box 122 Dulce NM 87528

BRZOZOWSKI, RICHARD JOSEPH
PAINTER
b New Britain, Conn, Sept 9, 32. *Study:* Paier Art Sch, New Haven, Conn. *Work:* Grumbacher Collection, New York; Phoenix Mutual Inst, Hartford, Conn; Springfield Mus Art, Mass. *Exhib:* Allied Artists, New York, 80; Copley Soc, Boston, Mass, 80 & 81; Nat Acad Design, 81; Am Watercolor Soc, 83; Adirondacks Nat Exhib Am Watercolors, 83; and others. *Pos:* Art dir & graphics designer, Miller and Johnson Co, Meriden, CT, currently. *Awards:* Sagendorph Award, Copley Soc, 76; Samuel J Bloomingdale Mem Award, Am Watercolor Soc, 83; Paul Mowrey Mem Award, Adirondacks Nat Exhib Am Watercolors, 83. *Mem:* Am Watercolor Soc; Conn Watercolor Soc (bd dirs, 69-70); Nat Soc Painters Casein & Acrylics; Allied Artists Am; Copley Soc Boston. *Media:* Watercolor, Acrylic. *Mailing Add:* 13 Fox Rd Plainville CT 06062

BUBA, JOY FLINSCH
SCULPTOR, ILLUSTRATOR
b Lloyd's Neck, NY, July 25, 04. *Study:* Eberle Studio, New York; Staedel Kunst Inst, Frankfurt, Ger; Art Acad, Munich, Ger; also with Theodor Kaerner & Angelo Yank. *Work:* Metrop Mus Art, New York; Florence Sabin, Statuary Hall, Capitol Bldg, Washington, DC; Nat Portrait Gallery, Washington, DC; John D Rockefeller, Jr, Rockefeller Plaza, New York; Pope Paul VI, Vatican Mus; and others. *Mem:* Fel Nat Sculpture Soc. *Publ:* Illusr, Elephants, Proboscidea Memoir; Elephants, Rabbits, Frogs & Toads, Goldfish; Written in Sand; Lyrico, the Only Horse of His Kind. *Mailing Add:* 140 Hibben St Mt Pleasant SC 29465

BUCHANAN, JOHN EDWARD, JR
MUSEUM DIRECTOR, ADMINISTRATOR
b Nashville, Tenn, July, 24, 53. *Study:* Univ Col, Oxford Univ, England, 73; Univ South, BA(fine arts, hon), 75; Vanderbilt Univ, MA(art hist), 79. *Work:* Tenn State Mus, Nashville. *Pos:* Coordr mus develop, Tenn State Mus, 78-80; mus assessment prog coordr, Am Asn Mus, Washington, DC, 80-82; exec dir, Lakeview Mus Arts & Sci, Peoria, Ill, 82- *Mem:* Am Asn Mus; Midwest Mus Conf; Art Mus Asn. *Publ:* Auth, Resources for Small Museums and Historic Sites, Tenn State Mus, rev ed 79; auth, Professional Concern Checklist, Am Asn Mus, 80; auth, The new museum assessment program, Mus News, 7-8/80; auth, An applicant's map to the museum assessment program, Hist News, 9/80. *Mailing Add:* Lakeview Mus Arts & Sci 1125 W Lake Ave Peoria IL 61614

BUCHANAN, SIDNEY ARNOLD
EDUCATOR, SCULPTOR
b Superior, Wis, Sept 12, 32. *Study:* Univ Minn, Duluth, BA, 62; NMex Highlands Univ, Las Vegas, MA, 63. *Work:* Sheldon Mem Art Gallery, Univ of Nebr, Lincoln; Joslyn Art Mus, Omaha, Nebr; Springfield Art Mus, Mo; Jacksonville Art Mus, Fla; City Art Gallery, Manchester, Eng. *Comn:* sculpture, Security Nat Bank, Omaha, Nebr, 75; Tornado (memorial), Pipal Park, Omaha, Nebr; sculpture, Med Ctr Sculpture Garden, Univ of Nebr Med Ctr, 77; sculpture, City of Omaha, Cent Park Mall, 82; sculpture, Wayne State Col, 83. *Exhib:* Midwest Biennial, 64-70 & Nebr 75, 75, Joslyn Art Mus, Omaha, Nebr; Mid-Am Exhib, William Rockhill Nelson Gallery of Art, Atkins Mus of Fine Arts, Kansas City, Mo, 65-66; Colo/Nebr Exchange Exhib, Omaha & Denver, 67; Report on the Sixties, Denver Art Mus, 69; Northwestern Biennial, SDak Mem Art Ctr, 72; one-man show, Turner Park, Nebr, 80. *Pos:* Vis sculptor, Manchester Col of Art & Design, Eng, 69-70; artist-in-residence, Southern Ill Univ, Edwardsville, 72, Bemidji State Col, Minn, 75 & Plattsburg State Univ, 78. *Teaching:* Prof sculpture, Univ of Nebr, Omaha, 64- *Awards:* Purchase Awards, Midwest Biennial, Joslyn Art Mus, Omaha, Nebr, 64-66 & Western Wash State Col, 67; Nat Endowment for the Arts Grant, 75. *Bibliog:* Dr Judith Van Wagner (auth), Metal Paintings, Leonardo Mag, Spring 77 & Award Winning Sculpture, Margaret Harold Publ, 67. *Media:* Steel, Aluminum. *Dealer:* Gallery 72 2709 Leavenworth Omaha NE 68105. *Mailing Add:* 1202 S 62nd St Omaha NE 68106

BUCHER, FRANCOIS
HISTORIAN, EDUCATOR
b Lausanne, Switz, June 11, 27; US citizen. *Study:* Univ Bern, Switz, PhD, 55; Brown Univ, Hon MA, 61. *Pos:* Mem exec comt, Acad Spoleto, 65-; mem adv comt, NJ State Coun Arts, 68-70. *Teaching:* From instr to asst prof art hist, Yale Univ, 54-60; assoc prof, Brown Univ, 60-63 & Princeton Univ, 63-70; prof, State Univ NY, Binghamton, 70-77, co-dir, Ctr Mediaeval & Early Renaissance Studies, 73-76; prof, Fla State Univ, Tallahassee, 78- *Awards:* Guggenheim Fel, 58; Am Coun Learned Soc Grant, 59; Inst Advan Studies Fel, 62-63. *Mem:* Mediaeval Acad Am; Col Art Asn Am; Soc Archit Historians; fel Int Ctr Mediaeval Art. *Res:* Mediaeval architecture. *Publ:* Auth, Josef Albers, Despite Straight Lines, Yale Univ Press, 69, rev ed MIT Press, 77; auth, The Pamplona Bibles, Yale Univ Press, 70; auth, The Dresden sketch-book of vault projection, Acts 22nd Int Cong Art Hist, 71; auth, Nature in the visual arts of the Middle Ages, Tenth Ann Conf Ctr Medieval & Early Renaissance Studies, State Univ NY Press, 78; auth, Architector, Medieval Lodge-books, Abaris Press, 79. *Mailing Add:* Dept Art Hist Fla State Univ Tallahassee FL 32306

BUCHER, GEORGE ROBERT
EDUCATOR, SCULPTOR
b Sunbury, Pa, Oct 14, 31. *Study:* Univ Pa & Pa Acad Fine Arts, BFA, 57, MFA, 59; Barnes Found, Merion, Pa, 56-58. *Work:* Sioux Falls Col. *Comn:* Ornamental cross, Freeburg Lutheran Church of Christ, 74. *Exhib:* Bruce Mus, Conn, 82; Stamford Art Soc, Conn, 82; Arts & Craft Show, West Hartford, Conn, 82; 15th Arts & Crafts Festival, Middletown, Conn, 82;

Somerstown Gallery, NY, 82; and others. *Collections Arranged:* Med Exhibs, Wistar Inst Anat Mus, Philadelphia, 55; Mayan Art, 58, Phrygian Art, 59, Philadelphia Artists, 59, Copic Art, 60 & Ruins of Rome, 61, also designed permanent NAm Art exhibs, 61, Univ Pa Mus. *Teaching:* Artist, Wistar Inst Anat, 55-56; artist & asst to mgr exhibs, Univ Pa Mus, 58-61; instr & mech drawing, Salem High Sch, NJ, 59-60; instr & artist, Univ Pa Fine Arts Sch & Mus, 60-61; assoc prof art & chmn dept, Sioux Falls Col, 61-65; assoc prof art, Susquehanna Univ, 65- *Awards:* Third Prize Sculpture, Old Saybrook 19th Art Show, 82; First Prize, Greenwich Art Soc, 82; Carle J Blenner Prize, New Haven Paint & Clay Ann, 82. *Mem:* Col Art Asn Am. *Media:* Fibers, Polyester. *Collection:* Twine fiber sculpture. *Publ:* Auth, No Island is a Man (cartoon bk), 65; cartoon illusr, Book on Economics by Daniel McGowan, Rand McNally, 76; auth, Geoffrey Beene collection, Archit Dig, 9/79. *Mailing Add:* Freeburg PA 17827

BUCHMAN, JAMES WALLACE
SCULPTOR

b Memphis, Tenn, Dec 3, 48. *Study:* Dartmouth Col, BA; Skowhegan Sch Painting & Sculpture. *Exhib:* one-man shows, Sculpture Now Inc, 75 & Max Hutchinson Gallery, 79 & 83, New York; Sculpture Outdoors, Nassau Co Mus Fine Arts, Roslyn, NY, 75; Sculpture Invitational, Zabriskie Gallery, New York, 82. *Teaching:* Marlboro Col, 80-82. *Awards:* Guggenheim fel, 77; Nat Endowment Arts, 80. *Bibliog:* Robert Hughes (auth), Working on the rock pile, Time Mag, 4/7/75; Ingeborg Hoesteret (auth), Buchman (Sculpture Now), Art Int, 6/15/75; Donald B Kuspit (auth), James Buchman at Sculpture Now, Art in Am, 7-8/75. *Dealer:* Max Hutchinson Gallery 138 Greene St New York NY 10012. *Mailing Add:* Cottekill Rd Cottekill NY 12419

BUCK, ROBERT TREAT, JR
HISTORIAN, MUSEUM DIRECTOR

b Fall River, Mass, Feb 16, 39. *Study:* Williams Col, BA; NY Univ, with Dr Walter Friedlaender, MA. *Collections Arranged:* Sam Francis: Paintings 1947-1972 (with catalog), 72; Paintings by Auguste Herbin; Here and Now: 13 Young Americans; Modernist Painting; Pollock to the Present; Master Drawings from the Art Inst Chicago & Mus Mod Art; Homage to Albers; Max Bill, 74; Bradley Walker Tomlin: A Retrospective View, 75; Richard Diebenkorn: Paintings & Drawings 1943-1976, 76-77; Antoni Tapies: 33 Years of His Work, 77; Cleve Gray: Serial Paintings, 77; Sonia Delaunay: A Retrospective (with catalog), 80; and many others. *Pos:* Lectr-researcher, Toledo Mus Art, 64-65; asst cur & instr, Wash Univ, 65-67 & dir, Gallery of Art, 68-70; asst dir, Albright-Knox Art Gallery, Buffalo, 70-73, dir, 73-83; dir, Brooklyn Mus, 83- *Teaching:* Adj assoc prof Univ Toledo, 65-66; adj assoc prof 19th & 20th century art, Wash Univ, 66-70; adj assoc prof mus training, State Univ NY Buffalo, 72-73. *Awards:* NY State Coun Arts Traveling Fel, summer 71; Nat Endowment Arts Fel for Museum Professional, summer 75. *Mem:* NY Coun Humanities; Asn Art Mus Dirs. *Res:* Nineteenth century French painting; art of the twentieth century. *Mailing Add:* 74 Wellington Ct Brooklyn NY 11230

BUCKLEY, MARY L (MRS JOSEPH M PARRIOTT)
PAINTER, EDUCATOR

b New Haven, Conn. *Study:* Yale Univ Art Sch; also with Victor Candell & Hans Hoffman. *Work:* Yale Art Mus; Heckscher Mus, Huntington, NY; Lake Erie Col, Painesville, Ohio; Pratt Inst, New York. *Comn:* Murals, Philip Johnson, Seagrams Bldg, New York, 59; Color & Design, Philip Johnson, New York World's Fair Pavillion, 64; People I (sculpture), Paragon Oil, Melville, NY; State Symbols Standards & People II (sculpture), NY State Legislature Bldg, Albany. *Exhib:* Manhattan Community Col, 70; Nassau Community Col, 71; Midtown Gallery, New York, 77; Women's Inter-art Exhib, New York, 77; Munson Gallery, New Haven, Conn, 77 & 78; and many others. *Pos:* Dir, Margaret Gate Inst, 73- *Teaching:* Prof art & design, Pratt Inst, Brooklyn, 58-; adj prof, Union Col, Antioch, Ohio, 75- *Awards:* NY Coun Arts Grant; Nat Endowment Arts Grant; Am Psychiatric Award, Ittleson Found. *Mem:* Nat Asn Women Artists; Indust Designers Soc of Am; Eastern Arts Asn; fel MacDowell Asn; fel Royal Soc Art. *Media:* Oil, Plate Aluminum. *Publ:* Auth, Color Theory Bibliography, Gale Res; auth, Color Glimpses, UR Brooklyn J, 76. *Mailing Add:* Bay Crest Huntington NY 11743

BUCKNALL, MALCOLM RODERICK
PAINTER

b Twickenham, Eng, Feb 1, 35. *Study:* Univ Viswa-Bharati, West Bengal, India, 54-55; Chelsea Art Sch, London, Intermediate Nat Dipl Design, 58; Univ Tex, Austin, BFA(hon), 61; Univ Wash, Seattle, MFA, 63. *Work:* Butler Inst of Am Art, Youngstown, Ohio; Okla Art Ctr, Oklahoma City; Univ of Va Art Mus, Charlottesville. *Exhib:* Midyear Show, Butler Inst of Am Art, Youngstown, Ohio, 65-79; Eight State Show, Okla Art Ctr, Oklahoma City, 71, 72, 74 & 77; Artists Biennial, New Orleans Mus, La, 71, 75 & 77; Delta Show, Ark Art Ctr, Little Rock, 73, 74, 79 & 80; SW Biennial, Santa Fe Mus, NMex, 74 & 76; Betty Moody Gallery, Houston, Tex, 81; and others. *Teaching:* Instr drawing & design, Univ Wash, Seattle, 61-63. *Awards:* Best in Oil, Sun Carnival, El Paso Mus, Tex, 68; Nat Jury Show, Chautauqua Inst, NY, 72; Medal, Midyear Show, Butler Inst of Am Art, 72. *Bibliog:* Lisa Tuttle (auth), Risky Artist Wins Worthwhile Gamble, Austin Statesman, 6/76; Patricia Sharpe (auth), Different Strokes, Tex Mo, 10/76; Melissa Hirsch (auth), Malcolm Bucknall: Apprehension of Mystery, Dart Mag, spring 83. *Media:* Oil, Ink. *Mailing Add:* 808 West Ave Austin TX 78701

BUCKNER, KAY LAMOREUX
PAINTER, DRAFTSMAN

b Seattle, Wash, Dec 26, 35. *Study:* Sch of Art, Univ Wash, BA(art), 58; Claremont Grad Sch, MFA(painting), 61, study with Roger Kuntz & Phil Dike. *Work:* Olympic Col, Bremerton, Wash; First Nat Bank Ore, Portland; Ga-Pac Co, Portland, Ore; Emanuel Hosp, Portland, Ore; Great Western Nat Bank, Portland, Ore. *Exhib:* Frye Art Mus, Seattle, 79; Nat Small Painting Exhib, Ctr Contemp Art, Los Angeles, 80; Oregon Mus Art, Eugene, 81; NMex Int, Clovis, 81; Nat Landscape Art Exhib, Springfield Art Mus, Ill, 82. *Teaching:* Vis instr drawing, Univ Ore, Eugene, 76-79. *Awards:* First Prize Painting, 18th Nat Greater Fall River Exhib, Mass, 76; Honored by Ore Gov Atiyeh, Salem, 81; First Prize, NMex Int Exhib, 81. *Mailing Add:* 2332 Rockwood Ave Eugene OR 97405

BUCKNER, PAUL EUGENE
SCULPTOR, EDUCATOR

b Seattle, Wash, June 16, 33. *Study:* Univ Wash Sch of Art, BA(sculpture), 59; Claremont Grad Sch, MFA(sculpture), 61, study with Albert Stewart; Fulbright grant, Slade Sch, Univ Col, London, 61-62. *Work:* Olympic Col, Bremerton, Wash; Salem Civic Ctr, Ore; Leighton Pool, Univ Ore, Eugene, Ore; First Nat Bank Ore, Portland; Multnoma Athletic Club, Portland, Ore. *Comn:* Eight 8 ft wood reliefs, Cascade Manor, Eugene, Ore, 67; Centennial Medallion, Univ Ore, Eugene, 76; risen Christ, St Cecilia's Catholic Church, Beaverton, Ore, 82; wood carvings, carved doors, Sacred Heart Gen Hospital, Eugene, Ore, 82-83; sanctuary wall, United Church Christ, Forest Grove, Ore, 83. *Exhib:* Northwest Artists, Seattle Art Mus, Wash, 64; one-man show, Ore Mus Art, Eugene, 64; Sculpture 67, Seattle Art Mus, Wash, 67; Mainstreams Int, Marietta Col, Ohio, 71, 76 & 77; Sculptors of Ore, Ore Mus Art, Eugene, 74; Works in Wood by Northwest Artists, Portland Art Mus, Ore, 76; Mountain High III, Timberline Lodge, Ore, 81; Sculpture on the Green, Univ Portland, 82. *Teaching:* Prof sculpture, Univ Ore, Eugene, 62- *Awards:* Nat Sculpture Rev Prize, Nat Sculpture Soc, 77; Award of Distinction, Mainstreams 77, Marietta Col, Ohio, 77. *Bibliog:* Works in wood by Northwest artists, Portland Art Mus, 76; Mary Balcomb (auth), Paul Buckner: Sculptor, Am Artist, 6/80. *Mailing Add:* 2332 Rockwood Ave Eugene OR 97405

BUCZAK, BRIAN ELLIOT
PAINTER, SCULPTOR

b Detroit, Mich, Aug 25, 54. *Study:* Wayne State Univ; Ctr Creative Studies, Col Art & Design, BFA. *Work:* Kansas City Art Inst, Mo; Boymans-Van-Beuningen Mus, Rotterdam; Stedelijk Mus, Amsterdam; Galleria D'Arte Mod, Bologna, Italy; Sonja Henie-Neils Onstad Art Ctr, Oslo, Norway. *Comn:* Image Bank 1984 Mural (with Flaky Roseships), Image Bank, Vancouver, 73; portrait in landscape, comn by Carl Heiden, Elkson, Mich, 74; 26 assemblages (with Geoffrey Hendricks), comn by Francesco Conz, Asolo, Italy, 77; collaborative performance (with Geoffrey Hendricks), Cavriago Sound & Performance Festival, Italy, 77. *Exhib:* 2 performances, Feigenson-Rosenstein Gallery, Detroit, 78 & 79; Sound at PSI, New York, 79; 9th St Survival Show, New York, 81; Gowanus Monumental Show, Brooklyn, NY, 81; Wall Paper in Burnt-Out Building, Fashion Moda, Bronx, NY, 81; and many others. *Awards:* State Fair Mural Award, Mich State Fair, 71; Metro Show Award, Newark, 83. *Media:* Mixed Media. *Publ:* Auth, Flax, 77 & coauth, Saved, 78, Money for Food Press; contribr, Detroit Artists Mo, 78-79; auth, Unmuzzled Ox, 79; auth, Benzene, 83. *Dealer:* Barbara Braathen Gallery 76 Duane St New York NY 10007. *Mailing Add:* 486 Greenwich St New York NY 10013

BUDNY, VIRGINIA
SCULPTOR, WRITER

b Maui, Hawaii, April 15, 44. *Study:* Vassar Col, with Concetta Scaravaglione, AB, 65; Columbia Univ, with Peter Agostini, 65-66; Univ NC, Greensboro, with Peter Agostini, MFA, 70. *Work:* Smithsonian Inst; Vassar Col Art Gallery. *Exhib:* North Carolina Sculpture 79, Weatherspoon Gallery, Univ NC, Greensboro, 79; American Porcelain Traveling Exhib, Renwick Gallery, 80-83; Illusion, Southeast Ctr Contemp Art, Winston-Salem, NC, 83; Contemporary Trompe l'Oeil Painting and Sculpture, Boise Gallery Art & traveling, 83-85. *Teaching:* Asst prof sculpture, Univ NC, Greensboro, 73-80. *Awards:* Nat Endowment Humanities Summer Sem Col Teachers, 79; Spec Award, North Carolina Sculpture 79, Weatherspoon Gallery, Univ NC, Greensboro, 79; Yaddo Found Fel, 81. *Bibliog:* William Zimmer (auth), article, Arts Mag, 1/77; Jane D Scholl (auth), Witty and pretty ... American porcelain, Smithsonian Mag, 2/81; Marlene Jack (auth), Emerging talent southeast, NCECA J, 83. *Mem:* Col Art Asn Am. *Res:* Leonardo da Vinci's creative process studied through his composition sketches. *Publ:* Auth, The poses of the child in the composition sketches by Leonardo da Vinci for The Madonna and Child With A Cat ..., Weatherspoon Gallery Asn Bulletin, 80; auth, the sequence of Leonardo's sketches for The Virgin and Child with Saint Anne and Saint John the Baptist, Art Bulletin, 83. *Mailing Add:* 224 S Mendenhall St Greensboro NC 27403

BUECHNER, THOMAS SCHARMAN
MUSEUM DIRECTOR, PAINTER

b New York, NY, Sept 25, 26. *Study:* Princeton Univ, 44-45; Art Students League, 46-47; Ecole Beaux-Arts, Fontainebleau & Paris, France, 47-48. *Comn:* portrait of Paul Sheaffer, Brooklyn Hosp, 65; portrait of David Atwater, Grace Episcopal Church, 70; portrait of Joseph Hill, State Univ NY Downstate Med Ctr, 72; portrait of Alfred Gelhorn, Univ Pa; portrait of Robert Blum, Brooklyn Mus. *Exhib:* Ithaca Art Gallery, NY; Elmira Arnot Art Gallery, NY; Nat Acad Design; Colo Historical Soc; Denver Rotary Clubs Artists Am Exhib, Colo. *Collections Arranged:* Vincent Van Gogh,

Metrop Mus Art, 49; Glass 1959, Corning Mus Glass, 59; Levine-Shikler (cataloged), Brooklyn Mus, 71. *Pos:* Dir, Corning Mus Glass, 50-60, 75-; dir, Brooklyn Mus, 60-71; pres, Corning Glassworks Found, 71; pres, Steuben Glass, 72; mem bd, Parsons Sch of Design, New York, Lawrenceville Sch, NJ, Shelburne Mus, Inc, Vt & Boston Univ; illusr, Book World & Dubbings Electronics; mem adv bd, Nat Collection Fine Arts, 72. *Teaching:* Head dept art, Corning Community Col, 58-60; head painting & drawing, Heights Casino, Brooklyn, 65-68; prof drawing arts & social change, Salzburg Sem Am Studies, 71. *Awards:* Brooklyn Man of Year, Brooklyn Col, 63; Forsythia Award, Brooklyn Botanic Garden, 71; Gari Melcher's Gold Medal, Artist's Fellowship, 71. *Mem:* Louis Comfort Tiffany Found (trustee, 71); fel Royal Soc. *Res:* American illustration, emphasis on cover artists; glass history with emphasis on art glass. *Publ:* Auth, Glass Vessels in Dutch Painting in the 17th Century, 52; auth, Life and Work of Frederick Carder, 52; auth, A Guide to the Corning Museum of Glass, 55; contribr, A Guide to the Brooklyn Museum, 67; auth, Norman Rockwell: Artist and Illustrator. *Mailing Add:* Corning Glass Works Corning NY 14830

BUECKER, ROBERT
GALLERY DIRECTOR, PAINTER
b Pittsburgh, Pa, 1935. *Study:* Pa State; Carnegie Tech. *Exhib:* Solo exhibs, Richard Feigen Gallery, New York, 66 & 69 & Zolla/Lieberman Gallery, Chicago, 77; Other Ideas, Detroit Inst Arts, Mich, 69; Six Greek Crosses, 77 & Religious Work Retrospective, 79, Cathedral St John the Divine Mus Religious Art; and others. *Pos:* Owner, Buecker & Harpsichords, New York, 70- *Bibliog:* Suzy Gablic (auth), article, Art News, 1/64; Michael Andre (auth), article, Village Voice, 8/11/75; Tom Johnson (auth), article, Village Voice, 3/25/81. *Res:* Contemporary New York art history. *Specialty:* Contemporary American art. *Mailing Add:* Buecker & Harpsichords 465 W Broadway New York NY 10012

BUENO, JOSE (JOE GOODE)
SCULPTOR, PAINTER
b Oklahoma City, Okla, Mar 23, 37. *Study:* Chouinard Art Inst. *Work:* Mus Mod Art, New York; Pasadena Art Mus, Calif; Los Angeles Co Mus Art; Victoria & Albert Mus, London; Ft Worth Art Mus, Tex. *Exhib:* Solo exhibs, Nicholas Wilder Gallery, 66-; Contemp Arts Mus, Houston, 73; St Mary's Col, Los Angeles, 77, Tex Gallery, Houston, 79 & Charles Cowles Gallery, New York, 80; American Pop Art, Whitney Mus Am Art, 74; Chicago Art Inst, 74; California Painting and Sculpture: The Modern Era, San Francisco Mus Art, 76; Black and White Art Colors, Scripps Col, 78; American Painting in the Seventies, Albright-Knox Art Gallery, 78; Aspects of Abstract, Crocker Mus, 78; and others. *Awards:* Cassandra Found Grant; Am Fedn Arts Award. *Media:* Wood; Oil. *Dealer:* Charles Cowles Gallery New York NY. *Mailing Add:* 1153 E 71st Los Angeles CA 90001

BUERGER, JANET E
HISTORIAN, CURATOR
b Boston, Mass, May 30, 46. *Study:* Skidmore Col, BA, 68; Columbia Univ, MA, 69, PhD(art hist & archaeol), 78. *Collections Arranged:* Site Museum (Small Finds), Excavations under the Cathedral, Florence, Italy, 75-; French Daquerreotypes, 77, George Davison, 78, The Kodak Number 1: More than Just a Snapshot, 79, Pierre Petit, 80 & George Barnard, 81, George Eastman House, Int Mus Photog; Nineteenth Century Photography, 79- *Pos:* Curatorial intern, George Eastman House, Int Mus Photog, 75-76, res cur & exec asst to dir, 76-79, actg cur 19th century photog, 79-81, from asst cur to assoc cur photog collections, 81-; mem ed bd, Image, 78. *Teaching:* Adj asst prof hist photog, Univ Rochester, 79- *Awards:* Comt to Rescue Italy Art Fel, Florence, Italy, 72-73; Instituto Roberto Longhi Fel, 73-75. *Mem:* Col Art Asn; Am Asn Mus; Nat Trust Hist Preserv. *Res:* Nineteenth century French photography; late Degas; early photo-secessions and medieval archaeology. *Publ:* Auth, Ceramica smaltata tardo medievale della costa adriatica, Atti, Albisola, Convegno Int della Ceramica, 74; auth, Reperti dagli scavi di Santa Reparata, Archeol Medievale, 75; auth, Minor White 1908-76, 76 & Degas, solarized and negative photographs, 78, Image; auth, The medieval glazed pottery, Diocletian's Palace Joint Am-Yugoslav Excavations (part three), 79. *Mailing Add:* 1063 East Ave Rochester NY 14607

BUGBEE-JACKSON, JOAN (MRS JOHN M JACKSON)
SCULPTOR, EDUCATOR
b Oakland, Calif, Dec 17, 41. *Study:* Univ Mont; San Jose State Col, BA & MA; Art Students League, with R B Hale; Sch of Fine Arts, with Nat Acad Design; also with M Wildenhain, EvAngelos Frudakis, Joseph Kiselewski, Granville Carter & Adolph Block. *Work:* Cordova Pub Libr, Alaska. *Comn:* Bob Korn Commemorative Plaque, City of Cordova, Alaska, 74; wall murals, Anchorage Pioneer's Home, Alaska, 78; Bronze Medal, Alaskan Wildlife, 80; two sculpture murals, Alaska State Capitol Bldg, Juneau, Alaska, 81; Gruening & Bartlett busts, Alaska State Capitol Bldg, Juneau, 82. *Exhib:* One-woman show, Springvale, Maine, 70; Nat Sculpture Soc Ann, New York, 70-73; Allied Artists Am Ann, New York, 70-72; Nat Acad Design Ann, New York, 71 & 74; Joan Bugbee, Retrospective, New York, 72. *Teaching:* Instr design, De Anza Col, Cupertino, Calif, 67-68; instr pottery & glaze chem, Greenwich House Pottery, New York, 69-71; instr pottery, Univ Alaska, Cordova, 72-80 & Prince William Sound Community Col, Cordova, 80- *Awards:* Helen Foster Barnet Prize, Nat Acad Design, 71; Daniel Chester French Prize, Nat Sculpture Soc, 72 & C Percival Dietsch Prize, 73. *Bibliog:* Jim Seay (auth), A move for inspiration, Anchorage Daily News, 8/13/72; New Issues, Alaskan Medal Series, The Numismatist, 1/81. *Mem:* Fel Nat Sculpture Soc; Artists' Equity Asn. *Media:* Fired Stoneware Clay, Cast Bronze. *Publ:* Contribr, Nat Sculpture Review, winter 70-71, spring 71 & winter 81-82. *Dealer:* Jean Shadrach c/o The Artique Ltd Gallery 314 G St Anchorage AK 99501. *Mailing Add:* Box 374 Cordova AK 99574

BUITRON, DIANA M
CURATOR, HISTORIAN
b Quito, Ecuador, Apr 17, 46; US citizen. *Study:* Smith Col, BA, 69; Inst of Fine Arts, New York Univ, MA, 72 & PhD, 76; Am Sch of Classical Studies, Athens, Greece, 72-73. *Pos:* Curatorial asst, Fogg Art Mus, Harvard Univ, 70-72; Andrew Mellon & Chester Dale Fel, Metrop Mus of Art, New York, 73-75; Cur Greek & Roman art, Walters Art Gallery, Baltimore, Md, 76-, co-dir, Walters-Mo Excavations at Sanctuary of Apollo Hylates, Kourion, Cyprus, 78-80, 81. *Teaching:* Asst prof classics, John Hopkins Univ, 82-83. *Mem:* Archaeol Inst Am; Am Asn Univ Women; German Archaeol Inst. *Res:* Greek art, specializing in Greek vase painting. *Publ:* Auth, Attic vase painting in New England collections, 72 & A Greek bronze mirror, 73, Fogg Art Mus; auth, A bronze statuette of Hermes in the Metropolitan Museum, 77 & ed, Essays in honor of Dorothy Kent Hill, 77, J Walters Art Gallery; auth, ann reports, Report of the Department of Antiquities, Cyprus, 79, 81-83. *Mailing Add:* c/o The Walters Art Gallery 600 N Charles St Baltimore MD 21201

BUJESE, ARLENE
GALLERY DIRECTOR, PRINTMAKER
b Hillsdale, NJ, May 8, 38. *Study:* Corcoran Sch Art, 64-70; Hood Col, Md, AB, 75, MA, 78. *Work:* Parrish Art Mus, Southampton, NY. *Exhib:* Four Graphic Artists, Parrish Art Mus, 70; Nat Exhib Prints & Drawings, Okla Art Ctr, 72; 11 Contemp Printmakers, Int Monetary Fund, Washington, DC, 74; Printmakers of the Region, Guild Hall Mus, New York, 75; solo exhib, Arts Club Washington DC, 84. *Pos:* Dir & vpres, Phoenix II Gallery, Washington, DC, 81- *Teaching:* Instr design, Hood Col, Md, 81- *Awards:* First Prize for Graphics, Ann Student Exhib, Corcoran Sch, 69; Best in Any Media, Guild Hall Ann, 80; Exhib Comt Prize, Arts Club Washington DC, 82. *Mem:* Arts Club Washington DC; Guild Hall; Smithsonian Assoc. *Media:* Etching. *Specialty:* Contemporary American artists, primarily first generation abstract expressionists and New York school. *Publ:* Ed, 25 Artists: Hans Namuth and 24 Artists, Univ Publ Am, 82. *Mailing Add:* 519 Culler Ave Frederick MD 21701

BUKI, ZOLTAN
CURATOR, ADMINISTRATOR
b Pecs, Hungary, Oct 26, 29; US citizen. *Study:* Acad de Belle Arti, Rome; Art Inst Chicago, BFA; Wayne State Univ Grad Sch; Tulane Univ Grad Sch, MFA. *Collections Arranged:* George Rickey-James Seawright (with catalog), 69-70; Richard Anuszkiewicz & George Segal, 71; Responsive Environment, 72; For the Mind & The Eye, 77. *Pos:* Dir exhibs, Ark Arts Ctr, Little Rock, 63-68; chmn art dept, Humboldt State Col, 68-69; cur fine arts, NJ State Mus, 69- *Teaching:* Instr drawing & painting, Univ Southwestern La, 61-62; instr drawing & anat, Layton Sch Art, Milwaukee, 62-63. *Publ:* Coauth, The Trenton Monument Eakins Bronzes, 73. *Mailing Add:* NJ State Museum 205 W State St Trenton NJ 08625

BULLARD, EDGAR JOHN, III
MUSEUM DIRECTOR
b Los Angeles, Calif, Sept 15, 42. *Study:* Univ Calif, Los Angeles, BA, 65, MA, 68; Nat Gallery Art, Samuel H Kress Found Fel, 67-68; Harvard Univ Inst Arts Admin, 71. *Collections Arranged:* German Expressionist Watercolors in American Collections, 69, Mary Cassatt 1844-1926, 70 & John Sloan 1871-1951 (auth, catalog), 71, Nat Gallery Art, Washington, DC; Richard Clague 1821-1873, 74 & Zenga & Nanga: Paintings by Japanese Monks & Scholars, 76, New Orleans Mus Art; The Contemp South: Photog, US Info Agency, 77; The Wild West: Paintings and Sculpture by Frederic Remington and Charles M Russell, 79, Robert Gordy: Paintings and Sculpture 1960-80, 81 & Edward Weston and Clarence John Laughlin: An Introduction to the Third World of Photography (auth, catalog), 82, New Orleans Mus Art; and others. *Pos:* Asst cur, J Paul Getty Mus, Malibu, Calif, 67; mus cur, Nat Gallery Art, 68-70, asst to dir, 70-71, cur spec projs, 71-73; dir, New Orleans Mus Art, 73-; trustee, Ga Mus Art, Univ Ga, 75-80. *Awards:* Order Rep Egypt, 79. *Mem:* Am Asn Mus; Col Art Asn Am; Nat Arts Club; Asn Art Mus Dir. *Res:* Late 19th & 20th century American and European art. *Publ:* Auth, Mary Cassatt: Oils and Pastels, Watson-Guptill, 72; auth, A Panorama of American Painting (exhib catalog), 75; auth, American paintings from the John J McDonough Collection, Antiques, 11/77; auth, Two visions of the wild west: Frederic Remington & Charles M Russell, Southwest Art, 12/79; auth, The Kinetic Sculpture of Lin Emery (exhib catalog), 82; and others. *Mailing Add:* New Orleans Mus of Art PO Box 19123 New Orleans LA 70179

BULONE, JOSEPH DOMINIC
SCULPTOR
b Cleveland, Ohio, Nov 15, 22. *Study:* Cleveland Inst Art, 41-43; Cranbrook Acad Art, with Carl Milles, 48-52. *Work:* Cleveland Mus Art; Tex Southern Univ; Detroit Inst Art; Wayne State Univ Gallery; Oakland Univ Gallery. *Comn:* St Rose of Lima (ceramic), St Rose of Lima Church, Houston, 50; Juggler Clown (bronze), J L Hudson Co, Detroit, 56; Crucifix (stained glass), St Roche Church, Caseville, Mich, 62. *Exhib:* 16th Ceramic Nat, Syracuse Mus Art, 51; May Show, Cleveland Mus Art, 51-53; Fifth Nat Religious Art Exhib, Cranbrook Art Gallery, 66; Third Biennial Mich Art & Craft Exhib, Grand Rapids Art Mus, 68; 21st Ann Ohio Ceramic & Sculpture Show, Butler Art Inst, 69; 58th Exhib Mich Artists, Detroit Inst Art, 71. *Teaching:* Asst instr figure modeling, Cranbrook Acad Art, 51-52. *Awards:* First & Third Prizes, May Show, Cleveland Mus, 51; Tiffany Found Sculpture Grant, 66. *Bibliog:* Walter Mossberg (auth), The craftsmen, Wall St J, 8/16/73; Mike Tharp (auth), It's Still a Craftsman's World, Amepnka Press & Publ Serv, 75. *Media:* Wood. *Publ:* Auth, St Rose of Lima, Ceramic Monthly, 3/19/53. *Dealer:* Little Gallery 350 Big Beaver Rd Birmingham MI 48012. *Mailing Add:* 388 Greenwood St Birmingham MI 48009

BULTMAN, FRITZ
SCULPTOR, PAINTER
b New Orleans, La, Apr 4, 19. *Study:* With Morris Graves, 31; New Bauhaus, Chicago, 37-38; Hans Hofmann Sch Fine Arts, 38-41. *Work:* Whitney Mus Am Art; Rockefeller Art Gallery, Seal Harbor, Maine; Mus Art, RI Sch Design; Riverside Mus; Univ Nebr; and others. *Exhib:* Whitney Mus Am Art, 50 & 53; Chicago Art Inst; solo exhibs, Martha Jackson Gallery, 59, 73, 74 & 76, Delgado Mus, New Orleans, 59 & 74, Okla Mus, 74, Newport Art Asn, RI, 74 & Long Point Gallery, Provincetown, 77-79; Hans Hofmann and His Students, Mus Mod Art, New York, 63; and others. *Teaching:* Lectr, univs, cols, art clubs & mus; instr painting, Sch Educ, Pratt Inst, 58-63; instr painting, Grad Art Sch, Hunter Col, 59-63; instr & artist-in-residence, Fine Arts Work Ctr, Provincetown, Mass, 68-70. *Awards:* Prize, Art Inst Chicago, 64; Fulbright Res Grant, Paris, 64-65; Guggenheim Mem Award, 75-76; and others. *Publ:* Auth, article on Hans Hofmann, Art News, 63. *Mailing Add:* 176 E 95th St New York NY 10028

BUMBECK, DAVID A
PRINTMAKER, EDUCATOR
b Framingham, Mass, May 1, 40. *Study:* RI Sch Design, BFA, 62; Syracuse Univ, with Robert Marx, MFA, 66. *Work:* New York Pub Libr; Rochester Mem Galleries, NY; Brooklyn Mus, NY; Wiggin Collection, Boston Pub Libr. *Exhib:* Boston Printmakers Nat Exhib, 67-79; Living Am Artists & the Figure, Mus Art, Pa State Univ, 74; 31st Nat Print Exhib, Brooklyn Mus, 78; Nat Print Exhib, Philadelphia Print Club, 79; Nat Exhib, Soc Am Graphic Artists, 79. *Pos:* Dir, Christian A Johnson Gallery, 73- *Teaching:* Instr painting & printmaking, Mass Col Art, Boston, 66-68; asst prof printmaking, Middlebury Col, 68- *Awards:* Purchase Award, Everson Mus, 66; David Berger Mem Award, Boston Printmakers Nat Exhib, 68; Purchase Award, Soc Am Graphic Artists Nat Exhib, NY, 79. *Mem:* Boston Printmakers (mem exec bd, 68-); Soc Am Graphic Artists. *Media:* Intaglio. *Dealer:* Ainsworth Gallery 42 Bromfield St Boston MA 02108. *Mailing Add:* Drew Lane RD 3 Middlebury VT 05753

BUMGARDNER, GEORGIA BRADY
CURATOR, HISTORIAN
b Mt Kisco, NY, Dec 8, 44. *Study:* Wellesley Col, BA(art hist), 66. *Pos:* Cur graphic arts, Am Antiqn Soc, Worcester, Mass, 69- *Awards:* Fel, First Pub Humanities Inst, Mass Found Humanities & Pub Policy, 82. *Mem:* Am Hist Print Collectors Soc; Archives Am Art; Colonial Soc Mass; New Eng Mus Asn; Art Libr Soc. *Res:* Eighteenth and nineteenth century American prints. *Publ:* Auth, American Broadsides, 1680-1800, Imprint Soc, 71; coauth, Massachusetts Broadsides of the American Revolution, Univ Mass, 76; auth, Graphic arts: seventeenth-nineteenth century, Arts Am, 79; auth, Aspects of American book illustration: technology, natural science and literature, Imprint, Vol 5, No 2, autumn 80; auth, Vignettes of the Past: American Historical Broadsides through the War of 1812, Printing Hist, Vol IV, No 7-8; and others. *Mailing Add:* Am Antiqn Soc 185 Salisbury St Worcester MA 01609

BUMGARDNER, JAMES ARLISS
PAINTER, EDUCATOR
b Winston-Salem, NC, Mar 25, 35. *Study:* Univ NC; Salem Col, Winston-Salem; Richmond Prof Inst, BFA; also with Hans Hofmann. *Work:* NC Mus Fine Arts, Raleigh; Va Mus Fine Arts; Philip Morris & Co, Richmond; Chrysler Mus, Norfolk, Va; Sidney & Frances Lewis, Richmond, Va; and others. *Exhib:* Art USA, New York, 59; Va Artist's Show, var times, 59-77; Art Across America, New York, 65; Metarealities, Wash Project Arts, 80; South Eastern Ctr Contemp Art Invitational, 81; and others. *Pos:* Guest set designer, Va Mus Theater, Waiting for Godot, 80. *Teaching:* Prof drawing & painting, Va Commonwealth Univ, 58- *Awards:* Five Special Awards Painting, NC Mus Art, 57-62; four Cert of Distinction, Va Mus Fine Art, 59-63 & 77; Purchase Prize, Southeastern Ctr for Contemp Arts, 77; and others. *Bibliog:* A painter of deja-vu experiences, Va Visual Arts Publ; Metarealities rev, New Art Examiner, Vol 7, Number 7, 4/80; Beyond refinement, Images & Issues, Vol 3, winter 80-81; and others. *Media:* Oil. *Dealer:* Gallery K 2032 P St NW Washington DC 20023. *Mailing Add:* 406 N Allen Ave Richmond VA 23220

BUNDY, STEPHEN ALLEN
SCULPTOR
b Denver, Colo, Apr 10, 42. *Study:* Univ Colo, Boulder, BA(physics), 64, MA(physics), 67, MFA(painting & sculpture), 72. *Exhib:* Twelfth Midwest Biennial, Joslyn Art Mus, Omaha, Nebr, 72; Performance (with Hans Breder), Mus Art, Univ Iowa, Iowa City, 74; Midwest Fac Painters & Sculptors, Krannert Art Mus, Univ Ill, 76; one-man shows, Nancy Lurie Gallery, Chicago, Ill, 77, Jordan Gallery, London, Eng, 78; invitationals: O K Harris, New York, 77, Stage House II, Boulder, Colo, 82. *Pos:* Cur, Corroboree: Gallery of New Concepts, Univ Iowa, Iowa City, 76-80. *Teaching:* Asst prof sculpture & video, Univ Iowa, Iowa City, 73-79; head 4-D studies, Hornsey Col Art at Middlesex Polytechnic, London, Eng, 77-78. *Bibliog:* Art ed (auth), New Sculpture, Al-Mesa, Cairo, Egypt, 6/77. *Mem:* Col Art Asn Am. *Media:* Wood, metal. *Dealer:* Gombinski Gallery 46 Walker St New York NY 10013. *Mailing Add:* 1769 Coronado Pkwy Denver CO 80229

BUNIN, LOUIS
SCULPTOR
b Kiev, Russia, Mar 28, 08; US citizen. *Study:* Chicago Art Inst, 29; Acad Grande Chaumiere, Paris, 30-31; Art Educ Alliance, New York, 75-80. *Work:* Mid-Hudson Art Mus, Poughkeepsie, NY; Corcoran Gallery Art; Montreal Mus Fine Arts. *Exhib:* Retrospective, Younge Gallery, Chicago, 30; Wood

Carvings, ACA Gallery, New York, 66; Sculpture in Motion, Lytton Ctr Art & Sci, Los Angeles, 75; Puppet Heritage, Pratt Inst Gallery, 78 & Corcoran Gallery Art, 80; Ideal Type Casting in Sculpture, Bronx Mus, 78; Mid-Hudson Art Mus, Poughkeepsie, NY, 81; Animation Film, Montreal Mus Fine Arts, 82. *Teaching:* Artist in residence sculpture in animation film, Pratt Inst, 78-79; instr, Sch Visual Arts, 79- *Awards:* Elizabeth Erlanger Mem Award, Steel Dancer, Am Soc Contemp Art, 83. *Bibliog:* Seymour Peck (auth), article, New York Times, 53; Derek Hudson (auth), Type casting in sculpture, Constable, London, 54; Seamas Culhane (auth), Sculpture in Animation, Dell, 83. *Mem:* Am Soc Contemp Artists (mem bd dirs, 79); Artists Equity; Sculptors Alliance; Int Sculpture Ctr. *Media:* Steel, Stone. *Publ:* Auth, 3-D forms in animation film, Theater Arts Mag, 39; auth, article, Am Artist Mag, 11/81; auth, Sculpture on films, Close Up Mag, 82. *Mailing Add:* 790 Riverside Dr New York NY 10032

BUNKER, GEORGE
PAINTER, EDUCATOR
b Denver, Colo, May 27, 23. *Study:* Yale Univ, BA, 46; Art Students League, 46-47; Brooklyn Mus Art Sch, 47-49; also with Kuniyoshi, Reginald Marsh & Vytlacil, NY; and with Victor Candell, Brooklyn. *Work:* Philadelphia Mus Art; Rosenwald Collection, Nat Gallery, Washington, DC; Joseph Pennell Collection, Libr Cong; Univ NMex Art Mus; Corcoran Gallery, Washington, DC. *Comn:* Lithographs, Tamarind Inst, Albuquerque, 73; color lithograph, Print Club Philadelphia, 73. *Exhib:* Cincinnati Mus Art, 58; Philadelphia Mus Art Festivals, 59, 61 & 62; Prints of Two Worlds, Philadelphia Mus & Rome, Italy, 67; Am Color Print Soc, 73; NY Studio Sch Sculpture & Painting, 73 & 74. *Teaching:* From instr to prof painting, drawing & printmaking, Philadelphia Col Art, 55-73, chmn fine arts dept, 58-65, dean fac, 65-72; vis prof painting, Univ NMex, 73-74; prof painting & drawing & chmn dept art, Univ Houston, 74- *Awards:* Lessing J Rosenwald Award, Print Club of Philadelphia, 61; Am Color Print Soc Award, 73; Mid-Western Graphics Award, 73. *Mem:* Am Asn Univ Prof. *Media:* Oil, Lithograpy. *Publ:* Ed, Leon Karp Portfolio, 60; ed & contribr, Alexey Brodovitch & His Influence, 72; ed, Melnicoff Memorial Exhibit (catalog), 73; ed, Victor Candell Memorial Exhibit (catalog), 78. *Dealer:* Harris Gallery 110 Bissonnet Houston TX 77005. *Mailing Add:* 2028 Quenby St Houston TX 77005

BUNNELL, PETER CURTIS
EDUCATOR, CURATOR
b Poughkeepsie, NY, Oct 25, 37. *Study:* Rochester Inst Technol, BFA, 59; Ohio Univ, MFA, 61; Yale Univ, MA, 65. *Collections Arranged:* Photography as Printmaking, 68, Photography into Sculpture, 70, Clarence H White, 71, Mus Mod Art, New York; Lynton Wells: Paintings 1971-1978, 79; Harry Callahan, US Pavilion, Venice Bienale, 78; and others; Robert O Dougan Collection, 83; and others. *Pos:* Cur photog, Mus Mod Art, New York, 66-72; cur photog, Art Mus, Princeton Univ, 72-, dir, 73-78. *Teaching:* Vis lectr hist photog, Dartmouth Col, 68; vis lectr hist photog, Inst Film/TV, NY Univ, 68-70; McAlpin prof hist photog & mod art, Princeton Univ, 72-; vis lectr hist photog, Yale Univ, 73. *Awards:* Guggenheim Fel, 79. *Mem:* Soc Photog Educ (nat chmn, 72-77); Col Art Asn Am (bd dirs, 75-79); Friends of Photog (bd trustees, 74-80, pres, 80-); Am Fedn Arts (exhib comt, 78-). *Res:* History of photography with primary emphasis on the 20th century. *Publ:* Auth, Diane Arbus, 73; auth, John Pfahl, 81; auth, Paul Caponigro, 81; auth, Emmet Gowin, 83; ed, Edward Weston on Photography, 83; and others. *Mailing Add:* Dept Art & Archaeol Princeton Univ Princeton NJ 08544

BUNN-STADDEN, CECINE
PAINTER
b Springfield, Ill. *Study:* MacMurry Col, Jacksonville, Ill; Univ Colo; Univ Ill; also with Dan Umberger, George Post, Elliott O'Hara & Rex Brandt. *Work:* San Francisco Hall of Justice; Triton Mus, Santa Clara, Calif; Menlo Park Civic Ctr, Calif; Sheila Spenser Mem Fine Art Gallery, Univ Ark; Permanent Collection, Springfield Art Asn. *Comn:* Designed rug, Northern Calif Handweavers Conf, 71; designed plates for 25th Silver Anniversary, City Los Altos, Calif, 77. *Exhib:* San Jose Mus, Calif; De Young Mus, San Francisco, 69-71; Directors Choice Show, Triton Mus, 71; Cedar City Nat Invitational, 72; Catharine Lorillard Wolfe Art Club Ann, 79. *Awards:* Second Contemporary, Cal Expo, Calif State Fair, 70; Best of Show in Watercolor, Palo Alto Art Club, Palo Alto Holiday Show, Calif, 71; Best of Show in Watercolor, Sunnyvale Coun Arts, Calif, 73; and many others. *Mem:* Soc Western Artists; Palo Alto Art Club (vpres, 71); Nat League Am Pen Women; and others. *Media:* Transparent & Salt Watercolor. *Dealer:* Gallery Artique Carmel CA; Greenleaf Gallery Saratoga CA. *Mailing Add:* 381 First St No 5005 Los Altos CA 94022

BUNSHAFT, GORDON
COLLECTOR, ARCHITECT
Mr Bunshaft, b Buffalo, NY, May 9, 09. *Study:* Mass Inst Technol, BArch, 33, MArch(fel), 35; Univ Buffalo, Hon DFA, 62. *Comn:* Design of Lever House, New York; Beinecke Rare Bk & Manuscripts Libr; Yale Univ; Albright-Knox Art Gallery, Buffalo; Joseph H Hirshhorn Mus & Sculpture Garden, Washington, DC; L B Johnson Libr, Univ Tex, Austin; and many others. *Pos:* Chief designer, Skidmore, Owings & Merrill, 37-42, partner, 49-; mem, Pres Comt Fine Arts, 63-72; mem int coun & trustee, Mus Mod Art, New York, currently. *Awards:* Brunner Award, Nat Inst Arts & Lett, 55; Medal Honor, NY Chap Am Inst Architects, 61; Chancellor's Medal, Univ Buffalo, 69. *Mem:* Academician Nat Acad Design; Nat Inst Arts & Lett; Munic Art Soc New York; hon mem Buffalo Fine Arts Acad; fel Am Inst Architects. *Collection:* Contemporary art. *Mailing Add:* 200 E 66th St New York NY 10021

BUNTS, FRANK
PAINTER, EDUCATOR
b Cleveland, Ohio, Mar 2, 32. *Study:* Yale Univ; Cleveland Inst; Western Reserve, BA & MA. *Work:* Philadelphia Mus Art, Pa; Fine Arts Gallery, San Diego, Calif; Libr of Cong, Washington, DC; Corcoran Gallery Art, DC; Aldrich Mus Contemp Art, Ridgefield, Conn. *Exhib:* Nat Exhib, San Francisco Mus Art, 65; Brooks Mem Art Gallery, 67 & 73; Baltimore Mus Art, 70; Corcoran Gallery Art, 72; Painting & Sculpture Today, Indianapolis Mus Art, 76; Int Exhib, Mus Mod Art, Rijeka, Yugoslavia, 78; one-man shows, Catholic Univ Am, 78, Plum Gallery, Washington, DC, 79 & Street Exhib, Moscow, USSR, 82; and many others. *Teaching:* Cleveland Inst Art, 63-64; Ark State Univ, 65-67; Univ Md, College Park, 67-77, dir, Grad Art Studio Prog, 71-77; Art Studio, New York, 81- *Awards:* Purchase Prize, Cleveland Mus Art, 62; Exhib Award, Nat Acad Sci, 76. *Bibliog:* Robert Glauber (auth), Chicago Skyline, 10/18/72; Jo Ann Lewis (auth), article, Washington Star-News, 9/21/73 & Washington Post, 3/17/79. *Media:* Oil, Resins. *Mailing Add:* 15 W 24th St New York NY 10010

BUONAGURIO, EDGAR R
PAINTER, MURALIST
b Yonkers, NY, July 4, 46. *Study:* City Col New York, BA, 69; Teachers Col, Columbia Univ, MA, 72. *Work:* Joseph Hirshhorn Mus & Sculpture Garden, Washington, DC; Mint Mus Art; Bronx Mus Arts; Herbert F Johnson Mus Art, Cornell Univ; Continental Group, Stamford, Conn. *Comn:* Fantail (mural), The Continental Group, Stamford, Conn, 80-81; Da Capo II, The Grand Hyatt Hotel, New York, 80; Byzantine Dream, Continental Nat Bank, Ft Worth, 82; Labyrinth (mural), City Nat Bank, Baton Rouge, 83. *Exhib:* Va Mus Fine Arts, Richmond, 74; McNay Art Inst, Houston, 80; Alternative Mus, New York, 80-81; Mint Mus Art, 83; Everson Mus Art, Syracuse, 83; Bronx Mus Arts, 84. *Pos:* Critic, Arts Mag, New York, 77-80. *Teaching:* Instr painting, Hudson River Mus, Yonkers, NY, 69-74; instr art & art hist, Riverdale Country Sch, Bronx, NY, 69-79; adj prof painting, Col New Rochelle, NY, 74; adj prof painting, Westchester Community Col, 73. *Awards:* Creative Artists Pub Serv Prog Fel Painting, 81-82. *Bibliog:* Alan G Artner (auth), Paintings soar with splendor, Chicago Tribune, 80; Douglass Blau (auth), Edgar Buonagurio, Arts Mag, 80; Ellen Lubell (auth), Edgar Buonagurio at Andre Zarre, Art in Am, 83. *Media:* Acrylic, Canvas. *Dealer:* Andre Zarre Gallery 41 E 57 St New York NY 10022; Zolla-Lieberman Gallery 356 W Huron Chicago IL 60610. *Mailing Add:* 2104 East 177th St Bronx NY 10472

BUONAGURIO, TOBY LEE
SCULPTOR
b Bronx, NY, June 28, 47. *Study:* The City Col New York, BA(fine arts), 69, MA(art educ), 71. *Work:* Heckscher Mus, Huntington, New York; Everson Mus Art, Syracuse, NY; Mint Mus Art, Charlotte, NC; Alternative Mus, New York. *Comn:* Ceramic sculpture, The Footwear Council, New York, 80. *Exhib:* solo exhib, Gallery Yues Arman, New York, 82, Everson Mus Art, Syracuse, New York, 82, Bronx Mus Arts, New York, 83, Contemp Arts Ctr, New Orleans, 83, Ashes to Ashes: Visions of Death, Alternative Mus, New York, 83; Contemporary self-portraits, Allen Frumkin Gallery, New York, 83; and others. *Teaching:* Asst Prof, Art Dept, State Univ New York, Stony Brook, 76- *Awards:* Creative Artists Public Service Fel for drawing, 80-81. *Bibliog:* April Kingsley (auth), Toby Buonagurio, Arts Mag, 80; Robert Lubar (auth), Toby Buonagurio, Arts Mag, 82; Thomas Piche (auth), Toby Buonagurio, Am Ceramics, 82. *Media:* Ceramic; Mixed Media. *Publ:* Coauth, Ceramic directions: A contemporary overview, 83. *Dealer:* Gallery Yves Arman 817 Madison Ave New York NY 10021. *Mailing Add:* 2104 E 177th St Bronx NY 10472

BURCH, CLAIRE R
PAINTER, WRITER
b New York, NY, Feb 19, 25. *Study:* Wash Sq Col, NY Univ, BA, 47. *Work:* Butler Inst Am Art, Youngstown, Ohio; Guild Hall, East Hampton, NY; Birmingham Mus, Ala; Brooklyn Mus, NY; Beth Israel Hosp, New York; and others. *Exhib:* One-man shows, Ruth White Gallery, New York, 63, Galerie L'Antipoete, Paris, France, 63, Southampton Col, 64-65 & Roko Gallery, 64; Maniacal Laughter, Westbeth Gallery, New York, 71; Berkely Art Ctr, 81. *Pos:* Contribr ed, Network News. *Teaching:* adj prof, Union Experimenting Col, currently. *Awards:* First Prize for Representational Painting, Guild Hall, 65; First Prize for Watercolor, North Shore Community Art Ctr, 65; Third Prize for Watercolor, Brooklyn Mus, 65. *Mem:* New York Playwrights Coop. *Media:* Watercolor, Collage. *Publ:* Auth, You Be The Mother Follies & Solid Gold Illusion, Norwood Press; contribr, Life, Saturday Review, McCalls and other magazines; illusr, Alfonia, 82; auth, Postscript to the Livermore Thousand, 83; and others. *Mailing Add:* 2747 Regent St Berkeley CA 94705

BURCHARD, PETER DUNCAN
ILLUSTRATOR, PHOTOGRAPHER
b Washington, DC, Mar 1, 21. *Study:* Philadelphia Mus Sch Art, cert, 47. *Awards:* Christopher Award, 73. *Media:* Wash, Gouache; Black & White Film. *Publ:* Illusr, For Ma and Pa, 73 & auth & illusr, Whaleboat Raid, 77, Coward McCann & Geoghegan; illusr, Night Spell, Atheneum, 77; auth & illusr, Ocean Race, 78 & Chinwe, 79, G P Putnam's Sons. *Mailing Add:* 943 Boston Post Rd Madison CT 06443

BURCHESS, ARNOLD
PAINTER, SCULPTOR
b Chicago, Ill, June 7, 12. *Study:* City Col New York, BSS; also with George W Eggers & Robert Garrison. *Comn:* Three bas reliefs (with Robert Garrison), Radio City Music Hall New York, 35; portrait in bronze of Senator Edmund S Muskie, State Capital, Augusta, Maine, 74. *Exhib:* Am Watercolor Soc, New York, 55-; Birmingham Mus Art, Ala, 55; one-man show, Van Dimant Gallery, Southampton, NY, 57; Mus Mod Art, New York, 59; Maine Art Gallery, Wiscasset, 75; Saddleback Col, Mission Viejo, Calif, 81. *Teaching:* Lectr, Shapes in Clay, Metrop Mus Art, New York, 39; prof fine art & chmn dept, Fashion Inst Technol, New York, 59-74; vis prof figurative sculpture, Bowdoin Col, 75; instr, Saddleback Col, Calif, 79- *Awards:* Watercolor Prize, Birmingham Mus Art, 55. *Bibliog:* Article in La Rev Mod, 56; Arnold Burchess-watercolorist, Am Artist Mag, 59; Norman Kent (auth), 100 Watercolor Techniques, Watson-Guptill, 70. *Mem:* Am Watercolor Soc; Audubon Artists. *Media:* Watercolor; Ceramic Clay, Slate. *Publ:* Coauth, The Human Form, Anatomy, Avery Publ, 81. *Dealer:* Challis Gallery Laguna Beach CA. *Mailing Add:* 5299 Cantante Laguna Hills CA 92653

BURCHETT, DEBRA
ADMINISTRATOR, CURATOR
b Bremerhaven, Ger, Sept 26, 55; US citizen. *Study:* Univ Ky, Lexington, 74-75; Univ Calif, Irvine, with Craig Kauffman, Alexis Smith & Tony DeLap, BFA, 77, independent res under Melinda Wortz, BA, 78. *Collections Arranged:* Clothing Constructions, 79, Michelangelo Pistoletto, 79, Barry Le Va, New York Artist, Nat Endowment Arts Exhib, 80, Architectural Sculpture, Nat Endowment Arts Mus Prog, 80, Il Modo Italiano, Nat Endowment Arts Mus Prog, 83-84 & others, Los Angeles Inst Contemp Art. *Pos:* Gallery asst, Univ Calif, Irvine & Newport Harbor Art Mus, Newport Beach, Calif, 76-77; ed, Jour: A Contemporary Art Mag, 77-80; cur, Main & Entrance Galleries, Los Angeles Inst Contemp Art, 79-; develop asst, Fine Arts Gallery, Mount St Mary's Col, 81 & Calif State Univ, Los Angeles, 83. *Awards:* Nat Endowment Visual Arts Mus Prog Grant, 79; Critics Residency Grant, 79 & Artist Residency Grant, 80, Nat Endowment Arts; and others. *Bibliog:* Jennifer Seder (auth), Closet art, Los Angeles Times, 6/8/79; Germano Celant (auth), Culture, L'Europeo, Rome, Italy, 8/79; Melinda Wortz (auth), Clothing constructions, Art News, 9/79. *Mem:* Nat Asn Artists' Orgn (founding bd dirs, 82-83). *Publ:* Ed, Art and music, 70, issues 17-25, 77-80 & Another look at conceptualism, 79, J Southern Calif Art Mag; contribr, Visits: Kisch, Lere, Vogel & Scoops: Nordman, Irwin, Wheeler, 78 & ed spec issue, Art in Latin America (bilingual ed), 79, J Los Angeles Inst Contemp Art. *Mailing Add:* Los Angeles Inst Contemp Art 2020 S Robertson Blvd Los Angeles CA 90034

BURCHFIELD, JERRY LEE
PHOTOGRAPHER, EDUCATOR
b Chicago, Ill, July 28, 47. *Study:* Calif State Univ, Fullerton, BA(photo-commun), 71, MA(art, photo emphasis), 77. *Work:* Los Angeles Co Mus, Calif; St Louis Mus Art, Mo; Bibliot Nat, Paris; Minneapolis Inst Arts, Minn; Denver Art Mus; plus others. *Exhib:* Contemporary Photoworks, Fogg Mus, 80; Color Works, Zurich Art Mus, Switz, 80; Contemporary American Photography, Am House Berlin, WGer, 81; California: The State of the Landscape, Newport Harbor Mus Art, Newport Beach, 81; Color As Form; A History of Color Photography, George Eastman House, Rochester, NY, 82; Studio Work, Los Angeles Co Mus Art, 82; Staged Studio Events, Lijnbaacenter, Rotterdam, Netherlands, 83; and others. *Pos:* Asst dir, Newport Gallery, Newport Sch Photog, Calif, 73-75; dir co-owner, BC Space, Photog Gallery, Laguna Beach, Calif, 76- *Teaching:* Instr photog, Univ Calif, Irvine Exten, 73-75; lectr photog, Calif State Univ, Fullerton, 74, instr, 78-; instr, Saddleback Col, Mission Viejo, Calif, 79-; instr, Summer Workshop Photog, Colo Mountain Col, 80-83; instr, Tahoe Photog Workshops, Orange Coast Col, 81. *Awards:* Photographer's Fel, Nat Endowment Arts, 81; Numerous Purchase Awards. *Bibliog:* Lauri Pelissero (auth), Jerry Burchfield, photographer, Air Calif Mag, 12/79; Elaine Dines (auth), Jerry Burchfield, Photo Bulletin, 6-7/81; Linda Bellon (auth), Jerry Burchfield: An interview, Obscura, fall 82. *Mem:* Soc for Photog Educ; Visual Studies Workshop; Los Angeles Ctr for Photog Studies; Friends of Photog. *Media:* Photography. *Publ:* Auth, Color Solarization, 73 & Cameraless photography, 75, Peterson's Photogs; illusr/contribr, Basic Darkroom Book, Plume, 77; contrib ed, articles in Darkroom Photog Mag, Vol 1, No 3 & 6, 79; auth & illusr, Darkroom Art, Amphoto, 80; plus others. *Dealer:* G Ray Hawkins 7224 Melrose Ave Los Angeles CA; Carson Sapiro Denver CO. *Mailing Add:* PO Box 1502 Laguna Beach CA 92652

BURCKHARDT, RUDY
PHOTOGRAPHER, FILMMAKER
b Basel, Switz, Apr 5, 14; US citizen. *Study:* Ozenfant Sch, New York, 48; Brooklyn Mus Sch, 49; Acad Naples, 50-51. *Work:* Mus Mod Art, Metrop Mus Art, New York; Art Inst Chicago; Univ New Orleans. *Exhib:* Limelight Gallery, 58; Tanager Gallery, 59; Green Mountain Gallery, New York, 70 & 73; Gotham Bookmart, 72; Brooke Alexander Gallery, New York, 75. *Teaching:* Lectr filmmaking, Grad Sch Art, Univ Pa, Philadelphia, 65- *Bibliog:* Alex Katz (auth), article, Art News, 41; Lucy Lippard (auth), article, Art in Am, 75; Thomas B Hess (auth), article, New York Mag, 75. *Publ:* Illusr, Mediterranean Cities, 55; illusr, Mobile Homes, Z-Press, 79. *Dealer:* Brooke Alexander Gallery 26 E 78th St New York NY 10021; Blue Mountain Gallery (Coop) 121 Wooster St New York NY 10012. *Mailing Add:* 50 W 29th St New York NY 10001

BURCKHARDT, YVONNE HELEN See Jacquette, Yvonne Helene

BURDEN, CARTER
COLLECTOR
b Los Angeles, Calif, Aug 25, 41. *Study:* Harvard Univ; Columbia Univ Law Sch. *Pos:* Founder & pres, Studio Mus in Harlem, currently; mem exec comt, jr coun, acquisitions comt & int coun, Mus Mod Art, New York, currently. *Collection:* Works of the contemporary period, mainly American abstract paintings since 1950. *Mailing Add:* Studio Museum in Harlem 2033 Fifth Ave New York NY 10035

BURDEN, CHRIS
CONCEPTUAL ARTIST, SCULPTOR

b Boston, Mass, Apr 11, 46. *Study:* Pomona Col, BFA, 69; Univ Calif, Irvine, MFA, 71. *Work:* Long Beach Arts Mus, Calif; Mus Mod Art, New York. *Exhib:* One-man shows, Riko Mizuno Gallery, Los Angeles, 72, 74 & 75, Ronald Feldman Fine Arts, New York, 74 & 75, Hansen Fuller Gallery, 74 & Alessandra Castelli Gallery, 75; 112 Green St, Video-Performance, New York. *Teaching:* Instr avant-garde art, LaVerne Col, 73-74; vis artist, Fresno State Univ, 74. *Awards:* New Talent Award, Los Angeles Co Mus, 73; Nat Endowment for Arts Individual Artist Grant, 74. *Bibliog:* Sharp & Bear (auth), Church of human energy, Avalanche, summer-fall 73; R Hughs (auth), Young Sadhu, Time Mag, 2/24/75; Jan Butterfield (auth), Through the night softly, Arts Mag, 3/75. *Media:* Live Performance, Broadcast Television. *Mailing Add:* c/o Ronald Feldman Fine Arts 33 East 74th St New York NY 10021

BURDOCK, HARRIET
HISTORIAN, PRINTMAKER

b Buffalo, NY, June 21, 44. *Study:* Univ NMex, with Garo Antresian, BFA, 66; Newark State Col, MA, 69; Pratt Graphics Ctr, New Sch Social Research, with Clare Romano & Federico Castellon. *Pos:* Lectr, NJ State Mus, Trenton, 67-68; asst, Prints & Photog Div, New York Public Libr, 80- *Teaching:* Instr art hist, Bergen Co Col, Paramus, NJ, 78-79. *Mem:* Graphic Arts Coun, New York (co-founder & executive secy, 77-79); Col Art Asn Am; Am Asn Mus; Int Coun Mus; Nat Print Asn. *Publ:* Auth, Notes from Russia, Graphic Arts Coun NY Newsletter, 77; auth, Woodcuts in China, Print Collector's Newsletter, 81. *Mailing Add:* c/o Art, Prints & Photog Div NY Public Libr New York NY 10018

BURFORD, BYRON LESLIE
PAINTER, PRINTMAKER

b Jackson, Miss, July 12, 20. *Study:* Univ Iowa, BFA & MFA. *Work:* Worcester Art Mus, Mass; Walker Art Ctr, Minneapolis; Nelson/Atkins Gallery, Kansas City, Mo; Sheldon Art Mus, Lincoln, Nebr; High Mus Art, Atlanta, Ga. *Exhib:* Solo exhibs, Babcock Galleries, 66, 67, 69 & 75; Am Acad Arts Ann, New York, 66, 72 & 79; Venice Biennale, Italy, 68; Bienal Arte Coltejer, Colombia, 70; Kunsthaus, Zurich, Switz, 72; and others. *Teaching:* Prof painting, Univ Iowa, 47-; prof painting, Univ Minn & Univ Mass, summer 67. *Awards:* Guggenheim Found Fel, 60 & 61; Ford Found Award, 61, 62 & 64; Nat Inst Arts & Lett Grants, 67, 72 & 75. *Media:* Oil, Acrylic; Prints. *Mailing Add:* 113 S Johnson Iowa City IA 52240

BURFORD, WILLIAM E
DEALER, ADMINISTRATOR

b Lubbock, Tex, May 16, 36. *Study:* Tex Tech Univ, BA. *Pos:* Pres, Tex Art Gallery, Dallas, 76-; vchmn, Tex Comn on the Arts & Humanities, Austin, 76, chmn, 77-78; mem, Dallas City Art Comn, 77- *Specialty:* Predominately contemporary Western art with Americana, wildlife, landscapes, books, prints, sculpture and porcelains. *Mailing Add:* 10877 Crooked Creek Rd Dallas TX 75229

BURG, PATRICIA JEAN
PAINTER, PRINTMAKER

b Windsor, Ont, Jan 9, 34. *US citizen. Study:* Otis Art Inst, Los Angeles, MFA, 66. *Work:* IBM Co, Los Angeles; Art in Embassies, White House Loan Collection; Standard Oil Co, New York. *Comn:* Oil paintings, Latham & Watkins, Los Angeles, 75 & 79, Allison Corp, Los Angeles, 75, Roberts Scott & Co, San Diego, 76 & Carson City Hall, Calif, 77. *Exhib:* Third Ann Miniature Print, Pratt Inst, New York, 68; Northwest Printmakers, Seattle Art Mus, Wash, 69; Affect-Effect Exhib, La Jolla Mus Art, Calif, 69; Graphic Gallery Exhib, Oakland, Calif, 70; New Work-New Talent, Los Angeles Co Mus Art, Los Angeles, 74; Int Exchange, Pacificulture-Asia Mus, Pasadena, Calif, 76; New Works '79, Calif State Polytech Univ, Pomona, 79. *Pos:* Co-founder & dir, Triad Graphic Workshop, Los Angeles, 66-; co-owner, Art Source Gallery, Los Angeles, 75- *Teaching:* Instr drawing, Otis Art Inst-Parsons, Los Angeles, currently. *Awards:* Purchase Awards, Home Savings & Loan, Los Angeles, 64, Mus Fine Arts, Boston, 68 & Otis Art Inst, Los Angeles, 69. *Bibliog:* Bentley Schaad (auth), The Realm of Contemporary Still Life, Reinhold Press, 65; Thelma R Newman (auth), Innovative Printmaking, Crown, 75. *Mem:* Los Angeles Inst Contemp Art; Los Angeles Printmaking Soc (bd dirs, 76-77); Artists Econ Action. *Media:* Etching. *Specialty:* Modern art with emphasis on graphics and paintings. *Mailing Add:* 11326 Ventura Blvd Studio City CA 91604

BURGART, HERBERT JOSEPH
EDUCATOR, ADMINISTRATOR

b St Marys, Pa, Apr 27, 32. *Study:* Calif State Univ, Long Beach, BA, 54; Pa State Univ, MEd, 57, DEd, 61. *Work:* La State Univ Gallery Fine Arts, Baton Rouge; Cohen Mem Mus, Nashville; Univ Ga Fine Arts Mus; Anderson Gallery, Richmond, Va; Pa State Univ Gallery. *Teaching:* Prof art & chmn dept, La State Univ, 58-60; prof art & chmn dept, Univ Ga, 62-65; prof art & dean, Va Commonwealth Univ, 66-76; pres, Moore Col Art, 76-82; pres, Ringling Sch Art Design, 81- *Awards:* fel Am Coun Ed. *Mem:* Nat Asn Schs Art (secy, 75-81, bd dirs); Nat Coun Art Adminr (bd dirs); Nat Art Educ Asn (pres, Southeastern Region, 70-72); Nat Exhib by Blind Artists, Inc (pres, 79-81); Philadelphia Art Alliance (bd dirs, 76-81). *Res:* Creative process. *Publ:* Auth, Art in Higher Education, 61; auth, Creative Art: the Child & the School, 63; auth, The Development of a Visual-Verbal Measure of Creativity, 68; auth, Administration in Higher Education, 72; auth, Computer Assisted Instruction and Research, 74. *Mailing Add:* c/o Ringling Sch Art & Design 1191 27th St Sarasota FL 33580

BURGER, W CARL
EDUCATOR, PAINTER

b Baden, Ger, Dec 27, 25. *US citizen. Study:* NY Univ, BS, MA; Columbia Univ, prof dipl; Rutgers Univ; Parsons Sch Design. *Work:* Pub Service, Newark, NJ; Johnson & Johnson, Somerville, NJ; Trenton Mus, NJ; David Yunich Collection, Bambergers, NJ; Warner Communications. *Comn:* Space Mural, Lockheed Electronics, Woodbridge, NJ, 60. *Exhib:* Drawings USA, Ball State Univ, 70; Small Drawing Show, Philadelphia Mus, 74; Nabisco Galleries, Hanover, NJ, 77; Assoc Artists of NJ, Benedict Gallery, Madison, 78; Somerset Col, Tri-State Show, Somerville, NJ, 78; Watercolor Show, Holyoke Mus, Mass, 78; Newark Mus Triennial, 82. *Pos:* Set designer, Capemay Playhouse, 54-55 & Hillson's Theatre Stars, Binghamton, NY, 56. *Teaching:* Prof of design & drawing, Kean Col of NJ, Union, 60- *Awards:* Jocelyn Mus Award, Ball State Drawing Ann, Jocelyn Mus, 73; NJ State Coun Arts Grant, 81. *Bibliog:* Article, Art News, 9/83. *Mem:* Federated Art Asn of NJ (vpres, 77); NJ Watercolor Soc; Hunterdon Art Ctr (trustee, 69-72); Audubon Artists (nat acad); Assoc Artists NJ. *Media:* Watercolor, Ink. *Dealer:* Peter Jones Gallery E Broad St Flemington NJ 08822; Joseph Grippi Gallery 315 E 62nd St New York NY 10021. *Mailing Add:* Beacon Light Rd Box 322 RR 1 Califon NJ 07830

BURGESS, DAVID LOWRY
ENVIRONMENTAL ARTIST

b Philadelphia, Pa, Apr 27, 40. *Study:* Pa Acad Fine Arts, Philadelphia; Univ Pa; Inst Allende, San Miguel, Mex. *Work:* Houghton Libr; Harvard Univ, Cambridge, Mass; Mus Fine Arts, Boston; Smithsonian Collection, Washington, DC; Archives, Boston Pub Libr. *Exhib:* Earth, Air, Fire, Water, The Elements, Mus Fine Arts, Boston, 71 & Master Drawings of the 19th & 20th Centuries, 72; CAYAC Traveling Exhib, Spain, Peru, Arg & Chile, 72; Multiple Interaction Team, Chicago, San Francisco, Cincinnati & Philadelphia; Art Transition, Mass Inst Technol; Documenta 6, Kassel, Ger; Vienna Biennial, Austria, 79; Sky Arts Conference (co-ed catalog), Mass Inst Technol, 81; and others. *Pos:* Adv, Mass Coun Arts & Humanities, currently. *Teaching:* Prof & head grad MFA studies, Mass Col Art, Boston, 69- *Awards:* Nat Endowment Arts Individual Artist Grant, 77; Rockefeller Artist Grant, 79-80; Mass Artist Found Artist Fel, 83; and others. *Bibliog:* Baker (auth) & Kepes (auth), articles, Art of the Environment, 72; Starpits Waiting for Light Planes, Leonardo, winter 75; article, Boston Mag, 10/78. *Mem:* Arts Educ Am (adv bd, 78-); Nat Humanities Fac. *Publ:* Auth, Fragments, 69; auth, Looking and Listening, 72; auth, Memory, Environment and Utopia, 75. *Mailing Add:* 27 Sherman St Cambridge MA 02138

BURGESS, JOSEPH JAMES, JR
PAINTER, EDUCATOR

b Albany, NY, July 13, 24. *Study:* Hamilton Col, BA, 47; Yale Univ, MA, 48; Pratt Inst, 52-54; Cranbrook Acad Art, MFA, 54. *Exhib:* Recent Drawings USA, Mus Mod Art, New York, 56; Drawing Nat, Calif Palace Legion Hon, San Francisco, 59; two-person show, DeWaters Art Ctr, Flint, Mich, 64; Calif Design Ten Show, Pasadena Art Mus, 68; First Ann City of Angels Int Exhib Photog, 74; Santa Fe Festival of Arts, 79; one-man exhib, Historic Costume of the Orient, 83; and others. *Pos:* Dir, Blair Galleries, Ltd, Santa Fe, NMex, 76-79. *Teaching:* Asst prof fine arts & head dept, St Lawrence Univ, Canton, NY, 54-55; art instr, chmn dept & dir, DeWaters Art Ctr, Flint Community Jr Col, 56-65; asst prof design, Ariz State Univ, Tempe, 65-66; asst prof art, NMex Highlands Univ, 82- *Media:* Mixed. *Specialty:* Painting, sculpture and graphics. *Publ:* Auth, Four Chinese poems, translations from T'ang poetry, fall 61 & Some thoughts on non-communication in the arts, spring 63, Mich Voices; auth, A random poem, translation from the T'ang Dynasty poet Wang Wei, 10/12/73, A shining legend, 9/10/74, Asia's first iron-clad warship, 5/19/75, Christian Sci Monitor; and many others. *Dealer:* Robiard Galleries 202 E Cheyenne Mountain Blvd Colorado Springs CO 80906; DFC Gallery 150 E 58th St New York NY. *Mailing Add:* PO Box 2151 Santa Fe NM 87504

BURGESS, LINDA SUZANNE
PAINTER, PHOTOGRAPHER

b Coral Gables, Fla, May 14, 54. *Study:* Miami-Dade Community Col, AA, 74; Appalachian State Univ, BA, 77; Rutgers Univ, MFA, 79. *Exhib:* New Orleans Biennial, New Orleans Mus Art, 77; Shreveport-Art Guild Nat, Meadows Mus Art, La, 81; solo exhib, Southeastern Ctr Contemp Art, Winston-Salem, NC, 82; 16 Artists, 83 & Birmingham Biennial, 83, Birmingham Mus Art; The Arts Network: Southeastern Artists, Nexus Gallery, Atlanta, 83; New Orleans Triennial, New Orleans Mus Art, 83; End of the World: Contemporary Visions of the Apocalypse, New Mus, New York, 83. *Teaching:* Asst prof art, Judson Col, 79-83 & Birmingham-Southern Col, 81- *Bibliog:* Jim Nelson (auth), Linda Burgess has a thing about tornadoes, Birmingham News, 3/82; Susan Kalil (auth), 1983 New Orleans Triennial, Arts Quart, 4-6/83; Sonja Henderson (auth), article, Birmingham Post-Herald, 11/4/83. *Mem:* Birmingham Art Asn. *Media:* Oil. *Mailing Add:* 2984 Donita Dr Birmingham AL 35243

BURGGRAF, RAY LOWELL
PAINTER, EDUCATOR

b Mt Gilead, Ohio, July 26, 38. *Study:* Ashland Col, BS, 61; Cleveland Inst Art, BFA, 68; Univ Calif, Berkeley, MA, 69, MFA, 70. *Work:* De Kalb Col, Clarkston, Ga. *Exhib:* Artists of the Southeast & Texas, Isaac Delgado Mus Art, New Orleans, 71; 16th Nat Sun Carnival Art Exhib, El Paso Mus Art, Tex, 71; 12th Ann Calgary Graphics Exhib, Alta Col Art, 72; 13th Dixie Ann, Montgomery Mus Fine Arts, Ala, 72; 61st Ann Exhib, Laguna Gloria Art Mus, Austin, Tex, 72. *Teaching:* Asst prof painting & drawing, Fla State Univ, 70- *Awards:* Purchase Award, Mint Mus Art, 71; First Nat Bank Award, Mobile Art Patrons League, Ala, 71; Award, Ball State Univ, Muncie, Ind, 72. *Mem:* Col Art Asn Am. *Media:* Acrylic. *Mailing Add:* 1507 Marion Ave Tallahassee FL 32303

BURGUES, IRVING CARL
SCULPTOR, LECTURER
b Austria, Oct 16, 06; US citizen. *Study:* Vienna Arts Sch, BA(fine arts), 26; Brooklyn Mus; Sch of Indust Fine Arts, Newark, NJ; sculpture apprentice to Mollet, Paris; Art Students' League; Mod Sch of Art, New York. *Work:* White House Mus; Vatican; Kremlin; Smithsonian Inst, Washington, DC; Brooklyn Mus. *Comn:* New Testament mural, Rio de Janeiro, 30; Big Horn Sheep sculpture, State of Nev, 73; Am Wild Goat, State of Mont, 76. *Exhib:* Brooklyn Mus, NY, 35; Indianapolis Mus, 70; Mus of Sci & Indust, Chicago, 72; NJ State Mus, 74; Smithsonian Inst, 76. *Mem:* Artists Equity. *Mailing Add:* 183 Spruce St Lakewood NJ 08701

BURK, A DARLENE
DEALER, COLLECTOR
b Wheatland, Wyo, Dec 24, 29. *Study:* Calvin Goodman Sem, 76-80. *Pos:* Owner, Burk Gallery, currently. *Specialty:* Western art, Indian culture, landscape and wildlife. *Collection:* Painting, John Hilton, Jeff Craven, Reynald Brown, Jack Jordan; bronzes, Jasper D'Ambrosi, Don Rubin, Terry Gilbreth; woodcarvings, Don Ely. *Mailing Add:* Burk Gallery PO Box 246 Boulder City NV 89009

BURKE, DANIEL V
PAINTER, EDUCATOR
b Erie, Pa, Apr 21, 42. *Study:* Columbus Col Art & Design, 60-62; Mercyhurst Col, BA(art), 69; Edinboro State Col, MEd(art), 72; MacDowell Colony, Peterborough, NH, 70 & 73. *Work:* Del Mar Col Art Gallery, Corpus Christi; Laguna Gloria Art Mus, Austin, Tex; Southern Utah State Col; IBM Corp, Austin; NC Nat Bank, Boone; and others. *Exhib:* 18th Nat Chautauqua Art Asn Show, NY, 75; Drawings USA, Minn Mus Art, St Paul, 75; one-man shows, Williams Col Mus Art, Mass, 81, Erie Art Ctr, Pa, 82 & Rike Ctr Gallery, Univ Dayton, Ohio, 83. *Teaching:* prof art, Mercyhurst Col, 69-, dir dept art, 79- *Awards:* Best of Show, Greater New Orleans Int, 74; Purchase Award, Appalachian Nat Drawing Competition, 75; Chautauqua Art Asn Award, 18th Nat Show, 75. *Mem:* Northwestern Pa Artists Asn (co-exec chmn, 75-). *Media:* Acrylic. *Mailing Add:* 223 E Sixth St Erie PA 16507

BURKE, E AINSLIE
PAINTER, EDUCATOR
b Omaha, Nebr, Jan 26, 22. *Study:* Md Inst Fine Arts; McCoy Col, Johns Hopkins Univ; Inst Allende, San Miguel, Mex; Art Students League; Fulbright Fel, 57-58. *Work:* Springfield Mus, Mass; Nat Broadcasting Corp, 76; Everson Mus, Syracuse, NY, 77; Munson-Williams-Proctor Inst, Utica, NY; Lowe Art Gallery, Syracuse Univ; and others. *Exhib:* Seventeenth Biennial Int Exhib, Brooklyn Mus, NY; Pa Acad Fine Arts Ann, Philadelphia, 69; Finger Lake Exhib, Rochester Mem Gallery, NY, 69 & 71-73; Munson-Williams-Proctor Inst Ann, 70-71 & 74-76; solo exhibs, Oxford Gallery, Rochester, 77 & 81, Stonington Gallery, Maine, 77 & 78, Everson Mus, Syracuse, 79-80 & others. *Teaching:* Vis artist, Exeter Acad, 64-; vis artist, Sch Art, Syracuse Univ, 62-64; prof drawing & painting, 64-77, chmn studio arts dept, Col Visual & Performing Arts, 70-80. *Awards:* Paul Puzinas Mem Award, Nat Acad Design, 73; Creative Artists Pub Serv Grant in Painting, 77; Henry Wardranger Fund Purchase Award, Nat Acad Design, 78. *Mem:* Am Asn Univ Prof; life mem Art Students League; Woodstock Artists Asn (pres, 60-62); Deer Isle Artists Asn; Maine Coast Artists Asn; and others. *Dealer:* Kraushaar Galleries 724 5th Ave New York NY 10028 *Mailing Add:* RD 1 Eldredge Rd Manlius NY 13104

BURKE, JAMES DONALD
MUSEUM DIRECTOR, ADMINISTRATOR
b Salem, Ore, Feb 22, 39. *Study:* Brown Univ, AB, 62; Univ Pa, AM, 66; Fulbright-Hayes Fel, Holland, 68-69; Harvard Univ, PhD, 72. *Collections Arranged:* Charles Meryon (auth, catalog), 74-75. *Pos:* Cur, Allen Art Mus, Oberlin Col, 71-72; cur drawings & prints, Art Gallery, Yale Univ, 72-78; asst dir, St Louis Art Mus, 78- *Teaching:* Instr, Yale Univ, 72-78. *Awards:* Nat Endowment Arts Mus Fel, 73. *Mem:* Am Asn Mus; Col Art Asn; Print Coun Am. *Res:* Sixteenth and seventeenth century Dutch and Flemish art; contemporary and modern art. *Publ:* Auth, Jan Both: Paintings, Drawings & Prints, 75. *Mailing Add:* St Louis Art Mus Forest Park St Louis MO 63110

BURKE, MARGARET
HISTORIAN
b Hartford, Conn, Apr 13, 50. *Study:* Wheaton Col, Norton, Mass, BA, 72; Winterthur Prog in Early Am Cult, MA, 76; Univ Del, PhD, in progress. *Collections Arranged:* Daniel Putnam Brinley: the Impressionist Years (auth, catalog), Bowdoin Col Mus Art, 78 & An Ounce of Prevention ...Care and Conservation of Works of Art, 79. *Pos:* Cur, Bowdoin Col Mus Art, 77-80; panel mem, Mus & Conserv Panel, Maine State Comn on Arts & Humanities, 78-80; asst dir, Va Mus Fine Arts, 80- *Mem:* Am Asn Mus; Col Art Asn; Decorative Arts Chap, Soc Archit Historians. *Res:* Influence of Italian futurism in America, 1910-1915; 20th century American art; American furniture. *Publ:* Contribr, Avant-Garde Painting and Sculpture in America, 1910-1925, Del Art Mus, 75; auth, Joseph True and the piecework system of Salem, Massachusetts, Antiques, 77; Salem Craftsmen of the Federal Period, Essex Inst Hist Collections, 77; ed, Bowdoin College Mus of Art: Handbook of the Collections, Bowdoin Col Mus Art, 82; and others. *Mailing Add:* Va Mus Fine Arts Boulevard & Grove Ave Richmond VA 23221

BURKERT, ROBERT RANDALL
PAINTER, PRINTMAKER
b Racine, Wis, Aug 20, 30. *Study:* Wustum Art Ctr, Racine; Univ Wis-Madison, with John Wilde & Alfred Sessler, 48-55; Jacques Desjobert Atelier,

Paris, France, summer 70. *Work:* Metrop Mus Art, New York; Mus Fine Arts, Boston; Nat Collection Fine Arts, Washington, DC; Tate Gallery, London; Fogg Mus, Harvard Univ; plus others. *Comn:* Outdoor wall (with Derse Outdoor Advert), Mortgage Guarantee Ins Co, 72. *Exhib:* Recent Drawings, USA Exhib, Mus Mod Art, New York, 56; Presentation Artist, Boston Printmakers, 62; Butler Art Inst Ann, 65; New Talent Graphics Show, Assoc Am Artists, New York, 66; Univ Ill Graphics Invitational, Champaign-Urbana, 70; Okla Printmakers, 77; Camden Art, Centre, London, 80. *Pos:* Bd trustees, Milwaukee Art Mus. *Teaching:* Prof graphics & drawing, Univ Wis-Milwaukee, 56- *Bibliog:* James Schineller (auth), Art: Search and Self Discovery, Int Textbook Co, 69; Ross & Romano (auth), The Complete Printmaker, Macmillan Free Press, 72; Fritz Eichenberg (auth), Art of the Print, Abrams, 76; plus others. *Dealer:* Associated American Artists 605 Fifth Ave New York NY 10022; Bradley Galleries 2565 N Downer Ave Milwaukee WI 53211. *Mailing Add:* 3228 N Marietta Ave Milwaukee WI 53211

BURKHARDT, HANS GUSTAV
PAINTER, PRINTMAKER
b Basel, Switz, Dec 20, 04; US citizen. *Study:* Cooper Union, 25-28; Grand Cent Sch Art, 28-29; Arshile Gorky Studio, 29-36. *Work:* Los Angeles Co Mus Art, Los Angeles; Joslyn Art Mus, Omaha, Nebr; Hirshhorn Mus, Washington, DC; Corcoran Gallery, Washington, DC; Guggenheim Mus, New York; plus others. *Exhib:* American Painting Today, Metrop Mus Art, New York, 50; 46th Ann, Pa Acad Fine Arts, 51; Chicago Art Inst Ann, 52; Art in the Twentieth Century, San Francisco Mus, 55; Weihnachts Ausstellung, Kunsthalle, Basel, 64; Calif State Univ, Northridge, 73; Santa Barbara Mus of Art, Calif, 76; 40 yr retrospective, Schoelkopf Gallery, New York; Rutberg Fine Arts, Los Angeles, 82 & 83. *Teaching:* Prof painting & drawing, Univ Southern Calif, 59-60; asst prof, Univ Calif, Los Angeles, 61-63; assoc prof, Calif State Univ, Northridge, 63-73, emer prof, 73- *Awards:* Award for Oil, Jr Art Coun, Los Angeles Co Mus Art, 57; Ala Story Purchase Award for Oil, Santa Barbara Mus Art, 58; First Purchase Award for Oil, Howard Amhanson, 61. *Bibliog:* Artist in His Studio, 9/10/61 & Thirty-Year Retrospective, 4/21/62, KHJ-TV, Los Angeles; Rabbi William Kramer (auth), Hans G Burkhardt: Artist and Patron of the Arts, Santa Susana Press, 82. *Media:* Oil, Pastel; Linocut. *Collection:* Arnoldo Pomadoro sculptures; deKooning watercolors and lithographs; numerous works of Mark Tobeys; also prints by Picasso, Kollwitz, Tamayo, Raphael Sawyer, Rouault and many others; large collection of Gorky oils and drawings. *Publ:* Contribr, God Dead? Then Man Is Slain, 77. *Dealer:* Robert Schoelkopf Gallery New York NY; Jack Rutberg Gallery Los Angeles CA. *Mailing Add:* 1914 Jewett Dr Los Angeles CA 90046

BURKO, DIANE
PAINTER, EDUCATOR
b Brooklyn, NY, Sept 24, 45. *Study:* Skidmore Col, BS, 66; Univ Pa Grad Sch Fine Arts, MFA, 69; Brooklyn Mus. *Work:* Philadelphia Mus Art; DeCordova Mus, Lincoln, Mass; Reading Pub Mus; Am Tel & Tel; Wells Fargo Bank; and others. *Exhib:* Contemp Reflections, Aldrich Mus of Contemp Art, Ridgefield, Conn, 77; Pa Acad Fine Arts, 78; one-person shows, Skidmore Col, 79 & Pa Acad Fine Arts, 80; Nat Drawing Show, Rutgers Univ, Camden, NJ, 79; Phoenix Mus Art, 80; Taft Mus, Cincinnati, Ohio, 81; Carson/Sapiro Gallery, Denver, 81; Whitney Mus Am Art, Fairfield Co Br, Stamford, Conn, 81. *Pos:* Pres & founder, Philadelphia Focuses on Women in Visual Arts, 73-75. *Teaching:* Asst prof drawing, painting & design, Philadelphia Community Col, 69-81, head art dept, 80-, assoc prof, 81- *Awards:* Purchase Prize, Rutgers Nat Drawing, 79; Vis fel, Tamarand Inst, Albuquerque, NMex, 80 & 82; Pa Coun Arts Individual Artists Grant, 81. *Bibliog:* B Berland (auth), Diane Burko at Stefanotti and Pennsylvania Academy of Fine Arts, Art in Am, 81; R Boyle (auth), Allentown--Burko, Art News, 83; V Donohoe (auth), A lofty view of Pennsylvania, Philadelphia Inquirer, 83. *Mem:* Col Art Asn Am; Philadelphia Print Club; Women's Caucus Art (treas adv bd, 77-78 & 82-85); Muse Found Visual Arts. *Media:* Oil, Acrylic. *Dealer:* Marian Locks 1524 Walnut St Philadelphia PA 19102; Matlingly Baker 3000 McKinney Ave Dallas TX 75204. *Mailing Add:* 510 South 46th St Philadelphia PA 19143

BURKS, MYRNA R
PRINTMAKER, GALLERY DIRECTOR
b Chattanooga, Tenn, Oct 31, 43. *Study:* Ga State Univ, BFA, 71; Univ NMex, MA, 73, MFA, 76. *Work:* Hunter Art Mus, Chattanooga, Tenn; US Info Agency, various embassies; Univ NMex Fine Arts Mus, Albuquerque. *Exhib:* Third Hawaii Nat Print Exhib, Honolulu Acad Arts, 75; Northwest Int Small Format Print Exhib, Davidson Gallery, Seattle, Wash, 76; Women Artists '79: Paperworks, Art & Design Gallery, Univ Kans, Lawrence, 79; Selected Artists, Mulvane Art Ctr, Topeka, Kans, 79-80; Mo Works on Paper Traveling Exhib, 79-80. *Collections Arranged:* Artists Choose Artists, Univ Mo-Kansas City, 79 & Missouri Artists: Works on Paper (auth, catalog), 80. *Pos:* Cur, Tamarind Inst, Univ NMex, 72-73, printer, 77; co-owner & printer, North Light Editions, Portland, Ore, 81- *Teaching:* Instr art & dir gallery, Univ Mo-Kansas City, 78- *Awards:* Ford Found Res Fel, 76; Best of Show Award, Women Artists: Paperworks, 79. *Bibliog:* Donald Hoffman (auth), The history of the world traced through its scars, Kansas City Star, 9/79; Jan Schmitz (auth), The personal lure of Myrna Burks, Forum/Kansas City Artists' Coalition, 10/79; Leonard Koenig (auth), A portfolio of artwork, New Lett, Univ Mo-Kansas City, 79-80. *Mem:* Col Art Asn; Women's Caucus Art (adv bd Kansas City chap, 78-80); Kansas City Artist's Coalition (adv bd, 79-80). *Media:* Lithography, Mixed. *Publ:* Auth, Women artists, Forum/Kansas City Artists' Coalition, 12/79. *Mailing Add:* 2909 Northwest Thurman Portland OR 97210

BURNETT, BARBARA ANN
PAINTER, CONCEPTUAL ARTIST
b Kansas City, Kans, May 7, 27. *Study:* Primarily self taught; La Tech, 82-83. *Work:* Barnard Libr, La Crosse, Kans; Pub Libr, Coffeyville, Kans; City of Mission & City of Prairie Village, Kans. *Comn:* Mural, comn by Lloyd Wagner, Kans, 54. *Exhib:* Century II Kans Tri-State Exhib, Wichita, 81; Midwest Watercolor Soc, Burpee Art Mus, Rockford, Ill, 81; Salmagundi Open Exhib, New York, 82; Allied Artists Am, 82 & Catherine Lorillard Wolfe, 82-83, Nat Arts Club, New York. *Teaching:* Instr, The Pallette, Leawood, Kans, 70-75; workshop instr, Kans State Univ, Lawrence, 78. *Awards:* Hunt Award, Midwest Watercolor Soc, 81; Floral Still Life Awards, Catherine Lorillard Wolfe Club, 82 & 83. *Mem:* Kans Watercolor Soc; Nat League Am Pen Women; Whiskey Painters Am; Greater Kansas City Art Asn (bd mem, 73-82). *Mailing Add:* 5430 Lamar Ave Mission KS 66202

BURNETT, CALVIN
PAINTER, ILLUSTRATOR
b Cambridge, Mass, July 18, 21. *Study:* Mass Col Art, BFA & BS; Sch Boston Mus Fine Arts; Boston Univ, MFA; studied with George Lockwood. *Work:* Boston Mus Fine Arts, Mass; Oakland Mus, Calif; Fogg Art Mus, Harvard Univ; Wiggins Collection, Boston Pub Libr; Wellesley Col; plus others. *Exhib:* San Francisco Mus Art; Mus Fine Art, Boston; Smithsonian Inst Travelling Exhib; Taller de Graphico, Mex; Bazalel Nat, Israel; Brooklyn Mus. *Teaching:* Prof art, Mass Col Art, 56- *Awards:* First Award for Printmaking, Boston Printmakers, 64; Leipzig Int Book Illus Exhib Award, Ger, 65; First Award for Painting, Atlanta Univ Ann, 66. *Bibliog:* M Holsen (auth), Introducing some Boston printmakers, The Connoisseur, London, 67; V E Atkinson (auth), Black Dimensions in Contemporary American Art, New Am Libr, 71; F van Almelo (auth), article, Tuesday Mag, 71. *Media:* Oil; Mixed Drawing Media. *Publ:* Auth-designer, Objective Drawing Techniques, Van Nostrand Reinhold, 66; also auth & illusr of children's bks. *Dealer:* Leon Braithewaite 303 Columbus Ave Boston MA. *Mailing Add:* 87 Fisher St Medway MA 02053

BURNETT, DAVID GRANT
HISTORIAN, CURATOR
b Lincoln, Eng, Oct 1, 40; Can citizen. *Study:* Birkbeck Col, Univ London, BA, 65; Courtauld Inst of Art, MA, 67, PhD, 73, under M Kitson. *Pos:* Cur contemp Can Art, Art Gallery Ont, Toronto, 80. *Teaching:* Lectr art hist, Univ Bristol, England, 67-80; assoc prof art hist, Carleton Univ, Ottawa, Ont, 70-80. *Res:* Contemporary Art. *Publ:* Guido Molinari: Quantificateur, 79; auth, Guido Molinari: Drawings, 80; auth, Gorshon Iskowitz, 82; auth, Alex Colville, 83; auth, Contemporary Canadian Art, 83. *Mailing Add:* Art Gallery Ontario 317 Dundas St W Toronto ON M5T 1G4 Canada

BURNETT, PATRICIA HILL
PAINTER, SCULPTOR
b Brooklyn, NY. *Study:* Univ Toledo; Goucher Col; Corcoran Art Sch; Soc Arts & Crafts; Inst Allende, Mex; Wayne State Univ; Truro Sch Art; also with John Carroll, Sarkis Sarkisian, Wallace Bassford, Walter Midener & Seong Moy. *Work:* Detroit Inst Arts, Mich; Bloomfield Art Asn, Mich; Wayne State Univ; Wooster Col; Ford Motor Co Collection, Detroit. *Comn:* Oil portrait, Joyce Carol Oates, Windsor, Ont, 72; portrait, Benson Ford, Ford Motor Co, Detroit, 75; portrait of Gov William Milliken, State of Mich, 79; and many others. *Exhib:* Butler Mus Nat Art Show, Cleveland, Ohio, 72; Ms & Masters, Midland Ctr Arts, Midland, Mich, 75; and others. *Teaching:* Painting techniques, Univ Mich Exten Courses & sculpture techniques, Grosse Pointe War Mem, formerly. *Awards:* First Prize Painting, Figure Painting Show, Boston, 69; First Prize, Western Art Show, Albuquerque, NMex, 74; First Prize Painting, Scarab Club, 77. *Bibliog:* Christine Hinz (auth), Detroit artist: Feminist home-maker and painter, Daily News, Midland, Mich, 75. *Mem:* Mich Acad Arts; Detroit Soc Women Painters & Sculptors; Ibex Club (pres, 50-51); Sculptors Guild Birmingham. *Media:* Oil; Bronze, Clay. *Publ:* Contribr, Painting the Female Figure, Bassford, Watson-Guptill Founders Gallery, 73; auth, Will NOW and the Junior League ever meet?, Jr League Mag, 73; auth, Have women artists been brushed aside?, Women in the Arts Mag, 75; auth, The winds of change are blowing, Zonta Mag, Int, 75; auth, Women today in Russia, Israel, India & Thailand, PHP Int Mag, Japan, 75. *Dealer:* Portraits Inc Gallery 41 E 57th St New York NY 10022; Rubiner Gallery 621 S Washington Royal Oak MI 48053. *Mailing Add:* 18261 Hamilton Rd Detroit MI 48203

BURNHAM, JACK WESLEY
CRITIC
b New York, NY, Nov 13, 31. *Study:* Boston Mus Sch, 53-54 & 56-57; Wentworth Inst, Boston, AE, 56; Sch Art & Archit, Yale Univ, BFA, 59, MFA(sculpture), 61. *Pos:* Contrib ed, Artforum Mag, 71-72; assoc ed, Arts Mag, 72-76; contrib ed, New Art Examr, 74- *Teaching:* Prof art, Northwestern Univ, 62-; Dana prof fine arts, Colgate Univ, Hamilton, NY, 75-76; Clark prof art hist, Williams Col, Williamstown, Mass, 80. *Awards:* Guggenheim Fel, 73; Critics Award, Chicago Art Awards, 77 & 78. *Bibliog:* Albert Elsen (auth), Beyond modern sculpture, Artforum, 5/69; Tom Conley (auth), The radicality of modern art, Diacritics, spring 73; R Blazer (auth), Blazer on Burnham--great western salt works, Criteria, 11/74. *Res:* Contemporary criticism; art semiotics; the writings and art of Marcel Duchamp. *Publ:* Auth, Beyond Modern Sculpture, Braziller, 68; auth, Art in the Marcusean Analysis, Pa State Univ Press, 69; auth, The Structure of Art, 71 & Great Western Saltworks, 74, Braziller; coauth, Hans Haacke: Framing and Being Framed, NY Univ Press, 75. *Mailing Add:* 2150 Sherman Ave Apt 3C Evanston IL 60201

BURNHAM, LINDA FRYE
EDITOR, WRITER
b Bartlesville, Okla, Dec 3, 40. *Study:* Univ Southern Calif, Los Angeles, BA, 62; Univ Calif, Irvine, MFA, 74. *Collections Arranged:* Public Spirit, Lace Gallery & elsewhere, Los Angeles, 80; CHI/LA, performances and documentation by Paul McCarthy, Kim Jones & Rachel Rosenthal, Artemisia Gallery, Chicago, 82; Critical Perspectives, static work by Jeffrey Vallance, Marc Kreisel & Edie Ellis, PS1 Long Island, NY, 82; Live Art in Eldorado, Washington Proj Arts, Washington, DC, 82; Gold Coast, San Francisco Art Inst, 83. *Pos:* Founding ed & publ, High Performance Mag, 78-; co-owner, Astro Artz Publ, 80-83, mem bd dir, currently; staff writer, Artforum, 81-; bd mem, Highland Art Agents, Los Angeles & Espace DBD, Los Angeles, currently. *Teaching:* Vis instr, San Francisco Art Inst, 83 & NY Univ, 83. *Awards:* Nat Endowment Arts Grants, 80, 82 & 83. *Mem:* Woman's Building, Los Angeles; Franklin Furnace, New York. *Res:* Performance art. *Publ:* Auth, Leave her in Naxos, review of performance by Rachel Rosenthal, 6/81 & Apron: A covering worn in front to protect, review of performance by Jerri Allyn, 11/81, Artforum; auth, Live sex act: A human sexual response to the performances of Paul McCarthy and Barbara Smith, Flue, Franklin Furnace, summer 82; auth, Actmusikspectakle V, review of performance by Michael Peppe, Artforum, 4/83; auth, A Book on Paul McCarthy, Astro Artz (in prep). *Mailing Add:* 240 S Broadway Fifth floor Los Angeles CA 90012

BURNS, D HARRISON
PAINTER, INSTRUCTOR
b Burlington, NC, Jan 28, 46. *Study:* Atlanta Col Art, BFA, 69; Douglass Col, Rutgers Univ, MFA, 72. *Work:* Chase Manhatten Bank, New York; American Telephone & Telegraph Co, New York; Blue Cross Southern Calif, Los Angeles; Western Electric Co, New York; Deloite, Haskins & Sells, World Trade Ctr, New York. *Exhib:* One-man shows, Fischbach Gallery, 77, Galeria Se, Madrid, 80, Jackson Gallery Iolas, 81, New York & Galeria Cellorio, Granada, Spain, 81; Gold, Mus Mod Art, New York, 78-79; Alexander Carlson Gallery, New York, 80; Galeria Cellorio, Granada, Spain, 80-81; NJ State Mus, Trenton, 82. *Teaching:* Chmn, Art Dept, Rutgers Prep Sch, 74- *Bibliog:* Richard Howard (auth), Harrison Burns, Arts Mag, 11/77; John Ashber (auth), New York Mag, 10/29/79; Robert Glauser (auth), Harrison Burns, a new realism, a new symbolism, 3/82. *Media:* Acrylic, Collage. *Dealer:* Iolas/Jackson Gallery 52 E 57th St New York NY 10019. *Mailing Add:* 269 Bowery New York NY 10002

BURNS, G JOAN
LIBRARIAN
b Belleville, NJ, Mar 6, 18. *Study:* Newark State Col, BA(art educ), 39; Columbia Univ, 42-44; Rutgers State Univ, MLS, 63. *Pos:* Draftswoman, Archit Forum, 42-45; free-lance archit illusr, Progressive Archit, Archit Forum, Holiday, and others, 45-57; principal art librn, Newark Pub Libr, 68-; reviewer art titles, Libr J, 70-75 & Am Reference Bks Ann, 72- *Mem:* Art Libr Soc North Am; Victorian Soc in Am. Interest: Twentieth century architectural history and design. *Interests:* Twentieth century architectural history and design. *Publ:* Illusr, Forms & Functions of 20th Century Architecture, Columbia Univ Press, 52. *Mailing Add:* 5 Washington St Newark NJ 07101

BURNS, JEROME
PAINTER, PRINTMAKER
b Brooklyn, NY, Mar 26, 19. *Study:* Art Students League, 36-39; Hans Hofmann Art Sch, New York, 42; Brooklyn Mus Art Sch, 49. *Work:* Okla Mus; C W Post Col Mus, Long Island Univ; Metrop Mus Art, New York. *Exhib:* Nat Acad Exhib, New York, 63; Audubon Artists Exhib, New York, 64; Am Watercolor Soc, New York, 65; Allied Artists of Am, New York, 66; Nat Soc Painters in Casein & Acrylic, New York, 66- *Pos:* Pres, Brownstone Gallery Inc, Brooklyn, 69-76. *Teaching:* Instr painting, Brooklyn Mus Art Sch, 60-61. *Awards:* Samuel F B Morse Medal, Am Nat Acad, 63; Tesser Mem Award, Audubon Artists, 64; Dir Award, Nat Soc Painters in Casein & Acrylic, 66, Memory of Ada Award, 78. *Mem:* Artists Equity Asn; MacDowell Colony Fels; Nat Soc Painters in Casein & Acrylic; Appraisers Asn of Am. *Media:* Casein, Acrylic. *Dealer:* Weyhe Gallery 794 Lexington Ave New York NY. *Mailing Add:* 248 Garfield Pl Brooklyn NY 11215

BURNS, JOSEPHINE
PAINTER
b Llandudno, North Wales, July 2, 17. *Study:* Cooper Union Art Sch, grad, 39, BFA, 76; Art Students League, 49 & 50. *Work:* C W Post Col Mus, Long Island Univ; Okla Mus Art, Oklahoma City; Bristol City Art Gallery, Whitworth Art Gallery, Manchester Univ, England. *Exhib:* Brooklyn & Long Island Artists, Brooklyn Mus, 58; Nat Arts Club, New York, 58, 63 & 73; Nat Acad Design, 64; one-woman show, Alonzo Gallery, New York, 66; Community Gallery, Brooklyn Mus, 76, 77 & 80; Bergen Co Community Mus, 82; Mostyn Art Gallery, NWales, UK. *Pos:* Co-dir, Hicks Street Gallery, Brooklyn, 58-63; assoc dir, Brownstone Gallery, Brooklyn, 69-76. *Awards:* Resident Fel, MacDowell Colony, 60, 62, 64, 65 & 68; Resident Fel, Yaddo, Saratoga Springs, NY, 61. *Mem:* Artists Equity Asn, New York; MacDowell Colony Fels. *Media:* Oil, Pastel. *Mailing Add:* 248 Garfield Pl Brooklyn NY 11215

BURNS, MARSHA
PHOTOGRAPHER
b Seattle, Wash, Jan 11, 45. *Study:* Univ Wash, 63-65; Univ Mass, Amherst, 67-69. *Work:* Mus Mod Art, Metrop Mus Art, New York; Nat Mus Am Art, Smithsonian Inst; Ctr Creative Photog, Tucson; Seattle Art Mus. *Exhib:* Works on Paper, 75, Northwest '77 & New Acquisitions, 79, Seattle Art Mus;

Attitudes--Photography in the '70s, 79 & Sequence Photography, 80, Santa Barbara Mus Art, Calif; Awards in the Visual Arts, Nat Mus Am Art, Smithsonian Inst, 82; Outside New York: Seattle, The New Mus, New York, 83; one-person show, Portland Art Mus, Ore, 84. *Awards:* Photogr Fel, Nat Endowment Arts, 78; Awards in Visual Arts, Nat Mus Am Art, Southeastern Ctr Contemp Art, 81. *Bibliog:* Gretel Ehrlich (auth), Dreamers, pvt publ, 81; David Featherstone (auth), Postures, Friends of Photog, 82; Randy Sue Coburn (auth), Raising the veil on emerging artists, Smithsonian Mag, 5/82. *Mailing Add:* 627 First Avenue Seattle WA 98104

BURNS, PAUL CALLAN
PAINTER, INSTRUCTOR

b Pittsburgh, Pa. *Study:* Pa Mus Sch of Art, Philadelphia; Philadelphia Acad of Fine Art; Cape Cod Sch of Art, Provincetown, Mass. *Work:* Clearing House, New York; Supreme Court, NJ; John R Wanamaker Collection, Philadelphia; Permanent Collection of the Wilmington Acad of Fine Arts, Del; Permanent Collection of the Bergen Community Mus, Paramus, NJ. *Comn:* Justice Weintraub (portrait), NJ Bar Asn, Trenton, 74; Rockport Street (landscape), comn by John Jobs, Ridgewood, NJ, 74; Bishop Gibson (portrait, with Portraits Inc, New York), Diocese of Richmond, Va, 75; Dean Alvin Kernan (portrait, with Portraits Inc, New York), Princeton Univ, 77; recent portraits: David Rockefeller, Arnold & Winnie Palmer & members of Royal Family of Saudi Arabia, Chief Justice Richard Hughes, NJ. *Exhib:* Carnegie Art Mus, Pittsburgh, 35; Corcoran Art Gallery, Washington, DC, 36; Portrait Soc of Ireland, Dublin, 64; Portraits Inc, New York, 65-; Nat Acad of Design, New York, 77; one-man shows, Omaha Mus, Nebr, 76 & M & L Gallery Fine Arts, New York, 76. *Teaching:* Prof portrait painting & life-figure drawing, Ridgewood Art Asn, NJ, 63- *Awards:* Gold Medal, Nat Arts Club Exhib, New York, 69; Puzinas Award, Allied Artists of America Exhib, Nat Acad of Design, New York, 72; Newington Award, Hudson Valley Art Asn Exhib, New York, 73; Artist of the Year, Hudson Artists, 76. *Bibliog:* Susan Meyer (auth), Water Color Page, 73 & Joe Singer (auth), Painting Womans Portraits, 77, Watson-Guptill; Radio interview, KSIL Radio, Silver City, NMex, 77. *Mem:* Am Watercolor Soc (dir, 76-79); Artists Fel (trustee, 75-78); Allied Artists of Am (bd mem, 76-77); Hudson Valley Art Asn (bd mem, 76-77); Ridgewood Art Asn (bd mem, 76-77). *Media:* Oil, Watercolor. *Publ:* Contribr, Painting Portraits of Men, 77, Painting Portraits of Women & The Portrait Painters Problem Book, Paul C Burns (auth), Watson-Guptill. *Dealer:* Grand Cent Art Galleries 50 East 50th Street New York NY 10017; Portraits Inc 41 E 57th St New York NY 10022. *Mailing Add:* 248 Kenilworth Rd Ridgewood NJ 07450

BURNS, SHEILA
PAINTER, LECTURER

b Scotland; US citizen. *Study:* Detroit Soc Arts & Crafts; Wayne State Univ, BA. *Work:* Grand Rapids Mus, Mich; Wayne State Univ; Founders Soc Gallery Loan Collection, Detroit Inst Art. *Comn:* Children's Hosp Mich. *Exhib:* Mich Biennial Exhib Painters & Printmakers, Grand Rapids Mus; Mich Acad Sci, Art & Lett & Mich Regional Exhib, Univ Mich; Blue Water Int Exhib, US & Can, 74 & 75; Eastern Mich Int, 75; plus many others. *Teaching:* Instr, secondary schs. *Awards:* Purchase Award, Mich Biennial Painters & Printmakers, Grand Rapids Mus; Awards, Scarab Club Detroit. *Mem:* Am Asn Prof Artists. *Media:* Watercolor, Oil, Acrylic. *Publ:* Illusr, Detroit Free Press; illusr, Are Nursery Rhymes for Children? by Dr Edward Southern. *Dealer:* Galerie de Boicourt 250 Martin St Birmingham MI 48011. *Mailing Add:* 23036 Ardmore Park St Clair Shores MI 48081

BURNS, STAN
PAINTER, SCULPTOR

b Suitersville, Pa. *Study:* Wayne State Univ, BA & MA; Detroit Soc Arts & Crafts, with Reginald Bennett, Sarkis & Mary Chase Stratton; Pewabic Pottery. *Work:* Wayne State Univ; Ford Motor Co; Founders Gallery Loan Collection, Detroit Art Inst. *Comn:* Numerous pvt comns. *Exhib:* Mich Acad Sci, Art & Lett & Mich Regional Exhib, Univ Mich; Mich Artists Exhib, Detroit Inst Art; Mich Watercolor Soc; Blue Water Int Exhib, 73 & 74; Eastern Mich Int, 75; plus many one-man shows. *Awards:* Board of Directors' Award, Scarab Gold Medal Show, Detroit; Blue Water Int Exhib, Port Huron Mus, Mich; Eastern Mich Int Exhib Award. *Mem:* Nat Asn Prof Artists; Scarab Club. *Media:* Oil/Acrylic, Silver Point; Lost-Wax Bronze. *Mailing Add:* 23036 Ardmore Park St Clair Shores MI 48081

BURNS, TIMOTHY JOSEPH
GALLERY DIRECTOR, DEALER

b St Louis, Mo, April, 1950. *Study:* Acad Art, San Francisco, 69-70; Metrop State Col, Denver, 70-71; Webster Univ, St Louis, BA, 73. *Exhib:* Mid-America Five, St Louis Art Mus & Nelson Gallery, Kansas City, 74; Paper as Medium, Smithsonian Inst Traveling Exhib, 78-80; Chicago Int Art Expo, Navy Pier, Chicago, 83. *Pos:* Conservator fine arts, St Louis, 73-74; asst dir, Terry Moore Gallery, St Louis, 75-79; dir, Timothy Burns Gallery, 79- *Media:* Mixed. *Specialty:* Paintings, drawings, prints, photographs and sculpture by St Louis area artists. *Mailing Add:* 393 N Euclid Ave St Louis MO 63108

BURNSIDE, WESLEY M
HISTORIAN, PAINTER

b Mt Pleasant, Utah, Nov 6, 18. *Study:* Brigham Young Univ, BS, 41, MS, 49; Art Inst Chicago, 46; Art Students League, with Kenneth H Miller & Reginald Marsh, 49; Univ Utah, summers 50-54; Univ Calif, Los Angeles, 55-58; Ohio State Univ, PhD, 70. *Work:* Brigham Young Univ; Orem City Collection; Dixie Col Collection; Idaho State Univ Collection. *Pos:* Dir art acquisitions, Brigham Young Univ, 71- *Teaching:* Instr art & art hist, Idaho State Col, 48-55; prof art hist, Brigham Young Univ, 58- *Mem:* Nat Soc Lit & Arts. *Media:* Watercolor, Oil. *Res:* Utah artists; Maynard Dixon. *Collection:* Americana; Hudson River School & Western art. *Publ:* Auth, Maynard Dixon Artist of the West, Brigham Young Univ, 74. *Mailing Add:* c/o Brigham Young Univ Provo UT 84602

BUROS, LUELLA
PAINTER, DESIGNER

b Canby, Minn. *Study:* Teachers Col, Columbia Univ, 29-30 & 33-34; Rutgers Univ, 31-32; Ohio State Univ, 34-35. *Work:* Newark Mus, NJ; Montclair Art Mus, NJ; City Cape May, NJ. *Exhib:* Five Watercolor & Print Exhibs, Pa Acad Fine Arts, Philadelphia, 37-47; Contemp Exhib Painting & Sculpture, Golden Gate Int Expos, San Francisco, 39; Corcoran Biennial Art, Corcoran Gallery Art, Washington, DC, 39, 43 & 45; Four Int Exhibs of Watercolors, Art Inst Chicago, 40-43; Contemp Am Art Exhib, Artists for Victory, Metrop Mus Art, New York, 43. *Awards:* First Prize Watercolor, Contemp Va Oil & Watercolor Exhib, Norfolk Mus Arts & Sci, 44-45; Medal Honor Oil, Nat Asn Women Artists, Nat Acad, 53. *Mem:* NJ Watercolor Soc; Assoc Artists NJ (dir, 58-60); Nat Asn Women Artists; Philadelphia Watercolor Soc. *Media:* Watercolor. *Mailing Add:* 4651 E Coachlight Ln Tucson AZ 85718

BURPEE, JAMES STANLEY
PAINTER, INSTRUCTOR

b Oakland, Calif, Feb 12, 38. *Study:* San Jose State Col, BA, 58; Calif Col Arts & Crafts, with James Weeks, MFA, 60. *Exhib:* Wide Regional Ann Painting & Sculpture Exhib, Dallas Mus Fine Arts, Tex, 65 & 66; A Sense of Place: Artists & the American Land, Sheldon Mem Art Gallery, Lincoln, Nebr, 73-74; America 1976, Minneapolis Inst Arts, 77; one-man show, Col St Catherine, St Paul, Minn, 78; Figurative Painting, Macalaster Col, St Paul, 79; American Art; The Challenge of the Land, Pillsbury Co Sponsor, 81. *Teaching:* From instr to asst prof & chmn, Art Dept, Midwestern Univ, Wichita Falls, Tex, 60-67; from asst prof to assoc prof painting & drawing, Minneapolis Col of Art & Design, 67-; vis artist painting, Kansas City Art Inst, 74 & Calif Col of Arts & Crafts, 74 & 75. *Awards:* Individual Artist Grant, Minn State Arts Coun, 73; Nat Endowment Arts Artist-in-Residence, Volcanoes Nat Park, Hawaii, 73-74; Fel, MacDowell Colony, 76. *Media:* Acrylic. *Dealer:* Sunne Savage Gallery 105 Newberry St Boston MA. *Mailing Add:* 3208 Aldrich Ave S Minneapolis MN 55408

BURR, HORACE
CURATOR, SCULPTOR

b New Castle, Ind, Feb 9, 12. *Study:* DePauw Univ, BA; Univ Southern Calif, MA; Acad Fine Arts, Florence, Italy, cert; Univ Parma, Italy, Hon Dipl Merit, 81; Sem Int Mod & Contemp Art, Maestro di Pittura, 82; Accad D'Europe, hon degree, 83. *Exhib:* Eleven one-man shows & 81 exhibs in 42 cities & 14 states. *Teaching:* Prof hist Japanese art, Univ Va, 74-77; cur fine arts & art consult, James Madison Univ, Harrisburg, 77- *Awards:* Golden Centaur Prize, 82; Nations Prize, 83; Gold Medal Int Parliament, 83. *Bibliog:* The Ancient City (doc film), St Augustine Rec, 57; Sculpture of Horace Burr, 63; History of Contemporary Art, Accad Italia, 83. *Mem:* Albermarle Art Asn (pres, 55-65, emer pres, 65-). *Media:* Mixed Media. *Interests:* Developing permanent collections for exhibition and study in universities, colleges, museums and foundations. *Publ:* Seventy-six publications in fine arts. *Mailing Add:* Carrsgrove Stribling Ave Charlottesville VA 22902

BURROUGHS, MARGARET T G
LECTURER, PAINTER

b St Rose, La, Nov 1, 17. *Study:* Art Inst Chicago, BAE, 46, MAE, 48; Teacher's Col, Columbia Univ, 59-61; Lewis Univ, Hon PhD. *Work:* Atlanta Univ Art Collection; Howard Univ Art Collection; Ala A&M Univ Print Collection; Jackson State Col Art Collection, Miss; Johnson Publ Co. *Exhib:* One-woman shows, Mexico City, 52-53, USSR, 65, Poland, 65, South Side Art Ctr, Chicago, 72, 74 & 78 & YWCA, Chicago, 73. *Pos:* Founder & dir, Du Sable Mus African-Am Hist, Chicago, 61- *Teaching:* Art, Du Sable High Sch, Chicago, 46-69; teacher art hist, Art Inst Chicago, 68-69; teacher humanities, Kennedy-King City Col, 69-79. *Awards:* First Watercolor Award, Atlanta Univ, 55; Best in Show, Nat Conf Artists, Lincoln Univ, Jefferson City, Mo, 63; Third Place Sculpture, Atlanta Univ, 69. *Mem:* founder Nat Conf Artists (chmn, 61); founder Southside Art Ctr. *Media:* Watercolor, Oil. *Publ:* Contribr, Black World & Nat Conf Artists Bulletin; illusr, Jasper the Drummer Boy, Crowell, 50; illusr, What Shall I Tell My Children Who are Black?, 65 & For Malcolm, 67; auth, Did You Feed My Cow, 75. *Mailing Add:* 3806 S Michigan Ave Chicago IL 60653

BURROUGHS, MOLLY LUCE See Luce, Molly

BURROWS, SELIG S
COLLECTOR, HISTORIAN

b New York, NY, 1913. *Study:* Fordham Univ, grad, 33; NY Univ Law Sch, grad, 36. *Pos:* Trustee & chmn acquisitions comt, Norton Gallery, West Palm Beach, Fla, currently; trustee, Friends of Whitney Mus, currently. *Mem:* Soc Four Arts, Palm Beach, Fla. *Collection:* Late nineteenth and twentieth century American art; German expressionist and modern French paintings. *Mailing Add:* Serena Horseshoe Rd Mill Neck NY 11765

BURT, DAN
PAINTER

b Owensboro, Ky, Aug 17, 30. *Study:* Ramon Froman Sch Art, Cloudcroft, NMex; Simon Michael Sch Art, Rockport, Tex; also with Harold Roney, Joy Carrington & William H Earle. *Work:* Texaco Corp, Houston; Brownsville Art League Mus, Tex; Tex Tech Mus, Lubbock. *Exhib:* Knickerbocker Artists of

Am, New York, 79; Allied Artists Am, New York; Salmagundi Club, New York; Nat Arts Club, New York; Audubon Artists, New York; and others. *Teaching:* Outdoor oil & watercolor landscape painting, Hill Country Arts Foundation, Ingram, Tex, 76-82. *Awards:* Best of Show Award, Coppini Acad Fine Arts Exhib, San Antonio, 81; Gold Medal, Coppini Acad of Fine Arts, San Antonio, 76; Best of Show Award, Artists & Craftmen Associated Exhib, Dallas, 80. *Bibliog:* Harry Reed (auth), article, Southwest Art, 3/78; Harry Reed (auth), article, Art Voices S, 9-10/79. *Mem:* Coppini Acad Fine Arts, San Antonio (vpres, 71-72, pres, 73-74); Am Artists Prof League; Salmagundi Club; Tex Watercolor Soc; Southwestern Watercolor Soc. *Media:* Oil, Watercolor. *Dealer:* Raul Gutierrez Gallery 8940 Wurzbach Rd San Antonio TX. *Mailing Add:* 1304 Ford Kerrville TX 78028

BURT, DAVID SILL
SCULPTOR, WRITER
b Evanston, Ill, Feb 20, 17. *Study:* Harvard Univ, BA, 40. *Work:* Fine Art Ctr, Univ Wis-Milwaukee; US Art in Embassies Prog, Stamford Mus. *Comn:* Harvey Hubbell Co, 74; Phelps Dodge Co, 81; Waterway Tower, Dallas, 81; Century Plaza & Landmark Bldg, Stamford, Conn, 81; Excelsior Hotel, Tulsa, 81; and others. *Exhib:* Pa Acad Fine Arts Exhib, 64; New Eng Exhib, 65, 67, 69, 70, 77, 80 & 81; 18 one-man exhibs, New York, Conn, RI, Colo & Ireland. *Pos:* Promotion writer, Archit Forum, Indust Design & Interiors. *Mem:* Sculptors League; Silvermine Guild Artists. *Media:* Hammered & Braised Sheet Metal. *Publ:* Auth, Detour to sculpture, Am Artist Mag. *Mailing Add:* c/o Sculpture Ctr 167 East 69th St New York NY 10021

BURTCHAELL, DEANN See Jones, Claire

BURTON, SCOTT
SCULPTOR, CONCEPTUAL ARTIST
b Greensboro, Ala, June 23, 39. *Study:* Hans Hofmann Studio, Provincetown, 57-59; Columbia Univ, BA(magna cum laude), 62; NY Univ Grad Sch Eng, MA, 63. *Exhib:* One-Person Performance-Piece Exhibs, Whitney Mus Am Art, New York, 72, Mus Fine Arts, Boston, 73, Guggenheim Mus, New York, 76, Univ Calif, 80 & Weinberg Gallery, San Francisco, 80; Whitney Biennial, New York, 75; Parrish Art Mus, Southampton, NY, 76; Ten Artists/Artists Space, State Univ NY, Purchase, 79; Image and Object in Contemp Sculpture, Detroit Inst Arts, 79; and others. *Awards:* Nat Endowment Arts Visual-Arts Grants, 73 & 75; Creative Artists Pub Serv Prog Multi-Media Grant, 75; L C Tiffany Grant, 80. *Bibliog:* Athena T Spear (auth), Thoughts on Contemporary art, Allen Art Mus Bulletin, spring 73; Ronald Argelander (auth), Scott Burton's behavior tableaux, Drama Rev, NY, 9/73; article, Art-Rite Mag, NY, winter 75. *Media:* Miscellaneous, Found Objects; Live Performance. *Publ:* Auth, Instructions, In: Art in the Mind, Allen Mus, Oberlin, 70; auth, Street works 1969, Drama Rev, 3/72; auth, Three furniture works, Tri-Quarterly, winter 75. *Mailing Add:* c/o Max Protetch Gallery 37 W 57th St New York NY 10019

BUSA, PETER
PAINTER, SCULPTOR
b Pittsburgh, Pa, June 23, 14. *Study:* Carnegie Inst Technol, with Raymond Simboli, Sam Rosenberg, Alex Kostellow, Harry Sternberg & Thomas Hart Benton; Art Students League; Hans Hofmann Sch Fine Art. *Work:* Smithsonian Inst; Whitney Mus Am Art, Metrop Mus Art, New York; Walker Art Ctr; Tweed Gallery, Univ of Minn; plus others. *Exhib:* Art of the Century, Peggy Guggenheim, 46; Bertha Schaefer Gallery, New York, 49-51; Albright-Knox Art Gallery, Buffalo, NY, 54; Retrospective, Chrysler Art Mus, 59; Selections from Permanent Collections, Whitney Mus Am Art, 72; plus many others. *Pos:* Dir summer art prog, Southampton Col, 71. *Teaching:* NY Univ, 45-54; Cooper Union, 45-54; prof art, State Univ NY Col Buffalo, 54-57; prof art, Univ Minn, Minneapolis, 60-82, prof emer, 82- *Awards:* Spec Donor Award, Walker Art Ctr, 66; College of Liberal Arts Distinguished Teacher Award, Univ Minn, Minneapolis, 75; Guggenheim Award for Painting, US & Europe, 76-77. *Bibliog:* Peter Busa, Tweed Gallery, Univ Minn, 66; Sidney Simon (auth), Concerning the beginnings of the NY School, Art Int, summer 67. *Mem:* Col Art Asn Am; Artists Equity Asn (pres, Minn Chap, 62-65); life mem Art Students League. *Media:* Oil; Plaster, Wood. *Publ:* Auth, Creative Imagination in Science & Art, Univ Mich, 57; auth, Art to Eat & Diet, 67. *Mailing Add:* PO Box 1705 East Hampton NY 11937

BUSCAGLIA, JOSE
SCULPTOR, EDUCATOR
b San Juan, PR, Sept 15, 38. *Study:* Harvard Univ, BA(cum laude), 60; also with Enrique Monjo, sculptor, 58-62; Univ PR, MA, 77. *Work:* Robert Frost, Nat Portrait Gallery, Washington, DC; Dean Delmar Leighton, Harvard Univ; Autobiography of an Inspiration, Ponce Mus Art; Justice, US Fed Dist Court. *Comn:* Monuments (bronze), Rio Piedras, PR, 72 & Bar Asn Bldg, San Juan, PR, 73; Allegorical Figure (bronze), Munic Sch Bd 84, New York, 73; five sculptural groups (bronze, 11 ft high), Park of the Americas, San Juan, PR, 77; teachers monument, Univ PR, 83; and others. *Exhib:* One-man shows, Harvard Univ, Banco Popular at Rockefeller Ctr, Lisner Auditorium, George Washington Univ, 67; Thirty Years of Sculpture, Inst PR Cult, 76-77. *Pos:* Adv to minister of state, Develop of Intelligence, Rep of Venezuela, 79-; sr consult Bolt, Beranek & Newman Inc, Harvard-Venezuela Proj Intelligence, 79-83. *Teaching:* Prof art, Univ PR, Rio Piedras, 63-83; extension, Harvard Univ, 80. *Awards:* Gran Premio Puertorrigueno, Acad Arts & Sci PR, 67. *Bibliog:* Film, Not by Bread Alone, Esso Co, 65; cover story, Harvard Mag, 11-12/83. *Mem:* Acad Arts & Sci PR (bd mem, 64 & 69); Nat Sculpture Soc. *Media:* Bronze. *Publ:* Auth, Anatomia del proceso creativo, 66 & Creatiology as a new approach to the teaching of the arts, Acad Arts & Sci Bull, 67; La intuicion y la velosidad del reflejo, 71. *Mailing Add:* 23 Independence Rd Bedford MA 01730

BUSH, BEVERLY
PAINTER, SCULPTOR
b Kelso, Wash. *Study:* Univ Wash, BA; Nat Acad Design Sch Fine Arts; Art Students League. *Exhib:* Nat Asn Women Artists, 58; City Ctr, New York, 58; Art: USA, 59; Audubon Artists, 59; Seattle Art Mus, 64; and others. *Pos:* Ed, Nat News Letter, Artists Equity Asn, 58- *Awards:* Youth Friends Asn Scholar, Nat Acad Design, 54-55; Joseph Isador Merit Scholar, 55-57. *Mem:* Artists Equity Asn. *Mailing Add:* 3521 E Spruce St Seattle WA 98102

BUSH, CHARLES ROBERT See Robb, Charles

BUSH, DONALD JOHN
HISTORIAN, EDUCATOR
b San Francisco, Calif. *Study:* Ariz State Univ, BS, 59; Univ Notre Dame with Dr John Howett, MA(art), 64; Univ NMex with Clinton Adams, Van Deren Coke & Peter Walch, PhD(art hist), 73. *Teaching:* Teaching asst art, Univ Notre Dame, 63-64; chmn art dept, Univ Albuquerque, 64-75; assoc prof art hist & humanities, Ariz State Univ, 75-80; assoc prof design hist, Ariz State Univ, 80- *Mem:* Col Art Asn; Am Asn Univ Prof; Soc Architectural Historians. *Res:* Development of American industrial design and architecture. *Publ:* Auth, Streamlining and American industrial design, autumn 74; auth, The Streamlined Decade, George Braziller, 75; auth, Thorstein Veblen's economic aesthetic, Leonardo Mag, autumn 78; auth, Futurama--World's Fair as utopia, Alternative Futures, fall 79; auth, An Irish William Morris, Tiller, 84; and numerous art exhib catalogs & bk rev. *Mailing Add:* Dept of Design Sciences Ariz State Univ Tempe AZ 85281

BUSH, MARTIN H
MUSEUM DIRECTOR, HISTORIAN
b Amsterdam, NY, Jan 24, 30. *Study:* State Univ NY Albany, BA & MA, 58; Syracuse Univ, PhD, 66. *Collections Arranged:* Photo Realism: Rip-Off or Reality, 75; George Grosz, 75; Wayne Thiebaud, 75; Robert Goodnough, 75; Richard Pousette-Dart, 75; Duane Hanson, 76; W Eugene Smith, 77; Milton Avery, 78; Joan Miro, 78; Louise Nevelson, 78; Theodoros Stamos, 79; Kenneth Noland, 80; and many others. *Pos:* Dir, E A Ulrich Mus Art, Wichita State Univ, 71-, vpres acad resource develop, 74- *Teaching:* Instr, Syracuse Univ, 63-65, asst dean, 65-70. *Mem:* Am Asn Art Mus; Col Art Asn. *Res:* 20th century American art. *Publ:* Contribr, Isabel Bishop, Univ Ariz, 75; auth, Duane Hanson, 76; auth, Ernest Trova, 77; auth, Robert Goodnough, Abbeville, 82; auth, The Photographs of Gordon Parks, Ulrich Mus Art, 83; and many articles, brochures and catalogs. *Mailing Add:* Wichita State Univ Box 46 Wichita KS 67208

BUSH-BROWN, ALBERT
WRITER, EDUCATOR
b West Hartford, Conn, Jan 2, 26. *Study:* Princeton Univ, AB, 47, MFA(Woodrow Wilson Fel), 49, PhD, 58; Emerson Col, Hon LLD, 65; Providence Col, Hon HHD, 66; Mercy Col, Hon DFA, 76. *Pos:* Nat adv comt, Archives Am Art, 62-; mem, Nat Coun on The Arts, White House, 64-70; dir-at-large, Nat Coun Arts in Educ, 65-71; managing dir, Metrop Opera, 78-; dir, Barclays Bank, New York, 79-, chmn, 81-; pres, Nat Building Mus, 80- *Teaching:* Instr art & archaeol, Princeton Univ, 49-50; asst prof art & archit, Western Reserve Univ, 53-54; asst prof archit, Mass Inst Technol, 54-58, assoc prof & exec officer archit, 58-62; pres, RI Sch Design, 62-68; Bemis vis prof, Mass Inst Technol, 68-69; vpres, State Univ NY Buffalo, 69-71; chancellor, Long Island Univ, 71- *Awards:* Howard Found Fel, Brown Univ, 59-60; Ford Found Fel, 68-69; fel, Harvard Univ, John F Kennedy Inst & Joint Ctr for Urban Studies, 68-69. *Mem:* Century Asn; hon mem Am Inst Architects; Conference Bd; Coun Foreign Relations. *Publ:* Auth, Louis Sullivan, 60; co-auth, The Architecture of America: a Social Interpretation, 61; auth, Books, Bass, Barnstable, 67; auth, King Khalid Military City, Saudi Arabia, 78; auth, Louis Sullivan, Japan, 79; auth, numerous articles in encycl, art & archit journals, 52-65. *Mailing Add:* Piping Rock Rd Locust Valley NY 11560

BUSHMAN, DAVID FRANKLIN
PAINTER, EDUCATOR
b Toledo, Ohio, Aug 2, 45. *Study:* Univ Wis, BFA, 67; Univ Wis-Madison, MFA, 69; also with Al Leslie, Jack Beal, James Rosenquist & Richard Artschager. *Work:* Johnson Wax Co, Racine, Wis; Wis State J, Madison; Univ Wis-Madison; C M Bruckner Collection, New York; Madison Art Ctr, Wis; and others. *Comn:* Mural, Mr & Mrs G Lauderdale, Ft Lauderdale, Fla, 70; painting, H C Westerman, Brookfield Ctr, Conn, 73; portrait, Mr & Mrs S Crane, Chicago, 75; painting, Mr & Mrs James Stewart, Chicago, 75; painting, Racine Nat Bank, Wis, 80; and others. *Exhib:* One-man shows, Performing Arts Ctr, Ill Cent Col, Peoria, 80, Kans State Univ, Manhattan, 81; Gilman Gallery, Chicago, 80; Art Inst Chicago, 81; Reicher Gallery, Barat Col, Lake Forest, Ill, 81; Smithsonian Inst, Washington, DC, 82; Ill State Mus, Springfield, 83; Portland Art Mus, Ore, 83; and others. *Teaching:* Instr painting & drawing, Univ Wis-Madison, 67-69; asst prof painting & drawing, Univ Ill, Urbana-Champaign, 69-76, assoc prof, 76-; guest lectr, Louisville Art Ctr, Ky, 72; guest lectr, George Peabody Univ, 74, Univ Wis, 82. *Awards:* Cash Award, Nat Drawings, NY Univ, 69; Cash Award, Ill State Fair, 70; Award, Art Inst Chicago; and others. *Mem:* Col Art Asn; New Col Art Asn; Am Fedn Teachers. *Dealer:* Gilman Gallery 227 Ontario Chicago IL 60611. *Mailing Add:* Dept Fine Arts Univ Ill, Urbana Urbana IL 61801

BUSHMILLER, ERNIE PAUL
CARTOONIST
b New York, NY, Aug 23, 05. *Study:* Nat Acad Design. *Pos:* Cartoonist, syndicated comic strip, Nancy & Sun comic strip, Fritzi Ritz, United Features, 31- *Mem:* Soc Illusr; Nat Cartoonists Soc; Dutch Treat Club; Artists & Writers Asn. *Mailing Add:* 552 Haviland Rd Stamford CT 06903

BUSHNELL, KENNETH WAYNE
PAINTER, EDUCATOR
b Los Angeles, Calif, Oct 16, 33. *Study:* Univ Calif, Los Angeles, BA(art), 56; Univ Hawaii, MFA(painting), 60. *Work:* Honolulu Acad Art & State Found Cult & Arts, Hawaii; Mich State Univ, East Lansing; Bibliotheque Nationale, Paris; Corcoran Gallery, Washington, DC. *Comn:* Commemorative portrait, comn by colleagues of Dr H B Tukey, East Lansing, Mich, 68; portrait of Dr Richard Lee, comn by Sch Publ Health, Univ Hawaii, 69; three panel painting, comn by Dr & Mrs Thole, Philadelphia, 80; Hawaii Suite (five-color lithography), HMK Fine Arts Inc, New York, 81; paintings, Finance Factors Bldg, 83. *Exhib:* Painting USA: The Figure, New York Mus Mod Art, 62; Baltimore Mus Art, 62; Drawings USA, St Paul Art Ctr, Minn, 63; 158th Ann Exhib, Pa Acad Fine Arts, Philadelphia, 63; NW Printmakers Ann, Seattle Mus & Portland Mus, 64; New Talent in the West, Salt Lake City Art Ctr, 68; Calif/Hawaii Exhib, San Diego Mus, 70; Int Print Biennial, Krakow, Poland, 74; Int Print Biennial, Honolulu Acad Art, 78-82. *Pos:* Bd mem, Hawaii Artists League, 81. *Teaching:* Prof art painting, Univ Hawaii, 61-81; prof art painting, C W Post Ctr, Long Island Univ, 78-79 & 83. *Awards:* Purchase Award, Honolulu Acad Art, 68; First Award Painting, Calif/Hawaii Exhib, San Diego Mus, 74; John Wyatt Gregg Award, Honolulu Acad Art, 73. *Mem:* Honolulu Printmakers (pres, 71); Nat Arts Club New York; Hawaii Artists League. *Media:* All Media. *Dealer:* Sande Webster 2018 Locust St Philadelphia PA; Art Loft 637 Sheridan st Honolulu HI 96813. *Mailing Add:* 29 E 22nd St 7N New York NY 10010

BUSHNELL, MARIETTA P
LIBRARIAN
b Vienna, Austria, July 26, 32; US citizen. *Study:* Wheaton Col, Norton, Mass, BA(art hist); Drexel Univ, Philadelphia, MLS. *Pos:* Photograph librn, Mus of Fine Arts, Boston, 56-61; asst, Slide Dept, Mus of Art, Philadelphia, 68-72; librn, Pa Acad of Fine Arts, 75- *Mem:* Art Librn Soc NAm. *Mailing Add:* Pa Acad of Fine Arts Broad & Cherry Sts Philadelphia PA 19102

BUSINO, ORLANDO FRANCIS
CARTOONIST
b Binghamton, NY, Oct 10, 26. *Study:* State Univ Iowa, BA, 52. *Pos:* Cartoonist, Sat Eve Post, McCall's, Ladies Home Jour, Sat Rev, Look, True, Argosy, Boys' Life, Family Circle & other US & foreign mags. *Awards:* Best Mag Cartoonist of Year, Nat Cartoonists Soc, 65, 67 & 68. *Mem:* Nat Cartoonists Soc; Mag Cartoonists Guild. *Mailing Add:* 12 Shadblow Hill Rd Ridgefield CT 06877

BUSSABARGER, ROBERT FRANKLIN
SCULPTOR, PAINTER
b Corydon, Ind, Sept 17, 22. *Study:* Wittenburg Univ, with Ralston Thompson, AB, 44; Mich State Univ, with John de Martelli, Louis Raynor & Carl Schmidt, MA, 47; Ohio State Univ, with Paul Bogatay & Edgar Littlefield, 49-51. *Work:* Air India Collection, Bombay, India; Springfield Art Mus, Mo; Mo Hist Soc, Columbia. *Exhib:* Sculptors Gallery, St Louis, Mo, 66; Acad Fine Arts, Calcutta, India, 69; Am Cult Ctr, Bombay, India, 69; one-man show, Chemould Art Gallery, Bombay, India, 78 & Urja Art Gallery, Baroda, India. *Collections Arranged:* Univ Mo Fine Arts Gallery, 55-59 & 63-67; Indian art exhib based on Bussabarger & Robins Collections, Univ Mo, Stephens Col, Westminster Col & Carleton Col. *Teaching:* Teacher art, Benton Harbor Jr & Sr High Sch, Mich, 48-49; asst prof art, Stephen F Austin State Univ, Nacogdoches, Tex, 51-53; prof art, Univ Mo-Columbia, 53-, chmn dept, 70-73. *Awards:* Merit Award in Sculpture, 30th Springfield Ann, Mo, 60; Fulbright Fel India, 61-62; Hays Univ SAsia Ctr Fac Fel, 68-69. *Bibliog:* L Bhattacharia (auth), Robert Bussabarger, US Info Serv, 10/62; A B Pine (auth), Bussabarger & ceramic art, Mo Alumnus, 11/60. *Mem:* Mo Crafts Coun; Columbia Art League; Mid-Am Art Conf. *Media:* Ceramic, Metal; Pastel, Watercolor. *Publ:* ed, John Sloans Etchings, Univ Mo, 67; coauth & illusr, The Everyday Art of India, Dover, 68; coauth, The Makara, Archaeology, 1/70; coauth, Folk images of Sanjhi Devi, Atribus Asiae, 7/75; coauth, Mirrored Images, Splendors of Tamil Nadu, Marg, 80. *Mailing Add:* 1914 Princeton Columbia MO 65201

BUSTER, JACQUELINE MARY
DEALER, LECTURER
b Huntington, NY, Nov 1, 26. *Study:* Univ WVa; Bradley Univ, BA. *Pos:* Gallery dir, Peoria Art Guild, Ill, 70-72; dir & owner, Tower Park Gallery, Peoria Heights, Ill, 72- *Specialty:* Contemporary mid-western paintings and graphics and other contemporary artists. *Mailing Add:* Tower Park Gallery 4709 Prospect Rd Peoria Heights IL 61614

BUTCHKES, SYDNEY
PAINTER, COLLAGE ARTIST
b Covington, Ky, Oct 13, 22. *Study:* Cincinnati Art Acad, Ohio; Art Students League; New Sch Social Res, New York. *Work:* Metrop Mus; Brooklyn Mus, NY; Cincinnati Art Mus; Wadsworth Atheneum, Hartford, Conn; Nat Collection Fine Arts, Smithsonian Inst, Washington, DC; and others. *Comn:* Sculpture for lobby of Financial Progs Bldg, Denver, 69; hanging sculpture for bar of Ritz Carlton Hotel, Boston, 69; painting for lobby of Skidmore, Owings, Merrill, Chicago, 70; paintings, World Trade Ctr, NY & Continental Tel Co, Washington, DC. *Exhib:* Art for the Collector, San Francisco Mus Art, 65; Painting Without a Brush, Inst Contemp Art, Boston, 65; Painting Out from the Wall, Des Moines Art Ctr, Iowa, 67; Plastic as Plastic, Mus Contemp Crafts, New York, 69; Mus Acquisitions, Colorado Springs Art Ctr, 69. *Mem:* Abstr Am Artists. *Media:* Acrylic Paint; Acrylic Sheet. *Mailing Add:* Sagg Main St Sagaponack NY 11962

BUTERA, ANNE FABBRI
MUSEUM DIRECTOR, CURATOR
b Norristown, Pa. *Study:* Radcliffe Col, AB(cum laude); Bryn Mawr Col, MA(art hist), 71; Univ Calif, Berkeley, 79; Princeton Univ, NEH Scholar, Dept of Art & Archaeol, 80. *Collections Arranged:* Seven Afro-American Artists of the Delaware Valley (auth, catalog), 81; Tradition and Innovations, 81; Five Hispanic Artists of Pennsylvania (auth, catalog), 82; Social Realism and the Figure, 82; Celebration of New Jersey Artists (auth, catalog), 83; and others. *Pos:* Art critic & art ed, The Drummer, Philadelphia, 76-79; art critic, The Bulletin, Philadelphia, 79-80 & WXPN Express, 80-81; dir & cur, Alfred O Deshong Mus, Widener Univ, Chester, Pa, 80-82; Noyes Mus, Oceanville, NJ, 82- *Teaching:* Lectr hist art, Villanova Univ, Pa, 71-73 & Drexel Univ, Philadelphia, 74-76. *Bibliog:* Article, Art Matters, 6/83. *Mem:* Print Club, Philadelphia; MUSE Found Visual Arts; Int Asn Art Critics; Am Asn Mus; Col Art Asn. *Res:* art theory; mannerist art and iconography. *Publ:* Auth, Patience pays at Dr Barnes's Bks & Arts, 1/80; auth, Three sculptors, 1/80, auth, Harry Bertoia, 2/80 & auth, Judith Ingram, 3/80, Arts Mag. *Mailing Add:* 225 Church St 6F Philadelphia PA 19106

BUTLER, BYRON C
DEALER, COLLECTOR
b Carroll, Iowa, Aug 10, 18. *Study:* Univ Calif, Los Angeles, 36-69; Columbia Col Physicians & Surgeons, MD, 43, Columbia Univ, MedScD, 50. *Work:* Phoenix Art Mus, Ariz; NASA, Houston, Tex, Smithsonian Inst, DC; plus many others. *Comn:* Large canvas by R C Gorman of Hohokam Indians Masked Dancers, St Lukes Hosp, Phoenix, 71. *Exhib:* Am Indian Art Collection, Heard Mus, Phoenix, Oklahoma City Mus, Okla, Atlanta Mus, Ga, Northern Ariz Mus, Flagstaff & Millicent Rogers Mus, Taos, NMex, 57-73. *Collections Arranged:* Yaqui Indian Art, Heard Mus, 77. *Pos:* Mem bd dirs, Heard Mus, 68-74; dealer, Art Consult Ltd, Phoenix, currently. *Bibliog:* Clara Lee Tanner (auth), Southwest Indian Paintings, Univ Ariz Press, 73; Guy & Doris Monthan (auth), Art and Indian Individualists, 75 & Doris Monthan (auth), R C Gorman Lithographs, 78, Northland Press. *Specialty:* American Indian art; space art; classical French 19th century art; Yaqui art; Chinese art. *Dealer:* Art Consult Ltd 550 W Thomas Rd Phoenix AZ 85013. *Mailing Add:* 6302 N 38th St Paradise Valley AZ 85253

BUTLER, JAMES D
PRINTMAKER, PAINTER
b Ft Dodge, Iowa, Aug 30, 45. *Study:* Omaha Univ, Nebr, BS, 67; Univ Nebr, Lincoln, MFA, 70. *Work:* Brooklyn Mus, NY; Brit Mus, London, Eng; Tamarind Inst, Albuquerque, NMex; Libr of Cong, Washington, DC; Smithsonian Inst, Washington, DC. *Comn:* First Ill Print Comn, Ill Arts Coun, 73. *Exhib:* Corp Collections Show, Minn Mus of Art, St Paul, 72; Prints: Midwest Invitational, Walker Art Ctr, Minneapolis, 73; 19th Nat Print Exhib, Brooklyn Mus, 74; Mod Printmaking Exhib of Contemp Prints, Bevier Gallery, Rochester Inst of Technol, NY, 74; New American Colorists, World Print Coun, San Francisco, 81; 30 American Printmakers, Columbus, Ohio, 82; and others. *Teaching:* Asst prof, Southern Ill Univ, Edwardsville, 70-76; assoc prof, Ill State Univ, Normal, 76-81, prof, 81- *Awards:* Robert Cooke Enlow Award, 1971 Mid-States Art Exhib, Evansville Mus of Arts & Sci, Ind, 71; First Place, Fine Art of Printmaking, Lexington, Ky, Nat Soc of Arts & Lett, 71; Nat Endowment Arts, 75-76 & 79. *Bibliog:* Clinton Adams & Susan Ellis (auths), Drawing Color Separations on Surfaced Mylar, Tamarind Tech Papers, 74; Experiments in affordable custom lithography, Print News, Vol 3, 2-3/81. *Mem:* Mid-Am Col Art Asn; Col Art Asn. *Media:* Lithography; Drawing, Oil. *Dealer:* Associated American Artists New York NY. *Mailing Add:* 102 Warner Bloomington IL 61701

BUTLER, JOSEPH THOMAS
CURATOR, WRITER
b Winchester, Va, Jan 25, 32. *Study:* Univ Md, BS, 54; Univ Ohio, MA, 55; Univ Del, MA(Winterthur Fel), 57. *Collections Arranged:* Divided Loyalties, Philipsburg Manor, North Tarrytown, NY, 76-79 & Four Centuries of History, A Decade of Restoration. *Pos:* Cur, Sleepy Hollow Restorations, Tarrytown, NY, 57-; Am ed, The Connoisseur, 68-78; ed bd, Art & Antiques, 78- *Teaching:* Adj assoc prof archit, Columbia Univ, 71-81. *Mem:* Nat Arts Club; Furniture Hist Soc; Victorian Soc in Am; Am Ceramic Circle. *Res:* American decorative arts. *Publ:* Auth, Candleholders in America, 1650-1900, 67; coauth, The Arts in America, the 19th Century, 70; auth, Washington Irving's Sunnyside, 75; auth, Van Cortlandt Manor, 78; auth, Sleepy Hollow Restorations: A Cross Section of the Collection, 83; and others. *Mailing Add:* 222 Martling Ave Tarrytown NY 10591

BUTLER, MARIGENE H
CONSERVATOR
b Ann Arbor, Mich, July 20, 31. *Study:* Mt Holyoke Col, AB, 53; Fogg Art Mus, Harvard Univ, 53-55; Art Inst Chicago, 66-68. *Pos:* Asst conservator, Art Inst Chicago, 68-70, assoc conservator, 70-73; dir & head training, Intermuseum Lab Oberlin, Ohio, 73-78; head conserv, Philadelphia Mus Art, 78- *Mem:* Fel Int Inst Conserv Hist & Artistic Works; fel Royal Micros Soc; fel Am Inst Conserv Hist & Artistic Works; Quekett Micros Soc. *Publ:* Auth, Portrait of a lady by Frans Hals, Mus Studies 5, 70; auth, Technical note, In: Painting in Italy in the 18th Century: Rococo to Romanticism, Art Inst Chicago, 70; auth, Application of the polarizing microscopy in the conservation of painting and other works of art, Int Inst Conserv Hist & Artistic Works Bulletin, 71; auth, Technical note, In: Paintings by Renoir, Art Inst Chicago, 73; auth, An investigation of pigments and techniques in the Cezanne painting Chestnut Trees, Art Inst Chicago Bulletin, 73. *Mailing Add:* Philadelphia Mus of Art Box 7646 Philadelphia PA 19101

BUTTER, TOM
SCULPTOR, INSTRUCTOR
b Amityville, NY, Oct 19, 52. *Study:* Antioch Col, 70-71; Philadelphia Col Art, BFA, 75; Wash Univ, St Louis, Mo, MFA, 77. *Work:* Acad Fine Arts, Philadelphia; Metrop Mus Art, New York; Chase Manhattan Bank; Prudential Insurance Co Am. *Exhib:* Critical Perspectives, PS 1, LIC, New York, 82; American Abstraction Now, ICA Va Mus, 82; Language, Drama, Source and Vision, New Mus, New York, 83; one-person shows, Lawrence Oliver Gallery, Philadelphia, 83 & Grace Borgenicht Gallery, 83; and others. *Teaching:* Lectr 3-dimensional design, Philadelphia Col Art, 78- *Awards:* Nat Endowment Arts Grant, 80 & 82. *Bibliog:* Wade Saunders (auth), article, Art Am, 3/83; Kate Linker (auth), article, Artforum, 11/83; and others. *Dealer:* Grace Borgenicht Gallery Inc 724 Fifth Ave New York NY 10019. *Mailing Add:* 63 E Broadway New York NY 10002

BUTTERBAUGH, ROBERT CLYDE
SCULPTOR, EDUCATOR
b Freeport, Ill, May 28, 31. *Study:* Univ of the Pac, BFA, 54; Claremont Grad Sch, with Paul Darrow MFA, 62. *Work:* Sunderland Col Art, Eng. *Comn:* Sculpture relief (copper sheet), Temple Beth El, Salinas, Calif, 64; sculpture (welded corten steel), T Merrill Hall, Hartnell Col, Salinas, 65; fountain (redwood & cast bronze), Cent Plaza Bldg, 66; sculpture (redwood & plastic), Salinas City Hall Foyer, 68; sculpture group & low relief (cast concrete), Aquatic Complex, Hartnell Col, 73; Children's Playground (steel & concrete), Salinas, 80. *Exhib:* Midland Group Gallery, Nottingham, Eng, 69; Cerritos 70, Norwalk, Calif, 70; Form and the Inner Eye, Los Angeles, Calif, 71; Southern Ore Col Gallery, Ashland, 71; Univ Mich, Ann Arbor, 75; and others. *Teaching:* Prof art, Hartnell Col, 62-; lectr sculpture, Sunderland Col Art, 68-69. *Awards:* Fulbright-Hays travel grant, 68-69. *Media:* Plastics, Metals. *Mailing Add:* 908 Riker St Salinas CA 93901

BUTTERFIELD, DEBORAH KAY
SCULPTOR, EDUCATOR
b San Diego, Calif, May 7, 49. *Study:* Univ Calif, Davis, BA, 71, MFA, 73. *Work:* Whitney Mus Am Art, New York; San Francisco Mus Contemp Art, Calif; Israel Mus, Jeusalem; Walker Art Ctr, Minneapolis, Minn. *Exhib:* 2 Sculptors, Univ Mus Berkeley, Calif, 74; Whitney Biennial & The Decade in Review, Whitney Mus Am Art, New York, 79; 8 Sculptors, Albright-Knox Gallery, Buffalo, 79; Israel Mus, Jerusalem, 80; Arco Ctr Visual Art, 81; Walker Art Ctr, Minneapolis, 82; Dallas Mus Fine Arts, 82; Oakland, 83. *Teaching:* Asst prof sculpture, Univ Wis-Madison, 75-76; asst prof sculpture, Mont State Univ, Bozeman, 79- *Awards:* Nat Endowments Arts Grant, 77 & 80; Guggenheim Grant, 80. *Bibliog:* Thomas Albright (auth), Unique balance of realism, art, San Francisco Chronicle, 6/15/74; Alan G Artner (auth), Sculptor Butterfield plunges deeper into a substantial body of work, Chicago Tribune, 5/18/79; Kay Larsen (auth), Behold a pale horse (or two), Village Voice, 11/26/79. *Media:* Natural Materials, Steel. *Dealer:* O K Harris Gallery 383 W Broadway New York NY 10012; Zolla Lieberman Gallery 368 W Huron Chicago IL 60610. *Mailing Add:* 11229 Cottonwood Rd Bozeman MT 59715

BUTTS, H DANIEL, III
GALLERY DIRECTOR
b Pittsburgh, Pa, July 15, 39. *Study:* Yale Univ, BA, 60, BFA, 61; Pa State Univ, MA, 62. *Pos:* Dir, Arts & Crafts Ctr Pittsburgh, 65-68; dir, Mansfield Art Ctr, 68- *Teaching:* Instr hist art, painting & drawing, Shady Side Acad, Pittsburgh, 62-65. *Mailing Add:* c/o Mansfield Art Ctr 700 Marion Ave Mansfield OH 44903

BUZZELLI, JOSEPH ANTHONY
PAINTER, SCULPTOR
b Old Forge, Pa, May 6, 07. *Study:* Art Students League; Univ Southern Calif; Beaux-Arts & Grande Chaumiere, Paris, France. *Work:* Philadelphia Pub Libr, Pa. *Comn:* One Religion, Early New York City to Present & Man Striving for Peace (murals), Fed Detention House, New York, 44; The Pool, Wiltwyck Sch for Boys, 45. *Exhib:* Whitney Mus Am Art; Smithsonian Inst; Art USA, New York; Metrop Mus Art; Carnegie Art Inst; Anti-Pollution Exhib, Sarasota Art Asn, Fla, 78; The Future of SW Fla by Design or Default, Univ South Fla New Col, Sarasota; Environmental Art & Man, 80; and others. *Teaching:* Instr, Henry St Settlement House, Educ Alliance, Long Beach Art Ctr & Brooklyn Mus Wiltwyck Sch for Boys & Youth House, formerly. *Mem:* Artists Equity. *Media:* Enamels, Oil; Metals, Woods. *Mailing Add:* 608 N Casey Key Osprey FL 33559

BYARD, CAROLE MARIE
PAINTER, ILLUSTRATOR
b Atlantic City, NJ, July 22, 41. *Study:* Fleisher Art Mem, sculpture with Aurelius Renzetti; New York-Phoenix Sch Design, painting with Felix & Trini DeCosio, cert. *Comn:* Religious mural, House of Light, Ibaden, Nigeria, 72; panel for Kwanza celebration, Studio Mus, Harlem, NY, 73 & 74. *Exhib:* In Her Own Image, Fleisher Art Mem, Philadelphia, 74; Children of Africa, Am Mus Natural Hist, New York, 74-75; Sojourn, Carole Byard, Valerie Maynard, Gallery 1199, New York, 77; Amherst Univ, 77; Gallery 1199, New York, 78. *Pos:* Pres, Darshan, New York, 74-; mural artist, NJ State Coun on the Arts, 76; US artist partic, FESTAC, Lagos Nigeria, 77; artist-in-residence, NY Found Arts, 78. *Teaching:* Instr life drawing & basic drawing, New York-Phoenix Sch Design, 68-71; instr painting, First Fruits Prog, Metrop Mus Art, New York, 74- *Awards:* Ford Found Travel Grant, Inst Int Educ, 72; Unique New Yorker Art Award, 77; Coretta Scott King Award for Africa Dream, 78. *Bibliog:* Barbara Cohen (auth), Careers (filmstrip), Harcourt Brace Javanovich, 74; Marla Hoffman (auth), Two women who paint, World Mag, Long View Publ, 74; Helen King (auth), Carole Byard speaks with her art, In: What It Is, Let's Save the Children Inc. *Mem:* Westbeth Graphic Artist; Black Artist Guild. *Publ:* Illusr, The Sycamore Tree, African Folktales, Doubleday, 74; illusr, Under Christopher's Hat, Scribners, 72; illusr, Arthur Mitchell, 75, auth, Africa Dream, 77 & auth, I Can Do It By Myself, 78, Crowell. *Mailing Add:* 4463 West St New York NY 10014

BYARS, DONNA
SCULPTOR, COLLAGE ARTIST
b Rock Island, Ill. *Study:* Stephens Col, Columbia, Mo; Iowa State Univ, BA; Parsons Sch of Design, New York. *Work:* Va Mus of Fine Arts, Richmond. *Comn:* Site sculpture, Bard/Hudson Valley Studies, 78; site sculpture, New Wilderness Found, 78; site sculpture, Wave Hill, New York, 79. *Exhib:* Aldrich Mus Contem Art, Ridgefield, Conn, 75-76; one-person shows, AIR Gallery, 77 & 79; Alternative Mus, New York 80; Lunds Konsthall, Lunds, Sweden, 81; Schweinfurth Mus, Auburn, NY, 82; Kulturhust, Stockholm, Sweden, 82; and many others. *Teaching:* Instr drawing, Parsons Sch of Design, 76-; instr collage, New Sch for Social Res, New York, 77- *Awards:* Artist-in-residence grant, Palisades Interstate Park, Am the Beautiful Fund, Washington, DC, 76; Creative Artists Pub Serv Program Fel, 82. *Bibliog:* Ellen Lubell (auth), articles, 12/75, 3/76 & 9/77, Arts Mag; Lucy Lippard (auth), Overlay: Ancient Images and Contemporary Art, Pantheon, 83; Lynn Zelevansky (auth), article, Art News, 10/83; and many others. *Mem:* Col Art Asn. *Dealer:* AIR Gallery 63 Crosby New York NY 10012. *Mailing Add:* 5-7 Woodworth Ave Yonkers NY 10701

BYE, RANULPH (DEBAYEUX)
PAINTER
b Princeton, NJ, June 17, 16. *Study:* Philadelphia Col Art; Art Students League. *Work:* Mus Fine Arts, Boston; Munson-Williams-Proctor Inst, Utica, NY; Reading Pub Mus, Pa; Smithsonian Inst, Washington, DC; Pa Hist & Mus Comn, Harrisburg, Pa. *Comn:* Mine Force (paintings of naval base), US Navy Dept, Charleston, SC, 66. *Exhib:* Ann Exhibs, Allied Artists Am, Am Watercolor Soc, Philadelphia Watercolor Club, Salmagundi Club, Nat Arts Club New York & others. *Teaching:* Instr, Moore Col Art, Philadelphia, 49-79. *Awards:* Goldsmith Award, Am Watercolor Soc, 73; Eastman Prize Watercolor, 72, Louis E Seley Cash Purchase Prize, 78, Salmagundi Club. *Bibliog:* Wendy Buehr (auth), Station Closed, Am Heritage Press, 66. *Mem:* Salmagundi Club; Am Watercolor Soc; Allied Artists Am; assoc Nat Acad Design; plus others. *Media:* Watercolor, Oil. *Publ:* Auth, Seascapes and Landscapes, 56 & Watercolor Technique American Artists, 66, Watson-Guptill; auth, The Vanishing Depot, Livingston, 73 & Haverford House, 2nd ed 83; auth, Victorian Sketchbook, Haverford House, 80. *Mailing Add:* Mechanicsville PA 18934

BYNUM, E ANDERSON (ESTHER PEARL)
CURATOR, PRINTMAKER
b Henderson, Tex, Dec 19, 22. *Study:* Dallas Mus Fine Arts, 52; NTex State Univ, BA, 65; Univ Md, MA, 72, advan grad specialist cert, 73; also lithography with Tadeusz Lapinski. *Work:* US Civil Serv Bldg, Washington, DC; Montgomery Co Contemp Print Collection & Montgomery Co Pub Schs, Md. *Exhib:* New York Int Art Show, 70; Baltimore Mus, 73-74; Jersey City Mus, NJ, 74; 26th Ann Exhib, McNay Art Inst, San Antonio, 75 & 32nd Ann, 81, Tex Watercolor Soc; Lowe Art Mus, Univ Miami, Fla, 75. *Pos:* Cur, Four Oaks Gallery, Henderson, Tex, 80- *Teaching:* Teacher art, Montgomery Co Pub Schs, Rockville, Md, 65-75, elem art coordr, 75-79. *Mem:* Tex Watercolor Soc; Am Craft Coun; Graphics Soc. *Media:* Watercolor, Lithographs. *Publ:* Contribr, monthly visual arts article, Henderson Daily Newspaper. *Dealer:* Four Oaks Gallery 709 Hwy 43 Henderson TX 75652. *Mailing Add:* 711 Highway 43 Henderson TX 75652

BYRD, D GIBSON
EDUCATOR, PAINTER
b Tulsa, Okla, Feb 1, 23. *Study:* Univ Tulsa, with Alexandre Hogue, BA; Univ Iowa, MA. *Work:* Butler Inst Am Art, Youngstown, Ohio; Philbrook Art Ctr, Tulsa; Kalamazoo Art Ctr, Mich; Wright Art Ctr, Beloit Col; Madison Art Ctr, Wis. *Exhib:* Walker Art Ctr Biennial Exhib, Minneapolis, 58; 2nd Nat Drawing Exhib, Univ Wis-Green Bay, 70; Arts: USA II, Northern Ill Univ, 71; Wisconsin Directions, Milwaukee Art Ctr, 75; State of the Art: Wisconsin Painting and Drawing, Kohler Art Ctr, 82; and others. *Pos:* Dir, Kalamazoo Art Ctr, 52-55. *Teaching:* Prof art, Univ Wis-Madison, 55-; vis lectr, Sch Art Educ, Birmingham, Eng, 65-66. *Mem:* Col Art Asn. *Media:* Oil, Gouache. *Publ:* Auth, The artist-teacher in America, Col Art J, winter 63-64; auth, Theodore Robinson (exhib monogr), Univ Wis, 64; auth, Artist-teacher in America: John Sloan, Sch Arts Mag, 66; auth, Visiting artists: thoughts & second thoughts, Visual Arts Educ, 70; auth, Thomas Hart Benton (exhib catalog), Madison Art Ctr, 70. *Dealer:* Bradley Galleries 2565 N Downer Ave Milwaukee WI 53211; Edgewood Orchard Galleries Door County. *Mailing Add:* Dept of Art Univ Wis Madison WI 53711

BYRD, ROBERT JOHN
ILLUSTRATOR, INSTRUCTOR
b Atlantic City, NJ, Jan 11, 42. *Study:* Philadelphia Mus Col Art, BFA(graphic arts), 66. *Work:* Free Libr Philadelphia; Philadelphia Col Art. *Exhib:* Soc Illusr, New York, 71-77; Graphis Press, Zurich, Switz, 74-77; Philadelphia Art Alliance, 74; Bologna Worlds Children's Bk Fair, Italy, 75; Design & Illustration: USA, Teheran, Iran, 78; Graphis Poster & Ann, Zurich, 78-79. *Teaching:* Portfolio sem illusr, Philadelphia Col Art, 76-77; adj instr illus, Moore Col Art, Philadelphia, 77- *Awards:* Citation Merit, Soc Illusr, 76; Jr Lit Award for The Gondolier of Venice, 76 & The Detective of London, 78. *Bibliog:* Diana Klemin (auth), The portfolio of Robert Byrd, Am Artist,

71; Linda Munich & Marty Jacobs (producers), For Your Information, WKBS TV, 78. *Mem:* Philadelphia Children's Reading Round Table; Illusr Guild (Graphic Arts Guild). *Publ:* Illusr, Rebecca Hatpin, 73, Pinch Penny Mouse, 74, The Gondolier of Venice, 76 & The Detective of London, 78, Windmill Bks. *Mailing Add:* 409 Warwick Rd Haddonfield NJ 08033

BYRNE, CHARLES JOSEPH
CONSULTANT, GRAPHIC ARTIST
b Louisville, Ky, Oct 15, 43. *Study:* Univ Louisville, BS; Wayne State Univ. *Work:* Detroit Inst of Arts, Mich; Mus of Mod Art, New York. *Comn:* Various Exhib Designs, Detroit Inst of Arts, 73-80; wall graphic, Interior Designers Guild, San Diego, Calif, 77. *Exhib:* 15th Ann, Commun Arts Mag, Palo Alto, Calif, 74; Am Inst Graphic Arts Ann, New York, 75; Soc Typographic Arts, Chicago, 80 & 82; Cincinnati Mus Art Biennial, 81; Brodie Art Gallery, Univ Cincinnati, 81 & 82; New York Art Dirs Club, 82 & 83; and others. *Pos:* Cur, Dept of Fine Arts, Univ Louisville, Ky, 63-66, asst univ designer, 66-70; chief designer graphics & signage, Smith, Hinchman & Grylls Assoc, Inc, Detroit, 70-76. *Teaching:* Instr, Interior Designers Guild, San Diego, 77-78; instr, Cincinnati Acad Art, 80; adj fac, Univ Cincinnati, 81- *Awards:* Commun Arts Mag Award, 74 & 81; Commun Graphics Award, Am Inst of Graphic Arts, 75 & 82; Awards, Art Dirs Club Cincinnati, 79-83. *Bibliog:* Articles, Print Mag, 82 & 83, Graphis, Zurich, 82 & Signs of the Times Mag, 11/83. *Media:* Print Graphics. *Publ:* Coauth, Computer Graphics, Mich Soc Archit Bull, 4/75; coauth, Downtown vs Suburban Shopping Centers: a Clear Case of Identity, Detroit Free Press Mag, 2/76. *Mailing Add:* c/o Colophon 405 Lafayette Ave Cincinnati OH 45220

BYRNES, JAMES BERNARD
MUSEUM DIRECTOR, HISTORIAN
b New York, NY, Feb 19, 17. *Study:* Nat Acad Design, New York, 36-38; Am Artists Sch, New York, 38-40; Art Students League, 41-42; Univ Perugia, Rome, First Meschini, 51-52. *Collections Arranged:* Edgar Degas, His Family & Friends in New Orleans (with catalog), 65; Odyssey of an Art Collector--the Collection of Mr & Mrs Frederick S Stafford, Paris (with catalog), 66; Arts of Ancient & Modern Latin America (with catalog), 68; Rothko (with catalog), 74; Artist as Collector--Ethnic Art (with catalog), 75. *Pos:* Cur mod & contemp art, Los Angeles Co Mus, 46-54; dir, Colorado Springs Fine Arts Ctr, 54-56; assoc dir, NC Mus Art, 56-58, dir, 58-60; dir, New Orleans Mus Art, 61-72; dir, Newport Harbor Art Mus, Newport Beach, Calif, 72-75; consult fine arts. *Teaching:* Vis prof hist 20th century art, Univ Fla, 60-61. *Awards:* Knight in the Order of Leopold II, Belg Govt, 72. *Mem:* Asn Art Mus Dirs; Appraisers Asn Am; Am Asn Mus; Int Coun Mus; hon life mem Am Inst Designers; and others. *Res:* Nineteenth and twentieth century art; seventeenth century Dutch art; pre-Columbian and African art. *Mailing Add:* James B Byrnes & Assoc 7820 Mulholland Dr Los Angeles CA 90046

BYRON, CHARLES ANTHONY
DEALER
b Istanbul, Turkey, Dec 15, 19. *Study:* Ecole Libre Sci Polit, Paris, France; Univ Paris; Harvard Univ; BA, LLB & MA. *Pos:* Dir & owner, Byron Gallery, New York. *Mem:* Art Dealers Asn Am, Inc. *Specialty:* Contemporary and surrealist art. *Mailing Add:* 25 E 83rd St New York NY 10028

BYRUM, DONALD ROY
EDUCATOR, PRINTMAKER
b Hertford, NC, June 19, 42. *Study:* RI Sch Design, BFA, 67; Univ Mich, MFA, 69; spec studies with John Maggio, 79. *Work:* Minn Mus Art, St Paul; Chrysler Mus Art, Norfolk, Va; BYK Gulden Lomberg Chemische Fabrik GMBH, Konstanz, WGer. *Comn:* Etching & aquatints, comn by Donald Dryden, 76-79, color serigraph, 79. *Exhib:* Minn Printmakers, Minn Arts Coun, 69-70; Talent Six, Minn Mus Art, St Paul, 73; Eastern US Print Exhib, Spirit Sq Art Ctr, NC, 79-81; 8th Ann NC Artist Exhib, Fayetteville Mus Art, 79; Southeastern Ctr Contemp Art, Winston-Salem, NC, 80; Don Byrum/ Reflections Portfolio Traveling Exhib, 81-82; Mint Mus Art, 81; New Am Graphics US State Dept Tour, 82-83; and others. *Pos:* Dir & cur, Lincoln Art Gallery, Mankato State Univ, 69-74. *Teaching:* Asst prof printmaking, Mankato State Univ, 69-74 & Univ NC-Charlotte, 74-80; assoc prof printmaking, Univ NC, Charlotte, 80- *Awards:* Purchase Awards, Minn Printmakers, Minn Arts Coun, 70 & NC Artists, Asheville Mus, 77; Fayetteville Mus Art Award, 79. *Mem:* NC Print & Drawing Soc; Col Art Asn Am; Philadelphia Print Club; Southeastern Col Art Asn. *Media:* Etching & Lithography. *Dealer:* Donlad Dryden Gallery Amsterdam Ave at SW 78th New York NY 10028. *Mailing Add:* 4136 Woodgreen Terr Charlotte NC 28205

BYWATERS, JERRY
PAINTER, HISTORIAN
b Paris, Tex, May 21, 06. *Study:* Southern Methodist Univ, AB; Art Students League; study in Europe & Mex. *Work:* Mus Fine Arts, Dallas; Southern Methodist Univ, Dallas; Houston, Quanah, Farmersville & Trinity Post Off Bldgs, Tex. *Exhib:* Golden Gate Int Expos, San Francisco, 39; New York World's Fair, 39 & 40; City Art Mus, St Louis, Mo, 40; 53rd Ann Am Painting & Sculpture, Art Inst Chicago, 42; Am Painting & Sculpture, Metrop Mus Art, New York; retrospective, Southern Methodist Univ, Dallas, 76. *Collections Arranged:* 200 Years of American Painting, 46; Six Southwestern States, 47; Pre-Columbian Art, 50; Lasker Collection, 53; Otis Dozier, 56; Survey of Texas Painting, 57; Andrew Dasburg, 58; Religious Art of the Western World, 58; South American Art Today, 59; Century of Art & Life in Texas, 61; The Arts of Man, 62; Indian Art, 63; Texas Painting & Sculpture (coauth, catalog), 71. *Pos:* Art critic, Dallas Morning News, 33-39; dir, Dallas Mus Fine Arts, 43-64; dir, Pollock Galleries, Southern Methodist Univ,

65-70; regional archivist, Tex Proj, Archives Am Art, Smithsonian Inst, 75-77. *Teaching:* Asst prof painting, Southern Methodist Univ, 36-63, prof NAm arts, 64-71, emer prof, 71- *Awards:* First Prize, Tex Ann, Houston Mus, 40; Dealey Purchase Prize, Dallas Mus Fine Arts, 42; Caller-Times Purchase Prize, Corpus Christi Mus, 47. *Publ:* Auth, Twelve from Texas, Southern Methodist Univ, 52; co-auth, Everett Spruce, Univ Tex, 58; auth, Andrew Dasburg, Am Fedn Arts, 59; auth, Seventy-Five Years of Art in Dallas, Dallas Mus Fine Arts, 78. *Mailing Add:* 3625 Amherst Dallas TX 75225

C

CABLE, MAXINE ROTH
SCULPTOR
b Philadelphia, Pa. *Study:* Tyler Sch Fine Art, Temple Univ, AA; Corcoran Sch Art, George Washington Univ, AB; Am Univ, with Hans Hofmann. *Work:* Allied Chem Corp Gallery, New York; Nat Acad Sci, Washington, DC; George Washington Univ. *Comn:* Environ sculpture, Allied Chem Corp, 69-70; sculpture, Wolf Trap Farm Performing Arts, Va, 73. *Exhib:* Area Exhibs, Corcoran Gallery Art, 55-67; Artists Equity Traveling Exhib, Columbia Mus, SC, 73-74; one-woman shows, Adams Morgan Gallery, Washington, DC, 64, Hodson Gallery, Hood Col, Frederick, Md, 69, Gallery Ten, Washington, DC, 75, 76, 79 & 83 & Art Dept, Cath Univ Am, 83. *Pos:* Dir, Glen Echo Graphics Workshop, Md, 75. *Teaching:* Consult art, Montgomery Co, Md, 57-65 & Head Start Prog, Washington, DC, 70. *Awards:* Sculpture Award, David Smith, Corcoran Gallery Art, 55; First Prize in Painting, Smithsonian Inst, 67. *Bibliog:* Washington Artists Today, Artists Equity Asn, 67; Art for Public Places, Dept Housing & Urban Develop, 73. *Media:* Mixed Media, Natural and Man-Made. *Dealer:* Gallery Ten Ltd 1519 Connecticut Ave Washington DC 20036. *Mailing Add:* 7000 Buxton Terr Bethesda MD 20034

CABOT, HUGH
PAINTER, SCULPTOR
b Boston, Mass, Mar 22, 30. *Study:* Vesper George Sch Fine Arts; Boston Mus Fine Arts Sch; Col of Americas, Mexico City; Asmolean, Oxford Univ, Cambridge, England. *Work:* USN Dept Hist & Rec, USN Art Gallery, The Pentagon & Nat War Mus, Washington, DC; Harwood Found Art, Taos, NMex. *Exhib:* Korea, Mitsubichi Gallery, Tokyo, Japan, 58 & Tokyo Press Club; La Marine Americaine, Mus de la Marine, Paris, 63; Oper Palette, every major city in free world incl Nat Gallery Art. *Awards:* First, Second & Third Awards, Tex Tri State, 69; Artist of Yr, Scottsdale, Ariz, 78. *Bibliog:* Jim Newton (auth), Those Cabots, Phoenix Gazette, 74; Meet Hugh Cabot, Ariz Living, 75; Danny Medina (auth), Hugh Cabot, Ariz Art Talk, 82. *Mem:* Salmagundi Club. *Media:* Oil, Watercolor; Bronze. *Publ:* Auth-illusr, Korea one, Readers Dig, 54. *Mailing Add:* Casa de Anza Tubac AZ 85640

CADDELL, FOSTER
PAINTER, INSTRUCTOR
b Pawtucket, RI, Aug 2, 21. *Study:* RI Sch Design; pvt study with Peter Helck, Robert Brackman & Guy Wiggins. *Comn:* Off portraits of Sen Thomas J Dodd, Washington, DC & Judge L P Moore, US Circuit Ct Appeals, Second Dist, New York; portrait of Dr George S Avery, Brooklyn Botanical Gardens, NY; portrait of Carl Cuttler, Mystic Seaport Mus, Conn; relig paintings for many denominations incl Church of Eng; portraits of many bus & civic leaders. *Exhib:* Am Artists Prof League Grand Nat Exhib, 70-80; Am Watercolor Soc Ann, Nat Acad Galleries, 71; Slater Mus, Norwich Acad, 71-80; Nat Arts Club, New York, 71-80; one-man show, Slater Mem Mus, Norwich Free Acad, 76. *Pos:* Lithograph artist, Providence Lithograph Co, 39-52; artist with Far East Air Force, 43-46. *Teaching:* Instr, Foster Caddell's Art Sch, currently. *Awards:* Michael Guiheen Award, 75; Weber Wyeth Award, Int Soc Artists, 78; Award for pastel, Salmagundi Club, New York, 80; and others. *Bibliog:* Wendon Blake (auth), Creative Color, Watson-Guptill, 73; Foster Caddell--landscape painter, The Artist, London; David Lewis (ed), Oil Painting Techniques, Watson Guptill, 83. *Mem:* Providence Art Club; Am Artists Prof League; Acad Artists Am; Salmagundi Club; Pastel Soc Am; and others. *Media:* Oil, Pastel. *Publ:* Illusr, series sports bks, Little, Brown & Co; auth & illusr, Keys to Successful Landscape Painting, 76, Keys to Successful Color & auth, Keys to Painting Better Portraits, 82, Pitman & Sons, London & Watson-Guptill; and others. *Mailing Add:* Northlight Rte 49 Voluntown CT 06384

CADE, WALTER, III
PAINTER, COLLAGE ARTIST
b New York, NY, Jan 17, 36. *Study:* Inst Mod Art, New York. *Work:* Southeast Banking Corp; City of Miami Beach, Fla; Va Beach Art Mus; Rockefeller Found. *Exhib:* C W Post Col, Long Island Univ, Brookville, NY, 68; Art Ann, 69-70; Contemporary Black Artists in America, 71, Whitney Mus Am Art, New York; Huntington Twp Art League Show, Heckscher Mus, Huntington, NY, 69 & 71; Corcoran Gallery, Washington, DC, 72; Queens Cult Ctr Arts, New York, 73; one-man shows, Ocean Co Col, 77 & Jackson State Univ, 80. *Bibliog:* Jeanne Paris (auth), The ghetto sparkles, Long Island Sun Press, 5/7/72; article, Playboy Mag, 72; article, New York Amsterdam News, 5/6/72. *Media:* Acrylic, Collage. *Mailing Add:* c/o Studio Gallery 172-03 119th Ave Jamaica NY 11434

CADGE, WILLIAM FLEMING
DESIGNER, PHOTOGRAPHER
b Philadelphia, Pa, May 5, 24. *Study:* Philadelphia Mus Sch Art, 45-49. *Pos:* Freelance designer, Philadelphia, 49-50; asst art dir, Eve Bulletin, Philadelphia, 50-52 & Woman's Home Companion, 52-56; art dir, Doyle, Dane & Bernbach, New York, 56-57; assoc art dir, McCall's Mag, 59-61; art dir, Redbook Mag, 61-76; owner, Bill Cadge Inc, 76- *Awards:* Numerous Gold Medals & Awards, Art Dirs Club, NY, NJ & Philadelphia; Awards Excellence, CA Mag Show, 67 & 68; Gold Medal, Soc Illusr, 71 & 72. *Mem:* Soc Illusr; Art Dirs Club NY (exec bd, 66-68). *Mailing Add:* 33 Colonial Ave Dobbs Ferry NY 10522

CADIEUX, MICHAEL EUGENE
EDUCATOR, PAINTER
b Missoula, Mont, June 15, 40. *Study:* Univ Mont, BA & MA. *Work:* Univ Mont Fine Arts Collection, Missoula; Yuma Fine Arts Asn, Ariz. *Exhib:* Spokane-Pac NW Ann, Cheney Cowles Mus, 66; SW Yuma Fine Arts Arts, 66-68; Ariz Ann, Phoenix Art Mus, 67; Tucson Art Mus Ann, Ariz, 68; Mid-Am, Nelson-Atkins Mus, Kansas City, Mo, 72, 30 Miles, 75; Mid-Am, St Louis Art Mus, 72; Davidson Nat Drawing, Davidson Col Galleries, 75. *Collections Arranged:* Univ Wis Ctr Syst, 67; Univ Md, 67; Western Asn Art Mus Traveling Exhib, 69; fac shows, Spiva Art Ctr, Memphis Acad, 75-78; Mo Art Coun-Mid Am Arts Alliance Shows. *Pos:* Reviewer art publ, SE Asia in Rev, 76- *Teaching:* Instr painting & drawing, Ariz Western Col, Yuma, 66-69; assoc prof art hist, Kansas City Art Inst, Mo, 69- *Awards:* Third Place, 2nd Southwestern, Yuma Fine Arts, 67; Grant Study in India, US Off Educ, 71. *Bibliog:* Donald Hoffman (auth), Here's Art All in a Row, Kansas City Star, 72 & Michael Cadieux, Kansas City Star, 77. *Media:* Painting Collage. *Res:* Cross-cultural art history. *Publ:* Auth, The mural tradition in Indian painting, SE Asia in Rev, 77. *Mailing Add:* 5807 Locust Kansas City MO 64110

CADILLAC, LOUISE ROMAN
PAINTER, INSTRUCTOR
b Central City, Pa. *Study:* Univ Northern Colo, BA, 54, MA, 64; with Sylvia Glass, Calif, Gene Matthews, Colo & Chen Chi, New York. *Exhib:* Metropolitan Denver, Denver Art Mus, 60; Nat Watermedia, Foothills Art Ctr, Golden, Colo, 74, 75, 82 & 83; two-person exhib, Univ Northern Colo, 81; Nat Watercolor Soc, Palm Springs Mus Fine Art, Calif, 82 & 83; Ky Watercolor Soc Ann, Owensboro Mus Fine Art, 83; San Diego Watercolor Int, Atrium Imperial Bank, Calif, 83. *Teaching:* Instr sec & elem art, Jefferson Co Pub Sch, Lakewood, Colo, 57-67, adaptive art specialist, 74-83. *Awards:* Brass Cheque Award, Rocky Mountain Nat Watermedia, Brass Cheque Gallery, Denver, 83; Dortha Tompkins Mem, Ky Watercolor Soc, Louisville, 83; Award for a non-objective painting, San Diego Watercolor Int, 83. *Bibliog:* Watercolors for Grades 4, 5 & 6 (film), KRMA TV, Denver Pub Sch, 75. *Mem:* Nat Watercolor Soc; Rocky Mountain Nat Watermedia Soc; San Diego Watercolor Soc; Ky Watercolor Soc. *Media:* Watercolor. *Publ:* Auth, Adaptive art for the multiply handicapped student, In: Viewpoints: Dialogue in Art Education, Univ Ill Col Fine Arts, 76. *Mailing Add:* 880 S Dudley St Lakewood CO 80226

CADLE, RAY KENNETH
PAINTER, CRAFTSMAN
b Ravenswood, WVa, Aug 26, 06. *Study:* Dayton Art Inst; woodblock printing with Kiyoshi Saito & suiboku painting with Ryukyu Saito, Tokyo. *Exhib:* Hanga Group Exhib, Metrop Gallery, Ueno Park, Tokyo, 52; one-man shows, Int House Gallery, Tokyo, 54 & Centenary Col Gallery, Shreveport, La, 65; Morris Harvey Col, Charleston, WVa, 59; La State Mus, Shreveport, 75; Barnwell Art Ctr, Shreveport. *Pos:* Staff arts & crafts dir, Hq Fifth Air Force, Nagoya, Japan, 49-50, Hq Far E Air Forces, Tokyo, 50-57 & Hq Pac Air Forces, Honolulu, 54-58; command arts & crafts dir, Hq Second Air Force and Eighth Air Force, Barksdale AFB, La, 61-78. *Awards:* Nat Recreation & Park Asn Fel Arts & Crafts, 64; Sculpture Award, Men's Art Guild, Shreveport, 80. *Mem:* Allied Artists, WVa; Honolulu Printmakers; Men's Art Guild, Shreveport (bd mem, 66-, pres, 79-80); Int Suiboku Soc, Japan. *Dealer:* C C Hardman 712 Texas St Shreveport LA 71101. *Mailing Add:* Towne House Apt 501 726 Cotton St Shreveport LA 71101

CADMUS, PAUL
PAINTER, PRINTMAKER
b New York, NY, Dec 17, 04. *Study:* Nat Acad Design, 16-26; Art Students League, with Joseph Pennell, 28. *Work:* Whitney Mus Am Art, New York; Metrop Mus Art, New York; Mus Mod Art, New York; Fogg Art Mus, Cambridge, Mass; Smithsonian Inst, Washington, DC. *Comn:* Costumes & scenery, Filling Station Ballet, Ballet Caravan, 38; mural, Parcel Post Bldg, Richmond, Va, 38. *Pos:* Vpres, Bd Control, Art Students League, 35- *Awards:* Flora Mayer Witkowsky Prize, Art Inst Chicago, 45; Nat Inst Arts & Lett Grant, 61; Purchase Prize, Norfolk Mus Arts & Sci, 67. *Bibliog:* Paul Cadmus of Navy fame has his first art show, Life Mag, 3/29/37; Una E Johnson (auth), Paul Cadmus/prints and drawings, Brooklyn Mus, 68; Philip Eliasoph (auth), Paul Cadmus/Yesterday & Today, Miami Univ Art Mus, 81. *Mem:* Soc Am Graphic Artists; Am Acad & Inst Arts & Lett; academician Nat Acad Design. *Media:* Tempera. *Dealer:* Midtown Galleries 11 E 57th St New York NY 10022. *Mailing Add:* PO Box 1255 Weston CT 06883

CADY, DENNIS VERN
CONSERVATOR, PAINTER
b Portland, Ore, Nov 10, 44. *Study:* Portland State Univ; Brooklyn Mus Art Sch, printmaking & drawing with Rubin Tam; Pratt Inst Graphic Ctr; Empire State Col, BS, plus independent study of tech aspects of paper restoration;

Margo Fieden Galleries, New York, apprenticeship in restoration and preserv of works on paper, 74-77. *Comn:* Poster, 72, costumes for dance (with Frank Garcia), 74, costumes, 77, Phillis Lamhut Dance Co; poster, Emery Hermans Dance Theatre, 75. *Exhib:* Max Beckman Scholar Students Paintings, Brooklyn Art Mus, 69; one-man shows, Drawings & Prints, Renshaw Gallery, Linfield Col, Ore, 71 & Margo Fieden Gallery, New York, 76; South Street Seaport Mus, New York, 80; and others. *Pos:* Freelance restorer, New York, 77- *Awards:* Nat Scholastics Award, New York, 62. *Mem:* Portland Art Asn. *Media:* Oil, Watercolor. *Publ:* Auth, Block Prints by Dennis Cady, Hillside Ctr, Portland, Ore, 71. *Dealer:* Ellen Sragow 80 5th Ave New York NY 10003; Judith Selkowitz 65 E 55th St Suite 504 New York NY 10022. *Mailing Add:* 45 Orchard St New York NY 10002

CAFRITZ, ROBERT CONRAD
CURATOR
b New Haven, Conn, July 5, 53. *Study:* Columbia Col, Columbia Univ, New York, BA, 77, MA(art hist), 78. *Collections Arranged:* Okada, Shinoda & Tsutaka (ed, catalog), Washington, DC, Austin, Utica, 79-80; Leon Spilliaert (ed, catalog), Washington, DC, 80; Metrop Mus Art, NY, 80; Sam Francis: The 50's (ed, catalog), Washington, DC, 80; Braque: Late Paintings (ed, catalog), Washington, DC, San Francisco, Minn & Houston, 82-83. *Pos:* Asst cur, The Phillips Collection, Washington, DC, 78-83, assoc cur, 83- *Res:* Renaissance art & architecture; twentieth century art. *Publ:* Coauth, Master Paintings from the Phillips Collection, Penshurt Books, Inc, 81; coauth, Georges Braque, Artist's Limited Edition, 81; auth, The Great Late Braque, The Connoisseur, 11/82. *Mailing Add:* The Phillips Collection 1600 21st St NW Washington DC 20009

CAGE, JOHN
PRINTMAKER
b Los Angeles, Calif, Sept 5, 12. *Work:* Metrop Mus Art & Mus Mod Art, New York; Stedlijk Mus, Amsterdam, Holland; San Francisco Mus Mod Art; Mus Fine Arts, Houston. *Exhib:* One-man shows, Mus Mod Art, New York, 77, Mus Folkwang Essen, Ger, 78, Stadtisches Mus Monchengladbach, 78, Kolnischer Kunstverein, Cologne, 78 & Kunst Forum Bonn, 79; Int Biennial of Prints, Nat Mus Mod Art, Tokyo, 79 & Nat Mus Art, Osaka, Japan, 79. *Awards:* Grand Honor, Int Biennial Exhib Prints, Tokyo, 79. *Media:* Etching. *Dealer:* Margarete Roeder Fine Arts & Crown Point Press 545 Broadway New York NY 10012. *Mailing Add:* 101 W 18th St New York NY 10011

CAHILL, JAMES FRANCIS
HISTORIAN, EDUCATOR
b Fort Bragg, Calif, Aug 13, 26. *Study:* Univ Calif, Berkeley, BA, 50; Univ Mich, with Max Loehr, MA(Louise Wallace Hackney Scholar, 50-52), 53, PhD(Fulbright Scholar, 54-55), 58. *Collections Arranged:* Guest-dir, The Art of Southern Sung China (with catalog), Asia House Gallery, New York, 62, Fantastics and Eccentrics in Chinese Painting (with catalog), 67 & Scholar-Painters of Japan: The Nanga School (with catalog), 72. *Pos:* Cur Chinese art, Freer Gallery Art, Washington, DC, 58-65. *Teaching:* Prof hist art, Univ Calif, Berkeley, 65- *Awards:* Guggenheim Fel, 72-73; Charles Norton Prof Poetry, Harvard Univ, 78-79. *Mem:* Col Art Asn Am. *Res:* Chinese and Japanese painting; Chinese bronzes. *Publ:* Auth, Chinese Painting, Skira, Geneva, Switz, 60; coauth, The Freer Chinese Bronzes, 67; auth, Hills Beyond a River: Chinese Painting of the Yuan Dynasty, 76; auth, Parting at the Shore, Chinese Painting of the Early & Middle Ming Dynasty, 78. *Mailing Add:* 2422 Hillside Ave Berkeley CA 94704

CAIMITE (LYNNE RUSKIN)
PAINTER, ILLUSTRATOR
b Youngstown, Ohio, Jan 23, 22. *Study:* Syracuse Univ, 38-40; Cleveland Inst Art, 40-41; Western Reserve Med Sch, spec study in anat, 52-53. *Work:* Butler Inst Am Art, Youngstown, Ohio; Nat Gallery Guatemala; Nat Gallery Haiti; Elliott Mus, Fla. *Exhib:* One-woman shows, Butler Inst Am Art, Ohio, 62, Lord & Taylor Art Gallery, New York, 66 & Elliott Mus, Fla, 74; Inst Francaise, Haiti, 63; Ferre Mus, PR, 64; The Gallery, St Croix, 80. *Pos:* Med illusr, St Luke's Hosp, Cleveland & Res Dept, Western Reserve Med Sch, 52-62. *Bibliog:* Aubelin Jolicoeur (auth), Caimite exhibits, Haiti Sun, Port-au-Prince, 62-63; Aage Heinberg (auth), Voodo Manden, Berlingske Tidende, Denmark, 5/14/65; Emeline Paige (auth), Caribbean impressionist exhibiting..., Stuart Daily News, Fla, 11/17/74. *Media:* Oil, Watercolor. *Publ:* Auth, Don't Get Hit by a Coconut, Expo Press, 79. *Mailing Add:* PO Box 2719 Christiansted St Croix VI 00820

CAIN, DAVID PAUL
PAINTER, PHOTOGRAPHER
b Indianapolis, Ind, Oct 14, 28. *Study:* Univ NMex, Albuquerque, 48-49; Earlham Col, Richmond, Ind, BA, 50; Madison Art Sch, Conn, 79. *Work:* Old Jailhouse Found, Austin, Tex; Int Ctr Photog, New York. *Exhib:* US Army Art Show, European Command, Munich, Germany, 52; one-man shows, Richmond, Ind, 53 & Yale Univ, New Haven, Conn, 81. *Mem:* Salmagundi Club; Copley Soc of Boston; Am Artists' Prof League; Madison Art Soc, Conn (pres, 81-); Mt Carmel Art Asn. *Media:* Oil; Black & White. *Dealer:* Munson Gallery 33 Whitney Ave New Haven CT. *Mailing Add:* 20 Livingston St New Haven CT 06511

CAIN, J FREDERICK, JR
PRINTMAKER, CURATOR
b Philadelphia, Pa, June 24, 38. *Study:* Assumption Col, Mass, AB; Tyler Sch Art, Temple Univ, MFA; Laval Univ; Harvard Univ; Univ Pa. *Work:* Mus Mod Art; Los Angeles Co Mus; Lessing J Rosenwald Collection, Jenkintown,

Pa; Art Inst Chicago; Pasadena Art Mus; plus others. *Collections Arranged:* M C Escher, Prints from the Roosevelt Collection & Alfred Stieglitz, Key-Set on deposit with the Nat Gallery of Art, 72-76; Medieval Miniatures from the Rosenwald Collection, Nat Gallery, 74-75. *Pos:* Mus cur, Dept Graphic Arts, Nat Gallery Art, Washington, DC, 66-76; cur fine arts, Charleston Art Gallery, Sunrise, WVa, 77-78; guest cur, Heritage Plantation of Sandwich, Mass, 79-80. *Teaching:* Instr art hist, Smithsonian Inst, Washington, DC, 72-76. *Awards:* Ford Found Cur Training Grant, Tamarind Lithography Workshop, Los Angeles, 67; Eng Speaking Union Grant Study at Brit Mus, 68. *Mem:* Am Asn Mus; Col Art Asn Am; Southeastern Mus Conf (WVa rep, 78); Philobiblon Club; Philadelphia Print Club; and others. *Publ:* Designed illus sect, Fifteenth Century Engravings of Northern Europe (catalog), Nat Gallery Art, 67; contrib, l'Incisone Europa dal XV al XX Secolo, Museo Civico, Torino, Italy, 68; auth, Rodolphe Bresdin, a drawing and a print, Print Collector's Newsletter, Vol 1, No 3, 70; contrib, Recent Acquisitions of Sculpture, Drawings, Prints, Nat Gallery Art, Washington, DC, 74; ed, Bernie peace: Paintings & ed, Douglas Chadwick: Photographs, Charleston Art Gallery, Sunrise, WVa, 78. *Mailing Add:* 301 I St SW Washington DC 20024

CAIN, JOSEPH ALEXANDER
PAINTER, EDUCATOR
b Henderson, Tenn, May 27, 20. *Study:* Univ Calif, Berkeley, BA, 47, MA, 48. *Work:* Butler Inst Am Art, Youngstown, Ohio; Nat Watercolor Soc Collection; Witte Mus, San Antonio, Tex; Univ Utah Permanent Collection; Laguna Gloria Mus, Austin, Tex. *Comn:* Oil mural, CofC, Corpus Christi, Tex, 59; mosaic mural, comn by Freeman Martin, Spohn Hosp, 62; mosaic murals, comn by Joe Williams, Buccanneer Bowl, 65. *Exhib:* Philadelphia Watercolor Club Exhib, Pa Acad Fine Arts, 65; Butler Inst Am Art Mid-Year Ann, 65; Southwestern Watercolor Soc Regional Show, Dallas, 69; Nat Watercolor Soc Ann, Los Angeles, 69; Watercolor USA, Springfield Art Mus, Mo, 73; Am Painters in Paris, 75; Nat Acad of Design, New York, 77-78. *Pos:* Critic, Art News and Reviews, Corpus Christi Caller-Times, 56-74. *Teaching:* Prof art, Del Mar Col, 50-82, chmn dept, 66-82. *Awards:* Juror's Award of Merit, Pa Festival Art, Pa State Univ, 79; Best in Show, 7th Ann Div Show, Corpus Christi Art Ctr; Top Award, 68th Ann Nat Show, Tex Fine Arts Asn. *Mem:* Fel Royal Soc Arts; Nat Watercolor Soc; Tex Fine Arts Asn (third vpres, 77-78); Tex Watercolor Soc (third vpres, 71-72); Nat Soc Painters Acrylics & Casein; Tex Fine Arts Asn (regional dir, 70). *Media:* Acrylic, Watercolor. *Publ:* Auth, The Ten, Art Voices/South, 3/78. *Mailing Add:* 402 Troy Dr Corpus Christi TX 78412

CAIN, MICHAEL PETER
PAINTER, SCULPTOR
b Boston, Mass, July 3, 41. *Study:* Art Students League, 61-62; Harvard Col, AB, 64; Yale Sch Art, BFA(painting), MFA(painting), 67. *Work:* Gould Corp, Rolling Meadows, Ill; CBS Collection, Los Angeles; Guild Investment Corp, Malibu, Calif. *Comn:* Course of the Wind (triptych frieze segment), Hemmeter Home, Aspen, Colo, 81; In the Wave (relief mural), Bullock's, Los Angeles. *Exhib:* Public Garden, Boston, 68; Gallery, Yale Sch Art, 68, 70 & 72; Mus Mod Art, New York, 70; Automation House, New York, 71; Walker Art Ctr, 71; Stamford Univ, 71; Philadelphia Mus Art, 71; Calif Inst Arts, 71 & 72; Wadsworth Atheneum, 73 & 79. *Teaching:* Res assoc & lectr, Yale Sch Art, 67-73; prof art, Maharishi Int Univ, 73- *Awards:* Top Prize, Leverett House Arts Festival, Harvard Col, 64; Pulsa Graham Found Res Grant, 68-72. *Bibliog:* Lucy Lippard (auth), Pulsa, Arts Can, 12/68; Gregory Battcock (auth), Politics of space, Arts, 2/70; Melinda Wortz (auth), Living the simple life, Art News, 2/82. *Media:* Painted Relief Sculpture. *Dealer:* David Olenick Fine Arts 14 East 4th St New York NY 10012; Stella Polaris Gallery 303 Boyd St Los Angeles CA 90013. *Mailing Add:* Dept Art Maharishi Int Univ Fairfield IA 52556

CAISERMAN-ROTH, GHITTA
PAINTER, PRINTMAKER
b Montreal, Que, Mar 2, 23. *Study:* Parsons Sch Design, BA; Am Artists Sch; Ecole Beaux-Arts, with Albert Dumouchel. *Work:* Montreal Mus Fine Arts; Vancouver Art Gallery, BC; Confederation Art Gallery, Charlottetown, PEI; London Pub Libr & Art Mus, Ont; Beaverbrook Art Gallery, Fredericton, NB. *Comn:* Hommage a Dumouchel, Univ Que Press, 72. *Exhib:* Expo '67, 67; Joint Int Exhib, Soc Can Etcher-Painters & Engravers & Can Soc Graphic Arts, 70; group show, Can Embassy, DC, 70; one-person show, Waddington Galleries, Montreal, 70. *Teaching:* Instr art, Concordia Univ, 60; Queen's Univ, 63 & Saidye Bronfman Ctr, Montreal, 70. *Awards:* Can Govt Centennial Medal, 67; and others. *Mem:* Can Soc Painter Etchers; Can Soc Graphic Art; Royal Can Acad Art; Can Coun. *Media:* Acrylic, Oil; Mixed Media, Graphics. *Dealer:* Wallack Gallery 203 Bank St Ottawa ON K2P 1W7 Can. *Mailing Add:* 4266 de Maisonneuve W Montreal PQ H3Z 1K6 Canada

CAJORI, CHARLES F
PAINTER
b Palo Alto, Calif, Mar 9, 21. *Study:* Colorado Springs Fine Arts Ctr; Cleveland Art Sch; Columbia Univ; Skowhegan Sch Painting & Sculpture. *Work:* Corcoran Gallery Art; Mitchner Collection, Univ Tex, Austin; Walker Art Ctr, Minneapolis; Whitney Mus Am Art, New York; Metrop Mus, New York; and others. *Exhib:* One-man shows, Howard Wise Gallery, 63; Landmark Gallery, 75 & 81, Ingber Gallery, 76, New York & Gross McCleaf Gallery, Philadelphia, 83; Decade of American Drawings, Whitney Mus Am Art, 65; three-man show, Loeb Ctr, NY Univ, 70; Conn Painters, Wadsworth

Atheneum. *Teaching:* Instr drawing & painting, Cooper Union Art Sch, 56-65; instr drawing & painting, New York Studio Sch, 64-69; prof drawing & painting, Queens Col, Flushing, 65- *Awards:* Award in painting, Inst Arts & Lett, 70; Nat Endowment Arts Fel, 81; Benjamin Altman Figure Prize, Nat Acad, New York, 83. *Bibliog:* L Finkelstein (auth), Cajori: figure in the scene, Art News, 63; Teaching drawing: Cajori, Drawing Soc Rev, 79. *Mem:* Col Art Asn Am. *Media:* Oil, Acrylic. *Mailing Add:* Litchfield Rd Watertown CT 06795

CALAMAR, GLORIA
PAINTER
b New York, NY, Sept 7, 21. *Study:* Otis Art Inst, scholar, 39-43; Art Students League, scholar, 45-46; Orange Co Community Col, AA, 69; State Univ NY Col, New Paltz, BA(art hist), 70. *Work:* Cent Theatre, Oslo, Norway; Santa Barbara Mus, Calif; Mt St Mary Col. *Exhib:* Los Angeles Co Mus Art, 54; solo exhib, Mus Art Mod, Paris, 67, Univ Calif, Berkeley, 69, Georgetown Univ, 74, Parnassus Sq, Woodstock, NY, 78 & Ibiza, Balearic Islands, Spain, 78; Bertrand Russell Centenary Invitational, London, 72-73. *Teaching:* Instr studio courses & art hist, Orange Co Community Col, 63-68; instr art hist, Mt St Mary Col, 68-69. *Awards:* Nat Endowment Arts Grant, 80-81. *Bibliog:* A gift is indicated, Trumpeteer Mag, 49; Gloria Calamar has affinity for her subject, Am Artist Mag, 4/69. *Mem:* Woodstock Art Asn; Artists Equity Asn; Art Students League. *Media:* Watercolor, Acrylic. *Dealer:* George Furnemont 47 Rue Esperonniers Brussels Belg, Gallery Bolotin 1420 South Coast Hwy Laguna Beach CA 92651. *Mailing Add:* PO Box 844 Summerland CA 93067

CALAPAI, LETTERIO
PRINTMAKER, PAINTER
b Boston, Mass. *Study:* Mass Sch Art; Sch Fine Arts & Crafts; Art Students League; Am Artists Sch; also with Robert Laurent, Ben Shahn & Stanley Hayter. *Work:* Metrop Mus Art, New York; Fogg Art Mus, Cambridge, Mass; Art Inst Chicago; Bibliot Nat, Paris, France; Kyobashi Mus Mod Art, Tokyo, Japan; plus many other pub & pvt collections. *Comn:* Presentation Print, Soc Am Graphic Artists, 78; bookplate, Thomas Wolfe Collection, Libr St Mary's Col, Raleigh, NC, 79. *Exhib:* 20-yr retrospective of graphic work, touring univs & cols throughout the US, 72-73; Int Print Exhib, Rockford Col, 79; Selected Chicago Artists, Chicago Pub Libr & Cult Ctr, 79; 79th Nat Print Exhib, Univ Tex, Austin, 79; Boston Printmakers Exhib, Attleboro Mus, 79; plus many others. *Pos:* Founder-dir, Intaglio Workshop for Advance Printmaking, New York, 60-65. *Teaching:* Chmn graphic arts dept, Albright Art Sch, Univ Buffalo, 49-55; instr graphics, New Sch Social Res, 55-62; instr graphics, NY Univ, 62-65; vis assoc prof fine arts, Brandeis Univ, 64-65; instr, Univ Ill, Chicago Circle, 65. *Awards:* Tiffany Found grant, 59; Rosenwald Found, 60; plus others. *Mem:* Soc Am Graphic Artists; Audubon Artists. *Mailing Add:* PO Box 158 344 Tudor Glencoe IL 60022

CALCAGNO, LAWRENCE
PAINTER
b San Francisco, Calif, Mar 23, 13. *Study:* Calif Sch Fine Arts, San Francisco, 47-50; Acad Grande Chaumiere, Paris, France, 50-51; Acad Delgi Belli Arte, Florence, Italy, 51-52. *Work:* San Francisco Mus Art; Whitney Mus Am Art, New York; Brooklyn Mus; Nat Collections, Smithsonian Inst, Washington, DC. *Exhib:* Albright Art Gallery, Buffalo, NY, 56; Am Pavilion, Brussels World's Fair, 58; Carnegie Inst Mus Int, 61; Mus Fine Arts, Houston, 65; Nat Collection Fine Arts, Smithsonian Inst, 68; Whitney Mus Am Art, 70; SITES, 73-75; traveling retrospective, 82-83. *Teaching:* Vis Andrew Mellon prof painting, Carnegie-Mellon Univ, 65-68. *Awards:* Ford Found Grant, 65. *Mem:* Artists Equity Assoc. *Mailing Add:* 215 Bowery New York NY 10002

CALDWELL, BENJAMIN HUBBARD, JR
COLLECTOR, HISTORIAN
b Humboldt, Tenn, May 1, 35. *Study:* Vanderbilt Univ, BA, 57, MD, 60. *Collections Arranged:* Made in Tennessee, Tenn Fine Art Ctr, Cheekwood, 71. *Teaching:* Lectr, Winterthur Mus, 80 & 83, Tenn State Mus, 81 & Williamsburg Antique Forum, 84. *Res:* Tennessee silver; Tennessee silversmiths. *Collection:* Tennessee silver; 18th century American furniture; 19th and 20th century American art & American primitive art. *Publ:* Auth, Tennessee Silver & Checklist of Tennessee Silversmiths, Antiques, 71; Tennessee Silversmiths, Univ Va Press (in prep). *Mailing Add:* 329 22nd Ave W Nashville TN 37203

CALDWELL, ELEANOR
EDUCATOR, JEWELER
b Kansas City, Mo, May 1, 27. *Study:* Southwest Mo State Univ, Springfield, BS in Educ, 48; Columbia Univ, MA, 53, EdD, 59; study with Robert von Neuman, John Leary, Dr Edwin Zeigfield, Dr Jack Arends & Arthur Young. *Work:* Colo Women's Col, Denver; Ft Hays Kans State Col, Hays; Denver Pub Schs; Northern Ill Univ, DeKalb; Sheldon Mem Art Gallery, Lincoln, Nebr. *Comn:* Presidential medallion, Northern Ill Univ, 70. *Exhib:* Midwest 3rd Biennial Exhib of Utilitarian Design, Joslyn Art Mus, Omaha, Nebr, 55; 3rd Nat Exhib of Contemp Jewelers, Walker Art Ctr, Minneapolis, Minn, 55; Am Jewelry, Smithsonian Inst Travelling Exhib, 55-57; Handweaving II, Smithsonian Inst Travelling Exhib, 58-59; Ann Own Your Own Exhib, Denver Art Mus, Colo, 61-63 & 65-67; Jewelry & Precious Objects by Eight Am Women Metalsmiths, Wichita Art Asn, 72; 7th Ann Prints, Drawings &

Crafts Exhib, 74 & Toys Designed by Artists, 75, Ark Art Ctr, Little Rock; Am Metalwork 1976, Sheldon Mem Art Gallery, Lincoln, 76; The Metalsmith Int Exhib, Phoenix Art Mus, Ariz, 77. *Collections Arranged:* Nat Jewelry & Holoware Exhib (dir & auth, catalogue), Northern Ill Univ Art Gallery, DeKalb & Lakeview Ctr for the Arts & Sci, Peoria, Ill. *Pos:* Consult, Cult Heritage Ctr, Dodge City, Kans, 66-74; res grant, Grad Sch, Northern Ill Univ, 68-71. *Teaching:* Assoc prof jewelry & graphics, Ft Hays Kans State Univ, 54-57 & 64-67; assoc prof jewelry & graphics, Edinboro State Col, Pa, 60-62; prof jewelry & metals, Northern Ill Univ, 67-83, prof emer, 83-; prof jewelry & metals, Arrowmont Sch of Crafts, Univ Tenn, Gatlinburg, 74-77 & 82. *Awards:* Jewelry Award, 12th Nat Decorative Arts, Cent States Craftsmen's Guild, 57; Purchase Award, 5th Ann Own Your Own Exhib, Denver Pub Schs, 61. *Bibliog:* Meg Torbert (ed), American Jewelry, Design Quart, Walker Art Ctr, 59 & 61; Lois E Franke (auth), Handwrought Jewelry, McKnight & McKnight, 62; Jon Nelson (auth), American Metalwork 1976 (slide set), Sheldon Mem Art Gallery, Lincoln, 76. *Mem:* Soc of NAm Goldsmiths; Am Crafts Coun; Artists Equity. *Media:* Jewelry and related objects in gold and silver. *Publ:* Auth, 1970 Oakbrook Invitational Crafts Exhib, Crafts Horizons, 70. *Mailing Add:* 4509 E Camino De Oro Tucson AZ 85718

CALDWELL, JOHN
CURATOR, CRITIC
b Nashville, Tenn, Nov 16, 41. *Study:* Harvard Col, AB(cum laude; Harvard Nat Scholar), 63; Hunter Col, MA, 73; Yale Univ. *Collections Arranged:* Andrew Wyeth: Drawings and Watercolors, Metrop Mus Art, New York, 77; Recent Acquisitions in Contemporary Art, Part One, 83 & Part Two, 83 & Irwin Kremen: Collages 1967, 83, Mus Art, Carnegie Inst. *Pos:* Andrew W Mellon Fel, Metrop Mus Art, 75-77; asst cur, Metrop Mus Art, 77-80; art critic, regional ed, New York Times, 80-; adj cur contemp art, Mus Art, Carnegie Inst, currently. *Res:* Drawing in New York, 1800-1850: origins of Hudson River School style. *Publ:* Contribr, Sixteenth century Italian drawings: Form and function, Yale Univ, 74; contribr, American master drawings and watercolors, Whitney Mus Am Art, 76; contribr, A bicentennial treasury: American masterpieces from the Metrop Mus Art, 76 & American drawings, watercolors and prints, 80, Metrop Mus Art. *Mailing Add:* Mus Art Carnegie Inst 4400 Forbes Ave Pittsburgh PA 15213

CALDWELL, MARTHA BELLE
EDUCATOR, HISTORIAN
b Chapel Hill, NC, Dec 12, 31. *Study:* Cornell Univ, BA; Univ Miss, MA; Ind Univ, MA & PhD. *Teaching:* Instr art hist, Westhampton Col, Univ Richmond, 60-63 & Rice Univ, 66-68; from asst prof to prof art hist, James Madison Univ, 68- *Mem:* Southeastern Col Art Conf (pres, 81-82); Col Art Asn; Soc of Archit Historians; Am Comt for Irish Studies (mem exec bd, 81-83); Am Inst of Archaeol. *Res:* Nineteenth and twentieth century art and architecture. *Mailing Add:* 216 Governors Lane 10 Harrisonburg VA 22801

CALDWELL, SUSAN HAVENS
HISTORIAN, EDUCATOR
b Clinton, Okla, June 9, 38. *Study:* Washburn Univ, Topeka, Kans, BA, 61; Cornell Univ, Ithaca, NY, PhD, 74. *Teaching:* Asst prof art hist, Boise State Univ, 74-76; asst prof, Okla Sch Art, 76-81, assoc prof, 81- *Mem:* Col Art Asn Am; Midwest Art Hist Soc; Int Ctr Medieval Art; Medieval Acad; Am Soc Hispanic Art Hist Studies. *Res:* Medieval, specifically Spanish romanesque; portal development, liturgical relationships to sculpture; contemporary criticism. *Publ:* Auth, Experiencing the dinner party, Woman's Art Journal, 81; Realism or Illusionism, Art Voices, 81; Place of folk art in the art of an industrialized society & Folk painting in Oklahoma, Folk art in Oklahoma, 81; auth, Ken Dawson Little, Catalog of Works, 83. *Mailing Add:* Sch of Art Univ of Okla Norman OK 73019

CALE, ROBERT ALLAN
PRINTMAKER, EDUCATOR
b Stonington, Conn, Jan 9, 40. *Study:* RI Sch Design, BFA, 64; S W Hayter's Atelier 17, Paris, France, 69-70; Pratt Graphics Ctr, New York, 71-73. *Work:* Bibliot Nat, Paris; Santa Barbara Mus Art; Trinity Col & Wadsworth Atheneum, Hartford, Conn; Libr Cong, Washington, DC; Roseawald Col. *Comn:* ed of 225 three-color prints from several plates (with Will Barnet, artist & Elisabeth Egbert, asst), Ferdinand Roten Galleries, Baltimore, Md, 71-72; Richard Black, artist, Lakeside Studios, 74; collector's ed, Lakeside Studios, 76; nineteenth century etchings, Paul Victorius Inc, 78-83. *Exhib:* Atelier 17, A 50th Year Retrospective Traveling Exhib, 77-78; Innovations in Intaglio: S W Hayter and the Atelier 17 Traveling Exhib, 80-82; Pressed on Paper: Fish Rubbings and Nature Prints, Smithsonian Inst Traveling Exhib, 81-84; and others. *Teaching:* Instr printmaking, Printmaking Workshop, New York, 71-73, Pratt Graphics Ctr, 72-73; Lyme Acad Fine Arts, 81-82; vis artist, Trinity Col, 72-78. *Awards:* Conn Comn Arts Grant, 74; Purchase Award, 5th Biennial Exhib, Dickinson, NDak, 75; Tiffany Found Grant, 78-79; Louis Comfort Tiffany Found Grant in printmaking, 78-79. *Bibliog:* Linda P Hill (auth), Guide to New England, Stonington and Litchfield, Yankee Mag, 78; Mary S Aikins (auth), The Fishlady, Westworld, 79; Patricia Mandell (auth), feature article in Sunday Mag, Providence Sunday J, 79. *Mem:* Mystic Art Asn; Boston Printmakers; Nature Printing Soc. *Media:* All Printmaking. *Publ:* Auth, Description of methods involved in the prints of Robert A Cale in the Rosenwald Collection, 71. *Mailing Add:* 32 Gold St Stonington CT 06378

CALFEE, WILLIAM HOWARD
SCULPTOR, PAINTER
b Washington, DC, 09. *Study:* Ecole Beaux-Arts, Paris, France; Cranbrook Acad Arts; Am Univ, LHD, 79. *Work:* Nat Collection Fine Arts, Washington,

DC; Corcoran Gallery of Art, Washington, DC; Honolulu Art Acad; Metrop Mus Art, New York; Baltimore Mus Art. *Comn:* Eight murals & two sculptures, Sect Fine Arts, US Treas Dept, 36-41; font, altar & candlesticks, St Augustine Chapel, Washington, DC, 69; sculpture, Civic Ctr, Rockville, Md, 79. *Exhib:* One-man shows, Southern Vt Art Ctr, Manchester, Baltimore Mus Art, Corcoran Gallery Art, Washington, DC; Carnegie Int, Pittsburgh, Pa; Metrop Mus of Art, New York; Heritage of Am Art, Nat Archives; Loan Exhib of Washington Artists, Phillips Gallery; Nat Acad of Sci, Washington, DC; Retrospective, Nat Acad Sci, 79; and numerous others. *Teaching:* Instr drawing & painting, Phillips Gallery, Washington, DC; chmn dept painting & sculpture, Am Univ, 46-54; instr mural tech, Centre Art, Port au Prince, Haiti, 49; guest assoc prof painting, Univ Calif, Berkeley, 51; adj prof, Am Univ; instr painting, Kensington Workshop, currently. *Mailing Add:* 7206 45th St Chevy Chase MD 20015

CALHOUN, LARRY DARRYL
CERAMIST, EDUCATOR
b Revere, Mo, Oct 9, 37. *Study:* Iowa Wesleyan, BA(art); Univ Iowa, MA(ceramics). *Work:* Bowling Green State Univ, Ohio. *Comn:* Outdoor sculpture, Ill Arts Coun for Decatur, Ill, 78. *Exhib:* May Show, Cleveland Art Mus, Ohio; Ann Crafts Exhib, Butler Mus Art, Youngstown, Ohio; Designer Craftsman Biennial, Columbus Mus Art, Ohio; Ann Crafts Exhib, J B Speed Mus, Louisville, Ky & Evansville Mus Art, Ind; Invitational, Akron Art Inst, Ohio; Marietta Crafts Regional, Ohio. *Pos:* Ill craftsman-in-residence, Ill Arts Coun, Decatur, 77-78; owner, Village Pottery, 76- *Teaching:* Instr art, Westmar Col, Le Mars, Iowa, 61-63; asst prof art, Millikin Univ, Decatur, Ill, 63-70; assoc prof ceramics, Akron Univ, 70-76; from asst prof to assoc prof & chmn dept art, MacMurray Col, Jacksonville, Ill, 79- *Awards:* Prize, Ball State Univ Small Sculpture & Drawing Exhib. *Mem:* Nat Coun Educ in Ceramic Arts. *Mailing Add:* 320 S Diamond Jacksonville IL 62650

CALIFANO, EDWARD CHRISTOPHER
DEALER, PUBLISHER
b Italy; US citizen. *Study:* City Col New York, Romance lang & art; Fine Arts Acad, Naples & Rome, Italy. *Collections Arranged:* Cross-Currents, Barbizon Sch, 55, World Trade Fair, NY Coliseum, 58; Gems of Expressionism, Span Pavillion, Hall of Sci & Top of the Fair, New York World's Fair, 64; I Rice Pereira Retrospective, New York, 65; Jacques Lipchitz Retrospective, Hastings, NY, 68; Bicentennial Exhib, New York, 76. *Pos:* Art consult, Goulart Enterprises, Rio de Janeiro, Brazil, 54-55; owner-dir, Califano Art Gallery, New York, 49-57; dir, Galerie Int, New York, 57- *Awards:* Italian Lit & Art Award, Friends of Italy, 48; Aspects of French Painting Award, French Teachers Asn, 50. *Specialty:* Contemporary art. *Publ:* Ed, Men at Work, Leo Oelski, 64; ed, Artists International, 74, Art Guide Int, 75 & Bicentennial Issue Art Guide, 76, Galerie Int, plus work on several filmed art documentaries. *Mailing Add:* 1095 Madison Ave New York NY 10028

CALIFF, MARILYN ISKIWITZ
PAINTER, DESIGNER
b Memphis, Tenn, Apr 27, 32. *Study:* Memphis Acad Arts, BFA. *Work:* Brooks Mem Art Gallery, Overton Park, Memphis. *Comn:* Glass mosaic murals (with Barbara Shankman), Memphis Hebrew Acad, 62, Baron Hirsch Synagogue, 66 & Memphis Jewish Community Ctr, 68. *Exhib:* Delta Printing Exhib, Little Rock, Ark, 65-71; 4th Nat Exhib, Tyler, Tex, 67; Ann Mid-South Exhib, Brooks Mem Art Gallery, Memphis, Tenn, 62-73; 10th All-State Artists Exhib, Nashville, 70; Ball State Univ Drawing Exhib, 71. *Awards:* First in Oils, 13th Mid-South Exhib, Brooks League, 68; Three Purchase Prizes, First Tenn Artists & Craftsman Show, 72. *Media:* Oil, Collage. *Publ:* Auth, Your First Quilt, 72. *Mailing Add:* 5305 Denwood Ave Memphis TN 38119

CALKIN, CARLETON IVERS
PAINTER, RESTORER
b Grand Rapids, Mich, July 27, 14. *Study:* Univ SDak, BFA; Minneapolis Inst Art Sch; Chouinard Art Inst; Ohio Univ, MA; Univ Calif, PhD; Univ Michoacan, Mex; Inter-Am Univ, Panama. *Work:* SDak Hist Mus, Vermillion; Tex Christian Univ; Ohio Univ; Rio Hato AFB, Panama. *Exhib:* Regional exhibs, Ft Worth, Tex; local, regional & state fair shows, Ind. *Pos:* Cur, Hist St Augustine Pres Bd, 66-73; operating own studio & restoring paintings for museums and collectors, currently. *Teaching:* Instr art, Ohio Univ, Univ Calif & Tex Christian Univ, formerly; head dept art, Purdue Univ, Lafayette, 55-62, prof art hist, 62-66. *Publ:* Contribr, Latin Am art sect, In: Encycl Britannica, 57. *Mailing Add:* 265 Matanzas Blvd St Augustine FL 32084

CALKINS, KINGSLEY MARK
PAINTER, EDUCATOR
b South Lyon, Mich, May 13, 17. *Study:* Eastern Mich Univ, BS, 48; Univ Mich, MS, 49; Univ Mich & Detroit Soc Arts & Crafts, post grad study. *Work:* South Bend Mus, Ind; Dayton Mus Nat Hist; Ford Motor Co; Parke-Davis; Steelcase Corp. *Comn:* Watercolors, Ford Motor Co Publ, 65-75; murals, Mayflower Hotel, Plymouth, Mich; watercolor, Mich Heart Asn. *Exhib:* Col Art USA, Andover Acad; Audubon Artists, New York; Mich Show, South Bend, Ind; Mich Artists Ann; Mich State Fair. *Pos:* Coordinator of Volunteers, Medieval Fair, Ringling Mus, Sarasota, Fla, 80-81. *Teaching:* Instr adult educ, Univ Mich, 48-50; from instr to prof watercolor & head dept, Eastern Mich Univ, Ypsilanti, 50-79; adjunct prof, Univ Southern Fla, winter 81. *Awards:* Mich Watercolor Soc; Scarab Club; South Bend Mus. *Mem:* Nat Asn Art Adminr; Mich Watercolor Soc; Mich Art Educ Asn; Ann Arbor Art Asn. *Media:* Watercolor, Acrylic. *Publ:* Illusr, The scarlet ibis, Lincoln Mercury Times & Ford Times. *Dealer:* Nestor-De Luca 9865 Edwards Drive Brighton MI 48116. *Mailing Add:* 1327 Collegewood Ypsilanti MI 48197

CALKINS, ROBERT G
HISTORIAN, EDUCATOR
b Oakland, Calif, Dec 29, 32. *Study:* Woodrow Wilson Sch Pub & Int Affairs, Princeton Univ, AB, 55; Harvard Univ, MA, 62, PhD, 67. *Collections Arranged:* A Medieval Treasury, An Exhib of Medieval Art from the Third to the Sixteenth Century, Andrew Dickson White Mus Art, Cornell Univ, Ithaca, NY & Munson-Williams Proctor Inst, Utica, NY, 68. *Teaching:* Prof medieval art & archit, Cornell Univ, 66-, chmn dept hist of art, 76- *Awards:* Grant, Am Coun Learned Soc, 73 & APS, 80. *Mem:* Int Ctr Medieval Art (mem bd adv, 71-, dir & vpres, 80-81, pres, 81-); Col Art Asn; Medieval Acad Am. *Res:* Fifteenth century manuscript illumination. *Publ:* Auth, The Master of the Franciscan Breviary, Arte Lombara, 71; auth, Medieval & Renaissance manuscripts in the Cornell University Library, Cornell Libr J, 72; auth, Distribution of Labor: The illuminators of the hours of Catherine of Cleves, Transactions Am Philos Soc, 79; auth, Monuments of Medieval Art, Dutton, 79; auth, Illuminated Books of the Middle Ages, Cornell Univ Press, 83. *Mailing Add:* Dept of Hist of Art Cornell Univ Ithaca NY 14850

CALLAHAN, HARRY
PHOTOGRAPHER
b Detroit, Mich, Oct 22, 12. *Study:* Mich State Col, 31-33; self-taught; RI Sch Design, Hon DFA, 78. *Work:* Int Mus Photog, George Eastman House, Rochester, NY; Metrop Mus Art, Mus Mod Art, New York; Nat Gallery of Can, Ottawa, Ont; Victoria & Albert Mus, London; and others. *Exhib:* Family of Man, Mus Mod Art, New York, 55; Retrospective, Int Mus Photog, George Eastman House, 58 & Mus Mod Art, 76; Mod Mus, Stockholm, Sweden, 78; one-man shows, Mass Inst Technol, 68, traveling exhib, George Eastman House, 71, Light Gallery, New York & Los Angeles, 80 & Colo Mountain Col, 81; The Magical Eye, Nat Gallery Can, Ottawa, 80. *Pos:* Head photog dept, Inst of Design, Ill Inst of Design, 49-61 & RI Sch of Design, 64-75. *Teaching:* Instr photog, Inst Design, Ill Inst Technol, Chicago, 46-49, photog dept head, 49-61, assoc prof, 61-64, prof, 64-77; chmn dept photog, RI Sch Design, 61-73; vis instr, Black Mountain Col, 51, Univ Calif Exten, Berkeley, 66 & Univ Mass, Boston, 74. *Awards:* Guggenheim Fel, 72; Photogr & Educator Award, Soc Photog Educ, 76; Hon Photogr, Rencontres Int de la Photog, Arles, France, 77. *Bibliog:* Harry Callahan: Photographs, El Mochuelo Press, 64; Sherman Paul (auth), The Photography of Harry Callahan, Mus Mod Art, 67; John Szarkowski (auth), Callahan, Museum of Modern Art, Aperture, 76. *Mailing Add:* 153 Benefit St Providence RI 02903

CALLAHAN, KENNETH
PAINTER
b Spokane, Wash, Oct 30, 05. *Work:* Whitney Mus Am Art, New York; Mus Mod Art, New York; Metrop Mus Art, New York; Pa Acad Fine Arts, Philadelphia; Brooklyn Mus; plus many other pub & pvt collections. *Comn:* Murals, US PO Bldgs, Centralia & Anacortes, Wash & Rugby, NDak; murals, Wash State Libr, Olympia, 60, Seattle Civic Theater, 62, Syracuse Univ, 64 & Wash Mutual Savings Bank, 70; plus others. *Exhib:* Many nat & int group & one-man shows. *Pos:* Panel selection, Tamarind Lithography Workshop, 59-69. *Teaching:* Vis artist, Syracuse Univ, Pa State Univ, Boston Univ, Univ Southern Calif, Skowhegan Sch Painting & Sculpture & others. *Awards:* Guggenheim Fel, 54-55; Nat Inst Arts & Lett Grant, 68; Am Acad Arts & Lett Purchase Award, New Orleans Art Mus, 72; plus others. *Mem:* Wash State Arts Comn; assoc mem Nat Acad Design. *Publ:* Auth, articles in Seattle Times, Art News, Art Digest, Creative Art & Am Mag Art. *Dealer:* Kraushaar Galleries 1055 Madison Ave New York NY 10021. *Mailing Add:* Box 493 Long Beach WA 98631

CALLE, PAUL
PAINTER, WRITER
b New York, NY, Mar 3, 28. *Study:* Pratt Inst. *Work:* Thomas Gilcrease Inst Am Hist & Art, Tulsa, Okla; Nat Cowboy Hall of Fame & Western Heritage Ctr, Oklahoma City; Nat Air & Space Mus, Washington, DC; NASA Fine Art Collection; US Dept Interior; and others. *Comn:* NASA, Cape Kennedy, Jet Propulsion Lab, Star City, Moscow, USSR, 68-75; Basic History of Iron & Steel, Basic Indust, 68-70; Nat Park Serv, Mesa Verde, Yosemite, Cape Hatterus, 70-74; Classics in Surgery, Schering Co, 71-73; and others. *Exhib:* 1st Convocation Western Art, Dallas, Tex; 2nd Convocation Western Art, Arlington, Tex; NASA Eyewitness to Space, Nat Gallery Art, Washington, DC; NASA Apollo-Soyuz, Moscow, 75; and others. *Awards:* Distinguished Western Art Gold Medal, Franklin Mint, 74; Hamilton King Award, Soc Illusr; Mill Pond Press Award, Northwest Rendezvous, 79 & 80; and others. *Mem:* Soc Illusr; Northwest Rendezvous Group. *Media:* Oil, Pencil. *Publ:* Auth & illusr, The Pencil, Watson & Guptill, 75. *Mailing Add:* 149 Little Hill Dr Stamford CT 06905

CALLICOTT, BURTON HARRY
PAINTER, CALLIGRAPHER
b Terre Haute, Ind, Dec 28, 07. *Study:* Cleveland Sch Art, cert, 31. *Work:* Brooks Art Gallery, Memphis, Tenn; Tenn Art Comn, Nashville; Miss Art Asn, Jackson; Ark Art Ctr, Little Rock; Addison Gallery Am Art. *Comn:* Three mural panels, Pub Works Admin Proj, 34-35. *Exhib:* New York World's Fair Exhib Am Painting, 39; Iron Horse in Art, Fort Worth Mus Art, Tex, 58; one-man shows, Brooks Art Gallery, 65, Miss Art Asn, 69 & Memphis Acad Arts, 71; Brooks Art Gallery, 74. *Teaching:* Prof drawing, painting & calligraphy, Memphis Acad Arts, 37-73. *Awards:* Purchase Award, Ark Art Ctr, 69 & Hors Concour Award, 70; Worthen Bank Award, Little Rock, 71. *Bibliog:* Edward Faiers (auth), catalog foreword, Memphis Acad Arts, 61; Sherwin Simmons (auth), catalog foreword, Brooks Art Gallery, Memphis, 74. *Media:* Oil. *Mailing Add:* 3395 Douglass Ave Memphis TN 38111

CALLISEN, STERLING
HISTORIAN, LECTURER
b New York, NY, Mar 30, 1899. *Study:* Princeton Univ, AB, 20; Harvard Univ, MA, 34, PhD, 36. *Pos:* Pres, Parsons Sch Design, 59-64, emer pres, 64-; dir, Col Art Asn Art Slide Proj, Ford Found, 71- *Teaching:* Asst fine arts, Harvard Univ, 34-36; asst prof, Rochester Univ, 36-41; assoc dean, Wesleyan Univ, 45-49; dean educ, Metrop Mus Art, 49-59; prof art hist, Pace Univ, 65-71; vis lectr, NY Univ, 72- *Mem:* Sch Art League; Col Art Asn Am; Scarsdale Art Asn; Am Asn Archit Historians; Mus Asn Clubs; and others. *Mailing Add:* 10 Ridgecrest W Scarsdale NY 10583

CALLNER, RICHARD
PAINTER, EDUCATOR
b Benton Harbor, Mich, May 18, 27. *Study:* Univ Wis, BS(art); Art Students League; Acad Julian, Paris, France, cert; Columbia Univ, MAFA. *Work:* Philadelphia Mus Art, Pa; Chicago Art Inst; Cincinnati Art Mus; Detroit Inst Art; Mus Painting & Sculpture, Israel. *Comn:* Tapestries, Mambush Tapestry Workshop, Ein Hod, Israel, 75-77. *Exhib:* Butler Inst Am Art Mid Yr Ann, Youngstown, Ohio, 57, 59, 61 & 62; Pa Acad Fine Arts Ann, Philadelphia, 58, 59, 61 & 63; DeCordova Mus, Lincoln, Mass, Ann Nat Print Exhib, Washington, DC; Watercolor Soc Ann, Washington, DC; Premio Int dell Arte, Sicily; one-man exhibs, US Info Serv, Italy, 67, Ger, 68 & 69 & Turkey, 73 & Bristol Mus, RI, 73. *Collections Arranged:* Kalamazoo Art Ctr, Mich, 64; Tyler Sch Art, 70; US Info Serv, Turkey, 73; Bristol Mus, RI, 75; State Univ NY Albany, 76. *Teaching:* Founding dir & prof painting, Tyler Sch Art, Temple Univ, Rome, Italy, 65-70; chmn dept art & prof painting, State Univ NY Albany, 75- *Awards:* Guggenheim Found Fel Painting, 59; Distinguished Fulbright Prof, 81. *Media:* Oil. *Mailing Add:* Art Dept State Univ NY Albany NY 12222

CALMAN, W(ENDY L)
PRINTMAKER, PHOTOGRAPHER
b New York, NY, Feb 23, 47. *Study:* Univ Pittsburgh, BA(art hist), 69; Tyler Sch Art, Temple Univ, MEd, 70, MFA(printmaking), 72. *Work:* Honolulu Acad Arts; Ark Art Ctr, Little Rock; Del Mar Col; Int Ctr Photog, George Eastman House, NY. *Exhib:* Photography Unlimited, Fogg Art Mus, Harvard Univ, 74; Photographer's Choice, Witkin Gallery, New York, 76; Photo/ Synthesis, Herbert F Johnson Mus, Ithaca, NY, 76; Uniquely Photographic, Honolulu Acad Arts, 79; 16th Joslyn Biennial, Joslyn Art Mus, 80; Photofusion, Pratt Manhattan Ctr Gallery, New York, 81; Sights Unseen, A I R Gallery, New York, 82. *Teaching:* Instr drawing & printmaking, Univ Tenn, Knoxville, 72-76; assoc prof printmaking, Ind Univ, Bloomington, 76- *Awards:* Best Graphic Award, 16th Joslyn Biennial, Joslyn Mus Art, 80. *Bibliog:* K Wise (auth), Photographer's Choice, Addison House Found, 76; Thelma Newman (auth), Innovative Printmaking, Crown Publ, 77; John Mayhill (auth), article, Indianapolis Monthly, 6/81. *Mem:* Col Art Asn; World Print Coun; Philadelphia Print Club. *Mailing Add:* Ind Univ Sch Fine Arts Bloomington IN 47405

CALROW, ROBERT F
INSTRUCTOR, PAINTER
b Lansing, Mich, Oct 20, 16. *Study:* Minn Sch Art, St Paul; Univ Minn, BArch; Minneapolis Sch Art. *Comn:* Hist montage watercolor, Kraft Foods Inc, New York, 71. *Exhib:* Am Watercolor Soc Annuals, Nat Acad Gallery, New York, NY, 70, 72, 77 & 83; Acad Artists Annuals, Springfield Mus, Mass, 72 & 73; Ann Juried Shows, Stamford Art Asn, Stamford Mus, Conn, 74 & 76; Rockport Art Asn, 83; and others. *Pos:* Dir, Caribbean and Maine Painting Tours & Cruises. *Teaching:* Teacher watercolor, Stamford & Greenwich, Conn & San Juan, PR, 68-75; workshops, Rockport, Mass, Bermuda, Puerto Rico, St Thomas & St John. *Awards:* Best of Show, Old Saybrook Conn Art Festival, 75; First Prize, Rowayton Ct Art Ctr Ann, 79 & 83; Katherine Howe Mem Award, Knickerbocker Artists, 79. *Mem:* Rockport Art Asn; Mamaroneck Art Guild; Conn Watercolor Soc; Acad Artists Inc, Springfield, Mass; Am Watercolor Soc; and others. *Media:* Transparent Watercolor, Ink. *Mailing Add:* 30 Glenbrook Rd Stamford CT 06902

CAMARATA, MARTIN L
EDUCATOR, PRINTMAKER
b Rochester, NY, June 10, 34. *Study:* NY State Univ Col Buffalo, BA, 56; NY Univ, MA, 57. *Work:* Mus Belles Artes, Caracas, Venezuela; Univ of the Pac; Calif State Col, Stanislaus. *Exhib:* Twenty-Second Painting Ann, Butler Inst Am Art, 57; Boston Printmakers Ann, 62-66; Philadelphia Print Club Ann, 65 & 66; Print-Drawing Ann, Pa Acad Fine Arts, 65, 66 & 68; Potsdam Ann Print-Drawing, NY, 74. *Teaching:* Prof drawing & printmaking, Calif State Col, Stanislaus, 64- *Awards:* First Prize Print, William J Keller Award, 56; Best of Show, Calif State Fair Art Exhib, 65; Print Award, Haggin Gallery-Mus, Calif, 66. *Bibliog:* T Albright (auth), rev in San Francisco Chronicle, 72 & 75. *Mem:* Calif Graphics (mem adv bd, 73-74). *Publ:* Auth, Lithography at Collectors Press, Artists Proof Mag, 72. *Mailing Add:* c/o Baum Gallery 2140 Bush St Suite 6 San Francisco CA 94115

CAMBLIN, BOB BILYEU
PAINTER
b Ponca City, Okla, Aug 1, 28. *Study:* Kansas City Art Inst, BFA, 54, MFA, 55; Fulbright study grant to Italy, 56-57. *Work:* Nelson-Atkins Mus Art, Kansas City, Mo; Joslyn Art Mus, Omaha, Nebr; Brooklyn Mus, NY; Yale Mus, New Haven, Conn; Fogg Mus, Harvard Univ, Cambridge, Mass. *Exhib:* Other Coasts (8 Tex Artists), Univ Calif, Long Beach, 71; Proj South/SW, Ft Worth Art Mus, Tex, 71; Extraordinary Realities, Whitney Mus Am Art, New York, 73; La State Univ, Baton Rouge, 76. *Bibliog:* N Laliberte & A Mogelon (coauths), Art in Boxes, Van Nostrand Reinhold, 74. *Media:* Watercolor, Pen & Ink. *Mailing Add:* c/o Moody Gallery 2015 J West Gray Houston TX 77019

CAMERON, BROOKE BULOVSKY
EDUCATOR, PRINTMAKER
b Madison, Wis. *Study:* Univ Wis, Madison, BS(art educ; honors); Univ Minn summer art hist tour of Europe with Prof Lorenz Eitner; Univ Iowa, with Maruicio Lasansky, MA(printmaking); NY Univ, viscosity printing workshop with Krishna Reddy, 82-83; Pratt Manhattan Graphics Ctr, litho & photo litho with James Martin & Ryo Watanabe. *Work:* Stephens Col, Columbia, Mo; Univ Wis Union, Madison; Mo State Hist Soc. *Comn:* Miss Willie, ed prints, Lakeside Studios, Mich, 77. *Exhib:* Mid-Am, St Louis Art Mus & Nelson-Atkins Mus, Kansas City, 68; Davidson Nat Print & Drawing Show, NC, 72; two-woman show with Nancy Bickford Bandy, US Info Agency/US Embassy, Turkey, 74-75; 3rd Ann Printmaking Competition, Tulsa City-Co Libr, Okla, 75; Women Printmakers, Univ Mo, Kansas City Fine Arts Gallery, 76; Women 77, Univ Mo Gallery, Kansas City, 77. *Teaching:* Instr art & art hist, Tex Christian Univ, Ft Worth, 66-67; from instr to assoc prof fine arts, Univ Mo, 67-, chmn dept art, 79-82. *Awards:* Printmaking Award, Crown Ctr Exhib Halls, Kansas City, Mo, 74. *Mem:* Col Art Asn Am; Women's Caucus Art. *Media:* Intaglio, Photo-intaglio. *Dealer:* Lakeside Studios 150 S Lakeshore Rd Lakeside MI 49116. *Mailing Add:* 923 College Park Columbia MO 65201

CAMERON, DUNCAN F
MUSEUM DIRECTOR
b Toronto, Ont, Feb 1, 30. *Work:* Royal Ont Mus, Toronto; Brooklyn Mus, NY; Glenbow-Alta Inst, Calgary; and many others. *Pos:* Sr adminr, Royal Ont Mus, Univ Toronto, 56-62; pres & chmn bd, Janus Mus Consult Ltd, Toronto, 62-71; nat dir, Can Conf Arts, Toronto, 68-71; dir, Brooklyn Mus, NY, 71-73; prin, P S Ross & Co, Mgt Consult, Toronto, 75-77; dir & chief exec officer, Glenbow-Alta Inst, Calgary, 77- *Teaching:* Occasional lectr museology, Royal Ont Mus, Univ Toronto, 71-76; adj prof art criticism, Univ Western Ont, London, 76-77. *Awards:* Samuel H Kress Found Res Grant, 74. *Mem:* Can Mus Asn; Coun Assoc Mus Dirs; Can Art Mus Dirs Orgn; Int Coun Mus; Commonwealth Asn Mus (pres, 83-). *Publ:* Auth, The Arts in Canada 1975: A Viewpoint, Can Coun, 75; auth, Gold for the Gods: A Review, Gazette, Quart Can Mus Asn, winter 77; auth, An Introduction to the Cultural Property Export and Import Act, Dept Secy State, Govt Can, 77; and others. *Mailing Add:* 130 Ninth Ave SE Ninth Ave & First St SE Calgary AB T2G 0P3 Canada

CAMERON, ELSA S
CURATOR, ADMINISTRATOR
b San Francisco, Calif, Nov 19, 39. *Study:* San Francisco State Univ, BA, 61 & MA, 65. *Collections Arranged:* Native American Ceramics: Contemporary Pueblo Works, 73, Works of Benemeno Serrano, 74, Food Show, 76, Foot Show, 76, Downtown Ctr & Downtown Dog Show, 78, M H de Young Mem Mus, San Francisco, Calif. *Pos:* Cur-in-charge, M H de Young Mem Mus Art Sch, Downtown Ctr, Fine Arts Mus of San Francisco, 66-80; chief cur for exhib & art collections, San Francisco Int Airport, 80-; consult for educ, Univ Art Mus, Berkeley; art consult, Gensler & Assoc Architects, San Francisco, 83. *Teaching:* Asst prof art education, Univ Southern Calif, 82-83. *Awards:* Nat Endowment Arts Fel, 73 & 76-77. *Res:* Writer and researcher in museum education and community arts. *Publ:* Contribr, Museum as educator, Univ Calif, Berkeley, 78. *Mailing Add:* San Francisco Int Airport Exhib Dept PO Box 8097 San Francisco CA 94128

CAMERON, ERIC
ADMINISTRATOR, PAINTER
b Leicester, Eng, Apr 18, 35. *Study:* Kings Col, Univ Durham, Newcastle, Eng, BA, 57, study with Lawrence Gowing, Victor Pasmore & Richard Hamilton; Courtauld Inst, Univ London, Acad Dipl(hist art), 59. *Work:* Coun, Art Bank, Ottawa, Ont; Art Gallery Ont, Toronto; Owens Art Gallery, Sackville, NB; Univ East Anglia, Norwich, Eng; Univ Leeds, Eng. *Exhib:* Woods II, Nat Gallery Can, 71 & Woods I, Art Gallery Ont, 71; Videoscape, Art Gallery Ont, 74; Video Show, Serpentine Gallery, London, Eng, 75; Int Video Exhib, Aarhus, Denmark, 76; Paintings in Mixed Exhib, Art Gallery NS, Halifax, 77; Newspaper Paintings & Lawn, Anna Leonowens Gallery, Halifax, NS, 77; Keeping Marlene Out of the Picture--and Lawn, Vancouver Art Gallery, BC, 78. *Pos:* Dir grad prog, NS Col Art & Design, Halifax, 76- *Teaching:* Lectr art & art hist, Univ Leeds, Eng, 59-69; assoc prof painting & video, Univ Guelph, Ont, 69-76. *Awards:* Can Coun grant collective projs, 71; Can Coun travel grant, 74; Can Coun video grant, 75. *Mem:* Univs Art Asn Can (Ont rep, 72-73, secy-treas, 73-76 & 76, vpres, 76-); fel Royal Soc Arts; Col Art Asn Am. *Media:* Oil, Acrylic. *Publ:* Auth, Lawrence Weiner: The Books, Studio Int, 74; auth, The Mysteries, 76, Dan Graham: Appearing in Public, 76, Art as Art and the Oxford Dictionary, Vanguard, 77 & Bill Beckley's Lies, 77, Artforum. *Dealer:* Art Metropole 241 Yonge St Toronto ON Can. *Mailing Add:* 5737 Southwood Dr 1991 Brunswick St Halifax NS B3H 1E6 Canada

CAMERON, JAMES H See Sepyo, James

CAMFIELD, WILLIAM ARNETT
HISTORIAN
b San Angelo, Tex, Oct 29, 34. *Study:* Princeton Univ, AB, 57; Yale Univ, MA, 61, PhD, 64. *Collections Arranged:* Francis Picabia Exhib (auth, catalog), Guggenheim Mus, New York, 70; Tabu Dada, Jean Crotti and Suzanne Duchamp (coauth, catalog), Kunsthall, Bern & Mus Fine Arts, Houston, 83; New Art from a New City--Houston (auth, catalog), Frankfurter Kunstverein, 83. *Teaching:* From asst prof to assoc prof mod Am & mod Europ art, Univ St Thomas, Houston, Tex, 64-69; from assoc prof to prof, Rice Univ, Houston, Tex, 69- *Awards:* Am Philos Soc Grant, 65; Am Coun

Learned Socs Grant-in-Aid, 68, Fel, 73-74; Nat Endowment Humanities Fel, 81. *Biblog:* F Will-Levaillant (auth), Picabia et la machine: symbole et abstraction, Rev l'Art, Paris, No 4, 69; Douglas David (auth), Big Dada, Newsweek, 9/70. *Mem:* Col Art Asn; founding mem Asn l'Etude Dada Surrealisme; co-founder, Tex Conf Art Historians. *Res:* Emphasis on Dada in Paris and art in France from about 1910 to 1925. *Publ:* Auth, Juan Gris and the golden section, 65 & The machinist style of Francis Picabia, 66, Art Bulletin; auth, Philip Renteria, Pelham-von Stoffler Gallery, 76; auth, Francis Picabia, Princeton Press, 79. *Mailing Add:* 1117 Milford Houston TX 77006

CAMHI, MORRIE
PHOTOGRAPHER, EDUCATOR
b New York, NY, Aug 16, 28. *Study:* Univ Calif, Los Angeles, BA, 56. *Work:* San Francisco Mus Mod Art; Ctr Creative Photog, Tucson; Oakland Mus; Israel Mus, Jerusalem; Magnes Mus, Berkeley. *Exhib:* Haiku, Camerawork, Christchurch, NZ, 76; Petaluma, San Francisco Art Inst, 77; Espejo, Ctr Contemp Photog, Chicago, 78, Oakland Mus, 78 & Ctr Creative Photog, Tucson, 83; Humanism, Consejo Fotografia, Mexico City, 79; Jews of Greece, Magnes Mus, Berkeley, 80; AD: Vantage, San Francisco Mus Mod Art, 83. *Pos:* Assoc ed, Photoshow Mag, 79-81. *Teaching:* Mem fac photog, San Francisco City Col, 69-; instr sem, Friends Photog & Univ Calif. *Awards:* Grants, Nat Endowment Arts, 77, Columbia Found, 78 & Magnes Mus, 80. *Biblog:* Milton Meltzer (auth), Eye of Conscience, Follett Press, 74; Don Owens (auth), articles, Picture Mag, 78 & 80. *Mem:* Soc Photog Educ. *Res:* Nature of medium; marketplace; international overview. *Publ:* Auth, Photography in China, Drakroom Mag, 81; auth, Back to basics, Camerawork Quart, 82; auth, Innovation over tradition, Photo Metro, 83. *Dealer:* Cityscape Gallery 97 E Colorado St Pasadena CA 91105. *Mailing Add:* 95 Marshall Ave Petaluma CA 94952

CAMINS, JACQUES JOSEPH
PAINTER, PRINTMAKER
b Odessa, Russia, Jan 1, 04; US citizen. *Study:* Paris, France; Art Students League; spec study with Jean Liberty & Byron Browne; Pratt Graphics Ctr, with Matsubara Naoka & Carol Summer. *Work:* Israel Mus, Jerusalem; Negev Mus, Bersheba, Israel; Fr Embassy Cult Inst in Israel; Copper-Hewitt Mus; Arnot Art Mus. *Exhib:* Veverly Gallery, New York, 64; Cript Gallery, Columbia Univ, 65; 50th Anniversary Audubon Artists at the Nat Acad Galleries, New York, 67; Artists Equity Asn Gallery, 71; Provincetown Art Asn, Mass, many years. *Teaching:* Instr painting, Lakewood, NJ Bd Educ, 67. *Biblog:* Frank Crotty (auth), profiles in Worchester Sunday Telegram & Provincetown Advocate, 65; Barbara Sloan (auth), profile in The Observer, 67. *Mem:* Artists Equity Asn; Provincetown Art Asn; Art Students League; Westbeth Graphics Workshop; Am Fedn Arts. *Media:* Oil. *Mailing Add:* 1065 98th St Studio 9 Bay Harbor Islands FL 33154

CAMLIN, JAMES A
PAINTER
b Hopkinton, Mass, Jan 16, 18. *Study:* Sch Practical Art, Boston; also with Aldro T Hibbard. *Exhib:* Acad Artists, Springfield Mus Fine Arts, Mass, 69; Allied Artists Am, Nat Acad Gallery, 70, Am Artists Prof League, Lever House, 70-75, Nat Art Club Ann Watercolor, 71, New York; Grand Prix de la Cote d'Azur, Cannes, France, 74. *Awards:* Diplome l'Honneur, Grand Prix de la Cote d'Azur, 73; Popular Award, Ogunquit Art Ctr, 73. *Mem:* Am Artists Prof League, New York; Ogunquit Art Ctr, Maine. *Media:* Watercolor. *Mailing Add:* 126 Franklin St Melrose MA 02176

CAMPANELLI, DAN
PAINTER
b Bronx, NY, Mar 18, 49. *Study:* Sch Visual Art, New York, grad, 69. *Work:* Portsmouth Mus Art, Va. *Exhib:* Am Drawings, El Paso Mus Art, Tex, 77, Albrecht Art Mus, St Joseph, 78, Yellowstone Art Ctr, Billings, Mont, 78 & Mint Mus Art, 78; Drawings Exhib 1977-79, Smithsonian Inst Traveling Exhib, major museums, 77-79; Temple Univ, Pa, 81; Art Gallery, Univ Ala; Cedar Rapids Art Ctr, Iowa. *Awards:* Distinguished Service Award, Am Artists Prof League-Grand Nat, 72 & Gold Medal Graphics, 73; Purchase Award, Portsmouth Mus, Va, 76. *Media:* Dry Brush Watercolor and Stone Lithography. *Publ:* Auth, cover article, Colonial Homes, 3-4/81. *Dealer:* Whistler's Daughter Gallery 88 S Finley Ave Basking Ridge NJ 07920. *Mailing Add:* Box 135 RD 1 Phillipsburg NJ 08865

CAMPANELLI, PAULINE EBLE
PAINTER
US citizen. *Study:* Ridgewood Sch Art, NJ, grad, 64; Art Students League, 65. *Exhib:* Catharine Lorillard Wolfe Art Club, Nat Arts Club & Nat Acad, New York, 75 & 77; Channel 39 On the Air Auction, Allentown Mus, Pa, 78; two-man show, Temple Univ, Pa, 81. *Awards:* Gold Medal Oils, 71 & 75 & Still Life Award, 72, Catharine Lorillard Wolfe Art Club; Distinguished Service Award, Am Artists Professional League, 72; and many others. *Biblog:* Cover article, rustic retreat, Colonial Homes Mag, 81. *Media:* Oils. *Publ:* Illusr, 4 Still-Life Oil Paintings, Scafa-Tornebene Publishers, 71. *Dealer:* Whistler's Daughter Gallery 88 S Finley Ave Basking Ridge NJ 07920. *Mailing Add:* Box 135 Rd 1 Phillipsburg NJ 08865

CAMPBELL, CHARLES MALCOLM
PAINTER, SCULPTOR
b Dayton, Ohio, Aug 27, 05. *Study:* Cleveland Art Inst, BA, 28. *Work:* Cleveland Mus Art, Ohio; Whitney Mus, New York; Phoenix Mus Art, Ariz. *Comn:* Paintings & murals for fed bldgs, Cleveland, Ohio, 35; post off murals, Kennedy, Tex, 36; mural panels for housing proj, Cleveland, 36; post off mural, Angola, Ind, 37. *Exhib:* 1st Biennial Exhib Contemp Am Sculpture,

Watercolors & Prints, Whitney Mus, New York, 33; Ferargil Galleries, New York, 42; Art Inst Chicago; Corcoran Gallery, DC; Brooklyn Mus; Mus Mod Art, DC; Metrop Mus Art, New York; Longview Mus & Art Ctr, Tex, 79; Lending Collection of Cleveland Mus; Rockefeller Ctr Munic Exhib. *Teaching:* Instr watercolor, Cleveland Art Inst, 28. *Awards:* May Show Awards, Cleveland, Ohio, 29-38. *Media:* Oil, Mixed Media. *Dealer:* Stewart Gallery 12610 Coit Rd Dallas TX 75230. *Mailing Add:* 2508 N 56th St Phoenix AZ 85008

CAMPBELL, COLIN KEITH
VIDEO ARTIST
b Reston, Man, Can, June 15, 42. *Study:* Univ Man, Winnipeg, BFA, 66; Claremont Grad Sch, Calif, MFA, 69. *Work:* Art Gallery Ont, Toronto. *Exhib:* Art/Video/Confrontation, Musee d'Art Moderne de la Ville de Paris, 74; Videoscape, Art Gallery Ont, 75; Video Art, Inst Contemp Art, Philadelphia, 75; Video Int, Aarhus Mus Art, Denmark, 75; Southland Video Anthology, Long Beach Art Mus, Calif, 77; Documenta 6, Kassel, Ger, 77. *Bibliog:* Eric Cameron (auth), Colin Campbell--The Story of Art Star, Vie des Arts, 76; Peggy Gale (auth), Colin Campbell--Windows & Mirrors, Video by Artists, 77 & Video art in Canada, Studio Int, 77. *Media:* Video. *Mailing Add:* c/o Art Metropole 241 Yonge St Toronto ON Canada

CAMPBELL, DAVID PAUL
PAINTER
b Takoma Park, Md, Mar 31, 36. *Study:* Art Students League, 57-58 & 61. *Work:* Mus Fine Arts, Boston. *Comn:* Painting, Gillette Co, Boston, 80. *Exhib:* A Sense of Place, Univ Nebr & Joslyn Mus, 73; Watercolor USA, Springfield Art Mus, 74; The Delaware Water Gap, Corcoran Gallery, 75; Directions in Realism, Danforth Mus, Framingham, Mass, 80; Brockton Art Mus Triennial, Mass, 80; Perspectives on Contemporary American Realism, Pa Acad Fine Arts, 82 & Art Inst Chicago, 83; Six From Around Town, Rose Art Mus, Waltham, Mass, 83. *Awards:* Purchase Award, Watercolor USA, Hallmark Inc, 74. *Bibliog:* Peter Merchant, John Pennington & Wendy Mason (dirs), David Campbell, Words and Watercolors (videotape), Somerville Educ TV, 84. *Media:* Watercolor, Ink. *Dealer:* Thomas Segal Gallery 73 Newbury St Boston MA 02116. *Mailing Add:* 22 Everett Ave Somerville MA 02145

CAMPBELL, DOROTHY BOSTWICK
PAINTER, SCULPTOR
b New York, NY, Mar 26, 1899. *Study:* Study with Eliot O'Hara, Washington, DC & Marilyn Bendell, Cortez, Fla. *Work:* Mystic Mus, Conn; Pioneer Gallery, Cooperstown. *Exhib:* Cooperstown Art Asn, var group & one-man shows, 65; var shows, Sarasota Art Asn, Fla & Pioneer Gallery, Cooperstown; Cortez Art Sch, Fla, 72. *Awards:* Purchase Prize Watercolor, Cooperstown Art Asn, 65; Merit Award for Oils, Cortez Sch Art Exhib, 72; Reasner Special, 75. *Mem:* Am Art League; Am Fedn Arts; Cooperstown Art Asn; Sarasota Art Asn; Longboat Art Asn, Fla. *Publ:* Auth & illusr, Passing Thoughts, Bks 1-14, 67-81. *Mailing Add:* 4315 Mangrove Pl Sarasota FL 33581

CAMPBELL, JEANNE BEGIEN
PAINTER, EDUCATOR
b Cincinnati, Ohio, Oct 21, 13. *Study:* Colorado Springs Sch Painting & Sculpture; Skowhegan Sch Painting & Sculpture; Richmond Sch Art, Col William & Mary. *Work:* Va Mus Fine Arts; Univ Richmond; Univ Va; Hollins Col; Roanoke Mus. *Exhib:* Va Mus Fine Arts; Phillips Gallery; Mint Mus Art. *Teaching:* From instr to assoc prof studio art, Univ Richmond, 44-83, cur, Marsh Gallery, 68-83, assoc prof emer, 83- *Awards:* Cite Artes, Paris, 68. *Media:* Acrylic, Oil. *Mailing Add:* 3715 Douglasdale Rd Richmond VA 23221

CAMPBELL, JEWETT
EDUCATOR, PAINTER
b Hoboken, NJ, Aug 10, 12. *Study:* Cooper Union; Art Students League; Skowhegan Sch Art, Maine; Hans Hofmann Sch of Art. *Work:* Mus Mod Art, New York; Va Mus Fine Arts, Richmond; Univ Va, Charlottesville. *Comn:* Mural, Va Educ Asn, Richmond, 50; mural, Chesapeake Corp, West Point, Va, 65. *Exhib:* One-man shows, Va Mus Fine Arts, Richmond, 43-70; Va Mus Fine Arts, Biennials, 48-70; Corcoran Biennial, Washington, DC; Art of the Armed Forces, Nat Gallery, Washington, DC, 44; retrospective, Anderson Gallery, Va Commonwealth Univ, 84. *Collections Arranged:* Avant-Garde Exhib, Richmond Artists Asn, 58. *Teaching:* Instr painting, Univ Richmond, 51-57 & Exten, Univ Va, 55-60; prof painting, Va Commonwealth Univ, 48-82, prof emer, 83- *Awards:* Purchase Awards, Va Mus, 40 & 60. *Media:* Oil. *Dealer:* Marc Moyens 2109 Paul Springs Rd Alexandria VA 22307; Gallery K 2032 P St NW Washington DC 20036. *Mailing Add:* 3715 Douglasdale Rd Richmond VA 23221

CAMPBELL, KENNETH FLOYD
HISTORIAN, SCULPTOR
b Ogden, Utah, Sept 17, 25. *Study:* Univ Utah, BFA, 50, MFA, 51; Univ Iowa, MA, 53; Univ San Carlos, Guatemala, cert, 56; Univ Wis, Eau Claire, BA, 70; Oxford Univ, England, dipl, 73, BLitt, MLitt, 77, DPhil, 81. *Work:* W G Skelley Mem, Tulsa Fairgrounds; Okla Art Ctr; Philbrook Art Ctr, Tulsa; Nat Indian Hall Fame, Anadarko, Okla. *Comn:* Judge Tillman D Johnson Sculpture, Utah Bar Asn, Salt Lake City, 51; Gov Warren Knowles Sculpture, Friends Warren Knowles, Madison, Wis, 65; small sculpture, Univ Wis, Eau Claire, 67; Old Abe Sculpture, Wilson Park Comn, Eau Claire, Wis, 69; Jim Thorpe Sculpture, Sac-Fox Tribal Coun, Shawnee, Okla, 79. *Exhib:* Eighth Midwest Biennial, Joslyn Art Mus, 64; Jewelry 64, Plattsburgh Col, NY, 64; Walker Art Ctr Biennial, 64; Okla Ann, Philbrook Art Mus, Tulsa, 67; 14th

Ann Drawing & Small Sculpture Exhib, Ball State Univ, 68; Nat Exhib Painting & Sculpture, Jersey City Mus, NJ, 69 & 70; Nat Sculpture Invitational, Okla Art Ctr, 70. *Teaching:* Chmn art dept, E Cent State Col, 53-64; chmn art dept, Univ Wis, Eau Claire, 64-67, prof art hist, 67- *Awards:* Purchase Award Sculpture, Fifth Ann Southwest Exhib, 63 & All-Okla Exhib, 64, Okla Art Ctr & Okla Ann, Philbrook Art Ctr, 64. *Bibliog:* Margaret Harold (auth), Prize Winning Graphics, 63 & Prize Winning Sculpture, 64, Margaret Harold Publ. *Mem:* Eau Claire Regional Arts Coun. *Media:* Stone, Bronze. *Res:* Skin-covered masks of Cross River region of Nigeria--Cameroun. *Publ:* Illusr, Men of Influence in Nuristan, Sem Press, London, 74; illusr, Nuristan, Akad Druck, Graz, Austria, 79; contribr, Le leopard, le serpent, et le crocodile, Arts d'Afrique Noire, France, 81; contribr, Kunst aus dem Alten Afrika, Staatlichen Mus, Munchen, Ger, 82; contribr, Nsibidi actualise, Arts d'Afrique Noire, France, 83. *Mailing Add:* 628 E Tyler Ave Eau Claire WI 54701

CAMPBELL, (JAMES) LAWRENCE
PAINTER, WRITER
b Paris, France, May 21, 14. *Study:* London Cent Schs Arts & Crafts; Acad Grande Chaumiere, Paris; Art Students League. *Work:* Joseph H Hirshhorn Mus & Sculpture Garden, Washington, DC. *Exhib:* One-man show, Contemp Arts, New York, 51; Am Fedn Arts Traveling Exhib, 55-56; Pa Acad Fine Arts Ann, Philadelphia; Weatherspoon Gallery, Univ NC; Realist Shows, circulated through State Univ NY, 70-72; plus others. *Pos:* Ed assoc, Art News Mag, 49-75; dir publ, Art Students League, 50- *Teaching:* Assoc prof studio art, Brooklyn Col, prof, 72-; vis prof art hist, Pratt Inst, 68- *Mem:* Int Asn Art Critics (mem, Am Sect); Art Students League. *Media:* Oil, Watercolor. *Res:* 19th & 20th century European and American painting; also Ruskin; history of Art Students League. *Publ:* Auth, Thomas Sills, 65; ed, The Elements of Drawing, Dover, 71; auth, articles, Art News, Art in Am & others. *Mailing Add:* 215 W 98th St New York NY 10025

CAMPBELL, MARJORIE DUNN
PAINTER, EDUCATOR
b Columbus, Ohio, Sept 14, 10. *Study:* Ohio State Univ, BS & MA; Claremont Col Grad Inst Art; Teachers Col, Columbia Univ; also with Hans Hofmann, Emil Bisttram & Millard Sheets. *Teaching:* Instr appl art, Univ Mo, 42-45; asst prof fine arts, Ohio State Univ, 45-49; asst prof art, Univ Northern Iowa, 49-71, assoc prof, 71-79, prof emer, 79- *Mem:* Art Educ Asn Iowa; Int Soc Educ through Art; Western Art Asn; Nat Art Educ Asn. *Publ:* Contribr, Sch Arts, Art Educ J & Everyday Art Mags. *Mailing Add:* Dept of Art Univ Northern Iowa Cedar Falls IA 50613

CAMPBELL, RICHARD HORTON
PAINTER, PRINTMAKER
b Marinette, Wis, Jan 11, 21. *Study:* Cleveland Sch Art; Art Ctr Sch, Los Angeles; Univ Calif, Los Angeles. *Work:* Theater Guild Am, New York; Hilton Hotel, Denver. *Exhib:* Los Angeles Co Mus, Calif; Denver Mus; Frye Mus, Seattle, Wash; Oakland Art Mus, Calif; De Young Mus, San Francisco. *Awards:* Second Prize, Los Angeles All-City Exhib, 51; First Prize, Cleveland May Show, 54; First Prize, 7th Festival of Arts, Los Angeles, 58. *Mem:* Nat Watercolor Soc; Los Angeles Art Asn; fel Int Inst Arts & Lett. *Media:* Oil. *Mailing Add:* 643 Baylor St Pacific Palisades CA 90272

CAMPBELL, VIVIAN (VIVIAN CAMPBELL STOLL)
COLLECTOR, WRITER
b Belmont, Mass, May 20, 19. *Pos:* Asst cur, Fogg Art Mus, Harvard Univ, 37-42; dir, Harry Stone Gallery, New York, 42-44; prod mgr & art ed, Woman's Press Mag, 44-47; ed art publ, UNESCO, Paris, 48-50; art reporter & ed, Life Mag, Paris & New York, 48-66; freelance writer, 60- *Mem:* ARC Directions; New York Printmakers Workshop (bd dirs, 69-); Inroads (bd dirs, 83-). *Collection:* Early and contemporary American painting and miniature portrait before 1830. *Publ:* Auth, A Christmas Anthology of Poetry & Painting, 47; contribr, Art Int, L'Oeil, Am Scholar & others. *Mailing Add:* 408 W 20th St New York NY 10011

CAMPBELL, WILLIAM HENRY
PAINTER
b Philadelphia, Pa, Sept 14, 15. *Study:* La France Art Inst, 28-30; Fleisher Art Mem, 30-33; Univ Pa, 33-34; Philadelphia Col Art, with Earl Horter, Franklin Watkins & Alex Bradevitch, dipl, 37. *Work:* Univ Del, Newark; Harcum Col & Ithan Valley Sch, Bryn Mawr, Pa; Container Corp Am, Chicago; Typographic Serv Inc, Philadelphia. *Exhib:* Pa Acad Fine Arts, Philadelphia, 35; Art Inst Chicago, 45; one-man shows, Philadelphia Art Alliance, 48 & 56 & Philadelphia Sketch Club, 60; Philadelphia Mus Art, 62; Artists Equity Asn, Civic Ctr, Philadelphia, 68, 71, 75 & 78; and many others. *Pos:* Art dir, Pa Railroad, Philadelphia, 53-58. *Teaching:* Instr illus, Moore Col Art, Philadelphia, 50-52; instr water media, Philadelphia Col Art, 63-65. *Awards:* Best Show, Wayne Art Ctr, 80; First Prize, Main Line Ann, 81; Prize, Ambler, Pa, 81. *Bibliog:* Paul Theobald (auth), Modern art in advertising, Container Corp, 46; Egbert Jacobson (auth), Good design, Graphis, Vol 6, 50; article, Art Direction, 12/58. *Mem:* Life mem Pa Sketch Club; Philadelphia Watercolor Club. *Media:* Gouache, Acrylic. *Mailing Add:* 552 North 23rd St Philadelphia PA 19130

CAMPOLI, COSMO
SCULPTOR, EDUCATOR
b South Bend, Ind, Mar 21, 22. *Study:* Art Inst Chicago, grad, 50, Anna Louise Raymond traveling fel to Italy, France & Spain, 50-52. *Work:* Mus Mod Art, New York; Va Mus Fine Arts; Unitarian Church, Chicago; City of Chicago Park Dist; Exchange Nat Bank, Chicago; and many pvt collections. *Exhib:*

The New Images of Man, Mus Mod Art, New York, 59; US Info Agency Show, Moscow & Petrograd; The Chicago School Exhibition, Galerie due Dragone, Paris; Festival of Two Worlds (sculpture exhib), Spoleto, Italy; 30-yr retrospective, Mus Contemp Art, Chicago, 71; and many others. *Teaching:* Instr adult art group, Hull House, 47-49; instr sculpture, Contemp Art Workshop, Chicago, 52-69; assoc prof sculpture, Inst Design, Ill Inst Technol, 53-69, chmn dept sculpture, 55-69; vis prof, Univ Chicago, summers 63-65; lectr original artist-mkt-concept, Conf World Affairs, Univ Colo, 72. *Awards:* Bronze Medal, Deleg Nat Educ-Fisica, Madrid, 69; Automotive Asn Spain Award, An Expression of the Automobile Obsession, 69; Knight of Mark Twain, 71; and others. *Bibliog:* Harold Haydon (auth), article, Chicago Sun-Times, 5/19/71; Franz Schulze (auth), article, Chicago Daily News, 5/29/71; Rev of 30-yr Retrospective, Fr TV, 6/71; and many others. *Publ:* Auth, Artists Market, Alumni Asn Newspaper, Sch Art Inst Chicago, 71. *Mailing Add:* 1150 E 54th Chicago IL 60615

CAMPUS, PETER
PHOTOGRAPHER, VIDEO ARTIST
b New York, NY, May 19, 37. *Study:* Ohio State Univ, BS, 60. *Comn:* Mass Inst Technol, 80. *Exhib:* Projected Art II, Corcoran Gallery Art, 71; Whitney Mus Am Art, 73, 75 & 76; Revision, Contemp Arts Mus, Houston, Tex, 73-74; Walker Art Ctr, 74 & 79; one-man exhibs, Everson Mus Art, Syracuse, 74, Film & Video, Whitney Mus Am Art, 78, Paula Cooper Gallery, New York, 81 & 82 & McIntosh-Drysdale Gallery, Washington, DC, 81; San Francisco Mus Art, 76; Projects Gallery, Mus Mod Art, New York, 77; Extended Photography, Int Biennale, Asn Visual Artists, Vienna, Austria, 81; Post Minimalism, Aldrich Mus Contemp Art, Ridgefield, Conn, 82; Festival of the Arts, Ctr Arts, Muhlenberg Col, Pa, 83; and others. *Teaching:* Fel, Mass Inst Technol, Cambridge, 76-78; RI Sch Design, 82-83. *Awards:* Guggenheim Fel, 75; Nat Endowment Arts Fel, 76. *Bibliog:* Bruce Kurtz (auth), Fields, Peter Campus, Arts Mag, 5/73; Roberta Smith (auth), About faces, the new work of Peter Campus, Art in Am, 3-4/77. *Media:* Photographs; Video Tape. *Mailing Add:* c/o Paula Cooper Gallery 155 Wooster St New York NY 10012

CANADAY, JOHN EDWIN
CRITIC
b Ft Scott, Kans, Feb 1, 07. *Study:* Univ Tex, BA; Yale Univ, MA; Ecole Louvre, Paris; Univ Rochester, LHD, 74; Tulane Univ, LHD, 83. *Pos:* Chief, Div Educ, Philadelphia Mus Art, 51-59; art critic, New York Times, 59-76. *Teaching:* Assoc prof art hist, Univ Va, 38-50; prof art hist & head, Sch Art, Newcomb Col, Tulane Univ, 50-52; vis prof, Univ Tex, Austin, 77. *Publ:* Auth, Mainstreams of Modern Art, Holt, 59, revised, 81; auth, Embattled Critic: Views on Modern Art, FS&G 62; auth, Culture Gulch, FS&G, 69; auth, Lives of the Painters, Norton, 69; auth, What is Art, Knopf, 80; coauth (with Katherine H Canaday), Keys to Art, Tudor, 64. *Mailing Add:* 25 Sutton Pl S New York NY 10022

CANADAY, OUIDA GORNTO
PAINTER, EDUCATOR
b Lake Wales, Fla, Apr 26, 22. *Study:* Univ Tampa; Atlanta Art Inst; Flat Rock Sch Art; Ga State Univ. *Work:* Ga State Univ; Eufaula Art Mus, Ala; Emory Univ; Mus Art, Greenville, SC. *Comn:* Acrylic, Morris Brown Col, 68; six batiks, Ga Tech Univ, 69; stained glass, Cobb Fed Bldg, Marietta, Ga, 69; Woodrow Wilson Commemorative, First Fed Bldg, Atlanta, 71; acrylic, US Corps Eng 200 Anniversary Commemorative, 75. *Exhib:* Mus Arts & Sci, Macon, Ga, 64 & 74; Southeastern Art Exhib, High Mus, Atlanta, 67 & Ga Artists Show, 72; Hunter Ann, Chattanooga, Tenn, 69; Calloway Gardens Art Show, Pine Mountain, Ga, 71. *Teaching:* Teacher, Studio Group Classes, 60-; teacher, Worldwide Painting Group Tours, 65-; mem fac art, Emory Univ, 68-73; mem fac art, Reinhardt Col, 72. *Awards:* Purchase Award, Eufaula Arts Festival; Honorable Mention, Calloway Gardens Art Show; Spec Award, Atlanta Beautiful Comn. *Bibliog:* Charlotte Hale Smith (auth), Ladies paint the world, 64, The wide world beckons, 65 & Doris Lockerman (auth), Painters world, 70, Atlanta J-Constitution Mag. *Mem:* Arts Festival Atlanta; Atlanta Artist Club; Ga Arts Comn; Fine Arts Comn. *Media:* Oil, Metallic. *Publ:* Georgia Sketchbook, Peachtree Publ, 81. *Dealer:* Ann Jacob Gallery Peachtree Ctr Atlanta GA 30303. *Mailing Add:* 2722 Rovena Ct Decatur GA 33034

CANBY, JEANNY VORYS
ARCHAEOLOGIST, CURATOR
b Columbus, Ohio, July 14, 29. *Study:* Bryn Mawr Col, BA, 50, PhD, 59; Oriental Inst, Univ Chicago, MA, 54. *Collections Arranged:* Egyptian Collection (rearranged), Walters Art Gallery, Baltimore, 65, Ancient Near Eastern and Egyptian Collection (re-installed new wing), 74-75; special exhibits, Ancients Seals, Egyptian Sculptor's Models & Sculpture from Sumer and Akkad (with catalog), 70; In Search of Ancient Treasure, 78; Ancient Persia, Art of an Empire, 78; Jewelry, Ancient to Modern (Egyptian & Near Eastern), 79; Egypt's Golden Age, 82. *Pos:* Asst cur ancient art, Walters Art Gallery, 64-71; cur ancient Near Eastern & Egyptian art, 71- *Teaching:* Vis lectr, Near Eastern archaeol, Johns Hopkins Univ, Baltimore, 60-64. *Mem:* Archaeol Inst Am; Am Oriental Soc; Am Res Ctr, Egypt. *Publ:* Auth, Decorated garments in Ashurnasirpalis sculpture, XXXII: 31-53, & The Stelenreihen at Assur, Tell Halaf & Massebot, XXXVIII: 113-128, Iraq; auth, Some Hittite figurines in the Aegean, Hesperia, XXXVIII: 14-149; auth, Walters Gallery Cappadocian tablet and the Sphinx in Anatolia in the Second Millennium, BC, J Near Eastern Studies, Vol 34 (1975): 225-248; The jewelry of the ancient Near East & The jewelry of ancient Egypt, In: Jewelry Ancient to Modern, 80. *Mailing Add:* 211 Haviland Mill Rd Brookeville MD 20833

CANDAU, EUGENIE
LIBRARIAN
b San Francisco, Calif, Jan 26, 38. *Study:* Fat City Sch Finds Art, MFA, 73; San Francisco State Univ, BA, 74; Univ Calif, Berkeley, MLS, 78. *Collections Arranged:* Kaethe Kollwitz, San Francisco Mus Art, 70; Hand Bookbinding Today, An International Art (traveling exhib), San Francisco Mus Mod Art, 78. *Pos:* Librn, Louise Sloss Ackerman Fine Arts Libr, San Francisco Mus Mod Art, 68- *Mem:* Col Art Asn; Art Libr Soc NAm; Int Inst Conserv; Man Mus Finds Art; Pac Ctr Bk Arts. *Interests:* Arts of the book; modern & contemporary art. *Publ:* Ed, Permanent Collection of Painting & Sculpture (catalog), San Francisco Mus Art, 70; contribr, bibliographies to San Francisco Mus Mod Art publ, 70-; auth, articles and reviews in Fine Print and Art Week, 76-; auth, Hand Bookbinding Today, An International Art (catalog), 78; contribr, P Selz, In: Art in Our Times, Abrams, 81; and others. *Mailing Add:* 2108 Derby St Berkeley CA 94705

CANFIELD, JANE (WHITE)
SCULPTOR
b Syracuse, NY, Apr 29, 1897. *Study:* Art Students League; James Earle & Laura Gardin Fraser Studio; Borglum Sch; also with A Bourdelle, Paris, France. *Work:* Whitney Mus Am Art; Cornell Univ Mus Art. *Comn:* Six animals in lead for gate posts, comn by Paul Mellon, Upperville, Va, 40; animals in lead for gym entrance, Miss Porters Sch, Farmington, Conn, 60; St John Apostle in stone, Church of St John of Lattington, Locust Valley, NY, 63; herons in stone, Mem Sanctuary, Fishers Island, 69; Canada geese in bronze for pool, Long Lake, Maine, 71. *Exhib:* Sculpture Pavilion, New York World's Fair, 39; one-man shows, Brit-Am Art Gallery, New York, 55 & Far Gallery, New York, 61, 65 & 74; Country Art Gallery, Locust Valley, 71. *Media:* Stone, Bronze. *Publ:* Auth, The Frog Prince, Swan Cove, Harper, 70. *Dealer:* Far Gallery 22 E 80th St New York NY 10021. *Mailing Add:* Guard Hill Rd Bedford NY 10506

CANIFF, MILTON ARTHUR
CARTOONIST
b Hillsboro, Ohio, Feb 28, 07. *Study:* Ohio State Univ, with Martha Schauer, James Hopkins, Ralph Fanning, Guy Brown Wiser & Hoyt Sherman, BA; Rollins Col & Univ Dayton, hon FAD, Ohio State Univ, LHD. *Work:* Metrop Mus Art, New York; Louvre (graphics), Paris, France; Air Force Mus, Dayton, Ohio; Nat Aviation Club, Washington, DC; Ohio State Univ Journalism Libr. *Comn:* Murals, Nat Aviation Club, 60, Flag Plaza, Pittsburgh, Pa, 68, Alumni House, 71 & Ohio Union, 79, Ohio State Univ; Conv Ctr, Dayton, 72. *Exhib:* Art of the Cartoon, Graphics Hall, Louvre, Paris, 66 & Lever Gallery, New York, 71; Cartoon Now, Kennedy Ctr, Washington, DC, 75; Felicia Gallery, New York, 83; Whitney Mus Am Art, 83; Gallery Cartoon Art, Rye Brook, NY. *Awards:* Reuben Award, Nat Cartoonists Soc, 47 & 72, Segar Award, 71; Cartoonist Hall of Fame, 79. *Bibliog:* Stephen Becker (auth), Comic art in America, Simon & Schuster. *Mem:* Nat Cartoonists Soc (pres, 48-50, hon chmn, 70-); Soc Illustrators. *Media:* Ink, Watercolor. *Publ:* Auth & illusr, Dickie Dare, 32-34; auth & illusr, Terry and the Pirates, syndicated newspaper feature, 34-46; auth & illusr, Male Call, US Serv Newspapers, 42-45; auth & illusr, Steve Canyon, syndicated newspaper feature, 47- *Dealer:* Toni Mendez 140 E 56th St New York NY 10022. *Mailing Add:* 333 E 45th St New York NY 10017

CANNIFF, BRYAN GREGORY
DESIGNER, DIRECTOR
b Minneapolis, Minn, Dec 26, 48. *Study:* Minneapolis Col Art & Design, BFA, 71. *Collections Arranged:* Designer, The Life of Florence Ziegfeld (and 40 other maj shows), New York City Mus, 75 & Bicentennial Exhib, South St Seaport Mus, 76. *Pos:* Art dir, New York City Mus, 72-75; designer, South St Seaport Mus, New York, 75-76 & Mus Mod Art, New York, 76-79; art dir, Saturday Rev Mag Corp, New York, 79-80, Panorama Mag, 81 & Boating Mag, 81-83; graphics dir, Popular Mechanics Mag, 83- *Awards:* Cert of Distinction, Art Direction Mag, 79, 82 & 83; Award of Merit, Soc Illusr, 82; Desi Awards, 82 & 83. *Mem:* Soc Publ Designers; Art Dirs Club; Soc Illusr. *Mailing Add:* 281 West 11th St New York NY 10014

CANNULI, RICHARD GERALD
PAINTER, GALLERY DIRECTOR
b Philadelphia, Pa, Feb 2, 47. *Study:* Villanova Univ, BFA, 73; Art Students League, 75; Pratt Inst, MFA, 79. *Comn:* Paintings, St Nicholas Tolentine Church, Bronx, 77-79, Assumption-St Paul Parish, Mechanicville, NY, 78 & St Augustine Prep Chapel, Richland, NJ, 80-81; Dedication Cross, Connelly Ctr, Villanova Univ, 80; Design the Chapel, Biscayne Col, Fla, 81. *Exhib:* Expressions, Earth Art, Mus Philadelphia Civic Ctr, 79; Creative Dimensions, Carrier Found, Bellmead, NJ, 79; Liturgical Art, Pavilion Gallery, Mt Holly, NJ, 81. *Teaching:* Instr studio art & hist, Msgr Bonner High Sch, Drexel Hill, Pa, 73-78; asst prof studio art & dir gallery, Villanova Univ, 79- *Media:* Oil, Fabric. *Mailing Add:* Art Gallery Connelly Ctr Villanova Univ Villanova PA 19085

CANO, MARGARITA
LIBRARIAN, PAINTER
b Havana, Cuba, Feb 27, 32. *Study:* Univ Havana, PhD, 56, MLibSc, 62; studies in art hist & mus conserv with Helmut Ruheman from Nat Gallery, London, Eng. *Work:* Mutual of Omaha Ins Co, Miami, Fla; Lowe Art Mus, Univ Miami, Coral Gables, Fla. *Exhib:* Mem Exhib, Ft Lauderdale Mus, Fla; Piedmont Graphics Ann, Mint Mus, Charlotte, NC; Hunterton Art Ctr, Clinton, NJ; Mem Exhib, Metrop Mus & Art Ctr, Miami, Fla; Pan-Am Exhib, Miami, Fla. *Collections Arranged:* Cintas Fellows, Paintings by Cuban Artists (auth, catalog), 77, Miami-Dade Pub Libr, Fla; Latin Am Graphics,

Permanent Collection, Miami-Dade Pub Libr Syst, 78; A Face is a Face is a Face, South Dade Regional Libr, 79; The Romance of an Era, Colonial Art in Cuba, Main Libr, 80; and others. *Pos:* Registr, Julio Lobo Found, Napoleonic Art Mus, 57-58; art librn, Miami-Dade Pub Libr, 63-80; art service adminr, Ctr Fine Arts & Main Libr, Dade, Fla, 80- *Teaching:* Instr contemp Latin Am art, Miami-Dade Community Col, South Campus, 77. *Awards:* Cintas Found Fel, 75-76. *Mem:* Art Libr Soc NAm. *Media:* Encaustic. *Res:* Contemporary Latin American art and keeping up-to-date materials on new artists. *Publ:* Auth, How to Bridge the Art Gap, Art Libr Soc NAm, 76; auth, Dictionary of Latin American Artists (bibliog), Cintas Found, 76; and others. *Mailing Add:* 501 SW 24th Ave Miami FL 33135

CANRIGHT, SARAH ANNE
PAINTER
b Chicago, Ill, Aug 20, 41. *Study:* Art Inst Chicago, BFA. *Work:* Kresge Found, New York; Art Inst Chicago; Nat Collection Fine Art, Washington, DC; Chase Manhattan Bank, London; Am Tel & Tel Corp, Richmond, Va; and others. *Exhib:* Whitney Biennial, New York, 74; Franklin Furnace, New York, 79; Phyllis Kind Gallery, Chicago, 79; Pam Adler Gallery, New York, 79-81; Walker Art Ctr, Minneapolis, 81; and others. *Teaching:* Instr, Princeton Univ, 78-; instr, Skowhegan Sch Painting & Sculpture, 80; vis sr lectr, Univ Tex, Austin, 82- *Awards:* Armstrong Award, Art Inst Chicago, 71; Nat Endowment Arts Fel Grant, 75 & 78; Creative Artists Public Serv Prog Grant, 77. *Bibliog:* Peter Frank (auth), article, Village Voice, 7/10/78; John Russell (auth), article, New York Times, 6/20/80; Rob Storr (auth), article, Arts Mag, 9/81. *Media:* Oil. *Dealer:* Pam Adler Gallery 37 W 57th St New York NY 10019. *Mailing Add:* 161 Mulberry St New York NY 10013

CANTIENI, GRAHAM ALFRED
PAINTER, ADMINISTRATOR
b Albury, Australia, Aug 26, 38; Can citizen. *Study:* Royal Melbourne Teachers' Col, sec teaching cert; Royal Melbourne Inst of Technol; Univ Melbourne; Univ Concordia. *Work:* Univ Montreal, Musee d'art Contemporain, La Soc Teleglobe Can, Montreal; Univ Sherbrooke, Que; Art Bank, Can Coun; and others. *Exhib:* New Brunswick Mus, St John, 71; Galerie de l'Anse-aux-Barques, Mus Que, 77; SGW Gallery, Univ Concordia, Montreal, 78; Galerie L'Aquatinte, Montreal, 79 & 81; Musee d'art de Joliette, 80; and many others. *Collections Arranged:* Concours d'estampe et de dessin, 77 & 79-81; Voir pour Voir, 80-81; Sherbrooke, 81; and others. *Pos:* Art dir, Cult Centre, Univ Sherbrooke, 76-83. *Teaching:* Art master practice & hist of art, Wesley Col, Perth, Australia, 67-68; animateur painting & graphics, Ateliers d'Animation Cult, Sherbrooke, 69-76; cert artistique, Univ Shebrooke, 74-76; vis prof, Univ Victoria, 83-84. *Awards:* Sr Bursary, Minister Cult Affairs, Que. *Bibliog:* Jean Tourangeau (auth), Graham Cantieni, polyphonies, Vie des Arts, Number 89, 77; Rene Viau (auth), Cantieni a la fois peinture et dessin, Cahiers 3, 79; Jules Arbec (auth), Imaginer le monde, DeVoir, 79. *Mem:* Regroupement des Artistes des Cantons de l'est (pres, 73-75); Soc des Artistes Prof du Que (vpres, 77); Societe des Musees Que; Asn Int des critiques d'art. *Media:* Oil, Ink. *Publ:* Auth, Les arts graphiques dans l'histoire, 79; auth, Pierrette Mondou, Vie des Arts, 80; auth, Biennales a la New Yorkaise, Cahiers, 81; auth, Olaf Hanel, dessins et sculptures, 81; and many others. *Dealer:* Warren Sanderson Fine Arts 4125 Blucridge Cres #43 Montreal PQ H3H 1S7 Can; Galerie Don Stewart 1460 ouest rue Sherbrooke Montreal PQ Can. *Mailing Add:* 3260 Quadra St Apt 208 Victoria BC V8X 1G2 Canada

CANTINE, DAVID
PAINTER
b Jackson, Mich, June 7, 39. *Study:* Univ Iowa, BA, 62, MA, 64. *Work:* Mazur Mus, Monroe, La. *Exhib:* One-man shows, Univ Saskatchewan, Univ Alberta & Northern State Univ, 66, 67 & 69, Mazur Mus, 72 & Kraushaar Galleries, New York, 77 & 82. *Mem:* Col Art Asn Am. *Media:* Oil, Acrylic Polymer. *Dealer:* Kraushaar Galleries 724 5th Ave New York NY. *Mailing Add:* 99 St Georges Crescent Edmonton AB T5N 3M7 Canada

CANTINI, VIRGIL D
PAINTER, SCULPTOR
b Italy, Feb 28, 20. *Study:* Carnegie Inst Technol, BFA, 46; Univ Pittsburgh, MA, 48; Duquesne Univ, Hon DFA, 81. *Work:* Wichita Mus Art, Kans; Carnegie Mus Art, Pittsburgh, Pa; Westmoreland Co Mus Art, Greensburg, Pa; Hillman Libr, Univ Pittsburgh; Point Park Col. *Comn:* Three sculptures & two tapestries, Hillman Libr, 69 & Nat Sci Bldg, 74, Univ Pittsburgh; Joy of Life (fountain sculpture), Urban Redevelop Authority, Pittsburgh, 69; Skyscape (enamel mural), Oliver Tyrone Co, Pittsburgh, 71; enamel murals, Univ Pittsburgh, 75 & 77. *Exhib:* Assoc Artists Pittsburgh, 45-70; Pittsburgh Int, Carnegie Mus Art, 61, 64 & 67; one-man shows, Westmoreland Co Mus Art, 62 & Pittsburgh Plan for Arts, 62, 67, 72, 75 & 78; Enamels 50/80, Brookfield Craft Ctr Gallery, Conn, 81. *Pos:* Vpres, Pittsburgh Coun for Arts, 68-70. *Teaching:* Prof art & chmn dept studio arts, Univ Pittsburgh, 52- *Awards:* Guggenheim Fel, 58; Pope Paul VI Bishop's Medal, 64; Davinci Medal-Ital Sons & Daughters Am, Cultural Heritage Found, 68. *Bibliog:* Dorothy Sterling (auth), article, Am Artist, 52; Helen Knox (auth), article in Pitt Mag, 64; Lloyd Davis (auth), article, Appalachian, 67. *Mem:* Assoc Artists Pittsburgh (pres, 62-64); Arts & Crafts Ctr (vpres, 55-57); Pittsburgh Plan for Arts; Col Art Asn Am; Am Crafts Coun. *Media:* Enamel. *Dealer:* Pittsburgh Plan for Arts 407 S Craig St Pittsburgh PA 15206. *Mailing Add:* Dept of Studio Arts Univ of Pittsburgh Pittsburgh PA 15260

CANTONE, VIC
CARTOONIST, WRITER
b New York, NY, Aug 7, 33. *Study:* Art Instr Schs, Inc, Minneapolis, dipl, 51; Sch Art & Design, New York, dipl, 52; Nassau Col, Garden City, NY, AA(cum laude), 78; Hofstra Univ, Hempstead, BA, 79. *Collections Arranged:* Cataloged Political Cartoons/Caricatures 1976-1983, Int Pavillion Humour, Montreal; Reins of Power, Mus of Cartoon Art, Portchester, NY, 79. *Pos:* Cartoonist, Newsday, Melville, NY, 54-59; political cartoonist, caricaturist, New York Daily News, 59-, Rothco Syndicate; Wall Street Journal Report (nat TV), 82-83; From the Editor's Desk (nat TV), 83. *Teaching:* Lectr, Nassau Col, NY, 77, Hofstra Univ, 79, New York Press Club, 80 & Asn Am Editorial Cartoonists, 83. *Awards:* Fourth Estate Award, Am Legion, 76; Recognition Award, Nat Conf Christians & Jews, 77; George Washington Honor Medal, Freedoms Found, 78; plus others. *Bibliog:* Marcia Ledwith (auth), In Search of Perspective, Chronicle, 79; cover story, Vic Cantone, Editorial Cartoonist, Illusr Mag, 79; Reach Out, Cable & Satellite, 5/83. *Mem:* Asn Am Ed Cartoonists; New York Press Club. *Publ:* Auth & illusr, Topo the Mouse, T S Denison & Co, 69; auth & illusr, The Sea Circus, Chicago Tribune, 70; auth & illusr, newspaper & mag articles; auth-illusr, More Women Cartoonists Sought, Ed & Publ Mag, 76. *Mailing Add:* PO Box 1345 Grand Cent Station New York NY 10017

CANTOR, B GERALD
COLLECTOR
b New York, NY, Dec 17, 16. *Study:* NY Univ, Hon DFA, 80. *Pos:* Chmn, Cantor, Fitzgerald, New York, Chicago, Boston, Dallas & Beverly Hills; trustee, Los Angeles Co Mus Art; mem pres coun, Col of the Holy Cross. *Mem:* Am Fedn Arts; Fine Arts Soc San Diego; Brooklyn Inst Arts & Sci; fel Metrop Mus Art; fel Cleveland Mus Art. *Interests:* Large scale donations, scholarships to museums and universities. *Collection:* Nineteenth and early twentieth century sculpture and paintings; major collection of Auguste Rodin; George Kolbe. *Mailing Add:* c/o Cantor Fitzgerald & Co Inc 1 World Trade Ctr New York NY 10048

CANTOR, FREDRICH
PHOTOGRAPHER, PAINTER
b New York, NY, July 8, 44. *Study:* Pratt Inst, 62-64, 66 & 67; San Francisco Art Inst, 66; Cooper Union, 69. *Work:* Pa State Mus; New Orleans Mus Art, La; Sheldon Mem Art Gallery, Univ Nebr, Lincoln; Univ Mass Mus Art, Amherst; Bibliot Nat, Paris, France. *Exhib:* City Landscape, Bibliot Nat, Paris, France, 74; one-man shows, Sheldon Mem Art Gallery, Univ Nebr, Lincoln, 79, Galeria Diaframma, Milan, Italy, 80, Galerie Delpire, Paris, France, 80 & 82 La Galerie Le Trepied, Geneva, Switzerland, 81 & Marcuse Pfeifer Gallery, New York, 81; and others. *Teaching:* Special instr photographic printing, St Martin's Sch Art, London, Eng, 71; adj lectr photog, Brooklyn Col, NY, 74-76; instr photog & drawing, Parsons Sch Design, New York, 77-78. *Awards:* Fels, Yaddo, Saratoga Springs, NY, 78, Va Ctr Creative Arts, 79 & 80 & McDowell Colony, 80. *Bibliog:* Gene Thornton (auth), Fredrich Cantor, Zoom Mag, Paris, 6/73 & 4/80; Madeleine Deschamps (auth), Fredrich Cantor, Art Press, Paris, 5/80; Hilton Kramer (auth), Fredrich Cantor, New York Times, 5/17/81. *Mem:* Col Art Asn. *Media:* Silver Gelatin & Kodalith Prints; Oil. *Publ:* Auth, Rome: Vol 1, 77 & auth, Paris: 1982, 82, pvt publ; illusr, Soul Survivors, Ticknor & Fields, 83. *Mailing Add:* 338 West 11th St New York NY 10014

CANTOR, MIRA (MIRA CANTOR-PIENE)
SCULPTOR, GRAPHIC ARTIST
b New York, NY, May 16, 44. *Study:* State Univ NY, Buffalo, BFA, 66; Univ Ill, Champaign-Urbana, MFA, 69. *Comn:* Portraits comn by Negroponte Family, Brookline, Mass, 78; portraits comn by Baumann Family, Dusseldorf, Ger, 79; portrait comn by Renate Bohmer, Essen, Ger, 79; portrait comn by Dieter Schroder, Dusseldorf, Ger, 79. *Exhib:* III Exposition Int de Dessins, Musee d'Art Moderne, Yugoslavia, 72; Norwegian Int Print Biennale, Fredrikstad, 76 & 78; one-person show, Galerie Lohrl, Ger, 78; Boston Invitational '78, Brockton Art Ctr, Mass, 78; Three Dimensional Possibilities, Rose Art Mus, Waltham, Mass, 79; Centerbeach, Ctr Advan Visual Studies, Mass Inst Technol, 79 & 80; and others. *Pos:* Consult, Massport, 81-82. *Teaching:* Instr painting & drawing, Univ Hawaii, Honolulu, 70-71; instr drawing, Mass Inst Technol, 78-80 & Northeastern Univ, 83- *Awards:* Ctr Advan Visual Studies Fel, Mass Inst Technol, 78-80; Artists' Found Award, State Mass, 79; Artist-in-residence Award, Univ Hawaii, 82; and others. *Bibliog:* Jill Jannows (auth), Prize winners at Brandeis--art of the state, Boston Globe, 7/78; Christine Temin (auth), Sonesta Beach, it was art as fun, Boston Globe, 9/79; Forsling (auth), Sun, sand and surfeit, Art News, 11/79. *Media:* Graphite, Charcoal; Soft Materials. *Mailing Add:* 1129 Beacon St Brookline MA 02146

CANTOR, ROBERT LLOYD
EDUCATOR, DESIGNER
b New York, NY, Aug 14, 19. *Study:* NY Univ, PhD. *Exhib:* One-man show, Charleston Art Gallery, WVa; Fashion Inst Technol; Sampson Naval Ctr, Geneva, NY; many group shows. *Pos:* Exec dir, Artists Equity Asn, New York; educ dir, Am Craftsmen Sch, New York; dir, Visions Gallery-4, Ft Monmouth, NJ; art critic, New Leader. *Teaching:* Prof fine & indust arts & head dept, WVa Inst Technol; vis prof, State Univ NY, NY Univ, City Col New York & Columbia Univ. *Mem:* Comn Art Educ, Mus Mod Art; Rutgers Univ Art Gallery Friends (bd dirs). *Publ:* Auth, Plastics for the Layman. *Mailing Add:* 15 Gulf Rd Lawrence Brook East Brunswick NJ 08816

CANTRELL, JIM
PAINTER, CERAMIST
b Sulpher, Okla, Nov 23, 35. *Study:* Univ Nebr, Lincoln, BFA, 58; Pa State Univ, 59; Univ Northern Colo, Greeley, MA, 65. *Work:* Sheldon Mem Art Gallery, Lincoln, Nebr; Utah Mus Fine Art, Salt Lake City; Owensboro Mus Fine Art, Ky; Austin Peay State Univ, Tenn; Miss Mus Art, Jackson; and others. *Exhib:* One-man shows, Sheldon Mem Art Gallery, 70, Hunter Mus of Art, Chattanooga, Tenn, 73 & Distelheim Galleries, Chicago, 75; Mainstream, Grover M Hermann Fine Arts Ctr, Marietta, Ohio, 74; Eight State Ann, Speed Art Mus, Louisville, Ky, 74; Sunne Savage Gallery, Boston, 79; Southern Realism, Miss Mus Art, Jackson. *Pos:* Resident artist, Berea Col, 70-71. *Teaching:* Guest instr art, Univ Northern Colo, summer 66; assoc prof art, John F Kennedy Col, 66-70. *Awards:* 12th Hunter Gallery Ann Award, Lincoln-Davies Insurance Co, 72; J B Speed Art Mus Eight State Ann Award, WAVE TV, Louisville, Ky, 74; Purchase Award, Mid-America Biennial, Tex Gas Corp. *Bibliog:* Jim Cantrell: an artist not by choice but by providence, Ky Artist & Craftsmen Mag, 76; Thelma Newman (auth), The Container Book, Crown, 77; Watercolorists, Beaux Arts Mag, 12/80; and others. *Mem:* Ky Guild Artists & Craftsmen (bd trustees, 73-75 & 78-79); Artists Equity; Piedmont Crafts, Inc; Ky Watercolor Soc. *Media:* Oil, Watercolor; Clay. *Publ:* Auth, Cut Decoration, Ceramics Mo, 75. *Dealer:* Bardstown Art Gallery PO Box 417 Bardstown KY 40004; Lazenby Assoc 300 D St SW Suite 503 Washington DC 20024. *Mailing Add:* PO Box 417 Bardstown KY 40004

CAPA, CORNELL
PHOTOGRAPHER, MUSEUM DIRECTOR
b Budapest, Hungary, Apr 10, 18. *Study:* Madach Imre Gymnasium, Budapest, 28-36. *Exhib:* Margin of Life, Ctr of Inter-Am Relations, New York, 74; Johnson Mus, Cornell Univ, Ithaca, NY, 75. *Pos:* Staff & contrib photogr, Life Mag, New York, 46-67; mem photogr, Magnum Photos, New York & Paris, 54-; guest dir, The Concerned Photographer, Riverside Mus, New York, 66; The Concerns of Roman Vishniac, Jewish Mus, New York, 73, Behind the Great Wall: China, Metrop Mus Art, New York, 72 & The Concerned Photographer Two, Israel Mus, Jerusalem, 73; ed, The Concerned Photographer One & Two, Grossman/Viking, 69-72; exec dir, Int Ctr of Photog, 74- *Teaching:* Lectr photog, NY Univ, 68-72 & Int Ctr of Photog, 74- *Awards:* Honor Roll, Am Soc Mag Photogr, 75; Joseph A Sprague Mem Award, Nat Press Photogr Asn, 76; New York Mayor's Award of Honor, 78. *Bibliog:* Feature prof, Who Am I?, NBC Television, Channel 4, 71; Center of Concern, CBS Television, 77; Richard Whelan (auth), Cornell Capa's lighthouse of photography, Artnews, 4/79. *Mem:* Magnum Photogs (pres, 57-60); Overseas Press Club of New York (exec comn, 67-70 & 69-73); Am Soc Mag Photogr. *Publ:* Coauth (with Maya Pines), Retarded Children Can Be Helped, Channel Press, 57; coauth (with Matthew Huxley), Farewell to Eden, Harper & Row, 64; coauth (with J M Stycos), Margin of Life, 73 & ed, International Center of Photography Library of Photographers (first six titles), 74, Grossman Publ. *Dealer:* Magnum Photog Inc 261 Park Ave South New York NY 10036. *Mailing Add:* 275 Fifth Ave New York NY 10016

CAPARN, RHYS (RHYS CAPARN STEEL)
SCULPTOR
b Onteora Park, NY, July 28, 09. *Study:* Bryn Mawr Col, 27-29; Ecole Artistique Animaux, with Edouard Navellier, 30; Archipenko Art Sch, New York, 31-33. *Work:* Morton May Collection, City Art Mus, St Louis; Riverside Mus Collection, Brandeis Univ; Fogg Mus; Whitney Mus Am Art, New York; Yale Univ Art Gallery. *Comn:* Figures on armillary sphere, Brooklyn Botanical Garden, 32; wall reliefs in concrete, bronze screen, drawings in ceramic tile & fountain head, Wollman Libr, Barnard Col, 58-59. *Exhib:* 15 Sculptors, Mus Mod Art Traveling Exhib, 41; Five Ann, Whitney Mus Am Art, 41-60; New York Six, Petit Palais, Paris, 50; Pa Acad, 51-53, 60 & 64; Unknown Political Prisoner, Tate Gallery, London, 53; Drawings, US Info Agency Exhibs, Europe & Far East, 56-57, Eight Americans, 57-58; Nat Inst Arts & Lett, 68 & 76. *Pos:* Mem Mayors Comt Beautification City of New York, 63-64; founding mem, Harlem Cult Coun, 64. *Teaching:* Instr sculpture, Dalton High Sch, New York, 46-55 & 60-72. *Awards:* Am Sculpture Second Prize, Metrop Mus Art, 51; Medals of Honor for Sculpture, Nat Asn Women Artists, 60 & 61. *Bibliog:* Robert Beverly Hale (auth), Rhys Caparn, Retrospective Press, 72. *Mem:* Fedn Mod Painters & Sculptors; fel Int Inst Arts & Lett. *Publ:* Illusr, Down the Mountain, 62. *Mailing Add:* RD 1 Taunton Hill Rd Newtown CT 06470

CAPES, RICHARD EDWARD
GRAPHIC ARTIST, INSTRUCTOR
b Atlanta, Ga, Nov 6, 42. *Study:* Univ Ga, Athens, BS, 65, MA, 69; Univ Ga, Cortona, Italy, 70. *Work:* Barnwell Mem Garden Art Ctr, Shreveport, La. *Comn:* 200 Years (painting), Collectors Wall Gallery, Sarasota, Fla, 76; graphic design, Laser Corp, Bradenton, Fla, 78; illus, Southside Sch, Sarasota, Fla, 83. *Exhib:* Nineteenth Drawing & Sculpture Show, Ball State Univ Art Gallery, 72; Two Southern Draughtsmen, Addison Gallery Am Art, 72; Brooks Mem Art Gallery, 72; Int Art Exhib, Stagecoach Gallery, Albuquerque, 73; 14th Ann Artist Salon, Okla Mus Art, 75; 51st Ann Nat Art Exhib, Springville Mus Art, 76; 31st Ann Fla Artist Group, Sarasota Art Asn, 80; 32nd Ann Exhib, Jacksonville Art Mus, Fla, 81. *Teaching:* Asst prof art educ, Univ Southern Miss, 71-73; asst prof art, Morehead State Univ, 73-74. *Awards:* Southeast Bank Award, 80 & Hamel Mem Award, 81, Fla Artist Group Inc; First Prize, Arvida State Fla, 83. *Bibliog:* Marcia Corbino (auth), Quality art at galleries, Sarasota J, 75; Linda Thomas Editor (auth), article, Fla Bus J, 83. *Mem:* Arts & Crafts Guild Inc (dir, 75-76); Sarasota Art Asn (vpres, 78-79); Fla Artist Group Inc; Art Uptown Inc (vpres, 83-); Fla Watercolor Soc. *Media:* Ink, Watercolor. *Publ:* Illusr, Sunburst Condominium Living News, 75; contribr, Focus on the visual arts, Fla Bus J, 83; illusr, Sarasota Art Asn Yearbook, 83. *Dealer:* Fla Sales Assoc 1203 Gulf Dr Bradenton FL 33501. *Mailing Add:* 2116 Florinda St Sarasota FL 33581

CAPLAN, JERRY L
SCULPTOR, EDUCATOR
b Pittsburgh, Pa, Aug 9, 22. *Study:* Carnegie-Mellon Univ, BFA & MFA; Art Students League; Univ NC. *Work:* NC State Art Gallery, Raleigh; Pittsburgh Bd Educ; Westinghouse Corp; US Steel; Alcoa; and others. *Comn:* Terra-cotta sculptures, Friendship Fed Plaza, Pittsburgh, 68; porcelain symbols, Westinghouse Ceramic Div, Derry, Pa, 72; terra-cotta, Kossman Group, Kossman Assocs, Pittsburgh, 72; symbol, Rockwell Corp, Pittsburgh, 72; ceramic panels, Temple Emanuel, 70, wood panels, 75. *Exhib:* Five shows, Butler Inst Am Art, 55-75; Kent State 69; Carnegie Inst, 71; Mainstreams, Marietta, Ohio, 74 & 75; Appalachian Corridors, Charleston, WVa, 75. *Teaching:* Instr sculpture & ceramics, Chatham Col, 59-; instr painting, Pittsburgh Ctr Arts, 62-; lectr, Frick Educ Comn, Pittsburgh, 64-, Hastack, 77, Santa Ana Col, 80 & 84. *Awards:* Purchase Award, Assoc Artists Pittsburgh, 65; Soc Sculptors Award, 70; Pittsburgh Artist of the Year, 75; and others. *Mem:* Assoc Artists Pittsburgh (pres, 65); Soc Sculptors (treas); Am Crafts Coun; Pittsburgh Craftsmen's Guild; Artists Equity. *Media:* Terra-cotta, Stoneware. *Publ:* Auth, articles in Ceramic Mo, 9/76 & 11/76. *Mailing Add:* 5812 Fifth Ave Pittsburgh PA 15232

CAPLAN, SANDRA (SANDRA CIARROCHI CAPLAN)
PAINTER
b Winnipeg, Man. *Study:* Univ Man, BFA, 57; Boston Univ, MFA, 60. *Work:* Winnipeg Art Gallery; J A MacAulay Collection, Toronto; Boston Mutual Life Insurance. *Exhib:* Landmark Gallery Invitational, New York, 73, 78 & 80; one-person exhib, Winnipeg Art Gallery, 74; Maine Coast Artists Exhibs, 74-77; Watercolour, Contemporary View, Fairleigh Dickinson Univ, 81; Views by Women Artists, Fordham Univ, 82; and others. *Teaching:* Instr art, Mus Mod Art, New York, 65-71; Village Community Sch, New York, 71-79 & Lenox Sch, New York, 79- *Awards:* Can Coun Award, 61-62; Woodstock Art Asn Award Watercolour, 83. *Bibliog:* John Graham (auth), article, Winnipeg Free Press, 74; John Perrault (auth), article, Soho Weekly News, 76. *Media:* Oil, Watercolor. *Publ:* Illusr, Fair Game--Hunter's Cookbook (Great American Cooking Schools), Irena Chalmers Cookbooks Inc, 83. *Dealer:* Sibley Gallery Nantucket MA. *Mailing Add:* 463 West St New York NY 10014

CAPLES, BARBARA BARRETT
PAINTER, PRINTMAKER
b Providence, RI, Oct 28, 14. *Study:* Smith Col, AB(magna cum laude), 36; Yale Univ Sch Fine Arts, 36-38; also with George Laurence Nelson & Ruth Starr Rose. *Work:* Smith Col Mus, Northampton, Mass; Univ Va, Charlottesville; Carlsbad Mus, NMex. *Exhib:* Soc Washington Printmakers, 68-; one-man show, Art League, Alexandria, Va, 70; Boston Printmakers, 71; Distinguished Mid-Atlantic Artists, Univ Del, 80; Carlsbad Mus, NMex, 82. *Teaching:* Instr art & art hist, Rye Country Day Sch, NY, 38-40; instr art, Walter Reed Hosp, Washington, DC, 43-45; instr serigraphy, YWCA, Alexandria, 65-75. *Awards:* Numerous Awards, Art League, Alexandria, 65-71; Honorable Mention, Fairfax Co Cult Asn, 71; NVa Fine Arts Assoc, 71 & 72; and others. *Mem:* Soc Washington Printmakers; Art League, Alexandria (mem bd, 69); NVa Fine Arts Asn; Washington Women's Art Ctr. *Mailing Add:* 1111 Roan Lane Alexandria VA 22302

CAPOBIANCO, DOMENICK
PAINTER, SCULPTOR
b St Louis, Mo, Dec, 22, 28. *Study:* Washington Univ, St Louis, Mo, BFA, 58; Skowhegan Sch Painting & Sculpture, 58 & 59. *Work:* Univ Dallas, Tex; Newark Public Libr, NJ; Mus Mod Art, Skopje, Jugoslavia; Mus Mod Art, Ljubljana, Jugoslavia; Graphische Sammlung Albertina, Vienna, Austria. *Comn:* Stage Sets: Experimental Death Unit #1, LeRoy Jones, St Marks Theatre, 64; Forensic & The Navigators, Sam Sheppard, Theatre Genesis, 67; Willy the Germ, Murray Mednick, Theatre Genesis, 68 & The Hunter, Murray Mednick, Theatre Genesis, 68. *Exhib:* Sky Piece over Mus Mod Art (skywriting drawing), 76; Brooklyn Mus Print Exhib, NY, 76; Tyler Mus Art, Tex, 76; Brooklyn Mus, NY, 78; Invitational Int Biennale Conde-sur-Escout-Bonsecours, Belgium, 80; Kyoto Municipal Mus Art, Japan, 80; Petit Format De Papier, Cul des Sarts, Couvin, Belgium, 81. *Teaching:* Instr painting, Washington Univ, St Louis, Mo, 57-58; lectr, Art Dept, Univ NC, Greensboro, 67; asst prof & chmn, Art Dept, Rutgers Univ, 67- *Awards:* Cassandra Found Award, Marcel Duchamp, 67; Creative Artists Public Service Program Grant, 76; 2 Purchase Awards, Int Exhib Graphic Art, Ljubljana, Jugoslavia, 77. *Bibliog:* Allen Tannenbaum (auth), Soho Weekly News, 10/74; Tiffany Bell (auth), Arts Mag, 5/79. *Media:* Oil, Canvas; Mixed Media. *Dealer:* Condeso/Lawler Gallery 119 West 25th Street New York NY 10001. *Mailing Add:* 133 Eldridge Street New York NY 10002

CAPONI, ANTHONY
SCULPTOR, EDUCATOR
b Pretare, Italy, May 7, 21. *Study:* Univ Flore, Italy; Cleveland Sch Art; Walker Art Ctr, Minn; Univ Minn, BS & MEd. *Work:* Minneapolis Inst Art; St Cloud State Col; Minn Mus Art. *Comn:* Sculpture, columns & figures, St Joseph Sch, Red Lake Falls, Minn; St Mary's Church, Warroad, Minn; St John's Church, Rochester, Minn; wax models for all bronze motifs in Eisenhower Libr, Abilene, Tex; two bronze relief sculptures, Ascoli, Italy; plus others. *Exhib:* Walker Art Ctr, Minneapolis, 47-58; St Paul Gallery Art, 47-58; Iowa State Teachers Col, 58; Minneapolis Art Inst Ann; Augustana Col, Sioux Falls, SDak, 71; and other group & one-man shows. *Teaching:* Prof art & chmn dept, Macalester Col, 58- *Awards:* Ford Found Grant & Four Prizes, Minneapolis Inst Art, 47-59; six Awards, Minn State Fair, 48-65; Awards, St Paul Gallery Art, 49 & 55. *Mem:* Artists Equity Asn; Soc Minn Sculptors. *Media:* Stone. *Publ:* Auth, Boulders & Pebbles of Poetry & Prose, Independence Press, 72. *Mailing Add:* Art Dept Macalester Col St Paul MN 55105

CAPONIGRO, PAUL
PHOTOGRAPHER
b Boston, Mass, Dec 7, 32. *Study:* With Benjamin Chin & Minor White. *Exhib:* Solo exhibs, Mus Mod Art, New York, 68, San Francisco Mus Art, 70, Art Inst Chicago, 73, Victoria & Albert Mus, London, 75, Albright-Knox Art Gallery, Buffalo, 76, Carl Siembab Gallery, Boston, 76, Mus Fine Arts, Santa Fe, 76, David Mirvish Gallery, Toronto, 77, Galerij Paule Pia, Antwerp, 81 & Photog Gallery, La Jolla, 81; American Masters, Smithsonian Inst, 74; Photography in America, Whitney Mus Am Art, 74; 14 American Photographers, Baltimore Mus Art & traveling, 75; Mirrors and Windows, Mus Mod Art, New York & traveling, 78-80; and many others. *Pos:* Consult photo res dept, Polaroid Corp, Cambridge, 60- *Teaching:* Instr creative photography, NY Univ, 67-71; instr photography, Yale Univ, 71-; lecturer at numerous universities & art schools throughout the US. *Awards:* Guggenheim Fel, 66 & 75; Nat Endowment Arts Grant, 71, 74 & 75; Art Dirs Club New York Award, 74. *Bibliog:* Joan Murray (auth), Caponigro and Heyman, Artweek, 8/23/75; Margaret R. Weiss (auth), Caponigro's sense of site, Saturday Rev, 5/15/76; Rolf Koppel (auth), Caponigro: A respect for the activities of existence, Santa Fe Reporter, 10/28/76. *Mem:* Founder Am Heliographers Asn. *Publ:* Portfolio Two, 73; Sunflower, Film Haus Inc, 74; Landscape: Photographs by Paul Caponigro, McGraw-Hill, 75; Portfolio Three: Stonehenge, 77. *Mailing Add:* Rte 3 Box 96D Santa Fe NM 87501

CARBAJAL G, ENRIQUE See Sebastian

CARD, GREG S
PAINTER, SCULPTOR
b Los Angeles, Calif, Aug 28, 45. *Study:* Independent study. *Work:* River Forest Bank, Chicago; NMex Mus Art; Am Tel & Tel, New York; Union Bank of Switz & Security Pac Bank, Los Angeles, Calif; and others. *Comn:* Act of Temporary Placement (process & environ sculpture), Univ Southern Calif, 74; Atlantic Richfield Corp/Anaconda, Denver, Colo, 79. *Exhib:* One-man shows, Galleria d'Arte del Cavallino, Venezia, Italy, 77, Newport Harbor Art Mus, Newport Beach, Calif, 78 & Koplin Gallery, Los Angeles, 82 and others; Sculpture in Calif, 1975-80, San Diego Mus Art, 80; Los Angeles Co Mus, 81; Palm Springs Mus, 83; and others. *Teaching:* Lectr, Ohio State Univ, Columbus, 79, Atlanta Col Arts, Ga, 79. *Awards:* Contemp Art Coun Award, Los Angeles Co Mus Art, 69; Purchase Award, Southern Ill Univ, Carbondale, 71; Individual Artists Fel, Nat Endowment Arts, 75. *Bibliog:* Peter Clothier (auth), Magic of the possible-five California artists, Artforum, 4/77; Merle Schipper (auth), Greg S Card, Catalog Essay, Newport Harbor Art Mus, 5/78; Lynn Gamwell (auth), Greg Card's illusions in reflections, Artweek, 6/78; and others. *Mailing Add:* c/o Koplin Gallery 8225 1/2 Santa Monica Blvd Los Angeles CA 90046

CARDINAL, MARCELIN
PAINTER
b Gravelbourg, Sask, Apr 26, 20. *Study:* Self-taught. *Work:* Quebec Mus, PQ; Can Coun, Ottawa; Hirshhorn Mus, Washington, DC; Musee d'Art Moderne, Dunkerque, France; Schniewind, Wuppertal, WGer. *Exhib:* Guggenheim Mus, New York, 54 & 58; Albright-Knox Art Gallery, Buffalo, NY, 60; 5th Int Art Fair, Basel, Switz, 74; Galerie Gilles Corbeil, Montreal, 75; Musee du Quebec, Quebec, 76; Musee d'Art Moderne, Dunkerque, France, 77; Musee d'Art Contemporain, Montreal, 77 & 78; Galerie Don Stewart, Due Sherbrooke, Montreal, Can. *Awards:* Creation et Recherche, Minister Cult Affairs, Quebec, 72, 73, 75 & 78. *Bibliog:* Christian Allegre (auth), article, Vie des Arts, 72; Profile: Marcelin Cardinal, Art Mag, 3/79; Germain Lefebvre (auth), Marcelin Cardinal, Temps, Espace Et Continuite--Vie Des Arts, 82. *Mem:* Soc Prof Artists Quebec (vprcs, 72-73); Can Conf Arts; Can Artists' Representation. *Media:* Oil, Acrylic. *Dealer:* Galerie Don Stewart 1460 Sherbrooke St W Montreal PQ Can. *Mailing Add:* 4897 Queen Mary Rd Montreal PQ H3W 1X1 Canada

CARDMAN, CECILIA
PAINTER
b Soveria Mannelli, Italy; US citizen. *Study:* Univ Colo, BFA; Inst Belli Arte, Naples, Italy; with Giuseppe Aprea, Naples; Nat Acad, New York, with Leon Kroll, Milford Zornes & E A Whitney. *Work:* Mesa Col, Grand Junction, Colo; Cathedral Rectory, Denver, Colo; Chapel House, Denver Art Mus. *Exhib:* One-man show, Naples, Italy & Grist Mill Gallery, Chester Depot, Vt; Nat Arts Club, Hammond Mus; Gallery North Star, Grafton, Va; Denver Art Mus; Knickerbocker Artists, Catharine Lorillard Wolfe Art Club; and others. *Teaching:* Instr, Mesa Col, Grand Junction; asst, Univ Colo; summer sch fac, Colo State Col Educ & Univ Calif. *Awards:* Shadows & Mexican Doorway, Jackson Heights Art Club. *Mem:* Jackson Heights Art Club; Catharine Lorillard Wolfe Art Club; Am Artists Prof League; Artists' Fel Inc; Salmagundi Club. *Media:* Watercolor, Oil. *Mailing Add:* Penthouse 34-06 81st St Jackson Heights NY 11372

CARDOSO, ANTHONY
PAINTER, INSTRUCTOR
b Tampa, Fla, Sept 13, 30. *Study:* Univ Tampa, BS(art); Art Inst Minn, BFA; Univ SFla, MA; Elysion Col, PhD. *Work:* Minn Mus Art, St Paul; Suncoast Credit Union Bldg, Tampa, Fla; and others. *Comn:* Sports Authority, Tampa Stadium Off, 71; sports theme paintings, Leto High Sch & Pierce High Sch, Tampa, 71; two murals, Sun Coast Credit Union Bldg, Tampa, Fla, 75; and many others. *Exhib:* Drawings USA, Minn Mus Art, St Paul, 71; Rotunda Gallery, London, Eng, 72; Rochester Festival of Art, NY, 73; Brussells Int, Belg, 73; Ringling Mus Archives, Sarasota, Fla, 78; Accademia Italia Exhib, Terme, Italy, 80; and many others. *Teaching:* Head art dept, Jefferson High Sch, 57-65; instr fine arts & head dept, Leto High Sch, 66- *Awards:* Prix de Paris Award, Raymond Duncan Galleries, 70; Drawings USA Purchase Award, Minn Mus Art, 71; Gold Medal Award, Accademia Italia Exhib, 80; and others. *Bibliog:* Bertrand Sorlot (auth), article in La Rev Mod, 71; articles, Tampa Tribune, 75-83 & Accad Italia, 80-83. *Mem:* Fla Arts Coun; Ringling Art Mus Archives. *Publ:* Contribr, La Rev Mod, 71 & 72, Accad Italia, 80-83 & Tampa Tribune, 83. *Dealer:* Warren Gallery 2710 MacDill Ave Tampa FL 33609. *Mailing Add:* 3208 Nassau St Tampa FL 33607

CARDOZO, PATRICIA VELEZ
ART DEALER
b Medellin, Colombia, Apr 1, 41; US citizen. *Study:* Escuela de Bellas Artes, Bogota, Colombia; Scuola di Belli Arti, Rome; Univ de Lausanne, Switz. *Pos:* Asst dir, Walter Randel Primitive Art, New York, 73-75; asst dir, Bykert Gallery, New York, 75-77; dir, Robert Elkon Gallery, New York, 77- *Mailing Add:* c/o Gransjean 32 Cansevoort St New York NY 10014

CAREY, ELLEN
PHOTOGRAPHER
b New York, NY, June 18, 52. *Study:* Art Students League, 70; Kansas City Art Inst, BFA, 75; State Univ NY, Buffalo, MFA, 78. *Work:* Albright-Knox Art Gallery; Fogg Mus; Mus Fine Art, Houston; Patrick Lannan Found, Palm Beach, Fla; Chase Manhattan Bank, New York. *Exhib:* Contemporary Photographs, Fogg Art Mus, 80; The New Photography, Contemp Arts Mus, Houston, 81; Figures: Forms and Expressions, Albright-Knox Gallery, 82; Painting, Pattern, Photograph, Addison Gallery Am Art, 82; Some Contemporary Portraits, Contemp Arts Mus, Houston, 82; Photo Start, Bronx Mus Arts, 82; Three Dimensional Photographs, Castelli Graphics, New York, 83; Contemporary Self-Portraiture in Photography, Hayden Art Gallery, 83. *Teaching:* Lectr photog, Int Ctr Photog, 82-; vis artist, RI Sch Design, 83 & Hartford Art Sch, Conn, 84. *Awards:* Creative Artists Serv Prog Grant, 79-80; Light Works Grant, 80; Polaroid Fel, 84. *Bibliog:* Shelley Rice (auth), Image making, Soho Weekly News, 5/24/79; Ben Lifson (auth), Redundant kisses, engaging ambiguities, Village Voice, 6/11-17/79. *Mem:* Visual Studies Workshop; Soc Photog Educ; Friends Photog; Col Art Asn. *Mailing Add:* c/o Pace-MacGill 11 E 57th St New York NY 10022

CAREY, JOHN THOMAS
EDUCATOR, HISTORIAN
b Wilmont, Minn, Aug 23, 17. *Study:* Milwaukee State Teachers Col, BA; Univ Wis, MS; Ohio State Univ, PhD; Harvard Univ. *Teaching:* Art instr, Univ Wis-Madison, 47-48; asst prof art, Ill State Univ, 49-51; instr art, Ohio State Univ, 53-54; asst prof art, Bowling Green State Univ, 54-56; prof art & chmn dept, Northern Ill State Univ, 56-66; vis prof, Rollins Col, 66-67; prof art, Univ West Fla, 67-, chmn art dept, 67-77; retired; vis prof, World Campus Afloat, Chapman Col, spring 69 & spring 73; vis prof, Univ Hawaii, Manoa, fall 77. *Awards:* Pac Cult Found Study Grant, Imperial Palace Collection Art, Taipei, Taiwan, spring 77. *Mem:* Col Art Asn Am; Southeastern Col Art Asn (pres, 75). *Res:* Introduction and development of lithography in America. *Publ:* Ed, Illinois Art Education Yearbook, 57; contribr, William Fendrick, Early American Lithographer, Libr Cong, 57. *Mailing Add:* 2320 Risen Dr Cantonment FL 32533

CARIOLA, ROBERT J
PAINTER, SCULPTOR
b Brooklyn, NY, Mar 24, 27. *Study:* Pratt Inst Art Sch; Pratt Graphic Ctr. *Work:* Fordham Univ; De Pauw Univ; La Salle Col; Hofstra Col; Topeka Pub Libr, Kans. *Comn:* Metal mural, altar & artifacts for St Gabriel's Church, Oakridge, NJ, 70-71; murals, Walker Mem Baptist Church, Bronx, NY, 75; two chapel murals, Mt St Mary Cemetery, Queens, NY, 77. *Exhib:* Boston Mus Printmakers Exhib, 62; Corcoran Gallery Art, Washington, DC, 63; Pa Acad Fine Arts, Philadelphia, 63; Vatican Pavilion, New York World's Fair, 64; Nat Acad Design, New York, 70. *Pos:* Art consult, Cath Youth Orgn, Rockville Ctr, NY, 67-; art coordr, St John's Cloister, Queens, NY, 72-74. *Teaching:* Instr art, La Salle Acad, Oakdale, NY, 63-65; instr art, Catholic Youth Orgn Summer Workshop; instr art, Huntington Twp Art League, 71. *Awards:* First Prize Painting, John Kennedy Cult Ctr Bankers Trust Award, 71; Grumbacher Cash Award, Silvermine Guild Artists, New Canaan, Conn, 76; Best in Show Award, Bayshore C of C Art Festival, 79. *Bibliog:* A V LesMez (auth), Cariola, Long Island Rev Mag, 64; Walt Carlson (auth), Vatican Pavilion gets Long Island exhibit, New York Times, 8/27/64; Jeanne Paris (auth), Cariola's works on exhibit at Merrick Gallery, Long Island Press, 5/28/67. *Mem:* Prof Artists Guild (pres, 69-70); hon mem Cath Fine Arts Soc. *Media:* Acrylic. *Publ:* Illusr, Writers's Ann, 58; illusr, Sign Mag, 71; contribr, Liturgical Arts Mag, 71-72. *Dealer:* Studio Art Gallery 12 2nd Floor Merrick Ave Merrick NY 11566; Contemporary Christian Art Gallery 1060-A Lexington Ave New York NY 10021. *Mailing Add:* 1844 Gormley Ave Merrick NY 11566

CARL, JOAN
SCULPTOR, DESIGNER
b Cleveland, Ohio, Mar 20, 26. *Study:* Cleveland Sch Art; Chicago Art Inst; Mills Col; with Dong Kingman, Bordman Robinson, Carl Morris & Albert Wein; New Sch Art, with Arnold Mesches & Ted Gilien. *Work:* NC Mus Art, Raleigh; Int Cult Ctr for Youth, Jerusalem, Israel; The Temple, Cleveland, Ohio; Sinai Memorial Park, Los Angeles; Capitol Nat Bank, Cleveland; and others. *Comn:* Steel Menorah, Eternal Light & Candlesticks, Temple Adat Ariel, Los Angeles, 69; bronze & steel relief, Repub Savings & Loan, Los Angeles, 74; mosaic wall, Mt Sinai Mem Park, Los Angeles, 75; designed & created awards, Los Angeles Hq City Asn, 77 & 78; aluminum pillars, Zinkal Office, Tel Aviv, 80; and others. *Exhib:* Laguna Beach Art Mus, 69; Fresno

Art Mus, 71; Linden-Kicklighter Gallery, Cleveland, Ohio, 71 & 73; Muskegon Community Col, 73; Chai (graphics), Nat & Int Traveling Show, 74-75; and other group & one-man shows. *Pos:* Teacher, Valley Ctr of Arts, Los Angeles, 59-64; lectr Title III Prog, San Bernardino, Inyo & Moro Co, Calif, 69-70; mem adv bd, Los Angeles Trade Tech. *Awards:* Honorable Mention, Nat Orange Show, San Bernardino, 58 & Calif State Fair, Sacramento, 70 & 72; Design Award, Ceramic Tile Inst, 75. *Bibliog:* Will H Tagress (auth), Valley sculptor believes in reflecting world around her, The News, 74. *Mem:* Artists Equity Asn (Los Angeles chap pres, 74-76); Calif Confederation of the Arts (bd mem). *Media:* Multimedia. *Publ:* Illusr, A World of Questions and Things, 50; illusr, Discovery Unlimited, A Guide to Raising a Creative Child, 81. *Mailing Add:* 4808 Mary Ellen Ave Sherman Oaks CA 91423

CARLBERG, NORMAN KENNETH
SCULPTOR, INSTRUCTOR
b Roseau, Minn, Nov 6, 28. *Study:* Brainerd Jr Col, Minn, 47-49; Minneapolis Sch Art, 50; Univ Ill, Urbana, 53-54; Yale Univ, BFA, 58, MFA, 61. *Work:* Addison Gallery Am Art, Phillips Acad, Andover, Mass; Whitney Mus Am Art, New York; Schenectady Mus, NY; Pa Acad Fine Arts, Philadelphia; Art & Archit Gallery, Yale Univ. *Comn:* Modular screen, Baltimore City Hosp, 65; four modular sculptures, Baltimore City Schs, Northern Parkway Jr High, 70-73 & for PS 39, 73-75; modular column, Harry Seidler, Trade Group Complex, Canberra, Australia, 73-75 & Black Widow (steel modular), 75-*Exhib:* Recent Sculpture USA, Mus Mod Art, New York, 59; Structured Sculpture, Galerie Chalette, New York, 60; one-man shows, Cath Univ, Santiago, Chile, 60 & Baltimore Mus Art, 68; Whitney Ann, Whitney Mus Am Art, 62. *Teaching:* Instr sculpture, Cath Univ, Santiago, 60-61; sculptor in residence, Rinehart Sch Sculpture, Md Inst Col Art, Baltimore, 61-*Awards:* Fulbright Teaching Grant, Santiago, Chile, 60; Purchase Award, Ford Found, 62; Mus Prize, Baltimore Mus Art, 66. *Bibliog:* Josef Albers (auth), The Yale School-Structured Sculpture, Art in Am, 61; George Rickey (auth), Constructivism, George Braziller, 67; Peter Blake (auth), Architecture for the New World, the work of Harry Seidler, Wittenborn & Co, 73. *Mailing Add:* 120 W Lanvale St Baltimore MD 21217

CARLIN, ELECTRA MARSHALL
DEALER
b Ft Worth, Tex. *Study:* George Washington Univ, BA. *Pos:* Dir, Carlin Galleries. *Mem:* Ft Worth Art Asn; Dallas Mus Art Asn. *Specialty:* American artists and craftsmen; Eskimo prints and carvings. *Mailing Add:* 710 Montgomery St Ft Worth TX 76107

CARLIN, JAMES
PAINTER
b Belfast, Ireland, June 25, 10; US citizen. *Study:* Belfast Munic Col, grad; London Art Schs; Newark Sch Fine & Indust Art; apprenticeship stained glass painting studios with German, English & Irish instrs. *Work:* Montclair Art Mus, NJ; also in pvt collections of Dore Schary, Los Angeles & many others. *Comn:* Design of stained glass windows (in collaboration), Londonderry Guild Hall & several prominent churches in Ireland, 26-28. *Exhib:* 12th Brooklyn Mus Int, NY, 41; Victory Exhib, Metrop Mus Art, New York, 42; Allied Artists Am Exhib, New York, 45; Portrait of America, Pepsi-Cola Co, New York, 45; Allied Artists Am Oils Exhib, Nat Acad Galleries, New York, 46. *Teaching:* Mem fac, Queen's Col; instr fine arts & head dept, Newark Sch Fine & Indust Art, 46- *Awards:* First Award, Watercolor, 77 & Purchase Award, 77, NJ State Show; First Award, Oil, Am Tel & Tel; First Prize in Oils, Audubon Artists. *Bibliog:* Norman Kent (auth), The Artist Speaks His Mind, 69 & Wendon Blake (auth), Acrylic Watercolor Painting, 71, Watson-Guptill; Michael Jenson (auth), Carlin and nature, Newark News, 71. *Mem:* Am Watercolor Soc; Philadelphia Watercolor Soc; NJ Watercolor Soc; Audubon Artists; Assoc Artists NJ; plus others. *Media:* Oil, Watercolor. *Dealer:* Grand Central Art Galleries 40 Vanderbilt Ave New York NY 10017. *Mailing Add:* 73 Cathedral Ave Nutley NJ 07110

CARLOS, (JAMES) EDWARD
PAINTER, ADMINISTRATOR
b Kingsville, Pa, Nov 8, 37. *Study:* Indiana Univ Pa, BS(art educ), 59; Colo Col, with Enrique Montenegro, summer 60; Cath Univ Am, with Ken Noland, Alexander Giampietro & Bernard Leach, MFA, 63; Univ Hawaii, with Gustav Ecke; Ohio Univ, fel & PhD. *Exhib:* Mainstreams '72, Marietta, Ohio, 72; Italy, Sweden & Scotland, 75; one-man show, Edinburgh Int Festival, Scotland, 76. *Pos:* Lectr various art groups & schs; Dir gallery & mus, Univ of the South, Tenn, currently. *Teaching:* Vis prof art, Portland State Col, summer 65; asst prof art, Western Ill Univ, 65-66; instr art, Ohio Univ, 67-69; from assoc prof to prof, Univ of the South, 69- *Awards:* Int Snapshop, East-Kodak, 71. *Media:* Oil. *Mailing Add:* Dept of Fine Arts Univ of the South Sewanee TN 37375

CARLOZZI, ANNETTE DIMEO
CURATOR
b Braintree, Mass, Dec 10, 53. *Study:* Brandeis Univ, BA(art hist), 75; Univ Minn, 75-77; Mus Mgt Inst, 83. *Collections Arranged:* New Works by Auston Artists (auth, catalog), 80-83; Dan Flavin: Flourescent Light Installations, 80; Sculpture Projects: Elyn Zimmerman, Nancy Holt, Clyde Connell, James Surls, 80-83; Five on Fabric: Kushner, MacConnel, Pindell, Samaras & Shapiro (auth, catalog), 81; Three Photographers: Barboza, Callis, Pfahl (auth, catalog), 81; Rafael Ferrer: Impassioned Rhythms (auth, catalog), 82; Invention: Designs by Buckminster Fuller, 83; Luis Jimenez (auth, catalog), 83; Surfaces in Contemporary Art, 83; Panorama Photographs by E O Goldbeck, 83. *Pos:* Rockefeller Found Fellow, Walker Art Ctr, Minneapolis,

76-78; project coordr, Art Pub Places, Nat Endowment Arts, Washington, DC, 79; cur exhibs, Laguna Gloria Art Mus, Austin, Tex, 79- *Publ:* Coauth & ed, American Images: New Works by 20 Contemporary Photographers, McGraw-Hill, 79; auth, Public art in Minnesota, Archit Minn, 9-10/79; auth, Rafael Ferrer: New paintings, Arts Mag, 2/84. *Mailing Add:* c/o Laguna Gloria Art Mus PO Box 5568 Austin TX 78763

CARLSON, CYNTHIA J
PAINTER, EDUCATOR
b Chicago, Ill, Apr 15, 42. *Study:* Chicago Art Inst, BFA; Pratt Inst, MFA. *Work:* Va Mus Fine Art, Richmond; Guggenheim Mus, New York; Philadelphia Mus of Art; Denver Art Mus; Allem Mem Art Mus, Oberlin, Ohio. *Exhib:* Artpark, 77; one-woman exhibs, Allen Mem Art Mus, Oberlin, Ohio, 80; Walls, Contemp Art Ctr, Cincinnati, 80; Rooms, Hayden Gallery, Mass Inst Technol, Cambridge, 81; Hudson River Mus, Yonkers, NY, 81; Lowe Art Mus, Coral Gables, Fla, 82; Milwaukee Art Mus, Wis, 82. *Teaching:* Assoc prof art, Philadelphia Col Art, 67-81, prof, 81- *Awards:* Nat Endowment Arts Grant, 75, 78 & 81. *Bibliog:* Patricia Stewart (auth), High decoration in low relief, Art in Am, 2/80; April Kingsley (auth), Cynthia Carlson: The subversive intent of the decorative impulse, Arts Mag, 3/80. *Media:* Acrylic, Oil. *Mailing Add:* 139 W 19th St New York NY 10011

CARLSON, GEORGE ARTHUR
SCULPTOR, PAINTER
b Elmhurst, Ill, July 3, 40. *Study:* Am Acad Art; Chicago Art Inst; Univ Ariz. *Work:* Denver Pub Libr, Colo; Indianapolis Mus Fine Arts; Genesee Mus, Rochester, NY. *Comn:* Monument of prospector, Washington Park, Denver, 77. *Exhib:* Denver Natural Hist Mus, Colo, 68; Denver Pub Libr, 68; Denver Art Mus, 68; Nat Acad Design, New York, 69; Nat Acad Western Art, Okla, 74-80; retrospective, Indianapolis Mus Fine Arts, Ind, 79-80; one-man show, Smithsonian Mus, 82. *Awards:* Gold Medals, Nat Acad Western Art, 74, 78 & 80 & Prix de West, 75. *Bibliog:* Patricia Broder (auth), Treasures of the American West: Selections from the Collection of Harrison Eiteljorg, 81; article, Smithsonian Mag, 4/82; article, Americana Mag, 1/83. *Mem:* Nat Acad Western Art; Nat Sculpture Soc. *Media:* Bronze; Mixed. *Publ:* Auth, The Tarahumara, pvt publ, 77. *Dealer:* Stremmel Galleries 1400 S Virginia St Reno NV 89502; Peters Corp 439 Camino del Monte Sol Santa Fe NM 87501. *Mailing Add:* 6675 Heartwood Drive Oakland CA 94611

CARLSON, JANE C
PAINTER
b Boston, Mass, Sept 1, 28. *Study:* Art Students League; Mass Col Art; study with Charles Kinghan & Robert Davis. *Exhib:* Allied Artists Am, 69-83; Am Artists Prof League, 70-83; Am Watercolor Soc, Nat Acad Design, New York, 71-83; Audubon Artists, 73-83. *Teaching:* Watercolor demonstrations. *Awards:* Gold Medals, Am Artists Prof League, 79 & 81; High Winning Medal, Am Watercolor Soc, 83. *Mem:* Am Watercolor Soc; Am Artists Prof League; Audubon Artists; Allied Artists Am; Hudson Valley Art Asn. *Media:* Oil, Watercolor. *Dealer:* Douglas Gallery 1117 High Ridge Rd Stamford CT 06901; Hobe Sound Gallery Hobe Sound Jupiter Island FL 33455. *Mailing Add:* 81 Park Ave Bronxville NY 10708

CARLSON, WILLIAM D
SCULPTOR, GLASS BLOWER
b Dover, Ohio, Feb 18, 50. *Study:* Art Students League, 70; Cleveland Inst Art, BFA, 73; State Univ NY Col, Alfred, MFA, 76. *Work:* Metrop Mus Art, New York; Kyoto Mus Mod Art, Japan; Hokkaido Mus Mod Art, Sapporo, Japan; Columbus Mus Fine Art, Ohio; Ill State Mus, Springfield. *Comn:* Glass sculpture, Chicago Bd Options Exchange, 83-84. *Exhib:* Contemporary Glass--Australia, Canada, USA and Japan, Kyoto Mus Mod Art & Tokyo Mus Mod Art, Japan, 81; Americans in Glass, Cooper Hewitt Mus, New York, 81; Contemporary Art, Detroit Inst Arts, 82; American Glass Art, Evolution and Revolution, Morris Mus Art, Morristown, NJ, 82; World Glass, Hokkaido Mus Mod Art, Sapporo, Japan, 82; Cleveland Inst Art: 100 Years, Cleveland Mus Art, 83. *Teaching:* Assoc prof glass sculpture, Univ Ill, Champaign, 76-; instr glass, Pewland Sch Crafts, 82 & Pilchuck Glass Ctr, 83. *Awards:* Hokkaido Glass Award, World Glass, Hokkaido Mus Mod Art, 82; Nat Endowment Arts Craftmens Fel, 82. *Bibliog:* Paul Hollister (auth), William Carlson: Light affecting form in space, Neues Glass, 2/82; Chloe Zerwick (auth), William Carlson: Balanced asymmetry, Am Crafts, 6-7/82. *Mem:* Glass Art Soc (bd dirs, 83-). *Media:* Glass. *Dealer:* Betsey Rosenfield Gallery 212 W Superior Chicago IL 60611; Heller Gallery 965 Madison Ave New York NY. *Mailing Add:* 808 W White St Champaign IL 61820

CARLSTROM, LUCINDA
PAINTER, PRINTMAKER
b Jamestown, NY, Sept 8, 50. *Study:* Ringling Sch Art, Sarasota, Fla, 68-70; Atlanta Col Art, Ga, BFA, 74; Inst Allende, San Miguel, Mex, 73. *Work:* Contemp Hotel, Walt Disney World, Lake Buena Vista, Fla; DeKalb Jr Col, McClatchey, Cody Rodgers & Regenstein, Atlanta, Ga; Barnett Banks, Barnett Holding Co, Jacksonville, Fla; Eldorado Hosp, Tucson. *Exhib:* Walt Disney World, Lake Buena Vista, Fla, 74-79; New Orleans Mus Art, 75; US Info Agency Traveling Exhib, 76-78; High Mus Art Gallery, Atlanta, Ga, 79-*Awards:* Best Graphics, Space Coast Arts Festival, Cocoa Beach, Fla, 75; Best Watercolor, Southeastern Arts & Crafts Festival, Macon, Ga, 76; Second Award, Art Festival Atlanta, 79. *Mem:* Artists Equity Asn; Univ Mich Artists Guild; Ga Watercolor Soc. *Media:* Watercolor; Etching. *Mailing Add:* 1075 Standard Dr NE Atlanta GA 30319

CARMEAN, E A, JR
HISTORIAN, CURATOR
b Springfield, Ill, Jan 25, 45. *Study:* MacMurray Col, BA(hist art); Univ Ill, with Allen Weller. *Collections Arranged:* The Collages of Robert Motherwell (with catalog); Friedel Dzubas (with catalog); Modernist Art 1960-1970 (with catalog); Morris Louis: Major Themes & Variations (with catalog); The Subjects of the Artist (with catalog); Mondrian: The Diamond Compositions (with catalog); Morton G Neumann Collection (with catalog); Picasso: The Saltimbanques (with catalog); Kadinsky: The Improvisations. *Pos:* Cur 20th century art, Mus Fine Arts, Houston, 71-74; cur 20th century art, Nat Gallery Art, 74- *Teaching:* Lectr art hist, Univ Ill, Urbana, 67-69; vis prof 20th century art, Rice Univ, 73-74; vis prof 20th century art, George Washington Univ, 75- *Awards:* Guggenheim Found Fel, 78-79. *Mem:* Col Art Asn; Am Asn Mus. *Res:* Picasso & cubism; abstract expressionism; modern sculpture. *Publ:* Auth, Julio Gonzalez, Mus Fine Arts Bulletin, 73; auth, Kenneth Noland and the compositional cut, 75, auth, Morris Louis and the modern tradition, 76 & auth, Juan Gris' Fantomas, 77, Arts Mag. *Mailing Add:* Nat Gallery Art Sixth St & Constitution Ave NW Washington DC 20565

CARMICHAEL, DONALD RAY
PAINTER, ADMINISTRATOR
b Elnora, Ind, Dec 26, 22. *Study:* Herron Art Inst, BFA, 51; Univ Tenn, Knoxville, MFA, 75; also with John Taylor & David Freidenthal, New York & Edwin Fulwider, Ford Times & Garo Antreasian, NMex. *Work:* Cheekwood Fine Arts Ctr, Nashville, Tenn; Jackson-Madison Co Pub Libr, Jackson, Tenn; Dyersburg Pub Libr, Tenn; Jackson Ment Health Ctr. *Comn:* Life size statue, Carl Smith Agency, Jackson, 67; official seal (engraving), Jackson State Community Col, 67; five panel mural, History of Jackson, McDonalds, Inc, 68. *Exhib:* Three-man show, Lynn Kottler Galleries, New York, 71; 23rd Grand Prix Int, Deauville, France & Palace of Fine Arts, Rome, Italy, 72; Watercolor USA, Springfield Art Mus, 74-75; Southeastern Collection of Contemporary Art, Mich Artrain Tour, 74; and others. *Pos:* Pres, Jackson Art Asn, 65-67; pres, Jackson Arts Coun, 68-70; chmn visual arts adv panel, Tenn Arts Comn, 72-75; field rep, 75-78; dir, Tarble Arts Ctr, Eastern Ill Univ, Charleston, 78-; bd mem, Cent Ill Arts Consortium, 78-; mem rev comt, Art in Archit, Capital Develop Bd, Ill, 79- *Teaching:* Instr painting, Shelbyville Art League, Ind, 51-55; instr art appreciation, Union Univ, Tenn, 64-66, instr drawing, painting & composition, 66-69; grad asst, Univ Tenn, Knoxville, 74-75; instr evening classes, Dyersburg State Community Col, Tenn, 76-77. *Awards:* Purchase Award, Enjay Chem Nat, 66; Tennessee Painting Today Purchase Award, Tenn Arts Comn, 67. *Bibliog:* Newman Jones (auth), Art leagues in small communities, Delta Rev, 68; William T Alderson (auth), Tennessee lives, Historical Rec Asn, 71; article, La Rev Mod, 72. *Mem:* Artists Equity Asn; Tenn Col Arts Coun; Tenn Watercolorist (dir & mem chmn, 71-); Southern Watercolor Soc; co-founder Tenn Watercolor Soc (pres, 74). *Media:* Watercolor, Oil. *Publ:* Contribr, Edward Betts, auth, Creative Seascape Painting, 81. *Dealer:* Main St Studio-Gallery 608 1/2 Jackson St Charleston IL 61920. *Mailing Add:* Tarble Art Ctr Eastern Ill Univ Lincoln & 7th Charleston IL 61920

CARMICHAEL, JAE
PAINTER, SCULPTOR
b Los Angeles, Calif, Aug 22, 25. *Study:* Mills Col, 42-44; Univ Southern Calif, BFA, 51, PhD(art & cinematography), 72; Claremont Grad Sch, MFA, 55. *Work:* Long Beach Mus Art; Oakland Mus; Frye Mus; Tate Gallery, London; San Francisco Mus Mod Art; plus many others including pvt collections. *Exhib:* Titanium One, Laguna Beach Art Mus, 71; Long Beach Mus & Palm Springs Mus, 79, 81 & 83; Edward-Dean Mus, 83; and many others. *Pos:* Spec cur, Galka Scheyer Children's Art Collection, Pasadena Art Mus, 54; dir, Wooden Horse Gallery, Laguna Beach, 62-66; cur photog arts, Pacificulture-Asia Mus, Pasadena, 71-72, dir, 72-75. *Teaching:* Instr drawing & painting, Pasadena Art Mus, 53-60, Rex Brandt Sch, Calif, 61-62 & Palos Verdes Community Art Asn, 66-72; instr drawing & painting, Pasadena Sch Fine Arts, 54-58 & 66-, dir, 70-; lectr art hist & cinema, Pasadena City Col, 68-71; lectr Renaissance art hist & film, Otis Art Inst, Los Angeles, 70-75; lectr & adj prof cinema, Univ Southern Calif, 77-80. *Awards:* Ann Award, 70 & First Award Sculpture, 73, Pasadena Soc Artists; Gold Crown Award Artist Yr, Pasadena Arts Coun, 78. *Bibliog:* Kim Blair (auth), Pacificulture Center becomes a reality, Los Angeles Times, 10/25/71; Ray McConnell (auth), More or less personal, 11/19/71 & Margaret Stovall (auth), Jae Carmichael fulfills dreams at Pacificulture Foundation, 12/11/71, Star News. *Mem:* Nat Asn Mus; Nat Watercolor Soc (pres, 76 & 80); Pasadena Soc Artists (mem bd, 58-60, 62 & 63, pres, 70-72); Women Painters West; Los Angeles Art Asn (mem bd, 65-). *Publ:* Auth, The Rug Culture, 72 & auth, A Joint Exhibition, Los Angeles Printmaking Society and the Korean Printmaking Society, 73, Pacific-Asia Mus; auth, NWS the first half-century, Nat Watercolor Soc, 75; dir, Heritage of Hope (film), 76; auth, Lighting and art direction, Am Cinematographers Mag, 11/82. *Mailing Add:* 985 San Pasqual St Pasadena CA 91106

CARNWATH, SQUEAK
PAINTER
b Abington, Pa, May 24, 47. *Study:* Goddard Col, 69-70; Calif Col Arts & Crafts, MFA, 77. *Work:* Oakland Mus; San Francisco Mus Mod Art. *Exhib:* Oakland Mus, 74; Sculpture Now, California Clay Routes, San Francisco Mus Art, 79; one-person exhibs, San Francisco Mus Art, 80, Fuller-Goldeen Gallery, San Francisco, 82, Brentwood Gallery, St Louis, 83 & Palo Alto Cult Ctr, Calif, 83. *Teaching:* Guest instr studio art, Univ Calif, Berkeley, 82-83 & Davis, 83-84. *Awards:* Nat Endowment Arts Grant, 80; Soc Encouragement Contemp Art Award, 80. *Bibliog:* S Winn (auth), Ramps & ghosts, Artnews, 11/80; S Boettger (auth), From the sunnyside, Art in Am, 1/83 & Impolite figure, Artforum, 10/83. *Media:* Oil. *Dealer:* Fuller Goldeen 228 Grant Ave San Francisco CA; Getler-Pall 50 W 57th St New York NY. *Mailing Add:* 291 Fourth St Oakland CA 94607

CARO, FRANCIS
DEALER
b New York, NY, Aug 22, 38. *Pos:* Dir, Frank Caro Gallery, New York, currently. *Specialty:* Antique arts of China, India and Southeast Asia. *Mailing Add:* c/o Frank Caro Gallery 41 E 57th St New York NY 10022

CARPENTER, ARTHUR ESPENET See Espenet

CARPENTER, DENNIS WILKINSON (BONES)
PHOTOGRAPHER, EDUCATOR
b Meridian, Miss, June 7, 47. *Study:* Univ Ky, BArch, 72; Univ Fla, MFA, 79. *Work:* Jacksonville Art Mus, Fla; Polaroid Corp, Clarence Kennedy Gallery, Cambridge, Mass; Polaroid Int, Amsterdam, Neth; St Petersburg Mus Fine Art, Fla; Univ Fla, Gainesville. *Exhib:* Graphics Invitational, Mint Mus, 80; solo exhib, Univ Denver, 82, Light Factory, Charlotte, NC, 83, Webster Univ, St Louis, 83 & Photogenesis Gallery, Albuquerque, 83; Photographers Choose Photographers, Name Gallery, Chicago, 83. *Teaching:* Assoc prof photog, Univ Ky, Lexington, 73-; grad teaching asst, Univ Fla, Gainesville, 77-79; dir photog, Penland Sch Crafts, NC, 83. *Awards:* Best of Show, The Landscape, Crealde Sch Art, 81 & Each Image Unique, Catskill Ctr Photog, 81; Nat Endowment Arts Fel, 83. *Mem:* Artists Equity; Col Art Asn; Soc Photog Educ; Philadelphia Print Club; Friends Photog. *Media:* Mixed. *Mailing Add:* Col Archit Univ Ky Lexington KY 40506

CARPENTER, EARL L
PAINTER
b Long Beach, Calif, Nov 13, 31. *Study:* Chouinard Art Sch, 1 yr; Art Ctr Col Design, 4 yrs. *Work:* Mus Northern Ariz, Flagstaff; Ariz Bank Collection State Traveling Exhibs; Valley Nat Bank Gallery Western Art, Valley Ctr, Phoenix; also in pvt collections of Olaf Weighorst, Sen Barry Goldwater, Walter Bimson, John P Sands & George Getz Jr. *Exhib:* Retrospective, Wyo State Arch & Hist Dept, 74; Gallery Western Art, Valley Nat Bank, Scottsdale, Ariz, 75; Grand Canyon Art, Northern Ariz Univ, Flagstaff, 78; Artist of the Rockies 10th Anniversary Exhib, Pueblo, Colo, 83. *Teaching:* Stable Art Gallery, Scottsdale, Ariz. *Awards:* Stacey Scholar, 67 & 69. *Media:* Oil on Canvas & Panel. *Publ:* Auth, My painting technique, Am Artist Mag, 68; illusr, paintings in Ariz Highways Mag, Phoenix, 73 & 74; auth, article in Artist of the Rockies Mag, winter/spring 76-77; article in Southwest Art Mag, 1/81 & Southwest Profile, 6/83; plus others. *Dealer:* Husberg Gallery Sedona AZ 86336; Wadle Gallery Box 1931 Santa Fe NM 87501. *Mailing Add:* Earl Carpenter Studio Pinewood Munds Park AZ 86017

CARPENTER, ETHEL
PAINTER
b Mianus, Conn, June 11, 17. *Study:* Nat Acad Design, with Mario Cooper; also with Edgar Whitney, Jane Carlson, Val Thelin, Claude Croney. *Comn:* Calendar & cards, New Eng Biol Lab, Point Judith, RI, 69; cover for calendar & watercolor pad, Aquabee, Bee Paper Co, Passaic, NJ, 69-70. *Exhib:* Nat Miniature Painters, Sculptors & Gravers Soc Show, Washington, DC, 69; Knickerbocker Artists, Nat Arts Club, 69-70; Nat Am Artists Prof League, Lever House, New York, 69-71; Catharine Lorillard Wolfe, Nat Gallery, NY. *Awards:* Salmagundi Scholar, Washington Square Art Exhib, New York, 68; NY Phoenix Sch Design Award, 69; Minor S Jamison Award, Nat Miniature Painters, Sculptors & Gravers Soc, 69; and others. *Mem:* Am Artists Prof League; Catharine Lorillard Wolfe Art Club; Int Soc of Artists; Bergen Co Artists Guild; Allendale Art Asn. *Media:* Watercolor. *Mailing Add:* 248 Wyckoff Ave Wyckoff NJ 07481

CARPENTER, GILBERT FREDERICK (BERT)
PAINTER, MUSEUM DIRECTOR
b Billings, Mont, July 14, 20. *Study:* Stanford Univ, AB; Chouinard Art Inst; Ecole Beaux Arts, Paris, France; Columbia Univ. *Work:* Honolulu Acad Art; Sheldon Mem Mus, Lincoln, Nebr; Weatherspoon Gallery, Univ NC, Greensboro; Kresge Found, Mich State Univ; Univ Mass, Amherst. *Exhib:* Honolulu Acad Art, 51 & 59-61; one-man shows, Calif Palace Legion Honor, 52, Joslyn Mus, Omaha, Nebr, 52 & 54, A M Sachs Gallery, 72, 77 & 80-83, Zabriskie Gallery, 70, 72 & 74 & Joy Tash Gallery, Scottsdale, Ariz. *Pos:* Dir, Weatherspoon Gallery, 74-; mem bd, Green Hill Art Gallery. *Teaching:* Instr art, Columbia Univ, 54-60; head dept art, Univ Hawaii, 60-64; prof art & head dept, Univ NC, Greensboro, 64-74; prof art, Weatherspoon Gallery, 74- *Publ:* Art critic, Honolulu Star Bull, 61-62. *Dealer:* A M Sachs Gallery 29 W 57th St New York NY 10019; Joy Tash Gallery Scottsdale AZ. *Mailing Add:* 2505 W Market St Greensboro NC 27403

CARPENTER, JAMES MORTON
HISTORIAN
b Glens Falls, NY, Dec 7, 14. *Study:* Harvard Univ, AB & PhD. *Pos:* Dir, Colby Col Art Mus, 59-66; bd govs, Skowhegan Sch Painting & Sculpture, 65-74; bd trustees, Haystack Mountain Sch Crafts, 68-73; mem, Maine State Comn Arts & Humanities, 68-73. *Teaching:* From instr to asst prof fine arts, Harvard Univ, 43-50; from assoc prof to prof art, Colby Col, 50-, chmn dept, 55- *Mem:* Col Art Asn Am. *Res:* Aspects of art theory; history of Maine art. *Publ:* Co-auth, Maine & Its Role in American Art, 63; co-auth, Color in Art; auth, Visual Art, 82. *Mailing Add:* 1 Edgewood Waterville ME 04901

CARR, SALLY SWAN
SCULPTOR
b Minong, Wis. *Study:* NY Univ; advan sculpture, Phoenix Sch Design; life sketch, Clay Club; also with John Hovannes, Frederick Allen Williams & wax tech with Paul Manship; Art Students League. *Work:* Am Numismatic Soc, New York; Basketball Hall Fame, Springfield, Mass; Cayuga Mus Art & Hist,

Auburn, NY; Florentine Craftsmen, New York. *Comn:* Great Seal of US (woodcarving), comn by M Ketchum, Jr, US Embassy, Rabat, Morocco, 59; Lion of St Marks (bronze relief), Marco Polo Club, Waldorf Astoria Hotel, New York, 60; Cardinal Virtues (cararra marble reliefs), Riverside Mem Park, St Joseph, Mich, 65; Dr A Schweitzer (bust), Town Hall, Kaysersburg & Gunsbach, France, 70; and others. *Exhib:* Nat Acad Design, Allied Artists, 69-70; Acad Artists, Springfield Mus Art, Mass, 70; Burr Artist, Metrop Mus Art, 77, Caravan Galleries, New York, 77; Goldboro Mus, NC, 77; Spec Award Winners Show, Nat Arts Club, New York, 78; and others. *Awards:* A H Huntington First Prize Trophy, Catharine Lorillard Wolfe Art Club, 70; Founders Prize & Plaque, Pen & Brush Club, New York, 70 & Bronze Medal, 79; and others. *Mem:* Archit League New York (mem exhibs comt, 60); Burr Artists (second vpres, 69-72); Catharine Lorillard Wolfe Art Club (first vpres, 66-71, pres, 71-74); Composers, Auth & Artists Am (dir & historian, 69-72); hon mem Smithsonian. *Media:* Stone, Wood. *Mailing Add:* 530 E 23rd St New York NY 10010

CARRERO, JAIME
PAINTER, INSTRUCTOR
b Mayaguez, PR, June 16, 31. *Study:* Polytechnic Inst, Columbia Univ, BA(art hist); Pratt Inst, MS. *Work:* Ponce Mus, PR; Mus Inst of of PR Art, San Juan; Univ PR, San Juan; Inter-Am Univ Collection, San German. *Comn:* Illus for bk, Cuentos Puertorriquenos, 73. *Exhib:* Univ PR, San Juan, 60 & 65; Inst Cult PR, San Juan, 62; Acad Fine Arts, Calcutta, India, 65; Ateneo Puertorriqueno, San Juan, 66; Ponce Mus, 68. *Teaching:* Assoc prof painting, drawing & art hist, Inter-Am Univ, 57-; assoc prof art hist, Rum, Mayaguez, PR, 74-75. *Bibliog:* Josemilio Gonzalez (auth), Jaime Carrero, Pintor, El Mundo, 60; Drawings by Jaime Carrero, El Corno Emplumado, Mex, Nos 26, 28 & 30, 64-66. *Media:* Acrylic, Watercolor. *Mailing Add:* A-26 Urb Interamericana San German PR 00753

CARR-HARRIS, IAN REDFORD
SCULPTOR, PHOTOGRAPHER
b Victoria, BC, Can, Aug 12, 41. *Study:* Queen's Univ, Kingston, Ont, BA(hon), 63; Univ Toronto, Ont, BLS, 64; Ont Col Art, Toronto, AOCA, 71. *Work:* Nat Gallery Can, Ottawa; Can Coun Art Bank, Ottawa; Art Gallery Ont, Toronto. *Exhib:* Contemp Ont Art, Art Gallery Ont, 74; 9th Biennale of Paris, Mus d'Art Mod, Paris, 75; Another Dimension, Nat Gallery Can, 77; Kanadische Künster, Kunsthalle, Basle, 78; Confrontations, Vancouver Art Gallery, 79; Int Sculpture Conf, Washington, DC, 80; Fiction, Art Gallery Ont, 82; solo exhib, Dalhousie Art Gallery, Halifax, 82 & 49th Parallel Gallery, 83; and others. *Pos:* Chief librn, Ont Col Art, Toronto, 71- *Teaching:* Instr contempr art, Ont Col Art, Toronto, 76- *Awards:* Can Coun Proj Cost Grant, 72, 75 & 82; Can Coun Art Grant B, 76 & 80. *Bibliog:* Alex Mogelon (auth), Art in Boxes, Van Nostrand Reinhold, New York, 74; P McGrath (auth), Ian Carr-Harris at Carmens, Vanguard, summer 81; D Nemiroff (auth), Ian Carr-Harris: A Demonstration, Parachute, winter 81. *Mem:* Univ Art Asn Can. *Media:* Various, Sound & Film. *Publ:* Contribr, Parachute, Montreal, 75 & 82- *Dealer:* Carmen Lamanna 840 Yonge St Toronto ON M4W 2H1 Can. *Mailing Add:* 68 Broadview Ave 4th Floor Toronto ON M4M 2E6 Canada

CARRICK, DONALD F
ILLUSTRATOR-CHILDREN'S BOOKS, PAINTER
b Dearborn, Mich, April 7, 29. *Study:* Colorado Springs Fine Arts Ctr, 48-50; Art Students League, 50-51; Vienna Acad Fine Art, 54. *Work:* Pa Acad Fine Arts; New York Bar Asn; Kerlan Collection, Univ Minn, Minneapolis; pvt collection of Roy Newberger, New York. *Exhib:* Painterly Realism, Am Fedn Arts Nat Traveling Exhib, 70; New England Paintings, Fleming Mus, Burlington, Vt, 71. *Awards:* New York Soc Illusr Ann Award, 70 & 71; Irma Simonton Black Award, 73; Am Inst Graphic Artists Cert Excellence, 75. *Media:* Watercolor, Ink; Oil. *Publ:* Illusr, Soundings at Sea Level, Houghton Mifflin Co, 80; illusr, Two Coyotes, 82, auth & illusr, Harald and the Giant Knight, 82 & illusr, Patrick's Dinosaurs, 83, Houghton Mifflin-Clarion; illusr, Alex Remembers, Green Willow, 83. *Dealer:* Tashtego Assoc Main St Edgartown MA 02539. *Mailing Add:* Box 1181 Edgartown MA 02539

CARRINGTON, JOY HARRELL
PAINTER, ILLUMINATOR
b Jacksonville, Tex. *Study:* Kansas City Art Inst, three years; Am Acad Art, Chicago; Nat Acad Chicago; Chicago Art Inst, with Pougialis; Art Students League, four years; also with Frank Peyraud, Highland Park, Ill & Robert Brackman, Noank, Conn. *Work:* Long Barrack Mus, Alamo; First Methodist Church, Jacksonville; Alamo Libr; Coppini Acad Fine Arts; San Antonio; State Capitol Bldg, Austin. *Exhib:* Meinhard Galleries, Houston, 67-72; Panhandle Plains Mus Ann, Canyon, Tex; Cent Tex Mus, Salado, Tex; McNamara O'Conner Mus, Victoria, Tex; Univ Tex, San Antonio, 76-78; and others. *Pos:* Com artist for Frank Bros, San Antonio, Hartman Furniture Co & Handelan & Staff Shoe Agency, Chicago & Loesers, Brooklyn. *Awards:* Coppini Acad Award for Oil Painting, Witte Mus, 57 & 82; Grumbacher Award for Oil Painting, Am Artists Prof League, 69; Sculpture Award, Kansas City Art Inst; Gold Merit Award, Univ Tex, San Antonio Watercolor Group, 76-77. *Bibliog:* Glenn Tucker (auth), Arts Rev, San Antonio Light, 8/63; Herweck (auth), article in The Record, spring 72. *Mem:* Am Artists Prof League; Nat Soc Arts & Letters; Coppini Acad Fine Arts; Kerrville Art Club; San Antonio Watercolor Group. *Media:* Oil. *Mailing Add:* T Anchor Ranch Rte 16 Box 30 Medina TX 78055

CARRINGTON, OMAR RAYMOND
PAINTER, INSTRUCTOR
b Philadelphia, Pa, Oct 16, 04. *Study:* Univ Md, BA, 28; Corcoran Sch Art, 31-35; Pa Acad Fine Arts, 35-36; Am Univ Grad Sch, 38-39; with Jack Tworkov, 55. *Work:* Dallas Mus Fine Arts, Tex; Mint Mus Art, Charlotte, NC; Md Federation Womens Clubs, Baltimore. *Exhib:* Regional Exhib, Richmond Mus Art, Va, 47; Biennial Exhib, Corcoran Mus Art, Washington, DC, 47, 49, 51, 53 & 55; Md Regional Exhib, Baltimore Mus Art, 47 & 49; Nat Exhib Am Art by States, Metrop Mus Art, New York, 50; State Dept Show in Europe, Paris, France & Switzerland, 53; one-man shows, Baltimore Mus Art, Mint Mus & Arts Club of Washington. *Pos:* Project dir, Graphics Div, US Dept of State, Washington, DC, 50-53. *Teaching:* Instr painting & drawing, Corcoran Sch Art, Washington, DC, 47-55; instr painter, Catholic Univ Am, Washington, DC, 47-50. *Awards:* Fel, Louis Comfort Tiffany Found of New York, 36; gold Medal for Landscape, Soc Washington Artists, 46; Prize for Best Paintings in Show, Regional Baltimore Mus, 48 & 49. *Mem:* Artists Equity Asn (treas, 65-67); Washington Watercolor Club (pres, 44-47); Soc Washington Printmakers. *Media:* Oil, Watercolor. *Mailing Add:* 3705 Taylor St Chevy Chase MD 20815

CARRON, MAUDEE LILYAN
PAINTER, SCULPTOR
b Melville, La. *Study:* Creative Arts Sch, Houston, scholar, with McNeill Davidson; Lamar Univ; & with Dr James McMurray. *Work:* Univ Tex Austin. *Comn:* Poster & stage sets for Glass Menagerie, Who's Afraid of Virginia Wolf? & Macbeth, Univ Tex Austin Drama Dept, 70 & 72. *Exhib:* 16 Southeastern States & Tex Exhib, New Orleans Mus, 63; Eight State Exhib, Okla Art Ctr, Oklahoma City, 68; one-man shows, Images, Univ Tex Fine Arts Gallery, 70; Environment 71, Univ Tex Austin, 71 & Et Cetera 3, Southwestern Univ, 72; All-Media Exhib 77, Univ Houston, 77. *Teaching:* Instr elements of visual design, Art & Alma's Art Ctr, 63-69; two workshops for Beaumont Art League, 72 & 73; visiting instr for Dick Bowling Pub Sch, 79. *Awards:* Miller Award for Incognito, Beaumont Art Mus, 68 & two awards for A Dangerous Game in Archaic Form, 70; Award for A Temple for All Delights, Tex Fine Arts Asn, 69. *Mem:* Tex Watercolor Soc; Tex Prof Sculptors Soc; Graphic Soc, Lamar Univ. *Media:* Metal, Acrylic. *Mailing Add:* Rt 6 Box 300 Beaumont TX 77705

CARSTENSON, CECIL C
SCULPTOR, LECTURER
b Marquette, Kans, July 23, 06. *Study:* Kansas City Art Inst; Univ Nebr; Art Inst Chicago; also with several sculptors in Italy. *Work:* Joslyn Mus, Omaha, Nebr; Phoenix Art Mus, Ariz; Med Ctr & Student Ctr, Univ Mo, Kansas City; Nelson Gallery Art, Kansas City; Jewish Community Ctr, Kansas City; plus others. *Exhib:* Mid America, Nelson Gallery Art; Joslyn Art Gallery Show; Mo Pavilion Exhib, New York World's Fair,; St Louis Mus Show; Denver Art Gallery Show. *Pos:* Comt mem, Mo Coun on Visual Arts, 68-72. *Teaching:* Instr sculpture, Univ Mo, Kansas City, 51-53. *Awards:* Purchase Award, Mid America, Nelson Gallery Art. *Media:* Wood. *Publ:* Auth, Film, sculpture, Nelson Gallery Art, 62; Craft and Creation of Wood Sculpture, Scribner, 71. *Dealer:* Pucker Safrai Gallery 171 Newbury St Boston MA 02116. *Mailing Add:* 1018 W 38th St Kansas City MO 64111

CARSWELL, RODNEY
PAINTER, EDUCATOR
b Carmel, Calif, Dec 15, 46. *Study:* Univ NMex, BFA, 68; Univ Colo, MFA, 72. *Work:* Univ NMex, Albuquerque; Univ Colo, Boulder; Ill State Mus, Springfield; Evansville Mus Art, Ind. *Exhib:* Chicago & Vicinity Show, Art Inst Chicago, 73, New Horizons in Art, Chicago, 73; Ill Invitational, Springfield, Ill, 73-74; Evansville Ann, Evansville Mus, Ind, 75; one-man shows, Not in New York Gallery, Cincinnati, Ohio, 76 & Roy Boyd Gallery, Chicago, 78; The Chosen Object, Joslyn Mus, Omaha, Nebr, 77; Carl Solway Gallery, New York, 77; Roy Boyd Gallery, Chicago, 79. *Teaching:* Asst prof painting & drawing, Ill State Univ, Normal, 72- *Awards:* Viewler Award, Art Inst Chicago, 73; Purchase Awards, Ill State Mus, 73 & Evansville Mus, 74. *Media:* Acrylic. *Dealer:* Roy Boyd Gallery 233 E Ontario St Chicago IL 60611. *Mailing Add:* Dept of Art Ill State Univ Normal IL 61701

CARTER, BERNARD SHIRLEY
PAINTER, INSTRUCTOR
b Boston, Mass, Oct 22, 17. *Study:* Art Students League, with Raphael Soyer & Arnold Blanch; Oqunquit Sch Art, Maine, with Bernard Karfiol. *Work:* Metrop Mus Art, New York; Boston Mus Fine Arts, Mass. *Exhib:* Int Watercolor Exhib, Brooklyn Mus, NY, 51; Am Watercolor Soc Ann, New York, 60 & 61; 100th Ann Exhib, Am Watercolor Soc, Metrop Mus Art, 67; Audubon Ann Exhib, Nat Acad Galleries, New York, 70. *Teaching:* Instr painting, Parsons Sch Design, New York, 46-65; instr painting & dir, Bedford Art Ctr, NY. *Awards:* Non-mem Award, Am Watercolor Soc, 60; Katonah Gallery Award, 65; First Prize Watercolor, Artists Northern Westchester, NY, 65. *Mem:* Am Watercolor Soc; Century Asn. *Media:* Watercolor. *Mailing Add:* 350 Cherry St Bedford Hills NY 10507

CARTER, (CHARLES) BRUCE
PRINTMAKER, EDUCATOR
b North Adams, Mass, May 15, 30. *Study:* Albright Art Sch, Buffalo, NY, dipl, 51; State Univ NY Buffalo, BS, 52; Pa State Univ, University Park, MEd & DEd, 58. *Work:* Nat Hist Mus, Univ Oslo, Norway; Philadelphia Mus Art; State Art Mus, Raleigh, NC; Amarillo Art Ctr, Tex. *Comn:* Painted mural, Narvik City Coun, Norway, 62 & mosaic mural, 63; mosaic mural, Kiruna, Sweden, 62; Painted Mural, Nat Mus, Gettysburg, Pa; mosaic mural, Nordsland Banken, Leknes, Norway, 68. *Exhib:* Soc Am Graphic Artists,

New York, 71; 2nd Triennial Int Exhib Contemp Xylography, Nat Mus Xylography, Carpi, Italy, 72; Hokkaido Print Asn Int Exhib, Sapporo, Japan, 72; 3rd Int Print Biennial Exhib, Art Mus, Epinal, France, 75; Return to the Crucible, The Pentagon, DC, 76; Wounded Knee: An Am Tragedy, Amarillo Art Ctr, Tex, 76; 6th Nat Print Exhib, Los Angeles, 78; Nat Hist Mus, Univ Oslo, Norway, 80; The Warsaw Woodcuts, Ghetto Fighters Mus, Israel, 81. *Pos:* Art consult, Poetry on the Buses, Pittsburgh, 76- *Teaching:* Prof printmaking-drawing, Carnegie Mellon Univ, Pittsburgh, 63- *Awards:* Purchase Prizes, Nat Mus Xylography, Carpi, Italy, 72 & Univ Wis-Madison, 75. *Mem:* Col Art Asn; Philadelphia Print Club; Artists' Equity Asn. *Media:* Woodcut, Lithography. *Publ:* Coauth, Wounded Knee: An American Tragedy (film), WQED-TV, 72. *Mailing Add:* RD 1 Saltsburg PA 15681

CARTER, CLARENCE HOLBROOK
PAINTER, DESIGNER

b Portsmouth, Ohio, Mar 26, 04. *Study:* Cleveland Sch Art, 23-27; with Hans Hofmann, Capri, Italy, summer 27. *Work:* Metrop Mus Art; Mus Mod Art; Whitney Mus Art; Philadelphia Mus Art; Cleveland Mus Art; and others. *Comn:* Murals, sect painting & sculpture, Treasury Dept, Portsmouth, Ohio & Ravenna, Ohio Post Off & Cleveland Pub Auditorium. *Exhib:* One-man shows, Mus Art, Carnegie Inst, 40, Minneapolis Inst Arts, 49, NJ State Mus, 74 & Univ Tex Art Mus, 77; plus many Europ, SAm, Can mus & others. *Pos:* Dir, FAP for Northeastern Ohio, 37-38. *Teaching:* Lectr art, mus, cols & art schs; asst prof painting & design, Carnegie Inst, 38-44; dir art, Chautauqua Inst, NY Univ, summer 42-43; guest instr painting, Cleveland Inst Art, summer 48; guest instr, Minneapolis Sch Art, fall 49; guest instr, Lehigh Univ, 54; guest instr, Ohio Univ, 55; guest instr, Atlanta Art Inst, 57; vis lectr, Lafayette Col, 61, artist-in-residence, 61-69; guest artist, Univ Iowa, spring 70, Iowa State, 75, Kent State 75. *Mem:* Assoc Nat Acad Design; Del Valley Art Asn (pres, 62-63); Am Watercolor Soc (bd dirs, 61-62, vpres, 62). *Publ:* Auth, chap, In: Work for artists; contrib, articles in Col Art J & Am Artist. *Dealer:* Gimpel & Weitzenhoffer Galleries 1040 Madison at 79th St New York NY 10021; Hirsch & Adler Galleries 21 E 70th St New York NY 10021. *Mailing Add:* RD 1 Box 119 Milford NJ 08848

CARTER, DAVID GILES
CONSULTANT, MUSEUM DIRECTOR

b Nashua, NH, Nov 2, 21. *Study:* Princeton Univ, with C R Morey & A M Friend, AB, 44; Harvard Univ Grad Sch Arts & Sci, with P Sachs, C R Post, C Kuhn & others, MA, 49; Inst Fine Arts, NY Univ, 51, with W Cook, E Panofsky, G Schoenberger & H Bober. *Collections Arranged:* Turner in America (with Wilbur D Peat), 56; The Young Rembrandt and His Times, 58; The G H A Clowes Collection, 59; Dynamic Symmetry, 61; El Greco to Goya (with Curtis Coley), 63; The Weldon Collection, 64; Masterpieces from Montreal, 66; The Painter and the New World, 67; Rembrandt and His Pupils, 69; Jan Menses, 76; and others. *Pos:* Curatorial asst, Metrop Mus Art, New York, 50-54; cur paintings & prints, John Herron Art Mus, 55-59; dir, Mus Art, RI Sch Design, 59-64; dir, Montreal Mus Fine Arts, 64-76. *Teaching:* Lectr, Ind Univ, Bloomington, 58-59. *Awards:* Gold Medal of Ital Cult, Ital Ministry Foreign Affairs, 63. *Mem:* ICOM; Mediaeval Acad; Grolier Club; Royal Soc Arts; plus others. *Res:* secondary interest in Mannerist and northern Baroque painting. *Publ:* Auth, Rencontre avec Valentin, l'Oeil, 70; auth, The Winnipeg flagellation and the master of the View of St Gudule, Miscellanea in Memoriam Paul Coremans (1908-1965), Bull de l'Institut royal du Patrimoine artistique, xv, 75; auth, Spanish itinerary, Apollo, 5/76; auth, Northern Baroque and the Italian connexion, Apollo, 5/76; auth, Montreal musee des beaux-arts, The Art Gallery, 4-5/76; and others. *Mailing Add:* 100 Edgehill Rd New Haven CT 06511

CARTER, DEAN
SCULPTOR, EDUCATOR

b Henderson, NC, Apr 24, 22. *Study:* Corcoran Sch Art; Am Univ, BA; Ogunquit Sch Painting & Sculpture; Indiana Univ, MFA; Ossip Zadkine Sch Art, Paris, France. *Work:* Cranbrook Acad Art, Mich; Charlotte Plaza, NC; Washington & Lee Univ; Wichita Art Asn Galleries, Kans; Harrisonburg Community Hosp, Va. *Comn:* Bronze portrait, Gropius, Col Archit, Va Polytech Inst, 65; welded bronze screen, Roanoke Mem Hosp, Va, 70; three piece bronze group, St Joseph's Preparatory Sch, Philadelphia, 70; welded bronze relief, First Colony Ins Co, Lynchburg, Va; bronze portrait, Stuart Cassell, Cassell Colesium, Va Polytech Inst, 77; plus others. *Exhib:* Pa Acad Fine Arts, Philadelphia, 54; Cini Found, Venice, Italy, 64; Smithsonian Circulating Exhib, 69-71; one-man show, Artists' Mart, Washington, DC, 70; Contemp Gallery Art Ann Sculpture Show, Winston-Salem, 71. *Pos:* Mem art adv bd, Va Highlands Community Col, Abigdon, 69-71 & Mountain Empire Community Col, Wise, 71-75; consult, US Fine Arts Surv, 72. *Teaching:* Founder art dept, Va Polytech Inst & State Univ, 63-; artist in residence, UGA Studies Abroad, Cortona, Italy. *Awards:* First Prize, Festival of Arts, Radford, Va, 79; Cert of Distinction, Roanoke Fine Arts Ctr, 79; Purchase Award, Bank of Va, Roanoke, 79; plus others. *Bibliog:* Ted Kliman (dir), A World of Sculpture (film), Va Polytech Inst & State Univ, 62; W M White, Jr (auth), Sculpturing by Dean Carter, Maelstrom, 66; W C Burleson (auth), On campus--Dean Carter, Context, summer 69. *Mem:* Soc Washington Artists; Southern Sculptors Asn (vpres, 66-68); Am Crafts Coun (state rep, 65); Col Art Asn Am; Am Fedn Art; plus others. *Media:* Bronze, Wood. *Dealer:* Area Landscape 4118 Olley Lane Fairfax VA 22039. *Mailing Add:* 1011 Highland Circle Blacksburg VA 24060

CARTER, DUDLEY CHRISTOPHER
SCULPTOR

b New Westminster, BC, May 6, 1891. *Study:* City Col San Fransisco, hon degree, 83. *Work:* Seattle Art Mus; Golden Gate Park, San Francisco; Evergreen East, Bellevue, Wash. *Comn:* Big Horn sculpture, San Francisco City Col, 40; totem column, Northgate Shopping Ctr, Wash, 53; carved relief, Schaefer Brothers Co, Aberdeen, Wash, 54; totem column, Shell Oil Refinery, Anacortes, Wash, 55. *Exhib:* Golden Gate Expos, San Francisco, 39; Seattle World's Fair, 61; David L Vaughn Exhib, Vancouver, BC, 72; US Dept Housing & Urban Develop, Washington, DC, 73; Native Craftsman, Yakima Valley Col, 76; Legend of the Moon, Marymoor Park, Wash, 77. *Awards:* Sculpture, Music & Art Found, Seattle, 48; Achievement Award for Sculpture, Past Pres Assembly, 62; Int Sculpture, US Dept Housing & Urban Develop, 73. *Bibliog:* Michael Minot (auth), BC Sculptors, F Cameron Wilkenson Co Ltd, 74. *Mem:* Seattle Art Mus; Can Fed Arts; Artists Equity Asn; BC Sculptors Asn (hon life pres). *Media:* Wood. *Mailing Add:* 3075 Bellevue Redmond Rd Bellevue WA 98008

CARTER, FREDERICK TIMMINS
PAINTER, ILLUSTRATOR

b Galveston, Tex, Sept 22, 25. *Study:* Franklin Sch Prof Art, New York, grad with hons, 45-48. *Work:* D D Feldman Collection Tex Artists, Dallas. *Comn:* Paintings, El Paso Natural Gas Co, Tex, 73, Ford Motor Co, Dearborn, Mich, 75. *Exhib:* Tex Ann Paintings Exhib, Dallas, Houston & San Antonio Mus, 53-58; Audubon Artists Nat Exhib, Nat Acad Galleries, New York, 55 & 70; Sun Carnival Nat Exhib, El Paso Mus Fine Art, 58-68; Nat Soc Painters in Casein, New York, 60; one-man show, Dos Pajaros Gallery, El Paso Int Airport, 75, 78 & 81. *Pos:* Staff artist, Wilkinson-Schiwetz & Tips, Houston, 50-55; art dir, Mithoff Advert, El Paso, 57-65, Frederick Carter Studio, 66- *Mem:* El Paso Co Hist Soc. *Media:* Acrylic. *Publ:* Illusr, Frank Mangan's Bordertown, 64, El Paso, 71 & Bordertown Revisited, 73; illusr, Ford Times Mag, 75; illusr, Fort Bliss History, 81. *Dealer:* Dos Pajaros Gallery Int Airport El Paso TX 79925; Frederick Carter Studio 5744 Beaumont El Paso TX 79912. *Mailing Add:* 5744 Beaumont El Paso TX 79912

CARTER, GRANVILLE W
SCULPTOR, INSTRUCTOR

b Augusta, Maine, Nov 18, 20. *Study:* Corburn Class Inst; Portland Sch Fine & Applied Art; New York City Sch Indust Art; Nat Acad Sch Fine Arts; Grande Chaumiere, Paris, France; Scuolo Circolare Int, Rome, Italy; Am Acad Rome. *Work:* Smithsonian Inst, Washington, DC; Thomas Alva Edison Mus, West Orange, NJ; Hall Fame Great Americans, NY Univ; Morristown Hist Mus, NJ; Maine State Mus, Augusta; and others. *Comn:* Monumental bust of Alexander Stewart, Garden City, NY, 69; West Texas Pioneer Family Monument (heroic bronze), Lubbock, Tex, 71; Brig Gen Casimir Pulaski Equestrian Monument (heroic bronze), Hartford, Conn, 76; heroic bronze bust of Charles Lindbergh, Garden City Hist Soc, 77; heroic bronze bust of Chiang Kai-Shek, St Johns Univ, 79; and others. *Exhib:* Am Acad Rome Ann, 55; Archit League, New York, 56-58; Int Expos Medals, Paris & Prague, 67 & 70; Am Artists Prof League Ann, New York, 70. *Pos:* Contribr, Hall of Fame for Great Americans Brochures, 63-72; deleg, Fine Arts Fedn New York, 72. *Teaching:* Instr sculpture, Nat Acad Design, 66-; lectr sculpture, Washington Cathedral & Hofstra Univ, 66- *Awards:* Saltus Award, Am Numismatic Soc, 76; Prize, Nat Acad Design, 80; Therese & Edward Richard Memorial Prize, Nat Sculpture Soc, 80. *Bibliog:* Charles Guy (auth), editorial in Lubbock Avalanche J, 6/10/71; Ford Mitchell (auth), West Texas Pioneer Family Monument (film), KCBD TV, 71; James M Goode (auth), Outdoor Sculpture of Washington, DC. *Mem:* Nat Sculpture Soc (pres, 79-81); Am Artists Prof League (bd dirs, 72-); academician Nat Acad Design; Coun Am Artists Socs (bd dirs, 69-, pres, 81-); Brookgreen Gardens, SC. *Media:* Stone, Metals. *Publ:* Contribr, Nat Sculpture Rev, spring 67. *Mailing Add:* 625 Portland Ave Baldwin NY 11510

CARTER, HARRIET (ESTELLE) MANORE
PAINTER

b Grand Bend, Ont, Mar 22, 29. *Study:* Dundas Valley Sch Fine Arts, Ont. *Work:* Sarnia Pub Libr & Art Mus, Ont; Art Gallery Brant, Brantford, Ont; Can Coun Art Bank; Hart House, Univ Toronto. *Exhib:* Traveling Exhib, 70-83 & Fifty Years, 75, Can Soc Pinters Watercolour; On View Traveling Exhib, Ont, 76-77; Can Watercolour Soc Japan & Can Exhib, 76-77; Ont Soc Artists Ann Exhib, Oakville Centennial Gallery, 77; Cloud Flowers Traveling Exhib, 81-82. *Pos:* Commercial designer, Dominion Glass Co, Wallaceburg, Ont, 49-52. *Awards:* Hon Award, Can Soc Painters Watercolour, 69; Ont Soc Artists 100th Ann Exhib Awards, 72; Purchase Award, London Pub Art Gallery & Mus, 72. *Bibliog:* Tom Thompson Memorial Gallery Museum of Fine Art Show, Art Mag, 71; Kay Kritzwiser (auth), Four exhibits mind stretching style, Toronto Globe & Mail, 72; Lenore Crawford (auth), Manore Carter art gets message across, London Free Press, 73. *Mem:* Can Soc Painters Watercolour; Ont Soc Artists; Royal Can Acad Arts. *Media:* Watercolour. *Dealer:* Nancy Pooles Gallery 16 Hazelton Ave Toronto ON M5R 2E2. *Mailing Add:* 78 MacLennan Ave Hamilton ON L8V 1X6 Canada

CARTER, JERRY WILLIAMS
MOSAIC ARTIST, MURALIST

b Wichita, Kans, Apr 19, 41. *Study:* Univ Md, BA, 68; Chicago Art Inst, 69; Acad Fine Arts Finland, 70; Centro Int Studi L'Insegnamento Mosaico, cert, 70; L'Ecole Nat Superieur Beaux Arts Paris, 71; Acad Belli Arti Ravenna, 72; Univ Studi Bologna, cert, 71; Nat Inst Design Finland, 73; Antioch Univ, Columbia Visual Arts Ctr, MFA, 81. *Work:* The Phillips Collection & Govt Employees Insurance Pub Collection, Washington, DC; Pinacoteca Comunale Ravenna, Italy. *Comn:* Seascape (mosaic collage venetian glass), Tomlinson Collection, Madison, Fla, 74; The Great Seal of the State of Florida (glass mosaic), House Rep, Tallahassee, 75; Descent of the Holy Spirit (venetian glass mosaic), Church Holy Spirit, Forrestville, Md, 78; Sointu (marble & glass mosaic), comn by James Bell, Washington, DC, 81; Cascade (ceramic & venetian glass mosaic sculpture), Vista Int Hotel, Washington, DC, 83. *Exhib:* Phillips Collection, Washington, DC, 69; Modern Mosaics, Loggetta Lombardesca, Ravenna, Italy, 72; Nat Mus Am Art, Smithsonian Inst, 75-83; The Am Painter's in Paris Show, Palais Cong, France, 76-77; Studio Int Mosaico Mod, Pinacoteca Comunale, Ravenna, Italy, 80; Royal Embassy Norway & Nat Wild Life Fedn Hq, Washington, DC, 81-82; Sign of Peace and Friendship Among Peoples, UNESCO, Ravenna, Italy, 83. *Collections Arranged:* Finnish Architecture Exhib, Am Inst Architects Headquarters, 77; Finnish Folk Art Exhib of 16th through 19th Century (auth, catalog), George Washington Univ, 78. *Pos:* Gallery asst, The Phillips Collection, Washington DC, 61-68; art dir, ABC-TV, Washington DC, 66-68. *Awards:* Ford Found Scholarship, 68; First Place, St Marks Art Festival, 75; Am Winner, Sign of Peace & Friendship Among Peoples Award, UNESCO, 83. *Bibliog:* Nick Addi (auth), Master of mosaics, Montgomery J, 11/27/81; Lars Hamberg (auth), Mosaikkonst i USA pa finländsk bas, Suomi-USA, 1/82; Peter Lancy (auth), Jerry Carter: Mosaicist, Artscapes, 1/82. *Mem:* Artist Equity; Int Asn Contemp Mosaicists; Montgomery Co Arts Coun. *Media:* Ceramic, Glass. *Publ:* Auth, Mosaic: Medium for the Times, Presso il centro stampa del comune di Ravenna, 80; auth, A Syllabus for Mosaic Art, Antioch Univ, 81. *Dealer:* J W Carter 10602 Bucknell Dr Silver Spring MD 20902. *Mailing Add:* 10602 Bucknell Dr Silver Spring MD 20902

CARTER, MARY
PAINTER
b Hartsdale, NY. *Study:* Art Students League, with Reginald Marsh, Robert Beverly Hale & E Dickenson, 51-55; Visual Arts, 68; Parsons Sch, 81. *Exhib:* Audubon Artists Ann, 54 & 72; Nat Acad Design, New York, 55 & 72; Hartford Atheneum Show, Conn, 55; Nat Competition, Springfield Art Mus, Mo, 66; Ann Drawings & Sculpture Show, Del Mar Col, Corpus Christi, Tex, 67; Hudson Guild Invitational, New York, 75- *Mem:* Art Students League. *Media:* Oil, Tempera. *Mailing Add:* 253 W 16th St New York NY 10011

CARTER, YVONNE PICKERING
PAINTER, EDUCATOR
b Washington, DC, Feb 6, 39. *Study:* Traphagen Sch, cert, 59; Howard Univ, AB, 62, MFA, 68. *Work:* NC Mus, Raleigh; Federal Reserve Bank, Richmond, Va; Gibbes Gallery, Charleston, SC; Miami-Dade Co Libr, Fla; Montgomery Co Print Collection, Md. *Exhib:* The Material Dominant: Some Current Artists & Their Media, Mus Art, Pa Univ, Univ Park, 77; New Dimensions: Art Works by Black American Artists, Miami-Dade Public Libr, Fla, 79; Reflections of a Southern Heritage Black Artists of the Southeast, Gibbes Art Gallery, Greenville Co Mus & Columbia Gallery Art, SC, 79-80; Alternatives by Black Artists, Washington Project Arts, 80; Bookworks: Washington DC, Washington Project Arts, 80; Elements of Art Line, Arlington Arts Ctr, Va, 80; Ten Plus Ten Plus Ten, Corcoran Gallery Art, 82; 47th Ann, Butler Inst Am Art, 83; and others. *Teaching:* Assoc prof design & painting, Univ District of Columbia, Washington, DC, 71- *Awards:* DC Commission Arts & Humanities Visual Arts Award, 81 & 82. *Bibliog:* Scott Lucas (auth), Washington Walkabout, New Art Examiner, 81; M Sunderland (auth), 3 Artists, 3 Ways, Ocular, fall 81. *Mem:* Col Art Asn; Washington Women's Art Ctr; Women's Caucus Art. *Media:* Watercolor, Acrylic. *Dealer:* Fendrick Gallery 3059 M St NW Washington DC 20007. *Mailing Add:* 1337 10th St NW Washington DC 20001

CARTLEDGE, ROSEANNE NIEMYT
GRAPHIC ARTIST
b Milwaukee, Wis, Mar 1, 39. *Study:* Alverno Col, Milwaukee, BA, 61; Okla Univ, Norman, MA(art educ), 69; Inst Allende, San Miguel de Allende, GTO, Mex, graphics & sculpture, summers 60 & 61. *Comn:* Five drawings for permanent display, US Forest Serv Hq, Williams, Ariz, 77. *Exhib:* 4th Colo Ann Exhib, Denver Art Mus, 76; 17 Ways to Draw a Picture, Harlan Gallery, Tucson, Ariz, 76; 12th & 16th Southwestern Invitationals, Yuma Art Ctr, Ariz, 78 & 82; Coconino Ctr Arts Holiday Exhibs, Flagstaff, Ariz, 81-83; Northern Ariz Invitational, Coconino Ctr Arts, 83. *Collections Arranged:* Ariz State Univ Mem Union Gallery (10-12 per yr), Tempe; A Technical Workshop, 4/74 & Design Awareness Seminar, 2/75, Ariz State Univ. *Pos:* Head of Exhib & Fine Arts Adv, Mem Union, Ariz State Univ, Tempe, 71-75. *Teaching:* Instr art, Homestead High Sch, Mequon, Wis, 61-63; instr art, Am Sch, Tegucigalpa, 63-65; asst prof design, Sch Home Econ, Okla Univ, 65-71; guest lectr, Yuma Art Ctr, 83. *Mem:* Prof Artists Northern Ariz; Asn Col Union Int (visual arts coordr region 13, 74-75); Coconino Co Comn Arts, Flagstaff, Ariz, 81. *Mailing Add:* 5 N Sunset Strip Williams AZ 86046

CARTMELL, HELEN
PAINTER, DIRECTOR
b Bridgeport, Conn, Jan 6, 23. *Study:* Detroit Soc Arts & Crafts, scholar; Wayne State Univ. *Work:* Wayne State Univ Collection; Chrysler Corp, Detroit; Int Nickel Co, New York; Ford Motor World Hq; Avon Corp; and many others. *Exhib:* Detroit Inst Arts; Willistead Gallery, Ont, Can; Grand Rapids Art Mus; one-woman shows, Arwin Galleries, Detroit, 70 & 75 & Mt Clemens Art Ctr, 75. *Pos:* Educ media art dir, Ctr Instrnl Technol, Wayne State Univ, 67-82. *Awards:* Silver Medal Award, Detroit Scarab Club; Best of Show Award, Int Exhib, Port Huron; Ferris Fitch Award. *Dealer:* Arwin Galleries 222 W Grand River Detroit MI 48226. *Mailing Add:* 21700 Winshall Rd St Clair Shores MI 48081

CARTWRIGHT, CONSTANCE B & CARROLL L
COLLECTORS
b US citizens. *Mem:* Mrs Cartwright, Am Fedn Arts (trustee & treas); Mus of Mod Art Int Coun; Mus of Mod Art (drawing comt); Mus of Fine Arts, Boston (visitor's comt Asiatic Art). *Collection:* Late 19th and 20th century drawings; Chinese blue and white porcelain. *Mailing Add:* 435 E 52nd St New York NY 10022

CARULLA, RAMON
PAINTER
b Havana, Cuba, Dec 7, 38; US citizen. *Study:* Self taught. *Work:* Detroit Inst Art, Mich; Mus Tamago, Mexico; Cincinnati Art Mus, Ohio; Mus Fine Art, Montreal, Can; CBS International, Miami, Fla. *Exhib:* one-man shows, Atelier Lukacs, Montreal, 77, Miami Laakes Public Library, Miami Fla, Schweger Gold Galleries, Birmingham, Mich, Atelier Gallery, Mexico, 81; Paper as a Medium, Fla Int Univ & Smithsonian Inst, 79-80; and others. *Teaching:* Guest lectr, Cranbrook Acad Art, Bloomfield Hills, Mich. *Awards:* Sixth Biennial of Graphic Latin Am Artists, San Juan, PR; Honorable Mention, 4th Ann Pan Am Exhib, 71-73; Cintas Fel Grant, 73-74 & 79-80; plus others. *Bibliog:* K Flanders (auth), article in Time Guide, 70-71; Helen Kohen (auth), Life Boundries, 80; Uva Clavijo (auth), Diario de las Americas, 80; R Pan Hosh (auth), The origins of Cuban art, Miami Herald, 10/81; Vanidades Magozie (auth), Ramon Caralla and the Latin American Expression, 10/82. *Mem:* Florida Artist Group; Artists Equity Asn. *Media:* Oil on Canvas. *Dealer:* Virginia Miller Galleries 3112 Commodore Plaza Coconut Grove FL 33133; Schweyer Galdo Galleries Birmingham MI & Morristown NJ. *Mailing Add:* 4735 NW 184th Terr Miami FL 33055

CARYL, JOAN LEONARD
PAINTER, SCULPTOR
b Fall River, Mass, Jan 21, 20. *Study:* Bennington Col, with Arch Lauterer & Paul Feeley, 42; Corcoran Sch Art, with Heinz Warneke, 61; Studio, with Andre L'Hote, Paris, France, 52; Georgetown Univ, MA, 77. *Work:* Washington Co Mus Fine Arts, Hagerstown, Md; West Liberty State Col, WVa; Wheeling Col, WVa; Art-in-Embassies Prog, Dept State. *Comn:* Christoglas, Registered & US Patent Office, Washington, DC, 63; 10 stained glass windows for chapel, Soc African Missions, Washington, DC, 64; logo for ROTC, US Navy, Washington, DC; John F Kennedy Bronze Head, Peace Corps Village, Peru, 70; paintings, Georgetown Univ Libr, 79, 80 & 83. *Exhib:* Corcoran Fac Show, Corcoran Gallery Art, Washington, DC, 62-65; 16th Area Exhib, Corcoran Gallery Art, Washington, DC, 63; George Washington Univ Gallery, Washington, DC, 64 & 65; Am Crafts Coun, New York, 67 & 68; one-woman shows, Corcoran Gallery Art, Washington, DC, 67, Agra Gallery, Washington, DC, 72-74, British Petroleum North Am, Washington, DC, 74 & 77 & Georgetown Univ Gallery, 78 & 84. *Teaching:* Instr 2-D design & sculpture, Corcoran Sch Art, 62-65; instr sculpture & drawing, Georgetown Univ, 65-70; guest prof, Univ Notre Dame Grad Sch, Georgetown Univ Summer Sch & others, 65-79; artist-in-residence art hist & studio, Georgetown Preparatory Sch, 74-76; private instr sculpture & drawing, 77- *Awards:* Third Prize, Smithsonian Inst, 63; Second Prize, Corcoran Sch Art, 65. *Mem:* Founding mem Artists Equity Asn, Washington, DC; Archaeol Inst Am. *Media:* Acrylics, Charcoal; Wood, Stone. *Dealer:* Rudy Agra Gallery 1061 31st St NW Washington DC 20007. *Mailing Add:* 4000 Cathedral Ave NW Washington DC 20016

CASANOVA, ALDO JOHN
SCULPTOR, EDUCATOR
b San Francisco, Calif, Feb 8, 29. *Study:* San Francisco State Univ, BA, 50, MA, 51; Ohio State Univ, PhD, 57. *Work:* Whitney Mus, New York; San Francisco Mus Art; Columbus Mus Fine Arts, Ohio; Sculpture Garden, Univ Calif, Los Angeles; Joseph Hirshhorn Collection, Washington, DC. *Comn:* Skidmore, Owings & Merrill, Archit, San Francisco, 66; Atlantic-Richfield Co, Los Angeles, 69; Washington Mutual Savings Bank, Seattle, 69; Calif Inst Technol, Pasadena, 74; Univ Judaism, Los Angeles, 81. *Exhib:* Pa Acad Ann, Philadelphia, 62-67; Art Dealers Asn Am, Parke-Bernet Gallery, New York, 64; one-man shows, Esther Robles Gallery, Los Angeles, 67, Santa Barbara Mus, Calif, 67 & Calif Inst Technol, 72; The New Vein, Smithsonian Inst, SAm travel tour, 68-70; New Acquisitions, Whitney Mus Am Art, New York, 70; State Univ NY, Albany, 81. *Teaching:* Asst prof sculpture, Temple Univ, 61-64; prof sculpture, Scripps Col, 66-, chmn art dept, 71-73; summer fac, Skowhegan Sch Painting & Sculpture, Maine, 74, head summer fac, 75; prof art & chmn art dept, State Univ NY, Albany, 81; prof sculpture, Claremont Grad Sch, 82- *Awards:* Rome Prize Fel Sculpture, Am Acad in Rome, 58-61; Louis Comfort Tiffany Award, 69. *Media:* Bronze, Casting; Carving, Stone or Wood. *Dealer:* Carl Schlosberg Fine Arts 15447 Valley Vista Blvd Sherman Oaks CA 91403; Van Doren Gallery San Francisco. *Mailing Add:* 691 W 12th St Claremont CA 91711

CASARELLA, EDMOND
SCULPTOR, PRINTMAKER
b Newark, NJ, Sept 3, 20. *Study:* Cooper Union, BFA, 42; Brooklyn Mus Art Sch, 49-51. *Work:* Whitney Mus Am Art, New York; Brooklyn Mus Art, NY; NJ State Mus, Trenton; Speed Mus, Louisville, Ky; Libr Cong, Washington, DC. *Comn:* Sculpture, Northern Valley Bank, Cresskill, NJ; sculpture, Unitarian Church, Louisville, Ky. *Exhib:* Brooklyn Mus, 52 & 58; Pa Acad Fine Arts, 53, 59 & 63; Libr Cong, 55, 56 & 58; Corcoran Gallery Art, 55, 56, 58, 59 & 63; Boston Mus Fine Arts, 57; Victoria & Albert Mus, 59; Whitney Mus Am Art, 59, 61, 62 & 63; Los Angeles Co Mus Art, 63; solo exhibs, Speed Mus, 68-69, Landmark Gallery, New York, 77 & 80 & Sculpture Ctr, New York, 77; retrospective, Allegheny Col, 78 & Edward Williams Col, 79; Terain Gallery, New York, 80; and many others. *Teaching:* Instr graphics, Brooklyn Mus Sch, 56-60, Norfolk Summer Art Sch, Yale Univ, 58, NY Univ, 62, Cooper Union, 63-70, Hunter Col, 63-, Columbia Univ, summer 63 & 64, Yale Univ, 64-, Rutgers Univ, 64-, Pratt Inst, 64-, Finch Col, 69-74, Manhattanville Col, 73-74 & Queens Col, 80; instr graphics, Brooklyn Mus Art, 56-60; instr graphics, Columbia Univ, summers; instr graphics & sculpture, Cooper Union, 63-70; instr, Pratt Inst, Yale Univ & Rutgers Univ, 64; instr graphics & sculpture, Finch Col, 70-79; instr, Manhattanville Col, Italy, summer 73 & Purchase, NY, summer 74. *Awards:* Fulbright Award for Graphics, Italy,

51-52; Tiffany Award Graphics, 55; Guggenheim Fel for Graphics, 59-60. *Bibliog:* Ross-Romano (auth), The Complete Printmaker, Macmillan Free Press. *Mem:* Sculptors Guild. *Media:* Steel, Bronze. *Mailing Add:* 83 E Linden Englewood NJ 07631

CASAS, FERNANDO RODRIGUEZ
PAINTER, DRAFTSMAN
b Cochabamba, Bolivia, Mar 25, 46. *Study:* Colo Col, BA; Rice Univ, MA, PhD; pvt training with Raul Prada. *Work:* Nat Mus Art, La Paz, Bolivia; Pinacoteca Nac, Cochabamba, Bolivia; Art of the Americas Collection (B Duncan), New York. *Comn:* Mural, Dominican Convent, Bolivia, 67; and others. *Exhib:* One-man show, Harriet Griffin Gallery, New York, 76; Ed La Humiere, Paris, France, 77; Toni Jones Gallery, Houston, 79 & 80; Heritage Gallery, Los Angeles, 79; Duveen Gallery, Houston, 79; and other group & one-man shows. *Awards:* First Nat Award Painting & First Nat Award Drawing, Concurso Nac de Artes Plasticas, City of Cochabamba, Bolivia, 72; First Nat Award Drawing, XXI Nat Art Contest, Pedro Domingo Murillo, City of La Paz, Bolivia, 73. *Bibliog:* Donna Tennant (auth), Restoring art to the people, Houston Chronicle, 10/16/80; and others. *Media:* Oil, Pencil & Ink. *Publ:* Illusr, Poetas Bolivianos, 66 & Indios en Revelion, 68, UTO, Bolivia; contribr (with Yves Froment), Rosee Aveugle, E Canelas, 68; and others. *Dealer:* Eidos Fine Art Inc 4906 Travis Houston TX 77002. *Mailing Add:* 1203 Bartlett 3 Houston TX 77006

CASAS, MELESIO
PAINTER, EDUCATOR
b El Paso, Tex, Nov 24, 29. *Study:* Univ Tex, El Paso, BA, 56; Univ of the Americas, Mex, MFA, 58. *Exhib:* Artlsts of the Southeast & Tex, Biennial Painting & Sculpture, 71; Tex Painting & Sculptures: 20th Century, 72; Mex-Am Art Symp, Trinity Univ, 73; 12 Tex Artists, Contemp Art Mus, Houston, 74; 1975 Biennial Contemp Am Art, Whitney Mus Art, 75; Dale Gas--Chicano Art of Tex, Contemp Arts Mus, Houston, 77; Showdown, Alternative Mus, New York, 83. *Pos:* Book reviewer, Choice Mag, Am Libr Asn, 54- *Teaching:* Prof art, design & painting, San Antonio Col, Tex, 61- *Awards:* Purchase Prize, 59 & Cash Award, 64, El Paso Art Mus; Cash Award, San Antonio Art League, 66. *Bibliog:* Jacinto Quiarte (auth), The Art of Mexican Americans, Univ Tex, 73; article, Art News, 12/77; Mimi Crossley (auth), Dale Gas at the Contemporary Art Museum, Art in Am, 1-2/78. *Mem:* Founding mem Con Safo Painters. *Media:* Acrylic. *Mailing Add:* 311 Breeden San Antonio TX 78212

CASCIERI, ARCANGELO
SCULPTOR, INSTRUCTOR
b Civitaquana, Italy, Feb 22, 02; US citizen. *Study:* Sch Archit, Boston Archit Ctr, 22-26; Boston Univ, 32-36. *Work:* Boston Col; Holy Cross Col; Buffalo Courier Express Bldg; Parlin Jr High Sch, Everett, Mass; Lexington Jr High Sch, Mass. *Comn:* Am War Mem World War I, Belleau Woods, France & World War II, Margraten, Holland; exterior Mem Auditorium, Lynn, Mass; exterior Boys' Stadium, Franklin Field, Dorchester, Mass; sculpture on fountain, Parkman Plaza, Boston; Duxbury Art Complex Mus, Mass; and many others. *Exhib:* Sculpture Exhib, Boston Mus Fine Arts; Sculpture Exhibs, New Eng Sculpture Asn; one-man exhib, Sch Design, Harvard Univ; Lit Arts Soc Exhib, New York. *Pos:* Asst dir sculpture & wood carving, W F Ross Studio, Cambridge, 23-41; sculptor & asst dir, Schwamb Assocs Studio, Arlington, 41-46, sculptor & dir, 46-52; partner studio for sculpture & decorations, Boston, 52- *Teaching:* Pvt classes, Boston, 32-37; instr design & head sch archit, Boston Archit Ctr, formerly; instr, Craft Ctr Sch, Boston, 39-40; instr design, New London Jr Col, Conn, 41-43. *Awards:* First Commun Award, New Eng Sch Art & Design, Hon Alumnus, 79; Citation Boston 200, 75; Silver Medal for Distinguished Pub Serv in the Arts & Educ, Boston Univ Alumni Asn, 76. *Mem:* Fel Am Inst Archit; hon mem Dante Alighieri Soc; hon mem Naples Asn Inst Archit & Engineers; New Eng Sculptors Asn; Mass Asn Archit; and others. *Mailing Add:* 500 Concord Ave Lexington MA 02173

CASE, ELIZABETH
PAINTER, WRITER
b Long Beach, Calif, July 24, 30. *Study:* Fr Inst, New York, with Mr Lee, 46; Art Students League, with Vlascov Vytlacil, Robert Hale, Reginald Marsh & Harry Sternberg, 48-49; Elmira Col, 49-51; Syracuse Univ; Chaffey Col, Ont, with Doug McClellan, 54; Scripps Col, with Dr Schardt, 54. *Work:* USN Combat Art Collection, Washington, DC; Elmira Col Ford Mus, NY. *Comn:* View Through Trees (mural), comn by Dr & Mrs S I Heller, New York, 75; Torpedo Loading (mural), Homecoming of USS Skate (mural) & NROTC Ball (mural), comn by Secy Navy Middendorf, USN Combat Art Collection, 75-76; Wall of Discovery (mural), Old Bridge Pub Libr, 77. *Exhib:* Am Freedoms Caravan Mural Design Exhib, Nat Arts Club, New York, 75 & Wilmington Opera House, 76; Nat Exhib Miniature Paintings, Nutley, NJ, 75; Inaugural Exhib, Ft Lee Libr, 75 & Ridgefield Pub Libr, 77; and other group & one-man shows. *Pos:* Asst animator, Walt Disney Prod, 56-58; sr copywriter/designer spec proj, Prentice-Hall Col Advert Dept, Englewood Cliffs, 75-77; creative dir, Gadfly Productions, Edgewater, NJ, 77-79; design/prom, Rutherford Mus, NJ, 79; sales prom mgr, M Grumbacher Inc, New York, 79-81. *Teaching:* Instr basic drawing & painting, Ft Lee Adult Sch, 75- *Awards:* Second Award, Wyn Rogers Gallery, Cliffside Park, NJ, 64; Award & Citation for Outstanding Achievement, Elmira Col, 76. *Bibliog:* Thomas Oat (auth), article, Groton News, Conn, 75; Judy Plummer (auth), article, Dolphin Newspaper, New London, Conn, 75; Roberta Roesch (auth), There's Always a Right Job for Every Woman, Berkeley, 76. *Mem:* Nat Soc Mural Painters Inc (secy, 75). *Media:* Egg Tempera, Oil. *Publ:* Auth, Nat Soc Mural Painters Brochure, 73; illusr cover, Weidenbaum's Business, Government and the Public, Prentice-Hall, 76; illusr cover & part openings, Algren & Hackworth's Programmed Algebra, Vols I & II, 77, Vol III, 79 & R Kimble's Use and Misuse of Statistics, 78, Prentice-hall. *Mailing Add:* Fine Arts Studio PO Box 58 Edgewater NJ 07020

CASEBERE, JAMES E
PHOTOGRAPHER, SCULPTOR
b Lansing, Mich, Sept 17, 53. *Study:* Mich State Univ, 71-72; Minneapolis Col Art & Design, BFA, 76; Calif Inst Arts, MFA, 79. *Work:* Neuberger Mus, Purchase, NY; Houston Mus Fine Arts; Allem Mem Mus, Oberlin Col. *Exhib:* Fabricated to be Photographed, San Francisco Mus Mod Art, Albright-Knox Gallery, Buffalo, NY, Newport Harbor Art Mus, Newport Beach, Calif & Univ NMex, Albuquerque, 79-80; solo exhibs, Franklin Furnace, New York, 81, Sonnabend Gallery, New York, 82 & CEPA Gallery, Buffalo, 82; Tableau: Nine Contemporary Sculptors, Contemp Art Ctr, Cincinnati, 82; Beauborg Mus, 83. *Awards:* Nat Endowment Arts Visual Artist Fel, 82. *Bibliog:* Roberta Smith (auth), Some things old, some things new, Village Voice; Hal Foster (auth), Mel Bochner and James Casebere at Sonnabend, Art in Am. *Dealer:* c/o Sonnabend Gallery 420 West Broadway New York NY. *Mailing Add:* 175 Ludlow St New York NY 10002

CASEY, ELIZABETH TEMPLE
CURATOR
b Providence, RI, Sept 24, 01. *Study:* Pembroke Col, Brown Univ. *Collections Arranged:* Exhibs from permanent collection of Mus Art, RI Sch Design, Providence. *Pos:* Mus asst, Mus Art, RI Sch Design, 26-35, cur textiles, 35-43, cur Aldrich Collection, 50-78, cur Oriental art, 56-78, emer cur, 78- *Res:* English, Chinese and Japanese ceramics; Oriental costumes and textiles; Japanese color prints. *Publ:* Auth, The Lucy Truman Aldrich Collection of European Porcelain Figures of the Eighteenth Century, 65. *Mailing Add:* 89 Ingleside Ave Cranston RI 02905

CASEY, JACQUELINE SHEPARD
ADMINISTRATOR, DESIGNER
b Quincy, Mass, Apr 20, 27. *Study:* Mass Col Art, BFA, 50; study of drawing with Hyman Bloom, 51-53. *Work:* Libr of Cong, Washington, DC; Mus Mod Art, New York; Cooper Hewitt Mus, New York. *Exhib:* Direction 1968, Philadelphia Col Art, 68; Mass Inst Technol Hayden Gallery Corridor, Cambridge, Mass, 72 & 79; Images of an Era, The American Poster, 1945-1975, Corcoran Gallery Art, Washington, DC, 76; Warsaw Biennale, Poland, 80; Lahti IV Poster Biennale, Finland, 81 & 83; and others. *Collections Arranged:* Ann Design for Printing and Commerce, Am Inst Graphic Arts; Typomundus 20 & 20 II; Creativity on Paper; New York Type Directors Club. *Bibliog:* Jean Coyne (auth), MIT Design Services Office, Commun Arts, 9-10/74; Stanley Mason (auth), Objective Graphic Design (MIT), Graphis, Zurich, Switz, 74-75; Important US Graphic Designers of the Last Twenty-Five Years, Silver Ann Issue, Idea Mag, Japan, 78. *Mem:* Alliance Graphique Int; Am Inst Graphic Arts. *Publ:* Contribr, A Primer of Visual Literacy, MIT Press, 73; contribr, Print Casebooks, RC Publ, 1st ed, 75, 2nd ed, 76; contribr, Images of an Era, MIT Press, 76; contrib, A History of Graphic Design, Van Nostrand Reinhold Co, 83; contrib, Top Graphic Design, ABC Verlag, Zurich, 83. *Mailing Add:* Mass Inst of Technol Design Servs Rm 5-133 77 Massachusetts Ave Cambridge MA 02139

CASEY, JOHN JOSEPH
EDUCATOR, SCULPTOR
b New London, Conn, June 27, 31. *Study:* Univ Ore, BA; Calif Col of Arts & Crafts, with Nathan Oliveira, MFA. *Work:* Univ Ore, Eugene; State of Ore, Salem & Pendleton; Coos Art Mus, Ore. *Exhib:* 68th Western Ann, Denver Art Mus, 62; The Painted Flower, Oakland Art Mus, Calif, 63 & 64; Supplement 66, Fountain Gallery, Portland, 66; Ore Artists Ann, Portland Art Mus, 67, 71-73, 75 & 77; 22nd Spokane Ann, Cheney Cowles Mus, Wash, 70, 72, 74 & 76; 32nd Ann NW Watercolor Exhib, Seattle Art Mus Pavilion, Wash, 71; and others. *Teaching:* Assoc prof drawing, painting & sculpture, West Ore State Col, Monmouth, 65- *Bibliog:* G E Guilbert (auth), The Art Forms Explosion, Spokane Spokesman-Rev, 7/72; Lorraine B Widman (auth), Sculpture: A Studio Guide to Concepts, Methods & Materials, Prentice-Hall (in prep). *Mem:* Artists Equity. *Media:* Plastic, Acrylic. *Mailing Add:* 289 S College Monmouth OR 97361

CASSANELLI, VICTOR VI
PAINTER, PRINTMAKER
b Dubrovnik, Yugoslavia, Feb 7, 20. *Study:* Inst Tecnico d'Arte, Fiume, Italy, 34-37; Art Students League, with Will Barnet & Julio Llort, 66-67. *Work:* Mus-Galerie Artte Mod, Santo Domingo; Ft Hays State Univ; Butler Inst Am Art, Youngstown, Ohio; St Lawrence Univ; Philadelphia Mus Art; and others. *Exhib:* Minn Mus Art, St Paul, 80; Nat Acad Design, New York, 80 & 81; Am Soc Contemp Artists, Salmagundi Club, New York, 81; Owensboro Mus Fine Art, Ky, 82; Birmingham Mus Art, 82; solo exhib, Polizzi Galleries, New York, 83. *Awards:* Michael M Engel Mem Award, Nat Acad Galleries, Audubon Artists, 78; Minn Mus Travel Award, 80; Silver Medal, AAA Am Acad, 82; and others. *Bibliog:* di Mario Albertazzi (auth), La geometria poetica di Cassanelli, Progresso Italo-Am, 11/7/70; Shannon King (auth), Museum exhibit renders artistic judgment of law, Minneapolis Star, 6/27/80. *Mem:* Am Soc Contemp Artists; Artists Equity Asn; Audubon Artists; Painters & Sculptors Soc NJ; Visual Artists & Galleries Asn. *Media:* Silkscreen; Oil. *Dealer:* Reece Galleries New York NY. *Mailing Add:* PO Box 144 Village Sta New York NY 10014

CASSARA, FRANK
PAINTER, PRINTMAKER
b Partinico, Sicily; US citizen. *Study:* Colorado Springs Sch Fine Arts, Colo; Univ Mich, MS(design); also spec study, Atelier 17, Paris, France. *Work:* Libr Cong, Washington, DC; Bibliot Nat, Paris, France; Stedelijk Mus, Amsterdam, Neth; Detroit Inst Arts; Free Libr Philadelphia. *Comn:* Murals, US Post Off, East Detroit, 39, Donald Thompson Sch (fresco), Highland Park,

Mich, 39, US Post Off, Sandusky, Mich, 40 & Water Conditioning Plant, Lansing, Mich, 41. *Exhib:* Seventh Int Exhib Lithography & Wood Engr, Art Inst Chicago, 39; Int Asn Plastic Arts, US Info Agency Tour, SAm, 59; 1st Int Calif Soc Etchers, San Francisco, 64; 1st Exhib Am Printmakers, Gallerie Nees Morphes, Athens, Greece, 65; 22nd Nat Exhib Prints, Libr Cong, 71; Atelier 17: A Retrospective, Elvehjem Art Ctr, Madison, Wis, 77. *Teaching:* Instr drawing, Detroit Soc Arts & Crafts, 46-47; prof printmaking, Univ Mich, 47- *Awards:* Over 50 in national and regional exhibitions; Rackham Res Grants, Univ Mich, 61, 68 & 74. *Media:* Intaglio. *Publ:* Contribr, Artists' Proof, A Collectors Edition, 71. *Dealer:* Forsythe Gallery 201 Nickels Arcade Ann Arbor MI 48104. *Mailing Add:* Sch of Art Univ of Mich Ann Arbor MI 48109

CASSELLI, HENRY C, JR
PAINTER

b New Orleans, La, Oct 25, 46. *Work:* Libr Cong; New Orleans Mus; Hunter Mus, Tenn; Greenville Mus, SC; Albany Mus, Ga. *Comn:* Mural, La State Univ, Baton Rouge, 78. *Exhib:* 24th Am Drawing Biennial, Chrysler Mus, Va, 72; Smithsonian Traveling Drawing Exhib, 72-75; one-man shows, Lauren Rogers Mus, 72 & Greenville Co Mus, SC, 80; Hunter Mus, Tenn, 81; Mint Mus, NC, 82. *Teaching:* Instr one-wk workshops watercolor & drawing, US, 74- *Awards:* Graphics Award, Hudson Valley Art Asn, 74; High Winds Medals, Am Watercolor Soc, 76-77 & 79; Dolphin Fel, Am Watercolor Soc. *Bibliog:* Doreen Mangan (auth), Henry Casselli, Am Arts; Susan Meyer (auth), 20 Figure Painters, Watson-Guptill, 79; article, Southern Accent Mag, 81. *Mem:* Am Watercolor Soc (vpres, 79-). *Media:* Watercolor, Pastels. *Publ:* Contribr, The Natural Way to Paint, Davis, 78. *Dealer:* Tex Art Gallery, Dallas; Trailside Galleries, Houston. *Mailing Add:* 4015 N LaBarre Rd Metairie LA 70002

CASSIDY, MARGARET CAROL (MRS JOHN MANSHIP)
SCULPTOR, LIBRARIAN

b Whitinsville, Mass. *Study:* Framingham State Col, BS, 44; Univ Mass, Amherst, MS, 49; Rosary Col Grad Sch Fine Arts, MA, 54. *Work:* Britain Mus Am Art, Conn; NY Univ Bobst Libr, New York; Holy Cross Col Libr, Worcester, Mass; Framingham State Col Libr, Mass; Vatican Collections, Rome. *Comn:* Madonna & St Joseph (sculpture), Holy Spirit Church, Kyoto, Japan, 61; Cardinal Newman, 63, Newman Ctr, Amherst, Mass, St Jude, 81; Risen Christ, St Anthony's Maronite Church, Springfield, 71 & St Mary's Church, Uxbridge, Mass, 75; Pres Clement Maxwell, Bridgewater State Col, Mass, 81. *Exhib:* Nat Acad Design Ann, New York, 66 & 79; three-man show, New Britain Mus, Conn, 71; Burr Artists, Metrop Mus Art, New York, 76. *Teaching:* Asst prof art, Bridgewater State Col, 64; artist-in-residence, Univ Southern Ill, Edwardsville, 76. *Awards:* Silver Medal, Pen & Brush Club, New York, 72; Bronze Medal, Catharine Lorillard Wolfe Art Club, New York, 72; Campidoglio D'oro, Burckhardt Acad, Rome, 78. *Mem:* Salmagundi Club; Catharine Lorillard Wolfe Art Club; Pen & Brush Club; Burr Artists; Rockport Art Asn. *Media:* Bronze; Stained Glass. *Res:* Card catalog of all American artists with professional qualifications. *Dealer:* Harbor Gallery 49 Main St Rockport MA 01966. *Mailing Add:* 10 Leverett St Gloucester MA 01930

CASSILL, HERBERT CARROLL
PRINTMAKER, EDUCATOR

b Percival, Iowa, Dec 24, 28. *Study:* State Univ Iowa, BFA, 48, MFA, 50, with Mauricio Lasansky. *Work:* Mus Mod Art, New York; Cleveland Mus Art; Brooklyn Mus; Libr Cong, Washington, DC; Oakland Art Mus, Calif. *Exhib:* Libr Cong, 52, 54 & 60; six shows, Philadelphia Print Club, 53-60; Int Exhib Graphic Arts (shown in Europe), Mus Mod Art, 54, Modern Art in the USA (shown in Europe), 55; Soc of Am Graphic Artists Overseas Exhib, US State Dept, 60. *Teaching:* Instr printmaking, State Univ Iowa, 53-57; head dept printmaking, Cleveland Inst Art, 57- *Awards:* Tiffany Found Fel Printmaking, 53; Purchase Prize, Philadelphia Print Club, 56; First Prize, Print Show, State Univ NY Col Potsdam, 61. *Media:* Intaglio, Wood. *Mailing Add:* 3084 Coleridge Rd Cleveland OH 44118

CASSYD, SYD
CURATOR, CRITIC

b NJ, Dec 28, 08. *Study:* Oxford Summer Inst, End, 29, Alliance Francaise, Paris, France, cert, 29; New Theatre Sch, 37; NY Univ, 43. *Work:* Theatre Arts Libr, Univ Calif, Los Angeles. *Exhib:* TV 1930-1974, Beverly Hills Libr, Calif. *Pos:* Actg cur television collection, Univ Calif, Los Angeles, 60-61; television cur, Hollywood Mus, 60-65; dir, New Horizons Broadcasting Sch, Ventura, Calif, 69; cur television collection, Hollywood Chap, Acad Television Arts & Sci, 75- *Teaching:* Asst instr motion picture, NY Univ, Washington Sq Col, 42-44. *Awards:* Pres Emmy, Acad Television Arts & Sci, 56, Gov Award Emmy, 73; Dove Award, Friendship Day Camp, 60. *Mem:* Life mem Acad Television Arts & Sci (pres, 50); Acad Motion Picture Arts & Sci; Found Motion Picture Pioneers; Hollywood Foreign Press Asn (vpres, 79-80); Calif State Coun Arts (exec vpres, 62-65). *Media:* Television. *Res:* Television; motion pictures; labor union's use of films; motion picture research; study of labor union's use of films. *Interests:* Impact of films and television as a world museum without walls, made possible by many years of mass communications impact. *Collection:* History of television, specifically history of television in California and the Academy of Television Arts and Sciences. *Publ:* Auth, 100 feature articles in Boxoffice Mag, 63-75; auth, An academy or a chamber of commerce, NAEB J, 64; auth, Emmy Awards confidential--how TV moved from motion pictures, Acad TV Arts & Sci, 76; auth, Peace has come to PBS, MAC Mag, 79. *Mailing Add:* 917 S Tremaine Ave Los Angeles CA 90019

CASTANIS, MURIEL (JULIA BRUNNER)
SCULPTOR

b New York, NY, Sept 27, 26. *Study:* Self-taught. *Work:* New Sch Social Res, New York; Martin Margolies Collection, Coral Gables, Fla; Gordon Hanes Collection, Winston-Salem, NC; Malcolm S Forbes Collection; Phillip Johnson Bldg, San Francisco; and others. *Exhib:* Contemporary Reflections, Aldrich Mus Contemp Art, 74; solo exhibs, Douglass Col Art Gallery, Rutgers Univ, 78, OK Harris Gallery, New York, 80 & 83 & OK Harris West, Scottsdale, Ariz, 81; Biennial, Va Mus Fine Art, 79; Icarus Odyssey, Guadalajara Int, Mex, 79; Women & Autobiography, Douglass Col Art Gallery, Rutgers Univ, 79; Human Forms, Moravian Col, Pa, 81; and others. *Teaching:* Instr advan sculpture, Cooper Union, New York, 78-79. *Awards:* Tiffany Found Sculpture Grant, 77; Award for Outstanding Design, Show Bus, 77; Award of Distinction, Va Mus Fine Art, 79. *Bibliog:* Lynn R Rigberg (auth), article, Artweek, 3/21; Grace Glueck (auth), article, New York Times, 8/7/81; Kim Levin (auth), article, Village Voice, 5/24/83; and others. *Publ:* Contribr, Speak out the arts & Behind every art, Village Voice, 3/70; contribr, Her story, Know Inc, 73; contribr, Women in the Year 2000, Arbor Press, 74; contribr, Are you a closet collector, Heresies Collective, winter 78. *Dealer:* O K Harris Gallery 383 W Broadway New York NY 10012. *Mailing Add:* 444 Sixth Ave New York NY 10011

CASTANO, ELVIRA
DEALER, HISTORIAN

b Cincinnati, Ohio, July 23, 32. *Study:* Emerson Col, AB; Villa Schifanoia, Florence, Italy; Univ Florence, Italy. *Pos:* Dir, Castano Art Gallery, Boston, 55- *Mem:* Boston Mus Mass. *Res:* Italian Renaissance art and the Macchiaioli school of art. *Specialty:* Traditional and Renaissance art. *Collection:* American, Dutch and Italian art. *Mailing Add:* 245 Hunnewell St Needham Heights MA 02194

CASTELLETT, MARISA See del Re, Marisa

CASTELLI, LEO
DEALER

b Trieste, Italy, Sept 4, 07. *Study:* Univ Milan; Columbia Univ. *Pos:* Dir, Leo Castelli Gallery, 57-; owner, Castelli Graphics, currently. *Awards:* Mayor's Award of Honor for Arts & Cult, New York, 76; Manhattan Cult Awards Prize, 80. *Specialty:* American vanguard painting and sculpture. *Mailing Add:* c/o Leo Castelli Gallery 420 W Broadway New York NY 10012

CASTER, BERNARD HARRY
PAINTER, ENAMELIST

b Wolcott, NY, May 27, 21. *Study:* Syracuse Univ, AA(fine arts), 56, BA, 60. *Work:* St Lawrence Univ; Newark Pub Libr, NY; Sch St Croixe de Neuilly, Paris, France. *Exhib:* 21st Ann Western NY Regional, Buffalo, 55; 19th Ceramic Nat, Syracuse Mus, 56; NY State Artists Exhib, NY State Fair, 58; The Kentucky Guild Train, 66; 14th Ann Rochester Festival of Religious Arts, 72. *Awards:* Marie Wilner Award, Cayuga Mus Hist & Art, Auburn, NY, 62, Ceramic Award, 64; Purchase Award, Four County Appleseed Collection, Wayne County Arts in Action, 83. *Mailing Add:* Box 154 South Butler NY 13154

CASTILE, RAND
GALLERY DIRECTOR

b North Carolina, July 15, 38. *Study:* Drew Univ, BA; Urasenke Tea Ceremony Hq, Kyoto, Japan; also study with Grand Master Sen Soshitsu, XV, diplomae. *Collections Arranged:* Four exhib per yr, Japan House Gallery, 71- *Pos:* Lectr, Japanese art & tea ceremony, US & Japanese Univs & mus; dir, Japan House Gallery, Japan Soc Inc, New York, 70-; consult-panelist, Nat Endowment Arts, 75; consult, Nat Endowment Humanities, 75-; bd adv, Japan Study Ctr, Columbia Univ. *Awards:* Fulbright Scholar, 66-67; Mayor's Award of Honor for Arts & Culture, New York, 82. *Mem:* Asn Art Mus Dirs; Metrop Mus Art (vis comt); Am Fedn Arts (Nat Exhib Comt); Am Asn Mus; US-Japan Educ & Cult Conf. *Publ:* Auth, numerous articles in Art News, Geijutsu Shincho, Bijutsu Techo & Print Collector's Newslett, 63-; auth, The Way of Tea, 72; auth, Ikeda & Ida: Two Japanese Printmakers, 74; auth, Japanese Art Now: Tadaaki Kuwayama & Rikuro Okamoto. *Mailing Add:* Japan House Gallery 333 E 47th St New York NY 10017

CASTLE, WENDELL KEITH
DESIGNER, SCULPTOR

b Emporia, Kans, Nov 6, 32. *Study:* Univ Kans, BFA & MFA; Md Inst Art, DFA. *Work:* Mus Mod Art, New York; Nordenfieldske Kunstindustrimus, Norway; Philadelphia Mus Art; Metrop Mus Art, New York; Renwick Gallery, Smithsonian Inst; and others. *Exhib:* Objects USA Traveling Show, US & Europe, 70-; Wooden Work, Smithsonian Inst, 72; 13th Triennale, Milan, Italy; Art & Relig, Vatican, Rome, 78; New Handmade Furniture, Mus Contemp Crafts, New York, 79; Alexander Milliken Gallery, New York; and numerous one-man shows. *Teaching:* Instr drawing, Univ Kans, 60-61; assoc prof furniture design, Rochester Inst Technol, 62-70; prof sculpture, Wendell Castle Workshop, 80- *Awards:* Louis Comfort Tiffany Found & NY State Grants, 72; Nat Endowment Arts Grants, 73, 75 & 76; and others. *Bibliog:* Wilson (auth), The Music Rack, produced by ACC, 66; Limber Timber, Newsweek, 5/13/68; Pierce (auth), Transitions (film), Nat Educ TV, 69. *Mem:* Am Craftsman Coun; NY State Coun Arts. *Media:* Wood. *Publ:* Auth, George Sugarman, 68, Mike Nevelson, 69 & Wharton Esherick, 71, Craft Horizons; auth, Complete Book of Lamination, Van Nostrand Reinhold, 79. *Dealer:* Alexander Milliken Gallery 98 Prince St New York NY. *Mailing Add:* 18 Maple St Scottsville NY 14546

CASTLEMAN, RIVA
CURATOR, HISTORIAN

b Chicago, Ill, Aug 15, 30. *Study:* State Univ Iowa, BA; Inst Fine Arts, New York Univ. *Collections Arranged:* Picasso Master Printmaker; Mus Mod 70; Jasper Johns, Lithographs, 70-71; Technics & Creativity: Gemini G E L, 71; The Prints of Edvard Munch, 73; Modern Prints Int Traveling Exhib, 73-75; Latin Am Prints from Mus Mod Art Int Traveling Exhib, 74-75; Impresario--Ambroise Vollard, 77; Modern Artists as Illustrators Int Traveling Exhib, 81-83; Printed Art: A View of Two Decades, 80; Prints from Blocks: Gaugin to Now (auth, catalog), 83. *Pos:* Curatorial asst, Art Inst Chicago, 51-55; cur, Calif Hist Soc, San Francisco, 56-57; from curatorial asst to cur, Mus Mod Art, New York, 63- *Mem:* Print Coun Am. *Res:* Contemporary prints. *Publ:* Auth, Contemporary Prints, 73; auth, Prints of the Twentieth Century: a History, 76. *Mailing Add:* Mus Mod Art 11 W 53rd St New York NY 10019

CASTORO, ROSEMARIE
SCULPTOR

b Brooklyn, NY, Mar 1, 39. *Study:* Mus Mod Art, New York, scholar, 54-55; Pratt Inst, BFA(cum laude), 56-63. *Work:* Berkeley Mus, San Francisco; Woodward Found, Washington, DC; Chase Manhattan Bank; Mus Mod Art, New York. *Comn:* Procession of Strokes, NY State Coun Arts, 72; Hexatryst, Gen Serv Admin, Topeka, Kans, 79; 24 Flashers, Art Park, Lewiston, NY, 79. *Exhib:* Solo shows, Tibor de Nagy Art Gallery, New York, 71-73, 75, 76, 78, 80 & 81 & Hal Bromm Gallery, New York, 78-81; Highlights of the 70-71 Art Season, Aldridge Mus Contemp Art, Conn, 71; Otis Art Inst, Los Angeles, Calif, 76. *Teaching:* Lectr, Boston Mus Sch, 71; Hunter Col, NY, 72, New Sch Social Res, 73; Calif State Univ, Fresno, 73; Philadelphia Col Art, 74; Mt Berry Col Art, Ga, 74; Syracuse Univ, NY, 75; Univ Colo, Boulder, 77 & Atlanta Col Art. *Awards:* NY State Coun Arts Grant, 72 & 74; Nat Endowment Arts Grant, 75; Tiffany Found, 77. *Bibliog:* E C Goosen (auth), Distillation, 11/66 & Lucy Lippard (auth), article, 5/72 & 2/74, Art Forum; Carter Ratcliff (auth), article, Art Int, 5/75. *Publ:* Auth, Artists transgress all boundaries, Art News, 1/72; ed, Art in the mind, 70; ed, Conceptual Art, 72; Tracks, 75; coauth (with Donald W Thalacker), The Place of Art in the World of Architecture, 80. *Dealer:* Tibor de Nagy Art Gallery 29 W 57th St New York NY 10019; Hal Bromm Gallery 90 W Broadway New York NY 10007. *Mailing Add:* 151 Spring St New York NY 10012

CASWELL, HELEN RAYBURN
PAINTER, WRITER

b Long Beach, Calif, Mar 16, 23. *Study:* Univ Ore Sch Fine Arts. *Comn:* Murals, Federated Church, Saratoga, Calif, 65; Mem Paintings, San Jose Hosp, Calif, 67 & Emanuel Lutheran Church, Saratoga, 69. *Exhib:* De Young Mus Show, Soc Western Artists, 61; one-man shows, Northwest Mo State Col, 66 & Rosicrucian Mus, San Jose, 70; Montalvo Cult Ctr, Saratoga, 68. *Awards:* James D Phelan Award for Narrative Poetry, 58; San Francisco Browning Soc Award, 66. *Media:* Oil. *Publ:* Auth & illusr, A Wind on the Road, 64 & A New Song for Christmas, 66, Van Nostrand Reinhold; Shadows from the Singing House, Charles Tuttle, 67; auth & illusr, Thank You for Being You, Gibson, 73; auth, Never Wed an Old Man, Doubleday, 75. *Dealer:* Gallery Americana Lincoln St & Sixth Ave Carmel CA 93921; Hardies Heritage Gallery 14515 Big Basin Way Saratoga CA 95070. *Mailing Add:* 13207 Dupont Rd Sebastopol CA 95472

CASWELL, JIM (JAMES DANIEL CASWELL-DAVIS)
SCULPTOR, CERAMIST

b St Boniface, Man, Nov 9, 48. *Study:* Calif State Univ, Northridge, with Peter Plagens, Marvin Harden, Walt Gabrielson, Karen Carson & Lance Richbourg, 66-71. *Exhib:* Scripps Ann, Lang Art Gallery, Claremont, Calif, 82; Pacific Currents, San Jose Mus Art, 82; Art and/or Craft, Kanazawa, Japan, 82; Clay for Walls, Renwick Gallery, 83; On and Off the Wall, Oakland Mus, 83. *Awards:* Nat Endowment Arts Fel, 83. *Media:* Ceramic. *Dealer:* Garth Clark Gallery Wilshire Blvd Los Angeles CA. *Mailing Add:* 1025 California Ave Santa Monica CA 90403

CATALAN, EDGARDO OMAR
PAINTER, EDUCATOR

b Valparaiso, Chile; US citizen. *Study:* Sch Fine Arts, Vina Del Mar, Chile, with Hans Soyka, MA, 60; Calif Col Arts & Crafts, Oakland, 67; lithography with Carlos Gonzalez, Stade, Ger. *Work:* Museo Bellas Artes, Vina Del Mar; Fine Arts Gallery, San Diego, Calif. *Exhib:* Santa Barbara Selection, Santa Barbara Mus Art, 74; Hist of Chilean Printmaking, Mus Art, Valparaiso, Chile, 76; Paintings, New Media Gallery, Ventura Col, Calif, 77; Drawings, Experimental Grafisch Werkcentrum, Orvelte, Holland, 77; and other group & one-man shows. *Teaching:* Prof painting & drawing, Acad Fine Arts, Vina Del Mar, Chile, 62-64; chmn fine arts dept, Thacher Sch, Ojai, Calif, 64-75. *Awards:* First Prize/Painting, Autumn Salon, Mus Art, Valparaiso, 64; First Prize/Poster, Cafe de Brasil, Brazilian Govt, 64; Calif Arts Coun grant, Artist-in-Residence Prog, Santa Barbara Pub Schs; and others. *Media:* Oil, Watercolor. *Mailing Add:* 2786 Ben Lomond Dr Santa Barbara CA 93105

CATALDO, JOHN WILLIAM
EDUCATOR, CALLIGRAPHER

b Boston, Mass, Nov 28, 24. *Study:* Mass Col Art, BSEd; Columbia Univ, MA & EdD; Sch Am Craftsmen, Rochester, NY, with L Copeland; Univ Calif, Los Angeles, with J P Jones; Teachers Col, Univ Buffalo; Pa State Univ. *Work:* Wichita Art Asn, Univ Mo; Albright-Knox Art Gallery, Buffalo, NY; NY State Crafts Fair, Ithaca; Teachers Col, Columbia Univ; Munic Art Ctr, Long Beach, Calif. *Comn:* Films on art, Nat Educ Asn, 61; screen-divider, Sheraton-Palace Hotel, San Francisco, 62; sculpture, Lithuanian Social Ctr, DuBois, Pa, 65; 30 films, Nat Inst TV, Bloomington, Ind, 70-72; five bronze sculptures, Boston Archit Ctr, 78. *Exhib:* Young Americans, USA, Contemp Crafts Show, 56; Wichita Art Asn Sculpture & Jewelry Show, 56 & 61; Albright-Knox Art Gallery Show, 60; Graphic Design, Syracuse Univ, 61; Ball State Drawing & Sculpture Ann, 63-64; Calligraphy, Mass Inst Technol Sch Archit. *Pos:* Assoc ed, Art Educ, 60-63; ed, Sch Arts, 62-67. *Teaching:* Assoc prof art, Teachers Col, Columbia Univ, 60-61; assoc prof art, Pa State Univ, 61-65; dir art educ & prof art, Philadelphia Col Art, 65-70; acad dean & instr calligraphy, Mass Col Art, 70-, prof & chmn media & performing arts dept, currently. *Awards:* Lacey Print Prize, Western NY Ann, 56 & Ceramic Sculpture Prize, 58, Albright-Knox Art Gallery; Words & Calligraphy, selected for AIGA 50 Best Books Award, Van Nostrand Reinhold, 70. *Mem:* Nat Art Educ Asn (bd dirs, 66-70, pres, Eastern Region, 68-70); Educ Press Asn; Am Asn Univ Prof; Col Art Asn Am. *Publ:* Auth, Lettering--a Guide for Teachers, David Publ, 58; auth, Graphic Design & Visual Communication, Intext, 66; auth, Words & Calligraphy for Children, Van Nostrand Reinhold, 69; auth, Pen Calligraphy, Davis Publ, 80. *Mailing Add:* 364 Brookline Ave Boston MA 02215

CATAN-ROSE, RICHARD
PAINTER, EDUCATOR

b Rochester, NY, Oct 1, 05. *Study:* Royal Acad Fine Arts, Italy, MFA; St Andrews Univ, London, LLD; Cooper Union Art Sch; also with Pippo Rizzo, Antonio Quarino, J Joseph & A Shulkin. *Work:* Our Lady Queen of Martyrs Church, Forest Hills, Long Island; Royal Acad Fine Arts, Italy. *Exhib:* Allied Artists Am, 39 & 40; Vendome Gallery, 39-41; one-man shows, Forest Hills, Long Island, 44-46 & Argent Gallery, 46; also in Europe. *Pos:* Pres, Catan-Rose Inst Art, Jamaica, Long Island. *Awards:* Gold Medal, Accademia Delle Arti, 81. *Mem:* Am Fedn Arts. *Res:* How the artist-designer will play a new role as major contributor to urban living and to improve the goal of the artist for our future civilization. *Mailing Add:* 72-72 112th St Forest Hills Flushing NY 11375

CATCHI (CATHERINE O CHILDS)
PAINTER, PRINTMAKER

b Philadelphia, Pa, Aug 27, 20. *Study:* Briarcliff Jr Col, 37; Commercial Illus Studios, 38-39; also with Leon Kroll, Harry Sternberg & Hans Hofmann & with Angelo Savelli, Positano, Italy; Accademia Int Medicea Bella Firenze, Positano, Italy, hon degree, 83. *Work:* Rosenberg Found; Hofstra Univ, Hempstead, NY. *Exhib:* One-person shows, Rayburn Hall, Washington, DC, 68 & 76, Gallerie Arte Spenetti, Florence, Gallery Coin d'Arte, Genoa, Galveston Art League, Tex & Galleria, Austin, Tex. *Awards:* Goldie Paley Award, Nat Asn Women Artists, 77; Winston Memorial Prize, 80; William Meyerowitz Memorial Prize, 82; and others. *Bibliog:* Nan Ickeringill (auth), Art & at home with Catchi, New York Times, 68; Doris Herzig (auth), She has painted since she was 12, Newsday, 68; Molly Sinclair (auth), Oil brush & canvas, Atlanta Constitution, 69. *Mem:* Nat Asn Women Artists (pres, 81-85); Audubon Artists; Int Platform Asn; New York Soc of Women Artists; Artists Equity, New York. *Media:* Oil, Watercolor; Stone, Cast Metals. *Publ:* Illusr (cover), La Vue Art Mag, France, 7/75 & 6/78; illus, doc book, Int Sculpture Symp, Tex, 76. *Mailing Add:* 2 Gristmill Lane Manhasset NY 11030

CATE, PHILLIP DENNIS
HISTORIAN, DIRECTOR

b Washington, DC, Oct 19, 44. *Study:* Rutgers Univ, BA(art hist), 67; Ariz State Univ, MA(art hist), 70. *Collections Arranged:* Meryon's Paris/Piranesi's Rome (with catalog), 71; Thomas Hart Benton, A Retrospective of His Early Years (with catalog), 72; The Ruckus World of Red Grooms (with catalog), 73; Japonisme: Japanese Influence on French Art, 1854-1910 (with catalog), 75; The Color Revolution, color lithography in France 1890-1900 (with catalog), 78; Circa 1800: The Beginning of Modern Printmaking, 1775-1835 (catalog), 80; Theophile Alexander Steinler, 1859-1923 (auth, catalog), 82. *Pos:* Asst to dir, Pa Acad Fine Art, 67-68; dir & cur, Fine Arts Collection & Univ Art Gallery, Rutgers Univ, 70- *Mem:* Print Coun Am; Printmaking Coun NJ (adv bd, 74-); Am Asn Mus; Col Art Asn. *Res:* 19th century French prints. *Mailing Add:* Jane Voorhees Zimmerli Art Mus Rutgers Univ New Brunswick NJ 08903

CATHCART, LINDA LOUISE
DIRECTOR, HISTORIAN

b Lafayette, Ind, Oct 20, 47. *Study:* Calif State Univ, Fullerton, BA(fine arts), 69; Hunter Col, City Univ New York, MA(art hist), 72; Cortauld Art Inst, London, postgrad study, 73-74. *Pos:* Curatorial asst, Whitney Mus Am Art, New York, 71-73; coordr spec progs, Brooklyn Mus, NY, 74-75; cur, Albright-Knox Gallery, 75-79; dir, Contemp Arts Mus, Houston, 79- *Teaching:* Instr art hist, Sch Visual Arts, New York, 73-75; instr, Cambridge Univ, Eng, 74; adj prof mus studies, State Univ NY Buffalo, 75- *Awards:* Nat Endowment for the Arts & Humanities Award, 71-72; Fulbright fel, 73-74. *Mailing Add:* 5216 Montrose Blvd Houston TX 77006

CATLIN, STANTON L
EDUCATOR, HISTORIAN

b Portland, Ore, Feb 19, 15. *Study:* Oberlin Col, AB; Acad Fine Arts, Prague, Czech; Am Sch Classical Studies, Athens; Fogg Mus, fel mod art; Inst Fine Arts, NY Univ, MA. *Pos:* Asst to dir circulating exhibs, Mus Mod Art, 39; secy comt art, Coordr Inter-Am Affairs, 41-42; supvr exhib contemp Am painting sent to S Am & Mexico by Mus Mod Art, 41; exec dir, Am Inst Graphic Arts, 46-50; from ed to cur Am art, Minneapolis Inst Art, 52-58; asst dir, Yale Univ Art Gallery, New Haven, Conn, 58-67; dir art gallery, Ctr Inter-Am Rels, NY, 67-71; dir, Lowe Art Gallery & Grad Mus Training Prog, Syracuse Univ, 74-77. *Teaching:* Prof NAm art, Fac Fine Arts, Univ Chile,

42-43; lectr hist art, Yale Univ, 62-64; dir art of Latin Am since independence, Yale Univ-Univ Tex, 65-67; vis assoc prof art, Hunter Col, 72-73; prof art, Col Visual & Performing Arts, Syracuse Univ, 74-82. *Mem:* Grolier Club; Am Asn Mus; Col Art Asn Am. *Res:* History of modern Latin American art. *Publ:* Auth, La peinture Mexicaine, 52; auth, articles, Art News & Art in Am; auth, Political iconography in Diego Rivera murals at Cuernavaca, In: Art and Architecture in Politics, MIT Press, 78; auth, Printmaking in Latin America, brief history and techniques, In: Artes Graficos, Panorama Artisfico, Mex, 80. *Mailing Add:* Lowe Art Gallery Syracuse NY 13210

CATOK, LOTTIE MEYER
PAINTER
b Hoboken, NJ. *Study:* New York Sch Appl & Fine Arts; also with Guy Wiggins, W Lester Stevens & Robert Brackman. *Work:* Fla Southern Col, Lakeland; Smith Col, Northampton, Mass; Bay Path Jr Col, Longmeadow, Mass; and many portraits in pub bldgs. *Comn:* Portrait of pres of Am Int Col, Springfield, 63; portraits of clergymen, churches & temples, Springfield, 63-80; portrait of Ted Shawn (ballet), Jacob's Pillow, Lenox, Mass, 64; portrait of med men, Med Ctr of Western Mass, 66-71; portrait of pres of Bay Path Jr Col, 80. *Exhib:* Grand Cent Art Galleries, New York, 55-57 & 77; North Shore Art Asn, Gloucester, Mass, 63-81; Hudson Valley Art Asn, White Plains, NY, 69-79; Allied Artists Am, New York, 70; Am Artists Prof League, New York, 70-80; Salute to the Met, Metrop Mus, New York, 79. *Awards:* Portrait Awards, Acad Artists, 76, 78, 80 & 83; Figure Award, North Shore Art Asn, 81; Portrait Awards, Ogunquit Art Asn, 81 & 82. *Bibliog:* Jack Steiner (auth), I know what I like, New York World Tel, 66. *Mem:* Copley Soc Boston; Royal Soc Art, London, Eng; Salmagundi Club; Acad Artists (pres, 69-70 & 75-80); Am Artists Prof League (dir, 75). *Media:* Oil, Watercolor. *Publ:* Contribr, Art News, 58; contribr, The Fifty American Artists' Book, 69; contribr, Robbins Reproductions, 69. *Mailing Add:* 45 May Fair Dr Springfield MA 01106

CATRON, PATRICIA D'ARCY
ADMINISTRATOR
b Memphis, Tenn. *Study:* Memphis Art Acad; Wittenberg Univ. *Collections Arranged:* Ralston Thompson--A Retrospective, 1933-74, Springfield Art Ctr & James Roy Hopkins, Ohio Artist, 1877-1969 (auth, catalogue), 77; The Barnitz Triad (auth, catalogue), 78. *Pos:* Managing dir, Springfield Art Ctr, Ohio, 70-72, dir, 72- *Mem:* Am Asn Mus; Ohio Mus Asn (mem bd trustees); Int Coun Mus. *Publ:* Contrib ed, The New Concept, 77. *Mailing Add:* 107 Cliff Park Rd Springfield OH 45501

CATTELL, RAY
PAINTER, DIRECTOR
b Birmingham, Eng, May 5, 21; Can citizen. *Study:* Birmingham Col Art, Eng; Univ Toronto. *Work:* London Art Gallery, Sarnia Art Gallery, Ont; Saskatoon Art Gallery, Alta; Windsor Pub Libr. *Exhib:* Royal Can Acad Art, 60-71; Ont Soc Artists, 60-71; Flint Inst Fine Arts, Mich, 65; Can Soc Painters in Watercolour, 66-72; Am Watercolor Soc, 72. *Pos:* Exec vpres, Royal Can Acad Art, 74-75. *Awards:* Watercolour Award, City of Toronto, 63; Hon Award, Can Soc Painters in Watercolour, 65, 68 & 72; Baxter Purchase Award, 66. *Mem:* Royal Can Acad Art; Ont Soc Artists (vpres, 67-68); Can Soc Painters in Watercolour (pres, 77); Arts & Lett Club; Art Dirs Club Toronto (pres, 64-65). *Media:* Acrylic, Watercolor. *Publ:* Auth, article on creativity, Marketing Mag, 60. *Dealer:* Allen Rubiner Gallery 621 S Washington Royal Oak MI; Gallery Moos 138 Yorkville Ave Toronto ON Can. *Mailing Add:* 21 Knightswood Rd Toronto ON M4N 2G9 Canada

CATTERALL, JOHN EDWARD
PAINTER, EDUCATOR
b Sheridan, Wyo, Jan 12, 40. *Study:* Univ Wyo, BA, 66; Wash State Univ, MFA, 68. *Work:* Brooklyn Mus; Detroit Inst Arts; Cranbrook Acad Art; Univ Colo, Boulder; Tex Tech Univ. *Comn:* Triptych, Barnett Winston Co, Jacksonville, Fla, 78; diptych, R J Reynolds Corp, Winston-Salem, NC, 80. *Exhib:* New American Graphics, Elvehjem Art Ctr, Madison, Wis, 75; Int Print Biennial, Ministry Cult & Art, Cracow, Poland, 76; Int Print Exhib, Cranbrook Acad Art, 80; solo exhib, Yellowstone Art Ctr, Billings, Mont, 80; Recent Acquisitions, Brooklyn Mus, 81; Western Skies--Western Eyes, Colo Inst Arts, Denver, 82; Int Print Invitational, Korean Print Soc, Seoul, 83. *Teaching:* Asst prof painting & printmaking, Univ SFla, 71-75; prof & dir, Mont State Univ, 75-82; prof & dept head, NMex State Univ, 82- *Awards:* Purchase Awards, Boston Printmakers Exhib, 70 & Potsdam Prints, State Univ NY, 75; Best of Show, Printmaking Exhib, Univ Colo, 75. *Bibliog:* Coke Van Deren (auth), The Painter & The Photographer, 72. *Mem:* Northwest Print Coun, Portland, Ore (bd mem, 80-82); World Print Coun; Col Art Asn; Nat Coun Arts Admin. *Media:* Acrylic, Oil. *Dealer:* Joan Hodgell Gallery Sarasota FL 33577; Austin Gallery Scottsdale AZ 85251. *Mailing Add:* 4130 Acacia Las Cruces NM 88001

CATUSCO, LOUIS
PAINTER, SCULPTOR
b Liberty, NY. *Study:* Brooklyn Mus Sch Art with John Ferren & Xavier Gonzalez, 47-50. *Work:* Santa Fe Mus Fine Art, NMex; US Bank Omaha Gallery, Nebr; Midland Bank, Denver. *Exhib:* Brooklyn Mus Fine Art; Mus Santa Fe Biennials, 64-76; Albuquerque Mus Fine Art, 66; Dallas Mus Fine Art, 66-70; Johnson Mus Fine Art, Albuquerque, 67; Joslyn Mus Fine Art, 70; El Paso Mus Fine Art, 70-73. *Awards:* Blumenschein, TAA Award Show, Helen Blumenschein, 66 & 67; Wurlitzer, TAA Award Show, Wurlitzer Found, 68; Gaspard Graphic, TAA Award Show, Dora Kaminsky Gaspard, 70-71. *Bibliog:* Tricia Jones (auth), The most private or lonely of men?, Southwest Arts Mag, 74 & Solitude is Catusco (objective), US Nat Bank of Omaha Art Gallery, 72. *Mem:* Taos Art Asn. *Media:* Acrylic, Oil; Construction, Wood. *Dealer:* Stables Art Gallery Taos NMex; Total Arts Gallery Taos NMex. *Mailing Add:* Box 1166 Taos NM 87571

CAVALIERE, BARBARA
CRITIC, HISTORIAN
b New York, NY. *Study:* State Univ NY Stony Brook, BA, 75; Queens Col, City Univ New York. *Pos:* Contrib ed, Arts Mag, New York, 77-; contribr, Acad Am Encycl, 21 vols, Arete Publ Co Inc, Princeton, NJ, 78-80; Contemp Artists, St Martin's Press. *Awards:* Helena Rubenstein Fel, Whitney Mus Am Art, 75; Art Critic's Fel, Nat Endowment Arts, 80. *Mem:* Int Asn Art Critics (chmn membership comt, 81-); Found Community Artists, New York; Nat Writer's Union. *Res:* 19th and 20th century art, especially abstract expressionism and contemporary art of 1940's to present. *Publ:* Auth, Theodoros Stamos in perspective, 12/77, auth, The making of omega, 10/80, auth, Vir heroicus sublimis: Building the idea complex, 1/81 & auth, Possibilities II, 9/81, Arts Mag; auth, Notes on Mark Rothko & auth, Early abstract expressionism: The 1940's, Flash Art, 1-2/79. *Mailing Add:* PO Box 531 Canal St Station New York NY 10013

CAVALLI, DICK
CARTOONIST
b New York, NY, Sept 28, 23. *Exhib:* Punch Exhib Humor, London, 53. *Pos:* Cartoonist, Syndicated Comic Strip, Winthrop, Newspaper Enterprise Asn, currently; mem founding fac, Famous Cartoonists Course, Famous Artists Schs. *Mem:* Nat Cartoonists Soc; Newspaper Comics Coun. *Publ:* Contribr cartoons, numerous bks, anthologies & cartoon collections; contribr cartoons in Sat Eve Post, Coller's, Look, This Week, True & many other US & foreign mags. *Mailing Add:* 90 Braeburn Dr New Canaan CT 06840

CAVANAUGH, JOHN W
SCULPTOR
b Sycamore, Ohio, Sept 20, 21. *Study:* Ohio State Univ, BFA; Univ Iowa, Iowa City; Sculpture Ctr, New York. *Work:* Colorado Springs Gallery Fine Art; Columbus Gallery Fine Arts, Ohio. *Comn:* Sculptured wall, Landmark, Baltimore, Md, 63; bull fighter & life-sized standing figure, Crown Towers, New Haven, Conn, 66; cross for altar, St Thomas's Church, Washington, DC, 74; Remembrance of Things Past (seven life-size panels), Swan St NW, 77; Ballet Dancer, Hunt Valley Mariott Hotel, Md, 81. *Exhib:* One-man shows, Antioch Col, Yellow Springs, Ohio, 56, Sculpture Ctr, New York, biennially 63-, Ohio State Univ, 64, Ball State Univ, Muncie, Ind, 67 & Univ Pa, 75. *Awards:* Ford Found Purchase Prize, Pa Acad Show; Richard Award, Nat Sculpture Soc. *Mem:* Sculpture Ctr, New York; Nat Sculpture Soc. *Dealer:* Swann's Way Gallery 1818 18th St Washington DC. *Mailing Add:* 1742 Corcoran St NW Washington DC 20009

CAVANAUGH, TOM RICHARD
PAINTER, EDUCATOR
b Danville, Ill, July 19, 23. *Study:* Univ Ill, BFA, 47, McLellan fel & MFA, 50; Fulbright grant to Italy, 56-57. *Work:* William Rockhill Nelson Gallery Art, Kansas City, Mo; Mulvane Art Mus, Topeka, Kans; Joslyn Art Mus, Omaha, Nebr; Ark Art Ctr, Little Rock; Isaac Delgado Mus Art, New Orleans. *Exhib:* Am Painting Today, Metrop Mus Art, New York, 50; Whitney Mus Am Art Ann, 51; Mo Annuals, St Louis Mus of Art, 52, 54 & 56; Kans State Col Biennials, 54 & 56; Colorado Springs Fine Arts Ctr, 54 & 55; New Orleans Mus, 58, 59, 60, 61 & 63; Provincetown Nat Art Festival, 58; Southeastern Annuals, High Mus, Atlanta, Ga, 58, 59, 60, 61, 62, 63 & 65; Birmingham Mus, 59; Dallas Mus, 59; Corcoran Biennial Exhibs, Washington, DC, 59 & 61; Maine: 100 Artists of the 20th Century, Colby Col, Waterville, 64; Am Painting, Va Mus Quadriennial, Richmond, 62. *Pos:* Art & educ dir, Springfield Art Asn, Ill, 47-49; dir, Bay St Studio, Boothbay Harbor, Maine, summers 50- *Teaching:* Instr painting & drawing, Kansas City Art Inst, 52-55 & Wash Univ Sch Fine Arts, 55-56; prof painting & drawing, La State Univ, 57-83, prof emer, 83- *Awards:* Painting Prize for Athletics, La State Univ Union, 69; Winner, mural competition, Govt Bldg, Baton Rouge, La, 78; Merit Award, 34th Ann La State Prof Artists Exhib, 79. *Bibliog:* Bartlett H Hayes (auth), Artist and advocate, Renaissance Ed, 68. *Media:* Oil, Encaustic. *Publ:* Auth, A city is not built in a day: the architecture of Springfield, Illinois, 1819-1949, 49; contribr, Maine Artists Calendar, 67. *Mailing Add:* Bay St Studio Boothbay Harbor ME 04538

CAVAT, IRMA
PAINTER, EDUCATOR
b New York, NY. *Study:* New Sch Social Res; Archipenko Art Sch; Acad Grande Chaumiere, Paris; also with Ozenfant, Paris & Hans Hofmann. *Comn:* Mural, Vodun, Port-au-Prince, Haiti, 48; wall of portraits, Fac Club, Univ Calif, Santa Barbara, 68; mural, pvt hotel, Athens, Greece, 70; wall piece, Los Angeles, Calif, 70. *Exhib:* Festival of Two Worlds, Spoleto, Italy, 58-59; Ten Americans, Palazzo Venezia, Rome, 60; one-man shows, Santa Barbara Mus, Calif & Phoenix Mus, Ariz, 66-67; and others. *Teaching:* Prof painting & drawing, Univ Calif, Santa Barbara, 64- *Awards:* Yaddo Fel, Trask Found, 50; Fulbright Fels, 56-58; Creative Arts Inst Award, Univ Calif, 70. *Media:* Oil, Mixed Media. *Dealer:* Kennedy Galleries New York NY. *Mailing Add:* Dept of Art Univ of Calif Santa Barbara CA 93106

CAVE, LEONARD EDWARD
SCULPTOR, EDUCATOR
b Columbia, SC, Oct 22, 44. *Study:* Furman Univ, BA; Univ Md, College Park, with Kenneth Campbell, MA. *Work:* Banker's Trust, Columbia, SC; Baptist Village, Waycross, Ga; George Meany Ctr for Labor Studies, Silver Spring, Md; Columbia Mus of Art, SC. *Comn:* Sculptural menorahs, Beth Torah Synagogue, Hyattsville, Md, 72; Duame Mem, Bells Mill Sch, Potomac, Md, 75. *Exhib:* Southeastern Mus Tour, Corcoran Gallery Art, 73; Wash Sculpture, Wolfe St Gallery, 77; one-man show, Greenville County Mus Art, SC, 79; Sculpture Ctr, New York, 79; and others. *Teaching:* Asst prof art,

Georgetown Univ, 70-77. *Awards:* Chaim Gross Sculptor's Exhib First Prize, Nat Young Sculptors Guild, 69. *Bibliog:* William Bradley (auth), Art, Magic Impulse & Control, Prentice-Hall, 73. *Mem:* Sculptors Guild; Artists Equity, Washington, DC (vpres, 73-75). *Media:* Stone; Wood. *Dealer:* Jen Hom Gallery 2121 P St NW Washington DC 20036; Sculpture Ctr 167 E 69th St New York NY 10021. *Mailing Add:* 10217 Old Field Dr Kensington MD 20795

CAVER, WILLIAM RALPH
SCULPTOR, PRINTMAKER
b Longview, Tex, Oct 11, 32. *Study:* NTex State Univ, BS; Univ Guanajuanto, MFA; Univ Barcelona. *Work:* Houston Mus Fine Arts; NTex State Gallery, Denton; Inst Allende Gallery, San Miguel de Allende, Mex. *Comn:* Sculpture, Louisville Libr, 71 & Texarkana Col Libr, Tex, 72; St James Church, Texarkana, Tex, 80. *Exhib:* Dallas Ann Libr Exhib, 63 & 64; Inst Allende Ann Show, 66; Texarkana Regional Art Show, 67-69; Denton Regional Art Show, 70; Paris, Tex Regional & Four States Regional, 74. *Teaching:* Instr art, Dallas Pub Sch Syst, 58-67; from assoc to prof art, Texarkana Col, 67- *Awards:* Second Prize, Four States Regional, 74, First Prize, 77 & 83. *Mem:* Tex Asn Art Schs. *Dealer:* Casa Del Bosque Texarkana TX 75501. *Mailing Add:* Rte 6 Box 453 Texarkana TX 75501

CAWEIN, KATHRIN
PRINTMAKER, ILLUMINATOR
b New London, Conn, May 9, 1895. *Study:* Art Students League, with George Bridgman, Allen Lewis & Harry Wickey; Oberlin Col Hon MA, 66; Pac Univ, Ore, Hon DFA, 81. *Work:* Metrop Mus Art, New York; Nat Gallery, Washington, DC; Oberlin Col, Ohio; Tampa Univ, Fla; Pa State Univ; and others. *Comn:* Illuminated manuscripts, St Marks Church, Van Nuys, Calif, St Andrew Church, Sarasota, Fla, Congregational Church, Colorado Springs, Colo, St John's Church, Pleasantville, NY & Pac Univ, Forest Grove, Ore. *Exhib:* Breezeway, Sarasota, Fla, 73; Tampa Univ, Fla, 73; Oberlin Col, 74; Berea Col, Ky, 76; Pac Univ, Forest Grove, Ore, 79-81; and many others. *Teaching:* Instr etching, Westchester Co Workshop, White Plains, 35-36; drawing for children, pvt studio, 50-55, workshop, Pacific Univ, 82. *Awards:* Prize non-mem, Soc Am Etchers; Etching Award, Nat Asn Women Artists; Hon Mention, Hudson Valley Women's Club, 52. *Mem:* Art Students League; Nat Asn Women Artists, New York; Am Soc Graphic Artists. *Mailing Add:* 35 Mountain Rd Pleasantville NY 10570

CAWOOD, GARY KENNETH
PHOTOGRAPHER
b Chattanooga, Tenn, Jan 17, 47. *Study:* Auburn Univ, BArchit, 70; E Tenn State Univ, MFA, 76. *Work:* Baltimore Mus Art, Md; New Orleans Mus Art, La; Libr Cong; Tenn Arts Comn, Nashville. *Exhib:* Solo exhibs, Sarah Reynolds Gallery, Univ NMex, Albuquerque & Contemp Art Ctr, New Orleans, 79; Works on Paper, Dallas Mus Art, Tex, 78; Photography in Louisiana, New Orleans Mus Art, 80; two-person exhib, Sioux City Art Ctr, Iowa, 82, Ascherman Gallery, Cleveland, Ohio, 82 & Project Art Ctr, Cambridge, Mass, 82; Recent Acquisitions, Baltimore Mus Art, 83. *Teaching:* Adj prof photog, Univ Del, 75-76; assoc prof, La Tech Univ, 76- *Awards:* Purchase Award, A Private Space, Contemp Art Ctr, New Orleans, 79; Visual Artist Fel Grant, Nat Endowment Arts, 82. *Bibliog:* Roger Green (auth), article, New Orleans Times/Picayune, 1/29/82. *Mem:* Soc Photog Educ. *Publ:* Contribr, Southern Eye, Southern Mind: A Photographic Inquiry, Memphis Acad Arts, 81; contribr, American Infrared Survey, Photo Survey Press, 82. *Dealer:* Rebecca Morgan 200 Arno NE #2 Albuquerque NM 87102. *Mailing Add:* 1605 S Barnett Springs Rd Ruston LA 71270

CECERE, GAETANO
SCULPTOR, LECTURER
b New York, NY, Nov 26, 1894. *Study:* Nat Acad Design; Beaux-Arts Inst Design; Am Acad Rome, 20-23. *Work:* Metrop Mus Art; Numismatic Mus, NY; Norfolk Mus Art. *Comn:* Plaques, US Capitol, Washington, DC; reliefs, Fed Reserve Bank, Jacksonville, Fla; war mem, Clifton, Plainfield & Princeton, NJ; and others. *Exhib:* Nat Sculpture Soc, 24-58; Nat Acad Design, 24-69; Allied Artists Am, 62-64; Knickerbocker Artists, 62-64; Audubon Artists, 62, 64 & 65; and others. *Teaching:* Lectr contemp & ecclesiastical sculpture; former dir sculpture dept, Beaux-Arts Inst Design; former mem fac, Mary Washington Col & Sch Fine Arts, Nat Acad Design. *Awards:* Award in Sculpture, Nat Arts Club, 68; Sculpture Award, Audubon Artists, 69; Therese Richard Mem Award, Allied Artists Am, 70; and others. *Mem:* Academician Nat Acad Design; Nat Sculpture Soc; New York Archit League. *Mailing Add:* c/o Cioffi 18 Green Glen Greenwich CT 06830

CECIL, CHARLES HARKLESS
PAINTER
b Kansas City, Mo, May 12, 45. *Study:* Haverford Col, Pa, BA(with honors), 67; Yale Univ Grad Sch, 67-69; with R H Ives Gammell, Boston, Mass, 69-71 & Richard F Lack, Minneapolis, Minn, 72-73. *Work:* Haverford Col Libr, Pa; West Bend Gallery Fine Arts, Wis. *Exhib:* Twin City Art Exhib, Minneapolis, Minn, 75; one-man show, Univ Club Chicago, Ill, 80; 154th & 155th Ann, Nat Acad Design, New York, 79 & 80. *Teaching:* Co-dir, Studio Cecil-Graves, Borgo San Frediano, Florence, Italy, currently; instr, Villa Schifanoia Grad Sch Fine Arts, Florence, Italy, currently. *Awards:* Benjamin Altman Second Prize Landscape, 155th Ann, Nat Acad Design, 80; Grant for Painting, John F & Ann Lee Stacey Found, 80; three ann grants, Elizabeth Greenshields Found, Montreal. *Media:* Oils. *Mailing Add:* 502 S Center Clinton IL 61727

CEDERSTROM, JOHN ANDREW
PAINTER, INSTRUCTOR
b Philadelphia, Pa, Apr 26, 29. *Study:* Philadelphia Col Art, study illus with Henry Pitz, painting with Gertrude Schell & watercolor with Ben Eisenstat; Pa Acad Fine Arts, study painting with Roswell Weidner. *Work:* Philadelphia Mus Art, Pa; Allentown Art Mus, Pa; UNICEF Collection, New York; Lehigh Univ, Bethlehem, Pa; Fed Reserve Bank, Philadelphia, Pa. *Comn:* Corp logo, Am Medicorp, Riverside Gen Hosp, NJ, 76 & FOCUS Orgn, Wallingford, Conn, 76; posters & logo, Nat Coun Arts & Educ, New York, 77; sketches jungle idol, Blue Lagoon, Columbia Pictures Inc, Hollywood, 79. *Exhib:* Ann Int, Pa Acad Fine Arts, Pa, 51; Regional Exhib, Philadelphia Mus Art, Pa, 54; one-man shows, Woodmere Art Gallery, Philadelphia, Pa, 69 & Philadelphia Art Alliance, 79; Audubon Artists, Nat Acad Design, New York, 76-78; The Artist Views the City, 76 & Print Show, 76, Philadelphia Art Alliance. *Collections Arranged:* Friends Collection 40th Anniversary: Ernest Lawson to Karel Appel, 71; Wildlife in Art: Benefit Philadelphia Zoo Wolf Woods, 73, A Child's World: Benefit Exhib, 74, Women in Art: 1776-1976, 76 & Surrealism, Fantasy & Sci Fiction: Dali to Miro, 77, Friends Cent Gallery, Philadelphia, Pa. *Pos:* Chief conserv, Hahn Gallery, Philadelphia, 75-; partner, Concepts Unlimited, Media, Pa, 81- *Teaching:* Dir art educ, Bryn Mawr Art Ctr, Pa, 53-63; chmn art & art hist, Friends Cent Sch, Philadelphia, Pa, 63-81. *Awards:* Charles K Smith Prize, 14th Ann Exhib, Woodmere Art Gallery, Philadelphia, Pa, 54; First Prize, First Ann Etchers Show, Philadelphia Sketch Club, Pa, 54 & 1975 Graphics Ann, Chester Co Art Asn, West Chester, Pa, 75. *Bibliog:* Eleanor Cederstrom (auth), A Poetry and Painting Festival, Gloucester Daily Times, Essex Co News, 77; Charles Movalli (auth), John Cederstrom, Looking for the infinite connection, Am Artist, 79. *Mem:* Artists Equity Asn, Philadelphia (vpres, 79-80); Am Color Print Soc; Philadelphia Print Club; Philadelphia Watercolor Club; Am Artists Prof League. *Media:* Oil, Silkscreen. *Dealer:* Hahn Gallery 8439 Germantown Ave Philadelphia PA 19118; School House Gallery Tarpon Bay Rd Sanibel FL 33957. *Mailing Add:* 518 Prescott Rd Merion Station PA 19066

CEGLIA, VINCENT
PAINTER, INSTRUCTOR
b Braintree, Mass, Mar 11, 23. *Study:* Brooklyn Mus Sch of Art; Pratt Inst. *Work:* Pa State Univ; Educ Testing Serv, Princeton, NJ; Rider Col, Trenton, NJ; Sun Oil Co, Philadelphia; Raccolta Arte Moderna, Florence, Italy; and others. *Exhib:* Philadelphia Mus of Art, 71; Philadelphia Art Alliance, 71 & 75; Butler Inst of Am Art, Youngstown, Ohio, 72; Am Watercolor Soc, 75-77; Cedar Rapids Art Ctr, Iowa, 77; Frye Mus, Seattle, Wash, 77; 154th Ann Exhib, Nat Acad Design, New York, 79; and others. *Teaching:* Asst prof visual arts, Trenton Jr Col, 60-68; assoc prof visual arts, Mercer Col, 68; dir painting, Gargonza Painting Workshop, Tuscany, Italy, summers, 75-78, Lake Maggiore, Italy, 79-84. *Awards:* 1st Patron Prize, Phillips Mill Ann Exhib, 68, 70, 75 & 76; Dana Prize, 79 & Zimmerman Prize, 81, Philadelphia Watercolor Club. *Mem:* Am Watercolor Soc; Philadelphia Watercolor Club; Salmagundi Club, NY; Artists Equity; Philadelphia Art Alliance; and others. *Media:* Watercolor, Acrylic. *Publ:* Illusr, A History of American Art Porcelain, Renaissance Ed, NY, 67; illusr, Vaughn Associates Architects, Vaughn Assoc, 69; auth & illusr, Watercolor Page, Am Artist Mag, 77, Am Artist Exec Calendar, 79 & Arte pui Arte, Milano, 81. *Mailing Add:* Mt Eyre Rd Washington Crossing PA 18977

CELENDER, DONALD DENNIS
HISTORIAN, CONCEPTUAL ARTIST
b Pittsburgh, Pa, Nov 11, 31. *Study:* Carnegie-Mellon Univ, BFA, 56; Univ Pittsburgh, MEd, 59, 60-63, PhD(A W Mellon Scholar), 63. *Work:* Centro Arte y Communicacion & Mus Arte Mod, Buenos Aires; Allen Mem Art Mus, Oberlin Col, Ohio; Latrobe Mus, Pa; Gen Mills Collection, Minneapolis. *Comn:* Stained glass panels, Children's Hosp, Pittsburgh, 61; moving water sculpture, Nokomis Br, stained glass mural, Main Br, & Eva Rhodes Freeman Mem (stained glass mural), Lake St Br, Minneapolis Pub Libr, 67; mem (stained glass panels), St James Lutheran Church, Minneapolis, 68. *Exhib:* Walker Art Ctr Biennial, 64; Art in the Mind, Allen Mem Art Mus, 70; 2,972,453, Ctr Arte y Comunicacion, Buenos Aires, 70; one-man shows, O K Harris Gallery, New York, 70-80; Art Systems I & II, Mus Arte Mod, Buenos Aires, 71-72. *Pos:* Cur, Nat Gallery Art, 61-63; dir educ & pub activities, Minneapolis Inst Arts, 63-64. *Teaching:* Edith M Kelso prof art hist, Macalester Col, 64- *Awards:* Ford Fel Humanities, 70-71; Bush Fel, 79-80; and others. *Bibliog:* Gareth Hiebert (auth), Grand Canyon sweet & other delicacies, St Paul Pioneer Press & Dispatch, 5/28/72; Max Kozloff (auth), article, Art J, fall 73; Marcel Jean (auth), article, La Quinzaine Litteraire, 2/15/75; and others. *Mem:* Col Art Asn Am; Am Mus Asn; Delta Phi Delta; Minn Arts Forum; Minneapolis Soc Fine Arts. *Res:* Development of conceptual art movements and ideas. *Publ:* Auth, articles on Bellows, Caneletto, Duccio, DeHooch, Grunewald, Manet & Turner for Nat Gallery Art, 61-63; auth, The Dance, 72; auth, Eight Conceptual Art Movements, 72; auth, Olympics of Art, 74; auth, Observation & Scholarship Examination for Art Historians, Museum Directors, Artists, Dealers & Collectors, 75; and others. *Dealer:* O K Harris Gallery 383 W Broadway New York NY 10012. *Mailing Add:* 15 Duck Pass Rd St Paul MN 55110

CELENTANO, FRANCIS MICHAEL
PAINTER, EDUCATOR
b New York, NY, May 25, 28. *Study:* NY Univ Inst Fine Arts, MA, 57; Acad Fine Arts, Rome, Italy, Fulbright Fel, 58. *Work:* Mus Mod Art, New York; Albright-Knox Art Gallery, Buffalo; Fed Reserve Bank, San Francisco; Seattle Art Mus, Wash; Rose Art Gallery, Brandeis Univ, Waltham, Mass. *Comn:* Painting, Hwy Bldg, Wash State Hwy Dept, 70; mural, Port of Seattle, Seattle-Tacoma Airport, 71; mural, Seattle City Light, 74; mural, Lincoln

Mutual Savings Bank, Seattle, 79. *Exhib:* The Responsive Eye, Mus Mod Art, New York, 65; Kinetic & Optical Art Today, 65 & Plus by Minus: Today's Half Century, 68, Albright-Knox Art Gallery; Whitney Ann, Whitney Mus Am Art, 67; Pacific Cities, Auckland City Art Gallery, New Zealand, 71; 1st Western States Bienniel Exhib, Nat Gallery Fine Arts, Washington, DC, 79. *Teaching:* Prof art, Univ Wash, 66- *Awards:* Int Artist's Sem Award, Fairleigh Dickinson Univ, 65. *Bibliog:* Moore (auth), Letters from 31 Artists, Albright-Knox Art Gallery, 70; Kingsbury (auth), Art, 1/70 & Kangas (auth), Francis Celentano, transcendence and negation, 81, Seattle Mag. *Media:* Acrylic on Plastic. *Dealer:* Fountain Gallery 117 NW 21st Ave Portland OR 97209; Greg Kucera Gallery 608 2nd Ave Seattle WA 98104. *Mailing Add:* 1919 1/2 Second Ave Seattle WA 98101

CELLI, PAUL
PAINTER, EDUCATOR
b Boston, Mass, May 8, 35. *Study:* Mass Col Art, BFA, 60; RI Sch Design, MFA, 62. *Exhib:* Providence Art Festival, RI, 61-69; New England Contemp Artists Asn, Boston, 63; Berkshire Mus, Pittsfield, Mass, 66; one-man shows, Bennett Col, Millbrook, NY, 67 & McIvor Reddie Gallery, Boston, 68 & 70. *Teaching:* Assoc prof 4D theory, Mass Col Art, 70- *Media:* Oil, Acrylic. *Mailing Add:* PO Box 109 Dover MA 02030

CELLINI, JOSEPH
ILLUSTRATOR
b Budapest, Hungary, June 13, 24; US citizen. *Study:* Acad Fine Art, Budapest, MA, 49. *Media:* Oil, Pencil. *Publ:* Illusr, The Great Adventure of Michelangelo, 65, illusr, The Miracle of Flight, 68 & illusr, Bayou Country, 69, Doubleday; illusr, Animal Fathers, Holiday House, 76. *Mailing Add:* 415 Hillside Ave Leonia NJ 07605

CENCI, SILVANA
SCULPTOR
b Florence, Italy, Aug 4, 26. *Study:* Manzoni Inst, Italy; Acad Fine Art, Italy, 49; Acad Grand Chaumiere, Paris, 49-50. *Work:* Uffizi Gallery Mod Art & Numero Gallery, Florence, Italy; Bundy Art Mus, Waitsfield, Vt; Metrop Boston Transit Authority; Merchants Bank, Manchester, NH; and others. *Comn:* Monumental sculpture, Pavilion Archit, New Haven, Conn, 61; two lions explosively formed, Graham Jr Col, Boston, 63; baptistry doors, Carter & Woodruff Archit, Keene, NH, 65; fountains, Western Front Restaurant, Cambridge, Mass, 67 & Sasha Montagu, Brookline, 69. *Exhib:* New England Art Today, Northeastern Univ, 62; Bristol Art Mus, RI, 67; New Eng Sculptors Asn, Boston City Hall, 69 & Contemporary Art-Italian Heritage, 75; ten-year retrospective, Bristol Art Mus, 77; and others. *Pos:* Artist-in-residence, City of Boston, 71-73. *Teaching:* Instr art, Brookline Art Ctr, 66-69. *Awards:* Gold Hammer Award, Medea, Italy, 58; First Honorable Mention, Design in Transit, Inst Contemp Art, 71; Blanche Coleman Award, 74. *Bibliog:* Al Kaliman (auth), Odyssey Implosion/Explosion, WBZ-TV, 64; John A Hughes (auth), Explosion in Northwood, NH Profiles, 64; Richard Hadley (auth), The state we are in, Channel 11 TV, NJ, 75. *Mem:* NH Art Asn; Artists Equity Asn. *Media:* Stainless Steel, 24-karat Gold. *Mailing Add:* Harmony Rte Northwood NH 03261

CERNUSCHI, ALBERTO C
DEALER, CRITIC
US citizen. *Study:* Univ Milan, PhD; Univ Lausanne, PhD; Kensington Univ, Calif, PhD. *Pos:* Founder, Cernuschi & Caravan de France Galleries, Paris, France, Tokyo & New York; trustee, Cernuschi Mus, Paris. *Teaching:* Lectr mod art, Ecole du Louvre, Mus Cernuschi. *Specialty:* Modern art. *Mailing Add:* Cernuschi Galleries 210 E 86th St New York NY 10028

CERVANTES, PEDRO
SCULPTOR
b Mexico City, Mex, Oct 10, 33. *Study:* Escuela Nac Artes Plasticas, San Carlos, Mex, 51-52. *Work:* Banco Fomento Cooperativo, Mex; Banco Attantico, Mex; Financiera Nuevo Leon, Mex; Leona Textil Bldg, Monterrey, Mex; Entrance to Port of Alvarado, Mex. *Comn:* Welded iron sculpture, Jorge Gonzalez Reyna, 62; iron sculpture, Inst Nac Vivienda, 65; Incongruente, chromed steel, Hojalata & Lamina Hylsa, 71; Euridice, steel, Club Industriales, A C, 72; Septentrion, chromed steel, Nylon Mex, 72. *Exhib:* New Values Show, Salon Plastica Mex, 62; Exhibition Young Artists Show, 65 & one-man show, 72, Mus Mod Art, Mexico City; Contemporary Mexican Painting, La Habana, Cuba, 65; Expo 67, Montreal, Que, 67. *Awards:* First Prize, Solar Exhib, Mex Ministry Educ, 68; First Prize, Ann Salon Sculpture & Engraving, Salon Plastica Mex, 72. *Bibliog:* Alfonso de Neuvillate & Luis Cardoza y Aragon (auths), Mexico pintura actual, Artes Mex; Raquel Tibol (auth), Pedro Cervantes o/a ahbivalencia, Excelsior, 2/72; Jorge Crespo de la Serna (auth), La escultura de Pedro Cervantes, Novedades, 3/72. *Media:* Welded Steel. *Mailing Add:* c/o Galeria de Arte Misrachi S A 20 Genova Mexico City 6 Mexico

CERVENE, RICHARD
PAINTER, CURATOR
b Ft Dodge, Iowa. *Study:* Grinnell Col, BA, 51; Univ Iowa, Iowa City, MFA, 53; Yale-Norfolk Art Sch, with Josef Albers, Nicholas Marsicano & Gabor Peterdi, 53. *Work:* Des Moines Art Ctr; Joslyn Art Mus; Coe Col, Iowa. *Exhib:* Nat Midyear Ann, Butler Inst Am Art, 66; Tenth Midwest Biennial Exhib, Joslyn Art Mus, 75; 45th Ann 17 State Show, Springfield Art Mus, Mo, 75; Iowa Artist Exhib, Des Moines Art Ctr, 76; Contemp Am Art, Am Acad & Inst Arts & Lett, New York, 79; Am Artists Exhib, US Embassy, Oslo, Norway, 80-81. *Collections Arranged:* Appel & Alechinsky, 81, Japanese Prints, 82, African Art: East & West, 83 & Giovanni Battista

Piranesi, 83, Grinnell Col. *Teaching:* Prof art, Grinnell Col, 56-, cur, Permanent Art Collection, 72- *Awards:* Grant Wood Prize, Iowa Art Exhib, Cedar Falls Art Mus, 62; First Award Painting, Iowa Artists Exhib, Des Moines Art Ctr, 65; Purchase Award, Tenth Midwest Biennial Exhib, Joslyn Art Mus, 68. *Mem:* Am Asn Art Mus; Am Asn Univ Prof; Col Art Asn Am; Am Soc Aesthetics. *Media:* Oil, Watercolor. *Mailing Add:* Dept Art Grinnell Col Grinnell IA 50112

CERVENKA, BARBARA
EDUCATOR, PAINTER
b Cleveland, Sept 28, 39. *Study:* Siena Heights Col, Studio Angelico, Adrian, Mich, 57-64, BA, 64; Wayne State Univ, Detroit, 67-69; Univ Mich, Ann Arbor, 69-71, MFA, 71. *Work:* Alumni Mem Mus, Univ Mich, Ann Arbor; Eastern Mich Univ, Sill Hall Art Collection, Ypsilanti. *Exhib:* Watercolor USA, Springfield, Mo, 69, 73 & 75; Mid-Mich Show, Midland, 71; Mich Watercolor Soc Show, Birmingham, 71, 72 & 74; Am Watercolor Soc Show, New York, 73; Toledo Area Artists Show, Ohio, 73. *Teaching:* Instr drawing & watercolor, Siena Heights Col, 71-78; adminr, Adrian Dominican Sisters, Mich, 78-82; instr watercolor drawing, Sch Art, Univ Mich, currently. *Awards:* Purchase Prize, Eastern Mich Univ, 71 & Watercolor USA, 73; First Prize, Toledo Area Artists Show, 73. *Mem:* Mich Watercolor Soc; Midwest Col Art Asn. *Mailing Add:* 1257 E Siena Heights Dr Adrian MI 49221

CETIN, ANTON
PAINTER, PRINTMAKER
b Bojana, Yugoslavia, Sept 18, 36; Can citizen. *Study:* Sch Applied Arts, dipl, 59; Acad Fine Arts, Masters dipl, 64. *Work:* Nat Libr France, Paris; United Nations Educ, Sci & Cult Orgn League, Japan; Imperial Oil, Toronto, Can; Univ Mich, Dearborn; Sony Collection, Tokyo, Japan; and others. *Exhib:* N Copernicus and His Thought, Mus Mod Art, Cracow, Poland, 72; Enrichissement du Cabinet des Estampes 1974-1978, Nat Libr France, Paris, 78; one-man shows, Salon XX, Bogota, Columbia, 81, Mannheimer Abenakademia, WGer, 81 & Gilman Galleries, Chicago, 83; and others. *Bibliog:* Dr Gordon McLennan (auth), The art of Anton Cetin, Art Mag, 78. *Mem:* Int Asn Art/UNESCO; Print Coun; World Print Coun; Visual Arts Ont. *Media:* Oil, Mixed Media; Etching, Aquatint. *Mailing Add:* 37 Hanna Ave 13A Toronto ON M6K 1W9 Canada

CHABOT, AURORE (MARTHA)
CERAMIST
b Nashua, NH, July 30, 49. *Study:* Pratt Inst, BFA, 71; Univ Colo, Boulder, MFA, 81. *Work:* Tweed Mus; Pratt Inst. *Comn:* Ceramic wall piece, comn by Thomas Head, Boulder, Colo, 82. *Exhib:* Marietta Col Crafts Nat, 81; solo exhib, Warm Gallery, Minneapolis, 82, Tweed Mus, 82, Francis Colburn Gallery, Univ Vt, Burlington, 83, Jane Hartsook Gallery, Greenwich House, New York, 83 & John Michael Kohler Art Ctr, Sheboygan, Wis, 84. *Teaching:* Artist in residence, Adirondack Arts & Crafts League, Broadalbin, NY, 75-76; coordr ceramics prog, Womens Interart Ctr, New York, 78-79; actg head ceramics, Univ Minn, Duluth, 81-82; asst prof, Univ Vt, Burlington, 82- *Awards:* Jurors Award, Marietta Col Crafts Nat, 81; grants, Nat Endowment Arts, 83 & Vt Coun Arts, 83. *Bibliog:* Gloria DeFilipps Brush (auth), article, New Art Examiner, 6/82; William Braun (auth), article, New England Art J, 6/83; Eleanor Heartney (auth), article, Arts Mag, 12/83. *Mem:* Col Art Asn; Nat Womens Caucus Art; Am Craft Coun; Nat Coun Educ Ceramic Arts. *Media:* Ceramics. *Dealer:* By Design Gallery 10 S Fifth St Minneapolis MN 55402. *Mailing Add:* 10 E Spring St Winooski VT 05404

CHADBOURN, ALFRED CHENEY
PAINTER, INSTRUCTOR
b Izmir, Turkey, Oct 5, 21; US citizen. *Study:* Chouinard Art Inst, Los Angeles, 40-42; Ecole des Beaux Arts, Paris, 47-50; Academie de la Grande Chaumiere, Paris, 47-51. *Work:* Adelphi Univ & Nat Acad Design, New York; Portland Mus Art, Maine; Boston Mus Fine Arts; Chicago Art Inst. *Exhib:* Salon des Independents, Mus Mod Art, Paris, 48-50; Ann, Los Angeles Co Mus, 50; Art Inst Chicago, 53; Pa Acad, Philadelphia Mus, 53-57; Nat Acad Design, New York, 53-54, 56-60, 70, 72-76, 76-81; Whitney Mus Art, New York, 56; Wadsworth Atheneum, Hartford, Conn, 58. *Teaching:* Instr, Queen's Col, New York, 53-56, Portland Sch Art, Maine, 56-58 & Westbrook Col, Portland, Maie, 73-81. *Awards:* Louis Comfort Tiffany Found, 59; Henry Ward Ranger Purchase Award, 64 & Emil & Dines Carlsen Award, 81, Nat Acad Design. *Mem:* Nat Acad Design. *Media:* Oil, Watercolor. *Publ:* Contribr, A direct approach to painting, N Light Publ, 80. *Dealer:* Barridoff Gallery Portland ME; Munson Gallery Chatham MA. *Mailing Add:* 4 Church St Yarmouth ME 04096

CHADDLESONE, SHERMAN
PAINTER, PRINTMAKER
b Lawton, Okla, June 2, 47. *Study:* Inst Am Indian Arts, Santa Fe, with Allan Houser, Fritz Scholder & Otellie Loloma, dipl, 67; Cent State Univ, Okla, with William Wallo, 72-73. *Work:* Dept Interior Bldg, Washington, DC; Southern Plains Indian Mus, Anadarko, Okla; Inst Am Indian Art Mus, Santa Fe; Mabee-Gerrer Mus, Shawnee, Okla; Mus NMex, Albuquerque. *Exhib:* Inst Am Ind Arts Student Exhib, NMex Fine Arts Mus, Santa Fe, 64; Scottsdale Ann Ivitational Exhib, Ariz, 65 & 66; Contemp Am Indian Art, Palace Fine Arts, San Francisco, 70; Inst Am Indian Arts Alumni Traveling Exhib, Amon Carter Mus Western Art, Ft Worth, New Orleans Mus Art & Okla Art Ctr, 73-74; Pintura Amerindia Contemporanea Traveling Exhib, US Communications Agency, SAm, 79; Ann Western Art Show & Auction, Mus Native Am Cult, Spokane, 82; Contemporary North American Indian Art, Smithsonian Inst, 82-83. *Collections Arranged:* New Kiowa Five, Inst Am Indian Arts Mus, 83. *Teaching:* Dir, Indian Arts Workshop, San Francisco

Art Comn, 70-71. *Awards:* Best of Show, Art From the Earth, 81 & First Place, Ann Kiowa Show, 82, Galeria, Norman, Okla; Second Place Painting, Gallup Ceremonial, 83. *Bibliog:* Maurice Boyd (auth), Kiowa Voices, Vol II, Tex Christian Univ Press, 82. *Media:* Acrylic, Pastel; Serigraph. *Dealer:* Okla Indian Art Gallery 2335 SW 44th St Oklahoma City OK 73119. *Mailing Add:* PO Box 1732 Anadarko OK 73005

CHADEAYNE, ROBERT OSBORNE
PAINTER
b Cornwall, NY, Dec 13, 1897. *Study:* Colgate Univ; Art Students League; also with C K Chatterton, Henry Martin Hoyt, George Luks & John Sloan. *Work:* Columbus Gallery Fine Arts; Butler Inst Am Art; Schumacker Collection, Capital Univ; and others. *Comn:* Broad & High St 1920 (painting), 64 & Central Ohio (painting), 65, Trautman Off Bldg, Columbus, Ohio; cityscape, Huntington Nat Bank, Columbus, 70. *Exhib:* Art Inst Chicago Ann; Pa Acad Fine Arts Ann; Nat Acad Design Ann, New York; Corcoran Biennial, Washington, DC; Butler Inst Am Art Midyear Nat Exhib, Youngstown, Ohio, 65-70. *Teaching:* Dir drawing & painting, Columbus Art Sch, 27-42; prof fine arts, Ohio State Univ, 42-63. *Awards:* Norman Waite Harris Medal, Art Inst Chicago, 20; Purchase Prize, Pa Acad Fine Arts, 20; IBM Medal for Contribution to World of Art. *Mem:* Columbus Art League; Columbus Gallery Fine Arts. *Dealer:* Capricorn Galleries 8003 Woodmont Ave Bethesda MD 20014. *Mailing Add:* 5578 Riverside Dublin OH 43017

CHAET, BERNARD
PAINTER, EDUCATOR
b Boston, Mass, Mar 7, 24. *Study:* Boston Mus Sch, with Karl Zerbe, 42-45; Tufts Univ, BS, 49. *Work:* Fogg Art Mus, Harvard Univ; Univ Calif Art Gallery, Los Angeles; Brooklyn Mus, NY; Addison Gallery Am Art, Andover, Mass; RI Sch Design Mus, Providence. *Exhib:* Univ Ill Biennial Am Painting, 51, 53 & 60; Golden Years of American Drawing 1900-56, Brooklyn Mus, 56; Recent Drawings USA, Mus Mod Art, New York, 56; Corcoran Biennial Am Painting, Washington, DC, 62; Pa Acad Fine Arts Ann, Philadelphia, 62. *Pos:* Auth mo article, Studio talk, Arts Mag, 56-69. *Teaching:* Prof drawing & painting, Yale Univ Art Sch, 51-; William Leffingwell prof painting, 79- *Awards:* Grant, Nat Found Humanities Arts, 66-67; Hassam & Speicher Fund Purchase Award, Am Acad & Inst Arts & Lett, 81. *Bibliog:* Margaret Mathews (auth), article, 9/82; Janice C Ovesman (auth), article, Arts Mag, 11/82. *Publ:* Auth preface, 20th Century Drawing (catalog), Yale Art Gallery, 55; auth, Artists at Work, Webb, 61; auth, The Art of Drawing, Holt, 71, 2nd ed 77, 3rd ed 83; auth, An Artist's Notebook: Techniques and Materials, Holt, 78. *Dealer:* Marilyn Pearl Gallery 29 West 57th St New York NY 10019; Alpha Gallery 121 Newbury St Boston MA 02116. *Mailing Add:* 141 Cold Spring St New Haven CT 06511

CHAFETZ, SIDNEY
PRINTMAKER, EDUCATOR
b Providence, RI, Mar 27, 22. *Study:* RI Sch Design, BFA, 47; Acad Julian, Paris, 47-48; L'Ecole Am Beaux Arts, Fontainebleau, 47; with Fernand Leger, Paris, 48 & S W Hayter, Atelier 17, 50-51. *Work:* Libr Cong, Washington, DC; Morgan Libr, NY; Dahlem-Staalesche Mus; Philadelphia Mus Art; British Mus. *Comn:* Dedication etching, Ohio State Univ Col Law, 64; Hawthorne Keepsake, Ohio State Univ, 64; Robert Lowell Poster, Int Poetry Forum, Pittsburgh, Pa, 67; F Scott Fitzgerald Keepsake, Fitzgerald Newslett, Ohio State Univ, 68; Poor Richards Almanacks Original Woodblock Portrait, Imprint Soc, Barre, Mass, 70. *Exhib:* Ten Years of American Prints, 1947-57, Brooklyn Mus, NY, 57; Young American Printmakers, Mus Mod Art, New York, 58-59; 9th Int Expos Gravure, Switz, Norway & Sweden, 66; 1st Biennial Int Gravure Sur Bois, Banska Bystrica, Czech, 70; 2nd Triennial Int Graphica Contemp, Capri, Italy, 72; 30-Year Retrospective, Antioch Col & throughout Ohio, 78-79. *Teaching:* Prof art, Ohio State Univ, 48-82, prof emer, 82-; vis prof art, Univ Ariz, spring 65, Univ Wis-Madison, summer 67 & Univ Denver, summer 71 & 79; Fulbright Sr lectr, Univ Belgrade, Yugoslavia, 80. *Awards:* Fulbright Fel, 50-51; Purchase Prize & Awards, 1st Biennial Int Gravure, Banska Bystrica, Czech, 70; MacDowell Colony Fel, 79. *Mem:* Soc Am Graphic Artists; Am Color Print Soc; Am Asn Univ Prof; Nat Acad Design. *Media:* Woodcut, Intaglio. *Dealer:* Assoc Am Artists 663 Fifth Ave New York NY 10022. *Mailing Add:* Dept of Art Ohio State Univ Columbus OH 43210

CHAHROUDI, MARTHA L
CURATOR
b Chicago, Ill, Nov 3, 46. *Study:* Col Wooster, BA, 68; NY Univ, MA, 70; State Univ NY, Buffalo, MFA, 81. *Collections Arranged:* Ansel Adams: 100 Photographs, 79-80, August Sander: Photographs of an Epoch, 80, The Spirit of an American Place, 80-81, The New West: Photographs by Robert Adams, 81, American Frontiers: The Photographs of Timothy H O'Sullivan 1867-1874, 81-82, Danny Lyon: Pictures from the New World 1962-1982, 82, Frederick H Evans: The Desired Haven, 82, Minor White, 83 & Tibet: The Sacred Realm, Photographs 1880-1950, 83, Philadelphia Mus Art. *Pos:* Asst managing ed, Afterimage, 78-79; admin asst, Alfred Stieglitz Ctr, Philadelphia Mus Art, 79-80, asst cur, 80- *Awards:* Visual Arts Prog Critics Fel, Nat Endowment Arts, 79. *Mem:* Soc Photog Educ. *Publ:* Auth, Snapshots: Open secrets of the self, 12/77 & Video reviews: Tapes by CAPS recipients, 4/78, Afterimage; auth, Photo-Booth Strips: Photographs by Carol Taback, Aperture 89, 82; auth, Tibet: The Sacred Realm, Photographs 1880-1950, Millerton, 83. *Mailing Add:* 6800 Scotforth Rd Philadelphia PA 19119

CHAIKIN, ALYCE (ALYCE CHAIKIN KLEINMAN)
GRAPHIC ARTIST, PAINTER
b New York, NY. *Study:* Parsons Sch Design, cert, 43; Silvermine Guild Ctr Arts, 79-81; Yale Univ Sch Art, with Robert Reed, 80-83. *Work:* Town of Fairfield, Conn; New Haven Paint & Clay Club, Conn; Univ Conn Health Ctr, Farmington. *Exhib:* Drawing Defined, Nat Arts Club, New York, 80; Mood of New England, Past & Present, Copley Artists, Boston, 80; Conn Invitational Exhib, Slater Mem Mus, Norwich, Conn, 81; solo exhib, Vassos Gallery, Silvermine Guild Ctr, Conn, 82; Conn Painters & Sculptors Ann, Stamford Mus, Conn, 83; Audubon Artists 41st Ann, Nat Arts Club, New York, 83. *Awards:* Best in Show, Summer Showcase, Ridgefield Guild Artists, 79; Silvermine Guild Award, 32nd New England Exhib, 81; Sharon Ortlip Mem Award, Sixth Open Show, Salmagundi Club, New York, 83. *Bibliog:* Kathie Beals (auth), Mamaroneck artists show, Westchester Weekend, 4/79; Betty Tyler (auth), People in the arts, Bridgeport Sunday Post, 2/82; Paula Reens (auth), Silvermine 60th anniversary, Art New Eng, 10/82. *Mem:* Silvermine Guild Ctr Arts; New Haven Paint & Clay Club; Conn Women Artists; Nat League Am Pen Women. *Media:* Pencil, Silverpoint. *Mailing Add:* 450 Holy Dale Rd Fairfield CT 06430

CHALKE, JOHN
CERAMIST, SCULPTOR
b Gloucestershire, Eng, Sept 28, 40; Can citizen. *Study:* Bath Acad of Art, Wiltshire, Eng, teacher's cert art educ, 62. *Work:* Esso Resources; Massey Found; Alta Art Found; Can Coun Art Bank. *Exhib:* Int Ceramics Exhib, Faenza, Italy, 70; Int Exhib of Ceramics, Victoria & Albert Mus, London, Eng, 72; Int Ceramics Exhib, Calgary, Alta, 73; 5th Int Ceramics Exhib, Vallauris, France, 76; 35th Concorso Int Della Ceramica d'Arte, Faenza, Italy, 77; and others. *Teaching:* Instr ceramics, var art schs in Southern Eng, 64-68; instr visual fundamentals, Univ Alta, Edmonton, 71-76; instr, Univ Calgary, Alta, currently. *Awards:* Avant-Garde Award, Can Crafts Exhib, Toronto, 70; Award of Excellence, Can Olympic Exhib, Montreal, 76; Dipl d'Honneur, 5th Int Ceramics Exhib, Vallauris, 76. *Bibliog:* E Lewenstein (auth), New Ceramics, Van Nostrand Reinhold, 75; R Fournier (auth), Illustrated Dictionary of Practical Ceramics, Van Nostrand Reinhold, 73; C Tyler (auth), Low-Fire Ceramics, 77. *Mem:* Acad Italia; Int Acad of Ceramics; Can Crafts Coun; Alta Crafts Coun; Alta Potter's Asn. *Media:* Clay. *Mailing Add:* 429 12th St NW Calgary AB T2N 1Y9 Canada

CHALLIS, RICHARD BRACEBRIDGE
DEALER
b London, Eng, Aug 12, 20. *Study:* King's Col Sch, London, 34-37; Chelsea Col, 38-39. *Collections Arranged:* Roger Kutz Retrospective, Laguna Beach Mus Art, Calif, 77. *Pos:* Founder & dir, Challis Galleries, 50-82, consultant, 83-; art dir, Los Angeles Home Show, 65-67. *Teaching:* Lectr, Marketing of Fine Art, Orange Co Dept Educ. *Mem:* Laguna Beach Mus Art; life mem Laguna Beach Fest Arts. *Specialty:* 20th century paintings and sculpture, representing R A Benson, Gerald Brommer, Philip Dike, Robert Frame, John Leeper, Frank M Hamilton & Polia Pillin. *Mailing Add:* 1390 S Coast Hwy Laguna Beach CA 92651

CHALMERS, E LAURENCE, JR
ADMINISTRATOR
b Wildwood, NJ, Mar 24, 28. *Study:* Princeton Univ, AB(psychol), 48, MA(exp psychol), 50, PhD(exp psychol), 51. *Pos:* Dean, Col Arts & Sci, Fla State Univ, 64-66, vpres, Acad Affairs, 66-69; chancellor, Univ Kans, 69-72; pres, Art Inst Chicago, 72- *Mailing Add:* Art Inst Chicago Michigan at Adams Chicago IL 60603

CHAMBERLAIN, CHARLES
CERAMIST, EDUCATOR
b Brockton, Mass, Aug 7, 42. *Study:* Mass Col Art, BFA; Col Ceramics, Alfred Univ, MFA. *Work:* Smithsonian Inst, Washington, DC; Archie Bray Found, Helena, Mont; Mass Col Art, Boston; Col Ceramics, Alfred Univ, NY. *Exhib:* Soc Arts & Crafts, Boston, 65; Artist, Craftsmen, Inst Art, Jacksonville, Fla, 73; one-man retrospective, NC Mus Art, Raleigh, 73; 27th Ceramics Nat, Everson Mus, Syracuse, NY, 74; Craft Multiples, Smithsonian Inst, Washington, DC, 75. *Pos:* Jury mem, Piedmont Craftsmen, Winston-Salem, NC, 74- *Teaching:* Instr ceramics, Worcester Art Ctr, Mass, 65; instr ceramics, Univ NH, 66-67; chmn art dept & assoc prof ceramics, East Carolina Univ, Greenville, NC, 67-82, chmn design dept, 82- *Awards:* Best in Show, Mass Assoc Craftsmen, 65; Merit Award, Emerging Craftsmen of New Eng, 65; Hon Mention, Piedmont Craftsmen Ann, 71. *Mem:* Piedmont Craftsmen; Carolina Designer Craftsmen; Am Crafts Coun. *Dealer:* Piedmont Craftsmen 300 S Main St Winston-Salem NC 27101. *Mailing Add:* 2307 E Third St Greenville NC 27834

CHAMBERLAIN, DAVID (ALLEN)
SCULPTOR
b Canton, Ohio, Aug 11, 49. *Study:* Princeton Univ, with Joe Brown & James Seawright, BA(archit design), 71; Colo Col, 72; Univ Pa, with Robert Engman & Neil Welliver, MFA(sculpture), 77. *Comn:* Sculpture (mahogany), Babson Col, Mass, 81. *Exhib:* Solo exhibs, Pucker-Safrai Gallery, Boston, 81, Gallery on the Green, Lexington, Mass, 82, Everson Mus Art, 83, New Acquisitions Gallery, Syracuse, NY, 83 & Concord Art Asn, Mass, 83; LaGrange Nat VII, Ga, 82; From Jerusalem to Boston, Mitchell Mus Art, Mt Vernon, Ill, 83. *Teaching:* Co-dir & artist in residence, Arts Col House Prog, Univ Pa, 75-77. *Awards:* Haas Fund Award, 74-75; Venture Fund Grant, Ford Found & Univ Pa, 75-77; Red Ribbon Award, Am Film Festival, 82. *Bibliog:* Margaret Wilson (auth), article, Art New England, 82; Thomas Piche (auth), Chamberlain's works compel, Syracuse Herald-Am, 83; Chamberlain at the Everson (film), WNPE-WNPI TV, Watertown, NY, 83. *Mem:* Artists Equity; Am Crafts Coun; Concord Art Asn. *Media:* Bronze, Marble. *Mailing Add:* c/o Pucker-Safrai Gallery 171 & 173 Newbury St Boston MA 02116

CHAMBERLAIN, JOHN ANGUS
SCULPTOR

b Rochester, Ind, Apr 16, 27. *Study:* Art Inst Chicago, 50-52; Univ Ill; Black Mountain Col, 55-56. *Work:* Albright-Knox Gallery, Buffalo, NY; Los Angeles Co Mus Art; Guggenheim Mus, Mus Mod Art, New York; Dallas Mus Fine Arts; and others. *Exhib:* One-man shows, Guggenheim Mus, New York, 71 & Galerie Heiner Friedrich, Cologne, 79; York Univ, Toronto, Ont, 69; Guggenheim Mus, 71; Painting & Sculpture Today, Indianapolis Mus Art, 72; Large Scale Sculpture Show, Pratt Inst, 74; Materials of Art: Plastic, Joseloff Gallery, Univ Hartford, 77; Art & the Automobile, Flint Inst Art, Mich, 78; Auto Icons, Whitney Mus Am Art, 79; and others. *Awards:* Guggenheim Fels, 66 & 77. *Bibliog:* Sam Hunter (ed), New Art Around the World: Painting & Sculpture, Abrams, 66; Wayne Craven (auth), Sculpture in America, Crowell, 68; Gregory Battcock (ed), Minimal Art: A Critical Anthology, Dutton, 68; and others. *Mailing Add:* 222 Bowery New York NY 10013

CHAMBERS, BRUCE WILLIAM
DEALER, HISTORIAN

b Cincinnati, Ohio, June 22, 41. *Study:* Yale Univ, BA, 63; Univ Rochester, MA, 70; Univ Pa, PhD, 74. *Collections Arranged:* Selections from the Robert P Coggins Collection of American Painting (auth, catalog), Univ Rochester, 76; Charles Burchfield: The Charles Rand Penney Collection (coauth, catalog), Smithsonian Inst, 78; Uncommon Visions (coauth, catalog), Univ Rochester, 79; David Gilmour Blythe, 1815-65 (auth, catalog), Nat Collection Fine Arts, 80. *Pos:* Asst dir curatorial serv, Mem Art Gallery, Univ Rochester, 76-, actg dir, 79-80; dir, Univ Iowa Mus Art, 80-81; assoc, Berry-Hill Galleries, New York, 82- *Teaching:* Asst prof art hist, Emory Univ, Atlanta, 70-76; adj prof, Univ Rochester, NY, 76-80. *Mem:* Col Art Asn; Am Asn Mus; Northeast Mus Conf; NY State Coun Arts. *Res:* Nineteenth and twentieth century American art and iconography. *Publ:* Auth, American Paintings in the High Museum of Art, High Mus Art, 75; auth, Pythagorean puzzle of Patrick Lyon, Art Bulletin, 6/76; auth, Thomas Cole and the ruined tower, Currier Gallery Bulletin, 11/83; auth, Continuities: American Figure Painting, 1900-1950, Berry-Hill Galleries, 83. *Mailing Add:* c/o Berry-Hill Galleries 743 Fifth Ave New York NY 10022

CHAMBERS, KAREN
HISTORIAN, CRITIC

b Madison, Ind, Sept 28, 48. *Study:* Wittenberg Univ, 66-70, BFA, 73; Case-Western Reserve Univ, study with Wolfgang Stechow; Univ Cincinnati, MA, 78. *Pos:* Cur asst, Dayton Art Inst, Ohio, 70-73; asst registr, Cincinnati Art Mus, 75; asst cur, Contemp Arts Ctr, Cincinnati, 75-77; asst dir, Sperone Westwater Fischer, New York, 77-79; asst dir, Droll/Kolbert, New York, 79-80; dir, Susan Caldwell, 81; ed, New Work, 83- *Mem:* Col Art Asn; Am Asn Mus; Glass Art Soc. *Res:* Glass arts. *Specialty:* Contemporary. *Publ:* Auth & ed, Selections from the Collection of the Vent Haven Museum, Contemp Arts Ctr, 77; auth, Jane Reece's portraits of artists, Exposure, 79; auth, Mission: Impossible--Dale Chihuli, spring 83 & Howard Ben Tre: An artist in time, summer-fall 83, New Work; auth, Fragments, Tangeman Ctr Fine Arts Gallery, Univ Cincinnati, 83. *Mailing Add:* 1 Sheridan St New York NY 10014

CHAMBERS, PARK A, JR
SCULPTOR, PAINTER

b Wheeling, WVa, Oct 29, 42. *Study:* Kent State Univ, BFA, 68, MFA, 70. *Work:* The Chicago-Tokyo Bank & Shatkin Trading Company, Chicago, Ill; Johnson & Johnson, Elmhurst, Ill; Kent State Univ, Ohio. *Comn:* Wrist Sculpture, comn by Fred Gordon, Skokie, Ill, 73; Installation/Performance, Focus on the Arts, Highland Park, Ill, 75. *Exhib:* 51st Ann, The Cleveland Mus Art, Ohio, 69; 22nd Ann, Butler Inst Am Art, Youngstown, Ohio, 70; Form in Fiber, Deson-Zaks Gallery, Chicago, Ill, 72; Sculpture in New Media, Ill State Mus, Springfield, 73; Fiber Forms, Cincinnati Art Mus, Ohio, 78; Fiber as Art, Metrop Mus, Manila, Philippines, 80. *Collections Arranged:* 6 X 6 Exhib, SAIC Gallery, 77. *Pos:* Juror, Univ Chicago, Ill, 72; lectr, Mus Contemp Art, 72; artist-in-residence, Highland Park High Sch, Ill, 74-75. *Teaching:* Instr metal & fiber, Kent State Univ, Ohio, 68-69; instr fiber, Akron Art Inst, Ohio, 69-70; assoc prof fiber & mixed media, Art Inst Chicago, Ill, 70- *Awards:* Research Grant, Kent State Univ Grad Sch, 69; Experiment Materials, Brunswick Corporation, Chicago, Ill, 69; Individual Grant, Nat Endowment Arts, 76. *Bibliog:* Judith Russi Kirshner (auth), The Art Gallery Mag, New York, 72; Franz Schulze (auth), Chicago Daily News, 72; Robert Glauber (auth), Skyline, Chicago, 72. *Media:* Rope, Wood; Photo Images, Gels. *Publ:* Contribr, Decorative Art in Modern Interiors, Studio Vista Limited, London, 71; contribr, Techniques of Rya Knotting, Van Nostrand Reinhold Co, 71; contribr, Soft Sculpture, Crown Publishers, 74; contribr, How to Create Your Own Designs, Doubleday & Co, 75; contribr, Hardcore Crafts, Ballantine Books, 76. *Mailing Add:* 95 Spring St Albany NY 12210

CHAN, PHILLIP PAANG
PAINTER, EDUCATOR

b Canton, China, July 11, 46; US citizen. *Study:* San Jose State Univ; Univ Calif, Berkeley, AB, 71; MFA, 76. *Exhib:* Third World Painting & Sculpture Exhib, San Francisco Mus Art, Calif, 74; All Iowa Artist Show, Des Moines Art Ctr, 78; Kans Generation Installation, Kans State Univ, Manhattan, 79; Mass Arts Fel Show, Artist Found, Boston, Mass, 80; Southeast Invitational Drawing Show, Huntsville Mus Art, Ala, 81; Five Views, Weber State Col, Ogden, Utah, 83. *Teaching:* Asst prof painting, Univ Northern Iowa, 77-78; Kans State Univ, 78-79; Long Beach State Univ, spring 82 & Univ Vt, fall 83; vis artist painting, Univ NC, 80-81; instr, State Univ NY, Purchase, 82-83. *Awards:* Summer Seminar Fel, Nat Endowment Humanities, 78 & 83;

Individual Artist Grant, Nat Endowment Arts, 79; Visual Fel, Fine Arts Work Ctr, 79. *Bibliog:* Robert Pineus (auth), Entries: Two cautionary tails, Arts Mag, 6/83. *Mem:* Col Art Asn Am. *Mailing Add:* 5225 Edgeworth San Diego CA 92109

CHANDLER, ELISABETH GORDON
SCULPTOR

b St Louis, Mo, June 10, 13. *Study:* Pvt study with Edmondo Quattrocchi; Art Students League, anat. *Work:* Columbia Univ Sch Law; Princeton Univ Sch Pub & Int Affairs & James Forrestal Res Ctr; Aircraft Carrier USS Forrestal; Gov Dummer Acad Libr; Storm King Art Ctr, Mountainville, NY. *Comn:* Bust of Owen R Cheatham, Founder, Georgia Pac Corp, bust of Albert A Michelson, Hall of Fame for Great Americans, NY Univ, 73; Adlai E Stevenson High Sch, 74; Messiah Col, Grantham, Pa, 75; statue of Queen Anne, Queen Anne's Co Courthouse Sq, Centerville, Md, 77. *Exhib:* Mattatuck Mus, Waterbury Conn, 49; Nat Acad Design Ann, New York, 50-83; Nat Sculpture Soc Ann, 53-83; Allied Artists Am, New York, 61-82; Smithsonian Inst, Washington, DC, 63; and others. *Pos:* Dir, Coun Am Artist Soc, 71-73; trustee, Lyme Acad Fine Arts, 76- *Teaching:* Instr portrait sculpture, Lyme Acad Fine Arts, Old Lyme, Conn, 76- *Awards:* Dessie Greer Prize, Nat Acad Design, 79; Tallix Foundry Award, Nat Sculpture Soc, 79; Gold Medal, Allied Artists Am, 82; and others; and others. *Mem:* Fel Nat Sculpture Soc (rec secy, 73-76); fel Am Artists Prof League (dir, 71-73); Nat Acad Design; Nat Sculpture Rev; Lyme Art Asn; and others. *Media:* Bronze, Marble. *Mailing Add:* Mill Pond Lane Old Lyme CT 06371

CHANDLER, JOHN WILLIAM
PAINTER, EDUCATOR

b Concord, NH, Sept 28, 10. *Study:* Exeter Sch Art, Boston; Manchester Inst Arts & Sci; St Anselm's Col, AB; Boston Univ, EdM(scholar), 60; Harvard Univ; Columbia Univ; study in Europe & with Aldro T Hibbard. *Exhib:* Pasadena Nat, 46; Currier Gallery Art Regional, 47; one-man show, Keene State Col, 51; De Cordova & Dana Mus, 52; Nebr Wesleyan Univ, 58. *Pos:* From asst to dir to actg dir, Currier Gallery Art, 42-52. *Teaching:* Exec dir & instr design & painting, Manchester Inst Arts & Sci, 33-44; assoc prof art & head dept, Lycoming Col, 52-70; instr painting, Concord Artists, Inc, 71-72; instr, Studio II, 72- *Awards:* First Watercolor Award, Currier Gallery Art, 47; Danforth Found Award, 52. *Mem:* Founding mem Concord Artists; charter mem NH Art Asn. *Publ:* Author various articles on glass & silver. *Mailing Add:* 2 Coolidge Ave Concord NH 03301

CHANNING, SUSAN ROSE
ADMINISTRATOR, PHOTOGRAPHER

b Englewood, NJ, Aug 16, 43. *Study:* Pa State Univ, BA(fine arts) & BA(gen arts & sci), 65; George Washington Univ, MFA, 67. *Work:* Polaroid Corp. *Exhib:* Eighteenth Ann Corcoran Gallery of Art Area Show, Washington, DC, 67; Camera Movements, Moore Col Art Gallery, Philadelphia, 83. *Collections Arranged:* Design in Transit, State Subway Station Competition, 71 & Points of View, Recent Work By Area Photographers (auth, catalog), 72, Inst of Contemp Art, Boston; Photography Fellowship Recipients, Enjay Gallery, Boston, 76; Prints & Drawings, Frank Tanzer Gallery, Boston, 77; Art of the State, Recipients & Finalists in Painting, Printmaking & Drawing, Rose Art Mus, Brandeis Univ, Waltham, Mass, 77 & 79; Photography Fellowship Recipients, Mass Inst of Technol Creative Photog Gallery, Cambridge, Mass, 78; and others. *Pos:* Performing arts prog coordr & art instr, Wadsworth Atheneum, Hartford, Conn, 68-70; dir urban action prog & spec proj, Inst Contemp Art, Boston, 70-72; asst dir, Mass Coun Arts & Humanities, Boston, 72-73; dir artists fel prog, Artists Found Inc, Boston, 73-82; consult, WGBH New TV Workshop, Boston, 78-79; dir, Prints in Progress, Philadelphia, 83- *Teaching:* Instr photog & serigraphy, Wadsworth Atheneum, Hartford, Conn, 68-70. *Publ:* Auth & ed, Art of the State--Massachusetts Photographers 1975-1977, Addison House, 78; ed, The Leather District and the Fort Point Channel, Artists Found, 82. *Mailing Add:* Prints in Progress 1406 Spruce St Philadelphia PA 19102

CHAPIAN, GRIEG HOVSEP
PAINTER, CONSERVATOR

b Varna, Bulgaria, May 27, 13; US citizen. *Study:* Cooper Union, 30-31; Nat Acad Design, 31-36, with Leon Kroll, Karl Anderson, Charles C Curran, Arthur S Covey, Francis Scott Bradford, Jr, Gifford Beal, Charles S Chapman & Ivan Olinsky. *Work:* Univ Eastern NMex; NMex State Fair Permanent Collection, Albuquerque. *Comn:* Two murals for Auto Racing Syndicate, Johannesburg, SAfrica, 39. *Exhib:* Pa Acad Fine Arts, Philadelphia, 37; NMex State Fair Art Exhib, Albuquerque, 71; Grand Nat Exhib, Am Artists Prof League, New York, 72; Int Art Show, Univ Eastern NMex, Portales, 75; Bicenntenial Art Show, Am Artists Prof League, New York, 76; Mountain Rd Galleries, Albuquerque, 83. *Pos:* Founder & dir, Albuquerque Inst Art, 74- *Teaching:* Dir hist art & landscape, Murray Art Schs, Scranton & Wilkes-Barre, Pa, 48-50; dean & dir figure drawing & painting, Cooper Sch Art, Cleveland, 50-55; dean fashion illus & philos of art, Pan-Am Art Sch, New York, 60-66. *Awards:* Grand Prize & First for Oils, Local One, CIO, 44; First for Oils & Best of Show for Graphics, NMex Art League, 69; Purchase Prize, NMex State Fair, 74. *Bibliog:* Louise Bruner (auth), Commercial shows now rival fine art, Cleveland News, 12/15/51; Flo Wilks (auth), Magic realism in noted artist's work reflects his wide range of interests, Albuquerque J, 6/14/70; Lynn B Villella (auth), Chapian work top winner, Albuquerque Tribune, 9/12/74. *Mem:* Am Artists Prof League; Southwest Watercolor Soc; Artists Equity Asn (pres, 73-74); Nat Art League; NMex Art League (mem bd dirs, 69-71). *Dealer:* Sussman Arthur Gallery Galeria 40 First Plaza Albuquerque NM 87102. *Mailing Add:* 1850 Gretta St NE Albuquerque NM 87112

CHAPLIN, GEORGE EDWIN
PAINTER, EDUCATOR

b Kew Gardens, NY, Aug 30, 31. *Study:* Yale Univ Sch Art, with Josef Albers, BFA & MFA. *Work:* Yale Univ Gallery; State Univ NY Col Cortland; Trinity Col, Conn. *Exhib:* Univ Conn, 74; Dept of State, Washington, DC, 76-80; New Britain Mus, Conn, 77; Mattatuck Mus, Waterbury, Conn, 78; Kent Sch Gallery, Conn, 80; Vassos Gallery, Silvermine Guild, Conn, 81; and others. *Teaching:* Head dept painting, Silvermine Col Art, 65-71; dir studio prog, Trinity Col, Hartford, Conn, 72-; prof fine arts, 78- *Awards:* David G Lyon Award, 31st New England Ann, Conn, 81; Faber Birren Award, 1st Ann Faber Birren Color Award Exhib, Stamford Art Asn, Conn, 81. *Media:* Oil; Pastel. *Mailing Add:* Box 488 ORS Oxford CT 06483

CHAPMAN, (M) ANNE
SCULPTOR, EDUCATOR

b Cleveland, Ohio, Oct 14, 30. *Study:* Cleveland Inst Art, BFA, 52; Cranbrook Acad Art, MFA, 54, post-grad, 55. *Work:* Cleveland Mus Art, Ohio; Everson Mus Art, Syracuse, NY; Univ Med & Dentistry, Rutgers Med Sch, NJ; Univ Art Mus, Univ NMex, Albuquerque; Utah Mus Fine Arts, Salt Lake City. *Comn:* The Four Elements (fountain, with Brian Watkins), Class of 1970, Montclair State Col, NJ, 77. *Exhib:* Women Artists 78, City Univ New York Grad Ctr, 78; North of New Brunswick--South of New York, Robeson Gallery, Rutgers Univ, NJ, 81; Paperworks 81, Ralph Wilson Gallery, Lehigh Univ, Pa, 81; Works: Paper, Seigfred Gallery, Ohio Univ, 82; On & Off the Wall, Newark Mus, NJ, 82; and others. *Teaching:* Instr, Univ Miss, Oxford, 54-57; guest instr ceramics & ceramic sculpture, Pa State Univ, 57; asst prof, Univ Fla, Gainesville, 57-59; instr, New York Univ, 59-65; asst prof, Hampton Inst, Va, 65-66; asst prof, Montclair State Col, NJ, 66-72, assoc prof, 72-80, prof, 80-; vis artist sculpture & drawing, Univ NMex, Albuquerque, 70. *Awards:* First Prize Sculpture, 17th Annual Ceramic Nat, Everson Mus, Syracuse, NY, 52; Special Earthenware Award Sculpture, 5th Ann Miami Nat Ceramic Exhib, Fla, 57; Purchase Award, Rutgers Nat Drawing, Rutgers Univ-Camden, NJ, 77. *Bibliog:* Michael Knigin and Murray Zimiles (auth), The Contemporary Lithographic Workshop Around the World, Van Nostrand Reinhold, 74; Judith E Stein (auth), Women artists 78, Art J, 78. *Mem:* Women's Caucus Art; Printmaking Coun NJ. *Media:* Paper, Varied Media. *Mailing Add:* 530 Valley Rd Upper Montclair NJ 07043

CHAPMAN, ROBERT GORDON
JEWELER, PAINTER

b Los Angeles, Calif, 26, 41. *Study:* Ventura Col; San Jose Univ, with Fred Spratt & J Richard Sorby, BA(painting), with David Hatch, John Leary & Dr Robert Coleman, MA(jewelry design), Pupil Scrv Credential(career coun in visual arts). *Work:* Metal Arts Guild, San Francisco; San Jose State Univ Gallery; San Jose Art League. *Comn:* Moon Pendant (commemorating first lunar landing), 68; Ring, comn by David San Jose, 69; plus pendants, rings, pins & body adornment comn by various individuals. *Exhib:* Art '65, Univ Santa Clara; Calif Expos of the Arts, 66-69; Crafts 10, 67; Western US Traveling Exhib, 68; Triton Mus, Santa Clara, Calif, 69; Eastside Fac Show, 81. *Pos:* Dir, Group 21 Gallery, Los Gatos, Calif, 72-73; mem art educ screening comt, San Jose State Univ, 73-; past bd dirs, San Jose Art League. *Teaching:* Instr art & chmn dept, Piedmont Hills High Sch, San Jose, 64-74; instr jewelry & metalsmithing, West Valley Col, Saratoga, Calif, 66-; coun visual arts, Santa Teresa High Sch, San Jose, 74- *Awards:* Ellen Brucker Jewelry Award, 69; Achiever of the Year in Art, Nat Pen Women Asn, 69; San Jose Regional Art Second Award, 75. *Mem:* Metal Arts Guild San Francisco; Calif Art Educators Asn. *Media:* Aqueous Media, Organic Material, Silver, Gold. *Publ:* Auth, An Analysis of Photomicrography as a Design Source for Lost-Model Jewelry, 69. *Mailing Add:* 6060 Loma Prieta Dr San Jose CA 95123

CHAPMAN, WALTER HOWARD
PAINTER, ILLUSTRATOR

b Toledo, Ohio, Dec 7, 12. *Study:* Cleveland Inst Art; John Huntington Polytech, Cleveland; Art Students League; study portraiture with Rolf Stoll, Cleveland and figure painting with Jon Corbino, New York. *Work:* Toledo Fedn Art Collection, Toledo Mus Art; Zanesville Art Mus, Ohio; Springfield Mus Art, Mo; Univ Toledo; Toledo Trust Co, Ohio. *Comn:* Three portraits, St Vincents Hosp, Toledo, 68; landscape, Toledo Hosp, 70; five portraits, Law & Sci Bldgs, Univ Toledo, 70 & 77; Bicentennial painting, Waterville Chamber of Commerce, Ohio, 76; three portraits, First Fed Bank, Toledo, 77. *Exhib:* Watercolor USA, Springfield Mus of Art, Mo, 72; Zanesville Mus of Art, 73 & Ella Sharp Mus, Jackson, Mich, 74; Springfield Art Ctr, Ohio, 74; Mid-Yr Ann, Butler Mus of Art, Youngstown, Ohio, 75; O'Briens Art Emporium, Scottsdale, Ariz; Toni Jones Gallery, Houston, Tex; and others. *Pos:* Illusr, New York, 39-42; combat artist, US Army, 43-45; creative dir, Phillipps Assoc, Toledo, 46-; owner, Chapman Art Gallery, Sylvania, 70- *Teaching:* Instr illus, Toledo Mus Sch Design, 50-54; instr portrait & figure, Toledo Artists Club, 55-64. *Awards:* First Awards, Watercolor USA, 71 & 72; First Award, Summer Show, Salmagundi Club, New York, 72; First Prize & Purchase Award, Mainstreams Ann, Marietta Col, Ohio, 73. *Bibliog:* Murray Kalis (auth), article in Art Rev, 68. *Mem:* Allied Artists Am; Salmagundi Club; Toledo Fedn Art Soc (pres, 54-56); Ohio Watercolor Soc (bd mem, 77); NW Ohio Watercolor Soc (pres, 71-72). *Media:* Watercolor, Oil. *Publ:* Contribr (cartoons), Stars & Stripes & Railsplitte, US Army newspapers, 45; illusr, Battle of Germany, Viking Press, 46; contribr ed cartoons, Toledo Monitor, 65; contribr, Prize Winning Art, Allied Publ, 66; contribr (cover art), Exhibit Mag, 67. *Dealer:* Chapman Art Gallery 5151 S Main St Sylvania OH 43560. *Mailing Add:* 6001 Gregory Dr Sylvania OH 43560

CHAPPELL, BERKLEY WARNER
PAINTER, PRINTMAKER

b Pueblo, Colo, Mar 21, 34. *Study:* Univ Colo, BFA, 56, MFA, 58. *Work:* San Francisco Mus Art; Henry Gallery, Univ Wash, Seattle; Tacoma Mus Art, Wash; Univ BC, Vancouver; Salishan Lodge, Gleneden Beach, Ore. *Exhib:* Young West Coast Artists, Pasadena, Calif, 59; Abstract Expressionism Today, San Francisco, 60 & Landscape Painting Today, 61; Am Printmaking Today, Ger, Greece, France, 69; Grand Gallerie, Seattle, 75. *Teaching:* Asst painting, Univ Colo, 56-58; instr to asst prof painting, Univ Puget Sound, Tacoma, 58-63; asst prof to prof painting & printmaking, Ore State Univ, Corvallis, 63- *Awards:* Purchase Awards, San Francisco Art Inst, 61 & Henry Gallery, Univ Wash, 64 & 69. *Media:* Oil; Engraving. *Mailing Add:* Ore State Univ Corvallis OR 97331

CHAPPELL, MILES LINWOOD
HISTORIAN, EDUCATOR

b Norfolk, Va, June 6, 39. *Study:* Col William & Mary, BS, 60; Univ NC, Chapel Hill, with Philipp Fehl, Frances Huemer & Joseph Sloane, PhD(art hist), 71. *Collections Arranged:* Capricci di Varie Figure (auth, catalog), Survey of Printmaking, 75, Rubens in Prints (auth, catalog), 77 & Arthur Strauss and the German Expressionists (auth, catalog), 78, Col William & Mary; Disegni dei Toscani a Roma 1580-1620 (coauth, catalog), Uffizi Gallery, Florence, 79; Drawings from the Herman Collection (auth, catalog), Muscarelle Mus Art, Col William & Mary, 83. *Pos:* Assoc ed, Studies in Iconography, 76-81, ed, 81-82. *Teaching:* Assoc prof fine arts, Col William & Mary, 71-; assoc fel, Harvard Univ Ctr Italian Renaissance, Florence, 80. *Awards:* Nat Endowment Humanities Fel, 83. *Mem:* Col Art Asn Am; Southeastern Col Art Conf (mem bd dirs, 78-84); Renaissance Soc Am; Kunsthistorisches Inst, Florence. *Res:* Renaissance and Baroque art; old master drawings; British and Colonial American painting. *Publ:* Auth, Crisfofano Allori's depictions of St Francis, Burlington Mag, 71; auth, Cigori, Galileo and Invidia, 75 & John Smibert's Italian sojourn, 82, Art Bulletin; auth, Missing paintings by Cigori, Paragone, 82; auth, Identification of S Coccapani drawing collection mark, Master Drawings, 83. *Mailing Add:* Dept Fine Arts Col William & Mary Williamsburg VA 23185

CHAPPELL, WALTER (LANDON)
PHOTOGRAPHER, CURATOR

b Portland, Ore, June 8, 25. *Study:* Frank Lloyd Wright Taliesin Fel, Ariz, 53-54. *Work:* Mus Mod Art, New York; Alfred Stieglitz Ctr, Philadelphia Mus Art, Pa; George Eastman House, Mus Photog, Rochester, NY; Smithsonian Inst; Contemp Photog Collection, Univ Ariz, Tucson. *Comn:* Treepeonies on Estate, comn by William Gratwick, Pavillion, NY, 57-60; M Edmond Kara (sculpture) & portraits Richard Burton & Elizabeth Taylor, Big Sur MGM Studios, Culver City, Calif, 64; portraits Sharon Tate, Filmways, New York, 64-68. *Exhib:* Photography at Mid-Century, George Eastman House Mus, Rochester, NY, 59; The Sense of Abstraction, Mus Mod Art, New York, 60; solo exhibs, Mus de Ville de Paris, France, 72 & The New Gallery, Taos, NMex, 82; Photography in America, 74 & Texture, A Photographic Vision, 75, Whitney Mus Am Art, New York; Mirrors and Windows, Mus Mod Art, New York, 79-81; 25 Years: Retrospective, Colo Ctr Photog Art, Denver, 80. *Collections Arranged:* Return to the Bud, Minor White Retrospective, Eastman House, 59; Photography at Mid-Century, Eastman House Mus, 59; A Quest for Light: F Bruguiere, Eastman House Mus, 59; Under the Sun, Poindexter Gallery, New York, 60; Heliography 101 Prints, Lever House Gallery, 63. *Pos:* Dir exhib, Photog Workshop Inc, Denver, 55-57; co-ed, Aperture Quart, Rochester, 57-60; cur exhib, prints & traveling shows, George Eastman House Mus, 57-61; artist in residence, Volcanoes Nat Park, Volcano Art Ctr, Hawaii, 77-78. *Teaching:* Lectr & sem instr, var US locations, 72-; instr camera vision workshop, Visual Studies Workshop, Rochester, 73. *Awards:* Photog Fel in Hawaii, 77 & in NMex, 80, Nat Endowment Arts. *Bibliog:* Lyons, Labrot, Chappell Under the Sun, Brazillier, 60 & Aperture, 70; Arthur Ollman (producer), Walter Chappell (video), 77; George Shaub (auth), Poet of light, Photogr Forum, 83. *Mem:* Santa Fe Ctr Photog; Friends of Photog, Carmel, Calif; Peer Awards in Creative Photog Prog. *Res:* History of photography; psychology in human nature pertaining to image formation and expression in art. *Publ:* Auth, ed & illusr, Gestures of Infinity, Wittenborn, 57; auth & ed, Logue and Glyphs, Poems 1942 to 1951, Glyph Press, 51; contribr, Aperture Quart, 57-81; auth & illusr, Collected Light, The Body of Work, Peregrine Smith, 84. *Dealer:* Scheinbaum & Russek Gallery Photog 615 Don Felix St Santa Fe NM 87501; Photog Gallery 7468 Girard Ave La Jolla CA 92037. *Mailing Add:* PO Box 8736 Santa Fe NM 87504

CHAPPELLE, JERRY LEON
CERAMIST, SCULPTOR

b Fredericktown, Mo, Nov 14, 39. *Study:* Murray State Univ, BS; Univ Minn, MFA. *Work:* High Mus Art, Atlanta, Ga; Greenville Co Mus Art, SC; Ga Coun Arts; La Sch Visual Impaired, Baton Rouge, La. *Comn:* Ceramic mural, Sally Julius Mem, Miller Libr, La Plume, Pa, 80; ceramic & stucco mural, St Gregory's Episcopal Church, Athens, Ga, 81. *Exhib:* Nat Ceramic Arts Exhib, Flagstaff, Ariz, 73; Fun and Fantasy, Xerox Corp Gallery, Rochester, NY, 73; Regional Invitational, Gallery Contemp Art, Winston-Salem, NC, 75; Hopkins Gallery Art, Ohio State Univ, Columbus, 80; Greenville Co Mus Art, SC, 81. *Pos:* Dir, Scorpio Rising Workshops, 70-77; vis artist, Ohio State Univ, winter 80. *Teaching:* Instr ceramics, Univ Minn, 69-70; asst prof ceramics, Univ Ga, 70-76. *Awards:* Two First Prizes, Atlanta Arts Comt, 75; Second Prize, Covington Arts Exhib, Covington Art Ctr, 74. *Bibliog:* Larry Smith (auth), Ceramic Art (film), Univ Ga, 74; Evolution of the Artist Craftsman in Georgia, Highlight of Contemporary Ceramics (film), Ga NEA-TV, 74. *Mem:* Am Crafts Coun; Piedmont Craftsmen Inc. *Media:* Clay, Glass. *Mailing Add:* Rte 3 Box 278 Farmington GA 30638

CHARLES, DURANT See Rizzie, Dan

CHARLES-SMITH, DONALD
PRINTMAKER, PAINTER
b Dexter, Mo, July 10, 35. *Study:* Univ Mo, BA & MA; Santa Reparata Graphic Art Ctr, Florence, Italy; also painting with Fred Conway & printmaking with Mauricio Lasansky. *Work:* Am Broadcasting Corp; Spiva Art Ctr, Joplin, Mo; Santa Reparata Stamperia d'Arte Grafica, Florence. *Exhib:* One-man shows, NW Mo State Univ, Maryville, 63, RI Col, 69, Wheelock Col, 71 & Lowell State Univ, 83; RI Painters Ann, RI Sch Design Mus, 82; and others. *Pos:* Dir, Spiva Art Ctr, Joplin, Mo, 60-64. *Teaching:* Prof painting, drawing & printmaking, RI Col, 64- *Awards:* Univ Fel, Univ Mo, 58; Faculty Res Grant, RI Col, 83-84. *Media:* Oil, Etching. *Publ:* Auth, Edwin Dickinson, draftsman/painter, Arts New England, 7-8/82. *Dealer:* Allan Stone Gallery 48 East 86th St New York NY 10028. *Mailing Add:* 132 Pine Hill Ave Johnston RI 02919

CHARLESWORTH, SARAH E
PHOTOGRAPHER, CONCEPTUAL ARTIST
b East Orange, NJ, Mar 29, 47. *Study:* Barnard Col, BA, 69. *Work:* Allen Mem Art Mus, Oberlin Col; Stedelijk Van Abbemuseum, Eindhoven, Holland. *Exhib:* Venice Biennale, Italy, 76; New York, New Wave, PS1, Long Island City, 81; solo exhib, Cepa Gallery, Buffalo, NY, 82; Art and Media, a Fatal Attraction, Renaissance Soc, Chicago, 82; Art and Social Change USA, Allen Mem Art Mus, Oberlin Col, 83. *Teaching:* Instr photog, NY Univ, 83- *Awards:* Creative Artists Pub Serv Fel, 77; Nat Endowment Arts Fel, 80 & 83. *Publ:* Contribr, Art in Am, 79 & Art Forum, 82; auth, A Lovers Tale, Wedge Press, 84. *Dealer:* Tony Shafrazi Mercer St New York NY 10012. *Mailing Add:* 591 Broadway New York NY 10012

CHARLOT, MARTIN DAY
PAINTER, MURALIST
b Athens, Ga, Mar 6, 44. *Work:* Bishop Mus, Honolulu. *Comn:* Murals, Hawaii State Sr Ctr, 78, Waipahu High Sch, 80, Kauai Intake Ctr, 80, Ala Moama Ctr, 83 & McDonalds, Kameohr, 83. *Exhib:* One-man shows, De Mena Gallery, New York, 67, Hawaii State Libr, Honolulu, 72, Volcano Art Ctr, 76, Contemp Arts Ctr, Hawaii, 79 & Kauai Libr, 80; and others. *Pos:* Illusr, Collins Assoc, New York, 69; art dir, Bravura Films, Mountain View, Calif, 70. *Teaching:* Lectr art & film, Univ Hawaii, 62-; lectr filmmaking, St John's Univ, 69; teacher cinema, Honolulu Acad Arts, 70; artist in residence, Doe Sch Syst, Hawaii, 75. *Mem:* Hawaii Painters & Sculptors League; Hawaii Film Bd. *Media:* Acrylic, Oil. *Publ:* Illusr, Mystery on the Rancho Grande, Young Scott Bks, 69; illusr & contribr, Our Hawaiian Music, 71; auth & illusr, Once Upon a Fishhook, 72 & Sunnyside Up, 72 & illusr, Felisa, 73, Island Heritage Press. *Mailing Add:* PO Box 161 Kaneohe HI 96744

CHARMATZ, BILL (WILLIAM ADOLPHE)
ILLUSTRATOR, PAINTER
b New York, NY, Nov 15, 25. *Study:* Ecole Beaux Arts, Paris, 49; Ecole Grande Chaumiere, Paris, 51-52. *Comn:* Mural, Union DC 37, New York, 75. *Exhib:* Art Dirs Club, New York, 49-79; Soc Illusr, New York, 47-79; Am Inst Graphic Art, New York, 65-68 & 73-76; solo exhib, Soc Illusr, New York, 78. *Teaching:* Instr, Sch Visual Arts, New York, 63-68. *Bibliog:* Ernst Lehrner (auth), Bill Charmatz's line, Publimondial, Paris, 50; Kichi Okasaki (auth), Bill Charmatz, Idea, Tokyo, 65; Jo Yanow (auth), Bill Charmatz, Graphics Today, 79. *Mem:* Soc Illusr; Am Inst Graphic Arts; Graphic Artists Guild (vpres, 76-78). *Media:* Ink, Gouache. *Publ:* Auth & illusr, The Little Duster, 69, auth & illusr, The Cat's Whiskers, 73 & auth & illusr, Troy Street Bus, 77, Macmillan; co-auth & illusr, My Darling Mao, Grosset & Dunlap, 70; auth & illusr, Endeerments, Ballantine, 72. *Dealer:* Arthur Brown & Bro Inc 2 West 46th St New York NY 10036. *Mailing Add:* 25 West 68th St New York NY 10023

CHASE, ALICE ELIZABETH
EDUCATOR, WRITER
b Ware, Mass, Apr 13, 06. *Study:* Radcliffe Col, with G H Edgell & P J Sachs, AB; Yale Univ, with Henri Focillon, Sumner Crosby & G H Hamilton, MA. *Pos:* Cur educ, Brooklyn Mus, 46-47. *Teaching:* Docent, Art Gallery, Yale Univ, 31-70, asst prof hist art, 46-70, emer prof, 70- *Awards:* Citations, Wilson Col & Radcliffe Col, 69. *Mem:* Archaeol Inst Am; Col Art Asn Am. *Publ:* Auth, Famous Paintings, An Introduction to Art for Young People, 51, 61 & 62 & Famous Artists of the Past, 64, Platt; auth, Looking at Art, Crowell, 66 & 74. *Mailing Add:* 18 Pleasant St Ware MA 01082

CHASE, ALLAN (SEAMANS)
SCULPTOR, MURALIST
Study: Univ Ga, BFA. *Comn:* Brass on steel, Sherwood Theatre, Gainesville, Ga, 66 & Oxford Chem Co, Atlanta, 67; welded steel, Woodward Acad, College Park, Atlanta, 68; 17 steel & polyester murals, Fla, 71-75. *Exhib:* 5th Biennial Nat Relig Art Exhib, Bloomfield, Mich, 66; Southeastern Ann Exhib, Atlanta, 66 & 68; Piedmont Park Arts Festival, Atlanta, 66-72; Mus Arts & Sci, Macon, Ga, 67; C & S Bank, Atlanta, 75. *Pos:* Designer, Gi-Gi's Restaurants, Fla & Rochester, NY, 65- *Teaching:* Instr, DeKalb Community Col, 80-81. *Media:* Steel, Other Metals; Relief Painting on Hardboard. *Dealer:* La Gallarie St Onge 3340 Peachtree Rd NE Atlanta GA 30326; Greenbrier Art Colony White Sulphur Springs WV. *Mailing Add:* 3779 Vermont Rd NE 3317 Piedmont Rd NE Atlanta GA 30319

CHASE, DORIS (TOTTEN)
FILMMAKER, VIDEO ARTIST
b Seattle, Wash, Apr 29, 23. *Study:* Univ Wash; also with Mark Tobey. *Work:* Mus Mod Art, Kobe, Japan; Art Inst Chicago; Smithsonian Inst; Nat Collection Fine Arts, Washington, DC; Mus Fine Arts, Boston; and many others. *Comn:* Monumental kinetic sculpture, Expo '70, Osaka, Japan, Atlanta Sculpture Park, Ga, Kerry Park, Seattle, Wash, four ballets, Seattle Opera Asn, Wash & Lakeside Park, Anderson, Ind. *Exhib:* One-man shows, Western Mus Asn Circulating Exhib, 70-72 & Henry Gallery, Univ Wash, Seattle, 71 & 78; Wadsworth Atheneum, Hartford, Conn, 73; Metrop Mus Art, New York, 74; Kennedy Ctr, 77; Univ Mich, Ann Arbor, 77 & 80; Calif Palace Legion Hon, 78; Hirshhorn Mus, 77; Mus Mod Art, New York, 78 & 81; Georges Pompidou Ctr, Paris, 82 & 83; AIR Gallery, New York, 83. *Awards:* Am Film Festival Awards, 72 & 79; Nat Endowment for Arts Fel, 76; NY State Coun Arts Grant, 80. *Bibliog:* Articles in Newsweek, 7/3/78, New York Times, 3/18/81 & Videography, 9/81. *Mem:* Women/Artist/Filmmakers (pres, 78); Asn Independent Video & Filmmakers; NY Film Coun. *Publ:* (Films), Circlis II, 72, Doris Chase Dance Series, 72-81, Dance Frame, 78, Jazz Dance, 79 & Doris Chase Concepts Series, 81-83. *Dealer:* Women Make Movies 19 W 21st St New York NY 10010; Erica Williams/Ann Johnson Gallery 3650 42nd NE Seattle WA 98105. *Mailing Add:* c/o Chelsey Hotel 222 W 23rd New York NY 10011

CHASE, JACK S(PAULDING)
SCULPTOR
b Burlington, Vt, Mar 4, 41. *Study:* US Military Acad, BS, 63; Univ Vt, Burlington, MS, 72. *Work:* Cathedral Church St Paul, Burlington, Vt. *Comn:* Assemblage, US Army Topographic Labs, Ft Belvoir, Va, 75; bronze tree, Heckler & Koch, Arlington, Va, 81; steel mobile, Security Arms Co, McLean, Va, 82; bronze mem trophy, Lake Champlain Yacht Club, Shelburne, Vt, 83; bronze tree, comn by Bishop Harvey Butterfield, South Burlington, Vt, 83. *Exhib:* Nat Vietnam Mem Design Winners, Am Inst Archit, Washington, DC, 81; Regional Exhib, Hopkins Ctr, Hanover, NH, 81; 33rd Nat Exhib, Wind River Valley, Dubois, Wyo, 81; 34th Ann Exhib, Am Veterans Soc Artists, New York, 81-82; NAm Sculpture Exhib, Foothills Art Ctr, Golden, Colo, 81 & 82. *Pos:* Owner, Chase Welded Sculpture, Jericho, Vt, 73-; ed, Soundings, Champlain Maritime Soc, 80-; co-owner & partner, Birch Pond Sculpture, Jericho, Vt, 82- *Awards:* Colonel Marshall Lefferts Award, Centennial Exhib, Seventh New York Regiment, 80; Most Popular Sculpture Award, Exhib Vt Artists, Norwich Univ, 80 & 82; Phillippe Citation Distinguished Pub Serv Art, Gen Electric Found, 82. *Bibliog:* Maggie Maurice (auth), Vietnam and Vermont, Free Press, 81; Donna Iverson (auth), Chase unveils project, News, 82 & Donna Carpenter (auth), Yankee artist, Monogram, 83, Gen Electric Co. *Mem:* Artists Equity; Am Veterans Soc Artists; Vt Coun Arts. *Media:* Welded Steel, Bronze. *Publ:* Coauth, The Phoenix, Champlain Maritime Soc, 81. *Dealer:* Barbara Gilmore 9 Piedmont Dr Rutland VT 05701. *Mailing Add:* RFD 1 Snipe Island Rd Jericho VT 05465

CHASE, JEANNE NORMAN
PAINTER, EDUCATOR
b Spokane, Wash, Feb 15, 29. *Study:* Calif State Col, BFA, 59. *Work:* LaGrange Col, Ga; Ringling Sch Art & Design. *Exhib:* Contemporary Am Art, Soc Four Arts, Palm Beach, 76, 78, 80, 81 & 83; 18th Ann El Paso Mus Painting Exhib; Group Invitational, Columbus Mus Art, Ga; Joan Miro Drawing Exhib, Miro Mus, Barcelona, Spain; Tex Traveling Exhib, Laguna Gloria Mus, Austin; and others. *Teaching:* Instr figure drawing & painting & chmn fine arts, Ringling Sch Art, Fla, 79- *Awards:* First Prize, Southeastern Art Exhib, 76; Merit Awards, Longboat Art Ctr Nat & Daytona Mus Art, 79. *Bibliog:* Linda Sherbert (auth), She sees subjects larger than life, Ft Lauderdale News, 76; Lorraine Huber (auth), Jeanne Norman Chase, painter, Fiesta Mag, 76. *Mem:* Am Prof Artist League; Artists Equity; Women's Caucus Arts; Fla Artists Group. *Media:* Pencil, Oil. *Publ:* Auth, Drawing in another dimension, Design Mag, 76; auth, Step by step painting, Palette Talk, 84. *Mailing Add:* 1602 Bay Rd Sarasota FL 33579

CHASE, LOUISA L
PAINTER
b Panama City, Panama, Mar 18, 51; US citizen. *Study:* Syracuse Univ, BFA, 73; Yale Univ Sch Art, MFA, 75. *Work:* Mus Mod Art, New York; Prudential Life Insurance; Morton Neumann Family Collection, Chicago, Ill; Am Can Company, Greenwich, Conn; Lehman Brothers, New York. *Comn:* Silkscreen print, Lincoln Ctr, New York, 81. *Exhib:* Painting of the Eighties, Grey Art Gallery, New York, 79; New Work, New York, The New Mus, New York, 80; Painting & Sculpture Today, Indianapolis Mus Art, Ind, 80; Whitney Biennial, Whitney Mus Am Art, New York, 81; Am Landscape, Whitney Mus, Fairfield Co, Conn, 81; New Visions, Aldridge Mus, Ridgefield, Conn, 81. *Teaching:* Instr painting, RI Sch Design, Providence, 75-79; instr painting, Sch Visual Arts, New York, 80-82. *Awards:* Nat Endowment Arts, 78-79; Creative Artists Public Serv Prog, 79-80. *Bibliog:* Deborah Phillips (auth), article, Arts, 1/81; Barry Yourgrau (auth), article, Art in Am, 4/81; Ellen Swartz (auth), Artists critics are watching, Art News, 5/81. *Media:* Oil. *Dealer:* Robert Miller Gallery 724 5th Ave New York NY 10019. *Mailing Add:* 17 White St New York NY 10013

CHASE, RICHARD ANDREW
PAINTER, ILLUSTRATOR
Columbus, Kans, Apr 19, 1891. *Study:* Carl Werntz Chicago Acad, 14-15; Art Inst Chicago, 26-29; Cape Cod Art Sch with Hawthorne & Miller, summers 28-29. *Work:* Chicago Hist Soc, Ill; City of Chicago Collection Art, Ill; Crawford Co Hist Mus, Girard, Kans; Univ Pittsburg, Kans; Valporaiso Univ, Ind. *Comn:* Glacier Nat Park, Great Northern Railroad, Chicago, 25; Mural (23 ft) Hall Sci, Journal Commerce, Chicago, 33; View Book Century Progress, R R Donnelly Printing, Chicago, 33; portraits, Encyclopedia Britannica, Chicago, 43. *Exhib:* Childrens Boat Watercolor, Art Inst Chicago, Ill, 24, Old Stuff Watercolor, 34 & Wabash Ave Viaduct, 34; Glacier Nat Park,

Washington Art Club, Washington DC, 28; 60 Yrs People & Places, Northern Ind Art Asn, Hammond, 81; Chicago Portrait, Chicago Hist Mus, Ill, 81; and others. *Pos:* Illusr, George Enos Throop Inc, 19-21; artist, McMillan Studios, 27-29. *Awards:* Mrs Julius Rosenwald Purchase Award, Art Inst Chicago, 29; Gold Medal, All Ill Art Soc, 36; Collectors Award, Ind Arts Asn. *Media:* Oil, Watercolor. *Mailing Add:* Story House Antiques 12306 Cline Ave Crown Point IN 46307

CHASE, ROBERT M
DEALER, COLLECTOR

b Chicago, Ill, Dec 5, 40. *Study:* Univ Wis, BS. *Pos:* Pres & ed newsletter, Merrill Chase Galleries, 64- *Mem:* Am Soc Appraisers; Mus Contemp Art, Chicago; Art Inst Chicago. *Specialty:* Old Master 19th century and 20th century fine prints; American and European paintings of the 20th century. *Collection:* Mixed media, Dali, Kipniss, Rembrandt, Durer, Addison, Renoir, Likan, Chagall & Picasso. *Publ:* Ed, Story of Prints, 77, Rediscovered Printmakers of the 19th Century, 78 & Manuel Robbe Catalog, Vol I, 79, Vol II, 80, Merrill Chase Galleries. *Mailing Add:* Merrill Chase Art Galleries 835 N Michigan Ave Chicago IL 60611

CHASE, W(ILLIAM) THOMAS
CONSERVATOR

b Boston, Mass, May 31, 40. *Study:* Oberlin Col, Ohio, BA, 62; NY Univ, MA, 67, conserv cert, 67; Brit Coun Course on conserv of antiquities, 69. *Pos:* Wadsworth Atheneum, Hartford, Conn, 62 & 63; conservator to Nemrud Dagh Excavations, Adiyaman Villayet, Turkey, 64; Chester Dale Fel in Conserv Dept, Metrop Mus Art, New York, 66; asst conservator, Freer Tech Lab, 66-68, head conserv, 68-; adv to John D Rockefeller 3rd Fund for Thai Bronze Treatment Proj, 73-75. *Mem:* Fel Int Inst Conserv Hist & Artistic Works; fel am Inst Conserv; Washington Conserv Guild (vchmn, 68-69, pres, 70). *Res:* Technical studies of Oriental art, particularly ancient Chinese bronzes and belt-hooks, mirrors and other objects; corrosion study and analysis. *Publ:* Coauth (with Gettens & Clarke), Two early chinese weapons with meteoritic iron blades, Freer Occasional Papers, 71; dir, Art of the Hyogushi (film), Freer Gallery, 73; auth, Bronze Disease and Its Treatment, Dept Fine Arts, Thailand, 75; co-ed, Corrosion and Metal Artifacts, Nat Bur Stand, 77; coauth (with U Franklin), Early Chinese Black Minnens and Patterns-Etched Weapons, Ars Orientals XI; and others. *Mailing Add:* c/o Freer Gallery of Art Smithsonian Inst Washington DC 20560

CHASE-RIBOUD, BARBARA See D'Ashnash-Tosi

CHATMAS, JOHN
PAINTER

b Marlin, Tex, Nov 1, 45. *Study:* Univ Tex, Austin, BFA, 68; Pratt Inst, MFA, 70. *Work:* Univ Tex, Austin. *Exhib:* Artists Biennial, New Orleans Mus Art, 73; Southwest Tarrant Co Ann, Ft Worth Art Mus, 77; Southwest Fine Arts Biennial, Mus Fine Arts NMex, Santa Fe, 78; Made in Tex, Univ Tex, Austin, 79; NTex Invitational, NTex State Univ, 79; Small Works, 80 WSE Galleries, NY Univ, 80; and others. *Teaching:* Instr art & art hist, McLennan Community Col, 70- *Awards:* Purchase Award, Waco Regional Art Exhib, Baylor Univ, 73; First Place Award, The Art Ctr, Waco, Tex, 77. *Bibliog:* Susie Kalil (auth), Houston galleries showcase new talent, Artweek, 7/28/79 & Texas ranges: Houston, from..., Art News, 12/82; Gordon McConnell (auth), The paintings of John Chatmas, Cult Activities Ctr, Temple, Tex, 10/83. *Media:* Acrylic, Oil. *Dealer:* Patrick Gallery Austin TX; Graham Gallery Houston TX. *Mailing Add:* 1315 N 34th St Waco TX 76710

CHAVEZ, EDWARD ARCENIO
PAINTER, SCULPTOR

b Wagonmound, NMex, Mar 14, 17. *Study:* Colorado Springs Fine Arts Ctr, Colo, with Boardman Robinson, Frank Mechau, Arnold Blanch & Peppino Mangravite; Tiffany Found painting grants, 48; Inst Int Educ, Italy, Fulbright grant, 51. *Work:* Libr of Cong Print Collection & Watkins Gallery, Washington, DC; Mus Mod Art, New York; Detroit Mus Art; Butler Inst Am Art, Youngstown, Ohio. *Comn:* Murals, Govt Art Com, Post Off, Center, Tex, 38, Post Off, Geneva, Nebr, Post Off, Glenwood Springs, Colo, West High Sch, Denver; mural, USA 200th Sta Hosp, Recife, Brazil. *Exhib:* Nat Inst Arts & Lett, New York; Whitney Mus Am Art, New York; Nat Acad Design, New York; Pa Acad Art Ann, Philadelphia; Am Art Exhib, Metrop Mus Art, New York. *Teaching:* Instr painting, Art Students League, 54-58; vis prof art, Colo Col, Colorado Springs, 59-60; prof art, Syracuse Univ Sch Art, 60-62. *Awards:* Tiffany Found Grant Painting, 48; Fulbright Grant Painting, 51; Childe Hassam Award for Painting, Nat Inst Arts & Lett, 53. *Mem:* Woodstock Art Asn; academician Nat Acad Design. *Mailing Add:* 370 John Joy Rd Woodstock NY 12498

CHAVEZ, JOSEPH ARNOLD
SCULPTOR, INSTRUCTOR

b Belen, NMex, Dec 25, 39. *Study:* Univ Albuquerque, BS(art educ), 63; Univ NMex, MA(art educ), 67, MA(art), 71; Univ Cincinnati, 74. *Work:* Slide Libr Collection, Univ Southern Ala; plus numerous works in pvt collections across the nation. *Exhib:* One-man shows, Jonson Gallery, Univ NMex, 71 & 76; NMex Arts & Crafts Fair Ann, Albuquerque; Southwest Arts & Crafts Fair Ann; Southwest Crafts Biennial, Santa Fe Folk Art Mus, 74; State Fair Dallas, Tex, 75; Gallery A, Taos, NMex; Aldridge Gallery, Albuquerque. *Teaching:* Art, Lincoln Jr High, Albuquerque, 63-70; supvr student teachers art educ, Univ NMex, 70-71; teacher art, Sandia High Sch, Albuquerque, 71-; instr art, Univ Albuquerque, summer 70; supvr student teachers art educ, Univ Cincinnati, 74; pvt tutoring, currently. *Awards:* Second Place, Pottery &

Sculpture Expos, Rio Grande Art & Crafts Fair, 74; Spec Merit, State Fair Tex, 75; Fourth Place, NMex State Fair Sculpture Exhib, 83. *Bibliog:* Dr Jacinto Quirarte (auth), Mexican-American Artists, Univ Tex, 73; The Man Who Fell to Earth, London Film Co, 75; Joseph Chavez (auth, videotape), The Art of Carving Stone. *Mem:* Designers & Craftsmen NMex (pres, 73). *Media:* Stone, Wood. *Publ:* Auth, Critique on art, Col St Joseph News, 64; auth, Space filled & fulfilled, Southwest Art, 4/82. *Dealer:* Gallery A Taos NM; Aldridge Gallery Albuquerque NM. *Mailing Add:* 4618 Sorrel Lane SW Albuquerque NM 87105

CHAVEZ-MORADO, JOSE
PAINTER, EDUCATOR

b Silao, Mex, Jan 4, 09. *Study:* Self taught. *Work:* Nat Mus Mod Art, Mexico City; Varsovia Art Mus, Poland; Mus Mod Art, New York; Haifa Mus, Israel; Mus Nat de Historia, Mexico City; and others. *Comn:* Glass mosaics, University City, Mexico City, 52; stone mosaics, Ministry of Pub Works, Mexico City, 54; frescoes & mixed mosaics, CIBA Labs, Mexico City, 55; oil mural & bronze pillar (with Tomas Chavez Morado in sculptural works), Mus Anthrop, Mexico City, 64; fresco & acrylic murals, Mus Alhondiga de Granaditas, Guanajuato, 55, 66 & 67. *Exhib:* Biennal of Sao Paulo, Brazil, 59; Portrait of Mexico Traveling Exhib, several countries, 60-70; Mus Nac Arte Mod, Mexico City, 61; Kunst der Mexikanishen Revolution, West Berlin, 74; 2 Salon Ann de Invitados, Presco Palacio Bellas Artes, Mex, 79. *Pos:* Inspector of art teaching, Inst Nac Bellas Artes, Mexico City, 34-36, head art educ, 36-40, dir art schs, 40-66. *Teaching:* Prof painting, Escuela Nat Artes Plasticas, Mexico City, 42-52. *Awards:* Medalla de Prata, 10th Salao Pan Americano, Inst Bellas Artes Rio Grande, Brazil, 58; Medalla Colaboration Gran Premio, 8th Biennal Sao Paulo, Brazil, 65; Mex Nat Price of Arts, 74. *Bibliog:* Antonio Rodriguez (auth), A history of Mexican mural painting, Thames & Hudson, London, 69; Raquel Tibol (auth), Apuntes de Mi libreta de Jose Chavez-Morado, Ed Cult Popular, 79. *Media:* Oil, Tempera. *Collection:* Pre-hispanic, Mexican colonial and folk art. *Dealer:* Ines Amor Galeria Arte Mexicano Milan 18, Mexico City, Mexico; Galeria de Arte Contemporaneo de Lourdes Chumacero Estocolmo 30 Mexico. *Mailing Add:* Pastita 158 Torre del Arco Guanajuato Mexico

CHEATHAM, FRANK REAGAN
PAINTER, DESIGNER

b Beeville, Tex, Feb 20, 36. *Study:* Art Ctr Col Design, BPA; Chouinard Art Inst; Otis Art Inst Los Angeles Co, study with Lorser Feitelson, Louis Danziger & Arthur Ames, BFA & MFA. *Work:* Los Angeles Co Mus Art; NMex Mus Fine Arts, Santa Fe. *Comn:* Catalog, Simon Rodia's towers in Watts, Los Angeles Co Mus Art, 62. *Exhib:* Los Angeles Munic Art Gallery Ann, Los Angeles Co Mus, 69; Sixth Ann Art Show, La Jolla Mus Art, 69; Ann Exhib, Long Beach Mus Art 70; Southwest Fine Arts Biennial, Mus NMex, 74. *Pos:* Creative dir, Porter, Goodman & Cheatham Design, Los Angeles, 61-73. *Teaching:* From assoc prof to prof design, Tex Tech Univ, Lubbock, 73- *Awards:* Cert of Merit, Art Dir Club New York, 60, 70 & 74; Award of Excellence, Am Inst Graphic Arts, 63, 65, 72 & 74; Purchase Award, Mus NMex Found, 74. *Mem:* Am Inst Arts; Am Craftsmans Coun. *Media:* Acrylic; Wood, Polychromed Ceramic. *Dealer:* Silvan Simone 11579 Olympic Blvd W Los Angeles CA 90064. *Mailing Add:* 2305 53rd St Lubbock TX 79412

CHEE, CHENG-KHEE
PAINTER, EDUCATOR

b Fujian, China, Jan 14, 34; US citizen. *Study:* Nanyang Univ, Singapore, BA, 60; Univ Minn, Minneapolis, MA, 64; studied watercolor painting with Dong Kingman & Edgar Whitney. *Work:* Univ Minn & 3-M Co, St Paul; Tweed Mus Art, Duluth, Minn; Purdue Univ, Calumet, Ind; Honeywell Inc, Minneapolis. *Exhib:* Am Watercolor Soc Ann, Nat Acad Design, New York, 75, 78, 79 & 81; Minn Mus Art, St Paul, 76; Rocky Mountain Nat Watermedia Exhib, Foothills Art Ctr, Golden, Colo, 76, 78 & 80; Midwest Watercolor Soc Ann, 77-83; Minneapolis Inst Arts, 78; Allied Artists Am Ann, Nat Art Club, New York, 80 & 82; Audubon Artists Ann, Nat Art Club, New York, 80 & 83. *Pos:* Sr librn, Univ Minn, Duluth, 65-78. *Teaching:* Instr, Univ Minn, Duluth, 78-80, asst prof, 81- *Awards:* Colo Centennial Award, Rocky Mountain Nat Watermedia Exhib, 76; Gold Medal, Allied Artists Am 67th Ann, 80; Bronze Medallion, Knickerbocker Artists 31st Ann, 81. *Bibliog:* Isadore Cohen (auth), Painting is his life, Duluth News Tribune, 10/28/79; Robert Ashenmacher (auth), For watercolorist Chee the work has just begun, Duluth News Tribune Accent North, 3/29/81; Joni Danzl (auth), Strokes of light in the wilderness, Lake Superior Port Cities, 12/82. *Mem:* Am Watercolor Soc; Midwest Watercolor Soc; Nat Watercolor Soc. *Media:* Watercolor, Chinese Ink. *Dealer:* J-Michael Galleries 3916 W 59th St Edina MN 55424. *Mailing Add:* 1508 Vermilion Rd Duluth MN 55812

CHEEK, RONALD EDWARD
PAINTER, INSTRUCTOR

b Greenville, SC, Dec 6, 42. *Study:* Ringling Sch Art & Design, BFA, 71; Art Students League, with Frank Mason, Theodoros Stamos & Charles Alston; New Sch Social Research, with Joseph Floch. *Work:* Columbia Mus Art, SC; Augusta Mus, Ga; The Citadel Mus, Charleston, SC; Banks Haley Art Mus, Albany, Ga; Jasper Rand Art Mus, Westfield, Mass. *Exhib:* Prize Winning Paintings of West Coast, Long Boat Key Art Ctr, Fla, 78; one-man shows, Jasper Rand Art Mus, Westfield, Mass, 79, Old Hyde Park Art Ctr, Tampa, Fla, 81, Cayuga Mus History Art, Auburn, NY, 81, The Citadel Mus, Charleston, SC, 81, Sioux Indian Mus, Rapid City, SDak, 82 & Manatee Jr Col, Bradenton, Fla, 83. *Teaching:* Art instr figure & drawing, Manatee Art League, Bradenton, Fla, 78-80; art instr all media & drawing, Manatee Area Vocational-Technical Ctr, 78-; art instr portrait & drawing, Sarasota Co Vocational-Technical Ctr, 78. *Awards:* Golden Jubilee Award, Sarasota Art

Asn, 78; First Place, Venice Area Art League, 79 & 81; First Place, Old Hyde Park Art Ctr, 82. *Bibliog:* Return of Color Refreshes, Columbia Record, 78; South Carolina Artists, SC Art Commission, 80; Drawings by Ronald Cheek, Sioux Indian Mus & US Dept Interior, 82. *Mem:* Old Hyde Park Art Ctr, Tampa, Fla; Art Ctr, St Petersburg, Fla. *Media:* Pastel. *Mailing Add:* 2434 Hickory Ave Sarasota FL 33580

CHEMECHE, GEORGE
PAINTER, SCULPTOR
b Baghdad, Iraq, May 11, 34; US citizen. *Study:* Avni Sch Fine Arts, Tel Aviv, 56-59; Ecole de Beaux Arts, Paris, 60-63. *Work:* Guggenheim Mus, New York; Denver Art Mus; Fogg Mus, Boston; San Francisco Mus Mod Art; Herbert F Johnson Mus Art, Cornell Univ, Ithaca, NY. *Exhib:* Mus Mod Art, Paris, 63; Tel Aviv Mus, 66; Jerusalem Mus, 76; Jewish Mus, New York, 77; Aldrich Mus Contemp Art, Ridgefield, Conn, 80 & 81. *Awards:* Award, Am-Israel Cult Found, 60. *Bibliog:* Jean Pierre Vandigaum (auth), Interview with the artist, Art Press, Paris, 77; John Perreault (auth), article, Soho News, 77; Ruth Bass (auth), article, Art News, 81. *Media:* Oil, Pastel; Metal. *Dealer:* Lillian Heidenberg Gallery 50 West 57th St New York NY 10024. *Mailing Add:* 222 West 23rd St New York NY 10011

CHEN, HILO
PAINTER
b Taiwan, Repub of China, Oct 15, 42; US citizen. *Study:* Chong Yen Col, BS(archit). *Work:* Guggenheim Mus. *Exhib:* Wadsworth Atheneum, Hartford, Conn, 74; Indianapolis Mus of Art, 74; Pa State Mus of Art, 74; Baltimore Mus of Art, 75; Lafayette Natural Hist Mus & Planetarium, La, 75; Edwin Ulrich Mus, Wichita State Univ, Kans, 76. *Collections Arranged:* New/Photo Realism, Wadsworth Atheneum, 74. *Bibliog:* Robert Hughes (auth), An omnivorous & literal dependence, Arts, 6/74; Andrea Mikotajuk (auth), American realists at LKM, Arts, 1/75; Dorothy Belden (auth), Realism exaggerated in Ulrich Art Exhibition, Wichita Eagle, 3/76. *Media:* Oil on Canvas; Watercolor on Paper. *Dealer:* Louis K Meisel 141 Prince St New York NY 10012. *Mailing Add:* 302 Bowery 3rd Floor New York NY 10012

CHEN, TONY (ANTHONY YOUNG)
ILLUSTRATOR, PAINTER
b Kingston, Jamaica, WIndies, Jan 3, 29; US citizen. *Study:* Art Career Sch, 49-51; Pratt Inst, BFA with honors, study with Richard Lindner & Dong Kingman, 55. *Work:* Univ Southern Miss, Hattiesburg; Kerlan Collection, Cedar Rapids, Minn; Fire House Gallery, Nassau Community Col, NY; plus numerous pvt collections. *Comn:* Bees, Defenders of Wildlife, Washington, DC, 74; Lyre Birds, 75 & Bamboo, 76, Nat Wildlife, Washington, DC; US Wildlife, Nat Geographic Soc, Washington, DC, 76; Siamang, Bronx Zoo, NY, 77. *Exhib:* One-man shows, Art Dir Club New York, 70, Uptown Gallery, New York, 73 & Sixth Estate Gallery, Brooklyn, NY, 77; Nat Collection of Fine Arts, Washington, DC, 74; Va Mus Fine Arts, Richmond, 75; Del Art Mus, Wilmington, 75; Wadsworth Atheneum, Hartford, Conn, 75; 200 Years of Am Illus, New York Hist Soc, 77; Naples Art Gallery, Fla, 81. *Collections Arranged:* Contemp Am Illustrators of Childrens Books, Soc Illus Ann, 69-80; 200 Years of Am Illustration, Am Artist Mag, 72; Children's Bk Showcase, 72 & 76. *Pos:* Art dir, Newsweek Mag, 59-70. *Teaching:* Instr drawing, Nassau Community Col, 72-74. *Awards:* Award for Excellence, Soc Illusr Show, 73; Award of Distinction, Educ Press Asn US, 77; Nat Sci Teachers Asn Award, 80. *Bibliog:* Dianna Klemin (auth), The Book Illustration of Tony Chen, Am Artist, 5/72; Anne Commire (auth), Something About the Author, Contemp Authors, 74; Hyatt Mayor (auth), Contemporary American Illustrators of Children's Books, 74. *Media:* Watercolor; Acrylic. *Collection:* Antique African art; early American folk art; Far and Near Eastern bronzes, paintings, and ceramics. *Publ:* Illusr, Hello Small Sparrow, 71 & auth-illus, Run, Zebra, Run, 72, Lothrop, Lee & Shepard; illusr, UNICEF Cookbook, T Y Crowell, 73; illusr, Honshi, Parents Mag Press, 74; illusr, About Owls, Scholastic Mag, 76; illusr, The Doubleday Illustrated Children's Bible, 83. *Mailing Add:* 53-31 96th St Corona NY 11368

CHEN CHI
PAINTER
b Wu-sih, China, May 2, 12. *Study:* Study in China. *Work:* Metrop Mus Art, New York; Pa Acad Fine Arts, Philadelphia; Butler Inst Am Art, Youngstown, Ohio; Fort Worth Art Mus, Tex; Charles & Emma Frye Art Mus, Seattle. *Exhib:* American Watercolors, Drawings & Prints, Metrop Mus Art, 52; Whitney Mus Am Art Ann, New York, 54-63; 24th Biennial, Corcoran Gallery Art, Washington, DC, 55; Contemporary American Painting & Sculpture, Univ Ill, Urbana, 57; Brooklyn Mus 22nd Int Watercolor Biennial, 63; one-man shows in museums & galleries throughout the US, 47- *Teaching:* Instr watercolor, St Johns Univ, Shanghai, 42-46; vis prof watercolor, Pa State Univ, 59-60; artist in residence, Ogden City Schs, Utah, 67 & Utah State Univ, 71. *Awards:* Nat Inst Arts & Lett Grant for Creative Work in Art, 60; Saltus Gold Medal of Merit, Nat Acad Design, 69; Bicentennial Gold Medal, Am Watercolor Soc, 76. *Mem:* Nat Acad Design (counr, 69-71); Am Watercolor Soc (dir, 56-59); Audubon Artists (dir, 64-69 & 72-); Allied Artists Am (dir, 58-60); Nat Arts Club (gov, 72-). *Media:* Watercolor, Oil. *Publ:* Illus, A Single Pebble, Readers Digest Condensed Bks, 56; illusr, Pageantry of VIII Winter Olympics, Squaw Valley, Sports Illus, 60; Two or Three Lines from Sketchbooks of Chen Chi, New York, 69; China from the Sketchbooks of Chen Chi, New York, 74; Chen Chi, Watercolors, Drawings, Sketches, New York, 80. *Dealer:* Grand Central Art Galleries 40 Vanderbilt Ave New York NY 10017. *Mailing Add:* 23 Washington Sq N New York NY 10011

CHENG, FU-DING
FILMMAKER, PAINTER
b Palo Alto, Calif, Feb 5, 43. *Study:* Sch Archit, Univ Southern Calif; Alliance Francaise, Paris; Univ Calif, Berkeley, BArch. *Exhib:* New Am Filmmakers, Whitney Mus Am Art, New York, 70; Yale Film Festival, 72; Belg Int Film Festival, 73; Media Ctr, New York, 75. *Teaching:* Instr art, Univ Calif, Los Angeles, 76-82. *Awards:* Second Place, Yale Film Festival, Yale Univ, 70; independent grant, Film Proj, Am Film Inst, 77; First Place, Foothill Nat Film Festival, Foothill Col. *Media:* Watercolor. *Publ:* Illusr, Solar Energy House, US Info Agency, 77; auth, Oasis Foods' Dehydrated Water, Wet Mag, 77. *Dealer:* Ed Lau 6015 Santa Monica Blvd Los Angeles CA 90038. *Mailing Add:* 209 Seventh Ave Venice CA 90291

CHEREPOV, GEORGE
PAINTER, INSTRUCTOR
b Lithuania, Mar 28, 09; US citizen. *Study:* With profs Konstantin Wisotzky, Riga, Latvia & Aalexis Hansen, Dubrovnic, Yugoslavia. *Work:* Mus, Kempten, WGer; Town Hall, Memmingen, WGer; State Bank, Munich WGer; Stamford Mus, Conn; Mus Art, Tucson, Ariz. *Exhib:* Allied Artists Am, New York; Acad Artists Asn, Springfield, Mass; Southern Vt Art Ctr, Manchester; Grand Cent Art Galleries, New York; Hudson Valley Art Asn. *Pos:* Fac, Painting Holiday Orgn, 73- *Awards:* Best in Show, First Award, Allied Artists Am, 68; Gold Medal, Hudson Valley Art Asn, 69; Medal of Honor, Kent Art Asn, Conn, 71. *Mem:* Fel Allied Artists Am; Hudson Valley Art Asn; Acad Artists Asn; Southern Vt Art Ctr; Am Artists Prof League Inc. *Media:* Oil. *Publ:* Auth, Discovering oil painting, 71; illusr, Landscape Painting in Oil, Watson-Guptill, 76; illusr, The Oil Painting Book, 79; illusr, Complete Guide to Landscape Painting in Oil, 81. *Dealer:* Newman Gallery 1625 Walnut St Philadelphia PA 19103; Grand Central Art Galleries Biltmore Hotel 40 Vanderbilt Ave New York NY 10017. *Mailing Add:* 1050 King St Greenwich CT 06830

CHERMAYEFF, IVAN
DESIGNER, PAINTER
b London, Eng, June 6, 32; US citizen. *Study:* Harvard Univ, 50-52; Inst Design, Ill Inst Technol, four Moholy-Nagy scholar, 52-54; Yale Univ Sch Design, BFA(Mohawk Paper Co Fel), 55. *Comn:* Exploding Triangles (shaped canvases), IBM Data Processing Hq, Harrison, NY, 70; Dimensional Abstractions (plastic laminate wall constructions), Bartholomew Consol Sch Corp, Columbus, Ind, 71; Abstraction I (Aubusson tapestry), Westinghouse Elec Corp, Pittsburgh, 72; Abstractions II & III, Philip Morris Inc, Richmond; Construction (wall with painted steel components), Am Repub Ins Co, Des Moines, Iowa. *Exhib:* Industry Sculpture Show, Butler Inst Am Art, Youngstown, Ohio, 71; Venice Biennale, 72; Va Mus Art, Richmond, 74; Jacksonville Art Mus, 75. *Pos:* Trustee & comt mem painting & sculpture, film, design, Mus Mod Art, New York, 65-; vpres, Yale Arts Asn, 68-; mem comt arts & archit, Yale Univ Coun, 71-; mem comt visual & environmental arts, Harvard Univ Bd Overseers, 72- *Teaching:* Instr design, Brooklyn Col, 56-57 & Sch Visual Arts, 59-65. *Awards:* Indust Arts Medal, Am Inst Architects, 67; Gold Medal, Philadelphia Col Art, 71. *Bibliog:* Douglas Davis (auth), article, Newsweek Mag, 71 & 200 American leaders, Time Mag, 74. *Mem:* Am Inst Graphic Arts (vpres, pres & bd dirs, 60-); Int Design Conf Aspen (vpres & co-chmn bd dirs, 67-); Indust Designers Soc Am; Alliance Graphique Int; Benjamin Franklin fel Royal Soc Arts. *Publ:* Auth, Observations on American Architecture, Viking, 72. *Dealer:* Pace Editions 115 E 23rd St New York NY 10010. *Mailing Add:* 830 Third Ave New York NY 10022

CHERNER, NORMAN
DESIGNER
b New York, NY, June 7, 20. *Study:* Columbia Univ, BS, 41, MA, 47. *Work:* Mus Mod Art, New York. *Comn:* Exhib house, US Dept Com, Vienna, 58; WVa pavilion, Pilgrim Glass, New York Worlds Fair, 65. *Exhib:* One-man shows, Am House, Mus Contemp Crafts, New York, 52-54; Inst Contemp Arts, Boston, 59; Akron Art Inst, Ohio, 61. *Pos:* Design consult, Marriott Corp, Washington, DC, 68-76, Mod Mode, Inc, Oakland, Calif, 78-, Risom/Marble Corp, Providence, RI, 78-81, Howe Furniture Corp, Norwalk, Conn, 80- & Gordon Russell Ltd, Worcestershire, England, 83- *Teaching:* Instr design, Mus Mod Art, 47-49; instr design & art educ, Teachers Col, Columbia Univ, 49-53. *Awards:* Design in Steel Citation, Am Iron & Steel Inst, 73; Roscoe Citation, Resources Coun, 82; Daphne Award, Hardwood Inst, 83. *Bibliog:* Mary Jo Weale (auth), Contemporary Designers, McGraw-Hill, 73. *Mem:* Indust Designers Soc Am. *Publ:* Auth, Make Your Own Modern Furniture, 53 & How to Build Children's Toys & Furniture, 54, McGraw-Hill; auth, Fabricating Houses from Component Parts, Reinhold, 58. *Mailing Add:* 9 Thomas Rd Westport CT 06880

CHERNOW, ANN
PAINTER
b New York, NY, Feb 1, 36. *Study:* Syracuse Univ, 53-55; NY Univ, BS, 57, MA, 69; with Irving Sandler, Jules Olitski, Hale Woodruff & Howard Conant. *Work:* New Britain Mus Am Art, Conn; Syracuse Univ Art Collection; Housatonic Mus Art, Bridgeport, Conn; Neuberger Mus, Purchase, NY; Univ Ariz Art Collection, Tucson. *Exhib:* One-woman shows, Alex Rosenberg Gallery, New York, 82 & 84; Schochet Gallery, Newport, RI, 81; Gallery Maag, Zurich, Switz, 80; Beall/Lambremont Gallery, New Orleans, 80, 81. *Teaching:* Instr studio work, Mus Mod Art, New York, 66-70; instr painting & drawing, Silvermine Col & Silvermine Guild, 68-80; instr art hist, Univ Conn, summer 69; asst prof, Norwalk Community Col, 82- *Awards:* Purchase Prize, Town of Westport, Conn, 79; State Conn Painting Fel, 80-81; Publishers Award, Old Lyme Art Works, 83. *Bibliog:* Article, New York

Times, 6/25/74; Barbara Cavaliare (auth), article, Arts Mag, 3/78; Hue Points Mag, spring-summer, 83. *Mem:* Silvermine Guild Art; Westport Weston Arts Coun. *Media:* Oil; Pencils. *Publ:* Auth, Let's remember, 69, Reuben Nakian, sculptor, 69, Palette, Mag of Conn Art Asn; auth (catalog), Odd Man In, Krushenick Exhib (catalog), Housatonic Mus Art, Conn, 75; art ed & contribr, Communitas, New Eng, 79. *Dealer:* Alex Rosenberg Gallery 20 W 57th St New York NY 10019. *Mailing Add:* 2 Gorham Ave Westport CT 06880

CHERNOW, BURT
INSTRUCTOR, MUSEUM DIRECTOR
b New York, NY, July 28, 33. *Study:* NY Univ, BA, 58, MA, 60; with Lawrence Alloway, Jules Olitski, Irving Sandler & Hale Woodruff. *Work:* Jacksonville Mus, Fla; Bridgeport Mus Art, Sci & Indust, Conn; Col Art Mus, Hampton, Va; Le Mus de L'Art Contemporain, Skopje, Yugoslavia; Housatonic Mus Contemp Art, Bridgeport, Conn. *Exhib:* Loeb Student Ctr, NY Univ; Bridgeport Mus; UN Pavilion, New York World's Fair, 64-65; US Info Agency Traveling Exhib; Silvermine Guild, New Canaan, Conn. *Collections Arranged:* 20th Century American & European Contemporary Art, Housatonic Mus Art; Christo Exhib (auth catalog), Wadsworth Atheneum, Hartford, Conn, 78; Abe Ajay Retrospective (auth catalog), Neuberger Mus, Purchase, NY, 78; Will Barnet Retrospective (auth catalog), Neuberger Mus, 79-80. *Pos:* Consult & writer, Educ Directions, 68-; dir, Housatonic Mus Contemp Art, 68- *Teaching:* Staff, Mus Mod Art, New York, 67-70; chmn art dept, Housatonic Community Col, Bridgeport, 68-; staff, Silvermine Guild Artists, 70- *Awards:* First Prize (sculpture), Barnum Art Festival, Bridgeport Mus, 60. *Bibliog:* M Bishop (auth), For arts sake, Conn Mag, 3/72. *Mem:* Westport-Weston Arts Coun, Conn (bd dirs, 69-); Conn Art Asn (bd dirs, 64-65); Silvermine Guild Artists; Appraisers Asn Am; Inst Asn Art Critics. *Publ:* Auth, Paper, paint & stuff, Educ Directions, Vols I & II, 69; auth, introd, In: Francisco Zuniga, Galerie D'eendt, Amsterdam, 80; auth, Gabor Peterdi Paintings, Taplinger, 82; auth, Drawings of Milton Avery, Taplinger, 84; and articles in Artnews, Intellect Mag, Craft Horizons, Conn Mag and others. *Mailing Add:* 2 Gorham Ave Westport CT 06880

CHERRY, HERMAN
PAINTER
b Atlantic City, NJ, Apr 10, 09. *Study:* Otis Arts Inst, Calif; Students Art League, Los Angeles, with Stanton MacDonald Wright; Art Students League, New York, with Thomas Hart Benton. *Work:* Brooklyn Mus; Univ Iowa, Iowa City; Univ Tex Mus, Austin; Southern Ill Mus, Carbondale; and others. *Comn:* Self-Help Community Ctr, Forest Hills, Queens, NY, 78; St Malachy's Church, New York, 79; Pomonok Community Ctr, Queens, NY, 79. *Exhib:* Mus Mod Art, New York; one-man shows, Stable Gallery, New York, 55, Pasadena Art Mus, 61, Oakland Art Mus, 61 & Univ Ky, Lexington, 67; Metrop Mus Art, New York; Walker Art Ctr; Corcoran Gallery, 77. *Teaching:* Vis prof painting, Univ Calif, Berkeley, 59 & 65; prof painting, Univ Minn, Minneapolis, 69; prof painting, New York Studio Sch, 74. *Awards:* Longview Found; Gottleib Found, 78; Am Video Artists Found, 82. *Media:* Oil. *Publ:* Auth, various articles on art in Arts Mag & Art News; auth, David Smith, Numero, Florence, 53; auth, On David Smith, Art Am, 67. *Mailing Add:* 121 Mercer St New York NY 10012

CHESHIRE, CRAIG GIFFORD
PAINTER, EDUCATOR
b Portland, Ore, Dec 31, 36. *Study:* Univ Ore, BA, 58, with David McCosh, MFA, 61; also with Francis Chapin. *Work:* Mus Art, Eugene, Ore; Univ Ore; Eastern Ore Col. *Exhib:* Northwest Artists Ann, Seattle; Artists of Ore Ann, 58-75; Northwest Painters, Smithsonian Inst Traveling Exhib, 59; Mus Art, Eugene, 61-74; Gallery West, Portland, 72; Visions & Perceptions Gallery, Eugene, 80. *Teaching:* Assoc prof drawing & painting, Portland State Univ, 63-81, prof, 81- *Awards:* Ina McClung Award in Painting, 61 & Ore Develop Fel, 62, Univ Ore; Purchase Award, Mus Art, Eugene & Ore Arts Comn, 74. *Mem:* Portland Art Mus; Am Asn Univ Prof. *Media:* Oil, Watercolor. *Mailing Add:* 3540 SW 108th Ave Beaverton OR 97005

CHESLEY, PAUL ALEXANDER
PHOTOGRAPHER, GRAPHIC ARTIST
b Red Wing, Minn, Sept 10, 46. *Study:* Ariz State Univ; Univ Minn; Colo Mountain Col. *Work:* Bell Mus of Natural Hist, Minn; Honolulu Acad, Hawaii. *Exhib:* One-man shows, Ecuador, Colorado Springs Fine Arts Ctr, 74 & Gargoyle Gallery, Colo, 75; Nature, Nishi Ginza Galleries, Tokyo, Japan, 75; Indians of the Andes, Birmingham Mus Art, Ala & Sci Mus Minn, 75; retrospective, James Ford Bell Mus Natural Hist, Minn, 75; Nature, Honolulu Acad Art, Hawaii, 76. *Bibliog:* Julia Scully (auth), Four photographers, Mod Photog, 7/77; Constance Brown (auth), It's always hot springs time in the Rockies, Smithsonian, 11/77 & Woman Alive, Quest, 11/77; and others. *Mem:* Am Soc Mag Photog. *Media:* Color Photography. *Publ:* Auth, Yellowstone abstracts, US Camera, 9/77; auth, Sawtooth range & Death Valley, In: National Geographic Book: Exploring America's Backcountry, 79; auth, Los Angeles new Santa Monica National Park, Smithsonian Mag, 7/79; auth, Hot springs bathing in Japan, Geo Mag/Ger, 80; auth, Along the Continental Divide, Nat Geographic Book; and others. *Dealer:* Putney Gallery Aspen CO 81611. *Mailing Add:* PO Box 94 Aspen CO 81612

CHESNEY, LEE R, JR
PRINTMAKER, PAINTER
b Washington, DC, June 1, 20. *Study:* Univ Colo, BFA, 46; Univ Iowa, MFA, 48; Univ Michoacan, Morelia, Mex; also with James Boyle, James Lechay & Mauricio Lasansky. *Work:* Rosenwald Collection, Nat Gallery Art, Washington, DC; Mus Mod Art, New York; Tate Gallery Art, London; Bibliot Nat, Paris; Nat Gallery Art, Stockholm, Sweden. *Comn:* Spec print ed, Honolulu Print Soc, 75; Honolulu Acad Art, 77; Univ Hawaii Centennial Comn, 82; Honolulu Printmaking Soc, 83. *Exhib:* Six Artists in Paris, Am Cult Ctr, Paris, 64; Epinal Print Biennial, France, 70-71; Cite Int des Arts, Paris, France, 79; Contemp Arts Ctr, Honolulu, 80; 10 yr retrospective, Fisher Gallery, Univ of Southern Calif, 68; BMIC Galerie, Paris, 81; Salon de Mai, Paris, 82; 75th Anniversary, Univ Hawaii, 82; and others. *Teaching:* Instr drawing, Univ Iowa, 48-50; prof painting & printmaking, Univ Ill, 50-67; assoc dean fine arts, Univ Southern Calif, 67-72; prof painting & printmaking, Univ Hawaii, 72-; Louis D Beaumont Vis Distinguished Prof, Washington Univ, 79. *Awards:* Vera List Purchase Award, Soc Am Graphic Artists, 65; Univ Hawaii/Ford Found Fac Enrichment Award, Paris, 78-80; Fondation Gardilanne-Moffat Studio Award, Cite Intern des Arts, Paris, 78-83. *Bibliog:* Wayne Miyamoto (auth), Lee Chesney--25 years of printmaking. *Mem:* Soc Am Graphic Artists; Col Art Asn Am; Los Angeles Printmaking Soc (adv bd, 67-); Hawaii Artists League; Honolulu Printmaking Soc. *Media:* Intaglio; Acrylic. *Publ:* Contribr, Printmaking today, Col Art J, Vol XIX, No 2; contribr, A brief glance at Ukiyo-e and Hanga, Japan Print Quart, winter 67; Teaching in art graduate programs, J Educ Perspectives, fall 77. *Dealer:* Downtown Gallery 125 Merchant St Honolulu HI 96813; Art Loft Honolulu HI 96813. *Mailing Add:* Art Dept Univ Hawaii 2444 Dole St Honolulu HI 96822

CHESNEY, LEE ROY, III
PRINTMAKER, EDUCATOR
b San Antonio, Tex, July 5, 45. *Study:* Univ Ill, with Dennis Rowan, Eugene Telez; Univ Calif, Los Angeles, with Ray Brown; Ind Univ, with Rudy Pazzatti, Marvin Lowe, MFA. *Work:* Honolulu Acad Arts; San Diego State Univ Mus; State Univ NY Potsdam; Dickinson State Col Mus, NDak; Graphic Chem & Ink Co Collection, Chicago. *Exhib:* Libr Cong, Nat Collection Fine Arts, Smithsonian, Washington, DC, 69 & 73; 1st Int Pratt Graphics, Bath, Eng, 73-74; Int Print Biennials, Epinal, France, 75 & 77; Boston Printmakers, 82; Prints USA, 82; Pratt Graphics, New York, 82; and others. *Pos:* Prog dir art dept, Univ Tex, 78-81, grad adv, 81- *Teaching:* Assoc instr printmaking & etching, Ind Univ, Bloomington, 69-72; instr design & prints, Univ Tex, Austin, 72-75, asst prof printmaking, 75-78, assoc prof art, 78- *Awards:* Graphic Chem & Ink Purchase Award, Soc Am Graphic Artists, 73; Honolulu Acad Arts Purchase Award, 73; Prints from Am Univs Purchase Award, US Info Agency, 74. *Mem:* Col Art Asn Am; The Graphic Soc (Int), Hollis, NH; Soc Am Graphic Artists, New York. *Media:* Intaglio, Mixed Media. *Mailing Add:* 3700 Werner Austin TX 78722

CHESTER, CHARLOTTE WANETTA
PAINTER, PRINTMAKER
b Columbus, Ohio. *Study:* Ft Wright Col, Wash, BFA; Capitol Univ; Oklahoma City Univ; Pa Acad Fine Arts, with Blackburn & Sloan; Philadelphia Col Art, with Niebert; also with Eric Irmer, Frankfurt, Ger, two years; numerous teachers and workshops in US and Europe. *Work:* Artist and Space, Nat Air & Space Mus, Smithsonian Inst, Washington, DC; The Barn, Millville, NJ; also in collection of Soovia Janis, New York. *Comn:* Many paintings. *Exhib:* Frankfurt Ger Juried Exhib, 65; Atlantic City Art Ctr, NJ, 65-70; Cult Art Ctr of Ocean City, 68; Kerr Mus, Okla, 70; plus numerous traveling exhibs. *Teaching:* Instr advan oil painting, Atlantic Community Col, 68-69; pvt art classes, 65- *Awards:* Too numerous to mention. *Mem:* Am Fedn Art; League South Jersey Artist (pres, 68-70); Fed Art Asn NJ (chmn South Jersey, 71); Green Co Art Asn; Watercolor Soc London; Printmaking Coun NJ; Allied Arts, Spokane; Wash Art Asn. *Publ:* Contribr, Yearbook Ocean City, 68. *Mailing Add:* RT 1 Box 53 Reardan WA 99029

CHESTNEY, LILLIAN
ILLUSTRATOR, PAINTER
b New Haven, Conn. *Study:* Pratt Inst Sch Fine & Appl Arts, study with Khosrov Ajootian, Alexander Kostello, Maitland Graves, William Gorham and others. *Work:* Grand Cent Galleries, New York; Bantam Bks Inc, New York. *Comn:* Bk covers, Theodore Driesers' An American Tragedy, The Charter House of Parma & De Maupassants' Boule De Suife; bk illus, Gullivers' Travels & Arabian Nights; plus others. *Exhib:* Grand Cent Galleries; Am Watercolor Soc; Soc of Illusrs; Allied Am Artists; Artists Guild of New York. *Awards:* Award, Mystic Seaport Mus; Three Cert Merit, Soc Illusrs. *Mem:* Allied Artists Am; Grand Cent Art Galleries. *Media:* Oil & Egg Tempera. *Mailing Add:* 21 Old Farm Rd Levittown NY 11756

CHETHAM, CHARLES
MUSEUM DIRECTOR
US citizen. *Pos:* Dir, Smith Col Mus Art, currently. *Teaching:* Prof art, Smith Col. *Mailing Add:* Smith Col Mus of Art Northampton MA 10160

CHETHLAHE (DAVID CHETHLAHE PALADIN)
PAINTER, DESIGNER
b Chinle, Ariz, Nov 4, 26. *Study:* Santa Fe Indian Sch; Art Inst Chicago. *Work:* William Penn Mem Mus, Harrisburg, Pa; US Dept Interior, Washington, DC; US State Dept, Washington, DC; UNICEF, New York. *Comn:* Sand painted mural, Howard Johnson's, Detroit, 69; four tapestries, comn by City of Phoenix, Phoenix Civic Plaza, 72. *Exhib:* One-man shows, William Penn Mem Mus, 69 & Martin Gallery, Scottsdale, Ariz, 71-81; Scottsdale Indian Nat, 69-72; American Indians Today, Mem Mus, Santa Ana, Calif, 70; Am Indian Art Ctr, New York, 75. *Pos:* Dir, Renaissance Acad Creative Develop, 75- *Teaching:* Dir fine arts workshop, Prescott Col, 71-74. *Awards:* First Prize, Scottsdale Nat, 70 & Grand Prize, 71; Gold Medal, Accad Italia, Lavoro, Italy, 80. *Bibliog:* Peterson (auth), Indian Art '70 & 3 Indians, 72, KAET-TV, Phoenix; Jules Power (auth), Chethlahe, Indian

Artist, Discovery '71, ABC-TV, 71. *Mem:* Am Craftsmen Coun; Artists Equity Asn; Am Indian Designer Craftsmen (pres, 68-69); Coun Am Indian Artists. *Media:* Acrylic, Mixed Media. *Mailing Add:* PO Box 11942 Albuquerque NM 87192

CHEW, PAUL ALBERT
ADMINISTRATOR, LECTURER
b Norristown, Pa, Apr 22, 25. *Study:* Univ Pittsburgh, BA, 50, MA(Henry Clay Frick Fine Arts Dept Grad Asst), 52; Univ Manchester, England, PhD(fel), 57; St Vincent Col, Latrobe, Pa, Hon DFA, 81. *Collections Arranged:* Recent Trends in American Art, 69; One-Man Show: Henry Koerner, 71; David Hanna, 77; New Am Still Life, 78; Kenneth Frazier Impressionist (auth, catalog), 78; Southwestern Pennsylvania Painters, 1800-1945 (auth, catalog), 81. *Pos:* Asst to dir, Carnegie Mus, 52-53; exec to dir circulating exhibs, Mus Mod Art, New York, 53-54; dir, Westmoreland Co Mus Art, 57-; adv comt mem, Gov Home, Harrisburg, Pa, 79-; trustee, Woods-Marchand Found, currently. *Teaching:* Instr art hist, Univ Pittsburgh, Greensburg, Pa, 63- *Awards:* Forbes Medal, Ft Pitt Assoc Inc, 83. *Mem:* Col Art Asn Am; Am Asn Mus; Nat Trust Hist Preserv. *Publ:* Ed, Permanent Collection of Westmoreland County Museum of Art (catalog), 78. *Mailing Add:* 208 N Maple Ave Greensburg PA 15601

CHIARA, ALAN ROBERT
PAINTER
b Cleveland, Ohio, May 5, 36. *Study:* Cooper Sch Art, Cleveland; Cleveland Inst Art. *Work:* Butler Inst Art, Youngstown, Ohio; Springfield Art Mus, Mo; Cent Nat Bank Cleveland; Bethany Col, Lindsborg, Kans; Nat Acad Design, New York. *Exhib:* Butler Inst Art, 68; Watercolor USA, Springfield, Mo, 68; Nat Art Exhib, Wichita, Kans, 70; Nat Acad Design, New York, 71; Am Watercolor Soc, New York, 72. *Pos:* Master designer, Am Greetings, Cleveland, 58-70; pres, Chiara Galleries, Cleveland, 69- *Awards:* Silver Medal Award, Am Watercolor Soc, 66; Adolph & Clara Obrig Prize, 67 & William A Paton Prize, 70, Nat Acad Design. *Mem:* Am Watercolor Soc; assoc Nat Acad Design. *Media:* Watercolor. *Specialty:* Living American artists. *Publ:* Auth, Watercolor page, Am Artist Mag, 11/67. *Mailing Add:* 21706 Altamira Ave Boca Raton FL 33433

CHIARENZA, CARL
PHOTOGRAPHER, HISTORIAN
b Rochester, NY, Sept 5, 35. *Study:* Rochester Inst Technol, AAS, 55, BFA, 57; Boston Univ, MS, 59, AM, 64; Danforth Found teacher grant, 66-68; Harvard Univ, PhD, 73. *Work:* Minneapolis Inst Arts, Minn; Fogg Art Mus, Cambridge, Mass; Mus Fine Arts, Houston; Int Mus Photog/George Eastman House, Rochester, NY; Princeton Univ Art Mus; and others. *Exhib:* Sense of Abstraction, Mus Mod Art, New York, 60; Photog in Am 1850-1965, Yale Univ Art Gallery, 65; Contemp Photogr I, George Eastman House, 67; one-man shows, Photog, Mus Art, Eugene, Ore, 67 & Selected Photog 1954-1979, Minneapolis Inst Arts, 79-80; Celebrations, Hayden Gallery, Mass Inst Technol, Cambridge, Mass, 74; Target Collection Am Photog, Mus Fine Arts, Houston, 77; Attitudes: Photog in the 1970's, Santa Barbara Mus Art, Calif, 79; plus many others. *Pos:* Ed, Contemp Photogr, Boston, 66-69; co-founder, Imageworks Ctr & Sch, Cambridge, Mass, 71-73; trustee, Visual Studies Workshop, Rochester, 75-; chmn, Dept Art Hist, Boston Univ, 76-81. *Teaching:* Prof art hist, Boston Univ, 63-; vis prof photog hist & theory, Visual Studies Workshop, Rochester, NY, 73-74; Harnish vis artist, Smith Col, 83-84. *Awards:* Mass Arts & Humanities Foun Fel, 75-76; Nat Endowment Arts Fel, 77-78. *Bibliog:* John Scarborough (auth), Eruptions of art..., Houston Chronicle, 5/29/76; S R Channing & E Jussim (coauth), Art of the State, State of the Art, Addison House, Danbury, NH, 78; David Robinson (auth), Carl Chiarenza, Am Photog, 12/83. *Mem:* Soc Photog Educ (bd dirs, 68-73); Photog Resource Ctr (bd trustees, 77-); Friends of Photog (adv trustee, 79-83). *Media:* Black and White Photography. *Res:* Twentieth century American photography. *Publ:* Auth, From Cliche-Verre to Vary Cliche, Light Gallery, New York, 79; auth, Notes toward integrated history of picturemaking, Afterimage, Vol VII, No 1/2, 79; auth, Siskind: Pleasures and terrors, NY Graphic Soc, Boston, 82; coauth, Heinecken, Friends Photog, 80; auth, Eye & mind: The seriousness of wit, Kenneth Josephson, Mus Contemp Art, Chicago, 83; and others. *Dealer:* Carl Siembab Gallery 162 Newbury St Boston MA 02116; Susan Harder Gallery 37 W 57th St New York NY 10019. *Mailing Add:* 725 Commonwealth Ave Boston MA 02215

CHICAGO, JUDY
PAINTER, SCULPTOR
b Chicago, Ill, July 20, 39. *Study:* Univ Calif, Los Angeles, BA, 62, MA, 64. *Work:* Brooklyn Mus; San Francisco Mus Mod Art; Oakland Mus; Pacific Sci Ctr. *Exhib:* Sculpture of the Sixties, Los Angeles Co Mus Art & Philadelphia Mus Art, 67; West Coast Now, Seattle Art Mus & San Francisco Mus Art, 68; Color as Structure, Whitney Mus Am Art, 70; Univ Wash, Seattle, 72; de Saisset Mus, Santa Clara, Calif, 73; Univ NDak, Grand Forks, 73; Western Wash State Col, Bellingham, 74; Cerritos Col, Newark, Calif, 75; The Dinner Party, San Francisco Mus Mod Art, 79; Brooklyn Mus; and others. *Teaching:* Instr, Calif State, Fresno, Cal Arts, Feminist Studio Workshop. *Bibliog:* Lucy Lippard (auth), exhib rev, Art Am, 4/80; John Perrault (auth), exhib rev, Soho News, 10/15/80; Jane Adams (auth), article, Horizon Mag, 3/81; and others. *Mem:* Women's Caucus Art. *Interests:* Porcelain painting. *Publ:* Auth, Through the Flower: My Struggle as a Woman Artist, Doubleday, 75 & 81; auth, The Dinner Party: a Symbol of Our Heritage, 79 & Embroidering Our Heritage: The Dinner Party Needlework, 80, Anchor/Doubleday. *Mailing Add:* PO Box 834 Benicia CA 94510

CHIEFFO, CLIFFORD TOBY
PAINTER, CONSERVATOR
b New Haven, Conn, July 23, 37. *Study:* Southern Conn State Univ, BS; Teachers Col, Columbia Univ, MA. *Work:* Baltimore Mus Art; Berkshire Mus Art; Georgetown Univ; US State Dept Art in Embassies Prog; Nat Mus Am Art, Washington, DC; plus others. *Exhib:* Corcoran Gallery Art, 63, 65 & 67; Baltimore Mus Art, 65 & 66; Four American Printmakers, Am Embassy, Ireland, 68; 45 group and one-man exhib. *Pos:* Tech ed, Am Artist Mag, currently. *Teaching:* Instr painting, drawing & silk-screen, Univ Md; Corcoran Sch Art; prof fine arts & cur, Georgetown Univ, currently. *Awards:* Distinguished Alumni Award, Southern Conn State Univ, 74; Nat Mus Art grant, 76-77; Award, Univ Tenn, 79; and others. *Mem:* Col Art Asn Am; Washington, DC Conservators Guild; Am Inst Conservators Hist Artistic Works. *Media:* Painting, Graphic. *Publ:* Auth, Silk-Screen as a Fine Art, Van Nostrand-Reinhold, 67 & paperback, 78; auth, Contemporary Oil Painters Handbook, Prentice-Hall, 76 & Van Nostrand Reinhold, 82. *Mailing Add:* 14 Riverwood Ct Potomac MD 20854

CHIEGO, WILLIAM JOSEPH
ADMINISTRATOR, CURATOR
b Newark, NJ, Sept 17, 43. *Study:* Univ Va, Charlottesville, BA(with distinction), 65; Case Western Reserve Univ, Cleveland, Ohio, MA(art hist), 68, PhD(art hist, Univ Fel, Bingham Travel Fel), 74; Mus Mgt Inst, summer 81; Resident Fel, Yale Ctr British Arts, spring 82. *Collections Arranged:* A Tribute to C S Price (auth, catalog), 76 & From Oregon Private Collections (auth, catalog), 77, Portland Art Mus, Ore; Art Advocates, 1966-76; Bonnie Bronson/Recent Works, 79; Master Prints from the Gilkey Collection, 80; The Phillips Taste in Portland, 80. *Pos:* Asst cur, Toledo Mus Art, Ohio, 73-74; assoc cur, 74-76; cur, Portland Art Mus, Ore, 76-83 & NC Mus Art, 83- *Mem:* Col Art Asn; Am Asn Mus; Decorative Arts Chap, Soc Archit Historians. *Res:* French art, 1750-1850, especially Gericault and Carle Vernet; British and American art of the 18th and 19th centuries; C S Price; American 20th century art. *Publ:* Auth, A boudoir scene by Le Prince, 74 & Two paintings by Fantin Latour, 74, Mus News, Toledo Mus Art; ed, Catalogue of European Paintings, Toledo, Pa State Univ Press, 76. *Mailing Add:* NC Mus Art 107 E Morgan St Raleigh NC 27611

CHIHULY, DALE PATRICK
GLASS ARTIST, EDUCATOR
b Tacoma, Wash, Sept 20, 41. *Study:* Univ Wash, Seattle, BA; Univ Wis, Madison, MS; RI Sch Design, MFA. *Work:* Metrop Mus Art, New York; Seattle Art Mus; Wadsworth Atheneum, Hartford, Conn; Philadelphia Mus Art; Victoria & Albert Mus, London; and others. *Exhib:* One-person shows, Univ Minn, Minneapolis, 76 & Hadler Galleries, Houston, Tex, 77; three-person shows, Seattle Art Mus, 77 & St Louis Art Mus, Mo, 83; Foster/White Gallery, Seattle, 78-83; Habitat Gallery, Detroit, 80-83; Charles Cowles Gallery, New York, 81-83; Betsy Rosenfield Gallery, Chicago, 81-83. *Teaching:* Chmn dept glass blowing, RI Sch Design, 67-80, chmn dept sculpture, 76-77; educ coordr & co-founder, Pilchuck Glass Ctr, Stanwood, Wash, 71- *Awards:* Louis Tiffany Found Award, 67; Fulbright Fel, Murano, Italy, 68; Master Craftsman-Apprenticeship Grant, Nat Endowment Arts, 75. *Bibliog:* David Manzella (auth), The Fluid Breath of Glass, Craft Horizons, 71; Roni Horn (auth), Dale Chihuly and the Glass Cylinders, Studio Potter, 76; Alexandra Anderson (auth), Bravura glass, Portfolio Mag, 82. *Media:* Glass. *Mailing Add:* 4301 N 33rd Tacoma WA 98407

CHILDERS, MALCOLM GRAEME
PRINTMAKER, PHOTOGRAPHER
b Riverside, Calif, Feb 19, 45. *Study:* Humboldt State Univ, Arcata, Calif, BA, 69; Fullerton State Univ, Calif, MA, 72. *Work:* Springfield Art Mus, Mo; Tenn State Mus, Nashville; Meadows Mus Art, Shreveport, La; Brooks Mem Art Gallery, Memphis, Tenn; Standard Oil Co-Ind, Chicago Corp Art Collection. *Exhib:* Hunter Mus Art Ann, Chattanooga, Tenn, 75; Appalachian Corridors Biennial Art Exhib 4, Charleston, SC, 75; Bradley Print Show, Peoria, Ill, 75-76; La Grange Nat Competition II, Ga, 75-76; Tenn Bicentennial Exhib, Nashville, Tenn, 76; and others. *Teaching:* Instr printmaking, Loma Linda Univ, Calif, 72-74; asst prof drawing, painting & printmaking, Southern Missionary Col, Collegedale, Tenn, 74- *Awards:* Purchase Awards, La Grange Nat II, La Grange Art Mus, 75, Mid-South Biennial, Brooks Mem Art Gallery, 75 & Tenn Bicentennial, State of Tenn, 76. *Dealer:* Assoc Am Artists 663 Fifth Ave New York NY 10022. *Mailing Add:* Dept of Art Southern Missionary Col Collegedale TN 37315

CHILDERS, RICHARD ROBIN
PAINTER
b El Paso, Tex, Nov 28, 46. *Study:* Dallas Mus Fine Arts Sch; Pa Acad Fine Arts; Northwood Inst. *Work:* Southwestern Med Ctr, Univ Tex, Dallas; Mus Mod Art, Paris; Texas Bank, Houston; and others. *Comn:* Energy stick (concrete sculpture), Dr & Mrs S Ainslie Shelburne, Cincinnati, 72. *Exhib:* Tex Painting & Sculpture Ann, Dallas Mus Fine Art, 71; 15th Ann Delta Art Exhib, Ark Art Ctr, Little Rock, 72; Eight State Exhib, Oklahoma Art Ctr, Oklahoma City, 74; solo exhib, New Orleans Mus Art, 74; First Ann Crossroads of Am Art Exhib, Chicago, Ill, 75; Dallas Art 78, Dallas City Hall. *Awards:* First Place, Tex Painting and Sculpture Ann, Dallas Mus Fine Art, 71; Grand Purchase Award, 15th Delta Art Exhib, Ark Art Ctr, 72; Purchase Prize, 1973 Artist Biennial, New Orleans Mus of Art, 73. *Bibliog:* Janet Kutner (auth), Richard Childers, Arts Mag, 9/77; Jim Stratton (auth), Pioneering in the Urban Wilderness, Urizen Books Inc, 77; Leellen Patchen (dir), Richard Childers (film), 78. *Media:* Acrylic on Canvas. *Publ:* Ed, First Saturday Art Magazine, 76. *Dealer:* SL Art Gallery 2133 Cedar Springs Rd Dallas TX 75201. *Mailing Add:* 842 First Ave Dallas TX 75226

CHILDS, BERNARD
PAINTER, PRINTMAKER
b Brooklyn, NY, Sept 1, 10. *Study:* Univ Pa, 28-30; Art Students League, with Kimon Nicolaides, 30; with Per Smed, 31 & Amadee Ozenfont, 47. *Work:* Stedelijk Mus, Amsterdam; Storm King Art Ctr; Achenbach Found Graphic Arts; Whitney Mus Am Art; Nat Mus Western Art, Tokyo. *Comn:* Grillwork, comn by Eric Cumine, Int Country Club, Hong Kong, 61. *Exhib:* Solo exhibs, Stedelijk Mus, Amsterdam, 59, Storm King Art Ctr, 69 & Honolulu Acad Arts, 82. *Awards:* Mus Occidental Art Award, Tokyo Int Print Biennial, 60; Purchase Awards, Cincinnati Int Print Biennial, 62 & 16th Nat Print Exhib, Brooklyn Mus, 68. *Media:* Oil. *Publ:* Auth, Nipponjin no Te: Hands of the Japanese, Art Int, 60; auth & illusr, Prints and impressions, Idea, Tokyo, 61; auth & illusr, Tropical noon: High speed presses and the unlimited edition, Artists Proof, Pratt Graphic Ctr, 70. *Mailing Add:* 222 W 23 St New York NY 10011

CHIN, RIC
LECTURER, PAINTER
b Hong Kong, July 16, 35; US & UK citizen. *Study:* State Univ NY; Art Students League; Sch Chinese Brushwork, New York; also with Barse Miller, Cheng Dai-Chien & Wang Chi-Yuan. *Work:* Nat Palace Mus, Taiwan; Penang Mus, Malaysia; Manhattan Savings Bank, Eastchester, NY; Houston's Ethan Allen Gallery, Greensboro, NC; Wantagh Sch Syst, NY. *Exhib:* Am Artists Prof League Grand Nat, Lever House, NY, 71-75; Nat Palace Mus Ann, Taiwan, 74; one-man shows, Winston-Salem Hyatt House, NC, 74 & Ctr Asian Studies, St John's Univ, NY, 75; United Va Bank. *Pos:* Dir, Bertrick Assoc Artists Inc, Seaford, NY, 65-74. *Teaching:* Lectr Chinese cult & art, Long Island Univ, 70-71; instr Chinese brushwork, var workshops, Southeastern US & Nat Art League, Douglaston, NY; nat painting & cooking lectr tour in 78 cities & on 34 TV shows, 77-78. *Mem:* Salmagundi Club (mem bd dir, 74 & 75); Am Artists Prof League; Sumi-E Soc Am; Nat Art League; Art League Nassau Co. *Media:* Watercolor; Water-Ink. *Res:* Rice paper. *Mailing Add:* 902 W Market St Greensboro NC 27401

CHINN, YUEN YUEY
PAINTER, PRINTMAKER
b Kwantung, China, Dec 24, 22; US citizen. *Study:* Columbia Univ, Brevoort Eickmeyer fel, 52-53, BFA, 53, study with Shahan, Heliker & Mangravite, 53-54, MFA, 54; Atelier 17, Paris with S Hayter, 58-59. *Work:* Nat Collection Fine Arts; Wadsworth Atheneum Mus; Fogg Art Mus; Nat Mus, Stockholm. *Comn:* Mural comn by Mrs Joanna Gunderson, 71. *Exhib:* Young American Printmakers, Mus Mod Art, New York, 53-54; Abstrakt Landskap, Nat Mus, Stockholm, 60; Salone de Mai, Musee Nat d'Art Mod, Paris, 61; 9 Europaische Kunstler, Haus Am Waldsee, Berlin-Zehlendorf, 63; 2e Salon Int Galeries Pilotes, Musee Cantonal Beaux Art, Lousanne, 66. *Teaching:* Adj teacher, Brooklyn Col, 75- *Awards:* Fulbright fel, 54-55; John Hay Whitney Fel, 56-57. *Bibliog:* C Von Wiegand (auth), The World of Abstract Art, 57; Alexander Watt (auth), In Paris the painter is at home, Studio, 60; Otto Hahn (auth), Review Art in Paris, Art Int, 5/64. *Media:* Oil, Gouache. *Dealer:* Galerie Karl Flinker 25 Rue de Tournon Paris France. *Mailing Add:* 80 N Moore St Apt 15J New York NY 10013

CHINNI, PETER ANTHONY
SCULPTOR, PAINTER
b Mount Kisco, NY, Mar 21, 28. *Study:* Art Students League; Acad Belle Arti, Rome, Italy; also with Roberto Melli, Rome & Felice Casorati, Turin. *Work:* Whitney Mus Am Art, New York; New Sch Social Res, New York; St Louis Art Mus, Mo; Nat Gallery Art, Smithsonian Inst, Washington, DC; Rockefeller Collection. *Exhib:* Carnegie Int, Pittsburgh, Pa, 64-65; Whitney Mus Am Art Ann, 64-65; New Sch Social Res, 69; Biennale Roma, 69; Gallery Mod Art, Rome, 70. *Awards:* Award Comn for Columbia, Mo Outdoor Steel Sculpture, 79. *Mem:* Sculptors Guild, NY; Artist's Equity, NY. *Media:* Bronze, Stainless Steel; Oil. *Mailing Add:* RFD 2 Pines Bridge Rd Katonah NY 10536

CHIPP, HERSCHEL BROWNING
EDUCATOR, CURATOR
b New Hampton, Mo, Nov 9, 13. *Study:* Univ Calif, Berkeley, BA & MA; Columbia Univ, PhD; Univ Paris; Fulbright fel to France, 51-52; Belg-Am Educ Found fel, 52. *Pos:* Dir, Univ Art Gallery, Univ Calif, Berkeley, 61-65; dir, Am Exhib, Paris Biennale, 63; mem selection comt, Fulbright-Hayes Prog & other agencies, Nat Endowment Humanities, 77- *Teaching:* Chmn art dept, Univ Calif, Berkeley, 61-63. *Mem:* Col Art Asn Am (dir, 61-65); Soc Hist Art Fr. *Publ:* Auth, The Human Image in German Expressionist Graphic Art, 81; auth, Guernica-Legado Picasso, 81; auth, Gaston Lachaise, 82; contribr, Theophile Alexandre Steinlen, 82; auth, Georges Braque: The Late Years, 82. *Mailing Add:* Dept of Hist of Art Univ of Calif Berkeley CA 94720

CHO, DAVID
DESIGNER, ASSEMBLAGE ARTIST
b Los Angeles, Calif, Aug 13, 50. *Study:* Calif State Univ, Los Angeles, BA, 72. *Work:* Long Beach Mus Art, Calif. *Exhib:* Long Beach Mus Art 10th Ann, 72; Small Environments, Southern Ill Univ & Wis Art Ctr, Madison, 72; The David Cho Show, Amerasia Gallery, Los Angeles, 74; Collage & Assemblage in Southern California, Los Angeles Inst Contemp Art, 75; William Grant Still Art Ctr, Los Angeles, Calif, 78; and others. *Bibliog:* Articles, San Francisco Chronicle, 71, Los Angeles Times Calendar Mag, 72 & Art Gallery Mag, 72. *Dealer:* Wood City 3626 W Jefferson Blvd Los Angeles CA 90016. *Mailing Add:* 716 Tularosa Dr Los Angeles CA 90026

CHODKOWSKI, HENRY, JR
PAINTER, EDUCATOR
b Hartford, Conn, Mar 20, 37. *Study:* Univ Hartford, BFA, 61; Yale Univ, MFA, 63. *Work:* Phillips Collection, Library Congress, Nat Collection Fine Arts, Washington, DC; Philadelphia Mus; DeCordova Mus, Mass. *Exhib:* One-man shows, J B Speed Art Mus, 68, 72 & 78, Duke Univ Mus, 72, Middendorf Gallery, Washington, DC, 75 & Allan Stone Gallery, New York, 79; Gallery Contemp Art, Winston-Salem, NC, 74; Nat Soc Painters in Casein & Acrylic 22nd Ann, Lever House, 75 & Hassam & Speicher Exhibition, Am Acad & Inst Arts & Letters, 82, New York. *Teaching:* Prof advan painting, Univ Louisville, 73- *Awards:* Polaroid Corp Grant, 68; Univ Louisville Res Grant, 67, 68 & 75; Award for Excellence in Teaching & Scholarship, Univ Louisville, 78. *Bibliog:* Jay Kloner (auth), The precisionist paintings of Henry Chodkowski, 10/75 & Henry Chodkowski, 3/79, Arts Mag. *Media:* Acrylic. *Dealer:* Kathleen Meyer Gallery 624 W Main Louisville Ky 40202. *Mailing Add:* 2015 Baringer Ave Louisville KY 40204

CHOO, CHUNGHI
METALSMITH, FABRIC DESIGNER
b Inchon, Korea, May 23, 38; US citizen. *Study:* Ewha Women's Univ, Seoul, Korea, BFA; Cranbrook Acad Art, Bloomfield Hills, Mich, MFA; Penland Sch Crafts; Tyler Sch Art. *Work:* Metrop Mus Art, New York. *Exhib:* Young Americans 1969, Mus Contemp Crafts, New York; one-woman show, Jack Lenor Larsen Show Rm, New York, 71; Fabric Vibrations, Eastern & Western Europe, Near & Far East & Pac Islands sponsored by Smithsonian Inst, 72-75; North American Goldsmith, Renwick Gallery, Washington, DC, 74; Forms in Metal, Mus Contemp Crafts, New York, 75; Dyers Art, Mus Contemp Crafts, New York, 76; Int Fiberworks, Cleveland Mus Art, Ohio, 77. *Teaching:* From assoc prof to prof metalworking & jewelry, Sch of Art & Art Hist, Univ Iowa, 68- *Bibliog:* Jack Lenor Larsen (auth), Dyer's Art, Reinhold; Textile surface, Craft Horizons, 4/76. *Mem:* Soc NAm Goldsmith; Am Crafts Coun. *Dealer:* Hardler Galleries 35-37 E 20th St New York NY 10003. *Mailing Add:* Sch of Art & Art Hist Univ of Iowa Iowa City IA 52242

CHOW CHIAN-CHIU
PAINTER, HISTORIAN
b Canton, China, Dec 23, 10. *Work:* Tsing Hwa Univ, Peking; Hopkins Ctr Art Galleries, Dartmouth Col, NH; Cernuschi Mus, Paris; Lawrence Univ, Canton, NY. *Exhib:* Yugoslavia traveling exhib, Kansas State Univ, Univ Calif, Berkeley, Stanford Univ, Calif, Univ Pittsburgh, Pa, Univ Rochester, NY & others; Art Mus Seattle, Wash; Dartmouth Col, Hanover, NH; and others. *Teaching:* Pres, Int Studio Chinese Art, 52-67; instr Chinese art, Grove Art Sch, Miami Art Ctr, Fla, 68-70. *Awards:* Respect Award, Inst Chinese Cult, New York, 70; Gold Medal & Jin Ding Award, Cent Gov Republic China, 80. *Bibliog:* Walter Foster (auth), Chinese Art, film, Wilbur T Blume, 62. *Mem:* Chinese Artist Asn, Nanking; Chinese Artist Asn, Hong Kong; hon mem Miami Artist Asn. *Publ:* Coauth, Easy Way to do Chinese Painting, 61; coauth, Chinese Painting No 2, 72; auth, The Biographies of Chinese Painting New School Founder in History, Libr Cong, 75; A Comprehensive Guide of Chinese Painting, 80. *Mailing Add:* 2740 Le Jeune Rd Coral Gables FL 33134

CHOW LEUNG CHEN-YING
PAINTER, CALLIGRAPHER
b Canton, China, Mar 20, 20. *Study:* Art Teacher Training Col, China. *Work:* Hopkins Ctr Art Galleries, Dartmouth, NH; Mus Cernuschi, Paris, St Lawrence Univ, Canton, N Y. *Exhib:* Dartmouth Col, Hanover, NH, Art Mus of Seattle, Wash, Kans State Univ, Manhattan, Stanford Univ, Calif & Univ Pittsburgh, Pa; and others. *Teaching:* Prof, Int Studio Chinese Art, 52-67; instr Chinese art, Grove Art Sch, Miami Art Ctr, Fla, 69-70; pres & prof, Chow Studio, 69- *Awards:* Gold Medal & Jin Ding Award, Cent Gov Republic China, 80. *Bibliog:* Foster (auth), Chinese Art (film), Wilbur T Blume, 62. *Mem:* Chinese Artist Asn, Hong Kong; hon mem Miami Artist Asn. *Publ:* Coauth, Easy Way to do Chinese Painting, 61; coauth, Chinese Painting No 2, 72; A Comprehensive Guide of Chinese Painting, 80. *Mailing Add:* 2740 Le Jeune Rd Coral Gables FL 33134

CHOY, TERENCE TIN-HO
PAINTER, EDUCATOR
b Hong Kong, Nov 26, 41; US citizen. *Study:* San Francisco State Univ, BA; Univ Calif, Berkeley, with David Hockney, Elmer Bischoff & Earl Loren, MA. *Work:* Alaska State Coun Arts, Anchorage; Alaska State Mus at Juneau; Univ Alaska, Anchorage; Univ Alaska, Fairbanks. *Exhib:* M H de Young Mem Mus, San Francisco, 69; Honolulu Acad Art, Hawaii, 76; Woodson Art Mus, Wausau, Wis, 76; Nat Collection Fine Arts, Washington, DC, 78; Univ Minn, Minneapolis, 80; Wing Luk Mem Mus, 81. *Pos:* Photographer, Univ Calif, Berkeley, 68-70; gallery coordr, Art Galleries, Univ Alaska, Fairbanks, 71-75. *Teaching:* Instr art, de Young Mus Art Sch, San Francisco, 69-70; prof art, Univ Alaska, Fairbanks, 70- *Awards:* Nat Endowment Humanities Grant, 79; Alaska State Coun Arts Grant, 79; Mellon Found Grants, 80 & 81. *Mem:* Col Art Asn; Nat Art Educ Asn; Alaska Asn Arts; Visual Art Ctr Alaska. *Mailing Add:* Dept of Art Univ of Alaska Fairbanks AK 99701

CHREPTOWSKY, ACHILLES N
COLLECTOR, PATRON
b Ukraine, June 6, 20; US citizen. *Pos:* Founder, pres & mem bd dirs, Ukranian Inst Mod Art, Chicago. *Mem:* Art Inst Chicago; Mus Contemp Art. *Interests:* Constructivism and abstract expressionism. *Mailing Add:* 950 N Columbian Ave Oak Park IL 60302

CHRISTENBERRY, WILLIAM
EDUCATOR, PAINTER
b Tuscaloosa, Ala, Nov 5, 36. *Study:* Univ Ala, Tuscaloosa, BFA, 58, MA, 59. *Work:* Corcoran Gallery Art, Washington, DC; Mus Mod Art, New York. *Comn:* US Gen Serv Admin, Washington, DC; southern wall, Fed Bldg, Jackson, Miss. *Exhib:* Photographs, Corcoran Gallery Art, Washington, DC, 73 & 78; Drawings and Small Works, Washington Gallery Art, Washington, DC, 73; one-man exhib, Baltimore Mus Art, 73; Zabriskie Gallery, New York, 76; Montgomery Mus Art, Ala, 79; Middendorf/Lane Gallery, Washington, DC, 81. *Teaching:* Assoc prof art, Corcoran Sch Art, Washington, DC, 68-74, prof, 74- *Awards:* Fel Nat Endowment Arts, 76. *Mailing Add:* Middendorf/Lane Gallery 2009 Columbia Rd NW Washington DC 20008

CHRISTENSEN, DAN
PAINTER
b Lexington, Nebr, 1942. *Study:* Kansas City Art Inst, BFA, 64. *Work:* Metrop Mus Art, Mus Mod Art, New York; Hirshhorn Mus, Washington, DC; St Louis Art Mus, Mo; Denver Mus Art. *Exhib:* Corcoran Biennial, Washington, DC, 69; Guggenheim Mus, New York, 69; Color & Field 1890-1970, Albright-Knox Gallery, Buffalo, NY, 70; The Structure of Color, Whitney Mus, New York, 71; Abstract Painting in the 70's, Boston Mus Fine Arts, 72; Meredith Long Contemp Gallery, New York, 78, 79 & 81; Harcus Krakow Gallery, Boston, 81; Douglas Drake Gallery, Kansas City, Kans, 81; Martha White Gallery, Louisville, Ky, 82; Ivory/Kimpton Gallery, San Francisco, 82; and others. *Bibliog:* Grace Glueck (auth), Like a beginning, Art in Am, 5-6/69; Emily Wasserman (auth), New York, Artforum, 9/69. *Publ:* Auth, Fine Young Artists Theodoron Awards, Guggenheim Mus, 69. *Dealer:* Andre Emmerich Gallery Inc 41 E 57th St New York NY 10022. *Mailing Add:* c/o Salander-O'Reilly Gallery 22 E 80th St New York NY 10021

CHRISTENSEN, HANS-JORGEN THORVALD
DESIGNER, SILVERSMITH
b Copenhagen, Denmark, Jan 21, 24. *Study:* Sch Arts & Crafts, Copenhagen, 39-44, dipl, 50; Georg Jensen Silver, apprentice; Col Tech Soc, Copenhagen, 51-53; Sch Arts & Crafts, Oslo, Norway, 52. *Work:* Johnson Wax Collection; Vatican Mus Contemp Art, Rome; and others. *Exhib:* Expo, Universal & Int Exhib, Brussels, Belg, 58; one-man shows, Albright-Knox Art Gallery, Buffalo, NY, 60 & Security Trust Co, Rochester, NY, 69; Johnson Wax Collection, Objects USA, traveled in US & Europe, 69; Radial 80, Xerox Art Show, Rochester, NY, 72. *Pos:* Head model dept, Georg Jensen Silver, Copenhagen, 52-54. *Teaching:* Instr design, Sch Arts & Crafts, Copenhagen, 52-54; instr silversmithing & design, Sch Am Craftsmen, Rochester Inst Technol, 54-59, assoc prof, 59-63, prof, 63-82, Charlotte F Mowris Prof contemp arts, formerly. *Awards:* Hertz Legazy, King Christian X of Denmark, 44; Damascene Plate of Leo Brom, Utrecht, Huntington Gallery, 55; Rochester Silversmith Guild Award, Mem Art Gallery, Rochester, 60; Fellow, Am Craft Coun, 79. *Bibliog:* Herald Brennan (auth), Why handmade?, Craft Horizons, 5-6/55; Talis Bergmanis (auth), Hans Christensen & the silver pots, Democrat & Chronicle, 68; Lee Nordness (auth), Objects USA, Viking, 70. *Media:* Sterling Silver, Metals. *Mailing Add:* 119 Faircrest Rd Rochester NY 14623

CHRISTENSEN, LARRY R
PAINTER, INSTRUCTOR
b Manti, Utah, Jan 18, 36. *Study:* Utah Tech Col, cert, 2 yrs. *Work:* Vernal High Sch, Utah; Cliff Lodge, Snowbird, Utah; Am Express Co, Salt Lake City; Veterans Admin. *Comn:* Idaho Telephone Dir Cover, Mountain Bell, 61. *Exhib:* Cody Country Regional Art Exhib, Wyo, 67-81; Springville Mus Art Nat, Utah, 69-79; Cedar City Nat Exhib, Utah, 72-77; two-man show, Phillips Gallery, 73, 74, 76, 79 & 82; Univ Utah Mus Fine Art, 76-79; plus others. *Pos:* Art dir, Mountain Bell, 71-79; instr, Watercolor Workshop, Salt Lake City, 75, 76, 79 & 80; instr, Div Continuing Educ, Univ Utah, 75, Photo Blue Workshop, 77- *Awards:* Silver 2nd Award, Utah State Expos, 70; First Place, Cody Country Art 70 & 81; Special Cash Award, Utah, 81. *Mem:* Assoc mem Am Watercolor Soc; Utah Watercolor Soc; Midwest Watercolor Soc; San Diego Watercolor Soc. *Publ:* Contribr, Art West, 72. *Dealer:* Brandywine Galleries Ltd 120 Morningside Dr SE Albuquerque NM 87108; Phillips Gallery 444 E 2nd Salt Lake City UT 84111. *Mailing Add:* 3534 Dover Hill Dr Salt Lake City UT 84121

CHRISTENSEN, RONALD JULIUS
PAINTER, PRINTMAKER
b Quincy, Mass, May 1, 23. *Study:* Sch Boston Mus Fine Arts, 47-50. *Work:* Rijksmuseum, Amsterdam, Holland; Springfield Mus Fine Art, Mass; Phoenix Art Mus, Ariz; Sloan Kettering Inst, New York; Bankers Trust, New York; and others. *Comn:* Three landscape murals, Celanese Corp Am, New York, 66; Americana Series painting, H B Hamilton Co, New York, 70; mural on acrylite, Boston Univ, 78. *Exhib:* Corcoran Biennial, Washington, DC, 59-60; Inst Contemp Art, Boston, 60; Nat Arts Club, New York, 76; Frank Fedele Fine Arts, New York, 79-83; Steve Rosendahl Gallery, Naples, Fla, 78-81; Museo Bogarin, El Tigre, Venezuela, 82; and others. *Pos:* Illusr, Original Print Collectors Group Ltd, New York, 73- *Bibliog:* Malcolm Preston (auth), Reminders of past masters of nature, Newsday, 70; S Barksdale (auth), Conductor of color orchestras, Emporium, 80. *Mem:* Nat Arts Club. *Media:* Oil, Acrylic; Serigraphy. *Dealer:* Frank Fedele Fine Arts 42 E 57 St New York NY 10022. *Mailing Add:* Box 157 Rt 3 Bean's Cove Clearville PA 15535

CHRISTENSEN, SHARLENE
PAINTER, INSTRUCTOR
b Fountain Green, Utah, Aug 24, 39. *Work:* Cliff Lodge, Snowbird, Utah; Salt Lake Surgical Ctr, Am Express Co & Vet Admin, Salt Lake City; Isabel M Haynes, Boseman, Mont. *Exhib:* Two-man show, Phillips Gallery, 73, 74, 76, 79 & 82; Audubon Artists 38th Ann, New York, 80; Watercolor West, Riverside, Calif, 80; San Diego Int Watercolor Exhib, 81; Watercolor West, Logan, Utah, 81; and many others. *Pos:* Artists-in-schs prog, Nat Found Arts & Utah Inst Fine Arts, 73-74; instr, Watercolor Workshop, Salt Lake City, 75-80. *Teaching:* Instr watercolor, Salt Lake Art Ctr, 72- *Awards:* Award of Merit, The Deseret News, 78; Best of Show, Cody Country Art Exhib, 78; Award of Merit, Utah State Fair, 82 & 83. *Mem:* Am & Utah Watercolor Soc; Midwest Watercolor Soc; assoc mem San Diego Watercolor Soc. *Media:* Transparent Watercolor. *Publ:* Contribr, Art West, 72 & Deseret News, 81. *Dealer:* Brandywine Galleries 120 Morningside Dr SE Albuquerque NM 87108; Phillips Gallery 444 E 2nd S Salt Lake City UT 84111. *Mailing Add:* 3534 Dover Hill Dr Salt Lake City UT 84121

CHRISTENSEN, TED
PAINTER, PRINTMAKER
b Vancouver, Wash, Mar 20, 11. *Study:* Art Ctr Sch, Los Angeles, with King & Feitelson; Mus Art Sch, Portland, Ore, with Givler & Bunce; Otis Art Inst, Los Angeles, with Hansen & Zornes. *Work:* Wurlitzer Found, Taos, NMex; City of Sausalito Collection, Calif; Harwood Found, Taos; Col of Marin, Kentfield, Calif; Vancouver High Sch Collection, Wash. *Exhib:* Los Angeles Co Mus Ann, Los Angeles, 45 & 46; Ore Soc of Artists, Portland Art Mus, 46 & 47; Painters & Sculptors Ann, Oakland Art Mus, Calif, 46-47 & 54; Int Ceramic Ann, Syracuse Mus of Art, NY, 49 & 50; one-man shows, Col of Marin, Kentfield, Calif, 54 & 63, Marin Mus, San Rafael, Calif, plus over 40 others. *Collections Arranged:* Paintings of Mendocino Area, Mendocino Hist Res Soc, Calif, 77. *Teaching:* Instr life drawing, Col of Marin, Kentfield, 52-60. *Awards:* First Prize, Ore Soc of Artists, Portland Art Mus, 46 & 47; First Prize, Marin Soc of Artists, Webb Gallery, Ross, Calif, 58. *Bibliog:* Mary Carrol Nelson (auth), Ted Christensen--Itinerant Painter, Am Artist, 12/76; Susan E Myer (auth), 20 Landscape Painters & How They Work, Watson-Guptill, 77; Acrylic painting in North America, Artists Mag, London, 11/78. *Mem:* Artist Equity; alumni Otis Art Inst; Mendocino Art Ctr. *Media:* Acrylic, Oil; Serigraph, Etcher-Woodcut. *Publ:* Auth, Mendocino Sketchbook, pvt publ, 72; illusr, Kitchen Magic with Mushrooms, San Francisco Mycological Soc, 63. *Dealer:* Village Gallery 2088 Sir Francis Drake Blvd Fairfax CA 94930. *Mailing Add:* 573 Third St E Sonoma CA 95476

CHRISTENSEN, VAL ALAN
PRINTMAKER, GALLERY DIRECTOR
b Valentine, Nebr, Jan 26, 46. *Study:* Univ Nebr-Lincoln, with Thomas P Coleman, BFA, 68; Wichita State Univ, MFA, 70. *Work:* Sioux City Art Ctr, Iowa; Sheldon Mem Art Gallery, Lincoln, Nebr; Kearney State Col, Nebr; Hastings Col, Nebr. *Exhib:* Thirty-fifth Nat Graphic Arts & Drawing Exhib, Wichita Art Asn, Kans, 71; 29th Nat Print Exhib, Silvermine Guild of Artists, New Canaan, Conn, 72; 3rd Ann Nat Print Exhib, Ga State Univ, Atlanta, 72; 43rd Ann Art Exhib, Springfield Art Mus, Mo, 73; Nebraska 75, Joslyn Art Mus, Omaha, 75; one-person show, Sheldon Mem Art Gallery, Lincoln, 76. *Pos:* Artist-in-sch, Grand Island Cent Cath, 75-79; panel mem, Community Arts Prog, Nebr Arts Coun, Omaha, 77-79; dir, Spiva Art Ctr, 79; asst prof of found prog, Mo Southern State Col, Joplin, 79- *Teaching:* Asst prof printmaking, Univ Nebr-Lincoln, 71-72; instr printmaking/drawing, Hastings Col, Nebr, 72-75. *Awards:* Vreeland Award, Univ Nebr-Lincoln Found, 67; Purchase Awards, 40th Ann Art Exhib, Springfield Art Mus, Mo, 70 & 33rd Ann Fall Show, Sioux City Art Ctr, 71. *Mem:* Mid-Am Col Art Asn; Col Art Asn; Grand Island Area Arts Coun (pres, 77-78). *Media:* Intaglio. *Mailing Add:* 426 N Pearl Joplin MO 64801

CHRISTIAN, WILLIAM
PAINTER, INSTRUCTOR
b Milwaukee, Wis, Nov 22, 32. *Study:* Self taught; also studied with Len Kolmetz & Jon Allen, 49-54. *Work:* Lagos Gallery Fine Art, Nigeria; North Side Savings & Loan, Milwaukee, Wis; Johnson Wax Co, Racine, Wis; Univ Wis, Madison; Roosevelt Univ, Chicago, Ill. *Exhib:* Black Statements, Racine Art Mus, Wis, 69; Afro-Work in Black, Afro-Workshop, New York, 70; The Graces, Perspective View Gallery, Milwaukee, Wis, 70; Contemp Black Artist in Am, Whitney Mus Am Art, New York, 71; Grace Lines, Miller Tour Ctr, Milwaukee, Wis, 80; Seven Artists, First Wis Bank Art Gallery, Milwaukee, 81. *Pos:* Bd dirs, Inner City Arts Coun, Milwaukee, Wis, 68-70; community arts specialist, Univ Extension, Madison, Wis, 75-77. *Teaching:* Milwaukee Public Schs, 70-72; instr, Univ Extension, Madison, Wis, 75-77; instr, Inner City Art Coun, Milwaukee, Wis, 79-81. *Awards:* Best in Shows, Art Fair, 61-62 & Inner City Arts Coun, 74. *Bibliog:* Jerold J Jackson (auth), His world is deceiving, Milwaukee J, 68; Cheik T Sylla (auth), Consistent charm, Milwaukee Courier, 81; Derral Blair (producer), Thinking Ebony (film), 81. *Media:* Oil, Charcoal. *Dealer:* Knoble Galleries 729 N Milwaukee St Milwaukee WI 53202. *Mailing Add:* 1315 W Wright Milwaukee WI 53206

CHRISTIANA, EDWARD
PAINTER, INSTRUCTOR
b White Plains, NY, May 8, 12. *Study:* Pratt Inst, dipl; Munson-Williams-Proctor Inst Sch Art, Utica, NY, with William C Palmer. *Work:* Currier Gallery Art, Manchester, NH; Syracuse Mus Fine Arts, NY; Worcester Mus, Mass; Albany Inst Hist & Art, NY; Cooperstown Art Asn, NY. *Exhib:* 53rd & 55th Watercolor & Drawing Ann, Art Inst Chicago, 42 & 44; Am Watercolor Soc Ann, New York, 45-50; Audubon Artists, New York, 50; 37th

Allied Artists Am Ann, New York, 50; 146th Painting & Sculpture Ann, Pa Acad Fine Arts, Philadelphia, 51; Oils & Watercolors, Munson-Williams-Procter Inst & Mus of Art, Utica, 78; Distinguished Mid-Atlantic Artists: Four Decades of Growth, Univ Del, 80. *Teaching:* Instr painting, drawing & design, Munson-Williams-Procter Inst Sch Art, Utica, 42-78, instr watercolor, 71- *Awards:* William Church Osborn Purchase Prize, Am Watercolor Soc, 49 & 51; 27th Ann Exhib Award, Assoc Artists Syracuse, 54; 21st Ann Upper Hudson Exhib Award, Albany Inst Hist & Art, 56. *Mem:* Cooperstown Art Asn. *Media:* Watercolor. *Mailing Add:* 6 Steuben St Holland Patent NY 13354

CHRISTIE, ROBERT DUNCAN
PAINTER
b Saskatoon, Sask, April 8, 46. *Study:* Univ Sask, BA, 67, hon degree(fine arts), 68, BEd, 70. *Work:* Mendel Art Gallery, Saskatoon, Sask; Edmonton Art Gallery; Norman Mackenzie Art Gallery, Sask Arts Bd, Regina; Can Coun Art Bank, Ottawa. *Exhib:* Canada X Ten, Edmonton Art Gallery, 74; Abstraction West, Nat Gallery Can, 76; solo exhibs, Edmonton Art Gallery, 78, Norman Mackenzie Art Gallery, Regina, Sask, 81 & Mendel Art Gallery, Saskatoon, 82. *Pos:* Gallery supvr, Univ Sask, Saskatoon, 73-82. *Teaching:* Lectr art, Univ Sask, Saskatoon, 83. *Bibliog:* Liz Wylie (auth), article, Artmag, Vol 12, No 50, 80; Nancy Tousley (auth), article, Calgary Herald, 82. *Media:* Acrylic on Canvas. *Dealer:* Can Art Galleries Calgary AB; Gallery One Toronto ON. *Mailing Add:* 725-13th St Saskatoon SK S7N 0M1 Canada

CHRISTISON, MURIEL B
MUSEUM DIRECTOR, EDUCATOR
b Minneapolis, Minn. *Study:* Univ Minn, BA & MA; Univ Paris Inst Art & Archaeol, dipl art hist; Univ Brussels, dipl art hist. *Collections Arranged:* The Impressionist & Post-Impressionists, 51, Goya, 53, Masterpieces of Chinese Art, 55, Les Fetes Galantes, 55, Masterpieces of American Silver, 60 & Sport & the Horse, 60, Va Mus Fine Arts, Richmond; Art of India & Southeast Asia, 63 & For Your Home, 66 & 70, Univ Ill; plus many others. *Pos:* Head educ dept, Minneapolis Inst Arts, 44-47; assoc dir, Va Mus Fine Arts, Richmond, 48-61; consult, Ark Art Ctr, 61; assoc dir & oper dir, Krannert Art Mus, Champaign, 62-71, dir, 71 & 75-82, dir emer, 82- *Teaching:* Instr art in civilization & Am art, Univ Minn, Minneapolis, 45-47; instr visual awareness, Univ Ill, Champaign, 71-72, instr art museology, 72-82; vis prof art mus studies, Col William & Mary, 83- *Awards:* Carnegie Scholar, Inst Int Educ, 36; CRB Fel, Belg-Am Educ Found, 38. *Mem:* Asn Art Mus Dirs; Col Art Asn Am; Am Asn Mus; Midwest Mus Conf; Int Coun Mus. *Publ:* Auth, circular on museum education: seven titles, 51-55; auth, The artmobile, an experiment in education, Art J, 55; auth, Le Museobus de Virginia Museum of Fine Arts, Va Mus Fine Arts, 55; auth, 25th anniversary in Virginia, 60 & The design game, 71, Mus News; plus others including articles and museum catalogs and bulletins. *Mailing Add:* 1184 Jamestown Rd No 5 Williamsburg VA 23185

CHRIST-JANER, ARLAND F
PAINTER, PRINTMAKER
b Garland, Nebr, Jan 27, 22. *Work:* Am Repub Ins Co, Des Moines, Iowa; Bankers Trust Co, New York; Hershey Foods Corp, Pa; Montclair Art Mus, NJ; Motion Picture Asn Am, New York; plus others. *Exhib:* Nat Print Competition, Auburn Univ, Ala; Nat Print & Drawing Exhib, Univ NMex; Columbia Art League, Mo; one-man shows, Carleton Col, 80, Columbia Col, 81; plus others. *Pos:* Col pres, Cornell Col, Boston Univ, New Col & Stephens Col, formerly. *Media:* Graphic. *Mailing Add:* The Royal St Andrew Apt 401 555 S Gulfstream Ave Sarasota FL 33577

CHRISTO
SCULPTOR
b Gabrovo, Bulgaria, June 13, 35. *Study:* Fine Arts Acad, Sofia, 52-56; Burian Theatre, Prague, Czech, work-study, 56; Vienna Fine Arts Acad, Austria, 57. *Exhib:* The Wall (wrapped Roman wall), Rome, 74; Ocean Front (polypropylene), Newport, RI, 74; Running Fence (nylon fabric), Sonoma & Marin Co, Calif, 76; Wrapped Walk Ways, Kansas City, Mo, 77-78; Surrounded Islands (polypropylene), Greater Miami, Fla, 80-83. *Bibliog:* Twelve books, 65-82. *Mailing Add:* 48 Howard St New York NY 10013

CHRYSLER, WALTER P, JR
COLLECTOR
b Oelwein, Iowa. *Exhib:* (Paintings from Walter P Chrysler, Jr Collection) Whitney Mus Am Art, New York; Metrop Mus Art, New York; Va Mus Fine Arts, Richmond; Mus Fine Arts, Dallas, Tex; Nat Gallery Can Ottawa; Portland Art Mus, Ore; Los Angeles Co Mus Art, Los Angeles, Calif; and others. *Pos:* Organizer, York Publ House, 26; pres & chmn bd, Cheshire House, 30; pres & trustee, Chrysler Mus, Provincetown, Mass, 58-71; trustee, Chrysler Mus, Norfolk, Va, 69-, pres, 71-, dir, 71-77. *Interests:* Every civilization and cultural effort of man. *Collection:* Encompasses most all of the important periods of painting. *Mailing Add:* c/o Chrysler Mus Norfolk VA 23510

CHRYSSA (VARDEA)
SCULPTOR
b Athens, Greece, 1933; US citizen. *Study:* Acad Grande Chaumiere, Paris, 53-54; Calif Sch Fine Art, 54-55. *Work:* Mus Mod Art, Whitney Mus Am Art & Guggenheim Mus, New York; Albright-Knox Art Gallery, Buffalo, NY; Walker Art Ctr, Minneapolis; plus others, incl major Europ mus. *Exhib:* One-man shows, Solomon R Guggenheim Mus, 61, Mus Mod Art, New York, 63, Pace Gallery, 66 & 67, Harvard Univ, 68, Galerie Rive Droite, Paris, 69 & Whitney Mus Am Art, New York, 72; Whitney Mus Am Art, New York,

72; Musee de l'Art Moderne de la Ville de Paris, France, 79; Kunsthaus, Zurich, 79; and others. *Bibliog:* Lucy R Lippard (auth), Pop Art, Praeger, 66; Gregory Battcock (ed), Minimal Art: A Critical Anthology, Dutton, 68; Diane Waldman (auth), Chryssa: Selected Works 1955-1957, Pace Gallery, 68; Sam Hunter (auth), Chryssa, Verlag Gerd Hatje, Stuttgart, WGer, 74; Pierre Restany (auth), Chryssa, Harry Abrams, New York, 77. *Mailing Add:* c/o Albright-Knox Art Gallery 1285 Elmwood Ave Buffalo NY 14222

CHU, GENE
PRINTMAKER, PAINTER
b China, Dec 8, 36; Can citizen. *Study:* Ont Col Art; Art Students League, with Harry Sternberg & Edwin Dickerson; Claremont Grad Sch, MFA. *Work:* Tom Thomson Mem Gallery & Mus Fine Art, Owen Sound, Ont; McMaster Univ; Art Bank of Can Coun, Ottawa; Soc Can Painter-Etchers & Engravers; Univ Guelph. *Exhib:* Art Gallery of Ont Traveling Exhib, 78; Rockford Int Print Competition, 79; Graphex 7, 7th Ann Exhib of Can Prints & Drawings, 79; Philadelphia Print Club Biennial Int Open Juried Exhib, 79; Boston World Art Exposition, 79; Image 79, 107th Ont Soc of Artists Ann Exhib, 80. *Teaching:* Instr drawing & printmaking, Mary Washington Col, 68 & 69; asst prof drawing & printmaking, Univ Guelph, 69- *Awards:* First Prize, Tom Thomson 7 Mem Gallery & Mus Fine Art Ann Exhib, 72; Jurors Award of Merit, Second NH Int Graphics Ann, 74; Editions Award, Art Gallery of Brant, 75. *Mem:* Soc Can Painter-Etchers & Engravers; Graphics Soc. *Media:* Lithography; Watercolor. *Mailing Add:* 9 Uplands Pl Guelph ON N1E 3R3 Canada

CHUEY, ROBERT ARNOLD
PAINTER, LECTURER
b Barberton, Ohio, Nov 15, 21. *Study:* Los Angeles Art Ctr Sch, 45-46; Los Angeles Co Art Inst, 47-49; Jepson Art Inst, with Rico LeBrun, 49-52. *Work:* Los Angeles Co Mus; City Mus St Louis. *Exhib:* Seven Los Angeles Co Mus Ann, 49-60; Carnegie Inst, Pittsburgh, 53; Sao Paulo Biennial, Brazil, 55; Pa Acad Fine Arts, Philadelphia, 58; Santa Barbara Mus Art, 57. *Teaching:* Lectr art, Los Angeles Co Art Inst, 54-56, Chouinard Art Inst, 58-63 & 67-68, Univ Calif, Los Angeles, 63-65 & 68-69, Univ Calif, Santa Barbara, 65-67 & Univ Southern Calif, 67-68. *Media:* Oil, Ink. *Publ:* Contribr, Realm of Contemporary Still-life, 63; contribr, Drawing--A Search for Form, 66; contribr, Painting Techniques, 68; contribr, The Art and Logic of Drawing, 75. *Mailing Add:* c/o Jacqueline Anhalt Gallery 748 1/2 N La Cienega Blvd Los Angeles CA 90069

CHUMLEY, JOHN WESLEY
PAINTER
b Rochester, Minn, Sept 12, 28. *Study:* Ringling Sch Art; Posey Sch Sculpture; Amaganset Art Sch; Pa Acad Fine Art. *Work:* Everhard Mus, Scranton, Pa; WTex Mus, Lubbock; Norfolk Mus, Va; R W Norton Gallery, Shreveport, La; Washington Co Mus, Hagerstown, Md. *Exhib:* Pa Acad Biennial, Philadelphia, 58; Nat Acad Arts & Lett, New York, 59; Carnegie Inst, Pittsburgh, Pa, 64; Twentieth Century Realists, San Diego, Calif, 68; Butler Art Inst, Youngstown, Ohio, 73 & 75; plus several one-man shows. *Pos:* Artist in residence, Ft Worth Art Ctr, Tex, 58-61. *Awards:* Philadelphia Watercolor Club Prize, 57; Hallgarten Prize, Nat Acad Arts & Lett, 59; Childe Hassam Award, Am Acad Arts & Lett, 59. *Mem:* Am Watercolor Soc; Philadelphia Watercolor Club. *Media:* Egg Tempera, Watercolor. *Mailing Add:* Rt 2 Box 285A Stephens City VA 22655

CHURCH, C HOWARD
PAINTER, PRINTMAKER
b South Sioux City, Nebr, May 1, 04. *Study:* Art Inst Chicago, with Boris Ainsfeld, John Norton & William P Welsh, 28-32, BFA, 35; Univ Chicago, BA, 38; Ohio State Univ, MA, 40. *Comn:* Murals, Morgan Park Mil Acad, Chicago, 32-36. *Exhib:* One-man shows, Mulvane Art Mus, Thayer Mus Art, Univ Nebr, Joslyn Art Mus & Kresge Art Ctr, East Lansing, Mich; and others. *Pos:* Dir, Morgan Park Sch Art, Chicago, 33-36; dir, Mulvane Art Mus, Washburn Univ, 40-45. *Teaching:* Head art dept, Washburn Univ, 40-45; head art dept, Mich State Univ, 45-60, prof, 60-72; retired. *Awards:* Mich Fine Arts Medal, 63 & Purchase Award, mem exhib, 66, Mich Acad Sci, Arts & Lett; Print Purchase Award, Mich Artists Exhib, Mich Educ Asn, 69 & 70; and others. *Mem:* Am Asn Univ Profs. *Mailing Add:* 271 Lexington Ave East Lansing MI 48823

CHURCHILL, DIANE
PAINTER, COLLAGE ARTIST
b Bronxville, NY, Jan 8, 41. *Study:* Wellesley Col, BA(art hist); Brooklyn Mus Art Sch; Hunter Col, MA(painting). *Work:* Chase Manhattan Bank Collection, New York; Reliance Group Inc, Mass; Jay Hambridge Art Found, Rabun Gap, Ga. *Exhib:* Soho 20 Gallery, 76, 78 & 80; Stevens Inst Technol Libr Gallery, 79; Robeson Gallery, Newark NJ, 81; NJ State Mus, Trenton, 80; Brookdale Community Col, Lincroft, NJ, 80; and others. *Pos:* Artist catalyst, Brigade-In-Action, New York, 68-73; publ & ed, Fourth St i, 71-73; field rep, Visual Arts Dept, NY State Coun Arts, New York, 76-77. *Teaching:* Art, Hudson Sch, Hoboken, NJ, 79-80. *Awards:* NJ State Coun Arts Fel, 79-80. *Bibliog:* Marian Courtney (auth), Artist & poet capture spirit of Pine Barrens, Jersey J, 12/30/80. *Mem:* Soho 20 Gallery Inc (secy, 75). *Media:* Mixed. *Dealer:* Soho 20 Gallery 99 Spring St New York NY 10012. *Mailing Add:* 57 Hudson Pl Weehawken NJ 07087

CHUTJIAN, SETA LEONIE See Injeyan, Seta L

CHWAST, SEYMOUR
DESIGNER, ILLUSTRATOR
b New York, NY, Aug 18, 31. *Study:* Cooper Union. *Work:* Mus of Mod Art, New York; Cooper-Hewitt Mus, Smithsonian Inst; Libr Congress; Israel Mus; Gutenberg Mus, Mainz, Ger. *Exhib:* Musee Des Arts Decoratif, The Louvre, Paris, France, 71 & 73; A Century of Am Illus, Brooklyn Mus, 73; Galerie Delpire, Paris, 81; Kunstgerverbe Mus, Zurich, 81; Gutenberg Mus, Mainz, Ger. *Pos:* Publ & art dir, The Push Pin Graphic Bi-Monthly Mag, 56-80; dir, Push Pin Studios, New York, 75-82; partner, Pushpin Lubalin Peckolick Inc, 82- *Teaching:* Instr design & illus, Cooper Union, 75- *Awards:* St Gardens Medal, Cooper Union; Several medals, NY Art Dir Club; Art Dir Club Hall of Fame, 83. *Bibliog:* T Nishio (auth), Seymour Chwast, Shinkosha Publ, Tokyo, 74; Mann Mit Nase (man with nose): Seymour Chwast, Frankfurter Allgemeine Zeitung, 81. *Mem:* Am Inst of Graphic Arts. *Publ:* Designer & illusr, Pancake King, Delacorte Press, 70 & Limerickricks, Random House, 72; designer, Sweetheart Book and Others, Avon Bks, 75; designer & illusr, Tall City, Wide Country, Viking Press, 83; co-ed, Art of New York, Harry N Abrams, 83. *Mailing Add:* c/o Push Pin Studios 67 Irving Pl New York NY 10003

CIANCIO, JUNE (KIRKPATRICK)
PAINTER, INSTRUCTOR
b Wilkinsburg, Pa, June 26, 20. *Study:* Carnegie-Mellon Univ, BFA, 42; Columbia Teachers Col; Hans Hoffman Sch; Art Students League, with Will Barnet. *Work:* Parrish Art Mus, Southampton, NY; Nassau Community Col, Garden City, NY; Citibank New York. *Exhib:* One-person shows, Parrish Art Mus, 74 & Long Beach Mus, NY; 38th Ann, Audubon Artists, New York, 80; 27th Ann, Nat Soc Painters Casein & Acrylic, New York, 80; 85th Ann, Catharine Lorillard Wolfe Art Club, New York, 81. *Teaching:* Instr watercolor, Parrish Art Mus, Southampton, NY, 76-79. *Awards:* Award of Excellence, Huntington Township Art League, 79; Grumbacher Silver Medal, Nat Soc Painters Casein & Acrylic, 80; Stefan Hirsch Award, Audubon Artists, 80. *Mem:* Guild Hall; assoc mem Audubon Artists; mem Nat Soc Painters Casein & Acrylic. *Media:* Acrylic, Watercolor. *Dealer:* Gallery East 257 Montauk Highway East Hampton NY 11937. *Mailing Add:* 13 W Argonne Rd Hampton Bays NY 11946

CIANFONI, EMILIO
CONSERVATOR, PAINTER
b Rome, Italy, Oct 9, 46; US citizen. *Study:* Studied drawing, painting & restoration with Giustino Caporali, 58-63, Manieri Art Inst, 60-63, Accad di Belle Arti, 64-66 & conserv of paintings at Inst Centrale del Restauro, 66-67, Rome; Art Students League, New York, 70-72; Baldwin Sch (glazes chemistry), New York, 73. *Comn:* Paintings, Lowenbrau Co, Munich, Bavaria, Ger, 67; painting & sculpture, Pacifici Family, Rome, Italy, 67; mural, Church Hosp Complex, Vilalba, Italy, 69; Bicentennial Coins Competition, Metrop Mus of Art, New York, 74. *Exhib:* Galeria Modigliani, 63, 20th Century Competition, City Bldg, 64 & Mus of Mod Art, 65, Rome; New Talent (2 shows), Betty Parsons Gallery, New York, 74; Primitive & Contemp Art, Tucson, Ariz, by Betty Parsons Gallery, 75; UN Group Am Exhib, New York, by Truman Gallery, 77. *Pos:* Design painter/conservator, Gucci Shops, Rome & New York, 68-70; sr craftsman, Alva Reproductions, New York, 70-72; restorer, Metrop Mus of Art, New York, 72-74; chief conservator, Vizcaya Mus & Gardens, 75- *Awards:* 1st Prize, 20th Anniversary of Italian Partisans Competition, Rome, 64; 2nd Prize, Ciac Poetry & Arts Competition, Rome, 66. *Mem:* Am Inst Conserv Hist & Artistic Work; Int Inst Conserv Hist & Artistic Work; Asn Preserv Technol. *Media:* Mixed Media. *Dealer:* Truman Gallery 38 E 57th St New York NY 10022. *Mailing Add:* 272 NW 36th St Miami FL 33137

CIARROCHI, RAY
PAINTER, INSTRUCTOR
b Chicago, Ill. *Study:* Chicago Acad Fine Arts; Wash Univ, BFA, with Fred Conway; Boston Univ, MFA. *Work:* Ciba-Geigy Collection, Ardsley, NY; Citibank, New York; Owens-Corning Glass Found; Am Tel & Tel; Brooklyn Mus. *Exhib:* One-man shows, Tibor De Nagy Gallery, 71, 72, 74, 76, 78, 80 & 83; Am Watercolors, 1800 to the Present, Brooklyn Mus, NY, 76; Artist's Choice--Figurative Painting in New York, Soho Ctr for Visual Arts, 77; Works on Paper from the Ciba-Geigy Collection, Neuberger Mus, Purchase, NY, 77; Nijinsky Series, Payson Gallery Art, Westbrook Col, Portland, Maine, 81; Painterly Realism, traveling exhib, Houston, Tex; and others. *Teaching:* Instr painting & drawing, Parsons Sch Design, New York, 66-71; adj prof, Sch Arts, Columbia Univ, 69-71 & 76- & Baruch Col, City Univ New York, 76-; instr painting, Md Inst Col Art, 71-72; instr, Brooklyn Col, 72-76. *Awards:* Fulbright Grant to Italy, 63-64; Tiffany Grant, 67; Ingraham Merrill Found Grant, 77 & 82-83. *Bibliog:* James R Mellow (auth) & Hilton Kramer (auth), rev in New York Times, 4/1/72 & 3/2/74; Nina Mallory (auth), article, Arts, 1/83. *Media:* Oil, Watercolor. *Dealer:* Tibor de Nagy Gallery 29 W 57th St New York NY 10019. *Mailing Add:* 463 West St New York NY 10014

CIARROCHI, SANDRA See Caplan, Sandra

CICANSKY, VICTOR
SCULPTOR
b Regina, Sask, Feb 12, 35. *Study:* Univ Sask, Saskatoon, BEd; Univ Regina, BA; Univ Calif, Davis, MFA, with Bob Arneson & Roy DeForrest. *Work:* Sask Govt Arts Bd; Can Coun Art Bank; Sacramento State Col; Mus of Mod Art, Tokyo, Japan; Mus of Mod Art, Montreal. *Comn:* Sask Grain Bin (group scultpure), COJO-Olympic Comt, Montreal, 76; The Old Working Class (sculpture), Sask Govt, Saskatoon, 77; My World (sculpture), CIS, Regina, 79. *Exhib:* Contemp Ceramics, Mus of Fine Arts, Kyoto, Japan, 71; Int Ceramics, Victoria & Albert Mus, London, Eng, 72; Trajectories 73, Musee de Art Moderne de Ville de Paris, France, 73; Cicansky, Espace 5, Montreal, Que, 74; Fired Clay Show, Greater Victoria Art Gallery, Victoria, BC, 75; New York Clay, Monique Knowlton Gallery, New York, 75. *Teaching:* Assoc prof art, Univ Regina, Sask, 70-78. *Awards:* Can Coun grants/travel & work, 68, 69, 71 & 74; Kingsley Ann Award/Sculpture, Sacramento, 69; Royal Albert Award, Ceramic Sculpture, Toronto, 71. *Media:* Clay. *Publ:* Contribr to Arts Mag, Fall 70, Mus of Mod Art J, Amsterdam, 4/71; Arts Can, 5/73; Art & Artists, 8/73; Time, 4/73 & ArtsCan, 230/231. *Mailing Add:* Box 79 Craven SK S0G 0W0 Canada

CICCONE, AMY NAVRATIL
LIBRARIAN
b Mich, Sept 19, 50. *Study:* Wayne State Univ, 68-72, BA(art hist); Univ Mich, 72-73, AMLS, specializing in art librarianship. *Pos:* Librn, Norton Simon Mus, Pasadena, Calif, 74-81; ed, Art Librs Soc of NAm Directory of Members, 75-77; contribr of articles in Art Libr Soc NAm Newsletter, 75-77; librn, Chrysler Mus, Jean Outland Chrysler Libr, Norfolk, Va, 81- *Mem:* Art Libr Soc NAm (mem chmn, 75-77, mem coordr, 79). *Mailing Add:* 2249 Rose Hall Drive Virginia Beach VA 23454

CICERO, CARMEN L
PAINTER
Study: Newark State Col, NJ, BS; Hunter Col, New York. *Work:* Guggenheim Mus, New York; Larry Aldrich Mus, Conn; Hirshhorn Mus, Washington, DC; Neuberger Mus, Purchase, NY; Montclair Mus, NJ. *Exhib:* Whitney Mus Ann, 55-66; one-man shows, Peridot Gallery & Leslie Rankow Gallery, New York; Premiere Bienale de Paris, France. *Teaching:* Mem fac, Sarah Lawrence Col, 59-68; instr, Montclair State Col, 60- *Awards:* Guggenheim Found Fel, 57 & 63; Purchase Prize, Ford Found, 65. *Media:* Oil, Acrylic. *Dealer:* Rankow Gallery 108 E 78th St New York NY 10021. *Mailing Add:* 278 Bowery New York NY 10012

CICERO, JAN (JANICE PICKETT)
DEALER
b Chicago, Ill. *Study:* Wheaton Col, BA, 59; Northwestern Univ, MA, 69. *Pos:* Dir, Jan Cicero Gallery. *Mem:* Chicago Art Dealers Asn. *Specialty:* Contemporary painting, sculpture, drawings and prints. *Mailing Add:* 437 N Clark St Chicago IL 60610

CIFOLELLI, ALBERTA (ALBERTA CARMELLA LAMB)
PAINTER, EDUCATOR
b Erie, Pa, Aug 19, 31. *Study:* Cleveland Inst Art, dipl(painting), 53; Kent State Univ, BS(art educ), 55; Fairfield Univ, MA, 77. *Work:* Cleveland Art Asn Rental Collection, Cleveland Mus Art; First Nat Bank of Pa, Erie; Housatonic Mus Art, Bridgeport, Conn; Swissre Holding Inc, New York; Marketing Corp Am, Westport, Conn. *Exhib:* Nat Soc Painters in Casein & Acrylic, Nat Acad Design, New York, 74; New Eng Ann, New Canaan, Conn; and others; Lyman Allyn Mus, New London, Conn; one-man shows, Noho Gallery, New York, 82 & Westport Weston Arts Coun, Conn, 78-79; dir, New Eng 31st Ann, New Canaan, Conn. *Teaching:* Instr painting & life drawing, Cleveland Inst Art, 67-70; assoc prof life drawing & design, Sacred Heart Univ, 79- *Awards:* Second Prize, Cleveland Mus Art, 59 & 65; Doris Kreindler Mem Award, Nat Soc Painters in Casein & Acrylic, 74; four grants, Conn Comn Arts. *Bibliog:* Renaissance of a City (film), Larner, 69; Joan Eagle (auth), Buying Art on a Budget, 68; J Moss (auth), article, Arts Mag, 4/82. *Mem:* Visual Artist & Gallery Asn; Westport Weston Arts Coun (vis arts chmn, 76-); trustee Silvermine Guild Artists (bd dirs, 78-83). *Media:* Acrylic, Pastel. *Dealer:* Kaber Gallery Ltd 900 1st Ave New York NY 10022; Branchville SoHo Gallery Old Main Hwy Georgetown CT 06829. *Mailing Add:* 8 Plover Ln Westport CT 06880

CIKOVSKY, NICOLAI
PAINTER, MURALIST
b Pinsk, Russia, Dec 10, 1894. *Study:* Royal Art Sch, Vilna; Tech Inst of Arts, Moscow. *Work:* Brooklyn Mus, NY; Art Inst Chicago; Cleveland Mus Art, Ohio; William Rockhill Nelson Gallery of Art, Kansas City, Mo; Los Angeles Co Mus Art, Los Angeles, Calif; and others. *Comn:* Murals, Interior Dept, Washington, DC & US Post Off, Towson & Silver Spring, Md. *Exhib:* Mus Mod Art, New York; Walker Art Ctr, Minneapolis, Minn; Carnegie Inst Int, Pittsburgh, Pa; Corcoran Gallery of Art, Washington, DC; Boston Mus Fine Art; Cleveland Mus Art, Ohio; Los Angeles Co Mus Art, Calif; one-man shows, Allied Artists of Am, 42-44 & 46 & ACA Gallery, 59, 63 & 67. *Teaching:* Instr, Ekaterinenburg Higher Tech Art Inst, Russia, Mus Arts & Crafts, Columbus, Ohio, St Paul Sch of Art, Art Acad of Cincinnati, Corcoran Sch of Art, Chicago Art Inst Sch & Art Students League, New York. *Awards:* Norman Wait Harris Bronze Medal, Art Inst Chicago, 32; Isaac N Maynard Prize, Nat Acad of Design, New York, 64; First Prize, Parrish Mus, Southampton, NY, 68. *Mem:* Nat Acad Design. *Media:* Oil, Watercolor; Graphic. *Dealer:* Am Contemp Artists Gallery 23 E 73rd St New York NY 10021. *Mailing Add:* Box 15 RFD 590 Noyac Rd Southampton NY 11968

CIKOVSKY, NICOLAI, JR
HISTORIAN, EDUCATOR
b New York, NY, Feb 11, 33. *Study:* Harvard Col, AB; Harvard Univ, AM & PhD. *Collections Arranged:* Sanford Robinson Gifford, Univ Tex Art Mus, 70-71; The White Marmorean Flock; Nineteenth Century American Women Neoclassical Sculptors, Vassar Col Art Gallery, 72. *Pos:* Dir, Vassar Col Art

Gallery, 71-74; cur Am art, Nat Gallery Art, Washington, DC, 83- *Teaching:* Assoc prof art, Vassar Col, 71-74; prof art, Univ NMex, 74-83. *Awards:* Guggenheim Fel, 78-79; Kress Sr Fel, Ctr Advan Study in Visual Arts, Nat Gallery Art. *Res:* Nineteenth & twentieth century American painting and sculpture. *Publ:* Auth, George Inness, 71 & Life & Work of George Inness, 77; ed, Samuel F B Morse's Lectures on the Affinity of Painting with the Other Fine Arts, 83. *Mailing Add:* Nat Gallery Art 4th St & Constitution Ave Washington DC 20565

CIMBALO, ROBERT W
PAINTER, PRINTMAKER
b Tiriolo, Italy; US citizen. *Study:* Pratt Inst, Brooklyn; Syracuse Univ; Sorita Dante Alighari, Belle Arte & Univ Studi Roma, Rome. *Work:* Kirkland Art Ctr, Clinton, NY; Munson-Williams-Proctor Inst, Utica, NY; Syracuse Univ; State Univ NY Col Cortland; Pratt Inst. *Teaching:* Assoc prof art hist & studio art, Utica Col, Syracuse Univ, 78- *Media:* All. *Publ:* Auth, East Utica, Munson Williams Proctor Inst, fall 71; auth, Frank, Catherine and Vito, Black Locust Press, 79. *Dealer:* FAR Gallery 746 Madison Ave New York NY 10021. *Mailing Add:* 1602 Harrison Ave Utica NY 13501

CINDRIC, MICHAEL ANTHONY
SCULPTOR, EDUCATOR
b Pittsburgh, Pa, Jan 2, 47. *Study:* Ind State Univ, BS, MS; NY State Col Ceramics, Alfred Univ, MFA. *Work:* R J Reynolds World Hq, Winston Salem, NC; NC Mus of Art, Raleigh; Krannert Art Gallery, Evansville, Ind; Huntington Galleries, WVa; J Patrick Lannan Found, Palm Beach, Fla. *Exhib:* Southeastern Ctr Contemp Art, Winston-Salem, NC, 78 & 80; Mus of Art, NC Cent Univ, Durham, 78; Wonderworks Three, Nashville Mus of Art, Tenn, 78; NC Artist Exhib Award Winners, Collectors Gallery, NC Mus Art, Raleigh, 79; Univ Pittsburgh, Johnstown, 79. *Collections Arranged:* Contemp Ceramic Sculpture, Ackland Art Ctr, Chapel Hill, NC, 77. *Teaching:* Asst prof ceramic sculpture, Univ NC, 75- *Awards:* Wulfmand Purchase Award, Exhib 280, Huntington Gallery, 76; First Prize Purchase Award/Sculpture, 76; Carolina Designer Craftsman Purchase Award, NC Artists Exhib, NC Mus of Art, Raleigh. *Mem:* Am Craftsmen Coun; Nat Coun Educ Ceramic Arts; Southern Asn Sculptors. *Media:* Sculpture, Clay. *Publ:* Contribr, Portable Museum Series, Am Craftsmen Coun. *Dealer:* Garden Gallery Hwy 70 W Raleigh NC. *Mailing Add:* Rte 3 Box 104A Hillsborough NC 27278

CINTRON, JOSEPH M
PAINTER, INSTRUCTOR
b Ponce, PR, Aug 4, 21. *Study:* Univ Dayton, BA, 43; Ohio State Univ; Cleveland Inst Art, dipl, 54; with Robert Brackman, Madison, Conn; Art Students League, with Sidney Dickinson, David Leffel & Howard Sanden. *Work:* Univ Hospitals Cleveland; La Fortaleza, San Juan, Puerto Rico; First Federal Bank, Cleveland; Lake Erie Col, Painesville, Ohio; Cleveland Play House; and others. *Comn:* Portrait, Eric Fromm, Case Western Reserve Univ, Cleveland, Ohio, 69; copy of Copley's Nathaniel Hurd, Edward A Hurd, Chicago, Ill, 73; portrait of Gov Luis a Ferre, La Fortaleza, San Juan, PR, 74; portrait of Capt Antoine Paulint of the Continental Army, W L L'Esperance, Columbus, Ohio, 78; portrait, Dr Dudley Allen, Univ Hospitals, Cleveland, 80; N W Shibley, pres, Ohio Bar Asn, 81; and others. *Exhib:* Canton Art Inst Regional, 65-69; Mid-Year Nat, Butler Inst Am Art, 70; Sch of Fine Arts, Willoughby, Ohio, 72; Cleveland Invitational, 73; Cleveland Athletic Club, 73-75; Int Platform Asn, Washington DC, 81; and others. *Teaching:* Prof painting & drawing, Cleveland Inst Art, 56-, Cooper Sch Art, 63-82, Sch Fine Arts, Willoughby, Ohio, 82- *Awards:* Painting Award, Cuyahoga Valley Art Ctr, 67 & 68; Silver Medal, 81 & Popular Award, 82, Int Platform Asn; and others. *Bibliog:* Marie Kirkwood (auth), Cintron trademark is realism, Sun Press, Cleveland, 8/5/71; Gloria Borras (auth), Pintar Rostros es Captar Almas, Puerto Rico Ilustrado, San Juan, 3/30/75. *Mem:* Int Platform Asn. *Media:* Multimedia. *Mailing Add:* 3853 Princeton Blvd South Euclid OH 44121

CISNEROS, FLORENCIO GARCIA See Garcia, Frank

CITRIN, JUDITH
PAINTER, SCULPTOR
b Chicago, Ill, May 29, 34. *Study:* Univ Ill; Am Acad Art; Art Inst Chicago; Adler Inst; Esalen Inst; Himalayan Inst; C G Jung Ctr. *Work:* Ruth Page Found, Chicago; Royal Palace, Rabat, Morocco; Mus Contemp Art, Chicago. *Exhib:* Art Inst Chicago, 77 & 81; Musee des Oudaias, Rabat, Morocco, 80; Nat Acad Design, New York, 82; Smithsonian Inst, Washington, DC, 82; Portland Art Mus, Wash; C G Jung Ctr, Chicago, 83. *Pos:* Contrib ed, New Art Examiner, 78. *Teaching:* Artist-in-residence, Cult Ministry, Marrakech, Morocco, 79-80; workshop facilitator, Oasis Ctr Human Potential, Chicago, Ill, 81; The Clearing House, Wilmette, Ill, 82- *Awards:* Ill Arts Coun Grant, 77; Royal Air Maroc Funding Grant, 80 & 81. *Bibliog:* Jean Goldman (auth), Anonymous image, Univ Chicago, 74; Donna Meilach (auth), Box Art, Crown, 75; C L Morrison (auth), article, Art Forum, 79. *Mem:* Arts Club Chicago. *Media:* Prismacolor Pencil; Clay. *Dealer:* Sonia Zaks Gallery 620 N Michigan Ave Chicago IL 60201. *Mailing Add:* 927 Noyes 220 Evanston IL 60611

CITRON, MINNA WRIGHT
PAINTER, PRINTMAKER
b Newark, NJ, Oct 15, 1896. *Study:* Brooklyn Inst Arts & Sci; New York Sch Appl Design; Art Students League; studied with K Nicolaides & Kenneth Hayes Miller; City Col New York; Atelier 17. *Work:* Nat Collection Fine Arts, Smithsonian Inst; Rosenwald Collection, Nat Gallery Art; The White House & US Info Agency, Washington, DC; Mus Mod Art, Whitney Mus Am

Art, New York; plus many others. *Exhib:* Dulin Gallery, Philadelphia, 66; Am Color Print Soc, Philadelphia Mus Art, 67; Calif State Col, Long Beach, 69; NJ State Mus, Trenton, 68 & 70; plus one-man shows throughout US, Europe & SAm. *Pos:* Rep, US Govt, Congres Int Educ Artistique, Paris, 47; mem, Washington Conf Women in Arts, Corcoran Gallery, 72. *Teaching:* Instr art, Brooklyn Mus, 40-44; lectr, US & abroad; instr art, Pratt Inst, Manhattan Ctr, 71-72. *Awards:* Soc Am Graphic Artists Award, Los Angeles Co Mus, 69; Awards, NJ State Mus, 68 & 70; Yaddo Fel, Artist in Residence, Lakeside Studio, Mich, 70; plus others. *Bibliog:* Herta Wecher (auth), Cimaise, Paris, 56; Adela Jaume (auth), El Diario de la Marina, Havana, Cuba, 57; Dario Suro (auth), Cuadernos Hispano-Americanos, 60; plus others. *Dealer:* AAA Gallery 663 Fifth Ave New York NY 10022; Marden Fine Arts Gallery New York NY. *Mailing Add:* 145 Fourth Ave New York NY 10003

CIUCA, EUGEN
SCULPTOR, PAINTER
b Miluan, Romania, Feb 27, 13. *Study:* Univ Cluj, Romania, 34-38; Univ Bucharest, Romania, 42-46. *Work:* Nat Mus of Art, Bucharest; Mod Galerija, Lubljiana, Yugoslavia; Forma Viva Open Air Mus, Kostanjevica, Yugoslavia; Nat Mus of Art, Budapest, Hungary; White House, Washington, DC. *Comn:* Festive Column, Herastrau Park, Bucharest, 64; Monument to the Partisans, Munic Kostanjevica, Yugoslavia, 68; Dante Alighieri Monument, Town Hall Pontelongo-Padova, Italy, 67; Dante Alighieri (monumental bust), Col Mus of Art Arsenale, Venice, Italy, 77; Heroes Monument, Venice, 83. *Exhib:* Exhib of Rumanian Art, Budapest, Hungary, 47; Int Exhib, Bucharest, 55; Divine Comedy in Images & Sculpture, Ravenna, Italy, 76; Int Exhib of Madrid, Spain, 77; Dante Alighieri Exhib, Rome, 77; Fourth Dimension in Art (travelling exhib), Rome, 77; and others. *Teaching:* Asst prof human anat drawing, Univ Bucharest, Romania, 43-50; prof arts & sculpture, Dowling Col, Oakdale, NY, 74-75. *Awards:* Gold Medal, Int Joint Exhib, Int Cult Ctr, Jesolo, 71; Gold Medal, one-man exhib, City of Ravenna, Italy, 76; Premio Cronaca, Int Archit TV-Art Info, Rome, 77. *Bibliog:* Marziano Bernardi (critic), La Stampa, Italy, 68; Carlo Giulio Argan (critic), article in Catalogo, Rome, 72; Paolo Rizzi (critic), article in Catalogo, Ravenna, Italy, 76. *Mem:* Int Asn Art. *Mailing Add:* 21 Shore Lane Bay Shore NY 11706

CIVALE, BIAGIO A
GRAPHIC ARTIST, PAINTER
b Rome, Italy, Aug 11, 35. *Study:* Acad Grande Chaumiere, Paris, 53-55; Fine Arts Acad, Rome, dipl(art educ), 58; NY Univ, 83. *Work:* Gabinetto Naz Stampe, Rome; Mod Sacred Art Gallery, Montecatini Mus, Florence, Italy; Argenton-Sur-Creuse Mus, France; Mus Espanol Arte Contemp Madrid, Spain; Mod Mus, Stockholm. *Comn:* Decoration for NCO Club, Ital Air Force, Cagliari, Italy, 58; Decoration for restaurant, NATO Ctr, Chateauroux, France, 62; Crucifixion for Sacrestia, Scarperia Church, Florence, Italy, 74; New Testament & Christmas, Dicomano Church, Florence, Italy, 75. *Exhib:* Naz Gioventu, Palazzo Barberini, Rome, 53-55 & 58; Ecole Francaise, Mus Beaux Arts, Paris, 55; Art Libre, Palais Beaux Arts, Paris, 55-57. *Bibliog:* Marzio Bugatti (auth), monogr, 70 & Puck Kroese (auth), Civale's Graphics (monogr), 70, Bugatti Ed; Luigi Servolini (auth), Incisori D'Italia, EIA, Milano, 74. *Media:* Etching, Serigraphy. *Dealer:* Franco Cardilicchia Via Adriani 15 Florence Italy 50126. *Mailing Add:* 311 Lee Ave Yonkers NY 10705

CIVITELLO, JOHN PATRICK
PAINTER
b Paterson, NJ, Aug 17, 39. *Study:* William Paterson Col, BA, 61; NY Univ, MA, 62. *Work:* NJ State Mus, Trenton; Monterey Peninsula Mus Art, Calif; 3M Co, St Paul, Minn; Nat Broadcasting Co Television, New York; Lloyd's Bank, Calif. *Exhib:* 30th Biennial of Am Art, Corcoran Gallery Art, Washington, DC, 67; What's Happening in Soho, Univ Md Art Gallery, 71; one-man show, Art Club Chicago, 74; Am Acad Arts & Lett Ann, 76; Drawing Today in New York, Sewall Art Gallery, Houston, Tex & Dayton Art Inst, Ohio; and others. *Pos:* Art project dir, Great Falls Historic District, Paterson, NJ, 78. *Awards:* Prix-de-Rome, Italy, 68-70; Creative Artists Pub Serv Grant, Cult Coun Found, 72; Childe Hassam Purchase Award, Am Acad Arts & Lett, 76. *Bibliog:* E Bilardello (auth), Pittori Americani a Roma, Margutta-Periodico d'Arte Contemporanea, Rome, 70; article in Arts Mag, 7/75. *Mem:* Am Acad Rome Alumni Asn; Foundation for the Community Artists, NY. *Media:* Acrylic. *Dealer:* Dubins Gallery 11948 San Vicente Blvd Los Angeles CA 90049. *Mailing Add:* 733 N King Rd Apt 22 Los Angeles CA 90069

CLAGUE, JOHN ROGERS
SCULPTOR
b Cleveland, Ohio, Mar 14, 28. *Study:* Cleveland Inst Art, BFA. *Work:* Cleveland Mus Art; Larry Aldrich Mus, Ridgefield, Conn; Princeton Univ Mus; Williams Col Mus; Smithsonian Archives Am Art. *Comn:* Limestone sculpture, Cleveland Recreation Ctr, 56; Israel (bronze sculpture), Jewish Community Ctr, Cleveland, 61; limestone motif, Child Guidance Ctr, Cleveland, 64; kinetic sound-making sculpture (stainless steel), Ashland Col, Ohio, 72. *Exhib:* Cleveland Mus Art May Show, 55-81; Whitney Mus Am Art Ann, New York, 64-65; Waddell Gallery, New York, 66; Highlights of 1966-1967 Art Season, Larry Aldrich Mus, 67; Int Monumental Sculpture Exhib, Blossom Music Ctr, 68. *Teaching:* Instr sculpture, Oberlin Col, 57-61 & Cleveland Inst Art, 56-71. *Awards:* Yale Norfolk Fel, 54; Catherwood Found Traveling Fel, 56; Nat Scholastic Mag Hall of Fame, 70. *Bibliog:* The Sculpture of the End of the 19th and the 20th Century, Editions Recontre, Paris; Nathan Knobler (auth), The Visual Dialogue, Holt, Rinehart & Winston, Inc; Richard Campen (auth), Outdoor Sculpture in Ohio, Summit Press. *Mem:* New Orgn for Visual Arts. *Media:* Stainless Steel, Bronze. *Mailing Add:* 11625 County Line Rd Gates Mills OH 44040

CLANCY, PATRICK
VIDEO ARTIST
b Hornell, NY, Oct 19, 41. *Study:* Pratt Inst, BS, 64; Yale Univ, BFA, 64 & MFA(painting), 67. *Exhib:* Spaces, Mus Mod Art, New York, 69 & 70; Works for New Spaces, Walker Art Ctr, Minneapolis, 71; Music with its Roots in Ether, Mills Col, Oakland, Calif, 71; Pulsa, Automation House, New York, 71. *Teaching:* Lectr & res assoc, Pulsa Sem, Yale Univ, 67-72; vis artist, Calif Inst Arts, 71 & 72; instr hist of cinema & environ art, Colgate Univ, NY, 73-80. *Awards:* Graham Found Grant, Advan Studies in Visual Arts, 68-72. *Publ:* Co-auth, Pulsa, Eye Mag, 5/68; auth, Proposal, Spaces Catalog, Mus Mod Art, 1/70; co-auth, Pulsa, radio interview, KPFA, Berkeley, Calif, 3/71; auth, The city as an artwork, Arts of the Environ, 72; Paseo video, anthology from the Center for Contemporary Music, Mills Col, 78. *Mailing Add:* 308 Harvard St SE Albuquerque NM 87106

CLAPSADDLE, JERRY
PAINTER
b Hastings, Nebr Dec 12, 41. *Study:* Drake Univ, Des Moines, Iowa, BFA, 64; Ind Univ, MFA, 66. *Work:* Chase Manhattan Bank, New York; Owens-Corning Fiberglass, Toledo, Ohio; Switzerland Embassy, Paris; Hyatt Regency, Baltimore & Crystal City, Va; Swiss Bank Corp, World Trade Ctr, NY. *Comn:* Mural, Artery Orgn, 82. *Exhib:* Max Protetch Gallery, Washington, DC, 77; Protetch-McIntosh Gallery, Washington, DC, 77 & 79; Md Biennial, Baltimore Mus Art, 78; The Emerging Generation, Washington Proj for the Arts, 79; Washington Light, Washington, DC, 80; Catholic Univ Am, Washington, DC, 80; McIntosh/Drysdale Gallery, Washington, DC, 81; and many others. *Pos:* Exhib organizer, Fine Arts Ctr, Univ RI, Kingston, 71-74; dir, Fine Arts Ctr Gallery, State Univ NY Col, Oneonta, 74-76. *Teaching:* From instr to asst prof studio art & printmaking, Univ RI, Kingston, 67-74; asst prof painting, Univ Md, College Park, 76-80; asst prof, Studio, George Mason Univ, Fairfax, Va, 81- *Awards:* Ben Forgey (auth), Jerry Clapsaddle at Montpelier, Washington Post, 4/11/83; Artists' Fel, Nat Endowment Arts, 80. *Bibliog:* Ben Forgey (auth), Clapsaddle's figures, Washington Star, 11/16/79; Paul Richard (auth), A Decade's Painted Daydreams, Washington Post, 8/30/80; Maeve Bee (ed), New Faces/New Images, Ocular, fall 80. *Mem:* Col Art Asn; Advocates Arts. *Media:* Acrylic-latex. *Publ:* Designer of exhib catalogues, Linda Benglis: Physical & Psychological Moments in Time, 75, Michelle Stuart, 75, State Univ NY & Maurice Prendergast: Art of Impulse & Color, 76 & From Delacroix to Cezanne: French Watercolor Landscapes of the 19th Century, 77 & The Public as Patron, 79, Univ Md. *Dealer:* McIntosh/Drysdale 2008 Peden Houston TX 77019. *Mailing Add:* 5807 Taylor Rd Riverdale MD 20737

CLARE, STEWART
RESEARCH ARTIST
b Montgomery City, Mo, Jan 31, 13. *Study:* Univ Kans, scholar, BA, 35; Iowa State Univ, MS(fel), 37; Univ Chicago, PhD(fel), 49; Kansas City Art Inst & Univ Mo, Kansas City, 46-49. *Work:* Work in libr & nat libr in US, Eng, Can, Australia & other countries. *Exhib:* The Science of Color & Design, 62-66, Chromatology: the Science of Color, 65-66, Scientific Illustrations & Diagrams, Designs & Writings, 68-70, on the theory of color & design: role of sci in art & vice versa, 79, at univs, cols & mus, US; Brit Asn for Advan Sci, Durham Mus & Art Ctr, 70; and others. *Pos:* Res artist sci of color, Kansas City Art Inst, Univ Mo, Kansas City, Univ Alta, Univ Adelaide, Union Col & others, 46-66; res in chromatology, Col Emporia, 67-74; color consult & info resource, Vol for Int Tech Assistance, 62-, Nat Referral Ctr for Sci & Technol, Libr Cong, 70- *Teaching:* Lectr, Dept Fine Art, Univ Alta, 50-53, Union Col, 58-61 & State Univ NY Col Twin Valleys, 62-66. *Awards:* Awards for Sci Illus, Univ Mo, Columbia, 29-31; Var Univ Res Grants, 46- *Mem:* Am Fedn Arts; Nat Art Educ Asn; Soc NAm Artists; Int Soc Educ Through Art; Inter-Soc Color Coun. *Res:* Science of color and design; technology in art; physical and chemical properties of earth pigments, gums, resins, adhesives and binders. *Collection:* Original and reproduced art, art objects and books. *Publ:* Contrib, sci illus in var periodicals & textbooks, 37-72; contribr, color design works in art publ & periodicals, 70-76. *Mailing Add:* 405 NW Woodland Rd Indian Hills in Riverside Kansas City MO 64150

CLARK, CAROL CANDA
CURATOR
b New York, NY, July 21, 47. *Study:* Univ Mich, AB(with distinction), 69, MA, 71; Cleveland Mus Art, Kress Found Fel, 72-75; Case Western Reserve Univ, PhD, 81. *Pos:* Registr, Univ Mich Mus Art, Ann Arbor, 71-72; cur paintings, Amon Carter Mus Western Art, Ft Worth, Tex, 77- *Teaching:* Instr art hist & mus studies, Tex Christian Univ, Ft Worth, 75-77. *Mem:* Am Asn Mus; Col Art Asn; Western Hist Asn. *Res:* American 19th century painting. *Publ:* Auth, Jean-Baptiste Simeon Chardin, still life with Herring, Bulletin Cleveland Mus Art, 11/74; coauth, Jasper Francis Cropsey, the narrows from Staten Island, Am Art Rev, 2/78; auth, American Impressionist and Realist Paintings and Drawings from the William Marshall Fuller Collection, Amon Carter Mus, 78; auth, Thomas Moran's Watercolors of the American West, Univ Tex Press, 80; auth, A Romantic Painter in the American West, Alfred Jacob Miller: Artist on the Oregon Trail, 82; and others. *Mailing Add:* Amon Carter Mus PO Box 2365 Ft Worth TX 76113

CLARK, CHARLES D
COLLECTOR, PATRON
b Peoria, Ill, May 28, 17. *Study:* Univ Mich, Ann Arbor, BA, LSA, 39. *Work:* Collection exhibited in Archer M Huntington Gallery, Univ Tex, Austin, Art Mus, Univ Calif, Berkeley, Whitney Mus Am Art, Philadelphia Mus Art & Univ Mich Mus Art, Ann Arbor. *Collections Arranged:* German Graphics of the 60s, 74, Swiss Concrete Art in Graphics, 75 & Finnish Constructivism,

79, Univ Tex Art Mus. *Pos:* Mem, Friends Coun, Univ Mich Mus, 68-75, Nat Comt, Art Mus, Univ Calif, Berkeley, 69-70 & Fine Arts Adv Coun, Univ Tex, Austin, 76- *Mem:* Am Fedn Arts; Arch Am Art. *Collection:* Charles and Dorothy Clark collection of contemporary prints. *Mailing Add:* 404 Lindberg McAllen TX 78501

CLARK, CLAUDE
INSTRUCTOR, PAINTER
b Rockingham, Ga, Nov 11, 15. *Study:* Philadelphia Mus Sch Art, dipl; Barnes Found, painting fel, 42-44; Sacramento State Col, BA; Univ Calif, Berkeley, MA. *Work:* Pa Mus, Philadelphia; Atlanta Univ; Oakland Mus, Calif; Fisk Univ; Nat Collection Art, Smithsonian Inst, Washington, DC. *Comn:* Freedom Morning (canvas interpretation), Philadelphia Orchestra Asn, 44. *Exhib:* Negro Artist Comes of Age, Brooklyn Mus, 45; Century of Uncle Tom's Cabin, Sorbonne, Paris, 53; Evolution of Afro-American Artists: 1800-1950, City Univ New York, 67; Amistad II: Afro-American Art Traveling Exhib, Fisk Univ, 75-76; Black American Artists 1750-1950 Traveling Exhib, Los Angeles Co Mus, 76-; Black Artists/South, 79. *Pos:* Artist, Fed Art Proj, Philadelphia, 39-42. *Teaching:* Assoc prof art, Talladega Col, Ala, 48-55; instr art, Alameda Co Schs, Calif, 59-68; instr art, Merritt Col, 68-81. *Awards:* Carnegie Found Grants Res, Painting & Ceramic Res, 49-50 & 51. *Bibliog:* David Driskell (auth), Retrospective Exhib, Fisk Univ, 72. *Media:* Oil. *Res:* African and African American art history; African art and culture in Ghana. *Publ:* Auth, A Black Art Perspective, 70. *Mailing Add:* 788 Santa Ray Ave Oakland CA 94610

CLARK, GARTH REGINALD
DEALER, HISTORIAN
b Pretoria, Republic SAfrica, May 15, 47. *Study:* Royal Col Art, London with Lord Queensberry & Edwardo Paolozzi, MA, 76. *Collections Arranged:* A Century of Ceramics in the US Traveling Exhib (auth, catalog), 79; The Contemporary American Potter Traveling Exhib (auth, catalog), Smithsonian Inst, 80; Michael Carden: A Portrait, NCECA Conference, 81; Ceramic Echoes: Historical References in Contemporary Ceramic Art (auth, catalog), Nelson Atkins Mus, 83. *Pos:* Dir, Inst Ceramic History, Los Angeles, 79-81. *Teaching:* Art historian ceramics, Univ Calif, Los Angeles, 78. *Awards:* Services to the Field, Nat Endowment Arts, 79; Art Critics Award, Nat Endowment Arts, 80; Morton Professor, Ohio Univ, 81. *Mem:* Decorative Art Soc; Inst Ceramic History. *Publ:* Co-auth, Potters of Southern Africa, G Struik, 73; ed, Ceramic Art: Comment & Review, E P Dutton, 78; auth, Century of Ceramics in the United States, 1878-1978, E P Dutton, 79; auth, American Potters, Watson Guptill, 81; auth, Ceramic echoes, Contemp Art Soc, 83. *Dealer:* Garth Clark Gallery 24 W 57th St New York NY. *Mailing Add:* 5820 Wilshire Blvd Los Angeles CA 90036

CLARK, JOHN DEWITT
SCULPTOR
b Kansas City, Mo. *Study:* Kansas City Art Inst; San Diego State Col, MA; also with Lowell Houser, Everett Jackson & John Dirks. *Work:* Palomar Col; Southwestern Col; La Jolla Mus Contemp Art. *Exhib:* 11 California Sculptors, Western Mus Asn, 62-64; Mex NAm Cult Inst, Mexico City, Mex, 66; Seven San Diego Artists, La Jolla Mus Contemp Art, 73; City is for People Exhib, San Diego Fine Arts Gallery, 74; Seider-Criegh Gal, Coronado, Calif, 78; plus numerous others. *Teaching:* Prof sculpture & design, Southwestern Col (Calif), 66- *Awards:* Southern Calif First Nat Bank Award, San Diego, 71; Med Growth Indust Award, San Diego, 71; M H Golden Construct Co Award, San Diego, 72. *Bibliog:* Rev in Artforum, 58. *Media:* Black Granite, Bronze. *Mailing Add:* c/o Art Dept Southwestern Col 900 Otay Lakes Rd Chula Vista CA 92010

CLARK, JON FREDERIC
EDUCATOR, GLASS BLOWER
b Waterloo, Wis, Aug 13, 47. *Study:* Univ Wis, BSc; Royal Col Art, London, MFA. *Work:* Royal Col Art, London, Eng; Archie Bray Found, Helena, Mont; Portnoy Ltd, New York; Hadler Galleries, New York; Lannan Found, Palm Beach, Fla. *Exhib:* New Am Glass, Focus WVa, Huntington, 76; Contemp Art Glass, Lever House, New York, 76; Art of Craft, The Am View, Ill State Univ, Normal, 76; Nat Glass III, Univ Wis, Madison, 76; Nat Craft Exhib, Del Mus of Art, Wilmington, 76; Philadelphia Craft Show, Philadelphia Mus of Art, 77. *Collections Arranged:* Cup Show, Fritz Driesbach, 76 & Eisch Retrospective, Littleton Collection, 77, Tyler Sch Art, Temple Univ, Philadelphia. *Teaching:* Glass technician, Calif Col of Arts & Crafts, Oakland, 73; assoc prof, Tyler Sch Art, 73-82. *Bibliog:* Judith Stein (auth), Exhibition Review, Vol 3 (1) & Richard Avidon (auth), Exhibition Review, Vol 4 (1), Glass Art Mag. *Mem:* Am Crafts Coun; Glass Art Soc; Nat Coun on Educ for Ceramic Arts. *Media:* Glass, Polyester. *Mailing Add:* 7703 Union Ave Elkins Park PA 19117

CLARK, MARK A
CURATOR
b Dayton, Ohio, Jan 20, 31. *Collections Arranged:* The Lipton Collection of Antique Tea Silver, 58; Glass from Area Collections, 66; The Folger Collection of Antique Silver Coffee Pots, 67; Paul Storr Silver in American Collections (with catalog), 72; Vermeil Collection (cataloger), White House, 72; A Tricentennial Celebration: Norfolk, 1682-1982 (catalog), 82; American Silver--A Survey of the Chrysler Museum Collection, 82; English Silver from the Chrysler Museum Collection, 83. *Pos:* Mus registr, Dayton Art Inst, 57-61, assoc cur decorative arts, 61-68, cur decorative arts & mus registr, 68-; cur dec arts, Chrysler Mus at Norfolk, 77- *Mem:* Norfolk Hist Soc; Decorative Arts Trust; Decorative Arts Soc. *Mailing Add:* 221 N Blake Rd Norfolk VA 23505

CLARK, MICHAEL VINSON
PAINTER
b Tex, Nov 20, 46. *Work:* Corcoran Gallery Art, Nat Collection Fine Art, Nat Gallery Art & Phillips Mem Collection, Washington, DC; Everson Mus, Syracuse, NY. *Exhib:* One-man shows, Mus STex, Corpus Christi, 78 & Harry Lunn Gallery, DC, 79; The Art of Organic Form, Smithsonian Inst, Washington, DC, 68; New Painting: Structure, Corcoran Gallery, 68; Nat Drawing Soc Show, Philadelphia Mus Art, Pa, 70; Ten Washington Artists 1950-1970, Edmonton Art Gallery, Can, 70; Washington Art: Twenty Years, Baltimore Mus of Art, 70; 75th Anniversary, Cooper-Hewitt Mus, New York, 77; Critics Choice 1977, Lowe Mus, Syracuse Univ, Syracuse, NY, 77; Dimock Gallery, George Washington Univ, DC, 79; Images of the 70's, Nine Washington Artists, Corcoran Gallery Art, DC, 80. *Awards:* Purchase Award, Nat Drawing Soc, Philadelphia Mus, 70; Purchase Award, 35th Corcoran Biennial Contemp Painting, 77. *Bibliog:* James Harithas (auth), Michael Clark, Everson Mus of Art, 73. *Publ:* Illusr, The Art of Organic Form, Smithsonian Inst, 68. *Dealer:* Harry Lunn Gallery Graphics Int Ltd 3243 P St NW Washington DC 20007. *Mailing Add:* 220 E 60th St Apt 6H New York NY 10022

CLARK, NANCY KISSEL
SCULPTOR, CONSULTANT
b Joplin, Mo, Jan 27, 19. *Study:* Mo Southern Col; Del Art Mus, with Henry Mitchell; Fleisher Art Mem, Philadelphia, with Aurelius Renzetti. *Work:* Woodmere Art Gallery; Univ Del, Newark; Pa Mil Col, Chester; Provident Nat Bank Gallery, Philadelphia. *Comn:* Francis, Camp Brisson, Childs, Md, 64; Steel sculpture, Walter Piel Mem, Corkran Gallery, Rehoboth, Del, 65; metal sculpture, Wood-Haven Kruse Sch, Wilmington, 66; Christ (5 ft), Notre Dame Brothers, St Edmon's Acad Chapel, Wilmington, 74; Holy Trinity Church & Barber Steamship Lines, Dallas, 79. *Exhib:* Nat Arts Club, New York, 67; June Week, US Naval Acad Mus, Annapolis, 69; Nat Sculpture Soc Ann, Lever House, New York, 71-73; Tex Sculpture Symp, Southern Methodist Univ Gallery, 78; Distinguished Mid-Atlantic Artists, Univ Del, 81. *Awards:* First Binswanger Award, Philadelphia Mus, 66; First Award, Nat League Am Pen Women Biennial, Tulsa, Okla, 66; Artist of the Year Award, Wilmington Coun Churches, 69. *Bibliog:* Louisa Turley (auth), Welded sculpture, Christian Sci Monitor, 68; Art in, National Competition, US Dept Housing & Urban Develop, 73; Archives, Am Art, Smithsonian Inst, 74 & Dallas Mus of Fine Arts, Tex, 78. *Mem:* Philadelphia Art Alliance; Artists Equity Asn, Philadelphia; Nat League Am Pen Women, Diamond State Chap. *Mailing Add:* 1015 Overbrook Rd Wilmington DE 19807

CLARK, ROBERT CHARLES
PAINTER, LECTURER
b Minneapolis, Minn, Aug 31, 20. *Study:* Minneapolis Sch Art; Walker Gallery Art Sch, Minneapolis. *Work:* Los Angeles Co Mus Hist, Sci & Art, Los Angeles; Norton B Simon Inc, Hunt's Foods & Industs Found, Los Angeles; Glendale Fed Collection of Calif Art. *Comn:* The Resurrection (mural), Forest Lawn Mem Park, Glendale, 65. *Exhib:* Artists of Los Angeles & Vicinity, Los Angeles Co Mus Art, 55-58; Illusion & Reality, Santa Barbara Mus Art, Calif, 56; one-man shows, Calif Palace of Legion of Honor, San Francisco, 56 & Rosicrucian Egyptian Mus, San Jose, 73; Charles & Emma Frye Mus, Seattle, Wash, 57-58. *Pos:* Background artist, Natural Hist Dept, Los Angeles Co Mus, 54-62. *Awards:* Artists of Los Angeles & Vicinity Award, Los Angeles Co Mus Art, 55; Purchase Award, Palos Verdes Estates Art Gallery, 56. *Bibliog:* Janice Lovoos (auth), The tempera paintings of Robert Clark, Am Artist, 12/69; William F Taylor (auth & producer), Robert Clark: An American Realist (film), 74; Elizabeth Rigby (auth), Robert Clark: A perfectionist's medium, Southwest Art, 1/79. *Media:* Tempera, Watercolor. *Dealer:* Zantman Art Galleries Ltd Sixth & Dolores Sts Carmel CA 93921; El Prado Gallery Art PO Box 1849 Sedona AZ 86336. *Mailing Add:* 2270 230th Pl Torrance CA 90501

CLARK, ROBERTA CARTER
ILLUSTRATOR, PAINTER
b St Louis, Mo, May 2, 24. *Study:* Purdue Univ; Ctr Creative Studies, Detroit, 48-51; Art Ctr Sch, Los Angeles, 53-54; Art Student's League, with Hirsch, 59; also studied with John Terslak, Don Stone & Charles Reid. *Work:* Brookdale Col, Lincroft, NJ; Rutgers Univ, New Brunswick, NJ; Freehold Area Hospital, Freehold, NJ; Margot Perot Women's and Children's Hospital, Dallas. *Exhib:* Soc Western Artists, De Young Mus, San Francisco, 54; Allied Artists, Nat Acad Design, New York, 76 & 82; Knickerbocker Artists, Nat Arts Club, New York, 81-83; Hudson Valley Art Asn, White Plains, NY, 81-83; Watercolor West, Riverside Art Mus, Calif, 83; Midwest Watercolor Soc, Davenport Art Mus, Iowa, 83. *Awards:* Silver Medals, NJ Watercolor Soc Ann, 78 & 81 & Knickerbocker Artists, Grumbacher Inc, 82; Strathmore Paper Co Award, Midwest Watercolor Soc, Strathmore Col, 83. *Mem:* NJ Watercolor Soc (secy, 76-78, pres, 79-82); Artists Fel; Catherine Lorillard Wolfe Art Club Inc; Rockport Art Asn. *Media:* Oil, Watercolor. *Publ:* Illusr, The Littles, ser of ten bks, Scholastic Inc, 70-83; auth & illusr, Portraits and How to Paint Them, Prentice-Hall (in prep). *Dealer:* Portraits Inc 985 Park Ave New York NY 10028. *Mailing Add:* 47B Cheshire Sq Little Silver NJ 07739

CLARK, TIMOTHY JOHN
PAINTER, INSTRUCTOR
b Santa Ana, Calif, June 30, 51. *Study:* Art Ctr Col Design, with Paul Marciel Souza & Harry Carmean, 69-70; Chouinard Art Inst, with Donald W Graham & Harold M Kramer, CFA, 72; Calif Inst Arts, BFA, 74; Calif State Univ, Fullerton, with Victor Joachim Smith, 75; Calif State Univ, Long Beach, with Joyce Wahl Treiman, MA, 78. *Exhib:* San Diego Watercolor Soc Nat Exhib,

Bard Hall, Calif, 79; 43rd & 44th Ann Midyear Show, Butler Inst Am Art, Youngstown, Ohio, 79 & 80; Rocky Mountain Nat Watermedia Exhib, Foothills Art Ctr, Golden, Colo, 80; Am Watercolor Soc Ann Exhib, Nat Acad Galleries, New York, 80; Nat Acad Design Ann Exhib, Nat Acad Galleries, New York, 80; Salmagundi Club Ann, New York, 82 & 83. *Teaching:* Instr drawing & painting, Orange Coast Col, Costa Mesa, Calif, 74-79; instr drawing, Saddleback Col, Mission Viejo, Calif, 76-77; instr drawing & painting, Coastline Col, Fountain Valley, Calif, 76-; dir, Timothy J Clark Watercolor Workshops, Hawaii, 81-; instr watercolor, Univ Hawaii, 82. *Awards:* Juror's Award, San Diego Watercolor Soc, 79; Mustardseed Award, Rocky Mountain Nat Watercolor Exhib, Mustardseed Gallery, 80; Purchase Award, Nat Competitive Graphics Exhibit, 83. *Bibliog:* Richard Reilly (auth), It's watercolors on parade, The San Diego Union, 7/22/79; Jane Summer (auth), The Art of Timothy J Clark, Showcase, The Santa Ana Register, 1/18/81; Joan Talmage Weiss (auth), Pastel colors and passionate song, Forum 50 Mag, 1/81. *Media:* Watercolor, Oil. *Dealer:* Challis Galleries 1390 S Coast Highway Laguna Beach CA 92652; Connoiseur's Gallery Maunalani PO Box 4000 Kawainae HI 96743. *Mailing Add:* 16320 Livingstone Fountain Valley CA 92708

CLARK, VICKY A
HISTORIAN, CURATOR
b Atlanta, Ga. *Study:* Univ Calif, Los Angeles, BA, 72; Univ Calif, Davis, MA, 74; Univ Mich (teaching fel, 75-77), PhD, 79. *Pos:* Cur educ, Mus Art, Carnegie Inst, Pittsburgh, 81- *Teaching:* Instr, Univ Toledo & Toledo Mus Art, 79; asst prof, Univ RI, 80; asst prof, Skidmore Col, Saratoga Springs, NY, 80-81; adj prof, Duquesne Univ, Pittsburgh, 82- *Mem:* Am Asn Mus; NE Mus Conf; Col Art Asn; Int Ctr Medieval Art; Medieval & Renaissance Collegium, Univ Mich. *Res:* Artistic, historical and cultural significance of astrological illustrations in the Middle Ages, the multi-faceted sources from which they are derived and the influence they exert on later works and beliefs. *Publ:* Contribr, The Meeting of Two Worlds: The Crusades and the Mediterranean Context, Univ Mich Mus Art, 81; auth, Collecting from the internationals, Carnegie Mag, Vol LVI, No 5. *Mailing Add:* Carnegie Inst Mus Art 4400 Forbes Ave Pittsburgh PA 15213

CLARK, WILLIAM W
HISTORIAN
b Tampa, Fla, Jan 17, 40. *Study:* Pa State Univ, BA(with hons); Columbia Univ, MA & PhD. *Teaching:* Assoc prof medieval archit, Queens Col, City Univ NY, Flushing, 67- *Mem:* Col Art Asn; Societe Francaise d'Archeologie; Int Ctr for Medieval Art; Centre des Recherches d'Archeologie Medievale; Soc of Archit Historians. *Res:* Twelfth-century early Gothic architecture, sculpture and manuscripts in North France, Normandy and England. *Publ:* Auth, The Central Portal of Saint-Pierre at Lisieux..., 72 & The Nave of Saint-Pierre at Lisieux..., 77, Gesta; auth, The Nave Vaults of Noyon Cathedral, 77 & Spatial innovations in the Chevet of Saint-Germain-des-Pres, 79, Soc of Archit Hist J; coauth (with R King), Laon Cathedral, London, 83-84. *Mailing Add:* 395 Riverside Dr 12-B New York NY 10025

CLARKE, ANN
LECTURER, PAINTER
b Norwich, Eng, Aug 27, 44; Can citizen. *Study:* Slade Sch Fine Art, Univ Col, London, dipl fine art & design. *Work:* Can Coun Art Bank; Westburne Collection, Montreal; Hill Trust Fund Collection, Calgary, Alta; Prov Courthouse Collection, Edmonton, Can; Queensland Art Gallery, Brisbane, Australia. *Exhib:* Abstraction West: Emma Lake and After, Nat Gallery, Ottawa, Ont & Mendel Art Gallery, Saskatoon, Sask, 76; Beaverbrook Art Gallery, Frederickton, NB, 76; Mus d'Art Contemporain, Montreal, Que, 76; Contemp Can Drawings, Mackenzie Art Gallery, Univ Regina, Sask, 77; Seven Prairie Artists, Art Gallery of Ont, 79; one-person shows, Latitude 53 Gallery, Edmonton, Edmonton Art Gallery, 77 & Southern Alberta Art Gallery, 79; and others. *Teaching:* Asst prof art, NS Col Art & Design, Halifax, 75-76; lectr art, Univ Alta, Edmonton, 76- & Red Deer Col, 79-80, Grant McEwan Col, 80- *Awards:* Can Coun Art Bank Award, 73 & 76; Govt Alta Cult Award, 74; Can Coun Art Award, 78-79. *Bibliog:* Article, Ken Carpenter (auth), Ann Clarke, Art Mag, 6/81. *Media:* Acrylic on Canvas. *Dealer:* Gallery One 121 Scollard St Toronto ON M5R 1G4; Martin Gerard 10416 80th Ave Edmonton AB T6E 5T7. *Mailing Add:* 8107 149th St Edmonton AB T5R 1B1 Canada

CLARKE, BUD (WARREN F)
DESIGNER, DIRECTOR
b Windsor, Vt, Jan 10, 41. *Study:* Art Students League, 59-63; Sch Visual Arts, with Milton Glazer. *Pos:* Art dir, McCalls Corp, 68-70; art dir, McGraw Hill Inc, New York, 70-; ed, Fleet Owner, 70- & Nat Petroleum News, 73-, McGraw Hill, Hunter Publ & Macmillan; owner-designer, Art Foundry, 77- *Teaching:* Instr mag design, Sch Visual Arts, 77, instr media commun, 78- *Awards:* Cert of Merit, Art Dir Mag, 78; Spec Issue Design, Soc Publ Designers, 79; Jesse H Neal Award, Am Bus Press, 80 & 82. *Bibliog:* Roy Paul Nelson (auth), Publication Design, William C Brown, 78. *Mem:* Soc Publ Designers; McGraw Hill Art Dirs Club (pres, 74-78). *Mailing Add:* 372 Central Park W New York NY 10025

CLARKE, JOHN CLEM
PAINTER
b Bend, Ore, June 6, 37. *Study:* Ore State Univ; Mexico City Col; Univ Ore, BFA, 60. *Work:* Whitney Mus Fine Arts, New York; Dallas Mus Fine Arts, Tex; Va Mus Fine Arts; Metrop Mus Art & Mus Mod Art, New York; Baltimore Mus Fine Arts, Md. *Exhib:* Whitney Mus, Bi-Ann, 67-73; Illusion and Reality, Australia; Realism in Am, touring USA; Mus Mod Art, New York; Art About Art, Whitney Mus, New York; Aspects of Realism, Can; and others. *Media:* Oil on Canvas. *Mailing Add:* 465 W Broadway New York NY 10012

CLARKE, JOHN R
EDUCATOR, CRITIC
b Pittsburgh, Pa, Jan 25, 45. *Study:* Georgetown Univ, AB, 67; Yale Univ, MA, 69, PhD, 73. *Teaching:* Asst prof hist art, Yale Univ, 75-80; asst prof, Univ Tex, Austin, 80-82, assoc prof, 82- *Mem:* Col Art Asn Am; Archaeol Inst Am. *Res:* History of Roman art; structuralism; American art and art criticism, 1960 to present. *Publ:* Auth, Roman Black-and White Figural Mosaics, NY Univ Press, 79; auth, Life/art/life, Quentin Crisp and Eleanor Antin: Notes on performance in the seventies, 79, Visual and conceptual structures in Susan Hall's painting, 79, The decorative revisited: Five on fabric, 82 & Up against the wall, transavanguardia!, 82, Arts Mag. *Mailing Add:* Dept Art Univ Tex Austin TX 78712

CLAYBERGER, SAMUEL ROBERT
PAINTER, EDUCATOR
b Kulpmont, Pa, Mar 26, 26. *Study:* Chouinard Art Inst, Los Angeles; Jepson Art Inst; study with Don Graham, Rico Lebrun & Richard Haines. *Work:* Pasadena Art Mus, Calif. *Exhib:* One-man shows, Pasadena Art Mus, 60, Laguna Beach Mus Art, Calif, 67, Whittier Art Asn, Calif, 70 & Orange Coast Col, Costa Mesa, Calif, 73; Otis Art Inst Gallery, Los Angeles, 73. *Pos:* Designer-colorist, UPA Pictures Inc, Burbank, 53-58 & Jay Ward Prod Inc, Los Angeles, 59-64. *Teaching:* Instr design, Chouinard Art Inst, 60; instr design & painting, Otis Art Inst of Los Angeles Co, 63-69, asst prof drawing & painting, 69- *Awards:* Nat Watercolor Soc, 56, 58, 60 & 69; Los Angeles All-City Exhib, Home Savings & Loan, 62. *Bibliog:* George De Groat (auth), Sam Clayberger eyes the human condition, Star News, Pasadena, 70. *Mem:* Nat Watercolor Soc; Artists Equity Asn. *Media:* Acrylic, Watercolor. *Mailing Add:* 486 Mavis Dr Los Angeles CA 90065

CLEARY, FRITZ
SCULPTOR, CRITIC
b New York, NY, Sept 26, 14. *Study:* St John's Univ; Nat Acad Design; Beaux-Arts Inst, with Alexander Finta. *Comn:* Presidential heads, Long Br Jr High Sch, NJ; Robert Mount Mem, Monmouth Col, NJ; World War II Mem, Point Pleasant, NJ; John F Kennedy Mem, Asbury Park, NJ; Rocco Bonforte Mem, Long Branch, NJ. *Exhib:* Nat Acad Design, New York; Pa Acad Fine Arts, Philadelphia; Oakland Art Mus, Calif; Nat Sculpture Soc, Allied Artists & Hudson Valley Art Asn Ann; also in col art mus & city mus in Eastern US. *Pos:* Art critic, Asbury Park Press, 45-62, Sun, 62-72; ed adv, Nat Sculpture Rev, 74-78. *Awards:* NJ Soc Archit Ann Award, 72; John Spring Award, Nat Sculpture Soc, 74; Anna Hyatt Huntington Award for Sculpture, Hudson Valley Art Asn, 75; and others. *Mem:* Allied Am Artists; fel Nat Sculpture Soc; Asbury Park Soc Fine Arts (pres, cur mus, 66-); and others. *Media:* Bronze. *Publ:* Auth & illusr, Sixty Days Around the World, 56; auth, editorials & articles, In: Nat Sculpture Rev, 72-81; and others. *Mailing Add:* 205 Grassmere Ave Interlaken Asbury Park NJ 07712

CLEARY, MANON CATHERINE
PAINTER, EDUCATOR
b St Louis, Mo, Nov 14, 42. *Study:* Wash Univ, BFA, 64; Temple Univ, MFA, 68. *Work:* Corcoran Gallery Art, Washington, DC; Mem Art Gallery, Univ Rochester, NY; Brooklyn Mus, NY; Ponce Mus, PR; Univ Va, Charlottesville. *Exhib:* Invitational Drawing Exhib, Fine Arts Gallery, San Diego, Calif, 77; Images of the 70's: 9 Washington Realists, Corcoran Gallery Art, Washington, DC, 80; Taft Menagerie, Taft Mus, Cincinnati, Ohio, 81; An Am Bestiary, Inst Contemp Art, Richmond, Va, 81; Am Drawings in Black & White, Brooklyn Mus, NY, 81; Perspectives on Contemporary American Realism: Works of Art on Paper from the Collection of Jalane and Richard Davidson, Pa Acad Fine Art & Chicago Art Inst, 82-83. *Pos:* Guest artist, Herning Hoiskoke, Denmark, 80. *Teaching:* Instr fine arts, State Univ NY, Oswego, 68-70; prof fine arts, Univ DC, Washington, DC, 70-82. *Awards:* Faculty Research Award, Univ DC, 83. *Bibliog:* Clair List (auth), Images of the 70's, 9 Washington Artists, Corcoran Gallery Art, 80; Frank Goodyear (auth), Contemporary Am Realism, NY Graphic Soc, 81; Gerrit Henry (auth), Manon Cleary at Iolas/Jackson, Art Am, summer 82. *Mem:* Col Art Asn. *Media:* Oil, Graphite. *Dealer:* Osuna Gallery 406 7th St NW Washington DC 20004; Iolas Jackson Gallery 52 East 57th St New York NY 10022. *Mailing Add:* 1736 Columbia Rd NW Washington DC 20009

CLEAVER, DALE GORDON
HISTORIAN, EDUCATOR
b Lafayette, Ind, June 24, 28. *Study:* Willamette Univ, BA, 50; Univ Chicago, MA, 52, Fulbright Res Grant Belg painting, 52-53, PhD, 55. *Pos:* Trustee, Dulin Gallery Art, Knoxville, 74-79; mem acquisitions comt, Hunter Mus, Chattanooga, 76- *Teaching:* Prof 19th & 20th century painting, sculpture & archit, Univ Tenn, Knoxville, 58- *Awards:* Lindsay Young Professorship Art Hist, 80; Outstanding Teacher Award, Univ Tenn Alumni, 81. *Mem:* Col Art Asn Am; Southeastern Col Art Asn. *Res:* Belgian 19th century painting; French landscape painting of the late 18th and early 19th centuries. *Publ:* Auth, Three combat scenes by Henri Leys, Bull Mus Royaux des Beaus-Arts de Belg, 6/53; auth, The concept of time in modern sculpture, summer 63 & auth, Girodet's deluge: a case study in art criticism, winter 79, Art J; auth, Art: an Introduction, 66, rev ed, 77 & coauth, Art and Music: an Introduction, 77, Harcourt Brace. *Mailing Add:* Dept of Art Univ of Tenn Knoxville TN 97316

CLEF, ROMAN A (HENRY E GUERRIERO)
WRITER, SCULPTOR
b Monroe, La, Mar 6, 29. *Study:* Royal Acad, London, 51-53; with Witol Klimowicz, Paris, 52; Inst Allende, Mexico, 55-56; Univ of the Americas, Mex, 56-59. *Work:* Univ Southern Calif; Ateneumin Taidemuseo, Helsinki;

Santa Barbara Mus Art, Calif; Kunsthaus, Zurich; Herbert F Johnson Mus, Cornell Univ; and others. *Comn:* The Arrangement (steel & bronze sculptures), Elia Kazan, 68; opera sets for Amerika, Western Opera Co, 72; Golden Needle (bronze sculpture), Paul Heller, 74. *Exhib:* One-person shows, John Whibley Gallery, Ltd, London, 69, Phoenix Art Mus, 71 & Loyola Marymount Univ, 74; Univ Southern Calif, 70-71; Leopold/Gold Gallery, 80; and others. *Bibliog:* M Leopold (auth), Henry Guerriero, Art Int, 73; Monika Henreid (producer), Roman A Clef: I'm a novel not a textbook (art doc film), 79. *Media:* Polyester Resin, Bronze. *Publ:* Auth, X-Art Manifesto, 68; auth, Age of Confrontation, 71; auth, Polarity, 75; auth, Roman A Clef on the works of Henry Guerriero with notes, Michael Leopold, 78; auth, Manifesto on transparent sculpture, 79; and others. *Mailing Add:* 3036 Veteran Ave Los Angeles CA 90034

CLEMENS, PAUL
PAINTER, WRITER
b Superior, Wis, Oct 29, 11. *Study:* Univ Wis, BA(art hist), 32; Chicago Art Inst, 33. *Work:* Metrop Mus Art, New York; Los Angeles Co Mus, Calif; Milwaukee Art Inst, Wis; Sterling Clark Mus, Williamstown, Mass; William Rockhill Nelson Gallery, Kansas City, Mo. *Comn:* Portraits of Frank Sinatra, Clare Booth Luce, Robert Six, Julie Andrews, Katherine Hepburn and others. *Exhib:* Am Show, Chicago Art Inst, 38; World Fair Expos, 38 & 40; Carnegie Inst Int, 39-43; Nat Acad Design, New York, 44-72; Show Am Artists, Metrop Mus Art, New York, 45. *Teaching:* Painting, Otis Art Inst, Los Angeles & Univ Wis-Superior. *Awards:* American Show, Chicago Art Inst, 37; Milwaukee Art Inst Medal, 37; Alman Prize for Figure Painting, Nat Acad Design, New York, 43. *Bibliog:* Articles in Time Mag, Art News & Life Mag. *Mem:* Academician Nat Acad Design. *Media:* Oil, Pastel. *Mailing Add:* Suite 3 11757 San Vicente Blvd Los Angeles CA 90049

CLEMENT, KATHLEEN (RUTH)
PAINTER, GRAPHIC ARTIST
b Ord, Nebr, May 28, 28. *Study:* Univ Nebr, BA, 50; with Frank Gonzalez, 67-69; Univ Am, with Toby Joysmith, 77-79; Mus Studies, Paris, 80. *Work:* Mus Mod Art, Isidro Fabela Cult Ctr & Inst North Am Cult Relations, Mexico. *Exhib:* Nat Mus Fine Arts, Mexico, 78; Triannual Latin American Grafics Exhib, Nat Salon of Exhibs, Buenos Aires, Arg, 79 & New Zealand, 79; Stuhr Mus, Grand Island, Nebr, 80; Mus Puebla, Mexico, 80; solo exhib, Rossi Gallery, Morristown, NJ, 83; and others. *Bibliog:* Jorge J Crespo de la Serna (auth), article, Novedades, 3/30/76; Berta Taracena (auth), article, Tiempo, 5/24/82. *Media:* Acrylic, Pen & Ink. *Dealer:* Margolis Galleries 100 E Meadow Dr Vail CO 81657. *Mailing Add:* Prolongacion de Nayarit 120 Colonia Progreso Tizapan Mexico DF 01080 Mexico

CLEMENT, SHIRLEY
PAINTER
b New York, NY July 7, 22. *Study:* Ringling Sch Art, two yrs; Amagansett Art Sch, Sarasota, Fla, two yrs. *Work:* Univ Fla, Gainesville; Davenport Munic Gallery, Iowa; Henry Ward Ranoer Fund, New York. *Exhib:* Am Watercolor Soc, Nat Acad, New York, 50-; Watercolor Show, Phoenix Mus, 68; Winterpark Sidewalk Art Festival, Fla, 71; Disneys Festival of the Masters, Lake Buena Vista, Fla, 74; Nat Acad Show, New York & High Mus, 74; Allied Artists, Nat Arts Club, New York, 74. *Awards:* Salmagundi Award, Am Watercolor Soc, 69; William A Paton Award, Nat Acad Design, 74; Verda Karen McCracken Young Award, Am Watercolor Soc, 77. *Mem:* Am Watercolor Soc; Fla Artist Group; Fla Watercolor Soc; Sarasota Art Asn; Manatee Art League. *Media:* Watercolor, Acrylic. *Mailing Add:* 3951 Red Rock Lane Sarasota FL 33581

CLEMENTS, ROBERT DONALD
SCULPTOR, EDUCATOR
b Pittsburgh, Pa, Dec 24, 37. *Study:* Carnegie-Mellon Univ, BFA(painting), 59; Pa State Univ, MA(art), 62, PhD(art educ), 64. *Work:* Nat Mus Am Arts, Smithsonian Inst, Washington, DC; Jacksonville Mus Arts; King & Spalding; Chase Manhattan Bank; Omni Int. *Exhib:* One-man show, Totems to Southerners & the South, Hunter Mus Art, Montgomery Mus & Asheville Mus; Nat Sculpture '80; MCCN '80; South Exhib, Palazzo Venezia, Rome, 84. *Pos:* Art consult, Arts & Humanities Prog, US Off Educ, 68-69. *Teaching:* Asst prof art, Ball State Univ, 64-68; assoc prof art, Univ Ga, 69-81, prof art, 81- *Awards:* Butler Inst Am Art Nat Show Award, 82; Energy Art Award, 82. *Bibliog:* Elliot Eisner (auth), Research on teaching the visual arts, In: Robert Travers, Second Handbook of Research on Teaching, 76; Joy Lee (auth), Wood sculpture, Arts/Crafts, spring 80; Charlotte von Glasersfeld (auth), article, Art Papers, 11/83. *Mem:* Nat Art Educ Asn; Ga Art Educ Asn; Southern Asn Sculptors; Int Sculpture Ctr. *Publ:* Auth, Art teachers' classroom questioning, Art Educ, 4/65; auth, The inductive method of teaching visual art criticism, J Aesthetic Educ, 7/79; auth, Modern architecture's debt to creativity education, Gifted Child Quart, summer 81; coauth, Evaluation of drama program on creativity, J Creative Behavior, 12/82; coauth (with Claire Clements), Art and Mainstreaming, Art Instruction for Exceptional Children in Regular Classrooms, Charles C Thomas, 83. *Dealer:* Fay Gold Gallery 3221 Cains Hill Pl NW Atlanta GA 30303. *Mailing Add:* 155 Bar H Ct Athens GA 30601

CLERK, PIERRE
PAINTER, SCULPTOR
b Atlanta, Ga, Apr 26, 28. *Study:* Loyola Col; McGill Univ; Montreal Sch Art & Design; Acad Julian, Paris; Acad Grande Chaumiere, Paris. *Work:* Mus Mod Art, Guggenheim Mus & Whitney Mus Am Art, New York; Nat Gallery Can, Ottawa, Ont; Mus Contemp Art, Montreal. *Comn:* City Walls, NY; Com Bank of Kansas City; First Wis Develop Corp, Milwaukee; Marine Midland

Bank, NY; sculpture, City Toledo, 83; and others. *Exhib:* One-man exhibs, Everson Mus of Art, Syracuse, NY, 77, Waterside Plaza, NY, 77, Monumental Outdoor Sculpture, NY, 77-78, Iran-Am Ctr, Tehran, Iran, 78 & Metrop Mus of Art, Manila, Philippines, 78; and many others. *Awards:* Us Info Serv Exhib Grant, 77; Munic Art Soc Grant, 77; US State Dept Travel Grant, 77-78; and others. *Mailing Add:* PO Box 188 Canal St Station New York NY 10013

CLERMONT, GHISLAIN
HISTORIAN, CRITIC
b Ste-Adele, PQ, Sept 30, 40. *Study:* Univ Montreal, DES(hist art); Univ BC, Vancouver. *Collections Arranged:* Second APAC Biennial Exhib, Serigraphs of Alex Colville, Moncton Collectors; various Canadian artists. *Pos:* Dir art gallery, Univ Moncton, 67-70. *Teaching:* Prof hist art, Univ Moncton, 67- *Mem:* Univ Art Asn Can. *Res:* 19th and 20th centuries Canadian art; James Wilson Morrice. *Publ:* Auth, articles in, Vie des Arts, Montreal, Rev Univ Moncton, Montreal-Medical, Racar & exhib catalogs. *Mailing Add:* 79 Portledge Moncton NB E1C 5S6 Canada

CLEVELAND, HELEN BARTH
ADMINISTRATOR, INSTRUCTOR
b Alliance, Ohio. *Study:* Mt Union Col, with George A Gibbs & Eric Johanson; Kent State Univ, with Novotny; Syracuse Univ, with George Sander Sluis & James A Smith; NY Univ; London Acad Art, Eng; Univ San Juan; Acad Arts Honolulu. *Work:* Art Gallery Ont, Toronto; Chautauqua Gallery Art, NY. *Comn:* Murals, Wildwood Gallery, Lake Orion, Mich, 67, Prendergast Libr, Jamestown, NY, 68 & Galerie 8, Erie, Pa, 69; natural hist murals, Hist Ctr, Gov Gilligan's Art Exhib, Alliance, 71. *Exhib:* Chautauqua Gallery Art Nat & Regional, 52, 56 & 63; Albright-Knox Regional, Buffalo, NY, 65; Cleveland Art Mus, Ohio, 67; Hemingway Gallery, New York & Jamestown, 68-70; Canton Cult Ctr, Ohio, 70. *Pos:* Pres & dir, Chautauqua Gallery Art, 63- *Teaching:* Instr art, Alliance Pub Schs, 27-; instr crafts, Syracuse Univ, Chautauqua & NY Univ, 50-52 & 61-64; instr art, Sierra Leone, Africa, 63. *Awards:* Chautauqua Art Asn Ribbons, Bestor Plaza Art Festival, 50, 54 & 57; Citation Winning Poster, State Ohio, 69. *Bibliog:* Lee Nelson (auth), Outstanding woman of today, Erie Times, Pa, 65-66; Jean Reeves (auth), The director, Chautauqua Gallery of Art, Buffalo Eve News, NY, 71. *Mem:* Am Fedn Art; Nat Educ Asn; life mem Ohio Educ Asn; Asn Am Univ Women; plus others. *Media:* Oil, Pastel. *Publ:* Coauth, Arts & Crafts, Grade Teacher, 55; coauth, Art in Poetry, Solvay Publ Co, 59; coauth, Creativity in Elementary Schools, 63-64; coauth, Arts Illustrated (children's ser), Rowe-Peterson, 65; coauth, Chautauqua Gallery of Art, Art Gallery Mag, 66. *Mailing Add:* 1192 Parkside Dr Alliance OH 44601

CLEVELAND, ROBERT EARL
ADMINISTRATOR, EDUCATOR
b Union, Miss, June 8, 36. *Study:* Miss Col, BA; Univ Miss, MFA; Univ Tenn, EdD. *Work:* Univ Miss Fine Arts Ctr, University, Miss. *Comn:* Redwood sculpture, Carson-Newman Col, 76. *Exhib:* Second Nat Print & Drawing Exhib, Dulin Gallery Art, Knoxville, Tenn, 67; Tenn Watercolor Exhib, Cheekwood Mus, Nashville, 75; Quinlan Ann Art Exhib, Gainesville, Ga, 76; Carroll Reece Mus, Johnson City, Tenn, 77; Owensboro Mus Fine Arts, Ky, 79; and others. *Pos:* Artist-illusr, Ling-Temco-Vought Inc, Dallas, Tex, 61-62. *Teaching:* Instr art, Univ Miss, Oxford, 63-64; prof art & chmn dept, Carson-Newman Col, Jefferson City, 64- *Awards:* First Prize Painting, Morristown Art Competition, Tenn, 66 & Macon Ann Arts Exhib, Macon Arts Coun, 73; First Prize Drawing, Oak Ridge Relig Art Exhib, Oak Ridge Art Ctr, Tenn, 76. *Mem:* Nat Asn Schs Art; Nat Coun Art Adminrs; Southeastern Col Art Conf; Tenn Watercolor Soc. *Media:* Oil, Watercolor. *Res:* Arts administration in higher education and art and law issues. *Publ:* Auth, Art and the Law, 77 & auth, The Art Department Chairperson: An Ambiguous Role, 78, Nat Coun Art Adminrs; auth, The Law: Public Aid and the Private Sector, 78 & auth, Art Administration in Pursuit of Efficacy, 83, Fac Studies. *Mailing Add:* Box 1901 Art Dept Carson-Newman Col Jefferson City TN 37760

CLIFF, DENIS ANTONY
PAINTER, INSTUCTOR
b Victoria, BC, Aug 8, 42. *Study:* Univ Victoria, BEd, 65; New Sch Art, 66-67. *Work:* Nat Gallery Can, Art Bank Gallery, Ottawa; Charlottetown Confederation Ctr Arts, PEI; Univ Sask, Saskatoon; Cobourg Art Gallery, Ont. *Comn:* Murals, Ostler Sch Nursing, Toronto, 70, Simcoe Bd Educ, Ont, 71, Eaton Ctr, Toronto, 78 & Fisher-Price, Toronto, 79. *Exhib:* New Blood, Rodman Hall Art Ctr, St Catherines, Ont, 73; Can Invitational, Can Consulate, Chicago, 77; Artists Coop Toronto at Nexus, Philadelphia, 78; Explorations, Thames Art Ctr, Chatham, Ont, 80; Toronto Exchange, Mem Univ, St Johns, Nfld, 81. *Teaching:* Artist in residence, Canador Col, North Bay, Ont, 72-74 & Arts Sake, Toronto, 77-79; vis prof, York Univ, Toronto, 79-82; asst prof, Univ Victoria, 82- *Awards:* Best Painting, 70 & Best in Show, 71, City Toronto Ann; Can Coun Grant, 79. *Bibliog:* Gail Habs (auth), Success story: ACT I, Artviews, 77; Sandra Shaul (auth), Altered egos: An exhibition of drawings by Denis Cliff, 77 & Diane Pugen (auth), article, 78, Art Mag. *Mem:* Royal Can Acad Art. *Media:* Acrylic on Canvas. *Dealer:* Artists Coop Toronto 424 Wellington St W Toronto ON N8A 2Y2. *Mailing Add:* 24 Lewis St Toronto ON M4M 2H3 Canada

CLIFFORD, JUTTA
DEALER, LECTURER
b The Hague, Holland; US citizen. *Study:* Univ Dallas, printmaking, 74 with Jurgen Strunck; Abitur Klosterscule, Hamburg, Ger, 64. *Pos:* Owner/dir, Clifford Gallery, 74- *Mem:* Dallas Print & Drawing Soc; Pratt Graphic Ctr. *Specialty:* Contemporary art--fine prints, sculpture and paintings; eight exhibitions annually. *Mailing Add:* 6610 Snider Plaza Dallas TX 75205

CLIFT, WILLIAM BROOKS
PHOTOGRAPHER
b Boston, Mass, Jan 5, 44. *Study:* Workshop Paul Caponigro, 59. *Work:* Metrop Mus Art, Mus Mod Art, New York; Art Inst Chicago; Mus Fine Arts, Boston; Nat Gallery, Canberra, Australia. *Comn:* Photographs, Old City Hall, Boston, Mass Coun Arts, 70, American County Courthouses, Joseph Seagrams & Sons, New York, 75-76 & American Images, Am Tel & Tel, New York, 78. *Exhib:* Solo exhibs, Old City Hall, Boston, Worcester Art Mus, Mass, 71 & Landscapes, Mus Fine Art, Santa Fe, 79, Phoenix Art Mus, 81 & Sheldon Mem Art Gallery, 81; Court House, 77, Mirrors and Windows, 78 & American Landscapes, 81, Mus Mod Art, New York; Counterparts, Metrop Mus Art, New York, 82. *Awards:* Fels, Nat Endowment Arts, 72 & 79 & Guggenheim Found, 74 & 80. *Mem:* Charter mem Asn Heliographers. *Publ:* Coauth, The darkness and the light, Aperture, 74; coauth, American Images, McGraw-Hill, 79. *Mailing Add:* PO Box 6035 Santa Fe NM 87502

CLIFTON, JACK WHITNEY
INSTRUCTOR, PAINTER
b Norfolk, Va, Feb 3, 12. *Study:* Art Inst Pittsburgh, 31-32; Pa Acad Fine Arts, Philadelphia, 33-39. *Work:* Va Mus Art, Richmond; Springfield Mus Art, Mass; Grumbacher Collection, New York; State Capitol Bldg, Richmond; Chrysler Mus, Norfolk. *Comn:* Portraits, Newport News Courthouse, Newport News Bar Asn, 46-; USS Enterprise Atomic Carrier, US Navy, Washington, DC, 63; Houses of Parliament, London Eng (hist painting), 68 & State Capitol, Richmond (painting), 74, Jamestown Found; State Capitol Bldg, Richmond (4ft x 7ft painting), Jamestown Found, 69-74. *Exhib:* Chrysler Mus Ann, Norfolk, 46-70; Va Mus Ann, Richmond, 46-70; Exhib of Unification, Pentagon, Washington, DC, 57; Springfield Ann, Springfield Mus Art, 60; Nat Biennial Exhib, Corcoran Gallery of Art, 62. *Teaching:* Instr basic art, Clifton Sch Art, 34-; instr basic art, Davis & Elkins Col, Elkins, WVa, 46; art prof life class, Christopher Newport Col, Newport News, 74-82. *Media:* Acrylic Polymer. *Publ:* Auth, Manual of Drawing & Painting, Watson-Guptill, 57; auth, Self-expression or self-indulgence, Am Artist Mag, 10/62; auth, The Eye of the Artist, Watson-Guptill, 73. *Dealer:* Chase Gallery 64th at Madison Ave New York NY. *Mailing Add:* 1615 Chesapeake Ave Hampton VA 23661

CLIFTON, MICHELLE GAMM
SCULPTOR, FILMMAKER
b Los Angeles, Calif, July 11, 44. *Study:* Yale Univ, summer scholar, 65; Univ Ill, Urbana, with Lee Chesney, BFA, 66; Pa State Univ, with Carol Summers, MFA, 68. *Work:* Mus City New York; Los Angeles Co Mus Art; Meany Ctr for Labor Studies, Silver Spring, Md; State Univ NY Col, Potsdam; US Info Agency, Washington, DC. *Comn:* Soft New York Times, comn by Carey Peck, A O Sulzberger at New York Times, 76; Bathroom Faucet (3-D billboard), Pasco Hernando Community Col, Brookville, Fla, 79. *Exhib:* Libr Cong, Washington, DC, 69; Fun & Fantasy, Xerox Ctr, Rochester, NY, 73; Renwick Gallery, Smithsonian Inst, Washington, DC, 74-75; Dayton Art Inst, Ohio, 77; two-person show, Cordy Gallery, New York, 77; Whimsy, Taft Mus & Cincinnati Inst of Fine Arts, 78; one-person shows, Great Am Foot Show, Mus Contemp Crafts, New York, 78 & US Military Acad, West Point, 81; Mus Art, Carnegie Inst, Pittsburgh, 79; and others. *Pos:* Art dir, Hardtimes Movie Co, Garrison, 72-; art dir & vpres, Hudson River Film Co, Garrison, 77-; art dir & production mgr, Henry Hudson's River: A Biography (film), 79. *Teaching:* Asst drawing & printmaking, Pa State Univ, 66-68. *Awards:* Hon Mention as Art Dir, Emmy Winner Christina's World, 77; Cine Golden Eagle Award, 79; Grand Award, Houston Int Film Festival, 79. *Bibliog:* Steven Lindstedt (auth), Soft Sculpture, Family Creative Workshop, 76; Erica Brown (auth), Bunking in a barnyard, New York Times, 12/25/77; Carol Sama (auth), Michelle Gamm Clifton lives in a material world, Houston Home & Garden, 5/77. *Mem:* Am Crafts Coun; Nat Acad TV Arts & Sci. *Media:* Fabric, Stuffing. *Publ:* Illusr series, Gerald Ford's America, San Francisco Pub TV, 75; auth & illusr cover, New York City couch, Art Now Gallery Guide, summer 77. *Mailing Add:* Avery Rd Garrison NY 10524

CLINE, CLINTON C
PRINTMAKER, EDUCATOR
b Granite City, Ill, Oct 21, 34. *Study:* ELos Angeles Col, AA, 62; Calif State Univ, Long Beach, BA, 65, MA, 68. *Work:* Univ Tex, Irving; Univ SDak; Downey Art Mus, Calif; Palm Springs Mus, Calif; Drake Univ, Des Moines, Iowa. *Exhib:* Ann Exhibs, Los Angeles Nat Printmaking Soc, 67 & 77-79; All Colo, Denver Art Mus, 74; Collagraph, A New Print Medium, Pratt Graphics Ctr, New York, 75 & traveling, 76-78; 15th Joslyn Biennial, Joslyn Art Mus, Omaha, Nebr, 78; 21st Nat Exhib, Okla Art Ctr, Oklahoma City, 79; Univ Tex Nat, Irving, 79. *Collections Arranged:* 1975 Governor's Awards for the Arts and Humanities, 75; In Their Own Image, Southern Conn State Col, 76. *Teaching:* Lithography, Univ Colo, Boulder, 69-, assoc prof, currently. *Awards:* Purchase Awards, Los Angeles Printmaking Soc, 79 & Vermillion Nat Print & Drawing, 79. *Bibliog:* Leonard Edmundson (auth), Etching, Van Nostrand Reinhold, 73. *Mem:* Los Angeles Printmaking Soc. *Media:* Lithography, Intaglio. *Publ:* Publisher, First National Colorado Print and Drawing, 74. *Dealer:* Emerson Gallery 23 E 74th St New York NY 10021. *Mailing Add:* 360 S 36th St Boulder CO 80307

CLINEDINST, KATHERINE PARSONS
PAINTER, LECTURER
b Stamford, Conn, July 13, 03. *Study:* Pratt Inst, with Jessie Leigh; China Inst, with Prof Wang. *Exhib:* Smithsonian Inst, Washington, DC; Springfield Mus, Mass; Asbury Park Mus, NJ; Hammond Mus, South Salem, NY. *Pos:* Asst mgr, Boston Soc Arts & Crafts, New York, 23-24. *Awards:* Hudson Valley Art Asn Award for Dr Woodrow, White Plains, NY, 63; Meridan Art Asn Award,

Conn, 67; Mt Vernon Art Asn Award, NY, 67. *Mem:* Ocean Co Art Guild NJ; Asbury Fine Arts Asn; Nat League Am Pen Women (pres, Westchester Br, 59-61); Kent Art Asn, Conn; Monmouth Art Asn. *Media:* Watercolor, Oil. *Mailing Add:* 951 A Argyll Circle Lakewood NJ 08701

CLINTON, PAUL ARTHUR
PRINTMAKER, INSTRUCTOR

b Salem, Ore, Nov 1, 42. *Study:* Ore State Univ, BA, 68; Tamarind Lithography Workshop, master printer, 70; Univ SFla, MFA, 77. *Work:* Mus Mod Art, New York; Brooklyn Mus; Pasadena Art Mus, Calif; Tex Technol Univ, Lubbock; Gruenwald Graphics Art Found, Univ Calif, Los Angeles. *Exhib:* Univ Wis, Madison, 75; Univ Dallas, Irving, 75; State Capitol Mus, Olympia, Wash, 78; Brooklyn Mus, 79; Okla Art Ctr, Oklahoma City, 81; Wash Painting & Sculpture, 83; and others. *Collections Arranged:* Collaboration, Prints by Major American Artists, Tacoma Art Mus, 81. *Pos:* Master printer, Tamarind Lithography Workshop, Los Angeles, 69-70; master printer, Gemini, Los Angeles, 70; master printer, Cirrus Ed, Los Angeles, 70-71; master printer, Graphicstudio, Univ SFla, Tampa, 71-76. *Teaching:* Asst prof, Univ SFla, Tampa, 71-76; Instr, Ft Steilacoom Community Col, Tacoma, Wash, 77- *Awards:* Printers Fel & Ford Found, 69. *Mem:* NW Print Coun; World Print Coun. *Media:* Lithography, Intaglio. *Publ:* Contribr, Printmaking: History and Process, Holt, Rinehart, Winston, 78. *Mailing Add:* 1603 Sequalish Steilacoom WA 98388

CLIPSHAM, JACQUELINE ANN
CERAMIST, EDUCATOR

b Welwyn Garden City, Hertfordshire, Eng, July 27, 36; US citizen. *Study:* Carleton Col, BA; Western Reserve Univ, MA; Cleveland Inst Art; Haystack Mountain Sch Crafts; study with Toshiko Takaezu, Shoji Hamada, Peter Voulkous, William McVey. *Comn:* Pvt collections. *Exhib:* Butler Inst Show, Butler Inst Am Art, Youngstown, Ohio, 63-65; Northeast Regional Exhib Am Crafts Coun, Del Art Ctr, Wilmington, 66; Craftsmen USA 1966, Mus Contemp Crafts, New York, 66; Brooklyn Mus Sch, 69-78; Ceramics Show, Pratt Inst, Brooklyn, 73; one-person show, Atlantic Gallery, Brooklyn, 76 & 77; and others. *Pos:* Proj coordr, Culpeper Found, Community Educ Dept, Metrop Mus Art, New York, 81-82. *Teaching:* Instr ceramics, Brooklyn Mus Art Sch, 69-79; dir art workshop, CORE Community Ctr, Sumter, SC, 65-66; instr ceramics, Essex County Col, 78-80. *Awards:* Award Ceramics, Butler Inst Am Art, 65; Nat Merit Award, Craftsmen USA 1966 Exhib, Mus Contemp Crafts, 66; NY State Coun Arts Artist Proj Grant, 82. *Bibliog:* William Neugebauer (auth), interview, New York Sunday News, 3/80; Pat Malacher (auth), interview, New York Times, 7/4/82; Reg Wells (interviewer), 9 on New Jersey (film), WOR-TV, New York, 9/7/82. *Mem:* Col Art Asn; Nat Conf Educ Ceramic Arts; Am Crafts Coun; Women's Caucus Art; Artists Equity, New York; and others. *Media:* Stoneware, Porcelain Clay. *Publ:* Auth, Crafts and the disabled, Part I & II, Crafts Report, 81. *Dealer:* Atlantic Gallery 458 W Broadway New York NY 10012. *Mailing Add:* PO Box 387 Califon NJ 07830

CLISBY, ROGER DAVID
CURATOR, HISTORIAN

b New York, NY, Feb 8, 39. *Study:* Pa State Univ, BA & MA. *Pos:* Chief cur, Crocker Art Mus, 70- *Teaching:* Instr Northern Renaissance art, Univ of Calif, Davis, 73; lectr gallery admn, Calif State Univ, Sacramento, 74-75. *Mem:* Sacramento Film Festival (bd dirs, 77-); Sacramento Regional Arts Coun. *Res:* General research on Italian, German, Dutch, French painting and drawing from Renaissance to the present. *Publ:* Auth, Roy De Forest: Recent Painting, Drawings and Constructions (catalog), 80; auth, Philip Menard: A Retrospective of Paintings and Drawings (catalog), 81; auth, Welcome to the Candy Store! An Exhibition of Paintings, Drawings and Sculpture from the Candy Store Gallery (catalog), 81; auth, Masterworks of Photography from the Rubel Collection (catalog), 82; auth, Wayne Theibaud: Landscapes and City Views (catalog), 83. *Mailing Add:* c/o Crocker Art Mus 216 O St Sacramento CA 95814

CLIVE, RICHARD R
PAINTER

b New York, NY, Jan 8, 12. *Study:* Nat Acad Design, 30; NY Univ, BFA, 35; also with Dan Greene & Harold Wolcott. *Work:* US Navy Combat Art Collection, Washington, DC; Munic Collection, Ossining, NY; Munic Collection, Gloucester, Mass; Addison-Gilbert Hosp, Gloucester, Mass; Fordham Univ Collection. *Comn:* WAVES at US Naval Training Ctr, Bainbridge, Md; Marines & Civilians, S Vietnam, Dept of Navy, Washington, DC. *Exhib:* Salmagundi Club Ann, 61-84; Am Friends Hebrew Univ Art Festival, 63-65; four presentations, Naval Art Coop & Liaison Comt, 63-72; Stevens Ctr Art Exhib, Stevens Inst Technol, 68; Society Animal Artists, 83; and others. *Teaching:* Elizabeth Seton Col. *Awards:* Portrait Prize, 67 & First Prize Graphic, 68, New Rochelle Art Asn; Lt Harry E Breng Award, Am Legion, 68; Purchase Award, Miniature Art Soc NJ. *Mem:* hon mem Salmagundi Club (pres, 79-81); Am Artists Prof League; Acad Artists Asn; Pastel Soc Am; Miniature Art Soc NJ; Soc Animal Artists. *Media:* Oil, Pastel. *Mailing Add:* 29 Holly St Yonkers NY 10704

CLIVER, KENDRA-JEAN (KENDRA-JEAN CLIVER KRIENKE)
DEALER, PAINTER

b Plainfield, NJ. *Study:* Drew Univ, with Lee Hall & Peter Chapin, BA, 69; Nat Acad Design, with Philip Isenberg, 69, watercolor with Nicholas Reale, 71. *Work:* Drew Univ Collection, Madison, NJ; Douglass Col Collection, New Brunswick, NJ. *Comn:* Portrait of retiring dean, Douglass Col, 70; Portrait--US Steel, Coun Tennant, Summit, NJ, 70; Christmas Card Design, Spaulding for Children, Westfield, NJ, 72; Drawing of AT&T Bldg, AT&T Int

Hq, Basking Ridge, NJ, 78; and others. *Exhib:* Group show, AT&T Hq Gallery, Basking Ridge, 79. *Collections Arranged:* Recent Works, Peter Sculthorpe, 79-81; Drawings & Paintings, Carroll N Jones III, 80-81; Recent Oils, A Hale Johnson, 81-82; Don Stone Recent Works, 81-82; Recent Watercolors, Philip Jamison, 81; Vermont Landscapes, Fred Swan, 82; American Paintings, 82; Ken Davies, Retrospective, 82; Recent Watercolors, David Armstrong, 83; Ray Ellis, Philip Jamison, Don Stone, 83; Gary Erbe, 84; and others. *Pos:* Free lance portrait artist, 70-75; art restorationist, Princeton Fine Arts; art restorationist, Whistler's Daughter Gallery, framer & designer, 72-, art dealer, 74- *Awards:* Purchase Award, Drew Univ, 68; Selection Award for Christmas Card, Spaulding for Children, 72 & Hon Mention, 73. *Bibliog:* Arden Melick (auth), Whistler's Daughter Gives Advise, Assoc Press, 74; David L Shirey (auth), Art sampler, New York Times, 80; Liz Matt (dir), State of the Arts (doc film), NJ Pub TV, 82; and others. *Media:* Watercolor, Mixed Media. *Specialty:* Fine 19th & 20th century paintings, including works by David Armstrong, Dan & Pauline Campanelli, Ken Davies, Ray Ellis, Gary Erbe, Philip Jamison, Vincent Nardone, Don Stone, Robert Vickery & Andrew Wyeth. *Publ:* Contribr, Art Lovers Cookbook, Summit Art Ctr, 75. *Mailing Add:* c/o Whistler's Daughter Gallery Inc 88 S Finley Ave Basking Ridge NJ 07920

CLOAR, CARROLL
PAINTER

b Earle, Ark, Jan 18, 13. *Study:* Southwestern Memphis, BA; Memphis Acad Arts; Art Students League, MacDowell fel, 40; DH, Southwestern Memphis, 77. *Work:* Metrop Mus Art, Mus Mod Art & Whitney Mus Am Art, New York; Brooks Mem Art Gallery, Memphis; Joseph H Hirshhorn Mus, Washington, DC. *Exhib:* Retrospective, NY Univ, Albany; Pittsburgh Int; Whitney Ann, New York; Pa Acad Fine Arts Ann, Philadelphia; Brooks Mem Art Gallery, Memphis. *Pos:* Bd trustees, Brooks Mem Art Gallery, 69-71. *Awards:* Guggenheim Fel, 46; Am Acad Arts & Lett Prize, 67. *Bibliog:* An Arkansas boyhood, Horizon, 11/58; Summer dies as slowly, Time Mag, 8/19/66; Growing up in the Arkansas Delta, Esquire, 6/69. *Publ:* Auth, Hostile Butterflies & Other Paintings, Memphis State Univ Press. *Dealer:* Forum Gallery 1018 Madison Ave New York NY 10021. *Mailing Add:* 235 S Greer Memphis TN 38111

CLOSE, CHUCK
PAINTER

b Monroe, Wash, July 5, 40. *Study:* Everett Community Col, Wash, 58-60; Yale Summer Sch Music & Art, Norfolk, Conn, 61; Univ Wash Sch Art, Seattle, BA, 62; Yale Univ Sch Art & Archit, New Haven, Conn, BFA, 63, MFA, 64; Acad Fine Arts, Vienna, Austria, Fulbright grant, 64-65. *Work:* Mus Mod Art & Whitney Mus Am Art, New York; Walker Art Ctr, Minneapolis; Neue Gallerie, Aachen, Ger; Art Gallery Ont, Toronto. *Exhib:* 22 Realists, Whitney Mus Am Art, 70; one-man shows, Los Angeles Co Mus, 71, Mus Contemp Art, Chicago, 71 & Mus Mod Art, New York, 73; Documenta V, Kassel, WGer, 72; George Pompidou Centre, Paris, 79; retrospective, Walker Art Ctr, Minneapolis, traveling, 80-81. *Teaching:* Instr art, Univ Mass Sch Art, Amherst, 65-67; Sch Visual Arts, New York, 67-71; NY Univ, 70-73. *Awards:* Fulbright Grant; 64-65; Nat Endowment Arts Grant, 73. *Bibliog:* Barbara Harshman (auth), An interview with Chuck Close, 6/78, Kim Levin (auth), Chuck Close: Decoding the image, 6/78 & Lisa Lyons (auth), Close portraits, 80, Arts Mag. *Media:* All Media. *Mailing Add:* 271 Central Pk W 32 E 57th St New York NY 10024

CLOSE, DEAN PURDY
DEALER, PAINTER

b Holmesville, Ohio. *Study:* Ohio Northern Univ; Ohio State Univ; also with Charles William Duvall. *Work:* Am Embassies, Japan & WGer & in many pvt collections. *Exhib:* Columbus Art League, Ohio, 38-50; Butler Art Inst Am, 40; Ogonquit, Maine, 40. *Pos:* Dir, Fifth Avenue Galleries, Columbus, Ohio, 61- *Media:* Oil, Acrylic. *Specialty:* American art. *Interests:* The status of American impressionism. *Collection:* Works of Croft, Leslie Cope, R Wagner and other fine American impressionists. *Mailing Add:* 3130 Glenrich Pkwy Columbus OH 43221

CLOTHIER, PETER DEAN
ADMINISTRATOR, CRITIC

b Newcastle-on-Tyne, Eng, Aug 1, 36; US citizen. *Study:* Cambridge Univ, England, BA & MA; Univ Iowa, PhD. *Work:* Los Angeles Co Mus of Art, Los Angeles; Univ Southern Calif. *Pos:* Dean col, Otis Art Inst, 76-79, actg dir, 77-79; dean, Col Fine & Communication Arts, Loyola-Marymount Univ, 81. *Teaching:* Asst prof comparative lit, Univ Southern Calif, Los Angeles, 68-76. *Awards:* Dart Award for Acad Innovation, Univ Southern Calif, 72; Art Critics Fel Grant, Nat Endowment for the Arts, 76-77; Rockefeller Found Humanities Fel, 80 & 81. *Bibliog:* Joseph E Young (auth), Re-evaluating the tradition of the book, Art News, 75. *Publ:* Auth, Parapoems, Horizon Press, 74; auth, Magic of the possible, Artforum, 77; auth, Bricks, barbells & brushes, 81 & Moving downtown, 81, Art in Am. *Mailing Add:* 2341 Ronda Vista Dr Los Angeles CA 90027

CLOUD, JACK L
GALLERY OWNER, PUBLISHER

b Fremont, Ohio, Mar 15, 25. *Pos:* Owner/pres, Litho-Graphics (publ), 72-80; owner/chmn bd, Odyssey Int Gallery, 75-80. *Mem:* Rockport Art Asn; Univ of Mich Artist Guild; Int Platform Asn; Am Printing Hist Asn; Check Collector Round Table. *Specialty:* Contemporary American art and limited edition graphics and prints. *Dealer:* Odyssey Int Gallery. *Mailing Add:* 4253 Brandywyne Dr Troy MI 48098

CLOUGH, CHARLES SIDNEY
PAINTER
b Buffalo, NY, Feb 2, 51. *Study:* Pratt Inst, Brooklyn, NY, 69-70; Ontario Col Art, Can, 71-72. *Work:* Albright-Knox Art Gallery & Burchfield Ctr, State Univ Col, Buffalo, NY; Buscaglia-Castellani Art Gallery, Niagara Univ, NY. *Exhib:* With Paper, About Paper, Albright-Knox Art Gallery, NY, 80 & Mus Fine Arts, Springfield, Mass, 81; Genius Loci, Pallazzo di Cotta, Ferrara, Italy, 80; Painting & Sculpture Today, Indianapolis Mus of Art, Ind, 80; Hallwalls, Five Years, New Mus, New York, 80; Abstraction--An Am Tradition, Henry Gallery, Univ Wash, Seattle, 81; New Directions: NY & Toronto, Toronto Art Fair, Can, 81. *Pos:* Co-Founder, Hallwalls Inc, Buffalo, NY, 74, pres bd dirs, 77-79. *Bibliog:* Valentin Tatransky (auth), Charles Clough, Arts Mag, 10/80. *Media:* Mixed. *Dealer:* Pam Adler Gallery 37 West 57th St New York NY 10019. *Mailing Add:* 124 Thompson St New York NY 10012

CLOWES, ALLEN WHITEHILL
COLLECTOR, PATRON
b Buffalo, NY, Feb 18, 17. *Study:* Harvard Univ, BS(fine arts), 39; Fogg Mus, with Chanler Post, Benjamin Rowland, Leonard Opdyke, Kuhn & Paul Sachs; Harvard Univ Grad Sch Bus Admin, MBA, 42; Franklin Col, Hon DFA, 64. *Pos:* Dir, Clowes Fund Collection Old Masters, Indianapolis Mus Art, 58-71, cur 71- *Collection:* Paintings by the Old Masters from the 14th to 19th Century, including Bellini, Bosch, Bruegel, Caravaggio, Clouct, Constable, Cranach, Duccio, Durer, El Greco, Goya, Hals, Holbein, Rembrandt, Rubens and Titian; Clowes Fund Collection originally formed by the late Dr G H A Clowes and now belongs to Clowes Fund, Inc, located in Clowes Pavilion, Indianapolis Museum of Art. *Mailing Add:* 250 E 38th St Indianapolis IN 46205

CLURMAN, IRENE
CRITIC
b San Francisco, Calif, Mar 2, 47. *Study:* Stanford Univ, BA(art hist; Phi Beta Kappa), 69. *Pos:* Art ed, Rocky Mountain News, Denver, 75- *Mem:* Dance Critics' Asn; Int Graphoanal Soc. *Publ:* auth, John DeAndrea, fall 78 & auth, Boulder Colorado: art on the verge, spring 79, Artspace Mag; Side glances, Fiberarts Mag, 9/81; auth, George Woodman, Arts Mag, 4/82; auth, The Children's Mus, Horizon Mag, 6/83; auth, Rosalea's Hotel, Artspace Mag, summer 83; and others. *Mailing Add:* Box 6713 Denver CO 80206

CLUTZ, WILLIAM
PAINTER, INSTRUCTOR
b Gettysburg, Pa, Mar 19, 33. *Work:* Mus Mod Art & Chase Manhattan Bank, New York; Joseph H Hirshhorn Collection, Washington, DC; Fogg Art Mus, Cambridge, Mass; Metrop Mus Art, New York; plus many others. *Exhib:* Recent Painting USA: The Figure, Mus Mod Art, New York, 62; Pa Acad Fine Arts Ann, Philadelphia, 64-66; one-man shows, Bertha Schaefer Gallery, 63, 64, 66 & 69 & Graham Gallery, 72; Alonzo Gallery, 77, 78 & 79; Tatistchaff & Co, New York, 81 & 82; John C Stollert Co, Minneapolis, 83; and many others. *Teaching:* Instr, Parsons Sch Design, New York, 69- *Mailing Add:* 370 Riverside Dr New York NY 10025

CLYMER, ALBERT ANDERSON
PAINTER
b Memphis, Tenn, Feb 16, 42. *Study:* Tex A&M Univ, with Joseph Donaldson. *Work:* White House, Washington, DC; Newport Mus Mod Art, Calif; Oakland Mus Mod Art, Calif; Berkeley Mus Mod Art, Calif; San Francisco Mus Mod Art, Calif. *Comn:* Ten paintings for Army Recruiting, US Army Reserve, Mountain View, Calif, 77. *Exhib:* Dallas Mus Fine Arts, Tex, 65; Newport Mus Mod Art, 69; Exhib of Am Art, Chautauqua, NY, 69-71; Univ Berkeley Mus, Calif, 71; Mus Mod Art, Roseville, Calif, 72; plus 152 one-man shows. *Pos:* Bd dir, Depot Gallery, Yountville, Calif, 81- *Awards:* First Prize in Mod Oil, Vintage 76 Int, 68 & Santa Rosa Statewide Ann, 71 & 72. *Bibliog:* Stephens (auth), Albert Anderson Clymer, La Rev Mod, Paris, 66 & 74; Paul Gillette (auth), The Single Man's Indispensable Guide Handbook, Playboy Press, 73. *Mem:* Berkeley Arts Crafts Coop. *Publ:* Illusr, Oakland Redevelopment Agency's Annual Report, Abby Press, 66; illusr, Bodega Bay, Nut Tree, 75; illusr (catalog), Works by Albert Anderson Clymer, Arlene Lind Gallery, 78. *Dealer:* Depot Gallery in Vintage 1870 Yountville CA 94599; Greenleaf Gallery 14753 Big Basin Way Saratoga CA 95070. *Mailing Add:* PO Box 2278 Yountville CA 94599

CLYMER, JOHN F
PAINTER, ILLUSTRATOR
b Ellensburg, Wash, Jan 29, 07. *Study:* Vancouver Sch Art; Ont Col Art; Wilmington Acad Art; Grand Cent Art Sch, with Harvey Dunn. *Work:* Glen Bow Found, Calgary; Mont Hist Soc, Helena; Cowboy Hall of Fame, Oklahoma City; Whitney Gallery Western Art, Cody, Wyo. *Comn:* Series of three large paintings, comn by Winchester Firearms Co, Winchester Gun Display, Buffalo Bill Hist Ctr & Whitney Gallery Western Art, 69. *Exhib:* Soc Animal Artists, 62-72; Whitney Gallery Western Art, 69; Cowboy Artists Am, 69-83; Mont Hist Soc, Helena, 72-73; Animals in Art, Royal Ont Mus, Toronto, 75. *Awards:* Silver Medals, 69 & 76-81, Gold Medals, 70, 72-77 & 79, Best of Show, 79, Cowboy Artists Am; Prix de West Award, Nat Acad Western Art, 76. *Mem:* Soc Animal Artists; Salmagundi Club; Ont Soc Artists; Cowboy Artists Am; Nat Acad Western Art; and others. *Mailing Add:* Box 369 Teton Village WY 83025

COATES, ANN S
SLIDE CURATOR, HISTORIAN
b Louisville, Ky. *Study:* Univ of Louisville, BA, 63, MA, 69; New York Sch Interior Design, Cert, 65; Arrowmont Sch Arts Crafts, Tenn. *Work:* Brown-Forman Distillers Corp; James G Brown Regional Cancer Center; Actors' Theatre Louisville; Baldwin-United. *Exhib:* Eight States Sculpture, J B Speed Mus, Louisville; Southeastern Invitational Exhib of Work in Handmade Paper, Univ Ga, Athens; 80 Biennial Exhib of Piedmont Crafts, Mint Mus, Charlotte; Mid-States Craft Exhib, Mus Arts Science, Evansville; Southeast 81 Craft Competition, Lemoyne Art Found, Tallahassee; Thread and Fiber, Alexandria Mus, La; Handmade Paper Nat Invitational, Liberty Gallery, Louisville. *Collections Arranged:* Edward Weston 1986-1958, 68. *Pos:* Cur slides, Univ Louisville, 69- *Teaching:* Instr mod art, Univ Louisville, 69-; lectr, Univ Ky, Lexington & Louisville Craftsmen's Guild. *Awards:* Bronze Medal, Great Quilts of America, Good Housekeeping, 78. *Bibliog:* Sarah Lansdell (auth), Paper works show uncovers artist's passion for the medium, The Courier Journal, 7/20/80; Karen Hisle (auth), Ann Coates mixes work with pleasure, Scripps-Howard Press, 7/9/80; Fiber Arts Design Book, Hasting House, 80. *Mem:* Col Art Asn; Art Libr Soc NAm; Soc Archit Historians. *Media:* Papermaking; Quilting. *Res:* Conservation; preservation; women artists. *Publ:* The Female Image in the Nineteenth Century (film), Univ Louisville, Women's Studies Ctr, 78. *Dealer:* Swearingen Gallery 4806 Brownsboro Center Louisville KY 40207. *Mailing Add:* 1819 Woodbourne Louisville KY 40205

COATES, ROSS ALEXANDER
HISTORIAN, PAINTER
b Hamilton, Ont, Can, Nov 1, 32. *Study:* Univ Mich; Art Inst Chicago, BFA; NY Univ, MA & PhD. *Work:* Chase Manhattan Bank, New York; NY Univ; Univ Calif, Berkeley; Schenectady Mus; Univ Alta. *Exhib:* Mus Art, Pullman, Wash, 78; Eastern Wash Univ, Cheney, 79; Diablo Valley Col, Calif, 82; Whatcom Mus, Bellingham, 83; Space Gallery, Los Angeles, 84; and others. *Teaching:* Art tutor, Canon Lawrence Col, Uganda, EAfrica, 68-70; chmn dept fine arts, Wash State Univ, 77- *Mem:* Col Art Asn Am. *Media:* Oil. *Res:* Non-Western art, particularly Africa; occult and how it relates to contemporary art. *Publ:* Coauth, Some potential values of primary art education, Educ in Eastern Africa, 71; coauth, New cattle sculpture of Uganda, African Arts, 73; auth, Some thoughts on the problems of the artist in contemporary Africa, J African Studies, Univ Calif Los Angeles, fall 78. *Mailing Add:* Dept Fine Arts Wash State Univ Pullman WA 99164

COBB, RUTH
PAINTER
b Boston, Mass, Feb 20, 14. *Study:* Mass Col Art, cert. *Work:* Boston Mus Fine Arts; Va Mus Fine Arts, Richmond; Butler Inst Am Art, Youngstown, Ohio; Munson-Williams-Proctor Inst, Utica, NY; Brandeis Univ, Waltham, Mass. *Exhib:* Am Watercolor Exhib, Metrop Mus Art, New York, 52; 22nd Biennial Int Watercolor Exhib, Brooklyn Mus, NY, 63; Am Watercolor Soc Ann, 68-77 & 80-83; Watercolor USA, Springfield Art Mus, Miss, 80; 35 Years in Retrospect, Butler Inst Am Art, 71; 45th Ann, Butler Inst Am Art, 81; and others. *Awards:* Purchase Award, Nat Acad Design, 68; Emily Lowe Award, 74 & Emily Goldsmith Award, 75, Am Watercolor Soc; Adolph Obrig Award, Nat Acad Design, 82. *Bibliog:* Article & reproductions in Am Artist Mag, 4/79; auth, Watercolor Bold and Free, Watson Guptill, 80; Artist at Work, Channel 5 TV, Boston, 81; and others. *Mem:* Am & Boston Watercolor Soc; Allied Artists Am; Nat Acad Design. *Dealer:* Midtown Gallery New York NY. *Mailing Add:* 38 Devon Rd Newton Center MA 02159

COBB, VIRGINIA HORTON
PAINTER, LECTURER
b Oklahoma City, Okla, Nov 23, 33. *Study:* Colo Univ; Community Col of Denver; additonal study with William Schimmel, Chen Chi & Edward Betts. *Work:* Foothills Art Ctr, Golden, Colo; Nat Acad of Design, New York; NMex Watercolor Soc, Albuquerque; St Lawrence Univ, Canton, NY. *Exhib:* Am Watercolor Soc, Nat Acad Galleries, New York, 73-; Butler Inst Am Art, Youngstown, Ohio, 75; Nat Acad Design, New York, 78-; San Bernadino Co Mus, 78; Nat Watercolor Invitational, 81; one-person exhib, Stuhr Mus, Grand Island, Nebr, 82; and others. *Teaching:* lectr & demonstr, Emphasis-KRDO Channel 13, Colorado Springs, Colo, 77; instr, Crafton Hills Col Master Seminars, Yucaipa, Calif, 77, 78 & 81; instr, Univ Alaska, Anchorage, 81; lectr & demonstr, Pub Broadcasting Serv, KAKM, Anchorage, 81. *Awards:* Walter Biggs Mem Award, Nat Acad Design, 78 & 81; High Winds Medal, 81; Silver Medal Honor, Am Watercolor Soc, 83; and others. *Bibliog:* Southwest Art Mag, 11/79; Todays Art Mag, 3/79; Houston Home & Garden, 2/80. *Mem:* Assoc Nat Acad Design; Dolphin fel Am Watercolor Soc; Rocky Mountain Watermedia Asn. *Media:* Mixed Watermedia; Graphics. *Publ:* Contribr, Am Artist Mag, 1/79. *Dealer:* Jack Meier Gallery Houston TX. *Mailing Add:* 3507 Roseland Houston TX 77006

COBER, ALAN E
ILLUSTRATOR, PRINTMAKER
b New York, NY, May 18, 35. *Study:* Univ Vt, 52-54; Sch Visual Arts. *Work:* Minn Mus Art, St Paul; Nat Air & Space Mus, DC; Albrecht Art Mus, St Joseph, Mo; New Britain Art Mus, Conn; Dept of Interior/Nat Park Serv, Harpers Ferry, WVa. *Comn:* Mural, Mus Am History, Smithsonian Inst, 82. *Exhib:* Drawings USA, Minn Mus Art, St Paul, 68 & 73; Century of Am Illus, Brooklyn Mus, NY, 72; Color, Whitney Mus Am Art, New York, 74; 200 Yrs Am Illus, NY Hist Soc, 76; Printmaking in Mod Am Illus, Pratt Graphic Ctr, New York, 79. *Collections Arranged:* The Forgotten Society Traveling Exhib (auth & illusr, catalog), 75-80; Same/Size Circus, John & Mabel Ringling Mus Art, 79. *Teaching:* Pres fac illus & design, Illusr Workshop, Noroton, Conn,

Tarrytown, NY, Monterey Calif & Paris, France, 74-81. *Awards:* Gold Medals, Soc Illusr, 68-77 & Art Dirs Club, New York, 73, 76 & 77; John Taylor Arms Award, Audubon Artists, 71. *Bibliog:* Dugald Stermer (auth), Alan E Cober: Illustrator, Reporter and Social Historian, Communication Arts, 1-2/75; Nick Meglin (auth), Alan E Cober, Graphis 192, Graphis Press, 11/77; Steve Heller (auth), Bold ink, Rocky Mtn Mag, 11/79. *Mem:* Soc Illusr (vpres, 68); Graphic Artists Guild. *Media:* Pen and Ink, Watercolor; Etching. *Publ:* Illusr, The Forgotton Society, Dover, 75; illusr, Slaughter House Five, 78 & illusr, Exile and the Kingdom/Camus/Etchings, 80, Franklin Libr; auth & illusr, Cober's Choice, E P Dutton/Unicorn 79. *Mailing Add:* Croton Dam Rd Ossining NY 10562

COBURN, RALPH (M H)
PAINTER, DESIGNER
b Minneapolis, Minn, Aug 10, 23. *Study:* Mirski Art Sch, with Esther Geller, Carl Nelson, Barbara Swan & John Wilson, 46-49; Mass Inst Technol, 47; Acad Julian, 50. *Work:* Stedlijk Mus, Amsterdam; Mus Mod Art, Caracas, Venezuela; Brockton Art Mus, Mass; Chase Manhattan Bank, New York; Smithsonian Inst. *Pos:* Graphic designer, Mass Inst Technol. *Media:* Oil, Acrylic; Pen and Ink, Watercolor. *Dealer:* Alpha Gallery 121 Newbury St Boston MA 02116. *Mailing Add:* 1269 Washington St Gloucester MA 01930

COCHRAN, DEWEES (DEWEES COCHRAN HELBECK)
DESIGNER, PAINTER
b Dallas, Tex, Apr 12, 1892. *Study:* Walnut Hill, Natick, Mass; Gunston Hall, Washington, DC; Sch Indust Art, Philadelphia; Acad Fine Arts, Philadelphia; spec study in Ger, Austria & France; anthrop with Prof Preuss & art hist with Oscar Fischel, Berlin. *Exhib:* Marie Sterner Galleries, New York, 32; Philadelphia Print Club, 32; Salzburg Festivals, Austria, 32; 17th Ann Women's Nat Expos, Grand Cent Palace, New York, 38; Women's Int Expo, 71st Armory, New York, 59. *Teaching:* Dir design, Sch Am Craftsmen, Educ Coun, 46-47. *Awards:* Award for Excellence, United Fedn Doll Collectors USA, 62-70. *Bibliog:* Jerry Fairbanks (auth), 3 Paramount Shorts, USA & Worldwide, 37-50; publ by King Features Syndicate, 50-51; Mazlin (auth), Woman of Tomorrow, TV documentary. *Mem:* Hon mem Doll Collectors Am Inc, Boston; assoc Int Inst Arts & Lett; Montalvo Asn, Saratoga, Calif; Nat Inst Am Doll Artists (pres, 67-69, dir, 75-). *Media:* Graphic; Watercolor, Oil. *Collection:* Dolls. *Publ:* Auth, Toward Design, articles, Crafts Horizons, 45 & 46; auth, As If They Would Speak, Paperweight Press, 78. *Mailing Add:* 155 Quail Hollow Rd Felton CA 95018

COCHRAN, GEORGE MCKEE (REDBIRD)
PAINTER, WRITER
b Stilwell, Okla, Oct 5, 08. *Work:* Pac Western Traders Art Gallery, Folsom, Calif; Pan Am Gallery, Pan Am Highway, Albuquerque, NMex; Northern Plains Indian Mus, Browning, Mont. *Comn:* Series of 40 Indian life drawings, Warm Springs Indian Reservation, KahNeeTah Lodge, Ore, 64; I Am an American (oil), Starline Corp, Albuquerque, 71; portraits of Pacific NW Indians, Western Equipment Co, Eugene, Ore, 73; Black & Whites & Sepias series of caricatures (oil), Nighthorse Studio Dee's Indian Supply, Sacramento, 75; First Sight of Sacramento Valley (oil), Am River Col Libr, Sacramento, 75. *Exhib:* Indian Festival Arts, LeGrande, Ore, 60-61; American Indian Days, Sheridan, Wyo, 61-62; America Discovers Indian Art Show, Smithsonian Inst, Washington, DC, 67; Univ Calif Med Ctr, San Francisco, 74; NMex State Fair, Indian Village, 71 & 75. *Teaching:* Instr drawing in native American studies, Univ Calif, Berkeley, 73-74. *Awards:* Am Eagle Feather Award, 60, Indian Festival Arts, 60-61 & American Indian Days, Sheridan, Wyo, 61-62, Am Indian Coun. *Bibliog:* Flo Wilks (auth), Indian artist seeks understanding, Albuquerque J, 10/71; Hubert Guy (auth), George Cochran-Cherokee artist, Indian Trader, 3/75; Mary Shearly (auth), He paints his people's history George Cochran, Southwest Art Mag, Vol 4 No 2. *Media:* Oil, Watercolor. *Publ:* Auth & illusr, ABC Book, 47; co-auth, The Celiloh Indians, 49; auth & illusr, Indian Portraits of the Pacific Northwest, 59; illusr, Who did it First?, 59; illusr cartoons, The Indian Trader, 75. *Mailing Add:* PO Box 1598 Tahlequah OK 74464

COCKRILL, SHERNA
PAINTER, INSTRUCTOR
b Chicago, Ill. *Study:* Univ Ark, BA & MA; Malden Bridge Sch Art, 67 & 68; also study with R Y Goetz, 65-69; with Albert Handell, 80-81. *Work:* Smithsonian Inst Archives Am Art, Washington, DC; Ozark Art Ctr, Springdale; First Nat Bank, Little Rock; Mid-Am Mus, Hot Springs, Ark; Arts Ctr Ozarks. *Comn:* Many portrait comn. *Exhib:* Greater New Orleans Nat Exhib, 73; Tex Fine Arts Asn Ann, Austin, 73-74; Governor's Distinguished Artists Exhib, 76; Five State, Univ Ark, 79-83; Art Expo 83, Dallas; and others. *Teaching:* Instr oil painting, Ozarks Arts Ctr, 72-75; also pvt classes. *Awards:* Grand Prize, Arkansas State Festival Art, 73; First Prize in Art, Little Rock Ten State Arts Fair, State of Ark, 73; Top Award Ark Festival Art, 73 & 74 & Top Award Ark Festival & Art Invitational, 75. *Mem:* Ozark Artists & Craftsmen (bd dir, 75-). *Media:* Oil, Acrylic. *Publ:* Auth, Women artists in mid-USA, Feminist Art J, Brooklyn, 74-75. *Dealer:* Fine Arts of Houston 60 Woodlake Sq Houston TX; Moulton Gallery Ft Smith AR 72701. *Mailing Add:* Sunrise Mt Rd Fayetteville AR 72701

CODE, AUDREY
PAINTER
b Pittsburgh, Pa, Oct 6, 37. *Study:* Carnegie Mellon Univ, with Balcomb Greene, BFA, 59, MFA, 61; Provincetown Workshop, Mass, 61. *Work:* Aldrich Mus Contemp Art, Ridgefield, Conn; Chautauqua Art Mus, NY; Fulton Co Arts Coun, Gloversville, NY. *Comn:* Murals, St John's Church, 62 & Sr Citizens Ctr, 75, Pittsburgh, Pa; mural, Cyclerama, Los Angeles, 70.

Exhib: Contemporary Reflections, Aldrich Mus, Ridgefield, Conn, 78; Arte Fiera, Bologna, Italy, 78; PS1, New York, 78; solo show, Frank Marino Gallery, New York, 79; Herbert F Johnson Mus, Ithaca, NY, 81; Alchemy, Hankook Gallery, New York, 83; Eight, Esta Robinson Gallerry, New York, 83. *Teaching:* Vis artist, San Francisco Art Inst, 79; lectr, Stuyvesant Group, New York, 80-83. *Awards:* Creative Artists Pub Serv Fel, NY State Coun Arts, 81. *Bibliog:* Corinne Robbins (auth), Audrey Code's drawings, F Marino, 79; Diana Morris (auth), Eight, Women Artists News, 83; Alchemy, Artspeak, 83. *Mem:* Women Arts; Women's Caucus Art. *Media:* Miscellaneous Media. *Publ:* Illusr, Life Forms of the 70's, Independent Press, 75; auth & illusr, Eggplants and Other Murders, Chrome Press, 82; auth, Alchemy, Chrome Press, 83. *Dealer:* Scherer Galleries Marlborough NJ; Hankook Gallery 50 W 57th St New York NY. *Mailing Add:* 70 Grand St New York NY 10013

CODELL, JULIE FRANCIA
HISTORIAN, EDUCATOR
b Chicago, Ill, Sept 19, 45. *Study:* Vassar Col, AB, 67; Univ Mich, MA, 68; Ind Univ, with Bruce Cole, MA(art hist), 75, cert(renaissance studies), 77, PhD(comparative lit & arts), 78. *Collections Arranged:* Montana Women Artists and the Environment (auth, catalog), Missoula Mus Arts, 82. *Teaching:* Instr, Western Ill Univ, 68-71; Asst prof art hist & criticism, Univ Mont, Missoula, 79-83, head slide libr, Dept Art, 79-, assoc prof, 83- *Awards:* Renaissance Studies Grant, Ind Univ, 77; Univ Mont Grants, 81 & 83. *Bibliog:* D McNamer (auth), Julie Codell, art historian, Missoulian, 80. *Mem:* Col Art Asn. *Res:* Nature of art criticism and the methods and philosophies of critics of the 19th and 20th centuries. *Publ:* Auth, The Century Guild Hobby Horse, 1884-1894, Victorian Periodicals Rev, 83. *Mailing Add:* 155 Mount Missoula MT 59801

COE, ANNE ELIZABETH
PAINTER, VIDEO ARTIST
b Henderson, Nev. *Study:* Ariz State Univ, BA, 70, MFA, 80; Univ PR, 78. *Work:* Centro Arte Mod Guadalajara, Mex; NDak Mus Art, Grand Forks; Scottsdale Ctr Arts, Ariz; Smithsonian Inst; Fund Anthropologia El Ecuador, Quito. *Comn:* Mural & set design, Warner Brothers, Tempe, Ariz, 76. *Exhib:* Ariz Invitational, Centro Arte Mod Guadalajara, Mex, 82; Recent Works, Art West, Jackson, Wyo, 82; Continuing Frontiers, NDak Mus Art, Grand Forks, 82; Tucson Mus Art Biennial, 82; Whatever Happened to the Avant Garde, Ctr Contemp Art, Santa Ana, Calif, 83. *Pos:* Arts producer, KAGT-TV, Phoenix, 77-80; artist in residence, Ariz Comn Arts, 81-83. *Bibliog:* Carol Kotrozo (auth), Four Arizona women, 82 & Donald Lock (auth), Arizona invitational, 82, Artspace; Robert Ewing (auth), Esthetic badness, Artweek, 82. *Media:* Acrylic on Canvas. *Dealer:* Suzanne Brown Gallery 7160 Main St Scottsdale AZ 85251. *Mailing Add:* 144 S 85th St Mesa AZ 85208

COE, MATCHETT HERRING
SCULPTOR
b Loeb, Tex, July 22, 07. *Study:* Cranbrook Acad Art, with Carl Milles; Lamar Univ. *Work:* US Navy C B Mus, Port Hueneme, Calif; Am Numismatic Soc & Metrop Mus Art, New York; Carnegie Mus, Pittsburgh; Corcoran Gallery Art, Washington, DC. *Comn:* Bronze statues, Dick Dowling, State of Tex, Sabine Pass, 36 & The Texan, Vicksburg Nat Mil Park, 60; entrance to zoo (stone relief), City Houston, 52; 75th Issue, Soc Medalists, New York, 67; proposed bas-relief for Grotto of Libby Dam, 75. *Exhib:* Nat Sculpture Soc 75th Anniversary Exhib, 68 & Medals By Mem Show, Smithsonian Inst, 68; Am Numismatic Asn Conv, San Diego, Calif, 68; Fidem Exhib, Libson, Portugal, 79. *Awards:* First Place for Dick Dowling Monument, Nat Competition; First Place for Frieze on New London Sch Mem, State Competition; selected by noted panel of sculptors to design 75th Issue, Soc Medalists. *Bibliog:* Emma Lila Fundaburk (auth), Art in Public Places in the United States, 75. *Mem:* Nat Sculpture Soc. *Media:* Bronze, Stone. *Mailing Add:* 2554 Gladys St Beaumont TX 77702

COE, RALPH TRACY
MUSEUM DIRECTOR, CURATOR
b Cleveland, Ohio, Aug 25, 29. *Study:* Oberlin Col, BA, 53; Yale Univ, MA, 57. *Collections Arranged:* Many exhibs at Nelson Gallery, 59-79. *Pos:* Asst cur, Nat Gallery Art, 57-59; cur paintings & sculpture, Nelson Gallery Art, Kansas City, 59-64, asst dir, 65-77, dir, 77-82. *Teaching:* Lectr, Univ Kans. *Mem:* Asn Art Mus Dirs (trustee, 79-, pres 81-82); Am Asn Mus; Am Fedn Arts (trustee, 77-); Col Art Asn Am; Soc Archit Historians. *Res:* French 19th century painting; modern art; ethnology. *Publ:* Auth, Impressionist and post-impressionist paintings in Washington, Burlington Mag, 59; co-ed, American Architecture and Other Writings, Harvard Univ, 61; auth, Pissarro's Jardin des Mathurins, Nelson Gallery Art & Atkins Mus Bulletin, 63; auth, Sacred Circles: Two Thousand Years of North American Indian Art (catalog), 76; auth, Dale Eldred: Sculpture into Environment, Regents Press of Kans, 78. *Mailing Add:* Nelson Gallery of Art 4525 Oak St Kansas City MO 64111

COES, KENT DAY
PAINTER, DESIGNER
b Chicago, Ill, Feb 14, 10. *Study:* Grand Cent Sch Art, New York; Art Students League; NY Univ. *Work:* Frye Mus Art, Seattle; Montclair Art Mus, NJ; Holyoke Mus Fine Arts, Mass; Norfolk Mus Arts & Sci, Va; Nat Acad Design, NY. *Exhib:* Ann exhibs, Nat Acad Design, Allied Artists Am & Am Watercolor Soc, New York & Acad Artists Asn, Springfield, Mass; exchange exhibs, London, Mexico City, Ont, Can & Sydney, Australia. *Pos:* Art ed for several publ, McGraw-Hill, 47-75. *Awards:* Gold Medal Honor, Allied Artists Am, 59; Gerhard Miller Award, Am Watercolor Soc, 71; Silver Medal, NJ Watercolor Soc, 73. *Bibliog:* Kent Day Coes insists, Am Artist Mag, 10/57;

Norman Kent (auth), 100 Watercolor Techniques, 68 & Norman Kent & Susan Meyer (auth), Watercolorists at Work, 72, Watson-Guptill. *Mem:* Acadamecian Nat Acad Design (aquarelle); Am Watercolor Soc (dir, var terms 52-); Allied Artists Am (dir, secy, vpres, 50); NJ Watercolor Soc (founder-mem & pres, 47-48); Acad Artists Asn. *Media:* Watercolor. *Dealer:* Grand Cent Galleries 40 Vanderbilt Ave New York NY 10017; Baker Gallery Fine Art 1301 13th St Lubbock TX 79408. *Mailing Add:* 463 Valley Rd Upper Montclair NJ 07043

COFFEY, DOUGLAS ROBERT
PAINTER, EDUCATOR
b Cleveland Heights, Ohio, Dec 27, 37. *Study:* Cleveland Inst Art, dipl, 59; Univ Denver, BFA, 61; Western Reserve Univ, MA, 65. *Work:* Xerox Corp, New York; Kodak Corp, Rochester, NY; Cleveland Mus Art. *Exhib:* Butler Inst Am Art Exhib, Youngstown, Ohio, 63; Rochester Fingerlakes Exhib, 71; 13th Ann Rochester Festival of Relig Art, 71; 16th Nat Print Exhib, Hunterdon Art Ctr, 72; one-man show, Mem Art Gallery, 75. *Teaching:* Assoc prof fine arts, Rochester Inst Technol, 67-82. *Awards:* Sullivan Award for Painting, Fingerlakes Exhib, 70; First Award, 13th Ann Festival of Relig Art, 71; Painting Award, Mem Art Gallery, 75. *Media:* Polymer, Oil. *Dealer:* Mem Art Gallery 490 University Ave Rochester NY 14607. *Mailing Add:* 29 Cole Rd Pittsford NY 14534

COFFEY, JOHN WILLIAM, II
CURATOR
b Raleigh, NC, Mar 12, 54. *Study:* Univ NC, Chapel Hill, BA, 76; Williams Col, MA(hist art), 78. *Collections Arranged:* American Posters of WW1 (auth, catalog), Williams Col Mus Art, 78; Four Artists: Biederman, Maddrell, Ross, Saganic (auth, catalog), 81; Maine Artists Invitational (auth, catalog), 82 & Winslow Homer Watercolors, 83, Bowdoin Col Mus Art. *Pos:* Asst to dir, Williams Col Mus Art, 78-79, acting dir & instr art hist, 79-80; cur, Bowdoin Col Mus Art, 80- *Mem:* New England Mus Asn; Visual Arts Adv Panel, Maine State Comn Arts & Humanities; Maine Festival Arts (vpres, 82-83, pres, 83-). *Res:* Twentieth century American art. *Publ:* Contribr, The Lawrence H Bloedel Collection of American Art, Int Exhibs Found, 81. *Mailing Add:* 3264 Maquoit Rd Brunswick ME 04011

COGGESHALL, CALVERT
PAINTER
b Whitesboro, New York, 07. *Study:* Univ Pa, 29. *Work:* Yale Univ Art Gallery, New Haven, Conn; NY State Collection, Albany; Albright-Knox Art Gallery, Buffalo; Chase Manhattan Collection; plus others. *Exhib:* Abstract painting and Sculpture in America, Mus Mod Art, New York, 54; Toledo Art Mus, Ohio, 54; Whitney Mus Am Art Painters Ann, New York, 67; Pittsburgh Plan for Art, Pa, 68; Univ Colo, Boulder, 68; plus one-man shows. *Bibliog:* Reviews in Art News, summer 67, 2/69 & 5/70, New York Times, 5/6/67 & 12/14/68 & Arts Mag, 2/69. *Media:* Oil, Casein. *Dealer:* Jack Tilton Gallery 24 West 57th Street New York NY 10019. *Mailing Add:* Newcastle ME 04553

COGGINS, JACK BANHAM
INSTRUCTOR, PAINTER
b London, Eng, July 10, 14; US citizen. *Study:* Grand Cent Sch Art Students League, New York. *Work:* Reading Pub Mus & Art Gallery & Philadelphia Maritime Mus, Pa; Air & Space Mus, Smithsonian Inst, Washington, DC. *Teaching:* Instr, Hunter Col, New York, 48-53; instr, Wyomissing Inst Fine Arts, Pa, 59- *Mem:* Citizens Arts Pa. *Publ:* Auth & illusr, Arms & Equipment of the Civil War, Doubleday, 62; auth & illusr, Ships and Seamen of the American Revolution, Stackpole, 69; auth & illusr, Campaign for Guadalcanal, Doubleday, 72; auth & illusr, Campaign for North Africa, Doubleday, 80; auth & illusr, Marine Painter's Guide, Van Nostrand Reinhold, 83. *Mailing Add:* PO Box 57 Boyertown PA 19512

COGGINS, ROBERT P
COLLECTOR
b Marietta, Ga, May 7, 24. *Study:* Emory Univ, AB, 47; Med Col Ga, MD, 51. *Exhib:* Works from Collection of Dr R P Coggins, Madison-Morgan Cult Ctr, Madison, Ga, 79; Selections from Coggins Collection of Women Paintings, Agnes Scott Col, Shorter Col, Barrows Co Hist Soc & Banks Haley Gallery, Ga; and many others. *Pos:* Mem bd of adv, Univ Ga Mus, Athens, 78-; mem adv bd, Col Arts & Sci, Emory Univ, Atlanta, Ga, 78- *Collection:* Nineteenth and twentieth century American art with an emphasis on the Southern aspect of American art; women artists. *Mailing Add:* 413 St Mary's Lane Marietta GA 30064

COGSWELL, DOROTHY MCINTOSH
EDUCATOR, PAINTER
b Plymouth, Mass, Nov 13, 09. *Study:* Yale Univ, BFA & MFA. *Work:* Springfield Mus Fine Arts, Mass; Wisteriahurst, Holyoke Mus, Mass; Newport Art Asn; Mt Holyoke Col. *Comn:* Mural, Libr, 44, mural, Buckland Hall, 61 & mural & relief, Torrey Hall, 63, Mt Holyoke Col. *Exhib:* New Haven Paint & Clay Club, 29-; New York Watercolor Soc, 32-; Am Watercolor Soc, 33-; Conn Acad, 37; New York World's Fair, 39; and others. *Pos:* Dir Holyoke Col, 70-74. *Teaching:* Prof art hist, Mt Holyoke Col, 39-74, emer prof, 74- *Awards:* First Prize in Watercolor, Eastern States Exhib, 41; Fulbright lectr, Nat Art Sch, Sydney, Australia, 57-58; Purchase Prize, Holyoke Bicentennial, 76. *Mem:* Springfield Art League (pres, 42-43); Manatee Art League (vpres, 81-83); Mt Holyoke Friends Art (chmn, 47-60). *Publ:* Auth, A visitor's impressions of Australian art, Soc Artists, Sydney, 58; auth, Mt Holyoke College art collection, Col Art J, 72. *Mailing Add:* 3860 Ironwood Lane Apt 402 G Bradenton FL 33505

COGSWELL, MARGARET PRICE
ADMINISTRATOR
b Evanston, Ill, Sept 15, 25. *Study:* Wellesley Col, BA, 47; Pratt Inst; Art Inst Chicago; Columbia Univ; Art Students League. *Collections Arranged:* Communication Through Art, 64; The American Poster (ed, catalog), 68; American Exhib, 34th & 35th Venice Biennales, 68 & 70; Explorations, 70; The Audio-Visual Magazine, 72; George Catlin's American Indians, 74; Images of an Era: The American Poster (with catalog), 75. *Pos:* Head dept publ & assoc foreign exhib, Am Fedn Arts, 55-66; ed, The Am Artists Series, 59-63; chmn, 50 Bks of the Yr, Am Inst Graphic Arts, 64; dep chief, Off Prog Support, 66-80, Nat Collection Fine Arts, Smithsonian Inst, 66-, mem, Women's Coun, 77-81, vchmn, 79, deputy cur of exhibs, 81- *Teaching:* Smithsonian Inst, 70. *Awards:* Gold Medal for Printmaking, Am Artist Mag, 53. *Mem:* Am Asn Mus; Ben & Abby Grey Found, St Paul (trustee, 63-79). *Publ:* Ed, The Ideal Theater: Eight Concepts, 63; co-ed, The Cultural Resources of Boston, 64; ed, Sao Paulo 9, 67; Images of an Era: the American Poster 1945-75, 76. *Mailing Add:* 2929 Connecticut Ave NW Washington DC 20008

COHELEACH, GUY JOSEPH
PAINTER, SCULPTOR
b New York, NY. *Study:* Cooper Union, with Don Eckelberry, grad; Col William & Mary, Hon Dr Arts, 75. *Work:* Nat Wildlife Gallery, Washington, DC; Nat Audubon Soc; Am Mus Natural Hist; Dean Amadon Collection; Beware, presented to President of US. *Comn:* Snowy Egrets, Nat Audubon Soc, 68; American Eagle, US Govt, presented to Vice President Agnew, 71; Elephant, African Safari Club, Washington, DC, for President of US, 72; Leopard & Elephant, World Wildlife Fund, 72. *Exhib:* Wildlife Art of America, Louisville, Ky, 68 & 72; Linnean Soc Exhib, Am Mus Natural Hist, New York, 69; Bird Artists of the United States, Graham Gallery, New York, 72; Bird Artists of the World, Tryon Gallery, London, 72. *Awards:* Guy Coheleach, Prints Mag, 79 & Mich Outdoors, 79; Master Artist, Leigh Yawkee Art Mus, Wis, 83. *Bibliog:* Roger Caras (auth), Ouest: An Artist & His Prey. *Mem:* Soc Animal Artists; Explorer's Club; African Safari Club; Adventurer's Club. *Media:* Oil, Tempera. *Interests:* First occidental artist to exhibit in post-WWII Peking. *Publ:* Illusr, Sat Eve Post, 67; illusr, Nat Wildlife Mag, 67-; illusr, Readers Digest, 67-; illusr, Int Wildlife Mag, 71-; auth, The Big Cats-The Paintings of Guy Coheleach, Harry Abrams, 82. *Dealer:* Pandion Art Box 728 Jensen Beach FL 33457. *Mailing Add:* c/o Regency House Art Inc Box 147 Plainview NY 11803

COHEN, ADELE
SCULPTOR, PAINTER
b Buffalo, NY. *Study:* Art Inst Buffalo; Albright Sch Buffalo; Parsons Sch Art, New York. *Work:* Burchfield Ctr, Western NY Forum Am Art, State Univ NY Col Buffalo; Newark Mus, NJ; Univ Mass, Amherst; Charles Rand Penny Collection, Lockport, NY. *Comn:* Fando & Liz stage sets, NY State Theatre, Buffalo Fine Arts Acad & Workshop Repertory Theatre, 67; Gorge Legend Arbor (sculpture), Art Park & Co, Lewiston, NY, 78; Chesterwood (sculpture), Nat Trust Hist Preserv, Stockbridge, Mass, 83. *Exhib:* Burchfield Ctr, Western NY Forum Am Art, State Univ NY Col Buffalo; Albright-Knox Art Gallery, Buffalo; Art Across Am Inst Contemp Art, Boston; Foreign Inst Group Exhib, Dartmund, WGer; Kanazawa Art Exhib Exchange Show, Japan; and others. *Teaching:* Instr drawing, State Univ NY Col Buffalo, 74-75. *Awards:* Paul Lindsay Sample Award, 10th Chautauqua Exhib Am Artists, NY, 67; Buffalo Courier Express Award, 32nd Western NY Exhib, Albright-Knox Art Gallery, 69; Janet E Turner Prize, 88th Ann Exhib Nat Asn Women Artists, 77. *Bibliog:* Jane Marinsky (auth), Adele Cohen: Tracing Her Inner Image, 77; Elaine Hancock Jones (auth), Adele Cohen: Gorge Legend Arbor, In Process, 78; Ethel Moore (auth), The Inner Image: Adele Cohen 1960-80, 80. *Mem:* Nat Asn Women Artists. *Dealer:* FARS Ltd 32 Union Sq New York NY 10003. *Mailing Add:* 66 Burbank Dr Snyder NY 14226

COHEN, ARTHUR A
BOOK DEALER, HISTORIAN
b New York, NY, June 25, 28. *Study:* Univ Chicago, BA & MA. *Pos:* Organizer of opening exhib, The Hebrew Bible in Christian, Jewish & Muslim Art, Jewish Mus, 63; managing ed, The Documents of 20th Century Art, Viking Press, 68-72; founder, Ex Libris for the Documentation of 20th Century Art. *Collection:* Primitive and ancient arts; modern painting and rare books, Dada and Constructivism. *Publ:* Auth, Sonia Delaunay, Abrams, 75; auth, Motherwell, 77; auth, The New Art of Color: The Writings of Robert & Sonia Delaunay, Viking, 78. *Mailing Add:* 160 E 70th St New York NY 10021

COHEN, CHARLES E
HISTORIAN, EDUCATOR
b New York, NY, July 11, 42. *Study:* Columbia Univ, AB, 63; Princeton Univ, MFA, 65; Harvard Univ, PhD, 71. *Teaching:* From asst to full prof, Univ Chicago, 70-, chmn, Art Dept, 76- *Awards:* Delmas Found Fel, 80; Nat Endowment Humanities Summer Stipend, 83; Guggenheim Found Fel, 83-84. *Mem:* Col Art Asn Am; Midwest Art Hist Soc. *Res:* Venetian & North Italian painting and drawing in the Renaissance. *Publ:* Auth, Pordenone's painted facade on the Palazzo Tinghi in Udine, Burlington Mag, 74; auth, I disegni di Pomponio Amalteo, GEAP, 75; auth, Pordenone's Cremona Passion Scenes & German Art, Arte Lomberda, 76; auth, The Drawings of Giovanni Antonio da Pordenone, La Nuova Italia, 80; auth, Pordenone not Giorgione, Burlington Mag, 80. *Mailing Add:* 5540 S Greenwood Ave Chicago IL 60637

COHEN, ELAINE LUSTIG
PAINTER, DESIGNER
b NJ, Mar 6, 27. *Study:* Tulane Univ, 45-46; Univ Southern Calif, BFA, 48. *Work:* Mus Mod Art, New York; Am Tel & Tel; Chase Manhattan Bank; Newark Mus; Atlantic Richfield, Calif. *Comn:* Graphic designs for Am Fedn Arts, Philip Johnson (architect), Lincoln Ctr, Fed Aviation Agency & Meridian Bks. *Exhib:* Greetings Exhib, Mus Mod Art, New York, 66; Fifty Years Graphic Arts in America, Am Inst Graphic Arts, 66; Exhib Galerie Carl van der Voort, Basel, Switz, 78; Am Painting: The Eighties, Grey Gallery, NY Univ, 79; Mary Boone Gallery, New York, 79; Janus Gallery, Los Angeles, 81 & 82; plus others. *Pos:* Designer (with Alvin Lustig), until 55; freelance designer, 55-67; mem adv comt art & archit, Yale Univ Sch Design, 57-62. *Mailing Add:* 160 E 70th St New York NY 10021

COHEN, GEORGE MICHAEL
EDUCATOR
b Sept 24, 31. *Study:* Harvard Univ, AB, 55, AM, 58; Boston Univ, PhD, 62. *Teaching:* Assoc prof, Hofstra Univ, 70- *Publ:* Auth, The bird symbolism of Morris Graves, Col Art J, 58; auth, The paintings of Charles Sheeler, 59 & auth, The lithographs of Thomas Hart Benton, 62, Am Artist; auth, The sculpture of John B Flannagan, Artvoices, 65; auth, The art of George Catlin, Art & Antiques, 81; and many others. *Mailing Add:* 80 Wintercress Lane East Northport NY 11731

COHEN, HAROLD
ARTIST-THEORIST, EDUCATOR
b London, Eng, May 1, 28. *Study:* Univ London, DipFA, 51. *Work:* Tate Gallery, London; Stedelijk Mus, Amsterdam, Holland; Victoria & Albert Mus, London; Los Angeles Co Mus Art, Calif; Walker Art Ctr, Minneapolis, Minn. *Comn:* Wallhanging, Milan Triennale, 63; tapestry, Brit Petroleum Co, 65. *Exhib:* Documenta, Kassel, WGer, 64 & 77; 33rd Venice Biennale, 66; one-man shows, Mus d'Art Contemporain, Montreal, Que, 67, Victoria & Albert Mus, 68 & Stedelijk Mus, 77; Three Behaviors for the Partitioning of Space, Los Angeles Co Mus Art, 72; Retrospective, Scottish Arts Coun Gallery, Edinburgh, 76; Harold Cohen: Drawing, San Francisco Mus Mod Art, 79; Computers & the Visual Arts: The Research & Drawings of Harold Cohen, Sierra Nevada Mus Art, 79; and others. *Pos:* Vis scholar, Artificial Intelligence Lab, Stanford Univ, 73-75. *Teaching:* Instr art, Univ Col London, 61-65; prof art, Univ Calif, San Diego, 68-, chmn visual arts dept, 68-69, dir, Ctr Art/Sci Study, 74- *Awards:* Harkness Fel of Commonwealth Fund, 59-61; Purchase Award, Gulbenkian Found, 61; Nat Endowment Arts Workshop Grant, 76. *Publ:* Auth, The making of a tapestry, 67, Apropos work in progress, 68 & On purpose, 74, Studio Int; auth, The material of symbols, First Ann Symposium on Symbols & Symbol Processing, Univ Nev, 76; auth, What is an Image?, Int Joint Conf Artificial Intelligence, Tokyo, Japan, 79. *Mailing Add:* 921 Eolus Ave Leucadia CA 92024

COHEN, HAROLD LARRY
DESIGNER, EDUCATOR
b Brooklyn, NY, May 24, 25. *Study:* Pratt Inst Art Sch, Brooklyn; Northwestern Univ; Inst Design, BA. *Pos:* Dir, Inst Behav Res, Silver Spring, Md, formerly; dean sch archit & environ design, State Univ NY, Buffalo. *Teaching:* Lectr; prof design, chmn dept & dir design res & develop, Southern Ill Univ, Carbondale, formerly. *Awards:* Five Good Design Awards, with Davis Pratt; Mus Mod Art Awards, 49-53. *Mailing Add:* Sch of Archit & Environ Design State Univ NY Buffalo NY 14214

COHEN, HY
PAINTER
b London, Eng, June 13, 01. *Study:* Nat Acad Design; City Col New York, BS. *Work:* Hirshhorn Mus. *Exhib:* Brooklyn Mus; Art Inst Chicago; Metrop Mus Art; St Louis Mus; Los Angeles Mus; Am Watercolor Soc; Washington Univ; Pa Acad Fine Arts; Carnegie Inst; Walker Art Ctr. *Pos:* Organized & moderated, Let's talk about art, weekly radio prog, 45-46. *Mem:* Artists Equity Asn New York (pres, 63-70, hon pres, 70-); life mem Am Watercolor Soc. *Mailing Add:* 166 W 72nd St New York NY 10023

COHEN, JEAN
PAINTER, MURALIST
b New York, NY, Aug 1, 27. *Study:* Pratt Inst, Brooklyn, 44-45; Cooper Union Art Sch, New York, 46-49; Skowhegan Sch Painting & Sculpture, Maine, summer 50. *Work:* Ciba-Geigy Corp, Ardsley, NY; Hampton Inst Mus, Va; Bocour Color Collection, Garnersville, NY; Colby Col Mus, Waterville, Maine; Wright State Univ Mus. *Exhib:* Contemp Artists, Riverside Mus, New York, 63; Pa Acad Regional, Philadelphia, 64; Visual R&D, Univ Tex Art Mus, Austin, 73; Contemp Am Painting, Randolph-Macon Col, 74; West Bronx Art League, Bronx Mus, 75. *Pos:* Consult, West Bronx Art League, 69-75; founder, Landmark Gallery, New York. *Teaching:* Instr painting & design, Cooper Union, spring & summers, 51-63; lectr painting, Philadelphia Col Art, 62-69; lectr painting, Queens Col Art Dept, 72-75; Jersey City State Col & Philadelphia Col Art, 81-82. *Awards:* Landscape Painting Prize, Skowhegan Sch Painting, 50; Creative Artists Pub Serv Grant, 80. *Mem:* Women in Arts; Am Abstract Artists. *Media:* Oil, Compressed Charcoal. *Dealer:* Cape Split Place Addison ME 04606. *Mailing Add:* 20 Cornelia St New York NY 10014

COHEN, JOAN LEBOLD
HISTORIAN, PHOTOGRAPHER
b Highland Park, Ill, Aug 19, 32. *Study:* Smith Col, BA, 54. *Work:* Smith Col Mus Art; Harvard Law Sch; Atlantic Richfield Corporation Collection. *Exhib:* LaChine, Centre Culturel De L'Ambassade De France, Peking, 81; Shadows of Mt Huang, Univ Art Gallery, Berkeley, Calif, 81; Detroit Inst Arts, 81; Univ Texas, Austin, 81; Art Mus, Princeton, 82; and others. *Teaching:* Lectr, Dept Pub Educ, Mus Fine Arts, Boston, 65-71; lectr Asian ideas & images, China, Japan & India, Sch of Mus Fine Arts, Tufts Univ, Boston, 68- *Awards:* Two awards for bk, China Today & Her Ancient Treasures, 74 & 75. *Res:* Words and images of the cultural history of Asia. *Publ:* Auth, Angkor--Monuments of the God-Kings, Abrams, 75; contrib, The Domestication of the Fourth Dimension. Abrams, 75; auth & illusr filmstrips, Ancient Art & History in People's China & Art Today in People's China, Mass Commun, 77; frequent contrib writing & photog, Asian Wall Street J, Hong Kong; auth, Painting the Chinese Dream, Chinese Art Thirty Years After the Revolution, 82. *Dealer:* Daniel Wolf Gallery 30 West 57th St New York NY 10019; The Gallery North Truro Mass. *Mailing Add:* 50 East 89th Street New York NY 10028

COHEN, LYNNE G
PHOTOGRAPHER, LECTURER
b Racine, Wis, July 3, 44. *Study:* Univ Wis, Madison, BS(art); Slade Sch Art, London, Eng; Univ Mich, Ann Arbor, grad study; Eastern Mich Univ, MA(art). *Work:* Int Mus Photog, George Eastman House, Rochester, NY; Art Inst Chicago; Univ NMex Art Mus; Nat Gallery Can, Ottawa; Bibliot Nat, Paris, France. *Exhib:* Photog: Midwest, Walker Art Ctr, Minneapolis, 73; one-person shows, Univ NMex, Albuquerque, 75, Int Ctr Photog, New York, 78 & Lightwork, Syracuse, NY, 79; Photogr Choice, Witkin Gallery, New York, 76; Room's, Mus Mod Art, New York, 76-77; Recent Acquisitions, Nat Gallery Can, 77; Cult Ctr, Nantes, France, 81; and others. *Teaching:* Lectr photog-art, Eastern Mich Univ, Ypsilanti, 69-73; lectr photog, Ottawa Univ, 74- *Awards:* Logan Award, 71st Chicago & Vicinity Show, Art Inst Chicago, 68; Can Coun Proj Grant, 77; Can Coun Arts Grant, 78-79. *Bibliog:* William Jenkins (auth), Portfolio, Image, 9/74; Geoffrey James (auth), Rooms with a viewfinder, Canadian, 77; Gary M Dault (auth), Destination Europe, Artscanada, 77. *Publ:* Contribr, Image, George Eastman House, 74; contribr, The Photographer's Choice, Addison House, 75; contribr, The Female Eye, Nat Film Bd Can, 75; contribr, The Banff Purchase, John Wiley, 79. *Mailing Add:* 316 Metcalf Apt 3 Ottawa ON K2P 1R1 Canada

COHEN, MICHAEL S
CERAMIST
b Boston, Mass, Mar 7, 36. *Study:* Mass Col of Art, BFA, 57; Cranbrook Acad of Art, Bloomfield Hills, Mich, 61; Haystack Mountain Sch of Crafts, Deer Isle, Maine, 61. *Work:* Mus of Mod Art, New York; Mus of Contemp Crafts, New York; Johnson Collection of Contemp Crafts, Wis; Everson Mus, Syracuse, NY; Addison Gallery, Andover, Mass. *Exhib:* Syracuse Int, Everson Mus, 62, 64 & 66; Am Studio Pottery, Victoria & Albert Mus, London, Eng, 63; 10th Int Exhib of Ceramic Art, Smithsonian Inst, Washington, DC, 65; one-man shows, Soc of Arts & Crafts, Lexington, Mass, 74 & Gallimaufry, Croton-on-Hudson, NY, 76; Objects USA, Mus of Contemp Crafts, New York, 70; Crafts 1970, Boston City Hall, Mass; Potter's Wheel, DeCordova Mus, Lincoln, Mass, 76; and others. *Awards:* Nat Endowment for the Arts grant, 74; Master Craftsman grant, Nat Endowment for the Arts, 75; 2nd Int Symposium, Tenn, 75. *Bibliog:* Peter Sabin (auth), Studio Production, Studio Potter, 76. *Mem:* Am Crafts Coun; Mass Asn of Craftsmen; Asparagus Valley Potters Guild (pres, 75-76). *Media:* Stoneware. *Mailing Add:* RR 2 Amherst MA 01002

COHEN, MILDRED THALER
DEALER, GALLERY DIRECTOR
b New York, NY, Oct 30, 21. *Study:* Hunter Col, New York, BA, 42; Pratt Inst Libr Sch, Brooklyn, NY, BLS, 43. *Collections Arranged:* Nell Choate Jones, 79; Frederic Taubes, 81; Three Generations of Wiggins: Carleton, Guy C, Guy A, 81; Robert Hallowell, 83. *Pos:* Librn, Mus French Art, French Inst, New York, 43-45; dir, The Marbella Gallery, Inc, New York, 71- *Mem:* Appraisers Asn Am Inc. *Specialty:* Nineteenth and early twentieth century American paintings. *Mailing Add:* 28 E 72nd St New York NY 10021

COHEN, RONNY H
CRITIC, HISTORIAN
b New York, NY, Apr 19, 50. *Study:* Finch Col, BA, 72; Inst Fine Arts, MA, 74, PhD, 79. *Collections Arranged:* Media Relief, John Weber Gallery, New York, 81; 7 Energist Painters, PS1 22, New York, 81; The First Energist Drawing Show, Stefanotti Gallery, New York, 81; Energism, PS1 Critical Perspectives, 82; Energism, Arthur Roger Gallery, New Orleans, 82; Ceramic Forms in Art, Zim-Lerner Gallery, New York, 83; Still-Life: A Thematic Survey, Zim-Lerner Gallery, New York, 83. *Awards:* Danforth Found Fel, 72-79; Fulbright-Hays Fel, US & Italian Govt, 76-77. *Bibliog:* Owen Findsen (auth), Energism: Becomes a New Buzz Word for Art, Artists, The Cincinnati Enquirer, 10/2/81; Jeffry Deitch (auth), Who has the Power, Flash Art, 11/81; Roger Green (auth), Energism peps things up, Times-Picayune, New Orleans, 9/19/82. *Publ:* Auth, Energism: An attitude, 9/80 & Alexandra Exter's designs for the theater, 9/81, Artforum; auth, Art and letters, Art News, 12/81; auth, Drawing the Meticulous Realist Way, Drawing, 3-4/82; and others. *Mailing Add:* 521 E 82nd St New York NY 10028

COHEN, WILFRED P
COLLECTOR, PATRON
b New York, NY, Aug 24, 1899. *Study:* NY Univ; City Col New York. *Awards:* Award, Nat Conf Christians & Jews, 64. *Collection:* Giacometti, Arps & California painters, exhibited collections at Country Art Gallery, Westbury, Long Island & Galerie Chassaing, Paris, France. *Mailing Add:* 1290 Avenue of the Americas New York NY 10019

COHN, FREDERICK DONALD
DEALER, GALLERY DIRECTOR
b Monroe, Mich, May 3, 31. *Study:* Univ Wis, BA, 54; Detroit Col Law, LLB, 57. *Pos:* Art dealer, Images Gallery, Toledo, Ohio, currently. *Mem:* Appraisers Asn Am; Toledo Mod Art Group (mem bd, currently). *Specialty:* Nineteenth and twentieth century American painting, print and sculpture. *Mailing Add:* Images Gallery 4324 W Central Ave Toledo OH 43615

COHN, MARJORIE B
CONSERVATOR, HISTORIAN
b New York, NY, Jan 10, 39. *Study:* Mt Holyoke Col, BA, 60; Radcliffe Col, AM, 61. *Collections Arranged:* Albrecht Durer, 1471-1528 (auth, catalogue), Mt Holyoke Col, 71; Wash & Gouache, Watercolor at Harvard, Fogg Art Mus, Harvard Univ, 77; Ingres Collection (auth, handbook), Fogg Art Mus, 81. *Pos:* Conservator works of art on paper, Fogg Art Mus, Harvard Univ, 62-; mem bd examr (paper), Am Inst for Conserv, 76-78, mem nominating comt, 77 & ed jour. *Teaching:* Guest lectr print hist, Boston Univ, 73; vis lectr print hist, Wellesley Col, 73; vis asst prof print hist, Brown Univ, 75; sr lectr fine arts, Harvard Univ, 77- *Mem:* Fel Int Inst for Conserv; fel Am Inst for Conserv. *Res:* Materials and techniques of traditional graphic arts. *Publ:* Contribr, Technical Appendix, Ingres Centennial Exhibition, Fogg Art Mus, 67; contribr, A Note on Media and Methods, Tiepolo, A Bicentenary Exhibition, Fogg Art Mus, 70; Wash & Gouache: A Study of the Development of the Materials of Watercolor, Fogg Art Mus, 81; contribr, Pursuit of Perfection: Works by J A D Ingres, J B Speed Mus, 83. *Mailing Add:* Fogg Art Mus Harvard Univ Cambridge MA 02138

COHN, MAX ARTHUR
PAINTER, PRINTMAKER
b London, England, Feb 3, 03; US citizen. *Study:* Art Students League, New York, 21-25; Colarossi Acad, Paris, 27. *Work:* Nat Mus Am Art, Washington, DC; Metrop Mus, New York; Philadelphia Mus; William Rockhill Nelson Gallery Art, Kansas City; Dallas Mus, Tex. *Exhib:* One-man shows, ACA Gallery, New York, 34; Delphic Studios, New York, 36; Couturier Galleries, Conn, 64 & Lucinda Galleries, NJ, 68; Biennial Watercolor, Brooklyn Mus, NY; Prints & Paintings, Mus Mod Art, New York. *Mem:* Life mem Art Students League; Del Valley Artists Asn (treas 47-62); Whiskey Painters Am, New York. *Media:* Oil, Watercolor. *Publ:* Co-auth, Silk Screen Stenciling as a Fine Art, McGraw-Hill, 42; co-auth, Silk Screen Techniques, Dover Press, 58. *Dealer:* Martin Diamond 1014 Madison Ave New York NY 10021. *Mailing Add:* 311 W 24th St New York NY 10011

COHN, RICHARD A
DEALER
b New York, NY, Feb 20, 24. *Study:* Univ Wis. *Pos:* Pres, Richard A Cohn Ltd, New York, 65-; partner, Kimmel/Cohn Photography Arts, New York, 74- *Specialty:* Twentieth century German Expressionism, Old Master paintings, drawings and prints. *Mailing Add:* Richard A Cohn Ltd One W 64th St New York NY 10023

COHOE, GREY
PRINTMAKER, PAINTER
b Tocito, NMex, Sept 9, 44. *Study:* Haystack Mountain Sch Crafts, Deer Isle, Maine; Univ Ariz, printmaking with Andrew Rush & Lynn Schroder & painting with Bruce McGrew, BFA, 72 & MFA, 74. *Work:* Pvt collections of Robert Putsch, Parker, Colo, John Humphrey, Cleveland, Ohio, Chris Isentberg, Pasadena, Calif, John Espy, New Orleans, La & Carl F Diener, Tucson, Ariz. *Comn:* NMex State Parks & Recreation Emblem, State NMex, 66; Mountain Bell Calendar, Mountain Bell Tel Co, Denver, Colo, 70. *Exhib:* The Am Indian Heritage Art Exhib, Nat Cowboy Fall of Fame, Oklahoma City, Okla, 66; Am Discovers Indian Art Show, Exhib, Smithsonian Inst, Washington, DC, 67; Scottsdale Nat Indian Arts Exhib, Ariz, 67; Biennial Exhib of Am Indian Arts & Crafts, Washington, DC, 67; Ariz State Mus, Tucson, 68. *Teaching:* Instr, Inst Am Indian Arts, Santa Fe, NMex, formerly. *Media:* Oil, Acrylic; Intaglio. *Publ:* Illusr, The King of Thousand Islands, Doubleday, 72. *Dealer:* Los Llanos Gallery of Contemporary Art 72 East San Francisco St Santa Fe NM 87501. *Mailing Add:* PO Box 5512 Coronado Sta Santa Fe NM 87502

COINER, CHARLES TOUCEY
PAINTER
b Santa Barbara, Calif, Aug 20, 1897. *Study:* Chicago Acad Fine Arts; Art Inst Chicago. *Work:* Philadelphia Mus Art & Pa Acad Fine Arts, Philadelphia; Whitney Mus Am Art; Univ Wichita, Kans; Syracuse Univ; Nat Acad. *Exhib:* One-man shows, Philadelphia Art Alliance, Pa Acad Fine Arts, Fleisher Mus & Midtown Galleries; also nat open shows & regional exhibs in Pa. *Pos:* Art dir & vpres, N W Ager, Philadelphia. *Mem:* Philadelphia Art Alliance; New York Art Dirs Club; Nat Acad Design; Pa Acad Fine Arts. *Media:* Oil. *Publ:* Auth articles on painting & conserv of wildlife, In: Esquire, Can, 9/63, Ireland, 2/65 & Scotland, 2/68. *Dealer:* Midtown Galleries 11 E 57th St New York NY 10022. *Mailing Add:* Mechanicsville PA 18934

COKE, F VAN DEREN
PHOTOGRAPHER, CURATOR
b Lexington, Ky, July 4, 21. *Study:* Univ Ky, BA; Ind Univ, MFA; Harvard Univ. *Work:* Mus Mod Art, New York; Int Mus Photog, Rochester, NY; Nat Gallery Can, Ottawa, Ont; San Francisco Mus Mod Art; Sheldon Mem Art Gallery, Lincoln, Nebr. *Exhib:* Witkin Gallery, New York, 74; Oakland Mus, 75; Galerie die Brucke, Vienna, 75; Schoelkopf Gallery, New York, 76; Art Mus, Univ NMex, 82; and many others. *Pos:* Dir, Univ NMex Art Mus, 62-67 & 72-79; dir, George Eastman House, 70-72; dir dept photog, San Francisco

Mus Mod Art, 79- *Teaching:* Asst prof photog & art hist, Univ Fla, 58-61; assoc prof, Ariz State Univ, 61-62; prof, Univ NMex, 62-70 & 72-79, chmn dept art, 62-70; lectr, St Martin's Sch Art, London, 71; prof art hist, Univ Rochester, 71-72; vis prof, Univ Calif, Berkeley, 73; distinguished vis prof, Univ Calif, Davis, 74. *Awards:* Int Competition Awards, Mod Photog Mag, 56 & US Camera Mag, 57, 58 & 60; New Talent USA Award, Art in Am, 60; Guggenheim Fel, 75. *Bibliog:* Joan Murray (auth), Two views of the West, Artweek, 1/22/72; A Frankenstein (auth), A creative photographer, San Francisco Chronicle, 1/13/72; Robert Routh (auth), An interview with Van Deren Coke, Peterson's Photo Mag, 4/11/76. *Mem:* Col Art Asn Am (bd dir, 72-76); Int Folk Art Found (bd dir, 68-76); Guadalupe Found (bd dir, 76-79); Soc Photog Educ (bd dir, 67-70). *Res:* The use of photographs by artists; twentieth century American painters; contemporary photographers. *Publ:* Auth, Fabricated to be Photographed, 79; auth, The Markers, 81; auth, Avant-garde Photography in Germany 1919-1939, 83; Bret Weston Photographs: 1925-1930 and 1980-1982, 83; Val Zelberg, 83; and others. *Mailing Add:* San Francisco Mus of Mod Art McAllister St at Van Ness Ave San Francisco CA 94102

COKENDOLPHER, EUNICE LORAINE
PAINTER, INSTRUCTOR
b Sonora, Tex, April 17, 31. *Study:* Tex Womans Univ, 48-50; studied with Don Stone, Edgar Whitney, Zoltan Szabo, George Cherepov, Bud Biggs, Naomi Brotherton & Howard Wexler, 75-83. *Work:* Southern Guild Artists & Craftsmen, Bowling Green, Ky; Baptist Med Ctr Found, Oklahoma City. *Comn:* Noah and the Ark, First United Methodist Church, Burkburnett, Tex, 81. *Exhib:* Texas Fine Arts Citation Exhib, Laguna Gloria Mus, Austin, Tex, 80; The Best of Southwest Watercolor Society, Brookhaven Col, Dallas, 81; 22nd Nat Sun Carnival Art Exhib, El Paso Mus Art, 82; Southern Watercolor Soc Seventh Ann, Asheville Art Mus, NC, 83; Ga Watercolor Soc Fifth Nat Exhib, Valdosta State Col Fine Arts Bldg, 84. *Teaching:* Instr watercolor, Vernon Regional Col, 84 & Wishing Well Studio, Burkburnett, Tex, 84. *Awards:* Award Merit, Aqueous 79, Ky Watercolor Soc Nat Exhib, 79; Mary Jo Weale Award, Southern Watercolor Soc Nat Exhib, 83. *Mem:* Tex Fine Arts Asn; Watercolor Soc, Southwestern, Ky, Southern & WTex. *Mailing Add:* 1200 Clover Dr Burkburnett TX 76354

COKER, CARL DAVID
PAINTER, EDUCATOR
b Greensboro, NC, Feb 8, 28. *Study:* Art Students League, with Robert Beverly Hale; Univ NC; Univ NMex, with Raymond Jonson, Richard Diebenkorn & Enrique Montenegro, BFA & MA; Ill State Univ. *Work:* Philbrook Mus, Tulsa; Performing Arts Ctr, Tulsa; Univ Okla Mus, Norman; Jonson Gallery, Univ NMex, Albuquerque; Mus of NMex, Santa Fe. *Comn:* Welded steel altarpiece, Holloman Air Force Hosp Chapel, USAF, 67; three paintings, Hillcrest Hosp, Tulsa, Okla, 71; painting, Farmers & Merchants Bank, Tulsa, 75; fiberglass painting, 76 & welded steel sculpture, 77, Hicks Park, City of Tulsa. *Exhib:* Tex Ann, Dallas Mus of Fine Arts, 60; Ill Print & Drawing Show, Art Inst Chicago, 63; Nat Drawing Show, Bucknell Univ, 65; Five NMex Artists, Pronaf Mus, Juarez, Mex, 65; NMex Sculptors, 66 & NMex Painters, 67, Mus of NMex, Santa Fe; Instituto Cultural Peruano Norte Americano, 79; Galeria Forum, Lima, Peru, 80; and others. *Teaching:* Instr painting, ETex State Univ, Commerce, 56-61; asst prof painting-sculpture, NMex State Univ, Las Cruces, 64-68; prof painting, Univ Tulsa, 68-; guest artist, Escuela Nacional de Bellas Artes, Lima, Peru, 79-80. *Awards:* First Prize Sculpture, 14th Ann, Quincy, Ill, 63; Grand Award, Okla Ann, Philbrook Mus, Tulsa, 73; Fulbright Teaching/Res Grant, Lima, Peru, 79-80. *Mem:* Mid-Am Col Art Asn; Asociacion Peruana de Artistas Plasticas. *Media:* Acrylic, Fiberglass. *Dealer:* Tally Richards Gallery of Contemp Art 1 Ledoux St Taos NM 87571. *Mailing Add:* 1135 S Gary Pl Tulsa OK 74104

COLARUSSO, CORRINE CAMILLE
PAINTER, INSTRUCTOR
b Boston, Mass, Mar 22, 52. *Study:* Yale Summer Sch Art & Music, 72; Univ Mass, BFA, 73; Tyler Sch Art, Temple Univ, Philadelphia, MFA, 75. *Exhib:* Corcoran Gallery Art, Washington, DC, 75; Inst Contemp Art, Recife, Brazil, 76; O'Kane Gallery, Univ Houston, Tex, 77; 30 Women Artists, Peachtree Ctr, Atlanta, Ga, 78; one-person show, Oglethorpe Univ, Atlanta, 78; Personal Statements: Drawing, Southeastern Ctr Contemp Art, Winston-Salem, NC, 79; Atlanta Women's Invitational, Agnes Scott Col, 79. *Teaching:* Asst drawing, Univ Mass, Amherst, 72-73; grad teaching asst, Tyler Sch Art, 74-75; fac mem found design & drawing, Atlanta Col Art, 75-, dept head found studio, currently. *Awards:* MacDowell Colony Fel, 77 & 79; Fulbright-Hayes Res Grant, India/Nepal, 78. *Mailing Add:* 344 Elmira Pl NE Atlanta GA 30307

COLBURN, FRANCIS PEABODY
PAINTER
b Fairfax, Vt, Oct 20, 09. *Study:* Univ Vt, PhB, 34; Bennington Col; Art Students League, scholar; Univ Vt, Hon DFA, 74. *Exhib:* One-man shows, Carnegie Inst, Corcoran Gallery, Whitney Mus Am Art, Nat Acad Design & Cordova Mus, Boston; and others. *Teaching:* Resident artist, Univ Vt, 42-, chmn art dept, 46-75, emer prof art, 75- *Awards:* Springfield Mus Fine Arts, Mass, Award; Calif Palace Legion Honor Award; Distinguished Serv to the Arts Award, Vt Coun Arts, 68. *Mem:* Vt Art Teachers Asn; Vt Coun Arts; Artists Equity. *Mailing Add:* 118 S Willard St Burlington VT 05401

COLBY, BILL
PRINTMAKER, EDUCATOR
b Beloit, Kans, Jan 8, 27. *Study:* Univ Denver, BA, 50; Univ Ill, Champaign, MA, 54. *Work:* Libr Cong, Pennell Print Collection, Washington, DC; Seattle

Art Mus; Wichita Art Mus, Kans; Portland Art Mus, Ore; Tacoma Art Mus, Wash. *Comn:* Painting, Kilworth Chapel, Univ Puget Sound, Tacoma, Wash, 67; prints, Weyerhauser Corp, Seattle, 82. *Exhib:* Seattle Art Mus, Wash, 71; State Capitol Mus, Olympia, Wash, 74, 76, 78 & 80; solo exhibs, Kittredge Gallery, Tacoma, 79 & J Nina Miller Gallery, Seattle, 81; Art Alliance Gallery, Philadelphia, 79; Bellevue Art Mus, Wash, 79 & 83; and others. *Teaching:* Prof printmaking, Univ Puget Sound, Tacoma, Wash, 65-, dir Kittredge Gallery, Univ Puget Sound, 58-65 & 83- *Mem:* Am Color Print Soc, Philadelphia; Col Art Asn; Tacoma Arts & Crafts Asn; NW Printmakers. *Mailing Add:* 3706 North Union Ave Tacoma WA 98407

COLBY, JOY HAKANSON
CRITIC
b Detroit, Mich. *Study:* Detroit Soc Arts & Crafts; Wayne State Univ, BFA. *Pos:* Art critic, Detroit News, 50-; art consult, Kasle/Colby, 76-80. *Mem:* Mich Coun Arts (adv, 72-79); Detroit Coun Arts; New Detroit Inc Arts Comt; Bloomfield Hills Arts Coun. *Publ:* Auth, Art & A City, 56; auth, Arts and Crafts in Detroit, Detroit Inst Arts, 76. *Mailing Add:* Detroit News 615 W Lafayette Detroit MI 48231

COLBY, VICTOR E
SCULPTOR, EDUCATOR
b Frankfort, Ind, Jan 5, 17. *Study:* Corcoran Sch Art; Ind Univ, AB, 48; Cornell Univ, MFA, 50. *Work:* Ithaca Col Mus; Munson-Williams-Proctor Inst, Utica, NY; St Lawrence Univ, Canton, NY; State Univ NY Col Cortland; Roberson Mus, Binghamton, NY. *Comn:* Wall sculpture, Wilson Nuclear Physics Lab, Cornell Univ, 68. *Exhib:* One-man shows, Hewitt Gallery, 58, The Contemporaries, 66 & Hartley Gallery, 74. *Teaching:* Prof sculpture, Cornell Univ, 50-82; retired. *Media:* Wood. *Mailing Add:* 642 Peruville Rd Groton NY 13073

COLE, BRUCE
HISTORIAN, EDUCATOR
b Cleveland, Ohio, Aug 2, 38. *Study:* Western Reserve Univ, BA, 62; Oberlin Col, MA, 64; Bryn Mawr Col, PhD, 69. *Teaching:* Asst prof art hist, Univ Rochester, NY, 69-73; assoc prof art hist, Ind Univ, Bloomington, 73-77, prof art hist, 77- *Awards:* Nat Endowment Humanities Fel, 72-73; Guggenheim Fel, 75-76; Am Coun Learned Societies Fel. *Res:* Painting of the 14th & 15th centuries in Florence. *Publ:* Auth, A popular painting from the Trecento, Apollo, 75; auth, Giotto & Florentine Painting 1280-1375, Harper, 76; auth, Agnolo Gaddi, The Clarendon Press & Oxford Univ Press, 77; auth, Masaccio and The Art of Early Renaissance Florence, Ind Univ Press, 80; auth, Sienese Painting from its Origins to the Fifteenth Century, Harper, 80. *Mailing Add:* Dept of Fine Arts Ind Univ Bloomington IN 47401

COLE, DONALD
PAINTER
b New York, NY, Oct 31, 30. *Study:* Bucknell Univ, BS(civil eng); Univ Iowa, MFA. *Exhib:* One-man exhibs, Wake Forest Univ, Winston-Salem, 79, Va Commonwealth Univ, 81 & Univ Ga, Athens, 81; Painting & Sculpture Today, Indianapolis Mus Art, 72, 74 & 78, Animals in American Art: 1880's-1980's, Nassau County Mus Fine Art, Roslyn, NY, 81; and others. *Teaching:* Pres, Parsons Sch Design, NY, 77- *Awards:* Creative Artists Pub Serv Grant/Painting, NY State Coun on the Arts, 75; Artist-in-residence grant, Nat Endowment for the Arts, State Univ NY, Plattsburgh, 77, Artists Fel Grant, 78. *Bibliog:* Caril Dreyfuss McHugh (auth), Donald Cole, Arts Mag, 5/81; Ellen Lubell (auth), article in Arts Mag, 73, 75 & 78; Robert Berner (auth), Donald Cole, Arts Mag, 4/82. *Media:* Acrylic, Oil Stick. *Mailing Add:* 328 Grand Ave Brooklyn NY 11238

COLE, HAROLD DAVID
HISTORIAN, EDUCATOR
b Tulsa, Okla, Feb 28, 40. *Study:* Univ Tulsa, BA, MA(art criticism), with Alexander Hogue & Harry A Broadd; Ohio State Univ, MA(art hist), PhD, with Franklin Ludden & Maurice Cope. *Work:* Art Gallery, Univ Tulsa, Okla; Art Gallery, Baldwin-Wallace Col, Berea, Ohio; Art Gallery, Cumberland Col, Williamsburg, Ky; Art Gallery, Nicholls State Univ, Thibodaux, La. *Exhib:* 32nd Ann Springfield Ann Ten-State Exhib, Springfield Art Mus, Mo, 62; 12th Ann Own Your Own Exhib, Denver Art Mus, Colo, 68; 51st Ann May Show, Cleveland Mus Art, Ohio, 69; one-man shows, Cumberland Col, 70 & 72 & Nicholls State Univ, 71. *Collections Arranged:* Kenneth R Weedman Exhib (auth, catalog), 73. *Pos:* Mem visual art panel, Ohio Arts Coun, 77-79. *Teaching:* Assoc prof art hist, Baldwin-Wallace Col, 66- *Awards:* Special Jury Mention, Cleveland Mus Art May Show, 69. *Mem:* Col Art Asn; Midwest Art Hist Asn; Int Ctr of Medieval Art; Monument Historique. *Res:* Thirteenth century French sculpture and architecture; 19th century French painting. *Publ:* Auth, Kenneth R Weedman Sculpture Exhibition, Crafts Horizons, 72; co-auth, Grant Reynard: His Life & Work, Baldwin-Wallace Col, 75. *Mailing Add:* 28 E Fifth Ave Berea OH 44017

COLE, HERBERT MILTON
HISTORIAN, PHOTOGRAPHER
b Newton, Mass, Apr 15, 35. *Study:* Williams Col, BA, 57; Columbia Univ, MA, 64, Ford Found foreign area fel, 65-68, William B Cutting fel, 66-67, PhD, 68; Nat Endowment for Humanities fel, 71-72; Creative Arts fel, 74. *Collections Arranged:* African Arts of Transformation (auth, catalog), Univ Calif, Santa Barbara, 70; The Arts of Ghana (auth, catalog), Mus Cult Hist, Univ Calif, Los Angeles, 75-77. *Pos:* Consult ed, African Arts, Univ Calif, Los Angeles, 70- *Teaching:* Prof African art hist, Univ Calif, Santa Barbara, 68- *Media:* Photography. *Res:* Arts of tropical Africa. *Publ:* Ed, African Art and Leadership, Univ Wis-Madison, 73; auth, The art of festival in Ghana, African

Arts, Vol VIII, No 3, 75; auth, North American Indian, African and oceanic art, In: Art Through the Ages, sixth ed, 75; auth, The Arts of Omaha, Univ Calif, Los Angeles, 77; auth, Mbari: Art and Life Among the Owerri Igbo, Ind Univ Press, 80; plus many others. *Mailing Add:* Dept of Art Univ of Calif Santa Barbara CA 93106

COLE, JOYCE
PAINTER
b New York, NY. *Study:* Finch Col, BA(art hist); Art Students League; Sch Visual Arts. *Work:* Aldrich Mus Contemp Art, Ridgefield, Conn; Guggenheim Mus; Oklahoma Art Ctr. *Exhib:* Andre Emmerich Gallery, NY, 72; Whitney Mus Am Art Biennial, New York, 73; Contemporary Reflections, Aldrich Mus Contemp Art, 73; Galerie Denise Rene, New York, 73; Soho Ctr Visual Arts, New York, 74; Susan Caldwell Gallery, New York, 77; Gloria Luria Gallery, Fla, 78. *Bibliog:* April Kingsley (auth), New York letter, Art Int, 10/73; Lawrence Campbell (auth), Reviews & previews, Art News, 9/73; Peter Frank (auth), article, Art News, 10/77. *Mailing Add:* 11 W 20th St New York NY 10011

COLE, MAX
PAINTER
b Hodgeman Co, Kans, Feb 14, 37. *Study:* Univ Ariz, Tucson, MFA, 64. *Work:* St Paul Art Ctr; Santa Barbara Mus Art. *Exhib:* Contemp Painting & Sculpture, Krannert Art Mus, Univ Ill, 69; Visible/Invisible, Long Beach Art Mus, Calif, 72; Whitney Mus Am Art Biannual, 75; New Abstract Painting, Los Angeles, Los Angeles Co Mus, 76; 35th Biannual, Corcoran Gallery Art, 77; one-person exhibs, Sidney Janis Gallery, New York, 77 & 79, Los Angeles Louver Gallery, 79, 80 & 83 & Miami/Dade Col, 82; Santa Barbara Mus Art, 80. *Teaching:* Asst prof painting, Pasadena City Col, Calif, 67-79. *Awards:* May Lieberman Award, Frye Mus Art, 66; Purchase Award, Laguna Beach Art Asn, Calif, 69; Nat Endowment Arts Artists Fel, 83. *Mailing Add:* 195 E 3rd St New York NY 10009

COLE, STEPHANIE KIRSCHEN
COLLAGE ARTIST
b New York, NY, Mar 28, 45. *Study:* Univ Md, BA, 68, MA, 70; Md Art Inst, MFA, 72. *Work:* Nat Collection Fine Arts, Smithsonian Inst; Baltimore Mus, Md; Hirshhorn Collection; Pasadena Mus, Calif; Mem Art Gallery, Rochester, NY. *Exhib:* Solo exhib, Mem Art Gallery, Rochester, NY, 72; Curators Choice, Mem Art Gallery, Rochester, NY, 73; Odda Stamp & Collage Traveling Exhib; Creative Artists Pub Serv Prog, Albany Mus, New York; Rochester Inst Technol, NY. *Awards:* Gov Award, Baltimore Mus Regional, 71; Juror's Award, Rochester Mem Mus Regional, 72. *Dealer:* Watson de Nagy Houston TX. *Mailing Add:* c/o Tibor de Nagy Art Gallery 29 W 57th New York NY 10019

COLE, SYLVAN, JR
DEALER, WRITER
b New York, NY, Jan 10, 18. *Study:* Cornell Univ, BA, 39. *Pos:* Pres & dir, Assoc Am Artists, New York, 58-; adv bd, Pratt Graphics Ctr, 64- *Mem:* Art Dealers Asn Am (vpres, 68-74); Print Coun Am (dealers adv comt, 66-76). *Specialty:* Original prints. *Publ:* Auth, Raphael Soyer: Fifty Years of Printmaking, 67; auth, The Graphic Work of Joseph Hirsch, 70; auth, Will Barnet--Prints 1932-1972, 72, supplement, 73-79; auth, The Lithographs of John Stuart Curry, A Catalog Raisonne, 76. *Mailing Add:* Associated American Artists 663 Fifth Ave New York NY 10022

COLEMAN, A(LLAN) D(OUGLASS)
CRITIC, LECTURER
b New York, NY, Dec 19, 43. *Study:* Hunter Col, Bronx, NY, BA, 64; San Francisco State Col, MA, 67. *Pos:* Vpres, Photog Media Inst, Inc, 77-; founder/organizer, Conf on Photog Criticism, 77-; photog columnist, Latent Image, Village Voice, 68-73; photog critic, New York Times, 70-74; contribr ed, Camera 35, 75-; bd dirs, Photog Resource Ctr, 78-; critic in residence, International Ctr Photog, NY, spring 79. *Teaching:* Instr photog, Dept of Film/TV, NY Univ, 78-82, asst prof, 83-; mem fac photog criticism, New Sch for Social Res, New York, 79- *Awards:* Nat Endowment for Arts Art Critics fel, 76. *Bibliog:* Norman Schreiber (auth), Who Is A D Coleman, Camera 35, 3/72; Tom Dugan (auth), Photog Between Covers, Impressions, 79; Video interview, Video Databanic, Sch Art Inst, Chicago, 77. *Mem:* Soc for Photog Educ; Authors Guild; PEN Am Ctr. *Publ:* Auth, The Grotesque in Photography: A Critical Survey, Ridge Press/Summit Books, 77; auth, Light Readings: A Photography Critic's Writings, 1968-1978, Oxford Univ Press, 79 & Galaxy Paperback, 82; auth, Lee, Model, Parks, Samaras, Turner: Five Interviews Before the Fact, Photographic Resource Ctr, 79; co-auth, The Photography A-V Program Directory, PMI, Inc, 80; auth, Confirmation, ADCO Enterprises, 82. *Mailing Add:* 465 Van Duzer St Staten Island NY 10304

COLEMAN, EDWARD H
DEALER, COLLECTOR
b Allentown, Pa, Aug 6, 28. *Pos:* Bd of dirs, Lehigh Valley Ctr Performing Arts, 76-78; bd of trustees, Valley Arts Coun, 78- *Specialty:* 15th to 20th century sculpture, paintings, prints and watercolors. *Collection:* French impressionists, Mexican realists, naive painters and social realists. *Mailing Add:* 1509 Hamilton St Allentown PA 18102

COLEMAN, FLOYD WILLIS
EDUCATOR, PAINTER
b Sawyerville, Ala, Jan 13, 39. *Study:* Ala State Univ, with Hayward L Oubre, BA, 60; Univ Wis, with Robert Burkert, MS, 62; Univ Ga, with Edmund B

Feldman, PhD, 75. *Work:* Oakland Mus, Calif; High Mus Art, Emory Univ, Spelman Col, Atlanta Univ, Atlanta, Ga. *Exhib:* Am Drawing Ann, Norfolk Mus Arts & Sci, Va, 62; 18th Southeastern Ann, High Mus Art, Atlanta, Ga, 63; 4th Dixie Ann, Montgomery Mus Fine Arts, Ala, 65; 30 Contemporary Black Artists, Minneapolis Inst Arts, Minn, 68; Spiral: Afro-American Art of the Seventies, Mus Nat Ctr Afro-Am Artists, Boston, 80. *Teaching:* Asst prof, Clark Col, Atlanta, Ga, 65-71; assoc prof, Southern Ill Univ, Edwardsville, 76-80, prof, 81- *Awards:* Fels, Ford Found, 68-70, Esso Found, 71 & Nat Endowment Humanities, 76-77. *Mem:* Col Art Asn Am; Nat Conf Artists (co-chmn, 70-71). *Res:* African continuities in Afro-American art; Mexican influences on Mayan architecture. *Publ:* Auth, African influences on Black American art, 76 & auth, Toward an aesthetic toughness in Afro-American art, 78, Black Art Quart; auth, Popular images in Afro-American art, J Soc Ethnic & Special Studies, 80. *Mailing Add:* 516 Chapman St Edwardsville IL 62025

COLEMAN, GAYLE (GAYLE COLEMAN MACDONALD)
RESTORER, LECTURER
b Allentown, Pa, Mar 15, 54. *Study:* Lehigh Univ, Bethlehem, Pa, BA; Art Restoration Tech Inst, cert & apprenticeship. *Pos:* Art conservator, Lehigh Univ, Bethlehem, Pa, 76-; freelance art restorer, Pa; partner, Coleman Art Gallery, Allentown, 76-; lectr at var cols & univs. *Mem:* Am Inst for Conserv of Hist & Artistic Work; Asn for Preservation Technol. *Res:* Microchemical analysis of art work. *Mailing Add:* 1509 Hamilton St Allentown PA 18015

COLEMAN, JACQUI (JACQUELYN F)
PAINTER
b Weleetha, Okla, July 17, 27. *Study:* Calif Col Arts & Crafts, Oakland, 50; Univ Calif, Berkeley, 60-62; Nat Acad, New York; landscape with Geo Post, San Francisco, Calif; also still-lifes with Charles Reid, Conn. *Comn:* Connecticut Scenes (watercolor), Architects, Kaufman & Black, New Canaan, 81; mural, Saugatuck Congregational Church, Westport, Conn, 82. *Exhib:* Soc Western Artists, M H DeYoung Mem Mus, San Francisco, Calif, 70; Am Watercolor Soc Ann, Nat Acad, New York, 76-79; Conn Watercolor Soc, Atheneum Mus, Hartford, 78; Nat Acad Design, New York, 80. *Awards:* General Electric Prize, 78; President's Prize, Silvermine Art Sch, New Canaan, Conn, 79; Honorable Mention, M H DeYoung Mem Mus, San Francisco, Calif. *Mem:* Am Watercolor Soc, New York; San Francisco Women Artists, San Francisco, Calif, (pres). *Media:* Watercolor, Acrylic. *Mailing Add:* 14 Old Redding Rd Weston CT 06883

COLEMAN, M L (MICHEAL LEE)
PAINTER, INSTRUCTOR
b Livingston, Mont, May 11, 41. *Study:* Univ Wyo, BS, 63; with James Disney, Loveland, Colo, 69 & 75 & Hall Diteman, Billings, Mont, 77. *Work:* Northern Natural Gas, Omaha, Nebr; Iowa Beef Producers; several oil companies, Can. *Exhib:* Mus Native Am Cult Art Show & Auction, Spokane, Wash, 80 & 81; Sun Valley Western Art Auction & Exhib, Idaho, 80 & 81; Stockmen's Found Art Show & Auction, Calgary & Edmonton, Alta, 81; Art of the West, German Mus, Munich, 81. *Teaching:* Instr workshops, Sedona, Ariz & Yosemite Nat Park, Calif, currently. *Awards:* Best of Show, Stockmen's Found Art Show and Auction, Calgary, Alta, 81. *Bibliog:* Kathe McGehee (auth), M L Coleman's dramatic landscapes, Art West Mag, Vol III, No 6; Dale Burk (auth), A Brush with the West, Mountain Press, 80; Peggy & Harold Samuels (auths), Contemporary Western Artists, SW Art Publ, 82. *Media:* Oil. *Dealer:* Crimson Shadows 450 N Hwy 89A PO Box 2519 Sedona AZ 86336. *Mailing Add:* PO Box 2519 Sedona AZ 86336

COLEMAN, MICHAEL
PAINTER
b Provo, Utah, June 25, 46. *Study:* Brigham Young Univ. *Work:* Buffalo Bill Hist Mus, Cody, Wyo; Kennedy Gallery, New York. *Exhib:* Springville Mus Nat; Nat Acad Western Art, Nat Cowboy Hall of Fame, Oklahoma City. *Bibliog:* Diane Cochrane (auth), Romantic Western landscapes, Am Artist, 1/75; Susan Myers (auth), Twenty American Landscape Painters; Romantic Western painter, SW Art Mag, 2/77. *Media:* Oil. *Dealer:* Kennedy Gallery 40 W 57th St New York NY 10019. *Mailing Add:* 2875 Marrcrest E Provo UT 84601

COLESCOTT, ROBERT H
PAINTER, INSTRUCTOR
b Oakland, Calif, Aug 26, 25. *Study:* Univ Calif, Berkeley, AB & MA; & with Atelier Fernand Leger, Paris. *Work:* Metrop Mus, New York; Seattle Art Mus; Portland Art Mus, Ore; San Francisco Mus Art; Reed Col, Ore. *Exhib:* Third World Exhib, San Francisco Mus Art, 74; Unordinary Realities, Xerox Found, Rochester, NY, 75; Calif Painting & Sculpture, San Francisco Mus Art, 76 & Smithsonian Inst, 77; Northern Calif Artists, Huntsville Ala Mus, 77; Art About Art, Whitney Mus, New York, 78; Uncommon Visions, Univ Rochester, 79; solo exhibs, Hamilton Gallery, New York, 79 & Semaphore Gallery, New York, 80; Eight Black American Artists, Va Mus Fine Art, 80; Not Just for Laughs, New Mus, New York, 81; Crimes of Compassion, Chrysler Mus, Norfolk, Va, 81; Humor in Art, Los Angeles Inst Contemp Art, Calif, 81; Painting & Sculpture Today, Indianapolis Mus Art, 82; Biennial of Western States, Corcoran Gallery Art, 83; Biennial, Whitney Mus, 83; American Still Life 1945-1983, Contemp Arts Mus, Houston, 83; and others. *Pos:* Artist in residence, Am Res Ctr, Egypt, 64-65. *Teaching:* Assoc prof drawing & art educ, Portland State Univ, 57-66; assoc prof painting, Am Univ, Cairo, 66-67; prof art, Calif State Col, Stanislaus, 70-74; lectr, Univ Calif, Berkeley, 74-79; instr, San Francisco Art Inst, 79-; vis artist, Univ Ariz, Tucson, 83- *Awards:* Nat Endowment Arts Grant for Creative Painting, 76, 80 & 83. *Bibliog:* John Russell (auth), review, New York Times, 1/9/81 &

11/21/82; Peter Plagens (auth), The academy of the bad, Art in Am, 11/81; Daniel Cameron (auth), Biennial cycle, Arts Mag, 6/83. *Media:* Mixed. *Dealer:* Semaphore Gallery 462 W Broadway New York NY 10012. *Mailing Add:* Art Dept Univ Ariz Tucson AZ 85719

COLESCOTT, WARRINGTON W
PRINTMAKER, EDUCATOR
b Oakland, Calif, Mar 7, 21. *Study:* Univ Calif, Berkeley, BA & MA; Acad Grande Chaumiere, Paris; Slade Sch Art, Univ Col, London. *Work:* Metrop Mus Art & Mus Mod Art, New York; Brooklyn Mus, NY; Art Inst Chicago; Carnegie Mus, Pa; Whitney Mus Am Art. *Exhib:* 19th, 20th & 22nd Print Biennial, Brooklyn Mus, 74, 76 & 80; Dulin Nat Print & Drawing Competition, 75 & 79; Biennial Americana De Artes Graficas, Cali, Columbia, 81; Biennial Int, Ljubliana, Yugoslavia, 81; and others. *Collections Arranged:* New American Graphics, US Info Agency, 83. *Pos:* Co-dir, Mantegna Press, Hollandale, Wis; bd trustees, Elvehjem Mus Art, Madison, Wis. *Teaching:* Prof art, Univ Wis-Madison, 49-78, Leo Steppat prof art, 79-, dir, intaglio printmaking prog. *Awards:* Guggenheim Fel, 65; Ed Award, Soc Am Graphic Artists, 77; Nat Endowment for the Arts Artists Fel, 79 & 83-84. *Bibliog:* Warrington Colescott: Between tragedy and comedy, Am Artists, 5/78; Warrington Colescott's history of printmaking, Madison Art Ctr, 79; Mathias Mende (auth), Durer A-Z, Verlag H Carl, Nurnberg, 80. *Mem:* Soc Am Graphic Artists; Philadelphia Print Club; Am Colorprint Soc. *Publ:* Illusr, Death in Venice, Aquarlus Press, 71; illusr (covers), 30 Years of Printmaking, Brooklyn Mus, 76 & Art News Mag, 3/77. *Dealer:* Assoc Am Artists 663 Fifth Ave New York NY 10022; Perimeter Gallery 356 W Huron Chicago IL 60610. *Mailing Add:* Rte 1 Hollandale WI 53544

COLIN, GEORGIA T
COLLECTOR, DESIGNER
b Boston, Mass. *Study:* Smith Col; Univ Grenoble, Sorbonne, Paris, France; Ecole de Louvre. *Pos:* Pres, Talmey Inc, 54- *Mem:* Am Soc Interior Designers; Smith Col Mus Art (vis comt 51-70). *Collection:* With husband, Ralph F Colin, have for forty years collected paintings, sculpture, drawings and graphics mainly School of Paris 1890-1970. *Mailing Add:* 941 Park Ave New York NY 10028

COLIN, RALPH FREDERICK
COLLECTOR
b New York, NY, Nov 18, 1900. *Study:* City Col New York, BA, 19; Columbia Univ Law Sch, LLB, 21. *Pos:* Dir & gen counsel, Parke-Bernet Galleries, Inc, 59-64; founder, admin vpres & gen counsel, Art Dealers Asn Am, 62- *Mem:* Mus Mod Art, New York (trustee, 54-69, vpres 60-69, vpres & dir, Int Coun, 56-69); Fogg Art Mus; Am Fedn Arts (trustee, 45-56); Adv Comt on Arts Ctr Prog, Columbia Univ. *Collection:* Paintings, sculpture, drawings and graphics concentrated on School of Paris 1890-1970. *Mailing Add:* 941 Park Ave New York NY 10028

COLINA, ARMANDO G
DEALER
b Veracruz, Mex, Mar 30, 35. *Study:* Univ Mex, BA. *Collections Arranged:* Carlos Merida: Graphic Works, Mus de Monterrey, Nuevo Leon, Mex & traveling to New York, Washington, DC, San Francisco, Coral Gables, Fla, San Antonio, Tex & Puerto Rico; Gunther Gerszo: A Retrospective, Mus de Monterrey, Mex; Frost (Palle Seiersen): Metamorfosis, Mus de Monterrey, Mex; A Panorama of Mexican Art, Ctr Cult Vanguardia, Saltillo, Coahuila, Mex; Ocejo (Jose Garcia): Cariatides, Ctr Cult Vanguardia, Saltillo, Coahuila, Mex; Raul Anguiano: Recent Graphics, Oils & Tapestries, Ctr Cult Vanguardia, Saltillo, Coahuila, Mex. *Pos:* Rep, Contemp Mus Bogota, Colombia; art consult, currently; owner, Arvil Art Gallery, currently. *Specialty:* Contemporary art. *Publ:* Illusr, Toledo/Sahagun, 74; illusr, Toledo/ Chilam Balam, 75; Merida/Un Canto al Libro Sagrado, 78; illusr, Merida/ Cielos Luminicos, 79; Vlady-Rebolledo, 79. *Mailing Add:* c/o Galeria Arvil SA Cerrada de Hamburgo No 9 Mexico 6 DF Mexico

COLKER, EDWARD
PAINTER, GRAPHIC ARTIST
b Philadelphia, Pa, Jan 5, 27. *Study:* Philadelphia Col Art, grad; NY Univ, grad; spec study with E & J Desjobert, Paris. *Work:* Mus Art, Philadelphia; NJ State Mus, Trenton; New York Pub Libr Print Collection; Mus Mod Art, New York; New York Univ; and others. *Comn:* Lithography ed, Print Club, Philadelphia, 66, Int Graphic Art Soc, New York, 66 & 69 & Ill Arts Coun, 73. *Exhib:* One-man show, Kenyon Gallery, Chicago, 75; Stampe di due Mondi, Rome & Philadelphia Mus Art, 67; American Art Today, Pa Acad Fine Arts, Philadelphia, 68; Nat Collection Fine Arts, Washington, DC, 77; Words and Images, Pennsylvania, 81; Works on Paper, Yugoslavia, 82. *Collections Arranged:* Spec exhibs, Symbol & Vision, Calif Painters & Sculptors, 70, Depth & Presence, Environmental Sculpture, Corcoran Gallery Art, Washington, DC, 71. *Pos:* consult, Works on Paper, US Int Commun Agency, 82. *Teaching:* Assoc prof fine arts, Univ Pa Grad Sch Fine Arts, 68-70; prof & dir, Sch Art & Design, Univ Ill, Chicago Circle, 72-78, res prof art, 77-80; dean, visual arts, State Univ NY, Purchase, 80- *Awards:* Univ Ill Res Bd, 77; Graham Found, 77; Ill Arts Coun, 80. *Bibliog:* Zigrosser (auth), The Appeal of Prints (appreciation), 70. *Mem:* Col Art Asn Am; Caxton Club; Ctr for Book Arts. *Publ:* Contribr, Pablo Neruda (lithos), 77; contribr, The Fall (lithos), 77; contribr, From South Dakota (lithos), 78; contribr, Aesthetique du Rale (lithos), 78. *Mailing Add:* Visual Arts Div State Univ NY Col Purchase NY 10577

COLLAZO, CARLOS ERICK
PAINTER, GRAPHIC ARTIST
b Ponce, PR, June 28, 56. *Study:* Auburn Univ, Ala, 73-75; San Juan Art Students League, 75-77. *Work:* Mus Ft Lauderdale; Univ PR Art Mus, Inst PR Cult, San Juan; Ponce Mus Art. *Exhib:* Unesco Salons, Univ PR Mus, San Juan, 83; PR Atheneum Art Show, San Juan, 83; Gulf Exhib Young Artists, Inst PR Cult, San Juan, 83; Contemporary Art From Puerto Rico, Chase Manhattan Bank Hall, Hato Rey, 83. *Pos:* Exhib coordr, Inst PR Cult, 77-79. *Teaching:* Prof painting, San Juan Art Students League, 79-; prof drawing, Casa Candina, 81. *Awards:* First prize, Unesco Salon, 83 & PR Atheneum Art Show, 83; Second Prize, Gulf Exhib Young Artists, 83. *Bibliog:* Marimar Benitez (auth), El mundo irreal de Carlos Collazo, Nuevo Dia, 82; Myrna Rodriguez (auth), Carlos Collazo's lonely rooms, San Juan Star, 82; Samuel Cherson (auth), Bodegones teatrales, Nuevo Dia, 83. *Mem:* San Juan Art Students League (vpres, 76-77). *Media:* Oil, Ceramics. *Dealer:* Sharon Moya Cristo St # 207 Old San Juan PR 00901. *Mailing Add:* 2105 Torre Del Mar Condado PR 00907

COLLETT, FARRELL REUBEN
PAINTER, EDUCATOR
b Bennington, Idaho, Nov 13, 07. *Study:* Brigham Young Univ, BA & MA; Sch Fine Arts, San Francisco; Art Inst Chicago; Am Acad Art, Chicago; Art Ctr Col Design, Los Angeles; Art Students League; and with Paul Bransom. *Work:* Springville Mus Art, Utah; Brigham Young Univ; Grand Central Art Galleries, New York; Univ Calgary. *Comn:* Portrait of Pres, Weber State Col, 59; Wildlife-Cougars, Brigham Young Univ, 70; Ft Buenaventura (mural), Walker Bank, Ogden, Utah, 72; Wildlife, Va Bankshares, Richmond, 73; Wildlife-Bison, Franklin Mint, Pa, 73. *Exhib:* Utah State Inst Fine Arts Ann, 68-; Wildlife 71, Minneapolis, 71-72; Am Natural Hist Art Show, Univ Minn, Minneapolis, 71; Soc Animal Artists Ann, New York, 72; Dismal Swamp Art Exhib, Richmond, Va, 73. *Pos:* Chmn, Utah State Inst Fine Arts, 63-65. *Teaching:* Prof art, Weber State Col, 39-, chmn dept, 39-69; guest prof painting, Brigham Young Univ, summer 53; guest prof art hist & painting, Univ Calgary, summers 66 & 67. *Awards:* Best of Show for White Horse, Nat Invitational, Springville Mus Art, Utah, 63; Best of Show for Girl in the Black Hood, Ogden Outdoor & Sweepstakes Award, Prize-winning Paintings Only Exhib, Salt Lake City, 65; DH, Weber State Col, Ogden, Utah, 77. *Bibliog:* George S Dibble (auth), Collett's horses are exciting, Salt Lake Trib, 11/24/74; Donald Jardine (auth), Most unforgettable lecture, Illustrator; George Harrison (auth), Painting a bright future for Dismal Swamp, Nat Wildlife, 10-11/74. *Mem:* Soc Animal Artists; Salmagundi Club; Ogden Palette Club; Assoc Utah Artists; Utah Watercolor Soc. *Media:* Oil, Watercolor. *Publ:* Illusr, Pit Pony, Knopf, 46; illusr, Conserv Series Filmstrips, Chicago, 54; illusr, Annual report, Pepsi-Cola Co, 56; illusr, Calendar posters, Browning Ann, 59; auth, Felt tip diary, Illustrator, fall 69. *Dealer:* Grand Central Art Galleries 40 Vanderbilt Ave New York NY 10017. *Mailing Add:* 876 Ben Lomond Ogden UT 84403

COLLIER, ALAN CASWELL
PAINTER
b Toronto, Ont, Mar 19, 11. *Study:* Ont Col Art; Art Students League, with Howard Trafton. *Work:* Nat Gallery Can, Ottawa, Ont; Art Gallery Ont, Toronto; Art Mus London, Ont; Hamilton Art Gallery, Ont; Frye Mus, Seattle. *Comn:* Murals, Ryerson Polytech Inst, Toronto, 58 & 62, Bank Can, Toronto Agency, 59 & Ont Govt Bldg, Queen's Park, Toronto, 68; many portraits for educ & bus orgns. *Exhib:* 1st & 4th Biennial Can Art, Nat Gallery Can, 55 & 61 & Dept Can External Affairs, 57; Faces of Canada, Stratford, Ont, 64; Canadian Artists '68, Art Gallery Ont, 68. *Mem:* Ont Soc Artists (pres, 58-61); Royal Can Acad Art (hon treas, 65-72). *Media:* Oil. *Dealer:* Roberts Gallery 641 Yonge St Toronto ON Can; Kensington Gallery 006 513 8th Ave SW Calgary Alta Can. *Mailing Add:* 115 Brooke Ave Toronto ON M5M 2K3 Canada

COLLIER, ALBERTA
CRITIC, CONSULTANT
b Vicksburg, Miss, Oct 25, 11. *Study:* Newcomb Art Sch, 34-35; Arts & Crafts Club Sch, New Orleans, 36-37. *Pos:* Art critic, Times-Picayune, 46-76; consult, Hist New Orleans Collection, 77-82; retired. *Publ:* Auth, chap on art scene, The Past as Prelude-New Orleans 1718-1968, 68; auth introd, Boyd Cruise, Hist New Orleans Collection, 76. *Mailing Add:* c/o John M Collier 4436 Perrier New Orleans LA 70115

COLLIER, (ALAN) GRAHAM
WRITER, PAINTER
b Manchester, Eng, Sept 12, 23; US citizen. *Study:* Slade Sch Fine Art, Univ London, with Randolph Schwabe, dipl(painting). *Work:* Walker Art Gallery, Liverpool, Eng; Usher Art Gallery, Lincoln, Eng; Volunteer Park Art Mus, Seattle. *Comn:* Sir John Barbirolli (portrait), Halle Concerts Soc, Manchester, Eng, 50; Sir Reginald Thatcher (portrait), Royal Acad Music, London, 52; Hugo Rignold (portrait), Liverpool Philharmonic Soc, 53. *Exhib:* One-man shows, Piccadilly Galleries, London, 56; Leicester Galleries, London, 57; Vancouver City Art Gallery, BC, 61. *Teaching:* Dir art, Lancing Col, Sussex, Eng, 54-60; assoc prof art, Univ Conn, Storrs, 63-68; prof art, Univ Ga, Athens, 69- *Awards:* National Registered Designer, Royal Register of Designers, London, 52; Best Produced Book of Year, Am Typographical Award, New York, 68. *Bibliog:* Art of Graham Collier (radio prog), Can Broadcasting Co, 62. *Res:* Immediate interest in the psychological bases of inspiration and image-making; the teleology of art and the issues of sense and mind. *Publ:* Auth, Form, Space & Vision, 3rd ed, 71 & auth, Art and the Creative Consciousness, 72, Prentice-Hall. *Mailing Add:* Dept of Art Univ of Ga Athens GA 30601

COLLIER, JAMES MITCHELL
HISTORIAN, PAINTER
b Bellingham, Wash, Oct 31, 43. *Study:* Pacific Lutheran Univ, BA(hist), 65; Univ Ore, MA(art hist), 70; Univ Mich, PhD(art hist), 75. *Teaching:* Instr, Univ Mo, Kans City, 70-71; instr, Univ Mich, 73; assoc prof art hist, Auburn Univ, 75-; dir, Rome, Italy art hist, Auburn Univ, 79-82. *Mem:* Col Art Asn Am; Southeast Col Art Asn. *Media:* Oil. *Res:* Northern painting of the 15th century and Italian renaissance art (especially perspective). *Publ:* Illusr, The Kansas City Petrus Christus: Its Importance and Dating, Nelson Gallery & Atkins Mus Bulletin, 78; Brunelleschi's Baptistry Demonstration Recreated, SECAC Review, 81. *Mailing Add:* Rt 2 Box 174 Auburn AL 36830

COLLINGS, BETTY
SCULPTOR, WRITER
b Wanganui, NZ, Jan 15, 34. *Study:* Ohio State Univ, BFA, 71, MFA, 74. *Exhib:* Solo shows, Urdang Gallery, 79, 81 & 82, Antioch Univ, 82 & Grad Ctr, City Univ New York, 83; Generative Systems, Wright State Univ, 79; Triple Helix, Ohio Univ, Lancaster, 83. *Collections Arranged:* Contemporary Collection of Ohio State University, 75-80. *Pos:* Dir, Ohio State Univ Gallery Fine Arts, 74-80, ed, Acquisitions, 76-78; consult, Oberlin Col, 81-82; invited cur, Wright State Univ, 81-, Va Commonwealth Univ, 82 & Bard Col, 82. *Awards:* Sculpture Fel, 81-82 & Criticism Fel, 83-84, Ohio Arts Coun. *Bibliog:* Madeline Burnside (auth), Betty Collings, Arts Mag, 9/79; William Olander (auth), article, Dialogue, 9/82; Fred Kalister (auth), article, Dialogue, 9/83. *Mem:* Columbus Art League; Col Art Asn; Int Asn Art Critics; NZ-US Arts Found (mem bd trustees, currently). *Publ:* Auth, Judy Pfaff, Art Mag, 11/80; auth, George Woodman, Art Mag, 81; auth, John Davies, Art Mag, 9/81; auth, 13 articles on Ohio artists, Dialogue, 82-; auth, Judy Rifka, Art Mag, 4/83. *Mailing Add:* 1991 Hillside Dr Columbus OH 43221

COLLINS, CHRISTIANE C
HISTORIAN, LIBRARIAN
Study: Carleton Col, BA; Columbia Univ, MA & MLS. *Pos:* Cataloguing librn, Mus Mod Art, New York, 71-72; head librn, Parsons Sch Design, Adam L Gimbel Libr, New York, 73- *Awards:* Fulbright Teaching/Research Fel, Sch Archit City Planning, Technische Univ, Graz, Austria, 80-81. *Mem:* Art Libr Soc NAm; Soc Archit Historians; Col Art Asn. *Res:* City planning; late 19th century, contemporary, German expressionist architecture; 20th century design. *Publ:* Ed & coauth, Architecture of Fantasy, Praeger, 62; translr, Camillo Sitte's City Planning According to Artistic Principles, 65 & coauth, Camillo Sitte & the Birth of Modern City Planning, 65, Random House/Phaidon. *Mailing Add:* 448 Riverside Dr # 11-1 New York NY 10027

COLLINS, GEORGE R
HISTORIAN, EDUCATOR
b Springfield, Mass, Sept 2, 17. *Study:* Princeton Univ, BA, 39, MFA, 42; Univ Barcelona, Dr Hon Causa, 77. *Pos:* Chmn, Urban Studies Program, Columbia Col, 80- *Teaching:* From instr to prof art hist, Columbia Univ, 46-, Mathews lectr, fall 79. *Awards:* Guggenheim Fel, 62-63; Rockefeller Humanities Fel, 76-77. *Res:* Modern architecture and city planning; Spanish art and architecture. *Publ:* Coauth, Architecture of fantasy (transl & rev, Phantastische Architektur), 62; coauth, Camillo Sitte..., Random House & Phaidon, Eng, Vols I & II, 65; auth, The Drawings of Antonio Gaudi, 77; auth, Visionary Drawings of Architecture and Planning, 79; coauth, Fantastic Architecture, Abrams, 80. *Mailing Add:* 448 Riverside Dr New York NY 10027

COLLINS, HOWARD F
HISTORIAN
b Buffalo, NY, Oct 28, 22. *Study:* Albright Art Sch, Buffalo, with Charles Burchfield, Ralston Crawford & Isaac Soyer, dipl, 43; State Univ NY Col, Buffalo, BS, 47; Columbia Univ, MA, 54; Univ Pittsburgh, with William S Heckscher & Charles Seymour Jr, PhD, 70. *Teaching:* Assoc prof art hist, Kutztown State Col, 60-65; from assoc prof to prof, WVa Univ, 65-72, chmn div art, 69-71; prof, Univ Nebr, Lincoln, 72- *Mem:* Col Art Asn Am; Mid-Am Col Art Asn (treas, 76); Renaissance Soc Am; assoc Int Inst Conservation; Asn Historians Am Art. *Res:* Fifteenth century Venetian painting. *Publ:* Auth, Decor, function and contour in early Chinese bronzes, Oriental Art, summer 66; auth, Major narrative paintings by Jacopo Bellini, Art Bulletin, 9/82; auth, The Cyclopean Vision of Jacopo Bellini, Pantheon, 82; auth, Time, space and Gentile Bellini's Miracle of the Cross at Ponte S Lorenzo, Gazette Beaux Arts, 12/82. *Mailing Add:* Art Dept Univ Nebr Lincoln NE 68588

COLLINS, J(OSEPH) B
PAINTER, PHOTOGRAPHER
b Buffalo, NY, Feb 10, 33. *Study:* Fordham Col, AB, 55; Fordham Univ Sch Social Serv, MSSS, 60; Art Students League, with Robert Beverly Hale & Gustav Rehberger, 82-83. *Exhib:* Nat Soc Painters Casein & Acrylic Ann Exhib, 78, 81 & 82; Knickerbocker Artists Ann Exhib, 80; solo exhib, Barbados Mus, St Michael, 81; Audubon Artists Ann Exhib, 81; Salmagundi Club Non-Mem Exhib, 82; Gracie Sq Outdoor Art Show, New York, 82-83. *Awards:* First Prize, Village Art Show, Rockville Centre, NY, 78; New York Am Legion Award, Wash Sq Outdoor Art Show, 80. *Mem:* Composers, Authors & Artists Am; assoc mem Nat Soc Painters Casein & Acrylic; assoc mem Audubon Artists. *Media:* Acrylic. *Mailing Add:* 10 Park Ave #20L New York NY 10016

COLLINS, JESS See Jess

COLLINS, JIM
EDUCATOR, SCULPTOR
b Huntington, WVa, Sept 12, 34. *Study:* Marshall Univ, AB, 57; Univ Mich, Ann Arbor, MPH, 61; Ohio Univ, MFA, 66. *Work:* Wichita Art Asn, Kans; Univ SC, Columbia; Huntington Galleries, WVa; Am Repub Ins Co, Des Moines, Iowa; Milwaukee Art Ctr, Wis. *Comn:* Outdoor sculpture, St Augustine Church, Signal Mountain, Tenn, 70 & Arlen Realty, Chattanooga, 71; wall-relief, B'nai Zion Synagogue, Chattanooga, 75; series of five wall reliefs, St Jude Catholic Church, Chattanooga, 78. *Exhib:* Sixteenth Ann Delta Art Exhib, Ark Arts Ctr, Little Rock, 73; 8 State Ann: Painting, J B Speed Art Mus, Louisville; Mid-South Biennial Appalachian State Univ, Boone, NC, 75; Exhib: 21st Ann Drawing & Small Sculpture Show, Ball State Univ, Muncie, Ind, 75; Southern Asn Sculptors Traveling Exhib; Dixie Ann, Montgomery Mus Fine Arts, Ala, 75 & 76; Hunter Mus Art, Chattanooga, 78; Invitational, Miss Mus Art, Jackson, 78; and others. *Teaching:* Prof art, Univ Tenn, Chattanooga, 66- *Awards:* Tenn Drawings, 74 & Tenn Bicentennial Art Exhib, 76, Tenn Arts Comn; Best of Show, Chiaha Nat, Rome, Ga, 78. *Mem:* Southern Asn Sculptors (pres, 70-71). *Media:* Wood, Metals. *Publ:* Auth introd, A Handbook to British Landscape Painters, 70; auth, Women Artists in America, 18th Century to the Present, 75; auth, Women Artists in American II, 76. *Mailing Add:* 109 Louisiana Ave Signal Mountain TN 37377

COLLINS, JOHN IRELAND
PAINTER
b Atlantic City, NJ, Dec 31, 26. *Study:* Corcoran Sch Art, Washington, DC, grad; also with Karl Knaths, Provincetown, Mass. *Exhib:* Int Watercolor Show, Brooklyn Mus, NY, 66; one-man show, Farnsworth Mus, Rockland, Maine, 67; 20th Exhib of New England Artists, Silvermine Guild Artists, New Canaan, Conn, 69; Landscape I, 135 Watercolors by 45 New England Artists, De Cordova Mus, Lincoln, Mass, 70 & Landscape II, 90 Oils by 45 New England Artists, 71. *Awards:* Emily Lowe Award, 53; Thomas E Saxe Jr Award, Silvermine Guild Artists, 69; Guggenheim Mem Grant, 72. *Bibliog:* Lawrence Kent (auth), John Ireland Collins, artist in residence, Maine Digest, 66; Leo Chabot (auth), Nature artist at work, Bangor Daily News, 67; Jim Moore (auth), Cushing, mecca for art, awards, Portland Press Herald, 72. *Dealer:* Capricorn Galleries Bethesda MD; Joan Peterson Gallery 561 Boylston St. *Mailing Add:* Pleasant Point Cushing ME 04563

COLLINS, LOWELL DAUNT
PAINTER, DEALER
b San Antonio, Tex, Aug 12, 24. *Study:* Colorado Springs Fine Art Ctr, with B Robinson; Mus Fine Arts, Houston; Art Students League; Acad Grande Chaumiere, Paris; Univ Houston, BFA & ML. *Work:* Mus Fine Arts, Houston; Mus Fine Arts, Dallas; US Info Agency. *Comn:* Painting for Nelson Found. *Exhib:* Provincetown Arts Festival; New York World's Fair; Hemisfair, San Antonio; Columbia Biennial, SC; NZ Exchange Exhib; plus many others. *Pos:* Art ed, Tex Cancer Bull, 47-49; cur pre-Columbian art, Mus Nat Sci, Houston, 70-; dir, Lowell Collins Gallery, 70-; lectr, Int Conf Pre-Columbian Art, Archaeol Soc Am, St Louis Univ, 77 & Chicago, 79. *Teaching:* Instr art & archit, Univ Houston, 51-58; dean art dept, Mus Fine Arts, Houston, 58-66; dir art sch, Lowell Collins Gallery, 66- *Awards:* First Prize, Tex Fine Arts Asn, 49; Second Prize, D D Feldman Art Exhib, 56; First Prize & Purchase Award, Motorola Corp, 60. *Mem:* Sr mem Houston Philos Soc; sr mem Am Soc Appraisers & Int Soc Appraisers; hon mem Hanzen Col, Rice Univ; Archaeol Soc Am; Valuation Consortium. *Media:* Oil. *Specialty:* Pre-Columbian art; African art; Oriental art; contemporary paintings and sculpture. *Publ:* Illusr, Houston, Land of Big Rich, 51; illusr, Houston, The Feast Years, 61; illusr, The Galveston Era, 65; illusr, Unhappy Medium, 68. *Mailing Add:* 2903 Saint St Houston TX 77027

COLLINS, PAUL
PAINTER
b Muskegon, Mich, Dec 11, 36. *Study:* Self-taught. *Work:* Gerald R Ford Mus, Grand Rapids, Mich; Martin Luther King Jr Ctr Nonviolent Social Change, Atlanta, Ga; Joseph P Kennedy Found, Washington, DC; Puskin Mus, Moscow, USSR; Palace de la Presidence du Senegal, Dakar Senegal, Africa. *Comn:* Portrait of the pres of Senegal, US Embassy, 72; portrait of an African journey, Eerdmens Publ Co, Grand Rapids, Mich, 73; Black Struggle, Grand Rapids Pub Mus, 73; Portrait of Dr Martin Luther King, Dr Martin Luther King Ctr, Montgomery, Ala, 74; Life of the President of US, Kent Co Airport, 75; and many others. *Exhib:* American Artist, Butler Inst Art, Youngstown, Ohio, 71; Am Heritage Exhib, Corcoran Gallery, Washington, DC, 73; John F Kennedy Ctr Performing Arts, Washington, DC; Parthenon Mus, Nashville, Tenn; Mus Sci & Industry, Los Angeles; Children's Mus, Indianapolis, Ind; Avery Fisher Hall, Lincoln Ctr, New York; and many others. *Awards:* Spec Art Award, Stax Rec Co, 74; Award, Accademia della Arti e dell Lavoro, Italy, 80; and others. *Bibliog:* Bicentennial projects, Newsweek Mag, 75; Paul Collins painter of people, Am Artist, 75; and others. *Media:* Dry Oil, Own Media. *Publ:* Auth, Show down at Wounded Knee, Ebony Mag, 73; Twenty Figure Paintings and How They Work, Watson-Guptill, 79; and others. *Dealer:* Hefner's Art Gallery 1440 Wealthy St SE Grand Rapids MI 49503. *Mailing Add:* 709 Logan St SE Grand Rapids MI 49506

COLLINS, WILLIAM CHARLES
PAINTER, ADMINISTRATOR
b Cambridge, Mass, Jan 18, 25. *Study:* RI Sch Design, BFA; Univ Ill, Urbana, MFA; Akad Bildende Kunste, Munich; Portland Sch Art, LLD. *Work:* Wash Univ, St Louis; Cincinnati Art Mus; Univ Ill, Urbana. *Comn:* Mural, St John's Unitarian Church, 62; paintings, Hunter Savings & Loan, 66, Bethesda Hosp,

71, O K Transfer Corp, 72 & Stone Corp, Cincinnati, Ohio. *Exhib:* Dayton Art Inst, 63, 65 & 71; American Art, Whitney Mus Am Art, New York, 64; American Landscape, Fort Worth Art Ctr, Tex, 65; Mid-Am Exhibs, Butler Inst Am Art, Youngstown, Ohio; Portland Mus Art, Maine, 73-75. *Teaching:* Instr drawing, Albright Art Sch, Buffalo, 51-54; instr drawing & painting, Art Acad Cincinnati, 54-67; vis prof drawing & painting, Wash Univ, 67-72; dir, Portland Sch Art, Maine. *Awards:* Morton D May Purchase Prize, City Art Mus, St Louis, 57; Fulbright Fel, Ger, 57-58; Painting Prize, Interior Valley Exhib, Contemp Art Ctr, Cincinnati, 61. *Media:* Acrylic, Oil. *Dealer:* Carl Solway Gallery 204 W Fourth St Cincinnati OH 45202. *Mailing Add:* Portland Sch Art 97 Spring St Portland ME 04101

COLLYER, ROBIN
SCULPTOR, VIDEO ARTIST
b London, Eng, Mar 7, 49; Can citizen. *Study:* Ont Col Art, Toronto, 67-68. *Work:* Nat Gallery Can & Can Coun Art Bank, Ottawa. *Exhib:* Carmen Lamanna Gallery, Toronto, Ont, 71, 72, 74, 76, 78, 79, 81 & 83, Mt Allison Univ, 76 & Etherington Art Ctr, 82; Nat Gallery Can, Ottawa, 73; Kunsthalle Basel, Switzerland, 78; Seven Toronto Artists, Artists' Space, New York, 80; and others. *Teaching:* Instr, Ont Col Art, Toronto, 75; NS Col Art, Halifax, 77. *Awards:* Can Coun Grants, 69-71, 73, 74 & 76-69; Can Coun Senior Arts Grant, 80. *Bibliog:* David Burett & Marilyn Schiff (auths), Contemporary Candian Art, Hurtig Publ, Edmonton, 83. *Mem:* Can Coun Adv Art Panel; Trinity Square Video (bd dirs, 79-82). *Media:* Mixed Media; Photography, Video. *Publ:* Contribr, Impulse, summer 80; co-prod & co-dir, The Girl Can't Fly It (film), A Space & Broadcast Serv, Toronto, 80; co-prod & co-dir, Darn These Hands (film), A Space & Rogers Cable TV, Toronto, 80; co-prod, Sculpture of Here and Now (film), Toronto. *Mailing Add:* Carmen Lamanna Gallery 840 Yonge St Toronto ON M4W 2H1 Canada

COLMAN, VIRGINIA O'CONNELL
SCULPTOR, DESIGNER
b Manhasset, Long Island, NY. *Study:* Columbia Univ, BS(art), 47; Teachers Col, Columbia Univ, MA(art), 68; sculpture with Minoru Niizuma; watercolor with Edgar A Whitney & George Post. *Exhib:* Painters & Sculptors Soc NJ, Jersey City Mus, 69, 72, 73 & 74; Nat Acad Galleries, New York, 74-75, & 79; Silvermine Guild Artists, New Canaan, Conn, 75; Newark Mus, NJ, 77 & 79; solo exhib, Bergen Community Mus, Paramus, NJ, 78; Morris Mus Arts & Sci, Morristown, NJ, 83; and others. *Pos:* Art ed & staff artist, Collier's Encycl, 49-52; art dir, Girl Scouts USA, New York, 52-56; promotion art dir, MacFadden Publ, New York, 56. *Teaching:* Teacher stone carving, Sculpture Ctr, New York, summer 80. *Awards:* Ellin A Ross Mem Prize, NJ Painters & Sculptors, 69, 72 & 73; Silver Medal, Audubon Artists Ann, 79. *Mem:* Catharine Lorillard Wolfe Art Club; Sculptors Asn NJ (corresp secy, 74-76); Stone Sculpture Soc NY (corresp secy, 78-80, treas, 80-). *Media:* Marble, Limestone. *Mailing Add:* 105 Leonia Ave Leonia NJ 07605

COLOMBINI, SUSAN MURPHY See Murphy, Susan

COLOMBO, CHARLES
PAINTER
b Wilmington, Del, Nov 3, 27. *Study:* Pa Acad Fine Arts, Philadelphia; Art Students League with Charles DeFeo; privately with Frank E Schoonover. *Work:* Pvt collections throughout US & abroad including The Vatican, Rome, Italy, Prince Ranier, Monaco, former Vpres & Mrs Walter Mondale & Senator Joseph R Biden, Jr. *Comn:* Hagley Powder Mills, comn by State of Del for Pres J F Kennedy, 62. *Exhib:* Am Watercolor Soc, 66-81; Nat Arts Club, New York, 66-75; Charles & Emma Frye Mus, Seattle, 75; Colonnade Des Artes Gallery; Lake Buena Vista, Disneyworld, Fla. *Awards:* Watercolor Award, Pa Acad Fine Arts, 49; Scholar Award, Pa Acad Fine Arts; Watercolor Award, Del Art Mus, Wilmington, 56. *Bibliog:* Frederick Kramer (auth), Brandywine Tradition Artists, Great Am Ed, New York, 71; Nancy Mohr (auth), Charles Colombo, a part of the Brandywine tradition, Delaware Today, Wilmington, 71; article, Art News, 5/83. *Mem:* Am Watercolor Soc; Delaware Art Mus; Rehoboth Art League. *Dealer:* Parkway Gallery Wilmington DE; Maxwell Gallery San Francisco CA. *Mailing Add:* 101 E 13th St Wilmington DE 19801

COLORADO, CHARLOTTE (RUTH SATURNESKY)
PAINTER
b Denver, Colo, Jan 18, 20. *Study:* Colo Woman's Col; Otis Art Inst; Jepson Art Inst; Chouinard Art Inst. *Comn:* Auth & dir, three theatre pieces (with Alex Haye's Los Angeles Summer Theatre Piece Lab), 67; spec proj, Covina Parks & Rec, 71-72. *Exhib:* Pa Acad Fine Arts; Fine Arts Gallery San Diego; Long Beach Art Mus; Jewish Community Ctr; Signs of Neon Traveling Exhib, Mod Art Gallery, Washington, DC, 69-71; and others. *Pos:* Founder, Changes (theatre co), 67; dir, The Ensemble Group (exp art theatre), Los Angeles, currently. *Awards:* Prizes, Los Angeles Mus Art, 60; Westside Jewish Community Ctr, Los Angeles, 63 & First Methodist Church, Santa Monica, 63. *Mailing Add:* 120 Westminster Apt 6 Venice CA 90291

COLSON, CHESTER E
PAINTER, EDUCATOR
b Boston, Mass, June 17, 17. *Study:* Mass Sch Art, BS, 46; Teachers Col, Columbia Univ, MA, 49, with Edwin Ziegfeld; also pvt study. *Work:* Everhart Mus, Scranton, Pa; Wilkes Col, Wilkes-Barre, Pa; Norwich Univ, Northfield, Vt. *Exhib:* One-man show, Everhart Mus, 69; Fleming Mus, Burlington, Vt, 69; Norwich Armory Show, Northfield, Vt, 72; Wilkes Col, Wilkes-Barr, Pa, 80; Warehouse Art Gallery, Pittston, Pa, 81. *Teaching:* Chmn dept fine arts,

Wilkes Col, 59-72, prof emer, retired. *Awards:* Sordoni Prize, 62; Purchase Prizes, Everhart Mus, 68 & Vt Artists, Norwich Univ, 69; plus others. *Mem:* Nat Soc Painters in Casein & Acrylic; Philadelphia Watercolor Soc. *Dealer:* Nancy Messinger Main St Gallery Kingston PA 18704; Gallery of Arts 381 N Main St Pittston PA. *Mailing Add:* 122 Frangorma Dr Trucksville PA 18708

COLT, JOHN NICHOLSON
PAINTER, EDUCATOR
b Madison, Wis, May 15, 25. *Study:* Univ Wis, BS & MS. *Work:* Whitney Mus Am Art; Milwaukee Art Ctr; Munson-Williams-Proctor Mus, Utica, NY; Le Centre d'Art, Port au Prince, Haiti; Beloit Col, Wright Art Ctr, Wis. *Comn:* Murals, Marquette Univ, 59 & First Wis Ctr, 73. *Exhib:* Butler Inst Am Art Exhib Am Painting, Youngstown, Ohio, 55; Whitney Ann Exhib Am Painting, Whitney Mus Am Art, New York, 60; one-man shows, Milwaukee Art Ctr, Wis, 62 & 69, Minneapolis Inst of Art, 70, Bradley Gallery, Milwaukee, 73, 75, 77, 79, 81 & 83, Neil Gallery, New York, 77 & 79-81, Cincinnati Acad Art, 81 & Perimeter Gallery, Chicago, 83; Chicago Vicinity, Art Inst Chicago, 62 & 64; Walker Biennial, Walker Art Ctr, Minneapolis, 62, 64 & 66; Art Across America, Knodler Gallery, New York, 68. *Teaching:* Prof painting, Univ Wis-Milwaukee, 58- *Awards:* Medal of Honor, Milwaukee Art Ctr; Ford Found Award & Top Award, Walker Art Ctr. *Media:* Oil, Acrylic, Pastel. *Dealer:* Perimeter Gallery 356 W Huron St Chicago IL 60610. *Mailing Add:* 823 N 2nd St Apt 807 Milwaukee WI 53203

COLTON, JUDITH
EDUCATOR, HISTORIAN
b New York, NY, Mar 21, 43. *Study:* Smith Col, Northampton, Mass, BA, 63; Inst Fine Arts, New York Univ, MA, 65, PhD, 74. *Teaching:* Teacher art hist, Bennington Col, 71-72; instr art hist, Queens Col, City Univ New York, 72-73; asst prof art hist, Yale Univ, 73-78, assoc prof, 78- *Awards:* James L Clifford Prize, Am Soc 18th Century Studies, 78; Ingram Merrill Found, 79-80; Fel, Am Coun Learned Socs, 82-83. *Mem:* Col Art Asn Am; Am Soc 18th Century Studies; Garden Hist Soc. *Res:* 17th and 18th century art in Italy, France and England; concentrating on the history of sculpture and garden design. *Publ:* Contribr, Architectura, 74; contribr, Eighteenth-Century Studies, 76; auth, The Parnasse Francois: Titon du Tillet and the Origins of the Monument to Genius, Yale Univ Press, 79; contribr, Art the Ape of Nature: Studies in Honor of H W Janson, 81; contribr, Studies on Voltaire and The Eighteenth century, 80. *Mailing Add:* Dept Hist Art Yale Univ New Haven CT 06520

COLVILLE, ALEXANDER
PAINTER, PRINTMAKER
b Toronto, Ont, Aug 24, 20. *Study:* Mt Allison Univ, with Stanley Royle, BFA. *Work:* Nat Gallery Can; Mus Mod Art, New York; Wallraf-Richarts Mus, Cologne, Ger; Ctr Nat Art Contemporain, Paris; Boymans-Van Beuningen Mus, Rotterdam. *Exhib:* Gemeentmuseum Arnhem, Kunsthalle, Dusseldorf; Fischer Fine Art, London, 77; Art Gallery Ont, Toronto; Staatliche Kunsthalle, Berlin; Ludwig Mus, Cologne, 83. *Mailing Add:* PO Box 550 Wolfville NS B0P 1X0 Canada

COLWAY, JAMES R
PAINTER
b Oneida, NY, Nov 12, 20. *Study:* Syracuse Univ Sch Art, 45-48, Univ Col, 46-48. *Work:* US Embassy Prog, Washington, DC; Butler Inst Am Art, Youngstown, Ohio; Lyman Allyn Mus, Univ Conn, New London; St Lawrence Univ, Canton, NY; Eisenhower Col, Geneva, NY; plus others. *Exhib:* Grumbacher Show, Grand Cent Art Gallery, New York, 64; one-man shows, Chase Gallery, New York, 70, St Lawrence Univ, 70, Grand Haven Art Ctr, Mich, 70 & 75 & Arvest Galleries, Boston, 76. *Pos:* Art dir, Oneida Silversmiths, NY, 48-53, dir advert, 64-77, vpres, 77-81, senior vpres advert, 81- *Bibliog:* Show rev in Art News, 5/69; Grumbacher's Palette Talk, 78; Good Housekeeping's Country Living Mag, winter 79. *Media:* Watercolor, Acrylic. *Dealer:* Orleans Art Gallery Orleans MA. *Mailing Add:* 101 The Vineyard Oneida NY 13421

COMBES, WILLARD WETMORE
CARTOONIST
b Cleveland, Ohio, Dec 23, 01. *Study:* Cleveland Inst Art, grad, 24; Gottwalk Traveling Scholar, Europe, 24; Slade Sch, Univ London, Paris & Madrid, 24-25; Belgium & Holland. *Work:* Libr Cong; Cleveland Mus Art. *Comn:* Murals for churches & stained glass art. *Pos:* Ed cartoonist, Cleveland Press, 34-63. *Teaching:* Head dept art, Cleveland Inst Art, 26-44; instr, Archit Sch, Western Reserve Univ, 26-36. *Awards:* Pulitzer Prize, 38; Award for Best Art, Cleveland Newspaper Guild, 55; Cleveland Builders Award Best Art Mosaic Mural, Lutheran High Sch. *Mem:* Cleveland Soc Artists. *Mailing Add:* 1266 Oakridge Dr Cleveland OH 44121

COMES, MARCELLA
PAINTER, PHOTOGRAPHER
b Pittsburgh, Pa. *Study:* Carnegie Sch Fine Arts, Pittsburgh; Accademia Della Belle Arte, Florence, Italy; also with A Kostellow & Knath. *Work:* Brooklyn Mus; US Mil Acad, West Point; Cent Intel Agency; Naval Acad Annapolis, Md; Harvard Univ. *Comn:* Mural, Homewood Libr, Pittsburgh, Pa; mural, Stone Ridge Sch, Washington, DC; portrait Adm Nimitz, Nimitz Libr, Annapolis, 76; and numerous portraits. *Exhib:* Corcoran Biennial, Washington, DC; 18 Pittsburgh Artists, Carnegie Inst, Pittsburgh, Pa; Mus de la Marine, Paris, France; one-woman show, Brooks Mus, Memphis, Tenn & Gallery on the Green, Lexington, Mass, 81; Tuscan Art, Florence, Italy. *Collections Arranged:* Travel tour, Corcoran Mus, Washington Artists, 10

Southeastern Mus, 72. *Teaching:* Instr painting, Catholic Univ, Figurative, Chmn, Corcoran Benefit Art Tour, 60; juror, Nat Miniature Show, 67; Nat Ed, Artists Equity Newsletter, 75-79. *Awards:* Soc Washington Artists, Katherine Kuh, 61; Soc Washington Artists, NCFA, dir, Norfolk Mus, 62; Benedictine Art Award, Am Fedn Arts, 68. *Bibliog:* Jourdan Houston (auth), Not a portrait painter, Carroll Co Independent, 75; Phyllis Theroux (auth), Marcella Comes, Washingtonian Mag, 77; Robert Taylor (auth), Painter to writer, Boston Globe, 81. *Mem:* Artists Equity (nat vpres, 69-74); Artists Guild Prof Artists. *Publ:* Illusr, Robert Frost portrait, Wash Post, 62; auth, DC harbors underground painters, Art Scene Mag, 71; auth, Shock of the old, AEA Newsletter, 81. *Mailing Add:* 3106 P St NW Washington DC 20007

COMINI, ALESSANDRA
HISTORIAN, LECTURER
b Winona, Minn, Nov 24, 36. *Study:* Barnard Col, with Julius Held, BA, 56; Univ Calif, Berkeley, with Herschel Chipp, MA, 62; Columbia Univ, PhD, 69. *Teaching:* Asst prof art hist, Columbia Univ, 69-74; vis prof art hist, Yale Univ, 73; prof art hist & humanities, Southern Methodist Univ, 74- *Awards:* Am Asn Univ Women Traveling Fel, Vienna, 67-68; Charles Rufus Morey Book Award, Col Art Asn, 75; Distinguished Professor of Art History, Southern Methodist Univ, 83. *Mem:* Am Soc Composers, Auth & Publ; Tex Inst Letters. *Res:* Jugendstil and expressionism; changing image of Beethoven; foreign artists in Rome 1750/1914; Gothic revival and German romanticism. *Publ:* Auth, Command performance: Twenty fantasy exhibitions, Art J, 4/80; auth, State of the field 1980: The women artists of German Expressionism, 11/80 & The mirror of Venice: From titillation to Tiepolo, 6/81, Arts Mag; auth, When form followed feeling: Expressionism, A German institution, 11-12/80, Portfolio Mag; auth, A minute with Munter or how on-site research in German Expressionism can be done in the good old US of A, Iris, 2/82. *Mailing Add:* 2900 McFarlin Dallas TX 75205

COMITO, NICHOLAS U
PAINTER, ILLUSTRATOR
b Brooklyn, NY, Sept 30, 06. *Study:* NY Univ, BS; Nat Acad Design, New York. *Work:* Sch Com, NY Univ; Merck & Co, New York. *Comn:* Youngstown with Pen & Pencil, Kelly Printing, New York, 34; Maroon, Centennial Yearbk, Fordham Univ, New York, 41; History of Aviation Medicine, Res Bldg, Randolph Field, Tex, 45; Murals of Different Cities, Astorian Manor, NY, 58; Stations of the Cross, Church of the Most Holy Rosary, Roosevelt, NY, 64. *Exhib:* Art in the United States, Carnegie Inst, Pittsburgh, Pa, 43-45; one-man shows, Witte Mus, San Antonio, Tex, 44, Noonan-Kocian Galleries, St Louis, Mo 46 & Southern Vt Art Ctr, Manchester, 58; Exhib of paintings, Sheepshead Libr, 78, Exhib of prints, lithographs, watercolors & oils, 79; Distinguished Mid-Atlantic Artists, Univ Del, Newark, 80. *Teaching:* Instr drawing & painting, Comito Art Sch, Brooklyn, NY, 48-60. *Awards:* Julian Hallgarten Prize, Nat Acad Design, New York, 40; John Milton Jr Award, Painters & Sculptors Soc NJ, 45; First Prize (oil painting), Irvington Art & Mus Asn, NJ, 46. *Mem:* Audubon Artists, New York; Southern Vt Artists, Manchester; Mid-Vt-Chaffee Art Gallery, Rutland. *Media:* Oil, Watercolor. *Mailing Add:* 1747 Burnett St Brooklyn NY 11229

COMTOIS, LOUIS
PAINTER
b Montreal, Que, April 11, 45. *Study:* Ecole Beaux-Arts, Montreal, dipl, 68. *Work:* Albright-Knox Gallery; Art Gallery Ont; Mus Art Contemp, Mus Beaux-Arts, Montreal; Mus Que. *Exhib:* Solo exhib, Mus Art Contemp, Montreal, 75, Ctr Cult Can, Paris, 78, Art Gallery Ont, 80, Dalhousie Univ Art Gallery, Halifax, 80, Kitchener-Waterloo Art Gallery, Ont, 81 & Mendel Art Gallery, Saskatoon, Sask, 81. *Awards:* Can Coun Grant, 81. *Media:* Oil on Mixed Media. *Dealer:* Galerie Jolliet 279 Sherbrooke Ouest Montreal PQ H2X 1Y2. *Mailing Add:* PO Box 258 Canal St Sta New York NY 10013

CONANT, HOWARD SOMERS
PAINTER, EDITOR
b Beloit, Wis, May 5, 21. *Study:* Art Students League, with Kunyiyoshi; Univ Wis, BS & MS; Univ Buffalo, EdD. *Work:* Andrew Dickson White Gallery, Cornell Univ Ithaca, NY; Trenton State Col, NJ; Drury Col, Springfield, Mo; Tex Technol Col, Lubbock; Milton Col, Wis. *Comn:* Mural painting, Molloy Col, Rockville Center, NY, 70; environmental mural, Sperry High Sch, Henrietta, NY, 71; Art for schools: A study of children's responses to original works of art, comn by Ctr for Appl Res in Educ; environmental painting, Valley Nat Bank, Tucson, 80; environmental painting, Good Samaritan Hospital, Phoenix, 81. *Exhib:* Univ Cent Fla, Orlando, 79; Northern Ariz Univ, 80; Washington State Univ, 81; Western Ore Col, 81; Lima Col, Tucson, 81; and other group & one-man shows. *Pos:* Art ed, Intellect Mag, 72-76 & USA: Today, 76- *Teaching:* Prof art, State Univ NY Buffalo, 47-55; prof & chmn, Dept Art & Art Educ, NY Univ, 55-76; prof & head, Dept Art, Univ Ariz, Tucson, 76- *Awards:* Distinguished Serv to Art Educ, Nat Gallery Art, 66; Distinguished Alumnus, Univ Wis-Milwaukee, 68. *Mem:* Int Asn Art Critics; Col Art Asn; Nat Asn Schs Art & Design. *Media:* Acrylic, Ink. *Publ:* Coauth, Art in Education, 63; ed, Masterpieces of the Arts, 63; auth, Art Education, 64; auth, Seminar on Elementary and Secondary School Education in the Visual Arts, 65; ed, Lincoln Library of the Arts, 73; and others. *Dealer:* Art Concepts Inc Phoenix AZ; Gombiniski Gallery 46 Walker St New York NY 10013. *Mailing Add:* Dept of Art Univ of Ariz Tucson AZ 85721

CONANT, JAN ROYCE
PAINTER, ILLUSTRATOR
b Boston, Mass, Sept 14, 30. *Study:* Boston Mus Sch Fine Arts, 48-51; Cincinnati Art Acad, 51-53. *Exhib:* One-man shows, Conn Gallery Fine Arts, Hartford, 70, Conn Bank & Trust Co, 71 & The Village Studio, South Galstonbury, Conn, 73; Jamaica by Jan, Runaway Bay Hotel, West Indies, 80; Animals in Art, Salt Box Gallery, West Hartford, Conn, 81 & Lyme Art Gallery, Conn, 81. *Media:* Oil, Pastel. *Publ:* Illusr, The Judge and the Junior Exhibitor, Duel, Sloan & Pearce, 64; auth & illusr, Half Pint and others, Book Press, 66; illusr, The Chronicle of the Horse, 68-79; illusr, Hunter Seat Equitation, Doubleday, 71; illusr, Designing Courses & Obstacles, Houghton Mifflin, 78. *Dealer:* The Crossroads of Sport Inc 5 East 47th St New York NY 10017. *Mailing Add:* Runaway Bay PO Jamaica Jamaica

CONAWAY, GERALD
SCULPTOR, PAINTER
b Manson, Wash, Feb 15, 33. *Study:* Everett Jr Col, Wash, ABA; Univ Wash, Seattle, with George Tsutakawa & Everett Dupen, BA(art educ), MFA(sculpture). *Work:* Anchorage Fine Arts Mus, Alaska; Alaska Methodist Univ, Anchorage; Nat Gallery Art. *Comn:* William H Seward (marble monument), Mutual Ins Co, New York & Anchorage Centennial, Anchorage, 67; concrete wall sculptures, Raymond Lawson, AIA, 73; aluminum sculptures, Gen Serv Admin Fed Bldg, Fairbanks, Alaska, 79 & Pub Safety Bldg, Fairbanks, Alaska, 81; Benny Benson Mem (aluminum), Anchorage, 83. *Exhib:* All Alaska, Anchorage, 65-70; Western Regional Craft Show, Portland, 67; Sculpture Northwest, Seattle, 68. *Pos:* Sign writer & artist, Univ Wash, 54-65; graphic artist, Boeing Airplane Co, 57. *Teaching:* Instr art, Northshore Sch Dist, Wash, 57-65; from assoc prof to prof art, Alaska Methodist Univ, 65-76. *Awards:* Sculpture Award, All Alaska, 65-70; Jewelry Award, Western Regional Craft Show, 67. *Mem:* Nat Art Educ Asn. *Media:* Wood, Stone. *Dealer:* Francine Seders Gallery 6701 Greenwood Ave N Seattle WA 98103. *Mailing Add:* 2457 Cottonwood Anchorage AK 99508

CONAWAY, JAMES D
PAINTER, EDUCATOR
b Granite City, Ill, Oct 9, 32. *Study:* Southern Ill Univ, Carbondale, Ill, BA; Univ Iowa, Iowa City, MA, MFA. *Work:* Am Embassy Collection; Waterloo Munic Art Gallery, Iowa; Davenport Munic Art Gallery, Iowa; Gen Mills, Minneapolis, Minn; 3M Company, St Paul, Minn. *Comn:* Painting, Texaco Oil Co, Houston, 81. *Exhib:* Walker Biennial, Walker Art Ctr, Minneapolis, 67; Art for the Embassies, Smithsonian Inst, Washington, DC, 67; Midwestern Ann Competition, Joslyn Art Mus, Omaha, 73; Mid Year Biennial, Butler Inst Am Art, Youngstown, Ohio, 74; Manisphere, Winnepeg Art Ctr, 74; Marietta Int Painting Exhib, Ohio, 76; Palace of Fine Arts, Santiago, Chile. *Teaching:* Asst prof, Univ Wis, Stevens Point; prof painting & drawing, Anoka Ramsey Col, Minneapolis, currently; prof painting, Hamline Univ, St Paul, currently. *Awards:* Purchase Award, Davenport Munic Art Gallery, 63, Waterloo Munic Art Galleries, 65; Donors Prize, Walker Art Ctr Biennial, 66. *Bibliog:* James Conaway, Artists of the Rockies, Fall 80; By the time he got to Phoenix, Arizona Arts and Lifestyle, Spring 81; James Conaway (auth), Minneapolis-Santa Fe connection, Southwest Profiles, 5/83. *Mem:* Mid-Am Col Art Asn (treas, 77-78); Artist Equity. *Media:* Oil. *Dealer:* C G Rein Galleries 3646 W 70th St Minneapolis MN 55435; Harris Gallery 110 Bissonnet Houston TX 77005. *Mailing Add:* 2758 Benjamin St Minneapolis MN 55418

CONDESO, ORLANDO
PRINTMAKER
b Lima, Peru, Dec 31, 47. *Study:* Visual Arts, Lima; Pratt Graphics Ctr, New York. *Work:* Nat Mus Hist, Repub China; Harlem Art Collection, New York; Orgn Am States, Washington, DC; Braniff Int, Lima; Cult Peruvian NAm Inst, Lima. *Exhib:* Second Biennial of Latin Am Prints, San Juan, PR, 72; 2nd Int Print Exhib, Mus Mod Art, Sao Paulo, Brazil, 72; 18th Nat Print Exhib, Brooklyn Mus, NY, 72; Young Artists 1973, Int Play Group Inc, New York, 73; Calif Palace Legion Honor, San Francisco, 73; Nat Mus Hist, Repub China, 73; 2nd Miami Graphics Biennial, Fla, 75. *Awards:* First Prize, 5th Nat Print Competition, USA Embassy, Lima, 70; Award, 5th Ann Exhib, Pratt Graphics Ctr, 72; Purchase Award, 2nd Miami Graphics Biennial, 75. *Media:* Acrylic, Silkscreen. *Dealer:* Condeso/Lawler Ltd. *Mailing Add:* 32 Grand St New York NY 10013

CONDRON, BRIAN JAMES
PHOTOGRAPHER
b Toronto, Ont, Nov 23, 49. *Study:* Sheridan Col, Oakville, dipl(photog), 71; York Univ, Toronto, BFA, 76. *Work:* Nat Photo Collection, New York; Nat Film Bd Can, Art Bank, Can Coun, Ottawa; Queensland Col Art, Brisbane, Australia; Ont Arts Coun, Toronto. *Exhib:* Focal Point, Art Gallery Ont, 77; Slowly I Turned ..., York Univ Art Gallery, Toronto, 81; The Taking of Niagara, Buscaglia-Castellani Art Gallery, Niagara Falls, NY, 82; Autobodies, Optica Ctr Contemp Art, Montreal, 82; Latitudes & Parallels, Winnipeg Art Gallery, 83; solo exhib, Queensland Col Art, Brisbane, Australia, 83. *Teaching:* Artist in residence, Queensland Col Art, Brisbane, Australia, 82. *Awards:* Can Coun Grants, 78 & 82; Ont Arts Coun Grant, 81. *Bibliog:* Gary Michael Dault (auth), Wish you were here, Saturday Night Mag, 78; Maia-Mari Sutnik (auth), Slowly I turned ..., Photo Communique, 82. *Mailing Add:* 123 Braemar Ave Toronto ON M5P 2L3 Canada

CONE, GERRIT CRAIG
ADMINISTRATOR
b Denver, Colo, May 23, 47. *Study:* Univ NMex, 65-68; Long Beach City Col, AA, 69; Calif State Univ, Long Beach, BA, 72. *Pos:* Gallery coordr, Tucson Art Ctr, 72-73; actg dir, Tucson Mus Art, 73-74, cur collections & asst dir, 74-80. *Mem:* Am Asn Mus; Western Regional Conf Am Asn Mus (Ariz state rep, 74-76, first vpres); Western Asn Art Mus (first vpres); Arch Am Art; Art Libr Soc Ariz (chmn, 75-76); and others. *Publ:* Ed, Western Regional Conf Am Asn Mus Newslett, 75-77. *Mailing Add:* 1300 Massachusetts Ave NW Suite 505 Washington DC 20005

CONESA, MIGUEL A
PAINTER, ILLUSTRATOR
b Ponce, PR, Sept 29, 52; US citizen. *Study:* Jose Azaustre Acad, Ponce, PR, 67-68; Escuela Artes Plasticas, San Juan, PR, 72; Augusta Col, Ga, 75-77. *Work:* Carnegie Libr, Ex-Libris Collection, San Juan, PR; Libr Univ Rio Piedras, PR; Ponce Art Mus, Luis A Ferre Found, PR; McDuffie Co Mus, Thomson, Ga. *Exhib:* First Am Painters in Paris, Argraf Asn Paris, France, 75-76; South Eastern Artist, High Mus, Atlanta, Ga, 76; Retrospective, Ponce Art Mus, PR, 80; Ann Show, Inst Cultura, San Juan, PR, 80; Gallery II/ RSVP, Charlottesville, Va, 83; Cayman Gallery, New York, 83. *Pos:* Post card designer, Graficas Nativas, Domingo Cabrera, Rio Piedras, PR, 71-72; illusr, Korsevish Advertising Agency, Atlanta, Ga, 77-78; illusr, TASC Federal Government, Ft Gordon, Ga, 81-83; creative dir, MC Studio Mod Design, Hato Rey, PR, currently. *Awards:* Best of Show Scholar Award, Luis Ferre Found, 70-71; Best of Show, Ga Depot Art Festival, McDuffie, 75; Bailies' Award, Augusta Col, Bailies' Studio, Augusta, 75. *Bibliog:* Antonio Molina (auth), History of Painting in Puerto Rico, Gran Enciclopedia de PR, vol 8, 73; Fay Rice (auth), Profile on Miguel Conesa, Art Voices South, 5-6/81. *Mem:* Int Platform Asn, Cleveland, Ohio. *Media:* Mixed Media, All Media. *Mailing Add:* 709 Second Ext A-5 Rambla Ponce PR 00731

CONE-SKELTON, ANNETTE
PAINTER, DEALER
b LaGrange, Ga, Oct 20, 42. *Study:* LaGrange Col, Ga; Atlanta Col of Art, Ford Found scholar, BFA. *Work:* High Mus of Art, Atlanta, Ga; Hunter Mus of Art, Chattanooga, Tenn; Am Tel & Tel Collection, New York & Chicago; Herbert F Johnson Mus, Cornell Univ, Ithaca, NY; Emory Univ, Atlanta. *Exhib:* Southeastern Ann Exhib, High Mus of Art, Atlanta, 67 & 68; Hunter Mus of Art Ann, Chattanooga, 67, 70 & 76; Ga Artists Show, High Mus of Art, Atlanta, 71, 72 & 74; 8th Grand Prix de Peinture, de la cote d'Azur, Paris, France, 72; 13th Atlanta Artists, Penha Gallery, Ft Lauderdale, Fla, 73; one-person shows, Image S Gallery, 74 & 75 & Heath Gallery, 77, 78, 79 & 80, Atlanta; Galleries Int, Winter Park, Fla, 75; 13 Women Painters, Festival of Women in the Arts, Ga State Univ, Atlanta, 75; 35 Artists in the SE, High Mus of Art, Atlanta, 76, Birmingham Mus, Ala, 77, Greenville Co Mus, SC, 77, Hunter Mus, Chattanooga, Tenn, 78 & Southeastern Ctr for Contemp Art, Winston-Salem, NC, 78; Mint Mus, Charlotte, NC, 79; Avant-Garde: 12 in Atlanta, High Mus Art, 79. *Pos:* Art consult, Arnold Gallery, Atlanta, 77-; managing ed, Contemp Art/SE, Atlanta, 77-79; dir, Heath Gallery, 79- *Awards:* Merit Award, Southeastern Ann, High Mus of Art, Atlanta, 67; Merit Award, Ga Inst of Technol, Atlanta, 68; Purchase Award, 15th Hunter Ann, Hunter Mus, Chattanooga, Tenn, 76. *Bibliog:* L'Art a l'Etranger, La Revue Mod, 71. *Mailing Add:* Heath Gallery 416 E Paces Ferry Rd Atlanta GA 30305

CONFORTE, RENEE
DEALER
b Belgrade, Yugoslavia, US citizen. *Study:* Mt Holyoke Col, BA(magna cum laude); Univ Paris I, Sorbonne; Ecole du Louvre, Paris. *Pos:* Admin asst, Marlborough Gallery, New York, 68-72; dir, David McKee Gallery, New York, 74- *Specialty:* Contemporary American art. *Mailing Add:* c/o David McKee Gallery 41 E 57th St New York NY 10021

CONFORTI, MICHAEL PETER
HISTORIAN, CURATOR
b Bradford, Mass, Apr 3, 45. *Study:* Trinity Col, Conn, BA, 68; Harvard Univ, MA, 73, PhD, 77. *Pos:* Cur sculpture & decorative arts, Fine Arts Museums of San Francisco, 77-80; chief cur & Bell Mem Cur, Minneapolis Inst Arts, 80- *Awards:* Fel Art Hist, Am Acad Rome, 75-77. *Mem:* Am Asn Mus; Decorative Arts Soc; Am Ceramics Circle; Silver Soc; English Ceramic Circle. *Res:* Sculpture and decorative arts, 17th to 19th centuries. *Mailing Add:* Minneapolis Inst Arts Minneapolis MN 55404

CONGDON, WILLIAM (GROSVENOR)
PAINTER
b Providence, RI, Apr 15, 12. *Study:* Provincetown Sch Art, with Henry Hensche; Demetrious Sch Sculpture, Boston & Folly Cove, Mass. *Work:* Metrop Mus Art, Whitney Mus Am Art & Mus Mod Art, New York; Cleveland Mus, Ohio; Vatican Mus Contemp Art, Vatican City; and others. *Comn:* Bronze head, Stephen O Metcalf, RI Sch Design, Providence Mus, 39. *Exhib:* Landmarks, American Painting--50 years, Wildenstein Gallery, New York, 50; Painters under 35, Metrop Mus Art, 50; Biennale Venezia, 52 & 58; Carnegie Inst Int, Pittsburgh, Pa, 52 & 58; New Decade, Whitney Mus Am Art, 55; Palazzo, Diamanti, Ferrara, Italy, 81. *Awards:* Temple Gold Medal, Pa Acad Fine Arts, 51; Purchase Prize, Univ Ill, 52; Clark Award, Corcoran Gallery Art, 53. *Bibliog:* Dorothy Seiberling & George Hunt (auth), William Congdon, Life Mag, 4/30/51; Peggy Guggenheim (auth), Pittore di Venezia, Biennale Venezia, 2/53; Emily Genauer (auth), Congdon converted, New York Herald Tribune, 8/21/68. *Media:* Oil, Pastel. *Publ:* Auth, In My Disc of Gold, Reynal, 62; auth, An Artist, His Art & the Christian Community, 72 & Esistenza-Viaggio di Pittore Americano, 75, Jaca Bk, Italy; and others. *Mailing Add:* Monastero Benedettino 20094 Buccinasco Milan Italy

CONGER, CLEMENT E
CURATOR
b Rockingham, Va, Oct 15, 12. *Study:* Strayer Col, grad, 32; George Washington Univ, 33-34; Adjutant Gen Officer's Candidate Sch, grad, 43; Col William & Mary, DHL, 77. *Pos:* Cur, Diplomatic Reception Rooms, US State Dept, 61-, cur, The White House, 70-; trustee, Va Mus Fine Arts, Richmond & Treasury Hist Asn, currently. *Awards:* Thomas Jefferson Award, Am Soc Interior Designers, 78; Gold Medal of Hon, Nat Arts Club, 80; Distinguished Serv Award & Medal, US State Dept, 81; Distinguished Honor Award, Dept State, 81. *Mem:* Nat Trust for Hist Preserv. *Mailing Add:* 320 Mansion Dr Alexandria VA 22302

CONGER, WILLIAM
PAINTER, EDUCATOR
b Dixon, Ill, May 29, 37. *Study:* Art Inst Chicago, 56-57; Univ NMex, with Elaine deKooning, BFA, 61; Univ Chicago, MFA, 66. *Work:* Mus Contemp Art, Chicago; Art Inst Chicago; Ill State Mus, Springfield; DePaul Univ, Chicago; Northern Ill Univ, DeKalb. *Exhib:* Chicago & Vicinity, Art Inst Chicago, 63, 71, 73, 78 & 80-81; one-man shows, Krannert Ctr Performing Arts, Urbana, Ill, 76 & Zaks Gallery, Chicago, 78, 80 & 83; Visions-Painting & Sculpture of Distinguished Alumni 1945 to present, Art Inst Chicago Sch Gallery, 76; Abstract Art in Chicago, Mus Contemp Art, 76; Chicago Connection, Crocker Art Gallery, Sacramento, Calif, 77; Chicago Abstract Painting, Sonoma State Univ, Calif, 82; Chicago: Some Other Traditions Nat Traveling Show, 83-85; and others. *Pos:* Mem bd dirs, Oxbow, Saugatuk, Mich, 83- *Teaching:* Prof art, DePaul Univ, Chicago, 71-, chmn dept, 71-77, 80- *Awards:* Bartels Prize, 71 & Cluseman Prize, 73, Art Inst Chicago. *Bibliog:* C L Morrison (auth), article, Artforum, 76 & 78; Franze Schulze (auth), Chicago, Artnews, 79; M Gedo (auth), article, Arts Mag, 82 & 83. *Mem:* Col Art Asn Am. *Media:* Oil on Linen or Wood. *Dealer:* Zaks Gallery 620 N Michigan Ave Chicago IL 60611. *Mailing Add:* 3014 W Hollywood Ave Chicago IL 60659

CONKLIN, GLORIA ZAMKO
PAINTER
b Detroit, Mich, Feb 6, 25. *Study:* Am Acad Art, Chicago, cert, 45; Art Inst Chicago, 46; Critique Professional Artists with Theodoros Stamos, 71-81; Art Students League, 76. *Work:* Smithsonian Collection, Washington, DC; Peat, Marwick & Mitchell, New York; Higgins & Johnson, New York; Scarsdale Bank, Scarsdale, NY; Greenwich Develop Corp, Conn. *Exhib:* Bruce Mus, Greenwich, Conn, 74; 23rd Ann Juried Exhib, White Plains, NY, 76; Bridge Gallery Westchester, White Plains, NY, 78; Ikones Group, Stamford Mus, Conn, 79; 155th Ann, Nat Acad Design, New York, 80; Nat Asn Women Artists, New York, 80 & 83. *Bibliog:* Helen Thomas (auth), article, Arts Mag, 10/77. *Mem:* Nat Asn Women Artists; Artists Equity New York. *Media:* Acrylic, Pastel. *Dealer:* Marden Fine Arts 41 Union Square W No 301 New York NY 10003. *Mailing Add:* 7 Whippoorwill Rd Chappaqua NY 10514

CONLEY, ZEB BRISTOL, JR
COLLECTOR, GALLERY DIRECTOR
b Andrews, NC, Feb 12, 36. *Study:* Mars Hill Col, 55-57; Col William & Mary, 57-61; NMex Highlands Univ, 63. *Pos:* Dir, Jamison Galleries, Santa Fe, 73-; bd mem, 74-, pres, 81- *Specialty:* Traditional Southwestern art, specializing in Taos and Santa Fe masters. *Mailing Add:* PO Box 2534 Santa Fe NM 87501

CONLON, JAMES EDWARD
SCULPTOR, HISTORIAN
b Cincinnati, Ohio, Dec 9, 35. *Study:* Ohio State Univ, BSc(art educ), 59, MA(fine arts), 62. *Work:* Fine Arts Mus South Mobile. *Exhib:* Southern Asn Sculptors Traveling Exhib, Smithsonian Inst; Competition 75, Mobile, Ala, 75; two-person show, Fine Arts Mus South-Mobile, 77; Montgomery Mus Art, 78 & 79; Alabama Sculptors Invitational, 80. *Teaching:* Instr, Ind Univ, Bloomington, 62-65; from asst prof to assoc prof, Univ S Ala, Mobile, 65-73, prof, 74- *Awards:* Award to Develop the Ethnic American Art Slide Library, Samuel H Kress Found, 72-75; Award to Produce a Research Index of Afro-American Art, Am Revolution Bicentennial Comn, 73; Univ Res Grant, 76-77. *Mem:* Southern Asn Sculptors; Southeastern Col Art Asn (vpres, 74-75). *Media:* Woods, Limestone; Cast & Laminated Plastics. *Res:* An investigation of stylistic development in Afro-American, Mexican American and Native American art from 1800 to the present. *Publ:* Coauth, An Afro-American slide project, Col Art Asn J, winter 70. *Mailing Add:* PO Box 781 Middle Earth Rd Citronelle AL 36522

CONN, DAVID EDWARD
PRINTMAKER, PAINTER
b Jersey City, NJ, Apr 10, 41. *Study:* Newark Sch Fine Arts, NJ; Md Inst Col Art, Baltimore, BFA; Univ Okla, Norman, MFA with Peter Milton. *Work:* Ark Art Ctr, Little Rock; Ft Worth Art Mus, Tex; Univ Okla Mus Art, Norman. *Exhib:* 20th Exhib of Southwestern Prints & Drawings, Dallas Mus of Art, 75; 5th Ann Nat Print, Drawing & Photog Exhib, Second St Gallery, Charlottesville, Va, 77; Kans 3rd Nat Small Painting, Drawing & Print Exhib, 78; Joslyn Art Mus, 78; NTex State Univ, 81; and others. *Teaching:* Asst prof art-printmaking, Tex Christian Univ, 69- *Awards:* Cash Award, 5th & 6th Monroe Ann, Masur Mus, 68-69; Cash Award, 29/Okla Artist Ann, Philbrook Art Ctr, Tulsa, 69; Purchase Award, Ark Print, Drawing & Crafts, Ark Art Ctr, 71. *Bibliog:* American Printmakers 74--Graphics Group, Arcadia, Calif, 74. *Media:* Intaglio, Crayon. *Mailing Add:* 3311 Cockrell Ft Worth TX 76109

CONN, RICHARD GEORGE
CURATOR
b Bellingham, Wash, Oct 28, 28. *Study:* Univ Wash, Seattle, BA, 50, MA, 55. *Collections Arranged:* Approx 40 temporary exhibs, EWash State Hist Soc, Spokane, 59-66; Robes of White Shell and Sunrise (auth, catalog), Denver Art Mus, 74; Circles of the World (auth, catalog), Denver Art Mus, 82. *Pos:* Cur of native art, Denver Art Mus, 55-59 & 71; dir, EWash State Hist Soc, Spokane, 59-66; chief of human hist, Man Mus, Winnipeg, Can, 66-70. *Teaching:* Adj prof native art, Univ Colo, Denver, 73- *Awards:* John J McCloy Found fel, 79. *Mem:* Am Asn Mus. *Res:* Native American art, all geographic areas, with special emphasis on native clothing and decoration. *Publ:* Auth, Native American Art in the Denver Art Museum, 79. *Mailing Add:* Denver Art Mus 100 W 14th Ave Pkwy Denver CO 80204

CONNEEN, JANE W
PRINTMAKER, MINIATURIST
b Montclair, NJ, April 19, 21. *Study:* With George Parker, Emily Hatch, Sally Kugelmeyer & David Sander; Lehigh Univ; Haverford Col. *Work:* Hunt Inst Botanical Doc, Pittsburgh, Pa; Mus City New York; Am Tel & Tel Long Lines, Bedminster, NJ. *Comn:* Drawings, Allentown Art Mus, Pa, 75 & Pa Chamber Commerce, Harrisburg, 76. *Exhib:* Solo exhib, Kemerer Mus, Bethlehem, Pa, 76 & Saylor Park Cement Indust, Coplay, Pa, 79; Miniature Painters Sculptors & Gravers Soc, Washington, DC, 76-83; Philadelphia Print Club, 82; Royal Soc Miniature Painters, London, 83. *Awards:* Best in Show & First in Graphics, Am Nat Miniature Show, Laramie, Wyo, 80; First in Graphics, Miniature Painters, Sculptors & Gravers Washington, DC, 83 & Miniature Art Soc Fla, 84. *Bibliog:* Nessa Mines (auth), Jane Conneen, botanical artist, Miniature World, 78; Lee Whitfield (auth), Herbs in miniature, Whitchappels Herbal, 80; Louis Bondy (auth), Miniature Books, Sheppard Press, London, 81. *Mem:* Impressit-Printmakers Group; fel Int Guild Miniature Artisans; Printmaking Coun NJ; Guild Natural Sci Illusr; Philadelphia Print Club. *Media:* Hand-Coloured Etchings; Pen and Ink, Watercolour. *Publ:* Illusr miniature books, Wildflowers I & II, French Cooking & A Medicinal Herbal, Borrowers Press, 77-80; Auth, Member of the issue, Northlight Mag, 78; coauth, Etching through the ages, Nutshell News Mag, 79. *Mailing Add:* The Little Farm 820 Andrews Rd Bath PA 18014

CONNER, BRUCE
PAINTER, FILMMAKER
b McPherson, Kans, Nov 18, 33. *Study:* Wichita Univ; Univ Nebr, BFA; Brooklyn Mus Art Sch; Univ Colo. *Work:* Guggenheim Mus, Whitney Mus Am Art, Mus Mod Art, New York; Art Inst Chicago; Los Angeles Co Art Mus. *Comn:* Poster, New York Film Festival, Am Fedn Arts, 65. *Exhib:* The Art of Assemblage, Mus Mod Art, New York, 60; Whitney Biannual, Whitney Mus Am Art; Retrospective, Inst Contemp Art, Univ Tex, 67 & de Young Mem Mus, San Francisco, 74; American Sculpture of the Sixties, Los Angeles Co Art Mus, 67; Belly-Button Art of the Seventies, Newport Harbor Art Gallery, 72; Tyler Mus Art, Tex, 74; Smith-Anderson Gallery, Palo Alto, Calif, 74; de Young Mem Mus, 75; The North Point Gallery, San Francisco, Calif, 80 & 81; plus others. *Pos:* Pres & founder, Rat Bastard Protective Asn, San Francisco, 58-61; dir, bd dirs, Canyon Cinema Coop, San Francisco, 69-70 & 71-72. *Teaching:* Instr film making, Calif Col Arts & Crafts, 65-66; undergrad sem, Wasted Time, San Francisco Art Inst, 66-67. *Awards:* Copley Found Award, 65; Gold Medal Award, Milan Biennale Nuovo Techniques in Arts, 67; Guggenheim Fel, 76. *Bibliog:* Carl Belz (auth), 3 films by Bruce Conner, Film Cult Mag, spring 67; Anthony Reveaux (auth), Bruce Conner (films), Film in the Cities, 81. *Publ:* Coauth, Bruce Conner/Mike McClure, Averhahn Press, 67; auth, The Dennis Hopper One-Man Show, Crown Point Press, Vols I-III, 71-73. *Mailing Add:* 45 Sussex St San Francisco CA 94131

CONNERY, RUTH M
PAINTER, INSTRUCTOR
b New York, NY. *Study:* Mills Col, AA; Art Students League, with William von Schlegell & Hans Hofmann. *Work:* First Nat Bank, Rye, NY. *Comn:* Portraits, comn by Mr & Mrs Peter Sellon, Rye, New York, Mrs & Mrs Victor Wouk, New York, Mr & Mrs Anthony Rizzo, Jupiter Island, Fla & Mr & Mrs H Canale, Larchmont, NY. *Exhib:* Nat Asn Women Artists, Nat Acad Design, New York, 49-69; one-person shows, Westchester Co, 60-69 & Forley & Wren Gallery, New York, 68; Mus Southern France, 67; Leger Bldg, Park Ave, New York, 67-68; Norton Gallery, West Palm Beach, Fla, 70-71; Scranton Mem Libr, Madison, Conn, 78. *Teaching:* Instr creative painting, Westchester Arts Workshop & Mamaroneck Artists Guild, 60-69, Palm Beach Adult Educ Inst, 70-72 & Recreation Comn, Madison, 77-78. *Awards:* Pres Prize, New Rochelle Art Asn, 65; Group Show Award, Westchester Arts Workshop, 67; One-Man Show Award, Contemporaries, Inc, New York. *Mem:* Nat Asn Women Artists (secy, 65); Artists Guild Norton Gallery, Palm Beach. *Media:* Oil, Acrylic. *Mailing Add:* 58 Beach Ave Madison CT 06443

CONNETT, DEE M
EDUCATOR, PRINTMAKER
b Mulvane, Kans, May 25, 35. *Study:* Kans State Teachers Col, BS(art educ), 53; Wichita State Univ, MA, 64; Am Univ, Mex, 64; art sem, Florence, Italy, 70; also with Mary Kretsinger & Dorothy MacCray. *Work:* Wichita Art Mus, Kans; Nebr Wesleyan Univ, Lincoln; Centre House, Swannanoa, NC; MacCray Gallery, Western NMex State Univ, Silver City. *Comn:* Paintings commissioned by Harry Litwin, Litwin Enterprises, Wichita, 70. *Exhib:* 5th Ann Midwestern Print and Drawing Show, Tulsa, Okla, 78; Juror's Selection Kansas Post Card ACACK Series II, Topeka, Kans, 79; 15th Ann Nat Drawing and Small Sculpture Show, Del Mar Col, Corpus Christi, Tex, 81;

and many more; Juried Show for Kans Artists, 82; Tom Millea Photographic Competition, Danbury, Conn, 83. *Pos:* Mem, Fine Arts Coun Comt, Wichita, 66-81; bd mem, Wichita Art Mus, 66-; mem, Century II Sculpture Planning Comt, Wichita, 70-72; mem, Metrop Arts Bd, Wichita, 78-81. *Teaching:* Instr art, Wichita Pub Schs, 57-64; chmn dept art & assoc prof, Friends Univ, Wichita, 66-; Wichita Art Mus, 69-70. *Awards:* Outstanding Teacher of Year Award, Friends Univ, 70; Juried Show for Kans Artists Merit Award, 82; hon mention, Tom Millea Photographic Competition, Danbury, Conn, 83. *Bibliog:* Dorothy Belden (auth), Wichita Eagle, 8/81; Reimer & Brooks (auth), Framing the Artist: A Social Portrait of Mid-American Artists, 82. *Mem:* Artist Guild Wichita; Kans Artist-Craftsmen Asn; Wichita Area Mus Asn. *Publ:* Illusr, Errol Elliot's Sing the Faith, 75 & Deepening Stream, 82; illusr, Friends and the Visual Arts, 82; illusr, Mennonite Mag, Can, 83. *Dealer:* Sales & Rental Gallery, Wichita Art Mus Wichita KS 67203; Art Works Gallery 2906 E Central Wichita KS 67214. *Mailing Add:* 1635 N Sheridan Wichita KS 67203

CONNOLLY, JEROME PATRICK
PAINTER, MURALIST
b Minneapolis, Minn, Jan 14, 31. *Study:* Univ Minn, BS(art educ); also with Francis Lee Jaques. *Work:* Diorama backgrounds & murals in more than 20 mus, incl Carnegie Mus, Pittsburgh, James Ford Bell Mus, Minneapolis, Vanderbilt Mus, Long Island, George C Page Mus, Los Angeles, Smithsonian Mus Nat Hist & many others. *Exhib:* Sportsman's Gallery of Art & Bks, New York; Crossroads of Sport, New York; Abercrombie & Fitch, New York & San Francisco; Petersen Gallery, Los Angeles; one-man show, Abercrombie & Fitch, New York, 72; and others. *Pos:* Staff artist, Ill State Mus, Springfield, 58-60; staff artist, Natural Sci Youth Found, Westport, Conn, 60-65. *Mem:* Soc Animal Artists. *Media:* Oil. *Publ:* Illusr, Adelbert the Penguin, 69; illusr, The Deer Family, 69; illusr, Aise-ce-bon: a Raccoon, 71; illusr, Saga of a Whitetail, 81; illusr, 15 children's books & contribr, Audubon Mag, Nat Wildlife & Hartford Life Insurance Co calendar. *Mailing Add:* 105 Sunset Dr Nokomis FL 33555

CONNOR, LINDA STEVENS
PHOTOGRAPHER, INSTRUCTOR
b New York, NY, Nov 18, 44. *Study:* RI Sch of Design, BFA, with Harry Calahan; Inst of Design, Ill Inst of Technol, MS, with Aaron Siskind. *Work:* Boston Mus of Fine Arts, Mass; Art Inst Chicago; Int Mus of Photography, George Eastman House, Rochester, NY; William Hayes Fogg Art Mus, Harvard Univ, Cambridge, Mass; Mus of Mod Art, New York. *Exhib:* Pvt Realities, Boston Mus Fine Arts, 74; 14 Am Photogr, Baltimore Mus, Md & Long Beach Mus, Calif, 74-75; 8x10, Ten Am Photogr, Dallas Mus of Fine Arts, Tex, 76; one-person shows, Visual Studies Gallery, Rochester, NY, 76, Ctr Photographic Studies, 76 & de Young Mem Mus, San Francisco, 77; Vision Gallery, Boston, 81; Light Gallery, New York, 81; Corcoran Gallery Art, Washington, DC, 82; Calif Mus Photog, Riverside, 83; and others. *Teaching:* Instr photog, San Francisco Art Inst, 69-, co-chmn, 73-75; instr photog, San Francisco State Univ, 72 & Calif Col of Arts & Crafts, Oakland, 73; Sch Mus Fine Arts, Boston, fall 78. *Awards:* Union Independent Col Art Fac Fel, 73; Nat Endowment Arts Grant, 76; Guggenheim Fel, 79. *Mem:* Soc for Photographic Educ. *Media:* Photography. *Publ:* Contribr, Darkroom, Lustrum, 77; American Images, McGraw-Hill, 79; contribr, Photographers in the national parks, Solos, 79; contribr, Linda Connor, Corcoran Gallery Art, 82; contribr, Calif Mus Photog Bulletin, Vol 2, No 2; and others. *Dealer:* Light Gallery 724 Fifth Ave New York NY 10019. *Mailing Add:* 87 Rutherford San Anselmo CA 94960

CONOVER, CLAUDE
SCULPTOR, CERAMIST
b Pittsburgh, Pa, Dec 15, 07. *Study:* Cleveland Inst Art, grad cert. *Work:* Cleveland Mus Art, Ohio; Everson Mus Art, Syracuse, NY; Utah Mus Fine Arts, Salt Lake City; Philadelphia Mus Art; Minn Mus Art, St Paul; and others. *Exhib:* Ann Exhib Works by Artists & Craftsmen of the Western Reserve, Cleveland Mus Art, 14 yrs; Ceramic Nat, Everson Mus Art, four biennials; Ann Ohio Ceramic & Sculpture Show, Butler Inst Am Art, Youngstown, Ohio, 12 shows; Beaux Arts Designer/Craftsmen Biennial Exhibs, Columbus Mus Art, Ohio, four shows; Objects USA Traveling Exhib, US & Europe; plus numerous one-man & invitational group exhibs. *Pos:* Graphic designer, several art studios in Cleveland, Ohio, 30-57; sculptor, 30-57; sculptor/ceramist, pvt studio, 57- *Awards:* Governor's Award, Exhib 68, Columbus Mus Art, 68; 10 Spec Jury Awards, Ann Shows, Cleveland Mus Art; Visual Arts Award, Cleveland, 83. *Bibliog:* Roger Bonham (auth), Claude Conover, Ceramics Monthly, 5/66. *Mem:* Am Crafts Coun. *Mailing Add:* 1860 Oakmount Rd Cleveland OH 44121

CONOVER, ROBERT FREMONT
PRINTMAKER, PAINTER
b Trenton, NJ, July 3, 20. *Study:* Philadelphia Mus Sch Art; Art Students League; Brooklyn Mus Sch. *Work:* Smithsonian Inst, Libr Cong, Washington, DC; Mus Mod Art, Pub Libr, Whitney Mus Am Art, New York; and others. *Comn:* Print ed, 200 woodcuts, 57 & 75 woodcuts, 61, Int Graphic Art Soc; print ed, 75 woodcuts, Hilton Hotels, 62; print ed, 30 woodcuts, Assoc Am Artists Galleries, 69; print ed, 60 relief prints, Ferdinand Roten Galleries, 71. *Exhib:* Painters of the 20th Century, Mus Mod Art, New York, 50; Whitney Mus Am Art Ann, 50-54; Carnegie Int, Pittsburgh, 54; Pa Acad Fine Arts Painting Ann, 54; one-man show, New Sch Social Res, New York, 68 & 74; Brooklyn Mus Print Biennial, 70 & 75. *Teaching:* Instr painting & graphics, New Sch Social Res, 51-; instr painting, Brooklyn Mus Sch, 60-; instr graphics, Newark Sch Fine & Indust Arts, 67- *Awards:* Purchase Prizes, Brooklyn Mus, 54, Soc Am Graphic Artists, Assoc Am Artist Gallery, 67 & Philadelphia Print Club. *Bibliog:* Article, Art in Am, 57; Seuphor (auth),

Dictionary of Abstract Painting, 58; Jules Heller (auth), Printmaking Today, Holt, 72. *Mem:* Soc Am Graphic Artists; Am Abstract Artists. *Media:* Oil, Graphics; Woodcut. *Dealer:* Assoc Am Artists Gallery 663 Fifth Ave New York NY 10022. *Mailing Add:* 162 E 33rd St New York NY 10016

CONRAD, GEORGE
EDUCATOR, PRINTMAKER
b Newark, NJ, Feb 10, 16. *Study:* Newark Sch Fine & Indust Arts; NY Univ, BS; Columbia Univ, MA & EdD. *Work:* Butler Inst Am Art; La Jolla Mus Art; Univ Ga; Columbus Pub Libr, Ohio; Univ Ore; and others. *Exhib:* Artists from NJ, Newark Mus; Independent, New York; NJ Art in Cols, State Mus, NJ. *Pos:* Ed, 62-72; mem, NJ Arts Coun, 66-71. *Teaching:* Prof art educ, Ill State Univ, 49-58; prof art hist, Glassboro State Col, 58-, chmn dept art, 78- *Mem:* NJ Art Educ Asn (pres, 69); Eastern Arts Asn (coun, 69); Nat Art Educ Asn (state assembly, 69). *Media:* Multiprint Media, Photography. *Publ:* Auth, Process of Art Educ, Prentice-Hall, 64. *Mailing Add:* 163 N Mansfield Blvd Cherry Hill NJ 08034

CONRAD, JOHN W
EDUCATOR, CERAMIST
b Cresson, Pa, Aug 3, 35. *Study:* Ind Univ of Pa, BS; Carnegie-Mellon Univ, Pittsburgh, MFA(ceramics); Univ Pittsburgh, PhD. *Work:* Mesa Col, San Diego, Calif. *Exhib:* Tiffany Invitational, New York, 65; one man show, Sculpture Gallery, San Diego, Calif, 76; Small Sculptures: National Cypress Fine Arts Gallery, Cypress, Calif, 76; Ceramics Design 76, Sculpture Gallery, San Diego, 76; Soup Tureens--1976, Campbell Mus, Camden, NJ, 76. *Teaching:* Instr crafts, Penn Hills Sr High Sch, Pittsburgh, Pa, 59-64; prof ceramics & chmn dept, Mesa Col, San Diego, 66- *Mem:* Col Art Asn; Nat Coun Educ Ceramic Arts; Int Guild Craft Journalists, Authors & Photogrs. *Publ:* Auth, Ceramic Formulas: The Complete Compendium, Macmillan, 73; auth, Contemporary Ceramic Techniques, Prentice-Hall, 77; auth, Ceramic Manual, Prentice-Hall, 84; auth, Contemporary Ceramic Formulas, Macmillan, 80; auth, Advance Ceramic Manual, Prentice-Hall, 84. *Mailing Add:* 3675 Syracuse Ave San Diego CA 92122

CONRAD, NANCY R
PAINTER
b Houston, Tex, Jan 29, 40. *Study:* Houston Mus Fine Arts; Randolph Macon Woman's Col, BA. *Work:* Randolph Macon Collection Am Women Painters, Lynchburg, Va; El Paso Mus Fine Arts, Tex; Continental Oil Co Collection & Dresser Indust Collection, Houston; Aviation Am Bldg, Love Field, Dallas; Allied Bank Group. *Exhib:* Sun Carnival Exhib, El Paso Mus Fine Arts, 73-75; Tex Painting & Sculpture, Dallas Mus Fine Arts; 52nd Ann Nat Exhib, Shreveport, La, 74; Nat Women's Year Exhib, 79; Women & Their Work, touring show, 80-81; and others. *Awards:* Foley Award, Foley's of Houston, 70; First Place Jurors Choice, Assistance League of Houston, 72; Purchase Award, El Paso Mus Art, 73. *Bibliog:* Articles in Southwest Art Mag, Art Mag, Art Voices South, & Artweek Newspaper. *Mem:* Art League Houston (vpres, 74-75); Artists Equity Asn. *Media:* Watercolor, Oil. *Dealer:* Adelle M Taylor Fine Arts 3317 McKinney Ave Dallas TX; Fine Art Consultants 1744 Norfolk Houston TX. *Mailing Add:* 819 Wade Hampton Houston TX 77024

CONRAD, PAUL FRANCIS
CARTOONIST
b Cedar Rapids, Iowa, June 27, 24. *Pos:* Ed cartoonist, Denver Post, 50-64, Los Angeles Times, 64-; cartoonist, Los Angeles Times Syndicate; lectr, Cooke-Daniels Lectr Tours, Denver Art Mus, 64. *Awards:* Sigma Delta Chi Award, 63, 69 & 71; Pulitzer Prize Ed Cartooning, 64 & 71; Overseas Press Club Award, 69. *Mailing Add:* Times Mirror Sq Los Angeles CA 90053

CONSEY, KEVIN E
MUSEUM DIRECTOR, ADMINISTRATOR
b New York, NY, Jan 15, 52. *Study:* Hofstra Univ, BA, 74; Univ Va, Charlottesville, 75; Univ Mich, Ann Arbor, MA(mus practice), 77. *Collections Arranged:* African Art (auth, catalog), Art Mus, Univ Mich, 76 & 77; Real, Really Real, Super Real, 81. *Pos:* Dir, San Antonio Mus Art, 80-83 & Newport Harbor Art Mus, 83- *Teaching:* Instr art hist, Univ Toledo, 75-76; asst prof & dir, Emily Lowe Gallery, Hofstra Univ, 77-80; vis prof, Univ Tex, San Antonio, 81-83. *Mem:* Asn Am Mus Dirs; Am Asn Mus; Col Art Asn; Visual Arts Panel, Tex Comn Arts; Int Coun Mus. *Res:* Twentieth century American art, expecially art of 30s and 40s and sculpture. *Publ:* Coauth, Pompeii as style, In: Pompeii as Source and Inspiration, Univ Mich, 77; ed, Art for the People--New Deal Murals on Long Island, Hofstra Univ, 78; ed, Off the Wall--Environments and Installations, San Antonio Mus Mod Art, 81. *Mailing Add:* 850 San Clemente Dr Newport Beach CA 92660

CONSTANTINE, GREG JOHN
PAINTER, EDUCATOR
b Windsor, Ont, Can, Feb 14, 38. *Study:* Andrews Univ, Mich, BA; Mich State Univ with Angelo Ippolito, MFA; Univ Calif, Los Angeles. *Work:* Grand Rapids Art Mus, Mich. *Exhib:* Arkansas Nat, 69; Chicago & Vicinity, Chicago Art Inst, 71; Michigan Artists, Detroit, 71; Philbrook Art Ctr, Tulsa, Okla, 75; LaGrange Nat, Ga, 75. *Teaching:* Chmn dept painting & art hist & prof art, Andrews Univ, 63- *Awards:* W & B Clusman Prize, Chicago Vicinity Show, Chicago Art Inst, 71. *Bibliog:* J Heriksen (auth), Artist, Insight Mag, 70; O Young (auth), Editor, Focus Mag, 75. *Mem:* Mus Contemp Art, Chicago; Col Art Asn; Mid-Am Art Asn. *Media:* Acrylic; Photography. *Publ:* Auth, article, Spectrum Mag, 75. *Dealer:* James Yu Gallery 393 West Broadway New York NY 10012. *Mailing Add:* Dept of Art Andrews Univ Berrien Springs MI 49104

CONSTANTINE, MILDRED
HISTORIAN

b Brooklyn, NY, June 28, 14. *Study:* NY Univ, MA, 38. *Collections Arranged:* The Olivetti Company, 52, The Package, 59, The Object Transformed, 66, Word & Image, 68 & Wallhangings, 69, Mus Mod Art, New York; art collections for Am Tel & Tel & Union Camp. *Pos:* Asst keeper, Archiv Hispanic Cult, Libr Cong, Washington, DC, 40-42; assoc cur, Dept Archit & Design, Mus Mod Art, 49-71; consult art, archit & design, 71- *Teaching:* Instr hist graphic design, Parsons Sch Design, 71-; vis fac, Banff Centre Arts. *Mem:* Col Art Asn; Latin Am Studies Asn. *Res:* Latin American art from pre-Columbian to modern; modern art, architecture and design. *Publ:* Co-ed, Art Nouveau, Mus Mod Art, 59, 2nd ed 75; coauth, Beyond Craft: The Art Fabric, Van Nostrand, 73; coauth, Soviet Revolutionary Film Posters, Johns Hopkins Univ Press, 74; auth, Tina Modotti, A Fragile Life, Paddington Press, 75. *Mailing Add:* 307 East 44th St Rm 1218 New York NY 10017

CONTINI, ANITA (ANITA O'NEILL-CONTINI)
ADMINISTRATOR, CURATOR

b Cleveland, Ohio, Jan 16, 44. *Study:* Cleveland Music Settlement, scholar, 60; Elizabeth Seton Col, Yonkers, NY, AAS, 64; Hofstra Univ, Long Island, NY, BA, 66. *Collections Arranged:* Ruckus Manhattan by Red Grooms (auth, catalog), 75-76, Ruckus Manhattan, 81 & Art on the Beach (auth, catalog), 82, Creative Time Inc. *Pos:* Exec dir & pres, Creative Time Inc, New York, 73-; pres & bd mem, Athena Found Inc, New York, 78- *Awards:* Certs Merit, Ruckus Manhattan, 76 & Masstransiscope, 81, Munic Art Soc. *Bibliog:* Deborah C Phillips (auth), New faces in alternative spaces, Art News, 11/81; Grace Glueck (auth), New home, new look for Ruckus Manhattan, New York Times, 12/18/81; Carrie Rickey (auth), Taking care of artists' business, Village Voice, 1/5/82. *Mem:* Arts & Bus Coun New York. *Mailing Add:* Creative Time Inc 66 West Broadway New York NY 10007

COOK, AUGUST CHARLES
PAINTER, PRINTMAKER

b Philadelphia, Pa, Mar 15, 1897. *Study:* Pa Acad Fine Arts; Harvard Univ. *Work:* La Salle Col, Philadelphia; Libr Cong; Butler Mus Am Art, Youngstown, Ohio; Gibbs Art Gallery, Charleston, SC; SC Art Comn Collection. *Exhib:* Pa Acad Fine Arts; Soc Am Graphic Artists; Libr Cong Print Exhib; Nat Acad Design, New York; Carolina 25th Ann, Gibbs Art Gallery. *Teaching:* Prof fine arts & head dept, Converse Col, Spartanburg, SC, 24-66, emer, 67- *Awards:* Purchase Prize, Furman Univ, Greenville, SC. *Bibliog:* Jack Morris (auth), Contemporary Artists of South Carolina, 70. *Mem:* Guild SC Artists. *Media:* Oil; Wood Engraving. *Mailing Add:* RR 3 Box 214 Chesnee SC 29323

COOK, CHRISTOPHER CAPEN
ADMINISTRATOR

b Boston, Mass, May 28, 32. *Study:* Wesleyan Univ, BA, 54; Univ Ill, MFA, 59. *Exhib:* De Cordova Mus, Lincoln, Mass, 64; Boston Fine Arts Festival, 64; Northeastern Regional Mead Corp, Smith Col Mus Art, 65; Mus Mod Art, New York, 70; Ctr Art & Commun, Buenos Aires, Arg, 70; Kyoto, Japan, 71; solo exhib, Inst Contemp Art, Boston, 73; Sch Mus Fine Arts, Boston, 78. *Pos:* Asst dir, Addison Gallery Am Art, Andover, Mass, 64-69, dir, 69-; dir, Inst Contemp Art, Boston, 71-72; visitor visual & environ studies, Harvard Univ, 74-79. *Teaching:* Instr art, Colby Jr Col, 56; instr art, Univ NH, 59-63, asst prof, 63-64; vis prof, Lesley Col, Cambridge, 75-78; vis artist teacher, Sch Mus Fine Arts, Boston, 78- *Mem:* Coun Mus & Educ in Visual Arts; Nat Humanities Fac; Archiv Am Art (adv bd, 72-76). *Publ:* Auth, Possibles, 69; auth, Book of Instants, 70; auth, Poem System-Anytime, 71. *Mailing Add:* c/o Dir, Addison Gallery Am Art Phillips Acad Andover MA 01810

COOK, JOHN (ALFRED)
SCULPTOR, MEDALIST

b Excelsior, Minn, June 2, 30. *Study:* Ariz State Univ, BA(with distinction), 55; State Univ Iowa, with H Albrizio, MFA(sculpture), 56; Akad Bildenden Kuenste, Munich, Fulbright Scholar, 62-63. *Work:* Brit Mus, London; Smithsonian Inst; Estense Gallerie, Modena, Italy; Nat Gallery, Budapest; Royal Coin Cabinet, Nat Mus, Stockholm. *Comn:* La Vie Sculpture Award, Assoc Students, Pa State Univ, 80; Frivolity, Vanity (medal), Soc Medallists, Danbury, Conn, 81; Faculty Scholar Medal, 81, Atherton Sculpture Relief, 82 & Eos Medal Merit, 83, Pa State Univ. *Exhib:* Solo exhibs, Art Gallery, Eastern Ky State Univ, 78, Union Gallery, Purdue Univ, 79 & Kipp Gallery, Ind Univ Pa, 82; 19th Esposizione Int Medaglie Contemp, Palazzo Medici-Riccardi, Florence, Italy, 83; Am Medallic Sculpture Asn Exhib, New York, Colorado Springs, Colo & San Francisco, 83-84. *Collections Arranged:* Dora De Pedery Hunt (auth, catalog), Medals and Sculpture, Pa State Univ, 82; Fedn Int Medaille Int Exhib Medallic Art (auth, catalog). *Teaching:* Instr sculpture, Cornell Univ, 56-58 & Univ Ariz, 58-62; prof, Pa State Univ, 64- *Awards:* Inst Arts & Humanistic Studies Award, 81-83. *Bibliog:* Margo Russell (auth), Cook should have a medal, Coin World, 3/83; Ed Reiter (auth), US medal is planned for international shows, New York Times, 6/13/83; Barbara Snavely (auth), Sculptor of medallions, Research, Pa State Univ, 9/83. *Mem:* Am Medallic Sculpture Asn (mem bd dirs, 82-); Fedn Int Medaille (mem exec coun, 83-). *Media:* Cast Bronze. *Publ:* Contribr, Future American directions, 1/84, The amuletic medal, 1/84 & American University prepares for medals workshop, 1/84, Medailles, Paris. *Mailing Add:* PO Box 181 Lemont PA 16851

COOK, LIA
TAPESTRY ARTIST, EDUCATOR

Study: Univ Calif, Berkeley, BA, 65, MA, 73. *Work:* Am Craft Mus, New York; Galerie de la Tapisserie et d'Art Textile, Beauvais, France. *Comn:* Embarcadero Ctr, San Francisco, 74; City Hall, Fairfield, Calif, 76; Art in Archit Prog, US Gen Serv Admn, Richmond, Calif, 76; Morrison & Foerster Law Offices, San Francisco, 77; Rensselaer Polytechnic Inst, 79. *Exhib:* Solo exhibs, Renwick Gallery, Nat Mus Am Art, 80 & San Jose Mus Art, Calif, 80; The Art Fabric: Mainstream, San Francisco Mus Mod Art, traveling, 81-84; Celebration 25, 81 & The Pattern Show, 82, Am Craft Mus, New York; Jacquard Textiles, Cooper-Hewitt Mus, New York, 82; Fiber Directions, Brunnier Gallery and Mus, Iowa State Univ, 82; retrospective, Galerie Nat de la Tapisserie et d'Art Textile, Beauvais, France, 83. *Teaching:* Prof art, Calif Col Arts & Crafts, Oakland, 76- *Awards:* Fels, Nat Endowment Arts, 74-75 & 77-78; Special Proj Grant, Nat Endowment Arts, 81. *Media:* Rayon. *Mailing Add:* c/o Allrich Gallery 251 Post St San Francisco CA 94610

COOK, MICHAEL DAVID
PAINTER, VIDEO ARTIST

b Ramey, PR, July 16, 53. *Study:* Fla State Univ, BFA, 75; Univ Dallas, MA, 76; Univ Okla, MFA, 78. *Exhib:* 77th Ann Exhib by Artists of Chicago & Vicinity, Art Inst Chicago, 78; New Dimensions--Time, Mus Contemp Art, Chicago, 80; Working Drawings, Hunter Gallery, New York, 81; War Games, Kitchen, New York, 82; solo exhib, NAME Gallery, Chicago, 82 & Grayson Gallery, Chicago, 83; The End of the World, New Mus Contemp Art, New York, 83; System and Structure, Allen Priebe Art Gallery & travelling, 83-84. *Teaching:* Vis artist painting & drawing, Video Univ Ill, Champaign-Urbana, 78-80; asst prof, Univ Ill, Chicago, 80-82; vis lectr, Univ Calif, Berkeley, currently. *Awards:* Ford Found Fac Res Grants, 78 & 79; Ill Arts Coun Fel, 82. *Bibliog:* Janet Kutner (auth), Graf-feet-i, glitter and crab claws, Artnews, 79; Pat Tomson (auth), article, New Art Examiner, 82. *Mailing Add:* 1636 Oakview Ave Kensington CA 94707

COOK, PETER (GEOFFREY)
PAINTER

b New York, NY, June 10, 15. *Study:* Princeton Univ, BA(archit), 37; Nat Acad Design, Pulitzer Traveling Scholar, 37-39; Art Students League, 37-40. *Work:* US Supreme Court; Wells Col. *Comn:* Portraits, Princeton Univ, Simmons Col, Boston, New Eng Merchants Bank, Exeter Acad, Harvard Univ & St Mark's Sch. *Exhib:* Nat Acad Design Ann, 43-; one-man shows, Vose Galleries, Boston & Richmond, Va, 52; Ogunquit Arts Ctr, 55-69; Boston Art Festival, 67. *Awards:* Governor's Prize, State of Maine, 61; Bronze Medal, Nat Arts Club, 65; Century Asn Medal, 67. *Mem:* Nat Acad Design; Century Asn. *Media:* Oil. *Dealer:* Portraits Inc 41 E 57th St New York NY 10022. *Mailing Add:* Box 202 Heathcote Farm Kingston NJ 08528

COOK, ROBERT HOWARD
SCULPTOR, MEDALIST

b Boston, Mass, Apr 8, 21. *Study:* Demetrios Sch, 38-42; Beaux Arts, Paris, under Marcel Gaumont, 45. *Work:* Whitney Mus Am Art, New York; Pa Acad Fine Arts, Philadelphia; Va Mus Fine Arts, Richmond; Hirshhorn Collection, Washington, DC; State Univ NY, Oneida. *Comn:* Lifeline, Sun Co, Radnor, Pa, 78; Off the Water, Sun-Co, 79; Emerging, Saudi Arabia, 81; Camel, Saudi Arabia, 82; Stretch, Saudi Arabia, 82. *Exhib:* One-man shows, Inst Contemp Art, Boston, 51, Birmingham Mus Fine Arts, Ala, 67, Mint Mus Art, Charlotte, NC, 68, Va Mus Fine Art, Richmond, 68 & Schenectady Mus Art, NY, 77; Pa Acad of Fine Arts; Whitney Ann; Nat Acad Design; Boston Art Festival; Univ Ill; Biennale Venezia, Italy, 51; and other group & one-man shows. *Awards:* Second Prize, Prix de Rome, Am Acad of Rome, 42; Cash Award & Best-of-Show, Nat Acad of Arts & Lett, 48; Tiffany Award, Tiffany Found, 48. *Bibliog:* Tracy O'Kates & Arnold Eagle (auth), World of Robert Cook (27-minute doc on his work), Beechtree Productions, 77. *Mem:* Sculptors Guild. *Media:* Bronze, Wood. *Publ:* Auth, Family Album in Bronze (photographs by Franco Romagnoli), 76, Twelve commissions, 78 & In motion, 80, Jasillo. *Dealer:* Sculpture Ctr 167 E 69th St New York NY 10021. *Mailing Add:* Piazza Borghese Rome 02186 Italy

COOK, STEPHEN D
PRINTMAKER, DRAFTSMAN

b Jackson, Miss, Sept 10, 51. *Study:* Miss Col, BA, 73; Univ Miss, MFA, 75; Royal Col Art, London, cert, 76. *Work:* Victoria & Albert Mus, London; Southern Graphics Coun Print Arch, Oxford, Miss; Miss Sch Supply Co, Jackson; Meridian Mus Art. *Exhib:* Mid-South Biennial, Brooks Mem, Memphis, 74; one-man shows, Miss Art Asn Gallery, Jackson, 77 & Meridian Mus Art, 79; Comparisons & Contrasts, Soviet Union Tour, 79-81; Southeast Mo State Univ Nat Print Invitational Exhib, 81; Southern Graphics Council Member Touring Exhib, 81-82. *Pos:* Artist-in-residence, Tupelo, Miss, 77-78. *Teaching:* Chmn dept printmaking, Miss Mus Art Sch, 77-78; instr printmaking & drawing, Univ Miss, Oxford, 78; instr, Hinds Junior Col, Raymond, 80, Miss Col, Clinton, 83-; adj instr, Jackson Pub Schs, 82. *Awards:* Bellamann Mem Found Ann Award, 75; ITT Corp Int Fel, London, 75-76; Award of Merit, Miss Artists Competitive, 78. *Mem:* Southern Graphics Coun. *Media:* Etching in Line & Aquatint; Charcoal, Pastel. *Publ:* Contribr, J Royal Col Art, 76. *Mailing Add:* 303 East St PO Box 720 Clinton MS 39056

COOKE, JODY HELEN
PAINTER, EDUCATOR

b Windriver, Wyo, Oct 25, 22. *Study:* Univ Calif, Berkeley, BA(fine arts); Univ Minn, Minneapolis, MA; Calif Col Arts & Crafts; Univ Ore, Eugene, with C Bryan Ryan, Robert James, June King McFee, Gordon Kensler & Vincent Lanier, PhD; Calif State Univ. *Work:* Calif State Univ, Hayward;

Alaska State Mus, Juneau; Anchorage Hist Fine Arts Mus. *Exhib:* One-man show, Anchorage Hist & Fine Arts Mus, 79; three-man show, Allied Arts Gallery, Sacramento, 67; All Alaska Exhib, Alaska Hist & Fine Arts Mus, Anchorage, 76 & 77; Contemp Arts of Alaska, Smithsonian Inst, Washington, DC, 78; On and Of Paper, Alaska, 81 & travelling exhib, 83-84. *Teaching:* Head art dept, Col Siskiyous, 64-67; asst prof art & educ, Univ Iowa, Iowa City, 69-70 & Ore State Univ, Corvallis, 70-73; lectr art educ, Calif State Univ, Sacramento, 73-74; assoc prof & dir exhib, Univ Alaska, 74-, chmn art dept, 76-77. *Awards:* Merit Award, Auburn Arts Festival, Calif, 66; Purchase Award, All Alaska Competition, 77 & Alaska State Bank, 81. *Bibliog:* Reid Hastie (auth), Encounter With Art, 61. *Mem:* Visual Arts Ctr Alaska; Anchorage Adv Arts Comn; Alaska Art Educ Asn. *Media:* Oil, Acrylic. *Collection:* Drawings, prints, paintings and pottery of contemporary artists. *Mailing Add:* 2802 W 30th Ave 8 Anchorage AK 99503

COOKE, JUDY (JUDY HANSON)
PAINTER, COLLAGE ARTIST
b Bay City, Mich, July 8, 40. *Study:* Boston Mus Sch Fine Arts, Hons dipl, 63; Tufts Univ, Medford, Mass, BFA, 65; Reed Col, Portland, Ore, MAT, 71. *Work:* Boston Mus Sch of Fine Arts; City of Seattle; Portland Art Mus, Ore; Ranier Bank & Pac Northwest Bell, Seattle; Itell Corp, San Francisco. *Exhib:* 14 Women Survivors, Henry Gallery, Univ Wash, Seattle, 72; Prospect: Northwest 72, Seattle Art Mus Pavilion, 72 & Northwest Ann, 73 & 74; 80th Anniversary Invitational, Portland Art Mus, Ore, 73; In Touch: Nature, Ritual & Sensuous Art from the Northwest, Portland Ctr for Visual Arts, 76; Aesthetics of Graffiti, San Francisco Mus Mod Art, 78. *Pos:* Founding mem, Blackfish Gallery, 79- *Teaching:* Instr basic design, Portland State Univ, 77- *Awards:* Purchase Award, Portland Art Mus, 73; Painting Award, Seattle Art Mus Pavilion, 73; Boston Mus traveling fel, 74. *Bibliog:* Judy Cooke/Canvas Constructions, Portland Art Mus, 73; Lucy Lippard (auth), Northwest passage, Art in Am, 7-8/76; Bruce Guenther (auth), Fifty Northwest Artists, Chronicle Bks. *Mem:* Portland Ctr for Visual Arts; Artists' Equity, Inc, Portland (pres, 75-76). *Media:* Acrylics; Drawing Mediums. *Dealer:* Blackfish Gallery 325 NW Sixth Portland OR 97209; Traver/Sutton Gallery 2219 Fourth Ave Seattle WA 98121. *Mailing Add:* 2317 NW Quimby St Portland OR 97210

COOKE, SAMUEL TUCKER
PAINTER, EDUCATOR
b Gainesville, Fla, Dec 4, 41. *Study:* Stetson Univ, with Fred Messersmith, BA; Univ Ga, with Lamar Dodd & Howard Thomas, MFA. *Work:* Asheville Art Mus, NC; Mint Mus Art, Charlotte, NC; Univ Ga Collection; Hunter Gallery Art, Chattanooga, Tenn; Davidson Col, NC. *Exhib:* Nat Drawing & Small Sculpture Exhib, Ball State Univ, 72-74; Davidson Col Nat Print & Drawing Exhib, 74-75; Gallery Contemp Art Realist, Winston-Salem, NC, 74-75; Southeastern Drawing Invitational, Mint Mus, Charlotte, 79; one-man shows, New Morning Gallery, Asheville, 78, Somerhill Gallery, Durham, 79 & 81 & Asheville Art Mus, 80. *Teaching:* Chmn dept art, Univ NC, Asheville, 68-79. *Awards:* 3rd Davidson Nat Drawing & Print Award, Knight Publ Co, 74; 39th Southeastern Painting & Drawing Award, Wachovia Bank NC, 74; Mint Mus Award for Realism in North Carolina, NC Arts Coun, 74. *Dealer:* New Morning Gallery 3 1/2 Kitchen Pl Asheville NC 28803; Somerhill Gallery 5504 Chapel Hill Blvd Durham NC 27707. *Mailing Add:* 65 Kenilworth Rd Asheville NC 28804

COOLEY, ADELAIDE N
PAINTER, WRITER
b Idaho Falls, Idaho, Apr 18, 14. *Study:* Stephens Col for Women, Columbia, Mo, AA; Univ Wis-Madison, BS; Bradley Univ, Peoria, Ill. *Work:* Peoria Art Guild Collection, St Paul's Episcopal Cathedral Collection, Carson Pirie Scott & Co, Peoria, Ill. *Comn:* Altar paraments, Univ United Methodist Church, Peoria, Ill, 67. *Exhib:* 24th Ann Invitational, Ill State Mus, 71; paintings & pottery with floral motifs, Peoria Pub Libr, 78; paintings & pottery, Western Ill Univ, Macomb, 79; retrospective exhib paintings, pottery and small sculpture, Peoria Art Guild, 79; Ill Crafts, Ill State Mus, Springfield, 77. *Pos:* Art consult, Peoria Hist Soc, 83-; art critic, Appraisals, 83- *Awards:* Outstanding Woman in Art, YWCA, Peoria, Ill, 73; Arts Award, YWCA, Peoria, Ill, 78. *Bibliog:* Edward Barry (auth), Art notes, Chicago Sun Tribune, 2/25/68; Don J Anderson (auth), Four women and the circle, Chicago Am, 2/18/68; Barbara Mantz (auth), Getting to know Adelaide Nation Cooley, Peoria J Star, 1/6/74. *Mem:* Peoria Art Guild (pres, 61-63); Ill Art League; Lakeview Mus Arts & Sci; Peoria Fine Arts Soc. *Media:* Oil, Watercolor. *Publ:* Auth, History of Art in Peoria, 1800-1975, Peoria Jaycees Mag, 75; auth, Joseph Petarde, immigrant stone carver, Ill Mag, 76; auth, The Monument Maker, Biography of Frederick Ernst Triebel, Expo Press, 78; auth, Reviews of art exhibits, The New Art Examiner, Chicago, 81. *Dealer:* Lakeview Art Mus Shop 1125 W Lake Ave Peoria IL 61611; Peoria Art Guild 1831 N Knoxville Peoria IL 61603. *Mailing Add:* 808 Chalon Dr Peoria IL 61604

COOLEY, WILLIAM, JR
COLLECTOR, PATRON
b Peoria, Ill, Aug 29, 10. *Study:* Northwestern Univ, BA, 32, MD, 36. *Bibliog:* Jerry Klein (auth), Collecting as art, Peoria Jour Star, 5/10/70. *Mem:* Peoria Art Guild; Lakeview Ctr Arts & Sci; Mus Contemp Art, Chicago; Chicago Art Inst; Smithsonian Inst. *Interests:* Support to Bradley Univ Sch Art, Lakeview Ctr, Peoria Art Guild & individual artists. *Collection:* About 300 works collected over a 30 year period, including most of the major 20th century artists, mainly drawings, sculpture and signed original prints of museum quality. *Mailing Add:* 808 Chalon St Peoria IL 61614

COOLIDGE, JOHN
HISTORIAN
b Cambridge, Mass, Dec 16, 13. *Study:* Harvard Univ, BA, 35; NY Univ, PhD, 48. *Pos:* Dir, Fogg Art Mus, Harvard Univ, 48-82; trustee, Mus of Fine Arts, Boston, 48-77, pres bd, 76-77, emer pres bd, 77- *Teaching:* Prof fine arts, Harvard Univ, 47- *Mem:* Col Art Asn Am; Soc Archit Historians. *Res:* History of American architecture, Italian renaissance architecture. *Publ:* Auth, Mill & Mansion, 42; auth, The Villa Guilea, Art Bulletin, 42. *Mailing Add:* 24 Gray Gardens Boston MA 02138

COONEY, BARBARA (MRS CHARLES TALBOT PORTER)
ILLUSTRATOR, WRITER
b Brooklyn, NY, Aug 6, 17. *Study:* Smith Col, BA, 38; Art Students League, 40. *Awards:* Caldecott Medal, 59 & 80; Smith Col Medal, 76; Nat Book Award, 83. *Publ:* Illusr, Wynken, Blynken & Nod, Hastings, 70; illusr, When the Sky is Like Lace, Lippincott, 75; illusr, The Donkey Prince, Doubleday, 77; illusr, I am Cherry Alive, the Little Girl Sang, Harper & Row, 79; illusr, Ox-Cart Man, Viking, 79; and many others. *Mailing Add:* Damariscotta ME 04543

COONEY-CRAWFORD, THOM M
PAINTER, SCULPTOR
b Boston, Mass, Sept 23, 44. *Study:* Provincetown Workshop, 63 & 64; Spring Hill Col, Mobile, Ala, BS, 66-62; Syracuse Univ, MFA, 66-67; RI Sch Design, 69. *Comn:* Interior & Exterior (painting & sculpture), Prickly Mt Architectural Project, Warren, Vt, 67; Exterior (painting & sculpture), Bundy Art Mus, Waitesfield, Vt, 69. *Exhib:* Post Modernism Metaphors, Alternative Mus, New York, 81; New Visions, Aldrich Mus Contemp Art, Ridgefield, Conn, 81; New York Visions, Janus Gallery, Los Angeles, 83; Queens Mus, 83; PS 1, Proj Rm, New York, 83; Monique Knowlton Gallery, New York, 84. *Awards:* Creative Artists Pub Serv Prog Fel, 82-83. *Bibliog:* Alexandra Anderson (auth), Review, Village Voice, 6/19/78; Peter Frank (auth), Review, Village Voice, 7/10/78; David K S Kermani (auth), New faces/new images, Ocular Mag, 81. *Media:* Oil, Bronze. *Publ:* Auth & illusr, Raising of the Heart, Limited Ed, Queen City Eds, 72. *Dealer:* Monique Knowlton Gallery 153 Mercer St New York NY 10012. *Mailing Add:* 12-07 Jackson Ave New York NY 11101

COOPER, ANTHONY J
PAINTER
b Chicago, Ill, Feb 28, 07. *Study:* Chicago Art Inst, grad(fel); spec study with Boris Anisfeld; summer study at Julienne Acad, Paris, France. *Work:* Ill State Mus; Balzekas Mus, Chicago; Chicago Corp; Standard Fed Savings & Loan, Chicago; Beverly Art Ctr, Chicago; Dr Stola Drag, Basel, Switz; and others. *Comn:* St Anthony (oil painting), Lady of Vilna Church, Chicago, 67; portrait of Mrs Switalski, comn by John Switalski, Berkeley, Calif, 69; St Sebastian (oil painting), Lithuanian-Am Jesuit Fathers, Chicago, 70; Chicago Landscapes (oil painting), comn by Dr Paul Egel, Chicago, 73; Still Life (oil painting), comn by Dr Leonard Lesko, Univ Calif, Berkeley, 77. *Exhib:* Ill State Fair, Springfield, 75; Mitchell Mus, Mt Vernon, Ill, 75; Traveling Bicentennial Show, Balzekas Mus & Ill Arts Coun, 76-77; Corcoran Gallery, Washington, DC; Nat Acad Design, New York; Discovering Workers Culture in Am Soc, Ann Arbor, Mich, 80; and others. *Teaching:* Instr landscape & oil painting, Chicago Art Club, formerly. *Awards:* William B French Award, 31; Munic Art League Award, Chicago Munic Art League, 64; First Place for Landscape Oils, Am-Lithuanian Artists, Balzekas Mus, 75. *Bibliog:* Harold Haydon (auth), Fine exhibits over town, Chicago Sun-Times, 3/14/71. *Media:* Oil, Watercolor. *Dealer:* Chicago Art Inst Art Rental/Sales Gallery Michigan & Adams Chicago IL 60603. *Mailing Add:* 4545 N Hamilton Ave Chicago IL 60625

COOPER, MARIO
PAINTER, INSTRUCTOR
b Mexico City, Mex, Nov 26, 05. *Study:* Otis Art Inst, Los Angeles, 24; Chouinard Art Sch, Los Angeles, 25; Grand Cent Art Sch, New York, 27-37; and with F Tolles Chamberlin, Louis Trevisco, Pruett Carter & Harvey Dunn. *Work:* Metrop Mus Art; Col USAF; Butler Inst Am Art; NASA; and others. *Comn:* Painting of Atlas ICBM & planes, USAF, Marianas Hall, Armed Serv Staff Col, Norfolk, Va; comn by USAF to paint the capitals of Europe, 60; invited by Nat Gallery to doc flight Apollo 10 & 11 for NASA, 69. *Exhib:* Shows & exhibs in Japan, Gt Brit, Europe, Can, Mex & Australia. *Pos:* Deleg to US Comn, Inter-Am Press Asn, 54-; in charge team artists to Japan, Korea & Okinawa, USAF, 56 & in charge team artists to Japan, 57; art consult, USAF, 60. *Teaching:* Instr, Art Students League, 57-; instr, Nat Acad Design Sch Fine Arts, City Col New York, 61-68. *Awards:* Audubon Artists Gold Medal of Honor, 74; Samuel F B Morse Gold Medal, Nat Acad Design; Am Watercolor Soc High Winds Medal, 79 & 81. *Bibliog:* History of the American Watercolor Society, 69 & History of watercolor painting in America, USAF, 66; The romance in Mario Cooper's watercolors, article in Am Artist, 9/79. *Mem:* Academician Nat Acad Design; Am Watercolor Soc (pres, 59-); Audubon Artists (pres, 54-58); hon mem Royal Watercolour Soc Gt Brit; Century Asn. *Publ:* Auth, Drawing & Painting the City, 67 & Painting with Watercolor, 71, Van Nostrand Reinhold; illusr, short stories of, P G Wodehouse, Quentin Reynolds & many others; auth, Watercolor by Design, Watson-Guptill, 80; auth, Flower Painting in Watercolor & Painting in Watercolor, 81 & The Art of Drapery, 83, Van Nostrand Reinhold. *Mailing Add:* Am Watercolor Soc 1083 Fifth Ave New York NY 10028

COOPER, MARVE H
PAINTER, CURATOR
b Bronx, NY, Jan 1, 39. *Study:* Caton Rose Inst, New York, 54; Cooper Union, 59; Pratt Inst; Queens Col, NY. *Exhib:* Sch of Fine Arts, Boston, 68; Art Asn of Newport, RI, 69 & 75; Southeastern Mass Univ Regional Exhib, 77; Drawings, DeCordova Mus, Mass; Hypergraphics V, RI Col, 81; and others. *Pos:* Printer, Universal Art Ltd Ed, East Islip, NY, 59-63; free-lance artist, corp design, 65-74; dir, Cooper & French Gallery, Newport, 74-; cur visual arts, Art Asn Newport, RI, 79- *Teaching:* Instr painting, Queens Col, NY, 67; lectr art, Sch Fine Arts, Boston, 68. *Awards:* First Prize & Hon Mention, Art Asn Newport, Drury, 68; First Prize, Prints, South Co Art Asn, 69. *Mem:* Art Asn Newport (coun mem, 75-); RI State Coun Arts (mem adv panel, 77-); Benefactors Arts. *Specialty:* Crafts. *Publ:* Contribr, Nine Independent Artists USA, Art Int, 68; auth, Painting and Sculpture, Language of the Specialists, Funk & Wagnalls, 66. *Dealer:* Asuna Gallery Washington DC; Marion Louis Gallery Philadelphia PA. *Mailing Add:* 46 Second Newport RI 02840

COOPER, PAULA
DEALER
b Mass, Mar 14, 38. *Study:* Pierce Col, Athens, Greece; Sorbonne, Paris; Goucher Col; Inst Fine Arts, NY Univ. *Pos:* Asst, World House Galleries, New York, 59-61; dir, Park Place Gallery, 68-; dir, Paula Cooper Gallery, 68- *Specialty:* Contemporary art. *Mailing Add:* 155 Wooster St New York NY 10012

COOPER, REBECCA
DEALER, COLLECTOR
b Philadelphia, Pa, July 11, 47. *Study:* New York Univ, BA, 69, MA, 71. *Pos:* Owner & dir, Rebecca Cooper Fine Art, 74- *Teaching:* Lectures given in var univs & mus groups on a regular basis. *Collection:* Eclectic. *Mailing Add:* 929 Park Ave New York NY 10028

COOPER, RON
ENVIRONMENTAL ARTIST, PHOTOGRAPHER
b NY, July 24, 43. *Study:* Happy Valley Sch, Chouinard Art Inst, Los Angeles. *Work:* Chicago Art Inst; Kaiser Wilhelm Mus, Krefeld, West Ger; Stedelijk Mus, Amsterdam, Netherlands; Whitney Mus Am Art, New York. *Comn:* Floating Volume Atmosphere, Libr Cong Dept Copyright & Artist, 68; Large Floating Volume of Light, Ft Worth, Tex, 71. *Exhib:* Whitney Ann Painting, 69; Theodoran Awards, Guggenheim Mus, 71; Documenta V, Kassel, WGer, 72; The State of California Painting, Brigham Young Univ Gallery, Utah, 73; Light, Lang Art Gallery, Scripps Col, Calif, 74; California Light, Cedars Sinai Med Ctr, Los Angeles, 77; Attitudes: Photography in the 70's, Santa Barbara Mus Art, 79; one-man show, Rosamund Felsen Gallery, Los Angeles, 79. *Pos:* Bd dir, Los Angeles Inst Contemp Art, 81- *Awards:* Los Angeles Co Mus Art Purchase Award, 68; Nat Endowment Arts Award, 70; Theodoran Purchase Award, Guggenheim Mus, 71. *Mem:* Artist Equity Asn (bd dir, 80-81). *Mailing Add:* 1310 Main St Venice CA 90291

COOPER, THEODORE A
DEALER
b Cleveland, Ohio, Feb 20, 43. *Study:* Muskingum Col, BA, 65; Ind Univ, MA, 67. *Pos:* Asst dir, IFA Galleries, 68-70; dir, Studio Gallery, 70-71; pres & dir, Adams Davidson Galleries, Inc, 71- *Teaching:* Teaching asst introd art, Ind Univ, 65-67. *Mem:* Am Soc Appraisers. *Specialty:* 19th century American and European Masters; early 20th century Masters. *Mailing Add:* 3233 P St NW Washington DC 20007

COOPER, WAYNE
PAINTER, GRAPHIC ARTIST
b Depew, Okla, May 7, 42. *Study:* Valparaiso Univ; Famous Artist Sch; Gary Artist League. *Work:* Art Inst Gallery, Chicago; Ft Wayne Mus Gallery, Ind. *Comn:* Story of Flight (oil), Parkview Hosp, Ft Wayne, 65; Crucifix (oil), Assembly of God Church, Hebron, Ind, 66; Christ Descending (oil), Endtime Tabernacle, Tulsa, Okla, 69; Painting of Christ, Church of God, Depew, Okla, 74; lithograph ed, Am Express Co, New York. *Exhib:* Country Beautiful, Minn, 68; Nat Show, Tyler, Tex, 69; Ft Wayne Mus, 75; Valparaiso Univ, 75; Gilcrease Mus, Tulsa. *Awards:* Best of Show, Twas Bay Show, Gilcrease Mus, Tulsa, 69; First Place for Oils, Southern Shores, Gary, Ind, 70; First Place for Watercolor, Ft Wayne Mus, 75. *Mem:* Mid-Am Art Asn; Ind Artists & Craftsmen; Am Artists Prof League; Fla Fedn Artists; Cowboy Hall of Fame. *Media:* Oil, Watercolor; Pencil, Charcoal. *Mailing Add:* 126 W 1025S Kouts IN 46347

COOPER, WENDY ANN
CURATOR
b Newark, NJ, July 28, 45. *Study:* Pembroke Col, Brown Univ, BA, 67; Univ Del, Winterthur Prog, MA(Winterthur Fel), 71; Attinham Summer Sch, Eng, 72. *Collections Arranged:* Herreshoff Collection, Bristol, RI, 69-71; Paul Revere's Boston: 1735-1818 (coauth, catalog), 75 & Copley, Stuart and West: In America and England (contribr, catalog), 76, Mus Fine Arts, Boston; In Praise of America, Nat Gallery Art, 80. *Pos:* Asst to dir, RI Hist Soc, Providence, 67-69; Mellon Fel, Brooklyn Mus, 71-72, asst cur, 72-73; spec asst, Mus Fine Arts, Boston, 73-75, asst cur, 75-77; guest cur, Nat Gallery Art, 79-80. *Teaching:* Lectr Am decorative arts, Boston Pub Libr, Mass, 75-76 & Shelburne Mus, Univ Vt, summer 76 & 77. *Mem:* Nat Trust; Decorative Arts Chap, Soc Archit Historians; Victorian Soc of Am (treas, New Eng Chap, 77). *Res:* Eighteenth century American furniture and silver, especially in New England. *Publ:* Auth, The furniture and furnishings of John Brown of Providence, Antiques, 73; auth, American Chippendale chairback settees, Am Art J, 77; auth, In Praise of America, American Decorative Arts, 1650-1830, Knopf, 80. *Mailing Add:* 313 Commonwealth Ave Boston MA 02115

COOPERSMITH, GEORGIA A
GALLERY DIRECTOR, CURATOR
b Phillipsburg, NJ, May 19, 50. *Study:* Syracuse Univ, 68-70, MFA, 77; Rochester Univ Technol, BFA, 73. *Pos:* Dir, Brainerd Art Gallery, Potsdam, NY, currently; asst cur, Mem Art Gallery, Rochester, 79-81. *Teaching:* Instr mus studies & gallery practices, State Univ & Col Arts & Science, Potsdam, 81-83. *Mem:* Am Asn Mus; Northeast Mus Conf; Col Art Asn. *Publ:* Auth, Paintings & Photographs, Moholy-Nagy, Mem Art Gallery, 78; auth, Drawings & Watercolor, Mem Art Gallery, 79; auth, Sculpture from the Johnson Atelier, Brainerd Art Gallery, 82; auth, The Twentieth Anniversary Exhibition of the Vogel Collection, 82. *Mailing Add:* 21 Cedar St Potsdam NY 13676

COPE, LOUISE TODD
WEAVER, INSTRUCTOR
b Ventnor, NJ, June 17, 30. *Study:* Syracuse Univ, BA(fine arts); Grinnell Col; Haystack Mountain Sch Crafts. *Work:* Australian Crafts Coun; NC Mus Art, Raleigh; Del Art Mus, Wilmington; Kutz State Col Collection, Pa; Riggs, Councilman, Michaels & Downs Ins Co, Baltimore; and others. *Comn:* Weaving, comn by Irving Grief, Stevenson, Md, 69; weaving, Kutztown State Col, 71. *Exhib:* Weaving Unlimited, DeCordova Mus, Mass, 71; Art in Fiber, Knoll Int, Washington, DC, 73; Invisible Artist, Philadelphia Mus Art, 73-74; Women's work, American Art, Civic Ctr Mus, Philadelphia Nat Exhib, 74; 2nd & 3rd Int Miniature Exhib; Thread Poem Traveling Show, Australia, 78; NC Mus Hist, 83. *Teaching:* Teacher fibers, Haystack Sch Crafts, 69; chmn dept textiles, Moore Col Art, 70-74; teacher textiles, Penland Sch Crafts, NC, summers 70-72 & 81-83; tutor textiles, Wincester Sch Art, Eng, summer 73; teacher fibers, var workshops in US, Eng & Can. *Awards:* NC Mus Art Purchase Award, 71; Del Art Mus Purchase Award, 70; NC Mus Art Award, 83. *Bibliog:* Donald J Willcox (auth), Body Covering: International Perspectives, Regnery, 73; Virginia Harvey (auth), article, Threads in Action, 72. *Mem:* World Crafts Coun; Am Crafts Coun; Philadelphia Coun Prof Craftsmen. *Media:* Fiber. *Publ:* Auth, Clothing, Shuttle, Spindle & Dyepot Mag, 72. *Mailing Add:* Box One 1625 Spruce St Penland NC 28765

COPELAND, LILA
PAINTER, PRINTMAKER
b New York, NY. *Study:* Art Students League, with George Grosz; Pratt Graphic Art Ctr. *Work:* Brit Mus, London, Eng; Bibliot Nat, Paris, France; Nat Collection Fine Arts, Washington, DC; Philadelphia Mus Art, Pa; Boston Mus Fine Arts, Mass; and others. *Exhib:* Art Inst Chicago; De Pauw Univ; Okla Mus Art; Staten Island Mus; Wis State Univ. *Awards:* Norman Waite Harris Bronze Medal & Prize, Art Inst Chicago. *Bibliog:* Joan Hess Michel (auth), Children--the drawings of Lila Copeland, Am Artist, 12/70; Joyce Hill (auth), Sketch of Lila Copeland, Lower Cape Artisan, 12/12/72. *Mem:* Provincetown Artists Asn. *Media:* Oil, Crayon; Lithography. *Dealer:* Harbor Gallery 24 W 57th St New York NY 10019. *Mailing Add:* 31 W Ninth St New York NY 10011

COPLANS, JOHN (RIVERS)
PHOTOGRAPHER
b London, Eng, June 24, 20. *Work:* Metrop Mus, New York; Biblioteque Nat, Paris; San Francisco Mus Art; Minneapolis Inst Arts; Mus Mod Art, New York. *Exhib:* One-person show, Art Inst Chicago, 81; Counterparts, Metrop Mus, New York, 82; Biennial, Whitney Mus, 83. *Pos:* Ed-at-large, Artforum Mag, 62-66, assoc ed, 66-70, ed, 71-; dir, art gallery, Univ Calif, Irvine, 65-68; cur, Pasadena Art Mus, 67-70; dir, Akron Art Inst, 78-81. *Awards:* Guggenheim Fel, 69; Frank Jewitt Mather, 74; Nat Endowment Arts Fel, 75 & 81. *Bibliog:* Ben Lifson (auth), Recent photographs by Bill Burne & John Coplans, Polaroid Close Up, 11/82; Charles Hagen (auth), Faces photographed, Artforum, 2/83. *Publ:* Auth, Roy Lichtenstein, Praeger, 72; auth, Ellsworth Kelly, Abrams, 72; Decisions, Decisions, 75, Norton; auth, Weegee: Tater und opfer, Schirmer/Mosel, 78; contribr, Artforum, Art News, Art in Am, Art Int; and others. *Dealer:* Pace-McGill Gallery New York NY. *Mailing Add:* 125 Cedar St New York NY 10006

COPLEY, WILLIAM NELSON
PAINTER
b New York, NY, Jan 24, 19. *Study:* Self-taught; Yale Univ, 42; Phillips Acad, Andover, Mass. *Work:* Mus Mod Art; Whitney Mus Am Art; Chicago Art Inst; Mus Mod Art, Paris; Los Angeles Co Mus Art, Los Angeles; and many others. *Comn:* Murals, Gov Rm, New York Cult Ctr. *Exhib:* One-man shows, Brooks Jackson Gallery, New York, 80 & 81, Centre George Pompidou, Paris, 81; Colorado Springs Fine Arts Ctr, Colo, 81; Mus Fine Arts, St Petersburg, Fla, 80; Ideal/The Fantastic, Whitney Mus Am Art, 80; Phyllis Kind Gallery, New York & Chicago; and others. *Bibliog:* Articles by Roland Penrose, Patrick Waldberg & Robert Melville. *Media:* Multimedia. *Mailing Add:* Phyllis Kind Gallery 139 Spring St New York NY 10012

COPPEDGE, ARTHUR L
PAINTER, EDUCATOR
b Brooklyn, NY, Apr 21, 38. *Study:* Brooklyn Mus Art Sch, with David Levine & Isaac Soyer; Art Students League; Pratt Graphic Ctr. *Work:* Brooklyn Mus, NY; Studio Mus Harlem, New York. *Comn:* Mural painting, Servo-Mation Corp, New York, 67; paintings & drawings, US Dept of Interior, DC, 75-76; paintings, Am the Beautiful, NY, 77. *Exhib:* Am 1976, Corcoran Gallery of Art, DC, 76, Fogg Mus, Boston, 77 & Ft Worth Art Mus, Tex, 77; Ann, Audubon Artist, New York, 77; Drawing Collection, Brooklyn Mus, NY, 78; Smithsonian Inst, DC; Ann Awards, Am Acad Arts & Letts, New York; Nat Gallery Jamaica, Us Embassy, Jamaica, 83. *Pos:* Bd mem, Found for Community of Artists, dir exhib dept, New Muse Mus, 76-78;

consult, African-Am Caribbean Cult Ctr, Brooklyn, New York. *Teaching:* Instr protriature, painting & drawing, Brooklyn Mus, 73-78; instr painting & drawing, Ethical Cult Soc, 76- *Awards:* Jerome Straka Award, Nat Arts Club, 77. *Bibliog:* Film of work, Nat Video Industs; film of paintings, Brooklyn Mus. *Mem:* Art Students League; Allied Artists; Brooklyn Arts & Cult Asn (consult, 78, bd mem re-grant prog, 81-82); Brooklyn Consortium Artists & Arts Inc. *Media:* Oil, Watercolor. *Publ:* Contribr, Attica Book; illusr, Intimate Portrait of Martin Buber, Viking Press; illusr, Essence Mag; auth, Found for Community of Artists; contribr, Cult Post, Nat Endowment Arts, Artspeak. *Dealer:* Brooklyn Consortium for Artists & the Arts 135 Eastern Parkway Brooklyn NY 11238. *Mailing Add:* 135 Eastern Pkwy Brooklyn NY 11238

COPPOLA, ANDREW
SCULPTOR, DRAFTSMAN
b Cophaigue, Long Island, NY, Jan 6, 41. *Study:* Hartford Art Sch & Hillyer Col, BFA, 63; studio study with Wolfgang Behl & James Van Dyke; Fulbright Hays Fel in Sculpture, Florence, Italy, 64-65. *Work:* Slater Mus, Norwich Free Acad, Conn; and pvt collections in Conn, Ariz, Fla, Colo, Italy & Calif. *Comn:* Wall relief models, West Point Military Acad, 68; Star Dancer, (cast aluminum sculpture), Berlin Town Hall, Conn, 75; Black Odesey (commemorative bronze), Amistad Resource Ctr, Hartford, Conn, 76; bronze sculptures, Nat Jewish Found, Boston, 76; granite fountain, Tower Park, Winsted, Conn, 77; and numerous others. *Exhib:* One-man shows, Stairwell Gallery, Manchester, Conn, 70 & Norwich Free Acad, 74; three-man show, New Britain Mus Am Art, Conn, 73; Lion's Gallery of the Senses, Wadsworth Atheneum Mus, 77; Architectural Sculpture: 50 Sculptors, NJ Mercer Co Community Col & traveling, 79-80. *Collections Arranged:* Head and Portrait in Sculpture 1900-1980, Farmington Valley Art Ctr, Conn, 81. *Pos:* Mem, Inst Int Educ to select Fulbright Fels, 83- *Teaching:* Instr sculpture, Univ Hartford, Hartford Art Sch, 70-71 & 84 & Hartford Jewish Community Ctr, West Hartford, 70-83. *Awards:* Painting Prize, Northwestern Community Col, Winsted, Conn, 72; Conn Comn Arts Individual Artist's Grant, 77; Art in Public Places Grant, Conn Comn Art, 78. *Bibliog:* Sigfried Halus (auth), Photographic survey of artist and work, 73; Health Hazards in the Arts & Crafts (videotape), Con Lunt Asn & Conn Comn Arts, WFSB TV, 75. *Media:* Mixed. *Mailing Add:* 262 Hudson St Hartford CT 06106

CORAL R (FLAVIANO EZEQUIEL CORAL REVELO)
PAINTER, MURALIST
b Ipiales Narino, Colombia, Dec 27, 29. *Study:* Nat Sch Art, Bogota, Colombia, 51-53; Sch Painting & Sculpture, Mexico City, 54-59. *Work:* Mus Mod Art, Toluca, Mex. *Exhib:* Contemporary Art, Mus Mod Art, Toluca, Mex, 72; one-person exhib, Nat Autonomous Univ Mex, 73; Permanent Collection of Contemporary Art, Mus Mod Art, Toluca, Mex, 77; The Forest in Art, Palace Fine Arts, Mexico City, 77; Univ Mex, Mexico City, 83. *Bibliog:* Juan Crespo de la Serna (auth), article, 9/2/70, Luis Rubluo (auth), Magnificent abstract painting, 11/15/78 & Awakening humanity, 8/21/83, Excelsior. *Media:* Oil. *Dealer:* Galeria Mer Kup Moliere 328 Colonia Polanco Mexico DF. *Mailing Add:* Ave Manuel Gutierrez Zamora 196 Col Las Aguilas Mexico 20 DF Mexico

CORBIN, GEORGE ALLEN
HISTORIAN, WRITER
b Detroit, Mich, Oct 23, 41. *Study:* Oakland Univ, Rochester, Mich, BA(art hist), 63; Bucknell Univ, Lewisburg, Pa, MA, 68; Columbia Univ, MA(art hist), 71, PhD(primitive & pre-Columbian art), 76. *Teaching:* From asst to assoc prof & chair art, Lehman Col, New York, 69- *Mem:* Col Art Asn. *Res:* Art of the South Pacific Islands, particularly Melanesia and Polynesia; African, North American Indian and pre-Columbian art. *Publ:* Auth, The art of the Baining: New Britain, Exploring the Visual Art of Oceania, Univ Press Hawaii, 79. *Mailing Add:* 41 W 96th St Apt 8D New York NY 10025

CORBINO, MARCIA NORCROSS
CRITIC, WRITER
b Tulsa, Okla. *Study:* Duke Univ, BA, 49; Art Students League, 50. *Pos:* Writer & photogr, Sarasota Jour, 74-77; critic, Sarasota Herald Tribune, 77-82. *Awards:* Nat Endowment Arts Critic fel, 80. *Mem:* Int Asn Art Critics; Am Theatre Critics Asn. *Res:* Contemporary art. *Publ:* Contribr, Two achievers, Christian Sci Monitor, 75; contribr, Ben Stahl: teaching art through television, Am Artist, 77; contribr, Common ground, Art Papers, 82; contribr, Contemporary art criticism, Am Artist, 83. *Mailing Add:* 1111 N Gulfstream Ave No 6B Sarasota FL 33577

CORDINGLEY, MARY BOWLES
PAINTER
b Des Moines, Iowa, Jan 1, 18. *Study:* Minneapolis Sch Art & Design; Minneapolis Art Inst; Univ Minn; Colorado Springs Fine Arts Ctr; also with Steve Rettegi, New York, Hilton Leech, Fla, Paul Olsen, Minneapolis, Robert E Wood, Zoltan Szabo, Carleton Plummer & Tony Couch. *Work:* In over 200 pvt collections. *Exhib:* Traveling Exhibs, 66 & 67 & Print Show, 70, Mont Inst Arts; Nat League Am Pen Women Nat Biennial, Washington, DC, 67 & 70; Jr League Print Shows, Great Falls, Mont; and over 30 one-man shows incl C M Russell Mus, Great Falls, 67 & 71, C M Russell Auction, 71, Univ Mont Mus Rockies, 70 & Univ Minn. *Pos:* Creator & owner, Orig Pioneer Prints Notepaper Co. *Mem:* Mont State Arts Coun; Mont Inst Arts; Prof Women Artists Mont. *Media:* All Media. *Mailing Add:* 42 Prospect Dr Great Falls MT 59405

CORDY-COLLINS, ALANA (KATHLEEN)
CURATOR, EDUCATOR
b Los Angeles, Calif, June 5, 44. *Study:* Univ Calif, Los Angeles, BA(art hist), 70, MA(archaeol), 72, PhD(archaeol), 76. *Pos:* Mem chmn, Archaeol Inst Am, San Diego Chap, 77-78, pres, 79-81; cur, Latin Am Collections, San Diego Mus of Man, 79. *Teaching:* Instr archaeol, Univ Calif, Los Angeles Exten, 72-74; instr art & archaeol, Univ Calif, San Diego Exten, 74-79 & San Diego Mesa Col, Calif, 75-80; asst prof anthropology, Univ San Diego, 80- *Awards:* Altman Art Award, Univ Calif, Los Angeles, 72. *Res:* Iconographic study of Chavin & Peru art; shamanic art; function of art in culture. *Publ:* Auth, The dual divinity concept in Chavin art, In: El Dorado, 78; ed, Pre-Columbian Art History, Selected Readings, Vol 2, 82; auth, The Cerro Sechin massacre: Did it happen?, Mus of Man Ethic Technotes #18, 83; auth, Ancient Andean art as explained by Andean ethnohistory: An historical review, 83 & coauth (with D D McClelland), Upstreaming along the Peruvian north coast, 83, Brit Archaeol Reports. *Mailing Add:* Mus of Man Balboa Park San Diego CA 92101

CORISH, JOSEPH RYAN
PAINTER
b Somerville, Mass, Apr 9, 09. *Study:* Boston Univ, JD, 32; Harvard Univ, Adj in Arts, 38; Bridgewater State Col, Hon Dr, 81. *Work:* US Naval Acad Mus; US Naval War Col; Boston Univ; also in var state capitols, foreign embassies & Brit, Ger, Span, Japanese, Portuguese & US Navies. *Exhib:* Jordon Exhib Contemp New Eng Artists, Boston Mus Fine Arts; Etajima Mus, Japan; one-man shows, Deutsches Mus, Munich, Ger, Barcelona Mus, Spain, Bergen, Norway, Birmingham Mus Art, Ala; and many others. *Pos:* Art dir, Castle Hill Found, 58-63; US Navy combat artist & hon artist-in-residence, US Navy. *Teaching:* Guest lectr, Harvard Univ, Regis Col, Univ Conn & other cols, mus & art asns. *Mem:* Charter mem Am Soc Marine Artists; Salmagundi Club; Am Artists Prof League. *Media:* Oil. *Publ:* Magazine covers for US Naval War Col Rev. *Mailing Add:* 421 Highland Ave Somerville MA 02144

CORKERY, TIM (TIMOTHY JAMES)
PAINTER, EDUCATOR
b Washington, DC, Oct 30, 31. *Study:* Univ Chicago Univ Col, 55-59; Art Inst Chicago, BFA, 60; Inst Allende Univ Guanajuato, Mex, MFA, 64. *Work:* Baltimore Mus Art; Idaho First Nat Bank, Boise; Alcoa Aluminum Co, Pittsburgh; Johnson & Johnson Inc, Newark, NJ. *Comn:* Mural for pub housing, Dept of Housing & Community Develop, Baltimore, 73; indoor mural for Univ Baltimore, Mayor's Adv Comt for Art & Culture, 79; indoor mural for Arts Tower, Baltimore, 80. *Exhib:* Eighteenth Area Exhib, Corcoran Gallery Art, DC, 67; one-man shows, Royal Marks Gallery, New York, 69 & 70 & Max Hutchinson Gallery, New York, 73 & 74; Univ Md, Baltimore Co, 75; Univ Ore Mus Art, 78. *Collections Arranged:* Seventeenth Area Exhib (cataloged), Corcoran Gallery Art, DC, 65; Washington 20 Years (cataloged), Baltimore Mus Art, 70; Mem Gallery, Albright-Knox Gallery, 70 & 75; New Washington Painting (cataloged), Hayden Gallery, Mass Inst Technol, 71; Washington Art, Richmond Mus Exten, 71; Artists Making Art, Baltimore Mus Art, 72; Synergy-Artists One Plus One Equals Three (cataloged), Thorpe Intermedia Gallery, Sparkill, NY, 82. *Teaching:* Instr fine arts & painting, Corcoran Sch Art, DC, 65-67; instr painting, Md Inst Col Art, Baltimore, 67-77; vis artist painting, Univ Ore, Eugene, 77-78; vis artist painting, Sch Art Inst Chicago, fall 78. *Awards:* Purchase Awards, Baltimore Mus, 70 & Macht Found, 70; Munic Art Soc Award, 72. *Bibliog:* Sidra Stich (auth), Five Washington artists, Art Int Mag, 12/71; Carter Ratcliff (auth), article, Art Spectrum Mag, 2/75; Ellen Lubell (auth), article, Arts Mag, 2/75. *Mem:* Col Art Asn Am. *Media:* Oil on Canvas. *Mailing Add:* 49 W 19th St #5 New York NY 10011

CORMACK, MALCOLM
CURATOR, HISTORIAN
b Birmingham, Eng, Dec 6, 35. *Study:* Courtauld Inst Art Univ London, BA, 59; Cambridge Univ, Eng, MA, 65. *Pos:* Asst keeper, City Birmingham Mus & Art Gallery, Eng, 59-62; from asst keeper to keeper, Fitzwilliam Mus, Cambridge, 62-76; cur paintings, Yale Ctr Brit Art, 76- *Teaching:* Instr art hist, Cambridge Univ, 62-76; instr, Yale Univ, 76- *Mailing Add:* Yale Ctr for Brit Art Box 2120 Yale Sta New Haven CT 06520

CORMIER, ROBERT JOHN
PAINTER, LECTURER
b Boston, Mass. *Study:* R H Ives Gammell Studios, cert. *Work:* Maryhill Mus, Goldborough, Wash; Superior Courthouse, Cambridge, Mass; Univ Sch, Shaker Heights, Ohio; Salem Courthouse, Mass; Suffolk Co Courthouse, Boston, Ma. *Comn:* Portraits for St Michael's Church, Charleston, SC, 60, Cent Savings Bank, Lowell, Mass, 72 & Univ Sch, Hunting Valley Campus, 73-75; John Hancock Mutual Life Insurance Co, 81; Mass Appellate Court, Boston, 83; and others. *Exhib:* New Eng Artists Contemp Ann, 54-69; Am Artists Prof League Grand Nat, 59-69; Guild of Boston Artists, 60-83; Boston Arts Festival, 62; Coun Am Artists Socs, New York, 66; Springfield Mus, Mass, 79. *Pos:* Mem, City Art Comn, Boston, 82- *Teaching:* Instr drawing & painting, Vesper George Sch Art, 69-83; private instruction, studio and art associations. *Awards:* Grand Prize, Boston Arts Festival, 62; Gold Medal of Honor, Coun Am Artists Socs, 65; Greenshields Found Award, 70. *Mem:* Guild Boston Artists (secy, bd gov, 70-80); Copley Soc Boston (vpres, 70-77); Acad Artists; Portraits, Inc. *Mailing Add:* 30 Ipswich St Boston MA 02215

CORNELL, DAVID E
CERAMIST, SCULPTOR
b Kalispell, Mont, Feb 24, 39. *Study:* Mont State Univ, BS(art); Archie Bray Found, with Kenneth Ferguson & David Shaner; Corcoran Sch Art, with

Teuro Hara & Richard LaFean; Alfred Univ, MFA(ceramics), with Bob Turner, Val Cushing & Daniel Rhodes. *Work:* Greenville Art Mus, SC; Charles M Russell Gallery, Great Falls, Mont; Libby Dam, Treaty Tower, Vis Ctr, Libby, Mont; Archie Bray Found, Helena, Mont; Mont State Univ, Bozeman. *Comn:* Ceramic fountain fixtures, Mont State Univ Libr, 64; Treaty Panel (sculpture), US Army Corps 18 Engineers & Mont Hist Soc, 75. *Exhib:* Tenth Int Exhib Ceramic Art, Smithsonian Inst, Washington, DC, 66; Norfolk Mus Art, Va, 66; Harriman Gallery, Orange Co Community Col, Middletown, NY, 69; Handblown Glass Exhib, Corning Glass Ctr, NY, 69; Mint Mus Art, NC, 70; Appalachian Corridors: Exhib 2, Charleston, Wva, 70; NW Crafts Show, Henry Gallery, Seattle, Wash, 71; Cheney Cowles Mem Mus, Spokane, Wash, 73; Mont State Hist Soc Exhib, Poindexter Gallery, Helena, 75. *Pos:* Artist-in-residence, Penland Sch of Crafts, 69-70; dir, Archie Bray Found, 70-77; owner-mgr, Pear Blossom Pottery, Talent, Ore; pres, Clayfolk, Inc, 78-79. *Awards:* First Prize, Univ Exhib, Mont State Univ, 64; Jury Award, 11th Biennial NW Ceramics, Ore Ceramics Studio, 65; Best of Show, 11th Ann Own Your Own, Southern Colo State Col, 74. *Bibliog:* Mary Lou O'Neil (auth), Archie Bray Found, Mountain Lines, Mountain Bell Tel & Tel, 11/70; David Depew (auth), Archie Bray Found, Ceramics Mo, 5/72; Jerry Metcalf (auth), Today at the Bray, Mont Arts, Mont Inst of Arts, 76. *Mem:* Helena Arts Coun (vpres, 73); Mont Art Gallery Dir Asn (secy, 75-76); Nat Coun Educ in Ceramic Arts; Am Crafts Coun; Glass Art Soc. *Media:* Ceramic. *Mailing Add:* 2316 S Pacific Hwy Talent OR 97540

CORNELL, THOMAS BROWNE
PAINTER, PRINTMAKER
b Cleveland, Ohio, Mar 1, 37. *Study:* Amherst Col, Mass, BA, 59; Yale Univ, 59-60. *Work:* Mus Mod Art, New York; Princeton Univ Libr; Lessing J Rosenwald Collection, Nat Collection Fine Arts, Washington, DC; Cleveland Mus Art, Ohio; Harvard Univ, Cambridge, Mass; and others. *Comn:* Mural, Bowdoin Col, Brunswick, Maine, 64; bronze plaques, Maine State Comn on Arts & Humanities, 68; Dionysus (bronze plaque), J Walter Thompson Inc, New York, 70; portrait, Bowdoin Col, Maine, 79; portrait, Va Engineering Found, 81. *Exhib:* Contemp Painters & Sculptors as Printmakers, Mus Mod Art, New York, 66; Young New Eng Painters Traveling Exhib, 69; Living Am Artists & the Figure, Pa State Univ, 74; 30 Yrs of Am Printmaking, Brooklyn Mus, NY, 76; one-man show, A M Sachs Gallery, New York, 79; Santa Barbara Mus Art, Calif, 80; A M Sachs Gallery, 81; and others. *Collections Arranged:* Thomas Cornell Drawings & Prints, Bowdoin Col, 71. *Teaching:* Instr art, Univ Calif, Santa Barbara, 60-62; lectr visual arts prog, Princeton Univ, NJ, 69-71; prof present art & chmn art dept, Bowdoin Col, 63-82, prof art, currently. *Awards:* Nat Inst Arts & Lett Grant, 64; Nat Found Arts & Humanities Grant, 66-67; Ford Found Grant, 70; and others. *Mem:* Col Art Asn; Union of Maine Visual Artists. *Media:* Oil, Pastel; Etching, Monotype. *Publ:* Illusr, The Monkey, pvt publ, 59; illusr, The Defense of Gracchus Babeuf, Gehenna Press, 64, Univ Mass, 67 & Schocken Press, 71; illusr & ed, Frederick Douglass, 64, illusr & ed, William Lloyd Garrison, 64 & illusr, Composed for Dying, 64, Tragos Press. *Dealer:* A M Sachs Gallery 29 W 57th Ave New York NY 10019. *Mailing Add:* c/o Art Dept Bowdoin Col Brunswick ME 04011

CORNETTE, MARY ELIZABETH
DEALER, PAINTER
b Russellville, Ky, Sept 9, 09. *Study:* Bowling Green Col Com, BS; Western Ky State Univ, MS; WTex State Univ, with Dr Emilio Caballero; also with Dirk Van Driest, Taos, NMex. *Pos:* Dir & pres, Canyon Art Gallery, Inc, Tex, 65- *Awards:* WTex CofC Cult Achievement Award, 72. *Bibliog:* Norman Nadel (auth), Mary Elizabeth Cornette brings Tenkei Tachibana wall screens to US as gift to people of US, Scripps-Howard Publs, 10/17/72. *Media:* Watercolor, Oil. *Specialty:* Representational art of Southwestern United States, especially of Texas. *Mailing Add:* 2710 Fourth Ave Canyon TX 79015

CORNIN, JON
PAINTER
b New York, NY, Mar 24, 05. *Study:* NY Univ; Art Students League; and with Raphael Soyer. *Exhib:* Palace of Legion of Honor, San Francisco; Los Angeles Co Mus; de Young Mem Mus, San Francisco; Sweat Mem Mus, Portland, Maine; J B Speed Mus, Louisville, Ky; San Francisco Mus Art; and others. *Awards:* Second Prize for Church Art, Grace Cathedral, San Francisco. *Media:* Oil, Casein Tempera. *Mailing Add:* 812 Northvale Rd Oakland CA 94610

CORPRON, CARLOTTA M
EDUCATOR, PHOTOGRAPHER
b Blue Earth, Minn, Dec 9, 01. *Study:* Eastern Mich Univ, BS, 25; Teachers Col, Columbia Univ, MA, 26; Art Ctr, Los Angeles, 26; study with Gyorgy Kepes on light, 44. *Work:* Mus Mod Art, New York; Art Inst Chicago; Mus Fine Arts, St Petersburg, Fla; New Orleans Mus Art, La; Univ Ariz Ctr Creative Photog, Tucson. *Exhib:* One-person shows, Carlotta Corpron, Dallas Mus Fine Arts, 48, Light as a Creative Medium, Art Inst Chicago, 53, Marcuse Pfeifer Gallery, New York, 77 & Galleria del Milione, Milan, 78; Abstraction in Photography, Mus Mod Art, New York, 52; Design in Nature, 52 & Women in Art, 53, Contemp Arts Asn, Houston; Women of Photography, An Hist Survey, San Francisco Mus Art, 75; Int Ctr Photog, New York, 79. *Teaching:* Instr design & hist of art, Univ Cincinnati, 28-35; assoc prof design, hist of art design & photog, Tex Woman's Univ, Denton, 35-68. *Media:* Photography. *Publ:* Contrib, Gyorgy Kepes' The New Landscape, 44; contribr, Moholy-Nagy's Vision in Motion, 46; contribr, Katherine Kuh's Art Has Many Faces, 51; contribr, Margaretta K Mitchell's Recollections: Ten Women of Photography, 79. *Dealer:* Marcuse Pfeifer Gallery 825 Madison Ave New York NY 10021. *Mailing Add:* 206 Forest Denton TX 76201

CORR, JAMES DONAT
PAINTER, GALLERY DIRECTOR
b Missoula, Mont, Feb 13, 31. *Study:* Western Mont Col, BS(art); Univ Mont, ME(art); also with Peter Volkous & Walter Hook. *Work:* Western Gallery, Dillon; Univ Collection, Missoula; Heritage Gallery, Great Falls; Co High School, Dillon; Copper City Mus, Anaconda, Mont. *Exhib:* Electra II, Helena, Copper Camp Festival, Butte, Mont. *Pos:* Gallery dir, Western Gallery, Dillon, Mont, 70-81, assoc prof art, 81- *Awards:* Mary Baker Emerick Art Chair. *Mem:* Mont Watercolor Soc; Mont Inst Arts; Beaver Head Watercolor Soc. *Media:* Multimedia. *Mailing Add:* 515 South Dakota Dillon MT 59725

CORREA, FLORA HORST
PAINTER
b Seattle, Wash, Feb 16, 08. *Study:* Univ Wash, BA(art); also with Kenneth Callahan, Sergei Bongart, Richard Yip, Raymond Brose, Mark Tobey & Rex Brandt. *Work:* Seattle First Nat Bank Collection; Craftsman Press, Seattle; Pac First Fed Savings & Loan Asn, Seattle; Rainier Bank, Seattle; Krusteaz Centennial Mills Collection, Oberto, Trident Seafoods. *Exhib:* Puget Sound Area Exhib, Frye Art Mus, 64-65, 67-68 & 75; Univ Ore Invitationals, 67 & 71-72; Northwest Watercolor Ann, Seattle, 64-67 & 72-75; Watercolor Exhib, Seattle Pac Col, 75; Grand Galleria Exhib, 75. *Awards:* First in Watercolor, Penwomen's Wash State Biennial, 79, Second in Watercolor, 81, First in Oils, 70 & Second in Oils, 81. *Bibliog:* Linda Plumb (auth), Flora Correa's distinctive collage art, View Northwest, 5/75. *Mem:* Northwest Watercolor Soc (secy, 67); Women Painters of Wash (pres, 69-70); Nat League Am Penwomen (vpres, Artist Div, Seattle Br, 74-77); Olympic Art Asn, Seattle (pres, 74-77). *Media:* Acrylic, Watercolor, Oil, Collage. *Mailing Add:* 8253 SE 29th St Mercer Island WA 98040

CORSO, SAMUEL (JOSEPH)
STAINED GLASS ARTIST, PAINTER
b Monroe, La, Jan 11, 53. *Study:* La State Univ, Baton Rouge, BFA, 75, MFA, 77; studied mosaics, sumi-e & bronze sculpture with Paul A Dufour, 77 & 79. *Work:* Dura-Vent Corp, Redwood, Calif; McWane Corp, Birmingham, Ala; Riverside Centroplex Munic Collection, Baton Rouge, La; Arrowmont Sch Arts & Crafts, Gatlinburg, Tenn; La State Univ, Baton, Rouge. *Comn:* Our Lady Queen Heaven Cath Church, Lake Charles, La, 76; Univ Methodist Church, Baton Rouge, La, 77; Cath Prep Sch, Baton Rouge, La, 77; Centreville Baptist Church, Miss, 79; St Mary Pines Cath Church, Shreveport, La, 80. *Exhib:* Mint Mus Art, Charlotte, NC, 78 & 80; Mus Fine Arts, St Petersburg, Fla, 79; Jacksonville Art Mus, Fla, 79; Crown Ctr, Kansas City, Mo, 80; Int Trade Ctr, New Orleans, 80; LeMoyne Art Found, Tallahassee, Fla, 80 & 81; Contemporary Glass Art, Art Ctr, Lafayette, La, 82; Rebirth of a Medium, Univ Tex, San Antonio, 83; and others. *Teaching:* Instr, Arrowmont Sch Arts & Crafts, Gatlinburg, Tenn, 78 & 81; asst prof, La State Univ, Baton Rouge, 81, instr, 83-84. *Awards:* 1st Place & Purchase Prize, Ala Watercolor Soc, McWane Inc, 80; 2nd Place, Fragile Art 80, Glass Mag, 80; La State Arts Coun Fel, 82-83. *Bibliog:* Albert Lewis (auth), Stained glass goes to college, Glass Mag, Vol 5, No 4, 78; Norman Temme (auth), On the wall, Stained Glass J, summer, 81. *Mem:* LA Crafts Coun; La State Arts Coun; La Watercolor Soc; Ala Watercolor Soc; Am Crafts Coun. *Media:* European Glass, Domestic Glass; Sumi-e, Gouache. *Publ:* Contribr, Robert Jenson's & Patricia Conway's Ornamentalism, Clarkson N Potter, 81; auth, New glass review #4, Corning Mus, 82; auth, Spectrum, Glass Mag, 12/82. *Dealer:* Perception Galleries 2402 Sunset St Houston TX 77005; Baton Rouge Gallery 205 North Fourth St Baton Rouge LA 70802. *Mailing Add:* PO Box 336 Baton Rouge LA 71201

CORTELLA, GLORIA CHARLENE
DEALER
b Salt Lake City, Utah, Apr 12, 29. *Study:* Univ Utah, 46-48; Salt Lake City Art Barn, 48-50; Otis Art Inst, MFA, 57. *Pos:* Dir, Contemp Gallery, Salt Lake City, 50-52; asst dir, Paul Kantor Gallery, Beverly Hills, Calif, 58-62 & Everett Ellin Gallery, Los Angeles, 62-64; cur, Tamarind Lithography Workshop, Los Angeles, 64-66; registrar, coordr collections & admin asst, Los Angeles Co Mus Art, Los Angeles, 66-72; dir exhib, Art Index, Los Angeles, 70-73; dir, Symphony Graphics, New York, 73-74; Galerie Ariadne, New York, 74-76 & Gloria Cortella Inc, 76-78; dir & pres, GHJ Graphics, Inc, 78- *Mem:* Comt to Rescue Italian Art (exec secy, Southern Calif Chap). *Specialty:* Contemporary art specializing in contemporary drawing. *Mailing Add:* 157 East 57th New York NY 10022

CORTESE, DON F
PRINTMAKER, INSTRUCTOR
b Chicago, Ill, Dec 30, 35. *Study:* Art Inst Chicago, BFA; Syracuse Univ, MFA. *Work:* Libr Cong, Washington, DC; Art Inst Chicago; Boston Pub Libr; Hougton Libr, Harvard Univ; Univ Mass, Amherst. *Comn:* Intaglio Print, Impressions Workshop, Boston, Mass, 71; Etching & Handset Type, Kirkland Col, Hamilton, NY, 71; etching on experimental paper, Boise Cascade, 80. *Exhib:* The 58th Conn Acad Fine Arts Exhib, Wadsworth Atheneum, Hartford, 68; Nat Print & Drawing Exhib, Northern Ill Univ, 70; Int Print Competition, Seattle Art Mus, Wash, 71; Graphics 71 Nat Print Exhib, Western NMex Univ, 71; Print Exhib, State Univ NY Brockport, 72; Artists of Cent NY, Munson-Williams-Proctor Inst Mus, Utica, NY, 76; Breaking the Bindings/American Book Art Now, Elvehjem Mus, Univ Wis, 83. *Collections Arranged:* New England Land Grant Universities Workshop, 81; June Exhib of Visiting Printmakers, Herter Gallery; Univ Mass Botany of Papermaking Invitational, Mo Botanical Garden Libr, St Louis, 81. *Teaching:* Prof printmaking, Sch Art, Syracuse Univ, NY, 65- *Awards:* One-Man Show Award, Nat Print Competition, Springfield Col, Mass, 70; Purchase Prize, Nat Print Competition, Western NMex Univ, 71; Ford Found Grant, Hand Papermaking, Print & Book, 80. *Mailing Add:* 8062 Cazenovia Rd Manlius NY 13104

CORTESE, EDWARD FORTUNATO
ADMINISTRATOR, ILLUSTRATOR
b Philadelphia, Pa, Jan 11, 22. *Study:* Temple Univ, 50; Philadelphia Col Art, with Henry Pitz, BFA, 51. *Exhib:* Bk Fair, Pa Acad Fine Arts, Philadelphia, 55. *Pos:* Art dir, John C Winston Co-Holt Rinehart Winston, Philadelphia, 50-60, Pa Lithographic Co, Philadelphia, 61-62, Curtis Publ Co, Philadelphia & Indianapolis, 63-79 & Benjamin Franklin Lit & Med Soc Inc, Indianapolis, 79- *Teaching:* Instr illus, Philadelphia Col Art, 65-70. *Media:* Watercolor, Ink. *Publ:* Illusr, The Adventures of Tom Sawyer, Robinson Crusoe, King Arthur, Black Beauty & To the Shores of Tripoli, 58-59, John C Winston Co, Philadelphia. *Mailing Add:* 2719 Embassy Row Indianapolis IN 46224

CORTOR, ELDZIER
PAINTER, PRINTMAKER
b Richmond, Va, Jan 10, 16. *Study:* Art Inst Chicago, 36 & 41; Inst Design, Ill Inst Technol, 42-43; Columbia Univ, New York, 47. *Work:* Smithsonian Inst, Washington, DC; Am Fedn Art, Mus Mod Art & Int Bus Machines, New York; Mus du Peuple Haitien, Port au Prince, Haiti. *Comn:* Painting, comn by Julius Rosenwald Fel, Chicago, 45-47; painting, comn by John Simon Guggenheim Fel, New York, 49-50. *Exhib:* Young American Painters, Metrop Mus Art, New York, 50; Reality Expanded, Studio Mus, New York, 73; Jubilee, Boston Mus Fine Art, 75; Migrations, Museo de Arte Moderno LaTertulia, Cali, Columbia, 76; Southern Heritage, Columbia Mus Art, SC, 80. *Teaching:* Instr, Ctr Art, Port au Prince, Haiti, 49-51; instr, Pratt Inst, Brooklyn, 72-74. *Awards:* Bertha A Florsheim Award, Am Artists, 45 & William H Bartels Award, Chicago Artists, 46, Art Inst Chicago; Hon Mention, Painting USA, Carnegie Inst, Pittsburgh, 47. *Bibliog:* Cedric Dover (auth), American Negro Art, New York Graphic Soc, 60; Elton C Fax (auth), 17 Black Artists, Dodd Mead Co, 71; Elso Honig Fine (auth), The Afro-American Artist, Holt-Rinehart-Winston, 73. *Mem:* Soc Am Graphic Artists, New York. *Media:* Oil. *Dealer:* Assoc Am Artists 663 5th Ave New York NY 10022. *Mailing Add:* 35 Montgomery St New York NY 10002

CORTRIGHT, STEVEN M
PRINTMAKER, PAINTER
b Detroit, Mich, Mar 18, 42. *Study:* Stanford Univ, BA & MA; Univ NMex, Tamarind Workshop artist-teacher fel. *Work:* Brooklyn Mus Art; Univ Colo; Seattle Art Mus; Achenbach Found, Calif Palace Legion of Honor, San Francisco; Calif Inst Technol. *Exhib:* 18th & 19th Nat Print Exhib, Brooklyn Mus Art, 72 & 74; World Print Competition, 73, San Francisco Mus Art, 73; 1st & 2nd Colo Print/Drawing Competition, Univ Colo, 74 & 75; Prints California, Oakland Mus Art, 75. *Teaching:* Assoc prof studio art & lithography, Univ Calif, Santa Barbara, 66- *Awards:* Numerous purchase awards from various exhibitions over the last ten years. *Mailing Add:* c/o Hank Baum Gallery 2140 Bush San Francisco CA 94115

CORWIN, SOPHIA M
SCULPTOR, PAINTER
b New York. *Study:* Nat Acad Sch Fine Arts; Art Students League; Hoffman Sch; Archipenko Sch; Phillips Gallery Art Sch, Washington, DC, with Karl Knaths, scholar, 45; NY Univ, BA & MA(creative arts). *Exhib:* Women Artists 78, City Univ New York Grad Ctr; Corcoran Gallery; Federal Plaza, 83; Fordham Univ, 83; Conn Col, 83; Baltimore Mus; and others. *Pos:* Juror, NY State Coun Arts, 70 & Queens Coun Arts, 73. *Teaching:* Grad asst related arts, NY Univ, 61-62; from instr to dir, Studio Workshop, Bronx House, NY, 62-73; lectr art hist, Coop Col Ctr Westchester, State Univ NY Col Purchase, 71-73; lectr art, New York City Drug Rehabilitation Ctr & Bedford Hills Women's Prison. *Awards:* Nat Competition Award for One-Man Show, Creative Arts Gallery, 54; Nat Sculpture Competition Award, US Dept Housing & Urban Develop. *Mem:* Nat Soc Women Artists; Am Soc Contemp Artists; Women's Caucus on Art; Visual Artists Coalition; Sculptors League. *Media:* Steel, Marble; Oil, Acrylic. *Mailing Add:* 79 Franklin Ave Yonkers NY 10705

COSGROVE, STANLEY
PAINTER
b Montreal, PQ, Dec 23, 11. *Study:* Beaux-Arts, Montreal; Art Asn Montreal; also with Orozco, Mex. *Work:* Nat Gallery Can; Vancouver Art Gallery; Mus Mod Art, New York; Winnipeg Art Gallery. *Exhib:* Yale Univ; UNESCO; Montreal Mus Fine Arts; Quebec Provincial Mus; Nat Gallery Can, Ottawa, Ont; and others. *Teaching:* Ecole des Beaux Arts, Montreal, 44-58. *Awards:* Medal, Beaux-Arts, Montreal; Provincial Govt Scholar, 40-44; Travel Scholar in France, Federal Govt, 53. *Mem:* Royal Can Acad Arts. *Mailing Add:* Box 11 RR 1 Hudson PQ J0P 1M0 Canada

COSSITT, FRANKLIN D
SCULPTOR, EDITOR
b La Grange, Ill, Oct 16, 27. *Study:* Univ Mich, 51; Univ Florence, Italy, cert, 50. *Work:* Va Mus Fine Arts, Richmond; Chrysler Mus at Norfolk, Va. *Comn:* Room divider, St Mary's Hosp, Richmond, Va, 63; sculpture, Carborundium Corp, Niagara Falls, NY, 65; sculpture, Reynolds Metals Co, Richmond, Va, 70; outdoor sculpture, City Chesapeake, Va, 75 & City Portsmouth, Va, 77. *Pos:* Art ed, Richmond Times-Dispatch, 65- & Norfolk Virginian Pilot, 65- *Teaching:* Lectr art, Norfolk State Col, Va, 65-76; lectr art hist, Va Wesleyan Col, Richmond, 77-82. *Media:* Sculpture. *Dealer:* Franz Bader 2001 I St NW Washington DC 20001. *Mailing Add:* 1712 Buford Rd Richmond VA 23235

COST, JAMES PETER
PAINTER
b Philadelphia, Pa, Mar 3, 23. *Study:* Univ Calif, Los Angeles, BA, 50; Univ Southern Calif, MS, 59. *Work:* R W Norton Mus, Shreveport, Mass; Monterey Mus Art; Reader's Digest Collection. *Exhib:* Artists Guild Gallery Am, Carmel, Calif, 61-63; Mus Fine Arts, Springfield, Mass, 65 & 73; Nat Arts Club, New York, 66; one-man shows, Northwood Inst, Midland, 71 & R W Norton Gallery, Shreveport, 71; plus others. *Pos:* Owner, James Peter Cost Gallery, 64- *Teaching:* Instr art, Los Angeles City Sch Dist; lectr art, Northwood Insts, Midland, Mich & Dallas, 71. *Awards:* Gold Medal, Franklin Mint, 75. *Mailing Add:* PO Box 3638 Carmel CA 93921

COSTANZA, JOHN JOSEPH
SCULPTOR, CERAMIST
b New York, NY, June 24, 24. *Study:* Tyler Sch Fine Arts, Temple Univ, BFA, 49; Univ Pa, cert, 43. *Work:* Philadelphia Col Performing Arts; Harcum Jr Col, Bryn Mawr, Pa. *Comn:* Ceramic murals, University City High Sch, Philadelphia Sch District, Pa; Paragon Industry, West Orange, NJ, Ampacet Corp, Mt Vernon, NY; Monsanto Corp, Montvale, NJ; Rauch, Duban & Venturi, Architects & Shubert Theatre, Philadelphia. *Exhib:* Nat Ceramic Competition, Everson Mus Art, Syracuse, NY, 58, 60, 62 & 64; New York World's Fair Invitational, 64-65; Smithsonian Drawing Nat, Washington, DC & traveling, 64-67; Painting, Drawing & Sculpture Invitational, Univ Del, Newark, 66-68; Philadelphia Regional Art Show, Philadelphia Mus Art, 67; Ceramics Invitational, Philadelphia Civic Ctr Mus, 67, 70 & 73; Ceramics Invitational, Mus Contemp Crafts, New York, 68, 75 & 77. *Pos:* Designer, Potters of Wall St, New York, 50-51. *Teaching:* Art, Devereux Sch, Devon, Pa, 51-53 & Sayre Jr High Sch, Philadelphia, 53-57; teacher ceramics, West Chester High Sch, Pa, 57-63; prof ceramics, Moore Col Art, Philadelphia, 63-73. *Awards:* Purchase Award, Univ Del Art Show, 65; Purchase Prize, Temple Univ Alumni Show, 68; First Prize, Sculpture, William Penn Mem Mus, Harrisburg, Pa, 71. *Bibliog:* Jack Bookbinder (dir), Black History, The Making of a Mural (film), Philadelphia Sch District, 75; Dr Burton Wasserman (auth), Exploring the Visual Art, Davis Publ, 76; Louis G Redstone (auth), Public Art-New Directions, McGraw Hill, 80. *Mem:* Artists Equity Asn; Am Craftsman Coun. *Media:* Clay. *Publ:* Ed, Gerry Williams's Nine Philadelphia Potters, Daniel Clark Found, 73. *Dealer:* Hahn Gallery 8439 Germantown Ave Philadelphia PA 19118. *Mailing Add:* 737 Polo Rd Bryn Mawr PA 19010

COSTIGAN, CONSTANCE CHRISTIAN
PAINTER, DESIGNER
b NJ, July 3, 35. *Study:* Boston Mus Sch Fine Arts; Simmons Col, BA; Am Univ, MA; Univ Va; Univ Calif, Berkeley, work in ceramics; ceramics with Eric Gronberg; fiber with Ron Goodman. *Work:* Phillips Collection, Washington, DC; Hirshhorn Mus, Washington, DC; Univ Iowa Mus; Dimock Gallery, George Washington Univ; also pvt collections in US & Gt Brit. *Exhib:* 19th Area Exhib, Corcoran Gallery Art, 74; Phillips Collection, 77; Label: Women, Women's Caucus for Art, Washington, DC, 79; 25 Washington Artists, Realism & Representation, Foundry Gallery, Washington, DC, 80; Del Mus Art, Wilmington, 80; Surface/Structure: Fiber Innovations, Arlington Arts Ctr, Va, 82; 10 Years, A Retrospective, Northern Va Community Col, 83. *Collections Arranged:* Elements of Art: line, (auth, catalog), Arlington Arts Ctr, Va, 80. *Pos:* Exhib designer, Smithsonian Inst, 57-59. *Teaching:* Instr studio art & crafts, Arlington Co Pub Sch, 70-76; asst drawing, design & painting, Smithsonian Inst, Washington, DC, 70-76; asst prof, George Washington Univ, 76-; distinguished vis prof, Am Univ in Cairo, Egypt, 80-81. *Awards:* Grant Award, Lester Hereward Cooke Found, Washington, DC, 78. *Bibliog:* Lenore Miller (auth), Constance Costigan, Phillips Collection, Washington, DC, 77. *Mem:* Am Crafts Coun; fel Royal Soc Arts; fel MacDowell Colony; fel Ossabow Island Project. *Media:* Pastel, Oil; Graphite, Mixed Media. *Dealer:* Franz Bader Gallery 2001 Eye St NW Washington DC 20006. *Mailing Add:* 603 S Carolina Ave SE Washington DC 20003

COSTIN, FRANK
DEALER
Can citizen. *Pos:* Dir, Gallery One, currently. *Specialty:* Contemporary North American painting and sculpture. *Mailing Add:* 121 Scollard St Toronto ON M5R 1G4 Canada

COSTLEY-JACOBS, AVERILLE ESTHER
DEALER, GALLERY DIRECTOR
b Washington, DC, Mar 24, 47. *Study:* Univ DC, 70-74; Northeastern Univ, Boston, 74-75. *Pos:* Art dealer & asst gallery dir, Galerie Triangle, Washington, DC, 78-; cur, First Am Bank Washington, DC, 82- *Awards:* Andre Shashaty (auth), Swann Street's Galerie provides an alternative, Rock Creek Monitor, 6/26/80; Schroeder Cherry (auth), Home galleries, Palavra Arts Publ, winter 81-82; Delmar Lipp (auth), A reporter-at-large, Hill Rag, 5/1/81. *Specialty:* Contemporary traditional arts in all media. *Publ:* Contribr, Building an art collection for less, Sol, Julia Jones, 83. *Mailing Add:* 1206 Carrollburg Pl SW Washington DC 20024

COTHREN, MICHAEL WATT
EDUCATOR
b Nashville, Ark, Apr 9, 51. *Study:* Vanderbilt Univ, BA, 73; Columbia Univ, MA, 74, PhD, 80. *Pos:* Pa regional dir, Census Stained Glass Am, 1840-1940, 80- *Teaching:* Asst prof art hist, Swarthmore Col, 78- *Mem:* Col Art Asn; Int Ctr Medieval Art; Medieval Acad Am; Soc francaise d'archeologie. *Res:* Twelfth to fourteenth century stained glass. *Publ:* Auth, A Re-evaluation of the Iconography and Design of the Infancy Window from the Abbey of Saint-Denix, Gesta, XVIII, 78; auth, Cistercian Tile Mosaic Pavements in Yorkshire: Context and Sources, In: Studies in Cistercian Art and Architecture, 81. *Mailing Add:* 406 N Swarthmore Ave Swarthmore PA 19081

COTTER, HOLLAND
CRITIC, EDITOR
b Caanan, Conn, April 9, 47. *Study:* Harvard Col, BA, 70. *Pos:* Ed in chief & art & book critic, New York Arts J, 76-80. *Publ:* Auth, Dark utopia: Works of Alex MacFarlane, 83, Jene Highstein, 83 & Max Coyer, 83, Arts Mag; auth, Jennifer Bartlett, 83 & Surreal and pop culture: Pages from the furnace, 83, Artworld. *Mailing Add:* 96 St Marks Pl #7 New York NY 10009

COTTINGHAM, ROBERT
PAINTER
b Brooklyn, NY, Sept 26, 35. *Study:* Pratt Inst, New York, 59-64, AA, 62. *Work:* Guggenheim Mus Art, Whitney Mus Am Art, New York; Nat Mus Am Art, Hirshhorn Mus & Sculpture Garden, Washington, DC; Philadelphia Mus Art; and others. *Exhib:* New Photo Realism, Wadsworth Atheneum, 74; Signs of Life: Symbols in the City, Renwick Gallery, Washington, DC, 75; Recent American Etchings, Nat Collection Fine Art, 75; Super Realism, Baltimore Mus Art, 75; Thirty Years of American Printmaking, Brooklyn Mus, 76; America as Art, Nat Collection Fine Art, 76; Recent Acquisitions, Whitney Mus Am Art, Hirshhorn Mus & Sculpture Garden, 77; Watercolor USA, 1978, Springfield Art Mus; Prospectus--Art in the Seventies, Aldrich Mus Contemp Art, Conn, 79; solo exhibs, Aldrich Mus, Conn, 79, Delta Gallery, Rotterdam, Neth, 79, Getler-Pall Gallery, New York, 79, Thomas Segal Gallery, Boston, 80, Fendrick Gallery, Washington, DC, 81 & Coe Kerr Gallery, New York, 82; and others. *Pos:* Art dir, Young & Rubicam Advertising, New York, 59-64 & Los Angeles, 64-68. *Teaching:* Instr, Art Ctr Col Design, Los Angeles, 69-70. *Awards:* Nat Endowment Arts Grant, 74-75. *Bibliog:* Udo Kultermann (auth), New Realism, Tubingen, Ger, 72; Peter Schjeldahl (auth), Too easy to be art, New York Times, 5/74; Toni Del Renzio (auth), Robert Cottingham--the capers of the signscape, Art & Artists, London, 2/75; Jane Cottingham (auth), Techniques of three photorealist painters, Am Artist, 2/80. *Dealer:* Coe Kerr Gallery 49 E 82nd St New York 10028. *Mailing Add:* 16 Blackman Rd Newtown CT 06470

COUCH, URBAN
PAINTER, CURATOR
b Minneapolis, Minn, Apr 27, 27. *Study:* Minneapolis Sch Art, BFA, 51; Skowhegan Sch Painting & Sculpture, 51; Cranbrook Acad Art, MFA, 59; Kyoto, Japan, 64-65. *Work:* Minneapolis Inst Arts; Walker Art Ctr, Minneapolis; Sioux City Art Ctr, Iowa; Cranbrook Mus, Bloomfield Hills, Mich; Gray Found Collection; plus others. *Exhib:* Walker Art Ctr, 59; Neville Mus Invitational, Green Bay, Wis, 67; Art in the Embassies, US State Dept, Sophia, Bulgaria & Canberra, Australia, 68-71; Minneapolis Inst Arts Faculty Exhib, 68; Difference of a Decade, Lee Nordness Galleries, New York, 69; plus others. *Pos:* Graphic designer, USN, Calif, 45; alumni dir, Minneapolis Col Art & Design, 57; design consult, Control Data Corp, 60-62; consult-examiner prog, Comn on Cols & Univs, Chicago, 62-63; consult & examiner, NCent Asn, 63-; Cur, Galleries & collection, WVa Univ, 81- *Teaching:* Instr art, Minneapolis Col Art & Design, 55-70, chmn found prog, 59-62, actg dir, 62-63, asst to dir, 63-64, actg chmn fine arts div, 65-66, chmn painting dept, 68-71; instr advan painting, Walker Art Ctr, 57-61; instr art, Kingswood Sch, Bloomfield Hills, Mich & Bloomfield Hills Art Ctr, 58-59; grad workshop, Univ Minn, 59-61; instr advan painting, Minnetonka Art Ctr, Minneapolis, 59-61; artist in residence, Minn Jr Cols, summers 67-69; instr grad painting, Calif Col Arts & Crafts, summer 70; prof painting, WVa Univ, 71- *Mailing Add:* Creative Art Ctr WVa Univ Div Art Morgantown WV 26506

COUGHLIN, JACK
PRINTMAKER, SCULPTOR
b Greenwich, Conn, Feb 19, 32. *Study:* Art Students League; RI Sch Design, BFA, 54, MS, 61. *Work:* Metrop Mus Art & Mus Mod Art, New York; Norfolk Mus Arts & Sci, Va; Staedelsches Kunst Inst, Frankfort, Ger; Nat Collection Fine Arts, Washington, DC. *Comn:* Ed original prints, Assoc Am Artists, 62-79, Int Graphic Arts Soc, 66 & 68, Silvermine Guild Artists, New Canaan, Conn, 67, Graphic Studio, Dublin, Ireland, 71 & Franklin Mint, Pa, 77. *Exhib:* Am Drawing Biennials, Norfolk Mus Arts & Sci, 62, 64 & 66; Contemp Artists Eligible for Awards, Nat Inst Arts & Lett, New York, 70; 17th Biennial Am Printmaking, Brooklyn Mus Art, NY, 70; 2nd San Diego Nat Print Exhib, Fine Arts Gallery San Francisco, 71; 51st & 57th Print Exhibs, Soc Am Graphic Arts, New York, 71-79. *Teaching:* Prof drawing & printmaking, Univ Mass, Amherst, 60- *Awards:* Madson Award for etching, Nat Exhib, Soc Am Graphic Artists, 77; William H Leavin Prize, 155th Nat Exhib, Nat Acad Design, 80 & 82; NJ State Mus Art Prize, 24th Nat Print Exhib, Hunterdon Art Ctr, Clinton, NJ, 80. *Bibliog:* Robin Skelton (auth), Imagination of Jack Coughlin, 70; Jack Coughlin: Irish portraits, 72 & Jack Coughlin: A Perspective View, 80, Malahat Rev, Univ Victoria, BC. *Mem:* Assoc Nat Acad Design; Soc Am Graphic Artists; Boston Printmakers. *Publ:* Illusr, Mnemosyne Lay in Dust, 66 & Synge-Petrarch, 71, Dolmen Press, Dublin, Ireland; illusr, Grotesques, 20 Etchings by Jack Coughlin, Aquarius Press, 70; illusr, 13 Irish Writers, Etchings, Godine Press, 73. *Dealer:* Assoc Am Artists 663 Fifth Ave New York NY 10022; David Hendriks Gallery 119 St Stephen's Green Dublin Ireland. *Mailing Add:* N Leverett Rd Montague MA 01351

COUGHTRY, GRAHAM
PAINTER, SCULPTOR
b St Lambert, Que, 1931. *Work:* Mus Mod Art, New York; Detroit Inst Art; Nat Gallery Can; Art Gallery Ontario; Philadelphia Mus Art; and others. *Comn:* Wall sculpture, Beth David Synagogue, Toronto, 58; mural, Toronto Int Airport, 62; sculpture, Yorkdale Plaza, Toronto, 63. *Exhib:* One-man exhibs, Isaacs Gallery, 56-83; two-man exhib, Montreal Mus Fine Arts, 58; New Acquisitions, Mus Mod Art, New York, 61; Albright-Knox Gallery, Buffalo, NY, 62 & 71; Coughtry Markle Rayner Traveling Exhib, Nat Gallery Canada, 68; 12th Winnipeg Show, Winnipeg Art Gallery, 70; Modern Painting in Canada, Edmonton Art Gallery, 78; Painting 82, Art Gallery Harbourfront, 82; and others. *Awards:* First Prize, Vancouver Art Gallery, 62; Can Coun Fel, 65; Can Coun Sr Grants, 73, 76-77 & 80-81. *Mailing Add:* c/o Isaacs Gallery Ltd 832 Yonge St Toronto ON M4W 2H1 Canada

COUPER, CHARLES ALEXANDER
PAINTER, INSTRUCTOR
b Portsmouth, NH, Feb 19, 24. *Study:* Vesper George Sch Art, Boston, cert; Cape Sch Art, Provincetown, Mass, with Henry Hensche; Ernest Lee Major Studio, Boston. *Work:* Greenshields Mus, Montreal; Attleboro Mus, Mass; Heritage Mus, Provincetown, Mass. *Comn:* Pastel portrait, Judge Phillip, Wolaver QC, NS, Can, 80. *Exhib:* One-man shows, Cape Cod Art Asn, 73 & Guild Boston Artists, 73; Allied Artists of Am, New York, 74; Grande Prix Int, Cannes, France, 74; Deauville Int, France, 75. *Pos:* Mem, Provincetown Art Comn, Mass, 78-79. *Teaching:* Instr life drawing & painting, Vesper George Sch Art, 55-; instr, Swain Sch Design, New Bedford, Mass, 65-68. *Awards:* Gloria Layton Mem Award, Allied Artists Am, 68; Elizabeth T Greenshields Found Mem Grant, Montreal, 69; Medal of Distinction, Grande Prix Int de Pientre de la Cote Azur, 75; and others. *Bibliog:* Critical rev in La Rev Mod, Paris, 69. *Mem:* Allied Artists Am; Artist de Pientre's de La Cote Azur; Visual Arts NS. *Media:* Oil, Pastel. *Dealer:* Grand Cent Art Galleries Madison Ave & 43rd New York NY; Market House Gallery Annapolis Royal NS Can. *Mailing Add:* RR 1 Bear River NS B0S 1B0 Canada

COUPER, JAMES M
PAINTER, EDUCATOR
b Atlanta, Ga, Nov 21, 37. *Study:* Atlanta Art Inst; Ga State Univ; Fla State Univ. *Work:* Fla State Univ; Miami Art Ctr; John & Mable Ringling Mus Art; Ft Lauderdale Mus, Fla; Dept Natural Resources, Fla. *Comn:* Mural, 20th Century Fox, 68. *Exhib:* Isaac Delgado Mus Art Nat, New Orleans, 66; Drawings 72, Ft Lauderdale, Fla, 72; Fla State Dept, 72; one-man shows, Fornal Gallery, New York, 78 & Metrop Mus & Art Ctrs, Fla, 81. *Collections Arranged:* Art of the Asian Mountains, 69; The Artist & The Sea, 69; Art of Italy, 69; Up & Out, 69-70. *Pos:* Asst to dir, Miami Art Ctr, 67-70; gallery dir, Fla Int Univ, 77-80. *Teaching:* Instr painting, Miami-Dade Jr Col, 64-68; instr painting, Miami Art Ctr, 65-72; from instr to assoc prof painting, Fla Int Univ, 72-, chmn art dept, 77-78. *Awards:* Hand Hollow Fel, 81; Fla Int Univ Found Grant, 81; Fla Fine Arts Coun Grant, 81. *Bibliog:* Reviews, Art News, Dec, 80 & Miami News & Miami Herald, Apr, 80. *Dealer:* Virginia Miller Galleries 169 Madeira Ave Coral Gables FL 33134. *Mailing Add:* 7845 SW 118th St Miami FL 33156

COURT, LEE WINSLOW
PAINTER
b Somerville, Mass, Dec 10, 03. *Study:* Mass Col Art; and with Aldro T Hibbard, Rockport, Mass & Harry Leith-Ross, Philadelphia, Pa. *Work:* Polar Archives, Nat Arch, Washington, DC; Farnsworth Mus, Rockland, Maine; Audubon Collection; Frye Mus, Seattle, Wash; Harvard Med Sch, Boston. *Comn:* Cat-Bow Farm, comn by Sinclair Weeks, Lancaster, NH, 66; Beech Aircraft Co, Wichita, Kans, 67; M S Lindblad, Explorer, comn by Lars-Eric Lindblad, Norway, 70. *Exhib:* Salmagundi Club, New York, 53-; Acad Artists Asn, Springfield, Mass, 55-; Am Artists Prof League, New York, 58-; Guild Boston Artists, Mass, 65-; Southern Vt Artists, Manchester, 69- *Pos:* Dir, Coun Am Artists Socs, New York, 56-59; producer, Int Trade Fairs, 57-62; pres, Copley Soc, Boston, 57-67, hon mem, 77- *Awards:* Award, Acad Artists Asn Nat, 77; John Singleton Copley Medal, 81; Copley Master, 81; and others. *Bibliog:* Lee Winslow Court Paintings, Farnsworth Art Mus, 83. *Mem:* Am Artists Prof League (dir, 58-62); Guild Boston Artists; Salmagundi Club; Acad Artists Asn; Southern Vt Artists, Inc. *Media:* Oil, Watercolor. *Publ:* Ed, An Appreciation, Joseph Rodover De Camp, 25. *Mailing Add:* Rte 30 West Townshend VT 05359

COURTNEY, BARBARA WOOD
PAINTER
b Pratt, Kans, Nov 12, 29. *Study:* Okla State Univ, 47-49; Famous Artist Course, cert, 67; studied with John C Pellew, 81-83. *Work:* Ponca City Art Asn, Okla; Phillips Petroleum Co, Bartlesville, Okla; Salina City Off, Kans; CCI Bldg, Utica Deed Trust Co Nat Bank, Tulsa. *Exhib:* Okla Mus Art & Art Gallery Ann, Oklahoma City, 80 & 83; Mayfest, Tulsa Arts & Humanities Coun, 81-83; Arts, Crafts & Design Fair, Montessori Soc, Little Rock, Ark, 81-83; Wichita Falls Spring Fling, Wichita Falls Art Mus, Tex, 81-83; Austin Fine Arts Mus Festival, Tex, 82 & 83. *Awards:* Best of Show, Okla Mus Art, 80 & Eastern Trails Art Show, Uinita Okla Art Asn, 82. *Mem:* Bartlesville Art Asn; Grove Art Asn. *Media:* Oil. *Mailing Add:* RR #1 Box 150 C Eucha OK 74342

COURTNEY, KEITH TOWNSEND
ADMINISTRATOR
b Oshawa, Ont, July 23, 49. *Study:* Waterloo Lutheran Univ, BA(English & art hist). *Pos:* Cur, Art Gallery Hamilton, Ont, 74-77, community relations officer, 77- *Mem:* Ont Asn Art Galleries; Hamilton Pub Relations Asn. *Mailing Add:* c/o Art Gallery Hamilton 123 King St W Hamilton ON L8P 4S8 Canada

COURTRIGHT, ROBERT
COLLAGE ARTIST, PAINTER
b Sumter, SC, Oct 20, 26. *Study:* St John's Col, Annapolis, Md; New Sch Social Research, New York, 47-48; Art Students League, 48-52. *Work:* Phillips Collection, Washington, DC; Metrop Mus Art, New York; Thyssen-

Bornemisza Collection, Lugano, Switzerland; Wadsworth Atheneum, Hartford, Conn; Collection de l'Etat, Paris, France. *Exhib:* Smithsonian Inst, Washington, DC, 56; Mus Mod Art, New York, 57; Carnegie Int, Carnegie Inst, Pittsburgh, Pa, 59; Festival Int de la Peinture, Cagnes-sur-Mer, France, 76; Am & Europe, A Century Mod Masters from Thyssen-Bornemisza Collection, traveled in Australia & New Zealand, 79-81. *Bibliog:* Calvin Tompkins (auth), Robert Courtright, Andrew Crispo Gallery, NY, 79; Ralph Pomeroy (auth), Light and substance: The collages of Robert Courtright, Arts Mag, 12/79; Jeffrey Robinson (auth), Robert Courtright: Collage-Masks, Andrew Crispo Gallery, NY, 81. *Media:* Papier Mache, Acrylic. *Mailing Add:* Andrew Crispo Gallery 41 East 57th St New York NY 10022

COUTURIER, MARION B
DEALER, COLLECTOR
b US citizen. *Study:* Univ Lausanne, Switz, cert de Francais et Langues; Univ Dijon; Columbia Univ. *Pos:* Owner, Couturier Gallery, 61- *Specialty:* Young international painters, sculptors and graphic artists. *Interests:* Work with major private and museum collections, selecting works from the modern to the contemporary. *Collection:* Contemporary artists in all media; Latin American artists for merit and variety of their work. *Mailing Add:* c/o Couturier Gallerie 1814 Newfield Ave Stamford CT 06903

COVE, ROSEMARY
SCULPTOR, PAINTER
b New York, NY, Jan 11, 36. *Study:* Parsons Sch Design, 54-56; Art Students League, 64-65; with Knox Martin, 66-70. *Work:* Weatherspoon, NC; New York Times; Grenoble Knitwear Inc; Tallix Inc; CIBA Geigy, NY. *Exhib:* Works on Paper, Brooklyn Mus, 75; Int Women Artists Slide Exhib, Ford Found, 76; 22 Drawings & Small Sculptures, Ball State Univ, 76; Small Sculpture Show, Weatherspoon Gallery Art, NC, 77 & Works on Paper, 78; Kite Show, Danforth Mus, 78; Guild Hall, East Hampton, 81 & 82; and others. *Bibliog:* Allen Ellingswieg (auth), Rosemary Cove, Arts Mag, 75; Dorothy Beskind (auth), Rosemary Cove (film), 77; Natalie Edgar (auth), Rosemary Cove, Arts Mag, 78. *Mem:* Women in the Arts. *Media:* Terra-Cotta, Corten Steel; Oil, Ink. *Dealer:* Ingber Gallery 460 W Broadway New York NY 10012. *Mailing Add:* 128 Ft Washington Ave New York NY 10032

COVEY, VICTOR CHARLES B
CONSERVATOR, ADMINISTRATOR
b Morehead City, NC, Nov 28, 16. *Study:* Baltimore City Col, 38; jewelry design & casting with Alvin Schmidt, 38-39; Corcoran Gallery, painting conserv with Russel Quandt, 53-59; NY Univ Conserv Ctr, materials of art & archeol, 68. *Work:* Conservator, Wurtzburger Collections Pre-Columbian, African, Oceanic & Mod Sculpture, Baltimore Mus Art & Collection Contemporary Japanese & Italian Paintings, Roland Gibson Art Found, Potsdam, NY. *Exhib:* Conservator, US Pavilion Biennale, Venice, Italy, 60, US Dept State Tour Exhib Archaeol Finds of People's Repub China, US & Peking, 75 & US Dept State Conserv Holy Crown of St Stephen & Coronation Regalia, US & Budapest, Hungary, 77-78. *Pos:* Master template draftsman, Glenn L Martin Aircraft Co, Baltimore, 40-49; supt bldgs & art technician, Baltimore Mus Art, 49-53; chief conservator art, Baltimore Mus Art, 55-72; chief conserv, Nat Gallery Art, Washington, DC, 72-83, chief conserv emer, 83-, sr conservator spec proj, 83- *Mem:* Fel Int Inst Conserv Hist & Artistic Works; Washington Conserv Guild (pres, 74-); Am Inst Conserv (dir bd, 75); Nat Conserv Coun (vpres, 78-); fel Am Inst Conserv Hist & Artistic Works. *Mailing Add:* 3717 Rexmere Rd Baltimore MD 21218

COVI, DARIO A
HISTORIAN
b Livingston, Ill, Dec 26, 20. *Study:* Eastern Ill State Col, BEd, 43; State Univ Iowa, MA, 48, with William S Heckscher; Univ Louisville, with Richard Offner, PhD, 58. *Pos:* Mem exec comt, Ky Arts Comn, 65-70. *Teaching:* From instr to prof art hist, Univ Louisville, 56-70; prof, Duke Univ, 70-75; Hite prof, Univ Louisville, 75- *Awards:* Am Coun Learned Socs Fel, 64; Fulbright-Hays Fel, 68-69; Gladys Krieble Delmas Found Grant, 79. *Mem:* Col Art Assn Am; Southeastern Col Art Conf; Renaissance Soc Am; Midwest Art Hist Soc. *Res:* Italian Renaissance art. *Publ:* Auth, Prints...from the Allen R Hite Art Institute Collection (exhib catalog), 63; contribr, McGraw-Hill Dict Art, Art Bulletin, Burlington Mag, Renaissance Quart & other nat art publ. *Mailing Add:* Hite Art Inst Univ of Louisville Louisville KY 40292

COVINGTON, HARRISON WALL
PAINTER, EDUCATOR
b Plant City, Fla, Apr 12, 24. *Study:* Univ Fla, 42-43; Hiram Col, 43; Univ Fla, BFA(hons), 49, MFA, 53. *Work:* Herron Mus Art, Indianapolis, Ind; Mead Corp, Atlanta, Ga; Everson Mus Art, Syracuse, NY; John & Mable Ringling Mus Art, Sarasota, Fla; Jacksonville Mus Art, Fla. *Exhib:* Museum Director's Choice, circulated throughout Southeastern US, 56 & 59; Nat Home Furnishings Show, New York, 59; Painting USA: The Figure, Mus Mod Art, New York, 62; New York World's Fair, 64; Florida 17, Pan-Am Union, Washington, DC, 68. *Teaching:* Instr art, Univ Fla, 49-61; prof art, Univ SFla, 61-82, chmn visual arts prog, 61-67, dean, Div Fine Arts, 67-72, dean, Col Fine Arts, 77-82, prof emer, 82- *Awards:* Sloan Found Grant, 47; Guggenheim Fel, 64. *Media:* Acrylic, Plastic. *Mailing Add:* Col Fine Arts Univ of SFla Tampa FL 33620

COWAN, AILEEN HOOPER
SCULPTOR, PAINTER
b Windsor, Ont, June 11, 26. *Study:* Univ Toronto, BA; Queen's Univ, Kingston, Ont; Univ Toronto. *Work:* Univ Western Ont; McLaughlin Art Ctr,

Oshawa. *Exhib:* Art Gallery Hamilton, 73; Agnes Etherington Gallery, Queen's Univ, Kingston, Ont, 74; Merton Gallery, Toronto, 79; McDowell Gallery, Toronto, 80; Sculptors Soc BC, Robson Sq Media Ctr, Vancouver, 80; and many other group and solo exhibs. *Teaching:* Univ Toronto, Ont. *Awards:* Augusts Kopmanis Mem Award, 80. *Bibliog:* Article, Athens News, Greece, 7/72; article, Art Mag, Toronto, Vol 5, No 15, 73. *Mem:* Sculptors Soc Can (vpres, currently). *Media:* Bronze, Welded Steel; Acrylic, Watercolor. *Dealer:* Wayne Gallery Windsor ON; Atlantic Art Gallery Halifax NS. *Mailing Add:* 357 Glencairn Ave Toronto ON M5N 1V2 Canada

COWIN, EILEEN
PHOTOGRAPHER
b Brooklyn, NY, Aug 17, 47. *Study:* State Univ NY, New Paltz, BS, 68; Ill Inst Technol, with Aaron Siskind & Arthur Siegel, MS, 70. *Work:* Mus Mod Art, New York; Los Angeles Co Mus Art; Nat Gallery Can; Fogg Mus; Santa Barbara Mus Art. *Exhib:* New Voices, Allen Mem Art Mus, Oberlin, Ohio, 81; California Photography, Mus Art, RI Sch Design, 82 & San Francisco Mus Art, 84; Studio Work, Los Angeles Co Mus Art, 82; The Diaristic Mode, Univ NMex Art Mus, Albuquerque, 83; The Image Scavengers, Inst Contemp Art, Philadelphia, 83; Mus Mod Art, Paris, 83; Whitney Biennial, Whitney Mus Art, 83. *Teaching:* Prof art, Calif State Univ, Fullerton, 75-; vis artist photog, Art Inst Chicago, 80. *Awards:* Nat Endowment Arts Fel, 79 & 82. *Mem:* Soc Photog Educ. *Dealer:* G Ray Hawkins Gallery 7224 Melrose Ave Los Angeles CA 90046; H F Mane's Gallery 177 Prince St New York NY 10012. *Mailing Add:* 1396 Rose Ave Venice CA 90291

COWLES, FLEUR
PAINTER, WRITER
Study: Pratt Inst, New York; Elmira Univ, LLD. *Work:* Seattle Art Mus, Wash; Museu Arte Mod, Sao Paulo, Brazil; Fisher Found, Iowa; Dart Indust, Orlando, Fla. *Comn:* Murals, Hotel Hilton, London, Eng & Athens, Greece. *Exhib:* One-man exhibs, Seattle Mus Art, 70, Museu de Arte Mod, Sao Paulo, 72; Cranbrook Mus, Bloomfield Hills, NJ, 74; Singer Mus, Laren, Holland, 77; Hammer Galleries, New York, 78 & Partridge Galleries, London, 83; and many others. *Pos:* Assoc ed, Look Mag, 48-55; ed-in-chief, Flair Mag, 50-52. *Mem:* Royal Soc Arts; Univ Art Mus Coun, Berkeley, Calif. *Media:* Acrylic. *Publ:* Auth, Bloody Precedent, 52; auth, The Case of Salvador Dali, 59; auth, The Hidden World of the Hadhramoutt, 63; auth, Friends and Memories, 76; auth, All Too True, 81; auth, The Flower Game, 83. *Mailing Add:* A5 Albany Piccadilly London England United Kingdom

COWLEY, EDWARD P
PAINTER, EDUCATOR
b Buffalo, NY, May 29, 25. *Study:* Albright Art Sch; Buffalo State Col, BS, 48; Columbia Univ, MA, 49; Nat Col Art, Dublin, Ireland, Ford Found Fel, 55. *Work:* Albany Inst Hist & Art, NY; Schenectady Mus, NY; Smith Col, Northhampton, Mass; Colgate Univ, Hamilton, NY; Berkshire Mus, Pittsfield, Mass. *Teaching:* Prof art & chmn dept, State Univ NY Albany, 56-75, prof art, 76- *Awards:* State Univ NY Res Grant, 66 & 74. *Media:* Oil, Pastels. *Mailing Add:* Box 198 Altamont NY 12009

COX, E MORRIS
COLLECTOR
b Santa Rosa, Calif, Feb 5, 03. *Study:* Univ Calif, AB; Harvard Univ Grad Sch Bus, MBA. *Pos:* Pres, San Francisco Mus Contemp Art, 55-60, trustee, currently; treas, Calif Acad Sci, 63-67, chmn bd trustees, 67-70; dir, Bay Area Educ TV Asn, currently. *Collection:* Contemporary sculpture and painting. *Mailing Add:* 2361 Broadway San Francisco CA 94115

COX, ERNEST LEE
SCULPTOR, EDUCATOR
b Wilmington, NC, June 1, 37. *Study:* Col of William & Mary, BA(fine arts); Cranbrook Acad of Art, Bloomfield Hills, Mich, MFA(sculpture); Mich State Univ, Oakland. *Work:* St Petersburg Pub Libr, Fla; Eckerd Col, St Petersburg; Univ SFla, Tampa; 1st Nat Bank of Atlanta, Ga; 1st Nat Bank of Tampa, Fla. *Comn:* Steel sculptures, Wesley Manor Retirement Village, Jacksonville, Fla, 64, Fed Deposit Ins Corp, Washington, DC, 65 & Gulf Life Ins Co, Jacksonville, 67. *Exhib:* The 17th Va Artists Exhib, Va Mus of Fine Arts, Richmond, 58; 24th Ann NC Artists Exhib, NC Mus of Fine Arts, Raleigh, 61; 20th-22nd Southeastern Ann Exhibs, High Mus of Art, Atlanta, Ga, 65-67; Fla 17, Pan Am Union, Washington, DC, 68; 15 Fla Artists Sculpture Exhib, Gallery of Contemp Art, Winston-Salem, NC, 70; one-man show, Jacksonville Mus of Art, Fla, 73. *Teaching:* From instr to prof sculpture, Univ SFla, Tampa, 62-, chmn art dept, 71-73. *Awards:* Second Prize, Fla Sculptors 7th Ann Exhib, 63; First Prize, Fla State Fair Fine Arts Exhib, 65; Purchase Prize, Southeastern Sculpture Exhib, Atlanta Chamber of Commerce, 69. *Media:* Welded, forged steel; mixed-media. *Dealer:* J Camp 380 W Broadway New York NY. *Mailing Add:* Rt 2 Box 1604 Lutz FL 33549

COX, GARDNER
PAINTER
b Holyoke, Mass, Jan 22, 06. *Study:* Art Students League, 24; Harvard Univ, 24-27; Boston Mus Sch, 28-30; Mass Inst Technol, 29-31. *Work:* Nat Gallery Art & Nat Portrait Gallery, Washington, DC; Boston Mus Fine Arts; Fogg Art Mus, Harvard Univ, Cambridge, Mass; Addison Gallery Am Art, Andover, Mass. *Comn:* Portraits, Lessing Rosenwald, Nat Gallery Art, Hon Dean Acheson, State Dept, Washington, DC, 50, Robert Frost, Frost Libr, Amherst Col, Mass, 57, Justice Felix Frankfurter, Harvard Univ Law Sch, 60 & Robert F Kennedy, Nat Portrait Gallery, 68. *Exhib:* Carnegie Int, Pittsburgh, 41; Va Mus Fine Arts, Richmond, 46; Art Inst Chicago, 48, 49 & 51; Metrop Mus Art, New York, 50; Corcoran Gallery Art, Washington, DC,

75. *Pos:* Exec comt, Boston Arts Festival, 55-65; exec comt, Mass Art Comn, 65- *Teaching:* Head dept painting, Boston Mus Sch, 54-56. *Awards:* M V Kohnstamm Prize, Am Exhib Watercolors, Art Inst Chicago, 49 & Norman Wait Harris Bronze Medal, 60th Am Exhib, 51; Popular Prize, Boston Arts Festival, 60. *Bibliog:* Portrait painters, Life Mag, 2/3/41; Experiments in New England, Time Mag, 7/21/52; Portraits by Cox, Newsweek Mag, 6/15/53. *Mem:* Nat Inst Arts & Lett; Nat Acad Design; Am Acad Arts & Sci; Am Acad in Rome (trustee, 63); Cambridge Art Asn. *Media:* Oil, Watercolor, Tempera. *Dealer:* Portraits Inc 41 E 57th St New York NY 10022. *Mailing Add:* c/o Fenway Studios 30 Ipswich St Boston MA 02215

COX, JOHN ROGERS
PAINTER
b Terre Haute, Ind, Mar 24, 15. *Study:* Univ Pa, BFA; Pa Acad Fine Arts, 38. *Work:* Cleveland Mus; Butler Inst; Springfield Mus, Mass & pvt collections. *Exhib:* Carnegie Inst; Pa Acad Fine Arts; Metrop Mus, New York; Boston Inst Art; Cleveland Mus; retrospective exhib, Swope Art Gallery, 82; and others. *Pos:* Dir, Swope Gallery, 41-43. *Teaching:* Instr figure drawing & painting, Art Inst Chicago, 48-60, asst prof figure drawing & painting, 60-65. *Awards:* Prizes, Metrop Mus, 42 & Carnegie Inst, 43 & 44. *Mailing Add:* 919 First St Wenatchee WA 98801

COX, MARION AVERAL
PAINTER, INSTRUCTOR
b Washingtonville, Ohio. *Study:* With H Gauguin, W Goodrich, H Radio, B I Payne, C Wallace, J M Jehu, N Bel Geddes, Max Reinhardt (Ger), and many others. *Exhib:* Sixty Text Books, Am Inst Graphic Arts, Grand Cent Palace, 44 & 54; 13th Ann Ohio Artists & Craftsmen, Massillon Mus, 48; 14th New Years Show, Butler Art Inst, 49; American Painting Today, Metrop Mus Art. *Pos:* Art dir, Universal Studios, Universal City, Calif, 28-30. *Teaching:* Art theory & practice, Art-O-Technix Inst, Carefree, Ariz, 75- *Mem:* Am Asn Advan Sci. *Media:* Mixed. *Publ:* Illusr, E T Smith (auth), Exploring Biology, 38. *Mailing Add:* Box 325 Cave Creek AZ 85331

COX, RICHARD WILLIAM
HISTORIAN, WRITER
b Los Angeles, Calif, July 13, 42. *Study:* Univ Calif, Los Angeles, BA(hist), 64, MA(hist), 66; Univ Wis, Madison, MA(art hist), 70, PhD(art hist), 73. *Teaching:* Instr Am art, Univ Wis, River Falls, 71-74; from asst prof to prof Am art & hist prints, La State Univ, 74- *Awards:* Solon Buck Award for Best Article, Minn Hist, 75; Nat Endowment Humanities Fel, 75. *Bibliog:* Matthew Baigell (auth), The American Scene: American Painting of the 1930s, Praeger, 74; James Dennis (auth), Grant Wood, A Study in Art & Culture, Viking, 75. *Mem:* Col Art Asn; Art Educ Asn; La Hist Soc. *Res:* American painting and graphic arts in 1900-1945 period; contemporary art. *Publ:* Auth, Wanda Gag and the Bite of the Picture Book, Minn Hist, 75; auth, Art Young: Cartoonist from the middle border, Wis Mag Hist, 77; auth, Caroline Durieux: The lithographs of the 1930s and 1940s, La State Univ Press, 77; auth, Adolf Dehn--jazz age satirist, Arch Am Art J, 78; auth, Southern works on paper, 1900-1950, Southern Arts Fedn, 80; and others. *Mailing Add:* Dept of Fine Arts La State Univ Baton Rouge LA 70803

COYER, MAX R
PAINTER, DEALER
b Hartford, Conn, Jan 12, 54. *Work:* Hospital Corp Am, Nashville. *Exhib:* Painting From the Mind's Eye, C W Post Ctr, Long Island Univ, 83. *Pos:* Dir, Bouckaert Gallery, New York, 81- *Bibliog:* Helena Harrison (auth), article, New York Times, 3/6/83; Holland Cotter (auth), article, 4/83 & Stephen Westfall (auth), article, 9/83, Arts Mag. *Specialty:* Contemporary American art. *Mailing Add:* c/o Harm Bouckaert Gallery 100 Hudson St New York NY 10013

COYNE, JOHN MICHAEL
PAINTER, EDUCATOR
b St Stephen, NB, 1950. *Study:* Mt Allison Univ, BFA, 75; Univ Regina, MFA, 77. *Work:* NS Art Bank, Halifax; Univ Regina, Sask; Acadia Univ Art Gallery, Wolfville, NS; Labatt's Breweries Ltd, St John, NB; Owens Art Gallery, Mt Allison Univ, Sackville, NB. *Exhib:* Art Gallery NS, Halifax, 80; retrospective, Acadia Univ Art Gallery, Wolfville, NS, 83; Owens Art Gallery, Sackville, NB, 83; Univ Col Cape Breton, Sydney, NS, 83; St Mary's Univ Art Gallery, Halifax, NS, 83. *Teaching:* Asst prof, Acadia Univ, Wolfville, NS, 77-, actg head, Art Dept, 83- *Awards:* Grant, Greenshield's Found, Montreal, 76. *Bibliog:* C MacLauglin (auth), Atlantic lines, Heritage Can Mag, 2/79; Dr Helen J Dow (auth), Michael Coyne: A Retrospective, Acadia Univ Art Gallery, 83. *Media:* Oil. *Mailing Add:* Dept Art Acadia Univ Wolfville NS B0P 1X0 Canada

CRABLE, JAMES HARBOUR
MULTI-MEDIA ARTIST, INSTRUCTOR
b Bronx, NY, Aug 30, 39. *Study:* State Univ NY Col Buffalo, BS, 62; Rochester Inst Technol, NY, MFA, 66; Chelsea Sch Art, London, Eng, HDA, 70. *Work:* Mem Art Gallery, Rochester, NY; Equitable Life Assurance Collection; AT&T Collection, DC; R J Reynolds Collection, NC; State Univ NY Art Collection, Albany. *Exhib:* One-man shows, Va Mus Fine Arts, Richmond, 76, Southeastern Ctr Contemp Art, Winston-Salem, 78 & Gallery K, Washington, DC, 79 & 82; 35 Artists in the Southeast, High Mus Art, Atlanta, Ga, 76-77; Continuum VII, Dulin Gallery Art, Knoxville, 82. *Teaching:* Assoc prof art survey, drawing & art educ, State Univ Col Brockport, NY, 66-69; lectr found studies, Croydon Col Art, Surrey, Eng,

70-71; assoc prof drawing & art survey, James Madison Univ, Harrisonburg, Va, 73- *Awards:* NEA Southeastern Artists Fel, 79; James Madison Univ Fac Res Fel, 80; Best in Show Award, Light Images 83, Chrysler Mus, Norfolk, Va, 83. *Mem:* Col Art Asn Am. *Media:* Photo-collage. *Mailing Add:* 261 Green St Harrisonburg VA 22801

CRACKER JACK KID (CHARLES D WELCH)
PRINTMAKER, GRAPHIC ARTIST
b Kearney, Nebr, Oct 5, 48. *Study:* Kearney State Col, BA(art educ), 70, MS(art educ), 74. *Work:* Chicago Art Inst; Galerie Diagonele, Paris; Workspace Gallery, Univ Maine, Orono; Arch Small Press & Commun, Antwerp, Belg; Kearney State Col. *Exhib:* Nat Exhib Xerox Art, Ga State Univ, Atlanta, 80; Artists Publ Exhib, Tweed Mus Art, 80; Sao Paulo Bienale, 82; 17th Biennial, Joslyn Art Mus, 82; Sixth Ann Art Educr Show, Nebr Wesleyan Univ, 82; Seoul Int Mail Art Exhib, Korea, 82; Nouveau Mixage Gallery, Caen, France, 82; and others. *Pos:* Proprietor, Sandbar Willow Handmade Paper Mill, Omaha, 78- *Teaching:* Chmn art dept, Bellevue Sr High Sch, 74- & Bellevue W High Sch, 77-84; Instr, Bellevue Col, 78-80. *Awards:* Fulbright Hayes Grant, 76; Hilda Maehling Fel, Nat Educ Asn, 80; Nat Exhib Xerox Art Merit Award, Ga State Univ, 80. *Bibliog:* Randy Harrellson (auth), SWAK, Workman Publ Co, 82; Judith Hoffberg (auth), article, Umbrella Mag, 83. *Mem:* Nat Educ Asn; Bellevue Educ Asn; Int Soc Copier Artists; Friends Dard Hunter Soc. *Publ:* Illusr, Tenth and Eleventh Assembling, Richard Kostelanetz, 79-80; contribr, Arte Postale, Vittore Baroni. *Mailing Add:* 2468 S 3rd Plaza Omaha NE 68108

CRAFT, DAVID RALPH
PAINTER, PRINTMAKER
b Elberton, Ga, July 31, 45. *Study:* ETenn State Univ, BS, 67. *Work:* Appalachian State Univ; Blount Inc, Montgomery, Ala; Tenn Arts Comn, Nashville; Hunter Mus Art. *Exhib:* Nat Print & Drawing Competition, Davidson Col, NC, 74 & 75; Art USA: The South, New Orleans Mus, 75-77; Smithsonian Inst, touring, 76; 11th Ann Nat Drawing & Small Sculpture Competition, Del Mar Col Art Ctr, 77; Am Drawings I, II & IV, Portsmouth Arts Ctr, 78 & 82; More Than Land and Sky: Art from Appalachia, Nat Mus Am Art, Washington & touring, 82-84. *Teaching:* Instr, Hunter Mus Art, 75- *Awards:* Purchase Awards, Dulin Gallery Nat, 76, Mt Holyoke Nat, 76 & Lauren Rogers Regional, 79. *Media:* Oils. *Dealer:* Margaret Townsend Gallery 406 High St Chattanooga TN 37403. *Mailing Add:* 1109 1/2 Mississippi Ave Chattanooga TN 37405

CRAFT, DOUGLAS D
PAINTER, EDUCATOR
b Greene, NY, Oct 20, 24. *Study:* Univ Iowa; Univ Chicago; Art Inst Chicago, BFA; Syracuse Univ; Univ NMex, MA. *Work:* Mus Mod Art & Whitney Mus Am Art, New York; Art Inst Chicago; Univ Ky, Lexington; Newark Mus, NJ; Univ Calif, Santa Cruz. *Comn:* Paintings, comn by Mr & Mrs Daniel Weinstein for Edward Weinstein Ctr Performing Arts, Nat Col Educ, Evanston, Ill, 72. *Exhib:* One-man shows, Mus Art, Carnegie Inst, Pittsburgh, Pa, 68, Twentieth Century West Galleries, Ltd, New York, 68, Fischbach Galleries, New York, 73 & Jersey City Mus, 78, 55 Mercer Gallery, New York, 80. *Pos:* Vis artist in residence, Univ Ky, 64; Am artist in residence, Royal Col Art, London, Eng, 64-65; vis artist-critic, Sunderland Col Art, Eng, 65 & Gloucestershire Col Art, Cheltenham, Eng, 65. *Teaching:* Assoc prof painting, Art Inst Chicago, 55-66 & Carnegie Inst Technol, 66-69; vis artist, Cooper Union, 69-71; prof painting, Col New Rochelle, 71- *Awards:* Harry Allison Logan Mem Award, Chautauqua Inst, NY, 63; Logan Bronze Medal & Prize, Art Inst Chicago, 66; Jury Award/Distinction in Painting, Mus Art, Carnegie Inst Int, 68. *Bibliog:* Max Wykes-Joyce (auth), Douglas Craft, Arts Rev, London, 64; Cordelia Oliver (auth), Exhibitions at Edinburgh, Guardian, 65; D L Shirey (auth), Douglas Craft Show in Jersey City, New York Times, 78. *Mailing Add:* 240 Ogden Ave Jersey City NJ 07307

CRAFT, JOHN RICHARD
MUSEUM DIRECTOR
b Uniontown, Pa, June 15, 09. *Study:* Phillips Acad, Andover, Mass; Yale Univ; Art Students League; Univ Paris, 36-38; Acad Julien; and with Andre l'Hote; Am Sch Classical Studies, Athens, Greece, 37-39; Johns Hopkins Univ, MA & PhD. *Pos:* Dir, Washington Co Mus Fine Arts, Hagerstown, Md, 40-49; dir, Columbia Mus Art, SC, 50-77, dir emer, 77- *Mem:* Am Asn Mus; Southeastern Mus Conf (pres, 52-55); SC Fedn Mus (pres, 70-71); Am Inst Designers. *Mailing Add:* 712 Kipling Dr Columbia SC 29205

CRAIG, NANCY ELLEN
PAINTER
b Bronxville, NY. *Study:* Acad Julien, Paris, France; Art Students League, New York; Hans Hofmann Sch, Provincetown, Mass. *Work:* Metrop Mus Art, New York; Baltimore Mus; New Britain Art Inst. *Comn:* Portraits comn by Assoc Justice Stanley Reed, Supreme Ct Bldg, Washington, DC, Gov & Mrs Herbert Lehman, New York, Mrs Franklin D Roosevelt, Jr, New York, Duke of Argyll, 69 & Princess Marie Luise of Prussia, 74. *Exhib:* Nat Acad Design, New York; Audubon Artists, New York; Allied Artists Am, New York; one-woman shows, Graham Gallery, New York & Galeria Betica, Madrid, Spain. *Awards:* First Benjamin Altman Figure Prize, Nat Acad Design, 57; Gold Medal of Honor, Allied Artists Am; Patron's Prize, Audubon Artists. *Bibliog:* Nardi Campion (auth), Nancy Ellen Craig & her portraits, Am Artist. *Media:* Oil on Canvas. *Publ:* Auth, Portrait painting in oil, 60. *Dealer:* Grand Central Galleries Hotel Biltmore Madison Ave & 43rd St New York NY 10017; Galeria Betica General Goded 12 Madrid Spain. *Mailing Add:* Box 57 Truro MA 02666

CRAIG, SUSAN V
LIBRARIAN
b Newton, Kans, Nov 11, 48. *Study:* Univ Kans, BA, 70; Emporia State Univ, MLS, 71. *Pos:* Indexer, Art Index, H W Wilson Co, New York, 71-74; art hist & classics librn, Univ of Calif, Berkeley, 75-81; art librn, Univ Kans, 81- *Teaching:* Instr art bibliog, Univ Calif, Berkeley, 81. *Mem:* Art Libr Soc NAm (secy 75-77). *Res:* Kansas artists; art librarianship. *Mailing Add:* Art Library Spencer Mus Art Univ Kans Lawrence KS 66045

CRAMER, RICHARD CHARLES
PAINTER, EDUCATOR
b Appleton, Wis, Aug 14, 32. *Study:* Layton Sch Art, BFA; Univ Wis-Milwaukee, BS, Univ Wis-Madison, MS, 61, MFA, 62. *Work:* Pa Acad Fine Arts; Everhart Mus, Scranton, Pa; Everson Mus, Syracuse, NY; Univ Wis; Philadelphia Mus; plus others. *Exhib:* Drawing Biennial, Norfolk Mus Art, 65; Drawings, Smithsonian Inst Traveling Exhib, 65; one-man shows, Gloria Cortella Gallery, New York, 77-78, Barbara Fiedler Gallery, Washington, DC, 77 & Pa Acad Fine Arts, Philadelphia, 78; Chromatic Structure, Philadelphia Col Art, 80; Geometric-Abstraction, Inst Contemp Art, Boston, 81; plus others. *Teaching:* From instr to assoc prof painting & drawing, Tyler Sch Art, Temple Univ, 66-79, prof, 79- *Awards:* Prizes, Milwaukee Art Inst, 54, Syracuse Allied Artists, 64 & Munson-Williams-Proctor Inst, Utica, NY, 65; and others. *Media:* Acrylic. *Mailing Add:* 723 Chestnut St Philadelphia PA 19106

CRANDALL, JERRY C
PAINTER
b La Junta, Colo, Apr 1, 35. *Study:* Woodbury Col, Los Angeles, Calif, 60. *Work:* Favell Mus, Klamath Falls, Ore; Koshare Indian Mus, La Junta, Colo; Bianchi Mus, Temecula, Calif. *Comn:* Robert Conrad as Pasquinelle in Centennial, comn by Robert Conrad, Malibu, Calif, 78; Wild Bill Hickok, Petersen Publ Co, Beverly Hills, Calif, 75; Custer's Last Stand, comn by Dr Larry Frost, Monroe, Mich. *Exhib:* Round Up of Western Art Ann, Saddleback Western Art Mus, Santa Ana, Calif, 74-; John Selmon Mem Art Show, Stamford, Tex, 76-77, 79 & 84; Portraits from Life, Art Cottage, Corona, Calif, 82 & 83; C M Russell Show, Great Falls, Mont, 83 & 84; O S Ranch Art Exhib, Post, Tex, 83 & 84. *Pos:* Historical technical adv, Universal Studios filming of Centennial, 78 & Columbia Pictures filming of The Mountain Men, 79; speaker, Professional Motivation in the Arts, Univ Calif, Riverside, 80-81. *Awards:* Silver Medal, Western Artists Am Ann Exhib & Sale, 81; Gold Medal, Western Artists Am Ann Exhib & Sale, 81. *Bibliog:* Jerry Crandall of Riverside, Art Voices South, 2/80; Phylllis Barton (auth), Creative credibility, Southwest Art, 10/80; Historical authenticity in art, In: Man at Arms, 11/83. *Media:* Oil, Acrylic. *Publ:* Illusr, Marsielles, Star of Africa, 69 & Battle of Britain, 70, JWC Publ; illusr, Guns of the Gunfighters (cover), Petersen Publ Co, 75; illusr, General Custer and the Battle of the Little Big Horn, Garry Owen Press, 76. *Dealer:* Eagle Editions Ltd PO Box 1830 Sedona AZ 86336. *Mailing Add:* PO Box 2606 Sedona AZ 86336

CRANDALL, JUDITH ANN
PUBLISHER, WRITER
b Milwaukee, Wis, Aug 20, 48. *Study:* El Camino Jr Col; Univ Ariz. *Collections Arranged:* Eleventh Ann Membership Show for Women Artists of the American West, 83. *Pos:* Staff writer, Southwest Art Mag, Houston, 74-; dir, Saddleback Western Art Gallery, Calif, 78-80; owner, Eagle Ed, Sedona, Ariz, currently. *Publ:* Auth, The Custer centennial, 76 & Women artists of the American West, 82, Southwest Art. *Mailing Add:* PO Box 2606 Sedona AZ 86336

CRANE, BARBARA BACHMANN
PHOTOGRAPHER, EDUCATOR
b Chicago, Ill, Mar 19, 28. *Study:* Mills Col, with Alfred Neumeyer, 45-48; NY Univ, BA(art hist), 50; Inst of Design, Ill Inst Technol, with Aaron Siskind, MS(photog), 66. *Work:* Libr Cong, Washington, DC; Int Mus Photog, George Eastman House, Rochester, NY; Art Inst Chicago; Pasadena Mus Art, Calif. *Comn:* 26 photomurals, Baxter Travenol Labs, Deerfield, Ill, 75; Chicago Epic (photomural), Chicago Bank Commerce, Standard Oil Bldg, Chicago. *Exhib:* One-woman shows, Friends of Photog, Carmel, Calif, 69 & 75, Limited Image Gallery, Chicago, 71, People of North Portal, Mus of Sci & Indust, Chicago, 72, Univ Iowa Mus, Iowa City, 73 & 75 & Vision Gallery, Boston, 80; retrospective traveling exhib, Ctr Creative Photog, Univ Ariz, Tucson, 80. *Teaching:* Prof photog, Sch Art Inst Chicago, 67-; vis prof photog, Philadelphia Col of Art, 77 & Sch Mus Fine Arts, Boston, 79. *Awards:* Nat Endowment for Arts grant, 75. *Bibliog:* Shelley Rice (auth), article, Camera 35 Mag, 12/79; Connie Lauerman (auth), Tempo, Chicago Tribune, 10/27/81; Deborah Bright (auth), article, Afterimage, 10/81. *Mem:* Soc Photog Educ (mem bd, 72-76); Friends of Photog (trustee, 75-81). *Publ:* Auth, Portfolios, Popular Photog, 67 & 74; auth, Portfolio, Creative Camera, 74; auth, Portfolio, Lightwork, 74. *Mailing Add:* 3164 N Hudson Chicago IL 60657

CRANE, JAMES
PAINTER, CARTOONIST
b Hartshorne, Okla, May 21, 27. *Study:* Albion Col, BA; State Univ Iowa, MA; Mich State Univ, MFA. *Work:* Walker Art Ctr, Minn; Joslyn Mus, Omaha; Times Publ Co, St Petersburg; Wis State Univ, River Falls; St Cloud State Col, Minn. *Exhib:* 28th Biennial, Corcoran Gallery Art; 149th Ann, Pa Acad Fine Arts, Philadelphia; Mich Artists, Detroit Art Inst; Painting of the Year, Smithsonian Inst; Ringling Mus, Sarasota; Joslyn Mus, Omaha; Walker Art Ctr, Minneapolis; Arts in Embassies Prog, Lima, Peru & Katmandu, Nepal. *Teaching:* Prof art, Eckerd Col, currently. *Awards:* Awards, Fla State

Fair, 65, Soc Four Arts, Palm Beach, Fla, 67 & Tampa Mus, Tampa Bay, 82; plus others. *Media:* Acrylic Collage, Plexiglas. *Publ:* Auth, On Edge, 65, Great Teaching Machine, 66 & Parables, 71, John Knox; auth, Inside Out, 67; illusr, A Funny Thing Happened on the Way to Heaven, 69; plus others. *Mailing Add:* Dept of Art Eckerd Col St Petersburg FL 33733

CRANE, JEAN
PAINTER
b Battle Creek, Mich, July 25, 33. *Study:* Syracuse Univ, BFA, 55. *Work:* Wustum Art Mus, Racine, Wis; Madison Art Ctr, Wis; Bergstrom Art Mus, Neenah, Wis; Springfield Art Asn Gallery, Ill. *Exhib:* Watercolor Wisconsin, Wustum Art Mus, Racine, Wis, 79; Watercolor USA 81, Kohler Art Ctr; Wisconsin Biennale 81, Sheyboygan, 81; Am Watercolor Soc, New York, 81; Art Inst Chicago Bales Gallery, 81; and others. *Awards:* Second Place, Wustum Art Mus, 79; Emily Lowe Award, Am Watercolor Soc, New York, 81. *Bibliog:* Review, New Art Examiner, Chicago, 3/81. *Mem:* Wis Watercolor Soc; Wis Painters & Sculptors; Chicago Artists Coalition. *Media:* Watercolor. *Mailing Add:* 2671 N Lake Dr Milwaukee WI 53211

CRANE, MICHAEL PATRICK
PHOTOGRAPHER, PERFORMANCE ARTIST
b St Louis, Mo, Dec 24, 48. *Study:* Art Inst Chicago, MFA(design & commun), 76. *Work:* Fluxus W Arch, San Diego, Calif; Jean Brown Arch, Tyringham Inst, Mass; Arch Sohm, Markgroningen, WGer; Mus Contemp Art, Univ Sao Paulo, Brazil; Mod Mus, Stockholm, Sweden. *Exhib:* 03-23-03, Nat Gallery Can, Ottawa, Ont, 77; Open Ring Gallery, Sacramento, 79; Micro Gallery, Ltd, Sacramento, 79; Berry Col, Mt Berry, Ga, 79 & 80; Union Gallery, San Jose, 80; La Mamelle, San Francisco, 81; and others. *Pos:* Original mem & co-dir, Name Gallery, Chicago, 73-74; ed, Running Dog Press, San Jose, 74-; adminr, All the Chicago Fog Performance Gallery, Chicago, 75-76; res fel, Inst Advan Studies in Contemp Art, San Diego, Calif, 77-78; gallery dir, Calif State Univ, Sacramento, 78-79; gallery dir, San Jose State Univ, 79-83; gallery & mus dir, Arvada Ctr Arts & Humanities, Colo, 83- *Teaching:* Vis artist, Univ Chicago & Calif State Univ, Sacramento, 77; vis lectr, San Diego State Univ, 78; lectr, Calif State Univ, Sacramento, 78-79; vis artist, Sch of Art Inst, Chicago, 79; vis lectr, Ariz State Univ, 79; lectr, San Jose State Univ, 79-83. *Media:* Posters, Live Performances. *Publ:* Contribr, Anti-Object Art, Northwestern Univ Press, 74; auth, Fill in This Space, 75 & Landscapes I'd Love to Perform/Do, 76, Running Dog Press; ed, Correspondence Art, Contemp Arts Press, 83. *Mailing Add:* 7720 Missy Ct St Louis MO 63123

CRARY, JONATHAN KNIGHT
CRITIC
b New Haven, Conn. *Study:* San Francisco Art Inst, BFA, 73; Columbia Univ, BA(Hon Pres Fel), BA, 75, MA, 78, PhM, 80. *Pos:* Contrib ed, Arts Mag, New York, 76-; New York corresp, D'Ars Mag, Milan, Italy, 79- *Teaching:* Instr art hist, Columbia Univ, New York, 80-82; vis lectr, Univ Calif, San Diego, 83. *Awards:* Art Critics Fel Grants, Nat Endowment Arts, 78 & 79. *Mem:* Am Sect Int Asn Art Critics. *Res:* Contemporary art and culture. *Publ:* Auth, Passage from virgin to bride, 77 & auth, Real estate opportunities, 77, Arts Mag; auth, Boundary works, 78 & auth, Delirious operations, 78, Artforum; auth, Joseph Beuys: New York, D'Ars Mag, 80. *Mailing Add:* 310 West 106th St New York NY 10025

CRAVEN, ROY CURTIS, JR
GALLERY DIRECTOR, EDUCATOR
b Cherokee Bluffs, Ala, July 29, 24. *Study:* Univ Chattanooga, BA, 49; Art Students League, 49-50, with George Grosz, Yasuo Kuniyoshi & Byron Browne; Univ Fla, MFA, 56. *Work:* Va Mus Art, Richmond; Mus Arqueolgia y Etnologia Guatemala, Guatemala City; Esso Standard Oil Collection, New York; New Col, Sarasota, Fla; Chattanooga Art Asn, Tenn. *Exhib:* American Prints & Watercolors, Metrop Mus Art, New York, 50; Forecast, 57-58 & Painting of the Year, 61-62, Am Fedn Arts touring exhibs, US; also exhibs at Delgado Mus, New Orleans, La & Four Arts Club, Palm Beach, Fla, several yrs. *Pos:* Dir univ gallery, Univ Fla, 66-, dir, Ctr Latin Am & Tropical Arts, 72- *Teaching:* Prof art, Univ Fla, 54- *Awards:* Fulbright sr res scholar to India, 62-63; four Ctr Latin Am Studies travel grants to Cent Am, 68-75; Am Philos Soc Res Travel Grant, India, 76. *Mem:* Am Asn Mus; Int Coun Mus Southeastern Mus Conf (bd mem, ed jour, 67-); Asia Soc; Asn Asian Studies; fel Royal Soc Arts. *Res:* Publications in ancient and contemporary art of India; pre-Columbian art. *Publ:* Auth, Ceremonial Centers of the Maya, 74; auth, A Concise History of Indian Art, London, 76. *Mailing Add:* 6818 NW 65th Ave Gainesville FL 32601

CRAVEN, WAYNE
HISTORIAN, WRITER
b Pontiac, Ill, Dec 7, 30. *Study:* John Herron Art Sch, Indianapolis, Ind; Ind Univ, BA, 55, MA, 57; Columbia Univ, PhD, 63. *Collections Arranged:* Co-cur, Exhib Celebrating the Creative American (sculpture sect), White House, Washington, DC, 65; guest cur, 200 Years of American Sculpture, Whitney Mus Am Art, New York, 76. *Pos:* Mem bd ed, The Am Art J, New York, 74-; mem adv bd, Daniel Chester French Papers, Nat Trust, Washington, DC, 75- *Teaching:* Instr art hist, Wheaton Col, Norton, Mass, 58-60; prof art hist, Univ Del, Newark, 60- *Mem:* Col Art Asn; Victorian Soc in Am (mem adv comt, 72). *Res:* Eighteenth and nineteenth century American painting and sculpture. *Publ:* Auth, Sculpture in America, T Y Crowell, Co, New York, 68; co-auth, Britannica Encycl Am Art, Chanticlair Press, 74; plus many jour articles on Am art. *Mailing Add:* Art History Dept Univ Del Newark DE 19711

CRAWFORD, BILL (WILBUR OGDEN)
ILLUSTRATOR, ADMINISTRATOR
b Northfield, NJ, Oct 5, 41. *Study:* Hussian Sch Art, AST, 65. *Exhib:* Bakers Art, Mus Contemp Crafts, New York; Christmas Exhib, Smithsonian Inst; Illustration, Philadelphia Art Alliance & Soc Illusr, New York; National Parks, First Bank US, Philadelphia; Design, Art Directors Show, New York. *Teaching:* Instr advert design, Hussian Sch Art, 65-83, asst dir design, 74-83, asst dir bus art, 83- *Awards:* Gold Award, Neo Graphics, 74; Award Merit, Illusr Show, Soc Illusr, 77; Gold Award, Artist Guild Philadelphia, 78. *Bibliog:* Raymond Ballinger (auth), Design with Paper, Van Nostrand Reinhold, 82. *Mem:* Philadelphia Watercolor Club; Artist Guild Del Valley (pres, 74-75, exec off, 76-83); Art Dir Club Philadelphia. *Media:* Paper Sculpture, Watercolor. *Publ:* Contribr, Cookies and Breads--The Bakers Art, Reinhold, 67; contribr, Illustrator 20, Hastings House, 78. *Mailing Add:* 220 Locust St 26-A Philadelphia PA 19106

CRAWFORD, CATHERINE BETTY
PAINTER
b Ingersoll, Ont, Feb 5, 10. *Study:* Univ Toronto, BA; summer study with Eliot O'Hara & at Doon Sch & Queen's Univ; also study with Gordon Payne, E*H Varley & Carl Schaeffer. *Work:* London Art Gallery, Ont; Arch Can Painter-Etchers, Hamilton, Ont; Woodstock Art Gallery, Ont. *Exhib:* Western Art League Shows, London, Ont & Soc of Can Painter-Etchers, various yrs; one-man shows, London, Burlington & Woodstock, 48-67 & London, 73; Brantford, 73. *Awards:* Purchase Award, London Women's Comt at Gallery, 53; First Prize for Watercolor, Western Fair, London, 64. Gallery, 74. *Mem:* Print & Drawing Coun, Can. *Media:* Watercolor. *Mailing Add:* 1 Duke Lane Ingersoll ON N5C 2L1 Canada

CRAWFORD, JOHN MCALLISTER, JR
COLLECTOR, PATRON
b Parkersburg, WVa, Aug 6, 13. *Study:* Brown Univ, AB, 37, LittD, 64; Harvard Univ Sch Educ; Syracuse Univ, LHD, 67. *Exhib:* Chinese Calligraphy & Painting Collection shown at Morgan Libr, New York, 62, Fogg Art Mus, Harvard Univ, 63, William Rockhill Nelson Gallery Art, Kansas City, Mo, 63; Victoria & Albert Mus, London, Eng, 65; Nat Mus, Stockholm, Sweden, 65; Mus Cernuschi, Paris, France, 66. *Pos:* Trustee, Asheville Sch, NC, 50-74; libr comt, Brown Univ, 58-73; vis comt, Fogg Art Mus, Harvard Univ, 61-66; mem coun friends, Columbia Univ Librs, 67-; mem art adv comt, Brown Univ, 74-; trustee & mem acquisition comt, Metrop Mus Art, New York, 82- *Mem:* China Inst Am (chmn art comt, 67-77, trustee, 71-); Friends of the Asia House Gallery (treas, 64-69); fel Morgan Libr; Century Asn; Grolier Club. *Interests:* Chinese art in calligraphy, painting, also early bronzes, gilt bronzes, sculpture, jade & ceramics. *Collection:* Chinese calligraphy & painting; William Morris & the Kelmscott Press; Medieval manuscripts; early printed books; other printed masterpieces & modern painting. *Publ:* Chinese calligraphy, Philadelphia Mus, 71; Friends of Wen Cheng-Ming, China Inst, 74; auth, William Morris and the Art of the Book, Morgan Libr, 76; contribr, Wango Weng, auth, Chinese Caligraphy & Painting--Crawford Collection, Dover, 78. *Mailing Add:* 46 E 82nd St New York NY 10028

CRAWLEY, WESLEY V
SCULPTOR, EDUCATOR
b Akron, Ohio, Mar 1, 22. *Study:* Chicago Art Inst, 37; Univ Ariz, 47-48; Univ Ore, AB, 52, MS, 59. *Work:* Greenville Art Ctr, NC; ECarolina Univ, Greenville; Pembroke State Univ, NC. *Comn:* Cascades (stone carving), Bethel Sch Dist, Ore, 58; Tomorrow (life size bronze), People's Bank & Trust Co, 65; Garden Figure (cast lead), Wright Chem Corp, Acme, NC, 66; portrait, comn by Anthony Brannock, II, Raleigh, NC, 74; and many other garden sculptures & portraits. *Exhib:* Pac Northwest Inst Sculpture, Portland Art Mus, Ore, 56 & Vancouver Art Mus, BC, 58; NC Artists Traveling Show, Raleigh Art Mus & through state, 64; Southern Asn Sculptors Traveling Show, galleries of the South & Southwest, 67; Art & Academia, NC Nat Bank Traveling Exhib, 73 & 74. *Teaching:* Prof drawing & sculpture, East Carolina Univ, 59-, coordr I found, 72- *Awards:* Contemp Southern Sculpture Purchase Award, Univ SC, 68; Small Southern Sculpture Purchase Award, Southern Asn Sculptors, 67; Purchase Award, NC Nat Bank Show, 74. *Bibliog:* J Hall (auth), Hall Marks, Raleigh News & Observer, 8/4/63; L Holmes (auth), article, Rocky Mount News & Observer, NC, 56; L Siegel (auth), article, Art Rev, summer 66. *Mem:* Southern Asn Sculptors. *Mailing Add:* 104 Dogwood Dr Greenville NC 27834

CREATORE, MARY-ALICE
SUMIE ARTIST, PAINTER
b New York, NY, Aug 11, 20. *Study:* Nat Acad Design; Art Students League; Nippon Club, New York; also studies in Japan. *Comn:* Japanese wall murals, KiKu Restaurant, 74. *Exhib:* Sumie Soc Am, 64 & 73; Nippon Club, 68 & 69. *Awards:* Cup of Japanese Consulate (First Prize), 64; Silver Cup, Charles Gracie Award (First Prize), 68; Silver Cup, Nippon Club Award (First Prize), 69. *Mem:* Sumie Soc Am (treas, 74). *Media:* Brush on Rice Paper; Watercolor, Oil. *Mailing Add:* 2333 Hudson Terr Ft Lee NJ 07024

CREECH, FRANKLIN UNDERWOOD
SCULPTOR, GRAPHIC ARTIST
b Smithfield, NC, Oct 14, 41. *Study:* Univ NC, Chapel Hill, summers 63 & 64; Duke Univ, BA, 64; Fla State Univ, MS, 66; Det Danske Selskab, Holbaek, Denmark, printing with Hugo Arne Bock. *Work:* Duke Univ Art Mus; NC Nat Bank; Appalachian State Univ; Rauch Indust; Mint Mus, Charlotte, NC. *Exhib:* 1971 Crafts Exhib, Gallery Contemp Art, Winston-Salem, NC, 71; 8th Int Grand Prix du Cote d'Azur, Cannes, France, 72; 1972

Regional Painting Exhib, Lauren Rogers Mus Art, Laurel, Miss, 72; dedication of the Storyteller, Gastonia, NC, 78; solo exhib, Goldsboro Arts Ctr, 80; and others. *Pos:* Chmn, Johnston Tech Col, 80- *Teaching:* Instr pottery, design & graphics, Gaston Col, Dallas, NC, 66-, chmn dept, 69-77; vis instr, Duke Univ, spring, 81; instr, Atlantic Christian Col, 81; chmn commercial art dept, Johnston Tech Col, currently. *Awards:* Purchase Award, Piedmont Drawing & Graphic Show; First Place, Appalachian Nat Drawing Competition, 77; Second Place, First Sofa Exchange, 77. *Bibliog:* Artist in the 33rd North Carolina Artists exhibition, La Rev Mod, 10/71; feature in Profiles, Art Voices of the South, 78 & NC State Mag, 12/79. *Mem:* Am Crafts Coun; World Crafts Coun; Nat Art Educ Asn. *Media:* Multi-Media. *Publ:* The development of art departments in the community college, Art Teacher Mag, 1/76. *Dealer:* Art Maker 312 S Fourth St Smithfield NC 27577. *Mailing Add:* 312 South Fourth Smithfield NC 27577

CREESE, WALTER LITTLEFIELD
EDUCATOR
b Danvers, Mass, Dec 19, 19. *Study:* Brown Univ, AB; Harvard Univ, MA & PhD; Columbia Univ. *Pos:* Ed, J Soc Archit Historians, 50-53; chmn, Louisville & Jefferson Co Planning & Zoning Comt, 54-55. *Teaching:* Fel, Harvard Univ, 44-45; instr, Wellesley Col, 45; instr, Univ Louisville, 46-47; asst prof, 47-52, assoc prof, 52-55, prof, 56-58; prof, Univ Ill, Urbana, 58-63, prof archit & chmn archit hist, 68-; vis prof, summer sch, Harvard Univ, 61-63; dean sch archit & allied arts, Univ Ore, 63-68. *Awards:* Guggenheim Fel, 72-73; Rockefeller Fel, 76-77; Cult Achievement Award, US Dept Interior, 79. *Mem:* Soc Archit Historians (pres, 58-59); hon mem Am Inst Archit; Col Art Asn Am (dir, 51-55). *Mailing Add:* Dept of Architecture Univ of Ill Urbana IL 61801

CREIGHTON, GWEN LUX See Lux, Gwen

CRELLY, WILLIAM RICHARD
HISTORIAN
b St Louis, Mo, Mar 15, 24. *Study:* Washington Univ, St Louis, Mo, BA, 49; Fulbright Scholar Study in Paris, 50-51; Am Coun Learned Soc, 58; Inst Fine Arts, NY Univ, PhD, 58; Morse Fel Study in Italy, 61-62. *Pos:* Lectr & instr, Washington Sq Col, NY Univ, 52-56; from instr to assoc prof, Yale Univ, 56-65; prof art hist, Emory Univ, Atlanta, Ga, currently. *Mem:* Col Art Asn Am. *Res:* Marcello Giovanetti, poet of the Roman baroque. *Publ:* Auth, Simon Vouet's allegory of victory, Bulletin John Herron Art Inst, 61; auth, The Painting of Simon Vouet, Yale Univ Press, 62; contribr, French Art of Sixteenth Century (exhib catalog), Cummer Gallery Art, Fla, 6/64; contribr, The Iconography of the Elian Graces (essays in hon of Walter Friedlaender), Marysas Mag, 65; contribr, Two allegories of the seasons by Simon Vouet and their iconography, In: Art the Ape of Nature, Prentice-Hall, 81. *Mailing Add:* Emory Univ Art Hist Dept Atlanta GA 30322

CRENSHAW, KAREN BRUCE
CONSERVATOR
b Baltimore, Md, Oct 29, 52. *Study:* Univ Del, Newark, BA(art hist & chem), 74; Intermuseum Laboratory, Oberlin, Ohio, cert, 77; Oberlin Col, Ohio, MA(art conserv), 79. *Pos:* Asst painting conservator, Cleveland Mus Art, Ohio, 77-81; conservator, Mus Art, Carnegie Inst, Pittsburgh, Pa, 81- *Awards:* Historic Deerfield Summer Fel, Mass, 74; Andrew W Mellon Fel, Conservation of Paintings, Cleveland Mus Art, 79-81. *Mem:* Prof assoc mem Am Inst Conserv Hist Artistic Works; assoc mem Int Inst Conserv Hist Artistic Works; Midwest Regional Conserv Guild. *Res:* Conservation research, study of 18th and 19th century American painting techniques and materials. *Publ:* Auth, A Study of Texture Modifications, Interlining Materials, Support Fabrics, and Cushioning Materials, 78 & auth, A Study of George Inness' Painting Technique, 81, Am Inst Conserv Hist Artistic Works. *Mailing Add:* c/o Mus Art Carnegie Inst 4400 Forbes Ave Pittsburgh PA 15213

CRESPO, MICHAEL LOWE
PAINTER, EDUCATOR
b New Orleans, La, Jan 3, 47. *Study:* La State Univ, BA; Queens Col, with James Brooks, John Ferren, Paul Georges, Louis Finklestein, Charles Cajori, MFA. *Comn:* Mural, Diversified Indust, Baton Rouge, La, 74; mural, Brown-Eagle Corp, Baton Rouge, 76; large painted floor covering, pvt residence, Baton Rouge, 77. *Exhib:* La Bicentennial Exhib, Masur Mus, Monroe, La, 73; Exhib of Drawings, Del Mar State Col, Corpus Christi, Tex, 73; solo exhibs, Purdue Univ Art Gallery, 74, Southern Mo State Univ, 76 & La State Univ Union Art Gallery, 77; 20th Exhib Southwestern Prints & Drawings, Dallas Mus Fine Arts, Tex, 75; and others. *Teaching:* Instr painting, Univ Southwestern La, 71; prof, La State Univ, 71-; vis artist painting, Purdue Univ, 74. *Mem:* Col Art Asn; Am Asn Univ Prof. *Media:* Oil on Canvas, Gouache. *Dealer:* Dixon Smith 1655 Lobdell Ave Baton Rouge LA 70808. *Mailing Add:* 535 Cornell Ave Baton Rouge LA 70808

CRESS, GEORGE AYERS
PAINTER, EDUCATOR
b Anniston, Ala, Apr 7, 21. *Study:* Emory Univ; Univ Ga, BFA, MFA. *Work:* Tenn Fine Arts Ctr; High Mus, Atlanta, Ga; Ford Motor Co; Birmingham Mus, Ala; Mint Mus, Charlotte, NC; plus many others. *Exhib:* Pa Acad Fine Arts; Springfield Watercolor Ann; one-man shows, Grand Cent Moderns, NY, Addison Gallery Am Art 20 Yr Retrospective, Hunter Gallery & var southeastern mus; Nat Mus Am Art, Washington DC; Bampton Arts Centre, Oxon, Eng; plus many other group & one-man shows. *Pos:* Chmn, Tenn Col Arts Coun, 66-68. *Teaching:* Instr art, Judson Col, Marion, Ala, 45-46, Mary Baldwin Col, Staunton, Va, 46-47, Univ Md, 47-48, Univ Ga, 49, 65 & 69,

Univ Tenn, 49-51, Ont Dept Educ, 63 & Univ SC, 67; Guerry prof art & head dept, Univ Tenn, Chattanooga, 51- *Awards:* Southeastern Ann, Birmingham Mus Ann & Atlanta Arts Festival; plus many others. *Mem:* Southeastern Col Conf (pres, 65-); Col Art Asn Am. *Mailing Add:* Dept of Art Univ of Tenn Chattanooga TN 37404

CRETARA, DOMENIC ANTHONY
PAINTER, EDUCATOR

b Chelsea, Mass, Mar 29, 46. *Study:* Boston Univ Sch Fine Arts, BFA(magna cum laude), 68, MFA, 70, Tanglewood Inst, summer 68. *Exhib:* Contemporary Naturalism, Doll and Richards Gallery, Cambridge, Mass, 80; Duxbury Art Complex, Mass, 82; Contemporary Portraits, Boston Univ Art Gallery, 84; Selections 21, Drawing Ctr, New York, 84; Works on Paper, Weatherspoon Art Gallery, Greensboro, NC, 84; and others. *Teaching:* Instr painting & design, DeCordova Mus Art, Lincoln, Mass, 71-74; chmn dept fine arts & prof painting & drawing, Art Inst Boston, 73- *Awards:* Fulbright-Hayes grant, Italian & US govts, 74-75; Camargo Found Grant Artist-in-Residence, Cassis, France, 78-79. *Mem:* Boston Visual Artist's Union; Asn Artist Run Galleries. *Media:* Oil, Pencil. *Publ:* Contrib, Figure Drawing, 76, The Art of Responsive Drawing, rev ed, 77 & Painting: Perceptual and Technical Fundamentals, 79, Prentice Hall. *Dealer:* First Street Gallery 386 W Broadway New York NY; Creiger-Sesen Assoc 10 Post Office Sq Boston MA. *Mailing Add:* 23 Grosvenor Park Lynn MA 01902

CRILE, SUSAN
PAINTER

b Cleveland, Ohio, 42. *Study:* Bennington Col, Vt, 61-62 & 64-65; NY Univ, 62-64; Hunter Col, 71-72. *Work:* Phillips Collection, Hirshhorn Mus, Washington, DC; Brooklyn Mus, NY; Albright-Knox Art Gallery, Buffalo, NY; Carnegie Inst, Pittsburgh. *Exhib:* Whitney Ann Exhib Am Paintings, Whitney Mus Am Art, New York; Art Inst Chicago Ann, 72; group show, 72, The Way of Color, 33rd Corcoran Biennial, 73, Corcoran Gallery Art, Washington, DC; Works on Paper, Va Mus Fine Arts, Richmond, 75; MacDowell Colony Artists, James Yu Gallery, New York, 76; solo exhibs, Droll/Kolbert Gallery, New York, 78 & 80, Nina Freudenhaim Gallery, Buffalo, 80 & Ivory Kimpton Gallery, San Francisco, 81; Am Drawing in Black & White 1970-1980, Brooklyn Mus, NY, 80; Geometric Abstraction: A New Generation, Inst Contemp Art, Boston, 81; 22nd Nat Print Exhib, Brooklyn Mus, NY, 81; Van Straaten Gallery, 83. *Pos:* Vis critic, Univ Pa, Philadelphia, 80. *Teaching:* Instr painting, Princeton Univ, 74-76, Sch Visual Arts, New York, 76- & Sarah Lawrence Col, 76-78. *Biblig:* Barbara Rose (auth), American Painting of the Eighties, 79; Elizabeth Frank (auth), Susan Crile: The Shapes of Change 1973-1979, Bennington Review, 80; Clark V Poling (auth), Geometric Abstraction: A New Generation, 81. *Media:* Oil, Gesso. *Mailing Add:* 325 West End Ave New York NY 10023

CRIMI, ALFRED D
PAINTER, INSTRUCTOR

b San Fratello, Italy, Nov 21, 24; US citizen. *Study:* Nat Acad Design; life drawing with Ivan Olinsky, Beaux Arts Inst; Preparatory Sch Ornamental Arts; fresco painting & Pompeian encaustic with Prof Venturini Paperi, Rome, Italy. *Work:* Ulrich Mus Art, Wichita State Univ, Kans; Butler Inst Am Art, Youngstown, Ohio; Smithsonian Inst, Washington, DC; Syracuse Univ, NY; Springfield Mus Fine Arts, Ma; and others. *Comn:* Fresco, Post Off Dept, Washington, DC, 37-38; oil mural, Northampton, Mass, 38-39; mosaic, comn by New York Bd Educ, Einstein Jr High Sch, 66-67 & Adlai Stevenson High Sch, 68-69. *Exhib:* Mus Mod Art, New York, 36; Art Inst Chicago, 36; Whitney Mus Am Art, 46 & Metrop Mus Art, New York, 52-53; First Int Exhib Liturgical Art, Trieste, Italy, 61. *Teaching:* Instr, City Col New York, 47-53; instr, Pratt Inst, 48-51; instr, Pa State Univ, 63; also instr, lectr & critic, cols & univs, 44- *Awards:* Mainstream Int, Marietta Col, Ohio, 69 & 70; top purchase award, Butler Inst Am Art, 69; Gold Medal of Honor, Audubon Artists, 71; plus others. *Biblig:* Mechanical brains (artist's drawings of war machinery), Life Mag, 1/21/44; Carrie Timpano (photographer & collabr), The making & fascination of fresco painting (color film), 57-59. *Mem:* Audubon Artists; Allied Artists Am (bd dir, 47-72); Am Watercolor Soc; Fedn Mod Painters & Sculptors. *Media:* Oil, Watercolor. *Publ:* Auth, articles in, Am Artist Mag, 1/57 & 2/62; auth, Art of Abstract Dimensional Painting, Grumbacher Libr, 77. *Mailing Add:* 615 Pelham Pkwy N Bronx NY 10467

CRIMMINS, JERRY (GERALD GARFIELD)
SCULPTOR, ASSEMBLAGE ARTIST

b Minneapolis, Minn, Feb 9, 40. *Study:* Minneapolis Col Art, BFA, 65; Pratt Inst, MFA, 67. *Work:* Philadelphia Mus Art; Minneapolis Inst Arts; Pratt Inst, Brooklyn, NY; Southern Ill Univ, Carbondale. *Exhib:* Twenty-three Sculptors, Philadelphia Mus Art, 72; The Artists' Book, Univ Calif San Diego at La Jolla, 77; Selections from the Collection of Richard Brown Baker, Squibb Gallery, Princeton, NJ, 79; Words & Images, Philadelphia Col Art, 79; Southern Alleghenies Mus, Pa; Imaginary Lands, Rotterdam Arts Found, Neth, 83; and one-man shows. *Teaching:* Prof basic arts & sculpture, Moore Col Art, 67- *Awards:* Purchase Award, Cheltenham Painting Show, Philadelphia Mus Art, 79; Bk Grant, Coun Arts & Nat Endowment Arts, 80; Nat Endowment Arts Grant, 83. *Biblig:* Jo Ann Lewis (auth), article, Washington Post, 9/11/81; John Russell (auth), article, New York Times, 4/21/80; Peter Frank (auth), Artists' stamps and stamp images, Art Express, 11/7/81. *Media:* Multimedia, Sculpture. *Publ:* Auth & illusr, Anatomical Notes, pvt publ, 75; auth & illusr, Thicker than Blood, Cold Chair Press, 76; auth & illusr, The Song of the Fair Haired, pvt publ, 77; Visitors Guide to La Republique de Reves, Synapse Art Press, 80; The Secret History of La Republique de Reves, Reverian Govt, 83. *Dealer:* Reverian Galleries 153 Roberts Ave Glenside PA. *Mailing Add:* 153 Roberts Ave Glenside PA 19038

CRIMP, DOUGLAS
CRITIC, HISTORIAN

b Coeur d'Alene, Idaho, Aug 19, 44. *Study:* Tulane Univ, BA(art hist); City Univ New York, MPhil. *Pos:* Curatorial staff, Solomon R Guggenheim Mus, 68-71; ed assoc, Art News, 71-76; managing ed, Oct Mag, 77- *Teaching:* Instr art hist, Sch Visual Arts, New York, 70-76. *Awards:* Art Critics Fel, Nat Endowment Arts, 73; Chester Dale Fel, Ctr Advan Study Visual Arts, Nat Gallery Art, 83-84. *Publ:* Auth, Richard Serra: Sculpture exceeded, fall 81, The new French culture: An interview with Guy Hocquenghem, winter 81 & Fassbinder, Franz, Fox, Elvira, Erwin, Armin and all the others, summer 82, October; auth, Drawings for sale, Arq, Quebec, 7-8/82; auth, Appropriating appropriation, In: The Image Scavangers: Photography, Inst Comtemp Art, Philadelphia, 83. *Mailing Add:* 93 Nassau St New York NY 10038

CRIQUETTE (RUTH DUBARRY MONTAGUE)
PAINTER, WRITER

b Paris, France; US citizen. *Study:* Ecole Beaux Arts, Paris; Univ Nev, MFA; seminars at Metrop Mus Art; Lumis Art Acad; also with Roland Pierson Prickett. *Exhib:* Da Vinci Exhib Artes, Rome, Italy, 69; Repertorium Artis Exhib, Monaco, 70; Int Exhib Artes, Rome, 71; 14th & 15th Int Exhib, Gallerie Int, New York, 72; Int Inst Arts & Lett Perpetual Exhib, Switz. *Pos:* Dir, Montague Studio-Gallery, Orlando, Fla, 71-73; dir, Sea Cliff Studio, Otter Rock, Ore, 74-76; dir, Blue Ridge Studio, Sterling, Va, 76- *Teaching:* Dir & instr oil painting, Prickett Sch Color, 60-64 & Montague Sch Painting, Washington, DC, 65-68; instr oil painting, Ecole Marsan, Vernon, Normandy, France, 69-70; instr, field studios, Calif, Va, Fla, 71- *Mem:* Int Arts Guild, Monte Carlo, Monaco; hon rep Centro Studi E Scambi Int, Rome; hon rep Acad Int Leonardo Da Vinci, Rome; life fel Int Inst Artes et Lett, Switz. *Media:* Oil. *Publ:* Contrib, Let's live, 60-61; auth & illusr, Bahamian ah-h-h, 69; auth & illusr over 100 monogrs in oil painting field, 71-72. *Mailing Add:* Blue Ridge Studio PO Box 344 Sterling VA 22170

CRISPO, ANDREW J
DEALER, COLLECTOR

b Philadelphia, Pa, Apr 21, 45. *Study:* St Joseph's Col, Pa. *Collections Arranged:* Pioneers of American Abstraction (with catalog), 73; Richard Pousette Dart: Paintings (with catalog); Ten Americans: Masters of Watercolor (with catalog), 74; Edward Hicks: A Gentle Spirit (with catalog); Twelve Americans: Masters of Collage, 77; Lowell Nesbitt: An Autobiography; Matta: A Totemic World (with catalog); Lowell Nesbitt: Flowers (with catalog); America and Europe: A Century of Modern Masters from the Thyssen-Bornemisza Collection (with catalog); Douglas Abdell: Recent Sculpture (with catalog); Jon Carsman: Paintings and Watercolors (with catalog); Robert Courtright: Collages (with catalog). *Pos:* Assoc dir, ACA Gallery, 69-72; owner & dir, Andrew Crispo Gallery, Inc, 73-, Metrop Appraisers of Am & Crispo Graphics Ltd. *Biblig:* Reviews in New York Times, New York Post, Time Mag, Arts Mag & Art Gallery Mag. *Specialty:* American and European art of the 19th and 20th centuries. *Collection:* Morris Louis, John Marin, Georgia O'Keeffe, Helen Frankenthaler, Edward Hicks, Horace Pippin, Robert Motherwell, William de Kooning, Jackson Pollock, Edward Hopper, Tom Wesselmann & Robert Rauschenberg. *Mailing Add:* 41 E 57th St New York NY 10022

CRISPO, DICK
PAINTER, PRINTMAKER

b Brooklyn, NY, Jan 13, 45. *Study:* Ariz Sch Art; Carmel Art Inst; Monterey Peninsula Col; Hartnell Col; St Sophia Divinity Sch; also with Victor DiGesu, Sam Colburn, Jan Hannah, Alexander Napote, Kay Rodgers & others. *Work:* Libr Cong, Washington, DC; Bibliot Nat, Paris, France; Inst Nac de Bellas Artes, Mexico City, Mex; Mus Western Art, Tokyo, Japan; Nat Libr Ireland, Dublin; plus others. *Comn:* Ecology (mural), Monterey High Sch, Calif, 72; Ecology, Robert Louis Stevenson Sch, Pebble Beach, Calif, 72; Spirit of Youth, Carmel Youth Ctr, Calif, 73; History of the Migrant Worker (mural), Opportunity Indust Ctr, Salinas, Calif, 74; Twelve Master Teachers of the World (mural), Church of Antioch, Pacific Grove, Calif, 75. *Exhib:* Calif State Fair, Sacramento, 64; Small Painting Biennial, Purdue Univ, 68; Univ Calif, Berkeley, 72; Pan-Am Graphics, Mexico City, 72; Western Graphics, Tokyo, 73. *Pos:* Chmn, Fine Arts Div, Monterey county Fair, 72-74; co-founder, Mus on Wheels, Monterey, 74-; exhib dir, Pacific Grove Art Ctr, 74-; art counr, Monterey Co Probation Dept, 75- *Teaching:* Instr arts & crafts, York Sch, Monterey, 71-73; instr folk & ethnic arts, Monterey Peninsula Col, 74-75; instr folk & ethnic arts & art hist, St Sophia Divinity Sch, Pacific Grove, 75- *Awards:* All Calif Watercolor Competition Third Prize, Pacific Grove, 67; San Juan Bautista Invitational Second Prize, Calif, 68; Gold Medal, Acad Italy, 79; plus others. *Biblig:* Pat Griffith (auth), An artist with a sense of humor, Carmel Valley Outlook, Carmel, Calif, 72; Robert Miskimon (auth), Social consciousness of art, Pine Cone, Carmel, 73. *Mem:* Artists Equity; Carmel Art Asn; Pacific Grove Art Ctr; Pac Art Asn (chmn); Art Workers United. *Res:* Eclectic study of world folk art. *Collection:* Folk and eccentric art from over 40 countries. *Publ:* Auth, Contemporary Print Making Renaissance in Japan, 69. *Mailing Add:* c/o 417 Cannery Row Monterey CA 93940

CRIST, WILLIAM GARY
SCULPTOR, EDUCATOR

b Pocatello, Idaho, Jan 17, 37. *Study:* Univ Wash, Seattle, BA(art educ), 66; Cranbrook Acad Art, Detroit, MFA(sculpture), 71; study with Michael Hall, Julius Schmidt, Joseph Beuys, Nam June Paik & Klaus Rinke; Staatliche Kunstakademie, Dusseldorf, WGer, 81 & 83. *Work:* Cameron Univ, Lawton, Okla; Univ Mo, Kansas City; Guggenheim Mus; Whitney Mus; Gen Serv Admin, Washington, DC. *Exhib:* 23 at 10, Soho, New York, 77; one-man exhib, Organic Pneumatics, Cranbrook Art Galleries, 71, Umbilical, Contemp

Arts Found, Oklahoma City, Okla, 74 & 7E7 Gallery, Lawrence, Kans, 78; Noho Gallery, New York, 79 & 80; Staatliche Kunstakademie, Dusseldorf, WGer, 81; and others. *Teaching:* Asst prof art, Wesleyan Col, Macon, Ga, 71-72; instr art, Cameron Univ, Lawton, Okla, 72-74; asst prof sculpture, Univ Mo, Kansas City, 74-79, assoc prof sculpture, 79- *Awards:* Univ Mo Res Coun Awards, 76-79. *Mem:* Kansas City Artists Coalition (vpres, currently). *Media:* Mixed Media. *Publ:* Auth, Towards an evaluation of American folk art, NY State Hist Soc, 72; auth, Coherent light and electronics as creative mediums, Okla State Arts Comn, 73; auth, Metaphysical sculpture, Mid-Am Col Art Asn, 81; auth, Interview with Joseph Bevys, Forum Mag, 82; auth, Underground art in Poland, Col Art Asn, Toronto (in prep). *Dealer:* Noho Gallery Inc 542 LaGuardia Pl New York NY 10012. *Mailing Add:* Dept of Art & Art Hist Univ Mo-Kansas City Kansas City MO 64110

CRISTIN-POUCHER, LILLI FONG
DESIGNER
b Shangahi, China, Feb 19, 47; US citizen. *Study:* Univ Calif, Irvine, BA, 69; Univ Calif, Los Angeles, 69-71. *Comn:* Catalog, poster, publ or exhib design; Atlantic Richfield Corp, Los Angeles, Chrysler Art Mus, Norfolk, Va, Timken Art Gallery, San Diego, Los Angeles Co Mus Art & Norton Simon Mus, Pasadena, and others. *Pos:* Exhibs & publ assoc, Los Angeles Co Mus Art, 69-74; dir publ & graphic design, J Paul Getty Mus, Malibu, Calif, 74-77; designer art mus & galleries, Lilli Cristin Design, Los Angeles, 74-; head graphic artist, Los Angeles Co Mus Art, 78, 79 & 83. *Teaching:* Lectr & designer, Calif State Univ, Long Beach, 79-82. *Awards:* Cert Merit, Printing Industs Am, 77, 79 & 82; Award of Excellence, Art Mus Asn, 82; Publications Award, Am Asn Mus, 82 & 83. *Publ:* Ed, Giovanni di Francesco and the Master of Pratovecchio, 74, ed, The Conservation of Ancient Marble, 76 & ed, Guidebook, 78, J Paul Getty Mus, Malibu, Calif. *Mailing Add:* 755 Luton Dr Glendale CA 91206

CRITE, ALLAN ROHAN
PAINTER, ILLUSTRATOR
b Plainfield, NJ, Mar 20, 10. *Study:* Boston Mus Fine Arts Sch; Mass Sch Art; Boston Univ, CBA; Harvard Univ, BA; Suffolk Univ, Hon DH, 79. *Work:* Boston Mus Fine Arts; Spelman Col, Atlanta, Ga; Addison Gallery Am Art, Andover, Mass; Marine Hosp, Carville, La; Villanova Col, Pa; and others. *Comn:* Insignia, USS Wilson; mural, Grace Church, Martha's Vineyard, Mass; stations of the cross, Holy Cross Church, Morrisville, Vt, 57; Allan Crite Wing, Blackstone Sq Community Sch, Boston; and others. *Exhib:* One-man shows, Boston Mus Fine Arts, Fogg Mus Art & Farnsworth Mus Art; Religious Art Festival, Brandon, Vt, 61; Festival Arts, Ecumenical Youth Assembly North Am, Ann Arbor, Mich, 61; and others. *Pos:* Artist-historian, Semitic Mus, Harvard Univ, formerly. *Teaching:* Lectr Christian art, Oberlin Col, 58 & Regis Col, formerly. *Awards:* Boston Mus Fine Arts Sch & Seabury Western Theol Sem Award, 52; Fourth Prize, Franklin Mint Bicentennial Medal Design; HDH, Suffolk Univ, 79. *Publ:* Auth & illus, Cultural heritage of the United States, 68 & Were you there when they crucified my Lord, McGrath, 69; contribr to magazines, bulletins & religious books. *Mailing Add:* 410 Columbus Ave Boston MA 02116

CROCKETT, GIB (GIBSON M)
CARTOONIST, PAINTER
b Washington, DC, Sept 18, 12. *Study:* Studied watercolor under several nationally known artists; illustration with Harry Anderson. *Work:* Represented in many pvt collections. *Exhib:* Landscape painting in local & nat exhibs. *Pos:* Mem staff, Washington Eve Star, 33-, ed cartoonist, 47-75, sport cartoonist, 40-46, retired, 75; free lance illusr, 43-; art dir, Am Publ Co, Washington, 45- *Awards:* Cartoon Awards from Headliner Asn & Freedoms Found. *Mem:* Washington Landscape Club; Olney Art Asn; Ed Cartoonists Asn; Baltimore Watercolor Soc. *Mailing Add:* 4713 Great Oak Rd Manor Club Rockville MD 20853

CROFT, MICHAEL FLYNT
GOLDSMITH, EDUCATOR
b Minneapolis, Minn, Oct 11, 41. *Study:* Univ NMex, Albuquerque, BFA; Southern Ill Univ, Carbondale, MFA. *Work:* Southern Ill Univ Art Mus, Carbondale; Renwick Gallery, Smithsonian Inst, Washington, DC; Tucson Art Mus, Ariz. *Comn:* Offertory basin, All Saints Episcopal Cathedral, Indianapolis, 65. *Exhib:* 10th & 11th Ann Southern Tier Crafts Exhib, Corning Mus Glass, NY, 73 & 74; Marietta Col Crafts Nat, Ohio, 75; Craft Multiples, Renwick Gallery, Smithsonian Inst, Washington, DC, 75; Contemp Enamel Work, Huntsville Mus Art, Ala, 76; The Metalsmith, Soc NAm Goldsmiths Exhib, Phoenix Art Mus, 77; Nat Invitational Metalwork Exhib, Pittsburgh Ctr for Arts & Crafts, Pittsburgh, Pa; and others. *Pos:* Dir, Copper, Brass & Bronze Competition, Univ Ariz Art Mus, Tucson, 77 & 80. *Teaching:* Asst prof jewelry & metalsmithing, Univ Wis, Milwaukee, 65-72; assoc prof, Univ Ariz, 72- *Awards:* Endicott Award, First Hon Mention, 12th Ann Kans Designer Craftsmen, 65; State Award, Marietta Col Crafts Nat, Ariz Comn Arts & Humanities, 75; McCullogh Award, Ariz Biennial, 82. *Bibliog:* James Schineller (auth), Art: Search & Self Discovery, Int Textbook Co, 2nd ed 68; Oppi Untracht (auth), Jewelry Concepts and Technology, Doubleday, 82. *Mem:* Soc North Am Goldsmiths (vpres, 82-); Am Crafts Coun. *Media:* Precious Metals. *Mailing Add:* 1441 N Day Rd Tucson AZ 85715

CRONBACH, ROBERT M
SCULPTOR
b St Louis, Mo, Feb 10, 08. *Study:* St Louis Sch Fine Arts, with Victor Holm, 25-26; Pa Acad Fine Arts, with Charles Grafly & Albert Laessle, 27-30; Cresson scholar to Europe, 29-30. *Work:* Nat Collection Art, Smithsonian Inst, Washington, DC; St Louis Art Mus; Springfield Art Mus, Mo; Walker Art Ctr, Minneapolis; Mus Fine Arts, Skopje, Yugoslavia; and others. *Comn:* Bronze & steel wall sculpture, UN Gen Assembly Bldg, New York, 60; fountain, Fed Off Bldg, St Louis, 63; fountain, Kanawha Co Pub Libr, Charleston, WVa, 66; Tribute to Leroy Grumman (stainless steel sculpture), Long Island Asn Hall Fame, 72; fountain, Libr Cong, Washington, DC, 74. *Exhib:* Whitney Mus; HemisFair, San Antonio, Tex; Pa Acad Fine Arts; Houston Mus Fine Arts; Brooklyn Mus; and many other group & one-man shows. *Pos:* Chmn bd gov, Skowhegan Sch Painting & Sculpture; mem, Nassau Co Fine Arts Comn; mem, Mayor's Comt Beautification of New York. *Teaching:* Instr, Adelphi Univ, 48-62, vis assoc prof, 74 & 75; instr, N Shore Community Art Ctr, 50-55 & Skowhegan Sch Painting & Sculpture, 59-60, 64-65 & 72. *Awards:* Nat competition for sculpture for Social Security Bldg, Washington, DC, 39; competition for sculpture for UN Bldg, New York, 60; Reynolds Metals Sculpture Trophy, 61; and others. *Bibliog:* John I H Baur (auth), Revolution and Tradition in Modern American Art, Harvard Univ Press, 59; Minor L Bishop (auth), Fountains in contemporary architecture, Am Fedn Arts, 65; Louis G Redstone (auth), Art in Architecture, McGraw-Hill, 68. *Mem:* Sculptors Guild; Munic Art Soc; Archit League New York; Fedn Mod Painters & Sculptors; Artist-Craftsmen New York. *Publ:* Auth, New New Deal Art Projects, An Anthology of Memoirs, Smithsonian Inst Press, 72. *Mailing Add:* 420 E 86th St New York NY 10028

CRONIN, ROBERT (LAWRENCE)
SCULPTOR
b Lexington, Mass, Aug 10, 36. *Study:* RI Sch Design, BFA, 59; Cornell Univ, MFA, 62. *Work:* Worcester Art Mus, Mass; Boston Mus Fine Arts; Brooklyn Mus; Mus Art, RI Sch Design; Mus Art, Univ Okla, Norman. *Comn:* On Speculation (sculpture), Lippincott Co, 81-; R S Reynolds Mem Award, 82. *Exhib:* Inst Contemp Art, Boston, 71; Gimpel Fils, London, 82; Gimpel & Weitzenhoffer Ltd, New York, 82; Watson DeNagy, Houston, 83; Gimpel-Hanover & Andre Emmerich Galerien, Zurich, 83. *Teaching:* Instr painting, Bennington Col, 66-68; instr art, Sch Worcester Art Mus, 71-79. *Awards:* First Prize in Painting, Boston Fine Arts Festival, 63; Mass Arts & Humanities Grant, 75; Mass Artists Found Grant, 79. *Bibliog:* Hilton Kramer (auth), New talent, New York Times, 6/17/73; Hilton Kramer (auth), article, New York Times, 9/21/74; Max Wykes-Joyce (auth), Robert Cronin, Gimpel Fils, London Arts Rev, 4/9/82. *Media:* Light Metals, Wire. *Dealer:* Gimpel-Weitzenhoffer 1040 Madison Ave New York NY 10021. *Mailing Add:* 325 W 15th St 4W New York NY 10011

CROOKS, W SPENCER
PAINTER, LECTURER
b Ireland, July 26, 17; US citizen. *Study:* RI Sch Design, cert, Shrivenham Am Univ, Eng, cert; summer sem with Edgar Whitney; RCA Scholar (scenic design), Berkshire Music Ctr. *Work:* RI Sch Design Fine Art Mus; Boston Symphony Hall, Mass; Pawtucket Boys Club, RI; Mayor's Office, City Hall, Providence, RI. *Comn:* Watercolor, covers for RI Providence J, 61-65; watercolor, Old Colony Banks, RI, 71-73; watercolor, Indust Leasing Corp, Indust Nat Bank, Providence, RI, 72; Irish Cult Exchange Comn RI, 82. *Exhib:* Watercolor, USA, Springfield, Mo, 64; Am Watercolor Soc Ann, Nat Acad Art Gallery, 67, 72 & 75; Springfield Mus Fine Arts, 75; one-man show, Rockport Art Asn, 75 & Trinity Col, Dublin, Ireland, 82. *Pos:* Creative artist, Hallady, Inc, Providence, RI, 52-58; creative artist, Hassenfeld Inc, Central Falls, 59-60; art dir, Cardono Inc, Pawtucket, 60-61; demonstr, watercolor, Grumbacher's Palette Talk, 75. *Teaching:* Instr Watercolor, Brown Univ Exten Sch, 68-74; instr watercolor, Cranston East High Sch (adult educ), 65-68; teacher graphic art, RI Col, 72- & instr watercolor, 74-75. *Awards:* Spec Serv Award, All-Southern England Open, US Army, 44; Travel Award, Washington Sq Show, New York, Forbes Mag, 67; James G Geddes Mem Award, Rockport Art Asn, 71. *Mem:* Providence Art Club; Providence Watercolor Club, Rockport Art Asn, Mass; Salmagundi Club, New York; Philadelphia Watercolor Club. *Media:* Watercolor; Pen, Ink. *Publ:* Illusr, Providence J Mag Sect, 61-65; ed, DeCordova Mus Gallery (catalog), 62; RI Sch Design Alumni Bull, 75; illusr, Palette Talk, Grumbacher Artist Material, NY, 75; Yankee Mag, Dublin, NH, 82. *Dealer:* Art Shanty Inc 7 Main St Wickford RI 02852. *Mailing Add:* 84 Davis Ave Cranston RI 02910

CROPPER, M ELIZABETH
HISTORIAN, LECTURER
b Dewsbury, Yorkshire, England, Aug 11, 44. *Study:* Newnham Col, Univ Cambridge, BA(hon), 67; Bryn Mawr Col, PhD, 72. *Teaching:* Prof art hist, Temple Univ, 73- *Awards:* Leverhulme Trust Res Fel, Univ Cambridge, 71-72; Arthur Kingsley Porter Prize, 76; fel, Villa I Tatti, Harvard Univ & Leopold Schepp Found, 78-79. *Mem:* Col Art Asn; Renaissance Soc Am. *Res:* Italian renaissance and baroque art. *Publ:* Auth, Bound theory and blind practice, 71 & Virtue's wintry reward, 74, J Warburg & Courtauld Insts; auth, On beautiful women, 76 & Poussin and Leonardo, 80, Art Bulletin; auth, The Ideal of Painting, Princeton Univ Press, 84. *Mailing Add:* 3918 Cloverhill Rd Baltimore MD 21218

CROSBIE, HELEN BLAIR See Blair, Helen

CROSBY, RANICE W
MEDICAL ILLUSTRATOR, EDUCATOR
b Regina, Sask, Apr 26, 15. *Study:* Conn Col, AB; Johns Hopkins Med Sch, under Max Broedel; also under Robert Brackman; Johns Hopkins Univ, MLA. *Pos:* Illusr for N J Eastman, Johns Hopkins Hosp, currently. *Teaching:* Assoc prof & dir dept art as appl to med, Johns Hopkins Med Sch, 44- *Mem:* Asn Med Illusr; Am Asn Univ Prof. *Publ:* Illustrator for medical textbooks and journals. *Mailing Add:* 3926 Cloverhill Rd Baltimore MD 21218

CROSMAN, CHRISTOPHER BYRON
MUSEUM EDUCATOR, EDUCATOR
b Chicago, Ill, June 25, 46. *Study:* Washington & Lee Univ, BA, 68; Oberlin Col, 70-72. *Pos:* Regional auditor, New York State Coun Arts, 77-80; cur educ, Albright-Knox Art Gallery, 80- *Teaching:* Instr art hist, Empire State Col, Buffalo, NY, 79-81. *Mem:* Am Asn Mus; New York State Educ Dept--Advisory Coun Adult Learning Services; Nat Art Educ Asn. *Publ:* Auth, Video Tripping in Great Britain, Audio-Visual Communications, 77; co-auth, A Cure for Video Phobia, Mus News, 77; co-auth, A Conversation with George Segal, Albright-Knox Art Gallery Studies, 78; co-auth, Speaking of Tomlin, Art J, 79; auth, Concepts of Constructionism, Albright-Knox Art Gallery, 79. *Mailing Add:* 793 Bird Ave Buffalo NY 14209

CROSS, WATSON, JR
PAINTER, VIDEO ARTIST
b Long Beach, Calif, Oct 10, 18. *Study:* Chouinard Art Inst, scholar, 38-42. *Comn:* Illustrations of Air Bases, USAF, Alaska, 63. *Exhib:* San Francisco Mus Art Ann, 47-48; Calif Watercolor Soc Traveling Exhib, Riverside Mus, New York, 48; John Herron Art Inst, 48; Los Angeles Co Mus Art Ann, 53-54; seven video performance pieces, Calif State Univ, Northridge, 80-83. *Teaching:* Prof drawing & painting, Chouinard Art Inst, 44-71; assoc prof, Calif State Univ, Northridge, 75-81; instr drawing, Art Ctr Col of Design, Pasadena, Calif, 75-79; instr, Otis Art Inst of Parsons Sch Design, Los Angeles, 80-83. *Mem:* Life mem Nat Watercolor Soc (secy, 51-53, pres, 53-54). *Media:* Watercolor; Oil; Video. *Publ:* Contribr, Content of Watercolor, Van Nostrand Reinhold, 69; illusr (cover), Westways Mag, 8/78. *Mailing Add:* 1238 E Workman Ave West Covina CA 91790

CROSSGROVE, ROGER LYNN
PAINTER, EDUCATOR
b Farnam, Nebr, Nov 17, 21. *Study:* Kearney State Col; Univ Nebr, BFA; Univ Ill, MFA; Univ Michoacan. *Work:* Butler Inst Am Art, Youngstown, Ohio; Montclair Art Mus, NJ; Des Moines Art Ctr, Iowa; New Britain Mus Am Art; Inst Mex-Norteamericano Relac Cult, Mexico City. *Exhib:* Whitney Mus Am Art, New York, NY, 56; Pa Acad Fine Arts, Philadelphia, 64; Audubon Artists, New York, 68; Conn Watercolor Soc, Wadsworth Atheneum, Hartford, Conn, 70; Monotypes, Pratt Graphics Ctr, New York, 72; New Am Monotypes, SITES, 78. *Pos:* Contribr & ed, Artists Proof, 67- *Teaching:* Prof art & assoc chmn dept graphic arts, Pratt Inst, 52-68; prof art, Univ Conn, 68- *Awards:* Emily Lowe Award, 51; Gold Medal, Nat Arts Club, 67; Am Watercolor Soc Award, 67. *Bibliog:* Henry N Rasmusen (auth), Printmaking with Monotype, Chilton, 60. *Mem:* Col Art Asn Am; Am Watercolor Soc; Conn Acad Arts; Conn Watercolor Soc; Am Asn Univ Prof. *Media:* Pastel, Watercolor. *Publ:* Contribr, Paperbound Books in Print, 63. *Mailing Add:* PO Box 99 Storrs CT 06268

CROTTO, PAUL
PAINTER, SCULPTOR
b New York, NY, Oct 24, 22. *Study:* Art Students League; Beaux-Arts, Florence, Italy; also with Fernand Leger, Paris. *Work:* Villeneuve-sur-Lot Mus, France; Mus Art Int, San Francisco; Galerie Grave, Munich, Ger. *Comn:* Portraits, L E Kaplan, New York & Robert Aries, Paris. *Exhib:* Mostra Artisti Am, Florence, 51; Mostra Int, Bordighera, Italy, 53; Am Painters in France, Galerie Craven, Paris, 53; Salon Automne, Paris, 56; Salon Comparaisons, Mus Mod Art, Paris, 68. *Awards:* Prix Int de Peinture, Villeneuve-sur-Lot, 63. *Bibliog:* T Ehrenmark (auth), American Artist in Sweden, Dagens Nyheter, 63; A Blasco Ibanez (auth), American artist in Paris, Los Angeles Herald Examr, 68; Betty Werther (auth), Art, Time-Life, Paris, 69. *Mem:* Soc Coop Entre Aide Artistes. *Media:* Oil. *Mailing Add:* 19 Rue Cauchois Paris France

CROUCH, NED PHILBRICK
SCULPTOR, CURATOR
b Nashville, Tenn, Mar 14, 48. *Study:* Austin Peay State Univ, Clarksville, Tenn, BS(art), 72; Cranbrook Acad Art, Bloomfield Hills, Mich, MFA(sculpture), 74. *Work:* Tenn Fine Arts Comn, Nashville; Cheekwood Fine Arts Ctr, Nashville; Ark Arts Ctr, Little Rock; Montgomery Bell Acad, Nashville; Austin Peay State Univ, Clarksville. *Exhib:* Michigan II, Flint Inst Arts, Flint, Mich, 74; Mid-South Biennial, Brooks Mem Art Gallery, Memphis, Tenn, 75; Artists Biennial, New Orleans Mus Art, La, 75; Nat Sculpture USA, Huntsville Mus Art, Ala, 75; 18th Ann Delta Exhib, Ark Arts Ctr, Little Rock, 75; Tenn Bicentennial, Brooks Mem Art Gallery, Memphis, 76; Invitational, Southeastern Ctr Contemp Art, Winston-Salem, NC, 77. *Pos:* Guest cur, Am Folk-Exhib of 20th Century Quilts, Drawings & Sculpture, Vanderbilt Univ, Nashville, 76-; consult spec proj, Cheekwood Fine Arts Ctr, Nashville, 77- *Teaching:* Instr sculpture, Austin Peay State Univ, Clarksville, 74-75. *Awards:* Hon Mention, Delta Exhib & Purchase Award, Toys by Artists, 75, Ark Arts Ctr, Little Rock; Purchase Award, Tenn Bicentennial, Tenn Fine Arts Comn, 76. *Mem:* Col Art Asn Am; Midwest Regional Conservation Guild. *Media:* Welded steel; wood. *Mailing Add:* 187 Maplemere Dr Clarksville TN 37040

CROUSE, MICHAEL GLENN
EDUCATOR, PRINTMAKER
b Grand Rapids, Mich, June 20, 49. *Study:* Kendall Sch Design, Grand Rapids, dipl, 70; Atlanta Col Art, BFA, 77; Univ Mich, Ann Arbor, MFA, 79. *Work:* Ga Dept Educ, Atlanta; Huntsville Mus Art. *Exhib:* Serial Imagery, Huntsville Mus Art, Ala, 82; Southeastern Graphics Int, Mint Mus Art, 82; Wesleyan Second Int Exhib Prints & Drawings, Macon Mus Arts & Sci, Ga, 82; Ninth Int Miniature Print Competition, Pratt Graphics Ctr, New York, 83; Second Int Miniature Print Exhib, Space Group Seoul, SKorea, 83; Red Clay V, Huntsville Mus Art, Ala, 83. *Teaching:* Instr art, Ill Col, 79-80; asst prof printmaking, Univ Ala, Huntsville, 80- *Awards:* Charles Brand Machinery, Pratt Graphics Ctr Int Miniature Print Competition, 79; Purchase Award, LaGrange Nat VI, LaGrange Col, 81 & 24th NDak Print & Drawing Show, Univ NDak, 81. *Mem:* Col Art Asn; Southeastern Col Art Conf. *Media:* Mixed Media. *Dealer:* Absteins Gallery Art & Framing 1139 Spring St Atlanta GA 30309. *Mailing Add:* 3215 Bradley SW Huntsville AL 35805

CROUTON, FRANCOIS (LAFORTUNE)
ADMINISTRATOR, PHOTOGRAPHER
b Montreal, Que, Mar 9, 21. *Study:* Col Montreal, BA & DLibrarianship. *Work:* Municipal Libr Montreal; Libr Can Inst, Quebec; Pub Libr Serv, Quebec; Quebec Mus; Musee Nicephore Niepce, de Chalon-Sur-Saone, France. *Exhib:* Toronto Univ, 49; Laval Univ; Municipal Libr Montreal, 50; All Art Ctr, Que. *Pos:* Librn, Municipal Libr Montreal, 48-52; chief librn, Libr Can Inst, Quebec, 53-60; asst dir, Pub Libr Serv, Quebec, 60-75; conservator, Quebec Mus, 75- *Publ:* Auth, Ou La Lumiere Chante, Laval Univ with Toronto Univ, 66; Les Photographes--Photographies, Crouton. *Mailing Add:* 809 Ave Levis Quebec PQ G1S 3E2 Canada

CROW, CAROL (WILSON)
SCULPTOR
b Christiansburg, Va, July 31, 15. *Study:* Columbia Univ, with Oronzio Maaldareli, 58; Beartsi Foundry, Italy, 65; Univ Calif, with Peter Vaulkos, 68. *Work:* Cannery Row, Monterey, Calif; Rose Garden Am, La. *Exhib:* Fine Arts Asn Show, Ft Worth Art Ctr, Tex, 60; Tex General Art Competition, Dallas Mus, 60-62; Tex General, Laguna Gloria Mus, Austin, Tex, 61; Pennisula Artists, Mus Fine Arts, Calif, 70; Invitational Sculpture Show, San Francisco Mus, Calif, 70; Houston Art Women, Alley Theater Gallery, Tex, 79; Fire, Contemp Art Mus, Houston, 80; Images of Childhood, Houston Mus Fine Arts, Tex, 81. *Teaching:* Sculpture, Sunset Ctr, 69-71; portraits, Art League Houston, 79-81. *Awards:* Bute Award, Mus Fine Arts, 52; First Prize, Monterey Jazz Festival, 69-70. *Mem:* Artists Equity of Houston; Tex Soc Sculptors; Women's Caucus Art (bd dirs, 80). *Media:* Clay, Bronze. *Mailing Add:* 1601 S Shepherd #115 Houston TX 77019

CROWELL, DAVID LEE
DEALER, CRITIC
b Detroit Lakes, Minn, Nov 28, 40. *Study:* Univ Mont, 70. *Pos:* Owner, Art West Gallery, Scottsdale, Ariz, currently; owner & publ, Scottsdale West Mag, currently. *Mem:* Am Soc Appraisers; Cert Western Art Appraisers. *Specialty:* Western art. *Publ:* Auth, Montana's Own, Gateway Press, 70; contribr, The Ace Powell Book, 74; contribr, A Brush with the West, Mountain Press, 79; auth, Majorie Reed--Dedicated chroniclee of the Butterfield Overland Stage, Art West Mag, 81. *Mailing Add:* Art of the West Gallery 7340 Scottsdale Mall Suite A Scottsdale AZ 85251

CROWELL, LUCIUS
PAINTER, SCULPTOR
b Chicago, Ill, Jan 22, 11. *Study:* Williams Col; Chicago Acad Art; Pa Acad Fine Arts; Barnes Found; Acad De la Grande Chaumiere, with Arthur B Carles & Franklin Watkins; Philadelphia Col Art; Tyler Sch, Temple Univ. *Work:* Boston Mus Fine Art; Philadelphia Mus Art; Pa Acad Fine Arts, Philadelphia; Columbus Mus; Univ Pa. *Comn:* Fresco secco mural, comn by Oskar Stonorov, Hopkinson House & mosaic mural, Venice Island, Philadelphia; oil mural, Overbrook Golf Club, Philadelphia; lobby paintings, Parker Pen Co, Janesville, Wis; portrait, Univ Pa Law Sch. *Exhib:* Art Inst Chicago; Whitney Mus Art; Philadelphia Mus Art; Boston Mus Art; Worcester Mus; Pa Acad Fine Arts; Nat Acad Art; Calif Palace of the Legion of Honor, San Francisco; one-man shows, Boston, Philadelphia, Chicago, Milwaukee, New York, Wilmington, Beloit & Lawrenceville, NJ. *Teaching:* Instr oil painting, Studio Group, Wilmington, Del, 50-63; instr painting, Chester Co Art Asn, 63-78. *Awards:* Medal of Honor, Concord Mus, Mass; Popular Prize, Worcester Mus, Mass; May Audubon Post Prize Fel, Pa Acad Fine Arts, 83. *Mem:* Philadelphia Art Alliance; Col Art Asn; fel Pa Acad Fine Arts; Artists Equity Asn; Philadelphia Watercolor Club. *Media:* Oil; Ceramic. *Dealer:* Coe Kerr Gallery 49 E 82nd St New York NY 10028. *Mailing Add:* 119 Charlestown Rd Phoenixville PA 19460

CROWN, KEITH ALLEN
PAINTER, EDUCATOR
b Keokuk, Iowa, May 27, 18. *Study:* Art Inst Chicago, 36-40, 45-46, BFA, 46. *Work:* Ackland Mus, Chapel Hill, NC; Long Beach Mus, Calif; Univ NMex, Albuquerque; Univ Tex Art Mus, Austin; The Phillips Collection, Smithsonian Inst, Washington, DC. *Exhib:* Lyric View, Lang Gallery, Scripps Col, 74; one-man shows, Ariz State Univ Mus Art, Tempe, 78, Univ Utah Mus Art, Salt Lake City, 78, Univ Calif, 79 & Univ Ariz Mus Art, Tucson. *Teaching:* Prof painting & drawing, Univ Southern Calif, 46-; prof painting, Univ NC, 79 & Univ Ill, 70-71 & 77-78. *Awards:* Purchase Awards, Nat Watercolor Soc, 60, 63 & 71; Purchase Award, Rio Hondo Col, 71; Watercolor USA, Springfield Mus, Mo, 74. *Bibliog:* Article, Am Artist Mag, fall 1978. *Mem:* Taos Art Asn Inc, NMex; Artists Equity Asn (mem bd dirs, 47 & 48); Nat Watercolor Soc (vpres, 58, pres, 59); Col Art Asn Am. *Media:* Watercolor, Oil. *Publ:* Contribr, Content of Watercolor, Van Nostrand Reinhold, 69; contribr, Transparent Watercolor, Brommer Davis Publ, 73; contribr, Master Class in Watercolor, 75, Mastering Color and Design in Watercolor, 80 & Watercolor Bold and Free, 81, Watson-Guptill. *Dealer:* Abraxas Gallery 428 31st St Newport Beach CA 92663. *Mailing Add:* 1713 S Catalina Ave d Redondo Beach CA 90277

CROYDON, MICHAEL BENET
SCULPTOR, EDUCATOR
b Woodford, Eng, July 2, 31. *Study:* Goldsmiths Col Art, London, 50-51; Ealing Col Art, London, 51-53; Royal Col Art, London, with John Nash, ARCA, 56. *Work:* Victoria & Albert Mus, London; Nat Collection of Kenya, Nairobi; Royal Col Art, London; Ill State Mus, Springfield; First Nat Bank Chicago. *Comn:* Bronze mem figure, by Gen Ojukwu, Lagos, Nigeria, 75; 65ft Corten & stainless steel monument, Fogelson Co Inc, Chicago, 76-77. *Exhib:* Brit Art from African Collections, Sorsbie Gallery, Nairobi, 64; 3 Sculptors, Suburban Fine Arts Gallery, Highland Park, Ill, 73; New Horizons in Sculpture, 500 N Michigan, Chicago, 73-74; Prof Mem Show, Arts Club Chicago, 74; Recent Sculpture & Drawings by Michael Croydon, Donnelley Gallery, Lake Forest, Ill, 77. *Collections Arranged:* Graven Image--the Prints of Ivan Albright (auth, catalog), Lake Forest Col, 79. *Pos:* Art reviews-radio, Voice of Kenya, Nairobi, 64-67; dir pub TV, Voice of Kenya (two programs), Nairobi, 64-68; design consult, Ministry Commerce & Indust, Govt of Kenya, 67-68. *Teaching:* Head dept design, Univ EAfrica, Nairobi, Kenya, 62-68; prof art, Lake Forest Col, Ill, 68-, artist-in-residence, 69-71. *Awards:* Sculpture Prize, Ealing Col Art, London, 53; Inland Steel-Ryerson Award, 81. *Bibliog:* Carol Ray (dir), Michael Croydon (doc film), Voice Kenya TV, 64; Laura Watters (auth), Artist's sculptural reality, The Herald, 11/16/77; Garrett Holg (auth), Michael Croydon--Richard Hunt, New Art Examiner, 6/9/82. *Mem:* Arts Club Chicago; Col Art Asn Am. *Media:* Bronze, Terra-cotta. *Publ:* Auth, Ivan Albright, Abbeville Press, 78; contribr, Colliers Encycl, Humanities, Mcmillan Educ Corp, 79. *Dealer:* Grayson Gallery 256 W Huron St Chicago IL 60610. *Mailing Add:* Dept Art Lake Forest Col Lake Forest IL 60045

CROZIER, RICHARD LEWIS
PAINTER, EDUCATOR
b Honolulu, Hawaii, Dec 28, 44. *Study:* Univ Wash, Seattle, BFA(painting), 68; Univ Calif, Davis, with Wayne Thiebaud, MFA(painting) 74. *Work:* Am Embassy, Zaire. *Comn:* Paintings Juvenile Court Bldg, Charlottesville-Albemarle Comt Arts, Va, 80-81; Cover, Am Libr Asn J, Chicago, 75. *Exhib:* Calif Landscape, Oakland Mus, 75; Va Artists, Va Mus Fine Arts, Richmond, 77; Sacramento Valley Landscape, Univ Calif, Davis, 79; Realist Invitational, Southeastern Ctr Contemp Art, Winston-Salem, 79 & 81; New York Realists 1980, Thorpe Intermedia Gallery, Sparkill, 80; Am Realism since 1960, Pa Acad Fine Arts, Philadelphia, 81. *Teaching:* Assoc prof studio art, Univ Va, 74- *Awards:* Purchase Award, Southeastern Ctr Contemp Art, 77. *Media:* Oil. *Dealer:* Peter Tatistcheff 50 W 57th St New York NY 10022. *Mailing Add:* 624 Preston Pl Charlottesville VA 22903

CROZIER, WILLIAM K, JR
CRAFTSMAN, DESIGNER
b Stanwood, Wash, Mar 23, 26. *Study:* Wash State Univ, BFA; Univ Wash, MFA(silversmithing, design). *Exhib:* Contemp Craftsmen of the Far West Mus Contemp Crafts, 61 & Craftsmen USA 66, 66; Northwest Craftsmen's Exhib, Henry Gallery, Seattle, 61, 65, 67, 71 & 77; The Kentucky Guild Train, State Ky, 67; Calif Crafts VI Pac Dimensions, E B Crocker Art Gallery, Sacramento, 69; Am Crafts Coun NW Metal Traveling Exhib, 73-75. *Pos:* Cur slides & visuals, Sch Art, Univ Wash, 59-61. *Teaching:* Asst prof design, jewelry, Ore Col Educ, 61-66; assoc prof art educ & dir art educ prog, Ore State Univ, 66-69, prof jewelry & metal design, 66- *Awards:* Nat Merit Award, Am Crafts Coun, 66; Ore State Univ Grad Sch Res Grant, 70, Gen Res Grant, 77; Spec Recognition Award, Ore Summer Festival Arts, 74. *Bibliog:* Paul Soldner (auth), Craftsmen USA '66/pt 2, Crafts Horizons, 66; R Phillips (ed), Faculty Section, Ore State Univ Summer Bull, 72. *Mem:* Northwest Designer Craftsmen; Am Crafts Coun; World Crafts Coun. *Media:* Sterling Silver; Gold, Pewter. *Mailing Add:* Dept Art Ore State Univ Corvallis OR 97331

CRUCHET, JEAN-DENIS See Jandeni

CRUMBO, MINISA
PAINTER, GRAPHIC ARTIST
b Tulsa, Okla, Sept 2, 42. *Study:* Wasatch Acad; Tex Western Col, El Paso; Univ Colo; Taos Acad Fine Art, NMex, with Ray Vinella; Sch Visual Arts, New York, with Harvey Dinnerstein; Soc of Illusrs, with Daniel Schwartz. *Work:* Heard Mus, Phoenix, Ariz; Gilcrease Inst Am Hist & Art, Tulsa; Philbrook Art Ctr, Tulsa; Univ Tulsa; Oklahoma City Univ. *Exhib:* Two-person show, with Woody Crumbo, Pottawatomi Agency & Cult Ctr, Shawnee, Okla; Gov's Spec Showing, Tulsa, 76; Adobe Gallery, Las Vegas, Nev, 77; one-person shows, Tulsey Town Gallery, Tulsa, Gilcrease Inst Am Hist & Art, 77 & traveling show, Moscow, Leningrad & Kiev, USSR, 78; First Am Indian Art Show, USSR, 78-79; Oklahoma City Univ, 80; Baker Univ Fine Arts Festival, 81; Indian Art Week, Oklahoma City Univ, 81; and many others. *Teaching:* Vis instr art, Taos Pueblo Day Sch Ctr. *Awards:* Oil Award & Graphics Award, 29th Am Indian Exhib, Philbrook Art Ctr, 74; Distinguished Alumni Award, Wasatch Acad, 80; Distinguished Serv Award, Baker Univ, Kans, 82. *Bibliog:* Cover & feature, American Indian Artist Exhibits in Moscow, Pravda Feature, 12/10/78; articles, US Mag, 5/79 & Soviet Life Mag, 6/79. *Mailing Add:* 5800 E Skelly Dr Tulsa OK 74135

CRUMBO, WOODY
PAINTER, PRINTMAKER
b Lexington, Okla, Jan 31, 12. *Study:* Am Indian Inst, Wichita, Kans; Wichita Univ, 33-36. Univ Mus, 36-38. *Work:* San Francisco Mus Art; Metrop Mus Art, New York; Smithsonian Inst, Washington, DC; Gilcrease Inst Am Hist & Art, Tulsa, Okla; Philbrook Art Ctr, Tulsa. *Comn:* Stained glass windows, Rose Chapel, Bacone Col, Muskogee, Okla, 36-38; Buffalo Hunt, Peyote Birds

& Symbols, Flute Player & Wild Horses (murals), US Dept of Interior, Washington, DC, 39-41; Rainbow Trail (mural), Post Office, Nowata, Okla, 43. *Exhib:* Two-person exhib, with Minisa Crumbo, Pottawatomi Agency & Cult Ctr, Shawnee, Okla; over 1200 one-man shows, including, Gilcrease Inst Am Hist & Art. *Pos:* Dir art, Bacone Col, Muskogee, 38-41; cur & assembler, Am Indian art Collection, Gilcrease Inst Am Hist & Art, 45-48; asst dir, El Paso Mus Art, Tex, 60-68, dir & chief cur, 68-74; state chmn, Okla Indian Bicentennial Comn, 76. *Awards:* Julius Rosenwald Fel, 45; Okla Hall of Fame, 78. *Media:* Painting; Silkscreen; Etching. *Mailing Add:* West Star Rt Box 770 Checotak OK 74426

CRUMP, WALTER MOORE, JR
PRINTMAKER, PAINTER
b Winston-Salem, NC, Mar 18, 41. *Study:* Gilford Col, NC, 61-64; Harvard Univ Exten, 64-66; Boston Univ, BFA, 70; additional study with Walter Murch, David Aronson & Susan Smiley. *Work:* DeCordova Mus, Lincoln, Mass; Philadelphia Mus Art; Nat Mus Am Art, Smithsonian Inst; Boston Univ; NC Mus Art, Raleigh. *Exhib:* Davidson Nat Drawing & Print Exhib, NC, 73; Color Print USA, Tex Tech Univ, Lubbock, 75; Artists Under 36, DeCordova Mus, 76; Nat Print & Drawing Exhib, Miami Univ, Ohio, 77; Int Miniature Print Exhib, Pratt Graphics Ctr, New York, 77; Boston Printmakers Nat Exhib, Mus Fine Arts, Boston, 75, Boston Ctr Arts, 76 & DeCordova Mus, 77 & 79; Korean Exchange Print Exhib, Seoul, 78; Silvermine Nat Print Exhib, New Canaan, Conn, 78, 80 & 83; Color Print USA, Lubbock, Tex, 78; one-man shows, Plum Gallery, 78, 80 & 82. *Teaching:* Chmn art dept & instr printmaking, Commonwealth Sch, Boston, 72-; lectr & slide presentations, DeCordova Mus, 78 & Nat Collection of Fine Arts, DC, 79. *Awards:* Purchase Prize & First Prize, Dulin Nat Print & Drawing Competition, Knoxville, Tenn, 78 & 79; A P Hanks Mem Purchase Prize, Print Club Int Biennial, Philadelphia, 79; Purchase Prize, Boston Printmakers Exhib, 76-79. *Mem:* Boston Visual Artists Union; Boston Printmakers. *Media:* Collagraph, Intaglio; Oil. *Mailing Add:* 59 Delle Ave Roxbury MA 02120

CRUTCHFIELD, WILLIAM RICHARD
PAINTER, PRINTMAKER
b Indianapolis, Ind, Jan 21, 32. *Study:* Herron Sch Art, Ind Univ, Indianapolis, BFA, 56; Tulane Univ, La, MFA, 60. *Work:* Mus Mod Art, New York; Art Inst Chicago; Cleveland Mus Art; Philadelphia Mus Art; Libr of Cong, Washington, DC. *Comn:* Countdown II (watercolor), Skylab II, NASA, 73; Alphabet Spire VI (laminated wood sculpture), Westfarms, West Hartford, Conn, 74; Countdown (wood sculpture), Newark, NJ; Punctuation Spire (wood sculpture), Los Angeles. *Exhib:* Minneapolis Inst Art, 67; Ft Lauderdale Mus Arts, 71; NJ State Mus, Trenton, 71 & 72; California Prints 1972, Mus Mod Art, New York, 72; Dorsky Gallery, New York, 72, 73 & 75. *Awards:* Mary Milliken Award for Travel in Europe, Herron Sch Art, Ind Univ, Indianapolis, 56; Fulbright Scholar, State Art Acad, Hamburg, Ger, 61. *Bibliog:* Jane Livingston (auth), Crutchfield phenomena, Art in Am, 1-2/71; article in Horizon, winter 72; Howard E Wooden (auth), Sage of machine wit, Studio Int, 74. *Media:* Watercolor; Lithography, Screenprints. *Publ:* Illusr, Americana, 67, Owl Feathers, 70, Air, Land, Sea, 70, Six Rainbow Trains, 71 & A Report on the Art & Technology Program of the Los Angeles County Museum of Art 1967-1971, 71. *Mailing Add:* PO Box 591 San Pedro CA 90733

CRYSTAL, BORIS
PAINTER
b Poland, Dec 25, 31; US citizen. *Study:* Plocer's Sch Fine Arts, 62-63; Acad Fine Arts, Israel, 63-64. *Work:* Israel Mus, Tel-Aviv; Journalist House Art Gallery, Tel-Aviv; Herzl Inst, New York; Nicholas Roerich Mus, New York; Mus Mod Art, New York; and numerous other museums. *Exhib:* Journalist House Art Gallery, Tel-Aviv, 66; Herzl Inst Art Gallery, New York, 68; Nicholas Roerich Mus, New York, 70; Mus Mod Art, New York, 72; Lerner Art Gallery, New York, 75; La Galerie Mouffe, Paris, France, 77; and numerous others. *Collections Arranged:* Herzl Int Exhib USA, 65; Human Relations Coun in Coop with Art League USA, 68; Int Group Exhib of Paintings, Sculpture & Graphics, New Haven, Conn, 71. *Awards:* Int Award, Crown Art Gallery, 71; Vallombreuse Prize, Biarritz, France, 76; Gold Medal, Accad Italia, 80. *Bibliog:* Max Founry (auth), article, Art News, 69. *Mem:* Artists Equity Asn; Art League New York. *Media:* Oil, Watercolor. *Dealer:* Ella Lerner 241 E 76th St New York NY 10021. *Mailing Add:* 65-10 108th St Forest Hills NY 11375

CSOKA, STEPHEN
PAINTER, PRINTMAKER
b Gardony, Hungary, Jan 2, 1897; US citizen. *Study:* Budapest Royal Acad Art, 22-27. *Work:* Budapest Mus Art; Libr Cong; Brit Mus Art; Metrop Mus Art; Norfolk Mus Art; plus others. *Exhib:* One-man shows, Philadelphia Art Alliance, 43, Mus de Arte de Ponce, PR, 76; Carnegie Inst, 43-45; Corcoran Gallery Art, 45; retrospective, Pacem in Terris Gallery, New York, 68; 50 Year Retrospective, Fashion Inst of Technol, New York, 79; one-man retrospective, Gallery Odin, Port Washington, NY, 81; and others. *Teaching:* Instr, Fashion Inst Technol; instr, Nat Acad Design Sch Fine Arts; retired, 80. *Awards:* Acad Arts & Lett Grant; Gold Medal, Arpad Acad, Cleveland, Ohio, 71 & Pannonia Art Soc, New York, 71; plus others. *Mem:* Academician Nat Acad Design; Soc Am Graphic Artists; Audubon Artists. *Publ:* Auth, Pastel Painting, 62. *Mailing Add:* 85-80 87th St Woodhaven NY 11421

CUEVAS, JOSE LUIS
PAINTER, ILLUSTRATOR
b Mexico City, Mex, Feb 26, 34. *Study:* Sch Painting & Sculpture (La Esmeralda, Inst Nac Bellas Artes), Mexico City. *Work:* Mus Mod Art & Solomon R Guggenheim Mus, New York; Brooklyn Mus, NY; Mus of Albi & Lyons, France; plus others. *Exhib:* Biennial Venize, Italy, 72; Palais Beaux Arts, Brussels, Belg, 74; Warsaw Gallery, Poland, 75; Ludwig Mus, Cologne, Ger, 78; Mus Mod Art, Mexico City, 79; World Print Awards, San Francisco Mus Art, 83; and others. *Teaching:* Resident artist, Philadelphia Mus Sch Art, 57; lectr art, San Jose State Col, 70, Fullerton Col, 75 & Wash State Univ, 75. *Awards:* First Int Prize for Drawing, V Biennial of Sao Paulo, Brazil, 59; First Int Award, Mostra Bianco e Nero, 62; Award Excellence, 29th Ann Exhib, Art Dir Club, Philadelphia, 83. *Bibliog:* Carlos Fuentes (auth), Los mundos de Jose Luis Cuevas, Misrachi Gallery, Mexico City, 70; Daisy Ascher (auth), Revelando a Jose Luis Cuevas, Madero, Mex, 79; J B Ponce (auth), Jose Luis Cuevas: Genio O Farsante?, Ed Signos, 83. *Publ:* Illusr, Cuevas Charenton, Tamarind Workshop, 65; auth, Cuevas by Cuevas, Era, Mexico City, 65; illusr, Crime by Cuevas, Lublin Ed, 68; illusr, Homage to Quevedo, 69 & Cuevas Comedies, 71, Collectors Press; plus others. *Mailing Add:* c/o Tasende Gallery 820 Prospect St La Jolla CA 92037

CULBERTSON, JANET LYNN (MRS DOUGLAS KAFTEN)
PAINTER, INSTRUCTOR
b Greensburg, Pa, Mar 15, 32. *Study:* Carnegie Inst Technol, BFA, 53; Art Students League, 54; NY Univ, MA, 63; Pratt Graphic Arts Inst, 64-65. *Work:* Univ Mass, Amherst Mus Collection; AT&T, Chicago; Westinghouse Corp, Pittsburgh; Heckscher Mus, New York. *Exhib:* Lerner-Heller Gallery, New York, 71, 73, 75 & 77; Philadelphia Mus Art, 74; Brooklyn Mus, 75; Benson Gallery, Bridgehampton, NY, 78, 81 & 83; Visitors to Arizona, Phoenix Art Mus & Tucson Mus Art, 80; Animals in the Arsenal, Dept of Parks, New York, 81; and many others. *Teaching:* Instr art, Pace Col, 64-68; adj prof, Pratt Art Inst, 73-74 & Southampton Col, NY, 76. *Awards:* Award, Palos Verdes Mus Ann, 70; Creative Artists Pub Serv Prog Graphics Award, 79; NY Abstract Award, Guild Hall, 79. *Bibliog:* John Gruen (auth), article, New York Mag, 6/21/71; Mary Vaughn (auth), article, Arts Mag, 4/77; Helen Harrison (auth), article, New York Times, 6/1/80 & 11/9/80. *Mem:* Womens Caucus Art; Women in Arts. *Media:* Ink & Charcoal; Acrylic, Oil. *Dealer:* Benson Gallery Bridgehampton NY. *Mailing Add:* 525 E 82nd St New York NY 10028

CULBRETH, CARL R
SCULPTOR, EDUCATOR
b Mineola, NY, Dec 2, 52. *Study:* Nassau Community Col, AA(studio art), 73; Univ Vt, BS(art educ), 75; Syracuse Univ, with Margie Hughto, 76-77; Univ Del, MFA(ceramic sculpture), 79. *Work:* Syracuse Univ. *Exhib:* Ten Artists Under 30, Fine Arts Mus Long Island, Hempstead, NY, 81; Wards Island Sculpture Site, New York, 81; Brooklyn Mus, 81; East Coast Clay, Sculpture Ctr, New York, 82; The Figure: New Form, New Function, Arrowmont Sch Gallery, Gatlinburg, Tenn, 83; Ancient Inspirations, Contemporary Interpretations, NY State Mus, Albany, 83. *Pos:* Resident ceramist & gallery dir, Clayworks Studio Workshop, New York, 79- *Teaching:* Adj assoc prof art, Long Island Univ, 80-; coordr ceramics prog, Parsons Sch Design, 80- *Bibliog:* Donna Harkavay (auth), article, Am Ceramics, 8/82; Martin Ries (auth), article, Re-Dact, 11/83. *Mem:* Am Crafts Coun; Nat Coun Educ Ceramic Arts; Col Art Asn. *Media:* Clay. *Mailing Add:* 161 Henry St Brooklyn Heights NY 11201

CULKIN, JOHN MICHAEL
ADMINISTRATOR, EDUCATOR
b Brooklyn, NY, June 21, 28. *Study:* Woodstock Col, STL, 61; Harvard Univ, EdD, 64. *Pos:* Dir, Ctr for Commun, Fordham Univ, 63-69; dir & founder, Ctr for Understanding Media, New York, 69- & Media Studies Prog, New Sch for Social Res, 74- *Teaching:* Asst prof commun, Fordham Univ, New York, 63-69; lectr media studies, New Sch for Social Res, New York, 74- *Mem:* Am Film Inst (trustee, 68-73); Media Educators Asn (founder, 70); Art, Educ & Americans (media adv). *Publ:* Auth, A Schoolman's Guide to Marshall McLuhan, Saturday Rev, 67; ed, Trilogy--An Experiment in Multi-Media, Macmillan, 68; contribr, Summerhill--For and Against, Hart, 68; coauth, Films Deliver, Citation, 69; auth, The New Literacy: From the Alphabet to Television, Media & Methods, 77. *Mailing Add:* 69 Horatio St New York NY 10014

CUMMENS, LINDA TALABA See Talaba, L

CUMMING, GLEN EDWARD
MUSEUM DIRECTOR
b Calgary, Alta, July 2, 36. *Study:* Alberta Col Art, 4 yr dipl. *Collections Arranged:* Nine Out of Ten, A Survey of Contemporary Canadian Art 1974-75; Ontario Now: A Survey of Contemporary Art 1976; Karel Appel, The Complete Graphic Collection (1957-1977), 77; Contemp Art of Senegal, 79; Viewpoint Twenty-nine by Nine, 81 & 82. *Pos:* Cur, Regina Pub Libr Art Gallery, Sask, 67-69; dir, Kitchener-Waterloo Art Gallery, Kitchener, Ont, 69-72; dir, Robert McLaughlin Gallery, Oshawa, Ont, 72-73; dir, Art Gallery Hamilton, Ont, 73- *Awards:* Queen Elizabeth Prize, Govt Alberta, 60. *Mem:* Ontario Asn Art Galleries (pres, 74-75); Asn Art Mus Dir; Can Art Mus Dirs Orgn (pres, 81-83); Can Mus Asn; Am Mus Asn; and others. *Publ:* Auth, The Graphic Work of Karel Appel, 77; auth, Contemporary Art of Senegal, 79; Viewpoint: 29 by 9, 81; El Dorado, Gold from Ancient Colombia, 82. *Mailing Add:* 222 Jackson St W 1502 Hamilton ON L8P 4S5 Canada

CUMMING, ROBERT H
ARTIST, PHOTOGRAPHER
b Worcester, Mass, Oct 7, 43. *Study:* Mass Col Art, Boston, BA, 65; Univ Ill, Champaign, MFA, 67. *Work:* Mus Fine Arts, Houston; Mus Mod Art, New York. *Comn:* Outdoor sculpture, Walker Art Ctr, Minneapolis, Minn, 70; Nation's Capitol Documentation, Corcoran Gallery, Washington, DC. *Exhib:* Art by Telephone, Mus Contemp Art, Chicago, 69; 9 Artists/9 Spaces, Walker Art Ctr, Minneapolis, Minn, 70; 24 Young Los Angeles Artists, Los Angeles Co Mus, 71; Narrative Art, Palais des Beaux Arts, Brussels, Belg, 75; Whitney Biennial, New York, 77 & 81; Paris Biennale, Mus d'Art Mod, France, 77; Mirrors and Windows, Mus Mod Art, New York; and others. *Teaching:* Instr painting & drawing, Univ Wis, Milwaukee, 67-70; lectr photography, Univ Calif, Los Angeles, 74- *Awards:* Frank Logan Prize, Chicago Art Inst, 69; Nat Endowment Arts Awards, 72, 74 & 83; Guggenheim Fel, 80. *Bibliog:* M Jochimsen (auth), Story Art, Mag Kunst, Mainz, Ger, 2/74; C Hagen (auth), Robert Cumming's Subject/Object, Artforum, summer 83. *Media:* Multimedia. *Publ:* Auth, Picture Fictions, Anaheim, Calif, 71; auth, The Weight of Franchise Meat, Anaheim, Calif, 71; auth, A Training in the Arts, Toronto, Can, 73; auth, A Discourse on Domestic Disorder, Irvine, Calif, 75; auth, Equilibrium and the Rotary Disc, Meriden, Conn, 80. *Mailing Add:* 1604 N Grand West Suffield CT 06093

CUMMINGS, DAVID WILLIAM
PAINTER
b Okmulgee, Okla, July 15, 37. *Study:* Kansas City Art Inst, Mo, BFA, 63; Univ Nebr, Lincoln, MFA, 67. *Work:* Whitney Mus Am Art, New York; Los Angeles Co Mus Art, Los Angeles, Calif; Phoenix Art Mus, Ariz; Mus Contemp Art, Antwerp, Belg; Aldrich Mus Contemp Art, Ridgefield, Conn; and others. *Exhib:* Lyrical Abstraction, Philadelphia Mus Art, Pa, 70 & Whitney Mus Am Art, 71; 20th Century Am Artists, Corcoran Gallery Art, Washington, DC, 71; Contemp Reflections, Aldrich Mus Contemp Art, 71-72; one-man shows, Allan Stone Gallery, New York, 74-77 & 82, Gallery Alexandra Monett, Bruxelles, Belg, 75, 77, 79 & 82, Ericson Gallery, New York, 80 & Shahin Requicha Gallery, Rochester, NY, 83; Galerij Tremerie, Huise, Belg, 79; one-man shows, Ericson Gallery, New York, 80, Gallery Alexandra Monett, Bruxelles, 82 & Allan Stone Gallery, New York, 82; and others. *Pos:* Vis artist, Ohio State Univ, Columbus, 74, Univ Iowa, Iowa City, 76 & Univ NDak, Grand Forks, 81; coordr painting symposium, Colo Mountain Col, Vail, 76-78. *Teaching:* Instr, State Univ NY, 67-71; asst prof, City Univ New York, 71- *Awards:* Purchase Award, Nelson Gallery, Kansas City, Mo, Ford Found, 63; John Lehmann Award, St Louis Mus Art, Mo, 65; Woods Found Fel, Univ Nebr, 66-67. *Bibliog:* Jacques Meuris (auth), David Cummings, Plus Minus Zero, 11/79; Theodore F Wolff (auth), The colorist's art, The Christian Sci Monitor, 9/10/80; Susan Dodge Peters (auth), A master of color, Rochester City News, 4/28/83. *Media:* Oil, Pastel. *Dealer:* Allan Stone Gallery 48 E 86th St New York NY 10028. *Mailing Add:* 106-108 Hopkins Ave Jersey City NJ 07306

CUMMINGS, FREDERICK JAMES
ADMINISTRATOR, HISTORIAN
b Floydada, Tex, Aug 19, 33. *Study:* Willamette Univ, BA, 54; Harvard Univ, MA, 56; Univ Chicago, PhD(hons), 66; Courtauld Inst Art, Univ London, 60-61. *Collections Arranged:* American Decorative Arts from the Pilgrims to the Revolution, 67; Art in Italy, 1600-1700, 65; Romantic Art in Britain: Paintings & Drawings, 1760-1860; Painting in France, 1774-1830. *Pos:* Actg dir, Mus Art & Archaeol, Univ Mo, 63-64; asst dir & cur European art, Detroit Inst Arts, 64-73, dir, 73-; ed, Art Quart, 66-69. *Teaching:* Instr art hist, Univ Mo, 61-64; adj prof, Wayne State Univ, 65- *Awards:* Hon Fine Arts Silver Medal Award, Mich Acad Sci, Arts & Lett, 72. *Mem:* Col Art Asn Am (bd dirs, 71-); Am Asn Mus; Am Soc 18th Century Studies. *Res:* Romantic painting in Western Europe. *Publ:* Auth, Charles Bell & anatomy of expression, Art Bulletin, 64; auth, Wright's Boothby, Rousseau, & the romantic malady, Burlington Mag, 68; auth, Folly & mutability in Joseph Wright's alchemist & Democritus, Art Quart, 70; contribr, Proc, Am Soc 18th Century Studies, 72. *Mailing Add:* Detroit Inst of Arts 5200 Woodward Ave Detroit MI 48202

CUMMINGS, PAUL
CURATOR, EDITOR
b US. *Study:* Univ Minn; Univ London. *Collections Arranged:* David Smith: The Drawings (auth, catalog), 79-80 & Willem de Kooning: Retrospective (auth, catalog), 83, Whitney Mus Am Art. *Pos:* Consult, var corporations & foundations, 62-; dir oral hist, Arch Am Art, 67-78, ed jour, 74-78; founder, Print Collectors Newslett, 70; adj cur drawings, Whitney Mus Am Art, 76-; pres, Drawing Soc, 78-, ed, Drawing, 79-; publ, Catchwork Papers, 83- *Res:* Twentieth century American art; drawing. *Publ:* Auth, American Drawings: The Twentieth Century, Viking Press, 76; ed, Fine Arts Market Place, R R Bowker, 3rd ed, 77; auth, Artists in Their Own Words, 79 & Dictionary of Contemporary American Artists, 4th rev ed, 81, St Martin's Press. *Mailing Add:* 945 Madison Ave New York NY 10021

CUMMINS, KAREN GASCO
ADMINISTRATOR, MUSEOLOGIST
b Trenton, NJ, Jan 30, 45. *Study:* Goucher Col, BA; Temple Univ, MEd; NY Univ. *Collections Arranged:* NJ traveling art exhibs, Intaglio Printmaking, Planographic Printmaking, Relief Printmaking, Merci (prints & posters by Ben Shahn), For the Sake of a Single Verse (by Ben Shahn), Olympic Games Posters, The Dreigroschen Film, Eleven Pop Artists & two portfolios by John Randolph Carter. *Pos:* Sr mus technician, NJ State Mus, Trenton, 67-68, coordr traveling exhib & pub info officer, 68-73; asst to dir, 73- *Mem:* Mus Coun NJ (chmn, 73-75); Northeast Mus Conf; Am Asn Mus. *Mailing Add:* NJ State Mus 205 W State St Trenton NJ 08625

CUNINGHAM, ELIZABETH BAYARD (MRS E W R TEMPLETON)
DEALER
b New York, NY. *Study:* Bronxville Sch, NY; Vassar Col, Poughkeepsie, NY; Finch Col, NY, BA; Hunter Col, New York, MA(art hist). *Pos:* Exec secy, Olana Preserv Inc, New York, 65-66; dir publicity, Comt to Rescue Italian Art, New York, 66-67; asst to pres, Nat Trust for Hist Preserv, 68-70; asst dir, Reese Palley Art Gallery, New York, 70-72; pres, Cunningham Ward Inc, 72-78; Betty Cuningham Gallery, 78- *Mem:* Drawing Soc Inc (exec comt, 70-80); Art Dealers Asn, 79-81. *Specialty:* Contemporary painting. *Mailing Add:* Betty Cuningham Inc 94 Prince St New York NY 10012

CUNNINGHAM, (CHARLES) BRUCE
PAINTER
b Bayonne, NJ, Mar 30, 43. *Study:* Baylor Univ, BFA; Univ Tex, Austin; Univ Calif, Berkeley, MA & MFA; also with Erle Loran, Elmer Bischoff & David Simpson. *Work:* Aldrich Mus Art, Ridgefield, Conn; Am Tel & Tel Co, NJ; Oppenheimer & Co, New York; Dallas Mus Fine Art, Tex; Gen Instrument Corp, New York. *Exhib:* One-man shows, Projects II, Dallas Mus Fine Arts, 75, Watson de Nagy Gallery, Houston, 77, Contemp Gallery, Dallas, 77, Inst for Art & Urban Resources, PS 1, New York, 79, Soho Ctr Visual Arts, New York, 81 & 55 Mercer St Gallery, New York, 82; plus others. *Pos:* Artist-in-residence, Tex Comn Arts & Humanities, Longview Mus & Arts Ctr, 74-75; Southwestern Univ, Georgetown, Tex, 81 & John Dewey High Sch, Brooklyn, NY, 81-82. *Teaching:* Instr painting & drawing, Baylor Univ, 72-74; asst prof painting & drawing, Univ Tex, Arlington, 75-77; vis prof painting, Univ Tex, Austin, 80-81; mem fac, Summit Art Ctr, NJ, 83. *Awards:* Nat Endowment Arts Fel, 75; Amarillo Two-Dimensional Three State Exhib Cash Award, Amarillo Art Mus, 75; First Award in Painting, Southwest/Tarrant Co Ann, Ft Worth Art Mus, 76. *Media:* Oil, Charcoal. *Mailing Add:* 40 Great Jones St New York NY 10012

CUNNINGHAM, CHARLES C, JR
ADMINISTRATOR
b Boston, Mass, May 25, 34. *Study:* Harvard Univ, AB, 56, MBA, 60. *Pos:* Chmn, Overseers Comt to Visit Harvard Univ Art Mus, 71-; trustee, Mus Fine Arts, Boston, 72- *Mem:* Fel Pierpont Morgan Libr, New York. *Mailing Add:* Rm 923 1 Boston Pl Boston MA 02108

CUNNINGHAM, FRANCIS
PAINTER, INSTRUCTOR
b New York, NY, Jan 18, 31. *Study:* Art Students League, with Edwin Dickinson & Robert Beverly Hale. *Exhib:* Butler Inst Am Art, Youngstown, Ohio, 67, 72 & 74; one-man shows, Berkshire Mus, Pittsfield, Mass, 69, Distelheim Galleries, Chicago, 70, Mickelson Gallery, Washington, DC, 71 & Welles Gallery, Lenox Libr, Mass, 71; two-man exhib, Forum Gallery, 79; and others. *Pos:* Co-founder & pres, New Brooklyn Sch Life Painting, Drawing & Sculpture Inc, 80- *Teaching:* Instr painting & drawing, Brooklyn Mus Art Sch, 62-80; instr painting & drawing, Art Students League, New York, 80- *Awards:* Berkshire Art Asn Purchase Award, Berkshire Mus, 68; Louis Comfort Tiffany Found Grant, 73; Minnie R Stern Award, Audubon Artists Ann, 78; and others. *Mem:* Art Students League; Audubon Artists. *Media:* Oil, Pencil. *Publ:* Coauth, Polykleitos' Diadoumenos: Measurement & animation, Art Quart, summer 62; illusr, Fundamentals of Roentgenology, 64. *Mailing Add:* 789 West End Ave New York NY 10025

CUNNINGHAM, J
SCULPTOR
b Greenwich, Conn, Sept 18, 40. *Study:* Kenyon Col, BA, 62; Yale Sch Art & Archit, BFA, 63 & MFA, 65. *Work:* Hirshhorn Mus; and others and many pvt collections. *Exhib:* Structured Sculpture, Galerie Chalette, New York, 68; Baltimore Mus, 70; Lenox Hill Show, Gimbel's East & Denis Rene Gallery, 72, New York & others; one-man shows, Betty Parsons, New York, 78 & 79 & Barbara Fiedler Gallery, Washington, DC, 79. *Teaching:* Vis critic design, Williams Col, spring 68 & Union Col, spring 71; instr sculpture, Inst Arts & Sci, Williamstown, Mass, summer 68 & Skidmore Col, summer 69; vis lectr, Saratoga Performing Arts Ctr, 71; assoc prof art, Skidmore Col, Saratoga Springs, 75- *Awards:* Fel in Sculpture, Univ Pa, 66. *Mailing Add:* Dept of Art Skidmore Col Saratoga Springs NY 12866

CURMANO, BILLY
CONCEPTUAL ARTIST, SCULPTOR
b 1949; US citizen. *Study:* Univ Wis, Milwaukee, BFA, 73, MS, 77; Art Students League, 82. *Work:* Metronom, Barcelona, Spain; Temple Univ, Philadelphia; Univ Wis, Milwaukee; Children's Theater, Minneapolis, Minn; Col St Teresa, Minn. *Exhib:* Artists Proposals, Milwaukee Art Mus, 71; Eighth Tyler Nat, Tyler Mus Art, Tex, 72; Triangulation, Dean Gallery, Minneapolis, 74; 23rd Chautauqua Nat, NY, 80; Irretrievable Statements, Krasl Art Ctr, St Joseph, Mich, 81; Orange County 16th Ann, Brea Civic Cult Ctr, Calif, 82; and others. *Bibliog:* Don Morrison (auth), Curmano kidding on square, Minneapolis Star, 8/15/74; In depth performance, Assoc Press, 9/18/83; Phil McCombs (auth), Getting down to it, Washington Post, 10/12/83. *Media:* Mixed. *Publ:* Contribr, Format, Seven Oaks Press, 79; contribr, Libres D'Artista--Artists Books, Metronom, 81; contribr, Mail Art Book, Japan Artists Union, 82; contribr, High performance, Astro Artz, 81-83. *Dealer:* Screening Room 68 Lafayette Winona MN 55987. *Mailing Add:* Rt 1 Box 116 Rushford MN 55971

CURRAN, DARRYL JOSEPH
PHOTOGRAPHER, PRINTMAKER
b Santa Barbara, Calif, Oct 19, 35. *Study:* Ventura Col, AA, 58; Univ Calif, Los Angeles, BA, 60 & MA, 64. *Work:* Mus Mod Art, New York; Nat Gallery Can, Ottawa; Int Mus Photog, George Eastman House, Rochester, NY; Royal Photog Soc, London. *Exhib:* Vision & Expression, George Eastman House, 68; Photog into Sculpture, Mus Mod Art, New York, 70; Photog into Art, Brit Arts Comn, 73; one-man shows, Focus Gallery, San Francisco, Calif, 74, Midway Studios, Univ Chicago, 75, Art Space, Los Angeles, 78 & Chaffey Col, 82. *Collections Arranged:* Graphic/Photographic (auth, catalogue), Art Gallery, Calif State Univ, Fullerton, 71; 24 From LA (auth, catalogue), San Francisco Mus Mod Art, 73; Photo Visionaries, Floating Wall Gallery, Santa Ana, Calif, 76; Los Angeles Perspectives, Secession Gallery, Victoria, BC, 76. *Pos:* Bd dir, Los Angeles Center for Photog Studies, 73-77, pres, 80-, juror & chmn, Los Angeles Olympic Organizing Comt Photog Comn Proj for 1984 Olympic Games. *Teaching:* Assoc prof creative photog, Calif State Univ, Fullerton, 67-; vis artist photog, Sch of Art Inst Chicago, spring 75. *Awards:* Phelan Award in Photog, James Phelan Trust, Oakland Mus, 71; First Place in Photog, 76 Calif Art Expo, Calif State Fair, 76; Nat Endowment for the Arts Photographers Fel, 80. *Bibliog:* Robert Stuart (auth), Light & Substance, Univ NMex, Coke/Barrow, 74; Lewis/Alger (auth), Darryl Curran Photographs 1967-1981 (exhib catalog), Chaffey Col, 82. *Mem:* Soc Photog Educ (bd dir, 75-79). *Publ:* Contribr, Revolution in a Box, Univ Calif, Riverside, contribr, Untitled 11, Emerging Los Angeles Photographers, Friends of Photog, Carmel, Calif; contribr, Object, Illusion, Reality, Calif State Univ, Fullerton, 79; contribr, L A Issue, Los Angeles Ctr Photog Studies, 79. *Dealer:* G Ray Hawkins Gallery 7224 Melrose Ave Los Angeles CA 90060. *Mailing Add:* 10537 Dunleer Dr Los Angeles CA 90064

CURRAN, DOUGLAS EDWARD
PHOTOGRAPHER
b Seaforth, Ont, Aug 7, 52. *Study:* Ryerson Polytechnical Inst, Toronto, BAA, 77; Banff Sch Fine Arts, Alta, scholar, 79. *Work:* Nat Film Bd Can, Ottawa; Alta Art Found, Edmonton; Walter Phillips Gallery, Banff Ctr, Alta; Olden Camera Gallery, New York; Edmonton Art Gallery. *Comn:* Alberta 1980, PhotoProject, Alta 57th Comn, Edmonton, 80; Metis Settlements of Alberta, Fedn Metis, Edmonton, 81. *Exhib:* Recent Acquisitions, Nat Film Bd Can, Ottawa, 79; Seven, Walter Phillips Gallery, Banff, Alta, 81; Folk Concepts of Outer Space, Edmonton Art Gallery, 81 & traveling, 81-83; Primary Colour, Harbourfront, Toronto, 82; Document, Nat Film Bd Can, Ottawa, 83. *Teaching:* Sessional instr photog, Univ Alta, Edmonton, 83-84. *Awards:* Grants, Can Coun, 77 & 78. *Bibliog:* Doug Clark & L Wedman (auth), Keepsake, Artswest Publ, 82. *Mailing Add:* 12525 104 Ave #5 Edmonton AB T5N 0V5 Canada

CURRIE, BRUCE
PAINTER, PRINTMAKER
b Sac City, Iowa, Nov 27, 11. *Work:* Nat Acad Design, New York; State Univ NY Albany; Butler Inst Am Art, Youngstown, Ohio; Colorado Springs Fine Arts Ctr; Kalamazoo Inst Arts, Mich. *Exhib:* Butler Inst Am Art, Ann Exhibs, 53-74 & 78; Audubon Artists, 62-83; Albany Inst Hist & Art, 65, 68, 70 & 75; Nat Acad Design, 69-83; Colorado Springs Fine Arts Ctr, Colo, 71; Nat Soc Painters Casein & Acrylic, 73-83; plus many others incl one-man shows. *Awards:* Benjamin Altman Figure Prize, Nat Acad Design, 79; Grand Prize, 46th Ann Exhib, Cooperstown Art Asn, 81; Audubon Artists Medal of Honor, 82. *Mem:* Nat Acad Design; Nat Soc Painters in Casein & Acrylic; Am Watercolor Soc; Audubon Artists; Woodstock Artists Asn. *Media:* Oil, Acrylic; Woodcuts. *Mailing Add:* RFD Box 284 Woodstock NY 12498

CURTIS, DOLLY POWERS
TAPESTRY ARTIST, SCULPTOR
b Bronx, NY, April 25, 42. *Study:* Pa State Univ, BS(educ), 60-63; NY Univ, MA(educ), 63-65; Brookfield Craft Ctr, Conn, 73-83. *Work:* Southern Conn State Univ; Choate Sch Art Dept; Marymount Col; Gov Residence, State Conn. *Comn:* Knotted sculpture, Landplan Partnership, Southport, Conn, 77; numerous comns for private residences, northeast US, 77-; woven wall, Richard Bergmann Architects, New Canaan, Conn, 80; weavings, Naperville Corp Ctr, Ill, 82; woven hanging, Coopers & Lebrand CPA, Hartford, Conn, 83. *Exhib:* Solo exhibs, Woven Folds--Fabric Drawing in Space, Pindar Gallery, New York, 80, 81 & 82 & Woven Environmental Sculpture, Wesleyan Univ, Conn, 82; Art in Craft Media Traveling Exhib, 81-83; Pa State Univ Mus Art, 82; Fiber: The Artist's View, C W Post Ctr, Long Island Univ, 83; and others. *Pos:* Owner, Archit Textiles, Easton, Conn, 73- *Teaching:* Instr weaving, Brookfield Craft Ctr, Conn, 77, Haystack Mt Sch, Deer Isle, Maine, 77 & others. *Awards:* State Conn Grant, 76; Outstanding Achievement Design, Women in Design Int, 83. *Bibliog:* Patricia Hubbell (auth), Her weavings soar thru space & Kossia Orloff (auth), Reforming fabric, Women Artists News, fall 82; Martha B Scott (auth), article, Art Voices, 1-2/81. *Mem:* Artists Equity Asn; Am Crafts Coun; Womens Caucus Art; Surface Design Asn; Artist-Craftsmen New York. *Media:* Fiber, Textiles. *Publ:* auth, State grant: A two way street, Shuttle, Spindle, Dyepot, fall 77; contribr, Architectural Ornament, Van Nostrand Reinhold, 82; contribr, Designing for Weaving, Hastings House Publ, 82; contribr, Fiberarts Design II, Lark Publ, 83; contribr, Women Working Home, Rodale Press, 83. *Dealer:* Bernice Steinbaum Gallery 903 Madison Ave New York NY 10021. *Mailing Add:* 35 Flat Rock Rd Easton CT 06612

CURTIS, MARY CRANFILL
PRINTMAKER, PAINTER
b Ft Worth, Tex, Aug 6, 25. *Study:* Columbia Univ, BS; Southern Methodist Univ, MFA; ETex State Univ; also workshops in NMex & San Miguel de Allende, Mexico. *Work:* Dallas Mus Fine Arts; Okla Art Ctr, Oklahoma City; Southern Methodist Univ; Mobil Oil Collection; Heard Mus Natural Hist, McKinney, Tex; and others. *Comn:* Portraits, Austin Col, 57; designed rug showing Tex hist, 63, designed glass murals, 65, Grayson Co State Bank,

Sherman, Tex. *Exhib:* Davidson Nat Print & Drawing, NC, 74; Int Miami Graphics Biennial, Fla, 75 & 77; Libr of Cong & Nat Collection Fine Arts Nat Exhib Prints, Washington, DC, 75; Los Angeles Printmaking Nat, 75; three-person show, Masur Mus Art, Monroe, La, 76; Print Exhib, Visual Arts Ctr Alaska, Anchorage, 79. *Teaching:* Instr art, Austin Col, 55-57 & 65-67; instr art, Sch Continuing Educ, Southern Methodist Univ, 68-75 & Artists Courtyard, Dallas, 75- *Awards:* First Graphics Prize, Univ Tex, Arlington, 73; Midwestern Graphics Purchase Award, Tulsa City-County Libr, Okla, 75; Juror's Commendation, Boston Printmakers, 75. *Media:* Etching; All Media. *Dealer:* Assoc Am Artists 663 Fifth Ave New York NY 10022. *Mailing Add:* 328 Sutton Pl Richardson TX 75080

CURTIS, PHILIP CAMPBELL
PAINTER
b Jackson, Mich, May 26, 07. *Study:* Albion Col, BA, 30; Univ Mich Law Sch; Yale Univ Sch Fine Arts, cert, 35; Harvard Univ, 41; Albion Col, hon DFA, 71; Ariz State Univ, hon doctorate, 79, DHL, 81. *Work:* Curtis Room, Phoenix Art Mus. *Exhib:* San Francisco Mus Art, Calif, 49; Calif Palace Legion Honor, 66; Galerie Krugier, Geneva, Switz, 67; Amon Carter Mus, Ft Worth, Tex, 70; Univ Calif, Los Angeles, 72; one-man show, Galerie Ariadne, Vienna, 74; Phillips Collection, Washington, DC, 78; and 17 others. *Pos:* Supvr mural painting, Works Progress Admin Proj, New York, 35; founder & first dir, Phoenix Art Ctr & Phoenix Art Mus, Ariz, 36-39; Designer, WPA Art Proj, DeYoung Mus, San Francisco, Calif, 38; mem staff, Des Moines Art Ctr, 39-41. *Awards:* Distinguished Achievement Awards, Nat Soc Arts & Letters, 76 & Ariz State Univ, 79; Governor's Award, Artist of the Year, 83. *Bibliog:* Jose Bermudez (auth, film), The Time Freeze, 74; article, Esquire Mag, 12/82. *Mem:* Benjamin Franklin fel, Royal Soc Arts. *Media:* Oil. *Mailing Add:* 109 Cattle Track Scottsdale AZ 85253

CURTIS, ROBERT D
SCULPTOR
b Susanville, Calif, Mar 28, 48. *Study:* Univ Ariz, BFA(sculpture), 70; Ariz State Univ, MFA(sculpture & design), 72. *Exhib:* Wis Directions 2, Milwaukee Art Mus, 78; Anita J Welch Mem Nat Competition & Sculpture Exhib, Scottsdale Ctr Arts, Ariz, 79; Wis Sculpture, Wustum Mus Fine Arts, Racine, 79; two-person exhib, Arts Club Chicago, Ill, 82; one-person exhib, Kit Basquin Gallery, Milwaukee, 82; Int Art Expo, Navy Pier, Chicago, 82 & 83. *Pos:* Consult restoration & installation of large scale sculpture, Bradley Family Found, Milwaukee, Wis, 78-; consult restoration & installation of large scale sculpture, Milwaukee Art Mus, 79. *Teaching:* Instr design & sculpture, Univ Wis, Milwaukee, 72-73; instr drawing, 3-D design, sculpture, Mt Mary Col, 75- *Awards:* Shapes of 77 Stainless Steel Sculpture Competition, Vollrath Co, Wis, 77; Grant-in-Aid, Wis Arts Bd, 78; First in Sculpture Competition, City Madison, 83. *Bibliog:* Judith M Kaiser (auth), New Dimensions in Wisconsin Art: Robert Curtis, Exclusively Yours, The Patten Co, 80; Karen Thorsen-Collins (auth), Opening exhibition: Kit Basquin Gallery, New Art Examiner, 12/81. *Mem:* Int Sculpture Ctr; Col Art Asn; Wis Painters & Sculpture Inc (pres, 76-78). *Media:* Steel, Stone. *Mailing Add:* 3307 N Newhall Milwaukee WI 53211

CURTIS, ROGER WILLIAM
PAINTER, DEALER
b Gloucester, Mass, Dec 20, 10. *Study:* Exten courses, Boston Univ, Harvard Univ, Mus Sch Boston; pvt study with Aldro T Hibbard; Burdett Col. *Work:* Concord Art Asn Permanent Collection; Raytheon Corp; Nat Shawmut Bank, Boston; Eastern Gas & Fuel, Boston; Mellon Bank, Pittsburgh, Pa; and others. *Exhib:* Jordan Marsh Exhib, 45-75; Arts Atlantic Exhib, NShore Arts Asn, Gloucester, 47-75; Sheldon-Swope Mus, Terre Haute, Ind; Symphony Hall Exhib, Boston, 65-70; Acad Artist Asn, Springfield, Mass, 72-75. *Pos:* Pres, Burlington Art Asn, Mass, 60-64; adminr, Ledgendsea Gallery & Riverview Gallery, currently. *Teaching:* Instr painting, pvt classes, 53- *Awards:* North Shore Arts Mem, 80; Gordon Grant Mem, 81; Saunders Award, 83. *Mem:* NShore Arts Asn (pres, 52-58, treas, 65-); Am Artists Prof League; Cape Ann Festival Arts (treas, presently); co-founder, Coun Mass Art Asn; Academic Artists Asn; and others. *Media:* Oil. *Publ:* Auth & illusr, How to Paint Successful Seascapes, 75 & Color in Outdoor Painting, 77, Watson-Guptill. *Mailing Add:* c/o New England Artists 30 Riverview Rd Gloucester MA 01930

CURTISS-TRUETSCH, GEORGE CURT (GEORGE C CURTISS)
PAINTER, GALLERY DIRECTOR
b Rasnov, Romania. *Study:* Acad Art, Milan, Italy, BFA; Acad Fine Arts, Berlin, Ger, BFA & MA; also with Prof Holst & Erik Richter. *Work:* Mus Mod Art, Munich; Mus Art, Vienna; Mus Sci & Natural Hist, Miami; Galeria del Sagrato, Milan; Artist's Arch, Thieme-Becker Int Artist's Lexicon, Heilbronn, WGer; plus others. *Comn:* Murals, Galeria del Sagrato, Milan, Italy, 50, murals, Am Red Cross, Salzburg, Austria, 51; posters, Teatro Lirico, Milan, Italy, 57; exhibits, backgrounds & murals, Mus Sci & Natural Hist, Miami, 57-64; scenery designs, Cinetron Film Co, Miami, 68. *Exhib:* Mus Sci & Natural Hist, Miami, 57-68; El Centro Gallery Art, Coral Gables-Miami, 59; Loft Gallery Arts, Hollywood, 63; Montmartre Art Galleries, Palm Beach, 67; exhib in most of Europe. *Collections Arranged:* As cur of exhib of the Mus of Sci & Natural Hist, planned, designed & executed over one hundred exhibits, including painting the backgrounds in oil in various sizes. *Pos:* Scenery & costume designer, Ballett-Revue Carise, Vienna-Milan, 48-51; cur, Mus Sci & Natural Hist, 57-64; dir, Loft Gallery Art, Hollywood, 64-67; dir, R Gallery Art, Miami, 52-75. *Teaching:* Art teacher portrait, Channel 4, WTVJ, Miami, 52-57; instr drawing, Mus Sci & Natural Hist, 57-64. *Awards:* Gold Medal, Acamemia, Italia; Medal, Galeria Del Sagrato, Milan, Cert Honor, Mus Sci & Natural Hist, 61; First Prize, The R Gallery Art, Miami

Beach, Fla, 63 & 64; and others. *Bibliog:* Artist's Archives, Heilbronn, 70; Thieme-Becker (auth), International Artists, Bonn, 71; May H Edmonds (auth), Local Authors & the Florida Scene, 71; plus others. *Mem:* Am Fedn Arts; Artists Equity; Int Soc Artists; Visual Artists & Gallery Asn; United Inventors & Scientists Am & Int. *Media:* Oil, Graphics. *Specialty:* Promotion of local American artists. *Publ:* Illusr, Who Smiles with Us, 49; illusr, The Illustration, 52; contribr, Artist's See Themselves, 59; auth & illusr, Li'l Piccolo's Adventures with Music & Instruments, Univ Miami, 71; auth, Multiple Painting Compositions. *Mailing Add:* 832 NE 124th St North Miami FL 33161

CUSHING, BARBARA
EDUCATOR, PAINTER
b Queens, NY, Feb 18, 48. *Study:* Skidmore Col, BS, 70; Pa State Univ, MFA, 72. *Work:* Fogg Art Mus, Harvard Univ, Cambridge, Mass. *Exhib:* Ariz Nat, Scottsdale Ctr Arts, 77; LaGrange Nat III & IV, LaGrange Col, Ga, 77 & 78; All Maine Biennial, Bowdoin Col Mus Art, Brunswick, 79; Barbara Cushing--Landscapes, State House, Augusta, Maine, 80; one-woman show, Univ Maine, Orono; and others. *Teaching:* Instr studio art, Otterbein Col, Westerville, Ohio, 72-74; assoc prof painting & drawing, Univ Maine at Orono, 75- *Awards:* MacDowell Fel, 77; Yaddo Residence, 78; Univ Maine at Orono Summer Res Award, 80. *Media:* Oil. *Mailing Add:* Dept of Art Univ of Maine Orono ME 04469

CUSICK, NANCY TAYLOR
PAINTER
b Washington, DC. *Study:* Am Univ, with Gates, Calfee, D'Arista & Summerford, BA, 59, MA, 61; Corcoran Art Sch, 68; Univ Calif, with Lindgren, 71. *Exhib:* Washington Artists Ann, Smithsonian Inst, 60-69; Corcoran Gallery Art Area Exhib, 67; Label: Women Show, Washington, DC, 79; Feminist Show, Washington Womens Arts Ctr, 80; two-person show, Collages & Masks, Studio Gallery, Washington, DC, 79; Women Artists Exhib, Converse Col, Spartanburg, SC, 80; solo exhib, Anne Hathaway Gallery, Folger Shakespeare Libr, Washington, DC, 83. *Pos:* Exec dir, Washington Womens Arts Ctr, 79-80; contrib ed, Women Artists News, New York, 80- *Teaching:* Instr painting & art hist, Dunbarton Col Holy Cross, 66-72; instr art, Prince George's Col, 72-77. *Awards:* First Prize Painting, Soc Washington Artists, 66; Best in Show, Hagerstown Mus, 67. *Bibliog:* Ruth Dean (auth), Networking from here to Copenhagen, Washington Star, 7/80; Pamela Kessler (auth), Masks, the myths and the magic, Washington Post, 10/81; Karen Alexis (auth), Nancy Cusick, illustrated woman series, Women Artists News, summer 83. *Mem:* Artists Equity Asn; Col Art Asn; Coalition Womens Art Orgn; Womens Caucus Art; Soc Washington Artists. *Media:* Collage, Oil. *Mailing Add:* 614 Laura Dr Falls Church VA 22046

CUTFORTH, ROGER
CONCEPTUAL ARTIST
b Lincolnshire, Eng, 1944. *Study:* Nottingham Col Art, Eng, 62-63; Ravensbourne Col Art, Eng, 63-66. *Work:* Walraf-Richartz Mus, Cologne, Ger; Metrop Mus Art, New York. *Exhib:* Mus Mod Art, New York, 70 & 80; Int Cult Ctr Mus, Antwerp, Belg, 75; Contemp Art Mus, Zagreb, Yugoslavia, 76; Vienna Int Biennale, Austria, 81. *Bibliog:* Valentin Tatransky (auth), article, Arts Mag, 78; Loredana Parmesani (auth), article, Segno, 79; Jean Fisher (auth), article, Aspects, 81. *Media:* Color. *Publ:* Auth, The Empire State Building, private publ, 69; auth, The Visual Book, private publ, 70; auth, Cleopatra's Needle/Eiffel Tower/Empire State Building, private publ, 71. *Dealer:* Hal Bromm Gallery 90 West Broadway New York NY 10007. *Mailing Add:* 330 East 33rd St 14K New York NY 10016

CUTHBERT, VIRGINIA
PAINTER
b West Newton, Pa, Aug 27, 08. *Study:* Syracuse Univ, BFA, 30; Acad Grande Chaumiere, Acad Colarossi, Paris, France & Chelsea Polytech Inst, Eng, Augusta-Hazard fel, 32; study with George Luks, 32; Univ Pittsburgh, 33-34; Carnegie Inst Technol, 34-35. *Work:* Albright-Knox Art Gallery, Buffalo, NY; Princeton Univ Art Mus, NJ; Rutgers Univ Libr Collection, NJ; Burchfield Ctr, Buffalo, New York; Everson Mus, Syracuse, NY; and others. *Comn:* Fortune Mag covers, 51 & 56; Southwestern Rev cover, 52; State Univ New York, Buffalo; Marine Midland Bank. *Exhib:* Metrop Mus Art, New York, 43, 44 & 50; 7 Whitney Mus Am Art Ann, New York, 44-53; South Western Pa Paintings, Greenburg; Retrospective, Burchfield Ctr, Buffalo, NY, 71; Members Gallery, Albright-Knox Gallery, Buffalo, NY. *Pos:* Art columnist, Buffalo Courier Express, 54-55. *Teaching:* Instr painting, Albright Art Sch, 42-54; instr painting, Univ Buffalo, 42-54; instr painting, State Univ NY Buffalo, 54-66. *Awards:* First Prize, Western NY Exhib, Albright-Knox Art Gallery, 46-52; Nat Inst Arts & Lett Grant for Painting, 54; Small Paintings USA, 74. *Media:* Oil, Watercolor; Drawing. *Publ:* Auth, spec art rev in, Buffalo Eve News, 54-56. *Dealer:* More-Rubing Gallery Bullalo New York. *Mailing Add:* 1240 Delaware Ave 114 Buffalo NY 14209

CUTLER, ETHEL ROSE
PAINTER, DESIGNER
b New York, NY, Mar 13, 15. *Study:* Hunter Col, BA; Columbia Univ, MA; Sch Prof Arts, cert advert & interior design; NY Univ; Univ Mo; Inst Design, Ill Inst Technol; Am Artist Sch; New Sch Social Res, with Yasuo Kuniyoshi & Alexei Brodovitch; Walden Univ, Inst Advan Studies, PhD. *Exhib:* New York City Center Gallery; Young American Artist Group, New York; Lynn Kottler Galleries, New York; Artist Equity Exhib, New York; East Galleries, NY Univ; and others. *Pos:* Design consult, artist & designer, Cutler Designs, 50- *Teaching:* Instr fine arts, Women's Col, Univ NC, Greensboro, 43-47;

instr, Adelphi Col, 47-50; asst prof interior design & related arts, Univ Mo-Columbia, 50-55; asst prof surface design, RI Sch Design, 55-59. *Awards:* Award for Boats, New York City Ctr Gallery, 59; Award for Brothers, Macy's Gallery; Grant, Metrop Mus Art, New York, 68; Grant, Walden Univ. *Mem:* Col Art Asn Am; Artists Equity Asn; Allied Bd Trade; Am Soc Interior Designers; Advertising Dir Club, Women in Design. *Media:* All media. *Res:* Techniques of William Morris and the arts and crafts movement of the Beaux Arts, the Bauhaus and other influences of the 19th century; the garden as an aesthetic experience, its influence on selected artists. *Mailing Add:* 230 E 88th St New York NY 10028

CUTLER, GRAYCE E
PAINTER, WRITER
b Salt Lake City, Utah. *Study:* Univ Utah; Art Students League, New York, with Kuniyoshi & Morris Kantor; New York Sch Design, cert; Hans Hofmann Sch Art, Provincetown, Mass; also with Eliot O'Hara. *Work:* Granite Schs Admin Art Collection, Salt Lake City; Pollard Collection, Greater Victoria Art Gallery, BC; Royal Family, Saudi Arabia; Utah State Arts Coun Collection. *Exhib:* Soc Western Artists Ann, De Young Mus, San Francisco, 66, 68 & 69; one-woman show, Rosicrucian Egyptian Mus & Gallery, San Jose, 68 & 71 & Kimball Art Ctr, 81; Watercolor W, Utah State Univ, Logan, 73; Metrop Mus of Art, New York, 78; Bertha Eccles Gallery, Ogden, Utah; Park City, Utah, 81; and others. *Awards:* First Prize, watercolor, Utah State Fair; Watercolor Award of Honor, Intermountain States Traveling Exhib, Utah State Inst Fine Arts; Watercolor Gold Award, Nat League Am Pen Women Biennial, Washington, DC; plus others. *Bibliog:* Articles in Rosicrucian Digest, 68 & 71 & Relief Soc Mag, 69. *Mem:* Soc Western Artists; Am Soc Interior Designers (pres, Utah Chap, 73-74); Nat League Am Pen Women; Asn Utah Artists; Burr Artists, NY; and others. *Media:* Watercolor, Oil. *Res:* Early writings and drawings as an art form. *Mailing Add:* 777 E South Temple St 8A Bonneville Towers Apts Salt Lake City UT 84102

CUTLER, RONNIE
PAINTER
b New York, NY, Jan 19, 24. *Study:* Columbia Univ Art Sch, 57; Brooklyn Mus Art, Art Sch, 58; Art Students League, 59-60. *Work:* Art Students League Collections, New York. *Exhib:* Artists of Manhattan, Whitney Mus, New York, 54; 54th Ann Competition, Delgado Mus, New Orleans, La, 55; 5th Ann Competition, Berkshire Mus, Pittsfield, Mass, 56; Alumni Show, Brooklyn Mus, New York, 56 & 58; Casein Soc, Riverside Mus, New York, 57; Audubon Artists, Nat Acad Design, New York, 58; one-woman show, Bodley Gallery, New York, 79. *Awards:* One-woman show, City Ctr, 55; Alumni Purchase Award, Art Students League, 60; Best of Show, Southern Berkshire Community Arts Coun, 79 & 80. *Media:* Oil. *Mailing Add:* 175 W 12th St New York NY 10011

CUTLER-SHAW, JOYCE
CONCEPTUAL ARTIST, EDUCATOR
b Detroit, Mich. *Study:* New York Univ, BA, 53; Columbia Univ, 53-54; Univ Calif, San Diego, MFA, 72. *Work:* Applied Sci Bldg, Univ Calif, San Diego; Univ Calif, Santa Barbara. *Comn:* Namewall for Los Angeles Int Airport, Los Angeles Bd Airport Commissioners, Calif, 74; charity namewall for New Orleans Charity Hospital, New Orleans Downtown Development District, La, 80. *Exhib:* Three Directions, Newport Harbor Art Mus, Calif, 76; Am Narrative Art, Contemp Art Mus, Houston, Tex, 77; Un Espace Parle, Galerie Gaetan, Geneva, Switzerland, 78; Other Child Book, Palace of Culture and Sci, Warsaw, Poland, 79; Arteder 82, Bilboa, Spain, 82. *Pos:* Dir, Art & Artists: Video/Audio Archive, 74-; TV interviewer/project dir, Art & Artists, KPBS-TV, San Diego, Calif, 79-80; chairwoman, Public Art Advisory Coun, San Diego, Calif, 78. *Teaching:* Vis fac contemp art, San Diego State Univ, Calif, 78-80; vis fac contemp art, Univ Calif, Irvine, 79-80. *Awards:* Project Patronage, Survival/Evolution, UNESCO, 79-80; Art & Artists Project Grant, San Diego State Univ Art Coun, 79-80; Nat Endowment Arts Media Grant, Video Portrait, 81-82. *Bibliog:* Moira Roth (auth), An Interview with Joyce Cutler-Shaw, Univ Southern Calif, 76; Lucy Lippard (auth), Three Directions, Newport Harbor Mus, 76; M Vogel (auth), Die Dame und der Vogel, Vaterland Luzern, Switzerland, 10/4/79. *Mem:* Col Art Asn; Woman's Caucus Arts; Landmark Art Projects (founding mem & secy, 78-). *Media:* Multi-Media. *Publ:* Auth, We The People: Proposal for an Artwork, self publ, 75; auth, Survival--Evolution Proposal for a Public Art Project, self publ, 77; contribr, The Lady and the Bird Odyssey, Sun & Moon, 77; auth, The Lady and the Bird, self publ, 77-79; auth, Name Pictures, Remont, Warsaw, Poland, 79. *Mailing Add:* 7245 Rue De Roark La Jolla CA 92037

CUTTLER, CHARLES DAVID
HISTORIAN, WRITER
b Cleveland, Ohio, Apr 8, 13. *Study:* Ohio State Univ, BFA & MA; Inst Art & Archeol, Paris, France; Univ Bruxelles; Inst Fine Arts, NY Univ, PhD. *Exhib:* Cleveland May Show, Ohio, 35-36; Philadelphia Watercolor Ann, Pa, 37. *Teaching:* Asst instr art hist, Ohio State Univ, 35-37; from instr to asst prof art hist, Mich State Univ, 47-57; from assoc prof to prof, Univ Iowa, 57-83, res prof, 65-75, emer, 83-; guest lectr, Sem Europ Art & Civilisation Belg, Ghent, summer 69. *Awards:* Ann Watercolor Competition Award, Ohio State Univ, 35; CRB Fel, Brussels, 53-54; Fulbright-Hays Sr Fel, 65-66. *Mem:* Col Art Asn Am; founding mem Midwest Art Hist Soc; Renaissance Soc Am; Medieval Acad Am; Int Ctr Medieval Art. *Res:* Netherlandish and German art of the 14th to 16th centuries; art of Hieronymus Bosch. *Publ:* Auth, Some Grünewald sources, Art Quart, 56; auth, Lisbon Temptation of St Anthony by Jerome Bosch, Art Bulletin, 57; auth, Northern painting, from Pucelle to Bruegel, XIVth, XVth & XVIth Centuries, 68; auth, Bosch & the Narrenschiff: A problem in relationships, Art Bulletin, 69; auth, Two aspects of Bosch's Hell imagery, Miscellanea F Lyna (Scriptorium, 23), 69. *Mailing Add:* 1691 Ridge Rd Iowa City IA 52240

CYRIL, R
PAINTER, PRINTMAKER
b New York, NY. *Study:* Art Students League; New Sch Social Res; NY Univ; Sorbonne, Inst Art & Archeol, Paris, Fulbright fel; and with Jacques Villon & S W Hayter. *Work:* Metrop Mus, New York; Smithsonian Inst; Fogg Art Mus; Nat Gallery Art; Victoria and Albert Mus, London; and others. *Exhib:* Deitsch Gallery, New York; Von Drecjan Gallery, New York; Circle & Squary Gal, New York; Victoria & Albert Mus, London; La Guilde de la Gravure, Paris; Biblioteque Nat, Paris; plus 50 one-man shows, US & Europe; many group shows. *Teaching:* Instr painting, graphics, design & crafts, Adelphi Univ, 63-66. *Awards:* First Prize Purchase Award, Dallas Mus Art, Tex; First Prize, Philadelphia Mus; First Prize, Delgado Mus, New Orleans. *Media:* Oil, Watercolor; Acrylic, Multi Media. *Mailing Add:* 800 West End Ave New York NY 10025

CZARNIECKI, M J, III
MUSEUM DIRECTOR, PHOTOGRAPHER
b San Francisco, Calif, May 28, 48. *Study:* Xaverius Col, Antwerp, Belg, dipl, 67; Wabash Col, Ind, BA, 71; Art Inst Chicago, 71-72; Columbia Col, Chicago, 73. *Collections Arranged:* Masters of Twentieth Century Photography (co-cur), Ringling Mus, 76; Before Its Too Late: The Photography of Edward S Curtiss (cur, catalog), 78 & Dance Image: A Tribute to Serge Diaghilev (dir), 79, Miss Mus Art; Southern Realism (dir), Miss Mus Art/Southern Arts Fedn, 78-81; Russian Stage Designs: Scenic Innovation, 1900-1930, Miss Mus Art, 82. *Pos:* Dir, Miss Mus Art, 76-; consult, Nat Endowment Arts & Inst Mus Services, 78- *Teaching:* Instr photog, Wabash Col, Ind, 70-71; lectr hist photog, Art Inst Chicago, 72-74; dir educ, Ringling Mus Art, 74-76; field fac, Goddard Col, Vermont, 79-80. *Mem:* Miss Mus Asn (vpres, 78-81); Miss Inst Arts & Letters (founding dir, 79-); Am Asn Mus; Int Coun Mus; Art Mus Assoc. *Media:* Photography. *Mailing Add:* PO Box 1330 Pascagoula at Lamar Jackson MS 39205

CZESTOCHOWSKI, JOSEPH STEPHEN
MUSEUM DIRECTOR
b Brooklyn, NY, Aug 8, 50. *Study:* Univ Ill, Champaign-Urbana, BA, 71, MA, 73; Jagiellonian Univ, Cracow, Poland, dipl, 71. *Collections Arranged:* A Question of Regionalism, American Collections, Brooks Mem Art Gallery, Memphis, Tenn, 75; Arthur B Davies Retrospective, M Knoedler & Co, Inc, New York, 75; Polish Graphic Art & Design, Baltimore, 78; Charles Burchfield - Charles Rand Penney Collection, Mem Art Gallery, Rochester, 78; Marvin D Cone--Retrospective, Cedar Rapids Mus Art, 80; Atelier 17-- New Directions, Cedar Rapids Mus Art, 81; Mauricio Lasansky, Cedar Rapids Mus Art, 82; Cedar Rapids Art Asn 1905-1981 Permanent Collection Handbook, 83. *Pos:* Student asst, Krannert Art Mus, Univ Ill, 72; art ed, Perspectives Inc, Washington, DC, 72-; cur collections, Brooks Mem Art Gallery, Memphis, Tenn, 73-75; dir, Decker Gallery, Md Inst, Col Art, 75-78; exec dir, Cedar Rapids Mus Art, 78- *Awards:* Fel Comt Relig & Art in Am, 76; Smithsonian Inst Foreign Currency Prog Res Award, 76-; Nat Endowment Arts, 1A Arts Coun, 78- *Mem:* Am Asn Mus; Am Asn Art Mus Dir; Col Art Asn; Int Coun Mus; Am Coun Arts. *Res:* Nineteenth & early twentieth century American paintings, drawings and prints; contemporary American painters and printmakers; Polish art. *Publ:* Auth, Hassam Prints, Dover, 80; auth, John Stewart Curry & Grant Wood, Univ Mo, 81; auth, Am Landscape Tradition, E P Dutton, 82; auth, Graphics Catalogue Raisonne Arthur B Davies, Am Art J, 83; auth, Gerald Geerlings Graphics Catalogue, Cedar Rapids Mus Art, 83. *Mailing Add:* Cedar Rapids Museum Art 324 Third St SE Cedar Rapids IA 52401

CZIMBALMOS, MAGDOLNA PAAL
PAINTER, INSTRUCTOR
b Esztergom, Hungary. *Study:* Art Schs, Hungary & Ger. *Work:* Staten Island Mus, NY; Mus Int Inst, Detroit; Carnegie Inst Int Centennial, NY; Nat Gallery Budapest, Hungary; City Mus, Esztergom, Hungary. *Comn:* Portraits, Most Rev Daniel Ivancho & Nicholas Elko, Bishops, Msgr Ernest Dunda, Jacqueline Kennedy & family of Congressman John M Murphy, NY. *Exhib:* One-man shows, UN Plaza, New York, Pulitzer Gallery, New York, Univ Del, 80 & Le Salon, Paris & Monaco; and other group and one-man exhibs in US and abroad. *Pos:* Founder & dir, Hungarian Doll & Handicraft Factory, Reichenbach, Bavaria, formerly. *Teaching:* Czimbalmos Pvt Art Sch, 65- *Awards:* Staten Island Mus Gold Medal, 58, 62, 63, 66 & 69; Italian Cult Award, 67; Szinnyei Merse Gold Medal, New York, 71. *Mem:* Pannonia World Orgn of Hungarian Artists (dir, currently); Staten Island Mus (dir exec bd, currently). *Mailing Add:* Czimbalmos Art Studio 31 Bayview Pl Ward Hill Staten Island NY 10304

CZIMBALMOS, SZABO KALMAN
PAINTER, EDUCATOR
b Esztergom, Hungary, 1914. *Study:* Royal Hungarian Acad Fine Arts, Budapest, grad, 36; also with J Haranghy & E Domanowsky, Vienna, Prague, Munich, Paris, London & Rome. *Work:* Nat Gallery Budapest; City Mus Esztergom, Hungary; Staten Island Mus, NY; Staten Island Community Col. *Comn:* Murals 32 churches US; Hungarian Govt & pvt owners. *Exhib:* Pulitzer Art Gallery, NY; Int Inst, Detroit; Univ Del, 80; Staten Island Mus; Le Salon, Paris; one-man shows & group exhibs in Hungary, Germany, France & Monaco. *Pos:* Owner, Czimbalmos Art Studio, Esztergom, 37-38, studio, Reichenbach, Ger, 45-49 & Staten Island, NY, 50-; art dir & partner, Hungarian Doll & Handcraft Factory, Reichenbach, formerly; art dir, Hungarian Relief, New York, 50; dir, Czimbalmos Pvt Art Sch, 55- *Awards:* Hungarian Art Award, Budapest, 34; Staten Island Mus Prize, 62, 64, 67 & 71; St Stephan Gold Medal, Pannonia Exhib, 71. *Mem:* Bavaryan Fine Art Soc; Staten Island Mus Art (vpres art sect, 61-62, pres, 63-64, exec bd, 63-75); Pannonia World Orgn Hungarian Artists (chmn bd dirs, 67-). *Media:* All. *Mailing Add:* Czimbalmos Art Studio 31 Bayview Pl Ward Hill Staten Island NY 10304

CZUMA, STANISLAW J
HISTORIAN, CURATOR

b Warsaw, Poland, Oct 26, 35; US citizen. *Study:* Jagiellonian Univ, BA & MA; Paderewski Found Scholar studies in India, 58-60; Nat Defense Foreign Lang Fel studies in India, 65-67; Banaras Hindu Univ, with Vasudeva S Agrawala; Univ Calcutta, with S K Saraswati; Sorbonne, with Louis Renou; Univ Mich, with Walter Spink, PhD, 68. *Collections Arranged:* Cambodian Art, Asian House Gallery, New York (with catalog), 69; Permanent Indian Gallery, Brooklyn Mus; Indian Art from the George P Bickford Collection, Cleveland Mus (with catalog), 75. *Pos:* Ford Found curatorial trainee, Cleveland Mus, 68-70; cur Oriental art, Brooklyn Mus, 70-72; cur Indian art, Cleveland Mus, 72- *Teaching:* Res asst Oriental art, Univ Mich, Ann Arbor, 62-64; adj prof, Case Western Reserve Univ. *Mem:* Asn Asian Studies; Asia Soc. *Res:* Art of India and Southeast Asia, especially Kushan, Gupta and Medieval India. *Publ:* Auth, Gupta style bronze Buddha, 2/70, A masterpiece of early Cambodian sculpture, 4/74, Mathura sculpture in the Cleveland Mus Collection, 3/77 & Mon-Dvaravati Buddha, 9/80, Bulletin Cleveland Mus. *Mailing Add:* Oriental Dept Cleveland Mus East Blvd Cleveland OH 44106

D

DABLOW, DEAN CLINT
PHOTOGRAPHER

b Superior, Wis, Aug 26, 46. *Study:* Univ Wis, Stevens Point, BS(educ), 69; Univ Iowa, MA, 72, MFA, 74. *Work:* New Orleans Mus Art, La; Kansas City Art Inst, Mo; Mus Art, Univ Okla; US Information Agency Am Embassies Int; Baltimore Mus Art. *Exhib:* 19 Portfolios, Milwaukee Art Ctr, Wis, 72; Contemporary Photography, Sheldon Mem Mus, Lincoln, Nebr, 72; one-man shows, Sioux City Art Ctr, Iowa, 79 & Project Art Ctr, Cambridge, Mass, 82; Photography in Louisiana 1900-1980, New Orleans Mus Art, 80; US Biennial, Mus Art, Univ Okla, 82; Photographic Illusion, Ithaca Col, NY, 82; and others. *Teaching:* Assoc prof photog, La Tech Univ, Ruston, 76- *Awards:* Purchase Award, US Biennial, Univ Okla, 82; Artist Fel Grant Color Photog, La Arts Coun, 82; Purchase Award, 16th Ann Prints, Drawings & Crafts, Ark Art Ctr, 83. *Mem:* Soc Photog Educ; Friends of Photog. *Publ:* Contribr, Creative Camera International Yearbook, Coo Press, London, 77; contribr, New Photographics/78 (cover), Cent Wash State Col, 78; contribr, Camera, C J Bucher Ltd, Lucerne, Switzerland, 9/81. *Dealer:* Carol Loewenstern Gallery 6135 Kirby Houston TX 77005. *Mailing Add:* 1202 Greenwood Dr Ruston LA 71270

DA CUNHA, JULIO
EDUCATOR, PAINTER

b Colombia, South Am, Mar 18, 29; US citizen. *Study:* Nat Univ Bogota, Colombia; Univ Fla, Gainesville, BA(archit), 52; Cranbrook Acad Art, Bloomfield Hills, Mich, MFA, 54. *Work:* Bloomsburg State Col, Pa. *Exhib:* Ann Regional Exhib, Del Art Mus, Wilmington, 56- & Univ Del, 61-; Four Del Artists, Del Art Mus, 64; Am Painters in Paris Bicentennial Exhib, France, 76; retrospectives, Haas Gallery, Bloomsburg State Col, Pa, 76 & Del Art Mus, 77. *Teaching:* Prof art, Univ Del, 56- *Awards:* Purchase Award, Univ Del, 63 & Del Art Mus, 62. *Bibliog:* A Profile: J Da Cunha, 71 & Clint Collins (auth), Paradoxes of J Da Cunha, 77, Del Today Mag. *Media:* Acrylic, Charcoal. *Dealer:* Pleiades Gallery 152 Wooster St New York NY 10012. *Mailing Add:* PO Box 893 Newark DE 19711

D'AGOSTINO, PETER PASQUALE
VIDEO ARTIST, EDUCATOR

b New York, NY, July 29, 45. *Study:* High Sch of Art & Design, New York, dipl, 63; Acad of Fine Arts, Italy, 65; Sch of Visual Arts, New York, BFA, 68; San Francisco State Univ, MA, 75. *Work:* San Francisco Mus Mod Art; Long Beach Mus Art, Calif; Oakland Mus, Archives of Calif Art, Calif Col Arts & Crafts, Oakland; San Francisco Pub Libr, Calif Resource Proj. *Comn:* Passages: Ft Point, Floating Mus, San Francisco, 76; Performances: Angel Island, San Francisco Mus Mod Art, 77; Alpha Week of Int Performances, Mus Mod Art, Bologna, Italy, 77; San Francisco BART, San Francisco Mus Mod Art, 78; DC Metro, Washington Proj for Art, 79. *Exhib:* Solo exhibs, Mus Mod Art, San Francisco, 77, Mus Mod Art, New York, 79, Kitchen Ctr Video, Music & Dance, New York, 82 & Franklin Furnace, New York, 83; Comings & Goings, Mus Mod Art, New York & Contemp Arts Ctr, Cincinnati, 79; Time/Space/Sound: 1970's, San Francisco Mus Mod Art, 80; 1981 Biennial, Whitney Mus Am Art; Paris Biennale, 82; New American Video, Kunsthaus Zurich, Switz, 83; Art Video: Perspectives and Retrospectives, Palais Beaux Arts, Belg, 83. *Teaching:* Instr art, Lone Mountain Col, San Francisco, 73-76; instr, San Francisco Art Inst, 76-77; asst prof art & art hist, Wright State Univ, Dayton, Ohio, 77-80; vis prof art, Univ NC, Chapel Hill, 82; asst prof commun, Temple Univ, 82-; fel, Ctr Advan Visual Studies, Mass Inst Technol, 83- *Awards:* Ohio Arts Coun Fel, 80; NY State Coun Arts Grant, 81; Pa Arts Coun Fel, 82. *Bibliog:* Kristine Stiles (auth), Trans-Europ Express/Expressed, 77; Rae Blakeney (auth), Syntactics and the ongoing work of Peter D'Agostino, Midwest Art, 11/77; Hal Fischer (auth), Cinematic structures, Afterimage, Summer 78. *Mem:* Col Art Asn Am; Int Network for Arts. *Media:* Video, Film Photography. *Publ:* Contribr, Photography and Language, 76 & co-ed, Photography: The Problematic Model, 80, NFS Press; ed, Alpha, Trans, Chung: Semiotics, Film and Interpretation, Wright State Univ Press, 78; contribr, Proposal for QUBE, Los Angeles Inst of Contemp Art J, 79. *Mailing Add:* Art Dept Mass Inst Technol 77 Massachusetts Ave Cambridge MA 02139

DAGYS, JACOB
SCULPTOR

b Lithuania, Dec 16, 05; Can citizen. *Study:* Kaunas Art Sch, Lithuania. *Work:* Balzekas Mus, Chicago, Ill; Ciurlionis Gallery, Chicago. *Comn:* Crucifix, sacre coeur & others, St Monicas Church, Toronto, Ont, 58; St Anthony & others, Church Resurrection, Toronto, 67, Chicago, 73 & Cleveland, 77; Christ, the Teacher, Church Saviour, Cincinnati, 82. *Exhib:* Sculptors Soc Can Traveling Exhib, Toronto, London, Brussels & Paris, 78; one-man show, Hamilton, Can, 81. *Teaching:* Instr art, Raseiniai High Sch, Lithuania, 32-44. *Bibliog:* Dagy's Sculptures & Paintings, Am Lithuanian Art Asn, 67. *Mem:* Sculptor Soc Can. *Media:* Wood, Bronze. *Publ:* Articles about art for Lithuanian Press. *Mailing Add:* 78 Chelsea Ave Toronto ON M6P 1C2 Canada

DAHILL, THOMAS HENRY, JR
PAINTER, EDUCATOR

b Cambridge, Mass, June 22, 25. *Study:* Tufts Col, BS, 49; Harvard Univ, summer 53; Sch Mus Fine Arts, Boston, dipl, 53, cert, 54; Skowhegan Sch Painting & Sculpture; Am Acad in Rome, fel, 55-57; Max Beckmann Gesellschaft, Murnau, Ger, resident, 56; Emerson Col, AM, 67. *Comn:* Mural, Unitarian Church, Brockton, Mass, 58; film strips, ser of paintings on Old & New Testaments, 61-62; film strip, life of George Washington Carver, 61; portrait, Dr Richard D Pierce, 74. *Exhib:* Boston Art Festival, 55, 56 & 63; Archit League, NY, 58; Int Bienale Relig Art, Salzburg, Austria, 58-59; Emerson Col, 64 & 67; Drawings of N Africa exhibited through Mus Fine Arts Boston to galleries of New Eng Prep Schs, 67-69; plus others. *Teaching:* Lectr gen art hist & contemp use of art in churches; instr hist art, Tufts Univ, 54-55 & 60-65; instr dept drawing, Sch Mus Fine Arts, Boston, 58-71; prof fine arts & chmn dept, Emerson Col, 67-, summer sch abroad, Europe, Africa & Asia, 67-82; guest, Minister of Cult, Moscow, USSR, summer 74. *Awards:* Abbey Mem Fel to Am Acad in Rome, 55-57. *Mem:* MacDowell Colonists; Alumni Asn, Sch Mus Fine Arts, Boston; Gibson House Victorian Mus; Soc Fel Am Acad in Rome. *Media:* Acrylic on Canvas. *Mailing Add:* 223 Broadway Arlington MA 02174

DAHLBERG, EDWIN LENNART
PAINTER

b Beloit, Wis, Sept 20, 01. *Study:* Art Inst Chicago, grad, John Quincy Adams fel. *Work:* Charles & Emma Frye Mus, Seattle, Wash; Wesleyan Univ. *Exhib:* Am Watercolor Soc Ann, 54-; Nat Acad Design; Pa Acad Fine Arts, 54-61; Art Inst Chicago, 54-61; Royal Soc Watercolor Painters, London, Eng, 66. *Awards:* Medal of Merit for Best in Show for All Media, Knickerbocker Artists, 70; Gold Medal of Hon, Am Watercolor Soc, 72; Gold Medal of Hon for Watercolor, Hudson Valley Art Asn, 74. *Bibliog:* Edwin L Dahlberg seeks mood in a motif, Am Artist, 2/65; Norman Kent (auth), 100 Watercolor Techniques, Watson-Guptill, 68; Edwin L Dahlberg Paints a Watercolor on Location (film), Electrographic Corp Am, 71. *Mem:* Am Watercolor Soc (bd dirs, 65-68); Allied Artists Am (bd dirs, 67-71); Hudson Valley Art Asn; Knickerbocker Artists; assoc Nat Acad Design. *Media:* Transparent Watercolors. *Mailing Add:* 6 South Boulevard Nyack NY 10960

DAILEY, CHUCK (CHARLES ANDREW)
MUSEOLOGIST, PAINTER

b Golden, Colo, May 25, 35. *Study:* Univ Colo, BA(art), 61; study in Western Europe, 62-63. *Work:* Mus NMex Permanent Collection, Santa Fe; Vincent Price Collection, Hollywood, Calif. *Exhib:* Fiesta Biennial, 64 & 65 & Southwest Biennial, 68, Mus NMex; NMex State Fair, Albuquerque, 68; one-man show, Gallery 5, Santa Fe, 64. *Collections Arranged:* Afro-Arabic World, 66-67, New Mexican Santero, 70-71 & World of Folk Costume, 71-72, Museum International Folk Art, Three Culture-Sculpture Exhibition & Rain Cloud Callers (Indian art), Fine Arts Mus & Spanish Endure (Spanish hist in Southwest), Palace of Governors, Mus NMex; Indian Arts & Crafts, J F Kennedy Ctr Performing Arts, Washington, DC, 73; One with the Earth traveling exhib, US & Can, 76- *Pos:* Mus preparator, Univ Colo Mus, 59-61; exhibs tech, Mus Northern Ariz, Flagstaff, 62-63; cur-in-charge exhib div, Mus NMex, 64-71; mus workshop presentations, NMex, Alaska, Okla, Ariz & Wash & Smithsonian Inst. *Teaching:* Mus training dir, Inst Am Indian Arts, Santa Fe, 71- *Bibliog:* Catherine Wenzell (auth), Artists of Santa Fe, privately publ, 68. *Mem:* NMex Asn Mus; Am Indian Mus Asn; Am Asn Mus; Midwest Mus Asn; Far West Mus Asn. *Media:* Acrylic. *Publ:* Auth, Creating a Crowd, NMex Asn Mus, 72; auth, Bringing a unique perspective to museum work, Mus News, 5-6/77; auth, A selection of contemporary art by Native Americans from the Museum of the Institute of American Indian Arts, Ohio Univ Press, 81; auth, Major influences in the development of 20th century Native American art, 82 & Many ways of seeing: The anniversary of the Institute of American Indian Arts, 83, IAIA Press. *Mailing Add:* 412 Sosaya Lane Santa Fe NM 87501

DAILEY, DAN (DANIEL OWEN)
SCULPTOR, DESIGNER

b Philadelphia, Pa, Feb 4, 47. *Study:* Philadelphia Col Art, BFA(glass); RI Sch Design, MFA(glass). *Work:* Corning Mus of Glass, NY; Metrop Mus Art, New York; Smithsonian Mus, Washington DC; Nat Gallery Victoria, Melbourne, Australia; Nat Mus Mod Art, Kyoto, Japan. *Comn:* Glass window (8ft x 8ft), Lovett & Linder Co, Providence, RI, 72; illum family portraits & glass & bronze sculptures, comn by the Otto Piene family, Cambridge, Mass, 78; glass and aluminum figurative wall relief, comn by Ron Abramson, Rockville, Md, 82; glass and aluminum figurative wall relief, comn by Michael Brillson, Chicago, 83. *Exhib:* One-man shows, Mass Inst Technol Gallery, 75 & 77, Theo Portnoy Gallery, New York, 77 & 79-82, Habatat Galleries, Detroit, Mich, 81 & 83; New Glass, Corning Mus Glass, NY, 79; Nat Mus

Mod Art, Tokyo, Kyoto, Japan, 81; Hokkaido Mus Mod Art, Sapporo, Japan, 82; Mus Arts Decoratifs, Paris, 82. *Pos:* Guest designer, Fabrica Venini, Murano, Venice, Italy, 72-73; designer & freelance artist, Cristallerie Daum, Nancy, France, 77- & Steuben Glass, New York, 82. *Teaching:* Teaching fel glass, RI Sch Design, Providence, 70-72; assoc prof glass, Mass Col Art, Boston, 73-, chmn three-dimensional fine arts dept, 74-79, dir glass prog, 74-; res fel sculpture & glass, Mass Inst Technol, 75-80; Pilchuck School, Stanwood, Wash, 77- *Awards:* Fulbright-Hays Grant as Designer, Fabrica Venini, Murano, Italy, 72-73; Nat Endowment for the Arts Fel, 79; Mass Coun Arts Fel, 80. *Bibliog:* Cover, feature article, ArtCraft, 6-7/80; feature article, American Craft, 2-3/81; feature, Art Express, 5-6/81. *Mem:* Glass Art Soc Am (mem bd dirs, pres, chmn bd, 80, 81-82). *Media:* Glass, Metal. *Dealer:* Kurland/Summers Gallery 8742 A Melrose Ave Los Angeles CA 90069; Betsy Rosenfeld Gallery 212 W Superior Chicago IL 60610. *Mailing Add:* 122 Market St Amesbury MA 01913

DAILEY, JOSEPH CHARLES See Jocda

DAILEY, MICHAEL DENNIS
PAINTER, EDUCATOR
b Des Moines, Iowa, Aug 2, 38. *Study:* Univ Iowa, BA & MFA. *Work:* Smithsonian Inst, Washington, DC; Munic Gallery Mod Art, Dublin, Ireland; Seattle Art Mus, Wash; Mercyhurst Col, Erie, Pa; Mus of Mod Art, New York. *Exhib:* Art Across Am, San Francisco Mus Art, 65; Ultimate Concerns Drawing Exhib, Ohio Univ, Athens, 65; one-man shows, Tacoma Art Mus, Wash, 66 & 75, Fountain Gallery, Portland, 71, 73, 77 & 81, William Sawyer Gallery, San Francisco, 72, 74, 76 & 82; Drawings USA, St Paul Art Ctr, Minn, 66 & 68; 73rd Western Ann, Denver Art Mus, Colo, 71; Art of the Pacific Northwest, Smithsonian Inst, 74. *Teaching:* Prof drawing & painting, Univ Wash, 63- *Awards:* Purchase Award, Mercyhurst Nat Graphics Exhib, Erie, Pa, 65; First Pl Award in Painting, Wash State Ann Art Exhib, 67; Northwest Watercolor Soc Award, 30th Ann Northwest Watercolor Exhib, Seattle Art Mus, 70. *Media:* Oil, Watercolor. *Mailing Add:* 5805 17th Ave NE Seattle WA 98105

DAILEY, VICTORIA KEILUS
DEALER
b Los Angeles, Calif, Jan 21, 48. *Study:* Univ Calif, Los Angeles, BA, 70. *Collections Arranged:* Chemical Printing: The Invention of Lithography (auth, catalog), 80; The Poltroon Press: 10th Anniversary Retrospective (auth, catalog), 80; Joby Baker: Prints, Drawings Monotypes (auth, catalog), 80; Auguste Lepere Woodengravings (auth, catalog), 81; Terry De Lapp: Recent Still Life Paintings, 81. *Mem:* Printing Historical Soc; Bibliographical Soc Am; Rounce and Coffin Club, Los Angeles; Graphic Arts Coun; Antiquarian Booksellers Asn Am (bd govs, 80-). *Specialty:* 19th century prints and drawings, mainly French and English; art and illustrated books. *Publ:* Ed, Frijoles Canyon Pictographs, Pegacycle Press, 81; ed, Henri Riviere, Peregrine Smith, 83. *Mailing Add:* 8216 Melrose Ave Los Angeles CA 90046

DAILY, EVELYNNE MESS
PAINTER, PRINTMAKER
b Indianapolis, Ind, Jan 8, 03. *Study:* Herron Sch Art, Ind Univ; Art Inst Chicago; Butler Univ; Ecole Beaux Arts, Fontainebleau, France, dipl; Wayman Adams Sch Portrait Painting, New York; also Bauhaus with Moholy-Nagy, Chicago; Colo State Christian Col, Hon PhD, 73. *Work:* Indianapolis Mus Art; Ft Wayne Mus; Richmond Art Asn; Libr Cong, Washington, DC; Philadelphia Mus Art. *Exhib:* Nat Acad Design, New York; Pa Acad Fine Arts; Brooklyn Mus, NY; Libr Cong Exhib Prints; Los Angeles Mus. *Teaching:* Instr drawing & painting, pub & pvt schs, Indianapolis, 40-60; instr painting & printmaking, Oxbow Acres Summer Art Sch, Brown Co, Ind, 64-80. *Awards:* P R Mallory Co Prize for Lithograph, 75; United Farm Bur Insurance Co Prize for Painting, 77; Honorable Mention, Ind State Art Exhibit, 80. *Mem:* Nat Soc Arts & Lett; Ind Artists Club; Nat League Am Pen Women Inc; Hoosier Salon; Brown Co Art Gallery Asn Inc. *Mailing Add:* 6237 Central Ave Indianapolis IN 46220

DALE, WILLIAM SCOTT ABELL
HISTORIAN, EDUCATOR
b Toronto, Ont, Sept 18, 21. *Study:* Univ Toronto, BA & MA; Harvard Univ, PhD. *Pos:* Res cur, Nat Gallery Can, Ottawa, Ont, 51-57; cur, Art Gallery Toronto, 57-59; dir, Vancouver Art Gallery, BC, 59-61; asst dir, Nat Gallery Can, 61-66, dep dir, 66-67. *Teaching:* Prof art hist, Univ Western Ont, 67- *Mem:* Col Art Asn Am; Mediaeval Acad Am; Royal Soc Arts; Int Ctr Medieval Art. *Res:* Romanesque ivories; sculptures of Chartres West; Exeter Cathedral. *Publ:* Contribr, Arts in Canada, 58; contribr, Oxford companion to art, 70; contribr, The British Museum Yearbook, 76. *Mailing Add:* Dept of Visual Arts Univ of Western Ontario London ON N6A 5B7 Canada

D'ALESSIO, GREGORY
CARTOONIST, ILLUSTRATOR
b New York, NY, Sept 25, 04. *Study:* Art Students League, New York, with Walter Jack Duncan, Kimon Nikolaides & George Bridgman. *Work:* Syracuse Univ, NY; Univ Ill. *Exhib:* Metrop Mus of Art, New York; Gallery of Mod Art, New York; Mus of the City of New York. *Pos:* Vpres, Art Students League, New York, 37-44; syndicated cartoonist, These Women, 40-62. *Teaching:* Instr drawing, anat & compos, Art Students League, New York, 62- *Awards:* Am Soc Graphic Arts Award, 51; Reuben Award, Nat Cartoonists Soc, 61. *Mem:* Life mem Art Students League New York; life mem Soc Illusr New York; Nat Cartoonists Soc, New York (secy, 46-48); Soc Classic Guitar (vpres, co-ed, illusr & writer, Guitar Rev, 22 yrs). *Media:* Multimedia. *Publ:* Cartoonist & illusr, New Yorker, Esquire, Saturday Evening Post, Colliers, Look & many others. *Mailing Add:* Art Students League 215 W 57th St New York NY 10019

D'ALESSIO, HILDA TERRY See Terry, Hilda

DALEY, WILLIAM P
CERAMIST, SCULPTOR
b Hastings-on-Hudson, NY, Mar 7, 25. *Study:* Mass Col Art, BS; Columbia Univ Teachers Col, MA. *Work:* St Louis Mus, Mo; Everson Mus Art, Syracuse; Dienst Beeldende Kunst, Kruithuis, Neth. *Comn:* Ceramic screen abacus, comn by Int Bus Machines Corp, Seattle World's Fair, 61; ceramic & copper modular wall, SAfrican Airlines, New York, 70; ceramic wall, Fairfield Maxwell Corp, New York, 72; ceramic screen (10ft x 20ft), Ritz Theatre, Philadelphia, 78. *Exhib:* Nat Ceramic Exhib, Everson Mus, Syracuse, NY, 62 & 68; Philadelphia: Three Centuries of Am Art, Philadelphia Mus Art, 76; solo exhib, Ctr Contemp Clay, Univ Iowa, 81 & Helen Drutt Gallery, Philadelphia, 83; A Century of Ceramics in the United States, Everson Mus, Syracuse & Renwick-Smithsonian, DC; retrospective, Selected Works 1954-1982, Mass Col Art. *Pos:* Mem adv bd, Clay Studio, Philadelphia & NY State Col Ceramics, 80- *Teaching:* Prof ceramics & design, Philadelphia Col Art, 57-, chmn crafts dept, 66-69; guest prof ceramics, Univ NMex, 72. *Awards:* Purchase Awards, Am Wing, Philadelphia Mus Art, 76 & Soup Toureen 1976, Campbell Mus, 76; Nat Endowment Arts Grant, 77; Distinguished Achievement Arts Award, Mass Col Art, 80. *Bibliog:* Article, Am Crafts Mag, 12/80-1/81. *Mem:* Hon life mem Nat Coun Educ Ceramic Arts. *Publ:* Auth, Notes on sources: A presentation, Nat Coun Educ Ceramic Arts J, Vol 1, No 1, 80; auth, On drawing, Am Ceramics, Vol 1, No 1, 82; auth, The geometry of residence, Nat Coun Educ Ceramic Arts J, Vol 4, 83. *Dealer:* Drutt Gallery 305 Cherry St Philadelphia PA 19106. *Mailing Add:* 307 Ashbourne Rd Elkins Park PA 19117

DAL FABBRO, MARIO
SCULPTOR, WRITER
b Cappella Maggiore, Italy, Oct 6, 13; US citizen. *Study:* Inst Indust Art, Venice, Italy; Magistero Art, Venice. *Work:* Museu Arte Sao Paulo, Brazil; Mus Art, Sci & Indust, Bridgeport, Conn; Allentown Art Mus, Pa; Museo Civico Revoltella Trieste, Italy. *Exhib:* One-man shows, Allentown Art Mus, Pa, 72 & Mus Art, Sci & Indust, Bridgeport, 78; New Eng Exhib, Silvermine Art Ctr, 77; Stamford Mus & Nature Ctr, 77; Mus Art Sci & Indust, 77. *Awards:* First Prize, Woodmere Art Gallery, Philadelphia, 74; First Prize Sculpture, Stamford Mus, Conn, 81; Gold Medal, Nat Art Exhib, Polpet-Boito Belluno, Italy, 81. *Mem:* Int Acad Tommaso Campanella, Rome, Italy; Silvermine Guild Artists. *Media:* Wood. *Publ:* Auth, Costruzione e funzionalita' del mobile moderno, Hoepli, Italy, 50; auth, Furniture for Modern Interiors, Van Nostrand Reinhold, 52; auth, How to Make Built-in Furniture, McGraw-Hill & Ceac, Spain, 55; auth, How to Build Modern Furniture, 57 & auth, Upholstered Furniture, Its Design & Construction, 69, McGraw-Hill, Hoepli & Ceac. *Mailing Add:* 67 Sherman Ct Fairfield CT 06430

DALI, SALVADOR
DESIGNER, PAINTER
b Figueras, Spain, May 11, 04. *Study:* Sch Fine Arts, Madrid, 21-25. *Work:* Centre Georges Pompidou, Paris; Tate Gallery, London; Guggenheim Mus, Mus Mod Art, New York; Cleveland Mus Art. *Exhib:* Solo exhib, Mus Mod Art, New York, 41 & 42, Philadelphia Mus Art, 55, Denver Art Mus, 55, M Knoedler & Co, New York, 72, Städtisches Galerie/Stadelsches Kunstinstitute, Frankfurt, 74, Sammlung Levy, Hamburg, 77, Tate Gallery, London, 80 & Caja de Ahorros, Madrid, 82; Retrospective 1920-1980, Centre Georges Pompidou, Paris, 80; A Century of Modern Drawing, Brit Mus, London & traveling, 82; and many others. *Awards:* Huntington Hartford Found Award, 57. *Bibliog:* A Reynold Morse (auth), The Draftsmanship of Dali, 70; David Larkin (ed), Dali, London, 74; A Reynold Morse (auth), Dali: A Guide to His Works in Public Museums, 74. *Publ:* Auth, The Tragic Myth of Millet's Angelus, 63; auth, Diary of a Genius, 64; auth, Dali de Draeger, Paris, 68; auth, Dali by Dali, 70; auth, The Unspeakable Confessions of Salvador Dali, 76; and others. *Dealer:* Knoedler & Co 21 E 70th St New York NY 10021. *Mailing Add:* Hotel St Regis New York NY 10022

DALLMANN, DANIEL FORBES
PAINTER, PRINTMAKER
b St Paul, Minn, Mar 21, 42. *Study:* St Cloud Univ, BS, 65; Univ Iowa, MA, 68, MFA, 69. *Work:* Nat Collection Fine Arts, DC; Art Inst Chicago; Yale Univ Art Mus, New Haven, Conn; Chemical Bank, New York; J B Speed Art Mus, Louisville, Ky; and others. *Exhib:* Contemporary Naturalism, Works of the 70's, Nassau Co Mus Fine Arts, Roslyn Heights, NY; Mint Mus Art, 77; Real, Really Real, Super Real: Directions in Contemporary Realism, Tucson Art Mus, Indianapolis Mus Art, Carnegie Inst; one-man show, Robert Schoelkopf Gallery, New York, 80; New Vistas: Contemporary American Landscape, Hudson River Mus, Yonkers, NY, 84. *Teaching:* Prof drawing & printmaking, Tyler Sch Art, 69- *Media:* All. *Dealer:* Robert Schoelkopf Gallery 825 Madison Ave New York NY 10021. *Mailing Add:* 947 Horsham Rd North Wales PA 19454

D'ALMEIDA, GEORGE
PAINTER
b Paris, France, June 30, 34; US citizen. *Exhib:* Fairweather Hardin Gallery, Chicago, 70, 72 & 74; Meredith Long & Co, Houston, 71 & 74; Gloria Luria Gallery, Miami, 75 & 76; Drian Galleries, London, 75; Rolly-Michaux Gallery, New York, 79, 81 & 83, Boston, 80 & 82; and others. *Media:* Multimedia. *Dealer:* Rolly-Michaux 943 Madison Ave New York NY 10021; Fairweather Hardin Gallery 101 E Ontario Chicago IL 60611. *Mailing Add:* Casina di Selvole 53017 Radda in Chianti Siena Italy

DALTON, HARRY L
COLLECTOR, PATRON
b Winston-Salem, NC, June 13, 1898. *Study:* Duke Univ, AB; Brit Univ; NY Univ; Duke Univ, LHD. *Mem:* NC Art Soc; Mint Mus; NC Mus; NC Arts Coun; Weatherspoon Gallery. *Collection:* Various schools of European and American art; collection has been loaned to numerous galleries. *Mailing Add:* 322 East Over Rd Charlotte NC 28207

DALY, KATHLEEN (KATHLEEN DALY PEPPER)
PAINTER
b Napanee, Ont, May 28, 1898. *Study:* Ont Col Art, assoc, with Arthur Lismer, J E H MacDonald & J W Beatty; Acad Grande Chaumiere, Paris; Ont Col Art; also woodcuts with Rene Poitier, Paris. *Work:* Nat Gallery Can, Ottawa, Ont; Art Gallery Ont, Toronto; Banif Libr & Archive Can Rockies, Ont; McMichael Mus, Kleinburg, Ont; Dept Northern Affairs, Ottawa. *Comn:* Portraits, Dr Thomas Cullen, Baltimore, 41, Premier Herbert Greenfield, 46 & Senor Hach, Tetuan, Morocco. *Exhib:* Group of Seven, 31; Brit Empire Exhib, 37-38; Great Lakes Exhib, 38-39; New York World's Fair, 39; Ann, Ont Soc Arts, Royal Can Acad & Can Group Painters. *Awards:* Gold Medal, Academia Italia delle Arti e del Lavoro, 81. *Bibliog:* Life in Eskimoland, London Press, 62. *Mem:* Royal Can Acad; Ont Soc Artists; Toronto Helicomian Club; Zonta Club Toronto; Can Group Painters. *Media:* Oil, Crayon; Lithograph. *Publ:* Co-illusr, Kingdom of Saguenay, 36; illusr, North, Dept Northern Affairs, 62; auth, Morrice, Clarke, Irwin, Toronto, 66. *Mailing Add:* 561 Avenue Rd Apt 1101 Toronto ON M4V 2J8 Canada

DALY, NORMAN
PAINTER, SCULPTOR
b Pittsburgh, Pa, Aug 9, 11. *Study:* Univ Colo, BFA; Ohio State Univ, MA; grad study, Paris, Inst Fine Arts & NY Univ. *Work:* Rochester Mem Art Gallery, NY; Herbert F Johnson Mus Art, Ithaca, NY; Everson Mus Art, Syracuse; Univ Wash, Seattle; St Paul Mus Art, Minn. *Comn:* Stained glass windows, Mt Savior Monastery, Pine City, NY; bas-relief, Meditation Rm, Student Union, NY State Univ Col Cortland. *Exhib:* One-man show, City Hist Mus, Boctium, WGer, 74; Inst Contemp Art, Philadelphia, 80; Temple Univ, Philadelphia, 80; Roberson Art Ctr, 82; Rotterdam Coun Arts Touring Exhib, Holland, 83; and others; Inst Contemp Arts, Univ Pa, 80; Tyler Sch Art, Temple Univ, 81. *Teaching:* Prof art, Cornell Univ, 42- *Awards:* Yaddo Fel, 71 & 76; Nat Endowments Arts Fel, 74; Cornell Distinguished Teaching Award, 81; and others. *Bibliog:* Charles Michener (auth), The fabulous Llhuroscians, Newsweek, 2/28/72; Kenneth Evett (auth), Llhuros, New Repub, 1/12/72; David Galloway (auth), The Civilization of Llhuros, Cleveland, 9/72. *Publ:* Illusr, Epoch, 71; contribr, Abrazas Press, 72; auth, The Civilization of Llhuros, 72; auth, Llhuros-Eine Entdeckte Kiltur-1974. *Mailing Add:* 110 N Quarry St Ithaca NY 14850

DALY, STEPHEN JEFFREY
SCULPTOR, EDUCATOR
b Governors Island, NY, July 4, 42. *Study:* San Jose State Univ, Calif, BA, 64; Cranbrook Acad Art, Mich, MFA(sculpture), 67. *Work:* Oakland Art Mus, Calif; Texas A&M Univ; Am Acad Rome, Italy; Bank San Antonio; Shasta College, Redding, Calif. *Exhib:* Zellerback Mem Sculpture, Calif Palace Legion Honor, San Francisco, 65; 85th San Francisco Art Inst Ann, M H DeYoung Mem Mus, Calif, 65; Objects USA, Smithsonian Mus, Washington, DC, 69; The Metal Experience, Oakland Art Mus, Calif, 71; one-man shows, Fairtree Gallery, New York, 72, Am Acad, Rome, 75, Triton Mus, Santa Clara, Calif, 77 & Graham Gallery, Houston, 83; Cooper/Daly, Patrick Gallery, Austin, 83; and many others. *Pos:* Art & Archit Panel, Tex Comn Arts, Austin, 80- *Teaching:* Univ Minn, Minneapolis, 67-69, Humboldt State Univ, 69-79, Univ Tex, San Antonio, 79-81, Univ Tex, Austin, 81- *Awards:* Prix de Rome, Am Acad Rome, Italy, 75; Louis Comfort Tiffany Award Sculpture, 77; Centennial Fel Fine Arts, Univ Tex, Austin, 83-84. *Mem:* Tex Sculpture Symposium (coordr, 81-). *Media:* Metals, Synthetics. *Mailing Add:* Univ Tex Dept Art Austin TX 78712

DAMAST, ELBA CECILIA
PAINTER
b Pedernales, Venezuela, Aug 11, 44. *Study:* Escuela Eloy Palacios, Maturin, Venezuela, BA, 59; Escuela Arturo Michelena, Valencia, MFA, 62. *Work:* Escuela Arturo Michelena, Gobernacio DF, Caracas, Biblioteca Del Estado, Valencia & Galeria El Parke, Valencia, Venezuela; Venezuelan Consulate, New York. *Exhib:* Salon Arturo Michelena, Valencia, 71; Joven Actualidad Venezolana, Studio Actual, Caracas, Venezuela, 71; 24th New Eng Exhib, Silvermine Guild, New Canaan, Conn, 73; Spanish Am Painters & Sculptors, Bronx Mus, New York, 74, Brooklyn Mus, 75 & Metrop Mus Art, New York, 76; NY Botanical Garden Mus Show, New York, 76. *Awards:* Premio, Arturo Michelena, Cristobal Rojas, 71. *Bibliog:* Tibisay Useche (auth), Talentos d Emitierra, Carabobeno, Venezuela, 70; Rafael Rondon Tarchetti (auth), Arte en New York, Valencia, 76. *Media:* Acrylic. *Mailing Add:* 115 W 23rd St New York NY 10011

D'AMATO, JANET POTTER
ILLUSTRATOR, CRAFTSMAN
b Rochester, NY. *Study:* Pratt Inst; Harriet FeBland Workshop. *Bibliog:* Anne Commire (auth), Something About the Author, Gale Publ, 75; Carmel Marchionni (auth), Lifestyles, Westchester Gannett Publ, 75 & 77. *Media:* Acrylic, Collage; Soft Sculpture. *Res:* Primitive and folk art and crafts, American Indian and African. *Publ:* Auth & illusr, Gifts to Make for Love or Money, Golden, 73; Colonial Crafts for You to Make, Messner, 75; Quillwork, Craft of Paper Filigree, 75 & Italian Crafts, 77, Evans; Indians, 79; Horns, Bones and Antlers, Messner, 82. *Mailing Add:* 32 Bayberry St Bronxville NY 10708

DAMAZ, PAUL F
WRITER, ARCHITECT
b Portugal, Nov 8, 17; US citizen. *Study:* Ecole Speciale Archit, Paris, France, BA(arch); Inst Urbanisme, Sorbonne, Paris, MA(town planning). *Pos:* Coun mem, Arts Acquisition Comt, State Univ NY Stony Brook, 70; dir, Fine Arts Fedn New York, 72-75. *Teaching:* Design critic archit, Columbia Univ, 52-53; adj prof, NY State Univ, Stony Brook, 83- *Awards:* Arnold Brunner fel, Archit League New York, 58. *Bibliog:* Anne Le Crenier (auth), Names, Archit & Eng News, 67. *Mem:* Am Inst Archits; Am Inst Planners; Ordre Architectes, France; Archit League New York; Munic Arts Soc. *Res:* Integration of art in modern architecture; art in public spaces. *Collection:* Contemporary art, mostly North and Latin American. *Publ:* Auth, Art in European architecture, 56 & Art in Latin American Architecture, 62, Van Nostrand Reinhold. *Mailing Add:* 302 E 88th St New York NY 10028

D'AMICO, AUGUSTINE A
COLLECTOR, PATRON
b Lawrence, Mass, May 15, 05. *Study:* Colby Col, BS, MA & Hon DFA. *Exhib:* Paintings & graphics, 61 & contemp ceramics, 63, Univ Maine, Orono; paintings & graphics, Colby Col Art Mus, Waterville, Maine, 63 & 78; contemp ceramics, Lincoln Co Mus, Wiscasset, Maine, 65; selected graphics from collection, tour sponsored by Maine Comn Arts & Humanities, 71. *Pos:* Trustee, Haystack Mountain Sch Crafts, Deer Isle, Maine; mem art adv coun, fel & former trustee, Colby Col, Waterville; chmn, patron fine arts, Univ Maine; mem, Maine State Comn Arts & Humanities. *Awards:* Distinguished Art Patron Award, Skowhegan Sch Painting & Sculpture, 74. *Mem:* Am Fedn Arts; Mus Mod Art; Am Craftsmen Coun; World Craft Coun. *Interests:* Advancement of art and craft programs in teaching institutions. *Collection:* 20th century paintings, graphics and ceramics. *Mailing Add:* 201 Broadway Bangor ME 04401

DAMRON, JOHN CLARENCE
PAINTER, ILLUSTRATOR
b Brooklyn, NY. *Study:* Pratt Inst, NY; Grand Cent Sch Art, with Harvey Dunn; with Edmund Oppenheim & Henry Gasser. *Comn:* Portraits, chmn bd US Banknote Corp, 66, pres Bloomfield Col, NJ, 69 & pres Barrington Col, RI, 71; and others. *Exhib:* Six Exhib: Am Artists Prof League Grand Nat, Lever House, NY, 68-81; Hudson Valley Art Asn 43rd Ann, White Plains, NY, 71; NJ Watercolor Soc, Brookdale Col, Lindcroft, 73, 75 & Morris Mus, Morristown, 74 & 77; Daughters of the Am Revolution Bicentennial, New York, 76; and others. *Teaching:* Instr portraiture, Art Ctr Sch, East Orange, NJ, 65-; instr portraiture & landscape, Summit Art Ctr, NJ & Art Guild South Orange, Maplewood. *Awards:* Am Artists Prof League Grand Nat First Award for Oil, 71 & 73; Art Ctr of NJ First Award for Watercolor, 72; Am Artists Prof League NJ State Show First Award for Watercolor, 71; and many others. *Mem:* Fel Am Artists Prof League (secy & dir nat bd, 70-); Grand Cent Art Galleries; Art Ctr of NJ (pres, 66, hon dir, 71-); NJ Watercolor Soc; and others. *Media:* Oil, Watercolor. *Publ:* Illusr, covers for Colliers & Liberty Mag, 43 & Capper's Farmer Mag, 46; illusr, Toronto Star Weekly, 46; illusr, New York Life Insurance Co calendars, 74 & 75. *Dealer:* Grand Central Art Galleries 24 W 57th St New York NY 10019. *Mailing Add:* 742 Sterling Dr Orange NJ 07050

DANBY, KEN
PAINTER, PRINTMAKER
b Sault Ste Marie, Ont, 1940. *Study:* Ont Col Art, Toronto, 58-60. *Work:* Nat Gallery Can, Ottawa, Ont; Mus Mod Art, New York; Montreal Mus Art, PQ; Art Inst Chicago; Univ Calif Art Gallery, Berkeley. *Comn:* Designer Series III Can Olympic Coins 1976 Olympics, Montreal. *Exhib:* Living Am Artists & the Figure, Pa State Univ, 74; 3rd Bienal Americana de Artes Graphicas, Colombia, 76; Aspects of Realism, Rothman's Touring Can Exhib, 76-78; Can Sport Art Collection, 76 Olympics, Montreal; 1st Bienniel of Am Graphics, Maracibo, Venezuela, 77; and others. *Awards:* First Recipient of R Tait McKenzie Chair for Sport 1975, Nat Sport & Recreation Ctr, Ottawa; Ont Arts Coun Editions Award, 76; Queen's Can Silver Jubilee Medal, 77. *Bibliog:* Rex Bromfield (producer), Ken Danby (film), 71; Paul Duval (auth), High Realism in Canadian Art, Clarke-Irwin, 74; Paul Duval (auth), Ken Danby, Clarke-Irwin, 76. *Mem:* Royal Can Acad Arts. *Media:* Egg Tempera. *Mailing Add:* RR #4 Guelph ON N1H 6J1 Canada

DANCE, ROBERT BARTLETT
PAINTER, PRINTMAKER
b Tokyo, Japan, May 31, 34; US citizen. *Study:* Philadelphia Col Art, with Henry C Pitz & W Emerton Heitland. *Work:* NC Mus Fine Art, Raleigh; R J Reynolds Indust, Winston-Salem, NC; Hanes Dye & Finishing, Winston-Salem; Miss Mus Art, Jackson; Wachovia Bank & Trust, Winston-Salem. *Exhib:* NC Artists Ann, 58-62 & NC Printmakers Traveling Show, 60, NC Mus Fine Arts, Raleigh; one-man show, Roanoke Fine Arts Ctr, Va, 62; Realist Invitational, Southeastern Ctr Contemp Art, Winston-Salem, NC, 71-81; Northwestern Open Carolina Art Competition, Winston-Salem, NC, 74; two-man show, Southeastern Ctr Contemp Art, Winston-Salem, 76; NC Watercolor Soc Exhib, Asheville Art Mus, NC, 76; R J Reynolds Indust NC Collection, Winston-Salem, 77; Reynolda House Am Art, Winston-Salem, 77; Funds Adv Co, Houston, Tex. *Awards:* First Place, NC Watercolor Soc, 73, 74 & 77, Assoc Artists Winston-Salem, 72, 73 & 74 & Northwestern Open Carolina Art Competition, Northwestern Bank, 74. *Bibliog:* Susan E Meyer (auth), 40 Watercolorists and How They Work, Watson-Guptill, 76 & Sir Isaac Pitman & Sons Ltd, Great Brit, 76; Wendon Blake (auth), The Alkyd Painting Book, Watson-Guptill. *Mem:* NC Watercolor Soc; Assoc Artists Winston-Salem. *Media:* Watercolor, Acrylic; Woodcut. *Publ:* Illusr (cover), The World of the Coyote, Lippincott, 64; illusr,

Things Invisible to See, Advocate Publ Group, 79; illusr cover, Wildlife in NC, 7/79; illusr cover, Artist Mag, London, Eng, 1-2/80; illusr cover, Yankee Mag, 9/80; plus others. *Dealer:* Southeastern Ctr for Contemp Art 750 Marguerite Dr Winston-Salem NC 27106. *Mailing Add:* 320 Anita Dr Winston-Salem NC 27104

D'ANCONA, MIRELLA LEVI
HISTORIAN, WRITER

b Florence, Italy; US citizen. *Study:* Univ Florence, PhD, 41, dipl(arch & paleography), 46; Bryn Mawr Col, MA, 49. *Teaching:* Asst prof art hist, Hunter Col, City Univ New York, 61-67, assoc prof, 67-72, prof, 72-; assoc prof, Inst Fine Arts, NY Univ, 67-68. *Mem:* Soc Studio Della Miniatura (mem bd dirs, 83); Soc Storia Dell'arte Lombarda. *Res:* Italian book illumination; iconography. *Publ:* Auth, The Immaculate Conception in the Middle Ages and Early Renaissance, Princeton Univ Press, 57; auth, Miniatura E Miniatori A Firenze Nel XIV E XV Secolo, 62, The Wildenstein Collection of Italian Book-Illuminations, 70, The Garden of the Renaissance, 77 & Botticelli's Primavera: A Botanical Interpretation, 83, Florence Olschki. *Mailing Add:* 360 E 72nd St New York NY 10021

D'ANDREA, JEANNE
CONSULTANT

b Chicago, Ill, Dec 9, 25. *Study:* Art Inst Chicago; Colo Col, with Rico Lebrun; Univ Chicago, with Joshua Taylor, Ulrich Middledorf & Carlos Castillo, PhB & MA. *Collections Arranged:* Gericault, Los Angeles Co Mus Art, 71; Women Artists: 1550-1950, 76; Treasures of Mexico, 78; and others. *Pos:* Designer sets, costumes, Turnau Opera Co, NY & Arlington Opera Theatre, Arlington, Va, 59-72; head educ dept, Ringling Mus Art, Sarasota, Fla, 60-62; coordr exhibs & publ, Los Angeles Co Mus Art, 69-81, ed & design consult, 81- *Mem:* Am Asn Mus; Col Art Asn Am. *Mailing Add:* 547 Alandele Ave Los Angeles CA 90036

DANE, BILL
PHOTOGRAPHER

b Pasadena, Calif, Nov 12, 38. *Study:* Univ Calif, Berkeley, BA(art & polit sci), 64 & MA(painting), 68. *Work:* Mus Mod Art, New York; Nat Gallery Can, Ottawa. *Exhib:* One-man shows, Painting, Sculpture, Snapshots, Reese Palley Gallery, San Francisco, 70, Unfamiliar Places, A Message from Bill Dane, Mus Mod Art, New York, 73, Ctr Creative Photog, Univ Ariz, Tucson, 76 & De Young Mus, San Francisco, 77; Landscape Discovery, Hofstra Univ, Long Island, NY, 73; Recent Am Still Photog, Edinburg Art Ctr, Scotland, 76; Concerning Photog, Photogr Gallery, London, 77. *Awards:* Fel in Photog, Guggenheim Mem Found, 73-74; Nat Endowment for the Arts photog fel, 76 & 78. *Publ:* Contribr, The Snapshot, Aperture Publ, 74; contribr, On Time, Mus Mod Art Calendar, 75. *Mailing Add:* 410 Washington Ave Point Richmond CA 94801

DANE, WILLIAM JERALD
LIBRARIAN

b Concord, NH, May 8, 25. *Study:* Drexel Inst Technol, MLS; NY Univ Inst Fine Arts; Sorbonne, Paris, France; Attingham Park Summer Sch, Eng; Palladio Studies, Vicenza, Italy, 80; Victorian Soc Summer Sch, London, 81. *Collections Arranged:* Fine Print Collection, Newark Pub Libr; 150 Years of Graphic Art in New Jersey; Silkscreen, A Survey Show of Serigraphs & Screenprints for the NJ State Coun on Arts; Rabin & Krueger Archives. *Pos:* Supvr art & music libr, Newark Pub Libr, 67- *Mem:* Grolier Club; Victorian Soc Am (nat bd mem, 74-80, chmn NY chap, 72-74); Coalition Arts & Humanities NJ, (vpres, 79-); Art Nouveau Chap (chmn, 80-); Newark Arts Coun (bd mem, 81-). *Publ:* Auth, Picture Collection Subject Headings, 69; contribr, Arts in America: A Bibliography, Smithsonian Inst Press, 79; auth, Networking and the art library, Drexel Libr Quart, fall 83; auth, Standing orders for an art library, Art Documentation, 12/83. *Mailing Add:* 5 Washington St Newark NJ 07101

DANHAUSEN, ELDON
SCULPTOR

US citizen. *Study:* Art Inst Chicago, James Nelson Raymond Foreign Traveling Fel, BFA, 47. *Work:* Hackley Art Gallery, Muskegon, Mich; Civic Ctr, New Orleans, La; Standard Club Chicago; Roosevelt Univ, Chicago. *Comn:* Sculpture, Int Minerals & Chem Corp, Skokie, Ill, 60; sculpture, Home Mutual Appleton, Wis, 63; sculpture, WOC TV, Davenport, Iowa, 64; sculpture, Civic Ctr, New Orleans, 67; sculpture, 150 N Wacker Dr Bldg, Chicago, 71. *Exhib:* Downtown Gallery, New York; Chicago Ann Show, Art Inst Chicago, 45-60; Rivinia Festival Art Exhib, 57, 59 & 60; American Business & the Arts, San Francisco Mus Art, 61; Sculpture 70, Art Inst Chicago, 70. *Teaching:* Assoc prof sculpture, Art Inst Chicago, 48- *Awards:* Linde Co Prize, Chicago Ann Show, Art Inst Chicago, 60; Citation for Art in Architecture, Am Inst Archit Iowa Chap, 63. *Bibliog:* Something to talk about in Chicago, Mademoiselle Mag, 1/54; Art in Chicago, CBS TV, 67; Meilach & Seiden (auth), Direct Metal Sculpture, Crown. *Publ:* Auth, Art in the market place, sculptor's viewpoint, Chicago Mkt Scene, 3/70; contribr, Contemporary Stone Sculpture, Crown. *Mailing Add:* 1418 N LaSalle St Chicago IL 60610

DANIEL, SUZANNE GARRIGUES
HISTORIAN

b New York, NY, May 15, 45. *Study:* Lindenwood Col, St Charles, Mo, BA(art), 67; Univ de las Am, Mex, MA(Latin Am art hist), 70; Johns Hopkins Univ, with Phoebe Stanton, MA(art hist), 75; Univ Md, with James B Lynch, PhD(art hist; grad fel), 83. *Collections Arranged:* Christine Neill: Recent Watercolors, C Grimaldis Gallery, Baltimore, 81. *Pos:* Mem archaeol team,

Las Pilas, Morelos, Mex, 73 & Xochicalco, Morelos, 78; asst area supervisor, Joint Archaeol Exped to Caesarea Maritima, Israel, summer 79. *Teaching:* Asst prof art hist, Morgan State Univ, 70- *Awards:* Fac grant-in-aid res, Morgan State Univ, 71, 72, 75 & 82. *Mem:* Col Art Asn Am; Latin Am Studies Asn; Soc Am Archaeol; Baltimore Mus Art; Res Ctr Arts, Univ Tex, San Antonio. *Res:* Iconography of highland Olmec and lowland Izapa monumental art; Wilfredo Lam and contemporary Cuban painting. *Publ:* Auth, The National Museum of Anthropology in Mexico City, The Museum of Modern Art in Mexico City & The Gold Museum in Bogota, Colombia, In: Art Museums of The World, Greenwood Press, 83. *Mailing Add:* 10 W Madison, Apt 1 Baltimore MD 21201

DANIELI, FIDEL ANGELO
PAINTER, CRITIC

b Ironwood, Mich, June 15, 38. *Study:* Pasadena City Col, with Leonard Edmondson, AA; Univ Calif, Los Angeles, with Jan Stussy & William Brice, BA & MA. *Exhib:* One-man shows, Orlando Gallery, Encino, Calif, 69-75 & Suburban Sections, Los Angeles Valley Col, 73; Magic Machine Traveling Exhib, Univ Calif, Berkeley, 74; Munic Gallery, Barnsdall Park, Los Angeles, 75. *Collections Arranged:* Inaugural Exhib, Brand Art Ctr, Glendale, Calif, 69; Nine Senior Southern California Painters, Los Angeles Inst Contemp Art, Century City, 74-75. *Pos:* Ed, Los Angeles Artists' Publ, 72-73. *Teaching:* From assoc prof to prof art, Los Angeles Valley Col, 61- *Awards:* Nat Endowment Humanities Grant for Jr Col Teachers, 74. *Dealer:* Orlando Gallery 17037 Ventura Blvd Encino CA 91316. *Mailing Add:* 7858 Goodland Ave North Hollywood CA 91605

DANIELS, DAVID M
COLLECTOR, PATRON

b Evanston, Ill, Apr 10, 27. *Study:* Yale Univ; Curtis Inst Music. *Pos:* Trustee & accessions comt, Minneapolis Inst Fine Arts, 65-; pres, Drawing Soc, 71-79. *Collection:* Drawings and sculpture of all periods; medals and paintings. *Publ:* Contribr, Drawings of Morris Graves, New York Graphics, 73. *Mailing Add:* 4 Sutton Pl New York NY 10022

DANIELSON, PHYLLIS I
ADMINISTRATOR, TAPESTRY ARTIST

b Marion, Ind. *Study:* Ball State Univ, BA(art), 53; Mich State Univ, MA, 60, EdS, 66; Ind Univ, EdD, 68. *Work:* Mint Mus Art, Charlotte, NC. *Exhib:* Weatherspoon Gallery, Greensboro, NC, 69 & 70; Stitchery, Pa, 71 & Iowa, 75; Matrix Gallery, Bloomington, Ind, 72; one-person shows, Jewish Community Ctr, Indianapolis, Ind, 72 & Eye-Opener Gallery, Cincinnati, Ohio, 72; Mint Mus Art, 74; Herron Art Gallery, Indianapolis, 74; Sloane O'Stickey Gallery, Cleveland, Ohio, 74; Women in Art, West Bend, Wis, 76. *Pos:* Pres, Kendall Sch Design, Grand Rapids, 76- *Teaching:* Asst prof art, Ball State Univ, Muncie, Ind, 66-67; asst prof art educ, Univ NC, Greensboro, 68-70; assoc prof educ & art, Herron Sch Art, Indianapolis, 70-76. *Bibliog:* Kathleen Fisher (auth), Women in Action, Asn Art Hist Educ Bulletin, 75. *Mem:* Nat Art Educ Asn; Nat Coun Art Adminr; Nat Asn Sch Art; Col Art Asn. *Media:* Fabric, Fiber. *Publ:* Auth, Art for the Second & Third Grades, Kimball/Hunt, 66; auth, Paper mache and the elementary teacher, Arts & Activities, 12/70; auth, Selected teacher characteristics of art student teachers, Studies Art Educ, winter 71; auth, Art education: An international survey, Educ Studies, 72; auth, The woman administrator in art, Col Art J, 76; and others. *Mailing Add:* 6137 Chamonix Ct SE Grand Rapids MI 49506

DANIKIAN, CARON LE BRUN
CRITIC, DEALER

b Rochester, NY, May 2, 42. *Study:* Marymount Manhattan Col, BA, 64. *Pos:* Art ed & critic, Boston Herald Traveler, Mass, 66-72 & Boston Herald Am, 72-73; art critic, Christian Sci Monitor, 73-; vpres, Arvest Galleries, Inc, Boston. *Res:* Turn of the century American impressionists, New England artists & 19th & 20th century European artists. *Publ:* Contribr, Sunday Herald Traveler Mag, Boston Arts Mag, Europe Mag, Sunday Herald Am Mag, Christian Sci Monitor, Quincy Patriot Ledger & Boston Herald. *Mailing Add:* 770 Boylston St 21E Boston MA 02199

DANK, LEONARD DEWEY
MEDICAL ILLUSTRATOR, CONSULTANT

b Birmingham, Ala, Dec 21, 29. *Study:* Cornell Univ, BA, 52; Sch Med Illus, Mass Gen Hosp, Boston, cert, 55; Art Students League; Jules Laurents Studio, New York. *Work:* McGraw-Hill Publ Co, New York; Stravon Educ Press Inc, New York; H S Stuttman Co Inc, New York; Proj-in-Health, New York; Doubleday & Co Inc, New York. *Comn:* Diabetes (animated film), Synapse Inc, Greenwich, Conn, 74; The Brain in Hypertension, Parts I & II (animated films), Merck Sharp & Dohme, 78. *Pos:* Staff artist, Plastic Surgery Clin, Manhattan Eye & Ear Hosp, New York, 55-57 & Eye Bank for Sight Restoration, New York, 57-59; owner, Leonard Dank Studio, New York, 59-61; owner, Medical Illus Co, New York & Cutchogue, NY, 61-; consult med illusr, St Luke's-Roosevelt Hosp Ctr, New York. *Awards:* First Prize Motion Picture, Am Col Surgery, 59 & 62; Better Teller Award, Asn Indust Advertisers, 73. *Mem:* Asn Med Illusr; Guild Natural Sci Illusr. *Media:* Multimedia. *Publ:* Illusr, Cells: The Basic Structure of Life, Franklin Watts, 70; coauth, Clinical Obstetrics & Gynecology, Harper & Row, 73-76; co-auth, Gynecologic Operations, Harper & Row, 78; illusr, The Male His Body, His Sex, Anchor Press/Doubleday, 78; illusr, Dr Fishbein's Illustrated Medical Encyclopedia, Doubleday, 79. *Mailing Add:* 114th St & Amsterdam Ave New York NY 10025

DANOFF, I MICHAEL
CRITIC, MUSEUM DIRECTOR
b Chicago, Ill, Oct 22, 40. *Study:* Univ Mich, BA, 62; Univ NC, Chapel Hill, MA, 64; Syracuse Univ, PhD, 70. *Collections Arranged:* Art in Our Time, traveling exhib, 80; Image in American Painting & Sculpture: 1950-1980 (co-auth, catalog), Akron Art Mus, 81. *Pos:* Cur collections, Dickinson Col, 70-73; cur Michener Collection, Univ Tex, 73-74; cur collections & exhibs, Milwaukee Art Ctr, 74-; assoc dir/chief cur, Milwaukee Art Mus, 74-80; dir, Akron Art Mus, 80- *Teaching:* Asst prof 19th & 20th century & contemp art, Dickson Col, 70-73, Univ Tex, Austin, 73 & Univ Wis-Milwaukee, 75- *Awards:* Nat Endowment Arts mus prof fel, 73. *Bibliog:* Rev, New York Times, 10/2/77; Helen Cullinan (auth), Italionate-Palazzo-Post Office, Art News, 9/81; Hilton Kramer (auth), An audacious inaugural, New York Times, 9/20/81. *Mem:* Col Art Asn Am; Midwest Art Hist Soc; Am Asn Mus; Asn Art Mus Dir. *Res:* Contemporary art history & criticism. *Publ:* Auth, Gallery Guides to Collections, Milwaukee Art Ctr, 74-75; auth, Mary Nohl: sophisticated naive, Midwest Art, 75; auth, Europe in the Seventies, Art in Am, 1/78; auth, Paintings that make your retinas dance, Art News, 11/81; and others. *Mailing Add:* Akron Art Mus 70 E Market St Akron OH 44308

DANTZIC, CYNTHIA MARIS
EDUCATOR, PAINTER
b Brooklyn, NY, Jan 4, 33. *Study:* Bard Col, 50 52; Yale Univ, with Josef Albers & Jose de Rivera, BFA, 55; Pratt Inst, MFA, 63. *Work:* Brooklyn Mus; Adelphi Univ Gallery; Univ Mass Gallery, Amherst; Edson Tool Bldg, Belleville, NJ. *Comn:* Modular paintings, New York Soc Gen Semantics, 68 & Springbok Ed, Kansas City, Kans, 74; stained glass windows, Church Resurrection, Lakeland, Fla, 75; portrait Mary Susan Miller, Berkeley Inst, Brooklyn, 79; Above and Beyond (ed photog collages), Brooklyn Art & Cult Asn, 83. *Exhib:* Solo exhibs, Modular Paintings, East Hampton Gallery, New York, 66 & The Expanded Field, Resnick Gallery, Long Island Univ, 83; The With of It, Delgado Mus, New Orleans, 72; Affect-Effect, La Jolla Mus Art, 79; Interior-Exterior, 80 & 100 New Acquisitions, 81, Brooklyn Mus; Common Ground: New York Abstract, Galerie Arts Visuels, Que, 82. *Collections Arranged:* Art Festival for NAACP Legal Defense (auth, catalog), Brooklyn Mus, 63. *Teaching:* Asst prof art, Brooklyn Ctr, Long Island Univ, 65-70, assoc prof, 70-75, prof, 75-, chmn dept, 77- *Awards:* Stipend Award Animation, Brooklyn Art & Cult Asn, 82. *Bibliog:* Talk of the town, New Yorker, 5/28/66; Marie Avona (auth), Cynthia Dantzic, multi-media artist, Pratt Reports, 6/79; Herbert Keppler (auth), Expand your view: Cynthia Dantzic's photo collages, Mod Photog, 1/84. *Mem:* Col Art Asn; Am Asn Univ Prof. *Media:* Acrylic, Pencil. *Publ:* Auth, A teacher of art looks at education, Gen Semantics Bulletin, 64; auth & illusr, Stop Dropping Bread Crumbs on My Yacht, 74 & Sounds of Silents, 76, Prentice-Hall; auth, An invitation to the butterfly ball, New York Times Book Rev, 5/76; illusr, Biography, Confrontation, Long Island Univ, 79. *Mailing Add:* 910 President St Brooklyn NY 11215

DANZIGER, AVERY C
PHOTOGRAPHER
b Chapel Hill, NC, June 25, 53. *Work:* Bibliot Nat, Paris; Corcoran Gallery Art; Mus Mod Art, New York; Nat Mus Am Art; Stedelijk Mus Mod Art, Amsterdam. *Exhib:* Hot Shots, Southeastern Ctr Contemp Arts, Winston-Salem, NC, 79; New Acquisitions, Corcoran Gallery, 81; Color as Form: A History of Color Photography, Int Mus Photog, Rochester, NY, 82; 20th Century Contemporary Photography, Seibu Mus, Tokyo, 83; one-man shows, Arco Ctr Visual Arts, Los Angeles, 83 & Ctr Contemporary Arts, Santa Fe, 83. *Teaching:* Instr photog, Los Angeles Harbor Col, 81-82, East Los Angeles Community Col, 81-82 & Univ Calif, Los Angeles Exten, 82. *Awards:* Purchase Award, 39th Ann Artists Exhib, NC Mus Art, 76; Nat Endowment Arts Fel, 79; Photog Competition Award, Reynolds Industries, 79. *Bibliog:* Suzanne Muchnic (auth), Avery Danziger's art about art, Los Angeles Times, 2/1/80; Neal Menzies (auth), Visions of empathy, Artweek, 10/31/83; MaLin Wilson (auth), article, Art Lines, 10/83. *Mem:* Soc Photog Educ. *Media:* Cibachrome. *Dealer:* McLain/Davis Gallery 2818 Kirby Dr Houston TX 77098. *Mailing Add:* PO Box 481192 Los Angeles CA 90048

DANZIGER, JOAN
SCULPTOR
b New York, NY, June 17, 34. *Study:* Cornell Univ, BFA, 54; Art Students League, 54-55; Acad Fine Arts, Rome, cert art, 56-58. *Work:* Nat Mus Am Art, Smithsonian Inst, Washington, DC; Jacksonville Mus Arts & Sci, Fla; Nat Mus Womens Art, Washington, DC; NJ State Mus, Trenton; Plaza Americas Hotel, Dallas. *Comn:* Suspended sculpture, Md Fine Arts Comn & Frostburg State Col, Md, 75; two sculptures, AFL-CIO Labor Studies Ctr, Silver Springs, Md, 76. *Exhib:* Drawing Soc Nat Exhib, Philadelphia Mus Art, 70; 26th St Playground Show, Baltimore Mus Art, 72; Suspended Sculptures, New Orleans Mus Art, 73; one-man shows, Jacksonville Mus Art & Sci, 79 & Terry Dintenfass Gallery, New York, 80; Images of the Seventies, 9 Washington Artists, Corcoran Gallery, DC, 80; A New Bestiary, Va Mus Fine Arts, Richmond, 81; Masks, Folk & Craft Mus, Los Angeles, Calif, 81; and many others; NJ State Mus, Trenton, 82; Joy Horwich Gallery, Chicago, 82; and others. *Pos:* Visual arts panelist, DC Comn Arts & Humanities, 74-80. *Teaching:* Instr sculpture, Smithsonian Inst, 70- *Bibliog:* Constance Dodge (auth), Fantasy Sculpture, Albany News, NY, 78; Maryse Pailla (auth), Profile, Art Voices, 81; Joanna Shaw Eagle (auth), American women in sculpture, Harpers Bazaar, 81; Cynthia Nadelman (auth), article, Art News, 80. *Mem:* Artists Equity; Washington Sculptors Group. *Media:* Mixed-Media Sculpture. *Dealer:* Barbara Fendrick Gallery 3059 M St NW Washington DC 20007; Terry Dintenfass Gallery 50 W 57th St New York NY 10019. *Mailing Add:* 2909 Brandywine St NW Washington DC 20008

DAPHNIS, NASSOS
PAINTER, SCULPTOR
b Krokeai, Greece, July 23, 14; US citizen. *Work:* Mus Mod Art, New York; Whitney Mus Am Art, New York; Albright-Knox Gallery Art, Buffalo; Carnegie Inst, Pittsburgh; Hirshhorn Mus. *Comn:* Wall paintings, City Walls Inc, 70 & Nat Environmental Arts, 71; art environment, Arlen Realty Develop Corp, 71. *Exhib:* One-man exhibs, Mint Mus, Charlotte, NC, 49; Leo Castelli Gallery, New York, 59-, Work Since 1951, Albright-Knox Mus, Buffalo, NY, 69, Everson Mus, 69, Andre Zarre Gallery, New York, 74 & 76 & numerous others; Corcoran Gallery Biennial, 59, 63 & 69; Ann Exhib Painting, Whitney Mus Am Art, 59, 61, 64, 65 & 67; Purist Painting, 61 & Geometric Abstraction in America, 62, Walker Art Ctr; Ann Exhib Sculpture & Drawing, Whitney Mus Am Art, 62; Am Abstract Expressionists & Imagists, Guggenheim Mus, 61; Highlights of the 68-69 Season, Aldrich Mus, 69; Pittsburgh Int, Carnegie Inst, Pa, 70; Birmingham Festival of Art, Birmingham Mus Art, 76; Provincetown Painters 1890s-1970s, Everson Mus Art, 77. *Awards:* Nat Found Arts & Humanities Award, 66; Nat Endowment Arts Grant, 71; Guggenheim Mem Found Fel, 77. *Bibliog:* Hilton Kramer (auth), The Corcoran Biennial, 2/23/69 & 12 artists join in an uncommon show, 3/18/71, New York Times. *Mem:* Am Abstract Artists. *Media:* Epoxy, Plexiglas. *Dealer:* Leo Castelli Gallery 420 W Broadway New York NY 10012. *Mailing Add:* 362 W Broadway New York NY 10013

DARBOVEN, HANNE
CONCEPTUAL ARTIST, GRAPHIC ARTIST
b Munich, Ger, Apr 29, 41. *Study:* Hochscule for Bildende Kunst, Hamburg. *Work:* Stedelijk Mus, Amsterdam, Holland; Kaiser Wilhelm Mus, Krefeld, WGer. *Exhib:* Eight Contemp Artists, Mus Mod Art, New York, 74; one-person shows, Leo Castelli Gallery, New York, 73-75, 78 & 80, Kabinett fur Akutelle Kunst, Bremerhaven, Kunstmuseum, Basel, Switz, 74-75, Stedilijk Mus, 75 & Kunstmuseum Lucerne, Switz, 75; Projekt 74, Kunsthalle, Cologne, 74; and others. *Bibliog:* J Collins (auth), Reviews: Hanne Darboven, Castelli Downtown, 9/73, Lucy R Lippard (auth), Hanne Darboven: Deep in numbers, 10/73 & Max Kosloff (auth), Transversing the field: Eight contemporary artists at Museum of Modern Art, 12/74, Artforum. *Publ:* Contribr, 6 Manuskripte 69, Kunstzeltung, Dusseldorf, 69; auth, Ein Jahrhundert, Amsterdam, 71; auth, Words, Avalanche, spring 72. *Dealer:* Leo Castelli Gallery 420 W Broadway New York NY 10012. *Mailing Add:* c/o Sonnabend Gallery 420 W Broadway New York NY 10012

D'ARCANGELO, ALLAN M
PAINTER
b Buffalo, NY, June 16, 30. *Study:* Univ Buffalo, AB(hist); City Col New York; Mexico City Col. *Work:* Whitney Mus Am Art, Mus Mod Art, New York; Albright-Knox Mus, Buffalo; Gemeente Mus, The Hague; Joseph H Hirshhorn Mus, Washington, DC. *Comn:* Poster, Olympic Games, Munich, 72; Bicentennial poster & print, Mobil Oil, 75. *Exhib:* One-man show, Albright-Knox Art Gallery, Buffalo, NY; Am Landscape Painting, Mus Mod Art Traveling Exhib, USA & Spoleto, Italy, 64; New Forms, Stedelijk Mus, Amsterdam, Holland, 66; Environ USA, Biennial of Sao Paulo, Brazil, 67; L'art Vivant Am, Found Maeght, St Paul de Vence, France, 69; Nat Acad Design, New York, 73; Inaugural Exhib, Hirshhorn Mus, DC, 74; Images of an Era: The American Poster 1945 75, Smithsonian Inst, 75-77. *Teaching:* Instr painting, Sch Visual Arts, New York, 63-68, Cornell Univ, 68, Syracuse Univ, 71 & Univ Wis, 72; prof art, Brooklyn Col, 73- *Awards:* Artist in residence, Aspen Inst Humanistic Studies, 65 & 67; Nat Inst Arts & Lett Ann Award, 70. *Bibliog:* N Calas (auth), Icons and Images of the Sixties, Dutton, 71; Dore Ashton (auth), A Reading in Modern Art, Case Western Reserve Univ, 69; Lawrence Alloway (auth), Topics in American Art since 1945, Norton, 75. *Mem:* Soc Am Graphic Artists; City Walls Inc. *Mailing Add:* PO Box 33 Kenoza Lake NY 12750

D'ARISTA, ROBERT
PAINTER, EDUCATOR
b Pelham, NY, July 2, 29. *Study:* Washington Sq Col, NY Univ; Columbia Univ; Acad Grande Chaumiere, Paris, France; Fulbright scholar, Florence, 55. *Work:* Yale Univ Art Gallery, New Haven, Conn; Toledo Mus Art, Ohio; Hirshhorn Collection, Washington, DC; Neuberger Collection; Nat Collection Fine Arts, Washington, DC. *Exhib:* Carnegie Inst, Pittsburgh; Solomon R Guggenheim Mus, New York; Whitney Mus Am Art, New York; one-man shows, four Nordness Gallery, New York, 64-72, & Boston Univ, 73. *Teaching:* Prof art, Am Univ, 61-; distinguished vis artist, Boston Univ, springs 73 & 78. *Awards:* Rosenthal Found Award, Inst Arts & Lett, 67. *Media:* Oil. *Publ:* Auth, Reflections on painting, In: Painters on Painting, Grosset & Dunlap. *Mailing Add:* 3125 Quebec Pl NW Washington DC 20015

DARLING, SHARON SANDLING
CURATOR, HISTORIAN
b Mitchell, SDak, Feb 28, 43. *Study:* NC State Univ, BA; Duke Univ, MAT; Winterthur Summer Inst, Am Dec Arts. *Collections Arranged:* Chicago Metalsmiths, 77, Chicago Ceramics and Glass (auth catalog), 80; Chicago Furniture: Art, Craft & Industry, 1833-1983 (auth, catalog), 84, Chicago Hist Soc. *Pos:* Cur dec arts, Chicago Hist Soc, 75- *Res:* Decorative arts of Chicago and the Midwest. *Publ:* Contribr, Silver Mag, 75 & 77; coauth (with Gail Farr Casterline), Chicago Metalsmiths, 77 & auth, Arts & crafts shops in the fine arts building, Chicago Hist, 77, Chicago Hist Soc; auth, Chicago metalsmiths, Am Art Rev, 78. *Mailing Add:* c/o Chicago Hist Soc Clark St at North Ave Chicago IL 60614

DARRIAU, JEAN-PAUL
EDUCATOR, SCULPTOR
b New York, NY, Nov 24, 29. *Study:* Pratt Inst, scholar, 47-48; Brooklyn Col, BA, 51; Univ Minn, MFA, 54. *Work:* Hirshhorn Mus & Sculpture Garden; Ind Univ Fine Arts Mus; Colorado Springs Art Ctr; Minneapolis Inst Art; Albert List Collection. *Comn:* Man and Woman (aluminum), Jersey City State Col, 69; Adam and Eve I (bronze), 68, Adam and Eve II (bronze), 73 & four portrait busts, 76, Ind Univ Campus; Red, Blond, Black and Olive (limestone), City Bloomington, Ind, 80. *Exhib:* One-man show, Grippi Gallery, New York, 62; Sculptors Guild, New York, 70-72; FAR Gallery, New York, 72-73; Privileges and Silences, Ind Univ, Bloomington, 82 & Univ Chicago, 83. *Teaching:* Instr, State Col, Arkadelphia, Ark, 53, Oberlin Col, 54 & Colo Col, 57-61; instr, Ind Univ, Bloomington, 61-, head sculpture dept, 61-72. *Awards:* Fulbright Grant, 55-57 & 66-67; res grants, Colo Col, 59 & Ind Univ. *Mem:* Col Art Asn. *Publ:* Contribr, Visions and Voice of the New Midwest, James A Rock & Co, 78. *Mailing Add:* Dept Fine Arts Ind Univ Bloomington IN 47401

DARRICARRERE, ROGER DOMINIQUE
SCULPTOR, STAINED GLASS ARTIST
b Bayonne, France, Dec 15, 12; US citizen. *Study:* Ecole des Beaux-Arts, Bayonne, 30-35; Ecole Nat Super Decoratifs Paris, dipl, 38; Inst Metiers, Paris, 45. *Comn:* Spatial kaleidoscope, Lytton Ctr, Los Angeles, 59; revolving steel & glass sculpture depicting moving picture indust; leaded glass window wall, World's Fair Contest, St Stephen's Lutheran Church, Granada Hills, Calif; Columbia Savings & Loan Asn, Los Angeles, 66; massive bronze sculpture, Atlantis, Lytton Savings & Loan Asn Northern Calif, Oakland, 67; plus others. *Exhib:* Pasadena Art Mus, 59-63; Otis Art Inst, Los Angeles, 61-65; New York World's Fair, 64-65; Mus Contemp Crafts, New York, 66; Craftsman USA, Los Angeles Co Mus, Los Angeles, 66; plus others. *Teaching:* Instr, interior design & painting, Coe Col, 48-51; workshop prof glass in archit, Calif State Col, Long Beach, 68-69; lectr stained glass & sculpture, Mt St Mary's Col, spring 69; conducts sem stained glass, Chartres, France, summers. *Awards:* Fine Arts & Craftsmanship Awards, Am Inst Architects, 58, 59, 61 & 63; First Prize, Nat Competition stained glass panel, New York World's Fair, 64-65; Nat Merit Award, Craftsman USA, 66; plus others. *Media:* Steel, Glass. *Mailing Add:* 217 Windward Ave Venice CA 90291

DARROW, PAUL GARDNER
PAINTER, EDUCATOR
b Pasadena, Calif. *Study:* Colorado Springs Fine Art Ctr; Claremont Grad Sch & Univ Ctr. *Work:* Pasadena Art Mus, Calif; Times-Mirror Collection, Los Angeles; US Navy, Washington, DC; Lytton Savings & Loan Collection, Los Angeles; Long Beach Mus Art, Calif. *Comn:* Murals, Air France, Los Angeles, 61, Balboa Yacht Club, 63 & Newport Bank, Calif, 71. *Exhib:* Los Angeles Co Mus Art, 51-54; San Francisco Mus Art, 52 & 53; Seattle Art Mus, 53; Butler Inst Am Art, 53 & 54; Pa Acad Fine Art, 54; Denver Art Mus, 54; Corcoran Gallery, 54; Smithsonian Inst, 55; Oakland Art Mus, Calif, 64; solo exhibs, Newport Harbor, 72 & Gallerie Forma, El Salvador, 75; retrospective, Scripps Col, 73; Southern California 100, Laguna Beach Mus Art, 77; California Photographers, Claremont Galleries, 78; and many others. *Teaching:* Prof art & chmn dept, Scripps Col, 60-; prof art, Claremont Grad Sch, 70- *Awards:* Purchase Award, Pasadena Art Mus, 58; Res Grant, Ford Found, 69; Nat Endowment Humanities Grant, 73. *Bibliog:* Bently Schaad (auth), The Realm of Contemporary Still Life Painting, 62 & Edmondson (auth), Printmaking, 72, Van Nostrand Reinhold. *Mem:* Calif Watercolor Soc; founding mem Los Angeles Printmaking Soc. *Media:* Graphic. *Publ:* Illusr, Aldous Huxley, Paris Rev, 62; illusr, The Concrete Wilderness, Meredith, 67; illusr, The Guide for the Married Man, Price Stern, 68; illusr, Psychological Perspectives, C G Jung Inst, 70. *Dealer:* Comara Gallery La Cienega Los Angeles CA 90034. *Mailing Add:* 690 Cuprien Way Laguna Beach CA 92651

DARROW, WHITNEY, JR
CARTOONIST
b Princeton, NJ, Aug 22, 09. *Study:* Princeton Univ; Art Students League. *Pos:* Cartoonist, New York Mag, 33- *Media:* Pencil, Charcoal. *Publ:* Auth, You're Sitting On My Eyelashes, 43, Please Pass the Hostess, 49 & Stop Miss, 57, Random House; auth, Give Up, Simon & Schuster, 66; illusr, Walter, the Homing Pidgeon, Harper & Row, 81; and others. *Mailing Add:* 331 Newtown Tpk Wilton CT 06897

DARTON, CHRISTOPHER
PAINTER
b New York, NY, Dec 9, 45. *Study:* New York Inst Technol, BFA, 69; Pratt Inst Grad Sch, MFA, 71. *Exhib:* Daniel Weinberg, San Francisco, Calif, 79; Mary Boone Gallery, 80. *Media:* Acrylic Paint. *Publ:* Auth, Matter as subject, Arts Mag, 11/77. *Mailing Add:* 9 E 16th St 4th Floor New York NY 10003

DASENBROCK, DORIS (NANCY) VOSS
DESIGNER, PAINTER
b Horicon, Wis, Nov 6, 39. *Study:* Wis State Univ, Oshkosh, BS, 62; Fla State Univ, Tallahassee, MFA, 67; Univ Md, 79. *Work:* Fla State Univ Fine Arts Collection, Tallahassee; Mus Art, Ft Wayne, Ind; US House Rep, Washington, DC. *Comn:* Contemporary design, St Matthew's Episcopal Church, St Petersburg, 69; altar, Bowie, Md, 70, stained glass designs, 79, All Saints Lutheran Church, Bowie, Md. *Exhib:* Am Acad Arts & Lett, New York, 69 & 70; West Bend Galley Fine Art, Wis, 76; St Paul Mus Art, Minn, 77; Tweed Mus Art, Duluth, Minn, 77; South Alleghenies Mus, Loretto, Pa, 78; Mus Tex Tech Univ, Lubbock, 78; Fed Bldg, Washington, DC, 79. *Collections Arranged:* Artists Today Traveling Exhib, Prince George's Col,

Marlboro Gallery, 79; Photography 79, Capital Ctr Gallery, 79. *Pos:* Exhib specialist, Capital Park Planning Comn, Riverdale, Md, 78-79; designer & illusr, Sterling Inst, Washington, DC, 79; media designer & coordr, Am Investment Corp, Rockville, Md, 79- *Teaching:* Instr, Montgomery Col, Takoma Park, Md, 69-70; instr, Bowie State Col, Md, 75-76. *Awards:* Childe Hassom Purchase Award, Am Acad Arts & Lett, 69; Art Purchase Award, Benedictine Corp, 76; Award Excellence, Simpson Paper Co, 80. *Bibliog:* Brian Abbott (auth), Artist profile, Bowie Blade, Md, 6/3/76. *Mem:* Washington Women's Art Ctr; Women's Caucus Art; Artists Equity Asn; Md Fedn Art; Southern Watercolor Soc. *Media:* Watercolor, Oil; Pen & Ink. *Publ:* Illusr, Probing the physical world: Excursions, Fla State Univ, Tallahassee, 67; illusr, Air Conditioning, Refrigeration and Heating, Nat Res Inst, Washington, DC; 73; illusr, Householder's Appliance Repair Course, McGraw-Hill, 74; illusr, Job Assessment and Career Development Guide, Sterling Inst, 79. *Dealer:* Jansson Art Gallery Rte 6A Barnstable MA 02637. *Mailing Add:* 1407 Pennington Lane Bowie MD 20716

DASH, HARVEY DWIGHT
ADMINISTRATOR, PAINTER
b Brooklyn, NY, June 28, 24. *Study:* Pratt Inst; Tyler Sch Fine Arts, Temple Univ, BFA, BSEd & MFA; Rutgers Univ; Columbia Univ; Montclair State Col. *Exhib:* Pa Acad Fine Arts, Philadelphia; Temple Univ; one-man shows, Fairleigh Dickinson Univ & Brighton Gallery, New York. *Pos:* Supvr art, Bound Brook Bd Educ, 48-51; dir creative arts, Paramus Sch Syst, 53-67; dir, Lighthouse Art Gallery, Nyack, NY, 67-69; dir, Dash Sch of Art (formerly Lighthouse Sch Art), Grandview, NY, 67-78. *Teaching:* Instr fine art, Temple Univ, 46-47; chmn dept art, Tenafly High Sch, 51-57 & Paramus High Sch, NJ, 57-63. *Awards:* Paramus Bd Educ grants, 65 & 66. *Mem:* NY State Art Teachers Asn; Nat Art Educ Asn. *Media:* Oils, Watercolor. *Mailing Add:* 654 Rte 9W Nyack NY 10960

DASH, ROBERT (WARREN)
PAINTER
b New York, NY, June 8, 34. *Work:* Brooklyn Mus, NY; Hirshhorn Mus; Pittsburgh Mus Art; Joslyn Art Mus, Omaha, Nebr; Philadelphia Mus Art; and others. *Comn:* Centennial, Cheesebrough-Pond's Inc. *Exhib:* The New York Season, 60-61; Yale Univ Exhib, 61; Landscapes by Five Americans, Festival of Two Worlds, Mus Mod Art Traveling Exhib, 66; Inform & Interpret, Am Fedn Arts Traveling Exhib, 68; The New Realism, Hirschl & Adler Galleries, New York, 81; New Acquisitions, Hirshhorn Mus, 83. *Teaching:* Adj prof advan painting, Southampton Col, spring 70, 75, 77 & 81. *Bibliog:* Gerrit Henry (auth), The making of the new Utopia, Art Int, spring 73; article, Am Artist, spring 74; The new realists, Art in Am, 9-10/81. *Media:* Oils, Pastels. *Dealer:* Prescott Schutz 205 W 57 St New York NY. *Mailing Add:* Sagg Main Sagaponack NY 11962

D'ASHNASH-TOSI (BARBARA CHASE-RIBOUD)
SCULPTOR, WRITER
b US, June 26, 39. *Study:* Temple Univ, BFA, PhD; Yale Univ, MFA. *Hon Degrees:* TempleD. *Work:* Mus Mod Art, New York; Berkeley Mus, Univ Calif; Newark Mus, NJ; Beaubourg Mus, Paris; NY State Off Bldg; and others. *Comn:* Fountain, Wheaton Plaza Ctr, Washington, DC; multi-colored bronze sculpture, Lannan Found, Fla; bronze & silk sculpture, Metrop Mus, New York. *Exhib:* One-man shows, Detroit Art Inst, 73, Indianapolis Art Mus, 73, Mus Mod Art, Paris, 74, Kunstmuseum, Dusseldorf, 74, Kunstmuseum, Baden-Baden, 79 & Bronx Mus, New York, 81. *Pos:* Lectr, US State Dept, Tunisia, Senegal, Mali, Ghana, Ivory Coast, and others, currently. *Awards:* Nat Endowment Arts Individual Grant, 73; John Hay Whitney Fel. *Bibliog:* Francoise Nora (auth), Another country, Art News, 72; Waller (auth), Textile sculptures, Studio Vista, 73; The Originals: American Women Artists, Munro, 80. *Media:* Miscellaneous. *Publ:* Auth, Sally Hemings--A Novel, (French, Ger, Ital, Spanish & Swed transl), Viking, 79. *Dealer:* Hessmayling Corp 45 Blvd St Michel Bruxelles Belg. *Mailing Add:* 3 Auguste-Comte 75006 Paris France

DASKALOFF, GYORGY
PAINTER
b Sofia, Bulgaria, May 15, 23; US citizen. *Study:* Acad Fine Arts, Sofia, grad. *Work:* Metrop Mus Art, New York; Nat Mus, Sofia; Royal Libr, Brussels, Belg; Butler Inst Am Art, Youngstown, Ohio. *Comn:* Mural, comn by ARA, Ann Arbor, Mich; portrait of Judge Theodor Levin, Detroit Bar Asn, 71; An American Family (mural), comn by Amos Cahan, New York, 73. *Exhib:* Bulgarian Art in Berlin, 58, Moscow, 59 & Prague, 59; Int Biennial Graphic Arts, Ljubljana, 59; Int Exhib Graphics, Leipzig, 60; Comparisons, Paris, 65-67. *Awards:* First Prize for Graphics, Bulgaria, 54 & 59. *Bibliog:* Pierre Rouve (auth), article, Arts Rev, London, 6/3/61; L L Sosset (auth), article, Les Beaux Arts, Brussels, 5/6/65; Pierre Lubecker (auth), article, Politiken, Copenhagen, 5/25/67. *Media:* Oil. *Mailing Add:* 46 Great Jones St New York NY 10012

DASS, DEAN ALLEN
PRINTMAKER, EDUCATOR
b Hampton, Iowa, Nov 16, 55. *Study:* Univ Northern Iowa, Cedar Falls, BA, 78; Tyler Sch Art, Temple Univ, MFA, 80. *Work:* Nat Collection Poland, Krakow; Brooklyn Mus, NY; Charlotte Printmaker's Soc, NC; Kansas State Univ, Laurence; Univ Dallas, Irving, Tex. *Exhib:* Intergrafia, Katowicz, Poland, 80; Int Print Biennale, Krakow, Poland, 80; Knots and Fetishes, World Print Coun, San Francisco, 81; Nat Print Exhib, Brooklyn Mus, NY, 81; 59th Ann Int Exhib, Print Club, Philadelphia, 83; Impressions: Experimental Prints, Inst Contemp Art, Richmond, Va, 83; Artist as Printmaker, Brooklyn Mus, NY, 83. *Teaching:* Supervisor, Info Conserv Inc,

Horsham, Pa, 80-83; instr printmaking & drawing, Kutztown Univ, Pa, 83-
Awards: Purchase Award, Vermillion 80, Univ SDak, 79. *Bibliog:* Ann
Jarmusch (auth), article, Art News, 5/83. *Mem:* Philadelphia Print Club; Col
Art Asn. *Dealer:* Assoc Am Artists 1614 Latimer St Philadelphia PA 19103.
Mailing Add: 766 Rock Lane Elkins Park PA 19117

DATER, JUDY
PHOTOGRAPHER, WRITER
b Hollywood, Calif, June 21, 41. *Study:* Univ Calif, Los Angeles, 59-62; San
Francisco State Univ, BA, 63, MA, 66. *Work:* San Francisco Mus Mod Art;
Ctr Creative Photog, Tucson, Ariz; Bibliot Nat, Paris; Boston Mus Fine Arts;
Mus Mod Art, New York. *Exhib:* Solo exhibs, Art Inst Chicago, 72, Oakland
Mus, Calif, 74, Atlanta Gallery, Ga, 81, Catskill Ctr Photog, Woodstock, NY,
81, Camera Obscura Gallery, Denver, 81, Spectrum Gallery, Fresno, Calif, 81
& Yuen Lui Gallery, Seattle, 82; Photography in America, Whitney Mus, 74;
Women of Photography, San Francisco Mus Art, 75; Mirrors and Windows
Traveling Exhib, Mus Mod Art, New York, 78-80; and others. *Collections
Arranged:* Imogen Cunningham: A Portrait Traveling Exhib, (auth, catalog),
New York Graphic Soc, 79. *Teaching:* Instr photog, San Francisco Art Inst,
Calif, 74-78. *Awards:* Dorothea Lange Award, Oakland Mus, 74; Nat
Endowment Arts Fel, 76; J S Guggenheim Mem Found fel, 78. *Bibliog:* Hal
Fisher (auth), Bay area photography, Picture Mag, 6/79; Gilles Walinski
(auth), Judy Dater and Jack Welpott, Zoom, Paris, 11-12/79; Richard S Street
(auth), Judy Dater, Pac Sun, 2/1/80. *Mem:* San Francisco Camerawork; Soc
Photog Educ. *Publ:* Coauth, Women and Other Visions, Morgan & Morgan,
75. *Dealer:* Collected Images PO Box 5154 Berkeley CA 94705. *Mailing Add:*
Box 709 San Anselmo CA 94960

DAUDELIN, CHARLES
SCULPTOR
b Granby, Que, Can, Oct 1, 20. *Study:* Ecole du Meuble de Montreal, 41-43;
with Fernand Leger, New York, 43-44, Paris, 46-48; with Henri Laurens,
Paris, 46-48. *Work:* Nat Gallery, Ottawa, Can; Mus D'Art Contemp,
Montreal; Mus Quebec; McGill Univ, Montreal. *Comn:* Iron fountain
sculpture, Prov Govt, Charlottetown, PEI, 66; Place Des Arts (bronze),
Montreal, 67; Nat Art Ctr (bronze), Ottawa, 69; Chaos (corten fountain),
Quebec, 73; Bronze mural, Notre Dame Church, Montreal. *Exhib:* Innovation
65, Art Gallery Mus Beaux Arts, Montreal, 65; Naissance D'Une Sculpture,
Art Contemp, Montreal, and traveling, 69-72; Panorama de la Sculpture 45-
70, Mus Art Contemp, Montreal & Paris, 70; Biennale Middelheim, Anvers,
Belgium, 71; retrospectives, Art Contemp Mus, Montreal, 74 & Mus Quebec,
74. *Teaching:* prof allied arts, Univ Que, Montreal, 64-68 & 73-, Univ Que,
Chicoutimi, 71-73 *Awards:* Prix de la Province for Painting, Que Govt, 46;
Allied Arts Award for Sculpture, Royal Archit Inst Can, 73; Bene Merenti de
Patria, Philippe Hebert Award, Soc St Jean Baptiste, Montreal, 81. *Bibliog:*
Louis Jacques Beaulieu (auth), Daudelin toujours vivant, Vie des Arts,
summer 64; B P Dozol (auth), Amenagement D'Une Chapelle a Quebec, In:
Structures, Art Chretien, France, 67; Pierre Moretti (dir), Bronze (film), Nat
Film Bd, Montreal, 69. *Mem:* Contemp Art Soc; Collaboration with Archit;
Conseil Sculpture Quebec; Royal Can Acad Arts. *Media:* Bronze, Stainless
Steel. *Dealer:* Michel Tetreault 4260 Rue St Denis Montreal PQ Can H2J
2K8; Galerie Fucito 5283 Ave du Parc Montreal PQ Can H2V 4G9. *Mailing
Add:* 17166 Chemin Ste-Marie Kirkland PQ H9J 2K9 Canada

DAUGHERTY, MARSHALL HARRISON
SCULPTOR, ADMINISTRATOR
b Macon, Ga, Sept 6, 15. *Study:* Ringling Art Sch; Mercer Univ, Macon, Ga;
Yale Sch Fine Arts & Cranbrook Acad Art, with Carl Milles et al, 31-38.
Work: Solomon R Guggenheim Mus, New York; Hay House Mus &
Washington Libr, Macon, Ga; Middle Ga Col, Cochran. *Comn:* Numerous
portrait busts and small sculptures, comn by orgns & individuals, 30-77; Royal
Monument, Royal Singing Convention, Mystic, Ga, 55; John Wesley
Monument (heroic size, bronze & granite), United Methodists, Savannah, Ga,
69; The Praying World, Macon Bicentennial Comn, Macon Coliseum, 76; and
others. *Exhib:* Grand Cent Galleries, New York, 37; Detroit Art Mus, Mich,
40; Houston Mus Art, Tex, 50; Mint Mus Art, Charlotte, NC, 61. *Pos:* Pres,
Ga Art Teachers Asn, 44 & Asn Ga Artists, 44; chmn dept art, Mercer Univ,
Macon, Ga, 45-; pres, Macon Art Asn, 48; vpres, Southern Asn Sculptors,
64-67. *Teaching:* Instr sculpture, Wesleyan Sch Fine Arts, Macon, Ga, 40-45;
prof art, Mercer Univ, Macon, Ga, 45- *Awards:* Yaddo Fel, Saratoga Springs,
NY, 39; Carnegie Grant, 46 & 47. *Mailing Add:* 1831 Upper River Rd Macon
GA 31211

DAUGHERTY, MICHAEL F
EDUCATOR, SCULPTOR
b Seattle, Wash, Sept 30, 42. *Study:* Univ Wash, Seattle, 60-62; Univ
Barcelona, Spain, 64-65; Univ Wash, Seattle, BA(sculpture), 69; Univ Tenn,
Knoxville, MFA(sculpture), 71. *Comn:* Outdoor fountains, comn by Walter
H Stevens, Knoxville, 70, Genevieve Stoughton, Oak Ridge, 71, Alvin
Rotenberg, Baton Rouge, 73, Janice Sachse, Baton Rouge, 74 & Derwood
Facundus, Baton Rouge,, 76. *Exhib:* 16th Joslyn Biennial, Joslyn Art Mus,
Omaha, Nebr, 80; Nat Drawing and Sculpture Exhib, Del Mar Art Gallery,
Corpus Christi, Tex, 81; Nat Sculpture Exhib, Westwood Ctr Arts, Los
Angeles, Calif, 81; Biennial Five State Exhib, Fine Arts Gallery, Port Arthur,
Tex, 81; Art for Arts Sake, Contemp Arts Ctr, New Orleans, La, 81; and many
others. *Teaching:* Asst, Univ Tenn, 69-71; instr, Art Ctr, Oak Ridge, Tenn,
70; assoc prof sculpture, La State Univ, 71- *Awards:* Purchase Award, Tenn
Sculpture 1970, Tenn Arts Comn, 71; Purchase Award, 7th Ann Mobile Art
Exhib, Mobile, Ala, 72; Second Place Award, Biennial Five State Exhib, Port
Arthur, Tex. *Mem:* Southern Asn Sculptors; Col Art Asn; Int Sculpture Ctr;
Southeastern Col Art Asn. *Dealer:* Adelle M Taylor Gallery 3317 McKinney
Ave Dallas TX 75204. *Mailing Add:* 5246 N Chalet Ct Baton Rouge LA
70808

DAUGHTERS, ROBERT A
PAINTER, PRINTMAKER
b Trenton, Mo, Feb 17, 29. *Study:* Kansas City Art Inst & Sch Design, Dipl,
53. *Work:* Koshore Indian Mus, Lajunta, Colo; Valley Nat Bank, Phoenix,
Ariz; NMex State Fair, Albuquerque; Maytag Found, New York. *Exhib:*
NMex State Fair, Albuquerque, 72; Taos 6 Exhib, Philbrook Mus, Tulsa,
Okla, 76; Western Heritage Sale, Shamrock Hilton Hotel, Houston, Tex, 78;
The Driscol Collection Am Western Art, Beijing Exhib Ctr, China, 81; Soc
Am Impressionists, 83. *Pos:* Partner, Moyer Crandall Art Studio, Kansas City,
Mo, 54-70. *Awards:* Best of Show & Gov Purchase Award, NMex State Fair,
72. *Bibliog:* Elizabeth Rigby (auth), 1980, Southwest Art (Anniversary Issue),
5/81; Don H Jones (auth), Robert Daughters, artist, Santa Fean Mag, 12/82;
Trica Hurst (auth), Robert Daughters--Contemporary American
Impressionist, NMex Mag, 8/83; and others. *Mem:* Nat Soc Art Dir. *Media:*
Oil. *Publ:* Illusr, New Mexico Magazine's Distinguished Artist Calendar-84,
Works by Robert Daughters, 84. *Dealer:* Trailside Gallery Scottsdale AZ;
Taos Art Gallery Taos NM. *Mailing Add:* 704 San Antonio PO Box 1754
Taos NM 87571

D'AULAIRE, EDGAR PARIN
ILLUSTRATOR, PAINTER
b Munich, Ger, Sept 30, 98; US citizen. *Study:* Kunstgewerbeschule; Hans
Hofmann Sch; Ecole Andre Lhote; Ecole Pola Gaugin, Paris. *Comn:* Fresco
in church, Drammen, Norway; Hopkin Ctr, Hanover, NH. *Exhib:* Salon
d'Automne, Paris; Galerie Wang, Oslo, Norway. *Awards:* Caldecott Medal,
Am Libr Asn, 40; Regina Award, Cath Libr Asn, 70. *Bibliog:* Esther Averill
(auth), Caldecott Medal Books, Vol II, Horn, 57; B Hurlimann (auth), Die
Welt im Bilderbuch, Atlantis Verlag, Zurich, 65; L B Hopkins (auth), Books
Are by People, Citation, 69. *Mem:* Artists Guild. *Media:* Mixed. *Publ:* Coauth
& co-illusr, Ola, 32, Greek Myths, 62, Norse Gods & Giants, 67, Trolls, 72,
Terrible Troll Bird, 76, Doubleday; and many others. *Mailing Add:* 74 Mather
Rd Georgetown CT 06829

D'AULAIRE, INGRI (MORTENSON) PARIN
PAINTER, WRITER
b Kongsberg, Norway, Dec 27, 04; US citizen. *Study:* Kunstindustriskolen,
Oslo, 23-24; Hans Hofmann Sch Art, Munich, Ger, 24-25; Acad Lhote; also
with Pola Gaugin & Scandinaie, Paris, 25-29. *Work:* Hopkin Ctr, Hanover,
NH. *Exhib:* Salon d'Automne, 27-29. *Awards:* Caldecott Medal, Am Libr
Asn, 40; Regina Medal, Cath Libr Asn, 70. *Bibliog:* L B Hopkins (auth), Books
Are by People, Citation, 69. *Mem:* Authors Guild Am. *Media:* Oils, Pastels.
Publ: Coauth & co-illusr, Ola, 32, Abraham Lincoln, 39, Greek Myths, 62,
Trolls, 72, & Terrible Troll Bird, 76, Doubleday; and others. *Mailing Add:* Lia
Farm 74 Mather Rd Georgetown CT 06829

DAUTERMAN, CARL CHRISTIAN
HISTORIAN, LECTURER
b Newark, NJ. *Study:* Newark Sch Fine & Indust Art; Newark Mus
Apprentice Training Course; NY Univ, BA; Columbia Univ, MA(art hist).
Collections Arranged: Numerous exhibs in decorative arts, especially
ceramics. *Pos:* Mgr spec exhibs, Cooper Union Mus Arts of Decoration,
38-42; catalog writer decorative objects, Parke-Bernet Galleries, 46-53; spec
admin consult to the dir, Metrop Mus Art, 53-55, from assoc cur to cur
Western Europ arts, 55-73, emer cur, 73- *Teaching:* From lectr to adj prof
Europ & Am decorative arts, Columbia Univ, 51-; vis prof art hist, Winterthur
Mus, Univ Del, 73-74. *Awards:* Guest archaeologist, Mex Govt Field Exped,
Monte Alban, Oaxaca, 36; Award for Outstanding Achievement, Sch Gen
Studies, Columbia Univ, 75. *Mem:* Am Friends Attingham Summer Sch; Am
Ceramic Circle; Wedgwood Int Sem; Decorative Arts Chap, Soc Archit
Historians; Am Soc 18th Century Studies. *Res:* Extensive analysis in 18th
century archives of Manufacture Nationale de Sevres. *Publ:* Auth, Sevres, 69;
coauth (with Sir Francis Watson), Catalogue of the Wrightsman Collection
III: Furniture, Snuffboxes, Silver, 70; auth, Catalogue of the Wrightsman
Collection IV: porcelains, 70; auth, Sevres Porcelain: Makers and Marks, 18th
Century, Metrop Mus Art, 84; auth, Sevres Porcelain: Makers and Their
Marks, XVIII Century, Metrop Mus Art, 84. *Mailing Add:* 1326 Madison
Ave New York NY 10128

DAVENPORT, RAY
PAINTER, PRINTMAKER
b Rockville Centre, NY, May 5, 26. *Study:* Pratt Inst, cert(advan design), 48;
Univ SC, Columbia, 80. *Work:* SC Permanent Collection, Columbia; Erskine
Col, SC; Calhoun Co Mus, St Matthews, SC. *Comn:* Sumter Skyline (wall
mural), First Fed Savings & Loan, SC, 72; Sumter County (wall mural),
Sumter Co, SC, 74; Bicentennial (oil painting), First Fed Savings & Loan,
Sumter, SC, 75. *Exhib:* Twenty-Fifth SC Artists Exhib, Gibbes Art Gallery,
72; 14th Hunter Ann, Hunter Mus Art, 74; Nat Soc Painters Casein & Acrylic
Ann, Nat Acad Galleries, New York, 77 & Am Acad & Inst Arts & Lett, New
York, 79; First Ann Non-Member Exhib, Salmagundi Club, New York, 78;
SC Watercolor Soc First Ann, Columbia Mus Art, SC, 78; Allied Artists Am
80th Ann, Nat Arts Club, New York, 83. *Awards:* Saul Alexander Found
Award, 25th SC Artists Exhib, 72; Ralph Fabri Award, Nat Soc Painters
Casein & Acrylic 20th Ann, 73; Atto Newer Award, Allied Artists Am 80th
Ann, 83. *Mem:* Nat Soc Painters Casein & Acrylic; Allied Artists Am;
Southern Graphics Coun; Guild SC Artists (secy & treas, 77-78); SC
Watercolor Soc. *Media:* Acrylic, Watercolor; Lithography. *Dealer:* G
McKenna Gallery 1521 Providence Rd Charlotte NC 28207. *Mailing Add:*
274 Keels Rd Sumter SC 29154

DAVENPORT, REBECCA READ
PAINTER, LECTURER
b Alexandria, Va, June 29, 43. *Study:* Pratt Inst, Brooklyn, NY, BFA(with honors), 66-70; Univ NC, Greensboro, MFA, 70-73. *Work:* Baltimore Mus Art, Md; Corcoran Gallery Art, Washington, DC; Chrysler Mus, Norfolk, Va; Federal Reserve Bank, Richmond, Va. *Exhib:* Selected 20th Century Nudes, Harold Reed Gallery, New York, 78; Mus d'Art Mod de la Villes de Paris, France, 78; Taft Menagerie, Taft Mus, Cincinnati, Ohio, 80; Images of the 70's, Corcoran Gallery Art, Washington, DC, 80; Inside Out, Newport Harbor Art Mus, Newport Beach, Calif, 81; Real, Really Real, Super Real, San Antonio Mus, Tex, 81; Contemp Am Realism Since 60, Pa Acad Fine Art, Philadelphia, Pa, 81. *Awards:* Cert of Distinction, Va Mus, Richmond, 73; Third Gold Palette, IV Festival IX de la Peinture, Cagnes Sur Mir, France, 77; Artist Fel, Nat Endowment Arts, 79. *Bibliog:* Theodore F Wolff (auth), Solving the mystery of the missing subject, Christian Sci Monitor, 10/1/80; Aubyn Kendall (ed), Real, Really Real, Super Real, San Antonio Mus Asn, 81; Frank H Goodyear (auth), Contemporary American Realism Since 1960, New York Graphic Soc, 81. *Media:* Oil. *Dealer:* Osuna Gallery 406 Seventh St NW Washington DC; Aberbach Fine Arts 988 Madison Ave New York NY. *Mailing Add:* 3110 Mt Pleasant St NW Washington DC 20009

DAVEY, RONALD A
HISTORIAN, EDUCATOR
b United Kingdom. *Study:* Wallasey Sch Art; Courtauld Inst, Univ London; Ecole Hautes Etudes, Univ Paris. *Teaching:* Asst lectr art, Slade Sch Fine Art, Univ London, 54-58; lectr, Univ Newcastle upon Tyne, 58-64; principal, West Sussex Col Art, 64-67; prof art & design, Univ Alta, 67-, chmn, 67-76. *Mem:* Fel Royal Soc Arts. *Mailing Add:* Dept Art & Design Univ Alta Edmonton AB T6G 2E1 Canada

DAVID, CYRIL FRANK
GRAPHIC ARTIST
b London, Eng, July 13, 20; US citizen. *Exhib:* The Nude, Himelfarb Gallery, Water Mill, NY, 80; Art of Drawing, Staempfli Gallery, New York, 80; Members Selections, Corcoran Gallery Art, Washington, DC, 80; one-man show, Capricorn Galleries, Washington, DC, 81; Ann Exhib, 82 & Joint Awards Exhib, 83, Guild Hall Mus, East Hampton, NY; and others. *Awards:* Nat Endowment Arts Fel, 80; Best Miniature Work, Guild Hall Mus, 82; Creative Artists Pub Serv Fel, NY State Coun Arts, 83. *Bibliog:* Valentin Tatransky (auth), article, Art Int, 81; Ruth Bass (auth), article, Art News, 80; Helen Harrison (auth), article, New York Times, 81. *Mem:* Drawing Soc. *Media:* Pencil. *Dealer:* Capricorn Galleries 4849 Rugby Ave Bethesda Md 20014. *Mailing Add:* PO Box 100 Sag Harbor NY 11963

DAVID, DON RAYMOND
PAINTER, INSTRUCTOR
b Springbrook, Ore, May 2, 10. *Study:* Art Ctr Sch Los Angeles; Chouinard's, Los Angeles; Hans Hoffman Sch, New York. *Work:* Corcoran Gallery Art, Washington, DC; Ciba Geigy Corp; IBM Corp. *Exhib:* One-man shows, Webb Gallery, Los Angeles, 47, Camino Gallery, New York, 56, 58 & 60, New Sch Social Res, New York, 65, Baruch Col, 72 & Alonzo Gallery, New York, 69, 70, 72 & 78; The New American Still Life, Westmoreland Co Mus Art, Greensburg, Pa, 79; Still Life, Lamont Gallery, Phillips Exeter Acad, NH, 81. *Teaching:* Instr drawing, Art Ctr Sch Los Angeles, 46-48; instr hist pictorial art & illus, Newark Sch Fine & Indust Art, NJ, 68-; instr, Parson's Sch Design, New York, 83. *Bibliog:* Article in Am Artist Mag, 8/79. *Media:* Acrylic, Watercolor. *Dealer:* Alonzo Gallery 26 E 63rd St New York NY 10012. *Mailing Add:* 521 East 14th St Apt 9B New York NY 10009

DAVIDEK, STEFAN
PAINTER
b Flint, Mich, May 15, 24. *Study:* Flint Inst Arts, with Jaroslav Brozik; Art Students League, with Morris Kantor; Cranbrook Acad, with Fred Mitchell. *Work:* Detroit Inst Arts, Mich; Flint Inst Arts, Mich; Muskegon Community Col & Hackley Art Mus, Mich; Albion Col. *Comn:* Dioramas, Carol Churchill Pierson Children's Gallery, Flint, 65-72 & 77-; mosaic, St Luke Cath Church, Flint, 69; sanctuary wall, Luke M Powers Sch, Flint, 70; interior murals, Zehnders, Frankenmuth, Mich, 80 & 81. *Exhib:* Mich Artists Show, 46-61; Flint Ann, 46-75; Butler Midyear Show, 59; Pa Acad Fine Art 9; Flint Invitational, 70. *Awards:* Founder's Prize, 61 & Lou R Maxon Prize, Detroit Inst Art. *Media:* Oil, Watercolor. *Dealer:* Forsythe Galleries 201 Nickels Arcade Ann Arbor MI 48108. *Mailing Add:* 5391 W Coldwater Rd Flint MI 48504

DAVIDOVICH, JAIME
PAINTER
b Buenos Aires, Arg, Sept 27, 36; US citizen. *Study:* Univ of the Republic, Uruguay, scholar, 59; Sch Visual Arts, New York, 63. *Work:* Mus Arte Mod, Buenos Aires; Mus Belas Artes, Rio de Janiero, Brazil. *Comn:* Carroll Wall Proj, John Carroll Univ, Cleveland, Ohio, 71. *Exhib:* One-man show, Retrospective 1962-1972, Drake Univ, Des Moines, Iowa, 71; Exp in Art & Technol Show, Lake Erie Col, Ohio, 71; Five Artists, New Gallery, Cleveland, Ohio, 72; Arte de Sistemas, Mus Mod Art, Buenos Aires & Mus Fine Arts, Santiago, Chile, 72; Akron Art Inst, Ohio, 72. *Pos:* Off rep to US, Di Tella Found, 63-64; coun mem, Int Soc Educ Through Art, 63-; pres, Artists TV Network, 77- *Teaching:* Prof painting, Sch Visual Arts, Bahia Blanca, Arg, 61-62. *Awards:* Di Tella Found grant to rep Arg at Int Cong Educ Through Art, Montreal, 63; Creative Artists Pub Serv grant, video, 75; Nat Endowment Art Artists Fel, 78. *Bibliog:* R Squirru (auth), International art exhibit, Mus Art Mod, Buenos Aires, 60; R Welchans (auth), Carroll project 1971, Fine Arts Mag, 71. *Mailing Add:* 152 Wooster New York NY 10012

DAVIDOWITZ (DROR), MOSHE
HISTORIAN, WRITER
b New York, NY, July 19, 34. *Study:* Jewish Theological Seminary, 59; New York Univ, PhD, 76. *Collections Arranged:* See and Sanctify: On Jewish Symbols (auth, catalog), Yeshiva Univ Mus, New York, 79. *Pos:* Dir, Spertus Mus Judaica, Chicago, 68-71. *Teaching:* Fac Jewish art, New York Univ, currently; fac Jewish art, New Sch, New York, currently; fac Jewish art, Hofstra Univ, Hempstead, Long Island, currently; dean art sch, Ramat Haneger Col, Yeroham, Israel, currently. *Mem:* Nat Coun Art Jewish Life (pres, 68-78). *Res:* Symbols in Jewish art; development of Judaic arts using high technology techniques. *Publ:* Ed, Readings on Jewish Art, six vols, 70-78 & ed, First Jewish Art Annual, 80, Nat Coun Art Jewish Life; auth, Exploring Jewish Symbols, Yeshiva Univ, 79. *Mailing Add:* Ramat Hanegev Col Yeroham Israel

DAVIDSON, ABRAHAM A
WRITER, PHOTOGRAPHER
b Dorchester, Mass, June 27, 35. *Study:* Harvard Univ, AB, 57; Hebrew Teachers Col, Boston, BJed, 60; Boston Univ, AM(art hist), 60; Columbia Univ, PhD(art hist), 65. *Work:* Insurance Co North Am; Bank Leumi; Sch Pharmacy, Temple Univ; Villanova Univ; Lehigh Univ. *Exhib:* One-man shows, Paley Libr, Temple Univ, 72, Painted Bride Art Gallery, Philadelphia, 74, Burlington Co Community Col, NJ, 78 & Gloucester Co Col, NJ, 79. *Teaching:* Instr art hist, Wayne State Univ, 64-65; asst prof, Oakland Univ, 65-68; from asst prof to prof, Tyler Sch Art, Temple Univ, 68- *Awards:* Group 17 Prize for Photog, Detroit Inst Arts, 69. *Bibliog:* Burt Wasserman (auth), People and places come to life in collection of photographs, NJ Courier Post, 11/10/79; Mary T Gregory (auth), Two artists display works, Villanovan, 2/19/82; Burt Wasserman (auth), Abraham Davidson, New Art Examiner, 4/83. *Res:* History of 19th and 20th century American painting and sculpture. *Publ:* Auth, The Story of American Painting, Abrams, 74; auth, Two from the second decade: Manierrc Dawson & John Covert, Art in Am, 9-10/75; auth, The Eccentrics & Other American Visionary Painters, Dutton, 78; auth, Demuth's poster portraits, Artforum, 11/78; auth, Early American Modernist Painting 1910-1935, Harper & Row, 81. *Mailing Add:* Tyler Sch Art Temple Univ Beech & Penrose Ave Elkins Park PA 19126

DAVIDSON, ALLAN ALBERT
PAINTER, SCULPTOR
b Springfield, Mass, Feb 24, 13. *Study:* Sch Mus Fine Art, Boston; Ecole Beaux Arts, Paris; Fogg Mus, BA; Maitre Arts. *Exhib:* NShore Art Asn; Provincetown Art Asn; Berkshire Mus; Fitchburg Mus; Boston Mus Fine Arts; Nat Acad; and others in US and Europe. *Pos:* Pres, Cape Ann Soc Mod Art, formerly; set designer, S Shore Playhouse, Cohasset, Mass, 41; corresp, Stars & Stripes, World War II, formerly. *Awards:* Charles Francis Adams Prize for Bronze Sculpture, Raytheon Co; Salmagundi Club; Am Artists Prof League; and others. *Mem:* Am Watercolor Soc; Boston Watercolor Soc; Am Artists Prof League; Rockport Art Asn; Concord Art Asn; and others. *Media:* Watercolor, Oil; Marble, Bronze. *Mailing Add:* 8 Dean Rd Box 7 Rockport MA 01966

DAVIDSON, ELIZABETH H DONNALLY
DEALER
b Newport, RI, Mar 28, 48. *Study:* Reed Col, BA, 70, MA, 71; Harvard Univ, arts mgt cert, 77; Portland State Univ. *Pos:* Dir mem & develop, Portland Art Mus, Ore, 75-78; dir artist-in-residence, Ore Arts Comn, Salem, 1/78-9/78; dir, Blackfish Gallery, Portland, 79-; owner, Donnally/Hays Books, Seattle, currently. *Specialty:* local and national artists working in photography, painting and drawing. *Mailing Add:* 85 Yester Way Seattle WA 98104

DAVIDSON, HERBERT LAURENCE
PAINTER, PRINTMAKER
b Green Bay, Wis, Sept 6, 30. *Study:* Art Inst Chicago, Anna Raymond Foreign Traveling Fel, 56. *Work:* Kemper Ins Co; Playboy Mag; Pullman Bank of Chicago; Rahr West Mus, Manitowoc, Wis. *Exhib:* Butler Inst Am Art, Youngstown, Ohio, 65; Alta Col of Art, Calgary, 76; Mendel Art Gallery, Saskatchewan, Can, 77; Chicago Cult Ctr, 79; Syracuse Univ, Lubin Hall, 80; Sao Paolo Mus, Brazil; and others. *Bibliog:* Article, Am Artist Mag, 7/80. *Media:* Oil; Lithography. *Dealer:* Merrill Chase Galleries Chicago IL 60610; Watertower Pl Chicago IL 60610. *Mailing Add:* 406 W Webster Ave Chicago IL 60614

DAVIDSON, IAN J
COLLECTOR, PATRON
b Toronto, Ont, July 21, 25. *Study:* Univ BC, BA;. *Pos:* Dir, Vancouver Art Gallery, 70-74; mem adv art comt, Can Coun, 75-; dir, Community Arts Coun, Vancouver. *Teaching:* Archit at Univ Toronto, Univ BC, Carleton Univ & Bezalel Acad, Jerusalem, Israel. *Awards:* Awards in architecture in every major design award program. *Mem:* Assoc Royal Can Acad Art; fel Royal Archit Inst Can. *Interests:* Commissioning original works by major artists in the non-objective and conceptual fields. *Mailing Add:* 1152 Mainland St Suite 120 Vancouver BC V6B 2T9 Canada

DAVIDSON, J LEROY
HISTORIAN
b Cambridge, Mass, Mar 16, 08. *Study:* Harvard Univ, AB; Inst Fine Arts, NY Univ, MA; Yale Univ, PhD. *Teaching:* Asst prof Asian art, Yale Univ, 47-55; prof Asian art, Claremont Grad Sch, 56-61; prof Asian art, Univ Calif, Los Angeles, 61-76, emer prof, 76-; vis distinguished Maude I Kerns prof, Univ Ore, 76. *Res:* Oriental art. *Publ:* Numerous articles and books on Asian art. *Mailing Add:* Art Dept Univ Calif Los Angeles Los Angeles CA 90024

DAVIDSON, MARSHALL BOWMAN
CRITIC, WRITER
b New York, NY, Apr 26, 07. *Study:* Princeton Univ, BS, 28. *Pos:* Asst cur, Am Wing, Metrop Mus Art, New York, 35-41, assoc cur, 41-47, ed publ, 47-60; ed, Horizon Bks, 61-64; ed, Horizon Mag, Am Heritage Publ Co, New York, 64-66, sr ed, 66- *Teaching:* Lectr Am decorative graphic & fine arts. *Awards:* Carey-Thomas Award for Creative Publishing, 51. *Publ:* Auth, The World in 1776 & Fifty Early American Tools, 75; auth, Bantam Book of Early American Furniture, 80; auth, Guide to the American Wing, Metrop Mus Art, 80; auth, The Drawing of America; Eye Witnesses to History, 83; auth, A History of Art (for children), 84. *Mailing Add:* 140 E 83rd St New York NY 10028

DAVIDSON, MAXWELL, III
DEALER
b New York, NY, Feb 8, 39. *Study:* Williams Col, BA(art hist), 61. *Pos:* Owner, Maxwell Davidson Gallery, 76- *Mem:* Art Dealers Asn Am. *Specialty:* 19th & 20th century masters and contemporary painters. *Mailing Add:* Maxwell Davidson Gallery 43 E 78th St New York NY 10021

DAVIDSON, NANCY
PAINTER
b Chicago, Ill. *Study:* Univ Ill, Chicago Circle, BA, 72; Art Inst Chicago, MFA, 75. *Comn:* Wall installation, City Chicago, 80. *Exhib:* Abstract Art in Chicago, Mus Contemp Art, Chicago, 76; Ten Painters, Walker Art Ctr, 77; 100 Years 100 Artists, Art Inst Chicago, 79; New Dimensions Surface, Mus Contemp Art, Chicago, 79; Works on Paper, Albright-Knox Gallery, 80. *Teaching:* Asst prof, Univ Ill, Champaign, 77-79 & Williams Col, Mass, 80- *Awards:* Fels, Nat Endowment Arts, 78, Yaddo Found, 80 & Mass Coun Arts, 81. *Publ:* Ed, NAME Book I: Artists Statements on Art, Name Gallery, 77. *Mailing Add:* 53 Pearl Brooklyn NY 11201

DAVIDSON, SUZETTE MORTON
PATRON, COLLECTOR
b Chicago, Ill, Aug 24, 11. *Study:* Vassar Col, AB, 34; Art Inst Chicago, 36-40. *Exhib:* Printing Design by Suzette Morton Zurcher (former name), Chicago Pub Libr, Albion Col, Mich & Univ Calif, Santa Barbara. *Pos:* Life Trustee, Art Inst Chicago; life trustee, Newberry Libr; trustee, Morton Arboretum, Lisle, Ill; owner, The Pocahontas Press, 37-; trustee, Santa Barbara Mus Art. *Awards:* Five Selections, 50 Bks of the Year Award, Am Inst Graphic Arts, 42-67. *Mem:* Am Fedn Arts. *Collection:* From classical antiquity to Picasso, with emphasis on seventeenth century Italian painting, pre-Raphaclite paintings and drawings; pre-Columbian gold. *Publ:* Designer numerous exhib catalogs, Art Inst Chicago. *Mailing Add:* 780 Riven Rock Rd Santa Barbara CA 93108

DAVIDSON, THYRA (CLAIRE THYRA WEXLER)
SCULPTOR, DRAFTSMAN
b Brooklyn, NY, Oct 15, 26. *Study:* Nat Acad Design, with John Corbino, 43-45; Brooklyn Mus Art Sch, with Milton Hebald, 45; New Sch Soc Res, with Robert Gwathmey, 45-47. *Work:* Albany Inst Hist Art, NY. *Exhib:* Riverside Mus, New York, 60; Soc Am Graphic Arts Int Print Show, traveling around the world, 60-62; Artists of Mohawk-Hudson Region, Albany Inst & Schenectady Mus, NY, 71-75 & 80; NY Figurative Painting & Sculpture, First St Gallery, New York & Swain Sch, New Bedford, Mass, 71; Brooklyn Col Art Dept, Davis Long & Schoel Kopf Galleries, New York, 77; First St Gallery, New York, 79 & 82; and others. *Teaching:* Adj lectr sculpture, Brooklyn Col, NY, 72-76. *Awards:* Purchase Prize, Albany Inst, 73. *Bibliog:* Gabriel Laderman (auth), Unconventional realists, Artforum Mag, 71. *Media:* Bronze, Plaster. *Dealer:* Mod Art Consult 390 West End Ave New York, NY 10024. *Mailing Add:* 359 Springtown Rd New Paltz NY 12561

DAVIEE, JERRY MICHAEL
ADMINISTRATOR, CURATOR
b Oklahoma City, Okla, Mar 29, 47. *Study:* San Francisco Art Inst, 65-66; Oklahoma City Univ, BA, 69; Univ Tex, Austin, MA, 77. *Collections Arranged:* Argentine Painting & Drawing, Univ Tex Art Mus, 75; Young Texas Artists Series, 77-78, Amarillo Competition, 79 & Jack Boynton: Retro/Spectrum, 80, Amarillo Art Ctr, Tex; Manuel Neri: Drawings & Bronzes, 81 & Sam Francis: Paintings on Paper & Monotypes, 83, Art Mus Asn, San Francisco. *Pos:* Registr, Univ Tex Art Mus, Austin, 74-77; cur, Amarillo Art Ctr, Tex, 77-80; cur, Art Mus Asn Am, San Francisco, 80-81, exhib prog dir, 80-83; planning & development dir, 83- *Mem:* Am Asn Mus; Col Art Asn. *Res:* Contemporary art. *Publ:* Auth, American Paintings 1900-1970, 79, Nancy Chambers, 80, Before Columbus, 80 & Jack Boynton, 80, Amarillo Art Ctr, Tex; auth, Stanton Macdonald-Wright, Art Mus Asn Am, 82. *Mailing Add:* Art Mus Asn Am 270 Sutter St San Francisco CA 94108

DAVIES, HAYDN LLEWELLYN
SCULPTOR, PAINTER
b Rhymney, Wales, Nov 11, 21; Can citizen. *Study:* Ont Col Art, AOCA, 47. *Work:* Mus d'Arte Mod, Venice, Italy; City Hall West Vancouver, BC; Galleria Nazionale d'Arte Mod e Contemporanea, Rome, Italy; Mus Royaux des Beaux-Arts de Belgique Art Mod, Brussels, Belg; Nat Mus Wales, Cardiff. *Comn:* Homage (laminated cedar), Lambton Col Arts & Technol, Sarnia, Ont, 74; Space Composition Red (fabricated aluminum), Govt of Ont, Windsor, 78; Space Composition for Rebecca (fabricated aluminum), Burlington Cult Ctr, Ont, 78; Composition with Five Elements (fabricated welded steel), Gulf Can Ltd, Toronto, 80; plus others. *Exhib:* Toronto-Dominion Ctr, Ont, 78; McIntosh Art Gallery, Univ Western Ont, London, 80; Centenary Exhibition of the Royal Canadian Academy of Arts, 80; Contemporary Sculpture at the

Guild, Toronto, 82; Bridges Exhibition, Pratt Inst, New York, 83; and others. *Teaching:* Artist in residence, Indian River Community Col, 82-83. *Awards:* Sculptor's Soc Can Award, On View, 76. *Bibliog:* Pat Fleisher (auth), Chronology of a sculpture, Artmag, 10/75; Lola Chester McCaffrey (auth), Haydn Davies, Sculptor's News Exchange, 3/79; Nicholas Roukes, Masters of Wood Sculpture, Watson-Guptill, 80. *Mem:* Royal Can Acad Arts. *Media:* Wood, Steel, Wood/Steel. *Mailing Add:* 10 Rose Park Crescent Toronto ON M4T 1P9 Canada

DAVIES, HUGH MARLAIS
HISTORIAN, GALLERY DIRECTOR
b Grahamstown, SAfrica, Feb 12, 48; Brit citizen. *Study:* Princeton Univ, AB, MFA & PhD. *Collections Arranged:* Artist & Fabricator, Univ Mass, 75-; Richard Fleischner (auth, catalog), 77; Stephen Antonakos (auth, catalog), 78; Sam Gilliam (auth, catalog), 78; Al Souza (auth, catalog), 79; John Walker (auth, catalog), 79; George Trakas (auth, catalog), 80; Prints of Barnett Newman (auth, catalog), 83. *Pos:* Asst dir, Monumenta Int Sculpture Exhib, Newport, RI, 74; dir, Univ Gallery, Univ Mass, Amherst, 75-77, La Jolla Mus Contemp Art, 83- *Teaching:* Vis prof, Amherst Col, 80-83. *Awards:* Nat Endowment Arts Fel, 81-82. *Mem:* Am Asn Mus; Col Art Asn. *Res:* 20th century American and European painting, sculpture and photography. *Publ:* Auth, Pop Prints: New Acquisitions, Rec Art Mus, Princeton Univ, 72; coauth, Scale in Contemporary Sculpture, Monumenta, 74; auth, Bacon's Black triptychs, Art Am, 75; Francis Bacon: The Early and Middle Years, 1928-1958, Garland Press; coauth, Sacred Art in a Secular Century (with Norton Davies), Liturgical Press; and others. *Mailing Add:* 2788 Bordeaux Ave La Jolla CA 92037

DAVIES, KENNETH SOUTHWORTH
PAINTER, INSTRUCTOR
b New Bedford, Mass, Dec 20, 25. *Study:* Mass Sch Art, Boston; Yale Sch Fine Art, BFA, 50; New Eng Sch Law, DFA, Boston. *Work:* Wadsworth Atheneum, Hartford, Conn; New Britain Mus Am Art, Conn; Detroit Inst Arts; Springfield Mus Fine Arts, Mass; Univ Nebr, Lincoln. *Comn:* US Postage Stamp commemorative for pharmacy, US Postal Serv, 72, chemistry, 76; Metrop Opera, 83. *Exhib:* American Symbolic Realism, London, Eng, 50; Carnegie Inst Int, 52; Whitney Mus Am Art Ann, 52; Univ Ill Ann, 52; 25 yr retrospective exhib, New Britain Mus Am Art, 71. *Teaching:* Dean drawing, painting & perspective, Paier Sch Art, Hamden, Conn, 53-81, vis prof & dean emer, 81- *Awards:* Louis Comfort Tiffany scholar, 50; Purchase Award, Berkshire Mus, Pittsfield & Springfield Mus, Mass, 50. *Mem:* Silvermine Guild Artists; New Haven Paint & Clay Club (vprcs, 69); Conn Acad Fine Arts (coun mem, 70, pres, 74-76). *Media:* Oil. *Publ:* Auth, Painting Sharp Focus Still Lifes, 75 & Ken Davies--Artist at Work, 78, Watson-Guptill. *Mailing Add:* PO Box 902 Madison CT 06443

DAVIES, THEODORE PETER
PRINTMAKER, PAINTER
b Brooklyn, NY, Oct 9, 28. *Study:* Sch Mod Photog, New York, 52; Art Students League, with George Grosz & Harry Sternberg, John Sloan Merit Scholar, 57-60. *Work:* Mus Mod Art, New York; Nat Gallery Art, Washington, DC; Philadelphia Mus Art; Art Students League; Queens Mus, NY. *Comn:* Six woodcuts on process of papermaking, Scott Paper Co, 60; three ed, woodcuts of New York financial dist, Picture Decorator, 68. *Exhib:* Silvermine Guild Ann; The Sense of Abstraction, Mus Mod Art, New York, 59; East End Arts Coun, NY, 80; Romana Kramoris Gallery, Sag Harbor, NY, 80; Parrish Art Mus, Southampton, NY, 80; Guild Hall, East Hampton, NY, 80; and others. *Awards:* First Prize Graphics, Atlantic City Ann Art Exhib, 59; Creative Artists Pub Serv Fel in Graphics, 73-74. *Bibliog:* Laurence Campbell (auth), article, Art Students League News, 12/61; Gene Paris (auth), article, Long Island Press, 4/23/67; and others. *Mem:* Life mem Art Students League ; Print Coun Am; Print Club Philadelphia; Queens Coun Arts; Jamaica Art Mobilization. *Media:* Woodcut, Serigraphy; Multimedia. *Publ:* Contribr, Woodcuts, 60; contribr, Realistic Abstract Drawing, 60; illusr, Picture Framing, 60. *Dealer:* Assoc Am Artists 663 Fifth Ave New York NY 10022. *Mailing Add:* 87-38 Santiago St Hollis NY 11423

DAVILA, CARLOS
PAINTER, PRINTMAKER
b Lima, Peru, Feb 1, 35. *Study:* Nat Sch Fine Art, Lima. *Work:* Pan Am Union, Washington, DC; Mus Mod Art, Miami; Univ San Marcos, Lima; Mint Mus Art; Mus Arte, Lima. *Comn:* Restoration pre-Colombian archaeol monuments, Chan-Chan, Peru, 63-65. *Exhib:* Fifth Biennale, Mus Mod Art, Paris, 65; Living Arts & Sci Ctr, Loch Haven, Fla, 77; Mus Art, Univ Fla, Gainesville, 77; Pensacola Art Ctr, Fla, 78; Kornbluth Gallery, NJ, 80; Enrique Camino Brent Galeria de Arte, Lima, Peru, 80. *Awards:* First Award, Soc Hebraica Nat Competition, 64; First Award, Jovenes Artistas, Univ San Marcos, 67; First Award, Adela Investment, Mus Arte, 68. *Publ:* Auth, articles, Artes Visuales Mag, Washington, DC, 66-67. *Dealer:* Nabis Fine Art Inc 276 Park Ave S New York NY 10010. *Mailing Add:* 4410 Broadway New York NY 10019

DAVIS, ALONZO JOSEPH
VISUAL ARTIST, ADMINISTRATOR
b Tuskegee, Ala, Feb 2, 42. *Study:* Pepperdine Univ, BA, 64; Otis Art Inst, Los Angeles, BFA, 71, MFA, 73. *Work:* Afro-Am Studies Ctr, Univ Calif, Los Angeles; Libr Collection, Calif Polytechnic Inst, Pomona. *Comn:* Group mural, 50th & Crenshaw, Los Angeles, Calif, 73-75; sculpture, Rogers Recreational Ctr, Los Angeles, 74; mural-retainer wall, Santa Monica Freeway underpass at La Brea, Los Angeles, 75; west wall mural, Watts Towers Neighborhood Arts Ctr, 76; north wall mural, Brockman Gallery

Productions, Los Angeles, 82. *Exhib:* One-man shows, Mod Nordisk Konst, Sweden, 79; Univ Southern Calif, Los Angeles, 80; Am Ctr, Helsinki, Finland, 80; Watts Towers Neighborhood Art Ctr, 81 & Brockman Gallery, Los Angeles, 82; and others. *Collections Arranged:* Brockman Gallery, Los Angeles, ten mo installations, 67-73. *Pos:* Exec dir, Brockman Gallery Productions, Los Angeles, 73-82. *Teaching:* Instr African art, Calif State Univ, Northridge, 76-78; instr, Otis Art Inst, 78-79. *Bibliog:* J Edward Atkinson (auth), Black Dimensions in Contemp Am Art, 71; Lewis & Waddy (auth), Black Artists on Art, Vol II, Pub Contemp Crafts Inc, 71; Elton Fax (auth), Black Artists of the New Generation, Dodd Mead, 77. *Mem:* Artists for Econ Action; Calif Confedn of the Arts (bd mem); Nat Conf of Artists; Am Mus Asn; Smithsonian Assoc. *Publ:* Auth (catalogue introd), Varying Directions of Contemporary Black Artists, State of Calif, 75. *Dealer:* Sol Del Rio Gallery 1020 Townsend Ave San Antonio TX 78209. *Mailing Add:* c/o Brockman Gallery 4334 Degnan Blvd Los Angeles CA 90008

DAVIS, BEN H
ENVIRONMENTAL ARTIST, PAINTER
b Syracuse, NY, June 5, 47. *Study:* Stetson Univ, Fla, ABA; Univ Fla, BS(commun); Fla State Univ, MFA. *Work:* Ctr Creative Photog, Univ Ariz, Tucson; Mus Mod Art, New York; Ctr Creative Photography, Tucson, Ariz; Atlanta Col Art; Mixage Gallery, Caen, France, 81; and others. *Comn:* Marianas Islands (doc film), Am Bicentennial Comn, 75. *Exhib:* Mass Inst Technol, 81; Mail Art, Pieter Brattinga Gallery, Amsterdam, 81; Not Sold in Stores, Atlanta Women's Art Collective, 81; Middendorf/Lane, Washington, DC, 82; Hvidovre Art Libr, Falling, Denmark, 83; Sky Art Conf, Munich, 83. *Pos:* Illusr, Fla State Archives & Mus, 74-75; dir, Senoj, Inc, Atlanta, Ga, 76- *Teaching:* Head dept video & instr photog, Atlanta Col Art, 75-; fac mem, Int Art Network, New York, formerly, Art Inst Chicago, 77; lectr, Sch Visual Arts, 79 & Univ Ill, 80. *Media:* Electronic Media, Crayon. *Publ:* Auth, Role of the artist, Community TV Rev, 4/81; contrib ed, Q/LSSEPA Environmental News, Nova Scotia, 82-83. *Mailing Add:* c/o Atlanta Col Art 1280 Peach St NE Atlanta GA 30301

DAVIS, BERTHA
PAINTER
b Vilno, Lithuania, July 15, 18; US citizen. *Study:* San Miguel Allende Pan Am Col, 60-61; with Fred Samuelson, Harold Phenix 72-73, Ed Whitney, 78 & Ed Betts, 79. *Work:* Luisville City Bank, Tex; Shell Oil Co, Houston, Tex; La Ciudadela, Mex; Inst de Relaciones Culturales, Mex; and 150 pvt collections. *Exhib:* Butler Inst Am Art, 79; one-woman shows, Univ Tex Health Sci Ctr, Dallas, 79 & Jewish Community Gallery, 81; Gallery 13, Dallas; North Lakes Col, Irving, Tex, 82; Simon & Lucet Gallery, Dallas, 83; and others. *Awards:* Honorable Mention, Salmagundi Art Club, 79; Signature Mem, Southwest Watercolor Soc, 81; Second Prize, Tex Fine Arts, 83. *Mem:* Southwest Watercolor Soc, Dallas; Texas Fine Art Asn; Western Art Asn; Watercolor Art Soc, Houston. *Media:* Acrylic, Watercolor. *Publ:* Contribr, La Revue Momderne des Artes de La Vie, 65, 68 & 69; contribr, Repartorium Artis Guide Eropean des Beaux Arts, 66-67 & Vision Mag, 82. *Dealer:* Nimbus Gallery 1135 Dragon St Dallas TX 75207. *Mailing Add:* 715 Gaylewood Dr North Dallas Richardson TX 75080

DAVIS, BRAD (BRADLEY DARIUS)
PAINTER
b Duluth, Minn, Apr 24, 42. *Study:* St Olaf Col, 61; Univ Chicago, 62; Art Inst Chicago, 63; Univ Minn, BA, 66; Hunter Col, 70. *Work:* Neue Galerie, Sammlung Ludwig, Aachen, WGer; Walker Art Ctr, Minneapolis; Whitney Mus Am Art, Mus Mod Art, New York; Saarland Mus, Saarbracken, WGer; and others. *Exhib:* Biennial, 64 & two-person show, 66, Walker Art Ctr, Minneapolis; Ann Exhib, 72 & Am Drawings '63-'73, 73, Whitney Mus Am Art; solo exhibs, Holly Solomon Gallery, New York, 75, 79, 81 & 83; The New Bestiary: Animal Imagery in Contemp Art, Inst Contemp Art, Va Mus, Richmond, 81; Friends of Corcoran Gallery 20th Anniversary Exhib, Corcoran Gallery Art, 81; New Work in Black and White, 81 & A Penthouse Aviary, 81, Art Lending Serv, Mus Mod Art, New York; Decoration and Representation, Alta Col Art Gallery, Can, 82; New Decorative Works from the Collection of Norma & William Roth, Loch Haven Art Ctr, Orlando & Jacksonville Art Mus, Fla, 83; New Decorative Art, Berkshire Mus, Pittsfield, Mass, 83; Back to the USA Traveling Exhib, Kunstmus, Lucerne, Switz, Rheinische Landesmus, Bonn & Kunstverein, Stuttgart, Ger, 83-84; and many others; Landscape/Cityscape, Art Gallery, State Univ NY Potsdam, 78; Pattern & Decoration, Sewall Art Gallery, Rice Univ, 78; Green Magic, Rutgers Univ Gallery, 79; Dekor, Kunstverein, Mannheim, Ger, 80; Am Drawings, Venice Biennale, Italy, 80; and many others. *Awards:* First Prize & Spec Jury Award, Minneapolis Inst Art Biennial, 65; Second Prize & Purchase Prize, Walker Art Ctr, 66. *Bibliog:* Alexandra Anderson (auth), Clay gardens, Portfolio, 3-4/82; Klaus Ahrens (auth), Schreie und Flustern, Stern Mag, Hamburg, Ger, 5/83; Klaus Honnef, New York Aktuelle, Kunstforum Int, 5/83. *Media:* Mixed. *Mailing Add:* c/o Holly Solomon Gallery 724 Fifth Ave New York NY 10019

DAVIS, D JACK
EDUCATOR, ADMINISTRATOR
b Canton, Tex, May 17, 38. *Study:* Baylor Univ, BA, 59, MA, 61; Univ Minn, PhD, 66, studies with Reid Hastie, Paul Torrance & Malcolm Myers. *Pos:* Assoc dir & dir evaluation, Aesthetic Educ Prog, Arts in Gen Educ Proj, Cemrel Inc, St Louis, Mo, 69-71; ed, Studies in Art Educ, Nat Art Educ Asn, 75-77. *Teaching:* Instr art, Wayland Col, Plainview, Tex, 61-63; prof art, Tex Tech Univ, 65-69; prof & assoc vpres acad affairs, NTex State Univ, Denton, 71- *Mem:* Life mem Nat Art Educ Asn (chmn higher educ div, 73-75); Tex Art Educ Asn; Nat Coun Art Adminrs; Decorative Arts Trust; Tex Asn Sch

Art. *Publ:* Coauth, The Artist in the School, Cemrel Inc, 70; auth, Research in art education, Art Educ, 71; ed, Behavioral Emphasis in Art Education, Nat Art Educ Asn, 75; contribr, Arts & Aesthetics: An Agenda for the Future, Cemrel Inc, 77; The visual arts: A classroom myth or an accountable program?, Nat Asn Sec Sch Principals Bulletin, 11/79. *Mailing Add:* 2007 Locksley Lane Denton TX 76201

DAVIS, DAVID ENSOS
SCULPTOR
b Rona de Jos, Romania, Aug 27, 20; US citizen. *Study:* Beaux Arts, Paris, France, 45; Cleveland Inst Art, BFA(scholar), 48; Case Western Reserve Univ, MA, 61. *Work:* James Michener Collection; Cleveland Mus Art, Ohio; Col Jewish Studies, Cleveland, Ohio; Kent State Univ; Akron Art Inst. *Comn:* David-Berger Monument, Jewish Community Ctr, Cleveland, 73; outdoor sculpture, Progressive Insurance Co; outdoor sculpture, Beck Cult Ctr, Lakewood, Ohio; outdoor sculpture, Case Western Reserve Univ, 82. *Exhib:* May Show Ann, Cleveland Mus Art, 72-79; Ohio Painting & Sculpture, Dayton Art Inst, 74; Materials & Techniques of 20th Century Artists, Cleveland Mus Art, 77; Ten Collages & One Sculpture in the Harmonic Grid, Akron Inst Art, Ohio, 78; Recent Sculpture & Collages, New Gallery Contemp Art, Cleveland, 78; plus others. *Pos:* Staff artist, Am Greetings Corp, Cleveland, 48-49, dir creative dept, 49-54, asst to vpres creative dept, 54-58, vpres creative dept, 58-61. *Awards:* Major Sculpture Cash Prize, May Show, Cleveland Mus Art, 77. *Bibliog:* Terry Breen (auth), Profile of a sculptor, New Rev, 1/76; Gerry O Patno (auth), Portrait of a welder as an artist, Welding Design & Fabrication, 4/76; Edward B Henning (auth), The art of David E Davis, Art Int, 11-12/78. *Mem:* Trustee Cleveland Inst Art; Artists Equity. *Media:* Mixed. *Mailing Add:* 19425 Van Aken Blvd #207 Shaker Heights OH 44122

DAVIS, DONALD ROBERT
PAINTER, DEALER
b Toronto, Ont, July 30, 09; US citizen. *Study:* Syracuse Univ; Art Students League. *Work:* Berkshire Mus, Jamaica, West Indies; also in many pvt collections. *Comn:* Prehistoric Lascaux cave fresco, Bandag, Inc, Jamaica, West Indies. *Exhib:* Berkshire Art Asn Ann Exhib, 67 & 68; one-man shows, Berkshire Mus, 67 & Tyringham Gallery, Mass, 69; Albany Inst Art Regional Exhib, NY, 68. *Pos:* Owner & dir, Tyringham Gallery. *Mem:* Am Asn Mus; Berkshire Art Asn. *Media:* Mixed Media, Oil, Acrylic. *Specialty:* Paintings, sculpture, prints and objets d'art. *Publ:* Auth, article in Am Artist Mag. *Mailing Add:* Tyringham Art Gallery Tyringham MA 01264

DAVIS, DOUGLAS MATTHEW
ARTIST, CRITIC
b Washington, DC, Apr 11, 33. *Study:* Abbott Art Sch, Washington, DC: Am Univ, BA, 56; Rutgers Univ, New Brunswick, MA, 58. *Work:* Metrop Mus Art, New York; Ludwig Mus, Cologne, Ger; DAhlem Mus, WBerlin; Venice Biennale Archive, Italy; Hirschorn Mus & Sculpture Garden, DC; and others. *Exhib:* Retrospective, Everson Mus, Syracuse, 72; Projekt 74, Kunstverein & Kunsthalle, Cologne, Ger, 74; San Francisco Mus Art, 75; Projected Video, Whitney Mus Am Art, New York & San Paulo Biennale, 75; Documenta 6, Kassel, WGer, 77; Arbeiten, Works 1970-1977, Berlin 1977-78; Neuer Berliner Kunstverein, 78 & Neue Galerie, Aachen, WGer, 78; Centre Georges Pompidou, Paris, 81; Whitney Mus Am Art, 81. *Collections Arranged:* Wallraf-Richartz Mus, Cologne; Finch Col Mus; De Saisset Art Gallery; Everson Mus Art; Panza di Biuma, Milan. *Pos:* Contribr ed, Am Art, 68-70; art critic, Newsweek Mag, 70-77, sr writer archit & photog, 77-; artist in residence, TV Lab, WNET-TV, New York; res fel, Mass Inst Technol Ctr Advan Visual Studies, 74-75; artistic dir, Int Network for Arts, New York, 76- *Teaching:* Vis artist, Corcoran Sch Art, 70 & 71; State Univ NY Buffalo, 73; art critic in residence, NY Univ, 75; regents lectr, Univ Calif, San Diego, 76; instr advanced video & performance, Int Network Arts, State Univ NY Purchase, Philadelphia Col Art, 76-, Columbia Univ, Univ Calif, Los Angeles. *Awards:* Nat Endowment Arts Grants, 70 & 75; NY State Coun Arts Grant for Creative Work in Mixed Media, 70; Chairman's Grant, Nat Endowment Arts, 81. *Bibliog:* Irving Sandler (auth), Questions NY-Moscow, San Francisco Mus Mod Art, 76. *Mem:* Artists Equity; Authors Guild. *Media:* Videotape, Printmaking. *Publ:* Auth, Media/art/media, Arts Mag, 9/71; auth, Video obscura, 4/72 & What is content, 10/73, Artforum; auth, Art and the Future, Praeger, 73; auth, Fragments for a New Art of the Future, 75; co-ed, The New Television, Mass Inst Technol Press, 76; auth, Artculture: Essays on the Post-Modern, Harper & Row, 77. *Dealer:* Ronald Feldman Fine Arts 33 E 74th St New York NY 10012. *Mailing Add:* 80 Wooster St New York NY 10012

DAVIS, ELLEN N
HISTORIAN
b Hackensack, NJ, July 20, 37. *Study:* Inst Fine Arts, NY Univ, with Peter H Von Blanckenhagen, PhD, 73. *Teaching:* Assoc prof ancient art hist, Queens Col, City Univ New York, 66- *Awards:* Arlt Award, Coun Grad Studies. *Mem:* Archaeol Inst Am; New York Soc (pres, 80-83); New York Bronze Age Colloq. *Res:* Aegean metalworking, painting and connections with Egypt. *Publ:* Auth, The Vapheio cups: One Minoan & one Mycenean?, Art Bulletin LVI, 74; ed, Symposium on the Dark Ages, Archaeol Inst Am, 74; auth, The Vapheio Cups and Aegean Metalware, Garland Press, 76; auth, Aegean art, In: Suppl McGraw-Hill Encycl, 83; auth, The iconography off the Thera Ship fresco, In: Greek Art and Iconography, Univ Wis Press, 83. *Mailing Add:* 225 E 76th St New York NY 10021

DAVIS, GENE
PAINTER

b Washington, DC, Aug 22, 20. *Study:* Univ Md; Wilson Teachers Col. *Work:* Mus Mod Art, New York; Whitney Mus Am Art; Tate Gallery, London, Eng; San Francisco Mus Art; Corcoran Gallery Art, Washington, DC; plus many others. *Comn:* Mural, South Mall Proj, NY State Capitol Bldg, Albany, 69; mural, Neiman-Marcus, Bal Harbour, Fla, 70; off poster, Liszt Found, Lincoln Ctr Concert Ser, New York. *Exhib:* One-man shows, Corcoran Gallery Art, 64, 68, 70 & 77, San Francisco Mus, 68, Jewish Mus, New York, 68 & Univ Utah Art Mus, Salt Lake City, 72; Walker Art Ctr, Minneapolis; Whitney Ann Exhib Am Painting, Whitney Mus Am Art, 67 & 68; plus many other one-man and group shows. *Teaching:* Asst prof painting, Corcoran Gallery Sch Art, 67-68 & 70-; instr painting, Am Univ, 68-70; artist in residence, Skidmore Col, summer 69 & Univ Va, spring 72. *Awards:* Bronze Medal for Painting & Am Painting Biennial Award, Corcoran Gallery Art, 65; Nat Coun Arts Grant, 67; Guggenheim Fel, 74. *Bibliog:* Donald Wall (auth), The micro-paintings of Gene Davis, Artforum, 12/68; Barbara Rose (auth), Coversation with Gene Davis, Artforum, 3/71; Donald Wall (ed), Gene Davis, Praeger, 75; plus others. *Publ:* Auth, Statement by the artist, Art Now, 2/70; auth, Random thought on art, Studio Int, 11/70. *Mailing Add:* 4120 Harrison St NW Washington DC 20015

DAVIS, GERALD VIVIAN
PAINTER

b Brooklyn, NY, Sept 8, 1899. *Study:* Ecole des Beaux Arts, Paris, France; Julian Acad, cert; Acad Grande Chaumiere, Paris; also with Dechenaud & Royer. *Comn:* President of Danish Engineers (portrait), Soc Danish Eng, Copenhagen, 38; Rev Dr Clayton Williams (portrait), Am Church in Paris, France, 40; Dr Knutson (portrait), Dir Watkins Hosp, Univ Kans, Lawrence, 51; Father Leopold Bruekberger (portrait), Paris, 69; Sir Ove Arup (portrait), Arup & Partners, London, 70; and others. *Exhib:* Trenton Art Mus, 68; Newark Mus, NJ, 68; Galt's Gallery, Chatham, NJ, 74; Hait Gallery, Maplewood, NJ, 74-; one-man shows, Chatham Libr, NJ, 79 & Caldwell Col, 79. *Teaching:* Instr art, Univ Ill, Champaign, 25-28; asst prof art, Univ Kans, 47-51. *Awards:* Contemp NJ Artists, 60; NJ State Show, East Orange Art Ctr, 68 & Summit Art Ctr, 69. *Mem:* Assoc Soc Nat Beaux Arts. *Media:* All. *Mailing Add:* 86 Elm St Summit NJ 07901

DAVIS, HARRY ALLEN
PAINTER, EDUCATOR

b Hillsboro, Ind, May 21, 14. *Study:* Herron Sch Art, Ind Univ-Purdue Univ, Indianapolis, BFA, 38; Am Acad Rome, FAAR, 41. *Work:* Butler Inst Am Art, Youngstown, Ohio; Springfield Art Mus, Mo; Evansville Mus Arts & Sci, Ind; Grover M Hermann Fine Arts Ctr, Marietta Col, Ohio; Carroll Reece Mus, Johnson City, Tenn; plus others. *Comn:* One Virginia Avenue, Ind Nat Bank, 69; Union Station, Am Fletcher Nat Bank, 73; Pathology Building, Surgeons' College, Ind Mus Med Hist, Indianapolis, 74; four historic landmarks, Lafayette Life Insurance Co, 80; History of Clay County (mural), Brazil, Ind. *Exhib:* Eight Butler Midyear Exhibs, Youngstown, 61-78; twelve Watercolor USA, Nat Watercolor Exhibs, Springfield, Mo, 65-79, Mainstreams Int Exhibs, Marietta, Ohio, 68-77; Bicentennial Traveling Show, Ind State Mus, Indianapolis Mus Art, plus others, 76-77; The Italian Influence Traveling Exhib, 83; and others. *Teaching:* Artist in residence, Beloit Col, 41-42; prof painting & drawing, Herron Sch Art, Ind Univ-Purdue Univ, Indianapolis, 46-83, prof emer, 83-; artist in residence, Evansville Mus Art & Sci & Univ Mo, 81. *Awards:* Second Medal, Butler Midyear Exhib, 78; Best of Show, Anderson Five-State Winter Show, 82; Strouse Award, Evansville Midstates Regional, 82. *Bibliog:* Mendelowitz (auth), Drawing: Guide to Drawing, Holt, 66; and others. *Mem:* Fel Am Acad Rome; Ind Artists Club (pres, 55-56, dir, 72); Ind Acad; and others. *Media:* Multimedia. *Mailing Add:* 6315 Washington Blvd Indianapolis IN 46220

DAVIS, J RAY
PAINTER, PRINTMAKER

Study: Cent State Univ, Okla, BA; Univ Okla, MFA(painting & printmaking). *Work:* State of Okla Collection & Traveling Exhib. *Exhib:* Kans State Univ Exhib to Grad Midwestern Univs, 69; one-man shows, Painting Prints & Vacuum Forms, Contemp Arts Found, Oklahoma City, 70 & Graphic Retrospective, Emporia, Kans, 70; 31st Ann Exhib Okla Artists, Philbrook Art Ctr, Tulsa, 71; Okla Featured Artist of Month, Okla Art Ctr, 4/72. *Teaching:* Instr art, Okla Sci & Arts Found, 67-70; assoc prof art, Oklahoma City Univ, 69-; instr art, state supported art classes for all fifth graders in Oklahoma City Pub Sch Syst, 71-72. *Awards:* Graphics Awards, 30th & 31st Ann Exhib Okla Artists, Tulsa, 70 & 71 & 57th Ann Tulsa Regional Exhib, 71. *Mailing Add:* Dept Art Oklahoma City Univ Oklahoma City OK 73106

DAVIS, JAMES GRANBERRY
PAINTER

b Springfield, Mo, 31. *Study:* Wichita State Univ, Kansas, Mo, BFA, 54, MFA, 60. *Work:* Wichita Art Mus, Kans; State Art Mus Jalisco, Guadalajara, Mex; Tucson Mus Art, Ariz; Phoenix Art Mus. *Comn:* Large painting, Container Corp Am, New York, 65. *Exhib:* Ninth Mid-West Biennial, Joslyn Art Mus, Omaha, Nebr, 66; solo exhibs, Tucson Mus Art, Arix, 75 & Scottsdale Ctr Arts, Ariz, 79; Nat Drawing Exhib, Santa Rosa, Calif, 78; 1st Western States Biennial, Denver, Wash, San Francisco, 79-80. *Teaching:* Instr painting & printmaking, Univ Mo, Columbia, 67-69; asst prof painting, Univ Ariz, Tucson, 69-70, assoc prof, 70- *Awards:* Purchase Award, Kans Artists Ann, 62 & Tucson Art Ctr, 74. *Bibliog:* Anita Winegate (auth), James G Davis, Artspace, 1/79; Barbara Cortright (auth), Interview with James G Davis, Phoenix Mag, 1/80; Carol Cratoza (auth), James G Davis, Art Voices S, 3/80. *Media:* Oil; Lithography, Monotype. *Dealer:* Yares Gallery 3625 Bishop Lane Scottsdale AZ 85251. *Mailing Add:* Rancho Linda Vista Oracle AZ 85263

DAVIS, JAMES ROBERT
CARTOONIST

b Marion, Ind, July 28, 45. *Study:* Ball State Univ. *Pos:* Artist, Groves & Assoc Advert, Muncie, Ind, 68-69; asst to cartoonist, Tumbleweeds (comic strip), 69-78; cartoonist, Garfield (comic strip), 78- *Mem:* Nat Cartoonists Soc; Newspaper Comics Coun. *Publ:* Auth, Garfield Mix & Match Storybook, 82 & Garfield the Knight in Shining Armor, 82, Random House; auth, Garfield Takes the Cake, 82, The Garfield Treasury, 82 & Garfield Weighs In, 82, Ballantine. *Mailing Add:* 104 Elm Muncie IN 47305

DAVIS, JAMES WESLEY
PAINTER, WRITER

b Los Angeles, Calif, Oct 9, 40. *Study:* Calif Col Arts & Crafts, BA(educ) & BFA; Univ Colo, MA & MFA(Inst Arts & Humanities Fel), 67. *Work:* Minn Mus Art; Ill State Mus; Alberta Col Art; Mulvane Art Mus; Laguna Gloria Mus; and others. *Exhib:* Mid-America 4, St Louis Art Mus & Nelson/Atkins Mus, 72; Smithsonian Inst Traveling Show, 73-74; Calgary Int Biennial, Alta Col Art Gallery, 74; Mid-Year Ann, Butler Inst Am Art, 74 & 75; 19th Mid-South Biennial, Brooks Mem Gallery, 75; Irwin Collection, Kvannert Mus, 80. *Teaching:* Instr painting & art hist, Univ Ark, 67-69; prof painting & drawing, Western Ill Univ, 69-; vis prof, Univ Colo, 82; head art dept, ETex State Univ, 83- *Awards:* Sworovski Int Award, Sworovski of Belg, 67; James D Phelan Award, 73. *Bibliog:* S W Semaj (auth), Memories, Structure, Vol 2, No 3; Alfred Frankenstein (auth), Visual, surreal acrobatics, San Francisco Chronicle, 1/74; Sylvia Brown (auth), Editorial highlights, City Mag, 2/16/74. *Mem:* Col Art Asn Am. *Media:* Acrylic, Watercolor. *Publ:* Auth, Self-actualized sculpture, Sculpture Int, Vol 3, No 2; auth, Unified drawing by means of hybrids and grids, Leonardo, Vol 5, No 1; auth, Some perceptual considerations on Vermeer and op art, Studies in the 20th Century, 73; auth, Revival in the slumbering cornfield, Art J, fall 74; auth, On mounds, Studio Int, 4/74. *Dealer:* Joy Horwich Gallery 226 E Ontario Chicago IL 60611. *Mailing Add:* Rt 1 Box 124-E Commerce TX 75428

DAVIS, JERROLD
PAINTER

b Chico, Calif, Nov 2, 26. *Study:* Univ Calif, Berkeley, BA, 53, MA. *Work:* Carnegie Inst Int, Pittsburgh; Santa Barbara Mus Art, Calif; Los Angeles Mus Art; San Francisco Mus Art; Oakland Mus Art; and others. *Exhib:* One-man shows, Calif Palace of Legion of Honor, 60-64, Flint Art Inst, 64, Newport Harbor Art Mus, Newport Beach, Calif, 73 & retrospective, Richmond Art Ctr, Calif, 80; Especially for Children, Los Angeles Co Mus, 65; Univ Ariz, 67; Lytton Ctr, Los Angeles, 67 & 68; A Sense of Place, 74; and others. *Teaching:* Instr, Univ Calif, summer 67. *Awards:* Guggenheim Fel, 58-59; Am Fedn Arts-Ford Found artist in residence grant, Flint, Mich, 64; Prizes, Calif Palace Legion Honor, 60 & 62; and others. *Mailing Add:* 66 Twain Ave Berkeley CA 94708

DAVIS, JOHN HAROLD
GALLERY DIRECTOR, ILLUSTRATOR

b Milwaukee, Wis, Feb 8, 23. *Study:* Layton Art Inst, Milwaukee; Art Inst Chicago, BFA. *Comn:* Stations of the Cross, Mt St Frances, Iowa, 49; new altar & reconstruct of church, Monsefu, Peru, 64-66; Veracruz (tapestry applique), Chimbote, Peru, 68; mural of cast concrete, San Antonio de Padua, Lima, Peru, 69; decoration of interior, Church of San Juan de Miraflores, 70. *Exhib:* Am Printmakers, Philadelphia, 45-55; Art Ctr, Lima, 56, 58 & 70; Charles Allis Art Libr, Milwaukee, 71 & 79; Inst Cult Peruano Norteamericano, Lima; Munson-Williams-Procter Inst, Utica, NY; and many others. *Collections Arranged:* Fifteen Impressionists, 50; Spanish painting included in prog exhibs, Iowa Art Ctr & Syracuse Univ, 52; Folk Art of Peru, Los Angeles Co Fair, 68; Peruvian Crafts Exhibition, Fardoms & Masions, London, Eng; 1st & 2nd Biennial Crafts of Peru (Artesania del Peru), Museo Arte Lima, 68 & 70; and others. *Pos:* Dir painting & drawing, Inst Art Ctr Gallery & Shop, Miraflores, 55-; dir & founder, Ctr Craft Develop, Peru, currently. *Teaching:* Instr painting & drawing, Syracuse Univ, 48-55. *Bibliog:* Petterson (auth), Folk Art of Peru, Scripps Col; Serven Rodman (auth), South American of the Poets & The Peru Traveler, Meredith. *Mem:* World Crafts Coun (dir for Latin Am, 68-72); founder, Asn Nac Artesanos Peru; Inst Art Ctr; Fundacion Peruana Pro-Arte y Educacion (pres, 65-74); and others. *Publ:* Illusr, Mis Antepasados, 54; illusr, Manuel Pardo Rivadeneyra, 55; illusr, Conquest of Peru, New Am Libr Ed, 58. *Mailing Add:* 2500 E Shorewood Blvd Milwaukee WI 53211

DAVIS, JOHN SHERWOOD
POTTER, ADMINISTRATOR

b Kingstree, SC, Jan 24, 42. *Study:* Univ SC, BFA(art), 71, grad work dept art, 73; Harvard Inst Art Admin, 76. *Exhib:* Artists Guild of Columbia, Columbia Mus Art, SC, 73; Piedmont Crafts Exhib, Mint Mus Art, Charlotte, NC, 74; Southeastern Ctr for Contemp Art, Winston-Salem, NC, 74; Am Crafts Coun Regional Exhib, Am Crafts Coun Mus, New York, 74; Marietta Col Crafts Nat, Ohio, 75; 26th Ann Exhib, Guild SC Artists, Greenville Mus Art, SC, 76. *Collections Arranged:* Alan Davis Drawing Exhib, 76, Mike French Jewelry Exhib, 76, Depression Glass, 77, An Artist Collects (Jasper Johns Collection), 77 & Guild of SC Artists Exhib, 77, Columbia Mus Art, SC. *Teaching:* Instr painting, Richland Art Sch, 69-70, instr ceramics, 71-72; teaching asst ceramics, Univ SC, 72-74. *Awards:* Merit Award, Guild SC Artists, Greenville Co Mus Art, SC, 72; Purchase Awards, Artist Guild Columbia, 74 & Piedmont Crafts Exhib, Mint Mus, Charlotte, NC, 74. *Mem:* Guild SC Artists (pres, 76-77); SC Fedn Mus (vpres, 76-78); Am Asn Mus; Artists of Columbia. *Media:* Clay. *Dealer:* Objects Gallery 410 Meeting St W Columbia SC 29169. *Mailing Add:* 7119 Gray Columbia SC 29209

DAVIS, L CLARICE
BOOK DEALER, COLLECTOR
b Akron, Ohio, Jan 30, 29. *Study:* Univ Akron, BA(fine arts), 55; Univ Calif, Los Angeles, MLS, 61, MA(art hist), 68. *Pos:* Chief librn, Los Angeles Co Mus Art, 63-68; owner & mgr, Davis Art Book Store & Gallery, Los Angeles, 71-79, partner, Davis & Schorr Art Books, 79-; actg unit head, Art Libr, Univ Calif, Los Angeles, 73-75. *Teaching:* Asst prof mod art hist, Calif State Univ, Northridge, 61-63 & 68-69; lectr, Otis Art Inst, Los Angeles, 69-70. *Mem:* Col Art Asn Am; Art Libr Soc NAm; Antiquarian Booksellers Asn Am. *Specialty:* Out of print books and exhibition catalogues; original prints, drawings and paintings . *Publ:* Contribr bibliog catalog, R B Kitaj, 65 & Peter Voulkos, Sculpture, 65, Los Angeles Co Mus Art; contribr introd, Pornography in Fine Art From Ancient Times, Los Angeles Elysium, 69; auth, Annuals of auction sales, Am Libr Soc NAm Newsletter, 12/76. *Mailing Add:* 5928 Cantaloupe Ave Van Nuys CA 91401

DAVIS, MARIAN B
HISTORIAN, CURATOR
b St Louis Co, Mo, Sept 24, 11. *Study:* Washington Univ, BA, 32, MA, 35; Radcliffe Col, MA, 39, PhD, 48. *Collections Arranged:* Sch of Fontainebleau, 65; plus many others. *Pos:* Chief cur & actg dir, Art Teaching Gallery, Univ Tex, Austin, 63-78. *Teaching:* Instr art hist, Worcester Art Mus, 41-44; from instr to prof, Univ Tex, Austin, 44-78, emer prof, 78- *Mem:* Col Art Asn (dir, 51-55); Soc Archit Historians; Archaeol Inst Am; Renaissance Soc; Nat Trust Hist Preserv. *Res:* Italian Renaissance; United States architecture. *Publ:* Auth, Two eighteenth century paintings, Worcester Art Mus Ann V, 46; auth, Summer travel for students, Col Art J, 54; auth, Some first impressions of Sicily, Tex Trends Art Educ, autumn 59; auth, Art history--contribution to understanding, Western Arts Asn Bulletin, 61. *Mailing Add:* 2701 Wooldridge Dr Austin TX 78703

DAVIS, MEREDITH J
GRAPHIC ARTIST, EDUCATOR
b Pittsburgh, Pa, May 15, 48. *Study:* Pa State Univ, BS, 70, MEd, 74; Cranbrook Acad Art, with Katherine & Michael McCoy, MFA, 75. *Work:* Mead Libr Ideas, Dayton, Ohio; Am Inst Graphic Arts, New York. *Exhib:* Am Inst Graphic Arts, New York, 75 & 83; Mead Ann Report Competition, New York, 80; Virginia Designers, Va Mus Fine Arts, 80; Soc Typographic Arts, Women in Design, Chicago, 81; New York Art Dir Club, 81 & 83; New York Type Dir Club, 82 & 83; Next Show, Va Mus Fine Arts, 83. *Pos:* Cur educ, Hunter Mus Art, 75-76; partner, Communication Design Inc, Richmond, Va, 79- *Teaching:* Assoc prof & asst chmn communication arts & design, Va Commonwealth Univ, 76- *Awards:* Excellence in Ann Report Design, Mead Libr Ideas, 81; Excellence Visual Communication, Designers Choice, Indust Design Mag, 82 & Creativity 13, New York Art Dir, 83. *Bibliog:* Annual reports: Business as usual?, Art Direction Mag, 81. *Mem:* Am Inst Graphic Arts. *Publ:* Coauth, Problem Solving in the Man-Made Environment, Cranbrook Environmental Educ Proj, 75; contribr, Trends in Annual Reports, S D Warren Co, 83; contribr, The role of education in research, Design J, 83. *Mailing Add:* 1705 Avondale Ave Richmond VA 23227

DAVIS, MICHAEL A
SCULPTOR
b Los Angeles, Calif, Apr 30, 48. *Study:* Calif State Univ, Fullerton, MA, 71. *Work:* Albuquerque Art Mus. *Comn:* Newport Harbor Art Mus, Calif, 78; Muckenthaler Ctr, Fullerton, Calif, 79; Calif State Univ, Los Angeles, 80; Calif Inst Technol, Pasadena, 80; Creative Time, New York, 80. *Exhib:* Architectural Sculpture, Los Angeles Inst Contemp Art, 80; one-man show, Gallery U, Nagoya, Japan, 80; Fed Reserve, Washington, DC, 80; Creative Time Inc, New York, 80; Visual Arts Ctr Alaska, Anchorage, 81; and others. *Pos:* Co-founder & dir, 58F Plaza Gallery, Orange, Calif, 71-75; dir, Santa Ana Col Gallery, Calif, 73-75; guest artist, Chapman Col, Orange, Calif, 74; dir, artist-in-residence prog, Los Angeles Inst Comtemp Art, 78-79; artist-in-residence, Calif State Univ, Northridge, fall 81; guest artist, Claremont Grad Sch, Calif, spring 82. *Awards:* Artist Fel, Nat Endowment Arts, 80. *Bibliog:* Melinda Wortz (auth), Crawling, like Alice, down the rabbit hole, Art News, 79. *Media:* Steel, Wood. *Dealer:* Roy Boyd Gallery 170 S La Brea Los Angeles CA 90036. *Mailing Add:* 748 12th St Los Angeles CA 90021

DAVIS, PHILIP CHARLES
PHOTOGRAPHER, WRITER
b Spokane, Wash, Oct 15, 21. *Study:* Albright Art Sch, Buffalo, NY, cert. *Work:* Mus Art Inst Chicago; Int Mus Photog, Rochester, NY; Detroit Art Inst; Mus Mod Art, New York. *Comn:* Outdoor exhib photos, Univ Mich Sesquicentennial Comt, 66. *Exhib:* One-man show photographs, Kalamazoo Art Ctr, Mich, 62; The University, Univ Mich, Ann Arbor, 66; three-man show photographs, 831 Gallery, Birmingham, Mich, 71; Group Invitational, Kresge Art Ctr, Mich State Univ, 72 & 79; Midwest Invitational, Walker Art Ctr, Minneapolis, Minn, 72; The Art of the Photogravure, Colo Photog Arts Ctr, Denver, 79. *Teaching:* From instr to prof art, Univ Mich, Ann Arbor, 48- *Awards:* Gold Medal, 59, Silver Medal, 60 & Bravo Gold Medal, 61, Art Dirs Club Detroit. *Bibliog:* Irving Desfor (auth), Camera angles, Assoc Press Newsfeatures, 72. *Mem:* Soc Photog Educ. *Publ:* Auth & illusr, The university, 67, Take Photography Step by Step, 70, Photography, 72, revised 79 & The Dexter Portfolio (50 set ed), 72. *Dealer:* The Halstead Gallery 560 N Woodward Birmingham MI 48011. *Mailing Add:* Art Dept Univ Mich Ann Arbor MI 48109

DAVIS, RONALD WENDEL
PAINTER, PRINTMAKER
b Santa Monica, Calif, June 29, 37. *Study:* San Francisco Art Inst, 60-64. *Work:* Los Angeles Co Mus; Mus Mod Art, New York; Tate Gallery, London; Albright-Knox Art Gallery, Buffalo; San Francisco Mus Art. *Exhib:* A News Aesthetic, Washington Gallery Mod Art, DC, 67; Documenta 4, Kassel, Ger, 67; Whitney Mus Am Art Ann, New York, 67; Color, Univ Calif, Los Angeles Art Galleries, 69; Venice Biennial, Italy, 72; Four Contemp Painters, Cleveland Mus Art, 78; and others. *Teaching:* Instr, Univ Calif, 67. *Awards:* Nat Endowment Arts, 68. *Bibliog:* M Fried (auth), Ronald Davis: Surface and illusion, Artforum, 4/67; R Hughes (auth), Ron Davis at Kasmin, Studio Int, 176, 12/68; B Rose (auth), American painting, Vol 2, 70. *Media:* Polyester Resin, Fiberglas. *Collection:* Contemporary art. *Dealer:* Nicholas Wilder Gallery 8225 1/2 Santa Monica Los Angeles CA 90046. *Mailing Add:* 29715 W Cuthbert Rd Malibu CA 90265

DAVIS, (MR & MRS) WALTER
COLLECTORS, PATRONS
Mr Davis, b New Orleans, La; Mrs Davis, b Natchez, Miss. *Study:* Mr Davis, Tulane Univ Law Sch; Mrs Davis, Newcomb Art Sch. *Pos:* Mr Davis, Bd New Orleans Opera, Mrs Davis, trustee & women's bd, New Orleans Mus Art; women's bd, New Orleans Symphony & New Orleans Opera. *Collection:* Drawings by Mary Cassatt, Louis Valtat, Chagall & Krebs; gouaches by Tamayo, Raoul Dufy, Cuevas; sculpture by Henry Moore, L Nierman & L Wercollier; watercolors by John Marin, Raoul Dufy, David Smith, Jean Dufy, Merida & Montenegro; oils by Modigliani, R Dufy, de Chirico, Vassarely, Roualt, Utrillo, Harold Carney, Merida, Montenegro & Guayasmin; sculpture by George Rickey & Oswaldo Guayasamin. *Mailing Add:* 1819 Octavia St New Orleans LA 70115

DAVIS, WALTER LEWIS
PAINTER, COLLAGE ARTIST
b Americus, Ga, Jan 12, 37. *Study:* NY Community Col; Abracheff Sch Art, New York. *Work:* Detroit Bd Educ, Mich; NY State Brookdale Hosp, Brooklyn; NY State Lincoln Hosp, Bronx. *Exhib:* One-man shows, Arts Extended Gallery, Detroit, Mich, 66-67 & 71 & Mt Vernon Coop Col Ctr, NY, 74; Childe Hassam Found Purchase Exhib, Am Acad Arts & Lett, New York, 69; Contemp Black Artists Am, Whitney Mus, 71. *Awards:* Purchase Award Painting, Okinawa Art Ctr, 57; First Place, Greenwich Art/Music Festival, Conn, 80. *Bibliog:* William Tall (auth), Walter Davis' Totems for Charlie Parker, Detroit Free Press, 71. *Mem:* NY Artists Equity Asn. *Media:* Oil, Acrylic. *Mailing Add:* 801-12 Tilden St Bronx NY 10467

DAVIS, WAYNE LAMBERT
PAINTER, ILLUSTRATOR
b Oak Park, Ill, Jan 3, 04. *Study:* Art Students League, with Joseph Pennell; Columbia Univ; NY Univ, State NY cert art teacher; Quinabaug Valley Community Col, 83. *Work:* Smithsonian Inst, Washington, DC; First Nat City Bank New York; Newman Galleries, Philadelphia; plus others. *Comn:* Mural of skiing, Vail, Colo, comn by Vernon Taylor, Denver, 68; Stairway murals of Brooklyn Bridge area, 53rd St Br, First Nat City Bank New York, 69; Gallery Americana, Carmel, Calif; O'Brien's Emporium, Scottsdale, Ariz; Artists Bank, Conn Comn Arts, Hartford. *Exhib:* One-man shows, Kennedy Galleries, 67, Country Art Galleries, 69 & Hunter Gallery, Aspen, Colo, 69. *Pos:* Art dir & staff artist, Grumman Aircraft Eng Corp, Bethpage, NY, 41-53. *Teaching:* Instr art, Hit Sch Art, Locust Valley, NY, 53-63; instr watercolor, Great Neck High Sch, NY, 54- *Awards:* First in watercolor for The Lobster Weir, Stony Brook Mus, NY, 68; First in oil for The Salmon Run, Oper Democracy, Locust Valley, 71. *Mem:* Nassau Art League. *Media:* Tempera, Watercolor; Etching. *Publ:* Illusr, Fortune & Liberty, 43, Vanity Fair, 44 & Sportman Pilot, 45; auth, Pathway to expression (color film), privately publ, 66. *Dealer:* Country Art Gallery The Plaza Locust Valley NY 11560. *Mailing Add:* RFD 1 Five Mile River Rd Putnam CT 06260

DAVIS, WILLIAM D
MUSEUM DIRECTOR, PAINTER
b Erie, Pa, Oct 6, 36. *Study:* Edinboro Univ, BS, 59; Bucknell Univ, with Neil Anderson, 59; Pa State Univ, MFA, 80. *Work:* Milton Shoe Collection Contemp Am Prints & Drawings, Pa; Sanford Gallery, Marwick-Boyd Fine Arts Ctr, Clarion, Pa; Kipp Gallery, Ind Univ, Pa; Bruce Gallery, Edinboro Univ, Pa; Lock Haven Univ Gallery, Pa. *Comn:* Lithograph, Friends Mus Art, Pa State Univ. *Exhib:* Two-person show, Forum Gallery, New York, 74, 77 & 80; Drawing Exhib, Haslem Gallery, Washington, DC, 77; one-person show, Butler Inst Am Art, 80; Pa Graphic Invitational, Southern Alleghenies Mus Art, Loretto, Pa, 81; Traditions: The Region, The World, Mich Art Train, Detroit, 81; Painting Invitational, Mus Art, Pa State Univ, 82-83. *Collections Arranged:* Living American Artists and the Figure (auth, catalog), 74, Materials Dominant (auth, catalog), 77, Intimate Worlds of Faust and Titolo (auth, catalog), 79, Sidney Goodman Paintings, Drawings, Graphics, 1959-1979, 80 & Jerome Witkin Paintings and Drawings: A Decade of Work, 83, Mus Art, Pa State Univ. *Pos:* Asst dir, Mus Art, Pa State Univ, 72-82, assoc dir, 82-83, interim dir, 83- *Teaching:* Art, Pa pub schs, 59-60 & 62-71. *Awards:* Graphics Award, Cent Pa Festival Arts, 69, 73 & 79; Purchase Award, Art Alliance, State Col, Pa, 74. *Bibliog:* John Russell (auth), article, New York Times, 6/6/74; article, Ind Penn, 4/7/76; Gerrit Henry (auth), article, Art News, 9/77. *Mem:* Northeast Mus Asn. *Media:* Graphite, Watercolor. *Mailing Add:* 382 Park Lane State College PA 16801

DAVISON, BILL
EDUCATOR, PRINTMAKER
b Burlington, Vt, Sept 23, 41. *Study:* Albion Col, BA, 63; Univ Mich, MFA, 66. *Work:* Libr Cong, Washington, DC; Dartmouth Col, Hanover, NH; Univ Southern Calif, Los Angeles; Franklin Furnace Arch, New York; Wesleyan Univ, Middletown, Conn. *Exhib:* Solo exhibs, var univ mus, Fla, 70-81, Kathryn Markel Gallery, New York, 78 & Roy Boyd Gallery, Chicago, 79; Brooklyn Mus, New York, 77; Contemporary American Prints, Tokyo, 79; Baltimore Mus, 79; Mod Gallery, Ljubljana, Yugoslavia, 81. *Teaching:* Assoc prof, Univ Vt, Burlington, 68-81. *Awards:* Horace H Rackham Fel, 66; Artists Fels, Nat Endowment Arts, 75 & Vt Coun Arts, 79. *Mailing Add:* 183 East Broadway New York NY 10002

DAWDY, DORIS OSTRANDER
WRITER, HISTORIAN
b Minn. *Study:* MacPhail Sch Music, Minneapolis; Colo State Univ; Los Angeles City Col. *Res:* American Indian paintings; artists of the American West born prior to 1900. *Publ:* Auth, Annotated Bibliography of American Indian Painting, Heye Found, 68; auth, Artists of the American West, Swallow, 74, reprinted, 80, Vol II, 81, Ohio Univ Press, Vol III (in press); auth, The Wyant Diary: An Artist with the Wheeler Survey in Arizona 1873, Ariz and the West, Univ Ariz Press, 80. *Mailing Add:* 3055 23rd Ave San Francisco CA 94132

DAWLEY, JOSEPH WILLIAM
PAINTER, DEALER
b Nashville, Ark, June 19, 36. *Study:* With Raymond Froman, 58-61; Southern Methodist Univ, BFA, 59; Dallas Mus Fine Arts, 60; Art Students League, 61. *Work:* Mus Arts & Crafts, Columbus, Ga; Davenport Mus Art, Iowa; Henderson Arts Coun, Tex; Southern Methodist Univ, Dallas, Tex; plus others. *Exhib:* Allied Artists Show, New York, 69 & 70; Acad Artists Show, Springfield, Mass, 69 & 70; Hudson Valley Art Show, White Plains, NY, 69 & 70; Am Artists Prof League, New York, 69-71; Salmagundi Club Show, New York, 70 & 72. *Pos:* Creator comic strip, Chief, 64-67; owner, Joseph Dawley Gallery, 77- *Awards:* Figure or Portrait Anonymous Award, Acad Artists, 69; William Collins Award, Hudson Valley Art Asn, 69; Jane Peterson Portrait Award, Allied Artists, New York, 70. *Bibliog:* Kolbe (auth), Dawley reasserts realism, Am Artist Mag, 70; Singer (auth), Meet the artist--Joseph Dawley, Suburban Life Mag, 70; Calaway (auth), Bringing sanity back to art, Southwest Scene Mag, 70. *Mem:* Allied Artists Asn; Hudson Valley Art Asn; Am Artists Prof League; Acad Artists; Salmagundi Club. *Media:* Oil. *Publ:* Auth, Character Studies in Oil, 72, The Painters' Problem Book, 73, Painting Western Characters, 75 & Painters' Problem Book II, 78, Watson-Guptill. *Dealer:* Grand Central Gallery 40 Vanderbilt Ave New York NY 10017. *Mailing Add:* 13 W Holly St Cranford NJ 07016

DAWSON, BESS PHIPPS
PAINTER, GALLERY DIRECTOR
b Tchula, Miss. *Study:* Belhaven Col; Southwest Miss Jr Col; workshops, Allisons Art Colony, Way, Miss & Miss Art Colony, Laurel. *Work:* Art in Embassy Prog, Taiwan; Old Capitol Hist Mus, Jackson, Miss; Miss Art Asn Gallery, Jackson; Miss State Col Women, Columbus; First Nat Bank Miss Collection, Jackson. *Comn:* Murals, Church God, McComb, Miss, 58, Delta Elec Co, Greenwood, Miss, 58, First Nat Bank, McComb, Miss, 59 & Hankins Container Corp, Magnolia, Miss, 59; painting, Order Eastern Star, Jackson, 69. *Exhib:* Delgado Mus Art, New Orleans, La, 67; Brooks Mem Gallery, Memphis, Tenn, 69; Ark Arts Ctr, Little Rock, 70; Art Asn Gallery, Jackson, 70; Lauren Rogers Mus, Laurel, Miss, 80; Secy State Building, Jackson, Miss, 80. *Pos:* Co-owner & dir, Gulf South Galleries, 71-; dir, Miss Art Colony, 77- *Teaching:* Supvr art, McComb Pub Schs, 68-71. *Awards:* Award of Merit, 71 & First Award of Merit, 74, Miss Art Colony; Purchase Award, Cottonlandia Mus, 83. *Mem:* Southwest Miss Art Asn (secy, 66-); Miss Art Colony (bd dirs, 62-); Miss Art Asn (coordr state bd, 68-69). *Specialty:* Mississippi artists in all media. *Publ:* Coauth, Manual for classroom teachers, 69 & illusr, Elementary Art (TV doc), 69, McComb Pub Schs. *Dealer:* Gulf South Galleries 1413 Aston Ave McComb MS 39648. *Mailing Add:* PO Box 32 Summit MS 39666

DAWSON, JOHN ALLAN
PAINTER
b Joliet, Ill, Sept 12, 46. *Study:* Northern Ill Univ, BFA, 69; Univ NMex; Ariz State Univ, MFA, 74. *Work:* Ulrich Mus Art; Phoenix Art Mus, Ariz; Wichita State Univ; Ark Art Ctr, Little Rock; Okla Art Ctr, Oklahoma City. *Exhib:* Ariz Invitational 75, Phoenix Art Mus, 75; one-man shows, Ark Art Ctr, Little Rock, 79, Okla Art Ctr, Oklahoma City, 79, Springfield Mus Art, Mo, 80 & Sheldon Mem Collection, Univ Nebr, Lincoln, 80; Wedding Series, Elaine Horwitch Gallery, Scottsdale, Ariz, 82; and others. *Pos:* Artist in residence, Mesa Pub Schs, Ariz Comn Art, 74. *Awards:* Purchase Award, Del Mar Col, 73 & El Paso Mus Art, 75. *Bibliog:* H Broadly (auth), Portraits Paraphrasis, Art News, 4/75; C D Kotrozo (auth), article, Art Voices South, 5/79; A Johns (auth), The wedding series, Ariz Arts & Lifestyle, winter 82. *Media:* Oil. *Dealer:* Elaine Horwitch Gallery N Marshall Way Scottsdale AZ 85251; Segal Gallery 63 E 57th St New York NY 10022. *Mailing Add:* 10246 E Brown Rd Mesa AZ 85207

DAY, CHON (CHAUNCEY ADDISON)
CARTOONIST
b Chatham, NJ, Apr 6, 07. *Study:* Art Students League, with Boardman Robinson & John Sloan. *Exhib:* Metrop Mus Art, 42; Pa Acad Fine Arts. *Awards:* Best Gag Cartoonist, Nat Cartoonists Soc, 56, 61 & 70. *Mem:* Nat Cartoonists Soc. *Publ:* Auth & illusr, I Could Be Dreaming, 45, What Price Dory, 55, Brother Sebastian, 57, Brother Sebastian Carries On, 59 & Brother Sebastian at Large, 61; contribr cartoons, New Yorker, Good Housekeeping, Ladies Home J & others. *Mailing Add:* 22 Cross St Westerly RI 02891

DAY, GARY LEWIS
PRINTMAKER, PAINTER
b Great Falls, Mont, Sept 29, 50. *Study:* Mont State Univ, BA, 75; Fla State Univ, MFA, 76. *Work:* Ariz State Univ, Tempe; Sheldon Mem Gallery, Lincoln, Nebr. *Exhib:* Thirty Yrs Am Printmaking, Brooklyn Mus, NY, 76; one-man show, Ga Tech Univ, Atlanta, 77; two-person shows, Gallery 72, 78 & Joslyn Art Mus, 81, Omaha; Young Am Printmakers, Univ Maine, Orono, 80; Small Works, New York Univ, 80. *Collections Arranged:* Drawing Invitational (auth, catalog), Univ Nebr, Omaha, 79. *Teaching:* Instr art, Metrop Tech Community Col, Omaha, 77-79; vis lectr lithography, Creighton Univ, Omaha, 79; asst prof drawing, Univ Nebr, Omaha, 79- *Awards:* Purchase Awards, Southeastern Ctr Contemp Art, 75, Appalachian State, 79 & Joslyn Mus, 80. *Mem:* Col Art Asn; Print Club. *Media:* Intaglio, Lithography. *Publ:* Contribr, Colleagues: An Inter-Media Anthology of Artists, Pittore Euforico, 79; contribr, Another Normal Conception, Univ Ill, 80; contribr, An American Portfolio, Univ Ariz, 81. *Mailing Add:* 3221 Poppleton Ave Omaha NE 68105

DAY, HOLLIDAY T
CRITIC, CURATOR
b Nashville, Tenn. *Study:* Wellesley Col, Mass, BA; Univ Chicago, MA. *Pos:* Writer, New Art Examiner, Chicago, 76-79, contrib ed, 79-; cur Am art, Joslyn Art Mus, Omaha, Nebr, 80- *Awards:* Nat Endowment for the Arts critic's travel grant, 78-79; and others. *Mem:* Col Art Asn. *Res:* Surfaces of David Smith's sculpture. *Publ:* Auth, Fotografia Polska, 1839-1979, Indianapolis, Cincinnati and Dayton, summer 79 & Art in Am, 1/80; auth, Dematerialized art materialized, New Art Exam, 10/79; auth, Stacked, Packed, and Hung (catalogue), Name Gallery, 80; auth, I-80 Series, numerous catalogs, Joslyn Art Mus, 80-82; auth, Shape of Space: The Sculpture of George Sugarman, Joslyn Art Mus, 81; and others. *Mailing Add:* 18 South Park St Hinsdale IL 60521

DAY, HORACE TALMAGE
PAINTER, DIRECTOR
b Amoy, China, July 3, 09; US citizen. *Study:* Art Students League, 28-32; with Kimon Nicolaides & Kenneth H Miller; Tiffany Found, Oyster Bay, 30-35. *Work:* Va Mus Fine Arts, Richmond; Norfolk Mus, Va; Philip Morris Collection; Randolph-Macon Woman's Col Collection, Lynchberg, Va; Fleming Mus, Burlington, Vt. *Comn:* Mural, Tenn Treas Dept, 38; three paintings, Dept Reclamation, US Dept Interior, Washington, DC, 69. *Exhib:* Whitney Mus Am Art Ann, New York, 39-41 & 44; one-man shows, Bodley Gallery, New York, 58 & Fine Arts Am, Richmond, Va, 83; Biennial Am Painting, Va Mus Fine Arts, 58; Biennial Am Drawing, Norfolk Mus, 70; Bicentennial of Vt Painting Exhib, 76. *Pos:* Dir painting, Herbert Inst Art, Augusta, Ga, 36-41; dir, Northern Va Fine Arts Ctr, Alexandria, 72- *Teaching:* Prof art, Mary Baldwin Col, Staunton, Va, 42-63; instr painting, Kansas City Art Inst, 47-48. *Mem:* Southern Vt Art Asn. *Media:* Oil, Watercolor. *Publ:* Contribr, Art in the armed forces, Hyperion, 45; illusr, Staunton in the Valley of Virginia (folio), McClure, 47. *Dealer:* Jamison Gallery 111 E San Francisco Santa Fe NM 87501; Fine Arts Am 404 W Franklin St Richmond VA. *Mailing Add:* 113 N Fairfax St Alexandria VA 22314

DAY, JOHN
PAINTER, EDUCATOR
b Malden, Mass, May 27, 32. *Study:* Yale Univ, BFA(design), 54, MFA, 56; study with Josef Albers, Burgoyne Diller & James Brooks. *Work:* Mus Mod Art, New York; Whitney Mus Am Art, New York; Metrop Mus Art, New York; Newark Mus, NJ; Montclair Art Mus, NJ; and others. *Exhib:* Painting Exhib, Lyman Allyn Mus, New London, Conn, 61; Recent Acquisitions, Whitney Mus Am Art, New York, 67; l'Art Vivant 1965-1968, Found Maeght, St Paul De Vence, France, 68; Director's Choice, Brooklyn Mus Community Gallery, 72; Acquisitions Recentes, Mus Cantini, Marseille, France, 72; l'Art de Trois Villes, Mus Pompidou, Paris, 77; 1st Biennial, NJ Artists, Newark Mus, NJ, 77; Transitions-Recent Paintings, Parrish Art Mus, Southampton, NY, 79; and others. *Teaching:* Assoc prof painting, Univ Bridgeport, Conn, 58-70; prof painting, William Paterson Col, NJ, 70- *Awards:* Artists Award, 50 States of Art, Burpee Mus Art, Rockford, Ill, 65; First Prize, 20th New Eng Exhib, Silvermine Guild Artists, Conn, 69; First Prize, Members Exhib Abstract Painting, Guild Hall, East Hampton, Conn, 77. *Bibliog:* Daniel Abadie (auth), John Day, l'Americano deo luogi immaginari, le Arti, Milan, Italy, 9/71; Henry Galy-Carles (auth), Clefs pour John Day, Lettres Francaise, Paris, 3/71; Karl Lunde (auth), John Day, Arts Mag, 3/77; David L Shirey (auth), Works like painted music, New York Times, 11/18/79. *Media:* Oil, Collage. *Publ:* Auth, Art, Student Art Asn, William Paterson Col, 75; auth, The Artery, William Paterson Col, 77. *Mailing Add:* c/o Gallery Gemini 245 Worth Ave Palm Beach FL 33480

DAY, LARRY (LAWRENCE JAMES)
PAINTER, EDUCATOR
b Philadelphia, Pa, Oct 29, 21. *Study:* Tyler Sch Fine Arts, Temple Univ, BFA & BS(educ). *Work:* Philadelphia Mus Art, Pa; Miami-Dade Col, Fla; Philadelphia Col Art, Pa; Fleischer Art Mem, Philadelphia; Corcoran Gallery Art, Washington, DC. *Exhib:* Realism Now, Vassar Col; The Figure in Recent Am Painting Traveling Show (coauth, catalog), Westminster Col, Pa, 74; The Realist Revival, Am Fedn Arts Travelling Show; Bicentennial Exhib, Philadelphia Mus Art, 76. *Teaching:* Prof painting, drawing & theory, Philadelphia Col Art, Pa, 53- *Awards:* Temple Univ Alumni Cert Honor, 80; Hazlett Award for Excellence in the Arts, Pa, 82. *Media:* Oil, Watercolor. *Publ:* Coauth, American Figure Drawing (catalog), Victorian Col Art, Melbourne, Australia, 76; and others. *Dealer:* Gross-McCleaf Gallery 1713 Walnut St Philadelphia PA 19103. *Mailing Add:* 310 Myrtle Ave Cheltenham PA 19012

DAY, ROBERT JAMES
CARTOONIST
b San Bernardino, Calif, Sept 25, 1900. *Study:* Otis Art Inst, 18-27. *Exhib:* Many cartoon exhibs throughout US & Europe. *Interests:* Line & wash drawings. *Publ:* Illusr, The Mad World of Bridge, 60, Over the Fence is Out, 61, What Every Bachelor Knows, 61, Rome Wasn't Burned in a Day, 72 & many others; contribr to New Yorker & other nat mags. *Mailing Add:* c/o The New Yorker Magazine 25 W 43rd St New York NY 10036

DAY, WORDEN
SCULPTOR, PRINTMAKER
b Columbus, Ohio, June 11, 16. *Study:* Randolph-Macon Womans Col, BA; NY Univ, MA; also with Jean Charlot, Emilio Amero, Maurice Sterne, Vaclav Vylacil, Hans Hofmann & Stanley William Hayter. *Work:* Nat Gallery Art & Libr Cong, Washington, DC; Philadelphia Mus Art; Metrop Mus Art & Whitney Mus Am Art, New York; and others. *Exhib:* Nat Print Exhibs, Libr Cong, Brooklyn Mus & Philadelphia Mus Art, 48-62; Int Print Exhibs, Europe, Asia & Mex, 50-62; Abstract Painting and Sculpture in Am, Mus Mod Art, New York, 51; Third Carnegie Inst Int, Pittsburgh, 53; Int Watercolor Exhib, Brooklyn Mus, NY, 62. *Teaching:* Instr design, Pratt Inst, 55-56; vis artist, Iowa State Univ, 61; instr woodcut & watercolor, New Sch Social Res, 61-66; instr multimedia, Art Students League, 66-70 & Univ Wis, currently. *Awards:* Va Mus Fine Arts Grant, 40-42; J Rosenwald Awards, 42-44; Guggenheim fel, 51-52 & 61-62. *Bibliog:* Printmakers USA (film), US Info Serv, 61; Three Mid-Atlantic Artists, Kalamazoo Art Ctr, 63. *Mem:* Fedn Mod Painters & Sculptors; Montclair Art Mus; MacDowell Colony; Art Students League; Sculptors Guild. *Media:* Multimedia. *Mailing Add:* Studios 21/28 427 Bloomfield Ave Montclair NJ 07042

DEADERICK, JOSEPH
PAINTER, EDUCATOR
b Memphis, Tenn, Jan 17, 30. *Study:* Univ Ga, BFA, 52; Cranbrook Acad Art, MFA, 54; Ind Univ, 58-59. *Work:* Kalamazoo Col, Mich; numerous pvt collections. *Comn:* Ceramic tile mural, Univ Wyo, Laramie, 68; faceted glass window, Lutheran Campus Ctr, Laramie, 68. *Exhib:* Sixth Midwest Biennial, Joslyn Art Mus, Omaha, Nebr, 60; Brooklyn Mus Biennial Print Show, 64; Drawing USA Traveling Show, St Paul, Minn, 66-68; one-man show, Colorado Springs Fine Arts Ctr, 67; Fedn Rocky Mountain States Traveling Show, 66-72; 20 yr retrospective, Univ Wyo Art Mus, 78. *Teaching:* Instr design, Ind Univ, Bloomington, 56-59; prof art, Univ Wyo, Laramie, 59-. *Awards:* First Place Award Design, Franklin Mint, 72; Nat Award Excellence in Design, Printing Indust Am Graphic Arts Competition, 72. *Media:* Multimedia. *Publ:* The Stage: A Series of Poetic Drawings by Joseph Deaderick, Univ Wyo, 78. *Mailing Add:* Art Dept Univ Wyo Laramie WY 82070

DEAK, EDIT
CRITIC, FILMMAKER
b Albania, Sept 16, 48; US citizen. *Study:* Columbia Univ, BA(art hist); Whitney Mus Educ Dept, 73-74. *Pos:* Mus intern, Whitney Mus, 73-74; co-publisher & ed, Art-rite Mag, 73-; asst dir, Comt Visual Arts, 74-75; contribr, Art in Am, 73-79, Data, Italy, 74-76, Artforum, 77- *Awards:* NY State Coun Arts Grant, 74-75; Nat Endowment Art Critic Fel, 76; Nat Endowment Art Service to the Field Film Grant, 80; and others. *Bibliog:* Gary Wright (dir), Edit, (film), NY Univ Inst Film, 69; Grace Gluck (auth), article, New York Times, 80; interview, East Village Eye, 81; and others. *Mem:* Int Art Critics Asn; Col Art Asn. *Interests:* Surfacing nascent ideas and work of young avant-garde artists. *Mailing Add:* 149 Wooster St New York NY 10012

DEAL, JOE
PHOTOGRAPHER, EDUCATOR
b Topeka, Kans, Aug 12, 47. *Study:* Kansas City Art Inst, BFA, 70; Univ NMex, MA, 74, MFA, 78, study with Van Deren Coke. *Work:* Mus Mod Art, New York; Mus Fine Arts, Houston; Int Mus Photog at George Eastman House, Rochester, NY; Ctr Creative Photog, Tucson; Oakland Mus. *Exhib:* Ten Am Photogrs, The Photogrs Gallery, London, 74; New Topographics: Photographs of a Man-Altered Landscape, Int Mus Photog at George Eastman House, Rochester, Princeton Univ & Otis Art Gallery, Los Angeles, 75-76; Contemp Am Photographs, Mus Fine Arts, Houston, 77; The Great West: The Real & The Ideal, Univ Colo, Boulder, 77. *Teaching:* Lectr photog, San Francisco Art Inst, summer, 76; assoc prof photog, Univ Calif, Riverside, 76- *Awards:* Nat Endowment Arts Photogr Fel, 77 & 80; Guggenheim Fel, 83. *Bibliog:* Carter Ratcliff (auth), Route 66 revisited: The new landscape photography, Art in Am, 1-2/76; Joe Deal: New Topographics, Northlight Five, Ariz State Univ, 77. *Mem:* Soc Photog Educators. *Dealer:* Light Gallery 724 Fifth Ave New York NY 10019. *Mailing Add:* 3540 Watkins Dr Riverside CA 92507

DEAN, JAMES
PAINTER
b Fall River, Mass, Oct 14, 31. *Study:* Swain Sch Design, New Bedford, Mass. *Work:* Nat Aeronaut & Space Admin, Dept Interior, Washington, DC. *Exhib:* American Artists & Water Reclamation, Nat Gallery Art, Washington, DC, 72; Smithsonian Inst Traveling Exhib, 72-73; Corcoran Gallery Art, Washington, DC, 74; 107th Ann, Am Watercolor Soc, New York, 74; Washington Area Art, US Info Agency Worldwide Tour, 75-76; Nat Air & Space Mus, Washington, DC, 81-83. *Pos:* Dir fine arts prog, Nat Aeronaut & Space Admin, 61-74; cur art, Nat Air & Space Mus, 74-80. *Awards:* Cert Merit, Nat Acad Design, NY, Award of Excellence, Com Arts Mag, 76 & 77; Citation of Excellence, Am Inst Graphic Arts, 76-77. *Bibliog:* R J Williams (auth), James Dean painter of the past, Southern Living Mag, 6/73; Alice

Laurich (auth), James Dean, Focus Mag, 9-10/75; Jack Perlmutter (auth), Duality of James Dean, Art Voices South, 7-8/79. *Mem:* Hereward Lester Cooke Found (vchmn bd trustees, 73-); Torpedo Factory Artists Asn (pres, 83-84). *Media:* Watercolor. *Publ:* Coauth, Eyewitness to Space, Abrams, 72; auth, Artist and space, Interdisciplinary Sci Rev; auth, Artist and the space shuttle, NASA, 81. *Dealer:* Franz Bader Gallery 2124 Pennsylvania Ave Washington DC 20037; Maurice Sternberg 140 E Ontario St Chicago IL 60610. *Mailing Add:* 4804 King Richard Dr Annandale VA 22003

DEAN, NAT(ALIE CAROL)
PAINTER, CONSTRUCTIONIST
b Redwood City, Calif, Jan 13, 56. *Study:* Calif Inst Arts, 71-76; Cooper Union Advancement Sci Art, 75; San Francisco Art Inst, BFA, 77. *Work:* Fukuoka Cultural Ctr, Japan; San Francisco Mus Mod Art; Univ Manitoba, Winnipeg. *Comn:* Box-Book, Jean Brown Archive, Tyringham, Mass, 82. *Exhib:* Aesthetics of Graffitti, San Francisco Mus Mod Art, 78; Bookworks, Walker Art Ctr, 81; Int Mail Art, Fukuoka Cultural Ctr, Japan, 81; Selections from Eaton/Shoen, H C Price House & E S Gallery, Ariz & Calif, 81; Bookworks, Univ Ariz Art Mus, Tucson, 81; Stories Your Mother Never Told You, White Plains Publ Libr Mus, NY, 82; 1960-1981 Artist Book Survey, Ben Shahn Gallery, Patterson, NJ, 82. *Pos:* Owner, Ruta Zinc Fine Arts, San Francisco, 78- *Teaching:* Instr artist bus & survival, Col New Rochelle, 80, Sch Visual Arts, 81; San Francisco Art Inst, 81 & 82 & State Univ NY, Potsdam, 82. *Awards:* Merit Award, Calif Inst Arts, 76; Merit Award, San Francisco Mus Mod Art, 77. *Bibliog:* Robert Atkins (auth), Bay area artists, LAICA J, 81; Janet Tyson (auth), review, Artweek, 81; Michael (auth), rev, Arts Mag, 82. *Mem:* Ctr Book Arts; Col Art Asn. *Media:* Acrylic; Paper, Cloth. *Mailing Add:* 3435 Army Street Suite 214 San Francisco CA 94110

DEAN, NICHOLAS BRICE
PRINTMAKER, PHOTOGRAPHER
b Huntington, NJ, July 20, 33. *Study:* Dartmouth Col; Harvard Col, with Ansel Adams & Minor White. *Work:* Int Mus Photog, George Eastman House, Rochester, NY; Mus Mod Art, New York; Univ Calif, Los Angeles; Portland Mus Art, Maine; Lessing J Rosenwald Col, Jenkintown, Pa. *Comn:* Poster, Maine State Comn on the Arts & Humanities, 70; poster, Maine Film Alliance, Augusta, 77. *Exhib:* Photog at Mid-Century, 59, Photog, 63 & Three Photogr, 63, George Eastman House; The Sense of Abstraction, Mus Mod Art, New York, 60; Sixth Minn Biennial, Minn Art Inst, 67; Photo in the 20th Century, Nat Gallery Can, Ottawa, Ont, 67; Into the Seventies, Ohio Art Inst, Akron, 70; Realists Invitational, SE Ctr for Contemp Art, Winston-Salem, NC, 73; one-man show, Univ Ga, Athens, 75. *Pos:* Res craftsman, Penland Sch Crafts, 72-73; artist-in-residence, Sandhills Community Col, Southern Pines, NC, 73-74. *Teaching:* Head photog dept, Portland Sch Art, Maine, 68-72; instr photog, Penland Sch Crafts, NC, summers 69, 71, 72, 78 & 79; instr graphics, Haystack Sch Crafts, Deer Isle, Maine, summer 72, 78 & 79. *Media:* Silkscreen, Intaglio; Silver Print. *Publ:* Illusr, Bulfinch's Boston, Oxford Univ Press, 64; auth, Lubec, Identity, Cambridge, Mass, 67; co-auth (with Jonathan Williams), Blues & Roots/Rue & Bluets, Grossman, New York, 71; illusr, A Social History of the Boston Private Clubs, Barre, 71; illusr, Portland, Greater Portland Landmarks, 72. *Dealer:* Carl Siembab Gallery 172 Newbury St Boston MA. *Mailing Add:* RFD 1 Box 242 River Rd North Edgecomb ME 04556

DEAN, PETER
PAINTER
b Berlin, Mont, July 9, 39. *Study:* Cornell Univ; Univ Wis, BA; Pratt Graphic Art Ctr; also with Andre Girard. *Work:* Madison Art Ctr, Wis; Mus Mod Art, New York; Chicago Art Inst; Los Angeles Co Mus, Los Angeles; Nat Collection Washington, DC. *Exhib:* One-man show, Allan Stone Gallery, New York, 70, 73, 78 & 80 & Alexandre Monett Gallery, Bruxelles, 76, 78 & 80; 32nd Corcoran Biennial Am Painting, Washington, DC, 71; Madison Art Ctr, Wis, 78; Darthea Speyer Gallery, Paris, 81; Venice Biennele, Italy, 84; and others. *Pos:* Artist in residence, La State Univ, 74. *Teaching:* Vis artist, Yale Univ, Colgate Univ, NDak Univ, Univ Wis, Princeton Univ, Univ Tex & Tulane Univ. *Awards:* NY Coun Arts Grant, 76; Nat Endowment Arts Fel Grant, 81. *Media:* Oil, Watercolor. *Dealer:* Galeri Bellman 41 E 57 St New York NY 10022; Bienville Gallery 1800 Hasting Pl New Orleans LA 70130. *Mailing Add:* 2 Spring St New York NY 10012

DE ANDINO, JEAN-PIERRE M
DEALER, COLLECTOR
b San Juan, PR, June 11, 46. *Study:* George Washington Univ; Univ NC. *Pos:* Pvt dealer, 72-77; dir-vpres, Osuna Gallery, Washington, DC, 77-81; pres, Crowley de Andino & Holmes Inc, Washington, DC, 81-82; pres, de Andino Fine Arts, currently. *Specialty:* Nineteenth and twentieth century masters and contemporary art. *Collection:* Unique images on paper. *Mailing Add:* 2853 Ontario Rd NW Washington DC 20037

DEANGELIS, JOSEPH ROCCO
SCULPTOR
b Providence, RI, Apr 22, 38. *Study:* RI Sch Design, BFA, 66; Syracuse Univ, NY, MFA, 68. *Work:* Art Gallery London, Ont. *Comn:* Windsor Pub Libr, Ont, 75; City North Vancouver, BC, 77; Essex Civic Ctr, Ont, 77; Prov Ont Govt Bldg, Windsor, 78. *Exhib:* Ontario Now, traveling, 76; Spectrum Canada, Montreal Olympics, 76; London Art Gallery, Ont, 77; Canadian Place, Toronto, Ont, 77; Art Gallery Windsor, Ont, 78; Agnes Etherington Gallery, Kingston, Ont, 81; and others. *Teaching:* Lectr, Univ Mich, Ann Arbor, 69-70; assoc prof, Univ Windsor, Ont, 70- *Awards:* Sculpture Award, Art Gallery London, 75; Grant, Ont Arts Coun, 77. *Bibliog:* Ann Rosenberg (auth), Wood sculpture of the Americas, Capilano Review, No 12, 77; Arthur

Perry (auth), Vancouver: Wood sculpture of the Americas, Art Mag, 10-11/77; David Quintner (auth), Angelic sculptural work suspends tactile senses, Windsor Star, 3/81. *Media:* Mixed. *Mailing Add:* 1690 Front Rd LaSalle ON N9J 2B6 Canada

DEARCANGELIS, GLORIA
SCULPTOR
b Munich, Ger, Jan 15, 57; US citizen. *Study:* Philadelphia Col Art, BFA, 78; Univ Wash, Seattle, MFA, 81. *Work:* City Seattle Portable Works Collection. *Exhib:* Crafts: Contemporary Perspective, Bellevue Art Mus, Wash, 83; NAm Sculpture Exhib, Foothills Art Ctr, Golden, Colo, 83; Reno-Seattle Exchange, Sheppard Gallery, Univ Reno, 83; solo exhibs, Pittsburg State Univ & Okla State Univ, 83 & Traver-Sutton Gallery & Univ Wash, Bellingham, 83. *Teaching:* Vis asst prof ceramics, Okla State Univ, Stillwater, 82-83; asst prof sculpture, Vanderbilt Univ, 83- *Awards:* Westland Award, NAm Sculpture Exhib, 83. *Bibliog:* Matthew Kangas (auth), Gloria DeArcangelis at Traver-Sutton, Art in Am, 11/82. *Mem:* Ctr Contemp Art, Seattle (mem bd dirs, 82-83). *Media:* Mixed. *Mailing Add:* c/o Traver-Sutton Gallery 2219 Fourth St Seattle WA 98101

DE ARMOND, DALE B
PRINTMAKER
b Bismark, NDak. *Study:* Study with Dannie Pierce, Carol Summers & Jules Heller. *Work:* Alaska State Mus; Anchorage Hist & Fine Arts Mus, Alaska Methodist Univ, Anchorage. *Exhib:* Charles & Emma Frye Art Mus, Seattle, Wash, 70; Alaska State Mus, Juneau, 75; Anchorage Hist & Fine Arts Mus, 77; Mus of Sci, Boston, 78. *Awards:* Purchase Award, Alaska Centennial, 67; First Prize, Woodblock, All-Alaska Show, Exxon Corp, 75. *Bibliog:* Pat McCullough (auth), Alaskan Artist, Alaska J Hist & Art, 76; article, Am Artist, 4/82. *Media:* Woodblock, Wood Engraving. *Publ:* Auth, Juneau A Book of Woodcuts, 73, Raven, 75 & Dale De Armond, A First Book of Prints, 79, Northwest Publ. *Dealer:* Artique Ltd 314 G St Anchorage AK 99501. *Mailing Add:* 422 Calhoun Ave Juneau AK 99801

DEATON, CHARLES
SCULPTOR, ARCHITECT
b Clayton, NMex, Jan 1, 21. *Comn:* Designs for sculptured bank, Key Savings & Loan, Littleton, Colo, 67 & sculptured stadia (with Kivett & Meyers, Architects), Jackson Co Sports Complex Authority, 72. *Exhib:* Photographs of sculptured house, Mus Mod Art, New York, 79. *Teaching:* Instr design, Franklin Sch Prof Art, 45-48; also lectr var art & archit depts, 60- *Bibliog:* Len Leddington (auth), Architecture as sculpture, Today Show, NBC TV, 66; Hermine Mariaux (auth), Freedom in space, Town & Country, 67; Mary Roblee Henry (auth), Live-in sculpture, Vogue, 70. *Media:* Concrete, Mixed Media. *Publ:* Auth, The sculptured house, Art Am, 66. *Mailing Add:* Genesee Mountain Golden CO 80401

DEATS, MARGARET (MARGARET DEATS BOTT)
DEALER, WRITER
b Houston, Tex, May 27, 42. *Study:* Univ Houston; Univ St Thomas, Houston. *Collections Arranged:* Gulf Coast Invitational Sculpture Exhib, 76; Houston Festival Sculpture Invitational, 79. *Pos:* Fine Arts writer, Galveston Daily News, 71-75; owner-pres, Loft-on-Strand Gallery, 71-78; pvt dealer, 78- *Bibliog:* Gay McFarland (auth), Living on The Strand, Sculptor & Wife Preserve Old Building, Houston Post, 5/73; Dancie Perugini (auth), Loft-on-Strand, Houston Town & Country Mag, 4/76. *Mem:* Galveston County Cultural Arts Coun (bd mem, 73-74). *Specialty:* Contemporary paintings, sculpture, conceptual art and process installations. *Publ:* Auth, Painter Frank Freed mirrors human foibles, Galveston Daily News, 72; auth, Nancy Hanks, the gentle persuader brings art to all people, United Press Int, 73; auth, Piled sugar, sacrificed painting are Michael Tracy's statements, Galveston Daily News, 74; auth, The arts of Galveston, Galveston Mag, 75. *Mailing Add:* 5400 Memorial #703 Houston TX 77007

DE BASSI, SOFIA CELORIO See Bassi

DE BELLIS, HANNIBAL
SCULPTOR, MEDALIST
b Accadia, Italy, Sept 22, 1894; US citizen. *Study:* Univ Ala, MD, 20; also with Gaetano Cecere, Jean De Marco & George Lober. *Work:* Navy Art Mus, Navy Combat Mus, Pentagon, Smithsonian Inst, Washington, DC. *Comn:* Portrait medallions of Adm King, Burke & Richets & Navaquila, Navy eagle, US Navy; Groedal Medal, Am Col Cardiol, 49; bronze plaques for St Vincent's Hosp & Med Ctr, New York; Adm Arleigh Burke Fleet Trophy, Navy Mus, Washington, DC; Salmagundi Club Honor Award Medal, 72. *Awards:* Salmagundi Sculpture Prizes, 60 & 71; Adm A Burke Sculpture Award, 62; Am Artists Prof League Award, 64. *Mem:* Medalist Soc; Nat Sculpture Soc; Am Artists Prof League; Salmagundi Club. *Media:* Bronze. *Mailing Add:* 10 Holder Pl Forest Hills NY 11375

DE BLASI, ANTHONY ARMANDO
PAINTER, EDUCATOR
b Alcamo, Italy, Jan 1, 33; US citizen. *Study:* Art Students League, with Sidndey Dickenson, Univ RI, BA; Ind Univ, Bloomington, with William Bailey, James McGarrell, Henry Hope & Albert Elsen, MFA. *Work:* Riverside Mus Collection, Rose Art Mus, Brandeis Univ; Wichita State Univ Mus Fine Arts, Kans; Detroit Art Inst; Ind Univ, Bloomington; Bethany Col, WVA. *Exhib:* Midyear Show Contemp Am Art, Butler Inst, Youngstown, Ohio, 67; Mus Mod Art, New York, 68; one-man shows, Spectrum Gallery, New York, 68, 69, 71 & 73; Detroit Art Inst, 72 & Razor Gallery, New York, 75 & 77; 33rd Corcoran Biennial Contemp Am Painting, Corcoran Gallery,

Washington, DC, 73; Wake Forest Univ, Winston-Salem, NC, 80; and others. *Teaching:* Chmn & artist in residence, Washington & Jefferson Col, 63-66; prof painting & drawing, Mich State Univ, 66- *Awards:* Louis Comfort Tiffany Found Grant, 66-67; Founders Purchase Prize, Detroit Art Inst, 70; Individual Artist Grant, Mich Coun Arts, 83. *Bibliog:* Emily Wasserman (auth), rev, In: Artforum, 4/68; Atirnomis (auth), rev, In: Arts Mag, 12-1/70; Gene Baro (auth), The 33rd Corcoran Biennial (catalog), 73; and others. *Mem:* Art Students League. *Media:* Acrylic. *Mailing Add:* Dept of Art Mich State Univ East Lansing MI 48824

DE BOSCHNEK, CHRIS (CHRISTIAN CHARLES)
PAINTER, PRINTMAKER
b Cannes, France, Apr 24, 47; US citizen. *Study:* Cleveland Art Inst; Akron Univ. *Work:* Weiskoff, Silver & Co, New York; Newark Mus, NJ; Kelly, Drye & Warren, Stanford, Conn; US Steel Co, Pittsburgh, Pa; Sherman & Sterling, New York. *Exhib:* One-man show, Akron Art Inst, Ohio, 71; Tibor de Nagy Gallery, New York, 73; OK Harris Gallery, New York, 79; Josef Gallery, New York, 81; Allentown Mus, Pa, 81; and others. *Awards:* Yaddo Fel, 80. *Mailing Add:* 28 East 18th St New York NY 10003

DE BRETTEVILLE, SHEILA LEVRANT
DESIGNER, INSTRUCTOR
b Brooklyn, NY, Nov 4, 40. *Study:* Barnard Col, Columbia Univ, BA(art hist); Yale Sch Art & Archit, MFA(graphic design). *Work:* Am Inst Graphic Arts, New York; Design Collection, Mus Mod Art, New York; Woman's Bldg, Community Gallery, Los Angeles. *Comn:* 40 under 40 show, Archit League, New York, 65; catalog of the Art of Latin America since Independance (with Alvin Eisenman), Yale Art Gallery, 66; book design, Canavese, Olivetti, Milan, Italy, 68; poster design, Calif Inst Arts, Valencia, 70; spec issue design, Art Soc Wis, 70. *Exhib:* Communications Graphics, Am Inst Graphics Art, 72; 5e Biennale des Arts Graphiques, Brno Czech, 72; Color, Am Inst Graphic Arts, Whitney Mus, 74; Poster from the Vietnam Years, New York, 75; Women and the Printing Arts, Woman's Bldg, Community Gallery, 75. *Pos:* Typographer, Yale Univ Press, New Haven, Conn, 65-68; designer, Olivetti, Milan, Italy, 68-69; designer, Calif Inst Arts, 69-74; co-founder & pres, Woman's Bldg Community Gallery, 73-; judge, Nat Endowment Arts-Civil Serv Comn, 75; co-founder, ed & designer, Chrysalis Mag, 77-; design dir, Los Angeles Times, 78-81; chmn, Dept of Commun, Design & Illus, Otis Art Inst of Parsons Sch of Design, Los Angeles, 81- *Teaching:* Dir inst & graphic design dept, Calif Inst Arts, 70-74; lectr at var cols & univs. *Awards:* Grand Award Excellence, Soc Publ Designers, 71; Communication Graphics Awards, Am Inst Graphic Arts, 72; IBM Fel, Int Design Conf Aspen, 74. *Bibliog:* Gilles de Bure (auth), Right on Sheila, Creations Recherches Esthetiques Europeenes, 73. *Mem:* Am Inst Graphic Arts. *Publ:* Ed, Calif Institute of the Arts: prologue to a community, Vol 7 No 2 & A reexamination of some aspects of the design arts from the perspective of the women designer, Arts Soc, 74; auth, A reevaluation of design, Icographic 6, 73; auth, Habitability, In: Proc of the Calif Chap Am Inst Archit, 74; auth, Feminist Design, Space & Soc, 6/83. *Mailing Add:* 8067 Willow Glenn Rd Los Angeles CA 90046

DECAPRIO, ALICE
PAINTER, DESIGNER
b Marshall, Mich, Feb 10, 19. *Study:* Mich State Univ, AB; Northwestern Univ, MA; also watercolor with Arthur Barbour, Nicholas Reale and Valfred Thelin. *Work:* Ocean Co Col, NJ; US Navy; RCA Corp Hq, New York; Chatham Savings & Loan; Ringling Mus, Sarasota, Fla. *Comn:* Carousel Horse (drawing), Ringling Mus, Sarasota, 78; US Navy-NY Harbor Oper Sail activities, 76-77; Navy Women at Work on Board USS Vulcan, 79; coloring books, Ringling Mus, Sarasota, Fla, 80; brochure, Albaz Corp, Riyadh, Saudi Arabia, 81; and others. *Exhib:* one-person shows, Nat Arts Club, 77, SVt Art Ctr, 77; AT&T Corp Hq, NJ, 80 & Friends of Arts & Sci, Sarasota, Fla, 80; Heritage Plantation, Sandwich, Mass, 81; and others. *Teaching:* Instr watercolor, Madison-Chatham Adult Sch, 68-76, instr outdoor sketching, 70-81, Creative Learning Workshop, Rockport, Mass, 77-82. *Awards:* Exhib Comn Award, Nat Arts Club Open Watercolor Show, 75; Grumbacher Award, NJ Watercolor Soc, 77; Naval Art Coop & Liaison Comt Bronze Medal for Achievement in Watercolor, Salmagundi Club, 78. *Mem:* Salmagundi Club; NACAL; Int Soc Marine Painters; Fla Watercolor Soc; NJ Watercolor Soc. *Media:* Watercolor, Charcoal; Pastel Drawings. *Mailing Add:* 3963 Country View Dr Sarasota FL 33583

DECARAVA, ROY RUDOLPH
PHOTOGRAPHER, EDUCATOR
b New York, NY, Dec 9, 19. *Study:* Cooper Union Art Sch, 38-40. *Work:* Metrop Mus Art, Mus Mod Art, New York; Mus Fine Arts, Houston; Ctr Creative Photog. *Comn:* The Nation's Capitol in Photographs, Corcoran Gallery Art, 76; American Images, Am Tel & Tel, New York, 78. *Exhib:* Always the Young Strangers, Mus Mod Art, New York, 53; The Family of Man, Mus Mod Art, New York, 53; The Photographers Eye, Mus Mod Art, New York, 64; Photography in the Fine Arts, Metrop Mus Art, New York, 64; Thru Black Eyes, Studio Mus Harlem, 69; Photography in America, Whitney Mus Am Art, 74; solo exhib, Mus Fine Arts, Houston, 75 & Clarence Kennedy Gallery, Boston, 82; Mirrors & Windows, Mus Mod Art, New York, 78; Silver Sensibilities, Newhouse Gallery, Staten Island, 80; The Sound I Saw, Studio Mus Harlem, 83. *Teaching:* Dir photog, Kamoinge Workshop, New York, 63-66; adj instr, Cooper Union Art Sch, 69-72; prof, Hunter Col, 75- *Awards:* Guggenheim Fel Photog, 52-53; Outstanding Achievements in Photography, Int Black Photogr, 79; Spec Citation Photojournalism, Am Soc Mag Photogr, 83. *Bibliog:* A D Coleman (auth), Roy DeCarava, Popular Photog, 70; Elton Fax (auth), Seventeen Black Artists, Dodd, Mead Co, 73;

Pat Leighton (auth), Roy DeCarava, Photograph, Vol 1, No 3, 77. *Mem:* Friends Photog (mem bd trustees, 82-); Photo Resource Ctr. *Publ:* Coauth (with Langston Hughes), The Sweet Flypaper of Life, Simon & Schuster, 55. *Dealer:* Witkin Gallery 41 E 57 St New York NY 10022. *Mailing Add:* 81 Halsey St Brooklyn NY 11216

DE CHAMPLAIN, VERA CHOPAK
PAINTER, PRINTMAKER
b Ger; US citizen. *Study:* Art Students League; spec studies with Edwin Dickinson. *Work:* Butler Inst Am Art, Youngstown, Ohio; Slater Mus, Norwich, Conn; Ga Mus Art, Athens; Evansville Mus Art & Sci, Ind; Smithsonian Inst Arch Am Art, Washington DC; and others. *Exhib:* Artists Equity Gallery, New York, 70, 72 & 75; Avery Fisher Hall, Lincoln Ctr, New York, 79, 81 & 83; NY Univ, 79; Metrop Mus Art, New York, 79; Muriel Karasik Gallery, Westhampton, NY, 80; B Altman Gallery, New York, 82; and others. *Teaching:* Art dir & instr oil painting, Emanu-El Ctr, New York, 68- *Awards:* Twilight & Onteora Club Award, Haines Falls, NY, 65; US Investor Award, 69; and others. *Bibliog:* Samuel M La Corte (auth), Creative images, Clifton Leader, 70. *Mem:* Fel Royal Soc Arts; Artists Equity Asn New York; Kappa Pi; Nat Soc Arts & Lett (art chmn Empire State, 69-); Art Students League; and others. *Media:* Oil, Watercolor. *Mailing Add:* 230 Riverside Dr New York NY 10025

DECHAR, PETER
PAINTER
b New York, NY, Apr 19, 42. *Work:* Mus Mod Art & Whitney Mus Am Art, New York; Larry Aldrich Mus, Conn; Walker Art Ctr, Chicago; Fiberglas Tower Art Collection. *Exhib:* Highlights from the 1967 Season, Larry Aldrich Mus, Conn, 67; Contemp Painting & Sculpture, Krannert Art Mus, 67; Whitney Mus Am Art Ann, New York, 67 & 69; one-man shows, Cordier & Ekstrom Gallery, New York, 67, 69 & 75; Twentieth Century Art from the Rockefeller Collection, Mus Mod Art, New York, 69. *Media:* Oil. *Mailing Add:* c/o Cordier & Ekstrom Gallery 417 E 75th St New York NY 10021

DECOCK, LILIANE (LILIANE MORGAN DECOCK)
PHOTOGRAPHER, EDITOR
b Antwerp, Belgium, Sept 11, 39; US citizen. *Study:* Studied photog with Ansel Adams, 63-72. *Work:* Art Inst Chicago; Amon Carter Mus Western Art, Ft Worth; Detroit Inst Art, Mich; Princeton Univ, NJ; Ctr Creative Photog, Phoenix. *Exhib:* RI Sch Design, Providence, 72; Amon Carter Mus Western Art, Ft Worth, 73; Hudson River Mus, Yonkers, 73; Witkin Gallery, New York, 75; Milwaukee Ctr Photog, 79. *Awards:* Guggenheim Fel Photog, 73. *Publ:* Ed, Ansel Adams, 73, ed, Wynn Bullock--Photography A Way of Life, 73, ed, Russell Lee--Photographer, 78, coauth, Morgan & Morgan Darkroom Book, 80 & ed, Photo-Lab-Index, 83, Morgan & Morgan. *Mailing Add:* RR 2 Box 264 Pound Ridge NY 10576

DE COUX, JANET
SCULPTOR
b Niles, Mich. *Study:* Carnegie Inst Technol, two yrs; NY Sch Indust Design; RI Sch Design; Art Inst Chicago; asst to C Paul Jennewein, A B Cianfarani, Gozo Kawamura, Alvin Meyer & James Earl Fraser. *Comn:* William Penn, William Penn Mem Mus, Harrisburg, Pa; Madonna (black granite), Manhasset, Long Island, NY; St Benedict, St Vincent's Archabbey, Latrobe, Pa; St Benedict sculpture proj, Liturgical Art Soc; five pieces sculpture, St Scholastica's Church, Aspinwall, Pa; plus many others. *Exhib:* One-man show, Carnegie Inst; Artist of Year Show, Arts & Crafts Ctr, Univ Pittsburgh. *Teaching:* Resident instr art, Cranbrook Acad Art, 42-45. *Awards:* Guggenheim Fel; Widener Gold Medal, Pa Acad Fine Arts; Lindsay Mem Prize, Nat Sculpture Soc. *Mem:* Nat Acad Design; Nat Sculpture Soc; Pittsburgh Assoc Artists. *Media:* Stone, Wood. *Mailing Add:* Gibsonia PA 15044

DE CREEFT, LORRIE J See Goulet, Lorrie

DEDINI, ELDON LAWRENCE
CARTOONIST
b King City, Calif, June 29, 21. *Study:* Hartnell Col, AA; Chouinard Art Inst, Los Angeles. *Work:* Achenbach Collection, Legion of Honor, San Francisco; Libr of Cong, Washington, DC; NY Univ. *Exhib:* Nat Cartoonists Soc Group Exhib, New York; Int Cartoonale, Heist-Duinbergen, Belg, 64-66; Three Cartoonists Show, Richmond Art Mus, Calif, 68; Three Cartoonists Show, Monterey Peninsula Mus Art, 83. *Pos:* Cartoonist, Salinas-Index-Jour, Calif, 40-42; story cartoonist, Disney Studios, Burbank, Calif, 44-46; cartoonist-gagman, Esquire, Inc, Chicago, 46-50; cartoonist, New Yorker Mag, 50-; cartoonist, Playboy, Inc, Chicago, 60- *Awards:* Best Mag Cartoonist, Nat Cartoonists Soc, 58, 61 & 64. *Mem:* Nat Cartoonists Soc; Mag Cartoonists Guild (2nd vpres, 71). *Publ:* Contribr, Esquire, 43-50, New Yorker, 50-80 & Playboy Mag, 60-80; auth, The Dedini Gallery, 61 & illusr, La Clef, 70, Holt. *Mailing Add:* PO Box 1630 Monterey CA 93940

DE DONATO, LOUIS
PAINTER, INSTRUCTOR
b New York, NY, Aug 29, 34. *Study:* Art Students League, with Frank Reilly, 55-61. *Work:* Abe Sharp Found, Maine; Navy Art Combat and Laison, Washington, DC. *Exhib:* Allied Artists Am 68th Ann, Nat Arts Club, New York, 81; Soc Animal Artists Exhib, Acad Natural Sci, Philadelphia, 82 & Topeka, Kans, 83; Am Artists Prof League, New York, 83; Greenwich Workshop Gallery Miniature Show, 83. *Teaching:* Instr life drawing & painting, Salmagundi Club, New York, 72- *Awards:* First Prize, NY & Conn Am Artists Prof League Show, 79; Maggie Bower Award, Knickerbocker

Artists Asn, 80; Franklin B Williams Fund Prize, Salmagundi Club, 83. *Mem:* Soc Animal Artists (bd dirs, 76-82); Allied Artists Am; Salmagundi Club (bd dirs, 70-82); Am Artists Prof League; Hudson Valley Artists Asn. *Media:* Oil. *Publ:* Illusr, National Institute of Art & Design, Northwest Sch, Inc, 64. *Dealer:* Hobe Sound Galleries Hobe Sound FL; Husberg Fine Arts Gallery Sedona AZ. *Mailing Add:* 47 Fifth Ave New York NY 10003

DEE, ELAINE EVANS
HISTORIAN
b Cleveland, Ohio, Jan 11, 24. *Study:* Oberlin Col, with Wolfgang Stechow, BA, 45; Radcliffe Col, with Jakob Rosenberg, MA, 51. *Collections Arranged:* Old Master Drawings (contribr, catalogue), 60; Nineteenth Century Master Drawings, Newark Mus, NJ, 61; Nineteenth and Twentieth Century European Drawings (auth, catalog), Am Fedn Arts, 65; Views of Florence & Tuscany, Washington, DC, 68; Master Printmakers from the Cooper-Hewitt Museum (auth, catalog), New York, 70; Winslow Homer, A Selection from the Cooper-Hewitt Museum (auth, catalog), Washington, DC, 72; An American Museum of Decorative Art & Design (contribr, catalog), Victoria & Albert Mus, London, Eng, 73; Etchings of the Tiepolos, Ottawa, Ont, 75. *Pos:* Asst cur drawings, Fogg Art Mus, Harvard Univ, 45-51 & 52-53; asst cur drawings & prints, Cleveland Mus Art, Ohio, 51-52 & Pierpont Morgan Libr, New York, 61-68; cur drawings & prints, Cooper-Hewitt Mus Design, New York, 68- *Awards:* Samuel H Kress Found Traveling Fel, 73; Nat Endowment Arts Mus Prof Fel, 76. *Mem:* Int Comt Cur Pub Collections Graphic Arts; Am Fedn Arts; Print Coun Am; Am Mus Asn. *Res:* Eighteenth century French and Italian drawings, particularly the artists Gilles-Marie Oppenord and Guiseppe Zocchi. *Publ:* Contribr, One Hundred Master Drawings, Harvard Univ Press, 49. *Mailing Add:* c/o Cooper-Hewitt Mus Design 2 E 91st St New York NY 10028

DEE, LEO JOSEPH
PAINTER
b Newark, NJ, July 8, 31. *Study:* Newark Sch Fine & Indust Art, with Hans Weingartner, Benjamin Cunningham, James Rosati & Ruben Nakian, dipl. *Work:* Newark Mus Art; Springfield Mus Art, Mass; Cooper-Hewitt Mus, New York; NJ State Mus, Trenton; Yale Univ Art Gallery. *Exhib:* Drawing Soc Regional, Philadelphia Mus, circulated by Am Fedn Arts, 65-66; Meticulous Realism, Tawes Art Ctr, Univ Md, 66; NJ State Mus, Trenton, 66-70; 4th Invitational Painting & Sculpture, Van Deusen Gallery, Kent State Univ, 70; one-man show, Coe Kerr Gallery, 75. *Teaching:* Instr drawing & painting, Newark Sch Fine & Indust Art, 58- *Media:* Oil. *Dealer:* Coe Kerr Gallery 49 E 82nd St New York NY 10028. *Mailing Add:* 38 Ridgewood Terr Maplewood NJ 07040

DEEM, GEORGE
PAINTER
b Vincennes, Ind, Aug 18, 32. *Study:* Sch of the Art Inst of Chicago, BFA, 58, with Paul Wieghardt & Boris Margo. *Work:* Indianapolis Mus Art, Ind; Ludwig Collection, Neue Galerie, Aachen, WGer; Evansville Mus Arts & Sci, Ind; Albright-Knox Art Gallery, Buffalo, NY; Allen Mem Art Mus, Oberlin Col, Ohio. *Exhib:* One-man shows, Paintings & Drawings by George Deem, Indianapolis Mus Art, 74-75 & Witte Mem Mus, San Antonio, Tex, 75; Art About Art, Whitney Mus Am Art, New York, 78; Mona Lisa in the 20th Century, Wilhelm-Lehmbruck Mus, Duisburg, WGer, 78; The Making of a Masterpiece: George Deem, recent paintings, Evansville Mus of Arts & Sci, Ind, 79; Contemporary American Realism Since 1960, Pa Acad fine Arts, Philadelphia, 81; Artist's Studio in America PTG, Allentown Art Mus, Pa, 83; Inaugural Exhib, Fort Wayne Mus Art, Ind, 84; and others. *Pos:* Artist-in-residence, Evansville Mus Arts & Sci, 79; secy exec comt, MacDowell Colony Fels 82-84; vis artist, Ill State Univ, Normal, 82. *Teaching:* Instr, Sch Visual Arts, New York, 65-66; instr painting, Leicester Polytechnic, Eng, 66-67; instr painting, Univ Pa, Philadelphia, 67-68. *Bibliog:* Ronald Vance (auth), Painting Lists, Art & Artists, London, Eng, 2/68; Edgar Buonagurio (auth), George Deem, Arts Mag, New York, 11/77; Udo Kultermann (auth), Vermeer and Contemporary American Painting, Am Art Rev, Los Angeles, 11/78. *Media:* Oil on canvas; drawing, various media. *Publ:* Auth, AANABABCAC, Sun & Moon, fall 79; auth, A Painting For Babies, Benzene, Fall 81; auth, Extra Genre, White Walls, summer 81; auth, Mona Lisa Washington, Zone, spring 80; auth, Actual Size, Benzene, fall-winter 83-84. *Dealer:* Sid Deutsch Gallery 20 W 57th St New York NY 10019; Merida Gallery Inc 2007 Frankfort Ave Louisville KY 40206. *Mailing Add:* 10 W 18th St New York NY 10011

DEFEO, JAY
PAINTER, PHOTOGRAPHER
b Hanover, NH, Mar 31, 29. *Study:* Univ Calif, Berkeley, BA, MA; San Francisco Art Inst, Hon Dr, 82. *Work:* Oakland Mus Art, Calif; San Francisco Mus Art; Pasadena Mus Art, Calif. *Exhib:* Sixteen Americans, Mus Mod Art, New York, 58; Pasadena Mus Art, 68; San Francisco Mus Art, 70; Poets of the Cities, Dallas Mus Fine Arts & San Francisco Mus Art, 75; Calif Painting & Sculpture, San Francisco Mus Art, 76 & Nat Gallery, Washington, DC, 77; Perceptions of the Spirit--20th Century Am Art, Indianapolis Mus Art, Ind, 77; Mod Era, Bay Area Update, Huntsville Mus Art, Ala, 77. *Teaching:* Instr drawing & painting, San Francisco Art Inst, 62-70, Sonoma State Col, 81-, Mills Col, currently. *Awards:* Sigmund Martin Heller Fel, 51; Nat Endowment for the Arts, 73; Adaline Kent Award, 83. *Bibliog:* Bruce Conner (auth, film), The Rose, 64. *Media:* Acrylic, Mixed-Media. *Mailing Add:* c/o Gallery Paule Anglim 14 Geary San Francisco CA 94108

DE FOIX-CRENASCOL, LOUIS
HISTORIAN, CONSULTANT
b Italy, June 2, 21; US citizen. *Study:* Maffeo Vegio State Col, Italy, MA; Pontif Univ St Anselm, Rome, LLD; Inst Archaeol & Art Hist, Univ Rome, with Cesare Brandi, dipl. *Collections Arranged:* Joseph Stella Retrospective, 64, Haitian Artists, 65, Religion in the Art of Haiti, 68, Imperial China, 72, Shapes & Techniques of Oriental Pottery, 78, Japanese Swords & Sword Fittings, 79 & Chinese Ritual Bronzes, 80, Seton Hall Univ. *Pos:* Inspector antiq & fine art, Ital Govt, 53-57; dir art gallery, Seton Hall Univ, 63-68, dir art ctr, 74-77; founder & cur, Wang Fang-yu Collection of Oriental Art, 77- *Teaching:* Prof art hist, Seton Hall Univ, 61-, chmn dept art, 68-77, prof art market & law, 80- *Awards:* Fulbright scholar, 65; Knight Comdr SS Mauritius & Lazarus (Italy), Knight of Malta. *Mem:* Asn Int Archeol Classique; Nat Trust Hist Preserv. *Res:* Italian Renaissance painting and architecture; Indian and Far Eastern art; art market, art law. *Publ:* Co-auth, Franchino Gaffurio (1451-1522), 51; auth, The Pallavicino Chorals and the Lombard Miniature of the 15th Century, 55; auth, The Incoronata of Lodi, 56; also contribr to many Europ & Am art jour & mag. *Mailing Add:* Dept of Art Seton Hall Univ South Orange NJ 07079

DE FOREST, ROY DEAN
PAINTER, SCULPTOR
b North Platte, Nebr, Feb 11, 30. *Study:* Yakima Jr Col, 48-50; Calif Sch Fine Arts, 50-52; San Francisco State Col, BA, MA. *Work:* San Francisco Mus Art; Art Inst Chicago; Joslyn Art Mus, Omaha, Nebr; Philadelphia Mus Art; Whitney Mus Am Art, New York; plus others. *Exhib:* Albright-Knox Gallery, 63; Walker Art Ctr, 63; solo exhibs, Hansen-Fuller Gallery, 71, 73, 75 & 78, Darthea Speyer Gallery, 74 & 77 & Clark/Benton Gallery, Santa Fe, 77; Extraordinary Realities, Whitney Mus Am Art, 73; retrospective, San Francisco Mus Art, 74; Painting and Sculpture in California: The Modern Era, San Francisco Mus Art, 76; 6 from California, Wash State Univ, 76; New in the Seventies, Univ Tex, Austin, 77; Roy de Forest, Robert Hudson, Inst Contemp Art, Boston, 77; Dog Images through the Century, Downtown Ctr, San Francisco Mus Art, 78; Dir, Larsen Gallery, Yakima Jr Col, 58-60. *Teaching:* Calif, 63-65; prof painting & drawing, Univ Calif, Davis, 65- *Awards:* Nealie Sullivan Award, San Francisco Art Asn, 64; Purchase Prize, La Jolla Art Mus, 65; Nat Endowment Arts Grant, 72. *Bibliog:* Thomas Albright (auth), Wildest of funk art, San Francisco Chronicle, 2/6/69; Charles Johnson (auth), The new symbolism, Sacramento Bee, 4/13/69. *Mem:* San Francisco Art Asn. *Dealer:* Hansen-Fuller Gallery 228 Grant Ave San Francisco CA 94108; Allan Frumkin Gallery 50 West 57th St New York NY 10019. *Mailing Add:* PO Box 47 Port Costa CA 94569

DEGENEVIEVE, BARBARA
PHOTOGRAPHER, EDUCATOR
b Wilkes-Barre, Pa, May 21, 47. *Study:* Wilkes Col, Wilkes-Barre, Pa, BFA, 69; Southern Conn State Col, New Haven, MS(art educ), 73; Univ NMex, Albuquerque, studied with Betty Hahn, Sandi Fellman, Van Deren Coke and Beaumont Newhall, MFA(photog, teaching asst), 80. *Work:* Univ NMex Fine Arts Mus, Albuquerque; Independent Press Archive, Visual Studies Workshop, Rochester, NY; Spurgeon Gallery, Cent Wash Univ, Ellensburg; Erie Art Ctr, Pa; Calif Inst Arts, Valencia. *Exhib:* Photoworks, Bellevue Art Mus, Wash, 79; Funny Photographs, Marcuse Pfeiffer Gallery, New York, 80; Krannert Art Mus, Champaign, Ill, 80-83; Midwest Mus Am Art, Elkhart, Ind, 81; Sights Unseen, AIR Gallery, New York, 82; and others. *Collections Arranged:* Women in the Southwest (auth, catalog), 78 & 79; Intimate Statements, 79; Work by Women, 81; Altered States (auth, catalog), 82. *Teaching:* Teacher arts & crafts, Bridgeport, Conn, Yonkers, NY & Dedham, Mass, 69-77; asst prof, Univ Ill, Champaign, 80-, chairperson photog, 83- *Awards:* 1st Prize, No Dumb Photographs, Calif Inst Arts, 81; 3rd Award, Midwest Mus Am Art, 81; Univ Ill Faculty Res Bd Grant, 81 & 83. *Bibliog:* Catherine Lord (auth), New Mexico: Work by women outside of the mainstream, 10/79 & Meridel Rubenstein (auth), Women and photography, 1/80, Afterimage; Chuck Nicholson (auth), Barbara DeGenevieve's novelettes, Artweek, 2/7/81; Lynne Brown (auth), Looking in/looking out, Catskill Ctr Photog Quarterly, Vol 4, 83. *Mem:* Soc Photog Educ; Women Arts (pres, 81-82); Albuquerque United Artists. *Publ:* Contribr, New American Nudes, Morgan & Morgan, 81; auth, Sex as subject, Exposure, Vol 20, No 4, 83. *Dealer:* Traction Gallery 800 Traction Ave Los Angeles CA 90013. *Mailing Add:* PO Box 292 2272 E Lincoln St St Joseph IL 61873

DE GERENDAY, LACI ANTHONY
SCULPTOR
b Budapest, Hungary, Aug 17, 11. *Study:* SDak Sch Mines; Ursinus Col; Nat Acad Design; Beaux Arts Inst, New York. *Work:* Salle d'Honneur, Mus Africa, Algiers; Adm Farragut Medal, NY Univ Hall of Fame Mus. *Comn:* Wood reliefs, Fed Govt, Tell City, Ind, 39 & Aberdeen, SDak, 41; gold medal, Soc Elec Engrs, 60; bronze relief, St Francis of Assisi Sch, Torrington, Conn, 65; medal, Soc Medalists, 81; self-portrait, Nat Acad Design, 82. *Exhib:* Pa Mus, Philadelphia; Gold Medal Exhib, Archit League, New York; Boston Mus; Mus Mod Art Nat Sculpture Soc Ann; Allied Artists Ann; two-man show, Art Ctr, Lyme, Conn; and others. *Teaching:* Instr sculpture, Lyme Acad Fine Arts, 80- *Awards:* Lindsey Morris Mem Awards, Allied Artists Am, 69, 76 & 78; Nat Sculpture Soc, 81; two Ellen Speyer Prizes, Nat Acad Design; and others. *Mem:* Nat Arts Club; Nat Acad Design; Nat Soc Lit & the Arts; Fel Nat Sculpture Soc; Allied Artists Am. *Media:* Wood, Bronze. *Mailing Add:* Mill Pond Lane Old Lyme CT 06371

DE GOGORZA, PATRICIA (GAHAGAN)
SCULPTOR, PRINTMAKER
b Detroit, Mich, Mar 17, 36. *Study:* Smith Col, BA, 58; S W Hayter's Atelier 17, Paris, France, 58-60; Goddard Col, Plainfield, Vt, MA, 75. *Work:* Collection Ville de Paris (Louvre), France; Victoria & Albert Mus, London, Eng; Boston Mus Fine Arts; Provincetown Art Asn & Mus, Mass; Bard Col, Annandale-on-Hudson, NY. *Exhib:* Salon des Realites Nouvelles, Mus Art Mod, Paris, France, 58-61 & Paris Biennale, 61; Vt Artists Bundy Mus, Waitsfield, Vt, 67 & 76; Arts Festival, White Mountain Art Festival, Jefferson, NJ, 78; one-man shows, First Branch Gallery, Chelsea, Vt, 78, Wood Art Gallery, Montpelier, Vt, 81 & Bundy Mus, Waitsfield, Vt, 82. *Pos:* Bd mem, Printmaking Workshop, New York, 70-74. *Teaching:* Asst prof print & sculpture, Bard Col, 66-69; insfr sculpture, Goddard Col, 77-79; instr drawing, Univ Vt, 80-81. *Awards:* First Prize Sculpture, Norwich Ann, Vt, 78. *Mem:* Soc Am Graphic Artists; Art Resource Asn (pres, 76-82); Provincetown Art Asn. *Media:* Wood, Stone; Color Etching, Copper. *Mailing Add:* Box 116 RFD East Calais VT 05650

DEGROAT, DIANE L
ILLUSTRATOR, DESIGNER
b Newton, NJ, May 24, 47. *Study:* New York Phoenix Sch Design, summer 64; Pratt Inst, 65-69, BFA. *Exhib:* Soc Illusr Ann Nat Exhib, New York, 72 & 75; Insides, 74 & Ann Bk Show, 77, Am Inst Graphic Arts, New York; Poster USA/74, Art Dir Club, 74; Master Eagle Gallery, New York, 81 & 83; Gallery at Hastings-on-Hudson, Hastings, N Y, 82; and others. *Pos:* Designer & art dir, Holt, Rinehart & Winston, New York, 69-72; lectr, Pelham Art Ctr, New York, 81. *Bibliog:* Upcoming illustrator, Art Dir Mag, 74; article, New York Times (Westchester), 8/29/82; article, Westchester Spotlight, 6/83. *Publ:* Illusr, Who Needs a Bear?, 81 & Tough Luck Karen, 82, Morrow; illusr, The Toad Intruder, Houghton-Mifflin, 82; illusr, Toad Food and Measle Soup, Dial, 82; illusr, The Ewoks Join the Fight, Random House, 83; and others. *Mailing Add:* 44 Crawford St Yonkers NY 10705

DE GROAT, GEORGE HUGH
PAINTER, PRINTMAKER
b Newark, NJ, Jan 7, 17. *Study:* Newark Sch Fine Arts, 34-38; Newark Prep Col, BA, 40; Art Sch Detroit Soc Arts, 54-56. *Work:* Monterey Penninsula Mus Art, Calif; Downey Mus Art, Calif. *Exhib:* Solo exhibs, Monterey Penninsula Mus Art, 72 & 82 & Loyola Marymount Univ, 74; Faculty Exhib, Otis Art Inst, Los Angeles Co, 72; San Bernardino Co Mus Art, 82; Brand Gallery, Glendale, Calif, 82. *Pos:* Art critic, Pasadena Star-News, 68-70; artist-in-residence, Monterey Peninsula Mus Art, 77- *Teaching:* Instr painting, Calif State Col, San Diego, 66-67; instr painting, Art Ctr Col Design, Los Angeles, 68-71; instr life drawing & painting, Otis Art Inst, Los Angeles Co, 68-78. *Awards:* First Prize, Fourth Ann Southern Calif Exhib, Long Beach Mus Art, 66; McBride Award, Pasadena Art Mus, 69; Ford Found Grant Color Field Painting, 77. *Bibliog:* Mugnaini (auth), Drawing--A Search for Form & Oil Painting Techniques, Van Nostrand-Reinhold. *Mem:* Am Asn Univ Prof; Los Angeles Art Asn (bd gov, 70-). *Media:* Oil on Canvas; Intaglio on Copper Plates. *Publ:* Auth, article, Am Artist Mag, 73. *Dealer:* Fireside Gallery Carmel CA 93921; Phyllis Lucas Gallery Second Ave New York NY. *Mailing Add:* 3474 San Juan Canyon Rd San Juan Bautista CA 95045

DE GUATEMALA, JOYCE (JOYCE BUSH VOURVOULIAS)
SCULPTOR
b Mexico City, Mex, Feb 25, 38; Guatemalan. *Study:* Univ Mex, 58; Univ Wis, 59; Silpakorn Univ, 60-62. *Work:* Lehigh Univ, Bethlehem, Pa; Cedar Crest Col, Allentown, Pa; Ringling Mus, Sarasota, Fla; Mus Mod Art Latin Am, Washington, DC; Mus Hist & Art of Guatemala, Guatemala City. *Comn:* Chamber of Industry of Guatemala, Guatemala City, 74; The Nat Fine Arts Sch of Guatemala, Guatemala City, 75; Oas & Mus Mod Art Latin Am, Washington, DC, 77; Exmibal-El Estor, Exmibal, Guatemala, 77; Kensington Town House Project, Redevelopment Authority of Philadelphia, Pa, 81. *Exhib:* Latin American Horizons 1976, Ringling Mus Art, Sarasota, Fla; one-woman shows, XIII Int Biannual Sao Paulo, Brasil, 75 & Mus Mod Art Latin Am, Washington, DC, 77; XVII Int Biannual Sao Paulo, Brazil, 83; Noyes Mus, 83; and others. *Pos:* Vpres, Asociacion Tikal, 68-73; dir, Fine Art Comt, Patronatd de Bellas Artes, 72-75. *Awards:* First Prize of Latin Am, Francisco Matarazzo, 75; Order of Garcia Granados, Guatemalan Govt, 76. *Bibliog:* Jose Castaneda (auth), Joyce y la degradacion del mito, La Semana, 70; Ricardo Mata (auth), Ante 54 artistas, Guatemaltelos, 73; Margarita Carrillo (auth), Escultura, Vanidades Continental, 79. *Media:* Stainless Steel. *Dealer:* Marian Locks Gallery 1524 Walnut St Philadelphia PA 19107. *Mailing Add:* Fairview Rd Rd #2 Box 506 A Glenmoore PA 19343

DE GUZMAN, EVELYN LOPEZ
PAINTER
b New York, NY, June 14, 47. *Study:* City Univ New York, BA, 70; Hunter Col, Grad Sch, MA, 74; Pratt Inst; Parsons Sch Design. *Work:* Museo del Barrio & Bronx Mus, New York; Museo de Arte y Historia, San Juan, PR; Museo de Ponce, PR. *Exhib:* Museo del Barrio, New York, 78; Bridge Between Islands, traveling, New York, 78; Puerto Rican Artists, Bronx Mus, New York, 81. *Teaching:* Instr, high school & elementary systems. *Bibliog:* Grace Glueck (auth), Art: Puerto Rican show in the Bronx, New York Times, 1/26/79; Elaine Wechsler (auth), Space: The inside, the outside, Artspeak, 11/81; Juan Bujan (auth), La Geometria Dinamica de Evelyn Lopez de Guzman, La Voz, 12/3/81. *Mem:* Women Arts; Women's Caucus Art; Asn Artist Run Galleries; Brooklyn Arts Cult Asn Inc. *Media:* Acrylic, Paste. *Publ:* Contribr, New York Art Yearbook, Noyes Art Books, 75-; contribr, Puerto Rico: Its people, its artists, Lightsource, 77. *Dealer:* Noho Gallery 168 Mercer St New York NY 10012; Cayman Gallery 381 West Broadway New York NY. *Mailing Add:* 2136 East 27th St Brooklyn NY 11229

DEHN, VIRGINIA
PAINTER
b Nevada, Mo. *Study:* Stephens Col, Columbia, Mo; Traphagen Sch of Design, New York; Art Students League, with George Grosz, Julian Levi & John Hovannes; additional study with Adolf Dehn. *Work:* Columbus Gallery of Fine Arts, Ohio; Univ Calif, Berkeley; Columbia Univ, New York; New York Pub Libr. *Exhib:* Butler Inst of Am Art, Youngstown, Ohio; Mus of Fine Arts, Springfield, Mass; Jewish Mus, New York; Am Acad & Inst of Arts & Lett, Nat Acad of Design; Pratt Inst & Graphic Art Ctr Travelling Exhib; Ten Artists Foreign & Am, Lafayette Col, Pa. *Awards:* Oil Painting Award, Nat Acad of Design, Salmagundi Club, 68. *Bibliog:* Mary Carroll Nelson (auth), Virginia Dehn Paints Inscapes, Am Artist Mag, 77. *Mem:* Artists Equity; Audubon Artists. *Media:* Oil, Mixed Media. *Mailing Add:* 443 W 21st St New York NY 10011

DEHNER, DOROTHY
SCULPTOR, PRINTMAKER
b Cleveland, Ohio, Dec 23, 01. *Study:* Univ Calif, Los Angeles; Skidmore Col, BS; Art Students League, with Nicolaides, K H Miller & Jan Matulka; Atelier 17, New York; Skidmore Col, Hon Degree, 82; Womans Art Caucus, Hon Degree, 83. *Work:* Metrop Mus Art & Mus Mod Art, New York; Seattle Art Mus, Wash; Minn Art Mus, Minneapolis; Cleveland Mus Art, Ohio. *Comn:* Aluminum grill, 59 & bronze room divider, 61, James Marston Fitch, Stony Point, NY; Plexiglas relief, NY Med Col, Valhalla, 72; bronze sculpture, Union Camp Corp, Wayne, NJ, 72; bronze sculpture, Rockefeller Ctr, New York; bronze sculpture, Am Tel & Tel, Basking Ridge, NJ. *Exhib:* Whitney Mus Am Art, New York, 49-63; Recent Sculpture, Mus Mod Art, New York; Hirshhorn Collection, Guggenheim Mus, New York, 61; Carnegie Inst Ann, 63; one-man retrospective, Jewish Mus, New York, 65; Boston Mus Fine Arts; Baltimore Mus Art; Dallas Mus Contemp Art; San Francisco Mus Art; Los Angeles Co Mus; Rutgers Univ Mus, 84. *Awards:* Sculpture Prize, Art USA, 68; Tamarind Lithography Inst Artist in Residence, 70-71; Yaddo Found Fel, 71. *Bibliog:* Voau Martee (auth), article, Womans Art Mag, 80. *Mem:* Sculptor's Guild (bd mem, 60-62); Fedn Mod Painters & Sculptors; Artists Equity Asn. *Media:* Bronze, Wood; Paper. *Publ:* Auth, Making & fabricating Plexiglas sculpture, 68 & John Graham, 69, Leonardo; auth, Foreword for John Graham's System & Dialectrics of Art, Johns Hopkins Press, 71; auth, David Smith's medallions, Art J, 1/78; contribr, Jake Matulka Catalogue, Whitney Mus & Nat Gallery. *Dealer:* Associated American Artists 663 Fifth Ave New York NY 10022; A M Sachs 29 W 57 St New York NY 10019. *Mailing Add:* 33 Fifth Ave New York NY 10003

DE KERGOMMEAUX, DUNCAN
PAINTER, EDUCATOR
b Premier, BC, July 15, 27. *Study:* Banff Sch Fine Art; Inst Allende, Mex; Hans Hofmann Sch Fine Art. *Work:* Nat Gallery Can; London Pub Art Gallery; Art Gallery of Ontario; Can Coun Art Bank; and others. *Comn:* Exterior wall mural, Vanier Post Off, Dept Pub Works, Can, 70; Man Centennial Caravan, Dept Secy State & Man Govt, 70; shaped banners, Schoeler, Heaton Archit, Univ Ottawa, 71; mall environment, Schoele, Heaton Archit, Garneau Sch, Orleans, Ont, 71; and others. *Exhib:* 3rd & 6th Biennials Can Art, Nat Gallery Can, Can Painting, Albright Knox Gallery, 66; DeKergommeaux-DeNiverville Touring Exhib, Nat Gallery Can, 67-68; London Pub Art Gallery, 71 & 80; Loranger Gallery, Toronto, 80 & 81; Take Two Touring Exhib, 80-84; and others. *Pos:* Dir, Can Pavilion Art Gallery, Expo 67, Montreal, 66-67; chmn dept visual arts, Univ Western Ontario, 81-*Teaching:* Assoc prof drawing & painting, Univ Western Ont, 70-80; vis prof drawing & painting, Banff Sch Fine Arts, summer 74-75; vis prof, NS Col Art, summer 80. *Awards:* Monsanto Can Art Competition, 57; Purchase Award, Minneapolis Biennial, Boutels, 58; Art Wall Competition, Benson & Hedges, 71. *Bibliog:* Groves (auth), DeKergommeaux at the Blue Barn, Can Art, 63. *Mem:* Univ Art Asn Can; Royal Can Acad Arts. *Dealer:* Mira Goddard Gallery 22 Hazelton Ave Toronto ON. *Mailing Add:* 437 Everglade Ct London ON N6H 4M8 Canada

DE KNIGHT, AVEL
PAINTER
b New York, NY, 33. *Study:* Ecole Beaux-Arts, Acad Grande Chaumiere & Acad Julien, Paris. *Work:* Metrop Mus Art, New York; Walker Art Inst, Minneapolis, Minn; Norfolk Mus Arts & Sci, Va; Springfield Art Mus, Mo; Massillon Art Mus, Ohio. *Exhib:* Afro-American Artists, Boston Mus Fine Arts, 70; Black American Artists, Ill Arts Coun, 71; Projected Art/Artists at Work, Finch Col Mus, New York, 71; Nat Acad Design, 72 & Mus Mod Art, 72, New York. *Pos:* Art critic, France-Amerique, 58-68. *Teaching:* Instr painting, Nat Acad Design, currently. *Awards:* Gold Medal Grand Award, Am Watercolor Soc Centennial, 67; William A Paton Prize, 71; Palmer Mem Prize, 78. *Mem:* Academician Nat Acad Design; Am Watercolor Soc. *Media:* Gouache, Oil. *Dealer:* Babcock Galleries 20 East 67th St New York NY 10021. *Mailing Add:* 81 Perry St New York NY 10014

DE KOONING, ELAINE MARIE CATHERINE
PAINTER, WRITER
b New York, NY, Mar 12, 20. *Study:* With Willem de Kooning & Arshile Gorky; Moore Col Art, Philadelphia, Pa, DFA; Western Col Women, DFA. *Work:* Mus Mod Art, New York; NY Univ; Elmira Col, NY; Greenville Mus, SC; Drew Univ, Madison, NJ. *Comn:* Portrait of Casey Stengel & Eddie Robinson, Baltimore, Md, 58; portrait of Joseph Hirshhorn, comn by Mr Hirshhorn, 62; portrait of John F Kennedy, Truman Libr, Independence, Mo, 62-63; two portraits of John F Kennedy, John F Kennedy Libr, 62-63; portrait of Allen Ginsberg, Channel 13, NET-TV, 71. *Exhib:* 4th Int Exhib, Tokyo, Japan, 54; Sixty American Painters, Walker Art Ctr, 60; Carnegie Inst Int, 60; Whitney Mus Am Art Ann, New York, 62; Figure Painting, Mus Mod Art, New York, 63. *Teaching:* Prof painting, Yale Univ Grad Sch, 67-68; Mellon chair painting, Carnegie-Mellon Univ, 69-70; prof painting, Univ Pa Grad Sch, Wagner Col, NY, 71, NY Studio Sch summer prog, Paris, 74-78, Parsons Sch Fine Art, 74-76 & Empire State Col, Urban Studies Ctr, 74-76; artist-in-residence, Brandeis Univ, 75 & Rice Univ, 76; vis Melon Prof, Cooper Union, 76; Lamar Dodd Chair, Univ Ga, Athens, 76-79. *Awards:* Hallmark Award. *Bibliog:* In quest of a famous likeness, Life Mag, 64; Lawrence Campbell (auth), Elaine de Kooning paints a picture, Art News. *Mem:* Artists Equity. *Media:* Oil. *Dealer:* Gruenebaum Gallery 60 Thomas St New York NY 10013. *Mailing Add:* 51 Raynor St Freeport NY 11520

DE KOONING, WILLEM
PAINTER
b Rotterdam, Holland, Apr 24, 04. *Study:* Acad Beeldende Kunsten ed Technische Wetenschappen, Amsterdam, 16-24. *Work:* Art Inst Chicago; Metrop Mus Art, Mus Mod Art, Whitney Mus Am Art, New York; Walker Art Ctr, Minneapolis, Minn; and others. *Comn:* Murals, New York World's Fair, 39, French Line Pier (with Fernand Leger), New York & Williamsburg Housing Proj, New York. *Exhib:* Retrospectives, Stedelijk Mus, Amsterdam, 68 & Carnegie Inst, Pittsburgh, 79; The New American Painting and Sculpture, Mus Mod Art, 69; Whitney Mus Am Art Ann, 69 & 70; one-man exhibs, Richard Gray Gallery, Chicago, 80 & Richard Hines Gallery, Seattle, 80; Grimaldis Gallery, Baltimore, Md, 81; Guild Hall, East Hampton, NY, 81; and many others. *Teaching:* Instr, Black Mt Col, 48; instr, Yale Univ, 50-51. *Awards:* Mr & Mrs Frank G Logan Medal, Art Inst Chicago, 51; President's Medal, 63; Andrew W Mellon Prize, 79; and others. *Mem:* Nat Inst Arts & Lett. *Publ:* Auth, articles in popular and prof publ. *Mailing Add:* c/o Fourcade Droll Inc 36 East 75th St New York NY 10021

D'ELAINE (D'ELAINE A HERARD JOHNSON)
PAINTER, INSTRUCTOR
b Auburn, Wash, Mar 19, 32. *Study:* Cent Wash Univ, BFA(scholar), 54; Univ Wash, MFA, 56. *Work:* Nova Scotia Art Mus, Can; Prince/Princess Eleski, Russia; Int Foreign Govt, Japan, Sweden & Germany; Vancouver BC Mus, Can; Whatcom Mus, Bellingham, Wash. *Comn:* Wall mural, New York Life, Seattle, Wash, 58; sea books illus, comn by Dept Navy for USS Bremerton submarine. *Exhib:* Seattle Art Mus, Wash, 62; Featured Artist, Whatcom Mus, Bellingham, Wash, 75-85; State Capital Mus, Olympia, Wash, 76-80, Shoreline Mus, Wash, 78-80; Vancouver BC Maritime Mus, Can, 82, Corvallis State Univ, 82; and many others. *Teaching:* Instr drawing & painting, Mus Hist & Industry, 54-56, Edmonds Adult Classes, 54-59 & Seattle Pub Schs, 54-78. *Mem:* Kappa Pi; Nat Artist Equity Asn. *Media:* Waterbase. *Mailing Add:* 16122 72nd Ave W Edmonds WA 98020

DE LAMA, ALBERTO
PAINTER, PRINTMAKER
b Havana, Cuba. *Study:* De La Salle Sch, Havana; Univ Havana; Am Acad Art, Chicago, with William Mosby & Joseph Vanden Broucke, AA; Northeastern Ill Univ, Chicago, BA. *Work:* Pullman Bank Art Collection, Chicago; Home Fed Savings Art Collection, Chicago; Stop Publicidad, Caracas, Venezuela; Jim Walter Corp, Tampa, Fla. *Exhib:* Ill State Fair Prof Art Exhib, 67 & 70; Munic Art League Chicago, 66 & 70; Galeria Sans Souci, Caracas, 73 & 76; Wildlife Gallery, Minocqua, Wis, 73-79; Talisman Gallery, 76; and others. *Teaching:* Instr painting & drawing, Am Acad Art, 69-74. *Awards:* Diamond Awards 70 & 71 & Gold Medal, 70 & 75, Palette & Chisel Acad Fine Arts; Harriet Bitterly Mem Award, Chicago, Ill, 76. *Mem:* Palette & Chisel Acad Fine Arts (bd dirs, 70-); Regent Art League, Chicago, Ill; Municipal Art League, Chicago, Ill. *Media:* Oil; Etchings. *Dealer:* Wildlife Art Galleries Inc Rt 3 Brule Lake Iron River MI 49935; de Lama Gallery Box 17 Chicago Ill 60690. *Mailing Add:* PO Box 17 Chicago IL 60690

DELAMONICA, ROBERTO
PRINTMAKER, EDUCATOR
b Ponta Pora, State of Mato Grosso, Brazil, 33. *Study:* Sao Paulo & Rio de Janeiro. *Work:* Mus Mod Art, Rio de Janeiro & New York; Nat Mus La Paz, Bolivia; Stedelijk Mus, Amsteram, Holland; Metrop Mus Art, New York; and others. *Exhib:* Brazilian Art Today, Royal Col Art, London, Eng, 64; New Talent in Printmaking, Assoc Am Artists Gallery, New York, 67; one-man shows, Pan Am Union, Washington, DC, Walker Art Ctr, Minneapolis, Minn & Columbia Mus, SC. *Teaching:* Instr graphics, Mus Mod Art, Rio de Janeiro, Nat Sch Fine Arts, Lima, Peru, Univ Santiago, Chile, Cath Univ, Santiago, Sch Fine Arts, Valparaiso, Chile, Minneapolis & Pratt Graphics Ctr, New York, formerly; instr, Art Students League, currently. *Awards:* Best Brazilian Printmaker, Seventh Sao Paulo Biennale; Grand Prize, Second Biennale of Santiago, Chile, 65; Guggenheim Fel, 65. *Mailing Add:* 11 Riverside Dr New York NY 10023

DELANO, JACK
PHOTOGRAPHER, FILMMAKER
b Kiev, USSR, Aug 1, 14; US citizen. *Study:* Pa Acad Fine Arts, Philadelphia. *Work:* Libr Cong, Washington, DC; New York Pub Libr; George Eastman House, Rochester, NY; Univ Ky Photog Arch, Louisville. *Exhib:* Family of Man, 55 & The Bitter Years, 62, Mus Mod Art, New York; A Vision Shared, Witkin Gallery, New York, 76; Masters of the Camera, Int Ctr Photog, New York, 76; Spoleto Festival, Charleston, SC, 77; Inst PR Cult, San Juan. *Pos:* Artist-photographer, Farm Security Admin, 40-43; photographer, Govt of PR, 46-47, dir films, 47-52, dir educ TV, 57-69. *Awards:* Guggenheim Fel, 46; Cresson Travelling Scholar, Pa Acad Fine Arts, 36. *Bibliog:* Roy E Stryker (auth), In This Proud Land, New York Graphic Soc, 73; Hank O'Neal (auth), A Vision Shared, St Martin's Press, 76; article, Combinations, J Photog, Vol 1, No 4. *Dealer:* Sonnabend Gallery 420 W Broadway New York NY 10012. *Mailing Add:* RD 2 Box 8BB Rio Piedras PR 00928

DELAP, TONY
SCULPTOR, EDUCATOR

b Oakland, Calif, Nov 4, 27. *Study:* Menlo Jr Col, Calif; Calif Col Arts & Crafts, Oakland; Claremont Grad Sch, Calif. *Work:* Mus Mod Art, Whitney Mus Am Art, New York; Walker Art Inst, Minneapolis; San Francisco Mus Art; Tate Gallery, London, Eng. *Comn:* Thirteen sculptures, Carborundum Abrasive Mkt Awards, Niagara Falls, NY, 69; sculpture-fountain complex, CCH Bldg, San Rafael, Calif, 70. *Exhib:* Whitney Mus Am Art, 64; Chicago Art Inst, 64; Mus Mod Art, New York, 64, 65 & 67; solo exhibs, Robert Elkan Gallery, 65-, Newport Harbor, 77, Casat Gallery, La Jolla, 77, Calif State Col, Chico, 79 & Janus Gallery, Venice City, 79; Contemporary American Sculpture, Whitney Mus Am Art, 66; American Sculpture of the Sixties, Los Angeles Co Mus Art, 67; California Painting and Sculpture: The Modern Era, San Francisco Mus Art, 76; Corcoran Biennial, 78; and others. *Teaching:* Lectr fine arts, Univ Calif, Davis, 63-64; prof fine arts, Univ Calif, Irvine, 65- *Awards:* Am Fedn Arts & Ford Found Grants, Mus in Residence Prog, Haverford, Pa, 66; Purchase Prize, Long Beach Mus Art, 69; First Prize Sculpture, Los Angeles Dept Airports, 76. *Biblig:* Alan Solomon (auth), Tony DeLap: The Last Five Years, Univ Calif, Irvine, 68; Gene Cooper (auth), DeLap, The Edge as Form and Metaphor, 77. *Dealer:* Janus Gallery 8000 Melrose Ave Venice CA 90046; Robert Elkon Gallery 1063 Madison Ave New York NY 10028. *Mailing Add:* 225 Jasmine St Corona Del Mar CA 92625

DE LARIOS, DORA
SCULPTOR, POTTER

b Los Angeles, Calif, Oct 13, 33. *Study:* Univ Southern Calif, BFA, 57. *Work:* Oakland Art Mus, Calif; Craft & Folk Art Mus, Los Angeles; Security Pacific Bank Collection. *Comn:* Ceramic mural (8ft x 40ft), Compton Co Libr, Calif, 73; cement mural (8ft x 10ft), Security First Nat Bank, 76; ceramic mural (8ft x 16ft), Norwood Co Libr, Calif, 77; ceramic mural (2ft x 173ft), Lynwood Co Libr, Calif, 77; two sculptural wall panels, Camarillo City Hall, Calif, 77. *Exhib:* Am Crafts at the White House, Renwick Gallery, Smithsonian Inst, Washington, DC, 77 & Contemp Craft Mus, New York, 77; Craft & Folk Art Mus, Los Angeles, 77; Kohler Art Ctr, Wis, 77; Everson Mus, Syracuse, NY, 77; Indianapolis Mus Art, Ind, 78. *Teaching:* Vis instr ceramics, Univ Southern Calif, Los Angeles, 58 & 79. *Awards:* Purchase Award for Ceramic Sculpture, Calif State Fair, 61. *Mailing Add:* 8635 W Washington Blvd Culver City CA 90230

DELAURO, JOSEPH NICOLA
SCULPTOR, EDUCATOR

b New Haven, Conn, Mar 10, 16. *Study:* Yale Univ, BFA(Alice Kimball Fel, Tiffany Fel & Elizabeth Pardee Scholar), 41; Univ Iowa, MFA, 47; also in Italy, 53, 62, 66 & 71. *Work:* In private collections of Dr D Corradini, Quito, Ecuador, Dr B Clemente, Akron, Ohio, Rev Ralph Kowalski, Detroit & Bishop Ernest Primeau, Manchester, NH. *Comn:* Mankato stone sculpture, St Columba Cathedral, Youngstown, Ohio, 59; glass & plastic mural, Windsor Bd Educ, Ont, 64; bronze sculpture, Hiram Walker & Sons, Ltd, Ont, 67; bronze sculpture, Detroit Pub Libr, Mich, 67; bronze sculpture, Jewish Community Centre, Windsor, Ont, 70. *Exhib:* Walker Gallery, Minneapolis, 47; Mich Regional Exhib, Detroit, 48; Ecclestical Art Guild, Detroit, 50; Fine Arts Dept Fac Exhib, Art Gallery Windsor, Ont, 70-72; Biannale de Fiorino, Florence, Italy, 71. *Teaching:* Prof sculpture & drawing, Marygrove Col, Detroit, 47-59; prof, Univ Windsor, formerly. *Mem:* Fel Royal Soc Arts; Nat Sculpture Soc; Col Art Asn Am; Mid Am Col Art Asn; Univ Art Asn Can. *Media:* Bronze, Marble. *Mailing Add:* 7560 Birchlan St Canton MI 48187

DE LA VEGA, ANTONIO
PAINTER, DESIGNER

b El Paso, Tex, July 13, 27. *Study:* NY Univ; Art Students League; also study in Mex, Spain, France, Italy & Port. *Exhib:* Pintores Nuevos, Galeria Ciga, Buenos Aires, Arg, 60; Antonio de la Vega, Galeria Fuentes, Mexico City, Mex, 61; Spanish Impressions, Galeria Gran Via, Madrid, Spain, 62; Portugal Viejo, Galeria Sesimbra, Lisbon, 66; de la Vega, Galeria Botto, Rome, Italy, 68. *Pos:* Art dir & designer, Cushing & Nevell, Inc, New York, 51-62 & Persons Advertising Inc, New York, 63-74; free-lance art dir, designer & illusr advert, 74- *Mem:* Nat Asn Portrait Painters; Am Artists Prof League; Am Inst Graphic Arts; Artists Guild New York (vpres, 64-65); Southwest Art Found. *Media:* Oil, Acrylic. *Mailing Add:* 2500 Johnson Ave Riverdale NY 10463

DE LA VEGA, ENRIQUE MIGUEL
SCULPTOR, DESIGNER

b Los Angeles, Calif, June 13, 35. *Study:* Los Angeles City Col, AA, 60; Los Angeles Co Art Inst, MFA, 64; study of sculpture with Renzo Fenci and of drawing & design with Joe Magnani. *Comn:* Two monumental symbolic forms, South West Produce Ctr, Nogales, Ariz, 65; Resurrection (22 ft monument), Nat Shrine of the Millenium, Doylestown, Pa, 67; bronze equestrian monument, Robert Atkinson Mem Park, Cascade, Mont, 68; Birds in Flight (bronze forms), Air Force Village, San Antonio, Tex, 72; 15 ft sculpture/mosaic design, St Francis of Assisi Church, South Windsor, Conn, 75. *Exhib:* Group Exhib, Simon Patrich Gallery, Los Angeles, 67; one-man show, Galeria Teatro Casa de la Paz, Mexico City, Mex, 69; Valyermo Ann Art Festival (relig art), St Andrew's Priory, Valyermo, Calif. *Pos:* Art ed, Larchmont Chronicle, Hancock Park, Los Angeles, Calif, 65-70. *Awards:* Harriman Jones Portrait Award, Harriman Jones Clinic, Long Beach, Calif, 65; Nat Design Award, St Francis of Assisi Church, South Windsor, Conn, 75. *Biblig:* Obras del la Vega, Am Embassy Mag, Mexico City, 68; Enrique de la Vega, Designers West Mag, 69; The Siesta Is Over (sculptures by de la Vega), KNX-TV Interview, Los Angeles, Calif, 72. *Mem:* Artists Equity Asn. *Media:* Miscellaneous Media. *Mailing Add:* 4507 Atoll Ave Sherman Oaks CA 91403

DE LA VERRIERE, JEAN-JACQUES See J J

DE LEEUW, LEON
PAINTER, SCULPTOR

b Paris, France, May 5, 31; US citizen. *Study:* Art Students League; NY Univ, with Philip Guston; also with Hans Hofmann. *Exhib:* One-man shows, Fairlong Libr, 71, Rivercel Gallery, 75 & NJ Inst Technol, Newark, 76; Fullerton Gallery, 78-81; Montclair Mus, 82; and others. *Teaching:* Instr painting & sculpture, Wilson Col, 59-60; assoc prof painting & drawing, Montclair State Col, 63- *Dealer:* Fullerton Gallery 13 S Fullerton Ave Montclair NJ 07042. *Mailing Add:* 317 N Fullerton Ave Montclair NJ 07042

DELEHANTY, SUZANNE E
HISTORIAN, MUSEUM DIRECTOR

b Southbridge, Mass. *Study:* Skidmore Col, BA(art hist); Univ Pa. *Collections Arranged:* Grids, 72; Nancy Graves: Sculpture & Drawing 1970-72, 72; Agnes Martin (with catalog), 73; Six Visions (with catalog), 73; Robert Morris/Projects, 74; Cy Twombly: Paintings, Drawings, Constructions 1951-1974 (with catalog), 75; Video Art (with catalog), 75; George Segal: Environments, 76; Pieces & Performances, 76; Improbable Furniture (with catalog), 77; Paul Thek/Processions (with catalog), 77; Dwellings, 78; On Sculpture/Christo, di Suvero, Irwin & Segal, 79; Richard Artschwager/Themes (with catalog), 79; Soundings (with catalog), 81. *Pos:* Curatorial asst, Inst Contemp Art, Univ Pa, 68-71, dir, 71-78; dir, Neuberger Mus, State Univ NY, Purchase, 78- *Mem:* Am Asn Mus dir; Am Fedn Arts. *Mailing Add:* Neuberger Mus State Univ NY Col Purchase NY 10577

DE LESSEPS, TAUNI
SCULPTOR, PAINTER

b Paris, France, Mar 10, 20; US citizen. *Work:* Three bronzes, The White House; Lausanne Mus, Switz; Hirshhorn Mus, Washington, DC; also works in pvt collections of Princesa Jose de Baviera y Borbon, Madrid, Spain, Mr & Mrs Nicholas du Pont, Capt J Y Cousteau; plus others. *Comn:* Headless Horseman (metal), Sleepy Hollow Country Club, Scarborough, NY; Scenic View of London (mural), Cumberland Ct, London, Eng; entire collection in solid 18-karat gold & silver, F J Cooper, Philadelphia, Pa; sculptures, Baccarat Crystal of France; three fountains, Spastic Children's Hosp, Kuwait. *Exhib:* Osawa Gallery, Tokyo, Japan, 75; one-man shows, Bruce Mus & Bell Gallery, Greenwich, Conn, 77; Kottler Gallery, New York, 78; French Embassy, New York, 78; Vernay-Jussel Galleries, New York, 78; plus others. *Awards:* Nominated Academician of Italy with Gold Medal, Belli Arte, Beaux Arts, 79. *Mem:* Soc Illusr; Nat Art Mus of Sport. *Media:* Miscellaneous. *Mailing Add:* Aiken Rd Greenwich CT 06830

DELGADO-GUITART, JOSE LUIS
PRINTMAKER

b Tanger, Spain, Sept 24, 47. *Study:* Univ Madrid; Univ Cincinnati; Pratt Graphics Ctr, New York; Univ Mass, BA(visual commun). *Work:* McDowell Colony Collection, NH; Galeria Circulo 2, Madrid, Spain; also many works in pvt collections. *Exhib:* Galeria Panorama, Port, 70; Nommo Gallery, Uganda, 71; IV Expos Internationale de Dessins, Yugoslavia, 74; Philadelphia Art Alliance, Pa, 75; Univ Mass, 77, 78 & 80. *Pos:* Founder & dir, Tamiz Graphics, Boston; visual arts dir, Areyto, Boston; co-founder, Galaxy Theater, Boston; publ, Imaginary News. *Teaching:* Art, Univ Mass & Mass Col Art. *Awards:* Pratt Graphics Ctr Fel, 73; Edward McDowell Fel, 73-74. *Mailing Add:* 16 Oakridge St Boston MA 02126

DELIHAS, NEVA C
SCULPTOR

b New Haven, Conn, Dec 29, 40. *Study:* Univ Conn; Southern Conn State Col; Empire State Col, BA. *Work:* Assoc Univs, Brookhaven Nat Lab, Upton, NY; Pittsfield City Bank, Mass. *Exhib:* Aldrich Mus, Ridgefield, Conn 76; Cent Hall Gallery, 76, Monumental Sculpture Exhib I & II, 81, Guild Hall Mus, 82, Hecksher Mus, 83 & Islip Art Mus, 83, Long Island, NY; Artists Equity Asn, New York, 75; 32nd & 34th Ann Nat Exhibs, Nat Arts Club, New York; Aldrich Mus, Ridgefield, Conn, 76; Norman Kramer Gallery, Danbury, Conn, 76; Cent Hall Gallery, 76 & Monumental Sculpture Exhib I & II, 81, Long Island, NY; B J Spoke Gallery, 79; plus many others. *Awards:* Silvermine Guild Artists 50th Ann Award, 72; Sculpture House Award, West Chester Art Soc, 73; Award of Excellence, Huntington Art League, 74. *Mem:* Artists Equity Asn; E End Arts Coun. *Mailing Add:* 25 Locust Rd Brookhaven NY 11719

DE LISIO, MICHAEL
SCULPTOR

b New York, NY. *Work:* Joseph H Hirshhorn Collection; Minneapolis Inst Arts; Wichita Mus, Kans; Christ Church Col, Oxford Univ; Smith Col Mus Art, Mass. *Exhib:* One-man shows, Minneapolis Inst Arts, 71 & Brooke Alexander Gallery, New York, 68; Addison Gallery Am Art, Andover, Mass, 73; Princeton Univ Libr, 73; Smith Col Mus Art, Northampton, Mass, 74; and others. *Biblig:* Anthony Clark (auth), Michael de Lisio, Minneapolis Inst Arts Catalogue, 1/71; Robert Phelps (auth), article, Life Mag, 1/29/71. *Media:* Terra Cotta, Bronze. *Mailing Add:* 32 E 64th At New York NY 10021

DELL, ROBERT CHRISTOPHER
SCULPTOR, PAINTER

b Nyack, NY, Feb 22, 50. *Study:* NY State Univ Col, Oneonta, BS(educ), 72; NY State Univ Col, New Paltz, MFA(sculpture), 75. *Work:* Syracuse Univ & Collaboration Art, Sci & Technol, Inc, Syracuse, NY; NY State Univ Col, Oneonta, NY; MacDowell Colony, Peterborough, NH; Archives of Smithsonian Inst, Washington, DC; and others. *Comn:* Sculpture, Arts Coun Rockland, Spring Valley, NY, 78. *Exhib:* Selection 74, Touring Exhib, State Univ NY Colleges, 75; solo shows, Vorpal Gallery, Chicago, 78, Soho, New

York, 81 & New Acquisitions Gallery, Syracuse, NY, 83; Sculpture 1980, Meyerhoff Gallery, Md Art Inst, Baltimore, 80; Everson Mus, Syracuse, NY, 83; and others. *Pos:* Mem, Archit and Community Appearance, Bd of Review, Town of Orangetown, 79-84. *Awards:* Collaboration Art, Sci & Technol Grant, Syracuse, NY, 78; Artist-in-Residence, Vriesland West Hudson Art Ctr, Pearl River, NY, 80; MacDowell Colony Fel, Peterborough, NH, 80. *Bibliog:* Nancy Stesin (ed), New York Review of Art, Two Centuries Publ, New York, 78; and others. *Media:* Metal, Mixed Media; Watercolor. *Dealer:* Vorpal Gallery 465 W Broadway New York NY 10012 & San Francisco CA 94102. *Mailing Add:* Two N Mary Francis St Orangeburg NY 10962

DELLA-VOLPE, RALPH EUGENE
PAINTER, EDUCATOR
b NJ, May 10, 23. *Study:* Nat Acad Design; Art Students League. *Work:* Chase Manhattan Bank Collection, New York; Treas Bldg, Washington, DC; Slater Mus, Norwich, Conn; Pennell Collection, Libr of Cong, Washington, DC; Wichita Art Asn, Kans. *Exhib:* Pa Acad Fine Arts, Philadelphia, 52; Butler Inst Am Art, Ohio, 63; Final, Nat Inst Arts & Lett, New York, 63 & 64; Columbia Mus, SC, 76; Seattle Art Mus, Wash; Berkshire Mus, Pittsfield, Mass; and others. *Teaching:* Prof drawing & painting & artist in residence, Bennett Col, 49-77; prof drawing & painting, Marist Col, Poughkeepsie, 77- *Awards:* Wichita Art Asn Purchase Award, 50; Libr of Cong Purchase Award, 52; Berkshire Mus Drawing Prize, 54. *Bibliog:* Articles, New York Times, Art News & Arts, 60-63; Arts 7: New York art world, Art Dig, 64. *Media:* Oil. *Mailing Add:* South Road Box 51 Millbrook NY 12545

DELLIS, ARLENE B
CRAFTSMAN, MUSEOLOGIST
b Brooklyn, NY, Apr 12, 27. *Study:* Antioch Col; Univ NC, Greensboro, BA. *Pos:* Head lending serv, Brooklyn Mus, NY, 49-55; head traveling exhibs & registr, Solomon R Guggenheim Mus, New York, 55-63; registr, Gallery Mod Art, New York, 64; registr, Marlborough-Gerson Gallery, New York, 64-67; registr, ed-designer & dir circulating exhibs, Bernard Danenberg Galleries, New York, 69-72; asst to dir, La Boetie Gallery, New York, 72-77; assoc dir, Helios Gallery, 78-79; registr & designer craftsman fine leather, Lowe Art Mus, Univ Miami, Coral Gables, Fla, 79- *Publ:* Ed, Max Weber Drawings, 72; ed, Kurt Seligmann: His Graphic Work, 73; ed & designer, Hans Bellmer: Graphic Work, 74; auth, Kurt Seligmann Graphics, Mus Fine Arts, Springfield, Mass, 74. *Mailing Add:* Lowe Art Mus 1301 Stanford Dr Coral Gables FL 33146

DELONEY, JACK CLOUSE
PAINTER, ILLUSTRATOR
b Enterprise, Ala, Nov 2, 40. *Study:* Auburn Univ, BFA, 64. *Work:* First Nat Bank, Montgomery, Ala; First Ala Bank, Birmingham; Coca Cola Co, Montgomery, Ala; Pope & Quint Co, Mobile, Ala; Fla Gas Corp, Winter Park, Fla. *Exhib:* Seventh Juried Art Exhib, Mobile Art Mus, 72; Mainstreams 73 & 76; Hudson Valley 46th Nat, 74; WTex Watercolor Asn Nat, 75; Rocky Mountain Nat Watermedia, Colo, 76; Okla Nat Watercolor Exhib, Okla Mus Art, 76; and group and one-man shows. *Pos:* Book designer, Methodist Publ House, Nashville, Tenn, 64-65; illusr & painter, Ft Rucker, Ala. *Awards:* Purchase Award, People's Bank & Trust, Tupelo, 72; Best Landscape, NJ Miniature Art Soc, 73; Purchase Award, Bluff Park Show, Birmingham, Ala, 77. *Mem:* Ala Watercolor Soc; La Watercolor Soc; Southern Watercolor Soc; assoc mem Am Watercolor Soc; assoc mem Allied Artists of Am. *Publ:* article, North Light, 4/78. *Mailing Add:* Rte 4 Box 560 Ozark AL 36360

DELONGA, LEONARD ANTHONY
SCULPTOR, EDUCATOR
b Cannonsburg, Pa, Dec 18, 25. *Study:* Univ Miami, BA, 50; Univ Ga, MFA, 52. *Work:* Del Art Mus, Wilmington; Lowe Art Gallery, Univ Miami, Coral Gables, Fla; Montclair Mus, NJ; Ga Mus Art, Athens; Nat Collection Fine Arts, Smithsonian Inst, Washington, DC. *Comn:* Marshalltown Iowa Community Ctr. *Exhib:* Nat Inst Arts & Lett, New York, 61; one-man exhibs, Univ Mass, Amherst, 65 Allentown Art Mus, Pa, 65 & Univ NH, Durham, 67; Univ NH, Durham, 67; Humanism in Sculpture, DeCordova & Dana Mus, Lincoln, Mass, 70. *Teaching:* Head dept art, Tex Wesleyan Col, Fort Worth, 54-56; instr art, Univ Ga, 56-62; asst prof art, 62-64; prof art, Mt Holyoke Col, 65-81, David B Truman Distinguished Prof, 81- *Bibliog:* Leonard DeLonga (catalogues of one-man exhibs), Kraushaar Galleries, 61, 64, 67, 70, 76 & 81. *Media:* Multimedia. *Dealer:* Kraushaar Galleries 724 5th Ave New York NY. *Mailing Add:* 23 Woodbridge St South Hadley MA 01075

DE LOOPER, WILLEM
PAINTER, CURATOR
b The Hague, Neth, Oct 30, 32. *Study:* Am Univ, BA, 57. *Work:* Phillips Collection, Hirshhorn Mus & Sculpture Garden, Washington, DC; Fed Reserve Bank, Richmond, Va & Miami, Fla; Nat Sci Found; and others. *Exhib:* Washington 20 Years, Baltimore Mus Art, 70; solo exhibs, Protetch-McIntosh Gallery, 75-78 & 80 & Sarah Y Rentschler Gallery, New York, 79; Nat Acad Sci, 77; retrospective, Fed Reserve Bd, Washington, DC, 78; Galerie L, Hamburg, WGer, 79; and many others. *Collections Arranged:* Franz Kline--The Paintings in Color, 78; Philip Guston-The Last Works, 81. *Pos:* Assoc cur, Phillips Collection, Washington, DC, 74- *Bibliog:* Article, Art News, summer 74 & 12/79; An interview with Willem de Looper, Art Int, 12/77. *Media:* Acrylic Emulsion. *Dealer:* McIntosh-Drysdale Gallery 406 7th St NW Washington DC 20004. *Mailing Add:* 2219 California St NW Washington DC 20008

DELORY, PETER
PHOTOGRAPHER, INSTRUCTOR
b Cape Cod, Mass, Oct 2, 48. *Study:* San Francisco Art Inst, BFA(photog), 71; Univ Colo, MFA(photog), 74. *Work:* Minneapolis Inst Art, Minn; William Hayes Fogg Art Mus, Harvard Univ, Cambridge, Mass; Mass Inst Technol, Cambridge; Nat Gallery of Can, Ottawa, Ont; Addison Gallery Am Art, Andover, Mass. *Exhib:* Mass Inst Technol, 72; Boise Mus Fine Art, Idaho, 72; two-man show, Addison Gallery Am Art, 74; Carl Siembab Gallery Photog, Boston, Mass, 76; Sheldon Mus Art, Lincoln, Nebr, 77; The West: Real & Ideal, Univ Colo, 77. *Pos:* Dir photog dept, Sun Valley Ctr Arts & Humanities, 75- *Teaching:* Instr photog, Ctr Eye Sch, Aspen, 69-71; asst photog, Minor White Workshop, Hotchkiss, Conn, 72-73; instr advan photog, Sun Valley Ctr Arts & Humanities, Idaho, 74-78; instr, Sch Art Inst Chicago, Ill, 80 & Portland Sch Art, Maine, 83. *Awards:* Western States Art Found Fel, Boise Art Gallery, 76-77; Nat Endowment Arts Photographer's Fel, 79. *Bibliog:* Alex Sweetman (auth), Peter deLory Photographs, An Afterimage, Visual Studies Workshop, Rochester, NY, 11/76. *Mem:* Soc Photog Educ. *Publ:* Contribr, Aperture, Inc, 73; contribr, Creative Camera, English, 12/73. *Mailing Add:* Box 3799 Ketchum ID 83340

DEL RE, MARISA (CASTELLET)
DEALER
b Rieta, Italy; US citizen. *Study:* Univ Naples, graduate. *Pos:* Owner, Marisa del Re Gallery, New York, currently. *Mem:* St Jude's Sch (trustee). *Specialty:* European and American paintings, sculptures and drawings by contemporary masters. *Mailing Add:* c/o Marisa del Re Gallery 41 East 57th St New York NY 10022

DELSON, ELIZABETH
PAINTER, PRINTMAKER
b New York, NY, Aug 15, 32. *Study:* Pa Acad Fine Arts; Smith Col, BA, 54; Hunter Col, MA, 72. *Work:* New York Pub Libr; Boston Pub Libr; Univ Southern Ill; Columbia Univ; Brooklyn Mus. *Comn:* Etchings comn and distributed by Assoc Am Artists, Collector's Guild Ltd, Landmarks Collection & Framemakers, Ltd, The Calvin Collection. *Exhib:* 100 Artists Honor the Prospect Park Centennial, 66; one-man shows, Hicks Street Gallery, 64, Paerdegat Libr, 72 & 74, Park Gallery, 73, Brownstone Gallery, 74 & Long Island Univ, 71; Brooklyn Mus Nat Print Biennials. *Teaching:* Instr printmaking, Pratt Inst, 62-66. *Awards:* Audubon Artists Medal of Honor for Graphics, 61. *Mem:* Soc Am Graphic Artists; Contemp Artists Guild (vpres, 71-75). *Media:* Oil Reliefs, Etchings. *Mailing Add:* 625 Third St Brooklyn NY 11215

DE LUCA, JOSEPH VICTOR
EDUCATOR, SCULPTOR
b Niagara Falls, NY, Mar 1, 35. *Study:* Bowling Green State Univ, BS, 57 & MA, 58; Mich State Univ with Angelo Ippolito, MFA, 65. *Work:* Renaissance Ctr, Detroit, Mich; Toledo Mus Art, Ohio; Univ Omaha, Nebr; Grand Rapids Mus, Mich; Ford Motor Company, World Headquarters, Dearborn, Mich. *Comn:* Cyma & Dyptich (oils & aluminum on canvas), Renaissance Ctr, Detroit, Mich, 76; Revival (aluminum & polyester on canvas), Kingscott Assoc, Inc, Kalamazoo, Mich, 81; Big Red (painting), pvt collection. *Exhib:* One-man shows, Century Ctr, South Bend Art Ctr, Ind, 78, Bim Haus, Amsterdam, the Netherlands, 80; two-person exhib, Gallery Artemus, Ghent, Belgium, 81; Midwest Sculptors & Painters, Krannert Mus, Univ Ill; Mich Artists, Southwest Regional, Kalamazoo Inst Arts, Mich, 80. *Collections Arranged:* Works by George Ortman (auth, catalog), 69; Works by Angelo Ippolito (auth, catalog), 70; Works by Harry Brorby (auth, catalog), 71; Works by Clifton McChesney (auth, catalog), 72; Works by Graduates & Undergraduates, Bowling Green, Western Mich Univ, 73. *Pos:* Gallery dir (part time), Gallery Two, Western Mich Univ, Kalamazoo, 67-71; Danforth Assoc, Nat Invitational Educators Asn, 76- *Teaching:* Instr art, Findlay High Sch, Ohio, 58-62; instr drawing, painting & art educ, Central Mich Univ, Mount Pleasant, 62-66; prof drawing & painting, Western Mich Univ, Kalamazoo, 66- *Awards:* First Award, Battle Creek Civic Art Ctr, 79; First Award, South Bend Art Ctr, 76; Purchase Award, Krasl Art Ctr, 83. *Bibliog:* Rick Campbell (auth), Sculptor Opens Art Exhibit, Grand Rapids Press, 11/78; Vern Berry (auth), WMU artists in Hope Show, Kalamazoo Gazette, 11/12/78; Cathy Wilhelm (auth), WMU instructor takes top honors with altar pieces, Battle Creek Enquirer & News, 6/10/79. *Mem:* Col Art Asn; Kalamazoo Inst Arts. *Media:* Mixed Media. *Dealer:* Willem Mudde Salon Eindhoven Netherlands. *Mailing Add:* 2222 Tipperary Road Kalamazoo MI 49008

DE LUE, DONALD
SCULPTOR
b Boston, Mass, Oct 5, 1897. *Study:* Boston Mus Fine Arts Sch. *Comn:* Two heroic figures (golden bronze), State La Mem, 71 & two-figure group (bronze), State Miss Mem, Gettysburg, Pa; four 8 ft bronze figures for The Alamo, San Antonio, Tex; Thomas Jefferson (bronze figure), Jefferson Parish, La, Bicentennial; Firestone Mem Exedra (granite), Akron, Ohio; and many others. *Awards:* Am Artists Prof League Gold Medal; Sculptors of the Yr Award, Am Numismatic Asn, 79; Medal, Brookgreen Gardens, 79. *Mem:* Academician Nat Acad Design; fel Nat Sculpture Soc (past pres, hon pres); Nat Inst Arts & Lett; Am Artists Prof League; Royal Soc Arts. *Media:* Bronze, Marble. *Mailing Add:* 82 Highland Ave Leonardo NJ 07737

DELUIGI, JANICE CECILIA
EDUCATOR, PAINTER
b Indianapolis, Ind, Nov 27, 15; Italian & Am citizen. *Study:* Art Inst Chicago; Univ Chicago; studied with Oskar Kokoschka and Marino Marini; Pope Pius

Inst, Florence; Art Inst Venice with Tito Guido. *Work:* Ill Bell Tel Co, Chicago; Art Inst Chicago; Civic Mus Revltella, Trieste, Italy. *Comn:* Sculpture in memory of John F Kennedy & Robert F Kennedy, Community of Milano, Italy, 69; stained glass windows, San Giorgio Maggiore, Benedictine Monastery, 73 & painting of St John Morosini, 77; stained glass windows, Cini Found & Benedictine M Nuovalese, 73; artistic glass sculpture of Murano for the best film presented at the VII Festival Int Film of Sch & Fiction, Trieste, 69. *Exhib:* Venice Biennale, 72 & 74; La Cappella, Art Ctr, Trieste, 75; The Women of Today, Italian Inst Cult, Vienna, 75; Engravings, Int Ctr Grafics, Venice, 75; Fourth Festival Films & Art, Asolo, Italy, 76. *Collections Arranged:* Exhibition of the Nude, Art Inst Venice, 75; 34th, 35th & 36th Biennales, Int Art Exhib, Venice, 68, 70 & 72. *Teaching:* Prof painting, Mercyhurst Col, Erie, Pa, in Venice, 66-; prof glass sculpture, mosaics & art hist Venetian painters, NY Univ, in Venice, 66- *Awards:* First Prize Int Painting & Sculpture, Fruili-Venezia Guilia, 71; Silver Medal for Painting, Pope Paul VI, 73. *Mem:* Arts Club Chicago; Renaissance Soc Univ Chicago; Artists Equity; Alumni Asn Sch Art Inst Chicago. *Media:* Multimedia. *Mailing Add:* Piscina San Moise 2053 San Marco 30124 Venice Italy

DEL VALLE, JOSEPH BOURKE
DESIGN CONSULTANT
b New York, NY, Feb 6, 19. *Study:* Cooper Union Art Sch, cert; Fulbright Grant Painting & Graphic Design, Paris; Inst Fine Arts, NY Univ. *Pos:* Sr publ designer, Mus Mod Art, New York, 64-68; sr designer, Orgn Comt, XIX Olympic Games, Mex, 69; publ design & prod consult, Whitney Mus Am Art, 70-76, design consult & art dir, currently. *Awards:* 50 Best Bks (three awards), Am Inst Graphic Arts; My Best Work, Mead Libr Ideas, 71; Cert Award, Printing Indust Am, 74. *Publ:* Designed: Treasures of the Philadelphia Museum of Art, 73, Great American Nude, 74, In Praise of Hands, 74 & Catalogue of the Collection Whitney Museum of American Art, 75; Western Collection, Stark Mus of Art, Orange, Tex, 78; The Smithsonian Illustrated Library of Antiques (15 vols), Cooper-Hewitt Mus, 79. *Mailing Add:* 41 Union Square W New York NY 10003

DE MARCO, JEAN ANTOINE
SCULPTOR
b Paris, France, May 2, 1898; US citizen. *Study:* Ecole Nat Arts Decoratif, Paris. *Work:* Sculpture, Brooklyn Mus, NY; engraving print, Metrop Mus Art, New York; sculpture, Norfolk Mus Art & Sci, Va; sculpture, Nat Art Collection, Smithsonian Inst, Washington, DC; prints, Joslyn Art Mus, Omaha, Nebr. *Comn:* Sculpture for two chapels and three heroic size statues, Nat Shrine Immaculate Conception, Washington, DC; two heroic size marble portrait medallions, House of Cong, Washington, DC; sculpture for West Coast Mem World War II, comn by Am Comn Battles Monuments, Presidio, San Francisco; two marble statues, House of Theology, Centerville, Ohio; twelve reliefs relative to St Benedict for Abbey, Monte Cassino Libr, Italy; and others. *Exhib:* Nat and regional exhibs and in mus in US. *Teaching:* Instr sculpture, Columbia Univ, Boston Mus Fine Arts Sch, Nat Acad Design & Bennett Jr Col, formerly; instr bronze casting & drawing, Iowa State Univ, formerly. *Awards:* Nat Inst Arts & Lett Grant, 50; Medal of Merit, Am Acad Arts & Lett, 59; Saltus Gold Medal & Elizabeth Watrous Gold Medal, Nat Acad Design; and others. *Mem:* Am Acad & Inst Arts & Lett; Nat Acad Fine Arts; emer mem Nat Sculpture Soc. *Mailing Add:* Cervaro 03044 Prov-Frosinone Italy

DEMAREE, BETTY (ELIZABETH ANN)
PAINTER, INSTRUCTOR
b Denver, Colo, Oct 19, 18. *Study:* Cooper Union Sch Art; with Robert E Wood, Calif; with Edgar A Whitney, Herb Olsen & Mario Cooper, New York; also with Milford Zornes, Utah & Charles Reid, Conn. *Work:* Kissinger Oil Bldg, Denver; Van Schack, Littleton, Colo; Marathon Oil Bldg, Littleton; Los Alamos Nat Lab; Rocky Mountain Energy Co, Broomfield, Colo; and others. *Comn:* Ceramic plaque of oil scene, Indust of Lowell Williamson, Calgary, Can, 62; ceramic, Off Gov of Colo, 62; watercolor scenes of Denver bldgs, Cassidy Paint & Hilb & Co, 69-72; Old Main (painting), Colo State Univ, Ft Collins, 70; watercolor portraits of children, James F Kuhns, Dallas, Tex, 71-72; Chilcott Portfolio Marquit, Fort Collins, Colo, 80. *Exhib:* Southwestern Watercolor Soc, Dallas, 69-75 & Albuquerque, NMex, 72; Am Watercolor Soc Traveling Exhib, 76-79; Watercolor West Traveling Exhib, Utah State Univ, 77-79; Allied Artists Am, New York, 78-81; Audubon Artists, New York, 79. *Teaching:* Instr pvt classes, 68-; lectr, demonstrations & workshops, 75- *Awards:* Emily Lowe Mem Award, Am Watercolor Soc, New York, 76; John Young-Hunter Award, Allied Artists Am, 77, Winsor & Newton Award, 78; First Place Award, Colo Artists Asn, Denver, 80. *Mem:* Allied Artists Am, New York; Colo Watercolor Soc; Southwestern Watercolor Soc; Assoc Am Watercolor Soc; Audubon Artists, New York; and others. *Media:* Watercolor, Pastel. *Publ:* Palette Talk & The Incredible Variety of Watercolor, 81, M Grumbacher. *Dealer:* Gallery A East Kit Carson Rd Taos NM 87571; Carson Gallery Seven N Last Chance Gulch Helena MT. *Mailing Add:* 4725 W Quincy #1403 Denver CO 80236

DE MARIA, WALTER
SCULPTOR
b Oct 1, 35; US citizen. *Study:* Univ Calif, Berkeley, MA, 59. *Work:* Mus Mod Art, Whitney Mus Am Art, New York; Basel Kunstmuseum, Basel, Switz. *Exhib:* Sculpture of the 60's, Los Angeles Co Mus, 67; Whitney Mus Am Art Sculpture Ann, 68; Information, Mus Mod Art, New York, 70; Vertical Earth Kilometer, Kassel, Ger, 77; Broken Kilometer, New York, 79; one-man exhib, Dia Art Found, New York, 79 & 80; Pier & Ocean, Hayward Gallery, London, 80; Venice Biennial, 80; and others. *Awards:* Guggenheim Fel, 69-70. *Bibliog:* D Bourdon (auth), Walter De Maria, the singular experience, Art Int, 12/68. *Media:* Earth. *Publ:* Contribr, Hard core (land film ed 100), 69. *Mailing Add:* PO Box 275 New York NY 10013

DE MARTINI, JOSEPH
PAINTER
b Mobile, Ala, July 20, 96. *Study:* Nat Acad Design, with Leon Krill & Ivan Olinsky. *Work:* Addison Gallery Am Art, Andover, Mass; City Art Mus St Louis; Boston Mus Fine Arts; Mus Mod Art; Metrop Mus Art; plus many others. *Exhib:* City Art Mus St Louis, 38, 41, 42 & 46; Corcoran Gallery Art, 41, 43 & 45; Va Mus Fine Arts, Richmond, 42, 44 & 46; John Herron Art Inst, 45; Nebr Art Asn, 45 & 46; plus many others. *Teaching:* Artist in residence, Univ Ga, 52-53. *Awards:* Prize, Nat Acad Design, 50; Guggenheim Fel, 51; Gold Medal, Pa Acad Fine Arts, 52; plus others. *Bibliog:* Rosamond Frost (auth), included in Contemporary Art: the March of Art from Cezanne until Now, Crown, 42; Emily Genauer (auth), included in Best of Art, Doubleday, 48; John I H Baur (auth), included in Revolution and Tradition in Modern American Art, Harvard Univ Press, 59; plus others. *Mem:* Assoc Nat Acad Design; Audubon Artists. *Mailing Add:* 103 W 27th St New York NY 10001

DEMARTIS, JAMES J
PAINTER
b Corona, NY, Mar 30, 26. *Study:* Acad Fine Arts, Florence, Italy, 50-54. *Work:* Pvt collections in Europe & US. *Exhib:* One-man exhib, Ward Eggleston Gallery, Ruko Gallery, Marcaleo Gallery, Artemis East Gallery & Hicks St Gallery. *Awards:* Emily Lowe Award Painting, 61. *Mem:* Artists Equity. *Dealer:* Brownstone Gallery 76 Seventh Ave Brooklyn NY 11217. *Mailing Add:* 161 Berkeley Pl Brooklyn NY 11217

DEMATTIES, NICK
PAINTER, PRINTMAKER
b Honolulu, Hawaii, Oct 19, 39. *Study:* Long Beach State Col, BA, 64; Inst Design, Chicago, with Misch Kohn, MS, 67. *Work:* Los Angeles Co Mus Art; Brooklyn Mus Art; Cabinet Estampes, Bibliot Nat Paris; Libr Cong; San Francisco Mus Mod Art. *Exhib:* Biennial 77, Phoenix Art Mus, Ariz; 16th Bradley Nat Print & Drawing Exhib, Peoria, Ill, 77; 19th Ann Nat Exhib & Drawings, Okla Art Ctr, 77; solo exhibs, Davidson Galleries, Seattle, 78, Univ WFla, Pensacola, 79 & Suzanne Brown Gallery, Scottsdale, Ariz, 81. *Pos:* Founder & dir, Pac Northwest Graphics Workshop, 70-75. *Teaching:* Instr printmaking & drawing, San Diego State Col, 67-69; asst prof, Mt St Mary's Col, Calif, 69-70; vis prof printmaking, Univ Ore, 72; instr, Albion Col, Mich, 73-74; asst prof printmaking & drawing, Ariz State Univ, Tempe, 74-76, assoc prof, 77- *Awards:* Juror's Award, Biennial 77, Phoenix Art Mus, 77; Cash Award, Scottsdale Fine Arts Festival, Ariz, 77; Western States Arts Found Fel Award, 79. *Bibliog:* Articles, Art Voices S, 11-12/79 & 9-10/81 & Portfolio Mag, 7-8/81; and others. *Dealer:* Kitchell/Newland 6125 E Indian School Rd Suite 1005 Scottsdale AZ. *Mailing Add:* c/o Dept of Art Ariz State Univ Tempe AZ 85281

DEMETRION, JAMES THOMAS
ADMINISTRATOR
b Middletown, Ohio, July 10, 30. *Collections Arranged:* Lyonel Feininger, 66; Egon Schiele & The Human Form, 71; 25 yrs Am Painting 1948-1973, 73; European Art: The Postwar Years 1945-1955, 78; Giorgio Morande: Retrospective, 81. *Pos:* Cur, Pasadena Art Mus, Calif, 64-66, dir, 66-69; dir, Des Moines Art Ctr, Iowa, 69-; mem mus adv panel, Nat Endowment for the Arts, 73-76, mem nat adv comt, Tamarind Inst, 78-; mem int adv comt, Stuart Found, La Jolla, currently. *Mem:* Asn Art Mus Dir (treas, 76-77, 1st vpres, 78-79, pres, 79-80). *Mailing Add:* Des Moines Art Ctr Greenwood Park Des Moines IA 50312

DE MILLE, LESLIE BENJAMIN
PAINTER, DEALER
b Hamilton, Ont, Apr 24, 27; US citizen. *Study:* Hamilton Tech Inst; Art Students League; also with John Franks, Laguna Beach, Calif. *Work:* Portraits, four former US Pres, Whittier Col Collection, Calif; Death Valley 49ers Collection. *Comn:* Portrait, Ronald Reagan, Calif, 67; paintings, US Sixth Fleet, Mediterranean (naval combat artist), 72 & Pearl Harbor, Hawaii painting, 73; portrait, Anchor Hocking Co, Ohio, 80. *Exhib:* Death Valley 49ers Exhib, Calif, 69-; Grand Nat Ann Exhib, Am Artists Prof League, New York, 71-; and others. *Pos:* Owner, Demille Gallery, Laguna Beach, Calif, currently; fac mem, Nat Portrait Seminar, New York, 81. *Teaching:* Organizer, dir & instr, sem for art orgn in US, 66-76; instr, Nat Portrait Seminar, 81. *Awards:* Best Show, 71 & Gold Medals, 76, 79 & 80, Am Artists Prof League, New York; Best Show, Death Valley 49ers Inc, 80; and others. *Bibliog:* Portraits in Pastel (series of half-hour programs), Pub Broadcasting System, 81-; Feature article, SW Art Mag, 10/81. *Mem:* Am Inst Fine Arts; Am Artists Prof League; Coun Traditional Artists Soc; Death Valley 49ers Inc; Am Portrait Soc. *Media:* Oil, Pastel. *Specialty:* Representational paintings and sculpture including American Western. *Publ:* Contribr, How to Draw Cats and Kittens, Walter Foster, 79. *Dealer:* Leslie B De Mille Galleries Laguna Beach CA; El Prado Galleries Inc Sedona AZ. *Mailing Add:* Fine Portraits and Paintings 1721 Orchard Dr Santa Ana CA 92707

DEMING, DAVID LAWSON
SCULPTOR, EDUCATOR
b Cleveland, Ohio, May 26, 43. *Study:* Cleveland Inst Art, with William McVey & John Clague, BFA; Cranbrook Acad Art, with Julius Schmidt, MFA. *Work:* Ft Worth Nat Bank, Tex; San Antonio Mus & Pub Libr Austin, Tex; Longview Mus Art, Tex; First City Ctr, Austin, Tex. *Comn:* Portraits of Clyde Littlefield, Ed Ole & D X Bible, Univ Tex. *Exhib:* One-man exhib, Univ Ark, Little Rock; Art Mus STex, Corpus Christi; Univ Tex-Austin; Southwest Tex State Univ; Patrick Gallery, Tex. *Teaching:* Instr sculpture, Sch Fine & Appl Arts, Boston Univ, 67-68; instr sculpture & drawing design, Univ Tex, El Paso, 70-72; assoc prof sculpture & drawing, Univ Tex, Austin, 72- *Awards:* Best of Show Foundation Award, Mus STex, Corpus Christi; Ford Found & Alcoa Found Grants. *Media:* Steel, Bronze. *Mailing Add:* 2504 Baxter Dr Austin TX 78745

DE MISKEY, JULIAN
SCULPTOR, PRINTMAKER
b Hungary; US citizen. *Study:* Art Students League; Cleveland Art Inst; Acad Grande Chaumiere, Paris. *Work:* Mus Mod Art, Metrop Mus Art, City Mus, New York; Nat Collection Fine Arts, Washington, DC. *Comn:* One hundred cover paintings, New Yorker Mag, 25-59. *Exhib:* One-man shows, Paris, 32-34 & Sculpture, Westbeth Galleries, 72; Artists for Victory Exhibs. *Awards:* Purchase Award for War Painting, Am Red Cross. *Bibliog:* D Z Meilach, Box Art, Crown, 75. *Mem:* Provincetown Art Asn. *Media:* Ceramics, Papier Mache, Oil, Lithographs. *Publ:* Illusr, What? no pie charts, New Yorker Mag, 27; illusr, Tim's Mountain, World, 59; auth & illusr, Piccole, Random House, 67; illusr, Chucaro, Harcourt, Brace; and others. *Mailing Add:* c/o Westbeth Studio D719 463 West St New York NY 10014

DE MONTE, CLAUDIA
EDUCATOR, CONCEPTUAL ARTIST
b Astoria, NY, Aug 25, 47. *Study:* Col Notre Dame, Md, BA; Cath Univ Am, MFA. *Work:* Mus Mod Art, New York; Indianapolis Mus Art, Indiana. *Comn:* Prudential Life Insurance, NJ, 81; Hyatt-Regency, Va, 81. *Exhib:* 19th Area Exhib, Corcoran Gallery of Art, Washington, DC, 74; Plus One, Corcoran Gallery of Art, Washington, DC, 76; 7th Int Encounter on Video, Centre d'Estudio d'Art Contemporani, Barcelona, Spain, 77; Contemp Arts Ctr, New Orleans, La, 78; one-person shows, Corcoran Mus Art, Washington, DC, 76, Miss Mus Art, Jackson, 80, Ft Worth Art Mus, Tex, 80, Marion Locks Gallery, Philadelphia, 80, Droll/Kolbert Gallery, NY, 80; and others. *Pos:* US rep sculpture, Int Women's Exhib, Olympia Art Ctr, Kingston, Jamaica, 75; dir art workshops, New Sch Social Research, New York, 80-82. *Teaching:* Instr drawing, design & painting, Bowie State Col, Md, 71-72; instr art survey, Prince George's Community Col, Largo, Md, 72; assoc prof design, Univ Md, College Park, 72- *Awards:* Creative award, Univ Md, summer grant, 74 & 77; Ariana Found Arts, 83. *Bibliog:* Artist Gives City Thanks in Very Big Way, New York Daily News, 11/70; Paul Richard (auth), Showy T-shirt trade-in, Washington Post, 4/76; David Tannous (auth), Five plus one at Corcoran, Art in Am, 1-2/77. *Mem:* Am Asn of Univ Prof; Washington Women's Art Ctr. *Media:* Mixed. *Publ:* Contribr, Women in the Arts: American Women and Social Change: Visual Arts, US Info Agency, 75; auth, Public Poet: Tom Jones, Andy Warhol's Interview, 1/77; coauth, The Height Report, 83. *Mailing Add:* 96 Grand St New York NY 10013

DE MONTEBELLO, PHILIPPE LANNES
ADMINISTRATOR, MUSEUM DIRECTOR
b Paris, France, May 16, 36. *Study:* Harvard Col, BA(magna cum laude), 58; New York Univ Inst Fine Arts, MA, 63; Lafayette Col, Hon LLD, 79; Bard Col, Hon LLD, 81. *Collections Arranged:* Greek Art of the Aegean Islands, 11/79; Clifford Still, 11/79; Horses of San Marco, 2/80; Seventeenth Century French Painting, 6/82; Cimabue, 1/82; Vatican, 1/83; Manet, 9/83; Summer Loan Exhibition, Metrop Mus Art. *Pos:* Asst cur to assoc cur Europ paintings, Metrop Mus Art, 63-69, vdir curatorial & educ affairs, 74-77, actg dir mus, 77-78, dir, 78-; dir, Mus Fine Arts, Houston, Tex, 69-74. *Teaching:* Lectr Fr art, romanticism & 18th century women painters. *Awards:* Woodrow Wilson Fellow, New York Inst Fine Arts, 61-62; Alumni Achievement Award, NY Univ, 78; Gallatin Medal & Fel, New York Univ, 81. *Mem:* Coun Mus & Educ Visual Arts; Am Asn Mus; Am Asn Mus Dirs. *Publ:* Auth, Peter Paul Rubens, McGraw, 68; contribr, Metrop Mus Art Bull & others. *Mailing Add:* Metrop Mus Art Fifth Ave at 82nd St New York NY 10028

DE MOURA SOBRAL, LUIS
HISTORIAN, CRITIC
b Viseu, Port, June 24, 43; Can citizen. *Study:* Univ Louvain, Belg, MA(art hist), 73, PhD, 76. *Collections Arranged:* Le surrealisme portugais (auth, catalog), Galerie UQAM, Montreal, 83. *Pos:* Cur, Montreal Mus Fine Arts, 71-75. *Teaching:* asst prof, Univ Montreal, 76-81, assoc prof, 81- *Mem:* Am Soc Hispanic Art Hist Studies; Asn Study Dada & Surrealism; Univ Art Asn Can; Int Coun Mus; Asn Port Mus. *Res:* Baroque painting; surrealism; Portuguese baroque painting; Iberoamerican colonial art. *Publ:* Auth, Deux nouveaux Valdes Leal au Louvre, Rev Louvre, 82; auth, Tres bodegones do Museu de Evora, Coloquio artes, 82; auth, L'iconographie de Vilallonga, Vie Arts, 83; ed, Surrealisme peripherique, Univ Mntreal, 83; auth, Le surrealisme portugais, Galerie UQAM, 83. *Mailing Add:* Dept Hist Art Univ Montreal PO Box 6128 Sta A Montreal PQ H3C 3J7 Canada

DEMPSEY, BRUCE HARVEY
MUSEUM DIRECTOR
b Camden, NJ, July 4, 41. *Study:* Fla State Univ, BA, MFA; study exten sch, Florence, Italy; Mozarabic manuscripts with Gulnar Bosch. *Collections Arranged:* Photons-Phonons (elec sculpture), 71; Lewis Comfort Tiffany, 72; Realizations and Figurizations, 72; Karl Zerbe Mem Exhib, 73; Photo Phantisists, 73; Colors (photog exhib), 74; Talent USA, 76; Elizabethan Portraiture, Nat Portrait Gallery, London, 76; New Realism, 77; New Floridians No 1, 77; The Florida Connection: Jim Rosenquist & Robert Rauschenberg, 77; Helen Frankenthaler, 77; New Floridians No 2, 78 & No 3, 79; The Flowing Word: Chinese Calligraphy, 79; Contemporary Stained Glass, 79; Duane Hanson, 80; Currents: A New Mannerism, 81; Joseph Raffael: Recent Works, 82. *Pos:* Dir art gallery, Fla State Univ, 68-74; dir, Jacksonville Art Mus, 75- *Teaching:* Instr fundamental art & art hist, Fla State Univ, 66-74. *Mem:* Am Asn Mus. *Publ:* Auth, Lewis C Tiffany--Beauty in Many Mediums, 72. *Mailing Add:* 2415 Mandarin River Lane Mandarin FL 32223

DEMPSEY, RICHARD WILLIAM
PAINTER, LECTURER
b Ogden, Utah, Sept 14, 09. *Study:* Sacramento Jr Col, Calif, 29-31; Calif Sch Arts & Crafts, Oakland, 32-34; Art Students League, 44. *Work:* Corcoran Gallery Art, Washington, DC; Atlanta Univ Gallery, Ga; Int Business Machines, New York; Bank Bogota, Columbia, SAm. *Comn:* Washington Juvenile Court, Washington DC; US Army Historical Ctr, Washington DC. *Exhib:* San Francisco Mus Art, 45; Ann Area Exhib, Corcoran Gallery Art, Washington DC, 50, 51 & 52; Nat Collection Arts Gallery, Smithsonian Inst, 54, 56 & 57; Franz Bader Gallery, Washington DC, 55, 59, 62, 74 & 77; Paintings from the Permanent Collection, Corcoran Gallery Art, Washington DC, 60; Luis-Angel Arengo Gallery, Bank Bogota, Columbia, SAm, 62; Centre d'Art Gallery, Port-au-Prince, Haiti; Inst Jamaica Gallery, Kingston, WIndes, 63; Howard Univ Gallery, Washington DC, 68. *Teaching:* Instr & lectr fine art, Corcoran Gallery Art, Washington DC; instr & lectr, Calif, currently. *Awards:* Julius Rosenwald Fel, Outstanding Am Negroes, 46; First Award, Corcoran Gallery, 49-51. *Mem:* Washington Watercolor Asn. *Media:* Oil, Watercolor. *Collection:* Haitian primitives, ultra modern world artists. *Dealer:* Franz Bader Gallery 20001 I St Washington DC 00037. *Mailing Add:* 6708 Poplar Ave Takoma Park MD 20012

DE NAGY, EVA
PAINTER
b Hungary. *Study:* Acad Royal Beaux-Arts, Brussels, Belg. *Work:* Color slides, Guild Libr, Church Archit Guild Am, Washington, DC. *Exhib:* Painters & Sculptors Soc NJ, 61 & 62; Am-Hungarian Art Asn, New York, 62 & 63; Catharine Lorillard Wolfe Art Club, 62 & 64; Provincetown Art Asn & Mus, 60-81; West 80's Art and the Law Traveling Exhib, Minn Mus Art, 80-81; and others. *Pos:* Owner-dir, Eva de Nagy Gallery, Provincetown, Mass; state art comn, NJ Fedn Women's Clubs, 60 & 62; mem art comn, Trenton State Mus, 60 & 62; chmn, Roebling-Boehm art scholar, 62 & 64. *Awards:* Prizes, NJ State Fedn Women's Club, 54 & 59; Bronze Medal, Seton Hall Univ, 56; Prize, NJ State Med Asn Convention Art Exhib, 58 & 60; plus others. *Mem:* Provincetown Art Asn; Cape Cod Art Asn; Am Artists Prof League; Painters & Sculptors Soc NJ. *Mailing Add:* 427 Commercial St Provincetown MA 02657

DE NAGY, TIBOR (J)
DEALER, COLLECTOR
b Debrecen, Hungary, Apr 25, 10; US citizen. *Study:* DEcon & PhD; Univ Frankfurt; Kings Col, Cambridge, Eng & Owens Col, Manchester; Univ Basel, Switz. *Pos:* Pres & dir, Tibor de Nagy Gallery, Inc, New York, 50- & Watson/de Nagy Gallery Texas, Houston, 73- *Awards:* Arts Award, Col Visual Arts, Syracuse Univ. *Mem:* Art Dealers Asn Am; Mus Mod Art. *Specialty:* Pioneer work to start out and promote contemporary talents, most of whom are Americans. *Collection:* Contemporary Americans. *Publ:* Auth, Di Ungarische National Bank, Duncker & Humlodt, Munich, 31; auth, The integrity of the artist, dealer and gallery, In: The Business of Art, Prentice-Hall. *Mailing Add:* Tibor de Nagy Gallery 29 W 57th St New York NY 10019

DENES, AGNES C
ENVIRONMENTAL SCULPTOR, GRAPHIC ARTIST
b Budapest, Hungary; US citizen. *Study:* City Univ New York; New Sch Social Res, New York; Columbia Univ. *Work:* Mus Mod Art, Whitney Mus Am Art, New York; Nat Collection Fine Arts, Washington, DC; Moderna Museet, Stockholm, Sweden; and others. *Comn:* Container Corp Am, 79; Wheatfield--A Confrontation (wheat planted downtown Manhattan), 82. *Exhib:* Whitney Mus Am Art, 71 & 73; Mus Mod Art, New York, 73 & 77; solo exhib, Corcoran Gallery Art, 74 & Hayden Gallery, Mass Inst Technol, 79; Venice Biennale, Italy, 78 & 80; Seibu Art Mus, Tokyo, 80; New Mus, New York, 80; Musee Nat d'Art Mod, Centre Georges Pompidou, Paris, 80; Master of Drawing, Kunsthalle, Nurnberg, Ger, 82; and others. *Teaching:* Instr fine arts, Sch Visual Arts, New York, 74-79; instr, Skowhegan Sch Painting & Sculpture, Maine, 79; guest lectr in numerous universities, museums & art centers. *Awards:* Creative Artists Pub Serv Grant, 72, 74 & 80; Nat Endowment Arts Grant, 74, 75 & 81; DAAD Fel, Berliner Kunstlerprogramm, 78; and others. *Bibliog:* Peter Selz (auth), Agnes Denes: The visual presentation of meaning, Art in Am, 3-4/77; Donald Kuspit (auth), Agnes Denes: The ironies of comprehension, Arts Mag, 12/81; Ronny H Cohen (auth), Agnes Denes: Triumph of the will, Print Collectors Newslett, 11-12/82. *Mem:* New York Artists Equity Asn (bd dirs, currently). *Media:* Mixed; All. *Publ:* Auth, Sculptures of the Mind, Univ Akron Press, 76; auth, Paradox & Essence, Tau/Ma Publ, Rome, Italy, 77; auth, Isometric Systems in Isotropic Space: Map Projections, Visual Studies Workshop, 79. *Mailing Add:* 595 Broadway New York NY 10012

DE NIKE, MICHAEL NICHOLAS
SCULPTOR
b Regina, Sask, Sept 14, 23; US citizen. *Study:* Nat Acad Fine Arts; also with Jean de Marco & Carl Schmitz. *Comn:* Albert Payson Terhune Mem, Collie Fanciers Am, Paramus, NJ, 71; Medallion, Int Chef's Asn, New York, 72; Stations of the Cross, Christ Church, Pompton Lakes, NJ, 75; Bicentennial Mural, Twp Wayne, NJ, 75; Young St Francis (bronze), St David's in Kinnelon, NJ; and others. *Exhib:* Nat Acad Design, New York, 64; Audubon Artists, 65; Knickerbocker Artists, 65; Nat Sculpture Soc Ann, 66; Am Artists Prof League, 74; and others. *Pos:* Dir, Am Carving Sch, Wayne, NJ, 74-75. *Teaching:* Instr woodcarving, Fair Lawn Adult Educ, 68-74; adj fac, Essex Co Col, Newark, NJ, 74-75; Passaic Co Col, 76-80. *Awards:* Dr Ralph Weiler Award, Nat Acad Design, 64; Herald-News Award, Passaic-Clifton, NJ, 69; Allied Artists Am Award, 75. *Mem:* Am Artist Prof League. *Media:* Wood, Stone. *Mailing Add:* 2343 Hamburg Turnpike Wayne NJ 07470

DENNEY, JIM (JAMES DAVID)
PAINTER
b Greenville, SC, May 13, 53. *Study:* Univ Ore, Eugene, BFA, 78; Univ Kans, Lawrence, MFA(Lockwood Fel), 80. *Exhib:* Solo exhib, Carnegie-Mellon Univ, 82; Urban Pulses--The Artist & the City, Frick Fine Arts, Pittsburgh, 83; Nature, Sch #33 Art Ctr, Baltimore, 83; Zaner Galery Nat, Rochester, 83; Three Painters, NAME Gallery, Chicago, 84; Young Pittsburgh, Carnegie Mus Art, Pittsburgh, 84; and others. *Teaching:* Asst prof art, Carnegie-Mellon Univ, 81- *Awards:* Proj Award, Urban Pulses, Vera Heinz Found, 83; Visual Arts Fel, Pa Coun Arts, 84. *Bibliog:* Elaine King (auth), article, New Art Examiner, 6/82; Harry Schwalb (auth), Teacher, teacher, Pittsburgh Mag, 3/83; William Homisak (auth), article, New Art Examiner, 11/83. *Media:* Oil. *Mailing Add:* 389 Bouquet Pittsburgh PA 15213

DENNIS, CHARLES HOUSTON
CARTOONIST
b Springfield, Mo, Nov 11, 21. *Study:* Art League Calif, San Francisco; Acad Art, San Francisco. *Pos:* Staff artist, Springfield Leader & Press, 39-42; free lance mag cartoonist, 50- *Publ:* Contribr, numerous mags, 50-; auth, Cartoon gag writing principles and techniques, 55. *Mailing Add:* 1831 Magnolia Way Walnut Creek CA 94595

DENNIS, CHERRE NIXON
PAINTER, ETCHER
b Raton, NMex. *Study:* Univ Tulsa, with Adah M Robinson; Univ NMex, with Emil Bisttram; Okla State Univ, with Doel Reed; also with Rexford E Brandt & Phillip L Dike. *Exhib:* Watercolor & Print Ann, Oakland Art Gallery, Calif, 42; Philbrook Art Ctr, Tulsa, Okla, 56; Nat Representational Art Ann, Thomas Gilcrease Inst, Tulsa, 58; Southwestern Biennial, Mus NMex, Santa Fe, 62; one-man show, Four Hills Gallery, Albuquerque, 74; and others. *Pos:* Pres & chmn bd, Adah M Robinson Mem Fund, Tulsa, 67-69. *Teaching:* Art instr etching & drawing, Philbrook Art Ctr, 40-41. *Awards:* First Award for graphics, Tulsa Art Ann, 35 & 36; Second Award for watercolor, Philbrook Art Ctr, 50; Graphic Awards, NMex Art League, 72. *Mem:* NMex Art League; Lake Region Arts & Crafts Colony. *Media:* Watercolor. *Dealer:* 12505 Summer NE Albuquerque NM 87112. *Mailing Add:* Lakeview on Gibson Rte 1 Box 655 Wagoner OK 74467

DENNIS, DON W
PAINTER, INSTRUCTOR
b Reading, Pa, Jan 21, 23. *Study:* Kutztown State Col, Pa, BS(art educ), 51; Pratt Inst, Brooklyn, NY, 51-52; with Edgar A Whitney 65-68; also with Barse Miller, 69-70 & 72. *Work:* Miami Univ, Oxford, Ohio; First Nat Bank of Cincinnati, Madeira, Ohio; Reading Mus, Pa; Utstein Kloster, Norway; Bell Telephone. *Comn:* 12 paintings (offshore oil rigs), Phillips Petroleum, Stavanger, Norway, 79. *Exhib:* One-man show, Reading Mus & Art Gallery, Pa, 68; Am Watercolor Soc Ann, Nat Acad, New York; Cincinnati Art Mus Invitational, Ohio, 77; All-Ohio Watercolor Show, Massillon Mus, Ohio, 78; Ohio Watercolor Soc Ann, Ohio, 79, 80 & 81; plus others. *Pos:* Art dir, Gibson Greetings, Cincinnati, 68-73; conductor watercolor workshops, Maine, Bahamas & Norway, 73-80; self-employed artist-teacher, 73- *Teaching:* Instr watercolor painting, Middletown Fine Arts Ctr, 70-79. *Awards:* Emily Lowe Mem Award, Am Watercolor Soc, 80; M Grumbacher Bronze Medallion, Ohio Watercolor Soc, 81; Walser Greathouse Medal, Am Watercolor Soc, 82; and others. *Bibliog:* The Watercolor Page, Am Artist, 8/82. *Mem:* Am Watercolor Soc (Midwest vpres, 76-77); Cincinnati Art Club (pres, 71-73); Ohio Watercolor Soc (trustee, 80-84); Cincinnati MacDowell Soc; assoc Nat Acad Design. *Media:* Watercolor. *Mailing Add:* 731 Brooks Ave Cincinnati OH 45215

DENNIS, DONNA FRANCES
SCULPTOR
b Springfield, Ohio, Oct 16, 42. *Study:* Carleton Col, BA, 64; Col Art Study Abroad, Paris, 65; Art Students League, with Stephen Greene, 66. *Work:* Geneva Art Mus, Switzerland; Neue Galerie-Sammlung Ludwig, Aachen, WGer. *Comn:* Entrance maze, Musical Theater, Kennedy Ctr, Washington, DC, 77; Mad River Tunnel (outdoor sculpture), Dayton City, Ohio, 81; River Resort (outdoor sculpture), Aberdeen, SDak. *Exhib:* Scale and Environment, Walker Art Ctr, Minn, 77; 1979 Biennial Exhib, Whitney Mus Am Art, New York, 79; Directions, Hirshhorn Mus, Washington, DC, 79; Les Nouveaux Fauves, Neue Galerie-Sammlung Ludwig, Aachen, WGer, 80; Painting & Sculpture Today, Indianapolis Mus Art, Ind, 80; Developments in Recent Sculpture, Whitney Mus, New York, 81; Aperto, Venice Biennale, Italy, 82; New York Now, Kestner Ges, Hannover, WGer, 82; Artists' Architecture, Inst Contemp Art, London, 83; New Art, Tate Gallery, London, 83; Ornamentalism, Hudson River Mus, Yonkers, 83. *Teaching:* Skowhegan Sch Art, Maine, 82. *Awards:* New York State Creative Artist Public Service Grant, 75 & 82; Nat Endowment Arts Grant, 77 & 80; John Simon Guggenheim Found Fel, 79. *Bibliog:* Francesca Alinovi (auth), Artists architecture, Domus Mag, 3/80; James Jordan (auth), Light: Adams, Dennis & Sonneman, Dialogue, 3-4/80; Robert Jensen & Patricia Conway (auths), Ornamentalism: The New Decorativeness in Architecture and Design, Clarkson N Potter, 82. *Media:* Mixed Media. *Publ:* Illusr, Hotels, Z Press, 74; auth, The presence of the past, Domus Mag, 10/80. *Dealer:* Holly Solomon Gallery 724 Fifth Ave New York NY 10019. *Mailing Add:* 131 Duane St New York NY 10013

DENNIS, GERTRUDE WEYHE
DEALER
Pos: Dir, Weyhe Gallery, New York. *Mem:* Art Dealers Asn Am. *Specialty:* American prints & drawings, 1920s & 1930s. *Mailing Add:* 794 Lexington Ave New York NY 10021

DENNIS, ROGER WILSON
PAINTER
b Norwich, Conn, Mar 11, 02. *Study:* Art Students League. *Exhib:* Lyme Art Asn; Conn Acad; Copley Soc, Boston. *Pos:* Conservator painting, Lyman Allyn Mus, New London, Conn, 45-78; retired. *Mem:* Lyme Art Asn; Copley Soc. *Media:* Oil, Watercolor. *Mailing Add:* 9 Columbus Ave Niantic CT 06357

DENNISON, KEITH ELKINS
MUSEUM DIRECTOR, HISTORIAN
b Oakland, Calif, Sept 20, 39. *Study:* San Francisco State Univ, BA; with Dr Ernest Mundt; spec training, M H de Young Mem Mus, San Francisco. *Collections Arranged:* Horizons, A Century of California Landscape Painting; La Pemdule Francaise, A Selected Survey of French Clocks 1750-1900; Ecclesiastical Arts 13th Through 17th Centuries. *Pos:* Asst cur educ, M H de Young Mem Mus, 68-70; visual arts adv, Calif Arts Comn, Sacramento, Calif, 70-71; dir, Haggin Mus, Stockton, Calif, 71- *Teaching:* Instr museology, Univ of the Pac, 74- *Publ:* Auth, Horizons, a century of California landscape painting, 70. *Mailing Add:* Haggin Museum 1201 N Pershing Stockton CA 95203

DENNISTON, DOUGLAS
PAINTER, EDUCATOR
b Cornwall-on-Hudson, NY, Nov 19, 21. *Study:* Col William & Mary, cert, 42; Univ NMex, BFA, 45, MA, 48. *Work:* Va Mus Fine Arts, Richmond; Denver Art Mus; Tucson Mus Art & Yuma Art Ctr, Ariz; Jonson Gallery, Albuquerque, NMex. *Exhib:* Am Watercolors, Prints & Drawings, Metrop Mus Art, New York, 52; Young Am Printmakers, Mus Mod Art, New York, 53; 18th Ann Watercolor Exhib, San Francisco Art Mus, 54; 67th & 73rd Western Ann, Denver Art Mus, 61 & 71; Southwestern Prints & Drawings, Dallas Mus Fine Arts, 52-62; Southwest Fine Arts Biennial, Mus Fine Arts, Santa Fe, NMex, 76. *Teaching:* Prof art, Univ Ariz, 59-83, prof emer, 83- *Awards:* Purchase Awards, Denver Artists Ann, Denver Art Mus, 53, Fifth & Seventh Southwestern, Yuma Art Ctr, Ariz, 70 & 72. *Media:* Watercolor, Oil. *Publ:* Illusr, Calendar, Baleen Press, 72. *Dealer:* Cob-Web Hall PO Box 2035 Prescott AZ 86301. *Mailing Add:* 1844 N Vine Ave Tucson AZ 85719

DENTON, PAT
PAINTER, INSTRUCTOR
b Scottsbluff, Nebr, July 20, 43. *Study:* Art Students Tour, Europe, 60; Univ Kans, 61; Univ Denver, cert painting, 62; studied with Virginia Cobb, John Pellew, Charles Reid, Lee Weiss & Buffalo Kaplinski. *Work:* Greeley Nat Bank, Colo; Wind River Collection, 80; Mus Tex Tech Univ; Hospital Building & Equipment, St Louis, Mo; United Banks Colo, Denver; and many in pvt collections. *Exhib:* Best of Show, Cody, Wyo, 80; Feature Show, Dubois, Wyo, 80; Feature Show, Maxims of Greeley, Colo, 81; Saxon's of Georgetown, 81; Scottsbluff Art League, Nebr, 82; and many other group & one-man shows. *Teaching:* Pvt lessons, Golden, Colo, 71-72; instr drawing, Foothills Art Ctr, Golden, 72; instr watercolor, 73; instr workshop, Parma Tyson Studio, 75, Wind River Artists Guild, Dubois, Wyo, 80, Studio West, 80-81, GI Sketch Club, Aurora, Nebr, 80-82; instr, Evridge's Studio West, 81-82 & Colo Inst Art, 83. *Awards:* First Prize in Watercolor, Nat Fetc, Scottsbluff, 73-77; Ida Becker Mem Award, Catharine Lorillard Wolfe Club, 74; Best of Show, Wind River Nat, Dubois, Wyo, 82; and others. *Bibliog:* B Hosicowa (auth), Art of Pat Denton, Empire Mag, Denver Post, 11/12/72; J Mills (auth), Dimensions, Denver Post; Con Marshall (auth), New York Award, Chadron Rec, Nebr & Scottsbluff Star Herald. *Mem:* Foothills Art Ctr; Southwestern Watercolor Soc; and others. *Media:* Acrylic, Watercolor. *Mailing Add:* 2948 Pierson Way Lakewood CO 80215

DEO, MARJOREE NEE
PAINTER
b Escanaba, Mich, Aug 27, 07. *Study:* Univ Wis, BA, 28; Grand Chaumiere, Paris, 32-33; Phillips Gallery Art Sch, with Karl Knaths, 44-45; Am Univ, with Boris Margo & Jack Tworkov, 46; Fine Arts Inst, Sarasota, Fla, with Afro, Guston, Marca-Relli, Rivers & Brooks, 64-67. *Work:* Corcoran Gallery Art; Univ Wis, Madison; Regis Col, Colo; Wagner Col, NY. *Comn:* Paintings, Bancroft Sch & Camp, Haddonfield, NJ & Owl's Head, Maine, 68, 70 & 73, Groom & Nordberg Attorneys, Washington, DC, 75, 77 & 80, Marco Island Hotel, Fla, 76, Tierra Verde Hotel, St Petersburg, Fla, 79 & Ellis Bank & Trust, Sarasota, Fla, 82. *Exhib:* Baltimore Mus Regional, 55, 57, 59 & 61; Turkey Imagined Traveling Exhib, Turkey & Washington, DC, 58 & 59; US Info Agency Int Tours, Europe, 59 & 60; Butler Inst Am Art Ann, 59-62; Pa Nat, Pa Acad Fine Arts & Detroit Mus, 60; Corcoran Gallery Art Biennial, 63; US Embassy Prog, 67- *Awards:* Sarasota Art Asn Award, 52, 53, 65, 77 & 83; First Prize, Corcoran Gallery Art Biennial, 63; Fla Artists Group Ann Award, 68 & 69-73. *Mem:* Artists Equity Asn; Sarasota Art Asn; Fla Artists Group. *Media:* Acrylic. *Dealer:* Howard Monroe Gallery Nine the Courtyard Chapel Hill NC 27514; Boca Grande Gallery Boca Grande FL 33921. *Mailing Add:* 35 Sandy Cove Rd Sarasota FL 33581

DEPAOLA, TOMIE
ILLUSTRATOR, DESIGNER
b Meriden, Conn, Sept 15, 34. *Study:* Pratt Inst, BFA, 56; Calif Col Arts & Crafts, MFA, 69; Lone Mountain Col, Doctoral Equivalency, 70; also with Ben Shahn & Richard Lindner. *Work:* Kerlan Collection, Univ Minn, Minneapolis; Worcester Art Mus, Mass; Osborne Collection, Toronto. *Comn:* Mural, Dominican Sisters Retreat House Chapel, Schenectady, NY, 58; two murals, Conception Abbey Retreat House, Mo, 59; renovation, design & murals, St Sylvester's Church, Graniteville, Vt, 61; murals, Glastonbury Monastery, Hingham, Mass, 62; altar painting, Newman Cult Ctr, Rensselaer

Polytech Inst, 68. *Exhib:* Children's Bk Illusr, Everson Mus, 77; Art and the Alphabet, 78 & A Peaceable Kingdom: Animals in Art, 82, Houston Mus Fine Arts; The Original Art Ann, Master Eagle Gallery, New York, 80-83; A Decade of The Original Art of the Best Illustrated Children's Books, 1970-1980, Univ Conn Libr, Storrs, 82; Illustrators Exhib, Metrop Mus Art & New York Pub Libr, 82-83; and others. *Collections Arranged:* Kerlan Collection, Univ Minn, Minneapolis, 81. *Pos:* Designer & tech dir speech & theater, Colby-Sawyer Col, 73-76. *Teaching:* Asst prof design & painting, Newton Col of Sacred Heart, Mass, 62-66; asst prof design, Lone Mountain Col, San Francisco, 67-70; instr art, Chamberlayne Jr Col, 72-73; assoc prof, Colby-Sawyer Col, 73-76; assoc prof design, illus & graphic design, New Eng Col, Henniker, 76-79. *Awards:* Art Bks for Children Award, Brooklyn Mus & Brooklyn Pub Libr, 75-76 & 78-79; Caldecott Honor Bk Award, Am Libr Asn, 76; Regina Medal, Cath Libr Asn, 83. *Bibliog:* Z Sutherland (auth), Children & Books, Scott Foresman, 5th ed, 77; Twentieth Century Children's Writers, St James/Macmillan, 83. *Mem:* Authors Guild; Soc Children's Bk Writers. *Media:* Mixed. *Publ:* Auth & illusr, Strega Nona, Prentice-Hall, 75; auth & illusr, The Clown of God, Harcourt Brace Jovanovich, 78; illusr, The Night Before Christmas, Holiday House, 80; auth & illusr, The Legend of the Bluebonnet, G P Putnam's Sons, 83; auth & illusr, Sing, Pierrot, Sing, Harcourt Brace Jovanovich, 83. *Mailing Add:* Redwing Farm New London NH 03257

DE PEDERY-HUNT, DORA
SCULPTOR, DESIGNER
b Budapest, Hungary, Nov 16, 13. *Study:* State Lyceum, Budapest, 32; Royal Sch Appl Art, Budapest, MA, 43. *Work:* Nat Gallery Can, Ottawa; Art Gallery Ont, Toronto; Smithsonian Inst; Royal Cabinet Medals, Brussels, Belg & The Hague, Netherlands; Mus Contemp Crafts, Charlottetown, PEI; and others. *Exhib:* Can Pavillion, Expo '67; Sculpture Symposium, Toronto, 78; Prince Arthur Gallerie, 78; Hamilton Art Gallery, 79; Gallery Stratford, 79; and others. *Awards:* Purchase Prizes, Uno-a-Erre, Arezzo, Italy, 64-66; Can Govt Centennial Medal, 67; Queen's Jubilee Medal, 72; and others. *Mem:* Royal Can Acad; Sculptors' Soc Can; Ont Soc Artists. *Mailing Add:* 65 Glen Rd Toronto ON M4W 2V3 Canada

DEPILLARS, MURRY N
ADMINISTRATOR, ILLUSTRATOR
b Chicago, Ill, Dec 21, 38. *Study:* Kennedy-King Community Col, AA(fine arts); Roosevelt Univ, BA(art educ) & MA(urban studies); Pa State Univ, University Park, PhD (art educ). *Work:* Paul Roberson Cult Ctr, Pa State Univ, University Park; Inst Positive Educ, Chicago, Ill; Consolidated Bank, Richmond. *Comn:* Mural, African & African-Am Studies Ctr, Univ Mich, Ann Arbor, 71; illusr, J Negro Educ, Howard Univ, 74; illusr, Destruction of Black Civilizations, 74 & Steps to Break the Circle, 75, Third World Press; illusr, Story of Kwanza, Inst Positive Educ, Chicago, 75. *Exhib:* Mus Sci & Indust, Chicago, 70; The Indignant Eye, Whitney Mus Am Art, New York, 71; Am Greeting Card Gallery, New York, 72; Rainbow Sign Gallery, Los Angeles, 74; World Expo '74, African-Am Pavilion, Spokane, 74; Huntsville Mus Art, 79; Miss Mus Art, Jackson, 80. *Pos:* Asst dir, Educ Asst Prog, Univ Ill, Chicago, 68-71, asst dean, Sch Arts, Va Commonwealth Univ, 71-76, dean, 76- *Teaching:* Instr, Chicago Comt of Urban Opportunity, 68; asst prof art, Va Commonwealth Univ, 76-, assoc prof fundamental drawing, 72-73. *Awards:* Outstanding Serv Award, Nat Conf Artists, 75; Elizabeth Catlett Mara Award of Excellence, 76; Man of Excellence Plaque, Rep China, 80; and others. *Bibliog:* F D Cossitt (auth), DePillars is Artist with message, Richmond Times Dispatch Newspaper, 6/15/70; Semella Lewis & Ruth Waddy (auth), Black artists on art, Contemp Crafts, Inc, Vol II; Robert Doty (auth), Contemporary Black Artists in America, Whitney Mus Am Art, 72. *Mem:* Nat Conf Artists (pres, 73-); Nat Art Educr Asn; Pan African Artists Alliance; and others. *Media:* Acrylic, Oil. *Publ:* Illusr, A People of the Sun, 73; auth, The Emerging Voice of the Black Visual Artists, Black Art, 76; auth, Art history and Black culture, 77 & Renaissance to Renaissance, 80, Minority Voices; auth, Wanted: A role for the Black visual artists, Western J Black Studies, 82. *Dealer:* Third World Press 7524 S Cottage Grove Chicago IL 60619. *Mailing Add:* 901 W Franklin St Richmond VA 23284

DE POL, JOHN
WOOD ENGRAVER, DESIGNER
b New York, NY, Sept 16, 13. *Study:* Art Students League; Sch Technol, Belfast, Northern Ireland. *Work:* Libr Cong; New York Pub Libr; Metrop Mus Art; Syracuse Univ Libr; Bucknell Univ Libr. *Comn:* Presentation prints, Woodcut Soc, 52, Miniature Print Soc, 53 & Albany Print Club, NY, 58-59. *Exhib:* One-man exhibs, Albany Print Club, Bucknell Univ, Syracuse Univ & Lycoming Col; Nat Acad Design Ann, 72. *Pos:* Free-lance art dir & design consult for var corp; illusr, Franklin Keepsake Ann Ser, ret, 81; free lance wood engraver, 81- *Awards:* Albany Print Club Purchase Prize, 68; John Taylor Arms Mem Prize, Nat Acad Design, 68; Nat Arts Club Purchase Prize, 68. *Bibliog:* P K Thomajan (auth), John De Pol, wood engraver, Print Mag, 8/54; Norman Kent (auth), The wood engravings of John De Pol, 3/56 & William Caxton, Jr (auth), A new chiaroscuro wood engraving by John De Pol, 2/68, Am Artist. *Mem:* Soc Am Graphic Artists; Albany Print Club; life mem Art Students League; academician Nat Acad Design; laureate, New York Printers Hall Fame, 80. *Media:* Wood. *Mailing Add:* 280 Spring Valley Rd Park Ridge NJ 07656

DEPUMA, RICHARD DANIEL
ARCHAEOLOGIST, HISTORIAN
b DuBois, Pa, May 15, 42. *Study:* Swarthmore Col, BA(art hist), 64; Bryn Mawr Col, MA(archaeol), 67, PhD(archaeol), 69. *Collections Arranged:* Etruscan & Villanovan Pottery (auth, catalog), Univ Iowa Mus Art, 71.

Teaching: Instr classical art, Univ Iowa, Iowa City, 68-69, asst prof, 69-74, assoc prof, 74- *Mem:* Archaeol Inst Am (pres, 71-75); Col Art Asn; Soc Promotion Roman Studies; Asn Int pour l'Etude de la Mosaique Antique. *Res:* Etruscan pottery & bronzes; Greek vase painting; mosaics. *Publ:* Auth, Unpublished Bucchero Pesante Pottery in Chicago, Studi Etruschi, 76; contribr, Greek Vase Painting in Midwestern Collections, Art Inst Chicago, 79; auth, A Prenestine Mirror with Telephos and Orestes, Romische Mitteil, 80; contribr, Animals in Ancient Art, Cleveland Mus Art, 81; contribr, A Guide to Etruscan Mirrors, Tallahassee, 82. *Mailing Add:* 409 Hutchinson Ave Iowa City IA 52240

DERGALIS, GEORGE
PAINTER, SCULPTOR
b Athens, Greece, Aug 31, 28; US citizen. *Study:* Painting with DeChirico, 48-50; Accad Belle Arti, Rome, MA, 51; Sch Mus Fine Arts, Boston, dipl, 59. *Work:* De Cordova Mus, Mass; Camara de Comercio & Museo de Arte, Medellin, Colombia; and others. *Comn:* Nine watercolors, Charlestown Savings Bank Boston, 78. *Exhib:* New England Drawing Competition, traveling, 79; Ariz Nat Sculpture Competition, 80; Museo de Arte de Medellin, Colombia, 80; West Art and the Law, traveling, 81-82; Tampa Mus, Fla, 83-84; and others. *Teaching:* Instr painting, De Cordova Mus, 61-; art instr, Sch Mus Fine Arts, Boston, 61-70; pvt art classes, Wayland, Mass, 69- *Awards:* Gold Medal, Accad Italia delle Arti e del Lavoro, 80. *Bibliog:* Thomas B Adams (auth), A New Nation, Pequot Press, 81. *Mem:* Accad Italia delle Arti e del Lavoro. *Media:* All. *Mailing Add:* 72 Oxbow Rd Wayland MA 01778

DE RIVERA, JOSE
SCULPTOR
b West Baton Rouge, La, Sept 18, 04. *Study:* With John W Norton, Chicago; Washington Univ, St Louis, Mo, hon doctorate, 74; also study in Spain, Italy, France, Greece & Egypt. *Work:* Mus Mod Art, New York; Art Inst Chicago; San Francisco Mus Art; Smithsonian Inst, Washington, DC; Tate Gallery, London, Eng; plus many others. *Comn:* Steel Century Two (sculpture), Am Iron & Steel Inst, 65. *Exhib:* Whitney Mus Am Art Ann, New York, 34-68; Grace Borgenicht Gallery, New York, 52-72; White House, Washington, DC, 66; Sculpture of the '60's, Los Angeles Co Mus Art, Los Angeles & Philadelphia Mus Art, 67; Retrospective 72, La Jolla Mus Contemp Art, Calif & Whitney Mus Am Art, 72; and many other group & one-man shows. *Teaching:* Instr sculpture, Brooklyn Col, 53; critic in sculpture, Yale Univ, 53-55; instr sculpture, Sch Design, NC State Col, 57-60. *Awards:* Watson F Blair Prize, Art Inst Chicago, 57; Nat Inst Arts & Lett Grant, 59; Creative Awards Medal, Brandeis Univ, 69; and others. *Mailing Add:* 435 E 57th St New York NY 10022

DERN, F CARL
SCULPTOR
b Salt Lake City, Utah, Apr 24, 36. *Study:* San Francisco Art Inst, with Richard Shaw & Fletcher Benton, 69; Univ Calif, Berkeley, with Robert Hudson & James Melchert, 71-72. *Work:* In many pvt collections. *Exhib:* San Francisco Art Inst Centennial Exhib, de Young Mus, 70; New Mus Mod Art, Oakland, 70-73; 1st & 2nd Soap Box Derby, San Francisco Mus Mod Art, 75 & 78; San Jose Mus Art, 78; Syntax Corp Outdoor Sculpture Exhib, 79-80; San Mateo Arts Coun, Proarts Gallery, Oakland, 80; Richmond Art Ctr, 81; and others. *Teaching:* Lectr sculpture, Univ Calif, Berkeley, 75 & Univ Calif, Davis, 83; lectr art, Sonoma State Univ, 77 & 78. *Awards:* Anne Bremer Prize in Art, Univ Calif, Berkeley, 69 & 72; First Prize, 1st Int Contemp, Jon Morehead Gallery, Chico, Calif, 71; Hand Hallow Found Fel, 82 & 83. *Mem:* Artists Equity. *Mailing Add:* 47 Oak Rd Fairfax CA 94930

DERNOVICH, DONALD FREDERICK
PAINTER, EDUCATOR
b Rock Springs, Wyo, April 9, 42. *Study:* Univ Wyo, BA(art educ), 66, MA(art), 67; Ft Hays State Univ, MFA(painting), 83. *Work:* Birger Sandzen Mem Gallery, Lindsborg, Kans; Halseth Co Community Arts Ctr, Rock Springs, Wyo; McCook Community Col, Nebr. *Exhib:* Ann Five State Exhib, West Nebr Arts Ctr, Scottsbluff, 78 & 80-82; Audubon Artists 38th Ann, Nat Arts Club, New York, 80; Rocky Mountain Nat Watermedia Exhib, Foothills Arts Ctr, Golden, Colo, 80 & 82; Burleson Art Exhib, Burleson State Bank, Tex, 82; Kans Three Art Exhib, Mulvane Art Ctr, Washburn Univ, Kans, 83. *Teaching:* Art dir & instr, McCook Community Col, Nebr, 75- *Awards:* Best of Show, Ninth Ann Nat Art Fete, WNebr Arts Ctr, 80 & Rock Springs Nat, Halseth Co Community Arts Ctr, 83. *Mem:* Assoc Am Watercolor Soc; Old Bergin Art Guild; life mem McCook Art Guild; Phi Kappa Phi. *Media:* Watercolor, Oil. *Mailing Add:* Box 163 210 Taylor Culbertson NE 69024

DEROUX, DANIEL EDWARD
PAINTER, PRINTMAKER
b Juneau, Alaska, Oct 25, 51. *Study:* NS Col Art & Design, Halifax, Can, 74-75. *Comn:* Drawing, Juneau Centennial Comn, Alaska, 79. *Exhib:* San Francisco Mus Mod Art, 79-80; New West Invitational, Suzanne Brown Gallery, Scottsdale, Ariz, 80; San Francisco Arts Comn, Capricorn Asunder, 81; Art of the State, Alaska State Arts Coun, Alaska State Mus, 81; 15th Ann Nat Small Sculpture & Drawing Exhib, Corpus Christi, Tex, 81; Collage & Assemblage, traveling exhib, 81-82; and many others. *Pos:* Cur visual arts, Alaska State Mus, 78-79. *Awards:* Best of Painting Award, Anchorage Hist & Fine Arts Mus, 79; Alaska Stat Counc Arts Grants, 79; and others. *Bibliog:* Margaret Firmin (auth), Only painting what he sees, Alaska Advocate, 2/79; art ed (auth), Whimsical images are his delight, Anchorage Times, 2/79; Marianna Woodward (auth), Dan DeRoux Juneau buckaroo, Alaska J, 1/80. *Dealer:* Bill Winn 513 East St Juneau AK 99801; Terry Shattuck Northern Images 301 Seward St Juneau AR 99801. *Mailing Add:* 1745 Beach St 5 San Francisco CA 94123

DE RUTH, JAN
PAINTER, WRITER
b Karlovy Vary, Czech, July 31, 22; US citizen. *Study:* Rotter Art Sch, Prague, Czech; Ruskin Sch Drawing, Oxford Univ, Eng; Art Students League; New Sch Social Res, New York; also with Frederic Taubes. *Exhib:* 72 nat juried exhibs, 14 mus one-man shows & 97 gallery one-man exhibs. *Teaching:* Instr figure painting, Carrizo Lodge, Ruidoso, NMex. *Awards:* Gold Medal, Allied Artists of Am & Nat Arts Club; Allied Artists Advan Art Award; Butler Inst Am Art Purchase Award, Audubon Artists. *Mem:* Allied Artists Am (vpres); Audubon Artists; Am Artists Prof League; artists fel Royal Soc Art, London; Knickerbocker Artists. *Media:* Oil. *Publ:* Auth, Portrait Painting, 64; auth, Painting the Nude, 68; auth, Painting Portraits, Nudes and Clothed Figures, Watson-Guptill, 81. *Mailing Add:* 1 W 67th St New York NY 10023

DESIND, PHILIP
DEALER, COLLECTOR
b New York, NY, Feb 28, 10. *Study:* City Col New York, BS, 34, MS, 38; Columbia Univ, work towards PhD. *Pos:* Dir, Capricorn Galleries, Bethesda, Md, 64- *Teaching:* Instr, Cath Univ & Univ Md, formerly; adj prof, Am Univ, Washington, DC, currently. *Specialty:* Contemporary American realism. *Mailing Add:* 4849 Rugby Ave Bethesda MD 20014

DESMARAIS, CHARLES JOSEPH
MUSEUM DIRECTOR, WRITER
b New York, NY, Apr 21, 49. *Study:* Western Conn State Col, 67-71; State Univ NY, Buffalo, BS, 75, MS, 77. *Collections Arranged:* The Portrait Extended (auth, catalog), Mus Contemp Art, Chicago, 80. *Pos:* Asst ed, Afterimage, Rochester, NY, 75-77; ed, Exposure: Quart J Soc Photog Educ, 77-81; dir, Chicago Ctr Contemp Photog, Columbia Col, 77-79; dir, Calif Mus Photog, Univ Calif, Riverside, 81- *Awards:* Art Critics Fel, Nat Endowment Arts, 79. *Bibliog:* College politics..., New Art Examiner, 6/79; interview, Museum dreams of future, Los Angeles Times, 7/5/81. *Mem:* Soc Photog Educ (bd dir, 79-83); Col Art Asn; Photog Hist Soc New York; Nat Stereoscopic Asn. *Res:* Contemporary photography and photographers. *Publ:* Auth, Roger Mertin: Records 1976-78, 78 & Michael Bishop, 79, Columbia Col, Chicago; auth of more than 30 articles in Afterimage, Art Am, Artwk, Mod Photog & others. *Mailing Add:* c/o Calif Mus Photog Univ Calif Riverside CA 92521

DESMIDT, THOMAS H
PAINTER, EDUCATOR
b Sheboygan, Wis, Sept 6, 44. *Study:* Lincoln Col, AA; Layton Sch Art, BFA; Syracuse Univ, MFA. *Work:* Milwaukee Art Inst, Wis; Francis & Sidney Lewis Collection Contemp Art; F&M Corp, Richmond, Va; Miller Brewing Co, Milwaukee, Wis; Everson Mus Art, Syracuse; and others. *Exhib:* Solo exhib, Mem Art Gallery, Univ Rochester, 72, Everson Mus, 73 & Va Mus Fine Arts, 78; James Yu Gallery, New York, 73 & 74; 19th Corcoran Biennial, Washington, DC, 74; Va Artists, Va Mus, Richmond, 77. *Teaching:* Instr painting, Va Commonwealth Univ, 70-73, dir, Art Found, 73-76, asst prof art, 73-, asst dean, 76- *Awards:* One-Man Exhib Award, Rochester Mem Gallery, 70; Fac Res Grant, Va Commonwealth Univ, 73. *Media:* Canvas, Acrylic. *Dealer:* OK Harris Works of Art 383 W Broadway New York NY 10013; James Yu Gallery 393 W Broadway New York NY 10012. *Mailing Add:* 7711 Woodman Rd Richmond VA 23226

DESON, MARIANNE (HERSTEIN)
DEALER
b Toronto, Ont. *Study:* Univ Toronto; Ind Univ; Ohio State Univ; Univ Chicago, with Joshua Taylor and Harold Rosenberg. *Teaching:* Lectr, Chicago Public Schs, pvt schs, Art Inst Chicago, currently. *Mem:* Renaissance Soc, Univ Chicago (pres, 82-84); Chicago Art Dealers Asn. *Specialty:* Contemporary with specialty in new movements; abstraction, installations & conceptual photography; major contemporary Italian artists. *Mailing Add:* Marianne Deson Gallery 340 W Huron Chicago IL 60610

DESOTO, RAFAEL M
PAINTER, ILLUSTRATOR
b Auadilla, PR. *Study:* Columbia Univ, 25; Pratt Inst, 33; Art Students League, 35-37; also with G Bridgeman, E Dickerson & I Soyer. *Work:* Bishop Mus, Bradenton, Fla; State Capitol Fla, Tallahassee; Mus Fine Arts, San Juan; State Univ NY, Greenly Mem Gallery, Farmingdale. *Comn:* Mural (fresco painted), Lens of Life, Westchester Med Ctr, NY, 38; mural, New World, Knights of Columbus Hall, Patchogue, NY, 66; monument, Lady of the Island (with Rock of Ages, Barry, Vt), comn by Montfort Fathers, Manorville, NY, 75. *Exhib:* Nat Soc Painters in Casein & Acrylic, Nat Arts Club, Gramercy Park, NY, 72; Am Artists Prof League, Lever House Bldg, New York, 72-74; solo exhibs, Ponce Mus Art, PR & San Juan Inst Cult, Mus Fine Arts, PR, 74; Lincoln Ctr for Performing Arts, Avery Fisher Hall, 75-79; and others. *Pos:* Illusr, various mag, pocket books, 33-60; asst art dir, Pop Publ Inc, 37. *Teaching:* Pvt instr, 58-; assoc prof art & design, State Univ NY Col Farmingdale, 62-82, prof emer, 82- *Awards:* Nat Poster Art Alliance Award, NY State Armory, 25; Great Seal State Fla, Former Gov Haydon Burns, 65; Emily Griffin Award, Nat Arts Club, 72; and others. *Mem:* Am Artists Prof League; Nat Arts Club; South Bay Art Asn. *Media:* Multimedia. *Mailing Add:* 23 Roosevelt Blvd Box 81 East Patchogue NY 11772

DESPORTES, ULYSSE GANDVIER
PAINTER, HISTORIAN
b Winnsboro, SC, Apr 12, 20. *Study:* Richmond Prof Inst, Col William & Mary, with Julien Binford, Marion Junkin & Theresa Pollack, BFA; Ecole Normale Superior Beaux-Arts, Paris, France, with Maurice Brianchon; Inst Art & Archeol, Univ Paris, with Pierre Lavedan & Andre Chastel. *Work:* Va Mus Fine Arts, Richmond; Washington & Lee Univ, Lexington, Va; Va Commonwealth Univ, Richmond. *Exhib:* Va Artists 1961 & Va Artists 1963, Va Mus Fine Arts; SC Artists, Gibbs Art Mus, Charleston, 62. *Pos:* Dir catalogues, Kende Galleries, New York, 46-48; dir, Florence Mus, SC, 57. *Teaching:* Asst prof art hist & painting, Hollins Col, 57-62; prof art & chmn dept, Mary Baldwin Col, 62- *Awards:* Second Prize, SC Artists Asn, 62; Cert of Merit, Va Mus Fine Arts, 63. *Media:* Oil. *Res:* Neoclassic art; sculptor Guiseppe Ceracchi; painter Louis David. *Publ:* Contribr, Bulletin Mus Bernadotte, 62; contribr, Princeton Libr Chronicle, 62; contribr, Art Quart, 63 & 64; contribr, Antiques Mag, 69. *Mailing Add:* 322 N New St Staunton VA 24401

DES RIOUX (DE MESSIMY), DEENA (COTY)
PAINTER, DESIGNER
b Cambridge, Mass, Dec 7, 41; French & US citizen. *Study:* RI Sch Design, 59-62; Brown Univ, 60-62; Ecole de la grande Chaumiere, Paris, 61; Univ Paris I at Sorbonne, 61 & 63. *Exhib:* Berkshire Mus Ann Exhib, Pittsfield, Mass, 74; Nashua Arts & Sci Ctr, NH, 74; Organic Visions, Design Around US Gallery, Boston's Mus Sci, 77-78; one-person show, Ward-Nasse Gallery, New York, 78; Ethel Scull-Collectors Choice, Pleiades Gallery, New York, 83; and others. *Pos:* Designer package & corp image, free-lance illus & design, Boston, 65-69; lectr, Lesley Col, Mass Col Art & Harvard Grad Sch Design, 75 & 78; founder & dir, Seven at Large, NE Women Artists' Collab, 75-80; dir, Future Figurations, New York, 81- *Awards:* RI Sch Design Scholar, 59-61; Painting Award, New Mem Show, Cambridge Art Asn, 73; Full Funding, Organic Visions, Boston's Mus Sci, 77. *Bibliog:* Garry Armstrong (auth), Boston Women Artists, WNAC-TV Channel 7 Spec Feature, Boston, 75; Mary Lou Kelley (auth), Organic visions, Christian Sci Monitor, 78; Joan Shepard (auth), Ethel Scull-Collectors Choice exhibit, Daily News, New York, 83. *Mem:* RI Sch Design Alumni Coun; Asn Artists Run Galleries, New York; Boston Visual Artists Union Inc (exhib coordr, Am Citifair, 74); Women Exhibiting Boston Inc. *Media:* Acrylic on textured canvas or flat museumboard. *Dealer:* Ward-Nasse Gallery 178 Prince St New York NY 10012. *Mailing Add:* 251 West 19th St Apt 3B New York NY 10011

DESSER, MAXWELL MILTON
PAINTER, DESIGNER
b New York, NY. *Study:* Queens Col, with Barse Miller; Pratt Inst; Cooper Union. *Work:* Sun Oil Co, Radnor, Pa; Brooklyn Jewish Hosp, NY; pvt collections. *Exhib:* Am Watercolor Soc Show, Nat Acad Design, New York, 68-81; Allied Artists of Am Exhib, 73-81 & Nat Acad Design Exhib, 76-81; Knickerbocker Artists Exhib, Nat Arts Club, New York, 75-81; Am Watercolor Soc Exchange with Mus in Australia, 76; Nat Soc Painters in Casein & Acrylic, Am Acad & Inst Arts & Lett, New York, 79; Salmagundi Club Mus Exhib, New York, 79-81. *Pos:* Free-lance filmstrip producer, McGraw-Hill Bk Co, New York, 55-; free-lance art dir, Dun & Bradstreet, New York, 55- & Pace Univ, New York, 79- *Awards:* Silver Medal of Honor, Am Watercolor Soc, 75; Silver Medals of Honor, Allied Artists of Am, 76 & Audubon Artists, 79. *Mem:* Am Watercolor Soc; Allied Artists Am; Audubon Artists (dir, 75-78 & 80); Nat Soc Painters in Casein & Acrylic; Salmagundi Club; and others. *Media:* Acrylic, Watercolor. *Mailing Add:* 85-28 168th Pl Jamaica NY 11432

DESSNER, MURRAY
PAINTER
b Philadelphia, Pa, Nov 11, 34. *Study:* Pa Acad Fine Arts, William Emlen Cresson Traveling Scholar, 65 & J Henry Schiedt Traveling Scholar, 66; also with Franklin C Watkins & Hobson Pittman. *Work:* Pittman Collection, Bryn Mawr Col, Pa; Penn Fed Collection. *Exhib:* Int Arts Festival PR, 69; two-man show, East Hampton Gallery, New York, 69; Cheltenham Ann, 69-72; one-man shows, Peale Galleries, Pa Acad Fine Arts, 70 & Marion Locks Gallery, Philadelphia, 72. *Teaching:* Instr painting, Pa Acad Fine Arts. *Awards:* Philadelphia Mus Art Purchase Prize, Cheltenham Art Ctr, 69. *Bibliog:* Two Philadelphians, Time Mag, 69; article, Art News, 69. *Dealer:* Marion Locks Gallery 1524 Walnut St Philadelphia PA 19103. *Mailing Add:* 802 Sansom St Philadelphia PA 19107

DETMERS, WILLIAM RAYMOND
EDUCATOR, PRINTMAKER
b Pontiac, Mich, June 20, 42. *Study:* Miami Univ, Ohio, BFA, 64, MEduc, 68; Cranbrook Acad Art, MFA, 70; Univ Cincinnati, EdD, 78. *Work:* Cranbrook Acad Art, Bloomfield Hills, Mich; Miami Univ, Oxford, Ohio; Southern Colo State Col, Pueblo; Nova Scotia Col Art & Design, Halifax; Herron Sch Art, Indianapolis. *Exhib:* Ann Midyear Show, Butler Inst Am Art, Youngstown, Ohio, 64; Ann Nat Graphics Exhib, Erie Art Ctr, Pa, 65; one-man shows, Bd Room, Nova Scotia Col Art & Design, 70, Gallery, Southern Colo State Col, Pueblo, 73 & Litho Constructs, Matrix Gallery, Ind Univ, Bloomington, 79; Miami Printmakers Rowan Hall, Miami Univ, Oxford, Ohio, 74. *Teaching:* Art Teacher, Preble Co Schs, Ohio, 65-68; vis instr printmaking, Nova Scotia Col Art & Design, summer 70; instr printmaking & art educ, Southern Colo State Col, 70-73; art teacher, Fredericktown, Ohio Schs, 73-74; vis lectr, Ind Univ, Bloomington, 76; prog chmn art educ, Herron Sch Art, Ind Univ-Purdue Univ, Indianapolis, 76-82. *Bibliog:* Mildred Monteverde (auth), Art display limited to plastic and wood, Pueblo Star J, 73; Lauretta Fox (auth), Litho Constructions and other prints by Detmers, Mt Vernon News, 75. *Mem:* Art Educ Asn Ind; Nat Art Educ Asn. *Media:* Lithography. *Publ:* Auth, A Conceptual Model for the Planning of Curricula for the Visual Arts in Higher Education, Dissertation Abstracts Int, 79; auth, A Conceptual Model for Curriculum Planning and Evaluating in Visual Arts, Studies in Art Educ, 80. *Mailing Add:* Sch Art 110 Foster Hall La State Univ Baton Rouge LA 70803

DE TURCZYNOWICZ, WANDA (MRS ELIOT HERMANN)
PAINTER
b Krakow, Poland, June 16, 08; US citizen. *Study:* Study with Earl of Tankerville, Northumberland, Britain; with Hetherington, La Jolla, Calif; Ont Col Art, Toronto, with Beach. *Work:* Art Mus Juarez; Vancouver Mus Art; Victoria, BC. *Comn:* Costume designs & sets for operas, San Diego Community Chest, Calif, 25-26, Gilbert & Sullivan, La Jolla, 25-26, Toronto Univ Opera, 27-29 & Victoria Opera, 30-34. *Exhib:* Vancouver Mus Art, 30-35; Sun Carnival Shows, El Paso Mus Art, 40-60; El Paso Mus Art, 60's; Santa Fe Bicentennial, NMex, 60's; El Paso Mus Art Asn Show, 71-83. *Pos:* Prog chmn, El Paso Art Asn, 45 & 64, vpres, 55 & 57, pres, 56; chmn, 6th Ann Sun Carnival, El Paso Mus Art, 62. *Teaching:* Pvt lessons all media, 30-; instr painting, drawing & sculpture, Boy Scouts Am, 61-83. *Awards:* Three Best of Show, 6 Firsts, 11 Seconds & many Hon Mentions, Don Purchase Prize, 79, El Paso Mus Art. *Bibliog:* Hudson Bay Co news coverage, Winnipeg, Can, 33; article in Hermosa Beach Women's Club Mag, Calif, 37; rev in Western Rev, Western NMex Univ, 67. *Mem:* El Paso Arts Alliance; life mem El Paso Art Asn. *Media:* Oil, Watercolor. *Mailing Add:* 4215 Santa Rita El Paso TX 79902

DEUTSCHMAN, LOUISE TOLLIVER
DEALER, CURATOR
b Taylorville, Ill, Sept 6, 21. *Study:* MacMurray Col, BA; Northwestern Univ Sch Journalism, Univ Paris. *Collections Arranged:* Seven Decades of Twentieth-Century Art From the Sidney and Harriet Janis Collection, Mus Mod Art & Sidney Janis Gallery Collection, La Jolla Mus Contemp Art & Santa Barbara Mus Art, Calif, 80. *Pos:* Assoc dir, Waddell Gallery, New York, 66-74; assoc cur, Sidney Janis Gallery, New York, 75-78 & 80-; dir, Alex Rosenberg Gallery, New York, 78-80. *Specialty:* Contemporary art; 20th century masters, American & European. *Mailing Add:* 36 E 68th St New York NY 10021

DE VECSEY, ESTHER BARBARA
EDUCATOR, MUSEUM DIRECTOR
b Pecs, Hungary, May 23, 44; US citizen. *Study:* Univ Calif, Los Angeles, with William Brice, John Paul Jones, Oliver Andrews, BA, 61, with Carlo Pedretti, MA, 75; Academia Di Belle Arti, Rome, cert, 66. *Collections Arranged:* Time After Time: Reflections Classical Past, 81, Aspects of Abstraction (auth, catalog), 81 & Variants: Drawings by Contemporary Sculptors (auth, catalog), 81, Sewall Gallery, Rice Univ. *Pos:* Res asst to dir, Los Angeles Co Mus, Calif, 76-77; coordr, Ace Gallery, Venice, Calif, 77; cur collections, Col Art Mus, Wooster, Ohio, 79-80; dir, Sewall Art Gallery, Rice Univ, Houston, Tex, 80- *Teaching:* Instr mus studies practicum, Col Wooster, Ohio, 79-80; instr mus studies practicum, Rice Univ, Houston, Tex, 80-81, asst prof art hist, 81- *Mem:* Am Asn Mus; Tex Asn Mus; Asn Univ & Col, Mus & Galleries. *Res:* Art, architecture and humanism in the Veneto, 16th century; contemporary art. *Mailing Add:* Rice Univ Dept Art & Art Hist Houston TX 77001

DEVEGATALES, JUGO (JOHN MAURICE THOMPSON)
SCULPTOR, EDUCATOR
b Los Angeles, Calif, May 25, 46. *Study:* Calif State Univ, Northridge, BA, 70; San Francisco Art Inst, 71; Tyler Sch Art, Temple Univ, MFA,73. *Work:* Int Acad Ceramics, Calgary; John Michael Kohler Arts Ctr Mus, Sheboygan, Wis. *Comn:* Ltd ed teapot, Helen Drutt Gallery, Philadelphia, 81. *Exhib:* New Photographics, Central Wash State Univ, Ellensburg, 76 & 77; Long Beach Mus Art, 77; 36th Ceramics Ann, Scripps Col, Pomona, Calif, 80; Homage to Josiah Wedgwood, Mus Philadelphia Civic Ctr, 80; John M Kohler Arts Ctr Mus, Sheboygan, Wis, 81; The Animal Image, Renwick Gallery, Smithsonian Inst, Washington, DC, 81; and others. *Teaching:* Asst prof, Moore Col Art, Philadelphia, 74-82. *Awards:* Cash Award & Medal, Int Acad Ceramics, 73; fel, Pa State Coun Arts, 81. *Bibliog:* Kent E Wade (auth), Alternative photographic processes, Morgan & Morgan Inc, Dobbs Ferry, NY, 78; Surreal genetics, Philadelphia Evening Bul, 4/27/80; Michael Monroe (auth), The Animal Image, Smithsonian Inst Press, 81. *Mem:* Bucks Co Coun Arts. *Media:* Acrylic. *Dealer:* Marian Locks Gallery 1524 Walnut St Philadelphia PA 18914. *Mailing Add:* 705 Almshouse Rd Chalfont PA 18914

DEVILLIER, CHARLES ARTHUR
DESIGNER, STAINED GLASS ARTIST
b Baton Rouge, La, July 23, 51. *Study:* La State Univ, BFA(glass design), 74, MFA(glass design), 77; summer scholar study in European workshops, 76. *Work:* Mint Mus Art, Charlotte, NC. *Comn:* Leaded glass panels, Holy Ghost Catholic Church, Hammond, La, 74-75; church furnishings, 76 & etched panel, 77, St Patrick Catholic Church, Lake Providence, La; leaded glass panels, Jackson St Presbyterian Church, Alexandria, La, 78; glass panels, Our Lady of the Lake Regional Med Ctr, Baton Rouge, La; and others. *Exhib:* Biennial Piedmont Crafts, Mint Mus Fine Art, Charlotte, NC, 78 & 80; Contemp Stained Glass, St Petersburg Mus Fine Arts, Fla, 79-80. *Pos:* Regional ed, Glass & Studio mags, Seattle, 79- *Teaching:* Instr flat glass & design, La State Univ, Baton Rouge, 79; instr flat glass, Arrowmont Sch Arts & Crafts, Gatlinburg, Tenn, summers 79, 80, 82 & 83. *Awards:* Purchase Awards, 1978 Biennial Piedmont Crafts, Mint Mus Art, & 34th Prof Exhib, State of La, Broussard Galleries, 79; Nat Endowment Arts Craftsman's Fel, 79. *Bibliog:* Albert Lewis (auth), Glass goes to college, Glass Mag, 5/75; Anne Price (auth), Artist receives endowment, Morning Advocate, 2/13/80. *Mem:* Am Craft Coun; Glass Art Soc. *Media:* Flat Glass, Furnishings; Aquamedia, Collage. *Mailing Add:* 8372 Imperial Dr Laurel MD 20708

DEVINE, WILLIAM CHARLES
DEALER, COLLECTOR
b Brooklyn, NY, Aug 22, 32. *Study:* Union Col, Cranford, NJ. *Pos:* Owner, D Fine Arts Inc, Westfield, NJ, currently. *Specialty:* Eighteenth and nineteenth century paintings and bronzes; Alois LeCoque; Harry Devlin. *Collection:* Work by Alois LeCoque, Thomas Gainsborough, J R Grabach, H Gasser, Eugene Gauss, Grant Wood, Louis Lozowick, Ben Sahn, Waldo Pierce & William Palmer. *Mailing Add:* D Fine Arts Inc 133 Harrison Ave Westfield NJ 07090

DEVLIN, HARRY
ILLUSTRATOR, PAINTER
b Jersey City, NJ, Mar 22, 18. *Study:* Syracuse Univ, BFA, 39; studied with Hans Hoffman, New York. *Comn:* Themes of Am Domestic Archit (44 paintings), Corp Hq, City Fed Savings, Hillsboro, NJ, 77. *Exhib:* Am Cartoonists, Metrop Mus Art, New York, 54; Am Children's Bk Illusr, Voorhees Gallery, Rutgers Univ, 76; one-man shows, Portraits of American Architecture, Morris Mus, NJ, 79 & Gen Elec World Hq Gallery, Fairfield, Conn, 80, Union League Club, New York, World Headquarter AT&T, NJ. *Teaching:* Instr hist fine arts, Union Col, Cranford, NJ, 70-74; instr hist Am domestic archit, 76- *Awards:* Best in Advert Cartooning, Nat Cartoonists Soc, 56 & 62; Arents Medal for Art & Lit, Syracuse Univ, 77; Chairman's Medal, Soc Illusrs Ann Exhib, 81. *Mem:* Soc Illusrs; Artists Equity; Nat Cartoonists Soc (pres, 56-57); Dutch Treat Club; Morris Mus Arts & Sci (trustee, 82-). *Media:* Oil. *Publ:* Coauth & illusr, Old Black Witch, 63, auth & illusr, To Grandfather's House We Go: A Roadside Tour of American Homes, 67, auth & illusr, What Kind of House Is That?, 69, coauth & illusr, Cranberry Thanksgiving, 71 & auth & illusr, Tales of Thunder & Lightning, 75, Parents Press. *Mailing Add:* 443 Hillside Ave Mountainside NJ 07092

DE WAAL, RONALD BURT
COLLECTOR, PATRON
b Salt Lake City, Utah, Oct 23, 32. *Study:* Univ Utah, BS, 55; Mexico City Col, summer 55 & 58; Univ Denver, MA, 58. *Collections Arranged:* Beethoven in the Arts, Univ Utah, 65 & Colo State Univ, 66, 67, 70 & 83. *Pos:* Humanities librn & exhibs chmn, Colo State Univ, Ft Collins, 66- *Awards:* John H Jenkins Award for best work of bibliography published in US during 74. *Mem:* Beethoven Soc; Col Art Asn Am; Nat Sculpture Soc. *Collection:* Beethoven statuary and paintings; pewter, porcelain, and wood figure sculptures; Sherlock Holmes statuary, paintings and prints. *Publ:* Auth, The World Bibliography of Sherlock Holmes and Dr Watson, New York Graphic Soc, 74; Bramhall House, 77; The International Sherlock Holmes, Shoe String Press, 80. *Mailing Add:* 5020 Hogan Dr Ft Collins CO 80525

DE WELDON, FELIX GEORGE WEIHS
SCULPTOR, ARCHITECT
b Vienna, Austria; US citizen. *Study:* Univ Vienna Sch Archit, BA, MA, MS & PhD; Oxford Univ; also study in Italy, Spain & France. *Work:* Air & Space Mus, Washington, DC; Truman Libr, Independence, Mo; Kennedy Libr, Boston. *Comn:* Flag raising on Iwo Jima, Marine Corps War Mem Found, Washington, DC, 54; Simon Bolivar (equestrian statue), Washington, DC, 58; Red Cross Monument, Washington, DC, 59; Truman Monument, Athens, Greece, 63; Nat Monument, Govt Malaysia, Kuala Lampur, 66. *Exhib:* Royal Acad, London, 36; Salon, Paris, 38; Archit League New York, 39; Mus Montreal, Can, 40; Art Asn, Newport, RI, 46. *Pos:* Comnr, Comn Fine Arts, 50-63; chmn, Comn Arts & Sci for President Eisenhower, 52-60; chmn, Arts & Sci Comt Taft Inst Govt, 71. *Teaching:* Dir, Newport Acad Fine Arts, 52-60. *Awards:* Medal of Honor for Arts & Sci, Austria, 62; Award for Outstanding Serv, Daughters Am Revolution, 72; Knight, Order of Malaysia Brit Commonwealth. *Bibliog:* Uncommon Valour (film), USN, 52; US Marines, Nat Geog Mag, 52; Tribute in transit, Life Mag, 54. *Mem:* Art Asn Newport, RI. *Mailing Add:* 219 Randolph Pl NE Washington DC 20002

DE YTURBE, ALEJANDRA R
DEALER
b Mexico City, Mex. *Pos:* Dir, Galeria de Arte Mexicano, currently. *Specialty:* Mexican artists, including contemporary. *Mailing Add:* Col Juarez Milan 18 Deleg Cuauhtemoc 006600 Mexico DF Mexico

DHAEMERS, ROBERT AUGUST
SCULPTOR, EDUCATOR
b Luverne, Minn, Nov 24, 26. *Study:* Calif Col Arts & Crafts, BFA, 52, MFA, 54. *Work:* City San Francisco Art Comn, Calif; First Christ Lutheran Church, Burlingame, Calif; San Jose State Col; Mills Col; St Catherine Indian Sch, Santa Fe, NMex. *Comn:* Wrought iron wall mural, Jerrys Restaurant, San Leandro, Calif, 60; sculpture crucifix, First Christ Lutheran Church, 61; fountain, Frank Hunt Archit, Oakland, Calif, 63; Sundial Cor-Ten (steel 2 ton), Sci Complex, Mills Col, 70; bronze tabernacle, Holy Cross Hosp, San Fernando, Calif, 77. *Exhib:* San Francisco Art Comn, Calif Palace Legion Honor, 61; M H DeYoung Mus, San Francisco, 62; Univ Columbia, 64; Mus Contemp Crafts, Creative Casting, NY, 64; Bertrand Russell Centenary Int, Nottingham, Eng, 73; Commissioned Arts in Archit, Civic Art Gallery San Jose, 74; Brigham Young Univ, Utah, 76; and others. *Teaching:* Asst prof art, Calif Col Arts & Crafts, 51-56; assoc prof art, Mills Col, 57-75, prof, 75-, actg head dept art, 63-64, head dept, 73-76 & 79-80; accrediting mem, Western Asn Schs & Col, 69-83. *Awards:* First Award Sculpture Gold Medal, Oakland Mus Art, 52; First Award Metal Work, Calif State Fair, 62; Mellon Foun Grant, 77, 80 & 83. *Bibliog:* Rose Slivca (auth), First congress of world craftsmen, Crafts Horizon, 65; Lunar suite, environmental sculpture, Look, 69; New talent, Art Am, 66. *Mem:* Western Col Asn (accreditation comt, 69-); Western Asn Schs & Cols; Accrediting Comn Sr Cols & Univs; Int

Sculpture Asn. *Media:* Metal. *Publ:* Coauth, Simple Jewelry Making for the Classroom, 58; contribr, Metal Techniques for Craftsmen, 68; contribr, Craftsmen of the SW, 65 & The Crafts of the Modern World, 68; contribr, Lunar Suite I, The Hamptons Publ Dans Papers Ltd, 7/81; contribr, Sculpture 12, Int Sculpture Ctr, 83. *Mailing Add:* Mills Col Box 9924 Oakland CA 94613

D'HARNONCOURT, ANNE
HISTORIAN, MUSEUM DIRECTOR
b Washington, DC, Sept 7, 43. *Study:* Radcliffe Col, BA, 65; Courtauld Inst Art, Univ London, MA, 67. *Collections Arranged:* Marcel Duchamp (auth, catalog), Philadelphia Mus Art, 73; Eight Artists, Philadelphia Mus Art, 78; Futurism and the International Avante-Garde (auth, catalog), Philadelphia Mus Art, 81. *Pos:* Cur asst, Philadelphia Mus Art, 67-69, cur dept 20th century art, 71-82, dir, 82-; asst cur 20th century art, Art Inst Chicago, 69-71. *Mem:* Col Art Asn Am; Smithsonian Coun; Am Asn Mus; Int Coun Mus; Am Asn Mus Dir. *Publ:* Coauth, Etant Donnes: Reflections on a New Work by Marcel Duchamp, 69; auth, A W Gallatin & the Arensbergs, pioneer collectors of 20th century art, Apollo, 7/74; auth, The cubist cockatoo: A preliminary exploration of Joseph Cornell's Homages to Juan Gris, Philadelphia Mus Art Bulletin, 6/78. *Mailing Add:* Philadelphia Mus Art PO Box 7646 Philadelphia PA 19101

DIAMOND, PAUL
PHOTOGRAPHER
b Brooklyn, NY, June 20, 42. *Study:* Pratt Inst, BFA, 65; Purdue Univ, MA, 80. *Work:* Int Mus Photog, George Eastman House, Rochester, NY; Nat Gallery Can, Ottawa, Ont; Fogg Art Mus, Cambridge, Mass; Boston Mus Fine Arts. *Exhib:* 60s Continuum, George Eastman House, 72; one-man shows, Sq Bromides, Gallery Optica, Montreal, Que, 73 & Floating Found of Photog, New York, 74; Peculiar to Photog, Univ NMex, 76; Five, St Charles on the Wazee, Denver, Colo, 77; Contemp Photog, Fogg Art Mus, 77. *Teaching:* Instr photog, Calif Col Arts & Crafts, Oakland, 77-78; guest lectr photog, Univ Colo, Boulder, 77; instr, Moore Col Art, Philadelphia, currently. *Awards:* Guggenheim Found Fel, 75-76; Nat Endowment for the Arts Grant, 78. *Mem:* Soc Photog Educ. *Publ:* Contribr, Photographer's Choice, Addison House, 75, Ctr for Creative Photog, Vol 4, Univ Ariz, 77 & Grotesque in Photography, Ridge Press, 77. *Dealer:* Witkin Gallery 41 E 57th St New York NY 10022. *Mailing Add:* 400 Diston St 9 Philadelphia PA 19135

DIAMONSTEIN, BARBARALEE
WRITER
Study: New York Univ, doctorate, 63. *Collections Arranged:* Buildings Reborn: New Uses, Old Places, traveling, 76-; American Architecture Now, Leo Castelli Gallery, New York, 81-; Visions and Images, Int Ctr Photog, New York, 81-; Handmade in America, Leo Castelli Gallery & Metrop Mus Art, New York, 83. *Pos:* Staff asst, White House, 63-66; writer, Saturday Rev, 65-68; Harper's Bazaar, 69-71; spec proj ed, Art News, 74-; Ladies Home J, 77-81; Int Commun Agency, 78; Partisan Rev, 78-79; Interiors, 80 & many others; interviewer & producer, ABC Art Cable Network, CBS-TV, WNYC-TV & Manhattan Cable Television; comnr, New York City Cult Affairs Comn, 74-, assoc Am Craft Mus, 81- *Teaching:* Adjunct assoc prof, City Univ New York, Hunter Col, 74-77; vis prof, Duke Univ, 78. *Awards:* Winifred Fisher Award, Distinguished Achievement as Teacher, 76; Rockefeller Found Fel, Aspen Inst, 79; Award, Am Archit Now. *Mem:* Munic Art Soc (mem bd dirs, 72-); Am Coun Arts, 83; Film Anthology Archives. *Publ:* Auth, American Architecture Now, 10/80, auth, Visions and Images: American Photographers on Photography, 11/81 & auth, Interior Design: The New Freedom, fall, 82, Rizzoli Int Publ; ed, Artists and Architects, Whitney Libr Design, 3/81; auth, Handmade in America, Harry N Abrams Publ, 83; and others. *Dealer:* Leo Castelli Gallery 420 West Broadway New York NY. *Mailing Add:* 720 Park Ave New York NY 10021

DIAO, DAVID
PAINTER
b Sichuan, China, Aug 7, 43; US citizen. *Study:* Kenyon Col, AB, 64. *Work:* Whitney Mus Am Art, New York; San Francisco Mus; Art Gallery Ont, Toronto; Va Mus, Richmond. *Exhib:* Eight Painters from New York, Mus Art, Univ Calif, Berkeley, 72; Painting & Sculpture Today, Indianapolis Mus, 74; New York Sch, State of Art, Albany, NY, 77; Arts Club Chicago, 79; plus others; and others. *Teaching:* Instr independent study prog, Whitney Mus, New York, 70- *Awards:* Guggenheim Fel, 73-74; Creative Artists Pub Serv Award, 78. *Bibliog:* Carter Ratcliff (auth), Painted vs painterly, Art News Ann, 71; Peter Schjeldahl (auth), Two on the move, New York Times, 3/19/72. *Mailing Add:* 72 Franklin New York NY 10013

DIAZ RIVERA, LOPE MAX See Max, Lope

DIBBLE, CHARLES RYDER
EDUCATOR, PAINTER
b Richmondville, NY, Apr 14, 20. *Study:* Syracuse Univ, BFA(fabric design), 41, MA(clothing & textiles), 50, PhD, 61; also with F Montague Charman. *Work:* Syracuse Univ; Everson Mus, Syracuse; Rochester Mem Art Gallery, NY. *Exhib:* Am Watercolor Soc; Munson-Williams Proctor Inst, Utica, NY; Rochester Mem Art Gallery; Everson Mus. *Collections Arranged:* Ruth H Randall Contemporary Japanese Ceramics, 63, African Sculpture (with M Peter Piening), 64, John R Fox Korean Ceramics, 65 & Romantic Painting in the University Collection, 66, Syracuse Univ. *Pos:* Designer, Etchcraft, Herkimer, NY, 41-42. *Teaching:* Prof fashion design, Syracuse Univ, 46-82, prof Japanese & other Oriental art, 61-82, asst dean acad affairs, Col Visual & Performing Arts, 71-82, chmn textile arts dept, 78-82; adj prof, State Univ

NY, Upstate Medical Ctr, 80- *Awards:* Purchase Prizes, Rochester Mem Art Gallery, 66 & Asn Artists Syracuse, 69; Florence Disaster (watercolor), Asn Artists Syracuse, 69. *Mem:* Ukioye Soc; Oriental Ceramic Soc; Am Ceramic Soc (exec comt, design div, 67-69, chmn, 68-70); Asn Asian Studies; Nat Trust Hist Preserv. *Media:* Watercolor, Pencil. *Res:* Oriental ceramics, mainly Japanese and Korean, especially the influence of Korean on Japanese. *Publ:* Auth, Contemporary Japanese Ceramics, 61; auth, The John R Fox Collection of Korean Ceramics, 66; contribr, Seventeen Prints, 68; contribr, Printmaking, 70. *Mailing Add:* 5865 E Seneca Turnpike Jamesville NY 13078

DIBBLE, GEORGE
PAINTER, WRITER
b Laie, Hawaii, Mar 29, 04; US citizen. *Study:* Art Students League with George Bridgman, Ivan Olinski & Howard Giles; Columbia Univ with Charles Martin, Arthur Young & Sallie Tannahill, BS & MFA. *Work:* Utah State Div Fine Arts, Salt Lake City; Univ Utah Mus Fine Arts; Utah State Univ, Logan; Southern Utah State Col, Cedar City; Granite Dist Sch & Davis Dist Sch, Utah. *Comn:* Watercolor collections of Hawaii, United Airlines, San Francisco Airport, Calif. *Exhib:* Utah Biennial, Salt Lake Art Ctr, 50; one-man show, Ogden Eccles Art Ctr, 67; Watercolor W, Utah State Univ, 74-76; Centennial Exhib, Utah Artists, Salt Lake City Art Ctr, 76; two-man show, Art Gallery, Univ Utah, 76; Eight-State Regional--Watercolor, Utah State Inst of Fine Arts; and others. *Pos:* Auth, weekly column, Art Scene, Salt Lake Tribune, 57- *Teaching:* Assoc prof watercolor, Univ Utah, 47-57, prof watercolor, 57-72, emer prof, 72- *Awards:* First Purchase Awards, Utah State Fair Asn, 35 & 38 & Utah State Inst of Fine Arts Watercolor, 52. *Bibliog:* One Hundred Years of Utah Painting, James Haseltine Salt Lake Art Ctr, 65. *Mem:* Utah Acad Sci, Arts & Lett. *Media:* Watercolor, Oil. *Publ:* Auth, Art and the Unadjusted School Child, Art Educ Today, Columbia Univ, 36; auth, Watercolor, Materials and Techniques, Holt, Rinehart & Winston, 66. *Mailing Add:* 2049 Wilmington Ave Salt Lake City UT 84109

DIBERT, RITA JEAN
PHOTOGRAPHER, EDUCATOR
b Flint, Mich, Feb 25, 46. *Study:* Flint Community Jr Col, AA(art), 66; Univ Mich, Flint Col, 66, Ann Arbor, BFA, 69, MFA, 71; Univ Calif, Los Angeles, 67-68. *Work:* Detroit Inst Art; Calif Mus Photog, Riverside; Munson-Williams-Proctor Inst; Polaroid Corp, Cambridge, Mass; WDIV-TV, Detroit. *Exhib:* Invisible Light, Smithsonian Inst Infrared Traveling Exhib, 80-84; Sleight of Hand, Fullerton Mus, Calif, 82; National Hand-Colored Photography Exhib, Lincoln Ctr Arts, Milwaukee, 83; Camera Movements, Moore Col Art, 83; Alternatives, Ohio Univ, Athens, 83 & 84; Magic Silver Show, Murray, Ky, 83. *Teaching:* Lectr & area coordr photog & printmaking, Residential Col, Univ Mich, Ann Arbor, 72-74; asst prof, Hartwick Col, 74-79; artist in residence, Pomona Col, 79-; asst prof arts, Claremont Grad Sch, 79- *Awards:* America the Beautiful Award, Photo Documentation, Upper Catskill Arts Coun, 76; Fac Res Grant, Pomona Col, 80-84; Materials Grant, Polaroid Corp, 83. *Bibliog:* Article, Trends Section, Time-Life, 82. *Mem:* Col Art Asn; Womens Caucus Art; Friends Photog; Soc Photog Educ; Calif Mus Photog. *Publ:* Illusr, Infrared photography, Rangefinder Mag, 12/81; illusr back cover, European Photography, Polaroid Corp, 83. *Mailing Add:* c/o Xochipilli Gallery 568 N Woodward Ave Birmingham MI 48011

DICE, ELIZABETH JANE
CRAFTSMAN, EDUCATOR
b Urbana, Ill, Apr 3, 19. *Study:* Univ Mich, BDesign, 41, MDesign, 42; Ind Univ, MA, 66; Int Sch Art, Mex; Inst Allende, Mex; Columbia Univ Teachers Col; Norfolk Art Sch; painting with Jerry Farnsworth; Penland Sch Crafts, 71 & 73. *Exhib:* Miss Art Asn, 48-51, 67 & 68; Nat Crafts Exhib, Wichita, Kans, 50; Nat Watercolor Show, Jackson, Miss, 51; New Orleans Art Asn, 55; Craftsmen's Guild Miss, 75; Path of the Weaver, Memphis, 78 & 80; and many others. *Teaching:* Assoc prof art, Miss State Col Women, 45-79, prof, 80-82; retired. *Awards:* Prizes, Jackson, Miss, 46 & 51; Miss River Craft Exhib Award, 63; Horn Lake Libr Purchase Award. *Mem:* Archaeol Inst Am; Handweavers Guild Am (state rep, 72-77); Miss Mus Art; Southeastern Col Art Conf; Columbus Art Asn. *Mailing Add:* 134 King St Columbus MS 39701

DI CERBO, MICHAEL
PAINTER, PRINTMAKER
b Paterson, NJ, 1947. *Study:* Pratt Inst, BFA & MFA. *Work:* Brooklyn Mus & Pratt Inst, Brooklyn, NY; NJ State Mus, Trenton; Columbia Univ, New York; Victoria & Albert Mus, London; and others. *Comn:* Mural, Next City Corp, 82 & In Business Corp, 82. *Exhib:* Brooklyn Mus, 78; Print Club, Philadelphia, 80; Sotheby Park, New York, 81; solo exhib, Union St Gallery, San Francisco, 82; New York Art Expos, 82; Utopia 84, Petit Palais, Paris, 83; and others. *Mem:* Print Club, Philadelphia. *Media:* Acrylic, Etching. *Dealer:* Union St Gallery 1909 Union St San Francisco CA 94123. *Mailing Add:* 33 Howard St New York NY 10013

DICKERSON, BRIAN S
PAINTER
b Middleburgh, NY, May 3, 51. *Study:* Private study with Charles Jahnke, 69-73; Pa Acad Fine Arts, 71-72. *Exhib:* One-man show, Del Co Community Col, Marple, Pa, 80; Nat Acad Design, New York, 80; Woodmere Gallery, Philadelphia, 80 & 81; Butler Mus Am Art, Youngstown, Ohio, 81; Hahn Gallery, Philadelphia, 82; Inst Man & Science, Rensselaerville, NY, 83; and others. *Pos:* Artist, Inst Man & Science, Rensselaerville, NY. *Awards:* First Prize, Woodmere Gallery; Medal of Merit, Nat Soc Painters Casein & Acrylic, 80. *Media:* Oil, Pastel. *Mailing Add:* 517 Burnham Rd Philadelphia PA 19119

DICKERSON, DANIEL JAY
PAINTER, EDUCATOR

b Jersey City, NJ, Dec 22, 22. *Study:* Cooper Union Art Sch, 41-43 & 45-46; Cranbrook Acad Art, BFA, 47, MFA, 49. *Work:* Joseph H Hirshhorn Collection; Adelphi Univ Mus; Ill Wesleyan Mus; Corcoran Gallery; Weatherspoon Gallery, Univ NC. *Exhib:* Whitney Mus Am Art Ann, 47; Pa Acad Fine Arts, 53; Audubon Artists Exhib, 64; Nat Inst Arts & Lett, 68; Nat Acad Design, 74; and others. *Teaching:* Lectr art, Manhattanville Col, 65-69; chmn dept art, Finch Col, 69-78; instr, Art Sudents League, 78-83. *Awards:* First Prize, Springfield Art Mus, 54; Emily Lowe Award for Painting, Audubon Artists, 64; Henry Ward Ranger Purchase Award, Nat Acad Design, 74; and others. *Media:* Acrylic, Oil. *Mailing Add:* 104 High St Leonia NJ 07605

DICKERSON, EDWARD TED
PAINTER, PRINTMAKER

b South Haven, Mich, June 10, 32. *Study:* Western Mich Univ, Kalamazoo, BS(art), 54; Univ Wis, Madison, MS(painting & printmaking), 57. *Work:* Smithsonian Inst, Washington, DC; Philadelphia Mus Art; St Louis Art Mus, Mo; Kalamazoo Inst Art, Mich. *Exhib:* Pa Acad Art, Philadelphia, 57; Contemporary American Prints, Libr Cong & US Info Agency, European tour, 57; Soc Washington Printmakers Nat Exhib, Smithsonian Inst, Washington, DC, 57 & 64; Atkins Mus Fine Art, Kansas City, Mo, 58; Univ Kans Mus Art, Lawrence, 58; Philadelphia Print Club, 62; Art Inst Chicago, 63 & 67; Butler Inst Am Art, Youngstown, Ohio, 64. *Pos:* Inventor, Dickerson Combination Press. *Teaching:* Instr painting, Univ Wis, Madison, 58-60; asst prof, Wis State Univ, Whitewater, 60-62; asst prof, Sch Art Inst Chicago, 63-65. *Awards:* 1st Prize, Philadelphia Print Club Nat Exhib, 56; Pennel Fund Purchase Award, Washington Printmakers Soc Nat Exhib, 57; Jenkins Mem Award, 70th Exhib Art Inst Chicago, 62. *Mem:* South Haven Community Art Orgn. *Media:* Oil, Watercolor; Woodblock, Lithography. *Mailing Add:* 28 Lake Shore Dr South Haven MI 49090

DICKERSON, WILLIAM J
DEALER

b Lexington, Ky, July 7, 43. *Pos:* Pres, O'Brien's Art Emporium, 78- *Specialty:* Contemporary-traditional American art. *Mailing Add:* 7122 Stetson Dr Scottsdale AZ 85251

DICKEY, HELEN PAULINE
PAINTER

b Cleveland, Ohio. *Study:* Mus Sch, Toledo Univ; Western Reserve Univ; Tampa Univ, with Harold Nosti; Cleveland Sch Art, with Carl Gaertner. *Work:* Fla Presby Col, St Petersburg; Merritt-Phinney-Southard, Cleveland; Fla Power Co, St Petersburg; Clearwater Fed, Fla; Raymond-James Investment Co; plus others. *Exhib:* Hunter Ann, Chattanooga, Tenn, 67; 22nd Southeastern Ann Exhib, High Mus, Atlanta, Ga, 67; one-person show, Weir Gallery, Vero Beach, Fla, 78; Fla Artist Group Exhib, Jacksonville Art Mus, 81; two-person shows, Scarborough Fair & Clearwater; and others. *Pos:* Dir Art Gallery, Main Pub Libr, St Petersburg, 68-78; dir, Arts Ctr Gallery, St Petersburg, 71-73. *Teaching:* Instr, Studio Four, 64-69; instr, Arts Ctr, St Petersburg, 71-72 & 75; instr, Art Club St Petersburg, 72; instr painting, Adult Educ Prog, St Petersburg Jr Col, 79-81. *Awards:* Many state awards, 62- *Bibliog:* Mariane Kelsey (auth), Artist says, I paint for myself, 67; Charles Benbow (auth), reviews, In: St Petersburg Times, 67-; Jeanette Crane (auth), interview, 74 & rev, 75, In: Times Independent, St Petersburg. *Mem:* Fla Artist Group; Fla League Arts; Arts Ctr Asn St Petersburg (vpres, 71-72); Fine Arts Mus. *Media:* Polymers, Oil. *Publ:* Contribr & illusr, A brighter dawn awaits the human day, Churchman Mag, 12/68. *Mailing Add:* 1723 Lakewood Dr S St Petersburg FL 33712

DICKINSON, DAVID CHARLES
PRINTMAKER, INSTRUCTOR

b Hendon, Middlesex, Eng, Jan 3, 40. *Study:* Chelsea Sch Art, London, 56-61; Statens-Kunst-og-Handverks Industrie Skoolen, Oslo, Norway, 61-62; Rochester Inst Technol, MFA, 72. *Work:* Southampton Civic Ctr, Eng; Mem Art Gallery, Rochester, NY; Sheldon Mem Art Gallery, Lincoln, Nebr; Kansas City Art Gallery. *Comn:* Portfolio of Prints, Cold Cream Alley, Rochester, 73; EGR Commun, Rochester, 73 & 74. *Exhib:* Espinale International, France, 75 & 77; two-man shows, Univ Mo, Columbus, 76 & Shoe String Gallery, Rochester, 79; Printmaker's Invitational, Rochester Inst Technol, NY, 78; Southern Univ NY, Geneseo, 82; and others. *Pos:* Mem Art Gallery visiting artist in NY high schs, 73-75. *Teaching:* Asst prof printmaking & drawing & chmn fine arts dept, Rochester Inst Technol, 72- *Awards:* Best in Show, Big Bend Nat Exhib, 68; Purchase Award, Comn Arts, Atlanta, 71; Purchase Award, Finger Lakes Regional Exhib, 73. *Mem:* Rochester Printmakers. *Media:* Intaglio, Non-Silver Photographic Processes. *Dealer:* Shoestring Gallery 2180 Monroe Ave Rochester NY 14618. *Mailing Add:* 6825 Rte 408 Mt Morris NY 14510

DICKINSON, ELEANOR CREEKMORE
PAINTER, VIDEO ARTIST

b Knoxville, Tenn, Feb 7, 31. *Study:* Univ Tenn, with C Kermit Ewing, BA, 52; San Francisco Art Inst, with James Weeks, 61-63; Calif Col Arts & Crafts, MFA, 82. *Work:* Libr Cong, Nat Collection Fine Arts, Corcoran Gallery Art, Washington, DC; San Francisco Mus Art; and others. *Exhib:* One-artist shows, San Francisco Mus Mod Art, 65, Fine Arts Mus, San Francisco, 68 & 75, Corcoran Gallery Art, 72, Poindexter Gallery, New York, 72- 74, J B Speed Art Mus, Louisville, Ky, 72, Wash State Mus, 75, Cheney Cowles Mus, Spokane, Wash, 75, Smithsonian Inst Travelling Exhib, 75-81 & Oakland Mus, 79; Tenn State Mus, 81-82; and others. *Pos:* Trustee, San Francisco Art Inst, 63-66; dir galleries, Calif Col Arts & Crafts, Oakland, 71-; cur, Tenn State Mus, 80-82. *Teaching:* Vis lectr drawing & painting, Univ Calif, 69-71; assoc prof life drawing & gallery mgt, Calif Col Arts & Crafts, Oakland, 71- *Awards:* San Francisco Women Artists Pres Prize, San Francisco Mus, 59; Purchase Award, Butler Inst Am Art, 60; Graphics Prize, City of San Francisco, 74; and others. *Bibliog:* Aline Saarinen (dir), Revival!, NBC Today Show, 70; James R Mellow (auth), Eleanor Dickinson, New York Times, 72; Walter Hopps (auth), Introduction to Revival!, Harper, 74; and others. *Mem:* Artists Equity Asn Northern Calif; Women's Caucus Art; Col Art Asn; Coalition Women's Art Orgns. *Media:* Mixed; Video Tapes. *Publ:* Auth, Tennessee revival services, Libr Cong Arch Folk Song, 71; illusr, Complete Fruit Cookbook, Scribner, 72; auth, Revival!, 74; auth, That Old Time Religion, 75, Harper; and others. *Dealer:* Poindexter Gallery 1160 Fifth Ave New York NY 10029; William Sawyer Gallery 3045 Clay St San Francisco CA 94115. *Mailing Add:* 2125 Broderick St San Francisco CA 94115

DICKINSON, WILLIAM STIRLING
LECTURER, ADMINISTRATOR

b Chicago, Ill, Dec 22, 09. *Study:* Princeton Univ, BA(cum laude); Art Inst Chicago; Fontainebleau Ecole des Beaux Arts, France. *Pos:* Dir, Univ Sch Fine Arts, San Miguel de Allende, 38-51; pres, Inst Allende, 51-, dir libr, 51- *Teaching:* Lectr, Inst Allende, San Miguel de Allende, Mex, 45- *Publ:* Coauth & illusr, Mexican odyssey, 35; coauth & illusr, Westward from Rio, 36; coauth & illusr, Death is Accidental, 37; coauth, San Miquel de Allende, 71; translr, Imperial Cuzco, 71. *Mailing Add:* Inst San Miguel de Allende Guanajuato Mexico

DICKSON, JENNIFER JOAN
PHOTOGRAPHER, PRINTMAKER

b Piet Retief, Repub SAfrica, Sept 17, 36; Can citizen. *Study:* Goldsmith's Col Sch Art, Univ London, 54-59; Atelier 17, Paris, with S W Hayter, 60-65. *Work:* Victoria & Albert Mus, London; Nat Gallery Can, Ottawa; Metrop Mus Art, New York; Montreal Mus Fine Arts; Smithsonian Inst; and many others. *Comn:* The Secret Garden (collabr: Henry J Kahanek & Ray Van Dusen), 76 & Paradise, 80, Nat Film Bd Can. *Exhib:* Salon des Realites Nouvelles, Musee d'Art Moderne, Paris, 62 & 66; Biennale de Paris, Mus Mod Art, Paris, 63; Modern Prints, 65 & Contemporary Prints, 68, Victoria & Albert Mus, London; Salon Internationale de la Gravure, Montreal Mus Fine Arts, 71; Folio Seventy Three Traveling Exhib, San Francisco Mus Art, 74; Forum 76, Montreal Mus Fine Arts, 76; Celebration of the Body, Agnes Etherington Art Centre, Queen's Univ, Ont; Tendances Actuelles au Quebec, 79 & L'estampe au Quebec 1970-1980, 80, Musee d'Art Contemporain, Montreal; 14th Int Biennial of Graphic Art, Ljubljana, Yugoslavia, 81; solo exhibs, Il Tempo Classica, Saidye Bronfman Centre, Montreal, 82, A Journey to Cythere, Wallack Art Ed, Ottawa, 82, Jennifer Dickson: A Continuum, Edward Monaghan Art Consult, Ottawa, 83 & Versailles: Through the Crystal Wall, Wallack Galleries, Ottawa, 83. *Collections Arranged:* Imprint 76 (current Can graphic art), Ont Arts Coun. *Teaching:* Vis prof fine arts, Univ Wis, Madison, 72; vis artist fine arts, Queen's Univ, Kingston, Ont, 77-78; instr dept visual arts, Univ Ottawa, currently. *Awards:* James A Reid Award, Can Painters-Etchers & Engravers, 73; Special Purchase Award, World Print Competition, San Francisco Mus Art, 73; Prize, 5th Norwegian Int Print Biennale, 80; and others. *Bibliog:* Michael Rothstein (auth), Frontiers of Printmaking, Studio Vista, 70; Anthony Gross (auth), Etching, Engraving & Intaglio Printing, Oxford Univ Press, 72; Edward-Lucie Smith (auth), Art in Seventies, Phaidon/Cornell Univ Press, 80; and others. *Mem:* Academician Royal Acad Arts; Print & Drawing Coun Can; Can Artists Representation; academician Royal Can Acad Arts; fel Royal Soc Painter-Etchers & Engravers. *Media:* Etching. *Dealer:* Wallack Galleries 203 Bank St Ottawa ON K2P 1W7 Can. *Mailing Add:* 508 Gilmour St Ottawa ON K1R 5Z4 Canada

DIEBENKORN, RICHARD
PAINTER

b Portland, Ore, Apr 22, 22. *Study:* Stanford Univ, 40-43; Univ Calif, 43-44; Calif Sch Fine Arts, 46; Univ NMex, MA, 52. *Work:* Toronto Mus; Corcoran Gallery Art, Washington, DC; Albright-Knox Gallery, Buffalo; Metrop Mus Art, New York; San Francisco Mus Art; and many others. *Exhib:* Five shows, Whitney Mus Am Art Ann, 55-70; one-man shows, DeYoung Mem Mus, San Francisco, 63, Jewish Mus, 65 & Los Angeles Co Mus, Los Angeles, 69 & 72; Venice Biennale, 68; 20th Nat Print Exhib, 77; and many other group & one-man shows. *Teaching:* Prof art, Univ Calif, Los Angeles, 66-73. *Awards:* Purchase Prize, Olivet Col; Gold Medal, Pa Acad Fine Arts, 68; Skowhegan Medal Painting, Skowhegan Sch Art, 79. *Bibliog:* David M Mendelowitz (auth), A History of American Art, Holt, 61; Lee Nordness (ed), Art: USA, C J Bucher, 62; Alfred Neumeyer (auth), The Search for Meaning in Modern Art, Prentice-Hall, 64; and others. *Mem:* Am Acad Arts & Lett. *Publ:* Auth, Drawing, 65. *Mailing Add:* c/o M Knoedler & Co Inc 19 East 70th St New York NY 10021

DIEHL, GUY LOUIS
INSTRUCTOR, PAINTER

b Pittsburgh, Pa, Feb 1, 49. *Study:* Calif State Univ, Hayward, BA, 73; San Francisco State Univ, MA, 76. *Work:* City Hall Bldg, Oakland, Calif. *Exhib:* One-man shows, Hank Baum Gallery, San Francisco, Calif, 79 & 80, Shasta Col, Redding, Calif, 79 & Shepard Art Gallery, Univ Reno, Nev, 80; Works on Paper, Univ Purdue, Lafayette, Ind, 79; Spokane Falls Col, Wash, 81. *Teaching:* Instr painting, Diablo Valley Col, Pleasant Hill, Calif, 79; instr painting, Chabot Col, Livermore, Calif, 80. *Awards:* Purchase Award, Alameda Co Art Commission, 72. *Bibliog:* Thomas Albright (auth), A photorealist paradox, 3/10/79 & Landscapes that dazzle the eye, 11/29/80, San Francisco Chronicle; Andree Marechal (auth), Suspenseful suburbia, Artweek, 12/13/80. *Media:* Acrylic, Watercolor. *Mailing Add:* c/o Hank Baum Gallery 2140 Bush St San Francisco CA 94115

DIEHL, SEVILLA S
PAINTER
b Philadelphia, Pa, May 15, 17. *Study:* Fleisher Art Mem, Philadelphia, 35-37; Philadelphia Mus Sch, 66-67; Barnes Found, 66-68; pvt studies with Hobson Pitman, Chinese brush painting with Pheobe Shih, mixed media with Ithzak Sankowsky & watercolor with Edgar Whitney. *Work:* Thomas Jefferson Univ; Widener Col; RCA Radio Corp, Washington, DC. *Exhib:* Woodmere Art Gallery 31st Ann Exhib, Chestnut Hill, Pa, 71; Catharine Lorillard Wolfe Art Club 66th Ann Show, Gramercy Sq, New York, 72; Nat Soc Painters in Casein & Acrylic 18th Ann, 72; three-woman show, 73 & Regional Oil & Acrylic Show, 75, Philadelphia Art Alliance; and numerous others. *Awards:* Shiva Artists Colors Award, Catharine Lorillard Wolfe Art Club, New York, 72; Best of Show, 74 & Jury Selection Award, 74, Maine Line Ctr Arts, Haverford. *Bibliog:* Marion Guthrie (auth), article, Montgomery Post, Norristown, Pa, 6/10/70; Dorothy Grafly (auth), articles, Philadelphia Sunday Bulletin, 8/2/70 & Art-in-Focus, Philadelphia, 1/75. *Mem:* Artists Equity, Philadelphia Chap; Philadelphia Art Alliance; Philadelphia Watercolor Club. *Media:* Mixed. *Mailing Add:* c/o The Gallery 21st on Central Ave Barnegat Light NJ 08006

DIENES, SARI
ASSEMBLAGE ARTIST, PRINTMAKER
b Debrecen, Hungary, Oct 8, 1898; US citizen. *Study:* With Fernand Leger, Amadee Ozenfant & Andre Lhote, 30-34. *Work:* Albright-Knox Mus; Mus Mod Art, New York; Brooklyn Mus. *Comn:* Mural, Albany State Legislature. *Exhib:* Art of Assemblage, Mus Mod Art, 50s; Year of the Women, Bronx Mus, 75; solo exhibs, Betty Parsons Gallery, 50-59, Donnell Libr, New York, 81, AIR Gallery, New York, 82 & 83 & Hopper House, Nyack, NY, 83; Ha Ha Ha: For the Fun of It, Thorpe Intermedia, Spark Hill, NY, 83. *Pos:* Dir, Amadee Ozenfant Sch, London, 35-39. *Teaching:* Instr, Brooklyn Mus Sch & Parsons Sch Design, formerly. *Awards:* Gold Medal, Accad Ital Arti Lavoro, 79; Gottlieb Found Grant, 80; Nat Endowment Arts Grant, 80 & 82. *Bibliog:* Elenor Munro (auth), Originals: American Woman Artists, 79; Like any other masterpiece ..., People Mag, 80; Bill Moyers (auth), Creativity & Garbage, PBS & Smithsonian Mag, 82. *Mem:* Womens Caucus Art; Women in the Arts. *Media:* Assemblage; Mixed Media. *Dealer:* AIR Gallery 63 Crosby St New York NY 10012. *Mailing Add:* RR 1 Box 405 Stony Point NY 10980

DIETRICH, BRUCE LEINBACH
MUSEUM DIRECTOR, ADMINISTRATOR
b Reading, Pa, Oct 10, 37. *Study:* Kutztown State Col, BS, 60; State Univ NY, MS, 69. *Collections Arranged:* The Sea, 76, Winter Winds, 78, Master Prints, 78, Spectrum, 78 & Director's Choice, 83, Reading Pub Mus & Art Gallery. *Pos:* Dir, Reading Planetarium, 69-; dir, Reading Pub Mus & Art Gallery, 76-. *Mailing Add:* 500 Museum Rd Reading PA 19611

DIETZ, GARY ALLAN J
DEALER
b Bridgeport, Conn, Aug 27, 44. *Study:* Emerson Col, BS, 66; Fairfield Univ, MA, 68. *Pos:* Art dealer, Wilton Gallery, currently. *Teaching:* Instr theatre/speech, Bridgeport Univ, 67-68; assoc prof theatre/speech, NY Univ, 68-72. *Specialty:* Nationally prominent, contemporary representational artists. *Mailing Add:* Wilton Gallery Inc Old Ridgefield Rd Wilton CT 06897

DI FATE, VINCENT
ILLUSTRATOR, PAINTER
b Yonkers, NY, Nov 21, 45. *Study:* Phoenix Sch Design, cert, 67; Sch Visual Arts, 68; Art Students League, 68-70. *Work:* NASA Mus, Smithsonian Inst, Washington, DC. *Exhib:* Solo shows, Reading Pub Mus, Pa, 78 & Mus Sci & Natural Hist, St Louis, Mo, 82; New Brit Mus Am Art, Conn, 80; Bronx Mus Arts, NY, 80; Stadthalle Limburg, WGer, 80. *Teaching:* Instr, Univ Bridgeport, Conn, 79. *Awards:* Hugo Award, World Sci Fiction Asn, 78; Frank R Paul Award, Nashville Sci Fiction Asn, 78. *Bibliog:* George Magnan (auth), Science Fiction Art, Today's Art & Graphics, 3/81; Ellen Datlow (auth), Stellar Technician, Omni Mag, 5/81; Brian M Fraser (auth), All the colors of space and time, Questar Mag, 10/81. *Mem:* Soc Illus; Graphic Artists Guild; Asn Sci Fiction/Fantasy Artists (pres, 80). *Media:* Acrylic, Oil. *Publ:* Co-auth & illusr, Di Fate's Catalog of Science Fiction Hardware, Workman Publ, 80; contribr, The Science Fiction Reference Book, Starmont House, 81. *Mailing Add:* 12 Ritter Dr Wappingers Falls NY 12590

DIFRANZA, AMERICO M
PAINTER
b Boston, Mass, Feb 24, 19. *Study:* Mass Col Art, BFA, 42; Art Students League NY & Nat Acad Design, 73-78. *Exhib:* Pastel Soc Am Ann, Nat Arts Club, New York, 76-83; Hudson Valley Art Asn, Co Ctr, White Plains, NY, 76-83; Salmagundi Ann Open, New York, 78-80; Audubon Artist Ann, Nat Acad, New York, 78-80; Berkshire Art Asn Ann, Berkshire Mus, Pittsfield, Mass, 79 & 80; New Eng Art Exhib, Silvermine Guild Ctr, Conn, 80 & 81; Ann Invitational Exhib, Katonah Gallery, NY, 82 & 83. *Awards:* Stefan Hirsch Mem Award for Portraiture, Audubon Artists Ann, 77; Bachman Award for seascape, Pastel Soc Am Ann, 80; VanderVoort Award for Oil Portraiture, Hudson Valley Art Asn Ann, 81. *Bibliog:* Ron Lister (auth), Drawing with Pastels, Prentice-Hall, 80. *Mem:* Art Students League NY (bd control, 78-79, vpres, 80-81, pres & chmn bd, 81-83); Pastel Soc Am; Artists Fel Inc, NY. *Media:* Pastels, Oils. *Dealer:* North Salem Gallery Ltd Route 116 North Salem NY 10560. *Mailing Add:* 10 Tanglewild Rd Chappaqua NY 10514

DIGIORGIO, JOSEPH J
PAINTER
b Brooklyn, NY, Jan 1, 31. *Study:* Cooper Union, BFA, 58. *Work:* 3-D Int, Houston; Bank of Calif, San Francisco; Security Pac Bank, Los Angeles; Western Elec, NJ; Shell Oil Co, Houston. *Comn:* Cherry Blossoms (oil), AT&T, Basking Ridge, NJ; Sierra Nev Mountains, comn by Victor Shaio, New York; Calif Coastline, Blue Cross of Calif, Los Angeles; After the Storm, comn by Victor Nevhaus, Houston. *Exhib:* US/Japan Exchange, US State Dept, Tokyo, 63; Biennial Exhib, Whitney Mus Am Art, 75; Large Scale Paintings, Security Pac Nat Bank, Los Angeles, 76; A Cur Collects, Art Inst Chicago, 77; 6 Sensibilities', Cornell Univ, Ithaca, NY, 78; A M Sachs, 80 & 81; Minn Art Mus, St Paul; and others. *Teaching:* Instr drawing, New York Univ, 80. *Bibliog:* John Russell (auth), Whitney finds this land is its land, New York Times, 75; John Gruen (auth), Michael Walls exhibit, Soho Weekly News, 75; Tram Combs (auth), Arts Mag, 81. *Mem:* Artists Equity of NY. *Media:* Oil, Watercolor. *Mailing Add:* 269 Bowery New York NY 10002

DIGIUSTO, GERALD N
SCULPTOR
b New York, NY, June 30, 29. *Study:* Mass Col Art, 49-50; Boston Mus Sch, dipl, 57; Yale Univ Sch of Art, BFA, 58; Univ Florence, Italy, 58-60. *Work:* Munson-Williams-Procter Inst Mus, Utica, NY; Schenectady Mus, NY; State Univ NY Collection, Albany; Everson Mus, Syracuse, NY. *Comn:* Bronze screen, Honors Col, Univ Ore, Eugene, 62; Great Am Eagle, Everson Mus, Syracuse, NY, 69; laminated wood sculpture, Marine Midland Computer Ctr, Syracuse, NY, 69; wood relief, State Off Bldg, Watertown, NY, 71-72; steel relief, Pub Sch 116, Bronx, NY, 74. *Exhib:* Inst Contemp Art, Boston, Mass, 57; Seattle Art Mus, Wash, 60; San Francisco Mus Art, 61; Carpenter Ctr, Harvard Univ, Cambridge, Mass, 74; Mus Fine Arts, Boston, Mass, 77; DeCordova Mus, Lincoln, Mass, 77; one-man exhibs, Munson, Williams, Proctor Inst Mus, 66 & State Univ NY Albany, 75; Stockton State Col, New York, 81; and others. *Teaching:* Asst prof, Univ Ore, 60-62; assoc prof sculpture & drawing, Syracuse Univ, 62-66; prof sculpture & drawing, State Univ NY Cortland, 66- *Awards:* Mrs David Hunt Scholar for study abroad, Boston Mus Sch, Mass, 58-60; State Univ NY Res Award, 77. *Media:* Steel. *Mailing Add:* 10 Hill St Cortland NY 13045

DIGNAC, GENY (EUGENIA M BERMUDEZ)
SCULPTOR, ENVIRONMENTAL ARTIST
b Buenos Aires, Arg, June 8, 32; US citizen. *Work:* Mus Mod Art, Cali, Colombia; Galeria Banco Cent, Quito, Ecuador; Latin Am Art Found, San Juan, PR. *Exhib:* Some More Beginnings, Exp in Art & Technol, Brooklyn Mus, NY, 68; IX Festival of Art, Cali, Colombia, 69; Earth, Air, Fire, Water, Elements of Art, Boston Mus Fine Arts, 71; Arte de Sistema, Centro de Arte y Communicacion, Mus Mod Art, Buenos Aires, 71; III Biennial of Art Coltejer, Medellin, Colombia, 72; many one-woman shows, 67-71 & produced 19 fire gestures, US, Europe & SAm, 70-80. *Awards:* Uranus II (light & plastic sculpture), IX Festival of Art, Mus Mod Art, Cali, 69. *Bibliog:* J Bermudez (producer), Dignac, 67-68 & Three fire gestures (films), 70-71; R Osuna (producer), D Dig Dignac (film), 68; Salt River Fire Gesture, KAET (PBS), Tempe, Ariz, 80. *Media:* Light, Plastics; Fire, Temperatures. *Publ:* Auth, Three Fire Gestures, 70. *Dealer:* Osuna Gallery 406 7th St NW Washington DC 20037. *Mailing Add:* 4109 E Via Estrella Phoenix AZ 85028

DIKE, PHILIP LATIMER
PAINTER
b Redlands, Calif, Apr 6, 06. *Study:* Chouinard Art Inst; Art Students League; Am Acad, Fontainebleau, France; also with Clarence Hinkle, F Tolles Chamberlin, George Luks & M St Hubert. *Work:* Hearne Collection, Metrop Mus Art, New York; Butler Inst Am Art, Youngstown, Ohio; Pennell Collection, Libr Cong, Washington, DC; Springfield Mus; Phoenix Art Mus. *Comn:* Painted altar piece, First ME Church, Redlands, Calif, 46; ceramic tile, Gladding McBean, Los Angeles, 51; ceramic tile entrance, San Antonio Col Fine Arts Ctr, 52; ceramic tile pool area, Scripps Col, 52; mosaic, chapel, Claremont Community Congregational Church, 62. *Exhib:* Calif Watercolor Soc Nat, 26-71; Am Watercolor Soc, New York, 29-72; one-man & juried exhibs, Los Angeles Co Mus, Los Angeles, 31-55; Carnegie Inst Int, Pittsburgh, Pa, 36-58; Nat Acad Design Exhib, 51; solo exhib, Calif Palace Legion Hon, San Francisco. *Pos:* Color coordr, Walt Disney Prod, 34-44. *Teaching:* Instr painting, Chouinard Art Inst, 30-49; prof painting, Scripps Col & Claremont Grad Sch, 49-69, emer prof painting, 70- *Awards:* First Prize Oil, Los Angeles Co Mus, 31; First Prize Watercolor, Butler Inst Am Art, 59; Purchase Prizes, Nat Watercolor Exhibs, Springfield, 67-72. *Mem:* Nat Acad Design; Am Watercolor Soc (hon vpres, 57); Nat Watercolor Soc (Calif pres, 38-39); West Coast Watercolor Soc (hon vpres), 64). *Media:* Watercolor, Oil. *Publ:* Auth, Watercolors, Am Artist Mag, 11/40 & 9/12/79. *Dealer:* Richard Challis Gallery 1390 S Coast Hwy Laguna Beach CA 92652. *Mailing Add:* 2272 N Forbes Ave Claremont CA 91711

DILL, GUY GIRARD
SCULPTOR
b Duval Co, Fla, May 30, 46. *Study:* Chouinard Sch Art, Los Angeles, BFA. *Work:* Guggenheim Mus, Mus Mod Art, Whitney Mus Am Art, New York; Calif State Univ, Long Beach; Long Beach Mus Art, Calif. *Comn:* Prudential Ins Co, Canoga Park, Calif, 77; and many pvt comns. *Exhib:* Guggenheim Mus, 71; Ace Gallery, Los Angeles, 71, 73 & 77; Felicity Samuel Gallery, London, Eng, 72; Pace Gallery, New York, 74 & 76; Biennial Show, Whitney Mus Am Art, 74; Sculpture Made in Place, Walker Art Ctr, Minneapolis, Minn, 76; Arco Ctr Visual Arts, Los Angeles, Calif, 77; and others. *Teaching:* Instr, Univ Calif, Los Angeles, 77-82. *Awards:* Theodoron Award, Guggenheim Mus, 71; Nat Endowment Arts Fel, 74; First Prize, Am Show, Chicago Inst Art, 74. *Bibliog:* Bill Packer (auth), Interview with Guy Dill, Art & Artists, London, 72. *Media:* Mixed. *Dealer:* Flo Ace Gallery Los Angeles CA. *Mailing Add:* 819 Milwood Ave Venice CA 90291

DILL, LADDIE JOHN
PAINTER, SCULPTOR
b Long Beach, Calif, Sept 14, 43. *Study:* Chouinard Art Inst, BFA, 68. *Work:* Norton Simon Mus, Pasadena, Calif; San Francisco Mus Mod Art, Calif; Smithsonian Inst, Washington, DC; Oakland Mus Art, Calif; Chicago Art Inst. *Exhib:* One-man shows, Pasadena Mus Mod Art, Calif, 71, Portland Univ Gallery, Ore, 71, Sonnabend Gallery, New York, 72, Calif Inst Technol, 82, Laica, 82 & Charles Cowles, 83; Recent Acquisitions, Pasadena Mus Mod Art, 71; 15 Abstract Artists, Santa Barbara Mus Art, Calif, 74; The Mod Era, San Francisco Mus Mod Art, 76 & Smithsonian Inst, Washington, DC, 77; Calif Painting & Sculpture, San Francisco Mus Mod Art, 77; Painting of the 70's, Albright-Knox Gallery, Buffalo, 78-79; Corcoran Biennial, 83-84. *Teaching:* Lectr painting, Univ Calif, Los Angeles, 75- *Awards:* Nat Endowment Arts Grant, 75 & 82; Guggenheim Fel, 80. *Bibliog:* Robert Hughes (auth), Los Angeles, Time Mag, 71; Judy Goodman (auth), Laddie Dill new work, Arts Mag, 75; Michael Smith (auth), Laddie John Dill, Baxter Art Gallery, Calif Inst Technol, Pasadena, 78. *Media:* Cement, Polymer, Glass; Oil on Canvas. *Dealer:* James Corcoran Gallery 8221 Santa Monica Blvd Los Angeles CA 90046; Charles Cowles 420 W Broadway New York NY 10025. *Mailing Add:* 9 Wavecrest Ave Venice CA 90291

DILLINGHAM, DOROTHY HOYT See Hoyt, Dorothy

DILLINGHAM, RICK (JAMES RICHARD), II
CERAMIST, DEALER
b Lake Forest, Ill, Nov 13, 52. *Study:* Calif Col Arts & Crafts, 1 yr; Univ NMex, BFA; Scripps Col, MFA. *Work:* Sheldon Mem Art Mus, Lincoln, Nebr; Scripps Cols Art Collection, Claremont, Calif; Univ Art Collections, Ariz State Univ, Tempe; Utah Mus Fine Arts, Salt Lake City; Mus Albuquerque. *Exhib:* David Stuart Gallery, Los Angeles, Calif, 76; Marietta Col Crafts Nat, Ohio, 77; Clarke-Benton Gallery, Santa Fe, NMex, 79, 80; Hadler-Rodriquez Gallery, New York, 81; Sheldon Mem Art Mus, Lincoln, Nebr, 81; and others. *Collections Arranged:* Pueblo Pottery & Demonstration, Dewey-Kofron Gallery, Santa Fe, NMex, 77; Seven Families in Pueblo Pottery (auth, catalogue), Maxwell Mus Anthrop, Univ NMex, 74; The Vessel, 12 Contemp Ceramic Artists, Delahunty Gallery, Dallas, Tex, 80. *Teaching:* Asst prof ceramics, Calif Col Arts & Crafts, 76, 79; ceramics workshop, Tucson Mus Art, Ariz, 76; plus numerous other national workshops and lectures. *Awards:* Best of Show & Purchase Award, Craft 5, Mus Albuquerque, 75; Purchase Award, Pottery 5, Calif Polytech State Univ, San Luis Obispo, 75. *Bibliog:* Hal Riegger (auth), Primitive Pottery, Van Nostrand Reinhold, 72; Susan Weghsler (auth), Low fire ceramics, Am Craft Mag, 11/81. *Mem:* Am Crafts Coun. *Media:* Ceramics. *Specialty:* American Indian art. *Collection:* American Indian art, contemporary ceramics and lithography. *Publ:* Nine Pueblo potters, Studio Potter, 77; auth, The Pottery of Acoma Pueblo, Am Indian Art, 77. *Dealer:* Hadler-Rodriquez Gallery 38 E 57th New York NY 10021 & 20 Pinedale Houston TX 76006; Clarke-Benton Gallery 149 E Alameda Santa Fe NM 87501. *Mailing Add:* Box 2601 Santa Fe NM 87501

DILLON, C DOUGLAS
ADMINISTRATOR, COLLECTOR
b Geneva, Switz, Aug 21, 09. *Study:* Harvard Univ, AB. *Pos:* Trustee, Metrop Mus Art, 51-, pres, 70-78, chmn, 78-83; mem bd, Nat Mus Servs, 78-83, chmn, 82-83; mem bd, Nat Counc Arts, 83- *Collection:* French impressionist painting; 18th century French furniture and decorative objects; Chinese paintings. *Mailing Add:* 767 Fifth Ave New York NY 10022

DILLON, MILDRED (MURPHY)
PRINTMAKER
b Philadelphia, Pa, Oct 12, 07. *Study:* Philadelphia Col Art, 25-28; Pa Acad Fine Arts, 28-29; Barnes Found, with Henry McCarter & Earle Horter, 29-31. *Work:* Philadelphia Mus Art; Barnes Found, Merion, Pa; Free Libr Philadelphia; Arch Can Painters & Etchers; Am Colorprint Soc Collection, Philadelphia. *Exhib:* Libr Cong Nat, 57; Contemp Graphics Overseas, Mus Bellas Artes, Caracas, Venezuela, 60; Color Prints of the Americas, NJ State Mus, 70; one-man show, Philadelphia Art Alliance, 75, & Woodmere Art Gallery, 82; and others. *Pos:* Vpres, Am Color Print Soc, Philadelphia, 55-; chmn, Rittenhouse Sq Outdoor Exhib, 58-70; demonstr, Print Club Philadelphia, 61-70. *Awards:* Harrison Morris Prize, Pa Acad Fine Arts, 53; George Lear Mem Prize, Woodmere Art Gallery, 58; Klein Prize, Print Club Philadelphia, 67. *Mem:* Philadelphia Art Alliance (mem bd dirs, 60-73); Pa Acad Fine Arts; Alumnae Philadelphia Col Art. *Media:* Serigraphy, Woodcut. *Mailing Add:* 7720-C Stenton Ave Philadelphia PA 19118

DILLON, PAUL SANFORD
PAINTER
b Newport, Vt, Aug 5, 43. *Work:* Los Angeles Co Mus Art, Los Angeles, Calif; La Jolla Mus Art, Calif; Cheney Cowles Mus, Spokane, Wash; Security Pac Bank Collection, Los Angeles; Prudential Insurance Co Collection, Los Angeles. *Exhib:* Los Angeles Six, Los Angeles Co Mus Art, 74; Biennial of Am Painting, Whitney Mus Am Art, New York, 75 & Corcoran Gallery Art, Washington, DC, 77; Los Angeles Painting, Mus Mod Art, New York, 77; Collector's Choice, Los Angeles Inst Contemp Art, 77; San Francisco Mus Mod Art; one-man shows, Jack Glenn Gallery, Newport Beach, Calif, 75, Tortue Gallery, Los Angeles, 77 & 78, Iolas Gallery, New York, 78 & 79 & Newport Harbor Art Mus, 79. *Awards:* New Talent Award, Los Angeles Co Mus Art, 74; Purchase Award, Contemporary Painting, Cheney Cowles Mus, 77. *Media:* Acrylic, Collage. *Dealer:* Iolas Gallery 52 East 57th St New York NY 10022; Asher/Faure Gallery 8221 Santa Monica Blvd Los Angeles CA 90021. *Mailing Add:* 3660 W Pico Blvd Los Angeles CA 90019

DILLOW, NANCY E (NANCY ELIZABETH ROBERTSON)
ADMINISTRATOR, HISTORIAN
b Toronto, Ont, June 26, 28. *Study:* Univ Toronto, BA. *Collections Arranged:* J E H MacDonald, R C A, 1873-1932 (catalog), 65; Piet Mondrian and the Hague Sch of Landscape Painting (catalog), 69; Saskatchewan: Art and Artists (catalog), 71; Nugent-Godwin (catalog), 72; Marilyn Levine-Donovan Chester (catalog), 74; Frank Nulf (catalog), 76; Sheila Butler Recent Works (catalog), 80. *Pos:* From asst cur to cur exten & educ, Art Gallery Ont, 56-67; dir, Norman Mackenzie Art Gallery, 67-79; chief cur, Winnipeg Art Gallery, 80- *Teaching:* Prof hist Can art, Univ Regina, 72- *Mem:* Can Art Mus Dir Orgn (secy, 71-75, vpres, 75, pres, 76-78); fel Can Mus Asn (coun, 67-70); Sask Mus Asn (vpres, 75, pres, 76-78); Western Art Asn (exec, 70-72); Col Art Asn. *Res:* Canadian art history. *Mailing Add:* Winnipeg Art Gallery 300 Memorial Blvd Winnipeg MB R3C 1V1 Canada

DI MEO, DOMINICK
PAINTER, SCULPTOR
b Niagara Falls, NY, Feb 1, 27. *Study:* Art Inst Chicago, four year dipl, 50, BFA, 52; Univ Iowa, MFA, 53. *Work:* Art Inst Chicago; Whitney Mus Am Art, New York; Ill Bell Tel Co, Chicago; Univ Mass, Amherst; Nat Collection Am Art, Smithsonian Inst. *Exhib:* Ann Exhib Contemp Am Painting, Whitney Mus Am Art, 67-68; Fantasy & Figure, Am Fedn Arts, New York & Traveling Show, 68-69; Violence in Recent American Art, Mus Contemp Art, Chicago, 68-69; The Crowd: Exhibit of Sculpture, Paintings & Graphics, Arts Club Chicago, 69; Visions/Painting & Sculpture: Distinguished Alumni 1945-Present, Art Inst Chicago, 76; 16th Joan Miro Int Drawing Prize Competition, Barcelona, Spain & Sala de Cult de la Caja de Ahorros de Navarra, Pamplona, 77; 100 Artists--100 Years, Alumni of the School of the Art Institute of Chicago, Centennial Exhibition, Art Inst Chicago, 79-80; Arteder 82: Int Graphic Arts Exhib, Feria int Muestras Bilbao, Spain, 82; and others. *Teaching:* Instr, Chicago Acad Fine Arts, 67-69; vis artist, Art Inst Chicago, 77. *Awards:* Guggenheim Mem Found Fel Graphics, 72-73; Nat Endowment Arts Sculpture Fel, 82-83. *Bibliog:* Whitney Halstead (auth), Introduction, In: Di Meo, Work: 1959-1966, Galaxie, 67. *Media:* Mixed Media. *Mailing Add:* 429 Broome St New York NY 10013

DIMOND, TERRY JARRARD
SCULPTOR, EDUCATOR
b Slater, SC, July 3, 45. *Study:* Winthrop Col, BA, 69; Clemson Univ, MFA, 79. *Work:* Pickens Co Art Mus, SC; SC State Art Collection. *Comn:* Fiber murals, comn by Harold Cooledge, Clemson, SC, 75 & Richland Mem Hosp, Columbia, SC, 83. *Exhib:* Assemblages & Collage, Southeastern Ctr Contemp Art, Winston-Salem, NC, 81; Convergence 1982, Seattle, Wash, 82; Woven Works: Tradition & Innovation, Univ Wis; two-artist exhib, Spirit Sq, Charlotte, NC; solo exhib, Ashville Art Mus, NC, 84. *Pos:* Dir, Pickens Co Art Mus, 79-81. *Teaching:* Instr weaving, Greenville Co Mus Art, 76-78, instr weaving, intro design (two & three dimensional) & sculpture, 81-; instr drawing, Anderson Col, SC, 81; instr matrix, Lander Col, 83- *Awards:* Merit Awards, Shelby Art League Juried Exhib, NC, 82 & NC/SC Fiber Competition, Charlotte, NC, 83; Special Merit Award, First Spartanburg Exhib, SC, 83. *Bibliog:* Sharyn Hyatt & Teresa Mangum (auths), The ceremonial structures of Terry Jarrard-Dimond, Fiber Arts Mag, 7-8/82. *Mem:* Guild SC Artists; Southeastern Women's Caucus Art (pres, 83-); Women's Caucus Art. *Media:* Miscellaneous. *Dealer:* Eve Manneg 288 E Paces Ferry Rd Atlanta GA 30305; Artistic Sass Inc 14 Greenwood Dr #1406 Hilton Head SC 29928. *Mailing Add:* 225 N Clemson Ave Clemson SC 29631

DIMONDSTEIN, MORTON
SCULPTOR, PAINTER
b New York, NY, Nov 5, 20. *Study:* Am Artists Sch, New York, 37-39; Art Students League, 39-41; Otis Art Inst, Los Angeles, 45-48; Inst Nac, Mexico City, Mex, 50-51. *Work:* World Bank, Washington, DC; Libr Cong; Pushkin Art Mus, Moscow, USSR; Seattle Art Mus, Wash; Portland Art Mus, Ore. *Exhib:* Solo exhibs, Jacqueline Anhalt Gallery, Los Angeles, 67-72, James Willis Gallery, San Francisco, 75-76, Roko Gallery, New York, 77, Gallery Nuance, Amsterdam, 80 & Brand Libr, Glendale, Calif, 84. *Pos:* Staff artist, Patzcuaro, Mex, 52-53. *Teaching:* Instr all media, Sch Fine Art, Los Angeles, 63-72; instr drawing & sculpture, Univ Southern Calif, 64-68. *Mem:* Soc Am Graphic Artists. *Publ:* Mexico (portfolio of woodcuts), Posada Graphics, 54. *Dealer:* James Willis Gallery 109 Geary San Francisco CA 94108; Roko Gallery 816 Broadway New York NY 10003. *Mailing Add:* 749 Longwood Ave Los Angeles CA 90005

DIMSON, THEO AENEAS
DESIGNER, ILLUSTRATOR
b London, Ont, Apr 8, 30. *Study:* Ont Col Art, Toronto. *Work:* Typomundus 20, France. *Exhib:* Am Inst Graphic Arts, New York; Graphica Club Toronto; Graphica Club Montreal; Int Poster Art, Bulgaria; one-man poster show, Toronto, 78; and others. *Pos:* Vpres creative design, Art Assocs Ltd, Toronto, 59-65; pres & creative dir, Dimson & Smith Ltd, Toronto, 65- *Awards:* Medal Awards, Graphica Club Toronto, 66 & Graphica Club Montreal, 71; Award of Excellence, Am Inst Graphic Arts, 71. *Bibliog:* Hara (auth), Designers, Graphic Design Mag, 62; Republic of Childhood, Oxford Univ, 67. *Mem:* Graphica Club Toronto; Am Inst Graphic Arts; assoc Royal Can Acad Arts. *Media:* Graphic. *Publ:* Illusr, The Sunken City, 60 & The Double Knights, 63, Oxford; illusr, Rubaboo Five, Sage, 65. *Mailing Add:* Dimson & Smith Ltd 172 Davenport Rd Toronto ON M5R 1J1 Canada

DINARDO, JOSEPH E
MEDALIST, SCULPTOR
b Schenectady, NY, Jan 17, 38. *Study:* Boston Univ, with Alphonse A Kolb, BS, 63. *Work:* Am Numismatic Soc Mus, New York; Albany Inst Hist & Art; Am Numismatic Asn Mus, Colorado Springs; Smithsonian Inst. *Comn:* Fortieth Anniversary Medal, Albany Numismatic Soc, 76; 30th Anniversary Medal, Long Island Coin Club, Flushing, NY, 82. *Exhib:* The Birth of a Medal, Empire State Numismatic Asn, Rochester, NY, 65; The Sculptured Model, Albany Numismtic Soc, Albany Inst Hist & Art, 73; Banker and Wife, Am Numismatic Soc, New York, 83. *Pos:* Owner & artist, Dinardo Medal Art Co, 67- *Mem:* Am Medalic Sculptors Asn. *Media:* Bas Relief. *Collection:* Domestic and foreign high relief medalic art. *Mailing Add:* PO Box 62 Schenectady NY 12301

DINE, JAMES
PAINTER, SCULPTOR
b Cincinnati, Ohio, June 16, 35. *Study:* Univ Cincinnati; Boston Mus Sch; Ohio Univ, BFA, 58. *Work:* Whitney Mus Am Art, Mus Mod Art, New York; Tate Gallery, London, Eng; Nat Collection Fine Art; Albright-Knox Art Gallery, Buffalo. *Exhib:* Solo exhibs, Mus Mod Art, New York, 67, 69 & 78, Calif State Univ, Long Beach, 79, Galerie Alice Pauli, Lausanne, 80, Janie C Lee Gallery, Houston, 80 & Harcus-Krakow Gallery, Boston, 80; American Drawings, 1963-1973, Whitney Mus Am Art, 73; Poets of the Cities, Dallas Mus Fine Art, 74; Drawings of the 70's, Chicago Art Inst, 77; Drawings about Drawing, Univ NC, 79; and many others. *Teaching:* Vis prof, Oberlin Col, 65 & Cornell Univ, 67. *Awards:* Norman Harris Silver Medal & Prize, Art Inst Chicago, 64. *Bibliog:* Christopher Finch (auth), Jim Dine, Abrams. *Publ:* Illusr, The Poet Assassinated, 68; auth & illusr, Welcome Home Lovebirds, 69; coauth, Work from the Same House, 69; co-auth & illusr, The Adventures of Mr & Mrs Jim & Ron, 70. *Mailing Add:* c/o The Pace Gallery 32 E 57th St New York NY 10022

DINEEN, TOM (FORGA)
PAINTER
b Port Washington, Wis, June 19, 48. *Study:* Layton Sch Art, Milwaukee, BFA, 71; Univ Wis-Madison, grad study, 74; Prix de Rome finalist, 75. *Work:* Corcoran Gallery Art, Washington, DC. *Comn:* 42 inches x 360 inches drawing, Cafe Des Artistes, Washington, DC. *Exhib:* 19th Area Exhib, Corcoran Gallery Art, DC, 74; US Info Agency Embassy Tour, Mid-East & N Africa, 75-76; Works on Paper, Nat Collection Fine Art, DC, 77; Art Fiesta 78, Int Exhib Festival, Bologna, Italy, 78; and others. *Awards:* Prix de Rome finalist, Am Acad Rome, 75; MacDowell fel, Peterborough, NH, 76-78; Yaddo fel, Saratoga Springs, NY, 79. *Media:* Charcoal; Oil, Magna Acrylic. *Mailing Add:* c/o Middendorf Lane 2009 Columbia Rd NW Washington DC 20009

DINGUS, RICK
PHOTOGRAPHER, WRITER
b Appleton City, Mo, Jan 3, 51. *Study:* Univ Calif, Santa Barbara, BA, 73; Univ NMex, MA, 77, MFA, 81. *Work:* Biblioteque Nat, Paris; Detroit Inst Arts; Nat Gallery Art, New Zealand; Mus Mod Art, New York; San Francisco Mus Mod Art. *Exhib:* Attitudes: Photography in the 1970's, Santa Barbara Mus Art, 79; solo exhib, PS 1 Gallery, Long Island City, 80 & Janet Lehr Inc, Bertha Urdang, New York, 83; The Markers, San Francisco Mus Mod Art, 81; Contemporary Western Landscapes, Light Factory, Charlotte, NC, 81; Radical/Rational--Space/Time, Henry Art Gallery, Univ Wash, Seattle, 83. *Teaching:* Lectr photog, NMex Tech, Socorro, 79-81; vis lectr, Univ Colo, Boulder, 81-82; asst prof, Tex Tech Univ, 82- *Awards:* Nat Endowment Arts Photog Survey Grants, 78-79 & 81-83; Juror's Award, Contemporary Photoworks, Albuquerque United Artists, 81 & NTex Ann Photo Competition, NTex State Univ, 82. *Bibliog:* Michael Costello (auth), Alternate views: A recent film by Roger Sweet and Rick Dingus, Artspace, summer 78. *Mem:* Soc Photog Educ; Friends Photog. *Publ:* Auth, The Photographic Artifacts of Timothy O'Sullivan, Univ NMex Press, 82. *Dealer:* Janet Lehr Inc Gracie Sq Sta PO Box 617 New York NY 10028. *Mailing Add:* Art Dept Box 4720 Tex Tech Univ Lubbock TX 79409

DINNERSTEIN, HARVEY
PAINTER
b Brooklyn, NY, Apr 3, 28. *Study:* With Moses Soyer, 44-46; Art Students League, 46-47; Tyler Art Sch, Temple Univ, cert art, 50. *Work:* Metrop Mus, Whitney Mus Am Art & Martin Luther King Labor Ctr, New York; New Britain Mus Art, Conn; Fleming Mus, Univ Vt, Burlington. *Exhib:* Contemp Am Painting, Whitney Mus Am Art, New York, 55; Contemp Drawings, Whitney Mus Am Art, 64; Childe Hassam Award Exhib, Am Acad & Inst of Arts & Lett, New York, 74; Living Am Artists & the Figure, Pa State Univ Mus Art, University Park, 74; 3 Centuries of Am-Nude, New York Cult Ctr, 76; Bicentennial Exhib of Am Illus, New York Hist Soc, 76; one-man show, Sindin Galleries, New York, 83; plus many others. *Pos:* Academician, Nat Acad Design, New York, 74. *Teaching:* Instr drawing & painting, Sch Visual Arts, New York, 65-80, Nat Acad Design, 75-, Art Students League, 80- *Awards:* Temple Gold Medal, Pa Acad Fine Art, 50; Hassam & Spelcher Purchase Award, Am Acad & Inst of Arts & Lett, 74 & 78; Ranger Purchase Award, Nat Acad Design, 76. *Bibliog:* Susan E Meyer (auth), 20 Figure Painters and How They Work, Watson-Guptill, 79; How We Lived, Esquire Mag 50th Anniversary Issue, 6/83; The Seasons, Am Artist Mag, 8/83. *Mem:* Audubon Artists; Allied Artists. *Media:* Oil, Pastel. *Publ:* Coauth, New look at protest, the eight since 1908, Art News, 2/58; illusr, Drawings of the Montgomery Bus Boycott, 12/64 & illusr & auth, The face of protest, 12/68, Esquire Mag; illusr, A Portfolio of Drawings, Kenmore Press, 68; illusr & auth, Harvey Dinnerstein--Artist at Work, Watson-Guptill, 78. *Dealer:* Sindin Galleries 1035 Madison Ave New York NY 10021. *Mailing Add:* 933 President St Brooklyn NY 11215

DINNERSTEIN, LOIS
HISTORIAN, LECTURER
b New York, NY, Oct 24, 32. *Study:* NY Univ Wash Sq Col, BA, 53; NY Univ Inst Fine Arts, MA, 60; City Univ New York Grad Ctr, PhD, 79. *Pos:* Res cur, Benjamin Sonnenberg Collection, NY, 57-58; res cur, Daniel & Rita Fraad Collection, NY, 62-63; res cur, Montclair Art Mus, NJ, 75-76. *Teaching:* Instr art hist, Vassar Col, 59-61; instr, City Univ New York Brooklyn Col, 64-77; adj prof, Brooklyn Ctr, Long Island Univ, 82-84. *Awards:* Rockefeller Found fel, City Univ New York, 77. *Mem:* Asn Historians Am Art. *Res:* Eighteenth and 19th century American art. *Publ:* Auth, The iron worker and King Solomon: Some images of labor in American art, 9/79, Beyond revisionism: Henry Lerolle's The Organ, 1/80 & The industrious housewife: Some images of labor in American art, 4/81, Arts Mag; auth, John Singleton Copley's Portrait of Elizabeth Allen Stevens (art mus catalog), Res Supplement, Montclair, 79; auth, Artists in their studios, Am Heritage, 2/83; and others. *Mailing Add:* 933 President St Brooklyn NY 11215

DINNERSTEIN, SIMON A
PAINTER
b Brooklyn, NY, Feb 16, 43. *Study:* City Col New York, BA, 65; Brooklyn Mus Art Sch, with David Levine & Louis Grebenak, 64-67; Hochschule für Bildende Kunst, Kassel, Ger, Fulbright fel, 70-71. *Work:* Munson-Williams-Proctor Inst, Utica; Univ Md Art Mus, College Park; Minn Mus Art, St Paul; Albrecht Mus, St Joseph, Mo; Univ Mo, Columbia; Pa State Univ, University Park. *Exhib:* Childe Hassam Mem Exhib, Am Acad Arts & Lett, 75-78; New Sch, 76 & 79; one-man shows, Staempfli Gallery, 75 & 79, Inst Int Educ, 76-77 & 79, Am Acad in Rome, 77 & New Sch, 81; and others. *Teaching:* Instr painting, Brooklyn Mus Art Sch, 71-72; instr painting & drawing, The New Sch, New York, 75-; instr, New York Community Col, 79. *Awards:* Louis Comfort Tiffany Grant, 76; Prix de Rome, Italy, 76-78; Ingram Merrill Award for Painting, 78-79. *Bibliog:* Attenzione Mag, summer, 81; Museum purchase, Pa State Press, 12/16/82; Museum acquires triptych, Centre Daily Times, Pa, 12/16/82. *Media:* Miscellaneous. *Dealer:* Staempfli Gallery. *Mailing Add:* 415 First St New York NY 11215

D'INNOCENZO, NICK JEROME
SCULPTOR, EDUCATOR
b Rochester, NY, Dec 12, 34. *Study:* State Univ NY Buffalo, BS(art educ), 60; Cranbrook Acad Art, MFA(sculpture), 63. *Work:* State Univ NY Buffalo; Smith-Corona-Marchant Corp, Syracuse, NY. *Comn:* Welded bronze reliefs, State Univ NY Col Oswego, City of Oswego & Oswego Co Savings Bank. *Exhib:* Artists of Finger Lakes, Mem Art Gallery, Rochester, NY, 65-; Graphics USA, NY State Fairgrounds, Syracuse, NY, 70; Mirrors, Motors & Motion, Albright-Knox Art Gallery, Buffalo, 71; Artists of NY, Everson Mus, Syracuse, 75; Univ Artists, State Univ NY Albany, 76; Artists of NY State, State Fairgrounds, Syracuse, 81; and others. *Teaching:* Prof sculpture & design, State Univ NY Col Oswego, 63- *Awards:* Chancellor's Award for Excellence in Teaching, State Univ NY, 79. *Bibliog:* George Stark (auth), Artists/Teachers, Sch Arts, 66. *Mem:* NY State Art Teachers Asn. *Media:* Brazed Steel, Vacuum-Formed Styrene. *Mailing Add:* Edwards Circle RD 3 Oswego NY 13126

DINTENFASS, MARYLYN
SCULPTOR, LECTURER
b New York, NY, Sept 26, 43. *Study:* Queens Col, NY, BAFA, 65; Jerusalem, Israel, 65-66. *Comn:* sculpture, Benton & Bowles Inc, New York, 78; sculpture, INS Co NAm, Philadelphia, 79; sculpture, Int Bus Machines, Charlotte, NC, 81; sculpture, comn by Wayne Hurdman, New York, 81; sculpture, Int Bus Machines, San Jose, Calif, 83. *Exhib:* Solo show, Queens Mus, New York, 76; Bronx Mus, New York, 78; Philadelphia Mus, 78; Nat Acad Design, New York, 78; Bowdoin Col Mus Art, 81; Scnectady Mus, NY, 82; Nat Mus Am Art, Smithsonian Mus, 83-84; and others. *Pos:* Bd mem, Nat Comt on Apprenticeship, 78- *Teaching:* Mem fac, Haystack Mountain Sch, Deer Island, Maine, 78 & 80; Mem fac, Haystack Mountain Sch, Deer Island, Maine, 78 & 80, Parsons Sch Design, New York, 80-, Radcliff Col, 81, Brookhaven Col, 83, Montclair St Col, 83. *Awards:* Nat Endowment Arts Grants, 78 & 82; Award, Women Design Int Competition, 81; and others. *Bibliog:* Contemporary International Ceramics, Buchhandlung Reuffel, WGer, 80; Electric Kiln Ceramics, Chilton, 81; Profile, Am Ceramics, Vol 2, No 2, 83; and others. *Media:* Architectural Ceramics. *Mailing Add:* 50 Webster Ave New Rochelle NY 10801

DINTENFASS, TERRY
DEALER
US citizen. *Pos:* Dir, Terry Dintenfass, Inc. *Specialty:* Contemporary American Art. *Mailing Add:* 50 W 57th St New York NY 10019

DIODA, ADOLPH T
SCULPTOR, INSTRUCTOR
b Aliquippa, Pa, Sept 10, 15. *Study:* Carnegie Inst Technol; Barnes Found. *Work:* Carnegie Mellon Mus, Pittsburgh, Pa; Pa Acad Fine Arts, Philadelphia; Ogunquit Mus Art, Maine; Westmoreland Mus Art, Greensburg, Pa. *Comn:* Figure, comn by Dahlen K Ritchey, Pittsburgh, 51; crucifix & stations of the cross for chapel, St Joseph's Prep Sch, Philadelphia, 72. *Exhib:* Whitney Mus Am Art Ann, New York, 40; Sculpture Int, Philadelphia Mus Art, 40-49; Carved in Stone, Bucholtz Gallery, New York, 45; Pa Acad Fine Arts Ann, 46, 47 & 69; 60th Am Exhib Am Paintings & Sculpture, Art Inst Chicago, 51. *Teaching:* Instr sculpture, Tyler Sch, Temple Univ, 59-69; instr wood & stone carving, Haverford Col, 62-69; instr wood & stone carving, Pa Acad Fine Arts, 62-; instr wood & stone carving, Philadelphia Col Art, 78-81. *Awards:*

Guggenheim Found Grant, 45; George D Widener Medal, Pa Acad Fine Arts, 47; Eben Demarest Fund grant, Carnegie Inst Technol, 48. *Mem:* Artists Equity Asn, Philadelphia Chap. *Media:* Wood, Stone. *Mailing Add:* 411 Healy St Jenkintown PA 19046

DIODATO, BALDO
PAINTER, SCULPTOR
b Naples, Italy, Feb 16, 38. *Study:* Liceo Artistico, Naples, Italy; Accad Belle Arti, Naples; Accad Albertina, Turin. *Work:* Milton Brutten Collection, Philadelphia; Philadelphia Mus Art. *Comn:* Mural, Military Hosp, Turin, Italy, 62; facade, Church San Martino Valle Caudina, Benevento, Italy, 63-64; facade, windows & door, Chiaiano, Naples, 60. *Exhib:* Artists Equity Exhib, Philadelphia Civic Ctr, 74; RI Univ, 74; NJ State Mus, Trenton, 75; Susan Caldwell Gallery, New York, 81; Baker Gallery, La Jolla, Calif, 82; and others. *Teaching:* Prof sculpture, Mattia Preti, Liceo Artistico, Reggio Calabria, 67-68; prof sculpture, Cheltenham Art Ctr, Philadelphia, 75. *Awards:* Mostra d'Autunno, City Naples, Italy, 64; Best Int Exhib, State NJ, 69-71. *Bibliog:* Lea Vergine (auth), Intervista Sulla Cultura a Napoli, Marcatre Ed, Lerici, 65 & 66 & Dieci Anni de Cultura, Almanaco Letterario, Bompiani, 68; Achille Bonita Oliva (auth), Scultura a Palazzo Reale, Ente Turismo, Naples, 68. *Mem:* Artists Equity Asn. *Media:* Mixed. *Mailing Add:* 93 Greene St New York NY 10012

DIPASQUALE, DOMINIC THEODORE
SILVERSMITH, EDUCATOR
b Buffalo, NY, Feb 21, 32. *Study:* State Univ NY Col Buffalo, BS(art educ); Sch Am Craftsmen, Rochester Inst Technol, MFA(metal design). *Work:* In over 500 pvt collections. *Comn:* Inaugural medallion, State Univ NY Col Oswego, 66; inaugural medallion, Worcester State Col, Mass, 75; Coat of Arms, comn by Bishop J F Cunningham, Syracuse Diocese, NY, 75. *Exhib:* Silversmiths of NY, Univ Mex, 75; 2nd Biennial Int Exhib, Tweed Mus, Duluth, 75; Nat Art Slide Competition, Fla, 75; Enamels 78, Torpedo Factory, Arlington, Va, 78; Prof Produce Invitational, Craftsmens Gallery, Scarsdale, NY, 79; Cooperstown Nat Art Exhib; Invitational, Kipp Gallery, Indiana, Pa; and others. *Teaching:* Prof jewelry & metals, State Univ NY Col Oswego, 63-, chmn dept art, 74- *Awards:* First Prize, Las Vegas Nat Art Round-Up, Nev, 69; First Prize, NY State Fair, Syracuse, 73; Jurors Award for Most Provacative in Show, Arnot Gallery, Elmira, NY, 79. *Mem:* Soc NAm Goldsmiths; York State Crafts Asn; Buffalo Craftsmen; Am Crafts Coun; Col Art Asn Am. *Media:* Gems, Precious Metals. *Publ:* Auth, Jewelry Making: An Illustrated Guide to Technique, 75. *Dealer:* David Church 71 Main St Saranac Lake NY 12983. *Mailing Add:* 24 W Fifth St Oswego NY 13126

DIPERNA, FRANK PAUL
PHOTOGRAPHER, INSTRUCTOR
b Pittsburgh, Pa, Feb 4, 47. *Study:* Ctr of the Eye, Aspen, Colo, with Gary Winogrand, 71; Visual Studies Workshop, Rochester, NY, with Ralph Gibson, Syl Labrot, Nathan Lyons & Alice Wells, 71-72; Goddard Col, MA(photog), 77. *Work:* Polaroid (Europa), Amsterdam, The Netherlands; Libr Cong, Smithsonian Inst, Corcoran Gallery Art, Washington, DC; Bibliot Nat, Paris; and others. *Exhib:* Va Photogr, Va Mus Fine Arts, 73 & 75; Eye of the West: Camera Vision & Cult Consensus, Hayden Gallery, Mass Inst Technol, Cambridge, 77; One of a Kind (traveling exhib), Mus Fine Arts, Houston, Univ Ariz, Los Angeles Inst Contemp Arts & Art Inst Chicago; one-man shows, Bushes, 74 & Color Photographs, 77, Corcoran Gallery Art, Photographs, Diane Brown Gallery, Washington, DC, 77 & 81 & Color Photographs, Sebastian Moore Gallery, Denver, Colo, 78; Kathleen Ewing Gallery, Washington, DC, 82; Washington Photography: Images of the Eighties, Corcoran Gallery Art, 82; and others. *Teaching:* Instr photog, Northern Va Community Col, Alexandria, 73-78; instr photog, Corcoran Sch Art, 74-78, asst prof & chmn dept, 78- *Awards:* Cert of Distinction, Va Photog, 73; Artist-in-Residence fel, Camargo Found, Cassis, France; Artist-in-Residence Fel, Lightwork, Syracuse, NY, 82. *Bibliog:* Mark Power (auth), Washington, Photographers and the Contact Print, Washington Rev Arts, winter 76; David Taunous (auth), Frank DiPerna at the Corcoran, Mark Power at Diane Brown, Art in Am, 1-2/78; Owen Edwards (auth), SX-70: Land's painless epiphany machine, Sat Rev, 7/22/78. *Publ:* Auth, Color photographs, Corcoran Gallery Art, 77; auth, One of a kind: Recent Polaroid color photography, Godine; auth, SX-70, Lustrum Press, 79; contribr, Washington Photography: Images of the Eighties (catalog), Corcoran Gallery Art, 82. *Dealer:* Kathleen Ewing Gallery 3615 Ordway St NW Washington DC 20016. *Mailing Add:* 9101 Jackson Ln Great Falls VA 22066

DIRUBE, ROLANDO LOPEZ
PAINTER, SCULPTOR
b Havana, Cuba, Aug 14, 28; US citizen. *Study:* Univ Havana Col Archit & Eng, 48; Art Students League, with George Grosz & Kuniyoshi, 49; Brooklyn Mus Art Sch, with Gabor F Peterdi & Max Beckman, 50; Escuela Nac Artes Graficas, Madrid, Spain, 51-52. *Work:* Metrop Mus Art, New York; Philadelphia Univ, Pa; Nat Mus, Havana, Cuba; Mus Mod Art, Madrid, Spain; Ponce Mus, PR. *Comn:* Nat Asn Architects, 58; Nat Theatre & Nat Sport Coliseum, Cuban Govt, Havana, 58; Int Theatres, GHG Enterprises, San Juan, PR, 70; One Biscayne Tower, GHG Enterprises, Miami, Fla, 72; outdoor sculpture, comn by Am Govt, Perrine Park, Fla. *Exhib:* I Bienal Hispanoamericana Arte, Madrid, 51; Lateinamerikanische Kunst Gegenwart, Ger, 51; II Bienal Sao Paulo, Brazil, 53; Int Colour Woodcut Exhib, Victoria & Albert Mus, London, 54-55; IX Biennale Int Art Menton, France, 72; one-man show, Mus Contemp Art, Caracas, Venezuela, 71. *Teaching:* Prof design anal, Inter-Am Univ PR Sch Archit, 64-65; lectr design, Sch Archit, Univ PR, San Juan, 67; prof painting, Art Students League, San Juan, 68- *Awards:* First

Prize Woodcut, I Bienal Hispanoamericana Arte, 51; Gold Medal in Painting & Gold Medal in Woodcut, Univ Tampa, 51; First Prize Sculpture, R J Reynolds Tobacco Co, 79. *Bibliog:* R Guastela (auth), Dirube painter & sculpture (film), Viguie Guastela, 68; J Gomez Sicre (auth), San Juan muralists, Pan Am Union Rev Am, 71; R Pau Llosa (auth), Dirube, Ala Art Editions. *Publ:* Illusr, En la Habana ha muerto un turista, 63; illusr, Los combatientes, 68. *Mailing Add:* PO Box 929 Catano PR 00632

DISKA
SCULPTOR
b New York, NY. *Study:* Vassar Col, BA; Acad Jullian, Paris. *Work:* Cornell Art Mus, Ithaca, NY; Mus Art & Indust St Etienne, France; Int Sculpture Parks, Austria, Israel, Czech, Yugoslavia & France; Palm Springs Art Mus, Calif; and others. *Comn:* Over 20 commissioned works in stone, wood, cast iron and brick for public spaces in France, including eight fountains & seven sculptures. *Exhib:* One-man shows, Galerie Suzanne de Coninck, Paris, 65, Galerie Les Contards, Lacoste, 65, Southern Methodist Univ, Dallas, Tex, 65, Galerie Jacques Casanova, Paris, 66, Ruth White Gallery, New York, 69; and others. *Teaching:* Instr sculpture, Sarah Lawrence Summer Sch, Lacoste, France, 74 & 75. *Awards:* Competition for fountain, New Town Melun-Senart, France, 79; Portes-les-Valence, France, 83; Sorgue, France, 83. *Bibliog:* Marjorie Hichisson (auth), article, Archit Asn J, London, 65; Dona Meilach (auth), Contemporary Stone Sculpture, Crown Publ, 70; article, Archit d'Aujourd'hui, Paris, 73. *Mem:* Sculptor's Guild; French Syndicat Sculptors. *Media:* Mixed. *Mailing Add:* 305 W 28th St New York NY 10001

DI SUVERO, MARK
PAINTER, SCULPTOR
b Shanghai, China. *Study:* Univ Calif, BA. *Work:* Wadsworth Atheneum, Hartford, Conn; Whitney Mus Am Art; Hirshhorn Mus; Dallas Mus Fine Arts; Art Inst Chicago. *Exhib:* Art Inst Chicago, 63; American Sculpture of the Sixties, Los Angeles Co Mus Art, 67; Whitney Mus Am Art, New York, 67, 75 & 80; San Francisco Mus Art, 69; Gov State Mus, Park Forest, Ill, 80; Landmark Ctr, Minn Mus Art, St Paul, 80; San Diego Mus, 80; Nat Col Fine Art, Washington, DC, 80; ConStruct, Chicago, 80. *Awards:* Longview Found Grant; Walter K Gutman Found Grant; Art Inst Chicago Award, 63. *Bibliog:* Robert Hughes (auth), Truth amid steel and elephants, Time, 7/71; Carter Ratcliff (auth), article, Artforum, 11/72; E C Baker (auth), Mark Di Suvero's Burgundian Season, Art Am, 5-6/74. *Mailing Add:* c/o Richard Bellamy 333 Park Ave S New York NY 10010

DITZION, GRACE
SCULPTOR, PAINTER
b Montreal, Que; US citizen. *Study:* Hunter Col, BA, 33; NY Univ, MA, 36; Art Students League; Mus Mod Art. *Work:* Grad Ctr, City Univ NY; Univ Hawaii, Hilo; City Milford, Conn; Cayuga Co Community Col. *Comn:* Sculptures (marble), comn by Joseph Borome, New York, 77 & Bernard Zelechow, Toronto, 79. *Exhib:* Allied Artists Am, 76 & 78 & Ann Exhib Nat Acad Design, 78, Nat Acad Design, New York; solo exhib, Salmagundi Club, New York, 78; Nat Arts Club 80th Anniversary Prize Winners Art Exhib, New York, 78; Hudson Valley Art Asn, Westchester Co Ctr, New York, 80; and others. *Awards:* First Prize, Nat Arts Club, 76 & Salmagundi Club, 77; Peggy Eagan Award, Hudson Valley Art Asn, 80. *Bibliog:* Patricia Keane-Mason (producer & interviewer), One-Woman Exhibit (TV show), Mus of Air, Channel D, Cable TV, New York, 10/75; Richard Roffman (producer), Richard Roffman Focus Show, Channel C & D, Cable TV, New York, 6/17/77; Bill Boggs (interviewer), Mid-Day Live Prog, WNEW TV, New York, 5/12/78. *Mem:* Salmagundi Club; Am Artists Prof League; Am Portrait Soc; Hudson River Contemp Artists; Composers, Artists & Authors. *Media:* Marble, Alabaster; Oil, Pastel. *Publ:* Auth, Rebirth of a widow, Hallandale Digest, 2/1/79; auth, The cloud of uncertainty, Asn Human Relations Publ, 4/23/81; auth, The creative impulse, Wash Sq Outdoor Art Exhib 50th Anniversary Issue, 5/25/81. *Dealer:* Gloria Salm Inc 35 Sutton Pl New York NY 10022. *Mailing Add:* 3635 Johnson Ave New York NY 10463

DIVOLA, JOHN MANFORD, JR
PHOTOGRAPHER
b Santa Monica, Calif, June 6, 49. *Study:* Calif State Univ, Northridge, BA, 71; Univ Calif, Los Angeles, MA, 73, MFA, 74. *Work:* Mus Mod Art, New York; Int Mus Photog, George Eastman House, Rochester; New Orleans Mus Art; Fogg Mus Art, Mass; Univ Calif, Los Angeles. *Comn:* 11 photographs, US Info Agency, 74. *Exhib:* 24 from Los Angeles, San Francisco Mus Art, 73; Mirrors & Windows, Mus Mod Art, New York, 78; New Presences at the Fogg, Fogg Mus Art, Mass, 78; Madison Art Ctr, Wis, 79; New Acquisitions, San Francisco Mus Mod Art, 79; Color: A Spectrum of Recent Photography, Part 2, The Romantic Vision & Beyond, Milwaukee Art Ctr, Wis, 79; one-man shows, Vision Gallery, Boston, 79, Blue Sky Gallery, Portland, Ore, 79, Freidas Gallery, New York, 80, New Image Gallery, Harrisonburg, Va, 80 & Photographers Gallery, Melbourne, Australia, 80; Young Hoffman Gallery, Chicago, 80; fac exhib, Loyola Marymount Univ, 80; and many others. *Teaching:* Instr photog, Loyola Marymount Univ, Los Angeles, 76-80; instr photog, Calif Inst Arts, 78-80. *Awards:* Endowment Arts Photography fels, 73, 76 & 79. *Bibliog:* Joan Murray (auth), Memorable visions, Artweek, 9/8/79; Photography Year 1980, Time-Life, 80; Andy Grundberg & Julia Scully (auths), Currents: American photography today, Mod Photog, 10/80; Mark Johnstone (auth), article in Camera, 11/80. *Publ:* Illusr, Three images reproduced, New West Mag, 11/6/78. *Mailing Add:* 245 Ruth Ave Venice CA 90291

DIXON, JENNY (JANE HODLEY)
ADMINISTRATOR
b Montreal, Que, Oct 1, 50; US citizen. *Study:* Univ Colo, BFA, 72; Univ Stranieri, Perugia, Italy, 72. *Collections Arranged:* Adminr & organizer of temporary installations of large-scale sculpture by: Jean Dubuffet, Isamu Noguchi, Jeffrey Owen Brosk, Mrvin Torffield, Richard Serra,, Linda Howard & Sandro Martini; also assisted in installation of work by: Arthur Weyhe, George Sugarman, Pierre Clerk & others. *Pos:* Dir, Pub Art Fund Inc, 76-; moderator & producer of weekly radio prog, Artists in the City, WNYC-AM, 79- *Publ:* Ed, Walking tour guide of public art in Lower Manhattan, Pub Arts Coun, 76. *Mailing Add:* c/o Pub Arts Coun 25 Central Park W New York NY 10023

DIXON, KENNETH RAY
PAINTER, GALLERY DIRECTOR
b St Clair, Mo, May 30, 43. *Study:* Drury Col, Springfield, Mo, BA, 65; SW Mo State Univ, Springfield, 66; Univ Ark, Fayetteville, MFA, 68, with David Durst & Howard Whitlach. *Work:* Utah State Univ, Logan; Baldwin-Wallace Col Art Gallery, Berea, Ohio; Kalamazoo Inst Arts, Mich; Mus Mod Art, Miami, Fla; Ky State Univ, Frankfort; plus others. *Exhib:* One-man shows, Camden Inst, London, 73, Kalamazoo Inst Arts, 75 & Utah State Univ Gallery, 78; Univ Okla Gallery, 80; 11th Nat Works on Paper, San Marcos, Tex, 81; Nat Works on Paper, Stephen F Austin Univ, Tex, 81; New Figurative Drawing in Texas, San Antonio Inst, 83. *Pos:* Gallery dir, Baldwin-Wallace Col, 69-72 & Tex Tech Univ, 77- *Teaching:* Instr painting, Kalamazoo Col, 66-69 & Baldwin-Wallace Col, 69-72; assoc prof painting, Tex Tech Univ, 75- *Awards:* First Award in Watercolor, 36th Nat Southern Utah State Univ, 77; Purchase Award, Miami Graphics Int, Mus Mod Art, Miami, 77; First Award, Abilene Art Mus, 83. *Media:* Watercolor, Gum Bichromate. *Publ:* Auth, Loretta longed to leave, Artspace, fall 82. *Mailing Add:* 2007 31st St Lubbock TX 79411

DMYTRUK, IHOR
PAINTER, INSTRUCTOR
b Ukraine, Feb 11, 38; Can citizen. *Study:* Univ Alta; Vancouver Sch Art. *Work:* Alta Art Found; Univ Calgary, Alta; Ukranian Inst Mod Art, Chicago; Art Gallery, Windsor, Ont; Art Bank, Can Coun; plus others. *Exhib:* Alta Contemp Drawings, Edmonton Art Gallery, 73; Landscape Abbreviations, Art Gallery Greater Victoria, 74-75; Commonwealth Games Visual Arts Proj Exhib, Latitude 53 Gallery, Edmonton, 78; Students Union Art Gallery, Univ Alberta, 79; Alberta Art Found, Hokkaido Mus Mod Art, Japan, 79; one-man show, Latitude 53 Gallery, 75 & 77. *Teaching:* Instr drawing & painting, Fac Exten, Dept of Art, Univ Alta, formerly. *Awards:* All Alberta 1966 Award, Reeves & Sons Ltd; Can Coun Travel Grant, 66 & Art Bursary, 72 & 74. *Bibliog:* E N Yates (auth), Four Edmonton artists, 10/69 & Myra Davies (auth), Recent work by Ihor Dmytruk, 10-11/71, Arts Can; Karen Wilkin (auth), A report on the West, Art Am, 5/72. *Media:* Multimedia. *Mailing Add:* 9803-92 Ave Edmonton AB T6E 2V4 Canada

DOBARD, RAYMOND GERARD
HISTORIAN, PAINTER
b New Orleans, La, Sept 13, 47. *Study:* Xavier Univ La, with Numa Rousseve, BA, 70; Johns Hopkins Univ, with Penelope Mayo, MA, 73 & Phoebe B Stanton, PhD, 75. *Work:* Tougaloo Col Gallery, Miss; Howard Univ Gallery, Washington, DC. *Exhib:* Ann Fac Exhib, Gallery Art, Howard Univ, 76-80; Sign of the Times Gallery, 77; one-man show, Evans-Tibbs Gallery, Washington, DC, 80. *Teaching:* Assoc prof art hist & archit hist, Howard Univ, Washington, DC, 75-82. *Awards:* Mellon Scholar in Residence, Tougaloo Col, 81. *Mem:* Col Art Asn. *Media:* Watercolor, Oil. *Res:* Death iconography in the works of Kaethe Kollwitz; German expressionism; iconography of Romare Bearden. *Publ:* Contribr, This Place: Works by Doris Colbert, Howard Univ, 79. *Dealer:* Evans-Tibbs Collection 1910 Vermont Ave NW Washington DC 20001. *Mailing Add:* 3816 Davis Pl NW Washington DC 20007

DOBBS, JOHN BARNES
PAINTER
b Passaic, NJ, Aug 2, 31. *Study:* RI Sch Design; Brooklyn Mus Art Sch, with Gregorio Prestopino; Skowhegan Sch Painting & Sculpture, with Jack Levine. *Work:* Syracuse Mus Art, NY; Fairleigh Dickinson Univ; Butler Inst Am Art, Youngstown, Ohio; Univ Mass; Springfield Mus Art, Mass; and others. *Exhib:* One-man shows, ACA Gallery, New York, 64, 66, 68, 70, 72, 75, 80 & 83, Long Island Univ, 71 & Wesleyan Univ, 71; Nat Acad Design, New York, 67, 68, 71, 74, 75 & 78; Nat Inst Arts & Lett, New York, 68-71 & 77; Washington Irving Gallery, New York, 82. *Teaching:* Instr, Brooklyn Mus Art Sch, 56-59; instr, New Sch Social Res, 65-; instr, City Col New York, 70-71; assoc prof, John Jay Col Criminal Justice, 72-, Art Students League, 82-83. *Awards:* Ranger Fund Purchase Prize, Nat Acad Design, 74 & 80; Thomas Proctor Prize, 74 & Benjamin Altman Prize, 78, Nat Acad Design. *Mem:* Academician Nat Acad Design. *Media:* Oil. *Publ:* Illusr, Death and Justice Frescoes, 70; illusr, Fortune Mag, 70; illusr, Liberation Mag, 4/72; illusr, Common Elligies, 78 & What Rhymes with Cancer, 82, New Rivers Press. *Dealer:* ACA Gallery 25 E 73rd St New York NY 10014. *Mailing Add:* 463 West St New York NY 10014

DOBIE, JEANNE
PAINTER, INSTRUCTOR
b Philadelphia, Pa. *Study:* Philadelphia Col Art; Rangemark Masterclass, Maine, with Barse Miller, Edward Betts & Chen Chi. *Work:* Lewis Univ, Lockport, Ill; NC Nat Bank; Frye Mus, Seattle; First Pa Bank, Philadelphia; Celanese Corp, Charlotte, NC. *Exhib:* Am Watercolor Soc, New York, 69-80;

Nat Watercolor Soc, Los Angeles, 70 & 81; Columbia Mus Art, NC, 77; Nat Arts Club Show of Past Prize Winners & Jurors, New York, 78; Nat Acad Design Ann, 79. *Teaching:* Instr watercolor, Rangemark, Maine, summers 74-77; instr watercolor workshops throughout US, Hawaii & Europe, 76-; mem fac, Moore Col Art, Philadelphia, 79-81. *Awards:* Charles Taylor Pres Award, Philadelphia Watercolor Club, 76; High Winds Medal, Am Watercolor Soc, New York, 80; D'Arches Award, Nat Watercolor Soc, 81. *Mem:* Am Watercolor Soc; Nat Watercolor Soc; Philadelphia Watercolor Club. *Publ:* Contribr, Watercolor, the Creative Experience, Van Nostrand Reinhold; auth, Painting with watercolor, Am Artist Mag, 9/80. *Mailing Add:* 160 Hunt Valley Circle Berwyn PA 19312

DOBKIN, JOHN HOWARD
MUSEUM DIRECTOR
b Hartford, Conn, Feb 19, 42. *Study:* Yale Univ, BA, 64; Inst d'Etudes Politiques, Paris, France, 65; NY Univ, JD, 68. *Collections Arranged:* Paintings of the Figure, Nat Acad Design, 79; Landscape Paintings, Nat Acad Design, 80; Edwin Dickinson: Draftsman Paints, 81; Artists by Themselves, 83. *Pos:* Exec asst to secy, Smithsonian Inst, Washington, DC, 68-71; adminr, Cooper-Hewitt Mus Design, 71-78; dir, Nat Acad Design, New York, 78-; adv comt, Archives Am Art, New York; bd dir, Municipal Art Soc & Arthur Ross Found, currently. *Awards:* Exceptional Serv Award, Smithsonian Inst, 71. *Mailing Add:* c/o Nat Acad of Design 1083 Fifth Ave New York NY 10028

DOCKSTADER, FREDERICK J
HISTORIAN, CONSULTANT
b Los Angeles. Calif, Feb 3, 19. *Study:* Ariz State Univ, AB & MA; Western Reserve Univ, PhD. *Work:* Cleveland Mus Art, Ohio. *Exhib:* Cranbrook Acad Art, Bloomfield Hills, Mich, 48; Cleveland Mus Art, 49-51. *Collections Arranged:* Specialized in exhib installation & reorganization at Cranbrook Inst Sci, Dartmouth Col Mus & Mus Am Indian. *Pos:* Staff ethnologist, Cranbrook Inst Sci, 46-53; cur anthrop, Dartmouth Col Mus, 53-56; asst dir, Mus Am Indian, 56-59, dir, 59-75; comnr, US Indian Arts & Crafts Bd, 56-68, chmn, 61-68. *Teaching:* Instr silversmithing, Cranbrook Acad Art & NH League Arts & Crafts, 52-55; prof art & archaeol, Columbia Univ, 61-64, mem adv coun, 61-; lectr silversmithing, American Indian art & arts & crafts; distinguished vis prof, Art Dept, Ariz State Univ, 82, adj prof, 83- *Awards:* Second Prize in Silversmithing, Cleveland Mus Art, 50, First Prize in Silversmithing, 51; Lotos Award, Lotos Club, New York, 72. *Mem:* Cosmos Club, Washington, DC; Century Club, New York. *Publ:* Auth & illusr, The Kachina and the White Man, 54 & 84; auth & illusr, Indian Art in America, 61, Indian Art in Middle America, 64, Indian Art in South America, 67, Indian Art of the Americas, 73 & North American Indian Weaving, 78; contribr, articles on arts & crafts to various nat publ. *Mailing Add:* 165 W 66th St New York NY 10023

DODD, ERIC M
GALLERY DIRECTOR, EDUCATOR
Can citizen. *Study:* Univ Durham, BA, 49, dipl(educ), 50; Ohio State Univ, MA, 51. *Teaching:* Prof art, Univ Calgary, 60-, head dept, 68-73. *Mailing Add:* Dept Art Univ Calgary 2500 Univ Dr NW Calgary AB T2N 1N4 Canada

DODD, LAMAR
PAINTER, EDUCATOR
b Fairburn, Ga, Sept 22, 09. *Study:* Ga Inst Technol, 26-27; Art Students League, with George Luks, Boardman Robinson, John Steuart Curry, Jean Charlot & George Bridgeman, 29-33; LaGrange Col, LHD, 47; Univ Chattanooga, DFA, 59; Fla State Univ, DFA, 68. *Work:* Atlanta Art Inst; Art Inst Chicago; Metrop Mus Art; Montclair Art Mus; Pa Acad Fine Arts; plus others. *Exhib:* Am Acad Arts & Lett; Am Fedn Arts; Art Inst Chicago; Am Watercolor Soc; Brooklyn Mus; plus others. *Pos:* Pres, Col Art Asn Am, 54-56; mem, US Dept State Comt Arts Tour, India, Thailand, Belg, Japan, Korea, Manila & others, 58; NASA artist, Apollo 7 & 10, 68-69. *Teaching:* Lectr, US, Denmark, Ger, Turkey, Italy, Austria & Greece; assoc prof art, Univ Ga, 37-29, head dept art, 38-73, regent's prof art, 48-76, chmn fine arts div, 60-76, Lamar Dodd prof art, 70-76, regent's prof emer art, chmn emer fine arts div & Lamar Dodd prof emer, 76-; lectr, United Chap Phi Beta Kappa, 67-68. *Awards:* Award, Nat Arts Club, 54; Purchase Prizes, Pa Acad Fine Arts & Whitney Mus Am Art, 58; plus others. *Bibliog:* Monroe Wheeler (auth), Painters and Sculptors of Modern America, Crowell, 42; Ray Bethers (auth), How Paintings Happen, Norton, 51; John I H Baur (auth), Revolution and Tradition in American Art, Harvard Univ, 59; plus others. *Mem:* Assoc Nat Acad Design; Col Art Asn Am; Southeastern Art Asn; Asn Ga Artists; Athens Art Asn; plus others. *Publ:* Illusr, The Savannah and the Santee, Rivers of Am Series; contribr, Col Art J, Bk Knowledge & others. *Mailing Add:* Dept of Art Univ of Ga Athens GA 30602

DODD, LOIS
PAINTER, EDUCATOR
b Montclair, NJ, Apr 22, 27. *Study:* Cooper Union, with Byron Thomas & Peter Busa. *Work:* Cooper Union Mus, New York; First Nat City Bank, New York; Kalamazoo Art Ctr, Mich; Ciba-Geigy Chem Corp, Ardsley, NY; Chase Manhattan Bank Collection, New York; and others. *Exhib:* Green Mountain Gallery, New York, 69-71 & 74-76; Fischbach Gallery, New York, 78 & 80-82; Cape Split Place, Maine, 77, 79 & 83; Lyman Allyn Mus, New London, Conn, 80; NJ State Mus, Trenton, 81; and other group & one-man shows. *Pos:* Co-founder, Tanager Gallery, New York. *Teaching:* Instr, Philadelphia Col Art, 63 & 65 & Wagner Col, 63-64; instr, Brooklyn Col, 65-72, assoc prof, 75- *Awards:* Ital Govt Study Grant, 59-60; Longview Found Purchase Award, 62; Ingraham, Merrill Found Grant, 71. *Dealer:* Fischbach Gallery 29 W 57th St New York NY 10019. *Mailing Add:* 30 E Second St New York NY 10003

DODDS, ROBERT J, III
COLLECTOR, MUSEUM DIRECTOR
b San Antonio, Tex, Sept 19, 43. *Study:* Yale Univ, BA, 65; Univ Pa Sch Law, LLB, 69. *Pos:* Term trustee, Mus Art, Carnegie Inst, 71-82; pres, Pittsburgh Plan Art, Pa, 82-; trustee, Westmoreland Co Mus Art, Greensburg, Pa, 83- *Collection:* Pre-World War II American art; post-minimal and conceptual art. *Mailing Add:* 747 Union Trust Bldg Pittsburgh PA 15219

DODGE, JOSEPH JEFFERS
PAINTER
b Detroit, Mich, Aug 9, 17. *Study:* Sch Fine Arts, Harvard Col, BS(hons), 40; also study with Yasuo Kuniyoshi, Woodstock, NY, 44. *Exhib:* Artists of the Upper Hudson, Albany Inst Hist & Art, NY, 42-61; 64th Am Art Exhib, Art Inst Chicago, 61; Realist Invitational, Gallery Contemp Art, Winston-Salem, NC, 69; Florida Creates, var mus, 71-72; retrospective, Cummer Gallery Art, 75; plus others. *Pos:* Cur, Hyde Collection, 41-62; dir, Cummer Gallery Art, 61-72; treas, Art Celebration I and II, 73-74 & 81. *Teaching:* Instr drawing & painting, Hyde Collection, 41-62; substitute prof art hist, Hamilton Col, 47; instr art hist, Adirondack Community Col, 61-62. *Bibliog:* Cover & article, Am Artist, 6/83. *Media:* Oil, Pencil. *Collection:* Nineteenth century realists and academic; drawings; small sculpture; contemporary. *Dealer:* Art Sources 1253 S Shore Dr Orange Park FL 32073; Harmon Galleries Am Art 1415 Main Sarasota FL 33577. *Mailing Add:* 6910 Silver Lake Terr Jacksonville FL 32216

DODRILL, DONALD LAWRENCE
PAINTER, GRAPHIC ARTIST
b Richwood, Ohio, Aug 28, 22. *Study:* Marion Bus Col, cert, 41; Ohio State Univ, Columbus, BFA(cum laude), 49; Syracuse Univ, MFA(illus), 75. *Work:* Schumacher Gallery, Capital Univ; Zanesville Art Ctr, Ohio; Wagnall Found Gallery, Lithopolis, Ohio; Ger Village Soc Hist Mus, Columbus. *Comn:* Union Station (painting), Ohio Bell Tel, Columbus, 78; Neil House (painting), Columbus Dispatch, 81; paintings, Huntington Bank, Washington Court House, Ohio, 81, E V Bischoff Co, Columbus, 83 & Borden Co, Columbus, Ohio, 83. *Exhib:* Watercolor USA, Springfield Art Mus, Mo, 74; Nat Watercolor Soc Exhib, Palm Springs Desert Mus, Calif, 81 & Laguna Beach Mus Art, Calif, 82; Salmagundi Club Fifth Ann Open, New York, 82; Ohio Watercolor Soc Exhib, Nationwide Gallery, Columbus, 83; Ky Watercolor Soc Aqueous Exhib, Owensboro Mus Fine Art, 83; and others. *Pos:* Partner, Dodrill Design, 54-; dir, Windon Gallery, 80- *Teaching:* Instr graphic design, Capital Univ, 76-83; instr watercolor, Adult Educ Prog, 77- & Sr Citizen Prog, 83-, Upper Arlington, Ohio. *Awards:* Permanent Pigments Award, 79 & Ruppel Award, 80, Ohio Watercolor Soc; Knickerbocker Award, Slmagundi Club Fifth Open, 82. *Bibliog:* Helen McClave (auth), Artist likes to have people identify with his pictures, Upper Arlington News, 7/11/74; Mary Bridgeman (auth), Dodrill paints natures moods, Columbus Dispatch, 7/9/78; Pat Smith (auth), Dodrill's real & unreal, Columbus Art Mag, 9/81. *Mem:* Watercolor Soc, Nat, Ohio & Ky; Cent Ohio Watercolor Soc (vpres, 68, pres, 69); Bexley Area Art Guild (pres, 80). *Media:* Watercolor. *Publ:* Illusr cover, Columbus Bus Forum, 75 & 76, Better Living Mag, 75 & 76 & Ohioana Libr Quart, 76-83. *Dealer:* Windon Gallery 1644 W Fifth Ave Columbus OH 43212. *Mailing Add:* 2442 Northwest Blvd Columbus OH 43221

DODWORTH, ALLEN STEVENS
MUSEUM DIRECTOR
b Long Beach, Calif, Nov 19, 38. *Study:* Stanford Univ, BA(fine arts & design); Portland State Univ; Univ Utah. *Collections Arranged:* Ann Exhibs for Artists of Idaho, 69-75, Painters of the Idaho Scene, 72 & American Masters in the West, 74, Boise Gallery Art; Am Abstracts, 76; The Grand Beehive, 80. *Pos:* Chmn, White Gallery, Portland State Univ, 67-69; dir, Boise Gallery Art, Boise Art Asn, 69-76; dir, Salt Lake Art Ctr, 76-81; dir, Western Colo Ctr Arts, 81- *Awards:* Mus Prof Fel, Nat Endowment Arts, 73. *Mem:* Western Asn Art Mus (trustee, 74-79); Am Asn Mus. *Mailing Add:* Western Colo Ctr Arts 1803 N 7th St Grand Junction CO 81501

DOGANCAY, BURHAN CAHIT
PAINTER, SCULPTOR
b Istanbul, Turkey, Sept 11, 29. *Study:* Acad Grande Chaumiere, Paris, France. *Work:* Guggenheim Mus, New York; Ga Mus Art; Brooklyn Mus; Mus Mod Art, New York; Los Angeles Co Mus Art; plus many others. *Exhib:* Kunstsalon Wolfsberg, Zurich; Palais des Beaux-Arts, Brussels; Gallery Engstrom, Stockholm; Galerie Baukunst, Cologne, 82; Centre Georges Pompidou, Paris; and many others. *Awards:* City New York Cert Appreciation, 64; Tamarind Lithography Workshop Fel, 69; Golden Palette Award, Turkey, 83. *Bibliog:* Louise Schultz (auth), Dogancay and His Work, 71; E G Bowles & Tonny Russell (auth), This Book is a Movie, 71; Dogancay (monogr), Alpine Fine Arts Collection Ltd, New York, 83. *Mailing Add:* 220 E 54th St New York NY 10022

DOHANOS, STEVAN
ILLUSTRATOR, PAINTER
b Lorain, Ohio, May 18, 07. *Study:* Cleveland Sch Art. *Work:* Whitney Mus Am Art, New York; Cleveland Print Club; Avery Mem, Hartford, Conn; New Britain Inst; Dartmouth Col. *Comn:* Murals, Charlotte Amalie, St Thomas, VI, Forest Serv Bldg, Elkins, WVa & US Post Off, West Palm Beach, Fla. *Exhib:* New Britain Mus Am Art, Conn, 72. *Teaching:* Founding fac mem, Famous Artists Sch, Westport, Conn. *Awards:* Medal, Philadelphia Watercolor Club; Art Dirs Club; Hall of Fame, Soc Illusr New York, 71. *Mem:* Soc Illusr (pres, 61-63); Am Watercolor Soc. *Mailing Add:* 271 Sturges Hwy Westport CT 06880

DOHERTY, MICHAEL STEPHEN
EDITOR, PRINTMAKER
b New Orleans, La, Mar 9, 48. *Study:* Knox Col, Galesburg, Ill, BA, 70; Cornell Univ, Ithaca, NY, MFA, 72. *Work:* Smithsonian Inst. *Exhib:* Young Printmakers, Herron Sch Art, Indianapolis, 70; Bradley Nat Print & Drawing, Bradley Univ, Peoria, Ill, 77. *Pos:* Art critic, WHCUAM, Ithaca, NY, 72-76; copy supervisor & ed, Advance Process Supply Co, 77-78; ed in chief, Am Artist Mag, New York, 79- *Teaching:* Adj prof art, Tompkins-Cortland Community Col, 73-76; instr art & art hist, Knox Col, Galesburg, Ill, 76-77. *Mem:* Am Soc Mag Ed; Col Art Asn. *Media:* Screen Printing. *Res:* Artist profiles; printmaking. *Publ:* Auth, A screen printed color mixing project, Sch Arts, 79; auth, Techniques of photo screen printing, Graphics, 79; auth, The romance in Mario Cooper's Watercolors, 79, Robert Cottingham: An unabashed realist, 79 & Working with light-sensitive materials, 80, Am Artist. *Mailing Add:* Am Aritst Mag 1515 Broadway New York NY 10036

DOHERTY, ROBERT J
MUSEUM DIRECTOR, EDUCATOR
b Everett, Mass, Jan 16, 24. *Study:* RI Sch Design, BFA, 51; Yale Univ, MFA, 54; Fulbright travel grant to Ger, 65-66. *Comn:* Design & supvr construction, Rice River House, Louisville, Ky, 62. *Collections Arranged:* Graphic Design, Allen R Hite Art Inst, 61; USA-FSA Photo Exhib, Univ Louisville, 61, 19th Century Photographs, 64; The Remote Transmitted Image, 76; Walter Dorwin Teague Designs Cameras, 76; The Photo-Pictorialists, 82; The Japanese Prints from the Arthur Wesley Dow Collection, 82; Moishe Smith Retrospective, 82; and others. *Pos:* Dir graphic design, Reynolds Metals Co, 53-57; dir develop, RI Sch Design, 57-59; art ed, Landscape Archit, 60-62; actg dir, Allen R Hite Art Inst, 64-65, dir, 67-72; graphic designer, Firma Dorland GmbH, Munich, Ger, 65-66; dir, Int Mus Photog, George Eastman House, Rochester, NY, 73-80; dir, Salt Lake Art Ctr & Sch, 81-; dir, Int Arch Photography, 81- *Teaching:* Assoc prof fine arts, Univ Louisville, 59-65, prof, 65-72, chmn dept, 67-72; instr, Free Univ, 70-72; prof, Univ Rochester, 73-80; prof, Rochester Inst Technol, 73-79; Univ Utah, 82- *Awards:* Aluminum Foil Design Award, Lithographers & Printers Nat Asn, 60; Fulbright Travel Grant, 65; Award for Educ, Photog Adminrs, 79; and others. *Mem:* Royal Photog Soc; Deutches Gesellschaft für Photographie; Am Asn Mus; Am Printing Hist Asn. *Res:* Visual controls for streets & highways. *Publ:* Auth, Foto, 64; picture ed, Documenting a Decade, 72; auth, Preservation, 73; auth, Social Documentary Photography, 74; Auth, The Complete Photographic Work of Jacob Riis, Macmillan, 82. *Mailing Add:* Salt Lake Art Ctr & Sch 20 South West Temple Salt Lake City UT 84101

DOLAN, MARGO
GALLERY DIRECTOR, DEALER
b Philadelphia, Pa, Mar 19, 46. *Study:* Conn Col, BA(art hist). *Collections Arranged:* Philadelphia Teaches Printmaking, 78; The Second Empire and The Etching Revival, 78; Sam Maitin: New Directions, 79; French Lithography Before 1850, 80; Philadelphia Connections 1880-1950, 80; The Prints of Lucas van Leyden, 81; Morris Blackburn Retrospective, 83; Lotte Jacobi Retrospective, 83; The Master Print: American Since 1960, 83; Impressions: Experimental Prints, 84. *Pos:* Docent, Univ Mus, Philadelphia, Pa, 68-70; asst dir, Print Club, 70-73, dir, 73-77; dir, Assoc Am Artists, Philadelphia, 78- *Mem:* Art Dealers Asn Am; Philadelphia Art Dealers Asn (vpres, 82-84); The Print Club, Philadelphia; Art Alliance, Philadelphia; Printmaking Coun NJ. *Specialty:* Original prints, drawings and photographs. *Publ:* Contribr, Jerome Kaplan prints, 73; contribr, Home is where the art is, 74; contribr, Folio 76, 75; contribr, intro, Charlotte Printmakers' Soc exhib catalog, 79. *Mailing Add:* 1614 Latimer St Philadelphia PA 19103

DOLE, WILLIAM
PAINTER, EDUCATOR
b Angola, Ind, Sept 2, 17. *Study:* Olivet Col, AB, 38; Mills Col, 40 & 49; Univ Calif, Berkeley, MA, 47; Olivet Col, Hon DFA, 78. *Work:* Fogg Art Mus, Boston; Joseph H Hirshhorn Mus, Washington, DC; Pa Acad Fine Arts, Philadelphia; Santa Barbara Mus Art; Walker Art Ctr, Minneapolis; plus others. *Exhib:* M H de Young Mem Mus, San Francisco, 51; Staempfli Gallery, New York, 74, 76, 78 & 80; Fine Arts Gallery, San Diego, Calif, 76; Hirschhorn Mus, 77; Allentown Art Mus, 79; Indianapolis Mus Art, 79; Phillips Collection, Washington, DC, 79; and many others. *Pos:* Artist-in-residence, Tamarind Inst, Albuquerque, NMex, 71. *Teaching:* Lectr, Univ Calif, Berkeley, 47-49; instr art, Univ Calif, Santa Barbara, 49-51, asst prof, 51-58, assoc prof, 58-63, chmn dept, 58-63 & 71-74, prof, 63- *Awards:* Art Award, Am Acad & Inst of Arts & Letters, 78. *Bibliog:* John Russell (auth), New Collage by William Dole, New York Times, 11/12/76; Henry Seldis (auth), William Dole, Arts Mag, 12/76; Gerald Nordland (auth), William Dole, Art Int, summer 79. *Publ:* Auth, The Wu Wei to Collage, Art Spectrum, 2/75; co-auth, The Collage of William Dole, Visible Language, IX, 75. *Dealer:* Staempfli Gallery 47 E 77th St New York NY 10021; Mekler Gallery 651 N La Cienega Los Angeles CA 90069. *Mailing Add:* Dept of Art Univ Calif Santa Barbara CA 93106

DOLL, DONALD ARTHUR
EDUCATOR, PHOTOGRAPHER
b Milwaukee, Wis, July 15, 37. *Study:* St Louis Univ, BA, MA. *Work:* Sheldon Art Gallery, Lincoln, Nebr; Mid-Am Arts Alliance, Kansas City, Mo; Rochester Inst Technol, NY. *Exhib:* Crying for a Vision, A Rosebud Sioux Trilogy (traveling exhib), Nat Endowment Arts, 76-78. *Teaching:* From assoc prof photog to prof, Creighton Univ, 69-, chmn fine & performing arts dept, 76- *Awards:* World Understanding Through Photog, Univ Mo Sch Journalism, Nat Press Photog Asn & Nikon, 76. *Mem:* Soc Photog Educ; Nat Press Photog Asn. *Publ:* Coauth & ed, Crying for a Vision, Morgan & Morgan, 76; contribr, Photojournalism, Nat Geographic & Nikon, 76. *Mailing Add:* Dept of Fine & Performing Arts Creighton Univ Omaha NE 68178

DOLL, LINDA A
PAINTER, PRINTMAKER
b Brooklyn, NY, May 5, 42. *Study:* Palomar Col, AA; San Diego State Univ, BA(art), 77; Univ Calif, San Diego, cert(teaching), 78; studied with Rex & Joan Irving Brandt, Millard Sheets & Robert E Wood. *Work:* Scripps Hosp, La Jolla, Calif. *Exhib:* San Diego Int Exhib, 78, 79, 82 & 83; La Int Exhib, New Orleans, 82; Nat Arts Club Ann Exhib, New York, 82; Allied Artist Ann Exhib, Salmagundi Club, New York, 82; Adirondacks Nat Exhib Am Watercolors, Old Forge, NY, 83; and others. *Teaching:* Instr workshops & sems, Calif, 78-; instr drawing & painting, Poway Unified Sch Dist, 78-82 & Palomar Col, 80- *Awards:* Third Place Jurors Award, Watercolor Art in All Media, Del Mar, Calif, 81; Second Place Jurors Award, Watercolor West, Riverside Mus, 82. *Mem:* San Diego Watercolor Soc (bd mem, 79-83, pres, 80-81); La Jolla Art Asn (vpres, 79-80); Artist Equity. *Media:* Watermedia. *Dealer:* Grays Gallery Escondido CA; Brandon Gallery Fallbrook CA. *Mailing Add:* 17490 Matinal Dr Rancho Bernardo CA 92127

DOMAREKI, JOSEPH THEODORE
PAINTER, SCULPTOR
b Newark, NJ, May 17, 14. *Study:* Newark State Col, BS, 37; Univ Iowa, MA, 47; NY Univ, 48-50. *Work:* Norfolk Mus Arts & Sci, Va; Navy Dept, Pentagon Bldg, Washington, DC; Montclair Mus, NJ; Columbia Mus Art, SC; Broad Nat Bank, Newark; Monmouth Col, West Long Branch, NJ. *Comn:* Bronze & stone wall mural, Sinclair Res Ctr, Tulsa, Okla, 63; hammered lead relief sculpture (exterior side), St Luke's Episcopal Church, Haworth, NJ, 65; oil painting, Newark Brush Co, Kenilworth, NJ; Corten free-standing sculpture (exterior), Clean-Way Laundry, South Orange, NJ; multi-media painting, Secord Mem, Columbia High Sch, Maplewood, NJ. *Exhib:* Newark Mus Biannual, 54-73; Newark Mus Triennial State Exhib, 62-71; Art Gallery 64, Hall of Educ, New York World's Fair, 64-65, American Art Today, Pavilion Fine Arts, 64; Silvermine Ann Exhib, Conn, 65; NJ Artists Ann, Trenton State Mus, 66, 68 & 70. *Teaching:* Head dept art, Sch Dist South Orange & Maplewood, NJ, 64-74; retired. *Awards:* Medal of Hon/Sculpture, Knickerbocker Artists Ann, 55 & 64; Medal Hon Painting, 64 & Medal Hon Sculpture, 75, Audubon Artists Ann; plus others. *Mem:* Audubon Artists (pres, 64-68); hon mem Salmagundi Club, New York; Assoc Artists NJ (vpres, 58-60); Nat Soc Painters & Sculptors (vpres, 56-58); NJ Watercolor Soc; Knickerbocker Artists. *Media:* Oil; Steel, Bronze. *Dealer:* Gallery Madison/90 1248 Madison Ave New York NY 10028. *Mailing Add:* 11 Sunset Lane Monmouth Beach NJ 07750

DOMBEK, BLANCHE M
SCULPTOR
b New York, NY. *Study:* With Alexandre Zeitlin & Leo Amino. *Work:* Brooklyn Mus, NY; Keene State Col, NH; Randolph-Macon Woman's Col; MacDowell Colony; Louis Armstrong Community Arts Mus. *Comn:* Many pvt collections. *Exhib:* Sculpture Ctr, New York Sculptors Guild, 80; Canton Art Inst, Ohio, 81; New York Botanical Garden, 81; Gallery 84, New York, 81; St Gauden's Mem, Nat Hist Site, Cornish, NH, 81; and many others. *Awards:* MacDowell Colony Award, 81; and others. *Bibliog:* Evelyn Eaton (auth), Progression (film), Draco Found, 65; American visitor's sculpture helps launch new play, Stroud Daily, Glos, Eng, 12/8/71; Kate Kendall (auth), Sculptor's range to mark Dombek show, Peterborough Transcript, 1/23/69; and others. *Media:* Multimedia. *Mailing Add:* RFD 1 Box 751 Hancock NH 03449

DOMINIQUE, JOHN AUGUST
PAINTER
b Virserum, Sweden, Oct 1, 1893; US citizen. *Study:* Portland Art Asn Sch, 13; San Francisco Inst Art, 15-16; Van Sloan Sch Painting, 17; Santa Barbara Sch Arts, 21 & 27-29; also with Colin Campbell Cooper, Armin Hanson & Carl Oscar Borg. *Work:* Univ Va Art Gallery. *Exhib:* Portland Art Mus, Ore, 36; Oakland Art Mus, Calif, 41; Los Angeles Art Mus, Calif, 44; Calif Watercolor Soc, Pasadena Art Mus, 61; Charles & Emma Frye Art Mus, Seattle, Wash, 62. *Awards:* Painting Award for Covered Bridge, Ore State Fair, 40, Painting Award for Oregon Landscape, 41; Painting Award for Peach Tree in Bloom, Glendale Art Asn, 50. *Bibliog:* Arthur Millier (auth), article in Los Angeles Times, 10/8/33; Maxine Buren (auth), article in Ore Statesman, 10/9/38; Melba Meredith (auth), article in Ojai Valley News, 7/5/62. *Mem:* Nat Watercolor Soc. *Media:* Oil, Watercolor. *Mailing Add:* 216 N Pueblo Ave Ojai CA 93023

DOMIT, MOUSSA M
MUSEUM DIRECTOR, HISTORIAN
b Lebanon, May 24, 32; nat US. *Study:* Ohio State Univ, BA(art hist); Southern Conn State Col, MS(art educ); Yale Univ. *Collections Arranged:* Sculpture of Thomas Eakins, Corcoran Gallery Art (with catalog), 69; Art of Wilhelm Lehmbruck, Nat Gallery Art, Washington, DC, 72; and others. *Pos:* Cur intra-univ loan collection & registrar collections, Yale Univ Art Gallery, 66-68; assoc dir, Corcoran Gallery Art, 68-70; mus cur, Nat Gallery Art, 70-72; assoc dir, NC Mus Art, Raleigh, 72-74, dir, 74-80; bd adv, Univ Ga Mus Art, Athens, 77-80; freelance consult, 81- *Teaching:* Instr hist art, Columbus Col Art & Design, Ohio, 62-64; lectr art appreciation, Corcoran Sch Art, Washington, DC, 68-70; lectr art hist, Hood Col, 71-72; adj prof art, Univ NC, Chapel Hill, 76-77. *Mem:* Asn Art Mus Dir; Am Asn Mus; Nat Soc Lit & Arts. *Res:* American impressionist painting. *Publ:* Auth, George Lee: Recent Color Photography, Corcoran Gallery Art, 69; auth, American Impressionist Painting, Nat Gallery Art, 73; auth, Art of Saliba Douaihy, NC Mus Art, 78. *Mailing Add:* 4117 Huckleberry St Raleigh NC 27612

DOMJAN, JOSEPH (SPIRI)
PAINTER, GRAPHIC ARTIST
b Budapest, Hungary, Mar 15, 07. *Study:* Hungarian Royal Acad Fine Arts, BFA & MA; also study in Italy, Ger & France. *Work:* Metrop Mus Art, New York; Nat Mus Mod Art, Paris; Brit Mus, London; Smithsonian Inst & Libr of Cong, Washington, DC; Mus Mod Art, Tokyo; 175 museum collections. *Comn:* Cards & calendar, UNICEF, 60-63; Fifteen Battles (bd & album of originals), Limited Ed Club, 69 & 70; silver snowflake & gold star, 71-75; silver & gold heart, 78 & angel, rooster, hearts, 83-84, Metrop Mus Art. *Exhib:* retrospective, NJ State Mus, Trenton, 66 & 73; Triennale Int Xilografia, Carpi, Italy, 69 & 72; Print Club, Albany, NY, 68; US Capitol; Int Exhib Exlibris, Marlboro, 75; Mint Mus Art, Charlotte, NC, 78; 500 one-man shows on four continents. *Teaching:* Vis lectr, coast to coast, 56- *Awards:* Rockefeller Found Grant, 58; George Washington Award, 70; Bela Bartok Commemorative Medal, 81; and others. *Bibliog:* Pierre Mornand (auth), Domjan in the Forest of the Golden Dragon, Opus, 73; Evelyn Domjan (auth), Edge of Paradise, 79 & Pavologia, 84. *Mem:* Fel Metrop Mus Art; Soc Illusr; Soc Am Graphic Arts; Soc Encouragement Progress, Paris; Nat Acad Design. *Media:* Oil; Wood, Tapestry. *Publ:* Illusr, Faraway Folk Tales, Holt, Rinehart & Winston, 72; Artist and the Legend, Eagle Woodcuts, Domjan, 76; Eternal Wool, 80; Sun Gates, 80. *Dealer:* Domjan Studio W Lake Rd Tuxedo Park NY 10987. *Mailing Add:* West Lake Rd Tuxedo Park NY 10987

DONAHUE, PHILIP RICHARD
PAINTER, EDUCATOR
b Detroit, Mich, Apr 1, 43. *Study:* St Peters Col, AB(art hist), 69; Spring Hill Col, MA, 72; Grad Theological Union, PhD, 83. *Comn:* Donahue Painting Series, Soc Jesus, New Orleans, La, 70-82; St Ignatius Mural, St Charles Col, Grand Coteau, La, 72; Presidential Series, Spring Hill Col, Mobile, Ala, 74; Ordination Card Series, Jesuit Sch Theology, Berkeley, Calif, 74-82; covers (Japanese poetry bk), Tokyo, 82-83. *Exhib:* Allied Arts Competition, Metrop Mobile Mus, Ala, 74; The Holy in Art, St Alberts Col, Oakland, Calif, 75; Religious Art Ann, Grad Theological Union, Berkeley, Calif, 75-82; Emergence Art Xian Thought, Grace Cathedral, San Francisco, Calif, 76; one-man show, Jesuit Art Ctr, Baltimore, Md, 78; Graduate Theological Union, Berkeley, 83. *Collections Arranged:* Artworks 82, Int Hunger Project, 82; Link Art Int, Tokyo, Osaka, Hiroshima, 82 & Hakuhodo, Sapporo, 83. *Pos:* Artist-in-residence, St Charles Col, Grand Coteau, La, 70-72; artist-in-residence, Jesuit Sch Theology, Berkeley, Calif, 74-82; dir special events & art educ, Link Art Int Ltd, Oakland, 82- *Teaching:* Asst instr art hist & drawing, St Peters Col, Jersey City, NJ, 64-68; asst prof painting, Spring Hill Col, Mobile, Ala, 72-74. *Awards:* Full Patronage, Soc Jesus, 70-82; First Place, Asn Educ Tech, 72; First Place, Allied Artist Council, 74. *Bibliog:* C J McNaspy (auth), American Jesuits in the Arts, The Jesuit, fall 76; K G Connolly (auth), Art & belief, New Catholic World, 1-2/80; T Anzai & A Donahue (auth), Link art international, Motions, Tokyo, 11/81. *Media:* Oil, Slides. *Res:* Iconological hermeneutics: symbolic interpretation of the levels of meanings in paintings. *Publ:* Illusr, Bom Pastor, Brazil, Catholic Voice, 77; auth, Iconological Hermeneutics, Am Acad Religion, 80, auth, Visual Art, Society & Religion, New Catholic World, 80; auth, Greco-Roman Influences in Early Xian Iconology, Calif Classic Asn, 81. *Dealer:* Link Art Int Ltd 3700 Verden Ave Oakland CA 94619. *Mailing Add:* 3700 Virden Ave Oakland CA 94619

DONALDSON, JEFF R
PAINTER, ADMINISTRATOR
b Pine Bluff, Ark, Dec 15, 32. *Study:* Univ Ark, Pine Bluff, BA(studio art); Ill Inst of Technol, MS(art educ); Northwestern Univ, PhD(art hist). *Work:* Studio Mus in Harlem, New York; Corcoran Gallery of Art & Nat Collection of Fine Art, Washington, DC; Fisk Univ, Nashville, Tenn; Univ Ark, Pine Bluff. *Comn:* P B S Pinchaback portrait, State of Ill Hist Soc, 63; Wall of Respect, Miles Col, Birmingham, Ala, 69. *Exhib:* Mus la Tertulia, Cali, Colombia, 71; Studio Mus in Harlem, New York, 75; Nat Ctr for Afro-Am Art, Boston, Mass, 75; Southside Art Ctr, Chicago, 75; Herbert Johnson Mus, Cornell Univ, Ithaca, NY, 76; Howard Univ, Washington, DC, 76; Afro-Am Hist/Cult Mus, Philadelphia, Pa, 77. *Collections Arranged:* Directions in Afro-Am Art, Johnson Mus, Cornell Univ, 75. *Pos:* Bd dir, Nat Ctr for Afro-Am Artists, 70-; vpres USA/Can zone, FESTAC 77, Lagos, Nigeria, 75-; art dir, Jazz Am Marketing, 81- *Teaching:* Lectr art hist, Northwestern Univ, Evanston, Ill, 68-70; chmn art dept, Howard Univ, Washington, DC, 70-76. *Awards:* First Place/Painting, Art & Soul Exhib, Westside Gallery, 68; First Place/Painting, Black Expressions, Southside Art Ctr, Chicago, 69; E Catlett-Mora Award, Nat Conf of Artists Ann, 77. *Bibliog:* Harold Hayden (auth), Right On Art Lovers, Chicago Sun-Times, 9/70; Edward S Spriggs (auth), Africobra; Paul Richard (auth), A Bright New School, Washington Post, 3/76. *Mem:* Nat Conf of Artists; Africobra-Farafindugu. *Media:* Opaque and transparent watercolor. *Publ:* Auth, Civil Rights Yearbook, Henry Regenry, 63; illusr, Riot, Broadside Press, 68; ed, Directions 69, Ill Art Educ Asn, 69; illusr, Book of Life, Broadside Press, 74. *Mailing Add:* 504 T St NW Washington DC 20001

DONALDSON, MARJORY (ROGERS)
CURATOR, PAINTER
b Woodstock, NB, Mar 22, 26. *Study:* Univ NB Summer Sch, 45, with Pegi Nicol MacLeod; Mt Allison Univ, BFA, 51; City & Guilds of London Sch, Eng, 63-64. *Work:* Prov NB Art Bank, Fredericton; NB Mus, St John; Mt Allison Univ, Sackville, NB; City Hall, St John, NB. *Comn:* Seventy portraits, NB Sports Hall of Fame, 69-77; official portraits, Univ NB, 71-77; official portrait of ex-pres, St Thomas Univ, 77 & Acadia Univ, 77. *Exhib:* One-person shows, Univ NB, Fredericton & NB Mus, St John, 64-76, Mem Univ Nfld Art

Gallery, 71, Atlantic Prov Art Galleries Asn (traveling exhib), 71-72 & Art Gallery of NS (traveling exhib of prov), 76; Can Soc Painter-Etchers & Engravers; Calgary Graphics. *Pos:* Art mistress, Edgehill Sch for Girls, Windsor, NS, 48-50; actg dir, Univ NB Art Centre, Fredericton, 54-55, asst to dir, 64-70, cur, 70- *Teaching:* Printmaking, Univ NB, Fredericton, 65- *Awards:* O'Keefe Brewery Award, Toronto, 50. *Mem:* Can Mus Asn; Atlantic Prov Art Galleries Asn (secy & treas); Asn of Mus of NB; Atlantic Can Inst (dir). *Media:* Oil, Intaglio. *Publ:* Illusr, Atlantic Advocate, 50-60; illusr (four cover designs. *Dealer:* Morrison Art Gallery 221 Union St St John NB Can. *Mailing Add:* c/o Univ NB Art Ctr Fredericton NB E3E 5A3 Canada

DONATI, ENRICO
PAINTER, SCULPTOR
b Milan, Italy, Feb 19, 09; US citizen. *Study:* Univ Pavia, Italy, Dr, 29; Art Students League, 40; New Sch Social Res, New York, 41. *Work:* Albright-Knox Art Gallery, Buffalo, NY; Univ Art Mus, Univ Calif, Berkeley; Mus Mod Art, New York; Whitney Mus Am Art, New York; Baltimore Mus Art. *Exhib:* Eight Carnegie Int Exhibs, 45-61; Embellished Surfaces, Mus Mod Art, New York, 53-54; Younger American Painters, Solomon R Guggenheim Mus, 54-55; Palais des Beaux-Arts, Brussels, Belg, 61; Friends Collection, Whitney Mus Am Art, 64, Staempfli Gallery, New York, 62-82 & Grand Palais, Paris, 80. *Pos:* Mem adv bd, Brandeis Univ, Waltham, Mass, 56-72; mem pres coun arts & archit, Yale Univ, 62-72; chmn nat comn, Univ Art Mus, Univ Calif, Los Angeles, 70-72. *Teaching:* Vis lectr & critic, Yale Univ, 62-72. *Bibliog:* John Gruen (auth), Enrico Donati, Mus de Poche, 65. *Dealer:* Gimpel & Weitzen Hoffer 1040 Madison Ave New York NY 10021. *Mailing Add:* 222 Central Park S New York NY 10019

DONDE, OLGA
PAINTER, PRINTMAKER
b Campeche, Mex, May 23, 37. *Study:* Self-taught. *Work:* Latin Am Contemp Mus, Washington, DC; Banamex Bank, London; Nat Mus, La Habana, Cuba; Mus Mod Art, Mexico City; Inst Panameno de Arte, Panama. *Comn:* Stained glass door, Arvil Gallery, Mexico City, 74; cover design & monotype, RCA Victor, 74; costume & stage designs, Las Tandas Del Tlancualejo, Nat Autonomous Univ Mex, 75. *Exhib:* Pape Mus, Monclova, Mex, 79; Montevideo Mus, Uruguay, 80; Inst Politecnico Nac, Mex, 80; Kunstlerhaus Bethanien, Berlin, WGer, 81; Stockholm Int Art Expos, Suecia, 81; and others. *Pos:* Founder, Editorial Domes, Mexico, 75- *Bibliog:* Olga Donde and Her Visceral Painting (film), Nat Broadcast, Mex, 74; James Fortson (dir), Face to Face (film interview), Nat Broadcast, Mex, 79. *Mem:* Contemp Art Forum, Mexico City (founder). *Media:* Mixed Media, Oil; Charcoal. *Dealer:* Misrachi Art Gallery Genova No 20 Mexico 6 DF. *Mailing Add:* Angel Urraza 523-1019 Col del Valle 03100 Del Benito Juarez Mexico DF Mexico

DONHAUSER, PAUL STEFAN
SCULPTOR, WRITER
b Berlin, Ger, May 6, 36; US citizen. *Study:* Univ Wis-Milwaukee, BS(art); Univ Wis-Madison, MS(art); Ill State Univ, PhD(art). *Work:* Int Mus Ceramics, Faenza, Italy; Nat Mus Art, Gdansk, Poland; Maison des Metiers d'Art Francais, Paris; Everson Mus Art, Syracuse, NY. *Comn:* Relief mural (6ft x 15ft), Student Union, Wis State Col, Oshkosh, 71; series of five free standing outdoor sculptures, Univ Wis Campus, 78. *Exhib:* Wis Directions, Milwaukee Art Ctr, 76; Landscape: New Views, Johnson Mus, Cornell Univ, Ithaca, NY, 78; Int Biennial Exhib of Ceramic Sculpture, Ballauris, France, 78; Clay & Fiber, Wustum Fine Arts Mus, Racine, Wis, 78; Donhauser Retrospective: 1957-1977, Paine Art Ctr, Oshkosh, 77; one-man show, Bergstrom Art Ctr, Neenah, Wis, 77; and many others. *Teaching:* Instr ceramic sculpture, Madison Area Tech Col, Wis, 60-63; instr drawing & ceramics, Ill State Univ, Normal, 63-65; prof ceramic sculpture, Univ Wis, Oshkosh, 65- *Awards:* Nat Award for Ceramic Sculpture, 8th Miami Ceramic Nat Exhib, Coral Gables Art Asn, Fla, 72; Grand Prize of Faenza, 35th Int Exhib of Ceramics, Int Mus of Ceramics, 76; Scandoli Mem Prize, Nat Exhib, Burpee Art Mus, Rockford, Ill, 77. *Bibliog:* Sergio Cavina (auth), Emilia Romagna, Regione, Bologna, Italy, 9/76; Linda Witt (auth), Donhauser wins Italy's top ceramic prize, People Weekly, 10/11/76; James Auer (auth), Uncommon clay, Milwaukee J, 9/77. *Mem:* Int Acad of Ceramics, Geneva, Switz; Am Crafts Coun; Wis Designer Craftsmen. *Publ:* Co-auth, New Ceramics, St Martins, London, 74; auth, History of American ceramics, The Studio Potter, Kendall/Hunt, 78. *Dealer:* Gilman Galleries 201 E Ohio St Chicago IL 60611. *Mailing Add:* Dept of Art Univ of Wis Oshkosh WI 54901

DONNELLY, MARIAN CARD
HISTORIAN, EDUCATOR
b Evanston, Ill, Sept 12, 23. *Study:* Oberlin Col, AB, 46, MA, 48; Yale Univ, PhD, 56. *Pos:* Art librn, Univ Rochester, 51-53; res assoc, Art Inst Chicago, 56-57. *Teaching:* Instr art hist, Upsala Col, 48-50; from asst prof to prof art hist, Univ Ore, 66-; retired. *Mem:* Archaeol Inst Am; Nat Trust Hist Preserv; Royal Soc Arts, London; Soc Archit Historians (dir, 64-67, 78-, second vpres, 72-74, first vpres, 74-76, pres, 76-78). *Res:* Vernacular and technological architecture in North Europe and America, particularly during the sixteenth, seventeenth and eighteenth centuries. *Publ:* Auth, Astronomical Observatories in New England, Old Time New Eng, 60; auth, New England Pyramids, J Soc Archit Historians, 60; auth, New England Meeting Houses of the Seventeenth Century, Wesleyan Univ Press, 68; auth, Materials in Early New England, Old Time New England, 71; auth, A Short History of Observatories, Univ Ore Bks, 73. *Mailing Add:* 2175 Olive St Eugene OR 97405

DONNESON, SEENA
SCULPTOR, GRAPHICS ARTIST
b New York, NY. *Study:* Pratt Inst; Art Students League, with Morris Kantor; Pratt Graphic Arts Ctr, with Michael Ponce de Leon. *Work:* Mus Mod Art, New York; Brooklyn Mus; Los Angeles Co Mus Art; Smithsonian Mus, Washington, DC; Norton Gallery of Art, Palm Beach, Fla. *Comn:* Ed of prints, Touchstone Press; tapestry design, Equitable Life & Insurance Co, New York, 76; ed prints, Ft Lauderdale Mus Fine Arts, Fla, 77; Outdoor sculpture for Snug Harbor Cult Ctr, Grow-Kiewit-Mk, New York, 79; outdoor sculpture, Jersey City State Col, NJ, 81. *Exhib:* 15th & 19th Biennale, Brooklyn Mus, 65 & 75; Projected Art: Artists at Work, Finch Col, 71; San Diego Mus, Calif, 75; Reflections/Refractions, Ft Lauderdale Mus Fine Art & Marymount Col, New York, 77-78; Sculpture in Color, New York, 78. *Pos:* app mem, Nassau Co Fine Arts Comn, 70-; exhib coordr, Dept Parks, Recreation & Cult Affairs, New York, 72-74. *Teaching:* Lectr hist mod art, NY Univ, 61-63; in-sch-artist, Nassau Co Cult Coun, 71-79; lectr, New Sch Social Res, 74-, New Hampshire Col, painting & drawing, 80-82. *Awards:* Tamarind Lithography Workshop, 68; Clayworks, 81; Creative Artists Serv Prog Grant, NY State Coun Arts, 83-84. *Bibliog:* John Perreault (auth), Up the river, Soho Weekly News, 78; Grace Glueck (auth), Sculpture under a city sky, New York Times, 78. *Mem:* Artists Equity Asn NY; Nat Asn Women Artists; Womens Caucus; Women in Art; Womens Interart Ctr. *Media:* Metals; Clay, Handmade Paper. *Dealer:* Grippi Gallery New York NY. *Mailing Add:* 319 Greenwich St New York NY 10013

DONOHOE, VICTORIA
HISTORIAN, CRITIC
b Philadelphia, Pa. *Study:* Rosemont Col, BA; Univ Pa Grad Sch Fine Arts, MFA; Pius XII Inst Fine Arts Advan Study, Florence, Italy, cert(scholar), 53; Am Fedn Arts Workshop Art Criticism, scholar, 68. *Collections Arranged:* Religious & Liturgical Art from the Eastern US, Philadelphia Civic Ctr, 63. *Pos:* Art critic, Standard & Times, Philadelphia, 59-62; art critic, Philadelphia Inquirer, 62-; guest cur, Into Storage Exhib, Univ Mus, Univ Pa, 74; corresp, Art News, 75-; dir for selection, Exhib Liturgical Art, 41st Int Eucharistic Cong, Philadelphia, 76; adv, Philadelphia Craft Show, 77; adv fac, Franklin & Marshall Col, 79. *Teaching:* Lab asst studio art & art hist, Rosemont Col, 50-52, lectr, 54-55. *Awards:* Award, Catholic Fine Arts Soc, 76. *Mem:* Int Asn Art Critics/Am Sect; Soc Archit Historians; Irish Georgian Soc, Dublin; Medieval Acad Am; Am-Italy Soc. *Res:* Late 19th & early 20th century American sculpture; figurative painting & sculpture; contemporary crafts; American architecture. *Publ:* Contribr, Sculpture of a City: Philadelphia's Treasures in Bronze and Stone, 74; contribr, Knight-Ridder Newswire, 73-; also contribr to anthologies, mags, encyclopedias & Sunday supplements. *Mailing Add:* 34 Narbrook Park Narberth PA 19072

DONSON, JEROME ALLAN
GALLERY DIRECTOR, DEALER
b New York, NY, Mar 20, 24. *Study:* Univ Southern Calif, with Prof DeErdely & Prof Don Goodall, BA, 49, MSEd, 50; Am Grad Sch, Denmark, Jean Hershholt Fund Scholar, 50; Univ Copenhagen, with Johannes Brondsted & Dr Vagn Poulsen, 51; New Sch Social Res, with Seymour-Lipton & Camillo Egas; Univ Calif, Berkeley, with Prof Herschel Chipp & Clark Winter, MA(art), 57. *Pos:* Dir, Florence Mus, SC, 54-56; munic art dir, Long Beach, Calif, 56-61; exec dir, Off Cult Affairs, New York, 63-64; ed, Col Art News Art J, 64-70; exec dir, Fine Arts Ctr, Anderson, Ind, 66-68; dir, Louisville Sch Art & Art Ctr Asn, 72-; dir, Collectors' Showroom, Chicago, 77-78; exec dir, Art Collectors Ctr, Chicago, 78- *Teaching:* Lectr mod art hist, Univ Calif, Los Angeles, 58-60; dir art & assoc prof art hist, Fairleigh-Dickinson Univ, 62-63; prof & art consult, Long Island Univ, 65; vis prof visual hist, Inst Design, Ill Inst Technol & Chicago Bd Educ, 70-72; prof, Louisville Sch Art, 72-82. *Awards:* First Prize in Sculpture, Guild SC Artists, 55; Cult Award of Yr, Long Beach CofC, 61; Award of Merit, Prof Photog Calif, 62. *Mem:* Col Art Asn Am; Am Coun Educ; Am Asn Higher Educ; Western Mus League; Western Asn Art Mus Dirs (adv). *Res:* Scandinavian arts, modern and contemporary, primitive. *Publ:* Auth, Light & shadow, ceramic exploration, Design, fall 60; auth, American vanguard exhibitions in Europe, Art J, summer 63; auth, New Bauhaus approach, New Art Asn, 71; auth, Eight by Eight, 73; auth, Community resource directory, Jefferson Co Bd Educ, 77. *Mailing Add:* 3150 N Sheridan Rd Chicago IL 60657

DOO DA POST (EDWARD FERDINAND HIGGINS III)
PAINTER, MAIL ARTIST
b LaCrosse, Wis, Nov 10, 49. *Study:* Western Mich Univ, Kalamazoo, BA(art), 72; Univ Colo, Boulder, MFA, 76. *Work:* Electroworks Collection, Eastman House, Rochester, NY; US Post Off, Boulder, Colo; Univ Mich, Ann Arbor; Artists Stamps & Stamp Images, Simon Frasier Univ Gallery, Burnaby, BC; Jean Brown Arch, Shaker Seed House, Tryingham, Mass. *Exhib:* Fourteenth Midwest Joslyn Art Mus, Omaha, Nebr, 76; Timbres, Et Tampons, E' Artistes Cabnet des Extampes, Mus d'Art & d'Histoire, Geneva, Switz, 76; 4th Denver Metro Show, Denver Art Mus, 76; Visual Poetics, Mus Arte Contemporarea, Sao Paulo, Brazil, 77; Electroworks, Eastman House Photog Mus, Rochester, 79-80. *Collections Arranged:* First New York City Stamp Invite (auth, catalog), 34 Artists' Stamp Images, 77; Commonpress Number 18 (auth, catalog), 79. *Bibliog:* Peter Frank (auth), Artists Stamps, Art Express 1, Vol 1, 81; Alexandra Anderson (auth), Portfolio 3, Vol 3, 5-6/81; Ronnie Cohen (auth), article, Art News, 12/81. *Media:* Oil; Color Xerox. *Publ:* Auth & illusr, To Grow an Asparagus (under pen name Sam Scotland), 70 & auth & illusr, A Piece of Licorice and Other White Elephants, 72, Glotco; contribr, The Rubber Stamp Album, Workman Publ, 78; auth, Artists' stamps, Print Collectors' Newslett, 11-12/79. *Dealer:* Gracie Mansion Gallery 337 E Tenth St New York NY 10009. *Mailing Add:* 153 Ludlow New York NY 10000

DOOLEY, HELEN BERTHA
PAINTER, DEALER
b San Jose, Calif, July 27, 07. *Study:* San Jose State Col, AB; Claremont Grad Sch, MA; Douglas Donaldson Sch Design; Calif Sch Fine Arts, San Francisco; Chouinard Art Inst, Los Angeles; Univ Calif, Berkeley; Teachers Col, Columbia Univ. *Work:* Univ Pac; Shimizu Mus, Japan; Liquid Paper Corp; Leonard Besinger Jr; Great Western Savings, Carmel. *Comn:* Portrait of Dr D Elton Trueblood (oil), 55-56; portrait of Mrs Lloyd Bertholf (oil), Stockton, 56; portrait of Dr Irving Goleman (oil), Irving Goleman Libr, Univ Pacific, Stockton, 62; Floral (oil), G Douglas Burck, Pres, Am Inst Foreign Studies, 69. *Exhib:* Pa Acad Fine Arts, Philadelphia, 41; Soc Western Artists, De Young Mus, San Francisco, 51 & 66; Am Watercolor Soc, Nat Acad Galleries, New York, 63; Lord & Taylor Galleries, New York, 69; Los Angeles Co Art Exhib & West Coast Watercolor Soc, Sacramento, Calif, 71 & 75; Carmel Art Asn Galleries, 73, 79 & 80; Royal Watercolor Soc, London, 78; plus others. *Pos:* Owner, Dooley Gallery, Carmel, Calif, 64- *Teaching:* Instr art, Oakland City Schs, 28-30; com artist, Hale Bros, San Jose, 31-32; adult educ instr art, San Jose City Schs, 33-37; instr art, Scripps Col, 37-39; supvr art, Kern Co Schs, Bakersfield, Calif, 39-47; prof art, Univ Pac, 48-68. *Awards:* Award for Mist on the Bay (watercolor), Soc Western Artists, 51; Award for How Green the Valley (oil), Calif State Fair, 65; Award for Festival (oil), Monterey Peninsula Mus Art, 67. *Mem:* Carmel Art Asn; West Coast Watercolor Soc. *Media:* Oil, Watercolor. *Publ:* Auth, Figure Drawing Teaching Charts, 48-49; auth, Elementary Crafts in a Nutshell, 63. *Mailing Add:* Dooley Gallery Box 5577 Carmel CA 93921

DOOLIN, JAMES LAWRENCE
PAINTER
b Hartford, Conn, June 28, 32. *Study:* Philadelphia Col of Art, BFA, 54, with Henry Pitz; Univ Calif, Los Angeles, MFA, 71, with Richard Diebenkorn. *Work:* Long Beach Mus of Art, Calif; Univ Vt, Burlington; Nat Gallery of Victoria, Melbourne, Australia; Gallery of NSW, Sydney; Australian Nat Gallery, Canberra. *Exhib:* One-man shows, Los Angeles Municipal Gallery, 77 & De Young Mus, San Francisco, 77; The Field, Victorian Nat Gallery, Melbourne, 68; two-man show, Palos Verdes Art Mus, Calif, 72; Shopping Mall--A Conceptual Perspective Traveling Exhib, 78-79; New Realism: Eight Calif Painters, Nev Art Gallery, Reno, 78; and others. *Teaching:* Instr drawing & painting, Prahran Tech Col, Melbourne, Australia, 65-66; lectr, Univ Calif, Los Angeles, 72-80; instr drawing & painting, Otis-Parsons Art Inst, Los Angeles, 77 & 79-80. *Awards:* Purchase Prize, 9th Ann Southern Calif Exhib, Long Beach Mus of Art, 70; Guggenheim Found Fel, 80-81; Nat Endowment Arts Grant, 81-82. *Bibliog:* Santa Monicao Mall: Jim Doolin, Dumb Ox Mag, fall 77-spring 78; Gary Catallano (auth), The Years of Hope, Oxford University Press, 80. *Media:* Oil, Acrylic. *Mailing Add:* 321 E Third St Los Angeles CA 90013

DORFMAN, BRUCE
PAINTER, INSTRUCTOR
b New York, NY, Aug 15, 36. *Study:* Art Students League, with Yasuo Kuniyoshi & Arnold Blanch; Univ Iowa, BA, 58. *Work:* Butler Inst Am Art, Youngstown, Ohio; Arco Ctr Visual Art, Los Angeles; Com Trust Co Found; Rockefeller Found; Govt Israel; and others. *Comn:* Rockefeller Found, RF Illustrated, 79 *Exhib:* Butler Inst Am Art, 71, 72 & 75; Kennedy Galleries, New York, 72; Nassau Community Col, New York, 76-77; Nobe Gallery, New York, 78; New Sch Soc Res, 81; Arras Gallery, New York, 81. *Teaching:* Guest artist, Norton Mus, W Palm Beach, Fla, 62-64; Schenectady Mus, 65-66, Everson Mus, Syracuse, NY, 72; instr painting & drawing, Art Students League, Woodstock, NY, 64-72; coordr & moderator Friday Noon Forum, 68-71; resident artist, Syracuse Univ, 71; instr, Art Students League, New York, 69-; mem fac art workshops, New Sch Soc Res, 79- *Awards:* New York World's Fair Exhib Award, State of Fla, 64; Friends of Am Art Purchase Award, Butler Inst Am Art Ann, 72; Award, Sharon Creative Arts Found, Conn, 78; and others. *Bibliog:* John Canaday (auth), article, New York Times, 10/67; David L Shirey (auth), article, New York Times, 1/77; Gerrit Henry (auth), Bruce Dorfman, Artnews, 1/83; and others. *Mem:* Life mem Art Students League. *Publ:* Auth, Color Mixing, Grosset & Dunlap, 67. *Dealer:* Arras Gallery 29 West 57th St New York NY 10019. *Mailing Add:* Art Students League 215 W 57th St New York NY 10019

DORFMAN, FRED
DEALER
b Chicago, Ill, Feb 19, 46. *Study:* Am Univ, 69; Chicago Art Inst, 71-72. *Pos:* Owner, Dorfman Gallery, currently. *Mem:* Visual Artist & Gallery Asn; Int Art Dealers Asn. *Specialty:* Twentieth century American and South American original art; sculpture, drawings, paintings and multiples. *Publ:* Article, New York Arts J, 79. *Mailing Add:* Dorfman Gallery 831 Broadway New York NY 10003

DORN, PETER KLAUS
DESIGNER, GRAPHIC ARTIST
b Berlin, Ger, June 30, 32. *Can citizen. Study:* Journeyman compositor, Berlin; Ont Col Art, Toronto; Hochschule für Grafik & Buch Kunst, Leipzig. *Work:* Toronto Pub Libr Fine Arts Sect; Douglas Libr, Kingston. *Exhib:* Royal Can Acad, 70; Agnes Etherington Art Ctr, Kingston, 71; Look of Books, 74, 76 & 77; Design Can, 75; Spectrum Can, 76; Group Exhib, Toronto, 79; and others. *Pos:* Proprietor, Heinrich Heine Press, Toronto, 63; typographer, Univ Toronto Press, 66-71; dir, Graphic Design Unit, Queen's Univ, 71. *Teaching:* Teaching master typography, St Lawrence Col, Kingston, 78-; guest lectr, NS Col Art & Design, Univ Man, Sheridan Col, 80. *Awards:* Awards, Ont Asn Art Galleries, 80-83; Awards, Am Inst Graphic Arts, 80 & 83; and others. *Mem:* Royal Can Acad; Guild Hand Printers (dir); Graphic Designers Can (nat past pres, Kingston past pres); Am Inst Graphic Arts; Am Asn Univ Presses. *Mailing Add:* 207 Stuart St Ridean Bldg Kingston ON K7L 3N6 Canada

DORN, RUTH (DORNBUSH)
PAINTER
b Leipzig, Ger, Feb 16, 25; US citizen. *Study:* Studied in Ger & Bolivia; Brooklyn Mus; Brooklyn Col; Nat Acad Fine Arts. *Exhib:* Brooklyn Mus, 69 & 77; Artists League of Brooklyn, Metrop Mus Art, New York, 77; Brooklyn Come to the Met, Hudson Valley Art Asn, 77; Nat Arts Club, New York; Allied Artists of Am, 78; Cork Gallery, Lincoln Ctr, New York, 78; Union Carbide Corp, New York, 78. *Awards:* First Prize, 74 & Nell Van Hook Memorial Prize, 75, Composers, Authors & Artists Am. *Mem:* Composers Authors & Artists Am; Am Artists Prof League; Burr Artists; Deerfield Valley Art Asn; Leverett Craftsmen & Artists, Mass. *Media:* Oil. *Mailing Add:* Cherry Lane Amherst MA 01002

DORR, (VIRGINIA) NELL
PHOTOGRAPHER
b Cleveland, Ohio, Aug 27, 1893. *Study:* Studied under her father, Jacob Becker. *Work:* Int Ctr Photog, Mus Mod Art, New York. *Exhib:* Mus Mod Art, New York, 55; San Francisco Mus Art, 75; Recollections Traveling Exhib, 79. *Bibliog:* Grace Mayer (auth), Interview with Nell Dorr, Infinity, 63; Margretta Mitchell (auth), article, Popular Photog, 75. *Mem:* Royal Photog Soc. *Publ:* Auth, In a Blue Moon, G P Putnam & Sons, 39; auth, Mother and Child, Harper, 54; auth, The Bare Feet, 62 & Night and Day, 68, New York Graphic; coauth, Life Dance, Alleluia Press, 78. *Mailing Add:* c/o Marcuse Pfeifer Gallery 825 Madison Ave New York NY 10000

DORRA, HENRI
HISTORIAN, EDUCATOR
b Alexandria, Egypt, Jan 17, 24; US citizen. *Study:* Univ London, BSc, 44; Harvard Univ, MS & MA, 50, PhD, 53, Student Fel, Metrop Mus Art, 51-52; Nat Endowment Humanities Fel, summer 75; Guggenheim Fel, 78-79. *Collections Arranged:* Visionaries and Dreamers & Ryder, Corcoran Gallery Art, San Francisco Mus Art & Cleveland Mus Art, 55-60; Years of Ferment, Univ Calif, Los Angeles, 65. *Pos:* Asst dir, Corcoran Gallery Art, 54-61; asst dir, Philadelphia Mus Art, 61-62; exec vpres, Indianapolis Art Asn, 62-63; trustee, Santa Barbara Mus Art. *Teaching:* Lectr art hist; mem fac, Univ Calif, Los Angeles, 63-65; prof art, Univ Calif, Santa Barbara, 65- *Awards:* Bowdoin Prize, Harvard Univ, 49. *Mem:* Col Art Asn Am. *Publ:* auth, Seurat, Beaux-Arts, Paris, 60; auth, The American Muse, Burlington Mag, 61; auth, Art in Perspective, 73; contribr, Gazette Beaux-Arts, Metrop Mus Art Bull & others. *Mailing Add:* Dept of Art History Univ of Calif Santa Barbara CA 93106

DORRIEN, CARLOS GUILLERMO
SCULPTOR
b Buenos Aires, Arg, Oct 8, 48; US citizen. *Study:* Univ de la Plata, Arg, 67; Lowell Technol Inst, Mass; Montserrat Sch Visual Art, Mass, BFA, 73. *Work:* Bentley Col, Waltham, Mass; John Hancock Insurance Co, Boston; Mus 20th Century, Medellin, Colombia. *Comn:* Portal (sculpture), Bentley Col, Waltham, Mass, 78; Cutting Object (marble), City Medellin, Colombia,81; Granite Ribbon, Mass Transit Authority, Porter Sq Sta, Cambridge, Mass, 82. *Exhib:* Arts on the Line, Hayden Gallery, Mass Inst Technol, Cambridge, 79; Art in Public Places, Carpenter Ctr, Harvard Univ, Cambridge, Mass, 80; Biennial Art Medellin, Colombia, 81; Mus 20th Century, Colombia, 81; Brocton Art Mus Trienial, Mass, 83. *Pos:* Guest sculptor, City Medellin, Colombia, 81. *Teaching:* Lectr, Sch Mus Fine Arts, Boston, 80-81; instr sculpture, Art Inst Boston, 82- *Awards:* Traveling Grant, Partners Am, 81; Purchase Award, IV Biennial Art Medellin, Colombia, 81; WBZ-TV Fund for the Arts Grant, 83. *Bibliog:* Mary Sullivan (auth), Carlos Dorrien: An interview, Back Bay View, Vol 3, 78; Gerald Ryan (auth), Sculptures for business, Boston Today, 9/79. *Media:* Granite, Bronze. *Dealer:* Clark Gallery Lincoln Sta Lincoln MA 01773. *Mailing Add:* 32 Robinwood Ave No 6 Boston MA 02130

DORSKY, MORRIS
HISTORIAN, EDUCATOR
b New York, NY, July 8, 18. *Study:* Brooklyn Col, BA, 40; NY Univ, MA, 66. *Teaching:* Prof art hist, Brooklyn Col, City Univ New York, 48-, chmn dept art, 70- *Res:* Ben Shahn. *Mailing Add:* 120 W 70th St New York NY 10023

DORSKY, SAMUEL
DEALER
b Brooklyn, NY, May 7, 14. *Specialty:* 20th century art. *Mailing Add:* 58 W 58th St 730 Fifth Ave New York NY 10019

DORST, CLAIRE V
PAINTER, EDUCATOR
b Plymouth, Wis, June 4, 22. *Study:* Beloit Col, BA, 49; Univ Iowa, MA, 53; Univ Wis-Madison, United Lutheran Church Am Scholar, 62-63, MFA, 63. *Work:* Univ Iowa; Univ Wis; also in pvt collections. *Exhib:* Wisconsin at Work, 50 & Wisconsin Painters & Sculptors Ann, 64, Mem Mus, Milwaukee; Fla State Fair Show, Tampa, 65; Nat Exhib Contemp Painting, Soc Four Arts, Palm Beach, Fla, 66 & 70; Hortt Mem Exhib, Mus Arts, Ft Lauderdale, Fla, 68 & 70. *Teaching:* Asst prof studio art, Wayne State Col, 53-59; prof art & art hist & chmn dept art, Carthage Col, 59-64; prof studio art, Fla Atlantic Univ, 64-, chmn dept art, 68- *Awards:* Tellus Madden Award, Wis Spring Show, 63; First Prize in Painting, Winter Park Art Fair, 65; Atwater Kent Award, Soc Four Arts Nat Exhib, 66. *Mem:* Fla League Arts (mem bd dirs, 71-); Fla Craftsmen; Col Art Asn Am. *Mailing Add:* Dept of Art Fla Atlantic Univ Boca Raton FL 33432

DORST, MARY CROWE
COORDINATOR, ARTIST
b Wis. *Study:* Beloit Col, BA(art; cum laude); Northern Ill Univ, MA(drawing); Univ Wis. *Exhib:* Fla Craftsmen Ann Exhib, 65, 72 & 74; Nat Exhib, Soc of the Four Arts, Palm Beach, Fla, 68; Hortt Mem Exhib, Ft Lauderdale Mus Arts, 69; Piedmont Crafts Exhib, Mint Mus, Charlotte, NC, 71-75; Contemp Women Artists of the Gold Coast Traveling Exhib, 83-86. *Collections Arranged:* The Other Side of the Generation Gap, Constructions in Flexible Materials, Printmakers of the Americas & Edward S Curtis, Fla Atlantic Univ Art Gallery, 73-77; Florida Heritage, Contemporary Women Artists of the Gold Coast & Art in Fiber and Clay, Palmetto Gallery. *Pos:* Gallery dir, Fla Atlantic Univ, 73-77; art reviewer, Boca Raton News, Fla, 75-76; art dir, Palmetto Gallery, NCNB Banks, Boca Raton, 79- *Teaching:* Instr art, Marymount Col, Fla, 65-67, Fla Atlantic Univ, 67-68 & 77-78 & Broward Community Col, Fla, 73-75; adj instr, Palm Beach Jr Col, 75- *Awards:* Jewelry Purchase Prize, Univ Wis Student Exhib, 63; Fla Open Best in Show, 71 & 80 & Mem Ann Award, 83, Boca Raton Mus Arts. *Mem:* Fla Craftsmen (area dir, 75-78 & 82-84); Am Crafts Coun; Morikami Mus Japanese Cult; Palm Beach Co Coun Arts. *Publ:* Auth, A Day in Mino, Crafts Horizons, 6/71; auth, Kozo Futura: Living National Treasure, Innovations in Paper. *Mailing Add:* 618 NW High St Boca Raton FL 33432

DOTY, ROBERT MCINTYRE
ADMINISTRATOR
b Rochester, NY, Dec 23, 33. *Study:* Harvard Univ, AB; Univ Rochester, MA. *Collections Arranged:* Photo-Secession, 1960; Photography America, 65 & 74; Whitney Ann, 66-71; Adolph Gottlieb, 68; Human Concern/Personal Torment, 69; Contemporary Black Artists of America, 71; Lucas Samaras, 72; American Folk Art in Ohio Collections, 76. *Pos:* Dir, Currier Gallery Art, currently. *Mailing Add:* Currier Gallery of Art 192 Orange St Manchester NH 03104

DOUAIHY, SALIBA
STAINED GLASS ARTIST, CONCEPTUAL ARTIST
b Lebanon, Sept 14, 15; US citizen. *Study:* Ecole Nat Superieure et Spec des Beaux de Arts, Paris. *Work:* Guggenheim Mus; Mod Mus Art, New York; Albright-Knox Mus Art; Syracuse Univ; Birmingham Mus; and others; Guggenheim Mus. *Comn:* Eight panels on Plexiglas, Xerox Co, Stanford, Conn, 70; ten religious subjects in glass, Church of Annaya, Lebanon, 73; created subject in oil and one copy in glass, Our Lady of Lebanon Church, Brooklyn, NY, 75; ten paintings, comn by Dr Elias Saadi, Youngstown, Ohio, 77; 65 semi-abstract windows, Cedars of Lebanon Church, Jamaica Plain, Mass, 78. *Exhib:* Retrospective, NC Mus Art, Raleigh, 78; one-man shows, Contemporaries Gallery, New York, 64, Gallery One, Beirut, 71, Lermouth Gallery, New York, 76 & The Arts & Sci Ctr, Nashua, NH, 79; and others. *Teaching:* Prof art, Col de la Sagesse, Beirut, 46-48. *Awards:* Hon Mention, Pa Acad Fine Arts, 68. *Bibliog:* Victor Hakim (auth), Une Osmose Par Le Style, L'Imprimerie Catholique, 49; Arturo Garcia Formenti (auth), Destellos, El Universal, Mex, 11/22/54; Charlotte Willard (auth), The Language of Color, New York Post, 3/20/66. *Mem:* Artists Equity. *Media:* Oil, Acrylic, Encaustic. *Dealer:* Saliba Douaihy 74 Cornwall Gardens London SW 7 Eng. *Mailing Add:* 74 Cornwall Gardens London SW7 England 12496 United Kingdom

DOUDERA, GERARD
EDUCATOR, PAINTER
b Sharon, Conn, Dec 29, 32. *Study:* Hartford Art Sch, BFA; Univ Ill. *Work:* Wadsworth Atheneum, Hartford; Butler Inst Am Art, Youngstown, Ohio; New Britan Mus, Conn. *Exhib:* One-man shows, DeCordova & Dana Mus, Lincoln, Mass, 59; New Britain Mus Am Art, Conn, 61; Univ Hartford, 71. *Teaching:* Prof painting, Univ Conn, 62-, head art dept, 74-77. *Awards:* Grant, Tiffany Found, 58; First Hallgarten Award, Nat Acad Design, 58; Painting Award, Conn Acad Fine Arts, 75. *Media:* Oil, Watercolor. *Mailing Add:* Art Dept Univ Conn Storrs CT 06268

DOUGHERTY, RAY (RAYMOND EDWARD)
PAINTER, INSTRUCTOR
b Wildwood, NJ, June 15, 42. *Study:* Pa Acad Fine Arts, dipl, 68; Univ Pa Grad Sch Fine Arts, BFA, 70. *Work:* Ocean City Art Ctr, NJ; Noyes Mus, Ocean View, NJ. *Exhib:* 27th Nat Soc Painters Casein & Acrylic, Am Acad & Inst Arts & Lett, New York, 79; 111th Am Watercolor Soc, Nat Acad Design, New York, 78; 2nd Biennial, NJ State Mus, Trenton, 79; Audubon Artist Ann, Nat Arts Club, New York, 80-82; NJ Art Educr Exhib, Trenton State Col, 82. *Collections Arranged:* 20th, 21st & 22nd National Traveling Exhibition, Nat Soc Painters in Casein & Acrylic, 77-80; Old Bergen Art Guild, Bayonne, NJ Group Nat Tour, 79-80. *Teaching:* Instr fine arts, NJ Pub Schs, 70-78, Am Inst Ment Studies, Vineland, NJ, 79 & Secondary Parochial School System, 80. *Awards:* Delta Brush Award, Permanent Pigments Co, 79; Painting Award, Soc NJ Artists, 79; Cert Merit, Nat Soc Painters Casein & Acrylic, 83. *Mem:* Nat Soc Painters Casein & Acrylic (bd dirs, 79-); Cape May Co Art League (pres, 77-78); Audubon Artists; Nat Artists Equity; Painters & Sculptors Soc NJ; and others. *Media:* Oil & Acrylic; Demonstration & Criticism. *Dealer:* Visual Arts Ctr Studio 6401 New Jersey Ave Wildwood NJ 08260. *Mailing Add:* 7609 Pacific Ave Wildwood Crest NJ 08260

DOUGLAS, EDWIN PERRY
PAINTER, INSTRUCTOR
b Lynn, Mass, June 18, 35. *Study:* RI Sch Design, BFA; San Francisco Art Inst, MFA. *Work:* Montreal Mus Fine Arts, Can; San Francisco Art Inst Art Bank; Dayton Art Mus, Ohio; Cincinnati Art Mus; Lincoln Land Community Col Art Mus, Springfield, Ill. *Exhib:* San Francisco Art Inst Nat Painting & Sculpture Tour, 63; 81st Ann Spring Exhib, Montreal Mus Fine Arts, 64; 31st Ann Can Soc Graphic Art, Kingston, Ont, 64; Cincinnati Biennial, Cincinnati Art Mus, 69; Portland Mus Art, Maine, 74; and others. *Teaching:* Instr painting, Univ Man Sch Art, 63-64; instr drawing & painting, Cincinnati Art Acad, Ohio, 64-68; vis prof art, Wash Univ Sch Fine Arts, 69-72; vis lectr painting, Univ Cincinnati, 72-73; instr painting & drawing, Portland Sch Art, 73- *Bibliog:* Dialogue on Painting (film), Miami Univ TV, 67. *Mailing Add:* 993 Highland Ave South Portland ME 04107

DOUKE, DANIEL W
PAINTER, EDUCATOR
b Los Angeles, Calif, Sept 18, 43. *Study:* Pasadena City Col, AA, 66; Calif State Univ, Los Angeles, BA, 70, MA, 71. *Work:* Avco Savings & Loan, Newport Beach, Calif; Nicholas Treadwell Galleries, London, Eng; Gallerie des Quatre Mouvements, Paris, France. *Exhib:* Oakland Mus Art, Calif, 73; State Univ NY Col, Potsdam, 74; one-man shows, Jack Glenn Gallery, Newport Beach, 75, Warren Benedek Gallery, New York, 75 & Dobrick Gallery, Chicago, 76; Mus Mod Art, New York, 76; Los Angeles Inst Contemp Art, 77. *Collections Arranged:* Douglas Bond: Twelve Year Survey (auth, catalog), Calif State Univ, 78. *Pos:* Visual arts specialist, Cult Arts, Co of Los Angeles, 73-75; gallery dir, Calif State Univ, Los Angeles, 75- *Teaching:* Instr painting, Calif State Univ, Los Angeles, 75- *Awards:* James D Phelan Award in Painting, Oakland Mus, San Francisco Found, 73. *Mem:* Col Art Asn. *Media:* Acrylic. *Publ:* Auth, Project Outreach, Nat Endowment for the Arts, 74; co-auth, Ceramic Conjunction, Co of Los Angeles, 74-75; contribr, Bradley Smith, auth, Erotic Art of the Masters, Lyle Stuart, 75; contribr, Gregory Battcock, auth, Super Realism, Dutton, 75; contribr, Udo Kultermann, auth, New Painting 2nd Edition, Wasmuth, 76. *Dealer:* O K Harris Works of Art 380 W Broadway New York NY 10012. *Mailing Add:* 5151 State Univ Dr Los Angeles CA 90032

DOUMATO, LAMIA
LIBRARIAN, HISTORIAN
b Aug 26, 47; US citizen. *Study:* RI Col, BA; Pa State Univ, MA(art hist); Simmons Col, Boston, MLS; Boston Univ; Columbia Univ. *Exhib:* Retrospective 1972-1982: Women's Caucus For Art, Moore Col Art, 83. *Collections Arranged:* Rhode Island Architecture, Providence Pub Libr; Raphael, Nat Gallery Art Libr, 81. *Pos:* Art librn, Providence Pub Libr, 70-71; ref librn, Boston Univ Libr, 71-74; ref librn, Mus Mod Art Libr, New York, 74-78; reference librn, Nat Gallery Art, Washington, DC, 81- *Teaching:* Teaching asst art hist, Pa State Univ, 70; prof & head, Art & Archit Libr, Univ Colo, Boulder, 78-81; teacher res methods, Univ Colo, 79-81. *Awards:* Coun Creative Work Grants, Univ Colo, 79-80 & 80-81. *Mem:* Col Art Asn; Art Librn Soc NAm; Art Librn Soc Washington, DC. *Interests:* Illuminated manuscripts, architectural bibliography and women artists. *Publ:* Auth, American Drawings, Gale Publ, 79; contribr, Six Painters of the Figure, Univ Colo Art Gallery, 79; auth, Marcel Breuer: Architect, Designer, Archit Series Bibliog, 79; auth, Museum Design, Chicago Coun Planning Librn, 80; auth, Women in literature of art, Oxford Art J, Vol 3, 4/80; and others. *Mailing Add:* 2950 Van Ness St NW Washington DC 20008

DOW, HELEN JEANNETTE
HISTORIAN, EDUCATOR
b Ottawa, Ont, June 13, 26. *Study:* Univ Col, Univ Toronto, BA, 49; Bryn Mawr Col, Pa, MA, 51, PhD, 55. *Collections Arranged:* Selections (auth, catalog), Owens Collection, Montreal Mus Fine Art, 63; Works of Alex Colville (auth, catalog), Univ Alta, 70. *Pos:* Cur, Owens Mus, Mt Allison Univ, NB, 61-64. *Teaching:* Acting chmn art dept, Sweet Briar Col, Va, 60-61; assoc prof, Univ Iowa, Iowa City, 65-66; assoc prof, Univ Alta, Edmonton, 66; assoc prof art hist, Univ Guelph, 71-72, prof, 73-, chmn, Dept Fine Art, 73-74. *Awards:* Workman Fel, Bryn Mawr Col, 52; Brit Coun Scholar, 56; Can Coun Grant, 58. *Mem:* Univ Art Asn Can; Int Ctr Medieval Art; life mem Brit Coun Scholars Asn; life mem William Goodenough Fel, London; life mem Nat Art Collections Fund Gr Brit. *Res:* Medieval architecture and sculpture; Canadian painting. *Collection:* Works of Alex Colville; North American Indian art. *Publ:* Auth, The rose window, Warburg J, 57; auth, Van Gogh both Prometheus and Jupiter, Am J Aesthetics, 64; auth, Andre Beauneveu and . . . England, Peregrinatio, 71; auth, The Art of Alex Colville, McGraw-Hill Ryerson, 72; auth, The apse mosaic of San Apollinare in Classe, PMR Proceedings, 79. *Mailing Add:* Dept Fine Art Univ Guelph Guelph ON N1G 2W1 Canada

DOWDEN, ANNE OPHELIA TODD
PAINTER, ILLUSTRATOR
b Denver, Colo, Sept 17, 07. *Study:* Univ Colo; Carnegie Inst Technol; Art Students League. *Work:* Hunt Bot Libr, Pittsburgh, Pa; New York Botanical Garden; Brooklyn Botanical Garden. *Comn:* Paintings for reproduction as facsimile prints, Frame House Gallery, Louisville, Ky, 69-79; painting, three azaleas, Callaway Gardens, Pine Mountain, Ga, 71; painting, tulip tree flowers, New York Botanical Garden, 72; painting, rhododendron, Holden Arboretum, Cleveland. *Exhib:* American Textiles, Metrop Mus Art, New York, 48; Decorative Arts Today, Newark Mus, 48; Int Group Shows, Hunt Botanical Libr, 64, 68, 72 & 77; and other group & one-man shows. *Teaching:* Instr drawing, Pratt Inst, 30-32; head dept art, Manhattanville Col, 32-53. *Awards:* Tiffany Found Fel, 29-31. *Media:* Watercolor. *Publ:* Auth & illusr, Look at a Flower, 63, Wild Green Things in the City, 72 & The Blossom on the Bough, 75, Crowell; auth & illusr, This Noble Harvest, Collins, 77; illusr, Wild Flowers and the Stories Behind their Names, Scribner, 77; illusr, The Lore and Legends of Flowers, Crowell, 82; and many others. *Mailing Add:* 205 W 15th St New York NY 10011

DOWELL, JOHN E, JR
EDUCATOR, PRINTMAKER
b Philadelphia, Pa, Mar 25, 41. *Study:* Temple Univ Tyler Sch Art, BFA(printmaking, ceramics), 63; John Herron Art Inst, Indianapolis, advan lithography with Garo Antreasian, 63; Tamarind Lithography Workshop, Los Angeles, artist-printer fel, 63 & sr-printer fel, 66; Univ Wash, Seattle, MFA(printmaking, drawing), 66. *Work:* Mus Mod Art, New York; Brooklyn Mus Art, NY; Boston Mus Fine Art, Mass; Art Inst Chicago; Corcoran Gallery Art, DC; and many others. *Exhib:* One-man shows, Venice Biennale, 70; Corcoran Gallery Art, DC, 71 & Ft Worth Art Mus Ctr, Tex, 72; Whitney Biennial, 75 & Printmaking New Forms, 76; Whitney Mus Am Art; Recent Am Drawings, Mus Mod Art, New York, 76; 30 yrs Am Printmaking, Brooklyn Mus Art, NY, 76; Three Centuries Am Art, Philadelphia Mus Art, 76; Drawings of the 70's, 35th exhib of Soc Contemp Art, Art Inst Chicago, 77; Collectors Collect Contemp: A Selection from Boston's Collections, Inst Contemp Art, Boston, 77; A J Wood Galleries, Philadelphia, 80; and many others. *Teaching:* Assoc prof art & printmaking, Tyler Sch Art, Temple Univ, Rome, Italy, 71-74, Philadelphia, 74-76, prof, 76-82. *Awards:* Univ Ill, Champaign Fac Summer Fel, 70; Nat Endowment Arts Fel Painting, 74-75; Temple Univ Res Grant, 75-77; and others. *Bibliog:* Henry Martin (auth), Scribble, Art Int, 3/73; Donna Stein (auth), Musicianly painting, Art News, 11/73; John Dowell's sound perspective, Arts Exchange, 5/77; and others. *Mailing Add:* 716 N Third Philadelphia PA 19123

DOWLER, DAVID P
SCULPTOR, DESIGNER
b Pittsburgh, Pa, Feb 1, 44. *Study:* Syracuse Univ, BID, 69. *Work:* Leigh Yawkey Woodson Mus Art, Wausau, Wis; Corning Mus Glass, NY; Hokkaido Mus Mod Art. *Exhib:* Mus Mod Art, Kyoto, Japan, 81; Americans in Glass, Leigh Yawkey Woodson Art Mus, Wausau, Wis, 81 & Cooper-Hewitt Mus, New York, 81; Good As Gold, Smithsonian Inst, Washington, DC, 81; Production Lines, Philadelphia Col Art, 83; Glass Now, Hokkaido Mus Mod Art, 83. *Awards:* Furniture Design Award, Progressive Archit Mag, 82. *Bibliog:* Elliot Erwit (auth), Assignment in Glass (film), 78. *Mailing Add:* 120 East Third St Corning NY 14830

DOWNES, RACKSTRAW
PAINTER, CRITIC
b Kent, Eng, Nov 8, 39; US citizen. *Study:* Cambridge Univ, Eng, BA, 61; Yale Univ, BFA, 63, MFA, 64. *Work:* Hirshhorn Mus, Washington, DC; Pa Acad, Philadelphia; Whitney Mus Am Art, New York; Chase Manhattan Bank, New York; Witherspoon Mus, NC. *Comn:* Painting, US Dept Interior, 76. *Exhib:* Artist's Choice Mus Show, six NY Galleries, 79; 20 Artists Yale Sch Art, Yale Univ Art Gallery, Conn, 81; The Animal in Am Art, Nassau Co Mus, NY, 81; 1981 Biennial, Whitney Mus, New York, 81; The Americans, the Landscape, Contemp Arts Mus, Houston, 81; Real, Really Real, Super Real, San Antonio Mus, 81; Contemp Am Realism, Pa Acad, Philadelphia, 81; Carnegie Int, Carnegie Inst, 83. *Pos:* Gov, Skowhegan Sch Painting & Sculpture, 81. *Teaching:* Asst prof fine arts, Univ Pa, Philadelphia, 67-79. *Awards:* Creative Artists Public Service Award, 78, Individual Grant, Ingram Merrill Found, 75; Individual Grant, Nat Endowment Arts, 80. *Bibliog:* Linda Nochlin (auth), article, Art in Am, 1/76; Hilton Kramer (auth), Return of Realism, New York Times, 3/12/78; Peter Schjeldahl (auth), Realism on the comeback trail, Village Voice, 11/81. *Mem:* NY Artists Equity Asn. *Media:* Oil. *Publ:* Auth, What the sixties meant to me, Art J, 74; auth, The Meaning of the Landscape, Parenthese, 75; auth, Post-modernist painting, Tracks, 76; ed, Fairfield Porter: Art in its Own Terms, Taplinger, 79; auth, Claude's sermon on the mount, Art News, 10/81. *Dealer:* Hirschl & Adler Modern 851 Madison Ave New York NY 10021. *Mailing Add:* 536 W 111th St New York NY 10025

DOWNEY, JUAN
VIDEO ARTIST, ARCHITECT
b Santiago, Chile, May 11, 40. *Study:* Sch Archit, Cath Univ Chile, BArch, 61; Atelier 17, Paris, 63-65, printmaking with S W Hayter; Pratt Inst, 67-69. *Work:* Mus Mod Art, New York; Casa Americas, Havana, Cuba; Tel Aviv Mus, Israel; Bibliot Nat, Paris; Nat Collection Fine Arts, Washington, DC; and others. *Exhib:* Lucht-Kunst, Stedelijk Mus, Amsterdam, 71; Art & Science, Tel Aviv Mus, 71; Contemp Art Mus, Houston, Tex, 76; Whitney Mus of Am Art, New York, 76; Everson Mus of Art, Syracuse, NY, 77; Documenta 6, Kassel, Ger, 77; Anthology Films Archive, New York, 77; Mus Arte Contemporaneo, Caracas, Venezuela, 77; plus many others. *Teaching:* Asst prof archit, Pratt Inst, New York, 70- *Awards:* Guggenheim Found Fel, 71 & 76; Mass Inst Technol Fel, 73; Rockefeller Found Fel, 81; and others. *Bibliog:* Howard Wise (auth), Pollution Robot (film), 70. *Dealer:* Castelli Sonnabend Video 420 West Broadway New York NY 10012. *Mailing Add:* 146 W 26th St New York NY 10001

DOWNING, ROBERT JAMES
SCULPTOR, EDUCATOR
b Hamilton, Ont, Aug 1, 35. *Study:* Self-taught. *Work:* Art Gallery Ont; Montreal Mus Fine Art; Brit Arts Coun, London; Cult Resources Ctr, Huntington Beach, Calif; Confederation Ctr, Charlottetown, PEI. *Comn:* Relief walls, Univ Toronto, 66; sculpture group, Mohawk Col, Hamilton, Ont, 68; wall sculptures, Valley Bank Nev, Las Vegas, 74 & United Gas Pipeline Co, Houston, 76; hanging sculpture, Jefferson Mall, Louisville, Ky, 78. *Exhib:* Sculpture 67, Nat Gallery Can, 67; EAT Competition, Brooklyn Mus, 68; solo exhibs, Whitechapel Art Gallery, London, 69; York Univ Gallery, Toronto, 70 & Col Park, Toronto, 81; 11th Biennale Middelheim, Middelheim Park, Antwerp, Belg, 71; Calif State Univ, Long Beach Show, Long Beach Mus Art, 75. *Teaching:* Lectr, Univ Toronto, 67-69 & Calif State Univ, Long Beach,

74-78; instr sculpture, Fanshawe Col, London, Ont, 69-71, Banff Ctr Sch, summer 73 & Ont Col Art, 81-82. *Awards:* Purchase Award, Centennial 67, Ont Arts Coun, 67; Arts Bursary, Can Coun, 71; Edinburgh Festival Award, DeMarco Gallery, Brit Arts Coun, 76. *Bibliog:* Alan Walker (auth), article, Time, 68; Bryan Robertson (auth), article, Studio Int, 69; Edward Lucie-Smith (auth), article, Art in Britain 19/70, 70. *Mem:* Royal Can Acad Arts; Sculpture Soc Can; Ont Soc Artists (mem exec coun, 79-81); founding mem Can Artists Reps. *Media:* Welded Metal, Concrete. *Publ:* Auth, article, Art & Artists, England, 6/69. *Mailing Add:* c/o Stitt, Baker & McKenzie 112 Adelaide St E Toronto ON M5C 1K9 Canada

DOWNS, LINDA ANNE
CURATOR, EDUCATOR
b Detroit, Mich, May 30, 45. *Study:* Monteith Col, Wayne State Univ, PhB, 69; Univ Mich, MA(hist of art), 73; Mus Mgt Inst, Univ Calif, Berkeley, 79. *Collections Arranged:* Student Art Exhibs, 69-77; Barbara Chase Ribaud Sculpture, 72; Diaghilev & Russian Stage Design, 72; Caravaggio's Conversion of the Magdalene: An Analysis of the Painting, 73; African Art of the Dogon, 74, Detroit Inst of Arts; The Rouge: The Image of Industry in the Art of Charles Sheeler and Diego Rivera (auth, catalog), Detroit Inst Arts, 78. *Pos:* Spec asst, Proj Outreach, Detroit Inst Arts, Mich, 68-69, jr cur educ, 69-73, cur educ, 73-76, cur educ, 76- *Teaching:* Adj asst prof art hist, Wayne State Univ, Detroit, Mich, 76- *Awards:* Best Cult Film Award for Only Then Regale My Eyes, Midwest Pub Broadcasting Serv, 76. *Mem:* Am Asn Mus; Col Art Asn; Mich Mus Asn; Midwest Mus Asn; Midwest Art Hist Asn; and others. *Publ:* Auth, Claes Oldenburg's Giant Three-Way Plub and Chrysler Airflow, Bull Detroit Inst Arts, 71; producer, Only Then Regale My Eyes (60 minute color film produced for the exhib, French Painting 1774-1830: The Age of Revolution), WTVS, Detroit, 75; auth, Diego Rivera's Portrait of Edsel Ford, Bulletin Detroit Inst of Arts, 79. *Mailing Add:* Detroit Inst of Arts 5200 Woodward Ave Detroit MI 48202

DOYLE, JOE
PAINTER, EDUCATOR
b Manhattan, NY, Feb 27, 41. *Study:* San Francisco State Univ, Calif, BA, 69, MFA, 71. *Work:* Oakland Mus, Calif. *Exhib:* Option 73/30, Contemp Art Ctr, Cincinnati, Ohio, 73; Interstices, Cranbrook Acad Art, Bloomfield Hills, Mich, 75; 6 EBay Painters, Oakland Mus, Calif, 77; Aesthetics of Graffiti, San Francisco Mus Art, 78; one-man show, San Jose Mus Art, Calif, 79; Reality of Illusion, Denver Art Mus, Colo, 79; Three Bay Area Painters, Chico State Univ, Calif, 79. *Teaching:* Instr painting, Laney Col, Oakland, Calif, 71-73; co-chmn fine arts, Acad Art, San Francisco, 75-76; adj prof fine arts, Univ San Francisco, 75-76. *Mem:* Calif Fedn Art Teachers. *Media:* Mixed. *Dealer:* Foster Goldstrom 257 Grant St San Francisco CA 94108. *Mailing Add:* 324 13th Oakland CA 94612

DOYLE, JOHN LAWRENCE
PRINTMAKER, PAINTER
b Chicago, Ill, Mar 14, 39. *Study:* Art Inst Chicago, BAE, 62; Northern Ill Univ, MA, 68. *Work:* Libr Cong; Smithsonian Inst Collection Traveling Exhib; Art Inst Chicago. *Exhib:* Twenty-Second Boston Printmakers Exhib, De Cordova Mus, Lincoln, Mass, 70; Images on Paper, Miss Art Mus, Jackson, 70; Colorprints USA, Tex Tech Univ, Lubbock, 72; 73rd Chicago Show, Art Inst Chicago, 72; 24th Am Drawings Biennial, Norfolk Mus, 72; Prints & Drawings, Los Angeles Co Mus Art, Los Angeles, Calif, 73; Rahr W Mus, Manitowoc, Wis, 79; Scottsdale Art Ctr, Ariz, 79; and others. *Awards:* Eisendrath Prize, 73rd Chicago Show, Art Inst Chicago, 72; Purchase Prizes, 24th Am Drawings Biennial, Norfolk Mus Arts & Sci, 72 & Images on Paper, Miss Art Mus, 72. *Bibliog:* Mendelowitz (auth), Drawings (Illustration), Univ Iowa, 76; Ben Dallas (auth), Mysticism through visual metaphor, SW Arts Mag, 77; Scott E Dial (auth), John L Doyle, Art Voices S, 11/79. *Media:* Lithograph; Watercolor. *Dealer:* Fishy Whale Press 411 Lincoln Ave Rockford IL 61102. *Mailing Add:* RR 7 Box 85 Burnsville NC 28714

DOYLE, TOM
SCULPTOR, EDUCATOR
b Jerry City, Ohio, May 23, 28. *Study:* Ohio State Univ, BFA, 52, MA, 53, with Roy Lichtenstien & Stanley Twardewicz. *Work:* Brooklyn Mus; Carnegie Inst, Pittsburgh; Kley Collection, Ger; City Beautiful Project, Dayton, Ohio. *Comn:* Fiberglas sculpture, Pub Arts Coun, City of New York, 72; Federal Bldg & Courthouse, Fairbanks, Alaska, 80. *Exhib:* Kunsthalle, Bern, Switz, 64; Kunsthalle, Dusseldorf, Ger, 65; Dwan Gallery, New York, 66 & 67; Sculpture of the Sixties, Los Angeles Co Art Mus, Calif, 67; Primary Structures, Jewish Mus Mus, New York, 67; Hammarskjold Plaza, New York, 82; and others. *Teaching:* Instr sculpture, Brooklyn Mus Art Sch, 60-68; instr sculpture, New Sch Social Res, 61-68; assoc prof sculpture, Queens Col, 70- *Bibliog:* Lucy R Lippard (auth), Tom Doyle, Kunsthalle, Dusseldorf, 65 & Space embraced: Tom Doyle's recent sculpture, Arts, 4/66; Robert Pincus-Witten (auth), Tom Doyle: Things patriotic and union blue, Arts, 9/79; and others. *Mailing Add:* Max Hutchinson Gallery 138 Greene St New York NY 10013

DOYON, GERARD MAURICE
EDUCATOR, HISTORIAN
b Manchester, NH, Apr 6, 23. *Study:* Manchester Inst Arts, dipl(fine arts), 49; St Anselm's Col, AB, 51; Fulbright scholar to Paris, 51-52; Ecole Beaux-Arts, Paris, 52; Ecole Mus du Louvre, AE, 52; Boston Univ, MA, 54, PhD(Danforth Scholar), 64. *Teaching:* Chmn dept art, St Anselm's Col, 52-61 & Miami-Dade Jr Col, 61-64; assoc prof art hist & chmn art dept, Fla Atlantic Univ, 64-68; prof art hist & chmn dept art, Washington & Lee Univ, 68-; dir, Paris Atelier, France, formerly; vis prof, Taiwan Nat Acad, 77. *Awards:* Nat

Endowment Humanities in French Art, New York, 75 & Paris, 79. *Res:* French art of the 18th and 19th centuries, especially painting. *Publ:* Auth, The mural paintings of Theodore Chasseriau, Gazette Beaux-Arts, Paris, 69. *Mailing Add:* Dept of Art Washington & Lee Univ Lexington VA 24450

DRAKE, DOUGLAS ARNOLD
DEALER, CURATOR
b Chicago, Ill, Dec 9, 43. *Study:* Williams Col, BA, 65; Stanford Univ, MBA, 67. *Collections Arranged:* Selected Modern Masters (auth, catalog), 74; Continental Corp Collection Mod Art (coauth, catalog), 83. *Pos:* Exhib co-cur, Nelson Gallery, Kansas City, Sales & Rental Gallery Selections Comn, 70-73; dir, Douglas Drake Gallery, Kansas City, 74-; mem Visual Arts Adv Comt, Mo Arts Coun, 76-78. *Bibliog:* Article, Kansas City Star, 4/21/74; Kansas City success stories, Kansas City Mag, 9/82. *Mem:* Kansas City Art Inst; Contemp Art Soc; Kansas City Art Gallery Asn; Coun Soc Fels, Nelson Gallery; Kansas City Artists Coalition; and others. *Specialty:* Contemporary American painting. *Publ:* Contribr, Presences: Jim Sajovic (mailer/folder) & Spectrum 77 (painting/sculpture), catalog, 77, Kansas City Art Inst. *Mailing Add:* 4500 State Line Kansas City KS 66103

DRAKE, JAMES
PRINTMAKER, SCULPTOR
b Lubbock, Tex, Sept 12, 46. *Study:* Art Ctr Col of Design, fel, BFA with Hons, 69, MFA, 70. *Work:* El Paso Mus Art, Tex; Phoenix Art Mus, Ariz; Univ NMex Art Mus, Albuquerque; Univ Tex, El Paso; Mathews Art Ctr, Ariz State Univ, Tempe. *Exhib:* New Visions, Amarillo Art Ctr, Tex, 81; one-man exhib, Galveston Arts Ctr on the Strand, Tex, 82; Southern Fiction, Contemp Art Mus, Houston, 83; New Orleans Triennal, New Orleans Mus Art, 83; and others. *Teaching:* Instr life drawing, Art Ctr Col of Design, Los Angeles, 69-70 & Univ Tex, El Paso. *Bibliog:* Barbara Cortright (auth), Sculpture & graphics, Art Week, 2/76. *Mailing Add:* 5330 Gateway E El Paso TX 79905

DRAPELL, JOSEPH
PAINTER, SCULPTOR
b Humpolec, Bohemia, Czech, Mar 13, 40; Can citizen. *Study:* Cranbrook Acad Art, with Donald Willett & George Ortman, MFA, 70. *Work:* Guggenheim Mus; Mus Fine Arts, Boston; La Jolla Mus Contemp Art; Minneapolis Inst Art; Art Gallery Ont, Toronto. *Exhib:* New Acquisitions, Guggenheim Mus, 72; Ontario Now, Art Gallery Hamilton, Ont, 76; New Abstract Art, Edmonton Art Gallery, Alta, 77; Color Abstractions from MFA, Mus Fine Arts, Boston, 79; The New Generatin, Andre Emmerich Gallery, New York, 80; The Heritage of Jack Bush, R McLaughlin Gallery, Oshawa, Ont, 81; The Threshold of Color, Edmonton Art Gallery, Alta, 82; retrospective, Art Gallery Windsor, Ont, 84. *Teaching:* Instr artistic methods, York Univ, Toronto, 70-71; vis artist in residence, Syracuse Univ, 73. *Awards:* Can Coun Grant, 71; Ont Arts Coun Grants, 75 & 76. *Bibliog:* Ken Carpenter (auth), Joseph Drapell: Re-inventing abstraction, Art Int, Switz, 12/78; Kenworth Moffett (auth), The New Generation, Rhineburgh Press, 80; Karen Wilkin (auth), article, Arts Mag, 1/81. *Media:* Acrylic on Canvas; Bronze. *Dealer:* Meredith Long & Co Houston TX; Thomas Segal Gallery Boston MA. *Mailing Add:* 123 Bellwoods Ave Toronto ON M6J 2P6 Canada

DRAPER, JOSIAH EVERETT
PAINTER, INSTRUCTOR
b East Orange, NJ, Oct 17, 15. *Study:* Pratt Inst, Brooklyn, advert design & illus; Grand Cent Sch Art, New York, with Harvey Dunn; also with Edgar Whitney, Paul Strisik & John Pike. *Work:* Cummer Gallery Art, Jacksonville, Fla; Jacksonville Univ; US Navy; City of Bahia Blanca, Arg; Jacksonville Mus of Arts & Sci; and others. *Comn:* Painting, Jacksonville Area C of C, 72 & 81; ten paintings, Sea Pines Co, Amelia Island, Fla, 73; 5 paintings, Indian River Plantation, Stuart, Fla, 81; painting, District Court Appeals, Daytona Beach, Fla. *Exhib:* Am Watercolor Soc Ann, New York, 62-74; one-man shows, Fla Gulf Coast Art Ctr, Clearwater, 73 & Jacksonville Art Mus, 74; District Court Appeals, Tallahasee, Fla, 82; Indian River Plantation, Stuart, Fla, 83; and many others. *Pos:* Artist, Prudential Ins Co Am, 35-50, art dir, 51-72; retired; pres, J E Draper, AWS, Inc, 81. *Teaching:* Instr watercolor technique, Jacksonville Art Mus, 70-81; Univ NFla, 79; spec watercolor workshops in US, West Indies, Europe & Mexico. *Awards:* Ann Traveling Exhib, Am Watercolor Soc, 66 & 69 & Carolyn Stern Award, 69. *Mem:* Am Watercolor Soc; Fla Watercolor Soc (bd dirs, 72-81, pres, 77-78); St Augustine Art Asn (pres, 72-74, bd dirs, 75-81); Sarasota Art Asn; Art League Daytona Beach (bd trustees, 72-75). *Media:* Transparent Watercolor. *Dealer:* Ponte Vedra Club Ponte Vedra Beach FL 32082; Peregrine Gallery 5627 San Jose Blvd Jacksonville FL 32207. *Mailing Add:* 20 Ponte Vedra Circle Ponte Vedra Beach FL 32082

DRAPER, WILLIAM FRANKLIN
PAINTER, INSTRUCTOR
b Hopedale, Mass, Dec 24, 12. *Study:* Harvard Univ, 31-32; Nat Acad Design, 31-34; Grande Chaumiere, Paris, France, 35; Art Students League, 37; also with Jon Corbino, Leon Kroll & Henry Hensche. *Work:* Nat Portrait Gallery; Pavilion, Music Ctr, Los Angeles; Off Housing & Urban Develop; US Central Intelligence Agency; and others. *Comn:* Portraits, President John F Kennedy, 62, Shah of Iran, 67, Terence Cardinal Cooke, 71, Gen Lauris Norsted, 72, Ambassador Walter Annenberg, James Michener, 79, President Richard M Nixon for Nat Portrait Gallery & Mayor John V Lindsay for City Hall, NY, 81; and others. *Exhib:* Nat Gallery, London, Eng, 44; Metrop Mus Art, 45; Cent Asn Ann; Graham Gallery, New York, 69 & 71; Palm Beach Gallery, Fla, 72; Far Gallery, 77-79. *Teaching:* Instr, Art Students League, 65-82. *Mem:* Boston Allied Artists; Century Asn; Knickerbocker Club. *Media:* Oil.

Dealer: Portraits Inc 41 E 57th St New York NY 10022; Grand Central Art Galleries Madison Ave at 43rd St New York NY 10017. *Mailing Add:* 160 E 83rd New York NY 10028

DR BRUTE (ERIC WILLIAM METCALFE)
VIDEO ARTIST
b Vancouver, BC, Aug 22, 40. *Study:* Univ Victoria, BFA, 70. *Work:* Art Bank Can, Ottawa; Nat Gallery Can; Akad Kunst, West Berlin; Univ Calgary, Alta; Art Gallery Ont. *Comn:* Multi-media performance, 78 & video performance, 83, Music Gallery, Toronto. *Exhib:* Chair Show, Art Gallery Ont, 74; From This Point of View, Vancouver Art Gallery, 77; Off the Wall, A Space, Toronto, 77; Chair Show, And/Or, Seattle, 79; Manner SM, Vancouver Art Gallery, 82; Okanada, Akad Kunste, West Berlin, 83. *Pos:* Dir & cur performance art, Western Front, 73- *Awards:* Bursary, 73 & Video Production Award, 77, 80 & 83, Can Coun; JVC Corp Third Video Festival Award, 80. *Bibliog:* Balkind Shadbolt (auth), Visions, Douglas & McIntyre, 83; Peggy Gane (auth), Parachute, Colour Video, 83. *Media:* Video, Performance. *Dealer:* Art Meterpole Toronto ON. *Mailing Add:* 303 E Eighth Vancouver BC V5T 1S1 Canada

DREAPER, RICHARD EDWARD
DEALER, CONSULTANT
b Mobile, Ala, Aug 24, 35. *Study:* St Bernard Col; La State Univ; Univ Ariz; Univ Calif, BA. *Pos:* Asst to dir, Univ Ariz Gallery, Tucson, 59-62; assoc, Ancient Art, Laguna Beach, Calif, 63-80; mgr, Royal Athena Galleries, Beverly Hills, currently. *Teaching:* Lectr Chinese art hist, Univ Calif, Irvine, 76- *Specialty:* Chinese and Southeast Asian art; classical antiquities; 19th & 20th Century American & European paintings. *Mailing Add:* 415 N Orange Grove Ave Apt #9 Los Angeles CA 90036

DREIBAND, LAURENCE
PAINTER, LECTURER
b New York, NY, Nov 8, 44. *Study:* Chouinard Art Inst, Los Angeles, 61; Art Ctr Col Design, Los Angeles, BFA(with distinction), 67, fel & MFA, 68. *Work:* Home Savings & Loan Collection; Container Corp Am Collection; Chase Manhattan Bank. *Comn:* Great Ideas of Western Man, Container Corp Am, 70. *Exhib:* West Coast 70, E B Crocker Art Gallery, Sacramento, Calif, 70; Beyond the Actual, Pioneer Mus, Stockton, Calif, 70; one-man shows, David Stuart Galleries, 70-72, Los Angeles Inst Contemp Art, 80 & Allen Stone Gallery, New York, 81; California Artists, Long Beach Mus Art, 71; Galerie Quatres Mouvements, 74; Janus Gallery, 83. *Teaching:* Instr painting & photog, Art Ctr Col Design, 70-, chmn dept fine arts, 72- *Awards:* First Prize, Fine Arts Gallery San Diego, 70; Great Ideas of Western Man Purchase Award, Container Corp Am, 70; 19th All City Festival Purchase Award, Munic Art Gallery, Los Angeles, 71. *Bibliog:* Joseph Young (auth), Los Angeles artist--Laurence Dreiband, Art Int, 70; Barbara Witus (auth), Paintings of Laurence Dreiband, Los Angeles Free Press, 3/31/72; Udo Kulterman (auth), New Realism, New York Graphic Soc, 72. *Media:* Oil, Acrylic. *Publ:* Auth, Laurence Dreiband, Paintings and Drawings, David Stuart Galleries, 72. *Dealer:* Janus Gallery 8000 Melrose Ave Los Angeles CA 90046. *Mailing Add:* 2450 Yosemite Dr Los Angeles CA 90041

DRESKIN, JEANET STECKLER
PAINTER, EDUCATOR
b New Orleans, La, Sept 29, 21. *Study:* Newcomb Col, Tulane Univ, with Xanvier Gonzales, BFA, 42; Johns Hopkins Univ, med art cert, 43; John McCrady Sch, New Orleans; Clemson Univ, MFA. 73. *Work:* Nat Mus Am Art, Smithsonian Inst, Washington, DC; Ga Mus Art, Athens; Greenville Co Mus Art, SC; Guild Hall Mus, East Hampton, NY; Columbia Mus Art, SC. *Comn:* Gibbes Art Gallery, Charleston, SC; seals, painting & plaque, SC State Bd Health, Columbia, 57; painting, Fiber Industs, Imp Chem, Dorchester, Eng, 66; wood block print, SC Tricentennial Comn, Greenville, 70; McDonald Corp, Chicago, 82. *Exhib:* Piedmont Ann, Mint Mus Art, Charlotte, NC, 69-72; Nat Asn Women Artists, Nat Acad, New York, 70 & USA Traveling Exhib, 70-77; Chautauqua Exhib Am Art, NY, 70; 38th Ann Mid-Year Show, Butler Inst Am Art, Youngstown, Ohio, 74 & 83; Mainstreams Int, Marietta Col, Ohio, 75; Expressions of Art in Nature Bicentennial Exhib, Gibbes Art Gallery, Charleston, SC, 76; Nat Watercolor Exhib, Birmingham Mus Art, Ala, 78 & 81; San Diego Int Watercolor Exhib, 81; and many others. *Pos:* Staff artist, Am Mus Nat Hist, New York, 43-45; staff artist, Univ Chicago Med Sch, 45-50. *Teaching:* Painting & graphics, Greenville Co Mus Sch Art, 50-52 & 62-, head sch, 68-74; adj prof art, Univ SC, 73-80, Governor's Sch, 81-83. *Awards:* Owen H Kenan Mem Award of Merit, Am Contemp Exhib, Soc Four Arts, Fla, 68; W J Kaplan Award, Nat Exhib Painters in Casein & Polymer, 64; Merit Award, Int Grand Prix, Cannes, France, 73; and others. *Bibliog:* Jack A Morris, Jr (auth), Contemporary Artists of South Carolina, Tricentennial Comn, 70; Lucille Green (auth), Jeanet S Dreskin, artist-educator, Sandlapper, 3/70; Patricia Robbins (auth), Jeanet Dreskin, Art Voices S, 5-6/79; plus many others. *Mem:* Guild SC Artists (mem bd, 55-, treas, 68, vpres, 71, pres, 72); Nat Asn Women Artists (mem comt, 71-); SC Watercolor Soc (pres, 83-84); Nat Asn Med Illusr; Southern Graphics Coun (secy-treas, 74-76, mem bd, 79-82); plus others. *Media:* Polymers, Oils. *Publ:* Illusr, Anatomy of the Gorilla, Am Mus Nat Hist, Columbia Univ, 43-46; illusr, What's New, Abbot Labs (& Latin Am ed), 46, 47 & 49; illusr, Surgery of Repair, Lippincott, 50; illusr, Williams Obstetrics, Stander-Appleton, 50; illusr, Pediatric Orthopedic Surgery, Williams & Wilkins, 67; and many others. *Dealer:* Hampton III Gallery Ltd 11 Hampton Ctr Taylors SC 29687; Fay Gold Gallery 3221 Cains Hill Pl Atlanta GA 30306. *Mailing Add:* 60 Lake Forest Dr Greenville SC 29609

DRESKIN-HAIG, JEANET ELIZABETH
PAINTER, PRINTMAKER
b Greenville, SC, June 8, 52. *Study:* Smith Col, BA; Univ Mich, MFA. *Work:* SC State Art Collection, Columbia; Nat Gallery, Washington, DC; Chrysler Mus Art, Norfolk; Nat Mus Am Art, Washington DC; Greenville Co Mus Art. *Comn:* Ed of 60 lithographs, First Piedmont Mortgage Co, SC, 74. *Exhib:* Davidson Nat Print & Drawing Competition, 76; 25th Nat Exhib Prints, Libr Cong & Nat Gallery, 77; 20th NDak Ann, Univ NDak, 77; 25th Nat Exhib Prints, Smithsonian Inst, 77; one-person show, Florence Mus, SC, 77, Furman Univ, 80 & Columbia Mus Art, 81 & 82; Butler Ann, 82; and others. *Teaching:* Instr printmaking, Greenville Co Mus Sch Art, summer 74; teaching fel, Univ Mich, 75; asst prof printmaking, Univ Tex, Dallas. *Awards:* Purchase Award, SC State Invitational, Clemson, 74; Mich Artists Print Competition Award, 74; Purchase Award, Appalachian Corridor Exhib, 75; Purchase Award, NDak Nat Print & Drawing Ann, 82. *Mem:* Col Art Asn; Southern Graphics Soc; Nat Print Coun. *Media:* Lithography, Etching, Drawing. *Mailing Add:* 9323 Guernsey Ln Dallas TX 75220

DRESSER, LOUISA (LOUISA DRESSER CAMPBELL)
ADMINISTRATOR, HISTORIAN
b Worcester, Mass, Oct 25, 07. *Study:* Vassar Col, BA; Fogg Art Mus, Harvard Univ; Courtauld Inst, Univ London. *Collections Arranged:* New England Painting, 1700-1775, Worcester Art Mus, 43, Christian Gullager, 49, Edward Savage, 51, The Dial and The Dial Collection, 59. *Pos:* Assoc in decorative arts & cur decorative arts, Worcester Art Mus, 32-49, actg dir, 43-46, cur of collection, 49-72, trustee, 72-77, hon trustee, 77- *Mem:* Mass Hist Soc; Am Antiqn Soc; Salisbury Mansion Assocs (pres, 71-79); Worcester Craft Ctr (corporator, 64-78). *Res:* American painting of the 17th & 18th centuries, primarily New England. *Publ:* Auth, Early New England Printmakers, 39; coauth, Maine and Its Role in American Art, 63; auth, Portraits in Boston, 1630-1720, J Archives Am Art, 66; auth, The Background of Colonial American Portraiture, 66; ed, European paintings in the collection of the Worcester Art Mus, 74; and others. *Mailing Add:* c/o Worcester Art Mus 55 Salisbury St Worcester MA 01608

DREWAL, HENRY JOHN
HISTORIAN, EDUCATOR
b Brooklyn, NY, Mar 11, 43. *Study:* Hamilton Col, BA; Inst African Studies, Columbia Univ, cert, MA, PhD. *Collections Arranged:* Dimensions in Black Art, African, Afro-American & Afro-Brazilian Art at CSU, Cleveland State Univ, 75; Visions of Africa: an Exhibition of Prints & Textiles by Nigerian Artists, 75 & African Fabrics: Tradition and Change, 76, Cleveland State Univ; Traditional Art of the Nigerian Peoples: the Ratner Collection (auth, catalogue), Mus African Art, 77; African Artistry: Technique and Aesthetics in Yoruba Sculpture, High Mus Art, Atlanta, 80. *Teaching:* Asst prof African, Oceanic, Am Indian & Afro-Am art, Cleveland State Univ, 73-77, assoc prof, 77-81, prof & chmn, 82- *Awards:* Cleveland State Univ Research Grants, 74, 75, 76, 79, 80, 81; Georgia Council on the Arts & Humanities, 79; Nat Endowment Humanities Grant, 77-78 & 81. *Mem:* Col Art Asn; Triennial Symp Traditonal African Art; Midwest Art Hist Asn; Soc Study Visual Anthro; Art Coun African Studies Assoc. *Res:* History of art among the Yoruba, Fon and Ewe of West Africa and the African Diaspora of Brazil and Cuba; principles of performance structure and aesthetics; iconology. *Publ:* Auth, More powerful than each other: An Egbado classification of Egungun, African Arts, 78; ed, Special issue on the arts of Egungun among Yoruba peoples, African Arts, 78; auth, Pageantry and power in Yoruba costuming, In: Cordwell and Schwartz, The Fabrics of Culture, 79; auth, Gelede Art and Female Power Among the Yoruba, Ind Univ Press, 83; auth, Composing time and space in Yoruba art, In: Ben-Amos, The Relations Between Verbal and Visual Arts in Africa (in prep). *Mailing Add:* Dept of Art Cleveland State Univ Cleveland OH 44115

DREWELOWE, EVE
PAINTER, SCULPTOR
b New Hampton, Iowa. *Study:* Univ Iowa, BA, 23, MA, 24; Univ Colo, 54. *Work:* Univ Iowa Mus; Univ Colo, Boulder; Harkness House, London, Eng; Utah State Univ; Wartburg Col. *Comn:* Two oil paintings, First Nat Bank Fort Collins, 61. *Exhib:* Eighteenth Int Watercolor Exhib, Art Inst Chicago, 39; Midwestern Show, Nelson Gallery & Atkins Mus, Kansas City, Mo, 60; Denver Art Mus, 64-65, 67 & 69; The West--80 Contemporaries, Univ Ariz, Tucson, 67; solo exhib, Univ Iowa, Iowa City, 78; Retrospective Part I, Colo Women in the Arts, Univ Colo, 79; Retrospective, Images 1921-1979, Univ Colo, 79; Faces and Findings--The Past in the Present, Boulder City Grant Exhib, Univ Colo, 83; and others. *Teaching:* Instr, Engineering Col, Univ Colo, 27-28 & Fine Arts Dept Summer Session, 36 & 37. *Awards:* First Prize in Oil, Boulder Art Asn Regional, 63; Distinguished Alumni Serv Award, Univ Iowa, 79; Grant, City of Boulder, 81; plus others. *Mem:* Hon life mem, Nat Artists Equity Asn; Colo Chap Artists Equity (pres, Boulder Chap, 63-68, actg pres, 69); Boulder Artists Guild (pres, currently). *Media:* Mixed Media. *Publ:* Illusr, In Denim and Broadcloth, 53. *Mailing Add:* 2025 Balsam Dr Boulder CO 80302

DREWES, WERNER
PAINTER, PRINTMAKER
b Canig, Ger, July 27, 1899; US citizen. *Study:* Charlottenburg Technische-Hochschule, Berlin, Ger; Stuttgart Sch Archit, Ger; Stuttgart Sch Arts & Crafts; Weimar Staatliches Bauhaus, with Itten & Klee; Dessau Staatliches Bauhaus, with Kandinsky & Feininger. *Work:* Represented in more than 80 public collection in USA and abroad. *Exhib:* Carnegie Int, Pittsburgh, 45-47; one-man shows, Prints, Drawings & Painting, Cleveland Mus Art, Ohio, 61; Prints, Achenbach Found, Calif Palace of Legion of Honor, San Francisco, 62,

Paintings, Prints, Retrospective, Wash Univ, St Louis, 65 & Prints, Retrospective, Nat Collection Fine Arts, Washington, DC, 69. *Pos:* Founding mem, Am Abstract Artists, New York, 37-46. *Teaching:* Instr painting, drawing & printmaking, Columbia Univ, 37-40; instr design, Inst Design, Chicago, 45; dir design & first yr prog, Wash Univ Sch Fine Arts, 46-65. *Awards:* Plexiglas Sculpture Competition, Mus Mod Art, 39; Award for Autumn Harvest (painting), St Louis City Art Mus, 59. *Bibliog:* R Frost (auth), Werner Drewes, nature & abstract, Art News, 2/15/49; Germain Bazin (auth), History of modern painting, Hyperion, 51; Caril Dreyfuss (auth), Werner Drewes, woodcuts, Smithsonian Inst, 69. *Mem:* Washington Soc Printmakers. *Media:* Oil, Watercolor; Woodcut, Etching. *Dealer:* Assoc Am Artists 653 Fifth Ave New York NY 10022; Martin Diamond Fine Arts Inc 1014 Madison Ave New York NY 10021. *Mailing Add:* 11526 Links Dr Reston VA 22090

DREXLER, ARTHUR JUSTIN
DIRECTOR, CURATOR
b New York, NY, Mar 13, 25. *Study:* Cooper Union, New York. *Collections Arranged:* Eight Automobiles (auth, catalog), 51, Japanese House in Museum Garden (auth, bull), 53, Buildings for Business and Government (auth, bull), 57, Architecture of the Ecole des Beaux Arts (auth, bk), 75 & Transformations in Modern Architecture (auth, bk), 79, Mus Mod Art; Frank Lloyd Wright Drawings (auth, bk), Horizons, 62; Twentieth Century Engineering, 64. *Pos:* Designer, George Nelson Assocs, New York, 47-48; archit ed, Interiors Mag, New York, 48-50; cur, Dept Archit & Design, Mus Mod Art, New York, 51-56, dir, 56- *Awards:* AIA Medal, Am Inst Architects, 77. *Mem:* Soc Archit Historians; Soc Arts, Relig & Contemp Cult. *Publ:* Auth, The Architecture of Japan, Mus Mod Art, 55; auth, Ludwig Mies Van Der Rohe, Braziller, 60. *Mailing Add:* Mus Mod Art 11 W 53rd St New York NY 10019

DREXLER, LYNNE
PAINTER
b Newport News, Va. *Study:* Richmond Prof Inst, BFA; Hunter Col; Col William & Mary; Hans Hoffman Sch Fine Arts, scholar. *Work:* Prentice Hall Collection, Englewood Cliffs, NJ; Ciba-Geigy Collection, Hudson River Mus; Tamarind Print Collection, Mus Mod Art, New York; Univ Mass, Amherst. *Exhib:* One-man show, Tanager Gallery, 59; Norfolk Mus Regional Show, 60; Galleria, San Miguel de Allende, Mex, 62; Tetra-Centennial, Va Mus Fine Arts, Richmond, 66; Traveling Show, mus in West & South, 66; plus others. *Dealer:* Alonzo Gallery 26 E 63rd St New York NY 10021; Aldona Gobujas Degdras Ltd 215 E 79th St New York NY 10021. *Mailing Add:* Box 14 Monhegan ME 04852

DREYER, GAY
SCULPTOR
b Christiansburg, Va, July 31, 15. *Study:* Art Students League, with William Zorach, 33; Beaux Art Inst, with Eugene Steinhof, 34; Baylor Univ, BS, 57; Iowa Univ, MFA, 59. *Work:* Chrysler Mus, Norfolk, Va; Hermitage Foundation, Norfolk, Va. *Comn:* Eve at Gate of Paradise (bronze), Norfolk, Va, 82. *Exhib:* Pa Acad, Philadelphia, 40; Brooklyn Mus, NY, 62; Smithsonian Inst, Washington, DC, 63; Silvermine Guild, New Canaan, Conn, 64; Old Dominion Univ Gallery, Norfolk, Va, 81. *Teaching:* Instr sculpture, Baylor Univ, 54-59; chmn, Art Dept, Old Dominion Univ, Norfolk, Va, 69-79. *Awards:* Purchase Award, Southwestern Art Show, Dallas, 59; Best in Show, Womens Club, White Plains, NY, 63; Best in Show, Norfolk Festival Art, 81. *Media:* Mixed. *Dealer:* David Johnson 765 Grandy Norfolk VA 23501. *Mailing Add:* 1355 Bolling Ave Norfolk VA 23508

DRIESBACH, DAVID FRAISER
PRINTMAKER, EDUCATOR
b Wausau, Wis, Oct 7, 22. *Study:* Univ Ill; Beloit Col; Univ Wis; Pa Acad Fine Arts; State Univ Iowa; Atelier 17, with S W Hayter, 69. *Work:* Seattle Mus, Wash; Dayton Art Inst, Ohio; Columbus Gallery Fine Arts, Ohio; Bibliot Nat, Paris, France; Univ Windsor, Canada. *Comn:* Fiscal Flight (ed 150 color etching), Sears Roebuck Co, 67; series of bronze reliefs, Assoc Am Artists, NY, 68; color intaglio ed, Checker Cab Co, Kalamazoo, Mich, 74; color intaglio, Soc Am Graphic Artists; color viscosity, Gemarts, Knoxville, Tenn. *Exhib:* Contemporary Art in USA, Worcester Mus, Mass, 51; Young Printmakers of America, Mus Mod Art, New York, 53; Ten Printmakers of USA, Purdue Univ, 66; 162nd Ann Am Watercolors, Prints & Drawings, Pa Acad Fine Arts, 67; Grafica Contemporanea Americana, Venice, Italy, 77; Retrospective Show, Univ Md, Baltimore Co, 79; Seventh British Int Print Biennale, Bradford, England, 82. *Teaching:* Prof printmaking, Northern Ill Univ, 64- *Awards:* Ford Found Purchase Prize for Intaglio, 60; Carlton Col Prize for Intaglio, 66; Uris Bros Prize for Intaglio, 66. *Bibliog:* Bob White (auth), David Driesbach, Chicago Art Scene, 1/68; The complex world of David Driesbach, Northern Alumnus, 3/68. *Mem:* Midwest Col Art Asn; Soc Am Graphic Artists; Boston Printmakers. *Media:* Intaglio, Bronze. *Dealer:* Merrill Chase Galleries Chicago IL 60611; Neville-Sargent Gallery 1515 Sheridan RD Wilmette IL 60091. *Mailing Add:* Kingston Rd RR 1 Box 35 AA Kingston IL 60145

DRIESBACH, WALTER CLARK, JR
SCULPTOR, INSTRUCTOR
b Cincinnati, Ohio, July 3, 29. *Study:* Sch Dayton Art Inst, 47-52, with Robert Koepnick; studio asst to Joseph Kiselewski, New York, 54-55; Art Acad Cincinnati, 55-56, with Charles Cutler. *Comn:* St Anthony of Padua (limestone relief), St Anthony of Padua Church, Cincinnati, 59; Life of St Teresa (limestone entablature), St Teresa Church, Cincinnati, 62; The Lord's Supper (walnut relief), Good Shepherd Church, Cincinnati, Ohio, 64; Fireman Monument (granite figure), Cincinnati, Ohio, 68; Immaculate

Conception (oak figure), St Charles Borromeo Church, Dayton, Ohio, 81. *Exhib:* Ohio Sculptors, Akron & Canton Art Insts, 60; Northwest Territory Sculpture Show, Cincinnati Art Mus & John Herron Inst Art, Indianapolis, Ind, 61; Univ Cincinnati Regional Sculpture, 68; Invitational Exhib, Cincinnati Art Mus, Ohio, 72 & 81; Figure '82, Contemp Art Ctr, Cincinnatti, Ohio, 82; plus others. *Teaching:* Instr sculpture & drawing, Memphis Acad Arts, 56-58; instr sculpture, Dayton Art Inst Eve Sch, 58-60; instr sculpture & drawing, Wilmington Col, 63-66; instr sculpture, drawing & 3-D design, Univ Dayton, 66-72; instr drawing & sculpture, Thomas More Col, 70-71 & 78-; instr sculpture, 3-D design & found, Art Acad Cincinnati, 70-; instr sculpture, Col Mt St Joseph, 72; instr wood carving, Communiv, Univ Cincinnati, 80-81. *Awards:* Fleischmann Purchase Prize, Zoo Arts Festival, Cincinnati, 64; First Prize, Prof Sculpture Div, Ohio State Fair Fine Arts Exhib, 66, Second Prize, 68. *Mem:* Cincinnati MacDowell Soc. *Media:* Stone, Wood. *Publ:* Contribr, Contemporary Stone Sculpture, 70 & Creating Small Wood Objects as Functional Sculpture, 76, Crown; contribr, Masters of Wood Sculpture, Watson-Guptill, 80. *Dealer:* Heritage Gallery 3412 Telford St Cincinnati OH 45220. *Mailing Add:* 2541 Erie Ave Cincinnati OH 45208

DRIESSEN, ANGELA KOSTA See Kosta, Angela

DRIGGS, ELSIE
PAINTER
b Hartford, Conn, Aug 5, 1898. *Study:* Art Students League; also with Maurice Sterne, Rome. *Work:* Whitney Mus Am Art; Baltimore Mus Art; Metrop Mus, New York; Phillips Gallery, Washington, DC; Sheldon Mem Gallery, Lincoln, Nebr. *Comn:* Animal cartoons & WAfrican gold weights, Works Prog Admin, Harlem House, New York, 34; La Salle, Post Off, Huntsville, La, 35; Indian Village, pvt comn, New York, 38. *Exhib:* 35 Under 35, Mus Mod Art Opening Show, 30; Edward J Gallagher, III Collection, Baltimore Mus Art, 53; Root Collection, Metrop Mus Art, 54; The Precisionists, Whitney Mus Am Art, 63; NC Mus of Art, Raleigh, 72; Nat Collection of Fine Arts, Washington, DC, 76; Hirshland Adler Lines of Power, New York, 77; Royal Scotch Acad, Edinburgh, 77; Hayward Gallery, London, 77; Heckscher Mus, Huntington, NY, 78; Akademie Kunste, Berlin, 80; Mus Mod Art, San Francisco, 82; and others. *Pos:* Asst, Metrop Mus Art, 23. *Teaching:* Instr, 45-48. *Bibliog:* Samuel M Kootz (auth), Modern American Painters, Brewer & Warren, 30; Sheldon Cheney (auth), The Story of Modern Art, Viking, 41; The Art of New York, Abrams, 83. *Mem:* Nat Soc Lit & Arts. *Media:* Oil, Watercolor. *Dealer:* Martin Diamond Fine Arts Inc 1014 Madison Ave New York NY 10021. *Mailing Add:* c/o Martin Diamond Fine Arts 1014 Madison Ave New York NY 10021

DRISCOLL, EDGAR JOSEPH, JR
CRITIC
b Boston, Mass, Sept 1, 20. *Study:* Cambridge Sch Weston; Univ Iowa, with Grant Wood; Yale Univ Sch Fine Arts. *Pos:* Art critic, Boston Globe, 46-73; Boston corresp, Art News, 73- *Mem:* St Botolph Club; Yale Club; Harvard Club. *Mailing Add:* 75 Hancock St Boston MA 02114

DRISCOLL, JOHN PAUL
CURATOR, HISTORIAN
b Madison, Minn, Oct 28, 49. *Study:* Univ Minn, BA, 71; Pa State Univ, MA, 74. *Collections Arranged:* Charles Sheeler: Works on Paper (catalog), 74, Checklist of the Permanent Collection, 77, American Paintings from Collection of Daniel J Terra, 77, Arthur B Davies from the Brill Collection, 79 & All That Is Glorious Around Us, 81, Pa State Univ Mus Art; Paintings from William H Lane Foundation, Munson-Williams-Procter Inst, 78; Contemporary British Ceramics, Fitchburg Art Mus, 82. *Pos:* Registr, Pa State Univ Mus Art, 75-78; cur, William H Lane Found, 78-82; guest cur, Kensett Exhib, Worcester Art Mus, 83. *Teaching:* Fitchburg State Col, 79- *Bibliog:* Hilton Kramer (auth), Charles Sheeler, New York Times, 4/13/74; Outstanding exhibitions, Apollo Mag, 6/74. *Mem:* Col Art Asn; New Eng Mus Asn; Am Asn Mus; Am Antiqn Soc; Am Numismatic Asn. *Res:* Emphasis on American art with current focus on John F Kensett and Edwin Dickinson. *Publ:* Auth, William Trost Richards' woodland scene rediscovered, Am Art J, 78; auth, John F Kensett Drawings (exhib catalog), Pa State Univ Mus Art, 78; auth, Charles Sheeler's early work: Five rediscovered paintings, Art Bulletin, 80; auth, A Marsden Hartley of 1908, Am Art J, 80; auth, John Stuart Ingle: Paradigms of reality, Am Artist, 82. *Mailing Add:* 437 Blossom St Fitchburg MA 01420

DRISKELL, DAVID CLYDE
PAINTER, EDUCATOR
b Eatonton, Ga, June 7, 31. *Study:* Skowhegan Sch Painting & Sculpture, with Jack Levine & Henry V Poor, scholar, 53; Howard Univ, with James A Porter & Morris Louis, BA, 55; Cath Univ Am, with Nell Sonnemann & Ken Noland, MFA, 62; Riksbureau voor Kunsthistorisches Documentatie, The Hague, Neth, cert, 64. *Work:* Corcoran Gallery Art, Smithsonian Inst, Washington, DC; Birmingham Mus Art; Corcoran Gallery Art, Washington, DC; Carl Van Vechten Gallery Fine Arts, Fisk Univ, Nashville, Tenn; Ark Fine Arts Ctr, Little Rock; and others. *Comn:* Mountain and Tile Suite (10 woodcuts-color), Tenn Arts Comn, 72. *Exhib:* Baltimore Mus Area Exhib, 65; Corcoran Area Exhib, 66; Birmingham Festival Exhib, 74; Cent South Ann, Nashville, 72; Mid-South Exhib, Memphis, 75; and others. *Pos:* Mem bd adv, Mus African Art, 67-; mem visual arts adv panel, Tenn Arts Comn, 69-, mus adv bd, 73-; guest curator, Smithsonian Inst, 72; guest curator, Los Angeles Co Mus Art, 74-76; mus adv panel, Nat Endowment Arts, 74-77; bd gov, Skowhegan Sch Painting & Sculpture, 75- *Teaching:* Prof painting & art hist, Talladega Col, 55-62; prof painting & art hist, Howard Univ, 62-66; prof art & chmn dept, Fisk Univ, 66-76; vis prof, Univ Ife, Nigeria, 70; vis prof, Bowdoin Col, 73;

vis prof, Bates Col, 73; prof art, Univ Md, College Park, 76-82, chmn dept art, 78-82. *Awards:* John Hope Award in Art, Atlanta Univ, 59; Museum Donor Award, Am Fedn Art, 62; Graphics Art Award, Corcoran Gallery Art, 65. *Mem:* Col Art Asn; Nat Conf Artists; Am Mus Asn; Am Fedn Art. *Media:* Oil, Tempera. *Res:* Role of the black artist in American society and traditional African art, its impact on Afro-American art. *Mailing Add:* 4206 Decatur St Hyattsville MD 20781

DROEGE, ANTHONY JOSEPH, II
PAINTER, DRAFTSMAN
b Philadelphia, Pa, Sept 22, 43. *Study:* Pa State Univ, BA, 65; Univ Iowa, MA, 67, MFA, 68. *Work:* Kemper Ins Co Collection, Long Grove, Ill; Clara Eagle Gallery, Murray State Univ, Ky; Art in the Embassy Prog, US State Dept; Indianapolis Mus Art, Ind; South Bend Art Ctr, Ind. *Comn:* Numerous pub & pvt portrait comns. *Exhib:* Mid-Year Show, Butler Inst Am Art, Youngstown, Ohio, 70; Mainstreams, 5th Ann Marietta Col Int Competitive Exhib, Ohio, 72; The Emerging Real, Storm King Art Ctr, Mountainville, NY, 73; New Realism Re-Visited, Brainerd Hall Art Gallery, State Univ NY Col Potsdam, 74; Living American Artists & the Figure, Pa State Univ Mus Art, 74; The Big Show, J B Speed Art Mus, Louisville, Ky, 75; Am Painters in Paris, 76; Ind-Ill Bicentennial Painting Exhib, 76; Panorama Am Art, Midwest Mus Am Art, Elkhart, Ind, 79; Thirteenth Union League Club, Chicago Art Show, 81; 68th Ind Artists Show, Indianapolis Mus Art, 81; and others. *Teaching:* Instr painting & drawing, Murray State Univ, Ky, 68-71; assoc prof painting & drawing, Ind Univ, South Bend, 71- *Awards:* Commendation from Elmer Bishoff, Mid-Am Show, Joslyn Art Mus, Omaha, 68; First Place Painting, 7th Biennial Michiana Regional Art Competition, South Bend Art Ctr, 72; Best of Show at 8th Biennial Michiana Regional Art Competition, First Bank & Trust Co, 74. *Bibliog:* Byron Burford (auth), View from the Midwest, Readers & Writers, summer 68; Gene Porter (auth), Mirrors repeated in Droege paintings, Ft Wayne News-Sentinel, 4/73; Dennis Shapiro (auth), article, New Art Examiner, Chicago, 4/75. *Media:* Oil, Conte Crayon; Pastel, Oil Pastel. *Mailing Add:* 202 S Filbert St New Carlisle IN 46552

DROHOJOWSKA, HUNTER
CRITIC, WRITER
b Schenectady, NY, Sept 5, 52. *Study:* Ohio State Univ, Columbus, 70-72; Ariz State Univ, Tempe, 73-75; Inst Allende, San Miguel de Allende, Mex, BFA, 76. *Pos:* Art ed, Los Angeles Weekly, Calif, 80-; columnist, Los Angeles Herald Examiner, 83- *Mem:* Art Table; Int Asn Art Critics. *Publ:* Auth, The Pasadena case, Art in Am, 5/81; auth, Young Turks--the exhibition, Artforum, 2/82; auth, Transitional use: A surburban exhibition, Arts & Archit, fall 82; auth, Robin Winters, John Mandel, Raul Guerrero: reviews, Flash Art, 3/83; auth, James Croak, New Myths & Heroic Allegories (catalog essay), Otis Art Inst, Parsons Sch Design, 10/83; and others. *Mailing Add:* 131 N Union Ave Los Angeles CA 90026

DROWER, SARA RUTH
PAINTER, ILLUSTRATOR
b Chicago, Ill, Oct 15, 38. *Study:* Roosevelt Univ, BS, 59; Univ Ill, Chicago, MS, 61; Art Inst Chicago. *Work:* Ill State Mus, Springfield; Minn Mus Art, Minneapolis; Borg-Warner Corp, DePaul Univ, Standard Oil, Chicago. *Exhib:* Drawings USA '73, Minneapolis, 73; Mid-Western Graphics, Tulsa, Okla, 75; Marietta Col Crafts Nat, Ohio, 76; Lake Superior 77, Int Crafts Exhib, Duluth, Minn, 77; Craft Show Wearables .Exhib, Philadelphia Mus Art, Pa, 77; 4th Ann Fibers & Fabric Exhib, Springfield, Ill, 78; plus many others. *Pos:* Sci illusr, Turtox-Biol Supply, 62-64. *Awards:* First Prize Watercolors, Union League Club, Chicago, 72; Purchase Award Drawing, Field Enterprises, Chicago, 72; Best of Show, Fine Art Exhib, Artists Guild Chicago, 74. *Mem:* Surface Design; Am Crafts Coun; Nat Asn Handcraftsmen. *Media:* Watercolor. *Mailing Add:* 127 Laurel Wilmette IL 60091

DRUM, SYDNEY MARIA
PAINTER, PRINTMAKER
b Calgary, Alta, Can, Nov 20, 52. *Study:* Univ Calgary, BFA(with distinction in art), 74; York Univ, MFA, 76. *Work:* Mus Mod Art, New York; Philadelphia Mus Art, Pa; Nat Mus Am Art, Washington, DC; Univ Nebr, Lincoln; Can Coun Art Bank, Ottawa, Ont. *Exhib:* One-woman shows, Name Gallery, Chicago, Ill, 79, Getter/Pall Gallery, New York, 81, Hart House Art Gallery, Univ Toronto, Ont, 81, Gallery Pascal, Toronto, Ont, 81 & Jan Licero Gallery, Chicago, Ill, 82; World Print III, San Francisco Mus Mod Art, Calif, 80; and others. *Teaching:* Sessional lectr studio art, Univ Alta, Edmonton, Can, 76-77; instr studio art, Nova Scotia Col Art & Design, Halifax, Can, 77-78; asst prof studio art, Univ Ill, Chicago Circle, 78- *Awards:* Can Coun Arts Grant, 76-77; A-N-W Prof Prize, 55th Ann Members Show, Print Club, Philadelphia, Pa, 79; Artist Fel, Yaddo Found, 80. *Bibliog:* Nancy Tonsley (auth), Sydney Drum, Artscanada, 5-6/79; Joyce Zemans (auth), Beyond the border at Harbourfront Art Gallery, Artmag, 2-3/80; Liz Wylie (auth), Sydney Drum at Gallery Pascal & Hart House Art Gallery, Artmag, 5-6/81. *Mem:* Col Art Asn; Print Club; Print & Drawing Coun Can; Univ Art Asn Can; Boston Printmakers. *Dealer:* Getter/Pall Gallery 50 West 57th St New York NY 10021. *Mailing Add:* 722 W 18th St Univ Ill Chicago IL 60616

DRUMM, DON
SCULPTOR, CRAFTSMAN
b Warren, Ohio, Apr 11, 35. *Study:* Hiram Col; Kent State Univ, BFA & MA. *Work:* Akron Art Inst; Bowling Green State Univ; Columbus Gallery Fine Arts; Massillon Mus; and others. *Comn:* Reliefs, walls, aluminum & steel sculpture & fountains, Alcoa Co, Pittsburgh, Episcopal Diocese, Sao Paulo,

Brazil, Richard Gossar Mem Sculpture, Toledo, Ohio, Curtain Bluff Hotel, Antigua BWI & City of Akron, Ohio; and others. *Exhib:* Group shows, 64 & 65 & Traveling Exhib circulated by Am Fedn Arts, 65-67 & 72, Mus Contemp Crafts, New York; Cleveland Mus Art, 64-68; Columbus Gallery Fine Arts, 66 & 67; and others. *Teaching:* Instr sculpture, Akron Art Inst; artist in residence, Bowling Green State Univ, 66-71; instr, Penland Sch Crafts, 66-79. *Awards:* Purchase Prize, Cleveland Mus Art, 64; Prize, Nat Soc Interior Design, 65; Prize, Columbus Gallery Fine Arts. *Mem:* Ohio Designer Craftsmen; Am Craftsmen's Coun. *Res:* Investigation into the use of contemporary materials and construction techniques to create urban sculpture specializing in the use of cast aluminum and concrete. *Dealer:* Don Drumm Studios & Gallery 437 Crouse St Akron OH 44311. *Mailing Add:* 110 Corson Ave Akron OH 44302

DRUMMER, WILLIAM RICHARD
GALLERY DIRECTOR
b Ottawa, Ohio, Feb 17, 25. *Study:* Ohio State Univ, BA, 50, MA, 57. *Exhib:* Piranesi, Miss State Mus, Jackson, 80-81 & Brooks Mem Art Gallery, Memphis, 82. *Pos:* Dir, Gallery 539, New Orleans, 75- *Specialty:* Japanese woodblock prints, Piranesi etchings, fine architectural prints and drawings. *Mailing Add:* 539 Bienville St New Orleans LA 70130

DRUMMOND, SALLY HAZELET
PAINTER
b Evanston, Ill, June 4, 24. *Study:* Rollins Col, 42-44; Columbia Univ, BS, 48; Inst Design, Chicago, 49-50; Univ Louisville, MA, 52. *Work:* Mus Mod Art, New York; Whitney Mus Am Art; J B Speed Mus Art, Louisville; Metrop Mus Art, New York; Hirshhorn Mus, Washington, DC. *Exhib:* Am Artists Ann, Whitney Mus Am Art, New York, 60; Lyric Abstraction in America, Am Fedn Arts Traveling Exhib, 62-63; Americans 63, Mus Mod Art, New York, 63; Focus on Light, NJ State Mus, Trenton, 67; 21st New Eng Painting & Sculpture Ann, Silvermine, Conn, 70; Retrospective, Corcoran Gallery Art, Washington, DC, 72; and others. *Teaching:* Instr, Skowhegan Sch Art, 73. *Awards:* Fulbright Grant, Venice, 52; Guggenheim Grant, France, 67. *Bibliog:* Lawrence Campbell (auth), Dotted light, Art News Mag, 4/72. *Media:* Oil. *Mailing Add:* One Wilton Rd Ridgefield CT 06877

DRUTT, HELEN WILLIAMS
DEALER, LECTURER
b Winthrop, Mass, Nov 19, 30. *Study:* Tyler Sch Art, Temple Univ, BFA; Barnes Found. *Collections Arranged:* Two British Goldsmiths, Ramshaw & Watkins, 73; UICA: Craft Faculty, 74; Soup Tureens: 1976 (ed, catalog), 76; Olaf Skoogfors Retrospective, 79; Robert Arneson: Self-Portraits 1966-1978 (ed, catalog), 79; Ruth Duckworth & Claire Zeisler (ed, catalog), 79; Contemporary Ceramics: A Response to Wedgewood (ed, catalog); Robert L Pfannebecker (ed, catalog); Claus Bury (ed, catalog). *Pos:* Curatorial consult, Mus Philadelphia Civic Ctr, 67, 70 & 73; exec dir, Philadelphia Coun Prof Craftsmen, 67-73; dir, Helen Drutt Gallery, 74-; gallery consult, Moore Col Art, 78; consult, Nat Endowment Arts, 79- *Teaching:* Lectr mod craft hist, Philadelphia Col Art, 72-; adj instr, Moore Col Art, Philadelphia, 74- *Awards:* Award Merit Dedicated Serv Crafts, Philadelphia Col Art, 72; Award Advan Mod Ceramics, Int Ceramics Symp, 81. *Bibliog:* Carol Saline (auth), Crafty lady, Philadelphia Mag, 75; Professional Women (film), ABC-TV, Philadelphia, 76 *Mem:* Collab 20th Century, Philadelphia Mus Art; Am Crafts Coun (Pa state rep, 75-); Pa State Coun on the Arts (crafts panel, 75-78). *Specialty:* Twentieth century work in fiber, ceramics & metal; contemporary crafts. *Publ:* Contribr, Craft Horizons, Am Crafts Coun, 70. *Mailing Add:* c/o Helen Drutt Gallery 305 Cherry St Philadelphia PA 19106

DRUTZ, JUNE
PAINTER, EDUCATOR
b Toronto, Ont, Feb 14, 20. *Study:* Cent Tech Sch; Ont Col Art, grad(hons), 65. *Work:* McMaster Univ, Hamilton, Ont; Univ Waterloo, Ont; Royal Can Art Collection, Nat Gallery, Ottawa; Univ Guelph, Ont; London Trust Co, Ont; and many others. *Comn:* Seeds of Spring Returning (serigraph ann print), Glenhyrst Art Asn, Brantford, Ont, 68-69. *Exhib:* One-man shows, Rebecca Sisler Gallery, Toronto, 78 & Prince Arthur Gallery, Toronto, 79; Ont Soc Artists, 80; Univ Ind, Elkhart, 80; Can Soc Painters Watercolor, 81; and many others. *Teaching:* Instr, Ont Col Art, Toronto, 67-80; Ont Dept Educ, summers 68-72; Ryerson Polytech Inst, Toronto, 72-73 & Toronto Art Sch. *Awards:* Purchase Award, Graphex-3, Brantford, Ont, 75; Ian Griffiths Award Watercolor, 80 & Joseph E Seagrams Purchase Award, 80, Ont Soc Artists; and others. *Bibliog:* Robert Myers (auth), The youth cult maidens of June Drutz, Art Mag, Vol 6, No 24, 75. *Mem:* Royal Can Acad; Ont Soc Artists; Can Soc Painters Watercolor; Print & Drawing Coun Can; Can Soc Graphic Artists. *Media:* Tempera, Watercolor. *Dealer:* Prince Arthur Gallery 33 Prince Arthur Ave Toronto ON M5R 1B2 Can; Sussex Gallery Sussex Dr Ottawa ON Can. *Mailing Add:* 430 Annette St Toronto ON M6P 1R9 Canada

DRYFOOS, NANCY
SCULPTOR
b New Rochelle, NY. *Study:* Sarah Lawrence Col, sculpture with Oronzio Maldarelli & painting with Curt Roesch, dipl; Columbia Univ Sch Archit, with Oronzio Maldarelli, also sculpture with Jose de Creeft. *Work:* Brandeis Univ; Columbia Univ; Sarah Lawrence Col; Evanston Mus Fine Arts; NY Univ. *Comn:* Am Jewish Tercentenary, 54; reliefs for Kingsbridge House Synagogue, Home for Aged Hebrews, 57; Edel Award for Fine Arts, Wedgwood-Dickenson Col, 59; Naomi Lehman Mem Award, 62; Jos M Proskauer Bar Asn Award, NY, 62. *Exhib:* Allied Artists Am Ann, Nat Acad Design Gallery, 48-72; Pa Acad Fine Arts Biennale; Syracuse Mus Ann, NY,

54; Brooklyn Mus Ann, NY, 56; Nat Sculpture Soc Ann, New York, 65-80; eight solo shows, Washington, DC, Silvermine, Conn & New York, NY. *Awards:* Gold Medal of Honor, Allied Artists Am, 58; Second Prize, Knickerbocker Artists, 60; Constance K Livingston Award, Am Soc Contemp Artists, 70. *Mem:* Fcl Nat Sculpture Soc (secy, 72-, former rec secy & exhib chmn); NY Soc Women Artists (vpres, 71-73, pres, 77-79); Nat Asn Women Artists (mem jury, 71-73, chmn nominating comt); Allied Artists Am (juror, 72); Am Soc Contemp Artists (dir, 70-72). *Media:* Marble, Terra Cotta. *Publ:* Contribr, Nat Sculpture Rev, 70-71. *Mailing Add:* 45 E 89th St New York NY 10028

DRYSDALE, NANCY MCINTOSH
PATRON, DEALER
b Chicago, Ill, July 22, 31. *Study:* Northwestern Univ, BS, 53. *Pos:* Dir, McIntosh/Drysdale Gallery, currently. *Mem:* Washington, DC Art Dealers Asn. *Specialty:* Contemporary art, painting, drawing, sculpture; European and American. *Interests:* Integration of visual arts with the other arts and architecture. *Mailing Add:* 2008 Peden 406 Seventh St NW Houston TX 77019

DUBACK, CHARLES S
PAINTER, PRINTMAKER
b Fairfield, Conn, Mar 10, 26. *Study:* Whitney Sch Fine Arts, New Haven, Conn; Newark Sch Fine & Indust Arts, NJ; Skowhegan Sch Painting & Sculpture, Maine; Brooklyn Mus Art Sch. *Work:* Corcoran Gallery Art, Washington, DC; Emory Collection, Emory Univ, Atlanta, Ga; Columbia Mus Art, SC; Butler Mus Am Art; Am Tel & Tel, New York; and others. *Exhib:* Prints & Drawings, 53, Trends in Watercolor Today, 57, 20th Biennial Int Watercolor Exhib, 59 & Print Show, 70, Brooklyn Mus, NY; Whitney Ann Exhib of Contemp Am Painting, New York, 59-60; Mus Mod Art, New York, 62; 20th Ann Exhib Contemp Am Painting, Lehigh Univ, Bethlehem, Pa, 74; Works on Paper, Weatherspoon Art Gallery, Greensboro, NC, 75; Ft Wayne Mus of Art, Ind, 76; one-man show, Landmark Gallery, 79-82; New Dimensions in Drawing, Aldrich Mus, Conn, 81; and other group & one-man shows. *Collections Arranged:* Ten Painters of Maine, Landmark Gallery, New York, 77. *Bibliog:* Connie Smith (auth), A sentimental journey, Village Voice, 4/76; Laura Pipune (auth), Window exhibit at museum, Ft Wayne Jour-Gazette, 10/76; Holland Cotter (auth), Charles DuBack, Arts Mag, 11/77. *Media:* Multimedia. *Mailing Add:* 457 W Broadway New York NY 10013

DUBANIEWICZ, PETER PAUL
PAINTER
b Cleveland, Ohio, Nov 17, 13. *Study:* Cleveland Inst Art, grad(scholar), 35; Agnes Gund Traveling Scholar, 35; Mus Sch Fine Arts, Boston, Mass; Albert Whitin Traveling Fel, France, Ger & Italy, 38. *Work:* Ohio Bell Tel Co; Cleveland Mus Art; Ford Motor Co; St Paul's Episcopal Church; Butler Inst; plus many other pub & pvt collections. *Comn:* Mural, New Eastman Br Libr, Cleveland, 80. *Exhib:* Metrop Mus Art, New York; Ten-Thirty Art Gallery, Cleveland; Corcoran Gallery, Washington, DC; Springfield Mus, Mass; 39th Ann Mid Year Show, Butler Inst Am Art; plus many others. *Teaching:* Instr, Boston Mus Sch Fine Art, 38-41; instr, Cleveland Inst Art, 45-81, prof emer, 81-; lectr, Skowhegan Sch Painting & Sculpture; instr, Oberlin Col, winter 72. *Awards:* Buffalo Art Club Prize, 63; Second Prize, Int Platform Asn Show, 66; H M Newman Relig Art Show, Cleveland, Ohio, 70. *Publ:* Illusr, color cover, Cleveland Plain Dealer. *Mailing Add:* 3289 Fairmount Blvd Cleveland Heights OH 44118

DUBIN, RALPH
PAINTER, COLLAGE ARTIST
b New York, NY, Sept 2, 18. *Study:* Am Artist Sch, with Moses Soyer & James Lechay; New Sch Social Res, with Robert Gwathmey & Stuart Davis; Brooklyn Mus Art Sch, with Gabor Ptererdi & Ben Shahn; Brooklyn Col, BA; Hunter Col, New York, MA(art), 76; also with Hans Hofmann. *Work:* Pa Acad Fine Art, Philadelphia; Smithsonian Inst, Washington, DC; Drawing Collection, Cornell Univ. *Exhib:* Nat Inst Arts & Lett, New York, 68; Pa Acad Fine Arts; Cornell Univ; Whitney Mus Am Art; 8 one-man shows, Kraushaar Gallery, New York; Butler Inst Am Art, Youngstown, Ohio; and others. *Teaching:* Lectr art, Queen's Col, 61-68; instr art, New York Community Col, 65-68. *Mem:* Artist Equity Asn; Fedn Mod Painters & Sculptors. *Media:* Oil, Mixed Media. *Mailing Add:* 463 West St No 935-B New York NY 10014

DUBLAC, ROBERT REVAK
PAINTER
b Farmington, Conn, Nov 28, 38. *Study:* Hartford Art Sch, Univ Hartford, BFA, 63; Temple Univ, Rome, Italy, 68-69. *Work:* North Adams State Col, Mass; General Electric, Plainville, Conn; and collections of many other corp. *Exhib:* Conn Acad Fine Arts, Wadsworth Atheneum, Hartford, 70; Nat Acad Design, Acad Gallery, New York; Am Watercolor Soc, New York; Nat Soc Painters Casein & Acrylic, New York; New Haven Paint & Clay Club, Slater Mus, Conn; Nat Biennial, Monza Mus, Italy, 78. *Awards:* Margaret Cooper Mem Prize, Conn Acad Fine Arts, 70; North Adams State Col Purchase Award, Birkshire Art Asn, 79; Best in Show Award, The Sharon Creative Arts Found, 81. *Media:* Watercolor, Oil. *Mailing Add:* 62 Cottage St Farmington CT 06085

DUBOIS, ALAN BEEKMAN
CURATOR, ADMINISTRATOR
b Forest Glen, NY, Dec 14, 35. *Study:* State Univ NY, New Paltz, MS, 58; Ind Univ, MFA, 66. *Work:* Ringling Mus Art, Sarasota, Fla; New Orleans Mus Art. *Exhib:* Light Seven, Mass Inst Technol. *Collections Arranged:* European Glass 1700-1900, 77; On Assignment: Sam Shere, 78;

Contemporary Silversmiths, 79; Contemporary Blown Glass by Southeastern Artists, 82; Pachner Landscapes, 83; Upham Collection of Photographs, 83; Murano Glass, 83; Picasso Aquatints, 84. *Pos:* Dir, Wash Co Mus Fine Arts, 64-66; asst dir, Mus Fine Arts, St Petersburg, Fla, 66- *Awards:* Nat Endowment Arts Fel, 72 & 75. *Mem:* Col Art Asn; Soc Photog Educ; Fla Art Mus Dir Asn; Ctr Creative Photog; Friends Photog. *Res:* Photography. *Publ:* Auth, Photography: A Changing Art, Mus Fine Arts, St Petersburg, Fla, 78; auth, Andre Kertesz, Maitland Art Ctr, 81. *Mailing Add:* 6351 Second Ave S St Petersburg FL 33701

DUBOIS, MACY
ARCHITECT, DESIGNER
b Baltimore, Md, Dec 20, 29; Can citizen. *Study:* Md Inst; Tufts Univ, BSE; Harvard Univ, MArch. *Comn:* Ont Pavilion, Expo 67, Ont Govt, 66; Lakehead Sci Bldg, Lakehead Univ, 66; Albert Campbell Libr, Scarborough Pub Libr Bd, 73; George Brown Col Applied Arts & Technol, Toronto, 73; Govt Can Bldg, North York, Ont, 78. *Exhib:* Toronto City Hall Competition, 58; Sao Paolo Exhib, 64; Massey Medals for Archit, 64 & 67; Amsterdam City Hall Competition, 69. *Pos:* Archit critic, Can Architect, 63- *Mem:* Ont Asn Architects; fel Royal Archit Inst Can; academician Royal Can Acad Arts. *Mailing Add:* 76 Richmond St E Toronto ON M5C 1P1 Canada

DUCA, ALFRED MILTON
SCULPTOR, PAINTER
b Milton, Mass, July 9, 20. *Study:* Pratt Inst, 38-41; Boston Mus Fine Arts, 43-44. *Work:* Addison Gallery Am Art, Andover, Mass; Fogg Mus & Divinity Sch, Cambridge; Worcester Art Mus, Mass; Munson Procter Inst, Utica, NY; Boston Univ Sch Basic Studies; and others. *Comn:* Sculptures, Prudential Ins Co, Boston, 68-69, Standard Oil Co Ind Res Ctr, 71-72 & Computer Sphere, J F Kennedy Post Off, Boston, 71-72; steel screen, Proj 57, Boston, 71-72; sculpture, bronze screen, John McCormack Bldg, Boston, 75-76. *Exhib:* Local, regional & nat exhibs, 58-72. *Pos:* Beaux art dir, Brandeis Univ, 52-53; vis lectr, Boston Univ, 57-58; res assoc, Mass Inst Technol, 58-65; consult, White House Conf Children & Youth, 70-71; auth-dir, Dissemination network syst, Channel One; founder-prog dir, Gloucester Experiment & Channel One Prog. *Awards:* Grants, Rockefeller Found, 58 & Ford Found, 60; New Eng Res Ctr Educ Award, 72. *Bibliog:* Arch Am Art, Smithsonian Inst. *Mem:* Mass Coun Arts & Humanities. *Media:* Polymer; Metal. *Res:* Development of polymer processes for painters and sculptors; development of foam vaporization process for casting metal for sculpture. *Publ:* Auth, Polymer Tempera, Significant Teaching Aid, 54; auth, Art casting, Mass Inst Technol J, 62; coauth, Plastics as Art Form, Newman, 64; coauth, Synthetic Pating Media, Jensen, 64; ed & contribr, Facilitator's guide to channel one programming, 81. *Mailing Add:* Annisquam Gloucester MA 01930

DUCKWORTH, RUTH
SCULPTOR, CERAMIST
b Hamburg, Ger, Apr 10, 19. British citizen. *Study:* Liverpool Sch Art, 36-40; Hammersmith Sch Art, 55; Cent Sch Art & Crafts, London, 56-58; De Paul Univ, Hon Dr, 81. *Work:* Windsor Castle, Eng; Smithsonian Inst, Washington, DC; Philadelphia Mus Art; Art Inst Chicago; Utah Mus Fine Arts; and others. *Comn:* Mural, Hodag Chemical Co, Skokie, Ill, 78; porcelain wall panels, Perkins & Will, Architects, Chicago, 81; three part wall piece, Main Bank of Chicago, 81; Beth Israel Synagogue, Hammond, Ind, 82; mural, Animal Care Ctr, Chicago, 83; and others. *Exhib:* One-woman shows, Hadler Gallery, New York, 78, Boyman's Mus, Rotterdam, 79 & Exhib A, Chicago, 80; Century of Ceramics, Traveling Exhib, 79; Am porcelain, Renwick Gallery, Washington, DC, 80; and many others. *Teaching:* Instr ceramics, Cent Sch Arts & Crafts, London, 59-64; asst prof ceramics, Midway Studio, Univ Chicago, 64-77. *Awards:* Third Prize, Int Handicrafts Exhib, Stuttgart, Ger, 62; Third Prize, Int Crafts, Istanbul, Turkey, 67; First Prize for Foreign Craftsmen, Nippon Gendai Kohgei Bijutsuka, Kyokai, Japan, 68. *Bibliog:* Tony Birks (auth), The Art of the Modern Potter, Country Life, 67. *Mem:* Arts Club Chicago; Am & World Crafts Couns. *Media:* Stoneware, Porcelain. *Dealer:* Alice Westphal Exhibita 233 E Ontario St Chicago IL 60601 *Mailing Add:* 3845 N Ravenswood Ave Chicago IL 60613

DUFF, ANN MACINTOSH
PAINTER, PRINTMAKER
b Toronto, Ont. *Study:* Cent Tech Sch; Queen's Univ Summer Sch Fine Arts. *Work:* Nat Gallery Can, Ottawa; Art Gallery Ont, Toronto, Agnes Etherington Gallery, Queen's Univ; City Toronto Arch. *Comn:* Watercolor painting, Reader's Digest for Expo 67, Montreal. *Exhib:* Five Toronto Painters, Montreal Mus Fine Art; Six Ways with Watercolor, London Art Gallery, Ont; Can Soc Painters in Watercolour & Am Watercolor Soc Joint Exhib, 72; Fifty Years, Art Gallery, Ontario, 75; Watercolours Japan-Canada, Tokyo-Montreal, 76-77; eleven one-man shows in Toronto. *Awards:* J Grant Glassco Purchase Award, Can Soc Painters Watercolor, 68 & John Labatt Award, 73; Curry Award, 80 & 81. *Bibliog:* Frances Duncan Barwick (auth), Pictures from the Douglas M Duncan Collection, Univ Toronto, 75; Rebecca Sisler (auth), Passionate spirits, Clarke Irwin, Toronto, 80. *Mem:* Royal Can Acad Arts; Can Soc Painters Watercolour (exec, 70-75); Can Soc Graphic Art (treas, 67-69); Print & Drawing Coun of Can. *Media:* Watercolor. *Dealer:* Gadatsy Gallery 45 Stephanie St Toronto. *Mailing Add:* 133 Imperial St Toronto ON M5P 1C7 Canada

DUFF, JAMES H
MUSEUM DIRECTOR, ADMINISTRATOR
b Pittsburgh, Pa, Oct 11, 43. *Study:* Washington & Jefferson Col, BA, 65; Univ Mass, MA, 70. *Collections Arranged:* Wildlife in Art, Brandywine River Mus, Chadds Ford, Pa, 73; Maxfield Parrish: Master of Make-Believe, 74; Harvey

Dunn, 74; Peter Hurd, 77; The Collection of Amanda K Berls & Ruth A Yerion, 80; Wyeth at Olsons, 81; N C Wyeth's Still-lifes and Landscapes, 82. *Pos:* Dir, Mus Hudson Highlands, 66-73; consult, NY State Coun Arts, 70-72; dir, Brandywine River Mus, 73-; NE Mus Conference (pres, currently); and others. *Mem:* Asn Art Mus Dirs; Am Asn Mus; NE Mus Conf (Pa gov, 76-). *Mailing Add:* PO Box 297 Chadds Ford PA 19317

DUFF, JOHN EWING
SCULPTOR
b Lafayette, Ind, Dec 2, 43. *Study:* San Francisco Art Inst, BFA, 67; with Manuel Neri, Paul Harris & Ron Nagle. *Work:* Kaiser Wilhelm Mus, Krefeld, Ger; Guggenheim Mus Art, Whitney Mus Am Art & Mus Mod Art, New York; Inst Contemp Art, Boston, Mass. *Exhib:* Anti-Illusion, Procedures & Materials Show, Whitney Mus, 69, David Whitney Gallery, 70 & 71, John Meyers Gallery, 72 & 73 & Willard Gallery, 75, 76, 77 & 78, New York; Irving Blum Gallery, Los Angeles, 72; Danial Wienburg Gallery, 73, 75, 77, 79 & 81; Margo Leavin Gallery, Los Angeles, Calif, 81; Development in Recent Sculpture, Whitney Mus Am Art, 81. *Awards:* Theodor Award, Guggenheim Mus, 77. *Bibliog:* Barbara Rose (auth), Where we are & what we like, New York Mag, 4/72 & 4/75; John Russell (auth), current shows in New York Times, 3/75; J Tannenbaum (auth), rev in Arts Mag, 6/75. *Media:* Fiberglas, Wood. *Publ:* Contribr, Art Now: New York, 72. *Mailing Add:* 5 Doyers New York NY 10013

DUFFY, BETTY MINOR
DEALER
Pos: Dir, Bethesda Art Gallery. *Specialty:* American Fine Prints from the first half of the 20th century. *Mailing Add:* c/o Bethesda Art Gallery 7950 Norfolk Ave Bethesda MD 20014

DUFOUR, PAUL ARTHUR
PAINTER, DESIGNER
b Manchester, NH, Aug 31, 22. *Study:* Univ NH, BA, 50; Yale Univ, BFA, 52; also with Takahiko Fujita & Ikuo Hirayama, Japan, 64. *Work:* Masur Mus Art, Monroe, La; Springfield Art Mus, Mo; La State Collection, Baton Rouge; La Bicentennial Collection; Centraplex Munic Collection, Baton Rouge. *Comn:* Stained glass sculpture & mosaic, St Joseph Prep Sch, Baton Rouge, La, 68; stained glass windows, Holy Ghost Church, Hammond, La, 74; stained glass windows & bronze sculpture, Our Lady of Mercy, Baton Rouge, 74; stained glass, St Patrick Church, Lake Providence, La; glass windows & bronze doors, St Mary of Pines, Shreveport, La, 79; and many others. *Exhib:* Stained Glass Invitational, Mus Fine Arts, Jacksonville, Fla, 79; 20 Year Retrospective, La State Univ Art Gallery, 79; Glaskunst, Int Expo of Glass, Kassel, Ger, 81; Vicointer, Glass Invitational Expo, Valencia, Spain, 83; A Rebirth of A Medium, Nat Glass Invitational, Univ Tex, San Antonio, 83; 21st through 34th Ann State Exhib Prof Artists, 66-79; Contemporary Glass, Corning Mus, 79 & 80; Southeast Craft, Lemoyne Art Found, 80; Am Glass Invitational, Kansas City, Mo, 80; Int Glass Art Exposition, Kassel, Germany, 80; and many others. *Pos:* Supvr educ, Currier Gallery Art, Manchester, NH, 52-55; artist in residence, Viterbo Col, 68. *Teaching:* Asst prof painting, St John's Univ, 55-58; vis prof design, Sienna Heights Col, 57; prof design & stained glass, La State Univ, Baton Rouge, 58- *Awards:* Top Award, La Int Watercolor Exhib, 69; First Purchase Award, 4th Int Watercolor, 72; Hon Mention, Vicointer, Valencia, Spain, 83. *Bibliog:* Corning Mus Glass Microfiche Prog, 78; New Glass Rev I, Corning Mus Glass, 80; Jensen & Conway (auths), Ornamentalism, Potter, 82. *Mem:* Am Glass Guild; Col Art Asn; Am Craft Coun; La Watercolor Soc. *Media:* Multimedia. *Dealer:* Baton Rouge Gallery 205 N Fourth St Baton Rouge LA 70801; Matrix Gallery 912 W 12th St Austin TX 78713. *Mailing Add:* Sch Art Col Design La State Univ Baton Rouge LA 70803

DUGMORE, EDWARD
PAINTER
b Hartford, Conn, Feb 20, 15. *Study:* Hartford Art Sch, scholarship, 4 years; Calif Sch Fine Arts; Univ Guadalajara, Mex, MA. *Work:* Albright-Knox Art Gallery, Buffalo; Ciba-Geigy Corp, Ardsley, NY; Walker Art Inst, Minneapolis; Des Moines Art Ctr, Iowa; Mus Purchase Fund, New York. *Exhib:* Solomon R Guggenheim Mus, New York, 61; San Francisco Mus Art, Calif, 63; Albright-Knox Permanent Collection Show, 72; A Period of Exploration, San Francisco 1945-50, Oakland Mus, 73; one-man shows, Stable Gallery, 53, 54 & 56, Howard Wise Gallery, 61, 62 & 63 & Green Mountain Gallery, 71 & 73; Painting & Sculpture in Calif, The Modern Era, San Francisco Mus Mod Art, 76; Nat Collection of Fine Arts, Smithsonian Inst, 77; plus others. *Teaching:* Vis artist, Mont Inst, Great Falls, 65; vis artist, Univ Minn, Minneapolis, spring 70; vis artist, Des Moines Art Ctr & Drake Univ, 72. *Awards:* Guggenheim fel, 66-67; Nat Endowment Arts fel, 76-77; Award, Am Acad Inst Arts & Letters, 80; and others. *Bibliog:* Harold Rosenberg (auth), Art on the Edge, Macmillan, 75; Mary Fuller McChesney (auth), A Period of Exploration San Francisco 1945-1950; Irving Sandler (auth), Painters and Sculptors of the Fifties, Harper & Row, 78; plus others. *Media:* Oil. *Mailing Add:* 118 W 27th St New York NY 10001

DUHME, H RICHARD, JR
SCULPTOR, EDUCATOR
b St Louis, Mo, May 31, 14. *Study:* Pa Acad Fine Arts, 32-38; Univ Pa, 34; Barnes Found, Marion, Pa, 40-41; Am Sch Classical Studies, Athens, Greece, summer 51; Wash Univ, BFA, 53. *Comn:* Mo Sesquicentennial Medallions (silver & bronze), Sesquicentennial Comt, 71; St Martin & the Beggar (monumental bronze group), Bishop of Erie, Pa, 71; Chautauqua, New York Centennial Medallions (silver & bronze), 74; Airmen (bronze sculpture), US Air Force Mus, Dayton, Ohio, 80; St John Baptist De La Salle (cold cast

bronze), Christian Brothers, St Louis, 80. *Exhib:* Pa Acad Fine Arts Ann, Philadelphia, 38-41 & 50; Metrop Mus Art Summer Sculpture Show, New York,42; St Louis City Art Mus Group Show, 49-50 & 52; Cincinnati Art Mus, Ohio, 61; Expos Int Medaile Contemporaine, Nat Mus, Athens, Greece, 66. *Teaching:* Prof sculpture, Wash Univ, 47-82, prof emer, 82-; head dept sculpture, Chautauqua Inst Summer Schs, 53-; head dept sculpture, Syracuse Univ Chautauqua Ctr, 53-69. *Awards:* Cresson Foreign Travel Award, 35, Lewis S Ware Foreign Fel, 38 & May Audubon Post Prize Fel, 41, Pa Acad Fine Arts; First Hon Mention, Prix de Rome, Am Acad Rome, 39. *Mem:* Fel Nat Sculpture Soc; Allied Artists Am. *Media:* Bronze, Stone, Terra Cotta. *Mailing Add:* 8 Edgewood Rd St Louis MO 63124

DUIS, RITA (RITA DUIS ASTLEY-BELL)
PAINTER
b New York, NY. *Study:* Nat Acad Design; Art Students League; Banff Sch Fine Arts, Univ Alta; China Inst; also with Rex Brandt, Edgar Whitney, George Post & Robert Wood. *Exhib:* Nat Collection Fine Arts, Smithsonian Inst, Washington, DC, 63; Am Watercolor Soc, Nat Acad Design, New York, 70, 71, 73, 76, 78 & 81; Watercolor USA, Springfield Mus, Ill, 70; Am Cult Ctr, Jerusalem, Israel, 81; Am Cult Ctr, Cairo & Alexandria, Egypt, 81; Allied Artists, 81; and many others. *Awards:* Bronze Medal, Nat Arts Club, 71; Merit Award & Award for Excellence in Watercolor, Midwest Watercolor Soc, Tweed Mus, 78; Grumbacher Silver Medal, Nat Asn Women Artists, New York, 80; and others. *Mem:* Salmagundi Club; Nat Arts Club; Am Watercolor Soc; Nat Asn Women Artists; Am Artists Prof League. *Media:* Watercolor, Oil. *Mailing Add:* 207 E 74th St New York NY 10021

DU JARDIN, GUSSIE
PAINTER, PRINTMAKER
b San Francisco, Calif, Feb 19, 18. *Study:* Univ Colo, BA; Univ Iowa, MA. *Work:* NMex Mus Art, Santa Fe; NMex Highlands Univ; Univ Iowa; Roswell Mus, NMex; Univ Colo Mus. *Exhib:* Butler Inst Am Art 26th Ann, 61; NMex Biennial, 71, 73 & 75; Mus NMex Southwest Biennial Exhib, 72, 74 & 76, Invitational, 78; NMex Southwest Biennial, 78; one-woman exhib, Roswell Mus, 78, Gov Gallery, NMex State Capitol, Santa Fe, NMex, 79. *Pos:* Artist-in-Residence Prog, Roswell Mus, 77- *Awards:* First Purchase Award, Mus NMex, 61. *Media:* Acrylic, Oil. *Mailing Add:* RT 1 Box 245 Roswell NM 88201

DULAC, MARGARITA WALKER
PAINTER, WRITER
b Asheville, NC. *Study:* Art Inst Chicago, summer 38, 40, 54 & 55; Acad Andre Lhote, Paris, France, Woolley Fel, 38-39, cert, 39; Northwestern Univ, scholar & BS(cum laude), 42; Univ Chicago, MA, 44. *Work:* New Trier High Sch, Winnetka, Ill; Northwestern Univ, Evanston. *Comn:* Portraits, Hans Lange, dir, Chicago Symphony Orch, 37, Gen de Gaulle, Paris, 44 & Candy Bergen, 72; and others. *Exhib:* Chicago Artists Exhib, Art Inst Chicago, 35, 36 & 38; Salon Tuileries, Paris, 39 & 50; Nat Arts Club, 74-79; Bergen Mus, Paramus, NJ, 80; and many others. *Teaching:* Head dept art, De Kalb High Sch, Ill, 37-38; instr painting, Acad Dulac, 79- *Bibliog:* Winning honors easy for artists, Chicago Am, 7/13/38; Andre Lhote (auth), Un peintre Americain, Nouvelle Rev Francaise, 6/1/60; Artistic talent-one family, Jersey J, 1/21/74; plus others. *Mem:* Jersey Painters & Sculptors Soc; Poetry Soc Am. *Media:* Oil, Pastel. *Publ:* Auth, Cyclorama, Univ Chicago, 42; auth, Ivan Albright--mystic-realist, 1/66, Raymond Katz, master of mixed media, 1/69, Werner Groshans, realism and fantasy, 6/70, & Marisol, 84, Am Artist; and others. *Mailing Add:* Box 334 Murray Hill Sta PO New York NY 10016

DUMAS, ANTOINE
PAINTER, EDUCATOR
b Quebec City, Que, Can, Dec 8, 32. *Study:* Col des Jesuites, Quebec City, Baccalaureate Rhetorique, 53; Ecole des Beaux-Arts, Quebec City, dipl, 58; Acad Art Col, San Francisco, 69-70; Ecole des Arts Visuels, Univ Laval, Titular, 81. *Work:* Imperial Oil Art Collection, Toronto, Ont; CIL Art Collection, Rothman Permanent Collection, Montreal; Mus du Sem, Mus du Que, Quebec City. *Comn:* Stained glass mural, Dorval Airport, Montreal, 60; painted mural, RSW & Assoc Consult Ingeneers, Montreal, 75; three stamps, Can Post, Ottawa, 76, 78 & 79; tapestry, Aetna Can Bldg, Montreal, 83. *Exhib:* Forum 76, Montreal Mus Fine Arts; Traveling Exhib, Nancy Poole's Studio, Toronto, 80, Rodman Hall, St Catharines, 80, Laurentian Univ Mus, Sudbury, 80, & Univ Western Ont, 80; Livres d'Artistes, Bibliot Nat du Que, Montreal, 82; and others. *Teaching:* Prof graphic design, Ecole des Beaux-Arts, Quebec City, 62-65; prof graphic design, Ecole des Arts Visuels, Univ Laval, 70-74, prof illus design, 70- *Awards:* Lt Gov's Silver Medal, Ecole des Beaux-Arts, Que State Dept, 58. *Bibliog:* Germain Lefebvre (auth), catalog, Ed Chema, 80; Michele Marchand (auth), Painters Series (film), Can Broadcasting Corp TV, 81; Roland Bourneuf (auth), Antoine Dumas, Ed Int Stanke, 83. *Mem:* hon mem Soc Graphistes du Que; Royal Can Acad Art. *Media:* Oil, Acrylics; Serigraphy. *Publ:* Auth, A l'Enseigne d'Antan, Ed Pelican, 70. *Dealer:* Galerie Bernard Desroches 1444 Sherbrooke W Montreal PQ Canada H3G 1K4. *Mailing Add:* 1100 Marguerite Bourgeoys Sillery PQ G1S 3X9 Canada

DUNBAR, JILL H
CRITIC, WRITER
b New Haven, Conn, Feb 10, 49. *Pos:* Mem staff, Betty Parsons Gallery, New York, 75-76; mem staff, Truman Drawing Inc, 76-78; art critic, The Villager, Byron Publ, 76-; contrib ed, ArtWorld, 76-78; contrib ed, 57th St Rev, 76-77; contribr, Womanart, Mag, 77-; contribr, Phoenix, 77- *Mailing Add:* 250 W 12th St New York NY 10014

DUNBAR, MICHAEL AUSTIN
ADMINISTRATOR, SCULPTOR
b Santa Paula, Calif, Sept 21, 47. *Study:* Ill State Univ, Normal, BS, 71, MS, 78; Sangamon State Univ, Springfield, MA, 74. *Work:* Ill State Mus; Ill Bell Collection, Chicago; Mitchell Mus, Mt Vernon; Western Ill Univ, Springfield; Ill State Univ, Normal; and others. *Exhib:* Ill Arts Coun Traveling Exhib, Chicago, 78; Mayor Byrne's Mile of Sculpture, Ill, 79; Mid-American Art Exhib, Owensboro Mus Art, Ky, 79; one-man shows, Milikin Univ, Decatur, 80 & Augustana Col, Rock Island, 80; and others. *Collections Arranged:* Illinois Image, Danville, Ill, 76; Springfield & Vicinity Show, Ill State Mus, 80; The Illinois Collection, State of Ill Ctr, Chicago; and others. *Pos:* Dir, Ill State Fair Prof Art Show, 73-74; exec dir, Galesburg Arts Coun, 75-76. *Awards:* Blick Purchase Award, Dick Blick Corp, 78; Lois Irwin Award, 29th Quincy Art Show, 78; Governor's Award, Ill Arts Coun, 79. *Mem:* Chicago Sculpture Soc; and others. *Media:* Steel, Bronze. *Mailing Add:* 400 S Walnut Springfield IL 62704

DUNBAR, RUSSELL RAYMOND
PAINTER, SCULPTOR
b Akron, Ohio, June 5, 27. *Study:* Pratt Inst, Brooklyn, NY, BID, 53. *Exhib:* Mich Artists Show, Detroit Art Inst, 66-68, 70; Print Int, Seattle Art Mus, DC, 71; 1st All Mich Exhib, Flint Art Inst, 71; Cleveland Painting Sculpture Ann, Cleveland Art Inst, Ohio, 71 & 72; Butler Ann, Butler Mus Am Art, Youngstown, Ohio, 72-76 & 79; Palm Beach Nat, Four Arts Plaza, Fla, 72-79; Ann Exhib, Nat Soc Painters Casein & Acrylic, New York, 78-79 & 80. *Awards:* Collyer Purchase Prize, B F Goodrich Co, 70; Ralph Fabri Medal & Prize, 78 & Arches-Cason-Rives Award, 79, Nat Soc Painters Casein & Acrylic. *Mem:* Artist Equity; Nat Soc Painters Casein & Acrylic. *Media:* Multimedia. *Dealer:* Robert L Kidd Assoc/Galleries 107 Townsend Birmingham MI 48011. *Mailing Add:* 29232 Wellington Farmington Hills MI 48018

DUNCAN, HARRY ALVIN
PRINTER, DESIGNER
b Keokuk, Iowa, Apr 19, 16. *Study:* Grinnell Col, BA, 38, Hon DLitt, 73; Hawthorn Hse, apprenticeship, 41. *Work:* Amherst Col Libr, Mass; Sheldon Mem Art Gallery, Lincoln, Nebr; Pierpont Morgan Libr, New York; Houghton Libr, Cambridge, Mass; Univ Nebr, Omaha Special Collection. *Comn:* I Rise in Flames, collab with Paul Wightman Williams New Directions, Norfolk, Conn, 51; Terence Illustrated, Chapin Libr, Williamstown, Mass, 55 & Dickens in Italy, Pierpont Morgan Libr, New York, 56; Journey to a Known Place, comn by J Laughlin, Norfolk, Conn, 61; The Poets Go Along, comn by Charles Antin, New York, 65. *Exhib:* Fifty Books of the Year, Am Inst Graphic Arts, New York; Cummington Press, Book Club Calif, San Francisco, 64 & Grolier Club, New York, 76; one-man show, Grinnell Col, Iowa, 73; Abattoir Ed/Cummington Press, Sheldon Mem Art Gallery, Lincoln, Nebr, 79. *Pos:* Founder, dir & pres, Cummington Press, Omaha, 42-; founder, dir & ed, Abattoir Ed, Omaha, 72- *Teaching:* Prof typography, Univ Iowa, Iowa City, 56-72; prof fine art arts press, Univ Nebr, Omaha, 72- *Awards:* Outstanding Research & Creative Activity, Univ Neb, 81. *Bibliog:* Mary L Richmond (auth), The Cummington Press, Books at Iowa, 69; K K Merker & Kay Amert (auth), Harry Duncan, Maker of Books, Fine Print, 78; Joseph Blumenthal (auth), The Printed Book in America, 143-144, David R Godine, 77. *Publ:* Auth, The Cummington Press, New Colophon, 51; auth, The Technology of Hand Printing, Abattoir, 80; contribr, Collegiate Book Arts Presses, Fine Print, 82; auth, Doors of Perception, Essays in Book Typography, Austin, 83. *Mailing Add:* 1803 S 58th St Omaha NE 68106

DUNCAN, (ELEANORE) KLARI DE SZECSANYI
PAINTER, PRINTMAKER
b Hungary; US citizen. *Study:* Pratt Graphic Ctr; Acad Grande Chaumiere, Paris, France, 5 yrs with Prof Jean Aujame; New York Phoenix Sch Design, NY State scholar. *Work:* Ulmann Collection, Paris; Ecole de France, Paris; Cornell Club, New York. *Exhib:* Galerie Andre Weil, Paris, 64; Mus Art Mod, Paris, 64-65; Expos Intercontinentale de Monaco, 68; Maitland Art Ctr, Fla, 72-73; solo exhib, Cornell Club, New York, 75; Metrop Mus Art, New York, 77; Nat Arts Club, New York, 79. *Teaching:* Instr painting classes, SHAPE, Paris & Cape Cod, Mass, 73- *Mem:* Nat Arts Club; Burr Artists, New York; E G Lee Gallery Found. *Media:* Oil, Watercolor; Woodcut, Etching. *Mailing Add:* 342 E 81st St New York NY 10028

DUNCAN, RICHARD (HURLEY)
PRINTMAKER, DRAFTSMAN
b Daytona Beach, Fla, Feb 11, 44. *Study:* Southern Ill Univ, BA, 66, MFA, 73. *Work:* Aukland City Art Gallery, NZ; Springfield Civic Collection, Ill; Southeast Ctr Contemp Art, Winston-Salem, NC; Printclub Albany, Cooperstown Art Asn, NY. *Comn:* Two lithographs, Verein Originalgraphik, Switz, 74. *Exhib:* 35 Artists of the Southeast, High Mus & travelling, 76-78; Worldprint 77, San Francisco Mus Mod Art, 77; one-person exhib, Hunter Mus, 77; 25th Nat Exhib Prints, Nat Collection Fine Arts & Libr Cong, 77-78; 100 Worldprints, Smithsonian Travelling Exhib, 77-79; 40 Artists of the South, Russia-US Exchange, 80-82; Nat Painting & Drawing Exhib, Soc Four Arts, Palm Beach, Fla, 81 & 83; Honolulu Nat Print Exhib, Hawaii, 82. *Teaching:* Instr printmaking, Univ South, 73-78; assoc prof printmaking & drawing, Fla Int Univ, 78- *Awards:* Merit Award, 18th Nat Printmaking & Drawing Exhib, Okla Arts Ctr, 76; Purchase Awards, 44th Semi-Ann Printmaking, Drawing & Photog Exhib, Southeast Ctr Contemp Art, 76 & Dulin Nat Printmaking & Drawing Exhib, Dulin Gallery, Knoxville, 78. *Bibliog:* Coleman, Richardson & Smith (auths), Basic Design: Systems, Elements, Applications, Prentice-Hall, 83. *Mem:* Col Art Asn Am; Worldprint Soc. *Media:* Etching. *Dealer:* Sandy Garcia 22400 Old Dixie Hwy Miami FL. *Mailing Add:* 8760 Ridgeland Dr Miami FL 33157

DUNCAN, RUTH
PAINTER
b Greeley, Colo, Feb 19, 08. *Study:* Stephens Col, AA; Univ Okla, BFA; and with Harold A Roney, Simon G Michael & Warren Hunter. *Work:* Stephens Col, Columbia, Mo; San Antonio Col Libr, Tex; Royal Bldg, Dallas; Bexar Co Court House, San Antonio; Republic Bank, San Antonio; and others. *Comn:* Many. *Exhib:* 50 one-man shows & many group shows; Exposition Intercontinentale, Congres des Palais, Monaco; Smithsonian Inst; Witte Mem Mus, San Antonio; Univ Tex, Austin; San Antonio Main Libr, 68 & 75. *Awards:* Coppini Acad Fine Arts Award for Best Conserv Painting, 72, River Art Group; Order of the Rose Award for Achievement & Success in Chosen Field with nat & int acclaim, Delta Gamma Sorority, 73; Medal of Honor, Coppini Acad Fine Arts, 79; and others. *Mem:* Fel Am Artists Prof League; Coppini Acad Fine Arts (rec secy, 60-66, bd dirs, 75-); River Art Group, San Antonio; Soc Western Artists, San Francisco. *Media:* Oil, Watercolor. *Mailing Add:* 1511 Fulton Ave San Antonio TX 78201

DUNKELMAN, LORETTA
PAINTER
b Paterson, NJ, June 29, 37. *Study:* Douglass Col, BA, 58; Accad Belle Arti, Florence, Italy, 60-61; Hunter Col, MA, 66. *Work:* Chase Manhattan Bank; Bellevue Med Ctr, New York; Dana Art Ctr, Colgate Univ; Univ Cincinnati; Univ Kans Art Mus. *Exhib:* Whitney Biennial Contemp Art, 73 & Am Drawings 1963-73, Whitney Mus Am Art, New York; one-artist shows, AIR Gallery, NY, 73, 74, 78, 81 & 83; Waves: An Artist Selects, Cranbrook Acad Art, Bloomfield Hills, Mich, 74; Cornell Artists Past & Present, Johnson Mus, 77; New York Now, Phoenix Art Mus, 79; Structure, Narrative, Decoration, McIntosh-Drysdale Gallery, Washington, DC, 80; Konsthall, Lund, Sweden, 81; and others. *Teaching:* Vis artist, Univ Cincinnati, 74; asst prof art, Univ RI, 74-75; asst prof art, Cornell Univ, 77-80. *Awards:* Nat Endowment Arts Fel, 75 & 82; Creative Artists Pub Serv Fel, 75-76; Am Asn Univ Women Fel, 76-77. *Bibliog:* Ellen Lubell (auth), article, Arts Mag, 5/74; Peter Frank (auth), Gifts of the imagi, Village Voice, 1/8/79; Tiffany Bell (auth), article, Arts Mag, 2/79. *Media:* Oil on Canvas. *Dealer:* AIR Gallery 63 Crosby St New York NY 10012. *Mailing Add:* 151 Canal St New York NY 10002

DUNKELMAN, MARTHA LEVINE
HISTORIAN, EDUCATOR
b Cincinnati, Ohio, May 17, 47. *Study:* Wellesley Col, BA, 69; NY Univ, Inst Fine Arts, with Irving Lavin, MA, 71, with H W Janson, PhD, 76. *Teaching:* Instr art hist, Rider Col, Trenton, NJ, 75-76; asst prof, Wright State Univ, Dayton, Ohio, 76-80; assoc prof, 81- *Awards:* Alumni Asn Award for Teaching Excellence, Wright State Univ, Dayton, Ohio, 79. *Mem:* Col Art Asn; Midwest Art History Soc; Foundations Art: Theory & Educ. *Res:* Italian fifteenth century painting and sculpture. *Publ:* Auth, Michelangelo's Earliest Drawing Style, Drawing, 79; auth, Donatello's influence on Mantegna's early narrative scenes, Art Bulletin, 80; auth, The Holy Family with St John the Babtist: Nosadella or Tibaldi, Perceptions, Indianapolis Mus, 81; auth, Central Italian Painting 1400-1465, G K Hall. *Mailing Add:* Wright State Univ Dayton OH 45435

DUNLAP, LOREN EDWARD
PAINTER, INSTRUCTOR
b Anderson, Ind, Feb 2, 32. *Study:* Herron Art Sch, BFA; Oqunquit Sch of Painting & Sculpture; Tulane Univ, MFA. *Work:* Addison Gallery Am Art, Andover, Mass; Santa Barbara Mus, Calif; Univ Calif Collection; New York Times Bk Collection; Fine Arts Ctr, Anderson, Ind. *Comn:* Mural, comn by Jane Blaffer Owen, Blaffer Trust, New Harmony, Ind, 65; three panel paintings, comn by Jane Arneberg, New York, 70; painting, Pfizer Chemical Co, New York, 74. *Exhib:* One-man shows, Purdue Univ, West Lafayette, Ind, 59 & Santa Barbara Mus Art, Calif, 63; Drawing Ann, Norfolk Mus, Va, 60; Albright-Knox Art Gallery, Buffalo, NY, 60; Boston Mus Contemp Arts, Mass, 60; Univ Calif Fac Show, 63; and others. *Teaching:* Instr studio & art hist, Herron Sch, Indianapolis, 58-62; lectr studio & art hist, Univ Calif, Santa Barbara, 63-65. *Awards:* Louis Comfort Tiffany Grant, 55 & 65. *Media:* Oil, Multimedia. *Publ:* Auth, Traditions of the East, Revolutions of the West, Herron J, 60. *Dealer:* James Bokynack Co 17 East 57th St New York NY 10022. *Mailing Add:* Box 332 Sagg Rd Sagaponack NY 11962

DUNN, CAL
PAINTER, FILMMAKER
b Georgetown, Ohio, Aug 31, 15. *Study:* Cincinnati Art Acad, 27; Cent Acad Commercial Art, 32-34. *Work:* Ford Motor Co, Detroit; Allstate Ins Co, Chicago; Am Artists Group, New York; Tavern Club Chicago. *Exhib:* Am Watercolor Soc Exhibs, New York, 55-56 & Traveling Exhib, 63; Chicago & Vicinity Exhib, Art Inst Chicago, 57; 100 American Watercolorists, Royal Gallery, London, 63; Santa Fe Festival Arts, NMex, 80; and many others. *Pos:* Animation art dir, USAAF, Wright Field, Dayton, Ohio, 43-44; art dir, Sarra Inc, 44-47; pres, Cal Dunn Studios, Chicago, 47-; illusr watercolor story assignments, Ford Times--Lincoln Mercury Times, Ford Motor Co, 50-62. *Awards:* Am Artists Mag Medal, 56; Emmy Award for TV Art Direction; and over sixty major film awards. *Mem:* Am Watercolor Soc; hon mem Art Guild Chicago (pres, 55-57); Dir Guild Am. *Media:* Watercolor. *Dealer:* Munson Gallery Santa Fe NM. *Mailing Add:* c/o The Squash Blossom 1888 First St Highland Park IL 60035

DUNN, NATE
PAINTER, INSTRUCTOR
b Pittsburgh, Pa, July 4, 1896. *Study:* Carnegie Inst Technol, with Arthur Sparks, Alfred Taylor & Geo Sotter. *Work:* Thiel Col; Pa State Univ. *Exhib:* Butler Inst Am Art, Youngstown, Ohio; Mansfield Col; Playhouse,

Pittsburgh, Pa; Canton Art Gallery, Ohio; Trumbull Art Guild, Warren, Ohio; and others. *Teaching:* Instr painting & drawing, Girls Buhl Club, 58-83; retired. *Awards:* Purchase Prizes, Butler Inst Am Art Area Shows, 64 & Steubenville Art Asn, 72 & 74-75; St John's Episcopal Church Award, 66. *Mem:* Friends Am Art, Youngstown; Steubenville Art Asn; fel Royal Soc Arts. *Media:* Mixed. *Dealer:* Queen's Gallery Cleveland OH 44101; Bogarad Fine Art Gallery 326 Penco Rd Wierton WV 26062. *Mailing Add:* c/o John XXIII Residence Shenango Freeway Hermitage PA 16148

DUNN, PHILLIP CHARLES
EDUCATOR, ADMINISTRATOR
b Chicago, Ill, Mar 1, 47. *Study:* Univ Ill, BFA(art educ), 68; Inst Design, Ill Inst Techol, MS(visual educ), 70; Ball State Univ, EdD(art educ), 78. *Exhib:* Photog 79, Ariz State Univ Gallery, Tempe, 79; four-person show, Presbyterian Col, Clinton, SC, 79; two-person show, McKissick Mus, Columbia, SC, 79; Columbia Col Gallery, SC, 80; one-person show, USC Coastal Gallery, Conway, SC, 82. *Teaching:* Instr photog, Col DuPage, 71-76; vis prof photog, St Xavier Col, 74-76; assoc prof art educ, Univ SC, 78-, dir grad studies in art, 80- *Awards:* Mary J Rouse Award, 81; Higher Educator of the Year, SC Art Educ Asn, 81. *Mem:* Nat Art Educ Asn; Guild SC Artists; Columbia Artist Guild; SC Art Educ Asn (treas, 80-82). *Media:* Photo-Related Processes. *Publ:* Auth, The position of art and art ed in public ed today, Undergrad Ed, 79; auth, Evaluation and the arts, Design Mag, 81; coauth, Briding the gap between teaching and research in art, Sch Arts, 82; coauth, Finding A Job in Art Education, 83. *Mailing Add:* 9515 Martindale Rd Columbia SC 29206

DUNN, ROGER TERRY
HISTORIAN
b Bethesda, Md, Feb 24, 46. *Study:* Am Univ, Washington, DC; Pa State Univ, BA(art & painting); Pratt Inst, MFA(painting), 70; Northwestern Univ, PhD(art hist), 78. *Collections Arranged:* Quilts from the Plymouth Antiquarian Soc, 74; John J Enneking: American Impressionist (ed catalog), 75; The Boston Painting Invitational, 75, Michael Mazur: Vision of a Draughtsman, 76; Craftforms (ed catalog), 76; American Pastimes (ed catalog), 77. *Pos:* Cur, Brockton Art Ctr, Mass, 74-77; dir, Gallery at OUI, Boston, 76-80. *Teaching:* Asst prof art hist, Bridgewater State Col, 80- *Mem:* Col Art Asn; New Eng Appraisers Asn. *Res:* Monet and his symbolist circle; exhibition research on 19th century American art. *Publ:* Auth, Lawrence Kupferman: A Retrospective Exhibition, 74; ed, Landscape and Life in 19th Century America, 74; The Ikat weavings of Joan Hausrath, Fiberarts, 11/81. *Mailing Add:* c/o Dept Art Bridgewater State Col Bridgewater MA 02324

DUNNIGAN, MARY CATHERINE
LIBRARIAN
b Shawvers Mill, Va, May 7, 22. *Study:* Mary Washington Col, BA; Columbia Univ, MLS. *Pos:* Librn, Col of Archit, Va Polytech Inst, Blacksburg, 66-73; librn, Fiske Kimball Fine Arts Libr, Univ Va, Charlottesville, 73- *Mem:* Soc Archit Historians; Art Libr Soc NAm; Asn Archit Sch Librn (pres, 80-81); Spec libr Asn Arts & Humanities Div (chmn mus, 73-74). *Interests:* Development of research library for support of art, architecture and drama curriculum. *Mailing Add:* Fiske Kimball Fine Arts Libr Bayly Dr Univ of Va Charlottesville VA 22903

DUNNINGTON, WALTER GREY
COLLECTOR, PATRON
b Long Branch, NJ, Aug 17, 10. *Study:* Smith Col, BA; Bryn Mawr Col. *Pos:* Treas, women's comt, Philadelphia Mus Art, 38-41; pres bd trustees, Parrish Art Mus, Southampton, NY, 64-70; dir, NY Horticulture Soc, formerly. *Collection:* Furniture, porcelain, paintings, drawings. *Mailing Add:* 3 E 77th St New York NY 10021

DUNWIDDIE, CHARLOTTE
SCULPTOR
b Strasbourg, France. *Study:* Acad Arts, Berlin, Ger, with Wilhelm Otto; also with Mariano Benlliure y Gil, Madrid, Spain & Alberto Lagos, Buenos Aires, Arg. *Work:* Cardinal's Palace, Buenos Aires; Church of Good Shepherd, Lima, Peru; Marine Corps Mus, Washington, DC; Mus Brookgreen Gardens, SC; Mus New Britain, Conn. *Exhib:* Salon Bellas Artes, Buenos Aires, 40-45; Allied Artists Am, 56-72; Nat Sculpture Soc, 58-72; Am Artists Prof League, 59-70; Nat Acad Design, 59-80. *Awards:* Speyer Award, 69, Artists Fund Prize Best Show, 72 & 74, Nat Acad Design; Lindsey Mem Prize, Nat Sculpture Soc, 70; and 15 gold medals. *Mem:* Academician & fel Nat Sculpture Soc (vpres, 79-81, pres, 81-); Royal Soc Arts; Am Artists Prof League (dir, 60-); Allied Artists Am. *Mailing Add:* 35 E Ninth St New York NY 10003

DU PEN, EVERETT GEORGE
SCULPTOR, EDUCATOR
b San Francisco, Calif, June 12, 12. *Study:* Univ Souther Calif, with Merril Gage; Yale Univ Sch Fine Arts, with George Eberhard, George Snowden & Alexander Archipenko, BFA(Tiffany Fel, Clara Kimball English Traveling Fel), 37. *Work:* Seattle Art Mus; Washington Mutual Savings Bank, Seattle; Univ Wash Faculty Club; Aberdeen City Hall, Wash; Bell Telephone Co. *Comn:* Crucifix & wall carving, St John Episcopal Church, Seattle, 63; carved walnut screens, Munic Bldg, City of Seattle, 63; heroic bronze portrait, pres Univ Wash, 73; bronze group, Dallas, Tex, 82; bronze, Edmonds, Wash, 83-84; and others. *Exhib:* Nat Acad Design, New York, 50, 59, 72 & 76-77; Seattle Art Mus Northwest Ann, 47-63; Pa Acad Fine Art, 50, 54 & 58; Nat Sculpture Soc, 50, 59, 72, 75 & 77; Mainstreams 72, Marietta Col, 72; one-man shows, Seattle Art Mus, 50, Seattle Mutual Bank, 78 & 79. *Pos:* Sculpture

mem, Munic Art Comn, Seattle; sculpture adv, Art Adv Bd Seattle World's Fair, 60-62. *Teaching:* Asst sculpture, Carnegie Inst Technol Art Sch, 39-40; asst sculpture, Wash Univ Art Sch, 40-42; from instr to prof sculpture, Univ Wash Sch Art, 45-82, prof emer,82- *Awards:* Saltus Gold Medal, Nat Acad Design; Univ Wash Grad Sch Grants, 55 & 57. *Bibliog:* Minor L Bishop (auth), Fountains in contemporary architecture, Am Fedn Arts, 65; Louis G Redstone (auth), articles in Art Archit, 68 & Nat Sculpture Rev. *Mem:* Fel Nat Sculpture Soc; academician Nat Acad Design. *Media:* Wood, Bronze. *Mailing Add:* 1231 20th Ave E Seattle WA 98112

DUPUY, JEAN
MULTIMEDIA ARTIST

b Moulins, Allier, France, Nov 22, 25. *Study:* Ecole des Beaux-Arts, Paris, 45-46. *Work:* Phoenix Mus Art, Ariz; P Lannon Found, Fla; Mus Elec in Life, Minneapolis; Mus Mod Art, Paris; Centre Pompidou, Paris; and others. *Exhib:* The Machine, 68 & 15-16-Chorus for Six Hearts Traveling Exhib, 69, Mus Mod Art, New York; Sonnabend Gallery, Paris & New York, 69-72; Mus d'Art Mod, Paris, 70; Motion Pictures, 70 & Sunday Afternoon on a Revolving Stage, 76, Whitney Mus Am Art; Scragow Gallery, New York, 77; Multiples Gallery, New York, 78; Performances/Minute, Musee du Louvre, Paris, 78; and many others. *Teaching:* Instr, Sch Visual Arts, New York, 70-72. *Awards:* First Prize for Heart Beats Dust, Mus Mod Art, New York, 68; Nat Endowment Arts Grant, 77-80. *Bibliog:* Maurice Tuchman (auth), A Report on the Art & Technology Program of the Los Angeles County Museum of Art 1967-1971, 71; Suzanne Page (auth), Ecouter par les yeux, ARC, Paris, 80. *Publ:* Auth, Conversation a Trois, Opus Int, Paris, 4/70; ed, Collective Consciousness--Art Performance in the 70s, 81. *Mailing Add:* 537 Broadway New York NY 10012

DUREN, STEPHEN D
PAINTER, INSTRUCTOR

b Fairfield, Calif, Apr 8, 48. *Study:* San Francisco Art Inst, BFA, 74; Calif State Univ, Sacramento, MA, 77. *Comn:* Painting, Steelcase Corp, Grand Rapids, Mich, 83; poster design, Grand Rapids Arts Coun, 83. *Exhib:* TFAA Nat Exhib, Laguna Gloria Art Mus, Austin, Tex, 81; Corporate Art & Renaissance 81, Grand Rapids Art Mus, 81; Nat Exhib Am Art, Chautauqua Galleries, NY, 81; Six Michigan Artists, San Jose Inst Contemp Art, Calif, 82; solo exhib, Corcoran Gallery, Muskegon, Mich, 84. *Teaching:* Asst prof painting, drawing & color, Kendall Sch Design, Grand Rapids, Mich, 79- *Awards:* Purchase Award, Festival Fine Arts, Grand Rapids Art Mus, 80; First Place Purchase Award, Livonia Invitational, Livonia Art Comn, 81; Third Place Purchase, Mich Artists Competition, Battle Creek Art Ctr, 83. *Bibliog:* Sylvie Roder (auth), Six from Michigan, Artweek, 3/20/82. *Media:* Oil, Acrylic. *Publ:* Contribr, Works Exchange, San Jose Inst Contemp Art, 82. *Mailing Add:* 11080 68th Ave Allendale MI 49401

DURHAM, WILLIAM
PAINTER, PRINTMAKER

b Flint, Mich, Mar 14, 37. *Study:* Mich State Univ, BA, 60; painting with Morris Kantor, Boris Margo & Abraham Rattner. *Work:* Guild Hall, East Hampton, NY; Warnaco Inc, Park Ave, New York; Mich State Univ, East Lansing; Kidder Peabody Inc, New York; Butler Inst Am Art. *Comn:* Painting, New York World's Fair, 64. *Exhib:* One-man shows, Benson Gallery, Bridgehampton, NY, 67, 71, 72 & 74 & Art Placement Int, New York, 81; Am Acad Arts & Lett, New York, 74; Hecksher Mus, Huntington, NY, 74; Artist of the Hamptons, Guild Hall, Easthampton, NY, 75; Chicago Art Inst. *Bibliog:* Article in New York Herald Tribune, 64 & New York Times, 64-75. *Media:* Acrylic; Serigraphy. *Dealer:* 25 Perry St New York NY 10014. *Mailing Add:* Main St Amagansett NY 11930

DURIEUX, CAROLINE WOGAN
PRINTMAKER

b New Orleans, La, Jan 22, 1896. *Study:* Newcomb Col, BA(art educ), 17; Pa Acad Fine Arts, fel, 18-20; La State Univ, MA, 49. *Work:* Rosenwald Collection, Nat Gallery Art, Washington, DC; Mus Mod Art, New York, NY; Philadelphia Mus Fine Arts, Pa; Bibliot Nat, Paris, France. *Exhib:* Libr Cong Print Ann, Washington, DC, 46; Print Coun Am, Europe & Far East, 62; 2nd Nat Lithography Exhib, Fla State Univ, 66; one-person shows, Baton Rouge Gallery, La, 76, New Orleans Hist Collection, La, 76 & Loyola Univ, 77; and others. *Pos:* Consult, Fed Art Proj, Works Proj Admin, 38-43. *Teaching:* Instr life class painting, Newcomb Col, 20-21 & 38-43; from asst prof to prof graphics, La State Univ, Baton Rouge, 43-65, emer prof, 65- *Awards:* La State Univ Coun Res Grants, 51-60 & 72-73; Women's Caucus Art Award, 80. *Bibliog:* Salpeter (auth), About Caroline Durieux, Coronet, 37; Caroline Durieux, La State Univ, 49 & 78; Zigrosser (auth), The appeal of prints, NY Graphics, 70. *Publ:* Illusr, Gumbo Yaya, Houghton, 38; illusr, New Orleans City Guide, Works Proj Admin, 38; coauth, Mardigras Day, Holt, 48; coauth, Caroline Curieux--Lithographs of the Thirties and Fourties, La State Univ, 78. *Dealer:* Taylor Clark Prints 2623 Government St Baton Rouge LA 70806. *Mailing Add:* c/o Taylor Clark Prints 2623 Government St Baton Rouge LA 70806

DURR, PAT (PATRICIA BETH)
PAINTER, PRINTMAKER

b Kansas City, Mo; Can citizen. *Study:* Univ Kans, BA(educ), 61; Univ Southampton, 62; Kansas City Art Inst, 63; Ottawa Sch Art, with Duncan deKergommeaux, 65. *Work:* Can Coun Visual Art Bank, Algonquin Col Art Collection & Capitol Region Congress Ctr, Ottawa, Ont; Robert McLaughlin Public Art Gallery, Oshawa, Ont; Toronto Dominion Bank Art Collection, Ont. *Comn:* Mural, Ottawa Sch Bd, First Ave Sch, Ont, 79; 75th anniversary portfolio, Royal Trust Co, Ottawa, Ont, 80. *Exhib:* Paint, Gairloch Public Gallery, Oakville, Ont, 81; Regional Exhib, Agnes Etherington Art Ctr, Kingston, Ont, 81 & 83; Monuments Nat Show, Off Centre Centre, Calgary, Alta, 81; Machine Hand Made-Nat Exhib Xerography, Beaver House Gallery, Alta Culture, Edmonton, 83; Minatures Show, London Regional Art Gallery, 83; and others. *Pos:* Consult, Mayors Adv Comt on Arts & Culture, 80-82; consult, Revenue Can Visual Arts Adv Bd on Customs Regulations, 80-82; consult, Ottawa Visual & Performing Arts Ctr Steering Comt, 81-82. *Teaching:* Fine arts coordr, Algonquin Col Visual Art, Ottawa, Ont, 75-78, teaching master painting, 79-82. *Awards:* Artist In The Schools, Ont Arts Coun, 79; Travel Grant, Can Coun, 81-82. *Bibliog:* Anna Babinska (auth), Paint--The Expressive Touch, Gairloch Public Gallery, 7/81; Doris Finta (auth), Oakville, Artmag, 11-12/81-1/82; Valerie Knowles (auth), Pat Durr, pres de la nature, Vie Des Arts, Autonme, 82. *Mem:* Can Artists Representation/Les Front des Artistes Canadians (pres, Ottawa, 79-80, nat vpres, 80-82); Visual Arts Ont; Print & Drawing Coun Can (nat pres, 82-84); Visual Arts Ottawa (activities chmn, 74-76). *Media:* Acrylic & Mixed Media; Serigraphy & Colour Xerography. *Publ:* Auth, Canada Council Art Bank today, CARFAC News, 2-3/83. *Dealer:* Wells Gallery 459 Sussex Drive Ottawa ON Can K1N 6Z4. *Mailing Add:* 167 First Ave #1 Ottawa ON K1S 2G3 Canada

DUSARD, JAY
PHOTOGRAPHER, WRITER

b St Louis, Mo, Feb 18, 37. *Study:* Univ Fla, BA(archit), 61. *Work:* New Orleans Mus. *Exhib:* Two-man exhib, Addison Gallery Am Art, 75; New Landscapes Part I, Friends Photog, Carmel, Calif, 80; The North American Cowboy: A Portrait, Phoenix Art Mus, 82, Glenbow Mus, Calgary, Alta, 84 & Colorado Springs Fine Arts Ctr, 84. *Pos:* Designer & lithographer, Northland Press, Flagstaff, Ariz, 66-68. *Teaching:* Asst prof photog, Prescott Col, Ariz, 68-74. *Awards:* Guggenheim Mem Found Fel Photog, 81. *Bibliog:* Harry Redl (auth), Jay Dusard: Documenting the cowboy, Ariz Highways Mag, 82; Steve Torbeck (producer), Cowboy Photographer (TV film), KPNX-TV, Phoenix & NBC Overnight, New York, 83; Michael Saltz (producer), segment, MacNeil-Lehrer News Hour (TV film), PBS-TV, 83. *Mem:* Friends Photog. *Publ:* Auth & illusr, Visions from the southwest, Plateau Mag, Mus Northern Ariz, 80; auth & illusr, The cowboy photographer, Ariz Mag, 82; illusr, Living portrait of the North American cowboy, Am West Mag, 83; contribr, Cowboy: The Enduring Myth of the Wild West, Stewart, Tabori & Chang, 83; auth & illusr, The North American Cowboy: A Portrait, Consortium Press, 83. *Dealer:* Photog West Gallery PO Box 4829 Carmel CA 93921; Folio Gallery 328 Tenth St NW Calgary AB T2N 1V8. *Mailing Add:* 2221 View Dr Prescott AZ 86301

DUSENBERY, WALTER
SCULPTOR

b Alameda, Calif, 1939. *Study:* San Francisco Art Inst, 61; ceramics with Marguerite Wildenhain, 62-66; Calif Col Arts & Crafts, MFA, 71. *Work:* Carnegie Inst, Pittsburgh; Columbus Mus Art, Ohio; Guggenheim Mus, New York; Metrop Mus Art, New York; San Francisco Mus Mod Art. *Comn:* Sculpture, Justice Ctr, Portland, Ore, 83; sculpture, Dept Art, Univ Northern Iowa, in prep. *Exhib:* Guggenheim Mus, New York, 77; Metrop Mus Art, New York, 79; Int Sculpture Conf, Washington, DC, 80; Yorkshire Sculpture Park, Bretton Hall, England, 81-82; Hamilton Gallery, New York, 81; Grad Sch Design, Harvard Univ, 82; Anderson Gallery, Va Commonwealth Univ, 83; Laumeier Sculpture Park, St Louis, 83; and many others. *Teaching:* Instr ceramic sculpture, Univ Calif, San Francisco, 69; vis sculptor, Sch Landscape Archit, Grad Sch Design, Harvard Univ, 79- *Awards:* Grants, Creative Artists Pub Serv, 80 & Nat Endowment Arts, 80. *Bibliog:* Nina Ffrench-Frazier (auth), Walter Dusenbery, Arts Mag, 6/78; David L Shirey (auth), Creations that defy the passage of time, New York Times Long Island Ed, 9/13/81; Ann Sargent-Wooster (auth), Dusenbery at the Nassau County Museum, Art in Am, 1/82. *Mem:* Artists Equity Asn; Archit League. *Publ:* Auth, The Story of the Bed, Natoma Soc, Santa Barbara, Calif, 70; auth, Dusenbery interviewed by Howard Greenfeld, 57th St Rev, 1/76. *Mailing Add:* 216 Lafayette St New York NY 10012

DUTTON, ALLEN A
PHOTOGRAPHER, PAINTER

b Kingman, Ariz, April 13, 22. *Study:* Art Ctr Schs, Los Angeles; Ariz State Univ, BA, MA, 49. *Work:* Mus Mod Art, New York; Bibliot Nat, Paris; Tokyo Col Photog Mus, Japan; Il Diaframma, Milano, Italy; Santa Barbara Mus Art. *Exhib:* Solo exhibs, Il Diaframma Gallery, Milano, Italy, 71; Northlight Gallery, Ariz State Univ, 79, Photog Southwest Gallery, Scottsdale, Ariz, 79; Shinju Gallery, Tokyo, 79 & New House Gallery, Staten Island, 80. *Pos:* Art ed & photog head, Phoenix Point West Mag, 63-66. *Teaching:* Prof photog & head dept, Phoenix Col, Ariz, 61-82; prof, Tokyo Col Photog, Japan, 72-73. *Awards:* John Hay Fel, 60. *Bibliog:* A D Coleman (auth), Grotesque in Photo, Ridge Press, 78; Jim Stone (auth), Darkroom Dynamics, Curtain & London, 79. *Mem:* Soc Photog Educ. *Publ:* Auth, The Great Stone Tit, Little Wonder Press, 72; auth, A A Dutton's Compendium, Buse Publ, 74; coauth, Arizona Then and Now, AQ2 Press, 82. *Dealer:* Photog Southwest Gallery 7130 Stetson Dr Scottsdale AZ 85251. *Mailing Add:* 15235 N 11th St Phoenix AZ 85022

DUTTON, PAULINE MAE
LIBRARIAN

b Detroit, Mich. *Study:* Calif State Univ, Fullerton, BA(art), with Jerry Samuelson; Univ Southern Calif; Univ Calif, Los Angeles, with Joel Schecter. *Pos:* Fine arts librn, Pasadena Pub Libr, 71-80, res librn & art consult, 81- *Mem:* Art Libr Soc NAm; Am Film Inst. *Interests:* Antiques, painting, picture file. *Mailing Add:* 954 Arroyo Drive South Pasadena CA 91030

DWORZAN, GEORGE R
PAINTER
b New York, NY, Mar 28, 24. *Study:* Cooper Union, with Morris Cantor; Art Students League, with Harry Sternberg; Acad Grande Chaumiere, Paris, France; Acad Leger, Paris, with Fernand Leger. *Work:* NY Univ; Chase Manhattan Bank, New York; Univ Mass, Amherst; Ohio State Univ; Herron Mus Art, Indianapolis, Ind. *Exhib:* Salon Realities Nouvelles, Mus Art Mod, Paris, 48-49; Art USA, Coliseum, NY, 59; Nat Print Competition, AAA Gallery, New York, 60; Contemp Arts Soc Ann, Herron Mus, 64 & 68; Univ NC Ann, Chapel Hill, 68. *Teaching:* Asst prof painting & drawing, NY Univ, currently. *Media:* Mixed. *Dealer:* East Hampton Gallery 305 W 28th St New York NY 10025. *Mailing Add:* 17 Bleecker St New York NY 10012

DWYER, EUGENE JOSEPH
HISTORIAN
b Buffalo, NY, Sept 14, 43. *Study:* Harvard Univ, BA(classics, cum laude); NY Univ Inst Fine Arts, MA, 67, PhD, 74. *Teaching:* Assoc prof art hist, Kenyon Col, Gambier, Ohio, 73- *Awards:* Tatiana Warsher Award for the Archaeol of Pompeii, Herculaneum & Stabia, Am Acad Rome, 73-74; Nat Endowment Humanities Fel, 80-81. *Mem:* Col Art Asn Am; Archaeol Inst Am; Am Numismatic Soc. *Res:* Greek and Roman art and classical tradition. *Publ:* The subject of Durer's four witches, Art Quart, 71; Augustus and the Capricorn, Roemische Mitteilungen, 73; auth, Sculpture and its display in houses of Pompeii, In: Pompeii and the Vesuvian Landscape, 79; auth, Pompeian Oscilla Collections, Roemische Mitteilungen, 81; auth, Pompeian Domestic Sculpture, 82. *Mailing Add:* Dept of Art Kenyon Col Gambier OH 43022

DWYER, GARY COLBURN
ENVIRONMENTAL ARTIST, SCULPTOR
b Denver, Colo, Oct 1, 43. *Study:* Syracuse Univ, BSLA & BFA, 67; State Univ NY, BLA, 67; Sch Art, Univ Denver, MA, 70; Akad Bildende Kunst, Salzburg, 80. *Work:* Atlantic Richfield, Los Angeles; May D & F Corp, Denver; Cert Life Underwriters, Chicago; US Financial Corp, Dallas. *Comn:* Steel sculpture, First Interstate Bank, Denver, 74; stone sculpture, City Los Angeles, 82; earth sculpture, Cuesta Col, San Luis Obispo, 83. *Exhib:* Nat Gallery Art, 73; Elizabeth Fortner Gallery, Santa Barbara, 77; Univ Landes Hessen Kassel, WGer, 81; Nat Gallery Mod Art, Lisbon, Portugal, 81; Oakland Mus, Calif, 82; Musee Granit, Isle de Vassiviere Limousin, France, 83. *Pos:* Landscape architect, HOH Assoc, Denver, 69-70; sr designer, Roark Assoc Architects, Denver, 72-73; fountain consult, Irvine Corp, Costa Mesa, Calif, 78. *Teaching:* Instr art, Univ Denver, 70; asst prof, Colo Womens Col, 70-72; prof landscape archit, Calif Polytech State Univ, 73- *Awards:* Sculpture Competition Winner, Dept Housing & Urban Develop, Washington, DC, 73; Pac Garden Mall, Santa Cruz, 77 & French Ministry Cult, Paris, 83. *Bibliog:* Charles Kuralt (interviewer), Sunday Morning (film), CBS TV, 82; Sandy Nelson (auth), Sculpture by the bay, Images & Issues, 82; Sculpteurs de Granit (film), French Nat TV, 83. *Mem:* Am Inst Architects; Design Arts Prog, Nat Endowment Arts; Guild Master Craftsmen, Sussex, England; Partners for Livable Places. *Media:* Earth, Plants; Stone. *Publ:* Contribr, Playgrounds for Free, MIT Press, 73; contribr, Supermannerism, E P Dutton, 77; contribr, Fountains as Sculpture, Univ Tulsa, 84. *Dealer:* Space Gallery 6015 Santa Monica Blvd Los Angeles CA 90038. *Mailing Add:* 444 Indian Knob Rd San Luis Obispo CA 93401

DWYER, JAMES
PAINTER, EDUCATOR
b Tulsa, Okla, Oct 24, 21. *Study:* Art Inst Chicago, BFA, 47; Acad Grande Chaumiere, Paris, 47-48; Syracuse Univ, MFA, 50; Univ Chicago; De Paul Univ; study with Boris Anisfeld. *Work:* Everson Mus, Syracuse, NY; Munson-Williams-Proctor Inst, State Univ, Utica, NY; Syracuse Univ, NY; Ashland Col, Ohio. *Comn:* 3100 sq ft mural decoration, Onondaga Co Civic Ctr, Syracuse, NY, 76. *Exhib:* Art Inst Chicago, 47; Metrop Mus Art, New York, 51; City Ctr Gallery, New York, 55; Silvermine Guild Artists Conn, 56; Univ Maine, Portland-Gorham, 74; Lubin House, New York, 77; solo exhib, Krasner Gallery, New York, 81; and others. *Teaching:* Prof painting & drawing, Syracuse Univ, NY, 49-82. *Media:* Acrylic. *Mailing Add:* 223 DeForest Rd Syracuse NY 13214

DWYER, MELVA JEAN
LIBRARIAN, HISTORIAN
b Kamloops, BC, Oct 29, 19. *Study:* Univ BC, BA, 42, MA, 61; Univ Toronto, BLS, 53. *Pos:* Head librn fine arts div, Univ BC, Vancouver, 53- *Teaching:* Hon lectr fine arts bibliog & res methods, Univ BC, Vancouver, 67- *Mem:* Can Art Libr Sect Can (chairperson, 70-78); Univ Art Assn Can; Art Libr Soc NAm; Col Art Asn. *Res:* A study of the enclosed choir in Norfolk churches; art bibliography and acquisitions. *Interests:* Medieval architecture and art; art bibliography and acquisitions. *Mailing Add:* 603-2233 Allison Rd Vancouver BC V6T 1T7 Canada

DYCK, PAUL
PAINTER, DIRECTOR
b Chicago, Ill, Aug 17, 17. *Study:* With Johann Von Skramlik, Florence, Italy, Prague, Czech, Rome, Italy & Paris, France, 26-33. *Work:* Phoenix Art Mus, Ariz; Mus Northern Ariz, Flagstaff; Whitney Gallery Western Art, Cody, Wyo; Franklin Inst, Philadelphia; and pvt collections in US, Can & Europe. *Comn:* Indians of the Overland Trail (painting), sponsored by pub mus, 56; Flame of Man (painting), F O Hess, Franklin Inst, Philadelphia, 70. *Exhib:* One-man exhibs, Southwest Mus, Los Angeles, Calif, Mont Hist Soc, Helena, Chicago Mus Nat Hist, Phoenix Art Mus & Ariz State Univ Mus, and many others. *Pos:* Dir, Paul Dyck Res Found Am Indian Cult. *Awards:* Artist

Commendation, US Navy, 45. *Mem:* Life mem Buffalo Bill Hist Ctr, Cody, Wyo; Manuscript Soc; Appraisers Asn Am. *Media:* Oil; Sumiye Watercolor. *Publ:* Auth, Brule, Sioux People of the Rosebud, 69; contribr, Montana, Mag of Western Hist, 72; contribr, Buffalo Bill Hist Ctr, 72; contribr, Persimmon Mag, 83. *Dealer:* Elaine Horwitch Galleries 4222 North Marshall Way Scottsdale AZ 85251. *Mailing Add:* PO Box 217 Rimrock AZ 86335

DYENS, GEORGES MAURICE
SCULPTOR, HOLOGRAPHER
b Mar 18, 32; Fr & Can citizen. *Study:* Ecole Nat Superieure Beaux Arts, Paris, dipl, 61; Acad Grande Chaumiere, with Ossip Zadkine; Concordia Univ, Montreal, MFA; Premier Grand Prix Rome. *Work:* Mus Mod Art & Hotel Hilton, Paris; Grotte de Lourdes, France; Univ Que & Mus Art Contemp, Montreal. *Exhib:* Symp Eur Sculptors, Berlin, 62; Mus Art Mod, Paris, 63 & 65-67; Biennial Int Piccolo Bronzo, Padova, Italy, 64-66; Mus Rodin, Paris, 66; Int Biennial New Delhi, India, 68; solo exhib, Mus Que, 81. *Pos:* Cur, Mus Saidye Bronfman Ctr, Montreal, 72-79; artist-in-residence, Mus Holography, New York. *Teaching:* Prof sculpture, Univ Que, Montreal, 69- *Awards:* Ger Critic Prize, Berlin, 62; Prix Susse, Biennial Paris, 63. *Bibliog:* Diulio Morosini (auth), La Revincita Della Vida, Paese Sera, Rome, 7/1/65; Gerald Gassiot-Talabot (auth), Dyens, Arts, Paris, 10/20/65; Yves Robillard (auth), Les metamorphoses lentes, Vie des Arts, Montreal, 6/80. *Mem:* Asn Sculpteurs Que, Montreal; Asn Arts & Techniques Holographics, Paris; Mus Holography, New York. *Media:* Wax, Multi Media; Holography. *Mailing Add:* CP 8888 Succ A Dept Plastic Arts Univ Que Montreal PQ H3C 3P8 Canada

DYER, CAROLYN PRICE
CRITIC, TAPESTRY ARTIST
b Seattle, Wash, Dec 19, 31. *Study:* Univ Wash, Seattle; Mills Col, Oakland, Calif, BA, 53, MA, 55, with Alfred Neumeyer, Ilse Schultz Hiller. *Comn:* Moon Clearing, Mary Blaylock, 78; Suns on a Wide Horizon, Tokio Marine, 80; Orange Wood, Chula Vista Dental Group, 81; Gen Electric logo, EPCOT, Fla, 83; Ocean Edge, Pepperdine Univ, 83; and others. *Exhib:* Craft & Folk Art Mus, Los Angeles, 68; Southern Calif Designer Crafts, Galeria del Sol, Santa Barbara, Calif, 76; China--A Personal View, Pac Asia Mus, Pasadena, 79; Flower Fields and Forests, Four Oak Gallery, San Marino, Calif, 81; Fiber Invitational, Univ Utah, 82; and others. *Pos:* Critic, Artweek, Oakland, Calif, 76-; contrib ed, Fiberarts, Asheville, NC, 77- *Teaching:* Instr art hist, Los Angeles Trade/Tech Col, 69-76. *Awards:* Textiles/Tapestries Awards, NW Craftsmen's Exhib, Seattle, 64 & Pac NW Arts & Crafts Exhib, Bellevue, Wash, 68; Gold Crown Award, Pasadena Arts Coun, 83. *Bibliog:* Judy Haddad (auth), Carolyn Dyer, Tapestries (videotape), Pasadena City Col, 76; Maria Bishop (auth), Fiber workspaces: in a room of your own, Fiberarts, 77. *Mem:* Southern Calif Designer-Crafts Inc; Am Crafts Coun; World Crafts Coun; Pasadena Arts Coun (trustee, 77-78); Int Guild Craft Journalists, Authors & Photogr. *Media:* Wool, Silk. *Mailing Add:* 28 N Marengo Pasadena CA 91101

DYSON, BRIAN
CURATOR, WRITER
b Leeds, Eng, Oct 4, 44. *Study:* Leeds Col Art, with Derek Hyatt, dipl AD, 66. *Exhib:* Remade Readymades & related work, Artons, Calgary, Alta, 77; toured Poland, 78; Canadians Nat touring, Mt Allison Univ, NS, 78; Artists' Polaroid NAm touring, Open Space, Victoria, BC, 78. *Collections Arranged:* One Eye Open, One Eye Closed, Photo: Belloq Krims (cataloged), 76; Mac Adams, Bill Beckley, James Collins, Photo-Narrative (ed, catalog), Alta Col Art, 77; Marcel Duchamp: a European Investigation (ed & contribr, catalog), 79 & Videonet, International Video/Performance (ed & co-auth, catalog), 79. *Pos:* Cur, Alta Col Art Gallery, Calgary, 75-80; juror, Video Sect, Can Coun, 79; founder/dir, Syntax, Calgary/Int Artists Contact Ctr. *Teaching:* Photog, Simon Fraser Univ, British Columbia, 70. *Awards:* Can Coun Travel Grant, 78; Can Coun Project Cost Grant, 79. *Bibliog:* Paul Woodrow (auth), Brian Dyson--Remade Ready-mades, Centerfold, 78 & Brian Dyson--Looking Both Ways at Once, Parachute, 78. *Media:* Mixed Media. *Publ:* Ed, Jan Swidzinski--Art, Society and Self-Consciousness, Alta Col Art Gallery, 79; ed, Les Levine, Media: the Biotech Rehearsal for Leaving the Body, 80. *Mailing Add:* 321 9A St NW Calgary AB T2N 1T7 Canada

DYSON, JOHN HOLROYD
PAINTER
b Folkestone Co, Kent, Eng, Jan 10, 10; Can citizen. *Study:* Heatherley Sch Art, London, Eng; Vancouver Sch Art, BC, Can; study under Algernon Newton in London & Jack Shadbolt in Vancouver. *Work:* Numerous pvt collections. *Comn:* Bethlehem Copper Mine, Bethlehem Copper Corp, Ashcroft, BC, 67 & 68; two Western Mines, Western Mines Ltd, Vancouver, BC, Can, 69; Can Arthritis Soc, Vancouver, 82. *Exhib:* one-man shows, in Vancouver at Danish Art Gallery, Alexander G Harrison Galleries & Alex Fraser Galleries, 60-70 & Pub Libr, Kelowna, BC, Can, 64; Prince George Art Gallery, BC, Can, 70-77 & 80-81; and many others. *Bibliog:* Eric Green (auth), Valemount Artist Has Ties With Chilcotin, Williams Lake Tribune, BC, 8/76; and others. *Media:* Oil. *Dealer:* Danish Art Gallery 3757 W Tenth Ave Vancouver BC Can. *Mailing Add:* Box 21 Valemount BC V0E 2Z0 Canada

DYYON, FRAZIER
PAINTER, SCULPTOR
b Ft Meyers, Fla, May 2, 46. *Work:* Mus Mod Art & Whitney Mus Am Art, New York; Larry Aldrich Mus, Conn; Case Western Reserve Univ. *Exhib:* Cleveland Top Artists, In Town Club, 69; Int Exhib Art, Cleveland, 70; Whitney Mus Am Art Ann, 72; Reflections, Larry Aldrich Mus, 72-73; one-man show, Mather Gallery, Case Western Reserve Univ, 83. *Awards:* T R Montalbano, 79; Printmaker Workshop Bd Scholar, New York, 82. *Mailing Add:* 155 W 73rd St New York NY 10023

DZIGURSKI, ALEX
PAINTER
b Stari Becej, Vojvodlina, Yugoslavia, May 15, 11; US citizen. *Study:* Sch Art, Belgrade, Yugoslavia; Acad Art, Munich, Ger. *Work:* Boston Mus Fine Arts; Norton Gallery, Shreveport, La; Franklin Mint Am Art, Pa; Okla Art Ctr, Oklahoma City; Belgrade Art Mus, Yugoslavia. *Comn:* Altars in Serbian churches, Cleveland, Ohio, 52, Aliquippa, Pa, 55 & Canton, Ohio, 56; interior church & altar, St Sava Serbian Church, Milwaukee, Wis, 58; altar in Serbian church, Kansas City, Kans, 59. *Exhib:* Soc Western Artists Exhib, De Young Mus, San Francisco, 72 & 73; Findlay Galleries, Chicago, Ill, 74. *Awards:* Gold Medal, Biennale Venice, Italy, 48; First Prize, Popular, Soc Western Artists, De Young Mus, San Francisco, 65; Gold Medal, Franklin Mint Bicentennial, Pa, 73. *Mem:* Prof League Am Artists; Soc Western Artists; fel Fine Art Inst, Los Angeles. *Media:* Oil. *Dealer:* Findlay Galleries 814 N Michigan Chicago IL 60611. *Mailing Add:* 1141 Lincoln Dr Mountain View CA 94040

DZUBAS, FRIEDEL
PAINTER
b Berlin, Ger, Apr 20, 15; US citizen. *Work:* Metrop Mus Art, Solomon R Guggenheim Mus, New York; Boston Mus Fine Arts, Mass; Mus Fine Arts, Houston; Hirschhorn Mus. *Comn:* Nat Shawmut Bank, Boston, 75. *Exhib:* Color and Field, Albright-Knox Gallery, Cleveland Mus & Dayton Art Inst, 70-71; Abstract Painting in the 70's, Boston Mus Fine Arts, 72; retrospectives, Mus Fine Arts, Houston, 74 & Boston Mus Fine Arts, 75; 34th Biennial, Corcoran Gallery, Washington, DC, 75; New Works in Clay, Everson Mus, 76; solo exhibs, John Berggruen Gallery, San Francisco, 77 & 79, M Knoedler & Co, New York, 77-80, Kunsthalle, Bielefeld, 77 & Dart Gallery, Chicago, 78; and others. *Teaching:* Artist in residence, Dartmouth Col, 62; vis artist critic, Inst Humanistic Studies, 65-66; vis artist critic, Univ Pa, 68-69; vis artist critic, Cornell Univ, 69-74. *Awards:* Guggenheim Fel, 66 & 68; Nat Coun Arts Award, 68. *Bibliog:* John Elderfield (auth), Abstraction in the 70's, summer 72 & Kenworth Moffett (auth), Recent paintings by Friedel Dzubas, 5/75, Art Int; Roald Nasgaard (auth), Friedel Dzubas, Arts Mag, 5/75. *Media:* Acrylic; Oil. *Publ:* Auth, Statement & color plate, Art in Am, 67 & Art Now, 72. *Dealer:* M Knoedler & Co 19 E 70th New York NY 10021; David Mirvish Gallery 596 Markham St Toronto ON Can. *Mailing Add:* 119 The Knoll Ithaca NY 14850

E

EADES, LUIS ERIC
PAINTER, EDUCATOR
b Madrid, Spain, June 25, 23; US citizen. *Study:* Bath Sch Art, Eng; Slade Sch, Univ London; Inst Polytech Nac, Mexico City, Mex; Univ Ky, Lexington, BA. *Work:* Whitney Mus Am Art, New York; Mus Fine Arts, Houston; Dallas Mus Fine Arts; Ft Worth Art Ctr; Mus Fine Arts, Holyoke, Mass. *Comn:* Airport mural, Govt Honduras, Toncontin, Tegucigalpa, 48. *Exhib:* Recent Painting USA: The Figure, Mus Mod Art, New York, 62; Forty Artists Under Forty, Whitney Mus Am Art, 62; State of Man, New Sch Social Res, New York, 64; 2nd Intermountain Biennial Exhib, Salt Lake Art Ctr, Utah, 65; Colorado Springs Fine Arts Ctr, 69. *Teaching:* Prof painting & drawing, Univ Tex, 54-60; prof painting & drawing, Univ Colo, 61. *Media:* Oil, Acrylic. *Publ:* Illusr, The Precipice, Univ Tex, 69. *Dealer:* Carlin Galleries 710 Montgomery Fort Worth TX 76107; Carson-Sapiro Gallery 2601 Blake St Denver CO 80202. *Mailing Add:* 1627 Fifth St Boulder CO 80302

EAGERTON, ROBERT PIERCE
PRINTMAKER, PAINTER
b Florence, SC, Mar 17, 40. *Study:* Atlanta Sch Art, BFA; Acad Fine Arts, Vienna, Austria; Cranbrook Acad Art, Bloomfield Hills, Mich. *Work:* Nat Collection Fine Art, Smithsonian Inst, Washington, DC; Art Inst Chicago; Lessing J Rosenwald Collection, Jenkintown, Pa; Sheldon Swope Gallery Art; Norman McKenzie Mus Art, Regina, Sask. *Exhib:* Biennale Int l'Estampe, Paris, France, 70; Contemporary American Prints, Krannert Mus, Univ Ill, 71; Lithographs de la Collection Mourlot, PR, 71; one-man show, Norman McKenzie Mus Art; Prints: USA 1974, Univ Pittsburgh; and others. *Pos:* Co-founder, Transfigurations Press, Sarasota, Fla, 64-66; owner, Cloud Race Press, currently. *Teaching:* Assoc prof lithography, Herron Sch Art, Ind Univ-Purdue Univ, Indianapolis, 66-78, head dept printmaking, 69-78, prof printmaking & chmn printmaking prog, 78-, prof lithography, 81-82; guest artist printmaking, Univ Ill, Champaign, 70; vis prof printmaking, Tyler Sch Art, summer 72. *Awards:* Southeastern Arts Grant, Atlanta Arts Comn, 65; First Prize, Ann Ind Print Exhib, Indianapolis Mus, 68; Res Grant, Ind Univ, 70. *Dealer:* Associated American Artists Gallery 663 Fifth Ave New York NY 10022. *Mailing Add:* 3111 N Meridian Indianapolis IN 46208

EAMES, JOHN HEAGAN
ETCHER, PAINTER
b Lowell, Mass, July 19, 1900. *Study:* Harvard Univ, AB, 22; Royal Col Art, with Malcolm Osborne & Robert Austin, 33, 35 & 37. *Work:* Metrop Mus Art, New York; Libr of Cong, Washington, DC; Albany Inst Hist & Art, NY. *Exhib:* Royal Acad, London, Eng, 35, 37 & 40; New York World's Fair, 39; Int Print Exhib, Art Inst Chicago, 39; Biennial Exhib, Venice, Italy, 40; Contemp Am Drawings, Metrop Mus Art, New York, 42 & 52. *Awards:* Kate W Arms Mem Prize, Soc Am Graphic Artists, 52, 54 & 57, John Taylor Arms Prize, 53, Henry B Shope Prize, 57. *Mem:* Soc Am Graphic Artists; Nat Acad Design; Royal Soc Painters-Etchers, London, Eng. *Mailing Add:* Boothbay Harbor ME 04538

EARL, JACK EUGENE
SCULPTOR
b Uniapolis, Ohio, Aug 2, 34. *Study:* Bluffton Col, BA; Ohio State Univ, MA. *Work:* Butler Mus Art, Youngstown, Ohio; Columbus Gallery Fine Arts, Ohio; Everson Museum of Art, Syracuse, NY; Museum of Contemp Crafts, New York, NY. *Comn:* Mural, Kohler Co, Kohler, Wis, 76. *Exhib:* Objects USA, Smithsonian Inst, Washington, DC, 69; Mus Contemp Crafts, New York, 71, 72 & Clay Works by 20 Americans, 72; Ft Wayne Mus Art, Ind, 71; Int Exhib Ceramics, Victoria & Albert Mus Art, London, Eng, 72; First World Crafts Exhib, Toronto, Ont, 74; Clay Things, Whitney Mus of Am Art, New York, 74; The Object as Poet, Renwick Gallery, Washington, DC, 76. *Collections Arranged:* Ojbects USA, 68; The Plastic Earth, John Michael Kohler Arts Ctr, Sheboygan, Wis; Decade of Ceramic Art, San Francisco Mus of Art, Calif, 73. *Teaching:* Instr ceramics, Toledo Mus Art, 63-72; from asst prof to assoc prof ceramics, Va Commonwealth Univ, 72-77. *Awards:* Nat Coun Educ Ceramic Arts Prize, Emerson Art Ctr, 68; Merit Award, Louisville Art Ctr, 68-70; Purchase Award, Columbus Gallery Fine Arts, 72. *Bibliog:* Down Home, Arts in Va, 74; Art in industry, Crafts Horizon, 74. *Mem:* Nat Coun Educ Ceramic Arts. *Media:* Ceramic. *Mailing Add:* c/o Theo Portnoy Gallery 56 West 57th New York NY 10019

EARLE, EDWARD W
CURATOR, HISTORIAN
b New Orleans, La, Aug 19, 51. *Study:* Univ Notre Dame, BA, 74; Visual Studies Workshop, State Univ NY, Buffalo, MA(mus studies), 78. *Collections Arranged:* Points of View (ed, catalog), 79; Hand Camera in History, 82; The Orient Viewed, 82; Philip Brigandi, Photographer, 83; Prof Joseph Jastrow, 84. *Pos:* Cur, Visual Studies Workshop, Rochester, NY, 77-79; librn & archivist, Photog Resource Ctr, Boston, 80-82; cur, Calif Mus Photog, Univ Calif, Riverside, 82- *Teaching:* Instr photog, Swain Sch Design, New Bedford, Mass, 79-80; instr hist photog, Boston Col, Chestnut Hill, 82-83. *Mem:* Col Art Asoc; Soc Photog Educ; Am Cult Asn. *Res:* History of photography, relating aesthetic trends to social and cultural conditions. *Publ:* Contributing articles in Afterimage and New England J Photog, 77-; Points of View, The Stereograph in America: A Cultural History, VSW Press, 79; ed, Philip Brigandi, Calif Mus Photog Bulletin, 83; contribr, The Photographic Vision (TV ser), KOCE-TV for PBS. *Mailing Add:* 4010 Fifth St Riverside CA 92501

EARLE, WILLIAM HENRY
PAINTER, INSTRUCTOR
b Norwalk, Conn, July 12, 25. *Study:* Art Students League, with Frank V Dumond & Robert B Hale, 45-49; Grand Chaumier & Beaux Arts, Paris, 50-52; State Univ NY & Southern Conn State Univ, 77. *Work:* Bruce Mus, Greenwich, Conn; Nat Arts Club, New York; Wichita Art Mus, Kans. *Comn:* E R Squibb Co, Salo Paulo, Brazil, 54; 9 war mem murals, Norwich Univ, Northfield, Vt, 60; Weider Assocs Lobby Murals, New York, 63; decorative murals, comn by Mrs B Rockefeller, New York, 63; Indian Murals, Mus Art & Sci, Bridgeport, Conn, 70. *Exhib:* One-man shows, Huntington Art Mus, Long Island, Grand Cent Galleries, New York, 72, Wadsworth Atheneum, Hartford, Conn, 73, Wichita Art Mus, Kans, 75, Cranston Gallery, New York & Vera Lazuk Gallery, Cold Springs Harbor, NY; and others. *Teaching:* Head dept art, US State Dept, 52-54; head dept art, New Canaan Country Sch, 63-76; asst instr, Froman Art Sch, 70- *Awards:* First Pl Awards, Hudson River Valley Art Asn, White Plains, Nat Arts Club, New York & Artists & Craftsmen of Dallas. *Mem:* Am Watercolor Soc; Salmagundi Club; Hudson River Valley Art Asn; Artists & Craftsmen of Dallas; Artists Fel. *Media:* Oil, Watercolor. *Publ:* Four articles in Artist Mag, 70; Art, Music and Education, privately publ, 78. *Mailing Add:* 228 Catalpa Rd Wilton CT 06897

EARLS, PAUL
ENVIRONMENTAL ARTIST
b Springfield, Mo, June 9, 34. *Study:* Eastman Sch Music, BM(cum laude), 55, MM, 56; Univ Rochester, PhD, 59. *Exhib:* Musical Sculpture, Vancouver Art Gallery, BC, 73; Centerbeam, Documenta 6, Kassel, Ger, 77; Expansion, Secession, Vienna, Austria, 78; Five Artists--Five Technologies, Grand Rapids Art Mus, Mich, 78; Modulations, Hayden Gallery, 81; Ars Electronica 82, Bruckenhaus, Linz, Austria, 82; Electra, Mus Mod Art, Paris, 83. *Teaching:* Lectr sound, Mass Col Art, 72-78; lectr environmental art, Mass Inst Technol, 78-81. *Awards:* Premier Award, Bienale Coltejar, Colombia, 73; Gold Medal, Dreamstage, Am Psychiatric Asn, 78; First Int Water Sculpture Competition Award, La World Exposition, 82. *Media:* Music, Lasers. *Publ:* Auth, Sounding Space, Musical Sculpture, UAG, Can, 74. *Mailing Add:* 40 Massachusetts Ave Cambridge MA 02139

EAST, N S, JR
DESIGNER, SCULPTOR
b Delaware Co, Pa, Mar 21, 36. *Study:* Philadelphia Col Art, 62-65; also with Herman Cohen. *Work:* Glassboro State Col, NJ; Tilden Jr High Sch, Bell Telephone Co, Univ City Arts League, Philadelphia. *Exhib:* Sculpture 68, Grabar Gallery, Philadelphia, 68; Nat Forum Prof Artists, Philadelphia, 68-72; two-man show, Wood-Type Workshop, 72; Oh-Ho, Franklin Inst Symmetry Exhib, 75. *Pos:* Pres, NE Design Consults, 70-; founder, 5000 Willows Design Ctr, 77-80. *Teaching:* Instr AV art, Philadelphia Sch Syst, 65-67; instr lang of art, Bell Tel Co & Univ City Arts League, 67-70; instr welding, Univ City Arts League, 70-73; prof art, Glassboro State Col, 75-82. *Awards:* Silver & Bronze, Nat Ornamental and Miscellaneous Metals Asn, 78; Gold Top Job Award, Nat Ornamental and Miscellaneous Metals Asn, 80. *Mem:* Univ City Arts League (vpres, 65-66); Nat Forum Prof Artists; and others. *Publ:* Auth, The Language of Art/Toward Another Bauhaus, 67; auth, Beachhead of the Stars, Apollo Mission, 69; auth, Design and the Social Dimension, 69; auth, The Combined Graphics Department, 70; auth, In Pursuit of Ultimates, 79. *Mailing Add:* 5008 Warmington Ave Hatfield PA 19143

EASTERWOOD, HENRY LEWIS
EDUCATOR, TAPESTRY ARTIST
b Villa Rica, Ga, Oct 29, 34. *Study:* West Ga Col, 53-55; Memphis Acad Arts, BFA, 58, spec studies in Europe & Scandinavia, 65. *Work:* Brooks Mem Gallery Art, Memphis; Miss Art Asn, Jackson; State of Tenn Collection of Crafts, Nashville; Fall Creek Falls State Park, Tenn. *Comn:* Three panel triptych, Mayo Clin, Rochester, Minn, 70; two tapestries, Tupperware Int, Orlando, Fla, 71; tapestry, Vanderbilt Univ, 74; four tapestries, Memphis Mem Gardens, 74. *Exhib:* Fiber, Clay & Metal, St Paul Mus, Minn, 59, 61 & 63; Craftsmen USA, Mus Contemp Crafts, New York, 66; Miss Art Asn, 72. *Pos:* Craft adv, Tenn Arts Comn, 72. *Teaching:* Assoc prof textiles & chmn dept, Memphis Acad Arts, 59- *Awards:* Miss River Crafts Award, 65, 67 & 69; Nat Merit Award, Am Craftsmen's Coun, 66; Am Inst Archit Gold Medal, 69; and others. *Mem:* Am Craftsmen's Coun (Tenn rep, 63-65); Tenn Craftsmen's Asn; hon mem Memphis Weavers Guild. *Dealer:* Fairweather Hardin Gallery 101 E Ontario St Chicago IL 60611; Jean Efron & Associates 2440 Virginia Ave NW Washington DC 20037. *Mailing Add:* 694 N Trezevant Memphis TN 38112

EASTMAN, GENE M
PAINTER
b Council Grove, Kans, Jan 1, 26. *Study:* Univ Kans, BFA; Art Inst Chicago; Univ Iowa, with Stuart Edie, MFA. *Exhib:* Houston Mus Fine Arts, Tex, 58 & 61; Dallas Mus Fine Arts Ann, 59, 63 & 66; Seven States Artists Ann, Delgado Mus, New Orleans, 61; Watercolor USA, Springfield, Mo, 64; 24-64 Nat Exhib Small Paintings, Purdue Univ, 64. *Teaching:* Prof drawing & painting, Sam Houston State Univ, 58-, chmn art dept, 72-79; guest instr drawing & painting, Mus Fine Arts Sch, Houston Mus Fine Arts, 68-70. *Awards:* First Prize, Painting, Tex Fine Arts Asn, 58; Purchase Award, Okla Printmaker Soc, 64; First Prize, Painting, Tri-State Exhib, Beaumont Mus, Tex, 67. *Media:* Oil, Watercolor. *Mailing Add:* 24004 S Sam Houston Ave Huntsville TX 77340

EATON, PAULINE (FRIEDRICH)
PAINTER, INSTRUCTOR
b Neptune, NJ, Mar 20, 35. *Study:* Dickinson Col, Carlisle, Pa, BA, 57; Northwestern Univ, Evanston, Ill, MA, 58; seminars with Ed Betts, Glenn Bradshaw & Alex Nepote. *Work:* Butler Inst Am Art, Youngstown, Ohio; St Mary's Col, Md. *Comn:* Paintings, Empire Savings Banks, Colo, 77-79; landscapes, Host Inns, Phoenix Airport, Ariz, 78; six paintings, Mercy Hosp, San Diego, 81. *Exhib:* Nat Acad Design, New York, 75 & 77; solo exhib, Nat Arts Club, New York, 77; San Diego Mus Art, 77-79 & 81; Butler Inst Am Art, Youngstown, Ohio, 77-79 & 81; Laguna Beach Mus Art, Calif, 78 & 80; Palm Springs Desert Mus, Calif, 79; and others. *Teaching:* Lectr & demonstr, San Diego Art Inst, San Diego & Watercolor Soc, 77-; instr, Miracosta Col, Oceanside, Calif, 80-81 & Idyllwild Sch Mus & Arts, 83- *Awards:* Golden Award, Foothills Art Ctr, Colo, 78; Strathmore Award, Butler Inst Am Art, 81; Third Award, Western Fedn Exhib, 82. *Bibliog:* Barbara Nechis (auth), Creative Watercolor, 79 & Edward Betts (auth), Creative Seascape Painting, 80, Watson-Guptill; Martin E Peterson (auth), On view: Pauline Eaton, Applause Mag, 80. *Mem:* Nat Watercolor Soc; San Diego Watercolor Soc (pres, 76-77); Nat Soc Painters Casein & Acrylic (western regional chmn, 80-81); Artists Guild San Diego Mus Art (pres, 82-83); Watercolor West (bd mem, 79-). *Media:* Watercolor, Acrylic. *Mailing Add:* 10 Alta Mira Ave Kentfield CA 94904

EATON, THOMAS NEWTON
CARTOONIST, ILLUSTRATOR
b Wichita, Kans, Mar 2, 40. *Study:* Univ Denver, 58; Univ Kans, BFA, 62. *Comn:* Mag covers, Jr Scholastic, Scholastic Voice, Scholastic Scope, Child Life, and others; posters, Scholastic Mag Inc, 74-79; plus others. *Pos:* Artist/writer contemp cards dept, Hallmark Cards, Inc, Kansas City, Mo, 62-66; art ed, Scholastic Mag Inc, New York, 66-68; free lance cartoonist/writer, 68- *Awards:* Cert of Excellence for Cover, Catch the Eye, 75, Am Inst Graphics Arts. *Bibliog:* Eleanor Van Zandt (auth), A cartoonist looks at the comics, Practical Eng Mag, 68. *Media:* Pen, Ink. *Publ:* Auth & illusr, Flap, Delacorte Press, 72; auth & illusr, Tom Eaton's Book of Marvels, 76, Holiday Greeting Cards, 78 & Super Valentines, 79, Scholastic Bk Serv; auth & illusr, Rufus and the Earth Patrol, Sat Eve Post, 78; plus numerous others. *Mailing Add:* 911 W 100th St Kansas City MO 64114

EAUCLAIRE, SALLY
ART CRITIC
b Cornwall, NY, Aug 15, 50. *Study:* Univ Rochester, NY, BA, 72, MS, 81. *Collections Arranged:* The New Color: A Decade of Color Photography, Everson Mus, Syracuse, NY, 80-81; Midwest Photo 81, Mus Am Art, Elkhart, Ind, 81. *Pos:* Art critic, Democrat & Chronicle, Rochester, NY, 73-79; guest cur, Everson Mus Art, Syracuse, NY, 80-81. *Teaching:* Guest lectr, Int Ctr Photog, Notre Dame, Kalamazoo Inst Arts, Rochester Inst Technol & others, 80- *Awards:* Fel, Nat Endowment Humanities, 78. *Mem:* Int Asn Art Critics. *Publ:* Auth, The New Color Photography, Abbeville Press, New York, 81. *Mailing Add:* 18 East 94th St New York NY 10028

EBERMAN, EDWIN
ADMINISTRATOR, EDUCATOR
b Black Mountain, NC, Feb 20, 05. *Study:* Carnegie-Mellon Col Fine Arts, BA. *Pos:* Art dir, Arts & Decorative Mag, 33-35; art dir, McCalls Mag, 36-38; art dir, Look Mag, 41-46; dir & co-founder, Famous Artists Schs, 47-65. *Teaching:* Dir educ, painting, illustrating & cartooning, Famous Artists Schs, 48-65. *Publ:* Coauth, Techniques of the Picture Story, 45; auth, Nantucket Sketchbook, 46; coauth, numerous textbooks for Famous Artists Sch, 48-65. *Mailing Add:* 370 Wahackme Rd New Canaan CT 06840

EBIE, WILLIAM DENNIS
ADMINISTRATOR, PAINTER
b Akron, Ohio, Feb 7, 42. *Study:* Akron Art Inst Sch Design, scholar, 60, Univ Akron & Akron Art Inst Sch Design, BFA, 64; Calif Col Arts & Crafts, scholarships, 67-68, MFA, 68. *Work:* Calif Col Arts & Crafts Gallery. *Exhib:* The Figure: An Invitational Painting Exhibition, Kans State Col Gallery, Pittsburg, 75; Territorial Gallery, Roswell, NMex, 76 & 78; Summer Arts Festival, Sally Port Inn, Roswell, 78; 20th Nat Sun Festival, El Paso Mus Art, Tex, 79; Santa Fe Festival of Arts, 79. *Pos:* Ceramic specialist, Peace Corps, Cuzco, Peru, 64-66; graphic artist, Alameda Co Health Dept, Oakland, Calif, 67-68; asst dir, Roswell Mus & Art Ctr & managing dir, Roswell Mus Artist in Residence Prog, 71- *Teaching:* Instr painting, Fla A&M Univ, 69-70; instr painting, Roswell Mus Adult Educ, NMex, 71- *Mailing Add:* Rte 1 Box 244 A Roswell NM 88201

EBSEN, ALF K
CALLIGRAPHER, LECTURER
b Berlin, Ger, July 29, 08; Can citizen. *Study:* Kunstgewerbeschule, Hamburg, Ger, 2 yrs. *Comn:* Honour scrolls, IBM Can, STELCO & many prof orgn; design of advert, Volkswagen AG, Ger; Mem Plaque, Windsor Libr, Ont; Medieval Studies Advertising, Univ Toronto. *Exhib:* Continual exhibs in Ontario. *Pos:* Dir graphic arts, Eddy Match Co, Ontario, 55-63. *Teaching:* Instr calligraphic design at community cols in Ontario & Alberta; lectr, Univ Toronto, 68-70. *Bibliog:* The Review, Vol 62, Number 2, Issue 340, Imperial Oil Ltd, 78. *Mem:* Handwriters Guild of Toronto (founder, 76); Royal Can Acad Arts; Graphic Designers Can. *Media:* Paper, Vellum. *Publ:* Auth, Calligraphy Practice Book of the Canadian System, pvt publisher. *Mailing Add:* 60 Logandale Rd Willowdale ON M2N 4H4 Canada

ECHOHAWK, BRUMMETT
PAINTER, ILLUSTRATOR
b Pawnee, Okla, Mar 3, 22. *Study:* Sch Arts & Crafts, Detroit, 44; Art Inst Chicago, 44-48. *Work:* Gilcrease Mus Am Hist & Art, Tulsa. *Comn:* Truman Mem Libr (mural, with Thomas Hart Benton), Independence, Mo, 59-60. *Exhib:* Gilcrease Mus, Tulsa; Amon Carter Mus, Ft Worth, Tex; M H De Young Mem Mus, San Francisco; Imperial War Mus, London; Karl May Theater Mus, Bad Segeberg, WGer; Art Through the Embassies, US State Dept, Pakistani, India. *Pos:* Auth & illusr, articles in Western Horseman, Colorado Springs, 50-, Tulsa Sunday World, 50- & Okla Today, 60-; bd mem, Gilcrease Mus Am Hist & Art, Tulsa, 80- *Bibliog:* Whose Children Are These (film), ABC-TV Network, New York. *Media:* Oil, Tempera. *Publ:* Auth & illusr, Blue book, McCalls Mag, 49. *Mailing Add:* PO Box 1922 Tulsa OK 74127

ECKE, BETTY TSENG YU-HO See Tseng Yu-ho

ECKELBERRY, DON RICHARD
PAINTER
b Sebring, Ohio, July 6, 21. *Study:* Cleveland Inst Art. *Comn:* Bird postage stamp, British Honduras, 62; murals, Adirondack Mus, 60. *Exhib:* One-man shows, New York, 43, 46 & 56 & Louisville, Ky, 70; Cleveland Inst Art, 70. *Pos:* Staff artist, Nat Audubon Soc, 43-45; free lance artist, 45- *Mem:* Fel Am Ornithol Union; Audubon Artists Soc; Cooper Ornithol Soc; Soc Animal Artists; Wilson Ornithol Soc. *Mailing Add:* 180 Woodsome Rd Babylon NY 11702

ECKERSLEY, THOMAS CYRIL
EDUCATOR, ADMINISTRATOR
b Detroit, Mich, Nov 23, 41. *Study:* Ohio Univ, with Clarence White, Jr, BFA, 66, MFA, 69. *Work:* Erie Art Ctr, Pa; Creative Eye Photo Gallery, Calif. *Exhib:* Washington Sq E Gallery, New York, 78; The Syracuse Show, NY, 78; Coos Art Mus, Ore, 79; Parkersburg Nat, WVa, 81; Mystic Photo Three, Conn, 81; and others. *Pos:* Studio mgr & admin asst, Josten's Am Photog, 67-68; photogr, WOSU-TV, Ohio State Univ, 68-69. *Teaching:* Instr photog, Columbus Col Art & Design, 69-70; assoc prof art & chmn art dept, State Univ NY Col Oswego, 70- *Awards:* Hon Mention, Des Moines Int, 74; First Prize, Oswego Art Guild, 75; Patron Purchase, Erie Art Ctr. *Media:* Silver Prints, Gum-Bichromate Prints. *Publ:* Coauth, Jewelry Making: An Illustrated Guide to Technique, 75. *Mailing Add:* Box 44 Hannibal NY 13074

ECKERT, LOU
PAINTER
b Lancaster, Pa, Jan 27, 28. *Study:* Univ Rochester, with John Mennihan, BA; workshops under Jan Horton, Univ Nebr, Ida Kohlmeyer, Univ New Orleans, Richard Brough, Univ Ala & Stuart Purser, Univ Fla; also with Marie Hull, Jackson, Miss, Andrew Bucci, Washington, DC. *Work:* Miss Art Asn Munic Gallery, Jackson; Greater Gulf Coast Art Asn Collection, Biloxi, Miss; and others. *Exhib:* Mid-South Ann, Brooks Mem Art Gallery, Memphis, Tenn, 65 & 69; one-man shows, Percy H Whiting Art Ctr, Fairhope, Ala, 69, New Orleans Theatre Performing Arts, 77 & Gulf South Galleries, McComb, Miss, 79-83; Second Greater New Orleans Nat Exhib, 72; five-man show, Gulf South Galleries, Macomb, Miss, 78; and others. *Pos:* Owner & operator, 22 Ltd Gallery, New Orleans, 73. *Awards:* First Nat Bank Award (Miss Collection), 67; Grand Hotel Purchase Award, Biloxi, 75. *Bibliog:* Jan Horton (auth), Art for the Day (film), ETV Ctr, Jackson, 70. *Mem:* Miss Art Asn, Jackson; New Orleans Art Asn; La Watercolor Soc, New Orleans. *Media:* Oil, Watercolor. *Mailing Add:* 3631 Post Oak Ave New Orleans LA 70114

ECKERT, WILLIAM DEAN
PAINTER, HISTORIAN
b Coshocton, Ohio, Oct 10, 27. *Study:* Ohio State Univ, BA(with distinction), BFA(cum laude) & MA; Univ Iowa, PhD. *Work:* Butler Inst Am Art, Youngstown, Ohio; State Hist Soc Mus, Columbia, Mo. *Exhib:* Quincy Art Ctr Regional, Ill, 74; Mid-South Biennial, Brooks Gallery, Memphis, 75; Mainstreams '76, Marietta Col, Ohio; Missouri Photographers, 1976, St Louis Art Mus; May Show, Spiva Art Ctr, Joplin, Mo, 77; 22nd Delta Art Exhib, Ark Art Ctr, Little Rock, 79; and others. *Teaching:* Assoc prof art hist, Western Ill Univ, Macomb, 59-65; assoc prof art hist, Union Col, Schenectady, NY, 65-68; prof art hist, Lindenwood Cols, 68-, chmn art dept, 75-78 & 80- *Awards:* Award in Painting & Graphics, Akron May Show, 54; First Prize in Graphics, Ohio State Fair Exhib, 56; Third Award in Painting, Quincy Art Ctr Regional, Ill, 71. *Mem:* Col Art Asn Am; Soc Archit Historians; Midwest Art Hist Soc; Decorative Arts Trust. *Media:* Acrylic. *Res:* Renaissance stage in Italy; evolution of the perspective scene. *Publ:* Contribr, The college gallery & the liberal arts, Symposium, summer 67. *Mailing Add:* 1302 Musket Hollow St Charles MO 63301

ECKHARDT, FERDINAND
HISTORIAN, MUSEUM DIRECTOR
b Vienna, Austria; Can citizen. *Study:* Univ Vienna; Univ Man, hon LLD, 71. *Pos:* Head educ, State Mus, Vienna; dir, Winnipeg Art Gallery, 53-74, emer dir, 74. *Awards:* Austrian Cross of Honor for Sci & Art, 72; Order of Canada, Can Govt, 76. *Mem:* Can Mus Asn; Can Art Mus Dirs Asn; Int Coun Mus, Can; Am Asn Art Mus Dirs. *Publ:* Auth, Das Graphische Werk von Walter Gramatte, Leipzig, 32; auth, Das Betrachten von Kunstwerken, Wien, 48; auth, Walter Gramatte, three vols, Winnipeg, 81; auth, Ferdinand Eckhardt (father), ein Wiener Graphiker, Winnipeg, 82; auth, Auswahl der Briefe von Walter Gramatte, Berlin, 83; and others. *Mailing Add:* 54 Harrow St Winnipeg MB R3M 2Y7 Canada

ECKSTEIN, RUTH
PAINTER, PRINTMAKER
b Nuremberg, WGer, May 11, 16; US citizen. *Study:* New Sch Social Res, New York, with Stuart Davis; Art Students League, with Harry Sternberg, Julian Levy & V Vitlacyl; Pratt Graphic Ctr, New York, with Seong Moy & Roberto Delamonica. *Work:* Philadelphia Mus Art; Brooklyn Mus; Columbia Univ; City of Nuremberg; Everson Mus, Syracuse, NY. *Exhib:* Prints & Watercolors, Pa Acad Fine Arts, Philadelphia, 59, 64 & 65; Triennial of Original Colored Graphics, Grenchen, Switz, 64; one-woman shows, Alonzo Gallery, New York, 68, 70, 72, 75 & 77, Kunsthalle, Nuremberg, 74-75, Nassau Co Ctr Fine Arts, 75, Benson Gallery, NY, 76 & 81, Galeria de Arte 9, Lima, Peru, 80, Adelphi Univ, 80; Silvermine Guild Ctr, 84; and others. *Awards:* Village Art Ctr Award, New York, 63; Audubon Artists Award, 77 & 78; Art of Northeast USA Award, 83. *Bibliog:* Interview (video), Port Washington Libr, 78; Review, New York Times, 11/80 & Newsday, 6/82. *Mem:* Am Abstr Artists (secy, 70-80); Soc Am Graphic Artists; Audubon Artists. *Dealer:* Payson-Weisberg 822 Madison Ave New York NY 10021. *Mailing Add:* 5 Cricket Lane Great Neck NY 11024

EDDY, DON
PAINTER
b Long Beach, Calif, Nov 4, 44. *Study:* Univ Hawaii, Honolulu, BFA, 67; MFA, 69; Univ Calif, Santa Barbara, 69-70. *Work:* Cleveland Mus Art, Ohio; Toledo Mus Art, Ohio; St Etienne Mus, France; Neue Galerie, Aachen, Ger; Williams Col Mus Art, Williamstown, Mass. *Exhib:* Fogg Art Mus, Harvard Univ, Cambridge, Mass, 73; Storm King Art Ctr, Mountainville, NY, 73; New York Avant-Garde, Saidye Bronfman Centre, Montreal, Que, 73; Hyperrealisme Americaine, Realism Europ, Centre Nat d'Art Contemporain, Paris, 74; Wadsworth Atheneum, Hartford, Conn, 74; Tokyo Biennial, Japan, 74; Baltimore Mus Art, Md, 76; Realist & Illusionist Art Traveling Exhib, Australia, 77; and others. *Bibliog:* Udo Kulterman (auth), New realism, NY Graphic Soc, 72; Peter Sager (auth), Realismus, Verlag M DuMont Schauberg. *Media:* Acrylic. *Dealer:* Nancy Hoffman Gallery 429 W Broadway New York NY 10012. *Mailing Add:* 30 Christopher St Apt 3F New York NY 10014

EDELHEIT, MARTHA
PAINTER, FILMMAKER
b New York, NY. *Study:* Columbia Univ Teachers Col, BS, 56; Univ Chicago. *Exhib:* (Paintings) Figure Show, Wadsworth Atheneum, Hartford, Conn, 64; Eleven From the Reuben, Guggenheim Mus, New York, 65; Sons & Others, Queens Mus, New York, 75; Three Centuries of the Am Nude, New York Cult Ctr, 75 & Minneapolis Inst Arts, Minn, 75; Works on Paper, Brooklyn Mus, NY, 75; (Films) Graz Mus, Austria, 74; Mus 20th Century, Vienna, Austria, 74; Portland Mus, Ore, 76; Brooklyn Mus, 77; Mus Mod Art, New York, 77; and others. *Teaching:* Vis artist, Feminist Art Prog, Calif Inst of the Arts, 73; artist-in-residence painting, Wilson Col, Chambersburg, Pa, 75; artist-in-residence film, Univ Cincinnati, Ohio, 76; artist-in-residence painting & drawing, Art Inst Chicago, 76; guest lectr film, New Sch Social Res, New York, 77. *Bibliog:* Dennis Adrian (auth), In Evanston, A fuss over nudes, Chicago Daily News, 6/6/74; Margaret Walters (auth), The Nude Male: A New Perspective, Paddington Press, 78; Bradley Smith (auth), Erotic Art of the Masters, Gemini-Smith Inc. *Mem:* Women/Artist Filmmakers Inc (vpres, 74, pres, 75-77); Women in the Arts; Women's Caucus Art; Col Art Asn. *Media:* Mixed. *Publ:* Contribr, Women in the Year 2000, Arbor House, 74; contribr, Anonymous Was a Woman, 74 & Art: A Woman's Sensibility, 75, Calif Inst of the Arts; auth, The Invention of the Albino Queen, ANIMA, Conococheague Assoc, 75; auth, Georgia O'Keefe: A reminiscence, Women Artists Newsletter, 12/77. *Mailing Add:* 1140 Fifth Ave New York NY 10028

EDELMAN, RITA
PAINTER
b New York, NY, Nov 2, 30. *Study:* Traphagen Sch Design, cert, 51; Silvermine Col Art, 67; also with Victor Candell, Leo Manso & Robert Reed. *Work:* General Electric, Fairfield, Conn; Fairfield Univ, Conn; Gen Foods, White Plains, NY; Deloitte Haskins & Sells, Stamford, Conn; Westport Hist Soc, Conn. *Exhib:* Stamford Mus, Conn, 73, 77, 78 & 82; Silvermine Guild Artists, New Canaan, Conn, 76, 80, 81, & 83; solo exhibs, Silvermine Guild Galleries, New Canaan, Conn, 76 & 81 & Pindar Gallery, New York, 78, 80 & 82; Butler Inst Am Art, Youngstown, Ohio, 79; Grey Galleries, New York, 80; Aldrich Mus Contemp Art, Ridgefield, Conn, 81; and others. *Awards:* Judges Choice, Greenwich Art Soc, 72; First Prize, New Haven Paint & Clay Club, 75; Painting Award, New Eng Exhib Painting & Sculpture, Silvermine Guild Artists, 80. *Bibliog:* George Albert Perret (auth), essay, 10/80 & Robert Yoskowitz (auth), review, 12/80, Arts Mag; Cynthia Nadleman (auth), rev, Art News Mag, 1/81. *Mem:* Westport Weston Arts Coun; New Haven Paint & Clay Club; Silvermine Guild Artists. *Media:* Oil, Acrylic. *Dealer:* Pindar Gallery 127 Greene St New York NY 10012. *Mailing Add:* 7 Manitou Ct Westport CT 06880

EDELSON, GILBERT S
ADMINISTRATOR, LECTURER
b New York, NY, Sept 15, 28. *Study:* NY Univ, BS, 49; Columbia Univ Sch Law, LLB, 55. *Pos:* Mem, Comt Art, Asn Bar, City New York, 64-67, 72-75; dir, Artforum Mag, 70-77 & Art Quart, 78- *Mem:* Col Art Asn Am; Art Dealers Asn Am; Am Fedn Art (trustee, mem exec comt, 82-); NY Univ Inst Fine Arts. *Mailing Add:* 575 Madison Ave New York NY 10022

EDELSON, MARY BETH
CONCEPTUAL ARTIST
b East Chicago, Ind. *Study:* Art Inst Chicago, 53-54; DePauw Univ, BA, 55; NY Univ, MA, 59. *Exhib:* One-woman shows, Cycles II, Univ Cincinnati, 80, Cycles, Herter Gallery, Univ Mass, Amherst, 80, Mary Beth Edelson, Recent Work, Albright-Knox Gallery, Buffalo, 81, Unfinished Plans for Utopia, Elise Meyer, New York, 81, Superwoman: A Photographic Survey of Mary Beth Edelson's Work, Wright State Univ, Ohio, 81, The Trickster Rabbit, Max Hutchison Gallery, New York, 81; Art on Paper, Corcoran Gallery Art, Washington, DC, 79; The Presence of Nature, Whitney Mus Am Art, 79; New Dimensions in Drawing, 1950-1980, Aldrich Mus Contemp Art, 81; Contempary American Landscapes, Whitney Mus Am Art, 81; and many others. *Teaching:* Instr, Corcoran Sch of Art, 71-76. *Awards:* Visual Artist Grant, Nat Endowment Arts, 81. *Bibliog:* Jack Burnham (auth), Mary Beth Edelson's Great Goddess, 11/75; Karen Peterson & J J Wilson (coauths), Women Artists, Harper & Row, 76; Lucy Lippard (auth), From the Center, E P Dutton & Co Bks, NY, 76. *Mem:* Founder Conf Women in Visual Arts, Washington, DC. *Media:* Mixed. *Publ:* Auth, Seven Cycles: Public Rituals, 80. *Mailing Add:* 110 Mercer St New York NY 10012

EDELSTEIN, J M
LIBRARIAN, EDUCATOR
b Baltimore, Md, July 31, 24. *Study:* Johns Hopkins Univ, AB, 47; Fulbright travel grant to Italy, 49-50; Univ Mich, MALS, 53. *Pos:* Chief librn, Nat Gallery of Art, 72- *Teaching:* Lectr rare bks, Univ Calif Los Angeles, 66-72 & Cath Univ, DC, 75- *Mem:* Bibliog Soc Am (ed, 64-81); Jargon Soc (bd dirs, 76-); Wallace Stevens Soc (ed, 76-); Am Libr Asn. *Publ:* Auth, Bibliographical Checklist of Writings of Thornton Wilder, Yale Univ, 59; ed, A Garland for Jake Zeitlin, Dahlstrom-Marks, 67 & Books from Library of Don Cameron Allen, Univ Calif San Diego, 68; auth, Wallace Stevens: a Descriptive Bibliography, Univ Pittsburgh, 74; auth, A Jargon Society Checklist 1951-79, Books & Co, 79. *Mailing Add:* Nat Gallery of Art Sixth St & Constitution Ave NW Washington DC 20565

EDELSTEIN, TERI J
ADMINISTRATOR, HISTORIAN
b Johnstown, Pa, June 23, 51. *Study:* Univ Pa, BA, 72, grad fel, Stouffer Col House, 72-74, teaching fel hist art, 73-75, Penfield scholar, 75-76, MA, 77, PhD, 79. *Pos:* Asst dir dept acad prog, Yale Ctr Brit Art, New Haven, Conn, 79-83; dir, Art Mus & Skinner Mus, Mt Holyoke Col, 83- *Teaching:* Lectr art hist, Univ Guelph, Ont, 77-79. *Mem:* Col Art Asn; Am Soc Eighteenth-Century Studies; Williamstown Regional Art Conserv (bd dirs, currently). *Res:* Iconology of British art of the nineteenth century. *Publ:* Auth, The yellow-haired fiend--Rosetti and sensation novel, Libr Chronicle, 79; auth, They sang the song of the shirt, the visual iconography of the seamstress, Victorian Studies, 79; auth, Review of German Romanticism and English art by William Vaugh, J Pre-Raphaelite Studies, 80; auth, Vauxhall Gardens (exhib catalog), Yale Ctr Brit Art, 83; auth, Augustus Egg's triptych: A narrative of Victorian adultery, Burlington Mag, 83. *Mailing Add:* Yale Ctr for Brit Art 1080 Chapel St New Haven CT 06520

EDEN, GLENN
DRAFTSMAN
b Atlanta, Ga, 51. *Study:* DeKalb Community Col, AA, 71; Ga State Univ. *Work:* Gibbes Mus, Charleston, SC; Macon Mus, Ga. *Exhib:* Wizard of Oz Drawings, Mint Mus, 76; Artists in Ga, High Mus Art, Atlanta, 81; The Human Figure, New Orleans Contemp Art Inst, La, 82; Ten Pens, Southern Arts Fedn, Atlanta, Ga, 82; Narrative Drawings, Nexus Gallery, Atlanta, 83. *Awards:* Atlanta Department of Cultural Affairs Grant, 82. *Bibliog:* Jeff Kipnis (auth), Glenn Eden at the Gibbes, Art in Am, 81; Jeff Kipnis (auth), Profile, Art Voices, 81. *Media:* Ballpoint Pen, Prisma Color. *Mailing Add:* 639 Cooledge Ave Atlanta GA 30306

EDER, JAMES ALVIN
PRINTMAKER, PAINTER
b Buffalo, NY, Jan 9, 42. *Study:* State Univ NY, Buffalo, BS, 63; Univ Nebr, Lincoln, MS, 66; Northern Ariz Univ, Flagstaff, MA, 75. *Work:* Valley Nat Bank, Mesa, Ariz; First Interstate Bank, Honeywell Corp & Talley Industries, Phoenix, Ariz; Quanex Corp, Houston, Tex; and others. *Exhib:* one-man shows, Univ Ariz, Tucson, 80 & Scottsdale Community Col, Ariz, 81; NDak Print & Drawing Ann, Univ NDak, Grand Forks, 81; PACT Printmakers Invitational, 83; Window to the Future, Scottsdale, Ariz, 83; and others. *Teaching:* Instr art, Evening Div, Phoenix Col, 78-81. *Awards:* First Place Printmaking, Ariz State Fair, 76, 77 & 81. *Bibliog:* Jim Eder: A unique western artist, Sedona Life Mag, winter 78; Mary Carroll Nelson (auth), James A Eder profile, Art Voices, 9-10/81; Mary Carroll Nelson (auth), Jim Eder: Making woodcut prints, Am Artist, 11/81. *Media:* Woodcut, Collagraph; Acrylic. *Dealer:* Gekas-Nicholas Gallery 6538 E Tanque Verde Rd Tucson AZ 85715. *Mailing Add:* 6402 South 42nd St Phoenix AZ 85040

EDGE, DOUGLAS BENJAMIN
SCULPTOR, PAINTER
b Fennimore, Wis, Aug 4, 42. *Study:* San Fernando Valley State Col, BA. *Work:* Mus Mod Art, New York; Arco, Washington, DC; Security Bank, Los Angeles; Patrick Lannon Mus, Fla. *Comn:* Constructionist Pagoda, Imperial Bank, Costa Mesa, Calif, 79. *Exhib:* West Coast Now, Seattle Art Mus, 68; Violence in Am Art, Mus Contemp Art, Chicago, 69; Continuing Surrealism, La Jolla Mus Art, 71; Calif Prints, Mus Mod Art, New York, 72; Separate Realities, Los Angeles Munic Art Gallery, 73; Santa Barbara Mus, 77. *Teaching:* Instr sculpture, Calif Inst Art, Valencia, 70-72; instr painting workshop, Art Ctr Sch Design, Los Angeles, 73-74; lectr sculpture & drawing, Univ Calif, Santa Barbara, 75-76. *Awards:* Cassandra Found Grant, 70. *Bibliog:* Thomas Garver (auth), rev, 10/69 & Peter Plagens (auth), rev, 11/73, Artforum; Milinda Terbell (auth), Art News, 10/73. *Mailing Add:* 635 N Alisos St Santa Barbara CA 93103

EDMISTON, SARA JOANNE
EDUCATOR, DESIGNER
b Independence, Mo, June 21, 35. *Study:* Univ Kans, BAE; ECarolina Univ, MA. *Work:* NC Mus Art, Raleigh; NC Nat Banks, several cities in NC; Wachovia Banks, several cities in NC; Duke Univ. *Comn:* Door knocker, NC Nat Bank, Charlotte, 74; and others. *Exhib:* NC Mus Art, Raleigh, 65-67, 71, 73 & 76; Enamels 70 Nat, Crafts Alliance, St Louis, Mo & William Rockhill Nelson Gallery Art, Kansas City, Mo, 70; Piedmont Crafts, Mint Mus Art, Charlotte, 70-73; Crafts Invitational, Jacksonville Mus, Fla, 72; Southeastern Crafts Exhib, Greenville Co Mus, SC, 74; New Directions in Fabric Design, Fine Arts Gallery, Towson State Univ, 76; and others. *Teaching:* Prof textiles & design, ECarolina Univ, 66- *Awards:* Purchase Award, 5th Ann Piedmont Graphics Exhib, Mint Mus Art, 69; Purchase Award, 39th Ann NC Artists Exhib, NC Art Soc, 76. *Mem:* Surface Design Asn (treas & nat mem chmn, 76-80); Am Crafts Coun; Piedmont Craftsmen Inc; Carolina Designer-Craftsmen; NC Crafts Asn (mem bd dirs, 76-79). *Media:* Dye, Enamel. *Dealer:* Piedmont Craftsmen Inc Sales Gallery 936 West Fourth St Winston-Salem NC 27101. *Mailing Add:* 406 West Fourth St Greenville NC 27834

EDMONDSON, LEONARD
PRINTMAKER
b Sacramento, Calif, June 12, 16. *Study:* Univ Calif, Berkeley, AB, 40, MA, 42. *Work:* Metrop Mus Art, New York; Bibliot Nat, Paris, France; New York Pub Libr; San Francisco Mus Art; Pasadena Art Mus. *Comn:* Edition of etchings, Int Graphic Arts Soc, NY, 60, Hilton Hotel, NY, 62, Ferdinand Roten Galleries, Inc, NY, 66 & US Info Agency, Washington, DC, 67. *Exhib:* American Watercolors, Drawings & Prints, Metrop Mus Art, 52; Younger American Painters, Guggenheim Mus, 54; American Prints Today, Print Coun Am, 62; Int Triennial of Original Colored Graphics, Switz, 64; Graphics '71 West Coast USA, Univ Ky, 71. *Teaching:* Prof art, Calif State Univ, Los Angeles, 64-74; chmn dept printmaking, Otis Art Inst, Los Angeles, 74-80. *Awards:* Purchase Prize for Oil, Univ Ill, 55; Purchase Prize for Etching, Brooklyn Mus, 56; Purchase Prize for Etching, Pasadena Art Mus, 58. *Bibliog:* Mugnaini (auth), Oil Painting, Techniques & Materials, 69 & Reep (auth), The Content of Watercolor, 69, Van Nostrand; Heller (auth), Printmaking Today, Holt, 71. *Publ:* Auth, Etching, Van Nostrand, 73. *Mailing Add:* PO Box 26765 Los Angeles CA 90026

EDMONSTON, PAUL
EDUCATOR, EDITOR
b Newton, Mass, Nov 15, 22. *Study:* Mass Sch of Art, with Ernest L Major & Cyrus Dallin; Boston Univ, AB(Eng lang & lit), with William Jewell, Edgar Brightman, Gerald Brace & Edward A Post; Fla State Univ, MA(art educ), with Karl Zerbe & Ivan Johnson; Ohio State Univ, PhD(fine art), with Hoyt Sherman, Sydney Chafetz, Manuel Barkan, Jerome Hausman & Ross L Mooney; Post Doctoral Fel, 68; Univ Pa, SAsian studies, 72-73. *Pos:* Ed, Apelles: Ga Art J, 79- *Teaching:* Instr art, Ohio State Univ, 56-60; from assoc prof to prof art appreciation, printmaking & art ed, Pa State Univ, 60-77; prof art appreciation, drawing & painting & art educ, Univ Ga, 77- *Awards:* Can Embassy Fac Enrichment Grant, 80-81; Ford Found Summer Research Grants, 78 & 81; Artist in Residence, Program, Cortona, Italy, 81. *Mem:* US Soc for Educ Through Art (vpres, 79); Nat Art Educ Asn (res sem, 70-); Asn for Asian Studies; Ga Art Educ Asn (pres, 81-83); World Future Soc; and others. *Media:* Watercolor; Brush & Ink on Rice Paper. *Res:* Studio way of learning, nature of creative teaching. *Publ:* Auth, Photography taken as a creative act, Art Ed, 75; auth, A conceptual model of creative visual intelligence, J Creative Behavior, 75; auth, Myth and symbol in Indian art, Int Art Sem 76, Franklin Perkins Sch, Mass, 76; contribr & ed, An Anthology of Faculty Papers: 1976-77, Pa State Univ, 77. *Mailing Add:* Dept of Art Univ Ga Athens GA 30602

EDMUNDS, ALLAN LOGAN
PRINTMAKER, ADMINISTRATOR
b Philadelphia, Pa, June 7, 49. *Study:* Tyler Sch Art, Temple Univ, Philadelphia & Rome; also with Romas Viesulas & John Dowell, BFA & MFA. *Work:* Philadelphia Mus Art; Nat Collection of Fine Art, Libr of Cong; First Pa Bank; Yale Univ; Philadelphia Savings Fund Soc. *Comn:* Photosilkscreen ed, Philadelphia Mus Art, 71-72. *Exhib:* Silkscreen: History of a Medium, Philadelphia Mus Art, 71-72; Expanded Photograph, Philadelphia Civic Ctr Mus, 72; one-man show, Univ Md, Baltimore Co, 72; Second World Black & African Festival Art & Cult, Univ Pa Mus, 74; Nat Invited Print Exhib, Cent Wash State Univ, 75; traveling exhib, Smithsonian Inst, 81-82. *Pos:* founder-pres, Brandywine Graphic Workshop, Inc, 72-; visual arts panelist, Pa Coun Arts, 82-; vis artist, Bloomsburg State Col, 80-; mem adv panel, William Penn Mus Fine Arts Collection, 81; partner, A L Edmunds Assoc, 81. *Teaching:* Instr graphics, Haystack Mountain Sch Crafts, Maine, 74; lectr printmaking, Philadelphia Col Art, 75; art coordr, Parkway Prog Sch Dist Philadelphia, 72-; adj instr, Philadelphia Col Art, 80- *Awards:* Philadelphia Civic Ctr Award Painting, 67; Temple Univ Scholar Study in Rome, 70. *Bibliog:* Baltimore Sun, 11/12/72; Philadelphia Inquirer, 11/15/72; Philly Talk Mag, 3/74. *Mem:* Artists Equity Asn; Philadelphia Print Club; Pa New Art Examiner Asn. *Res:* Continuous research project on the history of the Black graphic artist; collection of slides, manuscripts and original works as well as developing video documentation. *Dealer:* Hahn Gallery 8439 Germantown Ave Philadelphia PA 19118. *Mailing Add:* 1520-22 Kater St Philadelphia PA 19146

EDVI ILLES, EMMA
DEALER, CONSULTANT
b Budapest, Hungary; US citizen. *Study:* NY Sch Interior Design, 58; Int Asn Color Consults, dipl, 59; Sogetsu Sch Flower Design Tokyo, prof degree, 62. *Pos:* Owner & founder, Academia de Decoration, Caracas, Venezuela, 56; lectr & consult, Channel 2 & 4 TV, Caracas, 58-66. *Awards:* Dipl de Honor, Ministerio de Educ, Caracas, 66. *Publ:* Auth, Teoria de Color, 2 vols, 59; auth, Commercial Flower Design, 2 vols, 61. *Mailing Add:* 130 26th St Apt 407 Atlanta GA 30309

EDVI ILLES, GEORGE
PAINTER, SCULPTOR
b Budapest, Hungary, Apr 29, 11. *Study:* Acad Fine Arts Budapest; also with Oscar Glatz, Stephan Bosznay & Ede Telcs. *Work:* High Mus Art; Hungarian Nat Mus. *Comn:* Portrait (oil), Andres Eloy Blanco, Capitolium Caracas, 63; portrait (oil), Otto Habsburg Crownprince; cast gold medallion of Mrs Jacquelyn Kennedy; portrait, President Jimmy Carter. *Exhib:* One-man show, Budapest, Hungary, 29; Nat Mus Caracas, Venezuela; competition of posters, Hungarian Thermal Resort, Hajduszoboszlo, 39; competition for poster, Nepszava Newspaper, 46. *Awards:* First Prize, Thermal Resort Hajduszoboszlo, 39; Commemorative Medal Albert Schweitzer, 75; Albert Schweitzer World Prize, Wilmington NC, 76. *Media:* Oil, Pastel. *Mailing Add:* 3734 Peachtree Rd NE Atlanta GA 30319

EDWARDS, ELLENDER MORGAN
PRINTMAKER, PHOTOGRAPHER
b Hagerstown, Md. *Study:* Tyler Sch Art; pvt study art hist in Europe; Md Inst Col Art, BFA, 58; Art Students League, with Jean Liberte; Hunter Col, grad study; Corcoran Art Sch, George Washington Univ; also with Reuben Kramer & Victor D'Amico. *Exhib:* 29th & 30th Cumberland Valley Artists, Washington Co Mus Art, Hagerstown, Md, 61 & 62; Md Regional, Baltimore Mus Art, 61 & 76; 21st Ann Life in Baltimore, Peale Mus, Md, 61; Denim Art, Mus Contemp Crafts, New York, 74; Focus 76 Photo Competition, Amarillo Civic Ctr, Tex, 76; Bicentennial Competition, Goldman Fine Arts Gallery, 76. *Pos:* Secy, Montgomery Co Art Educators Asn, Rockville, Md, 70-73, treas, 73-75; treas, Glen Echo Graphics, 73- *Awards:* Second Prize Watercolor, Waterford Found, Inc, Va, 60; First Prize Graphics, Shepherd Col, 71; Honorable Mention, Int Platform Asn, 73 & 74 & Goldman Fine Arts Gallery, 76; plus others. *Mem:* Nat League Am Penwomen; Int Platform Asn. *Mailing Add:* Box 415 Arnold MD 21012

EDWARDS, ETHEL (MRS XAVIER GONZALEZ)
PAINTER
b New Orleans, La. *Study:* Newcomb Col Art Sch; also with Xavier Gonzalez. *Work:* Chase Manhattan Bank, New York; Commerce Trust Bank, Kansas City; Baltimore Mus Art, Md; Nat Gallery Art, DC; Newark Mus, NJ; Univ Nebr. *Comn:* Ser paintings, comn by Dept Interior, Colo & NMex. *Exhib:* Whitney Mus Am Art, 64 & 65; Watercolor: USA, Springfield, Ill, 67-69; Cape Cod Art Asn, 69; Nat Gallery, Washington, DC; Am Embassy, Paris; Galerie Jeanne Boucher, Paris; Mus Mod Art, New York; Pa Acad, Philadelphia. *Teaching:* Instr, Truro Ctr Arts. *Awards:* Larry Aldrich Prize, Silvermine Guild Artists; Prizes, Watercolor: USA, Springfield, Ill, 67 & Ball State Univ, Muncie, Ind, 67. *Mem:* Fel McDowell Colony. *Mailing Add:* 222 Central Park S New York NY 10019

EDWARDS, JAMES F
VIDEO ARTIST, PAINTER
b New York, NY, July 25, 48. *Study:* Univ Calif, Santa Barbara, BA, MFA. *Work:* Everson Mus Art, Syracuse, NY; SC State Arts Collection; Univ Calif, Santa Barbara; and others. *Comn:* Collage, Huntsville Mus Art. *Exhib:* one-man shows, Greenville Co Mus Art, Greenville, SC, 76 & Everson Mus Art, Syracuse, NY, 77 & others; Contemp Media Study Ctr, Dayton, Ohio, 79; Huntsville Mus Art, Ala, 81; Southeastern Ctr Contemp Art, Winston-Salem, NC, 81; and others. *Pos:* Cur video gallery, Univ SC, 77-79. *Teaching:* Assoc prof drawing & video, Univ SC, 78- *Awards:* Nat Endowment Arts Fel,

74-75; Proj Grant, SC Arts Comn, 76-77; Individual Artist Fel, SC Arts Comn, 81; and others. *Bibliog:* Kenneth Friedman (auth), James Edwards video tapes, Grossmont Col, El Cajon, Calif. *Mem:* Southeastern Col Art Conf. *Media:* Color Xerox; Miscellaneous. *Publ:* Auth, Getting into video, Contemp Art/SE, 77; auth, Art, language and criticism, Contemp Arts/SE, Vol II, Number 4-5. *Dealer:* Heath Gallery 416 East Paces Ferry Rd Atlanta GA 30305; Hodges-Taylor Gallery 227 N Tryon St Charlotte NC 28202. *Mailing Add:* Dept of Art Univ SC Columbia SC 29208

EDWARDS, PAUL BURGESS
EDUCATOR, PAINTER
b Moulton, Iowa, Feb 18, 34. *Study:* Iowa Wesleyan Col, with S Carl Fracassini, BA, 55; Wichita Art Asn Sch Art, with Jack Pharo, 57; Wichita State Univ, with Robert Kiskadden, MA, 59. *Work:* Wichita Art Mus; Miami Beach Pub Libr; Iowa Wesleyan Col; Citizens Libr, Washington, Pa. *Comn:* Mosaic mural, Sisters St Joseph, Halstead, Kans, 58; mural, Tasco Mining Co, Washington, Pa, 79. *Exhib:* Nat Small Painting Show, Purdue Univ, 66; 19th Ann Nat Decorative Arts Show, Wichita Art Asn, 66; Second Nat Polymer Exhib, Eastern Mich Univ, 68; solo exhib, Spectrum Gallery, New York, 70; 36th Ann Midyear Show, Butler Inst Am Art, 72; 13th Ann Three Rivers Arts Festival, Gateway Ctr, Pittsburgh, Pa, 72. *Collections Arranged:* W & J Nat Painting Show, 68- & Malcolm Parcell Retrospective, 82, Olin Art Ctr. *Teaching:* Instr ceramics, Wichita State Univ, summer 62; asst prof sculpture, West Liberty State Col, 63-65; chmn painting & drawing, Washington & Jefferson Col, 65- *Awards:* First Prize Painting, Bethany Col Ann, 64; First Prize, Oglebay Inst Summer Show, 64; Best of Show Award, Huntington 180, Huntington Gallery, 65. *Mem:* Am Asn Art Adminr; Wichita Artist Guild (pres, 61-62); Arts Coun Washington, Pa (pres, 69-72). *Media:* Acrylic. *Publ:* Contribr, Topic: 17 A liberal arts miscellany, Topic Mag, 69; illusr, Nonverbal Communication, Marcel Dekker Inc, 74. *Mailing Add:* 268 E Wheeling Washington PA 15301

EDWARDS, STANLEY DEAN
PAINTER, GRAPHIC ARTIST
b Joliet, Ill, Dec 5, 41. *Study:* Art Inst Chicago; Univ Chicago; BFA; Saugatuck Summer Sch. *Work:* Ball State Univ Art Gallery. *Exhib:* 12 Chicago Painters, Walker Art Ctr, 65; Corcoran Biannual, Washington, DC, 65; Protest & Hope Group Show, New Sch Social Res, 67; Butler Ann, Youngstown, Ohio, 68; Violence in Art, Mus Contemp Art, Chicago, 69; and others. *Teaching:* Instr art, Trinity Sch, New York, 69-70; instr, Chicago Acad Fine Arts, 72. *Awards:* Purchase Prize, Corcoran Gallery, 65; Vanderbilt Purchase Fund, 69. *Bibliog:* Whitney Halsted (auth), article, Artforum, 66; Franz Schultz (auth), articles, Panorama Mag & Chicago Daily News, 65-69. *Mailing Add:* c/o Fairweather-Hardin Gallery 101 E Ontario Chicago IL 60611

EDWARDS-TUCKER, YVONNE (LEATRICE YVONNE TUCKER)
CERAMIST, EDUCATOR
b Chicago, Ill, Jan 19, 41. *Study:* Univ Ill, Urbana, BFA(art educ; summa cum laude), 62; Univ Calif, Los Angeles, 62-64; Otis Art Inst, BFA, MFA, 68. *Work:* Evans-Tibbs Collection, Vermont Ave Gallery, Washington, DC; Otis Art Inst; Ala State Univ, Montgomery; Tenn State Univ, Nashville; Univ Ill, Urbana. *Exhib:* Contemporary African-American Crafts, Brooks Mem Art Mus, 79; Power Objects: Ancient & to the Future, Howard Univ Art Gallery, 80; Dimensions & Directions: Black Artists of the South, Miss Art Mus, 80; Forever Free: Art by African-American Women, 1862-1980, Joslyn Art Mus, Montgomery Mus Fine Arts, Indianapolis Mus & others, 81-82; Magic of Clay, Calif Mus Afro-Am Hist & Cult, Los Angeles, 82; Traditional Crafts, Mus Nat Ctr Afro-Am Artists, Boston, 82; and others. *Collections Arranged:* Florida Craftsmen, 73, Impact 79: Afro-American Women Artists, 79 & Tallahassee Tribute, 81, Fla A&M Univ Art Gallery. *Teaching:* Asst prof ceramics & drawing, Miami-Dade Community Col, 68-73; adj prof art, Miami Exten, Shaw Univ, 72-74; assoc prof ceramics, Fla A&M Univ, 73- *Awards:* Award Ceramic Sculpture, Fiftieth Anniversary Exhib, Otis Art Inst, 69; Blue Ribbon Ceramic Sculpture, Clay Glaze Miami 70, Metrop Mus & Art Ctr, Miami, 70; Best in Show, Clay Works 72, Grove House Gallery, Miami, 72. *Bibliog:* Ellen A Ashdown (auth), Afro-Raku: The ceramics of Yvonne & Curtis Tucker, Black Art Int Quart, winter 79 & The ceramics of Yvonne & Curtis Tucker, Art-Craft, 2-3/80. *Mem:* Fla Arts Coun Afro-Am Affairs (rec secy, 81-82); Nat Conf Artists; Kuumba Artists Asn Fla; Nat Conf Educ Ceramic Arts; founding mem Harambee Arts Coun. *Media:* Clay, Mixed Media. *Res:* African and Afro-American folklore; Black art of the South; Black aesthetics; folk art. *Publ:* Illusr, Le theme de la violence, African Arts, Arts d'Afrique, Vol 1, No 1, 67; contribr, African, Indian & Oriental Influences in the Aesthetics of Two Contemporary Craftspeople: First National African-American Crafts Conference: Select Writings, Shelby State Community Col, 80. *Dealer:* Vermont Ave Gallery 1910 Vermont Ave Washington DC 20001. *Mailing Add:* 3007 Kevin St Tallahassee FL 32301

EFRAT, BENNI
SCULPTOR, PAINTER
b Lebanon, Aug 13, 36; Israeli citizen. *Work:* Guggenheim Mus, Mus Mod Art, New York; Albright-Knox Art Gallery, Buffalo, NY; Stedelijk Mus, Amsterdam, Holland; Israel Mus, Jerusalem. *Comn:* Barbara (sculpture), Nelson Rockefeller, Albany, NY, 72; sculpture, Haifa Auditorium, Israel, 73. *Exhib:* Paris Biennale, France, 65-69; one-man shows, Concrete, Israel Mus, 72, On Paper, Stedelijk Mus, 74; Palais des Beaux Arts, Brussels, Belg, 76; Whitney Mus Am Art, New York, 77; Dokumenta 6, Kassel, WGer, 77 & Wadsworth Atheneum, Hartford, Conn, 78. *Awards:* Sandberg Found Prize, 71. *Bibliog:* Barbara Reise (auth), article, Studio Int, 69; R Pincus-Witten (auth), article, Arts Mag, 77. *Mailing Add:* 280-290 Lafayette St New York NY 10012

EGELI, PETER EVEN
PAINTER, ILLUSTRATOR
b Miami, Fla, Apr 19, 34. *Study:* Corcoran Sch Art; Md Inst, BFA; Art Students League; George Washington Univ; 3 yrs study with Jacques Maroger. *Work:* US Dept Agriculture; US State Dept; US District Court, Washington, DC; Maryland State Capitol; Maryland Senate Office Bldg. *Comn:* Portrait of Bayless Manning, Coun Foreign Relations, 78; portrait of Dr Thomas Bonner, Union Col, 79; Jerry McAfee, Gulf Oil Co, 81; James Higgins, Mellon Bank, 81; and others. *Exhib:* Two-man show, Md Fedn Arts, Annapolis, 70; one-man show, Bendann Art Galleries, Baltimore, 74; Franklin Mint Distinguished Am Marine Painting, Media, Pa, 74; 3rd Ann Exhib, Am Soc Marine Artists, 80-83. *Pos:* Illusr, Marine Corps Inst, Washington, DC, 53-56. *Teaching:* Instr painting, St Mary's Col of Md, 61-67. *Awards:* Gold Medal for Distinguished Am Marine Painting, Franklin Mint, 75; Best of Show, Mystic Int Marine Art Show, 81. *Bibliog:* Bonnie Ayres (auth), Portrait of Peter Egeli, Md Mag, 71. *Mem:* Am Soc Marine Artists. *Media:* Oil, Watercolor. *Res:* 17th century English ships, 19th and early 20th century Chesapeake Bay craft. *Dealer:* Bendann Art Galleries 105 E Baltimore St Baltimore MD 21202; Portraits Inc 41 E 57th St New York NY 10022. *Mailing Add:* Westbank Drayden MD 20630

EGLESON, JIM (JAMES DOWNEY)
PRINTMAKER, PAINTER
b Capelton, PQ, Mar 12, 07; US citizen. *Study:* Swarthmore Col, BS, 29; Mass Inst Technol, 29-30; apprenticeship with Jose Clemente Orozco, Mex, 35-36. *Work:* Pub Lib Print Collection, Metrop Mus Art, New York; Addison Gallery Am Art, Mass; Fairfield Univ. *Comn:* 12 panel frescoes, Swarthmore Col, 38; fresco lobby, US Post Off, Marysville, Ohio, US Treas Dept, 39-40. *Exhib:* one-man shows, Mattatuck Mus, Waterbury, Conn, 76 & Dreck Gallery, New Orleans, 79; Connecticut Printmakers-200 Years, Bridgeport, 75; Slater Mus, Norwich, Conn, 77; Metrop Mus & Art Ctr, Miami, Fla, 77; and others. *Pos:* News artist, CBS-TV, 48-50; freelance sci illusr, Sci Am Mag, McGraw-Hill & others, 50- *Teaching:* Instr intaglio, Silvermine Guild Artists, 72- *Awards:* Prize, New Haven Festival of Arts, 68; Purchase Prize, Springfield Col, 69; Anonymous Prize, Nat Acad Design Ann, 71. *Mem:* Soc Am Graphic Artists; Conn Acad Fine Arts; Silvermine Guild Artists. *Dealer:* Assoc Am Artists 663 Fifth Ave New York NY 10022. *Mailing Add:* 22 Dock Rd Norwalk CT 06854

EGLITIS, LAIMONS
PAINTER, EDUCATOR
b Asite, Latvia, Nov 15, 29; US citizen. *Study:* With Joblovskis, 46-47; Tyler Sch Art, BFA, 69, MFA(fel), 71. *Work:* Philadelphia Mus Art; Virginia Beach Art Ctr Collection; Ottawa Art Collection; Albright Col Collection. *Exhib:* New Directions, Civic Ctr Mus, Philadelphia, 71; New Acquisitions, Philadelphia Mus Art, 71; Baltimore Film Festival Invitational, Baltimore Mus Art, 75; Md Regional Water Color, Johns Hopkins Univ, 75 & 80; Bicentennial Events, Univ Pa Mus, 76; Overseas Artists, Riga Mus, Latvia, 81. *Teaching:* Assoc prof art, Catonsville Community Col, 71- *Awards:* Hon Award Visual Arts, Latvian Global Cult Found, 73; Bronze Medal Award, Md Regional Watercolor Exhib, 80; and many others. *Bibliog:* Arnolds Treibergs (auth), Laimons Eglitis--a painter in exile, Latvju Maksla, Latvian Inst, 12/75. *Media:* Oils, Watercolors. *Mailing Add:* 8 Arbutus Ave Catonsville MD 21228

EGRI, RUTH (RUTH EGRI HOLDEN)
PAINTER
b New York, NY, April 23, 11. *Study:* Nat Acad Design, New York, 26; Art Students League, New York, 32; Master Inst Roerich Mus, scholar, 34. *Work:* Del Art Mus, Univ Del, Wilmington; Du Pont Co; Blue Cross & Blue Shield Del; pvt collections of Greta Garbo & William Smith. *Comn:* Painting, Works Proj Admin, Lincoln Hosp, Bronx, 38. *Exhib:* Lynch Scene, Mus Mod Art, New York, 41; Corcoran Gallery Art, 43; NJ State Mus, 50; Girl With Bird, Isaac Delgado Muss, New Orleans, 57; solo exhib, Philadelphia Art Alliance, 75 & Ware Gallery, Arden, Del, 81. *Bibliog:* Articles, Del Today Mag, 76 & Am Artist, 12/77; Twenty Figure Painters and How They Work, Watson-Guptill, 79. *Media:* Acrylic, Pen and Ink. *Mailing Add:* 301 Andross Rd Wilmington DE 19809

EGRI, TED
SCULPTOR, PAINTER
b New York, NY May 22, 13. *Study:* Master Inst Roerich Mus, dipl, 31-34; Duncan Phillips Mem Gallery Art Sch, 42; Hans Hofmann Sch Art, New York & Provincetown, Mass, 48. *Work:* William Rockhill Nelson Mus, Kansas City, Mo; Mus NMex, Santa Fe; Simon Wiesenthal Holocaust Mus, Los Angeles; Roswell Mus, NMex; Northern Iowa Univ; and others. *Comn:* Fountain, Exec Life Bldg, Beverly Hills, Calif, 66; monument on pedestal, City Albuquerque, NMex, 69; menorah & eternal light, Temple Shalom, Dallas, Tex, 72; 8ft mem, Temple Sinai, Denver, 76; 10 sculptures, Temple B'Nai Israel, Albuquerque, 79. *Exhib:* Colorado Springs Fine Arts Ctr, Colo, 50 & 52; Stables Gallery, 53-81; Pa Acad Fine Arts Ann, Philadelphia, 53; Art: USA 58, Madison Sq Garden, New York, 58; Religious Art Western World, 58 & Southwestern Art Show, 60, Dallas Mus Fine Arts, Tex; Roswell Mus, NMex, 58, 72 & 81; Shidoni 6th & 7th Ann Outdoor Show, Tesuque NMex, 80 & 81; and others. *Teaching:* Instr oil painting & life drawing, Kansas City Art Inst, 48-50; lectr art sculpture, life drawing & painting, Univ Wyo, 59-60; vis lectr art, Univ Ill, 60-61; Nat Endowment Arts artist-in-residence, Taos Co Schs, 72-74; lectr, Las Palomas, Taos Art Asn & freelance. *Awards:* A I Friedman Award, Audubon Artists Ann, 47; Top Award for Sculpture & Honorable Mention for Drawing, Mus NMex, 65; Top Award for Sculpture, Mus NMex Five-State Regional, 69. *Bibliog:* Louis G Redstone

(auth), Art in Architecture; John Baldwin (auth), Contemporary Sculpture Techniques; John Rood (auth), Sculpture with a Torch; and others. *Mem:* Artists Equity Asn (nat vpres, 67-68 & 71-72); Taos Art Asn. *Media:* All Media. *Dealer:* Galeria Sigala Taos NM 87571. *Mailing Add:* N of El Prado Taos NM 87571

EGUCHI, YASU
PAINTER
b Japan, 1938. *Study:* Horie Art Acad, Japan, 58-65. *Work:* Frye Art Mus, Seattle; Heidenheim, WGermany; Giengen, WGermany; Am Embassy, Paris; and others. *Comn:* Paintings & relief, Sandpiper Golf Course, Santa Barbara, Calif, 72; painting, Deer Valley, Park City, Utah, 81; collage, Eye Bank Sight Restoration Inc, 81. *Exhib:* Austin Gallery, Scottsdale, Ariz, 68-83; City of Heidenheim, WGer, 80; Everson Mus Art, Syracuse, NY, 80; Nat Acad Design, New York, 80-83; Artique Ltd, Anchorage, Alaska, 81-83; and many others. *Awards:* Artist of the Year Award, Santa Barbara Arts Coun, 79; Honorary City Award, Heidenheim, WGer, 80; Adolph & Clara Obrig Prize, Nat Acad Design, 83. *Bibliog:* America's sunset coast, Nat Geographic, 78; article, Arts Mag, 78; article, Santa Barbara Mag, 78; article, American Artist, 80. *Mem:* Nat Acad Design, New York. *Media:* Watercolor, Oil. *Publ:* Auth, Der Brenz Entlang, City of Heidenheim and Austin Gallery, 80. *Mailing Add:* PO Box 30206 Santa Barbara CA 93130

EHRESMANN, DONALD LOUIS
HISTORIAN, EDUCATOR
b Newark, NJ, Oct 11, 37. *Study:* Rutgers Univ, BA, 59; NY Univ, MA, 63, PhD, 66; study with Willibald Sauerlander & Wolfgang Lotz. *Teaching:* Asst prof & chmn dept art hist, Bloomfield Col, NJ, 64-69; assoc prof art hist, State Univ NY Col Brockport, 69-71; assoc prof art hist, Univ Ill, Chicago Circle, 71-, chmn dept art hist, 73-77. *Awards:* Fritz Thyssen Found Res Fel, Ger Nat Mus, Nurenberg, WGer, 63-64; Alexander von Humboldt Found Res fel, Ger Nat Mus, Nurenberg, WGer, 67-68. *Mem:* Col Art Asn Am; Mid-West Art Hist Soc. *Res:* Medieval art and architecture; fine arts bibliography. *Publ:* Auth, articles & rev, Art Bull, Art J & Art Quart, 68-; auth, Fine Arts--A Bibliographic Guide to Basic Reference Works, Histories and Handbooks, 75, 2nd ed, 79; auth, Applied and Decorative--A Bibliographic Guide to Basic Reference Works, Histories and Handbooks, 77; auth, Architecture--A Bibliographic Guide to Basic Reference Works, Histories & Handbooks, 83. *Mailing Add:* 217 N Third St Geneva IL 60134

EHRLICH, GEORGE
HISTORIAN
b Chicago, Ill, Jan 28, 25. *Study:* Univ Ill-Urbana, BS, 49, MFA, 51, PhD, 60. *Pos:* Chmn dept art & art hist, Univ Mo-Kansas City, 64-75. *Teaching:* Prof art hist, Univ Mo-Kansas City, 54- *Mem:* Mid-Am Col Art Asn (pres, 75); Col Art Asn Am; Soc Archit Historians (pres, Mo Valley chap, 71 & 72); Landmarks Commission, Kansas City, Mo. *Res:* Architectural history of Kansas City, Missouri; interrelationship of art to science and technology. *Publ:* Auth, Robert Henri and Sissy, Ga Mus Art Bulletin, 76; auth, George Caleb Bingham as ethnographer: A variant view of his genre works, Am Studies, fall 78; auth, Kansas City, Missouri: An Architectural History, 1826-1976, Hist Kansas City Found, 79; Partnership practice and the professionalization of architecture in Kansas City, Mo, Mo Hist Rev, 7/80; auth, An atypical Walt Kuhn watercolor, Source, Notes in Hist Art, spring 82. *Mailing Add:* 5505 Holmes Kansas City MO 64110

EICHEL, EDWARD W
PAINTER, DRAFTSMAN
b Brooklyn, NY, June 8, 32. *Study:* Art Inst Chicago, BFA(G & I Brown Fel), 58; Oskar Kokoschka Acad, Salzburg, Austria, 59. *Work:* Lyman Allyn Mus, New London, Conn; New York Drawing Soc. *Exhib:* Young Painters Int Biennale, Mus Mod Art, Paris, France, 61; Animal Drawings from the 15th to 20th Centuries, Seiferheld Gallery, New York, 62; Drawing & Print Club Exhib, Detroit Inst Art, Mich, 66; Painters & Sculptors 27th Ann, Jersey City Mus, NJ, 68; Drawings: A Reinvestigation, Joseloff Gallery, Univ Hartford, Conn, 75; 156th Ann Exhib, Nat Acad Design, New York, 81; 43rd Anniversary Exhib, Fedn Mod Painters & Sculptors, 83. *Teaching:* Instr painting & drawing, Eastern Mich Univ, Ypsilanti, 65-66; instr drawing & illustration, Hartford Art Sch, Univ Hartford, Conn, 81-82. *Awards:* Tiffany Found Grant, 67; 27th NJ Ann Medal Merit, Syndicate Mag, 68. *Bibliog:* Sketches of a journey: Israel on the line of a pen, L'Arche, Paris, 7/61; Stuart Hilton (auth), Medal of merit in New Jersey Annual, Today's Art, 12/68. *Mem:* Fedn Mod Painters & Sculptors; Westbeth Artists Community; Creativity Laboratories (dir, 70-); Am Artist-Therapist Asn (hon bd mem, 79-). *Media:* Oil, Watercolor; Pencil, Pen & Ink. *Publ:* Illusr, The Glass Cage: The Eichmann Trial, Hakibbutz Hameuchad, 62; illusr, Israel Sketchbook, Dvir, 62; illusr, The Beast Book, Harper & Row, 64. *Dealer:* Allan Stone Gallery 48 E 86th Street New York NY 10028. *Mailing Add:* Studio A-1106 463 West St New York NY 10014

EICHENBERG, FRITZ
ILLUSTRATOR, PRINTMAKER
b Cologne, Ger, Oct 24, 01; US citizen. *Study:* State Acad Graphic Arts, Leipzig, MFA, 23; Southeastern Mass Univ, hon degree, 72; Univ RI, hon degree, 74; Pratt Inst, hon degree, 76; Calif Col Arts & Crafts, hon degree, 78. *Work:* Metrop Mus Art, New York; Vatican Art Collection, Rome; Rosenwald Collection, Nat Gallery Art, Washington, DC; Bibliot Nat, Paris, France; Arts of the Book Arch Collection, Yale Univ. *Comn:* Illustrations of more than one hundred classics, children's bks, comn by publ in the US & abroad. *Exhib:*One-man show, Pratt Manhattan Ctr, New York, 72, Int Exhib Found Traveling Exhibs, 80-81; Klingspor Mus, Offenbach, Ger, 75; Boston Pub Libr, Mass, 76; Assoc Am Artists, New York, 77; plus others. *Pos:* Dir emer, Pratt Graphic Arts Ctr, 56-72; mem, Pennell Comt, Libr Cong, 59-65; ed, Artist's Proof Ann, Pratt Inst, 60-72; sr adv, US Graphics Exhib, US Info Agency, USSR, 63; graphic survey Southeast Asia, J D Rockefeller, III Fund, 68. *Teaching:* Prof art & chmn dept, Pratt Inst, 56-63; chmn dept art, Univ RI, 66-69, mem fac art, 69-72; mem fac art, Albertus Magnus Col, 72. *Awards:* Joseph Pennell Medal, Pa Acad Fine Arts, 44; Distinguished Serv Medal, Ltd Ed Club; S F B Morse Medal, Nat Acad, 73; RI Governor's Art Award & Medal, 81. *Bibliog:* An artist's career, Idea Mag, Tokyo, Japan, 74; Kay Cassill (auth), Fritz Eichenberg, the gentle touch of humanity, Am Artists, 75; Emily Chewning (auth), Eichenberg's confessions, Print Mag, 76; and many others. *Mem:* Soc Am Graphic Artists; Nat Acad Design; Royal Soc Arts. *Media:* Graphics. *Res:* Graphic arts, printmaking, art education, art history. *Publ:* Auth & illusr, The Wood and the Graver, Clarkson N Potter, 77; auth & illusr, Yours in Peace, FOR, 77; auth & illusr, Endangered Species and Other Fables with a Twist, Stemmer House, 79; auth & illusr, Grimmelshausen's The Adventure of Simplicissimus, Limited Ed Club, 81; auth & illusr, Another Dance of Death, Abbeville Press, 82. *Dealer:* Associated American Artists 663 Fifth Ave New York NY 10022. *Mailing Add:* 142 Oakwood Dr Peace Dale RI 02883

EICHNER-DIXON, PETER
PAINTER, PRINTMAKER
b Mehring, WGer, Aug 3, 44. *Study:* Univ Erlangen, WGer, PhD(art hist, lit & philos), 80. *Work:* Wichita Art Mus, Kans; Town Burghausen, WGer; Colo Heritage Ctr Mus, Denver; Foothills Art Ctr, Golden, Colo; pvt collection of Prince Charles, London. *Exhib:* Royal Inst Painters in Watercolours, London, 80 & 81; Butler Inst Am Art Midyear Exhib, 81; Watercolor USA, Springfield Art Mus, Miss, 81; Rocky Mountain Nat Watermedia Exhib, Foothills Art Ctr, Golden, Colo, 81 & 82; Artists of America, Heritage Mus, Denver, 83; Recent Works, Wichita Art Mus, Kans, 83. *Awards:* Medal Best Painting by Non-Member, Ann Exhib Royal Inst Painters Watercolours, London, 81; First Prize, Rocky Mountain Nat Watermedia Exhib, Foothills Art Ctr, 82; Fel Worpswede, Govt Bremen, WGer, 83. *Bibliog:* Radiance of Stillness (video tape for TV), TV Studio Bad Homburg, fall 80; Bruce Wilson (auth), Contemporary watercolour, Art Mag London, England, spring 81. *Mem:* Royal Inst Painters Watercolour, London. *Media:* Watercolor, Acrylics; Lithography. *Publ:* Auth, Watermedia page, Am Artist, 5/82. *Dealer:* Carson Gallery Western Am Art 730 17th St Denver CO 80202; Joanne Lyon Gallery 525 E Cooper Ave Aspen CO 81611. *Mailing Add:* 1116 13th St Apt 2 Boulder CO 80302

EIDE, JOHN
PHOTOGRAPHER
b Minneapolis, Minn, Jan 28, 43. *Study:* Lawrence Univ, BA; Univ Minn, MFA; also with Jerome Liebling, Elaine Mayes & Allan Downs. *Exhib:* One-man shows, Photo Gallery, Portland Sch Art, 79 & Brockton Arts Ctr, Mass, 80; Cyanotypes--Boston Visual Artists Union; Thayer Acad, Braintree, Mass; Worchester Art Mus, Bowdoin Col, Brunswick, Maine, 79; and others. *Pos:* Hon cur photog, Portland Mus Art. *Teaching:* Area head photog, Portland Sch Art, 70- *Mem:* Soc Photog Educ. *Publ:* Contribr, Io Mag, Earth Geog Issue, No 2, 72. *Mailing Add:* 464 Cumberland Ave Portland ME 04101

EIDE, PALMER
SCULPTOR, DESIGNER
b Sioux Falls, SD, July 5, 06. *Study:* Augustana Col, BA; Art Inst Chicago; Harvard Univ; Yale Univ; Cranbrook Acad Art; St Olaf Col, DFA, 68. *Work:* Civic Fine Arts Ctr, Sioux Falls; Mem Art Gallery, Brookings, SDak. *Comn:* Mosaic, First Presby Church, Sioux Falls, 54; sculpture, First Lutheran Church, Sioux Falls, 62; sculpture, Jehovah Lutheran Church, St Paul, Minn, 64; sculpture, St Philips Lutheran Church, Minneapolis, 66; Augustana Col, 75; plus others. *Exhib:* Palmer Eide Retrospective Exhib, SDak Mem Art Ctr, Brookings, 77; Dakota Prairie Mus, 77; Civic Fine Arts Ctr, Sioux Falls, SDak, 77; Lee Fine Arts Ctr, Univ SDak, Vermillion, 77; Dahl Fine Arts Ctr, Rapid City, SDak, 77. *Teaching:* Prof painting, Augustana Col, 31-71, emer prof, 71-; Fulbright prof art, Nat Col Art, Lahore, WPakistan, 64-65; guest sculptor, Univ Northern Ariz, Flagstaff, spring 80 & 83. *Awards:* Award in Sculpture, Fine Arts in Serv Church, Seattle, 63; Award in Painting, 29th Ann Fall Show, Sioux City Art Ctr, 66; Governor's Award in Arts for Creative Achievement, SDak, 76. *Bibliog:* Mary Roche (auth), New ideas & inventions, New York Times, 3/14/48; Louis G Redstone (auth), Art in Architecture, McGraw, 68. *Mem:* Col Art Asn; Midwest Col Art Asn. *Media:* Oil, Acrylic; Wood, Stone. *Mailing Add:* 201 W 33rd Street Sioux Falls SD 57105

EIDELBERG, MARTIN
HISTORIAN
b New York, NY, Jan 30, 41. *Study:* Columbia Univ, BA, 61; Princeton Univ, PhD, 65. *Pos:* Ed, Decorative Arts Soc Newslett (quart mag), 78-80. *Teaching:* Prof art hist, Rutgers Univ, New Brunswick, 64- *Awards:* Robert C Smith Award, Decorative Arts Soc, 82. *Mem:* Decorative Arts Soc; Soc Archit Historians. *Res:* 18th century French painting and drawing; modern decorative arts. *Publ:* Coauth, The Arts and Crafts Movement in America, 1876-1916, Princeton Univ, 72; coauth, Japonisme-Japanese Influence on French Art, 1854-1910, Cleveland Mus, 75; auth, Watteau's Drawings: Their Use and Significance, Garland Press, 77; auth, E Colonna, Dayton Art Inst, 82; coauth, Cranbrook , A Vision of Design in America, Abrams, 82. *Mailing Add:* 15 West 72nd St New York NY 10023

EIKERMAN, ALMA
JEWELER, DESIGNER
b Pratt, Kans. *Study:* Kans State Col; Kans Univ; Columbia Univ, MA; spec study with Karl Gustav Hansen (silversmith), Baron Eric Fleming (metalsmith), Ossip Zadkine (sculptor) & Michael Wilm (goldsmith). *Work:* Smithsonian Inst, Washington, DC; Mus Contemp Crafts, New York; Sheldon Gallery Art, Univ Nebr, Lincoln; Hans Hansen Solvemedie, Kolding, Denmark; Home Galleries, Toulouse, France. *Comn:* Sterling silver plaque honoring Dean Wilfred Bain's yrs of serv to Ind Univ Music Sch, Bloomington; plus pvt comns. *Exhib:* Midwestern Crafts Exhib, Art Inst Chicago, 58; Soc NAm Goldsmiths Show, Minn Mus of Art, St Paul, 70, Renwick Gallery, Washington, DC, 74 & Henry Gallery, Univ Wash, Seattle, 77; 4th Int DeBijoux d'Art Contemporain, Toulouse, France, 73-74; Forms in Metal, 275 Yrs of Metalsmithing, Mus Contemp Crafts, New York, 75; Outstanding Jewelry Sch in USA, Nat Goldsmiths Show, Melbourne, Australia, 76; Objects USA, Smithsonian Traveling Exhib, Europe, 68-72. *Collections Arranged:* Creative Silversmithing Workshop I & II, summer 55 & 56 & Carnegie Grant for Graduate Student Experimental Silversmithing Project (with booklet & film), 68, Fine Arts Ctr, Ind Univ, Bloomington. *Teaching:* Asst prof design & jewelry, Kans State Univ, Wichita, 41-43, 45-46; head jewelry dept, Ind Univ, 47- *Awards:* Nat Endowment for the Arts Craft Award, 75; numerous travel grants for res. *Bibliog:* Lee Nordness (auth), Objects USA, Viking, 70; Phillip Morton (auth), Contemp Jewelry, Holt Rinehart & Winston, 76; Oppi Untracht (auth), Contemporary Craftsman, 78. *Mem:* Nat Soc Am Goldsmiths; Am Asn Univ Prof; Nat Soc Arts & Lett; Col Art Asn; Ind Craftsmen. *Media:* Gold; Silver; Copper, Brass. *Collection:* African sculpture, small Oriental and contemporary bronzes, enamel, ceramics, contemporary glass, paintings and prints. *Mailing Add:* 2007 E Second Ind Univ Bloomington IN 47401

EILERS, FRED (ANTON FREDERICK)
PAINTER, DESIGNER
b Wilmington, NC. *Study:* William & Mary Col, BS; Richmond Prof Inst, with Theresa Pollack. *Work:* Owensboro Mus, Ky; Old Nat Bank, Citizens Bank, Evansville; Ind State Univ; and others. *Comn:* Mural, Colonial Nat Bank, 69. *Exhib:* one-man shows, Univ Evansville, Old Gallery, Evansville, Hoosier Gallery, Indianapolis & Thor Gallery, Louisville; and others. *Pos:* Bd dirs, Evansville Mus, 58-60. *Teaching:* Instr portrait painting, Univ Evansville, 42-, instr figure drawing, 50-82. *Awards:* Bronstein Purchase Award, 60 & Graphics Purchase Award, 68, Evansville Mus; Hoosier Salon Merit Award, 65. *Media:* Oil. *Dealer:* Risley Evansville IN 47708; Lobster Pot Gallery Nantucket MA 02554. *Mailing Add:* 2140 E Chandler Ave Evansville IN 47714

EINO (EINO ANTTI ROMPPANEN)
SCULPTOR
b Mynamaki, Finland, Feb 6, 40; US citizen. *Comn:* Christ, Ga Marble Co, Tate, 66; memorial portrait, Univ Southern Calif, Los Angeles, 73; freeform marble, Sculpture Garden, Church of Perfect Liberty, Japan, 73; Sunset Vine Tower, 80; Valio, Helsinki, Finland, 80. *Exhib:* Gallerie Juarez, Los Angeles & Palm Springs, 70; Calif Expos, Sacramento, 71; Opening Exhib, Palm Springs Desert Mus, Calif, 76; one-man exhib, Nat Endowment Arts, Century City, Calif, 78; Calif Inst Technol, 79. *Teaching:* Instr sculpture, Pepperdine Univ, 69; instr TV credit course, Theta Cable, 71. *Bibliog:* Stan Pantovic (auth), The earth is shaking (Eino), The Geijutsu Seikatsu, Japan, 75; Stan Pantovic (auth), Eino: More than marble, Small World, winter 80-81; and others. *Media:* Marble. *Mailing Add:* 32926 Mulholland Hwy Malibu CA 90265

EINREINHOFER, NANCY ANNE
CURATOR, MUSEUM DIRECTOR
b Paterson, NJ, Sept 8, 43. *Study:* William Paterson Col, NJ, BA & MA, 78; apprenticed with Ivan Karp, New York, 78. *Collections Arranged:* Five Views (auth, catalog), William Paterson Col, NJ; Bladen, Kipp, Witkin (auth, catalog), 79; Illusion and Material (auth, catalog), 79; New New York (auth, catalog), 80; Language in the Visual Arts (auth, catalog), 81; Painting About Painting (auth, catalog), 81; Anti-Apocalypse (auth, catalog), 82; The Vogel Collection (auth, catalog), 82; Aspects of Contemporary Realism (auth, catalog), 83; The Great Illusionists (auth, catalog), 83. *Pos:* Dir, Ben Shahn Gallery, William Paterson Col, Wayne, NJ, 78-79, dir/cur, 79- *Res:* Contemporary art. *Mailing Add:* Ben Shahn Gallery William Paterson Col Wayne NJ 07470

EINSTEIN, GILBERT W
DEALER
b New York, NY, June 27, 42. *Study:* Columbia Univ, AB, 63, MBA, 68. *Pos:* Pres, G W Einstein Co, Inc, New York, 70- *Specialty:* Twentieth century American art. *Mailing Add:* G W Einstein Co Inc 243 E 82nd St New York NY 10028

EISENBERG, JEROME MARTIN
DEALER, COLLECTOR
b Philadelphia, Pa, July 6, 30. *Study:* Boston Univ, AB, 51; Columbia Univ, with Otto Brendel, Edith Porada & Henry Fischer, 60-63; Pa State Univ, with Jiri Frel, 69-71, PhD, 83. *Pos:* Dir, Royal-Athen Galleries, 58-; founder, Eisenberg Mus Biblical Archaeol, Louisville, 61; chmn, Herodium Archaeol Expedition Fund, 62. *Teaching:* Lectr forgery & fraud in ancient art, NY Univ, 69-70. *Bibliog:* Barbara Pollack (auth), Royal-Athena: Access to antiquities, Collectors Quart, 63. *Mem:* Archaeol Inst Am; Appraisers Asn Am. *Specialty:* Egyptian, Near Eastern, Greek, Roman, Pre-Columbian, Oriental and tribal art. *Collection:* Ancient Egyptian faience figurines; Egyptian stone vessels; South Italian pottery; Roman glass; Pre-Columbian and tribal art. *Publ:* Auth, A Guide to Roman Imperial Coins, 57; auth, Art of the Ancient, World, 65 & 67. *Mailing Add:* Royal-Athena Galleries 153 E 57th St New York NY 10022

EISENBERG, MARVIN
HISTORIAN, EDUCATOR
b Philadelphia, Pa. *Study:* Univ Pa, BA, 43; Princeton Univ, MFA, 49, PhD, 54. *Pos:* Mem, Inst for Advan Study, winter 70; mem adv comt, Ctr Advanced Study Visual Arts, Nat Gallery, Washington, DC, 79-83; mem vis comt, Freer Gallery Art, Washington, DC & Dept Fine Arts, Harvard Univ, 75-80; ed, Bulletin Mus Art & Archeol, Univ Mich, currently. *Teaching:* Instr art hist, Univ Mich, 49-53, asst prof, 54-58, assoc prof, 58-61, prof, 61-, chmn dept, 61-69; vis prof, Stanford Univ, 73. *Awards:* Guggenheim Fel, 59; Star of Solidarity, Ital Govt, 61. *Mem:* Col Art Asn Am (pres, 68-69); Benjamin Franklin Fel Royal Soc Arts. *Res:* Italian late medieval painting. *Publ:* Auth, articles on early Italian painting in journals and museum bulletins. *Mailing Add:* Dept of Hist of Art Univ of Mich Ann Arbor MI 48109

EISENBERG, SONJA MIRIAM
PAINTER
b Berlin, Ger; US citizen. *Study:* NY Univ, BA, 54; Nat Acad Sch Fine Arts, with Leon Kroll, 61; also with Daniel Dickerson, 62-68 & Sidney Delevante, in 60's. *Work:* Palm Spring Desert Mus; Fordham Univ Mus, New York; World Fedn UN Asn, New York; Archives Am Art, The Jewish Mus, New York. *Comn:* Designer, WF UNA Cachet, UN Water Conf, 77; designer mag cover, Our Planet Earth, Planetary Citizens, UN, 78; designer cover, Discovering Fire for the Second Time, Nat Conf of Christians & Jews, New York; designer cachet for United Nations, Int Year Disabled Persons. *Exhib:* One-woman shows, Galerie de Sfinx, Amsterdam, 74 & Am Mus Hayden Planetarium, New York, 80; Am Watercolor Soc 108th Ann Exhib, New York, 75; Archives of Am Art, Smithsonian Inst, 78; Betty Parsons Gallery, 81; Cathedral St John Divine, New York, 83. *Awards:* Accademia Italia delle Arti e del Lavoro, Medaglio d'Oro, 81; Gold Medal for artistic merit, Int Parliament Safety & Peace, 83. *Bibliog:* Jan deCarpentier (auth), Kijk's kunst, De Typhoon, 6/74; Gordon Brown (auth), Sonja Eisenberg, Art Mag, 4/75; Nina Brodsky (auth), Miniature Collector, 4/82. *Media:* Oil, Watercolor; Color Pencil. *Dealer:* Bodley Gallery 1063 Madison Ave New York NY 10028. *Mailing Add:* 1020 Park Ave New York NY 10028

EISENSTAT, BENJAMIN
PAINTER, ILLUSTRATOR
b Philadelphia, Pa, June 4, 15. *Study:* Fleisher Art Mem; Pa Acad Fine Arts; Albert Barnes Found. *Work:* Philadelphia Mus Art; Fleisher Art Mem, Philadelphia; Springfield Art Mus, Mo; Woodmere Gallery, Philadelphia; Jefferson Hosp, Philadelphia. *Comn:* Official painting of nuclear ship Savannah, US Maritime & NY Ship Comn, Washington, DC, 59; mural, First Bank NJ, Philadelphia, 60; mural, Provident Mutual Life Ins Co, Philadelphia, 62; mural, Burlington Co Trust Co, Moorestown, NJ, 63; mural, Oreland Episcopal Church, Pa, 70. *Exhib:* Artists for Victory, 45 & Nat Drawing Show, 55, Metrop Mus Art, New York; Watercolor USA, Springfield, Mo; Nat Acad Design Ann, New York; Am Watercolor Soc Ann, New York; Rutgers Nat Drawing Show, Rutgers Univ, Camden, NJ, 77; Ann, New York Soc Illusr, 79 & 80; and others. *Teaching:* Assoc prof painting & drawing, Philadelphia Col Art, 46-69, prof painting & drawing & chmn illustrating dept, 69-80, prof emer, 80-; instr watercolor, Philadelphia Mus Art, 62-66; instr illus, Cambridge Col Arts & Technol, Eng, 76; lectr Am illus, Royal Col Art, London, Eng, 76; lectr hist Am illus, Parsons Sch Design, NY, 76-81 & Syracuse Univ, Masters Prog, 81. *Awards:* Ann Medal Achievement, Philadelphia Watercolor Club, 62; Harrison Morris Prize, Fellowship, Pa Acad Fine Arts; Watercolor USA Prize, 72. *Bibliog:* Hugh Scott (auth), Mural on Market Street, Today Mag, 6/12/60; Henry Pitz (auth), Documentary drawings of Benjamin Eisenstat, Am Artists, 12/65. *Mem:* Am Watercolor Soc; Philadelphia Watercolor Club; Philadelphia Art Alliance (bd dirs, 62-68); Artists Equity (bd dirs, 67-71); fel Pa Acad Fine Arts (bd dirs, 55-60). *Collection:* Original illustrations. *Publ:* auth, Art of Murray Tinkelman, Southwest Art, 12/81; and others. *Dealer:* Newman Gallery 1625 Walnut St Philadelphia PA 19103; Mangel Gallery 1604 Locust St Philadelphia PA. *Mailing Add:* 438 Camden Ave Moorestown NJ 08057

EISENSTEIN, (MR & MRS) JULIAN
COLLECTORS
Mr Eisenstein b Warrenton, Mo, Apr 3, 21. *Study:* Mr Eisenstein, Harvard Univ, BS, 41, MA, 42, PhD, 48. *Pos:* Mr Eisenstein, Nat res fel, Oxford, 52-53; physicist, Nat Bureau Standards, 57-66; pres & trustee, Washington Gallery Mod Art, 61-65. *Teaching:* Mr Eisenstein, instr, Univ Wis, 48-52; from asst prof to assoc prof, Pa State Univ, 53-57; prof, George Washington Univ, 66- *Collection:* Contemporary art. *Mailing Add:* 82 Kalorama Circle NW Washington DC 20008

EISENTRAGER, JAMES A
PAINTER
b Alvord, Iowa, Sept 3, 29. *Study:* Augustana Col, Sioux Falls, SDak, BA, 51; Univ Md in Weisbaden, Ger, 52-53; Univ Northern Iowa, 55; Univ Iowa, Iowa City, MFA, 61; with Stewart Edie, Byron Burford & Mauricio Lasansky. *Work:* Univ Iowa, Iowa City; Sheldon Mem Art Gallery, Lincoln, Nebr; Millersville State Univ, Pa. *Exhib:* Ann Exhib, Springfield Art Mus, Mo, 64-72; one-man shows, Sheldon Mem Art Gallery, 66, Univ Del, Newark, 75 & Northern Ariz Univ Art Gallery, Flagstaff, 77; 31st Mid-Yr Show, Butler Inst Am Art, Youngstown, Ohio, 66; Mid-Am Exhib, William Rockhill Nelson Gallery of Art, Kansas City, Mo, 66 & 70; Mid-W Biennial, Joslyn Art

Mus, Omaha, Nebr, 66 & 70; Ten Artists West of the Mississippi, Colorado Springs Fine Art Ctr, 67. *Teaching:* Prof painting, Univ Nebr-Lincoln, 61-; prof & lectr, Vail Summer Workshop, Colo, 71-76; vis prof art, Univ Colo, Boulder, summer 67. *Awards:* Purchase Award, May Show, Sioux City Art Ctr, Iowa, 63; Best Painting Purchase Award, Nat Paper Nat Competition, Springfield Art Asn, Ill, 73; Jesse Loomis Award, Waterloo Ann, Waterloo Munic Gallery, Iowa, 73. *Mem:* Mid-Am Col Art Asn. *Media:* Polymer, Oil. *Mailing Add:* 5114 M St Lincoln NE 68510

EISINGER, HARRY
PAINTER
b Berlin, Ger, Apr 23, 32; US citizen. *Study:* Calif Sch Fine Arts, San Francisco, 57-59; also with Ralph Putzker, Nathan Oliveira & Wayne Thiebaud. *Work:* Slides, Whitney Mus, New York. *Comn:* Drawings, Territorial Gazette, San Francisco, 59; posters, Marin Co Art Ctr, Calif, 60. *Exhib:* One-man shows, Panoras Gallery, New York, 73 & Gallery 84, 77; 32nd & 33rd Nat Audubon Exhibs, Nat Acad Galleries, 74 & 75 & Allied Artists Am Exhib, 75; Gallery 84, New York, 75 & 77. *Awards:* Spinaker Award, Sausalito Mayor, Calif, 60. *Bibliog:* Herb Caen (auth), article, San Francisco Chronicle, 60. *Mem:* Allied Artists Am; Audubon Artists. *Media:* Oil. *Dealer:* Gallery 84 30 West 57th St New York NY 10019. *Mailing Add:* 330 E 19th St New York NY 10003

EISLER, LAWRENCE
PAINTER
b New York, NY, Mar 2, 19. *Study:* Brooklyn Col, BA, 40; Atelier Fernand Leger, Paris, 48-51; Acad Grande Chaumiere, Paris, cert, 53. *Comn:* Murals, US Army, Camp Lee, Va, 41. *Exhib:* WPA Artists, Metrop Mus Art, New York, 40; Galerie Beaux Arts, Paris, 51; Ecole Beaux Arts, Paris, 52; solo exhibs, Roberson Ctr Arts, Binghamton, NY, 72 & Greer Gallery, New York, 74 & 76. *Awards:* First Prize, Atelier Leger, 49 & 51. *Media:* Oil, Gouache. *Mailing Add:* c/o Washington Irving Gallery 117 E 17 St New York NY 10003

EISNER, DOROTHY (DOROTHY EISNER MCDONALD)
PAINTER, COLLAGE ARTIST
b New York, NY, Jan 17, 06. *Study:* Art Students League, 25-30; with Kenneth Hayes Miller & Boardman Robinson, 25-29; with Jack Tworkov, 49-52. *Work:* Colby Col Mus, Maine; Haughton Libr, Harvard Univ; Central Wyo Mus Art; Wichita State Univ, Kans; Whatcum Mus, Bellingham, Wash. *Exhib:* Brooklyn Mus; Corcoran Gallery Art; Chicago Art Inst; Pa Acad Fine Arts; Va Mus, Richmond; Fordham Univ, New York; Maine Coast Artists Gallery, Rockport; Skowhegan Art Gallery. *Awards:* Prize for Drawings, Dance Int, 38; Edith Penman Award, Nat Asn Women Artists, 39; Hassam Fund Purchase Award, Am Acad Arts & Lett, 76. *Bibliog:* Article, Art News, 30; Carl Little (auth), article, Arts Mag, 5/83. *Mem:* Founding mem Fedn Mod Painters & Sculptors. *Media:* Oil on Canvas. *Mailing Add:* 19 Eighth Ave New York NY 10014

EISNER, ELLIOT WAYNE
EDUCATOR
b Chicago, Ill, Mar 10, 33. *Study:* Roosevelt Univ, BA; Ill Inst Technol, MS; Univ Chicago, MA & PhD. *Teaching:* Instr art educ, Ohio State Univ, 60-61; asst prof educ, Univ Chicago, 61-65; prof educ & art, Stanford Univ, 65- *Awards:* Palmer Johnson Award, Am Educ res Asn, 67; Guggenheim Fel, 70; Sr Fulbright Fel, Australia, 79. *Mem:* Hon fel Nat Art Educ Asn (pres, 77-79); Am Educ Res Asn; Int Soc Educ Through Art. *Res:* Children's artistic development; the uses of art criticism for the study and evaluation of educational practice. *Publ:* Auth, Confronting Curriculum Reform, Little, 71; auth, Educating Vision, Macmillan, 72; auth, Conflicting Conceptions of Curriculum, McCutcheon, 76; auth, The Educational Imagination, Macmillan, 78; auth, Cognition and Curriculum, Longmans, 82. *Mailing Add:* Sch of Educ Stanford Univ Stanford CA 94305

EITELJORG, HARRISON
COLLECTOR, PATRON
b Indianapolis, Ind, Oct 1, 04. *Study:* Ind Univ Law Sch. *Mem:* Indianapolis Mus Art; Ind Art Comn; Contemp Art Soc; Decorative Arts Soc; Am Asn Mus. *Interests:* Sponsor of museum of western artifacts. *Collection:* Abstract and modern American art; school of Paris; western painting and bronzes; American Indian artifacts; African and oceanic. *Publ:* Treasures of the American West-Selections From the Collection of Harrison Eiteljorg. *Mailing Add:* 4567 Cold Spring Rd Indianapolis IN 46208

EITINGON, BRIGITTE
DEALER
b Paris, France, Sept 12, 27. *Study:* NY Univ, BA, 46; Sorbonne, Paris, Lic Lett, 48; Ecol du Louvre, Paris, dipl hist art, 48. *Pos:* Owner, Brigitte Eitingon Fine Arts Ltd, New York. *Specialty:* Nineteenth and twentieth century masters; specializing in Impressionists. *Mailing Add:* 245 E 63rd St New York NY 10021

EITNER, LORENZ E A
HISTORIAN, MUSEUM DIRECTOR
b Brünn, Czech, Aug 27, 19; US citizen. *Study:* Duke Univ, AB, 40; Princeton Univ, MFA, 48, PhD, 52. *Collections Arranged:* Masterdrawings, Guggenheim Mus, New York & Univ Gallery, Univ Minn, 60; Gericault, Los Angeles Co Mus, Detroit Inst Art & Philadelphia Mus Art, 71-72; numerous art exhibs at Stanford Mus. *Pos:* Dir, Stanford Mus, 63- *Teaching:* Prof art, Univ Minn, 49-63; prof art & chmn dept, Stanford Univ, 63- *Mem:* Col Art Asn Am (vpres, dir, 56-71 & 76-). *Res:* European painting of the latter half

of the eighteenth century and the beginning of the nineteenth century. *Publ:* Auth, Introduction to Art, Burgess, 60; auth, Gericault, Univ Chicago, 60; auth, Neoclassicism and Romanticism, Prentice-Hall, 69; auth, Gericault's Raft of the Medusa, Phaidon, 72; auth, Gericault, His Life and Work, Cornell Univ Press, 83. *Mailing Add:* Dept of Art Stanford Univ Stanford CA 94305

EKDAHL, JANIS KAY
LIBRARIAN
b Topeka, Kans, Dec 7, 46. *Study:* Occidental Col, BA, 68; Columbia Univ, MLS, 69. *Pos:* Art librn, Vassar Col, Poughkeepsie, NY, 71-81; asst dir, Mus Mod Art Libr, New York, 81- *Mem:* Art Libr Soc North Am (Eastern regional rep, 81-83); Art Libr Soc New York; Col Art Asn; Am Libr Asn. *Interests:* Modern and contemporary art; sculpture; American art and architecture. *Publ:* Auth, American Sculpture: A Guide to Information Sources, Gale, 77. *Mailing Add:* Mus Mod Art Libr 11 West 53rd St New York NY 10019

ELDER, DAVID MORTON
SCULPTOR
b Windsor, Ont, July 3, 36; US citizen. *Study:* Wittenberg Univ, BA, 57; Ohio State Univ Grad Sch, MA, 61. *Work:* Denver Art Mus, Colo; Long Beach Art Mus, Calif. *Comn:* Sculpture (metal), Gloria Christi Chapel, Valparaiso Univ, 62, St Paul Lutheran Church, Glenn Bermie, Md, 63, Coconut Grove Ambassador Hotel, Los Angeles, 69 & Barnsdall Park, Los Angeles, 74; sculpture (resin), Pac Home Burbank, 74. *Exhib:* Long Beach Mus Art, 66, 70 & 71; Calif Sky Scape Show, Calif Col Arts & Crafts, Oakland, 69; Calif Landscape Show, La Jolla Mus Art, 69; San Francisco Centennial Show, De Young Mus, 71; Last Plastics Show, Calif Inst Arts, Valencia, 72. *Teaching:* Asst prof sculpture, Calif State Univ, Los Angeles, 68-71; prof sculpture, Calif State Univ, Northridge, 71-, chmn dept 3-D art, 72-, assoc dean, Sch Arts, 74- *Awards:* Fourth Ann Long Beach Mus First Prize, 66; Purchase Award Comn, Southwestern Col, 67; Artist of the Year, Pasadena Arts Coun, 71. *Media:* Bronze, Polyester Resin. *Dealer:* Orlando Gallery 17037 Ventura Blvd Encino CA 91316. *Mailing Add:* Sch Arts Calif State Univ Northridge CA 91330

ELDER, MULDOON
PAINTER, DEALER
b Los Angeles, Calif, June 24, 35. *Work:* Long Beach Mus Art; Downey Mus Art; Pentagon Collection; Syntex Collection. *Exhib:* Long Beach Mus Art, 57; Houston Mus, 58; Dallas Mus Art, 58; Downey Mus Art, 60; San Francisco Mus Art, 69. *Pos:* Owner, Vorpal Gallery, presently. *Awards:* Purchase Awards, Long Beach Mus Art, Pentagon Collection & Downey Mus Art. *Media:* Multimedia. *Mailing Add:* c/o Vorpal Gallery 393 Grove St San Francisco CA 94102

ELDERFIELD, JOHN
HISTORIAN, CURATOR
b Yorkshire, Eng, Apr 25, 43. *Study:* Univ Leeds, BA & MPhil; Courtauld Inst Art, Univ London, PhD. *Collections Arranged:* Morris Louis (auth, catalog), London Arts Coun Gt Brit, 74; The Wild Beasts: Fauvism and Its Affinities (auth, catalog), 76, European Paintings from Swiss Collections: Post-Impressionism to World War II (auth, catalog), 76, Matisse in the Collection of the Museum of Modern Art (auth, catalog), 78, The Masterworks of Edvard Munch (auth, catalog), 79 & New Work on Paper (auth, catalog), 81, Mus Mod Art, New York. *Pos:* Harkness fel, Yale Univ, New Haven, Conn, 70-72; Guggenheim Found Fel, 72-74 & Studio Int Mag, 73-75; cur painting & sculpture, Mus Mod Art, New York, 75-, dir dept drawings, 80- *Teaching:* Lectr hist art, Winchester Sch of Art, Eng, 66-70. *Mem:* Int Asn Art Critics; Col Art Asn; fel Royal Soc Arts. *Res:* Twentieth century art. *Publ:* Ed, Hugo Ball (auth), The Flight from Time--A Dada Diary, Viking, 75; The Cutouts of Henri Matisse, Braziller, 78. *Mailing Add:* Mus Mod Art 11 W 53rd St New York NY 10019

ELDREDGE, CHARLES CHILD, III
MUSEUM DIRECTOR, HISTORIAN
b Boston, Mass, Apr 12, 44. *Study:* Amherst Col, BA, 66; Univ Minn, PhD, 71. *Collections Arranged:* The Arcadian Landscape: Nineteenth Century Am Painters in Italy (coauth & ed, catalogue), 72, Marsden Hartley Lithographs and Related Works (auth, catalogue), 72, Gene Swenson: Retrospective for a Critic (contribr & ed, catalogue), 71, John Ward Lockwood, 1894-1963 (auth, catalogue), 74, Am Imagination & Symbolist Painting (auth, catalogue) & Charles Walter Stetson: Color and Fantasy (auth, catalogue), 82, Helen Foresman Spencer Mus Art, Univ Kans, Lawrence. *Pos:* Cur collections, Univ Kans Mus Art, Lawrence, 70-71, dir & chief cur, Helen Foresman Spencer Mus Art (formerly Univ Kans Mus of Art), 71-; vis mus scholar, Nat Collection Fine Arts, Smithsonian Inst, 79, dir, Nat Mus Am Art, 82-; ed, Art J, 79-81. *Teaching:* Prof art hist, Univ Kans, 70-82. *Awards:* Smithsonian Fel, 79; Fulbright Scholar/New Zealand, 83. *Mem:* Am Asn of Mus; Asn of Art Mus Dirs (treas, 81-82); Col Art Asn; Mid-Continent Am Studies Asn (mem ed bd, 73-77). *Res:* American and 19th-20th century European art. *Publ:* Contribr, Works by John Rood: A Memorial Exhibition, Univ Minn, 74. *Mailing Add:* Nat Mus Art Smithsonian Inst Washington DC 20560

ELDREDGE, MARY AGNES
SCULPTOR
b Hartford, Conn, Jan 21, 42. *Study:* Vassar Col, with Concetta Scaravaglione & Juan Nickford, BA; Pius XII Inst, Florence, Italy, with Josef Gudics, MFA. *Work:* Dartmouth Col Collection. *Comn:* Stations of the Cross, Rising Christ, Church of Sts Joachim & Ann, Staten Island, NY, 76; Madonna & Child, Sanctuary Lamp, Mercy Hosp Chapel, Springfield, Mass, 76-77; Madonna &

Child, Calvary Hosp Chapel, Bronx, NY, 78; David, Church of the Good Shepherd, Lake Wales, 79; Ambry, Shrine of the Most Blessed Sacrament, Washington, DC, 81-82; and others. *Exhib:* Nat Arts Club Religious Art Exhib, New York, 66; Acad Artists Asn Nat Exhib, Springfield, Mass, 67; Modern Art and the Religious Experience, Fifth Ave Presby Church, New York, 68; 6th Biennial Nat Religious Art Exhib, Cranbrook Acad Art, 69; 42nd Nat Interfaith Conf Relig, Art and Archit, Chicago, 81; and others. *Awards:* Therese Richard Mem Prize, Nat Arts Club, 66; Acad Artists Asn Award, 67; Staten Island Chamber of Com Award, 77. *Mem:* Southern Vt Artists, Inc; Vt Coun on the Arts. *Media:* Multimedia. *Dealer:* Contemp Christian Art Inc 217 E 66th St New York NY 10021; Gallery 2 Woodstock VT 05091. *Mailing Add:* 520 Parker Hill Rd Springfield VT 05156

ELDREDGE, STUART EDSON
PAINTER
b South Bend, Ind, July 1, 02. *Study:* Dartmouth Col, AB; Art Students League, with Kimon Nicolaides; Beaux Arts Inst, New York. *Work:* Butler Inst Am Art, Youngstown, Ohio; Springfield Art Mus, Mass; Southern Vt Artists, Inc, Manchester; Dartmouth Col, Hanover, NH; Robert Hull Fleming Mus, Burlington, Vt. *Comn:* Murals, First Nat Bank, Springfield; mural, Springfield Hosp; Stations of Cross, St Joseph's Church, Chester, Vt; murals in textile bldg, World's Fair, New York, 39. *Exhib:* 9th Ann Print Exhib, Libr Cong, Washington, DC, 51; Philadelphia Watercolor Club, 52 & 53; Ind Artists 50th Ann Invitational, 57; Am Watercolor Soc, 61 & 63; plus others. *Teaching:* Instr drawing & painting, Cooper Union, 32-40 & Arts Students League Summer Sch, 34 & 35; prof drawing, Pius XII Inst, Florence, Italy, summer 64. *Awards:* Tiffany Fel, 32. *Mem:* Nat Soc Mural Painters; Southern Vt Artists (trustee, 50-78); Springfield Art & Hist Soc (trustee, 59-74). *Media:* Watercolor, Oil. *Dealer:* Gallery 2 Woodstock VT 05091. *Mailing Add:* 520 Parker Hill Rd Springfield VT 05156

ELENA, MARIA
PAINTER, PRINTMAKER
b New York, NY, May 5, 28. *Study:* Inst Nac Belles Artes Cuernavaca, with Alejo Jacobo, 59-61. *Work:* Mus Pintores Mex, Sonora; Mus Centro Medico, Mus Ciudad Mex, Mexico, DF; Mus Arte San Pedro, San Jose, Costa Rica; Mus Arte, San Salvador. *Comn:* Portraits, Luis Echeverria, 70, Gustavo Diaz Ordaz & Adolfo Lopez Mateas, Partido Revolucionario Inst, Mexico City, Felipe Rivera Crespo, City Cuernavaca, Morelos, Mex, 70 & Jack Nicklaus, Tabachines Golf Club, Cuernavaca, 72. *Exhib:* Friends Acapulco, Presidente Hotel, Mex, 68-82; Ferea de Arte, Am Embassy, Mexico City, 70-79; solo exhib, Mus Arte, San Salvador, 75; Las Calles de Cuernavaca, Jardin Borda, Mex, 77; Mus Art, Univ Ore, Eugene, 78; and others. *Awards:* First Prize, Dia Muerte, City Mexico, 69, Feria de la Flor, City Cuernavaca, Mex, 69-71 & Friends Acapulco, 69, 71, 74 & 75. *Mem:* Womans Caucus Art. *Media:* Acrylic, Oil. *Dealer:* Wollheim Rosequist 2843 N Cambell Tucson AZ 85719. *Mailing Add:* Apdo D-85 Acapulco 39359 Mexico

ELIAS, HAROLD JOHN
PAINTER, EDUCATOR
b Cleveland, Ohio, Mar 12, 20. *Study:* Art Inst Chicago, BFA, 50, MFA, 61; Mich State Univ; DePaul Univ; Univ Mich; Hamilton State Univ, Hon Dr, 73. *Work:* Ill State Mus, Springfield; Massillon Mus, Massillon, Ohio; Univ Idaho, Moscow, Idaho; Univ Ill, Champaign; Upjohn Collection, Kalamazoo, Mich. *Comn:* Michigan Scenes (painting), Fraternal Order Eagles Lodge, Muskegon, Mich, 53; Michigan Scenes (painting), Round Lake Lodge, Watervliet, Mich, 64; Medical Mobile, Mercy Hospital, Benton Harbor, Mich, 66; Trilogy Mobile, Catholic Church, Muskegon Heights, Mich, 67; wall murals, mobile & construction, Kilgore Col, Longview, Tex, 79. *Exhib:* American Art Today, Metrop Mus Art, New York, 50; Pittsburgh Int, Pa Acad Art, 51; Int Sculpture Competition, Brussels Mus, Belgium, 53; Baltimore Nat, Baltimore Mus, Md, 53; Detroit Exhib, Detroit Inst Art, Mich, 55; Creative Gallery Nat, New York, 55; US Embassies, worldwide, 76-78; over 200 one-man shows from coast to coast. *Pos:* Asst & acting dir, Hackley Art Gallery, Muskegon, Mich, 52-57; comnr, Tex Comn Arts, 70-77. *Teaching:* Asst prof art, Ambassador Col, Tex, 73-77, Stephen F Austin State Univ, 77-78; instr drawing, watercolor & advert art, Kilgore Col, Tex, 78-80; instr drawing & painting, Tarrant Co Jr Col, Tex, 80. *Awards:* Best of Show, Western Mich Artists, Grand Rapids Art Gallery, Mich, 52; Schiller Award, Mich Exhib, South Bend Art Gallery, Ind, 65. *Bibliog:* Esquire Exhib rev, Art News, 50; New talent, Art Am, 57. *Mem:* Tex Fine Arts Asn. *Media:* Oils, Watercolor. *Mailing Add:* 6008 Westridge Lane #512 Ft Worth TX 76116

ELIASON, SHIRLEY (SHIRLEY ELIASON HAUPT)
PAINTER, EDUCATOR
b Kanawha, Iowa. *Study:* Art Inst of Chicago, BAE; Univ Iowa, MFA with Mauricio Lasansky & James Lechay; Fulbright Scholar, Courtauld Inst of Art, Univ London, 2 yrs. *Work:* Des Moines Art Ctr, Iowa; Grinnell Col, Iowa; Yale Univ Art Gallery; Libr of Cong, Washington, DC; KWWL Collection, Waterloo, Iowa. *Comn:* Pvt comns. *Exhib:* Pratt Int Miniature Print Exhib, New York; Young Am Printmakers, Mus of Mod Art, New York; Nat Black & White Exhib, Erie, Pa; Joslyn Art Mus Biennial, Omaha, Nebr; Int Print Exhib, Libr of Cong; and numerous others. *Collections Arranged:* Am Prints 1950-1960 (auth, catalogue), Yale Univ Art Gallery, 60; and others. *Pos:* Docent, Yale Univ Art Gallery, 58-59, asst cur of prints, 59-61. *Teaching:* Instr, Univ Iowa, 54-55; prof drawing, painting & printmaking, Univ Northern Iowa, 66-, chairperson grad studies in art, 79-81, acting head, fall 82. *Awards:* Purchase Award, Iowa Artists, Des Moines Art Ctr, 54 & 56; Best-in-Show, All-Iowa, KWWL, 68. *Mem:* Midwest Col Art Asn; Col Art Asn. *Publ:* Auth, What makes a good studio teacher?, Col Art J, 56; Illusr (cover), The Burden of Memory, 69 & Iowa, Black Field, Bernini, 74, NAm Rev; Illusr, Iowa Review, 81; illusr & auth, Extended Outlook, Macmillan, 82; illusr, The bear who slept with his feet up, NAm Review, 83. *Mailing Add:* 803 Iowa Cedar Falls IA 50613

ELIASOPH, PAULA
PAINTER, WRITER
b New York, NY, Oct 26, 1895. *Study:* Pratt Inst; Columbia Univ; Art Students League; murals with Augustus Vincent Tack; paint, materials, technique with Dr Maximillian Toch. *Work:* Metrop Mus Art, New York; Brooklyn Mus, NY; New York Pub Libr; Libr Cong; Franklin D Roosevelt Libr; plus many others. *Comn:* Tree of Life, YMHA, 57; Tree of Life, Hillcrest Hollis Jewish Ctr, Jamaica, 60. *Exhib:* Am Watercolor Soc, 30-79; Philadelphia Soc Etchers, 40; Fedn Mod Painters & Sculptors, 40-71 & 79-80; Am Fedn Art Traveling Exhib, 55-57; Inst Mod Art, Boston, Mass, 64; plus many others. *Pos:* Secy, League of Am Pen Women, 50; researcher, Student Counseling Bur, Psychol Ctr, Univ Minn, 67-68; mem comt study art in educ, NY Univ, 69. *Teaching:* Instr pvt classes, 41-; instr art, Forest Hills Jewish Ctr, 49-66; instr & supvr art & art hist, Yeshiva of Cent Queens, 49-66. *Awards:* Award for Interior, Long Island Art League; Etchings of Trees in Central Park, YMHA & YMHA, 43, Award, Alexander Kriesel Art Gallery, 55. *Bibliog:* Carlyle Burrows (auth), On Paula Eliasoph, New York Herald Tribune, 31; E C Sherburne (auth), Form rhythms in space, Christian Sci Monitor, 32; Edward Alden Jewell (auth), On exhibition by Paula Eliasoph, New York Times, 32-57; plus others. *Mem:* Fedn Mod Painters & Sculptors (incorporating trustee, 41-, treas, 41-44); life mem Am Watercolor Soc; life mem Art Students League; life mem Long Island Art League. *Media:* Multimedia. *Publ:* Auth, Etchings & Drypoints of Childe Hassam, Smithsonian Inst, 33; auth, art educ articles in Yeshiva of Cent Queens Bull, 41-69; auth, article in Group Psycho Ther Mag, 68; plus others. *Mailing Add:* 83-33 Austin St Kew Gardens NY 11415

ELIOT, LUCY CARTER
PAINTER
b New York, NY. *Study:* Vassar Col, BA; Art Students League with Bridgman, Brackman, Raphael Soyer, William Von Schlegell & Kantor; Columbia Univ, with Ralph Mayer. *Work:* Rochester Mem Art Gallery, NY; Munson-Williams-Proctor Inst, Utica, NY. *Exhib:* Pa Acad Fine Arts, Philadelphia, 46, 48-50, 52 & 54; Va Biennial, Washington, DC, 47 & 51; Ringling Bros Mus, Sarasota, Fla, 58; Nat Acad Design, New York, 71 & 78; Butler Inst, Youngstown, Ohio, 65, 67, 69, 70, 72, 74 & 81; Upland Idyll, Everson Mus, Syracuse, NY, 76. *Pos:* Mem bd, Artists' Tech Res Inst, 75-79. *Teaching:* Instr painting & drawing, Occup Therapy Dept, Bronx Vet Hosp, New York, 50-52. *Awards:* Purchase Prize, Munson-Williams-Proctor Inst, 49; Painting of Indust Award, Silvermine Guild, 57; First Prize Painting, Cooperstown Art Asn, 78. *Mem:* NY Soc Women Artists (corresp secy, 70-73, pres, 73-75); Audubon Artists; Artists Equity Asn; Cooperstown Art Asn. *Media:* Oil, Casein. *Mailing Add:* 131 E 66th St New York NY 10021

ELISCU, FRANK
SCULPTOR
b New York, NY, July 13, 12. *Comn:* Inaugural medal, Pres Ford; inaugural medal, VPres Rockefeller; Astronauts, Headley Mus, Lexington, Ky; Cascade of Books (heroic bronze), James Madison Libr Cong, Washington, DC; John & Mable Ringling (portrait busts), Ringling Mus, Sarasota, Fla; and others. *Exhib:* Pa Acad Fine Arts; Conn Acad Fine Arts; Cleveland Mus Art; Springfield Mus Art; Detroit Inst Art; plus others. *Awards:* Prize, Archit League New York, 55, Silver Medal, 58; Henry Hering Award, 60; plus others. *Mem:* Fel Nat Sculpture Soc (pres, 67-70); academician Nat Acad Design; Archit League New York. *Publ:* Auth, Sculpture: Three Techniques-- Wax, Slate, Clay; auth, Direct Wax Sculpture. *Mailing Add:* 4707 Ocean Blvd Sarasota FL 33587

ELKIN, BEVERLY DAWN
DEALER, GALLERY DIRECTOR
b Chicago, Ill, Apr 23, 33. *Study:* Univ Ill, BA, 55, MA, 65. *Pos:* Co-owner & co-show mgr, House of Art, Champaign, Ill, currently. *Mem:* Prof Picture Framers Asn. *Specialty:* Contemporary midwestern American artist; painting, sculpture and ceramics. *Mailing Add:* 1103 W Green Champaign IL 61820

ELKINS, (E) LANE
EDUCATOR, CERAMIST
b McDonald Co, Mo, Mar 26, 25. *Study:* Southwest Mo State Col, BSEd(with hon); Columbia Univ, MAFA & FAEd, 50; with Marquerite Wildenhain, 56 & 63; Cranbrook Acad Art, MFA, 62. *Work:* Springfield Art Mus, Mo. *Comn:* Several jewelry comns for individuals. *Exhib:* Springfield Art Mus Ann Regional Show, 53-72; Wichita Art Asn Galleries Decorative Arts & Ceramics Exhib, 60 & 62; Ann Drawing & Sculpture Show, Ball State Univ Art Gallery, 63; American Jewelry Today, Ala Mus Fine Arts, 64; Am Craftsmen Show, Smithsonian Inst, 70. *Teaching:* Prof ceramics, Southwest Mo State Univ, 50-82, prof art, 82- *Awards:* Protective Image (cast bronze) Award, Edmund F Ball, Nat Sculpture Show, 63. *Mem:* Am Craftsman Coun; Mo Craftsman Coun. *Media:* Stoneware, Wood. *Publ:* Contribr, Walker Art Quart, spec issue, 59. *Mailing Add:* Rte 3 Box 198 Rogersville MO 65742

ELKINS, TONI MARCUS
PAINTER, DESIGNER
b Tifton, Ga, Feb 22, 46. *Study:* Boston Univ, 65-66; Univ Ga, ABJ, 68; Columbia Col, 78-80. *Work:* Parthenon Gallery, Nashville; Nancy Miller Gallery, Columbia, SC. *Exhib:* Knickerbockr Artists, Salmagundi Club, New York, 81; Birmingham Watercolor Show, Birmingham Mus, 81; Central South Art, Parthenon, Nashville, 81-83; Ga Watercolor Soc, Macon Mus, 82; Am Artists Prof League, Salmagundi Club, New York, 82; Rocky Mountain Nat, Foothills Art Ctr, Golden, Colo, 83; and others. *Collections Arranged:* SC First Miniature Show (auth, catalog), Cameo Gallery, 80. *Awards:* Traveling

Show Award, Ga Watercolor Soc, Macon Mus, 82; First Place Watercolor, SC State Fair, 82; Merit Award, Okla Patrons Guild, 83. *Bibliog:* Martha Beaver (auth), article, 81 & Margaret Corvini (auth), article, 83, State Newspaper. *Mem:* Watercolor Soc, Ga, SC, Southern & Nat; Nat League Am Penwomen. *Media:* Watercolor. *Mailing Add:* 4136 Sandwood Dr Columbia SC 29206

ELLENZWEIG, ALLEN BRUCE
CRITIC, CURATOR
b New York, NY, Nov 4, 50. *Study:* Cooper Union, with Dore Ashton, BFA, 73. *Collections Arranged:* Private Myths: Unearthings of Contemporary Art (auth, catalog), Queens Mus, NY, 78; Visual Diaries: A Personal Use of Words and Images (auth, catalog), Alex Rosenberg Gallery, 80. *Pos:* Contributing ed, Arts Mag, New York, 74-79; contributing reviewer, Art Am, 80-; moderator, Artists Talk on Art, Landmark Gallery, New York, 81. *Awards:* Writer in residence, Michael Karolyi Mem Found, Vence, France, 72 & Edward Albee Found, Montauk, NY, 79. *Bibliog:* John Russell (auth), When art imitates anthropology, New York Times, 4/9/78; Carrie Rickey (auth), Dear diary, The Village Voice, 2/11/80; Grace Glueck (auth), Visual diaries, New York Times, 2/22/80. *Mem:* Am Section Int Asn Art Critics. *Res:* Homoerotic themes throughout the history of photography. *Publ:* Auth, A Selection of American Art: The Skowhegan School 1946-1976, Inst Contemp Art, Boston, 76; auth, Artists Salute Skowhegan, Kennedy Galleries, 77; auth, The Homosexual Aesthetic, Am Photographer, 80; auth, The Hampton art scene: A mixed blessing, Long Island Life, 8/82; auth, Photo Fever on the Seine, Art Am, 4/83. *Mailing Add:* 200 West 15th St New York NY 10011

ELLER, EVELYN (EVELYN ELLER ROSENBAUM)
COLLAGE ARTIST, PAINTER
b New York, NY, Apr 17, 33. *Study:* Sch Art Studies, NY with Issac Soyer, 50-51; Art Students League, NY, with Morris Kantor & W Barnet, 51-54; Acad De Belle Arte, Rome Italy, 54-55. *Work:* Indianapolis Mus Fine Art, Ind; Miami Mus Mod Art, Fla; Queens Col, City Univ New York, Prudential Insurance Co & Irving Trust Co, New York. *Exhib:* Fulbright Painters, Whitney Mus & Smithsonian Inst, 58-59; Works on Paper/Women Artists, Brooklyn Mus, New York, 75; Queens Artists, Queens Mus, New York, 75; Arte Fiera 78, Palazzo Delle Esposioni, Bologna, Italy, 78; Breaking the Binds/American Book Art Now, Elvehjem Mus, Madison, Wis, 83; Small Works Annual, NY Univ, 79 & 83. *Pos:* Administrative asst, Art Sch Mus Mod Art, NY, 58-59. *Awards:* Fulbright Fel to Italy, US Govt, 54; Resident at Yaddo Saratoga Springs, NY, 57; Juror Award, Small Works Ann, 83. *Bibliog:* John Arthur Shanks (auth), Evelyn Eller, collages, Women Artists News, 4/81; John & Joan Digby (auths), Collage, State of the Art, Thames & Hudson, 84. *Mem:* Artists Equity; Found Community Artists; Organization Independent Artists; Crt Bk Arts. *Media:* Paper Collage; Oil, Acrylic. *Dealer:* Kathryn Markel Fine Arts 50 W 57th St New York NY 10019. *Mailing Add:* 71-49 Harrow St Forest Hills New York NY 11375

ELLINGER, ILONA E
PAINTER, EDUCATOR
b Budapest, Hungary, June 12, 13. *Study:* Royal Hungarian Univ Sch Art, MFA; Royal Swedish Art Acad; Johns Hopkins Univ, with David M Robinson & W F Albright, PhD; Univ Freiburg; Univ Wis. *Exhib:* Soc Washington Artists; one-man show, Am-Brit Art Ctr, George Washington Univ, 50; Silver Spring Art Gallery, 51; Corcoran Gallery Art, 58; Batiks, Gallery N, Setauket, 77; and others. *Teaching:* Prof art & head dept, Trinity Col, Washington, DC, 43-78; Fulbright hist art & archit, Nat Col Arts, Lahore, W Pakistan, 63-64; vis prof, State Univ NY Stony Brook, 69-79. *Mem:* Soc Washington Artists; Archaeol Inst Am; Phi Beta Kappa. *Mailing Add:* 67 Quaker Path Stony Brook NY 11790

ELLINGSON, WILLIAM JOHN
EDUCATOR, PRINTMAKER
b Forrestburg, SDak, Mar 29, 33. *Study:* Minneapolis Sch Art & Design, Minn, BFA, 60; Skowhegan Sch Sculpture & Painting, Maine; State Univ Iowa, Iowa City, MFA, 63; postgrad work, Univ Minn, Minneapolis. *Work:* Nelson Gallery, Kansas City, Mo; Springfield Art Ctr, Mass; Col S Idaho, Twin Falls; Permanent Collection, Hamline Univ, Minneapolis; plus numerous pvt collections in Denmark, Japan, Can, Ger & Eng. *Comn:* Ltd ed etching, Minn State Arts Coun, Minneapolis, 67 & New Eng Life Insurance Co, Wichita, Kans, 75-77; ltd ed silkscreen, Denmark Prog, St Cloud State Univ, 76. *Exhib:* Audubon Artists Inc, New York, 67; Pa Acad Fine Arts; 142nd Ann Exhib, Nat Acad Design, New York; Conn Acad Fine Arts, Hartford; Boston Printmakers 19th Ann, Boston, Mass; Nat Drawing Exhib, Okla Mus Arts; plus many others. *Teaching:* Prof print media, St Cloud State Univ, Minn, 63-; vis artist, Univ Saskatoon, Sask, 77. *Awards:* Edna Stauffer Award, Audubon Artists, Inc, 67. *Media:* Etching; Lithography; Woodcut; Silkscreen. *Dealer:* Fairweather Hardin Gallery 101 E Ontario Ave Chicago IL 60611. *Mailing Add:* 1723 Seventh Ave S St Cloud MN 56301

ELLIOT, CATHY J
CERAMIST, SCULPTOR
b New York, NY, July 26, 47. *Study:* Sarah Lawrence Col, BA, 69; Creative Arts Workshop, New Haven, Conn, 73; Otis Art Inst, Los Angeles, 76-77. *Comn:* Large outdoor sculpture, comn by Keith Williamson, Los Angeles. *Exhib:* Moon St Gallery, Westport, Conn, 74; Am Ceramics Soc, Brand Art Gallery, Los Angeles, 75; Otis Art Inst Group Show, Los Angeles, 77; one-man shows, RGA Gallery, Los Angeles, 77 & 26th St Gallery, Santa Monica, Calif, 79. *Teaching:* Instr ceramics, Moon St Pottery, Westport, Conn, 73; instr pvt ceramics lessons, 74-77. *Awards:* Purchase Award, Am Ceramic Soc Group Show, 75. *Mem:* Am Ceramic Soc; Artists Equity Asn. *Media:* Clay. *Mailing Add:* 530 Tigertail Rd Los Angeles CA 90049

ELLIOT, JOHN THEODORE
PAINTER, ILLUSTRATOR
b London, Eng, May 25, 29; US citizen. *Study:* Acad Fine Arts, Italy, 47-50; NY Univ, Film Sch, 51-54; Sch Visual Arts, 58-59; also pvt study in Europe. *Work:* Chesterwood Mus & Naumkeag, Trustees of Reservations, Stockbridge, Mass; Ala Space Ctr, Huntsville; Nat Trust Hist Preserv, DC; Newark Mus (file), NJ. *Comn:* DC French Public Monument (film), Nat Endowment Arts & Nat Endowment Humanities; Hist Preserv, comn by Mrs Onassis, K Hepburn, A Baxter & Nat Trust, New York, Los Angeles & DC; Thomas Watson Tribute, David Rockefeller & Adv Coun, New York; set design, Noonan's, A Coupla White Chicks Sitting Around Talking, 83; mural, Thomas J Lipton Inc, Englewood Cliffs, NJ, 83; and others. *Exhib:* French Retrospective, Metrop Mus Art, New York, 76, Nat Collection Fine Arts, Smithsonian Inst, 77, Detroit Inst, Mich, 77 & Fogg Art Mus, Cambridge, Mass, 78; 20th Ann Int, Soc Illustrators, New York, 77; Knickerbocker Nat, Nat Arts Club, New York, 79; Pastels Only, Copley Soc, Boston, 79; and others. *Pos:* Pres visual commun, Graphics for Industry Inc, Dover, Del & Tenefly, NJ, 67- *Teaching:* Instr, Art Ctr Northern NJ, Highmount Studios, currently. *Awards:* Gold Medal, Freedoms Found Valley Forge, 70; Ten Best Awards, Soc Illustrators, 77; Best Still Life Award, J&F Giffuni, Pastel Soc Am, 79. *Bibliog:* Freedom to innovate, Indust Photog, 7/70; G McConnell (ed), Illustrators XX, Hastings House, 79; Working with oil pastel, Am Artist, 83. *Mem:* Pastel Soc Am; Soc Illustrators; PSA Nat Arts Club; Oil Pastel Asn; Salmagundi Club. *Media:* Pastel and Oils. *Publ:* Illusr, Legend of John Henry, Troll Press, 70; illusr, Childrens Bible, Fawcett, 73; illusr, Childrens day magazine, Women's Day, 73-74; illusr, The Night the Animals Talked, Am Broadcasting Co, 75; illusr, American Phenomenon, Nat Found, 77. *Dealer:* Highmount Studios 304 Highmount Terrace Upper-Nyack-On-Hudson NY 10960. *Mailing Add:* c/o Graphics For Industry Box 554 Tenafly NJ 07670

ELLIOTT, B CHARLES, JR
CONSULTANT, HISTORIAN
b Grove City, Pa, Apr 9, 24. *Study:* Allegheny Col, BA, 47; Syracuse Univ, scholar, 52, 53 & 55, MA, 55; Univ Pittsburgh, travel grants, 53 & 56. *Collections Arranged:* Valfred Thelin (with catalog), 69; Joseph Domjan (with catalog), 70; George Papashvily (with catalog), 70; Gloria Vanderbilt (with catalog), 71; Carol Dudley Pritchett (with catalog), 73; Seaman Collection Fred Wagner Paintings, 83. *Pos:* Dir, Cult Exchange Prog, Univ Pittsburgh, 56-58; dir, Cheekwood Fine Arts Ctr, 59; dir, Reading Pub Mus & Art Gallery, 67-73, consult, 73- *Awards:* Eben Demarst Award, 63. *Res:* History of the fetes of Lorraine. *Publ:* Auth, Drinkhouse Embroidery Panel, Berk Co Hist Rev, 75. *Mailing Add:* 855 N Park Rd Wyomissing PA 19610

ELLIOTT, BRUCE ROGER
PRINTMAKER, EDUCATOR
b New York, NY, Aug 3, 38. *Study:* Silvermine Artists Guild; State Univ NY Buffalo, BS; State Univ NY Col Oswego; Univ Md, MA. *Exhib:* Graphics 68, Ultimate Concerns, Ohio Univ, 68; Graphics USA 1970, Clarke Col, 70; 13th Nat NDak Print & Drawing Exhib, Univ NDak, 70; 9th Ann Nat Print & Drawing Exhib, Olivet, Mich, 70; Nat Print & Drawing Exhib, Minot State Col, 70. *Teaching:* Chmn dept art, Kings Park High Sch, NY, 65-67; co-chmn, Grad Art Asn, Univ Md, College Park, 68-69; asst prof drawing & printmaking, Holy Cross Col, 71-77, sponsor spec studies, 71-; artist & photogr, Old Sturbridge Village, Archaeol Field Sch, 77-82. *Awards:* Lewisboro Fine Arts Comn Fine Arts Scholar, NY, 56; Fine Arts Award, State Univ NY Buffalo, 59; Graphics Award, 41st Nat Print & Drawing Exhib, Springfield, Mass, 70. *Mem:* Springfield Art League; Worcester Art Mus; Artists Equity Asn; Copley Soc Boston, Inc; Boston Visual Artists Union. *Publ:* Illusr, Digging the Past, Bruce Porell auth, Addison-Wesley, 79. *Dealer:* Franz Bader Galleries 2124 Pennsylvania Ave Washington DC 20037. *Mailing Add:* c/o The Galleries LTD 464 Washington St Wellesley MA 02181

ELLIOTT, DOROTHY BADEN
CONSERVATOR
b Brookfield, Md, July 18, 14. *Study:* Mt Holyoke Col, hons in course, AB, 36; Brooklyn Mus, prof training by Caroline Keck, 60-63. *Pos:* Asst to conservator, Whitney Mus, 61-62; assoc conservator, Brooklyn Mus, 62-63; conservator pvt studio, Sarasota, Fla, 63-; assoc conservator, Walters Art Gallery, Baltimore, 66-79. *Mem:* Fel Am Inst Conserv; fel Int Inst Conserv. *Mailing Add:* 3655 Egerton Circle Sarasota FL 33583

ELLIOTT, JAMES HEYER
MUSEUM DIRECTOR
b Medford, Ore, Feb 19, 24. *Study:* Willamette Univ, AB, 47; Univ de Paris, 47-48; l'Ecole du Louvre, 48; Harvard Univ, MA(hist art), 49; Fulbright scholar to Europe, 51-52. *Pos:* Chief cur & actg dir, Walker Art Ctr, 53-56; cur mod art & asst chief cur, Los Angeles Co Mus, 56-63, chief cur, 63-66; dir, Wadsworth Atheneum, Conn, 66-76; dir, Univ Art Mus, Univ Calif, Berkeley, 76-; mem adv panel, Nat Endowment for the Arts, 74-77; trustee, San Francisco Art Inst. *Teaching:* Teaching fel art hist, Harvard Univ, 50-51; assoc prof hist of art mus, Hunter Col, 66-67; adj prof art, Univ Calif, Berkeley, 76- *Mem:* Am Asn Mus; Asn Art Mus Dirs; Conn Comn on the Arts (comnr & vpres, 70-76); Col Art Asn; Int Comt Mus. *Publ:* Auth, title essay for catalog, Pierre Bonnard Exhibition, 65. *Mailing Add:* Univ Art Mus 2626 Bancroft Way Berkeley CA 94720

ELLIOTT, LILLIAN
WEAVER, TAPESTRY ARTIST
b Detroit, Mich. *Study:* Wayne Univ, BA; Cranbrook Acad Art, Bloomfield Hills, Mich, MFA. *Work:* Mus Contemp Crafts, New York; Detroit Inst Arts;

San Francisco City Art Collection; Objects, USA--Johnson's Wax Collection, Smithsonian Inst Traveling Exhib, 70-72; Univ Art Collections, Ariz State Univ, Tempe. *Exhib:* Calif Design Exhibs, Pasadena Art Mus, 62-71; Fabric Collage Invitational, Mus Contemp Crafts, New York, 65; Collagen--Collage Invitational Exhib, Kunstgewerbe Mus, Zurich, Switz, 68; Objects, USA--Johnson's Wax Collection, Smithsonian Inst Traveling Exhib, 70-72; Tapestry, Tradition & Technique Invitational, Los Angeles Co Mus Art, 71. *Pos:* Fabric designer, Ford Motor Co Styling Div, Dearborn, Mich, 56-59. *Teaching:* Instr art, Univ Mich Col Archit & Design, Ann Arbor, 59-60; lectr textiles, Univ Calif, Berkeley, 66-76. *Awards:* San Francisco Art Festival Purchase Award, 65 & 69; Founder's Soc Purchase Award, Mich Craftsmen's Show, Detroit Inst Arts, 69; Calif Arts Coun Grant/Artist in Residence, 79-80. *Media:* Textile. *Publ:* Auth, Chap, In: The New American Tapestry, Van Nostrand Reinhold, 68. *Mailing Add:* 1775 San Lorenzo Ave Berkeley CA 94707

ELLIOTT, PHILIP CLARKSON
PAINTER
b Minneapolis, Minn, Dec 5, 03. *Study:* Univ Minn, 21-23; Yale Univ, BFA, 26. *Work:* Univ Pittsburgh; Albright-Knox Art Gallery; Burchfield Ctr, State Col of NY at Buffalo; Charles R Penney Found, Rochester, NY; Chaloner Found, New York, NY; also in pvt collections. *Exhib:* Carnegie Inst, 43 & 45; Mus Mod Art, 52; NY State Fair, 62; Albright-Knox Art Gallery, 62-68; Western NY Exhib, 62-68; Retrospective, Burchfield Ctr, Buffalo, NY, 71; Patteran Traveling Exhib, Gallery Asn of NY; and others. *Pos:* Dir, Albright Art Sch, Buffalo, 41-54. *Teaching:* Lectr techniques of painting; asst prof fine arts, Univ Pittsburgh, 34-40; chmn, Dept Art, State Univ NY Buffalo, 54-71, prof painting & drawing, 54-74, emer prof, 74- *Awards:* Prizes, Albright Art Gallery, 49 & 52; Prize, Springville, NY, 62; Prize, Western NY Exhib, 65; and others. *Mailing Add:* 1240 Delaware Ave 114 Buffalo NY 14209

ELLIOTT, RONNIE
PAINTER
b New York, NY, Dec 16, 16. *Study:* Hunter Col; NY Univ; Art Students League. *Work:* Mus Mod Art, New York; Whitney Mus Am Art, New York; Carnegie Inst, Pittsburgh; Andrew Dickson White Mus, Cornell Univ; Jewett Arts Ctr & Farnsworth Mus, Wellesley Col; plus others. *Exhib:* Col Int Exhib, Mus Mod Art, New York, 48; Collage Retrospective, 1943-1963, 63; one-man shows, Rose Fried Gallery, New York, 58 & 67, Polo Gallery, Washington, DC, 76, Andre Zarre Gallery, New York, 77 & Nardin Gallery, New York, 79. *Awards:* Wellesley Col Purchase Award, Jewett Arts Ctr, 70. *Bibliog:* Michel Seuphor (auth), Dictionaire de la Peinture Abstraite, Paris, 57; Harriet Janis & Rudi Blesh (auth), Collage, 1961, Chilton, 61; Herta Wescher (auth), Die Collage, Harry N Abrams, NY; plus others. *Media:* Oil, Collage. *Mailing Add:* 68 E Seventh St New York NY 10003

ELLIS, FREMONT F
PAINTER
b Virginia City, Mont, Oct 2, 1897. *Study:* Art Students League. *Work:* El Paso Mus, Tex; Mus NMex, Santa Fe; Thomas Gilcrease Inst Am Hist, Tulsa, Okla; Univ Calif, Los Angeles; Stark Mus Art, Orange, Tex. *Comn:* S S America (mural). *Awards:* Rotary Award, Dean of SWestern Artists, 81; Gold Medal, Nat Acad Western Art, 81; Award of Merit, Gov Bruce King, 81; and others. *Mailing Add:* 553 Canyon Rd Santa Fe NM 87501

ELLIS, GEORGE RICHARD
MUSEUM DIRECTOR
b Birmingham, Ala, Dec 9, 37. *Study:* Univ Chicago, BA & MFA. *Pos:* Art supvr, Jefferson Co Schs, 62-64; former asst dir, Birmingham Mus Art; dir develop & asst dir, Mus Cult Hist, Univ Calif, Los Angeles, presently; consult ed, African Arts Mag; dir, Honolulu Acad Arts. *Mem:* Los Angeles Ethnic Art Coun; Am Mus Asn; Art Mus Dirs Asn. *Mailing Add:* Honolulu Acad Arts 900 S Beretania St Honolulu HI 96814

ELLIS, RAY G
PAINTER, LECTURER
b Philadelphia, Pa, Apr 24, 21. *Study:* Philadelphia Mus Sch Art, 39-42. *Work:* Farnsworth Mus, Rockland, Maine; Columbus Mus Art, Ga; Telfair Acad Art, Savannah, Ga; Morris Mus Arts & Sci, Morristown, NJ; Charles Russell Mus, Great Falls, Mont. *Comn:* One Man's Island (watercolor), McGraw-Hill Co, New York, 67; series of watercolors, Midlantic Bank, Newark, NJ, 68; Polo (watercolor), Dun & Bradstreet, New York, 73; River Man (watercolor), AT&T Co, Bedminster, NJ, 77. *Exhib:* One-man shows, Pa Acad Fine Arts, Philadelphia, 47, Columbus Mus Art, Ga, 72, Columbia Mus Art, SC, 72, Charles Russell Mus, Great Falls, Mont, 74, Morris Mus Arts & Sci, Morristown, NJ, 76 & MacCullough Mus, Morristown; Am Watercolor Soc, Nat Acad Design, New York, 65-71; Nat Arts Club Ann, New York, 72-77. *Awards:* Grumbacher Award, Am Watercolor Soc, 69; Winsor & Newton Medal, Audubon Artists, 72; Gold Medal of Honor, Hudson Valley Art Asn, 74. *Bibliog:* Norman Kent (auth), Watercolors of Ray G Ellis, Twin City Press, 71; Susan Meyer (auth), Watercolorists at Work, Watson-Guptill, 72; Dr Allan McNabb (auth), Ray G Ellis Paintings, Morris Mus, 76. *Mem:* Am Watercolor Soc; NJ Watercolor Soc (pres, 66-67); Salmagundi Club (first vpres, 72-73); Artists Fel Found (pres, 72-73); Philadelphia Watercolor Club. *Media:* Watercolor, Oil. *Mailing Add:* 126 W Harris St Savannah GA 31401

ELLIS, RICHARD
PAINTER, ILLUSTRATOR
b New York, NY, Apr 2, 38. *Study:* Univ Pa, BA. *Work:* New Bedford Whaling Mus; Philadelphia Zoological Garden; Denver Mus Natural Hist; Kendall Whaling Mus; Sea Life Park, Hawaii. *Comn:* Mural of whales, Denver Mus Natural History, 78. *Exhib:* Whale paintings, New Bedford Whaling Mus, 75, Mystic Seaport, 75 & Am Mus Natural Hist, 76; Animal Art Show, Los Angeles Co Mus, Los Angeles, 77; shark paintings, Am Mus Natural Hist, 78; Acad Natural Sci, Philadelphia, 81. *Pos:* Exhib designer, Am Mus Natural Hist, 65-68. *Teaching:* Lectr, Am Mus Natural Hist, 82-83. *Bibliog:* T Walker Lloyd (auth), Richard Ellis, Am Artist Mag; Steve Blount (auth), Richard Ellis, Sport Diver Mag. *Mem:* Soc Animal Artists; Explorers Club. *Media:* Mixed. *Publ:* Illusr, New York Mag, 74; illusr, The Great Whales, Audubon Mag, 75 & Sci Am, 75; auth & illusr, The Book of Sharks, Grosset & Dunlap, 76; auth & illusr, The Book of Whales, Knopf, 80; auth & illusr, Dolphins and Porpoises, Knopf, 82. *Dealer:* Sportsman's Edge Ltd 136 E 74th St New York NY 10021; Coast Gallery Hwy One Big Sur CA 93920. *Mailing Add:* 595 West End Ave New York NY 10024

ELLISON, NANCY
PAINTER, PHOTOGRAPHER
b Los Angeles, Calif, May 12, 36. *Study:* Finch Col, with Leon Kroll, BS(fine art). *Work:* Allen Mem Art Mus, Oberlin, Ohio; pvt collections of William de Kooning, Donald Sutherland, Mr & Mrs Joel Grey, Robert Goodnough, Athena Spear & Virginia Zabriskie. *Exhib:* Wadsworth Atheneum, Hartford, Conn; Zabriskie Gallery, New York, 66; Finch Col Mus, New York, 69; New York Cult Ctr, 73; New Sch Art Ctr, New York, 73; In Praise of Women Artists, 77. *Pos:* Free lance photojournalist. *Awards:* Leon Kroll Award, Finch Col, 56. *Media:* Oil. *Mailing Add:* 68 Malibu Colony Malibu CA 90265

ELLISON, ROBERT W
SCULPTOR
b Detroit, Mich, Dec 13, 46. *Study:* Mich State Univ, BFA, 69, MFA, 71. *Work:* Mich State Univ & Universal Steel Co, Lancing; City & Co San Francisco. *Comn:* Universal Steel, Lansing, Mich, 69; X Position, Wash State Univ, Pullman, 76; Slice, Syntex Corp, Palo Alto, Calif, 79. *Exhib:* New Ideas Expos, 70, Exhibs for Mich Artists, 70-72, Detroit Mus Art; 21st Ann All Calif Show, Laguna Beach Mus Art, 75; Outdoor Sculpture Exhib, Richmond Art Ctr, Calif, 75. *Collections Arranged:* Bourborbygmi, 28th Ann San Francisco Art Festival, 74; Grey Streak, 21st Ann Calif Show, 74; Riccochet, Palo Alto Outdoor Sculpture Exhib, 77; Four Times Daily, San Francisco Civic Ctr Plaza, 79; Arch Tworain, Donut Diorama, San Francisco Redevelopment Agency, 81. *Teaching:* Instr sculpture design & drawing, Mich State Univ, 70-71; instr sculpture design & drawing, Col Marin, Kentfield, Calif, 72-77. *Awards:* First Place, 21st Ann All Calif Show, 75. *Bibliog:* Gordon J Hazlitt (auth), Barometer of the unknown, Art News, 10/75; Four Times Daily (film), Bravura Films, 79; Donut Diorama (film), Chris Robson, 81. *Mem:* Artists Equity NCalif Region. *Media:* Welded Steel. *Mailing Add:* 6480 Eagle Ridge Rd Penngrove CA 94951

ELLOIAN, CAROLYN AUTRY See Autry, Carolyn

ELLOIAN, PETER
PRINTMAKER, GRAPHIC ARTIST
b Cleveland, Ohio, Apr 20, 36. *Study:* Cleveland Inst Art, BFA; Univ Iowa, MFA; Pratt Graphic Ctr. *Work:* NY Pub Libr; Libr Cong, Washington, DC; Philadelphia Mus of Art; Okla Art Ctr, Oklahoma City; Mus of Mod Art Gallery, Yerevan, Armenia. *Exhib:* Nat Exhib Prints, Libr Cong, 71 & 73 & 77; Soc Am Graphic Artists Nat Print Exhib, New York, 73, 77, 78 & 79; Calif Col Arts & Crafts World Print Competition '73, Int Biennial Exhib Graphic Art & Multiples, Segovia, Spain, 74; 14th & 15th Ann Biennial Graphic Art, Ljubljana, Yugoslavia, 81 & 83; and others. *Teaching:* Instr printmaking & drawing, Toledo Mus Art Sch, 66- *Awards:* Am Drawings III, Portsmouth, Va, 80; Award, Rutgers Nat 81 Works on Paper; Grand Diploma, Second Int Biennial Portrait Drawings, Tuzla, Yugoslavia, 82; and others. *Mem:* Soc of Am Graphic Artists; Philadelphia Print Club; Boston Printmakers. *Media:* Engraving, Drypoint. *Mailing Add:* 3348 Indian Rd Toledo OH 43606

ELMAN, EMILY
PAINTER, EDUCATOR
Study: Syracuse Univ, BFA; Hunter Col, MA. *Exhib:* Chicago Art Inst; Joselyn Art Mus, Omaha, Nebr; Sheldon Mem Art Gallery, Lincoln, Nebr; Nat Acad of Design, New York; San Francisco Mus; Pa Acad of Art, Philadelphia; one-person show, Kornblee Gallery, New York. *Awards:* MacDowell Colony Fel, Peterborough, NY; Creative Artists Pub Serv Grant, 76; Ingram Merrill Found Grant, 76. *Mailing Add:* c/o Kornblee Gallery 20 W 57th St New York NY 10019

ELOUL, KOSSO
SCULPTOR
b Jan 22, 20; US citizen. *Study:* Art Inst Chicago, 39-43; sculptor symposiums, Austria, 60, Yugoslavia, 61, Italy & Israel, 62, Berlin, Ger, 63, Montreal, 64 & Long Beach, Calif, 65. *Work:* Shalom 7 (painted steel), Rose Mus, Brandeis Univ; Art Gallery Ont, Toronto; Mus d'Art Contemp, Montreal; Mus Tel Aviv, Israel; Bezalel Mus, Jerusalem, Israel. *Comn:* Alat (sculpture), Greenwin of Toronto, 72; Swink Advert Head Off, Marion, Ohio, 73; Constella, J D S Investments, North York, Toronto, 75; Braha (stelcology), Steinberg's Miracle Food Mart, Rexdale, 76; Hommage to the Bull (Stelco steel), Bridlebrook Farms, Guelph, Ont, 78; and many others. *Exhib:* Calif Artists in US Mus, Lytton Art Ctr, Los Angeles, 67; The Sculpture Walk, Nat Arts Ctr, Ottawa, 78; Subterranea, Mus Arte Carillo Gil, Inst Nac Bellas Artes, Mexico City, 79; one-man shows, Koffler Ctr Arts, Toronto, 79 & Kosso Eloul: Celebration of the Arch, Art Gallery Hamilton, 80; and others. *Teaching:* Artist in residence sculpture, Calif State Univ, Long Beach, 65-66; artist in residence form & space, Univ Toronto Sch Archit, 69-70. *Awards:* Can Coun Sr Art Fel, 76; Medal of Accomplishment, Mexico City, 78; and

others. *Bibliog:* T H Heinrich (auth), The razor's edge, Vol 156/157 & Gilles Hemault (auth), article, Artscanada; Fernande St Martin (auth), Lettre de Montreal, Art Int, 11/64; Curt Oplinger (auth), article, Artforum, 1/66. *Mem:* L'Accademia Tiberina, Rome, Italy; hon fel Royal Acad Fine Art The Hague; Royal Can Acad Arts. *Media:* Stainless Steel, Concrete. *Dealer:* Arras Gallery 29 W 57th St New York NY 10019; Godard Mira Gallery 22 Hazelton Toronto ON Can. *Mailing Add:* 288 Sherbourne St Toronto ON M5A 2S1 Canada

ELOWITCH, ANNETTE
 DEALER
b Portland, Maine, Dec 24, 42. *Study:* Boston Univ, 61; Westbrook Col, Portland, Maine, AA, 63; Univ Maine. *Pos:* Co-owner, Barridoff Galleries, 75- *Specialty:* Nineteenth and twentieth century paintings. *Mailing Add:* 242 Middle St Portland ME 04101

ELOWITCH, ROBERT JASON
 DEALER
b Portland, Maine, Apr 8, 43. *Study:* Amherst Col, BA. *Pos:* Drama/film critic, Portland Press Herald & Eve Express, 67-69; drama/film critic, Maine Times, 70-75; owner, Barridoff Galleries, 75- *Mem:* Maine State Comn Arts & Humanities (comnr, 73-75); Skohegan Sch Painting & Sculpture (dir, 68-80); Portland Sch Art (sch comt mem, 74-75); United Portland Regional Orgn of Arts Resources (vchmn, 74). *Specialty:* 19th and early 20th century American oils and contemporary regional oils, watercolors, etc. *Interests:* Promotion and support of the arts in the state of Maine. *Mailing Add:* 242 Middle St Portland ME 04101

ELSE, ROBERT JOHN
 EDUCATOR, PAINTER
b Wayne, Pa, Nov 26, 18. *Study:* Columbia Univ, BS & MA. *Work:* Crocker Art Mus, Sacramento; Univ of Calif-Los Angeles Libr; Calif State Libr Prints Rm. *Exhib:* 4th Print Ann Exhib, Brooklyn Mus, 50; Kingsley Ann Exhib for Northern Calif Artists, Crocker Art Gallery, 50-64; Oakland Art Gallery's Ann Exhib, 51; Survey of Pac Coast Painting, Walnut Creek, Calif, 51; 17th Ann Watercolor Exhib, San Francisco Mus of Art, 53; Retrospective, Crocker Art Gallery, 77; Sacramento Valley Landscapes, Univ Calif, Davis, 79; and others. *Pos:* Coun mem, Comt on Art Educ, Mus of Mod Art, 49-52; mem joint bd trustees, Crocker Art Mus, 73-75; mem, Sacramento Metrop Arts Comn, 80-82. *Teaching:* Prof art pract, painting & drawing, Calif State Univ, Sacramento, 50-81, emeritus prof, 81- *Awards:* Purchase Award, 1st Int Biennial of Contemp Color Lithography, Cincinnati Mus of Art, 50; First Prize Oil Painting, Kingsley Club, 64. *Media:* Acrylic. *Mailing Add:* 5871 Shepard Ave Sacramento CA 95819

ELSEN, ALBERT EDWARD
 HISTORIAN
b New York, NY, Oct 11, 27. *Study:* Columbia Col, AB; Columbia Univ, MA & PhD; Dickinson Col, Hon DFA, 80. *Teaching:* Asst prof art hist, Carleton Col, 52-58; prof art hist, Ind Univ, Bloomington, 58-68; prof art hist, Stanford Univ, 68-75, Haas prof art hist, 75- *Awards:* Fulbright Fel, 49-50; Guggenheim Fel, 66-67; Nat Endowment Humanities Sr Fel, 73-74. *Mem:* Col Art Asn Am (bd dirs, 66-70, secy, 70-72, vpres, 72-74, pres, 74-76). *Res:* Modern art, principally modern sculpture. *Publ:* Auth, Paul Jenkins, Abrams, 73; auth, Origins of Modern Sculpture: Pioneers and Premises, 74; coauth (with John Merryman), Law, Ethics & the Visual Arts, 79; auth, Modern European Sculpture, 1918-1945, 79; auth, In Rodin's Studio, 80; and others. *Mailing Add:* 723 Alvarado Row Stanford CA 94305

ELSNER, LARRY EDWARD
 SCULPTOR, EDUCATOR
b Gooding, Idaho, 1930. *Study:* Utah State Univ, BS; Columbia Univ, MFA. *Work:* Ariz State Univ; Salt Lake City Art Ctr, Utah; Archie Bray Found, Helena, Mont; Utah State Univ. *Comn:* Wood relief, Edith Bowen Sch, Logan, 68; metal relief, Col Family Life, Utah State Univ, 69. *Exhib:* Intermountain Painting & Sculpture, Salt Lake Art Ctr, 63; 23rd Ceramic Nat, Everson Mus, Syracuse, NY, 64; Southern Sculpture, Columbia, SC, 67; Smithsonian Inst Show Sculpture, Washington, DC, 69; one-man shows, 100 Pieces of Pottery, Tokyo, Japan, 71, 74 & 76; World Ceramic & Flower Arrangement Exhib, Tokyo, Japan, 79. *Teaching:* Prof sculpture, Utah State Univ, 60- *Awards:* Ford Found Sculpture Purchase Award, 63; Purchase Award, Utah 83. *Mem:* Am Craftsmen Coun; Col Art Asn. *Media:* Wood; Ceramics. *Mailing Add:* 1229 Thrushwood Dr Logan UT 84321

ELWELL, CHIP
 MASTER PRINTER, PUBLISHER
b Kansas City, Mo, Dec 5, 40. *Study:* Columbia Col, 58-64; Columbia Univ, 64-65; Cooper Union, 65-70. *Comn:* Blue Crab (linocut), comn by Jack Beal, 78; Kiddo in the Garden (linocut), comn by Jack Beal, 79; Graceland Mansion (woodcut), comn by Jennifer Bartlett, 79; Poppies (stencil print), comn by Sondra Freckleton, 79; South Seas Kiss & other woodcuts, Richard Bosman, 81. *Exhib:* Sixth Brit Int Print Biennale, Bradford, Eng, 79. *Pos:* Cur, Bank St Atelier, 71-72. *Awards:* NY State Creative Artists Pub Serv Grant, graphics, 78. *Media:* Linocut, Woodcut; Pochoir Print. *Publ:* Artists and Printers, Art News, 3/81; printer & publ, Roberto Juarez's Sweet Sweat & Other Woodcuts. *Mailing Add:* 335 W 35th St New York NY 10001

ELZEA, ROWLAND PROCTER
 MUSEUM CURATOR
b Columbia, Mo, Sept 19, 31. *Study:* Univ Mo, BA & MA; Hunter Col, MSEd; also with Esteban Vicente, New York; Fel Mus Professionals, Nat Endowment Arts, 80. *Work:* Del Art Mus, Wilmington. *Collections Arranged:* American Painting Since World War II, 71; American Painting 1840-1940, 72; Golden Age of American Illustration: 1880-1914 (with catalog), 72; Howard Pyle: Diversity in Depth (with catalog), 73; Jean Dubuffet, 74; Avant-Garde Painting and Sculpture in America, 1910-1925, 75-; The Pre-Raphaelite Era: 1848-1914 (with catalog), The Am Mag, 1890-1940 (with catalog), 76. *Pos:* Cur collections, Del Art Mus, 58-, assoc dir, 80- *Teaching:* Instr art hist & painting, Sch Art & Design, Philadelphia, 69-71, pres, 69-70. *Publ:* Auth, Howard Pyle Collection, 71; auth, Samuel and Mary R Bancroft English Pre-Raphaelite Collection, 78; ed, The Correspondence Between Samuel Bancroft, Jr and Charles Fairfax Murray, 80. *Mailing Add:* 2013 Baynard Blvd Wilmington DE 19802

EMBREY, CARL RICE
 PAINTER, INSTRUCTOR
b Hamilton, Tex, Oct 28, 38. *Study:* Univ Tex, Austin, BFA, 63, with Everett Spruce, MFA, 64. *Work:* Contemp Art Mus, Houston; Marion Koogler McNay Art Inst, San Antonio; San Antonio Art League, Tex. *Exhib:* One-man show, Marion Koogler McNay Art Inst, San Antonio, 74; Am Arts Nat Exhib, Butler Inst, Youngstown, Ohio, 65; Artists of the Southeast & Tex, Isaac Delgado Mus, New Orleans, 67; 60 Tex Artists, Inst Texan Cult, San Antonio, 68; Tex Artists Invitational, Longview Mus, Tex, 68-70; Art Teachers, Witte Mem Mus, 77; and other group & one-man shows. *Collections Arranged:* Paintings of Carl Embrey (cataloged), Five Year Retrospective, 74. *Teaching:* Instr painting & drawing, San Antonio Art Inst, 64- *Awards:* Onderdonk Mem Award, San Antonio Art League, 65; Honorable Mention, Arts Nat, Tyler Mus, 67; Merit Award, Tex Artists Invitational, Longview Art League, 72. *Bibliog:* Gail Falbo Smith (auth), Embrey--A Documentary, Trinity Univ, 78; Nanette Simpson (auth), Carl Embrey, Southwest Art, Houston, 79. *Media:* Acrylic Emulsion, Pencil. *Dealer:* Meredith Long & Co 2323 San Felipe Rd Houston TX 77019; Harari & Johns Ltd 173 New Bond St London. *Mailing Add:* 9319 Nona Kay Dr San Antonio TX 78217

EMERSON, ROBERTA SHINN
 MUSEUM DIRECTOR
b Indianapolis, Ind, Feb 14, 22. *Study:* Northwestern Univ; Univ Chicago; Marshall Univ. *Collections Arranged:* WVa Artists on the Move (traveling exhib), 67; A Room Full of Ropes, 72; Ancient Art of Middle America, 74; New Am Glass: Focus WVa, 76; The Mining Life: Coal in Our History and Culture, 81; Beverly Pepper in Situ, Huntington Galleries, 83. *Pos:* Interim dir, Huntington Galleries, 67, dir, 71- *Teaching:* Asst prof art appreciation, Marshall Univ, 68-69. *Mailing Add:* Huntington Galleries Huntington WV 25701

EMERSON, WALTER CARUTH
 EDUCATOR, PAINTER
b Dallas, Tex, Jan 24, 12. *Study:* Aunspaugh Sch Art; with Olin Travis; Southwestern Sch Theatre; with John Knott; Southern Methodist Univ, BA. *Work:* Tex State Mus, Washington-on-the-Brazos, Tex; also in pvt collections. *Comn:* Life size full figure of Indian Chief Quanah Parker, Metrop Fed Savings, Dallas, 49; portraits of presidents, Repub Tex & portrait of Gen Santa Anna, Tex State Mus, 72. *Exhib:* Rainbowman Gallery, Santa Fe, NMex, 69; one-man show, Quadrangle Galleries, Dallas, 70, 72 & 79 & Tex State Mus, 73; Cushing Gallery, Dallas, 71. *Pos:* Art dir, Pollock Paper Corp, Dallas, 37-52; officer in chg, Art Dept, USN, Washington, DC, 41-45; art dir, Food & Drug Div, Hunt Oil Co, Dallas, 63-69; caricaturist, Plaza Am, Dallas, 82- *Teaching:* Instr art & art hist, Eve Div, Southern Methodist Univ, 40-63; conception, production & illustration, Pencil Personalities (TV series), 58; instr art, Christian Col Southwest, 69-70, Dallas Co Community Col Dist, 72-74 & Dallas Co Jail, 73-74; founder & dir, Art Acad Dallas, 74-; nat lectr, Kim Dawson Agency, 77- *Awards:* Best in Class, Cherokee Nat Mus, 76. *Bibliog:* Keith Kathan (auth), Walter Emerson Portraitist, Dallas Times Herald, 70; William Payne (auth), Portraits by Walter Caruth Emerson, Dallas Morning News, 73; Lorraine Haacke (auth), A guide to Dallas art galleries, Parade Mag, 74. *Media:* Miscellaneous Media. *Publ:* Editorial cartoons, Nationally Distributed, 37-56, Dallas Morning News, 41, NY Daily Mirror, 56-58; auth, American tragedy at Brussels, Am Mercury Mag, 10/58; auth & illusr, The Truth About Santa Anna, 73 & 75; auth, Art Alive (column), syndicated internationally, 79- *Mailing Add:* 3637 Haynie Ave Dallas TX 75205

EMERY, LIN (LIN EMERY BRASELMAN)
 SCULPTOR, KINETIC ARTIST
b New York, NY. *Study:* Ossip Zadkine Studio, Paris; Sculpture Ctr, New York. *Work:* Nat Collection Am Art, Washington, DC; New Orleans Mus of Art; Norton Art Galleries, West Palm Beach, Fla; Huntington Mus Art, WVa; Walter P Chrysler Mus, Norfolk, Va. *Comn:* Aquamobile, Fidelity Bank, Oklahoma City, 77; kinetic sculpture, Fed Bldg, Houma, La, 80; kinetic sculpture, Civic Ctr Lawrence, Kans, 82; Magnetmobile, SCent Bell, Birmingham, Ala, 72; kinetic & musical sculpture, InterContinental Hotel, New Orleans, 83; and others. *Exhib:* Pa Acad Fine Arts Ann, Philadelphia, 60 & 64; Sculpture: 1900-1965, DeWaters Art Mus, 65; G S A Art in Archit, Nat Collection Fine Art, 80; Int Sculpture Conference Exhib, 80; solo shows, Contemp Arts Ctr, New Orleans, 78 & 81 & Max Hutchinson Gallery, New York, 82; and others. *Pos:* Vis critic, Tulane Univ Sch Archit, 67-68; fel, Va Ctr Creative Arts, 81. *Teaching:* Vis artist, Newcomb Art Sch, Tulane Univ, 81. *Awards:* Mayor's Award Excellence in the Arts, New Orleans, 80. *Bibliog:* Moore & Allen (auth), Metal that moves, La Mag, 67; Pierce (auth), Lin Emery's aquamobiles, Art Int, 69; Roger Green (auth), The kinetic sculpture of Lin Emery, Arts Mag, 12/79. *Mem:* Sculptors Guild New York; Contemp Arts Ctr, New Orleans. *Media:* Kinetics, Metals. *Dealer:* Max Hutchinson Gallery 138 Greene St New York NY 10012. *Mailing Add:* 7520 Dominican St New Orleans LA 70118

EMIL, ARTHUR D
COLLECTOR
b New York, NY, Dec 29, 24. *Study:* Yale Univ; Columbia Law Sch. *Mem:* Int Coun Mus Mod Art; Am Fedn Arts. *Collection:* Modern painting; ancient sculpture. *Mailing Add:* 485 Madison Ave New York NY 10022

EMMERICH, ANDRE
DEALER, WRITER
b Frankfort, Ger, Oct 11, 24. *Study:* Amsterdam Lyceum, Neth; Kew Forest Sch, New York; Oberlin Col, BA, 44. *Pos:* Pres, Andre Emmerich Gallery, New York, 54- *Mem:* Art Dealers Asn Am (pres, 72-74); Century Club, New York; Am Asn Dealers Ancient, Oriental & Primitive Art; Tel Aviv Mus. *Specialty:* Contemporary art; pre-Columbian art; classical art. *Publ:* Auth, Art Before Columbus, Simon & Schuster, 63, 71, 78 & 83; auth, Sweat of the Sun and Tears of the Moon--Gold and Silver in Pre-Columbian Art, Univ Wash Press, 65 & 77; also numerous articles in Art Am, Arts, Am Heritage, Wash Post and many others. *Mailing Add:* 41 E 57th St New York NY 10022

EMONT-SCOTT, DEBORAH
CURATOR
b Passaic, NJ, Dec 1, 51. *Study:* Rutgers Univ, painting with Leon Golub, BA, 73; Oberlin Col, with Ellen Johnson, MA, 79. *Collections Arranged:* Veda Reed Paintings and Drawings 1955-80 & Alan Shields (auth, catalog), Memphis Brooks Mus Art, 83. *Pos:* Cur collections, Brooks Mem Art Gallery, 79-; Sanders Josland cur twentieth century art, Nelson-Atkins Mus Art, 83-; *Mem:* Col Art Asn. *Mailing Add:* Nelson-Atkins Mus Art 4525 Oak St Kansas City MO 64111

ENGEL, MICHAEL MARTIN, II
PAINTER, ILLUSTRATOR
b New York, NY, Mar 20, 19. *Study:* With A Katchemakoff; Art Students League, with Kimon Nicolaides & George Picken; Am Sch Design, with Cherkasoff. *Work:* Parrish Art Mus, Southampton, NY; St Lawrence Univ, Canton, NY; US Navy Combat Art Collection; Antioch Col, Yellow Springs, Ohio; Clayton-Liberatore Gallery, Bridgehampton, NY. *Exhib:* Hofstra Col Invitational, 59; Audubon Artists Ann; Salmagundi Club; Suburban Art League, NY; Nat Arts Club, New York. *Awards:* First Prize for watercolor, Suburban Art League, 64; Prof Award, Wall St Art Asn; Prize, Nat Arts Club, 77. *Mem:* Audubon Artists (historian, 45-79, pres, 62-63); Int Asn Arts (vpres, 70-73); Artists Fellowship (trustee, 63-, pres, 77-80); Nat Arts Club; life fel Royal Soc Arts; and others. *Media:* Watercolor. *Mailing Add:* 22 Lee St Huntington NY 11743

ENGEL, WALTER F
CRITIC, DEALER
b Vienna, Austria, June 11, 08; Can citizen. *Study:* Art & art hist with Oscar Lichtenstern, Vienna, 25-27; Joseph Floch, Paris, 28; Ludwig H Jungnickel, Vienna, 29-30. *Pos:* Art critic, Revista de las Indias, 41-51, El Tiempo, 44-55, Art Mag Plastica, 56-60 & El Espectador, 60-65, Bogota, Colombia; co-founder, critic & adv bd, Art Mag, Toronto, 69-79. *Mem:* Int Asn Art Critics; hon Soc Can Artists. *Res:* Twentieth century Latin American art, Canadian art, surrealism, and expressionism. *Specialty:* Contemporary art, with preference for Canadian, European and Latin American art, surrealism and figurative expressionism; Anishnawbe, Ontarian-Indian painting. *Publ:* Auth, Social Problems in the Visual Arts, 46; auth, The Painter Fernando Botero, 52; auth, Contemporary Colombian Paintresses, 59; auth, Wiedemann, 59; auth, The World of Frans Masereel (catalog), Art Gallery Windsor, Ont, 81 & Art Gallery Ont, Toronto, 82. *Mailing Add:* 350 Lonsdale Rd, Suite 201 Toronto ON M5P 1R6 Canada

ENGELHARDT, THOMAS ALEXANDER
EDITORIAL CARTOONIST
b St Louis, Mo, Dec 29, 30. *Study:* Denver Univ, 50-51; Ruskin Sch Fine Arts, Oxford Univ, 54-56; Sch Visual Arts, New York, 57. *Work:* State Hist Soc Mo, Columbia. *Comn:* Mural (humorous animals), Pediat Assoc, Mo, 73. *Exhib:* One-man shows, Fontbonne Col, Mo, 72 & Decade of the Environment 1970-1980, Old Courthouse, St Louis, 81; Sch Visual Arts Alumni Exhib, Hansen Gallery, New York, 75; plus numerous group shows. *Pos:* Free-lance cartoonist, New York, 57-60; editorial cartoonist, Newspaper Enterprise Asn, Cleveland, Ohio, 60-61 & St Louis Post-Dispatch, 62- *Media:* Pen & Ink, Crayon. *Publ:* Auth, Cartoonist Profiles, 69; auth, Dateline 1976, Overseas Press Club, 76. *Mailing Add:* 900 N 12th Blvd St Louis MO 63101

ENGERAN, WHITNEY JOHN, JR
PAINTER, EDUCATOR
b New Orleans, La, Feb 1, 34. *Study:* Spring Hill Col, BA & MA; St Louis Univ, STL; Art Students League. *Work:* Cunningham Mem Libr, Terre Haute, Ind; Vincennes Univ; Harold E Simon Collection; Hugh Kohlmeyer Collection. *Comn:* Fire ritual mural, St Marys Col, 62; suffering servant mural, Martin Army Hosp, Columbus, Ga, 66; Terre Haute First Nat Bank, 74. *Exhib:* Confractio, Shircliff Gallery, Vincennes, Ind, 74; Atmospheric Drawings, Barnwell Art Ctr, Shreveport, La, 75; Hands On--Hands Off (Review of 20 Yrs of Paintings & Drawings), Art Gallery, St Mary of the Woods Col, Terre Haute, Ind, 77; Tondo Paintings, Barnhart Loft Gallery, Terre Haute, Ind, 79; Turman Gallery, Terre Haute, Ind, 80 & 81; and others. *Collections Arranged:* Ida Kohlmeyer Retrospective, 72, Images of Our Time, 73 & American 6 Pak: Sic Bicentennial Exhibits, 74-75, Turman Gallery, Terre Haute; I Kohlmeyer Retrospective, Mint Mus, 82-84. *Pos:* Cur permanent collection & dir, Turman Gallery, 71-75. *Teaching:* Asst prof aesthet & chmn dept art, Loyola Univ, 66-68; assoc prof aesthet, Stephens Col, 68-71; prof art theory & criticism, Ind State Univ, Terre Haute, 71-,

chmn dept, 71-78. *Awards:* First Prize Watercolor, Kans Artists' Exhib, 62 & 65. *Bibliog:* Margaret Harold (ed), Prize Winning Watercolors of America, Allied Publ, 63. *Mem:* Col Art Asn Am; Nat Coun Art Adminr; Mid-Am Col Art Asn. *Media:* Enamel, Acrylics. *Publ:* Auth, Ida Kohlmeyer: A Retrospective Exhibition (catalog), High Mus, Atlanta, 12/71; auth, article, Arts Mag, 4/78; auth, article, Arts Update, 2/83; auth, Ida Kohlmeyer (catalog), Mint Mus, 12/83; auth, Decade of sculpture/Robert G Evans (monogr), Turman Gallery, Terre Haute. *Mailing Add:* 1509 S Center St Terre Haute IN 47802

ENGGASS, ROBERT
HISTORIAN, EDUCATOR
b Detroit, Mich, Dec 20, 21. *Study:* Harvard Univ, AB, 46; Univ Mich, MA, 50, PhD, 55. *Teaching:* Assoc prof art hist, Pa State Univ, 58-65, prof art hist, 66-71; prof art hist, Univ Kans, 71-78; Callaway prof art, Univ Ga, 79- *Awards:* Grants-in-Aid, Am Coun Learned Socs, 58, 70 & 76; Fulbright Res Scholar, Univ Rome, 63-64; Univ Kans Res Grants, 66-70. *Publ:* Auth, Tiepolo & the concept of the barocchetto, Atti del Congresso Int sul Tiepolo, Udine, 72; auth, Early Eighteenth Century Sculpture in Rome, Pa State Univ, 76; auth, Un probleme du baroque romain tardif, Rev Art, 76; co-ed, Nicola Pio, le vite de Pittori Scultori et Architetti, Vatican Libr, 78; auth, Visual counterpoint in 18th century Venetian painting, Art Bull, 82; and others. *Mailing Add:* 340 W Lake Dr Athens GA 30606

ENGLAND, PAUL GRADY
PAINTER, EDUCATOR
b Hugo, Okla, Jan 12, 18. *Study:* Carnegie Inst Technol, BA, 40; Univ Tulsa, MA, 59; Art Students League, 43-46; Zadkine Studio, Paris, 48 & 49. *Work:* Fitzwilliam Mus, Cambridge, England; permanent print collection, NY Pub Libr, NY; Heckscher Mus, Huntingtown, NY; State Collection, Oklahoma City, Okla; Bank of Okla, Tulsa; and others. *Exhib:* One-man shows, Creuze Gallery, Paris, 49, Iolas Gallery, New York, 51, Grand Cent Moderns, New York, 55, Philbrook Art Ctr, Tulsa, 71 & St Mary's Col Md, 72. *Teaching:* Assoc prof painting, Hofstra Univ, 59-81, prof, 81- *Awards:* Graphics Award, Joslyn Mus Art, 57; Grand Awards, Philbrook Art Ctr, 57 & 63; Award of Excellence, Smithtown Arts Coun, Long Island, 81. *Mem:* Art Students League New York. *Media:* Oil. *Publ:* Auth, Dust to dust, New Yorker Mag, 9/14/41; auth, Art critiques, France-Amerique, 55-57. *Mailing Add:* 359 Soundview Dr Rocky Point NY 11778

ENGLANDER, GERTRUD
CERAMIST
b Ger, Jan 29, 04; US citizen. *Study:* Kunstgewerbeschule Cologne; Craft Students League, YWCA, New York; NY Univ. *Exhib:* Designer-Craftsmen USA 1960, Mus Contemp Crafts, 60, Am Craftsmen's Coun Touring Exhib, 61; Craftsmen of Northeastern States, Worcester Art Mus, 63; Artist Craftsmen New York Ann, Lever House, 71. *Teaching:* Instr ceramics, Craft Students League YWCA, New York; instr ceramics, Little Art Workshop, New York, 53-55. *Awards:* Award of Merit for Outstanding Craftsmanship, Artist Craftsmen New York, 71; Award of Merit, Invitation Pen & Brush Club Show, 77. *Mem:* Artist Craftsmen New York; Am Craftsmens Coun; Craft Students League YWCA. *Mailing Add:* 345 E 52nd St New York NY 10022

ENGLE, BARBARA JEAN
PAINTER, JEWELER
b Grandin, NDak. *Study:* Honolulu Acad Arts, Hawaii; Chouinard Art Inst & Otis Art Inst, Los Angeles. *Work:* Amfac, Honolulu; Castle & Cooke Inc, Honolulu; Honolulu Acad Arts; State Found Cult & Arts; Dept of Educ, Honolulu. *Comn:* Three wall panels, Kauai High Sch, 73; gift print, Honolulu Printmakers, 74. *Exhib:* Nat Print Exhib, Honolulu Acad Arts, 71-79; one-woman shows, Silk Screen Prints, Honolulu Acad Arts, 71, Barbara Engle, Serigraphs, Santa Fe, NMex, 72 & Barbara Engle, Jewelry, Santa Barbara, Calif, 72 & Kauai Mus, 73; 10 Hawaii Printmakers, Honolulu Acad Arts, 78; Hawaii Craftsman Ann, Jewelry, 78 & 79; Hawaii Artists League Ann, Paintings, 78; Gimas Gallery, Jewelry, 79; Womens Exhib, Paintings & Prints, Downtown Gallery, 79; plus others. *Teaching:* Instr drawing, silkscreen printing & painting, Honolulu Acad Arts, 64- *Bibliog:* Ramona Solberg (auth), Inventive jewelry, Van Nostrand Reinhold Co, 73; J L Collins (auth), Women Artists in Am II, Univ Tenn, 75; Gerald F Brommer (auth), The Art of Collage, Davis Publ, Inc, Mass, 78. *Mem:* Hawaii Artists League; Hawaii Craftsmen; Honolulu Printmakers. *Media:* Oil. *Mailing Add:* 2231 Noah St Honolulu HI 96816

ENGLE, CHET
PAINTER
b Danville, Ill, June 25, 18. *Study:* Am Acad Art, Chicago; Art Ctr Sch Design, Los Angeles. *Work:* Calif State Collection Art, Sacramento; Air Mus, Smithsonian Inst, Washington, DC. *Exhib:* Paintings in the United States, Carnegie Inst Fine Arts, Pittsburgh, 49; Los Angeles Co Mus, 47, 50 & 55; one-man shows, Cowie Gallery, Los Angeles, 58, Manhattan Gallery, Pasadena, 59 & 60 & Maxwell Galleries, San Francisco, 63. *Pos:* Instnl advert artist, Lockheed Aircraft Corp, Burbank, Calif, 50-73. *Awards:* First Prize, Servicemans Show, Butler Inst Art, Youngstown, Ohio, 43; First Prize, Calif State Exhib, Sacramento, 49. *Media:* Oil, Tempera. *Publ:* Illusr, Lockheed Horizons, 65-70. *Dealer:* Jones Gallery Green Dragon Colony La Jolla CA 92037; Taos Art Gallery Inc PO Box 1007 Taos NM 87571. *Mailing Add:* PO Box 267 Manchester CA 95459

ENGLISH, JOHN ARBOGAST
PAINTER
b Trenton, NJ, Nov 7, 13. *Study:* Trenton Sch Indust Art; Trenton State Col, BS. *Comn:* Numerous marine paintings & yacht portraits comn by pvt individuals. *Exhib:* Miami Int Boat Show Marine Exhib, 74-75; Am Soc Marine Artists Ann Show, 78-79; Greenwich Workshop Ann Marine Show, 79; Mystic Seaport Ann Marine Show, 79; 3rd Ann Exhib, Am Soc Marine Artists, 81; and others. *Pos:* Publ lithographic reproductions marine subj, Riverside Studio, Island Heights, NJ. *Awards:* Gold Medal, Franklin Mint; First Award Oil Painting, Ocean Co Artist Guild; Second in Show, Miami Int Boat Show Exhib. *Mem:* Ocean Co Artist Guild; Grove House, Miami; Am Soc Marine Artists. *Media:* Oil. *Dealer:* Newman Galleries 1625 Walnut St Philadelphia PA 19103. *Mailing Add:* 236 Ocean Ave Island Heights NJ 08732

ENMAN, TOM KENNETH
PAINTER, MUSEUM DIRECTOR
b Salt Lake City, Utah, Feb 22, 28. *Study:* Univ Wash, Exten, 48-49; Chicago Acad Fine Arts, cert, 52; Cape Sch Art, Provincetown, Mass, scholar, 52; Calif Col Arts & Crafts, Oakland, 53-54; Univ Calif, Los Angeles, Exten, 58-61; Laguna Beach Sch Art, Calif, 69; also with Alex Villumsion & Playa Del Ray, Calif, 62. *Exhib:* 19th Newport Ann, Newport Beach, Calif, 64; Laguna Beach Art Gallery Ann Fall Mem, 64; All Calif Exhib, Laguna Beach, 65; 7th Nat Ann Art Round Up, Las Vegas, 66; Laguna Beach Art Asn Graphic & Drawing Exhib, 67. *Pos:* Dir, Artist Guild Laguna Beach, 64-65; dir, Laguna Beach Mus Art, 65-80; consul, Plein Air Painters Calif, Southland, 82. *Awards:* First in Graphic (pen & ink), 64 & hon mention in oil, 65, Laguna Beach Art Asn. *Mem:* Laguna Beach Art Asn (dir). *Media:* Oil, Watercolor. *Mailing Add:* 2160 S Coast Hwy Laguna Beach CA 92651

ENOS, CHRIS
PHOTOGRAPHER, LECTURER
b Calif, Aug 21, 44. *Study:* Foothill Col, AA, 65; Univ Am, Mexico City, 67; San Francisco State Univ, BA(sculpture), 69; San Francisco Art Inst, MFA(photog), 71. *Work:* George Eastman House, Rochester, NY; Bibliot Nat, Paris; Polaroid Corp, Amsterdam, Holland; Shaklee Corp, Calif; Seagrams Collection, NY; and many others. *Exhib:* Mass Inst Technol, Cambridge, 71, 73 & 80; San Francisco Mus Art, 71 & 80; Fogg Art Mus, 74, 76, 78 & 80; one-person shows, Mass Inst Technol, 74, Bibliot Nat, Paris, 75, Univ Colo, Boulder, 80 & 82 & Thomas Segal Gallery, Boston, 82; Recent Acquisitions, Boston Mus Fine Arts, 76; Univ Vt, Burlington, 80; Int Ctr Photog, New York, 81; Inst Contemp Art, Boston, 81 & 83; Sonnabend Gallery, New York, 81; and many others. *Pos:* Founder & pres, Photog Resource Ctr, Boston, 76-81; Gallery dir & coordr lect series, New Eng Sch Photog, 77-78; artist in residence, Lightwork Workshop, Syracuse Univ, 78 & Int Ctr Photog, New York, 80. *Teaching:* Instr photog, Sonoma State Univ, 71-73, San Francisco Acad Art, 72-73, Univ Calif, San Francisco, 72-73 & New Eng Sch Photog, 77-78; asst prof, Windham Col, 74 & Hampshire Col, 74-75; instr, Harvard Univ, 77 & MA prog, summer 80; vis artist, Univ Colo, Boulder, 80 & Smith Col, Northampton, Mass, 82-83; vis lectr, Univ Calif, Los Angeles, 83- *Awards:* Photog Fel, Nat Endowment Arts, 81; Phealen Award of Merit, San Francisco, 82; Proj Completion Grant, Artists Found, 83; and others. *Bibliog:* In/Sights, Godine Press; Eros In Photography, Camerawork Press; Popular Photography Annual, 81; and others. *Mem:* Soc Photog Educ; Visual Studies Workshop, New York; and others. *Publ:* Contribr, Octave of prayer, Aperture, 72; contribr, Camera 35 Mag, New York, 73; contribr, Camera Mag, Bucher/Switz, 75; contribr, Horticulture Mag, Boston, 77; contribr, Women See Women, Crowell, 77; and many others. *Mailing Add:* Univ Calif Dept Art 405 Hilgard Los Angeles CA 90024

ENRIQUEZ, GASPAR
DESIGNER, INSTRUCTOR
b El Paso, Tex, July 18, 42. *Study:* Univ Tex, El Paso, BA; printmaking with Loren Janzen & jewelry with Walt Harrison; NMex State Univ, metals with Kate Wayla & Peter Voris. *Work:* State Nat Bank; Univ Tex, El Paso. *Exhib:* Int Designers Craftsman, El Paso Mus Art, 70 & 75; Calif Int Artist of Year, Huntington Beach, Calif, 74; NMex State Univ, 76 & 77; NMex Designers Craftsman, Amazo, 78-79. *Teaching:* Instr art, El Paso Pub Schs & El Paso Community Col, 70- *Awards:* Hon mention, El Paso Designers Craftsmen, 79-80. *Mem:* Austin Contemp Vis Arts Asn; Int Designers Craftsman; Am Craft Coun. *Dealer:* Mi Casa Studio Gallery San Elizario TX 79849; Tiara Gallery 1500 Montana El Paso TX 79902. *Mailing Add:* Box 17112 El Paso TX 79917

ENSRUD, WAYNE
PAINTER, PRINTMAKER
b Albert Lea, Minn, Apr 4, 34. *Study:* Minneapolis Col Art & Design, BFA, 56; with Oskar Kokoschka, 56-79; with Ben Shahn, Joseph Albers & Vaclav Vitlacyl. *Work:* Bristol Mus Art, RI; New England Ctr Contemp Art, Brooklyn, Conn; French Inst Gallery, New York; Gallery Collection of the Governor of Trinidad, West Indies; Galleria of Contessa Borghese, Rome, Italy. *Comn:* Moses on Mt Sinai, Temple Emmanuel, Great Neck, NY, 77; life-size etched mirrors, Le Premier--Robert Pascal, New York, 77; engraved lucite wall, Nanni Il Valetto, New York, 78; The Last of the Blue Devils, Newport Jazz Festival, New York, 80; poster, Concert Management, New York, 80. *Exhib:* New England Ctr Contemp Art, Brooklyn, Conn, 81; Univ Conn, Storrs, 82; Buffalo Mus Sci, NY, 82; Slater Mus, Conn, 82; Old State House Mus, Hartford, Conn, 82; and others. *Pos:* Art dir, Univ Calif, Berkeley, 58-61; exec art dir, Channel 13 TV, New York, 64; art dir, Gemini Space Program, ABC, New York, 65-66. *Teaching:* Instr film animation, Pratt Inst, New York, 67-72; instr painting & drawing, Cumberland Sch, Great

Neck, NY, 67-79; guest prof figure painting, Simon's Rock Early Col, Great Barrington, Mass, 78. *Awards:* Second Award in Oils, Christian Themes Lever House, 66. *Bibliog:* Monika Pichler (auth), Wayne Ensrud: Life of an artist, In: Work in Progress, 81. *Mem:* Coffee House Club. *Media:* Oil, Watercolor; Lithography, Etching. *Mailing Add:* 65 Central Park West New York NY 10023

ENSTICE, WAYNE
CONCEPTUAL ARTIST, CRITIC
b Irvington, NJ, Dec 16, 43. *Study:* Pratt Inst, BFA, 65; Univ NMex, MA, 69. *Work:* Univ NC, Chapel Hill; Univ Ark, Art Gallery, Fayetteville; Yuma Mus Art, Ariz. *Exhib:* Twenty Ariz Artists, Phoenix Art Mus, 78; Nat Collage & Assemblage, Miss Mus Art, Jackson & traveling to six other museums, 81-84; Showdown, Alternative Mus, New York, 83; Alternative Space Coalition of Houston, 83. *Teaching:* Assoc prof contemp art, printmaking & drawing, Univ Ariz, Tucson, 70- *Awards:* Purchase Prizes, Tucson Mus Art, 78 & Ariz Commission Arts & Humanities, 78; Artist in Residence Grant, Roswell Mus & Art Ctr. *Bibliog:* Robert Murdock (auth), article, Univ Ark Press, 79; William Peterson (auth), article, Artspace, 80; John Perreault (auth), rev, Art in Am, 81. *Media:* Multi-Media. *Publ:* Auth, London and Tucson: Regional scenes compared, Artspace, 79; auth, Prologue: The splash factor, Re-Dact, 11/83; auth, Performance Art's Coming of Age, Dutton Press (in prep). *Mailing Add:* 7249 E Montecito Dr Tucson AZ 85710

ENTE, LILY
SCULPTOR, PRINTMAKER
b Ukrania, Russia, May 20, 05. *Work:* Hirshhorn Mus, Washington, DC; Mass Mus, Amherst; Phoenix Art Mus, Ariz; Safad Mus, Israel; Rose Art Mus, Waltham, Mass. *Exhib:* Claude Bernard Gallerie, Paris, France; Great Burlington Gallery, London, Eng; Whitney Mus Am Art, New York; Int Exhib 84 Artists, Bundy Art Gallery, Waitsfield, Vt; plus numerous one-person shows. *Mailing Add:* 400 Riverside Dr New York NY 10025

ENYEART, JAMES LYLE
HISTORIAN, DIRECTOR
b Auburn, Wash, Jan 13, 43. *Study:* Kansas City Art Inst, BFA, 65; Univ Santiago, Chile, cert(Orgn Am States Fel), 66-67; Univ Kans, MFA, 72. *Work:* Int Mus Photog, George Eastman House, Rochester, NY; Bibliot Nat, Paris, France; Sheldon Mem Gallery, Univ Nebr, Lincoln; Albrecht Mus Art, St Joseph, Mo; Nat Mus Am Art. *Comn:* Nineteenth Century archit of St Joseph, 74 & stained glass windows of St Joseph, 75, Albrecht Mus Art, St Joseph, Mo. *Collections Arranged:* Invisible in America: Photographs of Marion Palfi (auth, catalog), 73; Francis Bruguiere: A Retrospective, 77. *Pos:* Staff photog, Nelson Gallery Art, Kansas City, Mo, 65-66; charter dir, Albrecht Gallery Art, St Joseph, Mo, 67-68; cur photog, Helen Foresman Spencer Mus Art, Univ Kans, Lawrence, 68-76; dir, Ctr Creative Photog, Univ Ariz, 77-, ed, The Archive, 78-; leader hist sect, Rencontres Int de la Photog, Arles Festival, France, 79; consult, Polaroid Corp, 83- *Teaching:* Instr drawing & design, Mo Western State Col, Univ MO, 67-68; lectr art hist, Univ Kans, 68-70, asst prof 69-75, assoc prof 76, instr photog 71-75; adj prof art, Univ Ariz, 77- *Awards:* Prof Mus Fel, Nat Endowment for the Arts, 75; Photokina Obelisk Award for photog contrib, Cologne, WGer, 82. *Bibliog:* Alfred Frankenstein (auth), Francis Bruguiere, San Francisco Chronicle, 12/18/77; Bonnie Yochelson (auth), The picture is what you can do with the subject, Village Voice, 1/19/78; Photography's essential sixty, Am Photogr, 6/79. *Mem:* Nat Soc Photog Educ (bd dirs, 78-82); Friends Photog (exec dir, 76-77, vpres, 78-81). *Res:* Conservation and restoration of photographs; nineteenth and twentieth century photographers. *Publ:* Auth, intro to Charles Traub's Edge to Edge, Cardozo Inc, Minneapolis, 82; auth introd, Uncommon Reality (catalog), Photokina, 82; coauth, Three Classic American Photographs: Texts and Contexts, Am Arts Doc Ctr, Univ Exeter, Eng, 82; adv & contribr, Contemporary Photographers, St Martin's Press, 83; coauth, Non-destructive elemental analysis of photographic paper and emulsions by x-ray fluorescence spectroscopy, Hist Photog, 4-6/83; and many others. *Mailing Add:* 5860 N Genematas Dr Tucson AZ 85704

EPPINK, HELEN BRENAN
PAINTER
b Springfield, Ohio, Aug 19, 10. *Study:* Cleveland Art Inst; John Huntington Polytech Inst, Cleveland, Ohio; Colorado Springs Fine Art Ctr. *Work:* Wichita Art Mus, Kans; Kans State Univ, Manhattan; Kans Fedn Womens Clubs Collection; Topeka Public Libr. *Exhib:* 3rd Air Capitol Show, Wichita Art Mus, 56; Midwest Biennial, Joslyn Art Mus, Omaha, Nebr, 56; 8th Biennial Regional Exhib, Kans State Univ, 65; 22nd Ann Exhib Oils by Kans Artists, Manhattan, 70; two-man show, Topeka Pub Libr, 77. *Teaching:* Instr art, Col Emporia, 44-53, head dept art, 61-74; instr art, Ottawa Univ, Kans, 48-51 & Kans State Teachers Col, 51-52 & 60-61. *Awards:* Second Prize Watercolor, Midwestern Show, Kansas City Art Inst, 39; Purchase Prize Watercolor, Wichita Art Mus, 56; Purchase Prize Oil, 8th Biennial Exhib, Kans State Univ, 65. *Media:* Acrylic. *Mailing Add:* 2101 Canterbury Rd Emporia KS 66801

EPPINK, NORMAN R
PRINTMAKER, PAINTER
b Cleveland, Ohio, July 29, 06. *Study:* Cleveland Art Inst, BEA; Western Reserve Univ, MA. *Work:* Brit Mus, London; Metrop Mus Art, New York; Art Inst Chicago; Nat Gallery Art, Washington, DC; Cleveland Mus Art. *Comn:* Court of Romance (mural), comn by Lakewood Bd Educ for Harding Jr High Sch, Ohio, 30; indust mural, Mansfield Pub Libr, Ohio, 35. *Exhib:* 3rd Int Color Lithography, Cincinnati Art Mus, Ohio, 54; Pratt Inst Int Print Show, 64 & 68; one-man show, 101 Prints, Linda Hall Libr, Kansas City, Mo

& circulating exhib, Nat Gallery Art, Washington, DC, 68; two-man show, Topeka Pub Libr, 77. *Pos:* Med illusr, Cleveland Clin Found, 30-33; mem, Kans Cult Arts Comn, 66-67. *Teaching:* Instr art, Lakewood Pub Schs, 28-30; instr art, Cleveland Pub Schs, 35-37; instr art, Emporia State Univ, 37-75; head dept art, 47-68, prof art hist, 68-75, emeritus prof, 76- *Awards:* Second Prize Lithography, 53, First Prize, 54 & First Prize Color Lithography, 55, Cleveland Mus Art. *Bibliog:* Norman Eppink, printmaker, The Rotarian, 12/68. *Media:* Acrylic, Watercolor. *Res:* Printmaking processes. *Publ:* Auth & illusr, 101 prints, ltd ed, pvt press, 67, trade ed, Univ Okla Press, 71. *Mailing Add:* 2101 Canterbury Rd Emporia KS 66801

EPSTEIN, ANNABEL WHARTON
HISTORIAN
b New Rochelle, NY. *Study:* Univ Wis, Madison, BSc, 66; Univ Chicago, MA, 69; Courtauld Inst, London Univ, PhD, 75. *Teaching:* Res fel Byzantine art, Barber Inst, Univ Birmingham, Eng, 71-75; asst prof Medieval art, Oberlin Col, 75-78; asst prof Medieval art, Duke Univ, 79- *Awards:* Vis Fel, Dumbarton Oaks, Harvard Univ, 78-79; ACLS Fel, 81-82. *Mem:* Byzantine Studies Conf (bd pres); Inst Archit & Urban Studies, New York (bd mem); Int Ctr Medieval Art (bd mem). *Res:* Reevaluation of the aesthetic value of provincial art through a study of its function. *Publ:* Auth, Column Churches in Cappadocia: Arch & Ptng, Cahiers Archaeol, 75, 80 & 81; auth, Problems of Provincialism: Cappadocia and South Italy, J of Warburg & Courtauld Inst, 79; Byzantine churches of Kastoria, Art Bulletin, 80; Formulas for Salvation: Comparison of Byzantine Monasteries, Church Hist, 81; auth, Change in Byzantine culture in the 11th and 12th century, Univ Calif Press, 84. *Mailing Add:* 920 Dacian Durham NC 27701

EPSTEIN, MITCH (MITCHELL D)
PHOTOGRAPHER
b Holyoke, Mass, Aug 23, 52. *Study:* Union Col, Schenectady, NY, 70-71; RI Sch Design, 71-72; Cooper Union, New York, with Garry Winogrand, 72-74. *Work:* Australian Nat Gallery, Canberra; Bibliot Nat, Paris, France; Corcoran Mus Art, Washington, DC; Mus Mod Art, New York; Mus Fine Arts, Boston, Mass. *Exhib:* One-man shows, Light Gallery, New York, 79, 81 & 82 & Hampshire Col, Amherst, Mass, 83; Recent Acquisitions, Boston Mus Fine Art, Mass, 80 & Corcoran Gallery Art, Washington, DC, 80; Creative Artists Public Service Program Photog Traveling Exhib, NY state, 80; The New Color, Int Ctr Photog, New York, 81. *Teaching:* Lectr color photog, Carpenter Ctr, Harvard Univ, 77. *Awards:* Individual Photog Grant, Nat Endowment Arts, 78 & NY State Coun Arts, 80. *Bibliog:* Ben Lifson (auth), Americans abroad, Village Voice, 4/23/79; Andy Grundberg & Julia Sculky (auths), Currents: American photography today, Modern Photog, 6/80; Pepe Karmel (auth), Photography raising a hue: the new color, Art in Am, 1/82. *Publ:* Contribr, The New Color, 81 & Annie On Camera, 82, Abbeville Press. *Dealer:* H F Manes Gallery 177 Prince St New York NY 10012. *Mailing Add:* 424 West 119 St #67 New York NY 10027

EPTING, MARION AUSTIN
PRINTMAKER, EDUCATOR
b Forrest, Miss, Jan 28, 40. *Study:* Los Angeles City Col, AA; Los Angeles Co Art Inst, Otis, MFA, 69; also with Ernest Freed, Lee Chesney, Shiro Ikegawa & Charles White. *Work:* Oakland Mus, Calif; Seattle Art Mus; Libr Cong, Washington, DC; Auchebach Found, DeYoung Mus, San Francisco; Whitney Mus, New York; and others. *Comn:* Intaglio prints comn by John Wilson, Lakeside Studios, Mich, 72-74. *Exhib:* 1st Nat Print Exhib, San Diego Fine Arts Soc, 69; Northwest Printmakers, Seattle Art Mus, 69; Oakland Art Mus, 73; traveling exhib, Western Asn Art Mus, 73-75; Smithsonian Inst Traveling Exhibs, 80-84. *Collections Arranged:* Black Untitled III, Western Asn Art Mus; Chico Group, Old Bergen Art Guild, NJ. *Pos:* Resident artist, Lakeside Studios, Mich, 70-; art dir, J-Squared B-Squared Consult, Los Angeles, 71- *Teaching:* Prof art, Calif State Univ, Chico, 69- *Awards:* Calif South 7 Best of Show, San Diego Fine Arts Guild, 69; Northwest Printmakers Purchase Award, Seattle Art Mus, 69; First Place for Graphics, Cal Expo, Del Mar, Calif, 69. *Bibliog:* J Edward Atkinson (auth), Black Dimensions in Contemporary American Art, Times Mirror, 71; Theresa Dickason Cederholm (auth), Afro American Artists, Boston Pub Libr, 73; Wasy Lewis (auth), Art: African American, Harcourt Brace Jovanovich, 78. *Media:* Intaglio, Serigraphy. *Dealer:* Marquoit Galleries 710 Sansome St San Francisco CA 94111. *Mailing Add:* Art Dept Calif State Univ Chico CA 95929

ERBE, JOAN
PAINTER
b Baltimore, Md, Nov 1, 26. *Study:* Md Inst Col Art. *Work:* Munic Court, Washington, DC; Peale Mus, Baltimore; Baltimore Mus Art; Morgan Col. *Exhib:* Peale Mus, 51-61; seven shows, Baltimore Mus Art, 54-65; Smithsonian Inst, 56; Corcoran Gallery Art, 57-60; 20 one-person shows, IFA Galleries, Washington, DC, 58-80; Butler Inst Am Art, 60 & 61; Am Acad Arts, 76; and others. *Teaching:* Pvt lessons, 79. *Awards:* Artists Equity Asn, 60 & 61; Corcoran Gallery Art, 60 & 62; Baltimore Mus Art, 63, 64 & 66; plus others. *Mailing Add:* 103 Woodlawn Rd Baltimore MD 21210

ERBES, ROSLYN MARIA See Rensch, Roslyn

ERDELAC, JOSEPH MARK
COLLECTOR, PATRON
b Cleveland, Ohio. *Mem:* Life mem Cleveland Mus Art, Butler Inst Am Art, Youngstown, Ohio & Royal Photographic Soc Brit. *Interests:* Donor of art works to local and national museums, universities, schools and educational television. *Collection:* Oils, watercolors and graphics by local and national

Washington Project for the Arts artists; oils, watercolors, drawings and graphics by Rockwell Kent; watercolors, drawings and collages by Stephen Longstreet; also work by Henry Miller, Charles Bukowski, Kenneth Patchen and Udinotti. *Mailing Add:* 24414 Garden Dr Cleveland OH 44123

ERDLE, ROB
PAINTER, EDUCATOR
b Selma, Calif, Aug 17, 49. *Study:* Reedley Col, Calif, AA; Calif State Univ, Fresno, BA; Bowling Green Univ, Ohio, MFA. *Exhib:* Ala Nat Watercolor Exhib, Birmingham Mus Art, 75-76; Toledo May Show, Toledo Mus Art, Ohio, 75-76; Southern Watercolorist Nat Exhib, Cheekwood Arts Ctr, Nashville, Tenn, 77; Rocky Mountain Nat Watercolor Exhib, Foothills Arts Ctr, Golden, Colo, 77; one-man show, Del Mar Col, Corpus Christi, Tex, 77; Tex Fine Arts Nat Exhib, Laguna Gloria Art Mus, Austin, 77; and others. *Pos:* Dir, Chautauqua Inst Art Gallery, Chautauqua, NY, currently. *Teaching:* Asst prof watercolor works on paper, NTex State Univ, 76-80, assoc prof, 80- *Awards:* Outstanding Painting Award, May Show, Toledo Mus Art, 75 & 76; First Prize Purchase Award, Ala Nat Watercolor Exhib, Birmingham Mus Art, 76; Watercolor USA, Springfield Art Mus, 77. *Mem:* Nat Watercolor Soc, Los Angeles; Tex Watercolor Soc, San Antonio; Watercolor Soc Ala, Birmingham; Southern Watercolor Soc, Memphis; Southwestern Watercolor Soc, Dallas. *Media:* Mixed. *Mailing Add:* 1701 Greenwood Dr Denton TX 76201

ERES, EUGENIA
PAINTER
b Winiza, Ucrania, Apr 28, 28; US citizen. *Study:* Fine Art Sch, Sao Paulo, Brazil, with Prof Murillo, 54-58; Famous Artists Sch, Westport, Conn, with Norman Rockwell, Fletcher Martin & Doug Kingman, 66-69; Nat Acad Fine Arts, New York, with Hugh Cumpel, 70-71. *Work:* Galleria de Artes IV Centenario, Sao Paulo; Russian Am Hist Mus, Lakewood, NJ; pvt collection of Jacqueline Kennedy-Onassis and others. *Exhib:* Nat Art League, New York, 74-81; Knickerbocker Artists, 74-81; Pen & Brush, 77-79; Salmagundi Club, 77-78; Custom House Mus Area, World Trade Ctr, New York, 79-81; and others. *Awards:* First Prize, Russian Am Soc, 75-78; Gold Medal of Honor, Nat Art League, 77; Gold Medal, Accademia Italia, 79; and others. *Mem:* Life fel Am Artists Prof League; Knickerbocker Artists; Nat Art League; Catharine Lorillard Wolfe Art Club; Accademia Italia; and others. *Media:* Oil. *Mailing Add:* 86-10 109th St Apt CC2 Richmond Hill NY 11418

ERICSON, BEATRICE
PAINTER
b Paris, France; US citizen. *Study:* With Morris Davidson & Boris Margo, Provincetown, Mass; also with Max Schnitzler, New York. *Work:* NY Univ Fine Arts; Marist Col, Poughkeepsie, NY; Miami Mus Mod Art; Gov Nelson A Rockefeller Collection. *Exhib:* Silvermine Guild Artists, New Canaan, Conn; Norfolk Mus Arts & Sci; one-man shows, Letters to the Unknown, Brata Gallery, 67, Archaic Past, Caravan House, 72 & 77, Mythological Journey, Gallery 84, 81 & Solitary Journey, Gallery 84, 83, New York. *Bibliog:* Leo Soretsky (auth), article, FM Guide, 4/72; ArtSpeak, 10/81; Park F, 10/81. *Media:* Acrylics, Ink. *Dealer:* Gallery 84 30 W 57th St New York NY 10021. *Mailing Add:* 14 Watkins Ave Middletown NY 10940

ERIKSEN, GARY
SCULPTOR, MEDALIST
b Jackson, Mich, Sept 11, 43. *Study:* Oberlin Col, BA, 66; Kent State Univ, MA, 68; Univ Chicago, 71-73; Accad Belle Arti Roma, 73-77; Scuola Dell'Arte Medaglia, with Francesco Giannone & Guerrino Monassi, Rome, dipl licenza, 77. *Work:* Nat Gallery Art, Budapest; Smithsonian Inst Numismatics Collection; Cooper-Hewitt Mus, Am Numismatic Soc, New York; Zecca Roma, Italy. *Comn:* 100 Vestal Virgins, Chantal-Dubois, Rome, 76; James N Landis Medal, Am Soc Mechanical Engineers, New York, 78; American Eagle, Kurt Wayne Inc, New York, 80; Gargoyle Reconstruction, Grace Episcopal Church, New York, 81; Bishop O M Kelly Portrait, Church God in Christ, New York & Nashville, 81. *Exhib:* Fedn Int Editeurs Medailles Int Biennial, Nat Gallery Art, Budapest, 77 & Palazzo Medici Riccardi, Florence, 83; Nat Sculpture Soc Ann, Equitable Gallery, New York, 78; First Ann Open Sculpture Exhib, Salmagundi Club, New York, 82; Carnegie Mansion Embellishments, Cooper-Hewitt Mus, New York, 83. *Pos:* Consult hand tools design, Sculpture House Inc, New York, 81-82; book rev ed, Sculptworld News, New York, 83- *Awards:* First Prize, Salmagundi Club First Ann Open Sculpture Exhib, 82; Fountains Proj Grant, NY State Coun Arts, 82. *Bibliog:* Ed Reiter (auth), article, New York Times, 8/15/82. *Mem:* Am Medallic Sculpture Asn (pres, 82-83, mem bd dirs, 82-); New York Artists Equity Asn; Fedn Int Editeurs Medailles; Soc Artists & Anatomists. *Media:* Bronze, Terra Cotta. *Mailing Add:* 280 Mott St Apt 3FS New York NY 10012

ERIQUEZZO, LEE M
PAINTER
b Danbury, Conn. *Study:* Md Inst Art; Mus Mod Art; Art Students League; Cooper Union, scholar; Rome Acad Belle Arts, Ital Cult Soc travel scholar; also with Edwin Dickensen, Joseph Hirsch, Zolton Hecht & Frank Mason, Foster & E Mayan. *Work:* Slater Mus, Norwich, Conn; Art Students League, Nat Acad Design, Brooklyn Mus, NY. *Exhib:* Nat Arts Club, New York; Nat Acad Design; Audubon Soc, New York; Slater Mus; La Galerie Mouffe, Paris, France. *Awards:* Benedictine Award; Nat Art Club & Cooper Union Awards. *Mem:* Greenwich Art Soc. *Media:* Oil, Lithograph. *Publ:* Illusr, Rachael Karr book on Yoga, 74. *Mailing Add:* c/o I L Sell 245 E 21st St New York NY 10010

ERLIEN, NANCY BETH
DEALER, PATRON
b Milwaukee, Wis, June 4, 54. *Study:* Univ Colo, 72-74; Univ Wis, advanced glass educ with Harvey Littleton, BS(fine arts), 76. *Collections Arranged:* Contemporary Glass 79-81; Ten Major American Glass Artists, 79-81. *Pos:* Co-dir, D Erlien Gallery, Milwaukee, 78- *Mem:* Founding mem Milwaukee Fine Art Dealers Asn. *Specialty:* Original prints; Comtemporary American glass; investment and corporate collections; art conservation. *Mailing Add:* D Erlien Gallery Ltd 5623 N Lake Dr Milwaukee WI 53217

ERNST, JAMES ARNOLD
PAINTER, INSTRUCTOR
b New York, NY, Aug 5, 16. *Study:* Pratt Inst Sch Art, 37-39; Grand Cent Art Sch, 40. *Work:* Acad Arts, Easton, Md; Talbot Co Libr, Easton, Md; Elliot Mus, Stuart, Fla. *Exhib:* One-man shows, Veerhoff Galleries, Washington, DC, 76 & 83, Inst Cult Dominico-Americano, Santo Domingo, Dominican Repub, 76, Gallery by the Sea, Vero Beach, Fla, 79 & Elliott Mus, Stuart, Fla, 81. *Pos:* Specialist in design & line drawing, Batten, Barton, Durstine & Osborne, Inc, New York, 51-62. *Teaching:* Instr drawing, beginning & advan watercolor, City Col New York, 51-62. *Awards:* First Prize & Purchase Award, Land of Pleasant Living Exhib, 69; Best in Show, Lee Lawrie Award, Acad Arts, Easton, 75; Maritime Award, Baltimore Watercolor Soc, 78. *Mem:* Joint Ethics Comt; Rehoboth Art League, NJ; Baltimore Watercolor Soc; Vero Beach Art Club; Acad Arts, Md. *Media:* Watercolor, Oil. *Publ:* Drawing the Line, NY, Reinhold, 62. *Dealer:* Veerhoff Galleries 1512 Connecticut Ave Washington DC 20036; Calico Gallery St Michaels MD. *Mailing Add:* 3554 Ocean Dr PH1-N Vero Beach FL 32963

ERNST, JIMMY
PAINTER, EDUCATOR
b Cologne, Ger, June 24, 20; US citizen. *Study:* Altona Arts & Crafts Sch, 38. *Work:* Whitney Mus Am Art, Metrop Mus Art, New York; Brooklyn Mus; Wadsworth Atheneum; Art Inst Chicago; and many others. *Comn:* Plastic sculpture signature, NBC Producer's Showcase, 54; paintings, Abbott Labs, 55 & Fortune Mag, 55 & 61; mural, Continental Bank, Lincoln, Nebr, 58-59; relief mural, Envoy Towers, New York, 60; and others. *Exhib:* Pa Acad Fine Arts, 53, 55, 57 & 65; Bielefeld Mus, Ger, 64; one-man show, Grand Rapids Mus Art, 68; Whitney Mus Am Art Ann, 69 & 70; Guggenheim Mus Paris show, 72-78; Lucie Weil Gallery, Spiegel Gallery, Cologne, Ger, Yares Gallery, Scottsdale, Ariz, 77-78; plus many others. *Teaching:* Lectr contemp art, art asns & mus in US; prof art, Brooklyn Col, 51-82; vis artist, Univ Colo, summers 54 & 56; vis artist, Mus Fine Arts, Houston, 56; lectr, US Info Serv, USSR & Ger, 61 & 63. *Awards:* Norman Wait Harris Award, Art Inst Chicago, 54; Creative Arts Award, Brandeis Univ, 57; Guggenheim Found Fel, 61. *Dealer:* Borgenicht Gallery 1018 Madison Ave New York NY 10028. *Mailing Add:* Lee Ave East Hampton NY 11937

ERTMAN, EARL LESLIE
HISTORIAN, EDUCATOR
b Parma, Ohio, Nov 13, 32. *Study:* Univ Southern Miss, BS, 65; Case Western Reserve Univ, MA, 67; Cleveland Mus, Egyptian art with John D Cooney, 67-71; Univ Akron, classics with T T Duke, 67-70. *Pos:* Art historian & field photogr, Johns Hopkins Exped to pyramid area, Giza, Egypt, summer 72 & 74, Tell el Rataba, 78. *Teaching:* Instr Western art, Dept Art Hist & Educ, Cleveland Mus Art, 65-67; prof art hist, Univ Akron, 67-, head dept art, 81- *Bibliog:* Edward K Werner (auth), The Amarna period of 18th dynasty Egypt, bibliography supplement, 76, Am Res Ctr Egypt Newsletter, Numbers 101-102, 77; Pauline Albenda (auth), Landscape bas-reliefs in the Bit-Hilani of Ashurbanipal, Am Sch Oriental Res Bulletin, 77; Arielle Kozloff (auth), Nefertiti beloved of the living disk, Bulletin Cleveland Mus Art, 11/77. *Mem:* Am Asn Univ Prof; Archaeol Inst Am; Am Res Ctr Egypt. *Res:* Iconographic and stylistic analysis of ancient Egyptian art and documentation of Egyptian objects in minor collections in the United States. *Publ:* Auth, The oldest known three-dimensional representation of the God Ptah, J Near Eastern Studies, 72; auth, A manuscript fragment by the Parisian miniaturist Honore in Cleveland, Ohio, Sciptorium, Paris-Brussels, 73; auth, The cap-crown of Nefertiti: Its function and probable origin, J Am Res Ctr Egypt, 76; contribr, Recording and documentation of minor collections in the United States, 1st Int Cong Egyptology, Inst Hist & Archaeol, Munich, 76; coauth, Arts of Ancient Egypt: Treasures on Another Scale (catalog), pvt publ, 81; and others. *Mailing Add:* Dept Art Univ Akron Akron OH 44325

ESAKI, YASUHIRO
PAINTER, PRINTMAKER
b Omuta, Japan, June 8, 41. *Study:* Acad Art Col, BFA, 72; Lone Mountain Col, MFA(painting), 75, MFA(printmaking), 78. *Work:* Achenbach Found, Fine Art Mus, San Francisco; Boston Mus Fine Arts; Brooklyn Mus; Cincinnati Art Mus; Metrop Mus & Art Ctr, Miami, Fla. *Comn:* Etching, Mark Hopkins Hotel, San Francisco, 78. *Exhib:* MIX Graphic I, San Francisco Mus Mod Art, 73; Acquisition Shows, Achenbach Found, Fine Art Mus, San Francisco, 75, 78 & 79; Nat Drawing Exhib, Rutgers State Univ, Camden, 77; Third Int Graphic Biennial, Metrop Mus & Art Ctr, Miami, Fla, 77; Contemp Am Artist Exhib, Cent Mus, Tokyo, 78; 2nd Nat Drawing Competition, Miami Univ Mus, Oxford, Ohio, 78; 21st Nat Print Exhib, Brooklyn Mus, 79. *Teaching:* Instr printmaking, Acad Art Col, San Francisco, 78- *Awards:* Grand Prize, Third Miami Int Graphic Biennial, Metrop Mus & Art Ctr, 77; Purchase Prize, Belknap Mem Int Print Competition, Columbia-Greene Community Col, 78; Purchase Prize, Stockton Nat '78, Univ Pac & Pioneer Mus & Haggin Art Gallery, 78. *Bibliog:* Robert McDonald (auth), Drawing by Yasuhiro Esaki, Artweek, 77; Nancy C Pierce (auth), Third Miami graphic biennial, Graphics, 78; Gene Baro (auth), Twenty-First

National Print Exhibition, Brooklyn Mus, 79. *Mem:* Calif Soc Printmakers. *Media:* Acrylic, Color Pencil; Etching. *Dealer:* Asn Am Artists Gallery 663 Fifth Ave New York NY 10022. *Mailing Add:* 11 San Antonio Ct Walnut Creek CA 94598

ESAU, ERIKA
LIBRARIAN, HISTORIAN
b Santa Barbara, Calif, Apr 1, 49. *Study:* Colo Women's Col, Denver, BA, 71; Univ Denver, MA, 72; Bryn Mawr Col, Pa, Fel, 79. *Pos:* Asst humanities librn, Portland State Univ, Ore, 72-73; librn, Deutscher Werkbund, Darmstadt, Ger, 74; slide librn, Univ Tex, San Antonio, 75-77; librn, Kimbell Art Mus, Ft Worth, Tex, currently. *Awards:* Fulbright Scholar, Darmstadt, Ger, 73-74; Kress Fel, Vienna, Austria, 80-81. *Mem:* Art Libr NAm. *Res:* Nineteenth-century Austrian art; Dada. *Publ:* Auth, Index, Werk & Zeit Mag 1965-1977, Deutscher Werkbund, 78; coauth, The mermaid in Mexican folk art, Southwest Folklore, 5/81; contribr, Schwitters, Macmillan Encycl Archit, 82; contribr, International Art Periodicals, Greenwood Press (in prep); ed, Art Doc, Art Libr Soc NAm. *Mailing Add:* c/o Kimbell Art Mus PO Box 9440 Ft Worth TX 76107

ESCOBEDO, HELEN
ENVIRONMENTAL SCULPTOR
b Mexico City, Mex, July 28, 36. *Study:* Univ Motolinia, BA(humanities); ARCA, 3 yr scholar; also with Frank Dobson, John Skeaping & Leon Underwood. *Work:* Mus Mod Art, Mex; Prague Nat Gallery, Czech; Palacio de Bellas Artes, Mexico City; also in pvt collection of Stanley Marcus, US. *Comn:* Gateway to the Wind (concrete), Mex Olympic Games, Friendship Rte, 68; Signals (aluminum), Auckland, Golden Jubilee, NZ, 71; Coatl (steel), Univ Mex, 80; Reaseguradora Patria Bldg, 80; Barda Caida, Univ Mex, 81; and others. *Exhib:* One-man shows, Prague Nat Gallery, 69, Park Lazienkowsky, Stara Kordegarda, Warsaw, Poland, 70 & Mus Mod Art, Mexico City, 75; Kunstindustri Mus, Oslo, Norway, 70; Middelheim Sculpture Bienale, Antwerp, Belg, 71. *Pos:* Dir, Dept Mus & Galleries, Nat Univ Mex, 61-77 & res fel, Fac Humanities, Centre for Sculptural Space, Univ Mex, 78; tech dir, Mus Nat Arte, Mex, 82; dir, Mus Arte Mod, Mex, 83. *Teaching:* Artist in residence, Tulane Univ, 76, Hartnell Col, 77, Newcomb Col, 81, Kunsterhaus Betanien, Berlin, 81, Scripps Col, 83. *Bibliog:* 4 Shapes 4 Spaces, Nat Film Bd, NZ, 74; Alfredo Gurrola (auth), Helen Escobedo, Cent Univ de Estudios Cinematog, 75. *Mem:* Nat Sculpture Ctr, Lawrence, Kans (mem bd, 71-); Int Comn Mus (mem bd, 75-). *Media:* Multimedia. *Dealer:* Galeria de Arte Mexicano Milan 18 Mexico DF 6 Mexico. *Mailing Add:* AV San Jeronimo 162 Mexico DF Mexico

ESHOO, ROBERT
PAINTER
b New Britain, Conn, Apr 27, 26. *Study:* Boston Mus Fine Arts Sch Mass, cert & dipl; Vesper George Sch Art, Boston; Syracuse Univ, BFA & MFA. *Work:* Boston Mus Fine Arts; Wadsworth Atheneum, Hartford, Conn; Currier Gallery Art, Manchester, NH; Munson-Williams-Proctor Inst, Utica, NY; Addison Gallery Am Art, Andover, Mass; and others. *Exhib:* Recent Drawings USA, Mus Mod Art, New York, 56; Chicago Art Inst Ann, 57; Young Artists, Whitney Mus, 57; Selections 1959, 59 & View 1960, 60, Inst Contemp Art, Boston; American Painting 1962, Va Mus Fine Arts, Richmond, 62; The Dana Collection, 62 & Potlatch, 63, Inst Contemp Art, Boston; 28th Biennial, Corcoran Gallery, Washington, DC, 63; Northeastern Regional--Art Across America, 65 & Art for Embassies, 66, Inst Contemp Art, Boston; one-man shows, Rigelhaupt Gallery, 68, Pucker/Safrai Gallery, Boston, 72 & 75 & Manchester, NH, 76 & 79; Robert Eshoo: A Decade of Painting and Drawings, Currier Gallery Art, Manchester, NH, 81. *Teaching:* Sch Mus Fine Arts, Boston, 54-55, Syracuse Univ, 56-57, Phillips Acad, Andover, 60 & 62-64 & Derryfield Sch, 65-80; supvr, Currier Art Ctr. *Bibliog:* New Talents USA, Art in Am, 2/56; American artists coming to the fore, Harper's Bazaar, 3/60; Emerging reputations, Art in Am, summer 62. *Media:* Oil, Watercolor. *Mailing Add:* 47 Amoskeag Pl Manchester NH 03101

ESLER, JOHN KENNETH
PRINTMAKER, PAINTER
b Pilot Mound, Man, Jan 11, 33. *Study:* Univ Man, BEd, Univ Man Sch Art, BFA. *Work:* Mus Mod Art, New York; Victoria & Albert Mus, London; Albright-Knox Gallery, Buffalo; Nat Gallery Can, Ottawa; Montreal Mus Fine Arts. *Exhib:* Third Biennal Am Grababo, Santiago, Chile, 68; Third Int Gravure, Krakow, Poland, 70; Second Int Print Biennale, Bradford, Eng, 70; Premio Int Biella, Italy, 71; Int Buchkunst-Ausstellung, Leipzig, 71. *Teaching:* Assoc prof printmaking, Alta Col Art, Calgary, 64-68 & Univ Calgary, 68-80. *Awards:* C W Jefferies Award, Can Soc Graphic Arts, 68; First Purchase Award, Burnaby Biennial Print Exhib, 69; First Purchase Award, Graphic Exhib, Art Alliance Cent Pa, 70. *Media:* Etching, Collagraph. *Mailing Add:* Box 2 Site 7 SS 1 Calgary AB T2M 4N3 Canada

ESMAN, ROSA M
DEALER, GALLERY DIRECTOR
b New York, NY, Nov 29, 27. *Study:* Smith Col, BA. *Work:* Mus Mod Art, New York Int, Whitney Mus Am Art, Metrop Mus Art, New York; Brit Arts Coun, London. *Pos:* Pres & dir, Tanglewood Press, New York, 64-69 & 72-; dir, Abrams Original Editions, 69-72; pres & dir, Rosa Esman Gallery, 72- *Specialty:* Contemporary American paintings, drawings and sculpture; Russian avant-garde material, 1911-1923; American avant-garde painting of the 20's and 30's. *Collection:* Contemporary drawings, prints and paintings, with emphasis on New York artists of the 60's and 70's; also African and pre-Columbian art. *Publ:* Ed, Seven objects in a box, 66 & New York, 10/69, 69, Six drawing tables by Saul Steinberg, 71, Four Pochoirs by Helen Frankenthaler, 71 & No gas by Red Grooms, 72; and others. *Mailing Add:* 29 W 57th St New York NY 10019

ESPENET (ARTHUR CARPENTER)
CRAFTSMAN, LECTURER
b New York, NY, Jan 20, 20. *Study:* Dartmouth Col, BA. *Work:* City of San Francisco, Calif; San Francisco State Univ; Mus of Sci & Indust, Chicago; Oakland Mus, Calif; Johnson Wax Collection. *Comn:* Furniture, Stan Sobel, 70, Old St Mary's, 71, San Francisco; furniture, Mill Valley Libr, Calif, 72; furniture, Bishop O'Dowd Chapel. *Exhib:* Inst of Contemp Art, Boston, 49; Good Design Show, Mus of Mod Art, New York, 50-54; Mus of Contemp Crafts, New York, 56; Magnani Mem Craft Collection, San Francisco State Univ, 66; Mus of Contemp Crafts, New York, 66; Objects USA, Johnson Collection, 68; Wooden Works, Smithsonian Inst, Washington, DC, 72; E B Crocker Art Gallery, Sacramento, Calif, 73; Craft Multiples, Smithsonian Inst, 75; and others. *Teaching:* Lectr furniture, San Francisco State Univ, Univ Calif, Berkeley & Brigham Young Univ, formerly. *Bibliog:* Article, Am Crafts, 7/82; article, Fine Woodworking, 11/82; article, Britannica Encycl Am Art. *Mem:* Bolinas Craft Guild (pres, 77). *Media:* Wood. *Publ:* Auth, Eames Furniture, Craft Horizons, 73; auth, Artiture, Fine Woodworking, 2/83. *Mailing Add:* Lower County Rd Bolinas CA 94924

ESSER, JANET BRODY
HISTORIAN, EDUCATOR
b New Haven, Conn. *Study:* Univ Iowa, with John Rosenfield & William Heckscher, BFA, 51; Kent State Univ, BS, 53; Calif State Univ, Long Beach, MA, 70; Univ Calif, Los Angeles, with Rubin & Nicholson, PhD, 78. *Collections Arranged:* San Diego Collects: African Art, 78; Faces of Fiesta: Mexican Masks in Context, 80. *Teaching:* Lectr, Kent State Univ, 55-60 & Calif State Univ, Long Beach, 69-71; lectr, San Diego State Univ, 75-80, assoc prof, 80- *Awards:* Nat Endowment Humanities Summer Inst Fel, 78. *Mem:* Col Art Asn Am; Latin Am Studies Asn; Latin Am Art Historians Asn; African Studies Asn; Ethno-Historical Soc. *Res:* Pre-Columbian, European and African antecedents of masking traditions in contemporary rural Mexican cummunities; African imagery in Iberia. *Publ:* Auth, The Hortelanos: A Buffoon's Dance from Uruapan, Los Angeles, 71; auth, Actas Mexico del Congreso Internacional de Americanistas, 71; auth, Masks of Women from Michoacan, Masterkey, Vol 53, Southwest Mus, 79; auth, Tarascan Masking Traditions, Fabrics of Culture, Berlin, 79; auth, Mascaras rituales de la sierra tarasca, Michoacan, Inst Nac Indigenista, Mexico; and others. *Mailing Add:* 8057 Hillandale Dr San Diego CA 92130

ESTABROOK, REED
PHOTOGRAPHER, EDUCATOR
b Boston, Mass, May 31, 44. *Study:* RI Sch of Design, BFA, 69; Art Inst of Chicago, MFA, 71. *Work:* Mus Mod Art, New York; Art Inst Chicago; Int Mus Photog, Rochester, NY; RI Sch Design, Providence; Minneapolis Inst Arts, Minn. *Exhib:* Photo Synthesis, H F Johnson Mus, Cornell Univ, 76; Great West/Real: Ideal (travelling exhib), Univ Colo Mus of Art, Boulder, 77; Mirrors & Windows, Mus Mod Art, New York, 78; Attitudes, Santa Barbara Mus Art, Calif, 79; Hand Colored Photog, Philadelphia Col Art, 79; New American Nudes, Minneapolis Inst Arts, Minn; and others. *Teaching:* Instr photog, Univ Ill, Urbana-Champaign, 71-74; asst prof photog, Univ Northern Iowa, 74-78, assoc prof, 78-82; photog chmn, Kansas City Art Inst, 83- *Awards:* W R French Fel Competition, Art Inst Chicago, 71; First Place, Am Photographics, Andromeda Gallery, Buffalo, 76; Photog Fel, Nat Endowment Arts, 76. *Mem:* Soc for Photog Educ. *Publ:* contribr, Aura, Vol 1, 76 & Vol 2, 77, Andromeda Gallery; contribr, Creative Camera, Coos Press, Vol 153 (77); contribr, Darkroom Dynamics, Curtis & London, 79; contrib, New American Nudes, Morgan & Morgan, 81; contrib, Picture Mag #17, 81. *Mailing Add:* 1717 Wyandoite Kansas City MO 64108

ESTERN, NEIL
SCULPTOR
b New York, NY, Apr 18, 26. *Study:* Temple Univ, BFA & BS(educ), 47. *Work:* Brooklyn Mus; LaGuardia Community Col; Midwood High School. *Comn:* Portraits of LaGuardia, J Robert Taft, Danny Kaye, John F Kennedy, J Edgar Hoover, Pres Carter, Prince Charles, Lady Diana, Dolly Parton & Jack Nicholson; portrait bust of John F Kennedy, Kennedy Mem, Grand Army Plaza, Brooklyn, 65; Franklin D Roosevelt Memorial, Washington, DC. *Exhib:* Numerous one-man and group shows in Conn, New York, Philadelphia, NH & Italy. *Awards:* John Gregory Award, 66; Samuel F B Morse Gold Medal, 70; Award, Kent Art Asn, 81. *Mailing Add:* 82 Remsen St Brooklyn NY 11201

ESTEROW, MILTON
EDITOR, PUBLISHER
b New York, NY, July 28, 28. *Study:* Brooklyn Col, NY. *Pos:* Asst cult news dir, New York Times, 63-68; ed & publ, Art News, 72-; ed & publ, Art Newsletter, 75-; chmn, Art News Books, 79- *Teaching:* Lectr art, museums, colleges & universities. *Awards:* Silurians Award, 78; George Polk Award, 81; Nat Mags Award, 81; and others. *Publ:* Contribr, Art News, New York Times Mag & Atlantic Mag. *Mailing Add:* Art News 5 W 37th St New York NY 10018

ESTES, RICHARD
PAINTER
b Ill, 1936. *Study:* Chicago Art Inst, 52-56. *Work:* Whitney Mus Am Art, New York; Rockhill Nelson Mus, Kansas City, Mo; Toledo Mus, Ohio; Chicago Art Inst; Des Moines Art Ctr, Iowa. *Exhib:* Documenta V, Kassel, Ger, summer 72; Venice Biennale, Italy, summer 72; Whitney Mus Ann, 72; Twelve American Painters, Va Mus Fine Arts, Richmond, 74; Trends in Contemp Realist Painting, 75 & The Urban Landscape, 78, Boston Mus Fine Arts; and others. *Bibliog:* Peter Schjeldahl (auth), Flowering of the super-real,

3/2/69 & John Canaday (auth), Realism-waxing or waning, 7/13/69, New York Times; Mary Lou Kelly (auth), Popart inspired objective realism, Christian Sci Monitor, 4/1/74. *Media:* Oil. *Mailing Add:* 300 Central Park W New York NY 10028

ETCHISON, BRUCE
CONSERVATOR, PAINTER
b Washington, DC, Dec 19, 18. *Study:* Am Univ, BA; Yale Univ Sch Fine Arts, BFA & MFA. *Pos:* Dir, Washington Co Mus Fine Arts, 50-64; dir, Abby Aldrich Rockefeller Folk Art Collection, 64-66; conservator for pvt collectors mus, univs, cols, hist soc & the State of Pa, currently. *Mem:* Int & Am Insts Conserv Hist & Artistic Works; Washington Conserv Guild. *Publ:* Coauth, Roentgen Examination of Painting, 60; auth, Radiant Heat for Vacuum Tables, 69. *Mailing Add:* Bear Pond Studio 14072 Blairs Valley Rd Mercersburg PA 17236

ETIENNE, GUILLERMO C
PAINTER, PRINTMAKER
b Tampico Tamps, Mex, Oct 14, 38. *Study:* Self-taught. *Work:* Univ del Estado de Mex, Toluca; Diego Rivera Mus, Guanajuato; Univ N Aut d Mex. *Exhib:* Collective, McAllen Civic Ctr, Tex, 78; Collective, Anthropology Mus, Mex, 79; Lithographs & Drawing, J Guadalupe Posadas, Mex, 80; Etienne's Drawing, Univ N Aut de Mex, 81; Drawings & Lithographs, Diego Rivera, Guanajuato, 81; Collective, US Ambassador House, Mexico City, 81. *Media:* Charcoal, Pencil. *Publ:* Restoration and Cleaning of Paintings, private publ, 80. *Dealer:* Galeria Pavo Real Amberes 57 Mex 6 DF Mexico 06600. *Mailing Add:* Apdo 148 Cd Satelite Edo de Mexico Mexico

ETNIER, STEPHEN MORGAN
PAINTER
b York, Pa, Sept 11, 03. *Study:* Yale Art Sch; Pa Acad Fine Arts; also with Rockwell Kent & John Carroll; hon degrees from Bowdoin Col & Bates Col. *Work:* Metrop Mus Art; Boston Mus; Yale Univ; Toledo Mus; Duncan Phillips, Washington, DC. *Exhib:* Carnegie Inst; Corcoran Gallery Art; Pa Acad Fine Arts; Nat Acad Fine Arts; Milch Gallery, 31-64; Midtown Galleries, New York, 76; and others. *Awards:* Samuel F B Morse Gold Medal, Altman Prize & Saltus Gold Medal, Nat Acad Design. *Bibliog:* Howard Deoree & Ernest Watson (auths), Stephen Etnier, 56 & Betty Chamberlain (auth), Stephen Etnier, a long voyage home, 72, Am Artist; Stephen Etnier, artist, Maine Life, 9/81. *Media:* Oil. *Dealer:* Midtown Gallery 11 E 57th St New York NY 10022; P S Gallery 2525 Fairmount St Dallas TX. *Mailing Add:* Old Cove South Harpswell ME 04079

ETROG, SOREL
SCULPTOR, PAINTER
b Jassy, Romania, Aug 29, 33. *Study:* Inst Painting & Sculpture, Tel Aviv, Israel; Brooklyn Mus Sch Art. *Work:* Art Gallery Toronto; Mus Fine Arts, Mus Art Contemp, Montreal; Nat Gallery Can; Boymans Mus, Rotterdam, Holland; and many others. *Exhib:* Expo '67; one-man retrospective, Palazzo Strozzi, Florence, Italy, 68; Ont Cols Traveling Exhib, Art Gallery Toronto, 68-69; Fine Arts Mus, Montreal, 68; Winnipeg Art Gallery, Man, 71; 4th Int Exhib Contemp Sculpture, Mus Rodin, Paris, 71; and many others. *Mem:* Royal Can Acad Arts. *Mailing Add:* PO Box 5943 Terminal A Toronto ON M5W 1P3 Canada

ETS, MARIE HALL
ILLUSTRATOR, WRITER
b North Greenfield, Wis, Dec 16, 93. *Study:* NY Sch Fine & Appl Art, 16-17; Univ Chicago, PhB, 24; Art Inst Chicago; also with Frederick V Poole. *Work:* Kerlan Collection, Univ Minn Libr; Iowa City Pub Libr; Milwaukee Pub Libr. *Comn:* Set of illus, Childcraft & How & Why Libr. *Exhib:* 1st Ann Exhib Selected Bks for Children, Am Fedn Arts, 45; one-woman show, original drawings, Libr Exhib Gallery, Teachers Col, Columbia Univ, 63; Albright-Knox Gallery Art, 64. *Awards:* Hans Christian Andersen Award, Stockholm, Sweden, 56; Am Inst Graphic Arts Award, 58-60; Caldecott Award, 60. *Publ:* Auth & illusr, In the Forest, 44, Play With Me, 55, Nine Days to Christmas, 59, Gilberto and the Wind, 63, Just Me, 65, Viking Press; and many others. *Mailing Add:* c/o Viking Press Inc 625 Madison Ave New York NY 10022

ETTENBERG, FRANKLIN JOSEPH
PAINTER, DRAFTSMAN
b Brooklyn, NY, May 7, 45. *Study:* Univ Mich, BS(design), 66, with Milton Cohen, Fred Bauer & John Stephenson; Univ NMex, MA, 71, with John Kacere. *Work:* Detroit Inst Art, Mich; Univ NMex Fine Arts Mus, Albuquerque; Roswell Mus & Art Ctr, NMex; Fine Arts Mus, Santa Fe; Minnesota Mus Art, St Paul; and others. *Comn:* Paired Paintings, NMex Arts Comn, 77; Taos Watershed Mural, Mary Medina Bldg, Taos, NMex, 78. *Exhib:* 19th Exhib Southwestern Prints & Drawings, Dallas Mus Fine Arts, 72; Hill's Gallery, Santa Fe, 75; Horwitch Gallery, Santa Fe, 78; Cochise Fine Arts of Santa Fe, Bisbee, Ariz, 79; Taos to Tucson, Foundations Gallery, New York, 82; one-man show, Harris Gallery, Houston, 82; and others. *Pos:* Exec comt, Advocates for Contemp Art, Santa Fe, 73-75. *Teaching:* Instr, Santa Fe Workshops of Contemp Art, summer, 74; pvt painting instr, 79- *Awards:* Artist in Residence Grant, Roswell Mus & Art Ctr, 72; Purchase Award, Drawings/USA 77, Minn Mus of Art, St Paul, 77. *Dealer:* Harris Gallery 1100 Bissonnet Houston TX; Ellen Sragow Ltd 80 Fifth Ave New York NY. *Mailing Add:* 215 W San Francisco St Santa Fe NM 87501

ETTER, HOWARD LEE
PAINTER, LECTURER
b Moberly, Mo, Jan 22, 31. *Study:* Art League Calif, San Francisco; Acad Art, San Francisco. *Work:* Butler Inst Am Art, Youngstown, Ohio. *Exhib:* 37th & 39th Midyear Show, Butler Inst Am Art, 73 & 75; Nat Painting Show, Washington & Jefferson Col, 74; 17th Ann Delta Art Exhib, 74. *Teaching:* Lectr drawing, painting & watercolor, Lawrence Inst Technol, 68-77. *Awards:* Spec Jurors Award, Washington & Jefferson Col Painting Show, 74; 39th Butler Inst Midyear Show Purchase Award, Friends Am Art, 75. *Mem:* Mich Watercolor Soc; Artist Equity Asn; NMex Watercolor Soc; Midwest Watercolor Soc. *Media:* Watercolor, Egg Tempera; Acrylic. *Dealer:* Aldridge Fine Arts 110 San Felipe NW Old Town Albuquerque NM; Massachusetts House Lincolnville ME. *Mailing Add:* PO Box 198 Cherryfield ME 04622

ETTING, EMLEN
PAINTER, ILLUSTRATOR
b Philadelphia, Pa, Aug 24, 05. *Study:* Harvard Univ, BS, 28; Grande Chaumiere & Andre Lhote, Paris. *Work:* Whitney Mus Am Art, New York; Pa Acad Fine Arts, Philadelphia; Addison Gallery Am Art, Andover, Mass; Philadelphia Mus Art; Atwater Kent Mus, Philadelphia. *Comn:* Philadelphia Industries (oil), Market St Nat Bank, 47; oil, Italian Consulate, Philadelphia, 55. *Exhib:* Whitney Mus; Carnegie Inst, Pittsburgh; Corcoran Gallery Art, Washington, DC; Pa Acad Fine Arts; San Francisco World's Fair; Retrospectives, Fla Southern Col, Lakeland, 73 & Allentown Art Mus, Pa, 74. *Pos:* US artist-deleg, Second Int Cong Plastic Arts, Dubrovnik, 57. *Teaching:* Instr painting & drawing, Sch Indust Art, Philadelphia Mus Art; Philadelphia Col Art & Tyler Sch Art, Temple Univ. *Awards:* Chevalier, Legion d'Honneur, Fr Govt; Star Solidarity, Italian Govt. *Bibliog:* Mary Rupert (auth), Emlen Etting, Paintings of an American Romantic, London Studio, 39. *Mem:* Artists Equity Asn (nat pres, 55-58, hon pres & pres, Philadelphia Chap, 50-53); Nat Soc Mural Painters; Century Asn; Philadelphia Art Alliance; Alliance Francaise (hon pres); plus others. *Media:* Oil, Acrylic. *Publ:* Illusr & translr, Valery, Le Cimetiere Marin, Centaur Press, 32; illusr, Amerika & Ecclesiastes, New Directions, 40; illusr, Born in a Crowd, Crowell-Collier; auth & illusr, Drawing the Ballet, Studio Bks, 44. *Dealer:* Midtown Galleries 11 E 57th St New York NY 10022. *Mailing Add:* 1927 Panama St Philadelphia PA 19103

ETTINGER, SUSI STEINITZ
PAINTER, LECTURER
b Berlin, Ger, July 29, 22; US citizen. *Study:* Univ Louisville, BFA(cum laude art hist), 43; with Dr Justus Bier. *Work:* Springfield Art Mus, Mo; State Hist Soc Mo, Columbia; Sch of the Ozarks, Point Lookout, Mo; Greenwood Lab Sch, Springfield. *Exhib:* Women Artists 77 Exhib, Kansas City, Mo Univ, 77; Watercolor USA, 79; one-artist shows, Southwest Mo Univ, 80, 18th Ann Sch Ozarks Exhib, 81, Art on Paper, Mabee Art Ctr, Drury Col, 81; and many others. *Teaching:* Dir children's art classes, Springfield Art Mus, 60-66; lectr art, Southwest Mo State Univ, 64- *Awards:* Regional Ten State Competition Purchase Award, Springfield Art Mus, 69; First Prize Painting, Mo Col Fac Show, 70; Award in recognition of creative accomplishments in the visual arts, Am Asn Univ Women, 74; and others. *Media:* Acrylic, Charcoal. *Mailing Add:* 2020 S Ventura Ave Springfield MO 65804

ETTL, GEORG
PAINTER, SCULPTOR
b Nittenau, Ger, Mar 3, 31. *Study:* Sorbonne, Paris, France, 63-65; Wayne State Univ, BA, 65, MA, 67, MFA, 68. *Work:* Mus Abteiberg, Möchen Gladbach, Ger; Kaiser Wilhelm Mus, Krefeld, Ger. *Comn:* Amphitheater, 81 & Murals for City Co Bldg, Vierson, Ger, 83-84. *Exhib:* All Mich Exhib, Flint Inst Arts, 72; solo exhib, Mus Abteiberg, Mönchen Gladbach, Ger, 77-78; With a Certain Smile, Zurich, Switz, 79; Kick Out the Jams: Detroit's Cass Corridor 1963-77, Detroit Inst Arts & Mus Contemp Art, Chicago, 81; With a Certain Smile, Krefeld, Ger, 83. *Awards:* Purchase Prizes, 58th Exhib Mich Artists, Detroit Inst Arts, 70 & All Mich Exhib, Flint Inst Arts, 72. *Bibliog:* Johannes Cladders (auth), Georg Ettl, Städtisches Mus Mönchen Gladbach, 77; Julian Heyden (auth), Georg Ettl: Hausordnung, Krefelder Kunstmus, 83; Nena Dimitrijevic (auth), Sculpture and Its Double, Sculpture Show, Greater London Coun, 83. *Media:* All. *Dealer:* J Feigenson 310 Fisher Bldg Detroit MI 48202. *Mailing Add:* Rahserstr 14 Viersen Germany, Federal Republic of

ETTLING, RUTH (DROITCOUR)
PRINTMAKER, PAINTER
b Pittsburgh, Pa, Mar 30, 10. *Study:* RI Sch Design; Marshall Univ, BA; spec study with Charles Burchfield, Arnold Blanch, William Thon, Fletcher Martin, Victor Candell & Walter Murch. *Work:* Charleston Gallery Sunrise, WVa; Dayton Art Inst, Ohio; Hunterdon Co Art Ctr, Clinton, NJ; Huntington Galleries, WVa; WVa Arts & Humanities Collection, Charleston. *Exhib:* Hunterdon Co Nat Print Show, Clinton, 62; Ohio Printmakers, Dayton, 62; Exhib 180, Huntington, 70; Ruth Ettling's Recent Prints, Huntington Galleries, 71; Allied Artists WVa, Charleston, 72. *Teaching:* Instr drawing & painting, Huntington Galleries, 52-66; summer dir, print workshop, 72. *Awards:* Purchase Award, Tri-State Exhib, Huntington Galleries, WVa, 82; Merit Award, Cardinal Valley Show, Ashland, Ky, 83. *Mem:* Tri-State Arts Asn (pres, 72); Nat Art Educ Asn. *Publ:* Illusr, Dear Bob, love mother, 67. *Mailing Add:* 1475 Spring Valley Circle Huntington WV 25704

ETTLINGER, LEOPOLD DAVID
HISTORIAN
b Konigsberg, Ger, Apr 20, 13; Brit citizen. *Study:* Univs of Halle & Marburg, PhD, 37. *Pos:* Cur photog collection, Warburg Inst, Univ London, Eng, 48-56, lectr, 56-64. *Teaching:* Durning-Lawrence prof hist art, Univ London, Eng,

59-70; prof hist art, Univ Calif, Berkeley, 70-80, emer prof, 80- *Mem:* Fel Soc Antiquaries, London. *Publ:* Auth, The Sistine Chapel Before Michelangelo, Oxford Univ Press, 64; co-auth, Botticelli, Thames & Hudson/Oxford Univ Press, 76; auth, Antonio & Piero Pollaiuolo, Phaidon Press, 78. *Mailing Add:* Dept of Art Hist Univ Calif Berkeley CA 94720

EVANS, BRUCE HASELTON
MUSEUM DIRECTOR, HISTORIAN
b Rome, NY, Nov 13, 39. *Study:* Amherst Col, BA; NY Univ Inst Fine Arts, MA. *Collections Arranged:* The Paintings of Edward Edmondson, 72; Jean-Leon Gerome--The Paintings (with catalog), 72. *Pos:* Cur asst to dir, Dayton Art Inst, 65-67, chief cur, 68-72, asst dir, 72-74, dir, 75- *Mem:* Am Asn Mus; Asn Art Mus Dirs; Ohio Mus Asn (pres, currently). *Publ:* Auth, Fifty Treasures of the Dayton Art Institute, 69; auth, Edward Edmondson--A Biography and Critical Study of His Paintings, 72; and numerous articles in mus bulletins and exhib catalogs. *Mailing Add:* PO Box 941 Dayton OH 45401

EVANS, BURFORD ELONZO
PAINTER, LECTURER
b Golinda, Tex, July 20, 31. *Study:* Sorbonne Univ, cert 55. *Work:* Mus Fine Arts, Lubbock, Tex; Black Arts Ctr, Waco, Tex; Northwood Inst, Midland, Mich; Bishop Col, Dallas, Tex. *Comn:* Josephite Black Arts Calendar, Josephite Pastoral Ctr, Washington, DC, 74. *Exhib:* Mobile Arts Festival, Ala, 70; Discovery 70, Nat Black Arts Festival, Cincinnati, Ohio, 70; Nat Black Arts Festival, Normal, Ill, 73; one-man show, State Capitol, Austin, Tex, 73; Tex Fine Arts Festival, Houston, 74. *Awards:* Second Award, Dimension IV Houston Art League, Humble Oil Co, 68; Betty McGowan Award, Mobil Arts Festival, 70; Distinguished Artist Award, Nat Coun Negro Women, 72. *Bibliog:* James Kennedy (auth), Ethnic American Art, Slide Libr, Univ Ala, 70-75; Charolette Phelen (auth), Evans remembers June tenth, Houston Chronicle, 71; Theresa Dickason Cederholm (auth), Afro American Artist, Boston Pub Libr, 73. *Mem:* Art League Houston; Tex Fine Arts Asn; Contemp Arts Asn. *Media:* Multimedia. *Mailing Add:* 5327 Kreettyoaks Houston TX 77045

EVANS, DICK
CERAMIST, EDUCATOR
b Roswell, NMex, July 10, 41. *Study:* Tex Tech Univ, Lubbock, 59-62; Univ Utah, Salt Lake City, BFA, 64, MFA, 66. *Work:* Nat Mus Am Art, Smithsonian Inst; Sheldon Mem Art Gallery, Univ Nebr, Lincoln; Milwaukee Art Mus, Wis; Ariz State Univ, Tempe; Herbert F Johnson Mus Art, Cornell Univ, Ithaca, NY; and others. *Comn:* Ceramic mural, sculpture & fountain, City Club, Dallas, Tex, 68. *Exhib:* Solo shows, Bradley Galleries, Milwaukee, 76, 78 & 80 & Kohler Art Ctr, Sheboygan, Wis, 83; Landscape: New Views, Johnson Art Mus, Cornell Univ, Ithaca, New York, 78; American Porcelain: New Expressions in an Ancient Art Travling Show, Smithsonian Inst, 80-84; All Clay, Cheney Cowls Mem Mus, Spokane, Wash, 82; two-person show, Sheldon Mem Art Gallery, Univ Nebr, Lincoln, 82; and other group & one-man shows. *Teaching:* Instr ceramics, Texas Tech, Lubbock, 66-70; asst prof ceramics, Univ Tenn, Knoxville, 71-72 & Univ NMex, Albuquerque, 72-75; assoc prof ceramics, Univ Wis-Milwaukee, 75- *Dealer:* Bradley Galleries 2565 N Downer Ave Milwaukee WI 53211. *Mailing Add:* 2738 N Summit Milwaukee WI 53211

EVANS, GROSE
HISTORIAN, EDUCATOR
b Columbus, Ohio, Dec 14, 16. *Study:* Ohio State Univ, BFA, 38, MA, 40; Inst Fine Arts, NY Univ, 41-43 & 45-46; Johns Hopkins Univ, PhD, 53. *Pos:* From lectr to assoc cur, dept educ, Nat Gallery Art, 46-60, cur exten serv, decorative arts & index Am design, 60-70, cur exhibs & loans, 70-73, cur decorative arts, 73. *Teaching:* Prof lectr Baroque-mod art, George Washington Univ, 53-61, adj assoc prof art hist, 73-; prof lectr Am painting, Johns Hopkins Univ, 65; curric dir art teachers' training, George Washington Univ & Nat Gallery Art, 66 & 67. *Mem:* Col Art Asn Am. *Res:* Anglo-American art of the eighteenth century. *Publ:* Auth, Benjamin West and the Taste of His Time, Southern Ill Univ Press, 59; auth, Vincent Van Gogh, McGraw, 68. *Mailing Add:* 2308 Glasgow Rd Alexandria VA 22307

EVANS, HENRY
PRINTMAKER
b Superior, Wis, May 16, 18. *Work:* Albertina, Vienna; Libr Cong, Washington, DC; Hunt Bot Inst, Pittsburgh; Clark Libr, Calif, Los Angeles; Oakland Mus, Calif. *Exhib:* One-man shows, Royal Hort Soc, London, 65; Hunt Bot Inst, 66; Biomed Libr, Univ Calif, Los Angeles, 68, Calif Acad Sci, San Francisco, 70 & Oakland Mus, 71; and others. *Bibliog:* A Frankenstein (auth), Evans' botanical portfolios, San Francisco Chronicle, 8/25/68; staff (auth), Henry Evans, printmaker (doc film), KQED, 69; Johan Kooy (auth), Henry Evans, printmaker, Pac Discovery, 12/70. *Publ:* Illusr, Champagne and shoes, Peregrine Press, 62; illusr, Hortulus, 66; illusr, Flower pot gardens, Crowell Collier, 67; auth, illusr & printer, State flowers, Vol 1-5, Peregrine Press, 68-72; auth, Botanical Prints with Excerpts from the Artist's Notebooks, Freeman & Co, 77. *Mailing Add:* 555 Sutter Rm 306 San Francisco CA 94102

EVANS, JESSIE BENTON See Gray, Jessie Benton Evans

EVANS, JOHN
PAINTER, COLLAGE ARTIST
b Sioux Falls, SDak, Aug 24, 32. *Study:* Art Inst Chicago, BFA, 61, MFA, 63. *Exhib:* Pa Acad Fine Art Ann, 64; Key Gallery, New York, 79; Cordier &

Ekstrom, New York, 80 & 81; Visual Diaries-Alex Rosenberg Gallery, 80; Words & Numbers, Summit Art Ctr, NJ, 80; one-man show, Eastern Mont State Univ, Billings, 80 & Arts Club Chicago, 82; and others. *Bibliog:* Grace Glueck (auth), Visual diaries, New York Times, 2/22/80; Susan Grace Galassi (auth), article, Arts Mag, 3/80; Vivien Raynor (auth), A show that requires reading too, New York Times, 3/23/80. *Mem:* Artist's Equity. *Publ:* Auth, Collection of 38 Collage Books, privately publ, 76. *Dealer:* Luise Ross 171 W 12th New York NY 10011. *Mailing Add:* PO Box 1004 New York NY 10009

EVANS, LUCILE (LUCILE EVANS FERRELL)
PAINTER, PRINTMAKER
b Ogden, Utah, Oct 28, 1894. *Study:* Otis Art Inst, Calif with George Biddle, 30-40; Chouinard Art Inst, Calif, 32; Arthur Millier, Calif, 35. *Work:* Nat Mus Am Art, Phillips Collection, Art Collection of DC Superior Court & Howard Univ, Washington, DC. *Exhib:* Los Angeles Artists, San Francisco Mus, 40; The Pendulum of Art, Pasadena Mus, Calif, 41; Twelve Painters, Los Angeles Co Mus, 43; Washington Area Artists, Phillips Collection, Washington, DC, 48 & 62; Contemp Am Series 10, Corcoran Gallery, 50-51; 11th Nat Print Exhib, Libr Congress, Washington, DC, 53; Three Regional Painters, Baltimore Mus, Md, 55; Women in Washington Collections, Univ Md, College Park, 79. *Teaching:* Instr egg tempera, Pasadena Mus, Calif, 37-38; instr water media, Washington Workshop, 51-55. *Awards:* Saints Progress, Carl Zigrosser, 51; Unusual Spirits, Laamar Dodd, 52; Underground Passage, George Grosz, 53-54. *Media:* Acrylic, Collage; Stone Lithographs, Monotypes. *Dealer:* Franz Bader Gallery 2001 Eye Street NW Washington DC 20006. *Mailing Add:* 1345 27th St NW Washington DC 20007

EVANS, MINNIE
PAINTER
b Long Creek, NC, Dec 12, 1892. *Work:* Newark Mus, NJ; Ill Bell Tel, Chicago; L'Institut de L'Art Brut, Paris; Nat Collection Fine Arts; Whitney Mus Am Art; and others. *Exhib:* Solo shows, Davison Art Ctr, Wesleyan Univ, 69 & 70, Portal Gallery, London, Eng, 70, St John's Art Gallery, Wilmington, 70; Deson Zaks Gallery, Chicago, 75; Whitney Mus Am Art, 75; and others. *Bibliog:* Nina Howell Starr (auth), The lost world of Minnie Evans, Bennington Rev, summer 69; Diana Loercher (auth), Regaining a world lost to moderns, Christian Sci Monitor, 7/21/75; and others. *Media:* Crayon, Oil. *Mailing Add:* c/o Mrs Nina Howell Starr 333 East 68th St New York NY 10021

EVANS, RICHARD
PAINTER, EDUCATOR
b Chicago, Ill, Oct 1, 23. *Study:* Otis Art Inst, dipl; Calif Col Arts & Crafts; Studio of George Miller, New York; Univ Wyo, MA; Stacey Found Fel, 47; Tiffany Found Fels, 48 & 50. *Work:* San Francisco Fine Arts Comn; Univ Wyo; Col Southern Utah. *Comn:* Tile mural, Univ Wyo, 68; portrait of Sam S Knight, Univ Wyo Geol Mus; twenty sculptures of prominent personages for private comns. *Exhib:* one-man show, Yellowstone Art Ctr, Billings, Mont, 74; Retrospective, Univ Wyo Mus, 76; Santa Fe Art Festival, 77; Directions Gallery, Colo State Univ, 79; 57th Mid-Year, Butler Inst, 81; Drawing Ann, Rutgers Univ, 81; and others. *Teaching:* Instr drawing, Calif Col Arts & Crafts, Oakland, 50-52; instr drawing & painting, Miami Univ, Oxford, Ohio, 56-57; prof printmaking, drawing & painting, Univ Wyo, 57- *Awards:* Ford Found Grants, 64 & 66; 26th Cedar City Invitational Purchase Award, 66; Anonymous Donor Award, Otis Art Inst 50th Anniversary Exhib, 68. *Bibliog:* Victor Flach (auth), The Making of Ikon 13 (film & TV tape), Univ Wyo, 70; Victor Flach (auth), By these presents: Richard Evans, A retrospective, 76. *Media:* Oil, Acrylic; Intaglio. *Publ:* Auth, On large scale prints, Am Artist, 11/62. *Mailing Add:* Dept of Art Univ of Wyo Laramie WY 82070

EVANS, ROBERT GRAVES
SCULPTOR, EDUCATOR
b Rawlins, Wyo, Nov 19, 44. *Study:* Atlanta Sch Art, BFA; French Govt Fel, Paris, 69; with Stanley Hayter; Tulane Univ, with Julius Struppeck, MFA. *Comn:* Man of Year Award (sculpture), Atlanta, Ga, 69; Film Festival Award (sculpture), Atlanta, Ga, 69; bronze bust of Pres Rankin, Ind State Univ, 75; outdoor sculpture, Cent Mich Univ, 75. *Exhib:* Simonne Stern Galerie, New Orleans, 71; one-man shows, Bienville Gallery, New Orleans, 72, Swope Art Gallery, Terre Haute, Ind, 78 & Univ South, Tenn, 78; Mid-States Art Exhib, Evansville Mus Arts & Sci, Ind, 78. *Teaching:* Asst prof sculpture, Ind State Univ, Terre Haute, 72-78, assoc prof art, 78- *Awards:* Sculpture Acquisition, Swope Art Gallery, 77; Mus Guild Purchase Award, Evansville Mus Arts & Sci, 78; Beautification Award, Terre Haute CofC, 81. *Mem:* Southern Sculpture Asn; Arts Illiana; Col Art Asn. *Media:* Bronze, Aluminum. *Mailing Add:* Dept of Art Ind State Univ Terre Haute IN 47809

EVANS, ROBERT JAMES
PAINTER, MUSEUM CURATOR
b Chicago, Ill, May 2, 44. *Study:* Parsons Col; Univ Iowa; Northeast Mo State Univ, BEd; Drake Univ; Southern Ill Univ, Carbondale, MFA. *Work:* Southern Ill Univ, Carbondale; Western Ill Univ, Macomb; Ill State Univ, Normal; Quincy Art Club; Lakeview Mus Arts & Sci. *Exhib:* 16th Midwest Biennial, Joslyn Art Mus, Omaha, Nebr, 80; Irwin Collection, Krannert Art Mus, Univ Ill, 80; Watercolor USA, Springfield Art Mus, Mo, 80; one-man shows, Zaks Gallery, Chicago, Ill, 81 & 84; Chicago Int Art Expos, 82 & 84; Fabrications, Chicago Sculpture Soc, 83. *Collections Arranged:* Emergence of Modernism in Illinois 1914-1940, 76; Illinois Photographers, 1978, 80; Illinois Invitational, 71. *Pos:* Res asst, Univ Galleries, Southern Ill Univ, Carbondale, 69-70; cur art, Ill State Mus, Springfield, 70-, head art section, 81- *Teaching:* Instr drawing & painting, Springfield Art Asn, Ill, 71-76; adj

asst prof arts mgt, Sangamon State Univ, 73-78. *Awards:* Best in Show, Quincy Art Club Ann Exhib, 72 & 78; Governors Art Award, Ill Arts Coun, 80; Merit Award, Miss Corridors, Davenport Art Mus, Iowa, 81. *Bibliog:* David Elliott (auth), article, Chicago Sun Times, 6/21/81; Alan G Artner (auth), article, Chicago Tribune, 7/3/81. *Publ:* Auth, articles in Living Mus, 70-; auth, articles in Craft Horizons & Mus News; auth, numerous exhibit catalogs. *Dealer:* Zaks Gallery 620 North Michigan Ave Chicago IL 60611. *Mailing Add:* 2516 Churchill Rd Springfield IL 62702

EVEN, ROBERT LAWRENCE
EDUCATOR
b Breckenridge, Minn, June 7, 29. *Study:* Valley City State Col, BS; Univ Minn, MA & PhD; Art Inst Chicago; Minneapolis Col Art & Design. *Teaching:* Instr art, Univ Minn, 52-54; prof art, Northern Ill Univ, 63-, chmn dept, 74-82. *Awards:* Res Grant, State Ill, 64 & Dean's Fund, Northern Ill Univ, 65 & 73. *Mem:* Col Art Asn Am; Mid-Am Col Art Asn; Nat Coun Art Adminr; Nat Asn Sch Art. *Mailing Add:* 413 Fairmont De Kalb IL 60115

EVERETT, LEN G
PAINTER
b Burlington, Iowa. *Study:* State Univ Iowa, BFA & MFA; Art Students League, with Robert Brackman, Joseph Hirsch & Robert Hale; Nat Acad Design, New York, with Robert Philipp; also with Henry Hensche, Provincetown, Mass. *Work:* Washington & Jefferson Col, Washington, Pa; Butler Inst Am Art, Youngstown, Ohio; Slater Mem Mus, Norwich, Conn; Danforth Mus, Framington, Mass. *Exhib:* Butler Inst Am Art Midyear Ann, Youngstown, Ohio, 69, 72 & 77; Mainstreams 71, Marietta, Ohio, 71; Nat Art Round-Up, Las Vegas, Nev, 71; The New American Still Life, Westmoreland Co Mus of Art, Greensburg, Pa, 79; Nat Acad Design, New York, 81; and others. *Awards:* Best Still Life in Show Award, Am Artists Prof League, New York, NY, 77; First Tom Shoemaker Mem AWard, Silvermine Guild of Artists, New Canaan, Conn, 79; M Grumbacher Gold Medal, Allied Artists Am, 80; and 22 other awards. *Bibliog:* Ralph Fabri (auth), Medal of merit in Allied Artists Annual, Today's Art, 70. *Mem:* Allied Artists Am (exhib chmn, 76-78 & 80, treas, 81-84); Am Artists Prof League; Hudson Valley Art Asn; Audubon Artists (mem bd, 76-, sr vpres, 81-); Silvermine Guild of Artists, New Canaan, Conn. *Media:* Oil, Pastel. *Mailing Add:* 150 E 27th St New York NY 10016

EVERETT, RUSSELL HENRY
PAINTER, GRAPHIC ARTIST
b Washington, DC, Mar 3, 52. *Study:* Auburn Univ, BFA, 74; Univ Cincinnati, with Robert Knipschild, MFA, 76. *Work:* Butler Inst Am Art; Montgomery Mus Fine Arts; Rockford Col; Ball State Univ; Trenton State Col. *Exhib:* 40th Ann Midyear Show, Butler Inst Am Art, 76; West 81 Art and the Law, Minn Mus Art, 81; New Orleans Biennial, New Orleans Art Asn, 82; Rutgers Univ Nat, 83; Appalachian Nat, Appalachian State Univ, 83; NDak Print & Drawing Ann, Univ NDak, Grand Forks, 83; Springville Mus Art 59th April Salon, Utah, 83. *Teaching:* Adj instr drawing, Auburn Univ, Montgomery, 79-81 & DeKalb Community Col, 82-83; artist, elementary schs, Griffin, Ga & Symrna, Ga, 82-83. *Mem:* Art Asn Harrisburg, Pa. *Media:* Oil; Crayon, Pencil. *Mailing Add:* 528 W College Ave Decatur GA 30030

EVERHART, DON (DONALD NELSON), JR
MEDALIST, ILLUSTRATOR
b York, Pa, Aug 19, 49. *Study:* Kutztown State Univ, BFA(painting), 72. *Work:* Franklin Mint. *Comn:* Gold Coin for Govt Guyana, 77 & Balboa Gold Coin for Govt Panama, 80, Franklin Mint; Dance of The Dolphins, Soc Medalists, New York, 82; Martin Luther 500th Anniversary, Am Lutheran Publicity Bur, New York, 82; Liberty (ingot), Manfra, Tordella & Brookes, New York, 82. *Exhib:* One-man shows, York Univ, 79 & Batoff Gallery, Philadelphia, 79; Philadelphia Watercolor Show, Peale House, 80; Philadelphia Watercolor Club, Wyndemere Gallery, 81; Am Medallic Sculpture Asn, Am Numismatic Soc, New York & traveling, 83. *Pos:* Illusr, Int Design Orgn, Moorestown, NJ, 72-73; sculptor in residence, Franklin Mint, 73-80; freelance illusr & medalist, 80- *Awards:* First Prize for Crum Creek, Wallingford Art Ctr, 80; Second Prize, York Art Asn, 80 & Franklin Mint, 81. *Bibliog:* Ed Reiter (auth), Can bullion become a collectable?, New York Times Numismatic Sect, 9/82; Henry Sault (auth), Medal will celebrate Martin Luther's birth, Philadelphia Inquirer Coin Sect, 4/10/83; MTB unveils liberty bars, Coin World, 9/22/82. *Mem:* Medallic Sculpture Asn; Philadelphia Watercolor Club; Chester Co Art Asn. *Media:* Clay, Plaster. *Publ:* Illusr cover, To Touch the Deer, Westminster Press, 81; illusr cover, The Secret of the 100 MPG Automobile, Crest Serv, 81; illusr bas-relief cover, Mefoxin--A Comprehensive Summary, Merck, Sharpe & Dohme, 83. *Mailing Add:* 744 Marshall Drive West Chester PA 19380

EVERSLEY, FREDERICK JOHN
SCULPTOR
b Brooklyn, NY, Aug 28, 41. *Study:* Carnegie Inst Technol, BSEE, 63; Inst Allende, San Miguel de Allende, Mex. *Work:* Smithsonian Inst, Washington, DC; Whitney Mus Am Art, New York; Milwaukee Art Ctr, Wis; Oakland Art Mus, Calif; Guggenheim Mus, New York; and others. *Comn:* Plastic sculpture, San Francisco Int Airport, Calif, 70 & Lenox Sq Ctr, Atlanta, Ga; plastic sculpture fountain, Dallas Hyatt-Regency Hotel; kinetic stainless steel sculpture, Miami Int Airport, Fla; laser beam sculpture, Detroit Gen Hosp. *Exhib:* One-man shows, Sculpture Ann, 71 & 73, Whitney Mus Am Art, Los Angeles Inst Contemp Art, Calif, 76, Nat Acad of Sci, Washington, DC, 76 & 81 & Oakland Mus Art, Calif, 77; Permutations--Light and Color, Mus Contemp Art, Chicago, 70;; Art and Technology, Los Angeles Co Mus Art, Calif, 71; American Kunst 1950-1970, La Mus Contemp Art, Denmark, 71;

Andrew Crispo Gallery, NY; OK Harris Gallery, NY. *Pos:* Tech consult, Art & Technol Exhib, Los Angeles Co Mus Art, 71; first artist-in-residence, Nat Air & Space Mus, Smithsonian Inst, Washington, DC, 77-80. *Awards:* First Purchase Prize, 4th Ann Calif Small Images Exhib, Calif State Col, Los Angeles, 70; Nat Endowment Arts Fel, 72; Purchase Prize, 10th Ann Southern Calif Exhib, Long Beach Mus, 72. *Bibliog:* Henry Seldis (auth), Eversley show in New York, Los Angeles Times, 6/8/70; John Canaday (auth), article, New York Times, 4/7/71; Paul Richard (auth), The Space Museum's latest craft, Washington Post, 12/8/77. *Media:* Multicolored Cast Transparent Plastic, Stainless Steel. *Mailing Add:* c/o Engineered Aesthetics 1110 W Washington Blvd Venice CA 90291

EVERTS, CONNOR
PAINTER, PRINTMAKER
b Bellingham, Wash, Jan 24, 26. *Study:* Chouinard Art Inst, Los Angeles; El Camino Col, Calif, AA; Univ Wash; Mexico City Col, BA; Courtauld Inst, Univ London. *Work:* Mus Mod Art, San Francisco; Mus Mod Art, New York; Mus Mod Art, Tokyo, Japan; Pushkin Mus, Moscow, Soviet Union; Chicago Art Inst. *Comn:* Collage mural, El Camino Col, 58; mural, Goldwater Bldg, Calif, 63. *Exhib:* Brand Art Ctr, Calif, 73; Univ Southern Calif, 75; Cranbrook Art Mus, 80; World Print Coun Exhib, San Francisco, 82; Retrospective, Los Angeles Municpal Art Gallery, 83; and others. *Teaching:* Chmn graphic dept, Calif Inst of Art, 60-64; guest artist painting, San Francisco Art Inst, 64-65; head printmaking dept, Crambrook Acad Art, currently. *Awards:* Painting Award, Los Angeles Artists & Vicinity, Los Angeles Co Mus, Los Angeles, 55; Prize, 4th Int Young Artists Exhib, Tokyo, 67; Purchase Award, Southern Calif, Muckenthaler Found, 74. *Bibliog:* G Nordland (auth), Drawings of Connor Everts, Pasadena Art Mus, 60 & Self-Portraits 1949-1969, Western Asn of Art Mus, 69; D Brewer (auth), The Studies of Connor Everts, Brand Art Ctr, 73. *Mem:* Nat Adv Bd Print; Los Angeles Printmaking Soc (pres, 63-64); Nat Asn Univ Prof. *Media:* Aqua paint; collage. *Dealer:* Ruth Bachofner & Associates 335 S Almont Dr Beverly Hills CA 90211. *Mailing Add:* The Market 2351 Sonoma Torrance CA 90501

EVETT, KENNETH WARNOCK
PAINTER
b Loveland, Colo, Dec 1, 13. *Study:* Colo State Col, AB; Colo Col, MA; also with Boardman Robinson, George Biddle & Henry V Poor. *Work:* Amon Carter Mus, Ft Worth, Tex; Colorado Springs Fine Arts Ctr, Colo; Andrew Dickson White Mus, Cornell Univ, NY; Joslyn Mus, Omaha; Wichita Mus, Kans. *Comn:* Three murals for rotunda of Nebr State Capitol, 54. *Exhib:* Pa Acad Fine Arts, 52; Whitney Mus Am Art Ann, 52-54; Metrop Mus Art, 53; Corcoran Gallery Art Biennial, 54; Art Inst Chicago Biennial, 54; Nat Mus Am Art, 81; ten one-man exhibs, Kraushaar Galleries, 48-83. *Pos:* Art critic, New Republic, 72-77. *Teaching:* Prof art, Cornell Univ, 48-79, chmn dept, 74-77. *Awards:* Drawing Prize, Norfolk Mus, 66; Drawing Prize, Rochester Mus, 68; Purchase Prize, Munson-Williams-Proctor Inst, 68. *Media:* Watercolor, Oil. *Publ:* Auth, The New Realism, 72 & Literature and liberalism: 75 years of the New Republic, New Republic Mag. *Dealer:* Antoinette Kraushaar Galleries 724 Fifth Ave New York NY 10028. *Mailing Add:* 402 Oak Ave Ithaca NY 14850

EWALD, ELIN LAKE
DEALER, WRITER
b Raleigh, NC. *Study:* Students League with Edwin Dickinson; Am Acad Art; Art Inst Chicago; grad prog, New York Univ & Metrop Mus Art. *Pos:* Assoc, Gallery Mayer, New York; free-lance art writer, 70-72; pres, O'Toole-Ewald Art Assoc Inc, 74- *Mem:* Nat Asn Rev Appraisers; Am Soc Appraisers; Am Asn Mus; Int Coun Mus. *Specialty:* Consultants and fine art appraisers, antique and contemporary. *Interests:* For over 60 years, firm has arranged special exhibitions and assembled private collections for individuals, corporations and museums; additionally, it has arranged donations of individual works of art and collections to museums; specialists in damage/loss reports and appraisals of corporate collections. *Publ:* Auth, Hester Bateman and English Women Silversmiths of the 18th Century, Ms Mag, 76; and others. *Mailing Add:* 667 Madison Ave New York NY 10021

EWEN, PATERSON
PAINTER, EDUCATOR
b Montreal, Que, Can, Apr 7, 25. *Study:* Montreal Mus Sch Fine Art & Design, Can, dipl with high standing in painting, drawing & the teaching of child art; McGill Univ, Montreal. *Work:* Nat Gallery Can & Can Coun Art Bank, Ottawa, Ont; Amsterdam Civic Mus; Art Gallery Vancouver, BC; Mus de la Province de Que; Art Gallery Ont. *Comn:* Mural, Performing Arts Ctr, Univ Lethbridge, 81. *Exhib:* One-man shows, Carmen Lamanna Gallery, Toronto, 69, 72-74, 78, 80 & 82; Rutgers Univ Art Gallery, 75; Mt Allison Univ, 75; retrospective, London Pub Art Gallery, London, Ont, 77; Paterson Ewen: Recent Works Traveling Exhib, Nat Gallery Can, 77-78; Biennale Venezia, Venice, 82; Ten Canadian Artists in the 1970's Traveling Show, Art Gallery Ont, 80-81; 20th Century Canadian Painting Traveling Show, Nat Gallery Can, 81. *Teaching:* Asst prof painting & drawing, Univ Western Ont, London, 72- *Awards:* Purchase Award, Montreal Mus Fine Arts, 61; Sr Can Coun Award, Can Coun, 71; Purchase Prize, Queen's Silver Jubilee Art Collection, 77. *Mem:* Royal Can Acad; Can Artists' Rep. *Media:* Mixed Media. *Publ:* Contribr, Carmen Lamanna Gallery, Mt Allison Univ, Sackville, NB, 75; contribr, Paterson Ewen: Recent Works, Vancouver Art

Gallery, 77. *Mailing Add:* Carmen Lamanna Gallery 840 Yonge St Toronto ON M4W 2H1 Canada

EWING, BAYARD
ADMINISTRATOR, COLLECTOR
b Sorrento, Maine, Aug 19, 16. *Pos:* Trustee, RI Sch Design, 55-, chmn bd, 67-, actg pres, 75-77; dir, Am Fedn of Arts, 77-, pres, 78-80. *Collection:* Twentieth century painting and sculpture, chiefly American. *Mailing Add:* 2000 Hosp Trust Tower Providence RI 02903

EWING, EDGAR LOUIS
PAINTER
b Hartington, Nebr, Jan 17, 13. *Study:* Art Inst Chicago, grad, 35, Edward L Ryerson fel, 35-37 & also with Boris Anisfeld; two years European travel and study. *Work:* Richmond Mus Fine Arts, Va; Los Angeles Co Mus Art; Santa Barbara Mus; De Young Mem Mus, San Francisco; Nat Gallery, Athens, Greece. *Exhib:* Sao Paulo Mus Art Int, Brazil; Carnegie Mus Int, Pittsburgh; Art Inst Chicago; Metrop Mus Art, New York; Pa Acad Fine Arts, Philadelphia; one-man shows, Greek Nat Gallery, 73, Munic Gallery Los Angeles, 74 & Fisher Gallery, Univ Southern Calif, 78; 20 Yrs Retrospective, Palm Springs Desert Mus, 76-77. *Teaching:* Instr painting, Art Inst Chicago, 37-43; prof fine arts, Univ Southern Calif, 46-78, emer prof, 78-; Mellon prof painting, Carnegie Mellon Univ, 68-69. *Awards:* Samuel Goldwyn Award, Los Angeles Co Mus Art, 57; Los Angeles Libr Asn Award, 76; Floresheim Award, Art Inst Chicago. *Bibliog:* Schaad (auth), The Realm of Contemporary Still Life Painting, 62 & Mugnaini (auth), Oil Painting--Techniques and Materials, 69, Van Nostrand. *Mem:* Am Asn Univ Prof; Nat Watercolor Soc (pres); Col Art Asn; Los Angeles Mus Asn. *Media:* Oil. *Dealer:* Esther Bear Gallery 1125 High Rd Santa Barbara CA 93108. *Mailing Add:* 4226 Sea View Lane Los Angeles CA 90065

EWING, THOMAS R
PAINTER, INSTRUCTOR
b Pittsburgh, Pa, Nov 5, 35. *Study:* Corcoran Sch Art, 58; Pa Acad Fine Arts, 60-63. *Work:* Pa Acad Fine Arts, Philadelphia; Phoenix Art Mus, Ariz. *Exhib:* Ann Exhib Am Painting & Sculpture, Pa Acad Fine Arts, 64-68; Atlier Chapman Kelly Galleries, Dallas, 66; one-man show, Makler Gallery, Philadelphia, 69; Drawings, Univ Bordeux, France; 14 Sculptures, New York, 78. *Pos:* Court room artist, KYW TV, Philadelphia, formerly. *Teaching:* Instr painting, Pa Acad Fine Arts, 70-; instr painting & life drawing, Philadelphia Mus Art, 72- *Awards:* Emily Lowe Competition Award, 66; Louis Comfort Tiffany Grant, 72. *Dealer:* Hansen Gallery 72 Wooster St New York NY 10012; Reese Palley Fine Arts Inc 1911 The Boardwalk Atlantic City NJ 08401. *Mailing Add:* 507 S 48th Philadelphia PA 19143

EYEN, RICHARD J
DEALER, DESIGNER
b Lincoln, Nebr, Mar 24, 30. *Study:* Univ Calif, Los Angeles; Univ Cincinnati, BS(design). *Pos:* Owner & dir, Environment Gallery, New York, 63- *Mem:* Artist-Craftsmen Soc New York; Nat Soc Lit & Arts. *Specialty:* Contemporary American artists, especially sculptors. *Mailing Add:* Environment Gallery 405 E 54th St New York NY 10022

EYRE, IVAN
PAINTER
b Tullymet, Sask, Can, Apr 15, 35. *Study:* Univ Sask, 52; Univ Man, BFA, 57; Univ NDak, 58. *Work:* Nat Gallery Can, Ottawa, Ont; Montreal Mus Fine Arts, Que; Vancouver Art Gallery, BC; Winnipeg Art Gallery, Man; Art Bank, Ottawa, Ont. *Comn:* Ressurection, Can Cath Conf, Ottawa, Ont, 76; Black Arrow Plain, Can Indust & Com Bank, Edmonton, Alta, 80. *Exhib:* 6th Biennial Can Painting, Nat Gallery Can, Ottawa, Ont, 65, 7th Biennial Can Painting, 67, New Landscapes, 74, Landscape Can, 76; one-man shows, Nat Gallery Can, Ottawa, Ont, 78, Equinox Gallery, Vancouver, 81, Art Gallery Greater Victoria Traveling, 82 & Winnipeg Art Gallery, Calgary, 82; The Texture of Our Land, Art Gallery of Peterborough, 79; Encounters in the Imagination: Birdmen & Drawings, Brian Melnychenko Gallery, Winnipeg, 81; and others. *Teaching:* Prof drawing & painting, Univ Man, Winnipeg, 59-; prof painting, Banff Centre, Alta, summer 73. *Awards:* Sr Arts Awards, Can Coun, 66 & 78; Queens Silver Jubilee Medal, Gov Gen of Can, 77; Univ Man Jubilee Award, 82. *Bibliog:* E Zuk (producer), Visual Thinker (film), CBC, Winnipeg, 81; Doug Whiteway (auth), Out of sight, out of mind--the art of Ivan Eyre, Alumni J, Univ Man, autumn 82; Visions (film), TV Ont, 83; and many other films & articles in various mags. *Mem:* Royal Can Acad Arts. *Media:* Acrylic, Multimedia. *Publ:* Contribr, The Canadians, Fitzhenry & Whiteside, 79; contribr, One Hundred Years of Canadian Drawing 1880-1980, Metheun, 80; contribr, 1982 Printworld Directory, Ed Press, 82; contribr, K-6 Art, Man Dept Educ, 83; contribr, Visions: Contemporary Art in Canada, Douglas & McIntyre & TV Ont, 83. *Dealer:* Mira Godard Gallery 22 Hazelton Ave Toronto ON M5R 2E5 Can; Equinox Gallery 1525 W Eight Vancouver BC V6J 1T5 Can. *Mailing Add:* 1098 Trappistes St Winnipeg MB R3V 1B8 Canada

F

FABE, ROBERT
PAINTER, EDUCATOR

b Chicago, Ill, May 24, 17. *Study:* Art Acad Cincinnati, cert fine art, 38; Art Students League, with George Grosz, Arnold Blanch & Raphael Soyer, Out of Town Scholar, 38-39. *Work:* Cincinnati Art Mus; Univ Cincinnati; Miami Univ, Ohio; Procter & Gamble, Cincinnati; and other pub & pvt collections. *Comn:* Murals, Shrimp Boat Restaurant, Dayton, Otter Bein Press, Dayton & Highland Towers, Marvin Warner Corp, Cincinnati. *Exhib:* Butler Inst Am Art, Youngstown, Ohio, 40-68; Cincinnati Ann, 40-70 & Laser Art Exhib, 71, Cincinnati Art Mus; one-man shows, Mt St Joseph Col, Cincinnati, 70 & Ohio State Capitol, 71; and many other group & one-man shows. *Teaching:* Prof, Col Design Archit & Art, Univ Cincinnati, 58- *Awards:* Dayton Art Inst Purchase Award; Butler Inst Am Art Purchase Award; Ohio Univ Show Award. *Mem:* MacDowell Soc (pres, 70-72); Cincinnati Prof Artists (pres, 70-72). *Media:* Tempera, Watercolor. *Mailing Add:* 4235 Rose Hill Ave Cincinnati OH 45229

FABERT, JACQUES
PAINTER, EDUCATOR

b Paris, France, Apr 24, 25; US citizen. *Study:* Ecole Nat Super des Beaux Arts, Paris, grad, 46. *Work:* Butler Inst Am Art, Youngstown, Ohio; Norfolk Mus Art, Va; Univ Calif, Berkeley; Free Libr Philadelphia; Stedman Gallery, Rutgers Univ, Camden, NJ. *Comn:* Painting, San Francisco Theol Sem, Calif, 69; paintings, City San Francisco, 70; mural, Dr Boonswang, Easton, Pa, 78. *Exhib:* Invitational Shows, Calif Palace of the Legion of Honor, San Francisco, 62, 63, 67 & 75; one-man shows, E B Crocker Mus Art, Sacramento, Calif, 69 & Carroll Reece Mus, E Tenn State Univ, Johnson City, 74; Nat Int Arts & Lett Exhib, New York, 70; Nat Drawing '79, Stedman Gallery, Rutgers Univ, Camden, NJ, 79 & 81; and others. *Pos:* Dir, Mex Studies, Mex Exten, Calif Col Arts & Crafts, Morelia, Mex, 69-72. *Teaching:* Prof fine arts, San Francisco Acad Art, 63-70; prof fine arts, Calif Col Arts & Crafts, Oakland, 63-70; prof fine arts, Princeton Art Assocs, NJ, 79- *Awards:* Purchase Awards, Butler Inst Am Art, 68, Childe Hassam Fund, 70 & Stedman Gallery, Rutgers Univ, 79. *Bibliog:* Arthur Bloomfield (auth), article, San Francisco Chronicle, 67-69; Alfred Frankenstein (auth), article, San Francisco Examiner, 67-69. *Media:* Multimedia. *Dealer:* Langman Gallery 218 Old York Rd Jenkintown PA 19046. *Mailing Add:* PO Box 103 2682 Rte 413 Buckingham PA 18912

FACCI, DOMENICO (AURELIO)
SCULPTOR, PAINTER

b Hooversville, Pa, Feb 2, 16. *Study:* Roerich Acad Arts, 36. *Work:* Norfolk Mus Arts & Sci, Va; Fla Southern Col, Lakeland. *Comn:* St Rita (bronze sculpture), comn by Rambusch, St Rita's Church, Long Island City, NY, 66; figures of Martin Luther King, Abraham Lincoln, Mary McLeod Bethune & W Wilberforce and 16 corbels carved in situ on facade, Episcopalian Diocese, St Thomas' Church, New York, 71; Pablo Casals (bust), Pub Sch 181, New York, NY, 78; cartouche for lobby, Am Express Bldg, New York, NY, 78; cartouche for bronze doors, St Peter's Cathedral, Philadelphia, Pa, 78; and numerous others. *Exhib:* First Int Art Exhib, Fla Southern Col; Artists Equity Exhib, Whitney Mus Am Art; Butler Inst Am Art; Nat Acad, 78; Painters & Sculptors Soc, 78; Knickerbocker Artists, 78; Audubon Artists, 78; and numerous others. *Teaching:* Vis prof sculpture & stone carving, Fla Southern Col, 52-; instr sculpture & stone carving, Ridgewood Art Sch, NJ, 61-65; instr sculpture & stone carving, Craft Student League, New York, 66-72. *Awards:* Albert Dorne Prize, Audubon Artists, 56-61 & Cash Award, 78; Gold Medal, Knickerbocker Artists, 78; and numerous others. *Bibliog:* Domenico Facci, sculptor (film), WEDO-TV, Tampa, Fla, 70. *Mem:* Audubon Artists (pres, 66-77); Am Soc Contemp Artists; Sculptors League; League of Present Day Artists (treas, 65); fel Nat Sculpture Soc. *Mailing Add:* 248 W 14th St New York NY 10011

FACCINTO, VICTOR PAUL
PAINTER, FILMMAKER

b Albany, Calif, Oct 30, 45. *Study:* Calif State Univ, Sacramento, BA, 69, MA, 72; Creative Artists Pub Serv Prog Fel, NY, 77; NC Visual Artist Fel, NC, 81. *Work:* Film Study Collection, Mus Mod Art, New York. *Exhib:* New Am Filmmakers, Whitney Mus Am Art, New York, 72-74; Festival Animation, San Francisco Mus Art, Calif, 72; Arles Festival Art, France, 74; Cineprobe, Mus Mod Art, New York, 75; Retrospective Cut-out Animation, Mus Mod Art, New York, 78; Circulating Film Program, Am Fedn Arts, New York, 72-81; Artists Fellowship Exhib, NC Mus Art, 81. *Collections Arranged:* Gladys Nilsson Retrospective, Wake Forest Univ Art Gallery, 79. *Pos:* Gallery dir, Wake Forest Univ, 78- *Teaching:* Instr multi-media, Wake Forest Univ, Winston-Salem, NC, 81-82. *Bibliog:* Grace Glueck (auth), New York Times, 4/4/80; Linda Gross (auth), Darkside of Animated Film, Los Angeles Times, 9/30/78; Kay Larson (auth), Village Voice, 4/7/80. *Media:* Acrylic, Film; Video. *Dealer:* Phyllis Kind Gallery 139 Spring St New York NY 10012. *Mailing Add:* 2200 Faculty Dr 6-G Winston-Salem NC 27106

FADDIS, (WILLIAM) GEORGE
ENAMELIST, PAINTER

b Waynesburg, Pa, May 6, 20. *Study:* Pa State Univ, MA(art hist), 48; Skowhegan Sch Art, with Henry Varnum Poor & Jose de Creeft, 48; also with Charles Jeffrey, Cleveland, 55. *Work:* Butler Inst Am Art, Youngstown, Ohio; Massillon Mus, Ohio; Ind Univ Pa. *Exhib:* Butler Inst Am Art, Youngstown, Ohio, 49-55 & 58-70; Carnegie Mus, Pittsburgh, 61; one-man shows, Arts & Crafts Ctr, Pittsburgh, 65 & Hoyt Inst Art, New Castle, Pa, 73; Three Rivers

Ann/Carnegie Mus, Pittsburgh, 72; Rockport Art Asn, Mass, 78-82; and others. *Pos:* Exec dir, Hoyt Inst Art, New Castle, Pa, 67-68; cur, Rockport Art Asn, 81- *Teaching:* Asst prof, Westminster Col, New Wilmington, Pa, 48-53; instr art, Thiel Col, Greenville, Pa, 54-55; instr, Butler Inst Am Art, 54-76; instr, Pa State Univ Exten, Sharon, 62-63; lectr, Mahoning Co Med Soc, 62-63; res assoc, Carnegie Mus, Pittsburgh, 70-77; lectr art hist, Rockport Art Asn, Mass, 78-; speaker & juror, various New Eng art orgn, currently. *Awards:* First Prize, Pa Guild Craftsmen, 59; Realistic Painting Prizes, Assoc Artists Pittsburgh, 61 & Rockport Art Asn, 79. *Bibliog:* Design Quart, Walker Art Mus, Minneapolis, 56; Murray Bovin (auth), Jewelry Making for Craftsmen, 60; Norman Geske (auth), Blakelock in the West, Am Art Review J, 76. *Mem:* Northshore Arts Asn, Gloucester, Mass; Rockport Art Asn; Copley Soc, Boston. *Media:* Mixed Media; Oil. *Res:* Life and work of Ralph Albert Blakelock, including study of forgeries. *Dealer:* Stoffa Gallery Rockport MA 01966. *Mailing Add:* 26 Grapevine Rd Gloucester MA 01930

FADEN, LAWRENCE STEVEN
PAINTER, SCULPTOR

b Brooklyn, NY, Oct 21, 42. *Study:* Brooklyn Mus student scholar; Sch Visual Arts; NY Studio Sch; and with Nicholas Carone. *Work:* Chase Manhattan Bank, New York. *Exhib:* The Representational Spirit, Univ Art Gallery, State Univ NY Albany, 70; Painterly realism, Smith Col Mus Art, 70-72; New Images, Figuration in Am Painting, Queens Mus, 74; Artists Choice Figurative Art in New York, Bowery Gallery, 76-77; one-man show, G E Einstein Gallery, 80. *Bibliog:* Alfred Frankenstein & Ann Van Devanter (co-auth), The American Self Portrait?, Praeger, 75. *Mem:* Alliance Figurative Artists (prog dir, 75). *Media:* Windsor Newton Oil; Terra Cotta Clay. *Dealer:* G E Einstein Co 243 E 82nd St New York NY 10028. *Mailing Add:* 184 E Seventh St New York NY 10003

FAFARD, JOE (JOSEPH YVON)
SCULPTOR

b Ste Marthe, Sask, Sept 2, 42. *Study:* Univ Man, BFA; Pa State Univ, MFA. *Work:* Winnipeg Art Gallery, Man; Glenbow Mus, Calgary, Alta; Brock Collection, Vancouver; Montreal Mus Fine Arts; Nat Mus Manitoba, Ottawa; and others. *Exhib:* Joe Fafard's Pensee, Winnipeg, Calgary, Vancouver, Regina, 73; Joe Fafard: Recent Work, Edmonton, Calgary, Saskatoon, Surry, Lethbridge, Kingston, Hamilton, Banff, Oshawa, Charlottetown & Regina, 79. *Bibliog:* Mike McKinnery (auth), I Don't Have to Work that Big, Nat Film Bd, 73. *Media:* Mixed. *Dealer:* Susan Whitney Art Gallery 1627 Victoria Ave Regina SK Can; Downstairs Gallery 10154-103 St Edmonton AB Can. *Mailing Add:* Box 220 Pense SK S0G 3W0 Canada

FAGALY, WILLIAM ARTHUR
MUSEUM DIRECTOR, HISTORIAN

b Lawrenceburg, Ind, Mar 1, 38. *Study:* Ind Univ, Bloomington, BA, 62, MA, 67. *Collections Arranged:* Treasures by Peter Carl Faberge and Other Master Jewellers, New Orleans Mus Art, 72; Louisiana Folk Painting, Mus Am Folk Art, New York, 73; Art USA: The South, Cent & South Am, 75-78; David Butler: Louisiana Environmental Folk Sculptor, 76 & Five From Louisiana, 77, New Orleans Mus Art. *Pos:* Registrar, New Orleans Mus Art, 66-67, cur collections, 67-72, chief cur, 73-80, asst dir art, 81- *Teaching:* Assoc prof art hist, Delgado Col, 67-69; vis assoc prof, Univ New Orleans, 80. *Res:* African art; contemporary art; American contemporary folk art. *Publ:* Auth, Early Masters of Modern Art, New Orleans Mus Art, 68; auth, At Work: Tina Girouard, deVleeshal, Middleburg, Holland, 82; auth, The Victor K Kiam Collection at the New Orleans Mus Art, African Arts, 82; coauth, Southern fictions, In: Southern Fictions, Contemp Art Mus, Houston, 83; auth, An historical overview of Louisiana women's achievements in art, In: Louisiana Women in Contemporary Art, Univ Mus, Southern Ill Univ, 83. *Mailing Add:* New Orleans Mus Art PO Box 19123 City Park New Orleans LA 70179

FAGER, CHARLES J
EDUCATOR, CERAMIST

b Osage City, Kans, Feb 3, 36. *Study:* Kans State Univ, Manhattan, BArch, 59; Univ Kans, Lawrence, MA(ceramics), 63. *Comn:* Pub Libr, Trend Publ, First Financial Corp, Tampa, Fla; Gulf Life Ins Co, Jacksonville, Fla. *Exhib:* Piedmont Craftsman, Mint Mus, Charlotte, NC, 76; one-man shows, Stetson Univ, Deland, Fla, 63; Colo State Col, Greeley, 63; Pensacola Jr Col, Fla, 63; Fla Ctr Mod Art, Micapony, 70 & Univ N Fla, Jacksonville, 76; and many other group & one-man shows. *Pos:* Consult archit, Rowe Holmes Assoc Archits Inc, Tampa, Fla, 73-74. *Teaching:* Art instr, Kans State Univ, Manhattan, 60-61; grad asst instr, Univ Kans, Lawrence, 61-63; prof ceramics, Univ S Fla, Tampa, 63-82, prof visual arts, 82-; instr, Tampa Bay Art Ctr, 75. *Awards:* Irving Hill First Award for Ceramics, Ninth Ann Kans Designer-Craftsman Exhib, Lawrence, 62; Ceramics Purchase Award, Wichita Nat Decorative Arts & Ceramics Exhib, Wichita, 62; Award of Excellence, Ann State Fla Craftsmen Exhib, 76. *Bibliog:* Angelo Garzio (auth), Portfolio: Raku, Ceramics Monthly, 6/67; photograph of sculpture in Am Crafts Coun Newsletter, 1/70 & Art Week, 77. *Mem:* Col Art Asn; Southeastern Col Art Conf; Am Crafts Coun; World Crafts Coun; Nat Coun Educ Ceramic Arts. *Res:* Application of industrial clay form processes to art; slip casting ceramic figures from life; photoceramics. *Mailing Add:* Dept of Art Univ S Fla Tampa FL 33620

FAIERS, TED (EDWARD SPENCER)
PAINTER, PRINTMAKER

b Newquay, Eng, Oct 26, 08; Can citizen. *Study:* Univ Alta, with H G Glyde; Banff Sch Fine Arts; Arts Students League, with Will Barnet. *Work:* Willistead Gallery Art, Windsor, Ont; Glenbow Found, Calgary, Alta; Brooks Mem Art Gallery, Memphis, Tenn; Ark Art Ctr, Little Rock; Tenn Arts

Comn, Nashville. *Comn:* The Heritage of Tennessee, First Tenn Bank, Memphis. *Exhib:* Western Can Painters, 51; Mid-South Exhib Painting Awards, Memphis, 56 & 60; Delta Annual Awards, Little Rock, 61, 65 & 70; Six Americans, Ark Arts Ctr, Little Rock, 70; Retrospective, Memphis Acad Arts & Southwestern at Memphis, 72. *Pos:* Advert mgr, Western Can Hardware, Lethbridge, Alta, 40-50; chmn, Fedn Can Artists, Southern Alta Br, 48-50; mem, Cult Activities Bd, Prov Alta, 49-50; artist in residence, Univ Miss, summer 68. *Teaching:* Prof painting & printmaking & chmn painting dept, Memphis Acad Arts, 52-77, emer prof, 77- *Media:* Oil, Acrylic; Woodcut, Lithograph. *Publ:* Auth, An approach to painting in oils, Cult Activities Br, Prov Alta, 51. *Dealer:* Jean Effron 2440 Virginia Ave Washington DC 20037; Alice Bingham Graphics Inc 22 S Cooper Memphis TN 38104. *Mailing Add:* 3710 Friar Tuck Rd Memphis TN 38111

FAIRBANKS, JONATHAN LEO
CURATOR
b Ann Arbor, Mich, Feb 19, 33. *Study:* Brigham Young Univ & Univ Utah, BFA, 53; Univ Pa & Acad Fine Arts, MFA, 57; Univ Del, MA(Winterthur Fel), 61; Inst Patologia Libro, Rome, cert conservation, 68. *Pos:* Cur asst, Winterthur Mus, 61-62, asst cur, 62-67, assoc cur, 67-; cur Am decorative arts & sculpture, Mus Fine Arts, Boston, 71- *Teaching:* Teaching fel, Pa Acad Fine Arts, 55-57; adj prof, Univ Del, 61-70 & Am & New Eng Studies Prog, Boston Univ, 71- *Awards:* Mural Award, Acad Natural Sci; Ann Award Distinguished Serv Art & Antiques, Antiques Monthly, 83; Robert H Lord Award Excellence Hist Studies, Emmanuel Col, 83. *Mem:* Hon mem New Eng Chap, Am Soc Interior Designers; Soc Archit Historians; fel Am Inst Conserv; fel Pilgrim Soc; Colonial Soc Mass. *Publ:* Auth forward, Art and Commerce: American Prints of the Nineteenth Century, Univ Press Va, 78; ed, Boston Furniture of the Eighteenth Century, Colonial Soc Mass, Vol 48; coauth, American Furniture 1620 to the Present, Richard Marek Inc, 81; coauth, New England Begins, The Seventeenth Century, Boston Mus Fine Arts, 82; auth introd, Sam Maloof, Woodworker, New York, 83; and others. *Mailing Add:* Mus of Fine Arts Boston MA 02115

FAIRFIELD, RICHARD THOMAS
PRINTMAKER, EDUCATOR
b Peoria, Ill, Aug 7, 37. *Study:* Bradley Univ, BFA, 61; Univ Ill, MFA, 63. *Work:* Howard Univ, DC; St John's Univ, Jamaica, NY; B Carroll Reece Mem Mus, ETenn Univ, Johnson City; Ball State Univ, Muncie, Ind. *Exhib:* Drawing USA, St Paul Art Ctr, Minn, 67; Am Drawings, Mercyhurst Col, Erie, Pa, 69; Northwest Printmakers, Seattle Art Mus, 70; Ball State Small Sculpture & Drawings, Ball State Univ, Muncie, Ind, 73; Int Print Biennale, Cracow, Poland, 78. *Teaching:* Prof printmaking, Eastern Mich Univ, Ypsilanti, 63- & Santa Reparata, Florence, Italy, spring 74. *Awards:* Purchase Awards, NDak Ann, Univ NDak, 66, Imprint, Kutztown State Col, 67 & Drawing USA, St Paul Art Ctr, 67. *Media:* Etching. *Dealer:* Arwin Galleries 222 Grand River W Detroit MI 48226. *Mailing Add:* 1301 W Cross Ypsilanti MI 48197

FAIRWEATHER, SALLY H
DEALER
b Chicago, Ill, Sept 29, 17. *Study:* Art Students League, 36; Art Inst Chicago, BA, 39. *Pos:* Dir, Fairweather-Hardin Gallery, Chicago, 47-; dir, Art Dealers Asn Am, 62-63; dir, Found for Arts Scholarships, Chicago, 64-; co-founder, Chicago Art Dealers Asn, 66. *Teaching:* Instr life drawing, Katherine Lord Sch, Evanston, Ill, 39-43. *Specialty:* Modern paintings, graphics and sculpture. *Publ:* Auth, Picasso's Concrete Sculpture, Hudson Hills Press, 82. *Mailing Add:* 101 E Ontario St Chicago IL 60611

FAISON, SAMSON LANE, JR
HISTORIAN, MUSEUM DIRECTOR
b Washington, DC, Nov 16, 07. *Study:* Williams Col, BA, 29; Harvard Univ, MA, 30; Princeton Univ, MFA, 32; Williams Col, Hon LittD, 71. *Collections Arranged:* The New England Eye, 83, and other permanent collections & temporary exhibs, Williams Col Mus Art. *Pos:* Exec secy, Comt on Visual Arts, Harvard Univ, 54-55; dir, Williams Col Mus Art, 48-76. *Teaching:* From instr to asst prof art, Yale Univ, 32-36; from asst prof to prof art, Williams Col, 36-76, chmn dept, 40-69; vis prof, Univ Pa, NY Univ, Columbia Univ, Univ Calif, Berkeley & Harvard Univ, summers; vis res prof, Univ Ga, spring 68. *Awards:* Chevalier, Legion of Honor, Fr Govt, 47; Guggenheim Fel, 60-61. *Mem:* Col Art Asn Am; Asn Art Mus Dirs; Int Asn Art Critics; Mass Coun Arts & Humanities. *Res:* German eighteenth century architecture; nineteenth and twentieth century French and American painting. *Publ:* Auth, Dominikus Zimmermann, Mag Art, 52; auth, Manet, Abrams, 53; auth, Guide to Art Museums of New England, Harcourt Brace, 58; auth, Art Tours and Detours in New York State, Random, 64; auth, Art Museums of New England, Godine, 81. *Mailing Add:* Scott Hill Rd Williamstown MA 01267

FALFAN, ALFREDO
PAINTER, PRINTMAKER
b Mexico City, Mex, June 8, 34. *Study:* Escuela Nac De Arts Plasticas, 53-60; studied with Diego Rivera & Antonio Rodriguez Luna; Pratt Inst, Graphics Workshop, 69-70. *Work:* Mus Mod Art & Museo Rufino Tamaya, Mexico City. *Exhib:* Mus Mod Art, Paris, 66; Museo Genaro Perez, Cordoba, Argentina, 66; Mus Mod Art, Mexico City, 66 & 80; Museo Carrillo Gil, Mexico City, 78. *Teaching:* Prof painting, Escuela Nac De Artes Plasticas, 80- *Awards:* Spec Prize, Am Biennial III, Mus Genaro Perez, 66 & Gold Medal, Cordoba Munic Cult Mgt, 66; Purchase Prize, Excuela Mexicana, Nat Inst Fine Arts, Mexico City, 67. *Bibliog:* Toby Joysmith (auth), Iconographer of life's meaning, News, Mexico City, 3/17/68. *Mem:* Salon de la Plastica Mexicana; Asn Mexicana de Artes Plasticas. *Media:* Oils. *Dealer:* Merl de Kuper Moliere 328C Colonia Polanco Mexico DF. *Mailing Add:* Cosala 18 Dept 02 Mexico City 06140 Mexico

FALKENSTEIN, CLAIRE
SCULPTOR
b Coos Bay, Ore. *Study:* Univ Calif, Berkeley. *Work:* Addison Gallery Am Art, Andover, Mass; Baltimore Mus Art; Boston Mus Fine Arts; Solomon R Guggenheim Mus, New York; Los Angeles Mus Art. *Comn:* Floor to ceiling stair railing for Gallery Sapzio, Milan, Italy & for Gallery Stadler, Paris, France; fire-screen for Baron de Rothschild's chateau; fountain, Wilshire Blvd, Los Angeles; stained glass windows, rectory screen & doors, St Basil's Cath Church, Los Angeles; copper & fused glass fountain, Calif Fed Savings Bldg, Los Angeles. *Exhib:* Il Segno Gallery, Rome, Italy, 58; Inst Contemp Art, Boston, 59; Art for Use, Louvre, Paris, 62; Carnegie Inst, Pittsburgh, 64; Whitney Mus Am Art, New York, 64. *Media:* Glass. *Dealer:* Martha Jackson Gallery 32 E 69th St New York NY 10021. *Mailing Add:* 5 Great Jones St New York NY 10012

FALLER, MARION
PHOTOGRAPHER, EDUCATOR
b Passaic, NJ, Nov 5, 41. *Study:* Hunter Col, City Univ New York, BA; State Univ NY-Visual Studies Workshop, Rochester, MFA; additional study at William Paterson Col, NJ & New York Univ. *Work:* Carnegie Mus Art, Pittsburgh, Pa; Int Mus Photog, George Eastman House, Rochester, NY; Mus Fine Arts, Houston; Light Work, Inc, Syracuse, NY; Picker Art Gallery, Colgate Univ, Hamilton, NY; and others. *Exhib:* One-person show, Edith Barrett Gallery, Utica Col, NY, 81; Locations in Time, 77 & Acquisitions: 1973-1980, 80, Int Mus Photog, George Eastman House, Rochester, NY; New Photographics, Sarah Spurgeon Gallery, Cent Wash Univ, Ellensburg, 79; Explorations in Color Xerography, Picker Art Gallery, Colgate Univ, 79; The Image Considered: Recent Work by Women, Visual Studies Workshop, 79; US Eye, XIII Olympic Winter Games, 1980, traveling, Lake Placid, NY, 80; and many others. *Collections Arranged:* Edward S Curtis (auth), Photogravures--Volumes I & III from the North American Indian, 76 & Upstate Color: Photographs by Bishop, Block, Pfahl, 77, Everson Mus Art, Syracuse, NY. *Teaching:* Lectr photog, Dept Art, Hunter Col, New York, 71-74; lectr photog, Dept Art, Marymount Manhattan Col, New York, 73-74; asst prof photog & hist photog, Dept Fine Arts, Colgate Univ, Hamilton, NY, 74-82. *Awards:* Photogr's Grant, Light Work Visual Studies, Inc, Syracuse, NY, 76; Creative Artists Pub Serv Prog fel, NY, 77. *Bibliog:* Marion Faller, A Portfolio of Photographs, Creative Camera Mag, London, 7/74; Portfolio: Marion Faller, Ms Mag, 4/75; Connections: An invitational portfolio of images and statements by 28 women, Exposure, 81. *Mem:* Soc for Photog Educ; Photog Hist Soc NY. *Media:* Black & White, Color. *Publ:* Contribr, Messages/a Portfolio of Found Images, Rye Press, Chicago, 76; auth & illusr, A Resurrection of the Exquisite Corpse, Visual Studies Workshop Press, Rochester, 78; and others. *Mailing Add:* c/o Visual Studies Workshop Gallery 31 Prince St Rochester NY 14607

FALSETTA, VINCENT MARIO
EDUCATOR, PAINTER
b Philadelphia, Pa, Nov 5, 49. *Study:* Temple Univ, Philadelphia, Pa, BA, 72; Tyler Sch Art, Philadelphia, Pa, 72-73; Tyler Sch Art, Rome, Italy, MFA, 74. *Work:* Sheldon Swope Art Gallery, Terre Haute, Ind; Galleria Cavallno, Venice, Italy; Utah Mus Fine Arts, Salt Lake City; NTex State Univ, Denton; Utah Div Fine Arts. *Exhib:* Ind Artists Show, Indianapolis Mus Art, 77; Contemp Trends, Utah Mus Fine Arts, Salt Lake City, 77; 53rd Nat, Springville Mus Art, Utah, 77; Utah 77, Utah Mus Fine Arts, Salt Lake City, 77; Works on Paper: Southwest, Dallas Mus Fine Arts, Tex, 78; Made in Tex, Univ Art Mus, Austin, 79. *Teaching:* Asst prof painting & drawing, Ind Univ, Bloomington, 74-75; instr, Univ Utah, Salt Lake City, 75-77; asst prof, NTex State Univ, Denton, 77- *Awards:* Best Painting Award, Springville Mus Art, Utah, 77; First Place Drawing Purchase Awards, Miami Univ Oxford, Ohio, 77 & Ark Arts Ctr, 78. *Bibliog:* Jonathon Katz (auth), Unlikely visions, Bulletin, Philadelphia, 1/13/80; Bill Marvel (auth), Gallery humming with finely turned painting, Dallas Times Herald, 1/3/81; Robert Raczka (auth), Tackling a difficult game, Artweek, 1/17/81. *Media:* Mixed. *Dealer:* Mattingly-Baker Gallery 3000 McKinney Ave Dallas TX. *Mailing Add:* 151 Canal St New York NY 10002

FALTER, JOHN
ILLUSTRATOR
b Plattsmonth, Nebr, Feb 28, 10. *Study:* Kans City Art Inst, 28-30; Art Students League, New York (scholarship), 30-31; Grand Central Art Sch, New York, 30-31. *Work:* Harry S Truman Libr, Independence, Mo; Herbert Hoover Mus, Long Branch, Iowa; Mus City New York; Berkshire Mus; and others. *Comn:* Six major historical paintings to commemorate Bicentennial 1976, St Paul, Minn, 76; over 150 covers for the Saturday Evening Post. *Exhib:* Nat Acad Western Art, Cowboy Hall Fame, Okla, 75-81; Western Heritage Show, Houston, Tex, 80-81; Artists Am, Colo, 81. *Mem:* Soc Illustrators, New York. *Media:* Oil, Egg Tempera. *Publ:* Illusr, cover & profile, Newsweek Mag, 52; illusr, cover & profile, Today Mag, Philadelphia Inquirer, 77; illusr, profile, Saturday Evening Post, 71; illusr, profile, Artists of the Rockies, 76-77. *Mailing Add:* c/o American Legacy Gallery 5911 Main Street Kansas City MO 64113

FANE, LAWRENCE
SCULPTOR
b Kansas City, Mo, Sept 10, 33. *Study:* Harvard Univ, AB, 55; Boston Mus Sch, 56; with George Demetrios, 56-59. *Work:* Corcoran Gallery; Univ Mass Mus, Amherst; Mus Contemp Art, Udine, Italy; New York City Bd Educ; De Cordova Mus, Boston. *Comn:* Bronze & concrete fountain, comn by Villa Sam Lorenzo, Assizi, Italy, 66; portrait, Union of Am Hebrew Congregation, New York, 67; concrete sculpture, Trent Univ, Peterboro, Ont, 71; 8ft outdoor

sculpture, comn by Nichol Home, Milwaukee, 74; steel & concrete sculpture, Secker & Warburg Publ, London, 78. *Exhib:* One-man shows, Zabriskie Gallery, New York, 69, Marilyn Pearl Gallery, New York, 76, 78 & Duke Univ, Durham, NC, 77; Orgn Independent Artists, Wards Island, New York, 79; Marilyn Pearl Gallery, New York, 82; Four Artists and a Writer, Fed Hall, New York, 82; Aspects of Abstraction, Colby Col Mus, 83. *Teaching:* Instr design, RI Sch Design, Providence, 66-69; prof sculpture, Queens Col, NY, 69- *Awards:* Fels, Ingram Merrill Found, 73 & Dept Housing & Urban Develop, 74; Res Found, City Univ New York, 81. *Bibliog:* All Things Considered (film), City Univ New York, 73; Allan Ludwig (auth), Recycled sculpture, Arts Mag, 76; article, Arte Am Contemp, 80. *Mem:* Am Acad Rome (exec comt, 79-). *Media:* Steel, Bronze. *Dealer:* Marilyn Pearl Gallery 29 W 57th St New York NY 10019. *Mailing Add:* 355 Riverside Dr New York NY 10025

FANGOR, VOY
PAINTER
b Warsaw, Poland, Nov 15, 22; US citizen. *Study:* Warsaw Acad Fine Arts, MFA. *Work:* Guggenheim Mus, New York; Mus Mod Art, New York; Univ Calif Art Mus, Berkeley; Muzeum Sztuki, Lodz, Poland; Stedelijk Mus, Amsterdam, Holland. *Exhib:* The Responsive Eye, Mus Mod Art, 65; 34th Biennale Venezia, Padiglione Centrale, 68; Guggenheim Mus, 70. *Teaching:* Asst prof painting, Warsaw Acad Fine Arts, 53-61; prof painting, Fairleigh Dickinson Univ, 65. *Bibliog:* R C Kennedy (auth), Notes on Fangor, Art Int, 66; Jay Jacobs (auth), Pertinent and impertinent: illusionist, Art Gallery Mag, 69; John Canaday (auth), Fangors romantic op, New York Times, 2/15/70. *Media:* Oil. *Mailing Add:* Box 155 Summit NY 12175

FANNING, ROBBIE
WRITER, LECTURER
b West Lafayette, Ind, Jan 30, 47. *Study:* Knox Col, two yrs; State Univ NY, BS, 81; spec study with Constance Howard; Cal State, Dominguez Hills. *Pos:* Consult fiber art, 73-; fiber ed, Westart, Auburn, Calif, 73-76; ed/publ, Open Chain, 75-; mem adv coun, Ctr for Hist Am Needlework, Pittsburgh, Pa, 77-; columnist, Needle & Thread, 81- *Teaching:* Instr machine embroidery for artists & photog for textiles, Nat Standards Coun Convention, New Orleans, La, Fall 76; lectr self-publ for artists, Stanford Univ Pub Conf, Fall 77; workshop, W Coast Quilters Conf, Ore, summer 79; lectr writing, Calif Writers Conf, Stanford Univ, summer 79; lectr writing, San Jose State Univ, 80-82. *Mem:* Am Crafts Coun; Nat Standards Coun Am Embroiderers; Embroiderers Guild Am; Peninsula Stitchery Guild (chmn, 74-75); Int Guild Craft Auth, Journalists & Photogr. *Res:* The roots in traditional needlework that give rise to contemporary fiber and fabric art and craft. *Publ:* Auth, Stitches (weekly column), Country Almanac, Woodside, Calif, 73-; auth, West Coast Fiber Calendar (monthly), Westart, 73-76; auth, Decorative Machine Stitchery, 76 & co-auth, Here and Now Stitchery: Ethnic Embroidery & Applique, 78, Butterick Publ Co; coauth, The Complete Book of Machine Quilting, Chilton, 80. *Mailing Add:* PO Box 2634 Menlo Park CA 94025

FARAGASSO, JACK
ILLUSTRATOR, PAINTER
b Brooklyn, NY, Jan 23, 29. *Study:* Art Students League, with Frank J Reilly, 48-52. *Work:* George Washington Carver Mus, Tuskegee Inst, Ala. *Exhib:* Gallery Mod Art, New York, 69; Am Artists Prof League, 69-71 & 73-79. *Pos:* Illusr, many book co, 57- *Teaching:* Instr drawing, painting & illus & dir, treas & trustee, Frank Reilly Sch Art, New York, 67-68; instr drawing, painting & illus, Art Students League, 68-; instr drawing & painting, Woodstock Sch Art, 81. *Mem:* Art Students League; fel Am Artists Prof League; Am Portrait Soc; Artists Fel Inc. *Media:* Oil. *Interests:* Realistic school of painting, ranging from illustrative to surrealistic to malerisch. *Publ:* Auth, The Students Guide to Painting, North Light Publ, 79. *Mailing Add:* 340 E 55th St New York NY 10022

FARBER, DENNIS H
PAINTER, PHOTOGRAPHER
b Pittsburgh, Pa, Mar 8, 46. *Study:* Trinity Col, BA, 68; Claremont Grad Sch, MFA, 75. *Work:* Newport Beach Mus Art, Calif; San Diego Mus Mod Art; Honolulu Acad Art, Contemp Art Ctr Hawaii, Honolulu; State Found Arts, Hawaii. *Comn:* Mural painting, Prince Kuhio Hotel, Honolulu. *Exhib:* Los Angeles Abstract Painting, Univ NMex, Albuquerque, 79 & Univ Calif, Riverside, 79; Sleight of Hand, Calif State Univ, Fullerton, 82; Rancho de Taos: A Photographic History, Mus Fine Art, Santa Fe, Amon Carter Mus, Ft Worth, Colo Fine Art Mus, Colorado Springs & Univ Nebr, 82-83; Three Los Angeles Painters, Pepperdine Univ, 83 & Col Notre Dame, Calif, 83; Altered Photography, Arco Ctr Visual Arts, Los Angeles, 84. *Teaching:* Asst prof painting, Claremont Col, 75-76 & 82-83. *Awards:* Exhib award, Hawaii-Calif Biennial, San Diego Mus, 79 & From Santa Barbara to San Diego, 82. *Bibliog:* Meryl Schipper (auth), Dennis Farber, Los Angeles Inst Contemp Art J, 80; Ven Deren Coke (auth), Sleight of Hand, California St Univ, Fullerton, 82; Andree Marechal-Workman (auth), Controlled painterliness, Art Week, 82. *Media:* Acrylic, Oil. *Mailing Add:* 3328 Grand Ave Claremont CA 91711

FARBER, MAYA M
PAINTER
b Timisoara, Rumania, Jan 24, 36; US citizen. *Study:* Pratt Inst, with Edwin Oppler; Hunter Col; Hans Hoffman Sch; Art Students League, with Reginald Marsh. *Work:* Butler Inst Am Art, Youngstown, Ohio; Int Tel & Tel, New York; Columbia Mus Art, SC; Ga Mus Art, Athens; Jacksonville Art Mus, Fla. *Exhib:* Group shows, Great Expectations, Madison Ave, 78, Mountain Top Gallery, Windham, NY, 79 & Twilight Part Art Asn, Collage, 79; one-

woman shows, Rockefeller Ctr, New York, 79 & Mountain Top Gallery, 80; and others. *Awards:* Second Prize, Jamaica Festival Art, 67. *Media:* Oil, Acrylic. *Dealer:* Chase Gallery Inc 31 E 64th St New York NY 10021. *Mailing Add:* 435 E 52nd St New York NY 10022

FARES, WILLIAM O
PAINTER
b Compton, Calif, July 16, 42. *Study:* San Francisco Art Inst, BA & MFA. *Work:* Chase Manhattan Bank; Va Mus Fine Arts; State Univ NY Col Purchase; Yale Art Gallery; Muhlenberg Ctr for the Arts, Allentown, Pa. *Exhib:* Biennial, Whitney Mus Am Art, New York, 75; Albright-Knox Art Gallery, Buffalo, NY, 75; Paperworks, Mus Mod Art, New York, 76; Am Drawing 1927-1977, Minn Mus Art, St Paul, 77; one-man exhib, Zolla/Lieberman Gallery, Chicago, 77; Stamford Mus, Conn, 78; Va Mus Fine Arts, 79; Jefferson Co Hist Soc, Watertown, NY, 79; Tex Gallery, 79; and many others. *Awards:* Nat Endowment Arts Grant, 79-80. *Bibliog:* David Bourdon (auth), article, The Village Voice, 12/6/76; Barbara Cavaliere (auth), article, Arts Mag, 2/77; Kenneth Whal (auth), On abstract literalist works, Arts Mag, 4/77. *Media:* Acrylic. *Dealer:* Kathren Markel 50 W 57th St New York NY 10019. *Mailing Add:* 110 W 26th St New York NY 10001

FARIAN, BABETTE S
PAINTER, DESIGNER
b New York, NY, June 6, 16. *Study:* New York Sch Fine & Appl Art, two years; Cooper Union, three years; Art Students League, three months, with Bridgman; Mus Mod Art, three years; additional study with Donald Stacy, Addison Lamar, Joseph Margulies & Morris Kantor. *Work:* First Unitarian Church, Flushing, NY; Tamassee DAR Sch Gallery; US Fine Arts Registry; Women's Fine Arts Mus; also in many pvt collections. *Exhib:* Arts & Sci Mus, Stateville, NC, 68; Union Carbide, 76; Metrop Mus 81 St Gallery, New York, 77; Gov Mansion, Jackson, Miss, 80; Salmagundi Club, 81; Lever House, 83. *Pos:* Color consult, Addison Lamar, 37-40; textile designer-artist, Krasom Co, New York, 55-57; free-lance designer, 58-59; asst head studio, Manhattan Shirt Co, New York, 60-65; designer, Hanscom Fabrics. *Teaching:* Instr color & design, Cooper Union Art Sch, 40-41; pvt classes, 73-74. *Awards:* First Prize/Oil, Nat Art League, 79; Award of Merit, Nat League Am Pen Women, 79; First Prize Watercolor, Composers, Authors & Artists Am, 83. *Bibliog:* Photos of work in Artist Mag, 66; article in Vineyard Gazette & Queens Tribune, 74. *Mem:* Artist's Equity Asn; Burr Artists (catalogue chmn); Composers, Authors & Artists Am; Int Beaux Art; Nat Asn Am Pen Women (corresp secy). *Media:* Acrylic, Watercolor, Ink. *Publ:* Auth, The pendulum of time and the arts, 68; auth, article in Artist's Equity Mag, 75. *Dealer:* Mark A Gallery NJ. *Mailing Add:* 34-48 81st St Jackson Heights NY 11372

FARIS, BRUNEL DE BOST
PAINTER, EDUCATOR
b Oklahoma City, Okla, Aug 9, 37. *Study:* Univ Okla, BFA & MFA. *Work:* Univ Okla Art Mus, Norman; State Okla Collection; Philbrook Art Ctr, Tulsa, Okla; Barkouras Found, Oklahoma City; Privatklinik-Diabetiker, Bad Lauterberg, WGer. *Exhib:* Mid-Am Ann, Nelson Gallery Art, Kansas City, Mo, 65; 35th Ann Exhib, Springfield Art Mus, 65; 8 State Exhib Southwestern Art, Okla Art Ctr, Oklahoma City, 68 & 71; Okla Ann, Philbrook Art Ctr, Tulsa, 69 & 75; one-man shows, Univ Okla Art Mus, 74 & Barkouras Found, Okla, 77. *Pos:* Art dir, Okla Sci & Arts Found, 66-69. *Teaching:* Instr art, Tulsa Pub Schs, 61-64; instr art, Oklahoma City Pub Schs, 65-66; assoc prof art & chmn dept, Oklahoma City Univ, 69- *Mem:* Col Art Asn. *Media:* Collage, Assemblage. *Mailing Add:* 1012 N W 39th St Oklahoma City OK 73118

FARIS, PETER KINZIE
PAINTER, MUSEUM DIRECTOR
b Washington, DC, Oct 7, 43. *Study:* Nat Col Art, Lahore, Pakistan, 62; Colo State Univ, Ft Collins, BA, 65; Univ Colo, Boulder, MFA, 70. *Exhib:* One-man show, Hatton Gallery, Colo State Univ, Ft Collins, 79; 1974 All-Calif Exhib, Laguna Beach Art Mus; Aspen Art Found Exhib, Colo, 75; Assistance League All-Media Competition, Houston Art Mus, Tex, 76; 8-West Biennial, Western Colo Ctr for the Arts, Grand Junction, Colo, 76; and others. *Collections Arranged:* Pattern and Sources of Navajo Weaving, Navajo Rug Exhib, 77; Life on the High Plains (auth, catalog), Hist Photos from Black Hills, 78; Objects 79 (auth, catalog), Int Juried Crafts Biennial, 79. *Pos:* Gallery dir & educ progs coordr, Arvada Ctr for Arts & Humanities, Colo, 76-78; exec dir, Western Colo Ctr for Arts, Grand Junction, 78- *Teaching:* Instr fine arts, Prestonburg Community Col, Ky, 70-72; asst prof studio art, Chapman Col, Orange, Calif, 72-74; instr painting, Community Col Denver, Colo, 76. *Mem:* Future Soc Am; Western Asn Art Mus. *Media:* Acrylic; Pencil. *Mailing Add:* Western Colo Ctr Arts 1803 N Seventh Grand Junction CO 81501

FARM, GERALD E
PAINTER
b Grand Island, Nebr, Mar 8, 35. *Study:* Famous Artist Sch, Westport, Conn; Nebr State Col, BA(educ). *Work:* Deming Fed Savings, NMex; Olney Tex Savings & Loan; Bank of Beaver City, Okla; plus many pvt collections. *Exhib:* C M Russell Auction, Int Rodeo Finals, Great Falls, Mont, 73 & 75; The Real Show, Grand Cent Art Galleries, New York, 79; Preview '80, Tex Art Gallery, Dallas, 80; Preview, Tex Art Gallery, Dallas, 81; Santa Fe Festival Arts, 81. *Bibliog:* Helen Lally (auth), Gerald Farm--Guardian of our western heritage, Southwest Art, 74;; Byron Jones (auth), The story teller's art of Gerald Farm, Southwest Art, 79. *Media:* Oil. *Mailing Add:* 5609 Foothills Dr Farmington NM 87401

FARMER, JOHN DAVID
HISTORIAN, ADMINISTRATOR
b Washington, Ga, Jan 25, 39. *Study:* Columbia Univ, BA, 60; Univ NC, Chapel Hill, MA, 63; Princeton Univ, MFA, 65, PhD, 81. *Collections Arranged:* Virtuouso Craftsman (with catalog), 69; Concepts of the Bauhaus (with catalog), 72; German Master Drawings of the 19th Century (with catalog), 72-73. *Pos:* Curatorial asst, Worcester Art Mus, Mass, 67-69; curator, Busch-Reisinger Mus, Harvard Univ, 69-72; cur earlier painting, Art Inst Chicago, 72-75; dir, Birmingham Mus Art, 75-79; exec dir, Fulbright Comn, Belg, 79-80; dir, Univ Art Mus, Univ Calif, Santa Barbara, 81- *Teaching:* Instr art hist, Clark Univ, 68-69; lectr, Harvard Univ, 71; adj prof, Univ Calif, Santa Barbara, 81- *Mem:* Col Art Asn; Am Asn Mus. *Res:* Art of the Northern Renaissance, especially painting and decorative arts of early sixteenth century Low Countries. *Publ:* Coauth, Catalogue of European Paintings, Worcester Art Mus, 74; auth, Gerard David's lamentation and an anonymous St Jerome, Mus Studies, 75; auth, Ensor, Braziller, 77. *Mailing Add:* Univ Art Mus Univ Calif Santa Barbara CA 93106

FARNHAM, ALEXANDER
PAINTER, WRITER
b Orange, NJ, May 5, 26. *Study:* Art Students League, with George Bridgeman, W C McNulty & Frank Vincent DuMond; also with Van Dearing Perrine & Anne Steel Marsh. *Work:* Newark Mus, NJ; Nat Arts Club, New York; Monmouth Col; James A Michener Collection; Morgan Guaranty Trust Co, New York. *Comn:* Murals, Naval subjects, Naval Repair Base, New Orleans, 45; portrait of dir, Am Found for Blind, 50; painting of off bldg, NJ Mfrs Ins Co, Trenton, 69; Washington Crosses the Del (pewter plate design), Franklin Mint, 76. *Exhib:* Methods and Materials of the Painter, Montclair Art Mus, circulated in Can, 54; Nat Acad Design 135th Ann Exhib, New York, 60; Eastern States Art Exhib, Springfield, Mass, 65-67; NJ Award Artists Exhib, Montclair Art Mus, 66; NJ Artists, Newark Mus Invitational, 68. *Pos:* Artist, US Navy, 45-46. *Awards:* Agnes B Noyes Award, Montclair Art Mus, 50; NJ State Coun Painting Fel, 80; First Award, Summit Art Ctr Nat Exhib, 81. *Bibliog:* Diana Bainbridge (auth), art review and commentaries, NJ Mus & Arts, 6/69; Diane Hamilton (auth), Painters of the Valley, Country Mag, 12/81; Palette Talk #51, M Grumbacher Inc, 82. *Mem:* Assoc Artists NJ (pres, 72-77); Hunterdon Art Ctr. *Media:* Oil. *Publ:* Auth & illusr, Tool collectors handbook, 70, 72 & 75; auth, Architectural patterns, subjects for the artists brush, 74. *Dealer:* The Coryell Gallery 8 1/2 Coryell St Lambertville NJ; Golden Door Gallery New Hope PA. *Mailing Add:* RD 2 Box 365 Stockton NJ 08559

FARNHAM, EMILY
PAINTER, WRITER
b Kent, Ohio, May 27, 12. *Study:* Kent State Univ, BSc(educ); Art Students League; Cleveland Sch Art; Hans Hofmann Sch Fine Arts; Ohio State Univ, MA & PhD. *Comn:* Murals, Cine Sonora, Hermosillo, Sonora, Mex, 47. *Exhib:* one-man shows, Art Ctr, Salt Lake City, 40 & Univ Va, Charlottesville, 58; 6th Nat Exhib, Okla Printmakers Soc, Oklahoma City, 64; Traveling Show, Assoc Artists NC, 68; Street of Harbor, Provincetown, 81; and others. *Teaching:* Asst & instr design, Ohio State Univ, Columbus, 34-37, asst prof watercolor, 54-55; instr painting, Mich State Univ, East Lansing, 37; instr painting & drawing, Utah State Univ, Logan, 38-41; head dept design, Stout State Col, Menomonie, Wis, 42-45; asst prof painting & drawing, Southern Ill Univ, Carbondale, 47-53; prof painting & art hist, Mary Baldwin Col, Staunton, Va, 56-62; prof painting & art hist, E Carolina Univ, Greenville, NC, 62-77, chmn art hist dept, 68-73. *Bibliog:* Douglas MacAgy (auth), Charles Demuth: Behind a Laughing Mask by Emily Farnham, Sat Rev, 5/71. *Mem:* Provincetown Hist Asn; PEN; Provincetown Art Asn. *Media:* Mixed Media, Acrylics. *Res:* Abstract form resident in the great paintings of the past. *Publ:* Auth, Charles Demuth's Bermuda landscapes, Art J, New York, 65; auth, Charles Demuth: Behind a Laughing Mask, Univ Okla, Norman, 71. *Dealer:* Outermost Gallery Provincetown, MA 02657. *Mailing Add:* 208 Bradford St No 6 Provincetown MA 02657

FARNSWORTH, HELEN SAWYER See Sawyer, Helen

FARRENS, JUANITA G
PAINTER, INSTRUCTOR
b Philippine Republic; US citizen. *Study:* Bukidnon Inst, Mindanao, Philippines, BSE, 39; Md Univ Exten, Ankara, Turkey, 53-54; La Tech Univ, 83. *Work:* Westminster Abbey, Spencer, Mass; St Alphonso Church, Philippine Republic; St Dominic Church, Mother Cabrini High Sch, New Orleans; Colo Gold Mine Sch, Golden. *Comn:* Garden scene, comn by Joe Barhill, Boulder, 60; landscape, Shepherd Ctr, Mt Carmel Acad, New Orleans, 82. *Exhib:* Ann Exhib, Delgado Mus Art & New Orleans Mus Art, 57; Ann Gulf Coast Art Exhib, Masur Mus, Monroe, La, 70-72; Biennial Exhib Piedmont Painting & Sculpture, Mint Mus Art, 77-79; Joslyn Art Mus Ann, 78; Pastel Soc Am Ann, Nat Arts Club, New York, 78-80 & 83; Ga Second Ann Exhib, Columbus Mus Arts & Sci, 81; Aqueous, J B Speed Art Mus, 82; First Patron Watercolor Gala, Kresge Fine Art Ctr, Oklahoma City, 83. *Teaching:* Instr art, Farrens Art Sch, New Orleans, 60- & Sheperd Ctr, Mt Carmel Acad, New Orleans, 78-83; lectr & demonstr painting, New Orleans Art Asn, 64-83 & Holy Cross Col, 68. *Awards:* New Orleans Overture to the Cultural Season, New Orleans Art Asn, 69; First Award Impressionism, Second Ann Int Competition, Palm Beach Gallery, 83. *Mem:* Pastel Soc Am; Am Portrait Soc; founding mem La Watercolor Soc (vpres, 71-72); New Orleans Art Asn; Womens Caucus Art. *Media:* Oil, Pastel. *Dealer:* Reads Gallery 100A Bellemeade Blvd Gretna LA 70053. *Mailing Add:* 6164 Marshal Foch New Orleans LA 70124

FARRIS, JOSEPH
CARTOONIST, PAINTER
b Newark, NJ, May 30, 24. *Study:* Art Students League; Biarritz Univ; Whitney Sch Art. *Work:* Paintings in private collections. *Exhib:* One-man show, Ward Eggleston Gallery, New York. *Pos:* Contract artist, New Yorker. *Awards:* Emily Lowe Award. *Mem:* Cartoonists Asn. *Publ:* Contribr cartoons & covers to The New Yorker, Sat Eve Post, True, Ladies Home J, Playboy, Penthouse, Sat Rev, New Woman, Punch & other nat mag; illusr, Slave boy in Judea; illusr bk jackets for others; auth & illusr, Phobias & Therapies (cartoon bk), Grosset & Dunlap; contribr, Pilgrim's Progress (cartoon book), Thomas More Press. *Mailing Add:* Long Meadow Lane Bethel CT 06801

FARRIS, LINDA B
DEALER
b San Francisco, Calif, Mar 29, 44. *Study:* Univ Calif, Berkeley, BA, 66. *Collections Arranged:* Eight Seattle Artists, Los Angeles Inst Contemp Art, 81; Self Portraits, Los Angeles Munic Art Gallery, 83. *Pos:* Mem bd dirs, Henry Gallery, Univ Wash, 77- & Dance Theatre Seattle, 78-79; adv bd, Factory Visual Arts, Seattle, 78- *Bibliog:* Matthew Kangas (auth), Decade of excellence at Linda Farris, Argus, 8/10/79; article, Working Woman, 3/83; Farris Gallery celebrates 13 years of success, Seattle Times, 5/27/83. *Mem:* Contemp Art Coun; Henry Gallery Asn; Seattle Art Mus. *Specialty:* Seattle and nationally known artists of museum calibre; innovative works by Seattle artists; major exhibitions of Robert Rauschenberg, Louise Nevelson, Norie Sato, Sherry Markovitz & Jeffrey Bishop. *Mailing Add:* 322 Second Ave S Seattle WA 98104

FARRIS-LARSON, GAIL (THERESA GAIL LARSON)
METALSMITH, EDUCATOR
b Tulsa, Okla, Aug 23, 47. *Study:* Pittsburg State Univ, Kans, MA, 71; Ind Univ, Bloomington, with Alma Eikerman, MFA, 74. *Work:* Mus Plains Ind, Browning, Mont; Idaho First Nat Bank, Boise; Ind Mus Fine Arts, Bloomington; Pittsburg State Univ, Kans. *Exhib:* Goldsmith: 74, Renwick Gallery, Smithsonian Inst, Washington, DC, 74; Forms in Metal: 275 Years of Metalsmith, Mus Contemp Crafts, NY, 74; Contemp Crafts Am, Colo State Univ, Ft Collins, 75; Crafts for Am, Phillipines Design Ctr, Manila, 77; Copper, Bronze & Brass, Tuscon, Ariz, 77; Lake Superior Nat, Duluth Art Inst, Minn, 81. *Collections Arranged:* Marilyn Levine: Ceramics, 79; William Wiley Prints, 80. *Teaching:* Assoc prof metal & crafts, Idaho State Univ, Pocatello, 74- *Awards:* Cash Awards, Indianapolis Mus, 73 & Boise Art Gallery, 75 & 76. *Mem:* Prof mem Soc North Am Goldsmiths; Northwest Designer Craftsmen. *Media:* Gold, Silver. *Publ:* Contribr, Contemporary Jewelry, Holt Rinehart, 75; contribr, Contemporary Crafts of the Americas: 1975, Regnery, 75. *Mailing Add:* 340 S Lincoln Pocatello ID 83204

FARROW, PATRICK VILLIERS
SCULPTOR
b Los Angeles, Calif, Nov 27, 42. *Study:* Univ Calif, Los Angeles; Loyola Univ. *Work:* Norton Simon Mus, Pasadena, Calif. *Comn:* Crucifix, comn by Bruce Hubbard, Chicago, Ill, 83; sculpture, City Rutland, 84. *Exhib:* Dartmouth Col, Hanover, NH, 76; Allied Artists Am, Nat Art Club, Nat Acad Design & Am Acad Arts & Lett, 77-83; Nat Sculpture Soc Ann, New York, 78-83; Am Acad Arts & Lett, New York, 80-83. *Awards:* Award of Distinction, Allied Artists Am, 77; Bronze Medal, 78 & Edith & Richmond Proskauer Award, 80, Nat Sculpture Soc. *Bibliog:* Rex Reed (auth), article, Cosmopolitan, 68; Theodora Morgan (auth), articles, Nat Sculpture Rev, 78, 80 & 83; Joe Franklin (interviewer), WOR-TV, New York, 79. *Mem:* Nat Sculpture Soc; Allied Artists Am; Moonbrook Arts Union (bd dirs, 81-83); Rutland Area Art Asn (bd dirs, 83-84). *Media:* Steel, Bronze. *Publ:* Contribr, Sculpture Rev, 83. *Dealer:* Peel Gallery Danby VT 05739; O'Briens Art Emporium 7122 Stetson Dr Scottsdale AZ 85251. *Mailing Add:* 61 Killington Ave Rutland VT 05731

FARRUGGIO, REMO MICHAEL
PAINTER
b Palermo, Sicily, Mar 29, 06; US citizen. *Study:* Nat Acad Design, Beaux Arts Inst, Educ Alliance & Indust Art Sch, New York. *Work:* Metrop Mus Art, New York; Butler Inst Am Art, Youngstown, Ohio; Portland Mus Art, Ore; Santa Fe Art Mus, NMex. *Exhib:* Blues and Other Paintings, Julien Levy Gallery, New York, 39; Galleria Art Mod, Mexico City, 50; John Heller Gallery, New York, 55, 56 & 58; Schneider Gallery, Rome, Italy, 57; Nuovo Sagitario Gallery, Milano, Italy, 73-74. *Teaching:* Instr painting, Fedn Artists, Detroit, Mich, 40; teacher painting, Portland Mus Art Sch, 54-55. *Awards:* Award for Dear Old Southland, Detroit Art Inst, 43; Butler Inst Am Art Award, 57; Award for Rocks, Hyannis Art Asn, Mass, 70. *Mem:* Artists Equity; Am Fedn Arts & Lett. *Media:* Mixed. *Mailing Add:* 208 E Tenth New York NY 10003

FARWELL, BEATRICE
HISTORIAN, EDUCATOR
b Santa Barbara, Calif, Oct 9, 20. *Study:* Knox Col, BA(art), 42; NY Univ, MA(art hist), 65; Univ Calif, Los Angeles, PhD(art hist), 73. *Pos:* Mem bd trustees, Santa Barbara Mus of Art, 71-76. *Teaching:* Lectr & sr lectr, Metrop Mus Art, New York, 43-66; vis lectr art hist, Univ Calif, Santa Barbara, 66-67, lectr, 67-74, assoc prof, 74-77, prof, 77- *Mem:* Col Art Asn (bd dir, 77-81); Southern Calif Art Historians (vpres, 80-81); Arch Am Art. *Res:* French 19th century painting and graphic art; emphasis on realism and popular imagery. *Publ:* Auth, A Manet masterpiece reconsidered, Apollo, 7/63; auth, Courbet's Baigneuses & the rhetorical feminine image, Art News Ann, 72; auth, Manet's Nymphe Surprise, Burlington Mag, 4/75; auth, French Popular Lithographic Imagery 1815-1870, Vols 1-3, Univ Chicago Press, 81-83; auth, Manet and the Nude, Garland Press, 81; and others. *Mailing Add:* c/o Dept Art Hist Univ Calif Santa Barbara CA 93106

FASANO, CLARA
SCULPTOR
b Castellaneta, Italy; US citizen. *Study:* Cooper Union Art Sch; Art Students League; also with Prof Arturo Dazzi, Rome, Italy; Acad Julien & Colarossi Acad, Paris, France. *Work:* Metrop Mus Art, New York; Nat Collection Fine Arts, Smithsonian Inst, Washington, DC; Norfolk Mus Arts & Sci, Va. *Comn:* Sculpture for Middleport Post Off, Ohio, Richmond High Sch, Staten Island, NY & Tech High Sch, Brooklyn, NY; many portraits for pvt comns. *Exhib:* Whitney Mus Am Art, New York; Metrop Mus Art; Nat Acad Design, New York; Pa Acad Fine Arts, Philadelphia; Salon Automne in Paris, London, Rome & others. *Teaching:* Instr sculpture, Indust & Fine Arts Sch of New York & Adult Educ, Bd Educ, New York, 46-56; instr sculpture, Manhattanville Col, 56-66. *Awards:* Daniel Chester French Medal, 65, Dessie Greer Prize, 68, Nat Acad Design; Grant & Citation, Nat Inst Arts & Lett; and others. *Bibliog:* Fred Whitaker (auth), Clara Fasano and her terra cotta, Am Artist Mag, 2/57; and others. *Mem:* Academician Nat Acad Fine Arts; fel Nat Sculpture Soc (coun, 52 & 60-63); Sculptors Guild; Audubon Artists; Nat Asn Women Artists. *Media:* Terra-Cotta, Bronze. *Mailing Add:* Cervaro 03044 1083 Fifth Ave Prov Frosinone Italy

FASNACHT, HEIDE ANN
SCULPTOR
b Cleveland, Ohio, Jan 12, 51. *Study:* RI Sch Design, BFA, 73; NY Univ, MA. *Comn:* Storm Windows, New Gallery, Cleveland, Ohio, 81. *Exhib:* Paperworks 80, Hudson River Mus, New York, 80; May show, Cleveland Mus Art, Ohio, 81; one-artist show, New Gallery Contemp Art, Cleveland, 81 & Vanderwoude Tananbaum Gallery, New York, 83; Women Sculptors' Drawings, Max Hutchinson Gallery, New York, 82. *Teaching:* Adj asst prof drawing, State Univ NY, Purchase, 81- *Awards:* MacDowell Colony Fel, 81; Athena Found Fel, 83; Hand Hollow Found Fel, 83. *Bibliog:* Ronny Cohen (auth), article, Artforum, 10/80; John Russell (auth), Art: Sculpture on the beach at the battery, New York Times, 7/4/80; Grace Glueck (auth), Screens, New York Times, 10/19/82. *Mem:* Col Art Asn; Found Community Artists; Int Sculpture Soc. *Media:* Wood, Mixed Media. *Dealer:* Vanderwoude Tananbaum Gallery New York NY. *Mailing Add:* 4 White St New York NY 10013

FAUDIE, FRED
PAINTER, PHOTOGRAPHER
b DuBois, Pa, May 29, 41. *Study:* Cornell Univ, AB(art hist), 63; Univ Iowa, Iowa City, MA(painting), 65, with John Schulz, 67-68; Syracuse Univ, MFA(illus), 79. *Work:* Addison Gallery Am Art. *Exhib:* Brockton Triennial, Brockton Art Mus, Mass, 81; Profile of a Gallery, Addison Gallery Am Art, 81; Meadows Mus Art Nat Biennial, Shreveport, La, 82; Seeing Double, Visual Studies Workshop, Rochester, NY, 82; Boston Printmakers 35th Nat Show, Boston Univ, 83; Mus Sci 3-D Exhib, Boston, 83. *Teaching:* Assoc prof photog & art, Univ Lowell, 68-, chairperson art dept, 80-83. *Mem:* Boston Visual Artists Union; Lowell Art Asn. *Media:* Oil, Acrylic. *Dealer:* Martina Hamilton Gallery 19 E 71st St New York NY 10021; Andover Gallery 68 Park St Andover MA 01810. *Mailing Add:* 38 Wannalancit St Lowell MA 01854

FAULCONER, MARY (FULLERTON)
PAINTER, DESIGNER
b Pittsburgh, Pa. *Study:* Pa Mus Sch Art; also with Alexey Brodovitch. *Work:* Duchess of Windsor; plus many others. *Comn:* Paintings, UNICEF, 72; paintings, Steubin Glass; designed six stamps, US Postal Serv, 74; designed Rose stamp, US Postal Serv, 78; designed Love stamp, US Postal Serv, 82; and others. *Exhib:* Alex Iolas Gallery, New York, 55, 58 & 61; Philadelphia Art Alliance, 62; Bodley Gallery, New York, 64, 66, 69 & 72; Tenn Fine Arts Ctr, Nashville, 67; De Mers Gallery, Hilton Head, SC, 71-72. *Pos:* Art dir, Harper's Bazaar Mag, 40; art dir, Mademoiselle Mag, 45. *Teaching:* Instr advert, Philadelphia Mus Sch Art, 36-40. *Awards:* Distinctive Merit Award, 54, 57 & 61, Silver Medal, 58 & 59, Art Dir Club; Gold Medal, Am Rose Soc, 78. *Media:* Gouache. *Dealer:* ACA Galleries 21 E 67th Street New York NY 10021. *Mailing Add:* 20 Beekman Pl New York NY 10022

FAULKNER, FRANK
PAINTER
b Sumter, SC, July 27, 46. *Study:* Univ NC, Chapel Hill, BFA, 68, MFA, 72. *Work:* Hirshhorn Mus, Washington, DC; Nat Collection of Fine Arts, Washington, DC; Albright-Knox Art Gallery, Buffalo, NY; Smith Col, Northampton, Mass; Chase Manhattan Bank, New York. *Comn:* Urban wall proj, South Eastern Ctr Contemp Arts-Nat Endowment Arts, Winston-Salem, NC, 74; Orlando Int Airport, 81. *Exhib:* Whitney Mus Am Art Biennial, New York, 75; Material Dominant, Univ Pa, Philadelphia, 77; Southeast 7, Southeastern Ctr Contemp Art, Winston-Salem, NC, 77; Painters & Sculptors SE, High Mus Art, Atlanta, Ga, 77; Slocumb Gallery, Univ Tenn, 76; one-man shows, Knowlton Gallery, 76-81. *Awards:* Individual Artist Grant, Nat Endowment Arts, 75; Regional Artist Grant, South Eastern Ctr Contemp Arts-Nat Endowment Arts, 76; NC Architects Award, 76. *Bibliog:* William Zimmer (auth), Frank Faulkner, Arts Mag, 10/76. *Media:* Acrylic, Mixed Media. *Dealer:* Monique Knowlton Gallery 19 E 71st St New York NY 10021. *Mailing Add:* 150 W 26 St New York NY 10001

FAUNCE, SARAH CUSHING
MUSEUM CURATOR
b Tulsa, Okla, Aug 19, 29. *Study:* Wellesley Col, BA; Washington Univ, MA; Columbia Univ. *Collections Arranged:* New Black Artists, 69; Peruvian Colonial Painting, 71; Pearlman Collection of Post-Impressionist Painting, 74; Anne Ryan Collages (auth, catalog), 74; Folk Sculpture USA (contribr, catalog), 76; Belgian Art 1880-1914 (contribr, catalog), 80; The Edith and Milton Lowenthal Collection of Modernist American Art (contribr, catalog), 81; Northern Light: Realism and Symbolism in Scandinavian Paintings 1880-1910, 82; Carl Larsson (contribr, catalog), 82. *Pos:* Cur art collections, Columbia Univ, 65-69; exhib consult, Jewish Mus, 68-70; cur painting & sculpture, Brooklyn Mus, 69- *Teaching:* Lectr art theory & criticism, Barnard Col, 64. *Mem:* Col Art Asn Am; Victorian Soc; Am Asn Mus; Int Coun Mus. *Publ:* Auth, Anne Ryan Collages, 74; coauth, Masterpieces of American Paintings from The Brooklyn Museum, 76; auth, Seurat and the soul of things, In: Belgian Art 1880-1914, 80; auth, Modern French painting: Collecting in the 1920s, Apollo, 4/82; auth, The domestic art of Carl Larsson, In: Carl Larsson, 82. *Mailing Add:* c/o Brooklyn Museum Eastern Pkwy Brooklyn NY 11238

FAURER, LOUIS
PHOTOGRAPHER
b Philadelphia, Pa, Aug 28, 16. *Work:* Mus Mod Art, New York; New Orleans Mus; Seagram's Collections, New York. *Exhib:* Then and Now, 54, Photographs From the Mod Mus Collection, 59, Ben Schultz Mem Exhib, 68 & New Standpoints, 78, Mus Mod Art, New York; Whitney Mus Am Art, 78; Bologna Arts Fair, Italy, 78; New Acquisitions, Mus Fine Arts, Houston, Tex, 81; one-man show, Light Gallery, New York, 81; American Children, Lowe Art Mus, Univ Miami, Coral Gables, Fla, 81; and others. *Teaching:* Instr photog sem, Parsons Sch Design, New York, 75-77. *Awards:* Creative Artists Pub Serv Grant, New York, 78, Guggenheim Mem Found Fel, 79-80. *Publ:* Contribr, Art News, 50. *Mailing Add:* c/o Westbeth Group 464 West St Suite 520-H New York NY 10014

FAUSETT, (WILLIAM) DEAN
PAINTER, ETCHER
b Price, Utah, July 4, 13. *Study:* Brigham Young Univ; Art Students League; Nat Inst Archit Educ; Colorado Springs Fine Arts Ctr. *Work:* Metrop Mus Art; Mus Mod Art; Whitney Mus Am Art; Whitney Gallery of Western Art, Cody, Wyo; Toledo Mus Art. *Comn:* Murals, US Post Off, Augusta, Ga, Bldg for Brotherhood, New York, US Air Acad, Colorado Springs, Colo, Global Power, USAF & 4-H Nat Ctr, Washington, DC; plus many others. *Exhib:* Seven shows, Whitney Mus Am Art Ann, 32-46; one-man shows, Colorado Springs Fine Art Ctr, Colo, 70, Univ Ariz, Tucson, 71, Utah State Univ, Logan, 71, Inaugural Exhib, Tarble Art Ctr, 78; Eastern Ill Univ, Charleston Univ, 82; and many others. *Awards:* Prize, Salmagundi Club, 46; Distinguished Serv in Art Award, Brigham Young Univ, 69; Gold Medal & Cash Award, Franklin Mint, 76; and others. *Mem:* Nat Soc Mural Painters; Southern Vt Art Asn; Found Preserv Traditional Values Fine Arts. *Publ:* Auth, Address--special ceremony in Statuary Hall, US Capitol, Cong Rec, No 132, Part II, 9/21/82. *Mailing Add:* 1 W 67th St New York NY 10023

FAVRO, MURRAY
SCULPTOR, INVENTOR
b Huntsville, Ont, Dec 24, 40. *Study:* H B Beal Tech Sch, London, Ont, 58-64. *Work:* Art Gallery Ont, Toronto; Nat Gallery Can, Ottawa, Ont; Can Coun Art Bank, Ottawa, Ont. *Comn:* Sculpture, Ministry Transport Bldg, Cornwall, Ont, 78. *Exhib:* Musee D'Art Mod Ville Paris, 73; Carmen Lamanna Gallery, 74; Mt Allison Univ, 75; solo shows, Carmen Lamanna Gallery, 76 & 77; Montreal Mus Fine Arts, 76; Another Dimension, Nat Gallery Can, 77-78; retrospective, Art Gallery Ont, 83; A Response to the Environment, Rutgers Univ Art Gallery, New Brunswick, NJ, 75; Changing Visions: The Can Landscapes (traveling exhib), 76; London Art Gallery, Ont, 76; 10 Canadian Artists in the 1970's, traveling exhib, Europe, 80; one-man shows, 20/20 Gallery, London, Ont, 68, Carmen Lamanna Gallery, Toronto, 68, 71-72 & 76-78; and many others. *Awards:* Can Coun Grants, 68-72; Can Coun Senior Grant, 74, 78, 80 & 83. *Mem:* Can Artists Representation; Royal Canadian Acad. *Publ:* Auth, Heart of London, Ottawa, 68; Biographical Information About the Influences on My Work, 71, Windmill Electric Generator, 75 & The Flying Flea and Henri Mignet Its Designer, 77, Carmen Lamanna Gallery, Toronto. *Mailing Add:* c/o Carmen Lamanna Gallery 840 Yonge St Toronto ON M4W 2H1 Canada

FAX, ELTON CLAY
PAINTER, WRITER
b Baltimore, Md, Oct 9, 09. *Study:* Syracuse Univ Col Fine Arts. *Work:* US Navy & Marine Corps Exhib Ctr, Washington, DC. *Awards:* Louis E Seley Naval Art Coop & Liaison Comt Award, 72; Coretta Scott King Award, 72; Areana Players Award, 72. *Bibliog:* Brawley (auth), The Negro genius, 36; Locke (auth), The Negro in art, 37; Dover (auth), American Negro art, 61. *Mem:* Salmagundi Club (Naval Art Coop & Liaison Comt); Author's Guild Am; Poets, Essayists & Novelists. *Publ:* Auth, Seventeen black artists, 71; auth, Garvey, 72; auth, Through Black eyes, Dodd Mead & Co, 74; auth, Black Artists of the New Generation, Dodd Mead & Co, 77; auth, Hashar (illusr with drawings & paintings by the auth), Progress Publishers, Moscow, 80. *Mailing Add:* 51-28 30th Ave Woodside NY 11377

FAY, MING G
SCULPTOR, PAINTER
b Shanghai, China, Feb 2, 43. US citizen. *Study:* Columbus Col Art & Design, dipl, 65; Kansas City Art Inst, BFA, 67; Univ Calif, Santa Barbara, MFA, 70. *Work:* Columbus Art Mus, Ohio; Hong Kong Mus Art; NY State Univ Art Gallery, Potsdam; Sidney Lewis Found, Va; Mobile Hq, New York. *Exhib:* Int Print, Seattle Art Mus, Wash, 70; Drawing USA, Minn Mus, Minneapolis, 75; Chicago Int, Art Expo 80, Ill, 80; A Feast for Eyes, Heckscher Mus, Huntington, NY, 81; The Chinese Response, Hong Kong Mus Art; Selection 22, The Drawing Ctr, New York. *Teaching:* Instr sculpture, Columbus Col Art, 70-71; asst prof, Univ Pittsburgh, Pa, 71-74; vis asst prof 3-D, Pratt Inst, Brooklyn, NY, 78-80; vis artist, Semester at Sea, 82 & William Paterson Col, NJ, 83. *Media:* Mixed. *Mailing Add:* 365 Canal St New York NY 10013

FEAR, DANIEL E
DEALER, GALLERY DIRECTOR
b Tacoma, Wash, Mar 28, 49. *Pos:* Dir & pres, The Silver Image Gallery Inc, 73- *Mem:* Founding mem Asn Int Photog Art Dealers, Inc. *Specialty:* Contemporary photography; photography and posters. *Mailing Add:* The Silver Image Gallery Inc 92 S Washington St Seattle WA 98104

FEARING, WILLIAM KELLY
PAINTER, EDUCATOR
b Fordyce, Ark, Oct 18, 18. *Study:* La Tech Univ, BA; Columbia Univ, MA. *Work:* Dallas Mus Fine Arts; Ft Worth Art Ctr; Old Jail Found Mus, Albany, Tex; Mus Fine Arts Houston; Inst Contemp Arts, Boston; and others. *Exhib:* Solo exhib, Witte Mem Mus, San Antonio, Tex, 69; Du Bose Gallery, Houston, Tex, 77; L&L Gallery, Longview, Tex, 78; Spencer Gallery, Fine Arts Ctr, Univ Ark, Monticello, 81; Mary Moffett Gallery, La Tech Univ, 81; and many others. *Teaching:* Prof art, Univ Tex, Austin, 47-83, Ashbel Smith prof, 83- *Bibliog:* Allen S Weller (auth), The new romanticism, Art in Am, 60; New talent USA, Art in Am, 62; John Palmer Leeper (auth), The Texas hill country: Interpretations by 13 painters, Texas A & M Press, 81. *Media:* Multimedia. *Res:* Comparative arts: relationship between music and the visual arts. *Publ:* Coauth, Our expanding vision, 60, The creative eye, 69, 2nd ed, 79 & Art and the creative teacher, 71, Benson; ed, Creativity and the human spirit, Tex Quart, spring 73 & spec issue, 75; coauth, Helping children see arts and make art, Vol I & II, Benson, 82; and others. *Dealer:* Garner & Smith Gallery 509 W 12 Austin TX 78701; Ft Worth Gallery 901 Boland Ft Worth TX 76107. *Mailing Add:* 914 Calethea Austin TX 78746

FEATHERSTONE, DAVID BYRUM
CRITIC, CURATOR
b Iowa City, Iowa, Jan 23, 45. *Study:* Univ Calif, Berkeley, AB, 67; Univ Ore, Eugene, MA, 71. *Exhib:* Celebrations, Hayden Gallery, Mass Inst Technol, Cambridge, 74; Northwest Invitational, Seattle Art Mus, Wash, 75; Attitudes: Photog in 70's, Mus Art, Santa Barbara, Calif, 80. *Collections Arranged:* Bernard Freemesser, A Retrospective Exhib, 78; Photographs by Vilem Kriz, 79; The Diana Show, Pictures Through A Plastic Lens (auth, catalog), 80; Aerial Photographs by William Garnett, 80; Photographs by Marsha Burns (auth, catalog), 81. *Pos:* Cur photog, Historical Photog Collection, Univ Ore Libr, Eugene, 74-76; exec assoc, The Friends Photog, Carmel, Calif, 77- *Awards:* Nat Endowment Arts Art Critics Fel, 76 & 78; Residency Fel, Wurlitzer Found, Taos, NMex, 82. *Mem:* Soc Photog Educ. *Res:* Life & work of photographer Doris Ulmann (1874-1934); contemporary photography. *Publ:* Auth, Vilem Kriz, Photographs, 79, coauth, Photographs of the Columbia River & Oregon, 79 & contribr, 9 Critics/9 Photographs, 80, Friends Photog. *Mailing Add:* PO Box 2142 Carmel CA 93921

FEBLAND, HARRIET
PAINTER, SCULPTOR
b New York, NY. *Study:* Pratt Inst; NY Univ; Art Students League; Am Artists Sch; Atelier 17, Paris. *Work:* Westchester Co Court House, White Plains Civic Plaza; Cincinnati Art Mus; Emily Lowe Mus, Coral Gables, Fla; Metromedia, Los Angeles, Calif; Hempstead Bank of Long Island Collection of Am Art; and many others. *Exhib:* Retrospects, Hudson River Mus, NY, 63 & Silvermine Guild, Conn, 73 & 80; Mus Mod Art, Paris, 70; Alwin Gallery, London, 70; Women Choose Women, New York Cult Ctr, 73; Potsdam Plastics, State Univ NY, 74; and many others. *Teaching:* Instr & lectr, NY Univ, 60-62; instr & dir, Harriet FeBland's Art Workshop, Pelham, NY, 62-; instr, Westchester Art Workshop, White Plains, 65-72. *Bibliog:* Newman (auth), Plastics as sculpture, Chilton, 74; Dona Meilach (auth), Collage and assemblage, Doubleday, 75; Harriet FeBland (film), A K Haverly Found, 83; and others. *Mem:* NY Artists Equity Asn (vpres, 70-76, chmn & prog dir, 79); Am Soc Contemp Artists (pres, 81-83); Int Art Asn (secy, 80-82); Nat Asn of Women Artists; Fine Arts Fedn NY (deleg). *Media:* Acrylic; Metal, Plexiglas. *Mailing Add:* 245 E 63rd St Apt 408 New York NY 10021

FEDELE, FRANK D
DEALER, PUBLISHER
b New York, NY, May 23, 36. *Study:* Sch Art & Design/Indust Arts, serigraphy with Biegeleison and sculpture with Eliscu. *Pos:* Pres, Frank Fedele Fine Arts Inc, 73- *Specialty:* Exclusive agent and publisher of graphic works by Ronald J Christensen. *Mailing Add:* 42 E 57th St New York NY 10022

FEDELLE, ESTELLE
PAINTER, LECTURER
b Chicago, Ill. *Study:* Art Inst Chicago; Northwestern Univ; Inst Design; Am Acad Fine Arts; Colo State Christian Col, hon PhD, 73. *Exhib:* Grand Cent Galleries, New York; Barron Galleries, Chicago & Las Vegas; Kenosha Pub Mus, Wis; Chicago Pub Libr; Visual Arts Ctr; and others. *Pos:* Dir, Fedelle Art Ctr, Chicago & Park Ridge, Ill; auth, weekly column, The Leader Newspapers, 74- *Teaching:* Lectr, eastern & midwestern US on style & techniques in oil painting and demonstration of procedures. *Mem:* Life fel Royal Soc Arts London; Park Ridge Art League; Nat League Am Penwomen; Regent Art League (hon dir); Munic Art League; and others. *Publ:* How to Begin Painting for Fun, 65. *Mailing Add:* 1500 S Cumberland Park Ridge IL 60068

FEDER, BEN
DESIGNER, PAINTER
b New York, NY, Feb 1, 23. *Study:* Parsons Sch Design; Vet Ctr, Mus Mod Art, with Prestopino. *Exhib:* Stamford Mus Art, Conn, 60; Bodley Gallery, NY, 64; Inst Allende, San Miguel Allende, Mex. *Pos:* Designer & graphic arts consult, New Bk Knowledge, Grolier Inc; pres, Ben Feder Inc, New York; owner & design consultant, Clinton Vineyards Dutchess Co, NY. *Mailing Add:* 175 East 62nd New York NY 10021

FEDER, PENNY JOY
PRINTMAKER, LECTURER
b New York, NY, Oct 13, 49. *Study:* C W Post Col, Long Island Univ, Brookville, NY, with James Lewicki & Harry Hohen, BA(art educ), 71 & with Arthur Leipsig & Alfred van Loen, MA(printmaking), 72; Brooklyn Mus Art Sch, printmaking, 72. *Comn:* Catalog cover & poster design, Washington Sq Outdoor Art Exhib, New York, 75; woodcut, Collectors Guild, New York, 76; woodcut, Calhoun's Collectors Soc, Minneapolis, 81. *Exhib:* Brooklyn Artists, Contemp Gallery, Brooklyn Mus, 76; Ann, Philadelphia Print Club, 78 & 83; Long Island Printmakers, Galerijzolder, Belgium, 80 & Mus Düren, Ger, 80; Ann, Audubon Artists Soc, Inst Arts & Letts, 80, Ann, Nat Acad Design, 81 & Ann, Knickerbocker Artists, Nat Arts Club, 81, New York. *Teaching:* Lectr-demonstr, Suffolk Co Sch System, NY, 70; lectr-demonstr, var art groups in NY, 70-81; lectr-demonstr, Salmagundi Club, New York, 79. *Awards:* John Taylor Arms Award, Audubon Artists 39th Ann, 81; Knickerbocker Award, 32nd Knickerbocker Artists Ann, 81; Gold Medal, Salmagundi Club, 83. *Bibliog:* Jeanne Paris (auth), Diaries of creativity & Malcolm Preston (auth), Flourishing symbiosis, Newsday Newspaper, Long Island, NY, 2/77. *Mem:* Philadelphia Print Club; Audubon Artists Soc; Salmagundi Club; Knickerbocker Artists; Long Island Printmaking Soc. *Media:* Woodcuts, Etchings. *Mailing Add:* 302 7th St Brooklyn NY 11215

FEDERE, MARION
PAINTER, GRAPHIC ARTIST
b Vienna, Austria; US citizen. *Study:* Early art educ in Vienna with Frances Haendel; Brooklyn Col; Brooklyn Mus Beckman Scholar, two yrs; Charles Seiden's Workshop, two yrs; Pratt Graphics Ctr. *Work:* Butler Inst Am Art, Youngstown, Ohio; Philathia Mus Mod Art, London, Ont; Tel Aviv Mus, Israel; and others. *Exhib:* Brooklyn Mus Gallery, NY, 69, 72, 74, 75 & 76; United Nations Gallery, 75-77; Lincoln Ctr, 75-78; New York City Ctr Gallery; New York City Community Col; Long Island & Brandeis Univs; and several one-woman exhibs & traveling shows in USA mus, univs & librs. *Awards:* Floyd Bennett Field First Prize, First Place Prof Award, 69; Kashka Mem Award, Am Soc Contemp Artists, 76; Contemp Award, Am Soc Contemp Artists, 81; and others. *Bibliog:* Gordon Brown (auth), article in Arts Mag, 3/72; H G L (auth), Federe at Skylight, Park East, 3/16/72; Marion Federe, France-Amerique: Le Courier des Etats Unis, 3/23/72; plus others. *Mem:* Artists Equity Asn New York; Am Soc Contemp Artists (dir, 81-83); Metrop Painters and Sculptors; Contemp Artists Guild (treas); Womens Int Art Club, Eng. *Mailing Add:* 2277 E 17th St Brooklyn NY 11229

FEHER, JOSEPH
CURATOR, PAINTER
b Miskolcz, Hungary, Apr 23, 08; US citizen. *Study:* With Adolph Fenyes, Budapest, 23-24; Acad Fine Arts, Florence, Italy, Baron Hirsh Found Grant, 24-25; Acad Fine Arts, Budapest, scholar, 25-28; Art Inst Chicago, scholar, 28. *Work:* Abbott Labs, Chicago; Nemes Collection, Budapest; Honolulu Acad Arts; United Air Lines Collection, Chicago; Eli Lilly Collection, Indianapolis. *Comn:* Across the US (mural), United Air Lines, 46; The Navy in Micronesia-Documentation (watercolor drawings), US Navy, 50-51; Hawaii Statehood commemorative postage stamp, US Govt, 59. *Exhib:* Int Watercolor Exhib, Art Inst Chicago, 29; The US Navy in Micronesia, 51, Artists of Hawaii Ann Exhib, 57 & 58, three-man show, 68 & Fac Exhib, 72, Honolulu Acad Arts; two-man show, 70 & one-man show, 80, Downtown Galley, Honolulu; Honolulu Printmakers, 73; Printmakers Invitational Exhib, Contemp Art Ctr Hawaii, 73; Ryan Galleries, Kailua, Oahu, 81; retrospective, Honolulu Acad Arts, 82; and others. *Pos:* Designer publ, Honolulu Acad Arts, 49-, cur studio prog, 66-, sr cur, 77-; artist-historian, Bishop Mus, Honolulu, 55-69, ed & designer, Conch Shell, 63-68. *Teaching:* Instr, Chicago Art Ctr, 39-40 & Inst Design, Chicago, 42-44; instr, Art Sch, Honolulu Acad Arts, 47-66, dir, 62-66, instr studio prog, 66- *Awards:* Award Cert, Nat Offset-Lithography Competition, New York, 50; Award Excellence, 27th Ann Exhib, Soc Typographic Arts, Chicago, 54; Book Design Merit Award, Univ Hawaii Press, 67. *Media:* Oil. *Publ:* Auth, Tale Bearing Winds, Bishop Mus, 58; illusr, The Voyage of the Flying Bird, Dodd, 65; illusr, Claus Spreckels, Univ Hawaii Press, 67; auth, Hawaii: A Pictorial History, Bishop Mus, 69. *Mailing Add:* Honolulu Acad Arts 900 S Beretania St Honolulu HI 96814

FEHL, PHILIPP P
PAINTER, HISTORIAN
b Vienna, Austria, May 9, 20; US citizen. *Study:* Art Inst Chicago; Stanford Univ, BA & MA; Univ Chicago, PhD. *Work:* Neue Galerie Joanneum, Graz, Austria. *Exhib:* One-man shows, Mt Holyoke Col, 79, Univ Tel Aviv, 81, Dante Soc, Venice, 81, Wolfenbuettel Lib, 82 & Kiel Univ, 83. *Pos:* Art historian in residence, Am Acad Rome, 66-67; assoc, Ctr Advan Study, Univ Ill, 70-71, 80-81. *Teaching:* Prof hist art, Univ NC, Chapel Hill, 63-69; prof hist art, Univ Ill, Urbana-Champaign, 69- *Awards:* Res Fel, Warburg Inst, Univ London, 57-58; Nat Endowment Humanities fel, 77-78. *Bibliog:* Wilfried Skreiner (auth), Capricci by Philipp Fehl, Neue Galerie, Graz, 71. *Mem:* Col Art Asn Am (bd dirs, 68-71); Renaissance Soc Am; Am Soc Aesthetics & Art Criticism; Southeastern Renaissance Conf; Int Surv Jewish Monuments (pres). *Media:* Watercolor. *Res:* Renaissance art; history of the classical tradition in art; history of art criticism. *Collection:* Prints, Renaissance to modern. *Publ:* Illusr, The bird: a series of capricci, Finial Press, 70; auth, The classical monument, NY Univ Press, 72; ed, Franciscus Junius, Literature of Classical Art, Univ Calif Press, 82; auth, articles in Art Bull, Burlington Mag, J Warburg & Courtauld Inst, Gazette Beaux Arts & others; illusr, Voyager, Lillabulero & other mags. *Mailing Add:* Sch Art Univ Ill 408 E Peabody Champaign IL 61820

FEIFFER, JULES
CARTOONIST, WRITER
b New York, NY, Jan 26, 29. *Study:* Art Students League, 46; Pratt Inst, 47-51. *Pos:* Asst to syndicated cartoonist, Will Eisner, 46-51; cartoonist, Village Voice, 56-; cartoons publ weekly, London Observer, Eng, 58-66 & 72- & Playboy Mag, 59-; syndicated nationally, 59- *Awards:* Acad Award Animated Cartoon, Munro, 61; George Polk Mem Award, 62; Outer Circle Drama Critics Award, 69 & 70. *Mem:* Authors Guild. *Publ:* Auth, 11 collections cartoons including, Feiffer's Marriage Manual, 67, Feiffer on Nixon, 67, Tantrum: A Cartoon Novel, 79, Jules Feiffer's America: From Eisenhower to Nixon, 82 & Marriage is an Invasion of Privacy, 84; auth, plays & novels. *Mailing Add:* c/o Field Newspaper Syndicate 1703 Kaiser Ave Irvine CA 92714

FEIGEN, RICHARD L
DEALER, COLLECTOR
b Chicago, Ill, Aug 8, 30. *Study:* Yale Univ, BA, 52; Harvard Univ, MBA, 54. *Pos:* Pres, Richard L Feigen & Co, Inc, 57-; trustee, John Jay Homestead, Katonah, NY. *Mem:* Life fel Metrop Mus Art; life fel Minneapolis Soc Fine Arts; Art Dealers Asn Am; Cooper-Hewitt Mus (Friends Comt); Collectors Inst New Sch Art Ctr (adv comt). *Specialty:* Paintings, drawings and sculpture, 1400 to the present. *Collection:* Old Master paintings; Beckmann, Grosz, Kandinsky, Cornell, Dubuffet. *Publ:* Contribr, Arts Mag, 67; auth, Dubuffet and the Anticulture, 69; contribr, Office Design, 70; auth, George Grosz: Dada Drawings, 72. *Mailing Add:* 900 Park Ave New York NY 10021

FEIGENBAUM, HARRIET (MRS NEIL CHAMBERLAIN)
ENVIRONMENTAL ARTIST, SCULPTOR
b New York, NY, May 25, 39. *Study:* Art Students League; Nat Acad Sch Fine Arts; Columbia Univ. *Work:* Andrew Dickson White Mus, Cornell Univ; Colgate Univ Mus; Corcoran Gallery. *Exhib:* The Presence of Nature, Whitney Mus Am Art, New York, 78; Artyard, Brooklyn Mus, NY, 78; Art on the Beach, Creative Time, New York, 78 & 80; Architectural Sculpture, Los Angeles Inst Contemp Art, 80; one-person show, Marian Locks Gallery, Philadelphia, 81; The House That Art Built, Calif State Univ, Fullerton, 83; Land Marks, Edith Blum Art Inst, Annendale on Hudson, NY, 84; and many others. *Teaching:* Vis artist, Pratt Inst, 81 & 82. *Awards:* Palisades Interstate Park, Am the Beautiful Fun, 79; Pa Coun Arts Grant, 82; Scranton Area Found Grant, 83. *Bibliog:* James Beck (auth), article, Art in Am, 3-4/76; Eileen Thalenberg (auth), article, Artscanada, 10-11/77; Lucy Lippard (auth), article, Art in Am, 1-2/79. *Publ:* Auth, Bernini and Galileo, Art Bull, 3/77; Where Should Land Art Go?, Heresies, 81. *Dealer:* Marian Locks 1524 Walnut St Philadelphia PA 19102. *Mailing Add:* 11th Floor 49 West 24th St New York NY 10010

FEIGIN, MARSHA
PRINTMAKER, PAINTER
b New York, NY, June 17, 46. *Study:* Univ Hawaii, MFA; City Col New York, BA; Cooper Union; Syracuse Univ. *Work:* Brooklyn Mus; State Found Cult & Arts, Hawaii; De Cordova Mus, Mass; Nat Mus, Poland; Minneapolis Inst Arts. *Comn:* Etching, Creative Artists Pub Serv Prog, New York, 75. *Exhib:* 22nd Nat Exhib Prints, Libr Cong, 71; 18th Nat Exhib Prints, Brooklyn Mus, 72; 10th & 11th Biennial Graphic Art, Ljubljana, Yugoslavia, 73 & 75; 5th & 8th Int Biennial Graphic Art, Crakow, Poland, 74 & 79; 20th Nat Exhib of Prints, Brooklyn Mus, 76; 6th Int Biennial Graphic Art, Crakow, Poland, 76; Printmaking: New Forms, Whitney Mus Am Art, 76; Am Graphics in Venice, Galleria Bevilacqua La Masa, Venice, Italy, 77; Art Today: USA, Iran-Am Soc, Teheran, Iran, '77. *Pos:* Master-printer, Printmaking Workshop, New York, 71-72. *Teaching:* Teaching asst printmaking, Univ Hawaii, 69-71; instr life drawing & painting, Bishop Mus, 71; guest lectr printmaking, Rutgers Univ, 73; guest lectr, Fla Technol Univ, 77; instr printmaking, San Jose State Univ, 78-79. *Awards:* Creative Pub Serv Prog Printmaking Grant, NY State Coun Arts, 73 & 75; Nat Endowment Arts Printmaking & Drawing Grant, 75. *Mem:* Artists Equity Asn; Women's Caucus for Art; Col Art Asn; Graphic Arts Coun of NY; Printmaking Workshop, New York. *Media:* Mixed. *Dealer:* Assoc Am Artists 663 Fifth Ave New York NY 10022. *Mailing Add:* 200 E 84th St New York NY 10028

FEIN, B R
PAINTER, LECTURER
b Brooklyn, NY, Dec 11, 41. *Study:* Brooklyn Col, BA, 62; Univ Md, 64-66; City Univ New York, MA, 67, PhD, 69; Univ NH, 70-80. *Work:* New York Pub Libr; Seacoast Regional Coun Ctr, Portsmouth, NH; York Co Coun Ctr, Sanford, Maine; Deaconess Hosp, Boston; Kittery Art Asn, Maine. *Comn:* Child at a Circus (mural), USN Hosp, Portsmouth, 71. *Exhib:* Copley Soc, Boston, 69-75, Walt Kuhn Mem-Norton Hall Gallery, Cape Neddick, Maine, 69-76; Drawings '71, Minn Mus Art, Minneapolis, 71; 6th Ann Drawing & Small Sculpture Exhib, Del Mar Col, Corpus Christi, Tex, 72; Wadsworth Atheneum, Conn Acad Fine Arts, Hartford, 72; 33rd & 34th Ann Nat Art Exhib, Southern Utah State Col, Cedar City, 73 & 74. *Teaching:* Guest lectr abstract painting, Univ Maine, Orono, 71; vis lectr drawing & oil painting, Univ NH, Durham, 73-; assoc prof, NH Vocational Technol Col, Stratham, 82- *Awards:* Third Place Prof, Manchester Art Asn, NH, 70; First Place Oil-Acrylic & Hon Mixed Media, Newbury Port Art Asn, Mass, 71; Graphics Award, York Art Asn, Maine, 71, 73, 76 & 79. *Mem:* Maine State Art Asn (bd dir, 73-74); Copley Soc; Sharon Art Ctr; Boston Visual Artists Union; York Art Asn. *Media:* Watercolor; Pencil. *Publ:* Illusr, Dora Young's Tatting Manuals, 74 & 75; illusr, Single's Circle, 74; illusr, MCAT: New Medical Admissions Test, Barnes & Nobles, 81. *Dealer:* Kennedy Gallery New York NY; Fry Gallery York ME. *Mailing Add:* 4 Trefethen Ave Kittery ME 03904

FEIN, STANLEY
PAINTER, DESIGNER
b Brooklyn, NY, Dec 21, 19. *Study:* Parsons Sch Design; NY Univ. *Work:* NY Univ Collection; pvt collection Dr Timothy Costello, Pres Adelphi Univ. *Comn:* NY History (paintings), 71, Cities of NY (paintings), 72, Historic Interiors (paintings), 78 & Colleges of NY (paintings), Bank NY. *Pos:* Art dir, Doremus & Co, formerly; creative dir, Pesin Sydney & Bernard, currently. *Teaching:* Instr design & color, Pratt Inst, 56-58. *Awards:* Art Dirs Club NY, 56-65; Wall Street Art Asn, 60; Soc Illusrs, 70 & 71. *Media:* Multimedia. *Dealer:* Phoenix Gallery 30 W 57th St New York NY. *Mailing Add:* 313 DeGraw St Brooklyn NY 11231

FEINBLATT, EBRIA
HISTORIAN
b Hedera, Palestine; US citizen. *Study:* NY Univ; Inst Fine Arts; Univ Calif, Los Angeles, MA. *Collections Arranged:* Jacques Callot Prints & Drawings, 70; Honore Daumier: Prints, Drawings, Paintings & Sculpture, 58; Pieter Bruegel the Elder: Prints & Drawings, 61; Georges Rouault Prints, 62; Agostino Mitelli Drawings, 65; Picasso Prints, 65; Munch Prints, 69; Jacques Callot Prints, 70; Old Master Drawings, 76; Los Angeles Prints 1883-1980, 81; Marc Chagall: Early Graphics. *Pos:* Sr cur prints & drawings, Los Angeles Co Mus Art, currently. *Mem:* Print Coun Am. *Res:* Prints and drawings; 17th century Bolognese ceiling decoration. *Publ:* Auth, exhib catalogs and articles in Art Quart, Burlington Mag, Master Drawings & Drawing. *Mailing Add:* Los Angeles Co Mus Art 5905 Wilshire Blvd Los Angeles CA 90036

FEININGER, ANDREAS B L
PHOTOGRAPHER, WRITER
b Paris, France, Dec 27, 06; US citizen. *Study:* Bauhaus, Ger, 22-25; Bauschule, Ger, dipl(archit; summa cum laude), 28; studied with Le Corbusier, 32-33. *Work:* Metrop Mus Art, Mus Mod Art, New York; Victoria & Albert Mus, London; Bibliot Nat, Paris; Mus Folkwang, Essen, Ger. *Exhib:* One-man show, Shells, Am Mus Natural Hist, New York, 72, New York in the Forties, New York Hist Soc, 78 & Hamburg, Mus Kunst & Gewerbe, Ger, 80; retrospective, Int Ctr Photog, New York, 76, Mus Folkwang, Essen, Ger, 81 & Ctr Creative Photog, Tucson, 81. *Pos:* Staff photogr, Life Mag, 43-62. *Teaching:* Instr creative photocommunication, NY Univ, winter 72-73. *Awards:* Gold Medal Award, Art Dirs Club Metrop Washington, DC, 65; Robert Leavitt Award, Am Soc Mag Photogr, 66; Ehrenpreis, Touristische Buch, State of Vienna, 66. *Bibliog:* Fritz Gruber (auth), Grosse Photographen unseres Jahrhunderts, Econ, Dusseldorf, 64; Peter Pollack (auth), The Picture History of Photography, Abrams, 2nd ed, 69; Ralph Hattersley (auth), Andreas Feininger, Morgan & Morgan, 73. *Mem:* Charter mem Am Soc Mag Photogr. *Publ:* Auth, Feininger on Photography, Ziff-Davis, 49; auth, The Anatomy of Nature, Crown, 56; auth, The Complete Photographer, Prentice-Hall, 65; auth, Trees, 68 & The Mountains of the Mind, 77, Viking. *Dealer:* Daniel Wolf Gallery 30 W 57 St New York NY 10019. *Mailing Add:* 5 E 22 St Apt 26R New York NY 10010

FEININGER, T LUX
PAINTER, WRITER
b Berlin, Ger, June 11, 10; US citizen. *Study:* Bauhaus, Dessau, Ger, 26-32; stage design with Oskar Schlemmer; also with Paul Klee, W Kandinsky & Josef Albers, dipl, 29; Inst Fine Arts, NY Univ, with Salmony, Lopez-Rey, Cook & Friedlaender, 46-47. *Work:* Mus Mod Art, New York; Busch-Reisinger Mus & Fogg Art Mus, Harvard Univ; Altonaer Mus, Hamburg, Ger. *Exhib:* American Realists and Magic Realists, Mus Mod Art, New York, 43; Revolution and Tradition in Modern American Art, Brooklyn Mus, 51; Whitney Mus Am Art Ann, New York, 51; Four American Painters, Mass Inst Technol, 54; Retrospective, Busch-Reisinger Mus, 62; Wheaton Col, 73; Wamsutta Club, New Bedford, Mass, 74; Photographs of the 20's & 30's, Prakapas Gallery, NY, 80. *Teaching:* Instr design, Sarah Lawrence Col, 50-52; lectr drawing & painting, Harvard Univ, 53-62; instr, Boston Fine Arts Mus Sch, 62-75; retired. *Awards:* Hon mention, Arts & Crafts Club, New Orleans, 48; hon mention, Cambridge Art Asn, 63. *Bibliog:* Thomas B Hess (auth), Profile, Art News, 2/47; Feininger family, Life Mag, 11/51; E Bitterman (auth), Art in modern architecture, Van Nostrand Reinhold, 52. *Mem:* Westport Art Group. *Media:* Watercolor, Oil. *Publ:* Auth, The Bauhaus: evolution of an idea, Criticism, summer 60; auth, Lyonel Feininger: city at the edge of the world, Praeger, 65; auth, Address on modern art, Harvard Art Rev, 66; auth, The heritage of Lyonel Feininger, Am-Ger Rev, 66. *Mailing Add:* 22 Arlington St Cambridge MA 02140

FEINMAN, STEPHEN E
DEALER
b New York, NY, Sept 29, 32. *Pos:* Pres, Gary Arts Ltd, 65-72; pres, Multiple Impressions Ltd, 72- *Specialty:* Twentieth Century European and American prints; Haitian paintings. *Mailing Add:* 17 Greenwich Ave New York NY 10014

FEIST, HAROLD E
PAINTER, SCULPTOR
b San Angelo, Tex, 1945. *Study:* Univ Ill, Champaign-Urbana, BFA, 67; Col Art, Md Inst, MFA, 69. *Work:* Mus Fine Arts, Boston; Edmonton Art Gallery, Alta; Art Gallery Hamilton, Ont; Mendel Art Gallery, Saskatoon, Sask; Mem Univ Newfoundland Arts & Cult Ctr. *Exhib:* Canadian Canuas, Time-Life Inc & Edmonton Art Gallery, 74; Canada X Ten, Edmonton Art Gallery, 74-75 & Abstract Art Now, 77, Edmonton Art Gallery; Certain Traditions: Recent British and Canadian Art, Edmonton Art Gallery and travelling, 78-79; 25 Canadians, Birmingham Arts Festival, Ala, 79; The New Generation: A Curator's Choice, Andre Emmerich Gallery & travelling,

80-82. *Teaching:* Mem fac, Alta Col Art, Calgary, 68-74, Univ Regina, Sask, 74-75 & Mt Allison Univ, Sackville, NB, 75-78. *Bibliog:* Rene Micha (auth), Lettre de Paris, Art Int, 4/81; Terry Fenton (auth), 1981--the art year in review, Update, 1/82; Karen Wilken (auth), The paintings of Harold Feist, Art Mag, 2/82. *Media:* Acrylic on Canvas; Acrylic Sheet, Wood. *Dealer:* Gallery One 121 Scollard St Toronto ON; Harcus Gallery 7 Newbury St Boston MA. *Mailing Add:* 160 Langley Ave Toronto ON M4K 1B7 Canada

FEIST, WARNER DAVID
DESIGNER, PAINTER
b Augsburg, Ger, Dec 3, 09; Can citizen. *Study:* Bauhaus, Dessau, Ger, with Joseph Albers, Paul Klee, Oscar Schlemmer, Josef Schmidt & photog with Walter Peterhaus. *Work:* Concordia Univ, Montreal, Que; Montreal Mus Fine Arts. *Exhib:* One-man show, Goethe Inst, Montreal, 74; Early Photos, San Francisco Mus Mod Art; Mus Mod Art, New York; and others. *Pos:* Art dir, Harold F Stanfield Ltd, Montreal, 51-58 & Vickers & Benson Ltd, Montreal, 58-66; pres, Art Dir Club, Montreal, 58-60; design consult, Int Civil Aviation Orgn Bulletin, Int Air Transport Asn, 68- *Teaching:* Lectr basic principles art, Sir George Williams Univ, 63-68; lectr hist design, Concordia Univ, 82- *Mem:* Societe des Graphistes du Que. *Media:* Acrylic. *Mailing Add:* 592 Luck Ave Montreal PQ H4X 1S4 Can

FEITELSON, HELEN LUNDEBERG See Lundeberg, Helen

FEJES, CLAIRE
PAINTER, WRITER
b New York, NY, Dec 14, 20. *Study:* Art Students League with Jose de Creeft & Saul Balzerman; Univ Alaska, Dr Humanities. *Work:* Anchorage Mus, Alaska; Univ Alaska, Fairbanks; Alaska State Mus, Juneau; Noel Wien Libr, Fairbanks, Alaska; and others. *Exhib:* Contemporary Art from Alaska, Smithsonian Exhib, 78; one-woman shows, Bear Gallery, Fairbanks, 78 & 83, Collector's Gallery, Anchorage, 81 & Tokyo Metrop Mus, 83; Cork Gallery, Lincoln Ctr, 81; Artique Gallery, 83; and others. *Teaching:* Instr art, Fairbanks Public Sch, Alaska; instr art, Univ Alaska. *Awards:* Gold Medal for Excellence, Inst Human Potential, Philadelphia, Pa, 81. *Bibliog:* Nina Mollet (auth), Clair Fejes, Alaska Mag, spring 79. *Mem:* Artists Equity. *Media:* Oil, Watercolor. *Publ:* Auth & illusr, People of the Noatak, Alfred A Knopf, 66; auth & illusr, Enuk My Son, Pantheon, 69; illusr, Eskimo Story Teller, Univ Tenn, 75; auth, Villagers, Random House, 81. *Dealer:* Sindin Gallery 79th & Madison Ave New York NY 10021. *Mailing Add:* 924 Kellum St Fairbanks AK 99701

FELD, AUGUSTA
PAINTER, PRINTMAKER
b Philadelphia, Pa, Apr 18, 19. *Study:* Fleisher Art Mem & Music Settlement Sch, Philadelphia; Philadelphia Col Art, BA; Tyler Sch Fine Arts, Temple Univ; Pa Acad Fine Arts, MA. *Work:* Acad Fine Arts, Hahnemann Hosp, Sch Dist Permanent Collection, Woodmere Art Gallery, Philadelphia; Marple-New Town Libr, Broomall, Pa. *Comn:* Tree of Life (mural of wood inlays, gold paint and vinyl, with Joseph Brahim), Delaware Co Community Ctr, Springfield, Pa, 64; dance mural (oil painting), Melita Dance Studio, Philadelphia, 68. *Exhib:* Woodmere Art Gallery, 61-; Artist Equity Asn, Philadelphia, 74; Philadelphia Art Alliance, 74-75; Philadelphia Civic Ctr, 74 & 80. *Pos:* Dir art, Hillview-Trout Nursery Sch, Broomall, Pa, 61- *Teaching:* Instr art, Philadelphia, 54-65, Wallingford Art Ctr, Pa, 63-64 & Haverford, Pa, 63-65. *Awards:* First Prize for oils, Atlantic City CofC, 68; First Prize, print exhib, Cheltenham Art Ctr, 71; First Prize in Portraiture, La Lomita Mus, Mission, Tex, 79. *Bibliog:* Article, La Rev Mod, 64. *Mem:* Artists Equity Asn; Philadelphia Watercolor Soc. *Mailing Add:* 103 Forrest Ave Elkins Park PA 19117

FELD, MARIAN PARRY See Parry, Marian

FELD, STUART PAUL
DEALER
b Passaic, NJ, Aug 10, 35. *Study:* Princeton Univ, AB, 57; Harvard Univ, AM, 58. *Collections Arranged:* Three Centuries of American Painting, 65 & 200 Years of Watercolor Painting in American, 66, Metrop Mus Art; American Paintings & Historical Prints from the Middendorf Collection, Metrop Mus Art & Baltimore Mus Art, 67; and many others. *Pos:* Var curatorial positions leading to assoc cur-in-charge, Dept Am Paintings, Metrop Mus Art, 61-67. *Interests:* American and European art of 18th, 19th and 20th centuries. *Publ:* Coauth (with Albert Ten Eyck Gardner), American Paintings: Painters Born by 1815 (Catalogue of the Permanent Collection of the Metropolitan Mus of Art), Vol 1, NY Graphic Soc, 65; and more than fifty exhibition catalogues and articles about American paintings, decorative arts and architecture. *Mailing Add:* c/o Hirschl & Adler Galleries Inc 21 E 70th St New York NY 10021

FELDHAUS, PAUL A
EDUCATOR, PRINTMAKER
b Cincinnati, Ohio, July 19, 26. *Study:* Cincinnati Art Mus; Miami Univ, Oxford, Ohio, BFA, 50; Bradley Univ, Peoria, Ill, MA, 52; study with Edwin Fulwider & Ernest Freed, printmakers. *Work:* Carroll Reece Mus, ETenn State Univ; Friends Meeting House, Boston, Mass; Montomgery Mus Fine Arts, Ala; Mobile Pub Lbir, Ala; Ford Times Col. *Comn:* Mural, Mastin Sch Nursing, Mobile, Ala, 66; mural, Woman's Clinic, Mobile, Ala, 67. *Exhib:* Int Biennial Graphic Art, Mus Mod Art, Ljubljana, Yugoslavia, 75; Int Exhib Graphic Art, Frechen, WGer, 76; Seventh Premio Int Biella of Printmaking, Italy, 76; US Embassy Travelling Exhib, Yugoslavia, 83; Crocker-Kingsley Exhib, Sacramento, 83; and others. *Teaching:* Assoc prof art, Spring Hill Col,

Mobile, Ala, 52-71; prof printmaking & drawing & coordr printmaking dept, Calif State Univ, Chico, 71- *Awards:* First Place Purchase Award, Dauphin Island Nat Competition, 65, 66, 68 & 70; Flack Purchase Prize, 7th Dixie Print Ann, Montgomery Mus of Art, 66; First Place Graphics, Mobile Watercolor & Graphic Arts Show, 69. *Mem:* Col Art Asn; Graphics Soc; Ala Art League (pres, 69-70). *Media:* Lithography, Engraving. *Mailing Add:* 310 W Legion Ave Chico CA 95926

FELDMAN, ARTHUR MITCHELL
MUSEUM DIRECTOR
b Philadelphia, Pa, Dec 22, 42. *Study:* Villanova Univ, BS; Univ Pa with George Tatum; Univ Mo, MA(art hist & archaeol). *Pos:* Vis cur, Victoria & Albert Mus, London, Eng, 70-71; assoc cur & asst adminr, Renwick Gallery, Smithsonian Inst, Washington, DC, 71-73; dir, Spertus Mus of Judaica, 73- *Mem:* Am Asn of Mus; Soc of Archit Historians; Ethnic Preserv Coun. *Publ:* Auth, Jewish Artists of the 20th Century, 75, The Hill Page Collection, 75, The Jews of Yemen, 76 & Faith and Form: Synagog Architecture of Illinois, 76, Spertus Col Press; auth, The Sons of Zebulan: Jewish Maritime History, 79. *Mailing Add:* 618 S Michigan Ave Chicago IL 60605

FELDMAN, BELLA TABAK
SCULPTOR
b New York, NY. *Study:* Queens Col, City Univ New York, BA; Calif Col Arts & Crafts; Calif State Univ, San Jose, MA. *Work:* Oakland Mus, Calif; Berkeley Art Mus, Univ Calif. *Comn:* Sculptures, Marshal Tulin, Hydronautics Inc, Silver Spring, Md, 64, Sasaki-Walker Landscape Architects, Newport Shopping Ctr, Newport Beach, Calif, 65 & Royston Hanamoto Landscape Architects, Potrero Park, Richmond, Calif, 66. *Exhib:* Palace Legion Honor, San Francisco, 61; Summer Series, San Francisco Mus, 64; San Francisco Art Inst, 75; San Jose Mus Art, 82; Calif Mixed Media Traveling Exhib, Japan, 82-83; Fibre/Espace Biennale, Lausanne, Switzerland, 83; Gallerie Bernard Letu, Geneva, 83; and others. *Teaching:* Prof, Calif Col Arts & Crafts, 64-, grad dir, 75-79; lectr art, Makerere Univ Col, Fine Art Sch, Uganda, 68-70. *Awards:* Calif Mus Trustees Award, 67; First Prize, San Francisco Women Artists, 67; E L Cabot Trust Fund Award, Harvard Univ, 75. *Bibliog:* Gloria Frym (ed), Second Stories, Chronicle Bks; Jessica Scarborough (auth), Bella Tabak Feldman, Fiber arts Mag, spring 84. *Mem:* Women's Caucus Col Art Asn; Committee-West, East Bay. *Media:* Metal, Paper. *Mailing Add:* 12 Summit Lane Berkeley CA 94708

FELDMAN, EDMUND BURKE
EDUCATOR, CRITIC
b Bayonne, NJ, May 6, 24. *Study:* Newark Sch Fine & Indust Arts, with John R Grabach & Emile Alexay, dipl, 41; Syracuse Univ, BFA, 49; Univ Calif, Los Angeles, with Karl With, Stanton MacDonald Wright & Abraham Kaplan, MA(art hist), 51; Columbia Univ, with Lyman Bryson & George Counts, EdD, 53. *Pos:* Cur paintings & sculpture, Newark Mus, 53. *Teaching:* Assoc prof art, Livingston State Col, 53-56; assoc prof painting, sculpture & design, Carnegie-Mellon Univ, 56-60; chmn art div, State Univ NY Col New Paltz, 60-66; prof art, Ohio State Univ, summer 66; prof art, Univ Ga, 66-; vis prof, Univ Calif, Berkeley, winter 74. *Awards:* Named Alumni Found Distinguished Prof Art, Univ Ga, 73. *Mem:* Kappa Pi; Col Art Asn Am; Nat Art Educ Asn (pres-elect, 79-81); Nat Art Educ Asn (pres, 81-83). *Res:* Theory of art criticism. *Publ:* Auth, Art as Image and Idea, 67, Becoming Human Through Art, 70 & The Artist, 82, Prentice-Hall; auth, Varieties of Visual Experience, Prentice-Hall & Abrams, 72, second ed, 81. *Mailing Add:* 140 Chinquapin Pl Athens GA 30605

FELDMAN, RONALD
DEALER
Pos: Co-owner, Ronald Feldman Gallery, New York, currently. *Specialty:* Contemporary artists; European and American masters, painting, sculpture and prints from Impressionism forward. *Mailing Add:* 31 Mercer New York NY 10013

FELDMAN, WALTER (SIDNEY)
PAINTER, PRINTMAKER
b Lynn, Mass, Mar 23, 25. *Study:* Yale Univ Sch Fine Arts, BFA, 50, Sch Design, MFA, 51; also with W de Kooning, Stuart Davis & Josef Albers. *Work:* Addison Gallery Am Art, Andover, Mass; Metrop Mus Art, New York; Fogg Art Mus, Cambridge, Mass; Israel Mus, Jerusalem; Mus Mod Art, New York. *Comn:* Mosaic pavements, Temple Beth-El, Providence, RI, 57; stained glass windows, Sugarman Mem Chapel, Providence, RI, 61; World's Fair poster, IBM Corp, 63; Quezalcoatl (mural), Pembroke Col, Brown Univ, 66; 32 panel mural, Temple Emanu-El, Providence, RI, 68. *Exhib:* American Watercolors, Drawings and Prints, Metrop Mus Art, 52; Recent Drawings USA, Mus Mod Art, New York, 55; Mostra Int, Milan, Italy, 57; 26th Biennial, Corcoran Gallery, Washington, DC, 59; Nat Inst Arts & Lett, New York, 61; one-man show, Hopkins Ctr, Dartmouth Col, 78. *Teaching:* Instr painting & design, Yale Univ Sch Design, 50-53; prof painting & printmaking, Brown Univ, 53-; vis prof drawing, Harvard Univ, 68; artist in residence, Hopkins Ctr, Dartmouth Col, 78. *Awards:* Metrop Mus Art Award, 52; Gold Medal, Mostra Int, Milan, Italy, 57; First Painting Award, Boston Arts Festival, Mass, 64. *Bibliog:* G Y Loveridge (auth), Providence practitioner of ancient art, The Rhode Islander, 4/25/54; Michael Forster (auth), The color of Mexico is black, Nivel 41, German P Garcia (Mexico City), 5/25/62; Jane Shelton (auth), Walter Feldman, Harvard Art Rev, spring 66. *Mem:* Am Color Print Soc. *Mailing Add:* 107 Benevolent St Providence RI 02906

FELDSTEIN, MARY
COLLECTOR, LIBRARIAN

b Berlin, WGer, Dec 17, 51; US citizen. *Study:* City Col New York; Univ Mich; New Sch Social Res. *Work:* Univ Mich Undergrad Libr; New York Pub Libr. *Collections Arranged:* New York Pub Libr Permanent Video Collection; First Ann Video Art & Video Documentary Festival, Goddard Col, 77; Meet the Makers (video & film series), Donnell Libr Ctr, New York, 77 & 78. *Pos:* Media specialist & info asst, Bronx Bookmobiles, New York, 74-75; film/video historian, New York Pub Libr, 76- *Teaching:* Fac mem contemp trends in video art & doc, New Sch Social Res, 78- *Bibliog:* Carol Anshiem (auth), Video in New York state libraries, Videoscope, Vol 2 (1976); Marianne Cocchini (auth), Cataloging video art, Film Libr Quart, Vol 10 (1977); Victor Ancona (auth), Doings at Donnell, Videography, 10/77. *Mem:* Asn Independent Video & Filmmakers. *Res:* Original cataloging of video art, public access to films and video tapes; circulating video tapes in library context. *Interests:* Conceptual, minimal, architecture, video, film, holograms, multi-media, inter-media. *Mailing Add:* 155 E 76th St New York NY 10021

FELLER, ROBERT L
CONSERVATION SCIENTIST

b Newark, NJ, Dec 27, 19. *Study:* Dartmouth Col, AB, 41; Rutgers Univ, MS, 43 & PhD, 50. *Pos:* Head, Nat Gallery Art Res Proj, Carnegie-Mellon Inst Res, Pittsburgh, 50-76, dir, Ctr on the Materials of the Artist & Conservator, 76-; ed, Int Inst Conserv Hist & Artistic Works, Am Group Bulletin, 60-74. *Teaching:* Vis scientist, Conserv Ctr, NY Univ Inst Fine Arts, spring 61. *Awards:* Fel, Illum Eng Soc, 75; Pittsburgh Award, Am Chemical Soc, 83. *Mem:* Fel Int Inst Conserv Hist & Artistic Works (pres, Am Group, 64-66); Int Coun Mus, Comt Conserv (pres, 69-78); Nat Conserv Adv Coun (pres, 76-79); Inter Soc Color Coun; Fedn Soc Paint Technol; and others. *Res:* Picture varnishes; effects of light on museum objects; analysis of pigments in works of art. *Publ:* Co-auth, On Picture Varnishes and Their Solvents, 59, rev ed, 71. *Mailing Add:* Carnegie-Mellon Inst Res 4400 Fifth Ave Pittsburgh PA 15213

FELLOWS, FRED
PAINTER, SCULPTOR

b Ponca City, Okla, Aug 15, 34. *Comn:* Portfolio of prints, Winchester on the Frontier, Winchester Firearms. *Exhib:* Cowboy Artists Am Show, Phoenix & Okla, 68-; Cowboy Hall of Fame; Whitney Gallery; Gran Palais, Paris; First Western Art Show, China; Los Angeles Co Mus Art; Cowboy Artists Am Mus, Kerrville, Tex. *Pos:* Commercial artist & art dir. *Awards:* Gold Medal, Phippen Award, Cowboy Artists Am Exhib, 75; Award for Contrib to Fine Art in Am, Grumbacher, 76; Silver Medal, Cowboy Artists of Am, 78. *Bibliog:* Brave New Cowboy (doc), Nat Pub TV; Great Plains Massacre (doc), BBC; article, Southwest Art, 10/82. *Mem:* Cowboy Artists Asn (secy-treas & vpres, 74-75). *Publ:* Auth, Saddles of the early west, Mont Hist Soc Mag, 68. *Mailing Add:* Box 464 Bigfork MT 59911

FELS, C P
PAINTER, WRITER

b Kirksville, Mo, Aug 29, 12. *Study:* Univ Calif, Berkeley, with Margaret Petersen, 38; Univ Southern Calif, with Francis deErdely, BFA(painting), 49, with Jules Heller, MFA(graphics), 50. *Work:* Everett Gallery, Univ Wash; San Francisco Mus Art. *Exhib:* San Francisco Art Asn Ann, 54; Los Angeles Co Mus Ann, 56; Brooklyn Mus Print Exhib, 58; Hawthorne Art Ann, 67; Southbay Art Ann, 72; plus others. *Pos:* Exhib dir, Southbay Art Asn, Redondo Beach, Calif, 52-58; mem bd dirs, Downey Mus Art, 75- *Teaching:* Lectr painting & drawing, Univ Calif, Los Angeles, 50-54; asst prof art, Univ Southern Calif, 54-67; emer prof art, Calif State Univ, Los Angeles, 78- *Awards:* First Prize Watercolor, Hawthorne Art Asn, 67; Wurlitzer Fel, 70; plus many others. *Mem:* Artists Equity Asn Inc (secy-treas, 74-75, pres, Los Angeles Chap, 76-78, Nat Ethical Practice Chapter, 78-82); Artists Econ Action; Am Soc Aesthetics. *Media:* Oil, Woodcut. *Res:* Byzantine and Islamic art and architecture. *Publ:* Auth, Kieth Crown, 73, Presence of absence: Leonard Heath sculpture, 74 & Influences on Chicano art, 75, ASAAC; auth, Aesthetic reaction and autonomus choice, FWEPS, 74; auth, Folio of Mayan Silkscreen Prints, End Time, 83. *Dealer:* Meridith Hunter Fine Arts Santa Fe NM 87501; Song of the Wind Gallery Taos NM 87571. *Mailing Add:* PO Box 3165 Taos NM 87571

FELTER, JAMES WARREN
PAINTER, CURATOR

b Bainbridge, NY, Aug 25, 43; Can citizen. *Study:* Univ S Fla, Tampa, BFA(painting), 64; Univ Wash. *Work:* City of Vancouver, BC; BC Prov Collection, Can; Manawatu Art Gallery, NZ; Mildura Arts Centre, Australia; Cabinet des Estampes, Mus Art et Hist, Geneva, Switz; and others. *Comn:* Trademark, OCEPA-Ecuadorian Handcrafts, Quito, 65; posters, Seattle Opera Asn, Wash, 67; Simon Fraser Univ Arts Centre, Burnaby, BC, 70 & 72. *Exhib:* Timbers et Tampons d'Artistes, Cabinet des Estampes, Mus Art et Hist, Geneva, Switz, 76; The Seventies, Mus Mod Art, Sao Paulo, Brazil, 76; 37th Venice Biennale (ECART Invitational), Italy, 76; Four Can Artists, Moderna Galerija, Liubljana & touring Yugoslavia, 76-77; Sixth Int Miniature Print Competition, Pratt Graphics Ctr, New York & touring US, 77-78; and others. *Collections Arranged:* Simon Fraser Collection, Simon Fraser Univ; The British Columbia Craft Exhibition (with catalog), Vancouver, BC, 72; Artist's Stamps and Stamp Images (circulated 1975-80), 74. *Pos:* Dir, Galeria de Ocepa, Quito, Ecuador, 65-66; cur-dir exhib, Simon Fraser Univ, 70- *Teaching:* Vis artist, Escuela de Bellas Artes, Univ Cent Ecuador, 66; resident visual arts, Simon Fraser Univ, 69. *Awards:* Finalist-Major Work of Art Competition, Univ Calgary, Alta, 74; Winner, Trademark Competition, Craftsmen's Asn BC, 75; Can Coun grant, 79. *Bibliog:* Article, La Rev Mod, Paris, 8/63; Mario Leon Meneses (auth), James W Felter en la Galeria Siglo XX, El Comercio, Quito, 2/24/66; Francoise Le Gris (auth), article, Vie des Arts 69, Montreal, 73. *Mem:* Community Arts Coun Vancouver; Western Can Art Asn (chmn, 75-76 & 78-80); Can Mus Asn; Int Coun Mus. *Media:* Ink, Acrylic. *Res:* Pre-Columbian and native arts. *Publ:* Auth, 450 Desinos Del 500 DC, Span, Quito, 66; ed, Paul Rand 1896-1970, Vancouver, BC, 72; contribr, Contemporaries of Emily Carr in British Columbia, Vancouver, 74; contribr, Vehicule Art: in Transit, Montreal, PQ, 75. *Dealer:* Five/Cinq Aesthet Ltd PO Box 91519 West Vancouver BC Can. *Mailing Add:* 2707 Rosebery Ave West Vancouver BC V7V 3A3 Canada

FELTUS, ALAN EVAN
PAINTER, EDUCATOR

b Washington, DC, May 1, 43. *Study:* Tyler Sch Fine Arts, Temple Univ, Philadelphia, 61-62; Cooper Union, New York, BFA, 66; Sch Art & Archit, Yale Univ, MFA, 68. *Work:* Univ Va Art Mus; Dayton Art Inst, Ohio; Am Med Asn, Washington, DC; Hirshhorn Mus, Washington DC; NJ State Mus. *Exhib:* Washington Figurative Painters, Corcoran Gallery Art, 73-74; Forum Gallery, New York, 76, 80 & 83; Nat Acad Design, 77, 78 & 82; Am Acad & Inst Arts & Lett, New York, 77, 79 & 81; Okla Art Ctr, 78; Washington Painting, Corcoran Gallery Art, 82. *Teaching:* Instr art, Dayton Art Inst, Ohio, 68-70; assoc prof art, Am Univ, Washington, DC, 72- *Awards:* Rome Prize Fel Painting, Am Acad Rome, 70-72; Tiffany Found Grant, 80; Nat Endowment Arts Individual Grant, 81. *Bibliog:* Jim Brodey (auth), Alan Evan Feltus, Arts Mag, 4/77; Jill Wechsler (auth), Alan Feltus, Am Artist Mag, 4/80; Susan Ohle (auth), Alan Evan Feltus, Washington Rev Mag, 6/81. *Media:* Oil. *Dealer:* Forum Gallery 1018 Madison Ave New York NY 10021. *Mailing Add:* Rte 1 Box 344 Hughesville MD 20637

FENCI, RENZO
SCULPTOR

b Florence, Italy, Nov 18, 14; US citizen. *Study:* Royal Inst Art, Florence. *Work:* Permanent Gallery Mod Art, Florence; Santa Barbara Mus Art, Calif; Cedars Sinai Med Ctr, Los Angeles. *Comn:* Nine banks in Los Angeles area, Home Savings & Loan Asn; Dr Charles Leroy Loman Mem, Orthopedic Hosp, Los Angeles, 68; George C Page Bldg, Children's Hosp, Los Angeles, Calif, 76; portrait of Edwin Lester, Music Ctr, Los Angeles, 77; Kilroy Indust, Sea-Tac, Seattle, 80. *Exhib:* Art Inst Chicago, 41; Calif State Fair, 50; Los Angeles Co Mus Art, 55; Nat Exhib Contemp Arts US, Pomona, Calif, 56; one-man show, Santa Barbara Mus Art, 68. *Teaching:* Instr sculpture, Univ Wash, Pullman, 42; asst prof sculpture, Univ Calif, Santa Barbara, 46-54; prof sculpture & head dept, Otis Art Inst, 54-77. *Awards:* Calif State Fair Award, 47, 49 & 50; Los Angeles Co Mus Art Award, 55; Santa Barbara Mus Biennial Show Award. *Bibliog:* Bette Howell (auth), Twelve California sculptors, Am Artist Mag, 68; Dialogues in Art, ABC-TV, Los Angeles, 69. *Media:* Bronze. *Mailing Add:* 3206 Deronda Dr Los Angeles CA 90068

FENDELL, JONAS J
EDUCATOR, PAINTER

b Brooklyn, NY. *Study:* New Sch Social Res; Brooklyn Mus Art Sch; Syracuse Univ, BFA & MFA. *Work:* Print collection, Mus Mod Art, New York; painting, Baltimore Mus Art; print, Syracuse Univ; print, Univ Maine; IBM Collection; Southern Graphic Artists. *Exhib:* Butler Inst Am Art; Brooklyn Mus Print Show; Baltimore Mus Art; Whitney Mus Am Art; Mus Mod Art; Univ Md, 81. *Pos:* Asst dir, Syracuse Mus, 57-58. *Teaching:* Prof design, painting & printing, Hurdell/Designs, 56-57; instr design & materials, Md Inst Col Art, 58-; instr materials, Essex Col, 68- *Awards:* Purchase Award, Mus Mod Art, New York; Purchase Prize, Baltimore Mus Art; Artist of Distinction Award, Univ Md, 81. *Mem:* Col Art Asn Am. *Dealer:* IFA Gallery 2623 Connecticut Ave NW Washington DC 20008. *Mailing Add:* 1905 Dixon Rd Baltimore MD 21209

FENDER, TOM MAC
SCULPTOR

b Tyler, Tex, Oct 12, 46. *Study:* Baylor Univ, BFA, 69; Univ Calif, Los Angeles, MA, 75, MFA, 79. *Work:* Nat Mus of Mod Art, Kyoto, Japan; Europ Banking Co, Chicago, Ill; Security Pac Bank of Calif, Los Angeles. *Comn:* Wrapped & woven sculptures, Aramco Oil Corp, Houston, Tex, 75, Am Med Asn Hq, Chicago, 76 & Shaklee Corp, Oakland, Calif, 77. *Exhib:* Fiber Works: Am & Japan, Nat Mus of Mod Art, Kyoto & Tokyo, Japan, 77; Fiber/Metal, Boehm Gallery, Palomar Col, San Marcos, Calif, 77; Packages, Kaplan-Baumann Gallery, Los Angeles, 77; California, Riverside Art Ctr, Calif, 77; Fiber Structures/Fabric Surfaces, Herron Gallery, Indianapolis, 79; and others. *Teaching:* Teaching asst fiber structures, Univ Calif, Los Angeles, 73-75. *Bibliog:* Bernard Kester (auth), Tom Fender's fiber forms, Artweek, 11/76; Alfred Frankenstein (auth), Winning unique Packages by Tom Fender, San Francisco Chronicle, 11/19/76; Suzanne Muchnic (auth), article in Artweek, 11/77. *Media:* Fiber materials and homemade paper. *Dealer:* Allrich Gallery Two Embarcadero Ctr San Francisco CA 94111. *Mailing Add:* 634 1/2 S Detroit Los Angeles CA 90036

FENN, (FRANCES) ELIZABETH
PAINTER, GRAPHIC ARTIST

b Toronto, Ont, Can, Oct 15, 14; US citizen. *Study:* Sch Indust Art, Philadelphia, with Alexy Brodovitch, BA, 36; with Wallace Harrison, New York, 45-49; with Fernand Leger, 52 & William Hayter, 54-56, Paris; with Samuel Adler, New York, 71-72. *Work:* Folger Shakespeare Libr, Washington, DC; Mus Haitian Art, Port-Au-Prince; US Trust Co, New York; Bally Shoes, Switz. *Exhib:* Salon d'Automne, Grand Palais, Paris, 76-80; Exhib Am Artists, Mus Haitian Art, Port-Au-Price, 82; Homage a Alexi

Brodovitch, Grand Palais, Paris, 82; 70th Ann Exhib, Allied Artists Am, New York, 83; 68th Ann, Hudson River Mus, Yonkers, NY, 83. *Pos:* Art dir, J D Tarcher & Co, New York, 43-45; art dir & fashion illusr, Publicis, Paris, 56-63; art dir, fashion consult & illusr, Elvinger, Paris, 63-66. *Awards:* Gold Medal, Salon Int Indust Arts du Feu, 61; Prix du Papier, First Prize for Drawing, Salon de Versailles, 77; First Prize Abstract Painting, Grand Prix Int de Peinture des Cevennes, 79. *Bibliog:* B DuPlessis (auth), Nouvelle des Arts, L'Info Dentaire, 4/76; Emile de Bongnie (auth), Au Centre Culturel de Parly II: Elizabeth Fenn, J de Versailles, 11/4/76; Dorothy Friedman (auth), Paintings by Fenn, sculptures by Flanagan, Greenwich Times, 11/30/83. *Mem:* West Side Arts Coalition, New York. *Media:* Oil, Pastel; Charcoal, Lead Pencil. *Dealer:* Marianne Wyman 84 Round Hill Rd Greenwich CT 06830. *Mailing Add:* 51 W 81st St Apt 9G New York NY 10024

FENTON, ALAN
PAINTER, INSTRUCTOR
b Cleveland, Ohio, July 29, 27. *Study:* Pratt Inst, BFA; Art Students League; New Sch Social Res; also pvt study with Adolph Gottlieb & Jack Tworkov; Cleveland Sch Art. *Work:* Corcoran Gallery Art, Washington, DC; Hirshhorn Mus Art, Washington DC; Central Intelligence Agency, Washington DC; Herbert F Johnson Mus Art, Cornell Univ, Ithaca, NY; Norton Mus Art, West Palm Beach, Fla. *Exhib:* Fifth Ann Soc Encouragement Contemp Art Show, San Francisco Mus, 63; one-man exhibs, Larry Aldrich Mus, Ridgfield, Conn, 68, B Fiedler Gallery, Washington, DC, 73-80, NY Cult Mus, New York, 74, Houston Mus Art, 77, Isatan Gallery, Tokyo, Japan, 79 & Phillips Collection, Washington, DC, 80; Corcoran Gallery Art, 71-72. *Teaching:* Instr drawing, Pratt Inst, 69- & Housatonic State Col, 71-73; spec asst, Cleveland Inst Art, Ohio, 77-78. *Awards:* First Prize, Cleveland Mus Art, 60-61. *Bibliog:* Alan Fenton, Phillips Collection Catalog, 77; Contemp Art Mus Houston, Catalog, 77; also articles in New York Times, New York Post, Village Voice, New York & Art Int. *Mailing Add:* 333 Park Ave S New York NY 10010

FENTON, HOWARD CARTER
PAINTER, EDUCATOR
b Toledo, Ohio, July 2, 10. *Study:* Chouinard Art Inst; Univ Calif, Los Angeles, BA & MA; also with S McDonald Wright. *Work:* Santa Barbara Mus Art Calif; Univ Calif, Santa Barbara; Galleria Piazza di Spagna, Rome. *Exhib:* One-man shows, Santa Barbara Mus Art, 64, Esther Bear Gallery, 66 & 75, Univ Calif Art Galleries, 67, Galleria Piazza di Spagna, 67 & Alwin Gallery, London, 68. *Teaching:* Prof art, Univ Calif, Santa Barbara, 48-78, emer prof, 78- *Bibliog:* David Gebhard (auth), Howard Fenton, Haagen Press, 68. *Mem:* Col Art Asn Am. *Media:* Oil, Watercolor. *Collection:* Contemporary American artists. *Mailing Add:* 1000 Ladera Lane Santa Barbara CA 93108

FENTON, JULIA ANN
CONCEPTUAL ARTIST, LIBRARIAN
b Tupelo, Miss, Feb 11, 37. *Study:* Millsaps Col, Jackson, Miss, BA(relig), 58; Pa State Univ, grad study in philos & visual arts, 62-65; Atlanta Col of Art, 70-74. *Exhib:* Encuentro Int de Video 1977, Museo de Arte Contemporaneo de Caracas, Venezuela, 76-77; The Avant-Garde: 12 in Atlanta, High Mus Art, 79; Atlanta Women's Invitational, Agnes Scott Col, 79; Atlanta Women's Art Collective at AIR Gallery, New York, 80; one-man shows, Reductions, Atlanta Women's Art Collective, 80, Perspective, Atlanta Art Workers Coalition, 80 & Julia A Fenton, Redmont Gallery, Jackson, Miss, 83. *Pos:* Ed & vpres ed affairs & mem bd dirs, Contemp Art/Southwest, 76-77; dir activities & ed newspaper, Atlanta Art Workers Coalition, 77-78, dir info resources & bd dirs, 79-80, Southeastern Women's Caucus Art (prog chairperson, 79); ed, Southeast Mag, 75-77; ed, Atlanta Art Workers Coalition Newspaper, 77-78. *Mem:* Atlanta Art Workers Coalition; Atlanta Women's Art Collective; Independent Media Artists of Ga; Southeastern Women's Caucus for Art. *Media:* Video and multi-media installations. *Publ:* Contribr, John Y Fenton (ed), Theology and Body, Westminster, 74. *Mailing Add:* 397 Emory Dr NE Atlanta GA 30307

FENWICK, ROLY (WILLIAM ROLAND)
PAINTER, EDUCATOR
b Owen Sound, Ont, Feb 4, 32. *Study:* Mt Allison Univ, NB, with Alex Colville & Lawren Harris Jr, scholar, 54. *Work:* McIntosh Gallery, Univ Western Ont; Owens Mus, Mt Allison Univ, NB; London Regional Art Gallery, London Free Press, Ont; Sir George Williams Univ, Montreal. *Exhib:* Image of Man, McIntosh Gallery, London, Ont, 78; Masterworks on Paper, 78 & retrospective, 78, London Regional Art Gallery, Ont; Take Two, Hart House Gallery, Toronto, 83; Three Artists, Bau-Xi Gallery, Toronto, 83. *Pcs:* Art dir, Simpsons-Sears, Toronto, 56-66. *Teaching:* Assoc prof art, Univ Western Ont, 69- *Mem:* Univ Art Asn Can; Royal Can Acad; Ont Soc Artists. *Media:* Oil. *Publ:* Illusr, War and Other Measures, House Anansi, 77; illusr, Wintering Over, Quadraut Ed, 80. *Dealer:* Bau-Xi Gallery 340 Dundas St W Toronto ON M5T 1G5. *Mailing Add:* 810 Talbot St London ON N6A 2V6 Canada

FERBER, ELISE VAN HOOK
ADMINISTRATOR, CURATOR
b New York, NY. *Study:* Smith Col, BA; NY Univ Grad Sch. *Pos:* Asst to cur, Mus Mod Art, New York, 37-45; res asst, Am Inst Architects, Washington, DC, 54-56; mus cur, Nat Gallery Art, 56-70, cur art info serv, 72-; asst to dir, Dumbarton Oaks Res Libr & Col, 70-72. *Mailing Add:* Nat Gallery of Art Washington DC 20565

FERBER, HERBERT
SCULPTOR, PAINTER
b New York, NY, Apr 30, 06. *Study:* Beaux-Arts Inst Design; City Col New York; Columbia Univ. *Work:* Metrop Mus Art, Whitney Mus Am Art & Mus Mod Art, New York; Albright-Knox Art Gallery, Buffalo; Detroit Inst Art; plus others. *Comn:* Copper sculpture, John F Kennedy Off Bldg, Boston; copper & environ sculpture, Rutgers Univ; steel sculpture, Am Dental Asn Bldg, Chicago; steel sculpture, Ottumwa, Iowa; plus others. *Exhib:* Whitney Mus Am Art; Mus Mod Art, New York; Pa Acad Fine Arts; Boston Mus Fine Arts; Documenta 5, Kassel, Ger; plus others. *Teaching:* Vis prof sculpture, Univ Pa & Rutgers Univ; chair humanities, Rice Univ. *Bibliog:* Many articles in nat art periodicals. *Dealer:* M Knoedler & Co 19 E 70th St New York NY 10021. *Mailing Add:* 44 MacDougal St New York NY 10012

FERBER, LEE ALLAN
CRAFTSMAN, EDUCATOR
b Bakersfield, Calif, Aug 31, 41. *Study:* Univ Okla, BFA, 64; Univ Kans, MFA, 66. *Work:* Renwick Gallery, Smithsonian Inst, DC; Mus Art, Univ Okla Norman; Fisher Art Ctr, Marshalltown, Iowa. *Exhib:* Nineteenth Wichita Nat, Wichita Art Asn, Kans, 66; NCent Invitational, Midland Ctr Arts, Mich, 71; Craft Multiples, Renwick Gallery, Smithsonian Inst, DC, 76; Brunnier Gallery, Iowa State Univ, Ames, 76; Northwest Crafts III, SDak Mem Art Ctr, Brookings, 79; one-man show, Mus Art, Univ Norman, 79. *Teaching:* Prof art and ceramics, Drake Univ, Des Moines, Iowa, 66- *Awards:* Purchase Award, 12th Kans Designer Craftsmen, 66; First Award Metal, 19th Wichita Nat, 66. *Media:* Clay. *Publ:* Auth, Glaze trailing on plates, Ceramic Mo, 2/81. *Mailing Add:* 3616 Kingman Blvd Des Moines IA 50311

FERBER, LINDA S
CURATOR, HISTORIAN
b Suffern, NY, May 17, 44. *Study:* Barnard Col, New York, BA, 66; Columbia Univ, New York, MA, 68 & PhD(Wyeth Endowment Am Art fel), 80. *Pos:* Cur Am painting & sculpture, Brooklyn Mus, New York, 76- *Teaching:* Adj prof art hist, Columbia Univ, 78- *Mem:* Col Art Asn; Victorian Soc Am; Asn Historians Am Art; New York Asn Historians Am Art; Archives Am Art. *Res:* Am art with a special interest in painting and sculpture of the nineteenth century. *Publ:* Coauth, Masterpieces of American Painting from the Brooklyn Museum, 76; auth, William Trost Richards (1833-1905): American Landscape and Marine Painter, 79; coauth, American Light: The Luminist Movement, 1850-1875, Nat Gallery Art, 80; auth, Glorious Infinity: Notes on light and its significance in some drawings by William T Richards, Drawings, 1/80; auth, Themes in American Genre Painting: 1840-1880, Apollo, 4/82. *Mailing Add:* Dept Paintings & Sculpture Brooklyn Mus Brooklyn NY 11238

FERENCE, CYNTHIA
GALLERY DIRECTOR, PAINTER
b Harrisburg, Pa. *Study:* Art Inst Pittsburgh; Carnegie-Mellon Univ, Pittsburgh, BFA(Edgar Roth Scholar, Women's Alumni Scholar), 78. *Pos:* Dir, Forbes St Gallery, Pittsburgh, 76-77 & Hewlett Gallery, Carnegie-Mellon Univ, Pittsburgh, 77-79; exec dir, Green Hill Ctr NC Art, Greensboro, 79- *Mem:* Am Crafts Coun; Piedmont Craftsmen; NC Mus Coun; Handweavers' Guild Am; NC Fiber Arts Asn. *Specialty:* Contemporary visual arts of North Carolina. *Publ:* Auth, Arts is a 4 letter word, 3/80 & The Penland School of Crafts, 9/80, Arts J; auth catalog essay, A Survey of NC Fiber Arts & Textile Design, 82. *Mailing Add:* Green Hill Art Gallery 200 N Davie St Greensboro NC 27401

FERGUSON, BARCLAY (LORD OF LAMOND)
PAINTER, MURALIST
b St Andrews, Scotland, Sept 22, 24; Can citizen. *Study:* Glasgow Sch Art, dipl art, 51; Inst Allende, Univ Guanajuato, San Miguel de Allende, Mex, MFA, 59. *Work:* Monterey Peninsula Mus Art, Calif; Monterey Conf Ctr; Pacific Grove Art Ctr, Calif; Prudential Insurance Co of Am; The Morgan Flagg Corp. *Comn:* Curved mural, Can Westinghouse, Hamilton, Ont, 57; mural, Hist of the Popal Val, Inst Allende, Mex, 60; mural, Atomic Energy, Atomic Energy Can, Ltd, Toronto, 65. *Exhib:* One-man show, Boxes, Monterey Peninsula Mus Art, 73; Rainbow Show, De Young Mus, San Francisco, 75; Flag Show, Allentown Art Mus, Pa, 76; Robinson Gallery, Houston, 78; Lewis Newman Gallery, 79-80. *Pos:* Art adv & art dir, Atomic Energy Can, Ltd, 60-69; dir, Pacific Grove Art Ctr, 71. *Teaching:* Instr mural, Inst Allende, 68-69. *Awards:* Best of Show, Monterey Mus Art, 73; Calif State Fair, 80 & Int Platform Asn, Washington, DC, 81. *Bibliog:* Betty Ewing (auth), Tin toys and Barclay Ferguson, Houston Chronicle, 78; Abbe Slavin (auth), article, Houston Chronicle, 78; Jeffrey Whitmore (auth), Barclay Ferguson, Painter, Monterey Life, 11/81. *Mem:* Carmel Art Asn; Ont Art League; Glasgow Art Inst; The Arts Club of Washington, DC. *Media:* Oil, Acrylic. *Dealer:* Louis Newman Galleries 322 N Beverly Drive Beverly Hills CA 90210. *Mailing Add:* Box 1552 Carmel CA 93923

FERGUSON, CHARLES B
MUSEUM DIRECTOR, PAINTER
b Fishers Island, NY, June 30, 18. *Study:* Williams Col, AB; Art Students League, painting with Frank Dumond & graphics with Harry Sternberg; Trinity Col, MA. *Work:* New Britain Mus Am Art, Conn; Mattatuck Mus, Waterbury, Conn; DeCordova Mus, Lincoln, Mass; Amerind Found, Ariz; Scoville Corp, Waterbury, Conn. *Comn:* Stained glass window, Fishers Island, 71; murals, Williston Acad, Easthampton, Mass, Renbrook Sch, West Hartford, Conn & pvt home, Fishers Island, NY. *Exhib:* Conn Acad Fine Arts; Conn Watercolor Soc; Greater Hartford Civic Arts Festival. *Collections Arranged:* Aaron Draper Shattuck, 70; Robert B Brandegee, 71; William T

Richards, 73; Dennis Miller Bunker, 78; Three Generations of Wiggins, 1870's-1970's, 79; Three Centuries of Connecticut Art, 81; Allan Butler Talcott, Painter of Landscapes, 83. *Pos:* Dir, New Britain Mus Am Art, Conn, 65-; trustee, Hillstead Mus, Farmington, Conn, currently; pres, Henry L Ferguson Mus, Fishers Island, NY, currently. *Teaching:* Instr hist art & studio painting, Trinity Col & Loomis Sch. *Awards:* New Britain Herald Prize, 70; Sanford Low Prize, Conn Acad Fine Arts, 71; First Prize for Oils, Mystic Marine Exhib, Conn, 81. *Mem:* Conn Acad Fine Arts. *Mailing Add:* New Brit Mus Am Art 56 Lexington St New Britain CT 06052

FERGUSON, GERALD
PAINTER
b Cincinnati, Ohio, Jan 29, 37. *Study:* Wilmington Col, Ohio, BS, 62; Ohio Univ, Athens, MFA, 66. *Work:* Mus Mod Art, New York; Mus Stuzki, Lodz, Poland; Art Gallery Ont, Toronto; Glenbow Mus, Calgary, Alta; Art Gallery NS, Halifax. *Exhib:* Mus Mod Art, New York, 70; solo shows, Anna Leonowens Gallery, Halifax, NS, 74 & Art Gallery Ont, Toronto, 76 & 77; Galeria Foksal, Warsaw, Poland, 77; Glenbow Mus, Calgary, Alta, 81; and others. *Teaching:* Asst prof, Kansas City Art Inst, 67-68; prof, NS Col Art, Halifax, 68-; mentor art, Calif Inst Arts, Valencia, 73-74. *Bibliog:* Lucy Lippard (auth), Six Years..., Praeger, 73; Eric Cameron (auth), Gerald Ferguson, Studio Int, spring 75; Dennis Young (auth), Task Oriented Art, Dalhousie Univ, 76. *Media:* All Media. *Mailing Add:* 6134 Pepperell St Halifax NS B3H 2N9 Canada

FERGUSON, KATHLEEN ELIZABETH
SCULPTOR
b Chicago, Ill, Jan 31, 45. *Study:* Stephens Col, Columbia, Mo, 63-64; Layton Sch Art, Milwaukee, Wis, BFA, 69; RI Sch Design, Providence, MFA. *Work:* Russell Courthouse, Atlanta. *Exhib:* One-person shows, Smithsonian Inst, Washington, DC, 72, San Cicero Gallery, Chicago, 79, Ctr Contemp Art, Univ Ky, 80 & Univ Cincinnati, 81; Va Mus Fine Arts, Richmond, 73; Drawing Invitational, Rutgers Univ, NJ, 75; Biennial of Contemp Am Art, Whitney Mus Am Art, New York, 75; and others. *Teaching:* Vis artist, Conn Col, 79; vis artist, Univ Ky, 80-81. *Bibliog:* David Shirey (auth), article, New York Times, 78; John Yau (auth), article, Art Am, 79; William Zimmer (auth), article, Soho Weekly News, 79. *Media:* Mixed Media. *Publ:* Contribr, Milton Klonsky (auth), Speaking Pictures, Crown, 74; auth & illusr, Natti's Navigations, pvt publ, 78. *Mailing Add:* PO Box 54865 Lexington KY 40555

FERGUSON, LARRY SCOTT
PHOTOGRAPHER, CURATOR
b North Platte, Nebr, May 16, 54. *Study:* Univ Nebr, Lincoln, BFA, 77; Rochester Inst Technol, NY, sem 78. *Work:* Sheldon Mem Art Gallery, Lincoln, Nebr, Libr of Cong, DC; Western Heritage Mus, Omaha, Nebr; Univ Okla, Norman; Murray State Univ, Ky; and others. *Comn:* Photograph, collab Sachio Yamashita, Metrop Arts Coun, Omaha, Nebr, 79 & photograph, murals & sculpture, 79; photograph, Bldg Reborn, Smithsonian Inst, DC, 79; photograph, Tube Walkway, Omaha Airport Auth, Nebr, 80. *Exhib:* Am Vision, Nat Artists Alliance, NY Univ, 79; Juried Exhib, Friends of Photog Gallery, Carmel, Calif, 79 & Diana Camera Show, 80; Omaha: Then & Now, Western Heritage Mus, 79, Omaha: Then & Now II, 80 & Omaha: Then & Now III, 81; one-man shows, Sheldon Mem Art Gallery, Lincoln, Nebr, 79 & Southern Light Gallery, Amarillo, Tex, 80; Walker Art Ctr, Minneapolis, 81; and others. *Pos:* Cur photographs, Adams Co Hist Soc, Hastings, Nebr, 77-78; Nebr Arts Coun & Nat Endowment for Arts artist-in-residence grants & cur photographs, Bostwick-Frohardt Collection, Western Heritage Mus, Omaha, 78-81. *Teaching:* Instr photography, Univ Nebr, Omaha, 81-, Bellevue Col, 82- *Awards:* Jurors Award, Nat Artists Alliance, 79; Jurors Award, 2nd St Gallery, Charlottesville, Va, 80; Artist in residence Grant, Nebr Arts Coun, 81-82. *Bibliog:* Shawn P Leary (auth), Arts scan, 79 & Art Simmering (auth), Dodge Street, 80, Omaha Mag; Joanne Stanwick (auth), Suitable for framing, Omaha Mag, 81; article, Artweek, 9/5/81; and others. *Mem:* Soc Photog Educ; Friends of Photog; Visual Studies Workshop, Rochester, NY. *Publ:* Contribr, Twelve Photographers: A Contemporary Mid-America Document, Mid-Am Arts Alliance, 78; contribr, Self-Portrayal: The Photographers Image, 79 & Untitled Number 21, by Jim Alinder, 80, Friends of Photog; contribr, Object and Image, by George Craven, Prentice-Hall, 82. *Mailing Add:* 1402 William Omaha NE 68108

FERHOLT, ELEANORE HEUSSER See Heusser, Eleanore Elizabeth

FERIOLA, JAMES PHILIP
PAINTER, DESIGNER
b Great Notch, NJ, July 4, 25. *Study:* Phoenix Sch Design, New York, grad. *Work:* Nassau Co Mus, Syosset, NY; R Peerman Corp & H Butt Corp, Corpus Christi, Tex; Country Art Gallery, Locust Valley, NY; Forbes Mag. *Exhib:* Smithsonian Inst; Nat Acad Design, New York; New York World's Fair Fine Arts Pavilion; Hammond Mus; Prince Rainier III Palace, Monaco. *Pos:* Supvr art & exhib dept, Nassau Co Mus, presently. *Awards:* Gold Medal of Honor, Smithsonian Inst; Travel Grant to Europe, Greenwich Village Art Show; Silver Medal Honor, Am Vet Soc Artists. *Bibliog:* Famous People of Hempstead, NY (film). *Mem:* Am Watercolor Soc; Hudson Valley Artists; Am Artists Prof League; Am Vet Soc Artists; Art League of Nassau Co. *Media:* Watercolor, Acrylics. *Mailing Add:* 226 Perry St Hempstead NY 11550

FERN, ALAN MAXWELL
HISTORIAN, ADMINISTRATOR
b Detroit, Mich, Oct 19, 30. *Study:* Univ Chicago, AB, 50, MA, 54 & PhD, 60; Courtauld Inst, Univ London, res scholar. *Collections Arranged:* Diverse print, poster & photo shows, Libr Cong, 62-; Leonard Baskin, Nat Collection Fine Arts, Smithsonian Inst, 70. *Pos:* From asst cur to cur, asst chief to chief, Prints & Photographs Div, Libr Cong, 61-76, dir, Res Dept, 76-78, dir, spec collections, 78- *Teaching:* From asst to asst prof, Univ Chicago, 52-61. *Awards:* Fulbright Fel, 54-55; Chevalier, Ordre de la Couronne, Belgium, 80. *Mem:* Print Coun Am (dir, 63-, pres, 69-71); Col Art Asn Am; Am Antiquarian Soc; Double Crown Club, London; Spec Libr Asn. *Res:* History of prints, posters, book design, 19th and 20th century art. *Publ:* Auth, A note on the Eragny Press, Cambridge Univ Press, 57; co-auth, Art nouveau, 60 & auth, Word and image, 69, Mus Mod Art, New York; auth, Leonard Baskin, Smithsonian Press, 70; co-auth, Revolutionary Soviet film posters, Johns Hopkins Press, 74. *Mailing Add:* Res Serv Dept Libr of Congress Washington DC 20540

FERNANDEZ, RUDY M, JR
PAINTER, SCULPTOR
b Trinidad, Colo, Sep 21, 48. *Study:* Univ Colo, BA, 74; Wash State Univ, scholar, MFA, 77. *Work:* Smithsonian Inst, Washington, DC; Univ Ariz Art Mus, Tucson. *Exhib:* Denver Metrop Mus, 72; And/Or Gallery, Seattle, 75; Galeria de la Raza, San Francisco, 77; Heard Mus, Phoenix, 78; Alternative Mus, New York, 83; Univ Ariz Mus, Tuscon, 83. *Awards:* Scholar, Instituto Cultural Tenochtitlan, 75; Visual Arts Award, Ariz Comn Arts, 81. *Bibliog:* Carol Kotrozo (auth), Arizona: A guide to the art, Portfolio, 7-8/81; Barbara Perlman (auth), Reviews from Arizona, Art News, 12/81; Rudy Fernandez (auth), Secular santos, Arts, 6/83; and others. *Media:* Mixed Media; Wood. *Dealer:* Putney Gallery Aspen CO. *Mailing Add:* c/o Elaine Horwitch Gallery 4211 N Marshall Way Scottsdale AZ 85251

FERNIE, JOHN CHIPMAN
SCULPTOR, INSTRUCTOR
b Hutchinson, Kans, Oct 22, 45. *Study:* Colo Col, 63-65; Kansas City Art Inst, BFA, 68; Univ Calif, Davis, grant, 69, teaching fel & MFA, 70. *Exhib:* One-man shows, Nova Scotia Col Art, 74 & John Gibson Gallery, 77; group shows, Documenta 5, Kasel, Ger, 72; 8th & 9th Biennale de Paris; Israel Mus, 76; Houston Mus of Contemp Art, 77; Whitney Mus, New York, 78; Denver Art Mus, 78; Boulder Art Ctr, Colo, 79; plus others. *Teaching:* Asst, Univ Calif, Davis, 69; instr sculpture, Calif Col Arts & Crafts, 70-72; instr sculpture, Stephens Col, 72-75; instr sculpture, Nova Scotia Col Art & Design, 75- *Bibliog:* Richardson (auth), article in Arts Mag, 2/71; Albright (auth), Exciting, compelling show, San Francisco Chronicle, 7/1/71; Jochimsen (auth), Magazin Kunst, 7/74. *Media:* Wood, Cardboard, Photo, Plaster. *Publ:* Auth, Petit trianon, twikkel, I worship you, God bless your symmetry, 70; auth, Masters survey, 70. *Mailing Add:* 735 College Ave Boulder CO 80302

FERRARA, JACKIE
SCULPTOR
b Detroit, Mich. *Work:* Chase Manhattan Bank, Mus Mod Art, New York; Des Moines Art Ctr; Sol Lewitt Collection, Wadsworth Atheneum; La Mus, Copenhagen, Denmark. *Comn:* Outdoor sculptures, Minneapolis Col Art & Design, 78, City Beautiful Coun, Dayton, Ohio, 78, Gen Serv Admin, Carbondale, Ill, 80, Laumeier Sculpture Park, St Louis, 81 & NCent Ohio Arts Coun Norwalk, 84. *Exhib:* Biennial Exhib, Whitney Mus, 73 & 79; Drawings: The Pluralist Decade, Venice Biennale, Italy, 80; Painting & Sculpture Today, Indianapolis Mus Art, 80; solo exhib, Univ Mass, Amherst, 80 & Lowe Art Mus, Coral Gables, Fla, 82; Drawing Acquisitions, Whitney Mus, 81; Connections, Inst Contemp Art, Philadelphia, 83; Recent Acquisitions, Mus Mod Art, New York, 83. *Awards:* Grants, NY State Coun Arts, 71 & 75 & Nat Endowment Arts, 73 & 77; Guggenheim Found Fel, 76. *Bibliog:* Kate Linker (auth), Jackie Ferrara's il-lusions, Artforum, 11/79; Phil Patton (auth), Jackie Ferrara: Sculpture the mind can use, Artnews, 3/82. *Dealer:* Max Protetch Gallery 37 W 57 St New York NY 10019. *Mailing Add:* 121 Prince St New York NY 10012

FERRARI, VIRGINIO LUIG
SCULPTOR, EDUCATOR
b Verona, Italy, Apr 11, 37. *Study:* Scuola d'Arte, with N Nani; Acad Cignaroli, Verona. *Work:* Biennale Nazionale di Verona; High Mus Art, Atlanta, Ga; Univ di Parma Mus, Italy; Ravinia Park, Highland Park, Ill; Byer Mus, DePaul Univ, Ill. *Comn:* Bronzes, Pick Hall for Int Studies, Univ Miami, 75; Vanderbilt Univ Med Ctr Hosp, 80 & Northwestern Univ, Evanston, Ill; Being Born (sculpture), City of Chicago. *Exhib:* Art Inst Chicago, 68; Brooklyn Mus, 68; Sears Tower Bank, Chicago, 77; Seven Sculptors, DePaul Univ, 78; Ill for Art Dedication exhib, Springfield, 79; traveling exhibs, State Ill Arts Coun, 69 & Ill Bronzetto Italiano, 71; and others. *Pos:* Sculptor in residence, Univ Chicago, 66-76. *Teaching:* Asst prof sculpture, Univ Chicago, 67-76. *Awards:* Nostra Ministero Publica, Istruzione Roma, Italy, 64; Biennale Nazionale di Verona, 65; Ill Coun of Am Inst Architects Award, 77. *Bibliog:* Arturo Quitavalle (auth), Ferrari Gocce d'Amor Pop, Univ di Parma, 70; article, Cimaise Mag, 82. *Mem:* Sindacato Artisti; Arts Club Chicago. *Media:* Metal, Marble. *Mailing Add:* 5429 East View Park Chicago IL 60615

FERREIRA, (ARMANDO) THOMAS
EDUCATOR, SCULPTOR
b Charleston, WVa, Jan 8, 32. *Study:* Chouinard Inst; Long Beach City Col; Univ Calif, Los Angeles, BA & MA. *Work:* State Calif Collection; Univ Utah Art Mus. *Exhib:* Los Angeles Co Mus, 58, 60 & 66; Fine Arts Gallery, San Diego, 61, 69 & 73; Art Mus, Oakland, Calif, 63; Otis Art Inst Galleries, 65;

Pasadena Mus Art, 68; Univ Calif, Santa Barbara, 73; and other group & one-man shows. *Teaching:* Prof ceramic sculpture, Calif State Univ Long Beach, 57-; Fulbright lectr, Brazil, 81. *Awards:* Purchase Awards, Calif Expos, 61 & Wichita Art Asn, 66. *Mem:* Nat Asn Schs Art; Int Video Art Netwk. *Media:* Clay, Mixed Media. *Mailing Add:* c/o State Univ Dept Art 1250 N Bellflower Blvd Long Beach CA 90840

FERRELL, LUCILE EVANS See Evans, Lucile

FERRER, RAFAEL
PAINTER, SCULPTOR
b Santurce, PR, 1933. *Study:* Saunton Military Acad, Va, 48-51; Syracuse Univ, NY, 51-52; Univ PR, Mayaquez, with E Granell, 52-54. *Exhib:* Art of Latin Am, Pa Acad Fine Arts, Philadelphia, 67; Op Losse Schroven, Stedelijk Mus, Amsterdam, 69; Info, Mus Mod Art, New York, 70; Whitney Mus Am Art Ann, New York, 70; Depth & Presence, Corcoran Gallery Art, Washington, DC, 71; Biennial of Medellin, Colombia, South Am, 72; Whitney Biennial, 73; one-man shows, Philadelphia Mus Art, Pa, 70, Whitney Mus, 71, Nancy Hoffman Gallery, New York, 74, 75 & 82, Mus Mod Art, New York, 74, Hamilton Gallery, 79 & Frumkin & Struve, Chicago, 79; and others. *Bibliog:* Stephen Prokopff (auth), Rafael Ferrer, An interview, Art & Artists, London, 4/72; Kenneth Baker (auth), New York: Rafael Ferrer, Whitney Museum, Artforum, 3/72; J L Dunham (auth), article, Artweek, Oakland, Calif, 11/74. *Mailing Add:* c/o Nancy Hoffman Gallery 429 West Broadway New York NY 10012

FERRIS, EDYTHE
PAINTER, GRAPHIC ARTIST
b Riverton, NJ, June 21, 1897. *Study:* Philadelphia Sch Design for Women, dipl. *Work:* Free Libr Philadelphia; Philadelphia Mus Art; Archive Collection, Can Painters & Etchers, Toronto Mus; Randolph-Macon Woman's Col; Tinicum Nat Environ Ctr. *Exhib:* Norfolk Drawing Biennial, Va, 64; Artists Equity Asn Mem, Civic Ctr, Philadelphia, 68 & 71; Fibonocci Exhib, Art Alliance, Philadelphia, 72; Am Color Print Soc Ann, Philadelphia Art Alliance, 72 & 79; retrospective, Univ City Arts League, Philadelphia, 74. *Collections Arranged:* 78 exhibs of living artists of German origin or ancestry in Old Customs House for Carl Schurz Asn, 53-64; 20 traveling exhibs of original prints, German Expressionists, with notes & catalogue, 57-67. *Pos:* Art adv, Nat Carl Schurz Asn, 53-67; founder neighborhood rehabilitation proj, Friends of Clark Park, 75. *Teaching:* Dir crafts, adult educ, Cent YWCA, Philadelphia, 34-38; dir crafts, Fletcher Farm, Proctorsville, Vt, summers 34-36; instr crafts, Montgomery Co Day Sch, Wynnewood, Pa, 42-49; lectr art appreciation, Junto, Philadelphia, 50-54. *Awards:* J Lessing Rosenwald Prize for woodcut, Print Club, 55; hon mention, Am Automobile Asn, 70. *Bibliog:* Bet Jones (auth), Two bird pictures, Randolph Macon Woman's Col, 68; Janet Mowery (auth), The birds of Edythe Ferris and Morris Graves, 69. *Mem:* Am Color Print Soc; Artists Equity Asn; Moore Col Art Alumnae; Univ City Arts League (founder, 65). *Media:* Oil; Woodcuts. *Publ:* Contribr, American German Review, various years during 50's. *Dealer:* Sidney Rothman--The Gallery Bernegat Light NJ 08006. *Mailing Add:* Villa Ocotillo Apt 223 3327 N Civic Ctr Plaza Scottsdale AZ 85251

FERRIS, (CARLISLE) KEITH
ILLUSTRATOR, PAINTER
b Honolulu, Hawaii, May 14, 29. *Study:* Tex A&M Col; George Washington Univ; Corcoran Sch Art. *Comn:* Murals, Nat Air & Space Mus, Smithsonian Inst, Washington, DC, 76 & 81; and others. *Exhib:* USAF Exhib, New York Soc Illusr, 61-78; USAF Hq, The Pentagon, Washington, DC; one-man shows, Aerospace Hall, Nat Air & Space Mus, Smithsonian Inst, Washington, DC, 69-70, New York Soc Illusr, 70 & 79, Air Force Mus, 83 & US Air Force Acad, 83. *Pos:* Art dir/prod mgr, Cassell Watkins Paul Art Studio, St Louis, 52-56; chmn, Air Force Art Comt, Soc Illusr, 68-70 & 79- *Awards:* Citation of Merit, Soc Illusr, 66; Arts & Lett Award, Air Force Asn, NJ, 77; Citation of Honor, Air Force Asn, 78. *Mem:* Graphic Artists Guild; NY Soc Illusr. *Media:* Oil. *Mailing Add:* 50 Moraine Rd Morris Plains NJ 07950

FERRITER, CLARE
PAINTER, COLLAGE ARTIST
b Dickinson, NDak, June 18, 13. *Study:* Mass Col Art, Boston; Yale Univ, BFA; Stanford Univ, MA. *Work:* Butler Inst Am Art, Youngstown, Ohio; Harcourt, Brace, Jovanovich, Inc, New York; George Washington Univ; Massillon Mus, Ohio; Addison Gallery Am Art, Andover, Mass. *Comn:* Portrait of Miss H D Lamont, comn by Class of 1909 for Westover Sch, Middlebury, Conn, 59; portrait, Dr Vincent McKelvey, Friends US Geological Survey, 78. *Exhib:* One-man shows, Univ PR Mus, 62, Corcoran Gallery Art, Washington, DC, 63, Franz Bader Gallery, Washington, DC, 64 & 76 & Int Monetary Fund, Washington, DC, 73; Four Decades of Growth & Distinguished Mid-Atlantic Artists, Univ Delaware, 80. *Teaching:* Instr art, MacMurray Col, 36-38; instr art, Westover Sch, 40-42; lectr painting, Cath Univ Am, 66- *Awards:* Nat Asn Women Artists, 63 & 66; Baltimore Mus, 66; Soc Washington Artists, 64, 66 & 72. *Bibliog:* Barbara Martin Johnson (auth), Conversation with Clare Ferriter, Washington Rev, 45/79. *Mem:* Nat Asn Women Artists; Washington Watercolor Asn; Artists Equity Asn. *Publ:* Illustr, Manila lights and shadows (weekly page), Manila Sun Tribune Mag, 10/4/31-8/32; illustr, covers in Philippine Mag, 9/32-2/33. *Dealer:* Franz Bader Gallery 2001 Pennsylvania Ave Washington DC 20037. *Mailing Add:* 4722 Rodman St NW Washington DC 20016

FERRO, WALTER
PRINTMAKER, DESIGNER
b Brooklyn, NY. *Study:* Art Students League, 46-48; Brooklyn Mus Art Sch, color theory with John Ferren, 48-52. *Work:* Permanent print collection, Metrop Mus Art, New York; First Nat Bank, Chicago. *Exhib:* Audubon Artists, 53; Am Inst Graphic Artists, 56 & Soc Am Graphic Artists, New York, 59; United Nations Traveling Exhib, 66; one-man show, Kings Col, 67. *Awards:* Kenneth Hays Miller Mem Prize, Audubon Artists, 53; Kate W Arms Mem Award, Soc Am Graphic Artists, 59; Guggenheim Fel, 72. *Bibliog:* Norman Kent (auth), The woodcuts of Walter Ferro, Am Artist Mag, 1/62. *Media:* Woodcuts. *Publ:* illusr, Beowulf, Random, 62; illusr, Hold April, McGraw, 62; illusr, UN calendar, UN, 66; illusr, The invisible pyramid, Scribner, 70; illusr, Another Kind of Autumn, Scribners, 77. *Mailing Add:* RD 2 Hoyt Rd Pound Ridge NY 10576

FERRON, MARCELLE
PAINTER, GLASS ARTIST
Study: Prof-Agregee. *Work:* Mus Stedelick, Amsterdam; Mus Sao Paulo; Mus of British Arts, Montreal; Mus Quebec; Nat Gallery Can. *Comn:* Metro Govt Quebec, 67; metro-vendome, City of Montreal, 78; murals, La Portage, Can Govt, 74; sculpture, Int Aviation, 76; stained glass, church, Quebec; and others. *Exhib:* Antagnismes, Le Louvre, Paris, 59; Les Automatistes J Borduas, Grand Palais, Paris, 72; Peintres Canadians, Tate Gallery, London, 66; Silver Medals Biennial, Sao Paulo, 61; one-woman shows, Paris, 57, 60 & 72, Bruxelles & Munich, 58, 62 & 66. *Awards:* Silver Medal, Sao-Paolo; Gold Medal, Que. *Dealer:* Galerie Gilles Corbeil 2165 Crescent Montreal PQ H3G 2C1 Can; Walter Moos 139 Korkville Toronto ON. *Mailing Add:* 218 Bloomfield Outremont PQ H2V 3R4 Canada

FESSLER, ANN HELENE
BOOK ARTIST, PHOTOGRAPHER
b Toledo, Ohio, Oct 2, 49. *Study:* Ohio State Univ, Columbus, BA, 72; Webster Col, St Louis, MA(media), 75; Univ Ariz, MFA(photog), 82. *Work:* Whitney Mus Am Art; Ctr Creative Photog; Mus Contemp Art, Chicago; Franklin Furnace Book Arch, New York; Swedish Arch Artists Books, Bjarred. *Exhib:* Ctr Exploratory & Perceptual Arts, Buffalo, 82; Int Book Exhib, Ministerio Cult, Madrid, Spain, 82; Copycat Show, Franklin Furnace, New York, 82; Photography as Phantasy, Santa Barbara Mus, 82; Photography 1983, Pomona Col, 83; and others. *Teaching:* Instr photog & video, Webster Col, St Louis, 75-79; vis artist photog, Tyler Sch Art, 81-82; instr photog, film & books, Md Inst Col Art, 82- *Bibliog:* Articles, Afterimage, 2/83 & Am Photogr, 9/83. *Mem:* Soc Photog Educ. *Publ:* Auth, Guide to Coloring Hair, 82, First Aid For the Wounded, 82, Life Saving & Water Safety, 82, Horses, 82-83 & Animal Loco Motion Plastique, 83-84, pvt publ. *Dealer:* Books: Printed Matter New York NY; Washington Proj Arts Washington DC. *Mailing Add:* 2807 Goodwood Rd Baltimore MD 21214

FESSLER, MARY THOMASITA
SCULPTOR, EDUCATOR
b Milwaukee, Wis, Feb 23, 12. *Study:* St Mary's Acad; Univ Wis-Milwaukee, BE; Art Inst Chicago, BFA & MFA; Marquette Univ, DFA(hon), 76. *Comn:* Two wood mosaic murals, Marquette Univ Mem Libr; mahogany carved sanctuary crucifix, outdoor stone sculpture, rectory crucifix & wood mosaic stations of the cross for the Sisters' Chapel, St Cyprian's Church, River Grove, Ill; stained glass windows, St Xavier's Hosp, Dubuque, Iowa; and others. *Exhib:* New York, Washington, DC, Dayton, Ohio, Seattle, Wash, Chicago & many others. *Pos:* Mem Am deleg, 1st Int Cong Cath Artists, Rome, 50; Milwaukee Art Ctr Exhib Comt, 50-; bd mem, Milwaukee Children's Arts Prog, 52-; US rep, 4th Int Assembly Int Soc Educ through Art, Montreal, PQ, 63; Gov Coun on Arts, 63-; adv bd Arts & Activities Mag; adv bd, Wis Montessori Soc, 63- *Teaching:* St Anthony's High Sch, Sterling, Colo; St Mary's Acad, Milwaukee; chmn art dept, Cardinal Stritch Col, 47-; also summer sessions at Cath Univ Am, Univ Notre Dame, St Martin's Col, Maryhurst Col, Holy Name Col & Marquette Univ; also world-wide lect on liturgical art; summer art study tour dir to all parts of the world. *Awards:* Friends of Art Award, 64; Quota Club Women of Achievement Award, 64; Award of Excellence, Milwaukee Art Comm; plus others. *Bibliog:* Articles in Liturgical Arts, J Arts & Lett, Cath Art Quart & many others. *Mem:* Liturgical Arts Asn; Col Art Asn Am; Nat Art Educ Asn; Int Soc for Educ through Art; Wis Arts Comm; and others. *Publ:* Auth, articles in New World, Everyday Art, Cath Trends in Art Educ, Salesianum & Sch Arts; and others. *Mailing Add:* Studio San Damiano Milwaukee WI 53217

FETT, WILLIAM F
INSTRUCTOR, PAINTER
b Ann Arbor, Mich, Sept 22, 18. *Study:* Sch Art Inst, Chicago. *Work:* Mus Mod Art, New York; Mus Mod Art, Rome, Italy; Chicago Art Inst; Mus Mod Art, Mexico City; Weatherspoon Art Gallery, Univ NC, Greensboro. *Exhib:* Romantic Paintings in America, Mus Mod Art, New York, 43; one-man shows, Int Watercolor Show, Art Inst Chicago, 44, De Young Mus, San Francisco, 54 & Weatherspoon Art Gallery, Univ NC, Greensboro, 71; Seattle Art Mus, Wash, 45; Santa Barbara Mus Art, Calif, 45; Mex-Am Cult Inst, Mexico City, 65; Watercolor USA, Springfield Art Mus, Mo, 71. *Teaching:* Prof drawing & painting, Art Sch, Washington Univ, St Louis, Mo, 46-81, prof emeritus, 81- *Awards:* Anna Louise Raymond Grad Student Award, Art Inst Chicago, 41-43; Fulbright Scholar to Italy, US Govt, 50-51. *Media:* Watercolor, Oil; Charcoal. *Publ:* Articles in View Mag, View Inc, New York, 43; Dyn Mag, Wolfgang Paalen, Mex, 45 & Romantic Paintings in America, Mus Mod Art, New York, 44. *Mailing Add:* 152 Shadwell Drive San Antonio TX 78228

FEUERHERM, KURT K
PAINTER

b Berlin, Ger, Mar 22, 25. *Study:* Albright Art Sch; Univ Buffalo, BFA; Cranbrook Acad Art, MFA; Yale Summer Sch, Norfolk, Conn, with NaumGabo, Peter Blume & Ben Shahn; Yale Univ, with Josef Albers, Stuart Davis & Abraham Rattner. *Work:* Cranbrook Art Mus, Bloomfield Hills, Mich; Mem Art Gallery, Rochester, NY; Albright-Knox Art Gallery, Buffalo, NY; Henry Gallery, Univ Wash, Seattle; Am Fedn Art. *Comn:* Ceramic abstract mural, Midtown Plaza, Rochester, NY, 64; Stations on the Cross, Our Lady of Mercy Church, Rochester, 64; St John's the Evangelist Church, Rochester, 65; Liberty Pole (consult designer), City of Rochester, 66. *Exhib:* American Painting Today, Metrop Mus Art, New York, 50; Cranbrook Painting Exhib, Bloomfield Hills, Mich, 52; Columbia Mus of Art Painting Biennial, SC, 57; Everson Mus Art, Syracuse, NY, 57-70; one-man show, Henry Gallery, Univ Wash, Seattle, 69; New York Crafts, Munson-Williams-Proctor Inst, Utica, NY, 61; four-man show, Mem Art Gallery, Univ Rochester Fac Show, 70; and others. *Pos:* Conservator, Intermuseum Lab, Oberlin, Ohio, 71-72. *Teaching:* Asst prof painting, Univ Rochester, NY, 60-71; assoc prof studio arts, Empire State Col, Rochester, 73- *Awards:* Purchase Awards (painting & watercolor), Cortland Art Mus, 53; Award of Merit, Columbia Painting Biennial, 57; Henri Projansky Award, Rochester Finger Lakes Exhib, 69. *Media:* Collage, Acrylic. *Dealer:* Oxford Gallery 267 Oxford St Rochester NY 14607; Malton Gallery 2709 Observatory Ave Cincinnati OH 45208. *Mailing Add:* 431 1/2 South Ave Rochester NY 14620

FEUERSTEIN, ROBERTA
DEALER

b Los Angeles, Calif, Apr 16, 50. *Pos:* Dir-owner, Gallery West. *Specialty:* Contemporary prints, paintings and sculpture. *Mailing Add:* c/o Gallery West 107 S Robertson Blvd Los Angeles CA 90048

FICHTER, HERBERT FRANCIS
PRINTMAKER, PAINTER

b Jamaica, Long Island, NY, Dec 25, 20. *Study:* Sch Art League Scholar, New York Sch Fine & Applied Arts, 39; Corcoran Sch Art, Washington, DC; spec instr with Hal Reed, 75-76. *Work:* Pennell Collection, Libr Cong, Washington, DC; J F Kennedy Libr, Mass; MGM Grand Hotel, Las Vegas, Nev; Life/Time Mag Collection, New York; Parker Farms Collection, El Centro, Calif. *Comn:* Portrait of B De Klyn, comn by Dr Ward De Klyn, Danbury, Conn, 57; Oil-Scotch motif, Vince Dundee, Scotch Mist Restaurant, LaCanada, Calif, 65; portrait of Kathy Woodhouse, comn by R Woodhouse, Sunland, Calif, 65; Oil figure, Stockton Elec Co, Montrose, Calif, 66; three paintings for pub rels, comn by William Freelove for McDonalds, New Bern & Greenville, NC, 74-75. *Exhib:* Soc Am Etchers, Kennedy Gallery, New York, 52; Bi-Ann, Corcoran Gallery Art, Washington, DC, 53; Bi-Ann, Laguna Mus Art, Calif, 76; Nat Exhib, Fla Miniature Soc, Clearwater, 77; Nat Exhib, Soc Miniature Soc, Clinton, 78; two-man show, Burbank Creative Arts Ctr, Calif, 51; one-man show, Intalgio Graphics, Smithsonian Inst, Washington, DC, 51. *Pos:* Banknote Engraver, Bur of Engraving & Printing, Washington, DC, 41-54. *Teaching:* Instr in banknote engraving, Vignette Engraving, Jefferies Banknote Co, Los Angeles, 62- *Awards:* Purchase, Ann Pennell, Libr Cong, 51; Kate W Arms Mem, Kennedy Gallery, Soc Am Etchers, 52; First Graphics, Nat Exhib, Miniature Art Soc NJ, 78. *Bibliog:* Man of Steel, article in Ticor Mag, 74; Staff auth of Bank of Am, Traveler's Checques, Banking Bus, 72; American Print Collection, John Hopkins Press. *Mem:* Coun of Traditional Artists, Pasadena, Calif (bd mem), San Gabriel Fine Arts Assn; NJ Miniature Soc, 80; Laguna Art-A-Fair Festival, Calif. *Media:* Intaglio, Engraving through Mezzotint; Oils on Canvas & Panels. *Mailing Add:* c/o Jeffries Banknote Co 1330 W Pico Blvd Los Angeles CA 90015

FICHTER, ROBERT W
ARTIST, EDUCATOR

b Ft Myers, Fla, 1939. *Study:* Univ Fla, BFA(printmaking & painting), 63; Ind Univ, MFA, 66. *Work:* Int Mus Photog, George Eastman House, Rochester, NY; Pasadena Art Mus, Calif; Nat Gallery of Can, Ottawa; Mus Fine Arts, Boston, Mass; Princeton Univ, NJ; and others. *Exhib:* Contemp Photog from the Collections, Boston Mus Fine Arts, 74; Photog Unlimited, Fogg Mus, Harvard Univ, Cambridge, Mass, 74; The Art of Offset Printing, Sch Art Inst Chicago, 78; My Teacher, My Self, Susan Spiritus Gallery, Newport Beach, Calif, 79; Northlight Gallery, Tempe, Ariz, 81; Film in the City, St Paul, Minn, 81; Northern Ky State Col, 81; Whitney Biennial, Whitney Mus Am Art, 81; Robert Freidus Gallery, New York, 81; and many other group and one-man shows. *Teaching:* Prof art, Fla State Univ, 72- *Awards:* Fels, Nat Endowment Arts, 80 & Fla Visual Arts, 81. *Bibliog:* Robert Sobieszek (ed), Robert Fichter, Photography and Other Questions, Univ Mex Press, 83. *Dealer:* Robert Freidus Gallery Inc 70 Green St New York NY 10013. *Mailing Add:* 612 W Eighth Ave Tallahassee FL 32303

FIDLER, SPENCER D
PRINTMAKER

b Detroit, Mich, Nov 20, 44. *Study:* Calif State Univ, Northridge, BA, 66; Univ Iowa, MA, 76 & MFA, 78. *Exhib:* 12th & 13th Nat Print Exhib, The Silvermine Guild Artists, Conn, 78 & 80; Prix de Paris, Raymond Duncan Gallery, France, 79; Premio Int Biella per L'incisione, Italy, 80; Comparisons and Contrasts, Exchange exhib between the US & Soviet Union, 80-82; 24th Nat Print Exhib, Hunterdon Art Ctr, NJ, 81; Cabo Frio Int Print Biennial, Rio de Janiero, Brazil, 82-83. *Teaching:* Asst prof printmaking, NMex State Univ, Las Cruces, 78- *Awards:* First Prize, Westwood Art Asn Print Competition, 77; Purchase Award, Dulin Nat Print Competition, 78. *Mem:* Col Art Asn; Boston Printmakers; Southern Graphics Coun. *Dealer:* Miriam Perlman Inc Chicago IL. *Mailing Add:* 221 Oxford Dr Las Cruces NM 88001

FIELD, LYMAN
ADMINISTRATOR, COLLECTOR

b Kansas City, Mo, Oct 6, 14. *Study:* Univ Kans, AB, 36; Harvard Law Sch, LLB, 39. *Pos:* Founding mem, Mo State Coun on Arts, 65-75, chmn, 66-74; trustee, Samuel H Kress Found, New York, 65-; founding mem & 1st chmn, North Am Assembly of State & Prov Arts Agencies, 68-70; trustee & bd dir, Kansas City Art Inst, 69-74; mem bd dir, Findlay Galleries, Chicago, New York, Palm Beach, Fla & Paris, 72-76; participant, 46th Am Assembly on Art Mus, Arden House, Harriman, NY, 75; chmn, Thomas Hart Benton Homestead Mem Adv Comn of Mo, 75-, trustee Benton Testamentary Trusts; trustee, Mo Repertory Theater; co-chmn, Mid-West Regional Assembly on Future of Performing Arts, 79. *Mem:* Samuel H Kress Found, New York (trustee, 65-); Mid-Am Arts Alliance, Mo (mem bd dir, 71-); Kansas City Soc of Western Art (mem bd dir, 75-); Soc Fellows Atkins-Nelson Gallery of Art, Kansas City, Mo. *Collection:* Thomas Hart Benton paintings & lithographs; Jansem, Kluge, Michel Henry & Ardissone paintings. *Mailing Add:* 600 E 11th St Kansas City MO 64106

FIELD, PHILIP SIDNEY
PAINTER, PRINTMAKER

b Brooklyn, NY, Sept 17, 42. *Study:* Art Students League, with Arnold Blanch; Yale Norfolk Summer Sch Music & Art, 62; Syracuse Univ, BFA, 63; RI Sch Design, with Michael Mazur, MFA, 65; Vienna Acad Fine Arts, Fulbright Grant, 65-67. *Work:* Hunterdon Art Ctr, Clinton, NJ; Syracuse Univ; Univ Dallas; Tulsa City-Co Libr, Okla. *Exhib:* Prints, Drawings & Crafts Ann, 74 & 76 & Fantastic Images & Imaginary Worlds, 75, Ark Arts Ctr; Boston Printmakers Ann, Boston Mus Fine Arts, 75; Nat Print Show, Hunterdon Art Ctr, 75; Southwestern Prints & Drawings, Dallas Mus Fine Arts, 75; Miami Graphics Biennale, Fla, 75; Third Print Invitational, Univ Dallas, 76; Dulin Nat Print & Drawing Competition, Dulin Gallery Art, Knoxville, Tenn, 76 & 77; Nat Print & Drawing Competition, Okla Art Ctr, Oklahoma City, 76 & 77; and many other group and one-man shows. *Pos:* Critic, For Art's Sake, column, McAllen Monitor, 80-81. *Teaching:* Instr art studio, Juniata Col, Huntingdon, Pa, 69-70; from instr to asst prof, Pan Am Univ, 71-82. *Awards:* Augusta Hazard Award, Lowe Art Ctr, Syracuse Univ, 63; Merchants Prize, Corpus Christi Art Found Ann, 72; Purchase Award, Prints, Drawings & Crafts Ann, Ark Art Ctr, 74. *Bibliog:* Al Brunelle (auth), article, Art News, 5/73; Maurice Schmidt (auth), Reflections on art, 1/76 & Art, light and history 6/76, Corpus Christi Caller. *Mem:* Col Art Asn. *Media:* Intaglio; Oil. *Mailing Add:* 221 E Van Week St Edinburg TX 78539

FIELD, RICHARD SAMPSON
CURATOR, HISTORIAN

b New York, NY, Aug 26, 31. *Study:* Harvard Univ, AB, AM & PhD. *Collections Arranged:* 15th Century Woodcuts & Metalcuts from the National Gallery of Art (with catalog), 65; Jasper Johns: Prints 1960-1970 (with catalog), 70 & Silkscreen: History of a Medium (with catalog), 71, Philadelphia Mus Art; The Fable of the Sick Lion: A Fifteenth Century Blockbook (with catalog), 74, Gabriel de Sanit-Aubin (with catalog), 75, Jasper Johns: Prints 1970-1977, 78, Prints Drawings and Paintings by Philip Pearlstein, 79 & The Prints of Armand Seguin (1869-1903), 80, Davison Art Ctr, Wesleyan Univ; Fifteenth Century Woodcuts, Metrop Mus Art, 77. *Pos:* Asst to dir, Fogg Art Mus, Cambridge, Mass, 61-62; asst cur of prints, Alverthorpe Gallery-Nat Gallery Art, 62-68 & Philadelphia Mus Art, 69-72; cur, Davison Art Ctr, Wesleyan Univ, Middletown, Conn, 72-79; cur prints, drawings & photographs & assoc dir, Art Gallery, Yale Univ, New Haven, Conn, 79- *Teaching:* Assoc prof art, Wesleyan Univ, 72-79. *Awards:* Fulbright Grant, France, 59-60; Finley Fel, Nat Gallery Art, 65-67. *Mem:* Print Coun Am (dir, 70-72). *Res:* Fifteenth century woodcuts; Gauguin; contemporary prints. *Publ:* Auth, Gauguin's Noa Noa suite, Burlington Mag, 68; auth, Woodcuts from Altomunster, Gutenberg-Jahrbuch, 69; auth, Gauguin's Monotypes, 73; auth, The Prints of Richard Hamilton, 73. *Mailing Add:* Cedar Swamp Rd Deep River CT 06417

FIELD, ROBERT JAMES See Fish, Robert

FIELD, SAUL
PRINTMAKER, LECTURER

b Montreal, Que, Jan 12, 12. *Work:* Montreal Mus Fine Art; Philadelphia Mus Fine Art; Nat Libr Can; Dante Alighieri Soc, Rome; Nat Diet Libr, Tokyo. *Exhib:* Judaica Suite, Expo 67, Montreal, 67; Artists in Books, Nat Libr Can, Ottawa, 81; Tales of Heritage, Nat Arts Ctr, Ottawa, 81 & Can Embassy, Tel Aviv, Debut Mus, Beaux Arts, Budapest & Athens Col, Greece, 83; Joyce and Yeats, Can House, London, England & Sligo Art Gallery, Ireland, 83. *Teaching:* Lectr printmaking, Univ Toronto, 69-70 & York Univ, 70-79. *Awards:* Purchase Award, Glenhurst Art Gallery, Brantford, Ont, 64; Grand Prix Award, Second Int Miniature Print Exhib, 82. *Mem:* Ont Soc Artists; Printmakers Can (pres, 67-); Can Soc Graphic Artists; Can Painters & Etchers Soc. *Mailing Add:* 69 Banstock Dr Willowdale ON M2K 2H7 Canada

FIELDS, FREDRICA H
STAINED GLASS ARTIST, GLASS ENGRAVER

b Haverford, Pa, Jan 10, 12. *Study:* Landscape painting with Frank Morley Fletcher, 30 & Frank Logan, 31; Wellesley Col, 30-32; Art Students League, with Nicolaides, 33; stained glass with Mrs Orin Skinner, 38-39 & with George Sotter, 51. *Work:* Nat Cathedral, Washington, DC; YWCA, Greenwich; The Conn Hospice Inc, Branford; Concordia Col Chapel & Libr, Bronxville, NY; Asn Res & Enlightenment Prayer & Meditation Libr, Virginia Beach. *Exhib:* 9th & 11th Ann Area Exhibs, Corcoran Gallery of Art, Washington, DC, 55 & 56; Nat Conf on Relig Arch, New York, 67; Greenwich Art Soc Ann Exhibs, Conn, 68-78; Danbury Pub Libr, Conn, 74;

one-woman exhibs, Artist's Mart, Washington, DC, 55; First Presbyterian Church, Stamford, Conn, 76. *Teaching:* Instr stained glass, YWCA, Greenwich, 66-67 & pvt studio, 68-71. *Awards:* For stained glass, 4th & 6th Int Exhib of Ceramic Arts, Nat Collection of Fine Arts, 53 & 57; 9th & 11th Ann Area Exhib, Corcoran Gallery of Art, 55 & 56; work included in US Info Agency Traveling Exhib, 57. *Mem:* Stained Glass Asn Am; Greenwich Art Soc. *Publ:* Contribr, Stained Glass Asn Am Quart, 58-75; contribr, The Complete Book of Creative Glass Art, 74; contribr, Step by Step Stained Glass, 74; contribr, Decorating Glass, 76. *Mailing Add:* 561 Lake Ave Greenwich CT 06830

FIERO, GLORIA K
EDUCATOR, HISTORIAN
b New York, NY, May 19, 39. *Study:* Univ Miami, Coral Gables, AB, 60; Univ Calif, Berkeley, MA, 61; Fla State Univ, Tallahassee, PhD, 70. *Teaching:* Assoc prof art hist, Univ Southwestern La, 69- *Awards:* Woodrow Wilson Hon Fel, 60; Fulbright Fel to Belg, 66-67; Amoco Found Award Outstanding Teaching, 83. *Mem:* Col Art Asn Am; Southeastern Col Art Conf; Int Ctr Medieval Art. *Res:* Late medieval, northern renaissance painting and manuscripts; early 20th century painting. *Publ:* Auth, Dante's Ledge of Pride; literary pictorialism and the visual arts, J European Studies, 75; auth, Smith MS 36: A study of fifteenth century manuscript illumination, Courier, 76; auth, Courtier and commoner: Two styles of fifteenth century manuscript illumination, Explorations Renaissance Cult, 77; auth, The Humanistic Tradition: Chapters in the History of Culture to 1650, Univ Press Am, 81; auth, Geertgen tot Sint Jans and the Dutch manuscript tradition, Oud Holland, 82. *Mailing Add:* 327 Bacque Crescent Dr Lafayette LA 70503

FIFE, MARY (MRS EDWARD LANING)
PAINTER
b Canton, Ohio. *Study:* Carnegie Inst Technol, BA; Cooper Union; Acad Russe, Paris, France; Art Students League. *Exhib:* Metrop Mus Art & Whitney Mus Am Art, New York; Art Inst Chicago; one-man shows, Pen & Brush Inc, New York & Brooklyn Art Gallery, NY; and others. *Teaching:* Instr drawing, Kansas City Art Inst, Mo, 45-50; head dept art, Birch-Wathem Sch, New York, 61-70. *Awards:* Figure Prize, Nat Acad Design, 67; Elizabeth McGenius Award, 70; Doris Kreindler Prize, 79. *Mem:* Pen & Brush Inc; Nat Asn Women Artists. *Media:* Oil. *Mailing Add:* 82 State St Brooklyn NY 11201

FIFIELD, MARY
EDUCATOR
b Chicago, Ill, Apr 10, 46. *Study:* Clarke Col, AB; Univ Madrid; Art Inst Chicago; Pratt Inst, fel, 70-71, with Elaine de Kooning, Irving Sandler, Walter Rogalski & Ralph Wickiser, MFA; St Louis Univ, 83-84. *Exhib:* 26th Ill Exhib, Ill State Mus, 73; 37th Ann Midyear Show, Butler Inst Am Art, Ohio, 73; Small Paintings USA traveling exhib, Gallery North, 74; Mid South Biennial, Brooks Mem Art Gallery, Memphis, Tenn, 75; Contemporary Issues: Works on Paper by Women, Womens Bldg, Los Angeles, 77. *Pos:* Guest artist, SC Arts Comn, 74; design workshop dir, Lindenwood Cols, 74-75. *Teaching:* Asst prof design, color, drawing & printmaking, St Louis Community Col, 72-77, chmn dept, 77-81, assoc prof, 78- *Awards:* Positano Art Workshop Fel, Italy, 70; Ford Found Grant, 71; Leaders fo the 80s FIPSE Grant, 83. *Bibliog:* George Constable (auth), Show offers wide range of talent, Mansfield News J, 71; Mary King (auth), Painting, photographs by Forest Park Faculty, St Louis Post Dispatch, 74. *Mem:* Col Art Asn Am; Mid Am Col Art Asn; Am Asn Higher Educ. *Media:* Acrylic, Intaglio. *Publ:* Co-auth, Contemporary Women Artists, Forest Park Community Col, 74; coauth, Contemporary Black Artists, St Louis Community Col, 79; coauth, Advertising Design and Commercial Art: An Employer and Institutional Needs Assessment, 81; ed, Anger to action: A sex discrimination guidebook. *Mailing Add:* St Louis Community Col 5600 Oakland St Louis MO 63110

FILIPOVIC, AUGUSTIN
SCULPTOR, PAINTER
b Davor, Yugoslavia, Jan 8, 31; Can citizen. *Study:* Acad Fine Art, Rome. *Work:* Art Gallery Ont, Toronto; Ft William Libr, Ont; Palazzo Braschi, Rome, Italy; The Inn on the Park, Toronto, Ont; Montreal Mus Fine Arts, Can. *Comn:* Reclining figure (bronze), Parkin & Assocs for Don Mills Post Off, 69; poster 25th anniversary, Can Opera Co, 73. *Exhib:* Mostra Arte Lazio, Rome, Italy, 55; Nat Gallery Art, Ottawa, Ont, 62; Gallery Moos, Toronto, 67 & 73; Gallery Agnes Lefort, Montreal, PQ, 68; Bertha Schaefer Gallery, New York, 71 & 73. *Teaching:* Resident sculptor, Univ Toronto Sch Archit, 62; sessional lectr, Brock Univ, 77-81 & Guelph Univ, 81. *Awards:* Second Prize, Mostra Arte Lazio, Rome, 52; Prize of the Mayor of Rome, via Margutta, Rome, 58; Prize in Centennial Competition, Niagara Falls, 66. *Mem:* Sculpture Soc Can; Royal Canadian Acad. *Media:* Bronze. *Mailing Add:* c/o Gallery Moos 138 Yorkville Toronto ON Canada

FILIPOWSKI, RICHARD E
SCULPTOR, EDUCATOR
b Poland, May 29, 23; US citizen. *Study:* Inst Design, Ill Inst Technol, with L Moholy-Nagy, BA. *Work:* Addison Gallery Am Art, Andover, Mass; State St Bank & Trust Co & First Nat Bank, Boston; Boston Safe Deposit & Trust Co; Chase Manhattan Bank, New York. *Comn:* Sculptural ark, Temple B'rith Kodesh, Rochester, 62; sculptural cross, Trinity Lutheran, Chelmsford, Mass, 63; sculpture, Atlantic, Sheraton Corp, Prudential Ctr, Boston, 64; sculptural cross, Trinity Evangel Lutheran, Philadelphia, 65; sculpture, Echo, Revere Copper & Brass Corp, New York, 65. *Exhib:* Art for US Embassies, Inst Contemp Art, Boston, 66; Nat Exhib Art, Ogunquit, Maine, 67; one-man shows, Fitchburg Art Mus, Mass, 68 & State Univ NY Col Oneonta, 69;

Outdoor Sculpture Exhib, De Cordova Mus, Lincoln, Mass, 72; sculpture exhib, Mass Inst Technol, 84. *Teaching:* Assoc prof visual design, Mass Inst Technol, 53- *Awards:* First Prize Sculpture, Boston Arts Festival, 58; Aleck & Ruth McLean Award, Nat Exhib Art, Ogunquit, 67. *Bibliog:* Katherine Kuh (auth), Abstract and surrealist American art, Art Inst Chicago, 48; Patricia Boyd Wilson (auth), The home forum, Christian Sci Monitor, 65; Phoebe Cutler (auth), Richard Filipowski's sculpture, Harvard Art Rev, 67. *Media:* Bronze, Brass, Silver, Steel, Aluminum. *Mailing Add:* 10 Round Hill Rd Lexington MA 02173

FILKOSKY, JOSEFA
SCULPTOR, EDUCATOR
b Westmoreland City, Pa, June 15, 33. *Study:* Seton Hill Col, BA, 55; Carnegie-Mellon Univ, BFA, 63; Cranbrook Acad Art, MFA, 68; Art Inst Chicago, 68. *Comn:* Pipe Dream IX, Taubman Corp, Southfield; Pipe Dreams I & II, Oxford Merchandise Mart, Monroeville, Pa; Pipe Theme in Oranges II, Everson Mus, 76; Pipe Theme in Oranges II, St Lawrence Univ, NY, 76; Pipe Dream IV, Spirals in Blue, Pittsburgh, Pa, 82. *Exhib:* One-man shows, The Art Image In All Media, NY, 70, Ind Univ, 72 & Bertha Schaefer Gallery, New York, 73; two-man show, Pittsburgh Plan for Art, 71, 73 & 75; Sculpture in the Fields, Storm King Art Ctr, 74-76; Sculpture on Shoreline Sites, Roosevelt Island, New York, 79-80. *Teaching:* Prof art, Seton Hill Col, 56- *Awards:* Three Rivers Purchase Award, 72; Assoc Artists Pittsburgh Award, 76; Nat Grant, St Lawrence Univ, 76. *Bibliog:* Suzanne Vlamis (auth), Pipe Dream Nun, M D Mag, 5/72; Suzanne Benton (auth), Metal Sculpture, 75; Sandak Slide Set, Am Woman's Art, 74. *Mem:* Assoc Artists Pittsburgh; Sculptors Guild New York. *Media:* Aluminum, Steel Pipe. *Dealer:* Dorothea Silverman 500 E 83rd St New York NY 10028; Laudra Pharus Personalized Art Services Pittsburgh PA. *Mailing Add:* Seton Hill Col Greensburg PA 15601

FILLERUP, MEL
PAINTER
b Lovell, Wyo, Jan 28, 24. *Study:* Art Students League; study with Paul Bransom, Serge Bongart, William Reese, Conrad Schwiering & Robert Meyers. *Comn:* Husky dogs, Husky Oil Co; mural, Vis Ctr, Cody, Wyo. *Exhib:* Western States Show, Cody Country Art League, 65-75; Springville Art Mus Show, 70-75; C M Russell Auction, Great Falls, Mont; Wind River Artists Asn; New York Life Ann Calendar Competition; NAm Wild Animal Art Exhib, 79. *Teaching:* Oil painting, North West Community Col, 74-75. *Awards:* First Place, Cody Country Art League, 68 & 76; Gold Medal, Int Asn Art Critics, 81 & 82; Bronze Medal Watercolor, Western Artists Am Show, 83. *Mem:* Am Indian & Cowboy Artists; Cody Country Artist Asn (pres, 68-70); Soc Animal Artists. *Media:* Oil, Watercolor. *Mailing Add:* PO Box 938 Cody WY 82414

FILMUS, MICHAEL ROY
PAINTER
b New York, NY, May 12, 43. *Study:* Boston Univ, BA, 66; Art Students League. *Work:* Berkshire Mus, Pittsfield, Mass; Minneapolis Inst Art. *Exhib:* Drawings USA, Minn Mus Art, 75; solo exhib, Hirschl & Adler Galleries, New York, 75, 77 & 79; Albrecht Mus Art, 76; 200 Years of American Art, Berkshire Mus, Pittsfield, Mass, 76; Flint Inst Arts, Mich, 77; Art of the State, Rose Art Mus, Waltham, Mass, 79; Contemporary Naturalism, Nassau Co Mus Fine Art, Roslyn Harbor, NY, 80; and others. *Awards:* Purchase Prize, 40th Ann Midyear Show, Butler Inst Am Art, 76. *Mem:* Artists Equity; Art Students League. *Media:* Oil, Pastel. *Dealer:* David Findlay Jr Contemporary 41 E 57th St New York NY 10022. *Mailing Add:* 50 Bartlett Ave Pittsfield MA 01201

FILMUS, TULLY
PAINTER, LECTURER
b Otaki, Russia, Aug 29, 08; US citizen. *Study:* Pa Acad Fine Arts, Philadelphia; NY Univ; Barnes Found, Philadelphia; Art Students League; Crisson traveling scholar for study in Paris & Rome. *Work:* Metrop Mus Art & Whitney Mus Am Art, New York; Joslyn Art Mus, Omaha; Butler Inst of Art, Youngstown, Ohio; Univ of NC Permanent Collection; St Lawrence Univ Permanent Collection, Canton, NY; and others. *Exhib:* Whitney Mus Am Art, 40-46; Art Inst Chicago, 41; Carnegie Inst Int, Pittsburgh, 41-46; Pa Acad Fine Arts, Philadelphia, 41-46; Corcoran Gallery Art, Washington, DC, 42; Yeshiva Univ Mus, NY, 77; one-man shows, ACA Gallery, New York, 71, The Berkshire Mus, Pittsfield, Mass, 73 & 80 & ACA Gallery, Rome, Italy, 74. *Teaching:* Instr painting & drawing, Am Artists Sch, New York, 36-38 & Cooper Union Art Sch, New York, 38-50. *Awards:* Pa Acad Fine Arts Fel, 41; Salmagundi Prize, Audubon Artists, 69. *Bibliog:* Dr Alfred Werner (auth), The painter Tully Filmus, World Publs, 63; Tully Filmus--selected drawings, Jewish Publ, 71. *Mem:* Artist Equity NY; Audubon Artists; Art Comn Nassau Co, NY. *Media:* Oil. *Dealer:* ACA Gallery 21 E 67th St New York NY 10021. *Mailing Add:* 17 Stuart St Great Neck NY 11023

FINCH, RUTH WOODWARD
PATRON, PHOTOGRAPHER
b Rochester, NY, Feb 27, 16. *Study:* Bryn Mawr Col, BA(art hist), 37; Le Louvre, Paris, France; Photographic Workshop, New Canaan, Conn. *Exhib:* Indians of the SW, Silvermine Guild Artists, Norwalk, Conn, 76; threemedia show, Waveny Arts Ctr, New Canaan, Conn, 79; Arteder Int Graphic Arts Show, Bilbao, Spain, 82; Am Indian Exhib, W J Sloane, Washington, DC, 83. *Pos:* Chmn, Photographic Exhibits, New Canaan Libr, 76- *Awards:* Albert Jacobson Patron's Award, Silvermine Guild Artists, 72; Save the Children Award-Am Indian Section, 83. *Mem:* Silvermine Guild of Artists (mem artists bd); Rowayton Arts Ctr, Conn; Friends of Photog, Carmel, Calif; New Canaan

Soc for the Arts, Conn; Int Ctr Photography, New York. *Interests:* American sculpture and prints by American artists; donation of a sculpture prize annually at Silvermine Guild of Artists, New England Show. *Mailing Add:* 1081 Ponus Ridge Rd New Canaan CT 06840

FINCHER, JOHN H
PAINTER
b Hamilton, Tex, Aug 4, 41. *Study:* Tex Tech Col, BA, 64; Univ Okla, MFA, 66. *Work:* Dallas Mus Fine Arts; Univ Okla Mus Fine Arts; Wichita Mus Art; Honolulu Acad. *Exhib:* Long Beach Mus Art, 72; one-man shows, Robert Rice Gallery, Houston, Tex, 77 & Elaine Horwitch Gallery, Santa Fe, NMex, 80; Eight NMex Painters, Elaine Horwitch Gallery, Scottsdale, Ariz, 79; New Works--NMex: Sarah Campbell Blaffer Gallery, Univ Houston, Tex, 81; and many others. *Teaching:* Assoc prof art, Wichita State Univ, 66-77. *Awards:* Wurlitzer Found Grant, Taos, NMex, 72. *Media:* Oil, Ink. *Mailing Add:* 202 W Lupita Santa Fe NM 87501

FINCK, FURMAN J
PAINTER, INSTRUCTOR
b Chester, Pa, Oct 10, 1900. *Study:* Pa Acad Fine Arts, dipl; Ecole des Beaux Arts & Acad Julian, Paris; Am Acad, Rome; Muhlenberg Col, DFA. *Work:* Mass Gen Hosp; Temple Univ Health Sci Ctr; Nat Portrait Gallery; Toledo Mus; Dartmouth House, London. *Comn:* Med faculty (portrait ser), Temple Univ, 44; med clinics (ser), Med Schs US, 45; portrait of President Truman, Nat Dem Club, New York, 50; portrait of President Eisenhower, Union League, Philadelphia, 54; deans schs pharm US (ser), Wyeth Labs, 60-64. *Exhib:* Pa Acad Fine Arts Ann; Carnegie Inst Int; Nat Acad Design Ann; Corcoran Gallery Art Biennial; Portraits Inc Ann; retrospective, Woodmere Art Gallery, Philadelphia. *Teaching:* Instr sci paint & painting, Cheltenham Art Ctr, Pa, 67; dean, du Cret Sch Arts, Plainfield, NJ, 68-70; mem staff painting, Philadelphia Mus Art, 69-78; fac mem, Nat Acad, 83- *Awards:* Cresson European Traveling Scholar, Pa Acad Fine Arts, 24; First Altman Prize, Nat Acad Design, 55; Krindler Prize, Salmagundi Club Ann, 64. *Bibliog:* Henry Pitz (auth), Furman Finck, Am Artist Mag, 3/56; Martin Zipin (auth), Finck paints a portrait (film), produced by WFIL-TV. *Mem:* Salmagundi Club; Twenty Five Year Club of Temple Univ; Players; Artists' Fellowship, Inc (pres, 73-77). *Media:* All. *Publ:* Auth, The meaning of art in education, Columbia Univ Publ, 38; coauth, The Artist as Teacher, Appleton, 50; auth, The artist and the architect, Am Inst Architects J, 59; auth, Complete Guide to Portrait Painting, Watson-Guptill, 70. *Mailing Add:* 285 Central Park W New York NY 10024

FINDLAY, DAVID B, JR
DEALER
b Kansas City, Mo, June 30, 33. *Study:* Cornell Univ, BME & MBA. *Pos:* Dir, David Findlay Jr Fine Art, currently. *Mailing Add:* David Findlay Jr Fine Art 41 E 57th St New York NY 10022

FINDLAY, HELEN T
DEALER
b Kansas City, Mo, July 21, 09. *Study:* Vassar Col, AB, 30. *Pos:* Dir, Wally Findlay Galleries Int, currently. *Awards:* Distinguised Women Award, Northwood Inst, 82. *Specialty:* Contemporary art. *Mailing Add:* Wally Findlay Galleries 814 N Michigan Ave Chicago IL 60611

FINDLAY, JAMES ALLEN
LIBRARIAN
b Saginaw, Mich, Aug 13, 43. *Study:* Wayne State Univ, BA, 70, MSLS, 72; Univ Calif, Los Angeles, MA, 75. *Pos:* Reference & cataloging libr, Univ Calif, Los Angeles Art Libr, 75-79; Latin Am archivist, Mus Mod Art Libr, New York, 79-82; dir, RI Sch Design Libr, 82- *Mem:* Art Libr Soc NAm; Col Art Asn. *Res:* Modern Latin American art; design. *Interests:* Modern art; architecture. *Publ:* Auth, Modern Art of Latin America: A Bibliography, Greenwood Press, 83. *Mailing Add:* 20A Benefit St Providence RI 02904

FINE, JUD
SCULPTOR, EDUCATOR
b Los Angeles, Calif, Nov 20, 44. *Study:* Univ Calif, Santa Barbara, BA; Cornell Univ, MFA. *Work:* Minneapolis Inst Art; Los Angeles Co Art Mus; Pasadena Mus Mod Art; Art Inst Chicago; Yale Univ Art Mus; and others. *Exhib:* Los Angeles Co Mus, 72; solo exhibs, Ron Feldman Gallery, New York, 72, 73, 75, 76, 78 & 81; Dayton's Gallery 12, Minneapolis, 73 & 74 & Margo Leavin Gallery, Los Angeles, 77, 79 & 81; 71st Am Exhib, Art Inst Chicago, 74; Inst Contemp Arts, Boston, 74; Indianapolis Mus Art, 76; Santa Barbara Mus Art, 78; and many others. *Teaching:* Assoc prof art, Univ Southern Calif, 79- *Awards:* Contemp Art Coun New Talent Grant, Los Angeles Co Art Mus, 72; Laura Slobe Mem Award, Art Inst Chicago, 74. *Bibliog:* Articles, Arts Mag, 9/74 & 3/75 & Artforum, 4/75; Arts Mag, 5/72, 10/73, 9/74 & 3/75. *Media:* Mixed. *Publ:* Auth, Or: An Introduction, 74 & Walk, 75, pvt publ. *Mailing Add:* 110 Center St Los Angeles CA 90012

FINE, PERLE
PAINTER
b Boston, Mass, May 1, 08. *Study:* Atelier 17; studied with Hans Hofmann & printmaking with William Hayter. *Work:* Whitney Mus Am Art, New York; Los Angeles Co Mus; Mus Mod Art, New York; Solomon R Guggenheim Mus of Non-Objective Art, New York; Brooklyn Mus, NY. *Exhib:* Art of this Century, Peggy Guggenheim Gallery, New York; Geometric Abstraction in Am & Nature in Abstraction, Whitney Mus Am Art, New York; Mex Biennial, Palacio Bellas Artes, Mexico City; Art of Assemblage, Mus Mod Art, New York; Galerie Zabriskie, Paris, France; Marian Willard Gallery,

New York; Betty Parsons Gallery, New York; and others. *Teaching:* Vis prof fine arts, Cornell Univ; assoc prof fine arts, Hofstra Univ. *Awards:* Purchase Award for Wood-Collage, Brooklyn Mus; Am Acad Arts & Lett Grant for Painting, 74; Nat Endowment Arts Grant. *Bibliog:* Lyricism in Abstract Art. *Mem:* Am Abstract Artists; Fedn Mod Painters & Sculptors; Guild Hall, East Hampton. *Media:* Oil, Acrylic. *Mailing Add:* 538 Old Stone Hwy East Hampton NY 11937

FINGESTEN, PETER
GRAPHIC ARTIST, EDUCATOR
b Berlin, Ger, Mar 20, 16; US citizen. *Study:* Hochschule Bildende Kuenste, Berlin, prof dipl; Pa Acad Fine Arts, cert; Asia Inst, New York, MA. *Comn:* Archit relief, Villa Mantero, Como, Italy, 38; sculpture of Christ (bust), First Presby Church, Washington, DC, 48; portrait, Glycerine Corp Am, New York, 54; mem plaque, Pace Univ, New York, 68. *Exhib:* Int Exhib Black & White, Milan, Italy, 38; Art of Democratic Living, Am Fedn Arts Nat Traveling Show, 46. *Teaching:* Instr art hist, Manhattan Col, New York, 46-50; lectr Asian art, Asia Inst, 50-51; prof art hist, Pace Univ, 50-, chmn dept art, 68- *Awards:* First Sculpture Award, Int Exhib Black & White, 38; Louis Comfort Tiffany Grant, 48; and others. *Bibliog:* Fortunate Fingesten, Time Mag, 3/4/40; J K Reed (auth), Fingesten's 30th, Art Digest, 3/1/47. *Mem:* Am Soc Aesthetics; Col Art Asn Am. *Media:* Watercolor. *Res:* Symbolism of art. *Publ:* Auth, East is East, Muehlenberg Press, 56; auth, The Eclipse of Symbolism, Univ SC Press, 70; auth, Symbolism and Reality, J Psycholinguistic Res, 71; auth, Surrealism and the Symbolic Paradox, Humanitas, spring 72. *Mailing Add:* Pace Univ 41 Park Row New York NY 10038

FINK, ALAN
DEALER
b Chicago, Ill, July 17, 25. *Study:* Univ Ill, BA. *Pos:* Dir, Alpha Gallery Inc. *Mem:* Asn Boston Art Dealers (pres). *Specialty:* Contemporary American painting, sculpture and graphics; modern master prints. *Mailing Add:* c/o Alpha Gallery 121 Newbury St Boston MA 02116

FINK, HERBERT LEWIS
PAINTER, EDUCATOR
b Providence, RI, Sept 8, 21. *Study:* Carnegie Inst Technol, 41; RI Sch Design, BFA, 49; Yale Univ, MFA, 56; Art Students League; also with John Frazier, Gabor Peterdi, Arshile Gorky & Rico Lebrun. *Work:* Univ Mich; Univ Iowa; Baltimore Mus Art; Md Inst; Brown Univ; and others. *Comn:* Mural, RI Post Off Lobby, Providence, 59; metal sculpture, Sen Green Airport, 60; archit screen, Hartford Bank & Trust Bldg. *Exhib:* Am Color Print Soc, 59; Soc Am Graphic Artists, 59; Art Dirs Ann, 59; Libr Cong, 59; Philadelphia Mus Art, 59; and others. *Pos:* Print ed, Int Graphic Arts Soc; trustee, Tiffany Found. *Teaching:* Instr painting & drawing, RI Sch Design, 51-61; instr, Yale Univ, 56-61; prof art & chmn dept, Southern Ill Univ, Carbondale, 61- *Awards:* Purchase Prizes, Soc Am Graphic Artists, 59 & Libr Cong, 59; Purchase Prize, Libr Cong, 59; Guggenheim Fel, 65-66; and others. *Mailing Add:* 48 Hillcrest Dr Carbondale IL 62901

FINK, LARRY (LAURENCE B)
EDUCATOR, PHOTOGRAPHER
b Brooklyn, NY, Mar 11, 41. *Study:* With Lisette Model, 59; Coe Col; New Sch Soc Res. *Work:* Mus Mod Art, New York; Corcoran Gallery Art, Washington, DC; Mus Fine Arts, Boston. *Exhib:* Broxton Gallery, Los Angeles, 76 & Case Solway Gallery, Cincinnati, 77; one-man shows, Light Gallery, New York, 77 & 80, Lehigh Univ, Bethlehem, Pa, 78, Sander Gallery, Washington, DC, 78-79 & Mus of Mod Art, New York, 79; San Francisco Mus Art, 81. *Teaching:* Instr, Parson Sch Design, 67-72, Kingsborough Community College, City Univ New York, 69-73, Inst Contemp Photog, Lehigh Univ, 76, Int Ctr Photog, New York, 77; prof photog, Yale Sch Fine Arts, 77-78; prof, Cooper Union, 79. *Awards:* Creative Artists Pub Serv Fel, 71-72 & 73-74; Guggenheim Fels, 76-77 & 79-80; Nat Endowment Arts Photog Fel, 78-79. *Dealer:* Sander Gallery Inc 2604 Connecticut Ave NW Washington DC 20008; Light Gallery 724 Fifth Ave New York NY 10019. *Mailing Add:* PO Box 295 Martins Creek PA 18063

FINK, LOIS MARIE
HISTORIAN, CURATOR
b Michigan City, Ind, Dec 30, 27. *Study:* Capital Univ, BA, 51; Univ Chicago, MA, 55, PhD, 70; Capital Univ, Hon Dr Humanities, 82. *Collections Arranged:* Academy: The Academic Tradition in American Art (auth, catalog), Nat Collection Fine Arts, 75. *Pos:* Cur, Off Res & Fels, Nat Mus Am Art, 70- *Teaching:* Instr art hist & sociology, Lenoir Rhyne Col, 55-56; instr art hist & educ, Midland Col, 56-58; instr, Roosevelt Univ, 58-64; asst prof, 64-70. *Mem:* Col Art Asn; Am Studies Asn. *Res:* Nineteenth and early twentieth century American art; relationship of French art to American art. *Publ:* Auth, American artists in France, 1850-1870, Am Art J, 73; coauth, Academy: The Academic Tradition in American Art, Smithsonian, 75; auth, French art in the United States, 1850-1870, Gazette Beaux Arts, 78; auth, American participation at the Paris salons, 1870-1900, Int Comt Hist Art 24th Cong, 82; contribr, Elizabeth Nourse, 1859-1938: A Salon Career, Smithsonian, 83. *Mailing Add:* Nat Mus Am Art Smithsonian Inst Washington DC 20560

FINK, RAY (RAYMOND RUSSELL)
SCULPTOR, EDUCATOR
b Long Beach, Calif, July 8, 22. *Study:* Art Inst Chicago, BAE, 52; Ill Inst Technol, Chicago, MSAE, 55. *Work:* Nev Southern Univ, Las Vegas. *Comn:* Steel sculpture & six woodcuts, 50 & steel sculpture, 51, US War Bonds, US

State Dept; relief painting, Pittman & Moore, Chicago, 54; sculptural mural (in collab with Rip Woods), Nat Housing Indust, Phoenix, Ariz, 73 & Greyhoud Inc, Phoenix, 75. *Exhib:* US Steel's Iron in the Fire, Birmingham Mus Art, Ala, 54; one-man show, Am Univ, Washington, DC, 57; Int Sculpture, Contemp Art Mus, Houston, Tex, 57; Am Exhib, Art Inst Chicago, 57; Art USA 58, Madison Sq Garden, NY, 58; Seven State Regional Contemp Art Traveling Exhib, Fedn Rocky Mountain States Coun on the Arts & Humanities, 75; Ariz Comn Arts & Humanities Traveling Exhib, 77. *Teaching:* Instr metal sculpture, Art Inst Chicago, 53-55; instr sculpture, Inst Design, Chicago, 53-58; prof art, Ariz State Univ, Tempe, 58- *Awards:* First Prize, Momentum Mid-Continental, Momentum, 53; Walter M Campana Award, Chicago & Vicinity, Art Inst Chicago, 56; George Bright Mem Prize, Phoenix Art Mus, Ariz, 67. *Bibliog:* Watercolor Painting (videotape), KAET-TV, Ariz State Univ, 68. *Media:* Mixed Media. *Dealer:* Yares Gallery 3625 Bishop Lane Scottsdale AZ 85251. *Mailing Add:* 7036 N 22nd St Phoenix AZ 85020

FINKE, LEONDA FROELICH
SCULPTOR, DRAFTSMAN
b Brooklyn, NY, Jan 23, 22. *Study:* Art Students League; Educ Alliance; Brooklyn Mus Art Sch. *Work:* Norfolk Mus Arts & Sci, Va; Nassau Community Col; Port Washington Pub Libr; Plainview-Old Bethpage Pub Libr. *Exhib:* Pa Acad Fine Arts Painting & Sculpture Ann, 66; one-woman show, Nassau Co Mus, 73; Suffolk Mus, 74; Dallas Mus Fine Arts; Heckscher Mus; Images of Am, US Info Agency traveling exhib (bronze figure sculpture selected); New York Botanical Gardens, 81. *Teaching:* Adj prof sculpture & drawing, Nassau Community Col, 70- *Awards:* Medal of Honor, Nat Asn Women Artists, 80; Edith H & Richmond Proskauer Prize, Nat Sculpture Soc, 81; Tallix Foundry Prize, Audubon Artists, 81; Chaim Gross Found Award, Audubon Artists, 82. *Mem:* Nat Asn Women Artists; Audubon Artists; New York Soc Women Artists; fel Nat Sculpture Soc; Sculptors Guild. *Media:* Bronze, Wood; Ink, Silverpoint. *Dealer:* Grand Central Art Galleries 24 W 57th St New York NY; Fisher Galleries 1509-11 Connecticut Ave NW Washington DC 20036. *Mailing Add:* 10 The Locusts Roslyn NY 11576

FINKELSTEIN, LOUIS
EDUCATOR, PAINTER
b New York, NY, Mar 24, 23. *Study:* Cooper Union; Art Students League; Brooklyn Mus Art Sch. *Exhib:* Whitney Mus Ann; Pa Acad; Corcoran Biennial; Stable Ann; and many others. *Teaching:* Prof art, Philadelphia Col Art, 58-62; prof art, Yale Univ, 62-64; prof art, Queens Col, City Univ New York, 64-, chmn dept, 64-69. *Awards:* Fulbright Fel, Italy, 56-58; Distinguished Teaching Award, Col Art Asn, 78; Fulbright Grant, Brazil, 81. *Mem:* Col Art Asn Am (mem bd dir, 68-70); Int Asn Art Critics. *Media:* Oil. *Res:* Abstract expressionism; impressionism; art theory. *Publ:* Auth, Gotham news, 69 & Thoughts about painterly, 70, Art News; auth, Seeing Stella, Artforum, 73; auth, Al Held, Art in Am, 74. *Dealer:* Ingber Gallery 460 West Broadway New York NY 10012. *Mailing Add:* 459 W Broadway New York NY 10012

FINKELSTEIN, MAX
SCULPTOR, PAINTER
b New York, NY, June 15, 15. *Study:* Los Angeles City Col; Sculpture Ctr, New York; Calif Sch Art, Los Angeles; Univ Calif, Los Angeles. *Work:* Krannert Art Mus, Univ Ill, Champaign; Hirshhorn Mus, Washington, DC; Univ Calif Mus, Berkeley; Santa Barbara Mus Art, Calif; Los Angeles Co Mus Mod Art; and others. *Exhib:* Highlights of the 1967-1968 Art Season, Larry Aldrich Mus Contemp Art, Ridgefield, Conn, 68; one-man shows, La Jolla Mus Art, Calif, 68 & Esther Robles Gallery, 70; Microcosm, Long Beach Mus Art, 69; Painting & Sculpture Today, Indianapolis Mus Art, Ind, 70; and many others. *Teaching:* Instr sculpture, Univ Judaism. *Awards:* Los Angeles Munic Gallery, 65; Long Beach Mus, 65 & 67; Krannert Mus, Univ Ill, Champaign, 67. *Bibliog:* Ray Faulkner & Edwin Ziegfield (auths), Art Today, Holt, 69. *Media:* Metal. *Mailing Add:* 1308 Factory Pl Los Angeles CA 90013

FINKLER, ROBERT ALLAN
EDUCATOR, PAINTER
b Chicago, Ill, Nov 22, 36. *Study:* Ill Wesleyan Univ, with Rupert Rilgore & Fred Brian, BFA, 59; State Univ Iowa, with Byron Burford & Robert Knipschild, MFA, 62. *Work:* St Cloud State Col, Minn; Waldorf Col, Iowa; Wis State Univ, Oshkosh; Mankato State Univ; Gen Mills, Minn. *Exhib:* Drawings USA, St Paul Art Ctr, Minn, 66; Minn Artists Biennial, Minneapolis Art Inst, 67 & 70; Akron Art Inst, Ohio, 70; Rochester Art Ctr, Minn, 77; Minn Artists Competition, 79 & 81; and many others. *Teaching:* Prof art, Mankato State Univ, 61- *Awards:* Pres lectureship, Winter Holidays, Presidents Fund, Mankato State Univ, 77. *Mem:* Mid-Am Art Conf. *Mailing Add:* Dept of Art Mankato State Univ Mankato MN 56001

FINLEY, DONNY LAMENDA
PAINTER
b Goodwater, Ala, Oct 7, 51. *Study:* Jacksonville State Univ, BS, 75. *Work:* Birmingham Mus Fine Arts, Ala; Columbus Mus Arts & Sci, Ga; Fine Arts Mus of the South, Mobile, Ala; LaGrange Mus Fine Arts, Ga; Fayette Mus Fine Arts, Ala. *Comn:* Painting, Ala Cattleman's Asn, Talladega, 76. *Exhib:* Am Watercolor Soc, Nat Acad Design, New York, 78, 80 & 82; Donny Finley Watercolorist, Bot Hall, Cheekwood Mus Fine Arts, 78; Alabama Art, US Senate Bldg, 79; Watercolor USA, Springfield Art Mus, Mo, 80; Rocky Mountain Nat, Foothills Art Ctr, Golden, Colo, 81; and many others. *Awards:* Best in Show, Columbus Mus & Mus Art Exhib, Columbus Mus Arts & Sci, 77; Larry Quackenbush Mem Award, Am Watercolor Soc, 80; Strathmore Award, Nat Watercolor Soc, 83. *Bibliog:* Marda Kaiser Burton (auth), Just a country boy, Southwest Art, 79; Joyce Deaton (auth), Down home Donny, Birmingham Mag, 79. *Mem:* Southern Watercolor Soc; Ala Watercolor Soc; Birmingham Art Asn. *Media:* Watercolors, Egg Tempera. *Publ:* Contribr, The Tennessee Conservationist, Tenn Dept Conserv, 78, Southwest Art, Art Mag, 79 & Birmingham Mag, 79; illusr, A Catalogue of the South, Oxmoor House, 79; Watercolor page, Am Artist Mag, 81. *Dealer:* Bryant Allen c/o Bryant Galleries 826 R Lakeland Dr PO Box 4651 Jackson MS 39216. *Mailing Add:* 444M Indian Crest Dr Birmingham AL 35243

FINLEY, GERALD ERIC
HISTORIAN
b Munich, Ger, July 17, 31; Can citizen. *Study:* Univ Toronto, BA, MA; Johns Hopkins Univ, PhD. *Teaching:* Lectr art & archaeol, Univ Toronto, 59-60; lectr art, Univ Sask, Regina, 62-63, actg dir, Norman Mackenzie Art Gallery, 62-63; from asst prof to prof art hist, Queen's Univ, 63- *Awards:* Gustav Bissing Rotating Fel, Johns Hopkins Univ, 61; Inst Advan Studies Humanities Fel, Edinburgh Univ, 79-80. *Mem:* Royal Can Acad Art; Ont Soc Artists; Arts & Lett Club. *Res:* British late eighteenth and early nineteenth centuries painting; landscape, especially J M W Turner; history of ideas. *Publ:* Auth, J M W Turner's proposal for a royal progress, 75 & Turner, the apocalypse and history, 11/79, Burlington Mag; auth, Landscapes of Memory: Turner as Illustrator to Scott Scolar Press, London, Univ Calif Press, 80; auth, Turner and George the Fourth in Edinburgh, 1822, Tate Gallery, London, Edinburgh Univ Press, 81; auth, George Heriot: Postmaster Painter of the Canadas, Univ Toronto Press, 83. *Mailing Add:* c/o Queen's Univ Dept Art Kingston ON K7L 3N6 Canada

FINN, DAVID
PHOTOGRAPHER
b New York, NY, Aug 30, 21. *Study:* City Col of Univ New York, BA. *Exhib:* Oceanic Sculptures, Metrop Mus of Art, New York, 74; Henry Moore Photographs, l'Orangerie, Paris, France, 77. *Collections Arranged:* Exploring Sculpture, Canova (auth, catalog), & Cellini, Andrew Crispo Gallery, New York; Henry Moore Sculpture and Environment (photographs), Fischer Fine Art Ltd, London, 77; Large Two Forms (auth, catalog), Fairweather-Hardin Gallery, Chicago; Henry Moore, Am Cult Ctr, Madrid. *Awards:* Herbert Adams Mem Medal, Nat Sculpture Soc. *Mem:* MacDowell Colony (mem bd); Artists for Environ Found (mem bd); Int Ctr of Photog (mem bd dir & trustees); Parsons Sch of Design (mem bd overseers). *Publ:* Auth, Sculpture at Storm King, 79 & New Rochelle, Portrait of a City, 80, Abbeville Press; auth, The Florence Baptistery Doors, Viking Press, 80; auth, Henry Moore at the British Museum, Brit Mus Publ Ltd, 81; Monumental Greek Bronze Sculpture, Abbeville Press, 83. *Mailing Add:* 110 E 59th St New York NY 10022

FINNEGAN, SHARYN MARIE
PAINTER
b New York, NY, Aug 16, 46. *Study:* Art Students League, New York; Acad de Belli Arti, Rome, Italy; Marymount Col, Tarrytown, NY, BFA; NY Univ, studied with Esteban Vicente, MA. *Exhib:* Report from Soho, Grey Art Gallery, New York, 75; Artists' Choice: Figurative Art in New York, Bowery Gallery, and four others, New York, 76; one-woman exhibs, Roswell Mus & Fine Arts Ctr, NMex, 77 & Prince St Gallery, New York, 74, 75, 77 & 80; Painted Light, Queens Mus, 83. *Pos:* Gallery coordr, Prince St Gallery, New York, 74-75 & 77- *Teaching:* Instr art & art hist, Mt St Vincent's Col, New York, formerly. *Awards:* Artist-in-residence, Roswell Mus & Fine Arts Ctr, 76; Palisades Artist-in-Residence, NY, summer 79; Residency, MacDowell Colony, Peterborough, NH, 79. *Bibliog:* J Mellow (auth), Rev, New York Times, 1/74; P Frank (auth), Rev, Soho Weekly News, 1/74; J Dreiss (auth), Rev, Arts Mag, 4/74. *Mem:* Women in the Arts, New York; Col Art Asn. *Media:* Oil, Gouache. *Dealer:* Prince St Gallery 121 Wooster St New York NY 10012. *Mailing Add:* 515 W 111th St New York NY 10025

FINSON, HILDRED A
CHILDREN'S BOOK ILLUSTRATOR, PAINTER
b Warner, Okla, June 3, 10. *Study:* Univ Northern Iowa, Cedar Falls, AA, 30-32; Drake Univ, BS(elem art educ), 56; Ariz State Univ, Tempe, post-grad work, summers 65, 66, 69-70. *Work:* J C Clegg Pub Libr, Central City, Iowa; Iowa State Univ. *Exhib:* One-person shows, Gallery West, Jefferson, 73, Jefferson State Bank, 77 & Carroll Pub Libr, Iowa, 77; I-40 Expo Realistic Art Competition, Winslow, Ariz, 75. *Teaching:* Elem art teacher, Jefferson Community Schs, 39-62, art dir, 63-75, retired. *Media:* Oil, Watercolor; Pen & Ink. *Publ:* Auth & illusr, Klipspringer Twins, Carlton Press, 75; auth & illusr, Dik-Dik and Shrew, Dorrance, 77. *Mailing Add:* 304 S Wilson Jefferson IA 50129

FIORE, JOSEPH A
PAINTER, INSTRUCTOR
b Cleveland, Ohio, Feb 3, 25. *Study:* Black Mountain Col, with Josef Albers, Ilya Bolotowsky & William De Kooning, 46-48; Calif Sch Fine Arts, 48-49. *Work:* Whitney Mus Am Art; Corcoran Gallery, Washington, DC; Chase Manhattan Collection, New York; Colby Mus, Waterville, Maine; State Mus Art, Raleigh, NC. *Exhib:* Whitney Mus Am Art Ann, 59; solo exhibs, Staempfli Gallery, 60, Schoelkopf Gallery, 65 & 69, Green Mountain Gallery, 73, John B Myers Gallery, 74 & Fischbach Gallery, 77 & 81; Six Maine Artists, Farnsworth Mus, Rockland, 83. *Teaching:* Instr painting & drawing, Black Mountain Col, 49-56, chmn dept art, 51-56; instr painting, Philadelphia Col Art, 62-70; instr painting, Md Inst Col Art, 70-75; instr landscape painting, Nat Acad Design, NY, spring 79; instr landscape painting, Parsons Summer Painting Prog, France, 80. *Awards:* First Prize, Metrop Young Artists First Ann, Nat Arts Club, 58; Hassam-Speicher Fund Purchase

Award, 81; Nettie M Jones Fel, Ctr Music, Drama & Art, Lake Placid, 83. *Bibliog:* Fairfield Porter (auth), The Oriental in American Art, Art in its Own Terms, Taplinger, 79. *Media:* Oil, Watercolor. *Publ:* Contemporary American Painting & Sculpture, Univ Ill Press, 61. *Mailing Add:* 178 W 82nd St New York NY 10024

FIORE, ROSARIO RUSSELL
SCULPTOR
b New York, NY, Jan 5, 08. *Study:* Nat Acad Design; Beaux Arts Inst Fine Arts; Mech Inst. *Work:* Ft Dobbins, Ga; Home of Pres Suharto. *Comn:* Bronze sculptures, Interior Dept, Washington, DC, US Air Force, Ft Dobbins, Ga, Freeport Minerals Co, New York, White House, Washington, DC & Cornell Univ; heroic size bronze statue of Gen George C Marshall, Leesburg, Va; white bronze sculpture for Teamster Int Bldg, Washington, DC. *Exhib:* Grand Central Art Gallery & Archit League, New York; Montclair Exhib, NJ; Westchester Art Gallery, NY; Corcoran Art Gallery, Washington, DC. *Pos:* Visual info officer, US Army Exhibs, 42-47. *Teaching:* Instr sculpture, Jekyll Island Art Ctr, Ga, 69-70; instr sculpture, Glynn Art Ctr, St Simons, Ga, 70-72. *Awards:* Nat Acad Prize, 30; Anna V Huntington Award, Nat Acad, 31. *Mem:* Jekyll Art Ctr (vpres, 75); Ga Coun for Arts Panel; Nat Sculpture Soc. *Publ:* Auth, Fundamentals of Clay Modeling, House of Little Books, 46. *Mailing Add:* 5 Nelson Lane Jekyll Island GA 31520

FIRESTEIN, CECILY BARTH
PRINTMAKER, INSTRUCTOR
b Brooklyn, NY, Apr 25, 33. *Study:* Art Students League, with Yasuo Kuniyoshi-Woodstock, 40-; Adelphi Univ, BA, 53; with Hans Hofmann, New York, 54; New York Univ, with Hale Woodruff, MA, 55, cert advanced study, 58. *Work:* Housatonic Col Art Collection, Stratford, Conn; Spanish-Portuguese Congregation & Bronx Mus Hist, New York. *Comn:* Edition of rubbings & poster, Cathedral of St John the Divine, New York, 74 & 80; illustrations for handbook, The Central Synagogue, NY, 78 & 79; rubbing of monument, Tarrytown Historical Soc, NY, 79; art deco door, Miami Design Preservation League, Miami, Fla, 80; rubbing illusration for notepapers, South Street Seaport Mus, New York, 81. *Exhib:* One-woman shows, Phoenix Gallery, New York, 62-83, In Loving Mem, Mus City New York, 78, South Street Seaport Mus, New York, 81 & Spanish Inst, NYC, 83; Galerie Meissner, Hamburg, Ger, 83; and many others. *Pos:* Art consult, District 24 Valley Stream, NY, 53-60; arts coordr, Cent Synagogue NY, 75-78; critic, Artspeak, 82-83. *Teaching:* Lectr, many universities, 72-82; instr/lectr rubbings, Cooper Hewitt Mus, NY, 80, South Street Seaport Mus, New York, 81 & Parsons Sch Design, New York, 83. *Awards:* Traveling Exhib Am Art, Am Fedn Arts, 68; Grant, Unique New York, Nat Coun Arts, 74; Artist-in-Residence, Bronx Co Hist Soc, 75-81. *Bibliog:* Angela Taylor (auth), She teaches a modern form of an ancient art, New York Times, 76; Jerry Talmer (auth), Art among the headstones, New York Post, 78; Barbara B Buchholz, article, House & Garden Guides, 79. *Mem:* Life mem Art Students League; World Print Coun. *Publ:* Auth & illusr, Rubbing Craft, Quick Fox, NY, 77; auth & illusr, Rub a Landmark, Nat Trust Hist Preserv, 78; auth & illusr, Rubbing brass & stone, The New World Book of Knowledge, Grolier, Inc, 80; auth & illusr, The Art of making rubbings, Seaport Mag, 80; auth & illusr, Elevator doors, how to rub them the right way, New York Daily News, 81. *Dealer:* Phoenix Gallery Inc 30 West 57th St New York NY 10019. *Mailing Add:* 8 East 96th St New York NY 10128

FIRFIRES, NICHOLAS SAMUEL
PAINTER
b Santa Barbara, Calif, Nov 10, 17. *Study:* Los Angeles Art Ctr; Otis Art Inst, Los Angeles. *Work:* Riveredge Found Mus, Calgary, Can; Santa Barbara Hist Mus, Calif; Southwest Mus, Los Angeles; Univ Wyo Mus, Laramie. *Exhib:* Cowboy Artists Am, Cowboy Hall of Fame & Ariz Mus Art, 66-77; Western Art Show, San Antonio, Tex, 68-77; Stamford Art Found Exhib, Tex, 74-77; Trailside Galleries, Scottsdale, Ariz, 77; De Silva Gallery, Santa Barbara, Calif, 77. *Bibliog:* Ed Ainsworth (auth), The Cowboy in Art, World Publ Co, 68; Dorothy Harmsen (auth), Harmsen's Western Americana, Northland Press, 71; Royal B Hassrick (auth), Western Painting Today, Watson-Guptill, 75. *Media:* Oil, Watercolor. *Publ:* Illusr, The Vaquero, 64 & Conquering the Frontiers, 74. *Mailing Add:* 1330 Pepper Lane Santa Barbara CA 93108

FISCH, ARLINE MARIE
GOLDSMITH, EDUCATOR
b Brooklyn, NY. *Study:* Skidmore Col, BS(art); Univ Ill, Urbana, MA(art); Fulbright student grant to Denmark, Inst Int Educ, 56-57; Fulbright res grant to Denmark, Bd for Scholars, 66-67; Sch Arts & Crafts, Copenhagen, Denmark; also with Bernhard Hertz Guldvaerefabrik, Copenhagen. *Work:* Worshipful Company of Goldsmiths, London; Minn Mus Art, St Paul; Vatican Mus, Rome; Mus Contemp Crafts, New York; Royal Scottish Mus, Edinburgh. *Exhib:* California Design, Pasadena Art Mus Triennial, 65, 68, 71 & 76; Form and Quality, Int Handicraft Fair, Munich, Ger, 68-78; Schmuck-Objekte, Mus Bellerive, Zurich, Switz, 71; First World Crafts Exhib, Toronto, 74; Goldsmith, 74, 76 & 79; plus many solo exhibs. *Pos:* Mem, US Nat Comn UNESCO 77-, World Crafts Found, 81- *Teaching:* Instr design & weaving, Skidmore Col, 58-61; prof jewelry & weaving, San Diego State Univ, 61-; guest lectr design, Guldsmedshojskole, Copenhagen, Denmark, 67 & 71; vis lectr, Crafts Coun of Australia, 75; vis prof, Boston Univ, 75-76; Fulbright lectr, Inst Applied Arts, Vienna, Austria, 82. *Awards:* Gold Medal, Int Handicraft Fair, Munich, 71; Nat Endowment Arts Craftsman's Fel, 74-75 & Craftsman's Apprenticeship Grant, 77-78. *Bibliog:* Lee Nordness (auth), Objects: USA, Viking, 70; J Coyne (auth), The Penland Book of Jewelry, 75; O Emery (auth), Craftsman Lifestyle, The Gentle Revolution, 77. *Mem:* World Crafts Coun (dir, 74-, vpres for NAm, 76-81); founding mem Soc

North Am Goldsmiths (pres, 82-); fel Am Crafts Coun (Calif rep, southwest regional assembly, 69-72, craftsman-trustee, 72-75); Allied Craftsmen San Diego. *Media:* Precious Metals. *Publ:* Auth, Textile Techniques in Metal, Van Nostrand Reinhold, 75. *Mailing Add:* 4316 Arcadia Dr San Diego CA 92103

FISCHBACH, MARILYN COLE
DEALER, COLLECTOR
b New York, NY. *Study:* NY Univ; New York Sch Interior Design; painting with Nicolas Takis, Victor D'Amico & Peggy Bacon. *Pos:* Partner, Fischbach Gallery, New York. *Specialty:* Contemporary American art. *Collection:* Contemporary. *Mailing Add:* c/o Fischbach Gallery 29 W 57th St New York NY 10019

FISCHER, HAL (HAROLD ALAN)
WRITER, PHOTOGRAPHER
b Kansas City, Mo, Dec 18, 50. *Study:* Univ Ill, Champaign-Urbana, BFA, 73; San Francisco State Univ, with Jack Welpott, MA, 76. *Exhib:* Photospectus, Reading Mus Art, Pa, 77; Photo-Linguists, Santa Barbara Mus Art, Calif, 77; Camerawork Gallery, San Francisco, 78; Photo-Narratives, Lawson de Celle Gallery, San Francisco, 79; Photographs and Words, 81 & Photography in California, 1945-1980, 84, San Francisco Mus Mod Art; and others. *Pos:* Contrib ed, Artweek, 77-83; reviewer, Artforum, 78-; contribr, Advocate, 82-; develop assoc, Fine Arts Mus San Francisco, 82- *Teaching:* Lectr photog, Calif Col Arts & Crafts, Oakland, 78-80; instr, City Col San Francisco, 79-82. *Awards:* Art Critics Fel, 77 & Critic-in-Residence Grant, 81, Nat Educ Asn; Photogr Fel, Nat Endowment Arts, 80. *Bibliog:* Joan Murray (auth), Reading the structure of a subculture, 8/13/77 & Judith Dunham (auth), Messages on the skyline, 10/6/79, Artweek; Jeff Perrone (auth), Hal Fischer, Artforum, 10/19/77. *Mem:* Int Asn Art Critics. *Media:* Black & White Film. *Res:* Contemporary photography with specializaton on West Coast practitioners. *Publ:* Auth, Gay Semiotics, 78, auth, 18th Near Castro Street, 79 & contribr, The Still Photograph: The Problematic Model, 81, NFS Press; contribr, The Unnecessary Image, Tanam Press, 83. *Mailing Add:* 10 Lyon St No 211 San Francisco CA 94117

FISCHER, HENRY GEORGE
HISTORIAN, CURATOR
b Philadelphia, Pa, May 10, 23. *Study:* Princeton Univ, BA, 45; Univ Pa, PhD, 55. *Pos:* Asst, Eygptian Sect, Univ Mus, Univ Pa, 49-56; from asst cur to cur, Dept Egyptian Art, Metrop Mus Art, New York, 58-70, Wallace cur Egyptology, 70- *Teaching:* Adj prof Egyptian art & lang, Inst Fine Arts, NY Univ, 62-79. *Mem:* Am Res Ctr Egypt; corresp mem, Deutsches Archäologisches Inst; Egypt Explor Soc, London; Soc Francaise Egyptologie, Paris. *Res:* Palaeography; iconography; sculpture; minor arts of ancient Egypt. *Publ:* Auth, Ancient Egyptian Representations of Turtles, 68, auth, Egyptian Studies II: The Orientation of Hieroglyphs, Part 1: Reversals, 77 & auth, Ancient Egyptian Calligraphy, 83, Metrop Mus Art; auth, Dendera in the Third Millennium BC, J J Augustin, 69; coauth, Treasures of the Cairo Museum, Thames & Hudson, 70. *Mailing Add:* RR 1 Box 389 Sherman CT 06784

FISCHER, MILDRED (GERTRUDE)
DESIGNER, CRAFTSMAN
b Berkeley, Calif, Sept 15, 07. *Study:* Mt Holyoke Col, AB; Wiener Kunstgewerbe Schule; Art Inst Chicago; Cranbrook Acad Art; Wetterhoff Inst, Finland, cert in tapestry; tapestry with Martta Taipale, Finland & Else Halling, Oslo, Norway; papermaking with Eishiro Abe, Japan. *Work:* Mus Contemp Crafts, New York; Grand Rapids Art Mus, Mich; Weatherspoon Gallery, Univ NC Woman's Col, Greensboro; Federated Dept Stores, Inc; Cincinnati Art Mus. *Exhib:* Woven Wall Hangings by Eleven Americans, circulated by Victoria & Albert Mus, London, 62-63; Magic of Fibers, Grand Rapids Art Mus, 70; Exhibition '72, circulated by Columbus Art Gallery, 72; Miami Univ, Oxford, Ohio, 77; Louisville Sch of Art, Anchorage, Ky, 78; Ohio Designer Craftsmen, Ohio Fedn Arts, 79-81; and others. *Teaching:* Asst prof art & head dept, Knox Col, 46-49 & Lindenwood Col, 52-55; assoc prof design, Univ Cincinnati Col Design, Archit & Art, 55-72. *Awards:* Centennial Award in Fine Arts, Mt Holyoke Col Alumnae Asn, 72; Award, Cincinnati Art Mus Awards Exhib, 75; Achievement Award, Ohio Designer Craftsmen, 78. *Mem:* Ohio Designers/Craftsmen; Am Crafts Coun. *Media:* Fiber. *Dealer:* Miller Gallery 2722 Erie Ave Cincinnati OH 45208; Vincent Fitzgerald 11 E 78 St New York NY 10021. *Mailing Add:* 3423 Monteith Ave Cincinnati OH 45208

FISCHER, R M
SCULPTOR
b New York, NY, Mar 21, 47. *Study:* C W Post Col, Long Island Univ, NY, BA, 71; San Francisco Art Inst, Calif, MFA, 73. *Exhib:* Functional Art, Otis Art Inst, Los Angeles, Calif, 80; Usable Art, Danforth Mus & Queens Mus, 80-81; Energie, Centre d'echanges d'art Contemporain, Lyon, France, 81; Color Mass, Light, Hallwalls, Buffalo, NY, 81; Lampworks, Contemp Arts Ctr, Cincinnati, Ohio, 81; Figurative Aspects of Recent Art, Hayden Gallery, Mass Inst Technol, Cambridge, 81; Biennial Exhibition, Whitney Mus Am Art, 83. *Awards:* Nat Endowment Arts Award, 81; Creative Artists Pub Serv Prog Grant, 82. *Bibliog:* John Perreault (auth), Lamps on to feats, Soho Weekly News, 3/81; Ronnie Cohen (auth), R M Fischer, Art in Am, 9/81; Henry Garrit (auth), R M Fischer, Art Am, 10/83. *Mem:* Found Community Artists. *Dealer:* Daniel Weinberg Gallery San Francisco CA; Texas Gallery Houston TX. *Mailing Add:* 73 W Broadway New York NY 10007

FISH, ALICE GROSS See Gross, Alice

FISH, GEORGE A
PAINTER
b Cornwall, Eng; US citizen. *Study:* Nat Acad Design; Art Students League; Grand Cent Sch Art. *Comn:* Calendar Art for Provident Mutual Insurance Co, Philadelphia, 72 & NY Life Insurance Co, 73. *Exhib:* Audubon Artists, Allied Artists Am & Am Watercolor Soc Shows, Nat Acad Galleries, New York; Nat Arts Club & Salmagundi Club, New York; and many others. *Awards:* Nell Broadman Scholar, Washington Sq Outdoor Art Exhib, 66; Purchase Award, Salmagundi Club, 67; Best in Show, Hudson Artists, 68; and many others. *Mem:* Salmagundi Club; Am Watercolor Soc; Allied Artists Am; life mem Ariz Watercolor Asn; Am Artists Prof League; plus others. *Media:* Watercolor. *Mailing Add:* 13123 Whispering Oaks Dr Sun City AZ 85375

FISH, JANET I
PAINTER
b Boston, Mass, May 18, 38. *Study:* Smith Col, BA; Yale Sch Art & Archit; Skowhegan Summer Sch. *Work:* Whitney Mus Am Art, New York; Dallas Mus Art, Tex; Metrop Mus Art, New York; Art Inst Chicago; Pa Acad Fine Arts. *Exhib:* Art Inst Chicago, 72 & 74; Am Drawings 1963-1973, Whitney Mus Am Art, 73; Philadelphia Mus Art, 74; Art Inst Chicago, 74; The Liberation, Corcoran Gallery, Washington, DC & US Info Agency Traveling Exhib, Europe, 76-77; Am 76 (traveling exhib), Brooklyn Mus, NY & US Dept Interior, 76-78; Eight Contemp Am Realists, Pa Acad Fine Arts & NC Mus Art, 77; DeCordova Mus, 79; Butler Inst Am Art, 79; Westmoreland County Mus, 79; Centro Colombo Americano, 79; Art in Vice-President's House from Northeast Mus, 79-80; and others. *Awards:* MacDowell Fel, 68, 69 & 72; Harris Award, Chicago Biennale, 74; Australia Coun Arts Grant, 75. *Mem:* Artists Equity. *Media:* Oil, Pastel. *Dealer:* Robert Miller 724 Fifth Ave New York NY 10019. *Mailing Add:* 101 Prince St New York NY 10012

FISH, RICHARD G
PAINTER, ILLUSTRATOR
b Philadelphia, Pa, Apr 7, 25. *Study:* Univ Pa, BA(appl arts); Philadelphia Mus Sch Art, with Azio Martinelli, dipl(advert design); Haverford Col. *Comn:* Paintings, Dravo Corp, Pittsburgh, Pa, 69; Caleco, West Chester, Pa, 79-83. *Exhib:* One-man shows, Gross-McCleaf Gallery, Philadelphia, 75, 78 & 83; Del Art Mus, Wilmington, 68-70; Butler Inst of Am Art, Youngstown, Ohio, 68, 70 & 74; Norfolk Mus of Art, Va, 69; Philadelphia Mus of Art, 69; Cummer Gallery of Art, Jacksonville, Fla, 69; and others. *Pos:* Freelance designer & owner, Richard Fish Assoc, Ardmore, 52- *Awards:* Gold Medal, Philadelphia Graphic Arts, 62-65 & 76; Gold Medal, Philadelphia Art Dirs, 65; Silver Medal, Pennational Arts Ann, State of Pa, 65. *Mem:* Print Club, Philadelphia. *Media:* Ink, Watercolor; Egg Tempera, Acrylic. *Publ:* Illusr, Life & Death of the Salt Marsh, Atlantic Little Brown, 69; illusr, One Day in Summer, Random House, 69; auth, The Artist in Scotland, Small World/ Volkswagen of Am, 72; illusr, Pathways to Independence, Chatham Press, 75; illusr, Haym Salomon, Liberty's Son, Jewish Publ, 75. *Dealer:* Muson Gallery 653 Canyon Rd Sante Fe NMex 87501. *Mailing Add:* 1733 Academy Lane Havertown PA 19083

FISH, ROBERT (ROBERT JAMES FIELD)
SCULPTOR, EDUCATOR
b Kelowna, BC, July 24, 48. *Study:* Univ BC, BEd, with G Smith; Vancouver Sch Art; also apprenticeship with Michael Morris & Gary Lee Nova. *Work:* Nat Gallery Can, Ottawa; Art Bank. *Exhib:* Art Gallery of Ont, 75; Vancouver Art Gallery, 78; Biennale de Paris, 80. *Teaching:* Instr painting, Banff Sch Fine Arts, 72. *Awards:* Can Coun Grants, 73 & 77. *Mem:* Intermedia Soc. *Media:* Rubber. *Mailing Add:* Box 298 Sointula BC V0N 3E0 Canada

FISHER, CAROLE GORNEY
PAINTER, SCULPTOR
b Minneapolis, Minn. *Study:* Minneapolis Col Art & Design, BFA, 64; Pa State Univ, MFA, 66. *Work:* Roanoke Fine Arts Ctr, Va. *Comn:* Print ed, Minn State Arts Coun, 70; sculpture, Univ Minn, Morris, 73. *Exhib:* Pa State Univ, 72; Two Nations, Six Artists, Minn-Can, 74; Walker Art Ctr, Minneapolis, 74; Whitney Biennial Contemp Am Art, New York, 75; Woman as Viewer Exhib, Winnipeg Art Gallery, 75. *Pos:* Comnr, Minneapolis Art Comn, 75- *Teaching:* Instr printmaking & drawing, Minneapolis Col Art & Design, 68-69; artist in residence printmaking, Bemidji State Univ, 69-70; instr drawing, Col St Catherine, 73-82. *Bibliog:* Cindy Nemser (auth), Whitney Biennial, Changes, New York, 75; Amy Goldin (auth), The New Whitney Biennial, Art in Am, 5-6/75; Chris Kohlmann (auth), 1975 Whitney Biennial, Mid West Art, 5/75. *Mem:* Col Art Asn Am. *Media:* Miscellaneous Media. *Dealer:* One Hundred Eighteen: An Art Gallery 1007 Harmon Minneapolis MN 55400. *Mailing Add:* 2524 Stevens Ave S Apt 2 Minneapolis MN 55404

FISHER, ETHEL (ETHEL FISHER KOTT)
PAINTER
b Galveston, Tex, June 7, 23. *Study:* Univ Houston; Univ Tex, with Everett Spruce, Howard Cook & Ward Lockwood; Art Students League, with Morris Kantor & Will Barnet. *Work:* Peabody Mus, Tenn; Norton Gallery, Fla; Joe and Emily Lowe Gallery, Fla. *Exhib:* One-man shows, Norton Gallery & Mus, Fla, 58; High Mus, Atlanta, 58 & Nat Mus, Cuba, 58; Survey Show, Mus Mod Art, New York, 60; Expressionism Now & Cubism in West, M H DeYoung Mem Mus, San Francisco, 61; Am Protrait Show, Long Beach Mus, Calif, 71; Women Choose Women, New York Cultural Ctr, 73; Cityscapes, San Francisco Mus, Calif, 77. *Teaching:* Instr advanced painting, Brentwood Art Ctr, 80-81. *Awards:* Four Arts Award, Soc Four Arts, 60; Painting Award Grant, Louis C Tiffany Found, 65; Kulicke Award, Westchester Art Asn, 68.

Bibliog: Gerry Rosen (dir), Interviews with California Artists, 75; Martha Alf (auth), Buildings as icons, Art Week, 3/15/75; Roberta Loach (auth), Painting, Ethel Fisher, Visual Dialog Mag, 77. *Media:* Oil, Watercolor. *Mailing Add:* 14739 McKendree Ave Pacific Palisades CA 90272

FISHER, JAMES DONALD
SCULPTOR, MUSEUM DIRECTOR
b Houghton, Mich, July 24, 38. *Study:* Corcoran Sch Art, with Richard Lahey, 56-61; George Washington Univ, 68-73, with H Irving Gates, BA, 71, MFA, 73. *Exhib:* Washington Area Exhib, Corcoran Gallery Art, Washington, DC, 67; two-man show, Prince Georges Community Col, Largo, Md, 68. *Collections Arranged:* Dual Retrospective-Peter Hurd/Millard Sheets, Amarillo Art Ctr, 74, When You Say Cowboy-Survey of Western Art in Texas (with catalog), 74 & Elisabeth Ney in Austin, 81. *Pos:* Technician Mus Hist & Technol, Smithsonian Inst, 60-68; dir, Amarillo Art Ctr, 73-77; dir, George Washington Carver Mus, Elizabeth Ney Mus & O Henry Mus, 77- *Teaching:* Grad teaching asst & asst prof lectr design & drawing, George Washington Univ, 71-73. *Mem:* Col Art Asn; Soc Indust Archeol; Am Asn Mus. *Media:* Welded Steel, Vacuum-Formed Plastics. *Res:* 19th century industrial design and 20th century non-objective sculpture. *Publ:* Auth, The history of railroad station architecture, Smithsonian Inst, 68; auth, Two centuries of American quilts and coverlets, Amarillo Art Ctr, 76. *Mailing Add:* 1311 Westover Rd Austin TX 78703

FISHER, JOEL A
SCULPTOR
b Salem, Ohio, June 6, 47. *Study:* Kenyon Col, AB. *Work:* Butler Art Inst, Youngstown, Ohio; Va Mus Fine Arts; Victoria & Albert Mus, London, Eng; Tate Gallery, London; Ctr Pompidou, Paris. *Exhib:* One-man shows, Victoria & Albert Mus, London, 71, Stadt Mus Monchengladbach, 75, Mus Mod Art, Oxford, Eng, 77, Stedelijk Mus, Amsterdam, 78 & Kunst Mus, Luzern, 84; and others. *Bibliog:* Simon Field (auth), Joel Fisher on Paper, Art & Artists, 1/72; Lisa Bear (auth), Strong as a Spider's Web, Avalanche, 12/74; Robin White (auth), View Mag, 81. *Publ:* Auth, Double Camouflage, Mansfield Fine Arts Ctr, 70; auth, The Berliner Book, Berlin Kunstler Prog des DAAd, 73; auth, Instances of Change, Bonomo Diffusione, Bari, Italy, 75; auth, Dissolution, Stadt Mus Monchengladbach, 75; auth, An Image in Blankness, Mus Mod Art, Oxford, 77. *Mailing Add:* c/o Crown Point Gallery 1551 San Pablo Ave Oakland CA 94612

FISHER, KENNETH LEE
SCULPTOR
b Tacoma, Wash, April 28, 44. *Study:* Univ Ore, Eugene, BS(sculpture), 68, BFA(sculpture), 69, with Jan Zach, MFA(sculpture), 71. *Exhib:* Nov Ann, Coos Art Mus, Coos Bay, Ore, 81-83; Sept Competition, Alexandria Mus, La, 82; Great Garden Show Int, Sculptural Arts Mus, Atlanta, 82; Knickerbocker Artists 32nd Ann, Salmagundi Club, New York, 82; J K Ralston Mus Ann, Sidney, Mont, 82 & 83; Audubon Artists 41st Ann, Nat Arts Club, New York, 83; Salmagundi Club Second Non-Member Exhib Photog & Sculpture, New York, 83. *Awards:* Joseph A Cain Mem Purchase Award First Place, 16th Ann Nat, Del Mar Col, Tex, 82; M Grumbacher Bronze Medallion, Southports Second Nat Exhib, 82. *Mem:* Portland Art Asn, Ore; Cooperstown Art Asn, NY. *Media:* Cast Bronze, Aluminum. *Mailing Add:* 1656 SE Clatsop Portland OR 97202

FISHER, LEONARD EVERETT
PAINTER, ILLUSTRATOR
b New York, NY, June 24, 24. *Study:* With Moses Soyer, New York, 39; Art Students League, with Reginald Marsh, 41; Brooklyn Col, with Serge Chermayeff, 41-42; Yale Univ Sch Fine Arts, BFA, 49, MFA, 50. *Work:* Butler Inst Am Art, Youngstown, Ohio; Libr of Cong, Washington, DC; Univ Ore, Eugene; Mt Holyoke Col, South Hadley, Mass; New Brit Mus Am Art, Conn. *Comn:* Am Bicentennial (four block eight cent commemorative postage stamps), 72, Legend of Sleepy Hollow (ten cent commemorative postage stamp), 74, Liberty Tree (thirteen cent embossed envelope), 75 & Skilled Hands for Independence (four block thirteen cent commemorative stamps), 77, US Postal Serv, Washington, DC. *Exhib:* Painters Panorama, Am Fedn Arts Sponsored Tour, 54-56; New Eng Painting Ann, Silvermine Guild Artists, 68, 69 & 71; Butler Inst Am Art, Youngstown, Ohio, 73; one-man show, Rotunda, Free Libr Philadelphia, 76, Univ Hartford, Conn, 76, Gen Elec Corp, 76 & NY Hist Soc: 200 Yrs of Am Illus, 76. *Pos:* Illusr & auth, children's books for major publ, 54; deleg-at-large, White House Conf, Libraries & Info Serv, 79. *Teaching:* Dean studies, Whitney Sch Art, 51-53; instr art hist, painting & bk illus, Paier Sch Art, 66-78, dean acad affairs, 77-81, dean emer & vis prof, 81- *Awards:* Pulitzer Fel Art, 50; Christopher Medal, New York, 81; National Jewish Book Award, New York, 81. *Bibliog:* Joan Hess Michel (auth), Leonard Everett Fisher, illustrator and painter, Am Artist, 9/66; Charles M Daugherty (ed), Six Artists Paint a Still Life, North Light, 77; M Munce (ed), Magic and Other Realism, Hastings House, 81. *Mem:* Soc of Illusr; New Haven Paint & Clay Club; Authors Guild/Authors League Am; Silvermine Guild Artists (bd dir, 70-74); Audubon Artists. *Publ:* Auth & illusr, The Colonial Americans, Watts, Vols 1-19, 64-76; auth & illusr, The Death of Evening Star, Doubleday, 72; auth & illusr, The Art Experience: Oil Painting 15-19 C, Watts, 73; auth & illusr, Alphabet Art: Thirteen ABC's From Around the World, Four Winds, 79; auth & illusr, The Seven Days of Creation, Holiday House, 81. *Mailing Add:* 7 Twin Bridge Acres Rd Westport CT 06880

FISHER, ROB (ROBERT NORMAN)
SCULPTOR, ENVIRONMENTAL ARTIST
b Cleveland, Ohio, May 28, 39. *Study:* Mass Inst Technol, with Gyorgy Kepes, BSc, 61; State Sch Design, Oslo, Norway, cert, 62; Univ Rome, Italy, cert, 63; Syracuse Univ, with Arthur Pulos, MS(indust design), 65. *Work:* Indianapolis Mus Art; Joslyn Art Mus, Omaha, Nebr; Apollo Plastics Collection, Chicago. *Comn:* Mirror Images (two works), Prudential Insurance Corp, Newark, NJ, 77; Sybil's Sculptures, New York Hilton, 77; Atmospheres (environmental sculpture), Ball-Unimark Plastics Corp, Milroy, Pa, 80; Moon Columns (fountain), State of The Art Mfg Corp, State College, Pa, 82; Galaxy (suspended computer-aided sculpture), OBC Inc, Quincy, Mass, 83. *Exhib:* Opening Exhib, Chicago Mus Contemp Art, 67; New Horizons in Sculpture, Wrigley Bldg, Chicago, 68; one-man show, Light Sculpture, Indianapolis Mus Art, 69; 14th Midwest Biennial, Joslyn Art Mus, Omaha, 69; Nat Sculpture Exhib, Southern Asn Traveling Sculpture, 69; Akron Art Inst Ann, 70; Siggraph 82 Art Exhib, Expos Ctr, Boston, 82; Electra 83, Mus de Art Mod de La Ville, Paris, 83. *Pos:* Res fel, Materials Res Lab, Pa State Univ, 82-; nonresident fel, Ctr Advan Visual Studies, Mass Inst Technol, 83- *Teaching:* Instr visual design, Colo State Univ, Ft Collins, 65-67; asst prof sculpture, Univ Ill, Champaign-Urbana, 67-71; vis prof visual design, Pa State Univ, State College, 73-75. *Awards:* Fulbright Fel to Norway in Design, 61-62; Third Award, Nat Sculpture Exhib, Southern Asn Sculpture, 69; Merit Award, Vietnam Vet Mem Competition, 81. *Bibliog:* Mary S Cowen (auth), Have cosmos will travel, Christian Sci Monitor, 83; Sheila Donohue (auth), Sculptor merges tradition and technology, Computer Graphics News, 83; Alexandra Tana (dir), Galaxy (videotape), Sci Technol & Soc Prog, Pa State Univ, 83. *Media:* Metal, Plastic. *Publ:* Coauth, The Design Continuum, Van Nostrand Reinhold, 66; contribr, Art and Technology, Van Nostrand Reinhold, 71; coauth, Understanding Visual Forms, Van Nostrand Reinhold, 76; coauth, Computer-aided sculpture, Leonardo (in prep). *Dealer:* Creiger-Sesen Assoc 10 Post Office Sq Boston MA 02109. *Mailing Add:* 228 N Allegheny St Bellefonte PA 16823

FISHER, SARAH LISBETH
CONSERVATOR
b Washington, DC, Nov 1, 45. *Study:* Wellesley Col, BA(art hist), 67; Florence, Italy, with pvt painting conservator, 67-68; Inst Technol Paintings, Stuttgart, Ger, with Dr R Straub, 69-70; Swiss Inst Art Res, Zurich, Switz, with Dr T Brachert, cert in conserv, 72; with T Hermanes, Canton of Vaud, Switz, 69 & 70; Cent Inst Art Res, Amsterdam, Holland, with Dr J Mosk, 73; Inst Royal du Patrimoine Artistique, Brussels, Belg, with N Gortghebeur, cert in conserv, 75. *Pos:* Conservator & asst to the dir, Swiss Inst for Art Res, Zurich, Switz, 72-74; conservator, Intermus Lab, Oberlin, 75-77; Balboa Art Conserv Ctr, San Diego, Calif, 77-81 & Nat Gallery Art, Washington, DC, 81- *Teaching:* Instr painting conserv, Intermus Conserv Asn, Oberlin, Ohio, 75-77. *Mem:* Am Inst Conserv Hist & Artist Works; Int Inst Conserv Hist & Artistic Works; Western Asn Art Conserv; Washington Conserv Guild. *Publ:* Ed, Rubens' The finding of Erichthonius: Examination and treatment, Allen Mem Art Mus Bulletin, Oberlin Col, XXXVIII, No 1, 80-81. *Mailing Add:* 1405 35th St NW Washington DC 20565

FISHKO, BELLA
DEALER
b Russia; US citizen. *Study:* Hunter Col. *Pos:* Dir, Forum Gallery. *Mem:* Art Dealers Asn Am; Friends Whitney Mus Am Art. *Specialty:* American art of the 20th century, painting and sculpture. *Publ:* Contribr to var nat art mags. *Mailing Add:* 1018 Madison Ave New York NY 10021

FISK-HAYDEN, BONNIE
PAINTER
b Chicago, Ill, Sept 6, 43. *Study:* Wells Col, Aurora, NY, with Lawrence Adams, 61-62; Univ Calif, Berkeley, with Hassel Smith, Karl Kasten, Felix Ruvolo, Robert Hartman, Tom Akawie & Boyd Allen, BA(painting), 65. *Work:* Ctr Res Women, Stanford, Calif. *Exhib:* Calif Expos, 1975, Calif State Fair Bldg, Sacramento, 75; Concepts in Paper, Palo Alto Cult Ctr, Calif, 78; Images of Women, Kaiser Ctr Gallery, Oakland, Calif, 79; one person shows, Gallery Victor Pere, Oakland, Berkeley Art Co-op, 81, Richmond Art Ctr, Calif, 81; and others. *Mem:* San Francisco Women Artists (artist coun, 78-81); Berkeley Art Co-op, Calif; Marin Soc Artists, Ross, Calif; Artists Equity. *Media:* Watercolor, Acrylic. *Mailing Add:* 43 Chatsworth Ct Oakland CA 94611

FISKIN, JUDY (ANNE)
PHOTOGRAPHER, EDUCATOR
b Chicago, Ill, Apr 1, 45. *Study:* Pomona Col, with John Mason, BA, 66; Univ Calif, Berkeley, 66-67; Univ Calif, Los Angeles, MA(art hist), 69. *Work:* Bibliotheque Nat, Paris, France; Dallas Mus Fine Arts, Tex; Mus Contemp Art, La Jolla, Calif; Mus Fine Arts, Houston, Tex; Oakland Mus, Calif. *Exhib:* Los Angeles in the 70's, Ft Worth Art Mus, Tex, 77; Landscape Images, Mus Contemp Art, La Jolla, Calif, 80; Long Beach Photog Survey, Calif State Univ Mus, 80; More Stucco, Otis Art Inst, Los Angeles, Calif, 81; Recent Accessions, Mus Fine Arts, Houston, Tex, 81; State Landscape, Newport Harbor Art Mus, Newport Beach, Calif, 81; Four Calif Views, Oakland Mus, 81. *Pos:* Co-dir, Womanspace Gallery, 73-74. *Teaching:* Instr photog, Calif Inst Arts, Valencia, 77-, assoc dean, 79. *Awards:* Nat Endowment Arts Grant, 80. *Bibliog:* Gordon Hazlitt (auth), Verbal intentions, Artnews, 76. *Mem:* Soc Photog Educ; Los Angeles Ctr Photog Studies. *Media:* Black & White. *Dealer:* Newspace Gallery 5241 Melrose Ave Los Angeles CA 90038. *Mailing Add:* 10615 Blythe Ave Los Angeles CA 90064

FITCH, GEORGE HOPPER
COLLECTOR, PATRON
b New York, NY, Nov 29, 09. *Study:* Yale Univ, BA, 32. *Pos:* Gov bd, Yale Univ Art Gallery; first vpres & trustee, Fine Arts Mus San Francisco; comnr, Asian Art Mus, San Francisco. *Mem:* Mus Soc, De Young Mus & Calif Palace of Legion of Honor (chmn, 71-72); Art Comn City New York (vpres, 67-68); founder Art Collectors Club Am; fel Pierpont Morgan Libr (coun, 66-69); Royal Oak Found; Munic Art Soc New York (dir, pres, 58-60); Am Fedn Arts (trustee, 53-74, first vpres, 55-64). *Interests:* Increasing art appreciation. *Collection:* Twentieth century American watercolors; East Indian miniatures; Melanesian dagger handles; African bobbins. *Publ:* Auth, So You're Going to Heaven, 71. *Mailing Add:* 1960 Broadway San Francisco CA 94109

FITCH, STEVE (STEVEN RALPH)
PHOTOGRAPHER, INSTRUCTOR
b Tucson, Ariz, Aug 16, 49. *Study:* Univ Calif, Berkeley, BA, 71; San Francisco Art Inst, 77; Univ NMex, Albuquerque, MA, 78. *Work:* Mus Mod Art, New York; Mus Fine Arts, Boston; Fogg Art Mus; Oakland Mus; Houston Mus Fine Arts. *Exhib:* Light and Substance, Univ NMex Art Mus, Albuquerque, 73; solo exhib, Art Mus, Univ Calif, Berkeley, 75; 130 Years of Ohio Photography, Columbus Mus Art, 79; Silver and Ink, Oakland Mus, 79; Visiters to Arizona 1846 to 1980, Phoenix Art Mus, 80; The Aesthetics of Graffiti, 79 & Beyond Color, 80, San Francisco Mus Mod Art; Color as Form: History of Color Photography, George Eastman House, Rochester, NY, 82. *Teaching:* Instr, Assoc Students Univ Calif Studio, Berkeley, 71-77; teaching asst, Univ NMex, Albuquerque, 78-79; instr, Univ Colo, Boulder, 79- *Awards:* Nat Endowment Arts Fel, 73, 75 & 81. *Bibliog:* Lois Fishman (auth), article, Creative Camera, 8/77; Hal Fischer (auth), exhib rev, Art Forum, 5/80. *Mem:* Soc Photog Educ. *Publ:* Auth, Diesels and Dinosaurs, Long Run Press, 76; contribr, photogs, Bombay Duck, 76, Creative Camera, 77 & Picture Mag, 79; contribr, Personal notes on teaching the history of photography, Exposure, 81. *Mailing Add:* 801 LaFarge Louisville CO 80027

FITZGERALD, ASTRID
PAINTER, PRINTMAKER
b Wil, Switz, July 28, 38; US citizen. *Study:* Col St Agnes, Fribourg, Switz, 55; Art Students League, New York, 62; Fashion Inst Technol, New York, 68; Pratt Graphics Ctr, New York, 72. *Work:* Aldrich Mus, Ridgefield, Conn; Wellesley Col, Mass; Marymount Col, Tarrytown, NY; Rockefeller Ctr Collection & Union Carbide Collection, New York. *Exhib:* Albright-Knox Mus, Buffalo, NY, 73; Contemp Reflections, Alrich Mus, 78; 57th Soc Am Graphic Artists Nat Exhib, Parsons Sch, New York, 79; Atlantic Gallery, New York, 80 & 81; Galerie Steinfels, Zurich, Switzerland; Jayne H Baum Gallery, New York, 82-83. *Awards:* Michael M Engel Mem Award, Nat Soc Prevention Cruelty Animals Ann, 73; Charles Levitt Award, Nat Asn Women Artists Ann, 78; Juror's Award, Fourth Ann Small Works Competition, NY Univ, 80. *Dealer:* Jayne H Baum Gallery 12 W 37th St New York NY 10018. *Mailing Add:* 650 West End Ave New York NY 10025

FITZGERALD, EDMOND JAMES
PAINTER, LECTURER
b Seattle, Wash, Aug 19, 12. *Study:* Calif Sch Fine Arts; study with Eustace Zeigler & Mark Tobey. *Work:* Nat Acad Design, New York; Seattle Art Mus; New Brit Mus, Conn; George Washington Univ & USN Combat Art Collection, Washington, DC. *Comn:* Battle of Bear River, US Post Off, Preston, Idaho, 40; Man and the Land, Am Mus Natural Hist, New York, 50; Pasteur, White Lab, Kenilworth, NJ, 51; Long Island History, Jamaica Savings Bank, NY, 63; Normandy Invasion, Nat Maritime Union's Curran Plaza Bldg, New York, 70. *Exhib:* Am Watercolor Soc, New York, 39; one-man show, Seattle Art Mus, 41; Nat Acad Design, 53; Art USA, Madison Sq Garden, New York, 58; Metrop Mus Art, New York, 66. *Teaching:* Lectr watercolor, Parsons Sch Design, New York, 47-49; lectr anat & drawing, Nat Acad Sch Fine Arts, New York, 69-78. *Awards:* First Prize, Nat Soc Mural Painters, 46; Grand Prize, Art USA, 58; Winsor & Newton Prize, Am Watercolor Soc, 72. *Mem:* Am Watercolor Soc (hon pres, 71-); Nat Acad Design; Allied Artists Am (pres, 60-63); Nat Soc Mural Painters (vpres, dir); Artists Fel (vpres, dir). *Media:* Watercolor, Oil. *Publ:* Auth, Painting and Drawing in Charcoal and Oil, 59; auth, Marine Painting in Watercolor, 72. *Mailing Add:* 6585 Lisa Lane Cincinnati OH 45243

FITZGERALD, HARRIET
PAINTER, LECTURER
b Danville, Va, Sept 14, 04. *Study:* Randolph-Macon Womans Col, BA, 26, Hon Dr Humanities, 77. *Work:* Swope Gallery, Terre Haute, Ind; Lincoln Univ; Fed Reserve Bank, Richmond, Va; Westminster Col; Lawrence Col. *Comn:* Portraits, Samuel Hatcher, 55, William A Webb, 70 & Anne J Ribble, 72, Randolph-Macon Womans Col & John C Simpson, Stratford Col, 74; The Long Mill (landscape), Dan River Inc, Danville, Va, 82. *Exhib:* One-person exhibs, Va Mus Fine Arts, 42, Charles Barzansky Gallery, New York, 44-64 & traveling exhibs, 75-76 & 79-80; Butler Art Inst; and others. *Pos:* Dir, Abingdon Sq Painters, New York, 48-; lectr mod art, Va Univ Ctr, 49-51 & 60-62 & Arts Prog, Asn Am Col, 55-68. *Mem:* Artists Equity; Danville, Va Art Club; Abingdon Sq Painters. *Media:* Oil on Canvas, Oil on Paper. *Publ:* Auth, Art, philosophy and religion, 64, What kind of culture, 69 & Exploring new dimensions in creativity, Randolph-Macon Alumnae Bulletin; auth, American art between the wars, Randolph-Macon Col Mag, Vol 36, No 1; auth, What is religious art?, Reflection, Yale Divinity Sch, 81. *Mailing Add:* 720 Greenwich St #7N New York NY 10014

FITZGERALD, JOHN PHILIP
PAINTER, INSTRUCTOR
b Stocton, Calif, Aug 24, 50. *Study:* Hartnell Col, Salinas, Calif, AA, 71; San Francisco State Univ, Calif, BA, 73. *Work:* La Marida Civic Theatre, Calif; West Publishing Co, Minn; Cedar City Municipal Collection, Utah; Sun Telegram, San Bernadino, Calif; Bell Mem Student Union, Chico State Col, Calif. *Comn:* Mural landscape, Bell Mem Student Union, Chico, Calif, 74; Logo Trona Joint, Trona High Sch, Calif, 78. *Exhib:* Nat Watercolor Soc, Palm Springs Mus, Calif, 79; Nat Acad Design, New York, 79; West the Law, St Paul Mus, Minn, 79; Rocky Mountain Nat Watercolor Exhib, Foothills Art Ctr, Golden, Colo, 81. *Teaching:* Instr drawing & painting, Cerro Cosso Col, 76- *Awards:* Best of show, Nat Small Painting, Albuquerque, NMex, 79; Best of show, La Marida Festival Art, La Mirada, Calif, 80; First Place Watercolor, Calif State Fair, 81; 40 local, regional & nat awards. *Mem:* Nat Watercolor Soc. *Media:* Watercolor, Acrylics. *Dealer:* John Miller Gallery San Carlos & Ocean St Carmel CA 93921; Capricorn Galleries 4849 Rugby Ave Bethesda MD 20814. *Mailing Add:* 84629 11th St Trona CA 93562

FITZKEE, EUNICE AILES
DEALER
York, Pa, July 25, 46. *Study:* York Col; Miami Dade Univ, AA, 71; York Acad Fine Arts. *Pos:* Dir, Gallery 310, York, Pa, 78- *Mem:* Artists Equity. *Specialty:* Contemporary art. *Mailing Add:* 310 E Market St York PA 17403

FITZPATRICK, JOSEPH CYRIL
PAINTER, SCULPTOR
b Williamstown, Pa, Mar 14, 09. *Study:* Carnegie-Mellon Univ, Pittsburgh; Edinboro State Col, Pa, BS(art educ); Teachers Col, Columbia Univ, New York, MA; L'Ecole des Beaux Arts, Marseille, France. *Work:* Latrobe High Sch, Pa; Equitable Life Assurance Soc, New York. *Comn:* Oil paintings, Cats, Pittsburgh Playhouse Bd, 54, The Caliph, Univ Pittsburgh, 57 & Dejeuner, Pittsburgh Bd Pub Educ, 59; and many others. *Exhib:* Mountain Playhouse, Jennerstown, Pa, 53; two-man show, Slippery Rock State Col, Pa, 68; Regional Art Exhib, Westmoreland Co Mus Art, Greensburg, Pa, 70-79; one-man show, Gallery Upstairs, Pittsburgh; many Assoc Artists Shows, Carnegie Mus, Pittsburgh. *Teaching:* Art supervisor & teacher, Pittsburgh Bd Pub Educ, formerly; art dir & teacher, Carnegie Inst. *Awards:* Man of the Yr in Art, Pittsburgh Jr CofC, 62; Teacher of the Yr, Allegheny Asn Lawyers' Wives, 70; Artist of the Yr, Arts & Crafts Ctr, Pittsburgh, 73. *Bibliog:* Sam Hood (auth), Fitzpatrick's world of art, 57 & George Swetnam (auth), Art in the Open, 60, Pittsburgh Press; Artist on the Spot (film), KDKA TV, Pittsburgh. *Mem:* Assoc Artists Pittsburgh; Pittsburgh Watercolor Soc (pres, 54-55); Pittsburgh Soc Sculptors; Nat Art Educ Asn; Nat Soc Arts & Lett. *Media:* Oil, Watercolor; Welded Steel. *Publ:* Auth, Knights armor, and teenagers, Carnegie Mag, 53; auth, Art for the Classroom, Pittsburgh Teachers Bulletin, 53. *Mailing Add:* 2707 Fifth Ave Pittsburgh PA 15213

FITZPATRICK, ROBERT JOHN
ADMINISTRATOR
b Toronto, Ont, May 18, 40; US citizen. *Study:* Spring Hill Col, BA & MA; Woodrow Wilson Fel, Johns Hopkins Univ, 64-65. *Collections Arranged:* Roy Lichtenstein at CalArts--Drawings and Collages from the Artist's Collection, 77. *Pos:* Pres, Calif Inst Arts, 75-; vpres cultural affairs, Los Angeles Olympic Organizing Comt, 81- *Mem:* Nat Endowment Arts; Advocates for the Arts; Int Council Fine Arts Deans; Nat Asn Sch Art; Calif Arts Coun. *Mailing Add:* 24700 McBean Pkwy Valencia CA 91355

FIX, JOHN ROBERT
SCULPTOR, SILVERSMITH
b Pittsburgh, Pa, Oct 31, 34. *Study:* Rochester Inst Technol, Sch Am Craftsmen, BFA; Conn Col, MAT; study with Lawrence G Copeland, Hans Christianson, William A McCloy & Frances Felten. *Comn:* Host box, Glenwood Lutheran Church, Minn, 57; chalice, St Andrew's Episcopal Church, New Kensington, Pa, 62; chalice, 68 & menorah, 71, Harkness Chapel, Conn Col, New London; altar set, St Paul's Episcopal Church, Westbrook, Conn, 79; plus many pvt comn in sculpture & metalsmithing. *Exhib:* Assoc Artists Pittsburgh Ann, Carnegie Mus, 57-80; New England Invitational, DeCordova Mus, Lincoln, Mass, 62; RI Arts Festival, Providence, 64; Soc Conn Craftsmen Traveling Show, 66; Three Rivers Arts Festival, Pittsburgh, 71, 73 & 74; 25th Anniversary Exhib, Brookfield Craft Ctr. *Teaching:* Teacher metalsmithing, Norwich Art Sch, Conn, 60-; instr sculpture & hist art, Upward Bound, Conn Col, 69; dir young peoples art prog, Lyman Allyn Mus, New London, 74-; jewelry workshops, Guilford Handcraft Ctr, Conn. *Awards:* First Prize in Crafts, 58, Mrs Roy A Hunt Award, 61 & Jury Award for Distinction in Crafts, 68, Assoc Artists Pittsburgh Ann. *Bibliog:* John D Morris (auth), Creative Metal Sculpture, Bruce Pub Co, NY, 71; Shirley Charron (auth), Modern Pewter, Van Nostrand Reinhold Co, 73; Gold Smiths J, 79. *Mem:* Mystic Art Asn Inc (pres, 74); Assoc Artists Pittsburgh. *Media:* Silver, Gold, Pewter. *Mailing Add:* Box 167 Groton Long Point CT 06340

FLACH, VICTOR H
DESIGNER, WRITER
b Portland, Ore, May 31, 29. *Study:* Univ Ore, Sch Archit & Allied Arts, with Jack Wilkinson, BS & MFA; Univ Pittsburgh, Henry Clay Frick Fine Arts Dept, with Walter Read Hovey; also with R Buckminster Fuller, 53 & 59. *Comn:* Three-wall collage mural, with John Otto, Erb Mem Union, Univ Ore, 52; three-wall mural, Clearlake Sch, Eugene, Ore, 56; The Heritage Series Interview with American Painter Ben Shahn, PBS-TV, 65; two-wall, three-story mosaic tile mural, Sci Ctr, Univ Wyo, 67-68; The Arts in Practice, TV

prog, with Richard Evans, UW-TV, 71. *Exhib:* Six-state traveling shows, 4 by 4 Paintings & Counter-Encounter Photographs, 70-73; 12 experimental films exhibited at various locations, 70-74; 73rd Western Ann Inaugural, New Denver Art Mus, 71; photographs, macrographic drawings & visual-kinetic structures in group shows, Interaction, Praxis & Toward Diversity, Univ Wyo Art Mus, 74, 76 & 80; Contextualism: A Painting & Graphics from Five States, Black Hills Col, 82; and others. *Pos:* Ed, In/sert: Active Anthology for the Creative, 55-62. *Teaching:* Prof painting, Univ Wyo, 65- *Res:* Toward a comprehensive tetradic typologic systems programming as model for archetypal-prototypal iconographic and colorfielding structural morphology. *Publ:* Auth, By These Presents: Richard Evans Retrospective (1942-75), 76; auth, Prologue to The Stage: A Series of Poetic Drawings by Joseph Deaderick, 78; auth, The Indigenous Image, 79; auth, Contra/Verses: Selected Poems, 80; auth, Contextualist Manifesto, 82; and many others. *Mailing Add:* Dept Art Univ Wyo Laramie WY 82071

FLACK, AUDREY L
PAINTER, PHOTOGRAPHER
b New York, NY, May 30, 31. *Study:* Cooper Union, grad, 51; Cranbrook Acad Art; Yale Univ, scholar & study with Josef Albers. *Work:* Whitney Mus Am Art, New York; Mus Mod Art; Metrop Mus, New York; Guggenheim Mus; Smithsonian Inst, Washington, DC. *Comn:* Family portrait comn by Oriole Farb, Dir, Riverside Mus & Stuart M Speiser Collection. *Exhib:* 22 Realists, Whitney Mus Am Art, 70; Whitney Mus Am Art, 72 & 78; Tokyo Metrop Art Mus, 74 & 81; Toledo Mus Art, 75; Jacksonville Mus, Fla, 77; Australia Coun Traveling Exhib, through 78; Nat Gallery Art, 80; Guggenheim Mus, 81; Pa Acad Fine Arts, 81-82; and others. *Teaching:* Instr drawing, Pratt Inst, Brooklyn, NY, 65-71; instr anat, NY Univ, 68-71; instr drawing, Sch Visual Arts, NY, 71-74. *Awards:* Albert Dorne Prof, Univ Bridgeport, 75; Nat Exhib Paintings Second Prize, Butler Inst Am Art, 74; The Cooper Union Citation, 77. *Bibliog:* Articles, New York Times, 4/76, Art News, 11/77 & Arts Mag, 12/77; Edward Lucie-Smith (auth), Art in the Seventies, Phardon Press Ltd, 80; Louis K Meisel (auth), Photorealism, Harry N Abrahms Inc, 80. *Media:* Oil, Film. *Publ:* Illusr, Tokyo Biennale (catalog), 74; illusr, Art in Am, 74; illusr, Vanitas (exhib catalog), L K Meisel Gallery, 78; illusr, Super Realism, Phaidon Publ, 79; auth, Audrey Flack on Painting, Harry N Abrahms Inc, 81. *Mailing Add:* 110 Riverside Dr New York NY 10024

FLAKEY ROSE HIP (GLENN ALUN LEWIS)
ADMINISTRATOR, SCULPTOR
b Chemainus, BC, Oct 26, 35. *Study:* Vancouver Sch Art, Univ BC; and with Bernard Leach, Eng. *Work:* Winnipeg Art Gallery, Man; Vancouver Art Gallery, BC; Can Govt, Ottawa; Can Coun Art Bank, Ottawa; Nat Gallery, Ottawa. *Comn:* Ceramic wall mural, Can Govt Expo 70, Ottawa, 70; bronze dog, City Vancouver, 72; mural plastic boxes, Nat Sci Libr, Ottawa, 73. *Exhib:* One-man shows, Douglas Gallery, Vancouver, 68; Wall Graphs, Ace Gallery, 69 & 8 Closets, Vancouver Art Gallery, 70; Realisms, Montreal Mus Fine Art & Art Gallery Ont, 70; Can Trajectoires 73, Musee Mod Ville Paris, France, 73. *Pos:* Proj coordr, Intermedia Soc, 71-72; trustee, Vancouver Art Gallery, 73 & 75-76; pres & trustee, Western Front Soc, 75. *Teaching:* Instr ceramics, Univ BC, 64-67; vis prof ceramics, NY State Col Ceramics, Alfred Univ, 70-71; instr ceramics & sculpture, Univ BC, 71-74. *Awards:* Can Coun Art Bursary, travel to Japan, 67, study sculpture 68 & 70; Sr Can Coun Art Bursary, garden res, Italy, Iran & India, 76. *Bibliog:* Joan Lowndes (auth), Forest industry, Vancouver Sun Newspaper, 7/3/70; John B Mays (auth), Ottawa notebook, Proof Only, 2/22/74; Alex Mogelin & Normand Laliberte (co-auths), Art in Boxes, Reinholt, Van Nostrand, 75. *Media:* Multimedia. *Publ:* Illusr & contribr, BC Almanac, Nat Film Bd Can, 70; illusr & contribr, Is 13, 72 & Topiary & Artists Recipes (microfische cards), 73, Coach House; co-auth, Mondo Artie, episode 1681 Art's birthday and Hollywood decca dance, 74; illusr & contribr, Mondo Artie episode 1625, Source, 74. *Dealer:* Nova Gallery Vancouver BC Can. *Mailing Add:* 303 E Eighth Ave Vancouver BC V5T 1S1 Canada

FLAM, JACK D
HISTORIAN, EDUCATOR
b Paterson, NJ, Apr 2, 40. *Study:* Rutgers Univ, BA, 61; Columbia Univ, MA, 63; New York Univ, PhD, 69. *Collections Arranged:* Henri Matisse Paper Cut-Outs (auth, catalog), Nat Gallery, 77. *Teaching:* Instr art hist, Rutgers Univ, 62-66; assoc prof art hist, Univ Fla, 66-70; prof art hist, Brooklyn Col & Grad Ctr, City Univ New York, 75- *Awards:* Guggenheim Fel, 79-80. *Mem:* Int Asn Art Critics; Col Art Asn. *Res:* Currently working on a major critical study of Matisse and on a series of articles on early Modernist painting. *Publ:* Auth, Matisse on Art, Phaidon, 73 & Dutton, 78; auth, Graphic Symbolism in the Dogon Granary, J African Studies, 76; co-auth, Henri Matisse Paper Cut-Outs, Detroit Inst Arts & St Louis Art Mus, 77; ed, The Documents of 20th Century Art, G K Hall, 81; coauth, Robert Motherwell, Abbeville Press, 83. *Mailing Add:* 171 West 79th Street New York NY 10024

FLANNERY, THOMAS
CARTOONIST
b Carbondale, Pa, Dec 16, 19. *Study:* Pratt Inst, 39-40; Univ Scranton, 46-47. *Pos:* Staff cartoonist, Yank Mag, 43-45; polit cartoonist, Lowell Sun, Mass, 47-57; Baltimore Eve Sun, 57-73 & Baltimore Sun, 73- *Mem:* Am Soc Ed Cartoonists. *Mailing Add:* 518 Orkney Rd Baltimore MD 21212

FLATEMAN, IRA N
GALLERY DIRECTOR, CURATOR
b New York, NY, Jan 30, 53. *Study:* Queens Col, City Univ New York, with I Bolotowski, 71-73; RI Sch Design, with Jun Kneko & Dale Chihuly,

BFA(ceramics), 77. *Collections Arranged:* The Potter and the Painter, Woods Gerry Gallery, RI Sch Design, 82; Secrets, Stirrings of the Subconscious, Silvermine Guild Ctr Arts, 83. *Pos:* Dir exhibs, RI Sch Design, 80-83; gallery dir, Silvermine Guild Ctr Arts, 83- *Awards:* Best Painting, Queensboro Community Col, 72. *Mailing Add:* 120 Bennetts Farm Rd Ridgefield CT 06877

FLATTMANN, ALAN RAYMOND
PAINTER, INSTRUCTOR
b New Orleans, La, Aug 6, 46. *Study:* John McCrady Art Sch, 64-66. *Work:* Okla Art Ctr, Oklahoma City; Lauren Rogers Mus Art, Laurel, Miss; Miss Mus Art, Jackson; New Orleans Art Asn; S Cent Bell, Birmingham, Ala. *Comn:* Murals, Old Zion Baptist Church, New Orleans, 67 & Grace Episcopal Church, 72. *Exhib:* Biena de Arte, Bogota Mus Art, Colombia, 72; Mainstreams, Hermann Fine Arts Ctr, Marietta, Ohio, 72, 75 & 76; Am Watercolor Soc Ann, Nat Acad Design, New York, 72 & 76; Watercolor USA, Springfield Art Mus, Mo, 75; Allied Artists Am Ann, Nat Arts Club, New York, 76 & 77 & Pastel Soc Am Ann, 76, 77 & 79; plus others. *Teaching:* Instr painting & drawing, John McCrady Art Sch, New Orleans, 67-82; private workshops in oil & pastel. *Awards:* Elizabeth T Greenshields Found Grant Award, 73; New York Cent Co Award, Pastel Soc Am, 79; plus others. *Bibliog:* Marda Burton (auth), No subject too common, Southwest Art, 9/80; Joyce Kelly (auth), The Poetic Realism of Alan Flattmann, ACM Publ Co; Marda Burton (auth), Alan Flattmann, among unknown men, New Orleans Mag, 7/81. *Mem:* Pastel Soc Am. *Media:* Pastel & Oil. *Dealer:* Bryant Galleries 1855 Lakeland Dr Jackson MS 39216 & 524 Royal St New Orleans LA 70130. *Mailing Add:* Rte 2 Box 113B Covington LA 70433

FLAVIN, DAN
ARTIST, WRITER
b New York, NY, Apr 1, 33. *Study:* Self-educated as artist; Cathedral Col Immaculate Conception, 47-52; studied art hist, Univ Md Exten, Repub Korea, 54-55; New Sch Social Res, 56; Columbia Univ, 57-59. *Work:* Mus Mod Art, Whitney Mus Am Art, Guggenheim Mus, Metrop Mus Art, New York; Philadelphia Art Mus. *Comn:* Courtyard & inner arcade, Kunstmuseum Basel, 75; several platforms of Grand Cent Station, New York, 76; ultra-violet & blue fluorescent light, Kroller-Muller Mus, Eindhoven, 77; entranceway & gallery skylights, Hudson River Mus, Yonkers, 79; north facade, Fed Bldg & US Courthouse, Anchorage, 80. *Exhib:* Cornered installations in fluorescent light, Albright-Knox Art Gallery, Buffalo, 72; installations fluorescent light, Art Inst Chicago, 77 & Univ Art Mus, Berkeley, 78; drawn along the shores 1959-1976 & installations of fluorescent light, Parrish Art Mus, Southampton, NY, 78 & Hudson River Mus, Yonkers, 79; installation of fluorescent light, Nat Gallery Can, Ottawa, 79; The Reductive Object, Inst Contemp Art, Boston, 79; Laguna Gloria Art Mus, Austin, Tex, 80; Allen Mem Art Mus, Oberlin, Ohio, 80; Whitney Mus Am Art, 80; and others. *Teaching:* Lectr grad fac, Univ NC, Greensboro, spring 67; Albert Dorne vis prof, Univ Bridgeport, 73. *Awards:* William & Noma Copley Found Award, 64; Nat Found Arts & Humanities Award, 66; Skowhegan Medal for Sculpture, 76. *Mem:* Scenic Hudson Preserv Conf; Nat Trust Hist Preserv; Nat Audubon Soc. *Publ:* Auth, ...in daylight or cool white, 12/65, Some remarks..., 12/66 & ...on an American artist's education, 3/68, Artforum; auth, Several more remarks..., 4/69 & opening add for Donald Judd Exhib, 9-10/75, Studio Int. *Dealer:* Leo Castelli Gallery 420 W Broadway New York NY 10012. *Mailing Add:* PO Box 248 Garrison NY 10524

FLECKENSTEIN, OPAL R
PAINTER, CERAMIST
b Macksville, Kans, Nov 19, 11. *Study:* Eastern Wash State Col, BA & MA(educ); Univ Wash; Study with Guy Anderson, James Fitzgerald & Mark Tobey. *Work:* Cheney Cowles Mus, Wash. *Exhib:* Seattle Art Mus; one-man show, Watercolors & Oils, Seattle Art Mus; one-man retrospectives, Cheney Cowles Mus & Eastern Wash Univ, Cheney; Arts Centre South Hill Park, Bracknell, Berkshire, London, 81; All Hollows by the Tower, London, England, 83. *Teaching:* Assoc prof painting & humanities, Eastern Wash Univ, 49-75; guest instr art educ, Univ Sask, 57, 58 & 60; emer prof art, Int Prog, Guadalajara, Mex, 77-; workshops, Ore, Wash & BC, 77-79. *Awards:* Watercolor Purchase Prize, Seattle Art Mus, 50. *Media:* Oil, Watercolor. *Publ:* Prod 36 half hour TV progs, KSPS-PBS, Spokane, 71. *Mailing Add:* S 3118 Ultra Spokane WA 99204

FLECKER, MAURICE NATHAN
PAINTER, EDUCATOR
b Brooklyn, NY, Feb 27, 40. *Study:* State Univ NY Col, New Paltz, with Ilya Bolotowsky, Gabriel Laderman, George Wexler & George Wardlaw, BS; Brooklyn Col, with Philip Pearlstein, Ad Reinhardt, Carl Holty & R J Wolff, MFA; Art Students League, painting scholar; New Sch Social Res; Brooklyn Mus, painting scholar; Pratt Inst. *Work:* Fed Savings Bank, State Univ NY Col, New Paltz; Brooklyn Mus. *Exhib:* One-man shows, Aegis Gallery, New York, 62; Icarus Gallery, New York, 66; Bank Gallery, New York, 69 & First Street Gallery, New York, 77; Wadsworth Atheneum, Hartford, Conn, 65; W V Smith Art Mus, Springfield, Mass, 65; Brooklyn Mus, New York, 68-75. *Teaching:* Instr, Brooklyn Mus Art Sch, New York, 68-75; assoc prof life drawing & sculpture, asst head art, music & philos, 72-82; Suffolk Co Community Col. *Bibliog:* Amei Wallach (auth), One road to realism, Newsday, 77; Maria Latona (auth), Inspiration from life, Long Island Press, 77; Ellen Frisina (auth), Artist believes in taking time, Mid Island News, 10/18/79. *Mem:* Soho Ctr for Visual Arts; Col Art Asn. *Media:* Oil, Watercolor. *Dealer:* First Street Gallery 118 Prince St New York NY 10012. *Mailing Add:* 101 Cooper Ct Port Jefferson NY 11777

FLEISCHER, ROLAND EDWARD
HISTORIAN, EDUCATOR
b Baltimore, Md, Feb 12, 28. *Study:* Western Md Col, BA, 52; Johns Hopkins Univ, MA, 54, PhD, 64. *Teaching:* Assoc prof art hist, Univ Miami, Fla, 56-66; prof art hist, George Washington Univ, 66-74; prof art hist, Pa State Univ, 74-. *Awards:* Fulbright Award, Univ Amsterdam, 54-55. *Mem:* Col Art Asn. *Res:* Colonial painting in America; Dutch painting of the 17th century. *Publ:* Contribr, Philadelphia Painting and Printing to 1776, Pa Acad Fine Arts, 71; contribr, American Painting to 1776, Univ Va, 72; auth, An Altered Painting by Pieter de Hooch, Oud Holland, 76; auth, Ludolf de Jongh and the Early Work of Pieter de Hooch, Oud Holland, 78; auth, Three recently discovered portraits by John Hesselius, Antiques, 81. *Mailing Add:* 626 Hubler Rd State College PA 16801

FLEISCHMAN, LAWRENCE A
DEALER, COLLECTOR
b Detroit, Mich, Feb 14, 25. *Study:* Western Mil Acad, Alton, Ill; Purdue Univ; Univ Detroit, BS; St John's Univ, LHD, 78. *Pos:* Comn mem, Fine Arts Comt, US Info Agency, 57-59; pres, Arch Am Art, 59-66; pres, Detroit Inst Arts, 62-66; pres, White House Comt Fine Arts, 62-66; pres, Detroit Arts Comn; fel, Morgan Libr, New York, 68-; ed, Am Art J, 69-; pres & Owner, Kennedy Galleries Inc. *Awards:* Lotus Club Art Award, 67; Papal Knight of the Order of St Sylvester, 78; Copley Medal, Nat Portrait Gallery, 78. *Mem:* Arch Am Art (trustee); life mem Pa Acad Fine Arts; life mem Pa Hist Soc; Nat Acad Design; Metrop Mus Art. *Specialty:* 18th, 19th and 20th century American art. *Collection:* American art and Roman and Greek antiquities. *Mailing Add:* Kennedy Galleries Inc 40 W 57th St New York NY 10019

FLEISHER, PAT
EDITOR, PHOTO ARTIST
b Toronto, Ont. *Study:* Univ Toronto, BA; painting, Skowhegan, Maine; Ont Col Art; St Adele, Quebec; printmaking, York Univ, 72. *Exhib:* Palm Springs Desert Mus, 79; Koffler Ctr Arts, Toronto, 80; Idee Gallery, Toronto, 81; Spaces Gallery, Cleveland, 81; Gallery One, Toronto, 80 & 82; and others. *Collections Arranged:* Toronto Women Artists: Three Decades, 83. *Pos:* Founder/ed, Art Mag, 69-; pres, Artmagazine, Inc, 74-; founder, Toronto Int Art Fair, 80; publ & ed, The Art Post, currently; producer, Art Expo, Toronto, currently. *Teaching:* Lectr & art guide, Toronto & New York galleries & studios, 71- *Awards:* Award of Merit to Art Mag, Soc Publ Designers New York, 75; Queen Elizabeth Silver Jubilee Medal, awarded by Jules Leger, Gov Gen of Can, 78. *Mem:* Int Asn Art Critics (mem, Can Br). *Media:* Colour Xerox & Photography. *Publ:* Auth, Atlantic Provinces Journal, Artmagazine, 76; auth, A Western Pilgrimage, 77 & The mystery of the Maya, 79, Artmagazine; auth, The Woman as Artist, Avenue Mag, 83; auth, Artist Rose Lindzon: A profile, City & County Home Mag, 84. *Mailing Add:* 15 McMurrich, Apt 706 Toronto ON M5R 3M6 Canada

FLEMING, BETTY CORCORAN
DEALER
b Miami Beach, Fla, Feb 12, 47. *Study:* Syracuse Univ, BA. *Pos:* Owner, Betty C Fleming Fine Art Inc, Miami, Fla. *Mem:* Art Dealer's Asn SFla (treas, 79). *Specialty:* Contemporary American Art. *Mailing Add:* 34 La Gorce Circle Miami Beach FL 33141

FLEMING, LEE VIRGINIA
CRITIC, WRITER
b Philadelphia, Pa, Jan 26, 52. *Study:* Yale Col, BA, 72; Univ Toronto, MA, 74. *Pos:* Art reviewer & film ed, Washington Rev Arts, 79-; Washington contribr, New Art Examiner, 80-81; Washington ed, Images & Issues, 80-; Washington Correspond, Art News, 83- *Awards:* Washington, DC Comn Arts & Humanities Fel Lit & Criticism, 81. *Mem:* Col Art Asn. *Res:* Formal, mythic and psychosocial comparisons of prehistoric structures to contemporary sculpture; artists books; performance. *Publ:* Auth, Iconoclassicism: Eight Washington Women (catalog), Washington Proj Arts, 81; auth, On metaphor, Washington Rev, 82; auth, Biennial directions: Direction 1983, Art News, 83; auth, Art, Am Quart, 83; auth, What's at issue is the issue, Images & Issues, 83. *Mailing Add:* 1924 Park Rd NW Washington DC 20010

FLEMING, RONALD LEE
DESIGNER, ADMINISTRATOR
b Los Angeles, Calif, May 13, 41. *Study:* Pomona Col, BA, 63; Harvard Univ, MCP, 67. *Pos:* First chmn, Cambridge One Percent Pub Art Comn, 79- *Awards:* Merit Award, Am Soc Landscape Architects, 80; Commendation Design Excellence, Dept Transportation--Nat Endowment Arts, 81. *Mem:* Founding mem Cambridge Arts Coun (chmn, 74-79). *Publ:* Ed, Censored Laughter, Boston Publ, 76; coauth, Place Makers, Public Art That Tells You Where You Are, 81 & auth, Facade Stories, 82, Hastings House; coauth, On Common Ground, Harvard Common Press, 82. *Mailing Add:* 2 Hubbard Park Cambridge MA 02158

FLEXNER, JAMES THOMAS
WRITER, HISTORIAN
b New York, NY, Jan 13, 08. *Study:* Lincoln Sch, Teacher's Col; Harvard Col, grad (magna cum laude), 29. *Awards:* Guggenheim Fel, 53 & 80; Nat Bk Award, 74; Pulitzer Prize, 74. *Mem:* Century Asn; Am Inst Arts & Lett; Soc Am Historians (pres, 75-78); PEN Am Ctr (pres, 54-55). *Res:* American painting as an expression of American life. *Publ:* Auth, America's Old Masters, 39, rev ed, 79; auth, American Painting, First Flowers of Our Wilderness, 47, 69 & 79; auth, Pocket History of American Painting, 50; American Painting, the Light of Distant Skies, 54, 69 & 79; auth, American Painting, that Wilder Image, 62, 70 & 79; and others. *Mailing Add:* 530 E 86th St New York NY 10028

FLICK, PAUL JOHN
PAINTER, COLLECTOR
b Rock Island, Ill, Feb 5, 43. *Study:* Univ Minn, BA & MFA(printing & printmaking); studied with Herman Cherry & Mario Valpe. *Teaching:* Instr drawing & color, Bureau of Engraving, 72- *Mem:* Artist Equity Asn (pres, 76-77); Twin Cities Metrop Arts Alliance. *Media:* Assemblages. *Collection:* Primitive and African art. *Dealer:* Oxman's Art Gallery 639 Second Ave N Minneapolis MN 55803. *Mailing Add:* 4032 Lyndale Ave S Minneapolis MN 55409

FLICK, ROBBERT
PHOTOGRAPHER, EDUCATOR
b Amersfoort, Holland, Nov 15, 39; Can citizen. *Study:* Univ BC, BA, 67; Univ Calif, Los Angeles, MA, 70, with Robert Heinecken & Robert Fichter, MFA, 71. *Work:* Visual Studies Workshop, Rochester, NY; Nat Gallery Can, Ottawa; Art Inst Chicago; Seagrams Collection, New York; Ctr Creative Photog, Univ Ariz, Tucson; and others. *Exhib:* New Photographs of Ill, Chicago Art Inst, 74; Attitudes, Santa Barbara Mus Art, Calif, 79; New Landscapes, Friends Photog, Carmel, Calif, 80; Year 2000: New Views of Los Angeles, Mt St Mary's Col, 81; solo exhib, Barnsdall Municipal Art Gallery, Los Angeles, Calif, 82; Radical Space-Rational Time, Henry Art Gallery, Seattle, 83. *Teaching:* Instr photog, Univ Calif, Los Angeles Exten, 69-71; asst prof, Univ Ill, Champaign, 71-76; assoc prof, Univ Southern Calif, Los Angeles, 78- *Awards:* Can Coun Bursary Arts, 67 & 69; fel, Ctr Advan Studies, Univ Ill, 73; Nat Endowment Arts Survey Grant, 79; Nat Endowment Arts Individual Artist Grant, 83. *Bibliog:* Article, Afterimage, Vol 8, Number 5, 12/80; article, Journal, Southern Calif Art Mag #29. *Mem:* Soc for Photog Educ; Col Art Asn. *Media:* Silverprint. *Publ:* Contribr, Photographer's Choice, Addison House, 75; auth, Camera, Number 2, 2/81. *Dealer:* Tortue Gallery 2917 Santa Monica Blvd Santa Monica CA 90404. *Mailing Add:* 707 E Hyde Park Blvd Inglewood CA 90302

FLINN, ELIZABETH HAIGHT
EDUCATOR
b Ann Arbor, Mich. *Study:* Wellesley Col, BA; Inst Fine Arts, MA. *Pos:* Assoc mus educr, Jr Mus, Metrop Mus Art, 74- *Mem:* Am Asn Youth Mus. *Res:* Medieval manuscript, preparation of educational materials on the museum's collection for students and teachers. *Publ:* Auth, Medieval towns and guilds (sch picture set), auth, America: 1750-1789 (sch picture set) & auth, A magnificent manuscript--a historical mystery, the hour of Jeanne d'Evreux, Metrop Mus Art Bull, 71. *Mailing Add:* Jr Mus Metrop Mus Art 82nd St & Fifth Ave New York NY 10028

FLINT, JANET ALTIC
CURATOR, HISTORIAN
b Louisville, Ky, Aug 24, 35. *Study:* Louisville Art Ctr; Univ Louisville, BS(painting & art hist); Univ Minn, MA(art hist). *Collections Arranged:* And there was light, Studies by Abraham Rattner, 76; Jacob Kainen: Prints, A Retrospective, 77; Prints and Personalities; the American Theater's First Hundred Years, 79; Art for All: American Print Publishing Between the Wars, 81; Charles W Hawthorne: The Late Watercolors, 83. *Pos:* Assoc cur, Minneapolis Inst Arts, 59-66; asst cur & cur graphic arts, Nat Mus Am Art, Smithsonian Inst, 69- *Mem:* Print Coun Am. *Res:* American prints and drawings. *Publ:* Auth, George Miller and American Lithography, 76; auth, New Ways with Paper, 78; auth, The Print in the United States from the Eighteenth Century to the Present, 81; auth, The Prints of Louis Lozowick: A Catalogue Raisonne, 82; auth, Provincetown Printers: A Woodcut Tradition, 83. *Mailing Add:* Nat Mus Am Art Eighth & G Sts NW Washington DC 20560

FLOETER, KENT
SCULPTOR
b Saginaw, Mich, Oct 22, 37. *Study:* Boston Univ, BFA; Yale Univ, MFA. *Work:* Pangborn Found Collection, Hagerstown, Md; Etzold Collection, Stadtisches Mus, Monchengladbach, Ger. *Exhib:* Biennial Exhib Contemp Am Art, Whitney Mus Am Art, New York, 75; Drawings Series Number 3, Painters-Sculptors USA, Stadtisches Mus, Schlob Morsbroich, Levenkusen, Ger, 75; Soho Downtown Manhattan, Akad der Kunst, Berlin, Ger, 76; Selections, La Mus Mod Art, Humlebaeck, Denmark, 76; and other group and one-man shows. *Bibliog:* Carl Baldwin (auth), article, 6/75 & Robert Pincus-Witten (auth), Entries, 3/76, Arts Mag. *Mailing Add:* c/o Mary Boone 42 Bone St New York NY 10012

FLOETHE, RICHARD
ILLUSTRATOR, DESIGNER
b Essen, Ger, Sept 2, 01; US citizen. *Study:* Acad Appl Arts, Dortmund, Ger; Acad Appl Arts, Munich, Ger, with Willy Geiger & Edward Ege; Bauhaus Weimar, Ger, with Moholy-Nagy & Paul Klee. *Work:* Metrop Mus Art, New York; Libr Cong, Washington, DC; Philadelphia Mus Art, Pa; Kerlan Collection, Univ Minn; Spencer Collection, Fifth Ave Libr, New York; and others. *Comn:* Hist mural, Pressa, Cologne, Ger, 28. *Pos:* Art dir, Fed Art Proj, 36-39; art dir, New York City War Serv, 42-43. *Teaching:* Instr com design, Cooper Union, 41-42; instr illus, Ringling Sch Art, 55-67. *Awards:* Int Contest for Best Illus Bks award for Tyl Ulenspiegl, 35 & award for Pinocchio, 38, Limited Ed Club; Am Inst Graphic Arts Award for English is our Language, 50. *Bibliog:* Ronald K Floethe (auth), Kid Stuff, Gordon Kerckhoff Prod, 70; Ludwig Biclschowsky (auth), Richard Floethe, a German-American illustrator in Illustration 63, 74. *Media:* Woodcut, Serigraphy. *Publ:* Illusr, If I were Captain, 56, Blueberry Pie, 62, Jungle People, 71 & Fishing Around the World, 72, Scribner's; illusr, A Thousand & One Buddhas, Ariel, 67; plus many other titles, 32-80. *Mailing Add:* 1391 Harbor Dr Sarasota FL 33579

FLOMENHAFT, ELEANOR
MUSEUM DIRECTOR, HISTORIAN
b Brooklyn, NY, Aug 21, 33. *Study:* Willsey Inst, Hempstead, NY, 69; Hofstra Univ, Hempstead, NY, BA(art hist), 76; Queens Col, NY, 77- *Collections Arranged:* British Watercolors and Drawings 1750-1910 (auth, catalog), 80 & CoBrA, 81, Emily Lowe Gallery, Hofstra Univ; Gifts and Acquisitions, Fine Arts Mus, Long Island, NY, 82. *Pos:* Cur art, Emily Lowe Gallery, Hofstra, 78-80; dir, Fine Arts Mus, Long Island, NY, 81. *Bibliog:* David L Shirey (auth), Spontaneity in another age, New York Times, 2/10/80; Malcolm Preston (auth), Europeans of the CoBrA group, Newsday, 6/8/81; William Neugebauer (auth), Seeks new horizons in art, Daily News, 11/29/81. *Res:* Art of the CoBrA group 1948-1951; the abstract experimentalists of Europe. *Publ:* Auth, Intellect x Emotion-Sculpture, Linden Galleries, New York, 81; auth, The Unique Art of Harold M LeRoy, Profile Press, NY, 81. *Mailing Add:* 1294 Seawane Dr Hewlett NY 11557

FLOOD, EDWARD C
SCULPTOR, PAINTER
b 1944. *Study:* Art Inst Chicago. *Work:* Nat Mus Am Art, Washington, DC; Art Inst Chicago, Ill. *Exhib:* Painting & Sculpture Today, Indianapolis Mus Art, Ind, 70 & 72; XII Sao Paulo Bienal, Brazil, 73; Soc Contemp Art, Art Inst Chicago, Ill, 75; Approach/Avoidance, Queens Mus, Flushing, NY, 81; American Video Artists One, Nat Mus Am Art, Washington, DC, 82; Language, Drama, Source and Vision, New Mus Contemp Art, New York, 83; and others. *Awards:* Cassandra Found Grant, 70; Nat Endowment Artists Fel Grant, 78; Awards in Visual Arts/SEastern Ctr Contemp Art Fel Grant, 81. *Bibliog:* A Schoenfeld (auth), Edward Flood, Arts, 4/80; M Lolis (auth), Between painting and sculpture, Arts, 6/81. *Media:* Acrylic, Wood. *Mailing Add:* PO Box 64 Brooklyn NY 11211

FLOOD, RICHARD SIDNEY
WRITER, CURATOR
b Philadelphia, Pa, Nov 10, 43. *Study:* St Joseph's Col, BA, 65; Univ Pa, Annenberg Sch Commun, MA, 67. *Collections Arranged:* PSI (Inst Art & Urban Resources), Figuratively Sculpting, 81; Franklin Furnace, The Page as Alternative Space: The Last Decade, 81. *Pos:* Ed, Art Exchange, Philadelphia, Pa, 76-79; managing ed, Artforum, New York, 80, books ed, 81- *Res:* Contemporary art; particularly as it relates to popular culture. *Publ:* Contribr, Seven Artists, Neuberger Mus, 80; contribr, The Isdate Artist in America, 81 & auth, Ali Baba and the Forty Thieves, 81, Philadelphia Col Art; auth, Skied and grounded in Queens: New York/new wave, summer 81 & Paul Thek: Real misunderstanding, 10/81, Artforum. *Mailing Add:* 530 W 25th New York NY 10001

FLORA, JAMES ROYER
ILLUSTRATOR, PAINTER
b Bellefontaine, Ohio, Jan 25, 14. *Study:* Urbana Univ, Ohio, 31-33; Art Acad Cincinnati, 34-39; also study & asst to Carl Zimmerman (muralist) & Stanley William Hayter at Atelier 17. *Pos:* Art dir, Columbia Records, Bridgeport, Conn, 42-50, Park East Mag, New York, 51-53 & Computer Design Mag, Littleton, Mass, 62-80. *Media:* Ink; Watercolor, Acrylic. *Publ:* Auth & illusr, The Fabulous Firework Family, 55, The Day the Cow Sneezed, 57 & Leopold, the See-Through Crumbpicker, 61, Harcourt Brace; auth & illusr, The Great Green Turkey Creek Monster, 76 & Grandpa's Ghost Stories, 78, Atheneum; and many others. *Dealer:* Frank Lavaty 45 E 51st St New York NY 10022. *Mailing Add:* St James Pl Rowayton CT 06853

FLOWERS, THOMAS EARL
PAINTER, EDUCATOR
b Washington, DC, Feb 17, 28. *Study:* Furman Univ, BA; Univ Iowa, MFA. *Work:* Greenville Co Mus Art, SC; Columbia Mus Art, SC; Chase Manhattan Bank, New York; Vincent Price Enterprises, Chicago. *Comn:* Mural, Vince Perome, Greenville, SC, 62; mural, Saad Rug Co, Greenville, 63; mace & medallion, Furman Univ, Greenville, 65. *Exhib:* Eighteenth Ann Guild SC Artists Exhib, 68; 11th Ann Southern Contemp Art Exhib, Mobile, Ala, 69; 12th Ann Springs Art Exhib, Lancaster, SC, 70; Atlanta Artists Club, Nat 1, Ga, 70; Southeastern Painter's Choice Exhib, Ga Col, Milledgeville, Ga, 71. *Teaching:* Asst prof art & chmn dept, Ottawa Univ, 56-58; instr sculpture, E Carolina Col, 58-59; assoc prof art & chmn dept, Furman Univ, 59- *Awards:* Purchase Award, SC Arts Comn, 71; Second Award, Franklin Mint, 72; Art in Archit Award, SC Chap, Am Inst Architects, 77. *Bibliog:* Jack A Morris (auth), Contemporary artists of South Carolina, Greenville Co Mus Art, 70; R Smeltzer (auth), article, Southern Living Mag, 12/70; M Hays (auth), article, Furman Univ Mag, spring 72. *Mem:* Guild SC Artists (pres, 61-62, bd dirs, 71-72); Greenville Artists Guild (pres, 72-73); Southeastern Col Art Asn; Am Craftsman's Coun. *Media:* Mixed. *Publ:* Illusr covers, Furman Univ Mag, winter 67, summer 68 & 5/69; illusr cover, Springs Cotton Mill Ann Report, 69; illusr, Images, Univ NC, Asheville, summer 69. *Dealer:* Hampton III Gallery Ltd 10 Gallery Ctr Greenville SC 29601. *Mailing Add:* Box 28606 Furman Univ Greenville SC 29613

FLOYD, CARL LEO
SCULPTOR, ENVIRONMENTAL ARTIST
b Somerset, Ky, Oct 12, 36. *Study:* Kansas City Art Inst, BFA, 64; Cranbrook Acad Art, MFA, 67. *Work:* Praltown Park, Lexington, Ky; Vt Freeway, St Albans; Hogback Nature Park, Madison, Ohio; Mand Corning Prof, Holden Arboretum, Mentor, Ohio; Univ Vt Art Mus, Burlington. *Comn:* Steel & wood sculpture, Willoughby Fine Arts, Ohio, 72; Stone Earth, Inner City, Bad Kreuznach, WGer, 75; All People's Park, Lake Co Metrop Parks, 76-77; Earth-Stone, Cleveland Pub Libr, 79; One Acre Proj, Ohio Arts Coun, Madison, 80. *Exhib:* Contemp Sculpture, J B Speed Mus Art, Louisville, Ky,

68; Environ Sculpture, Dulin Gallery Art, Knoxville, Tenn, 69; 2nd Cincinnati Biennial, Cincinnati Art Mus, 69 & Biennial Awards Exhib, 70; Sculpture of New Era, Chicago Fed Plaza, 76; Sculpture on the Green, Columbus Arts Coun, Ohio, 79; Nature Environ, Minn State Univ, Bemidji, 79. *Teaching:* Instr sculpture & archit, Univ Ky, Lexington, 67-71; instr sculpture, Cleveland Inst Art, 71- *Mailing Add:* 7404 Doty Rd Madison OH 44057

FLUDD, REGINALD JOSEPH
PAINTER, CRAFTSMAN
b New York, NY, June 10, 38. *Study:* Ind Univ, BS(art); Queens Col, MS(art); study with Kenneth Campbell & Barse Miller; Art Inst Chicago; New York City Col. *Work:* Alcoa Aluminum Corp, New York; Norton Mus, Palm Beach, Fla; Nassau Community Col, Garden City, NY; Ocean City Cult Arts Ctr, NJ; Rose Art Mus, Brandeis Univ, Waltham, Mass; and others. *Exhib:* Am Drawing Biennial, Norfolk Mus, 71; Okla Art Ctr, Oklahoma City, 72; Aldrich Mus, Ridgefield, Conn, 74; New Britian Mus Contemp Art, Conn, 74; one-man show, Hecksher Mus, Huntington, NY, 75; and others. *Teaching:* Instr art, Syosset High Sch, NY, 64-; asst prof painting, Suffolk Community Col, 74- *Awards:* Best in Show, Bayshore CofC, 68 & Patchoque CofC, 70; Grand Prix, Locust Valley Art Show, Operation Democracy, 73. *Bibliog:* Laurie Anderson (auth), article in Art News, 1/72; Malcom Preston (auth), article in Newsday, 3/12/75; Jean Paris (auth), article in Long Island Press, 7/6/75. *Mem:* Nat Educ Asn; Nat Art Educ Asn; Huntington Art League; Huntington Group. *Media:* Oil; Rhoplex on Plywood. *Mailing Add:* 24 W Sanders Greenlawn NY 11740

FLUEK, TOBY
PAINTER, GRAPHIC ARTIST
b Czernica, Poland, Feb 20, 26; US citizen. *Study:* Art Students League, with Robert Beverly Hale; also with Joe Hing Lowe & Irving Koenig. *Exhib:* Bronx Mus Arts Ann, NY, 72, 74, 75 & 76; Am Artists Prof League Grand Nat Exhib at Lever House, NY, 72-76, 78 & 79; Hudson Valley Art Asn Ann, White Plains, NY, 73 & 75-83; Catharine Lorillard Wolfe Art Club, Nat Arts Club Gallery, 73-77; Knickerbocker Artists Exhib, Nat Arts Club, New York, 74; and many others. *Teaching:* Instr oil painting, Woodside Jewish Ctr, NY, 72. *Awards:* First Prize, Brush & Palette Soc, 71, 73, 75 & 78; Best Show, Art League Nassau Co, 79; and others. *Bibliog:* Bibliog: Jeanne Paris (auth), Art, Long Island Press, 10/8/72; Fern Allen (auth), Queen artist recalls Holocaust era by recreating vanished scenes, 9/23/79; Image Before My Eyes (doc film), Inst Jewish Res; and others. *Mem:* Am Artists Prof League; Art League Nassau Co; assoc mem Hudson Valley Art Asn; Catharine Lorillard Wolfe Art Club; New York Artists Equity Asn. *Media:* Oil, Charcoal. *Mailing Add:* 60-10 47th Ave Woodside NY 11377

FLUME, VIOLET SIGOLOFF
DEALER, RESTORER
b Huntington, WVa. *Study:* Trinity Univ, with Phillip Wilson. *Work:* Paintings & portraits in pvt collections, US & Mex. *Exhib:* San Antonio Art League, 64-70; one-woman shows, Southwestern Fine Arts Exhib, Univ Tex, 67, HemisFair, 68 & Trinity Univ, 68. *Pos:* Owner & dir, Wonderland Gallery, 66-72 & Wonderland Art Sch, 69-72; owner, Sigoloff Fine Art Galleries, 72- *Awards:* Watercolor & Miniature Award, Composers, Authors & Artists Exhib, New York, 65; San Antonio's Outstanding Woman in Art, San Antonio Express & Eve News, 67. *Mem:* Tex Fine Arts Asn; San Antonio Art League. *Media:* Oil. *Specialty:* Fine art, contemporary and antique paintings. *Mailing Add:* 8410 Tiffany Dr San Antonio TX 78230

FOGEL, SEYMOUR
PAINTER, SCULPTOR
b New York, NY, Aug 25, 11. *Study:* Art Students League, 29, with George Bridgeman; Nat Acad Design, 29-32. *Work:* Whitney Mus Am Art, New York; Joseph H Hirshhorn Collection, Washington, DC; Dallas Mus Art, Tex; Nat Archives of Am Art; City of St Louis Art Mus, Mo. *Comn:* Sand sculpture wall, Hoffmann-La Roche Res Tower, Nutley, NJ, 64; mosaic mural, US Customs Courts Bldg, New York, 68; mosaic mural, Intermediate Sch 29, New York, 71; stained glass screen, Bellevue Hosp, New York, 72; four mosaic murals, New Park West High Sch, New York, 78. *Exhib:* Houston Mus of Fine Arts, Tex, 51; Metrop Mus Art, New York, 51; M Knoedler & Co, 58; one-man shows, Mich State Univ, 61, Allen Stone Gallery, 63, Graham Gallery, New York, 80-83 & Stamford Art Mus, Conn, 81; Berlin & Hamburg, Ger, 80-81; many shows, Whitney Mus Am Art & Nat Gallery Art, Washington, DC. *Teaching:* Asst prof painting, design & mural, Univ Tex, Austin, 46-54; guest prof life drawing & grad painting, Mich State Univ, 61. *Awards:* First Prize, Gulf Carribean Int, Houston, 56; First Prize, Tex Gen, Dallas, 56; First Prize in Design, Archit League New York, 58. *Bibliog:* Zeigfield et al (auth), Art Today, Henry Holt; Ralph Pearson (auth), Modern renaissance in American art, Harper & Row, 54; Redstone (auth), Art & architecture, McGraw, 70. *Mem:* Archit League. *Publ:* Auth, Ethyl silicate & architecture, Archit & Engr News, 60; auth, Painter & architect, Am Inst Architects J, 60; auth, Art & the church, Liturgical Arts, 60; auth, Architect discovers painting & sculpture, Mich Am Inst Architects J, 61; auth, Painting & sculpture as architecture, Art in Am, 62. *Dealer:* Graham Gallery 1014 Madison Ave New York NY 10021. *Mailing Add:* Torandor 339 Georgetown Rd Weston CT 06883

FOGG-GERBER, MONICA
PAINTER, INSTRUCTOR
b Belaire, Tex. *Study:* Wash Univ, 73; Principia Col, Elsah, Ill, BA, 74. *Work:* General Mills, Minneapolis, Minn; Prudential Insurance Co Am, Plymouth, MN; Principia Col, Elsah, Ill; Honeywell, Minneapolis, Minn; Marathon Oil

Co, Midland, Tex. *Comn:* Minn Protective Life, Eden Prairie, 75; Woodhill Country Club, Wayzata, 82; AMFAC-City Ctr, Minneapolis, 82. *Exhib:* Metamorphose/One, Minn Mus Art, St Paul, 76; Midwest Watercolor Ann, Tweed Mus, Duluth, Minn, 77 & 78; Northstar Soc Ann, Minneapolis, 77-83; Aqueous Open, Pittsburgh Watercolor Soc, Pa, 78; one-woman show, Expressive of Alaska, Artique, Anchorage, 81; Minn Artist Asn, Minneapolis, 82; and others. *Teaching:* Instr, St Louis Watercolor Soc, 74, Northstar Watercolor Soc, 77, Univ Minn, 80-, Edina Art Ctr, 80-81, Fogg Gerber Studio, 81-83, Art Ctr Minn, 83. *Awards:* Second Prize, Minn 77, State Arts Coun, 77; Award Excellence, Northstar Watercolor Soc Ann, 77, 80, 82 & 83; Award of Excellence, Minn Artists Asn, 82; and others. *Bibliog:* Fredric Appel (auth), Watercolor: when it's good, Minn Star & Tribune, 78; Cindy Rumsey (auth), Artist on the move (film), WCCO-TV, Minneapolis, 81; Warren Martin (auth), Watercolor-An Art (film), WTCN-TV, Minneapolis, 81. *Mem:* Minn Soc Fine Arts; Northstar Watercolor Soc (treas, 78-81 & bd mem, 78-81); Midwest Watercolor Soc; Twin Cities Watercolor Soc. *Media:* Watercolor. *Dealer:* Fogg-Gerber Studio 18279 Minnetonka Blvd Deephaven MN 55371. *Mailing Add:* 5117 Washburn Ave S Minneapolis MN 55410

FOHR, JENNY
PAINTER, PRINTMAKER
b New York, NY. *Study:* Hunter Col, BA; Alfred Univ; Univ Colo, MA; City Col. *Work:* Norfolk Mus, Va; Long Beach Island Found Arts & Sci, NJ; Dr Wardell Pomeroy, New York; Oakland Mus, Calif; Charles Suter, Ciba-Geigy, New York. *Exhib:* One-man show, Chautauqua Art Asn Galleries, NY, 60 & Brooklyn Mus, 61; Nat Asn Women Artists, Chateau de la Napoule, France, 65; Nat Asn Women Artists Traveling Show, India, 66; NJ State Mus, Trenton, 68; Am Color Print Soc Traveling Show, 72. *Teaching:* Asst instr sculpture, Brooklyn Mus, 49-51; instr art, Beekman Hill Sch, 69- *Awards:* Samuel Mann Award, Am Soc Contemp Artists, 71; May Granick Award, Nat Asn Women Artists, 75; Doris Kreindlr Award, 81; and many others. *Bibliog:* Article, New York News, 76. *Mem:* Am Soc Contemp Artists (pres, secy, bd dir); Nat Asn Women Artists (secy, jury chmn, dir); Painters & Sculptors Soc NJ (selection jury, bd); Am Color Print Soc; New York Soc Women Artists (dir, cat chmn). *Media:* Multimedia. *Mailing Add:* 165 E 32 St New York NY 10016

FOLDA, JAROSLAV (THAYER), III
HISTORIAN
b Baltimore, Md, July 25, 40. *Study:* Princeton Univ, AB, 62; Johns Hopkins Univ, PhD, 68. *Teaching:* From asst prof to assoc prof medieval art, Univ NC, Chapel Hill, 68-78, prof, 78-83, chmn, 83- *Awards:* Dumbarton Oaks Ctr Fel, 67-68; Jr Humanist Award, Nat Endowment Humanities, 74-75; Nat Endowment Humanities, 81-83. *Mem:* Medieval Acad Am; Col Art Asn Am; Int Ctr Medieval Art; Am Schs Oriental Res; Soc Francaise d'Archeol. *Res:* Medieval art of the High and Late Middle Ages, especially Crusader art, 1099-1291. *Publ:* Auth, Manuscripts of the History of Outremer, Scriptorium Vol 27, 73; auth, Crusader Manuscript Illumination at St Jean d'Acre, Princeton Univ Press, 76; contribr, K M Setton (ed), A History of the Crusades, Vol 4, Univ Wis Press, 77; ed, Crusader art in the twelfth century, British Archeol Reports, Vol 152, 82; auth, Crusader frescoes at Crac des CheVolaliers and Marqab castle, Dumbarton Oaks Papers, v 136, 82. *Mailing Add:* Dept of Art 079A Univ of NC Chapel Hill NC 27514

FOLDS, THOMAS MCKEY
EDUCATOR, CONSULTANT
b Connellsville, Pa, Aug 8, 08. *Study:* Yale Col, BA, 30; Yale Univ Sch Fine Arts, BFA, 34. *Comn:* Mural, US Govt, Pub Works Admin, 34. *Exhib:* Painting a Mural & Art in Advertising, traveling exhibs for Am Fedn Arts. *Teaching:* Art dir, Phillips Exeter Acad, 35-46; prof art hist & chmn dept art, Northwestern Univ, 46-60; dean educ, Metrop Mus Art, 60-73, guest lectr, 73- *Mem:* Col Art Asn Am; Sch Art League New York (pres, 68-75). *Publ:* Auth, A critique of color reproductions, Col Art J, 48-49; co-auth, Masterpieces of painting in the Metropolitan Museum of Art, 70; auth, Abstract painting (exhib), Macmillan, 70. *Mailing Add:* 909-B Heritage Village Southbury CT 06488

FOLEY, KATHY KELSEY
DIRECTOR, HISTORIAN
b Perth Amboy, NJ, Aug 24, 52. *Study:* Trinity Col, Hartford, Fall semester in Rome, 72-73; Vassar Col, AB(hist art), 74; Nat Gallery Art, Washington, DC, internship cert, Summer 74; Johns Hopkins Univ, MA(hist art), 75. *Collections Arranged:* Mezzotints from the Collection of Edward Miller, 76 & Edward Weston's Gifts to His Sister (125 photographs), 78, Dayton Art Inst; Collaborations, Mary and Leigh Block Gallery, 80; Exploring Society Photographically, Mary and Leigh Block Gallery, 81; Chinese Ceramics from Chicago Collections, 82; Discoveries from Kurdish Looms, Block Gallery, 83. *Pos:* Asst cur, Dayton Art Inst, Ohio, 75-76, cur, 76-79; dir, Mary & Leigh Block Gallery, Northwestern Univ, Evanston, 79- *Teaching:* Inst, Brooklyn Mus, NY Dept Educ, Summer 73; lectr, Dept Art Hist, Northwestern Univ, 80- *Mem:* Am Asn Mus; Col Art Asn; Int Coun Mus. *Publ:* Co-auth, Selected Checklist of the Collection of the Dayton Art Inst, 76, auth, Handbook of the American Collection of the Dayton Art Inst, 76 & auth, Joseph Stella-Enigmatic Painter, Bulletin of Dayton Art Inst, 77, Dayton Art Inst; auth, Collaborations, Mary & Leigh Block Gallery, 80. *Mailing Add:* Mary & Leigh Block Gallery Northwestern Univ Evanston IL 60201

FOLEY, KYOKO Y
INSTRUCTOR, PAINTER
b Tokyo, Japan, Dec 23, 33; US citizen. *Study:* Mt San Antonio Col, AA, 69; Calif State Univ, Fullerton, BA & MA, 72; Claremont Grad Sch, MFA, 77.

Work: Mt San Antonio Col Gallery; Home Savings & Loan Asn, Calif; Security Pac Nat Bank, Culver City, Calif. *Comn:* Flower Garden 'n Forest, Amar Nursing Sch, Valinda, Calif, 74. *Teaching:* Instr drawing & painting, Scripps Col, Claremont, Calif, 78-79 & Claremont Grad Sch, 79-80; instr, Coast Line Community Col, Fountain Valley, currently. *Media:* Acrylic, Oil. *Mailing Add:* 21851 Newland St Space 33 Huntington Beach CA 92646

FOLKUS, DAN (DANIEL ALAN FREDRICKSON)
DESIGNER, ILLUSTRATOR
b Rice Lake, Wis, Oct 1, 46. *Study:* Lawrence Univ, BA(philosophy & art), 68; Southern Methodist Univ, 74; assisted muralist Granville Bruce, Dallas, 72. *Work:* Dallas Mus Natural Hist; Kenosha Pub Mus, Wis; Charleston Mus, SC. *Comn:* Murals & sculpture, NY Power Authority Mus, 82; Christmas murals, Lord & Taylor, New York, 82; sculpture, Ocean One, Atlantic City, 83; murals & sculpture, Azrak-Hamway, New York, 83; sculptures, Coca Cola-Seagrams 7, 83; and others. *Exhib:* Hermit Art, Water St Arts Ctr, Milwaukee, 77. *Pos:* Preparator, Dallas Mus, 72-74; freelance illusr, 74-78; cur exhibs; Kenosha Pub Mus, Wis, 78-79; chief exhibs planner/designer, Charleston Mus, SC, 79-80; asst film dir, WCBD-TV, SC, 80-81; pres, Visual Syntax, New York, NY & Collingswood, NJ, 82- *Mem:* Am Asn Mus. *Media:* Ink, Acrylic. *Publ:* Illusr, Pests Control, auth, Dr E P Cheatum, Prestige Press, 73; illusr, Hermit City (cartoon commentaries), Appleton Post-Crescent, 76; illusr, Dust storms of Mars, 77 & illusr, Phobos, 77, Astronomy Mag; and others. *Mailing Add:* 465 Haddon Ave Collingswood NJ 08108

FOLLETT, JEAN FRANCES
SCULPTOR, PAINTER
b St Paul, Minn, June 5, 17. *Study:* Univ Minn, AA; Hans Hofmann Sch Art, New York; Sch of Fernand Leger, Paris, France, 46-51. *Work:* Mus Mod Art, New York; Whitney Mus Am Art, New York; Univ Mass; Univ Calif; Univ Tex. *Exhib:* Group shows & four one-man shows, Hansa Gallery, New York, 51-59; Guggenheim Mus, 54; Leo Castelli Gallery, New York, 60; Soho Gallery, New York, 77; Landmark Gallery, New York, 77. *Awards:* Cash Award, Nat Found Arts & Humanities, 66. *Bibliog:* Fred W McDarrah (auth), The Artists World, E P Dutton & Co, 61; Irving Sandler (auth), The New York School, Harper & Row, 78; Tom Hess (auth), Art and Sexual Politics, Macmillan, 78. *Mailing Add:* 1510 English St St Paul MN 55106

FOLSOM, KARL LEROY
PRINTMAKER, INSTRUCTOR
b Seattle, Wash, Oct 18, 38. *Study:* Diablo Valley Col, Pleasant Hill, Calif, AA, 71, study with John Spence Weir; San Francisco State Univ, BA, 73, study with Jack Welpott & Don Worth, MA, 77, study with Dennis Beall & John Ihle. *Work:* Erie Cult Ctr, Pa; Univ Calif, Los Angeles; Palo Alto Cult Ctr, Calif. *Exhib:* Photography into Sculpture, Mus Mod Art, New York, 70; Erie Festival of the Arts, 74; 2nd NH Int Graphica Ann, 75; Bradley Print Show, Bradley Univ, Peoria, Ill, 75; Calif Invitational, Golden West Col, Huntington Beach, Calif, 75 & 76; 3rd & 4th Hawaii Nat Print Exhibs, 75 & 76; 30 Yrs of Am Printmaking, Brooklyn Mus, 76 & 77; and others. *Teaching:* Instr printmaking, Univ Calif Irvine Exten, San Francisco, 75-80; guest lectr, San Francisco State Univ, 79-80; adult educ instr photog & silkscreen, Acalanes Dist, Lafayette, Calif, 79-80; instr photog, Solano Community Col, Suisun, Calif, 80. *Awards:* Purchase Award, Refocus 74, Univ Iowa, 74. *Mem:* Calif Soc Printmakers (coun mem, 74-); Assoc Visual Dialogue Found. *Dealer:* van Straaten Gallery 646 N Michigan Ave Chicago IL 60611. *Mailing Add:* 3380 22nd St San Francisco CA 94110

FON, JADE
PAINTER, INSTRUCTOR
b San Jose, Calif, Sept 7, 11. *Study:* Northern Ariz Univ; Art Students League. *Work:* Trans-Am Corp, Los Angeles; Mus Sci & Art, Los Angeles; Lepersarium, Carlinville, Ill. *Exhib:* Soc Western Artists Ann, De Young Mus, San Francisco, 62; Am Watercolor Soc, New York, 69; Haggin-Pioneer Mus, Stockton, Calif, 72; Calif State Fair, Sacramento, 73; Franklin Mint Gallery Am Art, Pa, 74. *Pos:* Founder & dir, Asilomar Watercolor Workshop, 64. *Teaching:* Art teacher, Diablo Valley Col, 54-82, emer, 82- *Awards:* Foothills Ctr Cash Award, Golden, Colo, 77; Dalta Art Asn Best of Show, 83; Leroy Ulrich Mem Award, 83. *Mem:* Am & West Coast Watercolor Socs; Soc Western Artists. *Media:* Watercolor, Pastel. *Mailing Add:* 1237 Raymond Dr Pacheco CA 94553

FONDREN, HAROLD M
DEALER
b Canton, Ohio, Feb 5, 22. *Study:* Harvard Col, AB. *Pos:* Asst dir, Stable Gallery, 54-55; asst dir, Poindexter Gallery, 55- *Specialty:* Contemporary painting and sculpture. *Mailing Add:* Poindexter Gallery 1150 Fifth Ave New York NY 10028

FONTANA, BILL PATRICK
ENVIRONMENTAL ARTIST, CONCEPTUAL ARTIST
b Cleveland, Ohio, April 25, 47. *Study:* John Carroll Univ, 65-68; New Sch Social Res, BA, 70. *Comn:* Flight Paths Out to Sea, Newport Harbor Art Mus, Newport Beach, Calif, 80; Oscillating Steel Grids, Contemporary Art Ctr, Cincinnati, 80; Landscape Sculpture with Fog Horns, New Music Am, San Francisco, 81; Sound Sculpture with a Sequence of Level, 12th Int Sculpture Conf, Oakland, Calif, 82; Crossings Rochester Birds: 1983, Nat Shopping Ctrs, Rochester, NY, 83. *Exhib:* Sound Sculpture, Nat Gallery Victoria, Melbourne, Australia, 78; Space Between Sounds, San Francisco Mus Mod Art, 78; Fur Augen und Ohren, Akad Künste, West Berlin, 80; Ecouter par les Yeux, Mus Art Mod, Paris, 80; Soundings, Neuberger Mus, Purchase, NY, 81; Great East River Bridge, Brooklyn Mus, 83. *Teaching:* Guest artist,

Berliner Künstlerprogramm, Deutscher Akad Austauschdienst, 83-84. *Bibliog:* The Art of Sound, CBS News, 9/19/82. *Media:* Sound Sculpture. *Publ:* Auth, The music of sound, Village Voice, 83; auth, Brooklyn Bridge Sound Sculpture by Bill Fontana, Am Haus Berlin, 83. *Mailing Add:* PO Box 375 Berkeley CA 94701

FONTANINI, CLARE
EDUCATOR, SCULPTOR
b Rutland, Vt. *Study:* Col St Catherine, AB; Columbia Univ, with Josef Albers & Oronzio Maldarelli, MA. *Work:* Lamentations of Jerimiah (marble), Barnett-Aden Gallery, Washington, DC; Seat of Wisdom (walnut), Col St Catherine, St Paul, Minn; Copper Crucifix, Trinity Col Libr, Washington, DC. *Comn:* Madonna & Child (cherry wood), 69 & Rood Figures (carved), St Agnes & Ascension Episcopal Church, Washington, DC; Emily Reeder Mem, 72; Four Stations of the Cross, St Ann's Church, Manlius, NY; and others. *Exhib:* Mint Mus Art, Charlotte, NC; Walker Art Gallery, Minneapolis; Va Mus Fine Arts, Richmond; Corcoran Gallery Art, Washington, DC; Nat Collection Fine Arts, Smithsonian Inst, Washington, DC; and many others. *Teaching:* Instr design, Phillips Mem Gallery, Am Univ, Washington, DC, 46-47; asst prof sculpture, Cath Univ Am, 47-58, head dept art, 47-68, prof sculpture, 58-73, emer prof art, 73- *Awards:* First Prize Medal for Sculpture, Nat Christian Arts Festival, Univ Wis, 55; Frank E Jellef Award for Sculpture, Washington, DC, 57; First Prize for Sculpture, Corcoran Gallery Art Ann Area Show, 59. *Mem:* Artists Equity Asn; Soc Washington Artists (secy, 43-45, vpres, 47). *Media:* Stone, Wood. *Mailing Add:* 1029 Perry St NE Washington DC 20017

FOOLERY, TOM
ASSEMBLAGE ARTIST, PAINTER
b Green Bay, Wis, Aug 29, 47. *Study:* Self-taught. *Work:* Pierotti Pavillion, San Francisco; and others. *Comn:* Murals, St Francis Mem Hosp, San Francisco, 79-81. *Exhib:* Humor in Art, Los Angeles Inst Contemp Art, 81; one-man shows, William Sawyer Gallery, San Francisco, 81 & Jacqueline Anhalt Gallery, Los Angeles, 82; Dobrick Gallery, Chicago, 83; Anxious Interiors, Laguna Beach Mus Art, Calif, & traveling, 84; and others. *Bibliog:* Frank Cabulski (auth), Art of control, Artweek, 2/21/81; Neal Menzies (auth), Carrot Commentaries, Artweek, 11/27/82. *Media:* All. *Dealer:* Jacqueline Anhalt Gallery Los Angeles CA; Dobrick Gallery, Chicago. *Mailing Add:* 186 Clara San Francisco CA 94107

FOOSANER, JUDITH
EDUCATOR, PAINTER
b Sacramento, Calif, Aug 10, 40. *Study:* Univ Calif, Berkeley, BA, 64 & MA, 68. *Work:* Newport Harbor Art Mus, Newport Beach, Calif. *Exhib:* Laguna Beach Mus, Calif, 67; Calif Palace Legion Honor, San Francisco, 69; Bellevue Art Mus, Wash, 76; M H DeYoung Mem Mus, San Francisco, 77; Oakland Mus, Calif, 81. *Teaching:* Assoc prof fine arts, Calif Col Arts & Crafts, Oakland, 70-82; vis asst prof art, Univ Calif, Berkeley, 75-77. *Media:* Oil. *Mailing Add:* 5626 Ocean View Oakland CA 94618

FOOSE, ROBERT JAMES
PAINTER, DESIGNER
b York, Pa, Oct 17, 38. *Study:* Univ Ky, AB, 63. *Work:* J B Speed Art Mus, Louisville, Ky; Owensboro Mus Art, Ky; Springfield Art Mus, Mo; New York Pub Libr; Libr of Cong, Washington, DC; and others. *Comn:* Bks & bk jackets, Univ Ky Press, 60-78 & bk illus, 78; portraits, UK Law Alumni Asn, Univ Ky, 79, 81 & 83; posters & catalogs, Univ Ky Art Mus, 80. *Exhib:* 600 Years of American Watercolor Painting, J B Speed Art Mus, 77; one-person show, Kathulische Akademie Trier, WGer, 82; The Kentucky Tradition in American Landscape Painting, Owensboro Art Mus, Ky, 83; Kentucky Art 1983, Univ Ky Art Mus, 83; Kentucky Art, James Hunt Barker Galleries, New York, 83; and others. *Pos:* Founder & proprietor, Buttonwood Press, Lexington, Ky, 68- *Teaching:* Guest lectr watercolor, Western Ky Univ, 75; instr, Europ Summer Acad Fine Art, Trier, WGer, 80-81; asst prof graphic design, Univ Ky, currently. *Awards:* John Singer Sargent Award, Southern Watercolor Soc, 78 & 80; Grand Prize, Aqueous '79, Ky Watercolor Soc; First Place, Ky Watercolor Soc, 83. *Mem:* Ky Guild Artists & Craftsmen (pres, 69-73); Ky Watercolor Soc; Nat Soc Arts & Letters; Southern Watercolor Soc; and others. *Media:* Watercolor; All Print Media. *Publ:* Illusr, Uncle Will of Wildwood, 74 & Bestiary, 75, Univ Ky; illusr, The Trembling Land, Helecon Press, 80; and others. *Dealer:* Merida Galleries 2007 Frankfont Ave Louisville KY 40206. *Mailing Add:* 203 Tahoma Rd Lexington KY 40503

FOOTE, HOWARD REED
ARTIST, PRINTMAKER
b Richmond, Ind, Dec 15, 36. *Study:* Toledo Mus Art, Ohio, 54-55; Sch of Mus Fine Arts, Boston, 55-57; San Francisco Art Inst, BFA, 60; Stanford Univ, MA, 70; additional study with Nathan Oliveira. *Work:* Achenbach Found, Palace of the Legion of Honor, San Francisco; City of Leeds, Eng; City of San Francisco; Stanford Univ. *Exhib:* Bay Area Printmakers Soc Fourth Nat Exhib, Oakland Mus, Calif, 58; 1970 Peace Exhib, Philadelphia Mus Art, 70; San Francisco Art Inst Centennial Exhib, Palace of the Legion of Honor, San Francisco, 71; Four Printmakers, San Francisco Mus Art, 71; 18th Nat Print Exhib, Brooklyn Mus, NY, 72; San Francisco Area Printmakers, Cincinnati Art Mus, Ohio, 73; Interstices, San Jose Art Mus, Calif & Cranbrook Acad Art Mus, Bloomfield Hills, Mich, 75. *Teaching:* Instr printmaking, Acad Art, San Francisco, 70- & Calif State Univ, Hayward, 71-72; instr printmaking, drawing & 3-D design, Col Notre Dame, Belmont, Calif, 75- *Publ:* Contribr, Ramparts Mag, 6/70; contribr, BYTE, 9/81. *Mailing Add:* Box 462 Inverness CA 94937

FORAKIS, PETER
SCULPTOR
b Hanna, Wyo, Oct 2, 27. *Study:* Calif Sch Fine Arts, BFA, 57. *Comn:* Tower of the Lakotas (steel tubing sculpture), Williams Col, Williams, Mass, 66; Gateway (cast iron tubing sculpture), Great Southwest Corp, Atlanta, Ga, 66-67; Earth Handle (wood sculpture), Denver City Park, Colo, 68; Tower of the Cheyenne (corten steel tubing sculpture), Univ Houston, Tex, 72; Jack London (steel plate), Oakland Mus, 82. *Exhib:* New Forms New Media, Martha Jackson Gallery, New York; one-man show, Tibor de Nagy, New York, 63-64; American Artists Drawings, Guggenheim Mus, New York, 64; Primary Structures, Jewish Mus, New York, 65; Sculpture of the 60's, Los Angeles Co Mus, Los Angeles, 66. *Awards:* Nat Endowment Arts, 81. *Publ:* Auth & illusr, Grope Comics, Vol I & II, 63 & 66. *Mailing Add:* 7060 Bodega Ave Petaluma VT 94952

FORBES, DONNA MARIE
MUSEUM DIRECTOR
b Albion, Nebr, Mar 19, 29. *Study:* Mont State Univ; Pratt Inst; Eastern Mont Col, BS(art educ); Harvard Summer Inst in Arts Admin. *Collections Arranged:* 13th-16th Centuries Art of the Christmas Theme from the Metrop Mus, 78 & The Cowboy, 79, Yellowstone Art Ctr, Billings, Mont. *Pos:* Dir, Yellowstone Art Ctr, Billings, Mont, 74- *Teaching:* Instr design & art educ, Eastern Mont Col, 52-53. *Mem:* Western Asn Art Mus; Am Asn Mus; Mont Art Gallery Dirs Asn. *Mailing Add:* 1116 Eighth St W Billings MT 59102

FORBES, JOHN ALLISON
HISTORIAN, PAINTER
b Evansburg, Alta, Sept 19, 22. *Study:* Univ Alta, BEd, 48, MEd, 51; Univ London, associateship, 56; Univ Iowa, MA, 67. *Collections Arranged:* Bart Pragnell--Watercolours, Univ Art Gallery, Edmonton, 67; J B Taylor--Memorial (auth, catalog), Edmonton Art Gallery, 73. *Teaching:* Assoc prof art educ, Univ Alta, 49-65, prof art hist, 65- *Mem:* Royal Soc Arts, London; Univs Art Asn Can. *Media:* Watercolor, Acrylics. *Res:* Western Canadian landscape painters; military art. *Publ:* Coauth, Mountain landscapes of J B Taylor, Can Alpine J, Vol 57, 74; auth, Douglas Haynes (exhib catalog), Glenbow Art Gallery, Calgary, 74; auth, Robert Sinclair (exhib catalog), Aggregation Gallery, Toronto, 76. *Mailing Add:* 11523-77 Ave Edmonton AB T6G 0M2 Canada

FORCE, ROLAND WYNFIELD
MUSEUM DIRECTOR
b Omaha, Nebr, Dec 30, 24. *Study:* Stanford Univ, BA, 50, MA, 51, MA, 52 & PhD, 58; Hawaii Loa Col, Honolulu, DSc, 73. *Pos:* Assoc ethnology, Bishop Mus, 54-56, dir, 62-76; cur, Oceanic Archit & Ethnology, Field Mus, 56-61; dir, Mus Am Indian, 77- *Teaching:* Acting instr, Stanford Univ, 52-54; lectr, Univ Chicago, Ill, 56-61. *Mem:* Am Asn Mus; Int Coun Mus. *Publ:* Coauth, Art and Artifacts of the 18th Century, Bishop Mus Press, 68; coauth, The Fuller Collection of Pacific Artifacts, Praeger, 71. *Mailing Add:* Mus Am Indian Broadway & 155th St New York NY 10032

FORD, CHARLES HENRI
PAINTER, PHOTOGRAPHER
b Mississippi. *Work:* Univ Southern Ill, Carbondale; Univ Tex Arch, Austin. *Exhib:* Photographs, Inst Contemp Art, London, Eng, 54 & Carleton Gallery, New York, 75; Drawings & Paintings, Galerie du Dragon, 57 & 58, Paris; Color Photo-Lithos (poem posters), Cordier & Eckstrom, New York, 75; sculptures, prints & tapestries, New York Cult Ctr, 75; postcards to Charles Henri, Iolas Gallery, New York, 76; Layouts & Camouflages, Robert Samuel Gallery, New York, 80. *Bibliog:* Parker Tyler (auth), article, In: Screening the Sexes, Holt, Rinehart & Winston, 72. *Publ:* Auth, Spare Parts, 66; auth, Silver Flower Coo, 68; auth, Flag of Ecstasy, 72; auth, Om Krishna I: Special Effects, 79; auth, Om Krishna II, 81. *Mailing Add:* 1 W 72 St New York NY 10023

FORD, HARRY XAVIER
EDUCATOR, ADMINISTRATOR
b Seymour, Ind, Jan 12, 21. *Study:* John Herron Art Inst; Univ Calif Los Angeles, BA; Sacramento State Col, MA; Univ Calif Berkeley. *Pos:* Chmn dept teacher educ, Calif Col Arts & Crafts, 58-60, pres, 60- *Teaching:* Art, Placer Union High Sch, 51-53 & Stuttgart Am High Sch, Ger, 53-58. *Mem:* Nat Asn Schs Art (treas, 76-); Union Independent Cols Art (chmn, 72-74). *Media:* Oil. *Mailing Add:* 21 Humphrey Pl Oakland CA 94610

FORD, JOHN
PAINTER
b Washington, DC, Mar 2, 50. *Study:* Self-taught. *Work:* Oakland Mus Art; Prudential Insurance Co, Newark, NJ; Nashville Med Corp, Tenn. *Exhib:* Whitney Mus Am Art Biennial, 75; Aspects of Abstract, Crocker Art Mus, Sacramento, Calif, 79; Coastal Currents, Ctr Arts, Corpus Christi, Tex, 81; Sacramento Connection, Laguna Gloria Mus, Laguna Beach, Calif, 82; Jersey City Art Mus, NJ, 82; solo exhib, State Univ NY, Purchase, 82. *Teaching:* Lectr, Bakersfield State Univ, 77; Sacramento State Univ, 78 & C W Post Ctr, Long Island Univ, 83. *Awards:* Artists Fel, Nat Endowment Arts, 82. *Bibliog:* Thomas Albright (auth), Sleepers and spectacles, Art News, 9/79; Vivien Raynor (auth), article, New York Times, 82. *Media:* Acrylic, Oil. *Mailing Add:* 496 Broadway New York NY 10012

FORD, JOHN CHARLES
PAINTER
b Choudrant, La, Sept 29, 29. *Study:* La Polytech Inst, BFA, 50; Univ Tex; Austin Presby Theol Sem, BD, 53; Art Students League, 57; Univ Ore, MFA, 60. *Work:* Seattle Art Mus, Wash; Guggenheim Mus; Neuberger Mus, Purchase, NY; Hirschhorn Mus, Washington, DC; Corcoran Mus, Washington, DC; and others. *Exhib:* San Francisco Mus Art, 59 & 60; Seattle Art Mus, 63; Contemp Am Drawings, Smithsonian Inst, Washington, 63; Cambridge Sch Archit, Eng, 69; one-man shows, Guild Hall Mus, East Hampton, NY, 74, Neuberger Mus, Purchase, NY, 77 & Sid Deutsch Gallery, New York, NY, 77; plus many others. *Bibliog:* David Shirey (auth), Paintings that prod, New York Times, 2/6/77; John Russell (auth), article in New York Times, 12/2/77. *Mailing Add:* 121 Mercer St New York NY 10012

FORD, JOHN GILMORE
COLLECTOR
b Baltimore, Md. *Study:* Baltimore City Col, degree; Johns Hopkins Univ; Loyola Col; Md Inst Col Art, BFA. *Exhib:* Collection Indo-Asian art, Walters Art Gallery, Baltimore, 71. *Pos:* Nat vpres, Am Inst Interior Designers, 70- *Awards:* Citation of merit, Md Inst Col Art, 60. *Bibliog:* P Pal (auth), Indo-Asian art, 71, Walters Art Gallery, Apollo Mag & Connoisseur Mag. *Mem:* Am Fedn Arts; Asia Soc. *Collection:* Indian, Nepalese, Tibetan, Javanese, Chinese & Japanese bronzes, stone sculptures and paintings. *Mailing Add:* 2601 N Charles St Baltimore MD 21218

FORD, RUTH VANSICKLE
PAINTER
b Aurora, Ill, Aug 8, 1898. *Study:* Chicago Acad Fine Arts, cert; Art Students League; summers with John Carlson and spec classes with George Bellows, Guy Wiggins, Jonas Lie & Bruce Crane. *Work:* Pub Libr, YMCA, Aurora Col, Aurora, Ill; Lafayette Col, Ind; Northern Ill Gas Co. *Comn:* Portrait of Freeman for Freeman Room, Aurora YMCA, 68; portrait of head dept drama, Aurora Col, comn by sr class for gift to col, 69. *Exhib:* One-man show, Chicago Art Inst, 34; Grand Cent Galleries, New York, 47; Watercolor USA, Springfield, 62-63; Nat Acad Design; Am Artists, Chicago Art Inst; and many others. *Pos:* Pres-dir, Chicago Acad Fine Arts, 37-60. *Teaching:* Prof life class, Chicago Acad Fine Arts, 30-37; prof painting, Aurora Col, 64-70. *Awards:* Chicago Woman's Aid Prize, Chicago Art Inst, 31; Gold Medal Award for Oil Painting, Palette & Chisel Acad, 63; DFA, Aurora Col, 74; and many others. *Mem:* Am Watercolor Soc; hon mem Artist Guild Chicago; Am Artists Prof League; Palette & Chisel Acad; Rockport Art Asn, Mass. *Media:* Watercolor, Oil. *Dealer:* Schramm Galleries 215 SW Second St Ft Lauderdale FL 28315. *Mailing Add:* 69 Central Ave Aurora IL 60506

FORESTER, RUSSELL
PAINTER
b Salmon, Idaho, May 21, 20. *Study:* Inst of Design, Chicago, 50. *Work:* Guggenheim Mus, New York; La Jolla Mus Contemp Art, Calif; McCrory Corp, New York; Security Pacific Bank, Los Angeles; Cedars-Sinai Medical Ctr, Los Angeles, Calif; and others. *Exhib:* Houston Mus Fine Art, Tex, 62; Nat Drawing Exhib, San Francisco Mus Art, 70; Santa Barbara Mus Art, Calif, 74; Phoenix Art Mus, Ariz, 75; Sheldon Mem Art Gallery, 76; Fine Arts Gallery of San Diego, 76 & Drawing Show, 77; Everson Mus Art, Syracuse, NY, 77; New Acquisitions, Guggenheim Mus, 77, La Galerie, Paris, France, 77; San Diego Mus Art, 78; La Jolla Contemp Art, 79, 81 & 83; and others. *Bibliog:* Roland Anrig (auth), Russell Forester, Art Int, 1/73; Melinda Wortz (auth), articles, Art News, 9/79 & 4/83; Betty Brown (auth), article, Arts Mag, 1/83; and others. *Media:* Mixed media. *Mailing Add:* 2025 Soledad Ave La Jolla CA 92037

FORGE, ANDREW MURRAY
WRITER, PAINTER
b Hastingleigh, Kent, Eng, Nov 10, 23. *Study:* Camberwell Sch Art, London, 57-59, with William Coldstream & Kenneth Martin. *Work:* Tate Gallery, London; Arts Coun Gt Brit. *Exhib:* Retrospective, Bristol Mus, Eng, 64; Inst Contemp Arts, Boston, 75. *Pos:* Trustee, Tate Gallery, London, 64-72, Nat Gallery, London, 66-70, Am Acad Rome, 82- *Teaching:* Lectr painting, Slade Sch, London, 50-64; prof painting, Yale Sch Art, 75- *Awards:* Guggenheim Fel, 79-80. *Media:* Oil. *Res:* 19th and 20th century art. *Publ:* Auth, Soutine, 65; auth, Rauschenberg, Abrams, 69; auth, Monet, Abrams, 83. *Mailing Add:* 684 Whitney Ave New Haven CT 06511

FORGEY, BENJAMIN F
CRITIC
b Ashland, Ky, July 31, 38. *Study:* Princeton Univ, BA, 60. *Pos:* Art critic, Washington Star, 67-81, art/archit critic, Washington Post, 81- *Mem:* Int Art Critics Asn (Am sect). *Res:* 20th century art, architecture. *Publ:* Various articles in Art News Mag, 70-, Smithsonian Mag, 75-, Portfolio Mag, 78- & Aperture Mag, 79- *Mailing Add:* 2856 28th St NW Washington DC 20008

FORMAN, ALICE
PAINTER
b New York, NY, June 1, 31. *Study:* Cornell Univ, with Kenneth Evett & Norman Daly, BA; Art Students League, with Morris Kantor. *Exhib:* Whitney Mus Am Art, 60; White Mus Art, Cornell Univ, 61; Phoenix Gallery, NY, 66, 68, 71, 74 & 75; Marist Col, 68 & 71; Butler Inst Exhib, 72; Kornblee Gallery, 77 & 79; American Still Life, Contemp Arts Mus, Houston, 83; and others. *Teaching:* Lectr, Marist Col, 77; vis asst prof painting & drawing, Vassar Col, 80-81. *Awards:* Nat Student Asn Regional Awards; Daniel Schnackenberg Merit Scholar, Art Students League. *Media:* Oil. *Dealer:* Kornblee Gallery 20 W 57th St New York NY 10019. *Mailing Add:* 8 Croft Rd Poughkeepsie NY 12603

FORMAN, KENNETH WARNER
PAINTER, EDUCATOR
b Landour, India, June 5, 25; US citizen. *Study:* Wittenberg Col, AB, BFA; Ohio State Univ, MA. *Work:* Wittenberg Col, Springfield, Ohio; Univ RI, Kingston; Hartford CofC Festival Collection, Conn; Univ Conn Hon Ctr, Storrs. *Exhib:* Nat Drawing Exhib, Ball State Teachers Col, Muncie, Ind, 65; 12th Biennial Exhib Contemp Am Prints, Brooklyn Mus, 65; 23rd Int Exhib Soc Printmakers, US Nat Mus, 66; Contemp Am Painting, Mem Art Mus, Rochester, NY, 67; Nat Watercolor Exhib, Peoria Art Ctr, Ill, 67. *Teaching:* Instr media & techniques, painting, Am Archit & art hist, Univ Conn, 57-, prof art, 68- *Awards:* First Painting Award, Silvermine Guild Artists, 57; First Painting Award, Mystic Art Asn, Conn, 63; Hartford Art Festival Purchase Award, Hartford CofC, 72. *Mem:* Conn Watercolor Soc; Soc Archit Historians; Victorian Soc Am; Victorian Soc Eng; Am Fedn Arts. *Media:* Oil, Watercolor. *Res:* Victorian architecture in England and New England; traditional media with synthetic media in painting. *Publ:* Auth, Understanding in the Arts, 59 & illusr, 61, Fine Arts Mag; illusr, spec ed, Penny Paper, 64; auth, Salvador Dali's moustache, Floating Opera, 67; auth, Connecticut Architecture During the Growth of the Nation, William Benton Mus of Art, Univ Conn, 76. *Mailing Add:* 1010 Warrenville Rd Mansfield Center CT 06250

FORMICOLA, JOHN JOSEPH
PAINTER, EDUCATOR
b Philadelphia, Pa, Dec 27, 41. *Study:* Fleischer Art Mem, 56-59; Pa Acad Fine Arts, cert(Cresson Award, Schiedt Award), 63. *Work:* Philadelphia Mus Art; Cleveland Mus Art, Ohio; Miami Mus Mod Art, Fla; Mus Art, Carnegie Inst, Pittsburgh; Prudential Insurance Co Am. *Exhib:* Del Art Mus, Wilmington, 78; Contemporary Drawings, Philadelphia Mus Art & Pa Acad Fine Arts, 78; solo exhibs, Frank Marino Gallery, New York, 80 & Marian Locks Gallery, Philadelphia, 80; 20th Anniversary Del Biennial Exhib, Univ Del, Newark, 82. *Pos:* Owner & dir, Gallery Pane Vino, 65-68; dir, Marian Locks Gallery, Philadelphia, 68-73; designer & consult, Danhart-Heim Architects, 76-77. *Teaching:* Instr design, Drexel Univ, Philadelphia, 70-; instr painting, Cleveland Inst Art, Ohio, 79-80. *Awards:* First Hallgarten Award, Nat Acad Design, 65. *Dealer:* Frank Marino 489 Broome New York NY 10013; Marian Locks Gallery Philadelphia PA 19102. *Mailing Add:* 705 Federal St Philadelphia PA 19147

FORMIGONI, MAURI MONIHON
PAINTER, EDUCATOR
b Louisville, Ky, Nov 6, 41. *Study:* Kalamazoo Col, Mich, BA, 63; Art Inst Chicago; Sangamon State Univ, Springfield, Ill, MA, 72; Contemp Art Workshop, Chicago, with Cosmo Campoli. *Work:* Borg-Warner Corp, Chicago; Epcot Ctr, Disney World, Fla; Boromeo Collection, Pavia, Italy; Container Corp of Am; Playboy Enterprises, Chicago. *Exhib:* 36th Mid-States Exhib, Evansville Mus Art, Ind; Indiana Artists, Indianapolis Mus Art; 27th Invitational, Ill State Mus, Springfield; Galleria Podovini, Desenzano del Garda, Italy; Artists Invite Artists, Artemesia Gallery, Chicago; and others. *Pos:* Res asst for Bruno Bettelheim, Univ Chicago, 63-66; courtroom artist, ABC-TV, Chicago, 71. *Teaching:* Instr, Lincoln Land Community Col, Springfield, 71-75, 81-82; adjunct asst prof creative arts, Sangamon State Univ, 75- *Awards:* Ill Arts Coun Project Completion Grant, 82; Merit Award, Evansville Mus Art, 83. *Bibliog:* John Ratliff (auth), Pyrex (film), 72. *Mem:* Chicago Artists Coalition; Springfield Art Assoc. *Media:* Acrylic on plexiglass, Pastels. *Publ:* Illusr, Brainchild I, Women's Poetry Collective, 73; illusr cover, Down the Mississippi, Harcourt & Brace, 81; auth, An arts hazard story, Chicago Artists' Coalition Newsletter, 7/81. *Mailing Add:* 216 1/2 S Sixth St Springfield IL 62701

FORNAS, LEANDER
PRINTMAKER, INSTRUCTOR
b Gardner, Mass, June 18, 25. *Study:* Pratt Inst, cert, 50; Kunstgewerbeschule, Zurich, 51; Ateneum, Helsinki, 51-53; Univ Mass, MFA, 73 & currently. *Work:* Mus Mod Art, New York; Ateneum, Helsinki; Libr Cong; Rockefeller Collection; New York Pub Libr. *Comn:* Developed new glass engraving methods, Steuben Glass, New York, 55; graphic indust illus, portrait comns & misc design, Finland, 59-65; designed & instituted graphics facilities, Pratt Inst, NY, 58, Fine Arts Ctr, Univ RI, 66 & Holyoke Community Col, 72-75. *Exhib:* One-man shows, New Talent, Mus Mod Art, 55 & Sao Paulo Biennial Prints, 59; Curator's Choice, Print Club, Philadelphia, 56; Printmakers Soc Finland Traveling Exhib, US, Europe & Far East, 59-66. *Pos:* Dir, Design & Graphics Studio, Helsinki, 58-66. *Teaching:* Instr printmaking & drawing, Holyoke Community Col, 70-, chmn art dept, 70-74. *Mem:* Printmakers Soc Finland (bd dirs, 59-61). *Media:* All. *Mailing Add:* 2 Dudleyville Rd Leverett MA 01054

FORNELLI, JOSEPH
PAINTER, SCULPTOR
b Chicago, Ill, May 21, 43. *Work:* Cornell Univ, Ithaca, NY; Park Ridge Pub Libr, Ill; Jim Bridger Pub Sch System, Bridger, Mont. *Comn:* Dell Publ for Pres Nixon, New York, 74; Encycl Britannica for Pope Paul VI, Chicago, 74; Columbus Hosp, Chicago, 76; Italian Cult Ctr, Stone Park, Ill, 77; Ducks Unlimited, Chicago, 79. *Exhib:* Palette & Chisel Club, Chicago, 82; Denver Mus Natural Hist, 82; Nat Wildlife Fedn, Vienna, Va, 83; Acad Natural Sci Mus, Philadelphia, 83; Reflexes & Reflections, Vietnam Vet Arts Group, WPA Gallery, Senate Rotunda & US House Rep Rotunda, Washington, DC & LBJ Mus, Austin, Tex, 83; and others. *Pos:* Painter & sculptor, Richard Rush Studio, Chicago, 73-74; art dir, Monastery Hill Bindery, Chicago, 74-77; design coordr, Ducks Unlimited, Chicago, 79-83; bd dirs, Chicago Munic Art League, 79-; pres, Vietnam Veterans Arts Group, 81- *Awards:* Gold Medal, Chicago Munic Art League, 79; Award of Merit, Soc Animal Artists Denver Mus, 82; Blue Ribbon, Nat Wildlife Fedn, 83. *Bibliog:* Mary Ann Mills (auth), Art snares wild spirit, Chicago Tribune, 9/80; Art reflects Vietnam War, New York Times, 10/81; Joan Johnson (producer), Good Morning America, ABC TV, 10/81. *Mem:* Chicago Munic Art League; Chicago Artists Guild; Soc Animal Artists; assoc Am Watercolor Soc. *Media:* Watercolor, Oil; Bronze, Stone. *Publ:* Illusr, Sinclair Lewis' Main Street 1970, Inland Mag, 70; auth & illusr, Shield against time, 80 & illusr, Omens, 81, Ducks Unlimited Mag; illusr, America Outdoors, Izaak Walton League, 82; cover illusr, Rick Eilert's For Self & Country, Morrow Publ, 83. *Dealer:* Fornelli Studio 1017 S Prospect Park Ridge IL 60068. *Mailing Add:* 1017 South Prospect Park Ridge IL 60068

FORREST, CHRISTOPHER PATRICK
PRINTMAKER, PAINTER
b Trenton, NJ, Oct 2, 46. *Study:* Va Polytechnic Inst, BS, 68; NC State Univ, MS, 74. *Work:* Nat Acad Sci, Washington, DC; NJ State Mus, Trenton; Ferrum Col, Va; Metro Goldwyn Mayer, Los Angeles; Bausch & Lomb, Rochester, NY. *Exhib:* Easton Waterfowl Festival, Md, 80-83; Soc Animal Artists Exhib, Acad Nat Sci, Philadelphia, 81; one-man shows, Golden Door, New Hope, Pa, 81, Town Plaza, Brea, Calif, 83 & Chabot Galleries, Campbell, Calif, 83; Soc Animal Artists Ann, Denver Mus Nat Hist, 82; Nat Wildlife Fedn Wildlife in Art Show, Vienna, Va, 83; and others. *Pos:* Gen production mgr, Evergreen Publ Inc, 80-81. *Awards:* First Prize, Cary Arts Guild, NC, 73; Helen Richard Award for Best NC Scene, 73; Purchase Prize, NC Wildlife, Central Carolina Bank, 74. *Bibliog:* Member of the issue, North Light Mag, 8/79; Cathy Lyons Colletti (auth), All-enveloping moods, Southwest Art Mag, 81. *Mem:* Soc Animal Artists; Buzzard Coun Am. *Media:* Lithography, Intaglio; Acrylic, Oil. *Publ:* Illusr covers, Ducks Unlimited Mag, 78 & Readers Digest, 83. *Dealer:* Hang Ups 1319 W Katella Ave Orange CA 92667. *Mailing Add:* 31 Enter Turn Willingboro NJ 08046

FORREST, JAMES TAYLOR
MUSEUM DIRECTOR, EDUCATOR
b New Castle, Ind, Sept 22, 21. *Study:* Hanover Col, Ind; Ind Univ, Indianapolis; Univ Wis, BS, 48 & MS, 49. *Comn:* Art and artifacts for interior trapper room, Grand Teton Lodge, Jackson Lake, Wyo, 55. *Collections Arranged:* National Painting Exhibition, Gilcrease Inst, Tulsa, Okla, 59; Collector's Choice-European Art, Fine Arts Mus, Santa Fe, NMex, 61; Art of the American West, Fine Arts Mus, Santa Fe; Santa Fe Arts Festival, 81; and several retrospectives and others. *Pos:* Cur mus, Colo State Mus, Denver, 53-55; dir, Gilcrease Inst, 55-61; dir, Mus NMex, Santa Fe, 61-64; dir, Univ Wyo Art Mus, 68-; mem, Wyo Gov Coun Art in Pub Places. *Teaching:* Instr Am hist, Tulsa Univ, 58-60; instr Am art, Sheridan Col, Wyo, 66-67; instr, Am art hist, Univ Wyo, Laramie, 68- *Mem:* Am Asn Mus (secy, 79-82, nat coun mem, 83-86); Mountain-Plains Mus Conf (coun, 72-, vpres, 79-80, pres, 81); Colo-Wyo Asn Mus (chmn, 73-); Wyo Coun Arts (coun, 67-81, chmn, 71-73). *Res:* Art and artists of the American 19th century. *Publ:* Contribr, Keepers of the Past, Clifford Lord, Chapel Hill, 65; auth, Hans Kleiber-Artist of the Big Horns, 67 & Bill Gollings-Ranahan Artist, 69, Bradford Brinton Mem Ranch Mus, Big Horn, Wyo; auth, History of New Mexico, Teachers Press, Columbia, 72; auth, Bill Gollings--The Man and His Art, Northland Press, 79. *Mailing Add:* Box 3138 Univ Station Laramie WY 82071

FORRESTALL, THOMAS DE VANY
SCULPTOR, PAINTER
b Middleton, NS, Mar 11, 36. *Study:* Mt Allison Univ, 54-58; Can Coun grant to travel & study in Europe, 58-59, sculpture grant, 67. *Work:* Can Coun; Winnipeg Art Gallery; Art Gallery Windsor; Confederation Mem Gallery; Nat Gallery, Hungary; and others. *Comn:* Kennedy & Churchill Mem, Prov NB, 64; steel sculpture, Atlantic Pavilion, Expo 67; welded relief mural, Centennial Bldg Fredericton, 68; two large welded steel sculptures, Can Govt, Fed Bldg, Antigonish, NS, 70; mural abstract for playhouse, Beaverbrook Can Found, Fredericton, 72. *Exhib:* One-man shows, Montreal Mus Fine Arts, 72, Nat Mus Art, Bulgaria, 80, Nat Gallery Art, Romania, 81, Nat Mus Art, Transylvania, Nat Mus Art, Hungary, 81 & Bayard Gallery, New York, 81; and others. *Pos:* Asst cur, Beaverbrook Art Gallery, 59-60. *Awards:* Citation of Art Merit, Secy State, Commonwealth Mass, 72; Can Coun Lectr Tour Grants, 77-79; Queen's Jubilee Medal, 78. *Bibliog:* P Murphy (auth), Shaped paintings..., article, Art Mag, 78. *Mem:* Royal Can Acad Arts. *Media:* Tempera; Steel, Iron. *Publ:* Coauth, Shapes, 72. *Mailing Add:* c/o Three Oaks Corp 3 Albert St Dartmouth NS B2Y 3M1 Canada

FORRESTER, CHARLES HOWARD
SCULPTOR, EDUCATOR
b Jersey City, NJ, Sept 30, 28. *Study:* Univ Wash, BFA, 58; Univ Ore, MFA, 60. *Work:* Bundy Art Gallery, Waitsfield, Vt; Shakespeare Mem Theatre, Ashland, Ore; Medford Pub Parks, Ore; Western Ky Univ, Bowling Green. *Comn:* Sculpture (cast stone), Red Cross Bldg, Medford, Ore, 62; Five Sisters, Broughton Sch, Salford, Eng, 65; Two Figures, Mathews Co, Little Rock, Ark, 67; two sculptures (cast aluminum & cor-ten steel), PCA Bldg, Glasgow, KY, 74; Family Group, Bowling Green Hosp, Ky. *Exhib:* Mid-States Craft Exhib, Evansville Mus Art, 80; one-man show, Sweet Briar Col, 80; Small Sculpture/ Drawing, Ball State Univ, 80; Box Exhib, Arrowmont Sch Arts & Crafts, Gatlinburg, Tenn, 80; Capitol Arts Ctr, Bowling Green, Ky, 81; Del Mar Col, 82; Cafe Musee, J B Speed Mus, 83; and others. *Teaching:* Lectr sculpture, Salford Tech Col, Eng, 63-65; prof sculpture, Western Ky Univ, Bowling Green, 65- *Awards:* Citizens Nat Bank Purchase Award, Capitol Arts Ctr, Bowling Green, Ky, 81. *Bibliog:* Anon (auth), Some Younger Northwest Sculptors, NW Rev, 61; M Harold (ed), Prize-Winning Sculptures, Allied Publ Inc, 67. *Mem:* Southern Asn of Sculptors (vpres, 66-70). *Media:* Cast Metal, Fabricated Metal. *Mailing Add:* PO Box 102 Col Heights PO Bowling Green KY 42101

FORRESTER, PATRICIA TOBACCO
PAINTER, PRINTMAKER
b Northampton, Mass, Sept 17, 40. *Study:* Yale Summer Sch Music & Art, 61; Smith Col, BA, 62; Yale Univ Sch Art, BFA, 63, MFA, 65. *Work:* Brooklyn Mus; San Antonio Mus Art; Achenbach Found, Legion Hon; Oakland Mus; Mem Art Gallery, Univ Rochester. *Exhib:* Solo exhib, San Francisco Mus Art, 68 & M H De Young Mem Mus, 77; American Watercolors, Mitchell Mus & Cedar Rapids Art Ctr, Mt Vernon, Ill, 79; West Coast--Art for the Vice President's House, Washington, DC, 80; Real, Really Real, Super Real, San Antonio Mus Art, 81; Ten Plus Ten Plus Ten Washington Painters, Corcoran Gallery, 82; American Realism, Davidson Collection, Pa Acad Fine Arts, 83; Washington Watercolor, Corcoran Gallery, 84. *Teaching:* Asst prof printmaking, Calif Col Arts & Crafts, 72-81; guest artist painting, Kent State Univ, 81 & Art Inst Chicago, 82. *Awards:* Guggenheim Fel Printmaking, 67; Yaddo Fel, 79 & 81; MacDowell Colony Fel, 80. *Bibliog:* John Arthur (auth), Realist Drawings & Watercolors, New York Graphic Soc, 80; Ann Gerocimos (auth), article, Am Artist, 11/83. *Media:* Watercolor. *Dealer:* Kornblee Gallery 20 W 57th St New York NY 10019; Fendrick Gallery 3059 M St NW Washington DC 20007. *Mailing Add:* 2220 20th St NW Washington DC 20009

FORSMAN, CHUCK (CHARLES STANLEY)
PAINTER, EDUCATOR
b Nampa, Idaho, May 5, 44. *Study:* Univ Calif, Davis, study with Wayne Thiebaud & William Wiley, BA, 67; study with Gabriel Laderman, 70, MFA, 71. *Work:* Phoenix Art Mus, Ariz; Marion Koogler McNay Art Inst, San Antonio, Tex; Grinnel Col, Iowa; Wichita Art Mus; Denver Art Mus. *Exhib:* One-man shows, Tibor De Nagy Gallery, New York, 73, 75, 77, 79, 81 & 83, Watson De Nagy Gallery, Houston, 76, St Charles Gallery, Denver, 78, Wichita Art Mus, 81 & Yellowstone Art Center, Billings, Montana, 83; Nassau County Mus Fine Arts, Roslyn, NY, 80; Rahr-West Mus, Manitowoc, Wis, 82; Summit Art Center, NJ, 82; Boulder Center Visual Arts, Colo, 83; and others. *Teaching:* Asst painting & sculpture, Univ Calif, Davis, 70-71; assoc prof painting, Univ Colo, Boulder, 71- *Awards:* Nat Endowment Arts Grant, 79; Fac fel, Univ Colo, Boulder, 79; Mus Purchase, Am Acad Arts & Letters, 79. *Media:* Oil on Masonite. *Dealer:* Tibor De Nagy Inc 29 W 57th St New York NY 10019. *Mailing Add:* 511 Pleasant St Boulder CO 80302

FORST, MILES
SCULPTOR, EDUCATOR
b Brooklyn, NY, Aug 18, 23. *Study:* Mus Mod Art Vet Ctr; Art Students League, with Morris Kantor; Esquela Obrera, Mexico City; Hans Hofmann Sch Fine Arts. *Work:* Mus Mod Art, New York; Newark Mus, NJ; Mass Inst Technol, Cambridge; Chrysler Mus, Provincetown, Mass; Bowdin Col Mus. *Exhib:* Goldowsky-Bellamy Gallery, New York, 69; Sch Visual Arts, New York, 70; Otis Art Inst, Los Angeles, 74 & 79; 112 Green St, New York, 76; Los Angeles Contemp Exhib, 78; and others. *Pos:* Co-organizer, Exile Gallery, La, 81-82. *Teaching:* Instr painting & drawing, Sch Visual Arts, 63-71; assoc prof painting, San Francisco State Univ, 71-72; head, Intermedia Dept, Otis Art Inst, 71-79, chmn, Grad Sch, 80- *Awards:* Working artist award, Walter K Gutman Found, 60, 62 & 65; working artist award, Longview Found, 61 & 62; artist in residence, Ford Found, 65, 77-79. *Bibliog:* Article in Art Collectors Ann, 67; Kaprow (auth), Happenings, 68; Drs P & E Kronhausen (auth), Erotic Art, Grove, 69. *Dealer:* Richard Bellamy 157 Chambers St New York NY 10007. *Mailing Add:* 14 Westminster Ave Venice CA 90291

FORSYTH, CONSTANCE
PAINTER, PRINTMAKER
b Indianapolis, Ind, Aug 18, 03. *Study:* Butler Univ, BA; John Herron Art Sch, with W Forsyth & Clifton Wheeler, dipl; Pa Acad Fine Arts, with Henry McCarter & George Harding; Broadmoor Art Acad, Colorado Springs, Colo, with Ward Lockwood & Boardman Robinson. *Work:* Indianapolis Art Mus, Ind; Tex Fine Arts Asn; Ball State Teachers Col, Muncie, Ind; Joslyn Mem Mus, Omaha, Nebr; Dallas Mus Fine Arts; and others. *Exhib:* Watercolor, Bern, Switz, 57, Tokyo, Japan, 60, traveling print show to India, 65 & foreign exhib, Florence, Italy, 72, Nat Asn Women Artists; 16th Libr Cong Print Exhib, Esslingen on the Necker, Ger, 79. *Teaching:* Instr art, John Herron Art Sch, Indianapolis, 31-33; interim instr art, Western Col, Oxford, Ohio, spring 39; prof art, Univ Tex, Austin, 40-73, emer prof, 73- *Awards:* Naomi Goldman Prize for Surf (aquatint), Nat Asn Women Artists, 61; Maco Press Prize for Deluge (aquatint), John Herron Art Mus, 61; Purchase Prize for Up Close (watercolor), Tex Fine Arts Asn, 72. *Media:* Watercolor, Aquatint. *Publ:* Illusr, Friends, Steck Co, 51. *Mailing Add:* 7102 Kenosha Pass Austin TX 78749

FORSYTH, ILENE H(AERING)
EDUCATOR, HISTORIAN
b Detroit, Mich, Aug 21, 28. *Study:* Univ Mich, AB, 50; Columbia Univ, AM, 55, PhD, 60. *Teaching:* Lectr, Barnard Col, 56-58; instr, Columbia Univ, 59-61; asst prof, Univ Mich, Ann Arbor, 61-68, assoc prof, 68-74, prof, 74-84, Arthur F Thurnau prof, 84-; vis prof hist art, Harvard Univ, 80; Andrew W Mellon prof, Univ Pittsburgh, 81. *Awards:* Charles Rufus Morey Book Award, Col Art Asn, 74; Inst Advan Study Fel, 77. *Mem:* Col Art Asn (mem bd dirs, 80-, mem exec comt, 82-); Midwest Art Hist Soc (mem bd dirs, 79-81); Acad Arts, Sci & Belles Lett, Dijon; Int Ctr Medieval Art (vpres & dir, 81-); Soc Francaise Archeol. *Res:* Medieval art, especially Romanesque sculpture. *Publ:* Auth, Magi and majesty: Romanesque sculpture and liturgical drama, Col Art Asn Bulletin, 68; auth, Throne of Wisdom, Princeton Univ Press, 72; auth, Ganymede capital at Vezelay, Gesta, 76; auth, Cockfighting in Burgundian Romanesque sculpture, Speculum, 78; auth, Balaam in Romanesque sculpture, Gesta, 81. *Mailing Add:* 5 Geddes Heights Ann Arbor MI 48104

FORT-BRESCIA, BERNARDO M
ARCHITECT
b Lima, Peru, Nov 19, 51. *Study:* Princeton Univ, BA(archit), 73; Harvard Univ, MArch, 75. *Comn:* Babylon, Pacific Developers, Miami, Fla, 77; Atlantis, Stonecrest Development, Miami, Fla, 78; The Palace, Helmsley Enterprises, Miami, Fla, 78; Imperial at Brickell, Harlon Group, Miami, Fla, 79; Overseas Tower, Overseas Finance Corp, Miami, Fla, 80. *Exhib:* New Americans, Inst Archit & Urban Studies, Rome, Italy, 78; Work of Arquitectonica, Cooper-Hewitt Mus, New York, 79, Pa State Univ, 80 & Univ Va, 81; and others. *Pos:* Principal, Arquitectonica, Coral Gables, Fla, 77- *Teaching:* Vis prof archit, Univ Miami, Coral Gables, Fla, 75-77. *Awards:* Citation, Progressive Archit Ann Design Awards, 78 & 80. *Bibliog:* Articles, Wall St J, 7/7/83, Archit Rec, 7/83, Global Archit Document 7, 8/83 & others. *Mem:* Am Inst Architects; Architectural Club of Miami (pres, 78-80). *Mailing Add:* 4215 Ponce De Leon Blvd Coral Gables FL 33146

FORTESS, KARL E
PAINTER, PRINTMAKER
b Antwerp, Belgium, Oct 13, 07; US citizen. *Study:* Art Inst Chicago; Art Students League; Woodstock Sch Painting, with Yasuo Kuniyoshi. *Work:* De Cordova Mus; Mus Mod Art, New York; Brooklyn Mus; Nat Collection Fine Arts, Smithsonian Inst; Butler Inst Am Art; and many others incl pvt collections. *Exhib:* Art Inst Chicago; Mus Mod Art, New York; Whitney Mus Am Art; Nat Inst Arts & Letters; Nat Acad Design; plus many other group & one-man shows. *Pos:* Artist fed art projects, Works Proj Admin; contract with US Dept Health, Educ & Welfare for tape-recorded interviews with contemp Am artists (over 350 tapes). *Teaching:* Instr art, Art Students League, Brooklyn Mus Art Sch, La State Univ & Am Art Sch; vis artist, Ft Wright Col; from prof art to emer prof, Boston Univ Sch Arts. *Awards:* Nat Endowment Arts Grant; Salmagundi Club Prize, 73; Adolph & Clara Obrig Award, 79. *Bibliog:* Holger Cahill (auth), New Horizons in American Art; Ralph Pearson (auth), Modern Renaissance in American Art; Arthur Zaidenberg (auth), Prints & How to Make Them; plus many others. *Mem:* Artists Equity Asn; Soc Am Graphic Artists; Art Students League; Am Asn Univ Prof; Brit Film Inst. *Media:* Oil. *Res:* Participated in making a pictorial record of the Territory of Alaska for the US Dept of Interior. *Publ:* Auth, On the nature of things or the things of nature, In: Art of the Artist, Crown, 52; auth, Comics as non-art, In: Funnies: an American Idiom, Free Press, 63. *Mailing Add:* 311 Plochmann Rd Woodstock NY 12498

FOSTER, APRIL
PRINTMAKER, INSTRUCTOR
b Berwyn, Ill, Oct 9, 47. *Study:* Univ Ill, Champaign-Urbana, BFA, 70, MA(art educ; fel), 71; Tyler Sch Art, Temple Univ, MFA(printmaking; fel), 73. *Exhib:* Color Print USA, Tex Tech Univ, Lubbock, 73; Mem Exhib, Print Club, Philadelphia, 74; Cincinnati Exhib: Drawings & Prints, Cincinnati Art Mus, 74; All Ohio Graphics & Photography 1975, Dayton Art Inst; Works on Paper by Six Artists From the Midwest, San Diego Univ, 75. *Teaching:* Asst printmaking, Temple Univ, 71-72, instr printmaking, summer 73; instr printmaking & drawing, Art Acad Cincinnati, 73- *Mem:* Col Art Asn; Print Club, Philadelphia. *Media:* Lithography, Intaglio. *Mailing Add:* Art Acad Cincinnati Eden Park Cincinnati OH 45202

FOSTER, DON
SCULPTOR
b London, Eng, Sept 3, 32; US citizen. *Study:* Nottingham Col Art, Eng, 49-53; Royal Col Art, London, Eng, 55-58. *Work:* Memphis Acad Arts, Tenn; Univ Houston, Tex; Tex A&M Univ; Ferreira Collection, Barcelona, Spain. *Comn:* Bronze Doors, City Southend-on-Sea, Eng, 65; mural, Shell Oil Singapore, 67; mosaic mural, Bank West Africa, Lagos, 68; neon wall relief, Hyatt Regency Hotel, Houston, Tex, 72. *Exhib:* Neon Works, Waco Art Mus, Tex, 78; 72 Hour Private View, Robinson Galleries, Houston, Tex, 80; PV Series 100, Am Embassy, Mexico City, 81; Off the Wall, San Antonio Mus Art, Tex, 81; Recent Mixed with Neon Works, McAllen Int Mus, Tex, 82. *Teaching:* Tutor, Royal Col Art, London, Eng, 61-66; head fine art dept, Coventry Col Art, Eng, 66-70; guest lectr, Derby Col Art, Eng, 69; head design dept, Colchester Col Art, Eng, 70-72; guest lectr, Rice Univ, 71; vis artists, Mus Fine Arts, Houston, Tex, 75; guest artist, Edward Albee Found, 79. *Awards:* Traveling Scholarship, Royal Col, London, Eng, 59; First Prize, Fry-Drew Mural Co, 59. *Bibliog:* Art & Architecture, McGraw-Hill, 66; Plumb (auth), Houses Arch Live In, Vicking Press, 77. *Media:* Mixed Media, Neon. *Mailing Add:* c/o Robinson Galleries 1200 Bissonnet Houston TX 77005

FOSTER, DONALD ISLE
DEALER
b Seattle, Wash, July 9, 25. *Study:* Stanford Univ, BA, 47, MBA, 49. *Pos:* Owner, Foster/White Gallery, Seattle, 72- *Specialty:* Contemporary Northwest art. *Mailing Add:* 311 1/2 Occidental Ave S Seattle WA 98104

FOSTER, HOLLAND
PAINTER
b Caledonia, Iowa, Feb 15, 06. *Study:* Nat Acad Design; State Univ Iowa, BA & MA; Columbia Univ, also with John F Carlson, Sidney Dickinson, Alice Murphy & Wayman Adams; study in Eng, France, Spain & Holland. *Work:* Ames Col; Woodstock Guild Craftsmen, NY; Univ Iowa, also in many pvt collections. *Comn:* Portraits of family members, comn by Mrs Charlotte S McLean, Kingston, NY, 63, Mrs Nathan Katatsky, 69 & Dr David S Gerberg, 73; Grand Tetons (landscape), comn by Dr Norman F Foster, Denver, Colo, 74; Mont Blanc (landscape), comn by Mr Robert Foster, Foncenex, France, 75. *Exhib:* One-man show, Savings & Loan Asn, Kingston, 71; Woodstock Guild

Craftsman Exhib, Kleinart Gallery, 78- *Teaching:* Teacher special art, Kingston Schs, Kingston, NY, 45-65. *Awards:* Cert Merit, 75. *Mem:* Woodstock Guild Craftsmen. *Media:* Oil, Clay. *Publ:* Co-auth, Art in Kingston schools, 56; auth, The Ghost Town of Caledonia, 78. *Mailing Add:* 67-290 Mission Dr Palm Springs CA 92264

FOSTER, MAELEE THOMSON
EDUCATOR, PRINTMAKER
b Milford, Conn, Sept 19, 32. *Study:* Univ Bridgeport, BS(art educ), 64; Tyler Sch Art, Temple Univ, MFA, 69. *Work:* State Fla, State Senate Bldg, Tallahassee; Champion Paper Co, Stamford, Conn; Barnett Bank, Fla Artists Collection, Jacksonville; Trans-Co Company Public, Houston, Tex; Housatonic Community Col, Bridgeport, Conn. *Comn:* Collagraphs, Honeywell Int, Philadelphia, Pa, 69-74; cover & logo, Vupak Control System, Honeywell Int, Philadelphia, Pa; collage & cover designs, Technical Publ Co, Chicago, Ill, 71-72. *Exhib:* Six Nat Print Exhibs, 64-80 & five New England Ann, 65-79, Silvermine Guild Artists, Conn; Six Printmakers, Philadelphia Art Alliance, Pa, 70; Am Grafikk, Gallery 15, Oslo, Norway, 73; Lock Haven Art Mus, Orlando, Fla, 80; Prints USA: 1982 Traveling Exhib, Pratt Graphics Ctr, New York. *Pos:* Art dir, State Conn, Long Lane Sch, 64-67. *Teaching:* Instr drawing & design, Univ Bridgeport, Conn, 69-71; assoc prof graphic & design, Univ Fla, Col Archit, Gainesville, 71-81. *Awards:* First Prize, 64 & Best in Show, 66, Mus Arts & Sci, Bridgeport, Conn; First Prize, 67 & Purchase Prize, 68, New Haven Paint & Clay Club, Post Arts Gallery; Mixed Media Award, New England Ann Silvermine, John Kellam Assoc Award, 69. *Bibliog:* Articles, Philadelphia Inquirer, 4/27/69 & Times Picayune, 5/21/72. *Mem:* Am Color Print Soc; Artists Equity Asn; Intersoc Color Council; Silvermine Guild Artists; Print Club. *Media:* Collage, Collograph. *Publ:* Ed, An Introduction to Cards on the Table, concept drawings by the Architect, Richard England, MRSM Publ, Malta, Gt Brit, 81. *Dealer:* Galleries Int 401 B Park Ave N Winter Park FL 32789; Gallery Contemporanea Jacksonville FL. *Mailing Add:* 4030 NW 19th Pl Gainesville FL 32605

FOSTER, ROBERT STEPHEN
DEALER, PUBLISHER
b Greer, SC, Jan 3, 43. *Study:* Univ SC, BS, 64, MFA, 65. *Collections Arranged:* Louise Nevelson: Prints, 75, Carol Summers Print Retrospective (auth, catalog), 77, Gordon Mortensen: Woodcuts (auth, catalog) 78 & Edward S Curtis: Complete Works (auth, catalog), 78, ADI Gallery; Daniel Joshua Goldstein: Woodcuts (auth, catalog), Foremost-McKesson, 79. *Mem:* Am Marketing Asn; Nat Art Dealers Asn; Prof Picture Framers of Am. *Specialty:* Contemporary art; lithographs; screenprints; etchings. *Collection:* Contemporary artists. *Publ:* Contribr, Thirty Years of Printmaking (catalog), Brooklyn Mus, 77. *Mailing Add:* 388 Dolores St San Francisco CA 94110

FOSTER, STEPHEN C
HISTORIAN, WRITER
b Princeton, Ill, Dec 3, 41. *Study:* Northern Ill Univ, BA; Univ Ill, MA; Univ Pa, PhD. *Pos:* Co-dir, Corroberee, Gallery of New Concepts, Univ Iowa, Iowa City, 76-, dir, Fine Arts Arch, Dada Arch & Res Ctr. *Teaching:* Asst prof art hist, Bowdoin Col, Brunswick, Mass, 72-74; mem fac, Am Painting Summer Inst, 74 & 76; assoc prof art hist & criticism, Univ Iowa, Iowa City, 74-; mem fac, Dublin Seminars, Boston Univ, Dublin, NH, summer 76. *Awards:* Nat Endowment Arts Grants, 78-80; Nat Endowment Humanities Grant, 80-81; and others. *Mem:* Col Art Asn Am; Midwest Art Hist Soc; Midwest Col Art Asn Am. *Res:* Sociology of modern art with research emphasis in the areas of Dada and Abstract Expressionism; folk art. *Publ:* Auth, Dada Artifacts, 78; co-ed, Dada Spectrum, 78; co-ed, Intermedia, 78; auth, Critics of Abstract Expressionism, 81; and others. *Mailing Add:* Sch Art & Art Hist Univ Iowa Iowa City IA 52240

FOSTER, STEVEN DOUGLAS
PHOTOGRAPHER
b Piqua, Ohio, Sept 10, 45. *Study:* Nathan Lyons Home Workshop, Rochester, 64-66; Rochester Inst Technol, AAS, 65; Inst Design, Ill Inst Technol, BS, 68; Univ NMex, MFA, 72. *Work:* Art Inst Chicago; High Mus, Atlanta; Int Mus Photog at George Eastman House, Rochester; Visual Studies Workshop, Rochester; Univ NMex Art Mus. *Exhib:* Vision & Expressions, Int Mus Photog at George Eastman House, Rochester, 69; Artists in Ga, High Mus, Atlanta, 74; Wis Dirs II, Milwaukee Art Ctr, 78; Am Photog in the 70's, Art Inst Chicago, 79; Perception: Field of View, Los Angeles Ctr for Contemp Photog, 79. *Teaching:* Asst prof photog, Ga State Univ, Atlanta, 72-75; assoc prof photog, Univ Wis-Milwaukee, 75- *Awards:* Wis Arts Bd Visual Arts Fel, 77; Wis Arts Bd Project Grant-in-Aid, 78; Grad Sch Res Grant, Univ Wis-Milwaukee, 79. *Mem:* Soc Photog Educ. *Media:* Black and White Silver Print. *Publ:* Contribr, Vision and Expression, 69 & The City: American Experience, 71, Horizon Press; contribr, The Print, Time/Life Libr, 71; contribr, Nine Contemporary Photographers, Ga State Univ, 75; contribr, Wisconsin Directions II, Milwaukee Art Ctr, 78. *Dealer:* Frumkin Gallery 620 N Michigan Ave Chicago IL 60611. *Mailing Add:* 2924 N Prospect Ave Milwaukee WI 53211

FOULGER, RICHARD F
SERIGRAPHER, PAINTER
b Kamloops, BC, Apr 30, 49. *Study:* Alta Col Art, with Harold Fiest, 70; Vancouver Sch Art, with Don Jarvis, dipl fine art, 71; Notre Dame Univ, Nelson, Can, BFA, 74; Simon Fraser Univ, with Bob Crumlin, 75. *Work:* Alta Col Art; York Univ, Toronto; Vancouver Art Gallery, BC; and others. *Exhib:* Valley Visions Touring Exhib, Vallican Whole Community Centre, Vallican, BC & Langhorn Cult Centre, Kaslo, BC, 77; Exhib of BC Artists, Civic Centre, Nelson, BC, 77; one-artist show, Cobble Hill Loft Studio, Winlaw, BC, 78;

mixed-media exhib, Silverton Art Gallery, BC, 79; and many others. *Bibliog:* Article, In: Canadian Artists in Exhibition, Roundstone Press, Toronto, 74-75; article, In: Performance, Promotion Arts Enterprises, Vancouver, 75. *Mem:* Soc Can Painter-Etchers & Engravers; Malaspina Printmakers Soc; Can Artists Representation. *Publ:* Contribr, Waves, York Univ, 74; contribr, Playboard Mag, Archway Publ, 74; contribr, Three Hours Later, New Era Social Club, Vancouver, 74. *Dealer:* Bau-Xi Gallery 3003 Granville St Vancouver BC Can; Nancy Poole's Studio 16 Hazelton Ave Toronto ON Can. *Mailing Add:* Cobble Hill Loft Studio RR 1 Winlaw BC V0G 2J0 Canada

FOULKES, LLYN
PAINTER
b Yakima, Wash, Nov 17, 34. *Study:* Univ Wash, 52-54; Central Wash Col Educ, 53; Chouinard Art Inst, 57-59. *Work:* Whitney Mus Am Art, New York; Guggenheim Mus, New York; Art Inst Chicago; Mus Mod Art, New York; and others. *Exhib:* Fifth Paris Biennial, Mus Mod Art, Paris, 67; five exhibs, Whitney Mus Am Art, 67-77; 71st Am Exhib, Chicago Art Inst, 74; Los Angeles, Mus of Mod Art, New York, NY, 76; one-man shows, Willard Gallery, New York, 75, Gruenebaum Gallery, New York, 77 & Chicago Mus Contemp Art, 78; and others. *Collections Arranged:* Cur, Imagination, Los Angeles Inst of Contemp Art, Calif. *Teaching:* Prof painting & drawing & artist in residence, Univ Calif, Los Angeles, 65-71; resident painter, Painting Workshop, Art Ctr Sch, Los Angeles, 71-75. *Awards:* New Talent Purchase Grant, Los Angeles Co Mus Art, 64; Medal of France (first award for painting), 5th Paris Bienniale, Mus Mod Art, Paris, 67; Guggenheim Found fel, 77-78. *Bibliog:* Michael Compton (auth), Pop art, Movements Mod Art, 68; Henry Seldis (auth), Hollywood collects, Otis Art Inst, 70. *Media:* Oil, Acrylic. *Mailing Add:* 6010 Eucalyptus Lane Los Angeles CA 90806

FOURCADE, XAVIER
DEALER
b Paris, France, Sept 20, 26. *Study:* Politic Sci Sch, Paris; Univ Paris Law Sch; Sch Oriental Languages, Paris; Univ Paris Sch Advan Studies; Oxford Univ. *Pos:* Vpres & dir, M Knoedler & Co, Inc, New York, 66-72; pres, Fourcade, Droll, Inc, New York, 72-76; pres, Xavier Fourcade, Inc, New York, 76- *Specialty:* Twentieth century art and contemporary artists such as Baselitz, Crozier, De Kooning, Gorky, Newman, Tony Smith, Morley, Moore, Joan Mitchell, Catherine Murphy, Heizer, Hague, Westermann and others. *Mailing Add:* Xavier Fourcade Inc 36 E 75th St New York NY 10021

FOWLE, GERALDINE ELIZABETH
HISTORIAN
b Grand Rapids, Mich, Jan 3, 29. *Study:* Am Univ, 53-58; Univ Mich, Ann Arbor, MA(art hist), 60, PhD(art hist), 70. *Pos:* Newslett ed, Midwest Art Hist Soc, 77-80 & Soc Archit Historians, 80- *Teaching:* Asst lectr English art, Univ Manchester, England, 63-66; vis instr Baroque art, Univ Pittsburgh, 67; assoc prof, Univ Mo, Kansas City, 67- *Mem:* Col Art Asn; Soc Archit Historians; Midwest Art Hist Soc; Mid-Am Col Art Asn (treas, 74-75). *Res:* Sebastien Bourdon, French artist of the 17th century. *Publ:* Contribr, Two pendants by Sebastien Bourdon, Bulletin, Boston Mus Fine Arts, 73; contribr, Sebastien Bourdon's acts of mercy, Hortus Imaginum, 74; contribr, The lady who got Tassi thrown into prison, Helicon Nine, 80. *Mailing Add:* Dept Art & Art Hist Univ Mo Kansas City MO 64110

FOWLER, FRANK EISON
DEALER, CONSULTANT
b Chattanooga, Tenn, June 2, 46. *Study:* Univ Ga, BBA, 69. *Comn:* Produced Inaugural Portfolio, 76 & Presidential Portfolio, 80, comn by Pres Jimmy Carter. *Pos:* Art dealer, currently; mem adv bd, John F Kennedy Ctr Performing Arts, currently. *Mem:* Appraisers Asn Am; Int Soc Appraisers. *Res:* Represent Andrew Wyeth, Jamie Wyeth, Carolyn Wyeth & estate of N C Wyeth. *Mailing Add:* PO Box 247 Lookout Mountain TN 37350

FOWLER, MEL (WALTER)
SCULPTOR
b San Antonio, Tex, Nov 25, 21. *Study:* Univ Tex & Univ Md, 40; Norfolk Sch Art, with Linsey Ocheltree, 59; Southwestern Univ, with Bob Lancaster, 70; Acad Medicea Bela Arte di Firenze, Florence, Italy, 83. *Work:* State Health Dept Bldg, Homburg, Ger; St Helen's Cath Church, Georgetown, Tex, Town Park, Liberty Hill, Tex. *Comn:* sculpture of St Francis, St Francis Cath Church, Georgetown, Tex, 72; sculpture, Libertarian, Community of Liberty Hill, Tex, 76; sculpture, comn by Augusto Caiani, Florence, Italy, 77; sculpture, comn by David Winterman, Eagle Lake, Tex; sculpture, Reformed Jewish Temple, Memphis, Tenn, 82. *Exhib:* Abilene Fine Arts Mus, 77; Giornata Michaelangelo Int Exhib, Azzano, Italy, 78 & 79; Fire Exhib, Contemp Art Mus, Houston, Tex, 79; Scultura Alla Versilia, 82; Int Art Mus, 82; Wichita Falls Art Mus, 84; thirteen one-man shows, and many other national and international exhibitions. *Pos:* Prog dir, Liberty Hill Cult Affairs Coun, Tex, 75- *Awards:* First Prize, Tex State Art Fair, 74 & Laguna Gloria Art Mus, 74; Purchase Prize, Rosenberg Collection, Galveston, Tex, 76; and others. *Bibliog:* Beulah Hodge (auth), People and Ideas (video TV), 9/76; Bob Parvin (auth), A fine thing going, Tex Hwy Mag, 3/77. *Mem:* Artists Equity New York. *Media:* Marble, Negative Space. *Mailing Add:* Corner Main & Myrtle PO Box 255 Liberty Hill TX 78642

FOWLER, MEL
PAINTER, PRINTMAKER
b Chicago, Ill, July 29, 22. *Study:* Minneapolis Inst Art, scholarships, 39-40; Calif Sch Fine Art, with Ralph Stackpole. *Work:* Brit Mus, London; Klingspor Mus, Offenbach, Ger; Walker Mus, Minneapolis; Clark Libr, Univ Calif, Los Angeles; New York Pub Libr. *Comn:* Porcelain steel sculpture, M Mogenson,

Burlingame, Calif, 58; porcelain steel sculpture, Kaiser Hosp, Oakland, Calif, 59; hammered bronze sculpture, F Rosenthal, San Francisco, 59; porcelain steel mural, M Wornum, San Francisco, 59; aluminum sculpture, Cris Caras, Los Angeles, 65. *Exhib:* San Francisco Annual, 42 & 43; Mondrianna, Ann Arbor Film Festival & Mus Mod Art, 70; Museo de Ponce, PR, 73; Westbeth Graphic Arts Workshop, Belles Artes, Mexico City, Mex, 73-74 & traveling exhib sponsored by NY State Coun Arts, 74-75; plus ten one-man shows. *Pos:* Pres, Westbeth Painters, New York, 72-73. *Mem:* Fedn Mod Painters & Sculptors, New York. *Publ:* Illusr, Home for the Night, 64; illusr, Lyric Poems, Franklin Watts Co Inc, 68 & Psychiatry: What It Is, 69; illusr, Row With Your Hair, 69; illusr, The King of Numbers (childrens' bk), Jarrow, 71; and many others. *Dealer:* Brentano's The Roten Collection 9645 Gerwig Lane Columbia MD 21064; Multiple Impressions Gallery 17 Greenwich Ave New York NY. *Mailing Add:* Studio G-224 Westbeth 463 West St New York NY 10014

FOX, FLO
PHOTOGRAPHER, LECTURER
b Miami, Fla, Sept 26, 45. *Work:* Focus Gallery, San Francisco; Foto Gallery, New York. *Exhib:* Auto-Focus Photography, Foto Gallery, New York, 80, Boston Mus Fine Art, 82 & Philadelphia Mus Art, 83; Asphalt Gardens, Canon Gallery, Paris, 81, Camden Arts Ctr, England, 81, Image Gallery, Denmark, 82 & Focus Gallery, San Francisco, 83. *Teaching:* Instr photog, Lighthouse for Blind, New York, 79-80 & Human Resources Ctr, Albertson, NY, 80. *Awards:* Cert Merit, Boston Mus Fine Art, 82 & Philadelphia Mus Art, 83. *Bibliog:* Georgia Dullea (auth), A camera does the seeing, New York Times, 4/80; Elizabeth Mehren (auth), Trades sight for insight, Los Angeles Times, 9/81; Tony Guida (producer), Legally blind photographer, Today Show, 82. *Publ:* Contribr, Women See Woman, Thomas Y Crowell Co, 76; contribr, Women See Men, McGraw Hill Books, 77; contribr, The Decade of Women, Ms Books, 80; contribr, Asphalt Gardens, 81. *Mailing Add:* Twenty-First Century Fox 30 Perry St New York NY 10014

FOX, HOWARD NEAL
CURATOR, CRITIC
b Atlantic City, NJ, Oct 4, 46. *Study:* Univ Md, BA, 68; Univ Wis, Madison, MA, 70. *Collections Arranged:* Directions: Survey of Contemporary American Art (auth, catalog), 79 & Metaphor: New Projects by Vito Acconci, Siah Armajani, Alice Aycook, Lauren Ewing, Dennis Oppenheim & Robert Morris (auth, catalog), 81-82, Hirshhorn Mus, Washington, DC; Stacking/ Rigging/Binding: 10 Contemporary Sculptors (auth, catalog), Washington Proj Arts, Washington, DC, 80; 20 From DC (co-auth, catalog), Lawndale Annex, Houston, 82; US Projects: Jim Sanborn, Artists Space, New York, 82; International Survey of Contemporary Art, 1974-1984 (contribr, catalog), 84. *Pos:* Assoc cur exhibs, Hirshhorn Mus, Washington, DC, currently; art ed, Sun & Moon Press, 76-; mem bd dirs, Md Col Art Design, Silver Spring; chmn bd dirs, Washington Proj Arts, Washington, DC, 81-; consult, Nat Endowment Arts Visual Arts Program, 82-; consult, Gen Serv Admin, Art in Architecture Program, 82- *Res:* Modern art and critical theory, art in public places. *Publ:* Auth, The thorny issues of temporary art, Mus News, 79; contribr, The New Imagery, Pluralist Decade, Inst Contemp Art, Philadelphia, 80; auth, Kenneth Snelson (catalog), Albright-Knox Art Gallery, Buffalo, NY, 81; and others. *Mailing Add:* c/o Hirshhorn Mus Smithsonian Inst Washington DC 20560

FOX, JOHN
PAINTER
b Montreal, PQ, July 26, 27. *Study:* Montreal Mus Fine Arts; Slade Sch, London, Eng. *Work:* Nat Gallery Can, Ottawa; Montreal Mus Fine Arts; Mus Que, PQ; Beaverbrook Art Gallery, Frederickton, NB; Art Gallery Greater Victoria, BC. *Teaching:* Asst prof painting & drawing, Concordia Univ, 79- *Media:* Acrylic. *Mailing Add:* Art Dept, Concordia Univ 1455 deMaissoneuve W Montreal PQ H3G 1M8 Can

FOX, JUDITH HOOS
CURATOR
b Oakland, Calif, June 13, 49. *Study:* Bryn Mawr Col, BA, 71; Univ Minn, MA, 74. *Collections Arranged:* Catherine Murphy (auth, catalog), Inst Contemp Art, 75; Randy Stevens/Frances Cohen Gillespie (auth, catalog), 78, One Century: Wellesley Families Collect (with catalog), 78 & Sitework (auth, catalog), 80, Wellesley Col Mus; Art of the State: Sculpture 1975-80 (with catalog), Artists Found, Boston, 80; Catherine Wavvey Collection (auth, catalog), 83 & Furniture, Furnishings: Subject and Object (auth, catalog), 84, Mus Art, RI Sch Design. *Pos:* Cur intern, Walker Art Ctr, Minneapolis, 73-74; cur, Inst Contemp Art, Boston, 74-75; asst dir, Wellesley Col Mus, Mass, 77-82; cur painting & sculpture, Mus Art, RI Sch Design, Providence, 82- *Publ:* Contribr, Naives and Visionaries, Walker Art Ctr, 74; contribr, The Railroad in the American Landscape: 1850-1950, Wellesley Col Mus, 81. *Mailing Add:* 21 Myrtle St Jamaica Plain Boston MA 02130

FOX, LINCOLN H
SCULPTOR
b Morrilton, Ark, June 14, 42. *Study:* Univ Tex, Austin, with Charles Umlaf, BFA, 66; Univ Dallas, with Heri Barscht, MA, 67; Univ Kans, Lawrence, with Elden Tefft, MFA, 68. *Work:* El Paso Art Mus; Mus Southwest, Midland, Tex; Land of the Four Seasons Collection, Lake of the Ozarks, Mo. *Comn:* Child of Prague, Cistercian Prep Sch, Irving, Tex; Turn of the Century Cable Tool Workers, Permian Basin Petroleum Mus, Midland, Tex, 76; wall relief, First Christian Church, Ruidoso, NMex, 82. *Exhib:* One-man show, Smithsonian Inst, 75, Fine Arts Mus Albuquerque, 78 & El Paso Art Mus, 79; Nat Acad Western Art Ann, Nat Cowboy Hall Fame, Oklahoma City, 75, 79

& 80; Nat Sculpture Soc Ann Exhib, Equitable Bldg, New York, 82 & 83; Nat Western Artists First Ann Exhib, Civic Ctr, Lubbock, Tex, 82 & 83; and others. *Teaching:* Instr sculpture, Univ Kans, Lawrence, 67-68; instr sculpture & drawing, Amarillo Col, 69-71. *Awards:* Purchase Award, 60th Ann Nat Competition Am Art, 70; Bronze Medal, Solon Borglum Mem Sculpture Exhib, Nat Cowboy Hall Fame, 75; Misner Award, 49th Ann Exhib Nat Sculpture Soc, 82. *Bibliog:* Morgan Catherine Merrill (auth), Lincoln Fox: Mood, media and idea, Southwest Art Mag, 5/80; Peggy & Harold Samuels (auths), Contemporary Western Artists, Southwest Art Publ, 82; article, Nat Sculpture Rev, summer 82. *Mem:* Nat Sculpture Soc; Nat Western Artist Asn. *Media:* Bronze, Stone; Pastel. *Dealer:* Enthios Gallery 1111 Paseo de Peralta Santa Fe NM 87501; Driscol Gallery 555 17th St Suite 160 Denver CO 80202. *Mailing Add:* Box 95 Verano Loop Santa Fe NM 87501

FOX, MICHAEL DAVID
SCULPTOR, INSTRUCTOR
b Cortland, NY, Dec 29, 37. *Study:* State Univ NY Col, New Paltz, with Ilya Bolotowsky & Ken Green; State Univ NY Col, Buffalo, with Robert Davidson & George Stark, BS, 62, MS, 69; Brooklyn Mus Sch, with Tom Doyle, Rueben Tam & Toshio Odate, cert, 64. *Work:* State Univ Col NY, Buffalo, Cortland, Oswego & New Paltz; Brooklyn Mus. *Exhib:* Finger Lakes Ann, Rochester Mem Art Gallery, 63-83; Ann Prof Exhib, Brooklyn Mus, 64; J B Speed Art Mus, Louisville, Ky, 65-67; Cent NY Ann, Everson Mus, Syracuse, 68-78; Artists Cent NY, Munson-Williams-Proctor Inst, Utica, 68-80; State Univ Ark Nat, Univ Gallery, 73; Cooperstown Art Mus Nat, NY, 81. *Pos:* Dir, Popular Image Gallery, Oswego, NY, 73-; proj dir, Nat Endowment Arts Grant, State Univ NY Col, Oswego, 78- *Teaching:* Teacher art, Rochester City Schs, NY, 62-65; instr, Morehead State Univ, Ky, 65-67; assoc prof art, State Univ Col, Oswego, NY, 67- *Awards:* Sculpture Award, Ann Exhib, Brooklyn Mus, 64; Painting Awards, Finger Lakes Exhib, Rochester Mem Art Gallery, 78 & NY State Fair, Syracuse, 78-81. *Bibliog:* Sculpture (feature), CBS TV, 76; Sculpture (feature), Can Nat Television, 79; PM Mag (feature), CBS TV, 81; and others. *Media:* Plastic, Polyester Resin. *Mailing Add:* 7 W End Ave Oswego NY 13126

FRABEL, HANS GODO
SCULPTOR
b Jena, EGer, June 9, 41. *Work:* Smithsonian Inst & White House, Washington, DC; Wertheim Mus, WGer; Botanical Mus, Harvard Univ, Cambridge, Mass; Dusseldorf Mus, WGer. *Comn:* Gift to Deng Xiaoping, comn by City Atlanta, Ga, 79; gift to people of Berlin, comn by VPres Rockefeller, Washington, DC; Phoenix Award, Atlanta CofC, Ga; gift to Lord High Mayor, London, Delta Airlines, Atlanta, Ga, 79; gift to Pres Carter, Ga Democratic Party, Atlanta, Ga. *Exhib:* Jr Art Gallery, Louisville, Ky, 75; New Glass, traveling, 79-; Contemp Glass Gallery, New York, 80; Del Mano Gallery, Los Angeles, 81; Westlake Gallery, White Plains, NY, 81. *Awards:* Contemp Glass, Corning Mus Glass, 77. *Bibliog:* Sampling of contemporary picture, Cleveland Plain Dealer, 80; Creating art in glass, Dallas Times-Herald, 80; Frabel's glass meets the flame, Southern Living, 5/81. *Mem:* Glass Art Soc; Am Sci Glassblowers Soc. *Media:* Borosilicate Glass. *Dealer:* Frabel Gallery 231 Peachtree St NE Atlanta GA 30303. *Mailing Add:* c/o Bartlett Group 1483 Fairview Rd Atlanta GA 30306

FRACE, CHARLES LEWIS
ILLUSTRATOR, PAINTER
b Mauch Chunk, Pa, Feb 18, 26. *Study:* Philadelphia Col Art, Pa. *Work:* Nat Wildlife Fedn, Washington, DC. *Comn:* Official portrait of Morris the Cat, 9-Lives Cat Food, 76; paintings for reprod of ltd ed prints, Frame House Gallery, 73-80 & Am Masters Found, 81- *Exhib:* Soc Animal Artists, New York; Mus Sci & Space Transit Planetarium, Miami, Fla, 75-76; Mzuri Safari Found Conf, San Francisco, Calif, 76; Leigh Yawkey Woodson Art Mus, Wausau, Wis, 77; one-man show, Cumberland Mus & Sci Ctr, Nashville, 78 & 81; and others. *Awards:* Christopher Found Award Painting, 74. *Mem:* Soc Animal Artists, New York. *Media:* Oil, Acrylic. *Publ:* Illusr, Last Chance on Earth, Chilton 5096, 66; illusr, The Life of the Jungle, McGraw-Hill, 70; illusr, Wonders of Island Life & Animals in Action, Readers Digest, 72; illusr, The Wolf, Coward, McCann, 73. *Dealer:* American Masters Foundation 10688 Haddington Houston TX 77043. *Mailing Add:* 6011 Martingale Lane Brentwood TN 37027

FRACKMAN, NOEL
CRITIC, LECTURER
b New York, NY, May 27, 30. *Study:* Mt Holyoke Col, Sarah Williston Scholar, 48-50; Sarah Lawrence Col, BA, 52, MA(Eng lit), 53; Columbia Univ, 64-67; Inst Fine Arts, NY Univ, MA, 76. *Pos:* Lectr, Aldrich Mus Contemp Art, Ridgefield, Conn, 67-75; partic, Art Critics Workshop, Am Fedn Arts, 68; lectr, Gallery Passport Ltd, New York, 68-; contrib ed, Arts Mag, New York, 68-; cur educ, Storm King Art Ctr, Mountainville, NY, 73-75. *Awards:* Mademoiselle First Prize, Col Publ Contest, 61. *Publ:* Auth, Super-chair, Art Voices, fall 66; auth, The Stein family and the era of avant-garde collecting, 2/71 & The enticement of watercolor, 6/74, Arts Mag; auth, Jump into the New York art world, Harper's Bazaar, 2/72; plus art rev in Scarsdale Inquirer, 62-67, Patent Trader, 62-71 & Arts Mag, current issues. *Mailing Add:* 3 Hadden Rd Scarsdale NY 10583

FRAENKEL, JEFFREY ANDREW
DEALER, GALLERY DIRECTOR
b Shreveport, La, Jan 28, 55. *Study:* Antioch Col, BFA, 77. *Collections Arranged:* Carleton E Watkins, Photographs of the Pacific Coast 1873, 79; Timothy O'Sullivan, Photographs: 1864-1874, 80. *Mem:* Int Asn Photog Art Dealers. *Specialty:* 19th and 20th century photographs. *Mailing Add:* 55 Grant Ave San Francisco CA 94108

FRAME, ROBERT (AARON)
PAINTER

b San Fernando, Calif, July 31, 24. *Study:* With Henry Lee McFee, 47-50; Pomona Col, BA, 48; Claremont Col, MFA, 51. *Work:* Desert Art Mus, Palm Springs, Calif; State Calif, Sacramento; Nat Acad Design, New York; Munic Art Dept, City Los Angeles; Santa Barbara Art Mus, Calif. *Exhib:* Ill Biennial, Urbana, 58-65; American Painting, Richmond, Va, 65; De Young Mus, San Francisco; Los Angeles Co Mus; Otis Art Inst; Laguna Art Festival; David Findlay Galleries, New York; and 31 one-man exhibs. *Teaching:* Prof art, Santa Barbara City Col, Calif. *Awards:* Guggenheim Fel, 57-58; First Prize, James D Phelan Awards, 65; Purchase Prize, St Albans Home Savings & Loan, Los Angeles, 68. *Bibliog:* Schaad (auth), Realm of Contemporary Still Life, Reinhold, 61; Mugniani (auth), Oil Painting, Van Nostrand, 69. *Media:* Oil. *Dealer:* Austin Gallery 7103 Main St Scottsdale AZ 85251; Dubins Gallery 11948 San Vicente Blvd Los Angeles CA 90049. *Mailing Add:* 2102 Edgewater Way Santa Barbara CA 93109

FRAMPTON, HOLLIS
FILMMAKER

b Wooster, Ohio, 1936. *Study:* Phillips Acad, Andover, Mass, 51-54; Western Reserve Univ, Cleveland, Ohio, 54-57. *Exhib:* Info, Mus Mod Art, New York, 70; New Forms in Film, Guggenheim Mus, New York, 72; Retrospective, Walker Art Ctr, Minneapolis, Minn, 72 & Mus Mod Art, New York, 72; one-man shows, Sch Visual Arts, New York, 70, Yale Univ, New Haven, Conn, 70 & 71, Art Inst Chicago, 70, Carnegie Inst Int, Pittsburgh, 71, Mus Contemp Art, Chicago, 72 & Visual Studies Workshop, Rochester, NY, 72; and many others. *Collections Arranged:* Museum of Modern Art & Anthology Film Archives, New York; Carnegie Inst Int, Pittsburgh; Ger Film Arch, Berlin; Royal Film Arch Belgium, Brussels; and others. *Teaching:* Instr, Hunter Col & Cooper Union, New York, 69-71 & State Univ New York, Buffalo, 73-82. *Bibliog:* Simon Field (auth), Alphabet as Ideogram, Arts & Artists, London, 8/72; Simon Field & Peter Sainsbury (auths), Interview with Hollis Frampton, Afterimage, London, autumn 72; Mark Segal (auth), Hollis Frampton/Zorns Lemma, Film Cult, New York, 72. *Publ:* Auth: NY State Coun Arts. *Publ:* Auth, Meditations around Paul Strand, Artforum, Vol 10, 72; auth, Nostalgia: Voice-over narrations for a film of that same name, dated 1/8/71 & Notes on nostalgia, Film Cult, New York, Nos 53-55, 72; auth, A pentagram for conjuring the narrative, In: Form & Structure in Recent Film, Vancouver, 72; auth, Stan & Jane Brakhage talking, Artforum, Vol 11, 73. *Mailing Add:* c/o Anthology Film Arch 491 Broadway New York NY 10012

FRANCES, HARRIETTE ANTON
PAINTER, LITHOGRAPHER

b San Francisco, Calif. *Study:* San Francisco Sch Fine Arts, 42-45; Univ Pac, 55-57; San Fransico Art Inst, studied painting with James Weeks, 63 & 65-66; Univ Calif, summers 74-76. *Work:* Fresno Art Ctr, Calif; Charles D Clark Collection, McAllen, Tex; Achenbach Found Graphic Arts; San Francisco Legion of Honor. *Exhib:* James D Phelan Award Exhib, De Young Mus, San Francisco, 63 & Palace Legion of Honor, 65; Fifth Winter Show, Palace Legion of Honor, 64 & Calif Printmakers, 71; one-person shows, Calif Palace Legion of Honor, San Francisco, 68 & Western Asn Art Mus traveling one-man shows at mus & univ galleries throughout US, 68-70; New Sch Art Ctr, New York, 73; San Francisco Women Artists; Bicentennial Exhib, Mus of Mod Art, San Francisco, 76. *Teaching:* Instr life drawing, Exten, Univ Pac; instr lithography, Artists Proof Graphics Workshop, Larkspur, Calif; prog adv, Beacon Col, Wash. *Awards:* Calif State Fair Award, 64; James D Phelan Award in Art, 65; First Place, San Francisco Women Artists, 74. *Bibliog:* George Christy (auth), Are you with it, Town & Country Mag, 67; Martin Fox (ed), A graphic artist depicts her LSD trip, Print Mag, 67; Joan Lisetor (auth), Reviving an ancient art, Independent J, 75. *Mem:* San Francisco Women Artists; Calif Soc of Printmakers; Marin Soc Artists; Graphics Soc; World Print Council. *Media:* Lithography, Acrylic. *Publ:* Contrib, Ramparts Mag, 66; contribr, USA & Espanol issue, MD Mag, 66; contribr, Print Mag & Psychedelic Art, 67; Erotic Art of the Masters, 18th, 19th & 20th Centuries, Lyle Stewart Publ. *Dealer:* Contemporary Gallery 2425 Cedar Springs Dallas TX 75201. *Mailing Add:* 105 Rice Lane Larkspur CA 94939

FRANCIS, BILL DEAN
DESIGNER, EDUCATOR

b Salem, Ill, Oct 14, 29. *Study:* Ill State Univ, BS(art educ), 51; Univ Wis, MS(appl art), 52; Ind Univ, 56-63. *Comn:* Tapestry, Phillips Petrol Co, Phillips, Okla, 64 & Bank South Austin, Tex, 75. *Exhib:* Midwest Landscape Art Exhib, Ill State Fair, Springfield, 52; Exhib Momentum, Inst Design, Chicago, 53; 29th Ann Am Graphic Arts & Drawing Exhib, Wichita, Kans, 60; Tex Designer-Craftsman Exhib, Wichita Falls, 72; one-man exhib, Longview Mus, Tex, 73. *Teaching:* Asst prof sec & elem art methods, Drake Univ, 58-60; assoc prof sec & elem art methods, Univ Tex, Austin, 64-74, prof art & educ, 74-, assoc dean, Col Fine Arts, 78- *Mem:* Nat Art Educ Asn; Tex Art Educ Asn. *Publ:* Auth, Getting to Know Art (TV ser), KLRN, Tex, 70; auth, The Humanities in Retrospect, Kendall/Hunt, 74. *Mailing Add:* 1100 Yaupon Valley Rd Austin TX 78746

FRANCIS, JEAN THICKENS
ASSEMBLAGE ARTIST, PRINTMAKER

b Laurel, Miss, Mar 15, 43. *Study:* Millsaps Col, 61-63; Memphis Art Acad, BFA(sculpture), 66. *Work:* Bank Miss, Tupelo. *Exhib:* Papermakers & Paperusers, Southeastern Artists, Southeastern Ctr Contemp Art, Winston-Salem, NC, 80; Prints, Drawings & Crafts Show, Ark Art Ctr, Little Rock, 81; one-person shows, Artsite Invitational, New Orleans, La, 80 & Open Gallery, Miss Mus Art, 81; More Than Land or Sky: Art from Appalachia, Nat Mus Am Art, Smithsonian Inst & traveling, 81-84; The State of The Art: Mississippi, Contemp Art Ctr, New Orleans, La, 83; and others. *Pos:* Asst libr, Cleveland Inst Art, Ohio, 67-68; self-employed artist, currently. *Teaching:* Instr art, Memphis City Sch, Tenn, 66-67; instr sculpture, Memphis Acad Art, Tenn, summer 74; vis artist, Jackson City Sch, Miss, 76; guest artist, paper workshop, Alexandria Mus Art, La, 80; papermaking, Miss Mus Art, Jackson, 81; Univ Miss, Oxford, 81; Nat Mus Am Art, Smithsonian Inst & Kennedy Ctr, 81; papermaking & collage, Arrowmont Sch Arts & Crafts, Gatlinburg, Tenn, 82 & papermaking, Vanderbilt Univ, Nashville, Tenn, 83; instr, papermaking, Appalachia Ctr Crafts, Smithville, Tenn, 83; artist in residence, Tupelo City Sch, Miss, 83- *Awards:* Grand Prize, Miss Artist Competitive Exhib, Miss Art Asn, 76, Second Prize-Merit Award, 77; Merit Award, Greater New Orleans Int Art Exhib, 76-77; *Bibliog:* Annette Cone-Skelton (auth), Southeastern artists today: a cross section, Contemp Art/SE, 78; Gary Witt (auth), Ke & Jean Francis of Tupelo, Mississippi: A union of opposites, Art Voices/South, 5/79; Stephen Flynn Young (auth), A visit with Jean Thickens Francis, Art Papers, 82. *Media:* Mixed. *Mailing Add:* 512 Magnolia Dr Tupelo MS 38801

FRANCIS, MADISON KE, JR
SCULPTOR, PRINTMAKER

b Memphis, Tenn, Aug 19, 45. *Study:* Miss State Univ, Starkville; Memphis State Univ, Tenn; Memphis Acad Art, Tenn; Cleveland Inst Art, Ohio, BFA(sculpture), 69; Cape Sch Art, Provincetown, Mass, study painting with Henry Hensche. *Work:* Southeastern Ctr Contemp Art, Winston-Salem, NC; Meridian Mus Art, Miss; Cleveland Inst Art, Print Collection, Ohio; Unifirst Nat Bank Permanent Collection & Miss Art Asn Travelling Exhib, Jackson, Miss. *Comn:* Steel sculpture, People's Bank, Tupelo, Miss, 73; sculpture, Itawamba Jr Col, 78; time capsule sculpture, North Miss Med Ctr, Tupelo. *Exhib:* Mid-S Exhib, Brooks Mem Mus, Memphis, Tenn, 72; Drawings USA, Minn Art Ctr, St Paul, 74; Hunter Nat Painting Exhib, Hunter Mus, Chattanooga, Tenn, 74; Sixth Ann New Orleans Int Art Show, New Orleans Art Asn, La, 75; Mainstreams of Am Art, Marietta Col, Ohio, 77; Del Mar Nat Drawing Exhib, Del Mar Col, Corpus Christi, Tex, 77; Brooks Art Gallery, 79; one-person show, Roanoke Mus Fine Art, Va, 82; More Than Land or Sky, Smithsonian Inst, 82. *Teaching:* Instr, Cleveland Inst Art, 69-71; instr sculpture, Memphis Acad Art, summer 73; instr graphics, Penland Sch, NC, 78-79. *Awards:* Purchase Award, Southeastern Ctr Contemp Arts, Winston-Salem, 73; Second Prize Painting, New Orleans Art Asn, 75; Best in Show, Meridian Mus, Miss, 77. *Mem:* Guerilla Supermarket. *Media:* Miscellaneous Media; Intaglio, Silkscreen. *Dealer:* Arthur Roger Gallery 3005 Magazine New Orleans LA. *Mailing Add:* 512 Magnolia Dr Tupelo MS 38801

FRANCIS, SAM
PAINTER

b San Mateo, Calif, June 25, 23. *Study:* Univ Calif, Berkeley, BA, 43, MA, 50; Atelier Fernand Leger, Paris; Univ Calif, Berkeley, Hon DFA, 69. *Work:* Guggenheim Mus, NY; Mus Mod Art; Albright Art Gallery; Kunsthaus, Zurich, Switz; Dayton Art Inst; plus others. *Comn:* Murals, Kunsthalle, Berne, Switz, 57, Sofu Sch Flower Arrangement, Tokyo, Japan, 57 & Chase Manhattan Bank, New York, 59. *Exhib:* One-man shows, Seattle Art Mus, 59, San Francisco Mus Art, 59 & 67 & Mus Fine Arts Houston, 67; retrospective, Albright-Knox Art Gallery, Buffalo, NY, 72; Cantor-Lemberg Gallery, Birmingham, Ala, 80; Mills Col Art, Oakland, Calif, 80; Gallery 210, St Louis, Mo, 80; Du Bose Gallery, Houston, Tex, 80; Greenberg Gallery, St Louis, Mo, 80; and many other group & one-man shows, US & abroad. *Awards:* First Prize, Int Biennial Exhib Prints, Tokyo, 62; Dunn Int Prize, Tate Gallery, London, 63; Tamarind Fel, 63; and others. *Bibliog:* Werner Haftman (auth), Paintings in the Twentieth Century, Praeger, 60; Sam Hunter (ed), New Art Around the World: Painting & Sculpture, Abrams, 66; and many others. *Dealer:* Galerie Smith-Anderson 200 Homer St Palo Alto CA 94301. *Mailing Add:* 345 W Channel Dr Santa Monica Canyon Los Angeles CA 90402

FRANCIS, SHERRON
PAINTER

b Oct 28, 40; US citizen. *Study:* Univ Okla, 58-60; Kansas City Art Inst, BFA, 63; Ind Univ, MFA, 66. *Work:* Mus Mod Art & Everson Mus, NY; Denver Mus, Colo; Edmonton Art Gallery, Alta; Mus Southern Tex, Corpus Christi. *Exhib:* Whitney Biennial Exhib, Whitney Mus, New York, 73; New Abstract Art, Edmonton Art Gallery, Alta, 77; Am Acad & Inst of Arts & Lett, New York, 78; one-person shows, Barbara Kornblatt Gallery, Baltimore, 77; Tibor de Nagy Gallery, New York, 78 & 80; Bell Gallery, Brown Univ, 79 & Watson de Nagy & Co, Houston, 80; Douglas Drake Gallery, Kansas City, Mo, 81. *Bibliog:* Ann Holmes (auth), Two young Americans follow gallery's stars, Houston Chronicle, 10/3/74; New York letter, Art Int, 11/15/74; Kim Whee (auth), A personal definition of pictorial space, Arts Mag, 11/74; article, Art World, 2/15/80. *Dealer:* Tibor de Nagy Gallery 29 W 57th St New York NY 10019. *Mailing Add:* 16 Waverly Pl New York NY 10003

FRANCIS, TOM
PAINTER

b Sheboygan, Wis, Mar 12, 51. *Study:* Univ Wis, BS, 73, MA, 75, MFA(Henry Vilas Fel), 76. *Work:* State Ga, Atlanta; State Wis, Madison; Chase Manhattan Bank, New York; Omni Int, Atlanta; Europco Corp, Fla. *Exhib:* Generations, J M Kohler Art Gallery, Wis, 74; Walker Art Ctr, 75; Artists in Georgia, High Mus Art, 80; Columbia Mus, SC, 82. *Teaching:* Chmn dept painting, Atlanta Col Art, 78- *Media:* All. *Dealer:* Fay Gold Gallery 3221 Cains Hill Pl NW Atlanta GA 30305. *Mailing Add:* 1405 Woodland Hills Dr Atlanta GA 30324

FRANCK, FREDERICK S
PAINTER, WRITER

b Maastricht, Holland, Apr 12, 09; US citizen. *Study:* Belg, Eng & US; Univ Pittsburgh, hon DFA, 63. *Work:* Whitney Mus Am Art & Mus Mod Art, New York; San Francisco Mus Art, Calif; Stedelijk Mus, Holland; Mus Nat France, Paris; plus many others. *Comn:* Murals, Temple Beth-El, Elizabeth, NJ & Nat Mus Tokyo; stage designs for off-Broadway shows; drawings for New Yorker; Pacem in Terris. *Exhib:* Group shows in Whitney Mus Am Art & Metrop Mus Art, New York, Corcoran Gallery Art, Washington, DC, Butler Inst Am Art, Youngstown, Ohio, Calif Palace Legion of Honor, San Francisco & shows in Paris, Amsterdam, Geneva, London, Brussels, Rome & Japan; Foster/White Gallery exhib, Seattle, Wash, 77; Puget Sound Univ exhib, Tacoma, Wash, 78; plus many other group & one-man shows. *Awards:* Purchase Prizes, Carnegie Inst, Am Acad Arts & Lett & others; Living Arts Found Award, Maastricht Mus, Holland, 58; Medal of the Pontificate, Pope John, 63; plus others. *Mem:* Fel Int Inst Arts & Lett (dir); Soc Arts, Relig & Cult; Artists Equity Asn (hon dir, New York). *Publ:* Auth, The Zen of Seeing, Vintage Books, 73, Dutch transl, 83; The Awakened Eye, 79; auth, Art as 2 Way, a Return to the Spiritual Roots, 81, The Supreme Koan, Confessions on a Journey Inward, 82 & The Buddha Eye, 82, Crossroad Publ. *Mailing Add:* Rd 1 Box 165 Warwick NY 10990

FRANCO, BARBARA
CURATOR

b New York, NY, Mar 16, 45. *Study:* Bryn Mawr Col, BA; Cooperstown Grad Progs, MA. *Collections Arranged:* White's Utica Pottery (catalog), 69-70 & Shaker Arts & Crafts (catalog), 70-71, Munson-Williams-Proctor Inst, Utica, NY; Masonic Symbols in American Decorative Arts (catalog), Mus of Our Nat Heritage, 75-76; Decorated Masonic Aprons (catalog), Mus of Our Nat Heritage, 80-81. *Pos:* Cur decorative arts, Munson-Williams-Proctor Inst, 66-73; cur, Mus of Our Nat Heritage, 73- *Publ:* Auth, Stoneware made by the White Family in Utica, NY, 71 & auth, New York City furniture bought for Fountain Elms, 73, Antiques. *Mailing Add:* PO Box 519 Lexington MA 02173

FRANCO, ROBERT JOHN
PAINTER, EDUCATOR

b Yonkers, NY, Apr 12, 32. *Study:* Art Students League, 52; Franklin Sch Prof Art, NY, cert com art, 53; Silvermine Col Art, cert fine art, 60; Inst de Allende, San Miguel de Allende, Mex, 59. *Exhib:* New Eng Exhib Painting & Sculpture, 58-61, 68, 71, 75 & 76; Conn Watercolor Soc, The Atheneum, Hartford, Conn, 59, 60, 61, 76 & 77; one-man show, Silvermine Guild Artists, 59, 64, 68, 72 & 79. *Pos:* Exhib dir, Silvermine Guild of Artists, 69-71, dir, Sch of the Arts, 71-82. *Teaching:* Instr painting, drawing, watercolor & design, Silvermine Col Art, New Canaan, Conn, 58-71 & Silvermine Guild Sch of the Arts, Norwalk, Conn, 71- *Awards:* First Sculpture Award, New England Exhib, Olivetti Co, 68 & 76; Purchase Award, Conn Watercolor Soc, J M Ney Co, 77; Second Prize, Int Maritime Award Show, Mystic Seaport Mus, Conn, 80. *Mem:* Conn Watercolor Soc Inc; New York Artist Equity; Provincetown Art Asn; Cape Cod Art Asn. *Media:* Watercolor. *Dealer:* Miriam Perlman Inc Lakeside Drive Chicago IL; Bell Gallery Stamford CT. *Mailing Add:* PO Box 1243 Wellfleet MA 02667

FRANK, CHARLES WILLIAM, JR
WOOD CARVER, WRITER

b New Orleans, La, June 8, 22. *Study:* BChemEng. *Exhib:* New Orleans Mus Art, 75; Hillsborough Co Mus, Tampa, Fla, 76; Univ New Orleans Fine Arts Mus, 76; Huntsville Mus Art, Ala, 76-77; West Baton Rouge Hist Asn, 76; Nat Crafts Coun, Winston-Salem, NC, 77. *Pos:* Auth & contribr, NAm Decoys, 72-77; auth, La Duck Decoys, 75-79; auth, La Out of Doors, 77-78 & Ward Found Mag. *Awards:* Best of Show, Catahoula Lake Wildfowl Festival, 75 & 76; First Place, La Wildfowl Carvers Exhib, 76. *Bibliog:* Article in La Conservationist, State of La, 73 & 75; Phillips Petroleum Co (auth), Louisiana's Wetland Heritage, The Decoy, 76. *Mem:* La Crafts Coun; La Wildfowl Carvers & Collectors; Int Wildlife Carvers; Nat Wood Carvers Asn. *Media:* Wood painted with oils. *Collection:* Definitive collection of several thousand Louisiana and world wide duck decoys. *Publ:* Auth article, Am Shotgunner, 76; auth article, Southern Outdoors, 77; auth, Anatomy of a Waterfowl, Pelican Publ, 81. *Mailing Add:* 3112 Octavia New Orleans LA 70125

FRANK, DAVID
CERAMIST, EDUCATOR

b St Paul, Minn, Sept 13, 40. *Study:* Univ Minn, Duluth, with Glenn C Nelson, BS(art); Tulane Univ La, MFA. *Work:* Tweed Gallery, Duluth; Newcomb Art Sch Collection; Mid Tenn State Univ Collection, Murfreesboro; Miss Univ for Women, Columbus; Miss Dept Archives & Hist. *Comn:* Pohl Gym, Miss Univ for Women, Columbus & St Ignatius Catholic Church, Mobile, Ala. *Exhib:* Mid South Ceramics & Crafts Exhib, Tenn; 14th Ann Delta Art Exhib, Ark; Crafts Invitational, Univ of Ala; Invitational Exhib, Nat Endowment Arts; Miss River Crafts Exhib, Brooks Gallery, Memphis, Tenn. *Teaching:* Assoc prof art, Miss Univ for Women, 65- *Mem:* Craftsmen's Guild Miss; Am Craftsman's Coun. *Media:* Clay. *Mailing Add:* Dept of Art Miss Univ for Women Columbus MS 39701

FRANK, HELEN (GOODZEIT)
PAINTER, PRINTMAKER

b Jersey City, NJ, May 29, 30. *Study:* Tyler Sch Fine Arts, Temple Univ; Cooper Union; New Sch with Abraham Rattner & Seymour Lipton, 48; Art Students League, with George Grosz, 50. *Work:* NJ State Mus, Trenton; Newark Public Libr Print Collection, NJ; Am Mus Immigration, New York;

UNICEF; Overlook Hospital, Summit, NJ. *Comn:* Portfolio, Grant Union Co, NJ, 80-81. *Exhib:* NJ State Exhib, Montclair Mus, 63; Am Watercolor Soc, New York, 65; Pratt Graphic Int, New York, 75 & 77; Morris Mus, Morristown, NJ; NJ Watercolor Soc, Morristown; Rutgers Univ, NJ. *Teaching:* Artist-in-residence, Springfield Public Sch. *Mem:* Artists Equity. *Mailing Add:* 445 Meisel Ave Springfield NJ 07081

FRANK, JANE
PAINTER, SCULPTOR

b Baltimore, Md, July 25, 18. *Study:* Parsons Sch, New York, 38-39; with Hans Hofmann, Provincetown, Mass, 60; Rhinehart fel, Md Inst Art, 61. *Work:* Baltimore Mus Art & Turner Auditorium, Johns Hopkins Hosp, Baltimore, Md; Corcoran Gallery Art & Nat Gallery Fine Arts, Smithsonian Inst, DC; Fed Reserve Bank, Richmond, Va; New Ctr Adult Educ, Univ Col Md, College Park. *Comn:* Three-dimensional paintings, Mr & Mrs Alan Insley, Ruxton, Md, 70 & Charles Richter, Baltimore, 70; outdoor revolving sculpture, comn by Mr & Mrs David Halle, Baltimore, 72; three piece sculpture, City Baltimore Art, 76; tapestry, Citycorp, Inc, Baltimore, 79. *Exhib:* Three Man Show, Baltimore Mus Art, 58; one-woman shows, Corcoran Gallery Art, Washington, DC, 62; Retrospective, Towson State Univ, 74; A Decade of Sculpture, Philadelphia Art Alliance, 74; Philadelphia Mus, 76; Sculpture Outdoors, Temple Univ, Ambler, Pa, 77 & 78; Opening of Art Gallery, Mechanic Theater, Baltimore, 79; Franklin Plaza & the International Gardens, Franklin Town, Pa, 81; and others. *Pos:* Art psychotherapist, Springfield State Hosp, Sykesville, Md, 64-69 & Phipps Clin, Johns Hopkins Hosp, 80- *Awards:* Title of Award, Bicentennial Proj Univ Women, Evening Sun, 76. *Bibliog:* Dr Phoebe B Stanton (auth), Sculptural Landscape of Jane Frank, A S Barnes Co, 68; Julia Busch (auth), A Decade of Sculpture, Philadelphia Art Allinacc Press, 74; Josephine Novak (auth), Jane Frank acclaimed as sculptor-innovator, Features, Sunpapers, 75. *Mem:* Artist Equity Asn (chmn mem, 79-80). *Media:* Acrylic; Lucite and Outdoor Sculpture in Various Metals. *Publ:* Auth & illusr, Monica Mink, Vanguard Press, 44; illusr, The Further Adventures of Til Eulenspiegal, Thomas Yoseloff, 57; contribr, Aerial Perception, The earth as seen from aircraft and space craft and it's influence on Contemp Art, The Philadelphia Art Alliance Press, spring 82. *Dealer:* Cramer Gallery 21st & P Sts Washington DC 20002. *Mailing Add:* 1300 Woods Hole Rd Towson MD 21204

FRANK, PETER SOLOMON
CRITIC, CURATOR

b New York, NY, July 3, 50. *Study:* Columbia Col, BA(art hist), 72; Columbia Univ, MA(art hist), 74. *Collections Arranged:* Artists' books section of Documenta 6, Kassel, WGer, summer 77; Artists' Books USA Traveling Exhib, 78-80 & Mapped Art: Charts Routes Regions Traveling Exhib, 81-83, Independent Curators Inc. *Pos:* Art critic, SoHo News, 73-76, Village Voice, 77-79 & Diversion Planner, 83-; curatorial assoc, Independent Curators Inc, 74-81; assoc ed, Nat Arts Guide, 79-81; cur, Exxon Nat Exhib, 19 Artists-Emergent Americans, Guggenheim Mus, 81; contrib ed, Art Economist, 81-83; ed, Re Dact, 83- *Teaching:* Vis asst prof contemp arts, Pratt Inst, Brooklyn, NY, 75-76; adj assoc prof, Sch Arts, Columbia Univ, 78; adj lectr, Tyler Sch Art, Temple Univ, 83. *Awards:* Nat Endowment Arts Grant, 78 & 81. *Bibliog:* Diane Spodarek (auth), interview in Detroit Artists Mo, 6/78; Ken Friedman (auth), interview, Atlanta Art Workers Coalition Newspaper, 11/79; Grace Glueck (auth), How emerging artists really emerge: Getting the biennials together, Art News, 5/81. *Mem:* Int Asn Art Critics; Poets & Writers. *Publ:* Auth, Something Else Press: An Annotated Bibliography, McPherson & Co, 83; auth, Roger Selden, Edizioni del Naviglio, Milan, Italy, 83. *Mailing Add:* 712 Broadway 5 New York NY 10003

FRANKEL, DEXTRA
EDUCATOR, GALLERY DIRECTOR

b Los Angeles, Calif, Nov 28, 24. *Study:* Long Beach State Col. *Work:* Philadelphia Free Libr; La Jolla Art Mus, Calif; St Paul Art Ctr, Minn; Pac View Mem Park, Corona Del Mar, Calif; Kennecott Copper Co, Salt Lake City, Utah; also in pvt collections. *Exhib:* Los Angeles Co Mus Art, 59, 62 & 66; Cincinnati Art Mus; Newport Harbor Art Newport Beach, Mus, Calif; Butler Inst Am Art, Youngstown, Ohio; Calif Palace of Legion of Honor, San Francisco; Denver Art Mus; Seattle Art Mus, Wash; Portland Art Mus, Ore; San Francisco Mus Art; H M deYoung Mus, San Francisco; Smithsonian Inst; and many others. *Collections Arranged:* Recorded Images/Dimensional Media, 67, Intersection of Line, 67, Frazer/Lipofsky/Richardson, 68, Transparency/Reflection, 68 & others, Art Gallery, Calif State Univ, Fullerton; and numerous others. *Pos:* Dir art gallery, cur & designer exhib, Calif State Univ, Fullerton, 67- *Teaching:* From asst prof to assoc prof art, Calif State Univ, Fullerton, 64-79; prof art, 79- *Awards:* 8 Nat Endowment for Arts grants, 75, 77-82; Design Award, Soc Typographic Arts Union Bank Hist Mus, 81. *Mem:* Am Asn Mus; Am Craft Coun; Art Mus Asn. *Publ:* Auth, article, Pasadena Mus, 65 & 68 & Crafts Horizons Mag, 73. *Mailing Add:* Visual Arts Ctr Calif State Univ Fullerton CA 92634

FRANKENBERG, ROBERT CLINTON
ILLUSTRATOR, PAINTER

b Mt Vernon, NY, Mar 19, 11. *Study:* Art Students League, New York, 28-29; study with William McNulty. *Work:* War Mus, Washington, DC; St Patrick's Cath Collection, New York; Univ Ore Libr; Kerlan Collection of Children's Lit, Univ Minn. *Comn:* Murals, Pa State Bldg & NC Bldg, stage sets & dioramas, Chase Brass & Copper Exhib, New York World's Fair, 39. *Exhib:* Six one-man shows in New York, 53-70. *Pos:* Artist, Jenter Exhib, NY & NJ, 33-40; artist, US Army Signal Corps, 40-45. *Teaching:* Instr figure drawing, Sch Visual Arts, New York, 47-, head drawing dept, 58-67. *Awards:* Jews in Am 54 & Einstein, 56, Nat Filmstrip Award, Nat Jewish Coun for Audio

Visual Aids; First Merit Award for Teaching, Alumni Asn, Sch Visual Arts, 76. *Bibliog:* Nick Maglin (auth), On The Spot Drawing, Animals in Motion, Watson-Guptill Publ, 69; Anne Commire (ed), Something about the author, Gale Res Co. *Media:* Watercolor, Oil; Mixed Media. *Publ:* Illusr, Two Years Before the Mast, Doubleday, 49; illusr, The Christmas Book, 52 & The Easter Book, 54, Harcourt-Brace; illusr, Boston, Seabury, 67; illusr, Indians, Parents Mag Press, 68. *Dealer:* Hans Fybel Assoc 648 Kelton Ave Los Angeles CA 90024. *Mailing Add:* 601 E 20th St New York NY 10010

FRANKENTHALER, HELEN
PAINTER

b New York, NY, Dec 12, 28. *Study:* Horace Mann, Brearley & Dalton Schs; Bennington Col, BA, 49; also with Rufino Tamayo, Wallace Harrison, Paul Feeley & Hans Hofmann; twelve hon doctorates. *Hon Degrees:* DHL, Skidmore Col, 69, DFA, Smith Col, 73, Moore Col Art, 74, Bard Col, 76 & NY Univ, 79, DA, Radcliffe Col, 78 & Amherst Col, 79. *Work:* Brooklyn Mus, Cooper Hewitt Mus, New York Univ Art Collection, Solomon R Guggenheim Mus, Whitney Mus of Am Art, Metrop Mus Art & Mus Mod Art, New York; Art Inst Chicago; Cleveland Mus Art; Pasadena Art Mus, Calif; plus many others. *Exhib:* New York Painting & Sculpture: 1940-1970, Metrop Mus Art, New York, 69-70; one-person shows, Metrop Mus Art, New York, 73 & Guggenheim Mus, New York, 75; Retrospective, Whitney Mus Am Art, New York, 69 & Berggruen Gallery, San Francisco, Calif, 72; Albright-Knox Art Gallery, Buffalo, NY, 70; Abstract Painting in the 70's, Mus Fine Arts, Boston, 72; The Great Decade of Am Abstraction: Modernist Art 1960-1970, Mus Fine Arts, Houston, Tex, 74; Block Prints, Whitney Mus Am Art, 82; From Munch to Johns: Modern Prints from the Collection, Fogg Art Mus, 83; Changes: The 1960's into the 1980's, Aldrich Mus Contemp Art, 83; and many others. *Pos:* Trustee, Bennington Col, 67-; fel, Calhoun Col, Yale Univ, 68- *Teaching:* Instr contemp painting sem, Yale Univ, spring 70; instr contemp painting sem, Princeton Univ & Hunter Col, 70; plus many other lectures & seminars. *Awards:* Garrett Award, 70th Am Exhib, Art Inst; Nat Conf Christians & Jews Award, 78; Bennington Col Alumni Award, 79. *Bibliog:* Eugene C Goossen (auth), Helen Frankenthaler, Praeger, 69; Barbara Rose (auth), Frankenthaler, Abrams, 72; Hilton Kramer (auth), Helen Frankenthaler's art in the 50's, New York Times, 6/7/81. *Dealer:* Andre Emmerich Gallery 41 E 57th St New York NY 10022. *Mailing Add:* 173 E 94th St New York NY 10028

FRANKLIN, CHARLOTTE WHITE
PAINTER, SCULPTOR

b Philadelphia, Pa. *Study:* Tyler Art Sch, Temple Univ, BA, 45, BS(educ), 46, MFA, 47; Inst San Miguel Allende, Univ Guanajuato, 57; Mexico City Col, 58; Escuela Nat de Bellas Artes, Buenos Aires, Arg, 60; Goldsmith Col, Univ London, 62; Inst Cult Mex-NAm, Mex, 64; Tyler, Rome, Italy, 67; Univ Madrid, 68. *Comn:* Altar panel, St Augustine Church, Philadelphia; portrait, Cardinal Dougherty, Archdiocese of Philadelphia; 24 portraits, comn by Philadelphia Elec Co, 77; plus numerous portraits & paintings in pvt collections. *Exhib:* Bicentennial Women's Exhib, Penwalt Galleries, Philadelphia, 76; Artists of Pa, William Penn Mem Mus, 76; Radnor Mem Libr, Pa, 79; Distinguished Mid-Atlantic Artists, Univ Del, 80; Thomas Jefferson Univ, Commons Gallery, 81; and many other group & one-man shows. *Pos:* Lectr, Speaker's Bur Art, US Embassy, London, Sch District Philadelphia, Univ Pa. *Teaching:* Instr, Philadelphia Mus Art, 43-47; chmn sec educ art, Philadelphia Pub Schs, 51-; instr, Soc Brit Artists, Buenos Aires, 60; Fulbright fel art teacher, Grammar Sch Girls, Cheam, Eng, 61-62. *Awards:* Bessie Calhoun Bird Award, Les Beaux Arts, 40's; Am Asn Univ Women name grant to Nat Educ Found, Women's Univ Club, 77; Medal of Achievement, Accademia Italia, 80. *Mem:* Artists Equity Inc; Philadelphia Art Alliance; Provincetown Art Asn, Mass; Hispano-NAm Asn Cult, Madrid; Soc Brit Artists; and others. *Media:* Oil. *Mailing Add:* 24th St & Franklin Pkwy Philadelphia Apts Philadelphia PA 19130

FRANKLIN, GILBERT ALFRED
SCULPTOR, EDUCATOR

b Birmingham, Eng, June 6, 19; US citizen. *Study:* RI Sch Design, BFA, 46; Nat Mus Mexico City; Am Acad Rome, fel, 49. *Work:* RI Sch Design Mus Art; Hopkins Ctr Gallery, Dartmouth Col, NH; Boston Mus Fine Arts; Vassar Col Art Gallery, Poughkeepsie, NY; NC State Col, Greensboro; and others. *Comn:* Lincoln Mem Statue, Harvey Trust Comt, Providence, RI; Harry S Truman Mem, Harry S Truman Statue Comn, Independence, Mo; Orpheus ascending fountain, comn by Mrs Murray S Danforth, Providence & Daybreak--S O Metcalf Mem;; Bronze Group, Providence Col. *Exhib:* De Young Mem Mus Ann Am Art, San Francisco, 46; Whitney Mus Ann, New York, 50; Ann Sculpture & Painting, Pa Acad, Philadelphia, 52, 54 & 56; Inst Contemp Art, Boston, 59; Sculpture, De Cordova Mus, Lincoln, Mass, 64; Hopkins Ctr Gallery Retrospective Exhib, Hanover, NH, 75; plus others. *Pos:* Sculptor-in-residence, Am Acad Rome, 64-65 & Dartmouth Col, spring 75; co-dir, Europ Honors Prog, Rome, 69-71; trustee, Am Acad Rome, 75-80. *Teaching:* Lectr sculpture, Harvard Univ, 50-52 & Yale Univ, 52-54; prof sculpture, RI Sch Design, 56-, dean fine arts & design, 78- *Awards:* Prix de Rome, Am Acad Rome, 48; Grand Prize, Boston Arts Festival, 58; Providence Art Club Medal for Excellence in the Arts, 75. *Mem:* Providence Art Club. *Media:* Bronze, Marble. *Dealer:* Kanegis Gallery Newbury St Boston MA 02116. *Mailing Add:* 52 Angell St Providence RI 02906

FRANKLIN, PATT
SCULPTOR, PAINTER

b 1941. *Study:* Pratt Inst, BFA, 62; Tulane Univ, MFA, 70. *Work:* Bowdoin Col Mus Art, Brunswick, Maine; Boston Libr Print & Drawing Collection & New England Medical Ctr Lobby Collection, Boston, Mass; Int Telephone &

Telegraph, New York; Colby Col, Waterville, Maine; Gilette Corp, Boston. *Comn:* Painted murals, Doctors of Touro Hospital, New Orleans, La, 68. *Exhib:* Soup Tureens, Campbells Mus, Camden, NJ, 76-77 & Mus Contemp Craft, New York, 77; All New England Drawing, DeCordova Mus, Lincoln, Mass, 79-80; one-man show, State House, Augusta, Maine, 79-80; Lamont Gallery, Phillips/Exeter, NH, 81 & Bates Col, 83; Views, Impressions Gallery, Boston, Mass, 81. *Teaching:* Assoc prof drawing & ceramics, Univ South Maine, Gorham, 70-; instr ceramics, Haystack Sch Art & Crafts, Deer Isle, Maine, 77. *Awards:* Fellar Award, Silvermine Competition, 73. *Mem:* Am Craft Coun; Women's Caucus Art; Nat Coun Educ Ceramic Arts; Col Art Asn. *Media:* Pastels; Ceramic. *Mailing Add:* Box 94 Gorham ME 04038

FRANSIOLI, THOMAS ADRIAN
PAINTER, PRINTMAKER

b Seattle, Wash, Sept 15, 06. *Study:* Univ Pa, BArch; Art Students League. *Work:* Whitney Mus Am Art, New York; Seattle Art Mus, Wash; Dallas Mus Fine Arts, Tex; Farnsworth Mus, Rockland, Maine. *Comn:* Murals in dining rm, Aetna Life Bldg, Hartford, Conn, 62; four paintings of old New York, Univ Club, New York, 64; mural in stair hall, Princeton Club, New York, 66; mural in lobby, Brevoort East Hotel, New York, 67; painting of Brit Embassy, Washington, DC, comn by the Brit Ambassador to US, 75. *Exhib:* Boston Art Festival, 48-49; Whitney Mus Ann, New York, 48-52 & 58; Carnegie Inst, Pittsburgh, Pa, 49 & 52; Am Art Today, Metrop Mus Art, New York, 50; Maine & Its Role in American Art, Colby Col, Waterville, Maine & Whitney Mus Am Art, New York, 63. *Awards:* Purchase Prize, Boston Arts Festival, 52. *Media:* Oil, Acrylic. *Mailing Add:* 55 Dodges Row Wenham MA 01984

FRANZEN, JOAN C
ART ADMINISTRATOR

b Boston, Mass. *Study:* Bennington Col. *Pos:* Asst, J B Neumann, New York, 60-63; dir, Skowhegan Sch Painting & Sculpture, Maine & New York City, 64- *Mailing Add:* 329 E 68th St New York NY 10021

FRARY, MICHAEL
PAINTER, EDUCATOR

b Santa Monica, Calif, May 28, 18. *Study:* Univ Southern Calif, BA(archit), 40, MFA(painting), 41; Acad Grande Chaumiere, Paris, dipl, 50. *Work:* Nat Collection Fine Arts, Smithsonian Inst; Santa Barbara Mus, Calif; Butler Inst Am Art, Youngstown, Ohio; Dallas Mus Fine Art; Witte Mus, San Antonio, Tex. *Comn:* Murals, Brackenridge Hosp, Austin, Tex, 58 & Headliners Club, Austin, 62; tapestry, Hatfield Galleries, Los Angeles, 72; paint reclamation sites, US Dept of Interior, Colo & Wyo, 72; paint Psyche prize for best film Canada, San Antonio, Tex, 78. *Exhib:* Fifth Ann Exhib Southwest Am Art, Okla Art Ctr, Oklahoma City, 70; Water Reclamation, Nat Gallery Art, DC, 72; 24th Ann Mid-Yr, Butler Inst Am Art, Youngstown, Ohio; Ann Nat Watercolor Soc Exhib, Calif; 6th, 10th, 12th & 14th Ann Tex Watercolor Exhibs, McNay Art Inst, San Antonio. *Teaching:* Fac chmn painting, San Antonio Art Inst, 48-49; prof drawing & painting, Univ Tex, Austin, 54- *Awards:* Over 180 Purchase Prizes and Awards. *Bibliog:* Dorothy Blodgett (auth), Michael Frary: Person and palette-quicksilver, Southwestern Art Mag, 12/70;; Michael Frary, artist-teacher, Southern Living, 6/71; Beulah Hodge (producer), People and Ideas, Michael Frary (color video cassette), KLRN, 77. *Mem:* Calif Watercolor Soc (treas, 49); hon life mem Southwestern Watercolor Soc; Tex Watercolor Soc. *Media:* Watercolor, Acrylic. *Publ:* Coauth, Impressions of the Big Thicket, Univ Tex Press, 73; auth, Impressions of the Texas Panhandle, Univ Tex A&M Press, 77; illusr, Stolen steers, Univ Tex A&M Press, 78; contribr, Texas Gulf Coast, 79 & Texas hill country, 81, Univ Tex A&M Press; and others. *Dealer:* Hatfield Gallery Ambassador Hotel Los Angeles CA; Meredith Long Gallery 2323 San Felipe Houston TX 77019. *Mailing Add:* 3409 Spanish Oak Dr Austin TX 78731

FRASCONI, ANTONIO
ILLUSTRATOR, PAINTER

b Buenos Aires, Arg, Apr 28, 19. *Study:* Art Students League; New Sch Social Res. *Work:* Metrop Mus Art & Mus Mod Art, New York; Fogg Art Mus; Bibliot Nat, Paris, France; Brooklyn Mus. *Exhib:* Casa Americas, Havana, Cuba, 65-68; Venice Biennale, Italy, 68; Art of the Americas, Yale Univ; Smithsonian Inst, Washington, DC; var ann, Pa Acad Fine Arts, Philadelphia. *Teaching:* Mem art faculty, State Univ NY Col Purchase, currently. *Awards:* Premio La Habana, Casa Americas, 68; Conn Comn Grant, 74; Nat Acad Design Award, 79. *Bibliog:* Manuel Gasser (auth), A Frasconi, Graphis Press, Switz, 67; Frasconi--Against the Grain, Macmillan; Pablo Frasconi (auth), Antonio Frasconi--graphic artist (film), York Univ. *Publ:* Illusr, Twelve Fables of Aesop, 54; illusr, Bestiary, 65; illusr, Overhead the Sun, 69; illusr, Unstill Life, 69; illusr, On the Slain Collegians, 71. *Dealer:* Weyhe Gallery 794 Lexington Ave New York NY 10021; Terry Dintenfass Inc 50 W 57th St New York NY 10021. *Mailing Add:* 26 Dock Rd Norwalk CT 06854

FRASER, CAROL HOORN
PAINTER, DRAFTSMAN

b Superior, Wis, Sept 5, 30. *Study:* Gustavus Adolphus Col, St Peter, Minn, BS; Univ Minn, seminar with Jack Tworkov, MFA; painting with Yasuo Kuniyoshi. *Work:* Nat Gallery Can; Sir George Williams Art Galleries; Nat Portrait Gallery, Smithsonian Inst; Beaverbrook Art Gallery; and others. *Exhib:* Sixteen Minn Artists, Walker Art Ctr, 60; Montreal Mus Fine Art Spring Show, 62-63; Nat Gallery Can Biennials, 62-63 & 64; New Talent Festival, Midtown Galleries, New York, 74; Painting Now, 76-77, Agnes Etherington Art Ctr, 76; one-person show, Atlantic Provinces Art Circuit, travelling to five major inst, 65-67, Zwicker's Art Gallery, 80; one-person travelling show, eight provinces & inst, 77-78; and others. *Collections Arranged:* Drawing USA, St Paul Art Gallery, 63; Expo 67, Atlantic Pavilion,

67; Seven Artists Travelling Show, Dalhousie Univ Art Ctr, 69-70; Artists Media, Mt St Vincent Univ Art Ctr, 74; Montreal Olympics, Atlantic Gallery, 76. *Pos:* Actg dir, Dalhousie Univ Art Gallery, 78-79. *Teaching:* Instr drawing, Sch Archit, NS Tech Col, 62-69. *Awards:* First Prize & Purchase Award, Walker Art Ctr Biennial, 58; First Prize, Minn Inst Art, 59; Arts Award, Can Coun, 67. *Bibliog:* Felicity Redgrave (auth), Homage to Carol Fraser, Art Mag, Toronto, 77. *Mem:* Royal Can Acad Arts. *Media:* Oil; Black India & Colored Ink. *Publ:* Auth, Tim Zuck, spring 81 & Mark Gomes & Susanne Schelle, spring 81, Arts Atlantic; and others. *Dealer:* Dresden Gallery Birmingham St Halifax NS Can. *Mailing Add:* 6070 Oakland Rd Halifax NS B3H 1N8 Canada

FRATER, HAL
PAINTER
b New York, NY, Mar 3, 09. *Exhib:* Minnesota Mus, 80 & 82; Nat Acad Design; Brooklyn Mus; Allied Artists Am; Chrysler Mus, Provincetown, Mass; Seton Hall Univ; and others. *Teaching:* Instr, Sch of Art & Design, New York & Educ Alliance, New York. *Awards:* Jane Peterson Award, Allied Artists, 59. *Mem:* Painters & Sculptors Soc NJ; Allied Artists Am; Soc Illusr; Artists Equity Asn; Audubon Artists. *Mailing Add:* 215 Park Row New York NY 10038

FRAUCHIGER, FRITZ A
ADMINISTRATOR, DIRECTOR
Okla City, Okla, Sept 23, 41. *Study:* San Jose State Univ, Calif, BA, 69, MA, 72. *Collections Arranged:* Ed Ruscha New Work, 81; Paul Sarkisian Paintings (auth, catalog); 7 Little Known Artists (auth, catalog), Arco Biennial, 81 & 83; Deborah Butterfield Sculpture, 81; Joe Goode New Paintings (auth, catalog), 82; Art of the Movie Miniature (auth, catalog); Peter Alexander Velvets (auth, catalog); Larry Bell New Sculpture (auth, catalog), 83; Plank House Architecture of the Northwest Coast Indians (auth, catalog), 83. *Pos:* Registar's asst, Los Angeles Co Mus Art, Calif, 72-73; preparator, J Paul Getty Mus, Calif, 73-74; Southeby Park-Bernet, Los Angeles, 74-75; cur, ARCO Ctr Visual Art, Los Angeles, 76- *Mem:* Western Asn Art Mus; Los Angeles Inst Contemp Art. *Publ:* Contribr, Herbert Bayer: Photographic Works, ARCO Ctr Visual Art, 77; contribr, Traditional Textiles of Sumatra, From the Collection of Atlantic Richfield Co, ARCO Ctr Visual Art, 81. *Mailing Add:* 3484 Mandeville Canyon Rd Los Angeles CA 90049

FRAUGHTON, EDWARD JAMES
SCULPTOR
b Park City, Utah, Mar 22, 39. *Study:* Univ Utah, BFA, 62; studied under Dr Avard T Fairbanks & Justin Fairbanks. *Work:* Riveredge Found, Calgary, Can; Leanin' Tree Mus Western Art, Boulder, Colo; Valley Bank, Las Vegas, Nev; Nat Cowboy Hall of Fame & Western Heritage Ctr, Oklahoma City, Okla; Favell Mus Western Art, Klamath Falls, Ore. *Comn:* Mormon Battalion Monument, Sons of Utah Pioneers, Prisidio Park, San Diego, Calif, 69; Ben H Bohac (relief portrait), Talman Savings & Loan, Chicago, 70; All is Well, Family Monument, Sons of Utah Pioneers, Brigham Young Cemetery, Salt Lake City, 74; Truman O Angell Portrait, Church of Jesus Christ of Latter-day Saints, Salt Lake City, Utah, 77; Spirit of Wyo, 15 ft major monument, Capitol Grounds, Cheyenne, 80; Official Inaugural Medal, President Ronald Reagan. *Exhib:* Nat Acad Western Art, Oklahoma City; Nat Sculpture Soc, New York; Whitney Mus Western Art, Cody, Wyo; Bohemian Club, Bohemian Grove, Monte Rio, Calif; Nat Acad Design, New York; Artists of America, Denver. *Awards:* Lance Int Prize, Nat Sculpture Soc, 79; Artist of the West, San Dimas Festival of Western Arts, 81; The Tallix Foundry Prize, Spirit of Man, Nat Sculpture Soc, 81; and others. *Bibliog:* Pat Broder (auth), Bronzes of the American West, Abrams, 74; Peggy & Harold Samuels (auths), Contemporary Western Artists, Southwest Art Publ, 82; Profiles in American Art (film), Ken Meyer Prod. *Mem:* Soc Animal Artists; San Francisco Bohemian Club; Nat Sculpture Soc; Nat Acad Western Art. *Media:* Bronze & Stone Carving. *Mailing Add:* 10353 S 1300 West Riverton UT 84065

FRAZE, DENNY T
COLLAGE ARTIST, ADMINISTRATOR
b Weatherford, Tex, May 28, 40. *Study:* Univ Tex, Austin, BFA(studio, art hist), 62; Univ Colo, MFA(painting), 64, study with Luis Eades & Roland Reiss. *Work:* Univ Tex, Austin; Univ Colo, Boulder; Amarillo Col Collection, Tex. *Exhib:* One-man shows, Odessa Col, 80; Tarrant Co Jr Col, Tex, 81 & Mus Art, Norman, Okla, 83; Franklin Furnace Copycat Show, New York, 82; Kans 7th Ann Small Painting, Drawing & Print Exhib, Hays, 82. *Teaching:* Prof studio art & chmn dept, Amarillo Col, Tex, 65- *Mem:* Hon mem Tex Fine Arts Asn; Tex Asn Sch Art (pres, 70-72, bd mem, 70-74 & 83-); hon mem Amarillo Fine Arts Asn; Tex Coun Arts Educ (bd mem, 70-72); Nat Art Educ Asn. *Media:* Collage. *Collection:* 20th century prints. *Mailing Add:* 2219 S Hayden Amarillo TX 79109

FRAZER, JAMES (NISBET), JR
PHOTOGRAPHER, MURALIST
b Atlanta, Ga, Oct 6, 49. *Study:* Amherst Col, BA(cum laude), 71; Ga State Univ, MFA, 73; also with Fairfield Porter. *Work:* High Mus Art, Atlanta; Corcoran Gallery; Chase Manhattan Bank; Ackland Art Mus, Chapel Hill, NC; Smith Col Mus Art. *Comn:* Photomural design, Metro Atlanta Rapid Transit Authority, 78 & Southern Bell Telephone Co, 80; Veterans Admin Med Ctr, Atlanta, 83. *Exhib:* Artists Biennalle, New Orleans Mus Art, La, 75; The Southern Ethic, Nexus Gallery, Atlanta, 75; Arte EUA: El Sur (South Am traveling exhib), US Info Agency, 76-77; 35 Artists in the SE, High Mus Art, 76-78; Art Patron Art, Southeastern Ctr for Contemp Art, Winston-Salem, NC, 78; one-man shows, High Mus Art, 81 & Southeastern Ctr Contemp Art, Winston-Salem, NC, 81. *Pos:* Pres, Nexus Inc, Atlanta, 73-74,

mem bd dir, 73-81. *Teaching:* Instr photog, Atlanta Col Art, Ga State Univ, 72-76 & Mercer Univ, 77-81. *Bibliog:* Peter Morrin (auth), Jim Frazer: Hand-Colored Photographs, High Mus Art, Atlanta, 81. *Media:* Hand-Colored Photographs. *Interests:* Development special panoramic cameras. *Publ:* Contribr, The Southern Ethic, Inst for Southern Studies, 75; The Avant-Garde: 12 in Atlanta, High Mus Art, 79. *Dealer:* Heath Gallery 416 E Paces Ferry Rd Atlanta GA 30305; Kathleen Ewing Gallery 3243 P St NW Washington DC 20007. *Mailing Add:* Route 2 Box 285 Ranger GA 30734

FRAZER, JOHN THATCHER
FILMMAKER, PAINTER
b Akron, Ohio, Apr 2, 32. *Study:* Univ Tex, BFA; Yale Univ, MFA; with Joseph Albers; Wesleyan Univ, Hon MA. *Work:* Davison Art Ctr, Wesleyan Univ, Middletown, Conn; Libr of Cong, Washington, DC; Cullinan Collection, Houston Mus Fine Arts; Nicholson Mem Libr, Longview, Tex. *Exhib:* Tex Ann, Dallas Mus Fine Arts, 58; New Haven Arts Festival, Conn, 60; Boston Arts Festival, Mass, 61; Flaherty Film Festival, Lakeville, Conn, 66; Am Film Festival, New York, 68. *Teaching:* Prof art, motion pictures & drawing, Wesleyan Univ, 59- *Bibliog:* New talent, USA, Art in Am, 62; Bernard Chaet (auth), The Art of Drawing, Holt, 70. *Mem:* Am Asn Univ Prof; Col Art Asn Am; Am Film Inst. *Interests:* Motion pictures. *Publ:* Auth, Documentary films & books on documentary films, Choice Mag, 69; auth, Artificially Arranged Scenes, The Films of George Melies, G K Hall, 79. *Mailing Add:* Art Ctr Wesleyan Univ Middletown CT 06457

FRAZIER, PAUL D
SCULPTOR, EDUCATOR
b Pickaway Co, Ohio, May 6, 22. *Study:* Ohio State Univ, BFA; Cranbrook Acad Art, MFA; Skowhegan Sch Painting & Sculpture, with Jose de Creeft; Acad Grande Chaumiere, with Ossip Zadkine. *Work:* Cranbrook Mus; Skowhegan Sch Painting & Sculpture Collection; Munson-Williams-Proctor Inst; Rochester Mus Arts & Sci. *Exhib:* Primary Structures, Solomon R Guggenheim Mus, New York, 67; plus many other group & one-man shows. *Teaching:* Instr sculpture, ceramics & design, Univ Minn, 50-53; instr sculpture, Munson-Williams-Proctor Inst, 53-58; assoc prof 3-D area & drawing, Queens Col, 64- *Awards:* Gov Award, State of Ohio, 47; Cranbrook Found Medal for Sculpture, 49; First Prize for Sculpture, Cooperstown Mus, 57. *Bibliog:* Ralph Pomeroy (auth), Confirmed out-of-towner, Art Int, 10/28/68; Gregory Battcock (auth), Minimal Art, Dutton; Sam Hunter (auth), American Art in the 20th Century, Abrams. *Media:* Wood, Metal. *Mailing Add:* Box 33 Washington Depot CT 06794

FRECKELTON, SONDRA
PAINTER
b Dearborn, Mich, 1936. *Study:* Art Inst Chicago. *Work:* Amerada Hess Corp, Reader's Digest Asn, Inc & Sara Roby Found, New York; Best Products Co, Richmond, Va; Prudential Insurance Co, Newark, NJ. *Exhib:* Whitney Ann, Whitney Mus Am Art, New York, 64; Hand Colored Prints, Brooke Alexander, Inc, New York, 73; Brooke Alexander: A Decade of Print Publishing, Boston Univ Art, Mass, 78; Watercolor USA, Springfield Art Mus, Mo, 80. *Teaching:* Visiting artist & lecturer at many schools and universities. *Awards:* Ingram Merrill Grant; Bradford Print Prize. *Bibliog:* Judith Rosenthal (auth), article, Art Mag, 5/79; John Russell (auth), article, New York Times, 79; Jo Ann Lewis (auth), article, Washington Post, 80. *Media:* Watercolor. *Publ:* Contribr, Realist Drawings and Watercolors, NY Graphic Soc, 81; Contribr, Dynamic Still Life in Watercolor, Watson Guptill, 83. *Dealer:* Brooke Alexander Inc 20 West 57th St New York NY 10019. *Mailing Add:* 67 Vestry St New York NY 10013

FREDERICK, DELORAS ANN
PAINTER, INSTRUCTOR
b Fletcher, Okla, Jan 25, 42. *Study:* Central State Univ, 75; with Joseph Mugnaini, 79-80; with M Doug Walton, 79-80. *Work:* Presbyterian Hospital, Baptist Mem Hospital, Patrick Petroleum & CMI Corp, Oklahoma City, Okla; CCI Corp, Tulsa, Okla. *Exhib:* Artist Salon, Okla Mus Art, Oklahoma City, 75-80; Okla Territorial Mus, Guthrie, 78-80; Nat Small Painting Exhib, W F Mullaly Galleries, Birmingham, Mich, 78; The Miniature Painter, Sculptors & Gravers Soc, Art Club Washington, Washington, DC, 80; Ann Art Exhib, Mus Great Plains, Lawton, Okla, 80-81; and others. *Teaching:* Instr watercolor, Art Supply Shop, Oklahoma City, Okla, 75-79; instr, Workshops for Art Club in Okla, Oklahoma City, 77-81; instr watercolor, Nichels Hills Elementary Sch, Oklahoma City, Okla, 81. *Awards:* Best of Show, Mid-Del Art Guild, 77, 79 & 80; Founders Award for Best Still Life, Founders Arts Club, Washington, DC, 80; Artist Holiday Award, Tri State Kans, 83. *Bibliog:* Deloras Frederick, Okla Art Gallery Mag, 80; Peggy Ridgeway (auth), Deloras Frederick, Art Voices, 81. *Mem:* Mid-Del Art Guild (1st vpres, 76-77); Oklahoma Watercolor (1st vpres, 77-78); Watercolor Oklahoma (1st vpres, 78-79); Oklahoma Art Guild (1st vpres, 79-80); Nat League Am Pen Women, Inc. *Media:* Watercolor, Acrylic. *Dealer:* House Gallery 5536 N Western Oklahoma City OK 73116; Studio Gallery 2020 E Eleventh Tulsa OK 74104. *Mailing Add:* 7301 NW 13 Oklahoma City OK 73127

FREDERICK, EUGENE WALLACE
PRINTMAKER, EDUCATOR
b Washington, DC, Oct 29, 27. *Study:* Art Students League, New York; Corcoran Sch of Art & Howard Univ, Washington, DC. *Work:* Norfolk Mus Arts & Sci. *Exhib:* Ann Area Show, Corcoran Gallery of Art, Washington, DC, 59 & 75; 156th & 158th Ann Exhib, Pa Acad of Fine Arts, Philadelphia, 61 & 63; Va Artists, Va Mus, Richmond, 63 & 65; Am Drawing Biennial, Mus of Arts & Sci, Norfolk, 71; Invitational Exhib, Tatum Arts Ctr, Hood Col, Fredrick, Md, 74; Smithsonian Inst, traveling exhib ser, 75; US Info Agency,

Mid East traveling exhib, 77; one-man show, Va Mus, Richmond, 66; Washington Art 81, Washington, DC; and others. *Teaching:* Assoc prof printmaking, Corcoran Sch Art, Washington, DC, 64-; instr drawing, Montgomery Jr Col, Tacoma Park, Md, 70-74. *Awards:* Watercolor Prize, Ann Area Show, Corcoran Gallery of Art, 59; Awards of Distinction, Va Artists, Va Mus, Richmond, 65; Purchase Prize, Am Drawing Biennial, Norfolk Mus Arts & Sci, 71. *Bibliog:* Gil Golden (auth), Poor Mans America, Jerusalem Post, Israel, 75; Jack Perlmutter (auth), article, Washington, DC, Art Voices South, 78. *Media:* Engraving, Relief. *Mailing Add:* 6078 Belleview Drive Apt 102 Falls Church VA 22041

FREDERICK, SARADELL ARD See   Ard,   Saradell

FREDERICKS, MARSHALL MAYNARD
SCULPTOR
b Rock Island, Ill, Jan 31, 08. *Study:* John Huntington Polytech Inst, Cleveland; Cleveland Sch Art, grad, 30; Heimann Schule, Munich; Schwegerie Schule, Munich; Acad Scandinav, Paris; pvt studies in Copenhagen, Rome & London; Carl Milles Studio; Cranbrook Acad Art, fel. *Work:* Detroit Inst Arts, Mich; Cranbrook Mus Art, Bloomfield Hills, Mich; Milwaukee Pub Mus, Wis; City New York; US Govt. *Comn:* Emigrants Monument, Stavanger, Norway; Milles Garden, Stockholm, Sweden; Ministry Foreign Affairs, Copenhagen, Denmark; Brookgreen Gardens, Gibbes Gallery, Charleston, SC; Sterling Heights, Mich; and others. *Exhib:* Carnegie Inst Nat, Pittsburgh, Pa; Philadelphia Int; Art Inst Chicago Nat; Detroit Art Inst; Whitney Mus Am Art Nat; Cleveland Mus Art; and others. *Teaching:* Instr sculpture, Cranbrook Sch, 32-38, Kingswood Sch, 32-42 & Cranbrook Acad Art, 32-42. *Awards:* Fine Arts Gold Medal, Am Inst Archit, 52; Gold Medal Hon, Mich Acad Sci, Arts & Lett, 53 & Archit League New York, 56. *Mem:* Academician Nat Acad Design; fel Nat Sculpture Soc; hon mem Mich Soc Architects; fel Royal Soc Arts; fel Int Inst Arts & Lett. *Mailing Add:* 440 Lake Park Dr Birmingham MI 48009

FREDERICKSEN, BURTON BAUM
CURATOR, HISTORIAN
b Mitchell, SDak, Aug 6, 34. *Study:* Univ Calif, Los Angeles, BA & MA. *Exhib:* One-man show, CeeJe Gallery, Los Angeles, 64; two-man show, Long Beach Munic Art Gallery, 65; two-man show, Orange Coast Col, Costa Mesa, Calif, 69. *Collections Arranged:* Catalog of the Pre-Nineteenth-Century Paintings in the Los Angeles Co Mus. *Pos:* Cur, J Paul Getty Mus, 65-72, chief cur, 72-73 & cur of paintings, 73-; adj cur Renaissance & Baroque art, Los Angeles Co Mus Art, 69-73. *Media:* Oil. *Res:* Authorship and provenance of pre-nineteenth century Western European paintings. *Publ:* Auth, Census of Pre-Nineteenth Century Italian Paintings in North America, 72; auth, Giovanni de Francesco and the Master of Pratovecchio, 74. *Mailing Add:* 17985 Pac Coast Hwy Malibu CA 90265

FREDMAN, FAIYA R
ENVIRONMENTAL ARTIST, PAINTER
b Columbus, Ohio, Sept 8, 25. *Study:* Calif State Univ, San Diego; Univ Calif, Los Angeles. *Work:* Boehm Gallery Collection, Palomar Col, San Marcos, Calif; Univ Calif, San Diego; Ariz State Univ; La Jolla Mus Contemp Art, Calif; Security Pacific Bank, Los Angeles; and others. *Exhib:* Solo shows, La Jolla Mus Contemp Art, 68, 74 & 81 & Thomas Baveor Gallery, La Jolla, 81; Earth & Water, Women's Bldg, Los Angeles, 79; New Artists in New York, Alex Rosenberg Gallery, 79; Sao Paulo Mus Contemp Art, Brazil, 80; and others. *Teaching:* Instr, Exten, Univ Calif, San Diego, 77- *Awards:* US Dept Housing & Urban Develop Nat Community Art Competition Award, 73; 1st Prize, San Diego Pub Television, 78. *Bibliog:* Lucy Lippard (auth), Body, Nature & Ritual in Women's Art, Chrysalis Mag, 77; Jean Luc Bordeaux (auth), Unstretched surfaces Southern Calif, Los Angeles Inst of Contemp Art J, 11/77. *Media:* Sand. *Mailing Add:* 121 27th St Del Mar CA 92014

FREDRICKSON, DANIEL ALAN See Folkus, Dan

FREED, DAVID
PRINTMAKER, PAINTER
b Toledo, Ohio, May 23, 36. *Study:* Miami Univ; Univ Iowa; Royal Col Art, London. *Work:* Art Inst Chicago, Ill; Nat Collection Fine Arts, Washington, DC; Va Mus Fine Arts, Richmond; Victoria & Albert Mus, London; Mus Mod Art, New York; and others. *Exhib:* Photography in Printmaking, AAA Gallery, New York, 68-70; one-man shows, Franz Bader Gallery, Washington, DC, 68, 70, 73, 76 & 82 & Va Mus Fine Arts, Richmond; Albright-Knox Art Gallery, Buffalo, NY; Biennial Graphic Art, Moderna Galerija, Ljubljana, Yugoslavia; among others. *Teaching:* Prof printmaking, Va Commonwealth Univ, 66-78, prof, 78-; guest lectr etching, Cent Sch Art, London, 69. *Awards:* Fulbright grant, 63-64; Va Mus Fine Arts Fel, 83-84; Natie Marie Jones Fel, Lake Placid, NY, 83; and others. *Mailing Add:* 1825 W Grace Richmond VA 23220

FREED, DOUGLASS LYNN
PAINTER, EDUCATOR
b Garden City, Kans, Dec 24, 44. *Study:* Ft Hays Kans State Univ, BS, 67, MA, 68; Rotary Int Group Study Exchange to Italy, 78. *Work:* Univ Mo Mus Art & Archeol, Columbia; Ark Art Ctr, Little Rock; St Louis Art Mus; and others; Johnson Co Community Col, Kansas City; Mem Union Col, Univ Mo. *Exhib:* 8 State Regional, Okla Art Ctr, Oklahoma City, 71; Visions 81, 12 mus, 80-81; one-man shows, Art Res Ctr, Kansas City, 80 & Univ Mo, Kansas City, 81; Greenberg Gallery, St Louis, Mo, 81; Vorpal Gallery, New York, 81; and

many others. *Collections Arranged:* Works on Paper, Mo State Coun on Arts (contribr, assembled 12 sites), 80-81; Mid America Art Alliance, 24 sites, 82-83. *Teaching:* Chmn dept art, State Fair Community Col, Sedalia, Mo, 68- *Awards:* Mid-Am Art Alliance grant, Visions 81, 80. *Bibliog:* Susan Snieder, Conversations with Douglass Freed, KCTV Channel 19, 10/76; Pinky Case, Douglass Freed--Painter, Kans State Cable TV Network, 2/80; Andrew Kagan (auth), Douglass Freed in first maturity: The synthesis of classical structure and dynamic field, Arts Mag, 9/82; Gary Noland (auth), Douglass Freed interview, Forum Mag, 10/82. *Media:* Oil. *Dealer:* Vorpal Galleries 465 W Broadway New York NY 10012. *Mailing Add:* 1100 W Fourth Sedalia MO 65301

FREED, HERMINE
VIDEO ARTIST, WRITER
b New York, NY, May 29, 40. *Study:* Cornell Univ, BA, 61; NY Univ, with Irving Sandler & Lawrence Alloway, MA, 67. *Work:* Univ NC, Gainsborough; Smith Col, Northampton, Mass; Chicago Art Inst; Donnell Libr, NY; Univ Ga; and others. *Comn:* Videotape, Guild Hall, East Hampton, NY, 73; video portrait of pres Jill Ker Conway, Smith Col, Northampton, Mass. *Exhib:* Collector's Choice, Los Angeles Co Mus Art, 74; Video Art 1975, Corcoran Gallery, Washington, DC, 75; Projections, Whitney Mus Am Art, 75; Biennale de Paris, Mus Mod Art, Paris, 75; Changing Channels, Boston Mus Fine Arts, 76; Int Film Expos, LA Filmex, 77; Art About Art, Whitney Mus, 78; Custom and Culture, US Custom House, 79; one-woman shows, Everson Mus, Syracuse, NY, 78; Columbia Univ, Avery Hall, 79 & Stefanotti Gallery, NY, 80; Leo Castelli Gallery, NY, 81; and many others. *Pos:* Art rental cur, Inst Contemp Art, Boston, 63-65; asst cur, NY Univ Art Collection, 65-67. *Teaching:* Ideas in contemp art, NY Univ, 68-72; video art workshop, Sch Visual Arts, New York, 74-75. *Awards:* Nat Endowment Arts Grant, 74; Creative Artists Pub Serv Grant, NY State Coun Arts, 78; Rockefeller Found Grant, 78. *Bibliog:* Grace Glueck (auth), Video is replacing canvas, New York Times, 75; Margot Jefferson (auth), Veni, vedi, video, Newsweek Mag, 75; Ronny Cohen (auth), Hermine Freed: Information please, Print Collector's Newsletter, 5-6/81. *Media:* Videotape, Photography. *Publ:* Auth, Video and abstract expressionism, 12/74 & In time-of-time, 6/75, Arts Mag; auth, Where Did We Come From, Where Are We, Where Are We Going?, Harcourt, Brace, Jovanovich, 76; auth, Collecting video, Print Collector's Newsletter, 77. *Dealer:* Leo Castelli Gallery NY; Stefanotti Gallery NY. *Mailing Add:* 140 Fifth Ave New York NY 10011

FREED, WILLIAM
PAINTER
b Poland, July 28, 02; US citizen. *Study:* Art Students League, with Homer Boas & Richard Lahey; Hans Hofmann Sch Fine Arts. *Work:* Whitney Mus Am Art, Jewish Mus, Metrop Mus Art, NY Univ, New York; Chrysler Mus, Norfolk, Va. *Exhib:* One-man shows, James Gallery, New York, 52-62; Corcoran Art Gallery, Washington, DC, 60; Hans Hofmann and His Students Traveling Show, Mus Mod Art, New York, 62-65; 1st Major New Eng Show of the Seventies, Provincetown & Boston, 70; Free Abstract Form of the Fifties, Whitney Mus, 72; Provincetown, a Painter's Place, Everson Mus, Syracuse, NY & Provincetown Mus & Art Asn, Mass, 77; In Retrospect, Provincetown Art Asn & Mus, 81. *Teaching:* Instr art, 37-41; lending librn, Mus Mod Art, 59-62; instr painting & drawing, Bronx House, 74-75. *Awards:* Longview Found Award, 60; Chapelbrook Found Grant, 67-68; Best in Show, Goddard Col, Vt, 76. *Bibliog:* Ben Brook (auth), Painter's Kuchta-Seckler Day's Studio Then & Now, Provincetown Art Asn & Mus, 77. *Mem:* Artist Equity Asn New York. *Media:* Oil, Gouache. *Mailing Add:* 530 W 113th St New York NY 10025

FREEDBERG, SYDNEY JOSEPH
HISTORIAN, EDUCATOR
b Boston, Mass, Nov 11, 14. *Study:* Harvard Col, AB(summa cum laude); Harvard Univ, AM(Sachs Res Fel), 39, PhD, 40. *Pos:* Bd dirs, Col Art Asn Am, 62-66; nat vchmn, Comt to Rescue Italian Art, 66-71; dir, Save Venice, Inc, 71-; chmn, Univ Mus Coun, 77-80; chief cur, Nat Gallery Art, Washington, DC, 83- *Teaching:* Asst & tutor fine arts, Harvard Univ, 38-40; asst prof art, Wellesley Col, 46-49, assoc prof art, 50-54; vis lectr fine arts, Inst Mod Art, Boston, 47; assoc prof fine arts, Harvard Univ, 54-60, chmn dept, 59-63, prof, 60-79, Arthur Kingsley Porter prof fine arts, 79-83, prof emer, 83- *Awards:* Hon Mem, Order of the Brit Empire; Grand Officer, Order of Solidarity, Ital Repub; Grand Officer, Order of Merit, Italy. *Mem:* Fel Am Acad of Arts & Sci. *Publ:* Auth, Parmigianino: His Works in Painting, 50, auth, Painting of the High Renaissance in Rome & Florence, Vols I & II, 61, auth, Andrea del Sarto, Vols I & II, 63, Harvard Univ; auth, Painting in Italy, 1500-1600, Penguin Bks, London & Baltimore, 71. *Mailing Add:* Fogg Art Mus Harvard Univ Cambridge MA 02138

FREEDMAN, MAURICE
PAINTER
b Boston, Mass, Nov 14, 04. *Study:* Boston Mus Fine Arts, scholarship class, 19-21; Mass Normal Art Sch, with Andrew, Sharman & Porter, 21-25; Boston Mus Sch, 30; Acad Lhote, Paris, France, 30. *Work:* Nat Collection Fine Arts, Smithsonian Inst, Washington, DC; Carnegie Inst, Pittsburgh, Pa; City Art Mus, St Louis, Mo; Brooklyn Mus, NY; Los Angeles Co Mus, Calif. *Exhib:* Carnegie Int, 50; American Painting Today & American Watercolors, Metrop Mus Art, New York, 50-52; Am Acad Arts & Lett, New York, 70; Maurice Freedman Retrospective, Washington Univ Gallery Art, St Louis, 72; Contemp Am Oil Painting 23rd Biennial, Corcoran Gallery Art, Washington, DC; 32 one-man shows, Midtown Gallery, New York. *Awards:* Jane Peterson Medal, Audubon Artists, 72; Award, Audubon Artists, 82. *Bibliog:* Sheldon Cheney (auth), A primer of modern art, 45; A O Gruskin (auth), Painting in USA, 46. *Media:* Oil, Gouache. *Dealer:* Midtown Galleries 11 E 57th St New York NY 10022. *Mailing Add:* 121 Edgars Lane Hastings-on-Hudson NY 10706

FREELAND, WILLIAM LEE
PAINTER, SCULPTOR

b Pittsburgh, Pa, June 16, 29. *Study:* Philadelphia Mus Sch Art; Hans Hofmann Sch, Provincetown, Mass. *Work:* Wilmington Mus & Soc Fine Arts, Del; Int Tel & Tel Collection, NY. *Exhib:* One-man shows, Philadelphia Art Alliance, 56 & Touchstone Gallery, New York, NY, 78 & 80; 25th Corcoran Biennial Exhib, Washington, DC, 57; Color Show, Birmingham Mus, Ala, 63; Artists Tribute to J F K, Swarthmore Col, 64; Nat Watercolor Show, Pa Acad Fine Arts, Philadelphia, 69; Drawing Show, Montclair Mus, Montclair, NJ, 78; From the Winston Malbin Collection Traveling Exhib, 80. *Teaching:* Prof fine arts, Moore Col Art, 69- *Awards:* Purchase Awards, Univ Del, 71 & Montclair Mus, 78; Hereward Lester Cooke Found Grant, 78 & 79. *Media:* Gouache, Oil; Wood, Canvas. *Mailing Add:* Moore Col Art 20th & Race Sts Philadelphia PA 19103

FREEMAN, DAVID L
PAINTER, GRAPHIC ARTIST

b Columbia, Mo, Nov 10, 37. *Study:* Univ Mo, BA & MA; State Univ Iowa, MFA; Penland Sch Crafts & Penland Weavers. *Work:* Mint Mus Art, Charlotte, NC; Minn Mus Art, St Paul; SC Nat Bank, Columbia; SC State Art Collection; NCNB Corp, Charlotte, NC. *Exhib:* Eleventh Piedmont Painting & Sculptor Show, Mint Mus Art, NC, 71; three-man show, Mint Mus Art, NC, 78; Three SC Painters, Clemson Univ, 79; Bold Statement: Painting, Southeastern Ctr Contemp Art, Winston-Salem, 80; two-man show, Greenville Co Mus Art, SC, 81; one-man show, Florence Mus Art, SC, 82; Three SC Painters, Waterworks Gallery, Salisbury, NC, 82; and others. *Teaching:* Asst prof studio art, Univ Wis, Madison, 63-70; assoc prof studio art, Winthrop Col, 70- *Awards:* Purchase Awards, Drawings USA, Minn Mus Art, St Paul & 8th Ann Piedmont Graphics Exhib, Mint Mus Art, 71; Spring Mills Exhib & Traveling Show, New York, 78. *Mem:* Nat Col Art Asn. *Media:* Acrylic. *Dealer:* Southeastern Ctr for Contemp Art Winston-Salem NC 27102. *Mailing Add:* 630 University Dr Rock Hill SC 29730

FREEMAN, GERTRUDE
COLLECTOR

b Neward, NJ, July 20, 27. *Study:* Newark Sch of Fine & Indust Arts, NJ; Univ Miami, Fla, BA(art hist). *Pos:* Artist representative for sculptor Enzo Gallo, multi-media artist Leon Gordon Miller & renowned painter Ivy Volper; investment arts consult for corps & individuals; collector of contemp int art. *Mailing Add:* 6959 Sunrise Dr Coral Gables FL 33133

FREEMAN, MALLORY BRUCE
DEALER, CURATOR

b Tulsa, Okla, Jan 9, 38. *Study:* Univ Tulsa, BA, 61. *Pos:* Dir, Tortue Gallery, Santa Monica, Calif, presently. *Specialty:* Contemporary art. *Mailing Add:* c/o Tortue Gallery 2917 Santa Monica Blvd Santa Monica CA 90404

FREEMAN, MARK
PAINTER, PRINTMAKER

b Austria, Sept 27, 08. *Study:* Columbia Col, BA; Columbia Univ, MArch; Sorbonne, Paris, Int Inst Educ Fel, 30. *Work:* Libr Cong, Washington, DC; Philadelphia Mus Art, Pa; Norfolk Art Mus, Va; Hengelose Kunstzaal, Holland; Butler Art Inst, Ohio. *Exhib:* Int Biennial Color Lithography, Cincinnati Mus, 52-53; 80 Prints USA, State Dept Traveling Exhib, Europe & Africa, 54; Artists of the Region, Easthampton Guild Hall Mus, 56 & 66; Major Am Artists, Southampton Col, 68; Nat Inst Arts & Letters, 68 & 69. *Pos:* Ed-in-chief newsletter, New York Artists Equity Asn, currently. *Awards:* Gold Medal, Nat Soc Artists in Casein, 64; Medal, Audubon Artists, 69; Today's Art Medal, 73. *Bibliog:* Texture prints of Mark Freeman, Today's Art, 78; and others. *Mem:* Hon life pres Audubon Artists; Nat Soc Artists in Casein & Acrylic (pres, 74-); League Present Day Artists (pres, 75); Am Soc Contemp Artists (pres, 75-77); New York Artists Equity (vpres, 76-80 & 82-84). *Media:* Oil, Acrylic. *Mailing Add:* 117 E 35th St New York NY 10016

FREEMAN, ROBERT LEE
PAINTER, SCULPTOR

b Rincon Indian Reservation, Calif, Jan 14, 39. *Work:* Sioux Mus, Rapid City, SDak; Gonzaga Univ, Spokane, Wash; Valley Nat Bank, Phoenix, Ariz; US Dept Interior, Washington, DC; Heard Mus, Phoenix, Ariz; and others. *Exhib:* All-Am Indian Art Nat Exhib, Sheridan, Wyo; Red Cloud Indian Art Nat Show, Pine Ridge, SDak; one-man shows, Fifth Ave Gallery, San Diego, Calif, Sioux Mus, Rapid City, SDak & Gallery Am Indian, Sedona, Ariz. *Awards:* First Watercolor & First Graphics, Red Cloud Indian Art Nat, 74; Spec Award Misc, First Graphics & Second Prints, Nat Indian Exhib, Scottsdale, 75; Gold Medal drawing, Am Indian Cowboy Artists, 80; and others. *Media:* Pen & Ink; Oil. *Mailing Add:* 1697 Curry Comb Dr San Marcos CA 92069

FREEMAN, SARA
PAINTER, LECTURER

b Garfield, NJ. *Study:* William Paterson Col; Art Student's League; Provincetown Workshop. *Work:* Seton Hall Univ, South Orange, NJ; Paterson Mus, Barnert Hospital & St Joseph's Hospital, Paterson, NJ; Bergen Mus, Paramus, NJ. *Exhib:* Montclair Mus, NJ, 62; Trenton State Mus, NJ, 67; Ontario Libr & Mus, Can, 69; Summit Gallery Art, SC, 74; Nat Asn Women Artists, City Gallery, New York, 81. *Awards:* First Prize, St John's Ann Contemp Show, 76 & 79; Second Prize, Bergen County Art Exhib, 83; and others. *Mem:* Nat Asn Women Artists (adjudicator 80-82); Artists Equity; Mod Artists Guild (secy 74-76). *Media:* Acrylic, Found Materials. *Mailing Add:* 13-08 Bellair Ave Fair Lawn NJ 07410

FREEMAN, TINA
PHOTOGRAPHER, CURATOR

b New Orleans, La, May 5, 51. *Study:* Art Ctr, Col Design, BFA, 72; Rochester Inst Technology, 78; also with Helmet Gernsheim & Beaumont Newhall. *Work:* New Orleans Mus Art; Bibliot Nat, Paris. *Exhib:* Biannual, New Orleans Mus Art, 76. *Collections Arranged:* Paris After the Great War, 77; Diverse Images (auth, catalog), Photog Collection of New Orleans Mus Art, 78; Hard Times Farm Security Administration Photography, 79; Women in Photography, 80; Deep Ocean Photography (with assistance from US Navy), 80; Lisette Model: A Retrospective (auth, catalog), Washington, DC, 81; New Acquisitions: New Directions in Black and White, 81; The Photographs of Mother St Croix (auth, catalog), 82 & Leslie Gill: A Clinical Approach to Photography (auth, catalog), 83, New Orleans Mus Art. *Pos:* Assoc cur photog, New Orleans Mus Art, 77-79, sr cur, 79-, conservator, 82- *Teaching:* Lectr, Free Univ, New Orleans, 80. *Bibliog:* John Lawrence (auth), monograph, Women Artists News, 80; and others. *Mem:* Soc for Photog Educ; Am Soc Mag Photogrs. *Media:* Platinum, Silver. *Publ:* Contribr, Arts Quart, 78-; ed, Diverse Images, Amphoto, 79. *Dealer:* Galerie Simonne Stern Prytania & Washington New Orleans LA 70130. *Mailing Add:* 7927 Jeanette Pl New Orleans LA 70118

FREEMAN-APPELBAUM, MARGERY
SCULPTOR, ADMINISTRATOR

b Washington, DC. *Study:* Univ Md, BA(summa cum laude), 75, MFA(summa cum laude), 78. *Comn:* Fiber, hand made paper I, II, III & IV, Hyatt Regency Inc, Baltimore, Md, 81. *Exhib:* Md State Arts Council Fel Exhib II, 79; Md Biennale, Baltimore Mus Art, 79; Works on Paper, Corcoran Gallery Art, Washington, DC, 80; Maryland Biennale, Baltimore Mus Art, 83. *Pos:* Asst program dir, Div Performing Arts, Smithsonian Inst, Washington, DC, 75-76; visual arts prog dir, Arts Div, Md Nat Capital Park & Planning Comn, Riverdale, 78- *Awards:* Md State Fel, 79; Md Crafts Biennal Award, 83; Md Biennale Award, Baltimore Mus, 83. *Mem:* Artists Equity; Md State Arts Coun; Montgomery Co Arts Coun; Cultural Alliance Greater Washington. *Media:* Hand-Made Paper, Fiber. *Mailing Add:* 11305 Struttmann Terrace Rockville MD 20852

FREIFELD, ERIC
PAINTER, EDUCATOR

b Saratov, Russia, Mar 13, 19; Can citizen. *Study:* St Martin's Sch Art, London, Eng; Art Students League. *Work:* Montreal Mus Art, Can; Nat Gallery Can, Ottawa; Hamilton Art Gallery; Art Gallery Ont; Windsor Art Gallery. *Exhib:* Royal Can Acad Exhibs, 51-71; Brooklyn Mus Int Biennial, 59; solo exhibs, Edmonton Art Gallery, 66, Vancouver Art Gallery, 68, Saskatoon Art Gallery, 69, Hamilton Art Gallery, 69 & London Art Mus, Ont, 70; and many others. *Pos:* Chmn welfare comt, Ont Col Art Faculty Asn, 65-70, mem exec comt, 65-70, mem governing coun, Ont Col Art, 72-75, chmn dept fine art, 75-80. *Teaching:* Prof watercolor painting, figure drawing & artistic anat, Ont Col Art, 46- *Awards:* Carnegie Trust Fund scholar, 37; C W Jeffries Award, 57; Can Coun Sr Arts Fel, 61 & 71; and many others. *Bibliog:* Paul Duval (auth), High Realism in Canada, 74 & Eric Freifeld, Yaneff Gallery, 77; articles on Eric Freifeld in Toronto Star, 77, Globe & Mail, 78, Art Mag, 78, Can Forum, 78, Can Bus Quart, 78 & Canadian, 79. *Mem:* Can Soc Graphic Art; Can Soc Painters in Watercolour; Royal Can Acad Arts; hon fel Ont Col Art. *Media:* Watercolor, Carbon. *Mailing Add:* 48 Eccleston Dr Toronto ON M4A 1K7 Canada

FREILICH, ANN
PAINTER, COLLAGE ARTIST

b Czestochowa, Poland; US citizen. *Study:* Educ Alliance Art Sch. *Work:* Brooklyn Mus, New York; Peabody Mus, Nashville, Tenn; Univ of Wyo Art Mus, Laramie; Art Lending Collections, Philadelphia Mus Art & Mus Mod Art; Syracuse Univ. *Exhib:* Ten one-man shows, Roko Gallery, 54-78; Bucknell Univ Drawing Exhib, 65; Gallery Mod Art, Huntington Hartford Mus, 67; Am Acad Arts & Lett, 70-72; restrospective exhib, 78. *Teaching:* Santa Agata Art Workshop, Italy, 67; pvt art classes. *Awards:* Childe Hassam Purchase Award, Am Acad Arts & Lett, 72. *Media:* Oil, Watercolor. *Publ:* Contribr, Art from Found Objects, Lothorp, Lee & Shepard, 74. *Mailing Add:* 250 W 94th St New York NY 10025

FREILICHER, JANE
PAINTER, PRINTMAKER

b New York, NY, Nov 19, 24. *Study:* Brooklyn Col, BA; Columbia Univ, MA; Hans Hofmann Sch; art hist with Meyer Schapiro. *Work:* Brooklyn Mus, NY; Metrop Mus Art, Mus Mod Art, New York; Brandeis Art Mus, Mass; NY Univ. *Exhib:* Whitney Mus Am Art Ann, 55-; One-man shows, John Bernard Myers Gallery, New York, 71, Fischbach Gallery, New York, 75, 77 & 79 & Utah Mus Fine Arts, 79; 30 Yrs of Am Printmaking, Brooklyn Mus, 76; Am 1976, Dept of Interior Traveling Show, 76; Poets and Painters, Denver Mus Art, 79; Twentieth Century Acquisitions, Metrop Mus Art, 79. *Teaching:* Vis critic & lectr, Univ Pa Grad Sch Fine Arts, 68, Skowhegan Sch Art, 68, Carnegie-Mellon Inst, 71, Mus Fine Arts, Boston & Col Creative Studies, Univ Calif, Santa Barbara & others, formerly. *Awards:* Hallmark Int Art Award, 60; Am Asn Univ Women, 74; grant, Nat Endowment Arts, 76. *Bibliog:* Peter Schjeldahl (auth), Urban pastorals, Art News, 2/71; James Schuyler (auth), The painting of Jane Freilicher, Art & Lit, autumn 66; John Ashbery (auth), article, New York Mag, 1/79. *Mem:* Assoc Nat Acad Design. *Media:* Oil. *Publ:* Illusr, Turandot & Other Poems, 53 & Paris Review (portfolio of drawings), 65. *Dealer:* Fischbach Gallery 29 W 57th St New York NY. *Mailing Add:* 51 Fifth Ave New York NY 10003

FREIMAN, ROBERT J
PAINTER
b New York, NY, Mar 16, 17. *Study:* Nat Acad Design, New York, 38; L'Ecole Des Beaux-Arts, Fontainebleau, 50; Art Students League. *Work:* Boston Mus Fine Arts, Mass; New Britain Mus, Conn; Mus Municipal de St Paul de Vence, France; Kenneth Taylor Galleries, Nantucket, Mass. *Exhib:* Mus City New York, 57; Columbia Mus Art, SC, 60; Ga Mus Art, Athens, 60; Galerie Marcel Bernheim, Paris, France, 62; Bruce Mus, Greenwich, Conn, 65. *Awards:* First Prize, Fr Rep. *Bibliog:* Two worlds, 8/12/71 & article, 7/5/73, Inquirer & Mirror. *Mailing Add:* 360 W 55th St Apt 6E New York NY 10019

FREIMARK, ROBERT (MATTHEW)
PRINTMAKER, PAINTER
b Doster, Mich, Jan 27, 22. *Study:* Univ Toledo, BEd; Cranbrook Acad Art, MFA; independent study, Mex. *Work:* Nat Gallery, Prague, Czech; Smithsonian Inst, Libr Cong, Washington, DC; Los Angeles Co Mus, Calif; Brit Mus. *Comn:* Brenton Banks, Des Moines, 74; Kundalini Found, New York, 74; Impressions Workshop, Boston, 74-75; Am Micro Systs, Inc, Santa Clara, Calif, 75; created tapestry for Olympic Games, Moscow, 80. *Exhib:* Drawings of 12 Countries, Art Inst Chicago, 52; Pa Acad Fine Art Painting Ann, 52-53; Brooklyn Mus Biennial Watercolor Exhib, 64; Mich State Univ, E Lansing, 80; Ohlone Col, Calif, 81; Franz Wymans Gallery, Vancouver, BC, 81; Percival Gallery Ltd, Des Moines, Iowa, 82; Schrager Galleries, Saratoga, Calif, 82. *Pos:* Guest artist, Joslyn Mem Mus, Omaha, Nebr, 61; Huntington Galleries, WVa, 63 & Riverside Art Ctr, Calif, 64; guest artist & lectr, Columbia Univ, 63; vis prof, Harvard Univ, 72-73. *Teaching:* Instr drawing, Toledo Mus Art, 52-55; instr painting, Ohio Univ, 56-59; resident artist, Des Moines Art Ctr, 59-63; prof graphics, San Jose State Col, 64-. *Awards:* New Talent in USA Award, Art in Am, 57; Ford Found Grant, WVa, 65; Spec Creative Leave, Calif State Col Syst, 67. *Bibliog:* Chamberlain & Crockett (auth), Beyond Weaving, Watson-Guptill, 74; Roberta Loach (auth), In conversation with Robert Freimark, Visual Dialog, 76; Dan McGuire (auth), Kaleidoscope TV video for KTEH, 79-80. *Media:* Tapestry, Lithography. *Res:* Mexican popular culture; rehabilitation through art; environmental planning for contemporary living. *Interests:* Graphics, film and environmental art. *Mailing Add:* Rte 2 Box 539A Morgan Hill CA 95037

FREITAG, WOLFGANG MARTIN
LIBRARIAN, HISTORIAN
b Berlin, Ger, Oct 27, 24; US citizen. *Study:* Univ Freiburg, Ger, PhD; Simmons Col, Boston, MS(libr sci). *Pos:* Chief librn, Fine Arts Libr, Harvard Col Libr, Fogg Art Mus, 64- *Teaching:* Lectr bibliog & art historiography, Harvard Univ, 67-75, sr lectr bibliog & art historiography, 75- *Mem:* Col Art Asn; charter mem Art Libr Soc NAm (chmn, 80); Asn Col & Res Libr; Metrop Mus Art, New York; Syracuse Univ Sch Info Studies; and others. *Publ:* Auth, The proper study of librarians, Harvard Librn, 74; auth, Slides for individual use in the college library, 75 & ed, Music and art in the general library, 75, Libr Trends; auth, Tapping a serviceable reservoir: The selection of periodicals at art libraries, Art Libr J, 76; Early uses of photography in the history of art, Art J, 79. *Mailing Add:* Fogg Art Mus Cambridge MA 02138

FREL, JIRI
CURATOR
b Czech. *Study:* Charles Univ, Prague, PhD; Ecole Normale Superieure, Sorbonne. *Pos:* Assoc cur Greek & Roman art, Metrop Mus Art, New York, 70-72; cur antiq, J Paul Getty Mus, 73- *Teaching:* Prof hist of Greek & Roman art, Charles Univ, Prague, 48-68 & Univ Southern Calif, 74- *Mem:* German Archaeol Inst. *Res:* Greek and Roman sculpture and art. *Publ:* Auth, Les Sculpteurs Attiques Anonymes, Univ Prague, 69; Panathenaic Prize Amphoras, German Archael Inst, Athens, Greece, 73; The Getty Bronze, 78 & 82; The Death of a Young Hero, 84; ed, J Paul Getty Mus J, Vols 1, 2 & 5-11. *Mailing Add:* J Paul Getty Mus Malibu CA 90265

FRENCH, JARED
PAINTER, SCULPTOR
b Ossining, NY, Feb 4, 05. *Study:* Amherst Col, BA; Art Students League. *Work:* Whitney Mus Am Art, New York; Baltimore Mus Art, Md; Baseball Mus, Cooperstown, NY; Art Collection, Dartmouth Col; Columbia Mus Art, Bogota. *Comn:* Cavalry Fording Stream (mural), Parcel Post Off, Richmond, Va; food murals, Coxsachie, New York; mural, Plymouth Post Off, Pa. *Exhib:* Carnegie Inst Int, Pittsburgh, Pa & Realism Show, Rochester Mus, NY, 64; one-man shows, Banfer Gallery, New York, 68-69; Magic Realism Show & 20th Century Portraits Show, Mus Mod Art, New York; Whitney Mus Am Art Ann, New York; Four Anonymous Collectors, New York Cult Ctr, 72. *Awards:* Nat Inst Arts & Lett Award, 67. *Media:* Tempera; Cast Metals, Stone. *Publ:* Auth, Realism and Realities, 1940-1960, Rutgers Univ Art Gallery, 82. *Mailing Add:* Piazza Cucchi 3 Rome 00152 Italy

FRENCH, RAY H
PRINTMAKER, PAINTER
b Terre Haute, Ind, May 16, 19. *Study:* John Herron Art Sch; Ind State Univ; Univ Colo; Univ Iowa, BFA & MFA; Accad Belle Arte, Florence, Italy; Hobart Sch Welding Technol, Troy, Ohio; also study with Mauricio Lansansky & James Lechay. *Work:* Mus Mod Art, New York; Pennell Collections, Libr Cong; Victoria & Albert Mus, London; Nat Mus Am Art; Bibliot Nat, Paris. *Exhib:* Soc Am Graphic Artists Ann Exhib, Nat Acad, 47; A New Direction in Intaglio, the Work of Lasansky and His Students, Walker Art Ctr, Milwaukee, 49-53; Young Am Printmakers, Mus of Mod Art, New York, 53; Ray H French, 25 Yrs of Printmaking, Sheldon Swope Art Gallery, Terre Haute, Ind, 70; Forerunners of the American Print Renaissance, Pratt

Graphics Ctr, New York, 77. *Teaching:* Prof printmaking, DePauw Univ, Greencastle, Ind, 48-, head dept art, 70-78, cur, Univ Collection, 78. *Awards:* Art Asn First Prize, Indianapolis Mus Art, 56; Joseph Pennell Purchase Award for Etching, Philadelphia Free Libr, 60; Mus Purchase Award, Pasadena Mus, 70. *Mem:* Soc Am Graphic Artists; Print & Drawing Soc, Indianapolis Mus Art; Ind Artists Club (pres, 62-63); Ind Soc Printmakers (pres, 53-54). *Dealer:* Weintraub Gallery 992 Madison Ave New York NY 10021. *Mailing Add:* 106 E Seminary St Greencastle IN 46135

FRERICHS, RUTH COLCORD
PAINTER, LITHOGRAPHER
b White Plains, NY. *Study:* Conn Col, BA; Art Students League. *Work:* Thunderbird Bank, Phoenix, Ariz; First Nat Bank, Continental Bank, Valley Nat Bank, Ariz; permanent collection, Mus State Univ Southeastern Mo; and others. *Exhib:* Watercolor West Nat Exhib, Riverside, Calif, 72; Southwestern Fedn Watercolor Exhib, Mus Albuquerque, 76; Nat Watercolor Soc Ann, 76; Scottsdale Watercolor Biennial, Ariz, 78; Conn Col Alumni Exhib, New London, 78; and others. *Mailing Add:* 321 E Pomona Rd Phoenix AZ 85020

FREUDENHEIM, NINA
DEALER, COLLECTOR
Pos: Owner, Nina Freudenheim Gallery. *Specialty:* Contemporary, national and international art. *Collection:* Works by Pol Bury, Jules Olitski, Georges Noel, Lucas Samars, Fontana and many others. *Mailing Add:* 560 Franklin St Buffalo NY 14202

FREUDENHEIM, TOM LIPPMANN
MUSEUM DIRECTOR
b Stuttgart, Ger, July 3, 37; US citizen. *Study:* Harvard Col, AB; NY Univ, MA; Univ Md, Hon DFA, 82. *Collections Arranged:* Pascin (with catalog), 65 & Arnaldo Pomodoro (with catalog), 70, Univ Art Mus, Berkeley, Calif. *Pos:* Cur, Jewish Mus, New York, 62-65; asst dir, Univ Art Mus, Berkeley, 66-71; dir, Baltimore Mus Art, 71-78; dir, Mus Prog, Nat Endowment Arts, 78-82; Worcester Art Mus, 82- *Mem:* Col Art Asn Am; Am Asn Mus; Art Mus Asn (vpres, currently); Asn Art Mus Dirs. *Publ:* Auth, Myer Myers, American Silversmith, 65; auth, Illuminated Hebrew Manuscripts, 65; auth, Persian Faience Mosaic Wall, Kunst Orients, 68; Holocaust art, 78; ed, American Museum Guide, 83. *Mailing Add:* Worcester Art Mus 55 Salisbury St Worcester MA 01608

FREUND, HARRY LOUIS
PAINTER, ILLUSTRATOR
b Clinton, Mo, Sept 16, 05. *Study:* Univ Mo, 23-25; St Louis Sch Fine Arts, Washington Univ, 25-29; D H Wuerpel Travel Scholar, 29; Colarossi Acad, Paris, 29-30; Carnegie Fel, 40; Princeton Univ, 40-41; Colorado Springs Fine Arts Ctr, 46-47; Carnegie-Stetson Grant, Mex, 53; Stetson Univ Grant, Cent Am, 59, DFA, 79. *Work:* IBM Corp; Libr Cong, Washington, DC; Seattle Art Mus, Wash; St Louis Sch Fine Arts; Mus Fine Arts, Little Rock, Ark. *Comn:* Mural, Deland Mem Hosp, Fla; libr murals, Bishop Col & Shaw Univ; Centennial Mural, Eureka Springs, Ark, 79; plus many others in pub & pvt collections. *Exhib:* Contemp Am Art Exhib, New York World's Fair; Nat Acad Design; Pa Acad Design; Carnegie Inst; Corcoran Gallery Art; plus many others in mus, schs & libraries in US & abroad. *Pos:* Free lance illusr, Crowell Publ & Ford Motor Co Publs; mural designer, State of Mo at Chicago World's Fair, 33; mural artist, sect fine arts, US Treas Dept, 34-40; visual aids dir, Eighth Serv Command, US Army, 45-46. *Teaching:* Resident artist, Hendrix Col, 39-41, head dept art, 41-46; founder dept art, Little Rock Jr Col, 40; founder & dir, Art Sch Ozarks, 7 yrs; lectr & faculty artist vis, Asn Am Cols, 5 seasons; head dept art, Stetson Univ, 49-59, resident artist, 59-67. *Mem:* Fla Artist Group (past pres); Nat Soc Mural Painters; Eureka Springs, Ark Guild of Artists & Craftspeople; Fla Craftsmen (past pres). *Media:* Oil, Acrylic. *Mailing Add:* 31 Steel St Eureka Springs AR 72632

FREUND, TIBOR
PAINTER, MURALIST
b Budapest, Hungary, Dec 29, 10; US citizen. *Study:* Fed Tech Univ, Zurich, dipl archit, 32; Vilmos Aba-Novak Art Sch, Budapest, 34; studies Oriental techniques of mosaics, Meshed, Iran, 40. *Work:* Mus Fine Arts, Budapest; James A Michener Collection, Univ Tex, Austin; Goucher Col, Md; Ravinia Art Festival Asn, Chicago, Ill; Ball State Univ, Muncie, Ind. *Comn:* First moving mural on ridged surface, Bd Educ, Pub Sch 111, New York, 63; first moving mural on flat surface, Bd Educ Sch 162, New York, 70. *Exhib:* Seven one-man shows, New York, 60-76; Am Fedn Arts Traveling Exhibs, 63-65, 66-67 & 71-72; Abstract Art, Riverside Mus, New York, 65; An American Report on the Sixties, Denver Art Mus, Colo, 69; Painting & Sculpture Today, Indianapolis Mus Art, Ind, 70. *Awards:* Silvermine Guild Award, First Prize at 19th Ann New Eng Exhib, 68. *Bibliog:* John Canaday (auth), Tibor Freund, New York Times, 10/4/69; Peter Schjeldahl (auth), Fourth show in New York, 69 & Phyllis Derfner (auth), Sixth show in New York, 74, Art Int; and others. *Mem:* Fel Royal Soc Arts; Am Fedn Arts; Nat Soc Mural Painters. *Media:* Acrylic. *Res:* Developed motion painting from a crude nineteenth century invention called three-sided picture. *Publ:* Auth, Motion in painting-- a new art form, Am Artist Mag, 11/64. *Mailing Add:* 34-57 82nd St Jackson Heights NY 11372

FREUND, WILL FREDERICK
PAINTER, EDUCATOR
b Madison, Wis, Jan 20, 16. *Study:* Univ Wis, BS, MS; Univ Mo; Tiffany Found Fel, 40 & 49. *Work:* William Rockhill Nelson Gallery Art, Kansas City, Mo; Joslyn Mus Art, Omaha, Nebr; Okla Art Ctr, Oklahoma City; Mulvane Mus Art, Topeka, Kans; Univ Nebr Art Galleries, Lincoln; and

others. *Exhib:* Mo Pavilion, New York World's Fair, 64; New Talent USA, Art in Am Mag, 65; Watercolor USA, Springfield Art Mus, Mo, 70 & 72; Evansville Mus Art, Ind; Denver Art Mus; Butler Inst Art; Nat Gallery Art, Washington, DC; and others. *Teaching:* Instr art, Stephens Col, 46-64; prof fine art, Southern Ill Univ, Edwardsville, 64-81. *Awards:* Ruth Renfro Award (First Prize for Watercolor), St Louis City Art Mus, 63; Purchase Prize & Bronstein Award, Evansville Mus Art; First Prize Watercolor, Quincy's 24th Ann. *Bibliog:* Prize winners, Life Mag, 9/12/55; A B Louchheim (auth), Prize $, Art News, 10/56; Will Freund, painter, potter, woodworker, boombass player, Wis Alumnus, 1/61. *Media:* Oil, Watercolor. *Mailing Add:* Box 182 Watersmeet MI 49969

FREUNDLICH, AUGUST L
ADMINISTRATOR, COLLECTOR
b Frankfurt, WGer, May 9, 24; US citizen. *Study:* Antioch Col, BA, 49, MA, 50; New York Univ, PhD, 60. *Pos:* Consult, Nat Found Advancement Arts, currently. *Teaching:* Head art dept, Eastern Mich Univ, 54-58; chmn arts div, George Peabody Col, 58-64; dir & chmn art dept, Lowe Art Mus, Univ Miami, 64-70; dean sch art, Syracuse Univ, 70; dean, Col Visual & Performing Arts, 71-82; dean, Col Fine Arts, Univ SFla, 82- *Mem:* Int Coun Fine Art Deans; Col Art Asn; Am Asn Mus; and others. *Res:* Social commentary art, American & German; American graphics and sculpture. *Collection:* Self-portraits; 20th century prints. *Publ:* Auth, William Gropper, Ward, Richie Press, 63; auth, Frank Kleinholz, Univ Miami, 66; auth, Karl Schrag, 70 & 80; auth, Richard Florsheim, A S Barnes, 76; auth, Federico Castellon, Syracuse Univ, 78. *Mailing Add:* Timberlan Dr Lutz FL 33549

FREY, VIOLA
SCULPTOR, PAINTER
b Lodi, Calif, Aug 15, 33. *Study:* Delta Col, Stockton, Calif, AA; Calif Col Arts & Crafts, BFA; Tulane Univ, MFA. *Exhib:* Overglaze Imagery, Calif State Univ, Fullerton, 77; Soap Box Derby, San Francisco Mus Mod Art, 78; A Century of Ceramics in the US, Everson Mus Art, Syracuse, NY, 79; Renwick Mus, Washington, DC, 79 & Cooper-Hewitt Mus, New York, 79; Large Scale Ceramic Sculpture, Davis, Calif, 79; The Unpainted Portrait, Kohler Arts Ctr, Sheboygan, Wis, 79; and others. *Teaching:* Assoc prof ceramics, Calif Col Arts & Crafts, 65-, chmn dept ceramics, Noni Eccles Treadwell Ceramic Arts Ctr, currently. *Awards:* Nat Endowment for Arts fel grant, 78. *Bibliog:* Wenger (auth), Currant, Art Mag, 8/75; Garth Clark (auth), Commentary and Review. *Mailing Add:* Quay 254 Sutter St San Francisco CA 94108

FRIBERG, ARNOLD
ILLUSTRATOR, PAINTER
b Winnetka, Ill, Dec 21, 13. *Study:* Art Instr Schs; Chicago Acad Fine Arts; Am Acad Art, Chicago. *Work:* Tweed Mus, Duluth, Minn. *Comn:* The Ten Commandments (series 15 monumental paintings), Cecil B De Mille, 56; The Book of Mormon (series 12 paintings), Church of Jesus Christ of Latter-Day Saints, 60; 100 Years of American Inter-collegiate Football (series of paintings), Chevrolet Sports Art Collection, 69; The Northwest Mounted Police (series over 200 paintings), Northwest Paper Co, Tweed Mus, Duluth, Minn, 37-72; life size portrait of Prince Charles with horse Centenial, comn by Govt Northwest Territories, Can, 79. *Exhib:* Ten Commandments Series, toured every continent, 57-58; Motion Picture Indust Exhib, New York World's Fair, 64-65. *Pos:* Chief artist-designer, Cecil B De Mille, 54-57. *Teaching:* Lectr vitality in relig painting, art as serv & Russell & Remington. *Bibliog:* Vern Swanson (auth), Southwest Art Mag, 12/81; Ted Scharz (auth), Arnold Friberg, Northland Press, 84. *Mem:* Life mem Royal Soc Arts, London. *Publ:* Auth & illusr, The Ten Commandments, 57 & Arnold Friberg's Little Christmas Book, 58. *Mailing Add:* 5867 Tolcate Lane Salt Lake City UT 84121

FRICANO, TOM S
PAINTER, PRINTMAKER
b Chicago, Ill, Oct 28, 30. *Study:* Bradley Univ, BFA, 53; Univ Ill, Urbana, MFA, 56. *Work:* Libr Cong, Washington, DC; Philadelphia Mus; Art Inst Chicago; Los Angeles Co Mus Art; Detroit Inst Arts. *Exhib:* Art Inst Chicago, 67; Dong-A-Ilbo Int Print Show, Seoul, Korea, 70; Utah Mus Fine Art, Salt Lake City, 71; 3rd Brit Int Print Biennial, Bradford, Eng, 72; Am Colorprint Soc, Philadelphia, 74-79; one-man shows, Harmon Fine Art Center, Drake Univ, Des Moines, Iowa, 77, Quincy Col Art Gallery, Ill, 77, Fresno State Univ Gallery, Calif, 78, Mission Col, San Fernando, Calif, 78, Pepperdine Univ, Malibu, Calif, 79 & Univ NDak, Grand Forks, 80; Stockton Nat, Pioneer Mus & Haggin Art Gallery, Calif, 78; Footprint 78 Int, Davidson Gallery, Seattle, Wash, 78; 12th Nat Print Exhib, Silvermine Guild of Artists, New Canaan, Conn, 78; Twelve Ways of Giving, Cult Arts Ctr, Sylmar, Calif, 78; 8 Western Artists, Brooklyn Mus Art, 78; Ann Invitational Printmaking W, Utah Inst of Fine Arts, Utah State Univ, Logan, 78-79; Nat Print & Drawing Competition, Univ SDak, Vermillion, 79; Boston Printmakers, Copley Soc, 79; Nat Print Exhib, Austin, Tex, 79; 4th Invitational Watercolor Exhib, Springfield Art Asn, Ill, 80. *Teaching:* Instr painting & printmaking, Bradley Univ, Peoria, Ill, 58-63; prof painting & printmaking, Calif State Univ, Northridge, 63-; vis artist, Ohio State Univ, Columbus, 69, Univ Utah, 71, Univ Mont, Bozeman, & Art Inst Chicago, 75, Univ NDak, Grand Forks, Cranbrook Acad Art, Bloomfield Hills, Mich & Eastern Mich Univ, Ypsilanti, 80. *Awards:* Calif State Univ Found Res Grant, 66, 68, 74 & 78; John Simon Guggenheim Found Mem Fel, 69 & 70; Fulbright grant, Florence Italy, 60-61; Louis Comfort Tiffany Res Grant, 65. *Bibliog:* Leonard Edmondson (auth), Etching, Van Nostrand Reinhold, 73. *Mem:* Hon mem Los Angeles Printmaking Soc (vpres, 64-65). *Mailing Add:* 9820 Aldea Ave Northridge CA 91324

FRICK, JOAN
PAINTER
b Toronto, Ont, Mar 11, 42. *Study:* Ecole Beaux-Arts Montreal, dipl peinture, 63. *Work:* Art Gallery Ont; Gallery Stratford, Ont; Can Coun Art Bank, Ottawa; Can Art Arch, Vancouver Art Gallery; Norman McKenzie Art Gallery, Regina, Sask. *Comn:* Mural, Dixon Hall Community Ctr, Toronto, 72. *Exhib:* Ontario Now, Art Gallery Hamilton, Ont & Kitchener, Waterloo Art Gallery, Ont, 76; Abstractions, Place Bonaventure, Montreal, Gallery-Stratford, Ont & Can Cult Ctrs, London & Paris, 76; Summer Show, Royal Acad, London, 77; Markings, Can Embassy, Washington, DC, Ga State Univ Art Gallery, Atlanta & Can Consulates, Chicago & Boston, 78-79; Future Traditions Ontario 81 Travelling Exhib, 80-82. *Awards:* Can Coun Proj Costs Grants, 72, 74 & 80; Ont Arts Coun Grants, 75-79; Aviva Art Auction Third Prize, 79. *Bibliog:* Jim Tiley (auth), New drawings by Joan Frick ..., Artist Rev, 10/13/78; John Bently Mays (auth), Joan Frick's artistic vision isn't gun shy, Globe & Mail, 9/22/80; Cathy Arthur (auth), article, Artscanada, 12/80-1/81. *Dealer:* Aggregation Gallery Ltd 83 Front St E Toronto ON M5E 1B8. *Mailing Add:* 648 Richmond St W Toronto ON M6J 1C3 Canada

FRICK, ROBERT OLIVER
PAINTER, INSTRUCTOR
b Philadelphia, Pa, Feb 19, 20. *Study:* Pa Acad Fine Arts; also with Frank Benton Ashley Linton, Philadelphia; Daniel Garber, New Hope, Pa; Stanley Woodward, Rockport, Mass. *Exhib:* One-man shows, Chaffee Art Gallery, Chester Art Guild, Blue Hill Art Guild & Southern Vt Art Asn, 77-81; Salmagundi Club, 72-74; Concord Art Asn, Mass, 73-74; Saxtons River Art Assoc, 81. *Pos:* Trustee, Chaffee Art Gallery, Rutland, Vt, 71-74 & Southern Vermont Artists, Manchester, Vt, 80- *Teaching:* Instr oil & watercolor, Rutland Jr High, Vt, 68-80; instr oil & watercolor, Chester Art Guild, Vt, 68-; instr oil & watercolor, Southern Vt Art Ctr, 71-; instr, Saxtons River Art Asn, 69- *Awards:* Salmagundi Art Fund Award, 79; Kenneth Fitch Award, 79; Tuttle Memorial Painting Award, 83. *Mem:* Knickerbocker Artists Am; honorary life mem Saxtons River Art Asn, Chaffee Art Asn; Grand Central Art Gallery; Acad Artists Am; and others. *Media:* Oil, Watercolor. *Mailing Add:* Elm St Pittsford VT 05763

FRIDAKIS, GERA HESNESS
SCULPTOR
b New York, NY, May 5, 52. *Study:* Fashion Inst Technol, New York, AA(fine arts), 75; Nat Acad Design, New York; Frudakis Acad Fine Arts, Philadelphia, Pa. *Work:* Fashion Inst Technol, New York. *Comn:* Filter Square Ram (bronze), Philadelphia Dept Recreation, Pa, 81, Honey Bees (bronze), 82. *Exhib:* Nat Sculpture Soc Ann, New York, 80, 81 & 82; Nat Acad Design Ann, New York, 80 & 81; Allied Artists Am Ann, New York, 80 & 81; Salmagundi Club, New York, 81; Shidoni Gallery, Santa Fe, NMex, 82. *Pos:* Studio asst to EvAngelos Frudakis, Sculptor, 76-; adminr, Frudakis Acad, 76- *Teaching:* Instr sculpture & drawing, Frudakis Acad Fine Arts, Philadelphia, Pa, 76-80. *Awards:* Marguerite Hexter Prize, Allied Artists Am Ann Exhib, 80; Maurice Bittexter Prize, Nat Sculpture Soc, 80; Rachel Lean Armour Prize, Allied Artists, 81. *Mem:* Allied Artists Am; Nat Sculpture Soc. *Media:* Bronze. *Mailing Add:* Frudakis Gallery 1829 Chestnut Street Philadelphia PA 19103

FRIED, HOWARD LEE
SCULPTOR
b Cleveland, Ohio, June 14, 46. *Study:* Syracuse Univ, 64-67; San Francisco Art Inst, BFA, 68; Univ Calif, Davis, MFA, 70. *Work:* Cleveland Mus Art, Ohio; Syracuse Univ, NY; Univ Calif, Davis; Ft Worth Art Mus, Tex; San Francisco Mus Mod Art, Calif. *Comn:* Mural, Syracuse Univ, 66. *Exhib:* Looking West, Joslyn Art Mus, Omaha, Nebr, 70; The 80's, Univ Art Mus, Univ Calif, Berkeley, 70; Projection, Kunsthalle, Dusseldorf, Ger, 71 & Louisiana Mus, Denmark, 72; Documenta 5, Kassel, Ger, 72; and many others. *Teaching:* Instr sculpture, San Francisco Art Inst, 68-, chmn performance & video dept, 83- *Awards:* Augusta Hazard Award, Syracuse Univ, 66; Adeline Kent Award, San Francisco Artist's Comt, 71-72; Nat Endowment for Arts Grant, 75. *Bibliog:* Grace Glueck (auth), New York: Big thump on the bass drum, Art in Am, 5-6/71; Brenda Richardson (auth), Howard Fried: Paradox of approach-avoidance, Arts Mag, 6/71; Steve Davis (auth), Howard Fried installation piece, Art Week, 3/25/72. *Publ:* Auth, Inside the harlequin, Flash Art, 71; auth, Studio relocation, Breakthroughs in Fiction, 72; auth, Cheshire cat 4, Avalanche. *Mailing Add:* 16 Rose St San Francisco CA 94102

FRIEDBERG, RAY E (RACHEL)
PAINTER, INSTRUCTOR
b Brooklyn, NY, Jan 9, 29. *Study:* Art Students League, with Reginald Marsh; also with Leon Goldin & George Picken. *Exhib:* New Eng Exhib, Conn, 67, 70 & 72; Art from New Jersey, Trenton Mus, 71; Women in the Arts, Brooklyn Mus, 75; Aldrich Mus, Ridgefield, Conn, 75-76; Summerset Tri-State Exhib, 77; Women In Art, Paul Robeson Gallery, Rutgers, 79; Guild Hall, 80-81; and other group & one-man shows. *Pos:* Dir, Edward Williams Gallery, Fairleigh Dickinson Univ, 74- *Teaching:* Instr art, art hist & cult arts, Edward Williams Col, Fairleigh Dickinson Univ, 71-, artist in residence, 73- *Awards:* Northshore Competition First Prize, Mus Mod Art, 71; NJ Coun Arts Fel Painting, 83. *Bibliog:* Dona Z Meilach (auth), Box Art, Assemblage and Construction, Crown, 75; Eileen Watkins (auth), article, Newark Star Ledger, 1/78; Vivian Raynor (auth), article, New York Times, 12/16/79. *Mem:* Women Arts. *Media:* Encaustic, Multimedia. *Mailing Add:* 821 Summit Ave River Edge NJ 07661

FRIEDBERG, RICHARD S
SCULPTOR, EDUCATOR
b Baltimore, Md, Aug 10, 43. *Study:* Antioch Col, BA, 65; Yale Univ, BFA & MFA(Graham Found Fel), 68. *Work:* Citicorp Bank, Chase Manhattan Bank, New York. *Comn:* Sculpture, Rutgers Univ, NJ, 70; sculpture, Mobil Corp, Va, 79. *Exhib:* Whitney Ann, 71 & Whitney Biennial, 73, Whitney Mus Am Art, New York; Munson-Williams Proctor Inst, New York, 77; Storm King Art Ctr, NY, 79; Prospect Mountain Sculpture Show, Lake George, NY, 79; Alexander Milliken Gallery, New York, 81. *Teaching:* Assoc prof fine art, Fairleigh Dickinson Univ, Rutherford, 70- *Awards:* Nat Endowment Arts Fel, 74. *Bibliog:* Ellen Schwartz (auth), Richard Friedberg, Art News, 78; Carter Ratcliff (auth), Richard Friedberg, Arts Mag, 79. *Mem:* Col Arts Asn. *Media:* Steel, Aluminum. *Mailing Add:* c/o Alexander F Milliken Inc 98 Prince St New York NY 10013

FRIEDEBERG, PEDRO
PAINTER, SCULPTOR
b Florence, Italy, Jan 11, 37. *Study:* Iberoamerican Univ, Mex; sculpture with Mathias Goeritz. *Work:* Libr Cong, DC; Sci Mus, Toronto; Rose Art Mus, Brandeis Univ, Mass; Israel Mus, Jerusalem; Museums Mod Art, New York & Paris; plus others. *Comn:* Sculptures, garden of Andre Bloc, Paris, France, 63; mural, Hotel Camino Real, Mexico City, 68; several murals, pvt homes, Mexico City, 70-72. *Exhib:* Bienal Coltejer, Medellin, Colombia, 72; Bienal San Juan PR, 74 & 79; Bienal, Montevideo, Uruguay, 74; Three Mexican Artists, touring 7 mus Can, 73-74; Biennale of Tokyo, 79; plus others. *Pos:* Art ed, Mexico this Month, 60-64. *Awards:* Second Prize, Expos Solar, 68; First Prize, Bienal de Grabado de San Juan, PR, 79; Second Prize, Bienal Buenos Aires, 79. *Bibliog:* Ida Rodriguez (auth), Pedro Friedeberg, Programa Cult 19th Olimpiada, Mex, 68; Ida Rodriguez (auth), Pedro Friedeberg, Univ Mex, 72. *Mem:* Foro de Arte Contemporaneo; Salon Plastica Mex; founding mem Los Hartos. *Media:* Multimedia. *Publ:* Auth, Autobiography, Archit J, Archit Fantastique, Paris, 62; auth, Autobiography 2, Motive 62; auth, article, Dialogos Mag, 71. *Dealer:* Galeria Misrachi Genova 20 Mexico City 6 Mex; Galeria el Circulo Hamburgo 112 Mexico City 6 DF Mex. *Mailing Add:* Galeana 209 Acapantzingo Cuernavaca Morelos 62440 Mexico

FRIEDENSOHN, ELIAS
PAINTER, SCULPTOR
b New York, NY, Dec 12, 24. *Study:* Tyler Sch Fine Arts, Temple Univ, 42; with Gabriel Zendel, Paris, France, 46; Queens Col, BA, 48; NY Univ Inst Fine Arts, 49-51. *Work:* Whitney Mus Am Art; Art Inst Chicago; Minneapolis Mus Art; Walker Art Ctr; Sarah Roby Found Collection, Krannert Mus Art, Univ Ill; plus others. *Exhib:* Young American Painters, 59 & Whitney Mus Ann, 61-64, Whitney Mus Am Art; Art Inst Chicago Ann, 59 & 61; Corcoran Gallery Art Ann, Washington, DC, 62; Minneapolis Mus Art Drawing Ann, 71; Minn Mus, 80; Univ SFla, 80; Magnes Mus, Berkeley, 81; and 24 one-man shows. *Pos:* Chmn, Nat Screening Comt for Painting, Fulbright Prog, Inst Int Educ New York, 66-69, mem Cintas Award Comt, 75; chmn, Visual Arts, Univ Res Found Awards, City Univ New York. *Teaching:* Prof art, Queens Col, 59-; prof art & chmn arts div, Kirkland Col, 70-71. *Awards:* Guggenheim Fel, 60; Univ Res Found Award, City Univ New York, 81; NJ Coun Arts Award, 81. *Media:* Oil, Watercolor. *Dealer:* Terry Dintenfass 18 E 67th St New York NY 11210. *Mailing Add:* 209 Hillcrest Ave Leonia NJ 07605

FRIEDLAENDER, BILGE
SCULPTOR, PAINTER
b Istanbul, Turkey. *Study:* Robert Col, Istanbul, Turkey, BA, 55; Acad Fine Arts, Istanbul, Turkey, dipl, 58; NY Univ, MA, 59. *Work:* E F Hutton, Chase Manhattan Bank, New York; Prudential Insurance Co, Boston; Houghton Libr, Harvard Univ; Newark Mus, NJ. *Exhib:* Drawings USA Traveling Show, Minn Mus Art, 75-76; Painting and Sculpture Today, Indianapolis Mus Art, 76; Purchase Show, 76 & Book-Objects, 77, Albright-Knox Mus; Paper as Medium, Smithsonian Inst Traveling Exhib, 78-80; Artists Books Traveling Exhib, New England Found Arts, 80; Drawings, Sculpture and Unique Books, Pa Acad Fine Arts, 81; New American Paperworks, World Print Coun, San Francisco, 82-84. *Teaching:* Asst prof, Temple Univ, 80-81; instr basic design, Univ Pa, 83. *Bibliog:* Allen Ellenzweig (auth), Solo show at Kornblee, Arts Mag, 4/76 & 11/77; Jane Farmer (auth), Prints and the art of the book in America, In: American Prints & Printmaking 1956-1981, 81. *Media:* Watercolor, Pastel; Mixed Media. *Publ:* Illusr & contribr, War is a Boy Game, 81 & Amputee, 81, Esse Est Percipipress. *Dealer:* Victoria Munroe Gallery 57th St New York NY 19001. *Mailing Add:* 502 Westview St Philadelphia PA 19119

FRIEDLAND, SEYMOUR
PATRON, COLLECTOR
b New York, NY, Oct 8, 28; Can citizen. *Study:* Harvard Univ, PhD. *Pos:* Assoc ed, Financial Times Can, currently; prof finance & econ, York Univ, Toronto, currently. *Interests:* Art as investment. *Collection:* More than 200 pieces of painting and sculpture; emphasis on native art, including Amerindian, and nineteenth century Canadian watercolors. *Mailing Add:* 423 Avenue Rd No 2 Toronto ON M4V 2H7 Canada

FRIEDMAN, ALAN
SCULPTOR, DESIGNER
b Philadelphia, Pa, Sept 9, 44. *Study:* Rochester Inst Technol Sch Am Craftsman, BFA, 67; Univ Wis, Madison, MFA(sculpture), 69. *Work:* Univ Wis, Union Galleries, Madison, 69; Ind State Univ, Terre Haute, 72; Indianapolis Mus of Art, 77. *Comn:* Entrance doors (wood), St Paul's Univ Cath Church, Madison, 68; sculpture (plywood), Cunningham Mem Libr, Ind

State Univ, Terre Haute, 73. *Exhib:* retrospective, Wis Directions, Milwaukee Art Ctr, 75; Indianapolis Mus Art Traveling Exhib & Mus Gallery Exhib, 75-76; New Handmade Furniture, Mus Contemp Crafts, New York, 79; Contradictions, Fendrick Gallery, DC, 79; Fine Arts Comt Visual Arts, Program of the XIII Olympic Winter Games, Lake Placid, NY, 80; and others. *Pos:* Designer furniture, E A Roffman Co, New York, 72; dir, Alan Friedman Studios & Assoc, Hudson, NY, 80- *Teaching:* Vis asst prof art, Univ Wis, Madison, 69-70; assoc prof furniture design & sculpture, art dept, Ind State Univ, Terre Haute, 72-79. *Awards:* Grand Prize, Milwaukee Art Ctr, 69; Award, Indianapolis Mus Art, 75; Jurors Award, Marietta Col Crafts Nat Exhib, 75; Nat Endowment for the Arts Individual Fel Grant, 76-77. *Bibliog:* Thelma Newman (auth), Woodcraft, Chilton Bks, NY, 78; Nicholas Rookes (auth), Masters of Wood Sculpture, Watson-Guptill, NY, 80; Dona Meilach (auth), Woodworking, The New Wave, Crown, New York, 81. *Mem:* Am Crafts Coun. *Mailing Add:* RFD 2 Box 160 Hudson NY 12534

FRIEDMAN, ANN MARTI
HISTORIAN, MUSEOLOGIST
b New York, NY, Apr 20, 51. *Study:* Univ Calif, Santa Barbara, BA, 72; Courtauld Inst Art, Univ London, MA, 74; Bryn Mawr Col, PhD, 83. *Pos:* Registrar, Utah Mus Fine Arts, Salt Lake City, 75-76; acting dir, Tyler Gallery, State Univ NY, Oswego, 77-78; coordr, Morris Gallery, Pa Acad Fine Arts, Philadelphia, 78-81. *Teaching:* Lectr art hist, Univ Utah, Salt Lake City, 76-77; lectr mus studies, State Univ NY, Oswego, 77-78; asst prof art hist, Univ Minn, Duluth, 83-84. *Awards:* Jr Fel, Dumbarton Oaks, 81-83. *Mem:* Col Art Asn. *Res:* Seventeenth century French sculpture; history of gardens; Versailles. *Mailing Add:* Art Dept Univ Minn Duluth MN 55812

FRIEDMAN, B H
WRITER
b New York, NY, July 27, 26. *Study:* Cornell Univ, BA, 48. *Pos:* Adv coun mem, Cornell Univ Arts Col & Herbert F Johnson Mus; trustee, Am Fedn Arts, 58-64; trustee, Whitney Mus Am Art, currently; dir, Fine Arts Work Ctr, Provincetown, Mass. *Teaching:* Lectr Eng, Cornell Univ, 66-67. *Awards:* Fel, Coord Coun Lit Mag, 75; Nelson Algren Award, 83. *Publ:* Auth, Whispers, 72; auth, Jackson Pollock: Energy Made Visible (biog), 72; auth, Alfonso Ossorio (monogr), 73; auth, Museum, 74; auth, Almost a Life, 75; auth, Gertrude Vanderbilt Whitney (biog), 78; plus many others. *Mailing Add:* 435 E 52nd St New York NY 10022

FRIEDMAN, BENNO
PHOTOGRAPHER
b New York, NY, Mar 28, 45. *Study:* Brandeis Univ, BA. *Work:* Mus Mod Art, New York; Boston Mus Fine Arts; Fogg Mus, Cambridge, Mass; George Eastman House, Rochester, NY; Vassar Col Mus, Poughkeepsie, NY. *Exhib:* 60's Continuum, George Eastman House, 72; Octave of Prayer, Mass Inst Technol, 72; Light & Lens, Hudson River Mus, 73; one-man show, Light Gallery, 73 & 75; Private Realities, Boston Mus Fine Arts, 74. *Awards:* Mass Coun Arts & Humanities; grant, Creative Artists Publ Serv, NY State. *Publ:* Contribr, Art in Am, 70 & Aspen Mag; Idea, NY Photogr, 74; plus others. *Dealer:* Charles Lowles Gallery 420 W Broadway New York NY. *Mailing Add:* Kellogg Rd Sheffield MA 01257

FRIEDMAN, JOAN MARCY
CURATOR, LIBRARIAN
b New York, NY, Nov 30, 49. *Study:* Harvard Univ, AB(fine arts; magna cum laude), 71; Courtauld Inst of Art, London Univ, MA, 73; Columbia Univ, MS(honors), 74. *Collections Arranged:* Color Printing in England (auth catalog), Yale Ctr for Brit Art, 4-6/78. *Pos:* Summer intern, Metrop Mus of Art, New York, 70; asst res librn, Beinecke Libr, Yale Univ, 74-76; cur rare books, Yale Ctr for Brit Art, 76- *Teaching:* Instr book illus, Rare Book Sch, Columbia Univ Sch Libr Serv, summer 83. *Mem:* Asn Col & Res Libr Rare Bks & Manuscripts Sect (chair, 82-83); Bibliog Soc Am (mem coun, 82-). *Res:* English drawing manuals, 1600-1850; European illustrated books, 1650-1790. *Interests:* Books related to the visual arts in England. *Publ:* Auth, Every Lady Her Own Drawing Master, Apollo, 77; contribr, Book Collecting: A Modern Guide, Bowker, 77; auth, Color printing in England, Yale Ctr Brit Art, 78; auth introd, Hullmandel's Art of Drawing on Stone, 82 & Burch's Colour Printing and Colour Printers, 82, Garland. *Mailing Add:* Yale Ctr for Brit Art Box 2120 Yale Sta New Haven CT 06520

FRIEDMAN, MARTIN
MUSEUM DIRECTOR
b Pittsburgh, Pa, Sept 23, 25. *Study:* Univ Pa; Univ Wash, BA, 47; Univ Calif, Los Angeles, MA, 49; Columbia Univ, 56-57; Belg-Am Found Grant, Brussels, 57-58; Univ Minn, Am Art Fel, 58-60. *Collections Arranged:* Jean Dubuffet: Monuments, Simulacres, Practicables, 73; Nevelson: Wood Sculpture, 73; Naives & Visionaries, 74; Projected Images, 74; Oldenburg: Six Themes, 75; The River: Images of the Mississippi, 76; Scale and Environment: 10 Sculptors, 77; Noguchi's Imaginary Landscapes, 78; George Segal Sculptures, 78; Picasso: From the Future, Musee Picasso, Paris, 80. *Pos:* Fel, Brooklyn Mus, 56-57; sr cur, Walker Art Ctr, 58-60, dir, 61-; co-chmn mus panel, Nat Endowment Arts, 77-78. *Awards:* Ford Found Fel, 61-62. *Mem:* Am Fedn Arts; Nat Collection Fine Arts Comn; Asn Art Mus Dirs (pres, 78-79); Century Asn. *Publ:* Auth, Charles Sheeler, Watson-Guptill. *Mailing Add:* c/o Walker Art Ctr Vineland Pl Minneapolis MN 55403

FRIEDMAN, MARVIN ROSS
DEALER
b Minneapolis, Minn. *Study:* Univ Miami, BA, 63, JD, 66. *Bibliog:* Joan Kleinman (auth), The Art Market: Interview with Leading Dealers, Metrop Mus, 79; Tim Harris (auth), Great art dealers, Venture Mag, 9/83. *Specialty:* Major modern and contemporary pictures. *Mailing Add:* 2600 Douglas Rd Coral Gables FL 33134

FRIEDMAN, SALLY CEILA
PAINTER

b New York, NY, Jan 21, 32. *Study:* Queens Col, City Univ New York, BS, 53, MA, 59; Ruskin Sch Art, Oxford Univ, England, 62-64; Art Students League, 65-70. *Exhib:* Works on Paper, Brooklyn Mus, 75; Childe Hassam Fund Purchase Exhib, Am Acad & Inst Arts & Lett, New York, 77; Berkshire Mus Ann, Pittsfield, Mass, 77-80; Recent Paintings, Phoenix Gallery, New York, 78, 81 & 82; Still Lifes, Fairleigh Dickinson Univ, 82; Color Harmonious & Discordant, Marymount Manhattan Col, 83. *Pos:* Secy, Phoenix Gallery, New York, 80-81, pres, 82-83. *Awards:* Medal Hon, 75, Grumbacher Award, 80 & Sara Winston Mem Prize, 82, Nat Asn Women Artists Ann. *Bibliog:* Holland Cotter (auth), article, New York Arts J, 1/81; Phyllis Braff (auth), Still life that stirs imagination, New York Times, 4/10/83; Malcolm Preston (auth), Single theme, sextet of styles, Newsday, 4/13/83. *Mem:* Nat Asn Women Artists; Womens Caucus Art; Art Students League; Women in Arts. *Media:* Oil. *Publ:* Contribr, Art Now--color slides, Vol VI, No 3 & 4, 78. *Dealer:* Phoenix Gallery 30 W 57th St New York NY 10019. *Mailing Add:* 160 Riverside Dr Apt 14A New York NY 10024

FRINTA, MOJMIR SVATOPLUK
HISTORIAN, EDUCATOR

b Prague, Czech, July 28, 22; US citizen. *Study:* Col Fine & Appl Arts, Prague; Karlova Univ, Prague, BA; Ecole des Beaux Arts, Paris, France; Ecole du Louvre, Paris; Univ Mich, MA, 53, PhD(hist art), 60. *Pos:* Sr restorer, Metrop Mus Art, New York, 55-63. *Teaching:* Prof art hist, State Univ NY, Albany, 63- *Awards:* Nat Endowment Humanities Grant, 77-78 & 82-84. *Mem:* Col Art Asn; Int Inst Conserv Art; Int Ctr Medieval Art. *Res:* Late medieval & Byzantine painting & sculpture; early Netherlandish painting; art technology. *Publ:* Auth, Master of the Gerona martyrology & Bohemian illumination, 64, auth, Investigation of the punched decoration of medieval Italian & non-Italian panel paintings, 65 & auth, The quest for a restorer's shop of beguiling invention: Restorations and forgeries in Italian panel paintings, 3/78, Art Bulletin; auth, Genius of Robert Campin, Mouton, 66; auth, The puzzling raised decoration in the paintings by Master Theodoric, Simiolus, 76. *Mailing Add:* Dept of Art State Univ NY Albany Albany NY 12222

FRISBIE, AMY JONES See Jones, Amy

FRISCIA, ALBERT
PAINTER, SCULPTOR

b New York, NY, July 22, 11. *Study:* Nat Acad Design, 33-36; Black Mountain Col; Escuela Univ des Bellas Artes, Mex, 49. *Comn:* Bronze altar, Basilica St Mary, Montesanto, Rome, 75; bronze sculpture, Ministry of Post & Telecommunications Bldg, EUR, Rome, Italy, 77; bronze altar, Bernini Apse, St Peter's Basilica, Vatican, Rome, 80; bronze sculpture, Boccia Family Chapel, Rome, 81; bronze base relief, Parrocchia s Giustina, Auronzo di Cadore, Italy, 82; and others. *Exhib:* Light, Int Show Kinetic Art, Galleria Dell Obelisco, Rome, 67; 6th & 7th Int Biennial Sculpture, Carrara, Italy, 69 & 73; Seven Americans in Rome, Kinetic Projections, Gallery Mod Art, Rome, 70; Instanbul Izmir, Ankara, 73; 13th Int Biennial Sculpture, Civic Mus Padova, 81. *Pos:* Air dir, Case-Sheppard-Mann, 46-47; art dir, Pan Am Airways, 54-68. *Teaching:* Instr, Am Univ Rome, 80-83. *Awards:* Gold Medal of Merit, Mass of the Artists Asn, Rome, 72. *Bibliog:* Frank Popper (auth), L'art Cinetique, Gauthier-Villars, Paris, 70; Trecanni (ed), Lessico Universale Della Enciclopedia Italiana, Rome, 70; Corrado Maltese (auth), Contemporary Art in Italy, Presenza, Rome, 71. *Media:* Wax, Stone. *Mailing Add:* Via Margutta 54 Rome 00187 Italy

FRITZLER, GERALD J(OHN)
PAINTER

b Chicago, Ill, Aug 27, 53. *Study:* Am Acad Art, Chicago, AA(graphic art), 74, AA(fine art, scholar), 76. *Work:* Am Acad Art, Chicago; Am Western Art Collection, Peking. *Exhib:* Am Watercolor Soc, New York, 76-79; Nat Acad Western Art, Oklahoma City, 79; Rocky Mountain Nat Watercolor Exhib, Golden, Colo, 79, 81 & 82; First Am Western Art Exhib, Peking Exhib Hall, China, 81; one-man show, Western Colo Ctr Arts, Grand Junction, 81; Western Heritage Sale, Houston, 83-84. *Awards:* Strathmore Paper Award, Am Watercolor Soc, 79. *Bibliog:* Sally Ann Butler (auth), West goes east, Directions Mag, 4/81; Mary Caroll Nelson (auth), Western artists in China, Am Artist, 6/82. *Mem:* Salmagundi Club. *Media:* Watercolor. *Dealer:* Shriver Gallery 400 N Pueblo Rd Box 1237 Taos NMex 87571; Grapevine Gallery 304 NW 41st St Oklahoma City OK 73118. *Mailing Add:* PO Box 253 Mesa CO 81643

FROHLICH, M L (MINNETTE LEAH)
PAINTER, COLLECTOR

b St Louis, Mo. *Study:* Self-taught. *Work:* Western Union, Los Angeles, Calif. *Exhib:* 111th Ann Am Watercolor Soc Exhib, New York, 78; 155th Ann, Nat Acad Design, New York, 80; 61st Ann Nat Watercolor Soc, Palm Springs Desert Mus, Calif, 81; 115th & 116th Ann Am Watercolor Soc Exhib, New York, 82 & 83. *Awards:* Jury Selection Painting, Santa Paula C of C, 65; Caroline Stern Award, Am Watercolor Soc, 77; Merchandise Award, Am Artist Mag, New York, 78. *Mem:* Am Watercolor Soc; Nat Watercolor Soc. *Media:* Transparent Watercolor, Acrylic. *Collection:* Donald Teague, Robert E Wood, Francis deErdely, Eileen Monaghan Whitaker & H Traxler. *Mailing Add:* PO Box 51 Ambassador Station Los Angeles CA 90070

FROMAN, ANN
SCULPTOR, DESIGNER

b New York, NY, Apr 7, 42. *Study:* Fashion Inst Technol, NY, AA, 61; Palace of Fontainebleau Sch Fine Art, France, cert, 61; Nat Acad Sch Fine Art, New York; Art Students League. *Work:* Congregation Emanu-El of New York; Butler Mus Art, Youngstown, Ohio; Mus Fine Art, Springfield, Mass; Slater Mus, Norwich, Conn; Richmond Libr, Wichita, Kans. *Comn:* Queen Esther (bronze), Temple Israel, Wilkes Varre, Pa, 79; Women of the Bible (bronze), Temple DeHirsch Sinai, Seattle, Washington, 80; Swirl (bronze), Bankers Trust Co & Footwear Asn of New York, 82; Holy Family, St Raphael Church, Livingston, NJ, 83; American Bounty (bronze), Culinary Inst Am, Hyde Park, NY, 83. *Exhib:* New York Artists, Brooklyn Mus, 71; one-woman shows, Berkshire Mus, Pittsfield, Mass, 77, Col Misericordia, Dallas, Pa, Bennington Mus, Vt, 81 & Judaica Mus, Phoenix, Ariz, 82; US Customs Mus, New York, 80; and others. *Awards:* Mortimer C Ritter Award, Fashion Inst Technol, 71; Watson Guptill Award, Nat Art Club, 76; First Prize Sculpture, Salmagundi Club, Am Soc Contemp Artists, 80. *Bibliog:* Gerry Raker (auth), Life is cast realistically in bronze, Poughkeepsie J, 12/7/80; Joe Frisino (auth), Women of the Bible in bronze, Seattle Post, 4/17/80; Richard Lessner (auth), Bronze dance from sculptor's mind, Ariz Repub, 1/30/82. *Mem:* Am Soc Contemp Artists; Artists Equity Asn. *Media:* Bronze. *Dealer:* Irving Schwartz 2 Tudor City Place New York NY 10017. *Mailing Add:* S Anson Rd Stanfordville NY 12581

FROMBERG, LAVERNE RAY
INSTRUCTOR, PAINTER

b Duvall, Wash, May 6, 30. *Study:* Univ Wash, BFA, 51, MFA, 53; Univ NMex, 49-50; Art Students League, 51-52 & 63-64; Bradley Univ, study with Alexander Archipenko & Sherman E Lee, 69-70. *Work:* Libr Cong, Washington, DC; New Orleans Art Mus, La; Lakeview Ctr Arts & Sci, Peoria, Ill; Bradley Univ, Peoria; Employers Reinsurance Corp, Kansas City, Mo. *Comn:* Adoration of Shepherds and Wise Men (Triptych oil), Dillard Univ, New Orleans, 55. *Exhib:* New Orleans Art Mus Ann, 56; one-person shows, Fulton Gallery, New York, 64-66 & 69; Six Ill Painters Traveling Show, Ill Arts Coun, Ill & Mo, 67-69; Mus Mod Art Mem Floor, New York, 69; Butler Inst Am Art. *Collections Arranged:* Holiday Art Ann Elem Art Exhib, 73 & 74 & Impressions of a Teenage Art Exhib, Lakeview Ctr Arts & Sci, 74 & 75. *Pos:* Instr art, Lakeview Mus, 77- *Teaching:* Actg instr drawing, Bradley Univ, 54-57; lectr drawing, Ill State Univ, Normal, 69-71; instr painting, Ill Cent Col, 77-82. *Awards:* Prize for Painting, Three Times One, Am Painting & Sculpture Festival, Macon, Ga; Best in Show Purchase Prize Painting, Icon, New Orleans Art Asn; Carnegie Hall Art Award Painting, Art Students League. *Mem:* Midwest Mus Asn. *Media:* Encaustic Watercolor, Serigraph. *Publ:* Contribr, Art Let's Try It (TV series), Lakeview Ctr Art & Sci & Bradley Univ. *Dealer:* Tower Park Gallery 4709 N Prospect Peoria Heights IL 61614. *Mailing Add:* c/o Peoria Art Guild 1831 N Knoxville Peoria IL 61606

FROMBOLUTI, SIDEO
PAINTER

b Hershey, Pa, Oct 3, 20. *Study:* Tyler Sch Art, Philadelphia. *Work:* Cincinnati Art Mus, Ohio; Univ Mus, Southern Ill Univ, Carbondale; Mus Art, Providence, RI; Univ Ill Mus, Urbana; Philadelphia Mus Art; and others. *Exhib:* Speyer Gallery, Paris; Zabriskie Gallery, New York; Great Jones Gallery; Gross McCleaf Gallery; Landmark Gallery. *Bibliog:* Sandler (auth), article, Aujourd'hui; Oeri (auth), article, Quadrum; Kingsley (auth), article, Art Int. *Media:* Oil on Canvas. *Dealer:* Gross McCleaf Gallery 1713 Walnut St Philadelphia PA 19103. *Mailing Add:* 178 Prince St New York NY 10012

FROST, STUART HOMER
EDUCATOR, PAINTER

b Arendtsville, Pa, Nov 22, 25. *Study:* Pa State Univ, BA; Brooklyn Mus Sch; Skowhegan Sch Painting & Sculpture. *Work:* Pa Acad Fine Arts, Philadelphia; Butler Art Inst, Youngstown, Ohio; Dulin Gallery Art, Knoxville, Tenn; Mus Art, Pa State Univ, University Park; Mansfield State Col, Pa. *Exhib:* Am Watercolors, Drawings & Prints, Metrop Mus Art, 62; Recent Drawings USA, Mus Mod Art, 64; Watercolor USA, 66; Butler Art Inst Mid-Yr Show, 75; 9th Dulin Nat Print & Drawing Competition, 75. *Teaching:* Prof art, Pa State Univ, University Park, formerly. *Media:* Pen, Ink. *Mailing Add:* 139 E Hubler Rd State College PA 16801

FRUDAKIS, ANTHONY
SCULPTOR

b Bellows Falls, Vt, July 30, 53. *Study:* Apprentice to Evangeles Frudakis, 68-73; Pa Acad Fine Arts, cert, 76. *Comn:* Debbie (bronze portrait), comn by Dino Kartsonakis, Newport Beach, Calif, 79; Lovers (3-D bronze composition), comn by Ben Wienstock, Philadelphia, 80; Viking (bronze), Atlantic Co Bd Educ, Atlantic City, NJ, 80; Gods and Goddesses (bronzes), Garrison & Elliot, New York, 81-83; Pegasus (bas relief), Hammonton Libr, NJ, 83. *Exhib:* Nat Sculpture Soc, New York, 76-82; Nat Acad Design, New York, 77; Audubon Artists Ann, 81 & Allied Artists Am, 83, Nat Arts Club, New York. *Teaching:* Instr sculpture, Fashion Inst Technol, New York, 80-81. *Awards:* M B Hexter Award, Allied Artists Am Ann, New York, 82; Gold Medal, 82 & Gloria Medal, 83, Nat Sculpture Soc. *Mem:* Nat Sculpture Soc. *Media:* Bronze. *Mailing Add:* 10 S Oxford Ave Atlantic City NJ 08406

FRUDAKIS, EVANGELOS WILLIAM
SCULPTOR, INSTRUCTOR

b Rains, Utah, May 13, 21. *Study:* Greenwich Workshop, New York, 35-39; Beaux Arts Inst Design, New York, 40-41; Pa Acad Fine Arts, Cresson, Scheidt & Tiffany Scholar; Am Acad Rome, Italy, Prix de Rome Fel, 50-52. *Work:* Pa Acad Fine Arts, Philadelphia; Smithsonian Inst; Weizmann Inst,

Israel; Nat Acad Fine Arts, New York; Airlie Found, Va. *Comn:* John F Kennedy Mem Monument, Atlantic City, NJ; over-life size female figure in fountain, Philadelphia Civic Ctr; Fishing Bear Fountain, Philadelphia Zoo, 80; Naiad Fountain, Philadelphia Civic Ctr, 82; The Signer, Independence Nat Hist Park, Philadelphia, 82. *Exhib:* Nat Sculpture Soc Ann; Pa Acad Fine Arts Ann, 41-62; Nat Acad Design Ann, 48-63; Philadelphia Mus Art, 59 & 62 & Twenty-three Sculptors Exhib, 72; one-man shows, Atlantic City Art Ctr, 56 & 61, Woodmere Art Gallery, 57 & 62, Philadelphia Art Alliance, 58, Pa Acad Fine Arts, 62 & Briarcliff Col Mus Art, 74. *Teaching:* Instr, var art centers, NY, NJ & Pa, 41-63; instr, Nat Acad Fine Art, New York, 70-, Old Church Cult Ctr, Demarest, NJ, 75- & Frudakis Acad Fine Arts, Philadelphia, 76-; sr instr, Pa Acad Fine Arts, Philadelphia, 72- *Awards:* Herbert Adams Award, Nat Sculpture Soc, 76; Artist Fund Prize, Nat Acad Design, 77; Leonard J Meiselman Prize, 48th Ann, Nat Sculpture Soc, 81. *Mem:* Fel Pa Acad Fine Arts; fel Am Acad Rome; fel Nat Sculpture Soc; academician Nat Acad Design; Allied Artists Am. *Res:* Statues of the Roman Forum; Michelangelo's Rondanini Pieta. *Mailing Add:* Frudakis Gallery 1829 Chestnut St Philadelphia PA 19103

FRUDAKIS, ZENOS
SCULPTOR, PAINTER
b San Francisco, Calif, July 7, 51. *Study:* Pa Acad Fine Arts, Philadelphia, 73-76; Univ Pa, Philadelphia, BFA, 81, MFA, 83. *Work:* Bronze portrait, Afro-Am Mus, Philadelphia. *Comn:* Murals, Fairmount Farms Hosp, Roxborough, Pa, 76; portraits, Dilworth, Paxson & Kalish, Philadelphia, 80-81; Boy & Elephant (life size fountain sculpture), Burlington Mall, NJ, 81; Wolfhound & Wolf (lifesize bronze garden sculpture), private commission, Vineland, NJ. *Exhib:* Nat Sculpture Soc, 79-81, Allied Artists Am, 80-81 & Salmagundi Club, 81, New York; Inst Contemporary Art, Philadelphia, 81-83; Shidoni Gallery, Sante Fe, 82. *Teaching:* Instr, Frudakis Acad, Philadelphia, 78-79. *Awards:* John Spring Art Founder Award, Nat Sculpture Soc, 81; Gloria Medal, Nat Sculpture Soc, 81; Tallix Award, Nat Sculpture Soc, 82. *Mem:* Allied Artists Am; fel Pa Acad Fine Arts; Col Art Asn Am; Nat Sculpture Soc. *Media:* Bronze; Oil. *Dealer:* Frudakis Gallery 1829 Chestnut St Philadelphia PA 19103; Portraits Inc 985 Park Ave 10028. *Mailing Add:* 2316 Locust St Philadelphia PA 19103

FRUEH, JOANNA
CRITIC, EDUCATOR
b Chicago, Ill, Jan 18, 48. *Study:* Sarah Lawrence Col, BA, 70; Univ Chicago, MA, 71, PhD, 81. *Pos:* Dir, Artemisia Gallery & Fund, Chicago, 74-76. *Teaching:* Asst prof mod art, Oberlin Col, Ohio, 81-; vis asst prof contemp art & art criticism, Univ Ariz, Tucson, 83-84. *Mem:* Women's Caucus Art; Col Art Asn. *Res:* Contemporary art, with a special interest in women artists and feminist art theory. *Publ:* Auth, Chicago's emotional realists, Artforum, 78; auth, Sexuality in art, New Art Examiner, 79; auth, Janet Cooling: Born to be alive, Allen Mem Art Mus Bulletin, 81; auth, Re-vamping the vamp, Arts Mag, 82; auth, Brumas: A Rock Star's Passage to a Life Re-Vamped, Freshcut Press, 83. *Mailing Add:* Art Dept Oberlin Col Oberlin OH 44074

FRUMKIN, ALLAN
DEALER
b Chicago, Ill, July 5, 26. *Study:* Univ Chicago. *Pos:* Dir, Allan Frumkin Gallery, New York, currently. *Specialty:* Contemporary American artists; 19th and 20th century drawings. *Mailing Add:* 50 W 57th St New York NY 10019

FRUTCHEY, JERE (GERALD READ)
PAINTER
b Camden, NJ, Nov 6, 34. *Study:* Syracuse Univ, NY, BFA, 56; Sch Visual Arts, New York, 63. *Work:* A T & T, New York; IBM Corp, San Francisco, Calif; Delta Airlines, Dallas, Tex; C & S Bank & Fulton Nat Bank, Atlanta, Ga. *Comn:* First Union Nat Bank, Charlotte, NC, 73; Amelia Island Plantation, Pa, 80; series of 4 paper pieces, Alcan Corp, Atlanta, Ga, 81; Bank of South, Atlanta, 82. *Exhib:* Ga Artists Show, High Mus Art, Atlanta, Ga, 71; Biennial Piedmont Exhib Painting & Sculpture, Mint Mus Art, Charlotte, NC, 75; one-man show, Mint Mus Art, Charlotte, NC, 75; Watercolor USA, Springfield Mus Art, Mo, 77; Paperworks 80, Quinlain Art Ctr, Gainesville, Ga, 80. *Awards:* Graphic Arts Award, Printing Industries Am, 71; Silver Award, Nat Folding Carton Competition, 72 & 74; Merit Award, Printing Industries Am, 74. *Bibliog:* article, Art Voices South, 11-12/81. *Media:* Sprayed Acrylic, Colored Pencil. *Mailing Add:* c/o Image South Gallery 1931 Peachtree Rd NE Atlanta GA 30309

FRYBERGER, BETSY G
CURATOR
b Chicago, Ill, May 7, 35. *Study:* Bryn Mawr Col, BA, 56; Radcliffe Col, MA, 58. *Collections Arranged:* Gavarni: Prints (auth, catalog), Stanford Univ, 71, Toulouse-Lautrec: Prints and Drawings (auth, catalog), 72, Morris and Company (coauth, catalog), 75, Whistler: Themes and Variations (coauth, catalog), 78, Paul Klee: In Celebration of/50 Prints (coauth, catalog) 79 & Gwen John (coauth, catalog), 82. *Pos:* Asst cur prints & drawings, Art Inst Chicago, 60-67; cur prints & drawings, Stanford Univ Mus Art, 70- *Mem:* Print Coun Am (bd mem, 79-, vpres, 81-); Col Art Asn. *Mailing Add:* 2361 Middlefield Rd Palo Alto CA 94301

FUCHS, MARY THARSILLA
EDUCATOR, PAINTER
b Westphalia, Tex, Apr 19, 12. *Study:* Our Lady of the Lake Col, BA, 38; Columbia Univ, MA, 42; Univ Sch Handicrafts, 42; Art Inst Chicago, 45; Univ Tex, 49-51; with Buckley McGurrin, 50-54; NY Univ, 52; Pratt

Graphics Ctr, 69. *Comn:* Twelve faceted glass windows, St Timothy Church, San Antonio, Tex, 71. *Exhib:* Seventh & 8th Tex Gen, Witte Mus, San Antonio, 45 & 46; First Ann Tex Watercolor Soc, San Antonio, 50; San Antonio Press Club, 65. *Teaching:* Elem sch instr, St Joseph Acad, 32-37, high sch instr, 38-41; from instr to assoc prof art, Our Lady of the Lake Col, 42-68, chmn dept, 42-72, prof, 68- *Mem:* Col Art Asn; Nat Art Educ Asn; Tex Art Educ Asn; Tex Watercolor Soc; San Antonio Art League. *Media:* Watercolor, Oil. *Publ:* Designer, Toddler's Rosary, 54; auth, Rocky personalities, Sch Arts Mag, 3/57; auth, Religion worksheets for beginners, Confraternity of Christian Doctrine, 62. *Mailing Add:* 411 SW 24th St San Antonio TX 78285

FUERST, SHIRLEY MILLER
SCULPTOR, PRINTMAKER
b Brooklyn, NY, June 3, 28. *Study:* Brooklyn Mus Art Sch, with Reuben Tam; Pratt Ctr Contemp Printmaking; Art Students League, with Roberto DeLamonica; Hunter Col, MFA, 71. *Work:* James A Michener Found Collection of Twentieth Century Am Art, Univ Tex, Austin; Exxon Corp, NJ; Allentown Art Mus, Pa. *Exhib:* 32nd Mid-Yr Show, Butler Inst of Am Art, Ohio, 68; Contemp Artists, Brooklyn Mus, 71; The Women's Decade--The 1970's, Buecker & Harpsichords, New York, 80; Art and Technology, Col New Rochelle, 81; Arteder 82, Int Graphic Arts Exhib, Bilbao, Spain, 82; The Unexpected, Elaine Benson Gallery, Bridgehampton, NY, 82; Atlantic Gallery, New York, 84; and others. *Awards:* Oil Competition First Prize, Village Art Ctr, New York, 63; Merit Award with Distinction, Enjay Chem Co, NJ, 66; Eric Schwartz Graphics Award, Nat Asn Women Artists, 70. *Bibliog:* Sculpture for the Dance (videotape), Hudson River Mus, 73; John Gruen (auth), Shirley Fuerst, Soho Weekly News, 75; Conversation with an artist, Shirley Fuerst, Channel 31, 77. *Mem:* Women's Caucus for Art. *Publ:* Auth, A method of printing or painting using heat responsive inks, 71; auth, Health hazards in art, Art Workers News, 75; auth, videotape documentaries of women artists, 70 & Women Artists Newslett, 76; ed, Feminism and ecology, Heresies, 80. *Mailing Add:* 266 Marlborough Rd Brooklyn NY 11226

FUGATE-WILCOX, TERRY
SCULPTOR
b Kalamazoo, Mich, Nov 20, 44. *Study:* Ferris Inst. *Work:* Western Mich Univ, Kalamazoo; Dept of Parks, Guggenheim Mus, Mus Mod Art, New York; Nat Gallery of Australia, Canberra. *Comn:* Copper & aluminum sculpture, comn by J Patrick Lannon, West Palm Beach, Fla, 73; aluminum & magnesium sculpture, J Hood Wright Park, New York, 74; 300 copper & silver sculptures, Commodities Exchange Mkt, New York, 74; copper & aluminum sculpture, comn by Alan Stillman. *Exhib:* Detroit Inst Art, Mich, 68; Language IV, Dwan Gallery, New York, 69; First Battery Park Sculpture Show, New York, 71; Art in Evolution, Xerox Corp, Rochester, NY, 73; Fire Air Earth Water, Univ Wis-Milwaukee, 74. *Awards:* Creative Artists Pub Serv Prog Grant, 76; Nat Endowment Arts Grant, 76-77. *Bibliog:* Diane B Chichura & Thelma K Stevens (auths), Super Sculpture, Van Nostrand Reinhold, 74; Lawrence Alloway (auth), The public sculpture problem, Studio Int, 10/72; Ellen Lubell (auth), article, Arts Mag, 1/74. *Media:* All. *Mailing Add:* c/o Louis K Meisel Gallery 141 Prince St New York NY 10012

FUHRMAN, ESTHER
SCULPTOR, DESIGNER
b Pittsburgh, Pa, Feb 25, 39. *Study:* Pa State Univ, 56-57; Frick Dept Fine Arts, Univ Pittsburgh, BA, 60; also with Sabastiano Mineo & Hana Geber, New York. *Work:* Port New York Authority; World Trade Ctr, New York; Am Crafts Coun, New York; UAHC Architects Adv, New York; Deere & Co, Moline, Ill; and others. *Comn:* Gemstone & bronze memorial, Temple Sinai, Pittsburgh, 78; bronze memorial, Temple Keneseth Israel, Philadelphia, 79; pvt residential comns, New York, Philadelphia, Pittsburgh, Miami, NJ, Los Angeles, Paris, Sydney, 79-81; bronze figure, Scott Paper Co, Philadelphia, 81; and others. *Exhib:* Nat Asn Women Artists, New York; Sculptors League, New York; Reese Paley, Atlantic City, NJ; Equitable Life Assurance, New York; Lever House, New York; and others. *Teaching:* Lectr sculpture today, Sands Point Acad, Long Island, 71 & Kimberley Sch, NJ, 72; lectr studio secrets, Montclair Mus Art. *Bibliog:* Marilyn Goldstein (auth), Massive sculpture shapes her life, Newsday, 3/69; article, La Rev Mod, 3/72. *Mem:* Nat Asn Women Artists; Sculptors League (vpres, currently). *Media:* Bronze, Mixed Media. *Dealer:* Art Ventures 4710 Stenton Ave Philadelphia PA; J Barrett Galleries 3154 Markway Dr Toledo OH 43606. *Mailing Add:* 428 Newbold Rd Jenkintown PA 19046

FUKUHARA, (KAZUO) HENRY
PAINTER, INSTRUCTOR
b Los Angeles, Calif, Apr 25, 13. *Study:* with Edgar A Whitney, 72; with Rex Brandt, 74; with Carl Molno, 76. *Work:* Heckscher Mus, Huntington, NY; Palm Springs Desert Mus, Calif; Abilene Mus Fine Art, Tex; Nassau Community Col, Garden City, NY; Los Angeles Co Mus Art, Calif. *Exhib:* 108th Ann Am Watercolor Soc, New York, 75; one-man shows, Dowling Col, Oakdale, Long Island, 78 & Friends World Col, Lloyds Neck, NY, 80; Elaine Benson Gallery, Bridgehampton, NY, 79; Nat Invitational Watercolor, Zaner Gallery, Rochester, NY, 81. *Teaching:* Instr painting workshops, Cutchogue, Long Island, 81-83; Mont Miniature Art Soc, 82, Islip Art Mus, NY, 82, Parrish Art Mus, Southampton, 83. *Awards:* Purchase Award, Nassau Community Col, 76; Elise Brown Mem, Mamaroneck Art Guild, NY, 78; Best in Show Watercolor, Strathmore Paper Co, 79. *Bibliog:* Nancy Dustin Wall Moure (auth), Painting/Sculpture in Los Angeles, California 1900-1945, Los Angeles Co Mus Art; Helen A Harrison (auth), Paper is his palette for flowing colors, New York Times, 2/17/80; Frank Webb (auth), Watercolor energies, North Light, 83. *Mem:* Pittsburgh Watercolor Soc; Ala Watercolor Soc; Nat Watercolor Soc. *Media:* Watercolor. *Mailing Add:* 400 Half Hollow Road Deer Park NY 11729

FUKUI, NOBU
PAINTER

b Tokyo, Japan, June 2, 42. *Work:* Indianapolis Mus Art, Ind; Larry Aldrich Mus, Conn; Nat Mus Mod Art, Tokyo & Kyoto; Dartmouth Col, NH; and others. *Exhib:* Japanese Artists in Europe & America, Nat Mus Mod Art, Tokyo, 65; one-man shows, Max Hutchinson Gallery, 70, 72, 73, 75 & 79, Gallery Contemp Art, Pittsburgh, Pa, 71 & Watari Gallery, Tokyo, Japan, 77; Painting & Sculpture Today, Indianapolis Mus Art, 70, 72 & 74; and others. *Media:* Acrylic. *Mailing Add:* 141 W 26th St New York NY 10001

FULLER, DIANA
DEALER

b New York, NY, Jan 14, 31. *Study:* Sorbonne, art hist. *Pos:* Co-owner, Fuller Goldeen Gallery, 64- *Specialty:* Contemporary art. *Mailing Add:* c/o Fuller Goldeen Gallery 228 Grant Ave San Francisco CA 94108

FULLER, EMILY (EMILY FULLER KINGSTON)
PAINTER

b New York, NY, Aug 9, 41. *Study:* Garland Jr Col, Boston, Mass, Assoc BD, 62; Mus Sch Fine Arts, Boston, Mass, 62-66; Tufts Univ, BS(art educ), 66; Art Students League, New York, study with Richard Mayhew, 68-69. *Work:* Mus Mod Art, Chase Manhattan Bank, New York; Aldrich Mus Contemp Art, Ridgefield, Conn; Prudential Ins Corp Am; Indianapolis Mus Art, Ind; and others. *Exhib:* One-person shows, Soho 20, New York, 77 & Frank Marino Gallery, New York, 80; Art in Transition: A Century of The Mus Sch, Mus Fine Arts, Boston, Mass, 77; Paper as Medium, Smithsonian Inst Travelling Exhib Serv, 78-79; Gifts of Drawings: European Acquisitions, American Acquisitions, 79; and other group & one-person shows. *Bibliog:* Susan Heinemann (auth), articles, Artforum, 4/75; Michael Florescu (auth), Emily Fuller, article in Arts Mag, 4/79; John Russell (auth), Art: New drawings at the modern, New York Times, 8/10/79. *Media:* Acrylic. *Publ:* Contribr, Emily Fuller pioneers in art, Garland Mag, Garland Jr Col, 74. *Mailing Add:* 93 Mercer St New York NY 10012

FULLER, JEFFREY P
DEALER, GALLERY DIRECTOR

b Chicago, Ill, May 14, 50. *Study:* Univ Vienna, 70-71 & 73-74; Holy Cross Col, Mass, BA, 72. *Pos:* Dir, Jeffrey Fuller Fine Art, 79- *Mem:* Philadelphia Art Dealers Asn (treas, 82-83); Inst Contemp Art, Univ Pa; Philadelphia Art Alliance (bd mem, 82-); Swedish Am Hist Mus (art adv panel, 82-). *Specialty:* Twentieth century American and European art. *Mailing Add:* 2108 Spruce St Philadelphia PA 19103

FULLER, JOHN CHARLES
HISTORIAN, PHOTOGRAPHER

b Laconia, NH, Oct 7, 37. *Study:* Rochester Inst Technol, AAS; Syracuse Univ, AB & MA; Ohio Univ, PhD; study with J H Matthews. *Work:* Eastman Kodak Co; Ohio Univ; State Univ NY, Oswego. *Exhib:* Contemp Photog Nat, Univ Nebr, Lincoln, 72; Invitational, Univ of the S, Sewanee, Tenn, 72; Two Photographers, Eckerd Col, Fla, 73 & Johnson State Col, Vt, 73; NY State Super Fair, Syracuse, 74; and others. *Teaching:* Teaching fel fine arts, Ohio Univ, Athens, 64-67; asst prof art hist, State Univ NY Col Oswego, 67-69, assoc prof, 70-80, prof, 80- *Awards:* Develop grant photo criticism, 68 & res fel Victorian photog, 70, State Univ NY; Nat Endowment Arts & Humanities Awards, Col Teacher Seminar, 76. *Bibliog:* Irving Desfor (auth), Camera News, AP Newsfeatures, 1/58; Jacob Deschin (auth), Ex-Navy Photographer, Army-Navy-Air Force Times 6/59; Ralph Miller (auth), Camera Column, NY World Telegram-Sun, 1/60. *Mem:* Col Art Asn Am; and others. *Res:* History and criticism of photography and interrelationships of photography and painting. *Publ:* Auth, An un-Victorian photograph, 70 & Atget and Man Ray in the context of surrealism, 76-77, Art J; auth, A view through a window, Royal Photog Soc J, 70; auth, Frederick H Evans as late Victorian, Afterimage, 76; auth, O G Rejlander: From philistine to Forerunner, Exposure, 76. *Mailing Add:* 201 W Second St #313 Oswego NY 13126

FULLER, MARY (MARY FULLER MCCHESNEY)
SCULPTOR, WRITER

b Wichita, Kans, Oct 20, 22. *Study:* Univ Calif, Berkeley, AA, 43. *Work:* Yuba City Dept Motor Vehicles Bldg, Calif; Andrew Hill High Sch, San Jose, Calif; Children's Sculpture Garden, Community Ctr, Salinas, Calif; Univ Calif Med Ctr, San Francisco; Petaluma Pub Libr; and others. *Comn:* Dos Liones, San Francisco Art Comn, 74; Star Tail Lion, comn by Nancy Davidson Short, Yuba Totem, Yuba Lion, Calif Off State Architect; San Francisco Clean Water Proj, 83; Portsmouth Sq, San Francisco, 83; Cushing Lions, Squaw Valley, 83. *Exhib:* San Francisco Mus Art, 47-50 & 60; Gump's Gallery, San Francisco, 65; Calif State Univ, Sonoma, Cotati, 71; Santa Rosa City Hall, Calif, 74; Fremont, Calif, 80; Lafayette, Calif, 82. *Collections Arranged:* Period of Exploration (with catalog), Oakland Mus, 73. *Pos:* Researcher, Arch Am Art, 64-65; staff writer, Currant Mag, San Francisco, 75-76. *Awards:* First Prize Ceramic Sculpture, Pac Coast Ceramic Ann, 47 & 49; Merit Award, San Francisco Art Festival, 71; Nat Endowment Arts art critic grant, 75; and others. *Media:* Concrete. *Publ:* Auth, articles in Art Digest, 54, Artforum, 62, 63, 70 & 71, Art in Am, 63 & 64 & Craft Horizons, 73, 76, 77 & 78; auth, A Period of Exploration, 73. *Mailing Add:* 2955 Sonoma Mountain Rd Petaluma CA 94952

FULLER, SUE
SCULPTOR, PRINTMAKER

b Pittsburgh, Pa. *Study:* Carnegie Inst Technol, BA, 36; Columbia Univ Teachers Col, MA, 39; and with Hans Hofmann, S W Hayter & Josef Albers.

Work: Metrop Mus Art & Whitney Mus Am Art, New York; Nat Collection Fine Arts, Smithsonian Inst, Washington, DC; Tate Gallery, London; Guggenheim Mus, New York; plus others. *Comn:* String Composition 52, comn by M Greef for bd rm, Com Investment 200; String Composition T-250, Emerson Crocker Mem for Gail Borden Pub Libr, Elgin, Ill, 72; String Composition T252, All Souls Unitarian Church, New York, 79; String Construction #253, McNay Art Inst, San Antonio, 83. *Exhib:* First Biennial Sao Paulo, Brazil, 50; Abstract Art in America, Mus Mod Art, New York, 51; Edward Root Collection, Metrop Mus Art, New York, 53; Plastics USA, US Info Agency traveling exhib, USSR, 61; Responsive Eye, Mus Mod Art, New York, 65. *Teaching:* Instr mobile design, Mus Mod Art, New York, 45-47; guest artist, Univ Ga, 51-52; instr art, Columbia Univ Teachers Col, 52 & 58; instr two-dimensional design, Pratt Inst, 65-66. *Awards:* Guggenheim Fel, 49; Nat Inst Arts & Lett Grant, 50; Carnegie Mellon Univ Alumni Merit Award, 74. *Bibliog:* Rosalind Browne (auth), Sue Fuller: threading transparency, Art Int, 1/20/72; David Shirey (auth), Esthetic magic of geometry, New York Times, 4/23/78; Harry A Broadd (auth), The String Constructions of Sue Fuller, Arts & Activities, 4/82. *Mem:* Soc Am Graphic Artists (vpres Soc Am Etchers, 46-51); Artists Equity Asn New York (vpres, 52-53); Sculptor's Guild. *Media:* Plastic, String. *Publ:* Auth, Mary Cassatt's use of soft-ground etching, Mag Art, 2/50; auth, 20th century cat's cradle, Craft Horizons, 4/54; dir, String Composition (film), NY State Coun Arts, 70; co-dir (with film maker Maurice Amar), String Composition (video), 74. *Dealer:* Chalette Int 9 E 88th St New York NY 10028. *Mailing Add:* PO Box 1580 Southampton NY 11968

FULTON, FRED FRANKLIN
PAINTER

b Leslie, Idaho, Sept 27, 20. *Study:* Univ Fla; Mt San Antonio Col; spec study with Manuelito Leal, Guanajuato, Mex. *Work:* State Capitol & Cult Inst, Chihuahua, Mex; City Hall, Juarez, Mex; Pub Libr Juarez, Mex. *Exhib:* Cult Inst, Chihuahua, 72 & Mexicali, Mex, 74; Univ Guanajuato, 73; Museo Arte & Hist, Juarez, Mex. *Teaching:* Pvt studio, San Miguel, NMex & El Paso, Tex. *Mem:* Carlsbad NMex Art Asn; El Paso Tex Art Asn; Conserv, Exploration, Diving, Archeol, Mus Int. *Media:* Oil, Acrylic. *Res:* Coronado's expedition. *Mailing Add:* 5121 Harlan Dr El Paso TX 79924

FUMAGALLI, BARBARA MERRILL
PRINTMAKER

b Kirkwood, Mo, Mar 15, 26. *Study:* Univ Iowa, Iowa City, BFA, 48, MFA, 50, with Mauricio Lasansky; Univ NMex, 80-81, with Garo Antreasian & John Sommers. *Work:* Mus of Mod Art, New York; Nelson A Rockefeller Collection, New York; Univ Ill, Urbana; Univ Iowa, Iowa City; Hamline Univ, St Paul, Minn. *Exhib:* Walker Art Ctr, Minneapolis, Minn, 49, 56 & 63; Young Am Printmakers, Mus Mod Art, New York, 53; solo exhibs, Tweed Gallery, Univ Minn, 65 & 82, Concordia Col, Moorhead, Minn, 65, Suzanne Kohn Gallery, St Paul, 67, Hamline Univ, St Paul, 69 & 84 & Paine Art Ctr & Arboretum, Oshkosh, Wis, 73; Smithsonian Inst, traveling exhib, 66-68; NW Printmakers, Seattle Art Mus, Washington, 66-69; Drawing on Dance, Avery Fisher Hall, Lincoln Ctr, New York, 82. *Teaching:* Instr, Univ Wis, Stout, 79 & 81. *Awards:* Post Facto Prize, City Art Mus, St Louis, Mo, 47; Purchase Prize, Univ Ill, 54; Best in Show, Arrowhead Art Exhib, 63. *Bibliog:* Donald M Anderson (auth), Elements of Design, Holt, Rinehart & Winston, 61. *Media:* Engraving, Serigraphy. *Publ:* Illusr, Swing Around the Sun, Lerner Publ, 65. *Mailing Add:* Rte 4 Box 282A Menomonie WI 54751

FUMAGALLI, ORAZIO
EDUCATOR, SCULPTOR

b Taranto, Italy, Feb 21, 21; US citizen. *Study:* Univ Iowa, BA, 48, MFA, 50, PhD, 61. *Exhib:* Wis Sculptors, Madison Art Ctr, 65; Madison Art Salon, Univ Wis, 65; Biennial Painting & Sculpture, Walker Art Ctr, Minneapolis, 66; Computer Art, Tweed Mus, Univ Minn, Duluth, 71; Tweed Mus, Duluth, Minn, 80; Tier Garten Gallery, Hanover, Ger, 81; and others. *Pos:* Educ cur, Tweed Gallery, Univ Minn, Duluth, 54-57, cur, 57-60, assoc dir, 60-64; dir univ gallery, Univ Wis-Stout, 64- *Teaching:* Assoc prof art hist, Univ Minn, Duluth, 60-64; prof art & chmn dept, Univ Wis-Stout, 64-; exchange artist, Eng, 79-80. *Awards:* Fulbright Grant study in Italy, 50; Belg-Am Found Fel, 56. *Mem:* Col Art Asn; Mid-Am Col Art Asn; Wis Art Educ Asn; Am Asn Mus; Midwest Mus Conf. *Publ:* Auth & producer, A House Divided (film), Lincoln-Douglas Debates, 74; auth, Exhibition monographs on contemporary American artists and on thematic exhibitions, 74- *Mailing Add:* Dept Art Univ Wis-Stout Menomonie WI 54751

FUNK, CHARLOTTE M
WEAVER, TAPESTRY ARTIST

b Milwaukee, Wis, Sept 27, 34. *Study:* Univ Wis-Whitewater, BS, 71; Ill State Univ, Normal, MS, 75, MFA, 76. *Comn:* Planar Exchange (tapestry), Borg-Warner Corp, Chicago, Ill, 76; Passage to the Sea: Land, Sand & Sea, Corpus Christi Nat Bank, Tex, 81. *Exhib:* Seventh Int Biennial Tapestry, Lausanne, Switz, 76; Convergence, Carnegie Inst Int, Pittsburgh, 76; Clay, Fiber, Metal-- Women Artists, Bronx Mus Arts, New York, 78; New Art in Texas, Austin, 79; Contemporary Tapestry, Pratt Inst, New York, 80-81; and others. *Teaching:* Instr textiles, Tex Tech Univ, Lubbock, 78- *Awards:* Wis Designer/ Craftsmen Award, 57; Judges Choice Award, Contemp Crafts Americas, Handweavers Guild Am, 75. *Bibliog:* Article, Interweave Mag, winter 80-81. *Mem:* Am Craftsmens Coun; Handweavers Guild Am. *Media:* Wool. *Mailing Add:* 2312 58th St Lubbock TX 79412

FUNK, VERNE J
CERAMIST, SCULPTOR
b Milwaukee, Wis, July 19, 32. *Study:* Univ Wis-Milwaukee, BS, MS & MFA. *Work:* Milwaukee Art Ctr; Mus Contemp Crafts, New York; Lannon Found, Palm Beach, Fla; Columbus Gallery Fine Arts, Ohio; Ariz State Univ, Tempe; and others. *Comn:* Trophy, Gov Awards for the Arts, Wis, 69. *Exhib:* Objects: USA; Clayworks, 20 Americans, Mus Contemp Crafts, New York, 71; The Unpainted Portrait, Kohler, 79; Viewpoint: Ceramics 80, Grossmont Col, Calif; Hartford Art Sch, Conn, 81; and others. *Pos:* Pres, Wis Designer-Craftsmen, 64-66; chmn, Visual Arts II, Wis Arts Found & Coun, 67. *Teaching:* Instr, Carthage Col, 66-69 & Univ Wis-Whitewater, 69-73; guest artist ceramics, Calif State Univ, Fresno, 72; prof ceramics & dir art sch, Bradley Univ, Peoria, Ill, 73-77; assoc prof ceramics, Tex Tech Univ, Lubbock, 77-81, prof, 81- *Awards:* Beloit & Vicinity Show, 70; Wisconsin Designer-Crafts Award, Milwaukee Art Ctr, 70 & 72. *Bibliog:* Donald Key (auth), Prominent Wisconsin potters, Milwaukee J, 72. *Mem:* Am Craftsmen's Coun. *Media:* Clay. *Publ:* Contribr, New Ceramics, Hard Core Crafts, The Container Book, History of American Ceramics: The Studio Potter, Contemporary Ceramic Techniques, and others. *Mailing Add:* 2312 58th St Lubbock TX 79412

FURMAN, (DR & MRS) ARTHUR F
COLLECTORS, PATRONS
Dr Furman, b Scranton, Pa; Mrs Furman, b Hazleton, Pa. *Study:* Dr Furman, Temple Univ, DDS; Mrs Furman, Pa State Univ, BA. *Pos:* Trustees, Furman Family Trust; pres & vpres, Found Visual Arts. *Interests:* Arranging and exhibiting items from collection in various institutions, museums, galleries and schools. *Collection:* American contemporary masters painting and sculpture; ancient Thai, Cambodian and Indian bronzes; Chinese incense burners, Oriental artifacts. *Mailing Add:* 12308 Loch Carron Circle Ft Washington MD 20744

FURMAN, DAVID STEPHEN
SCULPTOR, EDUCATOR
b Seattle, Wash, Aug 15, 45. *Study:* Univ Ore, BA(ceramics), 69; Univ Wash, MFA(ceramics & glassblowing), 72. *Work:* Univ Puget Sound Mus Art; Marietta Col Art Mus; Brand Art Mus, Glendale, Calif. *Exhib:* 45 Sculptors, US Info Serv World Tour, 73; Clay (ceramic sculpture), Whitney Mus, 74; one-man shows, David Stuart Galleries, 74-75; Small Scale in Contemporary Art, Chicago Art Inst, 75; Hard and Clear, Los Angeles Co Art Mus, 75; and others. *Teaching:* Prof sculpture, Claremont Grad Sch, Pitzer Col, 73-; instr clay sculpture, Otis Art Inst, 75- *Awards:* Brand Art Ctr Purchase Award, Glendale, Calif, 75; Nat Endowment for Arts Fel, 75; Fulbright Fel, Peru, 79. *Bibliog:* C H Hertel (auth), David Furman-Biographical Narrative Sculpture, 74; W C Hunt (auth), David Furman-miniature environments, Ceramics Monthly, 1/75; and others. *Mem:* World Crafts Coun; Am Crafts Coun; Nat Coun Educ Ceramic Arts; Artists Equity. *Media:* Clay, Glaze. *Dealer:* David Stuart Galleries 748 N La Cienega Blvd Los Angeles CA 90069. *Mailing Add:* Pitzer Col Art Dept 1150 Mills Ave Claremont CA 91711

FURR, JIM
PAINTER, PRINTMAKER
b Camden, Tenn, Aug 14, 39. *Study:* Univ Tenn, BFA; Tulane Univ, MFA; Tamarind Inst Lithography. *Work:* Montgomery Mus Fine Arts, Ala; Equitable Life Assurance Soc US, Bank Am Corp; Kans State Univ, Lawrence; R J Reynolds Corp; IBM Corp; and others. *Comn:* Colony Sq Hotel Corp, Atlanta, 78; Loew's Anatole Hotel Corp, Dallas, 79; Cannon Chapel, Emory Univ, Atlanta, 81. *Exhib:* 35 Artists in the Southeast, traveling, High Mus Art, 76; Drawings, Mint Mus Art, NC, 79; Personal Statements: Drawings, Southeastern Ctr Contemp Art, 79-80; one-person show, Tex A&I Univ, Kingsville, 74 & Montgomery Mus Fine Arts, 81; Southeast Seven IV, Southeastern Ctr Contemp Art, 81; Continuum III, Dulin Gallery Art, Knoxville, Tenn, 81; and many others. *Teaching:* Sabbatical replacement printmaking, Tulane Univ, New Orleans, La, 73-74; vis artist printmaking, Tex A&I Univ, Kingsville, 74-75; asst prof lithography & drawing, Auburn Univ, Ala, 77- *Awards:* Southeastern Ctr Contemp Art/ Nat Endowment Arts Grant, 80; Nat Endowment Arts Indivvidual Artists Fel Grant, 81; Special Merit Award, Southeastern Exhib, Spartanburg, SC, 82. *Bibliog:* Mark Price (auth), Jim Furr, Artpapers, 3-4/81; Norman Pendergraft (auth), Southeastern Seven at SECCA, Art Voices, 7-8/81. *Media:* Oil; Charcoal, Oilstick. *Dealer:* Heath Gallery 416 E Paces Ferry Rd Atlanta GA 30305. *Mailing Add:* 1014 Auburn St Opelika AL 36801

FUSCO, LAURIE S
HISTORIAN, EDUCATOR
b Boston, Mass, Oct 31, 41. *Study:* Wellesley Col, Mass, with John McAndrew & Curtis Shell, BA(art hist), 63; NY Univ Inst Fine Arts, with Colin Eisler, Ludwig Heydenreich, Craig Smyth, Richard Krautheimer & Charles Sterling, MA & PhD(art hist), 77. *Pos:* Head acad affairs, J Paul Getty Mus, 78- *Awards:* Fulbright-Hays Grant, 72-73; Samuel H Kress Res Grant, 74-75; Harvard Fel, Villa I Tatti, 83. *Mem:* Col Art Asn Am; Art Historians of Southern Calif (secy-treas, 79-80). *Res:* Study and anatomy and movement by fifteenth century Italian artists. *Publ:* Ed, Antonio Pollaiuolo's use of the antique, J Courtauld & Warburg Inst, Vol 42, 257-263; auth, The use of sculptural models by painters in fifteenth century Italy, Art Bulletin, Vol 65, 175-194; auth, An unpublished Fra Filippo Lippi, J Paul Getty Mus J, vol 10, 1-16. *Mailing Add:* J Paul Getty Mus PO Box 2112 Santa Monica CA 90406

FUSCO, PETER RICHARD
CURATOR, HISTORIAN
b Englewood, NJ, Apr 24, 45. *Study:* Williams Col, BA, 67; NY Univ, MA, 71. *Collections Arranged:* European Bronzes, 78; The Romantics to Rodin, French Nineteenth Century Sculpture (co-auth, catalog), Los Angeles, 80. *Pos:* Chester Dale Fel, Metrop Mus Art, 70-72; David E Finley Fel, Nat Gallery Art, 72-75; cur Europ sculpture, Los Angeles Co Mus Art, 75-80, cur decorative arts & European sculpture, 81- *Teaching:* Instr baroque, Univ Southern Calif, 77. *Awards:* Nat Endowment Arts Fel. *Res:* European sculpture, Renaissance through the 19th century. *Publ:* Auth, L S Adam's bust of Neptune, 75, Falguiere, the Female Nude & La Resistance, 77, Los Angeles Co Mus Bull, Los Angeles; auth, Early eighteenth century sculpture in Rome, Art J, Vol 39, No 1, 79; auth, The Romantics to Rodin: French Nineteenth Century Sculpture, 80. *Mailing Add:* Los Angeles Co Mus Art 5905 Wilshire Blvd Los Angeles CA 90036

FUSSINER, HOWARD
PAINTER
b New York, NY, May 25, 23. *Study:* Am Peoples Sch, 38-42; Art Students League, 46-47; Cooper Union, 47-49; Hans Hofmann Sch, 48; NY Univ, 49-52. *Work:* Everhart Mus, Scranton, Pa; Staten Island Inst Mus, New York; Slater Mus, Norwich, Conn; Mattatuck Mus, Waterbury, Conn; Colby Jr Col, New London, NH. *Comn:* Mural, NY Univ, 51-52. *Exhib:* Pa Acad Fine Arts Biennial, Philadelphia, 62; Silvermine Guild Artists Ann, 62; Boston Arts Festival, 63; Hartford Plaza 7, 64; New Haven Arts Festival, 64; and others. *Teaching:* Instr humanities, Morehouse Col, 51-55; instr art, Colby Jr Col, 57-60; prof art, Southern Conn State Col, 60- *Awards:* Best in Show, New Haven Arts Festival, 64, Waterbury Arts Festival, 68 & Conn Artists, Slater Mus, 77. *Media:* Oil, Watercolor. *Publ:* Auth, Organic integration in Cezanne's painting, summer 56 & Use of subject matter in recent art, spring 61, Art J. *Dealer:* Munson Gallery 33 Whitney Ave New Haven CT 06510. *Mailing Add:* 1 Everit St New Haven CT 06511

G

GABE, RON See Partz, Feliz

GABIN, GEORGE JOSEPH
PAINTER, INSTRUCTOR
b Brooklyn, NY, Apr 16, 31. *Study:* Brooklyn Mus Art Sch; Art Students League, with Reginald Marsh, Ivan Olinsky & Will Barnett. *Work:* Repub Savings & Loan, Washington, DC; Bank Boston. *Exhib:* Nat Acad Design, Allied Artists Am & Audubon Artists, 60-83; one-man shows, Carl Seimbab Gallery, 63 & 67, Gallery 7, 65, Guild Boston Artists, 72, Doll & Richards Gallery, 75 & Montserrat Sch Art, 83; Am Fedn Arts Nat Traveling Show, 64-65. *Teaching:* Instr illus & drawing, New Eng Sch Art, Boston, 64-70; instr drawing & painting, Montserrat Sch Visual Arts, 70- *Awards:* Grumbacher Gold Award, Holyoke Art Coun, 81; Lindley Dean Mem Award, 81; Stow Wengenroth Award, Rockport Art Asn, 82; and others. *Mem:* Allied Artists Am; Guild Boston Artists; Rockport Art Asn (chmn arts comt, 65-69). *Media:* Oil. *Mailing Add:* 791 Tremont St #405 Boston MA 02118

GABLE, JOHN OGLESBY
PAINTER
b Frankfort, Ky, Mar 7, 44. *Study:* Univ Ky; Art Ctr Col Design, BS(indust design), 66. *Work:* Ford Col, Detroit; Ford Motor Co; Budd Co; IBM; Nat Bank Detroit. *Comn:* Watercolors, comn by Alan Bond, Australia, 83, Freedom Syndicate, Newport, RI & New York, 83 & Robert Mill, Boston Classical Orch, 83. *Exhib:* 46th Nat Ann, Butler Inst Am Art, 82; 157th Ann Exhib, Nat Acad Design, New York, 82; Coe Kerr Gallery, New York, 82; one-man show, Payson-Weisberg Gallery, New York, 83. *Awards:* Wurdemann Prize, Nat Watercolor Soc. *Bibliog:* Alexander Bridge (auth), article, Am Artist, 83; Philip Isaacson (auth), article, Maine Sunday Telegram, 83. *Mem:* Nat Watercolor Soc. *Media:* Watercolor, Egg Tempera. *Dealer:* Barridoff Galleries 242 Middle St Portland ME 04101. *Mailing Add:* S Maine St Kennebunkport ME 04046

GABLIK, SUZI
PAINTER, LECTURER
b New York, NY, Sept 26, 34. *Study:* Black Mountain Col, NC, summer 51; Hunter Col, BA, 55, with Robert Motherwell. *Exhib:* Terry Dintenfass, Inc, New York, 78. *Teaching:* Vis prof fine arts, Univ S, Sewanee, Tenn, fall 82. *Bibliog:* London Correspondent, article in Art in Am. *Mem:* Int Asn Art Critics. *Publ:* Coauth, Pop Art Redefined, 69 & auth, Magritte, 70, New York Graphic Soc; auth, Progress in Art, Rizzoli, 77; auth, Has Modernism Failed?, Thames & Hudson, 84. *Dealer:* Terry Dintenfass Inc 50 W 57th St New York NY 10022. *Mailing Add:* 5 Westmoreland St London W 1 England United Kingdom

GABRIEL, HANNELORE
GOLDSMITH
Study: Apprentice under Master Goldsmith-Essen, Ger, 4 yrs; Gewerblicke Unterrichtsanstalt, Essen, Ger. *Work:* Ft Lauderdale Mus of Fine Arts, Fla. *Comn:* Presentation piece, Cleveland Area Arts Coun, Ohio, 76. *Exhib:* Goldsmiths 77, Phoenix Art Mus, Ariz, 77; May Show, Cleveland Mus Art, Ohio, 78; Am Goldsmiths' Now, Washington Univ, 78; Der Ring, Goldschmiedehaus, WGer, 78; Beaux Arts Designer Craftsmen, Columbus

Mus Art, 79. *Teaching:* Pvt classes, 74-75; instr, Oberlin Col, 75 & Penland Sch Crafts, 78- *Awards:* Horace Potter Mem Award at May Show, Cleveland Mus Art, 79; Purchase Award, Ohio Artists & Craftsmen Show, Massillon Mus Art, Ohio, 80. *Mem:* Am Crafts Coun; distinguished mem Soc NAm Goldsmiths; Ohio Designer-Craftsmen. *Res:* Traditional jewelry in the Nepalese culture area. *Publ:* Auth, articles on Nepalese jewelry in Ornament Mag. *Mailing Add:* 1469 Rosena Ave Madison OH 44057

GABRIELSON, WALTER OSCAR
PAINTER, DRAFTSMAN
b Orr, Minn, July 25, 35. *Study:* Univ Calif Los Angeles, BS(econ), 58; Chouinard Art Inst, 61-63; Otis Art Inst, BFA, 63, MFA, 65. *Work:* Chase Manhattan Bank, New York; Crocker Bank, Los Angeles; Los Angeles Co Mus Art; Hilton Hotel, Hollywood; Cedars-Sinai Hosp, Los Angeles. *Exhib:* Drawing Show, Ft Worth Art Mus, Tex, 69; Newport harbor Art Mus, Calif, 72 & 75; Six Calif Artists, Saskatoon, Sask Mus, Can, 78; Los Angeles Mus Art, 82; Karl Bornstein Gallery, 82; and others. *Pos:* Printer, Tamarind Lithography Workshop, 64-66; writer, Artweek, Art in Am, 74-79; vis artist, Univ Hawaii, 79, Claremont Grad Sch, 80. *Bibliog:* Article, Artnews, 4/83; article, Images & Issues, 5/6/83; article, Los Angeles Times, 12/10/83; and others. *Mem:* Los Angeles Inst Contemp Art (chmn jour comt, 74-75). *Media:* Oil, Watercolor; Charcoal. *Publ:* Auth, 41 Airplanes, 70 & auth, Pop Dawson, the Formative Years, 71, Dawson Aircraft; auth, Why suck the mainstream if you don't live in New York, Art in Am, 1-2/74; auth, Winged Beauty, Air Progress, 11/75; auth, The ironic Los Angeles artist, LAICA J, 10-11/76. *Dealer:* Karl Bornstein Gallery 1662 12th St Santa Monica CA 90404. *Mailing Add:* 2029 State St Santa Barbara CA 93105

GACH, GEORGE
PAINTER, SCULPTOR
b Budapest, Hungary, Jan 27, 09; US citizen. *Study:* Hungarian Acad Fine Art, grad. *Work:* Hungarian Nat Gallery, Budapest; Suffolk Mus, NY. *Comn:* Bas reliefs, Methodist Church, Dallas, Tex, 69-70; 24 bronze bas reliefs of Okla hist, Liberty Bank Okla, 72. *Exhib:* Audubon Artists, Allied Artists, Nat Sculpture Soc; 25 one-man shows incl Hammer Galleries, New York, 75-77. *Teaching:* Instr sculpture, Acad Beirut Lebanon, 48-52. *Awards:* Gold Medals, Nat Sculpture Soc, New York, NY, 70, Art League of Long Island, NY, 77 & Nat Art League, New York, NY, 77; and others. *Mem:* Allied Artists Am; Nat Sculpture Soc; Nat Art League; Hudson Valley Art Asn; Nassau Art League. *Media:* Bronze, Wood; Oil. *Dealer:* Hammer Galleries 51 E 57th St New York NY 10022; Harbour Gallery Cold Spring Harbor NY. *Mailing Add:* 212 Willow Roslyn Heights NY 11577

GAGE, FRANCES M
SCULPTOR
b Windsor, Ont, Aug 22, 24. *Study:* Ont Col Art; Art Students League; Ecole Beaux-Arts, Paris, Royal Soc Can scholar. *Work:* Univ Western Ont Med Sch; Womens Col Hosp, Toronto; Univ Ottawa; McMaster Univ; Queens Univ, Ont. *Comn:* Crest, Ont Hydro Seaway, Cornwall; fountain head, Cancer Hostel, Toronto; fountain, Albright Gardens, London, Ont; figure & reliefs, Prov Inst Trades Bldg, London, Ont; memorial, Charles Lake Gundy, Mt Pleasant Cemetery, Toronto; and others. *Exhib:* Royal Can Acad Art; Sculptors Soc Can; Ont Soc Art; FIDEM Exhib, Florence, Italy, 83. *Mem:* Royal Can Acad of Art. *Mailing Add:* 60 Birch Ave Toronto ON M4V 1C8 Canada

GAGNON, CHARLES
PAINTER, PHOTOGRAPHER
b Montreal, Que, Can, May 23, 34. *Study:* Parsons Sch Design, 56-57; NY Univ, 57; New York Sch Design, 57-59. *Work:* Nat Gallery Can, Ottawa; Hirshhorn Mus, Smithsonian Inst, Washington, DC; Montreal Mus Fine Arts, Musee D'Art Contemp, Que; Art Gallery Ont, Toronto. *Comn:* Lester B Pearson Mem, Closed Competition, Can Government, Ottawa, Ont, 74-75. *Exhib:* 14 Canadians, Hirshhorn Mus, Smithsonian Inst, Washington, DC, 77; one-man shows, Montreal Mus Fine Arts, Que, 78, Nat Gallery Can, Ottawa, Ont, 79 & Art Gallery, Ont, Toronto, 80; Nat Award, Banff Ctr Arts, Alta, 81. *Teaching:* Assoc prof photog, Concordia Univ, Montreal, Que, 67-75; prof visual arts, Univ Ottawa, Ont, 75- *Bibliog:* Philip Fry (auth), Charles Gagnon, Montreal Mus Fine Arts, 78; Dore Ashton (auth), Charles Gagnon's point of view, Artscanada, 8-9/79; David Burnett (auth), Charles Gagnon--The Ambiguous Object, Vanguard & Vancouver Art Gallery, 79. *Media:* Oil. *Dealer:* Yajima Galerie 307 Ste Catherine W Montreal PQ Can H3X 2A3. *Mailing Add:* 3510 Addington St Montreal PQ H4A 3G6 Can

GAGNON, CHARLES EUGENE
SCULPTOR, CONSULTANT
b Minneapolis, Minn, Feb 24, 34. *Study:* Univ Minn, AA, 56, BS, 58 & MEd, 60; Minneapolis Sch Art, 59; with Berthold Schiwetz, Florence, Italy, 64-65 & with Jacques Lipchitz, 68. *Work:* Saint Marys Hosp, Rochester, Minn. *Comn:* Renaissance Man and Woman, Kenyon Col, Ohio, 73; Conrad N Hilton (sculpture), Mayo Clin, Rochester, 74; Hubert H Humphrey (life size portrait), New Govt Ctr, Worthington, Minn, 79; Mother and Child, Mayo Clinic, Rochester, Minn, 80; and others. *Exhib:* Nat Acad Galleries, New York, 62; Nat Arts Club, New York, 62; Walker Art Ctr Biennial, Minneapolis, 62; Minneapolis Art Inst, 63; one-man show, Defiance Col, 72. *Teaching:* Instr sculpture, Univ Minn, Rochester, 72; vis artist sculpture, Defiance Col, 72. *Awards:* One of ten students from US chosen to teach art in Europe, Univ Minn, 57-58; Purchase Award & Two-Man Show Award, Madison Ave Art Gallery, New York, 62. *Bibliog:* Kling (auth), The Sculpture of Charles E Gagnon, Preview, Collegeville, Minn, 68; Hardie (auth), Charles E Gagnon, Mohave, Kingman, Ariz, 73; Ehrbar (auth), A Ten-year Dance to

the Music of Bronze, Kenyon Col, 83. *Media:* Bronze. *Publ:* Contribr, An artist fulfilled, 71; contribr, Progeny, 73; contribr, Kenyon College, Its Third Half Century, 75; contribr, An Art Tour of Saint Mary's, 75; contribr, Voice of a New Age, 76. *Mailing Add:* PO Box 4 Rochester MN 55903

GAHAGAN, JAMES (EDWARD), JR
PAINTER, EDUCATOR
b New York, NY, Sept 20, 27. *Study:* Goddard Col, Plainfield, Vt, BA, 51; Hans Hofmann Sch Fine Art, New York, 52-58. *Work:* Provincetown Mus; Univ Calif Berkeley Mus; Metrop Mus Art, New York; Chrysler Mus, Norfolk, Va. *Exhib:* Hans Hofmann Students, Whitney Mus, New York, 63; 10th Street Days Co-ops of the 50's, Ward-Nasse Landmark Galleries, New York, 77; Days Lumberyard Studios Provincetown 1914-71; Provincetown Mus, Mass, 78 & 81; Tirca Karlis, Provincetown, Mass, 81; and others. *Pos:* Pres, Artist Tenants Asn, New York, 60-62 & 65-66; co-ed, New York Element, 68-72; bd trustees, Printmaking Workshop, New York, 70-76. *Teaching:* Instr painting & drawing, Pratt Inst, Brooklyn, NY, 64-71; instr painting, Columbia Univ Grad Sch, NY, 68-71; dir & instr painting & drawing, James Gahagan Sch Fine Art, Woodbury, Vt, 69-73; prof & chmn painting & drawing aesthetics, Goddard Col, Plainfield, Vt, 71-79; instr, Lesley Col, Cambridge, Mass, 81; instr, Vt Col, 83- *Awards:* Prize, Cape Cod Art Asn, Mass, 57; Longview Fund Purchase Grant, 58. *Bibliog:* Irving Sandler (auth), Thirteen Americans under thirty, Art News Mag, 58; Eileen Tolchin (auth), Action when enough people try, The Villager New York, 62; Gilbert Millstien (auth), New York: True North, Doubleday, 64. *Mem:* Art Resource Assoc, Woodbury, Vt (pres, 73-75, bd trustees, 73-79); Vt Coun Arts; and others. *Media:* Oil, Tempera. *Publ:* Illusr, Loaf of Earth, Spruce Mountain Press, 58; co-ed New York Element, 68-72; contribr, J Aesthetic Educ, Univ Ill Press, Urbana, 69; contribr, VizArt, 76-80. *Mailing Add:* RFD 1 Box 116 East Calais VT 05650

GAINES, ALAN JAY
PRINTMAKER, PUBLISHER
b New York, NY, Aug 23, 42. *Study:* NY Univ, BS, 65; New Sch, Parsons Sch Design, with John Ross, 72-74. *Work:* South Street Seaport Mus, Mus Gallery, New York; and others. *Comn:* Nantucket Whalers & New Bedford Whalers, 77 & Develop of Am Transportation, 78, Collector's Guild, New York; Gloucester Schooners (etching), Bk of Month Club & 260 Club, 77; marine etchings, 77 & two railroad etchings, 78, Graphics Guild, Div of Doubleday, New York; spec series five important & hist Am ships, Am Express, 78; America's Maritime Heritage (four etchings), Franklin Mint, Pa, 81; and others. *Exhib:* One-man shows, South Street Seaport Mus, 74, Oestreicher Gallery, New York, 74, Wiseman Gallery, Newport, RI, 76, Redwood Libr & Atheneum, Newport, RI, 79 & Providence Pub Libr, RI, 81. *Bibliog:* Joseph Patrick Henry (auth), Artist of the sea, The Franklin Mint Almanac, 7/75; article, RI Mag, 9/80. *Media:* Mixed. *Mailing Add:* 53 Everett St Newport RI 02840

GAINES, WILLIAM ROBERT
HISTORIAN, PAINTER
b Madison, Va, Aug 12, 27. *Study:* Pa Mil Col; Va Commonwealth Univ, BFA; Columbia Univ, MFA; and with Renato Guttuso. *Work:* Univ Va, Charlottesville; Va Polytech Inst & State Univ, Blacksburg; Retreat for the Sick, Richmond; Philip Morris Inc; First & Merchants Nat Bank. *Exhib:* Five Va Artists Biennials, 49-65; Abingdon Sq Painters, New York, 53; Va Beach Boardwalk Exhib, 58; Va Commonwealth Univ, 64; one-man exhib, Tappahannock, Va, 72. *Collections Arranged:* Art Nouveau (with catalog); Francisco Goya: Portraits in Paintings, Prints & Drawings (with catalog), 72; Sculpture by Willi Gutmann, 72; 12 American Painters (with catalog), 74. *Pos:* Registr, Va Mus, 51-53, artmobile cur, 53-54, supvr educ, 54-56, 57-62, head progs div, 62-; dir, Inst Contemp Art Va Mus. *Teaching:* Instr painting, drawing & art hist, Va Mus, Richmond, 54-56, 57 & 62; dir, Gov Sch Gifted, Mus Ctr, 73. *Awards:* Best in Show Awards, Va Beach Boardwalk Exhib, 58 & Thalhimers Invitational, 63; James R Short Award, SEMC, 81. *Mem:* Am Asn Mus; Assoc Coun Arts. *Media:* Oil, Acrylic. *Publ:* Auth, Art kits, Arts Va, Vol VI, No I; auth, Virginia Museum: Two pioneer programs, Mus News, Vol 50, No 2; producer, 12 American Painters (TV), 74 & Style & Expression: Encounter I (TV), 75. *Mailing Add:* Va Mus of Fine Arts Boulevard & Grove Ave Richmond VA 23221

GAITHER, EDMUND B
MUSEUM DIRECTOR, HISTORIAN
b Great Falls, SC, Oct 6, 44. *Study:* Morehouse Col, BA, 66; Ga State Col; Brown Univ, MA, 68. *Collections Arranged:* Afro-Am Artists: New York & Boston (with catalogue), Jamaica Art Since the Thirties, Henry O Tanner, A Romantic Realist, Home Folks Africa, For Us, Abdias Do Nascimento: A Brazilian Brother, African Gods in Brazil, Our Elders, Crite & Dames, Ah Haiti, Glimpses of Voudou, Haiti-Haiti, Bannister & Duncanson, Twentieth Century Afro-Am Artists, Mus Fine Arts, Boston. *Pos:* Dir & cur, Mus Nat Ctr Afro-Am Artists, Boston, 69-; dir visual arts prog, Elma Lewis Sch Fine Arts, Boston, 69-; spec consult, Mus Fine Arts, Boston, 69- *Teaching:* Asst prof art hist, Boston Univ, 70-78; lectr art hist, Wellesley Col & Harvard Col, 71-76. *Bibliog:* An American Collector, Mus Art, RI Sch Design, Providence, 68; Robert H Glauber (auth), Black American Artists, Ill Bell Tel Co, 71; Leo Twiggs (auth), Opinion, Mus News, 5/72. *Mem:* Nat Conf Artists; Col Art Asn; Pan-African Conf of Artists; Boston Black Artists Asn. *Res:* Historical and critical discussion of Afro-American art. *Publ:* Contribr, A new criticism needed, New York Times, 5/70; ed, Affairs of Black Artists, 71; contribr, Artists Proofs, The Annual of Prints and Printmaking, NY Graphic Soc, 72; contribr, Afro-American Art, in: Negro Reference Book, Phelps-Stokes Found, New York, NY, 73; and numerous others. *Mailing Add:* 598 Walk Hill St Mattapan MA 02126

GALAS, PHILIP-DIMITRI
CONCEPTUAL ARTIST, WRITER

b San Diego, Calif, July 21, 54. *Study:* Southwark Theatre Arts Lab, 72-74; Etienne Decroux, Paris, 74; Univ Calif, San Diego, BA, 74. *Work:* Salon Palazzo Capitano Popolo, Rome; Vanhan Galleria, Univ Helsinki, Finland; Western Front Gallery, Vancouver; Galerie Watari, Tokyo. *Comn:* Performance, Ctr Music Experiment, La Jolla, Calif, 77, 78, 81 & 83; Mail Art Exhib, PS II Gallery, San Diego, 82; performance, Open Space Gallery, Victoria, 83 & Cast Theatre, Hollywood, 83-84. *Exhib:* Art Cabaret Night, Western Front Gallery, Vancouver, 78; Baby D in Person, 544 Natoma St, San Francisco, 82; Performance Hell, Ctr Music Experiment, La Jolla, Calif, 83; Performance Hell #2, Open Space Gallery, Victoria, 83; Avante-Vaudeville, 80 Langton St, San Francisco, 83. *Collections Arranged:* Spotlight Technique, 81 & 82; Art-Cabaret Night, 81; Festival of New Arts (auth, catalog), 83. *Pos:* Pres, Exoti Cards, 79- & Avante-Vaudeville, 81-; performance cur, Sushi, San Diego, 81-83. *Teaching:* Lectr performance, Univ Calif, San Diego, 78-, San Diego State Col, 78- & San Diego Art Inst. *Awards:* Festival Award, Performance Hell, Partners for Livable Places, 83; Freeways Award, Avante-Vaudeville, Cast Theatre, 83. *Bibliog:* Thomas Bonn (auth), article, Paperback Quart, 4/82; Roger Rose (auth), New form of art, 2/83 & Hell business, 7/83, Los Angeles Times. *Res:* History of performance, especially 1890s to 1945; american art performance styles. *Publ:* Auth, Society general for extermination of Muriel Mathud, 76-77 & Bearded lady's manifesto, 79, Assassins; auth, Microphone: Loves of a star, Allos-Lingua, 80; auth, Exotic postcards, Calif Mag, 82; auth, Mona Rogers before she never got famous, Crawl Out Window, 83. *Dealer:* Patty Aande Gallery 660 Ninth Ave San Diego CA 92101. *Mailing Add:* 2425 First Ave San Diego CA 92101

GALE, PEGGY
WRITER, CURATOR

b Mackenzie, Guyana, May 18, 44; Can citizen. *Study:* Univ Toronto, 63-67; Univ degli Studi, Florence, Italy, 65-66; Univ Toronto, BA, 67. *Pos:* Educ officer, Art Gallery of Ont, Toronto, 67-74; asst film & video officer, Can Coun, Ottawa, 74-75; video dir, Art Metropole, Toronto, 75-79; exec dir, A Space, 79-81. *Teaching:* Instr, Nova Scotia Col Art & Design, Vancouver Art Gallery, Ont Col Art & Emily Carr Col Art; lectr video & performance art, var schs & galleries, 75- *Awards:* Canada Coun A Grant, 83. *Mem:* Int Asn Art Critics. *Res:* Media art in Canada, 1965-1985, specializing in performance, video, installations: chronology and thematic assessment. *Publ:* Auth, Video has captured our imagination, Parachute, summer 77; co-ed, Performance by Artists, 79 & Museums by Artists, 83, Art Metropole; auth, Earlier Askevold, In: David Askevold (catalog), Stedelijk van Abbemuseum, Eindhoven, 81; auth, History lesson, In: Performance and Multi-Disciplinarity: Post-Modernism, Parachute, 81; auth, Zu Performance und Mediakunst, In: Okanada (catalog), Akad der Künste, Berlin, 82. *Mailing Add:* 137 Summerhill Ave Toronto ON M4T 1B1 Canada

GALE, WILLIAM HENRY
PAINTER, DESIGNER

b Yonkers, NY, May 3, 15. *Study:* Columbia Univ; Art Students League; Nat Acad Design; Cooper Union; spec study with John Pike & Charles Kinghan. *Work:* Springfield Fine Arts Mus, Mass; Jasper Rand Mus, Westfield, Mass; Vt Art Ctr, Manchester; Manhattan Savings Bank, New York; Am Tel & Tel, New York; and others. *Comn:* Housatonic, NY, 70; Old Vt Landmarks, New York Life Ins Co, 72; Am Tel & Tel, New York; Merrill Lynch; Int Bus Machines; and others. *Exhib:* Nat Acad Design, 67-70; Am Watercolor Soc, New York, 68-73; Smithsonian Inst, 69; Mus Fine Arts, Springfield, Mass, 69-78; Rockport Art Asn, 70-79 & 82; Worcester Mus Fine Arts, Mass, 74-75; Allied Artists New York, 78; Butler Mus, 82; and others. *Pos:* Artist-designer, Ruth Ruthrauff & Ryan, New York, 35-40; art dir-designer, Batten Barton Durstine, Osborn, New York, 40-68. *Awards:* Quimby Award, Smithsonian Inst, 69; First Awards Mass Bicentennial, Springfield Fine Arts Mus, 75; Watercolor Award, Rockport Art Asn, 83; and others. *Bibliog:* Lee Sheridan (auth), New England painter, Springfield News, Mass, 63; Watercolorists, Festival of the Arts, Vt Art Ctr, 69. *Mem:* Am Watercolor Soc; Salmagundi Club; Rockport Art Asn; Acad Artists (vpres, 73-75); Hudson Valley Art Asn. *Media:* Watercolor, Oil. *Dealer:* Grand Central Art Gallery 40 Vanderbilt Ave New York NY 10017; Ellsworth Gallery 800 Hopmeadow Simsbury CT 06070. *Mailing Add:* 14 Hunting Lane Box 156 Wilbraham MA 01095

GALEN, ELAINE
PAINTER, SCULPTOR

b New York, NY, July 12, 28. *Study:* Philadelphia Mus Sch Art, dipl, 50; Univ Pa, BA, 51; Art Students League, 55-59; NY Univ, MA, 63; major study with Morris Kantor. *Work:* Philadelphia Mus Art; Mus Rigaud, France; Rey Collection, Perpignan, France; Atelier 45; and numerous others. *Exhib:* Whitney Mus Am Art Ann, New York, 61; Brooklyn Mus Int, 63 & 78; NJ State Arts Coun, 70; one-person show, Pa Acad Fine Arts, Peale House, 72; State Mus Ill, 74; Art Inst Chicago, 78; plus numerous solo exhibs and others. *Pos:* Consult & lectr-teacher, Developing Art Progs, NJ Schs, 68-72. *Teaching:* Lectr hist art, painting & drawing, NY Univ, 70-73, Prairie State Col, Chicago Heights, Ill, 74-, Lake Forest Col, 78-80, Manhattanville Col, 81- *Awards:* Nat Print Award, Hunterdon Ctr, NJ, 70; Am Iron & Steel Inst Award for Design Excellence, 72; plus others. *Mem:* Print Club, Philadelphia (artist mem); Col Art Asn; Col Art Asn Am; Women's Caucus Art. *Media:* Oil, Pencil-Ink; Stainless Steel. *Mailing Add:* Box 325 Millwood Rd RFD 1 Mt Kisco NY 10549

GALLAGHER, CAROLE
PHOTOGRAPHER, WRITER

b New York, NY, July 16, 50. *Study:* New Sch, with Philippe Halsman, 73; Hunter Col, City Univ New York, with Tony Smith, Robert Morris, Doug Ohlson & Rosalind Krauss, MA, 76. *Work:* Bibliot Nat, Paris; State Mus, Pazin, Yugoslavia. *Exhib:* Douglas Huebler Retrospective, Van Abbe Mus, Eindhoven, Holland, 79; Greenhouse, 81 & All the Time, 81, Leo Castelli Gallery; Surrealist Photography, Dept Cult, Vienna, 81; New New York, Fine Arts Gallery, Fla State Univ, Tallahassee, 82 & Phoenix Art Mus, 83. *Teaching:* Instr photog, Col New Rochelle, NY, 77-78 & Kingsborough Col, City Univ New York, 77-79. *Awards:* MacDowell Fel, 80 & 82. *Bibliog:* Paul Stimson (auth), Between the signs, Art in Am, 10/79; Rene Denizot & R Barry (auths), Il Est Temps--It's About Time, Yvon Lambert, Paris, 80; Carole Gallagher at Leo Castelli, Express, fall 81. *Publ:* Illusr, Muscles, 83 & Punch, 83, Avon. *Mailing Add:* 79 Mercer St New York NY 84770

GALLAGHER, MICHAEL B
PAINTER

b Los Angeles, Calif. *Study:* Univ Calif, Los Angeles, BFA, 67; Yale Univ, MFA(summer fel), 70. *Work:* Guggenehim Mus, New York. *Comn:* Mural, Swedish Indust Develop Corp, Conn, 74. *Exhib:* Art Scene, Swedish Mus, New York, 74; Abstract Illusionism, Mus Fine Art, Springfield, Mass, 78 & Ulrich Mus, Kansas City, 78; Abstract Painting, Pittsburgh Mus Art & Crafts, 78 & Aldrich Mus, Ridgefield, Conn, 79; Painting, Bassel Art Fair, Ger, 79; Reality of Illusion, Denver Art Mus, Colo, 79; Realist Space, C W Post Art Gallery, Greenvalde, NY, 79; Okla Art Ctr, 81. *Awards:* Eli Harwood Schless Draughtsmanship Award, Yale Univ Art Gallery, 70. *Bibliog:* Jay Richard DeBiaso (auth), Abstract Illusions, Mus Fine Arts, Springfield, Mass, 78. *Media:* Acrylic. *Dealer:* Louis K Meisel Gallery 141 Prince St New York NY 10012. *Mailing Add:* 84 Wooster St New York NY 10012

GALLANDER, CATHLEEN S
MUSEUM DIRECTOR

b San Antonio, Tex, Feb 4, 31. *Study:* Univ Tex, Austin, BA(sociol); Harvard Univ, scholar art hist; Harvard Bus Sch, Inst Arts Admin. *Pos:* Dir, Art Mus of S Tex, Corpus Christi; panelist, Nat Endowment for the Arts. *Mem:* Col Art Asn Am; Am Asn Mus; Am Fedn Arts; Western Asn Art Mus; Asn Art Mus Dir (trustee); Tex Mus Asn (trustee). *Mailing Add:* Art Mus of South Texas 1902 N Shoreline Corpus Christi TX 78402

GALLES, ARIE ALEXANDER
PAINTER, EDUCATOR

b Tashkent, Russia, Oct 29, 44; US citizen. *Study:* Temple Univ, BFA, 68; Univ Wis, MFA, 71. *Pos:* Dir, Madison Acad of Art & Morris Gallery, 77-80. *Teaching:* Asst prof art & chmn fine arts dept, Fairleigh Dickinson Univ, 72-81, assoc prof, 81- *Bibliog:* Article, Chicago Suns Times, 9/23/79; article, Phoenix Gazette, 12/27/80; Robert Paschal & Robert Anderson (auths), Advanced Air Brush Technique--The Art of the Dot, Van Nostrand Rineholt, 84. *Dealer:* OK Harris West 4200 N Marshall Way Scottsdale AZ 85251; Zolla/Lieberman Gallery 356 W Huron Chicago IL 60610. *Mailing Add:* 81 Ridgedale Ave Madison NJ 07940

GALLI, STANLEY WALTER
ILLUSTRATOR, PAINTER

b San Francisco, Calif. *Study:* Calif Sch Fine Arts, San Francisco; Art Ctr Sch, Los Angeles. *Work:* Air Force Mus, Colo; Baseball Hall of Fame Mus, Cooperstown, NY; Palm Springs Desert Mus; Hall Fame Soc Illusr, NY. *Comn:* Conserv series, Weyerhaeuser Co, Tacoma, Wash, 52-68; wildlife paintings, Calif Casualty Group Collection, San Mateo, 73-78. *Exhib:* One-man shows, Nut Tree Gallery, Calif, 76, Crocker Art Mus, Sacramento, Calif, 80, Robert Mondavi Winery, Calif, 81 & Charles & Emma Frye Art Mus, Seattle, 83; NY Hist Soc, 77; Oakland Mus, Calif, 78; two-man exhib, Palm Springs Desert Mus, Calif, 78; and others. *Pos:* Illusr, Saturday Evening Post, 50-68, Reader's Digest Mag & Condensed Bks, 60-78, McCall's Mag, 60-67 & US Postal Serv Stamp Design, 68-78. *Teaching:* Instr advert art, San Francisco City Col, 68-76. *Awards:* Silver Medal, Dillon Lauritzen Award, Los Angeles Art Dir Club, 58; Best US Postage Stamp of Yr, Postal Commemorative Soc, 68, 72 & 78. *Mem:* Soc Animal Artists; Soc Illusr New York; Soc Illusr, San Francisco. *Media:* Oil, Acrylic. *Mailing Add:* PO Box 66 Kentfield CA 94914

GALLO, ENZO D
SCULPTOR

b Italy, Oct 25, 27. *Study:* San Alejandro Univ/Fine Arts, Havana, Cuba, MFA; Senatus Univ Verae Arademirus, BA; study with Jose Sicri, sculptor & Augusto Valderama, painter, Havana. *Work:* Pagani Mus, Milan, Italy; Young Circle, Hollywood, Fla; Town of Padula, Italy. *Comn:* Sculpture & mosaic murals, Hollywood Mem Gardens, Fla; mosaic murals, Am Savings & Loan, Miami Beach; sculpture, Doral Beach Club, Miami Beach; sculpture (bronze), Hallandale Pub Libr. *Exhib:* Metrop Mus, Miami, 75; one-man shows, Heller Bldg, Miami, 77 & Hollywood Art & Cult Ctr, Fla; Latin Am Artist of the Southeastern US, Lowe Art Mus, Miami, 78; First Ann Art Competition, Nova Univ, 79. *Teaching:* Prof sculpture, San Alejandro Inst Fine Arts, Havana, Cuba & Broward Adult Educ, 62-65. *Awards:* Award of Merit, Am Inst Archit; First Prize Sculpture, Seven Lively Arts, Hollywood, Fla; Gold Medal, Fourth Nat Exhib, Campanine Gallery, 79. *Mem:* Fla Sculpture Asn; Artist Equity Asn Fla (pres, 75-78). *Media:* Marble, Bronze. *Mailing Add:* 500 N Ansin Blvd Hallandale FL 33009

GALLO, FRANK
SCULPTOR, EDUCATOR
b Toledo, Ohio, Jan 13, 33. *Study:* Toledo Mus Sch Art, BFA, 54; Cranbrook Acad Art, 55; Univ Iowa, MFA, 59. *Work:* Mus Mod Art, New York; Whitney Mus Am Art, New York; Art Inst Chicago; Los Angeles Mus Art; Cleveland Mus Art; plus others. *Comn:* Commemorative Medal for Civil Eng, Univ Ill. *Exhib:* Ann, Whitney Mus Am Art, 64-67, Young America, 65; Butler Inst Am Art, Youngstown, Ohio, 65; Toronto Int Sculpture Symposium, 67; Kennedy Mem Exhib; Venice Biennale, 68; Twelve Erotic Fantasies, Circle Gallery, Ltd, 74; plus others. *Teaching:* Prof sculpture, Univ Ill, 60- *Awards:* First Prize, Des Moines, 58; Prize, Interior Valley Competition, Cincinnati, 61; Guggenheim Found Fel, 66. *Mailing Add:* Dept of Art Univ Ill Urbana IL 61801

GALLO, WILLIAM VICTOR
CARTOONIST, ILLUSTRATOR
b New York, NY, Dec 28, 22. *Study:* Columbia Exten Cartoonists & Illusr. *Work:* Baseball Hall Fame, Cooperstown, NY. *Exhib:* One-man show, Spectrum Art Gallery, New York, 80. *Pos:* With NY Daily News, 41-, sports cartoonist, 60- *Awards:* Page One Awards, NY Newspaper Guild, 65, 68, 69, 70, 72, 73, 75, 77-81; Best Sports Cartoonist, Nat Cartoonist Soc, 68, 69, 70, 72 & 73; Outstanding Achievement, Alumni Soc Sch Visual Arts, 75; and others. *Mem:* Nat Cartoonists Soc; Soc Silurians; and others. *Mailing Add:* 1 Mayflower Dr Yonkers NY 10710

GAMBLE, KATHRYN ELIZABETH
MUSEUM DIRECTOR
b Van Wert, Ohio, Aug 19, 15. *Study:* Oberlin Col, AB, 37; Dayton Art Inst, 38; Newark Mus, cert, 41; New York Univ Grad Sch Fine Arts, MA, 48. *Collections Arranged:* Montclair in Manhattan, exhib of permanent collection, 61; American Painting Collection (with catalog), Montclair Art Mus; Asher B Durand Retrospective, 71; A B Durand (with catalog). *Pos:* Dir, Montclair Art Mus, 52-79, emer dir, 80. *Teaching:* Supvr art, Covington Pub Schs, Ohio, 38-40. *Mem:* Am Asn Mus; NJ Mus Coun; Int Coun Mus. *Mailing Add:* PO Box 847 Hernando FL 32642

GAMMON, JUANITA-LA VERNE
PAINTER, EDUCATOR
b McLeansboro, Ill. *Study:* Univ Ill, BFA & MFA. *Work:* Work in many pvt collections. *Comn:* Many pvt comns. *Exhib:* Dream Mus, Champaign, Ill, 70; McKinley Found, Urbana, Ill, 70; Nat Acad Design, New York, 70-71; Illini Union Gallery, Univ Ill, 71; Parkland Col, 75, 79-83; and others. *Pos:* Judge, local, regional & nat art exhibs, 67-; art lectr & critic & consult curric design, 67-; supvr, Champaign Co Art Show, 69- *Teaching:* Head dept Art & Commun Career Prog, Parkland Col, Champaign, 67- *Mem:* Ad Club Champaign-Urbana (treas, mem bd, 71-). *Media:* Acrylic, Oil, Watercolor; Graphic Design and Illustration. *Mailing Add:* 711 W Healey Champaign IL 61820

GAMMON, REGINALD ADOLPHUS
EDUCATOR, PAINTER
b Philadelphia, Pa, Mar 31, 21. *Study:* Philadelphia Mus Col Art, cert; Tyler Sch Fine Art, Temple Univ, one yr. *Work:* Chase Manhattan Bank, Fine Arts Div, New York; Denison Col, Ohio; Endicott Bd Educ, NY; plus numerous pvt collections. *Exhib:* New Voices--15 New York Artists, Am Greetings Gallery, New York, 68;; Afro-Am Artists Since 1950, Brooklyn Col, 68; 30 Contemp Black Artists, Minneapolis Inst Art, Minn (travel), 68-70; Afro-Am Artists, New York & Boston, Mus Fine Arts, Boston, 70; Blacks: USA: 1973, New York Cult Ctr, 73. *Pos:* Artist, Lifton, Gold & Asher Advert, New York, 55-64; artist in residence, New York Bd Educ, 67-69. *Teaching:* Assoc prof humanities, painting & drawing, Western Mich Univ, 70-82. *Awards:* Fac Res Fel & Grant, Western Mich Univ, 75. *Bibliog:* Eugene Redden (auth), Reggie (film), prod by Western Mich Univ, 71; Judith Wragge Chase (auth), Afro-American Art & Crafts, Van Nostrand Reinhold, 72; Barry Schwartz (auth), Humanism in 20th Century Art, Praeger, 74. *Mem:* Col Art Asn; fel MacDowell Colony. *Media:* Oil, Acrylic. *Mailing Add:* 2123 Amherst Ave Kalamazoo MI 49008

GANS, LUCY C
SCULPTOR, EDUCATOR
b Plainfield, NJ, Nov 18, 49. *Study:* Art Students League, 70; Lake Erie Col, BFA, 71; Pratt Inst, with Calvin Albert & George McNeil, MFA, 74. *Work:* Lehigh Univ, Westtown Sch, Pa. *Exhib:* May Show, Cleveland Mus Art, 74; Drawings USA, Smithsonian Inst Traveling Exhib, 76-79; solo exhib, Westchester State Col, Pa, 79; For the Love of Drawing, Kemerer Mus, Bethlehem, Pa, 81; Del Biennial, Univ Del, Newark, 81; Installation of Drawings & Sculpture, Muse Gallery, Philadelphia, 83. *Collections Arranged:* Womens Caucus Art Nat Exhib (auth, catalog), 84. *Teaching:* Vis lectr sculpture & drawing, Lake Erie Col, Ohio, 74-75; instr sculpture, Univ SAla, 76-77; asst prof sculpture, drawing & painting, Lehigh Univ, Pa, 81- *Mem:* Col Art Asn; Womens Caucus Art. *Dealer:* Muse Gallery 1915 Walnut St Philadelphia PA 19103. *Mailing Add:* 820 N 6th St Allentown PA 18102

GANTZ, ANN CUSHING
PAINTER, INSTRUCTOR
b Dallas, Tex, Aug 27, 35. *Study:* Memphis Acad of Art; Southwestern Univ, Memphis; Newcomb Col Tulane Univ, New Orleans, La, BFA, 55. *Work:* Dallas Mus Fine Arts, Tex; Denver Mus, Colo; Smithsonian Inst, Washington, DC; Boston Mus, Mass; Los Angeles State Mus. *Exhib:* Ann Exhib, Springfield Mus, Mass, 56 & 57; Painting Ann, Portland Mus, 56, 59 & 60; Oklahoma City Art Ctr, 56-58; Painting & Sculpture Ann, Nat Acad

of Design, New York, 57, 60; Norfolk Mus, Va, 58, 59; Printmaking Today, Brooklyn Mus, NY, 59; Ann Shows, Ark Art Ctr, Little Rock, 59, 60 & 61. *Teaching:* Instr printmaking & painting, Dallas Mus of Fine Arts Sch, 56-62; instr painting, printmaking & drawing, Cushing Galleries Sch of Studio Art, 62-79, instr, Cushing Studio, 79- *Awards:* TFAA Artist of Year Award, 79; Oak Award, 81; McMurray Found Award, 83. *Mem:* Dallas Print & Drawing Soc (pres, 58-60); YWCA Art Comt. *Media:* Oil, Acrylic. *Dealer:* Stewart Gallery 12610 Coit Rd Dallas TX 75251. *Mailing Add:* 4654 Edmondson Dallas TX 75209

GANTZ, JEANNE A
PRINTMAKER, ADMINISTRATOR
b Canton, Ohio, Nov 22, 29. *Study:* Goucher Col; Univ Calif, Berkeley; Crown Pt Press, apprenticed intaglio printing with Kathan Brown. *Comn:* Intaglio ed, comn by Marvin Spohn, 69-75, Arthur Okamura, 68-75, Beth Van Hoesen, 69-71, Robert Fried, San Francisco, 74-75 & Fritz Scholder, Scottsdale, Ariz, 75. *Pos:* Gallery dir, Artifactrie, Berkeley, 68-70; asst printer, Crown Pt Press, Berkeley, 69-71; dir/owner, El Dorado Press, Berkeley, 71- *Teaching:* Instr intaglio printing, Univ Calif Exten, Berkeley, 69-71. *Mem:* Calif Soc Printmakers (coun mem, 70). *Mailing Add:* 1516 Beverly Place Albany CA 94706

GANZ, SYLVIA SQUIRES See Tykie

GAONA ADAME, JOSE JULIO
PAINTER, PRINTMAKER
b Aguascalientes, Mex, Apr 12, 43. *Study:* Inst Aguascalentense de Bellas Artes, 59-63; Escuela Nac de Artes Plasticas, San Carlos, with Trinidad Osorio Ramirez, 63-67. *Work:* Inst Mex, Norteamericano de Relaciones Culturales; Inst Aguascalentense de Bellas Artes; Inst Jaliciense de Bellas Artes, Guadalajara; Salon de la Plastica Mexicana; Mus de Artes Plasticas de la Universidad Autonoma de Veracruz. *Exhib:* Mex-Art Int, La Jolla Gallery, Calif, 79; Paisaje, Sala Las Galerias, Mexico City, 80; Salon de Dibujo, Salon de la Plastica Mexicana, Mexico City, 80; Contemp Art Mex, Luther Ctr, San Antonio, Tex, 80; Nueva Escuela Mexicana, Art Mus, San Antonio, Tex, 81. *Teaching:* Art engraving, Escuela Nat de Artes Plasticas, San Carlos, 67-72. *Awards:* IV Concurso Nac de Pintura, Inst Nac dela Juventud Mexicano, 69. *Bibliog:* Luis Chavez (auth), Derroche de Poesia y Color, Revista Intamericana Vision, 81; Efrain Gutierrez (auth), Luz y Color de Gaona, 10/12/81 & Juan Servera (auth), Jose Julio Gaona--El Pintor y el Hombre, 9/21/81, El Nac. *Mem:* Salon de la Plastica Mexicana; Fomento Cultural Mexico. *Media:* Oil; Engraving. *Mailing Add:* Sol #58-58 Col Guerrero Del Cuauhtemoc 06300 Mexico DF Mexico

GARBATY, MARIE-LOUISE
COLLECTOR, PATRON
b Berlin, Ger, Mar 9, 10; US citizen. *Study:* Univ Berlin. *Mem:* Am Fedn Arts; Renaissance Soc Am; China Inst Am; Carnegie Inst; fel perpetuity Metrop Mus Art, New York; life fel Mus Fine Arts, Boston; benefactor & life mem Chrysler Mus; hon mem Allentown Mus Art. *Interests:* Patron to many museums, universities & colleges nationally. *Collection:* Fifteenth and seventeenth century Dutch and Flemish paintings; decorative art of the Renaissance; antique Syrian glass; fifteenth to eighteenth century blue white China; antique oriental textiles; old English silver; antique English furniture; Egyptian antiquities. *Mailing Add:* New York NY 10021

GARCHIK, MORTON LLOYD
PAINTER, PRINTMAKER
b Brooklyn, NY, June 25, 29. *Study:* Brooklyn Mus, painting with Max Beckmann & printmaking with Gabor Peterdi; Sch Visual Art, New York. *Work:* Minn Mus Art; Libr Cong. *Comn:* Book cover for Gimpel the Fool, Avon Paperback, 63. *Exhib:* One-man show, Union of Am Hebrew Congregations, 63; DePauw Univ 7th Ann Contemp Am Printmakers Exhib, 65; Ohio Univ 7th Ann, 66; Seattle Art Mus Int Exhibs, 66 & 67; two-man show, Art Corner, Milburn, NJ, 75; Artists Equity, New York, 78. *Pos:* Art dir, Commun Channels, Inc, New York, 72-77. *Awards:* First Prize, Drawing, Sch Visual Art, 55; Purchase Award, Olivet Col 5th Nat Print Exhib, 65. *Mem:* Artists Equity of New York. *Media:* Woodcut, etching, serigraph, lithograph; acrylic; wood, clay. *Publ:* Auth, Art Fundamentals: Basics of Drawing, Painting, Sculpture & Printmaking, Stravon Educ Press; auth, Creative Visual Thinking: How to Think Up Ideas Fast, Art Direction Bk Co; illusr, articles in Harpers, Avon paperback, Farrar, Straus & Cudahy, Parents Mag Press. *Dealer:* Assoc Am Artists 663 Fifth Ave New York NY 10022. *Mailing Add:* 21-25 34th Ave Long Island City NY 11106

GARCIA, FRANK (FLORENCIO GARCIA CISNEROS)
GALLERY DIRECTOR, HISTORIAN
b Victoria las Tunas, Cuba, Feb 1, 24; US citizen. *Pos:* Dir, Galeria Cubana, Havana, 52-59; dir, Sardio Gallery, Caracas, Venezuela, 55-57; dir, Cisneros Gallery, New York, 65-; publ & dir, Noticias de Arte, 76- *Awards:* Cintas fel, 54-55; Third Prize, Circulo de Escritores y Poetas Iberoamericanos, 78. *Bibliog:* G Chase (auth), Art in Latin America, Free Press, 70; D Bayon (auth), America Latina y sus Artes & Las Artes Plasticas en la America Latina. *Mem:* Circulo Pan Americano de Cult; Circulo Escritores y Poetas Iberoamericanos; Int Asn Art Critics. *Specialty:* Latin American art. *Publ:* Auth, Latin American painters in New York, 64; auth, Maternity in Precolumbian art, 70; auth, Jose Marti y las Artes Plasticas, 72; auth, Santos of Puerto Rico and the Americas, Blaine Etheridge Bks, 79. *Mailing Add:* 172 E 89th St Apt 5-A New York NY 10028

GARCIA, OFELIA
ADMINISTRATOR, PRINTMAKER

b Havana, Cuba, Feb 12, 41; US citizen. *Study:* Escuela Nacional de Bellas Artes, Havana, Cuba, 58-60; Manhattanville Col, BA, 69; Tufts Univ & Boston Mus Sch, MFA(printmaking), 72. *Work:* Princeton Univ Graphic Arts Col; NJ State Mus, Trenton; Free Libr Philadelphia; Museo Grafico, Inst Puerto Rican Culture, San Juan; Barnard Col, New York. *Exhib:* Third Miami Graphics Biennial, Metrop Mus & Art Ctr, Fla, 77; 53rd Ann Juried Show, The Print Club, Philadelphia, 77; NJ State Mus, Trenton, 78; Barnard Col, New York, 79; solo shows at Colegio Universitario, Santurce, PR, 70, Cohen Arts Ctr, Tufts Univ, 72 & Duke Univ Gallery, 74; Five Hispanic Artists, Deshong Mus, Pa, 82; and others. *Collections Arranged:* Putnam Art Ctr, Newton Col, 71-73; Boston Col Gallery, 75-76; Invitational Print Exhib in honor of Lessing J Rosenwald (auth, catalog), Print Club, Philadelphia, Pa, 80; Contemp Prints from LeHigh Univ Collection (auth, catalog), Bethlehem, Pa, 80; Recent Gifts: Prints at Univ Pa (auth, catalog), Grad Sch Fine Arts, 81; Printed by Women (auth, catalog), Philadelphia, Pa, 83. *Pos:* Dir, The Print Club, Philadelphia, 78- *Teaching:* Asst prof printmaking & drawing, 69-73, chmn art, 70-73, Newton Col; asst prof, Boston Col, 75-76; critic, Pa Acad Fine Arts, 82- *Awards:* First Prize, All-Sch Competition, Escuela de Bellas Artes, Havana, Cuba, 59; Am Bk Builders Scholar Prize, Boston Mus Sch, 69; Kent Fel, Danforth Found, 75-80. *Bibliog:* Ross Romano (auth), The Complete Collagraph, McMillan, 80; articles in Philadelphia Inquirer, 8/79 & Print Collector's Newsletter. *Mem:* Fel Soc Values Higher Educ; Woman's Caucus Art (pres, 84-86); Citizens Arts Pa; Afro-Am Historical & Cultural Mus (adv bd). *Dealer:* The Print Club 1614 Latimer St Philadelphia PA 19103. *Mailing Add:* c/o Print Club 1614 Latimer St Philadelphia PA 19103

GARCIA, RUPERT (MARSHALL R)
PAINTER, HISTORIAN

b French Camp, Calif, Sept 29, 41. *Study:* San Francisco State Univ, with John Gutmann, BA, 68, with Richard MacLean & Robert Bechtle, MA, 70; Univ Calif, Berkeley, with Peter Selz, Herschel Chipp & T J Clark, MA, 81. *Work:* Nat Collection Am Art, Smithsonian Inst, Washington, DC; Oakland Mus, Calif; Univ Art Mus, Berkeley, Calif; San Francisco Mus Mod Art, Calif. *Comn:* Posters, San Francsico Mus Mod Art, 74; Amnesty Int, San Francisco, Mex Mus, San Francisco, 76 & Nar Chicano Coun Higher Educ, Berkeley, Calif, 79; pastel painting, Ruben Libr, Sonoma State Univ, Rohnert Park, Calif, 79. *Exhib:* One-man show, Graphics, Oakland Mus, 70, Pastel Drawings, San Francisco Mus Mod Art, 78 & Univ Art Gallery, State Univ NY, Binghamton, 81; Images of an Era: The Am Poster 45-75, Nat Collection Fine Arts, Smithsonian Inst & Corcoran Gallery Art, DC, 75; Raices Antiquas/Visones Nuevas, Tucson Mus Art, Ariz, 77; Prelude to the Fifth Sun, Univ Art Mus, Berkeley, Calif, 77; Mex-Am Artists San Francisco Bay Area, Mex Mus, 78; Graphica Creativa '78, Alvar Aalto Mus Cent Finland, Jyvasklya, 78. *Collections Arranged:* Arte de la Revolucion Cubana: Silkscreens by Rene Mederos, Galeria de La Raza, San Francisco, 73; Realismo Chicano: Drawings by Juan Fuentes, Chicano Students Libr, Univ Calif, Berkeley, 76. *Teaching:* Lectr silkscreen, printmaking, painting & drawing, San Francisco State Univ, 78, 79 & summer 81; assoc art hist Mex, Univ Calif, Berkeley, 79-81; instr art hist Mex, San Francisco Art Inst, 80. *Awards:* Photo & Stencil Award, 75. *Bibliog:* Poster art reflects political ideology, San Francisco J, 77; Angel Rama (auth), El Arte de los Chicanos, El Nacional, Caracas, Venezuela, 77. *Media:* Pastel. *Res:* Art and culture of the Chicano and Mexican. *Publ:* Auth, Sources, Other Sources, San Francisco Art Inst, 76; co-auth, Recent Raza murals in the United States, Radical Am, 78; auth, Politics of Popular Art, Chismearte, Los Angeles, 78; coauth, Murales Recientes de La Raza en Estados Unidos, Plural, Mex, 79; auth, Mexican Movie Poster Art, Myth, Illusion, Deception, Galeria de la Raza, San Francisco, 79. *Dealer:* Simon Lowinsky Gallery 228 Grant Ave San Francisco, Calif. *Mailing Add:* 9607 Castlewood St Oakland CA 94605

GARDNER, ANDREW BRADFORD
PRINTMAKER, PAINTER

b Chicago, Ill, Nov 17, 37. *Study:* Antioch Col, BA, 61; Ohio State Univ, MA, 66; Escuela Cent Bellas Artes San Fernando, Madrid, Spain, 64. *Work:* Metrop Mus Art, New York; Johnson Wax Collection; Atlantic Richfield. *Exhib:* Door, Mus Contemp Crafts, New York, 68; Nat Print Exhibs, Brooklyn Mus, 68 & 72; New Talent in Printmaking-1969, Asn Am Artists Gallery, New York, 69; 2nd Biennale Int Estampe, Paris, France, 70; 4th Am Print Biennial, Santiago, Chile, 70. *Teaching:* Instr art & design, Rochester Inst Technol, 66-67; asst prof fine arts, Rutgers Univ, Newark, 67-76. *Media:* Silkscreen, Stencils; Spray Paint. *Publ:* Auth & illusr, The Artist's Silkscreen Manual, Grosset & Dunlap, New York, 76. *Mailing Add:* 365 Sackett Brooklyn NY 11231

GARDNER, JOAN A
PAINTER, PRINTMAKER

b Joliet, Ill, May 3, 33. *Study:* Univ Ill, BFA & MFA(Kate Neal Kinley Mem fel), 55; Norfolk Summer Art Sch, Yale Univ, with Rico Lebrun & Gabor Peterdi, fel, 56. *Work:* Univ Ill; Am Fedn Art; Art Inst Chicago; Yale Univ; Lyman Allyn Mus, New London, Conn. *Exhib:* Yale Univ, 70; New Britain Mus Art, Conn, 73; 55 Mercer Gallery, New York, 74-80; Slater Mem Mus, Norwich, Conn, 77; traveling show, New York State Coun Hearts, 74-75; retrospective, Lyman Allyn Mus, New London, Conn, 81. *Teaching:* Instr art, Southern Conn State Col, 65-77; asst prof, Univ New Haven, 78-81, assoc prof, 82-; assoc prof, Kent State Univ, 82. *Awards:* Conn Acad Fine Arts Award, New Britain Mus, 69; Fulbright-Hays Award, 74-75; Conn Comn Arts Grant, 79-80. *Mem:* Conn Acad Fine Arts. *Media:* Oil, Etchings. *Publ:* Coauth, Robot (film), Crowell Collier & Macmillan, 72; auth, Rooms (bk of drawings), 79; auth, If I Were, poetry-picture bk, 81. *Dealer:* Mercer Gallery 55 Mercer St New York NY 10013. *Mailing Add:* 547 S Lincoln Kent OH 44240

GARDNER, ROBERT EARL
PRINTMAKER, EDUCATOR

b Indianapolis, Ind, June 29, 19. *Study:* John Herron Art Sch, BFA, 48; Atelier 17, New York, 48-49; Cranbrook Acad Art, MFA, 52. *Work:* Carnegie Mus, Pittsburgh; Univ Okla Mus, Norman; Wichita Mus Art, Kans; Ohio Univ, Athens; Ga Comn Arts. *Exhib:* Pa Acad Fine Arts Exhibs; Brooklyn Mus Print Biennials; Libr Cong Print Exhibs; Northwest Printmakers Exhibs; Philadelphia Print Club Exhibs. *Pos:* Artisan-printer, Tamarind Lithography Workshop, Los Angeles, Calif, summer 62 & 63-64. *Teaching:* From assoc prof to prof printmaking, Carnegie-Mellon Univ, 53- *Awards:* Sixteen national & regional prizes & purchase awards. *Bibliog:* Michael Knigin & Murray Zimilis (authors), The technique of fine art lithography, Print Collectors Newslett, 9-10/70; Donald Saff & Deli Sacilotto (authors), Printmaking: History and process, Tamarind Papers, fall 78. *Media:* Intaglio, Lithography. *Mailing Add:* Dept of Art Carnegie-Mellon Univ Pittsburgh PA 15213

GARDNER, SUSAN ROSS
PAINTER

b New York, NY, Oct 25, 41. *Study:* Brooklyn Mus, 59; Antioch Col, BA, 63; Ohio State Univ, MA, 66. *Work:* Metrop Mus Art, New York; Southern Ill Univ; Northern Ill Univ; Atlantic Richfield Corp; Woman's Interart Ctr. *Exhib:* Seattle Art Mus, 71; DeCordova Mus, Lincoln, Mass, 71; Cook Gallery, Lincoln Ctr, 81; Brooklyn Mus, 72, 78, 79 & 82; 55 Mercer St, New York, 82; one-person shows, Webb & Parsons Gallery, Conn, 82 & Twinning Gallery, New York, 83; and others. *Teaching:* Asst prof studio & art hist, Manhattan Community Col, New York, 66-70; asst prof studio & art hist, Yeshiva Univ, 75-, Laguardia Community Col, 78 & Fordham Univ, 77-78. *Awards:* Purchase Award, Northern Ill Univ, 71. *Bibliog:* Wendy Schuman (interview), New York Times, 5/27/73; photo & article, Long Island Press, 4/27/73 & East Hampton Star, 5/73. *Mem:* Col Art Asn Am. *Media:* Acrylic, Rholpex. *Mailing Add:* 108 Wyckoff St Brooklyn NY 11201

GAREL, LEO
PAINTER

b New York, NY, Oct 8, 17. *Study:* Parsons Sch Art, NY; Art Students League, with George Grosz & Vaclav Vytlacil. *Work:* Norfolk Mus Arts & Sci; Chase Manhattan Bank Collection; Midland Bank Collection; NY Univ. *Exhib:* Albany Inst Hist & Art, NY, 61; one-man show, Berkshire Mus, Pittsfield, Mass, 67; Pa Acad Fine Arts, Philadelphia, 69; Montclair Art Mus, NJ, 75; Zabriskie Gallery, New York; Image Gallery, Stockbridge, Mass. *Teaching:* Instr painting, Austen Riggs Ctr, Stockbridge, Mass, 59-75. *Awards:* First Prize in Watercolor, Albany Inst Hist & Art, 61. *Media:* Watercolors, Gouache. *Mailing Add:* c/o Image Gallery Stockbridge MA 01262

GAREY, PAT
DRAFTSMAN, PAINTER

b State College, Miss, Nov 11, 32. *Study:* Tex Woman's Univ, BS(costume design & fashion illus); Tex Tech Univ, Lubbock, MFA, with Jim Howze, Terry Morrow, Lynwood Kreneck, Hugh Gibbons; Art Students League, 77. *Exhib:* 17th Ann Nat Exhib Prints & Drawings, Okla Art Ctr, 75; Santa Fe Festival of Arts, 79 & 80; Sangre Cristo Art Ctr, Pueblo, Colo, 79; one-woman shows, NMex Jr Col, Hobbs, 81 & Univ Tex Permian Basin, Odessa, 81; and many others. *Pos:* Artist in sch prog, HEW Emergency Sch Aid Proj, Hobbs, 74- *Teaching:* Instr drawing & painting, Col Southwest, NMex, 67-70, instr art hist, 74. *Awards:* Cash Award, Figure Study No 1, 72; First Prize Ceramics, 74 & First Prize Graphics, 75, Llano Estacado Art Asn. *Media:* Ink, Watercolor. *Mailing Add:* 315 E Alto Hobbs NM 88240

GARHART, MARTIN J
PRINTMAKER

b Deadwood, SDak, July 2, 46. *Study:* SDak State Univ, BA, 69; WVa Univ, MA, 70; Southern Ill Univ, Edwardsville, MFA, 72. *Work:* Libr Cong, Smithsonian Inst, Washington, DC; Cleveland Mus Art; Brit Mus, London; Calif Palace Legion of Honor, San Francisco. *Exhib:* Drawings USA, 72; Colorprint USA, 73; Bradley Print Show 15th Nat, 74; 2nd NH Int Print Competition, 74; Davidson Nat Print & Drawing Competition, 74. *Teaching:* From asst to assoc prof art, Kenyon Col, 72- *Awards:* Spec Purchase Award, Davidson Print & Drawing Competition, 74; Purchase Award, Bradley Print Show 15th Nat, 74; Jurors Award of Merit, 2nd NH Int. *Mem:* Col Art Asn Am; NH Graphic Soc. *Media:* Lithography. *Mailing Add:* 100 Woodside Gambier OH 43022

GARMAN, ED
PAINTER, WRITER

b Bridgeport, Conn, July 4, 14. *Study:* Self-taught. *Work:* Sheldon Mem Art Gallery, Univ Nebr, Lincoln; Mus NMex, Santa Fe; La Jolla Mus Art, Calif; Salt Lake Art Ctr, Utah; Ariz State Univ Art Collection, Tempe. *Exhib:* Painters & Sculptures of the Southwest Ann, Mus NMex, 41-44; Solomon Guggenheim Found 5th Ann, New York, 43; Lure of the West, Salt Lake Art Ctr, 70; Masterpieces from the Mus of NMex, Marion Koogler McNay Art Inst, San Antonio, Tex, 70. *Bibliog:* Marilyn Hagberg (auth), Hot Geometry of Ed Garman, San Diego Mag, 9/68. *Media:* Oil, Acrylic. *Publ:* Auth, Art of Raymond Jonson, Painter, 75. *Dealer:* Martin Diamond Fine Arts Inc 1014 Madison Ave New York NY 10021. *Mailing Add:* PO Box 1013 Imperial Beach CA 92032

GARNETT, WILLIAM ASHFORD
PHOTOGRAPHER, EDUCATOR
b Chicago, Ill, Dec 27, 16. *Work:* Smithsonian Inst, Washington, DC; Mus Mod Art, New York; George Eastman House, Rochester; and others. *Comn:* Photographic mural, Mus Mod Art & State Dept, US Pavillion, Osaka World's Fair; The Searching Eye (film), comn by Saul Bass & Eastman Kodak & From Here to There (film), comn by Saul Bass & United Airlines, NY World's Fair, 64-65; America Begins in New England (aerial essay), Life Mag, 67 & Splendors Where the Eagles Soar (aerial essay), 68. *Exhib:* William Garnett, Aerial Photography, Eastman House, Rochester; The Family of Man & Diogenes IV, Mus Mod Art; Photographer & the American Landscape & photography from mus collection, Mus Mod Art. *Teaching:* Prof design & photography, Univ Calif, Berkeley, 68- *Awards:* Ctr Advan Visual Studies Fel, Kepes, Mass Inst Technol, 67-68; Guggenheim Fel, 53, 56 & 75; Outstanding Achievement in Landscape Photog Award, Am Soc Mag Photogr, 83. *Bibliog:* Beaumont Newhall (auth), The History of Photography, Mus Mod Art; Peter Pollack (auth), The Pictorial History of Photography, Abrams; Walker Evans (auth), Over California, Fortune, 3/54. *Collection:* Aerial photography from US, Can, Mex, Japan, Hong Kong, Manila and Australia. *Publ:* Auth, The Extraordinary Landscape: Aerial Photographs of America, New York Graphic Soc, 82. *Mailing Add:* 1286 Congress Valley Rd Napa CA 94558

GARNSEY, CLARKE HENDERSON
HISTORIAN, EDUCATOR
b Joliet, Ill, Sept 22, 13. *Study:* Cleveland Inst Art, dipl, 47; Western Reserve Univ, BS(art educ), 47, MA(art hist), 48 & PhD(art hist), 62. *Comn:* Fourteen murals, Volusia Co Schs, Fla, 34-38 & series of etchings of historic locations, eastern Fla, WPA Fed Art Proj; watercolors, Amarillo Col, Tex. *Exhib:* Daytona Beach Art League Ann Exhib, 34-42; Southern States Art League Ann Exhib, 35-38; Wichita Art Asn Exhib, Kans, 37-38; May Show, Cleveland Mus Art, 49 & 58; Nat Exhib Relig Art, Rochester, NY, 69. *Pos:* Lectr, Cleveland Mus Art & Cleveland Inst, 57-59. *Teaching:* Chmn studio work, Amarillo Col, 49-63; chmn art hist, Wichita State Univ, 63-66; prof art, Univ Tex, El Paso, 66-79, emer prof, 79- *Awards:* Numerous awards and mentions nationally. *Mem:* Col Art Asn Am; Soc Archit Hist; Tex Fine Arts Asn; Int Designer Craftsmen El Paso; Rocky Mountain Coun Latin Am Studies. *Media:* Watercolor, Enamel. *Res:* Latin American colonial architecture with emphasis on Neo-Classicism. *Mailing Add:* 221 Carnival Dr El Paso TX 79912

GARRARD, MARY DUBOSE
HISTORIAN, EDUCATOR
b Greenwood, Miss, July 25, 37. *Study:* Newcomb Col, BA, 58; Radcliffe Col, MA, 60; Johns Hopkins Univ, PhD, 70. *Teaching:* From asst prof to prof art hist, Am Univ, Washington, DC, 64- *Mem:* Women's Caucus for Art (pres, 74-76); Col Art Asn Am (bd dirs, 77-81); Am Asn Univ Prof. *Res:* Sculpture of Jacopo Sansovino; painting of Artemisia Gentileschi; other aspects of 16th century and 17th century Italian art; women artists, 16th-20th century. *Publ:* Auth, Jacopo Sansovino's Madonna in South Agostino, Rome--an antique source rediscovered, J of Warburg & Courtauld Insts, London, 75; auth, Of men, women and art: some historical reflections, Art J, 76; auth, Artemisia Gentileschi's Self-portrait as the allegory of painting, Art Bulletin, 3/80; co-ed, Feminism and Art History: Questioning the Litany, Harper & Row, 82; auth, The liberal arts and Michelangelo's first project for the tomb of Julius II, Viator: Medieval & Renaissance Studies, 84; and others. *Mailing Add:* 2915 University Terr NW Washington DC 20016

GARRETT, STEPHEN
MUSEUM DIRECTOR
b Ashtead, Surrey, Eng. *Study:* Cambridge Univ, Eng, MA. *Pos:* dir, J Paul Getty Mus, 74-83. *Teaching:* Lectr design, Cent Sch Arts & Crafts, London, 54-64; sr lectr archit, Polytech Cent, London, 64-72. *Mem:* Assoc Royal Inst Brit Architects; Asn Art Mus Dirs. *Mailing Add:* 400 Aderno Way Pacific Palisades CA 90272

GARRETT, STUART GRAYSON
PAINTER, EDUCATOR
b Oklahoma City, Okla. *Study:* Cooper Union; Art Students League. *Work:* USN Hist Collection; Southern Vt Art Ctr; Factory Point Bank; Prudential Ins Co; Univ Md. *Exhib:* Nat Acad Design, New York; Am Watercolor Soc, New York; Am Artists Prof League, New York; Audubon Artists, New York; Mus Marine, Paris; and others. *Teaching:* Prof art, City Col New York, currently. *Awards:* Gold Medal, Am Artists Prof League, 59 & 60; Acad Artists Asn Awards, 59 & 78; Salmagundi Club Awards, 62, 63, 65 & 67; plus others. *Mem:* Am Watercolor Soc; Nat Soc Painters Casein & Acrylic; Southern Vt Artists; Salmagundi Club; Knickerbocker Artists. *Mailing Add:* RD 2 Salem NY 12865

GARRISON, EVE
PAINTER
b Boston, Mass, Apr 22, 08. *Study:* Art Inst Chicago, grad, 31; Wayne Univ; Lawrence Inst Technol; Lewis Inst Chicago. *Work:* Metrop Mus Art, Miami, Fla; Union League Club, Chicago; Drian Gallery, London; Roosevelt Univ Rehabilitation Hosp, Chicago; Nat Mus Art, Warsaw, Poland; and others. *Exhib:* Smithsonian Inst, 70-72; retrospectives, Ill Inst Technol, Chicago, 72 & Miami Mus Mod Art, 72; one-woman shows, Galerie Vallombreuse, Biarritz, France, 72 & Spertus Mus Chicago, 76. *Awards:* Awards for Old Colored Maid, Corcoran Mus, 34 & Bride & Groom, Union League Club, Chicago, 61. *Bibliog:* Dona Meilach (auth), Collage and found art, 65. *Mem:* Chicago Artists Coalition. *Media:* Oil, Casein. *Dealer:* Drian Gallery London Eng. *Mailing Add:* 1410B Sherwin Chicago IL 60626

GARSTON, GERALD DREXLER
PAINTER
b Waterbury, Conn, May 3, 25. *Study:* Johns Hopkins Univ, BA, 51; Art Students League, 52, painting with Louis Bouche & printmaking with Harry Sternberg. *Work:* Rose Mus, Brandeis Univ; Los Angeles Co Mus; William Rockhill Nelson Gallery Art, Kansas City, Mo; Philadelphia Mus Art, Pa; Wadsworth Atheneum, Hartford, Conn. *Exhib:* Poindexter Gallery, New York, 62; A M Sachs Gallery, New York, 65; Susan Morse Hilles Collection, Mus Fine Arts, Boston, 66; Graham Gallery, New York, 67; Pucker-Safrai Gallery, Boston, 71, 74, 76, 78, 80 & 82; Freedman Gallery, Albright Col, Reading, Pa, 77. *Media:* Oil. *Dealer:* Pucker-Safrai Gallery 171 Newbury St Boston MA 02116. *Mailing Add:* 131 Oliver Rd New Haven CT 06515

GARTEL, LAURENCE M
PHOTOGRAPHER, VIDEO-COMPUTER ARTIST
b New York, NY, June 5, 56. *Study:* Art Students League, with Knox Martin, 75; Sch Visual Arts, with Al Brunelle, George Trakas, Bill Beckley & Cora Kennedy, BFA, 77. *Exhib:* Video Still Photographs: Five Year Retrospective, Middle Tenn State Univ, 82; Points of View, Mus Art, Univ Okla, 82; Computer Images: Siggraph Computer Art Show, Detroit, 83; The Artist & the Computer, Long Beach Mus Art, 83; Art & Technology, Princeton Art Mus, 83. *Pos:* Cover artist video drawings, Computer Design Mag, Littleton, Mass, 81- *Teaching:* Instr manipulating photog images, Creative Photog Workshop, Sch Visual Arts, New York, 78-84, instr computer art, Computer Graphics Workshop, 83-; lectr, Graphic Computer Communications, Boston, 82 & Computer Conf, Univ Ottawa, 84. *Awards:* Video Art Grant, Intermedia Art Ctr, Bayville, NY, 83; Polaroid Corp Res & Develop Grant Electronic Imaging, 84. *Bibliog:* Helen Harrison (auth), Exploring new processes in photography, NY Times, 1/79; Stan Greene (ed), The tube is his canvas, Sunday Newsday Mag, 5/81; Phyllis Braff (auth), Video art: Ready for prime time?, Sunday New York Times, 83. *Publ:* Auth & illusr, Kunst, Diepuries Video, Panorama, Holland, 80; co-auth & illusr, Messing up the signals, Camera 35, 12/81; auth & illusr, The incubation of electronic imaging, Photomethods, 82; illusr, Laurence Gartel video, fantasy or future?, Camera Weekly, England, 82; coauth & illusr, Fantasia Ben Calcolata, PM Mag, Italy, 83. *Mailing Add:* 270-16B Grand Central Parkway Floral Park NY 11005

GARVAN, BEATRICE BRONSON
CURATOR, HISTORIAN
b New York, NY, Mar 9, 29. *Study:* Vassar Col, BA(hist art), 50; Barnes Found, 53-55; Univ Pa, MA(Am civilization), 65. *Pos:* Asst, Ed Dept, Art News Mag, 49; secy & asst, Van Diemen-Lilienfeld Gallery, 50-52; cur decorative arts, Philadelphia Mus Art, currently. *Teaching:* Lectr Am arts, Germantown Acad, Ft Washington, Pa, 65-71. *Mem:* Cliveden Coun, Nat Trust Hist Hist Preservation; Victorian Soc; Hist Soc Pa (mem bd, 64-); Soc Archit Historians & Decorative Arts; Am Crafts Coun. *Res:* American decorative arts of the 18th and 19th century; 18th century American architecture. *Publ:* Auth, A Craftsman's Handbook, Tinicum Press & Philadelphia Mus, 75; auth, Mathew Clark's Charts, Philadelphia Printmaking, Tinicum Press, 76; contribr, Philadelphia--300 Years of American Art, Philadelphia Mus Art, 76. *Mailing Add:* Box 304 Penllyn Pike Spring House PA 19477

GARVER, THOMAS H
ADMINISTRATOR, WRITER
b Duluth, Minn, Jan 23, 34. *Study:* Barnes Found, Merion, Pa; Haverford Col, BA; Univ Minn, MA. *Collections Arranged:* Rose Art Mus, Brandeis Univ; Bruce Conner; Assemblages, Drawings & Films; 12 Photographers of the American Social Landscape, Newport Harbor Art Mus; Just Before the War: Urban America From 1935-1941 as seen by Photographers of the Farm Security Administration; Robert Rauschenberg in Black and White; Tom Wesselman: Early Still Lifes, 1962-64; Wood, Sculpture of Gabriel Kohn; Edward Hopper: 15 Paintings; Don Potts: My First Car; New Art of Vancouver; Reginald Marsh Retrospective; George Tooker Retrospective, Fine Arts Mus San Francisco, 74; New Photography: San Francisco and Bay Area, 74; Representations of America (co-organized with Henry Geldzabler; co-auth, catalogue), traveling USSR, 77-78; Joseph Raffael, The California Years, 1969-78 (auth, catalogue), San Francisco Mus Mod Art, 78. *Pos:* Asst to dir, Krannert Art Mus, Univ Ill, 60-62; asst dir, Seattle World's Fair, 62; asst dir, Rose Art Mus, 62-68; dir, Newport Harbor Art Mus, Newport Beach, Calif, 68-72 & 77-80; consult art gallery design, Univ Chicago, Calif Inst Arts, 69 & ARCO Ctr Visual Arts, 73; cur exhibs, Fine Arts Mus San Francisco, 72-77; dir, Madison Art Ctr, Wis, 80- *Mem:* Art Mus Asn (bd trustees, 79 & pres, 79-82); assoc Int Inst Conserv Hist & Artistic Works; Asn Art Mus Dirs. *Res:* Contemporary American art. *Publ:* Contribr, An interview with George Sawchuck, Artscan, 69; contribr, Balboa & the fun zone, Art Am, 71; George Tooker, Am Art Rev, 74; contribr, Eros & photography: an exploration of sexual imagery and photographic practice, Camerawork/NSF Press, San Francisco, 78; auth catalogue essay, George Herms: The Prometheus Archives, Newport Harbor Art Mus, 79. *Mailing Add:* Madison Art Center 211 State St Madison WI 53703

GARVER, WALTER RAYMOND
PAINTER, INSTRUCTOR
b Medina, NY, Aug 29, 27. *Study:* State Univ NY Buffalo, BFA, 55; also with Charles Burchfield, 50. *Work:* Butler Inst Am Art, Youngstown, Ohio; Minn Mus Art, St Paul; Cincinnati Univ; Indiana Univ Pa; Mem Art Gallery, Rochester, NY. *Exhib:* Nat Acad Design, New York, 56, 60, 70, 71 & 75; Chautauqua Nat Jury Show, NY, 58-; one-man show, Albright-Knox Art Gallery, 72; Cooperstown Art Asn Am Nat Art Exhib, 73, 75 & 76; Okla Art Ctr Ann, Oklahoma City, 81-83; Audubon Artists Ann, New York, 83; and

many others. *Teaching:* Teacher art hist, drawing, painting & photog, Amherst Sr High Sch, Snyder, NY, 58-, chmn dept art, 78- *Awards:* Award Traditional Style Painting, E J Bellinger, Chautauqua Nat, 70-73 & 79; First Award Painting, Okla Art Ann, 82; Audubon Artists Medal Honor, 83; and others. *Mem:* Buffalo Soc Artists (pres, 64); Audubon Artists. *Media:* Oil on Masonite, Watercolor. *Publ:* Auth, I search for an idea, Am Artists Mag, 68; contribr, Creative Color (reproductions), 72; contribr, Creative Landscape Painting (reproductions), 78; auth, Portrait moods, Palette Talk, 82. *Dealer:* Zaner Gallery 100 Alexander St Rochester NY 14620. *Mailing Add:* 4230 Tonawanda Creek Rd East Amherst NY 14051

GARWOOD, AUDREY
PAINTER, PRINTMAKER
b Toronto, Ont, July 7, 27. *Study:* Ont Col Art; Rijksacad, Amsterdam, scholar; Le Chaumiere, Paris. *Work:* London Gallery & Art Mus, Ont; McLaughlin Art Gallery, Oshawa, Ont; Burnaby Art Gallery, BC; Hamilton Art Gallery, Ont; Ont Art Gallery, Toronto. *Exhib:* Royal Can Acad; Ont Soc Artists; Can Graphic Art Soc; Can Painters & Etchers; Nat Gallery Showcase. *Awards:* Can Graphic Art Soc Award; Sterling Trust Award, Can Painters & Etchers; J Forester Award, Ont Soc Artists. *Mem:* Royal Can Acad Art; Ont Soc Art; Can Graphic Art Soc; Can Painters & Etchers; Calif Soc Printmakers. *Media:* Oil; Silkscreen. *Mailing Add:* 46 Stephenson Ave Toronto ON M4C 1G1 Canada

GARY, DOROTHY HALES
COLLECTOR, WRITER
b San Francisco, Calif, Nov 21, 17. *Study:* Stanford Col. *Pos:* Owner, pvt gallery. *Specialty:* Abstract, contemporary art. *Collection:* Abstract art. *Publ:* Auth, Sun, Stones & Silence, Simon & Shuster, 63; coauth, Splendors of Asia, 65, coauth, Splendors of Byzantium, 67 & coauth, Morocco, Viking Press. *Mailing Add:* 1 East 66th St New York NY 10021

GARY, JAN (MRS WILLIAM D GORMAN)
PAINTER, PRINTMAKER
b Ft Worth, Tex, Feb 13, 25. *Study:* Art Ctr Sch, Los Angeles; San Antonio Art Inst, Tex; Art Students League. *Work:* Butler Inst Am Art, Youngstown, Ohio; Pensacola Art Ctr, Fla; Wis State Univ, Eau Claire; Brandeis Univ, Waltham, Mass; Rosenberg Libr, Galveston, Tex. *Exhib:* One-person show, Caldwell Col, NJ, 78; Am Acad Arts & Lett, 67-68; Four NJ Artists, Canton Art Inst, Ohio, 71; Cent Wyo Mus Art, Casper, 75; Charles & Emma Frye Mus Art, Seattle, Wash, 77; and others. *Pos:* Assoc dir, Old Bergen Art Guild, Bayonne, NJ, 62- *Awards:* M Grumbacher Purchase Award, Audubon Artists Ann, 66; Childe Hassam Fund Purchase Award, Am Acad Arts & Lett, 68; Dorothy F Seligson Mem Prize, Nat Asn Women Artists Ann, 75. *Bibliog:* Henry Gasser (auth), article, Am Artist, 10/70. *Mem:* Nat Soc Painters Casein & Acrylic; Audubon Artists; Assoc Artists NJ; Allied Artists Am. *Media:* Acrylic, Casein; Woodcut. *Mailing Add:* 43 W 33rd St Bayonne NJ 07002

GARZON-BLANCO, ARMANDO
DESIGNER, PAINTER
b Havana, Cuba, Feb 1, 41. *Study:* La State Univ, BA, 66, MA(design), 68, MA(art hist), 69, PhD(theatre-art), 76; Fulbright-Hays Res Grant, Spain, 72-73, La State Univ Coun on Res & Rodriguez-Acosta Fund Grants, Spain, 76. *Work:* Centroplex, Baton Rouge; Anglo-Am Mus & Univ Libr, La State Univ, Baton Rouge; Cath Student Ctr, Baton Rouge. *Comn:* Baptistry murals, St Paul Cath Church, Baton Rouge, 70; sanctuary & chapel, Christ the King Chapel, Baton Rouge, 73-75; altarpiece, St James Lutheran Church, Gonzales, La, 77. *Exhib:* Jay Broussard Mem Gallery, State La Dept Art, Hist & Cult Preserv, 72; US Cult Ctr of Am Embassy, Madrid, Spain, 73; Fundacion Rodriguez-Acosta Banco de Granada Gallery, Spain, 73. *Teaching:* From instr to prof design, painting & art hist, La State Univ, Baton Rouge, 68-77; prof design, painting & art hist & head art dept, Nicholls State Univ, Thibodaux, 77- *Awards:* Purchase Award, 2nd Ann Int La Watercolor Soc, 71. *Bibliog:* Miguel Rodriguez-Acosta Carlstrom (auth), Los artistas por el sureste espanol, Banco de Granada & Fundacion Rodriguez-Acosta, Spain, 73. *Mem:* La Watercolor Soc; SCent Renaissance Asn; Col Art Asn Am; Northeastern Mod Lang Asn; Nat Coun Art Adminr. *Media:* Watercolor, Mixed Media. *Res:* Interrelation of the theatre arts and visual arts; Spanish Jesuit theatrical practice in the 16th and 17th century; Afro-Cuban art. *Publ:* Auth, Note on the authorship of the Spanish Jesuit play of San Hermenegildo, Theatre Survey, 74; auth, The Tragedia de San Hermenegildo, Seville, 1590, Explorations in Renaissance Culture, 76; La Tragedia de San Hermenegildo en el teatro y en el arte, Estudios sobre literatura y arte dedicados al profesor, Emilio Orozco Diaz, II, Universidad de Granada, 79. *Mailing Add:* Dept of Art Nicholls State Univ Thibodaux LA 70301

GASPARIAN, ARMEN TIGRAN
INSTRUCTOR, PAINTER
b Abadan, Iran, Nov 25, 33; US citizen. *Study:* Calcutta Art Inst, India; Swain Sch Art, New Bedford, Mass; Univ Kans. *Work:* Univ Kans; Laguna Beach Mus, Calif; Denver Fine Arts Gallery, Colo. *Exhib:* All Calif Ann, 67-69 & 71-73; one-man shows, Martin Gallery, Scottsdale, Ariz, 68-72 & 74, Saks Gallery, Denver, 69, 71 & 73 & Laguna Beach Mus, 72; Hawaii-Calif Regional, San Diego Mus, 71. *Teaching:* Instr beginning & advan painting, Laguna Beach Sch Art, 71- *Awards:* First Prize, Inland V, 72; Purchase Award, All Calif Ann, 73; First Prize, Catalina Ann, 74. *Mem:* Laguna Beach Mus. *Media:* Oil. *Mailing Add:* 215 High Dr Laguna Beach CA 92651

GASPARRO, FRANK
SCULPTOR, INSTRUCTOR
b Philadelphia, Pa, Aug 26, 09. *Study:* Pa Acad Fine Arts; also with Charles Grafly. *Comn:* Designed reverse of Kennedy Half-Dollar, Am Numismatic Asn Medal, 69, obverse & reverse of President Richard M Nixon Medal, 69, obverse & reverse of Eisenhower Dollar & reverse of Lincoln Mem US One Cent; designed obverse & reverse of Susan B Anthony One Dollar, 79; also many medals for US mint. *Exhib:* Philadelphia Mus Art Sculpture Exhib, 40; Pa Acad Fine Arts, Philadelphia, 46; Medals at French Mint, Paris, 50; Spanish Int Medallic Art Exhib, Madrid, 52 & 68; Woman on the Medal, Int Medallic Exhib. *Pos:* Engraver, US Mint, Philadelphia, 42-65, chief engraver, 65-81. *Teaching:* Instr, Fleisher Art Sch, Philadelphia, 46-; instr, Pa Acad Fine Arts, 81- *Awards:* Order of Merit, Ital Repub (Cavaliere Ufficiale), 73; Percy Owens Award Outstanding Artist, Pa, 79; Citation for Super Performance of the US Treasury, 77; plus others. *Mem:* Soc Medalists; Pa Acad Fine Arts Fel (bd dirs, 58-); Fr Soc of the Medal. *Mailing Add:* 216 Westwood Park Dr Havertown PA 19083

GAST, CAROLYN BARTLETT (LUTZ)
ILLUSTRATOR, ILLUMINATOR
b Cambridge, Mass, Apr 30, 29. *Study:* Col Practical Arts & Lett, Boston Univ, BS(bk illus), 50. *Work:* Nat Mus Natural Hist, Smithsonian Inst & US Geol Surv, US Dept Interior, Washington, DC. *Exhib:* Seventeenth Area Exhib of Corcoran Gallery Art, Washington, DC, 65; Scientific Illus, Nat Mus of Natural Hist, Smithsonian Inst, 68; solo exhib & demonstration, Kotor, Yugoslavia, 70; Ann Exhibs of Asn of Med Illusr, 69-79; Nat Exhibs, Guild Natural Sci Illusr, 79 & 81-83. *Pos:* Scientific illusr, US Geol Surv, Dept Interior, 52-56; scientific illusr, Nat Mus Natural Hist, Smithsonian Inst, 59-; illusr, Proceedings of the US Nat Mus, 60-67; illusr, Proceedings of the Bio Soc of Washington, DC, 61-; illusr, Smithsonian Contributions to Zoology, 67- *Mem:* Founding mem Guild of Natural Sci Illusr (vpres, 71-73, pres, 73-75); Col Art Asn Am. *Media:* Mixed. *Publ:* Illusr, Mary S Gardiner's The Biology of the Invertebrates, McGraw-Hill, 72; illusr, numerous scientific publications and journals, 59-83. *Mailing Add:* 5730 First St S Arlington VA 22204

GAST, MICHAEL CARL
PAINTER
b Chicago, Ill, June 11, 30. *Study:* Sch Art Inst Chicago, BFA, 52; Univ Am, Mex, MFA(cum laude), 60. *Exhib:* Washington Watercolor Asn 66th Ann Nat Exhib, Smithsonian Inst, 63 & Metrop Area Exhib, Howard Univ, Washington, DC, 70; Soc Washington Artists 70th & 71st Ann Exhib, Smithsonian Inst, 63 & 64; four-man show, Mickelson Gallery, Washington, DC, 66; Foundry Gallery, Washington, DC, 80; Downtown Gallery, Del Art Mus, Wilmington, Del, 80. *Pos:* Mus technician, div ceramics & glass, Nat Mus Hist & Technol, Smithsonian Inst, 61-64 & mus specialist, Nat Collection Fine Arts, 69-71; contribr, Artists Equity Asn Nat Newsletter, 77-81. *Teaching:* Asst prof painting, George Washington Univ, 71. *Bibliog:* Andrea O Cohen (auth), article, Washington DC Gazette, 4/19/72. *Mem:* Artists Equity Asn (chap vpres, 73-77, nat secy-treas, 75-79, nat pres, 79-81); Col Art Asn Am. *Media:* Polymer, Oil. *Publ:* Contribr, Fed Art Patronage Notes, 77 & Ceramics Monthly, 78. *Mailing Add:* 5730 First St S Arlington VA 22204

GATEL, JEFF (JEFFREY STUART)
PHOTOGRAPHER
b Los Angeles, Calif, July 17, 49. *Study:* Mich State Univ, BA, 71; Univ Calif, Los Angeles, MA(photog & design), 73, MFA(photog & design), 75. *Work:* Victoria & Albert Mus; Bibliot Nat, Paris; Los Angeles Co Mus Art; Ctr Creative Photog, Tucson; Polaroid Collection, Amsterdam. *Exhib:* Solo exhib, Tyler Sch Art, 79, Univ Colo, Boulder, 80, Arco Ctr Visual Art, Los Angeles, 81 & Downey Mus Art, Calif, 83; Show II (Winter), Los Angeles Co Mus Art, 80; New American Photography, Chicago Ctr Contemp Photog, 81. *Pos:* Gallery dir, Cerritos Col, 81-83. *Teaching:* Instr photog, Otis Parsons Sch Design, 83- *Bibliog:* James Hugunin (auth), Finding a chink in the armor, Obscura Mag, Vol 1, No 4, 81; Colin Westerbeck (auth), article, Artforum, 4/82; Marlene Laskey (auth), When freeways come, Artweek, 10/15/83. *Mem:* Soc Photog Educ; Col Art Asn. *Publ:* Auth, In our path, U-Turn Mag, 83. *Mailing Add:* c/o Equivalents Gallery 1822 Broadway Seattle WA 98122

GATES, HARRY IRVING
SCULPTOR, EDUCATOR
b Elgin, Ill, Dec 8, 34. *Study:* Univ Ill, BFA, 58, MFA, 60. *Work:* Chase Manhattan Bank, New York; Corcoran Gallery Art, Washington, DC; Int Art Prog Div, Nat Collection Fine Art, Washington, DC; Washington Co Mus Fine Arts, Hagerstown, Md; Baltimore Mus Fine Art, Md. *Exhib:* One-man show, Baltimore Mus Fine Art, 64; Small Sculpture Purchases for Int Art Prog, Nat Collection Fine Art, 69; New Sculpture, Corcoran Art, Washington, DC, 70; Five Maryland Artists, Md Arts Coun, 72-73; Sculpture Invitational, Rochester Inst Technol, 75; The Object as Poet, Renwick Gallery, Washington, DC & Mus Contemp Crafts, New York, 77; 18 year retrospective, Washington Co Mus Art, Md, 78; two-man exhib, Dimock Gallery, George Washington Univ, 79. *Teaching:* Asst prof sculpture, George Washington Univ, 64-78, assoc prof, 78- *Awards:* First Prize, 21st Ann Contemp Art, Palm Beach, Fla, 59; Artists Coun Award, 25th Ann Exhib for Sculpture, 61; Gov Prize, Md Ann, 70. *Dealer:* Barbara Fiedler Gallery 1621 21st NW Washington DC 20009. *Mailing Add:* PO Box 766 Frederick MD 21701

GATES, JAY RODNEY
CURATOR, EDUCATOR
b Kansas City, Mo, Nov 21, 45. *Study:* Col Wooster, Ohio, BA, 68; Univ Rochester, NY, MA, 70. *Exhib:* Mitthoefer Collection of African Sculpture, Col Wooster Mus, Ohio, 74; Prints & Drawings by Sculptors, Cleveland Mus Art, Ohio, 75; Tenn Quilts, Brooks Mem Art Gallery, Memphis, 79; Arts of Ancient Egypt: Treasures on Another Scale, Memphis & Washington, DC, 81. *Pos:* Asst cur art hist & educ, Cleveland Mus, 73-76; cur educ, St Louis Art Mus, 76; dir, Brooks Mem Art Gallery, Memphis, 79-81; asst dir & cur Am art, Nelson Gallery, Atkins Mus, 81- *Teaching:* Instr art hist, Col Wooster, Ohio, 71-73; instr art hist, Case Western Reserve Univ, Cleveland, 73-76. *Mem:* Am Asn Mus; Col Art Asn. *Res:* Public education in art museums; American painting. *Publ:* Auth, Television from the galleries, Mus News, 75; co-auth, Teaching advanced placement art history in a museum, Art J, 75. *Mailing Add:* c/o Nelson Art Gallery 4525 Oak Kansas City MO 64111

GATES, THOMAS PAUL
EDUCATOR, CURATOR
b Cleveland, Ohio, Aug 21, 41. *Study:* Western Reserve Univ, BA, 67; Univ Southern Calif, MA, 70; Univ NMex, MA, 73. *Collections Arranged:* Man: The Music Maker (auth, catalog), Maxwell Mus, 73; Artists Proof/The Multiple Image, survey of printmaking, 77; A Shade of Light, history of int illum, 78; Ceramic containers, ceramic vessels, 79; American Still Lifes, paintings & prints, 79. *Pos:* Educ coordinator, Fine Arts Mus San Francisco Downtown Ctr, 75-80, acting dir, 80; registrar, M H De Young Mus Art Sch, San Francisco, Calif, 80-, libr asst, currently; mus educ consult, Univ Art Mus Berkeley, Calif, 81. *Teaching:* Lectr art hist, M H De Young Mus Art Sch, San Francisco, Calif, 75-79, Chabot Col, Livermore, Calif, 76-77 & Foothill Col, Los Altos Hills, Calif, 75-79. *Awards:* Rockefeller Fel, Fine Arts Mus San Francisco, 73-74. *Mem:* Col Art Asn; Am Asn Mus; Soc Architectural Historians; Nat Trust Historic Preserv. *Publ:* Auth, Community Murals in San Francisco, De Young Mus Art Sch, 77; ed, The Work Show, Fine Arts Mus San Francisco Downtown Ctr, 78. *Mailing Add:* De Young Mus Art Sch Golden Gate Park San Francisco CA 94118

GATEWOOD, MAUD FLORANCE
PAINTER
b Yanceyville, NC, Jan 8, 34. *Study:* Univ NC, Greensboro, AB; Ohio State Univ, MA; Univ Vienna; Fulbright grant, 62-63; Acad Appl Arts, Vienna; Harvard Summer Sch. *Work:* Mint Mus Art, Charlotte, NC; Nat Collection of Fine Arts, Washington, DC; NC Mus Art, Raleigh; pvt collections. *Exhib:* NC Artists Ann, NC Mus Art, 61-76; Peidmont Painting & Sculpture Ann, Charlotte, 65-71; Art on Paper, Greensboro, 65, 67, 79 & 80; Am Acad Arts & Lett & Nat Inst Arts & Lett, 72; Painting in the South, Va Mus, 83. *Teaching:* Prof, Averett Col, Danville, Va. *Awards:* Am Acad Arts & Lett Award, 72; Nat Endowment Arts/South Eastern Ctr Contemp Art Southeastern Seven, 81. *Media:* Acrylic. *Dealer:* Heath Gallery 416 E Paces Ferry Rd Atlanta GA 30305; Hodges-Taylor Gallery 227 N Tryon St Charlotte NC 28202. *Mailing Add:* Box 42 Yanceyville NC 27379

GATLING, EVA INGERSOLL
MUSEUM CONSULTANT, HISTORIAN
b Mobile, Ala, Dec 28, 12. *Study:* Richmond Prof Inst, Col William & Mary, cert art, 35; Univ Ala, BA, 41; Yale Univ, MA, 44. *Collections Arranged:* Eliel Saarinsen Mem Exhib (with catalog), Cranbrook Acad Art, 51; Whence Pop, 65, Moran Family, 65 & Salute to Small Museums, 70 (with catalogs), Heckscher Mus; collections of Helen Torr, 72, Ibram Lassaw, 73, Stanley Twardowicz, 74 & Fairfield Porter, 74-75; George Grosz Works in Oil, Heckscher Mus, 77. *Pos:* Dir exhib & supvr art equip, Duke Univ, 45-49; cur, Mus Cranbrook Acad Art, 49-54; asst dir, Des Moines Art Ctr, 59-61; dir, Heckscher Mus, 62-77. *Awards:* Katherine Coffee Award, Northeast Mus Conf, 79. *Mem:* Am Asn Mus; Soc Archit Historians. *Res:* American art, particularly after 1900; American architecture of the 19th and 20th centuries; Buddhist art. *Publ:* Contribr, Soc Art Historians J, 51; contribr, Art J, 55; contribr, Artibus Asiae, 57. *Mailing Add:* 206 Perdido St Fairhope AL 36532

GATRELL, MARION THOMPSON
EDUCATOR, PAINTER
b Columbus, Ohio, Nov 13, 09. *Study:* Ohio State Univ, BSEd, 31, MA, 32. *Work:* Butler Inst Am Art, Youngstown, Ohio; Columbus Gallery Fine Arts; Massillon Mus Art, Ohio; Otterbein Col, Westerville, Ohio; Schumacher Gallery, Capital Univ, Ohio. *Exhib:* Butler Art Inst Regional Ann, 50 & 57; Int Womens Competition, Cannes, France, 69; Florence & Naples, Italy, 72; retrospectives, Schumacher Gallery, Capital Univ, 80 & First Community Village, 80; Images of Age, Bowling Green, Ohio; and others. *Teaching:* From instr to assoc prof drawing & painting, Ohio State Univ, 43-76, emer prof, 76- *Awards:* Baldwin Purchase Award, Massillon Mus, 64; Pace Gallery Award, Schumacher Gallery, Capitol Univ, 68 & 74; Hengst Award, Columbus Art League Ann, 79. *Bibliog:* Mrs Jerry Baughman (auth), Keystones at Ohio State, Ohio State Univ Monthly, 3/72; cover article, 6/72 & article, 2/75, La Revue Moderne, Paris; Sara Carroll (auth), article in Columbus Dispatch, 2/25/79. *Mem:* Nat Asn Women Artists; Columbus Art League. *Media:* Graphics, Watercolor. *Mailing Add:* 2690 Berwyn Rd Columbus OH 43221

GAUCHER, YVES
PRINTMAKER, PAINTER
b Montreal, Que, 34. *Study:* Ecole des Beaux Arts, Montreal, 54-56. *Work:* Mus Mod Art, New York; Libr of Cong, Washington, DC; Victoria & Albert Mus, London, Ont; Mus d'Art Contemp, Montreal; Nat Gallery of Can, Ottawa, Ont. *Exhib:* Contemp Painters as Printmakers, Mus Mod Art, New York, 64; Expo 70, Japan, 70; Aspects of Can Art, Members Gallery, Albright-Knox Art Gallery, Buffalo, NY, 74; Thirteen Artists from Marlborough Gallery, New York, 74; one-man shows, Edmonton Art Gallery, Alta, 69, Sir George Williams Univ, Montreal, 70, Univ Man, Winnipeg, 71 & New York Cult Ctr, 75; and others. *Teaching:* Asst prof fine arts, Sir George Williams Univ, Montreal, 63-69, assoc prof, 70- *Awards:* First Prize, Nat Print Competition, Burnaby, BC, 61; Second Prize, Int Triennale of Colored Prints, Grenchen, Switz, 64; Grand Prize, Sandage 68, Montreal Mus Fine Arts, 68. *Bibliog:* William Withrow (auth), Contemp Can Painting, Toronto, 72; Michel Ragon (auth), Reveire de l'Absolu, Vie des Arts, Montreal, Que, spring 73; Dore Ashton (auth), Can Art in Review, Artscanada, 12/74. *Mailing Add:* c/o Marlborough Godard Gallery 1490 rue Sherbrooke-Ouest Montreal PQ H3G 1L3 Canada

GAUDIERI, ALEXANDER V J
MUSEUM DIRECTOR
b Columbus, Ohio, Apr 23, 40. *Study:* Ohio State Univ; Univ Paris, Sorbonne; Colgate Univ; Barton Kyle Yount Scholar, Am Grad Sch of Int Com; Inst of Fine Arts, NY Univ, with Robert Rosenblum, Francis Watson & James Parker. *Pos:* Dir, Telfair Acad Arts & Sci, 76-83 & Montreal Mus Fine Arts, 83- *Mem:* Asn Art Mus Dirs; Am Asn of Mus; Soc Archit Historians; Appraisers Asn of Am; and others. *Res:* European decorative arts--wood marquetry; development of geometric forms into curvilinear and floral motifs from circa 1715 to mid-century; French romantic painting--the horse paintings of Alfred de Dreux and the influence of Gericault on his oeuvre. *Collection:* Decorative arts including Georges II & III furniture, silver and porcelain. *Mailing Add:* 1227 Sherbrooke St W Montreal PQ H3G 1G1 Canada

GAUDIN, MARGUERITE
DESIGNER
b Philadelphia, Pa, Sept 13, 09. *Study:* Philadelphia Col Art, grad 30. *Exhib:* One-man shows, Philadelphia Art Alliance, Philadelphia Mus Col Art & Woodmere Art Gallery. *Pos:* Designer, Willet Stained Glass Studios, 31-, dir, 60-, vpres, 68- *Awards:* Alumnae Award, Philadelphia Col Art, 60; Honor Award in Ecclesiastical Arts, Church Archit Guild Am, 63; Award of Excellence in Ecclesiastical Art, Am Soc Church Archit, 64. *Mem:* Stained Glass Asn Am; Philadelphia Joint Apprenticeship Comt for Stained Glass Draft (secy); Guild for Relig Archit; Am Soc Church Archit; Philadelphia Watercolor Club. *Media:* Stained Glass. *Publ:* Goal of Life, WRCV TV, 11/17/63; Directions 65, ABC Network, 12/27/64. *Mailing Add:* 24 W Graves Lane Philadelphia PA 19118

GAUGH, HARRY F
EDUCATOR, CRITIC
b Indianapolis, Ind. *Study:* Ind Univ, AB, 60, MA, 63, MA(art hist), 66, PhD, 72. *Teaching:* Assoc prof, Skidmore Col, 66- *Awards:* Grants, Kress Found, 65 & 67; Noble Found Fel, Mus Mod Art, New York, 70; Fel, Nat Endowment Humanities, Princeton Univ, 80. *Mem:* Col Art Asn Am; Int Asn Art Critics. *Res:* Franz Kline and other abstract expressionists; Oskar Kokoschka and Thomas Mann; Rauschenberg; relationships between ancient and 20th century art; contemporary criticism and book reviews. *Publ:* Auth, Kline's transitional abstractions, 1946-50, 7-8/74 & auth, Urban vision of Richard Estes, 11-12/78, Art Am; auth, Franz Kline's romantic abstraction, Artforum, summer 75; auth, Franz Kline: The color abstractions, Phillips Collection, 79; contribr, The Greek Vase, Hudson-Mohawk Asn Cols & Univs, 81; auth, William de Kooning, Abbeville Press, 83. *Mailing Add:* c/o Dept Art Skidmore Col Saratoga Springs NY 12866

GAUVIN, CLAUDE E
PAINTER
b Bathurst, NB, June 14, 39. *Study:* Ecole Beaux Arts Montreal, dipl, 60; Univ Que, Montreal, BA(spec educ), 74; Tyler Art Sch, 76. *Work:* Banque Art NB, Fredericton; Consolidated Bathurst, Montreal; Univ Moncton, NB. *Exhib:* Solo exhib, Radio-Can, Moncton, NB, 80 & Rothmans Gallery, Moncton, NB, 83; Collections, Art Bank NB, Dieppe, 81; Univ Maine, 82; Art Collections, Univ Moncton, NB, 83. *Teaching:* Instr art, Montreal Sch Design, 60-63 & Philadelphia Sch Bd, 74-77; prof painting, Univ Moncton, NB, 78- *Awards:* Constance Carlston Award, Univ Maine, 82. *Bibliog:* Bernard Levy (auth), Le plaisir de l'objet, Vie Arts, 80. *Mem:* Can Art Rep, Fedn Artistes Can (secy, 81, exec secy, 82-83). *Mailing Add:* 185 Church St Moncton NB E1C 5A1 Canada

GAUVREAU, ROBERT GEORGE
PHOTOGRAPHER, EDUCATOR
b Renton, Wash, Aug 14, 48. *Study:* Cent Wash State Univ, BA, 70; Ariz State Univ, Tempe, MFA, 73. *Work:* Coos Art Mus, Coos Bay, Ore. *Exhib:* Phoenix Art Mus, Ariz, 73; Spectrum Gallery, Tucson, 76; Creative Eye Gallery, Sonoma, Calif, 76; Cent Wash State Univ, Ellensburg, 77; Coos Bay Mus, Ore, 78; and others. *Teaching:* Lectr photog, State Univ NY, New Paltz, 73-74; instr photog, Modesto Jr Col, Calif, 74- *Mem:* Soc Photog Educ. *Media:* Color. *Mailing Add:* 1425 Glenhaven Dr Modesto CA 95355

GAVALAS, ALEXANDER BEARY
PAINTER
b Limerick, Ireland, Jan 6, 45; US citizen. *Study:* Sch Art & Design, dipl, 63; Manhattanville Col, 69-71. *Work:* Tweed Mus Art, Duluth, Minn; and others. *Exhib:* One-man shows, Tweed Mus Art, Minn, 80, Western Ill Univ Libr Gallery, 81, Ft Wayne Mus Art, Ind, 82, Marycrest Col Eberdt Art Gallery, Iowa, 82, Arnot Art Mus, New York, 82 & Queens Col Art Ctr/Paul Klapper Libr, New York, 83. *Bibliog:* Matt Santoro (auth), At peace with his

environment, Queens Ledger, 80; Alan Garfield (auth), Alexander Beary Gavalas Recent Paintings & Drawings, Krasl Art Ctr, 80; Idealism, serenity mark Gavalas' landscapes, Ft Wayne Sentinel, 4/82. *Media:* Oil, Pen & Ink. *Publ:* Auth, articles in Irish Echo, 82 & 83, New York Daily News, 82 & Western Queens Gazette, 82. *Mailing Add:* 2578 34th St Astoria Long Island City NY 11103

GAWARECKI, CAROLYN ANN See Grosse

GAYLORD, FRANK CHALFANT, II
SCULPTOR, DESIGNER
b Clarksburg, WVa, Mar 9, 25. *Study:* Carnegie Inst Technol Col Fine Arts; Tyler Sch Fine Arts, Temple Univ, BFA. *Comn:* Firemen Mem (granite), Nyack, NY; Pioneer Family (granite), Akron, Ohio; Arthur Fiedler (granite portrait), Boston Univ Libr, 82; William Penn (granite figure), Pen Treaty Park, Philadelphia, 82; William Shakespeare (granite portrait), Old Globe Theater, San Diego, 83. *Exhib:* Nat Sculpture Soc Ann Exhib, 65 & 79. *Bibliog:* Article, The memorial sculpture of Frank Gaylord, Stone Am Mag, 4/82; The Stone Whistle (film), Barre Granite Asn. *Mem:* Assoc Nat Sculpture Soc. *Media:* Granite, Clay. *Publ:* Auth, Why Christ? & auth, A portrait of Hector, 68, Monumental News Rev. *Mailing Add:* 25 Delmont Ave Barre VT 05641

GEALT, ADELHEID MEDICUS
CURATOR, HISTORIAN
b Munich, Ger, May 29, 46; US citizen. *Study:* Ind Univ, PhD, 79. *Collections Arranged:* Italian Portrait Drawings, 1400-1800 from North American Collections Traveling Exhibit (auth, catalog), 83. *Pos:* Cur, Ind Univ Art Mus, Bloomington, 76- *Awards:* Nat Endowment Arts Cur Grant, 80; Nat Endowment Arts Planning & Implementation Grant, 81; Am Philos Soc Grant, 81. *Mem:* Ind Arts Comn(adv panelist, 78-81). *Res:* Primarily Italian painting and drawing from 1300-1800. *Publ:* Auth, Two Punchinello Drawings by Domenico Tiepolo, Arte Veneta, 80; contribr, Medieval Dictionary, Am Coun Learned Soc; Some Thoughts on the Minneapolis Nardo di Cione, Minn Inst Arts Bulletin, 10/81; The Uffizi lamentation, In: Gazette Beau-Arts, 4/83; auth, Looking at Art, A Visitor's Guide to Art Museums, R R Bowker, 83. *Mailing Add:* Ind Univ Art Mus Bloomington IN 47405

GEAR, JOSEPHINE
HISTORIAN, GALLERY DIRECTOR
b London, Eng, Nov 24, 38. *Study:* The English equivalent of a degree in museology; the dipl of Mus Asn Gt Brit, 65; Woodrow Wilson Dissertation fel, 73-74, Inst Fine Arts, NY Univ, scholar award, 75-76, PhD, 76; study with Bob Rosenblum & Gert Schiff. *Pos:* Dir, Univ Art Gallery, State Univ NY, Binghamton, 79- *Teaching:* Asst prof art hist, Briarcliff Col, NY, 75-77; asst prof art hist, State Univ NY, Binghamton, 79- *Mem:* Mus Asn Gt Brit; Col Art Asn Am (co-chmn Marxist caucus, 78). *Publ:* auth, Master or Servant?, A Study of Selected English Painters and Their Patrons of the Late 18th and Early 19th centuries, Garland, 77; coauth, The 70's Alternative View of Design: Danger from the Drawing Boards?, Contemp Art/SE, 77; auth, Trapped Women: The Work of Two Sister Designers, Margaret and Frances Macdonald, Heresies, 78; auth, Some alternative spaces in New York and Los Angeles, Studio Int, 80; and others. *Mailing Add:* 181 E 93rd St Apt 2A New York NY 10028

GEBER, HANA
SCULPTOR, INSTRUCTOR
b Praha, Czech, Feb 14, 10; US citizen. *Study:* Teachers Col, Prague; Art Students League; Sculpture Ctr, New York. *Work:* Yeshiva Univ Mus; Jewish Mus, New York; Rose Art Mus, Brandeis Univ; Mus Ethnography & Folklore, Ramat-Aviv, Israel; Lowe Art Mus, Univ Miami; and many others. *Comn:* Wedding altar, Temple Emanuel, Yonkers, NY; memorial, Verona High Sch, NJ; statue, Riverdale Temple, Bronx; statue, Temple Sinai of Long Island, NY; silver wallpiece, Free Westchester Synagogue; and others. *Exhib:* One-man shows, Montclair Art Mus, Union Am Hebrew Congregations, New York, Sculpture Ctr, New York, Am Jewish Hist Soc, Waltham & Boston, Mass & Pa Acad Fine Arts, Philadelphia; and others. *Teaching:* Mem fac, Sculpture Ctr; also pvt instr. *Awards:* Mem Found Jewish Cult Fel, 69; Gold Medal, Nat Asn Women Artists; First Prize, Am Soc Contemp Artists; and others. *Media:* Silver, Bronze. *Dealer:* Sculpture Ctr 167 E 69th St New York NY 10021; Rudolph Gallery 338 Sevilla Ave Coral Gables FL 33134. *Mailing Add:* 168 W 225th St New York NY 10463

GEBHARD, DAVID
MUSEUM DIRECTOR, HISTORIAN
b Cannon Falls, Minn, July 21, 27. *Study:* Univ Minn, BA, MA & PhD. *Collections Arranged:* Walker Art Ctr, 53; Purcell & Elmslie, Architects, 69; The Enigma of Ralph A Blakelock 1847-1919, 69, Art Galleries, Univ Calif, Santa Barbara, Charles Demuth, 71; Indian Art of the Northern Plains, 74; 200 Years of American Architectural Drawings (coauth, catalog), 77-78; The Architecture of Gregory Ain (auth, catalog), 80; Joseph Hoffmann, Design Classic (auth, catalog), 82; Santa Barbara, The Creation of a New Spain in America, (auth, catalog), 82. *Pos:* Dir, Roswell Mus & Art Ctr, 55-60; dir, Univ Calif Santa Barbara Art Mus, 61-80; cur, Archit Drawing Collection, Univ Calif, Santa Barbara, 80- *Teaching:* Instr art hist, Univ NMex, 53-55; prof art hist, Univ Calif, Santa Barbara, 61- *Mem:* Soc Archit Historians (pres, 80-); Nat Archit Accrediting Bd. *Res:* 19th and 20th century architecture; architecture of California; rock art of North America. *Publ:* Coauth, S & J C Newsom Victorian architectural imagery in California, 79; coauth, California Crazy, 80; coauth, Tulsa Art Deco, 80; coauth, Home Sweet Home, American Domestic Vernacular, 83; coauth, A Guide to Architecture in Los Angeles, 83. *Mailing Add:* 895 E Mountain Dr Santa Barbara CA 93108

GEBHARDT, HAROLD
SCULPTOR, PAINTER
b Milwaukee, Wis, Aug 21, 07. *Study:* Layton Sch Art. *Work:* Milwaukee Pub Libr; Univ Wis-Milwaukee; Los Angeles Mus Art; also in pvt collections. *Exhib:* Whitney Mus Am Art, New York; Los Angeles Co Mus Art; Chicago Art Inst; San Francisco Mus Art; Museu de Arte Moderna, Sao Paulo, Brazil; DeYoung Mem Mus, San Francisco; one-man shows, Occidental Col, Trinity Univ Gallery, Santa Barbara Mus, San Bernardino Col; and many others. *Teaching:* Prof sculpture, Univ Southern Calif, formerly, emer prof, currently. *Awards:* Milwaukee Art Inst Award, 37; Los Angeles Mus Art Award, 46 & 50; City of Los Angeles Award, 48. *Media:* Acrylic; Stone, Wood. *Mailing Add:* 13186 Glenoaks Blvd Sylmar CA 91342

GEBHARDT, PETER MARTIN
SCULPTOR
b Los Angeles, Calif, Dec 10, 43. *Study:* Univ Southern Calif, 61-65; San Fernando State Col, 62-66. *Exhib:* Southwest Craft Ctr, San Antonio, Tex, 73; Elements Gallery, Greenwich, Conn, 74; Studio Gallery, West Covina, Calif, 76; Philip Morris Gallery, Los Angeles, 77; Crafts & Folk Art Mus, Los Angeles, 77; and others. *Mailing Add:* 13186 Glenoaks Blvd Sylmar CA 91342

GEBHARDT, ROLAND
SCULPTOR, DESIGNER
b Paramaribo, Surinam, Sept 24, 39; US citizen. *Study:* Art Acad Hamburg, Ger, with Theo Ortner; Kuntsgewerbeschule, Zurich, Switz; also apprenticeship in stained glass, Marburg, Ger. *Work:* Art Acad, Hamburg; Brandeis Univ; Storm King Art Ctr, Mountainville, NY; City of Ludwigshafen, Ger; Neuberger Mus, Purchase, NY. *Exhib:* One-man sculpture & painting exhib, Hudson River Mus, 71; 20th Century Sculpture in Westchester Collection, Yonkers, NY, 72; one-man shows, Gallery 84, New York, 73 & Robert Freidus Gallery, 78; Carlton Gallery, New York, 74 & 77; Storm King Art Ctr, 75 & 76; The Minimal Tradition, Aldrich Mus, Ridgefield, Conn, 79. *Awards:* Annual Prize, Art Acad Hamburg, 62. *Bibliog:* Fred Salaff (auth), Roland Gebhardt--Sculptor (film), 72; Arlene Krebs (dir), Liniar Void (video), 78. *Media:* Metal, Stone; Fiberglass, Concrete. *Mailing Add:* 67 Vestry St New York NY 10013

GECHTOFF, SONIA
PAINTER
b Philadelphia, Pa, Sept 25, 26. *Study:* Philadelphia Mus Col Art, BFA, 50; Ford Found Fel, Tamarind Lithography Workshop, 63. *Work:* Guggenheim Mus, Mus of Mod Art & Metropolitan Mus Art, New York; Baltimore Mus of Art; San Francisco Mus Mod Art. *Exhib:* Am Painters, US Pavilion, Brussels Fair, Belg, 58; First Paris Bienale, France, 59; Calif Painting: Mod Era, San Francisco Mus of Art, 76 & Nat Collection of Fine Arts, Washington, DC, 76-77; Drawing Acquisition Shows, Mus of Mod Art, New York, 77 & Extraordinary Women & Am Drawn & Matched, 76-77; solo show, Gruenebaum Gallery, New York, 79, 80, 82 & 83; New Dimensions in Drawing, 1950-1980, Aldrich Mus Contemp Art, Conn, 81; and others. *Teaching:* Instr painting & drawing, Calif Sch Fine Arts, 57-58; adj asst prof art, NY Univ, 61-71; lectr art, Queens Col, 70-74; assoc prof art, Univ NMex, 74-75. *Awards:* Purchase Award, San Francisco Mus Art, 57; Drawing Prize, Four Corners States Bienale, Phoenix Art Mus, 75; plus others. *Bibliog:* Hilton Kramer (auth), Triumphant new work, 5/20/79 & Sonia Gechtoff's abstract drawing at its best, 10/31/80, New York Times; James Mellow (auth), Sonia Gechtoff: A different kind of knowledge, Arts Mag, 2/82. *Mem:* Archives Am Art. *Dealer:* Gruenebaum Gallery 38 E 57th St New York NY 10022. *Mailing Add:* 421 Hudson St New York NY 10014

GECK, FRANCIS JOSEPH
EDUCATOR, DESIGNER
b Detroit, Mich, Dec 20, 1900. *Study:* New York Sch Fine & Apl Art & Paris Atelier, France, dipl; Syracuse Univ, MFA, 46. *Exhib:* Washington Watercolor Club 54th Ann, Smithsonian Inst, Washington, DC, 50; Pavilion of American Interiors, New York World's Fair, 65; Boulder Nat Bank, Colo, 66; Village Theatre Lobby, Boulder, 67-74; Manufacturers Hanover Trust Gallery, New York, 71; and others. *Pos:* Interior architect & designer, William Wright Co, Detroit, 27-30; interior architect & consult, T Eaton Co, Toronto, 30; dir, Sherwood Art Gallery, Boulder, 37-40; dir exhib, Boulder Hist Soc, 44-55; cur exhib, Univ Colo, 47-57; dir exhib, Pioneer Mus, Boulder, 58-80; design consult, Mullins Plastics, 69-72. *Teaching:* Instr interior design, New York Sch Fine & Appl Art, Paris Atelier, France, 24-27; prof interior design, Univ Colo, Boulder, 30-69, prof emer, 69- *Awards:* Gold Medal Winner, Grand Nat Show, Am Artists Prof League, 53; Tommaso Campanella Silver Medal, Acad Int Lettre-Arti-Scienze, 70; and others. *Mem:* Boulder Artists Guild; Boulder Hist Soc; Am Inst Interior Designers; Interior Design Educ Coun; Am Soc Interior Designers. *Publ:* Auth, Exercises in Perspective, 48; auth, Introduction to Interior Decoration, 55; auth, Dial-a-Style: English Period Furniture, 66; auth, Interior Design & Decoration, 74; auth, French Interiors and Furniture--The Period of Francis I, 82; and others. *Mailing Add:* 407 16th St Boulder CO 80302

GEE, HELEN
ART CONSULTANT, CURATOR
US citizen. *Collections Arranged:* Guest cur, Stieglitz & the Photo-Secession, NJ State Mus, 78; Bank Tokyo, New York; Indust Bank Japan, New York; Photography of the Fifties (catalog), Ctr Creative Photog, Tucson. *Pos:* Owner & dir, Limelight Gallery. *Interests:* 19th and 20th century painting, sculpture and photography. *Mailing Add:* 263 W 11th St New York NY 10014

GEERLINGS, GERALD KENNETH
GRAPHIC ARTIST, ARCHITECT
b Milwaukee, Wis, Apr 18, 1897. *Study:* Univ Pa, BA(archit), 21, MA(archit), 22; Royal Col Art, London, two yrs. *Work:* Victoria & Albert Mus, London; Metrop Mus Art, New York; Libr Cong & Nat Collection Fine Arts, Washington, DC; Chicago Art Inst; plus others. *Exhib:* Royal Acad, London; Paris Int Exhib; New York Worlds Fair, 39; Nat Acad Design, New York; Philadelphia Acad Fine Arts; plus others. *Awards:* Gold Medal for Best Black & White of the Year, Philadelphia Acad Fine Arts, 31; First Prize for Best Etching, Chicago Worlds Fair, 33; Nat Arts Club Award, New York. *Mem:* Soc Am Graphic Artists; Am Inst Architects; Pastel Soc Am. *Media:* Pencil; Pastels, Watercolor. *Publ:* Auth & illusr, Metal Crafts in Architecture, 29 & 72, auth & illusr, Wrought Iron in Architecture, 29 & 72 & auth & illusr, Color Schemes of Adam Ceilings, 28, Scribners. *Dealer:* Uptown Gallery 1194 Madison Ave New York NY 10028; M Lee Stone 2101 Forest Avenue San Jose CA 95128. *Mailing Add:* 26 Gower Rd New Canaan CT 06840

GEESLIN, LEE GADDIS
PAINTER, EDUCATOR
b Goldthwaite, Tex, June 28, 20. *Study:* Univ Tex; New Orleans Art & Crafts; Art Inst Chicago, BFA & MFA. *Exhib:* Annually with local & regional shows of the Southwest; one-man shows, Brownsville, San Angelo, Houston, Corpus Christi, Brady, Lufkin, Dallas & Texarkana, Tex, also Shreveport, La, 63- *Teaching:* Prof art, Sam Houston State Univ, currently. *Mem:* Tex Watercolor Soc; Tex Fine Arts Soc; Tex Art Educ Asn; Am Asn Univ Prof; Col Art Asn Am. *Mailing Add:* Sch of Art Sam Houston State Univ Huntsville TX 77340

GEFTER, JUDITH MICHELMAN
PHOTOGRAPHER
b Gloversville, NY. *Study:* Pratt Inst, cert; NY Univ; Univ Fla; Fla State Univ; also with William E Parker & Wilson Hicks Conf, Univ Miami. *Work:* Mint Mus, Charlotte, NC; Jacksonville Art Mus, Fla; Tampa Art Inst, Fla. *Exhib:* Am Soc Mag Photogr Traveling Show, 62-63; one-woman shows, Pratt Inst, 66 & 67, Retrospect, Jacksonville Art Mus, 70, Breast & Face, Steiglitz Gallery, New York, 75, Jacksonville Univ-Phillips Gallery, Fla, 77 & Univ NFla, 78; There Is No Female Camera Traveling Show, Neikrug Gallery, New York, 75. *Bibliog:* Elizabeth Kaufman (auth), My life & my art, Arts Assembler, 11/75; portfolio, Charter Issue Kalliope, A Jour of Women's Art, winter 79; Challenge of Freelance Photography (audio-visual prog), Media Loft Inc, 80. *Mem:* Am Soc Mag Photogr, Soc Photogr in Commun (pres, NFla Chap, 65-70); Nat Soc Lit & Arts. *Publ:* Illusr, Jacksonville Calendar Diary Bicentennial Ed, 76; contribr, Longman Dict Mass Media & Communication, 82. *Mailing Add:* 1725 Clemson Rd Jacksonville FL 32217

GEHR, MARY (RAY)
PRINTMAKER, PAINTER
b Chicago, Ill. *Study:* Smith Col; Art Inst Chicago, with Paul Wieghardt; Inst Design of Ill Inst Technol, with Misch Kohn. *Work:* Art Inst Chicago; Philadelphia Mus; Libr Cong, Washington, DC; Nelson Rockefeller Collection; Free Libr, Philadelphia. *Comn:* Golden Santorini (intaglio-edition of 210 etchings printed by Leterio Calapai), Int Graphic Arts Soc, 67. *Exhib:* Chicago & Vicinity Exhibs & Soc Contemp Am Art, Art Inst Chicago; Brooklyn Mus Nat Print Exhib; Boston Printmakers, Mass; Print Club, Philadelphia; 54 one-man shows in US & Europe, 57-; 21 Views of China, Chicago Cult Ctr, 79. *Pos:* Mem artists adv comt, Art Rental & Sales Gallery, Art Inst Chicago, 64-83. *Teaching:* Lectr China, Art Inst Chicago, 79, 81 & 82. *Awards:* Print Fair Award, Philadelphia; First Purchase Award, Artist Guild Chicago; Award for Graphics, Old Orchard Festival, Chicago. *Bibliog:* John Fink (auth), The Greece of Mary Gehr, Chicago Tribune Mag, 67; T J Carbol (ed), The printmaker in Illinois, Ill Art Educ Asn, 71-72; plus many articles in local papers. *Mem:* Arts Club Chicago; Alumnae of Art Inst Chicago; Soc Typographic Arts. *Media:* Intaglio, Batik; Oil, Acrylics. *Publ:* Illusr, designer & art ed, Exploring the World of Archaeology, 66; illusr, designer & art ed, Exploring the World of Pottery, 67. *Dealer:* Joseph Faulkner 620 N Michigan Ave Chicago IL 60611. *Mailing Add:* 1829 N Orleans Chicago IL 60614

GEHRY, FRANK O(WEN)
ARCHITECT
b Toronto, Ont, Feb 28, 29; US citizen. *Study:* Univ Southern Calif Col Fine Arts, 49-51, Col Archit, BArch, 54; Harvard Univ Grad Sch Design, 56-57. *Work:* Mus Mod Art, Metrop Mus Art, New York; Los Angeles Mus Contemp Art; Philadelphia Mus Art. *Comn:* Cabrillo Marine Mus, City Los Angeles, San Pedro, Calif, 79; Loyola Law Sch, Loyola Marymount Univ, 81; Calif Aerospace Mus, State Calif, Los Angeles, 83; Frances Howard Goldwyn Regional Branch Libr, comn by Samuel Goldwyn Jr, Los Angeles, 83. *Exhib:* Chicago Tribune Late Entries, Inst Contemp Art, Chicago, 80; La Presenza del Passato, Biennale Venezia, Italy, 80; Documenta VII, Kasel, Ger, 82; Shape and Environment, Whitney Mus Am Art, 82; Ten New Buildings, Inst Contemp Art, London, 83; California Counterpoint, Nat Acad Design, New York, 83. *Teaching:* Vis critic, Rice Univ, 76; Univ Calif, Los Angeles, 79 & Harvard Univ, 83. *Awards:* William Bishop Chair, 79 & Charlotte Davenport Prof Archit, 82, Yale Univ; Arnold W Brunner Mem Prize Archit, Am Acad & Inst Arts & Lett, 83. *Bibliog:* Beyond Utopia, Michael Blackwood Productions, 83; Joseph Morgenstern (auth), The Gehry style, New York Times Mag, 5/16/83; Lindsay Stamm Schapiro (auth), A minimalist architecture of allusion, Progressive Archit, 6/83. *Mem:* Am Inst Archit. *Mailing Add:* Frank Gehrry & Assoc 11 Brooks Ave Venice CA 90291

GEIGER, EDITH ROGERS
PAINTER
b New Haven, Conn, July 13, 12. *Study:* Smith Col, BA, 34; Art Students League, 34-35; Yale Univ, with Joseph Albers. *Work:* Wadsworth Atheneum, Hartford; Tryon Art Mus, Smith Col; Springfield Art Mus, Mass; Art Mus, Ann Arbor, Mich; Bridgeport Univ Art Collection. *Exhib:* Brooklyn Mus 21st Int Watercolor Biennial; Detroit Nat Watercolor Exhib; Boston Art Festival; Providence Festival, RI; solo exhibs, Bodley Gallery, New York, 56, Ruth White Gallery, New York, 59 & 62, Naples Art Gallery, Fla, 69 & 70. *Awards:* Best in Show Awards, New Haven Festival Arts, 57 & 62; Woman's Award, Am Watercolor Soc, 62; Nat Asn Women Artists Award, 63. *Mem:* Am Watercolor Soc. *Media:* Mixed Media. *Mailing Add:* 2750 Gulf Shore Blvd N Naples FL 33940

GEIS, MILTON ARTHUR
PAINTER, DESIGNER
b Milwaukee, Wis, Jan 31, 26. *Study:* Univ Florence, Italy, 45; Columbia Univ, 45; Layton Sch of Art, dipl, 50; Webster Univ, BFA, 83. *Work:* Milwaukee Art Ctr, Milwaukee Art Inst; Zodok-Gimbel Wisconsin Collection; Tex Tech Univ Mus; Crestwood Govt Ctr. *Exhib:* Vicinity Ann, Art Inst Chicago, 54; Regional Ann, St Louis Artists Guild, Mo, 74-83; Butler Inst Am Art, 78, 80-81 & 83; Nat Soc Painters in Casein & Acrylic, 78, 80 & 83; Am Watercolor Soc, 81 & 83; Watercolor USA, 82; Nat Watercolor Soc, 82; and many others. *Pos:* Art dir, WBAY-TV, Green Bay, Wis, 52-56, WXIX-TV, Milwaukee, Wis, 56-60; dir design, KMOX-TV, St Louis, Mo, 60- *Awards:* Jean Despujols Award & Meadows Mus Purchase Award, 54th Ann Shreveport Nat, Friends of the Mus & Meadows Mus Guild, 76; Grumbacher Award, Nat Arts Club 80th Ann, 80; Strathmore Award, Nat Watercolor Soc 62nd Ann, 82. *Mem:* Audubon Artists Am; Nat Soc Painters Casein & Acrylic; St Louis Artists Guild: Broadcast Designers Asn. *Media:* Mixed. *Mailing Add:* 8978 Lindenhurst Dr St Louis MO 63126

GEISEL, THEODOR SEUSS (DR SEUSS)
ILLUSTRATOR, WRITER
b Springfield, Mass, Mar 2, 04. *Study:* Dartmouth Col, AB, 25, LHD, 56; Lincoln Col, Oxford Univ, 25-26; Am Int Col, 68. *Work:* Dr Seuss bk illus & mss in Libr of Univ Calif, Los Angeles. *Exhib:* One-man show, Fine Arts Gallery, San Diego, 58; 50th Anniversary Retrospective, Dartmouth Col, 75; Toledo Mus of Art, 75-76; La Jolla Mus of Contemp Art, Calif, 76-77. *Pos:* Advert illusr for indust firms; ed cartoonist, PM (newspaper), New York; publ, Bright & Early Bks; pres, Beginner Bk Div, Random House, Inc; designer children's furniture, Sears Roebuck; producer, animated cartoons for TV. *Teaching:* Lect on illustrating & writing children's bks. *Awards:* Legion of Merit for Educ & Info Films, World War II; Acad Awards for Best Doc Short, 46, for Best Doc Feature, 47 & for Best Animated Cartoon, 51. *Publ:* Auth & illus, The Foot Book, 68, I Can Lick 30 Tigers Today & Other Stories, 69, My Book About Me, 69, I Can Draw It Myself, 70, Mr Brown Can Moo, Can You?, The Lorax, 71 & Oh Say Can You Say, 79; plus many others. *Mailing Add:* c/o Random House 201 E 50th St New York NY 10022

GEISERT, ARTHUR FREDERICK
PRINTMAKER, ILLUSTRATOR
b Dallas, Tex, Sept 20, 41. *Study:* Concordia Teachers' Col, Seward, Nebr, BS, 63; Univ Calif, Davis, MA, 65; Chouinard Art Inst, Los Angeles; Otis Art Inst, Los Angeles; Art Inst Chicago. *Work:* Mus Art, Lodz, Poland; Freeport Art Mus, Ill; First Nat Bank Chicago; Standard Oil of Ind, Chicago; Calif Col Arts & Crafts, Oakland. *Comn:* Mural, First St Paul's, Chicago, 77. *Exhib:* Joslyn Biennial, Joslyn Art Mus, Omaha, Nebr, 78; West 79, The Law, Minn Mus Art, St Paul, 79; 5th Univ Dallas Nat Print Invitational, Univ Dallas, Tex, 79; one-man shows, Ill Art Coun Gallery, Chicago, 79 & Western Ill Univ, 79. *Teaching:* From instr to asst prof art, Concordia Col, River Forest, Ill, 65-70; asst prof art, Concordia Col, Seward, Nebr, 70-71; instr art, Clarke Col, 74- *Awards:* Purchase Awards, New Horizons, North Shore Art League, Chicago, 75 & 78; Ivah Thone Rostenbach Mem Award, Mid-Miss Exhib, Davenport Art Mus, 77. *Mem:* Chicago Artists Coalition; Artists Equity Asn Inc; North Shore Art League; Peoria Art Guild; Galena Artists' Guild. *Media:* Etching. *Publ:* Auth, The Orange Scarf (children's book), Simon & Schuster, 70; illusr, Prisoners of the Scrambling Dragon (children's book) & auth, F N Monjo, Holt, Rinehart & Winston, 80; auth & illusr, Pa's Balloon and Other Pig Tales, Houghton Mifflin, 84. *Mailing Add:* PO Box 3 Galena IL 61036

GEIST, SIDNEY
SCULPTOR, CRITIC
b Paterson, NJ, Apr 11, 14. *Study:* St Stephen's Col; Art Students League; Acad Grande Chaumiere, Paris. *Work:* Bard Col, Annandale-on-Hudson, NY. *Exhib:* Salon Jeune Sculpture, Paris, 50; one-man shows, Paris, 50, New York, 51, 57, 60, Bard Col, 69 & New York, 74, 76, 78 & 83; Pittsburgh Int, 58; Am Artists Ann, Chicago, 62. *Pos:* Dir, New York Studio Sch, 64-66; guest cur, Brancusi Retrospective, Guggenheim Mus, 69. *Teaching:* Instr sculpture, Pratt Inst, 61-65; instr sculpture, New York Studio Sch, 64-; instr sculpture, Vassar Col, 67-75, 76- *Awards:* Olivetti Award, Silvermine Guild, Conn, 60; Guggenheim Fel, 75-76. *Bibliog:* Thomas B Hess (auth), US sculpture: some recent directions, Portfolio, 59. *Mem:* Col Art Asn Am. *Media:* Wood, Stone. *Publ:* Auth, Brancusi: a Study of the Sculpture, Grossman, 68; auth, Constantin Brancusi: a Retrospective Exhibition, Guggenheim Mus, 69; Brancusi: Sculpture and Drawings, Abrams, 75; auth, Brancusi: The Kiss, Harpers, 78. *Mailing Add:* 310 W 106 St New York NY 10025

GEKIERE, MADELEINE
PAINTER, FILMMAKER

b Zurich, Switz; US citizen. *Study:* Art Students League, with Kantor; Brooklyn Mus Art Sch, with Tamayo; NY Univ, with Sam Adler. *Work:* Worcester Art Mus, Mass; Fogg Mus Art, Cambridge, Mass; NY Univ Collection; Brooklyn Mus, NY; Currier Gallery of Art, Manchester, NH; and others. *Exhib:* Univ Ga, 67; Western Carolina Univ, 72; Audubon Artists, New York; NY Univ Loeb Ctr; also many one-man shows in New York, Babcock Galleries, film showings, Millenium & Artists Space, The Collective for Living Cinema, NY & 2nd Int Women's Film Festival, New York Film Forum. *Teaching:* Asst prof painting, NY Univ, 58-67; prof painting, City Col New York, 67-; vis prof painting, Univ Ga, 67. *Awards:* Best Illustrated Book of Year, New York Times, 57, 59 & 63; Audubon Medal of Honor, 69; Childe Hassam Purchase Prize, Soc Art & Lett, 73. *Mem:* Artists Equity Asn. *Media:* Ink, Oil. *Publ:* Auth & illusr, Who Gave Us, 53; illusr, Switch on the Night, 57; auth & illusr, The Princess & the Frilly Lilly, 60; illusr, The Reason for the Pelican, 60; illusr, John J Plenty and Fiddler Dan, 63. *Mailing Add:* 427 W 21st St New York NY 10011

GELBER, SAMUEL
PAINTER, EDUCATOR

b Brooklyn, NY, Mar 14, 29. *Study:* Brooklyn Col, BA; NY Univ, MA. *Exhib:* Brooklyn Mus Biennial, 56; one-man shows, Green Mountain Gallery, New York, 72, 74, 76 & 79, A Sense of Place, Wichita Art Mus, Kans, 73, Springfield Art Mus, Mo, 74 & Joslyn Art Mus, Nebr, 74; Artist's Choice--Figurative Art in New York, 76; and others. *Teaching:* Instr drawing, Pratt Inst, Brooklyn, 62-65; prof painting & drawing, Brooklyn Col, 62- *Awards:* Crane & Co Award for Painting, Berkshire Mus, 66. *Bibliog:* Lee Wallin (auth), New Realism 70, St Cloud State Col, 70; Alan Gussow (auth), A Sense of Place--the Artist and the American Land, Friends of Earth, 72; Sanford Sintz Shannan (auth), An interview with Philip Pearlstein, Art in Am, 9/81. *Media:* Oil, Watercolor. *Mailing Add:* 215 W 98th St New York NY 10025

GELBURD, GAIL ENID
MUSEUM DIRECTOR, EDUCATOR

b New York, NY, Feb 24, 54. *Study:* Queens Col, City Univ New York, BA, 74; Ohio State Univ, MA, 77. *Collections Arranged:* Realism in American Art (with catalog), 80 & Light: Recent Issues in Illumination (with catalog), 82, Morris Mus Arts & Sci; Art & Psychological Warfare (auth, catalog), 82, Androgyny in Art (auth, catalog), 82 & The Blossoming of New Promises: Art of the Harlem Renaissance (auth, catalog), 84, Emily Lowe Gallery, Hofstra Univ. *Pos:* Cur, Morris Mus Arts & Sci, 78-80; dir, Emily Lower Gallery, Hofstra Univ, 81- *Teaching:* Lectr, Mus Mod Art, New York, formerly; instr art hist, Ohio State Univ, 75-77; lectr, Sch Visual Arts, 80-81; asst prof art hist & mus studies, Hofstra Univ, 81- *Mem:* Am Asn Mus; Col Art Asn. *Res:* American art influenced by the Far East; contemporary art; political art in America; art and philosophy. *Publ:* Contribr, Handbook of the Permanent Collection, Columbus Mus Fine Arts, 79; contribr, American Painting from Washington Museums, Smithsonian Inst, 80. *Mailing Add:* 140-66A Burden Crescent Jamaica NY 11435

GELDZAHLER, HENRY
CURATOR, HISTORIAN

b Antwerp, Belg, July 9, 35; US citizen. *Study:* Yale Univ, BA; Harvard Univ. *Pos:* Curatorial asst, Dept Am Paintings & Sculpture, Metrop Mus Art, 60-62; asst cur, 62-63, assoc cur, 63-67, cur, Dept 20th Century Art, 67-; comnr, Dept of Cult Affairs, City of New York, 78-82. *Publ:* Auth, American Painting in the Twentieth Century, Metrop Mus Art; auth, New York Painting and Sculpture 1940-1970, Dutton, 69. *Mailing Add:* Dept of Cult Affairs Two Columbus Circle New York NY 10019

GELINAS, ROBERT WILLIAM
PAINTER, EDUCATOR

b Springfield, Mass, Mar 1, 31. *Study:* Univ Conn; Univ Ala, BFA & MFA; also with Lawrence Calgagno & Tatsuiko Heima. *Work:* Kelley Fitzpatrick Mus, Montgomery, Ala; Mead Corp Collection, Atlanta, Ga; Fla House of Rep, Tallahassee; Mus Fine Arts, Little Rock, Ark. *Comn:* Chapel sculpture, Wesley Found Student Ctr, Memphis, 60. *Exhib:* Art USA, 58, New York, 58; 26th & 27th Corcoran Biennials, Washington, DC, 59 & 61; Painting of the Yr Ann, Mead Corp, Atlanta, 61; Bon Marche Nat Gallery Exhib, Seattle, Wash, 63; Fla Showcase, Rockefeller Ctr, New York, 64; Soc of Four Arts Exhibs, Palm Beach, Fla, 66, 72, 77, 78 & 79. *Pos:* Art dir, Tuscaloosa News, Ala, 55-57; artist in residence, Maitland Res Ctr, 65; artist in residence, Upham Studio, Naples, 66-69. *Teaching:* Guest artist instr, Allisons Wells Art Colony Workshops, Canton, Miss, 58-62; asst prof art, Memphis State Univ, 58-63; from assoc prof to prof art, Univ SFla, 63- *Awards:* First Purchase Prize, Mid South Ann, 61; 18th Ann Purchase Exhib Prize, Carrol Reese Mus, 67; Best of Show, Gulf Coast Art Exhib, Bellaire, Fla, 78. *Bibliog:* Benbow (auth), All out war, St Petersburg Times, 8/65; Gelinas the modern master, Tampa Tribune, 66. *Media:* Acrylic. *Dealer:* Virginia Miller Galleries Coconut Grove Miami FL 33133. *Mailing Add:* Rte 2 Box 1253 Odessa FL 33556

GELLER, ESTHER (ESTHER GELLER SHAPERO)
PAINTER, PRINTMAKER

b Boston, Mass, Oct 26, 21. *Study:* Mus Fine Arts Sch, Boston, dipl; also with Karl Zerbe. *Work:* Mus Fine Arts, Boston; Addison Gallery Am Art, Andover, Mass; Brandeis Univ; Walters Gallery, Regis Col; St Mark's Sch Gallery, Southboro, Mass. *Exhib:* Art Inst Chicago Ann; Boston Art Festivals; US Info Serv Circulating Exhibs in the US & Far East; one-man show, Am Acad Art Gallery, Rome, 71, Newton Art Ctr, 78, Artworks at the Wayne,

79; and others. *Teaching:* Instr painting & drawing, Sch Mus Fine Arts, Boston, 43, Boris Mirski Art Sch, 46-48, Natick Art Asn Sch, 55-61 & Wayland Art Asn, 83. *Awards:* Cabot Fel, 49; Fels, MacDowell Colony, Yaddo & Am Acad, 50-71. *Bibliog:* Pratt & Fizell (auth), Encaustic, Lear Publ, 49; Bern Chaet (auth), Artists at Work, Webb, 60; B Hayes (auth), The Layman's Guide to Modern Art; and others. *Media:* Encaustic, Watercolors. *Dealer:* Arts Wayland Gallery Loker St Wayland MA; Leonard Morse Art Gallery Natick MA 01760. *Mailing Add:* 9 Russell Circle Natick MA 01760

GELLIS, SANDY L
SCULPTOR

b New York, NY. *Study:* Sch of Visual Arts; City Col of New York; New Sch for Social Res, FTT (AAS). *Exhib:* Condensed Space, Nassau Co Mus Art, NY, 77; Breaking In, Creative Time, 48 Old Slip, New York, 80; Ten Sculptors, State Univ NY, Stony Brook, 81; 12th Anniversary, 55 Mercer, New York; Time Wall Installation, BACA, New York, 83; and others. *Awards:* Creative Artists Pub Serv Prog Grant, 78; MacDowell Colony Fel, 79; Nat Endowment Arts Fel, 79-80 & 81-82. *Bibliog:* Ellen Lubelli (auth), article, Soho News New York, 78; Jeanne Paris (auth), article, Newsday, 81; Jess Kipnis (auth), article, Atlanta Art Papers, 81. *Media:* Mixed Media. *Dealer:* Louise Ross 171 W 12th St New York NY; Actual Art Foundation Seven Worth St New York NY. *Mailing Add:* 39 Bond St New York NY 10012

GELMAN, MILTON
COLLECTOR

b Newark, NJ, Nov 3, 14. *Study:* Art appreciation under John R Grabach & Henry Gasser. *Collection:* Extensive collection of major works of: H Gasser, Robert Philipp, J Grabach, J Dawley, G Cimiotti, Burt Silverman, W Senoir and others. *Mailing Add:* 210 Crestwood Dr South Orange NJ 07079

GENAUER, EMILY
CRITIC, WRITER

b New York, NY. *Study:* Hunter Col, grad; Sch Jour, Columbia Univ, BLit; Nat Acad. *Pos:* Staff writer & art feature writer, New York World, 29-31; art critic & ed, New York World-Tel, 32-49; art critic, New York Herald Tribune, 49-66; art critic & ed, New York World Jour Tribune, 66-67; art commentator, Educ TV, New York, 67-77; art critic-columnist, Newsday Syndicate, 67-; adv bd, Sch Jour, Columbia Univ. *Awards:* New York Newspaper Women's Club Award for Outstanding Column in Any Field, 49, 56, 58, 60 & 69; Columbia Univ Jour Alumni Award, 60; Pulitzer Prize. *Mem:* Nat Coun Humanities; Int Asn Art Critics; New York Newspaper Women's Club. *Publ:* Auth, Toulouse-Lautrec (monogr), 53, Biography of Chagall, 57, Hommage a l'Ecole de Paris, 62, Biography of Tamayo 74, Metrop Mus Art, New York; auth, Chagall at the Met, 71; and others. *Mailing Add:* 243 E 49th St New York NY 10017

GENDERS, RICHARD ATHERSTONE
PAINTER, CRITIC

b London, Eng, Aug 3, 19; US citizen. *Study:* Herron Sch Art, Ind Univ-Purdue Univ, Indianapolis, with Edwin Fulwider, John Williams Taylor & Donald M Mattison, grad, 50. *Work:* US Navy Combat Art Collection, Washington, DC. *Comn:* Mural, Naval Sta, Dam Neck, Va, 55; McDonalds Corp Collection; Bank of Middlesex, Va; and others. *Exhib:* Operation Palette Worldwide Traveling Exhib, 50-82; Norfolk Mus Arts, Va, 58; Royal Scottish Mus, Edinburgh, 60; Mus Marine, Paris, France, 63; Asheville Art Mus, NC, 82. *Pos:* Illusr/art ed, Navy Aviation Safety Rev, 52-58, art dir, US Navy, Norfolk, Va & Washington, DC, 52-65; art dir, NASA, 65-66; art dir, Blair, Inc, Baileys Crossroads, Va, 66-67; dir prod div, Naval Facilities Eng Comd, Washington, DC, 69-75; auth, Arts and Artists, Sylva Herald, NC, 80-82; art critic & columnist, Asheville Citizen Times, NC, 82- *Teaching:* Instr fine arts, Indianapolis Art Inst, 48-51; instr com art, Atherstone's Studio, Indianapolis, 50-53; instr fine arts, Rappahannock Community Col, 77-78. *Awards:* First Prize for Watercolor, Ind Artist Club, 50; Postage Stamp Design, US Post Off, Washington, DC, 58; First Oil, Lancaster Art League, 80. *Bibliog:* Artist with a mission, Indianapolis Star Mag, 55; Operation palette, Chicago Tribune Mag, 64; Richard VanKleeck (auth), article in Asheville NC Times, 79. *Mem:* Tidewater Art Asn (pres, 55); Salmagundi Club; Northern Va Art League (vpres, 69); Jackson Co Art Coun, NC, 81- *Media:* Watercolor, Gouache. *Interests:* Motion picture producing and directing. *Publ:* Illusr & auth, Historic Buildings of Middlesex County, 77; illusr, Rosewell, Garland of Virginia, 78; ed, History of Urbanna, 79. *Dealer:* Betty Lawton Mustard Seed Art Gallery PO Box 704 White Stone VA 22578. *Mailing Add:* Rt 2 Box 145-A3 Whittier NC 28789

GENIUS, JEANNETTE (JEANNETTE M MCKEAN)
PAINTER, DESIGNER

b Chicago, Ill. *Work:* Ga Mus Art, Univ Ga; Columbus Mus Art, Ga; Jacksonville Art Mus, Fla; Univ Club, Orlando, Fla; Univ Cent Fla. *Exhib:* Currier Art Gallery, Manchester, NH; Nat Arts Club, New York; Nat Asn Women Artists, New York; Soc Four Arts, Palm Beach, Fla; Stetson Univ. *Pos:* Dir exhibs, Morse Gallery Art. *Awards:* First Prize, Fla Fedn Art, 48; Second Prize, Soc Four Arts, 50; First Prize, Pen & Brush Club, 58. *Mem:* Nat Asn Women Artists; Nat Arts Club; Artists Equity Asn; Soc Four Arts; NH Art Asn. *Media:* Oil, Pastel. *Mailing Add:* PO Box 40 Winter Park FL 32790

GENIUSZ, ROBERT MYLES
PRINTMAKER, FILMMAKER

b Milwaukee, Wis, Aug 30, 48. *Study:* Sch Fine Arts, Univ Wis, Milwaukee, BFA, 74, MFA, 76. *Work:* Kohler Art Ctr, Sheboygan, Wis; Sheboygan Pub Schs, Wis; Performing Art Ctr, Theatre Sch, Milwaukee. *Comn:* Puppet

Theatre, Kohler Art Ctr, Sheboygan, Wis, 76. *Exhib:* Strange Tales, Kohler Art Ctr, Sheboygan, Wis, 76; Ann Beloit & Vicinity, Wright Arts Ctr, Beloit, Wis, 76, 77 & 79; Artists/Toys, Milwaukee Art Ctr, 77 & 79; Toys Designed by Artists, Ark Arts Ctr, Little Rock, 78 & 27th Ann Delta Invitational, 79; Form, Fun & Fantasy, Mt Mary Col, Milwaukee 78; one-man show, Printed Worlds, Oshkosh Pub Mus, Wis, 79; Wisconsin Artists, Cudahay Gallery, Milwaukee Art Mus, 83; International Paper Conference, Kyoto, Japan, 83; and others. *Teaching:* Instr 3-D, 2D & drawing, Univ WisParkside, Kenosha, Jan, 78; instr filmmaking, Univ Wis-Milwaukee, Sept, 79; artist in residence filmmaking, Performing Art Ctr, Milwaukee, Wis, 79-80, Milwaukee Public Schs, 81-83. *Awards:* Nat Endowment Arts Grant, Artist-in-Residence Prog, 76-77 & 79-84. *Bibliog:* James Auer (auth), Geniusz's...universe, 2/8/79 & Roxanne Orgill (auth), PAC's Mini MGM, 9/16/79, Milwaukee J; Evelyn Terry Bridges (auth), Wisconsin artists make toys, Milwaukee, Vol 4, No 12, 12/79. *Mem:* Col Art Asn Am; Artists Equity Asn. *Media:* Lithography, Serigraphy; Super 8 Film, Paper. *Mailing Add:* 3150 S 39th St Milwaukee WI 53215

GENN, NANCY
PAINTER
b San Francisco, Calif. *Study:* San Francisco Art Inst, Calif; Univ Calif, Berkeley. *Work:* Albright-Knox Art Gallery, Buffalo, NY; San Francisco Mus Mod Art; Aldrich Mus, Ridgefield, Conn; Cincinnati Art Mus, Ohio; Oakland Art Mus, Calif. *Comn:* Bronze lectern & five bronze sculptures for chancel table, First Unitarian Church, Berkeley, Calif, 61 & 64; bronze fountain, Cowell Col, Univ Calif, Santa Cruz, 66; bronze menorah, Temple Beth Am, Los Altos Hills, Calif, 68; 17 murals in ceramic glazed tile & two bronze fountain sculptures, Sterling Vineyards, Caligosta, Calif, 72 & 73; bronze fountain sculpture, Expo 74, Spokane, Wash, 74. *Exhib:* Solo shows, M H De Young Mem Mus, San Francisco, 55 & 63, San Francisco Mus Art, Calif, 61, New Worlds, Oakland Art Mus, 71 & four exhibs, Los Angeles Inst Contemp Art, 76; Twentieth Century Drawings, Stanford Univ, Palo Alto, Calif, 55; Winter Invitational, Calif Palace Legion Hon, San Francisco, 60-63; Contemporary Reflections, 72-73, Aldrich Mus, Ridgefield, Conn, 72-73; Pioneer Printmakers, Contemp Graphics Ctr, Santa Barbara Mus, 74; Works on Paper, Mus Mod Art, New York, 76; The Handmade Paper Object, Santa Barbara Mus Art, 76; New Ways with Paper, Nat Collection Fine Arts, Washington, DC, 77; Paper as Medium, Smithsonian Inst Traveling Exhib, 78-80. *Awards:* Purchase Award Painting, State of Calif, 57; Honor Award for Design Excellence, US Dept Housing & Urban Develop, 68; US/Japan Creative Arts Fel, 78-79. *Media:* Working in handformed and embossed paper in multiple layers. *Mailing Add:* c/o Susan Caldwell Gallery 383 W Broadway New York NY 10012

GENTILE, GLORIA IRENE
DESIGNER, SCULPTOR
b New York, NY. *Study:* Cooper Union, New York, 47-50; Yale Univ, 51-54, BFA & MFA; study with Josef Albers, Will Barnet, Abraham Rattner, Marscicano, Stuart Davis, Buckminster Fuller, Philip Johnson, Frederick Kiesler, Louis Kahn, Frank Lloyd Wright & Alvin Lustig. *Exhib:* One-person shows, Harbrace Gallery, 67, Aleksandra Kierekieska Gallery, 68, Art Dir Club Gallery, 68, Young & Rubican Gallery, New York, 68 & Ogilvy & Mather Inc Gallery, 68; Sculpture Happening, Mus Mod Art, 72. *Pos:* Founder & dir, Gentile Studio Graphics, 75- *Teaching:* Instr concepts & promotion, Sch Visual Arts, New York, 68-74 & Parsons Sch Design, 72-; instr promotional design, Cooper Union, 74-; Queens Col, 78-79; instr, Fashion Inst Technology, 80-81 & Pratt Inst, 82-83. *Awards:* Graphic Design Desi Award. *Bibliog:* Article in New Worlds of Reading, Harcourt Brace Jovanovich, 69. *Media:* Articulated Bronze, Ball Joints. *Interests:* Working on jointed moveable figures with singing or talking installed within to be enlarged for street, building installments. *Mailing Add:* 333 E 46th St New York NY 10017

GENTLE, ESTHER
PAINTER
b New York, NY, Aug 22, 05. *Study:* Arts Students League, New York; with Michael Schindler, Calif, Hans Hofmann, New York & Abraham Rattner, New York. *Work:* Royal Art Acad, Scotland; Mus Nantes, France; Evansville Mus Art, Ind; Ark Art Ctr, Little Rock; Krannert Mus, Urbana, Ill; plus others. *Exhib:* Philadelphia Mus Fine Arts, 39; Les Petites Bronzes, Mus Mod Art, Paris, 61; one-man shows, Mus Mod Art, Salon Surindepedent, Paris, 64; Art & Cult Ctr, Hollywood, Fla, 79; Kresge Mus, East Lansing, Mich, 79; Mint Mus, Charlotte, NC, 79; Nat Fedn Temple Sisterhood, New York, 79; Abe Rattner Ctr Arts, Sag Harbor, NY, 79; Galerie Macler, Sarasota, Fla, 80; Mythemantics, Southampton Col Fine Art Gallery, NY, 81; and others. *Mailing Add:* 830 Greenwich St New York NY 10014

GENTRY (AUGUSTUS CALAHAN), JR
PAINTER, PRINTMAKER
b Tyler, Tex, Feb 5, 27. *Study:* Tyler Jr Col, AA, 48; Univ Tex, with Boyer Gonzales, Ralph White & Seymour Fogel, BFA, 52. *Work:* Am Nat Life Collection, Galveston, Tex; Shell Oil Collection, Houston; Repub Nat Bank, Dallas; First City Bank & InterFirst Bank, Tyler, Tex. *Comn:* McKittrick Canyon (16 pieces), comn by Donors of McKittrick Canyon Nat Park, Houston, 70. *Exhib:* New York Int, 70; Southwest Watercolor Soc 100 Best Ann, 73 & 74; Midwest Wildlife Art Show, Kansas City, Mo, 74-75; Outdoors in Ga, Nat Wildlife Show, 76-77 & 79-82. *Teaching:* Grad asst sculpture, Univ Tex, Tyler, 52-53, artist in residence, 80-, instr overseas grad studies in watercolor, 83; instr art, Tyler Independent Sch Dist, 53-59; instr watercolor, Tyler Jr Col, 70-73. *Awards:* Signature Mem Award, Southwest Watercolor Soc, 74. *Bibliog:* Wilkins (auth), The local Gentry, Chronicles, Smith Co Hist Soc, 70. *Mem:* Southwest Watercolor Soc; Graphics Soc. *Media:* Watercolor. *Publ:* Illusr, Chronicles of Smith Co, Tex, 70 & 71. *Mailing Add:* 623 S Chilton Tyler TX 75701

GENTRY, HERBERT
PAINTER
b Pittsburgh, Pa, July 17, 19. *Study:* NY Univ, 40-42; Acad Grande Chaumiere, 46-49. *Work:* Stedlijk Mus, Amsterdam, Neth; Moderna Museet, Stockholm, Sweden; Metrop Mus Art, New York; Butler Inst of Art, Youngstown, Ohio; Carnegie Inst Art; and others. *Exhib:* One-man shows, Galerie Andre Zarre, New York, 74, Royal Art Acad, Stockholm, Sweden, 75, Amos Anderson Mus, Helsinki, Finland, 76, Gallery Glaub, Cologne, Germany, 81 & Gallery Oscar, Stockholm, Sweden, 81; and many other group & one-man shows. *Teaching:* Vis instr, Montclair State Col, 80 & 82. *Mailing Add:* 222 West 23rd St New York NY 10011

GENTRY, WARREN MILLER
INSTRUCTOR, PAINTER
b Manville, Wyo, Oct 3, 21. *Study:* Ariz State Univ, BA, 50, MA, 55; Univ Calif, Berkeley, with Frank Lobdell, 64. *Work:* Munic Collection, Orange, France. *Exhib:* Ariz State Fair Fine Arts Exhib, 49-63; 1st Ariz Ann, Phoenix, 59; Fresh Paint Show, M H De Young Mus, 59; Old Phoenix Art Mus. *Teaching:* Prof art hist & painting, Glendale Community Col, 63- *Awards:* Valley Bank Purchase Award, 1st Ariz Ann, 59. *Mailing Add:* PO Box 4082 Scottsdale AZ 85258

GEOFFREY, SAYYID IQBAL (JAFREE)
ADMINISTRATOR
b Chiniot, Pakistan, Jan 1, 39. *Study:* Govt Col, Lahore, Pakistan, BA; Sangamon State Univ, MA; Harvard Univ, LLM; Read Univ, LLD. *Work:* Boston Mus Fine Arts; Philips Collection; Tate Gallery; Arts Coun Gt Britain; Cornell Univ Mus Art; and others. *Exhib:* Conceptual Occurrences, Hyde Park, London, 60; one-man shows, Arts Coun Pakistan, 64, Cent Wash State Col, 71, Cornell Univ, 72, Los Angeles Municipal Art Gallery, 73 & Everson Mus, Syracuse, NY, 74. *Pos:* Dir, Mus Conceptual Art, Lahore, 68-70; sr partner, Samundaronpar Geoffrey tey Khirtran, 83- *Teaching:* Prof fine arts, St Mary's Col, Ind, 67-68; prof fine arts, Cent Wash State Univ, 70-71; vis prof fine arts, Cleveland State Univ, 71-72. *Awards:* John D Rockefeller III Award Creative Painting, 64 & 65; Public Tribute by the President of Pakistan, 64; Arts Coun Gt Brit Award, 69; and others. *Bibliog:* Herbert Read-Janson (auth), Iqbal Geoffrey, Grand Central Moderns, 65; David Luisi (auth), Re: Iqbal Geoffrey, CWSC, 70; H W Janson (auth), Art of Iqbal Geoffrey, Abrams, 82. *Publ:* Grad ed, Harvard Art Rev, 65-66; auth, The Concept of Human Rights in Islam, 80; auth, How to Make Love to a Judge, 83. *Mailing Add:* 3410 W McLean Ave 12 E 65th St Chicago IL 60647

GEORGE, DAN
SCULPTOR
b Glens Falls, NY, July 5, 43. *Study:* Art Students League, Henry Schenckenberg Merit Scholar, 68-73; Academie v Schonekunsten, Antwerp, 70-71. *Work:* Hyde Collection, Glens Falls, NY; Queens Mus, Flushing, NY. *Comn:* Aluminum sculpture, Stewart-Scott Assoc, Poughkeepsie, NY; site project, Village of Lake George, NY. *Exhib:* Ten by Ten, Lowe Art Gallery, Syracuse, NY, 78; Contemp Reflections, Aldrich Mus, Ridgefield, Conn, 78; Prospect Mountain Sculpture Show, Lake George, 79; Usdan Gallery, Bennington Col, Vt, 79; PS 1, Long Island City, NY, 81; Sculpture at Columbia Plaza, Washington, DC, 80; Artpark, Lewiston, NY, 82; and others. *Awards:* Grant, NY State Coun Arts, 78 & Collaborations in Art, Sci & Technol, 78. *Bibliog:* John Ashbury (auth), Telling it on the mountain, New York Mag, 8/28/79; Ronny H Cohen (auth), Reviews, Artforum, 12/82. *Media:* Constructed Cast Metals. *Mailing Add:* 64 West 21st St New York NY 10010

GEORGE, RAYMOND ELLIS
PRINTMAKER, EDUCATOR
b Cedar Falls, Iowa, Sept 13, 33. *Study:* Univ Northern Iowa, BA, 55, MA, 62. *Work:* Smithsonian Inst, Washington, DC; Calif Palace of Legion of Honor, San Francisco; Victoria & Albert Mus, London, Eng; Libr Cong, Washington, DC; New York Pub Libr. *Comn:* Ceramic mural, Dubuque Pub Schs, Iowa, 60. *Exhib:* Contemporary American Prints, State Univ NY Col Oneonta, 69; 50th Nat Graphic Arts Ann, Wichita Art Mus, Kans, 71; Nat Drawing Exhib, Southern Ill Univ, Carbondale, 75; Biennial Int Open Competition, Print Club, Philadelphia, 75; Drawings USA 77, Minn Mus Art, St Paul, 77. *Teaching:* Prof art, Ill State Univ, Normal, 71-; artist in residence, Munson Williams Proctor Inst, Sch Art, Utica, NY. *Awards:* Purchase Awards, Eight-State Print Exhib, J B Speed Art Mus, 74 & 83 & Nat Drawing Exhib, Southern Ill Univ, Carbondale, 75; Fay Carter Drawing Purchase Award, Univ Colo, 74 & Owensboro Mus Fine Art, Ky, 80. *Mem:* Boston Printmakers; Print Club, Philadelphia; Col Art Asn. *Media:* Intaglio, Lithography. *Publ:* Auth, Graphite Lithography, Tamerind Tech Papers, 77. *Mailing Add:* 1907 Garling Dr Bloomington IL 61701

GEORGE, RICHARD ALLAN
PAINTER
b Chicago, Ill, Nov 28, 35. *Study:* State Univ NY Buffalo, with Larry Calcagno, BFA; Art Students League, with Frank Reilly; Miami Univ, Ohio, with Edwin Fulwider, MFA. *Work:* Massillon Mus, Ohio; Chase Manhattan Bank, New York; Del Mar Col, Corpus Christi, Tex; Cincinnati Bell, Ohio; Owensboro Mus of Fine Art, Ky. *Comn:* Painting, Ohio State Off Tower, Columbus, 74; 4 paintings, First Nat Bank, Hamilton, Ohio, 77 & 78; painting, Southwestern Ohio Steel Co, Hamilton, Ohio. *Exhib:* Ann Mid-Year Show, Butler Inst Am Art, Youngstown, Ohio, 72, 78 & 81; Biennial Contemp Art, Whitney Mus Am Art, New York, 75; Contemp Figure Painting in Midwest, Contemp Arts Ctr, Madison, Wis, 77; Surrealism Now, Spaces Gallery, Cleveland, 79; one man show, Osuna Gallery, Washington DC, 80; Chicago

Art Fair and Solway Gallery, 81-83; Interiors, Quay Gallery, San Francisco, 83. *Teaching:* Instr drawing & painting, Middletown Fine Arts Ctr, Ohio, 71- *Awards:* Best of Show, 73 & Award for Painting, 79, Ohio State Fair; First Award for Painting, Art League Regional, Indianapolis, 82. *Mem:* Art Students League; Nat Col Art Asn. *Media:* Acrylic, Oil. *Dealer:* Carl Solway Gallery 314 W Fourth St Cincinnati OH 45202; Osuna Gallery 2121 P St NW Washington DC 20037. *Mailing Add:* 4440 W Elkton Rd Hamilton OH 45011

GEORGE, THOMAS
PAINTER, DRAFTSMAN

b New York, NY, July 1, 18. *Study:* Dartmouth Col, BA, 40; Art Students League; Acad Grand Chaumiere, Paris; Ist Statale Arte, Florence, Italy. *Work:* Guggenheim Mus & Mus Mod Art, New York; Nat Collection Fine Arts, Washington, DC; Tate Gallery, London, Eng; and others. *Comn:* Tapestry, Slatkin Art Gallery, New York, 68; poster/print, US Olympic Comt & Kennedy Galleries, New York, 74. *Exhib:* Whitney Mus Am Art Ann, 60-62 & 65; Princeton Univ Art Mus, 75; Nat Collection Fine Arts, 77; Betty Parsons Gallery, 68, 70, 72, 74, 76, 78 & 81; Nat Gallery, Oslo; Okla Art Ctr, 74; plus many others. *Teaching:* Vis artist, Univ Tex, 78; artist-in-residence, Dartmouth Col, 79. *Awards:* Purchase Award Painting, 61 & Purchase Award Drawing, 62, Whitney Mus Ann; Salon Int Galeries Pilote, Lausanne, Switz, 66; Award, NJ State Mus, 72. *Bibliog:* Martica Sawin (auth), The nature of symbols of Thomas George, Art Int, 65; J Jacobs (auth), Norway series drawings, Art Gallery Man, 72. *Media:* Oil, Ink; Gouche; Woodcut. *Publ:* Illusr, A Line of Poetry, A Row of Trees, Jargon, 65; illusr, Kweilin's An American artist in China, 76; illusr, The Norway Series, Capellen, Oslo, 80. *Dealer:* Maxwell Davidson Gallery 43 E 78 St New York NY 10021. *Mailing Add:* 20 Greenhouse Dr Princeton NJ 08540

GERACI, LUCIAN ARTHUR
PAINTER, DEALER

b New Haven, Conn, Mar 13, 23. *Study:* Wesleyan Univ, Middletown, Conn, BA, 48; Skowhegan Sch Painting & Sculpture, Maine, scholar, 48; Beaux Arts Acad, Paris, cert, 49; Acad Julian, Paris, cert, 48-49; Ital Acad, Rome, cert, 50; RI Sch Design, BFA, 53. *Work:* Acad Julian, Paris; Accad Belli Arti, Rome; Armstrong Cork Company, Lancaster, Pa; Abraham Sharpe Found, New York; Conn Gen Life Insurance Co, Hartford. *Exhib:* Allied Artists, New York, 69; Nat Art Club, New York, 70-71; Knickerbocker Artists, New York, 76 & 77; Butler Art Inst, Ohio, 76 & 78; Salmagundi Club, New York, 70-81; Rockport Art Asn, Mass, 74-81. *Pos:* Owner, Art Gallery 123, Lancaster, Pa, 58-59; designer & stylist, Hygeine Co, New York, Maartex, Cannon Mills, New York, Armstrong Cork, Pa, 55-70; pres & owner, Geraci Galleries Ltd, Rockport, Mass, 78- *Awards:* Prix-Ann Concours, Acad Julian, Paris, 48; Ann Knickerbocker Artists, Delta Brush Company, NY, 77; Pres Award, Salmagundi Club, New York, 78. *Bibliog:* Lucian Geraci's Art Ctr, Gloucester D Times, Mass, 5/23/78; Kasha Gula (auth), Lucian Geraci's gallery--A work of art itself, Rockport Horizon, Mass, 6/16/78; Virginia Bohlin (auth), Where the art is, Boston Globe, 7/7/78. *Mem:* Salmagundi Art Club; Rockport Art Asn; North Shore Arts Asn. *Media:* Oil, Pastel. *Specialty:* Realist and modern eastern seaboard artists; large selection of woodblock prints by Winslow Homer and Gustave Dore. *Mailing Add:* Geraci Galleries & Art Ctr Ltd Six South Street Rockport MA 01966

GERALD, ELIZABETH BART See Bart, Elizabeth

GERAN, JOSEPH, JR
SCULPTOR, DESIGNER

b 1945. *Study:* San Francisco City Col, AA, 66; Calif State Univ, San Francisco, BA, 70; Calif Col Arts & Crafts, MFA, 73. *Comn:* Prints of movie stars, Oakland Mus, 74. *Exhib:* Los Angeles Co Mus, Los Angeles, 74; RI Sch Design, 75; Southeastern Mass Univ, 75; Bryant Col, 75; Univ Vt, 75; plus numerous group & one-man shows. *Pos:* Corp vpres, Col Inc, 70-71; processing chmn, FESTAC 74, 73-74; freelance jewelry designer. *Teaching:* Instr, EOC Summer Youth Prog, 69; lectr, Calif State Univ, San Francisco, 69-71; art consult & sch aide, Galileo High Sch, San Francisco, 70; instr, Booker T Washington Community Ctr, San Francisco, 71; asst prof painting, drawing & sculpture & co-dir ethnic studies div, Calif Col Arts & Crafts, 70-74; adj fac mem, Antioch Col West, 74; dean third world prog, RI Sch Design, 74-; prof art, Community Col RI, 81- *Awards:* Guy F Atkinson Found Award, 69-71; Ill State Univ Sculpture Award, 73; Distinguished Serv Award, Congressman Ron Dellums, 75. *Mem:* Nat Conf Artists; San Francisco Art Comn Screening Comt. *Publ:* Cover design, Black Art, Black Cult, issue, J Black Poetry, 72; photog of art work, Yardbird Reader, 73; cover design, Blacks on Paper, Brown Univ, fall 75. *Mailing Add:* 19 Academy Ave Providence RI 02908

GERARD, PAULA (MRS HERBERT RENISON)
PAINTER, GRAPHIC ARTIST

b Brighton, Eng; US citizen. *Study:* Pvt study in Florence & Venice, Italy; Univ Florence, with Toesca; Inst Francais, Florence, with Soulier; lithography & etching in Paris & Brussels; Art Inst Chicago; painting with Boris Anisfeld. *Work:* Libr Cong, Washington, DC; Smart Gallery, Univ Chicago; Ringling Mus, Sarasota, Fla; Ill State Mus, Springfield; London Branch, First Nat Bank of Chicago; and others. *Exhib:* One-man shows, Art Inst Chicago, 47, Montgomery Mus Fine Arts, Ala, 71 & Auburn Univ, 75; First Biennial Prints, Drawings & Watercolors, Art Inst Chicago, 61; Artists of Chicago & Vicinity, Art Inst Chicago, 77-78; Am Watercolorists 79, Mitchell Mus, Mt Vernon, Ill, 79; Three Artists, Fairweather Hardin Gallery, Chicago, 80; 33rd Invitational, Ill State Mus, Springfield, 81; and others. *Teaching:* Instr figure

drawing & anat, Layton Sch Art, Milwaukee, 45-62; vis instr graphics & printmaking, Midway Studios, Univ Chicago, 58-65; prof figure drawing & anat, Art Inst Chicago Sch, 62-75, emer prof, 75- *Awards:* Purchase Award, Ill State Mus, Springfield, 81; Honorary Award, Chicago Woman's Caucus Art, 83. *Bibliog:* Harold Haydon (auth), articles, Chicago Sun-Times, 6/7/74, 2/20/77 & 5/7/82. *Mem:* Alumni Asn Art Inst Chicago Schs; Renaissance Soc, Univ Chicago (mem bd, 64-75, hon bd mem, 75-); Artists Equity (dir, Chicago Chap, 72-77); Chicago Soc Artists; Arts Club, Chicago. *Media:* Watercolor, Silverpoint. *Publ:* Illusr, Is Your Contemporary Painting More Temporary Than You Think, 62; illusr, The Great Speckled Bird, Regnery, 64. *Dealer:* Fairweather Hardin Gallery 101 E Ontario St Chicago IL 60611. *Mailing Add:* 3764 N Magnolia Ave Chicago IL 60613

GERARDIA, HELEN
PAINTER, PRINTMAKER

b Russia; US citizen. *Study:* Art Students League; Brooklyn Mus Art Sch; Hans Hofmann Sch. *Work:* Arnot Art Mus, Elmira, NY; Nylander Art Mus, Caribou, Maine; Saginaw Art Mus, Mich; Slater Mem Mus, Conn; Nat Collection Fine Arts, Libr Cong, Washington, DC; Pori Art Mus, Finland. *Exhib:* Whitney Mus Am Art, New York; Corcoran Gallery Art Bienniel; Brooklyn Mus Print Ann; San Francisco Mus Art Painting Ann; Smithsonian Art Inst, Washington, DC, 59 & 64; Hermitage Mus, Norfolk, Va, 77; Mint Mus, Charleston, NC, 78; one-artist exhibs, Univ Wis, Whitewater, 78, State Univ NY, Alfred, 79 & 83, Univ Portland, Ore, 81 & Bemidje Univ, Minn, 82. *Awards:* Watson Guptill Prize in Graphics, Am Soc Contemp Artists, 79; Nelson/Whitehead Award, 81; Erlanger Mem Prize, Nat Asn Women Artists, 83; and others. *Bibliog:* Gordon Brown (auth), The new look in art, Art Voices Quart, spring 65. *Mem:* Nat Asn Women Artists (mem permanent adv bd, 74-); Int Asn Artists; Audubon Artists; Soc Am Graphic Artists (treas, 74-84). *Dealer:* Rudolph Galleries Woodstock NY & Coral Gables FL. *Mailing Add:* 490 West End Ave 4C New York NY 10024

GERBRACHT, BOB (ROBERT THOMAS)
PAINTER, INSTRUCTOR

b Erie, Pa, June 23, 24. *Study:* With Joseph Plavcan, 38-42; Yale Sch Fine Arts, with Rudolph Zallinger, Deane Keller & Josef Albers, BFA, 51; Univ Southern Calif, with Jules Heller, MFA, 52. *Comn:* Stations of the Cross (oil painting) & Creche (sculpture), Queen Apostles Church, San Jose, Calif, 63; portraits, Mrs Bruce Jenner, Malibu, Calif, 80 & 82; and others. *Exhib:* Contemporary Connecticut Artists, Wadsworth Atheneum, 50; 57th Ann Exhib Western Artists, Denver Art Mus, 51; Calif Col Students Exhib, Univ Vienna, Austria, 51; Fla Int Exhib, Fla Southern Col, 52; Graphic Arts USA, Univ Ill, Champaign-Urbana, 54; 13th Ann West Coast Oil Painting Exhib, Frye Mus, Seattle, 68; Second Ann Open Exhib, Salmagundi Club, New York, 79; and others. *Pos:* Vpres, Images West Gallery, Saratoga, Calif, 72. *Teaching:* Instr art, Col Notre Dame, Calif, 58-60 & San Jose City Col, 68-71; founder & instr, Nat Ann Portrait & Figure Painting Workshops, Univ Calif, Santa Cruz & Asilomar, Pacific Grove, Calif, 78- *Awards:* Andrews Nelson Whitehead Award, Pastel Soc Am, 79; Best of Show, 33rd Ann, Soc Western Artists, 82 & San Jose Art League's Ann All Calif Show, 83. *Bibliog:* George Magnan (auth), Gerbracht studies his subject, Todays Art & Graphics, 3/82. *Mem:* San Jose Art League; Soc Western Artists; Printmakers Southern Calif (pres, 51-52); Pastel Soc Am; Am Portrait Soc. *Media:* Pastel, Oil. *Publ:* Auth, Drawing what you see, Am Artist Mag, 82. *Dealer:* Portraits Inc 985 Park Ave New York NY 10028. *Mailing Add:* 1521 Parkview Ave San Jose CA 95130

GERDES, INGEBORG
PHOTOGRAPHER

b Merseburg, Ger, July 20, 38. *Study:* San Francisco Art Inst, MFA, 70. *Work:* Bibliot Nat, Paris, France; Fogg Mus Art, Harvard Univ; Washington Art Consortium, Whatcom Mus; San Francisco Mus Mod Art; Stanford Mus Art, Palo Alto, Calif; and others. *Exhib:* Women of Photog: An Hist Survey, San Francisco Mus Mod Art, 75; one-woman shows, Galerie Spectrum, Hannover, Ger, 76, Blue Sky Gallery, Portland, Ore, 76, Focus Gallery, San Francisco, 78 & Alaska State Mus, Juneau, 79; Henry Art Gallery, Univ Wash, Seattle, 81; and others. *Teaching:* San Francisco Art Inst, 78; Univ Calif, Santa Cruz, 81. *Awards:* Nat Endowment Arts Photogr Fel, 75 & 77, Photog Survey Grant, 78; Seattle Arts Comn Grant, 80; and others. *Publ:* Contribr, Camera, Lucerne, Switz, 75; contribr, Latent Image, 78; contribr, Camera Mainichi, Japan, 80; and others. *Mailing Add:* 3025 21st St San Francisco CA 94110

GERDTS, ABIGAIL BOOTH
CONSULTANT, HISTORIAN

b New Milford, Conn, June 20, 37. *Study:* Radcliffe Col, AB(fine arts), 60; Syracuse Univ, Sch Art, 62-63. *Collections Arranged:* Spec exhib, Charles Sheeler (auth, catalog), Nat Collection Fine Arts, Smithsonian Inst, 68; The Working American (auth, catalog), Dist 1199 & Smithsonian Inst Travelling Exhib Serv, 79. *Pos:* Mem secy, Corcoran Gallery Art, Washington, DC, 59-61; res asst painting dept, Mus Fine Arts, Boston, 61-62; asst cur exhib, Nat Collection Fine Arts, 64-70, coordr bicentennial inventory Am paintings, 70-77, coordr 19th century exhibs index, 77-78; spec asst to dir, Nat Acad Design, New York, 80- *Mem:* Am Asn Mus. *Publ:* Auth, Directory to the Bicentennial Inventory of American Paintings Executed Before 1914, Arno Press, 76; The Working American, Sites, 79. *Mailing Add:* 1120 Park Ave New York NY 10028

GERDTS, WILLIAM H
HISTORIAN, EDUCATOR

b Jersey City, NJ, Jan 18, 29. *Study:* Amherst Col, BA; Harvard Univ, MA. *Collections Arranged:* New Jersey Artists, 57; Nature's Bounty and Man's

Delight, 59; Old Master Drawings, 60; Nineteenth Century Master Drawings, 61; A Survey of American Sculpture, 62; Classical America 1815-1845, 63; The Golden Age of Spanish Still Life, 64; Women Artists America 1707-1964, 65. *Pos:* Dir, Myers House, Norfolk, Va, 53-54; cur painting & sculpture, Newark Mus, NJ, 54-66; dir gallery, Univ Md, 66-69; assoc with Coe Kerr Gallery, New York, 69-71. *Teaching:* Assoc prof, Univ Md, 66-69; assoc prof art, Brooklyn Col, 71-74, prof, 74-; lectr American art, collecting art & conservation & restoration, in cols, univs & adult schs. *Publ:* Ed, Drawings of Joseph Stella, 62; auth, Painting and Sculpture in New Jersey, Rutgers Univ, 65; contribr, Antiques, Art Quart & NJ Hist Soc Proc. *Mailing Add:* Dept of Art Brooklyn Col Brooklyn NY 11210

GERHOLD, WILLIAM HENRY
PAINTER, EDUCATOR
b Ashtabula, Ohio, Mar 30, 29. *Study:* Oberlin Col, with Jeanne Miles, BA; Ohio State Univ, MA. *Work:* Army-Navy Club, Charleston, WVa; Marshall Col, Ohio; Marshall Univ, WVa; WVa Univ, Morgantown. *Exhib:* Butler Midyear, Youngstown, Ohio; Appalachian Corridors II, Charleston; Perspectives, Cincinnati, Ohio, 70; Forest Festival, Elkins, WVa; Ohio State Fairs. *Teaching:* Assoc prof educ, Antioch Col, 57-58; assoc prof art, Marietta Col, 62- *Awards:* First Prize Watercolor, Appalachian Arts & Crafts Fair, 70; Best Prof & Best WVa Landscape, Forest Festival, 71-75. *Mem:* Cent Ohio Watercolor Soc; Am Artists Prof League; WVa Artists & Craftsmen Guild; Allied Artists; Am Watercolor Soc. *Publ:* Auth & illusr, Trinity Rev, 58; WVa Mag, 73 & 74. *Dealer:* Bonfoeys 1710 Euclid Ave Cleveland OH 44115. *Mailing Add:* 510 Caroline Ave Williamstown WV 26187

GERIN-LAJOIE, GUY
ARCHITECT
b Montreal, PQ, Can, May 6, 28. *Study:* McGill Univ, Montreal, BArch. *Exhib:* Physical Educ & Univ Ctr, Univ Ottawa, Ont; Sci Res Lab, Igloolik, NW Territories; New Montreal Int Air Terminal Bldg; Girls' Residence, Univ Montreal, Que; Off Bldg, Phase IV, Govt Can, Quebec; and many others. *Awards:* Award Nat Housing Design Coun, 62; Massey Medals, Quebec Pavilion, Expo 67, Montreal, 70; Ann Award, Can Archit Yearbk, Povungnituk Sch & Housing Proj, 73. *Mem:* Ont Asn Archit; Royal Acad Arts; Nat Design Coun; fel Royal Archit Inst Can; Royal Can Acad Arts. *Mailing Add:* 2001 University Suite 1100 Montreal PQ H3A 2A6 Canada

GERNHARDT, HENRY KENDALL
SCULPTOR, CERAMIST
b Salem, Conn, Aug 3, 32. *Study:* Norwich Art Sch, Conn; Sch Am Craftsmen, Rochester Inst Technol, NY, with Frans Wildenhain; Sch Art, Syracuse Univ, NY, BA & MFA; Sch Appl Arts, Helsinki, Finland, study with Kyllikki Salmenhaara, Fulbright Scholar. *Work:* Everson Mus Art, Syracuse, NY; Syracuse Univ; DePauw Univ, Greencastle, Ind; Chrysler Mus, Provincetown, Mass; Univ SDak, Vermillion. *Comn:* Pottery, Imperial House, New York, 60; tile mosaic, Syracuse Univ, 63; vase, State Univ NY, Cortland, 67; baptismal font, Lynnwood Reformed Church, Guilderland, NY, 69; sculpture, comn by Alexander E Holstein, Syracuse, 72. *Exhib:* Ceramic Nat, Everson Mus Art, 54-72; Int Trade Fair, Posen, Poland, 58; Contemp Crafts Exhib, Skidmore Col, Saratoga Springs, NY, 62, 71 & 75; Int Ceramic Exhib, Silvermine Guild Artists, New Canaan, Conn, 64; 22nd Ceramic Ann, Scripps Col, Claremont, Calif, 66. *Teaching:* Prof ceramics, Sch Visual & Performing Arts, Syracuse Univ, 60- & Sch Am Craftsmen, summer 71. *Awards:* Merle Alling Sculpture Award, Rochester Finger Lakes Exhib, Mem Art Gallery, 63 & 71; O Hommel Prize for Pottery, Ceramic Nat, Everson Mus, 68; 1st, 2nd & 3rd Awards, NY State Expos, Syracuse, 71. *Bibliog:* Lewenstein & Cooper (auth), New Ceramics, Van Nostrand Reinhold, 74; Rick Hirsch (auth), Raku, Watson Guptill, 75; article, Craft Horizons, 75. *Mem:* Nat Coun Advan Ceramic Arts; Am Crafts Coun; New York Craftsmen. *Media:* Clay, Glaze. *Mailing Add:* 2581 Webb Rd La Fayette NY 13084

GERSH, BILL
PAINTER, SCULPTOR
b Charleston, SC, July 15, 43. *Study:* State Univ New York, New Paltz, BS, 64; with Ilya Bolotowsky & Manuel Bromberg. *Work:* State Univ NY, New Paltz; Denver Art Mus, Colo. *Exhib:* New Paintings & Sculpture, State Univ NY, New Paltz, 63; The Armory Show, Santa Fe Armory Arts, NMex, 79; Sculpture, Md Inst Col Art, Baltimore, 80. *Awards:* Sante Fe Coun Arts Grant, 83. *Bibliog:* Steve Parks (auth), Interview, Art Lines, 80; William Peterson (auth), Smoke rings, Shinto shrines, Artnews, 80. *Media:* Acrylic, Collage. *Mailing Add:* PO Box 44 San Christobal NM 87564

GERSHINOWITZ, GEORGE
DRAFTSMAN, ILLUSTRATOR
b Stamford, Conn, Apr 26, 44. *Study:* Pratt Inst, Brooklyn, NY, BFA, 68, MFA, 73. *Work:* New York Historical Soc. *Comn:* Golden Jubilee Poster, Metrop Transit Authority, New York, 79. *Exhib:* Brooklyn Mus, NY, 71; one-man show, Forbes Libr Gallery, Northampton, Mass, 76; Artists by the Sea, Snug Harbor Cultural Ctr, Staten Island, NY, 79; Ann Competition, Nat Acad Design, New York, 79 & 80; Small Works, New York Univ, 80; The Original Art, Master Eagle Gallery, New York, 80 & 81. *Awards:* Outstanding Sci Books for Children, Nat Sci Teachers Asn & Children's Book Coun Joint Comt, 80. *Bibliog:* John Canaday (auth), John Canaday on art, New Republic Mag, 81. *Media:* Pencil, Watercolor. *Publ:* Illusr, Electric Fish, 80 & illusr, Midnight Prowlers, 81, Morrow, New York; illusr, The Goblin Market, David R Godine, Boston, 81. *Mailing Add:* PO Box 204 Old Chelsea Station New York NY 10011

GERSHOY, EUGENIE
SCULPTOR, PAINTER
b Krivoi Rog, Russia, Jan 1, 01; US citizen. *Study:* Art Students League, with Alexander Stirling Calder, Boardman Robinson, Kenneth Hayes Miller, John Sloan, 21-22. *Work:* Metrop Mus Art, Whitney Mus Am Art, New York; Nat Mus Am Art, Washington, DC; Syracuse Univ Mus Art, NY; San Francisco Mus Art, Calif. *Comn:* Polychromed papier mache sculptures, Cafe Soc, NY, 42 & San Francisco Art Comn, 65; polychrome papier mache portrait sculptures, Chelsea Hotel, NY, 67-77. *Exhib:* Whitney Mus Am Art Ann & Biennial Exhibs, New York, 31-; 15 Young Am Sculptors Traveling Exhib & 20th Century Portraits, Mus Mod Art, New York, 42; Sculpture Invitationals, Philadelphia Mus Art, Pa, 40 & 52; Artists for Victory, Metrop Mus Art, New York, 42; Ann Exhibs, San Francisco Mus, Calif, 48-65; Women Artists Am, Newark Mus, NJ, 64; one-man shows, Brooklyn Mus, Baltimore Mus, Dallas Mus, Wichita Mus, Delgado Mus, and others. *Teaching:* Instr painting & drawing, New Orleans Art Sch, 40-41; art instr, San Francisco Unified Sch, 46-65; art instr ceramic sculpture, Calif Sch Fine Art, San Francisco, 56-57. *Awards:* Gold Medal Fine Draughtsmanship, Augustus St Gaudens, 19; Purchase Prize, Metrop Mus Art, 42. *Bibliog:* Sidney Geist (auth), Prelude: The 1930's Art, Special Am Number, 56. *Media:* All. *Mailing Add:* Hotel Chelsea 222 W 23rd St New York NY 10011

GERSOVITZ, SARAH VALERIE
PRINTMAKER, PAINTER
b Montreal, Que. *Study:* McDonald Col; Montreal Mus Fine Arts; Concordia Univ, MA. *Work:* Am Embassy, Ottawa; Libr Cong, Washington, DC; New York Pub Libr; Nat Gallery SAustralia; l'Instituto Cultural Peruano, Lima; and many others. *Exhib:* One-man shows, Montreal Mus Fine Arts, 62 & 65, Int Biennale, Ljubljana, Yugoslavia, 75 & 79, Confederation Art Gallery, 76 & London Art Gallery, 82; Sixth Biennale Int Gabrovo, Bulgaria, 83; Fourth Seoul Int Biennale, 83; and others. *Teaching:* Instr painting & drawing, Saidye Bronfman Ctr, Montreal, 72- *Awards:* Purchase Awards, Mus du Que, 66, Nat Gallery S Australia, 67, Dawson Col, 74, Thomas More Inst, 77, l'Universite de Sherbrooke; and others. *Bibliog:* Guy Robert (auth), L'Art au Quebec depuis 1940; plus others. *Mem:* Royal Can Acad Arts. *Media:* Silkscreen. *Publ:* Illusr, cover, Figures in a Landscape, Oberon, 67; illusr cover, Feminin Pluriel, Masculin Singulier, 80. *Dealer:* Wallack Art Editions 204 Bank St Ottawa K2P 1N8. *Mailing Add:* 5173 Mayfair Ave Montreal PQ H4V 2E8 Canada

GERST, HILDE W
DEALER
US citizen. *Study:* Ploner Acad, Italy. *Pos:* Owner, Hilde Gerst Gallery, New York & Palm Beach, Fla. *Mem:* Am Asn Mus; Nat Soc Lit & Arts. *Specialty:* French painting from Impressionist to contemporary; sculpture. *Mailing Add:* c/o Hilde Gerst Gallery 681 Madison Ave New York NY 10021

GERSTEIN, DAVID STEVEN
FILMMAKER
b Cleveland, Ohio, Sept 23, 51. *Study:* Antioch Col, BA, 74; Art Inst Chicago; San Francisco Art Inst. *Exhib:* One-man shows, NAME Gallery, Chicago, 76 & Canyon Cinematheque, San Francisco, 78, 80 & 82; High Mus Art, Atlanta, Ga, 79; Anthology Film Archive, New York, 81; Newberger Mus, Purchase, NY, 81; Arsenal Cinema, Berlin; Austrian Film Mus, Vienna; and others. *Pos:* Bd dirs, Canyon Cinema Coop, San Francisco, 77-82, Found Art Cinema, 83- *Awards:* 3rd Place, San Francisco Art Inst Film Festival, 77; Ann Arbor Film Festival, 77; Hon Mention, Athens Int Film Festival, 78. *Bibliog:* Linda Dackman (auth), Kino-Frisco, Cinema News, Found Art Cinema, 77. *Media:* 16mm Film, Super-8 Film. *Publ:* Auth, Films of Joel Singer, 77, auth, A modest confutation, 78 & ed, Cinemanews. *Dealer:* Canyon Cinema Coop 2325 3rd St 338 San Francisco CA 94133. *Mailing Add:* 2050 Powell St No 4 San Francisco CA 94133

GERVASI, FRANK
PAINTER
b Palermo, Italy, Oct 5, 1895; US citizen. *Study:* New York Sch Indust Arts; Art Students League. *Work:* Brueckner Mus, Albion, Mich; Lubbock Mus, Tex; Okla Mus Art, Tulsa. *Comn:* Paintings, comn by George T Abell, Oil & Gas Mus, Midland, Tex. *Exhib:* Nat Acad Design, Allied Artists Am, Am Watercolor Soc & Audubon Artists, New York; Baker Fine Arts Gallery, Tex. *Awards:* Medal of Honor, Allied Artists Am, 57; First Prize Oil Painting, Salmagundi Club. *Mem:* Nat Acad Design; Allied Artists Am (pres, 55-57); Am Watercolor Soc; Audubon Artists; Salmagundi Club (vpres, 57-58). *Media:* Oil, Watercolor. *Mailing Add:* PO Box 415 Marfa TX 79843

GERZSO, GUNTHER
PAINTER, GRAPHIC ARTIST
b Mexico City, Mex, June 17, 15. *Study:* German Sch, Mexico City, 34; self-taught. *Work:* Alvar Carrillo Gil Collection, Mus Mod Art, Mexico City. *Comn:* Stained glass window, Hotel Aristos, Mexico City, 69. *Exhib:* FIAC Art Contemporain, Grand Palais, Paris, 78; Tamayo, Merida y Gerzso, First Ann Exhib, Inst Fine Arts, Mexico, 80; El Arbol Florido, traveling, 81-82; FIAC 82 Retrospective, Paris, 82; Mussee Petit Palais, 82; and others. *Awards:* Nat Prize Fine Arts, Mexico, 78; Guggenheim Fel, 73. *Bibliog:* L Cardoza y Aragon (auth), Gunther Gerzso, Nat Univ Mex, 72; Octavio Paz (auth), Gerzso: Centella Glacial, Visual Arts, Mus Mod Art, Mexico, spring 74; Gerzso, Merida, Tamayo, Instituto Nacional de Bellas Artes, Mexico, 79; John Golding & Octavio Paz (auths), Gerzso, Editions Griffon Neuchatel, 83. *Media:* Oil, Acrylic. *Mailing Add:* Fresnos 21 Deleg A Obregon San Angel Inn Mexico 01060 DF Mexico

GESKE, NORMAN ALBERT
MUSEUM DIRECTOR, EDUCATOR
b Sioux City, Iowa, Oct 31, 15. *Study:* Univ Minn, BA; NY Univ Inst Fine Arts, MA; Doane Col, hon DFA, 69. *Collections Arranged:* Ernst Barlach (first Am mus exhib), 55; American Participation, 34th Venice Biennale, 68; American Sculpture, 70; Ralph Albert Blakelock (auth, catalog), 75. *Pos:* Asst dir, Univ Nebr Art Galleries, 50-53, actg dir, 53-56, dir, 56-83, dir emer, 83. *Teaching:* Prof, Univ Nebr-Lincoln. *Awards:* Gov Art Award, 78; Distinguished Service Award, Kearney State Col, 80. *Res:* Nebraska Blakelock inventory. *Publ:* Auth, The Figurative Tradition in Recent American Art, 68; contribr, Int Art Exhibs, Arts Mag Yearbk No 10, 69; auth, Rudy Pozzatti, American Printmaker, 71; Ralph Albert Blakelock 1847-1919, 75; Light & Color, Images from New Mexico, 81. *Mailing Add:* Univ Neb Lincoln Sheldon Mem Art Gallery Lincoln NE 68588

GETLER, HELEN
DEALER
b New York, NY, May 30, 25. *Study:* Bryn Mawr Col, BA, 45. *Pos:* Co-dir, Getler/Pall Gallery, New York, currently. *Specialty:* Contemporary artists; works on paper, prints, paintings and drawings. *Mailing Add:* 50 W 57th St New York NY 10019

GETTINGER, EDMOND WALTER
EDUCATOR, PAINTER
b Geneva, Ill, July 9, 41. *Study:* Mo Valley Col, BS; Wichita State Univ, with David Bernard, MFA. *Work:* Wichita State Univ; Univ SDak, Springfield. *Exhib:* SDak Art Fac Exhib, Mitchell, 70; one-man shows, Mo Valley Col, Marshall, 71; Dickenson State Col, NDak, 72; Mt Marty Col, Yankton, SDak, 73 & Univ SDak, Vermillion, 74. *Teaching:* Asst prof multi-media, Univ SDak, 70-; guest artist painting, Mt Marty Col, 72. *Mem:* Nat Woodcarvers Asn. *Media:* Oil, Intaglio. *Mailing Add:* 1011 Pine Springfield SD 57062

GETTY, NILDA FERNANDEZ
EDUCATOR, SILVERSMITH
b Buenos Aires, Arg, June 2, 36; US citizen. *Study:* Archit at Buenos Aires Univ, Univ NC, Raleigh & Univ Pa; Stetson Univ, Deland, Fla, BFA(art); Univ South Fla, Tampa; Univ Ga, MFA(metalsmithing & printmaking). *Work:* Deland Mus, Fla; Univ South Fla; Denver Art Mus; Minn Mus of Art, St Paul; Colo State Univ. *Comn:* St Luke's Chalice, St Luke's Episcopal Church; eleven copper emblems, Larimer Co High Sch. *Exhib:* Goldsmiths Invitational (travelling exhib), Minn Mus Art, St Paul, 74; Metals Invitational, Fullerton Gallery, Calif, 75; two-person show, Gryphon Gallery, Denver, 75 & 77; Sheldon Mem Art Gallery, Lincoln, Nebr, 76; NAm Goldsmith Invitational, Phoenix Mus, Ariz, 76-77; Metals Invitational, Henry Gallery, Seattle, Wash, 77; solo exhib, Minn Mus Art, St Paul, 74; and others. *Teaching:* From instr to prof metalsmithing, Colo State Univ, Ft Collins, 70- *Bibliog:* Donald Willcox (auth), Body Jewelry: International Perspectives, Regnery, 73; Philip Morton (auth), Contemporary Jewelry, Holt, Rinehart & Winston, 2nd ed 76. *Mem:* Soc NAm Goldsmiths; Am Crafts Coun; World Crafts Coun. *Media:* Silver, Gold. *Publ:* Auth, Contemporary Crafts of the Americas, Regnery, 75; auth, articles, Contemporary Crafts, 75 & Ceramics Mo, 75; auth, Crafts in the Americas, Crafts Horizons, 74. *Mailing Add:* 1912 Mohawk Ft Collins CO 80521

GETZ, ILSE
COLLAGE ARTIST, ASSEMBLAGE ARTIST
b Nuremberg, Ger, Oct 24, 17; US citizen. *Study:* Art Students League, with Morris Kantor & George Grosz. *Work:* Carnegie Inst, Pittsburgh; Tel-Aviv Mus, Israel; Aldrich Mus, Ridgefield, Conn; Neuberger Mus, Purchase, NY; Hirshhorn Mus, Washington, DC; plus others. *Comn:* Designed set for Ionesco's The Killer, New York, 60. *Exhib:* Kostiner-Silvers Gallery, Montreal, 75; Retrospective, Neuberger Mus, Purchase, NY & Kunsthalle, Nuremberg, Ger, 78; Goethe Inst, New York, 81; Alex Rosenberg Gallery, New York, 81; and many others. *Teaching:* Instr art, Positano, Italy, summers 56 & 58. *Awards:* Yaddo Fel, 59. *Bibliog:* Collages & Constructions by Ilse Getz, Arts Mag, 4/80; and others. *Dealer:* Alex Rosenberg Gallery 20 W 57th St New York NY 10019. *Mailing Add:* Saw Mill Rd Newtown CT 06470

GHENT, HENRI
CRITIC, WRITER
b Birmingham, Ala, June 23, 26. *Study:* US Armed Forces Inst, Honolulu, Hawaii, 45-46; New Eng Conservatory, Boston, 47-51; Marian Anderson scholar, 51 & 52; Georges Longy Sch, Cambridge, 51-53; Martha Baird Rockefeller grant, 57; Univ Paris, 58-60; also pvt study in Ger & Eng; Vogelstein Found Fel, 78; Yaddo Found Fel, 79. *Collections Arranged:* The Invisible Americans: Black Artists of the 1930s, 69; 10 Afro-American Artists, Mt Holyoke Col, 69; 15 International Artists, Community Gallery, Brooklyn Mus, 69, Allusions, 2nd Anniversary Exhib, 70 & Native North American Art: Mixed Media Works by Contemporary American Indian Artists, 72; Afro-American Artists: Since 1950, Brooklyn Col, 69; 8 Afro-American Artists (catalog), Rath Mus, Geneva, Switz, 71; 1972 All-Ohio Painting & Sculpture Biennial, Art Inst, Dayton, 72. *Pos:* Consult, Nat Endowment Arts, Minn Mus Art, St Paul, Dayton Art Inst, Mt Holyoke Col, Rath Mus, Geneva & Mus d'Art Haitien, Port-au-Prince, Haiti; with Allen Univ; dir, Community Gallery, Brooklyn Mus, 68-72. *Teaching:* Vis lectr, Col Finger Lakes Series, 70-71 & Dayton Art Inst, Ohio; Queens Col, NY, 74; lectr, Teachers Col, Columbia Univ, 75-80. *Awards:* Ford Found Res-Travel Grant, 74-75; Crane Found Res-Travel Grant, 81-82; Cottonwood Found Grant, 83. *Bibliog:* Articles in Boston Sunday Globe, 12/7/75, Village Voice,

7/19/76, Los Angeles Times, 10/10/76, Artforum, New York Times, Cleveland Plain Dealer, and others; plus others. *Mem:* Smithsonian Assocs; Int Soc Educ Through Art; African-American Inst; Nat Art Educ Asn; Nat Soc Lit & Arts. *Interests:* Eclectic art with emphasis on contemporary painting, sculpture and graphics. *Collection:* Contemporary painting, sculpture & graphics. *Publ:* Auth, White is not superior, New York Times, 12/8/68; auth, Black creativity in quest of an audience, Art in Am, 5-6/70; The second generation, Art Gallery Mag, 6/74; auth, Spanish art in transition, Art Int, 10/15/75; plus others. *Mailing Add:* 310 E 75th St Apt 1-F New York NY 10021

GHIKAS, PANOS GEORGE
PAINTER, EDUCATOR
b Malden, Mass. *Study:* Yale Univ Sch Fine Arts, BFA, 43, MFA, 47; Akad der Bildenden Kunste, Stuttgart, Ger, with Willi Baumeister, 53-54. *Work:* Wadsworth Atheneum, Hartford, Conn; Walker Art Mus, Bowdoin Col; New Britain Mus Am Art, Conn; Colby Col; Art Mus, Waterville, Maine; and others. *Exhib:* Abstract & Surrealist Show, Chicago Art Inst, 47; 2nd Int Salon des Realites Nouvelles, Paris, France, 48; Annual of American Painting, Whitney Mus Am Art, 49; American Painting Annual, Univ Ill, 50; Worcester Mus Biennial Contemp Am Painting, 52. *Pos:* Asst conservator, Yale Univ Art Gallery, 57-59. *Teaching:* Vis artist design, Carpenter Ctr, Harvard Univ, 64-66; vis prof drawing, Bowdoin Col, 70-71; prof painting, RI Sch Design, Providence, 71-82. *Awards:* Fulbright Fel, 53; MacDowell Colony Fel, 67; Blanche E Colman Found Grant, 69. *Bibliog:* Chaet (auth), Artists at Work, Webb, 61. *Media:* Egg Tempera. *Publ:* Illusr, Tales of Christophilos, 54; illusr, Again Christophilos, 56; illusr, The Golden Bird, 57; illusr, The Golden Sword, 60. *Mailing Add:* 30 Ipswich St Boston MA 02215

GHIKAS, PATIENCE HALEY See Haley, Patience E

GIACALONE, VITO
PAINTER, HISTORIAN
b Newark, NJ. *Study:* Montclair State Col, BA, 60; Univ Iowa, MA, 65, MFA, 66. *Work:* Mus Univ Iowa. *Exhib:* Provincetown Art Asn & Mus, Mass, 69 & 80; Westbeth Gallery, New York, 70-72 & 79-83; solo exhib, Univ Ill, Urbana, 75; Orgn Independent Artists Exhib, PS1 Galleries & traveling, 78-79; Guild Hall Mus, East Hampton, NY, 82 & 83; and others. *Collections Arranged:* Chu Ta, Selected Paintings and Calligraphy (auth, catalog), Vassar Col Art Gallery, 72-73 & New York Cult Ctr, 73. *Teaching:* Assoc prof painting, Kean Col NJ, 66-; artist in residence, Univ Ill, Urbana, 75-; lectr Chinese painting, China Inst Am, New York, 78-80 & Inst Asian Studies, New York, 82- *Bibliog:* John Canaday (auth), article, New York Times, 71; Barbara Schwartz (auth), article, Art News, 71; Suzanne Frank (auth), article, Arts Mag, 72. *Mem:* China Inst Am. *Media:* Acrylic, Oil. *Res:* Chinese eccentric painting of the 17th and 18th centuries. *Publ:* Auth, Chu Ta (1626-1705): Towards an understanding of his art, 75, Wen Cheng Ming exhibition, 76 & Eight dynasties of Chinese painting, 81, Oriental Art Mag. *Mailing Add:* 463 West St B938 New York NY 10014

GIACOMANTONIO, ARCHIMEDES
ADMINISTRATOR, SCULPTOR
b Jersey City, NJ, Jan 17, 06. *Study:* Leonardo Da Vinci Art Sch, New York, 25; with Onorio Ruotolo, 25-26; with Vincenzo Gemito, 26-29; Royal Acad Art, Rome, 29; Jersey City State Col, Hon Dr Fine Arts & Lett, 83. *Work:* Jersey City Mus, NJ; Gaalleria D Arte Moderna Mus Rome, Italy; Royal Palace, Germany; Royal Palace Rome, Italy. *Comn:* Columbus Monument, Hoboken, NJ, 35; Columbus Monument, Hazelton, Pa, 37; Spanish-Am Soldier, Union City, NJ, 39; Columbus Monument, Jersey City, NJ, 50; Columbus (colossal bronze bust), Union City, NJ. *Exhib:* Many Pieces, Equitable Galleries, Allied Artists & Nat Sculpture Soc, New York, 36-81; Theodore Roosevelt, Metrop Mus, New York, 43; Nat Acad Design New York, 80. *Awards:* Gold Medal, Nat Acad Design, 80; Gold Medal, Nat Sculpture Soc, 81; Linsey Morris Mem, Allied Artist, 81. *Mem:* Allied Artists Am; Nat Sculpture Soc; assoc mem Nat Acad Design; life mem Lotus Club, NY. *Mailing Add:* c/o Jock Manton 42 W 67th St New York NY 10023

GIAMBERTONE, PAUL
SCULPTOR
b Italy; US citizen. *Study:* Beaux Arts Inst Design, New York, with Gaetano Cecere; Educ Alliance, New York, with Chaim Gross. *Work:* Safad Mus, Israel; Philothea Mus, London, Ont. *Exhib:* Nat Arts Club, New York, 57; Silvermine Guild Artists, New Canaan, Conn, 58; NJ Soc Painters & Sculptors, Jersey City Mus, 59 & 60; Am Soc Contemp Artists, Nat Arts Club, New York, 76-79; Salmagundi Club, 81. *Awards:* Ivan R Laskins Award for Sculpture, 80; First Prize Sculpture, Am Soc Contemp Artists, 82. *Bibliog:* Dorothy Hale (auth), article, Parkeast, 11/77 & 11/82; Palmer Poroner (auth), article, Artspeak, 3/80. *Mem:* Artists Equity Asn New York; League Present Day Artists (dir, 60-); Am Soc Contemp Artists (dir, 73-); Sculptors League, Contemp Artists Guild. *Media:* Welded and Cast Bronze. *Dealer:* Art for Indust 663 Fifth Ave New York NY 10022; Brownstone Gallery 76 Seventh Ave Brooklyn NY 11217. *Mailing Add:* 121 E 23rd St New York NY 10010

GIAMPIETRO, ISABEL (ISABEL A GIAMPIETRO KNOLL)
SCULPTOR, DESIGNER
b Marsicovetere, Potenza, Italy; US citizen. *Study:* Scuola Dell'Arte Della Medaglia, with G Romagnoli, dipl, 50; Fine Arts Acad, Rome, Italy, with Calori, Rivosecchi & Fazzini, dipl, 51; Konstfachskolan, Stockholm, Sweden,

glass with S E Skawonius, cert, 56. *Work:* Smithsonian Inst; Corning Glass Mus; Villa Essen Mus, Ger; and other mus in Europe and pvt collections. *Comn:* Seal of State of Va (bas-relief), Jr CofC, Oklahoma City, 52; portrait of George Washington (bronze relief), Eastman Kodak, Washington, DC, 76. *Exhib:* Triennale, Stedelijk Mus, Amsterdam, Holland, 57; two-person exhib, Leerdam New Glass, Utrecht Mus, Holland, 57; Expos Int, Brussels, Belgium, 58; Glass 1959, Metrop Mus Art, New York; Corcoran Gallery, Washington, DC; and others. *Awards:* Gold Medal, Triennale XI, 57; Grand Prix, Expo, Brussels, Belgium, 58; International Design Grant, Nat Endowment Arts, 78. *Bibliog:* Renzo Marchelli (auth), Portrait of an artist, Negozi e Vetrine, 57; The Metropolitan Museum of Art: Glass 1959, Corning Mus, 59; Geoffrey Beard (auth), International Modern Glass, Charles Scribner's & Sons, 76. *Mem:* Am Medallic Sculpture Asn. *Media:* Bronze, Glass. *Mailing Add:* 300 E 40th St New York NY 10016

GIANAKOS, CRISTOS
SCULPTOR
b New York NY, Jan 4, 34. *Study:* Sch Visual Arts, cert. *Work:* Mus Mod Art, New York; Moderna Museet, Stockholm; Nat Bank Boston; Brutten & Herrick Artworks; and others. *Exhib:* Whitney Mus Am Art, New York, 69; A Plastic Presence, Milwaukee Art Ctr, Wis & San Francisco Mus Art, Calif, 70; Mus Mod Art, New York, 71; New York Cult Ctr, 72; PS 1, Queens, NY, 78; one-man exhibs, Nassau Co Mus Fine Arts, New York, Hal Bromm Gallery, New York, 79 & 80 & Deson Gallery, Chicago, 80 & 81; and others. *Teaching:* Instr Sch Visual Arts, 65- *Awards:* Creative Artists Pub Serv Grant, 76-77 & 79-80; Nat Endowment Arts Award, 80. *Bibliog:* Images of an Era: The American Poster 1945-1975, Smithsonian Inst, 75; Peter Frank (auth), Where is New York, Art News, 80; Sarah McFadden (auth), Going places, part II: The outside story, Art Am, 80. *Media:* Mixed Media. *Mailing Add:* 93 Mercer St New York NY 10012

GIANAKOS, STEVE
SCULPTOR, PAINTER
b New York, NY, 1938. *Study:* Pratt Inst, Brooklyn, NY. *Exhib:* Theodoron Awards Exhib, Guggenheim Mus, New York, 77; Contemp Greek-Am Artists, Brooklyn Mus, NY, 77; one-man shows, Fischbach Gallery, New York, 68, The Clocktower, Inst for Art & Urban Resources, 74, Alessandra Gallery, New York, 76 & Droll-Kolbert Gallery, New York, 77 & 79; Contemp Arts Mus, Houston, Tex, 79; and many others. *Mailing Add:* c/o Droll/Kolbert Gallery Inc 724 Fifth Ave New York NY 10019

GIBALA, LOUISE
PAINTER
b Allegheny, Pa, May 2, 1897. *Study:* Art Students League, New York, 27-30; Nat Acad Design, 30-31; Nat Art League, 50-60. *Work:* Dutch Reformed Church, Flushing, NY; Christ Lutheran Church, Long Island, NY. *Exhib:* New York City Open Competition, Metrop Mus, 50; Ann Open Competition, Nat Art League, 55-83; Flower Painting Exhib, Parrish Mus, Southampton, NY, 64; Catharine Lorillard Wolfe Mem Exhib, Nat Acad Design, 67; 14th Ann Golden Age Art Exhib, World Trade Ctr Gallery, New York, 78; Non-Mem Exhib, Salmagundi Club, 81. *Collections Arranged:* Artists Exhib for 60 Years and Over, 56-78. *Teaching:* Instr landscapes & still life, Nat Art League, 48-70. *Awards:* Gold Medal for wash drawing, 68 & Claude Parsons Mem Award, 76, Am Artists Prof League; Gold Trophy, 14th Ann New York City Art Exhib, 78. *Mem:* Nat Art League (pres, 51-53 & 63-65); Catharine Lorillard Wolfe Art Club (dir, 81-82); Am Artists Prof League; Hudson Valley Art Asn; Knickerbocker Artists. *Media:* Oil. *Publ:* Auth, Art clubs of America: Art League of Long Island, Artist Mag, 57. *Mailing Add:* 251-24 51st Ave Little Neck NY 11362

GIBBONS, HUGH (JAMES)
PAINTER, EDUCATOR
b Scranton, Pa, Oct 26, 37. *Study:* Pa State Univ, with Elaine de Kooning & Robert Mallary, BA(painting), 59, MA(painting), 61. *Work:* WTex Mus, Lubbock; Bucknell Univ Collection. *Exhib:* One-man shows, Mus Fine Art, Carlsbad, NMex, 80, WTex Mus, Lubbock, 82, Northern Ariz State Univ, Flagstaff, 83, NMex Jr Col, Hobbs, 83 & Art Ctr, Amarillo, Tex, 83; and others. *Teaching:* Prof painting & drawing & MFA coordr, Tex Tech Univ, 63- *Awards:* First Prize, LEA Nat, 82. *Media:* Oil, Pencil. *Mailing Add:* 3312 20th St Lubbock TX 79410

GIBBS, TOM
SCULPTOR
b Dubuque, Iowa, Sept 17, 42. *Study:* Loras Col, BA(art); Univ Iowa, with Olivier Strabelle, MA(sculpture) & MFA; also with Walter Arno, Ger. *Comn:* Winged Victory (steel), Cent Col, Pella, Iowa, 75; four large scale steel sculptures, City of Dubuque, Iowa, 75-76; Broken From Whole (steel), Franklin Pub Libr, Des Moines, Iowa, 77; Western Electric Corp, 80; Esterville Public Libr, 81. *Exhib:* Int Art Exposition, 82 & Mayor Byrne's Mile of Sculpture, 82, Navy Pier, Chicago; Ill Sculptor's Invitational, Tarble Arts Ctr, 82; Vietnam Veteran's Mem Design Traveling Exhib, 82; Mile 2, Chicago Sculpture Int, Navy Pier, 83; and others. *Teaching:* Instr art, Clarke Col, 68-69; asst prof sculpture, Ariz State Univ, 70-72. *Awards:* Nat Community Art Competition Award, US Dept Housing & Urban Develop, 73. *Bibliog:* Articles, Chicago Sun Times, 6/29/80 & 5/23/82 & Art News, 11/80. *Media:* Welded & Cast Metal. *Dealer:* Zaks Gallery 620 N Michigan Ave Chicago IL 60611; Anton Gallery 415 E Capitol Washington DC 20003. *Mailing Add:* 1333 Kaufman Dubuque IA 52001

GIBRAN, KAHLIL GEORGE
SCULPTOR
b Boston, Mass, Nov 29, 22. *Study:* Boston Mus Sch, 40-43, painting with Karl Zerbe. *Work:* Chrysler Collection, Va Mus, Norfolk; Pa Acad Fine Art, Philadelphia; Cheekwood Art Ctr, Nashville, Tenn; Elmira Col, NY. *Comn:* Bronze wall mural, Forsythe Dental, Boston, 71; bronze plaque of Judge Francis Ford, Fed Ct House, Boston, 77; bronze plaque of poet Kahlil Gibran, Copley Sq, Boston, 77; Bronze Figure of Madonna, Jamaica Plain, Mass, 81. *Exhib:* Whitney Mus Am Art Ann, 56; Int, Trieste, Italy, 66; New Eng Artists, Provincetown Art Asn & Cyclorama, Boston, 71; one-man show of bronze sculpture, Cambridge Art Asn, 77; Cambridge Art Asn, Mass, 80; Boston Athenaeum, 81. *Teaching:* Wellesley Col, 58; Boston Univ, formerly. *Awards:* George Wiedner Medal, Pa Acad Fine Arts, 58; John S Guggenheim Fel, 59-61; Nat Inst Arts & Lett Award & Fel, 61. *Bibliog:* Gregory MacDonald (auth), Kahlil Gibran a Boston sculptor, Boston Globe Mag, 67; Nathan Hale (auth), Welded Sculpture, Watson-Guptill, 68; Donald Irving (auth), Sculpture Material and Process, Van Nostrand Reinhold, 70. *Mem:* Nat Sculpture Soc; New Eng Sculpture Soc; Cambridge Art Asn (vpres, 68); Provincetown Art Asn. *Media:* Steel. *Publ:* Auth, Sculpture in process, Nat Sculpture Rev, 70; auth, Sculpture Kahlil Gibran, 72; coauth, Kahlil Gibran-- His Life and world, New York Graphic Soc, 74. *Mailing Add:* 160 W Canton St Boston MA 02118

GIBSON, BENEDICT S
PAINTER, EDUCATOR
b Grand Rapids, Mich, Sept 21, 46. *Study:* Kendall Sch Design, dipl, 67; Aquinas Col, BA, 70; Univ Nebr, MFA, 73. *Work:* Albright-Knox Art Gallery, Buffalo, NY; Butler Inst Am Art, Youngstown, Ohio; Mem Art Gallery, Rochester, NY; Rutgers Univ, New Brunswick, NJ; Flint Inst Arts, Mich; and others. *Exhib:* 34th Western NY Exhib, Albright-Knox Art Gallery, 74; Midwest Invitational II, Springfield Art Mus, Mo, 74; Reo-Realist Exhib, Col St Catherine, St Paul, Minn, 74; Mich Surv, San Jose Art Gallery, Calif & Cranbrook Acad, Bloomfield Hills, Mich, 75 & 76; 41st Midyear Show, Butler Inst Am Art, Youngstown, Ohio, 77; Nat Drawing, Rutgers State Univ, NJ, Camden, 77; Hassam & Speicher Fund Exhib, Am Acad & Inst Arts, New York, 78; and others. *Collections Arranged:* Drawing Invitational (cataloged), 76; First Decade, Charles B Burchfield Ctr Col, 76; Penney Collection (cataloged), State Univ NY Upstate Med Ctr, 77; Three Painters, Millersville State Col, 77; Tenth Anniversary Exhibition, Kenan Ctr, Lockport, NY, 77. *Teaching:* Asst prof art, Damaen Col, Buffalo, NY, 73-76; assoc prof art, Edinboro State Col, Pa, 76- *Awards:* First Prize, Birge Co, Inc, 74, Chautauqua Inst, 74 & Edinboro State Col, 77; Best of Show, Ann Spring Show, Erie Art Ctr, 80; and others. *Bibliog:* Nancy Tobin Willig (auth), Gibson's Show: Superrealism with a plus, Buffalo Courier-Express, 74; Jean Reeves (auth), Gibson's craftsmanship produces mystery, illusion, 74 & Hal Crowther (auth), Gibson Art dominates 4-man show, 75, Buffalo Evening News. *Mem:* Patteran Artists Asn, Buffalo, NY; Col Art Asn Am. *Media:* Acrylic, Oil. *Mailing Add:* Edinboro State Col Art Dept Meadville & Normal Streets Edinboro PA 16412

GIBSON, GEORGE
PAINTER, ADMINISTRATOR
b Edinburgh, Scotland, Oct 16, 04; US citizen. *Study:* Edinburgh Col Art, Glasgow Sch Art, Scotland; W E Glover Scenic Studios, Glasgow; Chouinard Sch Art, Los Angeles; also with F Tolles Chamberlain, Pasadena, Calif. *Work:* Calif Nat Watercolor Soc Collection, Los Angeles Co Mus Art; Home Savings & Loan, Los Angeles; Laguna Beach Mus Art, Calif; Santa Barbara Mus Art, Calif; Santa Paula CofC, Calif. *Exhib:* Calif Nat Watercolor Soc Ann, 47-71; Am Watercolor Soc Ann, 49-72; Nat Acad Design, New York, 54-58; Phoenix Art Mus, Ariz, 72. *Pos:* Supvr scenic art prod, MGM Studios, Culver City, Calif, 34-69. *Awards:* Calif Nat Watercolor Soc 32nd Ann Award, 51; Nat Acad Design 134th Ann Watercolor Award, 59; Verda Karen McCracken Young Award, Am Watercolor Soc 105th Ann, 72. *Bibliog:* V Hewtschy (auth), From any angle, 10/54 & Ron Ross (auth), Cameraman's comments, 12/54, Int Photogr; G Gibson (auth), Scenic art in motion picture industry, Soc Motion Picture & TV Eng J, 10/62. *Mem:* Assoc Nat Acad Design; Am Watercolor Soc; Nat Watercolor Soc (secy, 47, first vpres, 49, pres, 51); West Coast Watercolor Soc; Acad Motion Picture Arts & Sci. *Media:* Watercolor. *Publ:* Contribr, Am Artist, 5/68 & 9/69. *Dealer:* A Huney Gallery 3746 Sixth Ave San Diego CA 92103. *Mailing Add:* 1449 Santa Maria Ave Los Osos CA 93402

GIBSON, JAMES D
EDUCATOR, PAINTER
b Milbank, SDak, Dec 13, 38. *Study:* Ill Wesleyan Univ, BFA; Ohio Univ, BFA. *Work:* State Univ NY Col, Fredonia; Univ NDak. *Comn:* Historic Panorama (mural, with Vic Runnels), First Nat Bank, Aberdeen, SDak, 76. *Exhib:* Artists of Montana, Senate Off Bldg, Washington, DC, 65; Hawaiian Nat Print Competition, 71; Nat Environ Print Show, Univ Wis, Green Bay, 71; 12th Midwest Biennial, Joslyn Art Mus, Omaha, Nebr, 72; Nat Print Show, Minot, NDak, 73. *Teaching:* Instr art, Eastern Mont Col, 65-67; prof art, Northern State Col, SDak, 67-, chmn dept art, 67-78. *Awards:* Purchase Award, Paintings, 68 & SDak Works on Paper, 71-72, SDak Mem Art Ctr; Res Grant, Northern State Col, 79. *Mem:* Nat Asn Sch Art (bd dirs, 71-72). *Media:* Acrylic, Ink. *Publ:* Illusr, Motive Mag, Methodist Church, 68-70; auth, Campus Call, Catholic Church, 68; illusr, Sunday Clothes, Arts Coun SDak, 73. *Mailing Add:* RR 1 Box 60 Westport SD 57481

GIBSON, RALPH H
PHOTOGRAPHER
b Jan 16, 39. *Study:* US Navy, studied photog, 56-60; San Francisco Art Inst, 60-61. *Work:* Mus Mod Art & Metrop Mus Art, New York; Int Mus Photog, George Eastman House, Rochester, NY; Fogg Art Mus, Cambridge, Mass; Ctr for Creative Photog, Univ Ariz, Tucson; Nat Gallery of Can, Ottawa, Ont; plus many others. *Exhib:* Photog for Collectors, 76, Rooms, 77 & Mirrors & Windows, 78, Mus Mod Art, New York; Recent Acquisitions, Stedelijk Mus, Amsterdam, Neth, 76; Baltimore Mus, Md, 76; Friends of Photog, San Francisco Mus Art, Calif, 77; The Great Am Foot, Mus Contemp Crafts, New York, 78; Bologna Art Fair, Italy, 78; Walker Art Ctr, Liverpool, Eng, 78; one-man shows, Mus Mod Art, Oxford, Eng, 77, Camera Obscursa, Stockholm, 78 & Castelli Uptown, New York, 78. *Teaching:* Lectr at var places including Ont Col of Art, Toronto, Sun Valley Ctr for the Arts, Idaho, Int Festival at Arles, France, Ansel Adams Gallery, Yosemite Valley, Calif & Tyler Sch of Art, Temple Univ, Philadelphia, Pa, 75 & Cranbrook Acad, Detroit, Mich, Inst of Contemp Art, London, Eng, Sydney Acad of Art Australia, Mus Fine Art, Houston, Tex & Frei Univ, Amsterdam, Neth, 77. *Awards:* Nat Endowment for the Arts Grant, 73 & 75; Creative Artists Pub Serv Grant, NY State Coun of the Arts, 77. *Bibliog:* Julia Scully (auth), article in Mod Photog, 6/75; Allan Porter (auth), article in Camera, Switz, 4/77; Ralph Gibson (auth), How he creates his fractional images, Popular Photog, 4/77. *Publ:* Auth, The Strip, Roger Kennedy Inc, 66; auth, The Hawk, Bobbs-Merrill Inc, 68; auth, The American Civil Liberties Union Calendar, 69; auth, The Somnambulist, 70, Deja-vu, 73 & Days at Sea, 75, Lustrum Press Inc; auth, Syntax, Lustrum Press, 83. *Dealer:* Castelli Uptown 4 E 77th St New York NY 10021. *Mailing Add:* 331 W Broadway New York NY 10013

GIBSON, ROLAND
COLLECTOR, CURATOR
b Potsdam, NY, Feb 4, 02. *Study:* Dartmouth Col, AB, 35; Columbia Univ, MA, 40, PhD(econ), 47. *Exhib:* Exhibs circulated by Roland Gibson Art Found, at col & univ art galleries throughout US, 64-74. *Pos:* Pres & treas, Roland Gibson Art Found, Inc, Potsdam, 65-75; dir, Roland Gibson Mus Art, Dunbarton, NH, 67-70; cur art, State Univ NY Col Potsdam, 70- *Collection:* 300 works of contemporary abstract painting, prints and sculpture; Japanese and Italian abstract art. *Publ:* Auth, Japanese Abstract Art Collected in Japan in 1963 (catalog), 64; auth, Italian Abstract Art Collected on a Visit to Italy in 1966 (catalog), 67; auth, A Retrospective of the Paintings of Mary Sloane (catalog), 69; auth, New New England Sculpture (catalog), 73; auth, Japanese Art of the Sixties (catalog), 73. *Mailing Add:* 9 Garden St Potsdam NY 13676

GIBSON, WALTER SAMUEL
HISTORIAN, WRITER
b Columbus, Ohio, Mar 31, 32. *Study:* Ohio State Univ, BFA, 57, MA, 60; res at Kunsthistorisch Inst Rijksuniversiteit, Utrecht, 60-61 & 64-66; Harvard Univ, PhD, 69. *Teaching:* Asst prof art, Case Western Reserve Univ, Cleveland, 66-71, chmn dept & assoc prof, 71-79, Andrew W Mellon Prof humanities, 78- *Mem:* Col Art Asn Am; Int Ctr Medieval Art; Midwest Art Hist Soc; Renaissance Soc Am; Medieval Acad Am. *Res:* Dutch and Flemish art of the 15th and 16th century; iconography. *Publ:* Auth, Hieronymus Bosch, Praeger, 73; Bruegel, Oxford Univ Press, 77; The Paintings of Cornelis Engebrechtsz, Garland, 77; Hieronymus Bosch: An Annotated Bibliography, G K Hall, 83; numerous articles in American & European journals. *Mailing Add:* Dept of Art Case Western Reserve Univ Cleveland OH 44106

GIFFORD, J NEBRASKA
PAINTER, SCULPTOR
b Omaha, Nebr, Nov 25, 39. *Study:* Bennington Col, BA; Atelier 17, Paris, with S W Hayter. *Work:* Owens-Corning Fiberglas Collection, Toledo, Ohio; NY Univ; Joslyn Art Mus, Omaha, Nebr. *Comn:* Acrylic painting, indoor wall, Omaha Community Playhouse, 61; oil & enamel painting, outdoor wall, Old Market, Omaha, 69. *Exhib:* Contemporary Reflections (1971-72), Aldrich Mus, Ridgefield, Conn, 72; Whitney Mus Am Art Ann, New York, 72; one-person shows, Louis K Meisel Gallery, 74 & 55 Mercer Gallery, 76, New York & Univ Nebr, Omaha, 77; Bridge of Cows, Madison Square Park, Animals in Arsenal, Arsenal Gallery & Saints, Harm Bovkaert Gallery, New York, 83; Terminal Show, 83; and others. *Pos:* Columnist, Gallery Mag. *Awards:* MacDowell Fel, 76. *Media:* Acrylic, Latex; Oil, Metal. *Publ:* Ed, Int Soc Copier Artists Newsletter; Article, New York Mag, 6/6/83; article, New York Times, 7/8/83. *Mailing Add:* 4 Great Jones St New York NY 10012

GIKAS, CHRISTOPHER
EDUCATOR, STAINED GLASS ARTIST
b Lincoln, Nebr, Jan 26, 26. *Study:* Okla State Univ, BFA; Univ NMex, stained glass with Hans Tatschl, MA. *Work:* Okla State Univ; Univ NMex; WTex State Univ. *Comn:* Granite & stainless steel Vietnam monument, Cannon AFB, Clovis, NMex, 74; lava stone & copper monument to Eastern NMex Univ veterans, 77. *Teaching:* Instr art, WTex State Univ, 55-62; prof art, Eastern NMex Univ, 62-, dir, Div Art, Theatre & Dance. *Awards:* Eastern NMex Univ Pres Faculty Award, 69. *Publ:* Coauth, Tole' Painting for the Decorative Artists, Vols I & II, 70 & 72; illusr, Journey Through the History of New Mexico (pub sch text), 72. *Mailing Add:* PO Box 600 Portales NM 88130

GILBERT, ALBERT EARL
PAINTER, ILLUSTRATOR
b Chicago, Ill, Aug 22, 39. *Work:* Am Mus Natural Hist, New York; Carnegie Mus, Pittsburgh; Ill State Mus, Springfield; Nat Audubon Soc, New York; du Pont Collection, Del Mus Natural Hist, Wilmington. *Comn:* Paintings of Am wildlife & plants, Nat Wildlife Fedn, Washington, DC, 67-74; Audubon bird proj (20 color plates of Am birds), Franklin Mint, Pa, 75. *Exhib:* Wildlife in Art, Brandywine River Mus, Chadds Ford, Pa, 73; SAm Birds, Am Mus Natural Hist, New York, 73; one-man show, Wildlife Portraits, Incurable Collector Gallery, New York, 74; Animals in Art, Royal Ont Mus, Toronto, 75; Bird Art Exhib, Leigh Yawkey Woodson Art Mus, Wausau, 75; and others. *Awards:* Winner, Fed Duck Stamp Competition, 78-79. *Bibliog:* B J Lancaster (auth), Gilbert's birds, Cornell Univ Lab of Ornithology Bulletin, 75; The artist--Al Gilbert, Prints Mag, spring, 79. *Mem:* Soc Animal Artists; Ridgefield Guild Artists. *Media:* Opaque Watercolors, Acrylics. *Publ:* Illusr, The Audubon Illustrated Handbook of American Birds, 68, The Red Book-- Wildlife in Danger, 68, Curassows and Related Birds, 73 & Birds of New York State, 74; auth, My studio is the jungle, Int Wildlife Mag, 9-10/76; and others. *Dealer:* Sportsman's Edge Ltd 136 E 74th St New York NY 10021; Steep Rock Wildlife Art Box 107 Bridgewater CT 06752. *Mailing Add:* Rt 67 Bridgewater CT 06752

GILBERT, ARNOLD MARTIN
COLLECTOR, PHOTOGRAPHER
b New York, NY, Mar 28, 21. *Study:* Univ of Chicago. *Exhib:* One-man shows, Monterey Peninsula Mus Art, Univ Wis, Milwaukee, Gilbert Gallery, Chicago, Ill & Prairie State Col, Chicago Heights, Ill. *Teaching:* Prof photography, Governors State Univ, Park Forest S, Ill, 74-82. *Mem:* Friends of Photography. *Collection:* Modern 20th century photography. *Mailing Add:* 1610 Butterfield Flossmoor IL 60422

GILBERT, CLYDE LINGLE
PAINTER
b Medora, Ind, Oct 15, 98. *Study:* Sch Appl Art, Battle Creek, Mich; Nat Acad Com Art, Chicago; Studio Fine Arts, Brazil, Ind. *Exhib:* Wawasee Art Gallery, Syracuse, Ind, 49; Howe Mil Sch, Ind, 49; one-man show, Weddleville Sch, Ind, 66; Battle Creek Sanatorium, Mich, 66; State-Wide Show, French Lick Hotel, Ind, 66. *Awards:* Gold Medal for Highest Packaging Honors, 38. *Mem:* Ind Fedn Art Clubs. *Media:* Oil, Watercolor. *Mailing Add:* 139 Riverview Ave Elkhart IN 46514

GILBERT, CREIGHTON EDDY
HISTORIAN, WRITER
b Durham, NC, June 6, 24. *Study:* NY Univ, with Walter Friedlaender, Richard Offner, Lionello Venturi, Erwin Panofsky, Meyer Schapiro & Richard Krautheimer, BA, 42, PhD, 55; Yale, Hon MA, 81. *Pos:* Cur, Ringling Mus, Sarasota, Fla, 59-61; ed in chief, Art Bulletin, 80- *Teaching:* Jr posts, Emory Univ, Univ Louisville, Ind Univ, Bloomington, 46-; from assoc prof to Sidney & Ellen Wien prof hist art, Brandeis Univ, 61-69; prof hist art, Queens Col, 69-77; vis prof, Univ Leiden, Netherlands, 74-75; Robert Sterling Clark vis prof, Williams Col, 76; Jacob Gould Schurman prof hist of art, Cornell Univ, 77-81; prof, Yale Univ, 81- *Awards:* Fulbright Sr Lectr, Univ Rome, 51-52; Mather Award for Best Art Criticism of Year, Col Art Asn Am, 64; Fel, Netherlands Inst Advan Study, 72-73. *Bibliog:* Interview, Amerikaanse Kunsthistoricus Creighton Gilbert, Rotterdam Courant- Handelsblad, 2/75. *Mem:* Fel Am Acad Arts & Sci; Col Art Asn Am. *Publ:* Transl, Complete Poems & Selected Letters of Michelangelo, 63, Mod Libr Ed, 65, Vintage, 70, 3rd Revised Ed, Princeton, 80; auth, Michelangelo, McGraw, 67; auth, Change in Piero della Francesca, Augustin, 68; auth, History of Renaissance Art, Abrams, 72; ed, Italian Art 1400-1500, Sources and Documents, Prentice-Hall, 79. *Mailing Add:* Hist Art 56 High St Yale Univ New Haven CT 05620

GILBERT, HELEN ODELL
PAINTER, PRINTMAKER
b Calif. *Study:* Mills Col, Oakland, Calif, AB, 43; Cent Sch Art, London, 60; Univ Calif, Berkeley; with J Frielander, Paris, Univ Hawaii, MFA, 68; Pratt Graphics, New York. *Work:* Univ Calif, Berkeley; San Diego Art Mus; Honolulu Acad Art; Bibliot Nat, Paris; Contemp Arts Ctr, Honolulu. *Exhib:* Hawaii Nat Print Exhib, Honolulu Acad Arts, 77, 80 & 83; L'Estampe Ajourd'hui, Bibliot Nat, Paris, 78; Soc Am Graphic Artists, New York, 79 & 83; Dusseldorf & Basel Art Fairs, 80, 81 & 83; Contemp Arts Ctr, Honolulu, 83; Meissner Gallery, Hamburg, 84; Maghi Bettini, Amsterdam, 84; and others. *Teaching:* Prof art, Univ Hawaii, 65-; vis exchange prof, Parsons Sch, New York, 78-79; vis prof, Pratt Inst, 83. *Awards:* Res Grant, Univ Hawaii, 69 & 70; Study & Res Grant, Pratt Graphics, Ford Found, 79. *Mem:* Am Abstract Artists Asn; Honolulu Printmakers Asn; Nat Arts Club; Hawaii Artists League. *Dealer:* Edward Meissner Norderstedt 200 Hamburg WGer; Artloft 637 Sheridan St Honolulu HI 98613. *Mailing Add:* 29 E 22nd St #7N New York NY 10010

GILBERT, HERB
PAINTER, GRAPHIC DESIGNER
b Brooklyn, NY, Oct 30, 29. *Study:* Art Career Sch, 48-51; Brooklyn Mus Art Sch, with Reuben Tam, 55-58; Pratt Inst with Walter Murch, Reuben Nakian & George McNiel, 56-57; Univ Calif, 73. *Work:* Mus NMex, Santa Fe; Motorola Corp, Phoenix, Ariz; Am Republic Insurance Co, Des Moines, Iowa. *Exhib:* Own Your Own Regional, Denver Art Mus, 64; Southwest Fine Arts Biennial, Mus NMex, 74; Invitational, Cochise Col, Douglas, Ariz, 77; Cochise Fine Arts, Bisbee, Ariz, 79; Lambert-Miller Gallery, Phoenix, Ariz, 81; and others. *Pos:* Art dir, Campbell Mithun Advert Agency, Denver, 64-65; art dir & graphic designer, Herb's Place, Denver, 65-71; graphic designer/ illusr, civil serv, 79-83. *Teaching:* Instr graphics, Inst Am Indian Arts, Santa Fe, 71-75. *Awards:* Three Distinctive Merit Awards, Two Gold Medals & Eight Honor Awards, Art Dirs Club Denver, 59-69. *Bibliog:* Michael Cadieux (auth), Herb Gilbert, Artspace, summer 83. *Mem:* Cochise Fine Arts Asn, Bisbee, Ariz. *Media:* Acrylic, Oil; Mixed Media, Collage. *Publ:* Contribr, Impressions of Arizona (painting), Art Am, 4/81. *Mailing Add:* PO Box 1294 Bisbee AZ 85603

GILBERT, LIONEL
PAINTER, INSTRUCTOR
b Newark, NJ, May 29, 12. *Study:* Newark Sch Fine & Indust Art, grad, 29; Acad Grande Chaumiere, Paris, 33; with Suzanne Valadon, Paris, 34; Chicago Sch Design, with Maholy-Nagy, 41; NY Univ, with Sam Adler, 55. *Work:* Chase Manhattan Bank, New York; Joslyn Mus Art, Omaha, Nebr; Slater Mus, Conn; Eureka Col Collection; Silver Springs Acad, Colo; also in many pvt & corp collections. *Exhib:* One-man shows, Gallery Contemp Art, Toronto, 58, New Sch Social Res, New York, 66 & Alonzo Gallery, New York, 68, 70, 71, 73, 75, 76 & 80; Childe Hassom Fund Exhib, Acad Arts & Lett, 69; Nat Acad Design; and others. *Teaching:* Instr drawing & painting, YMHA, New York, 67-; instr drawing & painting, NY Univ, 68-69; instr painting, Summit Art Ctr, NJ, 75- *Awards:* Certificate of Merit, Nat Acad Design, 75. *Media:* Oil. *Mailing Add:* 244 West 74th St New York NY 10023

GILBERTSON, CHARLOTTE
PAINTER, LECTURER
b Boston, Mass. *Study:* Boston Univ, BA; Art Students League; Pratt Inst, New York; studied with Fernand Leger, Paris. *Exhib:* E A T Show, Brooklyn Mus, New York, 68-69; Erik Nord Gallery, Nantucket, 75; Bodley Gallery, 75 & 77; Irving Galleries, Palm Beach, Fla, 77; Pace Univ Mus & St Peters Col Mus, 78; Galeria Bryna, Palm Beach, 80 & 81; plus many others. *Pos:* Gallery dir, Iolas Gallery, New York, 62-74; dir, Galeria Bryna, Palm Beach, 79-80; free lance lecturer, 80- *Mem:* Visual Arts Galleries Asn; Palm Beach Co Coun Arts; Am Fedn Arts; Int Women's Writing Guild. *Media:* Oil, Acrylic. *Dealer:* Iolas Gallery 15 E 55th St New York NY 10022. *Mailing Add:* Old Sch House Rd Harwich Port MA 02646

GILBOY, MARGARETTA
PAINTER, INSTRUCTOR
b Philadelphia, Pa, Aug 10, 43. *Study:* Philadelphia Col Art, BFA, 65; Univ Colo, Boulder, MFA, 81. *Work:* Univ Colo, Boulder. *Exhib:* Biennial, Joslyn Art Mus, Omaha, Nebr, 68; 5th Colo Ann, Denver Art Mus, 79; Colo Women Arts, Arvada Ctr Arts & Humanities, 79; Nat Painting Show, Washington & Jefferson Col, Washington, Pa, 80; Portraits, Philadelphia Col Art, Pa, 80; Colo Biennial, Colo Springs Art Ctr, 81. *Teaching:* Instr painting, Univ Colo, Boulder, 76-77 & 80- *Awards:* Award for Creative Work, Univ Colo, 81; Teaching Excellence Award, 81 & Eugene Kayden Colo Arts Award, 83, Univ Colo. *Bibliog:* Eve Medoff (auth), Realism plus, Am Artist Mag, 3/79. *Mem:* Artists Equity; Front Range: Women in the Visual Arts; Col Art Asn. *Media:* Oil. *Dealer:* Marian Locks 1524 Walnut St Philadelphia PA 19102. *Mailing Add:* 1502 Columbine Ave Boulder CO 80302

GILCHRIEST, LORENZO
CONSTRUCTIONIST, EDUCATOR
b Thomasville, Ga, Mar 21, 38. *Study:* Newark Sch Fine & Indust Arts, 57-58; Newark State Col, BA, 62; Pratt Inst, MS, 67; Md Inst, MFA, 75. *Work:* Newark State Col; Fairleigh Dickinson Univ. *Exhib:* Some Negro Artists, Fairleigh Dickinson Univ, 65; one-man shows, Univ Md, 70 & Morgan State Univ, 79; Md Regional, Baltimore Mus Art, 71; Black Art, Towson State Col, 75; three solo & many group shows, Argus Gallery. *Pos:* Assoc art dir, Sen Robert Kennedy Proj, Bedford Stuyvesant Youth in Action, Brooklyn, NY, 65-67. *Teaching:* Asst prof art, Towson State Col, 67-; guest prof sculpture, Cornell Univ, summers 72 & 73; teacher constructions, painting & drawing, Baltimore Mus Art, 73-74; guest prof print workshop, Morgan State Univ, summer 77. *Awards:* Afro American Slide Depository for Afro Americans, Samuel Kress Found, 71; Fel Int Arts Sem, Fairleigh Dickinson Univ, 62. *Bibliog:* Barbara Gold (auth), Blackmarks, Black art, Sun Paper Art Sect, 6/75. *Mailing Add:* 1013 Woodbourne Ave Baltimore MD 21212

GILCHRIST, ELIZABETH BRENDA
EDITOR
b Coulsdon, Eng; US citizen. *Study:* Smith Col, BA(art hist); Art Students League. *Pos:* Asst, Durlacher Brothers Art Gallery, New York, 54-57; art admin asst, Brussels World's Fair, Belg & New York, 57-58; fund raiser, Mus Mod Art, New York, 59-62; reporter, Show Mag, New York, NY, 62-64; staff writer, Am Heritage Publ Co, 64; sr art ed, Praeger Publ, New York, 65-75; ed publ, Cooper-Hewitt Mus, Nat Mus of Design, Smithsonian Inst, New York, 76-81; mem adv coun for continuing educ prog, Mus Collaborative Inc, 77-78, publ consult, 81- *Mem:* Drawing Soc (mem bd dirs, 60-81, mem exec comt, currently); Soc Archit Historians; Col Art Asn; Am Asn Mus; Victorian Soc Am. *Publ:* Translr, Jacques Lassaigne's Marc Chagall: The Ceiling of the Paris Opera, 66; ed, American Art & Artists series, Praeger, 71-75; gen ed, The Smithsonian Illustrated Library of Antiques, Cooper-Hewitt Mus, 76-81. *Mailing Add:* 175 W 93rd St New York NY 10025

GILDZEN, ALEX
WRITER, COLLECTOR
b Monterey, Calif, April 25, 43. *Study:* Wagner Col, with Kenneth Koch, 63; Kent State Univ, BA, 65, MA, 66. *Collections Arranged:* The Photographer's Art: An Exhibition of Prints and Books on Photography, 81. *Pos:* Assoc cur, Spec Collections, Libr, Kent State Univ, 77-, acting cur, Mus, 82-83; ed, Dress: J Costume Soc Am, 82- *Mem:* Costume Soc Am (region III pres, 82-). *Res:* Film history; costume history; photography; modern sculpture. *Collection:* Contemporary sculpture, drawings, prints and photographs. *Publ:* Ed, Six Poems-Seven Prints, Kent State Univ Libr, 71; auth, Haber's shattered landscapes: Studies in nature and time, In: exhib catalog, Kent State Univ, 77; auth, Partially buried woodshed: A Robert Smithson log, 78 & Ira Joel Haber: Poolside reflections on coming out of the box, 82, Arts. *Mailing Add:* 1129 Morris Rd Kent OH 44240

GILES, NEWELL WALTON, JR
PAINTER
b Flushing, NY, June 20, 28. *Study:* Wesleyan Univ, BA(art hist); New York-Phoenix Sch Design; also studied watercolor with Herb Olsen, Westport, Conn. *Comn:* Watercolor renderings, Stanwich Presby Church, Greenwich, Conn, 69 & main lobby, Innis Arden Golf Club, Old Greenwich, Conn, 71; Pan Ocean Oil Corp, New York, 72; and var pvt comns. *Exhib:* Greenwich Art Soc Ann Show, Greenwich Libr, 66-70; Hudson Valley Art Asn Ann Show, White Plains, NY, 66-77; Am Watercolor Soc Ann Show, New York, 68; Hammond Mus Exhib Contemp Am Art, North Salem, NY, 68; Am Artists Prof League Regional Show, New York, 72-77. *Pos:* Art dir, J M Mathes Inc, New York, 55-63; art & prod dir, J J Lane Inc, Advert, New York, 63-78; sr art dir advert, Kohler Co, Riverside, Conn, 78- *Teaching:* Pvt instr watercolor, 70-71. *Awards:* Puck Award for Newspaper Advert, New York J-Am, 60; First Prize for Watercolors, Greenwich Art Soc, 68 & Old Greenwich Art Soc, 70, 72, 75 & 77. *Bibliog:* Article, La Rev Mod, 69. *Mem:* Assoc Am Watercolor Soc; Am Artists Prof League; Hudson Valley Art Asn; Greenwich Art Soc; Old Greenwich Art Soc. *Media:* Watercolor, Oil. *Mailing Add:* 26 Mimosa Dr Cos Cob CT 06807

GILHOOLY, DAVID JAMES, III
SCULPTOR
b Auburn, Calif, Apr 15, 43. *Study:* Univ Calif, Davis, BA, 65, MA, 67. *Work:* Whitney Mus; Oakland Mus, Calif; Bronfman Collection Can Art, Nat Gallery, Ottawa, Ont; Stedelijk Mus, Amsterdam; San Francisco Mus Mod Art; and others. *Comn:* Seattle's Own Ark, Woodland Park Zoo, Wash, 79; Breadwall, Govt Can Bldg, Calgary, Alta; and others. *Exhib:* Funk Show, Inst Contemp Art, Boston, Mass, 67; Realisms '70, Montreal Mus Art & Art Gallery Ont, 70; Whitney Mus Am Art, 70, 74, 81 & 82; Matrix Gallery, Wadsworth Atheneum, Hartford, Conn, 76; Painting & Sculpture: the Mod Era, San Francisco Mus Art, Nat Collection Finc Art, Washington, DC, 77; Candy Store Gallery, Folsom, Calif, 64-83; Mus Contemp Craft, New York, 78; St Louis Art Mus; E B Crocker Art Mus, Sacramento, Calif, 81; and many others. *Teaching:* Instr drawings & watercolor, San Jose State Col, 67-69; instr ceramics & sculpture, Univ Sask, Regina, 69-71; instr ceramic sculpture, York Univ, 71-75 & 76-77; instr ceramics & drawing, Univ Calif, Davis, 75-76. *Bibliog:* Jeannette Arneson (auth), David Gilhooly, Crafts Horizon, 8/71; Gary Dault (auth), With David Gilhooly in the frogworld, spring 72 & Dale Conathy (auth), David Gilhooly's Mythanthropy, 6/75, Arts Can; and others. *Mem:* Royal Can Acad. *Media:* Clay, Wood. *Dealer:* Smith-Anderson Gallery 200 Homer Palo Alto CA 94301. *Mailing Add:* 26261 Omar Dr Ft Bragg CA 95437

GILKEY, GORDON WAVERLY
CURATOR, EDUCATOR
b Linn Co, Ore, Mar 10, 12. *Study:* Albany Col, BA, 33; Univ Ore, MFA, 36; Lewis & Clark Col, Hon DA, 57. *Work:* Metrop Mus Art, New York; Libr Cong, Washington, DC; Brit Mus, London; Bibliot Nat, Paris; San Francisco Art Mus; plus others. *Comn:* Etchings, Univ Ore Libr Construction, 36; etchings, New York World's Fair, 1939, New York World's Fair & Charles Scribner's Sons, 38-39. *Exhib:* Northwest Printmakers Int, 50-72; Soc Am Graphic Artists, New York, 52-80; Expos Int Gravure, Ljubljana, Yugoslavia, 65-73; Biennale Int Gravure, Cracow, Poland, 68-70 & 74; Expos in Dessins Originaux, Rijeka, Yugoslavia. *Pos:* Dir, Int Exchange Print Exhibs, US Prints in Europe & Africa, 56 & 65; importer contemp prints, 56-65, 69-72 & 75; trustee & chmn art comt, Portland Art Mus, 61-67, cur prints & drawings, 78-; chmn, Gov Planning Coun Arts & Humanities Ore, 65-67. *Teaching:* Instr art & studio, Stephens Col, 39-42; prof art hist & studio & head dept, Ore State Univ, 47-64, dean, Sch Humanities & Social Sci, 63-73, dean, Col Liberal Arts, 73-77; mem art fac, Pacific Northwest Col Art, 78. *Awards:* Off Order Palms Acad, Repub France, 69; King Carl XVI Gustaf's Gold Medal Art, Sweden, 77; Chevalier, Nat Order Legion Hon, France, 78. *Mem:* Soc Am Graphic Artists; Col Art Asn Am; Calif Soc Printmakers. *Res:* History of printmaking. *Collection:* Historical and contemporary prints. *Publ:* Auth, Etching Showing Construction Progress of the University of Oregon Library, 36; auth, Etchings: New York World's Fair, 1939, 39; auth, numerous articles on printmaking. *Mailing Add:* Portland Art Mus 1219 SW Park Ave Portland OR 97205

GILKEY, RICHARD CHARLES
PAINTER, SCULPTOR
b Bellingham, Wash, Dec 20, 25. *Study:* Self-taught with guidance of Mark Tobey, Morris Graves & Guy Anderson. *Work:* Seattle Art Mus; Wahtcom Mus Hist & Art, Bellingham, Wash; Port Seattle; Skagit Co Admin Bldg, Mt Vernon, Wash. *Comn:* Oil paintings, Western Wash Univ, 70, Peoples Nat Bank, Seattle, 74, Williams, Lanza, Kastner & Gibbs, Seattle, 76 & Pay N Save Corp, Seattle, 78. *Exhib:* Grantee Exhib, Acad Art Gallery, New York, 58; solo exhib, Seattle Art Mus, 60 & Bellevue Art Mus, Wash, 80; Artists West of the Mississippi, Seattle Art Mus Pavillion, 63; Exhibition of American Painters, Kobe Mus, Japan, 66; Washington Artists, Expo 70, Osaka, Japan, 70; Northwest Traditions, Seattle Art Mus, 79; Pacific Northwest Artists and Japan, Nat Mus Art, Osaka, Japan, 82. *Awards:* Guggenheim Fel Study & Travel Abroad, 58; Henry Rachen Awrd, Puget Sound Area Exhib, Frye Art Mus, 66; Norwegion Sesquicentennial Award Creative Arts, 75. *Bibliog:* Paul V Thomas (auth), Richard Gilkey artist, Seattle Times, 63; Robert C Arnold (auth), Travelling through Richard Gilkey's landscape, Argus, 78. *Media:* Oil. *Dealer:* Janet Huston 1816 Skagit City Rd Mt Vernon WA 98273. *Mailing Add:* 2278 Mann Rd Mt Vernon WA 98273

GILL, GENE
PAINTER, PRINTMAKER
b Memphis, Tenn, June 18, 33. *Study:* Memphis State Univ; Chicago Art Inst, Ill; Chouinard Art Inst, Los Angeles, BFA. *Work:* Los Angeles Co Mus, Los Angeles; Palm Springs Desert Mus, Calif; Atlantic Richfield Corp, Los Angeles; Home Savings, Los Angeles; Northrop Corp, Los Angeles. *Exhib:* All Calif Print Exhibs, Los Angeles, 69-71; 9th Ann Southern Calif Exhib, Long Beach Mus Art, 71; Laguna Beach Art Mus Exhib Ten, Calif, 71; Dimensional Prints, Los Angeles Co Mus Art, 73; Laguna Beach Art Mus, 77; Los Angeles Printmakers 1960-1980, Los Angeles Co Mus Art, 81; one-man shows, Comara Gallery, 70, 71 & 74. *Awards:* Purchase Award, Home Savings, 69; Purchase Award, Westside Jewish Community Ctr, 70; Jurors Award, Laguna Beach Art Mus, 70. *Bibliog:* Gatto, Porter & Selleck (auths), Exploring visual design, 78; George Magnan (auth), Today's art, 79; Gerald F Brommer (auth), Discovering Art History, 81. *Mailing Add:* 2430 Cascadia Dr Glendale CA 91206

GILL, JAMES (FRANCIS)
PAINTER, SCULPTOR
b Tahoka, Tex, Dec 10, 34. *Study:* San Angelo Jr Col; Univ Tex, fel, 60. *Work:* Mus Mod Art, Whitney Mus Am Art, New York; Art Inst Chicago; Univ Calif Mus Art, Berkeley; Mead Corp, Dayton, Ohio; and others. *Comn:* Cover painting, Time, Inc. *Exhib:* Art Inst Chicago, 64; Mus Mod Art, 65; San Francisco Art Inst, 65; Whitney Mus Am Art, 66-68; Sao Paulo, Brazil, 67; Nat Collection Fine Art Traveling Exhib, Europe, 68-69. *Publ:* Auth, Metamage, 69. *Mailing Add:* 1529 N Beverly Glen Rd Los Angeles CA 90024

GILLESPIE, DOROTHY MURIEL
PAINTER, SCULPTOR
b Roanoke, Va, June 29, 20. *Study:* Md Inst Col Art, Baltimore; Art Students League; Atelier 17, New York, with Stanley William Hayter; Caldwell Col, NJ, Hon DFA, 76. *Work:* Guggenheim Mus; Grey Art Gallery, NY Univ; Mus Art, Ft Lauderdale, Fla; Birmingham Mus Art; NC Mus Art, Raleigh. *Comn:* City Wall, City Walls Inc, New York, 75; Venetian Gardens (frieze), Housing & Urban Develop Proj, North Miami, Fla, 79; fountain sculpture, US Mission to UN, New York, 81; sculptural wall environment, Univ Ark Conf Ctr, Little Rock, 83; Summerscape (sculptural set), Cleveland Ballet, 83. *Exhib:* Solo exhibs, Del Art Mus, Wilmington, 83, Mus Art, Ft Lauderdale, Fla, 83, Wash Co Mus, Hagerstown, Md, 83 & Squibb World Hq, Princeton, NJ, 83; Philadelphia Col Art, 83. *Collections Arranged:* Women Artists Paint Women Artists, Virginia Miller Gallery, 78; Artist Choice, Clayworks Gallery, New York, 79; PCA: Invites, Philadelphia Col Art, 83. *Pos:* Co-coordr, Women's Interart Ctr, 73-76; dir, Art & Community Inst, New Sch Social Res, New York, 77- *Teaching:* Instr, Human Relations Ctr, New Sch Social Res, 72- *Awards:* Gov Ark Travelers Award, 83. *Bibliog:* David L Shirey (auth), article, 1/13/83 & Phyllis Braff (auth), Spirit of dance captured, 3/13/83, New York Times. *Mem:* Col Art Asn; Southeastern Conf Art Cols. *Media:* Painted Sculpture. *Publ:* Contribr, Professionalism & the woman artist, Womens Studies & Arts, 79 & Feminist Collage, 79; contribr, Overcoming barriers: The woman artist in the South, Southern Quart, 79. *Dealer:* Constance Kane 425 E 79th St New York NY 10021; City Wall Mercer & Houston St New York NY. *Mailing Add:* 549 West 52nd St New York NY 10019

GILLESPIE, GREGORY JOSEPH
PAINTER
b Elizabeth, NJ, Nov 29, 36. *Study:* Cooper Union Art Sch; San Francisco Art Inst, MFA. *Work:* Whitney Mus Am Art; NJ State Mus, Trenton; Hirshhorn Collection. *Exhib:* Ann, 66, 68 & 72 & Biennial, 73, Whitney Mus Am Art; Smith Col Mus Art, 71; Univ Ga, 71 & 78; Nat Acad Design, 72; Forum Gallery, New York, 75; Retrospective Exhib, Hirshhorn Mus, Washington, DC & Ga Mus Art, Univ Ga, Athens, 78; Univ Bridgeport, 80; and others. *Awards:* Am Acad Rome Award, 65-68; Fulbright Fel, 67; Nat Inst Arts & Lett Award, 69. *Bibliog:* Gregory Gillespie (paintings Italy, 1962-70), Forum Gallery, 71. *Mem:* Nat Acad Design. *Media:* Oil, Acrylic. *Mailing Add:* c/o Forum Gallery 1018 Madison Ave New York NY 10021

GILLETTE, W DEAN
PAINTER, DEALER
b Parsons, Kans. *Study:* Kansas City Art Inst, Kansas City, Mo; Univ Kans, Lawrence, BFA, 52; Univ London; Yale Univ, BFA, 55, MFA, 57 & study with Josef Alber, Conrad Marca-Relli, James Brooks & Burgoine Diller. *Work:* William Rockhill Nelson Gallery Art, Kansas City, Mo; High Mus Art, Atlanta, Ga; Ga Mus Art, Athens; Am Tel & Tel Collection, New York; Sheldon Mem Mus of Art, Lincoln, Nebr; and numerous pvt collections. *Exhib:* Ga Artists Show, High Mus, Atlanta, 71; William Rockhill Nelson Gallery of Art, Kansas City, Mo, 74; one-man shows, Galleria 88, Rome, Italy, 70, Bienville Gallery, New Orleans, La, 72, Montgomery Mus of Art, Ala, 74, Haslem Gallery, Washington, DC, 75, Mint Mus of Art, Charlotte, NC, 75, Hunter Mus of Art, Chattanooga, Tenn, 76, Sheldon Mus, Lincoln, Nebr, 76, ADI Gallery, Inc, San Francisco, Calif, 77; and numerous others. *Pos:* Owner-partner, Image South Gallery, Atlanta, 70-, Great American Gallery, Atlanta, 82-, Great American Glass Gallery, 82- *Awards:* Purchase Award, Watercolor USA, 79. *Bibliog:* Dean Gillette: Toward abstraction, Arts Mag, 12/76; Dean Gillette, Art Voices S, 7-8/78. *Mem:* Pa Acad Art. *Specialty:* Images of the current styles. *Dealer:* Galleries International Winter Park FL; Image S Gallery Atlanta GA. *Mailing Add:* Image South Gallery 1931 Peachtree Rd Atlanta GA 30309

GILLIAM, SAM
PAINTER
b Tupelo, Miss, 1933. *Study:* Univ Louisville, MA. *Work:* Mus African Art, Phillips Collection, Nat Collection Fine Arts, Corcoran Gallery Art & Howard Univ, Washington, DC; and many others. *Comn:* GSA, Art in Archit, Richard B Russell Fed Bldg, Atlanta, 79. *Exhib:* Works for New Spaces, Walker Art Ctr, Minneapolis, 71; Mus Mod Art, New York, 71; one-man exhibs, Galerie Darthea Speyer, Paris, 78, Middendorf/Lane Gallery, Washington, DC, 79, Dart Gallery, Chicago, 79 & 82 & Freudenheim Gallery, Buffalo, NY, 79; plus many other group & one-man shows. *Awards:* Norman Walt Harris Prize, Art Inst Chicago, 70; Longview Found Purchase Award, 70; Guggenheim Mem Found Fel, 71; and others. *Bibliog:* Benjamin Forgey (auth), Around the galleries: Encounters with high levels of energy and ambition, Washington Sunday Star, 2/12/78; Jay Kloner, Sam Gilliam: Recent black paintings, Arts Mag, 2/78; Richard Huntington (auth), Painter Sam Gilliam prescribes, practices artistic diversity, Buffalo Courier Express, 11/25/79. *Mailing Add:* c/o Middendorf/Lane Gallery 2009 Columbia Rd NW Washington DC 20010

GILLING, LUCILLE
PRINTMAKER
b Hamilton, Mo. *Study:* Kansas City Art Inst; New York Sch Fine & Appl Arts in Paris, France, Eng & Italy, dipl; Queens Univ. *Work:* Nat Libr Can, Ottawa; Montreal Mus Fine Art; Victoria & Albert Mus, London, Eng; Ohio State Univ; Wayne State Univ. *Exhib:* Soc Can Painters, Etchers & Engravers, Toronto, Ont, 56-; one-man shows, Pascall Gallery, Toronto, 66, Sobot Gallery, Toronto, 69 & Marjorie Kauffmann Graphics, 72; Can Fine Art Gallery, Toronto, 74; plus others. *Awards:* Sterling Trust Award, 59; Anaconda Award of Merit, 68. *Mem:* Toronto Heliconian Club (exec coun, 71-75). *Publ:* Portfolios of etchings, The Canterbury Tales, 66 & Don Quixote, 69, original signed etchings Ed 100. *Dealer:* Marjorie Kauffmann Graphics 5015 Westheimer Houston TX 77027. *Mailing Add:* 178 Alfred Ave Willowdale ON M2N 3J2 Canada

GILLINGWATER, DENIS CLAUDE
SCULPTOR, EDUCATOR
b Glendale, Calif, Feb 15, 46. *Study:* Univ Cincinnati, BFA, 68, MFA, 70. *Exhib:* Eighth West Biennial, Western Colo Ctr Arts, 74; Southwest & Rocky Mountain States Exhib, Scottsdale Fine Arts Comn, 75; solo exhib, Scottsdale Ctr Arts, 78; Ariz Sculpture, Northern Ariz Univ Art Gallery, Flagstaff, 80 & 81; Four Corners State Biannual, Phoenix Art Mus, 81; and others. *Teaching:* Asst prof intermedia, Ariz State Univ, 73-78, assoc prof, 78- *Awards:* Nat Endowment Arts Artist in Residence, Mesa, Ariz, 73; Acquisitions, Phoenix Art Mus, 77 & Scottsdale Ctr Arts, 75; and others. *Mailing Add:* 6701 East Clinton Scottsdale AZ 85254

GILLMAN, BARBARA SEITLIN
DEALER
b Miami, Fla, Jan 14, 37. *Study:* H Sophie Newcomb Col, 55; Univ Miami, with Dr Virgil Barker, BA(Am art), 58. *Collections Arranged:* Israel 25, contemp Israeli art (auth, catalog), Bacardi Bldg, City of Miami, 79. *Pos:* Panelist, State Fla Grant Panel. *Specialty:* Contemporary original art, paintings and sculpture. *Mailing Add:* 3886 Biscayne Blvd Miami FL 33137

GILMARTIN, F THOMAS
ADMINISTRATOR, CONSULTANT
b Palmer, Mass, Aug 6, 40. *Study:* Worcester Art Mus Sch, grad; Goddard Col, BA; Penland Sch Crafts, NC; AGFA Teknikum, Munich. *Pos:* Dir, Arts & Crafts Ctr, Ft Knox, Ky, 63-65; prog supvr, Arts & Crafts Ctr, Ft Eustis, Va, 68-70; civilian supvr, US Army Artist Team, Thailand, 70-71; dir, Asheville Art Mus, NC, 73-77; dir, Ga Coun Arts & Humanities, Appalachian Crafts Prog, 77-79; co-owner, Abtin Ltd, 79- *Teaching:* Instr exhib design & printmaking, Asheville Art Mus, NC, 73-77. *Mem:* Southeastern Mus Coun; Ga Designer-Craftsmen; Am Crafts Coun; Am Asn Mus. *Res:* Researched and authored, Contemporary Art History of the Eastern Cherokee Indians. *Mailing Add:* 9 College St PO Box 671 Weaverville NC 28787

GILMOR, JANE E
PAINTER, EDUCATOR
b Ames, Iowa, June 23, 47. *Study:* Iowa State Univ, Ames, BS(textiles), 69; Univ Iowa, Iowa City, MA(paint), 76 & MFA(painting), 77. *Work:* Hoover State Office Bldg, Des Moines, Iowa; Sioux City Art Mus, Iowa; Mus Contemp Crafts Libr, New York; Los Angeles Co Mus Libr, Calif; Augustana Col Collection, Rock Island, Ill. *Exhib:* 27th-34th Ann Iowa Artists, Des Moines Art Ctr, 75-83; La Grange Nat VII & VIII, Atlanta, 82-83; TFAA Nat, Austin, Tex, 82-83; Iowa State Univ, Design Ctr, 84; NAME Gallery, Chicago, 84. *Teaching:* Assoc prof art painting & drawing, Mount Mercy College, Cedar Rapids, Iowa, 74-; guest artist/lectr, Univ Iowa, Iowa City, 81; guest artist, Columbia Col, Mo, 83. *Awards:* Art in Architecture Purchase Award, Hoover State Office Bldg, Des Moines, Iowa, 77; Edith Younker Best in Painting, Des Moines Art Ctr, 77 & 81; First Place, Sixth Nat Small Painting Exhib, Birmingham, Mich, 83. *Bibliog:* N Givven (auth), Jellical cats, reviews, Art Week, 10/1/77; Jannick Storm (auth), Jeg Mar Moot Miss Iowa, Copenhagan Daily, 11/15/77; Lucy Lippard (auth), Overlay: Contemporary Artists and the Art of Prehistory, Pantheon Books, 83. *Media:* Multi-media. *Mailing Add:* Art Dept Mt Mercy Col Cedar Rapids IA 52402

GILMORE, ROGER
ADMINISTRATOR, CONSULTANT
b Philadelphia, Pa, Oct 11, 32. *Study:* Dartmouth Col, AB; Univ Chicago Divinity Sch, grad study. *Pos:* Dean, Sch Art Inst Chicago, 65- *Mem:* Soc Archit Historians; Nat Art Educ Asn; Col Art Asn; Int Coun Fine Arts Deans; Nat Trust Hist Preserv; life mem Nat Schs Art & Design. *Mailing Add:* 4371 Central Ave Western Springs IL 60558

GILPIN, HENRY EDMUND
PHOTOGRAPHER, INSTRUCTOR
b Cleveland, Ohio, Nov 10, 22. *Study:* Los Angeles City Col, 46-48; Univ Calif, Los Angeles, 49-50; Cleveland Inst Art, 51; Ansel Adams Yosemite Workshop, 59. *Work:* Monterey Peninsula Mus Art, Calif; Amon Carter Mus, Ft Worth, Tex; Utah State Univ Gallery, Logan; Currier Gallery, Manchester, NH; State Univ Calif, Long Beach. *Exhib:* Friends of Photog, Carmel, Calif, 72; Rockford Art Asn, Ill, 72; Sam Houston State Univ, 74; Art & Sci Mus, Nashua, NH, 78; Photo Gallery Int, Tokyo, Japan, 81. *Teaching:* Instr photog, Monterey Peninsula Col, 64-, Ansel Adams Yosemite Workshop, 67-73 & 81-82 & Friends of Photog, Carmel, 69- *Mem:* Friends of Photog (trustee, 69-79). *Dealer:* Susan Spiritis Gallery 522 Old Newport Blvd Newport Beach CA 92663; Josephus Daniels Gallery Su Vencino Ct Delores near 6th Carmel CA 93921. *Mailing Add:* 1353 Jacks Rd Monterey CA 93940

GIMBLETT, MAX(WELL)
PAINTER
b Auckland, NZ, Dec 5, 35; US & NZ citizen. *Study:* Ont Col Art, Toronto, 64; San Francisco Art Inst, 65. *Work:* Marion Koogler McNay Art Inst, San Antonio; Laguna Gloria Art Mus, Austin; Conn Col, New London; Lang Art Gallery, Scripps Col, Claremont, Calif; Bank Tex, Houston. *Exhib:* Modernism Gallery, San Francisco, 80 & 83; Power Gallery Contemp Art, Sydney Australia, 81 & 83; Color-Four Painters, Oscarsson Hood Gallery, New York, 82; Seven Painters/The Eighties, Auckland City Art Gallery, NZ, 83; Auckland City Art Gallery, NZ, 84; and others. *Teaching:* Vis artist printmaking, Ind Univ, Bloomington, 79; vis assoc prof, Pratt Inst, Brooklyn, 79-; vis lectr, Univ Canterbury, Christchurch, 81; vis assoc prof, Int Honors Program in Japan, India & Kenya. *Awards:* Grant, Queen Elizabeth II Arts Coun NZ, 80. *Bibliog:* Barbara Zabel (auth), Max Gimblett, Marion Koogler McNay Art Inst, 78; Ronny H Cohen (auth), Max Gimblett: A color visionary, 82 & Mary Lee Thompson, Max Gimblett's paintings on canvas and paper, 82, Modernism, San Francisco. *Media:* Oil, Acrylic Polymer. *Publ:* Contribr, In the presence, Art NZ, 80; contribr, Max Gimblett and Wystan Curnow, Modernism, San Francisco, 82. *Dealer:* Modernism 236 8th St San Francisco CA 94103; Galerie Nordenhake Malmo Sweden. *Mailing Add:* 231 Bowery New York NY 10003

GINNEVER, CHARLES
SCULPTOR
b San Mateo, Calif, Aug 28, 31. *Study:* With Zadkine & Hayter, Europe, 53-55; Calif Sch Fine Arts, San Francisco, BFA, 57; Cornell Univ, MFA, 59. *Work:* Wadsworth Atheneum, Hartford, Conn; Hirshhorn Mus, DC; Storm King Art Ctr, Mountainville, NY; Univ Mich, Ann Arbor; State Univ NY, Albany. *Exhib:* One-man shows, Dag Hammarskjold Plaza Sculpture Garden, New York, 73, Max Hutchinson Gallery, 78-79, Long Beach Mus Art, 78, Construct, Chicago, 79 & 81 & Storm King Art Ctr, 80. *Teaching:* Instr, Cornell Univ, 57-59, Pratt Inst, 63, New Sch Soc Res, 64, Brooklyn Mus Sch, 64-65, Newark Sch Fine & Indust Art, 65, Dayton Art Inst, 66, Aspen Sch Contemp Art, Colo, 66, Orange Co Community Col, NJ, 66 & Windham Col, 67-75. *Awards:* Guggenheim Fel, 74; Nat Endowment Arts Grant, 75. *Media:* Steel. *Dealer:* Max Hutchinson Gallery 138 Greene St New York NY 10012; ConStruct 233 E Ontario St Chicago IL 60611. *Mailing Add:* PO Box 411 Putney VT 05346

GINSBURG, ESTELLE
PAINTER, SCULPTOR
b St Louis, Mo, Mar 27, 24. *Study:* Univ Mo; Brooklyn Mus Art Sch; Cornell Univ. *Work:* C W Post Col, NY; Univ Mass, Amherst; pvt collections in Europe, SAm & US. *Exhib:* Ball State Univ, Muncie, Ind, 73; solo shows, Cent Hall Gallery, New York, 75, 77-79, Fine Arts Mus Nassau Co, NY, 77 & Royal Acad, Stockholm, Sweden, 79; invitational, York Col, Pa, 77; Brentano Gallery, New York, 79, 81 & 82. *Pos:* Dir, Aida Dornbrand Brentano's Gallery, Manhasset, NY. *Teaching:* Art lectr mus collections, North Shore Community Arts Ctr, New York, NY, 70-73; teacher, Five Towns Music & Art Found, New York, 73-83; Nassau Off Cult Develop, 74-77 & Art Resources Ltd, New York, 79-80. *Awards:* Mixed Media Award, Heckscher Mus, NY, 72; Sculpture Award, North Shore Art Exhib, 74; Painting Award, Port Washington Libr, 75. *Bibliog:* Malcum Preston (auth), Review of Work, Newsday, NY, 76-79; Jeanne Paris (auth), Review of Work, Long Island Press, 77 & 78; Woman art, New York Times, 79. *Mem:* Cent Hall Artists, NY; Prof Artists Asn NY (mem chmn, 74-76). *Media:* Wood, Paint; Mixed Media, Silkscreen. *Dealer:* Aida Dornbrand Brentano's Gallery 20-72 Northern Blvd Manhasset NY 11030. *Mailing Add:* 370 Longacre Ave Woodmere NY 11598

GINSBURG, MAX
PAINTER, ILLUSTRATOR
b Paris, France, Aug 7, 31. *Study:* Syracuse Univ, BFA; Nat Acad Design; City Col New York, MA. *Work:* New York Cult Ctr. *Exhib:* Allied Artists Am, 56-72; Am Vet Soc Artists, 61-72; Audubon Artists, 62-72; Harbor Gallery, Cold Spring Harbor, 66, 68, 69, 71 & 72. *Teaching:* Instr art, High Sch Art & Design, New York. *Awards:* Prize, 61 & Gold Medal, 62 & 65, Am Vet Soc Artists; Allied Artists Am, 61 & 72; Nat Art Club, 63. *Mem:* Allied Artists Am; Audubon Artists; Am Vet Soc Artists; Artists Equity Asn. *Mailing Add:* c/o Harbor Gallery 43 Main St Cold Spring Harbor NY 11724

GINZBURG, YANKEL (JACOB)
PAINTER, PRINTMAKER
b Alma-Ata, USSR, Mar 23, 45; US citizen. *Study:* Art Inst Israel, dipl, 61. *Work:* Israel Mus, Jerusalem; Hirshorn Mus; Bat-Yam Mus, Israel; Skirball Mus, Los Angeles; Tel Aviv Mus, Israel. *Comn:* Mural, City Jerusalem, 73; tapestry, Nat Jewish Coun, US, 76; outdoor mural, B'nai Brith Hq, Washington, DC, 79; Bicentennial Poster, Air & Space Mus, Washington, DC, 83. *Exhib:* One-man show, Washington Gallery Art, 69, Ep Gallery, Dusseldorf, Ger, 76, Benezit Gallery, Paris, 72, Walker Inst, 78 & Martin Lawrence Gallery, Los Angeles, 82; Modern Masters, Philadelphia Mus Art, 78; Works on Paper, Skirball Mus, Los Angeles, 78. *Awards:* Silver Medal, Biennale Rome, 62; First Prize, Bat-Yam Mus, Israel, 65. *Bibliog:* Betancourt (auth), New printmakers, Graphics Mag, 78; Eli Nisan (producer), film, 79. *Media:* Acrylic, Serigraph. *Mailing Add:* 2126 Connecticut Ave #75 Washington DC 20008

GINZEL, ROLAND
PAINTER, PRINTMAKER
b Lincoln, Ill, 1921. *Study:* Art Inst Chicago, BFA; State Univ Iowa, MFA; Slade Sch, London. *Work:* Univ Southern Calif; Univ Mich; Ill Bell Tel Co; Art Inst Chicago; US Embassy, Warsaw, Poland; and others. *Exhib:* Art Inst Chicago, 69; Madison, Wis, 69; Notre Dame Univ, 69; one-man show, Phyllis Kind Gallery, 69; Whitney Mus Am Art Biennial, New York, 75. *Teaching:* Prof printmaking, Univ Chicago, 57-58; prof prints & painting, Univ Ill, Chicago Circle, 58-69; instr painting, Univ Wis, 60; instr art, Saugatuck Summer Sch, 61-62. *Awards:* Print & Drawing Prize, 67 & Campana Prize, 69, Art Inst Chicago; Fulbright Fel to Rome, 62. *Dealer:* Phyllis Kind Gallery 226 E Ontario St Chicago IL 60611. *Mailing Add:* 412 N Clark St Chicago IL 60610

GIOBBI, EDWARD GIOACHINO
PAINTER, SCULPTOR
b Waterbury, Conn, July 18, 26. *Work:* Boston Mus Fine Arts; Whitney Mus Am Art, New York; Hirshhorn Mus; Art Inst Chicago; Albright-Knox Gallery; and others. *Exhib:* One-man exhibs, Neuberger Mus, 77 & Gruenebaum Gallery, New York, 78 & 79; Young America, Whitney Mus Am Art, 60; Recent Figure USA, Mus Mod Art, New York, 60; 40 Painters under 40, Whitney Mus Am Art, 62; and others. *Teaching:* Artist in residence, Memphis Acad, Tenn, 59-60 & Dartmouth Col, 72. *Awards:* Emily Lowe Award, 49; Ford Found Artist in Residence Prog, 66; Guggenheim Fel, 72. *Media:* Oil; Mixed. *Mailing Add:* 161 Croton Lake Rd Katonah NY 10536

GIRARD, (CHARLES) JACK
PAINTER, EDUCATOR
b Ft Knox, Ky, May 15, 51. *Study:* ECarolina Univ, BFA, 73, MFA, 76; Univ SC, 73. *Work:* SC Mus Comn, Columbia; Berea Col, Ky; Appalachian State Univ; ECarolina Univ; Coca-Cola Bottling Co, Atlanta. *Exhib:* Corcoran Gallery Art, 75; Seventh Ann Competition, Fayetteville Mus Art, NC, 79; two-person exhib, Columbia Mus Art, SC, 80; Eight State Ann, J B Speed Art Mus, 82; solo exhib, Morlan Gallery, Lexington, Ky, 82 & Clarion Univ, Pa, 84; Points of View, Headley-Whitney Mus, Lexington, Ky, 83. *Pos:* Asst, Walker Gallery, Columbia, SC, 76-78. *Teaching:* Vis artist, Carteret Tech Col, 78-79; instr painting, Berea Col, 79-80; asst prof painting, Centre Col, Ky, 80-81 & Transylvania Univ, 81- *Mem:* Am Asn Univ Prof; Col Art Asn Am; Found Art: Theory & Educ. *Media:* Oil, Acrylic. *Publ:* Auth, An introspective view of Columbia art, Columbia Scene, 77. *Mailing Add:* Box 147 Transylvania Univ Lexington KY 40508

GIRAUDIER, ANTONIO
PAINTER, WRITER
b Havana, Cuba, Sept 28, 26; US citizen. *Work:* Harvard Univ Libr; Am Poets Fel Soc, Charleston, Ill; Greenville Mus Art, SC; Maryhill Mus Fine Arts, Wash; Trinity Episcopal Church, Boston; also in pvt Am & foreign collections. *Exhib:* Congress Arts & Communications, IBC Gallery, Hyatt-Regency, Cambridge, Mass, 79; Congress Arts & Communications, IBC Gallery Krasuapolsky, Amsterdam, Holland, 80; Am Drawings I, Portsmouth Arts Council, Va, 76; one-man shows, Jefferson Market Libr, New York, 80 & NY Poetry Forum, Am Asn Univ Women, 80 & 81; plus others in US & abroad. *Pos:* Ed, Am Poetry Mag, 78-81. *Awards:* Academinician of Italy with Gold Medal, 80; Master of Painting, H C Accademia Italia, 82; Grand Prize of the Nations, Italy, 83. *Bibliog:* Reviews in Arts Mag, 12/71-1/72 & The Inner Loom, 72; art work reproduced in many publ, US & abroad. *Media:* Acrylic, Mixed Media. *Publ:* Auth, 127 definitive works in English, French & Spanish; contribr, many books & periodicals, US & abroad. *Mailing Add:* 215 E 68th St New York NY 10021

GIRONDA, R
ARCHITECT, SCULPTOR
b Brooklyn, NY, Dec 3, 36. *Study:* Pratt Inst, BFA; Nat Acad Design; Metropolitan Col, BS, 72; Art Students League. *Comn:* Sculptures, stainless steel, Kenneth Richardson, 69, stainless steel, Selma Wallace Assoc, 72, bronze, Selma Wallace, 72; and others. *Exhib:* Silvermine Guild, New Canaan, Conn, 63; Nat Acad Design Galleries, 72-75; Brooklyn Mus Show, 73-75; Caravan House, New York, 74; and others. *Awards:* First Prize, Brooklyn Mus, 73 & 75. *Mem:* Nat Acad Design; Am Inst Archit. *Media:* Carved Brass, Welded Stainless Steel. *Mailing Add:* 305 Degraw St Brooklyn NY 11231

GITLIN, MICHAEL
SCULPTOR, DRAFTSMAN
b Capetown, SAfrica, April 23, 43. *Study:* Hebrew Univ Jerusalem, BA, 67; Bezalel Acad Art, Jerusalem, dipl, 67; Pratt Inst, MFA, 72. *Work:* Guggenheim Mus; Stedelijk Mus, Amsterdam; Lenbachhaus, Munich; Israel Mus, Jerusalem; Wilhelm Lehmbruck Mus, Duisburg, WGer. *Comn:* Sculpture (corten steel), Schmela Gallery, Düsseldorf, 76; Adam's Gate (mahogany), Jerusalem Found, Israel, 83. *Exhib:* Pratt Prints, Brooklyn Mus,

73; Beyond Drawing, Israel Mus, Jerusalem, 74; Documenta 6, Kassel, Ger, 77; solo exhibs, Israel Mus, Jerusalem, 77 & ICC, Antwerp, Belg, 80; World Print III, San Francisco Mus Mod Art, 80; Interior Sculpture, Schellmann & Klüser, Munich, 80; Marking Black, Bronx Mus Arts, 80. *Teaching:* Instr art, Parsons Sch Design, 79- *Bibliog:* Susan Heineman (auth), article, Arts Mag, 5/76. *Media:* Wood, Mixed Media. *Dealer:* Schellman & Klüser Gallery 50 Greene St New York NY 10012. *Mailing Add:* 280 Lafayette St New York NY 10012

GIUSTI, GEORGE
DESIGNER, SCULPTOR
b Milan, Italy; US citizen. *Study:* Acad Brera, Milan. *Work:* Graphic Sect, Mus Mod Art, New York; also in several art cols, US & abroad. *Exhib:* New York, Philadelphia, Boston, Chicago, Los Angeles, Paris, London, Milan, Vienna, Latin Am, Japan & the Orient. *Teaching:* Instr, Cooper Union, New York. *Awards:* Art Dir Year, 58; Art Dirs Club Hall of Fame, 79; also many major awards & gold & silver medals. *Bibliog:* Articles in Graphis, Switz, Communication Art, US & Daily Tel Mag, London. *Mem:* Alliance Graphique Int; Am Inst Graphic Arts; Int Ctr Typographic Arts; Art Dirs Club New York. *Media:* Metal, Acrylic. *Publ:* Auth & illus, The Human Heart, 61; portfolios, Graphis, Switz, Idea & FAS, Japan, Pagina, Milan, Gebrauchsgrafik, Ger, Communication Art, US & Daily Tel Mag, London; illustrations in Fortune, Sat Eve Post, Time, Holiday, US Info Agency Publ & most publishing houses. *Mailing Add:* 20 Chalburn Rd West Redding CT 06896

GLADSTONE, BARBARA REGEN
DEALER, HISTORIAN
b Philadelphia, Pa. *Study:* Univ Pa; Hofstra Univ, BA, 68, MA, 70. *Pos:* Dir, Barbara Gladstone Gallery, New York. *Teaching:* Instr art hist & mod archit, Hofstra Univ, 71-75. *Specialty:* Contemporary painting, sculpture and photography; publisher of conemporary American prints and photographs. *Mailing Add:* 152 Wooster St New York NY 10012

GLADSTONE, M J
ADMINISTRATOR, PUBLISHER
b New York, NY, May 4, 23. *Study:* Harvard Univ, SB(anthrop), 44, MA(fine arts), 46. *Pos:* Ed, Print & Print Collector's Quart, 50-53; ed, Merriam-Webster Dictionary, 53-55; ed, Collector's Quart Report, 62-63; assoc dir publ, Mus Mod Art, New York, 63-64; consult, NY State Coun Arts, 67-73; dir, Mus Am Folk Art, New York, 69-70; dir, Publ Ctr Cult Resources, New York, 73- *Publ:* Contribr, Britannica Encycl Am Art, 73; auth, A Carrot for a Nose, Scribner, 74; auth, How to Know American Folk Art, Dutton, 77. *Mailing Add:* 310 E 75th St New York NY 10021

GLANZ, ANDREA E
ADMINISTRATOR, CURATOR
b New York, NY, Oct 14, 52. *Study:* Cornell Univ, BS(human develop & expressive arts); Stanford Univ, MA(art educ). *Pos:* Grad asst, Stanford Univ Mus Art, Calif, 74-75; cur educ, Triton Mus Art, Santa Clara, Calif, 75-77, dir, 77-78; from asst cur to cur, San Jose Mus Art, Calif, 78-79; asst dir, Continuing Prof Educ, Mus Collab, New York, 79- *Teaching:* Instr, West Valley Community Col, Saratoga, Calif, 76. *Mem:* Am Asn Mus; Mus Educators Roundtable; Col Art Asn; Nat Trust for Hist Preserv. *Publ:* Coauth, A Catalog of Paintings by Theodore Wores in the Collection of the Triton Museum of Art, 76 & Two Hundred Years of Santa Clara Valley Architecture: A Stylistic Survey, 76, Triton Mus Art. *Mailing Add:* 110 Bank St Apt 3J New York NY 10014

GLASCO, JOSEPH M
PAINTER, SCULPTOR
b Pauls Valley, Okla, Jan 19, 25. *Study:* Univ Tex, 41-42; study with Rico Lebrun, 46; study in Mexico City, 47; Art Students League, New York, 48. *Work:* Metrop Mus Art & Mus Mod Art, New York; Hirshhorn Mus & Sculpture Garden, Washington, DC; Whitney Mus Am Art, New York; Princeton Univ Mus, NJ. *Exhib:* One-man shows, Perls Gallery, New York, 51, Catherine Viviano Gallery, New York, 52, 55, 58, 60, 63, 67 & 70 & Gimpel & Weitzenhoffer Gallery, 79; 15 Americans, Mus Mod Art, New York; The New Decade, Whitney Mus Am Art; Metrop Mus Art, New York; Solomon R Guggenheim Mus; Art Inst Chicago; Corcoran Gallery Art; Dallas Mus Fine Arts; Los Angeles Co Mus Fine Arts. *Collections Arranged:* 15 Americans, Mus Mod Art, New York; The New Decade, Thirty-five American Painters & Sculptors, Whitney Mus Am Art, New York. *Mem:* Nat Soc Lit & Arts. *Dealer:* Gimpel & Weitzenhoffer Ltd Gallery 1040 Madison Ave New York NY 10021. *Mailing Add:* 2116 1/2 Strand Ave Galveston TX 77550

GLASER, BRUCE
HISTORIAN, EDUCATOR
b Brooklyn, NY, Sept 25, 33. *Study:* Columbia Col, BA; Columbia Univ, MA. *Pos:* Dir, Howard Wise Gallery, New York, 60-61; dir, Gallery of Israeli Art, Am-Israel Cult Found, New York, 65-68; exec dir, Art Ctr Northern NJ, Tenafly, 68-70. *Teaching:* Instr art hist, Pratt Inst, 61-62; instr, Hunter Col, 62-65; prof art hist, Univ Bridgeport, 70-, chmn dept, 70-77, dean, Col Fine Arts, 77-81. *Awards:* Mem Found for Jewish Cult Fel, 70-72. *Mem:* Col Art Asn Am; Int Coun Fine Arts Deans; Nat Coun Art Adminr; Int Coun Mus; Am Asn Mus. *Res:* Modern and contemporary art; Israeli art. *Publ:* Ed & coauth, Oldenburg, Lichtenstein, Warhol: A discussion, Artforum, 2/66; coauth, Questions to Stella & Judd, Art News, 9/66; ed & coauth, An interview with Ad Reinhardt, Art Int, 12/66; ed & coauth, Modern art and the critics, Art J, winter 70-71; auth, Robert Natkin, Arts, 6/78. *Mailing Add:* 211 Buena Vista Rd Fairfield CT 06432

GLASER, DAVID
PAINTER, SCULPTOR
b Brooklyn, NY, Sept 29, 19. *Study:* Art Students League, scholarship; New York Sch Indust Art; New York Sch Contemp Art, with Philip Evergood; Brooklyn Mus Art Sch, with Moses Soyer, Xavier Gonzales & Edwin Dickinson. *Comn:* Poster series for US Army, 43-44. *Exhib:* Nat Arts Club, 59; Art Directions, 59; City Ctr, New York, 60; Allied Artists Am, 60-71; three-man exhib, Heckscher Mus, Huntington, 64. *Pos:* Art dir & designer, 46-48; art dir, 54-60; dir & designer, Studio Concepts, 60- *Teaching:* Instr, Art Ctr Island Jewish Sch, 59. *Awards:* Monadnock Mills Graphic Excellence Award, 75; Cert of Merit, Vet Soc Am Artists, 79; Desi Graphics Award, 80 & 82; and others. *Mem:* Allied Artists Am; Vet Soc Am Artists; Art Dir Club of Long Island. *Media:* Mixed Media. *Res:* Experimental silk screen production for industry; new approaches in advertising and media including all communication skills. *Publ:* Illusr for Popular Sci, Popular Mechanix & Electronics Illustrated, 61-65; auth & illusr, My mother died dancing. *Mailing Add:* 33 Downhill Lane Wantagh NY 11793

GLASER, MILTON
DESIGNER, ILLUSTRATOR
b New York, NY, June 26, 29. *Study:* Cooper Union Art Sch, 51; Acad Fine Arts, Bologna, Italy, with Giorgio Morandi, Fulbright Scholar, 52-53; Minneapolis Inst Art, Hon DFA; Moore Col Art, Hon Degree; Philadelphia Mus Sch, Hon Degree; Sch Visual Arts, Hon Degree. *Work:* Mus Mod Art, New York. *Comn:* Mural, Fed Off Bldg, Indianapolis, 74; permanent exhib, Port Authority NY, World Trade Ctr, 75. *Exhib:* Push Pin Decorative Arts Show, The Louvre, Paris, 70; one-man show, Portland Visual Arts Ctr, Maine, 75, Mus Mod Art, New York, 75 & Wichita State Univ, 75; Pompidou Cult Ctr, Beaubourg, Paris, 77; Mus Mod Art, Liege, Belgium, 82. *Pos:* Pres, Push Pin Studios, New York, 54-74; chmn bd & design dir, New York Mag, 68-77; pres, Milton Glaser Inc Design Studio, 74-; vpres & design dir, Village C Voice, 75-77. *Teaching:* Instr design prog, Sch Visual Arts, New York; instr design prog, Cooper Union Art Sch. *Awards:* Gold Medal, Am Inst Graphics Arts, 72; Gold Medal, Soc Illusr, 78; Art Dirs Club Hall of Fame, 79. *Bibliog:* Article, Art News, 9/75; John Russell (auth), article, New York Times, 8/30/75; article, United Mag, 8/82. *Mem:* Int Graphic Alliance; Am Inst Graphic Arts (co-chmn, 73); Art Dir Club. *Publ:* Illusr, Cats and Bats and Things With Wings, 65; illusr, Fish in the Sky, 71; illusr, Don Juan, 72; illusr, Graphic Design, 73; illusr, Milton Glaser Poster Book, 77. *Mailing Add:* 207 E 32nd St New York NY 10016

GLASGOW, LUKMAN
MUSEUM DIRECTOR, SCULPTOR
b Richfield, Utah, Aug 27, 35. *Study:* Brigham Young Univ, BS(psychol of aesthetics), 61; Univ Calif, Santa Barbara, 69; Calif State Univ, Los Angeles, MA, 76. *Work:* E B Crocker Mus, Sacramento, Calif; Downey Mus Art, Calif; Brand Art Ctr, Glendale, Calif; Riverside Art Ctr, Calif; Laguna Beach Mus Art, Calif. *Exhib:* Calif Ceramic & Glass, Oakland Mus Art, Calif, 74; Surrealism in Clay, Utah Mus Fine Arts, Salt Lake City, 74; Impossible Skyscapes & Improbable Shadows, E B Crocker Mus, 75; 100 Artists Commemorate 200 Yrs, Xerox Exhib Ctr, Rochester, NY, 76; Calif Design 1976, Pac Design Ctr, Los Angeles, 76; Contemp Crafts of the Americas, Smithsonian Inst Traveling Exhib, 76-77; Illusionistic-Realism, Laguna Beach Mus Art, 77. *Pos:* Visual arts specialist, Los Angeles Co, Calif, 69-76; dir, Los Angeles Co Cult Arts Ctr, Calif, 76-77; exec dir, Contemp Crafts Gallery, Portland, Ore, 78-79; dir, Downey Mus Art, Calif, 79- *Teaching:* Mem fac ceramics, Calif State Univ, Fullerton, 79-80. *Awards:* Individual Artist Fel, Nat Endowment Arts Visual Arts Prog, 75-76. *Bibliog:* Diane Simons (auth), Lukman Glasgow--the sum of the parts, Designers West, 7/73; Judith Samuel (auth), Interviews with Lukman Glasgow, Currants, 76. *Mem:* Am Craftsman Coun; Am Mus Asn; Am Asn Mus. *Media:* Clay, Photography. *Publ:* Auth, Use of the hollow ring, Ceramic Monthly, 74; auth, Inner City Mural Program, Los Angeles Inst of Contemp Art J, 74; auth, Three neon sculptors, Art Week, 75; auth, Illusionistic-Realism (catalog), Laguna Beach Mus Art & Nat Endowment Arts, 77; auth, American Ceramic National Catalog, 83. *Mailing Add:* 5479 Dahlia Dr Los Angeles CA 90041

GLASGOW, VAUGHN LESLIE
CURATOR, HISTORIAN
b Apr 23, 44; US citizen. *Study:* La State Univ, BA; Borso di Studii, Centro Int Studii Archit A Palladio, Vicenza, Italy, cert, 68; Pa State Univ, MA(Nat Defense Act Title IV Grant), 70; Inst Mus Mgt, Univ Calif, Berkeley, fel, 79; Int Partnership Among Mus, La Rochelle, France, fel, 81. *Collections Arranged:* Permanent Collection, Anglo-Am Art Mus, La State Univ, 66-67; G P A Healy: Famous Figures and La Patrons (coauth, catalog), 76; Savoir Faire: The French Taste in Louisiana, 77; Played With Immense Success, 79; L'Amour de Maman: The Acadian Textile Heritage, 80. *Pos:* Reader youth grants, Nat Endowment Humanities, Washington, DC, 71-76; arts mgr, State Arts Coun, New Orleans, La, 73-75; chief cur, La State Mus, New Orleans, 75-83, assoc dir, 83- *Teaching:* Instr art hist & admin asst, Pa State Univ, 70-71; asst prof art hist, Middle Tenn State Univ, 72-73; lectr art hist, Tulane Univ, 74-79; lectr arts mgt, St Mary's Dominican Col, 81- *Awards:* Nat Sci Found Grant, Proj SoHo, 71. *Res:* European post-Renaissance period; Louisiana studies; architectural history; post-revolutionary French painting. *Publ:* Auth, Series of mus-related feature stories, var newspapers, 75-77; auth, G P A Healy and His Louisiana Portraits, Antiques Mag, 77; auth, Textiles of the Louisiana Acadians, Antiques Mag, 81; auth, L'Amour de Maman: l'heritage des Textiles Acadiennes en Louisiana, 83. *Mailing Add:* La State Mus 751 Chartres St Box 2458 New Orleans LA 70176

GLASIER, ALICE GENEVA See Kloss, Gene

GLASS, DOROTHY F
HISTORIAN
b New York, NY. *Study:* Vassar Col, BA, 64; Johns Hopkins Univ, PhD, 68. *Teaching:* Asst prof medieval art, Boston Univ, 69-74; assoc prof, State Univ NY, Buffalo, 74-81, prof, 81- *Awards:* Chancellor's Award Excellence in Teaching, State Univ New York, 77; fel, Am Coun Learned Socs, 79-80. *Mem:* Medieval Acad Am; Col Art Asn; Int Ctr Medieval Art (bd dirs, 80-). *Publ:* Auth, Studies on Cosmatesque Pavements, Oxford, BAR, 80; auth, Jonah in Campania: a late antique revival, Commentari, 76; auth, Romanesque sculpture in Campania: a problem of method, Art Bulletin, 74; auth, The archivolt sculpture at Sessa Aurunca, Art Bulletin, 69; auth, Italian Romanesque Sculpture: An Annotated Bibliography, Boston, G K Hall & Co, 83. *Mailing Add:* State Univ NY Buffalo NY 14214

GLASS, MICHAEL L
DESIGNER, EDUCATOR
b New York, NY, Dec 21, 45. *Study:* Clark Univ, Mass, BA, 68; Yale Univ, BFA, 69, MFA, 71. *Exhib:* Inst Graphic Arts & Art Dirs Club New York, 72-83; 32nd, 33rd and 34th Chicago Book Clinic, 81-83; Asn Art Museums, 82; The 100 Show, 83 & Ill Show, 83, Soc Typographic Arts. *Teaching:* Assoc prof visual commun, RI Sch Design, 71-77, Inst Design, Ill Inst Technol, 78-80 & Univ Ill, Chicago, 80- *Awards:* Three Awards, Am Asoc Mus, 83; Three Gold Awards, Soc Typographic Arts, Ill, 83. *Bibliog:* Bryan Fuermann (auth), On Chicago, Beaux Arts, 10/83. *Mem:* Soc Typographic Arts (bd mem, 80-82); Am Inst Graphic Arts; Art Dirs Club New York. *Mailing Add:* 213 W Institute Place Suite 702 Chicago IL 60610

GLASS, SYLVIA
PAINTER
b Baltimore, Md. *Study:* Univ Calif, Los Angeles, BA, 48; Calif State Univ, Northridge, MA, 71. *Work:* Security Pac Bank, Bonventura Hotel, Los Angeles, Springfield Art Mus, Mo; Laguna Beach Mus Art, Calif; Phoenix Art Mus. *Exhib:* Honored Artists Exhib, Birmingham Mus, 79; solo exhib, Scottsdale Ctr Arts, 80, Chautauqua Art Asn Galleries, NY, 81 & Brigham Young Univ, 81; Palos Verdes Art Ctr & Mus, Rancho Verdes, Calif, 82; Light, Allusion & Reality, Riverside Art Mus, Calif, 83. *Awards:* Top Award, Scottsdale Ctr Arts, 78, Rocky Mountain Nat, Golden, Colo, 78 & Chautauqua Exhib Am Art, NY, 79. *Mem:* Nat Watercolor Soc. *Media:* Acrylic on Paper or Canvas. *Publ:* Contribr, Creative Seascape Painting, Watson-Guptill, 81; contribr, Expressive Watercolor Techniques, 82 & Airbrush Painting Art, Techniques, Projects, 82, Davis. *Dealer:* Simard Gallery 323 S Towne Los Angeles CA 90013. *Mailing Add:* 23705 Crosson Dr Woodland Hills CA 91367

GLASS, WENDY D
DEALER, COLLECTOR
b New York, NY, Aug 28, 25. *Study:* Bard Col, study of art hist with Stefan Hirsch. *Collections Arranged:* Temple Shaaray Tefila, New York; Temple Israel, New Rochelle, NY; Temple Soc Advan of Judaism, White Plains, NY; Waldamar Cancer Res Found, Hilton Hotel, New York, 65. *Pos:* Dir & owner, Glass Gallery, 60- *Specialty:* Figurative art; American paintings and graphics, 20th Century; Japanese Ukiyo-e prints. *Interests:* Impressionistic graphics; South American graphics. *Collection:* Max Weber, Matisse, Picasso, Pascin, Chaim Gross, Raphael Soyer & Benny Andrews; contemporary 20th century painters; Ukiyo-e masters of the 19th century. *Mailing Add:* c/o Glass Gallery 315 Central Park W Apt 8W New York NY 10025

GLASSMAN, AUDREY LAVINE
PAINTER, PHOTOGRAPHER
b Trenton, NJ, June 12, 25. *Study:* Syracuse Univ, BFA, (Post Grad Fel), 46; Am Univ, MFA, 75. *Exhib:* Area exhibs, Corcoran Gallery, Washington, DC, 62-67; one-woman shows, Studio Gallery, Washington, DC, 68, 70 & 73 & Georgetown Art Gallery, Washington, DC, 78; Southeastern Mus Tour, Corcoran Gallery, Washington, DC, 73; two-person show, Intuitiveye Gallery, Washington, DC, 80. *Teaching:* Lectr, Northern Va Community Col, 77-; from asst prof to assoc prof painting, George Washington Univ, 78- *Mem:* Artists Equity Asn; Washington Womens Arts Ctr. *Media:* Oil, Watercolor. *Dealer:* Anne E Winkelman 8009 Overhill Rd Bethesda MD 20014. *Mailing Add:* 6124 Overlea Rd Bethesda MD 20016

GLASSMAN, JOEL A
VIDEO ARTIST, PHOTOGRAPHER
b New York, NY, Apr 10, 46. *Study:* Parsons Sch Design; Univ NMex, BFA; Hunter Col. *Work:* Ft Worth Art Mus, Tex; San Francisco Mus of Contemp Art; Everson Mus Art, Syracuse, NY; de Ssaiset Mus, Univ Santa Clara. *Exhib:* Kolnischer Kunstverein, Koln, Ger, 74;; La Jolla Mus Contemp Art, Calif, 74; Everson Mus Art Circuit Show, 74; Malmo Konsthall, Malmo, Sweden, 75;; Whitney Mus Am Art Biennial, 75; video retrospective 1970-1980, Univ Calif Berkeley Art Mus, 79. *Teaching:* Instr, San Francisco Art Inst, 81. *Awards:* Nat Endowment Arts Award Video Work, 75 & 77-78. *Bibliog:* Brenda Richardson (auth), New talent, Arts Mag, 70. *Publ:* Auth, Contemporary Video, Harcourt Brace, Janovich, 76; auth, California Performance, 81. *Dealer:* Electronic Art Intermix 84 Fifth Ave New York NY 10011. *Mailing Add:* 863 Florida St San Francisco CA 94110

GLASSON, LLOYD
SCULPTOR, EDUCATOR
b Chicago, Ill, Jan 31, 31. *Study:* Art Inst of Chicago, BFA, 57; Tulane Univ, MFA, 59. *Work:* New Brit Mus Am Art, Conn; George Walter Vincent Smith Mus, Springfield, Mass; Wichita Art Mus; Forma Viva Sculpture Garden, Slovenija, Yugoslavia. *Comn:* DeVane Mem, Yale Univ, 68; Shapiro Mem &

Herbert Portraits, Karen Horney Clin, New York, 67. *Exhib:* One-man shows, Dorsky Gallery, New York, 66 & 74 & Trinity Col, Hartford, Conn, 77; John Slade Ely House, New Haven, Conn, 75; Univ NH, Durham, 76. *Pos:* Manikin sculptor, Greneker Corp, New York, 59-60; exhib designer, Newark Mus, NJ, 60-61; sculptor, New York, 61-64. *Teaching:* Prof sculpture & drawing, Univ Hartford, West Hartford, Conn, 64- *Awards:* First Prizes, Art Asn Regional, Delgado Mus, New Orleans, 59 & Religious Art Exhib, New Orleans, 59; First Prize, St Timothy's, Hartford, Conn, 79. *Bibliog:* Jolene Goldenthal (auth), Adventurous Revivalist, Hartford Courant, 4/77; Anthony Padovano (auth), The process of sculpture, 81. *Mem:* Sculptors Guild (vpres); assoc Nat Acad Design. *Media:* Bronze and ceramic. *Dealer:* Dorsky Gallery 58 W 58th St New York NY. *Mailing Add:* Wilcox Hill Rd Portland CT 06480

GLAUBER, ROBERT H
CRITIC, CURATOR
b New York, NY, July 28, 20. *Study:* Harvard Univ. *Collections Arranged:* Violence in Recent American Art (with catalog), Mus Contemp Art, Chicago, 68; Decade of Accomplishment (with catalog), Chicago, 70; Black American Artists (with catalog), Univ Iowa, 71; Search for an American Image, Brooks Mem Gallery, Memphis, 74; Classic Revival, Realism in Recent American Drawings (with catalog), Chicago, 75; Mex Indian Dance Masks, Chicago, 81. *Pos:* Cur, Ill Bell Tel, Chicago, 66-78; art critic, Skyline, Chicago, 67-80; cur, Am Tel & Tel Co, New York, 72-77; cur, Western Elec, 78-81; cataloger, Print & Drawing Dept, Art Inst Chicago, 79-; critic, Arts Mag, 81-82; cur, Union League Club Chicago, 82- *Teaching:* Lectr, Univ Chicago, summer 80. *Mem:* Arts Club, Chicago; Asn Corp Art Mus Curs, Chicago. *Res:* American prints and drawings of the 20th century. *Publ:* Auth, Arts & language of China & Japan, Encycl Britannica Jr, 65; auth, Two centuries of US painting, Comptons Encycl, 75; auth, numerous magazine articles, 78- *Mailing Add:* 424 Melrose St Chicago IL 60657

GLENDINNING, PETER
PHOTOGRAPHER
b New York, NY, Sept 23, 51. *Study:* Syracuse Univ, BFA, 76, MFA, 78. *Work:* Int Mus Photog, Rochester, NY; Everson Mus Art & Light Work, Syracuse, NY; Marymount Col, Salina, Kans; Murray State Univ, Ky; Unicolor Corp. *Exhib:* Everson Mus Art, Syracuse, NY, 79; one-person shows, Lightsong Gallery, Tucson, 80, CEPA Gallery, Buffalo, NY, 81 & Foto Gallery, New York, 82; Fugitive Color, Slusser Gallery, Ann Arbor, Mich, 82; Proj Art Ctr, Cambridge, Mass, 82; Contemporary Photography as Phantasy Traveling Exhib, Univ Denver, 83. *Pos:* Dir, Light Fantastic Gallery, Mich State Univ, East Lansing, 78- *Teaching:* Assoc prof dept art & head photog, Mich State Univ, 78- *Awards:* Ford Found Grant, 78; Res Grant, Mich State Univ, 81; Unicolor Artist Support Grant, 82. *Mem:* Soc Photog Educ; Friends of Photog; Ctr Creative Photog. *Media:* Color. *Publ:* Contribr, Light/Color (exhib catalog), Ithaca Col, 81; contribr, Fugitive Color (exhib catalog), Univ Mich, 82. *Dealer:* Foto Gallery 492 Broome St New York NY. *Mailing Add:* c/o Art Dept Mich State Univ East Lansing MI 48824

GLENN, CONSTANCE WHITE
ADMINISTRATOR, HISTORIAN
b Topeka, Kans, Oct 4, 33. *Study:* Univ Kans, BFA; Univ Mo, Kansas City; Calif State Univ, Long Beach, MA. *Collections Arranged:* Lucas Samaras: Photo-Transformations (contribr, catalog), 75; Roy Lichtenstein: Ceramic Sculpture (auth, catalog), 77; George Segal: Pastels 1957-1965 (auth, catalog), 78; Frances Benjamin Johnston: Women of Class and Station (co-auth, catalog), 79; Jim Dine Figure Drawings: 1974-1979 (auth, catalog), 79; Frederick Sommer at Seventy-Five (contribr, catalog), 80; Nathan Oliveira: Print Retrospective (catalog), 80; Apropos Robinson Jeffers: Robert Motherwell/Renate Ponsold (catalog), 81. *Pos:* Co-dir, Jack Glenn Gallery, 70-73; assoc prof & dir, Mus Studies Cert Prog & dir, Art Mus & Galleries, Calif State Univ, Long Beach, 73-, dir, Ctr Southern Calif Studies Visual Arts, 79-; art consult, Archit Digest, 80- *Mem:* Am Asn Mus; Assoc Art Mus Dir; Col Art Asn; Southern Calif Bd Archives Am Art; Friends Photography. *Res:* American art since 1945. *Collection:* (Mr & Mrs Jack W Glenn); contemporary American art & American photography. *Publ:* Ed, Bryan Hunt: A Decade of Drawings (catalog), 83; auth, Jim Dine Drawings, fall 84. *Mailing Add:* Calif State Univ 1250 Bellflower Blvd Long Beach CA 90804

GLEZER, NECHEMIA
DEALER, CONSULTANT
b Vilno, Lithuania, 1910; US citizen. *Study:* Acad Fine Arts, Vilno; Stefana Batorego Univ, Vilno; Brera Acad Fine Arts, Milan, with Aldo Carpi. *Collections Arranged:* Fourteen Italian Artists, sponsored by Italian Ambassador to USA, Veerhoff Gallery, Washington, DC, 60; French Artists, C W Post Col, Long Island Univ, NY, 61; I Pailes, Maison Francaise, NY Univ, sponsored by French Cult Attache to USA, 63; Ferruccio Steffanutti, Vatican Pavilion, New York World's Fair, 64-65; Trento Longaretti, Casa Italiana, Columbia Univ, New York, 67; I Pailes, Maison Francaise, Columbia Univ, 72 & I Pailes Exhib, Yeshiva Univ Mus, New York, NY, 75. *Pos:* Pres, Nechemia Glezer Gallery, New York, 53- *Awards:* Award for Cult Enrichment, Fr Cult Attache, 63; Award for Introducing Italian Artists to USA, Ital Consul Gen, 69; Academician, Accad Tiberina di Rome, 72. *Bibliog:* Elspeth Flynn (auth), Southeby at Glezer Gallery, Brit Info Serv, 2/5/63; Mr Glezer from NY visits Museum at Casteleone, La Notte, Milan, 5/24/64; Mario Pescara (auth), Collection of Nechemia Glezer, Am Rev Art & Sci, 4/69. *Res:* Macchiaioli; Italian nineteenth century artists. *Specialty:* School of Paris artists; contemporary Italian artists. *Interests:* Bringing contemporary French and Italian art to the attention of the American public. *Mailing Add:* 760 West End Ave New York NY 10025

GLICK, PAULA FLORENCE
DEALER, COLLECTOR
b Baltimore, Md. *Study:* Am Univ; George Washington Univ, BA & MA; Columbia Univ. *Pos:* Assoc dir, Capricorn Galleries, 64- *Mem:* Col Art Asn Am; Soc Archit Hist. *Specialty:* Italian Renaissance and Baroque; the 30s & 40s; Americans and American contemporary realists. *Collection:* Contemporary American realists from 1900 to 1940. *Mailing Add:* 9536 Lawnsberry Terr Silver Spring MD 20901

GLICKMAN, ARTHUR
SCULPTOR
b New York, NY, Apr 29, 23. *Study:* With Issac Soyer, 53; Nat Acad Design, with Jeon DMarco & Envangelo Frudakis, 64-68; New Sch Social Research, with Bruno Luccesi, 69. *Work:* Bergen Community Mus, Paramus, NJ. *Comn:* Bird in Flight, IBM, NJ, 74; Freedom Series, comn by Roger Williams Mint, Providence, RI, 76. *Exhib:* Allied Artists Am, Nat Acad Gallery, New York, 70, 74, 78, 80 & 81; Nat Acad Design, Nat Acad Gallery, New York, 75; Nat Sculpture Soc, Equitable Life Assurance Soc, New York, 76; Newark Mus, NJ, 76; Sculptors Asn NJ, Madison Square Garden, New York, 76. *Awards:* First Prize in Sculpture, Bergen Co Artists Asn, 65 & West New York, NJ, 66; Second Prize in Sculpture, Washington Square, New York, 70. *Mem:* Allied Artists Am; Sculptors Asn NJ. *Media:* Bonded Bronze on Plexiglass. *Dealer:* Sculpture III 538 Rutland Ave Teaneck NJ 07666. *Mailing Add:* 538 Rutland Ave Teaneck NJ 07666

GLICKMAN, MAURICE
SCULPTOR, WRITER
b Jassy, Romania, Jan 6, 06; US citizen. *Study:* Educ Alliance Art Sch, New York, 21-26; Art Students League, 27 & 29-30. *Work:* Roberson Mem Art Ctr, Binghamton, NY; Albany Inst Hist & Art, NY; Hirshhorn Mus & Sculpture Garden; Queens Col, New York. *Comn:* Negro Mother & Child (bronze), Dept Interior, Washington, DC, 34; Construction (Philippine mahogany bas-relief), US Treas Dept, South River, NJ, 38; Mailmen (stone composition bas-relief), US Post Off, Northampton, Pa, 40. *Exhib:* One-man show, Morton Galleries, New York, 31; Govt in Art, Mus Mod Art, New York, 35; Carnegie Sculpture Invitational, Philadelphia Mus, 38; Whitney Mus Am Art Ann, New York, 38-61; Woman's Col Univ NC, 40; Artists for Victory, Metrop Mus Art, New York, 41; Florence Lewison Gallery, New York, 61, 65, 68 & 72; Sculpture by Maurice Glickman--A Selected Retrospective 1933-1963, Albany Inst Hist & Art, 63;; Heritage of American Art, Nat Archives Bldg Rotunda, Washington, DC, 71; and others. *Pos:* Founder-dir, Sch Art Studies, New York, 45-55. *Awards:* Guggenheim Fel, 34. *Bibliog:* Donald Johnson (auth), A visit with Maurice Glickman, Today's Art, 5/53; Cecil Roth (auth), Jewish Art, NY Graphic Soc, 71. *Mem:* Nat Sculpture Soc; founding mem Sculptors Guild (exec secy, 54-55). *Media:* Bronze, Wood. *Res:* Inter-relation of the arts with emphasis on the relation of sculpture and architecture, stressing the master sculptors' contributions. *Publ:* Auth, A lesson from history on sculpture and architecture, Archit Rec, 5/40; auth, The sculptor and his market, Mag Art, 41; auth, On wood carving, 43 & Techniques in sculpture, 60, Am Artists; auth, The tools of the sculptor, Design Mag, 49. *Dealer:* Florence Lewison Gallery 30 E 60th St New York NY 10022. *Mailing Add:* 165 E 66th St New York NY 10021

GLIMCHER, ARNOLD B
DEALER, WRITER
b Mar 12, 38; US citizen. *Pos:* Pres, Pace Gallery, New York, 63- *Specialty:* Twentieth-century art. *Publ:* Auth, Jean Dubuffet--Simulacres (catalog), 70 & Ernest Trova--Recent Sculpture (catalog), 71, Pace Ed; auth, Louise Nevelson, Praeger, 72; auth, Louise Nevelson, E P Dutton & Co, Inc, 76; coauth (with Paul Vitz), Modern Art and Modern Science: The Parallel Analysis of Vision, Praeger, 83. *Mailing Add:* Pace Gallery 32 E 57th St New York NY 10022

GLOBUS, DOROTHY TWINING
CURATOR
Study: Swarthmore Col, Pa, BA(art hist, magna cum laude). *Collections Arranged:* Immovable Objects I: Lower Manhattan From Battery Park to Bridge (auth, catalog), New York, 74; MAN transFORMS, 76; More than Meets the Eye (design & coordr), 77, Ornament in the 20th Century, 78, Gardens of Delight, Cooper-Hewitt Mus Decorative Arts & Design. *Pos:* Asst to dir, Wilcox Gallery, Swarthmore Col, Pa, 67-69; apprentice design & prod, Off of Exhib, Smithsonian Inst, Washington, DC, summer 68; exhib specialist res, design & coordr for spec exhib, DRUGS, 70-72, exhib specialist res & design on assignment to James S Ward Inc, New York, Smithsonian Inst, 72-73; exhib coordr, Cooper-Hewitt Mus Decorative Arts & Design, New York, 73- *Mailing Add:* 889 Broadway New York NY 10003

GLORIG, OSTOR
PAINTER
b New York, NY, Feb 14, 19. *Study:* Am Art Sch, New York, with Robert Brackman, Raphael Soyer & Gordon Samstag, four yr cert. *Work:* Mark Twain Portrait, Mark Twain Libr & Mem, Hartford, Conn. *Exhib:* One-man shows, Lynn Kottler Galleries, 56, 59, 61, 64 & 72; Clarksville Gallery, 65 & Col Mt St Vincent, 67; Nat Soc Arts & Lett Empire State Chap Showing, 69 & 79. *Awards:* Interior Design Cover Award, 51; Grumbacher Merit Award, 61. *Bibliog:* Elaine Israel (auth), From diamond to canvas, Long Island Star-J, 5/9/67. *Mem:* Life fel Royal Soc Arts Eng; life mem Nat Soc Arts & Lett; hon mem Kappa Pi. *Media:* Oil. *Dealer:* Lynn Kottler Galleries 3 E 65th St New York NY 10021. *Mailing Add:* 21-56 47th St Long Island City NY 11105

GLUCK, HEIDI
PAINTER, EDUCATOR
b Brooklyn, NY, Dec 30, 44. *Study:* Bennington Col, with D Smith, T Smith, Caro, Londo, Stroud & P Feely, BA, 66; Hunter Col, New York, with E Goosen, T Smith, R Humphrey & R Morris, 66-70. *Work:* Guggenheim Mus, New York; Israel Mus, Jerusalem; State Univ Ohio, Columbus; Picker Art Gallery, Colgate Univ, Hamilton, NY; Bennington Col, Vt. *Exhib:* Sensible Exploration, Univ Gallery Fine Art, Ohio State Univ, Columbus, 70; A Painting Show, PSI Projects Studios One, Inst Art & Urban Resources, NY, 77; A Brooklyn Portfolio, Brooklyn Mus, NY, 80; Contemp Drawings & Watercolors, Mem Art Gallery, Univ Rochester, 80; Creative Artists Public Service Program Grantees, Brooklyn Mus, NY, 81; 19 Artists--Emergent Am, Guggenheim Mus, New York, 81. *Teaching:* Vis artist painting, Princeton Univ, 80-82. *Awards:* Creative Artists Public Service Program Grant, 78-79. *Bibliog:* Robert Pincus-Witten (auth), Entries: Glück, Stephen, Acconci, Arts Mag, 3/78; Donald B Kuspit (auth), Heidi Glück, Arts Mag, 6/79; Donald B Kuspit (auth), Stops & starts in seventies art and criticism, Arts Mag, 3/81. *Media:* Oil, Acrylic. *Mailing Add:* 285 Livingston St Brooklyn NY 11217

GLUHMAN, JOSEPH WALTER
HISTORIAN, GRAPHIC ARTIST
b Corpus Christi, Tex, July 21, 34. *Study:* Johns Hopkins Univ, AB, 55; Western Reserve Univ, MA, 62; Fulbright fel, Ger, 68; Harvard Univ, PhD, 70. *Exhib:* Drawings USA, Minn Mus Art, St Paul, 71; 23rd-27th & 29th Nat Drawing/Sculpture, Ball State Univ, Muncie, Ind, 77-81 & 83; 4th Nat Potsdam Drawing, State Univ NY Potsdam, 79; Photoregional, J B Speed Art Mus, Louisville, Ky, 82; Southeastern Photogr, Greenville Art Mus, SC, 83; Nat Drawings, Trenton State Col, NJ, 83; and others. *Collections Arranged:* Lyonel Feininger: Nature Notes (auth, catalog), Watson Gallery, Norton, Mass, 70; Italian Drawings from Janos Scholz Collection (auth, catalog), 71 & Drawings '74 National Exhibition (auth, catalog), 74; Kazimieras Zoromskis: Recent Paintings (auth, catalog), Van Wickle Gallery, Easton Pa, 77; Regional Artists I: Tennessee, Ivan Wilson Gallery, Bowling Green, 79. *Teaching:* Prof & head, Dept Art, Western Ky Univ, 78- *Awards:* Nat Watercolor Soc Award, 14th Ann Del Mar Show, 80; 12th Ann Owensboro Photography Award, 83; 18th Ann Owensboro Guild Merit Award, 83. *Mem:* Col Art Asn; Southeastern Col Art Conf; Soc Archit Historians; Asn for Studies Cent Europ Art. *Res:* Nineteenth and twentieth century German painting. *Mailing Add:* 752 Richland Dr Bowling Green KY 42101

GLUHMAN, MARGARET A
GRAPHIC ARTIST, COLLAGE ARTIST
b Bethel Park, Pa. *Study:* Univ Pittsburgh; Cleveland Inst Art. *Work:* Rutgers Univ Art Mus; Meidinger Corp, Louisville, Ky. *Exhib:* Nat Drawing & Sculpture Exhib, Ball State Univ, 74, 79, 81 & 82; Mid-States Exhib, Evansville Art Mus, 78, 80, 81 & 83; Nat Drawing & Sculpture Exhib, Del Mar Col, 79-81; Appalachian Nat Drawing Exhib, Appalachian State Univ, 80 & 81; Mid-Am Nat, Owensboro Art Mus, Ky, 80 & 82; Kentucky Art, Univ Ky, Lexington, 81 & 83. *Pos:* Exhib coordr, Capitol Arts Ctr, Bowling Green, Ky, 81- *Media:* Paper, Collage. *Dealer:* Martha White Gallery 330 W Main St Louisville KY 40202. *Mailing Add:* 752 Richland Dr Bowling Green KY 42101

GLYDE, HENRY GEORGE
PAINTER, EDUCATOR
b Luton, Eng, June 18, 06. *Study:* Hastings Sch Art & Sci; Royal Col Art, London, hons; Can Arts Coun, sr fel, 58-59; Univ Alta, LLD, 82. *Work:* Edmonton Art Gallery; Nat Gallery Can; Glenbow Found, Calgary; Alta Col Art; Univ Alta; plus others. *Exhib:* Royal Brit Artists; Royal Acad, London; Can Group Painters; Can Soc Graphic Art; Royal Can Acad; plus others. *Teaching:* Instr, Borough Polytech, London; instr, Croydon Sch Art; instr, High Wycombe Sch Art; head art dept, Prov Inst Technol & Art, Alta; emer prof fine arts, Univ Alta & Banff Sch Fine Arts. *Awards:* Univ Alta Nat Award, 66. *Mem:* Royal Can Acad Arts. *Media:* Egg Tempera, Oils. *Mailing Add:* RR 1 Mackinnon Rd Pender Island BC V0N 2M0 Canada

GOBIN, HENRY (DELANO)
DIRECTOR, PAINTER
b Tulalip Indian Reservation, May 29, 41. *Study:* San Francisco Art Inst, BFA, 70; Sacramento State Col, MA, 71. *Work:* Am Embassy, Kenya, Africa; Am Embassy, Madrid, Spain. *Exhib:* Am Indian Hist Soc Mus, San Francisco, 68; Mus Nac Bellas Artes, Buenos Aires, Arg, 68; San Francisco Art Inst, 70; Civic Art Gallery, San Jose, Calif, 71; Jamison Gallery, Santa Fe, NMex, 71. *Teaching:* Asst prof native Am art, Sacramento State Col, 70-71; training instr humanities, Inst Am Indian Arts, 71-78, arts dir, 78-82. *Awards:* First Prize, NMex Wildlife Mag, 62; First Prize, 17th Ann Navajo Fair, Gallup, NMex, 63; First Prize, Scottsdale Nat Indian Art Exhib, Ariz, 64. *Bibliog:* Articles in Crafts Horizon, 64, Am Indian Hist Soc Mus, 68 & Artforum, 70. *Media:* Watercolor. *Mailing Add:* 2706 Galisteo Ct Santa Fe NM 87501

GOBUZAS, ALDONA M
DEALER, COLLECTOR
b Brooklyn, NY. *Study:* Notre Dame Col, St John's Univ, BA. *Collections Arranged:* Sponsored Stella Waitzkin New Works, Serious Literature, Calhoun Col, Yale Univ, 74 & Concepts in Small Format (auth, catalog), 79. *Specialty:* Contemporary American art. *Collection:* Contemporary paintings, sculpture, drawings, etchings. *Mailing Add:* Veydras 215 E 79th St New York NY 10021

GODDARD, DON (DONALD)
EDITOR, WRITER

b Cortland, NY, Apr 16, 34. *Study:* Princeton Univ, BA, 56. *Pos:* Writer & ed, McGraw-Hill Book Co, New York, 66-69; managing ed, ARTnews Mag, New York, 74-78, contrib ed, 78-; ed, Harry N Abrams Inc, 79- *Publ:* Auth, Tschacbasov, Am Arch of World Art, 64; auth, Mark di Suvero: an epic reach, ARTnews, 76; auth, Rothko's journey into the unknown, ARTnews, 79; auth, Harry Jackson, Harry N Abrams Inc, 81; auth, The professional fashion photographer, Amphoto, 81; and others. *Mailing Add:* 425 W Broadway New York NY 10012

GODDARD, VIVIAN
PAINTER

b San Francisco, Calif. *Study:* Calif Sch Fine Art; Art Students League; Stanford Univ, with Ed Farmer & Dan Mendelowitz; Art League San Francisco; Robert Brackman Summer Sch, Noank & Madison, Conn; Otis Art Sch, Los Angeles; Acad Grande Chaumiere, Paris; Simi Studio, Florence, Italy. *Work:* Pioneer Mus & Hagan Gallery, Stockton, Calif; Hall Justice, San Francisco; City Sacramento, Calif; Stanislaus State Col. *Comn:* Portraits, Richard Cragin, Alexander Capurso, Otto Kruger, Mrs Bernard McFadyen, Hubert Latimer and many others. *Exhib:* One-man shows, Windblad Gallery, San Francisco, Pioneer Mus, Hagan Gallery, Stanislaus State Col & Rosecrucian Mus, San Jose, Calif; Soc Western Artists, De Young Mus, 68-70; and others. *Pos:* Demonstrations, Soc Western Artists, Calif, Burlingame Art Asn, Calif, Fresno Art Asn, Calif & Am Fine Arts Asn, Los Angeles; juror. *Teaching:* Instr pvt studio, 69-71. *Awards:* First Award for Graphics & Award for Oil Portrait, Soc Western Artists, 67; Award for Portrait, Mother Lode Nat, 70; and others. *Mem:* Soc Western Artists; life mem Art Students League; Am Artists Prof League; life mem Am Inst Fine Arts; San Francisco Soc Women Artists. *Media:* Multimedia. *Dealer:* Portraits Inc 41 E 57th St New York NY 10022; Kertesz Gallery 521 Sutter St San Francisco CA 94108. *Mailing Add:* Metropolitan Club 640 Sutter St San Francisco CA 94102

GODFREY, ROBERT
PAINTER, EDUCATOR

b Mt Holly, NJ, Apr 17, 41. *Study:* Philadelphia Col Art, BFA, 66; Royal Acad Fine Arts, Copenhagen, post grad, 66-67; Ind Univ, MFA, 69. *Work:* Ind Univ Art Mus, Bloomington; Butler Inst Am Art; Hoyt Inst Fine Arts. *Exhib:* Painting & Photog, Something in Common, Fleisher Art Mus, Philadelphia, 72; Mid-Yr Show, Butler Inst Am Art, Youngstown, Ohio, 73, 74 & 81; Figure in Recent American Painting, traveling exhib, Pa & NY, 74-75; Am Figure Drawing (traveling exhib, Pa & Australia, 76; In Praise of Space, The Landscape in American Art, traveling exhib, Pa & NY, 76; Artists Choice, Figurative Art in NY, Green Mountain Gallery, New York, 77; plus many others. *Pos:* Dir, Artists' Choice Mus, New York, 79-80; ed, Artists' Choice Mus Newsletter, 80-82. *Teaching:* Prof art, painting, drawing & art hist, Westminster Col, New Wilmington, Pa, 72-; vis artist painting & drawing, Univ Pa, Philadelphia, 79-82. *Awards:* Drawing Award, Philadelphia Col Art, 66; Fulbright-Hays scholar, Denmark, 66-67; Buhl Found grant, 78. *Bibliog:* William Kelly (auth), An Individual Perception (monograph), Beaver Col, 79; James Ashbrook Perkins (auth), Presentational Immediacy (monograph), Butler Inst Am Art. *Media:* Oil, Pastel. *Publ:* Auth, Have museums slighted certain types of art--particularly figurative art?, Am Artists Mag, 79; auth, About sentimentality, Artists' Choice Mus J, 83. *Dealer:* Blue Mountain Gallery 121 Wooster St New York NY 10012; Noel Butcher Gallery 132 S 17th St Philadelphia Pa 19103. *Mailing Add:* c/o Blue Mountain Gallery 121 Wooster St New York NY 10012

GODFREY, WINNIE (WINIFRED M)
PAINTER, INSTRUCTOR

b Philadelphia, Pa, Nov 21, 44. *Study:* Marycrest Col, Iowa, 61-63; Art Inst Chicago, 62; Univ Wis, Madison, BS, 66, MFA, 70. *Work:* Ill State Mus, Springfield; Portland Mus, Ore; Borg-Warner Art Collection, Kemper Insurance Art Collection, Chicago; Rochester Art Ctr, Minn. *Comn:* Oil painting, State Ill, Danville, 83. *Exhib:* Midwest Biennial Exhib, Joslyn Art Mus, 72; solo exhib, Burpee Art Mus, Rockford, Ill, 76; Group Realist Exhib, Wutsum Art Mus, Racine, Wis, 76; two-person show, Art Inst Chicago Sales Gallery, 81; Soc Illusr Ann, New York, 82; Ill State Mus Invitational, Springfield, 83. *Teaching:* Artist in residence drawing & painting, Rochester Art Ctr, Minn, 70; vis lectr drawing, Univ Ill, Chicago, 75-76; instr portraits, Evanston Art Ctr, Ill, 80- *Awards:* Second Prize, New Horizons in Art, North Shore Art League, 75; First Prize, Milwaukee Lakefront, Milwaukee Art Ctr, 75 & 78; Best of Show, Arthur Baer Mem Competition, Beverly Art Ctr, 83. *Bibliog:* Richard Waller (auth), article, New York Gallery Guide, 5/82; Jim Hatfield (producer), Two on two, CBS, 83. *Mem:* Artists Equity; Chicago Artists Coalition; North Shore Art League. *Media:* Oil. *Publ:* Auth, article, New York Examiner, 81; auth, article, In: Gallery Guide, Art Now Inc, 82; contribr, The New York Art Review, Macmillan, 82; contribr, Illustrators 24, Madison Sq Press, 83. *Dealer:* Andre Zarre 41 E 57 St New York NY 10022. *Mailing Add:* 2647 N Orchard St Chicago IL 60614

GODSEY, GLENN
EDUCATOR, PAINTER

b Amarillo, Tex, June 1, 37. *Study:* Okla State Univ; Univ Tulsa, BA & MA; and with Alexandre Hogue. *Work:* Springfield Art Mus, Mo; Okla State Art Collection, Okla Arts & Humanities Coun, Oklahoma City; Magic Castle, Hollywood, Calif. *Comn:* Portrait, Univ Tulsa; The Petroleum Club, Tulsa; portrait, Oral Roberts Univ. *Exhib:* One-man show, Philbrook Art Ctr, Tulsa, 71; Okla Artists Ann, Tulsa, 75; Traveling Exhib of Okla Art, Washington, DC, 76; Saltillo, Mex, 77; two-man show, Univ Tulsa, 78. *Teaching:* Assoc

prof painting & art hist, Univ Tulsa, 67- *Awards:* Watercolor USA Purchase Award, SMo Mus Asn, 74; Okla Artist Ann Award, 72 & 74. *Bibliog:* Rev Blakey (auth), Delineating the mysterious, Univ Tulsa Mag; Maurice DeVinna (auth), Music & the arts, Tulsa World Mag, 71; Bill Donaldson (auth), Showcase, Tulsa Tribune, 71. *Media:* Acrylic, Watercolor. *Publ:* Auth, Hip generation, Univ Tulsa Mag, 68; illusr, Okla State Univ Lit Quart, Nimrod, Tulsa Mag & Univ Tulsa Mag. *Mailing Add:* Dept Art Univ Tulsa 600 S College Ave Tulsa OK 74104

GODSEY, JERRY & ANNE
COLLECTORS

Mr Godsey, b Tampa, Fla, July 18, 39; Mrs Godsey, b San Juan, PR, July 18, 41. *Study:* Mr Godsey, Univ Fla, MBA, 67, Mrs Godsey, BAE, 67. *Collections Arranged:* Oglethorpe Univ, 78; Creative Images of Japan, Handshake Gallery, Atlanta, Ga, 78 & 80; Elliott Mus, Stuart, Fla, 80. *Mem:* High Mus Art; Ga Coun Arts; Ga Asn Mus Galleries. *Collection:* Original, limited edition prints by contemporary Japanese artists recognized worldwide. *Mailing Add:* 470 N Harbor Dr NW Atlanta GA 30328

GODWIN, JUDITH WHITNEY
PAINTER

b Suffolk, Va. *Study:* Mary Baldwin Col, Staunton, Va; Va Commonwealth Univ, BFA; Art Students League, with Vaclav Vytlacil, Will Barnet & Harry Sternberg; Hans Hofmann Sch, Provincetown, Mass & New York. *Work:* Metrop Mus, New York; Milwaukee Art Ctr, Wis; San Francisco Mus Mod Art; Nat Mus Art, Osaka, Japan; Chase Manhattan Collection, New York; and others. *Comn:* Painter's Themes (fabric design), Bloomcraft Inc, New York, 76. *Exhib:* Nat Mus Art, Osaka, Japan; Recent Acquisitions, Ulrich Mus, Wichita, Kans, 77 & NC Mus Art, Raleigh, 77; Danforth Mus, Framingham, Mass, 77; Northern Mich Univ, 78; Past, Present and Peculiar, Ingber Gallery, New York, 79 & 81; and others. *Awards:* Popular Prize, Leache Mem Exhib, Norfolk, 51. *Bibliog:* Joyce E Davis (auth), Judith Godwin, Art Voices S, 5-6/79; Natalie Edgar (auth), Judith Goodwin, Arts Mag, 5/81; Cynthia Nadelman (auth), Judith Godwin, Artnews, 81. *Mem:* Am Fedn Arts; Col Art Asn; Women's Caucus Art. *Media:* Multimedia. *Dealer:* Ingber Gallery 460 W Broadway New York NY 10012; John Pence Gallery 750 Post St San Francisco CA. *Mailing Add:* 247 W 13th St New York NY 10011

GOEDICKE, JEAN
PAINTER, INSTRUCTOR

b DePass, Wyo, Sept 24, 08. *Study:* Taos Sch Art, NMex, with Emil Bisttram; Casper Col, with Ed Gothberg, AA; Univ Wyo, with James M Boyle & Richard Evans, BA & MA(with hon); also with Robert E Wood, Calif, Mario Cooper & Dale Meyers, NY & Milford Zornes, Utah; workshops with Richard Proctor, Univ Wash, Bud Shackelford, Calif & Carole Barnes, Colo. *Work:* Wyo State Art Gallery, Cheyenne; Wyo State Capitol, Cheyenne. *Exhib:* Wyo Traveling Art Exhib, 57-74; Univ Fed de Goias, Brazil, 69; eight state regional watercolor exhib, Fedn Rocky Mountain States, Inc, 69-71; Invitational, Nicolaysen Art Mus, Casper, Wyo, 79-81; Juried regional and national exhibs, Montana, Nebraska & Wyoming, 80-81; and others. *Teaching:* Instr watercolor & drawing, Mobile Art Symp, Wyo Coun Arts, 67-79, Friends of Artists, 75- *Bibliog:* Peggy Simson Curry (auth), A tool box & a talent, In Wyoming, summer 70; Jean Mead (auth), Wyoming in Profile, 82. *Mem:* Wyo Artists Asn (pres, 66-67); Casper Artists Guild (pres, 65); Soc Western Artists San Francisco; Scotch & Watercolor Soc, Wyo; and others. *Media:* Transparent Watercolor. *Dealer:* West Wind Gallery 1040 W 15th Casper WY 82604; Wild Goose Gallery 211 W 19th Cheyenne WY 82003. *Mailing Add:* 2125 S Coffman Casper WY 82601

GOEDIKE, SHIRL
PAINTER

b Los Angeles, Calif, 1923. *Study:* Univ Calif, Los Angeles; Art Ctr Sch, Los Angeles. *Work:* Los Angeles Co Mus Art; Louvre, Paris; Palm Springs Mus; Birmingham Mus Art, Ala; Hirshhorn Mus, Washington, DC; and others. *Exhib:* Los Angeles Co Mus, 55-56; Stanford Univ, 56; Whitney Mus Ann, 60; one-man shows, Palace Legion of Honor, San Francisco, Calif, 59 & Elysee Palace, Paris, 83; Santa Barbara Biennial, Santa Barbara Mus & Nat Tour, 59; 26th Biennial, Corcoran Gallery Art, Washington, DC; Pasadena Art Mus, Calif; Palm Springs Mus, Calif, 76. *Bibliog:* Alfred Frankenstein (auth), articles, San Francisco Chronicle, 59, 60 & 62; Henry Seldis (auth), articles, Los Angeles Times, 72; Alfred Frankenstein (auth), Shirl Goedike (monogr), Hammer Publ, 78. *Media:* Oil, Watercolor. *Mailing Add:* c/o Ankrum Gallery 657 N La Cienega Blvd Los Angeles CA 90069

GOELL, ABBY JANE
PAINTER, ASSEMBLAGE ARTIST

b New York, NY. *Study:* Art Students League, with Harry Sternberg & Charles Alston; Syracuse Univ, BA; NY Sch Interior Design, Cert; Columbia Univ, with Robert Motherwell, Stephen Greene & John Heliker, MFA(painting); Attingham Park, Shropshire, United Kingdom, 63; Pratt Graphic Ctr, 65. *Work:* Mus Mod Art, New York; Yale Univ Art Gallery; Chase Manhattan Bank Collection, New York; Kresge Art Ctr, Mich; Altantic Richfield Oil Co; and others. *Comn:* Original print, Pratt Graphics Ctr, 75. *Exhib:* Brooklyn Mus Print Biennial, 70; Hudson River Mus, Yonkers, NY, 71; Grey Gallery & Study Ctr, NY Univ, 77; one-man shows, US Mission, Havana, Cuba, 79-81 & Sculpture Ctr, NY, 81; TAGA-Pratt Exhib, Caracas, 82; and others. *Pos:* Co-publ, Arcadia Press, New York. *Teaching:* Instr art hist, Hunter Col, 67; lectr, Lab Inst Merchandising, 67-70. *Awards:* Yaddo Fel, Saratoga Springs, NY, 68; Va Ctr Creative Arts Fel, Sweet Briar, 81. *Mem:* Women's Caucus Art; sr mem Am Soc Appraisers; Victorian Soc in Am. *Media:* Oil, Serigraph, Lithograph, Collage. *Publ:* Ed, English Silver 1675-1825, Ensko & Wenham, revised ed, 80. *Mailing Add:* 37 Washington Sq W New York NY 10011

GOERITZ, MATHIAS
SCULPTOR, DESIGNER
b Danzig, Ger, Apr 4, 15. *Study:* Friedrich-Wilhelms Univ, PhD; Kunstgewerbeschule, Berlin-Charlottenburg. *Work:* Mus Arte Mod, Mexico City, Mex; Kunsthalle, Hamburg, Ger; Mus Mod Art, New York; Israel Mus, Jerusalem, Israel; Univ Ariz Art Gallery. *Comn:* El Eco (total environ), comn by Daniel Mont, Exp Mus, Mexico City, 52-53; environ sculpture, Towers of Satellite City, comn by L Barragan & M Pani, 57, Towers of Automex, comn by R Legorreta, Toluca, Mex, 63-64 & Pyramid of Mixcoac, Mexico City, 70-72; Route of Friendship (hwy environ), Mex Olympic Comt, Mexico City, 68; and others. *Exhib:* Art of Assemblage, Mus Mod Art, New York, 61; Pittsburgh Int Exhib, Carnegie Inst, 61; Concrete Poetry, Stedelijk Mus, Amsterdam, Holland, 70-71; Mathias Goeritz-Architecture Sculpture, Israel Mus, Jerusalem, 80; 11th Biennial, Open-Air Mus Sculpture, Middelheim, Belg, 71. *Pos:* Dir Sch Fine Arts & Indust Design, Iberoamericano Univ, Mex, 57-60; ed art sect, Arquitectura-Mex, 59-; artist in residence, Aspen Inst Humanistic Studies, Aspen, Colo, 70-72. *Teaching:* Prof design, Nat Univ Mex, 54- *Bibliog:* Olivia Zuniga (auth), Mathias Goeritz, Ed Intercontinental, Mexico City, 63; Clive B Smith (auth), Builders in the sun, Architectural, New York, 67; H Harvard Arnason (auth), History of Modern Art, Abrams, 68. *Publ:* Illusr, Los amantes y la noche, ed Eco, Mex, 53; auth & illusr, bks & articles. *Mailing Add:* Apartado 20-390 Mexico DF 01000 Mexico

GOERTZ, AUGUSTUS FREDERICK, III
PAINTER, PRINTMAKER
b Greenwich Village, New York, NY, Aug 15, 48. *Study:* High Sch of Music & Art, New York; Carnegie-Mellon Univ, Pittsburgh, Pa; San Francisco Art Inst, BFA; also with Tom Akawie, Jay Defeo, Augustus Goertz, Wally Hedrick, Bruce Nauman & Jim Rienekin. *Work:* San Francisco Art Inst; Chicago Art Inst; Aldrich Mus of Contemp Art, Ridgefield, Conn; New York Law Sch; Hyatt Collection, New York; and others. *Exhib:* Selections from The Collection, Aldrich Mus of Contemp Art, 78; Arte Fiera, Bologna, Italy, 78; Gallery of Emerging Am Artists, New York, 79; one-man shows, New York Law Sch, 77 & Sarah Rentschler Gallery, 78, 79, 80 & 82; Are You Experienced, Univ Brussels, Belgium, 81. *Collections Arranged:* Contemporary Reflections, Aldrich Mus of Contemp Art, Ridgefield, Conn, 73; Encounter, Warren Benedek Gallery, New York, 73. *Pos:* Dir, Art Time Found, New York. *Awards:* Spec Acheivement Award, New York Taxi Drivers, Robert Scull, 65; Honor Student Award, San Francisco Art Inst, 67. *Bibliog:* J Wiessman (auth), article, Art News, 75; Ellen Stern (auth), article, New York Mag, 78; Eleanor Blan (auth), article, New York Times, 80. *Mem:* Orgn of Independent Artists; New York WPA Artists Inc; San Francisco Art Inst Alumni Asn. *Dealer:* Sarah Y Rentschler 450 W 24th St New York NY 10013. *Mailing Add:* 319 Greenwich St New York NY 10013

GOETZ, EDITH JEAN
PAINTER, INSTRUCTOR
b Media, Pa, Oct 28, 18. *Study:* St Margaret's Sch, Waterbury, Conn, with Frederic Sexton; Cape Sch, Provincetown, Mass, with Henry Hensche; Art Students League with George Bridgeman, Arnold Blanch & Charles Chapman; Nat Acad, New York, with Charles Curran; Grand Cent Art Sch, with Mario Cooper. *Work:* Women's Col, Chickasha, Okla; Great Plains Mus, Lawton, Okla. *Exhib:* Okla Ann, Philbrook Mus, Tulsa, 65; one-man show, Okla Art Ctr, 70; Jamison Gallery, Santa Fe, NMex, 72; Am Artists Prof League, New York, 75; Three State Show at Lawton, Great Plains Mus, 75. *Teaching:* Portrait & figure drawing & painting, Goetz Art Sch, Oklahoma City, 65-75 & Santa Fe, summers 70-73. *Mem:* Am Artists Prof League; Grand Cent Galleries; Pastel Soc Am. *Media:* Oil, Pastel. *Dealer:* Grand Cent Galleries New York NY; Marbella Gallery New York NY. *Mailing Add:* 535 Bedford Ctr Rd Bedford Hills NY 10507

GOETZ, PETER HENRY
PAINTER, LECTURER
b Slavgorod, Russia, Sept 8, 17; Can citizen. *Study:* Waterloo Col, 45; Doon Sch Fine Art, with F H Varley; study watercolor in Japan. *Work:* London Pub Libr & Art Mus, Ont; Sarnia Pub Libr & Art Mus, Ont; Kitchener Waterloo Art Gallery; Univ Waterloo, Ont; Univ Guelph, Ont. *Comn:* Series of twelve paintings from around the world, Waterloo Co Health Bldg, 65; painting of Parliament bldgs, Nat Club, Toronto, 67; Peace Tower, comn by Sen John B Aird, Toronto, 69; painting of Budapest, CFTO-TV, Toronto, 69; View of Prague, Toronto Stock Exchange, 69. *Exhib:* Royal Can Acad; Ont Soc Artists; Can Soc Painters Watercolour; Nat Gallery Ottawa; Am Watercolor Soc, New York, 72. *Teaching:* Lectured and demonstrated adult education classes throughout Ontario for Department of Education. *Awards:* Watercolor Prize, Western Ont Exhib; First Prize, Brampton Ann Exhib; Purchase Award, Image 76, Ont Soc Artists, 76. *Mem:* Ont Soc Artists; Canada Soc Painters Watercolour; Soc Can Artists; Centro Studi & Scambi Int, Rome; fel Int Inst Arts & Lett; Am Fedn Art. *Media:* Watercolor. *Mailing Add:* 784 Avondale Ave Kitchener ON N2M 2W8 Canada

GOETZ, RICHARD VERNON
PAINTER, INSTRUCTOR
b Lawrenceburg, Tenn, Apr 6, 15. *Study:* Oklahoma City Univ; Univ Okla; Cape Sch Art; Nat Acad Design; Art Students League; with Robert Brackman, Henry Henche, George Bridgman, Sidney Dickenson & Jonas Lee. *Work:* Butler Inst Am Art, Youngstown, Ohio; Okla Art Ctr, Oklahoma City; Okla Hist Soc, Oklahoma City; Ft Smith Art Ctr, Ark. *Exhib:* Butler Inst Am Art, 68; Allied Artists Am, 68; Okla Mus Art, 68; Am Artists Prof League, 71; Okla-Tex Spring Ann, 72. *Teaching:* Dir, Goetz Art Schs, Oklahoma City, 46 & Santa Fe, 71-; co-dir, Malden Bridge Art Sch, New York, 64-71; instr, Art Students League, New York, currently. *Awards:* Best

in Show, Tex-Okla Spring Show, 68 & Am Artists Prof League, 69; McDonnough Award, Butler Inst Am Art, 68. *Mem:* Am Artists Prof League. *Media:* Oil. *Publ:* Auth, Painting a still life, Am Artist, 68. *Dealer:* Grand Central Art Galleries Vanderbilt & 44th St New York NY 10017; Fenn Galleries Santa Fe NM. *Mailing Add:* 535 Bedford Center Rd Bedford Hills NY 10507

GOETZL, THOMAS MAXWELL
LECTURER, EDUCATOR
b Chicago, Ill, May 31, 43. *Study:* Univ Calif, Berkeley, AB(psychology), 65 & Boalt Hall Sch of Law, JD, 69. *Pos:* Mem bd dirs, Ctr Visual Arts, Pac Basin Sch Textile Arts, currently; assoc mem, Nat Conf State Legislatures, Arts Task Force, currently. *Teaching:* Prof art and the law, Golden Gate Univ, Sch of Law, San Francisco, Calif, 72- *Mem:* Artists Equity Asn; Bay Area Lawyers Arts. *Publ:* Auth, Recent Arts Legislation-An Overview, Artweek & Glass Studio, 78; No Tainting the Painting: The California Art Preservation Act, 80; Legislative Masterpieces, Calif Art Legislation, Bay Area Lawyers Arts. *Mailing Add:* 1019 Keith Ave Berkeley CA 94708

GOFF, THOMAS JEFFERSON
SCULPTOR, MEDALIST
b Bristol, RI, Dec 22, 07. *Study:* RI Sch Design, study under Louise A Atkins, Hugo O E Carlborg & William A Heath, dipl, 30, 33-34. *Work:* US Naval Mus, Washington, DC; Smithsonian Inst, Washington, DC; Newport News Mus, Va; US Naval War Col Mus, Newport, RI; RI Hist Soc Mus, Providence. *Comn:* Armed servs insignia, Craven & Whitaker Co, Providence, 40-45; Bryant Col bronze seal, pres Bryant Col, Providence & Smithfield, RI, 62; Gordon Col bronze seal, Seal Comt, Wrentham, Mass, 71; Univ RI bronze podium seal, Foundry-Auburn Brass Foundry, Cranston, RI, 69; Jackson State Col bronze seal, Herff-Jones Co, Indianapolis, Ind, 70. *Exhib:* Nat Sculpture Soc Exhib, 49 & 62; Bristol Art Mus, 65; Int Exhib by Uno A Erre, Arezzo, Italy, 69; Int Exhib, Arezzo, Italy, 70. *Awards:* Steel Engraving, RI Sch Design, New Eng Jewelers & Silversmiths Asn, 34; Lunar 1969 Landing Award, Uno A Erre, Arezzo, Italy, 70. *Bibliog:* Wayne Worchester (auth), Designs ship's insignia, Providence J Co, 66; K Nelson (auth), Ship's insignia, an art, The Newport Navalog, 67; Rose Derosiers (auth), Heraldic art, Bulletin RI Sch Design, 12/73. *Mem:* Soc Medalists, Danbury, Conn; Orders & Medals Soc Am. *Media:* Wax, Modeling Clay; Bronze, Die Steel. *Dealer:* Block Artists' Material Co 129 Dyer St Providence RI 02901; Manufacturers Supply Co 171 Chestnut St Providence RI 02901. *Mailing Add:* 1227 Hope St Bristol RI 02809

GOHEEN, ELLEN ROZANNE
CURATOR, HISTORIAN
b New York, NY, Mar 30, 44. *Study:* Univ Kans, Lawrence, BA & MA. *Collections Arranged:* Masters of 20th Century Photography, 73, American Impressionism, 74, Friends of Art Retrospective, 76, Joseph Cornell, 77 & Jasper Johns in Kansas City 1967-1977, 78, Nelson Gallery-Atkins Mus, Kansas City, Mo. *Pos:* From asst cur to assoc cur Europ painting & sculpture, Nelson Gallery-Atkins Mus, 70-75, 20th century art, 75-81, sr lectr, 81- *Awards:* Sir George Trevelyan Scholar, Attingham Park Summer Sch, Shropshire, Eng, 73. *Mem:* Archaeol Inst Am (pres, Kans Chap, 74-77); Nat Trust Hist Preserv; Victorian Soc Am. *Res:* Twentieth century American and European art, European and American architecture. *Publ:* Auth, From romanticism to pop, Apollo, 12/72; contribr, European Painting & Sculpture, American 20th Century, Handbook, Nelson Gallery, 73; Christo: Wrapped Walk Ways, Abrams, 79. *Mailing Add:* 3681 Madison Ave Kansas City MO 64111

GOINGS, RALPH
PAINTER
b Corning, Calif, May 9, 28. *Study:* Calif Col Arts & Crafts, Oakland, BFA, 53; Calif State Univ, Sacramento, MA, 66. *Work:* Mus Mod Art, New York; Mus Contemp Art, Chicago; Neue Galerie, Essen, Ger; Kunstverein in Hamburg, Ger; Inst of Contemp Art, Univ Pa. *Exhib:* One-man exhibs, OK Harris, 70, 73, 77 & 80 & Mus Mod Art, New York, 77; Urban Aesthetics, Queens Mus, 76; Contemp Images in Watercolor, Akron Art Inst, Ohio, 76; Perspective 1976, Albright Col, 76; Illusion and Reality, Canberra, 77; and others. *Pos:* Chmn art dept, La Sierra High Sch, Carmichael, Calif, 59-70. *Teaching:* Instr, Del Norte High Sch, Crescent City, Calif, 55-59, Calif State Univ, Sacramento, 71 & Univ Calif, Davis, 72. *Bibliog:* Udo Kulterman (auth), New Realism, Tubingen, 72; Yusuke Nakahara (auth), Man Made Nature, Vol 5, Tokyo, 72; Linda Chase (auth), The connotation of denotation, Arts Mag, 2/74. *Media:* Oil, Watercolor. *Mailing Add:* c/o O K Harris Works of Art 383 W Broadway New York NY 10012

GOLBIN, ANDREE
PAINTER, ILLUSTRATOR
b Leipzig, Ger, June 4, 23; US citizen. *Study:* Art Students League; Parsons Sch Design; Hans Hofmann Sch Art; New Sch Social Res, Printmaking Workshop. *Work:* Indust Bank Japan; Wako Securities Co, Tokyo, Japan; Eastman Kodak; New York Port Authority, Klopman Mills; Printmaking Workshop. *Exhib:* Los Angeles Co Mus Art Ann, 49-50; Women Choose Women, New York Cult Ctr, 73; Works on Paper, Brooklyn Mus, 75; Noah Goldowsky Gallery, 76; solo exhibs, Camino Gallery, 56 & 58, Grand Cent Moderns Gallery, 64 & 65 & Contemp Arts Gallery, New York Univ, 71. *Pos:* Prom art dir, Mademoiselle Mag, 50-52. *Teaching:* Instr graphic design, Kean Col NJ, 79-80 & Fashion Inst Technol, 80-81; instr drawing, Parsons Sch Design, 79-83 & New York City Tech Col, 82- *Awards:* Grumbacher Prize, Nat Asn Women Artists, 49-50. *Bibliog:* Reviews in Art News, Arts Dig, New York Times, Art Forum, 3/73, Nation, 6/25/73. *Mem:* Artists Equity Asn

New York; Woman's Caucus for Art. *Media:* Acrylic, Oil; Pen & Ink. *Publ:* Illusr, New York Sunday Times gardening section, 74-75 & children's books publ by Lothrop, Lee & Shepard Co, 74, Rand McNally, Grossett & Dunlap. *Mailing Add:* 521 East 14th St Apt 9B New York NY 10009

GOLD, ALBERT
PAINTER, EDUCATOR
b Philadelphia, Pa, Oct 31, 16. *Study:* Philadelphia Mus Sch Art, dipl, 39. *Work:* Fogg Art Mus, Harvard Univ, Cambridge, Mass; Smithsonian Inst; Ford Motor Co; Standard Oil, NJ; Atwater Kent Mus; and others. *Comn:* Twelve paintings of Pa, Gimbel Brothers, 47-48; murals, Bur Agr; plus many others. *Exhib:* Nat Acad Design, New York, 40-68; Pa Acad Fine Arts Ann, 40-68; Venice Biennial, 41; Artists for Victory, Metrop Mus Art, New York, 42; Mus Galliera, Paris, 44. *Teaching:* Prof illus & materials of artist, Philadelphia Col Art, 46-, dir illus dept, 59- *Awards:* Prix de Rome, 42; Sesnan Gold Medal for Landscape, Pa Acad Fine Arts, 50; Smith Grant, Woodmere, Chestnut Hill, Pa, 73; plus others. *Bibliog:* Henry C Pitz (auth), Albert Gold, painter-draftsman, Am Artists, 11/56. *Mem:* Philadelphia Watercolor Club; Philadelphia Art Alliance (past chmn, 46-72, chmn watercolor, 49-65); Artists Equity; Am Watercolor Soc. *Media:* Oil, Watercolor. *Res:* History of American illustration. *Publ:* Illusr, Our Philadelphia, 50; illusr, The Commodore, 54; illusr, This Was Our War, 63; illusr, The Captive Rabbi, 65. *Dealer:* 252 Gallery 252 S 16th St Philadelphia PA 19103. *Mailing Add:* 6814 McCallum St Philadelphia PA 19119

GOLD, BETTY
ADMINISTRATOR, DIRECTOR
b San Francisco, Calif, July 17, 32. *Study:* Univ Calif, Berkeley & Los Angeles. *Pos:* Cur, Ford Found Fel, Tamarind Lithog Workshop, Los Angeles, 65; exhib comt, Newport Harbor Art Mus, Newport Beach, Calif, 65-70; owner, Betty Gold Gallery, Los Angeles, 70-75; dir, ARCO Ctr Visual Arts, 75-, mgr fine arts progs, Atlantic Richfield Co, 79- *Mailing Add:* Atlantic Richfield Co 515 S Flower St Los Angeles CA 90071

GOLD, LEAH
PAINTER, PRINTMAKER
b New York, NY. *Study:* With Ruth Reeves & Hans Hofmann. *Work:* Butler Inst Am Art; Birmingham Mus Art, Ala; Slater Mem Mus, Norwich, Conn. *Exhib:* Montclair Mus, NJ, 73-75; Tirca Karlis Gallery, Provincetown, Mass, 75-; Fordham Univ at Lincoln Ctr, New York, 75; Nat Art Mus of Sports, New York, 75; Cork Gallery, Lincoln Ctr, New York, 76- *Awards:* Mrs John T Pratt Prize for Woodcut, Nat Asn Women Artists, 57; Prize for Casein Painting, Painters & Sculptors Soc NJ 18th Ann, 59; Award for Stained Glass Sculpture, Brooklyn Soc Artists, 59; and others. *Mem:* Artists Equity Asn New York (bd dirs, 65-); Am Soc Contemp Artists; Metrop Painters & Sculptors, New York (publicity & exhib comt, 72-); Painters & Sculptors Soc NJ; League Present Day Artists. *Media:* Casein, Graphics; Stained Glass, Collages. *Mailing Add:* Apt 5-A 330 W 28th St New York NY 10001

GOLD, MARTHA B
SCULPTOR
b New York, NY, Sept 20, 38. *Study:* Univ Rochester; Barnard Col, Columbia Univ, BA; Columbia Univ, MA; Nat Acad Sch Fine Arts, cert. *Exhib:* NAm Sculpture Ann, Foothills Art Ctr, Golden, Colo, 80 & 83; Allied Artists Am, Am Acad Inst Arts & Letts, 80; Audubon Artists Ann, Nat Arts Club, 81 & Nat Sculpture Soc Ann, Equitable Life Insurance Bldg, 81, New York; Philadelphia Tricentennial, 82; and others. *Teaching:* Privately. *Awards:* Mem Award, Audubon Artists, 79; Youth Award, Nat Sculpture Soc, 79 & 80; Gold Medal Honor, Allied Artists Am, 80. *Mem:* Allied Artists Am. *Media:* Bronze, Clay. *Dealer:* Tyringham Gallery Tyringham MA 01264. *Mailing Add:* 315 E 91 St New York NY 10128

GOLD, SHARON CECILE
PAINTER, EDUCATOR
b Bronx, NY, Feb 28, 49. *Study:* Hunter Col, City Univ of NY, 68-69; Columbia Univ, 69-70; Pratt Inst, BFA(Acad Fel), 76. *Work:* McCrory Corp, Chase Manhattan Bank & Norsearch Indust, New York; Prudential Insurance Co Am, NJ; Best Products, Inc, Va. *Comn:* Painting on aluminum and fiberglass, Humbolt-Hospital Station, Niagara Frontier Transportation Authority, Buffalo, NY, 82-84. *Exhib:* Works on Paper, Mus Mod Art, Art Lending Serv, New York, 81; solo exhib, Anderson Gallery, Va Commonwealth Univ, 82; Contemp Abstract Painting, Ctr Arts, Muhlenberg Col, 83; Art of the Rapid Transit, Niagara Frontier Transportation Authority, Buffalo, 83; Tyler & Penrose Galleries, Tyler Sch Art, Philadelphia, 83; New York Painting Today, Three Rivers Arts Festival, Pittsburgh, 83; and many others. *Pos:* Assoc ed, Re-View Mag, New York, 77- *Teaching:* Guest lectr, La Guardia Community Col, City Univ New York, 77, Col New Rochelle, 77, C W Post, Long Island Univ, 78 & 81, Barnard Col, Columbia Univ, 78, Muhlenberg Col, 81, San Jose State Univ, 81 & Hunter Col, City Univ New York, 82; guest lectr, Pratt Inst Technol, 77-78 & 80, vis assoc prof, 80; adj lectr, Queensborough Community Col, City Univ New York, 77; vis artist, Univ Rochester, 79, San Francisco Art Inst, 81, Univ Colo, Boulder, 83 & Tyler Sch Art, 83; lectr, Princeton Univ, 79-80; vis assoc prof, Univ Tex, San Antonio, 80 & Syracuse Univ, 80-81; vis prof, Va Commonwealth Univ, 82; adj prof, NY Univ, 83. *Awards:* MacDowell Colony Fel, 72; Nat Endowment Arts Painting Fel, 81-82. *Bibliog:* Drawing invitational 1981, Arts Mag, 2/82; Art fashion, J Contemp Art Mag, summer 82; The 1983 Whitney Biennial: Who wasn't there, Nit & Wit, 9-10/83; and other articles and reviews. *Publ:* Auth, The cognitive create object: intuition and the creative process, Re-View Mag, fall 77; contribr, reviews in Artforum, 77; auth, Statement, Re-View Mag, 79; auth, The Texas Paintings/Modernism: Forms and Concepts, Univ Tex Press (in prep). *Mailing Add:* 10 Leonard St New York NY 10013

GOLDBERG, ARNOLD HERBERT
PAINTER, PRINTMAKER
b Brooklyn, NY, May 16, 33. *Study:* Univ Wis, BS(appl arts), 55; Pratt Inst, BArch, 59; Univ Houston, painting, 70-72. *Exhib:* Twelfth Midwest Biennial, Joselyn Mus, Omaha, Nebr, 72; 17th Ann Delta Art Exhib, Ark Art Ctr, 74; 16th Ann Eight State Exhib, Okla Art Ctr, 74; 52nd State Exhib, Shreveport Art Guild, 74; Corpus Christi Art Found Ann Exhib, Art Mus STex, 75; Corpus Christi Art Found Ann Exhib, Art Mus STex, 77. *Awards:* Dimension VI Award, Art League Houston, 71; Eighth Jury Award Art Exhib, Jewish Community Ctr, Houston, 72; Corpus Christi Art Found Grant, Art Mus STex, 75 & 77. *Media:* Acrylic; Silkscreen. *Mailing Add:* 425 Whitewing Houston TX 77079

GOLDBERG, CHAIM
PAINTER, SCULPTOR
b Kazimierz, Poland, Mar 20, 17. *Study:* Art High Sch-Krakow, with Zbigniew Pronashko; Acad Fine Arts, Warsaw, with Tadeusz Pruszkowski; Govt Poland fel study in Paris, 47. *Work:* Mus Mod Art, Metrop Mus Art, New York; Nat Collection Fine Art, Washington, DC; Mus Petit Palais, Geneva, Switz; Mus Fine Art, Boston, Mass; and others. *Comn:* Monument, Polanica Zdroj, Govt Poland, 54; mosaic fountain, 56 & embossed copper door, 57, Hotel Ramat Aviv, Tel Aviv, Israel; engravings, Govt Israel, 59-64. *Exhib:* One-man shows, Mus Yad Labanim, Israel, 66, Lys Gallery, New York, 67, St John's Univ (NY), 71 & Randall Galleries, New York, 79; Smithsonian Inst, Washington, DC; and others. *Awards:* Silver Medal, Artists Guild-Novosibirsk, 44. *Bibliog:* I Luden (auth), articles, Art Mag, Israel, 66; D Shirey (auth), article, New York Times, 71; Paul Scott (auth), Chaim Goldberg--An artist reborn, Southwest Art Mag, 7-8/75; plus others. *Media:* Oil, Watercolor; Wood. *Mailing Add:* 11007 Crestmore Houston TX 77096

GOLDBERG, JUDITH
DEALER
b New York, NY, Feb 22, 47. *Study:* City Col New York, BA, 71. *Pos:* Owner, Judith Goldberg Gallery, currently. *Specialty:* 19th and 20th century prints & drawings. *Mailing Add:* 25 E 83rd St New York NY 10028

GOLDBERG, MICHAEL
PAINTER
b New York, NY, Dec 24, 24. *Study:* Art Students League, 38-42; City Col New York, 40-42; Hans Hofmann Sch Art, 41-42 & 48-50; Art Students League, with Jose de Creeft, 46; City Col New York, 46-47. *Work:* Baltimore Mus Art; Albright-Knox Gallery; Walker Art Ctr; Art Inst Chicago; Nat Gallery Art, Washington, DC. *Exhib:* Smithsonian Inst, 66; Mus Mod Art, New York, 68; Corcoran Bienale, 69; solo exhibs, Young-Hoffman Gallery, Chicago, 78, Loyse van Oppenheim Gallery, Geneva, 78, Daniel Weinberg Gallery, San Francisco, 78, Sonnabend Gallery, New York, 79 & Thomas Segal Gallery, Boston, 79. *Teaching:* Instr art, Univ Calif, Berkeley, 61-62; Yale Univ, 67; Univ Minn, 68. *Dealer:* Paley & Lowe Inc 59 Wooster St New York NY 10012. *Mailing Add:* 222 Bowery New York NY 10012

GOLDBERG, ROSELEE
HISTORIAN, CURATOR
Study: Rand Univ, BFA, 68; Courtauld Inst Art, London, with John Golding, MA(art hist), 70. *Collections Arranged:* Record as Artwork, Royal Col Art Gallery, 73; Piero Manzoni, Royal Col Art Gallery, 74; IMPORTS (int performance series), The Kitchen Ctr, 78 & 79. *Pos:* Dir, Royal Col Art Gallery, London, 72-75; cur, The Kitchen Ctr, New York, 78-80. *Teaching:* Lectr performance hist, Archit Asn London, 77-78; lectr performance hist, Sch Visual Arts, New York, 80- *Awards:* Publ Award, Arts Coun Great Brit, 75; Nat Endowment for Arts Art Critic's grant, 79. *Mem:* Int Asn Art Critics; Col Art Asn; Nat Union Journalists, United Kingdom. *Res:* Thesis on Oskar Schlemmer and performance at the Bauhaus; specialist in history of performance art and related contemporary media. *Publ:* Ed & contribr, special issue, Studio Int on Archit/Art, 75; ed & contribr, special issue, Performance Studio Int, 76; contribr, Oskar Schlemmer's performance art, Artforum, 77; auth, Performance: Live Art 1909 to the Present, Harry N Abrams, 79; contribr, Performance: a Hidden History, In: Battcock's Anthology/Dutton, 80. *Mailing Add:* 40 Renwick Street New York NY 10013

GOLDEEN, DOROTHY A
DEALER, CONSULTANT
b San Francisco, Calif, Nov 12, 48. *Study:* Univ Calif, Berkeley, BA. *Pos:* Assoc, Dancer-Fitzgerald-Sample, San Francisco, 72-73; dir, Hansen Fuller Gallery, 72-79; vpres, Hansen Fuller Goldeen Gallery, 79-82 & Fuller Goldeen Gallery, 82- *Teaching:* Instr, Contemp Art Gallery, Col Marin, 75. *Mem:* San Francisco Art Dealers Asn (prog dir assoc). *Specialty:* Contemporary painting and sculpture. *Publ:* Auth, Hot mama of the west, City Mag, 9/19/73; auth, Art criticism as fiction, Artweek, 11/23/74; California Gold (catalog essays), US Embassy, 75; Joan Brown (catalog essay), Univ Akron, Ohio, 78; American Eight (catalog essay), Interpace Corp, NJ, 80. *Mailing Add:* Fuller Goldeen Gallery 228 Grant Ave San Francisco CA 94108

GOLDEN, EUNICE
PAINTER, FILMMAKER
b New York, NY. *Study:* Univ Wis; Brooklyn Col, MFA; New Sch Social Res; Art Students League; Empire State Col, BFA. *Comn:* Portrait of Poet Leon Herald, comn by Leon Herald, 71; murals, Dept of Parks & Recreation, New York, Dept of Cult Affairs, New York & Bronx Mus of Art; Bronx Community Col. *Exhib:* 148th Nat Acad Design Ann, New York, 73; Soho 20 Gallery, New York, 73; Painting & Sculpture Today, Indianapolis Mus &

Taft Mus, Cincinnati, 74; Works on Paper, Brooklyn Mus, NY, 75; Nothing But Nudes, Downtown Whitney, 77; film exhib, Gemeente Mus, The Hague, Holland, 79; plus others. *Pos:* Dir, Walk-On Community Art Proj, Dobbs Ferry, NY, 68. *Teaching:* Lectr erotic art, New Sch Social Res, 73; instr mural painting, Guggenheim Mus Prog, New York, summer 75; instr painting, Pratt Inst, 80-81; artist in residence, Univ SDak, 76. *Awards:* Hudson River Mus Purchase Award, 63; One of Outstanding Women, NY State Women's Unit Exec Chamber, Albany, 68; MacDowell Colony Fel, 69 & 71. *Bibliog:* Lucy Lippard (auth), From the Center, Feminist Essays on Women's Art, Dutton, 76 & Art in Am, 11/81; Carter Ratcliff (auth), Art Int, 3/77; Lucy Lippard (auth), Overlay, Random House, 83. *Mem:* Fel MacDowell Colony; Col Art Asn Am; Women's Caucus Art. *Media:* Oil, Acrylic. *Publ:* Illusr, MS Mag, 75; illus, A New Eros, 75; auth, article, Art Workers News, New York, 76; coauth, article, An Anti-Catalog, 77; auth, The male nude in womens art, Heresies, spring 81; and others. *Mailing Add:* 463 West St Apt 332B New York NY 10014

GOLDEN, JUDITH
PHOTOGRAPHER
b Chicago, Ill, Nov 29, 34. *Study:* Art Inst Chicago, BFA, 73; Univ Calif, Davis, MFA(Regents Graduate Fel), 75. *Work:* San Francisco Mus Mod Art, Calif; Oakland Mus, Calif; Ctr Creative Photog, Tucson, Ariz; Fogg Mus, Cambridge, Mass; Mus Mod Art, New York. *Exhib:* One-women shows, Art Inst Chicago, 77 & San Francisco Mus Mod Art, Calif, 81; Contemp Photog, Fogg Mus, Cambridge, Mass, 77; Silver & Ink, Oakland Mus, Calif, 78; Attitudes--Photog in the 70's, Santa Barbara Mus Art, Calif, 79; Erweiterte Fotografe, Wiener Int Biennale, 81; Photographer as Printmaker, Arts Coun Great Britian, 81; Autoportraits Photographiques, Ctr Georges Pompidou, Paris, France, 81; Ctr Creative Photog, Tucson, Ariz, 83; and many others. *Pos:* Bd mem, Los Angeles Ctr Photographic Studies, Calif, 77-79; bd mem, Camera Work, San Francisco, Calif, 81. *Teaching:* Vis lectr photography, Univ Calif, Los Angeles, 75-79; vis lectr photography, Univ Calif, Davis, 80; assoc prof photography, Univ Ariz, Tucson, 81- *Awards:* Nat Endowment Arts Individual Photographers Fel, 79. *Bibliog:* Serious Masquerades, Time-Life Books, 78; Katzman (auth), Photo-Transforms, San Francisco Mus, 81; Connections: An Invitational Portfolio of Images and Statements by Twenty-Eight Women, Exposure, fall 81. *Mem:* Soc Photographic Educ; Womens Caucus Arts; Friends of Photog; Camera Work. *Media:* Mixed Media. *Dealer:* Quay Gallery San Francisco CA; G Ray Hawkins Gallery Los Angeles CA. *Mailing Add:* 400 W Simpson No C Tucson AZ 85701

GOLDEN, LIBBY
PRINTMAKER, PAINTER
b New York, NY. *Study:* Cooper Union Art Sch, dipl, 34; Hunter Col, NY Univ & Art Students League, 34-42; Pratt Graphic Arts Inst, 58-60. *Work:* Philadelphia Mus Art; Detroit Inst Arts; Grand Rapids Mus Art; Colby Col Mus Art, Mass; US State Dept. *Exhib:* Silvermine Guild, Conn, 66-68; Boston Printmakers, Boston Mus Fine Arts, Mass, 66-69; Northwest Printmakers, Seattle Mus Art & Portland Mus Art, 68 & 69; Colorprint, USA, Lubbock, Tex, 71; Retrospective Exhib, Scottsdale Center Arts, Ariz, 82; plus seven one-man shows. *Awards:* Print Prizes, Mich State Fair, 65-69 & Nat Acad Design, New York, 69; Purchase Prize, Mich Painters & Printmakers & Colorprint USA. *Mailing Add:* 7527 N Del Norte Dr Scottsdale AZ 85258

GOLDEN, ROLLAND HARVE
PAINTER, PRINTMAKER
b New Orleans, La, Nov 8, 31. *Study:* John McCrady Art Sch, study with John McCrady. *Work:* Miss Mus Art; Masur Mus; New Orleans Mus Art; Pushkin Mus, USSR; Int House, New Orleans. *Comn:* Fifty watercolors, La State Hwy Dept, Baton Rouge, 59-60; four watercolors, comn by Gov John McKeithen, La, 65. *Exhib:* Seven Am Watercolor Soc Exhibs, New York, 65-78; Watercolor USA, Springfield, 66-79; Butler Inst Am Art, Youngstown, Ohio, 67-78; Nat Arts Club, New York, 68 & 72-81; Nat Soc Painters in Casein & Acrylics, New York, 72-81; many one-man shows, USSR & the US. *Awards:* Paul Remney Mem Award, Am Watercolor Soc, 79; Nat Arts Club, New York, 79, 80 & 81; Zinn's Award, Audubon Artists, New York, 80. *Bibliog:* Don Lee Keith (auth), Golden boy of watercolor, Delta Rev Mag, 68 & World of Rolland Golden, Royal Publ Co, 70; Jim Keyser (auth), Rolland Golden's Southland, WDSU TV, 73. *Mem:* Nat Arts Club; Am Watercolor Soc; Nat Watercolor Soc; Nat Soc Painters Casein & Acrylics; Allied Artists Am. *Media:* Watercolor, Acrylic. *Publ:* Auth, Watercolor page, Am Artist Mag, 71; contribr, Transparent Watercolor-Ideas and Techniques, 73; Southwest Art Mag, 5/7 & Art Voices South, 3-4/79 & 7-8/79. *Mailing Add:* Rt 1 Box 293 G Folsom LA 70437

GOLDFIELD, EDWARD L
DEALER, COLLECTOR
b Philadelphia, Pa, Dec 3, 30. *Pos:* Pres, Goldfield Galleries, Ltd, currently. *Mem:* Art Dealers Asn Southern Calif. *Specialty:* 19th and early 20th century American impressionists, ash can, Western paintings and sculpture. *Publ:* Contribr, Impressionism--The California View, Oakland Mus, 81; contribr, The West as Art, Palm Springs Desert Mus, 82; contribr, California: The State of Landscape 1872-1981, Newport Harbor Art Mus & Santa Barbara Mus Art, 81; contribr, Plein Air Painters of California, The Southland, Westphal Publ, 82; contribr, Americans in Brittany & Normandy 1860-1910, Amon Carter Mus, Phoenix Art Mus & Nat Mus Am Art, 83. *Mailing Add:* 8400 Melrose Ave Los Angeles CA 90069

GOLDFINGER, ELIOT
SCULPTOR
b New York, NY, Aug 14, 50. *Study:* Pratt Inst, BFA, 74; Nat Acad Sch, New York, 77-78. *Work:* Mus Natural Hist; Paganini Mus, Genoa, Italy. *Comn:* Bust of Mayor John Lindsay, 78, Mayor Abe Beame, 79, Mayor Robert Wagner, 80 & Mayor Ed Koch, Mus City New York, 81; Bust Leonid Brezhnev, comn by Newsweek for cover, 4/12/82. *Exhib:* Ann Exhib, Allied Artists Am, New York, 78 & 80; Ann Exhib, Nat Acad Design, New York, 79; Mem Exhibs, Salmagundi Club, New York, 79-81; Ann Exhib, Nat Sculpture Soc, New York, 80-81. *Teaching:* Instr animal sculpture & anatomy, NY Acad Art, 83. *Awards:* Gloria Medal, Nat Sculpture Soc, 80; Elliot Liskin Prize, Salmagundi Club, 80; Dr H Debellis Prize, Salmagundi Club, 81. *Bibliog:* John David Klein, Apple Polishers (film), WOR-TV News, 81; Jackie Perelson (auth), Standard Star, New Rochelle, 80; Sculpture in the News, Nat Sculpture Review, 81. *Mem:* Nat Sculpture Soc; Allied Artists Am; Soc Artists & Anatomists (trustee, 82-83). *Media:* Plastillene, Bronze. *Mailing Add:* 370 Columbus Ave New York NY 10024

GOLDIN, LEON
PAINTER
b Chicago, Ill, Jan 16, 23. *Study:* Art Inst Chicago, BFA, 48; Univ Iowa, MFA, 50. *Work:* Brooklyn Mus, NY; Va Mus Fine Arts, Richmond; City Mus St Louis, Mo; Pa Acad Fine Arts, Philadelphia; Munson-Williams-Proctor Inst, Utica, NY. *Exhib:* American Painting at Mid-Century, Metrop Mus Art, New York, 51; American Drawings, Mus Mod Art, New York, 56; Corcoran Gallery Art Biennial, Washington, DC, 62; Carnegie Inst Int, Pittsburgh, Pa, 64; Pa Acad Fine Arts Ann, 66. *Teaching:* Instr painting & drawing, Calif Col Arts & Crafts, 50-55; instr painting & drawing, Cooper Union, 61-64; from assoc prof to prof painting, Columbia Univ, 64-, chmn dept, 73-75 & 77-80. *Awards:* Guggenheim Fel, 59; Award in Painting, Nat Inst Arts & Lett, 68; Nat Endowment Arts Grant, 80; and others. *Media:* Oil, Gouache. *Dealer:* Kraushaar Galleries 724 Fifth Ave New York NY 10019. *Mailing Add:* 438 W 116th St New York NY 10027

GOLDMAN, JUDITH
WRITER, CRITIC
b Chicago, Ill. *Study:* Bard Col, Annandale-on-Hudson, NY, printmaking with Louis Schanker, BA(Lit), 64; Inst Design Ill Inst Technol, printmaking with Misch Kohn, 64. *Pos:* Managing ed, Artist's Proof, Pratt Graphics, New York, 67-69; ed, Print Collector's Newslett, New York, 70-72; managing ed, Artnews, New York, 73-75; contrib ed, 75-; adv, Print Collection, Whitney Mus Am Art, 76- *Teaching:* Adj instr graphics, Hunter Col, New York, 74-75; asst prof criticism, Pratt Inst, 76-78. *Awards:* MacDowell Colony Fel Criticism, summer 76; Nat Endowment Arts Grant Criticism, 78. *Res:* Twentieth century graphics and photography. *Publ:* Auth, Windows at Tiffany: The Art of Gene Moore, 80 & James Rosenquist, 82, Abrams. *Mailing Add:* 525 West End Ave New York NY 10024

GOLDMAN, RACHEL BOK
COLLECTOR, PATRON
b Philadelphia, Pa, Mar 28, 37. *Study:* Univ Pa, BA(hist art). *Pos:* Co-chmn, Friends Philadelphia Mus Art, 82-83; exhib selection comt, Morris Gallery, Pa Acad Fine Arts, 79-82; co-founder & secy, Samuel Yellin Found. *Mem:* Friends Philadelphia Mus Art; Pa Acad Fine Arts; Inst Contemp Art; Philadelphia Col Art; Inst Contemp Art, Boston; and others. *Collection:* Primarily living Philadelphia painters and watercolorists. *Mailing Add:* 1213 Waverly Walkway Philadelphia PA 19147

GOLDRING, ELIZABETH
WRITER, ENVIRONMENTAL ARTIST
b Forest City, Iowa, Feb 13, 45. *Study:* Smith Col, BA, 67; Harvard Univ, MEd, 72. *Exhib:* Artransition (coordr), Mass Inst Technol, Cambridge, 75; Inst Contemp Art, Boston, 76; Centerbeam (coordr), Documenta 6, Kassel, Ger, 77 & Smithsonian Inst, DC, 78; 5 Artists/5 Technologies (doc), Grand Rapids Art Mus, Mich, 79; Int Biennial Exhib Graphic & Visual Art (doc), Secession, Vienna, Austria, 79. *Collections Arranged:* Ars Electronica, 80, Sky Art Conference, 81 & Trio (with Keiko Prince & Edward le Poulin), 83, Ctr Advan Visual Studies, Mass Inst Technol; and others. *Pos:* Elem educ specialist, Nat Collection Fine Arts, Smithsonian Inst, 71-72; exhib developer, Childrens Mus, Boston, 73-75; fel art & environ, Ctr Advan Visual Studies, Mass Inst Technol, 75-, exhib & proj dir, 78- *Res:* Sky Art. *Publ:* Contribr, You are Here (exhib catalog), Mass Inst Technol, 76; ed, CAVS Report on Elemental Sculpture in Public-Predominantly Urban-Places, Nat Endowment Arts & Ctr Advan Visual Studies, Mass Inst Technol, 78; contribr, International Biennial Exhibition of Graphics and Visual Arts, 79; auth, Sky Art-That Flies, Flying Colors, Braniff, 79; ed & contribr, Centerbeam, Ctr Advan Visual Studies, Mass Inst Technol, 80. *Mailing Add:* Ctr for Advan Visual Studies Mass Inst Technol 40 Massachusetts Ave Cambridge MA 02139

GOLDRING, NANCY DEBORAH
GRAPHIC ARTIST, EDUCATOR
b Oak Ridge, Tenn, Jan 25, 45. *Study:* Smith Col, BA(art hist); Univ Florence, with Nina Gregori (Fulbright Fel), 67-68; NY Univ, MFA(graphics, NDEA Fel & Grad Teaching Fel), 69-70. *Work:* Eastman Kodak Mus; Int Tel & Tel Corp, NJ; pvt collections. *Exhib:* Drawings with foto-projections, Carlsson Memorial Gallery, Univ Bridgeport, 79; Solo Exhibition, Herzliya Mus, 82; Arteder: Feria Int Muestras, Bilbao, Spain, 83; Miss Mus Art, Jackson, 83; Inside Spaces, Mus Mod Art, 83. *Collections Arranged:* Photographs, Mus of Natural Hist, Nat Park Serv, 73; Celebrations II (photographs), Mass Inst Technol, Cambridge, 76; one-person shows, Haverford Col, Pa, 76 &

Knowlton Gallery, New York, 77. *Pos:* Co-founding dir, SITE, New York, 69-72 & Chamber, New York, 76- *Teaching:* Prof drawing, Montclair State Col, NJ, 72-; vis prof contemp art, RI Sch of Design, Providence, 74-75; vis prof, Haverford Col, Pa, 78. *Awards:* Rockefeller Brothers Fund, 70-73; NY State Council on Arts, 70-73 & 77-79. *Bibliog:* Talia Rappaport (auth), Drawing & Photography, Pavar, 81; article, Artspeak, 11/81; film, On the Road in Mississippi, PBS, 83; and many others. *Media:* Pencil, Gouach. *Publ:* Auth, Grant's Tomb Mosaic Project, New York City Star, 73; auth, Rebirth of a Tomb, The Paper, 73; auth, A Monument for the Living, Art & Artists, 73; auth, Grant National Memorial: A Monument to the Living, Art News, 74; auth, Celebrations II, The Speaking Monument, Mass Inst of Technol, 76. *Mailing Add:* 463 West St H659 New York NY 10014

GOLDSCHMIDT, LUCIEN
DEALER
b Brussels, Belg, Mar 3, 12. *Pos:* Pres, Lucien Goldschmidt, Inc. *Mem:* Art Dealers Asn Am. *Specialty:* Continental European art, circa 1500-1950, mainly prints and drawings. *Publ:* Coauth, Unpublished Correspondence of Henri de Toulouse-Lautrec, 69 & The Truthful Lens, 80. *Mailing Add:* 1117 Madison Ave New York NY 10028

GOLDSLEGER, CHERYL
PAINTER, DRAFTSMAN
b Philadelphia, Pa, Dec 16, 51. *Study:* Tyler Sch Art, Rome, 71; Philadelphia Col Art, BFA, 73; Wash Univ, MFA, 75. *Work:* Miss Mus Art, Jackson; Progressive Corp, Cleveland; Chase Manhattan Bank, Equitable Life Assurance Co, New York; State Ga, Atlanta. *Exhib:* Works on Paper, Dayton Art Inst, 80; Members Gallery Exhib, Albright-Knox Gallery, 81; Ohio Selections, New Gallery Contemp Art, Cleveland, 82; solo exhib, Miss Mus Art, Jackson, 83; Connections, Inst Contemp Art, Philadelphia, 83; Habitats, Wright Mus, Beloit, Wis, 84. *Teaching:* Asst prof painting, Western Carolina Univ, 75-77; instr art, Univ Ga, Athens, 78-; lectr drawing, Ga Southern Col, 81. *Awards:* Grants, Pa Coun Arts, 81, Ohio Arts Coun, 82 & Nat Endowment Arts, 82. *Bibliog:* Valerie McKenzie (auth), article, Atlanta Art Papers, 1/81; Gerrit Henry (auth), article, Art News, 2/82; Donal La Badie (auth), Artists merit corner, Memphis Commercial Appeal, 2/7/83. *Mem:* Col Art Asn; Southeastern Col Art Asn. *Media:* Oil. *Dealer:* Bertha Urdang Gallery 23 E 74th St New York NY 10021. *Mailing Add:* 170 Greenwood Dr Athens GA 30606

GOLDSMITH, BARBARA
WRITER, CRITIC
b New York, NY, May 18, 31. *Study:* Wellesley Col, BA, 53; Columbia Univ, MA, 55; Pace Univ, Hon DLit, 81; Syracuse Univ, Hon DLett, 81. *Pos:* Ed, Town & Country Mag & New York Mag, 66-71; sr ed, Harper's Bazaar, 70-74. *Awards:* Penny-Mo Award, 70; Trust Award, Brandeis Univ Libr, 80. *Mem:* Whitney Mus Am Art; Mus Mod Art, New York; Mus City New York (pres coun, 70-); Parks Coun City New York. *Publ:* Auth, articles, New York Mag, Esquire & Harpers Bazaar; auth, The Straw Man, 75; auth, Little Gloria, Happy at Last, 80. *Mailing Add:* c/o Lynn Nesbit ICM 40 W 57th St New York NY 10019

GOLDSMITH, BENEDICT ISAAC
GALLERY DIRECTOR, EDUCATOR
b New York, NY, Aug 1, 16. *Study:* NY Univ, BS, 40; Art Students League & Woodstock, NY, with Arnold Blanch; Teachers Col, Columbia Univ, MA, 50; Inst Del'Arte, Florence, Italy, 64. *Collections Arranged:* Potsdam Prints (with catalog), 63-74; Robert Mallary, 68; Sculpture, NY Six, 69; New Realism, 71; Women in Art, 72, New Realism, Revisited, 74; Potsdam Plastics, 75; African Sculpture Selections, Anspach Collection, 75; Maine Coast Artists Open, 79; Artists as Teachers, 79; Associates Selects, 79; Off the Wall, 80; & Painters, 80; Richard Derby Tucker Mem Retrospective, 80. *Pos:* Gallery dir, State Univ NY Col Potsdam, 65-78; exhib dir, Maine Coast Artists, 79 & 81- *Teaching:* Prof art, State Univ NY Col Potsdam, 50-78. *Mem:* Gallery Asn NY (exec comt); Asn Exhib & Gallery Dirs, NY (pres, 68-69). *Mailing Add:* Box 162 Camden ME 04843

GOLDSMITH, ELSA M
PAINTER
b New York, NY, Jan 26, 20. *Study:* Parsons Sch Fine & Appl Art, scholar award, BA; NY Univ; Pratt Graphic Ctr, (lithography); etching with Ruth Leaf; painting with Betty Holiday. *Exhib:* Am Drawing Biennial, Norfolk Mus, Va, 71; Palazzo Vechio, Florence, Italy, 72; Brooklyn Mus, NY, 75; M J Greene Gallery, Bridgehampton, New York, 81; Cayuga Mus, NY, 83; Syosset Libr, NY, 83; and others. *Pos:* Advert artist, Newsweek Mag, New York, 40-41; indust designer, Belle Kogan Assoc, New York, 41-48; freelance artist, Book & Magazine Illustrating, New York, 42- *Teaching:* Teacher, Elsa Goldsmith's Studio, 50-74 & North Shore Commun Ctr, 71-73; Great Neck, NY; teacher painting, Adult Educ, Sewanhake High Sch, Floral Manor, NY, 72-74. *Awards:* Int Goldmedal of Honor, Cannes, 69; Susan Kahn Award, Nat Asn Women Artists, New York, 74; Doris Krindel Award, 80; and others. *Mem:* Nat Asn Women Artists; Nat Art Asn; Women in the Arts, Inc (bd mem & bicentennial chmn, 74-76); North Shore Community Art Ctr (bd dir & art coordr, 73-, vpres, 76-77); UN Int Womens Year Arts Festival (bd mem, 75-76). *Mailing Add:* 52 Ruxton Rd Great Neck NY 11023

GOLDSMITH, LAWRENCE CHARLES
PAINTER, INSTRUCTOR
b New York, NY, Nov 22, 16. *Study:* Yale Univ Sch Fine Arts; Brooklyn Mus Art Sch, with Reuben Tam; Art Students League. *Work:* Lamont Gallery, Phillips Exeter Acad, NH; Univ Maine, Orono. *Exhib:* One-man shows,

Watercolors, Lamont Gallery, Phillips Exeter Acad, NH, 72 & Univ Maine, Orono, 80; San Diego Watercolor Soc Gallery, Calif, 79; Watercolors, Fresno Arts Ctr, Calif, 80; Georgia Watercolor Soc, 81; and others. *Teaching:* Guest instr watercolor, Art Students League, 65-69; lectr art, Queens Col, New York, 68-70; instr painting, Univ Vt Continuing Educ, 77- *Awards:* Winsor & Newton Award, 69. *Bibliog:* Susan E Meyer (auth), 40 Watercolorists and How They Work, Watson-Guptill Publ, 76; Edward Betts (auth), Creative Seascape Painting, Watson-Guptill, 81. *Mem:* Am Watercolor Soc; Artists Equity; Nat Arts Club. *Media:* Landscape in Oils and Watercolor. *Publ:* Auth, Watercolor page, American Artist, 75 & auth, Watercolor Bold and Free, 80, Watson-Guptill Publ. *Dealer:* Four Winds Gallery Ferrisburg VT 05456; Passepartout Gallery Winooski VT 05404. *Mailing Add:* RD 2 Fairfax VT 05454

GOLD STAR (WILLIAM MYERS WATKINS III)
CURATOR, PAINTER
b Memphis, Tenn, Aug 19, 47. *Study:* Univ Miss, summer 65; Delta State Univ, BSE(art), 69; Northeast La Univ, MA(painting & drawing), 71. *Work:* Miss Mus Art, Jackson & Meridian Mus Art, Meridian. *Exhib:* First Ann Fine Arts Competition, NY Univ, Buffalo, 69; 8th Ann Monroe Nat, Masur Mus, La, 71; Appalachian Nat Drawing Competition, Boone, NC, 76; Meridian Mus Art, Miss, 77; First Miss Competitive, Miss Mus Art, Jackson, 78; and others. *Collections Arranged:* Ann Bi-States, Meridian Mus, 73-79. *Pos:* Dir, Meridian Mus Art, 72-79; supervisor exhibs, Miss Mus Art, Jackson, 81- *Teaching:* Instr drawing, Masur Mus Art, Monroe, La, 70-71; instr drawing, Northeastern La Univ, Monroe, 70-71; instr painting, Meridian Jr Col, 74-79. *Awards:* Second Place, Appalachian Nat, Boone, NC, 76. *Bibliog:* David Nester (auth), Works by W Watkins, Meridian Mus, 79. *Collection:* Mississippi artists. *Publ:* Auth, Found object imagery, Thesis, 71. *Dealer:* Myles Frank Southern Exposure Meridian MS 39301. *Mailing Add:* 963 Bellevue Pl B Jackson MS 39205

GOLDSTEIN, CARL
EDUCATOR, SCULPTOR
b New York, NY, June 24, 38. *Study:* Brooklyn Col, BA, 60; Columbia Univ, MA, 62, PhD, 66. *Exhib:* Brooklyn Artists, Brooklyn Mus, 56; NC Sculpture, Weatherspoon Gallery, Greensboro, 79; Custom & Culture II, Custom House, New York, 79; NC Sculpture Invitational, Green Hill Gallery, Greensboro, 80; one-man show, Durham Art Guild, NC, 80. *Teaching:* Instr art hist, Wheaton Col, Norton, Mass, 66; asst prof, Brown Univ, 66-71; prof, Univ NC, Greensboro, 71- *Bibliog:* W Zimmer (auth), articles, Arts Mag, 1/77 & 5/77. *Mem:* Col Art Asn Am. *Media:* Wood. *Res:* Baroque art; twentieth century sculpture; history of academies of art. *Publ:* Auth, Studies in seventeenth century French art theory and ceiling painting, Art Bulletin, 65; auth, Observations on the role of Rome..., Art Quart, 70; auth, The erotic Baroque of Lachaise, Art Int, 74; auth, Towards a definition of academic art, Art Bulletin, 75; auth, Notes on realist sculpture, Arts Mag, 83. *Mailing Add:* 426 N Cedar St Greensboro NC 27401

GOLDSTEIN, DANIEL JOSHUA
PRINTMAKER, SCULPTOR
b Mt Vernon, NY, June 19, 50. *Study:* Brandeis Univ; Univ Calif, Santa Cruz, BA; St Martin's Col, London, Eng, post-grad study. *Work:* Brooklyn Mus, NY; Chicago Art Inst; Achenbach Found, San Francisco, Calif; Oakland Mus of Art, Calif; Carnegie Inst; and others. *Exhib:* Achenbach Found, 72; Prints Calif, Oakland Mus Art, 75; Nat Print Exhib, Brooklyn Mus, NY, 76 & 80; one-man shows, Getler-Pall Gallery, New York, 77, ADI Gallery, San Francisco, 77 & Brooklyn Mus, 83; New Talent in Printmaking, AAA Gallery, New York, 77; Calif Palace Legion Honor, San Francisco; 12th Nat Print Exhib, Silvermine Guild Artists, New Canaan, Conn, 78; RI Sch Design Mus, 79. *Dealer:* Fischbach Gallery 29 W 57th St New York NY 10019. *Mailing Add:* 224 Guerrero San Francisco CA 94103

GOLDSTEIN, GLADYS HACK
PAINTER
b Newark, Ohio. *Study:* Md Inst Art; Art Students League; Columbia Univ, New York; Pa State Univ, University Park; study with Hobson Pittman. *Work:* Baltimore Mus Art, Md; Pa State Univ; Univ Ariz; Goucher Col, Baltimore; Univ Md; and others. *Exhib:* One-man shows, Baltimore Mus Art, Goucher Col, Duveen-Graham Gallery, New York, Galerie Philadelphie, Paris, IFA Gallery, Washington, DC, Western Md Col, Newark Gallery, Del, Richter Gallery, Weisbaden, Ger, 65-75. *Pos:* Co-chmn art festival, City Baltimore, 71-74; art comt, Mayor's Ball, 73-74; exec comt, Mayor's Adv Comt for Arts & Cult, 74- *Teaching:* Instr painting, Md Inst Col Art, 60-65; instr art, Col Notre Dame, Md, 65- *Awards:* Third Award, Md Art Today, H K & Co, 72; First Award, 25th Ann of Israel, JCC, 74; Awards, Baltimore Mus Art & Pa State Univ. *Media:* Mixed Media, Oils. *Dealer:* IFA Gallery 2623 Connecticut Ave NW Washington DC 20008. *Mailing Add:* 2002 South Rd Baltimore MD 21209

GOLDSTEIN, HOWARD
PAINTER, EDUCATOR
b New York, NY, Feb 10, 33. *Study:* Albright Art Sch, cert; State Univ NY, Col Buffalo, BS; NY Univ, MA; Columbia Univ, EdD. *Work:* NJ State Mus, Trenton; Morris Mus Arts & Sci, Morristown, NJ; YMCA, New York; Univ Frankfurt, WGer; Imperial Chem Industs, US, Wilmington, Del. *Exhib:* 154th Ann Nat Exhib, Pa Acad Fine Arts, Philadelphia, 59 & 65; Ann NJ State Exhib, Newark Mus, 61, 64, 66, 68 & 77; Art from NJ, NJ State Mus, Trenton, 66-73; 32nd Ann Nat Painting Exhib, Butler Inst Am Art, Youngstown, Ohio, 67; Nat Show, Chautauqua Exhib Am Art, NY, 68 & 69; Ann New Eng Exhib, Silvermine Guild Artists, New Canaan, Conn, 70, 72

& 73; one-person exhib, Westbroadway Gallery, New York, 73, 74, 76, 77, & 79; Summer Art Ctr, NJ, 81 & 83. *Collections Arranged:* Geometric Art: An Exhib of Paintings & Constructions by 14 Contemp NJ Artists, NJ State Mus, 67; Westbroadway Gallery Group, Rundetarn Mus, Copenhagen, Denmark, 73; one-man exhib, NJ State Mus, 74; Viewpoint 76, Morris Mus Arts & Sci, Morristown, NJ, 76. *Teaching:* Prof painting, Trenton State Col, NJ, 60-, chmn art dept, 80- *Awards:* Emily Lowe Award, Emily Lowe Found Competition, 60; Videorecord Corp Am Award, 23rd New Eng Exhib, 72; Purchase Award, Art from NJ, State of NJ, 73. *Media:* Acrylic. *Dealer:* Westbroadway Gallery 431 W Broadway New York NY 10012. *Mailing Add:* 49 Rockleigh Dr Trenton NJ 08628

GOLDSTEIN, JACK
FILMMAKER, CONCEPTUAL ARTIST
b Montreal, Que, Sept 27, 45. *Study:* Chouinard Art Sch, Los Angeles, BFA, 70; Calif Inst of the Arts, MFA, 72. *Work:* Mus of Mod Art, Geneva, Switz. *Exhib:* Twenty-four Young Los Angeles Artists, Los Angeles Co Mus of Art, Calif, 70; one-man shows, Nigel Greenwood Gallery, London, England, 71, Francoise Lambert Gallery, Milan, Italy, 74, Kabinette für Aktuelle Kunst Bremerhaven, Ger, 76, Centre d'Art Contemporain, Cite Univ, Geneva, Switz, 77 & The Kitchen Ctr for Video & Music, New York, NY, 78. *Awards:* Can Coun Arts grant, 73-74; production grant, NY State Coun on the Arts, 77; Nat Endowment for the Arts Fel, 79-80. *Bibliog:* Germano Celant (auth), The Record as Artwork, Rome, Italy, 77; Morgan Fisher (interviewer), Talking with Jack Goldstein, Los Angeles Inst of Contemp Art J, 77; Douglas Crimp (auth), About pictures, Flash Art, Milan, Italy, 3-4/79. *Mailing Add:* 45 York St Fifth Floor Brooklyn NY 11201

GOLDSTEIN, JULIUS
PAINTER, INSTRUCTOR
b New York, NY, Mar 17, 18. *Study:* Brooklyn Mus Art Sch, with Rufino Tamayo & John Ferren, 46-47; Art Students League; travel & study in Europe, 48, 54, 66 & 67; England, 75. *Exhib:* Speed Art Mus Ann, Louisville, Ky, 57; Brooklyn Mus Int Watercolor Show, 61 & 63; Butler Inst Am Art Ann, Youngstown, Ohio, 66; Nat Inst Arts & Lett Contemp Painting & Sculpture, 70; Childe Hassam Fund Exhib, Am Acad Arts & Lett, 70; one-man exhib, Christ Hosp Col Art Ctr, Horsham, Sussex, Eng, 80. *Teaching:* From asst prof drawing & painting to assoc prof art, Hunter Col, 51- *Awards:* Yaddo Found Fel, Saratoga Springs, NY, 64-66. *Media:* Oil, Watercolor. *Dealer:* Babcock Galleries 805 Madison Ave New York NY 10021. *Mailing Add:* 26 W Tenth St New York NY 10011

GOLDSTEIN, MILTON
PRINTMAKER, EDUCATOR
b Holyoke, Mass, Nov 14, 14. *Study:* Art Students League, 46-49; also with Harry Sternberg, Morris Kantor & Will Barnet; Guggenheim Fel, 50. *Work:* Philadelphia Mus Art; Metrop Mus Art, New York; Mus Mod Art, New York; Smithsonian Nat Mus, Washington, DC; Brooklyn Mus, NY. *Comn:* Collection of etchings for Europe & US (200 ed), Int Graphic Arts Soc, New York, 52; collection of etchings (150 ed), 54. *Exhib:* Libr Cong, Washington, DC, 48; Smithsonian Inst, Washington, DC, 55; Outstanding Prints Produced in America, Brooks Mem Mus, Memphis, Tenn, 59; Am Printmakers in Italy, sponsored by Boston Pub Libr, 60; Masters Engraving Show, Queens Col, New York, 64; 30 Yrs of Am Printmaking, Brooklyn Mus, 77. *Teaching:* Prof printmaking, Adelphi Univ, 53- *Awards:* First Prize & Purchase Award, Philadelphia Mus, 52; First Prize & Purchase Award, Nat Print Show, Western NMex Univ, 71. *Bibliog:* Carl Zigrosser (auth), Fine Prints, Crown, 60; Jules Heller (auth), Printmaking Today, Holt, 60. *Mem:* Soc Am Graphic Artists (coun, 72); fel Royal Soc Arts, London; Am Color Print Soc; Kappa Pi; Print Club. *Publ:* Auth, How to Make an Etching (film), Almanac Films, 51; auth, A new color etching process, Everyday Art; auth, Reprint, Design Mag, 55. *Mailing Add:* 56-16 219th St Bayside NY 11364

GOLDSTEIN, NATHAN
WRITER, PAINTER
b Chicago, Ill, Mar 26, 27. *Study:* Art Inst of Chicago, BFA, MFA, with Louis Ritman; Art Students League, with Julian Levi. *Pos:* Chmn, Found Prog of Study, Art Inst of Boston, 73- *Bibliog:* Gerald Monroe (auth), Technical drawing: The personal approach of Nathan Goldstein, Drawing, 5-6/80 & Am Artist, 2/82. *Media:* Oil, Pen and Ink. *Publ:* Auth, The Art of Responsive Drawing, 73, 2nd ed, 77, 3rd ed, 83, Figure Drawing: The Structure, Anatomy and Expressive Design of Human Form, 76 & 81, Painting: Perceptual and Technical Fundamentals, 79, 100 American and European Drawings: A Portfolio, 82 & A Drawing Handbook, Themes, Tools, and Techniques, in prep, Prentice-Hall. *Mailing Add:* 99 Pond Ave Apt D514 Brookline MA 02146

GOLDSZER, BATH-SHEBA
PAINTER, GRAPHIC ARTIST
b Warsaw, Poland, Jan 26, 32; US citizen. *Study:* Hertzeliah Teachers Sem, BA(educ), 56; Art Students League, with Gustav Rehberger; also with Joe Hing Lowe & Ludmila Morosova. *Work:* Many pvt collections, US, Israel, Poland & Argentina. *Exhib:* Hudson Valley Art Asn, Westchester Co Ctr, 73-81; Catharine Lorillard Wolfe Arts Club, Nat Arts Club Gallery, 73-81; Nat Art League, Union Carbide Gallery 73 & Douglaston Gallery, 74-81; Chung-Cheng Art Gallery, Sun Yat Sen Hall, St John Univ, 78 & 79; plus others. *Awards:* First Prize in Oil, Nat Art League, 74 & 82, Queensboro Soc Arts, 74-77 & Art League Nassau Co, 78 & 79; and numerous others. *Bibliog:* Jack Besterman (auth), Big Six Art League, Chapel & Pension News, 2/72, An accomplished artist, 2/73 & Coop art scene, 4/74 & 5/79, Towers Reporter. *Mem:* Life fel Am Artists Prof League; Hudson Valley Art Asn; Catharine Lorillard Wolfe Arts Club; Nat Art League; Art League Nassau Co; and others. *Media:* Multimedia. *Mailing Add:* 46-10 61st St Apt 2H Woodside NY 11377

GOLUB, LEON ALBERT
PAINTER
b Chicago, Ill, Jan 23, 22. *Study:* Univ Chicago, BA(hist art), 42; Art Inst Chicago Sch, BFA, 49, MFA, 50. *Work:* Mus Mod Art, New York; Art Inst Chicago; Nat Collection Fine Arts, Smithsonian Inst; Mus Contemp Art, Chicago; Nat Gallery Victoria, Melbourne; and others. *Exhib:* One-man shows, Hayden Gallery, Mass Inst Technol, 70, San Francisco Art Inst, 76, State Univ NY Col, Stony Brook, 78; New Images of Man, Mus Mod Art, New York, 59; Sao Paulo Biennial, 62; 2nd Biennial Int Deporte Bellas Artes, Madrid, Spain, 69; Chicago Imagist Art, Mus Contemp Art, 72; Paris-New York, Centre Beaubourg, Paris, 77; plus many others. *Teaching:* Prof art, Mason Gross Sch Arts, Rutgers Univ, 70- *Awards:* Ford Found Grant, 60; Cassandra Found Grant, 67; Guggenheim Found Grant, 68. *Bibliog:* Franz Schulze (auth), Fantastic Images: Chicago Art since 1945, Follett, 72; Lawrence Alloway (auth), Leon Golub: art & politics, Artforum, 11/74; Donald Kuspit (auth), Leon Golub's murals of mercenaries: aggression, resentment and the artists will to power, Artforum, 5/81; plus others. *Media:* Acrylic. *Publ:* Auth, Bombs & helicopters, the art of Nancy Spero, Caterpillar I, 67; auth, Utopia/antiutopia, Art Criticism, 5/72; auth, 2D/3D, Art Forum, 3/73; auth, What works, Art Criticism, 2/79. *Mailing Add:* 530 La Guardia Pl New York NY 10012

GOLUBIC, THEODORE
SCULPTOR, DESIGNER
b Lorain, Ohio, Dec 9, 28. *Study:* Miami Univ, BFA; Art Students League, with Jon Corbino; Univ Notre Dame, asst to Ivan Mestrovic, MFA. *Comn:* Oracle Amanita (light-shadow work), comn by Vincent Mejer, South Bend, Ind, 60; Crypt Relief Series, Rock of Ages Corp, Barre, Vt, 65-67; Equinoctial Point (4-dimensional, sun/spectral), comn by Diane Dudley, Litchfield, Ill, 67; Nativity (limestone heroic relief), Cathedral Church of Nativity, Dubuque, Iowa, 68; Spectra-Cube (sun/time environ), comn by Josephine Davis, Escondido, Calif, 83. *Exhib:* Art USA, Madison Sq Garden, New York, 58; 134th Ann Exhib, Nat Acad Design, New York, 59; 2nd Biennial Am Painting & Sculpture, Detroit Inst Arts, 60; 155th Ann Exhibit, Pa Acad Fine Arts, Philadelphia, 61; 13th Ann Drawing & Small Sculpture Show, Ball State Univ, Muncie, Ind, 63; 34th Ann Exhib, Nat Sculpture Soc, New York, 67; Art for 1970, Southern Calif Expo, Del Mar, 70; one-man show, Roswell Mus in conjunction with Sunspot Observatory, NMex, 72. *Pos:* Sculpture consult, Rock of Ages Corp, 65-67; artist in residence, Roswell Mus & Art Ctr, NMex, 71-72. *Teaching:* Guest instr sculpture, Univ Notre Dame, summer 59; guest instr, Art Sch Air, Educ TV & ABC-TV, Elkhart, Ind, 62-63; invited artist/lectr, 28th Ann Conf Workshop, Am Soc Aesthetics, 70. *Bibliog:* Hatch (auth), article, West Art, 11/70; article, Roswell Mus & Art Ctr Bulletin, fall 71 & spring 72; Community Arts Program, US Dept Housing & Urban Develop, 73. *Mem:* Int Sculpture Ctr; Artists Equity Asn. *Media:* All; Sun-Time, Diffractives. *Publ:* Guest ed, 3/67, contribr cover & auth, In art there is victory, 4/67, Am Art Stone. *Mailing Add:* 3321 W Orchid Lane Phoenix AZ 85021

GOLUBOV, MAURICE
PAINTER
b Ukraine, Russia, May 25, 05; US citizen. *Study:* Nat Acad Design Art Sch, 21-24. *Work:* Metrop Mus Art, New York; Mint Mus, NC; Birla Acad, Calcutta, India; Mus Mod Art, New York; Mus Fine Arts, Houston. *Exhib:* One-man shows, Mint Mus, NC, 43 & 51 & Tibor de Nagy Gallery, NY, 76, 79 & 81; 50 Yrs of Abstract Paintings & Sculpture in Am, Mus Mod Art, New York, 51 & 62; The Non-Objective World--25 Yrs 1914-1939, Annely Juda Fine Arts, London, 78; Geometric Abstractions & Related Works, Newark Mus, 79; retrospective 1925-1980, Mint Mus, traveling, 80-81. *Bibliog:* John Ashbery (auth), From Russia with Golubov, New York Mag, 5/14/79; Vivien Raynor (auth), Art: Maurice Golubov, New York Times, 7/24/81. *Media:* Oil, Watercolor. *Dealer:* Tibor de Nagy Gallery 29 West 57th St New York NY 10019. *Mailing Add:* 1100 S Hillcrest Apt 309 Hollywood FL 33021

GOMEZ-QUIROZ, JUAN MANUEL
PAINTER, PRINTMAKER
b Santiago, Chile, Feb 20, 39; US citizen. *Study:* RI Sch Design, Fulbright Fel, 62-63; Yale Univ, Fulbright Fel, 63-64; invited by Gabor Peterdi; Pratt Graphic Art Ctr, Pan Am Union Fel, 64-66. *Work:* Guggenheim Mus; Metrop Mus Art, New York; Mass Inst Technol; Boston Mus Fine Arts; Mus Mod Art, New York; plus many others. *Exhib:* Int Print Exhib, Montreal Mus Fine Art, 71; Int Drawing Show, Bronx Mus, New York, 77; one-man shows, Schubert Gallery, Marbella, Spain, 77, Kornblee Gallery, New York, 78 & Sutton Gallery, New York, 80; DeArmas Gallery, Miami, Fla, 80; and many other one-man and group exhibs. *Teaching:* Lectr studio art, Univ Calif, Santa Barbara, 67-68; adj prof studio art, NY Univ, 69-; lectr, Summit Art Ctr, Summit, NJ, 72-77. *Awards:* Nat Endowment Arts Grant, 74; Grand Prize, IV Biennial Printmaking, San Juan, PR, 79; Prize Bienal Maracaibo Venezuela, 82. *Bibliog:* Gabor Peterdi (auth), Printmaking, Macmillan, rev ed 71; Gordon Brown (auth), article in Arts Mag, 4/71; David Shirley (auth), article in NY Sunday Times, 78. *Media:* Oil, Acrylic; Intaglio. *Mailing Add:* 44 Grand St New York NY 10013

GOMEZ-SICRE, JOSE
ADMINISTRATOR, CRITIC
b Matanzas, Cuba, 1916. *Study:* Univ Havana, dipl law, 40 & 41; Columbia Univ, 44; NY Univ, 44. *Collections Arranged:* Permanent Collection of Latin Am Contemp Art & Exhib Prog, Orgn Am States, 46-; assisted or directed assembling of collections for numerous mus & corp, incl Esso Standard Oil Collection, now property of Lowe Mus Art, Miami Univ. *Pos:* Art critic, El Mundo, Norte, Havana & New York, 42-50; organized exhibs Cuban art for

mus abroad & assisted in direction foreign & nat exhibs, Havana, 42-45; dir, Mus Mod Art Latin Am, Washington, DC, 46- *Teaching:* Lectr art hist & Latin Am art, cols, univs & mus throughout US, Latin Am & Europe, 50- *Res:* Contemporary Latin American art. *Publ:* Auth, Four Artists of the Americas, 57; auth, Cuevas, Art Int, 11/71; auth, Leonardo Nierman, Mexico, 73; auth, The true El Dorado: Colombian gold, Connoisseur, 5/75; auth, Torres-Garcia y la America arcaica, Mundo Hispanico, Madrid, 5/75; and others. *Mailing Add:* c/o Mus Mod Art Latin America 201 18th St NW Washington DC 20006

GONGORA, LEONEL
PAINTER, EDUCATOR
b Cartago, Colombia. *Study:* Wash Univ. *Work:* Pub Libr, Mus Mod Art, New York; Wash Univ Permanent Collection, St Louis, Mo; Staatsgalerie Mus, Stuttgart, Ger; Mus Mod Art, Bogota, Colombia. *Comn:* Paintings, comn by Fernando Gamboa for Mex Pavilion, Expo 67, Montreal, PQ & Expo 70, Osaka, Japan; lithographs, Lublin, Inc, New York, 69, Bank St Atelier, New York, 70 & Aquarius Press, New York, 71. *Exhib:* Confrontacion 66, Mus Bellas Artes, Mexico City, 66; Am Acad Arts & Lett, New York, 69; 1st Pan-Am Graphics Biennial, Mus Latertulia, Cali, Colombia, 71; 4th Int Miniature Print Exhib, AAA Gallery, New York, 71; 3rd Brit Int Print Biennale, Bradform Mus, Eng, 72. *Teaching:* Instr painting & drawing, People's Art Ctr, St Louis, Mo, 56-59; prof painting & drawing, Iberoamericano Univ, Mex, 60-61; prof painting & drawing, Univ Mass, Amherst, 63-74. *Awards:* First Prize in Drawing, Nat Mus, Bogota, 64; Nat Acad Arts & Lett Award in Painting, New York, 68; Tenth Nat Arte Prize in Lithography, Mus Latertulia, 70. *Bibliog:* Toby Joysmith (auth), Two painter poets, The News, Mexico City, 8/69; Roberto Paramo (auth), Gongora, el erotismo en persona, El, Mexico City, 10/71; Anna Mayo (auth), Never on Good Friday, Village Voice, New York, 11/71. *Publ:* Illusr, Mass Rev, 67; illusr, Minn Rev, 69; illusr, The intricate land, New Rivers Press, 70; illusr, Poemas podridos, Villa Miseria Press, 72; contribr, Requirements of yesterday and today, Spectrum, 72. *Mailing Add:* 122 Spring New York NY 10012

GONZALES, BOYER
PAINTER, EDUCATOR
b Galveston, Tex, Feb 11, 09. *Study:* Univ Va, BS(archit); studied with Henry Lee McFee, Charles Rosen, Eugene Speicher & Yasuo Kuniyoshi. *Work:* Rochester Mem Gallery, NY; San Antonio Mus; Dallas Mus Fine Arts; Seattle Art Mus; Texas Fine Arts Assoc; and others. *Exhib:* New York World's Fair, 39; Pa Acad Fine Arts Ann, 52; Corcoran Gallery Art Biennial, 52; Pac Coast Invitational, 62-63; Artists West of the Mississippi, Colorado Springs Fine Arts Ctr, Colo, 65; Retrospectives, Whatcom Mus, Bellingham, Wash, 78, Henry Art Gallery, Univ Wash, Seattle, 79 & Rosenberg Libr, Galveston, 81. *Pos:* Dir, Nat Asn Schs Art, 60-62, vpres, 62-63. *Teaching:* Instr painting, Univ Tex, Austin, 39-42, from asst to assoc prof painting, 46-54, chmn dept art, 46-48; prof painting, Univ Wash, 54-79, dir, Sch Art, 54-66, emer prof, 79- *Awards:* Northwest Ann Exhib Painting, Seattle Art Mus, 56; Governor's Award of Special Commendation, State of Wash, 75; Honors Award, King Co Wash Arts Comm, 80. *Media:* Oil. *Mailing Add:* 6525 51st Ave NE Seattle WA 98115

GONZALES, CARLOTTA (MRS RICHARD LAHEY)
PAINTER, SCULPTOR
b Wilmington, NC, Apr 3, 10. *Study:* Pa Acad Fine Arts; Nat Acad Design; Art Students League; Corcoran Sch Art; Ogunquit Sch Art. *Work:* Am Battle Monuments Mem, Honolulu; Francis Bangs Collection, Ogunquit Mus Art, Maine; Print Collection, Corcoran Gallery Art, Washington, DC; and others. *Comn:* The Heavens Above (star charts), 41, state seals, 45 & flags of America, 47, Nat Geographic Soc, Washington, DC; mural (battle maps), Am Battle Monuments Comns, 60; and others. *Exhib:* Nat Acad Design, New York, 30; Corcoran Gallery Art Biennial, Washington, DC, 36-38; Goucher Col, Towson, Md, 43; Montclair Art Mus, NJ, 46; Baltimore Mus, Md, 56. *Pos:* Staff artist, Nat Geographic Soc, 41-47. *Teaching:* Instr sculpture, Goucher Col, 35-37, Corcoran Sch Art, 35-45; instr pvt classes, 55-71. *Awards:* Sculpture, Nat Acad Design, 30. *Mem:* Ogunquit Mus Art. *Media:* Oil, Stone. *Publ:* Coauth, Life of Rembrandt & Life of Picasso, Stravon. *Mailing Add:* 9530 Clark Crossing Rd Vienna VA 22180

GONZALEZ, JOSE GAMALIEL
ADMINISTRATOR, DESIGNER
b Iturbide, Nuevo Leon, Mex, Apr 20, 33. *Study:* Chicago Acad Fine Arts; Univ Chicago; Am Acad Art, Chicago, dipl; Art Inst Chicago, BFA; Instituto Allende, San Miguel, Mex, study with Jaime Pinto; Univ Notre Dame, MFA candidate. *Collections Arranged:* Hispanic Festival of the Arts, Mus Sci & Indust, Chicago, 74-78; Mexposicion I-25 Paintings from Bellas Artes in Mexico, 76 & Mexposicion II-Agustin Casasola-1910 Mexican Revolution (photog), 77, Univ Ill, Chicago Circle; Anisinabe Waki Aztlan, Truman Col, Chicago, 77; La Mujer-Mexican Women of Mexico plus Midwest Latinas, Cult Ctr Chicago Pub Libr, 78; Raices y Visiones, Mus Contemp Art Chicago, 79. *Pos:* Art dir, Revista Chicano Riquena, Ind Univ NW, 73-80; art dir, Foxlady Mag, Chicago, 75-76; visual consult, Ill Arts Coun, 76-79 & Nat Endowment Arts, Washington, DC, 78-79; nominator, Chicago Art Awards, 78- *Teaching:* Instr mural painting, Ind Univ NW, Gary, 74; instr Mex crafts, Columbia Col, Chicago, 78- *Mem:* Chicago Artists Coalition; Movimiento Artistico Chicano (dir, 78-). *Media:* Acrylic, Mixed Media. *Publ:* Contribr, 450 Years of Chicago History, Albuquerque, NMex, 76; contribr, We Americans, 75 & Gallery, 76, Scott Foresman. *Mailing Add:* 567 W 18th St Chicago IL 60616

GONZALEZ, JUAN J
PAINTER
b Camagüen, Cuba, Jan 12, 45; US citizen. *Study:* Univ Miami, BFA, 69, MFA, 72. *Work:* Carnegie Inst, Pittsburgh, Pa; Indianapolis Mus Art; Vassar Col Art Gallery; Hirshhorn Mus & Sculpture Garden. *Exhib:* Whitney Mus Ann Exhib, 72; Painting and Sculpture Today, Indianapolis Mus Art, 74; Drawings, Del Mus, Wilmington, 76; Drawings Today in New York, Tulane Univ Mus, 77; Images of Horror, Fantasy, Bronx Mus, 77; Pastel in America, Grand Rapids Mus, Mich, 79; Faculty Invitational, Univ Art Gallery, Albany, NY, 79; Inside-Out: Self Beyond Likeness, Newport Harbor Mus, Calif, 81. *Teaching:* Instr painting & drawing, Sch Visual Arts, 77- *Awards:* Grants, Creative Artists Pub Serv, 76 & Nat Endowment Arts, 79. *Bibliog:* Nina French-Fraise (auth), Images of Horror & Fantasy, Abahams, 78; Nina French-Fraise (auth), article, 79 & Roney Cohen (auth), article, 83, Arts Mag. *Dealer:* Nancy Hoffman 429 W Broadway New York NY 10012. *Mailing Add:* 42 W 17 St New York NY 10011

GONZALEZ, XAVIER
PAINTER, SCULPTOR
b Almeria, Spain, Feb 15, 1898; US citizen. *Study:* Art Inst Chicago, 21-23. *Work:* Whitney Mus Am Art & Metrop Mus Art, New York; New Orleans Mus Art; Witte Mus, San Antonio, Tex; Mus Fine Arts, Seattle; plus others. *Exhib:* Grand Central Moderns, New York, 51-53; Pa Acad Fine Arts, Philadelphia; Carnegie Inst, Pittsburgh; Brooklyn Mus, NY; retrospective, Witte Mus, San Antonio, 68; plus many others. *Teaching:* Instr art, San Antonio, 24; prof, Newcomb Col, Tulane Univ, 30; instr, Brooklyn Mus, 45; lectr, Nat Col Asn, 46; Western Reserve Univ, 53-54; Summer Sch Art, Wellfleet, Mass; lectr, Metrop Mus Art, New York; instr, Art Students League. *Awards:* Am Acad Arts & Lett Grant; Guggenheim Fel, 47; Ford Found Grant, 65; Gold Medal & the 79 Artist Ann Award, Nat Art Club of New York, 78; plus others. *Mem:* Am Nat Acad; Nat Asn Mural Painters (pres, 68). *Publ:* Auth, Notes About Painting, 55. *Mailing Add:* 222 Central Park S New York NY 10019

GONZALEZ-TORNERO, SERGIO
PAINTER, PRINTMAKER
b Santiago, Chile. *Study:* Univ Santiago; Atelier 17, Paris, with S W Hayter. *Work:* Metrop Mus Art, New York; Mus Mod Art, New York; Libr Cong, Washington, DC; Minneapolis Inst Art, Minn; Smithsonian Inst, Washington, DC. *Exhib:* Int Bienale of Prints, Krakow, Poland, 66; Couturier Galerie, Stamford, Conn, 67; Stamford Mus, Conn, 67; Int Bienal of Prints, Epinal, France, 71; Painting & Sculpture Exhib, Silvermine, Conn, 73; Gruenebaum Gallery, New York, 75. *Awards:* Silver Nat Print Exhib, 71; Ture Bengzt Mem Award; Vera List Award for Printmaking, 83. *Mem:* Soc of Am Graphic Artists. *Media:* Oil. *Mailing Add:* c/o Couturier Galerie 1814 Newfield Ave Stamford CT 06903

GOO, BENJAMIN
SCULPTOR, PAINTER
b Honolulu, Hawaii, July 12, 22. *Study:* State Univ Iowa, BFA, 53; Cranbrook Acad Art, MFA, 54; Brera Acad Fine Art, Sch of Marino Marini, Milan, Italy, 54-55. *Work:* Phoenix Art Mus, Ariz; Ariz State Univ Art Collection, Tempe; plus others. *Comn:* Two non-objective white marble sculptures, Phoenix Civic Plaza, 71; bronze sculpture, Centennial Hall, City Mesa, Ariz, 80; City Hall, City Tempe, Ariz. *Exhib:* 155th Ann Exhib Am Painting & Sculpture, Pa Acad Fine Arts & Detroit Inst Art, 60; 24th Ann Drawing, Print & Sculpture Exhib, San Francisco Mus Art, Calif, 61; Creative Casting: Exhibit of Art in Bronze, Mus Contemp Crafts, New York, 63; 73rd Western Ann, Denver Art Mus, 71; Fed Int Medaille, Palazzo Medici Riccardi, Florence, 83. *Teaching:* Prof art, Ariz State Univ, 55-; Nat Endowment for the Arts artist in residence, Mesa, Ariz, 72-73; artist in residence, Roswell Mus & Art Ctr, NMex, 75-76. *Awards:* First Ann Southwestern States Purchase Award, Roswell Mus & Art Ctr, 62; 4th Southwestern Invitational Purchase Award, Yuma Art Ctr, 69; 21st Ann Tucson Festival Art Exhib Award, Tucson Art Ctr, 71. *Media:* Metals, Stone. *Publ:* Auth, Education and the craftsman, 1-2/62 & auth, Dick Seeger: Artist craftsman in plastics, 7-8/62, Creative Crafts Mag. *Dealer:* Elaine Horwitch Gallery 4200 N Marshall Way Scottsdale AZ 85251. *Mailing Add:* 506 W First St Tempe AZ 85281

GOOCH, DONALD BURNETTE
PAINTER
b Bloomingdale, Mich, Oct 17, 07. *Study:* Univ Mich Col Archit & Design, BS(educ), with J P Slusser, 32-39, MA(design), 39; Detroit Art Acad, with C F Lopez, 33-36; Fontainebleau Sch Fine Arts, France, 37. *Work:* Detroit Inst Arts; Ford Motor Co, Dearborn, Mich. *Comn:* Seven educ film strips, McGraw Hill, New York, 49-55; seven illus, Ford Times, Dearborn, 50-60; oil mural, Mich Consolidated Gas Co, Detroit, 51; oil painting, Mich Union, Ann Arbor, 56; literary map of Mich, Mich Coun Teachers Eng, 64. *Exhib:* San Francisco Watercolor Show, 40; Am Fedn Arts Traveling Show Selected Watercolors, 41; Pepsi Cola's Painting of the Year, 46; Pa Acad Fine Art, 47; Terry Nat Exhib, Miami, Fla, 52. *Teaching:* Instr design, Detroit Art Acad, 33-36; prof design, Univ Mich Col Archit & Design, Ann Arbor, 36-73, emer prof, 73- *Awards:* Alumni Prize, Collaborative Competition, Am Acad Rome, 35; Detroit Inst Arts Founders Prize, 47; Faculty Res Grants, Horace H Rackham Sch Grad Studies, Univ Mich, 60-65. *Mem:* Ann Arbor Art Asn (pres, 47-48); Mich Watercolor Soc (dir, 46-50); Mich Acad Sci, Arts & Lett (vchmn fine arts, 51-52); fel Int Acad Arts & Lett; Nat Soc Lit & Arts; plus others. *Media:* Watercolor, Tempera, Oil, Acrylic. *Res:* Pictographic techniques for communication with non-literates. *Publ:* Ed, Advertising to the American Taste, 56, ed, Search for Certainty in Advertising, 59, Univ Mich; ed & illusr, Theatre & Main Street, Univ Mich, 64; contribr, Picture talk in Kathmandu, Mich Acad Sci, Arts & Lett, 63. *Mailing Add:* 1633 Leaird Dr Ann Arbor MI 48105

GOOD, LEONARD
PAINTER

b Chickasha, Okla, June 25, 07. *Study:* Univ Okla, BFA, 27; Art Students League, with Nicolaides, 30; Univ Iowa, with Jean Charlot, 40. *Work:* Des Moines Art Ctr, Iowa; Milwaukee Art Ctr, Wis; Okla Art Ctr; Mabee-Gerrer Mus Art, Shawnee, Okla; City Hall, Kofu, Japan. *Comn:* Portrait, Okla Hist Mus, Oklahoma City, 49; two portraits, Univ Okla, Norman, 49-50; three portraits, Drake Univ, 54-60; portrait, Iowa Hist Mus, Des Moines, 62; series of Iowa scenes for Sun features, Des Moines Register, 65. *Exhib:* First & second Nat Exhibs Am Art, Metrop Mus Art, New York, 36 & 37; Gallery of States Touring Exhib, Am Fedn Arts, Washington, DC, 45; Mid America Annual, Joslyn Mus Art, Omaha, 55; Arts Ann, Tyler, Tex, 69; Am Painters in Paris Exhib, Palais des Congres, France, 75-76. *Collections Arranged:* Assembled permanent collection of paintings for Preferred Risk Life Ins Co Home Off Bldg, Des Moines, 69. *Pos:* Vis artist in residence, Iowa State Univ, 60-61; artist in residence, Nat Endowment Arts & Iowa Arts Coun, Shenandoah, Iowa, 70-71. *Teaching:* Prof painting & drawing, Univ Okla, 30-50; prof drawing & painting, Univ Wis, 50-52; prof art hist, Drake Univ, 52-77, head dept art, 52-68, emer prof art hist, 77- *Awards:* Purchase Prize for New Mexico Town (painting), Springville Mus Art, Utah, 74; Fourth Ann Nat Exhib Small Paintings First Prize, Iowa State Fair, 74; plus others. *Mem:* Delta Phi Delta (nat vpres, 54-58, nat pres, 58-60). *Media:* Multimedia. *Publ:* Illusr, A Certain Young Widow, Univ Okla, 30; illusr, instructional manuals for US Air Force, Tinker Field, Okla, 43-44. *Dealer:* Arts Place II 115 Park Ave Oklahoma City OK 73102. *Mailing Add:* 1320 Oregon Ave Chickasha OK 73018

GOODACRE, GLENNA
PAINTER, SCULPTOR

b Lubbock, Tex, Aug 28, 39. *Study:* Colo Col, BA; Art Students League. *Work:* Tex Tech Mus, Lubbock; Presby Hosp, Denver, Colo; Diamond M Found Mus, Snyder, Tex. *Comn:* Dr Harvie Pruitt, Lubbock Christian Col, 82; Patrick Haggerty, Tex Instruments, 82; Eric Sloan, 83; Erik Jonsson, Tex Instruments, 83; Cecil Green, Tex Instruments, 83. *Exhib:* Allied Artists Am, New York, 74, 77 & 78; Nat Acad Design, New York, 75, 78 & 79; Nat Acad Western Art, 77, 78 & 79; Beijing, China, 81; Thomas Gilcrease Mus Asn, 82. *Awards:* Johnson Atelier Award, Audubon Artists, 83; Joyce & Elliot Liskin Award, Pen & Brush, 83; Leonard J Meiselman Award, Nat Sculpture Soc, 83. *Mem:* Allied Artists of Am; Nat Sculpture Soc; Catherine Lorillard Wolfe Art Club. *Media:* Oil, Pastel; Bronze. *Publ:* Illusr, bronze relief for jacket, The Flamboyant Judge, 73 & Trank Tenny Johnson, 75; illusr, silver relief for jacket, Robbing Banks was My Business, 74. *Mailing Add:* 313 Foxtail Circle Boulder CO 80303

GOODE, JOE See Bueno, Jose

GOODMAN, BENJAMIN
PATRON

b Memphis, Tenn, Jan 18, 04. *Study:* Princeton Univ, AB, 24; Harvard Univ, LLB, 27; Memphis Acad Arts, Hon Doc Humanities, 78. *Pos:* Trustee & former pres, Memphis Acad Arts; chmn, Memphis Munic Art Comn, 60-76. *Mailing Add:* 115 S Rose Rd Memphis TN 38117

GOODMAN, BERTRAM
PAINTER

b New York, NY, Sept 21, 04. *Study:* Sch Am Sculpture, 23-24; Art Students League, 25. *Work:* Brooklyn Mus; Libr Cong; Abbott Labs, Chicago; Butler Art Inst, Youngstown, Ohio; Metrop Mus Art, New York; and others. *Exhib:* Mus Mod Art, New York; Whitney Mus Am Art; Carnegie Art Inst; Metrop Mus Art, New York; Nat Acad Fine Arts. *Awards:* First Prize Watercolor, Screen Publicists Guild, 46; Purchase Prize, Abraham Lincoln Gallery, 47; Jo & Emily Lowe Prize, 56. *Mem:* Artists Equity Asn (dir, 55-56); Brooklyn Soc Artists; Am Soc Graphic Artists. *Mailing Add:* 299 W 12th St New York NY 10014

GOODMAN, CALVIN JEROME
CONSULTANT, COLLECTOR

b Chicago, Ill, Mar 1, 22. *Study:* Harvard Univ, AB(hon), 49. *Pos:* Mgt consult in art, 60-; vpres, Tamarind Lithography Workshop, 59-74; nat consult, Artists Equity Asn, 74-76. *Teaching:* Instr bus methods for artists, Tamarind Lithography Workshop, 61-71; instr prof practices, Calif Inst Arts, 67-71; instr prof practices, Otis Art Inst, 68-71; also lectr seminar & workshops in marketing art for San Francisco Art Inst, Scripps Grad Sch of Art, Pratt Inst, among others. *Bibliog:* Antreasian & Adams (auth), The Tamarind Book of Lithography, Abrams, 71; The booming art market, Los Angeles Mag, 1/82. *Res:* Fine art market; operations of specialized schools of art and music; paper specialties market. *Publ:* Auth, Business Methods for a Lithography Workshop, Tamarind, 68; auth, Marketing Art, A Handbook for Artists and Art Dealers, 72; auth, Art Marketing Handbook, GeeTeeBee, 78; auth, Monotypes, Am Artist, 1/80; auth, Finding and Working with a Dealer, Am Artist, 6/83. *Mailing Add:* 11901 Sunset Blvd Suite 102 Los Angeles CA 90049

GOODMAN, JAMES NEIL
DEALER, COLLECTOR

b Rochester, NY, Apr 11, 29. *Pos:* Dir, James Goodman Gallery. *Specialty:* Modern American and European masters, including Calder, Cornell, de Kooning, Klee, Leger, Lichtenstein, Matisse, Moore, Picasso & Tanguy. *Mailing Add:* 1020 Madison Ave New York NY 10021

GOODMAN, MARIAN
DEALER, PUBLISHER

b New York, NY, June 15, 28. *Study:* Columbia Univ Grad Sch Art Hist, BA. *Pos:* Dir publ, Multiples Inc, 65-, pres, 74-; dir, Marian Goodman Gallery, currently. *Mem:* Art Dealers Asn. *Specialty:* Publishing limited editions and sometimes books, records, etc by prominent contemporary artists such as Arakawa, Lewitt, Rauchenberg, Rosenquist, Oldenburg, Warhol and many others. *Mailing Add:* Multiples Inc 24 W 57th St New York NY 10019

GOODMAN, MARK
PHOTOGRAPHER

b Boston, Mass, May 19, 46. *Study:* Boston Univ, BA, 70; also with Minor White, 70 & Bruce Davidson, 71. *Work:* Mus Mod Art, New York; Mus Fine Arts, Boston; Mus Art, Univ Okla, Norman; Spencer Mus Art, Univ Kans, Lawrence; Vassar Col Art Gallery. *Exhib:* Recent Acquisitions, Mus Mod Art, New York, 78-79; Likeness, Spencer Mus, Univ Kans, Lawrence, 80; solo exhib, George Eastman House, Rochester, NY, 80-81; American Children, Mus Mod Art, New York, 81; Millerton, NY, Vassar Col Art Gallery, 81; Contemporary Photographers IX, George Eastman House, Rochester, NY, 82; New American Photographs, Calif State Col Art Gallery, San Bernardino, 82. *Teaching:* Artist in residence photog, Apeiron Workshops Inc, Millerton, NY, 72-76; asst prof, Univ Tex, Austin, 80- *Bibliog:* Julia Scully & Andy Grundberg (auth), Currents: American photography today, Mod Photog, Vol 44, No 2, 80; James Kaufmann (auth), Works of love: The photographs of Mark Goodman, Exposure, Vol 20, No 1, 82. *Publ:* Contribr, Photographs of Millerton, NY, 1971-1975, Aperture, Vol 19, No 4, 75; contribr, Kansas Album, Addison House, 77; Photographing Children, Time-Life Books, 83. *Mailing Add:* 1503 Larkwood Austin TX 78723

GOODMAN, SIDNEY
PAINTER

b Philadelphia, Pa, Jan 19, 36. *Study:* Philadelphia Col Art, 58. *Work:* Art Inst Chicago; Libr Cong, Washington, DC; Whitney Mus Am Art, Mus Mod Art, New York; Hirshhorn Collection; and others. *Exhib:* The Figure in Recent American Painting Traveling Exhib, 74-75; Three Centuries Am Art, Philadelphia Mus Art, 76; Am 1976 Bicentennial Exhib, US Dept of Interior, Washington, DC, 76; Eight Contemp Am Realists, Pa Acad Fine Arts, 77; one-man exhibs, RI Col, 79 & Col William & Mary, 79; Contemp Drawing: Philadelphia II, Philadelphia Mus Art, 79; retrospective, Queens Mus, 80; 20th Century Drawings, Whitney Mus Am Art, 79-81; and others. *Teaching:* Instr drawing & painting, Philadelphia Col Art, 60-78; instr, Tyler Sch, Philadelphia, 77 & Pa Acad Fine Arts, 78- *Awards:* Guggenheim Fel, 64; Philadelphia Print Club Purchase Award, 65; Nat Endowment Arts Grant, 74; and others. *Dealer:* Terry Dintenfass Inc 50 West 57th St New York NY 10019. *Mailing Add:* 323 Harrison Ave Elkins Park PA 19117

GOODNOUGH, ROBERT
PAINTER

b Cortland, NY, Oct 23. *Study:* Syracuse Univ, Hiram Gell fel, 40, BFA; NY Univ, MA; New Sch Social Res; Ozenfant Sch Art; Hans Hofmann Sch Fine Arts. *Work:* Albright-Knox Art Gallery, Buffalo, NY; Solomon R Guggenheim Mus, Mus Mod Art & Metrop Mus Art, New York; Wadsworth Atheneum, Hartford, Conn; plus others. *Exhib:* One-man shows, Univ Minn, Univ Notre Dame & Arts Club Chicago, 64; Cayuga Mus Hist & Art, Auburn, NY, 69, Albright-Knox Art Gallery, Buffalo, NY, 69 & Syracuse Univ, 72; Nat Inst Arts & Lett, 64; New American Painting & Sculpture, Mus Mod Art, 69; Univ Ill, 69; Indianapolis Mus Art, 69; Venice Biennial, 70; Am Acad Arts & Lett, 71; plus many other group & one-man shows. *Pos:* Art critic, Art News, 50-57; secy, Documents of Mod Art, 51. *Teaching:* Instr painting, Cornell Univ, NY Univ & Fieldston Sch, New York. *Awards:* Ada Garrett Award, Art Inst Chicago, 61; Ford Found Purchase Prize, 63. *Mailing Add:* 38 W Ninth St New York NY 10011

GOODNOW, FRANK A
PAINTER, EDUCATOR

b Evanston, Ill, Dec 14, 23. *Study:* Northwestern Univ, Evanston; Art Inst Chicago, BFA; Anna L Raymond Traveling Fel, 48; also with Boris Anisfeld & Fernand Leger, 50. *Work:* Philadelphia Mus Art; NY State Univ; Univ Rochester; Everson Mus Art, Syracuse; Syracuse Univ. *Exhib:* Pa Acad Fine Arts, 53, 57 & 65; Whitney Mus Am Art, 55; Everson Mus Art, 60, 67, 74 & 75; one-man shows, Schuman Gallery, Rochester, 65, 69, 71 & 72; Oxford Gallery, Rochester, NY, 75, 77 & 82; Lubin House Gallery, New York, 76; Hanover Gallery, Syracuse, 79; Abstract Tradition, Munson-Williams-Proctor Inst, Utica, NY, 79. *Teaching:* Prof painting, Syracuse Univ, 50- *Awards:* B Forman Award, Rochester Mem Gallery, 69; First Prize, Cooperstown Nat Show, 71 & NY State Fair, 81; grant, Ford Found, 77, 79 & 80. *Dealer:* Oxford Gallery 267 Oxford St Rochester NY 14607. *Mailing Add:* 214 Dawley Rd Fayetteville NY 13066

GOODRICH, LLOYD
ADMINISTRATOR, WRITER

b Nutley, NJ, July 10, 1897. *Study:* Art Students League, with Kenneth Hayes Miller; Nat Acad Design; Cornell Col, Hon DFA, 63; Colby Col, Hon DFA, 64; RI Sch of Design, Hon DFA, 77. *Pos:* Res cur, Whitney Mus Am Art, 35-47, assoc cur, 47-48, assoc dir, 48-58, dir, 58-68, dir emer, 68-, hon mem bd trustees, currently; founder & dir, Am Art Res Coun, 42-; mem adv comt, Art for the White House, 60-63; bd dirs, Edward MacDowell Asn, 65-72; plus many other prior art positions. *Awards:* Award for Distinguished Serv to the Arts, Am Acad & Inst of Arts & Letters, 79; Archives of Am Art Award, 79; Award, Skowhegan Sch of Painting & Sci, 81. *Mem:* Hon mem Asn Art Mus Dirs; Art Students League; hon mem Am Inst Interior Designers; fel Am

Acad Arts & Sci. *Res:* American art and artists. *Publ:* Auth, Georgia O'Keefe, 70, Edward Hopper, 71, Raphael Soyer, 72, Reginald Marsh, 72 & Thomas Eakins, 82; and others. *Mailing Add:* Whitney Mus Am Art 945 Madison Ave New York NY 10021

GOODRICH, SUSAN
PAINTER
b La Crosse, Wis, Aug 23, 33. *Study:* Univ Wis, Madison, with Robert Grilley & John Wilde. *Exhib:* Mid-Yr Show, Butler Inst Am Art, Youngstown, Ohio, 65, 66, 76 & 79-82; Wis Painters & Sculptors, Milwaukee Art Ctr, Wis, 67; Art in the Embassies, State Dept, 67; one-person shows, Jewish Community Ctr, Milwaukee, 69, Milwaukee Art Ctr, 73 & Allan Stone Gallery, New York, 75; Nat Acad Design, New York, 72; Contemp Figurative Painting in the Mid-West, Univ Wis, Madison, 77; American Art-The Challenge of the Land, Pillsbury Int Hq, Minneapolis, Minn, 81; and others. *Awards:* Painting of the Yr, Art Across Am, Mead Paper Corp, 63; Major Award, Wis Painters & Sculptors, Milwaukee Art Ctr, 67 & Top Award, 73; Wis Artists Make Toys, Milwaukee Art Ctr, 77 & 79. *Bibliog:* Article in La Rev Mod, Paris, 65; Susan Braudy (auth), article in MS Mag, 8/73; feature prog, Wis Directions, Pub Broadcasting Station, Television film, Channel 10, Milwaukee, 75. *Media:* Oil. *Mailing Add:* c/o Allen Stone Gallery 48 E 86th St New York NY 10028

GOODRIDGE, LAWRENCE WAYNE
PAINTER, SCULPTOR
b Cincinnati, Ohio, Mar 18, 41. *Study:* Univ Cincinnati, BFA(with hon), 63; Univ Cincinnati & Art Acad Cincinnati, MFA, 67. *Exhib:* All-Ohio Painting & Sculpture Exhib, Dayton Art Inst, 67; Mid-States Art Exhib, Evansville Mus Arts & Sci, Ind, 70; one-man show & Louisville Biennial, J B Speed Art Mus, Ky, 71; 17th Ann Drawing & Sculpture Show, Ball State Univ, Muncie, Ind, 71. *Pos:* Toy designer, Kenner Prod Co, 63-65. *Teaching:* Instr found design & color theory, Art Acad Cincinnati, 69-, co-dean, 72- *Awards:* Second Prize, Eastern Fine Paper Graphic Design, 65. *Publ:* Auth & illusr, European diary, 70 & Truck stop, 71, Cincinnati Mag. *Dealer:* Richard Feigen Gallery 226 E Ontario St Chicago IL 60611. *Mailing Add:* Art Acad Cincinnati Eden Park Cincinnati OH 45202

GOODWIN, LOUIS PAYNE
CARTOONIST
b Flintville, Tenn, Oct 9, 22. *Study:* Ark Polytech Col, 41-42; Univ Chattanooga, BA, 48. *Pos:* Advert & ed cartoonist, Dispatch Printing Co, Columbus, 52-62; ed cartoonist, Columbus Eve Dispatch, 62- *Awards:* Cartoon Award, Freedoms Found, 62-69, 71 & 73; Cartoonists Award, Hwy Safety Found, 66. *Mailing Add:* 5158 Woodside Dr Columbus OH 43229

GOODYEAR, FRANK H, JR
HISTORIAN, CURATOR
b New York, NY, Jan 5, 44. *Study:* Yale Univ, BA, 66; Univ Del, Winterthur Prog, MA, 69. *Collections Arranged:* Pennsylvania Academicians (with catalogue), Pa Acad of Fine Arts, 73, The Beneficent Connoisseurs, Gibson, Harrison (with catalogue), 74 & In This Academy: The Pennsylvania Academy of the Fine Arts, 1805-1976 (with catalogue), 76; Thomas Doughty: An American Pioneer in Landscape Painting, 1793-1856 (with catalogue), Pa Acad, Corcoran Gallery of Art & Albany Inst, 73-74; American Paintings in the Rhode Island Historical Society, 74; Cecilia Beaux (1855-1942): Portrait of an Artist (with catalogue), Pa Acad & Indianapolis Mus of Art, 74-75; American Art: 1750-1800 Towards Independence, Yale Univ Art Gallery, 76; Eight Contemporary American Realists: Philip Pearlstein, Alfred Leslie, Stephen Posen, Janet Fish, Duane Hanson, Joseph Raffael, Neil Welliver & Sidney Goodman, 77; Seven on the Figure (with catalog), Pa Acad Fine Arts, 79; Contemporary American Realism since 1960 (with catalog), Pa Acad Fine Arts, 81. *Pos:* Cur, RI Hist Soc, 69-72; cur & ed exhib catalogs, Pa Acad Fine Arts, 72-, pres, 83-; actg cur, Am Painting & Sculpture, Yale Univ Art Gallery, 74-75. *Mailing Add:* Pa Acad Fine Arts Broad & Cherry Sts Philadelphia PA 19102

GOODYEAR, JOHN L
PAINTER, KINETIC ARTIST
b Los Angeles, Calif, Oct 22, 30. *Study:* Univ Mich, BD, 52, MD, 54. *Work:* Corcoran Gallery Art, Washington, DC; Guggenheim Mus, Whitney Mus Am Art, Mus Mod Art, New York; Princeton Univ Mus Art. *Comn:* State NJ, 81; IBM, Raleigh, NC, 81. *Exhib:* Responsive Eye, Mus Mod Art, New York, 65; Whitney Mus Am Art Ann, New York, 66 & 68; Radius 5 Touring Exhib, Smithsonian Inst, Washington, DC, 67-68; Albright-Knox Art Gallery, Buffalo, NY, 68; Boston Mus Fine Arts, 71; Mus Mod Art, New York, 72; one-man shows, Addison Gallery Am Art, Andover, Mass, 76, Mass Inst Technol Ctr Advan Visual Studies, Cambridge, 76; Slusser Gallery, Univ Mich, Ann Arbor, 81; NJ State Mus, Trenton, 81; and others. *Teaching:* Instr, Univ Mich, Grand Rapids, 56-62 & Univ Mass, Amherst, 62-64; prof design, Mason Gross Sch Art, Rutgers Univ, 64-, chmn dept, 76-79. *Awards:* Graham Found Fel, 62 & 70; Ctr Advan Visual Studies Fel, Mass Inst Technol, 70-71. *Bibliog:* David L Shirey (auth), Kinetics, New York Times Sun, 3/15/81. *Mem:* Am Abstract Artists. *Media:* Mixed. *Dealer:* Dumont-Landis Fine Art New Brunswick NJ. *Mailing Add:* Dept Art Walters Hall Rutgers Univ New Brunswick NJ 08903

GOOSSEN, EUGENE COONS
WRITER, EDUCATOR
b Gloversville, NY, Aug 6, 20. *Study:* Hamilton Col; Corcoran Sch Fine Arts; Sorbonne, Paris, cert; New Sch Social Res, BA. *Collections Arranged:* Kenneth Noland, Morris Louis & First Barnett Newman Retrospective,

Bennington Col, Vt, 58-61; Eight Young Artists, Hudson River Mus, NY, 64; The Art of the Real, Mus Mod Art, New York, Grand Palais, Paris, Kunsthalle, Zurich, Switz & Tate Gallery, London, Eng, 68-69; Helen Frankenthaler, Whitney Mus Am Art, New York, Whitechapel Gallery, London, Herrenhausen, Hanover & Kongresshalle, Berlin, Ger, 69; Ellsworth Kelly, Mus Mod Art, New York, 73. *Pos:* Art critic, Monterey Peninsula Herald, 48-58; dir exhibs, Bennington Col, 58-61. *Teaching:* Prof art, Bennington Col, 58-61; prof art & chmn dept, Hunter Col, 61-82, prof art hist, currently. *Awards:* Frank Jewett Mather Citation for Excellence in Art Criticism, 58; Guggenheim Fel, 70; City Univ New York Res Grant, 72. *Bibliog:* Article, Time Mag, 4/7/67; Michael Murphy (auth), The Art of the Real (film), US Info Agency, 68. *Mem:* Int Art Critics Asn; Am Asn Univ Prof; Col Art Asn Am. *Publ:* Auth, Ellsworth Kelly, 58; auth, Stuart Davis, 59; auth, The Art of the Real, Eng, Fr & Ger ed, 68-69; auth, Helen Frankenthaler, 69; coauth, Encyclopaedia of American Art, Chanticleer Press, 72. *Mailing Add:* RFD 1 Buskirk NY 12028

GORCHOV, RON
PAINTER
b Chicago, Ill, Apr 5, 30. *Study:* Art Inst Chicago, 47-50; Univ Ill, 50-51. *Work:* Whitney Mus Am Art, New York; Hartford Atheneum, Conn; Metrop Mus of Art, New York; Everson Mus Art, Syracuse, NY; Detroit Inst of Arts. *Teaching:* Asst prof art, Hunter Col, presently. *Media:* Oil on Canvas. *Dealer:* Marlborough Gallery New York NY. *Mailing Add:* Dept Art Hunter Col 6951 Park Ave New York NY 10021

GORDER, CLAYTON J
PAINTER, EDUCATOR
b Fargo, NDak, Mar 20, 36. *Study:* Concordia Col, Minn, BA; Univ Iowa, MFA. *Work:* San Francisco Mus Art; Des Moines Art Ctr, Iowa; Davenport Municipal Art Gallery, Iowa; Murray State Univ Gallery, Ky. *Exhib:* One-man shows, Des Moines Art Ctr, 72 & Arras Gallery, New York, 77; Col Marin Painting Exhib, Kentfield, Calif, 72; Striped & Shaped Canvases, Bronx Mus Arts, 74; Nine Artists at Work, Bronx Mus of Arts, New York, 75; Brunnier Gallery, Iowa State Univ, Ames, 76. *Teaching:* Assoc prof painting & drawing, Augustana Col, Ill, 63- *Awards:* First Prize Purchase Award, Container Corp Am, Rock Island, Ill, 63; Edmundson Award for Best Work in Show, 69, Esther & Edith Younker Award in Painting, 72, Ann Iowa Artists Exhib. *Bibliog:* Jerome Tarshis (auth), article, Artforum, 10/70; Alfred Frankenstein (auth), article, San Francisco Chronicle, 1/7/72; article, Arts Mag, 8/77. *Dealer:* William Sawyer Gallery 3045 Clay St San Francisco CA 94115; Arras Gallery 29 W 57th St New York NY 10019. *Mailing Add:* 424 Clark St Iowa City IA 52240

GORDIN, SIDNEY
SCULPTOR, EDUCATOR
b Cheliabinsk, Russia, Oct 24, 18. *Study:* Cooper Union, New York, 37-41, with Morris Kantor, Carol Harrison & Leo Katz. *Work:* Art Inst Chicago; Newark Mus, NJ; Walter T Chrysler Mus Art at Norfolk, Va; Southern Ill Univ; Whitney Mus Am Art, New York; and others. *Comn:* Sculpture, Temple Israel, Tulsa, Okla, 59 & Envoy Towers, New York, 60; sculpture, Davies Symphony Hall, San Francisco, Calif. *Exhib:* Metrop Mus Art, New York, 51; Whitney Ann, 52-57; Mus Mod Art, New York; Art Inst Chicago; Pa Acad Fine Arts, 54 & 55; Brooklyn Mus, NY; Newark Mus; San Francisco Mus Art, Calif; Oakland Art Mus, Calif; Philbrook Art Ctr, Tulsa, Okla, 60; one-man shows, New Sch Social Res, 57 & de Young Mem Mus, San Francisco, 57. *Teaching:* Instr, Pratt Inst, 53-58, Brooklyn Col, 55-58, New Sch for Social Res, 56-58, Sarah Lawrence Col, 57-58 & Univ Calif, Berkeley, 58- *Mailing Add:* 903 Camelia St 710 Montgomery St Berkeley CA 94700

GORDLEY, MARILYN CLASSE
PAINTER
b St Louis, Mo, Aug 4, 29. *Study:* Washington Univ, BFA; Univ Okla, MFA; Ohio State Univ. *Work:* Greenville Mus Art, NC; Spring Mills, Lancaster, SC; Univ Okla; NC Nat Bank, Greenville. *Comn:* Portraits of Gov Kerr Scott, Arthur Tyler, Henry Belk, Elmer Browning & Weldell Smiley, ECarolina Univ, 64-74. *Exhib:* XXII Am Drawing Biennial, Norfolk (Smithsonian traveling exhib), 67; Cent South Exhib, Nashville, Tenn, 69; Nat Drawing Exhib, Southern Ill Univ, Carbondale, 75; Miss Mus Art, Jackson, 78; Fayetteville Mus Art, NC, 79; Southern Exposure, Hanson Gallery, New Orleans, 80; and others. *Teaching:* Assoc prof drawing & painting, ECarolina Univ, 64- *Awards:* 18th Irene Leache Award, Norfolk Mus, 66; Spring Mills First Prize, 67; Cent South Exhib Award, 69. *Mem:* Am Asn Univ Women; Col Art Asn Am; NC Artists Asn. *Media:* Oil. *Mailing Add:* 105 Dalebrook Circle Greenville NC 27834

GORDLEY, METZ TRANBARGER
PAINTER
b Cedar Rapids, Iowa, May 24, 32. *Study:* Wash Univ, BFA; Univ Okla, MFA; Ohio State Univ; Univ NC, Chapel Hill. *Work:* Greenville Mus Art, NC; Nat Bank Collection, Charlotte; NC State Soc Print & Drawings, Raleigh; Univ Okla, Norman. *Comn:* Aycock portrait for E Carolina Univ. *Exhib:* One-man shows, Kate Lewis Gallery, ECarolina Univ, 74 & Mint Mus, Charlotte, NC, 78; two-person shows, High Point Exhib Ctr, High Point, NC, 77, Mark Twain S Co Bank, St Louis, Mo, 78 & Fayetteville Mus Art, NC, 79; 11th Ann Piedmont Graphics Exhib, Greenville Co Mus Art, SC, 74; 21st Ann Drawing & Small Sculpture Show, Ball State Univ Art Gallery, 75; 1975 Biennial Exhib Piedmont Painting & Sculpture, Mint Mus, Charlotte, NC; Razor Gallery, NY, 79; 44th Ann, Butler Inst Am Art, Youngstown, Ohio, 80; and others. *Teaching:* Prof painting, ECarolina Univ, 59-, actg dean, Sch of Art, 77. *Awards:* First Prize, NC Print & Drawing Soc, 66; Second Prize for

Watercolor & Second Prize for Oil, Kinston Art Show, 68. *Bibliog:* Emily Farnham (auth), Behind a Laughing Mask, Charles Demuth. *Mem:* Assoc Artists NC (bd mem, 66-67); Col Art Asn. *Media:* Oil. *Mailing Add:* 105 Dalebrook Greenville NC 27834

GORDON, ALBERT F
DEALER

b Antwerp, Belg, June 18, 34; US citizen. *Study:* Sorbonne, Univ Paris, cert, 53; City Col of New York, BA, 55; Columbia Univ, MA, 60. *Collections Arranged:* Aspects of the Doubled Image in African Art (auth, catalog), 76; Beauty and the Beast: A Study in Contrasts (auth, catalog), 77; Ekon Society Puppets: Sculptures for Social Criticism (auth, catalog), 77. *Pos:* Pres, Tribal Arts Galleries, Inc, New York, 68- *Bibliog:* Terry Trucco (auth), Primitive art, Art News, 4/81. *Mem:* Am Appraisers Asn; Explorers Club. *Specialty:* African art. *Mailing Add:* c/o Tribal Arts Gallery 84 E Tenth New York NY 10003

GORDON, DONALD EDWARD
HISTORIAN, EDUCATOR

b New York, NY, May 13, 31. *Study:* Harvard Col, BA, 52; Harvard Univ, MA, 53, PhD, 60. *Collections Arranged:* E L Kirchner Retrospective, Seattle, Pasadena & Boston Mus Fine Art, 68-69; Joseph L Katz Collection, Univ Pittsburgh Art Gallery, 71. *Teaching:* From asst prof to assoc prof mod art, Dickinson Col, 60-69, chmn dept fine arts, 61-69; prof mod art, Univ Pittsburgh, 69-, chmn dept fine arts, 69-74; vis prof 20th century art, Columbia Univ, 81-82. *Mem:* Col Art Asn Am; Art Students League, New York; Soc Arts, Relig & Contemp Cult (bd dirs, 74-83). *Res:* 20th century German and American painting. *Publ:* Auth, Ernst Ludwig Kirchner: The Paintings, Harvard Univ Press, 68; auth, Modern Art Exhibitions 1900-1916, 2 vols, Prestel, Munich, 74; auth, Pollock's bird, Art in Am, 10/80; auth, Expressionism: Art by antithesis, Art in Am, 3/81; auth, Marc and Friedrich again, Source, fall 81; and others. *Mailing Add:* Frick Fine Arts Bldg Univ Pittsburgh Pittsburgh PA 15260

GORDON, JOHN S
SCULPTOR, EDUCATOR

b Milwaukee, Wis, Nov 16, 46. *Study:* Antioch Col, BA, 70; Claremont Grad Sch, MFA, 73. *Exhib:* Whitney Mus Am Art, Biennial Contemp Am Art, New York, 75; Southland Video Anthology, Long Beach Mus Art, Calif, 75; Collage & Assemblage in Southern Calif, Los Angeles Inst Contemp Art, 75; 100 plus Current Concerns, Los Angeles Inst Contemp Art, 77; one-man show, Los Angeles Louver Gallery, Venice, Calif, 77; Los Angeles Show, San Francisco Art Inst Gallery, 78. *Teaching:* Instr ceramics, Mt St Mary's Col, Los Angeles, 73; assoc prof sculpture & ceramics, Univ Southern Calif, 73-; vis asst prof, Claremont Grad Sch, fall 79; dean, Univ Southern Calif, Sch Fine Art, 81. *Awards:* Cash Award, Calif-Hawaii Regional, San Diego, 72; Nat Endowment Arts Grant, 76; res & publ grant, Univ of Southern Calif, 77. *Bibliog:* Ted Forhead (auth), Clay sampler, Artweek, 4/23/74; NEA Artist's Grants, Art in Am, 11-12/76; Susan C Larsen (auth), John S Gordon, Arts Mag, 3/77. *Mem:* Col Art Asn Am. *Media:* Steel, Wood. *Mailing Add:* 1129 N La Brea Ave Inglewood CA 90302

GORDON, JOSEPHINE
PAINTER

b Walla-Walla, Wash. *Study:* Univ Guadalajara, with Maria Medina; Ariz State Univ, with Dr Harry Wood; Sedona Art Ctr, Ariz, with Nassan Abiskhairoun; also with A E Park, William Kimura & Wassily Sommer, Anchorage, Alaska; and with Perry Acher, Seattle, Wash. *Work:* Bank of North Anchorage & Miller Construction Co, Anchorage; Alaska Seafood Corp, Homer; and others. *Exhib:* All Alaska Exhib, 70 & 71; Artists of Alaska Traveling Show, 73-75; one-woman show, Artique Ltd, 73-75. *Bibliog:* Lael Morgan (auth), Jo Gordon, painter, Alaska J, fall 75. *Mem:* Alaska Artist Guild. *Media:* Watercolor, Acrylic. *Dealer:* Artique Ltd 314 G St Anchorage AK 99501. *Mailing Add:* 1521 McHugh Lane Anchorage AK 99501

GORDON, JOY L
MUSEUM DIRECTOR, EDUCATOR

b New York, NY, Jan 31, 33. *Study:* NY Univ, BA & MA. *Collections Arranged:* Contemporary Latino Americano Art, 72; Prints from the NYU Art Collection, Hudson River Mus, Yonkers, 73; Paintings & Sculpture from the NYU Art Collection, Art Gallery, Univ Notre Dame, 73; William Benton Mus Art, Univ Conn, 73; Contemporary Asian & Middle Eastern Art from the Grey Foundation Collection, 75; Report from Soho, 75; Aspects of Am Realism, 76; Prints & Techniques (with catalog), 76; Drawing & Collage (with catalog), 76; Contemp Israeli Crafts, 77; Am Impressionist Painting, 77; Am Still Life Paintings, 19th & 20th Centuries, 78; Containers, Mass Crafts, 79; Art in Process, 79; Directions in Realism: Boston, 80. *Pos:* Asst cur educ, cur & researcher pvt collections, NY Univ Art Collection, 72-74; cur, Grey Art Gallery & Study Ctr, NY Univ, 74-77; dir, Danforth Mus, Framingham, Mass, 77- *Mem:* Col Art Asn; Am Asn Mus; New Eng Mus Assoc; Bus & Prof Women. *Publ:* Auth, Introduction, Inaugural Catalog, Grey Art Gallery & Study Ctr, 75. *Mailing Add:* 180 Commonwealth Ave Boston MA 02116

GORDON, LEAH SHANKS
WRITER

b Sharon, Pa, May 16, 34. *Study:* Bryn Mawr Col, BA, 56. *Pos:* Art researcher, Time Mag, 64-69, deputy chief researcher, 69-76, chief of res, 76- *Res:* American folk art. *Publ:* Auth, Thomas Hoving: Boomer of the arts, 11/30/75 & Help wanted at the Met, search for the new director, 6/26/77, New York Times Mag; auth, Unschooled artists, deft craftsmen in a dazzling show, Smithsonian Mag, 2/74; auth, Vanes of the wind, Natural Hist; auth, Chalk-poor man's porcelain, Americana, 1/76. *Mailing Add:* 45 W 54th St New York NY 10019

GORDON, MARTIN
DEALER, COLLECTOR

b New York, NY, Aug 15, 39. *Study:* Rochester Inst Technol, BS. *Pos:* Owner & publ, Martin Gordon Gallery, currently; general partner, Sigma Art Fund. *Mem:* Print Dealers Asn of Am; Art Dealers Asn of Am; Graphic Arts Coun NY. *Specialty:* Mid-19th through mid-20th century original prints. *Mailing Add:* Martin Gordon Inc 1000 Park Ave New York NY 10028

GORDON, RUSSELL TALBERT
PAINTER

b Philadelphia, Pa, June 3, 36. *Study:* Temple Univ, Tyler Sch, BFA, 62; Univ Wis, MS, 66, MFA, 67. *Work:* Philadelphia Mus Art; Oakland Mus; Cincinnati Mus Art; Can Coun, Ottawa; Walker Art Ctr, Minneapolis. *Comn:* Philadelphia Print Club. *Exhib:* Printmakers Invitational, Oakland Mus, 70; Poetic Fantasies, San Francisco Mus Art, 71; Extraordinary Realities, Whitney Mus Am Art, 73; Afro-American Abstraction, Los Angeles Munic Art Gallery, 82; Selected Works by Five Twentieth Century American Artists, Hastings Gallery Art, Univ Calif, San Francisco, 82; Two Artists, The Chevron Gallery, San Francisco, Calif, 83; one-person exhibs, Miami Dade Pub Libr, Fla & Waddington Gallery, Montreal, 83; and many others. *Teaching:* Asst beginning drawing, Univ Wis, 65-67; asst prof printmaking & grad sem, Univ Utah, Salt lake City, 67-69; asst prof, Univ Calif, Berkeley, 69 & 72. *Awards:* Fac Res Grant, Limited Ed Bk, Univ Utah, 69; George Marshall Fel, Vikingsborg Kunst Mus, Am Scandinavian Found, 72; Nat Endowment Arts Grant for Painting, 81. *Bibliog:* The Artists Proof Vol XI, Pratt Graphics Ctr, 71; Edward Atkinson (auth), Balck dimensions in contemporary American art, New Am Libr, 71; Leonard Edmonson (auth), Etching, Van Nostrand Reinhold Co, 73. *Publ:* Auth, Images & Impressions, Printmaking Dept, Univ Utah, 69. *Dealer:* Theo Waddington Galleries 1504 Sherbrooke West Montreal PQ Canada H3G 1L3. *Mailing Add:* 3462 Ste Familie St Montreal PQ H2X 2K8 Canada

GORDON, VIOLET
ILLUSTRATOR, WRITER

b Buffalo, NY, May 22, 07. *Study:* Albright Fine Arts Acad, with Urqhart Wilcox, Harry Jacobs, Mildred Green & Franc Root McCreery, grad (with hons); Univ Buffalo, with Dr Charles LeClair, Dorothy Shay, Harvey Beverman & Catherine Koenig. *Work:* Grosvenour Libr, Buffalo, NY; State Univ NY Buffalo. *Exhib:* San Francisco Worlds Fair, 35; Buffalo Soc Artists, Albright Knox Art Gallery, 63; one-man shows, Roycroft-Elbert Hubbard Mus, East Aurora, NY, 66 & 81 & Lincoln Room, Wilcox Mansion, 75; Cork Gallery, Lincoln Ctr, 81 & 82. *Pos:* Fashion illusr, Buffalo Eve Times & News, 29-33; designer, Ed Muth Co, 30-35. *Teaching:* Instr art & critic teacher, var grade schs, high schs & univs, 30-68; instr art, Fosdick Masten Sr High Sch, 55-68; assoc teacher art, Univ Buffalo, 65. *Awards:* Outstanding Achievement Award, Assoc Arts Orgn, 73. *Bibliog:* Betty Ott (auth), About V Gordon, Courier-Express Newspaper, 73; Natalie Fiedler (auth), And who thought up Peter Rabbit?, Ariz Repub, 74. *Mem:* Nat League Am Pen Women; Buffalo Soc Artists. *Media:* Oil, Conte Crayon. *Publ:* Contribr & illusr, Col Humor Mag, 29-32; contribr, Sch Arts Mag & Arts & Activities Mag; yearbk ed, Herald, 64-67; auth & illusr, Who's Who at the Zoo, 72; recorded, Libr Cong, 75. *Dealer:* Bonnie Flickinger 31 Nottingham Terr Buffalo NY 14216. *Mailing Add:* 891 Amherst Buffalo NY 14216

GORDY, ROBERT P
PAINTER, PRINTMAKER

b Jefferson Island, La, Oct 14, 33. *Study:* La State Univ, BA & MA; State Univ Iowa; Yale Univ, with Hans Hofmann, Yale-Norfolk Fel, 53. *Work:* Whitney Mus Am Art, New York; Corcoran Gallery, Washington, DC; Ft Worth Art Ctr, Tex; Chicago Mus of Contemp Art. *Exhib:* Am Art Exhib, 67, New Acquisitions, 68 & Biennial Exhib, 73, Whitney Mus Am Art; Winners of Exhib Artists of Southeast & Tex, New Orleans Mus Art, 68 & 72; solo exhib, Delahunty Inc, Dallas, 77 & Phyllis Kind Gallery, New York, 79; 21st Nat Print Exhib, Brooklyn Mus, 78; The 1970's: New American Painting, Int Commun Agency, 79-80; Image into Pattern, Inst Art & Cult Resources, PS1, New York, 80; retrospective, New Orleans Mus Art, 81; and others. *Awards:* Purchase Prize, Dallas Mus Fine Arts, 69; Nat Coun Arts Grant, 67; Nat Endowment Arts Grant, 78. *Bibliog:* Joseph Mashek (auth), Interview with R Gordy, Studio Int, 12/69; The character of collecting-modern, Peoria Art Mus, 70; Ted Calas (auth), The art gallery guide, 5/72. *Media:* Acrylic, Ink. *Dealer:* Phyllis Kind 226 E Ontario Chicago IL 60611; Delahunty Gallery 2611 Cedar Springs Rd Dallas TX 75201. *Mailing Add:* 2630 Bell St New Orleans LA 70119

GORE, JEFFERSON ANDERSON
CURATOR

b Selma, Ala, April 25, 43. *Study:* Harvard Col, BA(visual studies), 65; Skowhegan Sch Painting & Sculpture, 66; Grad Sch Fine Arts, Univ Pa, MFA(sculpture), 70. *Collections Arranged:* Sesquicentennial of Railroad in the Arts (auth, catalog), 79; Exquisite Nomads: Seashells Real and in Art (auth, catalog), 80; Season of Mists (auth, catalog), 81; Spacetoys: Fifty Years of Fantasy, 82; Painted Light (auth, catalog), 83; Mushroom Magic: The R Gordon Wasson Collection of Mycological Art. *Pos:* Cur fine arts, Reading Pub Mus, Pa, 78- *Teaching:* Asst sculpture, Grad Sch Fine Arts, Univ Pa, 68-70; instr, Albright Col, Pa, 70-74. *Mem:* Citizens Arts in Pa; Philadelphia Art Alliance. *Res:* Cross-cultural influences between Europe and Asia in art and philosophy. *Mailing Add:* PO Box 194 Mohnton PA 19540

GORE, KEN (KENNETH LEON)
PAINTER
b Elvira, Ill, Oct 2, 11. *Study:* Meinzinger Art Sch, Detroit, 40-42; with George Rich, 40-45 & Aldro T Hibbard, 49. *Exhib:* Guild Boston Artists, 60-83; Spring Show, Hudson Valley Art Asn, White Plains, NY, 63-83; Nat Acad Design Invitational, New York, 76; solo exhib, Frye Mus, Seattle, 77; Salmagundi Club Ann, New York, 79-82. *Awards:* Mary F Salvia Mem Award, Salmagundi Club, New York, 79; Catherine McGovern Mem Award, Hudson Valley Art Asn, 83; Marguerite Pearson Gold Medal, Rockport Art Asn, Mass, 83. *Mem:* Guild Boston Artists (vpres, 70-80); Am Artists Prof League; Allied Artists Am; North Shore Arts Asn; Rockport Art Asn. *Media:* Oil. *Dealer:* Baker Gallery Lubbock TX; Gallery Southwest Taos NM. *Mailing Add:* Main St Gloucester MA 01430

GORE, SAMUEL MARSHALL
PAINTER, SCULPTOR
b Coolidge, Tex, Nov 24, 27. *Study:* Atlanta Sch Art, BFA; Miss Col, BA; Univ Ala, MA; Ill State Univ, EdD. *Work:* Hull Gallery, Hinds Jr Col, Raymond, Miss; Ill State Univ; Miss Univ Women; Aven Galleries, Miss Col. *Comn:* Mural, Van Winkle Methodist Church, Jackson, Miss, 74; portrait bust (bronze), US Sen John Stennis, Miss Wing, Civil Air Patrol, 74 & William Faulkner, Sta WJTV, Howard Lett, Jackson, Miss, 74. *Exhib:* One-man shows, Miss Art Asn, 57 & House Admin Comt Suite, US Capitol Bldg, 75; Nat Oils Show, 58 & Mem Show, 58, Miss Art Asn, Jackson; Sears Traveling Show, 63. *Teaching:* Prof drawing, painting & sculpture & head art dept, Miss Col, 52- *Bibliog:* Ruth Campbell (producer), Conversation with Sam Gore (video tape), Miss Educ TV, 11/75. *Mem:* Miss Art Asn (secy, 61, vpres, 62, pres 63); Nat Art Educ Asn; Southeastern Art Educ Asn. *Media:* Oil, Watercolor; Terra Cotta, Bronze. *Publ:* Illusr, Mississippi Game and Fish, 58-59; illusr, Freshwater species of Mississippi, 59. *Mailing Add:* Art Dept Miss Col Clinton MS 39058

GORE, TOM
CURATOR, PHOTOGRAPHER
b Victoria, BC, Aug 7, 46. *Study:* Univ Victoria. *Work:* Prov Collection, Parliament Bldgs, Victoria; Vancouver Art Gallery, BC; Univ Victoria, BC; City Seattle. *Comn:* Illusr, Earth Meditations, Mike Doyle, 70 & Vancouver Island Poetry Soft Press, 74. *Exhib:* Art Gallery Greater Victoria, 71, 75 & 82; one-man shows, Open Space Gallery, Victoria, BC, 76 & Mind's Eye Gallery, Idaho, 79; group show, Spokane Art Mus, 79; Works in Progress, Mind's Eye Gallery, Idaho, 79; and others. *Collections Arranged:* Victoria & Victoria Five, Secession Gallery; Polaroid Collaboratory, 78 & The Stereo Show, 80, Open Space; Latitudes and Parallels, Winnipeg Gallery, 81. *Pos:* Ed art mag, Tryste, 66-68; com photogr, 69-71; cur photog, Open Space, Victoria, 75-; ed, Rhino Press, 79-; consult, Winnipeg Art Gallery, 81. *Teaching:* Instr bio-illus, Univ Victoria, 71-, lectr photog, 77-; instr photog, Camosun Col, Victoria, BC, 73-78. *Awards:* Hon Mention, BC Photogr Show, Simon Fraser Art Gallery, 73; First Prize, Vancouver Island Juried Show, Art Gallery of Greater Victoria, 74; Can Coun Grants, 77 & 78. *Bibliog:* Glen Howarth (auth), Bio-article, Victoria Press, 70; Carolyn Leier (auth), article, Arts W, 76; Contemporary Personage, Padua, Italy, 80. *Mem:* Open Space Arts Soc (pres, 78-); Soc for Photog Educ, NW Region (chmn, 78-81). *Media:* Collage and photography. *Res:* Criticism of photography; John Thomson biography; the photograph as theatre; evolution of photographic landscape.. *Publ:* Contemporary Photography in British Columbia, Ryerson, 79; auth, Collecting the paradoxical magic mirror, Photo Communique, PI, 5/79; auth, In perspective: Vancouver art, Arts W, 1/79; Portfolio, Camera Mainichi, Tokyo, 10/81; George Craven's Objects and Images, New York, 81. *Mailing Add:* PO Box 5207 Sta B Victoria BC V8R 6N4 Canada

GOREE, GARY PAUL
INSTRUCTOR, PAINTER
b Jackson, Miss, Apr 8, 51. *Study:* Southwestern Okla State Univ, BFA, 72; Tex Tech Univ, MA(educ), 80. *Exhib:* Greater Fall River Nat, Mass, 78; Nat Cape Coral Ann, Fla, 79; Okla Art Ann, Tulsa, 80; Okla 81, Univ Okla, Norman, 81. *Pos:* Art supervisor, Tulsa pub schs, 82- *Teaching:* Instr art, Lewis & Clark Jr High, Tulsa, 73-81; teaching asst art, Tex Tech Univ, 77; instr watercolor, Tulsa Jr Col, Okla, 74- *Awards:* Okla Art Educr of Yr, 83. *Mem:* Nat Art Educ Asn; Okla Art Educ Asn; Southwestern Art Asn; Okla Art Guild; Tulsa Artist Guild. *Media:* Watercolor. *Publ:* Coauth, Found Object Design in Jewelry, 76, coauth, Weaving, Soft Sculpture & Natural Dyes, 77 & coauth, Plans, Projects and Processes, 80, Tulsa Pub Schs. *Dealer:* Margo Shorney 6616 N Olie Oklahoma City OK 74128. *Mailing Add:* 1112 E 17 Tulsa OK 74120

GORELEIGH, REX
PAINTER, PRINTMAKER
b Penllyn, Pa, Sept 2, 02. *Study:* Pvt study with Xavier J Barile, New York; Art Inst Chicago, with Francis Chapin; Andre L'Hote Acad, Paris; sculpture with Leo Z Moll, Berlin, Ger; Art Dept, Univ Chicago. *Exhib:* One-man show, Strindberg Gallery, Helsinki, Finland, 35; Am Artist Gallery, Chicago, 43; Watercolor Exhib NJ Artist, Trenton Mus, 50; NJ Artist, Montclair Art Mus, 53; Realities Expanded, Nat Ctr Afro-Am Artists, 73. *Pos:* Assoc dir, Community Ctr, Greensboro, NC, 38-39; dir, Southside Community Art Ctr, Chicago, 42-44; dir, Princeton Group Arts, NJ, 47-53; dir & owner, Studio-on-the-Canal, Princeton, 55- *Awards:* Certificate Award, NJ Coun Arts, 70; Award-Grant for Mural Design, NJ State Coun Arts, 77; and others. *Bibliog:* Alain L Locke (auth), The Negro in Art, Hacker Co, 40; Cedric Dover (auth), American Negro Art, New York Graphic Soc, 60; Elton C Fax (auth), 17 Black Artists, Dodd, Mead & Co, 72. *Mem:* Artists Equity NJ; Alain L Locke Soc Princeton Univ. *Mailing Add:* 6-H Avon Dr E Windsor Township NJ 08561

GORELICK, SHIRLEY
PAINTER, PRINTMAKER
b Brooklyn, NY, Jan 24, 24. *Study:* Brooklyn Col, BA; Teachers Col, Columbia Univ, MA. *Work:* Norfolk Mus, Va; Brooklyn Mus; Post Col; Housatonic Mus, Conn; Aldrich Mus, Ridgefield, Conn; and others. *Exhib:* 3rd Ann Contemporary Reflections, Aldrich Mus, Ridgefield, Conn, 74; 19th Nat Print Exhib, Brooklyn Mus, NY, 74; solo shows, Angelski Gallery, New York, 61, Cent Hall Gallery, Port Washington, NY, 74, 76 & 78, Soho 20 Gallery, New York, 75, 77 & 79 & Art Gallery, State Univ NY Stony Brook, 79; Nothing but Nudes, Whitney Mus of Am Art, New York, 77; Hassam Fund Exhib, Am Acad-Inst Arts & Letters, New York, 78; 43rd Nat Midyear Show, Butler Inst Am Art, Youngstown, Ohio, 79; Contemporary Naturalism, Nassau Co Mus, Roslyn, New York, 80; and many others. *Teaching:* Instr painting, NShore Community Arts Ctr, Great Neck, NY, 61-79; instr drawing, Nassau Co Off Cult Develop, 73-74. *Awards:* RI Arts Festival Award, 64; Purchase Award, Nassau Community Col, 72; Creative Artists Pub Serv Fel/Painting, NY State Coun on the Arts, 75-76. *Bibliog:* Yvette Jayson Sencer (auth), article, Arts, 79; Barbara Colin (auth), article, Arts, 82; Phyllis Brap (auth), New York Times, 83; and others. *Mem:* Women's Interart Ctr, New York ; Woman's Caucus Art; Prof Artist Guild (vpres, 71-75); Central Hall Artists (treas, 74-78); and others. *Media:* Acrylic. *Dealer:* Soho 20 Gallery 469 Broome St New York NY 10013. *Mailing Add:* 3 Mirrielees Circle Great Neck NY 11021

GORMAN, R C
PAINTER, DEALER
b Chinle, Ariz, July 26, 33. *Study:* Northern Ariz Univ, with Jack Salter & Ellery Gibson; Mexico City Col. *Work:* Heard Mus, Phoenix, Ariz; Philbrook Art Ctr, Tulsa, Okla; Northern Ariz Univ, Flagstaff; Gonzaga Univ, Spokane, Wash; Santa Fe Fine Arts Mus, NMex. *Comn:* Dance of the Hohokam Masked Figures, St Luke's Hosp, Phoenix, 71. *Exhib:* Muirhead Gallery, Costa Mesa, Calif, 78; Art Wagon Gallery, Scottsdale, Ariz, 78; Munic Mus, St Paul de Vence, France, 79; Navajo Turquoise Gallery, Paris, France, 80; Marjorie Kauffman Graphics Gallery, Houston, Tex, 80; and others. *Collections Arranged:* US Indian Arts & Crafts Bd, Washington, DC, 68. *Pos:* Owner, Navajo Gallery, Taos, currently. *Awards:* Grand Award, Am Indian Art Exhib, Oakland, 66; First Award, Scottsdale Nat Indian Exhib, 67; First Award, Heard Mus Guild Exhib, Phoenix, 68. *Bibliog:* Ronald Leal (auth), R C Gorman-the two worlds of a Navajo artist, Mankind Mag, 70; John Milton (auth), R C Gorman-interview-the American Indian speaks, SDak Rev, 70; Robert A Ewing (auth), An Indian artist & hist art-this is Gorman, NMex Mag, 71. *Mem:* Taos Art Asn. *Media:* Acrylic, Oil, Pastel. *Specialty:* Southwest art; Indian painters. *Interests:* Modern Indian painters. *Collection:* F Scholder, Tavlos, Pletka, C Counter, C Bissell, C Lovato, C Cannon, Kin-ya-onny Beyeh & Bob Hoasous. *Publ:* Contribr, 23 contemporary Indian artists, Art in Am, 72; contribr, American deserts, Nat Geog Mag, 72. *Dealer:* Jamison Galleries 111 E San Francisco Santa Fe NM 87501; Mary Livingston c/o Gallery II 1211 N Broadway Santa Ana CA 92701. *Mailing Add:* Navajo Gallery PO Box 1756 Taos NM 87571

GORMAN, WILLIAM D
PAINTER, GRAPHIC ARTIST
b Jersey City, NJ, June 27, 25. *Study:* Newark Sch Fine & Indust Arts, NJ. *Work:* Newark Mus; Butler Inst Am Art, Youngstown, Ohio; Montclair Art Mus, NJ; Colorado Springs Fine Art Ctr, Colo; US Dept State, Washington, DC. *Exhib:* One-man show, Philadelphia Art Alliance, 65; US Dept State Art in Embassies Prog, Europe, Africa & Orient, 67-75; NJ Artists, Newark Mus, 68; US Watercolor Invitational; Seven American Watercolorists, Davenport Mus, Iowa, 73; plus others. *Pos:* Dir, Old Bergen Art Guild, Bayonne, NJ, 62- *Awards:* Henry Ward Ranger Fund Purchase Prizes, Nat Acad Design, 65 & 71; Gold Medal of Honor, Allied Artists of Am, 73; Shiva Award, Audubon Artists, 79; plus others. *Bibliog:* Henry Gasser (auth), article in Am Artist, 10/70. *Mem:* Assoc Nat Acad Design; Audubon Artists; Am Watercolor Soc (1st vpres, currently); Allied Artists Am; Nat Soc Painters Casein & Acrylic; Assoc Artists NJ. *Media:* Casein Tempera; Pen & Ink. *Publ:* Auth, articles in Today's Art Mag & Am Artist. *Mailing Add:* 43 W 33rd St Bayonne NJ 07002

GORNEY, JAY PHILIP
DEALER
b Brooklyn, NY, Sept 26, 52. *Study:* Oberlin Col, with Ellen H Johnson, BA(art hist), 73; Whitney Mus Independent Study Prog, fall 72. *Collections Arranged:* City as a Source, Whitney Mus Am Art, 72-73; Matta: Totemic World (with Patricia Hamilton), Andrew Crispo Gallery, 75; Color & Structure, Hamilton Gallery, 79; New Biomorphism and Automatism, Hamilton Gallery, 83. *Pos:* Assoc dir, Hamilton Gallery of Contemp Art, New York, currently. *Res:* Contemporary painting, drawing and sculpture. *Publ:* Auth, Oberlin's tribute to Ellen Johnson, Art News, 4/75; auth, Cynthia Carlson, Arts Mag, 10/76; auth, Barbara Zucker, Arts Mag, 1/77; auth, Review of drawing today in New York, Col Art J, winter 76/77. *Mailing Add:* 302 W 12th St New York NY 10019

GORNIK, APRIL
PAINTER
b Cleveland, Ohio, Apr 20, 53. *Study:* Cleveland Inst Art, 71-75; Nova Scotia Col Art & Design, BFA, 75-76. *Work:* Nova Scotia Art Bank, Halifax, NS; Chase Manhattan Permanent Collection, London, Eng. *Exhib:* May Show, Cleveland Mus Art, Ohio, 74; Women's Invitational, Nat Organization Visual Arts, Cleveland, Ohio, 74; Butler Women's Invitational, Butler Inst Am Art, Youngstown, Ohio, 76; one-woman show, Edward Thorp Gallery, New York, 81; The Reality of Perception, Robeson Ctr Gallery, Rutgers Univ, Newark,

NJ, 81; Landscape, Davis Art Gallery, Univ Akron, Ohio, 81. *Bibliog:* Addison Parks (auth), article, Arts Mag, 81; Thomas Lawson (auth), article, Artforum, 81; Robert Berlind (auth), April Gornik at Thorp, Art in Am, 81. *Media:* Oil. *Dealer:* Edward Thorp Gallery 419 W Broadway New York NY 10012. *Mailing Add:* 77 Reade St New York NY 10007

GORSKI, DANIEL ALEXANDER
SCULPTOR, PAINTER
b Cleveland, Ohio, Oct 26, 39. *Study:* Cleveland Inst Art, dipl, 61; Yale Univ Sch Art & Archit, with Jack Tworkow & Al Held, BFA, 62 & MFA, 64. *Work:* Yale Univ. *Exhib:* Primary Structures, Jewish Mus, New York, 66; Cool Art, Larry Aldrich Mus, Ridgefield, Conn, 68; Hanging and Leaning, Emily Lowe Gallery, Hofstra Univ, 70; 26 x 26, Vassar Col Art Gallery, 71; Md Biennial Exhib, Baltimore Mus of Art, 76; Sculpture Outdoors, Temple Univ, Ambler, Pa, 77-80; Sculpture 81, Beaver Col; and others. *Teaching:* Instr design, painting & color, Md Inst Col Art, 71-; vis lectr art hist & fashion design, Drexel Univ, 72. *Awards:* Mr & Mrs Jules Horelick Award, Baltimore Mus of Art, 76; Ford Found Grant, Shelter Inst, summer 79. *Bibliog:* L Lippard (auth), Recent sculpture as escape, 2/66 & Escalation in Washington, 1/68, Art Int; U Kalterman (auth), The New Sculpture, Praeger, 68. *Mailing Add:* 1601 Guilford Ave Baltimore MD 21202

GORSKI, RICHARD KENNY
EDUCATOR, GRAPHIC ARTIST
b Green Bay, Wis, Apr 20, 23. *Study:* Northern Ill Univ, De Kalb, 62-65; Univ Wis, Milwaukee & Madison, MS(art educ), 50. *Work:* Milwaukee Pub Schs collection of Wis Artists. *Exhib:* Wisconsin Painters & Sculptors, Wis Union Gallery, Madison, 39, 47, 49 & 53-56; Minneapolis-Milwaukee Art Inst, 40, 46, 47, 49, 50, 53, 55-57 & 60; Walker Art Inst, 47 & 49. *Pos:* Cur & dir, Rahr Civic Ctr & Mus, Manitowoc, Wis, 50-53; illusr & designer, John Higgs Studios, Milwaukee, Wis, 56-57; art dir, United Educators Publ Inc, Lake Bluff, Ill, 60-61; dept head, art & design, Northern Mich Univ, Marquette, 65-75. *Teaching:* Instr art educ, Nat Col of Educ, Evanston, Ill, 57-60; assoc prof art educ, Northeastern Ill Univ, Chicago, 61-65; prof graphic design, Northern Mich Univ, Marquette, 65- *Awards:* Journal Purchase Award, Wis Painters Ann, Milwaukee J Pub Schs Collection, 57; Special Merit Award, Wis Gimbels Salon, Gimbels Inc, 50. *Mem:* Nat Art Asn; Mich Art Educ Asn. *Res:* Structural basis of visual communication. *Publ:* Auth, Color; an article in United Educators Encycl & auth, Painting; an article in The Wonderland of Knowledge Encycl, United Educ Publ, 60. *Mailing Add:* 1502 N Garfield Ave Marquette MI 49855

GORSLINE, DOUGLAS WARNER
PAINTER, ILLUSTRATOR
b Rochester, NY, May 24, 13. *Study:* Yale Univ Sch Fine Arts; Art Students League. *Work:* Butler Inst Am Art; Harvard Univ Houghton Libr; Libr Cong, Washington, DC; Lehigh Univ; St Paul Gallery Art, Minn; and others. *Comn:* Oil painting on basketball, Sports Illustrated, New York; oil painting on sports, Westvaco, New York; City Dijon, France, 79. *Exhib:* Pa Acad Fine Arts, 63; Am Acad Arts & Lett, 64; Butler Inst Am Art, 72; one-man shows, Mem Art Gallery, Rochester, 75, Palais des Etats de Bourgogne: Salon D'Appollon, Dijon, 79 & Foire Int de Grand, Belgium, 80; Art 83, Palais Fleurs Aix Bains, France; and others. *Teaching:* Instr art, Nat Acad Sch Fine Arts. *Awards:* Childe Hassam Fund Purchase Award, Am Acad Arts & Lett, 62; Henry Ward Ranger Fund Purchase Award, Nat Acad Design, 63; Tiffany Found Grant, 63. *Bibliog:* The new dimension of Douglas Gorsline Whitaker, Am Artist, 66; Pierre Bouhin (dir), Bleau Comme Ure Orange (film), 81. *Mem:* Nat Acad Design. *Media:* Oil, Watercolor. *Mailing Add:* Bussy le Grand 21150 Les Laumes 10031 France

GOSSAGE, JOHN RALPH
PHOTOGRAPHER
b New York, NY, Mar 15, 46. *Study:* Waldon Sch, 67-69. *Work:* Mus Mod Art, New York; Houston Mus Fine Art; San Francisco Mus Art; Philadelphia Mus Art; George Eastman House, Rochester, NY. *Comn:* Nation's Capitol in Photographs, Corcoran Gallery, 76; Photography in America, Am Tel & Tel, New York, 78; Photography and the City, Seattle Art Comn, 79. *Exhib:* 14 American Photographers, Baltimore Mus & travelling, 75; solo exhib, Castelli Gallery, New York, 76 & Lunn Gallery, Washington, DC, 80; Tenth Biennale Paris, Mus Mod Art, Paris, 77; Contemporary Photographic Works, Houston Mus Fine Arts, 77; Gardens, Werkstalt Photog, Berlin, 78; Photography & Sense of Order, Inst Contemp Art, Philadelphia, 81; History of Portrait Photography, Mus Art, Bonn, Ger, 82. *Pos:* Assoc ed, Aperture Mag, 82-; vpres, Columbia Arts Inc, 82- *Teaching:* Assoc prof photog & art, Univ Md, 77- *Awards:* Grants, Stern Found, 74 & Nat Endowment Arts, 74 & 78. *Bibliog:* Renato Dansse (auth), American Images, McGraw Hill, 79. *Publ:* Auth, Gardens, Castelli Graphics, 78; auth, The Pond, Aperture Publ, 84. *Dealer:* Castelli Uptown 4 E 77 St New York NY 10021. *Mailing Add:* 1875 Mintwood Pl NW #30 Washington DC 20009

GOTO, JOSEPH
SCULPTOR
b Hilo, Hawaii, Jan 7, 20. *Study:* Art Inst Chicago; Roosevelt Univ. *Work:* Art Inst Chicago; Ind Univ; Mus Mod Art, New York; Univ Mich; Union Carbide Corp. *Exhib:* Art Inst Chicago; J B Speed Art Mus, Louisville, Ky; Whitney Mus Am Art, New York; Retrospective, RI Sch Design, 72; solo exhibs, Honolulu Acad, 73, Contemp Arts Ctr Hawaii, Honolulu, 73 & Zabriskie Gallery, 73; and others. *Teaching:* Instr, Col William & Mary, 58-59, Univ Mich, 59-63, RI Sch Design, 63-65, Univ Ill, 65, Carnegie Inst Technol, 58 & Brandeis Univ, 70. *Awards:* Graham Found Fel, 57; John Hay Whitney Fel; Guggenheim Fel, 69. *Mailing Add:* 17 Sixth St Providence RI 02906

GOTTLIEB, CARLA
EDUCATOR, WRITER
b Cernauti, Bukovina, July 16, 12; US citizen. *Study:* Oltea Doamna, Cernauti, BA, 29; Carolina Univ, Cernauti, MA, 34; Columbia Univ, with Rensselaer Lee, Meyer Schapiro & Charles de Tolnay, PhD, 51. *Teaching:* Fac mem hist art, New Sch Social Res, 56-60; chmn dept, Ripon Col, 60-62; assoc prof, Univ Ill, Urbana-Champaign, 62-64. *Mem:* Am Asn Univ Prof; Authors Guild. *Res:* Modern and contemporary art; Greek architecture; symbolic and expressive meaning of motifs; principles of art. *Publ:* Contribr, The Meaning of Death, McGraw-Hill, 59 & 65; auth, Beyond Modern Art, E P Dutton, 76; auth, The Restoration of the Nereid Monument at Xanthos, 81 & The Window as a Symbol in Western Painting: From Divinity to Doubt, 83, Boian; auth, Self-Portraiture: From Ancient Egypt to World War II, E P Dutton, 83. *Mailing Add:* 246 West End Ave 10B New York NY 10023

GOTTSCHALK, FRITZ
DESIGNER, LECTURER
b Zurich, Switz, Dec 30, 37. *Study:* Kunstgewerbeschule, Zurich, Switz, dipl; Art Inst Orell Fussli, Zurich, dipl; Allgemeine Gewerbeschule, Basel, Switz, post-grad dipl, with E Ruder & A Hofmann. *Exhib:* The Visual Image of the Montreal Mus, Montreal Mus Fine Arts, Que, Can, 68; Swiss Design, Mus du Louvre, Paris, France, 71; Alliance Graphique Internationale: 107 Int Designers, Milan, Italy, 74; The Work of Gottschalk & Ash Ltd, Ryder Gallery, sponsored by Container Corp of Am, Chicago, 76. *Pos:* Designer, art dir & design dir, Gottschalk & Ash Int, Meilen, Zurich, Switz, 77-; dir design & quality control off, Organizing Comt of 1976 Olympic Games, 74-76. *Awards:* Award of Excellence, Swiss Contemp Design, Dept of Interior, Swiss Govt, 62; two Awards of Excellence, Soc Publ Designers, New York, 70; Bronze Medal, Foire Int du Livre, Leipzig, EGer, 77. *Bibliog:* Adrian Gatrail (auth), The Image Makers, The Gazette, Can, 70; Bill Bantey (auth), Gottschalk & Ash Ltd, Graphis, Switz, Vol 148 (1972); Midori Imatake (auth), Gottschalk & Ash Ltd, Idea (Japan), Vol 115 (1973). *Mem:* Que Soc Graphic Artists; Royal Can Acad; Asn of Swiss Graphic Artists; Alliance Graphique Internationale; Graphic Designers of Can. *Media:* Graphic Design, Books and Corporate Images. *Publ:* Auth & illusr, article, Idea, Seibundo Shinkosha Publ Co, Japan, Vol 115, 72; ed, article, Revue Suisse de l'Imprimerie, Zollikofer AG, Switz, 74; illusr & contribr, article, Communication Arts, Coyne & Blanchard, Inc, 75; ed, article, Graphis, Vol 185, 77. *Mailing Add:* Sonnhaldenstrasse 3 Zurich Switzerland

GOTTSCHALK, MAX JULES
DESIGNER, INSTRUCTOR
b St Louis, Mo, Dec 14, 09. *Study:* Painting, drawing & design with father, Max Gottschalk, also with Edmond Wurpel, Charles Quest, Fred Conway, E Ludwig, Goetsh, Hudson & Mylonas; Wash Univ, BA. *Work:* Agnese Udinotti, Scottsdale, Ariz; Robert Graham, New York. *Comn:* Nat indigenous product form, Newfoundland Comn Govt, 39-42; Scott Paper Towel Holder, Gerald C Johnson Assocs, New York, 44-48; new modular chassis systs, Hughes Aircraft, Tucson, Ariz, 52-60; first open frozen food refrigeration, electronic checkout, Hussmann Ligonier Co, St Louis; work on lunar escape vehicle, air cushion vehical, Bell Aerosysts, Niagara Falls, NY. *Exhib:* St Louis Artist Guild, 35 & St Louis Art Mus, 36; St John's, Nfld, 40-42; Mus Mod Art, New York, 48-50; Int Canvas Exhib, Tokyo, 75; Pima Col, Rosequrst Wohlheim Gallery, Tucson; and others. *Pos:* Pres Imagineering & vpres, Max Gottschalk Inc, currently. *Teaching:* Instr design, drawing & perception & chmn art & design dept, Pima Community Col, Tucson, 70-, instr functional design, interior decoration & graphics & chmn design, decorating & drafting dept, 75, chmn, Applied Design Dept, 81. *Mem:* Life mem Soc Audio Engineers. *Dealer:* Agnese Udinotti Scottsdale AZ; The Contemporary Craftsman 112 Don Gaspar Santa Fe NM. *Mailing Add:* 5620 N Campbell Tucson AZ 85718

GOUGH, GEORGIA BELLE
CRAFTSMAN, EDUCATOR
b Oklahoma City, Okla, Dec 21, 20. *Study:* Central State Univ, Okla, BS, 41; NTex State Univ, MS, 45; with Carlton Ball, 48; with Daniel Rhodes, 54; Univ Okla, PhD, 60. *Work:* Campbell Mem Collection, Am Craft Mus, New York. *Exhib:* Syracuse Mus, NY, 51 & 56; Wichita Decorative Arts & Crafts, Wichita Mus, Kans, 50, 51 & 53; Miami Nat Ceramic Exhib, Fla, 56; Dallas Craft Market, Tex, 81 & 82. *Teaching:* Prof ceramics, NTex State Univ, 47-75. *Awards:* Third Place, Tex Fine Arts Asn, 53. *Mem:* Am Craft Coun (trustee, 76-80); Nat Coun Educ Ceramic Arts (secy, 70-73); Am Ceramic Soc Design Sect Southwest Region (pres & secy); World Crafts Coun (US delegate, 78 & 80); honorary mem Tex Designer/Craftsmen. *Publ:* Auth, Use of native clays in high-grade pottery, Ceramic Industry, 53; auth, Computer data processing system calculations of glaze formulae, Am Ceramic Soc Bulletin, 65. *Dealer:* Creative Hands Gallery 3000 McKinney Dallas TX 75204. *Mailing Add:* 1813 Willowwood N T Station Denton TX 76201

GOUGH, ROBERT ALAN
PAINTER
b Quebec, PQ, Aug 13, 31; US citizen. *Study:* Am Acad Art, Chicago, with William H Mosby & J Allen St John. *Work:* Am Fedn Arts; Butler Inst Am Art; Univ Nebr; Sheldon Swope Art Gallery; Marietta Col. *Exhib:* Painting & Sculpture Today, Herron Mus Art, 66; one-man shows, Gilman Galleries, Chicago, 67 & 69; 35 Years in Retrospect, Butler Inst Am Art, 71; Mainstreams, Marietta Col, 74, 75 & 77; Art from Appalachia Traveling Exhib, Smithsonian Inst, 81-; and others. *Awards:* Henry Ward Ranger Purchase Prize, Nat Acad Design, 62; Judges Award, Marietta Nat, 78; Ohioana Libr Asn Citation, 81. *Bibliog:* Documentary, WBNS-TV, Columbus, Ohio, 70. *Media:* Oil, Pencil. *Dealer:* Foster Harmon Galleries Am Art 1415 Main St Sarasota FL 33577; Harmon Gallery 1258 Third St S Naples FL 33940. *Mailing Add:* 220 Brookside Dr Chillicothe OH 45601

GOULD, JOHN HOWARD
PAINTER, FILMMAKER

b Toronto, Ont, Aug 14, 29. *Study:* Ont Col Art, AOCA, 52; Acad Julian, Paris, 52. *Work:* Nat Gallery Can; Montreal Mus Fine Arts; Beaverbrook Mus, Fredericton, NB; and others in pvt collections. *Comn:* Portrait of Alan Jarvis, Head of Nat Gallery Can, Ottawa, 62; Pikangikum (drawn film of Indians), Nat Film Bd Can, 67; performance drawings of Marcel Marceau, City Ctr, New York, 71; drawn film of Marceau, Paris. 71. *Exhib:* Canadian Surrealism Today, touring exhib, 64; Focus on Drawing, Int Drawing Survey, 65 & The Work of Art, 79, Art Gallery Toronto; Retrospectives, Univ Toronto, 65 & The Drawn Image, traveling, 79; Can rep, Films on Art Category, Venice Biennale, 66; Flint Inst Arts Survey Exhib, 66. *Teaching:* Instr life drawing, Ont Col Art, Toronto, currently. *Awards:* Greenshield Award for Figurative Painting, Spain, 60; Can Coun Grants, Drawn Film of Peru, 67 & Drawn Film of Japan, 70. *Bibliog:* John Griffin (dir), John Gould on Drawing (film), Gesture Productions, 72; incl in The Nude in Canadian Painting, New Press, Can, 72; The Drawn Image, Roberts Gallery, 79. *Mem:* Royal Can Acad. *Dealer:* Roberts Gallery 641 Yonge St Toronto ON M4Y 1Z9 Can. *Mailing Add:* Moonstone PO Moonstone ON L0K 1N0 Canada

GOULD, KAREN KEEL
HISTORIAN, EDUCATOR

b Austin, Tex, Sept 26, 46. *Study:* Univ Tex, Austin, BS, 68, MA, 70, PhD, 75. *Teaching:* Vis asst prof art hist, Univ Ore, 80; Mellon Fel, Duke Univ, 80-81; lectr hist, Univ Tex, Austin, 81- *Mem:* Col Art Asn; Int Ctr Medieval Art; Southeastern Medieval Asn (mem exec coun, 81-83); Medieval Acad Am; Bibliographical Soc Am. *Res:* Manuscript illumination; history of manuscripts and printed books. *Publ:* Auth, Illumination and sculpture in thirteenth century Amiens, Art Bulletin, 77; auth, The Psalter and Hours of Yolande of Soissons, Medieval Acad, 78; auth, Sequences De Sanctis Reliquiis as Sainte-Chapelle Inventories, Mediaeval Studies, 81; auth, The Gutenberg Bible at Texas: An educational resource, Libr Chronicle, 83. *Mailing Add:* 2602 La Ronde Austin TX 78731

GOULD, PHILIP
HISTORIAN, EDUCATOR

b New York, NY, Oct 17, 22. *Study:* NY Univ, BA, 49; L'Univ Paris, Dr Univ, 53. *Teaching:* Instr art hist, Columbia Univ, 54-59, lectr, 56-62; prof, Sarah Lawrence Col, 59-; vis prof, Fordham Univ, spring 68, Pratt Inst, fall 73 & Col Chinese Cult, Taipei, Taiwan, 75-76. *Bibliog:* Nick Natanson (auth), The craft of teaching, Sarah Lawrence Col Bulletin, spring 83. *Mem:* Soc Archit Historians; Am Soc Aesthetics. *Res:* Chinese art in general and aspects of Chinese garden design and history in particular. *Publ:* Contribr, Encycl Am, 64; contribr, New Cath Encycl, 64; auth, Exhibition of Chinese Painting, Ming & Ch'ing (catalog), 73 & Exhibition of Chinese Folk & Provincial Ceramics (catalog), 76, Sarah Lawrence Col; contribr, Acad Am Encycl, 80. *Mailing Add:* 15 Claremont Ave New York NY 10027

GOULD, STEPHEN
SCULPTOR, COLLECTOR

b New York, NY, Dec 25, 09. *Study:* New Sch Social Res, with Manola Pascal. *Work:* Newark Mus, NJ; Morris Mus Fine Art, NJ; Miami Mus Mod Art, Fla; Washington Co Mus Fine Arts, Hagerstown, Md; Allen R Hite Art Inst, Univ Louisville. *Exhib:* Nat Exhib Prof Artists, New York, 65; New Sch Social Res, 67; Nat Soc Arts & Lett, New York, 69; Nat Coun Jewish Women, South Orange, NJ, 71; Salmagundi Club, 75; Nat Soc Arts & Letters Exhib, Metrop Mus Art, New York, 79. *Pos:* Art lectr, Bermuda Club, Tamarac, Fla, 74- *Awards:* Award of Month for Heart of Humanity, Washington Co Mus Fine Art, 70; First Prize for I Protest (bronze sculpture), Soc l'Ecole Francais, 71-72; First Prize for We are the Clay & Thou Lord our Potter, De Bellis, Salmagundi Club, 75. *Bibliog:* M Pescara (auth), Sculptor-Stephen Gould, Am Rev Art & Sci, 69. *Mem:* Royal Soc Arts; Nat Soc Arts & Lett; Artists Equity Asn; Salmagundi Club. *Media:* Clay. *Collection:* Oils, French impressionist and post impressionist; prints, lithographs, watercolors, numismatics, glass; violin collection. *Mailing Add:* 4905 Bayberry Lane Tamarac FL 33319

GOULDS, PETER J
DEALER, DESIGNER

b London, England, Oct 5, 48. *Study:* Walthamstow Sch Art, England, 65-67; Coventry Sch Art, England, 67-70; Sch Advan Studies, Manchester Polytechnic, Shell Fel, 72. *Pos:* Owner, LA Louver Gallery, Venice, Calif, 76- *Teaching:* Lectr commun design, Leeds Polytechnic, Yorkshire, England, 72; vis lectr video workshop & design, Univ Calif, Los Angeles, 72-75. *Awards:* Leverhulme Award, Uni-Lever Trust, 71; univ res grants, Univ Calif, 72, 73 & 74. *Specialty:* Contemporary American and English painting & sculpture. *Mailing Add:* c/o LA Louver Gallery 55 N Venice Blvd Venice CA 90291

GOULET, CLAUDE
EDUCATOR, PAINTER

b Montreal, Que, June 5, 25. *Study:* Univ Montreal, LScBioChem. *Work:* Mus Montreal, Que; Mus Que, Montreal; Nat Gallery Can, Ottawa; Cult Art Ctr Can, Paris; Yoseido Gallery, Tokyo, Japan. *Comn:* Mural, Univ Montreal, 67; mural, Negresco Nice, France, 66; mural, Radio Can, Montreal, 70; mural, Toronto Dominion, Ctr, Ont, 71; mobile sculpture, Thetford Mines, Asbestos Ctr, Que, 75. *Exhib:* Third Int Exhib, Cagnes-sur-Mer, France, 71; Can Cult Ctr, Paris, 71; Zwarte Panter Gallery, Anvers, Belg, 72; Neuilly-sur-Seine, Paris, 74; Galerie G Wolf, Deauville, France, 75. *Teaching:* Instr art environment, Univ Que, 75- *Awards:* Can Art Coun Grant, 70; Min Cult Affairs Grant, Prov Que, 71; Nat Prize, 3rd Int Festival, Cagnes-sur-Mer, France, 71. *Bibliog:* Articles, Vie Des Arts, 77. *Mem:* Royal Can Acad; Asn Prof Artists, Que (vpres, 65-69); Can Soc Artists. *Media:* Oil, Acrylic. *Mailing Add:* 15160 Notre-Dame Est Pointe Aux Trembles PQ H1A 1W6 Canada

GOULET, LORRIE (LORRIE J DE CREEFT)
SCULPTOR, INSTRUCTOR

b ˈverdale, NY, Aug 17, 25. *Study:* Inwood Potteries Studios, New York, 32-36, with Amiee Voorhees; Black Mountain Col, with Josef Albers; sculpture with Jose de Creeft, 43-44. *Work:* Sarah Roby Found; Joseph H Hirshhorn Collection; NJ State Mus; Sen William Benton; Ball State Univ Art Gallery. *Comn:* Ceramic relief, New York Pub Libr, Grand Concourse, Bronx, 58; ceramic relief, Nurses' Residence & Sch, Bronx Munic Hosp, 61; stainless steel relief, 48th Precinct Police & Fire Sta, Bronx, 71. *Exhib:* Dimensions 69, Temple Emein, NJ, 69; Outdoor Sculpture Show, Van Saun Park, NJ, 71; one-artist shows, Contemporaries Gallery, New York, 59, 62, 66 & 68, Kennedy Galleries, New York, 71, 73-75, 78 & 80; Summit Art Ctr, NJ, 78; Nat Arts Club, New York, 78; plus many other group & one-man shows. *Pos:* Guest demonstr, Around the Corner, New York Dept Educ, CBS-TV, 64-65. *Teaching:* Instr sculpture-var media & staff mem, Mus Mod Art, New York, 57-64; sculpture staff mem, Scarsdale Studio Workshop, 59-61 & New Sch Social Res, 61-75; staff instr sculpture, Art Students League, New York, 81. *Awards:* First Sculpture Prize, Norton Gallery, 49 & 50 & Westchester Art Soc, 64; Soltan Engel Mem Award, Audubon Artists, 67. *Mem:* Sculptors Guild; Audubon Artists; founding mem Visual Artists & Galleries Asn; Nat Comt Art Educ; Rye Art Ctr (bd dirs); Westchester Art Soc. *Media:* Stone, Wood; Metal. *Publ:* Contribr, 20th century sculptors look at their work, The Palette; auth article on greenstone, In: Slate & Soft Stones, 71. *Dealer:* Kennedy Galleries 40 W 57th St New York NY 10022. *Mailing Add:* 241 W 20th St New York NY 10011

GOUMA-PETERSON, THALIA
EDUCATOR, HISTORIAN

b Athens, Greece, Nov 21, 33; US citizen. *Study:* Mills Col, BA(art), 54, MA(art hist), 57; Univ Wis, PhD(art hist), 63. *Teaching:* Instr art hist, Univ Wis, 58 & Oberlin Col, 60-61; from asst prof to assoc prof, Col Wooster, 68-76, prof, 76- *Mem:* Nat Comt Byzantine Studies; Col Art Asn; Medieval Acad Am; Int Ctr of Medieval Art; Women's Caucus for Art. *Publ:* Auth, A Palaeologan Icon of St Nicholas, Byzantine, Greek and Russian Icons, Univ Col, Cardiff, Wales, 73; auth, The Pareeclesion of St Euthymios in Thessalonika: Art and monastic policy under Andronicos II, Art Bulletin, Vol 3 (1976) 168-183; auth, Piero della Francesca's Flagellation: An Historical Interpretation, Storia dell' Arte, Vol 28 (1976): 219-233; auth, Christ as Ministrant and the Priest as Ministrant Christ in a Palaeologan Program of 1303, Dumbarton Oaks Papers, 80; ed & coauth, Miriam Schapiro: A Retrospective 1953-1980, College Wooster, 80. *Mailing Add:* Art Dept Col of Wooster Wooster OH 44691

GOUREVITCH, JACQUELINE
PAINTER

b Paris, France, Oct 28, 33; US citizen. *Study:* Black Mountain Col, NC, 50; Art Students League, 52; Univ Chicago, BA, 54; Art Inst Chicago, 54-55. *Work:* Chase Manhattan Bank; Am Acad of Arts & Lett, New York; Univ NMex, Albuquerque; Wesleyan Univ, Middletown, Conn; Univ Art Mus, Berkeley, Calif. *Comn:* Conn Comn Arts, Western Conn State Univ, Danbury, 83. *Exhib:* One-woman shows, Tibor de Nagy Gallery, New York, 71, 72 & 73, Painting & Sculpture Today, Indianapolis Mus Art, 72, Wesleyan Univ, Conn, 74, 77 & 83, Wadsworth Atheneum, Hartford, Conn, 75 & Condeso/Lawler Gallery, New York, 80 & 82; De Cordova Mus, Lincoln, Mass, 71 & 78; Whitney Mus Am Art Ann, 73; MacNay Art Inst, San Antonio, Tex, 74; and others. *Teaching:* Artist in residence, Tamarind Inst, Albuquerque, NMex, 73; lectr, Hartford Art Sch, Univ Hartford, 73-78; vis artist, Univ Calif, Berkeley, 74, Vassar Col, 77, Univ Houston, 78 & Yale Univ, 82; artist in residence, Wesleyan Univ, 78- *Awards:* Artist in Residence, Tamarind Inst, Albuquerque, NMex, 73; Purchase Award, Am Acad Arts & Lett, New York, 73; grants, Nat Endowment Arts, 76 & Conn Comn Arts, 76. *Bibliog:* Andea Miller-Keller (auth), Notes on Notations Exhibition, Wadsworth Atheneum, 75; Article, Art/New England, 11/80; John Paoletti (auth), Activated and tenacious: The art of Jacqueline Gourevitch, Arts Mag, 11/82. *Media:* Oil. *Publ:* Auth, article, Art Now: New York, fall 71. *Mailing Add:* 13 Red Orange Rd Middletown CT 06457

GOUTMAN, DOLYA
EDUCATOR, PAINTER

b May 5, 18; US citizen. *Study:* Art Inst Chicago, BFA; Univ Pa, MFA. *Work:* Pa Acad Fine Arts; Phoenix Art Mus; Dallas Mus Art; Butler Inst Am Art; White House, Washington, DC. *Exhib:* Calgary Allied Arts Ctr; Univ Brit Columbia; Univ Man; Massillon Mus, Ohio; Washington Co Mus Fine Arts, Md. *Teaching:* Head painting dept, Moore Col Art, formerly, prof, currently. *Media:* Oil, Acrylic. *Mailing Add:* 314 Williams Rd Rosemont PA 19010

GOVAN, FRANCIS HAWKS
EDUCATOR, PAINTER

b Marianna, Ark, Dec 19, 16. *Study:* Hendrix Col, BA; Art Inst South, Memphis; Univ Wis; Layton Sch Art; Columbia Univ, MA; Univ Saugl, Mex. *Work:* Ark Art Ctr; Choo Gakuin Univ, Japan. *Exhib:* Am Watercolor Exhib, France, 53-55; one-man shows, Feigl Gallery, New York, 54, 55 & 56; retrospective, Brooks Mem Art Gallery, Memphis, 57 & 66; Kunst Am, 57-58; Art in the Embassies & Smithsonian Inst, 67-68. *Pos:* Instr & occup therapist, Rockland State Hosp, Orangeburg, NY, 52-54; freelance artist, New York, 54-55; educ dir, Brooks Mem Art Gallery, 55-56; cur exhibs, Memphis State Univ, 57-67. *Teaching:* Instr art & creative dramatics, Milwaukee Univ Sch, 43-45; assoc prof art, Hendrix Col, 45-52; prof art, Memphis State Univ, 56-82. *Awards:* First Prize in Watercolor, Memphis Biennial, 46; Carnegie Found Grants Res Ark Pottery Clays, 49 & Mus Fine Art, 50. *Media:* Oil, Watercolor. *Publ:* Illusr, Arkansas pioneer days, Ark Gazette Sun Suppl, 48-49; auth, Art--what is it?, 59 & My last duchess, 65, Educ Quest. *Mailing Add:* 540 Hawthorne Memphis TN 38112

GRABILL, VIN (E VINCENT, JR)
VIDEO ARTIST, ENVIRONMENTAL ARTIST
b Boston, Mass, Apr 4, 49. *Study:* Oberlin Col, BA(studio art), 71; Mass Inst Technol, Ctr Advanced Visual Studies, SM(visual studies; Mass Artists Found Fel & St Botolph's Grant), 81. *Work:* De Cordova Mus (paintings), Lincoln, Mass; Kunsthaus (videotape), Zurich, Switz. *Comn:* Mural painting, State St Bank, Quincy, Mass, 73; mural painting, Houghton Chemical Co, Cambridge, Mass, 74; Vermont Story (videotape), WGBH-TV, Boston, Mass, 81. *Exhib:* Sculpture in the Park, De Cordova Mus, 73; Video Nu, Stockholm Mus Art, Sweden, 81; Centervideo, Kunsthaus, Zurich, Switz, 81 & Kolnischer Kunstverein, Cologne, Ger, 81; Boston Now, Inst Contemp Art, Boston, 83; San Paolo Biennale, Brazil, 83. *Pos:* Chief designer, Akko Inc, Lawrence, Mass, 74-79; fel, Ctr Advanced Visual Studies, Mass Inst Technol, 81-83. *Awards:* New Stagings/Video Performance Grant, Coun Arts, Mass Inst Technol, 81. *Bibliog:* Florence Gilbard (auth), Interactive cable, In: Visions, Boston Film/Video Found, 81. *Media:* Video. *Publ:* Ed, Centervideo, 81 & Centerdisk/Skydisk (electronic videodisk catalog), 83, Ctr Advanced Visual Studies, Mass Inst Technol; ed, Communicodes, d'Video Reality, 81. *Dealer:* Dr Francine A Koslow PO Box 206 Newton MA 02159. *Mailing Add:* Ctr Advan Visual Studies Mass Inst Technol 40 Massachusetts Ave Cambridge MA 02139

GRADO, ANGELO JOHN
PAINTER, INSTRUCTOR
b New York, NY, Feb 17, 22. *Study:* Art Students League, with Robert Brackman; Nat Acad Design, with Robert Philipp & Frank Reilly. *Exhib:* Am Watercolor Soc Exhibs, 58-71; Allied Artists Am Exhibs, 61-78; Nat Acad Design, New York, 63; Am Artists Prof League, New York, 63-83; Hudson Valley Art Asn, 69-83; 14 one-man exhibs. *Teaching:* Pvt classes, Nat Art League. *Awards:* Salmagundi Club Prize, 69; Seven Am Artists Prof League Awards, 69-79; Hudson Valley Art Asn Awards, 69, 70 & 72; 20 Nat Awards. *Bibliog:* Billi Boros (auth), New talent, Art Times Mag, 64. *Mem:* Am Watercolor Soc; Am Artists Prof League (pres, 78-); Hudson Valley Art Asn; Pastel Soc Am; Fine Arts Fedn New York. *Media:* Oil, Watercolor, Pastel. *Dealer:* Harbor Gallery 24 W 57th St New York NY 10019; Alterman Art Gallery 2504 Cedar Springs Dallas TX 75201. *Mailing Add:* 641 46th St Brooklyn NY 11220

GRADY, RUBY MCLAIN
PAINTER, SCULPTOR
b Bedford Co, Va, Jan 11, 44. *Study:* Corcoran Sch Art, Washington, DC, with Richard Lahey; Md Univ, with Pietro Lazzari. *Work:* Am Fine Art Exhibs, Washington, DC; NASA Gemini Collection, Washington, DC; Imprimerie Arte Galerie Maeght, Paris, France; West Publ Co, St Paul, Minn. *Exhib:* Va Mus Art, Richmond; P K Fine Arts, Ltd, New York; Washington Sculptures Exhib, DC, 79; solo exhib, Jack Rasmussen Gallery, DC, 79 & Roanoke Fine Art Mus, Va, 80; Sculpture Exhib, Gallery K, Washington, DC, 81. *Pos:* Art illusr, FBI, Washington, DC, currently. *Awards:* Annapolis Fine Arts Exhib Award for Metal Sculpture, 74; Md Biennial Exhib, Baltimore Mus Art, 76; Washington Artist Photog Exhib, Corcoran Gallery, Washington, DC, 77. *Bibliog:* Allen Smith (dir), Solo Exhibit in Washington (film), WTTG-TV, 72; Ruth Dean (auth), Profile of artist Ruby Grady, Washington Star News, 72; article, Am Bar Asn J, Chicago. *Media:* Steel, Acrylic. *Publ:* Illusr, Virginia Beach Exhib Catalog, 60; contribr, Nat Community Arts Prog Publ, Govt Printing Off, 70, Am Inst Archit Yearbook, 73 & Art and The Law National Exhibition Book, West Publ, 82 & 83; contribr, Washington Artists Directory; contribr, Am Inst Archit Yearbk, 73. *Dealer:* Gallery K 2032 P St NW Washington DC 20036. *Mailing Add:* Potowmack Bay Studio 431 Broadcreek Dr Ft Washington MD 20744

GRAESE, JUDY (JUDITH ANN)
PYROGRAPHY, ILLUSTRATOR
b Loveland, Colo, Nov 8, 40. *Study:* Augustana Col, 58-59; Univ Colo, Boulder, 65-67. *Work:* Nat City Bank, Denver, Colo; Rose Medical Ctr, Denver, Colo; Kent-Denver Country Day Sch, Colo; Enid Libr, Okla. *Comn:* Ink on stone, 78 & woodetching, 81, Colo Contemp Dance; woodetching, comn by Hanya Holm, 7/81; ink on stone, Kent-Denver Country Day Sch, Colo, 83. *Exhib:* One-man shows, Two-Twenty Two Gallery, El Paso, Tex, 71-72 & 73, Artisan, Princeton, NJ, 72 & 74 & Bishop's Antiques & Gallery, Scottsdale, Ariz, 73-83; De Colores, Denver, 73-81; Reflections Gallery, St Louis, Mo, 73-74. *Pos:* Designer, display dept, May D&F, 67-69. *Teaching:* Instr contemp dance, Kent-Denver Country Day Sch, Colo, 68- *Bibliog:* Rena Andrews (auth), The fine arts, 11/25/73 & Robert Downing (auth), Ad Lib, 2/2/75, Denver Post Roundup Sect; Betty Harvey (auth), Judy Graese, Artists of the Rockies, 5/75. *Media:* Wood, Stone; Ink, Fire. *Publ:* Illusr, The Song of Francis, Northland Press, 73; illusr, The Treasure is the Rose, Pantheon Press, 73. *Mailing Add:* 2055 S Franklin Denver CO 80210

GRAFTON, RICK (FREDERICK WELLINGTON)
PAINTER
b Middletown, Conn, May 3, 52. *Study:* Calif Col Arts & Crafts, BFA(high distinction), 76. *Work:* Metrop Mus Art, Chase Manhattan Bank, New York; Art Inst Chicago; Arco Ctr Visual Art, Prudential Life Insurance, Los Angeles. *Comn:* Meridian Building (watercolor), comn by J Lee, San Francisco, 83. *Exhib:* Solo exhib, Grapestake Gallery, San Francisco, 80 & 83, Dominican Col, Calif, 82 & San Jose Mus Art, 82; Bay Area Works on Paper, Seoul-San Francisco Exchange, USIS Gallery, SKorea, 83; Dealers Choice, San Francisco-Los Angeles, Kirk de Gooyer Gallery, Los Angeles, 83. *Teaching:* Instr watercolor, Assoc Students Univ Calif, Berkeley. *Awards:* Watercolor Award, Calif State Expo, 78. *Mem:* Emeryville Artists Coop. *Media:* Watercolor on Paper, Acrylic and Oil on Canvas. *Dealer:* Grapestake Gallery 2876 California St San Francisco CA 94115. *Mailing Add:* 1420 45 St #30 Emeryville CA 94608

GRAHAM, BILL (WILLIAM KARR)
CARTOONIST, GRAPHIC ARTIST
b Coshocton, Ohio, Dec 14, 20. *Study:* Centenary Col, BS(social sci), 42. *Work:* Wayne State Univ; LBJ Library, Univ Tex; Centenary Col, La; Univ Cincinnati; Va Mil Inst. *Exhib:* Pavilion D'Humor, Montreal, 71; Nat Cartoonists Soc Traveling Exhib; Asn Am Ed Cartoonists Traveling Exhib. *Mem:* Nat Cartoonists Soc; Asn Am Ed Cartoonists. *Publ:* Ed cartoonist, Ark Gazette, 48- *Mailing Add:* Arkansas Gazette PO Box 1821 Little Rock AR 72203

GRAHAM, DANIEL H
CONCEPTUAL ARTIST, ENVIRONMENTAL ARTIST
b Urbana, Ill, Mar 31, 42. *Work:* Tate Gallery, London; Stadisches Mus, Monchengladbach, Ger; Allen Art Mus, Oberlin, Ohio; Van Abbemuseum, Eindhoven; Art Inst Chicago. *Exhib:* Information, Mus Mod Art, New York, 70; Documenta VI, Kassel, Ger, 76; Basel Kunsthalle, Swits, 77; Van Abbemuseum, Eindhoven, 77; Documenta VII, Kassel, Ger, 72; Berne Kunsthalle, Switz. *Teaching:* NS Col Art & Design, Halifax, summer 81. *Awards:* Artists-in-Berlin, Ger Acad Serv, 76; Nat Endowment Arts Visual Arts Grant, 80; Creative Artists Pub Serv Grant, 81. *Publ:* Auth, 1966, 70; auth, Performance, 70; auth, Films, 77; auth, Buildings and Signs, 80; auth, Theatre, 82; auth, Pavilions, 83. *Dealer:* Lisson Gallery 66-68 Bell St London NW1 Eng. *Mailing Add:* Box 380 Knickerbocker Sta New York NY 10002

GRAHAM, DOUGLAS J M
MUSEUM DIRECTOR, COLLECTOR
b US citizen. *Study:* Piarist Col, BA(humanities), 54; NY Inst Finance, 61. *Pos:* Pres & dir, Turner Mus, Denver, Colo, 72- *Awards:* Founder's Award, Turner Mus, 74. *Bibliog:* Eugene Levin (auth), Turner finds a second home, Times of London, 3/13/76; The world's first Turner Museum, Art News of New York, 11/77. *Mem:* Turner Soc, London (vpres, 78-). *Media:* Watercolor. *Collection:* Turner and Moran; most varied and extensive Turner print collection outside the British Museum. *Publ:* Auth, Durer and Domjan, Graham Collection, NY, 72; auth, Turner and Moran, 77 & auth, Turner's Hand: The Master Touch, 78, Turner Mus; auth, Turner on Paper In: Joseph Mallord William Turner, Dixon Gallery & Gardens, Mephis, Tenn, 79; auth, Love Beginnings (poems, illus), privately publ, 80. *Mailing Add:* Turner Mus 773 Downing St Denver CO 80218

GRAHAM, F LANIER
CURATOR, MUSEOLOGIST
b Shawnee, Okla, Mar 6, 40. *Study:* Kenyon Col, 58-60; Am Univ, 61-63; Columbia Univ, 63-66, MA, 66; NY Univ Inst Fine Arts, 66-67. *Work:* Chess set, Mus Mod Art, New York & Mus Arts Decoratifs, Paris. *Pos:* Mus asst, Phillips Collection, Washington, DC, 62-63; assoc cur, Mus Mod Art, New York, 65-70; deputy dir, Collections, Exhib & Publ & chief cur, Fine Arts Museums of San Francisco, 70-76; pres, Inst for Aesthetic Develop, 75-80; cur, Cult Resource Mgt Ctr, 75-81, Headlands Art Ctr, 82-83 & Australian Nat Gallery, 84-; dir, Calif Inst of Asian Studies, 77- *Teaching:* Adj mem grad fac, Inst Fine Arts, NY Univ, Univ Calif, Berkeley & John F Kennedy Univ. *Mem:* Col Art Asn Am (local chmn nat conv, 72); World Print Coun. *Publ:* Auth, Hector Guimard, Mus Mod Art, 70; Three Centuries of American Painting, 71 & 77 & Three Centuries of French Art from the Norton Simon Collections, 73 & 76, Fine Arts Mus San Francisco; ed, The Rainbow Book, Fine Arts Mus San Francisco-Shambhala, 75 & Vintage-Random House, 79; The Prints of LeRoy Neiman: A Catalogue Raisonne, Knoedler & Bk Month Club, 80. *Mailing Add:* Australian Nat Gallery Canberra, Art 2600 94118 Australia

GRAHAM, K M
PAINTER
b Hamilton, Ont, Can, Sept 9, 13. *Study:* Univ Toronto, BA. *Work:* Art Gallery Ont; Art Bank Can, Ottawa; Edmonton Art Gallery, Alta; Art Gallery, Univ Guelph, Ont; Toronto Dom Bank, Toronto, Ont & Montreal, Que; plus others. *Exhib:* Art Gallery of Ont, Toronto, 74; Montreal Mus of Fine Arts, Que, 76; Hirshhorn Mus, Washington, DC, 77; Art Gallery of Hamilton, Ont, 77; Beaverbrook Art Gallery, Fredericton, NB, 77; Norman MacKenzie Art Gallery, Regina, Sask, 77; Edmonton Art Gallery, Alta, 77; Watson de Nagy Gallery, Houston, Tex, 77; Galerie Wentzel, Hamburg, WGer, 77; Canada House, London; Cultural Ctr, Paris. *Awards:* Can Coun Travel Award, 74. *Bibliog:* Juliana Borsa (auth), Kay Graham, 12/76-1/77 & Washington: 14 Canadians: A critic's choice, 5-6/77, Arts Mag; Karen Wilkin (auth), The late blooming vitality of Toronto Art, Artnews, 2/80; and others. *Mem:* Royal Can Acad of Arts. *Mailing Add:* 26 Boswell Ave Toronto ON M5R 1M4 Canada

GRAHAM, LOIS (M GORD)
PAINTER
b Kewanee, Ill, Aug 27, 30. *Study:* Knox Col, BA(magna cum laude), 52; Washington Univ, with Paul Burlin; also with Jack Tworkov, Nathan Oliviera & Lothar Schall. *Work:* City Seattle Portable Works Collection, Wash; City Bellevue City Hall Collection, Wash; Santa Barbara Mus Art; Seattle Art Mus; Continental Bank, Chicago. *Comn:* Mural, Knox Col, Galesburg, Ill, 51; mural, Bellevue, Wash, 74; mural, Bellevue, Wash, 75; painting, pvt collection, Seattle, Wash, 79. *Exhib:* Seattle Art Mus, 58 & 80; Seattle Pac Univ, 79-81; solo show, Foster White Gallery, Seattle, 81 & 82; Bellevue Art Mus, Wash, 82 & 83; E R Squibb Galleries, Princeton, NJ, 82; Portland Ctr Visual Arts, 82; and others. *Awards:* First Prize, Blossom Time Festival, Canon City, Colo, 67; Hon Mention, Mercer Island Visual Arts League, Wash, 70; Purchase Award, Pac NW Arts & Crafts Exhib, Bellevue Arts Comn, 77. *Bibliog:* Matthew Kangas (auth), Lois Graham at Foster/White, Art Am, 12/81; Ron

Glowen (auth), Lois Graham at Foster/White, Images & Issues, 1-2/83; Betty Brown (auth), Southern California, Lois Graham at Kirk deGooyer, Arts, 2/83. *Media:* Oil, Monotype. *Dealer:* Foster/White Gallery 311 1/2 Occidental Ave S Seattle WA 98104; Kirk deGooyer Gallery 1308 Factory Pl Los Angeles CA 90013. *Mailing Add:* 9210 NE 25th St Bellevue WA 98004

GRAHAM, MARGARET BLOY
CHILDREN'S BOOK ILLUSTRATOR
b Toronto, Can, Nov 2, 20, US citizen. *Study:* Univ of Toronto, BA(fine arts); New Sch Soc Res, New York, with Alexey Brodovitch; New York Univ, with Stuart Davis. *Work:* Lilian Smith Collection, Toronto Pub Libr, Can. *Publ:* Auth & illusr, Be Nice to Spiders, 67, Benjy and the Barking Bird, 71, Benjy's Dog House, 73, Harper & Row; illusr, The Pack Rat's Day, Macmillan, 74; auth & illusr, Benjy's Boat Trip, Harper & Row, 77. *Mailing Add:* c/o Harper & Row 10 E 53rd St New York NY 10022

GRAHAM, RICHARD MARSTON
SCULPTOR, EDUCATOR
b Lynn, Mass, July 29, 39. *Study:* Boston Univ, with Hugh Townley & Walter Murch, BFA, 62; RI Sch Design, with Gilbert Franklin, MFA, 64. *Work:* Ithaca Col Mus Art, NY; Ft Wright Col, Spokane, Wash; First Nat Bank, Atlanta, Ga; Ark Art Ctr, Little Rock; St Norbert Col, De Pere, Wis. *Comn:* Playground sculpture, Minneapolis Parks & Recreation Bd & Minn State Arts Coun, Fair Oaks Park, Minneapolis, summer 72. *Exhib:* Toys designed by Artists, Ark Art Ctr, Little Rock, 75; J Hunt Gallery, Minneapolis, Minn, 77; St Norbert Col, De Pere, Wis, 77; Coffman Gallery, Univ Minn, Minneapolis, 78; Clough Hanson Gallery, Memphis, Tenn, 79; and others. *Teaching:* Chmn dept art, Cent Mich Univ, 78-80. *Awards:* Union Independent Cols Art Fac Res Grant, summer 72; fac res grant, Minneapolis Col Art & Design, summer 77. *Bibliog:* Duane Bradley (auth), Part art, part park, Minneapolis Tribune Picture, 12/12/71; Paul Hogan (auth), Playgrounds for Free, Mass Inst Technol, 74; Roukes (auth), Masters of Wood Sculpture, Watson-Guptill, New York, 81. *Mem:* Artists Equity Asn; Southern Asn Sculptors. *Media:* Wood. *Mailing Add:* 2709 Lyndale Ave S Minneapolis MN 55408

GRAHAM, ROBERT
SCULPTOR
b Mexico City, Mex, Aug, 38. US citizen. *Study:* San Jose State Col, 61-63; San Francisco Art Inst, 63-64. *Work:* Whitney Mus Am Art & Mus Mod Art, New York; Hirshhorn Mus & Sculpture Garden; Los Angeles Co Mus; Houston Mus Fine Arts; and many others. *Comn:* Franklin D Roosevelt Mem, Washington, DC; Crocker Ctr, Los Angeles, 83; Fed Reserve Bank San Francisco, Calif, 83; San Jose Fed Bldg, Calif, 84; Los Angeles Olympic Organizing Comt, 84. *Exhib:* Galerie Neuendorf, Hamburg, WGer, 79; one-man show, Walker Art Ctr Traveling, 81; Dorothy Rosenthal Gallery, 81; Sch Visual Arts, New York, 81; Robert Miller Gallery, New York, 82; and many other group & one-man shows. *Bibliog:* Carter Radcliff (auth), Beyond erotic, Saturday Rev, 3/82; Barbara Isenberg (auth), A Graham bronze for the Olympics, Los Angeles Times, Part IV, 10/5/82; Joseph Giovannini (auth), Architecture: Robert Graham, Archit Digest, 10/83. *Mailing Add:* 69 Windward Ave Venice CA 90291

GRAHAM, ROBERT C, JR
DEALER
b New York, NY, Sept 6, 41. *Study:* Middlebury Col, BA, 63. *Pos:* Vpres & dir, Graham Gallery, New York, 63-81. *Mem:* Art Dealers Asn Am. *Specialty:* American painting and sculpture. *Mailing Add:* Graham Gallery 1014 Madison Ave New York NY 10021

GRAHAM, ROBERT CLAVERHOUSE
DEALER, COLLECTOR
b New York, NY, Apr 28, 13. *Study:* Yale Univ, BFA, 36; NY Univ, 38-39. *Pos:* Dir, Graham Gallery. *Specialty:* Nineteenth and twentieth century American art. *Collection:* American and Oriental art. *Mailing Add:* 1014 Madison Ave New York NY 10021

GRAHAM, ROBERT MACDONALD, JR
PAINTER
b New Rochelle, NY, Nov 1, 19. *Study:* Kansas City Art Inst, Mo, with Thomas H Benton, dipl, 41; Hoger Inst voor Schone Kunsten, Antwerp, Belg, with Jules van Vlasslaer, cert, 49. *Work:* War Art Collection, Pentagon, Washington, DC; Witte Mus, San Antonio, Tex; Tex Fine Arts, Austin; Topeka Art Mus, Kans; Butler Inst Am Art, Youngstown, Ohio; Inland Steel Co, Chicago. *Exhib:* 53rd Nat Ann, Art Inst Chicago, 41; Univ Ill Nat Contemp Am Painting, Champaign, Ill, 48; Audubon Nat Ann Contemp Am Art, New York, 50; Dallas Mus Invitational, 52 & 53; Delgado Mus Invitational, New Orleans, La, 54; 38th Midyear Show, Butler Inst Am Art, Youngstown, Ohio, 74; Benedictine Art Awards Nat, New York, 75; 30th Ann Nat Soc Painters Casein & Acrylic, Nat Arts Club, New York, 83. *Teaching:* Instr painting & drawing, Univ Tex, Austin, 51-55; teaching assoc painting & drawing, Univ Mo, Kansas City, 58-75. *Awards:* Purchase Prize, Topeka Art Mus, 56; Purchase Prize, Butler Inst Am Art, 74; Pres Citation Merit, 30th Ann Nat Soc Painters Casein & Acrylic Exhib, 83. *Mem:* Nat Soc Painters Casein & Acrylic. *Media:* Multi-Media. *Dealer:* Capricorn Gallery 4849 Rugby Ave Bethesda MD 20014. *Mailing Add:* Rte 2 Box 239-A Greenwood MO 64034

GRAHAM, WALTER
PAINTER, SCULPTOR
b Toledo, Ill, Nov 17, 03. *Study:* Chicago Acad Fine Arts; Chicago Art Inst; plus pvt instruction. *Work:* Cent Wash Mus, Wenatchee; Douglas Co Mus, Waterville, Wash; Favell Mus, Klamath Falls, Ore. *Comn:* Murals & wildlife paintings for ocean-going ships, State of Alaska, 69-72; murals & paintings, Rocky Reach Dam, Wenatchee, 60; fountain sculpture, Lincoln Savings, Spokane, Wash, 70. *Exhib:* Ann Western Art Exhib, Russell Mus, Great Falls, Mont, 73-74; NW Indian & Western Art Show, Ridpath Hotel, Spokane, 74-75; Artists of the Old West, Oldfield Gallery-Tacoma Inn, Wash, 75; Soc Animal Artists Exhib, Columbus Gallery of Fine Art, Ohio, 76; Mem Show, Palette & Chisel Acad, Chicago & Art Inst of Chicago; and others. *Pos:* Owner, Nugent Graham Studios, Chicago, 39-50; mem, Wash State Art Comn, 60-62; pres, Cent Wash Mus, 60-65. *Awards:* First Prizes, Chicago Galleries, 37, 38 & 42; Gold Medal, Palette & Chisel Acad, Chicago, 40. *Bibliog:* Royal B Hassick (auth), Western Painting Today, Watson-Guptill, 75. *Media:* Oil, Watercolor; Bronze. *Mailing Add:* 201 S Eliott Wenatchee WA 98801

GRAHAM, WILLIAM ANDREW
DEALER, COLLECTOR
b Leon, Iowa, Dec 13, 39. *Study:* Univ Iowa, BA, 62; studied lithography under Ferdnand Mourlot, 69-74; photography in Paris, with Man Ray, 69-74; Studio Salon, with Jean Helion, 69-71 & Charles Lapicque, 69-76. *Collections Arranged:* Leopold Survage: Retrospective (auth, catalog), Vestart, New York, 69; Justino Alvez: Paintings (auth, catalog), Document A, Paris, 77; Figurative Painting: Six in America and Europe (auth, catalog), Graham Gallery, 81; Allen Jones: Print Retrospective, Sewall Art Gallery, 81. *Pos:* Dir & Europ buyer, Vestart, New York, 69-70; dir & co-owner, Galerie Balanci Graham, Paris, 72-77; coordr & asst dir, Sewall Art Gallery, Rice Univ, Houston, 80; dir, Graham Gallery, Houston, 81- *Teaching:* Pvt lectr collecting, Paris, 70-77; vis lectr, Rice Univ, Houston, 81- *Specialty:* Contemporary Americans and Europeans. *Collection:* 20th century American and European. *Mailing Add:* 2411 Bartlett Houston TX 77098

GRALEY, GARY JAMES
PHOTOGRAPHER
b Buffalo, NY, June 27, 51. *Study:* State Univ NY, Buffalo, BA, 73; Rochester Inst Technol, MFA, 75. *Work:* Int Mus Photog, George Eastman House, Rochester, NY; Albright-Knox Art Gallery, Buffalo, NY; Mus Mod Art, New York. *Comn:* The Desert Habitat, Ariz Dept Tourism, Phoenix, 79; Inside the Grand Canyon, Sierra Club, Flagstaff, Ariz, 80. *Exhib:* The Appalachian Trail, Int Mus Photog, George Eastman House, Rochester, NY, 76; The Inner Canyon, Los Angeles Inst Art, 79; Red Rocks of Sedona, San Francisco Art Inst, 80; Desert Landscapes, Ctr Creative Photog, Tucson, Ariz, 81. *Mem:* SW Asn Photog Art; Upstate NY Soc Photog; Am Soc Photog Expressionism. *Media:* Black & White, Color. *Dealer:* M M Cargill 8108 East Buena Terra Scottsdale AZ 85253. *Mailing Add:* 9459 E Jenan Dr Scottsdale AZ 85260

GRAMBERG, LILIANA
PAINTER, PRINTMAKER
b Treviso, Italy; US citizen. *Study:* Univ Rome, with Laurea; Escuela Nac Bellas Artes, Madrid; Ecole Nat Super Beaux Arts, Paris, Atelier Gravure, with Bersier; Atelier 17, Paris, with Hayter; Calif Col Arts & Crafts, MFA. *Work:* Mus Art Mod Ville Paris; Brit Mus, London; Nat Mus Am Art; Rosenwald Collection; Nat Gallery of Art, Washington, DC; and other mus in US & abroad. *Exhib:* Northwestern Printmakers; Silvermine Guild; Pa Acad Fine Arts; Libr Congress; one-man shows, Smithsonian Inst & Retrospective, Folkwang Mus, Essen, WGer; Seoul Int Print Biennale, 83; and others. *Teaching:* Prof fine arts, Trinity Col (DC), 67. *Awards:* Treadwell Award, Nat Asn Women Artists, 63; Silver Medal, Asn Incisori Italia, 64. *Bibliog:* Margarita Nelken (auth), El patetico grabado de Liliana Gramberg, Arte (Mex), 3/59; Cajide (auth), Tecnica y poesia de los grabados de Liliana Gramberg, Artes (Spain), 2/61. *Mailing Add:* 6322 32nd St NW Washington DC 20015

GRANDEE, JOE RUIZ
PAINTER, GALLERY DIRECTOR
b Dallas, Tex, Nov 19, 29. *Study:* Aunspaugh Art Sch, Dallas. *Work:* White House, Washington, DC; Xavier Univ Mus, Cincinnati, Ohio; Mont State Hist Soc Mus, Great Falls; Marine Corps Mus, Quantico, Va; Univ Tex, Arlington. *Comn:* Twenty Mules of Death Valley, US Borax Co, Hollywood, Calif, 65; Linda Bird & Chuck Robb Off Portrait, comn by Lyndon B Johnson family & friends, 67; portrait of Johnny Carson, comn by Rudy Tellez, Assoc Producer NBC, New York, 67; portrait of Robert Taylor, comn by US Borax Co for Robert Taylor, Hollywood, 68; portrait of Leander H McNelly, Texas Ranger, East Wing of White House, Washington, DC, 72. *Exhib:* Custer Exhib, Amon Carter Mus Western Art, Ft Worth, Tex, 68; one-man shows, Norton Art Gallery Mus, Shreveport, La, 71; El Paso Mus Fine Arts, Tex, 72 & Tex Ranger Mus Show, Waco, Tex, 72 & US Capitol, 74; and many others. *Pos:* Owner, Joe Grandee Gallery & Mus of Old West, currently. *Awards:* First Official Artist of Texas, Tex Legis & Gov, 71; Franklin Mint Gold Medal Western Art for Pursuit and Attack, 74; and others. *Bibliog:* Wayne Gard (auth), Joe Grandee--painter of the old west, Am Artist Mag, 67; Grandee Paintings (TV film), US Borax Co, 68; Joy Schultz (auth), The West Still Lives: Grandee, Heritage, 70. *Media:* Oil, Ink. *Res:* Ruizeem water medium. *Specialty:* Paintings, drawings and sculpture works of Joe Ruiz Grandee and displays of historical artifacts. *Publ:* Illusr, Indian Wars of Texas, 65, Pictorial History of The Texas Rangers, 69, The Grand Duke Alexis in the USA, 72 & The Life of Jim Baker (mountain man), 1818-1898, 72; contribr, Cowboy Series, In: Time-Life Bks, 72. *Dealer:* Gene McDaniel PO Box 433 Midland TX 79701; Bob Hoff PO Box 231 Houston TX 77001. *Mailing Add:* Joe Grandee Gallery & Mus Old West 606 S Center St Arlington TX 76010

GRANLUND, PAUL THEODORE
SCULPTOR, INSTRUCTOR
b Minneapolis, Minn, Oct 6, 25. *Study:* Gustavus Adolphus Col, BA, 52; Univ Minn; Cranbrook Acad Art, George A Booth scholar, 53, MFA, 54; Gustavus Adolphus Col, LHD, 71. *Work:* Walker Art Ctr, Minneapolis Inst Art, Minn; Cranbrook Acad Art; Va Mus Fine Arts; Sheldon Mem Mus Art Gallery, Lincoln, Nebr; and others. *Comn:* Sculpture, Gustavus Adolphus Col & Lutheran Church of the Good Shepherd, Minneapolis; 21 pub sculptures, Minneapolis & St Paul. *Exhib:* One-man shows, Calif Palace Legion Honor, 62, Univ Nebr, 64 & Washington Univ, 65; La State Univ, 64; Art of Two Cities, Minneapolis Sch Art, 65; and others. *Teaching:* Cranbrook Acad Art, 54; Minneapolis Col Art & Design, 55-57 & 59-71; sculptor-in-residence, Gustavus Adolphus Col, 71- *Awards:* Fulbright Fel, 54; Guggenheim Fels, 57 & 58. *Publ:* Auth, Granlund: The Sculptor and His Work, Kathryn Christenson & Kelvin W Miller (eds), Gustavus Adolphus Col, 78. *Mailing Add:* Route 1 Box 121 Gustavus Adolphus Col St Peter MN 56080

GRANSTAFF, WILLIAM BOYD
PAINTER, ILLUSTRATOR
b Paducah, Ky, May 17, 25. *Study:* Kansas City Art Inst, with Ross Braught & Ed Lanning, grad; Am Acad Art, with William Mosby & Bill Fleming. *Comn:* Mural, Cadet Club, Garden City, Kans, 45; Old Homeplace, B J Farless, Princeton, Ky, 70; Vietnam (painting), comn by Nat Am Legion, 75 & Korea (painting), 78; 1st Bank & Trust, Princeton, Ky. *Exhib:* Mid-S, Nashville, Tenn, 53; one-man show, Planters Bank, Hopkinsville, Ky, 72. *Pos:* Mem, Art Dirs Club, Nashville, 55-58. *Teaching:* Instr illus, Famous Artist Sch, 59-61. *Awards:* Brackman Blue Ribbon, Nashville, 53. *Bibliog:* Meet your instructors, Famous Artist Mag, 61. *Mem:* Audubon Soc. *Media:* Oil, Watercolor. *Publ:* Illusr, What's in a Word, Abingdon, 65; illusr, The Way Out, Moody, 70; illusr, Golden Treasury of Bible Stories, Southern, 71; illusr, Man-US & Americas, 72 & illusr, Americans All, 72, Benefic. *Dealer:* Heritage Gallery Rosemont Gardens Lexington KY 40503. *Mailing Add:* Old Eddyville Rd Rt II Box 7 Princeton KY 42445

GRANT, ART
CONCEPTUAL ARTIST, EDUCATOR
b San Francisco, Calif, June 22, 27. *Study:* San Francisco City Col, AA, 45-48; San Francisco State Univ, BA, 54, 54-55; San Francisco Art Inst, 55. *Work:* San Francisco Mus Mod Art; Oakland Art Mus; City Sausalito, Calif. *Comn:* Murals, Coleman Sch, San Rafael, Calif, 74, Martin Luther King Sch, Sausalito, Calif, 75, Univ Calif Exten, San Francisco, 75, Liberty Sch, Petaluma, Calif, 75 & Steffan Manor Sch, Vallejo, Calif, 76. *Exhib:* San Francisco Art Inst Show, De Young Mus, 62; Three Projective Sculptors, Oakland Art Mus, 63; Kinetic Forces, 65, Holiday Show, 65, 66 & 83 & Aesthetics of Graffiti, 78, San Francisco Mus Mod Art; Edible Art Show, Univ Calif Art Mus, Berkeley, 81 & 82; Found and Assembled, Matthews Gallery, Ariz State Univ, 82. *Teaching:* Assoc prof art, Lincoln Univ, Calif, 63-66 & 77-; instr art & art educ, Univ Calif Exten, San Francisco, 64-77 & Sonoma State Univ Exten, Rohnert Park, Calif, 68-79. *Awards:* Sculpture Prize, 77th Ann Painting & Sculpture Show, San Francisco Art Asn, 58, San Francisco Art Festival, 60 & 77 & Sausalito Art Festival, 62 & 63. *Bibliog:* Sarah Grissom (auth), article, Arts, 5/58; Mary Fuller (auth), article, Art in Am, No 3, 64; Americana, Time Mag, 3/5/79. *Mem:* Nat Soc Mural Painters. *Media:* Junk. *Publ:* Coauth, Sculpture from Junk, Van Nostrand Reinhold, 67. *Mailing Add:* 154 Ethel Ave Mill Valley CA 94941

GRANT, JAMES
SCULPTOR
b Los Angeles, Calif, 1924. *Study:* Univ of Southern Calif, BEd, 45, MFA, 50; Jepson Art Inst, Los Angeles, 47-49. *Work:* San Francisco Mus Art; Univ Pacific, Stockton, Calif; Pasadena Art Mus, Calif; Mary Washington Col, Fredericksburg, Va. *Exhib:* Los Angeles Co Mus Art; Mus Mod Art, New York; retrospective, Mills Col, Calif, 70; and others; and many others. *Teaching:* Instr, Pomona Col, 50-59. *Mailing Add:* c/o Hansen-Fuller Gallery 228 Grant Ave San Francisco CA 94108

GRASHOW, JAMES BRUCE
SCULPTOR, PRINTMAKER
b Brooklyn, NY, Jan 16, 42. *Study:* Pratt Inst, BFA, MFA. *Work:* Mus Mod Art, Pub Libr, New York; Greenville Mus, SC; Libr Cong; Iron Range Mus, Minn. *Comn:* Ballet stage sets, San Francisco Ballet Co, 76 & Nat Ballet Cuba, Havana, 78. *Exhib:* Made With Paper, 67 & Tombstones & Monuments, 67, Mus Contemp Crafts, New York; Human Concern, Personal Torment, Whitney Mus, 69; Hudson River Mus, NY, 72; Univ Conn, Storrs, 79; Ctr Arts, State Univ NY, Purchase, 82. *Teaching:* Assoc prof painting & figure drawing, Pratt Inst, 68-81. *Awards:* Fulbright Travel Grant, 63; Ital Govt Grant, 63; Tiffany Award Graphics, 65. *Bibliog:* Steven Heller (auth), article, Graphis, 81; Chauncey Howell (producer), Live at Five, NBC-TV, 82; Jane Cottingham (auth), article, Am Artist Mag, 5/82. *Media:* Fabric Mache; Woodcut. *Publ:* Illusr, Making Vegetables Grow, 75 & Twelve Moons Make a Year, 80, Knopf; illusr, New York Times Mag, 83. *Dealer:* Allan Stone Gallery 48 E 86th St New York NY. *Mailing Add:* 14 Diamond Hill Rd West Redding CT 06896

GRASS, PATTY PATTERSON
PAINTER
b Oklahoma City, Okla. *Study:* Univ Okla, BFA; Ecole Beaux-Arts, Fontainebleau, France; Taos Sch Art; Art Students League; Okla State Univ; additional study with Emil Bisttram, Robert E Woods, Milford Zarnes, George Post, Edgar Whitney & Millard Sheets. *Exhib:* One-woman show, Univ Okla Health Sci Ctr, 76; Mass Inst Technol; Oklahoma City Art Ctr; Art Students League; Okla Mus Art. *Teaching:* Instr art, Oklahoma City Schs & Oklahoma City Univ, 34-81. *Awards:* First Prize, Watercolor Okla, 75; Spec Award, Okla Art Guild, 75; Four Certs of Award for 100 Best Painters, Southwestern Watercolor Soc, Dallas, Tex, 71-80; and others. *Mem:* Okla Art Asn; Okla Watercolor Asn; Watercolor Okla; Southwestern Watercolor Soc; and others. *Mailing Add:* 2506 NW 66th St Oklahoma City OK 73116

GRASSO, DORIS (TEN-EYCK)
PAINTER, SCULPTOR
b Fremont, NY, May 3, 14. *Study:* Educ Alliance, New York, with Moses Soyer, Alex Dobkin & John Hovannes; N Hudson Arts Sch, with Fabian Zaccone; Rutherford Art Sch, with Lucille Hobbie. *Work:* Paul Whitener Mem Collection, NC Mus Art; George B Burr Collection, New York; Jersey City Mus Art; Staten Island Pub Schs Collection, NY; Women's Club Collection, Lynhurst, NJ. *Exhib:* Knickerbocker Artists Int, New York, 63-65; Painters & Sculptors Soc NJ Nat, 65-72; Nat Casein Soc, New York, 68; Acad Artists Regional, NJ, 68-71; Am Artists Prof League Nat, New York, 69-70. *Teaching:* Instr art, YWCA, Bayonne, NJ, 50-55, Doris Grasso Sch Fine Arts, 52-62 & Bayonne's Woman's Club Eve Dept, 65-68; instr, Doris Ten-Eyck Grasso Gallery & Studio, Gloucester, Mass, currently. *Awards:* Pauline Wick Award for Oils, Am Artists Prof League, 68; Golden Lady Award, Nat Women of Achievement (Art), Amita, Inc, 69; First Award for Sculpture, State Fedn Women's Clubs, 70; and others. *Mem:* Fel Am Artists Prof League (pres, NJ Chap, nat dir, 60-62); Painters & Sculptors Soc NJ (bd dirs & secy, 62-65); Burr Artists (pub rels, 66-68); assoc Rockport Artists; fel Int Arts & Lett, Ger & Switz; and others. *Media:* Oil, Watercolor. *Mailing Add:* 15 Langsford St Lanesville Cape Ann Gloucester MA 01930

GRASSO, SALVATORE FORTUNATO
PAINTER, CONCEPTUAL ARTIST
b Boston, Mass, April 27, 45. *Study:* Art Inst Boston, cert, 66. *Work:* DeCordova Mus, Lincoln, Mass; Suffolk Univ; Tom Nicholas Gallery, Rockport, Mass; Gallery OUI, Boston. *Exhib:* Nat Acrylic & Casein Exhib, Nat Acad Design, New York, 78; New England Watercolor Soc Exhib, 78-82; Nat Acad Design Exhib, New York, 79; DeCordova Mus Exhib, Lincoln, Mass, 79; Hudson River Artist Nat Exhib, 80. *Awards:* Rockport Art Asn Awards, 77-82; Frank & Annie Shikler Award, Nat Acad Design Ann Exhib, 79; Purchase Prize, DeCordova Mus, 79. *Media:* Acrylic. *Mailing Add:* 46 Langsford St Gloucester MA 01930

GRAUBARD, ANN WOLFE See Wolfe, Ann

GRAUER, MELANIE KAHANE See Kahane, Melanie

GRAUER, SHERRY
SCULPTOR, PAINTER
b Toronto, Ont, Feb 20, 39. *Study:* Wellesley Col, 56-59; Ecole Louvre, Paris; Calif Sch Fine Art, BFA(hon), 64. *Work:* Vancouver Art Gallery; Mus Art Contemp, Montreal; Ont Heritage Found, Can Coun Art Bank, Nat Gallery Can, Ottawa. *Comn:* Relief mural, Worldwide Int Travel, Vancouver, 69; ceiling panels (steel & fiberglass), DPW, Fed Bldg, Powell River, BC, 76; banners, City Vancouver, 76; Brave Birdmen (steel mesh ceiling sculpture), Ministry Transport, Cornwall, Ont, 80. *Exhib:* People in the Park, Rothmans Gallery, Stratford, Ont, 69; Art From Canada's West Coast, Vancouver Art Gallery, 71; Some Canadian Women Artists, Nat Gallery Can, 75; Current Pursuits, Vancouver Art Gallery, 76; retrospective, Surrey Art Gallery, 80; New Vancouver Art Gallery Inaugural Exhib, 83. *Bibliog:* Joan Lowndes (auth), Modalities of West Coast Painting, Artscanada, Vol XXXI, No 2, 74; Rosalie Staley (auth), article, Vanguard, 11/83. *Mem:* Royal Can Acad Art. *Media:* Canvas, Steel Mesh; Oil, Acrylic. *Dealer:* Bau-Xi Gallery 3045 Granville St Vancouver BC V6H 3J9 & 340 Dundas St Toronto ON M5T 1G5. *Mailing Add:* 4794 Belmont Ave Vancouver BC V6T 1A9 Canada

GRAUPE-PILLARD, GRACE
PAINTER, INSTRUCTOR
b New York, NY, Sept 28, 41. *Study:* City Univ NY, BA, 63; Art Students League, George Bridgman Scholar, with Marshal Glasier and Julien Levi, 64-68. *Work:* Roland Gibson Found, Potsdam, NY, Edward & Vivian Merrin Collection, New York; Malcolm Forbes Collection, New York; Bell Labs, Holmdel, NJ; Greg Lunt Collection; NJ State Mus, Trenton; and others. *Exhib:* Aldrich Museum, Ridgefield, Conn, 76; Women Artists 1978; City Univ New York Graduate Ctr, New York, 78; Alex Rosenberg Gallery, 80; New Drawings in America, Mus Mod Art, Venice, 83; one-person show, Bernice Steinbaum Gallery, 83. *Teaching:* Instr painting & life drawing, Monmouth Adult Educ Comm, 74-82, Monmouth Co Parks, 76- *Awards:* NMex Biennial Juror's Award, 73; Women in the Arts Honorarium, Rutgers Univ, 74; NJ State Coun Arts Grant, 82-83. *Bibliog:* Article, SoHo News, 12/1/81; article, Appearances No 8, 82; article, Arts, 6/83. *Media:* Oil. *Dealer:* Bernice Steinbaum Gallery 903 Madison Ave New York NY 10021. *Mailing Add:* PO Box 1032 Freehold NJ 07728

GRAUSMAN, PHILIP
SCULPTOR
b New York, NY, July 16, 35. *Study:* Syracuse Univ, BA(cum laude), 57; Skowhegan Sch Painting & Sculpture, summers 56 & 57; Cranbrook Acad Art, MFA, 59; Art Students League, with Jose de Creeft, 59. *Work:* Brooklyn Mus; Pa State Univ; Wadsworth Atheneum, Hartford; Univ Mich; Univ Conn, Storrs; and others. *Exhib:* Pa Acad Fine Arts, 60 & 62; Whitney Mus Am Art, 62, 64 & 66; Hartford Arts Festival, Wadsworth Atheneum, 74; A Mus Menagerie, Mus Mod Art, New York, 76; Am Drawing Exhib, Fine Arts

Mus San Diego, 77; Drawing USA 78, St Paul Art Ctr, Minn, 78; one-man shows, Wash Art Asn Commision, 78 & 81; Rockland Ctr Arts, New York, 79; Bethune Gallery, State Univ NY, Buffalo, 83; Robert Schoelkopf Gallery, New York, 83; and others. *Pos:* Artist in residence, Dartmouth Col, 72. *Teaching:* Instr design, Cooper Union, 65-67; instr design & drawing, Pratt Inst, 65-69; vis asst prof, Yale Univ, 73-76, vis critic archit drawing, Grad Sch Archit, 77-80. *Awards:* Rome Prize Fel, 62-65; Solon H Borgliem Award, Silvermine Exhib, 80; Dessie Greer Prize, Nat Acad Design, 81; and others. *Media:* Cast Metal. *Mailing Add:* c/o Robert Schoelkopf Gallery 825 Madison Ave New York NY 10021

GRAVES, BRADFORD
SCULPTOR, EDUCATOR
b Dallas, Tex, July 26, 39. *Study:* Sch of Visual Arts; New Sch for Social Res, with Seymour Lipton; Goddard Col, BA & MA. *Work:* NJ State Mus, Trenton; Corcoran Gallery, Washington, DC; Weatherspoon Art Gallery, Univ NC, Greensboro; Sheldon Mem Art Gallery, Lincoln, Nebr; Chase Manhattan Bank. *Comn:* Hwy sculpture, Adirondak Northway-Interstate 87, NY, 71; Vt Sculptor's Symposium, Interstate 89, 71 & Interstate 80, Nebr, 76; Scottish Sculpture Trust, 83. *Exhib:* Sculpture in the Fields, Storm King Art Ctr, Mountainville, NY, 74; First West Side Sculpture Exhib, New York, 76; one-man show, NJ State Mus, Trenton, 76; Whitney Counterweight, New York, 77; Forms in Focus, Co-op City, 77; and others. *Teaching:* Asst prof sculpture, Fairleigh Dickinson Univ, Madison, NJ, 69-; instr sculpture, Parsons Sch Design, New York, 74-80. *Awards:* Creative Artists Pub Serv Award, Hwy Sculpture, Vt, 71; Nat Endowment Arts Artist Fel, 80. *Bibliog:* Josh Cohn (auth), Between School and Castelli, Art in Am, 73; Barbara Rose (auth), Nebraska Highway Sculpture, Vogue, 76. *Media:* Stone sculpture and stone earthworks. *Publ:* Auth, John Coltrane, Doubleday & Co, New York, 73; auth, William Bronk--Poet, Occurrence Number 7, Philadelphia, 77; auth, John Taggart, In: Peace on Earth, Turtle Island Found, 81. *Mailing Add:* 799 Greenwich St New York NY 10014

GRAVES, (MRS) JOHN W
COLLECTOR
US citizen. *Collection:* Late 19th and early 20th century American paintings. *Mailing Add:* 67 Via Verde Wichita KS 67230

GRAVES, KA (KATHLEEN ROSE)
PAINTER, SCULPTOR
b Detroit, Mich. *Study:* Am Col Paris, AA, 74; Ariz State Univ, BFA, 76, MFA, 79. *Work:* Rutgers Univ; Scottsdale Ctr Arts, Ariz. *Comn:* Drawings, Mesa Mus, Ariz, 80. *Exhib:* Nat Drawing Exhib, Rutgers Univ, 77; Southwestern Invitational, Yuma Ctr Arts, Ariz, 78 & 79; Four Corners States Biennial, Phoenix Art Mus, 79; Mother, Daughter & Wholly Beastie, Scottsdale Ctr Arts, Ariz, 82; Arizona's Finest, Ctr Arts, Tempe, Ariz, 83. *Teaching:* Adj instr painting & drawing, Grand Canyon Col, Ariz, 83- *Bibliog:* Barbara H Perlman (auth), Phoenix: A sun palace ..., Art News, 12/81; Carol Donnell-Kotrozo (auth), The mythic core, Art Week, 6/5/82; Kathryn Coe (auth), Ka Graves, imaginative artist, Scottsdale Daily Progress, 4/15/83. *Media:* Mixed. *Mailing Add:* 921 W Lynwood Phoenix AZ 85007

GRAVES, KENNETH ROBERT
PHOTOGRAPHER
b Portland, Ore, June 27, 42. *Study:* San Francisco Art Inst, with Jerry Burchard & John Collier Jr, BFA, 70, MFA, 71. *Work:* San Francisco Mus Art; Nat Libr, Paris; Ann Bremer Mem Libr, San Francisco Art Inst; Mus Mod Art, New York; George Eastman House, Rochester, NY. *Exhib:* Three Photographers, San Francisco Mus Art, 71; New Photography in the Bay Area, M H De Young Mus, 73; Exchange DFW/SFO, Ft Worth Art Mus & San Francisco Mus Art, 75; Color as Form, George Eastman House & Corcoran Gallery, 82; solo exhib, Blue Sky Gallery, Portland, 82 & Portico Gallery, Philadelphia, 83. *Pos:* Photogr, Jeroboam Inc, San Francisco, 71- *Teaching:* Instr photog, San Francisco Art Inst & Photog Film Ctr West, Berkeley; asst prof, Pa State Univ, 77- *Awards:* First Award, Pa Festival Arts, 83; Purchase Award, Alternatives, 83. *Bibliog:* Joan Murray (auth), interview, Artweek, 1/22/72; Time-Life Photography, 75; Popular Photog Ann, 82. *Publ:* Coauth, American Snapshots, Scrimshaw Press, 78. *Dealer:* Portico Gallery 902 Spruce Philadelphia PA 19107. *Mailing Add:* 332 W Prospect State College PA 16802

GRAVES, MICHAEL
ARCHITECT, EDUCATOR
b Indianapolis, Ind, July 9, 34. *Study:* Univ Cincinnati, BSArch, 58; Harvard Univ, MArch, 59; Am Acad in Rome(fel), Prix de Rome, 62. *Work:* Mus Mod Art, Cooper-Hewitt Mus, New York; Berlin Mus, Ger; Vassar Col Art Mus, Poughkeepsie, NY. *Comn:* Murals, Gunwyn Ventures, Princeton, NJ, 71, XV Triennale, Milan, Italy, 73, Transammonia Inc, New York, 74, Assoc Metals & Minerals, New York, 79 & John Witherspoon Sch, Princeton, NJ, 81. *Exhib:* XV Triennale, Milan, Italy, 73; 200 Yrs of Am Archit Drawings, Cooper-Hewitt Mus, New York, 77 & Ornament in the 20th Century, 78-79; Roma Interrotta, Markets of Trajan, Rome, Italy & Cooper-Hewitt Mus, 78-79; one-man show, Max Protech Gallery, New York, 79 & Mus Mod Art, Rome, 81; Venice Biennale, 80. *Pos:* Dir visual studies prog, Princeton Univ, 70-72; architect-in-residence, Am Acad in Rome, Italy, 79. *Teaching:* Prof archit, Princeton Univ, NJ, 62-; vis prof archit, Univ Tex, Austin, 74, Univ Calif, Los Angeles, 77, Univ Houston, Tex, 78 & Univ NC, Charlotte, 79. *Awards:* Design Award, Progressive Archit, 70 & 75-80; Nat Honor Awards, Am Inst Archit, 75, 79 & 82; Arnold W Brunner Mem Prize, 80. *Bibliog:* Five Architects, Oxford Univ, 72; Ada Louise Huxtable (auth), A unified new

language of design, New York Times, 5/17/79. *Mem:* Fel Am Inst Architects; fel Soc for Arts, Relig & Cult. *Media:* Pencil, Ink. *Publ:* Auth, Thought Models, Sch Design, NC State Univ, 78; auth, Value of color, Archit Rec, 80; contribr, Catalogue Venice Biennale, 80; contribr, Speaking a New Classicism, Smith Col Mus Art, 81; auth, Le Corbusier's drawn references, In: Introduction to Le Corbusier Drawings, Acad Ed, London, 81. *Dealer:* Max Protech Gallery 37 W 57th St New York NY 10019. *Mailing Add:* 44 Patton Ave Princeton NJ 08540

GRAVES, MORRIS
PAINTER
b Fox Valley, Ore, Aug 28, 10. *Work:* Seattle Art Mus; Phillips Mem Gallery, Mus Mod Art, Whitney Mus Am Art & Metrop Mus Art, New York. *Exhib:* One-man shows, Seattle Art Mus, 36, Willard Art Gallery, 42-, Detroit Art Inst, 43, Los Angeles Co Mus, 48 & Art Inst Chicago, 48; Univ Mich, 65; Mus Mod Art, New York, 66; Minn Mus Art, 71; Albrecht Art Mus, St Joseph, Mo, 73; Nat Acad Design, 74; Morris Graves: Vision of the Inner Eye Touring Retrospective, Phillips Collection, Washington, DC, 83-84. *Awards:* Guggenheim Found fel, 46; Blair Prize, Art Inst Chicago, 48; Windsor Award, Duke & Duchess of Windsor, 57. *Bibliog:* Katherine Kuh (auth), The Artist's Voice, Harper & Row, 60; The Drawings of Morris Graves, NY Graphic Soc, 74; Morris Graves: Vision of the Inner Eye, Phillips Collection & George Braziller Inc, 83. *Mem:* Hon mem Am Watercolor Soc. *Media:* Tempera, Oil, Watercolor. *Mailing Add:* c/o Willard Gallery 29 E 72nd St New York NY 10021

GRAVES, NANCY STEVENSON
PAINTER, SCULPTOR
b Pittsfield, Mass, 40. *Study:* Vassar Col, BA, 61, fel, 71; Yale Univ Sch Art & Archit, BFA & MFA, 64. *Work:* Whitney Mus Am Art, Mus Mod Art, New York; Nat Gallery Ottawa; Albright-Knox Art Gallery, Buffalo, NY; Chicago Art Inst. *Exhib:* Whitney Mus Am Art, New York, 69; Mus Mod Art, New York, 71; A; Andre Emmerich Galleries, New York, 74 & 77 & Zurich, 77; Albright-Knox Art Gallery, Buffalo, 74 & 80; M Knoedler & Co, New York, 78-82; 200 Yrs of Am Sculpture, Whitney Mus Am Art, New York, 76; Documenta VI, Kassel, WGer, 77; Strata, Vancouver Art Gallery, BC, 77; 39th Venice Biennale, 80; Whitney Biennale, 83. *Awards:* Fulbright-Hays Grant painting, Paris, 64-68; Paris Biennale Grant, 71; Nat Endowment Arts Grant, 72. *Bibliog:* L Lippard (auth), article, Art in Am, 11/75; L Cathcart (auth), Nancy Graves: A Survey 1969-1980, 80; R Storr (auth), article, Art in Am, 3/83. *Mem:* Col Art Asn (bd dir, currently). *Dealer:* M Knoedler & Co 19 E 70th St New York NY. *Mailing Add:* 69 Wooster St New York NY 10012

GRAVES, ROBERT EDWARD
PAINTER, INSTRUCTOR
b Spokane, Wash, Feb 2, 29. *Study:* Whitworth Col, Spokane, BA, 52; Univ Wash, Seattle, MFA, 62; also with Gandy Brodie, 68 & Elaine de Kooning, 79. *Work:* Seattle Art Mus, Evergreen State Col & Bremerton Housing Authority, Wash; Portland Art Mus, Ore; NY Univ, Potsdam. *Exhib:* Northwest Ann, Seattle Art Mus, Wash, 57; Nat Printmakers Exhib, NY Univ, Potsdam, 61; Younger Washington Artists, Henry Gallery, Seattle, 62; Printmakers of Washington, Seattle Art Mus, Mod Art Pavilion, 78; Regional Photography and Printmaking, Gallery 4, Evergreen State Col, Olympia, Wash, 79-80; one-man shows, Seattle Art Mus, 79 & Kerns Gallery, Pa, 81; Governor's Invitational, State Capitol Mus, Olympia, Wash, 81. *Pos:* Dir, Gallery 76, Wenatchee, Wash, 76-78. *Teaching:* Instr fine art, Wenatchee Valley Col, 62-; lectr art & printmaking, Leicester Polytechnic, England, 70-71. *Awards:* K B Baker Mem Award, 43rd Ann, Seattle Art Mus, 57; First Award, Nat Printmaking Exhib, NY State Univ, Potsdam, 61; Printmaking Award, Edmonds Arts Festival, Old Nat Bank, 80. *Mem:* Northwest Print Coun, Portland; Wast State Art Educ Asn (pres, 64-66). *Media:* Oil, Printmaking. *Dealer:* Nancy Teague Gallery Seattle WA 98122. *Mailing Add:* 1412 Saddle Rocke Dr Wenatchee WA 98801

GRAY, CLEVE
PAINTER, SCULPTOR
b New York, NY, Sept 22, 18. *Study:* Princeton Univ, BA, 40. *Work:* Guggenheim Mus & Whitney Mus Am Art, New York; Phillips Collection, Washington, DC; Albright-Knox Art Gallery, Buffalo, NY; Univ Art Gallery, Berkeley, Calif. *Exhib:* Albright-Knox Art Gallery, 77; Columbus Gallery of Fine Art, Ohio, 77; Mus Art, RI Sch Design, Providence, 78. *Awards:* Purchase Award, Univ Ill, 51; Ford Found Award, 61; Neuberger Mus Mural Paintings, 73. *Bibliog:* Daniel Robbins (auth), Cleve Gray, Art Int, 3/64; Thomas Hess (auth), Cleve Gray 1967-1977, Albright Knox Art Gallery, 77; David Shirey (auth), article, New York Times, 6/12/79. *Publ:* Ed, David Smith, 68; ed, John Marin, 70; ed, Hans Richter, 71. *Dealer:* Irving Galleries 332 Worth Ave Palm Beach FL 33480. *Mailing Add:* Cornwall Bridge CT 06754

GRAY, DON
PAINTER, CRITIC
b San Francisco, Calif, June 16, 35. *Study:* Ariz State Univ, Tempe, BA, 57; Univ Iowa, Iowa City, MA, 62. *Exhib:* Lever House, New York, 82; Adelphi Univ, Garden City, NY, 82; Parrish Mus, Southampton, NY, 82; Art Students League, New York, 83; and others. *Pos:* Art critic, Applause Mag, 70-71, New York Arts J, 75-79, Times-Herald Record, Middletown, NY, 82-, Sunstorm Arts Mag, Long Island, NY, 82- & TV & Art World Mag, New York, 82-; producer & moderator, Artist & Critic, Manhattan Cable TV Show, 75- *Teaching:* Instr art, St Francis Col, Brooklyn, 67-70; asst prof art, Ladycliff Col, Highland Falls, NY, 71-80; assoc prof art, Pace Univ, Pleasantville, NY,

80- *Awards:* Grant, Inst Art & Urban Resources, 81. *Bibliog:* Malcolm Preston (auth), article, Newsday, 12/82; Phyllis Braff (auth), article, New York Times, 1/83; Lawrence Campbell (auth), article, Arts Mag, 12/83. *Mem:* Int Asn Art Critics; St Painters Group, New York. *Media:* Acrylic, Oil. *Publ:* Auth, Reassessing the New York School, 8/82 & Contemporary art, video games and ET, 3/83, Sunstorm Arts Mag; auth, Alfred Kubin's Leviathan, 4/83 & Stanley Spencer: Visionary sexuality, 5/83, Art World; auth, John Constable: The mating of flesh and spirit, Sunstorm Arts Mag, 7/83. *Mailing Add:* Box 573 Union Corners Rd Florida NY 10921

GRAY, GLADYS
PAINTER, MURALIST
b Truckee, Calif. *Study:* Fresno State Univ, Calif, AB; Univ Calif, Berkeley, grad study; Claremont Col, Calif; study with Eliot O'Hara, Phil Paradise, Rex Brandt, Jean Ames & others. *Work:* Long Beach Mus Art, Calif; Laguna Beach Mus Art, Calif; Utah State Univ; Calif State Polytech Univ; Art Ctr, San Luis Obispo, Calif. *Comn:* Murals depicting history of the area, comn by Morgan Flagg, Convalescent Hosp, Hacienda, San Luis Obispo, 63, Hacienda, Livermore, Calif, 66, Hacienda, Petaluma, Calif, 69, Hacienda, Roseville, Calif, 69, Hacienda, Porterville, Calif, 69 & Hacienda, Woodland, Calif, 69. *Exhib:* Three Women Painters, Crocker Art Gallery, Sacramento, Calif, 59; one-woman show, Laguna Beach Mus Art, 61 & 71; 21 Paint in Polymer, M Grumbacher Co Exhib, Grand Cent, NY, 65; Grand Prix de Peinture de la Cote d'Azur, 71; Watercolor West, Utah State Univ Gallery, 72. *Pos:* Vol, San Luis Obispo Art Ctr, 52-, bd trustees & secy, six yrs. *Awards:* Purchase Award for Triptych, Los Angeles Madonna Festival, 61; Spec Mention for Top Till, Grand Prix Int, Rome, Italy, 72; Award for Cycle Shapes, Grand Prix Int de Peinture de Deauville, 72. *Bibliog:* Myrtle Kerr (ed), Sketchbook of Kappa Pi, Int Art Fraternity, spring 66; Sandy Smith (auth), Mrs Gray, The Artist, Sociol of Arts, 68. *Mem:* Central Coast Watercolor Soc, (pres 81-82); fel Royal Soc Arts; hon life mem San Luis Obispo Art Asn. *Media:* Transparent Watercolor, Acrylic. *Mailing Add:* 133 Orange Dr San Luis Obispo CA 93401

GRAY, JESSIE BENTON EVANS
PAINTER, CRITIC
b Phoenix, Ariz. *Study:* Ariz State Univ, Tempe, BA, 60; State Univ Iowa, Iowa City, with Mauricio Lazansky, MA, 72. *Work:* Ariz State Univ, Tempe. *Exhib:* Silvermine Guild Artists, New Canaan, Conn, 81; Parrish Mus, South Hampton, NY, 81; Adelphi Col, Garden City, NY, 81 & 82; Art Students League, 81 & 83; Pace Univ, Briarcliff, NY, 82; Lever House, NY, 82; and many others. *Pos:* Assoc ed & art critic, New York Arts J, 75-80; auth, producer & interviewer, Personalities, WTBQ Radio, Warwick, NY, 75-80. *Teaching:* Instr art, Bd Coop Educ Serv, Goshen, NY, 68-69 & Warwick Art League, 71. *Awards:* Grant, Inst Art & Urban Resources, 81. *Bibliog:* Helen Harrison (auth), article, 82 & Phyllis Braff (auth), article, 83, New York Times; Lawrence Campbell (auth), article, Arts Mag, 12/83. *Mem:* Alliance Figurative Artists; Street Painters Figurative Expressionist Group. *Mailing Add:* PO Box 573 Union Corners Rd Florida NY 10921

GRAY, JIM
PAINTER, SCULPTOR
b Middleton, Tenn, June 4, 32. *Work:* Carnegie Libr, Regar Mus, Anniston, Ala; Brooklyn Navy Yard; Loyal Am Life Ins Co, Mobile, Ala; City-Co Bldg, Knoxville, Tenn; Winsor & Newton, Secaucus, NJ; and others. *Comn:* Design & sculpture for Bicentennial Medal, Sevier Co, Tenn; Gen John Sevier (bronze bust), Knoxville, Tenn; Dr Robert F Thomas (mem painting), Sevierville, Tenn. *Exhib:* Whiting Mus, Fairhope, Ala, 70, 73 & 75; Watercolor USA, Springfield, Mo, 70; Realist Invitational, Gallery Contemp Art, Winston-Salem, NC, 71; Am Soc Marine Artists Ann, Grand Cent Gallery, New York, 80 & Peabody Mus, Salem, Mass, 81; 400 Years of Seafaring, Fine Arts Mus, Mobile, Ala, 82; and others. *Teaching:* Instr painting, Buckhorn Art Workshop Ann, Gatlinburg, Tenn; instr watercolor, Atlanta Artist Club, Ga, 69-; lectr art & humanities, Univ Tenn, Knoxville, 70-71. *Awards:* Best in Show & Permanent Trophy, Azalea Trail Arts Festival, 57, 58 & 59; Best of Show, Hammel-Adams Glass, Mobile, 62 & 63. *Bibliog:* Am Artists Mag, 4/77; North Light Mag, 7-8/78; Pace Mag, Piedmont Airlines, 7-8/79; and others. *Mem:* Am Soc Marine Artists (bd dirs, 83-); Salmagundi Club; and others. *Media:* Watercolor, Oil; Clay, Bronze. *Dealer:* Jim Gray Gallery Parkway Gatlinburg TN 37738. *Mailing Add:* PO Box 189 Gatlinburg TN 37738

GRAY, LARRY
PAINTER
b Columbia, Tenn, Sept 19, 44. *Study:* Univ Ga, with Lamar Dodd, BFA, 67; Yale Univ, with Jack Tworkov, Al Held & Bernard Chaet, MFA, 69. *Work:* Mus Mod Art, New York; Chicago Art Inst; Brooklyn Mus; Seattle Art Mus; Achenbach Found, Calif Palace Legion of Honor, San Francisco. *Comn:* Oil painting, comn by His Majesty, the King of Saudi Arabia, 79. *Exhib:* New Works, Stanford Univ, Palo Alto, 73; one-man shows, ADI Gallery, San Francisco, 77-78, Foster/White Gallery, Seattle, 77-79, Mirage Gallery, Santa Monica, Calif, 79 & Getler-Pall, New York, 80; Am Painters, Tokyo Cent Mus Arts, Japan, 78; New Acquisitions, Brooklyn Mus, 79. *Teaching:* Assoc prof painting, Humboldt State Univ, 69-77. *Bibliog:* Robert McDonald (auth), Larry Gray's atmospheric paintings, 77, Landscapes sensitively interpreted, 78 & Landscape: macro and micro, 79, Artweek. *Media:* Dry Pigment and Pastel; Oil on Linen. *Dealer:* Foster/White Gallery 311 1/2 Occidental Ave S Seattle WA 98104. *Mailing Add:* 2054 44th Ave 530 McAllister St San Francisco CA 94116

GRAY, MARIE ELISE
PAINTER
b Bremanger, Norway; US citizen. *Study:* Derbyshire Sch Fine Art, 64-65; Cornish Sch Allied Art, 66-70; Olympic Col, 71; and with Rex Brandt, Sergei Bongart, Warren Brandon & Raymond Brose. *Work:* Frye Art Mus, Seattle, Wash; Univ Ore; Boeing Airplane Co, Seattle; US Steel Co, Seattle; AMFAC Inc, San Francisco. *Comn:* Four paintings (acrylic), Washington Mortgage Co, Seattle, 74. *Exhib:* Northwest Watercolor Exhibs, 61-75, Northwest Ann, 63 & 65 & 42nd Ann Int Print Exhib, 71, Seattle Art Mus; Northwest Watercolor Ann Exhib, Bellevue Art Mus, Wash, 80; Audubon Wildlife Exhib, Kirsten Gallery, Seattle, 81; Puget Sound Ann, Frye Art Mus, Seattle, 83; Northwest Marine Exhib, Kirsten Gallery, Seattle, 83; Wash State Art Biennial, Nat League Am Pen Women, Unitarian Gallery, Seattle, 83; and others. *Teaching:* Instr art, YWCA, Seattle, 68; instr art, Washington Athletic Club, Seattle, 73; instr art, Women's Univ Club, Seattle, 73. *Awards:* Top Award, Women Painters Wash Ann, Frederick & Nelson Gallery, Seattle, 81; First Award Oil Painting, Nat League Am Pen Women, Wash, 83; First Award Watercolor, Art Biennial, Unitarian Gallery, Seattle, 83. *Mem:* Northwest Watercolor Soc; Nat League Am Pen Women; Women Painters Wash; Olympic Art Asn. *Media:* Multimedia. *Dealer:* Kirsten Gallery 5320 Roosevelt Way NE Seattle WA 98105; Stillwater Gallery 1900 N Northlake Way #145 Mariner's Sq Seattle WA. *Mailing Add:* 7723 30th Ave NE Seattle WA 98115

GRAY, MAXINE CUSHING
EDITOR
b Brookline, Mass. *Study:* Stanford Univ, BA(cum laude), 30. *Pos:* Music critic, Seattle Post-Intelligencer, 51-53; arts ed, Argus, Seattle, 54-74; ed & publ, Northwest Arts (Seattle-biweekly), 75- *Awards:* Ford Found travel & study award for critics, 64; Ann Arts Award, King Co Arts Comn, Seattle, 74; Cert of Recognition, Gov Writer's Day Award, 78. *Mailing Add:* 538 NE 98th St Seattle WA 98115

GRAY, RICHARD
DEALER
b Chicago, Ill, Dec 30, 28. *Pos:* Owner & dir, Richard Gray Gallery. *Mem:* Art Dealers Asn Am (former dir); Chicago Art Dealers Asn (former pres); Col Art Asn Am. *Specialty:* Paintings, sculpture, drawings and prints by established European and American artists and the avante garde. *Mailing Add:* Richard Gray Gallery 620 N Michigan Ave Chicago IL 60611

GRAY, ROBERT HUGH
EDUCATOR, ADMINISTRATOR
b Dallas, Tex, Sept 22, 31. *Study:* Yale Univ, BFA(painting), 59, MFA(painting), 61. *Pos:* Dean, Visual Arts Div, State Univ NY Col, Purchase, 75-79; dean, Col Fine Arts, Univ Calif, Los Angeles, 80-; bd trustees, Sundance Inst Film & Craft & Folk Art Mus. *Teaching:* Instr design & visual commun, Cooper Union, New York, 60-66; instr drawing, painting & design & dean, Silvermine Col Art, Conn, 66-71; prof painting & head dept art, Pa State Univ, State Col, 72-75. *Awards:* Outstanding Educator Award, 73. *Mem:* Nat Coun Art Adminrs; Col Art Asn; Am Asn Higher Educ; Confederation Calif Arts; Nat Crafts Planning Comt. *Mailing Add:* Col of Fine Arts Murphy Hall Los Angeles CA 90024

GRAY, ROBERT WARD
ADMINISTRATOR
b Tallahassee, Fla, June 26, 16. *Study:* Univ Fla; Tri-State Col; Grad Sch Am Craftsmen, with Herbert H Sanders. *Collections Arranged:* Co-dir, New Eng Craft Exhib, 55. *Pos:* In charge pottery shop & coordr craft prog, Old Sturbridge Village, 49-51; dir, Worchester Craft Ctr, 51-61; dir, Southern Highland Handicraft Guild, 61- *Mem:* Fel Am Crafts Coun. *Mailing Add:* South Highlands Handicraft Guild PO Box 9545 Asheville NC 28805

GRAY, THOMAS ALEXANDER
CONSULTANT, COLLECTOR
b Winston-Salem, NC, Feb 7, 48. *Study:* Duke Univ, BA(hist art), 70; Am Cult Winterthur Prog, Univ Del, MA, 74; Summer Inst Arts Admin, Harvard Univ, 74. *Pos:* Dir, Mus Early Southern Decorative Arts, Winston-Salem, 76-79; consult, Graylyn Conf Ctr, Wake Forest Univ, 81- *Mem:* Hist Preservation Soc NC Inc (pres exec comt, 76-78); Hist Preservation Fund NC Inc (bd, 76-, vpres, 79-, pres, 80-82); Stagville Preservation Ctr, Durham, NC (bd, 77-); Piedmont Craftsmen Inc (bd, 77-79); Old Salem Inc (develop dir, 74-76, bd, 81-, exec comt, 82-). *Mailing Add:* 10 West St Winston-Salem NC 27101

GRAYSMITH, ROBERT
CARTOONIST, ILLUSTRATOR
b Pensacola, Fla, Sept 17, 42. *Study:* Calif Col Arts & Crafts, BFA, 65. *Pos:* Staff artist, Stockton Rec, Calif, 65-68; ed cartoonist, San Francisco Chronicle, 68- *Mailing Add:* San Francisco Chronicle Fifth & Mission Sts San Francisco CA 94119

GRAYSON, CASSANDRA
DEALER, PUBLISHER
b New York, NY. *Study:* Columbia Univ. *Pos:* Asst dir, Davis Galleries, New York, 59-61; pres, Gallery G Fine Arts, 65-, Galaxy Graphics & Taos Western Publ Corp, currently. *Mem:* Am Fedn of Arts. *Specialty:* Graphics, American painting of the 19th and 20th centuries; Western & Southwestern art. *Mailing Add:* Gallery G Fine Arts Ltd 6611 E Central Wichita KS 67206

GRAZIANI, SANTE
PAINTER, MURALIST
b Cleveland, Ohio, Mar 11, 20. *Study:* Cleveland Sch Art, 38-41; Sch Fine Arts, Yale Univ, BFA, 43, MFA, 48. *Comn:* Murals, Bluffton Post Off, Ohio, 41, Columbus Junction Post Off, Iowa, 42, Holyoke Pub Libr, Mass, 49-51, Am Battle Monument, Henri-Chapelle, Belg, 55-58 & Mayo Clin, Rochester, Minn, 69; and others. *Exhib:* One-man shows, Babcock Galleries, New York, six times, 62-71, Kanegis Gallery, Boston, 64-70, Allentown Art Mus, 70, Inst Arts & Sci, Manchester, NH, 81 & Jersey City State Col, 81; retrospective, Springfield Mus, Mass, 77; and others. *Pos:* Officer in charge arts & crafts, USA, Pac Theatre Operations, 45-46. *Teaching:* Instr drawing & painting, Sch Fine Arts, Yale Univ, 46-51; dean, Whitney Sch Art, 50-51; head, Worcester Art Mus Sch, 51-72, dean, 72-81, dean emer, 81- *Awards:* Pulitzer Scholar, 42; Boston Art Dirs Club Award, 54; Spec Drawing Award, Norfolk Mus, 61; and others. *Mem:* Nat Soc Mural Painters. *Dealer:* Babcock Galleries 805 Madison Ave New York NY 10021; Fairweather-Hardin Gallery 101 E Ontario St Chicago IL 60611. *Mailing Add:* Worcester Art Mus 55 Salisbury St Worcester MA 01608

GREACEN, RUTH NICKERSON See Nickerson, Ruth

GREAR, JAMES MALCOLM
DESIGNER, EDUCATOR
b Mill Springs, Ky, June 12, 31. *Study:* Art Acad Cincinnati, Ohio, 58, cert. *Comn:* Graphics for The New American Painting & Sculpture: The First Generation Exhibition (designer), Mus Mod Art, New York, 69; Henri Matisse Catalogue, Detroit Inst Art, Mich, 77; HHS Seal, Dept Health & Human Serv, Washington, DC, 80; Admin 50th Anniversary 15-cent Commemorative Stamp, US Postal Serv, Washington, DC. *Exhib:* New Eng Designers, Addison Gallery Contemp Art, Andover, Mass, 64; Commun by Design, Inst Contemp Art, Boston, 64; Malcolm Grear Designers Exhib, List Art Bldg, Bron Univ, 73, Am Inst Graphic Arts, New York, 74; Jorgensen Gallery, Univ Conn, 75 & others; Biennale of Graphic Design Brno 74, Czech; New Eng Bk Show, Boston, 76; Environmental Design: Signing & Graphics, Am Inst Graphic Arts, 77. *Pos:* Designer/consult publ, RI Sch Design, 63- & Guggenheim Mus, New York, 69-; design consult, Comt to Rescue Italian Art, 67-68; nat design chmn, Nat Asn Partners of the Americas, 70-; designer/consult publ, Fogg Art Mus, Cambridge, Mass, 71-76; design consult, RI Tall Ships 76, 75-76. *Teaching:* Prof graphic design, RI Sch Design, 61- *Awards:* Am Inst Graphic Arts Ann Award, 50 Best Bks Publ in US, 68, 70, 71, 74 & 77; Gov's Arts Award, RI State Coun Arts, 69; Art Libr Soc NAm Award, Henri Matisse: Paper Cut-Outs, 77. *Bibliog:* Walter Diethelm (auth), Signet/Signal/Symbol, ABC Ed, Zurich, 70; Graphis Posters, The Graphis Press, Zurich, Switz, 73; article, Idea Mag, Japan, 75. *Mem:* Am Inst Graphics, New York; Providence Art Club. *Publ:* Auth, Recombinant DNA, Light, Science of Musical Sounds, The Discovery of Subatomic Particles, Scientific American Series, 81; auth, Computer Graphics, Polaroid Corp, 81. *Mailing Add:* 391 Eddy St Providence RI 02903

GREAVER, HANNE
PRINTMAKER
b Copenhagen, Denmark, Aug 1, 33. *Study:* Kunsthaandvaerkerskolen, Copenhagen. *Work:* Beloit Col, Wis; Univ Ga; Univ Maine, Orono; Mich State Univ; Univ Nebr. *Exhib:* Univ Maine, Orono, 70; Five Women Printmakers, Kalamazoo Inst Arts, Mich, 69; Boston Printmakers, 76; Mich Printmakers, 77; Northwest Print Coun Inaugural Exhib, 82. *Awards:* Purchase Award, Boston Printmakers, 76. *Mem:* Northwest Print Coun. *Media:* Etching, Lithography. *Mailing Add:* Box 120 Cannon Beach OR 97110

GREAVER, HARRY
PAINTER, PRINTMAKER
b Los Angeles, Calif, Oct 30, 29. *Study:* Univ Kans, BFA & MFA. *Work:* Amherst Col, Mass; Univ Maine, Orono; New York Pub Libr; Norfolk Mus Arts & Sci, Va; Univ Utah Mus Fine Arts. *Exhib:* Drawings USA, St Paul, Minn, 63; Drawing & Small Sculpture Show, Ball State Univ, Ind, 68; 2nd Nat Print Show, San Diego, Calif, 71; Drawings by Living American Artists, Univ Utah Mus Fine Arts, 72-73; Small Print Exhib, Purdue Univ, 77. *Collections Arranged:* Paintings by American Masters, Kalamazoo Inst Arts, Mich, 66, Western Art, 67, The Surrealist, 71 & Reginald Marsh, 74; Harvey Breverman, 76. *Pos:* Dir, Kalamazoo Inst Arts, 66-78; dir, Greaver Gallery, 78- *Teaching:* Assoc prof art, Univ Maine, Orono, 55-66. *Awards:* Purchase Awards, Norfolk Mus, 63 & 64. *Media:* Watercolor; Lithographs. *Mailing Add:* Box 120 Cannon Beach OR 97110

GREAVES, JAMES L
CONSERVATOR, RESTORER
b Middletown, Conn, Jan 25, 43. *Study:* Col William & Mary, BS; Inst Fine Arts, NY Univ, MA(art hist), 70, dipl(art conserv), 70. *Pos:* Conserv intern, Los Angeles Co Mus Art, 68-70, conservator, 70; chief conservator, Detroit Inst Arts, 70-76; conservator, Los Angeles Co Mus Art, 77-, actg head conservator, 79-80, senior paintings conservator, 80-; consult conservator, Huntington Libr, Art Gallery & Botanical Gardens, 79- *Teaching:* Instr, Calif State Univ, Fullerton, 80-; vis lectr, Univ Calif, Los Angeles, 81- *Mem:* Fel Int Inst Conserv Hist & Artistic Works; fel Am Inst Conserv; Western Asn Art Conservators (pres, 78-79). *Publ:* Coauth, New findings on Caravaggio's technique in the Detroit Magdalen, Burlington Mag, 74. *Mailing Add:* Los Angeles Co Mus of Art 5905 Wilshire Blvd Los Angeles CA 90036

GRECO, ANTHONY JOSEPH
PAINTER, ADMINISTRATOR
b Cleveland, Ohio, Apr 24, 37. *Study:* Cleveland Inst Art, with Louis Bosa, BFA, 60; Kent State Univ, with Joseph O'Sickey, MFA, 66. *Work:* Kent State Univ; Ga State Art Comn. *Comn:* Urban Walls Atlanta, one of six inner-city walls. *Exhib:* Butler Inst Am Art Ann; Alumni from Twenty Years, 1949-1969, Cleveland Inst Art, 70; Mint Mus Art Biennial Exhib, 75; Artists in Ga, High Mus Art, Atlanta, 75 & 78; one-man shows, Armstrong State Col, Savannah, Ga, 76 & Javo Gallery, Atlanta, 78; Works on Paper, Kohler Arts Ctr, Sheboygan, Wis, 77; and others. *Teaching:* Chmn drawing dept, Atlanta Col Art, 66-75, chmn div advanced studio & asst to pres, 74-76, acad dean & instr, 75-; vis instr drawing & painting, Univ Wis-Madison, summer 69. *Awards:* Purchase Award, Butler Inst Am Art Midyear, 61; B F Goodrich Mem Award, Akron Art Inst Ann, 70; NC Bank Purchase Award, Mint Mus Art Biennial Exhib, 75. *Media:* Mixed. *Mailing Add:* Atlanta Col Art 1280 Peachtree St NE Atlanta GA 30309

GRECO, FRANK
PAINTER
b Trenton, NJ, Mar 14, 03. *Study:* Sch Indust Aht, Trenton, 22-27, with Henry R McGuiness, George Bradshaw & Harry Rosin; Indust Art Sch, New York; Am Artist Sch, New York, with Sol Wilson & the Soyer Brothers; Ozenfant GI Sch Fine Arts, New York. *Work:* Mus of Mod Art, New York; Nat Gallery, Washington, DC; NJ State Mus, Trenton; Mercer Co Community Col, Trenton, NJ. *Exhib:* Italian-Am Bicentennial, Philadelphia, 76; Then & Now--WPA Exhib of 200 Artists, New York, 77; Am Art of the 1930's, NJ State Mus, 79; retrospective, Trenton, NJ, 80; Sixteen Artists, Trenton Artists Workshop, 80; and many others. *Collections Arranged:* Hist of Modern Posters, Mus Mod Art, New York, 41; Direction Gallery, Darien, Conn & New York, 41; Artists for Victory, Mus Mod Art, New York, 42; Armenian War Relief, New York, 43. *Awards:* Fourth Prize, United Against Aggression, Mus Mod Art, New York, 41-42; Fourth Prize, Artist for Victory, Inc, 42. *Bibliog:* Carlyle Burroughs (auth), Greco work sure, Herald Tribune, 55; Linda Holt (auth), Are you the Greco who worked with Jackson Pollock?, Trentonian, NJ, 74; Elisabeth Stevens (auth), Still-growing artist--60 years later, Trenton Times, NJ, 77; Barbara Murphy (auth), Greco returns to Trenton after 42 years for inspiration, The Trentonian, 77. *Mem:* Artist Equity, Philadelphia Chapter; New York Works Progress Admin. *Media:* Oil, Watercolor. *Mailing Add:* 127 Kent Trenton NJ 08611

GRECO, JOSEPHINE G
GALLERY DIRECTOR, CURATOR
b Augusta, Italy, May 19, 40; US citizen. *Study:* Univ Naples, Italy, 57; Univ Siena, Italy, 58-59; Cath Univ, Hon Degree, 82-83. *Pos:* Dir, Osuna Gallery, Washington, DC, 81- *Specialty:* Contemporary American, South American and European art; old masters, 17th to 19th centuries. *Publ:* Auth, articles in Italian newspapers & mags, 59-63. *Mailing Add:* 1800 Old Meadow Rd Suite 1119 McLean VA 22102

GREELEY, CHARLES MATTHEW
PAINTER, INSTRUCTOR
b Teaneck, NJ, Sept 11, 41. *Study:* New York Sch Visual Arts, with George Ortman. *Work:* NMex Mus Fine Arts, Santa Fe; Mus Contemp Art, Houston, Tex; Longview Mus, Tex; Mus of Mod Art, San Francisco, Calif; Albuquerque Mus, NMex; and others. *Exhib:* Seven Year Retrospective, Capricorn Asunder Gallery, San Francisco, 71; two-person show, Contemp Arts Mus, Houston, Tex, 79; Ceramic Show, Glorieta Gallery, NMex, 79; Mariposa Gallery, Albuquerque, NMex, 81; Santa Fe Arts Festival, 81; and others. *Pos:* Screening judge, San Francisco Art Festival, 71. *Teaching:* Instr painting & ceramics, Glorieta Pass Inst, Glorieta, NMex, 73- *Awards:* Cash Award, Weatherhead Found, NY, 74; Purchase Prize, Longview Mus Competition, Tex, 75; First Prize Cash Award, Southwest Biennial Weatherhead Found, NY, 76; and others. *Bibliog:* Tom Albright (auth), The Visionaries, Rolling Stones Mag, 71; Dr Roland Fischer (auth), The art of madness & the madness of art: an altered state experience, Md Psychiat Res Ctr, 72; Charlotte Moss (auth), Art in the Southwest, Art News, 8/77. *Media:* Acrylic, Watercolor. *Publ:* Contribr, Visions of Elsewhere, San Francisco Art Inst, 71. *Mailing Add:* PO Box 42 Glorieta NM 87535

GREEN, ART
PAINTER
b Frankfort, Ind, May 13, 41; Can citizen. *Study:* Art Inst Chicago, BFA, 65. *Work:* Art Inst Chicago; Nat Gallery Can, Ottawa; New Orleans Art Mus; Mus Mod Kunst, Vienna, Austria; Can Coun Art Bank Collection, Ottawa, Ont. *Exhib:* Five-man group, The Hairy Who, Chicago, 66-68; Personal Torment-Human Response, Whitney Mus Am Art, New York, 69 & Extraordinary Realities, 73; three-man show, Darthea Speyer Gallery, Paris, France, 70; two-man show, Pa Acad Fine Arts, Philadelphia, 74; Can Canvas, Time Mag Travel Show, 75-76; Ann, San Francisco Art Inst, 77; Who Chicago Traveling Show, Sunderland Arts Ctr, Eng, 79; one-man shows, Phyllis Kind Galleries, 74-81. *Teaching:* Asst prof painting, NS Col Art, Halifax, 69-71 & Univ Waterloo, Ont, 77-80. *Awards:* Cassandra Award, Cassandra Found, Chicago, 70; Can Coun Arts Bursary, 71-73 & 76-77. *Bibliog:* A Adrian (auth), rev in Art in Am, 7-8/74; C Scher (auth), Arts Can, 3/75; T Gruber (auth), Arts Mag, 5/77. *Media:* Oil. *Dealer:* Phyllis Kind Gallery 226 E Ontario St Chicago IL 60611. *Mailing Add:* 5 Elizabeth St Stratford ON N5A 4Z1 Canada

GREEN, DAVID OLIVER
SCULPTOR, EDUCATOR

b Enid, Okla, June 29, 08. *Study:* Am Acad Art; Nat Acad Art. *Work:* Los Angeles Co Mus Natural Hist. *Comn:* Dragonfly Fountain, Welton Beckett Asn, Hillsdale Shopping Ctr, San Mateo, Calif, 55; five figure group, Lytton Savings & Loan Asn, Hollywood, 60; children's sculpture, Women's Club for Bruggemeyer Mem Libr, Monterey Park, Calif, 68; Owl Tree (wall relief), dedicated to daughters of Maurice Fletcher & Tree of Life (fountain), Guyer Mem, Altadena Libr, Calif, 69. *Exhib:* Los Angeles Co Mus Art Ann, 61; Tucson Art Ctr, Ariz, 63; Southern Calif Expos, San Diego Fair, Del Mar, 66; Citrus Col Invitational, Glendora, Calif, 68; 17th Ann All Calif Exhib, Laguna Beach Art Gallery, Calif, 71; Retrospective Exhib, Sculpture & Calligraphy, Walla Walla Col, Wash, 79. *Teaching:* Asst prof sculpture, Otis Art Inst, 47-73 & Scripps Col, 66; instr, Pasadena Art Mus, Calif, 56-59; instr calligraphy, Pasadena City Col, 74-76. *Awards:* First Prize for Sculpture, Laguna Beach Art Asn, 62 & 67 & Pasadena Soc Artists, 71 & 75. *Bibliog:* Jarvis Barlow (auth), David Green, Pasadena Independent, 7/13/47; Bev Johnson (auth), Owls, cats & bats, Los Angeles Times Sun Sect, 3/13/60; Peg Powell (auth), A way with animals, Independent Star-News, 12/15/63. *Mem:* Int Inst Arts & Lett; Pasadena Soc Artists; Soc Italic Handwriting (Western Am Br); Soc Calligraphy, Los Angeles. *Media:* Stone, Wood. *Mailing Add:* 176 W Jaxine Dr Altadena CA 91001

GREEN, DENISE G
PAINTER

b Melbourne, Australia, Apr 7, 46; US citizen. *Study:* Ecole Nat Superiere des Beaux Arts; Sorbonne Univ, Paris, BA, 69; Hunter Col, New York, MFA, 76. *Exhib:* Young Am Artists: 1978 Exxon National, Solomon R Guggenheim Mus, New York, 78; New Image Painting, Whitney Mus Am Art, New York, 78; Surfaces/Textures, Mus Mod Art, New York, 81; solo exhib, Ado Gallery, Bonheiden, Belgium, 82 & Gallery A, Sydney, Australia, 83; Contemporary Still Lifes Traveling Exhib, Mus Mod Art, New York, 82; Expatriate New York Works on Paper, City Art Inst, Paddington, Australia, 83; Premio Internazionale Biella per l'incisione 1983, Italy, 83; Extra-Critical Role, Gabrielle Bryers Gallery, New York, 83; and others. *Pos:* Reviewer, Arts Mag, 70-72. *Teaching:* Instr painting, Roger Willams Col, 72; instr studio & art hist, Fairleigh Dickinson Univ, 72-74; instr, Pratt Inst, 74; artist in residence, Ill State Uni, 76 & Art Inst Chicago, 77; instr, summer prog art, State Univ NY, Fredonia, 77; artist in residence, Va Commonwealth Univ, 81, Tyler Col Art, Temple Univ, 82 & Calif Inst Arts, 83. *Awards:* Ingram Merrill Found Grant, 72 & 73; Visual Arts Bd Grant, 74 & Traveling Grant, 77, Australian Coun Arts. *Bibliog:* Peter Frank (auth), article, Art News, 12/73; Ann Lauterbach (auth), article, Art in Am, 12/75; Mona da Vinci (auth), article, Art News, 1/77. *Publ:* Ed, Heresies, 2nd issue, 77. *Dealer:* Max Protetch Gallery 37 W 57th St New York NY 10019. *Mailing Add:* c/o Max Protetch Gallery 37 W 57th St New York NY 10019

GREEN, EDWARD ANTHONY
DIRECTOR, DESIGNER

b Milwaukee, Wis, Apr 20, 22. *Study:* Univ Wis-Madison, with Edward Boerner, Helmut Summ, Misch Kohn, Al Sessler, Dean Meeker & Warrington Colescott, BS & MS; Layton Sch Art, Milwaukee, 52; Univ Wis-Milwaukee, MFA, 66. *Work:* Alverno Col, Marine Bank & Manpower, Milwaukee; Cherokee Art Mus, Iowa; Univ Wis-Madison; Univ Wis-Milwaukee. *Comn:* Church for Baptist Mission, Bamenda, Brit Cameroons, 62; outdoor fountains, Conrad Mem, 66. *Exhib:* Wis Printmakers, 54-72; Beloit & Vicinity, Wis, 58-72; Wis Watercolor, 67-72; West Bend Art Gallery, Wis, 81; and others. *Collections Arranged:* Streets of Old Milwaukee; Hanseatic League; Hopi Pueblo; Kwakiutl Plank House; Guatemala Market; Japanese House & Garden; Moroccan House; Mexican Courtyard; European Village; and many others. *Pos:* Archit designer, Off Martin White, 40-42; archit model maker, Off Allen Wadsworth, 47-48; art dir, Milwaukee Pub Mus, 51-; art & landmarks comnr, City of Milwaukee, 67-; consult to mus in Minn, Iowa, Calif, Ill, Colo, NMex & others. *Teaching:* Instr watercolor & life drawing, Univ Wis-Milwaukee, 55-70; instr outdoor sketching, Whitnall Park, Milwaukee, 68-; instr watercolor, Cardinal Stritch Col, Milwaukee, 73- *Awards:* First Award for Watercolor, Grumbacher, 62; First Award for Serigraph, Wis Printmakers, 64; First Award for Watercolor, Wis State Fair, 67. *Bibliog:* Margaret Rahill (auth), article, Milwaukee Sentinel, 56; Jane Farley (auth), article, 63 & Lois Hagen (auth), article, 74, Milwaukee J. *Mem:* Milwaukee Art Comn (chmn, 67-); Am Asn Mus; Midwest Mus Asn; Am Asn Mus; Milwaukee Art Ctr. *Media:* Watercolor; Lithographs. *Publ:* Auth, Cleverly Rearranged Cabinets of Curios, Bowling Green Univ Press, 82; and others. *Dealer:* Bradley Gallery 2565 N Downer Ave Milwaukee WI 53211. *Mailing Add:* 3173 S 31st St Milwaukee WI 53215

GREEN, ELEANOR BROOME
CONSULTANT

b Covina, Calif. *Study:* Vassar Col, AB; George Washington Univ, MA & PhD. *Collections Arranged:* Edward Weston (with catalog), 67; Picasso since 1945, 67; Scale as Content (Tony Smith, Barnet Newman, Ronald Bladen, with catalog), 67; Al Held (with catalog), 68; Augustus Vincent Track (with catalog), 72; Photography Here and Now, 72; Masterpieces from the Musee de Grenoble, 73; The Apocalypse, 73; Tony Smith (with catalog), 74; Rockne Krebs, 75; Maurice Prendergast for Univ Md; Univ Mus, Austin, Tex; Des Moines Fine Arts Ctr; Columbus Gallery of Fine Arts; Johnson Mus, Ithaca, NY; Davis & Long Gallery (auth, catalog); French Watercolor Landscapes of the Nineteenth Century: From Delacroix to Cezanne at Univ Md, Speed Mus, Louisville; Univ Mich (with catalog); Rufino Tamayo (with catalog), 11th Int Sculpture Conf, Washington, DC, Marion Koogler McNay Inst, Guggenheim Mus. *Pos:* Cur, Washington Gallery Mod Art, DC, 64-66; cur contemp art,

Corcoran Gallery, Washington, DC, 66-69; dir, Art Gallery, Univ Md, 72-79. *Teaching:* Prof Am art, Univ Md, College Park, 72-80. *Mem:* Col Art Asn; Am Asn Mus. *Res:* Contemporary American artists. *Publ:* Discovering Museums: The Phillips Collection, Penhurst Books; Masterpieces from the Phillips Collection, Fine Arts Mus San Francisco. *Mailing Add:* 2101 Connecticut Ave Washington DC 20008

GREEN, GEORGE D
PAINTER

b Portland, Ore, June 24, 43. *Work:* Portland Mus of Art, Ore; Univ of Tex, MA, 68; Kansas City Art Inst, Mo. of Art, Austin; Everson Mus of Art, Syracuse, NY; Ft Worth Art Ctr Mus, Tex; Brainard Gallery, State Univ of NY, Potsdam. *Exhib:* Abstract Illusionism, Shore Gallery, Boston, Mass, 77; Photo Illusionism Abstract Illusionism, Tomasulo Gallery, NJ, 77; one-man shows, Triangle Gallery, San Francisco, 77, Louis Mus Am Art, Meisel Gallery, 78 & 79. *Teaching:* Instr Purchase Award for painting, Portland Art Mus, Ore, 77; 69, El Centro Jr Col, Dallas, 69-70 Found Grant & Fel for Abstract Illusionistic Paintings, 75-76 & 78-79. *Mailing Add:* c/o Louis K Meisel Gallery 141 Prince St New York NY 10012

GREEN, GLENDA
PAINTER, HISTORIAN

b Weatherford, Tex, Feb 4, 45. *Study:* Tex Christian Univ, BFA(magna cum laude), 67; Kress Fel, 67-70; Tulane Univ, MA(art hist), 70. *Work:* Mus City New York; Nat Mus Hist & Technol, Smithsonian Inst; Williams Col Mus Art; State of Okla Art Collection, Okla Art Ctr, Oklahoma City; Okla Hist Soc, Oklahoma City. *Comn:* Portrait of Hon Allen J Ellender, Ellender Mem, Houma, La, 72; portrait of A Hyatt Mayor, comn by sitter, Mus City New York, 74; portrait of S Lane Faison, Jr, comn by sitter & Williams Col, Williams Col Mus, 76. *Exhib:* 1975 Bicentennial Nat Art Exhib, Art Gallery, Univ Tex, Arlington, 75; Eight State Exhib of Painting & Sculpture, Okla Art Ctr, Oklahoma City, 76 & 77; Southwest Tarrant Co Ann, Ft Worth Mus Art, 76; 1976 SW Fine Arts Biennial, Mus of Fine Arts, Santa Fe, NMex, 76; Philbrook Art Ctr, Tulsa, 78; Art Expo West, Los Angeles, 80; Art Expo New York, 81- *Pos:* Res asst, Kimbell Art Mus, Ft Worth, 68-69; cur collections, Newcomb Col Sch Art, New Orleans, 69-72; artist in residence, Okla Arts & Humanities Coun, 77-78; dir, Q Co, Art Enterprizes, 79- *Teaching:* Instr art hist, Tulane Univ, 69-72; guest artist painting, Univ Okla, Norman, 72-75, vis instr art hist, 73-76. *Bibliog:* V Kimbell (auth), A new search for humanism in art: An interview with Glenda Youritzin, 1/74 & Jim Ramses (auth), A feminine humanist: Glenda Youritzin, 9/76, Southwest Art; Boo Browning (auth), More than meets the eye (the art of Glenda Youritzin), Okla Mo, 1/78. *Media:* Oil. *Mailing Add:* 8904-A Trone Circle Austin TX 78758

GREEN, JASHA
SCULPTOR, PAINTER

b Boston, Mass, May 1, 27. *Study:* Boston Mus Sch, 41, 46-47; with F Leger, Paris, France, 48-50. *Work:* Guggenheim Mus, New York; Brooklyn Mus; Philadelphia Mus Art; Kansas City Art Inst, Mo; Denver Art Mus. *Comn:* Steel Sculpture, Ottawa Steel Co, Grand Rapids, Mich, 77, Globe Iron Works, Norfolk, Va, 78, AVX Corp, Great Neck, NY, 79 & Midwestern Ins, Cincinnati, Ohio, 80; Peace Sculpture, Israel Govt, Jerusalem, 79. *Exhib:* One-man shows, Univ Calif, 77, Albrecht Mus, St Joseph, Mo, 77, Everson Mus, Syracuse, NY, 78, Chrysler Mus, Norfolk, 78, Okla Mus, Oklahoma City, 78, H F Johnson Mus, Cornell Univ, New York, 79 & St Peters Col, Jersey City, NJ, 79; plus others. *Bibliog:* Peter Frank (auth), Works of Jasha Green, Arts Mag, 76; Hilton Kramer (auth), J Greens' Gouaches, New York Times, 77; Harold Rosenberg (auth), Monumontage (catalog), 78. *Media:* Steel Sculpture; Oil Painting. *Mailing Add:* 117 E 18th St New York NY 10003

GREEN, MARTIN LEONARD
PAINTER, PRINTMAKER

b Monterey Park, Calif, Oct 4, 36. *Study:* Brandt-Dike Sch Painting, 53-54; Pomona Col, Calif, 54-58; Mexico City Univ Americas, 57; Orange Coast Col, Calif, 75-76. *Work:* Los Angeles Co Mus of Art, Los Angeles; Gruenwald Ctr for the Graphic Arts, Univ Calif, Los Angeles; Calif Palace Legion Honor; Standard Oil of Ind Arts Collections, Chicago; Fogg Mus Art, Harvard Univ; and others. *Comn:* Panels, Rockresorts/Kapalua Bay Hotel, Maui, Hawaii, 77-78; Double Tree Hotel, Houston; Boca Raton Hotel, Fla; King Fahd, Saudi Arabia; and others. *Exhib:* All-Calif Show, Laguna Beach Mus of Art, 75; Contemp Monotypes, Santa Barbara Mus of Art, Calif, 76; Brand V, Brand Libr Art Gallery, Glendale, Calif, 76; New Am Monotypes, Smithsonian Inst Travelling Exhib, 78-80; Los Angeles Mus Sci & Indust; and others. *Pos:* Lectr monotype hist & demonstr technique, Los Angeles Co Mus of Art, Santa Barbara Mus of Art & Glendale Col. *Bibliog:* Florence Goodman (auth), A blending of eastern & western philosophies and art, SW Art, 4/76; Brendan Gill (auth), The Dream Come True, Lippincott & Crowell, 80; Calvin J Goodman (auth), Monotype: A singular art form, Am Artist, 81. *Mem:* Los Angeles Printmaking Soc; Artists Equity. *Media:* Intaglio, Lithographs. *Dealer:* Louis Neuman Galleries 322 N Beverly Dr Beverly Hills CA 90210. *Mailing Add:* Star Rte Box 61 Banning CA 92220

GREEN, TOM
INSTRUCTOR, SCULPTOR

b Newark, NJ, May 27, 42. *Study:* Univ Md, BA, 67, MA(painting), 69. *Exhib:* New Sculpture: Baltimore-Washington-Richmond, Corcoran Gallery Art, Washington, DC, 70; Washington Sculpture, Philadelphia Art Alliance, 73; one-man show, Corcoran Gallery Art, 73; Whitney Biennial, Whitney Mus Am Art, New York, 75; North, East, West, South & Middle, Traveling Drawing Show, 75. *Teaching:* Asst prof sculpture & drawing, Corcoran Sch

Art, 69- *Bibliog:* Susan Sollins (auth), Washington report, Arts Mag, 9/73; David Tannous (auth), Tom Green: Words and images, Woodwind Mag, 12/11/73; Ben Forgey (auth), Washington: Pyramid shapes, Grenoble and theatrics, Art News, 1/74. *Mailing Add:* Corcoran Sch of Art 17th & New York Ave NW Washington DC 20006

GREEN, WILDER
ADMINISTRATOR, ARCHITECT
b Paris, France, Apr 17, 27; US citizen. *Study:* Yale Col, 45-47; Ill Inst Technol & Design Inst, Chicago, 47-48; Yale Univ Sch Archit, BArch, 52. *Pos:* Asst dir & cur, Dept Archit & Design, Mus Mod Art, New York, 57-61, coordr planning for bldg prog, 61-63, coordr prog, 63-67, dir exhib prog, 67-69, dep to actg dir, 69-70, dir exhib prog, 70-71; pres, Cunningham Dance Found, 69-72; dir, Am Fedn Arts, 71- *Teaching:* Asst prof, Yale Sch Archit, 56-57; Hunter Col, 67-68. *Mem:* Munic Art Soc New York; Archit League New York; Arch Am Art; Am Asn Mus; Drawing Soc (mem exec comt, 62-). *Mailing Add:* Am Fedn Arts 41 E 65th St New York NY 10021

GREENAMYER, GEORGE MOSSMAN
SCULPTOR, EDUCATOR
b Cleveland, Ohio, July 13, 39. *Study:* Philadelphia Col Art, BFA; Univ Kans, MFA. *Comn:* Steel column, comn by Malcolm Wells, Cherry Hill, NJ, 68; bell tower, Haystack Mountain Sch Arts & Crafts, Deer Isle, Maine, 70; steel mountain, Basteille-Neilly Architects, Boston, 72; steel sculpture, Mass Bay Transportation Authority, comn by Earl Flansburgh Assocs, Architects, Essex St Station; steel sculpture, Metro System, Miami, Fla, 81; sculpture, Am Electric Power Co, Columbus, Ohio, 83; sculpture, Sasaki Asn, Watertown, Mass, 83. *Exhib:* Sculpture Festival, 70 & New Work Four Artists, 72, Inst Contemp Art, Boston; Outdoor Sculpture Exhib, DeCordova Mus, Lincoln, Mass, 72, 75 & 78; Boston Visual Artist Union Exhib, Hayden Gallery, Mass Inst Technol, Cambridge, 73; Rose Art Mus, Waltham, Mass, 82; and others; one-man shows, Ctr Advan Visual Studies, Mass Inst Technol, Cambridge, Mass, 80, DeCordova Mus, 80, Am Sculpture, Saks 5th Ave, New York, 81, Bowdoin Col Mus Art, Brunswick, Maine, 81, Queens Mus, Flushing, NY, 81, Neill Gallery, New York, 81, & Sculpture Park, St Louis, Mo, 81; and many other group and one-man exhibs. *Teaching:* Chair, Dept Sculpture, Mass Col Art, 71-80, prof sculpture, 81- *Awards:* First Award, Greater Fall River Art Asn Ann Nat Exhib, Mass, 78; New Eng Exhib Award, Silvermine Guild of Artists, 29th Juried, 78; Ctr Advanced Visual Studies Res Fel, Mass Inst Technol, 79. *Bibliog:* Review in Christian Sci Monitor, 2/23/78; pictures in News Jour, 10/7/78 & 12/2/78; John Baker (auth), picture & pre-review essay, Arts Mag, 5/79; Christine Temin (auth), picture & review, 80 & Robert Taylor (auth), picture & review, 80, Boston Globe. *Mem:* Boston Visual Artists Union; New Eng Sculptors Asn. *Media:* Steel, Aluminum. *Dealer:* Lopookhive 10 Newbury St Boston MA 02116; Horne Company 151 Ponce de Leon Ave Atlanta GA 30308. *Mailing Add:* 994 Careswell St Marshfield MA 02050

GREENBAUM, DOROTHEA SCHWARCZ
SCULPTOR, GRAPHIC ARTIST
b New York, NY, June 17, 1893. *Study:* New York Sch Fine & Appl Art; Art Students League. *Work:* Whitney Mus Am Art, Acad-Inst Arts & Letters, New York; Baltimore Mus Art, Md; Pa Acad Fine Arts, Philadelphia; Princeton Mus Art, NJ. *Comn:* Princeton Pub Libr, NJ; Mus Art, Ogunquit. *Exhib:* 28 one-man shows. *Awards:* George Widener Mem Medal, 41; Gold Medal for Sculpture, Pa Acad Design, 47; Ford Found Grant, Asn Women Artists, 56; elected mem, Nat Inst Arts & Letters, 68. *Mem:* Am Acad Inst Arts & Lett. *Media:* Stone, Bronze; Intaglio Prints, Drawings. *Publ:* Auth, Friends and Foes from A to Z, Stories and Drawings, Castle Howard Press, 77. *Mailing Add:* 104 Mercer St Princeton NJ 08540

GREENBAUM, MARTY
PAINTER, SCULPTOR
b New York, NY, Mar 3, 34. *Study:* Univ Ariz, Tucson, BA, 56. *Work:* Picker Art Gallery, Colgate Univ, Hamilton, NY; Chrysler Mus at Norfolk, Va; Citibank, New York; The Print Club, Philadelphia. *Comn:* Unique bk, Lannan Found, Palm Beach, Fla, 67; Sept Calendar (centerfold), Changes Mag, New York, 71; eds of prints, Shenanigan Press at Jones Rd Print Shop, Barneveld, Wis, 74; graphics portfolio, Creative Artists Pub Serv Prog, New York, 75. *Exhib:* Personal Torment & Human Concern, Whitney Mus Am Art, New York, 69; 4th Ann Contemp Reflections, Aldrich Mus Contemp Art, Ridgefield, Conn, 75; 20th Nat Print Exhib, Brooklyn Mus, NY, 76; The Object as Poet, Renwick Gallery, Smithsonian Inst, Washington, DC, 76-77; New Ways with Paper, Nat Collection of Fine Arts, Smithsonian Inst, 77; Marty Greenbaum, Picker Art Gallery, Colgate Univ, 77; Paper as Medium, Smithsonian Inst Traveling Exhib, 78-80; Playground, installation, Inst Art & Urban Resources, PS 1, New York, 78; Book Forms, Dayton Art Inst, Ohio, 79; Visual & Scuptural Book Works, Montclair Mus, 79; Three Artists, Allan Stone Gallery, New York, 79. *Awards:* Creative Artists Pub Serv Prog Grants, 73 & 76; Nat Endowment Arts Grant, 74. *Bibliog:* Dorothea Baer (producer), Marty & Lulu's Playground, Independent Film, 65; David Bourdon (auth), Marty Greenbaum, Village Voice, 65. *Mem:* Ctr Bk Arts; Found Community Artists. *Dealer:* Allan Stone Gallery 48 E 86th St New York NY 10028; Aldona Gobuzas 215 E 79th St New York NY 10021. *Mailing Add:* 99 Maiden Lane New York NY 10038

GREENBERG, BLUE (BLUMA KAFKA)
EDUCATOR, CRITIC
b Portsmouth, Va, Oct 13, 26. *Study:* Duke Univ, AB, 47; Univ NC, Chapel Hill, MA, 78; Univ Ital Stranieri, Perugia, Italy, 79. *Pos:* Art critic, Durham Herald, NC, 75- *Teaching:* Instr art, Meredith Col, NC, 76-; lectr, Wesleyan

Col, NC & Cent Carolina Tech. *Awards:* Am Found Fel, Reynolda House, Winston-Salem, 82. *Mem:* Col Art Asn; Am Asn Univ Prof; Nat Fedn Press Women. *Res:* Role of regional artists as independent voices against the force of international art trends, especially in the South. *Publ:* Auth, North Carolina's Center Gallery, Art Voices, 80; auth, Embellished visions, Darkroom, 81; auth, NC artists at Hotel Europa, Art Voices, 82; auth, Southern Painting Exhibition, Am Artist, 12/83. *Mailing Add:* 2203 Stuart Dr Durham NC 27707

GREENBERG, ELENOR SIMINOW
PAINTER, PRINTMAKER
b Philadelphia, Pa, Jan 9, 14. *Study:* Pratt Inst, cert, 35; with Reuben Tam, 56-58; with Alberto DeLamonico, 70-71. *Work:* Collectors Am Art, New York; Mission Guinea, New York. *Exhib:* Printmakers Show, Brooklyn Mus, NY, 65; one-woman show, Artemis East, New York, 72 & Laguna Fed Savings Bank, Laguna Beach, Calif, 81; Statewide Juried Show, Rockland Found Arts, Nyack, NY, 74; Milford Fine Arts Coun Nat Show, Milford Libr, Conn, 75; 27th Ann New England Exhib, Silvermine Guild Artists, New Canaan, Conn, 76; Newport Beach Art Festival, Calif, 79. *Awards:* Nat Asn Women Artists Medal Honor, 78; Costa Mesa Art League, 79; Laguna Beach Mus Art, Richter Moore, 81. *Mem:* Nat Asn Women Artists; Laguna Hills Art Asn. *Media:* Oil, Watercolor; Color Etching, Woodcut. *Mailing Add:* 2004C Via Mariposa West Laguna Hills CA 92653

GREENBERG, GLORIA
PAINTER, DESIGNER
b New York, NY, Mar 4, 32. *Study:* Cooper Union Art Sch, cert, 52; Yale-Norfolk Art Sch, painting with Nicholas Marsicano, scholar, 52; Brooklyn Mus Art Sch, printmaking with Gabor Peterdi, scholar, 53. *Work:* Kennedy Airport; Int Business Machines Corp; Bankers Trust, Los Angeles. *Exhib:* Brooklyn Mus Print Ann, 53; Soc Beaux Arts Dordogne, France, 59; eight one-woman shows, Mercer Gallery, New York, 70-80; Report from Soho, Grey Art Gallery, New York, 75; Women in the Arts: Artists Choice, traveling exhib, 77; Women Invite Women, Warm, Minneapolis, Minn, 77; 15th Ann Drawing Show, Delmar Col, Corpus Christi, Tex, 80. *Pos:* Art consult & bk designer, Jr Bks Div, Harper & Row, 65-79. *Teaching:* Instr, Mid Westchester YWCA, Scarsdale, NY, 81; instr, Henry Street Settlement, 80-81, JASA, 81-83. *Awards:* Medal of Honor, Soc Beaux Arts Dordogne, France, 59. *Media:* Acrylic, Oil; Paper Works with Ink. *Publ:* Co-auth & illusr, Away We Go, 63 & Strange Plants & Animals, Harvey House, 64. *Dealer:* 55 Mercer Gallery 55 Mercer St New York NY 10013; Judith Selkowitz Fine Arts New York NY. *Mailing Add:* 118 E 17th St New York NY 10003

GREENBERG, IRWIN
PAINTER, INSTRUCTOR
b Brooklyn, NY, Apr 5, 22. *Study:* Art Students League; NY Univ, BS(art educ); study with Yasuo Kuniyoshi, Will Barnet, Hale Woodruff & Paul Gerchik. *Exhib:* Soldier Art, Nat Gallery, Washington, DC, 45; Mus Fine Arts, Boston, 45; Brooklyn Mus, 48; Springfield Mus, Mass, 60; Heckscher Mus, New York, 62; Birmingham Mus, Ala, 70-71; Allied Artists, 70; Nat Arts Club, 70-78; Le Nid Gallerie, Long Island, NY, 72, 73, 74 & 77; Audubon Artists, 75-77. *Teaching:* Instr life drawing, Baruch Col, City Col New York, 53-54; teacher painting & illus, High Sch of Art & Design, New York, 68- *Awards:* Mario Cooper Award, Am Watercolor Soc, 68; Award for Watercolor, Allied Artists, 70; President's Award for Oil Painting, Nat Arts Club, 76. *Mem:* Am Watercolor Soc. *Media:* Oil, Watercolor. *Publ:* Contribr, Soldier Art, Infantry J, 45; illusr, Reader's Digest Fun and Laughter, Reader's Digest, 67; auth, Much Depends on Attitude, Am Artist Mag, 69; auth, Max Ginsburg-Above Ground & Underground, Am Artist Mag, 70; contribr, Arts and Man, Scholastic Pub & Nat Gallery Art, 75-76. *Dealer:* Bobbie Law Le Nid Gallerie 72 Main St Northport Long Island NY 11768. *Mailing Add:* 17 W 67th St New York NY 10023

GREENBERG, RONALD K
DEALER, COLLECTOR
b St Louis, Mo, July 17, 37. *Study:* Washington Univ, St Louis, Mo. *Mem:* Art Dealers Asn Am. *Specialty:* Contemporary American art. *Collection:* Works by Lichenstein, Warhol, Stella, Kelly, Motherwell, Frankenthaler, Judd, Serra, Chamberlain and Rauschenberg. *Mailing Add:* The Greenberg Gallery 44 Maryland Plaza St Louis MO 63108

GREENBOWE, F DOUGLAS
PAINTER
b Bayonne, NJ, Sept 19, 21. *Study:* Art Students League, with Frank DuMond. *Work:* Butler Inst Am Art, Youngstown, Ohio; Dayton Art Inst, Ohio; Phoenix Mus Art, Ariz; Art Inst Chicago; Seattle Art Mus, Wash; and others. *Comn:* Paintings, Bank of Douglas, Tucson & Ariz Bank of Tucson. *Exhib:* Am Watercolor Soc Ann; Brooklyn Mus, NY; Pa Acad Fine Arts, Philadelphia; NJ Watercolor Soc; Am Acad Arts & Lett; and others. *Awards:* Medal, Nat Arts Club, 53; Two Medals, Ariz State Fair, 63. *Mem:* Am Watercolor Soc; Ariz Watercolor Asn. *Media:* Watercolor. *Mailing Add:* 7610 E McDonald Scottsdale AZ 85253

GREENE, BALCOMB
PAINTER
b Millville, NY, May 22, 04. *Study:* Syracuse Univ, AB, 26; NY Univ, AM, 40; Univ Vienna, 26-28. *Work:* Mus Mod Art, Whitney Mus Am Art, Metrop Mus Art, Guggenheim Mus, New York; Corcoran Gallery Art; and many others. *Exhib:* Whitney Mus Am Art Annuals; Art Inst Chicago; Walker Art Ctr; Brooklyn Mus; solo exhibs, Forum Gallery, 70 & 73-75, Fairweather Hardin Gallery, Chicago, 72 & 73, Harmon Gallery, Naples, Fla, 74-77, Int

Oceanographic Inst, Key Biscayne, Fla, 76 & ACA Gallery, New York, 77 & 79; and many others. *Pos:* Ed, Art Front, 35-36. *Teaching:* Instr art, Dartmouth Col, 28-31; assoc prof, Carnegie Inst Technol, 42-59. *Awards:* Carol H Beck Medal; Critic's Choice, Art News, four times. *Bibliog:* John I H Baur (auth), Balcomb Greene, Whitney Mus Am Art; Robert Beverly Hale (auth), The Art of Balcomb Greene, Metrop Mus Art. *Mem:* Am Fedn Arts; fel Int Inst Arts & Lett; Am Abstract Artists (first chmn, 36-37 & 38-41); Century Club. *Dealer:* ACA Gallery 21 E 67th St New York NY 10021; Harmon Gallery Naples FL. *Mailing Add:* 2 Sutton Pl S New York NY 10022

GREENE, ETHEL MAUD
PAINTER

b Malden, Mass, Nov 11, 12. *Study:* Boston Univ Sch Art; Sch Boston Mus; Mass Col Art. *Work:* Calif Western Univ, San Diego Mus Art & Fine Arts Collectors, Inc, San Diego; Southwestern Col, Chula Vista, Calif; La Salle Col, Philadelphia. *Exhib:* Artists of Los Angeles & Vicinity, Los Angeles Co Mus, 50, 52 & 55; two-person show, San Diego Mus Art, 61; solo shows, Feingarten Gallery, Los Angeles, 70, Ariz State Univ, Tempe, 72 & Taylor Gallery, Taos, NMex, 80; Newspace Gallery, Los Angeles, 78. *Awards:* San Diego Co Expos Awards, 48, 54, 63, 72, 78 & 81; La Jolla Mus Ann Award, 58; Two Californias Award, Calif Western Univ, 63. *Bibliog:* Marilyn Hagberg (auth), The visual puns of Ethel Greene, San Diego Mag, 7/70. *Mem:* San Diego Art Guild (pres, 56). *Media:* Acrylic. *Publ:* Illusr, A Dog Called Bum, 60 & 81. *Dealer:* Jefferson Gallery 3528 Herman St San Diego CA 92104. *Mailing Add:* 2940 Helix St Spring Valley CA 92077

GREENE, LOIS D
DEALER

b Cleveland, Ohio, Dec 11, 24. *Study:* Case Western Reserve Univ, MEduc. *Collections Arranged:* American Folk Art. *Pos:* Dir, The Piedmont Art Gallery, Augusta, Ky, 77- *Mem:* Bracken County Arts Coun (chmn). *Specialty:* Ohio, Indiana and Kentucky artists and craftspersons; contemporary art. *Mailing Add:* The Piedmont Art Gallery 115 Riverside Dr Augusta KY 41002

GREENE, STEPHEN
PAINTER

b New York, NY, Sept 19, 18. *Study:* Art Students League; State Univ Iowa, BFA, 42, MA, 45; also with Philip Guston. *Work:* Whitney Mus Am Art, Guggenheim Mus & Metrop Mus Art, New York; Tate Gallery, London; Corcoran Gallery Art, Washington, DC. *Exhib:* The New Decade, Whitney Mus Am Art, 55; Abstract Expressionists & Imagists, Guggenheim Mus, 61; VI Sao Paulo Bienal, Brazil, 61; Internatinale Der Zeichnung, Darmstadt, Ger, 64; L'Art Vivant aux Etats-Unis, Fondation Maeght, France, 71. *Teaching:* Artist in residence, Princeton Univ, 56-59; instr painting & drawing, Art Students League, 59-65; from asst prof to prof painting & drawing, Tyler Sch Art, Temple Univ, 68- *Awards:* Prix de Rome, Am Acad Rome, 49; Coun Arts & Lett Grant, 66; Inst Arts & Lett Award, 67. *Bibliog:* H W Janson (auth), Stephen Greene, Mag Art, 48; Michael Fried (auth), The goals of Stephen Greene, Arts Mag, 4-5/63; Barbara Rose (auth), Stephen Greene, Art Int, 4/63. *Media:* Oil. *Dealer:* Marilyn Pearl Gallery 38 E 57th St New York NY 10022. *Mailing Add:* 408A Storms Rd Valley Cottage NY 10989

GREENE-MERCIER, MARIE ZOE
SCULPTOR, DRAFTSMAN

b Madison, Wis, Mar 31, 11. *Study:* Radcliffe Col, Harvard Univ, AB(fine arts), 33; New Bauhaus, Chicago, with Moholy-Nagy, Archipenko & Gyorgy Kepes, 37-38. *Work:* Mus des Sables, Barcares, France; Ca Pesaro, Mus Mod Art, Venice, Italy; Hilles Libr, Radcliffe Col, Cambridge, Mass; Bauhaus-Arch Mus, West Berlin; First Nat Bank Chicago. *Comn:* Portrait in bronze of Rudolph Ganz, Ganz Hall, Roosevelt Univ, Chicago, 52; monumental chancel cross, First Baptist Church, Chicago, 67; monumental steel sculpture, French Govt, Barcares, 71 & Arras, 74; monumental steel sculpture, Homburg, WGer, 74. *Exhib:* Salon de Mai, Paris, 73-78; 39 solo shows, including 40 Yr Retrospective, Amerika Haus, W Berlin, 77 & Musee de Poche Gallery, Paris, 78; Bad Homburg, Summer Festival & Am Haus, Stuttgart, Ger, 79; Alliance Francaise, Washington, DC, 80; Art Inst Chicago, 82; and others. *Awards:* First Prize Composition, 68 & First Prize Mod Sculpture, 69, Semaines Int Femme, Cannes, France; First Prize Sculpture, Festival SGermain Pres, Paris, 75. *Bibliog:* Frank Elgar (auth), Greene-Mercier, Musee de Poche, Paris, 78; Lloyd Engelbrecht (auth), Art Int, spring 78; Germany-USA, Edelweiss Publ Co, 83. *Mem:* Artists Equity Asn (pres, Chicago Chap, 59-62, first nat vpres, 62-64); Arts Club Chicago; Renaissance Soc Univ Chicago; Amis du Louvre, Paris; Amis de Bourdelle, Paris. *Media:* Multimedia. *Publ:* Auth, 101 Disegni, 69, Salzburg, 101 Zeichnungen, 70 & Venezia, 101 Disegni, 70, Ed Libr, Italo Svevo, Trieste; auth, The role of materials in my sculpture, Leonardo, Vol 15, No 1. *Dealer:* International Film Bureau Inc 332 S Michigan Ave Chicago IL 60604. *Mailing Add:* 1232 E 57th St Chicago IL 60637

GREENFIELD, AMY
FILMMAKER, VIDEO ARTIST

b Boston, Mass, July 8, 40. *Study:* Radcliffe Col, with Anne Sexton & William Alfred, BA(hon), 62. *Work:* Lincoln Ctr Dance Collection, Mus Holography, New York. *Comn:* Resoled (film), 71 & For God While Sleeping (film), 71, Visual Learning Corp; One-O-One (film), comn by Duglas Dunn, New York, 76; Four Solos for Four Women (videotape), Artists TV Proj, New York, 80. *Exhib:* Solo exhibs, Womens Avant-Garde Film Festival, Whitney Mus Am Art, 72, New Videodance, Anthology Film Arch, New York, 77, 80 & 83, The Wave: Film & Holography, Hayward Gallery, London, 79 & Dance-Film-

Video, Mus Mod Art, New York, 83; Two Channel Video, Whitney Mus Am Art, 78; London Film Festival, Nat Film Theatre, 82; Edinburgh Film Festival, Edinburgh Arts Festival, Scotland, 82. *Teaching:* Instr film, Tufts Univ, 72-74; vis asst prof, Univ RI, 77-78 & Montclair State Col, 78-79. *Awards:* Nat Endowment Arts Grants, 75, 78, 81 & 84; Rockefeller Found Grant, 80. *Bibliog:* Robert Haller (auth), article, Millennium Film J, 80; Deborah Jowitt (auth), Prisoners of the lens, Village Voice, 80; John Gruen (auth), Dance visions, Dancemag, 83. *Media:* Film, Video. *Publ:* Auth, Verticle roll, Film Libr Quart, 78; auth, The Big Apple: First in video, 80 & The case of the vanishing videotape, 81, Am Film; auth, Video and film and video, Video Roma, 82; auth, Filmdance space, time, energy, Film Dance, 83. *Dealer:* Filmmakers Coop 175 Lexington Ave New York NY 10016. *Mailing Add:* 135 St Pauls Ave Staten Island NY 10301

GREENFIELD-SANDERS, TIMOTHY
PHOTOGRAPHER

b Feb 16, 52; US citizen. *Study:* Columbia Col, Columbia Univ, BA(art hist), 74; Am Film Inst, with Slavko Vorkapich, MFA(film fel), 77. *Work:* Mus Mod Art, Metrop Mus Art, Int Center Photog, New York; Australian Nat Gallery; Nat Portrait Gallery, Washington, DC. *Exhib:* One-man shows, New York Artists of the 50's in the 80's, Ohio State Mus Fine Art, 81, Syracuse Mus Art, 81, Marcuse Ffeifer Gallery, 81, Ark Art Ctr, 82, Edwin A Ulrich Mus, 82 & Weatherspoon Mus, 82. *Awards:* Fine Arts Photogr, Am Photogr Mag, 83. *Bibliog:* Hilton Kramer (auth), NY Artist of 50's in 80's, New York Times, 3/27/81; Robert Schwalberg (auth), Portfolio, Camera Arts Mag, 3/82; Dore Ashton (auth), Avenue, 11/82. *Publ:* Contribr, Barrons, 81-83 & Vogue, 83; auth, Downtown in the fifties, 81 & Art of the real, 83, Horizon; auth, Clarkson Potter, Artnews, 83. *Mailing Add:* 135 E 2nd St New York NY 10009

GREENLEAF, ESTHER (HARGRAVE)
PAINTER, PRINTMAKER

b Ripon, Wis. *Study:* Univ Minn, BS(archit); Andre L'Hote, Paris; Minneapolis Sch Art; Art Students League; also with Rudolf Rey, New York. *Work:* High Sch, Recreation House in Taylor Park, Millburn, NJ; Millburn High Sch Collection. *Comn:* Painting, Bd Room, Tex Distribr, Inc, Dallas, 74. *Exhib:* Cambridge Art Asn-Symphony Hall Show in Boston, 69; NH Art Asn 25th Ann Show, Currier Gallery, Manchester, 71; one-woman shows, Sharon Arts Ctr, 73, Kendal at Longwood, 78-79 & Crosslands, Kenneth Square, Pa, 80. *Teaching:* Instr design & art hist, Minneapolis Sch Art, 27-30; instr hist furniture & decoration, Univ Minn Sch Archit, 28-30; instr art hist, Cooper Union Sch Art, 32-34. *Awards:* Zuita Gerstenzang Award for Oils, Nat Asn Women Artists, 62; First Award for Oils & Alice Standish Buell Mem Prize for Graphics, Pen & Brush, 68. *Mem:* Chester Co Art Asn. *Media:* Stoneware ceramics; acrylic on gessoed linen with sand; serigraphy. *Mailing Add:* Crosslands Apt 190 Kennett Square PA 19348

GREENLEAF, KENNETH LEE
SCULPTOR, CRITIC

b Damariscotta, Maine, Aug 10, 45. *Work:* New Sch Social Res, Whitney Mus Am Art, New York; Houston Mus Fine Arts, Tex; Mint Mus Art, Charlotte, NC; Portland Mus Fine Art, Maine. *Exhib:* Contemp American Art, Whitney Mus Biennial, 73; one-man shows, Tibor de Nagy Galleries, New York, 73, 74, 76 & 78, Kelly Gallery, Chicago, 74, B R Konblatt Gallery, Baltimore, Md, 77, Park St Exhib, Lewiston, Maine & Barridoff Galleries, Portland, Maine, 80. *Pos:* Art reviewer, Maine Times, currently. *Media:* Various. *Mailing Add:* c/o Tibor de Nagy Gallery 29 W 57th St New York NY 10019

GREENLEAF, VIRGINIA (VIRGINIA KOCH)
PAINTER

b Chicago, Ill. *Study:* Yale Univ Sch Fine Arts; Am Univ; also with Ivan Olinsky, Robert Brackman & Gene Davis. *Exhib:* Phillips Collection, Washington, DC, 71; one-person shows, Studio Gallery, Washington, DC, 71-76, Main St Gallery Ann, Nantucket, 70-83, Parsons Dreyfuss Gallery, New York, Gallery 124, New York, 83 & Main St Gallery, Boston; Mus Fine Arts, Brazil. *Mem:* Artists Equity Asn. *Media:* Acrylic. *Dealer:* Main St Gallery Nantucket MA 02554. *Mailing Add:* 10 Pine St Nantucket MA 02554

GREENLY, COLIN
ENVIRONMENTAL ARTIST, CONCEPTUAL ARTIST

b London, Eng, Jan 21, 28; US citizen. *Study:* Harvard Univ, AB, 48; Columbia Univ Sch Painting & Sculpture, with Oronzio Maldarelli & Peppino Mangravite; Am Univ Grad Sch Fine Arts. *Work:* Mus Mod Art, New York; Corcoran Gallery Art, Washington, DC; Herbert F Johnson Mus, Ithaca, NY; Philadelphia Mus Art; Albright Knox Art Gallery, Buffalo; and others. *Comn:* Wall painting, Everson Mus, Syracuse, NY, 71; participatory murals, NY State Off Bldg, Utica, 73 & Creative Artists Pub Serv Prog, 75. *Exhib:* Young American Printmakers, Mus Mod Art, New York, 53; one-man exhib, Corcoran Gallery Art, 68 & Finch Col Mus, 74; Contemporary American Painting & Sculpture, Krannert Art Mus, Ill, 69 & 74; Images, Mus Mod Art, New York, 73; John Weber Gallery, New York, 75; Whitney Mus Am Art, New York, 78; and others. *Pos:* Vis artist, Cent Mich Univ, 72; artist in residence, Everson Mus, Syracuse, NY, 72 & Cazenovia Col, 72; Nat Endowment Arts & Humanities artist in residence, Finch Col, 74. *Teaching:* Dana prof art, Colgate Univ, 72-73. *Awards:* Nat Endowment Arts & Humanities Grant for Sculpture, 67; Creative Artists Pub Serv Prog Grant for Intangible Sculpture, New York, 72 & Creative Artists Pub Serv Fel, 78. *Mailing Add:* RD #1 Box 545 Campbell Hall NY 10916

GREENSPAN, (MR & MRS) GEORGE
COLLECTORS

Mr Greenspan, b New York, NY, May 17, 1900. *Collection:* Comprehensive collection of impressionist and post-impressionist drawings; contemporary American paintings. *Mailing Add:* 885 Park Ave New York NY 10021

GREENSPUN, REGINA RUTH
DEALER
b Melrose, Mass, May 20, 34. *Study:* Radcliffe Col, with Lux Feininger, served as his asst, 53-58, BA, 55, MA, 57. *Collections Arranged:* Art of the Synagogue (auth, catalog), Union Am Hebrew Congregations, 72-73. *Teaching:* Teaching fel fine arts, Harvard Univ, 55-58; instr fine arts, Emerson Col, Boston, 57-58. *Specialty:* Washington artists, European and American graphics. *Publ:* Auth, Herman Perlman: His Life and Art, Marvin Press, 82. *Mailing Add:* 6407 Dahlonega Rd Washington DC 20816

GREENSTEIN, ILISE
PAINTER, CONCEPTUAL ARTIST
b New York, NY, Nov 16, 28. *Study:* NY Univ, BA, 49; Harvard Univ, 49-51; Great Neck Adult Educ, 60-70. *Work:* New York Cult Ctr; Marine Midland Bank, Bear Stearns, New York; Stratford Col Mus; Southeast First Nat Bank, Miami & Orlando, Fla. *Comn:* Paintings, comn by Gwen Wishman, Miami, 82, Helene Weissner, Miami, 83, Selma Zelinka, Boca Raton, 83, Irene Seman, Boca Raton, 84 & Billy Saster, Miami, 84. *Exhib:* Women Choose Women, New York Cult Ctr, 73; Contemporary Reflections, Aldrich Mus, 74; Point of View: 19 Women Artists, Portland Mus, Maine, 74; Women Artists: Works on Paper, Brooklyn Mus, 75; Prof Women Artists Fla, Lowe Art Mus, Miami, 76; The Sister Chapel, PS1, Long Island, Syracuse Univ & State Univ NY, Stony Brook, 78-80; Women's Art-Miles Apart, Aaron Berman Gallery, New York, 82. *Teaching:* Vis artist, Long Island schs, 72-75; instr, Metrop Mus Miami, 76-80. *Awards:* First Prize Mixed Media, 31st Ann, Guild Hall, East Hampton, 69; First Prize Painting, 16th Ann, South Shore Community Arts Coun, 70. *Bibliog:* Sandra L Langer (auth), The Sister Chapel, Southern Quart, 78. *Mem:* Womens Caucus Art; Women Artists It's Time (pres, 75-76); Artist Equity (bd mem, 79-80). *Publ:* Auth, Full Circle, Hollywood Art & Cult Ctr, 80. *Mailing Add:* c/o Moos Art 4001 NE Second Ave Miami FL 33137

GREENSTONE, MARION
PAINTER
b Mar 30, 25. *Study:* Brooklyn Col, AB, 46; Columbia Univ Teachers Col, MA, 47; Cooper Union, dipl(fine arts), 54. *Work:* Art Gallery London, Ont; Queens Col, Kingston, Ont. *Comn:* Mural, comn by Bernard Rothzeid & Fine Arts Comn, New York, 76. *Exhib:* Brooklyn Mus Ann Print Show, 53; Whitney Mus Ann, 53; Pittsburgh Int, 55; Can Nat Exhib, 58; Ohio Univ Prints & Drawings Exhib, 63; Works on Paper, Brooklyn Mus, 75. *Teaching:* Adj assoc prof art, Pratt Inst, 68- *Awards:* Fulbright Award, 54-56; Montreal Mus Spring Show Award, 60; Baxter Found Award, 61. *Media:* Oil on Canvas. *Mailing Add:* 790 Carroll St Brooklyn NY 11215

GREENWALD, ALICE (ALICE MARIAN GREENWALD-WARD)
MUSEUM DIRECTOR, LECTURER
b Oceanside, NY, Jan 2, 52. *Study:* Univ Exeter, Devon, Eng, with Theo Brown, 71-72; Sarah Lawrence Col, Bronxville, NY, BA(anthrop & Lit), 73; Univ Chicago Divinity Sch, Ill, AM(hist relig), 75. *Collections Arranged:* Los Angeles Collects: Works on Paper and Graphic Art from Israel, 78-79; The Five Sense Show, 78; The Custom Cut: Jewish Papercuts, Past & Present, 79; Jewish Marriage Contracts: A Celebration in Art, 79; Bill Aron: Portraits of Life, The Elderly Jews of Venice, Calif, 79-80, The Realm of Torah, 81, Between Holy & Profane: Xerography by Dina Dar, 81, Huc Skirball Mus, Hebrew Union Col, Los Angeles, Calif; The Tallis as a Metaphor of Community: Fiber Sculptures by Laurie Gross, 82 & Odyssey of Freedom: The Canvas Diary of a Soviet Jewish Emigre (paintings & works on paper by Tanya Kornfeld), 83, Mus Am Jewish Hist, Philadelphia. *Pos:* Asst to cur, Spertus Mus Judaica, Chicago, Ill, 74-75; cur, Huc Skirball Mus, Hebrew Union Col, Los Angeles, 75-81; dir, Mus Am Jewish Hist, Philadelphia, Pa, 81- *Teaching:* Mus educator Jewish art, Hebrew Union Col, Los Angeles, Calif, 75-81. *Awards:* Nat Endowment Arts Fel Mus Prof, 81. *Mem:* Am Asn Mus; Int Coun Mus; Coun Am Jewish Mus. *Res:* All areas of Jewish art, emphasis on European ritual art and near eastern archaeology. *Publ:* Auth, The Mizrach: Compass of the heart, Hadassah Mag, 10/79; auth, The masonic Mizrach: Jewish ritual art as a reflection of cultural assimilation, J Jewish Art, Vol 10, 83. *Mailing Add:* 42 Nassau Pl Princeton Junction NJ 08550

GREENWALD, PAT
PRINTMAKER, PAINTER
b Westfield, NJ. *Study:* Art Students League, with Corbino Trafton, 46-50; Montclair State, NJ, with B Watkins, 74-77; Pratt Graphics Ctr, 75; NY Univ, with Reddi, 80. *Work:* Monmouth Col, NJ; Co Col Morris, Dover, NJ; IBM; Union Carbide; Am Airlines; and others. *Exhib:* Fry Art Mus, Seattle, 76; Westerly Mus, RI, 76; Hermitage Found, Norfolk, Va, 77; Cayuga Mus, Auburn, NY, 78; Mint Mus Art, Charlotte, NC, 78; Katonah Gallery, NY, 81-82; and others. *Pos:* Art dir, McCartin Advert, New York, 65-68. *Teaching:* Painting, Livingston Student Develop, NJ, 77-79; teacher printmaking, Livingston Arts Asn, NJ, 78- *Awards:* First Prizes, Hunterdon Arts Nat, 78, Carrier Found, 78 & Dean Warren E Bower, 81. *Mem:* Nat Asn Women Artists; NJ Print Coun; Summit Art Ctr, NJ; Philadelphia Prints Club. *Media:* Mixed. *Dealer:* S Rothman Barnegat Light NJ. *Mailing Add:* 23 Highland Dr Livingston NJ 07039

GREENWALD, SHEILA ELLEN
ILLUSTRATOR
b New York, NY, May 26, 34. *Study:* High Sch of Music & Art; Sarah Lawrence Col, BA, 56. *Media:* Pen, Ink. *Publ:* Auth & illusr, The Mariah Delany Lending Library Disaster, 77 & The Atrocious Two, Houghton Mifflin; illusr & auth, All the Way to Wits End, 79, It All Began with Jane Eyre, 80 & Give Us A Great Big Smile, Rosy Cole, 81, Atlantic Little Brown. *Dealer:* Harriet Wasserman Lit Agency 230 East 48th New York NY 10017. *Mailing Add:* 175 Riverside Dr New York NY 10024

GREER, JOHN SYDNEY
SCULPTOR
b Amherst, NS, Can, June 28, 44. *Study:* NS Col Art, dipl(bursary), 64; Montreal Mus Sch Art & Design, dipl(hon sculpture; scholar), 66; Vancouver Sch Art, dipl, 67. *Work:* Nat Gallery, Ottawa; Can Coun Art Bank; Art Gallery Ont; Owens Art Gallery, Mt Allison Univ, Sackville, NB; Art Gallery NS. *Comn:* Y D Klein (lithograph), NS Col Art & Design, 74; Olympic poster proposal, Artist's Athletics Coalition, 75 & John Greer-His Art (videotape), 76, Mt St Vincent Art Gallery, Halifax; silkscreen ed, Can Coun Art Bank, Grand Western Screen Shop, Winnipeg, 77. *Exhib:* Young BC Painters, Nat Gallery Can Traveling Exhib, 67; solo exhibs, Isaacs Gallery, Toronto, 70-, Eye Level Gallery, Halifax, 76- & Sculptural Objective 1968-1981 Traveling Exhib, Art Galley NS, 49th Parallel/49e Parallele, New York, Musee d'Art Contemporain, Montreal & others. *Collections Arranged:* The Isaacs Gallery (with catalog) & Investigations (with catalog), Owens Art Gallery, 74; Sceptical Spectacles (with catalog), Dalhousie Art Gallery, 74. *Teaching:* Assoc prof sculpture, NS Col Art & Design, currently. *Bibliog:* Victor Coleman (auth), John Greer-Eye Ear, Open Letter, Coach House Press, 72; Gary Dault (auth), Review, Arts Can, spring, 75. *Mem:* Eye Level Gallery, Halifax (vchmn, 75-); Can Artist Representation, Provincial, Nat. *Dealer:* Isaacs Gallery 832 Yonge St Toronto ON Can. *Mailing Add:* PO Box 130 La Have NS B0R 1C0 Canada

GREER, WALTER (MARION)
PAINTER
b Ware Shoals, SC, Aug 11, 20. *Study:* The Citadel, BS, 42; Clemson Univ, BS, 47; Atlanta Sch Art, 59 & 60; Nat Acad Design, New York, with Robert Phillipp; also with Ben Shute, Atlanta, 62 & study abroad. *Work:* Telfair Acad Arts & Sci, Savannah, Ga; SC State Collection, Columbia Mus Art; paintings, Sea Pines Plantation Co, Hilton Head Island, SC; Greenville Mus Art, SC; C & S Collection, Atlanta & Greenville, SC; and others. *Comn:* Oil landscape, Gov Mansion, Columbia, 67; three paintings, Phipps Land Co, Hilton Head Island & New York, 70; portrait of pres, Emory Univ, 71; triptych, Simmons Collection, Atlanta, Ga; ltd ed print for Marriott Hotels, 81. *Exhib:* Mead Paper Show, Atlanta, Ga, 60; Hunter Ann, Chattanooga, Tenn, 62; SC Invitational, 69; one-man shows, Columbia Mus Art, 73 & Telfair Acad Arts & Sci, 74, 76 & 82; Guild SC Artists, 81. *Teaching:* Instr pvt classes, 63-66, 78 & 81; instr spec art classes, USMC, Parris Island, SC, 64-65 & Savannah Art Asn Sch, 66. *Awards:* Savannah Arts Festival Award for Rivers, 66; SC Arts Coun Purchase Award for Pond, 69; SC Archit Award for Pond (Grey Phase), 71. *Bibliog:* Virginia Ball (auth), The man that got away, Atlanta Mag, 65; articles & 28 covers, Islander Mag; Jack Morris & Robert Smeltz (auth), Contemporary artists of South Carolina, 70. *Mem:* Guild SC Artists; hon life mem Beaufort Art Asn. *Media:* Oil, Acrylic. *Publ:* Cover and profile, Southern World Mag, 79 & 80; article, Southern Accents Mag, 82. *Dealer:* Tatler Gallery Hilton Head Island SC 29928. *Mailing Add:* 33 Willow Oak Rd W Hilton Head Island SC 29928

GREGG, RICHARD NELSON
MUSEUM DIRECTOR
b Kalamazoo, Mich, Sept 4, 26. *Study:* Western Mich Univ; Cranbrook Acad Art, BFA & MFA. *Pos:* Dir, Kalamazoo Inst Art; curatorial asst, Toledo Mus Art; head mus educ, Art Inst Chicago; dir, Paine Ctr & Arboretum; dir, Joslyn Art Mus; dir, Allentown Art Mus, Pa, 72- *Teaching:* Instr, Worcester Mus Art. *Mailing Add:* Box 117 Allentown Art Mus Allentown PA 18105

GREGOR, HAROLD LAURENCE
PAINTER, EDUCATOR
b Detroit, Mi Mich, Sept 10, 29. *Study:* Wayne State Univ, BSEd, 51; Mich State Univ, MS(ceramics, painting), 53; Detroit Soc Arts & Crafts, 55-57, with John Foster; Ohio State Univ, PhD(painting, art hist), 60; and with Hoyt Sherman. *Work:* Filipacci Collection, Paris, France; Xerox Collection, Stamford, Conn; Calif Col Arts & Crafts, Oakland; Rose Art Mus, Brandeis Univ; Govett-Brewster Gallery, New Plymouth, NZ. *Exhib:* One-man shows, Metrop State Col, Denver, 73 & Nancy Lurie Art Gallery, Chicago, 74 & 77-; Tibor De Nagy Gallery, New York, 77-82; Land, Sky, Water, Spokane World's Fair, 74; Contemp Am Realism Since 1960, Pennsylvania Acad Fine Arts, Philadelphia, 81; New Directions: A Corporate Collection Selected by Sam Hunter, Sloney Janis Gallery, New York, 81; Richard Gray Gallery, Chicago, 83. *Teaching:* Asst prof painting & art hist, San Diego State Univ, 60-63; asst prof painting, Purdue Univ, Lafayette, 63-66; assoc prof painting & art hist, Chapman Col, 66-70; prof painting & art hist, Ill State Univ, Normal, 70- *Awards:* Nat Endowment Arts Grant, 73. *Bibliog:* B Hayes (auth), New Directions: Contemporary American Artists, 81; A L Morgan (auth), rev, Art Int, 5-6/82; H Hanson (auth), Painterly Poet of the Prairie State, Chicago Mag, 9/82. *Dealer:* Richard Gray Gallery 620 N Michigan Chicago IL 60611; Tibor de Nagy Gallery 29 W 57th St New York NY 10019. *Mailing Add:* 107 West Market St Bloomington IL 61701

GREGOR, HELEN FRANCES
DESIGNER, TAPESTRY ARTIST
b Prague, Czech, June 28, 21; Can citizen. *Study:* Birmingham Col Art, Eng; Royal Col Art, London, Assoc. *Work:* Nat Gallery Can, Ottawa; Queens Univ, Kingston, Ont; Benson & Hedges; First Off Can Tapestry Collection, Dept External Affairs, Ottawa; First World Tapestry Collection. *Comn:* Hamilton Auditorium, 73; Hydro Bldg, Toronto, 75; Metrop Toronto Bd Trade, 79; Hyatt Regency, Jedda, 80; and others. *Exhib:* One-man shows, Architect Asn Toronto, 67, Royal Ont Mus, Toronto, 76 & Can Cult Centre, Paris, 77; 4th Int Biennial Tapestry, Lausanne, Switz & Paris, France, 69 & 8th Int Biennial, Lausanne & Lisbon, Port, 78; Fourth Triennial Textiles, Lodz, Poland, 81; Gregor Vermeite Staniszuis Traveling Exhib; and others.

Teaching: Head textiles & tapestry, Ont Col Art, 52-75. *Awards:* Can Coun Award for Spec Studies, 64 & 69. *Bibliog:* Tapestry Today (video), Can Art, Gt Brit, 74; Madeleine Jarry (auth), La Tapisserie, Art du XXeme Siecle, 74. *Mem:* Royal Can Acad Arts; Ont Soc Artists (exec, 72-73); Visual Arts Ont. *Media:* Natural Fibers, Metal. *Dealer:* Nancy Poole Studio Toronto ON Can; Equinox Gallery Vancouver BC Can. *Mailing Add:* 218 Glen Rd Toronto ON M4W 2X3 Canada

GREGOROPOULOS, JOHN
PAINTER
b Athens, Greece, Dec 16, 21; US citizen. *Study:* In Athens; Univ Conn, BA. *Work:* Minn Mus Art, St Paul; Ball State Found, Muncie, Ind; Slater Mus, Norwich, Conn; De Cordova Mus, Lincoln, Mass; Berkshire Mus, Pittsfield, Mass. *Exhib:* Whitney Mus Am Art Ann, 54 & Art USA, New York, 58; 1st Biennale Christlicher Kunst Gegenwart, Salzburg, 58; Drawings USA, Minn Mus Art, 71. *Teaching:* Prof art, Univ Conn, 53- *Awards:* Small Drawings & Sculpture Purchase Award, Ball State Teachers Col, 55; Grumbacher Award, Chautauqua Art Asn 2nd Nat, 59; Drawings USA, St Paul Art Ctr, 63. *Bibliog:* F Walkey (auth), John Gregoropoulos, Art in Am, 2/55; John Gregoropoulos, Zygos, Athens, 57; Art & the new patron, WEDN-TV, 68. *Publ:* Auth, Change in art, Nea Estia, Athens, 57. *Mailing Add:* 644 Wormwood Hill Rd Storrs CT 06268

GREGORY, ANGELA
SCULPTOR, EDUCATOR
b New Orleans, La, Oct 18, 03. *Study:* Art Sch, Newcomb Col, BDesign, Tulane Univ La, MA(archit); Parsons Sch, Paris & Italy, Newcomb Col scholar, cert, 25; Acad Grande Chaumiere, Paris; NY State Col Ceramics; also with Charles Keck, New York & Antoine Bourdelle, Paris. *Work:* Sculpture of the Western Hemisphere, IBM Collection. *Comn:* John McDonogh Monument, Works Progress Admin, Civic Ctr, New Orleans, 38; Bienville Monument, New Orleans, 55; Gen Hy Watkins Allen, State of La, Port Allen, 61; St Louis, Archdiocesan Bldg, New Orleans, 61; aluminum relief panels on walnut, John XXIII Libr, St Mary's Dominican Col, New Orleans, 67. *Exhib:* Nat Mus, Washington DC, 32; Whitney Mus Am Art, New York, 40; Salon d'Antomme, Paris, 30; one-man show, New Orleans Mus Art, 33-34; Int Exhib Contemp Medals, Numismatic Mus, Athens, Greece, 66; Retrospective, Art Sch Newcomb Col. *Pos:* State supvr, Work Proj Admin, New Orleans, 41-42; asst engr camouflage, Corps Engrs, New Orleans Dist, 42-43. *Teaching:* Artist in residence, Newcomb Col, Tulane Univ La, 40-41; sculptor in residence & prof art appreciation, St Mary's Dominican Col, 62-75, prof art, 75-76, emer prof, 76- *Awards:* Shell Co Found Grant, 72; St Mary's Dominican Col Distinguished Award Medal, 77; Chevalier de L'Ordre Arts & Lett, Minister of Cult, France, 82. *Bibliog:* Hilda P Hammond & Betsy Peterson (auth), Lady at Dominican, a tribute to a pope, Dixie-Roto, Times-Picayune, 67; M Roehl (auth), article, New Orleans State Item, 10/78; Al Rose (auth), Born in New Orleans, 83. *Mem:* Fel Nat Sculpture Soc; New Orleans Mus Art. *Media:* Mixed. *Mailing Add:* 630 Pine St New Orleans LA 70118

GREGORY, (ELEANOR) ANNE
EDUCATOR, CALLIGRAPHER
b Seattle, Wash, Jan 20, 39. *Study:* Reed Col, BA, 63; Univ Wash, MFA, 66; Columbia Univ Teachers Col, EdD, 78. *Work:* Portland Art Mus, Ore. *Comn:* Mural, Seattle Pub Sch, Wash, 70. *Exhib:* American Northwest Watercolor Show, Seattle Art Mus, Wash, 74 & 75; Calligraphy by New York Society of Scribes, Brooklyn Mus, 76; New Works by Anne Gregory, Art Galleries, Teachers Col, Columbia Univ, 79; American Calligraphy: New Directions, Purdue Univ Galleries, 80; Indiana Contemporary Artists, Ind State Mus, 80; Tippecanoe Biennial, Lafayette Mus Art, Ind, 82; 83rd Ann Watercolor Exhib, Nat Arts Club, New York, 83. *Pos:* Artist-illusr, Seattle Health Dept, Wash, 66-68; theatre costumer, ACT Theatre, Seattle, 69; ed, Calligraphy Jour, Soc Scribes, 81-82. *Teaching:* Art, Seattle Pub Sch, 70-75; vis asst prof art, NMex State Univ, 78-79; asst prof art, Purdue Univ, 79-82 & WTex State Univ, 82- *Mem:* Nat Art Educ Asn; Col Art Asn; New York Soc Scribes; Soc Italic Handwriting; Chicago Calligraphy Collective. *Media:* Watercolor, Mixed. *Res:* History of art education; gifted and talented in the arts; international art education; American calligraphy and handwriting. *Publ:* Auth, American calligraphy: New directions, In: Design in Arts Education, Helen Dwight Reid Found, 82; auth, Marion Quin Dix: A people picker and an innovator in American art education, 82, auth, Handwriting instruction and art education in the early grades, 82 & auth, Origins of the National Art Education Association: An interview with Ralph Beelke, 83, Art Educ. *Mailing Add:* Art Dept W Texas State Univ Canyon TX 79016

GREGORY, BRUCE
PAINTER, INSTRUCTOR
b Anadarko, Okla, June 27, 17. *Study:* Art Students League; Colorado Springs Art Ctr; and with Fernand Leger. *Comn:* Murals, UN, New York, 52 & Franklin D Roosevelt Sch, New York, 56; map murals, Civil Defense Hq, New York, 57. *Exhib:* Terry Art Inst, Miami, Fla, 51; Pa Acad Art, Philadelphia, 52; Art USA, New York, 58; Butler Art Inst Ann, 66; Fla State Fair, 66. *Pos:* Color & design consult, Harrison & Abramovitz, New York, 52-56; prof serv contractor, Fine Arts Evan, Gen Serv Admin, 73. *Teaching:* Instr painting, Union Col, 56-57; instr painting, John Herron Art Inst, Ind, 60-61; instr painting, color & design, Ringling Sch Art, Sarasota, Fla, 61- *Awards:* Kleinert Award, Woodstock Asn, 60; First Place All-Media Statewide, Glen Gallery, Sarasota, Fla, 83; Best of Show, Fla Artist Group, 83. *Bibliog:* Aline Louchhien (auth), UN murals, 9/7/52 & Kathleen Teltsch (auth), US painter does UN Coats-of-Arms, 4/30/53, New York Times; Gorden Brown (auth), Bruce Gregory, Arts Mag, 66. *Mem:* Sarasota Art Asn;

Fla Artists Group. *Media:* Oil, Acrylic. *Publ:* Auth, Leger's atelier & auth, UN murals, Col Art J, 62; contribr, New International Encyclopedia of Art, 67. *Dealer:* Van Straaten Gallery, 361 W Superior Chicago IL 60610; Expressions PO Box 251 Boca Grande FL 33921. *Mailing Add:* 2115 Lee Lane Sarasota FL 33581

GREGORY, ELEANOR ANNE
EDUCATOR, CALLIGRAPHER
b Seattle, Wash, Jan 20, 39. *Study:* Reed Col, Ore, with Lloyd Reynolds, BA, 63; Univ Wash, MFA, 66; Teachers Col, Columbia Univ, EdD, 78. *Work:* Portland Art Mus, Ore; Reed Col, Ore. *Exhib:* Univ Wash, Henry Gallery, 60; Northwest Watercolor Exhib, Seattle Art Mus, Wash, 60; Brooklyn Mus, New York, 77; Henry Street Settlement Gallery, New York, 78; Sun Festival, El Paso Art Mus, Tex, 79; Indiana 79 and Indiana 80, Lafayette Art Ctr, 79 & 80; Ind Contemp Artist's Exhib, Ind State Mus, Indianapolis, 80. *Collections Arranged:* American Calligraphy, New Directions (auth, catalog), 80 & Indiana Calligraphy I, II & III, 80-82, Watson's Crick Gallery, Purdue. *Pos:* Artist, Seattle Health Dept, Wash, 66-68; commercial artist, Rarig Films Production, Seattle, 68-69; costumer, ACT Theatre, Seattle, Wash, 69. *Teaching:* Secondary art teacher, Seattle Pub Sch, 70-75; instr art, Edmonds Community Col, Washington, 75; vis asst prof art, NMex State Univ, Las Cruces, 78-79; asst prof art & design & dir, Watson's Crick Gallery, Purdue Univ, West Lafayette, 79- *Mem:* Nat Art Educ Asn; Col Art Asn; New York Soc Scribes; Chicago Calligraphy Collective; Lafayette Calligraphy Guild. *Media:* Pen & Inks. *Res:* Documentation of American calligraphy movement. *Publ:* Ed, Calligraphy Journal, Soc Scribes, 81; Super Saturday, Sch Arts Mag, 82; An Interview with Marion Quin Dix, Women in Art Educ, 82; An Interview with Marion Quin Dix, Art Educ, 82. *Mailing Add:* Creative Arts Dept CA #1 Purdue Univ West Lafayette IN 47907

GREGORY, ELLNA KAY
PAINTER, PRINTMAKER
b Houston, Tex, Oct 3, 43. *Study:* Univ Okla, BFA, 65; NTex State Univ, MFA, 79. *Work:* Rockwell Int, Brown Found & Consult & Atlantic Richfield, Dallas, Tex; Ford-Renaissance Ctr, Detroit. *Exhib:* 29th Tex Watercolor Soc, McNay Art Inst, San Antonio, 78; Pastel Soc Am, Nat Arts Club, New York, 79; Watercolor Invitational, Birmingham Mus Art, Ala, 79; Tex Fine Arts Asn 65th Nat Exhib, Laguna Gloria Mus, Austin, 79; Southern Watercolor Soc, Univ Art Gallery, Denton, Tex, 79; one-man show, Eastfield Jr Col, 81; and others. *Teaching:* Art, Dallas Independent Schs, 65-79. *Awards:* Best Abstract Award, Pastel Soc Am, 79; Red Sable Award, Southern Watercolor Soc, 79; award, Southwestern Watercolor Soc, 79. *Bibliog:* Articles in Park E Publ, New York, 79 & Dallas Morning News, 79. *Mem:* Col Art Asn; Pastel Soc Am; Southern Watercolor Soc; Tex Watercolor Soc; Southwestern Watercolor Soc. *Media:* Watercolor. *Mailing Add:* 7214 Lane Park Dr Dallas TX 75225

GREGORY, JOAN
EDUCATOR, PAINTER
b Montgomery, Ala, Apr 1, 30. *Study:* Univ Montevallo, AB, 52; Peabody Col, MA, 53, EdD, 66; Inst Allende, San Miguel Allende, Mex. *Work:* NC Nat Bank; La State Art Comn; Springs Mills, Lancaster, SC; US Park Serv, Gatlinburg, Tenn. *Exhib:* Huntington Galleries, 56-61; one-woman shows, 63 & 13th Dixie Art Ann, Montgomery Mus Fine Arts; Southeastern Painting Show, Gallery Contemp Art, Winston-Salem, NC, 71 & 79; Ann NC Artists Exhib & Traveling Show, 71-72. *Teaching:* Instr art, Marshall Univ, 55-61; chmn dept art, Bloomsburg State Col, 63-64; prof art & head dept, Univ NC, Greensboro, 64- *Awards:* Purchase Awards, Dillard Collection, Weatherspoon Gallery, Univ NC, Greensboro, 66 & Springs Art Show, Lancaster, SC, 72; Merit Award, NC/Va Art Educators, Southeastern Ctr Contemp Art, 75. *Mem:* Nat Art Educ Asn (mem states assembly, 71-73); NC Art Educ Asn (pres, 71-75); Southeastern Col Art Conf (bd dirs, 74-78, secy-treas, 81-); Assoc Artists NC (bd dirs, 69-71). *Media:* Collage. *Mailing Add:* Dept of Art Univ of NC Greensboro NC 27412

GRELLE, MARTIN GLEN
PAINTER
b Clifton, Tex, Sept 17, 54. *Study:* Art Instruction Schs, 72; McLennan Community Col, 75. *Comn:* Bosque landscape, Bosque Co Mus, Clifton, Tex, 74; football mural, Cub Stadium, Clifton, Tex, 76; Bosque Autumn (painting), comn by King Olav IV of Norway, 82; mural, Trinity Lutheran Church, Clifton, Tex, 82. *Exhib:* Am Indian & Cowboy Artists Ann, Sandmas Calif, 77-83; Western Heritage, Houston, Tex, 79 & 81; Stamford Art Found, Tex, 79-83; Tex Art Gallery Preview, Dallas, 80-82; O S Ranch, Post, Tex, 80-82. *Awards:* Bronze Medal, Am Indian Cowboy Artists Exhib, 77; Gold Medal, Am Indian Cowboy Artists Exhib, 79; Best of Show, Am Indian Cowboy Artists Exhib, 79. *Bibliog:* rticle, Art West Mag, 1-2/83. *Mem:* Am Indian and Cowboy Artists (treas, 80-). *Media:* Acrylics, Oils. *Dealer:* Texas Art Gallery 1400 Main St Dallas TX 75202. *Mailing Add:* 1302 West 5th St Clifton TX 76634

GRESSEL, MICHAEL L
SCULPTOR
b Wurzburg, Ger, Sept 20, 02; US citizen. *Study:* Art Sch, Bavaria, with Arthur Schleglmünig; Beaux Art Inst Design, New York. *Work:* Bruckner Mus, Albion, Mich; Metrop Mus Art & Nat Theater & Acad, New York; Nat Theater, Washington, DC; County Trust Co, Mount Kisco, NY. *Comn:* Ivory relief portrait for Gen Eisenhower, 62; Emblem of Harvard Univ; Legend of Sleepy Hollow (centennial monument), Tarrytown, NY; bust, Charles Durning, Calif; portrait, George Meany, AFL Bldg, Washington, DC; and

others. *Exhib:* Hudson Valley Art Asn Ann, White Plains, 46-72; Valhalla High Sch, NY, 49; Allied Artists Am, Nat Acad Design, 71; Nat Sculpture Soc, New York, 72; Armonk Libr, NY. *Awards:* Mrs John Newington Award for Madonna, 63 & Gold Medal, 65; Gold Medal, Hudson Valley Art Exhib, 72; and others. *Mem:* Hudson Valley Art Asn (dir, 52-); Nat Sculpture Soc. *Mailing Add:* Gressel Pl Armonk NY 10504

GREY, ABBY WEED
COLLECTOR, PATRON
b St Paul, Minn. *Study:* Vassar Col, BA, 24. *Collections Arranged:* Turkish Art Today, traveling with American print show in Tehran; Minnesota Art Portfolio, traveling to Iran & Mediterranean countries. *Pos:* Trustee, Minneapolis Soc Fine Arts, 67-; pres, Ben & Abby Grey Found, 60-; originated cultural exchange program, Communication Through Art; sponsor of American Section of First and Second India Triennial of Contemporary World Art. *Interests:* Iranian contemporary art exhibited in the United States. *Collection:* Contemporary art from various countries, specializing in Middle East and South-Asian countries. *Mailing Add:* 497 Otis Ave St Paul MN 55104

GRIEDER, TERENCE
HISTORIAN
b Cedar Rapids, Iowa, Sept 2, 31. *Study:* Univ Colo, BA, 53; Univ Wis, MS(appl art), 56; Univ Pa, MA(art hist), 60, PhD(art hist), 62. *Teaching:* Instr art, Univ Wis, Milwaukee, 56-57 & Conn Col, New London, 60-61; from asst prof to prof art, Univ Tex, Austin, 61- *Awards:* US Govt Smith-Mundt Fel to Guatemala, 59-60; Am Coun Learned Soc Foreign Area Fel, 65-67. *Mem:* Col Art Asn; Soc Am Archaeol. *Res:* Archaeological study of the history of pre-Columbian art, emphasizing the Andean highlands of Peru. *Publ:* Coauth (with S L Catlin), Art of Latin America Since Independence, 66; auth, The interpretation of ancient symbols, Am Anthropologist, 75; auth, Art & Archaeology of Pashash, 78; auth, La Galgada: Peru before pottery, Archaeol, 81; auth, Origins of Pre-Columbian Art, 82. *Mailing Add:* 2603 Maria Anna Rd Austin TX 78703

GRIEFEN, JOHN ADAMS
PAINTER
b Worcester, Mass, Nov 24, 42. *Study:* Williams Col, BA, 66; Art Inst Chicago; Bennington Col; Hunter Col, 66-68. *Work:* Hirshhorn Mus & Sculpture Garden; Boston Mus Fine Arts; Whitney Mus Am Art & Mus Mod Art, New York; Brooklyn Mus; and others. *Comn:* Painting, Gerald Hines Interest, Framingham, Mass. *Exhib:* Lyrical Abstraction, Whitney Mus Am Art, New York, 71; NS Print Show, Mus Mod Art, New York, 74; Recent Aquisitions, Hirshhorn Mus & Sculpture Garden, DC, 77; Recent Aquisitions Contemp Art, Boston Mus Fine Arts, 77; solo exhibs, Diane Brown Gallery, Washington, DC, 78, Martha Jackson Gallery, New York, 79, Sunne Savage Gallery, Boston, 79, Galerie Wentzel, Hamburg, 80 & Williams Col, 80; and others. *Teaching:* Instr painting, Bennington Col, 67-68; pvt lessons, New York, 72-; instr sculpture, Great Neck Pub Schs, NY, 76- *Bibliog:* Larry Aldrich (auth), Lyrical Abstraction, Whitney Mus Am Art, 70; William Zimmer (auth), John Griefen, 76 & Earl Powell (auth), John Griefen, 78, Arts Mag; plus others. *Media:* Acrylics. *Dealer:* Salander-O'Reilly Galleries Inc 22 E 80th St New York NY 10021. *Mailing Add:* 57 Laight St New York NY 10013

GRIER, MARGOT EDMANDS
LIBRARIAN
b Washington, DC, May 15, 46. *Study:* Old Dominion Univ, with Parker Lesley, BA(magna cum laude), 71; Univ Md, MLS, 72. *Pos:* Serials librn, Nat Gallery Art, Washington, DC, 73- *Awards:* Hermitage Found Award, Norfolk, Va, 69 & 70. *Mem:* Art Libraries Soc North Am; Wasington Art Libr Resources Comt. *Res:* Art serials and auction catalog access systems. *Interests:* 20th century Mexican; contemporary; small press art magazines. *Publ:* Auth, Old St Paul's, Kent Co, Md, St Pauls Episcopal Church, 71; contribr, ARLIS/NA Newsletter, Art Libr Soc, 79-80; co-ed, Art Serials Union List, 81; contribr, Art Doc, 83- *Mailing Add:* c/o Nat Gallery Art Washington DC 20565

GRIGGS, MAITLAND LEE
COLLECTOR
b New York, NY, Sept 13, 02. *Study:* Christ Church, Oxford Univ. *Collection:* Hudson River School of painting (confined to views of and on the Hudson River); old Staffordshire china with Hudson River views; Oriental, African and pre-Columbian artifacts. *Mailing Add:* Ardsley-on-Hudson NY 10503

GRIGORIADIS, MARY
PAINTER
b Jersey City, NJ, June 23, 42. *Study:* Barnard Col, BA, 63; Columbia Univ, MA, 65. *Work:* Chase Manhattan Bank, Athens & Piraeus, Greece; First Nat Bank Chicago; Lincoln Hosp, New York; Prudential Insurance Co; Allen Memorial Art Mus, Oberlin, Ohio; and others. *Exhib:* One-woman shows, A I R Gallery, New York, 72, 75, 78 & 82, Gallery K, Washington, DC, 78 & Helen Shlien Gallery, Boston, 78, 81 & 83; Biennial Contemp Am Art, Whitney Mus Am Art, 73; Small Works, Albright-Knox Mus Art, 76-77; Pattern Painting, PS I, New York, 77; Douglass Col, 78 & 81; Islamic Allusions, Alternative Mus, New York, 80; Aldrich Mus Contemp Art, 81; Luuds Konsthall, Sweden, 82; and others. *Bibliog:* Hayden Herrera, reviews, Art in Am, 3-4/77; C Robins (auth), article in Arts Mag, 9/78. *Media:* Oil. *Dealer:* A I R Gallery 63 Crosby St New York NY 10012; Helen Shlien Gallery 14 Newbury St Boston MA. *Mailing Add:* 382 Central Park W New York NY 10025

GRIGSBY, JEFFERSON EUGENE, JR
EDUCATOR, PAINTER
b Greensboro, NC, Oct 17, 18. *Study:* Morehouse Col, with Hale Woodruff & Nancy Prophet, BA, 38; Am Artists Sch, with M Hebald, H Harrari & J Groth, 39; Ohio State Univ, with Prof Hopkins & R Fanning, MA, 40; Ecole Beaux Arts, Marseilles, 45; NY Univ, PhD, 63; Philadelphia Col Art, Hon DFA, 65. *Work:* Tex Southern Univ, Houston; Mint Mus, Charlotte, NC; Nat Mus Ghana, Cape Castle; Richmond Pub Schs, Va. *Exhib:* Am Negro Expos, Tanner Art Galleries, Chicago, 40; Baltimore Mus, 40; Ariz Ann, Phoenix Mus, 64; one-man show, Centennial Celebration, Morehouse Col, 67; Dimensions in Black, La Jolla Mus, Calif, 70; Dallas City Hall, 81. *Pos:* Head dept art, Carver High Sch, 46-54 & Phoenix Union High Sch, Ariz, 54-66. *Teaching:* Artist-in-residence, Johnson C Smith Univ, 40-41; prof art educ & drawing, Ariz State Univ, 66-, distinguished res scholar, 82-83. *Awards:* Medallion of Merit, Nat Gallery Art, 66. *Mem:* Nat Art Educ Asn (vpres, 72-74); Ariz Artists Guild; Col Art Asn Am; Nat Conf Artists; Ariz Artists Black Community. *Media:* Acrylic, Serigraph. *Res:* African art, its history, materials used and style. *Publ:* Auth, Ba Kuba art, In: Africa Seen by American Negroes, 58; auth, Encounters (exhib catalog), J C Smith Univ Exhib, 68; auth, Art & Ethnics, William C Brown Co; ed, Sch Arts Mag, 10/79. *Mailing Add:* 1117 N Ninth St Phoenix AZ 85006

GRIMES, MARGARET W
PAINTER, EDUCATOR
b New Bern, NC. *Study:* Gov State Univ, BA, 74, MA, 75; Notre Dame Univ, with Alice Neel, 77; Univ Pa, with Neil Welliver, Yvonne Jacquette, Rudy Burckhardt & John Button, MFA, 80. *Work:* Pittsburgh Plate Glass Co; Conn Insurance Group NAm, Philadelphia; Christian Sci Church Ctr, Boston. *Exhib:* Int Womens Art Festival, Walker Art Inst, 76; Woodmere Mus 37th Ann Exhib, Philadelphia, 77; Works on Paper, Provincetown Art Mus, Pa, 78; one-person exhibs, Green Mountain Gallery, New York, 79 & Blue Mountain Gallery, New York, 80-82; Painted Light Traveling Exhib, Reading Mus, Pa, 82; Queens Mus, New York & Butler Inst, 83; Women Painters Today, Rahr-West Mus, Manitowal, Wis, 83. *Teaching:* Instr drawing & design, Thornton Community Col, Chicago, 74-79; asst prof painting & graphic design, Western Conn State Univ, 80- *Bibliog:* Helen Thomas (auth), article, 5/79 & Robert Godfrey (auth), article, 11/80, Arts Mag. *Mem:* Col Art Asn; Am Asn Univ Prof. *Media:* Oil. *Publ:* Co-ed, New Art Asn Newsletter, 71. *Dealer:* Fischbach Gallery 29 W 57th New York NY 10019. *Mailing Add:* 25 Taunton Lake Rd RD3 Newtown CT 06470

GRIMLEY, OLIVER FETTEROLF
PAINTER, SCULPTOR
b Norristown, Pa, June 30, 20. *Study:* Pa Acad Fine Arts, William Emlen Cresson traveling scholar, 47, Henry J Scheidt traveling scholar, 50; Univ Pa, BFA & MFA. *Work:* Woodmere Art Galleries, Mus Art, Pa Acad Fine Arts, Philadelphia; Libr Cong, Washington, DC. *Comn:* Murals, Commonwealth Fed Savings & Loan, Norristown, 63, Continental Bank & Trust, 65 & Am Bank, Lafayette Hills, Pa, 72; papier-mache eagle, comn by Leonard Tose, Vet Stadium, Philadelphia, 71. *Exhib:* Whitney Mus Am Art, Libr Cong & Metrop Mus, 52-57; Pa Acad Fine Arts Watercolor Shows, 58-63; Philadelphia Mus Art. *Teaching:* Instr drawing, Hussian Sch Art, 60- & Pa Acad Fine Arts, 65- *Awards:* Ralph Pallen Coleman Prize for Illus, 73; First Prize for Sculpture, Regional Coun Community Arts Ctr, 74; J W Zimmerman Mem Prize for Work of Distinction, 79. *Bibliog:* Henry Pitz (auth), article, Am Artist, 71. *Media:* Pen & Ink, Watercolor; Miscellaneous. *Publ:* Auth, article, Am Artist, 50. *Mailing Add:* 16 W Township Line Norristown PA 19403

GRIMM, LUCILLE DAVIS
PAINTER, INSTRUCTOR
b Nashville, Tenn, Aug 20, 29. *Study:* George Peabody Col Teachers, Vanderbilt Univ, Nashville, BA, 51. *Work:* Fairfield Univ, Conn; Town Collection, Fairfield, Conn. *Comn:* McDonald's Corp, Bennington, Vt, 73; Heublin Inc, Hartford, Conn; Mo Electrochem, St Louis; painting, HEB Hospital, Euless, Tex. *Exhib:* Am Watercolor Soc 108th Ann, Nat Acad Galleries, New York, 75; Rocky Mountain Nat Watermedia Exhib, Foothills Art Ctr, Golden, Colo, 76; 32nd New Eng Exhib, Silvermine Ctr Arts, New Canaan, Conn, 81; Watercolor USA, Springfield Art Mus, Mo, 81; one-woman show, New Eng Ctr, Univ NH, Durham, 81; NH Art Asn 35th Ann, Currier Gallery, Manchester, 82. *Teaching:* Teacher art, Milford Area Sr High Sch, NH, 75-78. *Awards:* Award for Drawing, NH Art Asn Ann, 82; Printmaking Studio Scholarship Award, Old Lyme Art Works, Conn, 82; First Award, Greene Gallery Ann, Guilford, Conn, 82. *Bibliog:* Shirley Gonzales (auth), article, New Haven Register, Conn, 81. *Mem:* New Eng Watercolor Soc; NH Art Asn; Nat League Am Pen Women. *Media:* Watercolor, Acrylic. *Dealer:* Munson Gallery 33 Whitney Ave New Haven CT 06511; Puccio's Gallery West 13496 Clayton Rd St Louis MO 63131. *Mailing Add:* Box 554 235 E Main St Clinton CT 06413

GRIMM, RAYMOND MAX
SCULPTOR, GLASS ARTIST
b St Louis, Mo, June 20, 24. *Study:* Wash Univ Sch Fine Arts, BFA, 53; Southern Ill Univ, with F Carlton Ball in pottery, MS, 55. *Work:* Univ Ore Mus Art, Eugene; Contemp Crafts Gallery, & Fountain Gallery Art, Portland, Ore; Salem Civic Ctr, Ore. *Comn:* Design of 60ft x 12ft rock mosaic, Our Lady Queen of Peace Church, Portland, 65; ceramic plaque, 13ft x 3ft, Salishan Lodge, Gleneden, Ore, 65; hanging ceramic sculpture, 9ft x 6ft x 5ft, Sunriver Lodge, Bend, Ore, 69; brick mosaic, 60ft x 9ft, Mountain Park Recreation Ctr, Lake Oswego, Ore, 70; seven brick sculptures, Ore State Veterinary Teaching Hosp, Corvallis, 79. *Exhib:* One-man show, Contemp Crafts Gallery, Portland, 57-59, 63 & 75; Scripps Col Ceramic Exhib, Scripps

Col Gallery, Claremont, Calif, 61; Univ Ore W Coast Craft Show & Traveling Exhib, Eugene, 64; Fiber, Clay & Metal, St Paul Art Mus, Minn, 66; Int Exhib Ceramic Art, City Mus, Faenze, Italy, 66. *Teaching:* Prof art, ceramics & glass, Portland State Univ, 56- *Awards:* Jr League Award, St Louis Art Mus, 56; Harold Hirsch Award, Ore Ceramics Studio, 64; Merit Award, Mus Contemp Crafts, New York, 66. *Bibliog:* Catherine Jones (auth), Jere and Raymond Grimm, Creative Crafts Mag, 63; Polly Rothenberg (auth), The Complete Book of Ceramics, Crown Publ, 72; Lamar Harrington (auth), Ceramics in the Pacific Northwest, Univ Wash, 79. *Mem:* Am Craftsmen's Coun (state rep, 58-61). *Media:* Clay and Glass. *Mailing Add:* R 3 Box 186 G Sherwood OR 97140

GRINER, NED H
EDUCATOR, CRAFTSMAN
b Tipton, Ind, Dec 14, 28. *Study:* Ball State Teachers Col, BS; State Univ Iowa, MA; Ind Univ, MFA; Pa State Univ, DEd. *Work:* Evansville Mus Art & Ball State Univ Art Gallery, Muncie, Ind. *Exhib:* Midstates Craft Exhib, 66-67; Jewelry Exhib, Purdue Univ, 67; Indianapolis Mus Art, 75; Ind Univ Mus Art, Bloomington, 76; Ind State Mus, Indianapolis, 77; Ft Wayne Art Mus, Ind, 78. *Teaching:* Asst prof art, Ark State Col, 54-60; asst, Pa State Univ, 60-61; prof, Ball State Univ, 61-, head dept, 70- *Mem:* Nat & Ind Art Educ Asns; Col Art Asn Am; Ind Artist Craftsmen (pres, 66-68); Nat Coun Art Adminr. *Media:* Silver, Bronze, Brass. *Publ:* Auth, Jewelry is sculpture, Palette Mag, spring 62; coauth, Ned Griner: Artist teacher, Sch Arts, 9/63; auth, Individuality in the arts & crafts, Asn Am Women, 12/63; auth article, Quartet Mag, Vol 2, No 10; contrib, Art--search & self discovery, 68. *Mailing Add:* Dept of Art Ball State Univ Muncie IN 47306

GRIPPE, FLORENCE (BERG)
PAINTER, INSTRUCTOR
b New York, NY, Jan 6, 12. *Study:* Educ Alliance, 32-34; Works Proj Admin Art Courses, 34-38; pottery with William Soini, 39-41. *Work:* Rose Art Mus, Brandeis Univ. *Comn:* Portraits comn by Doris Brewer Cohen, Lexington, Mass, 69, Signora Attilio Roveda, Locarno, Switz, 70; Dr Luis Martinez & Julio Farinos Castillo, Valencia, Spain, 70 & Jose Marina Galvao Telles, Lisbon, Portugal, 71. *Exhib:* Brooklyn Mus, 51; Lower East Side Independent Artists 3rd Ann Exhib, 58; Guild Hall, Southampton, Long Island, 75; Provincetown Art Asn & Mus, Mass, 78; Himmelfarb Gallery, Long Island, 80-81; Burnside Gallery, Long Island, 81 & 83; and others. *Teaching:* Instr drawing, painting, sculpture & puppetry, United Art Workshops, Brooklyn Neighborhood Houses, NY, 47-54; instr design & pottery, Brooklyn Mus Art Sch, 51-57. *Awards:* Fulbright-Hayes, 78-79. *Bibliog:* S Sheridan (auth), Native handicrafts, New York Times Mag, 7/52; article in Daily Transcript, Boston, 7/19/79; article, Peconic Bay Shopper, Long Island, 10/81; and others. *Publ:* Auth, With the brush, Ceramic Age, 3/56; coauth, Art news from Boston, Art News, 61-63. *Mailing Add:* 28100 Main Rd Orient NY 11957

GRIPPE, PETER
SCULPTOR, PRINTMAKER
b Buffalo, NY, Aug 8, 12. *Study:* Albright-Knox Art Sch, 23-25; Art Inst Buffalo, with Edwin Dickinson, 29-35; Atelier 17, New York, with William Stanley Hayter, 44-48. *Work:* Albright-Knox Art Gallery, Buffalo, NY; Nat Gallery Art, Washington, DC; Whitney Mus Am Art; Philadelphia Mus Art; Brooklyn Mus; and others. *Comn:* two sculpture murals, comn by James B Bell & Assoc, PR Info Ctr, New York, 58; sculpture, Theodore Shapiro Forum, Brandeis Univ, 63; portrait of Composer Irving Fine, Brandeis Univ, 64; sculpture, Sci Bldg lobby, Simmons Col, Boston, 69; portrait, Marver H Bernstein, pres Brandeis Univ, 80; and others. *Exhib:* Painting, Drawing & Sculpture, Am Acad Rome, Italy, 65; Sculptors Guild, New York, 67; The New American Painting & Sculpture: The First Generation, Mus Mod Art, New York, 69; Boston Now, Inst Contemp Art, Boston, 69; Provincetown Art Asn & Mus, Mass, 78; Whitney Mus Am Art, 80; Boston Athenaeum, 80; Zabriskie Gallery, New York, 83; and others. *Teaching:* Instr design, Pratt Inst, 49-50; dir printmaking, Atelier 17, New York, 51-54; prof fine arts, Brandeis Univ, 53-80. *Awards:* Contemp Watercolors, Drawings & Prints Award, Metrop Mus Art, 52; Boston Arts Festival Award, Art Comn Boston, 55; Guggenheim Fel for Sculpture, 64. *Bibliog:* On sculpture, It Is, autumn 65; W V Anderson (auth), The city of Peter Grippe, Connection, 66; article, The Daily Transcript, Boston, 7/19/79; articles, Suffolk Times, New York Times & others. *Publ:* Contribr, Credo (Iconograph), 46; producer, ed & contribr, Twenty-one etchings & poems, Morris Gallery, New York, 58; contribr, Enter Mephistopheles with images, Art News, Vol 59, No 6; contribr, Contemporary American Painting & Sculpture, Univ Ill, 61; auth, Mots Trouvees (collage-poems), Nordness Gallery, New York, 63. *Mailing Add:* 28100 Main Rd Orient NY 11957

GRIPPI, SALVATORE WILLIAM
PAINTER, EDUCATOR
b Buffalo, NY, Sept 30, 21. *Study:* Mus Mod Art Sch, 44-45; Art Students League, 45-48; Atelier 17, 51-53; Inst Statale Arte, Florence, Italy, Fulbright Scholar, 53-55. *Work:* Whitney Mus Am Art, Metrop Mus Art, New York; Joseph Hirshhorn Collection, Washington, DC; St Lawrence Univ; Everson Mus, Syracuse, NY. *Exhib:* Biennials, Corcoran Gallery Art, 59 & 63; Whitney Mus Am Art Ann, 60; Walker Art Ctr, 60; Recent Painting USA, The Figure, Mus Mod Art, New York & throughout US, 62; Calif Palace Legion of Honor, 65; Drawing Invitational, Long Beach Mus, Calif, 66 & traveling exhib, Western Asn of Painters, 66-68; Selected American Painters, Phoenix Art Mus, Ariz, 67; Elvehjem Art Ctr, Univ Wis, 77 & traveling exhib to other mus; Brooklyn Mus, New York, 78; Everson Mus, Syracuse, NY, 78; Krasner Gallery, New York, 79 & 81; others in New York, Los Angeles &

Milwaukee. *Teaching:* Instr painting, drawing & 2-D design, Cooper Union Art Sch, 56-59; instr, Sch Visual Arts, 61-62; assoc prof art, Pomona Col & Claremont Grad Sch, 62-68; prof art, Ithaca Col, 68- *Bibliog:* Brian O'Dougherty (auth), Variety of exhibitions, New York Times, 3/22/62; Larry Campbell (auth), article, Art News, 10/64; Henry J Seldis (auth), Art walk: A critical guide to the galleries, Los Angeles Times, 5/29/70; and many others. *Mem:* Life mem Art Students League (treas, 61-62, bd control, 61-64); Col Art Asn Am. *Publ:* Auth, Visual impressions of Italy, Inst Int Educ Bull, 56; auth, Turntable kaleidoscope, Mus Mod Art, 56, 57 & 59; contribr, Twenty-one Etchings & Poems, 58. *Mailing Add:* 423 E Seneca St Ithaca NY 14850

GRISHAM, BARBARA JEAN
PAINTER
b Denver, Colo. *Study:* Mus Fine Arts, Glassell Sch, 82; studied with Dick Wray, 82. *Work:* Southeast Art Arts & Sci Ctr, Pine Bluff; Galerie Triangle, Washington, DC; Raju Collection, Secunderbad, India; Profile Collection, Houston; Gulf Southern Collection, Pasadena, Tex. *Comn:* Oil painting, Discovery Art, Houston, 83. *Exhib:* Twenty-Fifth Ann Exhib, Sidney Rothman Gallery, Barnegat Light, NJ, 82; 15th Ann Ark Exhib, Southeast Ark Sci Ctr, Pine Bluff, 82; Aqueous 82, J B Speed Art Mus, 82; Biennial Nat, Meadows Mus Art, Shreveport, La, 82; 37th Ann Open, Westmoreland Co Mus, Greensburg, Pa, 82; New Works, Discovery Art, Houston, 83. *Awards:* Bronze Medallion, Prix du Centenaire, Mus Duncan, Paris, 81; Grumbacher Best of Show, 15th Ann Ark Exhib, 82; Reliance-Universal Award, Aqueous 82, J B Speed Art Mus, 82. *Bibliog:* Robin Lewis (auth), Grisham earns awards, Broadcaster-Progress, 82; Cathy Cochran (auth), Odyssey, Pasadena Citizen, 82; Sarah Lansdell (auth), Aqueous 82 showcase, Courier-J, 82. *Media:* Oil. *Dealer:* Discovery Art 3718 Mt Vernon Houston TX; CAP 5613 Almeda Houston TX. *Mailing Add:* 1806 Whitebriar Deer Park TX 77536

GRISSOM, EUGENE EDWARD
EDUCATOR, HISTORIAN
b Melvern, Kans, May 15, 22. *Study:* Philippine Univ, 45; Kans State Teachers Col, Emporia, BS, 48; State Univ Iowa, with M Lasansky, MFA, 51. *Teaching:* Instr art educ, Kans State Teachers Col, summer 51; instr art, Univ Ky, 51-53; asst prof art, Univ Fla, 53-62, assoc prof, 62-65, chmn dept, 62-78, prof, 65-78. *Mem:* Col Art Asn Am; Southeastern Col Art Conf. *Res:* Drawing workshops of the early 15th century in Italy. *Mailing Add:* 4607 Clear Lake Dr Gainesville FL 32607

GRISSOM, FREDA GILL
PAINTER, GOLDSMITH
b Groom, Tex. *Study:* WTes State Univ, Canyon, BS; Univ Tex, Austin; also watercolor workshop. *Work:* Montgomery Mus Fine Arts, Ala. *Exhib:* Ann Dixie Exhib, Montgomery Mus Fine Arts, 68; Nat Art Roundup, Las Vegas, Nev, 68; Greater New Orleans Nat, 71; 9th Grand Prix Int, Cannes, France, 73; Galerie Rene Borel, Deauville, France, 73. *Pos:* Co-chmn, Nat Sun Carnival Art Exhib, El Paso, Tex, 65-71. *Awards:* Purchase Award, Montgomery Mus Fine Arts, 68; Second Prize, Greater New Orleans Nat Exhib, 71; Medaille de la Ville de Cannes, First Prize, Watercolor, 9th Grand Prix Int, Cote D'Azur, 73. *Mem:* El Paso Art Asn, Inc (dir, 64-65); El Paso Mus Art; Black Range Art Asn; Tex Watercolor Soc. *Media:* Transparent Watercolor, Acrylic, Oil; Gold, Silver. *Mailing Add:* Rte 1 Box 321-G Anthony TX 88021

GROAT, HALL PIERCE
PAINTER, MURALIST
b Syracuse, NY, Dec 31, 32. *Study:* Syracuse Univ, BFA, also Grad Sch Painting; spec summer session with Josef Albers. *Work:* Philatelic Mus, Geneva, Switz; Syracuse Univ & Syracuse Savings Bank, NY; Skaneatelles Savings Bank, NY; Merrill Ctr, Bangor, Maine. *Comn:* Hist mural, Merrill Trust Co, Bangor, Maine, 75; hist mural (five panels), Syracuse Savings Bank, 77; hist mural, Skaneatleles, NY, 79; mural, Miller Brewing Co, Fulton, NY, 80; mural, Bristol Laboratories, 81; and others. *Exhib:* Rochester Finger Lakes Exhib, Rochester Mem Art Gallery, NY, 59 & 63; Springfield Nat, Mass, 62; Everson Mus Regional, Syracuse, 64 & 70; Cooperstown Nat, NY, 67-83; Butler Inst Am Art, Youngstown, Ohio, 68. *Awards:* Berkshire Mus Purchase Award, Berkshire Art Asn, Pittsfield, 62; First Prize, Cent NY Art Open, 81; Int Award for UN stamp; and others. *Bibliog:* 32nd annual midyear show-- Butler, La Rev Mod, 2/68;; Review of selected artist, Art Rev, fall 68. *Mem:* Assoc Artists Syracuse; Sarasota Art Asn; Am Soc Mural Painters. *Media:* Acrylic. *Mailing Add:* 8364 Vassar Dr Manlius NY 13104

GROELL, THEOPHIL
PAINTER, INSTRUCTOR
b Pittsburgh, Pa, Feb 11, 32. *Study:* Carnegie Inst Technol, BFA, 53. *Work:* Randolph-Macon Women's Col, Va; Weatherspoon Gallery, Greensboro, NC. *Exhib:* The Contemporary Figure, Suffolk Mus, Stony Brook, NY, 71; Paintings Eligible for Childe Hassam Fund Purchase, Am Acad Arts & Lett, 73 & 74; Three Centuries of the Nude in American Art, New York Cult Ctr, 75 & traveling, 76; The Classic Revival, Ill Bell Tel Traveling Show, 75-76; Contemporary American Realism Since 1960, Pa Acad Fine Arts, 81-82; and other group & one-man shows. *Bibliog:* Cindy Nemser (auth), Representational painting in 1971, Arts Mag, 12-1/72. *Media:* Oil. *Mailing Add:* 37 3rd Pl Brooklyn NY 11231

GROGAN, KEVIN
MUSEUM DIRECTOR, MUSEOLOGIST
b Washington, DC. *Study:* Franklin & Marshal Col; Am Univ, grad. *Pos:* Asst cur, Phillips Collection, DC, 71-79; dir, Fine Arts Ctr, Cheekwood, Nashville,

Tenn, 80- *Teaching:* Lectr, Owen Sch Mgt & adj assoc prof, Dept Fine Arts, Vanderbilt Univ, currently. *Mem:* Am Asn Mus; Int Mus Coun of Nashville; Tenn Asn Mus; Southeast Mus Conf. *Res:* American art of the late 19th and early 20th centuries; American collectors of the same period. *Publ:* Contribr, The Phillips Collection in the Making: 1920-30, Smithsonian Inst, 79; auth, Karl Struss: A Retrospective (exhib catalog), 80; ed & auth foreword, Red Grooms: A Catalogue Raissone of his Graphic Work, 81; auth, The American Scene, 1900-1950 (exhib catalog), 83. *Mailing Add:* Fine Arts Ctr Cheekwood Nashville TN 37205

GRONBECK, JEAN
PAINTER
b Long Beach, Calif, Mar 22, 26. *Study:* Univ Mex, Mexico City, 43; also with Arden Von Dewitz, 61. *Work:* Nat Archives Am Art, Smithsonian Inst, Washington, DC; San Luis Obispo Co Collection, Calif; Bank of Am, Santa Barbara; many in pvt & pub collections. *Exhib:* Statler-Hilton Hotel, Beverly Hills, Calif, 62; 14th Ann Greek Theatre, Los Angeles, Calif, 62; Wilshire-Ebell Exhib, Los Angeles, 70; Santa Barbara Mus, Calif, 71-72; Fresno Art Ctr, Calif, 71-78. *Pos:* Gallery dir, Gronbeck Gallery, 72-78. *Awards:* Best of Show & Hon Mention, El Camino Art Asn, 63; 7th Ann Hawthorne, Hawthorne Art & Cult Soc, 66; Non-Purchase Award, Lompoc Art Asn, 74. *Bibliog:* Nonie Higgins (auth), Jean Gronbeck gives show, Los Angeles Times; Morris Cecil (auth), Prominent artist featured, Sun Newspaper, 6/65; Jim Hayes (auth), A bright airy look, Telegram-Tribune, 71. *Mem:* Am Inst Fine Arts; Nat Artists Equity Asn; Fresno Art Ctr. *Media:* Oil, Acrylic. *Specialty:* Contemporary impressionism in oil and watercolor. *Mailing Add:* 1000 N 8th, Sp 56 Reedsport OR 97467

GRONBORG, ERIK
SCULPTOR, CERAMIST
b Copenhagen, Denmark, Nov 12, 31; US citizen. *Study:* Univ Calif, Berkeley, BA, 62, MA, 63. *Work:* Oakland Art Mus, Calif; Everson Mus Art, Syracuse, NY; Mus Art, Basel, Switz; Univ Art Collections, Ariz State Univ, Tempe; Contemp Crafts Asn, Portland, Ore. *Exhib:* One-man shows, Mus Mod Art, Paris, France, 65 & Mus Contemp Crafts, New York, 69; Ceramics '70, Everson Mus Art, Syracuse, NY, 70; 73rd Western Ann, Denver Art Mus, Colo, 71; World Crafts Coun, Int Exhib, Toronto, Can, 74; Allied Craftsmen, San Diego Mus Art, Calif, 74, 77 & 79; Americana, San Francisco Mus Art, 76; Philadelphia Crafts Show, Philadelphia Mus Art, 78. *Teaching:* Asst prof ceramics & sculpture, Reed Col, Portland, Ore, 65-69; assoc prof, San Diego State Univ, Calif, 73-75; prof ceramics & sculpture, Mira Costa Col, Oceanside, Calif, 75- *Awards:* Grand Prix, Mus Mod Art, Paris, 63; Nat Endowment Arts Craftsman Grant, 73; Award, Victoria & Albert Mus, London, 73. *Bibliog:* Kent Hall (auth), Erik Gronborg: the history of the present, Univ Portland Rev, 66; Ida Rigby (auth), Erik Gronborg's accessible art, Artweek, 2/3/79; Judi Nicolaidis (auth), Erik Gronborg: Portrait in Clay (video), Nicolaidis, 79. *Mem:* Am Crafts Coun (state rep, 71-73); Allied Craftsmen of San Diego; Art Guild-San Diego Mus Art. *Media:* Mixed. *Publ:* Auth, The new generation of ceramic artists, Craft Horizons, 69; auth, Man and art in the urban environment, Nat Park & Conserv Mag, 72; auth, Address to World Crafts Council Conference, Mexico, Ceramic Rev, 77; contribr, Ceramic Art, Comment and Review, 1882-1977, Dutton, 78. *Mailing Add:* 424 Dell Ct Solana Beach CA 92075

GROOMS, RED
PAINTER, SCULPTOR
b Nashville, Tenn, June, 37. *Study:* Peabody Col; pvt study with J Van Sickle; New Sch Social Res; Art Inst Chicago; Hans Hofmann Sch, Provincetown, Mass. *Work:* Hirshhorn Mus & Sculpture Garden, Washington, DC; Art Inst Chicago; Mus Mod Art, New York; Museet Moderna, Stockholm, Sweden; Brooklyn Mus, NY; and others. *Comn:* Sets for Kenneth Koch's Red Robins, 78; mural (with Mimi Gross), Ctr for Mod Cult, Florence, Italy; Way Down East, Univ Northern Ky, 79; The Shoot Out, New Height Orgn, Denver, 82; sets for Kenwood Elmsley's City Junket, 80. *Exhib:* Twenty Americans, Art Inst Chicago, 66; Mus Mod Art, New York, 66; Guggenheim Mus, New York, 72; one-man shows, Ft Worth Art Mus, Tex, 76, Discount Store, Southern Univ NY Purchase, 78, Lowe Art Mus, Univ Miami, 80, Red Grooms: Works From the 60's, Colo State Univ, 80 & Ruckus Manhattan, Fuller Bldg, New York, 81; Whitney Mus Am Art, 73; plus many others. *Teaching:* Vis artist, Syracuse Univ, 80, Southern Ill Univ, 80 & Colo State Univ, 81; Albert Dorne Prof, Univ Bridgeport, 82. *Awards:* Lower Manhattan Cult Coun Award, 82. *Bibliog:* William Olander & Mark Gottlieb (auths), Welcome to Cleveland, New Gallery Contemp Art, 82; Carter Ratcliff & Carrie Rickey (auths), Red Grooms' Philadelphia Cornucopia, Inst Contemp Art, Univ Pa, 82; Jean Frumkin (auth), The Early Sixties: Red Grooms (catalog), Frumkin Gallery, 82; and others. *Mailing Add:* Marlborough Gallery Inc 40 W 57th St New York NY 10019

GROOT, CANDICE BETH
CERAMIST
b Berwyn, Ill, Mar 4, 54. *Study:* Gustavus Adolphus Col, BA, 76; Tex Tech Univ, with Verne Funk, MFA, 80. *Work:* Contemp Mus NMex, Santa Fe. *Exhib:* 9th Marietta Col Crafts Nat, Ohio, 80; Clay Work/New Work, D W Gallery, Dallas, Tex, 80; Clay Workers Guild, Ill, 81; Small Work Nat, Zaner Gallery, Rochester, NY, 81; Westwood Clay Nat, Calif, 81. *Teaching:* Asst prof ceramics, Gustavus Adolphus Col, St Peter, Minn, 81- *Awards:* Purchase Prize, Southwest Fine Arts Biennial, Hill Gallery, 78; Juror's Awards, Tex Col Art Show, 78 & Midland Col, 78. *Mem:* Am Crafts Coun; Nat Coun Educ Ceramic Arts. *Media:* Clay, Paper. *Mailing Add:* 1001 S Seventh St St Peter MN 56082

GROOVER, JAN
PHOTOGRAPHER
b Plainfield, NJ, Apr 24, 43. *Study:* Pratt Inst, BFA, 65; Ohio State Univ, MA, 70. *Work:* Metrop Mus Art, Mus Mod Art, Whitney Mus Am Art, New York; Baltimore Mus Art, Md; Mus Fine Art, Minneapolis, Minn. *Exhib:* One-man exhibs, Corcoran Gallery Art, 76, Baltimore Mus Art, Md, 77, Akron Art Inst, 79, Milwaukee Art Mus, 80 & Neuberger Mus, Purchase, NY, 82; two-man exhib, Mus Am Art, New York, 78; Mirrors and Windows, Mus Mod Art, New York, 78; Counter Parts, Metrop Mus Art, New York, 82. *Awards:* Creative Artists Pub Serv Award, NY State Coun Arts, 75; Photog Grant, Nat Endowment Arts, 78; Guggenheim Mem Found Grant, 79. *Publ:* Auth, Still life runs deep, Ben Lifson, Village Voice, 80; auth, Jan Groover: Color Photographs, Milwaukee Art Mus, 80; auth, The New Color Photography, Abbeville Press, 81; auth, Counterparts: Form & Emotion in Photographs, Metrop Mus Art, 82; auth, Jan Groover, Photographs, Neuberger Mus, 83. *Dealer:* Blum Helman 20 W 57th St New York NY 10019. *Mailing Add:* 189 Bowery New York NY 10002

GROSCH, LAURA
PAINTER, PRINTMAKER
b Worcester, Mass, Apr 1, 45. *Study:* Wellesley Col, Mass, BA(art hist), 63-67; Univ Pa, Philadelphia, BFA(painting), 68; study with Gertrude Whiting, James Rayen, Sigmund Abeles, Neil Welliver. *Work:* Libr Cong & Smithsonian Inst, Washington, DC; Brooklyn Mus, NY; Boston Mus Fine Arts, Mass; Calif Palace Legion Honor, San Francisco. *Comn:* Mural, Litchfield Plantation, Pawley's Island, SC, 69; paintings, McDonald's, Overstreet Mall, Charlotte, NC, 79. *Exhib:* 27th Ann Exhib Boston Printmakers, Boston Mus Fine Arts, 75; 20th Nat Print Exhib, Brooklyn Mus, NY, 77; Art USA: The South, United States Information Agency, 76-77; 4th Int Exhib, The Hunt Inst Botanical Documentation, Carnegie-Mellon Univ, Pittsburgh, 78; In Celebration of Prints, The Print Club & Philadelphia Art Alliance, Philadelphia, 80; one-women show, Hodges/Taylor Art Gallery, Charlotte, NC, 83; and others. *Awards:* First Nat Bank of Boston Purchase Award, Boston Printmakers, 75; Charlotte Printmakers Award, 78; Best Graphics Booth, Arts & Science Council Artists Showcase, Charlotte, 79; and others. *Mem:* Col Art Asn. *Media:* Acrylic; Litho Pencil. *Dealer:* Hodges Taylor Gallery 227 N Tryon St Charlotte NC 28202. *Mailing Add:* 497 S Main St Davidson NC 28036

GROSHANS, WERNER
PAINTER
b Eutingen, Ger, July 6, 13; US citizen. *Study:* Newark Sch Fine & Indust Art, grad; also with Bernar Gussow. *Work:* Newark Mus, NJ; Montclair Art Mus, NJ; Canton Art Inst, Ohio; New Britain Mus Am Art, Conn; William Benton Mus, Univ Conn, Storrs. *Exhib:* Whitney Mus Am Art, 48, 49 & 52; Carnegie Inst, 49; Metrop Mus Art, 50 & 52; Canton Art Inst, 71; Retrospective, New Britain Mus Am Art, New York, 73; Am Acad Inst Arts & Letters, 75, 80 & 82; Retrospective, Montclair Art Mus, NJ, 76; Nassau Co Mus Fine Art, 80; and others. *Awards:* Henry Ward Ranger Fund Purchase, 61 & 74; Painting Fel, NJ State Co Arts, 80; Hassam & Speicher Fund Purchase, Am Acad Inst Arts & Letters, 80; and others. *Bibliog:* Margarita Dulac (auth), Werner Groshans, painter of realism & fantasy, Am Artist Mag, 6/70; William D Gorman (auth), Werner Groshans, pastellist, Today's Art, Vol 26, No 9, 78; and others. *Mem:* Nat Acad Design (mem coun, 70-73); Audubon Artists; Allied Artists Am; Artists Equity; Conn Acad Fine Arts. *Media:* Oil, Pastel. *Dealer:* Babcock Galleries 20 East 67th St New York NY 10021. *Mailing Add:* RD 1, Box 57 Catskill NY 12414

GROSS, ALICE (ALICE GROSS FISH)
SCULPTOR
b New York, NY. *Study:* With Ruth Yates. *Work:* Berkshire Mus, Pittsfield, Mass. *Exhib:* Eastern States Exhib, Springfield, Mass, 64; Audubon Artists, Nat Acad Design, New York, 68 & Allied Artists Am, 69; Knickerbocker Artists, Nat Arts Club, New York, 71; New Rochelle Art Asn, Col New Rochelle, 71. *Awards:* Award for Duo, Allied Artists Am, 69; Award for Rhythm, Knickerbocker Artists, 70; Award for Who's the Fairest of Them All, Beaux Arts of Westchester, 71. *Mem:* Silvermine Guild Artists; Audubon Artists; Allied Artists Am; Knickerbocker Artists. *Media:* Multimedia. *Mailing Add:* 16 Sutton Pl New York NY 10022

GROSS, CHAIM
SCULPTOR, INSTRUCTOR
b Kolomea, Austria, Mar 17, 04; US citizen. *Study:* Kunstgewerbe Schulle; Educ Alliance, New York; Beaux-Arts Inst Design, with Elie Nadelman; Art Students League, with Robert Laurent; Franklin & Marshall Col, Hon DFA, 70; Yeshiva Univ, Hon LHD, 78; Adelphia Univ, hon degree, 80. *Work:* Metrop Mus Art, New York; Art Inst Chicago; Brooklyn Mus; Jewish Mus; Worcester Art Mus, Mass; and over 60 other mus & univs. *Comn:* Isaiah (large bronze sculpture), Holy Cross Col, 79; life size bronze sculpture for shopping ctr, Ft Lauderdale, Fla, 80; bronze sculpture, Jewish Community Ctr, Tenafly, NJ, 80; two sculptures, Palm Court Galleria, Ft Lauderdale, Fla, 81; Pillar of Faith (bronze sculpture), Community Ctr Palisades, NJ, 81; and others. *Exhib:* The Making of Sculpture, Mus Mod Art, New York, 61-62; Drawings by Sculptors, Smithsonian Inst, 61-63; retrospectives, Jewish Mus, 77, Univ Miami, Fla, 77 & Mt Clair Art Mus, NJ, 77; Exhib Watercolors & Drawings, Forum Gallery, New York, 80; 50 Years of Sculpture in Wood & Stone, Forum Gallery, New York & Wichita Art Mus, Kans, 82; and others. *Teaching:* Instr sculpture, Educ Alliance Art Sch, 27- & New Sch Social Res, 48-; instr, Mus Mod Art, 52-57. *Awards:* Award of Merit Medal, Nat Inst Arts & Lett, 63; Gold Medal, Nat Acad Design; several awards from Audubon Artists; and others. *Bibliog:* John I H Baur (auth), Revolution and Tradition

in Modern American Art, Harvard Univ, 65; Dr Alfred Werner (auth), Watercolors and Drawings, Abrams, 80; Frank Getlein (auth), Chaim Gross Sculpture, Harry Abrams; Eternal Light: Two Chaims (with Chaim Potok, film), Nat Broadcasting Co, 9/11/83; and others. *Mem:* Sculptors Guild; Educ Alliance Alumni Asn; Fedn Mod Painters & Sculptors; Nat Inst Arts & Lett; Artists Equity Asn. *Publ:* Auth, Fantasy Drawings, Beechhurst, 56; coauth, Tree Trunk to Head & A Sculptor Speaks (art films), 56; auth, Sculpture in Wood, Vista Press; contribr, The Poetry of Isaiah, 79 & The Song of Songs, 81, Ltd Ed; contribr, var art mag. *Mailing Add:* 526 La Guardia Pl New York NY 10012

GROSS, CHARLES MERRILL
EDUCATOR, SCULPTOR
b Cullman, Ala, Sept 18, 35. *Study:* Atlanta Col Art, BFA; Univ Guanajuato, Mex, MFA. *Work:* Jackson State Univ, Miss; Univ Southern Miss; Marion Military Inst, Ala; Miss Delta Jr Col. *Exhib:* Mid-South Exhib, Brooks Mem Art Gallery, Memphis, Tenn, 69, 70 & 72; Nat Arts & Crafts Exhib, Jackson, Miss, 69 & 71; Delta Art Exhib, Ark Arts Ctr, Little Rock, 69-71, 74-75 & 78; Regional Sculpture Exhib, Carroll Reece Mus, Jackson City, Tenn, 72; Monroe Nat Ann Art Exhib, Masur Mus Art, La, 73; plus others. *Teaching:* Instr drawing, painting & sculpture, Miss Col, 68-69; asst prof sculpture, Univ Miss, 69-73, assoc prof sculpture, 73-80, prof sculpture, 80- *Awards:* Merit Awards, 14th Mid-South Exhib, Seventh Ann Southeastern Competition, Rome, Ga & Fifth Nat Arts & Crafts Exhib, Jackson. *Mem:* Nat Art Educ Asn; Southern Asn Sculptors (regional vpres, 73-75). *Media:* Aluminum, Bronze. *Mailing Add:* 300 Longest Rd Oxford MS 38655

GROSS, EARL
PAINTER, LECTURER
b Sept 11, 1899; US citizen. *Study:* Westminster Col; Carnegie-Mellon Univ. *Work:* New Britain Mus Am Art; Atlanta Art Inst, Ga; Reading Mus, Pa; Ill State Mus; Art Inst Chicago; and others. *Exhib:* Two-man show, Art Inst Chicago, 50; Paintings of Past Decade, Metrop Mus, 52; one-man show, Butler Art Mus, 52; Am Watercolor Soc, New York, 58; Frank Oehlschlaeger Galleries, Chicago & Sarasota, Fla. *Pos:* Off combat artist, US Air Force, Far East, formerly; pres, Stevens-Gross Studios, Chicago, 26-62. *Teaching:* Prof painting, Longboat Key Art Ctr, Fla, New Orleans Acad Art & Highland Park Art Ctr, formerly; instr, Chicago Acad Fine Art, Ill & Am Acad, Chicago, formerly. *Awards:* Second Prize, Denver Mus, Colo & Cosmopolitan Mag Competition; First Prize, Chicago Artists Guild. *Bibliog:* Norman Kent (auth), Sea scapes & landscapes & Wendell Blake (auth), Acrylic watercolor painting, Watson Guptill. *Mem:* Am Watercolor Soc, Philadelphia & Washington, DC; Arts Club Chicago; Artist Guild Chicago; hon mem Chicago Art Dir Club. *Media:* Watercolor, Oil. *Publ:* Auth, Watercolor Series, 47, Illustrators Page, 51, Robert Addison, 58 & Polymer colors in depth, 67, Am Artist Mag; also articles in Art News & Chicago Tribune. *Dealer:* Oehlschlaeger Galleries 107 E Oak St Chicago IL 60611; Frank Oehlschlaeger Gallery 28 Blvd of the Presidents St Armands Key Sarasota FL 33578. *Mailing Add:* 1810 Calle de Sebastian A 4 Santa Fe NM 87501

GROSS, ESTELLE SHANE
DEALER
b New York, NY. *Study:* Pa State Univ, BA; Temple Univ, MA; Philadelphia Mus Art, studied with Hobson Pittman, eight yrs; Parsons Inst of Design. *Collections Arranged:* Rockwell Kent Graphics Exhib; Fairfield Porter Exhib; Adja Yonkers Graphics Exhib; Neil Welliver, Hobson Pittman, Jane Piper, Larry Day & Violet Oakley Exhibs; Paul Hogarth Exhib of Bk Illustrations. *Pos:* Pres, Gross-McCleaf Gallery, Philadelphia, 66- *Mem:* Fine Arts Appraisal Soc; Philadelphia Art Dealers Asn; Philadelphia Print Club; Philadelphia Art Alliance. *Specialty:* Philadelphia painters & sculptors, Martha Armstrong, Jan Baltzell, Larry Day, Louisa Matthiasdottir, Jane Piper, Nora Speyer, Susan Van Campen, and others; expertise in Japanese prints. *Publ:* Auth, Jane Piper: Recent Paintings, 81; auth, Bertha Leonard: Recent paintings, 83. *Mailing Add:* Gross-McCleaf Gallery 1713 Walnut St Philadelphia PA 19103

GROSS, SANDRA LERNER See Lerner, Sandra

GROSSBERG, JAKE
EDUCATOR, SCULPTOR
b Luban, Poland, Feb 13, 32; US citizen. *Study:* Columbia Univ, MA; Brooklyn Col, MFA. *Work:* Riverside Mus Collection, Columbia Univ, New York; Rose Art Mus, Brandeis Univ, Boston; Chrysler Mus, Provincetown, Mass; Stanford Mus Collection, Conn. *Comn:* Steel sculpture, Northern Ill Univ, DeKalb, 68. *Exhib:* Brooklyn Mus, New York, 58-60; Riverside Mus, New York, 60-67; Chrysler Mus, Provincetown, Mass, 62; Mus Mod Art, New York, 66; Philadelphia Art Alliance, 67; Central City Park, Atlanta, Ga, 76; Grey Art Gallery, New York Univ, 78. *Pos:* Dir, Milton Avery Grad Sch, Annondale-on-Hudson, NY, 80-83. *Teaching:* Prof fine arts, Bard Col, Annondale, NY, 69- *Media:* Steel. *Mailing Add:* c/o Frank Marino Gallery 489 Broome St New York NY 10013

GROSSE (CAROLYN ANN GAWARECKI)
PAINTER, INSTRUCTOR
b Rahway, NJ, Oct 30, 31. *Study:* Douglass Col, BA, 53; Univ Calif, Berkeley; Univ Colo. *Work:* City Falls Church, Va; Indust Col Armed Forces, Ft McNair, Washington, DC; First Va Bank; Holiday Inn Corp, Falls Church; Georgetown Univ. *Exhib:* First Ann Southern Watercolor Soc, Nashville, Tenn, 77 & Second Ann, Ga, 78; one-artist show, Atlantic Gallery, Washington, DC, 78, 79 & 81; Baltimore Watercolor Soc 3rd Ann 81; Va Watercolor Soc 2nd Ann, Richmond, 81; and others. *Pos:* Exhibits artist, Mus

Nat Hist, Smithsonian Inst, 56-57; partic, Art in Embassies Prog, US State Dept. *Teaching:* Instr art, Highland Park High Sch, NJ, 53-55; instr watercolor, City Falls Church, 66-; instr watercolor workshops, Md & WVa, currently. *Awards:* Best in Show Area, Metrop Area Show, Springfield Guild, 74; Award, Baltimore Watercolor Soc, 81; Potomac Valley Watercolorists Awards, 81-83. *Mem:* Assoc mem Am Watercolor Soc; Va Watercolor Soc & Art League; Washington Watercolor Soc; Southern Watercolor Soc; Potomac Valley Watercolorists (pres, 74-77). *Media:* Watercolor, Casein. *Dealer:* Atlantic Gallery Washington DC; Art League Gallery Alexandria VA. *Mailing Add:* 7018 Vagabond Dr Falls Church VA 22042

GROSSEN, FRANCOISE
SCULPTOR, INSTRUCTOR
b Neuchatel, Switz, Aug 19, 43. *Study:* Sch Archit, Polytech Univ, Lausanne, Switz; Sch Arts & Crafts, Basel, Switz, grad; Univ Calif, Los Angeles, with B Kester, MA. *Work:* Dreyfus Fund, GM Bldg, New York; Bank Tex, San Antonio; Mus Bellerive, Zurich, Switz; Am Dist Tel Co, New York. *Comn:* Thirty-eight elements in lobby-bar, O'Hare Regency Hyatt House, Chicago, 70; two lobby pieces, One Embarcadero Ctr, San Francisco, 72; Tensile-Ten, NTex State Univ, Denton, 75; two lobby pieces, Rudin Management, New York, 81; and others. *Exhib:* Wall Hangings, Mus Mod Art, New York, 68; Three Dimensional Fiber, New Plymouth, NZ, 74-75; one-person shows, Hadler Galleries, New York, 76 & Mus Bellerive, Zurich, 76; Fiberworks-The Americas & Japan, Nat Mus Mod Art, Tokyo & Kyoto, Japan, 77; Soft-art, Weich, Plastisch, Kunsthaus Zurich, 79; and others. *Pos:* Designer, Larsen Design Studio, 68-71. *Teaching:* Instr, New Sch Social Res, New York; instr fiber art, Kansas City Art Inst, summer 74 & Univ Calif, Los Angeles, summer 75. *Awards:* Women in Design Int Hon Award, 81. *Bibliog:* Jean-Luc Daval, article, Art Int, Vol 15, 71; Andre Kuenzi (auth), La Nouvelle Tapisserie, Bonvent, 73; Constantine & Larsen (auth), Beyond Craft, 73 & Art Fabric, Mainstream, 81, Van Nostrand Reinhold. *Media:* Fiber. *Mailing Add:* 135 Greene St New York NY 10012

GROSSER, MAURICE
PAINTER, WRITER
b Huntsville, Ala, Oct 23, 03. *Study:* Harvard Univ, BA, 24. *Work:* American Collection; Smithsonian Inst, Washington DC; Brooklyn Mus; Fogg Art Mus, Cambridge, Mass; Mus Mod Art, New York. *Comn:* Portrait of Dean of Grad Sch, comn by Dr Nina Garsoian, Princeton Univ, NJ, 79. *Pos:* Art critic, The Nation, 56-63. *Teaching:* Prof painting, Univ Ife, Nigeria, 70. *Awards:* Holden Fel, Harvard Univ, 25-27. *Media:* Oil. *Publ:* Auth, Painting in Public, Knopf, 48, reprint as Painting in Our Time, Bobbs-Merrill, 64; auth, The Painter's Eye, Rinehart, 51; auth, Critic's Eye, Bobbs-Merrill, 62; auth, Painter's Progress, Clarkson Potter, 71. *Dealer:* Fischback Gallery 29 W 57th St New York NY 10019. *Mailing Add:* 219 W 14th St New York NY 10011

GROSSMAN, MAURICE KENNETH
EDUCATOR, CRAFTSMAN
b Detroit, Mich, Sept 16, 27. *Study:* Wayne State Univ, Detroit, with J Foster, BS(art educ), 50; Alfred Univ, NY, with Dan Rhodes, 51; Ohio State Univ, Columbus, with Paul Bogatay, MFA(ceramics), 53. *Work:* Detroit Mus Art; Phoenix Mus Art; El Paso Mus; Utah State Mus, Salt Lake City; Albuquerque Mus Art, NMex. *Exhib:* Ceramic Nat, Everson Mus Art, Syracuse, 50-68; Clay Invitational, Smithsonian Inst, DC, 53 & 59; Designer-Craftsmen of the West, De Young Mus, San Francisco, 57; Western Artists, Denver Art Mus, 57; Krannert Mus Design, 64; Southwest Craftsmen, Santa Fe, NMex, 65; Crafts Invitational, Ark Art Ctr, Little Rock, 66; Eighth Ariz Ann, Phoenix Art Mus, 66; Objects Are, Mus Contemp Crafts, New York, 68. *Teaching:* Instr ceramics, Western Wash Col, Bellingham, 53-54; prof ceramics, Univ Ariz, Tucson, 55- *Awards:* Fac Recognition Award, Tucson Trade Bureau, 68; Creative Teaching Award, Univ Ariz Found, 78; and many others; Fulbright Fel, Japan, 54-55. *Bibliog:* Polly Rothman (auth), The Complete Book of Ceramics, Crown Publ, 72; John Conrad (auth), Contemporary Ceramic Techniques, Prentice Hall, 79. *Mem:* Am Crafts Coun (southwest area rep, 63-66), Ariz Designer-Craftsmen (pres, 60); Nat Coun Educ for Ceramic Arts (regional rep, 72); Tucson Art Ctr (bd dirs, 68); World Crafts Coun. *Media:* Ceramics. *Publ:* Auth, American ceramics, Tanko Mag, Kyoto, Japan, 56; auth, Clay in the Hand, an American in Japan, Inst of Int Educ, 56. *Dealer:* Wright Designs Assocs 1736 E Speedway Tucson AZ 85719. *Mailing Add:* Dept of Art Univ of Ariz Tucson AZ 85721

GROSSMAN, MAURIZIA M
DEALER, GALLERY DIRECTOR
b Udine, Italy, Aug 9, 43; US citizen. *Study:* Univ Florence, Italy, MA. *Collections Arranged:* The Native Traditions--19th Century Decorative Arts, 74-75;; several photog exhibs by maj 19th & 20th century photographers, Lunn Gallery, 75- *Pos:* Asst ed, Collector's Ed Ltd, New York, NY, 70-72; asst dir, Lunn Gallery/Graphics Int Ltd, Washington, DC, 72- *Specialty:* Photography of the nineteenth and twentieth century; twentieth century graphics. *Publ:* Auth, Catalogue 3--19th and 20th Century Prints and Photographs, Graphics Int Ltd, 73 & Catalogue 4--19th and 20th Century Prints and Photographs, 74. *Mailing Add:* c/o Lunn Graphics Int Ltd 406 Seventh St NW Washington DC 20004

GROSSMAN, MORTON
PAINTER
b 1926. *Study:* Art Students League, scholar, 44-47; Queens Col, NY, BA(hons), 48; Louis Comfort Tiffany Found fel, 49-50. *Work:* Cleveland Mus Art; Norfolk Mus Art, Va; Ball State Univ, Ind; Birmingham Mus Art, Ala; SS United States; plus many pvt collections. *Exhib:* Whitney Mus Am Art; Dallas Mus Fine Arts; Baltimore Mus Art; Walker Art Ctr; Seattle Art Mus;

Boston Mus Fine Art; San Francisco Mus of Art; Corcoran Gallery of Art; Okla Art Ctr; Inst Contemp Art, Boston; one-man shows, Albright-Knox Art Gallery, Miami Beach Art Ctr, Akron Art Inst, Canton Art Inst, Ohio, San Joaquin Mus, Calif, Grand Central Moderns Gallery, New York; plus many others. *Teaching:* At Queens Col, NY, 55-56, State Univ NY Col Buffalo, 56-60, Cleveland Inst Art, 61-64, Univ Md, 64-69 & Tyler Sch Art, Temple Univ, summers 67 & 68; prof painting, Kent State Univ, 69- *Awards:* Grand Award & Gold Medal, Am Watercolor Soc, 60; Audubon Artists Medal for Creative Aquarelle, 62; Arches Award, Watercolor USA, Springfield Art Mus, 69. *Media:* Acrylic, Watercolor. *Mailing Add:* 217 Crain Ave Kent OH 44240

GROSSMAN, NANCY
SCULPTOR, PAINTER
b New York, NY, Apr 28, 40. *Study:* Pratt Inst. *Work:* Whitney Mus Am Art, New York; Princeton Univ Art Mus; Univ Mus, Berkeley, Calif; Dallas Mus Fine Art; Israel Mus, Jerusalem. *Exhib:* Corcoran Gallery Art Biennial Exhib, Washington, DC, 63; Whitney Mus Am Art Sculpture Ann, 68 & Whitney Biennial, 73; Recent Figure Sculpture, Fogg Art Mus, Harvard Univ, 72; Perceiving Modern Sculpture, Grey Art Gallery, NY Univ, 80; bronze, Hamilton Gallery, 80; Drawing Acquisitions, Whitney Mus Am Art, 81; Figuratively Sculpting, PS1, 81; The Americans: The Collage, Contemp Arts Mus, Houston, 82; The Sculptor as Draftsman, Whitney Mus Am Art, 83; Terminal New York, 83. *Awards:* Guggenheim Mem Found Fel, 65; Am Acad Arts & Lett/Nat Inst Arts & Lett Award, 74; Commencement Honoree, Mass Col Art, 74. *Bibliog:* Corinne Robins (auth), Man is anonymous: the art of Nancy Grossman, Art Spectrum Mag, 2/75; Cindy Nemser (auth), Art Talk, Conversations with 12 Women Artists, Scribners, 75; Charlotte Streifer Rubenstein (auth), American Women Artists, Avon, 82. *Dealer:* Terry Dintenfass Gallery 50 W 57th St New York NY 10019. *Mailing Add:* 105 Eldridge St New York NY 10002

GROSSMAN, SHELDON
MUSEUM CURATOR, HISTORIAN
b New York, NY, Aug 30, 40. *Study:* Hunter Col, BA, 62; NY Univ Inst Fine Arts, MA, 66. *Pos:* Cur, Northern & Later Ital Paintings, Nat Gallery Art, Washington, DC, 71- *Awards:* Fulbright-Hays Travel Grant, 66; Ital Govt Study Grant, 66; Chester Dale Fel, Nat Gallery Art, 67-69. *Res:* Problems in Florentine painting in the late fifteenth and early sixteenth century; analysis of problems of style; archival research. *Publ:* Auth, National Gallery of Art report and studies in the history of art, 68; auth, Mitteilungen des kunsthistorischen institutes in Florenz, 69; auth, Master drawings, 72; auth, National Gallery of Art, Studies in the History of Art, 74; auth, Stadel-Jahrbach, 79. *Mailing Add:* 2312 Tunlaw Rd NW Washington DC 20007

GROSVENOR, ROBERT
SCULPTOR
b New York, NY, 1937. *Study:* Ecole des Beaux Arts, Dijon, France, 56; Ecole Superieure des Arts Decoratifs, Paris, 57-58; Univ Perugia, Italy, 58. *Work:* Whitney Mus, New York; Storm King Art Ctr, Mountainville, NY; Mus Mod Art, New York; Hirshorn Mus, Washington, DC; Walker Art Ctr, Minneapolis. *Exhib:* Sculpture for the 60's, Los Angeles Co Mus, 67; Plus by Minus, Albright-Knox Art Gallery, Buffalo, NY, 68; Sculpture Ann, Whitney Mus Am Art, New York, 68; Biennial Exhib Am Painting & Sculpture, 73 & 200 Yrs Am Sculpture, 76; 14 Sculptors: the Industrial Edge, Walker Art Ctr, Minneapolis, 69; Works on Paper, 31st Ann Exhib, Soc Contemp Art, Art Inst Chicago, 71; NY State Mus, Albany, 77; one-man shows, Galerie Eric Fabre, Paris, 77 & Paula Cooper Gallery, New York, 78 & 79; Private Images: Photographs by Sculptors, Los Angeles Co Mus Art, Contemp Art Galleries, Lytton Halls, 77-78; Drawings for Outdoor Sculpture: 1946-1977, Amherst Col, Mass, Univ Calif, Santa Barbara & Mass Inst Technol, 78; Minimal Tradition, 79 & postMINIMALism, 82, Aldrich Mus Contmep Art; and many others. *Awards:* Guggenheim Fel, 69; Nat Endowment Arts & Humanities Grant, 70; Nat Acad Arts & Lett Grant, 72. *Bibliog:* Jeremy Gilbert Rolfe (auth), Robert Grosvenor: Specific Clarity, Art in Am, 3-4/76; John Russel (auth), Critics Choice: Galleries, New York Times, 4/21/78; Deborah Perlberg (auth), Reviews in New York, Artforum, summer 78. *Mailing Add:* c/o Paula Cooper Gallery 155 Wooster New York NY 10012

GROSZ, FRANZ JOSEPH
PAINTER, DESIGNER
b New York, NY, Oct 7, 09. *Study:* Nat Acad Design, with Kroll, Olinsky & Nielson; Art Students League New York, with Boardman Robinson & Brackman; also with Hans Hofmann, New York. *Work:* Carnegie Mus; Nat Acad Design; Currier Mus Art; Pa Acad Fine Art; Corcoran Gallery Art; and others. *Comn:* Glass murals (mixed media), Joseph's Sch Auditorium, Astoria, NY & Manhasset Congregational Church, Nassau Co, NY, 60; glass murals, Salem Lutheran Church, Bridgeport, Conn, 61, US Coast Guard Acad, New London, Conn, 63 & St Anthony Shrine, Boston, Mass, 65; over 350 murals, 41-60. *Exhib:* Whitney Mus Am Art, New York, 48; one-man show, Galerie Visconti, Paris, France, 71; one-man show sponsored by Fr Embassy, Amsterdam, 73. *Awards:* Carnegie Int. *Media:* Oil, Glass. *Mailing Add:* 2100 Linwood Ave Ft Lee NJ 07024

GROTENRATH, RUTH
PAINTER, PRINTMAKER
b Milwaukee, Wis, Mar 17, 12. *Study:* State Teachers Col, Milwaukee, BA. *Work:* Philadelphia Mus Art; IBM Collection; Madison Union; Milwaukee Art Inst; Gimbel Collection. *Comn:* Murals, Post Off, Hart, Mich, Wayzata, Minn & Hudson, Wis & Timmerman Field Bldg. *Exhib:* One-man shows, Chapman Gallery, Milwaukee, 65; Bradley Gallery, 66, 69, 72, 74, 77, 78 & 80 & others; Milwaukee Art Ctr, 62; Cudahy Gallery, Milwaukee Art Ctr, 79;

Two-man show with Schomer Lichtner, Fish Creek, 83 & Bradley Gallery, 83, Wis; Bradley Gallery, Wis, 83. *Teaching:* Instr design, Univ Wis-Milwaukee, 61. *Awards:* William & Bertha Clusman Award, Chicago Art Inst, 63; Grand Rapids Art Gallery Award; Dayton Co Award, Minneapolis; plus others. *Dealer:* Bradley Galleries 2565 N Downer Ave Milwaukee WI 53211 *Mailing Add:* 2626A N Maryland Ave Milwaukee WI 53211

GROTH, BRUNO
SCULPTOR
b Stolp, Ger, Dec 14, 05; US citizen. *Study:* Otis Art Inst, Los Angeles. *Work:* Palm Springs Mus, Calif; Joseph H Hirshhorn Collection, New York. *Comn:* Bronze fountain pieces, Cities of Fresno & Crescent City, Calif; wood sculpture, Humboldt State Col. *Exhib:* One-man show, De Young Mus, San Francisco, 59; Brussels World's Fair; Santa Barbara Mus Art; Portland Art Mus; Mus Contemp Crafts, New York. *Media:* Welded Steel, Bronze. *Dealer:* Ankrum Gallery 657 N La Cienega Blvd Los Angeles CA 90069. *Mailing Add:* N Aspaas Rd PO Box 46C Cornville AZ 86325

GROTH, JOHN AUGUST
ILLUSTRATOR, PAINTER
b Chicago, Ill, Feb 2, 08. *Study:* Art Inst Chicago; Art Students League; Eastern Mich Univ, Hon DA, 76. *Work:* Mus Mod Art, Whitney Mus Am Art & Metrop Mus Art, New York; Brooklyn Mus, NY; Art Inst Chicago. *Pos:* Art dir, Esquire Mag, 33-36; art dir, Parade Mag. *Teaching:* Instr compos, Art Students League, 46-; artist in residence, Univ Tex, 70. *Mem:* Nat Acad Design; Soc Illusr; Am Watercolor Soc; Allied Artists; Audubon Artists. *Media:* Watercolor, Oil; Ink. *Publ:* Illusr, Gone with the Wind, 68; illusr, All Quiet on the Western Front, 71; illusr, Pudden' Head Wilson, 75; illusr, The Promise Kept, 75; illusr, Biography of the American Reindeer, 76; and numerous others. *Mailing Add:* 61 E 57th St New York NY 10022

GROTZ, DOROTHY ROGERS
PAINTER
b Philadelphia, Pa. *Study:* Univ Berlin, 29; Columbia Univ, MS, 45; Art Students League, 47. *Work:* Rochester Univ Mus Art; Santa Barbara Mus Fine Arts; Norfolk Mus Arts & Sci; Evansville Mus Arts & Sci. *Exhib:* Avery Libr, Columbia Univ, 50, Van Diemen Lilienfeld Gallery, 62-67 & Bodley Gallery, New York, 72; Univ Wis, 67; Columbus Gallery Fine Arts, Ohio, 72. *Bibliog:* Archives of Am Art, Smithsonian Inst, Washington, DC. *Media:* Oil. *Publ:* Auth rev in Archit Forum, 69 & Leonardo, 72. *Dealer:* Bodley Gallery 787 Madison Ave New York NY 10021; Sid Deutsch Gallery 20 W 57th St New York NY 10019. *Mailing Add:* 7 St Lukes Pl New York NY 10014

GROVE, EDWARD RYNEAL
MEDALIST, PAINTER
b Martinsburg, WVa, Aug 14, 12. *Study:* Nat Sch Art, Washington, DC, 33; Corcoran Sch Art, Washington, DC, with Schuler & Weisz, 34-40; also with Robert Brackman, Noank, Conn, 46. *Work:* Metrop Mus Art; Smithsonian Inst; Imperial Palace, Tokyo; Portsmouth Royal Naval Mus, England; Mus Medallic Art, Poland. *Comn:* Communion Saints mural, Church Holy Comforter, Drexel Hill, Pa, 58; Cong gold medal for Bob Hope, 63; alphabet medal, Soc Medalists, 73; An American Eagle (bronze Bicentennial monument), Palm Beach, Fla, 76; Am Express goldpiece, 82. *Exhib:* Watercolor Ann, Pa Acad Fine Arts, Philadelphia, 54; 2nd Philadelphia Arts Festival, Philadelphia Mus Art, 62; Nat Sculpture Soc, Lever House, New York, 67, 69 & 71; Florida Creates Traveling Exhib, 73-74; 16th & 17th Congress FIDEM, Krakow, Poland, 75 & Budapest, Hungary, 77 & Florence, Italy, 83. *Pos:* Secy, treas & pres, Steel & Copper Engravers League, Philadelphia, 50-62; sculptor-engraver, US Mint, Philadelphia, 62-65; official sculptor-engraver, Order St John of Jerusalem, Knights of Malta Hq, Shickshinny, Pa, 67- *Teaching:* Instr drawing & portraiture, Flagler Art Ctr, West Palm Beach, 72-73. *Awards:* Lindsey Morris Mem Prize, Nat Sculpture Soc, 67; Sculptor Yr Gold Medal, Am Numismatic Asn, 69; Louis Bennett Mem Prize, Nat Sculpture Soc, 71. *Bibliog:* T W Becker (auth), Edward R Grove, commitment to America, Franklin Mint Almanac, 11/69; V Culver (auth), The four best, Coins Mag, 6/70; C W Hill (auth), Edward Grove, man of many talents, Coin Monthly, Eng, 3/76. *Mem:* Artists Equity Asn (nat first vpres, 65-67); fel Nat Sculpture Soc; assoc Nat Acad Design; Token & Medal Soc; Fedn Int de la Medaille. *Media:* Clay, Bronze & Silver; Oil, Watercolor. *Publ:* Contribr, Design Handbook, Nat Philatelic Mus, 54; co-auth & illusr, The Communion of Saints (brochure), Church of the Holy Comforter, 58; illusr, Our Christian Heritage, Morehouse-Gorham, 59; auth & illusr, Assignment: Malta, Coin World, 65; auth & illusr, The making of a medal, Am Artist Mag, 1/72, reprinted, Numismatist, 7/78. *Mailing Add:* Sea-Lake Studio 3215 S Flagler Dr West Palm Beach FL 33405

GROVE, JEAN DONNER
SCULPTOR
b Washington, DC, May 15, 12. *Study:* Hill Sch Sculpture; Corcoran Sch Art; Cath Univ Am; Wilson Teachers Col, BS, 39; Cornell Univ; Philadelphia Mus Art; travel study in Europe; also with Clara Hill, Hans Schuler, Heinz Warneke & Fritz Janschka. *Work:* Rosenwald Collection, Philadelphia, Pa; Fine Arts Comn, City Hall, Philadelphia. *Comn:* Many portrait comn, 40-; The Communion of Saints (mural with E R Grove), Church of the Holy Comforter, Drexel Hill, 52-58; garden figures, fountains & other works in pvt collections, Washington, DC, Philadelphia, NJ, NC, Calif & WVa; Am Express goldpiece, 82. *Exhib:* Corcoran Gallery of Art, 43-47; Pa Acad Fine Arts Ann, Philadelphia, 47, 48 & 51, Regional, 53; Philadelphia Mus Art Regional Art Festivals, 55, 59 & 62; Nat Sculpture Soc Ann, 57, 74-78 & 83; Civic Ctr Mus, Philadelphia, 68; Flager Art Ctr, West Palm Beach, 73; Norton Gallery of Art, West Palm Beach, Fla, 74 & 81; Nat Acad Design, 78, 81 &

83; plus others. *Awards:* Competition Prize, Artists Equity Asn Philadelphia, 60; Tallix Foundry Award, Nat Sculpture Soc Bicentennial Exhib, New York, 76; Acad of Italy with Gold Medal, 79; plus others. *Bibliog:* E Williams (auth), The mural, Today Mag, 11/58; H H Reinhold (auth), Third dimensional encounters, Palm Beach illus, 2/82 & Grove team designs, Coin World, 2/2/83. *Mem:* Nat Sculpture Soc; Artists Equity Asn (dir, Philadelphia Chap, 64-66); Philadelphia Art Alliance; Soc Four Arts, Palm Beach, Fla; assoc Nat Acad Design, New York; and others. *Media:* Stone, Wood. *Mailing Add:* Sea Lake Studio 3215 S Flagler Dr West Palm Beach FL 33405

GROVE, MERRILL DALE
CURATOR, PAINTER
b Aituras, Calif, May 25, 54. *Study:* Shasta Jr Col, 74; Calif State Univ, Sacramento, BA, 77, MA, 79. *Pos:* Cur & dir, Aita Galleries, 80-82 & Chan Elliot Gallery, 82- *Awards:* Crocker Kingsley Purchase Award, 82. *Bibliog:* Karen Wilson (auth), Practically speaking, Arts Alive, 7/81; Jeff Kelly (auth), Disjunctive ambitions, Artweek, 82; Ellen Schlessinger (dir), Art, KYXL-TV. *Mem:* Sacramento Area Gallery Asn; Calif Rural Arts Coun. *Media:* Watercolor. *Specialty:* Contemporary art and emerging artists. *Mailing Add:* 727 1/2 J St Sacramento CA 95814

GROVE, SAMUEL HAROLD
ADMINISTRATOR, HISTORIAN
b Joliet, Ill, Mar 8, 25. *Study:* Northeastern Ill Univ, BA, 74; Art Inst Chicago. *Collections Arranged:* Shang Dynasty to Ching Dynasty, 75; Catlin Plains Indian Portraits, 75; Retrospective Exhibit, Clark Hulings, 78; Baroque European Painting, Amodeo Collection, 78; Contemporary Egyptian Art and Artifacts, 82. *Pos:* Sr sci illusr, Field Mus Natural Hist, Chicago, 68-75; dir, Mus Southwest, Midland, Tex, 75-79 & Mus Art Am West, Houston, 83- *Teaching:* Instr sci illus, Field Mus Natural Hist, Chicago, 68-75; instr art hist, Glassell Sch Art, Mus Fine Arts, Houston, 79- & Univ Houston, 79-80. *Bibliog:* Articles, Houston Post, 79 & Southwest Art Mag, 10/83. *Mem:* Adventurers Club, Chicago (mem bd of dirs, 72-74); fel Explorers Club, New York; Tex Asn Mus (coun mem, 75-78); Savage Club. *Res:* Rock art of the inner Sahara. *Mailing Add:* Mus Art Am West PO Box 13037 Houston TX 77219

GROVES, NAOMI JACKSON
WRITER, PAINTER
b Montreal, Que. *Study:* Rannows Art Sch, Copenhagen; Sir George Williams Col, McGill Univ, BA & MA; Heidelberg Univ; Univ Berlin; Univ Munich; Radcliffe Col, AM & PhD; McMaster Univ, DLitt, 72. *Exhib:* One-man shows, Radcliffe Col, Wheaton Col, McMaster Univ & Montreal Mus Fine Arts. *Pos:* Asst to dir, Nat Gallery Can, 42-43, consult, 63-64. *Teaching:* Lectr, Ernst Barlach as Sculptor, as Dramatist & Barlach in America, 64; lectr, The Group of Seven, Another Look, Nat Gallery Can, 69; lectr, McGill Univ, Wheaton Col, Carleton Col; assoc prof in charge fine arts, McMaster Univ. *Awards:* Gov Gen Gold Medal, McGill Univ, 33; Can Fedn Univ Women Traveling Fel, 36-37. *Mem:* Canadian Artists Representation; hon life mem E Barlach Soc, Hamburg. *Media:* Oil, Wood. *Publ:* Auth, The Transformations of God, Hamburg, 62; auth, A Y's Canada, Toronto, 68 & 69; auth, Ernst Barlach-Leben im Werk, 72; auth, Ernst Barlach-Life in Work, 81. *Mailing Add:* 2896 Highfield Crescent Ottawa ON K2B 6G5 Canada

GRUBAR, FRANCIS STANLEY
HISTORIAN, LECTURER
b New Britain, Conn, June 8, 24. *Study:* Univ Md, BA, 48, MA(educ), 49; Johns Hopkins Univ, MA, 52, PhD(art hist), 66. *Collections Arranged:* Consult, William Ranney Exhib, 60-61 & Richard Caton Woodville Exhib (auth, catalog), 67-68, Corcoran Gallery Art, Washington, DC. *Pos:* Chmn art dept, George Washington Univ, 72-73. *Teaching:* Asst prof art hist, Univ Md, 48-66; assoc prof Am art, George Washington Univ, 66-73; prof, 73- *Mem:* Col Art Asn; Columbia Hist Soc; Conn Hist Soc; Am Studies Asn. *Res:* History of painting and sculpture in America during the nineteenth century. *Publ:* Auth, William Ranney, Painter of the Early West, Potter, 62; contribr, Leila Mechlin, In: Notable American Women 1607-1950, Vol 2, Harvard Univ Press, 71; contribr, Minerva Chapman, retrospective exhib catalog, Adams-Davidson, 71; contribr, A J Dozar's R Tait McKenzie: Sculptor of Athletes, Univ Tenn Press, 75. *Mailing Add:* Dept of Art George Washington Univ Washington DC 20052

GRUBER, AARONEL DEROY
SCULPTOR, KINETIC ARTIST
b Pittsburgh, Pa. *Study:* Carnegie Inst Technol. *Work:* Smithsonian Inst; Rose Art Mus, Brandeis Univ; Butler Inst Am Art; DeCordova Mus, Lincoln, Mass; Aldrich Mus Cntemp Art; and others. *Comn:* Steelcityscope (steel sculpture), Fort Duquesne Blvd, Pittsburgh, 77; kinetic metal & plexiglas sculpture, Allegheny Int Inc, Pittsburgh; 32 ft cor-ten sculpture, Gen Mills Corp, Minneapolis, 71; two sculptures, comn by DeBartolo, Melbourne Sq Mall, Fla; and others. *Exhib:* Refracted Images, DeCordova Mus, Lincoln, Mass, 73; II Bienniale Int de la Petite Sculpture, Budapest Mus, Mucsarnok, Hungary; Everson Mus, Syracuse, NY, 73; Basil Art Fair, 76-77; Vancouver Art Gallery, Vancouver Mus, BC, 77; and many others. *Awards:* Six Sculpture Awards, Western Pa Soc Sculptors, 62-77, Allegheny Ludlum Indust Award, 77; Artist of the Yr, 81, Pittsburgh Arts Ctr, Pa; and others. *Bibliog:* Alex Mogelon & Norman LaLiberte (auths), Art in Boxes, Van Nostrand Reinhold, 75; Dr Thelma Newman (auth), Plastics as sculpture, 74; Evert & Gay (auths), Discovering Pittsburgh's Sculpture, 83; and others. *Mem:* Western Pa Soc Sculptors (pres, 74-78); Group A (pres, 79-); Assoc Artists of Pittsburgh (bd dirs, 67-69); Artists Equity Asn; Nat Soc Lit & Arts; and others. *Media:* Lucite, Plexiglass; Metals. *Dealer:* Peter Rose Gallery 200 E 58 St New York NY 10022; Gallery G 408 Blvd of Allies Pittsburgh PA 15219. *Mailing Add:* 2409 Marbury Rd Pittsburgh PA 15221

GRUCZA, LEO (VICTOR)
PAINTER, EDUCATOR
b Erie, Pa, Jan 3, 35. *Study:* Cleveland Inst Art, dipl, 57; Tulane Univ, MFA, 61, with George Rickey & others. *Exhib:* Corcoran Biennial Exhib, Washington, DC, 63; Art Inst Chicago, 80-81; Univ Malaya, 82; Ill Arts Consortium Traveling Show, 82-83; Zriny Gallery, Chicago, 83; Am Acad & Inst Arts & Letters, 83; Nihon Univ, Tokyo, 83; and others. *Teaching:* Asst prof painting, Univ Ill, Champaign, 66-70, assoc prof painting, 70- *Awards:* First Prize/Painting, Ann Exhib, Delgado Mus, New Orleans, 61; Tiffany Found grant, New York, 61; Nat Endowment Arts Grants, 82-84. *Media:* Oil. *Dealer:* Zriny Gallery 1963 N Halsted Chicago IL 60614. *Mailing Add:* 2204 Blackthorn Champaign IL 61821

GRUEN, JOHN
CRITIC, WRITER
b Enghien-les-Bains, France, Sept 12, 26; US citizen. *Study:* City Col New York; Univ Iowa, BA & MA. *Pos:* Critic of music & art, New York Herald Tribune, 62-68; art critic, New York Mag, 69-73; art critic, Soho Weekly News, 74-; contribr ed, Art News, 76-; sr ed, Dance Mag, 79- *Teaching:* Lectr, Metrop Mus Art, 79- *Publ:* Auth, The Party's Over Now--Reminiscences of the Fifties, 72, The Private World of Ballet, 74 & Erik Bruhn: Danseur Noble, 79, Viking Press; auth, Menotti: A Biography, Macmillan, 78; The World's Great Ballets, Abrams, 81. *Mailing Add:* 317 W 83rd St New York NY 10024

GRUNDBERG, ANDY (JOHN ANDREW)
CRITIC, EDITOR
b Bryn Mawr, Pa, June 25, 47. *Study:* Cornell Univ, BA, 69; Univ NC, Greensboro, MFA, 71. *Pos:* Picture ed, Mod Photog, 74-; photog critic, Soho Weekly News, 79-81 & New York Times, 81- *Mem:* Soc Photog Educ (bd dirs, 83-). *Res:* Twentieth century American photography, with emphasis on contemporary practice and theory. *Publ:* Contribr, the Camera Viewed, Dutton, 79; contribr, Reading into Photography, Univ NMex Press, 82. *Mailing Add:* Arts & Leisure New York Times 229 W 43 St New York NY 10036

GRUNDY, J(OHN OWEN)
PATRON, WRITER
b Jersey City, NJ, Mar 8, 11. *Study:* Cooper Union; Jersey City State Col, DHL, 83. *Pos:* Contrib ed, Jersey Rev, Jersey City, 28-34; free lance writer, 43-46 & 61-68; assoc ed & reporter, Villager, New York, 46-59; pres & ed, Greenwich Village News, 59-61; archivist, Jersey City Free Pub Libr, 68-72; city historian, Jersey City, 72-; chmn, Munic Hist Dist Comn, Jersey City, NJ, currently; mem gov bd, Washington Square Art Outdoor Exhib, New York, currently. *Awards:* Patron of the Arts Award, Hudson Artists, Inc; Local Historians Award, League Hist Soc NJ, 81. *Mem:* Jersey City Mus Asn (pres, currently); Munic Art Soc; Nat Trust Hist Preservation; Nat Soc Lit & Arts. *Interests:* Collector paintings, etchings, prints, autograph letters and pictures. *Mailing Add:* Free Pub Libr Jersey City 472 Jersey Ave Jersey City NJ 07302

GRUPP, CARL ALF
PAINTER, PRINTMAKER
b Moorhead, Minn, Sept 11, 39. *Study:* Minneapolis Col Art & Design, BFA, 64; Vrije Acad, Netherlands, Vanderlip Scholar, 65; Ind Univ, MFA(with hons), 69; and with Rudy Pozzatti, Urban Couch, Marvin Lowe, William Bailey & James McGarrell. *Work:* Minneapolis Inst Art; Univ Minn Gallery, Minneapolis; Am Embassy, London; Chicago Art Inst; SDak Mem Art Ctr, Brookings. *Exhib:* Joslyn Art Mus 12th Biennial, Omaha, Nebr, 72; Pratt Graphic Art Exhib, New York, 72-73; Am Printmakers, Ind Univ, US Info Agency Tour Eng, 73; Drawings USA, Minn Mus Art, St Paul, 75; Boston Printmakers, 81; plus many others. *Teaching:* Teaching asst lithography, Minneapolis Col Art & Design, 64-65; teaching asst intaglio printmaking, Ind Univ, Bloomington, 68-69; asst prof art, Augustana Col, 69-81, assoc prof art, 81- *Awards:* Gustave Krollman Award for Draftsmanship, Minneapolis Col Art & Design, 63; Purchase Awards, SDak Mem Art Ctr, 73 & Silvermine Guild, New Canaan, Conn. *Bibliog:* Spotted talents in America, Frasconi, Grupp, Tendensen, 11/65; Craig Volk (auth), Art of Carl Grupp (video tape), KUSD-TV, Univ SDak, 3/75. *Media:* Oil. *Dealer:* Assoc American Artists 663 Fifth Ave New York NY 10022; Miriam Perlman Inc 505 N Lake Shore Dr Chicago IL 60611. *Mailing Add:* 1614 S Phillips Ave Sioux Falls SD 57105

GRUPPE, CHARLES
PAINTER
b New York, NY, July 1, 28. *Study:* Yale Univ; Nat Univ Mex; Columbia Univ, BFA, 54, MFA(Brevoort Fel), 55; Huntington Hartford Found, Pacific Palisades, 56. *Comn:* Paintings, Am Pres Lines, Coolidge, Jackson & Wilson, 65; Yale Divinity Sch, New Haven, Conn, 65; Dolly O'Brien Estate, Palm Beach, 64; First Nat Bank, New Haven, 65; Apt Complexes, Palm Beach, 72-73. *Exhib:* Silvermine Guild Artists, New Canaan, Conn, 65 & 77; Provincetown Art Asn, 65 & 77 & Rockport Art Asn, Mass, 70 & 77; Butler Mus Am Art, Youngstown, Ohio, 72 & 75; Lord & Taylor, New York, 75; Witte Mus, San Antonio, Tex. *Awards:* Bronze Medal & Purchase Award, Arthritis Found, 81; Frederic Waugh Mem Award, Provincetown, Mass, 83; Art & the Law Nat Competition Award, 83. *Media:* Oil. *Mailing Add:* PO Box 841 Old Lyme CT 06371

GRUSHKIN, PHILIP
DESIGNER, CALLIGRAPHER
b New York, NY, June 1, 21. *Study:* Cooper Union Art Sch, BFA. *Exhib:* Calligraphy, Grolier Club, 58; Art Dirs Club, 60; Int Calligraphy & Lettering, Brown Univ, 61; and many others. *Pos:* Cartographer, US Geol Survey, 42-43

& Off Strategic Serv, USA, 43-45; designer, World Publ Co, 55-56; designer, Harry N Abrams, Inc, 57-59, art dir, 59-, vpres, 60-69; pres, Philip Grushkin Inc, Englewood, NJ, 69- *Teaching:* Instr lettering, calligraphy & illus, Cooper Union Art Sch, 46-68; dir bk workshop, Radcliffe Col Publ Procedures & Harvard Summer Sch, Cambridge, Mass, 66-79; adj asst prof graphic design, NY Univ, 66-78. *Awards:* Cert of Excellence, Print for Com Exhib, Am Inst Graphic Arts, 50; and others. *Mem:* Grolier Club, NY; Am Printing Hist Asn (bd trustees, currently); Typophiles, NY. *Publ:* Publ & calligrapher, Aesop's Fables, 46; publ, Christmas Carols, 48; contribr, Bouquet for Bruce Rogers, 50; contribr, Calligraphics, 55; and others. *Mailing Add:* 86 E Linden Ave Englewood NJ 07631

GRUSKIN, MARY JOSEPHINE
DEALER
b Trani, Italy; US citizen. *Pos:* Dir, Midtown Galleries. *Specialty:* Contemporary American artists. *Mailing Add:* 11 E 57th St New York NY 10022

GRYGUTIS, BARBARA
CERAMIST
b Hartford, Conn, Nov 7, 46. *Study:* Univ Ariz, BFA, 68, MFA, 71. *Work:* Tucson Mus Art, Ariz; Tucson Sch Dist 1; Lannan Found, Mus Folk Art, Los Angeles, Calif. *Comn:* Mural, Kino Community Hosp, Tucson, Ariz, 77; 12 place settings, Senate Wives Luncheon, The White House, Washington, DC, 77; fountain, Cochise Col, Sierra Vista, Ariz, 78; mural for Revenue Bldg, State Capital, Phoenix, Ariz, 79; murals, Flagstaff City Hall, 83; and others. *Exhib:* Am Crafts at the White House, Renwick Gallery, Smithsonian Inst, Washington, DC, 76; Mus Contemp Crafts, New York, NY, 76; Everson Mus of Art, Syracuse, NY, 76; Landscape, New Views, Herbert Johnson Mus, Cornell Univ, Ithaca, NY, 78; Women Artists: Clay, Fiber, Metal, Bronx Mus, NY, 78; plus numerous others. *Pos:* Artist in residence, Tucson Sch Dist 1, 73; artist-in-residence, Haystack Mountain Sch Crafts, Deer Isle, Maine, 78. *Awards:* Nat Endowment Arts grants, 73-74 & 77; Pat Mutterer Mem Award & Group Show Award, Tucson Mus of Art, 76; Purchase Award, Eleventh Southwestern Invitational, Yuma Fine Arts Ctr, Ariz, 76; and others. *Bibliog:* Leon Nigrosh (auth), Clayworks, Davis Publ, 75; Adina Wingate (auth), article in Craft Horizons, 6/75 & article in Ceramics Monthly, 2/76; James Hepworth (auth), article, Artspace, summer 81. *Media:* Clay. *Dealer:* Dinnerware Artists Cooperative Gallery Tucson AZ. *Mailing Add:* 273 N Main Tucson AZ 85705

GUADAGNOLI, NELLO T
DEALER
b Walsenburg, Colo, Dec 16, 29. *Pos:* Owner/dir, Kiva Gallery. *Specialty:* Paintings by Indian artists. *Mailing Add:* c/o Kiva Gallery 202 W Hwy 66 Gallup NM 87301

GUALTIERI, JOSEPH P
MUSEUM DIRECTOR, PAINTER
b Royalton, Ill, Dec 25, 16. *Study:* Norwich Art Sch, Conn, dipl; Sch Art Inst Chicago, Ill, dipl. *Work:* Pa Acad Fine Arts, Philadelphia; Wadsworth Atheneum, Hartford, Conn; RI Sch Design Mus Fine Arts, Providence; Lyman Allyn Mus, New London, Conn; Slater Mem Mus, Norwich, Conn. *Comn:* Wall mural, New London Co Mutual Ins Co, Norwich, Conn; portrait of Gov John Dempsey, State of Conn. *Exhib:* Chicago Art Inst, Ill, 41; Pa Acad Fine Arts, Philadelphia, 48 & 51; Whitney Mus Am Art, New York, 52; Corcoran Gallery Art, Washington, DC; Nat Acad Design, New York; Albany Inst Hist & Art, NY; Wadsworth Atheneum, Hartford, Conn; Calif Palace of the Legion of Honor, Lincoln Park, San Francisco. *Collections Arranged:* Seven or eight arranged annually. *Pos:* Dir, Slater Mem Mus, Norwich, Conn, 62- *Teaching:* Art teacher oil painting, figure & portrait, The Norwich Free Acad, Conn, 43-79. *Awards:* First Prize & Logan Medal, Chicago Art Inst, 41; Purchase Prize, Pa Acad of Fine Arts, 48 & 51; Conn Artists Eastern States Expo Award, 51. *Mem:* Conn Acad Fine Arts Asn; Am Asn Mus; New Eng Conf, Am Asn Mus. *Media:* Oil, Mixed Media. *Mailing Add:* 60 Warren St Norwich CT 06360

GUASTELLA, C DENNIS
PAINTER, INSTRUCTOR
b Detroit, Mich, July 8, 47. *Study:* Macomb Co Community Col, 67; Wayne State Univ, BFA, 72; Eastern Mich Univ, MFA, 75. *Work:* Sheldon Mem Art Galleries, Univ Nebr, Lincoln; NDak Univ, Grand Forks; SDak Mem Art Ctr, Brookings. *Exhib:* Northwest Biennial III, SDak Mem Art Ctr, Brookings, 76; Biennial, Joslyn Art Mus, Omaha, Nebr, 76, 78 & 80; one-man shows, Sheldon Mem Art Galleries, Univ Nebr, Lincoln, 76 & Univ Mich, Slusser Gallery, Ann Arbor, 81; Mich Artists 80/81, Detroit Inst Arts & Flint Inst Arts, 81; and others. *Teaching:* Asst prof art, SDak State Univ, Brookings, 75-80; instr visual arts, Washtenaw Community Col, Ann Arbor, Mich, 80- *Awards:* Purchase Award, Rutgers Univ, Camden, NJ, 75; Best of Show/ Purchase Award, 16th Joslyn Biennial, Joslyn Art Mus, Omaha, Nebr, 80. *Bibliog:* Interview, Detroit Artist Monthly, 11/77; Mike Odom (auth), Exhibit Reflexs 80's Mood, Uno Gateway, Univ Nebr, 1/23/81; Robert Igelhardt (auth), Close examination, distance needed to appreciate works, Ann Arbor News, 8/9/81. *Mem:* Col Art Asn; Midwest Col Art Asn. *Media:* Acrylic, String. *Mailing Add:* 1165 Carol Plymouth MI 48170

GUAY, NANCY ALLEN
TAPESTRY ARTIST, SCULPTOR
b Salem, Mass, Aug 21, 45. *Study:* Haystack Mountain Sch, 63, 67 & 76; Skidmore Col, BS(art), 67; Univ Wis-Madison, MA, 74, MFA, 76. *Work:* Mus Mod Art, New York; Stedelijk Mus, Amsterdam, Holland. *Exhib:* Wall Hangings: The New Classicism, Mus Mod Art, New York, 77; The Art Fabric: Mainstream, San Francisco Mus Mod Art, 81; Collections from the Mus, Stedelijk Mus, Amsterdam, 81; IV Textile Triennale, Central Mus Textiles, Lode, Poland, 81; Contemporary International Textile Art, Inst Kunstlerishe Textilgestaltung, Linz & Vienna, Austria, 81; Fiber Art: An Uncommon Thread, Mod Master Tapestries, New York, 81; The Jacquard Loom, Cooper-Hewitt Mus, New York, 82. *Teaching:* Instr textiles, Rhode Island Sch Design, 79-80. *Awards:* Finnish Govt Grant, 75; Fels, Am-Scandinavian Found, 75 & Artists Found, Boston, 79. *Media:* Fibers; Wood. *Dealer:* Mod Masters Gallery 11 E 57th St New York NY 11201. *Mailing Add:* 195 Congress St Brooklyn NY 11201

GUBERMAN, SIDNEY THOMAS
PAINTER, SCULPTOR
b Greenville, SC, Aug 24, 36. *Study:* Princeton Univ, with Stephen Greene, BA, 58; Univ Pa, with Robert Venturi, MA(archit), 67. *Work:* Nat Mus Am Art, Corcoran Gallery Art, Washington, DC; High Mus Art, Atlanta; Princeton Univ Art Mus; Birmingham Mus Art; and others. *Exhib:* One-man show, Greenville Co Mus, SC, 76 & Princeton Univ Art Mus, 83; William Seitz Mem, Princeton Univ Art Mus, NJ, 77; Artists in Ga, High Mus, Atlanta, 80 & 82; Small Sculpture, Del Mar Col, Corpus Christi, Tex, 81 & 83; Birmingham Biennial, 83. *Pos:* Exhib dir, Govt Services Savings & Loan, 76-79. *Teaching:* Prof painting, l'Ecole Cantonale Beaux Arts, Lausanne, Switz, 71-73; asst prof drawing, l'Ecole Polytech Fedn Lausanne, Switz, 73-75; vis lectr painting, Princeton Univ, NJ, 81-82. *Awards:* Individual Artist's Grant, Nat Endowment Arts, 80-81. *Bibliog:* Benjamin Forgey (auth), An exhilerating abstract painter, Washington Star, 10/78; Mary Swift (auth), Sidney Guberman, Art Voices South, 4/80; Iris Welch (auth), Sidney Guberman, Art Papers, 8/82. *Mem:* College Art Asn. *Media:* Oil, Acrylic; Steel, Wood. *Publ:* Auth, Frank Stella's polar coordinate series, Art Papers, 2/82. *Dealer:* Fay Gold 3221 Cains Hill Pl Atlanta GA 30305. *Mailing Add:* 3731 Stonewall Drive NW Atlanta GA 30339

GUDERNA, LADISLAV
PAINTER, ILLUSTRATOR
b Nitra, Czech, June 1, 21; Can citizen. *Study:* Tech Acad, Bratislava, Czech; Acad Creative Arts, Belgrade. *Work:* Nat Gallery, Prague; Nat Gallery, Bratislava; plus pvt collections in Czech, Holland, Venezuela, US, Ger, Can, Switz & Italy. *Exhib:* Exhibs in Zurich, New York, Vienna, Toronto & Ottawa, 75-77; Move Gallery, Vancouver; Galeria Ambito, Madrid, 80; XVI Biennial, Sao Paulo, 81; Canada House, London, Eng, 82. *Awards:* Gold & Silver Medal for Display, Expo '57; First Prize for Best Stamp, Ministry of Telecommunications, Prague, 65; Gold Medal for Paneau, Int Stamps Exhib, Prague, 67. *Bibliog:* Articles in Art Diary, Milan, Italy, 78 & Scarabeus, Toronto, 79; two portfolios in Gallery Press, Toronto, 78-79. *Media:* Tempera, Oils; Graphics. *Mailing Add:* 1234 Barclay St Apt 1207 Vancouver BC V6E 1H4 Canada

GUENTHER, PETER W
HISTORIAN
b Dresden, Ger, Mar 29, 20; US citizen. *Study:* Univ Breslau; Acad Fine Arts, Stuttgart, Ger; Univ Tex, Austin, MA & PhD. *Collections Arranged:* Edvard Munch (auth, catalog), Sarah Campbell Blaffer Gallery, Univ Houston, New Orleans, San Antonio & Dallas; German Expressionism, Toward a New Humanism (auth, catalog), Sarah Campbell Blaffer Gallery, Univ Houston. *Teaching:* Prof art, Univ Houston, 62-, chmn dept art, 62-72. *Awards:* Teaching Excellence Award, Univ Houston, 70; Master Teacher Award, Col Humanities & Fine Arts, Univ Houston, 82. *Mem:* Col Art Asn Am; Tex Asn Sch Arts (pres, 71-73); SCent Renaissance Conf (pres, 73); SCent Mod Lang Asn; Mid-Am Art Hist Asn. *Res:* Northern Renaissance; iconography; German expressionism. *Publ:* Auth, Destruction of Art Works During the Reformation, Renaissance Explor, 77; Renaissance and mannerism north of the Alps, In: Encycl World Art, suppl vol 18; Der junge Felixmüller, German Nat Mus, Nuremberg, 82. *Mailing Add:* 10013 Hazelhurst Houston TX 77080

GUERIN, JOHN WILLIAM
PAINTER, EDUCATOR
b Houghton, Mich, Aug 29, 20. *Study:* Am Acad Art, Chicago; Art Students League; Escuela Bellas Artes, San Miguel, Mex; Colorado Springs Fine Arts Ctr. *Work:* Dallas Mus Fine Arts; Chrysler Mus, Provincetown, Mass; Joslyn Art Mus, Omaha, Nebr; Colorado Springs Fine Arts Ctr; Houston Mus Fine Arts; and others. *Exhib:* One-man shows, Kraushaar Gallery, New York, 59, 63 & 68; Galeria Realities, Taos, NMex, 60; Corcoran Gallery Art, 61; Whitney Mus Am Art, New York; retrospective, Ft Worth Art Ctr, 64; and others. *Teaching:* Instr painting, Dallas Mus Fine Arts, 50-52; prof art, Univ Tex, Austin, 53-80, prof emer, 80-; artist in residence, Skowhegan Sch Painting & Sculpture, 60. *Awards:* Am Acad Arts & Lett Grant, 59; Univ Tex Res Inst Grant, 60 & 66; Ford Found Grant, 79; and others. *Mem:* Tex Fine Arts Asn; life mem Art Students League; assoc elect Nat Acad Design. *Dealer:* Carlin Galleries 710 Montgomery St Ft Worth TX 76107. *Mailing Add:* 3400 Stoneridge Rd Austin TX 78746

GUERRERO, JOSE
PAINTER, PRINTMAKER
b Granada, Spain, 1914; US citizen. *Study:* Escuela Superior Bellas Artes San Fernando, Madrid, Spain, 40-44; Ecole Beaux-Arts, Paris, 45-46. *Work:* Guggenheim Mus, Whitney Mus Am Art, New York; Art Inst Chicago; Calif Palace Legion Hon; Albright-Knox Art Gallery; and others. *Exhib:* Whitney Mus Am Art Ann, 58, 62 & 69; solo exhibs, Gruenebaum Gallery, New York, 78 & 80; retrospectives, Edificio Arbos, Madrid, 80 & Fundacion Miro,

Barcelona, 81; De Falla Cult Ctr, Granada, 81; Madrid Int Fair, 82; and others. *Teaching:* Instr painting, New Sch Social Res, 62-65; vis artist, Cleveland Art Inst, 74 & Iowa State Univ, 78. *Awards:* Graham Found Advan Studies in Fine Arts Grant, 59; Official Cross of Isabel La Catolica, Spain, 78; Officer, Order Arts & Lett, Fr Govt, 80. *Bibliog:* Alberto Portera (producer), Jose Guerrero Painter (film), Madrid, 70; Paintings & sculpture, Crucible Mag, 70; monogr, Jose Guerrero, Juana Mordo Gallery, 76. *Media:* Oil. *Dealer:* Gruenebaum Gallery 38 E 57th St New York NY 10021; Juana Mordo Gallery Costello 7 Madrid Spain. *Mailing Add:* 406 W 20th St New York NY 10011

GUERRIERO, HENRY E See Clef, Roman A

GUILMAIN, JACQUES
HISTORIAN, EDUCATOR
b Brussels, Belg, Oct 15, 26; US citizen. *Study:* Queens Col, City Univ New York, BS, 48; Columbia Univ, MA, 52, univ fel, 57, PhD, 58, and with Meyer Schapiro. *Teaching:* Vis asst prof hist art, Stanford Univ, 58-59; vis asst prof, Univ Calif, Riverside, 59-60; instr, Queens Col, 60-63; from asst prof to prof art hist, State Univ NY Stony Brook, 63-, chmn art dept, 70-76; vis prof, Columbia Univ, 68 & 70. *Awards:* Am Philosophical Soc Grant, 60; State Univ NY Res Found Grant, 64-79; and others. *Mem:* Col Art Asn Am; Int Ctr Medieval Art; Medieval Acad Am. *Res:* Early Medieval ornaments; Mozarabic manuscript illumination; Carolingian manuscript illumination; early Medieval metalwork. *Publ:* Contrib, American Watercolors, Drawings & Prints, 1952, Metrop Mus Art, New York; auth, Zoomorphic decoration and the problem of the sources of Mozarabic illumination, XXXV 60 & Illuminations of the Second Bible of Charles the Bald, XLI 66, Speculum; auth, Observations on some early interlace initials and frame ornaments in Mozarabic manuscripts of Leon-Castile, Scriptorium, XV, 61; auth, Enigmatic beasts of the Lindau Gospels lower cover, Gesta, X, 71; auth, On the chronological development and classification of decorated initials in Latin manuscripts of 10th century Spain, LXIII 81, Bulletin, John Rylands Univ Libr, Manchester; and others. *Mailing Add:* PO Box 363 Setauket NY 11733

GULLY, ANTHONY LACY
HISTORIAN, ADMINISTRATOR
b Orange, Calif, Feb 28, 38. *Study:* Univ Calif, Riverside, BA; Univ Calif, Berkeley, MA; Stanford Univ, PhD; with Jean Boggs, Jean Bony, Walter Horn, Lorenz Eitner & Albert Elsen. *Teaching:* Instr 17th-18th century art hist, Pomona Col, Claremont, Calif, 65-66; asst prof 19th-20th century art hist, Calif State Univ, Los Angeles, 66-68; assoc prof 18th-19th century art hist, Ariz State Univ, Tempe, 72-83, asst dean col fine arts, 81-, chair grad humanities prog, 83-84; vis prof, Stanford Univ, 81. *Awards:* Nat Defense Educ Act Award, Stanford Univ, 68-71; Mabel McLeod Fel, Rowlandson Study, London, Stanford Univ, 71-72; Nat Endowment Humanities Award, Yale Univ, 76; and others. *Bibliog:* J Hayes (auth), Rowlandson, Phaidon Art Bks, 72; R Paulsen (auth), Rowlandson: New interpretation, Yale Univ, 72; R Wark (auth), Rowlandson drawings in Huntington Libr, 75. *Mem:* Col Art Asn; Mid-Am Col Art Asn; Rocky Mountain Conf on Brit Studies (pres, 78-79); Nat Conf Brit Studies; Pacific Conf on Brit Studies. *Res:* Nineteenth century British art; John Sell Cotman, 1782-1842. *Publ:* Auth, Book reviews on eighteenth century art and aesthetics, Current Bibliog: 18th Century, 76; auth, Mr B and the cherubim: William Blake's descriptive catalog, 78, An unpublished sketchbook by Rowlandson, 79 & Milton's unholy trinity, 81, Phoebus; auth, Source of Goya's May 3, 1808, In: Studies in Iconography, 83. *Mailing Add:* 2618 S Country Club Way Tempe AZ 85282

GUMBERTS, WILLIAM A
COLLECTOR, PATRON
b Evansville, Ind, May 21, 1912. *Study:* Harvard Univ; Ohio State Univ. *Pos:* Bd dirs, Evansville Pub Mus, currently. *Mem:* Ind Arts Comn; charter mem Evansville Arts & Educ. *Collection:* Nineteenth century American oils; etchings of classical periods; moderns. *Mailing Add:* 3701 Washington Ave Evansville IN 47715

GUMMELT, SAMUEL
PAINTER
b Waco, Tex, Aug 28, 44. *Study:* NTex State Univ, BA, 68; Southern Methodist Univ, MFA, 71. *Work:* Dallas Mus Fine Arts; Am Tel & Tel, Chicago. *Exhib:* Proj South/Southwest, 71 & Focus: Sam Gummelt, 79, Ft Worth Art Mus; Interchange, Dallas Mus Fine Art, 72 & Walker Art Ctr, Minneapolis, 73; Exchange, Ft Worth Art Mus, 75 & San Francisco Mus Mod Art, 76; Recent Works on Paper by Contemp Am Artists, Madison Art Ctr, Wis, 77; Projects: Sam Gummelt, Art Mus STex, Corpus Christi, 78; Am Drawing in Black & White 1970-1980, Brooklyn Mus, NY, 80. *Awards:* Purchase Awards, 4th Ann Prints & Drawing Exhib, Ark Art Ctr, 70, 35th Tarrant Co Ann, Ft Worth Art Ctr, 73 & Tex Invitational, Beaumont Art Mus, 78. *Bibliog:* Jan Butterfield (auth), The young Texans: The phenomenon of interstitial art on America's last frontier, Arts Mag, 73; Jozanne Rabyor (auth), article, Art in Am, 74; Susan Platt (auth), Reviews: Houston, Art Forum, 79. *Media:* Oil & Wax on Canvas. *Dealer:* Janie C Lee Gallery 2304 Bissonnet Houston TX 77005. *Mailing Add:* 5909 Palo Pinto Dallas TX 75206

GUMMER, DON
SCULPTOR
b Louisville, Ky, 1946. *Study:* John Herron Art Inst, Indianapolis, 64-66; Sch Mus Fine Arts, Boston, 66-70; Yale Univ Sch Fine Arts, New Haven, BFA, 71, MFA, 73. *Work:* McCrary Corp & Chase Manhattan Bank collection, New York; HHK Found Contemp Art, Milwaukee; Commodities Corp,

Princeton, NJ. *Comn:* Interpretations 79, comn by Castle Clinton/Manhattan Cult Coun, Battery Park, NY, 79; outdoor installations, Dag Hammerskjold Plaza, 80 & Joseph E Seagram & Sons, 82, New York. *Exhib:* Eight Sculptors, Albright-Knox Art Gallery, Buffalo, NY, 79; Current/New York, Joe & Emily Lowe Art Gallery, Syracuse Univ, NY, 80; one-man show, Akron Art Mus, Ohio, 80; New Visions, Aldrich Mus Contemp Art, Ridgefield, Conn, 81; Artists Return to Artists Space, NY, 81; Chicago Arts Club, 82; and others. *Awards:* Grant, Nat Endowment Arts, 76; grant, Tiffany Found, 78; grant, Creative Artists Pub Serv Prog, 79. *Bibliog:* Margaret Sheffield (auth), Don Gummer, Castle Clinton, Artforum, 1/80; Phyllis Tuchman, Don Gummer, Art Am, 2/80; Carolyn K Carr (auth), An interview with Don Gummer, Dialogue, 11-12/80. *Media:* Wood, Stone. *Mailing Add:* c/o Sperone Westwater Fischer 142 Greene St New York NY 10012

GUMPEL, HUGH
PAINTER
b New York, NY, Feb 3, 26. *Study:* Columbia Univ; Art Students League. *Comn:* Mural, State of NY Pub Works Admin Bldg, 63. *Teaching:* Instr painting, Nat Acad Sch Fine Arts, 59-; instr watercolor, State Univ New York, Purchase, Westchester Art Workshop. *Awards:* Gold Medal of Honor, Am Watercolor Soc, 59. *Mem:* Nat Acad Design; Am Watercolor Soc. *Media:* Watercolor. *Mailing Add:* c/o Nat Acad Fine Arts 5 E 89th St New York NY 10028

GUMPERT, GUNTHER
PAINTER
b Krefeld, Ger, Apr 17, 19; US citizen. *Study:* Sch Fine Arts Krefeld; Sch Fine Arts, Wuppertal. *Work:* Metrop Mus Art, New York; Denver Art Mus, Colo; Phillips Collection, Washington DC; Victoria & Albert Mus, London; Albertina, Vienna, Austria; and others. *Comn:* Mural, Inter-Am Develop Bank, Washington, DC, 68. *Exhib:* Kaiser-Wilhelm Mus, 48, 49 & 52; Salon Realites Nouvelles, Paris, 58-60 & 62; Int Exhib Abstr Art, Pistoia, 61; Int Exhib Contemp Art, London, 62; Salon Mai, Paris, 62; and others. *Bibliog:* Jean Grenier (auth), Gumpert, Preuves, Paris, 60; Victor Summa (auth), Gumpert & The Evolution of His Art (film), Educ TV Asn, 63; Willy Huppert (auth), Gunther Gumpert, Kunst-und Kunstgewerbe Verein, Pforzheim, 64. *Dealer:* Franz Bader Gallery 2001 Eye St NW Washington DC 20006; Francine Seders Gallery 6701 Greenwood Ave N Seattle WA 98103. *Mailing Add:* 3752 McKinley St NW Washington DC 20015

GUNASINGHE, SIRI
EDUCATOR, HISTORIAN
b Ruanwella, Sri Lanka, Feb 20, 25. *Study:* Univ Ceylon, BA, 48; Univ Paris, Doctorate, 55. *Teaching:* Instr sanskrit, Univ Ceylon, 48-70; prof, Univ Victoria, BC, 70- *Awards:* Arts Fel, Govt Ceylon, 48; Fel, Rockefeller Found, 62; Sr Specialist, Univ Hawaii, 68. *Res:* History of Buddhist and Hindu art in India, Sri Lanka and Southeast Asia. *Publ:* Auth, La Technique de la Peinture Indienne, Univ Press France, 56; auth, Masks of Ceylon, Dept Cult Affairs, Colombo, 63; auth, Album of Buddhist Paintings from Sri Lanka, Nat Mus, Colombo, 78. *Mailing Add:* Dept Visual Arts Univ Victoria Victoria BC V8W 2Y2 Canada

GUNDELFINGER, JOHN ANDRE
PAINTER, COLLAGE ARTIST
b St Die, France, Oct 3, 37; US citizen. *Study:* Sch of Visual Arts, New York; NY Univ. *Work:* Chase Manhattan Bank, New York; Sara Roby Found; Int Bus Machines; Am Tel & Tel Co; Mus Fine Arts, Caracas, Venezuela. *Exhib:* One-man show, Sneed-Hillman Gallery, Rockford, Ill, 77; Am Drawing 1970-73, Yale Univ Art Gallery, 73; Galerie Stevenson et Palluel, Paris, France, 76; Weatherspoon Art Gallery, Univ NC, Greensboro, 77; Nightfall, Del River Valley, A M Sachs Gallery, New York, 81; and others. *Teaching:* Instr painting & drawing, Sch of Visual Arts, New York, 63- & Parsons Sch of Design, New York, 71- *Bibliog:* John Bernard Myers (auth), The Gouaches of John Gundelfinger, Sachs Gallery Publ, 75 & Recent Paintings--John Gundelfinger, Sachs Gallery & Art Inst Mag, Fall 77. *Media:* Oil, Gouache. *Mailing Add:* 10 White St New York NY 10013

GUNDERSHEIMER, HERMAN (SAMUEL)
HISTORIAN, EDUCATOR
b Würzburg, Ger, Apr 25, 03; US citizen. *Study:* Univ Munich; Univ Würzburg; Univ Berlin; Univ Leipzig, PhD, 26. *Pos:* Cur, Mus Ulm/Danube, Kunstgewerbe Mus, Frankfurt, Ger, 27-33; dir, Rothschild Mus, Frankfurt, 33-39. *Teaching:* From asst prof to prof art hist, Temple Univ, 41-70, prof & dir Temple Abroad, Tyler Sch Art, Rome, Italy, 70-73; guest prof, Univ Tel-Aviv, Israel, 73-74; prof, LaSalle Col, Philadelphia, 75- *Awards:* Lindbach Award for excellent teaching. *Mem:* Col Art Asn Am; hon mem Cambridge Art Soc, England; Renaissance Soc Am. *Res:* Renaissance and Baroque art; Jewish ceremonial art. *Collection:* American furniture, Piranesi and contemporary graphics. *Publ:* Contrib to journals & magazines & contributing editor to encyclopedias. *Mailing Add:* 1500 Locust St Apt 3305 Philadelphia PA 19102

GUNDERSON, BARRY L
SCULPTOR
b Baird, Tex, Feb 9, 45. *Study:* Augsburg Col, Minneapolis, BA; Univ NDak, Grand Forks; Univ Colo, Boulder, MFA. *Work:* Ball State Univ, Muncie, Ind; Minot State Col, NDak; Normandale Jr Col, Minneapolis; Augsburg Col, Minneapolis. *Comn:* Large outdoor sculptures, Kenyon Col, Gambier, Ohio, 77 & Downtown Plaza, Portsmouth, 79. *Exhib:* Colo Biennial, 71 & Denver Metrop, 72, Denver Art Mus; Drawings USA, Minn Mus Art, 75 & 77; Ceramic & Sculpture Exhibs, Butler Inst Am Art, Youngstown, Ohio, 76 &

77; 10th Dulin Nat Print & Drawing Competition, Dulin Art Mus, Knoxville, Tenn, 76; one-man show, Ohio Wesleyan Univ, Del, 77. *Teaching:* Asst prof sculpture, Kenyon Col, 74-, chmn dept, currently. *Mem:* Col Art Asn. *Mailing Add:* Box 515 Gambier OH 43022

GUNN, PAUL JAMES
PAINTER, EDUCATOR
b Guys Mills, Pa, June 21, 22. *Study:* Edinboro State Teachers Col, BS, 47; Calif Col Arts & Crafts, MFA, 48; wood block printing with Hideo Hagiwara, Tokyo, Japan, 61-62. *Work:* Portland Art Mus; Seattle Art Mus; Am Info Serv, Athens, Greece; Bibliot Nat, Paris, France; Victoria & Albert Mus, London, Eng. *Exhib:* Int Bordighera Biennial, Italy; Bay Printmakers Second Ann, Oakland Art Mus, Calif; Ann Northwest Artists, Seattle Art Mus; Western Artists Ann, Denver Art Mus; Ore Artists Ann, Portland Art Mus. *Pos:* Resident dir, Japan Studies Prog, Ore Study Ctr, Waseda Univ, Japan, 72-74. *Teaching:* Prof painting & printmaking, Ore State Univ, 48-, chmn dept art, 64-72. *Media:* Oil. *Mailing Add:* Dept of Art Ore State Univ Corvallis OR 97331

GUNSHOR, RUTH
PAINTER, INSTRUCTOR
b Brooklyn, NY. *Study:* Brooklyn Col, 51-53; Brooklyn Mus Art Sch, with Reuban Tam, Louis Finklestein & Fred Farr, merit scholar, 54-57; Educ Alliance Art Sch, with Alex Dopkin, merit scholar, 57-59. *Exhib:* Riverside Mus, New York, 62; Brooklyn Mus, NY, 69, 71, 72, 74 & 80; Nat Acad Design, New York, 71-78; Nat Arts Club, New York, 74 & 76-79; Saginaw Art Mus, Mich, 76; Cayuga Mus, Auburn, NY, 80; and others. *Teaching:* Instr fine arts, Adult Educ, New York City Bd Educ, 68-77. *Awards:* Jean Magio Leeman Mem Prize, 80; Gehner Watercolor Prize, 81; Ralph Mayer Mem Prize, Nat Asn Women Artists, 83. *Bibliog:* Sidney Tillim (auth), In the galleries, Arts Mag, 10/59; Dorothy Hall (auth), Art and artists, Park E, 3/73 & 4/79; Hirsch (auth), In the galleries, Westsider, 2/80. *Mem:* Am Soc Contemp Artists (bd dirs, 79-82); Contemp Artists Guild (vpres, 81-); Nat Asn Women Artists; New York Artists Equity Asn (bd dirs, 73-77); New York Soc Women Artists (bd dirs, 78-). *Media:* Acrylic, Watercolor. *Mailing Add:* 3820 Lyme Ave Brooklyn NY 11224

GUNTER, FRANK ELLIOTT
PAINTER, EDUCATOR
b Jasper, Ala, May 8, 34. *Study:* Univ Ala, BFA; Fla State Univ, MA. *Work:* Sheldon Swope Gallery, Terre Haute, Ind; Evansville Mus Arts & Sci, Ind; Ill State Mus, Springfield; Birmingham Mus Art, Ala; St Paul Art Ctr, Minn. *Comn:* Painting, Rochester State Bank, Ill, 74; painting of facade, Bank of Ind, Merrillville, 75. *Exhib:* Cult Ctr for Am Embassy, Paris, 71; Mus Art, Besancon, France, 72; Am Libr, Brussels, Belg, 73; Maison Descartes, Amsterdam, 73; Varieties of Visual Reality, Northern Ariz State Univ, 75; Am Exhib, Krannert Art Mus, Univ Ill, Urbana, 77. *Teaching:* Instr art, Birmingham Pub Schs, Ala, 56-58; asst prof art, Murray State Univ, 60-62; prof art, Univ Ill, Urbana-Champaign, 62-, chmn, Painting Programs. *Awards:* Second Award for Painting, Soc Four Arts, 73; Purchase Awards, Wabash Valley Ann, Terre Haute, 74 & Union League Club, Chicago, 74. *Bibliog:* Stephen Spector (auth), Super realists, Architectural Dig, 11/12/74; G A Rodetis (auth), Varieties of visual reality, Northern Ariz Univ Art Gallery 1-3/75. *Media:* Acrylic on canvas. *Dealer:* Joy Horwich Gallery 226 E Ontario St Chicago IL 60611. *Mailing Add:* 806 S Elm Blvd Champaign IL 61820

GUREWITSCH, EDNA P
DEALER, HISTORIAN
b New York, NY. *Study:* Pratt Inst; NY Univ, BA & Inst Fine Arts, with Richard Offner, Walter Friedlaender, Erwin Panofsky & Jose Lopez-Rey; Columbia Univ, MAEd. *Pos:* Vpres E & A Silberman Galleries, Inc, New York, 53-61; pres, E P Gurewitsch Works of Art Inc, New York, 73-. *Specialty:* Twentieth century European and American painting and sculpture. *Interests:* Formed collection for Rehabilitation Dept, Columbia Presbyterian Hosp, New York. *Mailing Add:* 55 E 74th St New York NY 10021

GURNEY, GEORGE
HISTORIAN, CONSULTANT
b Sharon, Conn, Nov 26, 39. *Study:* Brown Univ, BA, 62; Univ Pa, MA, 65; Univ Del, PhD, 78. *Collections Arranged:* Nineteenth Century Sculpture (auth, catalog), Nat Gallery Art, 74; Sculpture and the Federal Triangle, Nat Collection Fine Arts, 79. *Pos:* Guest cur, Nat Mus Am Art, Washington, DC, 77-82. *Teaching:* Teaching asst art hist, Univ Pa, Philadelphia, 64-65; instr art hist, Univ Hartford, Conn, 65-66 & Sweet Briar Col, Va, 66-69. *Awards:* Nat Gallery Art Samuel H Kress Fel, 73-74; Nat Mus Am Art Smithsonian Res Fel, 74-75. *Mem:* Col Art Asn Am; Soc Archit Historians; Nat Sculpture Soc. *Res:* Nineteenth and twentieth century American sculpture. *Publ:* Contribr, Sculpture of a City: Philadelphia's Treasures in Bronze and Stone, Walker & Co, 74; contribr, Sculpture and the Federal Traingle, Nat Sculpture Rev, 79; contribr, Cast and Recast: The Sculpture of Frederic Remington, Smithsonian Press, 81. *Mailing Add:* 2023 N Taylor St Arlington VA 22207

GURNEY, SUSAN ROTHWELL
LIBRARIAN
b Rockville Centre, NY, Nov 19, 51. *Study:* Conn Col, BA(art hist), 74; Univ Md, MLS, 80. *Pos:* Reference librn, Nat Mus Am Art/Nat Portrait Gallery Libr, Smithsonian Inst, 80-81, acting librn, 81-82, asst librn, 82- *Mem:* Art Libr Soc NAm (chap treas, 81); Col Art Asn. *Res:* Art serials and little magazines. *Interests:* American art. *Publ:* Auth, Bibliography of little magazines in the visual arts in the USA, Art Libr J, 81; coauth, Art Serials; Union List ..., Washington Art libr Resources Comt, 81. *Mailing Add:* Nat Mus Am Art/Nat Portrait Gallery Libr Smithsonian Inst Washington DC 20560

GURR, LENA
PAINTER, PRINTMAKER
b Brooklyn, NY, Oct 27, 1897. *Study:* Maxwell Training Sch Teachers, dipl, 17; Educ Alliance, New York, 19; Art Students League, study with John Sloan & Maurice Stern, two scholars, 20-22. *Work:* Metrop Mus Art, New York; Brasenose Col, Oxford, Eng; Smithsonian Inst, Libr Cong, Washington, DC; Brooklyn Mus, NY; and many others. *Exhib:* Painting in the USA, Carnegie Inst, Pittsburgh, 45 & 51; Contemporary American Sculpture, Watercolors & Drawings, Whitney Mus Am Art, New York, 53; Am Acad Arts & Lett, 58, 65, 66 & 69; 37 Contemporary Americans, Nat Coun Women, IBM Corp, 60; Art in Embassies Prog from ACA Galleries, Athens, Greece, 66-68. *Awards:* Medal of Honor, 54 & 61 & Marcia Brady Tucker Prize, 61, Nat Asn Women Artists; Jersey City Mus Medal, NJ Painters & Sculptors Soc, 69; and many others. *Bibliog:* Elizabeth Lips (auth), Artist Lena Gurr says studio should be neat like office, Brooklyn Eagle, 51; Frank Crotty (auth), Paints big city & Cape Cod scenes, Worcester Sun Telegram, 60. *Mem:* Artists Equity Asn New York (rec secy, 53, bd dirs, 63-65, vpres, 66-74); Nat Asn Women Artists; Soc Am Graphic Artists (mem coun, 67-68); Painters & Sculptors Soc NJ; Am Soc Contemp Artists; and many others. *Media:* Oil, Casein. *Dealer:* ACA Gallery 25 E 73rd St New York NY 10021. *Mailing Add:* 71 Remsen Ave Brooklyn NY 11212

GURRIA, ANGELA
SCULPTOR, STAINED GLASS ARTIST
b Mexico City, Mex. *Study:* Univ Mex, LittD; Mexico City Col; and with German Cueto. *Work:* Mus Mod Art, Mexico City; UN Orgn, New York. *Comn:* fountain, Unidad Popular, Acapulco, 70; obra oculta, Cent Dept, Tenayuca, Mex, 75; Esulltura Hotel, Presidente Chapultepec, Mex, 77; Citibank, Mex, 79; stained glass, Monterrey, Mexico, 81; and others. *Exhib:* Escultura Mexicana Contemp, Alameda, Mex, 60; Biennial Mexicana de Escultura, Mus Mod Art, Mexico City, 64 & 67; Contoy Isla de Caribe, 74; El Bosque, Fraccionamiento, Mex, 80; Angela Gurria, Palacio Bellas Artes, Mexico, 70. *Teaching:* Instr sculpture, Ibero-American Univ, Mex, 61-62; instr sculpture, Univ of the Americas, 62-63. *Awards:* First Prize, Escultura Integrada Arquitectura, 67; Women in the Arts Prize, Mex Inst Art, 64. *Bibliog:* Juan O'Gorman (auth), Angela Gurria, Mex Acad Arts, 74; Angela Gurria--Vitrales;; Piedras Vivas II, Mario Monteforte, Toledo. *Mem:* Mex Acad Arts. *Media:* Stone, Bronze. *Mailing Add:* Francisco Sosa 369 Coyoacan Mexico DF Mexico

GURSOY, AHMET
PAINTER
b Turkey, Mar 5, 29; US citizen. *Study:* Tech Univ Istanbul, Turkey, 47-52; Ill Inst Technol, 54-56; Art Students League, 58-63. *Work:* Chase Manhattan Bank; Cornell Univ; St Lawrence Univ; Grey Gallery, NY Univ; Ulrich Mus, Wichita, Kans. *Exhib:* Wells Col, Aurora, NY, 77; Niagara Arts Ctr, Niagara Falls, NY, 77; Mohawk Valley Community Col, Utica, NY, 77; Nassau Community Col, Garden City, NY, 77; Hyden Collection, Glen Falls, NY, 77; and many others. *Awards:* Painting Prize, 21st Ann New Eng Exhib, Silvermine, Conn, 70. *Bibliog:* Grace Glueck (auth), article, New York Times, 68; C Giuliano (auth), article, 68 & Gordon Brown (auth), article, 70, Arts Mag. *Mem:* Fedn Mod Painters & Sculptors (pres, 75-); Silvermine Guild Artists; Music for People (treas, 71-72). *Media:* Oil. *Publ:* Auth, Convergence of Engineering & Art, 70. *Mailing Add:* 490 Bellwood Ave North Tarrytown NY 10593

GUSELLA, ERNEST
VIDEO ARTIST
b Calgary, Alta, Can, Sept 13, 41. *Study:* Alberta Col Art, dipl; Art Student League; San Francisco Art Inst, BFA & MFA; Workshop in Mod Music Compos, State Univ New York, Buffalo, with John Cage. *Work:* Ctr Cult Canadien, Paris; Palais Des Beaux-Arts, Brussels; Mus Mod Art, New York; Tokyo Nat Univ; Neuer Berliner Kunstverein, Berlin, West Germany. *Exhib:* Stichting Kijhuis, The Hague, 81; Int Cult Ctr, Antwerp, 81; Musee D'Ixelles, Brussels, 81; Mus Mod Art, Liege, Belgium; Anthology Film Arch, New York, 82. *Teaching:* Lectr art hist, City Univ New York, 73-75; lectr film & drawing, Rutgers Univ, Newark, NJ, 74-77. *Awards:* Nat Endowment Arts Video Grant, 80-81; Guggenheim Found Fel, 82-83; Production Award, Montbelliard Video Festival, 83. *Bibliog:* Featured artist, Atlanta Video Festival, Atlanta Cable TV, 83; featured artist, Video Art, ABC Nightly News Broadcast, 83; featured artist, USA Cable Network, 83. *Mem:* Artists Equity; Assoc Independent Film & Video Makers. *Media:* Video, Performance. *Publ:* Contrib, Kunst Und Video Book, Dumont Buchverlag, Koln, 83. *Dealer:* Peter Nower Gallery Zurich Switzerland; Stiching Kijkhuis The Hague. *Mailing Add:* 118 Forsyth St Fourth Floor New York NY 10002

GUSSOW, ALAN
PAINTER, SCULPTOR
b Bronx, NY, May 8, 31. *Study:* Middlebury Col, BA, 52; Cooper Union, 52-53; Atelier 17 Graphic Workshop, 52-53. *Work:* Portland Mus Fine Art, Maine; Guild Hall, Easthampton, NY; Sheldon Mem Art Gallery, Lincoln, Nebr; Corcoran Gallery Art, Washington, DC; Montgomery Mus Fine Art, Ala. *Exhib:* A Sense of Place, Joslyn Art Mus & Sheldon Mem Art Gallery, Nebr, 73; Paintings of the Delaware Water Gap, Corcoran Art Gallery, Washington, DC, 75; Life Yard Project, Rockland Lake, NY, Santa Cruz, San Francisco, Minneapolis, Pittsfield, MA, 82; Shadow Project, New York, 82; Eight Sensibilities, Thorpe-Intermedia Gallery, Sparkhill, NY, 82; Common Ground, Gallery Am Indian Community House, New York, 83; Sea Strand Project, Dir, Huntington, New York, 83; and others. *Pos:* Consult arts, Nat Park Serv, US Dept Interior, 70- *Teaching:* Instr painting & drawing, Parsons Sch Design, 56-68, chmn dept, 59-68; instr painting & drawing, Sarah

Lawrence Col, 58-59; vis critic & lectr, Ohio State Univ, 74, Md Inst, Philadelphia Col Art, Minneapolis Col Art & Kansas City Art Inst, 75, Calif Col Arts & Crafts, 76 & Pace Univ, 77; vis artist & sr lectr, Univ Calif, Santa Cruz, 75 & 82. *Awards:* Prix de Rome in Painting, Am Acad Rome, Italy, 53-55; Award in Art, Am Acad & Inst Arts & Lett, 77. *Bibliog:* Diane Cochrane (auth), Alan Gussow revives the Hudson River School, Am Artist, 3/73; P Mainardi (auth), Alan Gussow: A sense of place, Art News, 11/75; M Sawin (auth), Alan Gussow, Arts, 4/80. *Media:* Oil, Pastel; Wood. *Publ:* Auth, The Use of Artists as Artists in the Struggle for Population Control, Population, Environment & People, McGraw, 72; auth, We Are What We See, In: Encycl of Ecol & Pollution, North Am Publ, 72; auth, The traumas and relief of leaving a gallery, Artworkers News, 2/81. *Dealer:* Sid Deutsch Gallery 20 W 57th St New York NY 10019. *Mailing Add:* 121 New York Ave Congers NY 10920

GUSSOW, ROY
SCULPTOR, ENVIRONMENTAL ARTIST
b Brooklyn, NY, Nov 12, 18. *Study:* With Archipenko, Chicago & Woodstock, NY, 46-47; Inst Design, Chicago, BS, 48, with Moholy-Nagy. *Work:* Whitney Mus Am Art, Mus Mod Art, Brooklyn Mus & Guggenheim Mus, New York; NC Mus Art, Raleigh. *Comn:* Steel sculpture, Xerox Corp, Rochester, NY, 69; steel sculpture, New York Family Ctr Bldg, New York, 72; sculpture, Combustion Engine Corp, Stamford, Conn, 76; sculpture, City Reading, Pa, 78; sculpture, City Harrisburg, Pa, 83; and others. *Exhib:* Sculpture 1951, Metrop Mus Art, New York, 51; Pa Acad, Philadelphia, 51-59; NC Artists, NC Mus Art, Raleigh, 52-61; Whitney Mus Am Art, 56 & 62-68; solo show, Borgenicht Gallery, 64, 71, 73, 77 & 80; Nat Gold Medal Exhib Bldg Arts, Archit League, New York, 62 & 65. *Teaching:* Instr design & sculpture, Bradley Univ, 48-49 & Colorado Springs Fine Arts Ctr, Colo, 49-51; prof design & sculpture, Univ NC Sch Design, 51-62; adj prof sculpture, Pratt Inst Sch Archit, 62-68, Columbia Univ Sch Art, 81- *Awards:* Purchase Awards, Ford Found, 60 & 62; First Prize, New York Family Ct Sculpture Competition, 72. *Mem:* Sculptors Guild (bd dirs, 67-, & pres, 76-80); NY Artists Equity Asn (bd dirs, 77-, & vpres, 80-82). *Media:* Stainless Steel, Bronze. *Dealer:* Borgenicht Gallery 724 Fifth Ave New York NY 10019. *Mailing Add:* 4040 24th St Long Island City NY 11101

GUSSOW, SUE FERGUSON
PAINTER, PRINTMAKER
b Brooklyn, NY, Aug 2, 35. *Study:* Cooper Union, with Will Barnett & Stefano Cusumano, dipl, 56; Columbia Univ, BS, 60; Tulane Univ, MFA, 64. *Work:* Cooper-Hewitt Mus, New York; Philadelphia Free Libr; Minn Mus Art, St Paul; Seattle Art Mus; Dallas Mus Fine Arts. *Comn:* Portrait Judge William O'Hara, Criminal Courts Bldg, New Orleans, 69. *Exhib:* Print Biennial, Brooklyn Mus, 64; Soc Wash Printmakers, Smithsonian Inst, DC, 64; Soc Amer Graphic Artists, Kennedy Galleries, New York, 71; Drawings in St Paul, Minn Mus Art, 71-72; Ten Years of Ten Downtown, Pub Sch 1, Queens, NY, 77; one-woman shows, New Orleans Mus Art, 66 & Newcomb Gallery, Tulane Univ, New Orleans, 77; Stanford Mus, Calif, 83; Loyola Marymount Univ, Calif, 83. *Teaching:* Asst prof drawing, Cooper Union, 71-; asst prof adj painting & drawing, NY Univ, 73-80. *Awards:* Solo Exhib Award, Artists of La, New Orleans Mus Art, 65; Purchase Prize, Drawings USA, Minn Mus Art, 66; Pamela Djerassi Vis Artist Grant, Stanford Univ, 82-83; and others. *Bibliog:* Doreen Mangan (auth), Sue Ferguson Gussow, Am Artist, 75; Susan Meyer (auth), Twenty Figure Painters, Watson-Guptill, 79; Ann Glenn Crowe (auth), A French heritage, Art Week, 7/2/83. *Media:* Oil, Pastel; Charcoal, Intaglio. *Dealer:* Associated American Artists 605 Fifth Ave New York NY 10017. *Mailing Add:* Cooper Union Sch Art Cooper Square New York NY 10003

GUTHMAN, LEO S
COLLECTOR
b Chicago, Ill. *Mem:* Gov life mem Art Inst Chicago; Soc Contemp Art, Chicago (dir); Art Collectors Club, New York; Art Club Chicago; Nat Collectors Comt, Nat Gallery Art, DC; and others. *Collection:* Contemporary painting, especially by Americans; international sculpture. *Mailing Add:* 1040 N Lake Shore Dr Chicago IL 60611

GUTHRIE, PERRI PIZER
DEALER
b Los Angeles, Calif, Apr 21, 58. *Study:* Univ Calif, Los Angeles, BA(design), 80. *Pos:* Trustee, Los Alamitos Art Mus, 76-77; dir, Bolen Gallery Inc, Santa Monica & Los Angeles, 80-83; dir, Robertson Gallery, Riverside, 83-; Co-owner, Robertson Publ, Riverside. *Teaching:* Juror, Rand Corp, Pac Palisades Art Asn and others. *Mem:* Los Angeles Co Mus Art; Riverside Art Ctr; US Bicentennial Art Comn Southern Calif. *Specialty:* Specializing in twentieth century American paintings, sculpture, original graphics and photgraphs. *Mailing Add:* 2500 E Willow St Unit 206 Signal Hill CA 90806

GUTKIN, PETER
SCULPTOR, DESIGNER
b Brooklyn, NY, 44. *Study:* Tyler Sch Art, Temple Univ, BFA, 66; San Francisco Art Inst, MFA, 68. *Work:* Temple Univ, Philadelphia; Oakland Mus, Calif; Best Products; Portland Mus Art, Ore; San Francisco Mus Mod Art; and others. *Exhib:* Contemp Am Sculpture Ann, Whitney Mus Art, New York, 68 & Contemp Am Painting & Sculpture Biennial, 73; one-man shows, San Francisco Mus Art, 72, San Francisco Art Inst, 83 & Modernism, San Francisco, 84; Contemporary American Painting & Sculpture, Krannert Art Mus, Champaign, Ill, 74; Menace, Mus Contemp Art, Chicago, 75; Sculpture in California 1975-1980, San Diego Mus Art, Calif, 80; In the Spirit of Constructivism 1980, Janus Gallery, Venice, Calif, 80; and others. *Teaching:*

Instr, Aspen Sch Contemp Art, Colo, 66 & Univ Calif, Berkeley, 72-74, San Francisco Art Inst, 78. *Awards:* Nat Endowment Humanities & Art Award, 66; Purchase Prize, C R Smith Collection, 72; Nat Endowment Arts Fel, 82. *Bibliog:* Thomas Albright (auth), An artist who shows dramatic development, San Francisco Chronicle, 10/1/77 & Compressed constructions, spiderweb sculptures, Art News, 12/77; Howard Junker (auth), San Francisco, Peter Gutkin at 170 Capp St, Art Am, 5/80. *Dealer:* Modernism San Francisco CA. *Mailing Add:* 170 Capp San Francisco CA 94110

GUTMANN, JOHN
EDUCATOR, PAINTER
b Breslau, Ger, May 28, 05. *Study:* State Acad Arts & Crafts, Breslau, BA; State Acad Berlin, MA. *Work:* Boston Mus Fine Arts; Amon Carter Mus; Mus Mod Art, New York; San Francisco Mus Art; Nat Gallery, Canberra. *Exhib:* San Francisco Mus Art; M H De Young Mem Mus Art; one-man shows, Light Gallery, New York, 74, As I Saw It, San Francisco Mus of Mod Art, 76, Castelli Gallerie, New York, 79 & 81 & Fraenkel Gallery, San Francisco, 80 & 83. *Teaching:* Prof art, Calif State Univ, San Francisco, 38-73, prof emer, 73- *Awards:* Guggenheim Fel, 78. *Mem:* Am Asn Univ Prof; Col Art Asn Am. *Publ:* Contribr, Life, Time, Asia, Sat Eve Post & other nat mag; producer & photographer of two documentary films on China, 50. *Mailing Add:* 1543 Cole St San Francisco CA 94117

GUTMANN, JOSEPH
HISTORIAN, LECTURER
b Würzburg, Bavaria, WGer, Aug 17, 23; US citizen. *Study:* Temple Univ, BS, 49; NY Univ, with C R Morey, MA, 52; Hebrew Union Col, PhD, 60. *Teaching:* Assoc prof art hist, Hebrew Union Col, 60-69; adj prof art, Univ Cincinnati, 61-67; prof art hist, Wayne State Univ, 69- *Publ:* Ed, Beauty in Holiness, 70 & No Graven Images, 71, Ktav; ed, The Temple of Solomon, Scholars Press, 75; Hebrew Manuscript Painting, G Braziller, 78; ed, Ancient Synagogues, Scholars Press, 81. *Mailing Add:* 13151 Winchester Huntington Woods MI 48070

GUTZEIT, FRED
PAINTER
b Cleveland, Ohio. *Study:* Yale Norfolk Summer Sch, 61; Cleveland Inst Art, Mary C Paige Traveling Scholar, 62; Hunter Col, MA, 79. *Work:* Aldrich Mus, Ridgefield, Conn; Alternative Mus, New York; Fashion Moda; Cleveland Art Asn. *Exhib:* Biennial, Butler Inst Am Art, 65; Contemporary Images in Watercolor, Akron Art Inst, 76; solo exhibs, NY State Artist Series, Herbert F Johnson Mus, Cornell Univ, 77 & Distinguished Alumnus, Cleveland Inst Art, 77; Personal Visions, Places/Spaces, Bronx Mus Arts, 78; May Show, Cleveland Mus Art, 82; A Look Back, A Look Forward, Aldrich Mus, 82. *Teaching:* Instr painting, Philadelphia Col Art, 79-82 & Brooklyn Mus Art Sch, 81- *Bibliog:* Patricia Eakins (auth), Fred Gutzeit: An organic approach to images, Am Artist Mag, 10/75 & article, Arts Mag, 4/77. *Media:* Mixed. *Mailing Add:* 264 Bowery New York NY 10013

GUZEVICH-SOMMERS, KRESZENZ (CYNTHIA)
PAINTER, INSTRUCTOR
b Munich, Ger, May 24, 23; US citizen. *Study:* Acad Art, Munich; also with Frank Gervasi, Paul Strisik, Louis Krupp, Helen Van Wyk, Ramon Froman & Ken Gore. *Work:* First Nat Bank, Las Cruces, NMex. *Exhib:* Overseas Press Club Am, New York; El Paso Mus Art Exhib, Tex; Grand Nat Exhib, New York; Southwest Intercult Exhib, El Paso; Artists Equity Show, Albuquerque, NMex. *Teaching:* Instr painting, workshops in var states & pvt studio, 65- *Awards:* Artist of Year & Best in Show Award, Black Range Artists, 68; Best in Show Award, NMex Art League, 69. *Mem:* Am Artists Prof League; El Paso Mus Art Asn; Artists Equity Asn; Accademia Italia Delle Arti e Del Lavoro. *Media:* Oil. *Mailing Add:* 1635 Country Club Circle Las Cruces NM 88001

GUZMAN-FORBES, ROBERT
PAINTER, ILLUSTRATOR
b New York, NY, July 11, 29. *Study:* Univ Va, with John Canaday, BFA; Art Instr Inst, scholar; Sch Visual Arts, with Al Werner & Burne Hogarth, cert. *Work:* Univ Va Mus Fine Arts, Charlottesville; Conn Humane Soc, Newington; Baltimore City Court House, Md. *Comn:* Animal portrait, comn by Mrs Anthony Biddle Duke, Jr, New York, 69; portrait of Alan H Murrell, attorney, 72 & Solomon Liss, Judge, 73, Saints & Sinners of Baltimore; portrait of Harris T Whittemore II, comn by Harris T Whittemore III, Middlebury, Conn, 75; animal portrait, comn by Kenneth E Keating, Simsbury, Conn, 79. *Exhib:* Old State House, Hartford, Conn, 80; Art Ctr, Old Lyme, Conn, 81; Saltbox Gallery, West Hartford, Conn, 81; Ethel Walker Sch Gallery, Simsbury, Conn, 81; Hartford Civic Ctr, Conn, 81; and others. *Pos:* Dir & artist in residence, Evergreen Art Gallery & Studio, Old Avon Village, Avon, Conn. *Bibliog:* K Cassidy (auth), The fine art of Robert G Forbes, Twin Circle Cath Newspaper, 71; article in Christian Sci Monitor; Mary E Renn (auth), Animal art, My Weekly Reader, Xerox Educ Group, 75. *Mem:* Portraits, Inc. *Media:* Pastel, Watercolor. *Dealer:* Evergreen Art Gallery & Studio Old Avon Village Avon CT 06001. *Mailing Add:* 23 Latimer Lane Simsbury CT 06070

GUZZARDI, BARONESS ELENA See Wurdemann, Helen

GWATHMEY, ROBERT
PAINTER
b Richmond, Va, Jan 24, 03. *Study:* NC State Col, 24-25; Md Inst, 25-26; Pa Acad Fine Arts, 26-30. *Work:* Brooklyn Mus; Carnegie Inst, Pittsburgh; Los Angeles Co Mus, Calif; Philadelphia Mus Art; Whitney Mus Am Art, New York. *Exhib:* Whitney Mus Am Art & Carnegie Inst Ann; Metrop Mus Art; Corcoran Gallery Art & Pa Acad Fine Arts Biennials; solo exhib, Terry Dintenfass, 61, 64, 68, 71, 74 & 76; Drawing--America, Albrecht Art Mus, 73; Ball State Univ Ann, 74; An Exhibition of Twentieth-Century Drawings, Skidmore Col, 75; retrospective, St Mary's Col Md, 76; and others. *Teaching:* Instr drawing & painting, Carnegie Inst Technol, 38-42; instr drawing, Cooper Union, 42-68; vis prof painting, Boston Univ, 69-70. *Awards:* Saltus Gold Medal, Nat Acad Design, 77; Adolph & Clara Obrig Prize, 78; Benjamin Altman Prize, 79. *Mem:* Artists Equity Asn; Nat Inst Arts & Lett; assoc Nat Acad Design. *Media:* Oil. *Dealer:* Terry Dintenfass Inc 50 West 57th St New York NY 10019. *Mailing Add:* Box 108 Amagansett NY 11930

GYERMEK, STEPHEN A
EDUCATOR
b Budapest, Hungary, Nov 9, 30. *Study:* Rijks Akad voor Beeldende Kunsten, Amsterdam, Holland, with Heinrich Campendonk; Academia de Bellas Artes Madrid, Spain; Univ Okla. *Comn:* Murals, Convent at Madrid, Spain, 55 & US Embassy, Spain, 55; stained glass windows, St Gregory's Abbey, Shawnee, Okla & St Benedict Church, Ada, Okla. *Exhib:* Amsterdam, 52-53; Madrid, 54; Okla Art Ctr, 60. *Collections Arranged:* Archaeology, Europe, Near & Far East, Egypt; American Indians & Central & South American Ethnology; Paintings from the Italian Renaissance; 19th Century American Paintings; plus others. *Pos:* Dir, Gerrer Mus & Art Gallery, Shawnee, Okla, 57-62; actg dir, Stovall Mus Sci & Hist, Univ Okla, 62-65; dir, Pioneer Mus & Haggin Art Galleries, Stockton, Calif, 65-70. *Teaching:* Lectr painting methods & religious art; asst prof art hist & art, Univ Okla; instr art hist, San Joaquin Delta Col, 67- *Awards:* Prizes & Van Alabbe Award, Amsterdam, Holland, 52. *Mailing Add:* 1870 Douglas Rd Stockton CA 95207

GYRA, FRANCIS JOSEPH, JR
INSTRUCTOR, PAINTER
b Newport, RI, Feb 23, 14. *Study:* RI Sch Design, dipl; Parsons Sch Design, Paris, cert advert illus & X Ital Res Sch; Brighton Col Arts & Crafts, Sussex, Eng; Froebel Inst, Roehampton, Eng; Univ Hawaii; McNeese State Col; Keene State Col, BS. *Work:* Providence Art Mus, RI; Tenn Fine Arts Ctr, Nashville. *Exhib:* Int Watercolor Exhib, Art Inst Chicago, 38 & 40; 1st Int Ann, Marietta Col, Ohio, 69; 1st Art Ann, Northern New Eng, Canaan, NH, 69; Stratton Arts Festival, Vt, 70; 8th Exhib Vt Artists, Norwich Univ, 71. *Pos:* Chmn, Vt Educ Asn Prog, 52; adv art & art educ, Aquinas Jr Col, Nashville, 66- *Teaching:* Supvr, Woodstock Union & Dist Schs, Vt, 49-69; dir art workshops, Vt State Dept Educ, 54-70; art educator, Woodstock Sch Dist, 69- *Awards:* First Prize, 3rd Ann Norwich Univ Art Exhib, 66; Eva Gebhard-Gourgand Found grants, 66-72; Vt State Teacher of Yr, 83. *Mem:* Vt Art Teachers Asn (secy-treas, 57-58); life fel Int Inst Arts & Lett. *Publ:* Coauth, Vermont Art Guide for the Classroom Teacher K-6, 69. *Mailing Add:* 6 Linden Hill PO Box A Woodstock VT 05091

GYSIN, BRION
PAINTER, WRITER
b Jan 19, 16; US citizen. *Study:* Downside Col, Eng, 32-34; Sorbonne, 34-35; Univ Bordeaux, France, 49-52; Univ Seville's Archivos de India, Spain, 50-52. *Work:* Mus Mod Art, New York; Mus Art, Phoenix, Ariz; Boston Fine Arts Mus, Mass; Centre Pompidou, Paris; Mus Mod Art, Paris; plus numerous pvt collections. *Exhib:* Poesie Graphie, Poesie Action, Univ Rouen, France, 68; Lettre-Signe, Swedish Cult Ctr, Paris, 73; Sontemp Villa Borghese, Rome, 73; Galerie Raph, Paris, 77 & 78; Galerie Stadler, Paris, 78; Galerie von Bartha, Basel, 79. *Awards:* Fulbright Res Scholarship, 49-52; Merrill Found Grant, 70. *Bibliog:* Articles in The Art Gallery, New York, 62 & Phantomas, Brussels, 63; Eduard Roditi (auth), article in Art Voices, New York, 64; Rolf-Gunter Dienst (auth), Vernissage, Das Kunstwerk, Baden-Baden, 64. *Publ:* Auth, Dreamachine, The Olympia Review, Paris, 62; auth, The Process, New York, London, 68; auth, Brion Gysin Let the Mice In, New York, 73; illusr, The William Burroughs Catalogue, London, 73; coauth with William Burroughs, The Third Mind, New York, 78. *Dealer:* Galerie zem Specht Basel. *Mailing Add:* 135 rue St Martin Paris 4 France

H

HAACK, CYNTHIA R
PAINTER, PRINTMAKER
b Eagle Bend, Minn. *Study:* St Cloud State Univ, Minn, AE, 53; Univ Wyo, Laramie, 54; Idaho State Col, Pocatello, 57-58. *Exhib:* Mariner's Mus, Newport News, Va, 68; Ann Print Exhib, Mint Mus Art, Charlotte, NC, 68; Ann Small Painting Exhib, Albany Inst Hist & Art, 69; Tidewater Artists Biennial, Chrysler Mus, Norfolk, Va, 70-74; Invitational, Winston-Salem Arts & Sci Mus, NC, 79. *Teaching:* Private lessons, 61-66; instr painting, Rawls Mus, Courtland, Va, 72-73; private lessons painting, 61-66. *Awards:* First Place, Va State Fair Art Show, 69; Best Graphic, Thalhimer's Salon, Richmond, Va, 70; First Place, Southside Artists, Rawls Mus, 73-74. *Bibliog:* Staff, Southside scenes, Daily Press Newspaper, 73; Barclay Sheaks (auth), Landscape illusion, 73; Lynn Bonney (auth), Travels inspire art, Emporia Gazette, 81. *Mem:* Petersburg Area Artists League (pres, 67-68); Flint Hills Arts & Crafts Asn (co-founder, secy, 80-81); Peninsula Arts Asn. *Media:* Acrylic. *Dealer:* Seaside Art Gallery PO Box 1 Nags Head NC 27959. *Mailing Add:* 2520 La Guna Ct Emporia KS 66801

HAACKE, HANS CHRISTOPH
SCULPTOR, CONCEPTUAL ARTIST
b Cologne, Ger, Aug 12, 36. *Study:* Staatl Werkakademie, Kassel, Ger, MFA; Atelier 17, Paris, with S W Hayter; Tyler Sch Art, Philadelphia. *Work:* Mus Mod Art, NY; Kaiser Wilhelm Mus, Krefeld, Ger; Mod Museet, Stockholm; Art Gallery Ont, Toronto; Nat Gallery Can, Ottawa; and others. *Exhib:* Mus Mod Art, New York, 70; Mus Mod Art, Oxford, 78; Stedelijk van Abbe Museum, Eindhoven, 79; one-man shows, Paul Maenz Gallery, Cologne, Ger, 71, 74 & 81; John Weber Gallery, New York, 73, 75, 77, 79 & 81; Mus Mod Art, Oxford, 78 & Stedelijk van Abbe Mus, Eindhoven, 79; Stedelijk Mus, Amsterdam, 82; and many others. *Teaching:* Prof art, Cooper Union, 67- *Awards:* Fulbright Fel, 61; Guggenheim Fel, 73; Nat Endowment Arts Fel, 78. *Bibliog:* Margaret Sheffield (auth), interview, Studio Int, London, 3-4/76; Framing and Being Framed, NS Col Art & Design Press & NY Univ Press, 75; Tony Brown (auth), interview, Parachute, Montreal, summer 81. *Publ:* Auth, Werkmonographie, DuMont, Cologne, 72; auth, Working conditions, Artforum, summer 81. *Mailing Add:* 463 West St New York NY 10014

HAAR, FRANCIS
PHOTOGRAPHER, FILMMAKER
b Csernatfalu, Hungary, July 19, 08; US citizen. *Study:* Nat Acad Decorative Arts, Budapest, Hungary, Master Photog. *Work:* Victoria-Albert Mus, London; Mus Mod Art, New York. *Comn:* The Arts of Japan (film), US Info Agency, Tokyo, Japan, 53; Ukiyoe, Japanese Print (film), Art Inst Chicago, 59; Hoolaulea (dance film), Honolulu Acad Arts, 60; Japan's Cultural History, Fuji TV Co, Tokyo, 64. *Exhib:* Ind Univ, Bloomington, 61; one-man shows, Honolulu Acad Arts, 70 & Contemp Arts Ctr, Honolulu, 71. *Teaching:* Lectr photog, summer courses, Univ Hawaii, 62- *Awards:* Golden Eagle Award for Pineapple Country Hawaii, 63 & Hawaii's Asian Heritage, 66, Coun Int Nontheatrical Events, Washington, DC. *Mem:* Painters & Sculptors League; Honolulu Printmakers; Honolulu Acad Arts. *Publ:* Auth, Around Mount Fuji, 41, Benlido Publ Co, Kyoto, Japan; auth, The Best of Old Japan, 49, coauth, Japanese Theatre in Highlights, 51 & Geisha of Pontocho, 53, C Tuttle Publ Co, Tokyo; coauth, Artists of Hawaii, Vols I & II, Univ Hawaii, 74. *Mailing Add:* 4236 Carnation Pl Honolulu HI 96816

HAAR, TOM
PHOTOGRAPHER
b Tokyo, Japan, June 2, 41; US citizen. *Study:* San Francisco State Col, BA, 64; Univ Hawaii, MFA, 67; Alexei Bradovitch Design Lab, scholar, 68; Int Ctr Photog Advan Workshop, scholar, 75. *Exhib:* Nine Photographers at Westbeth, New York, 80; solo exhibs, Amano Gallery, Osaka, Japan, 80, Green Collections Gallery, Tokyo, 80 & Capen Gallery, State Univ NY, Buffalo, 81; Hamanoya Gallery, Tokyo, 80; and others. *Teaching:* Instr photog, Haystack Mountain Sch Crafts, Maine, 73 & 80; instr photog, Univ Hawaii, 74. *Awards:* Grants, Japan Found & Ishibashi Found, 79. *Mem:* Print Club. *Publ:* Auth, Color Communication (film), Univ Hawaii, 67; asst dir, Artists of Hawaii (film), Honolulu, 9/75; producer & dir, Festival at Mizumi (film), Japan, 79. *Mailing Add:* 463 West St No H454 New York NY 10014

HAAS, ERNST
PHOTOGRAPHER, LECTURER
b Vienna, Austria, Mar 2, 21. *Work:* Mus Mod Art, New York; Eastman Kodak Mus, Rochester, NY; Mus of 20th Century, Vienna; Ctr of Photog, Bath, Eng; Int Ctr Photog, NY. *Comn:* Dye-Transfer Prints, E R Squibb & Son, Princeton, NJ, 74 & Volkswagon USA, Englewood, NJ, 69; E Leitz Inc, NJ, 75. *Exhib:* Color Photog, Mus Mod Art, New York, 62; The Creation, Photokina, Cologne, Ger, 72; Vienna 47-49, Mus of 20th Century, 75; In Ger, Photokina, Cologne, 78. *Teaching:* Vis lectr photog, Maine Photog Workshops, Rockport & Anderson Ranch Found, Aspen, Colo, 75-, Int Ctr Photography, 78-83 & St Louis-Mississippi River Workshop, 82-83. *Awards:* New House Award, Syracuse Univ, 58; Kultur Preis Award, Ger govt, 78. *Bibliog:* Cronell Capa, Concerned Photographer, Grossman, 72; The Great Photographers, 82. *Mem:* Am Soc Mag Photogr (pres, 60). *Media:* Color Photography; Audio-Visual Works. *Publ:* Auth, The Creation, 71 & In America, 75, Viking Press; auth, In Germany, Viking & Econ Verlag Viking, 77; co-auth, Time-Life Bk Ser; Hilalaya Pilgrimage, Viking, 78. *Mailing Add:* 853 Seventh Ave New York NY 10019

HAAS, RICHARD JOHN
PRINTMAKER, MURALIST
b Spring Green, Wis, Aug 29, 36. *Study:* Univ Wis, Milwaukee, BS, 59; Univ Minn, MFA, 64. *Work:* Mus Mod Art, Metrop Mus Art & Whitney Mus Am Art, New York; Yale Univ Art Gallery, New Haven, Conn; Walker Art Ctr, Minneapolis. *Exhib:* Contemporary American Art, Herron Mus Art, Indianapolis, 72; Printmaking Biennial, Brooklyn Mus, 74-76; one-man shows, Hundred Acres Gallery, 72, 73 & 74; Brooke Alexander, 73, 74, 77, 80, 81 & 82; Whitney Mus Am Art, 75 & Young Hoffman Gallery, Chicago, 78, 79 & 82; plus others. *Pos:* New York City Art Comn, 76-79. *Teaching:* Instr art, Univ Minn, 63-64; asst prof art, Mich State Univ, 64-68; instr printmaking, Bennington Col, 68-80; instr, Sch Visual Arts, 77- *Awards:* Medal Honor, Am Inst Archit, 77; Nat Endowment Arts Printmaking Grant, 78; Guggenheim Fel, 83. *Mem:* Archit League (vpres, 78-). *Media:* Intaglio; Watercolor. *Publ:* Auth, An Architecture of Illusion, Rizzoli Publ, New York, 81. *Dealer:* Brooke Alexander 24 E 78th St New York NY 10021; Young Hoffman Gallery 248 Superior St Chicago IL 60610. *Mailing Add:* 81 Greene St New York NY 10012

HABER, IRA JOEL
SCULPTOR, WRITER

b Brooklyn, NY, Feb 24, 47. *Work:* NY Univ Art Collection; Nueu Gallerie, Ludwig Collection, Aachen, Ger; Guggenheim Mus, New York; Hirshhorn Mus, Washington, DC; Albright-Knox Art Gallery, Buffalo, NY. *Exhib:* Information, Mus Mod Art, New York, 70; Whitney Mus Ann Sculpture Exhib, New York, 70; three one-man shows, Fischbach Gallery, New York, 71-74; Whitney Mus Contemp Art Biennial, 73; retrospective, Kent State Univ Art Gallery, 77 & State Univ NY, Stony Brook, 81; Tableaux Constructions, Univ Calif, Santa Barbara, 77; Pam Adler Gallery, New York, 78-80; Eight Sculptors, Albright-Knox Art Gallery, Buffalo; 1979 Street Sights, Inst Contemp Art, Philadelphia, Pa, 80. *Teaching:* Instr sculpture, Fordham Univ, 71-74; assoc prof, State Univ NY Stony Brook, 81. *Awards:* Creative Artists Pub Serv Grant, 74-75 & 76-77; Nat Endowment Arts Fel, 74-75 & 77-78. *Bibliog:* Corrinne Robins (auth), Ira Joel Haber, Arts Mag, 11/77; Robert Berlind (auth), Ira Joel Haber at Pam Adler, Art in Am, 12/79; April Kingsley (auth), article, Arts Mag, 9/80. *Media:* Mixed. *Publ:* Auth, Radio City Music Hall, 69; auth, Five stories of the Music Hall, St Marks Poetry Proj, 73; auth, Some thoughts on camouflage by John Perreault, Serif-Lit Quart, Kent State Univ, 74; M E Thelen Gallery Piece, Tri-Quarterly, 75; auth, Some reasons why I do what I do, Appearances, Vol 1, 77. *Mailing Add:* c/o Pam Adler Gallery 37 W 57th St New York NY 10001

HABER, WILLIAM
DEALER, COLLECTOR

b New York, NY, Feb 4, 21. *Pos:* Owner, William Haber Art Collections Inc. *Interests:* Since 1960, conducted art auctions and art shows in the US and Japan, and lectured and exhibited graphic art with presentation as an art form in itself. *Publ:* Ed, Moshe Gat's Mexico Spain Portugal Israel, United Artists Israel, 68; ed, Rubin's, Story of King David, 71; ed, Rattner's, In the Beginning..., 72 & People in Israel, 75, Mourlot, Paris. *Mailing Add:* William Haber Art Collection 139-11 Queens Blvd Jamaica NY 11435

HABERGRITZ, GEORGE JOSEPH
PAINTER, SCULPTOR

b New York, NY, June 16, 09. *Study:* Nat Acad Design; Cooper Union, grad; Acad Grande Chaumiere. *Work:* Butler Mus, Youngstown, Ohio; Wilberforce Univ, Ohio; Purdue Univ, Ind; Safad Mus, Israel; Jewish Mus, London. *Exhib:* Albright Mus Painting Ann, Buffalo, NY, 38-40; Va Biennial, Richmond, 40; Am Watercolor Soc Ann, 47-49; Nat Asn Painters Casein, 47-74; Nat Acad Design Drawing & Painting Ann, 48-51; Univ Mont; Okla State Mus; Evansville Mus, Ind; Detroit Gallery of Fine Arts; Gallery Meindel & El Callejon Gallery, Bogota, Colombia, 74-77. *Pos:* Dir, Sch Continuing Art Educ, 68- *Teaching:* Lectr artist in Africa, SPac & India, 57-; instr painting, Art Students League, 60-64 & Friend Sch Art, 65-69; instr new media, Workshop Prof Artists, 67- *Awards:* Gold Medal for Drawing, Nat Acad Design, 38; Grumbacher Awards, Nat Soc Painters Casein, 68, 70, 72 & 74. *Bibliog:* G Klotz (auth), Two American artists, Galerie Klotz, Stuttgart, 67. *Mem:* Nat Soc Painters Casein (pres, 63-64). *Mailing Add:* 32 Morton St 1B New York NY 10014

HACK, PHILLIP S & PATRICIA Y
COLLECTORS

Mr Hack, b Ill, Dec 8, 16; Mrs Hack, b Los Angeles, Calif, Dec 21, 26. *Study:* Univ Ariz; Stanford Univ; Oxford Univ; Ariz State Univ; Wabash Col; Purdue Univ. *Collection:* Contemporary paintings, sculpture, prints and drawings. *Mailing Add:* 2201 N Central Ave Phoenix AZ 85004

HACKENBROCH, YVONNE ALIX
CURATOR, WRITER

b Frankfurt, Ger, Apr 27, 12; US citizen. *Study:* Univ Frankfurt, 32-33; Univ Rome, 33-34; Univ Munich, PhD(summa cum laude), 36. *Pos:* Asst dept Brit & mediaeval antiq, Brit Mus, London, 36-45; cur, Lee Fareham Collection, Univ Toronto, 45-49; cur, Irwin Untermyer Collection & cur, Western European Arts, Metrop Mus Art, 49- *Awards:* Ford Found Grant, 63; Kress Found Grants, 64 & 65. *Res:* Decorative arts. *Publ:* Auth, seven catalogues of the Irwin Untermyer Collection; contribr, Connoisseur & other mag. *Mailing Add:* 7 E 85th St New York NY 10028

HACKETT, MICKEY
PAINTER, EDUCATOR

b Louisville, Ky. *Study:* Univ Louisville, Univ Tex, 48. *Work:* Brown-Williamson Corp, Brown Forman Distilleries, Univ Louisville, Ky; Philip Morris Corp; United Am Bank, Tenn; and others. *Comn:* Convention cover, Ky Bankers Asn, 81 & 83. *Exhib:* Evansville Mus Arts & Sci; Catherine Lorillard Wolfe, Nat Arts Club, New York; Patron's Gala, Okla; J B Speed Mus; Watermedia 83, Mont; Milford Fine Arts Ctr, Conn; and many others. *Pos:* Interior designer, George Fetter Co, Louisville, 65-69. *Teaching:* Instr adult educ, Jefferson Co Bd Educ, Ky, 76-; instr watercolor tech, Jefferson Community Col, Univ Ky, 78-82; instr, var workshops for artists, currently. *Awards:* Purchase awards, Olan/Mills, Tenn, 83, Midwest Acousti Corp, Ohio, 83 & Bank One, Ohio, 83. *Mem:* Whiskey Painters Am; charter mem Ky Watercolor Soc; life mem J B Speed Mus; Southern Watercolor Soc; Ala Watercolor Soc; and others. *Media:* Mixed. *Mailing Add:* 1901 Woodfield Rd Louisville KY 40220

HACKLIN, ALLAN DAVE
PAINTER, SCULPTOR

b New York, NY, Feb 11, 43. *Study:* Pratt Inst. *Work:* Whitney Mus Am Art, New York; Dallas Mus Fine Arts; Allen Mus, Oberlin, Ohio. *Teaching:* Instr painting, Pratt Inst, 69-70; instr painting, Calif Inst Arts, 70-77; vis prof, Cooper Union, 77-80; vis prof, RI Sch Design, 79-82, chmn, Painting Dept, 80-82. *Awards:* Nat Endowment Arts, 75 & 80. *Mailing Add:* E Jefferson Rd Jefferson NY 12093

HACKNEY, ALLEN L
PAINTER

b Madison, Ind, Aug 13, 38. *Study:* Ind State Univ, Terre Haute, BS, 62, MS, 64; with John Laska & Zoltan Sepeshy. *Work:* Chalmer's Gallery, London; Rose-Hulman Inst, Ind; Ind State Univ, Terre Haute; Indianapolis Public Schools, Ind. *Comn:* State Bird-Cardinal, State Ind, 70; Commemorative Painting, Lambda Chi Alpha Int Hq, Indianapolis. *Exhib:* Hoosier Salon, Indianapolis, 65-75; Mid-States Art Exhib, Evansville Mus Arts & Sci, Ind, 66-68; George Walter/Vicent Smith Mus Ann, 70; Retrospective, Ind State Univ, Terre Haute, 72; Ind Realists, Sheldon Swope Art Gallery, 78-79; Ind Realists, Ind State Mus, Indianapolis, 81. *Collections Arranged:* Indiana Realists, 78-81. *Awards:* Commemorative Medal, State Ind, 74. *Mem:* Nat Soc Painters in Casein & Acrylic; Ind Realists (pres 78-); Hoosier Salon Patrons Asn; Int Platform Asn; Brown Co Art Gallery. *Media:* Egg Tempera, Watercolor. *Dealer:* Brown Co Art Gallery 1 Artist's Drive Nashville IN. *Mailing Add:* RR 51 Box 655C Terre Haute IN 47805

HADEN, EUNICE (BARNARD)
PAINTER, ILLUSTRATOR

b Washington, DC, Oct 21, 01. *Study:* Oberlin Col, BA; Abbott Sch Art, with Hugo Inden; also with Eliot O'Hara. *Work:* In pvt collections only. *Exhib:* Nat Collection Fine Arts, 53-56; Burr Gallery, New York, 59 & 60; one-man show, Payne Gallery, Washington, DC, 64; Gallery on the Landing, Ft Wayne, Ind, 77; Art Contemp, Bathesda, Md, 81; and others. *Awards:* Awards, Arts Club Washington, 56, 59, 64 & 66; Miniature Painters, Sculptors & Gravers Soc Awards, 66, 68, 78 & 79; Second Prize, Nat League Am Pen Women, 81. *Mem:* Miniature Painter, Sculptors & Gravers Soc (pres, 60-64, recorder, 82-83); Arts Club Washington (chmn, 61-62, bd gov, 64-68); Nat Registrar (interim), 77-78, Nat League Am Pen Women; Order Descendants Colonial Gov (nat treas, 80-83). *Media:* Watercolor; Ink. *Publ:* Auth & ed, DAR Patriot Index, first vol, 67, suppl, 69 & 82, vol II, 80; auth & ed, Am Clan Gregor Soc Yearbks, 68-79 & 81-83. *Mailing Add:* 5112 Connecticut Ave NW Washington DC 20008

HADFIELD, TED LEE
SCULPTOR

b Flint, Mich, May 8, 50. *Study:* Mott Community Col, AA, 70; Colo State Univ, BFA, 78; Cranbrook Acad Art, MFA, 80. *Work:* Mott Community Col; Colo State Univ Art Gallery; Cranbrook Mus Art. *Exhib:* Marietta Nat, 79; Westwood Clay Nat, Otis Parsons Gallery, Los Angeles, 80; Variations in Clay, GMB Gallery, Birmingham, Mich, 82; Michigan Artists 80-82, Detroit Inst Art, 82; Cranbrook Ceramics 1950-1980, Cranbrook Mus, 83; Drawing with Space, Midland Mus, Mich, 84; New Vistas in Clay, Pewabic Pottery, Detroit, 84. *Pos:* Co-owner, Artpack & Transport Art Installations, 81- *Bibliog:* Exhibitions now showing, Am Crafts, 5/79; Michigan artists, Detroit News, 7/81; Artists studio, Detroit Free Press, 8/83. *Media:* Mixed. *Mailing Add:* 33642 Longwood Farmington Hills MI 48024

HADLEY, ROLLIN VAN NOSTRAND
MUSEUM DIRECTOR

b Westboro, Mass, Dec 13, 27. *Study:* Harvard Univ, AB, 49, MA, 81; St Anselm's Col, Hon PhD, 79. *Pos:* Trustee, Corning Mus of Glass, NY, 58-60; adminr, Isabella Stewart Gardner Mus, 63-70, dir, 70-; bd vis, Dept Art & Hist, Boston Univ, 77. *Teaching:* Mem fac Eng lit, Universita Bocconi, Milan, Italy, 60-62; vis scholar, Harvard Ctr for Italian Renaissance Studies, Florence, Italy, 72. *Awards:* Commander, Order of Merit, Ital Govt, 78. *Mem:* Save Venice Inc (chmn Boston Chap, 71-74, pres, 74-); Am Asn Art Mus Dirs; Boston Fulbright Comt (mem bd dirs, 74-). *Publ:* Auth, Drawings, Isabella Stewart Gardner Mus, 68 & contribr, Sculpture, Isabella Stewart Gardner Mus, 77, Mus Trustees; auth, Museums Discovered: Isabella Stewart Gardner Museum, Shorewood Fine Art Bks, 81. *Mailing Add:* c/o Isabella Stewart Gardmen Mus 2 Palace Rd Boston MA 02115

HADZI, DIMITRI
SCULPTOR, PRINTMAKER

b New York, NY, Mar 21, 21. *Study:* Cooper Union, cert, 50; Brooklyn Mus Art Sch, 48-50; Polytechnion, Athens, Greece, 50-51. *Work:* Mus Mod Art, Guggenheim Mus & Whitney Mus Am Art, New York; Fogg Art Mus, Harvard Univ, Cambridge, Mass; Hirshhorn Mus, Washington, DC. *Comn:* Arcturus, Fed Reserve Bank Bldg, Minneapolis, 71-72; basalt & granite intarsia, Johnson Wax, Racine, Wis, 78-79; Bishop's Triad, Dallas Ctr, Tex, 79-80; Propylaea (granite fountain), Owens-Illinois Co, Toledo, Ohio, 80-81; Copley Place (stone foundation), Boston, 82-83; and others. *Exhib:* Recent Sculpture USA, Mus Mod Art, New York, 59; Pittsburgh Int, Carnegie Inst, Pa, 61 & 64; Mekler Gallery, Los Angeles, 78 & Gruenebaum Gallery, New York, 78; Joseph H Hirshhorn Collection, Guggenheim Mus, New York, 62 & Art in Am Since World War II, 79; Middleheim Park, Antwerp, Holland, 71; Art from Northeast Mus, Vice-President's House, DC, 79; Sculptors, Boston Athenaeum, 82. *Teaching:* Artist in residence, Dartmouth Col, summer 69; Int Sculpture Symposium, Univ Ore, Eugene, 74; studio prof, Dept Visual & Environment Studies, Harvard Univ. *Awards:* Cooper Union Citation, 76; hon MA, Harvard Univ, 77; fel, Am Acad Arts & Sci, 78. *Bibliog:* Peter Hollander (auth), Dimitri Works in Black Wax (film), Kinesis Films, 52; Albert Elsen (auth), Sculpture with a memory, Art News, 9/78; A Conversation with Dimitri Hadzi, Harvard Mag, 3-4/81; and others. *Mem:* Am Acad & Inst Arts & Letters, 83. *Media:* Bronze, Stone. *Publ:* Illusr, Hellas, 71; illusr, The Venetian Vespers, Godine Press, 79. *Dealer:* Gruenebaum Gallery 38 E 57th St New York NY 10022; Mekler Gallery 651 N La Cienega Blvd Los Angeles CA. *Mailing Add:* Carpenter Ctr for Visual Arts Harvard Univ Cambridge MA 02138

HAERER, CAROL
PAINTER

b Salina, Kans, Jan 23, 33. *Study:* Doane Col; Univ Nebr, BFA; Art Inst Chicago; Univ Calif, Berkeley, MA. *Work:* Whitney Mus Am Art & Guggenheim Mus, New York; Oakland Art Mus, Calif; Sheldon Mem Art Galleries, Lincoln, Nebr; Univ Kansas, Lawrence; and others. *Exhib:* Salon des Realities Nouvelles, Paris, 55; San Francisco Art Mus, 60; Whitney Mus Am Art Ann, New York, 70 & 72; Critics' Choice, Syracuse Univ Mus, NY, 77 & Munson-Williams-Proctor Inst, Utica, NY, 78; Ford & Haerer, Usdan Gallery, Bennington Col, Vt, 78; Recent Acquisitions, Brooklyn Mus, 78; Oscarsson-Hood Gallery, New York, 81 & 83; Invitational Exhib, Bershire Mus, Pittsfield, Mass, 81; and many others. *Teaching:* Instr painting, Bennington Col Summer Workshops, 76-80 & Bennington Col, 83-; instr drawing & painting, Univ Vt, Burlington, 80- *Awards:* MacDowell Colony Fel, 69 & 79; Yaddo Residency, 82; Hand Hollow Fel, 83. *Bibliog:* Larry Aldrich (auth), Young lyrical painters, Art in Am, 11/69; article, Art Int, 1/74, Arts Mag, 5/81; April Kingsley (auth), Carol Haerer, Spiraling Through Space & Time, Arts Mag, 9/83; and others. *Dealer:* Oscarsson-Hood Gallery 41 W 57th St New York NY 10019. *Mailing Add:* Rte 2 Box 63B Hoosick Falls NY 12090

HAESSLE, JEAN-MARIE GEORGES
PAINTER, PRINTMAKER

b Alsace, France, Sept 12, 39. *Study:* Ecole Nat des Beaux Arts, Paris; Ecole de la Grande Chaumiere, Paris. *Work:* Albright-Knox Art Gallery, Buffalo, NY; Bibliot Nat, Paris, France; Nat Art Mus, China; Southern Ill Univ, Edwardsville. *Exhib:* Westbeth Graphic Show, Palace of Fine Arts, Mexico City, 72; Selected Graphic Show, Albright-Knox Art Gallery, Buffalo, 72; one-man shows, Westbroadway Gallery, New York, 73 & Nat Acad Sci, Washington, DC, 79; Young Talent Festival, Pace Gallery, New York, 77; Gabrielle Bryers Gallery, New York, 81; and others. *Bibliog:* Laurie Anderson (auth), reviews in Art News, 72; April Kingsley (auth), New York newsletter, Art Int, 73; Vivian Raynor (auth), review in Art in Am, 74. *Media:* Acrylic, Oil. *Dealer:* Gabrielle Bryers Gallery 110 Green St New York NY 10012. *Mailing Add:* 106-112 Spring St New York NY 10012

HAFF, BARBARA J E
PAINTER, INSTRUCTOR

b New York, NY. *Study:* With A Haff; Art Student's League, with Sydney Dickinson, Dan Greene & Mario Cooper. *Work:* Wall Street Transcript & Ackerman Realty Co, New York. *Exhib:* Pastel Soc Am, Nat Arts Club; Allied Artists Am, Nat Acad/Nat Arts Club, New York; Salmagundi Club Ann, New York; Knickerbocker Artists, Nat Arts Club/Salmagundi, New York; Hermitage Found Mus, Norfolk, Va, 83. *Teaching:* Pastel painting, Pastel Soc Am, Nat Arts Club, 82-83. *Awards:* Gold Medal of Honor, Wall Street Transcript; J Hunter-Young Award, Allied Artists, 82; B Cammer Award, Pastel Soc Am, 83. *Mem:* Allied Artists Am (awards chairperson, 79-); Pastel Soc Am (recording secy, 81-); Knickerbocker Artists; C L Wolfe Art Asn; life mem Art Student's League NY. *Media:* Pastel, Watercolor. *Mailing Add:* 23-38 31 Rd Astoria NY 11106

HAFIF, MARCIA
PAINTER, EDUCATOR

b Pomona, Calif, Aug 15, 29. *Study:* Pomona Col, BA(art), 50; Claremont Grad Sch; Univ Calif, Irvine, MFA, 71. *Comn:* Ohio Red (clay mural), Wright State Univ, Ohio, 77; painting, Sheldon Solow, NY, 80. *Exhib:* Marcia Hafif, La Jolla Mus Contmep Art, 75; Tendences Actuelles de la Nouvelle Peinture Americaine, Mus Art Moderne Ville Paris, 75; Wall Painting, Mus Contemp Art, Chicago, 79; Abstract Painting: 1960-69, PS1, 83; and many others. *Teaching:* Instr painting & color, Sch Visual Arts, New York, 74-76; artist-in-residence drawing, Wright State Univ, Dayton, Ohio, 77; instr, Sarah Lawrence Col, 78-80 & Hunter Col, 79; adj asst prof, Hunter Col, 82; vis artist, Univ Calif, Irvine, 83. *Awards:* Creative Artists Pub Serv Prog Grant, 76; Nat Endowment Arts, 80-81. *Bibliog:* Marisa Volpi (auth), Marcia Hafif, Data, 74; Rosalind Krauss (auth), Notes on the Index: Seventies Art in America Part II, October (mag), 10/78; Carter Ratcliff (auth), Mostly monochrome, Art Am, 4/81. *Mem:* Am Abstract Artists; Artist's Space. *Media:* All traditional paint media. *Publ:* Auth, A Fusion of Real and Pictorial Space, Arts Mag, 72; auth, Diversificazione dell'Avanguardia, d'Ars, 77; auth, Beginning again, Artforum, 9/78; auth, Robert Ryman: Another response, Art in Am, 9/79; auth, Getting on with painting, Art Am, 4/81. *Dealer:* Sonnabend Gallery 420 W Broadway New York NY 10012; Bluxome Gallery San Francisco. *Mailing Add:* 112 Mercer St New York NY 10012

HAGAN, FREDERICK
PRINTMAKER, PAINTER

b Toronto, Ont, May 21, 18. *Study:* Ont Col Art; Art Students League; also with George Miller, New York. *Work:* Nat Gallery Art, Ottawa, Ont; Art Gallery Hamilton, Ont; Grimsby Pub Art Gallery, Ont; McIntosh Gallery, London, Ont; MacDonald Stewart Art Ctr, Ont. *Comn:* Mural, Oakville Centennial Libr. *Exhib:* Ont Soc Artists; Can Soc Painters Watercolour; Can Group Painters; Nat Gallery Can; Libr of Cong; plus others. *Teaching:* Res artist, Pickering Col, Newmarket, Ont, 42-46; instr drawing & printmaking, Ont Col Art, 46-83. *Mem:* Ont Soc Artists; Print & Drawing Coun Can; and others. *Dealer:* Gadatsy Gallery 45 Stephanie St Toronto ON M5T 1B2; Madison Gallery 334 Sundas St Toronto ON M5T 1G5. *Mailing Add:* 53 Lundy's Ave Newmarket ON L3Y 3R9 Canada

HAGAN, JAMES GARRISON
SCULPTOR, INSTRUCTOR

b Pittsburgh, Pa, July 11, 36. *Study:* Carnegie-Mellon Univ, BFA; Iowa State Univ; Univ Pittsburgh, MA. *Work:* Column 5, Nat Gallery Art, Washinton, DC; Column 8, Princeton Univ, NJ. *Exhib:* One-man show, Zabriskie Gallery, 75; Nine Sculptures, Nassau Co Mus, NY, 76; Wood Works, Wadsworth Atheneum, Hartford, Conn, 77; Wood, Nassau Co Mus, NY, 77. *Teaching:* Assoc prof sculpture, Univ Va, Charlottesville, 63- *Media:* Wood. *Dealer:* Zabriskie Gallery 29 West 57th New York NY 10019. *Mailing Add:* Rte 1 Box 277 Charlottesville VA 22901

HAGE, RAYMOND JOSEPH
COLLECTOR, PATRON

b Huntington, WVa, Nov 28, 43. *Study:* Univ Ky; Marshall Univ, BBA, 66; Colgate Darden Grad Bus Sch, Univ Va, TEP, 71. *Pos:* Pres & chief exec officer, AA Benefit Corp, currently; trustee, Huntington Galleries, currently. *Collection:* Original American prints; other American art. *Mailing Add:* 2105 Wiltshire Blvd Huntington WV 25701

HAGEMAN, CHARLES LEE
EDUCATOR, JEWELER

b Clay Center, Kans, June 22, 35. *Study:* Univ of Kans, BFA, 57, MFA, 67. *Work:* Ill State Univ, Visual Arts Ctr, Normal, Ill; Univ of Mo, Columbia. *Comn:* Univ Mace, Pres Chain of Office & 6 Board of Regent's Medallions, comn by Pres of Northwest Mo State Univ, Maryville, 77. *Exhib:* Juried Craft Exhib, Ark Arts Ctr, Little Rock, 73 & J P Speed Art Mus, Louisville, Ky, 74; Invitational Craft Exhib, Albrecht Mus, St Joseph, Mo, 75; Prof Jewelry Exhib, Univ of Mo, Columbia, 76; Mid-Am Metalcrafts, Kansas City Pub Libr, Mo, 77. *Collections Arranged:* Mo Craftsman Exhib, Olive DeLuce Gallery, Maryville, Mo, 73. *Teaching:* Assoc prof of jewelry & metals, Northwest Mo State Univ, Maryville, 67-; instr summer jewelry workshop, NMex State Univ, Las Cruces, 74- *Awards:* Best in Metals, Designer-Craftsman Show, Kans, 67; Metals Award, Springfield Art Mus, 69; Best in Metals, Mo Craftsman Exhib, 70. *Mem:* Mo Craft Coun; Am Craft Coun; Soc of NAm Goldsmiths. *Media:* Pewter & Gold. *Mailing Add:* 722 W 2nd St Maryville MO 64468

HAGER, HELLMUT W
HISTORIAN

b Berlin, Ger, Mar 27, 26. *Study:* Univ Bonn, PhD, 59. *Collections Arranged:* Architectural Fantasy and Reality, Mus Art, Pa State Univ, 81-82. *Pos:* Asst to dir, Bibliot Hertziana, Rome, 59-63. *Teaching:* Prof art hist, Pa State Univ, 71-, dept head, 72- *Mem:* Col Art Asn Am; Soc Archit Historians; Am Soc 18th Century Studies; Am Inst Archaeol. *Res:* Baroque architecture in Italy and Germany. *Publ:* Auth, Filippo Juvarra e il concorso di modelli del 1715 bandito da Clemente XI per la nuovo sacrestia di S Pietro, 70; coauth, Carlo Fontana: The Drawings at Windsor Castle, 77. *Mailing Add:* 318 E Prospect Ave State College PA 16801

HAGERSTRAND, MARTIN ALLAN
MUSEUM DIRECTOR, ADMINISTRATOR

b Chicago, Ill, Nov 10, 11. *Study:* Metrop Theological Sem; Univ Richmond; Univ Va Exten; Univ Kans; US Army Command & Gen Staff Col; US Dept Defense Armed Forces Staff Col. *Collections Arranged:* Sponsored & administered numerous spec exhibs, Cherokee Nat Hist Soc & Cherokee Nat Mus since 69. *Pos:* Exec vpres, Cherokee Nat Hist Soc, Tahlequah, Okla, 63-; producer, Trail of Tears Drama, Theatre at TSA-LA-GI, Tahlequah, 69-; dir, Cherokee Nat Mus, Tahlequah, 75-; pres, Okla Summer Arts Inst, 76-78. *Awards:* Arts & Tourism Award, Okla Arts & Humanities Coun & State Dept of Tourism & Recreation, 72; Governor's Arts Award, 81. *Mem:* Am Asn of Mus; Mountain Plains Mus Asn; Okla Mus Asn (pres, 76-77); Am Asn of State & Local Hist; Nat Trust for Hist Preserv. *Interests:* Indian art. *Mailing Add:* Cherokee Nat Hist Soc Box 515 Tahlequah OK 74464

HAGUE, RAOUL
SCULPTOR

b Constantinople. US citizen. *Study:* Iowa State Col, 21; Beaux Arts Inst Design, New York, 26-27; Art Students League, 27-28; Courtauld Inst London, Guggenheim Fel, 50-51. *Work:* Albright Art Gallery; Whitney Mus Am Art, Mus Mod Art, New York; Art Inst Chicago. *Exhib:* Mus Mod Art, 33 & 56; Curt Valentin Gallery, 45; Whitney Mus Am Art, 45-48, 52, 57 & 58; Xavier Fourcade, 79. *Awards:* Ford Found Grant, 61; Am Arts & Letts, 73; Mark Rothro, 72. *Mailing Add:* Maverick Rd Woodstock NY 12498

HAHN, BETTY
PHOTOGRAPHER, EDUCATOR

b Chicago, Ill, Oct 11, 40. *Study:* Ind Univ, BA, 63, MFA, 66 with Henry Holmes Smith. *Work:* Mus Mod Art, New York; Smithsonian Inst; Nat Gallery Can, Ottawa; Art Inst Chicago; San Francisco Mus Mod Art; and others. *Exhib:* Photog in the 20th Century, Nat Gallery Can, 67; Betty Hahn & Gayle Smalley, Smithsonian Inst, 69; Photography: New Acquisitions, Mus Mod Art, New York, 70; Photo Media, Mus Contemp Crafts, New York, 71; Photog Into Art, Camden Arts Ctr, London, Eng, 72; Betty Hahn, Witkin Gallery, New York, 73; Festival du Photographie, Arles, France, 75; Am Family Portraits: 1730-1976, Philadelphia Mus of Art, 76; Nat Gallery Can, Ottawa, 80; Smithsonian Inst, 80; and others. *Teaching:* Asst prof photog, Rochester Inst of Technol, NY, 69-76; assoc prof photog, Univ NMex, 76-; lectr, numerous univs. *Awards:* Creative Artists Pub Serv Prog Grant, New York State Coun, 75; Res Grant, Univ NMex, 77; Nat Endowment Arts Grants, 78 & 83; and others. *Bibliog:* James N Miho (auth), More Than Real, Commun Arts, 72; R Sobieszek (auth), Photographer: Betty Hahn, Czech

Photo, 74 & Russian Photo Rev, 74. *Mem:* Soc for Photog Educ; Evidence Photogrs Int Coun. *Publ:* Auth, Speaking with a Genuine Voice: Henry Holmes Smith, IMAGE Eastman House, 73; contribr of chap on Gum Bichromate Printing, In: Darkroom, Lustrum Press, New York, 77. *Dealer:* Witkin Gallery 41 E 57th St New York NY 10022. *Mailing Add:* 1511 Kit Carson Ave SW Univ of NMex Albuquerque NM 87104

HAHN, GERALD
PAINTER, EDUCATOR
b Brooklyn, NY, Mar 1, 38. *Study:* Cooper Union Art Sch, with Morris Kantor, R de Harak & Walter Rosenblum, cert(fine arts), 58; Skowhegan Sch Painting & Sculpture, with Edwin Dickenson, summer 58; Yale Univ Art Sch, with James Brooks, C Marca-Relli, Jack Tworkov & Alex Katz, BFA, 60, MFA, 62. *Work:* Yale Univ Art Sch; Cooper Union Art Sch; Bucknell Univ; Dr Herman Goodman Found, New York; Estate of Sibyl Moholy-Nagy, New York. *Exhib:* 11th Ann Nat Drawing & Sculpture Exhib, Ball State Univ, 65; Nat Print Exhib, San Francisco Mus Art, 67; James Yu Gallery, New York, 75; Calligraphy Invitational for Cooper-Hewitt Mus, Cooper Union Art Sch, 76; Grosse Kunstausstellung, Hans der Kunst, Munich, WGer, 77; Landmark Gallery, New York, 79; Tower Gallery, Southampton, 79; plus others. *Pos:* Chmn drawing, Pratt Inst, 65-70; asst chmn dept art, Queens Col, 71-76; dep chmn dept, 78-80, chmn, MFA Program, 81-82. *Teaching:* Instr drawing, Sch Archit, Pratt Inst, Brooklyn, 65-70; assoc prof fine arts, Queens Col, NY, 70- *Awards:* Tiffany Found Award for Printmaking, 62-63; Purchase Prize, 1st Ann Nat Drawing Exhib, Bucknell Univ, 65; PSC-CUNY Research Found Award, 80-81. *Bibliog:* John Gruen (auth), On Art, Soho News, NY, 1/16/75; Robbie Ehrlich (auth), Review, Arts Mag, 4/79; Cynthia Saltzman (auth), Review, Art News Mag, 4/79. *Media:* Acrylic. *Publ:* Contribr, The Art of Drawing, Holt, 70; auth, Optical Artificials: Understanding Color Mixing, Saltwater Sportsman Publ, 79. *Dealer:* Tower Gallery 3 S Main St Southampton NY 11968. *Mailing Add:* 463 West St Apt H-521 New York NY 10014

HAHN, MAURICE & ROSLYN
DEALERS
US citizen. *Study:* Mr Hahn, Northwestern Univ, BS(bus); Mrs Hahn, Univ Pa, BA, grad studies in art hist; Temple Univ, Tyler Sch of Art. *Collections Arranged:* Benton Spruance, Retrospective, William Penn Mus, Harrisburg, Pa, 77; Benton Spruance Traveling Exhib, (coauth, catalog), with Dr Ricardo Viera, Lehigh Univ, 77-78; Alfred Bendiner, The Philadelphia Years, William Penn Mus, Harrisburg, 78; 17th, 18th and 19th Century Japanese Woodblock Prints, Longwood Gardens, Kennett Square, PA, 82. *Pos:* Dir, Hahn Gallery, Philadelphia. *Mem:* Philadelphia Print Club; Prints in Progress (Mrs Hahn, bd mem, 70-77); Philadelphia Art Dealers Asn; Friends of Artists Equity (Mrs Hahn, bd mem). *Specialty:* Twentieth century art and crafts, with special emphasis on American paintings and prints; Japanese woodblock prints. *Mailing Add:* c/o The Hahn Gallery Chestnut Hill Philadelphia PA 19118

HAHN, STEPHEN
DEALER
Pos: Dir, Stephen Hahn Gallery, New York, currently. *Specialty:* French paintings. *Mailing Add:* 817 Fifth Ave New York NY 10021

HAINES, RICHARD
PAINTER, MURALIST
b Marion, Iowa, Dec 29, 06. *Study:* Minneapolis Sch Art, 32-34; Ecole des Beaux Arts, Fontainebleau, France, 34. *Work:* Metrop Mus Art, New York; Corcoran Mus, Washington, DC; Los Angeles Co Mus; Dallas Mus, Tex; Kansas City Mus, Mo. *Comn:* Painted mural, Mayo Diag Clin, Rochester, Minn, 50; mosaic mural, Schoenberg & Knutson Hall, Univ Calif, Los Angeles, 54; painted mural, 3M Res Ctr, St Paul, 58; 3 large mosaic murals, Fed Bldg, Los Angeles Civil Ctr, 65; West Art and the Law Collection, 83. *Exhib:* Corcoran Biennial, Washington, DC, 51; Univ Ill, 50, 51 & 61; Am Painting, Metrop Mus, New York, 50; Carnegie Inst Int, 54; Third Biennial, Sao Paulo, Brazil, 55; retrospect 44-81, Brand Gallery, Glendale, Calif, 81; R H Love Galleries, Chicago, 83. *Pos:* Pres, Calif Watercolor Soc, 50. *Teaching:* Teacher painting, Minneapolis Sch Art, 41-42; head dept painting, Chouinard Art Inst, Los Angeles, 45-54; head dept painting, Otis Art Inst, Los Angeles, 54-74. *Awards:* First Prize in Oils, Los Angeles Co Mus, 45; First Prize Oils Ann, Calif State Fair, 48; Third Prize Oils, Biennial Nat, Corcoran Mus, 51. *Bibliog:* Feature article in, Am Artist Mag, 4/63; Prize Winning Oil Paintings, Allied Publ, 64; Louis Redstone (auth), Art in Architecture, McGraw-Hill, 68. *Media:* Oil, Mosaic. *Mailing Add:* 247 Amalfi Dr Santa Monica CA 90402

HALABY, SAMIA ASAAD
PAINTER, EDUCATOR
b Jerusalem, Palestine, Dec 12, 36; US citizen. *Study:* Mich State Univ, with Abraham Rattner & Borris Margo, MA, 60; Ind Univ, with James McGarrell, MFA, 63. *Work:* Solomon R Guggenheim Mus, New York; Speed Art Mus, Louisville; Indianapolis Mus of Art; Cleveland Mus of Art; Art Inst Chicago; and others. *Comn:* Lithograph, Cleveland Mus Print Club, 74. *Exhib:* Nine Conn Artists, Wadsworth Atheneum, 74; Recent Acquisitions, Solomon R Guggenheim Mus, 75; one-artist shows, Marilyn Pearl Gallery, New York, 78, 22 Wooster Gallery, New York, 82 & 83 & Tossan-Tossan Gallery, New York, 83; Kunstnernes Mus, Oslo, Norway, 81; Housatonic Mus, Bridgeport, Conn, 83; and others; and others. *Pos:* Artist in residence, Tamarind Lithography Workshop, 72. *Teaching:* Assoc prof painting & drawing, Ind Univ, Bloomington, 69-72 & Yale Univ, New Haven, 72-82. *Awards:* Creative Artists Pub Serv Prog Grant Painting, 79. *Bibliog:* Article, Newsday, 2/12/82; Art and liberation: Samia Halaby speaks, Aurora, spring 82; article, New York Times, 8/19/83. *Media:* Oil. *Mailing Add:* 103 Franklin St New York NY 10013

HALASZ, PIRI
HISTORIAN, CRITIC
b New York, NY, April 5, 35. *Study:* Barnard Col, BA, 56; Columbia Univ, MA, 76, PhD, 82. *Collections Arranged:* The Expressionist Vision: A Central Theme in New York in the 1940s, Hillwood Art Gallery, C W Post Ctr, Long Island Univ, 83-84. *Pos:* Contrib ed, Time Mag, 63-69; writer art sect, 67-69. *Teaching:* Adj art hist, C W Post Ctr, Long Island Univ, 76-77; adj assoc prof, Hunter Col, 82. *Mem:* Int Asn Art Critics. *Res:* Twentieth century European and American art, especially in New York in the 1940s. *Publ:* Auth, Figuration in the 40s: The other expressionism, Art in Am, 82; auth, Art criticism (and art history), in New York: The 1940s vs the 1980s, 83 & Abstract painting in general; Friedel Dzubas in particular, 83, Arts Mag. *Mailing Add:* 529 E 88th St New York NY 10128

HALBACH, DAVID ALLEN
PAINTER, INSTRUCTOR
b Santa Barbara, Calif, Jan 12, 31. *Study:* Chouinard Art Inst, cert grad; with Rex Brandt, Edward Reep & Robert Uecker. *Work:* Permanent Collection, Bank Calif, San Francisco, San Jose & Seattle, Wash; Favell Mus Western Art, Klamath Falls, Ore. *Exhib:* Cowboy Hall of Fame, Oklahoma City, 75, 77, 78, 79 & 81; Western Heritage Show, Houston, Tex, 78-81, 83 & 84; European tour, 83-; Biltmore Celebrity Show, Los Angeles, Calif, 81-84; Governor's Invitational, Cheyenne, Wyo, 81-84; Northwest Rendezvous, 83 & 84; Western Art Classic, Pillsbury Co & Northwest Airlines, 84. *Pos:* Illusr, US Navy, 52-54; with Walt Disney Studio, Burbank, 54-55; illusr & art ed, Cannon Elec Co, Los Angeles, 55-59; art dir, Mowinckle Advert, Los Angeles, 59-63. *Teaching:* Art teacher (adult educ); San Gabriel, Whittier & Covina High Schs, Calif, 65-73. *Awards:* Silver Medalist, Nat Acad-Cowboy Hall of Fame, 75. *Media:* Watercolor. *Publ:* Illusr, Orange County Illustrated, 75 & Southwest Art, 78. *Dealer:* Gateway Galleries Palm Beach FL; Reminisce Gallery Fort Worth TX. *Mailing Add:* 2722 Lema Dr Mesa AZ 85205

HALBERSTADT, ERNST
PAINTER, PHOTOGRAPHER
b Budingen, Ger, Aug 26, 10; US citizen. *Work:* Metrop Mus Art & Mus Mod Art, New York; New Brit Mus, Conn; Fogg Mus, Harvard Univ, Cambridge; Addison Gallery Am Art, Andover, Mass; Mus Fine Arts, Boston; and others. *Comn:* Murals, Rockingham Park, Salem, NH, 60 & Irving Trust Co, New York, 65; sculpture, Irving Trust Co, New York, 67 & 72 & Southside Hosp, Bayshore, Long Island, 74; murals (42 panels), Metrop Life Insurance Co, Warwick, RI, 77; and others. *Exhib:* Painting, Marion Art Ctr, 70; photog retrospective, S Rose Gallery, Boston, 79; one-man shows photog, Univ NH, 70, Traveling Show, DVA Assocs, Fla, 72 & NH Col, 77; and others. *Pos:* Dir, New Eng Artists Equity Asn, 49-52. *Teaching:* Head dept murals, Sch Mus Fine Arts, Boston, 47-51; instr photog, Penland, NC, 73; instr painting, Mass Maritime Acad, 74. *Awards:* Purchase Awards, US Govt, 41; Pepsi Cola Corp New Eng Area Fel Painting, 46; Medals, Art Dirs Club, Boston, 56-57. *Bibliog:* H Devree (auth), Newcomer, New York Times, 3/46; T Lyman (auth), E H, double vision--photographer-painter, Prof Photogr, 5/50; P S Hurd (auth), E Halberstadt--expectancy, Christian Sci Prof Monitor, 12/68. *Publ:* Illusr, Shore Road to Ogunquit, 69; and others. *Mailing Add:* Sunset Island Onset MA 02558

HALBROOK, ANNE-MIEKE PLATT
LIBRARIAN
b Dordrecht, Neth. *Study:* Rijksuniversiteit, Utrecht, Neth, Kandidaats, 66; Univ Mich, Ann Arbor, MLS, 72. *Pos:* Librn, J Paul Getty Ctr Hist Art & Humanities, 79- *Mem:* Art Libr Soc North Am; Art Librns Asn. *Interests:* Western European art and archeology. *Mailing Add:* J Paul Getty Mus 17985 W Pacific Coast Hwy Malibu CA 90265

HALBROOK, RITA ROBERTSHAW
PAINTER, PRINTMAKER
b Greenville, Miss, May 22, 30. *Study:* Miss Art Colony, with Ida Kohlmeyer, 77; Delta State Univ, BFA, 82. *Work:* Delta State Univ; William Carey Col, Miss; Pike Co Hosp, McComb, Miss; Northern Electric Co Laurel, Miss. *Comn:* October (abstract landscape), Holmes Co Bank, Lexington, Miss, 70; stained canvas, Fed Land Bank, New Orleans, 77; vestments, All Saints Cath Church, Belzoni, Miss, 78. *Exhib:* Mid-South Exhib, 66 & 67 & Artist Registry Show, 70, Brooks Men Mus; Miss Arts Festival, St Andrews Cath Gallery, Jackson, 70; Belzoni Group, Univ Fla, Gainesville, 71; Miss Gallery, Miss Mus Art, Jackson, 80-81; Wall Series, Cottanlandia Mus, Greenwood, Miss & Meridian Mus Art, Miss, 83. *Awards:* Best in Show, Miss Art Colony, 69, Crosstie Festival, 71 & Cottonlandia Competition, 83. *Bibliog:* Porioer (auth), Mississippi Artists, Univ Southern Miss Press, 78; Louis Dollahide (auth), Of Arts and Artists, Univ Miss Press, 81. *Mem:* Miss Art Colony (mem bd dirs, 80-). *Media:* Mixed Acrylic. *Dealer:* Gulf South Gallery Acton Ave McComb MS 39648. *Mailing Add:* PO Box 694 Belzoni MS 39038

HALBROOKS, DARRYL WAYNE
PAINTER, EDUCATOR
b Evansville, Ind, May 3, 48. *Study:* Univ Evansville, Ind; Murray State Univ, Ky; Southern Ill Univ. *Work:* Brooks Mem Art Gallery, Memphis, Tenn; Huntington Gallery, WVa; Evansville Mus Arts & Sci, Ind; Atlantic Richfield Corp; Millikin Univ; and others. *Exhib:* Dulin Nat Print & Drawing Exhib, Dulin Gallery, Knoxville, Tenn, 76; Exhib 280, 78 & 79; Watercolor USA, 79; one-man shows, Joy Horwich Gallery, Chicago, 79-81; Appalachian Nat, 80; and others. *Teaching:* Assoc prof painting, Eastern Ky Univ, Richmond, 72- *Awards:* Purchase Award, 72 Mid-S Exhib, Brooks Mem Art Gallery, Memphis, Tenn, 72; Purchase Award, Appalachian Corridors & Exhib 280,

Huntington, WVa, 74 & 77; Contemporary American Painting, Palm Beach, Fla, 81; and others. *Bibliog:* Marion Garmel (auth), Works on Paper, Indianapolis News, 5/74; article, Arts Mag, 5/77; article, New Art Examiner, Chicago, 10/81; and others. *Media:* Acrylic, Lithography, Film. *Dealer:* Joy Horwich Gallery 226 E Ontario Chicago 60611. *Mailing Add:* Box 948 Eastern Ky Univ Richmond KY 40475

HALE, KENNETH JOHN
LITHOGRAPHER, PAINTER
b Philadelphia, Pa, Nov 10, 48. *Study:* Calif State Univ, Long Beach, BA; Univ Ill, with Dan Socha, MFA. *Work:* Univ Colo Fine Arts Permanent Collection, Boulder; Watson Gallery, Wheaton Col; Southwest Tex State Univ; foreign US embassies. *Comn:* Three ed lithographs, US Info Agency, US Embassy Collections, 73; one ed lithograph, Ill Arts Coun, 73. *Exhib:* Potsdam Nat Print Exhib, NY, 72; 13th Ann Calgary Graphics Exhib, Can, 73; Color Print USA, Lubbock, Tex, 73; Drawings '74, Watson Gallery, Norton, Mass; Colo 2nd Print & Drawing Competition, Boulder, 75. *Teaching:* Instr lithography, Univ Tex, Austin, 73- *Awards:* Ford Found Grant, summer 75. *Media:* Mixed Media. *Mailing Add:* Art Dept Univ Tex Austin TX 78712

HALE, NATHAN CABOT
SCULPTOR, WRITER
b Los Angeles, Calif, July 5, 25. *Study:* Chouinard Art Inst, Los Angeles; Art Students League; Empire State Col, BS; Union Grad Sch, PhD. *Work:* Bronze madonna, St Anthony of Padua, East Northport, NY; bronze reliefs, Rose Assoc Bldg, Bronx, NY; also in mus & pvt collections. *Exhib:* Many group & one-man shows since 1947. *Pos:* Dir, Ages Man Found, 68-, sculptor, Cycle Life Chapel Sculpture Proj, 68- *Teaching:* Mcm fac, Pratt Inst, Brooklyn, 63-64; instr anat & drawing, Art Students League, 66-72. *Mem:* Art Students League; Audubon Artists. *Publ:* Auth, Welded Sculpture, 69, Embrace of Life--the Sculpture of Gustav Vigelund, 70 & Abstraction in Art & Nature, 72; auth, Birth of a Family, Doubleday, 79; also contribr to archit & art mags. *Mailing Add:* Ages of Man Found Sheffield Rd Amenia NY 12501

HALE, ROBERT BEVERLY
ADMINISTRATOR, INSTRUCTOR
b Boston, Mass, Jan 29, 01. *Study:* Columbia Univ Sch Archit; Fontainebleau, France; Art Students League. *Work:* Metrop Mus Art, Whitney Mus Am Art, New York; Univ Ariz, Tucson. *Collections Arranged:* Many collections arranged at the Metrop Mus Art. *Pos:* Cur Am art, Metrop Mus Art, 48-66, cur emer, 66- *Teaching:* Lectr & instr drawing & anat, Art Students League, 43-; adj prof anat, Columbia Univ, 45-67; lectr anat, Pa Acad Fine Arts, 69-80; prof art, Cooper Union, 71-80. *Awards:* First Mayor's Award for Art & Cult, City of New York, 77. *Mem:* Benjamin Franklin fel Royal Soc Arts; Tiffany Found (prcs, 56-66); hon life mem Art Students League. *Publ:* Auth, Drawing Lessons from the Great Masters, 64; ed & translr, Dr Paul Richer, Anatomie Artistique, 71; coauth (with Nike Hale), The Art of Balcomb Greene, 77; coauth (with Terry Coyle), Anatomy Lessons from the Great Masters, 77 & Albinus on Anatomy, 79, Watson-Guptill. *Mailing Add:* 2 W 67th St New York NY 10023

HALEY, JOHN CHARLES
PAINTER, SCULPTOR
b Minneapolis, Minn, Sept 21, 05. *Study:* With Cameron Booth, Minneapolis & Hans Hofmann, Munich & Capri. *Work:* Phillips Mem Gallery, Washington, DC; Metrop Mus Art, New York; San Francisco Mus Art; Oakland Art Mus; IBM Collection. *Exhib:* San Francisco Art Asn Ann, 30-60; 19th Int Watercolors Exhib, Chicago Art Inst, 40; Contemp Am Painting, Univ Ill, 48 & 51-53; Exhibs Oil Painting, 51 & Drawing, 52, Metrop Mus Art, New York; 149th Ann Painting & Sculpture, Pa Acad Fine Arts, 54; Int Biennial, Sao Paulo, Brazil, 55 & 62; Palace of Legion of Honor Winter Invitationals, 60-64; Mus Mod Art, New York, 63; one man show, M H De Young Mem Mus, San Francisco, 80. *Pos:* Mem bd dirs, San Francisco Art Inst, 59-62; mem, Inst Creative Arts, Univ Calif, 63-64. *Teaching:* Prof art, Univ Calif, Berkeley, 30-72, emer prof art, 72- *Awards:* Six Painting & Sculpture Awards, San Francisco Art Asn, 36-56; Watercolor Award, Calif Watercolor Soc, 56; Painting Award, Richmond Art Ctr, 56 & 58. *Media:* All media in painting and sculpture. *Mailing Add:* PO Box 31 Point Station Richmond CA 94807

HALEY, PATIENCE E (PATIENCE E HALEY GHIKAS)
PAINTER, CONSERVATOR
b Boston, Mass. *Study:* Oberlin Col, AB. *Work:* Addison Gallery Am Art, Andover, Mass; Smith Col Mus Art, Northampton, Mass; Ctr Arts, Wesleyan Univ, Middletown, Conn; Mus Art Ogunquit, Maine; Mus of Art, Lehigh Univ, Pa. *Comn:* History of Manchester, Conn (mural), Manchester Savings Bank. *Exhib:* One-woman shows, George Walter Vincent Smith Mus, Springfield, Mass, 60, DeCordova Mus, Lincoln, Mass, 57 & Radcliffe Inst, Cambridge, Mass, 71; New England Drawings, Lyman Allyn Mus, Conn, 57; Highlights of Am Hist, Addison Gallery, Andover, Mass, 58. *Pos:* Asst painting conserv, Dept Painting Restoration, Boston Mus, Mass, 73- *Teaching:* art instr, Abbot Acad, Andover, Mass, 56-59. *Awards:* Grant in Painting, Louis Comfort Tiffany Found, 61; Scholar in Painting, Radcliffe Inst, 69-71; Three Painting Fels, Yaddo & MacDowell Colony. *Bibliog:* Edward Betts (auth), Master Class in Watercolor, Watson-Guptill Publ, 75. *Mem:* Boston Watercolor Soc; Ogunquit Art Asn, Maine; Radcliffe Inst Fels, Inc. *Media:* Watercolor; Ink. *Mailing Add:* c/o Fenway Studios Rm 208 30 Ipswich St Boston MA 02215

HALEY, PRISCILLA J (PRISCILLA HALEY BILOUS)
PAINTER, PRINTMAKER
b Boston, Mass, June 22, 26. *Study:* Oberlin Col, Ohio, BA(fine arts), 48; Brooklyn Mus Art Sch, 52-53; with Kienbusch, Rogalski, 54. *Work:* Libr Congress, Washington, DC; Addison Gallery, Andover, Mass; Nat Acad Galleries, New York; Brooklyn Mus, NY; Philadelphia Mus Art, Pa. *Exhib:* Print Ann, Philadelphia Mus Art, Pa, 57; Print Show, Inst Contemp Art, Boston, Mass, 58; Print Ann, Libr Congress, Washington, DC, 60; Print Ann, Brooklyn Mus, NY, 60; Print Ann, Farnsworth Mus, Rockland, Maine, 63; Worcester Print Show, Worcester Art Mus, Mass, 64; New England Artists, DeCordova Mus, Lincoln, Mass, 65; Soc Am Graphic Artists Print Show, Kennedy Galleries, New York, 76. *Awards:* Medal of Honor & First Prize, Audubon Artists, 58; Tiffany Found Grant, 59; Graphics Award, Providence NJ Art Asn, 79. *Mem:* Soc Am Graphic Artists. *Media:* Etching, Intaglio; Watercolor. *Publ:* Contribr, The Print, Adele Lewis Publ, 59; illusr, The Island, P J Haley, 60. *Mailing Add:* 133 Livingston Ave Babylon NY 11702

HALEY RUSSO, SALLY FULTON
PAINTER
b Bridgeport, Conn, June 29, 08. *Study:* Yale Univ Sch Fine Arts, BFA, 31; studies with Prof Maxon, Munich, Ger, 33. *Work:* Portland Art Mus & City of Portland, Ore; State of Ore & Willamette Univ, Salem; Univ Wash, Seattle. *Comn:* US Post Office, Works Progress Admin, McConnelsville, Ohio, 39. *Exhib:* San Francisco Art Mus, 49; Reality & Fantasy, Walker Art Ctr, Minneapolis, 54; Denver Art Mus, 57 & 58; one-person shows, Portland Art Mus, 60, Maryhill Mus, Wash, 75 & Gov Off, State of Ore, 76; retrospective, Portland Art Mus, 75; Seattle Art Mus, 76; Women's Bldg, Los Angeles, 77. *Awards:* Gov Awards Poster, State of Ore, 82. *Media:* Acrylic, Egg Tempera. *Dealer:* Fountain Gallery 117 NW 21st Portland OR; Woodside/Braseth Gallery Seattle WA. *Mailing Add:* 3227 NW Thurman Portland OR 97210

HALFF, ROBERT H
COLLECTOR
b San Antonio, Tex, Dec 1, 08. *Study:* Wharton Sch, Univ Pa, grad; New Sch Social Res; NY Univ; Univ Calif, Los Angeles Exten. *Pos:* Chmn spec proj & chairperson acquisitions comt, Mod & Contemp Art Coun, Los Angeles Co Mus Art; bd trustees, Fels Contemp Art; mem bd, Los Angeles Inst Contemp Art. *Collection:* American contemporary and European art. *Mailing Add:* 1659 Waynecrest Dr Beverly Hills CA 90210

HALKIN, THEODORE
SCULPTOR, PAINTER
b Chicago, Ill, Mar 2, 24. *Study:* Art Inst Chicago, BFA, 50; Southern Ill Univ, MS(art), 52. *Work:* Art Inst Chicago; ButD. *Exhib:* 25th Biennial Contemp Am Oil Painting, Corcoran Gallery Art, Washington, DC, 57; Am Painting & Sculpture Ann, Pa Acad Fine Arts & Detroit Inst Arts, 58; one-man shows, Allan Frumkin Galleries, New York & Chicago, 61 & Phyllis Kind Gallery, Chicago, 70; Chicago Images Show, Mus Contemp Art, Chicago, 72. *Teaching:* Assoc prof art, Art Inst Chicago. *Awards:* 21st Ann Midyear Show Purchase Prize, Butler Inst Am Art, 56; Chicago & Vicinity Show First Prize for Sculpture, Art Inst Chicago, 65; Cass Andran Award, 72. *Bibliog:* Article, Art Int, 2/64; Franz Schulz (auth), Fantastic Images, Follett, 72. *Mailing Add:* c/o Phyllis Kind Gallery 313 W Superior St Chicago IL 60610

HALKO, JOE
SCULPTOR, PAINTER
b Great Falls, Mont, Aug 11, 40. *Study:* Col Great Falls, Mont. *Comn:* Mural, comn by C A Rumford, Great Falls Sporting Goods, Mont, 70; centennial sculpture, Great Falls Gas Co, Mont. *Exhib:* C M Russell Mus Art Show & Auction, Great Falls, 73, 75, 77-83; Mus of Native Am Cult, Spokane, Wash, 77-78; Fred Oldfield Show, Tacoma, Wash, 77-78; Soc Animal Artists, Sportsmans Edge, New York, 78 & Owens Gallery, Okla, 78; one-man show, C M Russell Mus Art, Great Falls, Mont, 82. *Awards:* Spec Award Western Art, Spokane Art Exhib, Wash State Hist Soc, 74; Best Sculpture, C M Russell Auction, 79 & 82; Mont Hist Soc Award Merit, 79 & 81. *Bibliog:* Verna Lund Praast (auth), Back home to wildlife, Billings Gazette, Mont, 4/73; Denise Mort (auth), Halko gives wildlife seminar, Great Falls Tribune, 3/78. *Mem:* Soc Animal Artists; Northwest Rendezvous Group. *Media:* Wax; Acrylic, Oil. *Publ:* Illusr, A Century in the Foothills 1876 to 1976, Fairfield Times, 76. *Dealer:* Settler's West Galleries Tucson AZ; Artist Union, Bozeman MT. *Mailing Add:* RR 1 South Box 2209 Cascade MT 59421

HALL, CARL ALVIN
PAINTER, INSTRUCTOR
b Washington, DC, Sept 17, 21. *Study:* Meinzinger Art Sch, Detroit, Mich, with Carlos Lopez. *Work:* Whitney Mus Am Art, New York, NY; Boston Mus Art, Mass; Springfield Art Inst, Mass; Swope Art Gallery, Terre Haute, Ind. *Exhib:* 66th Ann Western, Denver Art Mus, 60; 18th Artists West Miss, Colorado Springs, 61; Drawings USA, St Paul Gallery, Minn & Traveling Show, 61; Century 21, Seattle, Wash, 62; The West, 80 Contemporaries, Univ Ariz, 66; Bicentennial Exhib, Ore, 76-77. *Teaching:* Artist in residence, Willamette Univ, 48-72, assoc prof, 78- *Awards:* Nat Inst Arts & Lett Grant, 49; Newberry Prize, Detroit Inst Art, 49. *Bibliog:* Collection of drawings, Northwest Rev, 63; article in Alaska J, Vol 7, 77; Neglected generation: American realist painters 1930-1948, Wichita Art Mus, 5-6/81. *Publ:* Auth, Voyage of the eye, Malahat Review, 10/81. *Mailing Add:* 4626 Pettyjohn Rd S Salem OR 97302

HALL, JOHN (SCOTT)
EDUCATOR, PAINTER
b Edmonton, Alta, Jan 17, 43. *Study:* Alta Col of Art, dipl(fine arts); Inst Allende, Mex. *Work:* Nat Gallery Can; Montreal Mus Fine Arts; Can Coun Art Bank, Ottawa; Glenbow Alta Art Gallery, Calgary; Alta Art Found, Edmonton. *Exhib:* Realism: Emulsion & Omission, Agnes Etherington Art Centre, Kingston, Ont, 72; Alta Realists, Edmonton Art Gallery, 75; What's New, Edmonton Art Gallery, 76; Realism in Can, Norman MacKenzie Art Gallery, Univ Regina, 78; Nat Gallery of Canada, 79; Public School 1, New York, 80; Mendel Gallery, Saskatoon, Calgary; Aggregation Gallery, Toronto, 80-81; solo exhibs, Southern Alta Art Gallery, Lethbridge, 82 & Edmonton Art Gallery, 83. *Collections Arranged:* A Major Survey of the Rose Motif in Western Culture Traveling Exhib, Rose Mus, 73-74. *Teaching:* Vis instr painting & design, Ohio Wesleyan Univ, 69-70; instr painting & design, Alta Col of Art, Calgary, 70-71; asst prof painting & drawing, Univ Calgary, 71-81, assoc prof, 81- *Awards:* Proj grant, 73, travel grants, 75 & 77 & sr grant, 79, Can Coun. *Bibliog:* Corinne Mandel (auth), rev, Artscanada, 7-8/81; Derek Michael Besant (auth), John Hall--the artist as a tourist, Artsmag, 8-9/81; Otto Rapp (auth), article, Lethbridge Herald, 12/6/82. *Mem:* Royal Can Acad; Can Artists Representation; Alta Soc Artists (pres, 67-68). *Media:* Acrylic. *Dealer:* Aggregation Gallery 83 Front St E Toronto ON M5E 1B8. *Mailing Add:* 19 Rosetree Rd NW Calgary AB T2K 1M8 Canada

HALL, JOHN A
PAINTER, EDUCATOR
b Toronto, Ont, Oct 10, 14. *Study:* Ont Col Art. *Work:* Art Gallery Ont; Nat Gallery, Ottawa. *Comn:* Murals in porcelain enamel on steel panels, Delhi, Port Colborne & Simcoe, Ont & Expo '67, Montreal, Que. *Exhib:* Can Group Painters; Ont Soc Artists; Royal Can Acad; New York World's Fair, 39; Rio, 44 & 46; and others. *Collections Arranged:* Can Nat Exhib, Can Furniture Mart & Can Pavilion, Brussels, Belgium. *Teaching:* Instr, Art Gallery Toronto; instr painting, Ont Dept Educ, summer courses; assoc prof drawing & painting, Dept Archit, Univ Toronto; retired. *Awards:* Can Arts Coun Sr Artists' Award, 63. *Mem:* Print & Drawing Coun Can; Ont Soc Artists; Ont Asn Archit. *Media:* Oil, Watercolor. *Mailing Add:* Glencroft RRD 2 Newmarket ON L3Y 4V9 Canada

HALL, LEE
ADMINISTRATOR, PAINTER
b Lexington, NC, Dec 15, 34. *Study:* Univ NC, Greensboro, BFA; NY Univ, scholar, 65, AM & PhD; Warburg Inst, Univ London; Univ NC, Greenbro, DFA, 66. *Work:* Hudson River Mus; Montclair Art Mus; Drew Univ, NJ; Greenville Mus, SC; Citicorp; and others. *Exhib:* One-woman shows, Ruth White Gallery, 68, Drew Univ, 74 & Betty Parsons Gallery, 75, 77, 78, 80 & 82; RI Sch Design, 75; Phoenix Gallery, Washington, DC, 83. *Pos:* Chmn dept art, Drew Univ, Madison, NJ, 65-74; consult, Nat Endowment for Humanities, 69-75; dean visual arts, State Univ NY, Purchase, 74-75; pres, RI Sch Design, 75-83. *Awards:* Am Philos Soc Grant, 65 & 68. *Mem:* Col Art Asn Am. *Media:* Watercolor, Polymer Tempera. *Res:* History and theory of symbolism in 19th and 20th century art. *Publ:* Auth, Women artists in the academic world, Art & Sexual Politics, 73; auth, Ruth Vollmer's sculpture (catalog), Everson Mus, Syracuse, 74; auth, Art & sullen craft of portraiture, Craft Horizons, 74. *Dealer:* Harriet Lebish Gallery 50 W 57th St New York NY 10019. *Mailing Add:* RI Sch of Design Providence RI 02903

HALL, MICHAEL DAVID
SCULPTOR, EDUCATOR
b Upland, Calif, May 20, 41. *Study:* Western Wash State Col, 58-60; Univ NC, BA, 62; Univ Iowa, 62; Univ Wash, MFA(sculpture), 64. *Work:* Princeton Univ Art Mus, NJ; Jacksonville Art Mus, Fla; Univ Iowa Art Mus, Iowa City; J B Speed Art Mus, Louisville, Ky; Wright State Univ; and others. *Exhib:* Whitney Mus Am Art Ann Sculpture Exhib, New York, 68 & 73; American Sculpture, Sheldon Mem Art Gallery, Univ Nebr, Lincoln, 70; Hammarskjold Plaza, New York, 72; Sculpture Off the Pedestal, Grand Rapids, Mich, 73; Three Installations, Detroit Inst Arts, 77; Scale & Environment, Walker Art Ctr, Minneapolis, 77; Los Angeles Inst Contemp Art, 80; Nassau Co Mus, Roslyn, NY, 83; and others. *Teaching:* Instr ceramics & sculpture, Univ Colo, Boulder, 65-66; assoc prof sculpture, Univ Ky, 66-70; resident sculptor, Cranbrook Acad Art, 70- *Awards:* Guggenheim Found Fel, 73; Nat Endowment Art Fel, 74; Mich Found Arts Fel, 78. *Bibliog:* Articles, Arts Mag, 11/77, 2/78 & 6/79. *Mem:* Mus Am Folk Art; NY State Hist Asn; Visual Arts Div; Mich Coun Arts; Col Art Asn. *Media:* Steel, Aluminum. *Publ:* Auth, Icons of John Perates, Cincinnati Art Mus, 74; auth, The Artist as Collector, Brooklyn Mus, 76; auth, The Isolate Artist in America, Transmitters, Philadelphia Col Art, 81; The Hemphill Perspective, The Hemphill Collection, Milwaukee Art Mus, 81. *Dealer:* Hill Gallery 163 Townsend Birmingham MI 48011. *Mailing Add:* c/o Cranbrook Acad of Art 500 Lone Pine Rd Bloomfield Hills MI 48013

HALL, REX EARL
PAINTER, EDUCATOR
b Asbury, Mo, Feb 3, 24. *Study:* Washburn Univ, AB; Kansas City Art Inst; Univ Wichita, MFA. *Work:* Wichita Art Mus; Wichita State Univ. *Exhib:* Kans Ann, 56-63; Kans Biennial, 59-64; one-man shows, Birger Sandzen Gallery, 63, Kansas City Pub Libr, Mo, 63 & Wichita Art Mus, 64; and others. *Teaching:* Prof art, Kans State Teachers Col, 60-68; prof art & chmn dept, Emporia Kans State Col, 69- *Awards:* Wichita Air Capital Award, 57 & 58; Living with Art, Wichita, 60; Designer-Craftsmen Show Award, Lawrence, Kans, 62. *Mem:* Kans Fedn Art (vpres, 62); Kans Art Educ Asn; Col Art Asn Am; founder Index Art Group; Wichita Art Guild (vpres, 58-); plus others. *Publ:* Auth, A profile, Kans Art Educ Asn J, 61; auth, three booklets for Kans Art Educ Asn, 64-65. *Mailing Add:* Dept of Art Emporia Kansas State Col Emporia KS 66801

HALL, ROBERT L
CURATOR, PAINTER
b Miami, Fla. *Study:* Fisk Univ, BS(art); George Washington Univ, MAT(mus educ), 75. *Work:* Fisk Univ Mus Art; Carroll Reece Mus, ETenn State Univ. *Comn:* Mural, Miami-Dade Community Col, Cult Arts Ctr, Miami, 73. *Exhib:* Lowe Art Mus, Univ Miami, 70; Zale Mus, Bishop Col, Tex, 78; Black Artists South, Huntsville Mus Art, Ala, 79; Recent Works, Van Vechten Art Gallery, Fisk Univ, 82; Carroll Reece Mus, ETenn State Univ, 84. *Collections Arranged:* Lev Mills Prints (auth, catalog), 78; Betty Blayton (auth, catalog), 79; Recent Acquisitions (auth, catalog), Fisk Univ Mus Art, 80; Portraits by Carl Van Vechten Traveling Show (auth, catalog), 80; Anderson, Hyman and Wood (auth, catalog), 81. *Pos:* Cur collections & educ, Fisk Univ Mus Art, 73- *Teaching:* Instr, Fisk Univ, 76-79. *Mem:* Intermuseum Coun Nashville (bd mem, 80-82, treas, 81-82); Tenn Asn Mus. *Media:* Oil. *Mailing Add:* Art Mus Fisk Univ Box 2 Nashville TN 37208

HALL, SUSAN
PAINTER
b Point Reyes Station, Calif, Mar 19, 43. *Study:* Calif Col Arts & Crafts, Oakland, 62-65; Univ Calif, Berkeley, MA, 67. *Work:* Whitney Mus, New York; Brooklyn Mus, NY; Carnegie Inst, Pittsburgh, Pa; San Francisco Mus Art. *Exhib:* San Francisco Mus Art Ann, 66; one-woman shows, San Francisco Mus Art, 67, Whitney Mus, 72, Nancy Hoffman Gallery, New York, 75, Hamilton Gallery, 78-79 & 81 & Dart Gallery, Chicago, 81; Twenty-six Contemp Women Artists, Aldrich Mus Contemp Art, Ridgefield, Conn, 71; Womans Work: Am Art 1974, Philadelphia Civic Ctr, 74; Back to the USA, traveling in Ger & Switz, 83; and others. *Teaching:* Instr, Univ of Calif, Berkeley, 67-70, Sarah Lawrence Col, Bronxville, NY, 72-75 & Sch Visual Arts, 81- *Awards:* Nat Endowment Arts Award. *Bibliog:* Alfred Frankenstein (auth), Extraordinary Realities, San Francisco Chronicle, 11/73; John R Clarke (auth), Visual and conceptual structures in Susan Hall's painting, Arts Mag, 9/79; Klaus Honnef (auth), article, Kunstforum, 5/83. *Mailing Add:* 10 White St New York NY 10013

HALLAM, BEVERLY (LINNEY)
PAINTER, LECTURER
b Lynn, Mass, Nov 22, 23. *Study:* Mass Col Art, BSEd, 45; Cranbrook Acad Art, 48; Syracuse Univ, MFA, 51-53. *Work:* Everson Mus, Syracuse, NY; Corcoran Gallery Art, Washington, DC; Colby Col Art Mus, Waterville, Maine; Worcester Art Mus, Mass; Addison Gallery Am Art, Andover, Mass. *Exhib:* One-person shows, Inst Contemp Art, Boston, 56 & 77, Fitchburg Art Mus, Mass, 72, and others; View 1960, Inst Contemp Art, Boston; New England Watercolor Soc, Boston Mus Fine Arts, 61, 65 & 67; retrospective, Addison Gallery Am Art, 71; 76 Maine Artists, Maine State Mus, 76; Collectors Collect Contemporary, Inst Contemp Art, Boston, 77; Recent Acquisitions, Bowdoin Col Mus Art, 81; Selections from the Collection of Univ Maine, Orono, Farnsworth Mus Art & Libr, 82; Works by Contemporary Maine Artists, Portland Mus Art, Maine, 83; and many others. *Teaching:* Chmn art dept, Lasell Jr Col, 45-49; assoc prof painting & teacher educ, Mass Col Art, 49-62; lectr & demonstr, Use of Polyvinyl Acetate as Painting Medium, throughout Eastern US, 52- *Awards:* Pearl Safir Award for Outstanding Painting by a Woman, Silvermine Guild Artists, 55; Blanche E Colman Found Award, 60; New Eng Watercolor Soc, 60, 62 & 64; and others. *Bibliog:* Edward Betts (auth), Creative Landscape Painting, 78 & Creative Seascape Painting, 81, Watson-Guptill; Babbette Brandt Fromme (auth), Choice, Northeastern Edition, Crown Publ, 81. *Mem:* Ogunquit Art Asn (pres, 64); Barn Gallery Assoc. *Media:* Acrylic on Canvas. *Dealer:* Hobe Sound Galleries Hobe Sound FL 33455; PS Galleries Ogunquit ME 03909. *Mailing Add:* Surf Point Studio RR 1 Box 381 York ME 03909

HALLER, EMANUEL
PAINTER, PRINTMAKER
b Newark, NJ, Sept 7, 27. *Study:* Newark Sch Fine & Industrial Art, cert, 49. *Work:* NJ State Mus, Trenton; Newark Mus, NJ; Monmouth Col, West Long Branch, NJ; Rosenwald Collection, Jenkintown, Pa; Am Tel & Tel, Bedminster, NJ. *Exhib:* Pa Acad Art Open, Philadelphia, 66; Eastern Drawing Open, Philadelphia Mus Art, 70; Boston Printmakers, Boston Mus Art; NJ Ann, NJ State Mus, Trenton; NJ Ann, Newark Mus, 77. *Bibliog:* Loren Eisley (auth), All the Strange Hours, Scribner's, 75. *Media:* All. *Publ:* Auth & illusr, article on travel drawings, Am Artist Mag, 70. *Mailing Add:* 121 Greenbrook Rd North Plainfield NJ 07060

HALLIDAY, NANCY RUTH
ILLUSTRATOR
b Chicago, Ill, Mar 30, 36. *Study:* Mich State Univ, East Lansing, 54-56 & 58-61; Art Sch Soc Arts & Crafts, Mich, 56-57; Univ Okla, Norman, BSc, 62. *Work:* Payne's Prairie Visitor Ctr, Fla; Fla State Mus, Gainesville; Nat Mus Natural Hist, Smithsonian Inst; Hunt Inst Botanical Documentation, Pittsburgh, Pa; Visual Arts Gallery, Pensacola Jr Col, Pensacola, Fla. *Comn:* Watercolor poster, Rare Animal Relief Effort, Inc, New York, 81; five oil paintings, State Fla Dept Natural Resources, Gainesville, 81. *Exhib:* Two-person show, Mus Arts & Sci, Macon, Ga, 82; Visual Arts Gallery, Pensacola Jr Col, Fla, 83; Wildlife in Art, Nat Wildlife Fedn, Vienna, Va, 83; Windows Wildlife, Cincinnati Zoo, Ohio, 83; Ann Bird Art Exhib, Leigh Yawkey Woodson Art Mus, Wausau, Wis, 83; and many others. *Pos:* Receptionist & asst exhib preparator, Mus Mich State Univ, East Lansing, 57-60; asst, Mus Northern Ariz, Flagstaff, summer 63; artist, Nat Mus Natural Hist, Smithsonian Inst, 66-70; illusr dept natural sci, Fla State Mus, Gainesville, 73-81. *Teaching:* Instr, animal illus, Univ Fla, Gainesville, 77, 78 & 82. *Awards:* First Prize Color Wildlife, Guild Natural Sci Illusr Show, Hunt Inst Botanical Doc, Pa, 79; Second Prize for Watercolor, Wildlife in Art Show,

Nat Wildlife Fedn, 83. *Bibliog:* Peggy Thomson (auth), Fun behind the Smithsonian's walls, Potomac Supplement, Washington Post, 11/17/68. *Mem:* Soc Animal Artists; Guild of Natural Sci Illusr; Graphic and Scientific Illusr Asn (vpres, 80-81). *Media:* Watercolor; Pen & Ink. *Res:* History of biological illustration, history of animals in fine art. *Publ:* Illusr, Behavioral ecology of the Yucatan jay, Wilson Bulletin, 76; auth, Adventures of an illustrator on the island of Trinidad, Trinidad Naturalist Mag, 11-12/80; auth, Bird illustration, In: Handbook of Biological Illustration, Guild of Natural Sci Illusr & Van Nostrand Reinhold (in prep); illusr, Nannipus phlegon (mammalia, equidae) from the Pliocene (Blancan) of Florida, Bulletin Fla State Mus, Vol 25, No 1; illusr cover, Rare Animal Relief Effort Inc Ann Report, 81. *Mailing Add:* 629 NE Eleventh Avenue Gainesville FL 32601

HALLMAN, GARY LEE
PHOTOGRAPHER
b St Paul, Minn, Aug 7, 40. *Study:* Univ Minn, Minneapolis, BA, 66, MFA, 71. *Work:* Mus Mod Art, New York; Int Mus Photog, Rochester; Nat Gallery Can, Toronto; Fogg Art Mus, Harvard Univ; Princeton Univ Art Mus. *Comn:* Photo murals, Dayton-Hudson Corp, Minneapolis, 70. *Exhib:* 60's Continuum, Int Mus Photog, 72; Fight of the Image, Contemporary American Drawings, Paintings & Photographs, Mus Turin, Italy, 73; one-man shows, Int Mus Photog, George Eastman House, 74 & Light Gallery, New York, 75; Fourteen American Photographers, Baltimore Mus, 75. *Teaching:* Vis artist, Southampton Col, summer 72 & 73; asst prof photog, Univ Minn, Minneapolis, 70-76, assoc prof photog, 76-; vis adj prof photog, RI Sch Design, 77. *Awards:* Grad Sch Univ Minn Res Grant, 73 & 76; Nat Endowment Arts Photog Fel Grant, 75; Bush Found Fel for Artists, 76. *Bibliog:* E W Peterson (auth), The photography of Gary Hallman, Image, 9/75. *Mem:* Soc Photog Educ. *Dealer:* Light Gallery 724 Fifth Ave New York NY 10019. *Mailing Add:* 2932 Pierce St NE Minneapolis MN 55418

HALLMAN, H THEODORE, JR
CRAFTSMAN, DESIGNER
Study: Tyler Sch, Temple Univ, Sen scholar, BFA & BSEd; Fontainebleau Fine Arts, Pew scholar, cert, with Jacques Villon; Cranbrook Acad Art, West scholar, MFA(painting) & MFA(textile design); Bundestextilschule, Austria, cert; Univ Calif, Berkeley, PhD(educ); Self-awareness study with Kenneth G Mills, Toronto. *Work:* Smithsonian Inst; Chicago Art Inst; Victoria & Albert Mus, London; Metrop Mus Art, New York; Philadelphia Mus Art, Pa; and others. *Comn:* Translucent tapestry, Nieman Marcus, Dallas; room, St John's Church, Allentown, Pa. *Exhib:* Woven Structures, Camden Arts Ctr, London, 72; 1st Int Exhib Miniature Textiles, Brit Crafts Ctr, London, 74; one-man shows, Nicolaysen Art Mus, Casper, Wyo, 81, Sunset Ctr, Carmel, Calif, 81 & Southwest Ctr, San Antonio, Tex, 82; and others. *Pos:* Consult, ILO Textiles, Jamaica, summer 68; textile designer, var co. *Teaching:* Instr, Haystack Sch, Maine & Penland Sch Crafts, summers 58-69; prof textiles & chmn dept, Moore Col Art, 65-70; assoc prof textile design, San Jose State Univ, 72-75; lectr & workshop leader, US, Can & Eng (incl San Antonio, Vancouver, Ottawa & Mich, 77-78); instr design, Ont Col of Art, Toronto; guest lectr, World Craft Conf, Mex, 76. *Awards:* Tiffany Found Grant, 62; Textile Prize, Int Kunsthandwerk Expos, Stuttgart, 67. *Bibliog:* Neuman (auth), Plastics as an Art Form, Chilten, 68; Regensteiner (auth), Art of Weaving, 70 & Willcox (auth), Techniques of Rya Knotting, 71, Van Nostrand Reinhold; among others. *Mem:* Philadelphia Coun Prof Craftsmen ; Ont Craft Coun; hon mem Int Soc Arts & Lett; Nat Soc Lit & Arts. *Media:* Weaving, Textile Designing. *Mailing Add:* 202 Harleysville Pike Souderton PA 18964

HALLMARK, DONALD PARKER
HISTORIAN, MUSEUM DIRECTOR
b McPherson, Kans, Feb 16, 45. *Study:* Univ Ill, BFA(art hist), 67; Univ Iowa, MA(art hist), 70; St Louis Univ, PhD, 80. *Collections Arranged:* Richard W Bock Sculpture Collection (with catalog), Greenville Col, 75; Frank Lloyd Wright Decorative Arts Collection, Dana House, 81-82. *Pos:* Cur & dir, Richard W Bock Sculpture Collection, Greenville Col, 72-81; supt, hist site, Dana House, Springfield, Ill, 81-; lectr, Springfield Art Asn, 81-, Sangamon State Univ, 82- *Teaching:* Assoc prof art & fine arts, Greenville Col, 70-81, prof, 81- *Awards:* Kress Found Res Grant, Univ Iowa, 69; Shell Found Fac Improv Grant, 72-73; Nat Endowment Arts & Am Asn Mus Cur Seminar Scholar, 75 & 80. *Bibliog:* W R Hasbrouck (auth), Editors note, Prairie Sch Rev, Vol VIII, No 1, 71; H Allen Brooks (auth), Prairie Sch, Univ Toronto, 72; David Hanks (auth), Decorative Designs of Frank Lloyd Wright, Dutton, 79. *Mem:* Am Asn Mus; Col Art Asn. *Res:* Late 19th and early 20th century sculpture and architecture with emphasis on the Chicago School, 1880-1915. *Publ:* Auth, Richard W Bock, Sculptor, Prairie Sch Rev, 71; auth, Chicago's prairie sculptor, R W Bock, Univ Ill, 82. *Mailing Add:* 1613 Lowell Ave Springfield IL 62704

HALPERN, LEA
CERAMIST, PAINTER
Study: Acad in Amsterdam, with Bert Nienhuis; Reiman Art Sch, Berlin; Austrian Nat Art Sch, Vienna, with Prof M Powolny; Nat Res Sch Clay & Ceramic Indust, Gouda, Holland, with Dr Kurt Zimmerman, dipl. *Work:* Baltimore Mus Art, Md; Metrop Mus of Art, New York; Nat Collection Fine Arts, Washington, DC; Victoria & Albert Mus, London; Tel Aviv Mus, Israel. *Comn:* The City of Amsterdam; Wertheim & Gomperts Bank, Amsterdam; Synagogue, The Hague; Temple Emanu El, Birmingham, Ala; New Sch Bldg, Chizuk Amuno Congregation, Baltimore. *Exhib:* One-woman shows, The Stedelijk Mus, Amsterdam, Ryksmus, Huis Lambert Van Meerten, Delft, Phillips Collection, Washington, DC, Baltimore Mus Art, 76, Frans Hals Mus, Haarlem, Neth, and others. *Teaching:* Instr ceramics, New Art Sch,

Amsterdam, Univ NH, Westchester Co Ctr, White Plains, NY & privately. *Awards:* French Ministry of Fine Arts Prize for Holland, Int Exhib in the Jeu de Paume, Paris. *Bibliog:* Article, Art News; G Forsythe (auth), 20th Century Ceramics, London. *Mem:* Am Craft Coun; World Craft Coun; Md Craft Coun; Kiln Club of Washington; Artists Equity Asn. *Mailing Add:* 2714 Bartol Ave Baltimore MD 21209

HALPERN, NATHAN L
COLLECTOR
b Sioux City, Iowa, Oct 22, 14. *Study:* Otis Art Inst, Los Angeles; Univ Southern Calif, BA, 36; Harvard Univ Law Sch, LLB(cum laude), 39. *Pos:* Pres, TNT Commun Inc. *Collection:* French impressionist and post-impressionist art; Chinese ceramics; SE Asian art. *Mailing Add:* 993 Fifth Ave New York NY 10028

HALSEY, WILLIAM MELTON
PAINTER, EDUCATOR
b Charleston, SC, Mar 13, 15. *Study:* Univ SC; Sch Boston Mus Fine Arts, with Alexandre Iacovleff & Karl Zerbe, Paige Traveling Fel, 39-41; Univ Mex. *Work:* Baltimore Mus Art, Md; SC Arts Comn State Collection, Columbia; Mint Mus Art, Charlotte, NC; Gibbes Art Gallery, Charleston; Greenville Co Mus Art, SC. *Comn:* Three frescoes, Berkshire Mus Art, Pittsfield, Mass, 39; murals, Beth Elohim Synagogue, Charleson, 50 & Baltimore Hebrew Congregation Temple, 52; Container Corp Am, Ford Motor Co; and many portrait comn in pub bldgs. *Exhib:* Contemp Artists SC, Columbia Mus, Florence Mus, Greenville Mus & Gibbes Art Gallery; retrospective, four SC mus, 72-73; Art in Transition, Boston Mus Fine Arts, 77; Spoleto Festival USA, 82; Painting in the South, Va Mus, 83; Birmingham Mus, 84; Nat Acad Design, 84; Miss Mus, 84; J B Speed Art Mus, 84; New Orleans Mus, 85; and many others. *Teaching:* Asst prof painting & drawing, Col Charleston, 65-75, artist in residence, 76-; instr painting & drawing, Newberry Col, 68-70. *Awards:* Res Grant, SC State Art Comn, 74-75; SC Comt Humanities Grant, 82; Col Charleston Grant, 82. *Bibliog:* Jack Morris (auth), Contemporary Artists of South Carolina, 70 & William M Halsey: retrospective (monogr), 72, Greenville Co Mus Art. *Mem:* Guild SC Artists (pres, 58). *Media:* Oil, Casein. *Publ:* Coauth, A Travel Sketch Book, 71; auth, Maya Journal, 77. *Mailing Add:* 26 Archdale St Charleston SC 29401

HALVORSEN, RUTH ELISE
PAINTER, WRITER
b Camas, Wash. *Study:* Portland Art Mus Sch, Ore; Pratt Inst, Brooklyn; Columbia Univ; and with Walter Beck, Charles Martin & Albert Heckman. *Work:* Reed Col, Portland; Georgia-Pacific, Portland; Univ Ore, Eugene; Ft Sumner Marine Hosp, NMex; Portland Art Mus. *Exhib:* San Francisco World's Fair, 39; Henry Gallery, Univ Wash, 43; Rockefeller Ctr, New York, 48; Fifth Army Midwestern Travel Show, 55; Portland Art Mus Show, 71. *Teaching:* Instr art, Portland State Col, 40-60; art supvr, Portland Pub Schs, 43-62. *Awards:* Pratt Inst Alumni Award for Distinguished Serv in Art Educ, 72; Distinguished Serv Award, Nat Art Educ Asn, 74; Distinguished Fel Nat Art, 83. *Mem:* Portland Art Mus (mem bd, 47-53); Ore Contemp Crafts Asn (mem bd, 44-71); Nat Art Educ Asn (mem bd, 47-, vpres & pres, 59-63); Pac Art Asn (vpres & pres, 55-57); Contemp Crafts (mem bd & docent). *Media:* Watercolor, Oil. *Publ:* Co-auth, Painting in the Classroom, 62; contribr, Art J; also numerous articles for var art mags. *Mailing Add:* 422 NE Going St Portland OR 97211

HALVORSON, JILL BAKER See Baker, Jill

HAMADY, WALTER SAMUEL
GRAPHIC ARTIST, PAPERMAKER
b Flint, Mich, Sept 13, 40. *Study:* Wayne State Univ, BFA, 64; Cranbrook Acad Art, MFA, 66. *Work:* Numerous public and private collections. *Exhib:* Seventy from the Seventies: A Decade of Fine Printing, New York Pub Libr, 80; Paperworks: Art of Paper/Art on Paper, Belgrade, Yugoslavia, 81; and others. *Pos:* Proprietor, The Perishable Press Limited, 64- *Teaching:* Prof drawing, bk illus, typography & papermaking, Univ Wis-Madison, 66-81. *Awards:* Nat Endowment for the Arts Grants, 76-79; Howard Found Fel, 77-78; Wis Alumni Res Found Grants & Awards, 72-81. *Bibliog:* Joseph Blumenthal (auth), The Printed Book in America, Dartmouth/Godine, 77; Book Publishing in Wisconsin, Wis Hist Soc, 77; Jules Heller (auth), Papermaking, Watson-Guptill, 78. *Res:* Typecasting; Sequoyah Syllabary; Papermaking. *Publ:* Auth, The Plumfoot Poems, 69 & auth, Since Mary, 71, New Directions; auth, These Chairs, 71 & The Interminable Gabberjabbs, 74-75, Perishable Press; auth, Papermaking by Hand, A Book of Suspicions, 81. *Mailing Add:* PO Box 7 Mt Horeb WI 53572

HAMAGUCHI, YOZO
PRINTMAKER
b Wakayama-ken, Japan, Apr 5, 09. *Study:* Sch Fine Arts, Tokyo, 28-30; independent study, painting & engraving, Paris, 30-39. *Work:* Nat Mus Mod Art, Tokyo; Mus Mod Art, New York; Victoria & Albert Mus, London; Libr Cong & Nat Gallery, Washington, DC; Cleveland Mus Art. *Exhib:* One-man exhibs, Paris, Turin, Sao Paulo, New York & others, 58-72 & Cleveland Mus Art, Ohio, 73, San Francisco, 83; and others. *Awards:* 1st Int Prize, Sao Paulo Biennale, 57; Grand Prizes, Ljubljana Int Print Biennale, 61 & 72; Purchase Prize, Warsaw Nat Mus, 66 & 72. *Mem:* Acad Fiorentina Della Arti del Disegno. *Dealer:* Vorpal Gallery New York NY San Francisco & Laguna Beach Calif. *Mailing Add:* c/o Vorpal Gallery 393 Grove St San Francisco CA 94102

HAMANN, MARILYN D
EDUCATOR, PAINTER
b Los Angeles, Calif, Nov 24, 45. *Study:* Univ Calif, Berkeley, BA, 67, with Robert Hudson & Jim Melchert, MA, 70. *Work:* Univ Ky Art Mus, Lexington; Citizen's Fidelity Bank & Trust Co & Liberty Nat Bank, Louisville, Ky. *Exhib:* Whitney Mus Am Art, New York, 73; Everson Mus Art, New York, 74; Contemp Art Ctr, Cincinnati, 74; New Orleans Mus Art, 75; Oakland Mus Art, Calif, 75; J B Speed Art Mus, Louisville, Ky, 74, 77 & 81; Southeastern Ctr Contemp Art, Winston-Salem, NC, 81. *Teaching:* Assoc prof, Univ Ky, Lexington, 80- *Awards:* Purchase Award, J B Speed Mus Art, 77; Merit Award, 70th Ann, Birmingham Mus Art, 78. *Bibliog:* Sarah Lansdell (auth), article, Louisville Courier-J, 77; Jacqueline Rapp (auth), article, New Art Examiner, 78; Guy Mendes (producer), Kentucky Now, Ky Educ Television, 79. *Media:* Acrylics. *Dealer:* Nancy Lurie Gallery 1632 North LaSalle Chicago IL 60614. *Mailing Add:* 321 Grosvenor Ave Lexington KY 40508

HAMEL, BERNARD FRANKLIN
PAINTER
b Holyoke, Mass, May 29, 33. *Study:* Art Students League, 51-52; Pratt Inst, 56-59. *Exhib:* Ann Nat Exhib, Nat Acad Design, NY, 77; Nat Exhib, Acad Artists Asn, Springfield, Mass, 77-79; Ann Exhib, Conn Acad Fine Arts, Wadsworth Atheneum, 77 & 78; 42nd Nat Art Exhib, Cooperstown Art Asn, NY, 7/77; Nat Exhib, Nat Soc Painters in Casein & Acrylic, New York, 77-79; Knickerbocker Artists 30th Exhib, 80-81; Holyoke Mus Libr Exhib, 83. *Awards:* Creative Art Award, Audubon Artists, 81; Greenwich Award, Silvermine Guild Artists, 81; First Award, Nat Arts Club, 81. *Mem:* Nat Soc Painters in Casein & Acrylic, New York; Allied Artists Am, NY; Silvermine Guild Artists, New Canaan, Conn; Nat Arts Club, New York. *Media:* Acrylic; Pen & Ink. *Mailing Add:* 144 High St Holyoke MA 01040

HAMER, CHARLES JAMES
PAINTER, DESIGNER
b Elmira, NY, Jan 5, 31. *Study:* Rochester Inst Technol, with Ralph Avery & Hans Barschel, BS(art & design), 56. *Work:* Lake St Presby Church, Elmira, NY; also pvt collections. *Exhib:* Salmagundi Club Ann Non-Mem, New York, 79-81; Nat Arts Club Ann, New York, 80-81; 155th Ann, Nat Acad Design, New York, 80; Allied Artists Asn, World Trade Ctr, New York, 81; and others. *Awards:* 1st Prize Watercolor, US Postal Serv, New York, 78; and others. *Mem:* Nat Acad Design; Allied Artists Am Asn. *Media:* Watercolor. *Publ:* Illusr, Newsprint application of Webb offset colour, Penrose Ann, Hasting House, 59. *Mailing Add:* 133 E 35th St New York NY 10016

HAMES, CARL MARTIN
DEALER, COLLECTOR
b Birmingham, Ala, July 12, 38. *Study:* Birmingham Southern Col, BA, 58; Samford Univ, Birmingham, MA, 71, MSEd, 80, with Cornelia Rivers & Gene Smith. *Collections Arranged:* Decade of Effective Painting in Ala, Birmingham Centennial, 71, Eye Found Art--The Collection of the Eye Found Hosp (auth, catalog), 75-77, Rx Art: The Collection of the Spain Rehabilitation Ctr (auth, catalog), 75 & Collection of Altamont Sch, Town Hall Gallery, Birmingham; Heroes and Other Myths, Birmingham Southern Col, 78; Doris Wainwright Kennedy in Private Collections, Birmingham Southern Col, 79; Paintings by Gerald Davis, Town Hall Gallery, 80; Recent Followers of Edith Frohock, 83. *Pos:* Dir, Town Hall Gallery, Birmingham, 65-; co-ed, Birmingham Mus of Art Bulletin, 73-75; mem adv bd, Ala Alliance for Arts in Educ; comt chmn, Imagination Celebration, 81- *Teaching:* Teacher art/sci, Birmingham Pub Sch, 62-64; teacher art & organizer art dept, Birmingham Univ Sch, 64-75; asst headmaster, Altamont Sch, 75-81, dean students, 81- *Awards:* Silver Bowl Award for Art, Birmingham Festival of Arts. *Mem:* Birmingham Arts Mus Art Educ Coun; Birmingham Mus Art; Ala Mus Photog; Birmingham Art; and others. *Specialty:* Alabama Mus and southeastern artists. *Collection:* Prints by 20th century European and American masters; sculptures, paintings and contemporary photographs. *Publ:* Auth, A Patient and Discerning Eye: An Appreciation of Silvia Pizitz, B'ham Mus Art, 80; auth introd, Rosalie Pettus Price Retrospective (catalog), Birmingham Mus Art; contribr, Ida Kohlmeyer Nat Retrospective (catalog). *Mailing Add:* 3963 Montclair Rd Birmingham AL 35213

HAMILL, TIM J
PAINTER, PRINTMAKER
b Clinton, Iowa, Dec 2, 42. *Study:* Univ Wis, 60-62; L'Ecole Nat Superieure Beaux-Arts, Paris, 62-63; Boston Univ Sch Fine Arts, BFA, 65, MFA, 68; Akademie Bildenden Künste, Munich, 65-66. *Work:* Boston Mus Fine Arts & Boston Pub Libr, Mass; DeCordova Mus, Lincoln, Mass; Minn Mus Art, St Paul; Worcester Mus, Mass; and many others. *Comn:* Painting, comn by Stephen Alpert, Boston, 79; 11 paintings & 2 prints, Royal Palace, Riyadh, Saudi Arabia, 80. *Exhib:* One-man exhibs, Brockton Art Ctr, Mass, 69, Milton Acad, Mass, 71-80 & Gallery Naga, Boston, 78-83; Boston Printmakers, Rose Art Mus, Waltham, Mass, 70 & 72; DeCordova Mus, Lincoln, Mass, 73, 77, 80 & 82; Photography in Printmaking, Boston Mus Fine Arts, Mass, 75; Artists in Residence, Inst Contemp Art, Boston, 75; Art Complex Mus, Duxbury, Mass, 76-81; and many others. *Pos:* Founding mem, Boston Visual Artists Union, 72-, mem exec bd, 72-75. *Teaching:* Instr painting & drawing, Boston Univ, 68-71; instr painting & drawing, Milton Acad, Mass, 71-81. *Mem:* Boston Printmakers (vpres, 82-). *Media:* Oil, Acrylic; Silkscreen, Lithography. *Dealer:* Gallery Naga 67 Newbury St Boston MA 02116. *Mailing Add:* 345 Centre St Milton MA 02186

HAMILTON, CHARLES F
EDUCATOR, WRITER
b Fairmont, WVa, May 21, 47. *Study:* Art Ctr Col Design, Los Angeles; WVa Univ, Morgantown; Fairmont State Col, WVa, BA, 68. *Pos:* Vpres, Faster Than Light Indust Inc, Pittsburgh. *Teaching:* Dept head photog, Art Inst Pittsburgh, 72-80; dir educ, Art Inst Philadelphia, 80- *Bibliog:* articles, Int Television Asn, 5/80 & Portfolio Mag, 5/80; Timothy Woodcock (auth), USA: Nude photography, SLR Camera, London, 4/81. *Mem:* Art Dir Club Philadelphia; Am Soc Mag Photogr; Asn Multi-Image; Soc Photogr Educ. *Media:* Black & White. *Res:* Emphasis on structure, lighting. *Publ:* Auth & illusr, Photographing Nudes, 1/80 & auth & illusr, A Photographic Ideabook: The Nude (in press), Prentice-Hall. *Mailing Add:* 2300 Walnut St No 321 Philadelphia PA 19103

HAMILTON, FRANK MOSS
PAINTER, ARCHITECT
b Kansas City, Mo, June 26, 30. *Study:* With Eliot O'Hara; Stanford Univ, 2 years; Univ Kans, BA(archit), 54. *Work:* Favell Mus, Klamath Falls, Ore; Leanin' Tree Gallery, Boulder, Colo; Walter Bimson's Valley Nat Bank Collection. *Exhib:* Laguna Beach Festival of Arts, Calif, 49-68; Orange Co Fair, 51; Laguna Art Asn Gallery; Nat Orange Show, Pomona; Gold Medal Western Competition, Franklin Mint Yearly Western Show, 74. *Teaching:* Pvt art classes, 49-67. *Awards:* First Awards, Laguna Beach Art Festival, 63-65; First Prizes, Lake San Marcos Art Festival, 66 & 68; Third Place, Franklin Mint Bicentennial Medal Design, 72. *Media:* Watercolor, Oil. *Publ:* Illusr, Orange Co Illus Mag, Calif, 66, 69 & Jerome Arizona Cookbook, 72. *Mailing Add:* PO Box 733 Cambria CA 93428

HAMILTON, GEORGE EARL
PAINTER, EDUCATOR
b Pittsfield, Mass, Oct 10, 34. *Study:* Int Christian Univ, 56-58; with Dr Samine Tuyoda, Japan, 58-60. *Work:* Frye Art Mus, Seattle; Univ Wash; Kaiser Found & First Nat Bank, Portland, Ore; Royal Bank Can. *Exhib:* One-person shows, Am Watercolor Soc, New York, 75 & 76, North Western Watercolor Soc, Seattle, 75-79, Mus Art, Casper, Wyo, 76, Frye Art Mus, Seattle, 76 & 81, Portland Art Mus, 77 & Univ Mus Art, Eugene, Ore, 77-79. *Teaching:* Instr watercolor, Univ Wash, 76-; instr watercolor, Univ Idaho, 79-81. *Awards:* Am Watercolor Soc Award, 76. *Mem:* Ore Watercolor Soc; Northwest Watercolor Soc. *Media:* Watercolor, Collage. *Dealer:* Gallery West 4836 SW Scholls Perry Rd Portland OR 97225. *Mailing Add:* 41416 Rodger Mountain Rd Scio OR 97374

HAMILTON, GEORGE HEARD
MUSEUM DIRECTOR, HISTORIAN
b Pittsburgh, Pa, June 23, 10. *Study:* Yale Univ, BA, MA, PhD; Williams Col, D Litt, 77. *Pos:* Curatorial staff, Yale Univ Art Gallery, 36-66; dir, Sterling & Francine Clark Art Inst, Williamstown, Mass, 66-77, emer dir, 77-; vpres & trustee, Hill-Stead Mus, Farmington, Conn; trustee, Mus Mod Art, New York; vchmn & trustee, Joseph H Hirshhorn Mus & Sculpture Garden, Washington, DC, 71-75. *Teaching:* Mem dept hist art, Yale Univ, 36-66; Robert Sterling Clark vis prof art, Williams Col, 63-64, prof art, 66-75, emer prof, 75-; Slade prof fine arts, Cambridge Univ, 71-72; Kress vis prof, Nat Gallery Art, Washington, DC, 78-79. *Awards:* Wilbur Lucius Cross Medal, Yale Grad Sch Asn, 77; Fel, Am Acad Arts & Sci, 79. *Mem:* Col Art Asn Am (pres, 66-68). *Res:* 19th and 20th century European and American art. *Publ:* Auth, Manet & his Critics, 54; Russian Art & Architecture, 54; European Painting & Sculpture, 1880-1940, 67; coauth, Raymond Duchamp-Villon, 67; auth, 19th & 20th Century Art--Painting, Sculpture, Architecture, 70. *Mailing Add:* 121 Gale Rd Williamstown MA 01267

HAMILTON, LYDIA
PAINTER
b Philadelphia, Pa, Dec 12, 47. *Study:* Pa Acad Fine Arts, cert, 73. *Work:* El Paso Mus Art, Tex; Gerald P Peters Corp, Santa Fe, NMex; Union Planters Nat Bank, Memphis, Tenn. *Comn:* Pueblo Indian Ceremonies, NJ State Coun Arts, Trenton, 80. *Exhib:* Sun Carnival Exhib, El Paso Mus Art, Tex, 78 & 82; NJ Artists Invitation, NJ State Mus, Trenton, 80; 37th Ann Painting Competition, Abilene Fine Arts Mus, Tex, 81; one-person shows, Los Llanos Gallery, Sante Fe, 82 & Pavilion Gallery, Mt Holly, NJ, 83; and others. *Pos:* Evaluator for state fellowships, NJ State Coun Arts, Trenton, 81. *Teaching:* Artist in residence, NJ high schools, 83-84. *Awards:* Scheidt Mem Traveling Scholarship, Pa Acad Fine Arts, 73; Goldberg Mem Prize, Pa Acad Fine Arts, 74; Purchase Prize, El Paso Mus Art, 76. *Mem:* fel Pa Acad Fine Arts. *Media:* Acrylic, Monoprints. *Mailing Add:* 59 Potter St Haddonfield NJ 08033

HAMILTON, PATRICIA ROSE
DEALER
b Upper Darby, Pa, Oct 21, 48. *Study:* Temple Univ, BA, 70; Rutgers Univ, MA(art hist), 71. *Collections Arranged:* Ten Americans, Masters of Watercolor (with catalogue), 74, Edward Hicks, A Gentle Spirit (with catalogue), 75 & Malta: A Totemic World, 75, Andrew Crispo Gallery; Outdoor Sculpture 1974 (with catalogue), Merriewold West Gallery, Far Hills, NJ, 74. *Pos:* Curatorial asst, Whitney Mus Am Art, New York, 71-73; sr ed, Art in Am, New York, 73-; cur exhibs, Andrew Crispo Gallery, New York, 74-75; dir, Hamilton Gallery Contemp Art, 77- *Mem:* Artist's Cert Comt. *Specialty:* Contemporary art. *Mailing Add:* 39 Fifth Ave New York NY 10003

HAMILTON, SUSAN (SUSAN HAMILTON BOLT)
PRINTMAKER, PAINTER
b Edinburg, Tex, Aug 1, 49. *Study:* Tex Tech Univ, BFA, 71; Ind Univ, Bloomington, MFA, 74. *Work:* Libr Cong, DC; Honolulu Acad Arts; US Info Agency; Readers Digest Collection. *Exhib:* Boston Printmakers, De Cordova Mus, 75; 25th Nat Exhib Prints, Libr Cong, DC, 77; 3rd Miami Graphics Biennial, Metrop Mus & Art Ctr, Fla, 77; Colorprint USA, Tex Tech Univ, 78; 5th Nat Exhib, Los Angeles Printmaking Soc, 78; 21st Nat Print Exhib, Brooklyn Mus, 78-79; 15th Sao Paulo Bienal, Brazil, 79. *Collections Arranged:* New American Graphics, Madison, Wis, 75; Former Students Exhibition, Tex Tech Univ, 77; Philadelphia Teaches Printmaking, Assoc Am Artists, Pa, 79; New Talent in Printmaking, Assoc Am Artists, NY, 79; New Prints, Impressions Gallery, 79. *Awards:* Purchase Award, 23rd Nat Exhib Prints, Libr Cong, 73; Purchase Award, 2nd Hawaii Nat Print Exhib, 73; Purchase Award, Miami Graphics Biennial, Virginia Miller Galleries, 77. *Mem:* Col Art Asn. *Media:* Serigraphy; Watercolor, Mixed Media. *Dealer:* Assoc Am Artists 663 Fifth Ave New York NY 10022. *Mailing Add:* 10787 Bushire Dr Dallas TX 75229

HAMILTON, W PAUL C
EDUCATOR, HISTORIAN
b Toronto, Ont, Mar 13, 38. *Study:* Williams Col, BA, 59; Univ Toronto, MA, 64; Johns Hopkins Univ, PhD(Fel), 73. *Pos:* Coordr educ English, Educ Serv, Nat Gallery Can, Ottawa, 73-76. *Teaching:* Asst prof, Univ Sask, Saskatoon, 70-78, assoc prof & head dept, 78- *Awards:* Grant, Italian Govt, 65-66. *Mem:* Verein Kunsthistorisches Inst, Florence. *Publ:* Auth, Andrea del Minga's Assunta in S Felicita, Kunsthistorisches Inst, 70; coauth, Grandmaison, Henderson, Kenderdine, Univ Sask, 79; auth, Disegni di Bernardino Poccetti, Olschki, 80. *Mailing Add:* Dept Art & Art Hist Univ Sask Saskatoon SK S7N 0N6 Canada

HAMLETT, DALE EDWARD
EDUCATOR, PAINTER
b Memphis, Mo, Aug 15, 21. *Study:* Northeast Mo State Univ, BS(cum laude), 44; Am Acad Art, with William Mosby; Acad Appl Art, Chicago; Chicago Art Inst, with Charles Wilamoski; Univ NMex, with Ralph Douglass & Elaine de Kooning, MA(painting), 63; also with Robert Wood, Millard Sheets, George Post, Edgar Whitney, Morris Shubin, Charles Reid & Milford Zornes. *Work:* Univ NMex; State Fair Mus, Albuquerque; NMex Inst Mining & Technol; Eastern NMex Univ. *Comn:* Series of portraits, comn by Mrs William Givens, Socorro, NMex, 67; proposed redesigning of plaza, Mayor, City of Socorro, 68; drawings of 17 founders of Sigma Tau Gamma, Warrensburg, Mo, 71; painting, KOA Campgrounds, Las Vegas, NMex, 75. *Exhib:* Sun Carnival, El Paso Mus Art, Tex, 71; Eight State Regional Watercolor Exhibs, Fedn Rocky Mountain States, Inc, 71-72; 23rd Grand Prix Int de Peinture, Deauville, France, 73; Gran Premio della Citta Eterna Palazzo delle Esposizioni, Rome, Italy, 73; 14th Ann Artists Salon, Nat Show, Okla Mus Art, Oklahoma City, 75. *Pos:* Package designer, Montgomery Ward & Co, Chicago, Ill, 47-51; commercial artist, Ward Hicks Advert Agency, Albuquerque, 51-64; artist in residence, NMex Inst Mining & Technol, 64-69. *Teaching:* Instr art, NMex Inst Mining & Technol, 65-69; assoc prof art, Eastern NMex Univ, 69- *Awards:* Best of Show, La Junta, Colo, 78; Best of Show, Black Canyon Painters, Hotchkiss, Colo, 80; Purchase Prize, Cent States Exposition, Pratt, Kans, 80; and others. *Mem:* Artists Equity, Albuquerque Chap (pres, 81); NMex Watercolor Soc (eastern NMex rep, 72); Nat Arts Educ Asn; Clovis-Portales Arts Coun (mem bd dirs, 71, 73-74, vpres, 72 & 77-78, pres, 75); NMex Art League; and others. *Media:* Watercolor, Acrylic. *Mailing Add:* 2104 S Ave H Portales NM 88130

HAMMER, ALFRED EMIL
PAINTER, ADMINISTRATOR
b New Haven, Conn, Jan 11, 25. *Study:* RI Sch Design, BFA; Yale Univ, BFA & MFA; and with John R Frazier, Josef Albers, Willem DeKooning, Stuart Davis, Abraham Rattner, Alvin Lustig & John Howard Benson. *Work:* Nat JC Mus, Israel; Cleveland Art Asn; RI Sch Design; Portland Art Mus. *Exhib:* Newport Ann, RI, 60; Boston Art Festival, Mass, 60; Four Americans, La State Univ, 62; one-man shows, Melnychenko Gallery, Winnipeg, 80 & Univ Man, Winnipeg, 80; and others. *Pos:* Mem bd dirs, Hartford Arts Coun, 82- *Teaching:* Assoc prof painting, drawing, design & calligraphy, RI Sch Design, 53-69, chmn div grad studies, 63-65; vis lectr design & painting, Minneapolis Col Art, 67; dean inst, Cleveland Inst Art, 69-74; vis lectr design & painting, Case Western Reserve Univ, 70; dir sch art, Univ Man, 74-81; dir, Pac Northwest Col Art, 81; dean, Hartford Art Sch, Univ Hartford, 82. *Awards:* First Prize, RI Artists Ann, 53; Providence Art Club Ann, 54, 55 & 56 & Newport Ann, 60. *Media:* Oil, Watercolor. *Mailing Add:* Hartford Art Sch Univ Hartford 200 Bloomfield West Hartford CT 06117

HAMMER, ARMAND
COLLECTOR, DEALER
b New York, NY, May 21, 1898. *Study:* Columbia Univ, BS, 19, Col Physicians & Surgeons, MD, 21; hon degrees from Pepperdine Univ, 78, Southeastern Univ, 78, Columbia Univ, 78, Univ Colo, 79, Salem Col, 79 & Aix-en Provence Univ, France, 81. *Collections Arranged:* Exchange program between major American Mus & Russian Mus, 73-76. *Pos:* Pres, Hammer Galleries Inc, New York, 30-; chmn, M Knoedler & Co Inc, 72- *Awards:* Legion of Honor, France, 78; Royal Order Polar Star, King Sweden, 79; Award for Distinguished Contrib in World of Art & Antiques, Antique Monthly, New York, 80; and many others. *Bibliog:* Robert Considine (auth), The Remarkable Life of Dr Armand Hammer, Harper & Row, 75; Robert Considine (auth), Larger Than Life, W H Allen, 76. *Mem:* Los Angeles Co Mus Art (mem bd trustees, 68-); hon corresp mem Royal Acad Arts, London; James Smithson Soc; Corcoran Gallery Art, Washington, DC (bd dirs, 78-). *Collection:* Rubens, Rembrandt, Gilbert Stuart, Harnett, Sargent, Prendergast, Mary Cassatt, Thomas Eakins, Van Gogh, Gauguin, Monet, Pissaro, Degas, Renoir, Cezanne, Chagall, Picasso, Soutine, Mondigliani, Durer, Raphael, da Vinci, Michelangelo, Corregio, Fragonard, Watteau & Daumier. *Publ:* Ed mag, The Compleat Collector, Vols IV-VI, 44-46; auth, Quest of the Romanoff Treasure, Paisley Press, New York, 36. *Mailing Add:* Armand Hammer Found Los Angeles CA 90024

HAMMER, VICTOR J
DEALER
b New York, NY, Nov 1, 01. *Study:* Colgate Univ; Princeton Univ. *Pos:* Pres, Appraisers Asn Am, 64; dir, Hammer Galleries, currently. *Specialty:* Ninteenth and 20th century American art; Western American art, especially Charles M Russell and Frederic Remington; French impressionist and post-impressionist paintings; elegant genre paintings. *Mailing Add:* 781 Fifth Ave New York NY 10022

HAMMERBECK, WANDA LEE
PHOTOGRAPHER, SCULPTOR
b Lincoln, Nebr, Mar 24, 45. *Study:* Univ NC, Chapel Hill, BA, 67, MA, 71; San Francisco Art Inst, MFA, 77. *Work:* Mus Mod Art, New York; Fogg Mus, Harvard Univ, Cambridge, Mass; RI Sch Design, Providence; Univ Calif, Los Angeles; Ctr for Creative Photog, Tucson, Ariz. *Exhib:* One-woman shows, Photographs by Wanda Hammerbeck, San Francisco Mus Mod Art, 78 & O K Harris, New York, 79; Object Illusion & Reality, Calif State Univ, Fullerton, 79; Images Considered, Visual Studies Workshop, Rochester, NY, 80. *Collections Arranged:* California Views (auth, catalog), 79; Text and Context (auth, catalog), 79. *Pos:* Arch dir & founder, San Francisco Camera Work Inc, 78-80. *Awards:* Nat Endowment Arts Photogr Fels, 79 & 80 & Serv to the Field Award, 80. *Mem:* Soc for Photog Educ; Friends of Photog. *Publ:* Auth, Depositions, 78 & contribr, Problematic Photography, 80, NFS Press. *Dealer:* Jeffrey Fuller Fine Art Philadelphia PA. *Mailing Add:* 2829 Eleventh Ave Oakland CA 94610

HAMMERMAN, PAT JO
PRINTMAKER, PAINTER
b New York, NY, Oct 15, 52. *Study:* Queens Col, BA, 75; Hunter Col, MA, 78. *Work:* Grand Rapids Mus, Mich; Brooklyn Mus; Lockhaven Art Ctr, Orlando, Fla; Amarillo Art Ctr, Tex; Firehouse Gallery, Nassau Community Col, NY. *Comn:* Mural, Queensborough Community Col, 70; print, House of Future, Knoxville World's Fair, Tenn, 81; three-panel mural, Panell, Kerr, Foster, New York, 83. *Exhib:* Print Biennial, Brooklyn Mus, 81; Handmade Paper Books, Am Craft Mus, New York, 82; International Impact, Kyoto Munic Mus, Japan, 82; New American Graphics, Alaska State Mus, Juneau, 83; Artist Books, Tucson Mus Art, Ariz, 83; Making Paper, Columbus Mus Art, Ohio, 83; and others. *Teaching:* Asst prof fine art, Queensborough Community Col, 80- *Awards:* First Prizes, Firehouse Gallery, Nassau Community Col, 79, 26th Ann, Parrish Mus, 79 & Queensborough Community Col, 70. *Bibliog:* Peter Frank (auth), A passel of patterners, Village Voice, 2/79; John Fremont (auth), Paperworks, Am Craft Mag, 8/82; Ronnie Cohen (auth), Papermaking, Art News, 10/83. *Mem:* Col Art Asn; Women in the Arts. *Res:* Etching; Acrylic, Oil. *Dealer:* John Szoke 144 E 57 St New York NY 10022. *Mailing Add:* 91-06 104th St Richmond Hill NY 11418

HAMMERSLEY, FREDERICK
PAINTER
b Salt Lake City, Utah, Jan 5, 19. *Study:* Univ Idaho Southern Br, Pocatello, 36-38; Chouinard Art Sch, Los Angeles, 40-42 & 46-47; Ecole des Beaux Arts, Paris, France, 45; Jepson Art Inst, Los Angeles, 47-50. *Work:* Los Angeles Co Mus Art & La Jolla Art Mus; Butler Inst Am Art, Youngstown, Ohio; Santa Barbara Mus Art, Calif; Corcoran Gallery Art. *Exhib:* Responsive Eye, Mus Mod Art, New York, 62; Geometric Abstraction Am, Whitney Mus Am Art, New York, 62; Art Across Am, Mead Corp & Traveling Show, 65-67; one-man shows, Univ NMex, Albuquerque, 69 & 75 & L A Louver Gallery, Venice, Calif, 78 & 81; 35th Biennial, Corcoran Gallery, 77; Calif: Five Footnotes to Mod Art Hist, 77 & Private Images: Photographs by Painters, 77, Los Angeles Co Art Mus, Los Angeles; Fall Invitational, Roswell Mus & Art Ctr, NMex, 79; First Western States Biennial Traveling Exhib, 79-80. *Pos:* Guest artist, Tamarind Inst, Albuquerque, NMex, 73. *Teaching:* instr, Jepson Art Sch, Los Angeles, 48-51; lectr painting, drawing & design, Pomona Col, 53-62; instr, Pasadena Art Mus, 56-61; instr painting, drawing & design, Chouinard Art Inst, 64-68; vis assoc prof painting & drawing, Univ NMex, 68-71. *Awards:* Purchase Awards for Painting, Butler Inst Am Art, 61 & Los Angeles All City Ann, 64-66; Guggenheim Fel Painting, 73-74; Nat Endowment for the Arts for Painting, 75 & 77. *Bibliog:* Jules Langsner (auth), Four abstract classicists, Los Angeles Co Mus Art, 59; Lawrence Alloway (auth), West Coast hard edge, Inst Contemp Art, London, 60; Michel Seuphor(auth), Abstract Painting, Abrams, 62. *Publ:* Contribr, Classicism or hard-edge?, 60 & Los Angeles letter, 2/61, Art Int; auth, My first experience with computer drawings, 10/69 & My geometrical paintings, 4/70, Leonardo Mag; contribr & illus, Visual Art, Mathematics and Computers, Pergamon Press, 79. *Dealer:* L A Louver Gallery 55 N Venice Blvd Venice CA 90291; Hoshour Gallery 417 2nd St SW Albuquerque NM 87102. *Mailing Add:* 608 Carlisle SE Albuquerque NM 87106

HAMMETT, POLLY HORTON
PAINTER, INSTRUCTOR
b Oklahoma City, Okla, Jan 31, 30. *Study:* Univ Okla, 48-50; Union Col, BA, 78; study with Richard V Goetz & Eugene Bavinger. *Work:* Albuquerque Mus

Art; Houston Neurosensory Ctr; Women's Hosp-Houston; Houston Power & Lighting; Methodist Hospital, Houston, Tex. *Exhib:* Am Wtaercolor Soc Ann, Nat Acad Galleries, 76, 77, 80 & 82; Watercolor, Southwest Two, Tucson Mus Art, 76; Nat Watercolor Soc 56th Ann, Laguna Beach Mus Art, Calif, 76; two artist exhib, Foothills Art Ctr, Colo, 76; Western Federation Watercolor Socs, 81; and others. *Teaching:* Instr watercolor sem, Okla Arts Coun, 73; instr watercolor workshops, Colo, Okla & Tex, La, Calif, 69-81; originator workshop, The Art Experience, Tex Inst Child Psychiat, Houston, 74 & 75 & Houston Univ, Sch Continuing Educ Drug Abuse Prog, 76-77. *Awards:* Juror's Selection for Purchase, Eight-State Exhib Painting & Sculpture, Okla Art Ctr, 72; Mus Purchase Award & Merit Award Watercolor, Southwest One, Albuquerque Art Mus, 76; First Award, Watercolor Art Soc, Houston, 81. *Mem:* Nat Watercolor Soc; Am Art Therapist Asn; Watercolor Art Soc, Houston; Am Watercolor Soc. *Media:* Mixed Media, Printmaking. *Dealer:* Arts Place II 115 Park Ave Okla City OK 73102. *Mailing Add:* 351 N Post Oak Ln #610 Houston TX 77024

HAMMOCK, VIRGIL GENE
CRITIC, PAINTER
b Long Beach, Calif, Aug 5, 38; Can citizen. *Study:* San Francisco Art Inst, BFA, 65, with James Weeks; Ind Univ, MFA, 67, with James McGarrell. *Work:* Ind Univ, Bloomington; Univ Alta, Edmonton; Art Bank Collection, Can Coun, Ottawa, Ont; Univ Man, Winnipeg; Mt Allison Univ, Sackville. *Exhib:* The 84th Ann, San Francisco Mus Art, Calif, 65; Young Alta Painters, Alta Col Art, Calgary, 68; West-71, Edmonton Art Gallery, 71; Olympic Exhib, Montreal, 75; one-man shows, Owens Art Gallery, Sackville, NB, 73 & Drawings, Dalhousie Art Gallery, Halifax, NS, 77; two-man show with Arnold Saper, Gallery 111, Univ Man, Winnipeg, 74. *Teaching:* Instr design & drawing, Univ Alta, Edmonton, 67-68, asst prof drawing & art hist, 68-70; assoc prof art criticism, Univ Man, Winnipeg, 70-75; prof & head, Dept Art, Mt Allison Univ, 75-. *Awards:* Phelan Award, Trustees James D Phelan Awards Lit & Art, 65. *Mem:* Univs Art Asn Can (pres, 73-79); Int Asn Art Critics, Can Sect (pres, 76-79); Can Fedn Humanities (bd mem, 77-). *Media:* Oil, Pencil. *Res:* Contemporary Canadian painting. *Mailing Add:* c/o Mt Allison Univ Art Dept Sackville NB E0A 3C0 Canada

HAMMOND, GALE THOMAS
PRINTMAKER, EDUCATOR
b Lumberton, NC, Sept 27, 39. *Study:* Chicago Acad Fine Arts, com art dipl; ECarolina Univ, 62-64, BS & MAEd; Univ NC, Greensboro; Atelier 17, Paris, with S W Hayter, 77. *Work:* High Mus, Atlanta; NC Mus Art, Raleigh; Del Mar Col, Corpus Christi; Univ NC Sch Pub Health, Chapel Hill; Metrop Mus Art; and others. *Exhib:* Colorprint USA, Lubbock, Tex, 72; Ann Exhib, Davidson Col, NC, 73; Boston Printmakers, Mass, 75-79; New American Graphics, Madison Art Ctr, Wis, 75; Netherlands & Russian Exchange Exhibs of the Southern Graphics Coun; and others. *Teaching:* Assoc prof drawing & printmaking, Univ Ga, Athens, 70- *Awards:* Etching Award, Southeastern Ctr for Contemporary Art, NC, 68; Drawing Award, Ga Arts Comn, Atlanta, 71; Etching Award, Southeastern Printmakers, Western Carolina Univ, NC, 75. *Mem:* Southeastern Graphics Coun (pres, 74-76). *Media:* Etching, Multimedia. *Mailing Add:* Dept Art Univ Ga Athens GA 30602

HAMMOND, HARMONY
SCULPTOR, PAINTER
b Chicago, Ill, Feb 8, 44. *Study:* Jr Sch Art Inst Chicago, 60-61; Milliken Univ, 61-63; Univ Minn, BFA, 67; Alliance Francaise, Paris, summers 67 & 69. *Work:* Mus Contemp Art, Chicago; Indianapolis Mus of Art, Ind; Gen Mills Corp, Minn; Walker Art Ctr; Denver Art Mus. *Exhib:* International Feminist Art, Haags Gementemuseum, The Hague, 80; retrospective, Glen Hanson Gallery, Minneapolis, 81; Ten Years of Collecting, Denver Art Mus, 81; Extended Sensibilities, New Mus, 82; one-woman show, AIR Gallery, 82 & 84; The American Artist as Printmaker, Brooklyn Mus, 83; and many others. *Collections Arranged:* vis adj instr, Hunter Col, 82 & Feminist Art Inst, New York, 82-83. *Teaching:* Instr & visiting artist painting, Art Inst Chicago, 73; asst prof drawing & painting & vis artist, Tyler Sch Fine Art, Philadelphia, 77; asst prof, Univ NMex, Albuquerque, 78; vis lectr, Univ Va, Charlottesville, 80 & Univ NC, Chapel Hill, 81-82; vis artist & instr, Mason Gross Sch Art, New Brunswick, NJ, 82. *Awards:* Nat Endowment Arts, 79-80 & 83-84; MacDowell Colony fel artist-in-residence, 79 & 81; Creative Artists Pub Serv Grant, 82. *Bibliog:* Lucy Lippard (auth), Binding-bonding, Art in Am, 4/82; Sandra Langer (auth), Harmony Hammond: Strong affections, Arts, 2/83; article, Art News, 4/81. *Mem:* Heresies; New York Feminist Art Inst; Womens Caucus Art. *Media:* Oil, Gouache; Cloth. *Publ:* Auth, More on women's art: An exchange, Art in Am, 11/76; auth, Feminist abstract painting--a political viewpoint, Heresies, 12/77; A sense of touch, New Arts Examiner, summer 79; A Sense Touch: Women Identified Sexuality in Womens Art, Heresies, No 12, spring 81; Wrappings, Time & Space Ltd Press, 83. *Dealer:* AIR Gallery New York NY; Klein Gallery, Chicago, IL. *Mailing Add:* 129 W 22nd St New York NY 10011

HAMMOND, LESLIE KING
HISTORIAN, WRITER
b Bronx, NY, Aug 4, 44. *Study:* Queens Col, with Louis Finkelstein, Herb Aach, Paul Frazer, Marvin Belick & Harold Bruder, BA, 69; Johns Hopkins Univ, MA, 73, PhD, 75. *Collections Arranged:* 3400 on State, Baltimore Mus Art, 73; Baltimore Black Arts Calendar Retrospect, 1973-1978, Morris Mechanic Gallery, 78; Montage of Dreams Deferred (auth, catalog), Baltimore Mus Art, 79-80; Three Episodes in Black American Art, Harmon Found, Bronx & Queens Mus, 80; Celebrations: Myth & Ritual in African-American Art, Studio Mus Harlem, 82. *Pos:* Actg dir, Cult Arts, Youth in Action, Bedford, Stuyvesant, NY, 66; chmn art dept, Performing Art Workshops, Queens, NY, 67-69; guest cur & mem bd dir, Morris Mechanic Gallery, formerly. *Teaching:* Lectr art hist, Md Inst Col Art, 73-76, dean grad studies, 76-; doctoral supvr, Dept African Studies & Res, Howard Univ, 77-82; instr, Corcoran Sch Art, 82. *Awards:* New York City SEEK Grant, 66-69; Horizon Fel, 69-73; Kress Found Fel, 74. *Mem:* Nat Conf Artists. *Res:* Ninteenth and Twentieth century Afro-American art; cartoon and comic strip art; African Art; Ancient--Renaissance/Baroque Survey; women in history of art. *Publ:* Contribr, National Landmarks Registry, Dept Interior, 75; auth, Impact of roots on American society, African Directions, Fall 1977; auth, African-American aesthetics, Aura of the Arts, 2/78. *Mailing Add:* Maryland Inst Col Art 1300 W Mount Royal Ave Baltimore MD 21217

HAMMOND, NATALIE HAYS
PAINTER, MUSEUM DIRECTOR
b Lakewood, NJ, Jan 6, 04. *Study:* With Sergei Soudeikine. *Work:* The Luxembourg, Paris, France; Pittsfield Mus, Mass; also in pvt collections. *Exhib:* Royal Miniature Soc, Grieves Gallery, London, Eng, 27-29; one-man shows, Mem Gallery, Rochester NY, Brooklyn Mus, 27, Corcoran Gallery Art, Washington, DC, 29 & Philadelphia Art Alliance, 35; Pa Acad Fine Arts, Philadelphia, 28; plus others. *Pos:* Pres, Natalie Hammond Process Corp, 30-32; dir, Am Arbit Asn, 30; assoc mem, Royal Miniature Soc London, 27-39; founder & dir, Hammond Mus, North Salem, NY, 57- *Mem:* Mediaeval Acad Am. *Media:* Watercolor. *Publ:* Auth & illusr, Elizabeth of England, Kamin, 36; auth & illusr, Anthology of Pattern, Helburn, 49. *Mailing Add:* Hammond Mus Deveau Rd Rte 124 North Salem NY 10560

HAMMOND, PHYLLIS BAKER
SCULPTOR
b Elizabeth, NJ, Apr 13, 30. *Study:* Sch Mus Fine Arts, Boston, Mass, 60; Kyoto City Col Fine Arts, Japan, 62; Tufts Univ, BS, 64. *Work:* Mendocino Art Ctr, Calif; Neiman Marcus, Dallas, Tex; Univ Southern Conn. *Comn:* Isetan Dept Store, Hanneman, Japan, 79; Sculptures, Ikebania Soc, Tokyo, Japan, 79; Macy's, Kenneth Hanneman, New York, 79; Architectural Ceramics, Womans Interart Ctr. *Exhib:* Clay Sculpture, Hudson River Mus, NY, 76; New England Exhib Painting, Silvermine Art Ctr, Conn, 77; Prize Winning Artists of Westchester, Bridge Gallery, 78; Art in Transition, Boston Mus, Mass, 78; one-woman show, Briar Cliff Col, NY, 79; Katonah Art Gallery, NY, 80; Clay & Fiber, Summit Art Ctr, NJ, 80. *Collections Arranged:* Renaissance Festival, Westchester Coun Art, NY, 75 & 77. *Teaching:* Adj asst prof, Col New Rochelle Graduate Sch, 81; ceramic sculpture, Mendocino Art Ctr, Calif, 81 & 82. *Awards:* Clarissa Bartlett Traveling Fel, Boston Mus, 60; Second Prize, Mamaroneck Artist Guild, 73; Grant for Apprentice, National Endowment Arts, 76. *Bibliog:* Maxine Rosenberg (auth), Ceramics Monthly, 12/78; Aline Benjamin (auth), article, New York Times, 5/7/78; Robert Yoskowitz (auth), Arts Mag, 2/81. *Mem:* Artist-Craftsman New York; Nat Coun Apprenticeship; Int Laison; Visual Arts Affiliates of Westchester (vpres, 79-81). *Media:* Clay, Bronze. *Dealer:* Kendell Gallery Wellfleet MA; Pindar 127 Green St New York NY 10021. *Mailing Add:* 285 Scarborough Rd Briarcliff Manor New York NY 10510

HAMOUDA, AMY (AMY MIDDLETON HAMOUDA BICE)
SCULPTOR
b Edinburg, Ind. *Study:* Boston Mus Sch; Ohio State Univ, BFA; Inst Allende, Univ Guanajuato, study under David Alfaro Siqueiros, MFA; Ecole de la Grande Chaumiere, Paris; State Univ NY, Buffalo, MA, 78. *Work:* Novadecor Galleries, Cairo, Egypt; Birchfield Ctr, Buffalo. *Comn:* Metal cross, First Methodist Church, Boulder, Colo, 61; Venetian glass mural & cast concrete fountainheads, Colo State Univ, Ft Collins, 62; art appointments, St Albans Episcopal Church, Worland, Wyo, 63; kinetic sound sculpture, Spaulding Fibre Co, Buffalo, NY, 66; stained glass, Lutheran Church, Arvada, Colo. *Exhib:* Denver Art Mus, 61; Colorado Springs Fine Arts Ctr, 61; Albright-Knox Art Gallery, Buffalo, numerous exhibs; Experiments in Art & Technol, Brooklyn Mus, 68; J Fields Gallery, New York, 80; Creative Arts Public Serv, State Mus, Albany, New York, 81; Lowe Gallery, Univ Syracuse, 82; Black Mountain Gallery, State Univ NY, Buffalo, 83; and others. *Pos:* Artist in residence, Sculpture Space, Utica, NY, 82. *Teaching:* Instr sculpture, NY State Univ Col, Buffalo, 69-70, instr design, 82-83; instr art & soc structures, NY State Univ, Buffalo, 73-77. *Awards:* Grant sculpture, New York State Coun Arts, Creative Artists Public Serv, 80; Money for Women Fund, 82. *Media:* Multimedia. *Mailing Add:* 368 Voorhees Ave Buffalo NY 14216

HAMPSON, FERDINAND CHARLES
GALLERY DIRECTOR
b Detroit, Mich, June 26, 47. *Study:* Wayne State Univ, dipl, 71. *Collections Arranged:* Emergence Art in Glass (auth, catalog), Bowling Green Univ & Kent State Univ, 81-82; Glass: Artist and Influence Traveling Exhib (auth, catalog), 81-82; Kyohe: Fujita Blown Glass (auth, catalog), Leigh Yawkey Woodson Mus & Burgstrom Mus, 81-82; Four Artists Four Views (auth, catalog), Jesse Besser Mus, 82; The Fine Art of Contemporary American Glass (auth, catalog), Columbus Col Art & Design, 83. *Pos:* Dir, Habatat Galleries, 71- *Bibliog:* Mack Talaba (auth), Art craft--glass has come a long way, Artcraft, 8/80; Janet Koplos (auth), Habatat Gallery, Am Craft, 9/80; Maureen Michelson (auth), Inside Habatat, Glass Studio, 4/81. *Mem:* Glass Art Soc; Detroit Art Dealers Asn (vpres, 76, pres, 78-80); Am Craft Coun; Mich Glass Month (chmn, 80-83). *Res:* Written history of contemporary glass. *Specialty:* Exclusively artists who use glass. *Publ:* Auth, article, Glass Art J, 81; auth, article, Nues Glas, Verlagsanstalt Handweck, 81. *Mailing Add:* Habatat Gallery 28235 Southfield Rd Lathrup Village MI 48076

HAMPTON, AMBROSE GONZALES, JR
COLLECTOR
b Statesburg, SC, July 24, 26. *Pos:* Mem, SC State Mus Comn, 73-; pres, Columbia Mus Art, 75- *Collection:* Chiefly contemporary oils, graphics and sculpture, with emphasis on South Carolina artists. *Mailing Add:* 2750 Laurel St Ste 303 Columbia SC 29204

HAMPTON, GRACE
EDUCATOR, JEWELER
b Courtland, Ala, Oct 23, 37. *Study:* Art Inst Chicago & Univ Chicago, BAE, 61; Ill State Univ, MSEd, 68; Ariz State Univ, PhD(art educ), 76. *Exhib:* Traveling Crafts Show, State Ill Off Pub Instruction, Chicago, 72; Arizona Women, Tucson Art Mus, 75; Second World Festival of Black and African Arts and Culture, Lagos, Nigeria, 77. *Collections Arranged:* Dimension and Directions: Black Artists of the South (auth, catalog), Miss Mus Art, Jackson, 80. *Teaching:* Asst prof art educ, Univ Ore, Eugene, 76-78; fac mem art & chairperson dept, Jackson State Univ, 78- *Awards:* Nat Endowment Arts Expansion Arts Prog Fel, 78. *Bibliog:* Linderman & Herberholz (auths), Developing Artistic and Perceptual Awareness, 74 & Herberholz (auth), Early Childhood Art, 74, W C Brown. *Mem:* Nat Art Educ Asn; Nat Conf Artists; Col Art Asn. *Media:* Copper. *Publ:* Auth, Hayden House Program: Community involvement in the arts, Sch Arts, 79. *Mailing Add:* 1629 Columbia Rd NW Washington DC 20009

HAMPTON, JOHN W
PAINTER, SCULPTOR
b New York, NY, 1918. *Work:* The Cow Punchers, Cowboy Hall Fame, Oklahoma City. *Awards:* First Prize, World Telegram Artist Contest, 35; Gold Medal/Sculpture, Cowboy Artist of Am Show, 77, 79-81. *Mem:* Founder Cowboy Artists Am. *Publ:* Illusr in Ariz Hwys & Western Horseman & other mags & books. *Mailing Add:* PO Box 928 Scottsdale AZ 85252

HAMPTON, LUCILLE CHARLOTTE
SCULPTOR, MEDALIST
b Brooklyn, NY, July 22, 22. *Study:* Columbia Bible Col, SC; Brooklyn Col, NY; NY Univ. *Comn:* Western series, Lance Indust, Mass, 78, 79 & 80; St George & the Dragon, 80, Roundup, 81 & Pieta, 82, Donald C Cook, New York; Western, Wildlife Series and Mythological Themes, House of Renaissance, Worcester, Mass, 82 & 83; Medal, Pope John Paul II, 79. *Exhib:* Overland Trail Galleries, Scottsdale, Ariz & Jackson Hole, Wyo; Gateway Art Gallery, Palm Beach, Fla; Grand Cent Art Gallery, New York; Nat Acad Design, 71-77; Am Artists Prof League, Lever House, New York, 73-81; and others. *Awards:* Am Artists Prof League Award, 74, 80 & 81; Bronze Medal, Catharine Lorillard Wolfe Art Club, 81; Gold Medal, Accad Italia, Lavoro, Italy, 81. *Bibliog:* Pat Boder (auth), Bronzes of the American West, 75; William C Ketchum (auth), Western Memorabilia, 80. *Mem:* Catharine Lorillard Wolfe Art Club (treas, 74-76); fel Royal Soc Arts, London; fel Am Artists Prof League. *Publ:* Article in Southwest Art, 11/78; auth, The Chilmark Collection, Lance, 81. *Mailing Add:* 1270 Avenue of the Americas Suite 507 New York NY 10020

HAMPTON, PHILLIP JEWEL
PAINTER, EDUCATOR
b Kansas City, Mo, Apr 23, 22. *Study:* Citrus Jr Col, Glendora, Calif; Kans State Univ; Drake Univ; Kansas City Art Inst, BFA, 51, MFA, 52; Univ Mo-Kansas City. *Work:* Liberty Nat Bank, Savannah, Ga; Lincoln Univ, Jefferson City, Mo; South Co Bank, Clayton, Mo; Tuskegee Inst, Ala; Ga Southern Col, Statesboro, Ga; New Atlanta Life Bldg, Ga. *Comn:* Epitome of Home Economics, Savannah State Col, 56. *Exhib:* Nelson Gallery 2nd Mid-Am Ann, Kansas City, 52; 1st Nat Watercolor Competition, 64 & Nat Print & Drawing Competition, 65, Dulin Gallery, Knoxville, Tenn; Mid-Am Ann, Nelson Gallery, Kansas City & Art Mus, St Louis, 74; Huntsville Mus, Ala, 74; J B Speed Mus, Louisville, Ky, 82. *Pos:* Mem bd & chmn educ, Savannah Art Asn, 67-69. *Teaching:* Assoc prof art, Savannah State Col, 52-69; assoc prof painting & design, Southern Ill Univ, Edwardsville, 69-78, prof, 78-, coordr ethnic & spec studies workshop, 71-72. *Awards:* Teacher of Yr, Students Nat Educ Asn, 66; Award for Serv in Art to Community, Savannah Chap Links & Nat Conf Artists, Savannah Chap, 66. *Bibliog:* Alma Thomas (auth), article, Savannah Morning News & Eve Press, 3/12/67. *Mem:* Col Art Asn Am; Am Fedn Art; Nat Conf Artists. *Media:* Acrylic, Watercolor. *Res:* Investigating synthetic media and their application to painting developments. *Publ:* Auth, An approach to art for pre-adults, 63 & Modern art--the celebration of man's freedom, 66, Savannah State Col Faculty Res Bull; illusr, cover, Islander, 3/68; auth & designer, 3rd World Drawings 1979 (catalog), Soc Ethnic & Spec Studies Exhib, Los Angeles, 79; and others. *Mailing Add:* 832 Holyoake Rd Edwardsville IL 62025

HAMROL, LLOYD
SCULPTOR
b San Francisco, Calif, Sept 25, 37. *Study:* Univ of Calif, Los Angeles, BA, 59, MA, 63. *Work:* Pasadena Mus Mod Art, Calif; Los Angeles Co Mus Art, Los Angeles; Smithsonian Inst, Washington DC. *Comn:* City of Seattle, Wash, 78; Gen Serv Admin, Atlanta, 79; Univ NMex, Albuquerque, 80; Gallaudet Col, Washington DC. *Exhib:* Ann Sculpture & Prints, Whitney Mus Am Art, New York, 66; Am Sculpture of the Sixties, Los Angeles Co Mus Art, 67; Four Los Angeles Sculptors, Mus Contemp Art, Chicago, 73; Los Angeles in the Seventies, Ft Worth Art Mus, Tex, 77; one-man shows, La Jolla Mus Art, Calif, 68, Pomona Col, Calif, 69 & Calif State Univ, Fullerton, 70; Sculpture in Calif 1975-1980, San Diego Mus Art, Calif, 80; The Museum as Site: Sixteen Projects, Los Angeles County Mus Art, 81; and others. *Teaching:* fac, Calif Inst of the Arts, Valencia, 70-74; lectr sculpture, Univ Calif, San Diego,

77-78; lectr sculpture, Univ Calif Los Angeles, 78-79. *Awards:* Indiv Artist's Fel Grant, Nat Endowment for the Arts, 74; Individual Artist's Fellowship Grant, Nat Endowment Arts, 80. *Bibliog:* Ruth Iskin (auth), Public art as identity reinforcement: an interview with Lloyd Hamrol, Los Angeles Inst Contemp Art J, 1/76; Merle Schipper (auth), Public Sculpture and the Urban Community: Recent Work by Lloyd Hamrol, Journal: A Contemp Art Mag, 9-10/81. *Media:* Wood, Stone. *Mailing Add:* 901 Pacific Ave Venice CA 90291

HAMWI, RICHARD ALEXANDER
PAINTER, EDUCATOR
b Brooklyn, NY, June 11, 47. *Study:* Queens Col, BA(cum laude); Univ NMex, MA; Univ Calif, MFA; Pa State Univ, PhD; also with William Dole, Leonard Lehrer, Harry Nadler, James Brooks, Louis Finkelstein & John Ferren. *Work:* Pa State Univ; Queens Col; Nat Mus Am Art; Vassar Col; Ark Art Ctr. *Exhib:* Staempfli Gallery, 81; Phillips Collection, Washington, DC, 82; solo shows, Queens Col, 82, Carnegie-Mellon Univ, 82 & Mus Art, Pa State Univ, 82. *Teaching:* Asst, Univ NMex, 72-73, Univ Calif, 73-74; instr, Pa State Univ, 77- *Awards:* Purchase Award, Ball State Univ, 79; Mem Award, Chautauqua Nat Exhib, 81; Yaddo Fel, 83. *Mem:* Col Art Asn Am. *Media:* Ink, Watercolor. *Dealer:* Staempfli Gallery 47 E 77th St New York NY 10021; Marian Locks Gallery 1524 Walnut St Philadelphia Pa 19102. *Mailing Add:* 102 Visual Arts Bldg Sch Visual Arts, Pa State Univ University Park PA 16802

HANBURY, UNA
SCULPTOR
b England; US citizen. *Study:* Polytech Sch Art; Royal Acad Sch Art, grad; Acad Grande Chaumiere & Acad Julian, Paris, France; and with Frank Calderon, March Brothers & Jacob Epstein. *Work:* Nat Portrait Gallery, Washington, DC; Carmichael Auditorium, Smithsonian Inst, Washington, DC; The Mus NAriz; Long View Mus, New Orleans; Cornell Univ; and others. *Comn:* Julius Rudel, J F Kennedy Ctr, Washington, DC; marble monolith, Yugoslavia; Andre Segovia, Govt Spain; Pet Show (bronze), Childrens Mem Hosp, Memphis, Tenn, 83; Lioness with Cubs (bronze), Albuquerque Zoo, 83; Julius Rudel, J F Kennedy Ctr, DC. *Exhib:* Nat Sculpture Soc, Lever House, New York, 66 & 69-72; Mostra a' Arte Moderna, Camaiore, Italy, 70; retrospective, Folger Shakespearean Libr, Washington, DC, 71; Portraits of the American Stage, Nat Portrait Gallery, Washington, DC, 74; St Johns Col, Santa Fe, NMex, 73. *Pos:* Art ed, Faith & Form, 71-72. *Awards:* Best Show, Relig Art, Washington, DC, 65; George L Erion Award, Washington Soc Artists, 66; Landseer Price Sculpture Archit Setting & Gold Medal Portrait Bust, Royal Acad Art; and others. *Bibliog:* Andrea Cohen (auth), Una Hanbury, Washington, DC Gazette, 71; Patricia Broder (auth), Bronzes of the American West, 74; James M Goode (auth), Outdoor Sculpture of Washington, DC, 74; and others. *Mem:* Soc Animal Artists; Nat Sculpture Soc; Artists Equity Asn (vpres, 70). *Media:* Bronze, Stone. *Mailing Add:* 1108 Calle Catalina PO Box 245 Santa Fe NM 87501

HANCOCK, WALKER (KIRTLAND)
SCULPTOR
b St Louis, Mo, June 28, 01. *Study:* St Louis Sch Fine Arts; Washington Univ, 18-20, hon DFA, 42; Univ Wis, 20; Pa Acad Fine Arts, 21-25; Am Acad Rome, fel, 28. *Work:* Pa Acad Fine Arts; John Herron Art Inst, Indianapolis; Nat Portrait Gallery; Parrish Art Mus, Southampton, NY; Nat Gallery Art; plus many others. *Comn:* Eisenhower Inaugural Medals; Pa Railroad War Mem; portrait statue of Douglas MacArthur, US Mil Acad; portrait statue of John Paul Jones, Fairmount Park, Philadelphia; Statue of James Madison, Libr of Cong, Madison Bldg; plus many other medals, monuments & portrait busts throughout US & abroad. *Exhib:* Nat & int mus & galleries. *Pos:* Resident sculptor, Am Acad Rome, 56-57 & 62-63; sculptor in charge, Stone Mountain Mem, Ga, 64. *Teaching:* Lectr on sculpture; head sculpture dept, Pa Acad Fine Arts, 29-68. *Awards:* Proctor Prize, Nat Acad Design, 59; Medal of Achievement, Nat Sculpture Soc, 68, Medal of Honor, 81; plus many others. *Mem:* Nat Acad Design; fel Nat Sculpture Soc; Architectural League; Franklin Fel Royal Soc Arts; Nat Mus Am Art Comn; plus others. *Media:* Bronze, Stone. *Mailing Add:* Lanesville Box 133 Gloucester MA 01930

HAND, JOHN OLIVER
HISTORIAN, CURATOR
b New York, NY, Aug 17, 41. *Study:* Denison Univ, AB, 63; Univ Chicago, MA(art hist), 67; Princeton Univ, MFA(art hist), 71, PhD(art hist), 78. *Pos:* Docent, Nat Gallery Art, 65-69, cur, Northern European Painting, 73- *Teaching:* Teacher art & art hist, Denison Univ, 63 & Princeton Univ, 71. *Awards:* Samuel H Kress Found Fel, 71-72; Belg Am Educ Found Fel, 72-73. *Res:* Northern Renaissance painting; 15th and 16th century Northern Renaissance painting; Joos Van Cleve. *Publ:* Abstract painting and sculpture, In: American Arts Since 1960, Art Mus, Princeton Univ, 71; Joos Van Cleve and the Saint Jerome in the Norton Gallery and School of Art, Norton Gallery, 72; auth, Joos Van Cleve: The Early & Mature Paintings, Princeton Univ, 78. *Mailing Add:* Nat Gallery Art Washington DC 20565

HANDELL, ALBERT GEORGE
PAINTER
b Brooklyn, NY, Feb 13, 37. *Study:* Art Students League; Grande Chaumiere, Paris. *Work:* Bates Col; Brooklyn Mus Art, NY; Schenectady Mus Art, NY, Salt Lake City Mus Fine Arts; Art Students League. *Exhib:* One-man show, Berkshire Mus, Pittsfield, Mass; ACA Gallery, New York, 66 & Eileen Kuhlik Gallery, 72; group shows, Allied Artist Am, New York & Audubon Artist, New York; plus many other group & one-man shows. *Teaching:* Instr, Albert

Handell Pastel Workshops, 84- *Awards:* John F & Anna Lee Stacy Scholar Fund, 62-65; Ranger Fund Purchase Prize, Audubon Artist, 68; Elizabeth T Greenshields Mem Found, 72; over 50 awards, 58- *Bibliog:* Heather-Meredith-Owens (auth), The inner universe of Albert Handell, Am Artist Mag, 4/71; Joe Singer (auth), Pastel Portraits, Watson-Guptill; Leslie Trainer (auth), Pastel landscapes of Albert Handell, Am Artist Mag, 12/82; and others. *Mem:* Allied Artist Am; Salmagundi Club; Art Students League; Pastel Soc Am. *Media:* Pastels, Oils. *Publ:* Coauth (with Leslie Trainor), Oil Painting Workshop, 80 & Pastel Painting Workshop, 81, Watson-Guptill. *Dealer:* Eileen Kuhlik Gallery 23 E 67th St New York NY 10021; Albert Wadle Gallery 123 W Palace Santa Fe NM 87501. *Mailing Add:* 10 Lower Byrdcliffe Rd Woodstock NY 12498

HANDLER, AUDREY
GLASS BLOWER, EDUCATOR
b Philadelphia, Pa, Dec 9, 34. *Study:* Tyler Sch Fine Arts, Temple Univ, Philadelphia, 52-54; Boston Univ Sch Fine & Appl Arts, BFA, 56, study with David Aronson; Art Students League, New York, summer 55; Univ Ill, Champaign, 62; sr res fel, Royal Col Art, London, Eng, 67-68; Univ Wis-Madison, MS, 67, MFA, 70, study with Harvey Littleton. *Work:* Lannan Found, Palm Beach, Fla; Royal Col Art, London, Eng; Lobmeyr Mus, Vienna, Austria; Corning Mus Art, NY; Hastings Col Glass Collection; Ronald Abramson Glass Collection, Washington, DC. *Exhib:* Nat Collection Fine Art, Renwick Gallery, Smithsonian Inst, Washington, DC, 73; Am Glass Now, San Francisco Mus Art, Calif, 74; Glass 1976, Bergstrom Mus, Neenah, Wis, 76; New Glass, Corning Mus, 79, Toledo Mus, 79, Renwick Gallery, 80, Metrop Mus of Art, 80-81, Calif Palace of the Legion of Honor, 81, Victoria & Albert Mus, London, 81, Musee des Arts Decoratifs, Paris, 82 & Japan, 82; and many others. *Teaching:* Instr glass, Penland Sch Crafts, NC, 71-83 & Haystack Mountain Sch Crafts, Deer Isle, Maine, 73; instr painting, Madison Area Tech Col, Wis, 73- *Awards:* Juror's Awards, 46th & 59th Wis Designer Craftsmen Shows, Milwaukee, 66 & 71 & Madison Artists Exhib, Madison Art Ctr, Wis, 70; Master Craftsmen Apprenticeship Prog Grant, Nat Endowment Arts, 77-78 & 80-81. *Bibliog:* Paula Orth (auth), Blown Glass..., Milwaukee Sentinel, 72; Terri Gabriell (auth), Instructor Makes..., Hunterdon Co Dem, Flemington, NJ, 72; S K Oberbeck (auth), Glass Menagerie, Newsweek, 4/73. *Mem:* Glass Art Soc, Inc (mem bd, 76-78); Nat Coun on the Educ of Ceramic Arts; Am Crafts Coun; World Crafts Coun; Wis Designer Craftsmen Coun. *Media:* Blown Glass; Rare Wood. *Mailing Add:* 105 S Rock Rd Madison WI 53705

HANDVILLE, ROBERT T
PAINTER, ILLUSTRATOR
b Paterson, NJ, Mar 23, 24. *Study:* Pratt Inst, cert, 48; Brooklyn Mus Art Sch; also painting with Rubentam, 60-64. *Work:* J F Kennedy White House Collection; UNICEF; Univ Denver; Syracuse Univ; Univ Okla; and others. *Comn:* Design of Yellowstone Nat Park Commemorative US Postage Stamp, Presidential Citizens Adv Stamp Coun, 71-72; design of Alfred Verville Air Mail Commemorative US Postage Stamp, 81. *Exhib:* 200 Yrs Am Watercolor Painting, Metrop Mus Art, New York, 66; Exhib Olympic Games, Mus Acuarela, Inst Arte Mex, 68; New Eng Silvermine Guild, Conn, 70; Butler Inst Am Art, Youngstown, Ohio; Smithsonian Inst, Washington, DC; Champions of Am Sport Show, Nat Portrait Gallery, Washington DC, 81. *Teaching:* Mem fac, Fashion Inst of Technol, State Univ NY. *Awards:* 27th New England Exhib Am Can Co Award, Silvermine Guild Artists; Mary Pleissner Mem Award, 81; Speyer Prize, Nat Acad Design 157th Ann Exhib, 82. *Mem:* Am Watercolor Soc (dir, 73-75); Soc Illusrs; elect Nat Acad Design. *Media:* Watercolor, Acrylic; Ink, Oil. *Mailing Add:* 99 Woodland Dr Pleasantville NY 10570

HANES, JAMES (ALBERT)
PAINTER
b Louisville, Ky, Feb 5, 24. *Study:* Philadelphia Sch Indust Art; US Army Univ, France; Pa Acad Fine Arts; Barnes Found, Pa. *Work:* Pa Acad Fine Arts, Philadelphia; Univ Tampa, Fla; Yale Univ, New Haven, Conn; La Salle Col, Philadelphia; Nat Acad Design, New York. *Exhib:* Palazzo Venezia, Rome, Italy, 52; Palazzo Esposizione, Rome, 53; Nat Inst Arts & Lett, New York, 56; Univ Pittsburgh, 72; Peale House Galleries of Pa Acad Fine Arts, 79; Goldsmith Gallery, Memphis, Tenn, 80. *Pos:* Art ed, Four Quarters, 70- *Teaching:* Instr painting, Pa Acad Fine Arts, 80-81; asst prof painting & artist in residence, La Salle Col, 65- *Awards:* Cresson, Thuron & Lambert Awards, Pa Acad Fine Arts, 49; Tiffany First Award, 50; Prix de Rome, Am Acad in Rome, 51-54. *Bibliog:* Valerio Mariani (auth), Un pittore Americano, Idea, 8/16/53. *Mem:* Am Acad in Rome; fel Pa Acad Fine Arts. *Media:* Oil. *Mailing Add:* 415 W Stafford St Philadelphia PA 19144

HANEY, WILLIAM H
PAINTER, DRAFTSMAN
b Elizabeth, NJ, May 31, 50. *Study:* Univ Tampa, with Joe Testa-Secca, BFA, 73; Univ Ga, with Lamar Dodd & James Herbert, MFA, 75. *Work:* People's Repub China; Portsmouth Mus, Va; Grover H Hermann Mus, Marietta, Ohio; Westinghouse Corp Collection, Tampa, Fla. *Comn:* Painting, Am Steel Erectors Corp, South Plainfield, NJ, 77; drawings, Duquesne Light Corp, Pittsburgh, 77 & Pa State Govt, People's Repub China, 80. *Exhib:* US Info Agency Am Art Series, Embassy, Ankara, Turkey, 77; Artists Biennial, New Orleans Mus Art, 77; Mainstreams Int, Grover H Hermann Fine Arts Mus, Marietta, Ohio, 77; Am Drawings II, Portsmouth Ctr for Arts, Va, 78; Nat Drawing Exhib, Brainerd Art Gallery, Potsdam, NY, 79; Smithsonian Inst Traveling Exhib, 79-81; one-man shows, Carnegie Mus Art, Pittsburgh, 79 & Butler Inst Am Art, Youngstown, Ohio, 79. *Teaching:* From assoc prof to prof drawing, Carnegie-Mellon Univ, 75- *Awards:* Award of Artistic Distinction,

Mainstreams Int, Marietta Col, 76; Purchase Awards, Am Drawings II, Portsmouth Ctr for Arts, 79 & Potsdam Nat Drawing, State Univ NY Col Potsdam, 79. *Bibliog:* Donald Miller (auth), Machines and animals blend in his art, Pittsburgh Post-Gazette, 79; Clyde Singer (auth), Fantasy Theme at Butler Institute, Youngstown Press, 79; Harry Schwalb (auth), Wunderkind, Pittsburgher Mag, 80. *Media:* Conte Crayon; Acrylic on Paper. *Publ:* Illusr, Patricia Henley's Learning to Die, 3 Rivers Press; illusr, Perspective Mag, Duquesne Light Co, 77; illusr, Pittsburgher Mag, WQED, 77. *Mailing Add:* 109 Laurie Dr Pittsburgh PA 15235

HANFMANN, GEORGE M A
EDUCATOR, HISTORIAN
b Petersburg, Russia, Nov 20, 11; US citizen. *Study:* Univ Berlin, PhD, 34; Univ Jena; Munich Univ; Johns Hopkins Univ, PhD, 35; Harvard Univ, MA, 49. *Pos:* Cur classical art, Fogg Art Mus, 46-74, emer cur, 74-; dir, archaeol exploration, Sardis, 58-78; mem Inst Advan Study, Princeton Univ, 71-72. *Teaching:* From jr prize fel to asst prof, Harvard Univ, 35-43, asst prof, 45-49, assoc prof fine arts, 49-56, prof, 56-, John E Hudson prof archaeol, 71-82, emer, 82-; vis, classical dept, Mus Fine Arts, Boston. *Mem:* Soc Antiquaries, London; Ger Archaeol Inst; Archaeol Inst Am; Am Schs Oriental Res; Acad Inscriptions Belles Lett France; and others. *Mailing Add:* Fogg Art Mus Harvard Univ Cambridge MA 02138

HANKS, DAVID ALLEN
CURATOR, WRITER
b St Louis, Mo, Dec 13, 40. *Study:* Washington Univ, St Louis, AB & MA. *Collections Arranged:* American Art of the Colonies and Early Republic (auth, catalog), Art Inst Chicago, 71; The Arts and Crafts Movement in America, 1876-1916 (contrib, catalog), 73; The Decorative Designs of Frank Lloyd Wright, Renwick Gallery, Smithsonian Inst, 77-78; Innovative Furniture in America, Smithsonian Inst, 81. *Pos:* Asst cur, Art Inst of Chicago, 69-74; cur, The Philadelphia Mus of Art, 74-77; guest cur, Smithsonian Inst, 77- *Mem:* Decorative Arts Chap Soc Archit Hist (pres, 74-77); Philadelphia Chap Victorian Soc (pres 75-77). *Res:* American furniture of the 19th and 20th century. *Publ:* Auth, Isaac E Scott: Reform Furniture in Chicago, Chicago Sch of Archit Found, 74; co-auth, Daniel Pabst, Philadelphia Mus of Art, 77. *Mailing Add:* 800 Fifth Ave New York NY 10021

HANLEN, JOHN (GARRETT)
PAINTER, INSTRUCTOR
b Winfield, Kans, Jan 1, 22. *Study:* Pa Acad Fine Arts, three traveling fels; independent study with George Harding, muralist; Barnes Found, Merion, Pa. *Work:* Pa Acad Fine Arts, Philadelphia; Libr of Cong, Washington, DC; War Dept Collection of Combat Paintings, Washington, DC; Woodmere Gallery Art, Chestnut Hill, Pa. *Comn:* Mural, egg tempera (collaborated with George Harding), comn by Montgomery Co, John James Audubon Shrine, Mill Grove, Pa, 54-56. *Exhib:* Pa Acad Fine Arts Ann, Philadelphia, 48-; Philadelphia Mus Art, 55; Detroit Inst Art, 59; one-man shows, Pa Acad Fine Arts, Peale House Gallery, 65 & Woodmere Gallery Art, Chestnut Hill, Pa, 73; Am Drawing 1968, Moore Col Art, 68; Pennsylvania 71, William Penn Mem Mus, Harrisburg, 71 & 83. *Pos:* Mem bd, fel of Pa Acad Fine Arts. *Teaching:* Advan critic painting & drawing, Pa Acad of Fine Arts, Philadelphia, 53-; prof painting & drawing, Moore Col Art, Philadelphia, 54- *Awards:* First, Tiffany Award for Painting, Louis Comfort Tiffany Found, 50; 1st Award, Edwin Austin Abbey fel for Mural Decoration, 51; Pa Acad Fine Arts Fel. *Media:* Roplex (acrylic) with dry color and collage; gold and silver Mylar. *Mailing Add:* 2218 St James St Philadelphia PA 19103

HANNA, BOYD EVERETT
PAINTER, PRINTMAKER
b Irwin, Pa, Jan 15, 07. *Study:* Univ Pittsburgh, 25-28; Carnegie-Mellon Univ, 28-30. *Work:* Metrop Mus Art, New York; New York Pub Libr; Libr Cong Pennell Collection, Washington, DC; Carnegie Inst, Pittsburgh; Boston Pub Libr; and others. *Comn:* Presentation print, Hunt Inst, 72 & Print Club Albany, 75. *Exhib:* Seattle Art Mus, Wash, 41; Corcoran Gallery, Washington, DC, 42; Artists for Victory, Metrop Mus Art, 42; Denver Art Mus, Colo, 43; Brooklyn Mus, NY, 47; Nat Mus, Washington, DC, 47; Nat Acad Design 123rd Ann, New York, 49; Soc Am Graphic Artists Ann, New York, 48-56; Springfield Mus, Mo, 54; Hunt Inst, 73; Nat Acad, 73-74; Audubon Artists, New York, 73-74; one-man show, Print Club Albany, 75-83; Washington Miniature Soc, 75-83; Arena 76 Art Open, 76; and others. *Pos:* Graphic designer, Pullman-Swindell Co, Pittsburgh, 50-70. *Awards:* Purchase Prize, Print Club Albany, 72, First Award, 74; Second Place, Washington Miniature Soc, 76. *Bibliog:* Wood Engraving, Sander, Viking Press. *Mem:* Print Club Albany; Washington Miniature Soc. *Media:* Oil, Watercolor, Wood Engraving. *Publ:* Illusr, Longfellow's poems, Ltd Ed Club, 44; illusr, Compleat Angler, 47, Story of the Nativity, 49, Leaves of Grass, 51 & Sayings of Buddha, 57, Peter Pauper Press; illusr, Wild & Wily, Northland Press, 80; plus others. *Dealer:* Bellevue Gallery 60 Schubert St Binghamton NY 13905. *Mailing Add:* 1475 S Jones G-16 Tucson AZ 85713

HANNA, KATHERINE
MUSEUM DIRECTOR
b Cleveland, Ohio, Jan 25, 13. *Study:* Sweet Briar Col; Oberlin Col. *Collections Arranged:* Taft Art Collection; assembled, arranged & cataloged spec art & hist exhibs. *Pos:* Tech res, NBC-TV, Hollywood, Calif, 39-40; assoc to Harden deV Pratt, architect, Providence, RI & Tidewater, Va, 40-41; cur & dir, Taft Mus, Cincinnati, Ohio, 52-83; retired. *Mem:* Asn Art Mus Dirs; Am Asn Mus; Int Coun Mus; Nat Trust Hist Preserv; Midwest Mus Conf. *Res:* History of art and architecture; art appreciation. *Publ:* Ed, Taft Mus catalog, 57; contribr, Let's Go to An Art Museum, 60; ed, exhib catalogs & brochures; contribr, art magazines, mus bulletins, newspapers & periodicals. *Mailing Add:* 316 Pike St Cincinnati OH 45202

HANNA, PAUL DEAN, JR
PAINTER, PRINTMAKER

b Alice, Tex. *Study:* Austin Col, BA; Chouinard Art Inst; Tex Christian Univ, MFA. *Work:* Tex Tech Mus, Lubbock; Pace Collection, San Antonio; Bell Reproduction Collection, Ft Worth; Lubbock Art Asn, Tex; First Nat Bank, Hobbs, NMex. *Comn:* Six glass engraved windows & four stained glass windows, Covenant Presbyterian Church, Lubbock, Tex, 77- *Exhib:* Two-man show, Witte Mus, San Antonio, 68; Northwest Printmakers' Int, Seattle & Portland, 69; Southwestern Exhib Painting & Sculpture, Dallas, 71; Printmaking Now, Nat Print Exhib, 73; Longview Painting Exhib, 74; Tex Tech Univ, Lubbock, 77. *Teaching:* Prof painting & drawing, Tex Tech Univ, 69- *Awards:* Eight State Painting & Sculpture Award, Okla Art Ctr, 66 & 80; Longview Painting Award, 74; Juror's Award, 23rd Ann, Okla Art Ctr, 80. *Mem:* Tex Watercolor Soc; Tex Asn Schs Art (pres, currently). *Media:* Acrylic, Oil; Woodcut, Silkscreen. *Dealer:* Sol Del Rio Gallery Inc San Antonio TX 78209; The Baker Gallery 1301 13th Lubbock TX. *Mailing Add:* 2831 24th St Lubbock TX 79410

HANNAH, DUNCAN (RATHBONE)
PAINTER

b Minneapolis, Minn, Aug 23, 83. *Study:* Minneapolis Col Art & Design, 70; Bard Col, 71-73; Parsons Sch Design, BFA, 75. *Work:* Republic Bank Houston. *Exhib:* New Still Life, Mus Mod Art, New York, 72; New Talent, Albright-Knox Mus, 81; Soldes, Palais Beaux Arts, Brussels, Belg, 81; Face to Face, Alternative Mus, New York, 82; Faces Since the 50s, Ctr Gallery, Bucknell Univ, 83; Portrait Exhib, Ctr Gallery, Chicago, 83. *Bibliog:* Paul Bray (auth), Duncan Hannah, Daedalus Fine Art Press, 82; Simon Lane (auth), Simon Lane meets Duncan Hannah, Bomb Mag, 82; Walter Robinson (auth), Duncan Hannah: An appreciation, East Village Eye, 83. *Media:* Oil on Canvas. *Publ:* Illusr, Esquire, High Times, Interview, Rolling Stone & New York Times. *Dealer:* Semaphore Gallery 462 W Broadway New York NY 10012. *Mailing Add:* 160 W 71st St New York NY 10023

HANNAH, JOHN JUNIOR
PRINTMAKER, EDUCATOR

b Buffalo, NY, Mar 23, 23. *Study:* Univ Buffalo, BFA; Univ Ill, with Lee Chesney, MFA, 55; Albright Art Sch, with Letterio Calapai; Neth Royal Acad Painting & Sculpture, Fulbright grant, 60-61; Pratt Graphic Art Ctr, 67; also with Birgit Skiold Workshop, London. *Work:* Northwest Printmakers, Seattle Mus Art, Wash; Okla Printmakers Collection, Oklahoma City; 3-M Collection, Tweed Gallery, Duluth, Minn; Bradley Univ Collection, Peoria, Ill; Joslyn Art Mus, Nebr, Omaha; and others. *Comn:* Tourist, Friends of Art, Kans State Univ, 67. *Exhib:* Colorprint USA, Art Dept, Lubbock, Tex, 71 & 74; 1st Int Print Exhib, Hilo, Hawaii, 76; Three Decades of Am Printmaking, Brooklyn Mus, NY, 77; Nat Color Blend Print Exhib, Univ Miss, 77; 44th Ann Miniature Printers Sculptors & Gravers, Washington, DC, 77; Six Printmakers, Loyola Univ, Los Angeles, 77; and others. *Teaching:* Instr drawing, Ohio State Univ, Columbus, 56; assoc prof printmaking, Kans State Univ, Manhattan, 57-68; prof printmaking & drawing, Calif State Univ, Northridge, 69- *Awards:* Calif Art Coun Artist Grant, 78. *Mem:* Los Angeles Printmaking Soc (bd mem, 70-); Artists Econ Action (bd mem, 73-74). *Media:* Etching, Serigraphy. *Publ:* Contribr, Etching, Van Nostrand, 73; contribr, American Printmakers, 74 & California Graphics, 74, Graphis Group Arcadia, 74. *Mailing Add:* 665 Haverford Pacific Palisades CA 90272

HANNIBAL, JOSEPH HARRY
EDUCATOR, PAINTER

b Brooklyn, NY, May 4, 45. *Study:* Austin Peay State Univ, Clarksville, Tenn, BS, 68; Univ Tenn, Knoxville, MFA, 72. *Work:* Austin Peay State Univ; Univ Wis, Stout. *Exhib:* one-man show, 118 Gallery, Minneapolis, 80; Austin Peay, State Univ, 81; Los Angeles City Col, 82; Ontario Mus Art & History, Calif, 83; Laguna Beach Sch Art, 83; and others. *Teaching:* Head, Printmaking Area, Dept Art, Univ Wis-Stout, Menomonie, 72-81; head lithography dept, Cent Col Art & Design, London, Eng, 75-76; chmn art dept, Calif State Polytechnic Univ, Pomona, 81- *Awards:* Gold Medal, Italy, 81; Purchase Award, 12th Nat Drawing Exhib, Minot, NDak, 82; Cash Award, Multicultural Art Inst, San Diego, 82. *Mem:* Col Art Asn; Los Angeles Printmaking Soc. *Dealer:* 118 Gallery 1007 Harmon Pl Minneapolis MN 55403. *Mailing Add:* 1448 Lynoak Drive Claremont CA 91711

HANSEN, ARNE RAE
MUSEUM DIRECTOR, ADMINISTRATOR

b Fergus Falls, Minn, Mar 4, 40. *Study:* Pvt study, Misawa, Japan, 59-60 & Hof/Saale, Ger, 62-63; Black Hawk Col, Moline, Ill, AA, 68; Univ Tex, Austin, BFA, 70; Univ Okla, Norman, MFA, 72. *Work:* Jones Art Ctr, Univ Okla; Goddard Art Ctr, Ardmore, Okla. *Collections Arranged:* The Hoover Collection of Pre-Columbia Art, 73 & African Art in the Collection of Illinois State University (auth, catalog), Ill State Univ; African Textiles in the Girard Collection, 75, Colorado-New Mexico Contemporary Art, 75 & 10 take 10, Ten Contemporary Southwestern Retrospectives, 77, Colorado Springs Fine Arts Ctr. *Pos:* Asst dir mus, Ill State Univ, 72-73; dir mus, 73-75; dir, Colorado Springs Fine Arts Ctr, 75-79; dir, Rocky Mountain Regional Art Ctr, Univ Denver, 79- *Teaching:* Asst prof design, Ill State Univ, 72-75. *Mem:* Asn Art Mus Dir; Western Asn Art Mus (vpres, 77-79); Am Asn Mus; Mountain Plains Mus Asn; Art Mus Asn; and others. *Res:* American & primitive sculpture. *Publ:* Contribr, Hispanic Crafts, 77 & Ernest Blumenschein, A Retrospective, 78, Colorado Springs Fine Arts Ctr. *Mailing Add:* 6505 Hawkeye Circle Colorado Springs CO 80919

HANSEN, FRANCES FRAKES
EDUCATOR, PAINTER

b Harrisburg, Mo. *Study:* Univ Denver, BFA; Art Inst Chicago; Univ Northern Colo, MA; Univ Southern Calif; Univ Denver; Ecoles Art Am, Fontainebleau, France. *Exhib:* Joslyn Mus Biennial, Omaha, Nebr, 53 & 67; Gilpin Co Ann, Central City, Colo, 55-56, 66, 69 & 72; Mus NMex Ann Regional, Santa Fe, 59; William Rockhill Nelson Mus, Kansas City, Mo, 65; Denver Festival Arts, 69; Colo State Univ Centennial Exhib, 70; and others. *Pos:* Researcher & display designer, Am Indian, Denver Mus Natural Hist, 73-78; artist-mem ed bd, Denver Botanic Gardens, 77-; lectr Am Indian art. *Teaching:* Prof art, Colo Women's Col, 45-73. *Awards:* Painting Prize for Oils, Canyon Pastoral, Colo State Fair Prof Show, 65; Colo Women's Col Faculty Res Grant, 69; Painting Prize for Acrylic, Lights, Univ Northern Colo Centennial Exhib, 70; and others. *Mem:* Delta Phi Delta (Art Inst Chicago Chap); Am Asn Univ Prof; Nat Audubon Soc; and others. *Media:* Acrylic, Watercolor. *Publ:* Auth, Native arts in America, US Cult Bull, 66; illusr, Song of the Ghost Trains, Denver Symphony Guild, 81. *Mailing Add:* 700 Pontiac St Denver CO 80220

HANSEN, GAYLEN CAPENER
PAINTER, EDUCATOR

b Garland, Utah, Sept 21, 21. *Study:* Utah State Agricultural Col, BS, 52; Univ Southern Calif, Los Angeles, MFA, 54. *Work:* Wash State Univ, Pullman; Seattle Arts Comn; Utah State Permanent Collection, Salt Lake City. *Comn:* Painting on canvas, Art in Archit Prog, Moscow, Idaho, 80. *Exhib:* 57th Ann Exhib Western Artists, Denver, 50; solo exhib, Seattle Art Mus, 59 & Glenbow Mus, Calgary, Alta, 81; 81st Ann Painting Exhib, San Francisco Art Inst, 62; In Touch, Portland Ctr Visual Arts, 76; Sustained Visions, New Mus, New York, 79; Animals in American Art, Nassau Co Mus Fine Art, Roslyn, NY, 81; Contemporary Artist, Cleveland Mus Art, 81. *Teaching:* Instr painting & drawing, Univ Tex, Austin, 47-52; prof art, Wash State Univ, Pullman, 57- *Awards:* Purchase Prize, Utah State Fair Exhib, 44; First Prize, Fifth Ann Oil Exhib, Woessner Gallery, Seattle, 58; Second Prize, Northwest Watercolor Ann, Seattle Art Mus, 60. *Bibliog:* Ron Glowen (auth), Natural selection Gaylen C Hansen, Vanguard, 81; Theodore Wolfe (auth), The many masks of modern art, Christian Sci Monitor, 81. *Media:* Oil on Canvas. *Mailing Add:* c/o Monique Knowlton Gallery 19 E 71 St at Madison Ave New York NY 10021

HANSEN, HAROLD JOHN
EDUCATOR, PAINTER

b Chicago, Ill, June 18, 42. *Study:* Univ Ill, BFA, 64; Univ Mich, MFA, 66. *Work:* SC State Art Collection; Columbia Mus Arts & Sci; Univ South; Univ Pac; Carroll Reese Mus, E Tenn State Univ. *Exhib:* Mainstreams, Marietta Col, Ohio, 70; 17th Ann Drawing & Small Sculpture Exhib, Ball State Univ, 71; La Watercolor Soc 4th Ann Int Exhib, Baton Rouge, 72; 9th Ann Piedmont Graphics Exhib, Mint Mus Art, Charlotte, NC, 73; Drawings USA, 73 & traveling show, 73-75, Minn Mus Art, St Paul; plus others. *Teaching:* Instr art, Kendall Sch Design, Grand Rapids, Mich, 66-69; asst prof art, Ferris State Col, Big Rapids, Mich, 69-70; assoc prof art, design & painting & assoc head dept art, Univ SC, Columbia, 70- *Mem:* Col Art Asn Am; Southeastern Col Art Asn; Guild SC Artists. *Media:* Encaustic, Watercolor. *Res:* Technical investigation of the encaustic media to improve working characteristics and hardness. *Publ:* Auth, A method for modern encaustic painting, Southeastern Col Art Asn Rev, spring 76; auth, The development of new vehicle recipies for encaustic paints, Leonardo, 77. *Mailing Add:* 1314 Brentwood Dr Columbia SC 29206

HANSEN, JAMES LEE
SCULPTOR

b Tacoma, Wash, June 13, 25. *Study:* Portland Art Mus Sch. *Work:* San Francisco Art Mus; Seattle Art Mus; Portland Art Mus, Ore; Univ Ore Mus Art, Eugene. *Comn:* The Guardian, Clark Col, Vancouver, Wash, 77; Talos 2, Civic Transit Mall, Portland, Ore, 78; The Crescent Probe, Civic Ctr Fountain, Salem, Ore, 78; Stempost, Stadium Plaza, Wash State Univ, Pullman, 80; The Oasis, Bur Land Mgt Bldg, Medford, Ore, 80. *Exhib:* Whitney Mus Am Art Ann, 53; Artists Environ, Amon Carter Mus, Ft Worth, Tex, 62; one-man shows, Fountain Gallery, Portland, 69 & 77-81, Portland Art Mus, 71 & Friedlander Gallery, Seattle, 73 & 77; Art of the Pacific Northwest, 1930 to Present, Nat Col Fine Art, Smithsonian Inst, Washington, DC, 74; Hodges/Banks Gallery, Seattle, 83. *Pos:* Founder & 1st pres, Alliance of NW Sculptors, 77-80. *Teaching:* Prof sculpture, Portland State Univ, 64- *Awards:* Norman Davis Award for Neo Shang, Seattle Art Mus, 58; Am Trust Co Award, 56 & Award for Ritual, 60, San Francisco Art Mus. *Bibliog:* William Davenport (auth), Art treasures in the West, Lane, 10/66; J A Schinnelier (auth), Art/search & self discovery, Int Textbk, 12/67. *Dealer:* Fountain Gallery 117 NW 21st Ave Portland OR 97209; Hodges/Banks Gallery 319 First Ave S Seattle WA 98104. *Mailing Add:* 6423 NE 284th St Battle Ground WA 98604

HANSEN, ROBERT
PAINTER, EDUCATOR

b Osceola, Nebr, Jan 1, 24. *Study:* Univ Nebr, AB, BFA, 48; Escuela Univ Bellas Artes, San Miguel Allende, Mex, MFA, 49; also with Alfredo Zalce, Morelia, Mex, 52-53. *Work:* Mus Mod Art & Whitney Mus Am Art, New York; Los Angeles Co Mus Art; San Diego Gallery Fine Arts; Long Beach Mus Art. *Exhib:* Carnegie Int, Pittsburgh, Pa, 61 & 63; Painting USA: Figure, 62 & Tamarind: Homage to Lithography, 69, Mus Mod Art, New York; retrospectives, Long Beach Mus Art, Calif, 67 & Los Angeles Munic Gallery, 73; New Vein, organized & mounted in mus of nat capitols in Europe & SAm, Smithsonian Inst, 68-70; and numerous solo exhibs. *Teaching:* Prof art,

Occidental Col, 56- *Awards:* Guggenheim Fel, 61; Fulbright Sr Grant, 61; Tamarind Fel, 65. *Media:* Lacquer. *Publ:* Auth, This curving world: Hyperbolic linear perspective, J Aesthetics & Art Criticism, winter 73. *Mailing Add:* 1974 Addison Way Los Angeles CA 90041

HANSON, ANNE COFFIN
HISTORIAN
b Kinston, NC, Dec 12, 21. *Study:* Univ Southern Calif, BFA(painting), 43; Univ NC, Chapel Hill, MACA(painting), 51; Bryn Mawr Col, PhD(art hist), 62. *Pos:* Dir, Int Study Ctr, Mus Mod Art, 68-69, consult, 69-70; mem, Inst Advan Study, fall 83. *Teaching:* Instr drawing & painting, Albright Art Sch, Univ Buffalo, 55-58; asst prof art hist, Swarthmore Col, 63-64 & Bryn Mawr Col, 64-68; adj assoc prof, NY Univ, 69-70; prof art hist, Yale Univ, 70-78, dept chmn, 74-78, John Hay Whitney prof, 78- *Awards:* Nat Endowment for Humanities fel, 67-68; Resident Award, Acad in Rome, spring 74; Charles Rufus Morey Prize for Best Art Hist Bk, 77; Am Coun Learned Soc Fel, 83-84. *Mem:* Nat Comt, Comt Int de l'Hist de l'Art; Col Art Asn Am (bd dirs, 69-73, pres, 72-74). *Res:* Nineteenth century French painting, particularly the work of Edouard Manet; 15th century Italian sculpture, particularly the work of Jacopo della Quercia; problems in perspective and perception. *Publ:* Articles & reviews in Art Bulletin, Burlington Mag, and others, 60-; auth, Jacopo della Quercia's Fonte Gaia, Clarendon Press, Oxford, 65; auth, Edouard Manet: 1832-1883, Philadelphia Mus Art, 66; auth, Manet and the Modern Tradition, Yale Univ Press, London, 77. *Mailing Add:* 28 Lincoln St New Haven CT 06511

HANSON, DUANE
SCULPTOR, EDUCATOR
b Alexandria, Minn, Jan 17, 25. *Study:* Macalester Col, BA; Univ Minn; Cranbrook Acad Art, MFA; DHL Nova Univ, Ft Lauderdale, 79. *Work:* Whitney Mus; Wadsworth Atheneum, Hartford; Norton Gallery, West Palm Beach; Milwaukee Art Mus; Nelson Gallery, Kansas City, Mo. *Comn:* Businessman, for Melvin Kaufman, New York, 71; Dockman, Yellow Trucking Co, Kansas City, 79. *Exhib:* Whitney Mus Am Art Sculpture Ann, 70 & 78; Whitney Mus Am Art Biennial, 73; Mus Contemp Art, Chicago, 74; one-man shows, Va Mus of Fine Arts, Richmond, Corcoran Gallery Art, Washington, DC, 77 & Whitney Mus Am Art, New York, 78; Jacksonville Art Mus, 80; Lowe Art Mus, Miami, 81; Loch Haven Art Mus, Orlando, 81; Norton Gallery, West Palm Beach, Fla, 81; and others. *Teaching:* Asst prof art, Miami-Dade Jr Col, Miami, Fla, 65-69; adj prof art, Univ Miami, Fla, 79- *Awards:* Blair Award, Art Inst Chicago, 74; Ger Acad Exchange Serv Grant, West Berlin, 74; Ambassador Arts, Fla, 83. *Bibliog:* Varnedoe (auth), Duane Hanson retrospective and recent work, Art News, 1/75; John Canaday (auth), What is Art?, Knopf, 80; Chistine Lindey (auth), Superrealist Sculpture & Painting, Morrow, 80. *Media:* Mixed Media, Polyvinyl-acetate. *Dealer:* O K Harris Gallery 383 W Broadway New York NY 10012. *Mailing Add:* 6109 SW 55 Ct Davie FL 33314

HANSON, J B
SCULPTOR, WEAVER
b Gadsden, Ala, Oct 23, 46. *Study:* Md Inst, Col Art, 72-76. *Work:* Univ Md, College Park; Washington Co Mus Fine Art; Cloisters Children's Mus, Baltimore; Centre Int de la Tapisserie Ancienne et Moderne, Lusanne, Switzerland. *Comn:* 6 banners depicting the History of the Govans Community, City Baltimore, Md, 79; tapestry for Medfield Recreation Ctr, 79; mural, Mallory Ctr, Int Arts, Inc, 81. *Exhib:* Maryland Ann, Baltimore Mus Art, 72; Maryland Biennial, Baltimore Mus Art, 74; Miniatures, West Tex Mus Art, Lubbock, 76; 11th Int Sculpture Symp, Studio Gallery, Washington, DC, 80; American Clay 1981, Meredith Contemp Art, Md, 81; Fine Art Auction Exhib, Metrop Mus, Fla, 81; Art of Ceramics, Atheneum Mus, Va, 81. *Awards:* Sculpture Award, Baltimore Mus Art, 74; Sculpture Award, Md Crafts Coun, 78. *Bibliog:* David Tannous (auth), Baltimore art scene, Smithsonian Assoc Mag, 79; Thomas Haulk (auth), reviews, Craft Horizon Mag, 79; Elisabeth Stevens (auth), Pots full of wit: sculptor shows he has a way with animals, Baltimore Sun, 80. *Mem:* Artist Equity Asn (pres, 80-81, nat ECoast vpres, 81-83); Md Crafts Coun (pres, 76). *Media:* Clay; Fibers. *Mailing Add:* 806 Gorsuch Ave Baltimore MD 21218

HANSON, JEAN (ELPHICK)
PAINTER, PRINTMAKER
b Toronto, Ont, Sept 27, 34. *Study:* Ont Col Art. *Exhib:* Smithsonian Inst, 62-63; Art Gallery Hamilton, Ont, 63; Ont Soc Artists, 63-67; Hart House, Univ Toronto, 64; Can Soc Painters in Watercolour, 68; and many other group & one-man shows. *Mem:* Ont Soc Artists; Can Soc Painters in Watercolour. *Media:* Oil, Watercolor; Wool. *Mailing Add:* 1378 2 Side Rd RR 3 Campbellville ON L0P 1B0 Canada

HANSON, JO
SCULPTOR
b Carbondale, Ill. *Study:* San Francisco State Univ, MA(art), 73; Univ Ill, MA(educ). *Exhib:* Crab Orchard Cemetery, Corcoran Gallery Art, DC, 74; San Francisco Mus Mod Art, 76 & Pa Acad Fine Arts, Philadelphia, 77; Aesthetics of Graffiti, San Francisco Mus Mod Art, 78; Pub Disclosure: Secrets from the St, San Francisco Mus Mod Art & San Francisco City Hall, 80; USA Women Artists, Musue de Arte Contemporanea da Universidade de Sau Paulo, Brazil, 80; Photofusion, Pratt Manhattan Ctr Gallery, New York, 81; Illegal Sights/Sites, Int Sculpture Conference, San Francisco, 82; and many others. *Teaching:* Lectr sculpture, Univ Calif, Berkeley, 77-78; instr sculpture, Calif Col Arts & Crafts, Oakland, 78-79; lectr humanities sem, Otis Art Inst, Los Angeles, 78-79. *Awards:* Nat Endowment Arts Grant, 77; Nat Endowment Arts & San Francisco Neighborhood Art Prog Grant, 79. *Bibliog:*

Thelma R Newman (auth), Innovative Printmaking, Crown Publ Inc, NY, 77. *Mem:* Artists Equity Asn; Women's Caucus Art; Col Art Asn. *Media:* Multimedia. *Publ:* Auth, Messages from the Street, 80. *Dealer:* William Sawyer Gallery 3045 Clay St San Francisco CA 94118. *Mailing Add:* 201 Buchanan San Francisco CA 94102

HANSON, JUDY See Cooke, Judy

HANSON, LAWRENCE
SCULPTOR, EDUCATOR
b Winona, Minn, July 28, 36. *Study:* Univ Minn, BA, 59, MFA, 62; Univ Calif, Santa Barbara, with Stan Reiffel, 69. *Work:* Walker Art Ctr, Minneapolis; Henry Gallery, Univ Wash; La Jolla Mus Contemp Art; Seattle Art Mus; C M Russell Mus, Great Falls, Mont; and others. *Comn:* LaMar's Tape (sound tape), Henry Gallery, Univ Wash, 73; Soft Glow II (site sculpture with boulders & light), Henry Gallery, Univ Wash, 81. *Exhib:* Recent Acquisitions, Walker Art Ctr, 62; Recent Works, Univ Mont, 74; one-man exhib, 4 installations, Western Gallery, Western Wash Univ, 77; Mod Art Pavillion, Seattle Art Mus, 79; group exhib, William Rockhill Nelson Gallery, Kansas City, 84th San Francisco Ann, Mod Art Pavillion, Seattle Art Mus & Calif State Univ, Los Angeles; Fifth Ann Downtown Artists Show, Los Angeles Contemp Exhibs, 82; Kentwood Sculpture (stone, water & light), Kent High Sch, Wash, 83; and many others. *Collections Arranged:* George Segal, 67; Robert Irwin: Paintings, 67; Painting of the Sixties (with catalog), 68; Seven from Washington: Printmaking Today (with catalog), 69; Sculpture of the Sixties (with catalog), 69; Robert Morris: Earthworks & Projects, 74; Painting of the Seventies, 75. *Pos:* Dir, Western Gallery, Western Wash State Col, 66-77; artist & consult, Pike St Ltd, Seattle, 77; Earthworks Symp, King Co Arts Comn, Seattle, 79; guest artist, Calif State Univ, 81-82. *Teaching:* Teaching asst & instr sculpture & ceramics, Univ Minn, 59-62; assoc prof sculpture & contemp art, Western Wash Univ, 63-81, prof, 81- *Mem:* Western Asn Art Mus; Am Mus Asn; Wash Art Consortium (chmn, 75-77). *Media:* Multimedia. *Mailing Add:* Dept of Art Western Wash Univ Bellingham WA 98225

HANSON, PHILIP HOLTON
PAINTER, LECTURER
b Chicago, Ill, Jan 8, 43. *Study:* Univ Chicago, BA, 65; Art Inst Chicago, MFA, 69. *Work:* Mus des 20 Jahrhunderts, Vienna, Austria; Mus Contemp Art, Chicago. *Exhib:* Extraordinary Realities, Whitney Mus, 73; Contemp Figurative Photog in Midwest, Madison Art Ctr, 77; Contemp Chicago Painters, Univ North Iowa Gallery Art, 78; Fabrications, Univ Miami, Lowe Art Mus, 80; Some Recent Art from Chicago, Ackland Art Mus, Univ NC, Chapel Hill, 80; Show Chicago, London, Edinburgh and traveling, 80. *Teaching:* Vis Artist, Sch Art Inst Chicago, 72- *Awards:* Casandra Grant, 73; Nat Endowment Arts Grant, 78 & 83. *Dealer:* Phyllis Kind Gallery 313 W Superior Chicago IL. *Mailing Add:* 5008 N Hermitage Chicago IL 60640

HAPKE, PAUL FREDERICK
PAINTER, EDUCATOR
b Chester, Ill Sept 19, 22. *Study:* Ill Col, BA; Calif Col Arts & Crafts, with Leon Goldin, MFA; Univ Am, with Cueto & Justin Fernandez, MA. *Work:* Minneapolis Mus Art. *Comn:* Abstract duco mural, Unitarian Ctr Mankato, Minn, 59. *Exhib:* Exhibition Momentum, Chicago, 54; Ball State Univ Drawing & Sculpture, 57; Walker Art Ctr, Minneapolis, 58-64; Piccolo Formato, Florence, Italy, 61; Minneapolis Inst Art, 65. *Teaching:* Prof painting, Mankato State Univ, 55- *Awards:* First Prize, Galeria Numero, Florence, 61; Bertah Walker Award, Walker Art Ctr, 64 & Ford Found Award, 64. *Mem:* Col Art Asn Am. *Media:* Oil, Watercolor. *Mailing Add:* 35 Ridgewood Mankato MN 56001

HARA, KEIKO
PAINTER, PRINTMAKER
Japanese citizen. *Study:* Miss State Univ Women, BFA(painting), 74; Univ Wis, Milwaukee, MS(printmaking), 75; Cranbrook Acad Art, MFA(printmaking), 76. *Work:* Milwaukee Art Mus, Wis; Art Inst Chicago; Johnson Wax Coun House; St Paul Co, Minn; Muskegon Mus Art, Mich; and others. *Comn:* Equinocital Beat (monoprint), Autemburg, 79; lithography, Perimeter Press, Racine, Wis, 81. *Exhib:* Maru, Miyuki Gallery, Tokyo, Japan, 68; 30th Am Printmakers Invitational, 76 & 20th Nat Print Exhib, 76, Brooklyn Mus; one-person shows, Westum Mus Fine Art, Racine, Wis, 81 & Calerie in Den Vierlanden, Hamburg, WGer, 81-82; solo exhibs, Perimeter Gallery, Chicago, 82 & 83; Nat Prints & Photos by Women, Philadelphia Landing Mus, 83; and others. *Teaching:* Instr printmaking, Carthage Col, 79-80 & Univ Wis, River Falls, 80- *Awards:* First Prize, Mich Prints & Drawing, Detroit Inst Arts, 76. *Bibliog:* article, Print Newsletter, 82; Printed By Women, US, 83; article, Wis Acad Rev, 3/83. *Dealer:* Perimeter Gallery 356 W Huron Chicago IL 60610; Bradley Galleries 2629 N Downer Ave Milwaukee WI. *Mailing Add:* c/o Fine Art Dept Univ Wis River Falls WI 54022

HARARI, HANANIAH
PAINTER
b Rochester, NY, Aug 29, 12. *Study:* Syracuse Univ Col Fine Arts; Fontainebleau Ecole Fresque, France; also with Fernand Leger, Andre Lhote & Marcel Gromaire, Paris. *Work:* Metropolitan Mus Art, Whitney Mus, New York; Yale Univ Art Gallery; Mus Mod Art, New York; Philadelphia Mus Art; and others. *Exhib:* Whitney Mus Am Art Painting Ann, 42-47; American Realists & Magic Realists, Mus Mod Art, New York, 43; Pa Acad Fine Arts Ann, 46 & 49; Am Abstract Artists, Art Mus, Univ NMex, Albuquerque, 77; Decade of Transition 40-50, Whitney Mus, 81; and others. *Teaching:* Instr

painting, New Sch Social Res, 74 & Sch Visual Arts, New York, 74- *Awards:* First Hallgarten Prize, Nat Acad Design, 41; Emy Herzfeld Award, Audubon Artists, 45; Medal Award, Art Dir Club, Chicago, 50. *Bibliog:* Clement Greenberg (auth), article, Nation, 1/43; Doris Brian (auth), Who's who, Art News, 1/43; Alexander Eliot (auth), Double trouble, Time, 5/50. *Mem:* Artists Equity Asn NY. *Media:* Oil. *Dealer:* Martin Diamond Fine Arts Inc 1014 Madison Ave New York NY 10021. *Mailing Add:* 34 Prospect Pl Croton-on-Hudson NY 10520

HARBART, GERTRUDE FELTON
PAINTER, INSTRUCTOR
b Michigan City, Ind, Dec 25, 08. *Study:* Univ Calif; Univ Ill; Art Inst Chicago; Art Students League, NY; and with Aaron Bohard, Charles Birchfield & Hans Hofmann. *Work:* Purdue Univ; Ind Univ; Ind State Univ; South Bend Art Inst; Indianapolis Mus Art; plus others. *Comn:* In many private collections. *Exhib:* Art Inst Chicago; Corcoran Biennial, Washington, DC; Butler Inst Am Art, Youngstown, Ohio; Indianapolis Mus Art; Michiana Biennial, South Bend. *Teaching:* Instr art, South Bend Art Ctr; instr art, Dunes Art Found; instr art, Michigan City Art League, Michigan City Community Ctr for the Arts; Pima Col, Tucson, Ariz, 79-80; pvt art classes. *Awards:* Northern Ind Art Patrons Award, Hammond Art Ctr, 70; Sarasota Art Asn First Award, 74; First Award, Southern Ariz Watercolor Guild, 82. *Mem:* Ind Artists; Southern Ariz Watercolor Guild; Am Pen Women. *Media:* Acrylic, Watercolor. *Publ:* Auth, article, Art News, 6/55 & Sch Arts, 60. *Dealer:* Abba Gallery 2100 N Wilmot Suite 317 Tucson AZ 85712; Indianapolis Museum of Art IN. *Mailing Add:* 2201 Maryben Ave Long Beach Michigan City IN 46360

HARBUTT, CHARLES
PHOTOGRAPHER
b Camden, NJ, July 29, 35. *Study:* Marquette Univ, BS, 56. *Work:* Mus Mod Art, New York; Art Inst Chicago; Smithsonian Inst. *Exhib:* Photography as a Fine Art, Metrop Mus, New York, 60; Photography in the 20th Century, Eastman House, Rochester, NY, 67; Sao Paulo Biennale, Nat Collection Art, Washington, DC, 70; Photography in America, Whitney Mus Am Art, New York, 76; Photography, Beauborg Mus, Paris, 77; Tusen Och en Bild, Mod Mus, Stockholm, Sweden, 78; Mirrors and Windows, Mus Mod Art, New York, 78; one-man exhib, Univ Salford, Eng, 80. *Teaching:* Vis artist photog, Art Inst Chicago, 75, RI Sch Design, 76 & Mass Inst Technol, 79. *Awards:* Best Photog Book, Arles Festival, 74. *Bibliog:* Andy Grundberg (auth), Sympathetic Explorations, Plains Art Mus, 78; A Grundberg & J Scully (auth), Currents, Mod Photog, 79. *Publ:* Ed & contribr, American in Crisis, Holt Rinehart, 69; ed & contribr, The Plan for New York, New York Planning Comn, 70; auth, Travelog, MIT Press, 73; contribr, Sympathetic Explorations: Kertesz/Harbutt, Plains Art Mus, 78; contribr, I Grandi Photografi: Charles Harbutt, Editoriale Fabbri, 82. *Dealer:* Actuality Inc 1 Fifth Ave New York NY 10003. *Mailing Add:* c/o Archive Pictures Inc 111 Wooster New York NY 10012

HARCUS, PORTIA GWEN
DEALER, CONSULTANT
b Brockton, Mass. *Study:* Wheaton Col, BA. *Pos:* Dir, Harcus Krakow Gallery, 64-82; dir & pres, Harcus Gallery, 82- *Mem:* Art Dealers Asn Am; Asn Int Photog Art Dealers; Art Table Inc; Confederation Int Negociants Oeuvres D'Art. *Specialty:* Contemporary painting, sculpture, grahics and major 20th century works. *Mailing Add:* 7 Newbury Boston MA 02116

HARDAWAY, PEARL (PEARL HARDAWAY REESE)
PAINTER
b Brooklyn, NY, Apr 11, 17. *Study:* Brooklyn Col, BA(fine arts); Art Students League, with Vaclav Vytlacil, Will Barnet; Acad Bildenden Kunst, Munich, Ger. *Work:* Queens Col Art Collection, Flushing, NY; First Methodist Church, White Plains, NY; Queens Col Print Collection; First Methodist Church of Jamaica, NY; Community Presbyterian Church, Sand Hills, NJ. *Exhib:* One-woman shows, Arts Gallery, New York, 58 & Educ Testing Serv, Princeton, NJ, 76; Butler Inst Am Art, Youngstown, Ohio; Audubon Artists Ann, Acad Fine Arts, New York; New York Artists, Brooklyn Mus, NY; Monmouth Col Ann, West Long Branch, NJ; Phillips Mill Ann, New Hope, Pa; and others. *Teaching:* Pvt teaching. *Awards:* Emily Lowe Award, Ward Eggleston, New York. *Mem:* Art Students League; Sarasota Art Asn; Artists League Cent NJ; Hunterdon Art Ctr. *Media:* Multimedia. *Dealer:* Swansborough Gallery Wellfleet MA 02667; Avenue of the Arts Gallery Palm Harbor FL 33563. *Mailing Add:* 32 Norton Rd Monmouth Junction NJ 08852

HARDEN, MARVIN
PAINTER, EDUCATOR
b Austin, Tex. *Study:* Univ Calif, Los Angeles, BA(fine arts) & MA(creative painting); Los Angeles City Col. *Work:* Whitney Mus Am Art & Mus Mod Art, New York; Home Saving & Loan Asn, Los Angeles; Mus, Univ Calif, Berkeley; Metromedia Inc, Los Angeles; plus other pub & pvt collections. *Exhib:* Brooklyn Mus, 76; 15 one-man exhibs, incl Rath Mus, Geneva, Switz, 71, Whitney Mus of Am Art, New York, 71, Irvine Blum Gallery, Los Angeles, 72, Col Creative Studies, Univ Calif, Santa Barbara, 76, Calif State Col, Bakersfield, 77, James Corcoran Gallery, 78 & Newport Harbor Art Mus, 79; and many others. *Pos:* Co-founder, Los Angeles Inst Comtemp Art, 73, exhib comt mem, 73-74; bd dirs, Images & Issues, 80- *Teaching:* Instr drawing, Univ Calif, Los Angeles Exten, 64-68; instr drawing, Los Angeles Harbor Col, 65-68; prof painting & drawing, Calif State Univ, Northridge, 68- *Awards:* Nat Endowment Arts Fel, 72; Guggenheim Mem Found Fel, 83. *Media:* Pencil, Oil. *Dealer:* James Corcoran Gallery 8223 Santa Monica Blvd Los Angeles CA 90046; Dobrick Gallery 216 E Ontario St Chicago IL 60611. *Mailing Add:* PO Box 353 Chatsworth CA 91311

HARDER, ROLF PETER
DESIGNER
b Hamburg, Ger, July 10, 29; Can citizen. *Study:* Hamburg Acad Fine Arts, 48-52. *Exhib:* Design Collaborative Int Travelling Exhib, 70-78; Biennale of Graphic Design, Brno, 70, 74, 78, 80 & 82; Experimental Graphic Design, Venice Biennale, 72; group exhibs, Can, USA, Europe, South Am & Japan. *Teaching:* guest lectr, graphic design. *Awards:* Symbol Competition First Prize, Can Asn Retarded Children, 64; numerous nat & int awards, Am Inst Graphic Arts; Spec Prize, 4th Biennale Graphic Design, Brno, 70. *Bibliog:* Theodore Hilten (auth), Rolf Harder, 9/64 & Hans Kuh (auth), Design Collaborative, 9/70, Gebrauchsgraphic, Munich; Jean-Claude Leblond (auth), Rolf Harder, Vie des Arts, spring 74. *Mem:* Royal Can Acad Arts; Alliance Graphique Int; Am Inst Graphic Arts; Int Ctr Typographic Arts; Soc Graphic Designers Can. *Mailing Add:* Rolf Harder & Assoc 1350 Sherbrooke W Suite 1000 Montreal PQ H3G 1K4 Canada

HARDIN, ADLAI S
SCULPTOR
b Minneapolis, Minn, Sept 23, 01. *Study:* Art Inst Chicago; Princeton Univ. *Work:* Pa Acad Fine Arts; New Britain Mus Am Art, Conn; Medallic Art Co Collection Bronzes; IBM Collection Sculptures of Western Hemisphere. *Comn:* Murals, Interchurch Ctr, New York & Seamen's Bank Savings, New York; reliefs, McMaster Univ, Hamilton, Ont, Lutheran Acad Asn, Appleton, Wis & Princeton Univ, NJ; St Peter & St Paul (bronze figures), St Patricks Cathedral, New York. *Exhib:* Nat Acad Design, New York; Pa Acad Fine Arts; Nat Sculpture Soc; Art Inst Chicago; one-man show, New Britain Mus Am Art. *Awards:* Henry O Avery Award, New York Archit League; Saltus Gold Medal, Nat Acad Design; Lindsey Morris Mem Prize, Nat Sculpture Soc. *Bibliog:* Frederick Whitaker (auth), The sculpture of Adlai S Hardin, Am Artist, 60; Walker Hancock (auth), Adlai S Hardin past president, Nat Sculpture Rev. *Mem:* Nat Acad Design; fel Nat Sculpture Soc (pres, 57-60); Old Lyme Art Asn. *Media:* Wood, Bronze. *Mailing Add:* Cove Rd Old Lyme CT 06371

HARDIN, HELEN
PAINTER
b Albuquerque, NMex, May 28, 43. *Study:* Univ NMex; Spec Sch Indian Arts, Univ Ariz, Tucson. *Comn:* Illus for two children's bks, Clarke Indust, Albuquerque; Hist of the Am Indian (ser of coins), Franklin Mint. *Exhib:* Ann Am Indian Art Exhib, Wayne State Univ, Detroit, Mich; Inter-Tribal Indian Ceremonials, Gallup, NMex; Mus NMex, Santa Fe; Scottsdale Nat Indian Art Exhib, Ariz. *Teaching:* Lectr, Civil Serv Comn Sem, Colo, 70. *Awards:* Grand Award, Best Art Work in the Painting & Sculpture Category & Best in Acrylic Div, 11th Nat Indian Arts Exhib, Scottsdale, Ariz; First & Second Awards, Santa Fe Indian Market; Patrick Swazo Hinds Award for Excellence in Painting. *Bibliog:* Picture of work in Am Artist, 65. *Mem:* Pinon Br, Nat League of Am Pen Women. *Media:* Acrylic, Ink. *Mailing Add:* 805 Adams NE Albuquerque NM 87110

HARDIN, SHIRLEY G
DEALER
Pos: Co-dir, Fairweather-Hardin Gallery, currently. *Mailing Add:* 101 E Ontario St Chicago IL 60611

HARDING, ANN
PAINTER, EDUCATOR
b Minneapolis, Minn, Mar 16, 42. *Study:* Univ Minn, BA, 66; Univ Cincinnati, MFA, 71. *Work:* Ark Arts Ctr, Little Rock; 3-M Corp, Minn Mutual Life Insurance Corp, Minneapolis; Pan Am Life Ctr, New Orleans. *Exhib:* 20th Exhib Southwest Prints & Drawings, Dallas Mus Fine Arts, 75; one-person exhib, Friends Gallery, Minneapolis Inst Fine Arts, 81 & West Baton Rouge Mus, Port Allen, La, 83; 52nd Ann Ala Exhib, Montgomery Mus Fine Arts, 81; Nat Ann Midyear Show, Butler Inst Am Art, 81 & 82; Biennial Piedmont Painting & Sculpture, Mint Mus, 81 & 83; Southeast Seven V, Southeast Ctr Contemp Art, Winston-Salem, NC, 82; Louisiana Women in Contemporary Art Traveling Exhib, 83-84. *Teaching:* Instr painting & drawing, La State Univ, 73-76, asst prof, 76-80, assoc prof, 80- *Awards:* Purchase Award, 35th Ann Exhib, La State Art Collection, 80; First Place Purchase Award Painting, Extempo, 81; Nat Endowment Arts Fel, Southeast Seven V, 81-82. *Media:* Oil on Canvas, Acrylic on Paper. *Dealer:* Mario Villa Gallery 3908 Magazine St New Orleans LA 70115. *Mailing Add:* 2114 North Blvd Baton Rouge LA 70806

HARDING, NOEL ROBERT
VIDEO ARTIST, ENVIRONMENTAL ARTIST
b London, Eng, Dec 21, 45. *Work:* Art Gallery of Ont, Toronto; Nat Gallery of Can, Ottawa, Ont; Univ Guelph, Can; Kitchen Gallery, New York; Vehicule, Montreal. *Exhib:* Minneapolis Col Art & Design & Walker Art Ctr, Minneapolis, Minn, 72; Nat Gallery of Can, 77; Mus Mod Art, New York, 78; one-man videotape, Alta Col Art & Design, Calgary, 76; Ctr Georges Pompidou, Paris, France, 77 & Acme Gallery, London, 79; group exhib, videotapes, Washington Proj for the Arts, DC, 79 & Faculty Show, Univ Guelph, 79; and others. *Teaching:* Instr fine art video, Univ Guelph, 74-; instr independent 74-77, instr independent study utilizing video, 72-76, instr sr independent study utilizing any/all of film slide & video, 76 & instr experiments in art performance, 77; instr creative film/video, Photo Electric Arts Dept, Ont Col Art, 77; instr creative film video, Univ Guelph & Ont Col Art, 77-; plus many lectr in Can. *Awards:* Can Coun Arts Grant, 76 & 78-79, Travel Grant, 77 & Proj Grant, 78; Ont Arts Coun Grant, 77 & 79. *Bibliog:* Art Perry (auth), Noel Harding: once upon the idea of two, Vancouver in Rev, 1/78; Peggy Gale (auth), Temporal realities & Eric Cameron (auth), Video as

painting, Parachute, spring 78. *Media:* Videotape, Film, Live Video. *Dealer:* Videotape: c/o Art Metropole 217 Richmond St W Toronto ON M5V 1W2; Installations/Sculpture: John Gibson Gallery 392 W Broadway New York NY 10012. *Mailing Add:* 101 Niagara St Toronto ON M5V 1C3 Canada

HARDY, DAVID WHITTAKER, III
PAINTER, INSTRUCTOR

b Dallas, Tex, Oct 5, 29. *Study:* Austin Col; Southern Methodist Univ; Univ Colo; Laney Col; Am Acad; Art Students League; Sch Visual Art; Calif Col Arts & Crafts; and with Ramon Froman, William Moseby, Joseph Van Der Brock, Robert Beverly Hale & Frank Mason. *Work:* Pvt collections in US & abroad. *Exhib:* One-man shows, North Park, Dallas, 64 & Pantechnicon Gallery, San Francisco, 70; Hemisfair Art, Witte Mem Mus, San Antonio, 68; Soc Western Artists, M H De Young Mus, San Francisco, 70; San Francisco Ann, 71; Audubon Artists, Nat Acad, New York, 73; and others. *Pos:* Guest, Wurlitzer Found, Taos, NMex, 65; owner, 13th Street Crafts Garden, Oakland, 73-76. *Teaching:* Pvt art classes, 60-; instr art, Mendocino Art Ctr, Calif, 73-74; instr art, Calif Col Arts & Crafts, Oakland, 79- *Awards:* First Place Painting, Alameda Co Fair, 73 & Valley Artists Asn, 73. *Mem:* Berkeley Art Festival Guild (pres, 72-77); Soc Western Artists; Ctr Visual Arts (bd trustees, 74-78). *Media:* Oil, Pastel. *Res:* Old master painting techniques. *Specialty:* Portraits and figure paintings. *Dealer:* Arden Van Wijk Gallery 14320 Saratoga-Sunnyvale Rd Saratoga CA 95030; Neville-Sargent Gallery 511 Main Evanston IL 60202. *Mailing Add:* 4220 Balfour Ave Oakland CA 94610

HARDY, (CLARION) DEWITT
PAINTER, ADMINISTRATOR

b S Louis, Mo, June 25, 40. *Study:* Syracuse Univ, 58-62. *Work:* Bowdoin Col Mus Art, Brunswick, Maine; Kalamazoo Inst Art, Mich; St Lawrence Univ, Canton, NY; Mus Art Ogunquit, Maine. *Exhib:* Four New England Artists, Kalamazoo Inst Art, 63; New England Regional, Drawing Soc, 65; one-man shows, Frank Rehn Gallery, New York, 66-71 & Lehigh Univ, Pa, 71; Butler Inst Am Art, 69-70. *Collections Arranged:* Young American Draughtsmen, Mus Art Ogunquit, 69. *Pos:* Assoc dir, Mus Art Ogunquit, 64-77. *Awards:* First Prize for Drawing, Summit Art Ctr, NJ, 65; Purchase Award, Butler Inst Am Art, 69. *Media:* Watercolor. *Dealer:* Robert Schoelkopf 825 Madison Ave New York NY 10021. *Mailing Add:* Oak Woods Rd North Berwick ME 03906

HARDY, HOWARD (COLLINS)
PAINTER, INSTRUCTOR

b Baltimore, Md, July 26, 1900. *Study:* Md Inst Fine Art, dipl, 22; Art Students League, with Jean Charlot, 30-40; Alexander Archipenko Sculpture Studio, 30-40. *Work:* Dale Co War Mem Libr, Ala; Smithsonian Inst; US Air Force Acad. *Comn:* paintings (air force activities), US Air Force, West Coast US, 55 & Japan, 56. *Exhib:* Watercolor Show, Art Inst Chicago, 35; Cubist oils, Nicholas Roerich Mus, New York, 40's; Baltimore Mus Art, 45; Silvermine Guild, 50's; Am Watercolor Soc, Nat Acad Gallery, New York, 58-70 & Metrop Mus Art, New York, 67; Parrish Mus, Southampton, NY, 73; Guild Hall, East Hampton, NY, 75-81. *Teaching:* Instr composition & design, Sch Visual Arts, 50-52 & Pratt Inst, 54-57; dept head pictorial illus, Newark Sch Fine & Industrial Art, 59-75. *Awards:* Patrons Prize, Nat Soc Painters Casein, 58; First Prize, Emily Lowe Competition, 62; Celia Atkin Mem Award, Nat Soc Painters Casein, 67. *Bibliog:* Article, Baltimore Evening Sun, 22; Robert Winternitz (auth), Artists among us, Suffolk Times, 73; Patricia Wood (auth), article, Long Island Traveler, 75. *Mem:* Am Watercolor Soc; Allied Artists; Audubon Artists; Nat Soc Painters in Casein & Acrylics. *Media:* Acrylics, Watercolors. *Mailing Add:* Box 110-A Main Rd Mattituck NY 11952

HARDY, JOHN
PAINTER

b Tours, France; US citizen. *Study:* Ga State Univ, BFA, 69. *Work:* Brooklyn Mus, NY; Nat Mus Am Art/Art in Embassies, US State Dept, Washington, DC; Mint Mus, Charlotte, NC; Mus Art, Univ of Iowa; Grey Art Gallery, NY Univ; and others. *Exhib:* Nat Col Fine Arts, Washington, DC, 79; Brooklyn Mus, 80 & Sid Deutsch Gallery, 83, New York; One-man shows, Stanley-Schencke Gallery, Atlanta, 82 & Armstrong Gallery, New York, 84; Provincetowm Art Assoc & Mus, Mass, 83; and others. *Teaching:* Chmn visual arts, sch archit, Ga Tech, 69-75; vis artist painting, Rice Univ, Houston & La State Univ, Baton Rouge, 79; adj fac painting, NY Univ, 80-82. *Bibliog:* Tram Combs (auth), article, Art Am, 5-6/78; Renatta Karlin (auth), catalog essay, 6/81; Clyde Burnette (auth), article, Atlantic J, 2/82. *Mailing Add:* 130 W 26th St New York NY 10001

HARDY, ROBERT
GALLERY DIRECTOR, CERAMIST

b Millville, NJ, Aug 2, 38. *Study:* Calif State Univ, Long Beach, BA, MA; Univ Calif, Irvine; Scripps Grad Sch, Claremont, Calif. *Comn:* Numerous comns for interior designers in bas-relief ceramic sculptures. *Exhib:* Los Angeles Mus Sci & Indust, 62; Craftsmen USA, Lytton Gallery, Los Angeles Co Art Mus, Los Angeles, 66; Mus Contemp Crafts, New York, 66 & Ravinia Festival, Chicago, 67; Saginaw Art Mus, Mich, 68; Grand Rapids Art Mus, Mich, 68; Columbia Mus Art, SC, 68; Laguna Mus Art, Calif, 74. *Collections Arranged:* Religious Expressions in Art, 75, National Basketry Exhibition, 76, California Indian Basketry: An Artistic Overview (ed, catalogue), 76, June Wayne: Weaver of Tapestries, Painter & Printmaker, 77 & Year of the Horse: 4676, 78, Fine Arts Gallery, Cypress Col. *Pos:* Gallery dir, Fine Arts Gallery, Cypress Col, 66- *Teaching:* Prof ceramics, Cypress Col, 66- *Awards:* Merit Award, Craftsmen USA, Lytton Gallery, 66. *Mailing Add:* c/o Cypress Col Fine Arts Gallery 9200 Valley View Cypress CA 90630

HARDY, THOMAS (AUSTIN)
SCULPTOR

b Redmond, Ore, Nov 30, 21. *Study:* Ore State Univ, 38-40; Univ Ore, BA, 42, with Archipenko, summer 51, MFA, 52. *Work:* Whitney Mus Am Art, New York; Seattle Art Mus, Wash; San Francisco Mus Art; Neuberger Mus, New York; Portland Art Mus, Ore. *Comn:* Diving Birds, Fed Bldg, Juneau, Alaska, 64; Duck Fountain, Univ Ore, Eugene, 64; Flight, Dorothy Chandler Music Ctr, Los Angeles, Calif, 65; wall sculpture, State Dept Agr, Salem, Ore, 68; Bear, Univ Calif, Berkeley, 80. *Exhib:* 3rd Biennial, Sao Paulo, Brazil, 55; Am Watercolors, Drawings & Prints, Metrop Mus Art, 56; Mus Mod Art Sculpture Exhib, 63; Whitney Mus Am Art Sculpture Ann, 64; Exhib Cand Grants, Am Inst Arts & Lett, 68. *Teaching:* Lectr, Univ Calif, Berkeley, 56-58; instr, Calif Sch Fine Arts, San Francisco, 56-58; assoc prof sculpture, Tulane Univ La, 58-59; resident artist, Reed Col, 60-61; vis prof sculpture, Univ Wyo, 75-76. *Awards:* Award for Color Lithography, Soc Am Graphic Artists, 52; Seattle Art Mus Northwest Ann Sculpture Award, 55; Distinguished Serv Award, Univ Ore, 64. *Bibliog:* H Wurdemann (auth), Recent art of the West Coast, Art Am, 2/55; Metal sculptures by Tom Hardy, Am Artist, 4/55; L Jones (auth), Tom Hardy: sculptor-craftsman, Creative Crafts, 7/62. *Mem:* Portland Art Mus; Contemp Crafts Asn; Friends Mus Art, Univ Ore; Portland Ctr Visual Arts; Metropolitan Arts Comn (comnr, 81-85). *Media:* Welded Bronze. *Dealer:* Kraushaar Galleries 724 Fifth Ave New York NY 10019. *Mailing Add:* 1023 N Killingsworth Portland OR 97211

HARE, DAVID
SCULPTOR

b New York, NY, Mar 10, 17. *Study:* Studied in New York, Ariz & Colo. *Work:* Guggenheim Mus; Los Angeles Co Mus Art; Mus Mod Art, New York; Metrop Mus, New York; Whitney Mus Am Art; plus others. *Comn:* Sculpture for New York City, States of RI, Mass & Ill. *Exhib:* Dada, Surrealism and Their Heritage, 68 & The New American Painting and Sculpture, 69, Mus Mod Art, New York; one-man shows, Philadephia Mus Art, 69, Guggenheim Mus, 77 & Hamilton Gallery, New York, 79 & 80; Whitney Mus Am Art, 76; Nat Gallery Am Art, 76; Albright-Knox Art Gallery, 78; Contemp Arts Mus, Houston, 81 & 82; Mus Fine Art, Houston, 82. *Pos:* Ed, VVV (surrealist mag), 42-44. *Teaching:* Lectr extensively; guest critic & lectr, Md Inst Col of Art. *Bibliog:* Hilton Kramer (auth), David hare: A painter of the human psyche, New York Times, 9/30/77; Harold Rosenberg (auth), An American surrealist, New Yorker, 10/24/77; Katharine Kuh (auth), David Hare; American surrealist, Saturday Rev, 10/24/77; and others. *Mailing Add:* 151 Spring St New York NY 10012

HARI, KENNETH
PAINTER, PRINTMAKER

b Perth Amboy, NJ, Mar 31, 47. *Study:* Newark Sch Fine & Indust Arts, dipl, 66; Md Inst Art, BFA, 68; and with Leon Franks & John Delmonte. *Work:* Mus Mod Art, Barcelona, Spain; Baltimore Mus, Md; Nat Portrait Galleries, London, Eng & Washington, DC; Vatican, Rome, Italy; Brooklyn Mus. *Comn:* Portraits, W H Auden & M Moore, New York, 69, Pablo Casals, comn by Mrs Pablo Casals, Vt, 70, Salvador Dali, New York, 72, Ernest Hemingway, Hemingway House, Cuba, Michael York, & Aaron Copland, 82; Paul Robeson, for Paul Robeson Ctr, Rutgers Univ, 79. *Exhib:* Union Col, 69; Monmouth Col, 70; Newark Mus, 71; Trenton State Mus, 72; Va Polytechnic Inst, 74. *Pos:* Dir, NJ Art Festival, 64-69. *Awards:* Pulaski Award, Kusiosko Found, 63; Felice Found Award, 69; Trenton State Mus Award, 72. *Bibliog:* Art in the Hamptons, 69 & feature story, 73, New York Times; M Lenson (auth), Portrait of Casals, Newark News, 71; D Brown (auth), Poetess an artist, Home News, 72. *Media:* Oil, Graphite. *Publ:* Illusr, Vermont, 72, Folk Singer, 72 & Time for Peace, 72, H S Graphics; illusr, Abraham, 74 & Marcel Marceau, 75; and others. *Dealer:* C C Price Gallery 15 E 48th St New York NY 10017; H S Graphics Box 243 Keasbey NJ 08832. *Mailing Add:* 228 Sherman St Perth Amboy NJ 08861

HARJO, BENJAMIN, JR
PAINTER, PRINTMAKER

b Clovis, NMex, Sept 19, 45. *Study:* Inst Am Indian Arts, cert, 66; Okla State Univ, BFA, 74. *Work:* Inst Am Indian Arts, Santa Fe; McFarlin Libr Indian Collection, Univ Tulsa & Tulsa City Co Libr; US Embassy, Mogadiscio, Somalia; Mus Northern Ariz. *Exhib:* Young American Indian Artist, Riverside Mus, New York, 65-66; Nat Indian Arts Exhib, Heard Mus, Phoenix, Ariz, 66; Philbrook 30th Ann Am Indian Arts Exhib, Tulsa, 75; Ann Competition, 5 Tribes Mus, Muskogee, Okla, 76 & 80; Southern Plains Indian Mus, Anadarko, Okla, 80; Trail of Tears Ann, Cherokee Mus, Tahlequah, Okla, 81; Native Am Ctr Living Arts, Niagara Falls, NY, 81. *Pos:* Cult recreational coordr, Tulsa Indian Youth Coun, 74-76. *Teaching:* Jr gallery instr Indian cult, Philbrook Art Ctr, Tulsa, 76-77. *Awards:* First Place Seminole, Five Tribes Mus, 82; Second Graphics Division, Cherokee Mus, 82; Best of Division & First Place, 62nd Ann Indian Market, Sante Fe, 83. *Bibliog:* Peggy Ridgeway (auth), Benjamin Harjo Jr, Art Voice S, 81; Rennard Steickland (auth), Indians of Oklahoma, Okla Press, 81. *Media:* Oil, Acrylic; Etching, Woodblock. *Mailing Add:* 2813 NW 19th St 4955-J S Memorial Oklahoma City OK 73107

HARKINS, DENNIS RICHTER
ADMINISTRATOR, PHOTOGRAPHER

b Nelsonville, Ohio, July 20, 50. *Study:* Ohio Univ, BFA, 72, MA(int affairs), 73. *Collections Arranged:* African Art (with catalog), Ohio Univ, Alden Libr, 73. *Pos:* Educ chmn, Prof Photogr Guild Fla, 78-79 & bd dirs, 79. *Teaching:* Dir photog, Art Inst Ft Lauderdale, 74-81; dir educ, Art Inst Atlanta, 81- *Awards:* Cert Prof Photogr, 79; Lecture Award, Fla Prof Photogr Conf. *Mem:* Soc Photog Educators; Prof Photogr Am; Fla Prof Photogr; Prof Photogr Fla. *Mailing Add:* Art Inst Atlanta 3376 Peachtree Rd NE Atlanta GA 30326

HARLAN, ROMA CHRISTINE
PAINTER

b Warsaw, Ind. *Study:* Art Inst Chicago, Daughters Ind Scholar; Purdue Univ, Lafayette; and with Ralph Clarkson, Francis Chapin, Constantine Pougialis & Marie Goth. *Comn:* Portraits, Sen Kenneth S Wherry, US Capitol Bldg; John Davis, US Supreme Ct; Dean Stanley Brown-Serman, Va Theological Sem, Alexandria; Rev Thomas A Stone, Nat Presby Church, Washington, DC; Mr & Mrs Edwin Shelton, Children's Hospital Nat Med Ctr, Washington, DC; and many others. *Exhib:* One-man exhibs, Lake Shore Club, Chicago, Purdue Univ, Lafayette & George Washington Univ, Washington, DC; Hoosier Salon Ind; All Ill Soc Fine Arts; Arts Club Washington, DC; and others. *Bibliog:* Eleanor Jewett (auth), article, Chicago Tribune; Florence Berryman (auth), article, Washington Eve Star, 67; and others. *Mem:* Arts Club Washington; Ind Fedn Arts Clubs; Washington Forum Club; DC Fedn Women's Clubs; Zonta Club. *Media:* Oil. *Publ:* Auth, Rembrandt, Cong Rec, 57. *Mailing Add:* 1600 S Joyce St A-1607 Arlington VA 22202

HARLOW, ROBERT E
PAINTER

b Philadelphia, Pa, Mar 20, 14. *Study:* Pa Acad Fine Arts, Univ Pa, BFA, 36; Columbia Univ; Yale Univ. *Work:* Albany Inst Art & Hist; Dumbarton Oaks, Washington, DC; Miami Mus Mod Art; Conn Pub Insts; John Davis Hatch Collection. *Exhib:* Directions American Art, Carnegie Inst, 42; Artists for Victory, Metrop Mus Art, New York, 43; Artists & Engineers, Brooklyn Mus, 69; NJ State Mus Ann, Trenton, 71; IBM, Princeton, NJ, 73; one-man shows, Miami Mus Mod Art, 69 & Rutgers Univ, 71. *Pos:* Supvr & artist, Fed Art Proj, Pa & Conn, 43-44. *Teaching:* Instr art, Manville Pub Schs, NJ, 57-72; supvr art, Am Sch, Madrid, Spain, 66-67. *Awards:* Hon mention, Nat Drawing Ann, Nat Acad Design, 42; cover design award, Nat Drawing Ann, Albany Mus Art & Hist, 43. *Media:* Oil. *Res:* Discovery and authentication of Thomas Eakins' painting, Pushing for Rail, Yale Univ. *Mailing Add:* Fernan Gonzoles 66 Madrid 9 Spain

HARMAN, MARYANN WHITTEMORE
PAINTER

b Roanoke, Va, Sept 13, 35. *Study:* Univ Va, Mary Washington Col, BA; Va Polytech Inst & State Univ, MA. *Work:* Minn Mining & Mfg Corp, Minneapolis; Philip Morris Corp, Richmond, Va; Hunter Mus, Chattanooga, Tenn; Gen Motors, Detroit; Boston Mus Fine Arts; and others. *Exhib:* Irene Leach Mem Exhib, Chrysler Mus, Norfolk, 67-72; Butler Inst Art Nat Show, Youngstown, Ohio, 69 & 72; one-person shows, Andre Emmerich Gallery, New York, 76 & 78, Allen Rubiner Gallery, Detroit, 77 & 79, Meredith Long Gallery, New York, 80; Haber-Theodore Gallery, New York, 81; Osuna Gallery, Washington DC, 82; and many others. *Teaching:* Assoc prof painting & drawing, Va Polytech Inst & State Univ, 64-81, prof, 81- *Awards:* Purchase Awards, Hunter Mus, 74; Cert of Distinction, Va Mus Fine Arts, 74; Purchase Award, Mint Mus, 83. *Bibliog:* Barclay Sheaks (auth), Painting Natural Environment, Davis, 74 & Painting with Oils, Davis, 77; Marsha Miro (auth), rev, Detroit Free Press, 12/78; Edgar Buonagurio (auth), rev, Arts Mag, 5/80. *Mem:* Col Art Asn Am; Southeastern Col Art Asn; Va Mus Fine Arts; Am Fedn Arts. *Media:* Acrylic, Oil. *Dealer:* Haber-Theodore Gallery 29 W 57th St New York NY. *Mailing Add:* 602 Landsdowne Dr Blacksburg VA 24060

HARMON, BARBARA SAYRE
PAINTER, CHILDREN'S BOOK ILLUSTRATOR

b Yerington, Nev, Aug 8, 27. *Study:* Bisttram Sch Fine Art, painting & drawing; etching with Lawton Parker; Black Mountain Col, bookbinding with Johanna Jalowitz. *Bibliog:* Mary Carrol Nelson (auth), Barbara Harmon: magic & mastery, Am Artist Mag, 5/75; Kelly Malore Cribbs (auth), The tumpfce wood world of Barbara Harmon, Santa Fean Mag, 7/79. *Mem:* Exhib Artist Taos Art Asn. *Media:* Mixed; Lithography. *Publ:* Auth & illusr, Tabbigail's Garden, 67, The Little People's Counting Book, 68 & Monday's Mouse, 70, The Children's Gallery Press; auth & illusr, This Little Pixie, 69 & The Tumpfee Wood Acorn Book, 77, The Children's Gallery Press & The Baker Co. *Dealer:* Baker Gallery of Fine Art Box 1920 Lubbock TX 79408; Stables Gallery Box 198 Taos NM 87571. *Mailing Add:* Las Cruces NM 87571

HARMON, CLIFF FRANKLIN
PAINTER

b Los Angeles, Calif, June 26, 23. *Study:* Bisttram Sch Fine Art, Los Angeles, Calif & Taos, NMex, with Emil Bisttram; Black Mountain Col, NC, with Joe Fiore; Taos Valley Art Sch, with Louis Ribak. *Work:* Mus NMex, Santa Fe; Okla Art Ctr, Oklahoma City; Harwood Found, Taos, NMex. *Exhib:* NMex & Southwest Biennials, NMex Mus, 66, 70-72, Watercolor NMex, 74; 11th Midwest Biennial, Joslyn Art Mus, Omaha, Nebr, 70; 1st Four Corners Biennial, Phoenix Art Mus, Ariz, 71; Bertrand Russell Centenary Art Exhib, Rotundagallery, London, Eng, 72. *Pos:* Mem, NMex Arts Div Funding Adv Panel, 79-80. *Awards:* First Premium for Abstract Painting, NMex State Fair, 68; Hon Mention, NMex Mus & Phoenix Art Mus, 71. *Mem:* Taos Art Asn (first vpres, 68-69, pres, 78-79). *Media:* Acrylic, Watercolor. *Dealer:* Torreon Gallery Taos NM 87571; Total Arts Gallery Taos NM 87571. *Mailing Add:* PO Box 6584 Taos NM 87571

HARMON, FOSTER
DEALER, DIRECTOR

b Judsonia, Ark, Nov 5, 12. *Study:* Ind Univ; Ohio Univ; State Univ Iowa, BA, 35, MFA, 36. *Pos:* Pub relations dir, Ringling Mus Art, Sarasota, Fla, 58-59; dir, Oehlschlaeger Galleries, Asolo Sarasota, 61-70; bd trustees, Ringling Sch Art & Design; bd dirs, Asolo State Theatre; dir, Harmon Gallery, Naples, Fla, formerly, emer dir, currently; owner-dir, Foster Harmon Galleries of Am Art, Sarasota, Fla. *Teaching:* Instr drama & dir univ theatre prod, Ind Univ, Bloomington, 36-42. *Awards:* Award of Merit for Long Serv & Contrib to Art, Ohio Univ, 70. *Mem:* Am Fedn Arts; Fla League Arts; Ringling Mus Art; Sarasota Art Asn (pres, 59-60); Fla Artists Group; Archives of Am Art, Smithsonian Assocs. *Specialty:* Paintings, drawings and sculpture by major American artists of the 20th century. *Collection:* American art. *Mailing Add:* PO Box 6187 St Armands Sta Sarasota FL 33578

HARMON, LILY
PAINTER, WRITER

b New Haven, Conn, Nov 19, 12. *Study:* Yale Sch Art; Acad Colarossi, Paris; Art Students League. *Work:* Whitney Mus; Butler Art Inst, Youngstown, Ohio; Newark Art Mus, NJ; Tel Aviv Mus, Israel; Hirshhorn Mus, Washington, DC. *Comn:* Mural, Portchester Jewish Ctr, NY, 50. *Exhib:* Metrop Mus Art, New York, 43; Carnegie Inst, Pittsburgh, 44-49; Univ Ill, 49; 20 one-man shows, Int Salon, Palace Fine Arts, Mexico City, 44-73; 50 Year Retrospective, Wichita Art Mus, 81; Butler Inst Am Art, 82; Provincetown Art Asn & Mus, 83. *Teaching:* Teacher oil painting, Nat Acad Design, New York, 74- *Awards:* La Tausca Art Award, 47; Hallmark Art Award, 49; Pearl Safir Award, Silvermine Guild, 54; plus others. *Bibliog:* A Lily for a Lily, Limited Ed Club, 75; Art in boxes, Norman Laliberte, 75; Contemporary American Painting 1945 (catalog), Wichita Art Mus, 81. *Mem:* Provincetown Art Asn; Artists Equity; Nat Acad Design. *Publ:* Illusr, Jean Paul Sartre's Dirty Hands, 67, Kafka's Castle, 67 & Thomas Mann's Buddenbrooks, 67, Jap Publ; illusr, Guy de Mauppasant's Short Stories, Franklin Libr, 77; auth, Freehand, autobiography, Simon & Shuster, 81; and others. *Mailing Add:* 151 Central Park W New York NY 10023

HARMS, ELIZABETH
PAINTER

b Milwaukee, Wis, May 26, 24. *Study:* Art Inst Chicago, BFA & MFA. *Work:* Newark Mus, NJ. *Exhib:* Art Inst Chicago Ann, 61-64 & 66; one-man shows, Mus Art, Carnegie Inst, 69, Mercer Gallery, New York, 80 & Condeso/Lawler, New York, 82; Contemp Images in Watercolor Touring Show, 76; Eight Painters, Jersey City Mus, 80; Selected Women Painters, Castle Gallery, Col New Rochelle, 82; and others. *Awards:* Third Prize Nat Watercolor exhib, Smithsonian Inst, 63; Armstrong Prize, Art Inst Chicago, 63; Tiffany Found Grant for Painting, 77. *Bibliog:* Hilton Kramer (auth), Art: More from Dubuffet feast, NY Times, 9/27/75; David Shirey (auth), Unsensational art in a municipal office, NY Times, 11/11/79; William Zimmer (auth), Harms at Condeso/Lawler, Art GAllery Scene, 10/30/82. *Media:* Oil, Watercolor. *Dealer:* Condeso/Lawler 76 Green St New York NY. *Mailing Add:* 240 Ogden Ave Jersey City NJ 07307

HARNETT, (MR & MRS) JOEL WILLIAM
COLLECTORS

Mr Harnett, b New York, NY, Dec 3, 25. *Study:* Mr Harnett, Univ Richmond, BA; New Sch Social Res. *Pos:* Mrs Harnett, mem, NY State Coun Arts. *Mem:* Friends Whitney Mus Am Art; Art Table Inc. *Collection:* Works by Hopper, Burchfield, Marsh, Greene, Anuszkiewcz, Raphael Soyer, Rosenberg, Seley, Tooker, Jenkins, Pearlstein, Calder, Lamis and Fletcher Benton. *Mailing Add:* 2 Sutton Pl S New York NY 10022

HAROOTIAN, KHOREN DER
PAINTER, SCULPTOR

b Armenia, Apr 2, 09; US citizen. *Study:* Worcester Art Mus, Mass. *Work:* Metrop Mus Art & Whitney Mus Am Art; Worcester Art Mus; Billy Rose Collection, Bezalel Mus, Israel; Armenian Nat Mus, Erevan, Soviet Armenia. *Comn:* Sculptures, Scientist, Fairmount Park Art Asn, 50, Christ, Armenian Cathedral Comt, New York, 58, Beaver, Baruch Col, 60 & saints, Armenian Apostolic Church, Wynnewood, Pa, 73; bronze monument, Armenian Bicentennial Comt, Fairmount Park, Philadelphia, 75. *Exhib:* Whitney Mus Am Art Ann, New York, 45-66; Pa Acad Fine Arts, Philadelphia, 45-66; Fairmount Park Int Exhib, Philadelphia Mus, 48; Am Pavilion, Brussels World's Fair, Belg, 58; Royal Acad Arts Summer Exhib, Piccadily, London, Eng, 64 & 65; plus others. *Awards:* George D Widener Medal, Pa Acad Fine Arts, 54; Am Acad Arts & Lett & Nat Inst Arts & Lett Award & Citation, 54; Silver Medal, Gruppo Donatello, Florence, Italy, 62. *Bibliog:* Dorothy Grafly (auth), Prophet of man in his eternal battle against evil, Am Artist Mag, 11/46; Ralph M Pearson (auth), article in Modern Renaissance Am Art, Harper & Row, 54; article in, Current Biog, 1/55. *Media:* Watercolor; Bronze, Marble. *Mailing Add:* RFD Rte 9-W Castle Rd Orangeburg NY 10962

HARPER, ELEANOR O'NEIL
PAINTER

b Newburyport, Mass, Dec 23, 19. *Study:* Radcliffe Col, AB(fine arts); Sch Practical Art, Boston; also with Donald Stoltenberg, Betty Lou Schlemm & Arthur Pope. *Exhib:* Catharine Lorillard Wolfe Art Club Exhib, Nat Arts Club, New York, 72-73; Nat Exhib, Mus Fine Arts, Springfield, Mass, 75; Butler Mus, Ohio, 77-78; Guild Boston Artists; Hudson Valley Art Asn, 80-81; Allied Artists Am Ann Exhib, Nat Arts Club, New York, 83. *Pos:* Copywriter, Filene's, Boston, 42-43, dir advert, Br Shop, 43-45. *Teaching:* Instr, Painting workshops, Rockport, 74 & New York, 84. *Awards:* Carl R Matson Mem Award, Rockport Art Asn, 80; Morton Donald Catok Mem Award, Academic Artists Asn, 80; Margaret Fitzhugh Brown Mem Award, NShore Arts Asn, 83; and others. *Mem:* Rockport Art Asn; Copley Soc; Guild Boston Artists; Academic Artists Asn; Nat League Am Pen Women. *Media:* Oil. *Mailing Add:* Penzance Rd Rockport MA 01966

HARPER, PAULA (HAYS)
HISTORIAN, WRITER
b Boston, Mass, Nov 17, 38. *Study:* Hunter Col, New York, art hist with Leo Steinberg, studio art with Tony Smith, BA, 66, MA, 68; Stanford Univ, with Albert Elsen & Lorenz Eitner, PhD, 76. *Collections Arranged:* Against the Madness: Art from California Campuses, Dumbarton Gallery, Washington, DC, 70; War, Revolution and Peace, Propaganda Posters from the Hoover Institution Archives, 1914-1945 (auth, catalog), Stanford Univ, 71; Daumier's Lithographs, Stanford Art Gallery (with Lorenz Eitner & Betsy Fryberger), 72; Women's Weekend (paintings, sculpture, film), Franklin Sch Contemp Studies, London, 74. *Pos:* Dir, Hunter Arts Gallery, Hunter Col, New York, 77-78. *Teaching:* Asst prof 19th & 20th century painting & photog, hist women artists, Calif Inst Arts, 71-74; asst prof 19th century painting & 20th century art criticism, Stanford Univ, 79-80; asst prof 19th & 20th century art & art criticism, Mills Col, 80-81. *Mem:* Col Art Asn; Am Asn Univ Prof; Women's Caucus of Col Art Asn (founding mem, 72, pres New York chap, 76-77, nat adv bd, currently). *Res:* Work done on 20th century propaganda posters; World Wars I and II, Russian Revolution and women's suffrage posters; history, political & social commentary in prints. *Publ:* Contribr, Art and Architecture in the Service of Politics, MIT Press, 79; auth, Daumier's Clowns: New Biographical and Political Functions for a Nineteenth Century Myth, Garland Press, 80; coauth, Pissarro His Life and Work, Horizon Press, 80, Fr transl, Flammarion, Paris, 80, German transl, Atheneum, Berlin, 82. *Mailing Add:* 1955 Leavenworth San Francisco CA 94133

HARPER, WILLIAM
ENAMELIST, GOLDSMITH
b Bucyrus, Ohio, June 17, 44. *Study:* Western Reserve Univ, BS, 66, MS, 67; Cleveland Inst Art, cert, 67. *Work:* Vatican Mus; Columbus Gallery Fine Art; Metrop Mus, New York; Minn Mus; Cleveland Mus Art. *Comn:* Collar and Jewel of Office of the President, Yale Univ, 82. *Exhib:* Goldsmith, 74 & solo exhib, 77-78, Renwick Gallery; Landscape: New Views, Johnson Mus of Art, Cornell Univ, 77; Goldsmiths Hall, London, 78; Craft Art & Religion, Vatican Mus, 78; one-man show, Kennedy Galleries, NY, 81 & 82. *Teaching:* Vis artist enamels, Kent State Univ, 70-73; from assoc prof to prof metals & enamels, Fla State Univ, 73-; vis prof, Parsons Sch Design, New York, 79. *Awards:* Award for Crafts & Horace Potter Award for Excellence in Craftsmanship, Cleveland Mus Art, 73-74; Medallion of Limoges, Int Enamel Biennalle, 75; Craftsman's Res Fel, Nat Endowment Arts, 78-79. *Bibliog:* Elizabeth McClelland (auth), Enameling on the upbeat, Craft Horizons, 5/73; Penelope Hunter-Stiebel (auth), William Harper talismans for our time, Am Crafts, 8-9/81. *Mem:* Soc NAm Goldsmiths; Am Crafts Coun. *Publ:* Contribr, The Art of Cloisonne, Lowe Art Mus, Coral Gables, Fla, 72; auth, Step by Step Enameling, Western, 73; auth, The magic of cloisonne: William Harper, Craft Horizons, 6/77. *Dealer:* Galerie Am Graben, Vienna. *Mailing Add:* 3516 Trillium Ct Tallahassee FL 32312

HARRIES, MAGS (MARGARET L)
SCULPTOR
b Barry, SWales, Gt Brit, April 6, 45. *Study:* Leicester Col Art & Design, England, dipl, 67; Univ Southern Ill, MFA, 70. *Work:* Boston Mus Fine Arts; Univ Southern Ill. *Comn:* Asaroton 1976, City Boston, 76; Bellingham Square (bronze artifacts), City Chelsea, Mass, 78; Glove Cycle (bronze narrative), Mass Bay Transit Authority, Boston, 79-83; Three Gardens (topiary sculpture), DeCordova Mus, Lincoln, Mass, 81-82; Gateway (wood table), City Cambridge, Mass, 83. *Exhib:* The Presence & Absence of Realism, State Univ NY, Potsdam, 76; Collectors Collect Contemporary, Inst Contemp Art, Boston, 78; Impressions in Clay, Everson Mus, 79; Directions in Realism, Danforth Mus, Framingham, Mass, 81; Cast Illusions, Wellesley Col Mus, 82; solo exhib, DeCordova Mus, Lincoln, Mass, 82. *Teaching:* Instr sculpture, Sch Mus Fine Arts, Boston, 78- *Awards:* Bicentennial Sculpture Comn, City Boston, 76; Bunting Fel, Radcliffe Col, 77-78; Design Excellence Pub Art, Nat Endowment Arts & US Dept Transportation, 81. *Bibliog:* Nancy Stapen (auth), article, Art New England, 11/82; Pamela Allara (auth), article, Art News, 3/83. *Mailing Add:* 388 Walden St Cambridge MA 02138

HARRINGTON, LA MAR
WRITER, CURATOR
b Iowa, Nov 2, 17. *Study:* Iowa State Col, 35-36; Cornish Sch Fine Arts, Seattle, 45-50; Univ Wash, BA, 79. *Collections Arranged:* Art and Machines: Light, Motion and Sound, 69; Claes Oldenburg Icebag, 71; More Art for Public Places, 71; New Works from the Walker, 71; Kenneth Callahan: A Universal Voyage, 73; Adventures in Photography, 75; Another Side to Art: Ceramic Sculpture in the Northwest, 79; Washington Craft Forms: Creators and Collectors, 82; Historical Survey of Crafts in the Northwest, 83. *Pos:* Staff mem, Henry Gallery, Univ Wash, 56-75, assoc dir, 72-75; cur, Arch of Northwest Art, Univ Wash, 75-77; panel mem visual arts, Nat Endowment for the Arts, 76-78; bd trustees, Pilchuck Sch, Seattle, Wash. *Awards:* Governor's Art Award, Wash State Art Comn, 71 & 74; Woman of Achievement Award, Women in Commun Ann Matrix Table, 74; Governor's Writer's Award, Wash State Comn, 80. *Mem:* Western Asn Art Mus (bd trustees, vpres, 73, pres, 74 & 75); Pac Northwest Arts & Crafts Asn (life mem bd trustees, pres, 57 & 58); Pottery NW (bd trustees, vpres, 76 & 77). *Res:* Contemporary American art and handcrafts; history of Pilchuck School. *Publ:* Auth, Letter from Seattle, 63-68, First ann western craft competition, Craft Horizons, 7/64; contribr, 74th Western Annual (exhib catalog), Denver Art Mus, 73; auth, Ceramics in the Pacific Northwest: A History, Univ Wash Press, 79; Washington Craft Forms: An Historical Perspective, State Capitol Mus, Olympia, Wash, 82; auth, the making of a modernist metalworker, J Archives Am Art, 10/83. *Mailing Add:* 511 Galer Seattle WA 98109

HARRINGTON, WILLIAM CHARLES
SCULPTOR
b Chicago, Ill, June 20, 42. *Study:* Hartford Art Sch; Univ Ill, with Roger Majorowicz & Clyde Fern, BFA; Univ Hartford with Ted Behl & Lloyd Glasson, MFA. *Comn:* 15 ft concrete & steel, Cabot, Cabot & Forbes, Seattle, Wash, 75; 4 ft wood relief, Amalgamated Spirits & Provisions, Ames, Iowa, 75 & Cedar Rapids, Iowa, 76. *Exhib:* Des Moines Art Ctr, 76; Sweet Briar Col, 79; Second St Gallery, Charlottesville, Va, 80; Open Air Sculpture Exhib, Virginia Beach, 80-81; Bridgewater Col, Va, 82; and others. *Pos:* Workshop asst, George Rickey, East Chatham, NY, 65; mem, Combat Artists Team Vietnam, 68-69. *Teaching:* Asst prof sculpture & drawing, Ind State Univ, Terre Haute, 70-72; asst prof sculpture, Iowa State Univ, 74-78. *Mem:* Tri State Sculptors Guild. *Media:* Wood, Scrap Steel. *Mailing Add:* RR 1 Box 407 A Crozet VA 22932

HARRIS, ALFRED PETER
PAINTER, ADMINISTRATOR
b Toronto, Ont, Apr 4, 32. *Study:* Ont Col Art, Toronto, hon dipl. *Work:* Sir George Williams Univ, Montreal; Bronfman Collection, Montreal Mus Fine Art; Brascan Collection, Toronto; Can Coun Art Bank; Northern & Cent Gas Co. *Exhib:* Mem Gallery, Albright-Knox Gallery, Buffalo, 62; four-man exhib, London Pub Libr & Art Mus, 63-65; two-man exhibs, Dorothy Cameron Gallery, 64-65; two-man show, Roberts Gallery, Toronto, 70; Ann Exhib Contemp Can Art, Hamilton, 70-72. *Collections Arranged:* J W Morrice, J Chambers Retrospective & William Kurelec Retrospective, 66; Baker, Boyle & Hollenback, 67; John Newman, 68; Soul of Niagara, 69; John Boyle, Ed Fantinel, 70; Harvey Breverman & Niagara Now, 71. *Pos:* Dir, Rodman Hall Arts Ctr, 59-; pres, Ont Asn Art Galleries, 70-71. *Teaching:* Art instr, Ont Col Art, 59-60; instr gen art, Ridley Col, St Catharines, 63-65; spec lectr mod art, Brock Univ, 66. *Bibliog:* Harry Malcomson (auth), Artist, Toronto Life, 69. *Mem:* Can Soc Graphic Art; Ont Soc Artists; Ontario Arts Coun. *Media:* Oil. *Publ:* Contribr, Nude in Canadian Art, 72. *Dealer:* Roberts Gallery 641 Yonge St Toronto ON Can. *Mailing Add:* 165-901 Ontario St St Catharines ON L2R 5K4 Canada

HARRIS, ANN SUTHERLAND
HISTORIAN, ADMINISTRATOR
b Cambridge, Eng, Nov 4, 37. *Study:* Courtauld Inst Art, Univ London, BA(hon, first class), 61, PhD, 65; Eastern Mich Univ, Hon DA, 81. *Collections Arranged:* Women Artist 1550-1950 (coauth, catalog), Los Angeles Co Mus Art, Los Angeles, 76-77; Univ Art Mus, Univ Tex, Austin, 77; Mus Art, Carnegie Inst Int, Pittsburgh, 77; Brooklyn Mus, 77. *Pos:* Chmn acad affairs, Metrop Mus Art, New York, 77- *Teaching:* Asst prof art hist & archaeol, Columbia Univ, 66-71; vis lectr, Yale Univ, 72-73; asst prof art hist, Hunter Col, New York, 71-73; assoc prof, State Univ NY, Albany, 73-77; vis assoc prof, Inst Fine Arts, NY Univ, 74-75; adj prof, Juilliard Sch, 78-; Mellon prof, Univ Pittsburgh, spring 84. *Mem:* Col Art Asn Am (mem bd dir, 75-79); Women's Caucus for Art (pres & founder mem, 71-74, mem exec adv bd, 74). *Res:* Italian and French, 16th & 17th century painting and drawing. *Publ:* Co-auth, Die Zeichnungen von Andrea Sacchi & Carlo Maratta, Kataloge des Kunstmuseums, Düsseldorf, III, Düsseldorf, 67; ed, Selected Drawings of Gian Lorenzo Bernini, Dover Publ, 77; auth, Andrea Sacchi, Complete Edition of the Paintings, Phaidon, Oxford, 77. *Mailing Add:* 560 Riverside Dr New York NY 10027

HARRIS, CONLEY
PAINTER, INSTRUCTOR
b Kans, July 7, 43. *Study:* Univ Kans, BFA, 65; Univ Wis, MFA, 68. *Work:* Fogg Art Mus, Harvard Univ, Cambridge, Mass; Boston Mus Fin Art; DeCordova Mus, Lincoln, Mass; Wichita Art Mus, Kans; Portland Mus Art, Maine; and others. *Exhib:* Made in Boston, Fogg Art Mus, Harvard Univ, Cambridge, Mass, 80; 5 Artists in Amsterdam, Broekhoven Gallery, Holland, 81; Works on Paper, Boston Univ, 82; Figuration on Paper, Boston Mus Fine Arts, 83; one-person shows, Cutler/Stavaridis Gallery, Boston, 82, Barridoff Galleries, Portland, Mass, 83 & Newport Art Mus, RI, 83; American Drawings IV, Smithsonian Tour, 83-85; and others. *Teaching:* Vis artist drawing, Boston Univ, Mass, 69-70; assoc prof drawing & painting, Univ NH, Durham, 70- *Awards:* Wurlitzer Found Residence Grant, 75; Purchase Prize, Am Drawing, Portsmouth, Va, 76. *Bibliog:* Robert Taylor (auth), article, Boston Globe, 3/24/76; Pamela Allara (auth), The Boston art party, Art News Mag, 11/80; Nancy Stapen (auth), article, Art New England, 12/80. *Media:* Oil, Watercolor. *Dealer:* Bess Cutler Gallery 164 Mercer St New York NY. *Mailing Add:* PO Box 511 Portsmouth NH 03801

HARRIS, DOLORES ASHLEY
DESIGNER, EDUCATOR
b Tuskegee, Ala. *Study:* Tuskegee Inst, with Mathilda Schwalegch, BS, 51; Univ Wis, Madison, MS, 56; Sophio Univ, Tokyo, cert(art & cult), 65; Arrowmont Sch Arts & Crafts, with Meda Parker Johnson, 71. *Work:* Meharry Hubbard Hosp, Tenn State Mus, African-Am Mus, Nashville; George Washington Carver Mus, Tuskegee, Ala; Jackson City Sch Mus, Tenn. *Exhib:* Art Fibers and Fabrics, Univ Ctr Art Gallery, Cookeville, Tenn, 74; The Early Eighties, Tenn State Mus, Nashville, 81; Womans Perspective, Schenectady Mus, NY, 82-83; Wearable Art, Nashville Artist Guild Gallery, 83; Artist Guild Exhib, Cheekwood Fine Arts Mus, Nashville, 83. *Teaching:* Asst prof design, Prairie View Col, 64-66; prof, Tenn State Univ, Nashville, 67-; guest lectr, Murray State Univ, summer 73. *Awards:* Excellence in Teaching, Tenn State Univ, 74; Hanging Arts Award, Arts Jamboree, Fla State Univ, 80; Progression Award, Early 80s, Tenn State Mus, 82. *Bibliog:* Clara Hieronymous (auth), A time to live and a time to dye, 71 & Art is unifying factor, 75, Nashville Tennessean; Caroline McNeilly (auth), Three

figures, Nashville Banner, 81. *Mem:* Nashville Artist Guild; Nat Conf Artists; Tenn Arts Comn Panel Crafts; Am Soc Interior Designers. *Media:* Batik, Tie-Dye. *Publ:* Contribr, Contemporary Batik and Tie-Dye, Crown Publ, 73; contribr, Educators to Africa 75, Approaches to the Study of West Africa, Sch Educ, Howard Univ & African Am Inst, 75; contribr, The American Artist Today in Black, Vol 1, RNM Publ, 82. *Mailing Add:* PO Box 320 Tenn State Univ Nashville TN 37203

HARRIS, GLORIANE
PAINTER, EDUCATOR
b Santa Monica, Calif, Jan 7, 47. *Study:* Art Ctr Col Design, Los Angeles, 64; Univ Southern Calif, 64-66; El Camino Col, 65; Los Angeles City Col, 66; Otis Art Inst of Los Angeles Co, 66, BFA, MFA(fel), 70; Los Angeles Trade Tech Col, 78. *Exhib:* New Talent, New Work, Los Angeles Co Mus Art, Calif, 71; Video Los Angeles, Palais de Beaux Artes, Brussels, Belg, 77; Painting Show, Mount San Antonio Col, Walnut, Calif, 78; Painting, Newport Harbor Art Mus, Calif, 79; Hang 8: Artists from Southern California, Foundations Gallery, New York, 82; Self-Portrait Invitational, Am Gallery, Los Angeles, 82. *Pos:* Co-organizer, Experiments in Art & Technol, 68-71; co-organizer & founding mem, Los Angeles Inst Contemp Art, 73-75; tech asst, Documenta, Kassel, Ger, 77; photo typesetter, Future Studio, 78-79; typographer & graphic artist, Montage Publ, 80-81; dir art serv, Vintage Image, 81-83; freelance production artist & photo retoucher, 83- *Teaching:* Lectr painting, drawing & design, Cerritos Col, Calif, 70-72; lectr painting & drawing, W Los Angeles Col, Culver City, Calif, 71-74; lectr design & drawing, El Camino Col, Torrance, Calif, 74-78; lectr photo retouching, Otis Art Inst of Parsons, Los Angeles, Calif, 80-81. *Bibliog:* William Wilson (auth), article, Los Angeles Times, 6/14/74; Ronald Steen (auth), Gloriane Harris and Steven Semeyer, Artweek, 9/27/75; Peter Frank (auth), Unslick in Los Angeles, Art in Am, 9-10/78. *Media:* Oil, Watercolor. *Mailing Add:* 3742 Jasmine Ave Los Angeles CA 90034

HARRIS, HARVEY SHERMAN
PAINTER, EDUCATOR
b Hartford, Conn, Aug 31, 15. *Study:* Hartford Art Sch, dipl; Kansas City Art Inst, with Thomas Hart Benton & John de Martelly; Yale Univ, with Josef Albers & Willem de Kooning, BFA & MFA. *Work:* Speed Mus, Louisville, Ky; Southern Ill Univ Mitchell Gallery, Carbondale; State Univ NY Oswego Libr Art; La State Univ, Baton Rouge Libr Art. *Comn:* Illustrations for Look Homeward, Angel, 45; sets/costumes, Rockefeller Fund Louisville Symphony & Opera, 56 & 57. *Exhib:* Drawings, USA, Mus Mod Art, New York, 55; Pa Acad Nat Watercolor & Drawing Biennial, 58 & 59; Butler Inst Am Art Nat Mid-Yr Show, Youngstown, Ohio, 64; Norfolk Mus 21st Am Drawing Biennial & Smithsonian Inst Traveling Drawing Show, 65; Avanti Gallery, New York, 75. *Teaching:* Lectr basic studio graphic design, Louisville Art Ctr & Univ Louisville, 54-57; asst prof drawing & art hist, State Univ NY Oswego, 57-60; assoc prof, Southern Ill Univ, Carbondale, 60-67; prof painting & drawing, La State Univ, Baton Rouge, 67-82, prof emer, 82- *Awards:* Hon Mention, Conn Artist-Teachers, Yale Art Gallery, 49; Robert B Tunstall Prize, Norfolk Mus 21st Am Drawing Biennial, 65. *Media:* All Media. *Mailing Add:* 2209 Glendale Ave Baton Rouge LA 70808

HARRIS, JULIAN HOKE
SCULPTOR, ARCHITECT
b Carrollton, Ga, Aug 22, 06. *Study:* Ga Inst Technol, BS, 28; Pa Acad Fine Arts, 29-34. *Work:* IBM Collection, New York; High Mus Art, Atlanta, Ga; Univ Va Mus; Emory Univ, Atlanta; Nat Acad of Design, New York; also in many pvt collections. *Comn:* 50 sculptures for pub & pvt bldgs; 50 portrait & mem comns; 24 commemorative medallions including official inaugural medallion for President Jimmy Carter. *Exhib:* Painting & Sculpture From Sixteen Cities, Mus Mod Art, 33; Pa Acad Fine Arts Mus, 34; one-man shows, High Mus, Atlanta, 35, 39 & 69; Jewish Mus, New York, 52; Nat Sculpture Soc Ann, 70-72. *Pos:* Pres, Asn Ga Artists, 39-42; charter mem, Atlanta Citizens Adv Comt Urban Renewal, 58-71; charter mem, Atlanta Civic Design Comn, 65- *Teaching:* Emer prof, Ga Inst Technol Sch Archit; prof sculpture, Atlanta Sch Art, 46-52. *Awards:* Gov Award Arts, Ga, 80; First Prize, Nat Sculpture Soc, 80; Archdiochese Medal, Greek Orthodox America, 80. *Bibliog:* Many articles in, Nat Sculpture Rev, 53-72; Georgia Tech Alumnus, Ga Inst Technol, 53, 71 & 72; Julian Hoke Harris, Am Sculptors Ser, No 16, 54. *Mem:* Fel Nat Sculpture Soc; fel Am Inst Architects; Nat Acad Design; Atlanta Art Asn (sch adv comt, 72). *Publ:* Auth, Sculpture can be functional, WVa State Mag, 54; auth, Sculpture in architecture today, J Am Inst Architects, 55; auth, Architectural sculpture, Dixie Contractor, 55; auth, Environment, Atlanta Pub Sch Syst, 60. *Mailing Add:* 177 Fifth St NW Atlanta GA 30313

HARRIS, LAWREN PHILLIPS
PAINTER, EDUCATOR
b Toronto, Ont, Oct 10, 10. *Study:* Boston Mus Fine Arts; also with Lawren S Harris (father), Toronto. *Work:* War Records, Nat Gallery Can. *Comn:* Off war artist with Can Army, 43-46; prize, Atlantic Awards Exhib, 67. *Exhib:* Ont Soc Arts, 36-; Royal Can Acad Arts, 38-; Can Group Painters, 38-; New York World's Fair, 39; Can Soc Graphic Art, 39-41; and others. *Teaching:* Instr, N Voc Sch, Toronto, 38-40; instr, Trinity Col Sch, Port Hope, Ont, 40-41; emer prof fine arts & head dept, Mt Allison Univ, currently. *Awards:* Can Govt Overseas Fel, 57-58; Hon Fel, NS Col Art. *Mem:* Ont Soc Arts; Can Group Painters; Royal Can Acad Arts. *Mailing Add:* 29 Crichton St Ottawa ON K1M 1V5 Canada

HARRIS, LEON A, JR
COLLECTOR, PATRON
b New York, NY, June 20, 26. *Study:* Harvard Col. *Collection:* Paintings, drawings and prints. *Publ:* Auth, The great picture robbery, Young France, The fine art of political wit & Only to God: the life of Godfrey Lowell Cabot; articles in New York Times, New York Mag, Town & Country, Harper's Bazaar, Esquire, Good Housekeeping, McCalls & Encycl Americana. *Mailing Add:* 4512 Fairfax Dallas TX 45205

HARRIS, LUCILLE S
PAINTER, PRINTMAKER
b Stockton, Calif, Feb 11, 14. *Study:* Univ Calif, Berkeley, BA, 35; San Francisco State Col, 55; San Francisco Art Inst, 62. *Work:* Haggin Mus, Stockton, Calif; St Marys Col, Moraga, Calif; Oakland Art Mus; Helen Crocker Russell Libr, Mus Temple Emanuel, San Francisco. *Exhib:* One-person exhib, St Marys Col, Moraga, Calif, Haggin Mus, Stockton, Calif & Atheneum Found, Calif Palace Legion Hon; retrospective, Mus Temple Emanuel, San Francisco; Calif Palace Legion Hon First, Second & Third Invitationals; Artists of Hawaii, Honolulu Acad Art, 82-83; Oakland Art Mus; San Francisco Mus Art; De Young Mem Mus; NC Print & Drawing Ann. *Pos:* Gallery asst, Kahana Kii Fine Arts Gallery, 79- *Awards:* San Francisco Art Inst Ann First Award; San Francisco Women Artists Ann Award, San Francisco Mus. *Mem:* Artists Equity Asn; San Francisco Women Artists; Kauai Soc Artists; Garden Island Arts Coun. *Media:* Watercolor, Oil. *Dealer:* Kahana Kii Fine Arts Gallery 3178 Kuheo Hwy Sihue Kauai HI 96766. *Mailing Add:* RR 1 Box 253 Koloa HI 96756

HARRIS, MARIAN D
PAINTER
b Philadelphia, Pa, Apr 22, 04. *Study:* Pa Acad Fine Arts, 22-26, Cresson traveling scholar, 25, Acad Summer Sch, Chester Springs, Pa, 21-24 & 32; Hugh Breckenridge Summer Sch Art, East Gloucester, Mass, 26; with Wayman Adams, Elizabethtown, NY, 33, 35 & 38. *Work:* Albright-Knox Art Gallery, Buffalo, NY; Fellowship Pa Acad Fine Arts; Philadelphia Art Alliance; Gov Bacon Hosp, Del; YWCA, Wilmington, Del; among others. *Exhib:* Pa Acad Fine Arts Ann, 32; Art Inst Chicago Int Watercolor Exhib, 35; Newark Mus Triennial, NJ, 64; Am Artists Prof League Ann, 73 & 74; Garden State Art Ctr, NJ, 74; Cape May Co Art League, NJ, 74; NJ Fed Art Asn Asn, NJ State Cult Ctr, Trenton, 76 & 77; plus many others. *Teaching:* Instr painting, Wilmington Acad Art, Del, 27-32, 36-37; instr art, Atlantic City Friends Sch, NJ, 56-57; lectr art appreciation, Jewish Community Ctr, Margate, NJ, 59. *Awards:* George A Rhodes Prize, Wilmington Soc Fine Arts, 30; Public Choise, Triennial, South Jersey, 64; Best of Show, Atlantic City Art Ctr Ann, 68; and others. *Bibliog:* Benizet (auth), French Dictionary of Artists & Painters; Fielding (auth), American Artists from 1860. *Mem:* Fellowship Pa Acad Fine Arts; Am Watercolor Soc; League SJersey Artists; Atlantic City Art Ctr; Prof Artists SJersey . *Media:* Oil, Watercolor. *Dealer:* Charles Bertolino Gallery 406 Harrison Ave West Berlin NJ 08091. *Mailing Add:* 22 N Cornwall Ave Atlantic City NJ 08406

HARRIS, PAUL
SCULPTOR
b Orlando, Fla, Nov 5, 25. *Study:* With Joy Karen Winslow, Orlando; Univ NMex; New Sch Social Res, with Johannes Molzahn; Hans Hofmann Sch. *Work:* Los Angeles Co Mus Art; Mus Mod Art, New York; Univ NMex; Yale Univ. *Exhib:* Sculpture USA, 59 & Hans Hofmann & His Students, 64-65, Mus Mod Art, New York; Sculpture of the Sixties, Los Angeles Co Mus & Sao Paulo Biennial, 67; Soft Art, NJ Mus, 69; New Vein Show, Vienna, Cologne, Belgrade, Baden-Baden, Geneva, Brussels & Milan, 69-70; solo exhibs, San Francisco Mus Art, 72, Univ Calif, Santa Barbara, 72, Univ NMex, 73 & Ark Art Ctr, Little Rock, 74; and others. *Teaching:* Instr art, Univ NMex, Knox Col, BWI, New Paltz State Col, Calif Art Inst & Cath Univ Chile; prof art, Calif Col Arts & Crafts, presently. *Awards:* Resident MacDowell Colony, 77; Longview Found Grant, 78; Guggenheim Fel, 79. *Media:* Bronze, Cloth. *Publ:* Contribr, Art News & Art in Am; illusr, Dorothy Schmidt's Torso, 74; illusr, Pas de UN, 79. *Dealer:* Poindexter Gallery 24 E 84th St New York NY 10028. *Mailing Add:* Box 930 Bolinas CA 94924

HARRIS, PAUL ROGERS
MUSEUM DIRECTOR, EDUCATOR
b Dallas, Tex, Jan 2, 33. *Study:* NTex State Univ, BA, 54, MA, 56; NY Univ, 65-67. *Collections Arranged:* Fifteen from Dallas, 80, Emerging Texas Photographers (with catalog), 80, Mimi Smith: Television Drawings, 80 (with catalog), Nancy Chambers: Sculptures (with catalog), 81 & Hearts & Flowers (with catalog), 82; Three Photographers: The Human Presence, 82, Fun and Games, 82, James Dowell: Paintings, (with catalog), 83, Barbara Bell: Watercolors and Painted Objects (with catalog), 83, Gateway Gallery; Inaugural Exhibition, Dallas Mus Art, 84. *Pos:* Coordr educ servs, Mus Mod Art, New York, 66-70; dir, The Art Ctr, Waco, Tex, 74-; chmn visual arts & archit adv panel, Tex Comn on the Arts, 80-83. *Teaching:* Supvr art, Children's House, Dallas Mus Contemp Arts, Tex, 60-65; head dept art educ, Southern Methodist Univ, Dallas, Tex, 70-74. *Bibliog:* Janet Kutner (auth), Texas small museums discovering each other, Art News, 2/77; Charlotte Moser (auth), Texas museums: gambling for big change, Art News, 12/79; The state's small museums open doors for young artists, Tex Homes, 10/81. *Mem:* Am Asn Mus; Nat Art Educ Asn; Tex Arts Alliance. *Publ:* Auth, Gillian Bradshaw-Smith: Soft Sculptures & Drawings, 76, Richard Hunt: Sculpture, Drawings, Prints, 78, Pedro Friedeberg, 78 & many others. *Mailing Add:* c/o The Art Ctr 1300 College Dr Waco TX 76708

HARRIS, PAUL STEWART
CURATOR, MUSEUM DIRECTOR
b Orange, Mass, Mar 7, 06. *Study:* Antioch Col, BS; Harvard Col, SB(hist art); New York Univ Grad Sch Fine Arts. *Collections Arranged:* Assisted in installation of the Cloisters and medieval gallery displays, Metrop Mus Art; numerous exhibs, Des Moines Asn Fine Arts, Iowa & J B Speed Art Mus, Louisville, Ky, 33-62. *Pos:* Curatorial asst & asst cur, Metrop Mus Art, 33-38; dir & secy, Des Moines Asn Fine Arts, 38-40; sr cur, Minneapolis Inst Arts, 41-42 & 46; dir & cur, J B Speed Art Mus, 46-62; dep dir, H F du Pont Winterthur Mus, 62-67; dir collections, Henry Ford Mus & Greenfield Village, Mich, 67-71. *Teaching:* Lectr Am Art, Univ Minn, 46. *Mem:* Am Asn Mus; Col Art Asn Am; NH Hist Soc; Early Am Indust Asn. *Res:* Mediaeval European art, American art, European decorative arts and paintings, and modern art. *Publ:* Auth, Fourteen seasons of art accessions, J B Speed Art Mus, 60; also var articles in mus bulletins, 34-64. *Mailing Add:* RFD Chesham Marlborough NH 03455

HARRIS, ROBERT GEORGE
PAINTER, ILLUSTRATOR
b Kansas City, Mo, Sept 9, 11. *Study:* Kansas City Art Inst, with Monte Crews; Grand Cent Sch Art, with Harvey Dunn; Art Students League, with George Bridgeman. *Work:* Portraits, Phoenix Jr Col, Dept of Justice, Washington, DC, Seabury Western Theol Seminary, Chicago, Ill, Wabash Col, Crawfordsville, Ind & Franciscan Renewal Ctr, Scottsdale, Ariz; also in many pvt collections in US. *Exhib:* Soc Illusr; Art Dirs Club, 43-46; New Rochelle Art Asn, 49; Westport Artists, 50; one-man show of portraits, Phoenix Art Mus, 62. *Mem:* Soc Illusr; Phoenix Fine Art Asn; Phoenix Art Mus. *Media:* Oil. *Publ:* Illusr, McCall's, 39-60, Sat Eve Post, 39-61, Good Housekeeping, 40-60, Ladies' Home J, 40-61 & other nat mags. *Mailing Add:* PO Box 1124 Carefree AZ 85377

HARRIS, WILLIAM WADSWORTH, II
PAINTER, COLLAGE ARTIST
b Hamden, Conn, Mar 26, 27. *Study:* Yale Univ, BA; Univ Mich, MA; also with Richard Wilt, Deane Keller & Jerry Farnsworth. *Work:* Galerie Moos, Geneva, Switz; Toledo Mus Fine Arts, Ohio; Yale Univ Collection; Mattatuck Mus Arts & City Nat Bank, Waterbury, Conn; Northwestern Conn Col, Winsted; and in pvt collections in Europe, Mid East & US. *Exhib:* Ringling Mus Art, Sarasota, Fla, 61; Galerie Georges Moos, Geneva, Switz, 64-69; Hub Gallery, Pa State Univ, State College, 73; Conn Soc Fine Arts, Wadsworth Atheneum, Hartford, 74; Am Painters in Paris Exhib, France, 75-76; Berkshire Mus Fine Arts, Pittsfield, Mass, 77; Munson Gallery, New Haven, Conn, 80-83. *Awards:* Top Award, Conn Artists 23rd Ann, Slater Mus, Norwich, 66; Top Awards, Waterbury Arts Festival, Conn, 67 & 68; Winsted Award, 75 & Top Purchase Award, 79, Northwest Conn Art Asn. *Bibliog:* Prize Winning Art, Bk 7, Allied Publ, 67. *Mem:* New Haven Paint & Clay Club (bd dirs, 67-69); New Haven Festival Arts (bd dirs, 71-73). *Media:* Oil on Canvas, Collage in Mixed Media. *Dealer:* Munson Gallery 33 Whitney Ave New Haven CT 06511. *Mailing Add:* 156 Chestnut Hill Rd Killingworth CT 06417

HARRISON, (WILLIAM) ALLAN
PAINTER
b Montreal, Que, Dec 27, 11. *Study:* Art Students League, with Kimon Nicolaides, 31; studied painting with John Lyman, Montreal, 32-33; with Arpad Szenes, Paris, 47-48 & Andre Lhote, 56. *Work:* Montreal Mus Fine Arts; Musee du Que; Mus Bezalel, Jerusalem; Can Coun, Art Bank, Ottawa. *Exhib:* One-man exhibs, Montreal Mus Fine Arts, 45 & Inst dos Arquitetos, Rio de Janeiro, 47; retrospective, Montreal Mus Fine Arts, 78. *Pos:* Art dir, J Walker Thompson Co Ltd, Montreal, 40-46 & Rio de Janeiro, 46-47. *Teaching:* Instr graphic design, Sch Montreal Mus Fine Arts, 41-46 & Sir George Williams Col, Montreal, 60-65; instr drawing & design, Univ Que, Montreal, 71-72; lectr, Sch Archit, McGill Univ, Montreal, Mt Allison Univ, Sackville, NB & Alta Col Art, Calgary. *Bibliog:* Robert Stacey (auth), Allan Harrison, Artmag, 9/80; Joan Murray (auth), Mainstream realism, Toronto Calendar Mag, 11/81; Carolle Gagnon-Marior (auth), Allan Harrison, Vie des Arts, 12/82. *Mem:* Royal Can Acad Arts; Contemp Arts Soc, Montreal (secy, 39-48). *Media:* Oil. *Dealer:* Nancy Poole's Studio 16 Hazelton Ave Toronto ON; Galerie Art Francais Montreal PQ. *Mailing Add:* 201 Metcalfe Ave Westmount PQ H3Z 2H7 Canada

HARRISON, CAROLE
SCULPTOR
b Chicago, Ill, Oct 30, 33. *Study:* Cranbrook Acad Art, BFA, 55, MFA, 56; Cent Sch Art, London, with Robert Adams, Fulbright Scholar, 58. *Work:* Hackley Art Mus, Muskegon, Mich; Springfield Mus Art, Ill; New Wilderness Found, New York; Cranbrook Mus Art; Fine Arts Complex, Western Mich Univ. *Comn:* Unity and Growth (brass & copper), City Oak Park, Ill, 66; Seated Figure (cast brass), Kalamazoo Art Inst, 69; Fountain (welded brass), Steinman Real Estate, Kalamazoo, 70; Three Figures (welded brass), 72 & Motif (welded brass & copper), Western Mich Univ, 82. *Exhib:* Second Biennial Am Painting & Sculpture, Detroit Art Inst & Pa Acad Fine Arts, 59; New Horizons in Sculpture, McCormick Pl, Chicago, 61; Painting & Sculpture Today, Herron Mus Art, Indianapolis, 67; solo exhib, Women & Landscape, Kalamazoo Inst Arts, 76; 157th Nat Acad Design Exhib, New York, 82. *Teaching:* Assoc prof sculpture, Western Mich Univ, 60-74 & State Univ NY, Fredonia, 75-78. *Awards:* Tiffany Found Fel, 60; First Prize, New Horizons in Sculpture, McCormick Pl, Chicago, 61. *Bibliog:* Cesta Peekstok (producer), Art and Architecture in Kalamazoo (video), Western Mich Univ, 76; Marcia Wood (auth), Sculpture, Carole Harrison, Kalamazoo Col, 77; Cesta Peekstok (producer), Art is All Around Us (video), Western Mich Univ, 80. *Mem:* New York Artists Equity; Nat Asn Women Artists. *Media:* Brass, Copper. *Publ:* Auth, Building three figures, Western Mich Univ Press, 73. *Mailing Add:* 140 Hills Sta Rd Box EEE Southampton NY 11968

HARRISON, HELEN AMY
CURATOR, CRITIC
b Richmond Hill, NY, Dec 4, 43. *Study:* Adelphi Univ, Garden City, NY, AB(art), 65; Brooklyn Mus Art Sch, Max Beckmann Mem scholar in sculpture, 65-66; Hornsey Col Art, London, Eng, 66-67; Case Western Reserve Univ, Cleveland, MA(art hist), 75. *Collections Arranged:* Seven American Women: The Depression Decade (co-auth, catalog), 76; David Burliuk: Years of Transition, 1910-1931 (auth, catalog), 78; Dawn of a New Day: the 1939/40 New York World's Fair (auth, catalog), 80; Lithographs of George Bellows, 82; Larry Rivers: Performing for the Family (auth, catalog), 83. *Pos:* Cur, Parrish Art Mus, Southampton, NY, 77-78; art critic, New York Times, Long Island Weekly, 78-; guest cur, Queens Mus, Flushing, NY, 79-81; exec dir, Pub Art Preserv Comt, 81-82; cur, Guild Hall Mus, East Hampton, NY, 82- *Mem:* Cur Comt, Am Asn Mus; Int Asn Art Critics, Am Section; Am Studies Asn. *Res:* Federal art patronage projects of the New Deal era, especially mural painting; the 1939/40 New York World's Fair; contemporary American art. *Publ:* Contribr, Federal Art in Cleveland, 1933-1943 (exhib catalog), Cleveland Pub Libr, 74; auth, 20th Century Paintings from the Metropolitan Museum of Art (exhib catalog), Parrish Art Mus, 77; contribr, Art for the People: New Deal Murals on Long Island (exhib catalog), Hofstra Univ, 78; auth, John Reed Club artists and the New Deal, Prospects 5, 80; auth, Subway art and the PUAC, Archives Am Art J, fall 81. *Mailing Add:* Box 447A RD 1 Sag Harbor NY 11963

HARRISON, HELEN MAYER
ENVIRONMENTAL ARTIST, CONCEPTUAL ARTIST
b New York, NY. *Study:* Queens Col, BA; Cornell Univ; NY Univ, MA. *Work:* Powers Inst, Univ Sydney, Australia; La Jolla Mus Contemp Art, Calif; Mus Contemp Art, Chicago; Brooklyn Mus, New York; Arco, Dallas, Tex. *Comn:* Lagoon Cycle, Metromedia, 77-83; Baltimore Promenade, Md Ins Col Art, 81. *Exhib:* Ronald Feldman Gallery, 74-75, 78, 80 & 82; Venice Bienale, 76 & 80; Maps, Mus Mod Art, Penthouse Gallery, New York, 77; Southern Calif Artists, La Jolla Mus, 79; Dialogue, Discourse, Research, Santa Barbara Mus Art, 79; Guadalupe Meander, San Jose Mus, Calif, 82; and many other group & one-man shows. *Pos:* Consult, Presidential Task Force on Educ, Nat Endowment Arts, 79. *Teaching:* Prof visual arts, Univ Calif, San Diego, 81-, chmn visual arts dept, 83. *Bibliog:* Kim Levin (auth), Helen and Newton Harrison: New grounds for art, Vol 52, No 6 & Peter Selz (auth), Helen and Newton Harrison: Art as survival instructions, Vol 52, No 6, Arts Mag; Ann Schoenfeld (auth), Helen Mayer Harrison and Newton Harrison, Arts Mag, 6/80; and others. *Media:* Mixed. *Publ:* Illusr, San Diego as the center of the world, Los Angeles Inst Contemp Art J, 2/75; illusr, One full work and part of another, 12/77-1/78 & Great Lakes Meditations, summer 79, New Wilderness Lett, New York; auth, The book of the crab, In: Dialogue, Discourse, Research, Santa Barbara Mus Art, 79. *Dealer:* Ronald Feldman Fine Arts 33 E 74th St New York NY 10021. *Mailing Add:* PO Box 446 Del Mar CA 92014

HARRISON, JOSEPH ROBERT, JR
COLLECTOR, PATRON
b Chicago, Ill, June 20, 18. *Study:* Wabash Col, AB; Univ Chicago Law Sch. *Pos:* Pres bd trustees, Metrop Mus & Art Ctr, Miami, 74-77, chmn bd trustees, 76-79; mem, Metrop Dade Co Coun Arts & Sci, 76-78. *Mem:* Am Asn Mus (trustees comt). *Interests:* Museums, art education, sculpture. *Collection:* Late Cubist paintings and watercolors; late 19th century watercolors and drawings. *Mailing Add:* 3120 Munroe Dr Miami FL 33133

HARRISON, NEWTON A
ENVIRONMENTAL ARTIST, CONCEPTUAL ARTIST
b New York, NY, Oct 20, 32. *Study:* Yale Univ Sch Art & Archit, BFA & MFA. *Work:* Arco, Dallas, Tex; Powers Inst, Univ Sydney, Australia; La Jolla Mus Contemp Art, Calif; Mus Contemp Art, Chicago; Brooklyn Mus, New York; and others. *Comn:* Lagoon, Los Angeles, 73-74; Lagoon Cycle, Metromedia, 77-83; Baltimore Promenade, Md Inst, 81. *Exhib:* Art & Technology, Los Angeles Co Mus Art, 71; Earth, Air, Fire, Water: Elements of Art, Boston Mus Fine Art, Mass, 71; Maps, Mus Mod Art, Penthouse Gallery, New York, 77; Artists Investigate the Environ, Munic Art Gallery, Los Angeles, 78; Southern Calif Artists, La Jolla Mus Contemp Art, 79; Dialogue, Discourse, Research, Santa Barbara Mus Art, 79; Drawings, The Pluralist Decade, Venice Bienale, 80; and many others. *Pos:* Chmn Policy Panel, Nat Endowment Arts, Vis Arts Sect, 77-79. *Teaching:* Asst prof art, Univ NMex, 65-67; assoc prof art, Univ Calif, San Diego, 67-71; prof & chmn dept, 73-76, prof, 76- *Awards:* Award for E A T: Projects Outside Art; Nat Endowment Arts Grant, 75; US Dept Com Sea Grant, 74-76. *Bibliog:* Madeleine Burnside (auth), Helen Mayer Harrison and Newton Harrison, New York Rev Arts News, 4/78; Kim Levin (auth), Helen and Newton Harrison: New grounds for art, Vol 52, No 6 & Peter Selz (auth), Helen and Newton Harrison: Art as survival instructions, Vol 52, No 6, Arts Mag; and others. *Publ:* Illusr, San Diego as the center of the world, Los Angeles Inst Contemp Art J, 2/75; illusr, One full work and part of another, 12/77-1/78 & Great Lakes meditations, summer 79, New Wilderness Lett, New York; auth, The book of the crab, In: Dialogue, Discourse, Research, Santa Barbara Mus Art, 79. *Dealer:* Ronald Feldman Fine Arts 33 E 74th St New York NY 10021. *Mailing Add:* PO Box 446 Del Mar CA 92014

HARRISON, PAT (BROEDER)
PAINTER, MURALIST
b Houston, Tex, May 3, 41. *Study:* Tex Tech Univ, BA(fine arts); also with Sam Smith & Milford Zornes. *Work:* Nat Bank, Am Bank Com, Albuquerque; mural, Albuquerque Nat Bank. *Comn:* Designs for posters, tickets, progs, etc, Albuquerque Symphony Asn, 71-75; prog & logo for convention ctr opening,

Albuquerque City Comn, 72; mural, Asset Mgt Inc, Albuquerque, 79; mural, John Baker Elementary Sch, Albuquerque, 81. *Exhib:* Santa Fe Biennial, Mus Santa Fe, 68; NMex Rocky Mountain Fedn 8-State Traveling Exhib, 69-71; Catharine Lorillard Wolfe Art Club 76th Ann Exhib, Nat Arts Club, New York, 72; Am Artists Prof League Grand Nat Exhib, New York, 73 & 78; George Phippen Ann Mem Exhib, Prescott, Ariz, 75. *Awards:* Citation, Tex Fine Arts Asn, 68; Purchase Award Watercolor, NMex State Fair, 69; First Prize & Purchase Award, Nacimiento Mining Co Competition, Earth Resources Co, Dallas, Tex, 71. *Bibliog:* Jack Kirk (auth), Art and artists of New Mexico, Your Host, 11/71; Lois Duncan (auth), How our land feels to us, NMex Mag, 10/73; Alan Weisman (auth), Prescott art scene, Ariz Living, 7/74. *Mem:* Am Artists Prof League. *Publ:* Illusr, Menu Mates, 73. *Dealer:* Linda McAdoo Galleries 503 Canyon Rd Santa Fe NM 87501. *Mailing Add:* 11 Juniper Hill Rd NE Albuquerque NM 87122

HARRISON, TONY
PAINTER, EDUCATOR
b Gt Brit, Aug 18, 31; US citizen. *Study:* Northern Polytech England; Chelsea Sch Art, London; Cent Sch Arts & Crafts, London. *Work:* Aldrich Mus Contemp Art, Ridgefield, Conn; Achenbach Found at Calif Palace Legion Honor, San Francisco; Arts Coun Gt Brit, London; Royal Collection, Stockholm, Sweden; Nat Gallery S Australia; and many others. *Exhib:* One-man shows, San Francisco Mus Art, 64, Bertha Shaefer Gallery, New York, 68-69, 72 & 74 & Soho Ctr for Visual Artists, New York, 77; 10th Anniversary Exhib, Westmoreland Co Mus Art, Greensburg, Pa, 69; 3rd Kent Exhib Contemp Art, Ohio, 69; Nat Inst Arts & Lett, New York, 73; and others. *Teaching:* Instr drawing & printmaking, Columbia Univ, 71-; sr lectr painting, NY Univ, 72; Printmaking Workshop, New York, 74-75. *Awards:* Purchase Award, Soc Am Graphic Artists, 65; Nat Endowment Arts Grant, 75; Creative Artists Pub Serv Grant, 76. *Bibliog:* Robert Erskine (producer), Artists proof (film), St Georges Gallery, 57; Collectors Choice, produced on ITV, London, 62. *Media:* Acrylic, Mezzotint. *Mailing Add:* 106 Hopkins Ave Jersey City NJ 07306

HARRITON, ABRAHAM
PAINTER
b Bucharest, Rumania, Feb 16, 1893; US citizen. *Study:* Nat Acad Design, 08-15, with Emil Carlsen, Kenyon Cox, George DeForest Brush & Mielatz. *Work:* Whitney Mus Am Art, New York; Addison Gallery Am Art, Phillips Acad, Andover, Mass; Ein Harod Mus, Israel; Syracuse Univ Mus; Hirshhorn Mus, Washington, DC; and others in public & private collections. *Comn:* Mural, Louisville Post Off & Agr Bldg, Ga, 36. *Exhib:* Five Whitney Mus Am Art Ann, 36-41; 15 one-man exhibs, ACA Galleries, 36-72; Mus Mod Art, 40; Carnegie Inst, 41, 43, 45 & 46; Artists for Victory, Metrop Mus Art, 42; Am Painting Collection, Montclair Art Mus, 77. *Teaching:* Instr painting & drawing, WPA Art Sch, New York, 32-36; instr painting & drawing, Great Neck Art Asn, NY, 45-50. *Awards:* Marjorie Peabody Waite Award, Nat Inst Arts & Lett, 68-; Mark Rothko Found Grant, 74; Alice G Melrose Mem Award, Audubon Artists 40th Ann Exhib, 82. *Bibliog:* Harry Salpeter (auth), Ex-Picassoid, Esquire Mag, 1/46; Abraham Harriton discusses a system of glazing, Am Artist, 9/51. *Mem:* Audubon Artists (dir, 58); New York Whiskey Painters Am; Artists Inc. *Media:* All. *Res:* Technique of underpainting and glazing as based on Venetian masters. *Dealer:* Ellen Sragow Gallery 80 Fifth Ave New York NY 10011; Nancy Stein Gallery 711 Amsterdam Ave New York NY 10025. *Mailing Add:* 66 W Ninth St New York NY 10011

HARROUN, DOROTHY SUMNER
PAINTER, INSTRUCTOR
b El Paso, Tex, Nov 29, 35. *Study:* With Roderick Mead, 44-53; Univ NMex, BFA(Fulbright Scholar), 57; Univ Colo, MFA, 60; with Peter Hurd, 63. *Work:* Univ Colo Fine Arts Mus, Boulder; Mus Fine Arts, Carlsbad, NMex. *Comn:* Mural of Sandia Mountains, comn by Jon ver Ploegh, Albuquerque, 77. *Exhib:* Am Watercolor Soc 112th Ann, New York, 79; 19th Ann Nat Art Show, Coos Art Mus, Coos Bay, Ore, 80; Images of Albuquerque, Albuquerque Mus, 82; Ga Watercolor Soc Exhib, Atlanta, 83. *Pos:* Art dir, Wood-Reich Advert Agency, Boulder, Colo, 60-61. *Teaching:* Instr, Univ Colo, 61-62, San Francisco State Col, 63-65, Art Ctr Sch, Albuquerque, 75-79, Sanado Group, Sandia Base, Albuquerque, 78-80 & Univ NMex, 80-81. *Awards:* First Place Painting, Ouray Nat Show, Colo, 78; First Prize Watercolor, Carlsbad Area Art Asn, Carlsbad Fine Arts Mus, 80 & Black Canyon Nat Art Show, Hotchkiss, Colo, 80. *Mem:* Nat League Am Penwomen (pres Albuquerque branch, 82-84); NMex Watercolor Soc; Artists Equity Asn (pres Albuquerque chapter & mem nat bd, 77-79); Albuquerque United Artists (mem bd, 78-80); Am Asn Univ Women. *Media:* Oil, Egg Tempera. *Publ:* Auth & illusr, Take Time to Play and Listen, Chapman Press, 63; auth & illusr, Phun-y Physics, Living Vine Press, 75. *Mailing Add:* Star Route Box 982 Corrales NM 87048

HARSH, RICHARD
PAINTER, EDUCATOR
b Feb 6, 40. *Study:* Columbia Tech Inst, cert, 61; Univ Northern Iowa, BA, 65; Southern Ill Univ, MFA(scholar), 69; also with Siegfried Reinhardt; Harvard Univ, 74; Emmanuel Sem, 75; Calif Western Univ, PhD, 81. *Comn:* Bicentennial prints, Moravia, Iowa; Mich State Univ, 78. *Exhib:* 14th Ann Christian Art Show, Lansing, Mich; Flint Inst Art, Mich; one-man shows, Adrian Col, Mich, Grand Rapids Bible Col, Mich & Saginaw Valley State Col, Mich; plus other group & one-man exhibs. *Pos:* Asst, Fed Bur Invest, Washington, DC, 58-61; illusr, McGregor-Werner Co, 61; owner, Richard Harsh & Assoc Fine Art, currently. *Teaching:* Instr art, Community Unit II High Sch, Greenville, Ill, 66-68; asst to supvr dept painting, Southern Ill Univ,

68, instr workshop & grad asst, 69; instr art, Univ Northern Iowa, 70-71; asst prof art, Mackinac Col, 72; lectr var civic, relig & educ orgn; artist in residence, John Wesley Col. *Awards:* Purchase Awards, Third Nat Polymer Exhib, Eastern Mich Univ, 70 & Am Acad Arts & Lett, Hassam Found, 70. *Mailing Add:* 605 Pine Owosso MI 48867

HART, ALLEN M
PAINTER, ADMINISTRATOR
b New York, NY, June 12, 25. *Study:* Art Students League, with Anne Goldthwaite, Frank Vincent Dumond & Jean Liberte; Brooklyn Mus Art Sch, with Vincent Candell. *Work:* Butler Inst Am Art, Youngstown, Ohio; Univ Mass, Amherst; Slater Mem Mus, Norwalk, Conn; Children's Aid Soc, New York; Union Am Hebrew Congregations. *Exhib:* One-man shows, Visual Arts Ctr, 70, Boiborik Gallery, 76 & NJ Cult Arts Ctr, 78; Joseph & Betty Harlem Gallery; Lerner Heller Gallery, 73; and others. *Teaching:* Instr painting, Samuel Field YMHA & YWHA, Littleneck, NY, 62-68; dir painting, Visual Arts Ctr, 68-; dean visual arts, Union Am Hebrew Congregations, 70-, resident artist, 72-; art consult, Bd Coop Educ Serv, 71- *Bibliog:* NY illustrated, NBC-TV, 70; Ned Harris (producer), In the beginning (film), 70 & Shabbat (film), 72; Doris Freedman (auth), Artists in the City, WNYC-FM, 10/12/72. *Mem:* Life mem Art Students League. *Media:* Oil, Mixed Media. *Publ:* Auth, articles, Lower Manhattan Twp, 2/20/71 & Herald, 5/1/71. *Mailing Add:* 34 Jackson Rd Valley Stream NY 11581

HART, BETTY MILLER
PAINTER, GRAPHIC ARTIST
b East Orange, NJ, Apr 15, 18. *Study:* Van Deering Perrine; Syracuse Univ Sch Fine Arts; Newark Col Eng. *Work:* Monmouth Col; Henry Chaucey Conf Ctr, Princeton; Monmouth Med Ctr. *Comn:* Panoramic view of Mobile, Ala & oil landscape, comn by Everet Eaves, Shreveport, La, 65; self portrait, comn by James Elder, Washington, DC; landscape, Philip Desind Collection, Silver Spring, Md, 75. *Exhib:* Pa Acad Fine Arts, 69; Philadelphia Mus Art, 70; 36th Ann Nat Exhib of Audubon Artists, Nat Acad Design, New York, 78; 2nd Biennial NJ Artists, NJ State Mus-Newark Mus, Trenton, 79; Nat Drawings 79, Stedman Art Gallery, Camden Col of Arts & Sci, NJ, 79; Boulder Ctr Visual Arts, 82; Hunterdon Art Ctr, 82; and others; and many others. *Awards:* First Prize Drawings, Arts Coun Suburban Essex, 80; Drawing Award, Salmagundi Club, 81; and others. *Bibliog:* Feature, New York Sunday News, 61; Michael Lenson (auth), Realm of art, Newark Sunday News, 67; Florence Lonsford (auth), Spot light on Kappa artists, Key of Kappa Kappa Gamma, Vol 91 No 4. *Mem:* Guild Creative Art (pres, 70-71). *Media:* Oil, Pastel; Pencil, Ink. *Dealer:* Capricorn Galleries 4849 Rugby Ave Bethesda MD 20014. *Mailing Add:* 60 Little Silver Point Rd Little Silver NJ 07739

HART, JOHN LEWIS
CARTOONIST
b Endicott, NY, Feb 18, 31. *Pos:* Comic strip BC nat syndicated, 58-, The Wizard of Id, 64- *Awards:* Outstanding Cartoonist of Year, 68; Yellow Kid Award, Int Cong Comics for Best Cartoonist, Lucca, Italy; France's Highest Award Best Cartoonist of Year, 71. *Mem:* Nat Comics Coun; Nat Cartoonists Soc. *Publ:* The Peasants are Revolting; Remember the Golden Rule; There's a Fly in my Swill; The Wonderous Wizard of Id; The Wizard's Back; plus others. *Mailing Add:* 11 Halford Endicott NY 13760

HART, MORGAN DRAKE
PAINTER, INSTRUCTOR
b Shrub Oak, NY, Jan 8, 1899. *Study:* Nat Acad Design, with Charles Webster Hawthorne & Francis C Jones. *Work:* Maine Harbor; Trenton State Mus; Somerset Hosp, NJ; Hillsborough NJ Libr. *Comn:* Portrait of Dr A D Dunbar & landscape mural of George Washington (in auditorium), Peekskill High Sch, NY; Frank Demster Sherman, Poet (portrait), Peekskill Mil Acad; William R O'Neal (portrait), Rollins Col, Winter Park, Fla; portrait, Somerset Medico Ctr, NJ. *Exhib:* Montclair Mus State Show, 53, 59 & 63; Grand Nat Show, Lever House, 60, 65, 71 & 72; Ft Worth Mus, Tex, 65; Am Artists Prof League Traveling Show, Prince Rainier's Palace, Monaco, 67; one-man show, Ferargi Gallery, New York, 28. *Pos:* Color technician, Union Carbide Corp, Bound Brook, NJ, 48-64. *Teaching:* Instr art, Peekskill Eve Schs, 30-35 & Peekskill Mil Acad, 34; instr drawing, Ducret Art Sch, 67-68; instr pvt classes. *Awards:* Second Prize, All City Show, Somerville, NJ, 77; Best of Show, Raritan Valley Arts Asn, 77; First Prize, Sr Citizen's Exhib, Somerset Co, 77. *Mem:* Am Artists Prof League (secy nat bd, 60-72); hon mem Raritan Valley Arts Asn; Hunterdon Co Art Asn; hon fel Am Artists Prof League. *Media:* Oil, Acrylic. *Dealer:* M Knoedler & Co 21 E 70th St New York NY 10021; Swain Gallery 317 Front St Plainfield NJ 07060. *Mailing Add:* Hickory Dr Sunset Lake Pluckemin NJ 07978

HART, ROBERT GORDON
ADMINISTRATOR
b San Francisco, Calif, Dec 28, 21. *Pos:* Ed, Brooklyn Mus, NY, 59-61; gen mgr, Indian Arts & Crafts Bd, US Dept of Interior, 61- *Mem:* Am Asn of Mus; Conseil Int des Musees; NAm Crafts Adminrs Asn (chmn, 77); Am Crafts Coun; World Crafts Coun; Fed Interagency Crafts Comt (chmn, 74-). *Mailing Add:* 916 25th St NW Washington DC 20037

HARTAL, PAUL ZEV
PAINTER, WRITER
b Szeged, Hungary, April 25, 36. *Can citizen. Study:* Hebrew Univ Jerusalem, BA, 64, dipl, 66; Concordia Univ, Montreal, MA, 77; Univ Delle Arti, Salsomaggiore, Italy, Hon Dipl, 82. *Work:* Mus Fine Arts, Montreal; Nat Gallery, Ottawa; Guggenheim Mus; Israel Mus, Jerusalem; Galleria Naz Arte, Rome. *Exhib:* Festival Int Peinture, St Germain Pres, Paris, 78; Lyrical

Conceptualism, Acad Raymond Duncan, Paris, 78; Concrete Poetry, Vehicule Art, Montreal, 80; solo exhib, Painted Melodies, J Yahouda Meir, Montreal, 83; retrospective, Psycho-Soc, Univ Lausanne, Montreux, Switz, 83. *Awards:* Prix Paris, Acad Raymond Duncan, 78; Rubens, Antwerpen, Asn Belgo-Hispanica, 78. *Bibliog:* Roger Delneufcourt (auth), Les expositions, Nouveau J, Paris, 6/24/78; Tom Konyves (auth), Poetry corner, Montreal Star, 7/21/79; Kara Szathmary (auth), Cosmic Symbiosis, Artists/USA, 7th ed, 82. *Mem:* Int Soc Artists; Graphic Soc; Surindependants, Paris; founding mem Lyrical Conceptualist Soc (dir, 77-). *Publ:* Auth, A History of Architecture, R Mass, Jerusalem, 72; auth, Statement, Art in Am, 11-12/76; contribr, Artists/USA, 76-; auth, Painted Melodies, Lyrical Conceptualist Soc, 83. *Mailing Add:* Box 1012 St Laurent Montreal PQ H4L 4W3 Canada

HARTELL, JOHN
PAINTER
b Brooklyn, NY, Jan 30, 02. *Study:* Cornell Univ, BArch; Royal Acad Fine Arts, Stockholm, Sweden. *Work:* Herbert F Johnson Mus Art, Cornell Univ; Ill Wesleyan Univ; Munson-Williams-Proctor Inst, Utica, NY; Univ Nebr, Lincoln; Wake Forest Univ; and others. *Exhib:* Five exhibs, Mem Art Gallery, Rochester, NY, 43-71; Cincinnati Mus, 45; City Art Mus, St Louis, 45; Carnegie Inst, Pittsburgh, Pa, 45-47; four exhibs, Whitney Mus Am Art, 45-56; Munson-Williams-Proctor Inst, Utica, NY, 48-58; Chicago Art Inst, Ill, 51; Pa Acad Fine Arts, Philadelphia, 53; Mus of Fine Arts, Houston, 55; Mus Fine Arts, Dallas, 57; Walker Art Ctr, Minneapolis, Minn, 58; Mus Art, Indianapolis, 70; Lehigh Univ, 71; Butler Inst Am Art, Youngstown, Ohio, 77. *Teaching:* Prof archit & art, Cornell Univ, 30-68, chmn dept art, 39-59, emer prof archit & art, 68- *Bibliog:* Rosamund Frost (auth), Hartell: builder in paint, Art News, 10/15/45; Hartell: visiting artist, Munson-Williams-Proctor Inst Bull, 1/52; Verlaine Boyd (auth), John Hartell, Arts, 10/80. *Media:* Oil; Watercolor. *Dealer:* Kraushaar Galleries 724 Fifth Ave New York NY 10019. *Mailing Add:* 319 The Parkway Ithaca NY 14850

HARTER, JOHN BURTON
CURATOR, PAINTER
b Jackson, Miss, Oct 7, 40. *Study:* Hanover Col, Univ Louisville, BA(art hist); Univ Vienna; Univ Pa; grad archaeol, Hebrew Univ, Jerusalem; La State Univ, MA(studio art); Williamsburg Seminar. *Collections Arranged:* Louisiana Folk & Native Art, 75, Louisiana Portrait Gallery (coauth, catalog), 77 & Louisiana Landscape, 81, La State Mus. *Pos:* Cur paintings & graphics, La State Mus, 67-83. *Mem:* Am Asn Mus. *Media:* Oil, Acrylic. *Mailing Add:* c/o La State Mus 751 Chartres St New Orleans LA 70116

HARTFORD, HUNTINGTON
COLLECTOR, PATRON
b New York, NY, Apr 18, 11. *Study:* Harvard Univ, AB, 34. *Pos:* Patron, Lincoln Ctr for Performing Arts; founder, Huntington Hartford Found, 49; founder & bd dirs, Gallery Mod Art (now New York Cult Ctr), 64; ed-in-chief, Show Mag; mem, Nat Coun on Arts, 69; mem adv coun, dept art hist & archaeol, Columbia Univ. *Awards:* Art Man of Year, Nat Art Materials Trade Asn, 62; Am Artists Prof League Award, 64; Orgn Am States Award, 66. *Mem:* Hon fel Nat Sculpture Soc; Nat Arts Club; Salmagundi Club; Am Artists Prog League. *Collection:* Oriental and far Eastern Art. *Publ:* Auth, Art or anarchy?, 64. *Mailing Add:* 600 Third Ave New York NY 10016

HARTFORD, JANE DAVIS
TEXTILE ARTIST, CRAFTSMAN
b Erick, Okla, Aug 21, 27. *Study:* Univ Okla, Norman, BFA, 49; Univ Louisville, Ky, MA, 60; Parson's Sch Design; Univ Ill, art hist; Univ Hawaii, graphics with Jean Charlot; weaving with Lou Tate, Theo Moorman, Sallie O'Sullivan, Irene Waller, Mary Jane Leland & Jon Eric Riis. *Comn:* Eucharistic Vestments, St Mark's Cathedral, Salt Lake City, Utah, 67; ceremonial basket, Mrs LeRoy W Horne, Tulsa, Okla, 78; tapestry, Mr & Mrs Leonard Good, Chickasha, Okla, 82. *Exhib:* Utah Mus Natural Hist, Salt Lake City, 75, 77, 79, 81 & 83; Braithwaith Fine Arts Gallery, Cedar City, Utah, 81; Okla Mus Art, Norman, 81; Atrium Gallery, Salt Lake City, 82; Handweavers Guild Asn Convergence 82, Seattle, 82; and others. *Pos:* Bd dirs, Handweavers Guild Am Inc, 80-; bd dirs, Intermountain Weavers Conf, 79- *Awards:* Merit Award, Southwest Crafts Biennial, NMex Art Mus, 75; Fiber Award, Utah Arts Coun Exhib, 80; Cash Award, Intermountain Weavers Conf Exhib, 83. *Mem:* M M Atwater Weavers Guild Utah (pres, 74-75); Am Crafts Coun; Handweavers Guild Am (pres, 83-); Intermountain Weavers Conf; and others. *Publ:* Auth, Fashion Ballet, winter, 74, auth, Sheep to shawl, spring, 77, & coauth, Flight into fantasy, fall, 80, Shuttle, Spindle & Dyepot. *Mailing Add:* 211 Roundtoft Dr Salt Lake City UT 84103

HARTGEN, VINCENT ANDREW
PAINTER, EDUCATOR
b Reading, Pa, Jan 10, 14. *Study:* Sch Fine Arts, Univ Pa, BFA & MFA. *Work:* Mus Fine Arts, Boston; Wadsworth Atheneum, Hartford, Conn; Sheldon Swope Art Gallery, Terre Haute, Ind; Walker Art Ctr, Minneapolis, Minn; Wichita Art Mus, Kans. *Exhib:* One-man shows, Fla Gulf Coast Art Ctr, Clearwater, Kings Col, Wilkes-Barre, Pa & others; Artists of Maine, Am Fedn Arts Traveling Exhib, 64-66; Embassies Art Prog, Dept State, Washington, DC, 66-70; 200 Yrs Watercolor Painting Am, Metrop Mus Art, 67; Landscape I, De Cordova Mus, Lincoln, Mass, 70. *Collections Arranged:* Contemp Schs, USA, Contemp Churches, USA, 56-57, Ceramics & Dinnerware, 68 & Boxes, Sacks & Bags, 71, Univ Maine Art Gallery. *Pos:* Trustee, Haystack Sch Crafts, 50-55; comnr, Maine State Comn Arts & Humanities, 65-70; Dir art gallery & collection, Univ Maine, Orono, 46-82, emer cur, 82- *Teaching:* Prof art, Univ Maine, Orono, 46-62, Huddilston prof, 62-82, emer prof, 82- *Awards:* Creative Aquarelle Award, 65 & Silver Medal,

74, Audubon Artists. *Bibliog:* H J Seligmann (auth), Vincent Hartgen...artist & teacher, Downeast Mag, 60; Ralph Fabri (auth), Watercolorist for all seasons, Today's Art, 65; Norman Kent (auth), 100 Techniques of Watercolor Painting, 70. *Mem:* Am Asn Univ Prof; Col Art Asn Am; Audubon Artists; Am Watercolor Soc; hon mem Can Soc Painter-Etchers & Engravers. *Media:* Watercolor. *Publ:* Auth, Watercolor, Pen & Brush, 54; auth, Defending the middle ground of the semi-abstract, Am Artist, 67 & Maine Alumnus, 75. *Mailing Add:* 109 Forest Ave Orono ME 04473

HARTIGAN, GRACE
PAINTER
b Newark, NJ, Mar 28, 22. *Study:* Pvt art classes with Isaac Lane Muse; Moore Col, Philadelphia, Hon DFA; Md Inst Art, Baltimore, Hon DFA; Goucher Col, Hon DFA; Towson State Univ, Hon DFA. *Work:* Whitney Mus Am Art & Metrop Mus Art, New York; Walker Art Ctr, Minneapolis, Minn; Art Inst Chicago, Ill; Albright-Knox Art Gallery, Buffalo, NY; plus many others. *Exhib:* Carnegie Int, 61; American Vanguard, organized by Solomon R Guggenheim Mus for US Info Agency, Austria, England, Ger & Yugoslavia, 61-62; A Decade of New Talent, Am Fedn Arts Exhib, 64-65; one-man shows, Univ Chicago, 67 & Gertrude Kasle Gallery, Detroit, 68; plus many others. *Teaching:* Resident artist, Md Inst Grad Sch Painting, 65- *Awards:* Mademoiselle Mag Merit Award for Art, 57. *Media:* Oil, Watercolor; Collage. *Dealer:* Gruenebaum Gallery 38 E 57th St New York NY 10022. *Mailing Add:* 1701 1/2 Eastern Ave Baltimore MD 21231

HARTIGAN, LYNDA ROSCOE
CURATOR, HISTORIAN
b Scranton, Pa, Aug 26, 50. *Study:* Bucknell Univ, Lewisburg, Pa, BA(art hist), cum laude), 72; George Washington Univ, DC, MA(art hist), 75. *Collections Arranged:* James Hampton: The Throne of the Third Heaven of the Nations Millennium General Assembly, Walker Art Ctr; Natives & Visionaries (contribr, catalog), Whitney Mus Am Art, 74; 200 Years Am Sculpture Traveling Show (auth, catalog), 76-77. *Pos:* Curatorial asst, 20th Century Painting & Sculpture Dept, Nat Mus Am Art, Smithsonian Inst, Washington, DC, 74-76, asst cur, 76-, cur, Joseph Cornell Study Ctr, 78- *Awards:* Grad internship, Nat Collection Fine Arts, Smithsonian Inst, DC, 73-74; Nat Endowment Arts Res Grant, 76-78. *Bibliog:* Peggy Thomson (auth), Museum People, Prentice-Hall, 77. *Mem:* Col Art Asn; Southeastern Col Art Conf. *Res:* 20th century American art, especially sculpture 1930's to present, with major research conducted on Joseph Cornell; American folk art. *Publ:* Contribr, critical commentaries for Art Inc, American Paintings from Corporations, Montgomery Mus Fine Arts, Ala, 79; contribr, Joseph Cornell: A biography, monograph, Mus Mod Art, New York, 80; contribr, Yuri Schwebler: His Art and the Studio, catalog, Hudson River Mus, Yonkers, NY, 81; contribr, Perkins Harnly: From the Index of American Design, catalog, Nat Mus Am Art, Washington, DC, 81. *Mailing Add:* Nat Mus Am Art Eighth & G Sts NW Washington DC 20560

HARTLEY, PAUL JEROME
PAINTER, EDUCATOR
b Charlotte, NC, Dec 30, 43. *Study:* NTex State Univ, BA; ECarolina Univ, MFA. *Work:* Rausch Indust Collection; NC Art Soc, Raleigh. *Exhib:* One-man shows, Vanderbilt Univ Fine Arts Gallery, Nashville, Tenn, 73, Southeastern Ctr for Contemp Art, Winston-Salem, NC, 75, NC Mus Art, Collectors Gallery, Raleigh, 76 & G Walker Gallery, Columbia, SC, 76; Mint Mus Art, 501 Gallery, Charlotte, NC, 73; Am Inst Architects, Raleigh, NC, 75 & 76; Southeastern Artist Invitational, Southeastern Ctr for Contemp Art, Winston-Salem, NC, 75; and others. *Teaching:* Chairperson & assoc prof, ECarolina Univ, 75- *Awards:* Rausch Indust Award, Piedmont Graphics Exhib, Mint Mus Art, Charlotte, NC, 73; Purchase Awards, Southeast Regional Graphics Exhib, Southeast Ctr for Contemp Art & NC Nat Bank, 74. *Mem:* Col Art Asn Am. *Media:* Mixed. *Dealer:* NC Mus Art Collectors Gallery 107 E Morgan St Raleigh NC 27611. *Mailing Add:* 227 Woodstock Dr Greenville NC 27834

HARTLEY, W DOUGLAS
SCULPTOR, EDUCATOR
b Indianapolis, Ind, Nov 24, 21. *Study:* Ind Univ, Bloomington, BS, 48, MFA, 49; Kansas City Art Inst, MFA, 51; NY Univ, PhD, 71. *Comn:* Pres Frank H Sparks, Wabash Col Union, Crawfordsville, Ind, 58; Madonna & Child (sculpture), St Matthew's Episcopalian Church, Bloomington, Ill, 59; Jesse W Fell (bronze bust), City Hall, Normal, Ill, 76; Ambassador Adlai E Stevenson III, Adlai Stevenson Lect Comt, Bloomington, Ill, 78. *Teaching:* Asst instr sculpture, Kansas City Art Inst, 50-51; prof art hist, Ill State Univ, 54- *Media:* Bronze, Stone. *Publ:* Auth & illusr, Indian drawings of the Cimarron Country, Ford Times, 6/53; auth, The head I almost lost, Reader's Digest, 7/57; auth, The Search for Henry Cross: An Adventure in Biography, Ind Hist Soc, 66; co-ed, Readings in the Humanities, Xerox Corp, 76; auth, Things Invisible to See: An Introduction to Art Appreciation, Advocate Publ, 79. *Mailing Add:* 1001 S Fell Ave Normal IL 61761

HARTMAN, ROBERT LEROY
PHOTOGRAPHER, EDUCATOR
b Sharon, Pa, Dec 17, 26. *Study:* Univ Ariz, BFA & MA; Colo Springs Fine Arts Ctr, with Vaclav Vytlacil & Emerson Woelffer; Brooklyn Mus Art Sch. *Work:* Nat Collection Fine Arts, Smithsonian Inst, Washington, DC; Colorado Springs Fine Arts Ctr; Oakland Mus Art, Calif; Achenbach Found Graphic Arts, San Francisco; Henry Gallery, Univ Wash. *Exhib:* Contemp Am Painting & Sculpture Biennial, Krannert Mus, Univ Ill, 65; 4th Int Young Artists Exhib, Am-Japan, Tokyo, 67; Santa Barbara Mus Art, 73; Whitney Mus Biennial, New York, 73; photog, San Jose Mus Art, 83; and others. *Pos:*

Mem, Univ Calif Inst Creative Arts, 67-68. *Teaching:* Instr art, Tex Technol Col, 55-58; asst prof art, Univ Nev, Reno, 58-61; from assoc prof to prof art, Univ Calif, Berkeley, 61- *Awards:* Emanuel Walter Fund First Prize, 85th Ann San Francisco Art Inst, 67; hon mention, 4th Int Young Artists Exhib Am-Japan, 67. *Bibliog:* Peter Nabokov (auth), Flight patterns--photographs by Robert Hartman, Camera Arts, 1/83. *Media:* Color Photography, Oil. *Dealer:* Bluxome Gallery 173 Bluxome St San Francisco CA 94107; Brook House Box 1177 Orinda CA 94563. *Mailing Add:* 1265 Mountain Blvd Oakland CA 94611

HARTSHORN, WILLIS E
PHOTOGRAPHER, INSTRUCTOR

b Fairfield, Conn, Sept 9, 50. *Study:* Univ Rochester, NY, BA, 73; Pratt Inst, Brooklyn, NY, 75; Visual Studies Workshop, Rochester, NY, MFA, 81. *Work:* Visual Studies Workshop Archive, Rochester, NY. *Exhib:* The Finished Print, Art Guild Gallery, Farmington, Conn, 80; Light Factory, Charlotte, NC, 81; Light, Light Gallery, New York, 81; Contemporary Still Life Photography Traveling Exhib, 82-84; one-man show, Mass Inst Technol, 83; Washington Projects Arts, Washington, DC, 83; and others. *Pos:* Assoc dir exhibs, Int Ctr Photog, 82- *Teaching:* Instr photog, Int Ctr Photog, New York, 79-; teaching asst photog, Sch Visual Arts, New York, 79; grad fac, New York Univ/Int Ctr Photog, 82- *Awards:* Resource Access Development Project, State Univ NY, 79; Materials Grant, Polaroid Corp, 79; Major Fel in Photog, Nat Endowment Arts, 81. *Mem:* Soc Photog Educ. *Media:* Black & White. *Publ:* Auth, Printletter, Zurich, Switzerland, 80. *Mailing Add:* 40 Lispenard St New York NY 10013

HARTT, FREDERICK
HISTORIAN, EDUCATOR

b Boston, Mass, May 22, 14. *Study:* Nat Acad Design; Columbia Col, BA, 35; Princeton Univ, 35-36; NY Univ, MA, 37, PhD, 49. *Pos:* Asst, Yale Art Gallery, 41- 42; actg dir art mus, Smith Col, 46-47; bd dirs, Am Comt for Restoration Ital Monuments, 46-49; mem exec comt, Comt to Rescue Ital Art, 66-; dir, Univ Va Art Mus, 72-76. *Teaching:* Vis lectr art, Smith Col, 46-47; lectr fine arts, NY Univ, 48-49; from asst prof to prof, art hist, Wash Univ, 49-60; prof hist art, Univ Pa, 60-67, chmn dept art, 60-65; vis art historian, Harvard Renaissance Ctr, Florence, Italy, 65-66; McIntire prof hist art, Univ Va, Charlottesville, 67-, chmn art dept, 67-76. *Awards:* Guggenheim Fel, 48-49 & 54-55; Fulbright Res Grants, 54-55 & 65-66; Am Coun Learned Socs Fel, 65-66. *Mem:* Col Art Asn Am; Am Asn Univ Prof; Renaissance Soc Am ; hon academician Acad Arts Design, Florence, Italy. *Res:* Italian Renaissance art. *Publ:* Auth, Giulio Romano, Yale, 58 & History of Italian Renaissance Art, 69, Abrams; Donatello, Prophet of Modern Vision, 73; Art, History of Painting, Sculpture & Architecture, Abrams, 76; also many articles & rev in art periodicals. *Mailing Add:* 1007 Rugby Rd Charlottesville VA 22903

HARTWELL, PATRICIA LOCHRIDGE
ADMINISTRATOR

b Austin, Tex, Sept 22, 16. *Study:* Columbia Univ, MS; Wellesley Col, BA; Ariz State Univ; Univ Hawaii. *Collections Arranged:* Lew & Mathilde Davis, 72; Naive Art, Scottsdale & Honolulu, 72 & 73; Fibers '74, Dorothy Fratt Retrospective, 74; continuing exhibs, Civic Ctr Gallery, Scottsdale, Ariz & Arts Coun Gallery, Prince Kuhio Fed Bldg, Honolulu, Hawaii, 69- *Pos:* Dir, UN Children's Greeting Card Fund, 56-62; exec dir, Scottsdale Fine Arts Comn, 69-75; exec dir, Hawaii Coun for Cult & the Arts, 76-79; dir, Arts Coun Hawaii, 80- *Teaching:* Adj lectr, Univ Hawaii, Manoa, 83- *Awards:* Ford Found Study Arts Grant, 75. *Res:* Mainstreams in contemporary European, Middle European and American naive art. *Mailing Add:* 44-003 Aumoana Pl Kaneohe HI 96734

HARTWIG, CLEO
SCULPTOR

b Webberville, Mich, Oct 20, 11. *Study:* Western Mich Univ, AB; Int Sch Art, Europe; Art Inst Chicago, summers; carving with Jose de Creeft; Western Mich Univ, Hon MA & Hon DFA. *Work:* Detroit Inst Arts, Mich; Pa Acad Fine Arts, Philadelphia; Montclair Art Mus, NJ; Chrysler Mus at Norfolk, Va; Brookgreen Gardens, SC. *Comn:* Family Group (aluminum), Facade of Continental Casualties Bldg, New York, 52; Wild Ducks (terra-cotta), Cabin Class Lounge, SS United States, 52; bronze kneeling figure with dove, All Faiths Mem Tower, Paramus, NJ, 63. *Exhib:* Artists for Victory, Metrop Mus Art, New York, 42; Am Paintings & Sculpture Ann, Art Inst Chicago, Ill, 42; Pa Acad Fine Arts Ann, 45-54, 58 & 62; Fairmount Park Int Sculpture Exhib, Philadelphia Mus Art, 49; one-person shows traveling Can, 49-50, US, 65-66, Montclair Art Mus, NJ, 71 & Sculpture Ctr, New York, 81; Whitney Mus Am Art, New York; Denver Art Mus, Colo; Boston Mus Sci, Mass; Nat Acad Design; Nat Inst Arts & Lett; Smithsonian Inst. *Awards:* Two sculpture awards, Columbia Univ Law Sch Alumni, New York, 71; C Percival Dietsch Prize, Nat Sculpture Soc, 76; Ellin P Speyer Prize, Nat Acad Design, 79. *Bibliog:* Enid Bell (auth), Compatibles, Am Artist Mag, summer 68; Archives of American Art, Smithsonian Inst. *Mem:* Sculptors Guild (exec dir, 74-76, exec vpres, 80-); fel Nat Sculpture Soc; Audubon Artists (vpres for sculpture, 70-73); Nat Asn Women Artists (first vpres, 74-76); Artists Equity, New York (bd dirs, 83-). *Media:* Stone, Wood. *Publ:* Coauth, Direct carving in stone, Nat Sculpture Rev, summer 65. *Mailing Add:* 5 W 16th St New York NY 10011

HARVEY, (WILLIAM) ANDRE
SCULPTOR

b Hollywood, Fla, Oct 9, 41. *Study:* Univ Va, BA; additional study with Michael Anasse, Valauris, France & Charles Parks, Hockessin, Del. *Work:* Del Art Mus, Wilmington; Hunter Mus, Chattanooga; Greenville Mus Art, SC; Brandywine River Mus, Chadds Ford, Pa; Univ Va, Charlottesville. *Exhib:* Nat Sculpture Soc, New York, 75-77; Images of Am, US Info Agency, Moscow, London, Paris, 76-77; Del Art Mus, Wilmington, 76; Hunter Mus, Chattanooga, Tenn, 77; Greenville Art Mus, SC, 80; and others. *Bibliog:* John Caldwell (auth), The Sculpture of Andre Harvey, SW Art, 11/76; Lisa Lyons (auth), Andre Harvey, Art Voices S, 5-6/80; John Caldwell (auth), Andre Harvey, Southern Accents, fall 82; and others. *Mem:* Nat Sculpture Soc. *Media:* Bronze. *Dealer:* Frank Fowler 1213 Ft Stephenson Oval Lookout Mountain TN 37350. *Mailing Add:* Box 8 Rockland Rd Rockland DE 19732

HARVEY, DERMOT
KINETIC ARTIST, SCULPTOR

b Amersham, Eng, June 26, 41. *Study:* Univ Dublin, Trinity Col, MA; Univ London, MPhil. *Work:* Okla Art Ctr. *Comn:* Muse Aurora (liquid projections exhib operated by viewer), Brooklyn Children's Mus, 70; portable, multi-image aurora, Okla Art Ctr, 73; liquid projection exhib, Arnot Mus, Elmira, NY, 75; portable muse aurora, Continuum Mus, Ft Lauderdale, Fla, 76. *Exhib:* 24 Hour Technicolor Dream, Alexandra Palace, London, 67; Alliance of Light Artists, Fillmore East, New York, 69; Liquid Projections, Montreux Television Festival, Switz, 69; Projected Environments, New York Avant Garde Festival, 72, 74 & 75; Light Works, Intermedia Found, Garnerville, NY, 75. *Pos:* Dir theater of light prog, Intermedia Found, 74-; spec effects lighting for revue, Hot Stuff, Wailea Town Ctr, Maui, Hawaii, 80. *Teaching:* Instr kinetic & light art, Rockland Community Col, Suffern, NY, 75-77. *Awards:* Creative Artists Pub Serv Grant, NY Cult Coun, 71. *Bibliog:* Martha Geacintov (auth), He practices his art in the light side, 3/5/74 & Michael Hitzig (auth), Theater of light, 5/4/75, Journal News; Carol Lawson (auth), Film night with a Gothic twist, New York Times, 6/18/76. *Mailing Add:* 17 Church St Garnerville NY 10923

HARVEY, DONALD
PAINTER, PRINTMAKER

b Walthamstow, England, June 14, 30; Can citizen. *Study:* West Sussex Col Art, nat dipl painting; Brighton Col Art Eng, art teachers dipl. *Work:* Nat Gallery Can, Ottawa; Montreal Mus Fine Arts; Charlottetown Confedn Gallery, PEI; Seattle Art Mus, Wash; Albright-Knox Mus, Buffalo, NY. *Comn:* Large mural, BC Provincial Govt, Nelson, BC, 75. *Exhib:* Brit Print Biennial, Bradford, Eng, 68; Int Print Exhib, Seattle, 69; Art Gallery Greater Victoria, 79; Kyles Art Gallery, Victoria, 80; Can Nat Exhib, Toronto, 80; and others. *Teaching:* Prof painting, Univ Victoria, 61- *Awards:* Sadie & Samuel Bronfmann Purchase Prize, Montreal Mus, 63; First Prize, Vancouver Island Show, Art Gallery Gt Victoria, 64-66 & 69; First Prize, Exhib Can Art, Vancouver Art Gallery, 64. *Bibliog:* Tony Emery (auth), Canadian art today, Artscanada, 65. *Mem:* Royal Can Acad Arts. *Dealer:* Doris Pascal Gallery Pascal 334 Dundas St W Toronto ON Can; Kenneth G Heffel Inc Vancouver BC. *Mailing Add:* 1025 Joan Crescent Victoria BC V8S 3L3 Canada

HARVEY, DONALD GILBERT
SCULPTOR, INSTRUCTOR

b Louisville, Ky, June 25, 47. *Study:* Dixie Col, 65; Utah State Univ, BFA, 69; Univ Hawaii, MFA, 71. *Work:* Honolulu Acad Arts, Hawaii; State Found Cult & Arts, Honolulu; Utah State Univ; Honolulu Community Col; Honolulu Int Airport; and others. *Exhib:* Hawaii Craftsman, 69-70; Artist of Hawaii, 70; Easter Art Festival, Honolulu, 70-71; one-man show, Contemp Art Ctr Pac, 72; Artist Hawaii, Honolulu Acad Arts, 83. *Teaching:* Lectr art, Univ Hawaii, 70-71; instr art, Kamehameha High Sch, 71- *Awards:* Honolulu Acad Arts Purchase Award, 70; Purchase Award, Contemp Art Ctr, Hawaii, 78; Juror's Award of Excellence, Easter Art Festival, 79. *Bibliog:* Nicholas Roukes (auth), Masters of Wood Sculpture, Watson-Guptill. *Mem:* Hawaii Painters & Sculptors League; Nat Art Educ Asn. *Media:* Mixed Media. *Mailing Add:* c/o Kamehameha Sch Bernice Pauahi Bishop Estate Kapalama Heights HI 96820

HARVEY, JACQUELINE
PAINTER

b La Madeleine, France, Feb 2, 27; US citizen. *Study:* High Sch Mus & Art, New York, 42-45; New Sch Social Res, 45-46; also silversmith apprentice with Paul Lobel, 45-46 & studio training with Morris Davidson, New York, 45-46, Fernand Leger & Leopold Survage, Paris, 46-47 & William Hayter, New York, 48. *Work:* Birla Acad Art & Cult, Calcutta, India; Eggers Partnership, New York; also in pvt collections. *Exhib:* Art USA, Madison Sq Garden, New York, 58; Rose Fried Gallery, New York, 69-70 & Ruth Kurle Gallery, 78-79; Abreu Gallery, New York, 80; Sandra Bertsch Gallery, Oyster Bay, NY, 82-83; and others. *Mem:* Artists Equity Asn New York; Visual Artists & Galleries Asn. *Media:* Oil, Acrylic. *Mailing Add:* 279 Park Ave Manhasset NY 11030

HARVEY, ROBERT MARTIN
PAINTER

b Lexington, NC, Sept 16, 24. *Study:* Ringling Sch Art, with Elmer Harmes & Georgia Warren; San Francisco Art Inst, with Nathan Oliveira & Sonia Gechtoff. *Work:* Corcoran Gallery Art & Hirshhorn Collection, Washington, DC; Wichita Art Mus, Kans; Fine Arts Mus of the South, Mobile, Ala; Stanford Univ Mus, Calif; Crown-Zellerbach Found, San Francisco; and others. *Exhib:* American Painting, Va Mus Fine Arts, Richmond, 66; Butler Inst Am Art, Youngstown, Ohio, 66; Univ Ill, 67 & 69; Phoenix Art Mus; Centro Cult de Los Estados Unidos, Madrid, 77; Malacke Gallery, Malaga, Kresler Dos, Madrid, 79; and others. *Awards:* Award of Merit, San Francisco Art Festival, 63; Western Wash State Col Purchase Prize, 65; Mead Painting of the Year, 67; and others. *Dealer:* Gumps 250 Post St San Francisco CA 94108; Studio Galleries 602 Downing St Denver CO 80220. *Mailing Add:* La Huerta del Angel Macharaviaya Malaga Spain

HASELTINE, JAMES LEWIS
PRINTMAKER, PAINTER
b Portland, Ore, Nov 7, 24. *Study:* Portland Mus Art Sch, Ore, 47 & 49; Art Inst Chicago, 47-48; Brooklyn Mus Sch, 50-51. *Work:* Portland Art Mus, Ore; Oakland Art Mus, Calif; Mus Art, Univ Ore. *Exhib:* Libr Cong, Washington, DC, 51; Brooklyn Mus, NY, 51-52; Portland Art Mus, Ore, 51-58; Seattle Art Mus, Wash, 52, 53, 57 & 59; San Francisco Mus Art, Calif, 53-54; Evergreen State Col, 82. *Pos:* Dir, Salt Lake Art Ctr, Utah, 61-67; exec dir, Wash State Arts Comn, Olympia, 67-80. *Teaching:* Vis lectr art hist, Univ Utah, 64-65. *Awards:* Purchase Prize, Portland Art Mus, 53; best monogr, Mormon Hist Asn, 64-66); British Am Arts Asn (bd mem); Nat Assembly State & Prov Arts Agencies (exec comt, 68-70); Nat Endowment Arts (mus panel, 70-72 & visual arts policy panel, 77-79). *Media:* Oil; Intaglio, Woodcut. *Publ:* Auth, 100 Years of Utah Painting, 65; contribr, Mus News, 65; contribr, Utah Hist Quart, Dialogue & American West, 66. *Mailing Add:* 3820 Sunset Beach Dr NW Olympia WA 98502

HASELTINE, MAURY (MARGARET WILSON)
PAINTER, CONSULTANT
b Portland, Ore, May 7, 25. *Study:* Reed Col; Mus Art Sch, Portland; Eastern NMex Univ. *Work:* Salt Lake Art Ctr, Utah; Univ Ore Mus; Bell Tel Co, Portland; First Nat Bank, Portland; Preston, Thorgrimson, Ellis & Holman, Washington, DC. *Comn:* Assemblage collage mural, Donald Lloyd, Assoc Grocers Off, Salt Lake City, 65; Plexiglass collage, Columbian Optical Co, Seattle, Wash, 74. *Exhib:* New Accessions USA, Colorado Springs Fine Art Ctr, 64; Selected Painters 65, Mulvane Art Ctr, Topeka, Kans, 65; Our Land, Our Sky, Our Water, Spokane World's Fair, 74; Anacortes Art Festival, Wash, 75; Governor's Invitational, State Capitol Mus, Olympia, Wash, 79 & 81. *Teaching:* Instr oil painting, Salt Lake Art Ctr, 64-65; instr oil & acrylic painting, Creative Activities Ctr, State Capitol Mus, Olympia, Wash, 67-79. *Awards:* Southwest Fiesta Biennial Prize, Santa Fe, NMex, 66; 8th Utah Biennial Salt Lake Art Ctr Award, 66; 3rd Ann Painting & Sculpture Award, Tacoma Art Mus, 73. *Bibliog:* Charles Miller (producer), Way of art, KUTV, 65; Prize-Winning Graphics, Allied Publ, 66. *Media:* Oil, Acrylic. *Publ:* Contribr, Forms Upon the Frontier, Utah State Univ, 69. *Mailing Add:* 3820 Sunset Beach Dr NW Olympia WA 98502

HASEN, BURT STANLY
PAINTER, PRINTMAKER
b New York, NY, Dec 19, 21. *Study:* Art Students League, 40, 42 & 46, with Morris Kantor; Hans Hofmann Sch Fine Arts, 47-48; Acad Grande Chaumiere, Paris, 48-50, with Ossipe Zadkine; Accad Belli Arti, Rome, 59-60. *Work:* Walker Art Ctr, Minneapolis; Worcester Art Mus; Hampton Inst, Va; Crestview Col, Allentown, Pa; Muhlenberg Col, Allentown. *Comn:* Mural, YMHA & YWHA, New York, 47. *Exhib:* Salon Mai, Mus Art Mod, Paris, 51; Metrop Mus Art, New York, 53; Berlin Acad, WGer, 56; Whitney Mus Am Art Ann, New York, 63; Walker Art Ctr, 66. *Teaching:* Instr painting & drawing, Sch Visual Arts, 53-; instr painting, Col Art & Design, Minneapolis, 66. *Awards:* Three Purchase Prizes, Emily Lowe Found, 54; Fulbright Grant to Italy, 59-66; *Bibliog:* Allen S Weller (auth), Contemporary American Painting & Sculpture, Krannert Art Mus, 61; The Whitney Annual, Time, 63; Eric Protter (auth), Artists on Art, Grosset & Dunlap, 64. *Media:* Oil, Acrylic. *Publ:* Illusr, Contes del'Inattendu, 59, De la Terre a la Lune, 61, Voltaire, 61 & Moliere, 61. *Mailing Add:* 7 Dutch St New York NY 10038

HASKELL, BARBARA
CURATOR
b San Diego, Calif, Nov 13, 46. *Study:* Univ Calif, Los Angeles, BA(philos & art hist), 69. *Collections Arranged:* Claes Oldenburg: Object into Monuments (with book), 71; Larry Bell (with catalog), 72; John Mason (with catalog), 74; Arthur Dove, 74; Jo Baer (with catalog), 75; H C Westermann, Whitney Biennial, 77, 79, 81 & 83; Marsden Hartley, 80; Milton Avery, 82; and others. *Pos:* Cur painting & sculpture, Pasadena Mus Mod Art, 72-74, dir exhib & collections, 74; cur painting & sculpture, Whitney Mus Am Art, New York, 75- *Awards:* Woman of the Year, Mademoiselle Award, 73; Leadership Among Professional Women, Los Angeles Soroptimist, 73. *Publ:* Auth, Arthur Dove, New York Graphic Soc Ltd, 74; auth, Marsden Hartley, NY Univ Press, 80; auth, Milton Avery, Harper & Row, 82. *Mailing Add:* Whitney Mus 945 Madison Ave New York NY 10021

HASKIN, DONALD MARCUS
EDUCATOR, SCULPTOR
b St Paul, Minn, July 28, 20. *Study:* Univ Minn, study with Tovish, BA; Cranbrook Acad Art, MFA. *Comn:* Bronze figure, City Tucson, 72; stainless steel fountain, City Tucson, 72; sculpture, Univ Ariz, 73. *Exhib:* Contemp Crafts Mus, New York, 61; San Francisco Mus Art, 62; Preview '65, Alamo Gallery, Benicia, Calif, 65; Southwestern Invitational, Yuma Art Asn, 72-75; Tucson Mus Art, 75. *Teaching:* Lectr sculpture, Univ Calif, Berkeley, 63-65; prof sculpture, Univ Ariz, Tucson, 65-82, prof emer, 82. *Awards:* First Prize, Minn State Fair, 58; Purchase Award, City of Benicia, 65; Purchase Prize Award, Yuma Art Asn, 72. *Mailing Add:* 3242 N Kelvin Tucson AZ 85716

HASKINS, JOHN FRANKLIN
HISTORIAN, EDUCATOR
b La Junta, Colo, Nov 16, 19. *Study:* Univ Colo, Boulder, BFA, 47; NY Univ, PhD, 61. *Collections Arranged:* Near Eastern & Far Eastern Art from the Collections of Jay C Leff, New York (auth, catalog), 65; Imperial Carpets form Peking (auth, catalog), Univ Art Gallery, Pittsburgh & Duke Univ, Durham, NC, 73-74. *Teaching:* Instr art hist, Finch Col, New York, 57-58; asst prof, Columbia Univ, NY, 58-64; prof Oriental art hist, Univ Pittsburgh, 64- *Awards:* Guggenheim Mem Fel, 58 & 63. *Mem:* Col Art Asn; Am Oriental Soc; Soc Archit Historians; Asian Asn. *Res:* Art of Central Asia, the Far East and the Steppe nomads. *Publ:* Auth, Northern Origins of Sasanian Metalwork, Artibus Asiae, 52; auth, Er Targhyn--The Hero, Aq-Zhunus--The Beautiful & Peter's Siberian Gold, Ars Orientalis IV, 61; auth, The Mongolian Captivity of Lady Wen-Chi, and the Pazyryk Felt Screen, Bulletin Mus Far East, 63; auth, Nomads and Migrants in the Art of Early Europe, 22nd Cong Art Hist, Budapest, 69. *Mailing Add:* 5820 Elwood St Apt 4 Pittsburgh PA 15232

HASLEM, JANE N
DEALER
b Knoxville, Tenn, Dec 26, 34. *Study:* DePauw Univ, BA; Ind State Univ. *Collections Arranged:* Various nat & int exhibs. *Pos:* Dir, Jane Haslem Gallery, Chapel Hill, 60-65, Madison, Wis, 65-71 & Washington, DC, 69-71; pres, Haslem Fine Arts, Inc, Jane Haslem Gallery, Washington, DC, 71- *Teaching:* Instr art, Mecklenburg Co, NC, 58-59; resident assoc prog, Smithsonian Inst. *Mem:* Washington Print Club; Art Dealers Asn Washington DC (found mem). *Specialty:* Contemporary American paintings, prints and political cartoons; publisher of art catalogues. *Publ:* American Paintings & Graphics, 73; Woodcuts by Antonio Frasconi, 1943-1975, 76; Mark Tobey: Graphics, 79; American Prints, Drawings, Paintings, 81; Jane Haslem Gallery Newsletter. *Mailing Add:* 406 7th St NW Washington DC 20004

HA-SO-DE (NARCISO ABEYTA)
ILLUSTRATOR, PAINTER
b Canyoncito, NMex, Dec 18, 18. *Study:* Santa Fe Indian Sch, with Dorothy Dunn Kramer, 35-39; Am Indian Art Inst Am; Somerset Art Sch, Pa, 41-42; Univ NMex, with Johnson & Haas, BFA, 53. *Work:* Am Indian Art Dietrich Collection; Phil Brook Mus, Tulsa, Okla. *Comn:* Navajo Antelope Hunt (mural), Maisel Store Entrance, Albuquerque, NMex, 35. *Exhib:* Painting & Reproduction Exhib, Paris, France by Paul Coze, 35; Philbrook Mus, 35-53; Scottsdale Nat Indian Art Coun, 67-74; NMex Art & Crafts Fair, Albuquerque, 74; NMex State Fair, 75. *Teaching:* Instr silversmithing, Santa Fe Indian Sch, 47-48. *Awards:* Poster Antelope Hunt & Scholar, Indian Golden Gate Int Exposition Courts, San Francisco summer 39; First Prize Faun Hunt, NMex State Fair, 75. *Bibliog:* Jeanne O Snodgrass (auth), American Indian Painters, Heye Found, 68; J J Brody (auth), Indian Painters & White Patrons, Univ NMex, 75; Doris Monthan (auth), Up to date write up on Ha-So-De, Am Indian Art Mag. *Mem:* NMex Teacher-Counr Orgn. *Media:* Shiva Casein. *Res:* Early explorers in Ft Wingate; Navajo sand paintings, mythology and history. *Publ:* Illusr, Dorothy Dunn's American Indian Painting, Univ NMex Press, 68; illusr, Robert Ashton & Jozefa Stuart's Images of American Indian Art, Walker & Co; illusr, Arthur Silberman's 100 Years of Native American Painting, Okla Mus Art, 78; illusr, Jamake Highwater's The Sweet Grass Lives On, 81. *Dealer:* Kiva Gallery 202 W 66th Gallup NM 87301. *Mailing Add:* 102 Viro Circle Gallup NM 87301

HASSRICK, PETER H
MUSEUM DIRECTOR, HISTORIAN
b Philadelphia, Pa, Apr 27, 41. *Study:* Univ Colo, BA(hist & classics); Harvard Univ, classics; Univ Denver, MA(art hist). *Collections Arranged:* Albert Bierstadt, 72, Frederic Remington (auth, catalog), 73 & Peter Rindisbacher, 70, Amon Carter Mus, Ft Worth, Tex; The Rocky Mountains, Buffalo Bill Hist Ctr, Cody, Wyo, 83. *Pos:* Cur collections, Amon Carter Mus, Ft Worth, Tex, 69-75; dir, Buffalo Bill Hist Ctr, Cody, Wyo, 76- *Teaching:* Adj prof hist, Univ Wyo, Laramie, 80- *Mem:* Wyo Coun on the Arts (vchmn, 77). *Res:* Nineteenth and early twentieth century artists of the American West. *Publ:* Auth, Frederic Remington, 73 & The Way West: Art of Frontier America, 77, Harry N Abrams Inc; coauth (with Patricia Trenton), The Rocky Mountains: A Vision for Artists of the Nineteenth Century, Univ Okla Press, 83. *Mailing Add:* Box 1000 Cody WY 82414

HASTENTEUFEL, DIETER
SCULPTOR
b Krefeld, Ger, 1939; Can citizen. *Study:* Sch Applied Arts, Gelsenkirchen, Ger, 58-60; Werkkunstschule, Krefeld, 61; Werkkunstschule, Wuerzburg, 64; Acad Fine Art, Stuttgart, Ger, dipl, 68. *Work:* Art Gallery Ont; Art Gallery Hamilton; Art Gallery Peterborough, Ont; Sculpture Park, Liberty Hill, Tex; Can Coun Art Bank. *Exhib:* Art Bank Collection, Norman Mackenzie Art Gallery, Univ Regina, 81; Six Years Artsake, Harbourfront Art Gallery, Toronto, 82; solo exhibs, Art Gallery Windsor, Ont, 83, Burlington Cult Ctr, 83 & Kitchener-Waterloo Art Gallery, Ont, 83. *Awards:* Grants, Can Coun, 76, 79 & 82 & Ont Art Coun, 76-78 & 80-82. *Bibliog:* Gail Habs (auth), article, Artview, Toronto, spring 81; Joy Ilakanson Colby (auth), article, Detroit News, 4/24/83; Shirley Morriss (auth), article, Guardian, Brampton, Ont, 5/11/83. *Mailing Add:* 9 Davies Ave Toronto ON M4M 2A6 Canada

HASTIE, REID
EDUCATOR, WRITER
b Donora, Pa, Feb 14, 16. *Study:* Edinboro State Col, BS; WVa Univ, MA; Univ Pittsburgh, EdD. *Work:* Minneapolis Inst Arts; Minn Mus Arts. *Exhib:* State Fair Gallery, St Paul, Minn, 66; Northrop Gallery, Univ Minn, 67; Encounters with Artists, 70; Drawings, St Paul, 72. *Teaching:* Prof art & art educ, Univ Minn, 49-70; prof art & art educ, Tex Tech Univ, 70- *Awards:* Distinguished Art Educator, Minn Art Educ Asn, 66; Award of Merit, Nat Art Educ Asn, 69. *Mem:* Nat Art Educ Asn (pres, 57-59); Nat Soc Study Educ. *Media:* Acrylic, Watercolor. *Res:* Study of aesthetic theory and sensitivity; the creative process. *Publ:* Ed, Art Education, 65; auth, Encounter with Art, 69. *Mailing Add:* 3021 21st St Lubbock TX 79410

HASWELL, HOLLEE
LIBRARIAN, PAINTER
b Albany, NY, May 4, 48. *Study:* Russell Sage Col, Troy, NY, BA; Simmons Col, Boston, Mass, MLS. *Work:* Russell Sage Col. *Pos:* Art & music librn, Forbes Libr, Northampton, Mass, 73-78; librn, Worcester Art Mus, Mass, 78-81; librn, Sleepy Hollow Restorations, Tarrytown, NY, 81- *Mem:* Am Libr Asn; Art Libr Soc NAm. *Interests:* Development of resource collections to serve researcher and artist alike. *Mailing Add:* c/o Sleepy Hollow Restorations 150 White Plains Rd Tarrytown NY 10591

HATCH, JOHN DAVIS
CONSULTANT, HISTORIAN
b Oakland, Calif, June 14, 07. *Study:* Univ Calif, 26-28; Harvard Univ, 32; Princeton Univ, 38; Yale Univ, 40. *Collections Arranged:* Traveling Exhibs for Carnegie Corp, 36-37; American Drawings, 42; Thomas Cole, 43; pioneer exhib, Negro Artist Comes of Age, 45; Painting in Canada, 46. *Pos:* Exec secy, Seattle Art Inst, 28-29, dir, 29-31; vpres, Western Art Asn Mus, 30-31; asst dir, Isabella Stewart Gardner Mus, 32-35; dir, US art projs, New Eng States, 33-34; ed, Parnassus, 37-39; founder, Am Art Depository, 38; founder, Am Drawing Ann, 40; dir, Albany Inst Hist & Art, 40-48; ed, Albany Co Hist Asn Rec, 41-48; ed, Early Am Indust Chronicle, 42-49, pres, 46-47; dir, Norfolk Mus Art & Sci, 50-60. *Teaching:* Vis prof, Univ Ore, 48-49; vis prof, Univ Calif, summer 49; coordr adv & actg chmn fine arts div, Spelman Col, 64-70; vis prof, Univ Mass, summer 71. *Mem:* Master Drawing Asn (trustee, founder, 62); Am Drawing Soc; Berkshire Co Hist Soc; Col Art Asn Am; MacDowell Colonist. *Interests:* Life of John Vanderlyn, and a study of American drawings and draughtsmen. *Mailing Add:* Rt 183 Lenox MA 01240

HATCH, JOHN W
PAINTER, EDUCATOR
b Saugus, Mass, Nov 1, 19. *Study:* Mass Col Art; Sch Fine Arts, Yale Univ, BFA & MFA. *Work:* De Cordova & Dana Mus, Lincoln, Mass; Currier Gallery Art, Manchester, NH; Portland Mus Art, Maine; Addison Gallery Am Art, Andover, Mass; Pa Acad Art, Philadelphia; and others. *Comn:* Mural, Army Map Serv Bldg, Washington, DC; mural, Profile Bank, Rochester, NH; mural, Kingsbury Hall, Univ NH; mem window, Student Union, Univ NH; hist mural, Ledges, Durham, NH; and others. *Exhib:* US Info Agency Exhib, Russia, 61; Centennial Exhib of Land Grant Cols, Kansas City, Mo, 62; De Cordova & Dana Mus, 62 & 64; Boston Mus Fine Arts, 67-69; Addison Gallery Am Art; and others. *Teaching:* Prof art, Univ NH, currently. *Awards:* City Manchester Award, NH, 64; NH Art Asn Award, 82; Portland Mus Art Festivals Award; and others. *Mem:* NH Art Asn (pres, 58-60); Artist's Equity. *Media:* Acrylic, Watercolor. *Mailing Add:* Paul Creative Arts Ctr Univ of NH Durham NH 03824

HATCH, (MR & MRS) MARSHALL
COLLECTORS
Mr Hatch, b Seattle, Wash, Aug 26, 18; Mrs Hatch, b Seattle, Wash, July 7, 18. *Study:* Mr & Mrs Hatch, Univ Wash. *Pos:* Mr Hatch, pres, Seattle Art Mus, currently. *Collection:* Morris Graves, Mark Tobey, other Northwest artists, The Eight (Ashcan Group), Mexican paintings and ethnic art. *Mailing Add:* 4422 55th NE Seattle WA 98105

HATCH, MARY
PAINTER
b Saginaw, Mich, Dec 12, 35. *Study:* Skidmore Col, 51-53; Western Mich Univ, MA(painting), 72; studied with Harvey Breverman, 74-77. *Work:* Kalamazoo Inst Arts; Sturgis Coun Arts, Mich. *Exhib:* West 81 Art and the Law, Minn Mus Art, 81; one-person exhib, Inner Realities, CPL Cult Ctr, Chicago, 82; Allied Artists Am Ann, Nat Arts Club, New York, 82; New Talent--New Visions, Zolla/Lieberman Gallery, Chicago, 83; Selections from the Chicago Artists Coalition Slide Registry, Wustum Mus, Racine, Wis, 83; In Your Dreams, Marie Pellicone Gallery, New York, 83; and others. *Awards:* Third Place, Jubilee 75, Western Mich Univ, 75; Second Place, 78 Area Show, Battle Creek Art Ctr, Mich, 78; Susan Kahn Prize, Nat Asn Women Artists Ann, 83. *Mem:* Nat Asn Women Artists; Chicago Artists Coalition. *Media:* Oil. *Mailing Add:* 6917 Willson Dr Kalamazoo MI 49009

HATCH, W A S
PRINTMAKER, EDUCATOR
b Bridgeport, Conn, Mar 19, 48. *Study:* Syracuse Univ, BFA, 70; Pratt Inst, MFA, 72. *Work:* City Col New York; Kemper Collection, Chicago, Ill; US Info Agency Embassy Collection; Univ Leeds; San Diego Mus; and others. *Comn:* Spec ed prints, Pratt Graphic Ctr, New York, 73. *Exhib:* Brooklyn Mus 19th Nat Print Exhib, 74-75; 5th Int Drawing Show, Mus Mod Art, Riejka, Yugoslavia, 76; World Print Competition, 77; Am Printmakers, Venice, 77; New Talent Show, Allied Artists of Am, New York, 77; Self-Portrait, Kyoto, Japan, 77; and many others. *Teaching:* Asst prof printmaking, Bradley Univ, 73-79; instr drawing, Columbia Col, 79-80; adj prof, Widener Univ, 82- *Awards:* Purchase Award, Los Angeles 2nd Nat Print Exhib, 74; Merit Award, Boston Printmakers 26th Ann Exhib, 74; Purchase Award, Eastern Regional Drawing Exhib, 83. *Bibliog:* The European Graphic Biennale, Print Rev, 77. *Mem:* Del Ctr Contemp Arts (vpres, 82-83); Col Art Asn. *Media:* Intaglio, Lithography. *Dealer:* Assoc American Artists 663 Fifth Ave New York NY 10022; Sande Webster Gallery 2018 Locust St Philadelphia PA 19103. *Mailing Add:* 1326 Woodlawn Ave 663 Fifth Ave Wilmington DE 19806

HATCHETT, DUAYNE
SCULPTOR, EDUCATOR
b Shawnee, Okla, May 12, 25. *Study:* Univ Mo; Univ Okla, BFA & MFA. *Work:* Whitney Mus Am Art; Rochester Mem Mus, NY; Ft Worth Art Mus, Tex; Carnegie Inst, Pittsburgh, Pa; Albright-Knox Gallery, Buffalo, NY. *Comn:* First Nat Bank Tulsa, Okla; Trader's Nat Bank, Kansas City, Kans, 61; Tulsa Fire Dept Hq, Okla, 63; GSA-Fed Bldg, Rochester, NY, 75; Nat Endowment for the Arts, Flint, Mich, 78. *Exhib:* Whitney Mus Am Art Ann, 66-68; Am Sculpture of Sixties, Los Angeles Co Mus, 67; Pittsburgh Int, 67-71; 11th Int Biennial Sculpture, Middelheim Mus, Antwerp, Belg; one-man show, Albright-Knox Gallery, 74. *Teaching:* Assoc prof sculpture, Ohio State Univ, 64-68; prof art, State Univ NY Buffalo, 68- *Media:* Metal. *Mailing Add:* 347 Starin Ave Buffalo NY 14216

HATFIELD, DAVID UNDERHILL
PAINTER
b Plainfield, NJ, July 16, 40. *Study:* Miami Univ, BFA, 62; Sch Visual Arts, 63; Art Students League, 64. *Exhib:* Nat Acad Design Ann, New York, 70 & 73; Nat Arts Club Ann, New York, 69-72, 75 & 76; Am Artists Prof League Grand Nat, New York, 71-77; one man shows, Nat Arts Club, 76, Christopher Gallery, New York. *Awards:* Elizabeth T Greenshields Mem Found Grant, 73 & 74; Philip G Shumaker Mem Award, Rockport Art Asn, 81; Figure Award, Rockport Art Asn, 82. *Mem:* Salmagundi Club; Allied Artists Am; Rockport Art Asn; Am Artists Prof League; Knickerbocker Artists; and others. *Media:* Oil. *Publ:* Contribr, Am Artist Mag, 12/81; illusr, Prevention Mag, 1/82. *Dealer:* Grand Central Art Galleries 50 E 50th St New York NY 10017; Gallery Henoch 80 Wooster St New York NY 10012. *Mailing Add:* 9 River St Hoosick Falls NY 12090

HATFIELD, DONALD GENE
PAINTER, EDUCATOR
b Detroit, Mich, May 23, 32. *Study:* Northwestern Mich Col, AA; Mich State Univ, BA & MA; Univ Wis, MFA. *Work:* Jacksonville State Univ, Ala; Tuskegee Inst, Ala; Brandt Corp, New Orleans; South Cetral Bell, Birmingham; Southern Servs, Birmingham; and others. *Exhib:* Ala Art League, Mongomery, 81; Columbia Col, Mo, 83; Del Mar Col, 83; Ala Works on Paper, Auburn, Ala, 83; Competition for Spoleto, Marble Arch Gallery, Charleston, SC, 83; and others. *Teaching:* Elem art supvr, Auburndale Elem Sch Syst, Wis; instr jr & sr high art classes, Auburndale High Sch, 62-64; asst prof art, Auburn Univ, 64-71, assoc prof art, 71-81, prof art, 81-; part time instr hist archit & art, Tuskegee Inst, 68-69. *Mem:* Ala Art League (first vpres, 69-70, pres, 70-72); Opelika Arts Asn (bd trustees, 71-73); Ala Watercolor Soc; Birmingham Art Asn. *Media:* Watercolor. *Mailing Add:* 550 Forest Park Circle Auburn AL 36830

HATGIL, PAUL
SCULPTOR, EDUCATOR
b Manchester, NH, Feb 18, 21. *Study:* Mass Col Art, BFA; Columbia Univ, MFA; Harvard Univ, summer 50. *Work:* Fed Aviation Agency, Balboa, CZ; Litton Industs; Ft Worth Nat Bank; Mitchell Energy Corp; Tandy Corp. *Comn:* St Paul's Lutheran Church, Austin, Tex; Univ Tex Bus & Admin Bldg, Austin; Our Saviour's Lutheran Church, Victoria, Tex; Design Assocs Bldg, Dallas, Tex; Rio Bldg, Austin; plus others. *Exhib:* 4th-6th Int Invitational, Smithsonian Inst, Washington, DC; Int Invitational, Gulf-Caribbean Exhib, Houston, Tex; Philbrook Art Ctr Int, Tulsa, Okla; US World's Fair Pavilion, NY; Hemisphere 1969, Tex Pavilion, San Antonio, Tex; US Senate, St Petersburg, Jacksonville & Fla Mus; plus many others. *Teaching:* Instr, Columbia Univ; instr, San Antonio Art Inst; instr, Tex Fine Arts Asn, Austin; prof art, Univ Tex, Austin, 51- *Awards:* Univ Tex Res Inst Grants, 64 & 65. *Mem:* Am Craftsmen Coun; Col Art Asn Am. *Media:* Resin, Polyester. *Publ:* Auth, articles in, Ceramic Monthly, Sch Arts, Tex Trends Art Educ, La Rev Mod, Ceramic Age & Hellenic Chronicle. *Mailing Add:* 1401 Red Bud Trail Austin TX 78746

HATHAWAY, WALTER MURPHY
MUSEUM DIRECTOR
b Norfolk, Va, Feb 25, 39. *Study:* Richmond Prof Inst, BFA; Fla State Univ, MS. *Pos:* Art consult, State Dept Pub Instr, NC, 70-72; dir, Roanoke Fine Arts Ctr, Va, 73-77; dir, Columbia Mus of Arts & Sci, 77- *Teaching:* Instr art, Lake City Jr Col, Fla, 64-67; asst prof art & art educ, Longwood Col, Farmville, Va, 67-70. *Mem:* Am Asn Mus; Asn Art Mus Dir; Southeast Mus Conf. *Mailing Add:* Columbia Mus of Art & Sci Senate & Bull Columbia SC 29201

HATKE, WALTER JOSEPH
PAINTER
b Topeka, Kans, Jan 11, 48. *Study:* Apprentice to Jack Beal, 69 & 72-73; DePauw Univ, BA, 71; asst to Alexander Calder, 74-76; Univ Iowa, Iowa City, MA(Ingram Merrill Found Grant), 81, MFA, 82. *Work:* Chase Manhattan Bank, Chemical Bank, Lehman Brothers Kuhn Loeb, New York; Gen Foods, White Plains, NY; Sheldon Mem Art Gallery. *Comn:* Mobile sets, Calder Mem Comt & Orchestra of Our Time, New York, 77. *Exhib:* Gallery XV, McNay Inst, San Antonio, Tex, 81; Chicago Int Exposition Art, 83; American Realism 1930s-1980s, Summit Art Ctr, NJ, 83; Aspects of Contemporary Realism, William Patterson Col, 83; solo exhib, Swarthmore Col, 84. *Collections Arranged:* Realistic Directions (coauth, catalog), Pa State Univ, 83. *Pos:* Asst to dir, Perls Galleries, New York, 73-77. *Teaching:* Instr painting & drawing, DePauw Univ, 71-72 & Pa State Univ, 82-; grad asst painting, Univ Iowa, 80-81. *Bibliog:* John Russell (auth), The many faces of naturalism, New York Times, 8/11/80; Donald Lambert (auth), article, Am Artist, 10/82. *Mem:* Col Art Asn. *Media:* Oil. *Dealer:* Robert Schoelkopf Gallery 825 Madison Ave New York NY 10021. *Mailing Add:* 326 W Ridge Ave State College PA 16801

HAUG, DONALD RAYMOND
PAINTER
b Detroit, Mich, May 12, 25. *Study:* Mich State Univ, 46-47; Albright Art Sch, dipl, 52 & 53; State Univ NY, BS, 56, MS, 60; Univ Chicago, John Hay Whitney Found Fel, 62-63. *Work:* Butler Inst Am Art; Ball State Univ Art Gallery; Univ Rochester Mem Art Gallery; Charles R Penney Found Collection. *Exhib:* Butler Inst Am Art Ann Midyear Show, 56-79; Chautauqua Art Asn Nat Jury Show, NY, 59, 66 & 72-74; Cooperstown Art Asn Nat Ann, NY, 71-72 & 73-75; Drawing & Small Sculpture Ann, Ball State Univ, 72-75; Smithsonian Inst Traveling Show, 76-78; Third Nat Drawing Exhib, Emporia State Univ, 79. *Awards:* Purchase Award, Butler Inst Am Art, 70 & Drawing & Small Sculpture Show, Ball State Univ, 74; Manufacturers & Traders Trust Co Award, 39th Western NY Show, Albright-Knox Art Gallery, Buffalo, 82; plus others. *Media:* Oil. *Mailing Add:* 9267 W Lane Angola NY 14006

HAUGHEY, JAMES M
PAINTER
b Courtland, Kans, July 8, 14. *Study:* Univ Kans Sch Fine Art, 32-34; with Leroy Greene, 43-53. *Work:* Mont Inst Arts Permanent Collection in State Mus, Helena, Mont; Mont Hist Soc Mus, Helena; Yellowstone Art Ctr, Billings, Mont. *Exhib:* Allied Artists Am, 63; Am Artists Prof League, various galleries, New York, 71-82; Am Watercolor Soc Ann Exhib, Nat Acad Galleries, New York 61-80; Rocky Mountain Watercolor Painters, 13 western states, 75; retrospective, Yellowstone Art Ctr, 80. *Pos:* Pres, Yellowstone Art Ctr Found, 64-65; pres, Mont Inst Arts Found, 65-66. *Awards:* First Award Watercolor, Hockaday Ctr Arts, 73; Coun Am Artists Socs Award, Am Artists Prof League, 81; Governor's Award for Arts, 81. *Bibliog:* Dale A Burk (auth), The element of chance: James Haughey, New Interpretations, Western Life Publ, 69; Jeanne Rhodes (auth), James Haughey, The Arts in Mont, Mont Press Publ Co, 77; Weldon Blake (auth), James Haughey, Acrylic Watercolor Painting, Watson-Guptill. *Mem:* Am Watercolor Soc (vpres, 78-81); fel Am Artists Prof League; Kans Watercolor Soc (hon mem, 71); Midwest Watercolor Soc; hon mem Mont Watercolor Soc. *Media:* Watercolor, Acrylic. *Publ:* Auth, Calligraphy: The gracile art, 67 & The arts in our society, 73, Mont Arts, Mont Inst Arts; auth, The arts and the lawyer, Kansas Law Review, 81. *Mailing Add:* 2205 Tree Lane Billings MT 59102

HAUPT, SHIRLEY ELIASON See Eliason, Shirley

HAUSER, ALONZO
PAINTER, SCULPTOR
b La Crosse, Wis, Jan 30, 09. *Study:* Layton Sch Art; Univ Wis; Art Students League, with William Zorach; also with Amedeo Merli. *Work:* State Capitol Grounds, St Paul Gallery Art, St Paul, Minn; Walker Art Ctr, Minneapolis; Wustum Mus, Racine, Wis. *Comn:* Five figures & four reliefs, Greendale Fed Govt, Wis, 37-40; Christ figure (limestone), St Paul's Evangel Church, St Paul, 52; fountain (bronze), Vet Serv Bldg, St Paul, 52-56; fountain (bronze), Rice Park Woman's League, St Paul, 68. *Exhib:* ACA Gallery, New York, 36; Milwaukee Art Inst, Wis, 40; one-man retrospective, Walker Art Ctr, Minneapolis, 46; Rochester Art Ctr, 62; Las Cruces Community Art Ctr, NMex, 75. *Teaching:* Chmn & founder art dept, Macalester Col, St Paul, 44-49; critic, Sch Archit, Univ Minn, Minneapolis, 57-69. *Media:* Stone, Bronze. *Mailing Add:* Box 12037 Mesilla Park NM 88047

HAUSER, REINE I
CURATOR, DEALER
b Niagara Falls, NY, May 15, 56. *Study:* Sarah Lawrence Col, BA, 78; Columbia Univ MFA, 83. *Pos:* Ed, Downtown, Lower Manhattan Cult Coun, New York, 78-79; dir artists serv, Just Above Midtown Inc, 80-82; gallery dir, Soho 20, New York, 81-82; dir, Artemage, Tex & NY, 83- *Mem:* Found Community Artists (bd dirs, currently); Art Without Walls (bd dirs, currently). *Res:* Contemporary art. *Mailing Add:* 275 Bleeker St New York NY 10014

HAUSEY, ROBERT MICHAEL
PAINTER
b Baton Rouge, La, Nov 25, 49. *Study:* La State Univ, BFA, 71; Univ Pa, MFA, 74; Skowhegan Sch Painting & Sculpture, 75. *Work:* La State Univ, Baton Rouge; West Baton Rouge Art Mus, Port Allen, La. *Exhib:* Louisiana Landscapes, Contemp Art Ctr, New Orleans, 81; Art Ann Two, Okla Art Ctr, 81; Birmingham Biennial, Birmingham Mus, 81; 25th Exhib Am Art, Chautauqua Art Asn, NY, 82; Shreveport Biennial, Meadows Mus, La, 82; Piedmont Biennial, Mint Mus, 83; New Orleans Art Now, Laurel Mus, Miss, 83; Bodies and Souls, Artists Choice Mus, New York, 83. *Teaching:* Instr painting, Univ Tex, San Antonio, 76 & Sam Houston State Univ, 76-77; assoc prof, La State Univ, 77- *Awards:* Merit Award, Birmingham Biennial, Birmingham Mus, 81; Jean Despuljols Award, Meadows Mus Biennial, 82; Nat Endowment Arts--Southeastern Ctr Contemp Arts Fel, 83-84. *Bibliog:* Jeanie Thompson (auth), What's a fellow to do?, Los Angeles Life, 1/82; Linda Bofinger (auth), Solitary moments in time, Artspectrum, 7/82. *Media:* Oil on Canvas. *Dealer:* Galerie Simonne Stern 2727 Prytania St New Orleans LA 70130; More Gallery 1630 Walnut St Philadelphia PA 19103. *Mailing Add:* 9498 Hooper Rd Baton Rouge LA 70818

HAUSMAN, FRED S
SCULPTOR, DESIGNER
b Bingen on Rhine, Ger, Apr 27, 21; US citizen. *Study:* Pratt Inst; New Sch Social Res, with Stuart Davis. *Work:* Emily Lowe Collection, Univ Miami; Mus Mod Art, Bogota, Colombia; Evansville Mus; Rutgers Univ; Fordham Univ. *Exhib:* NY Univ, 66; Contemporary Art USA, Norfolk Mus, 67; Columbia Univ, 68; Black & White Show, Smithsonian Inst, 69-70; 2nd Biennial, Medellin, Colombia, 70. *Media:* Acrylic. *Dealer:* Bodley Gallery 1063 Madison Ave New York NY 10028. *Mailing Add:* 100 Pembroke Dr Stamford CT 06903

HAUSMAN, JEROME JOSEPH
EDUCATOR
b New York, NY, May 4, 25. *Study:* Pratt Inst, 42-43; Cornell Univ, AB, 46; Columbia Univ, 47-48; Art Students League, 48; NY Univ, MA, 51, EdD, 54. *Pos:* Mem arts & humanities panel, US Off Educ, 64-70; ed bd, J Aesthetic Educ, 68-80; consult, John D Rockefeller III Fund, 69-75; pres, Minn Alliance Arts Educ, 77-79; bd dirs, Arts, Educ & Americans, 79; bd trustees, Minn Mus Art, 79-82. *Teaching:* Instr art, Elizabeth Pub Schs, NJ, 49-53; assoc prof, Sch Fine & Appl Arts, Ohio State Univ, 53-58, actg dir, 58-59, dir, 59-68; vis lectr, Sch Art, Syracuse Univ, 57; vis prof art educ, Pa State Univ, 58; prof div creative arts, NY Univ, 68-75; pres & prof, Minneapolis Col Art & Design, 75-82; acad vpres & prof, Mass Col Art, 82- *Mem:* Nat Art Educ Asn; Nat Comn Art Educ (chmn); Am Soc Aesthetics; Western Arts Asn; Inst Study Art Educ. *Publ:* Ed, Research in Art Education (yearbk), Nat Art Educ Asn, 59; contribr, articles in prof jour; ed, Arts and the Schools, McGraw-Hill, 80. *Mailing Add:* Vpres Academic Affairs Mass Col Art Boston MA 02215

HAUSRATH, JOAN W
WEAVER, EDUCATOR
b Detroit, Mich, May 29, 42. *Study:* Bowling Green State Univ, Ohio, BS(educ), 64, with Philip Wigg, MFA, 66; Ohio State Univ, MA(art hist), 70. *Work:* Teradyne Inc, Nashua, NH; Nat Fire Prevention Agency, Quincy, Mass; Bowling Green State Univ, Ohio. *Exhib:* Marietta Col Craft Nat, G M Hermann Art Ctr, Ohio, 80 & 81; Crafts 81, Currier Art Gallery, Manchester, NH, 81; solo exhib, Signature Gallery, Boston, 82; Surface-Structure, Volid Gallery, Chicago, 82; Craftsmans Gallery, Scarsdale, NY, 82; American Crafts in Iceland, Kjarvalsstadir Mus, Reykjavik, 83. *Collections Arranged:* New England Weaving Invitational, 81 & European Costume in New Plimoth, 83, Bridgewater State Col, Mass. *Teaching:* Instr art hist, Ohio State Univ, Columbus, 70-71; from assoc prof to prof art, Bridgewater State Col, Mass, 71-, co-dir art gallery, 76-77, 80-81 & 83-84; craft instr weaving, Summer Workshops, Eastern Conn State Col, Willimantic, 79-81. *Awards:* Mass Artists Found Fel Crafts, 83. *Bibliog:* Roger Dunn (auth), The Ikats of Joan Hausrath, a painterly approach to weaving, Fiberarts Mag, 11-12/81. *Mem:* Mass Asn Crafts; Boston Soc Arts & Crafts. *Media:* Fiber. *Mailing Add:* 74 Union St East Bridgewater MA 02333

HAUT, CLAIRE (JOAN)
PAINTER, GRAPHIC ARTIST
US citizen. *Study:* Augustana Col; Am Acad Art, Chicago; Sch Design, Chicago, Lazlo Moholy-Nagy scholarship; Inst Design; also with Hin Bredendieck, John Kearney & Gyorgy Kepes. *Work:* Libr Cong, Washington, DC. *Comn:* Screen, woven and printed drapes, rug and upholstery, Teachers Rm & Home Econ Rm, Saarinens Crow Island Sch, Winnetka, Ill, 40; libr traveling display throughout S & Cent Am, Am Libr Asn, 40; and pvt comn. *Exhib:* Traveling Exhib Works Progress Admin Crafts, Chicago Art Inst, Mus Mod Art, New York, Corcoran Mus, San Francisco Mus, Mus St Louis & Toledo Mus; one-man show, Jonson Gallery, Univ NMex, Albuquerque, 79; Contemp NMex Fine Art Invitational, Sweeney Ctr & Santa Fe Festival of Arts, 79; Carlsbad Fine Arts Mus, NMex, 82; and others. *Pos:* Artist-designer, Experimental Design Workshop, Ill Art Project, Chicago, 39-42; art ed, Cudahy Packing Co, Chicago, 43-45; illusr, Sandia Labs, Albuquerque, 58-74. *Awards:* Pop Art Exhib First Prize, NMex Art League, 64; First Prize for Graphics, NMex State Fair Prof Artists Exhib, 67; First Purchase Prize for Crafts & Sculpture, Llano Estacado, 71; and others. *Mem:* Artists Equity (secy-treas, 73 & pres, 76, Albuquerque Chap); Albuquerque Designer Craftsmen; Nat League Am Pen Women (pres, Manzanita Br, 70-72, state chmn, Biennial Exhib, 75-76); NMex Art League. *Mailing Add:* 9836 McKnight NE Albuquerque NM 87112

HAVELOCK, CHRISTINE MITCHELL
HISTORIAN, EDUCATOR
b Cochrane, Ont, June 2, 24; US citizen. *Study:* Univ Toronto, AB; Radcliffe Col, AM; Harvard Univ, PhD(Charles Eliot Norton Fel), 52. *Teaching:* Prof art hist, Vassar Col, 53-, dir women's studies, 78-79, cur classical collection, currently. *Awards:* Am Asn Univ Women Fel, 58-59. *Mem:* Col Art Asn Am; Archeol Inst Am. *Res:* Greek sculpture of Hellenistic period. *Publ:* Auth, Hellenistic Art, W W Norton, rev ed 81. *Mailing Add:* Vassar Col Poughkeepsie NY 12601

HAVENS, JAN
SCULPTOR
b Norfolk, Va, May 7, 48. *Study:* Atlantic Christian Col, BS, 70; George Peabody Col, MA, 73. *Work:* Tenn Botanical Garden & Fine Arts Ctr, Nashville. *Comn:* Sculpture, Radio City Music Hall, New York, comn by, Governor Alexander, Nashville, Tenn, 81. *Exhib:* one-man show, Tenn Botanical Garden & Fine Arts Ctr, Nashville, 81 & Southeastern Ctr Contemp Art, Winston-Salem, NC, 83; Greenwood Gallery, Washington, DC, 81; The Animal Image: Contemporary Objects and the Beast, Renwick Gallery, Smithsonian Inst, Washington, DC, 81. *Bibliog:* Adele Pilsk (auth), article, Ceramics Monthly, 9/78; Sandy Seawright (auth), Clay fantasies by Jan Havens, Artcraft Mag, 80; Clara Hieronymus (auth), Artist to show clay creations, Tennessean, 2/3/80. *Mem:* Am Craft Coun; Tenn Artist-Craftsmen's Asn. *Media:* Clay. *Mailing Add:* 1121 Graybar Ln Nashville TN 37204

HAVERSAT, LILLIAN KERR
DEALER, WRITER
b New York, NY, Jan 12, 38. *Study:* Famous Artist Sch, cert com art; Trinity Col, Vt, BA, 83; also with David K Merrill & Patricia Reynolds. *Pos:* Art consult, Discovery Mus, Essex Junction, Vt, 74-; owner, Monk's House Art Serv & Gallery, Jericho, Vt, 74-; consult, Vt Educ Television Arts Auction, 75-78, state coordr, 75-76; consult, Lake Champlain CofC Regional Exhib, 77-79, coordr, 79; dir, Red Mill Gallery, Jericho, Vt, 81. *Awards:* Grants, Vt Coun Arts, 81-83. *Mem:* Northern Vt Artist Asn (pres, 73-78); founding mem Essex Vt Art League; founder Jericho Historical Soc Art Coun; Nat Pen Women. *Specialty:* Contemporary American art; contemporary and antique prints, sculpture, pottery; New England representative for David K Merrill. *Publ:* Auth, Artfully Speaking, 74; contribr, Northern Vt Artists Newsletter, 78-83; contribr, Jottings from Jericho, 77-83. *Mailing Add:* Box 351 Jericho VT 05465

HAWES, LOUIS
HISTORIAN
b Rochester, NY, Feb 25, 31. *Collections Arranged:* Presences of Nature: British Landscape 1780-1830, 82. *Teaching:* From instr to asst prof, Columbia Univ, 58-68; assoc prof, Indiana Univ, Bloomington, 68-73, prof, 73-; resident fel, Yale Ctr Brit Art, 78-79. *Awards:* Fulbright Fel to England, 57-58. *Mem:* Col Art Asn; Midwest Art Hist Soc; Walpole Soc; Victorian Soc; Turner Soc. *Res:* Later 18th and 19th century European and American painting; Romantic landscape painting. *Publ:* Auth, The American Scene: Landscape & Genre Painting 1820-1900, Ind Univ Art Mus, 70; auth, Turner's fighting temeraire, Art Quart 35, 72; auth, Constable's Stonehenge, Victoria & Albert Mus, 75; auth, Presences of Nature: British Landscape 1780-1830, Yale Ctr Brit Art, 82; auth, Constable's Hadleigh Castle & British Romantic ruin painting, Art Bulletin 65, 83. *Mailing Add:* 1329 S High St Bloomington IN 47401

HAWKES, ELIZABETH H
CURATOR
b Wilmington, Del, Aug 12, 43. *Study:* Mary Washington Col, BA, 65; Univ Del, MA, 69. *Collections Arranged:* Posters by Edward Penfield, Del Art Mus, 69; American Painting and Sculpture (auth, catalog), 75; The Poster Decade (auth, catalog), 77; Bertha Corson Day Bates (auth, catalog), 78; Magazine Illustrations for the American Magazine (auth, catalog), 79; City Life Illustrated (auth, catalog), 80. *Pos:* Asst cur, Del Art Mus, 69-79, cur, John Sloan Collection, 77-, actg cur mus, 80-81, assoc cur, 81- *Mem:* Asn Am Mus; Northeast Mus Conf; Col Art Asn. *Publ:* Contribr, Artists in Wilmington: 1890-1940, 80 & The Students of Howard Pyle, 80, Del Art Mus. *Mailing Add:* 2301 Kentmere Pkwy Wilmington DE 19806

HAWKINS, BARBARA
PAINTER
b Columbia, Mo, Feb 1, 47. *Study:* Univ Mo, Columbia, BA, 71, MA(teaching asst), 74. *Exhib:* Nat Painting Show, Butler Inst Am Art, Youngstown, Ohio, 80; Watercolor USA, Springfield Art Mus, Mo, 80; Ky Watercolor Soc Nat Ann, Art Ctr, Louisville, 80; Nat Watercolor Soc Ann, Laguna Beach Art Mus, Calif, 81; Kansas Three, Washburn Univ, 83; Mid-Four, Nelson Art Mus, Kansas City, Mo, 83. *Awards:* Top Cash Award, Kans Watercolor Soc Tri-State Ann, 81; Third Prize, Washburn Univ, 83; Lithography Grant, Kans Art Comn, 83. *Mem:* Nat Watercolor Soc. *Media:* Charcoal, Watercolor. *Publ:* Contribr, Literature and Graphics from US Small Press 1965-1977, Spirit That Moves Us Press, 81. *Dealer:* Kellas Gallery 7 E 7th Lawrence KS 66044. *Mailing Add:* 545 N 3rd Lawrence KS 66044

HAWKINS, MYRTLE H
PAINTER, WRITER
b Merrit, BC. *Study:* Harnell Col, AA; San Jose State Univ; Univ Calif; West Valley Col; also with Marshall Merrit, Maynard Stewart & Thomas Leighton. *Work:* Nat Easter Seal Soc, Chicago. *Comn:* Portrait, Rev John Foster, First Congregational Church, San Jose, Calif, 70; portrait, Rose Shenson, Triton Mus, Santa Clara, Calif, 71. *Exhib:* De Saisset Gallery, Santa Clara, 68; Am Artist Prof League Nat Exhib, Lever House, New York, 71; one-man shows, Triton Mus Art, 71 & Rosicrucian Mus Art, San Jose, 73 & 77; Harnell Col, 69. *Teaching:* Teacher painting, Calif State Dept Vocational Rehab, San Jose & Palo Alto, 69-71; also pvt painting lessons. *Awards:* First Place, Nat Easter Seal Soc, Chicago, 65; Gold Seal Award, de Saisset Art Gallery, 66; Best of Show, St Mark's Art Ann, Santa Clara, 68. *Bibliog:* Article in Rosicrucian Digest, 11/73; article, Grit, 8/28/77. *Mem:* Allied Artists Santa Clara Co (pres, 72-73); Am Artists Prof League; Soc Western Artists; Triton Mus Art. *Media:* Pastel, Oil. *Publ:* Illusr, The Adventures of Mimi, Books I & II, 66; auth, Art as Therapy and Rehabilitation for the Handicapped. 74. *Mailing Add:* 646 Bucher Ave Santa Clara CA 95051

HAWKINS, THOMAS WILSON, JR
PAINTER, INSTRUCTOR
b Los Angeles, Calif, May 15, 41. *Study:* Calif State Univ, Long Beach, BA(design) & MA(drawing, painting); Calif State Univ, Los Angeles, art hist, design & ceramics. *Work:* Overholt & Overholt Law Off, Los Angeles; Home Savings & Loan Art Collection; Dr Ambler Collection, Palos Verdes, Calif; Whittier Art Asn, Calif. *Exhib:* Southern Calif Expos, Del Mar, 67-77; Inland Exhibs, 68-77; Butler Inst Am Art, Youngstown, Ohio, 70; DaVinci Open Art Competition, New York, 70; Bertrand Russell Centenary Art Exhib, London & Nottingham, Eng, 73; and others. *Teaching:* Instr drawing & design & art gallery dir, Rio Hondo Col, Whittier, Calif, 67-; instr art, drawing & art hist, Long Beach City Col, 67-72; instr painting, Golden West Col, Huntington Beach, Calif, 72-78. *Awards:* Best Painting, Art in All Media, Southern Calif Expos, 67, Third Prize, 70; Second Award, Inland Exhib, San Bernardino Art

Asn, 71 & 73; Purchase Award 25th All City Los Angeles Art, Barnsdall, 77. *Mem:* Los Angeles Art Asn; Whittier Art Asn; Art Teachers Asn; Calif Teachers Asn; Nat Educ Asn. *Mailing Add:* 414 Fairview Ave Arcadia CA 91006

HAWORTH, B COGILL
PAINTER
b Queenstown, SAfrica; Jan 20, 04; Can citizen. *Study:* ARCA; Univ London, grad. *Work:* Nat Gallery Can; Art Gallery Ont; Art Gallery Hamilton; Art Gallery of Windsor; Art Gallery, SAfrica. *Exhib:* Royal Can Acad; Ont Soc Artists; Can Soc Painter Watercolour; Can Group Painters. *Awards:* Best in Show, Can Soc Painters Watercolor; Best in Show for Watercolor, Jessie Dow; Monsanto Award. *Mem:* Royal Can Acad; Ont Soc Artists; Can Soc Painters Watercolour; Can Group Painters. *Publ:* Illusr, Book of Remembrance, Guelph Agr Col. *Dealer:* Roberts Gallery 641 Yonge St Toronto ON Can. *Mailing Add:* 111 Cluny Dr Toronto ON M4W 2R5 Canada

HAWORTH, PETER
PAINTER, STAINED GLASS ARTIST
b Oswaldtwistle, Lancashire, England, Feb 28, 1889; Can citizen. *Study:* Manchester Sch Art; Royal Col Art, Univ London, ARCA, 23. *Work:* Nat Gallery Can, Ottawa; Art Gallery Ont, Toronto; Art Gallery Windsor, Ont; Art Gallery Hamilton, Ont; Art Gallery London, Ont. *Comn:* Stained glass windows, Toronto, Hamilton, Ont, Montreal, Oakville, Ont & Halifax, NS. *Exhib:* Royal Can Acad; Ont Soc Artists; Can Soc Painters Watercolor; retrospective, Art Gallery Windsor. *Teaching:* Dir art, Central Tech Sch, 27-55. *Mem:* Royal Can Acad; Ont Soc Artists; Can Soc Painters Watercolor; Royal Soc. *Media:* Mixed. *Dealer:* Roberts Gallery 641 Yonge St Toronto ON Canada. *Mailing Add:* 111 Cluny Dr Rosedale Toronto ON M4W 2R5 Canada

HAWTHORNE, JACK GARDNER
EDUCATOR, PAINTER
b Philadelphia, Pa, May 8, 21. *Study:* Philadelphia Col Art, BA, 43; Univ Pa, MSEd, 56, MFA, 58. *Teaching:* Dir art educ, Pub Schs, Pa & NJ, 43-50; instr drawing, Philadelphia Col Art, 43-53, asst dean & registr, 57-60; guest lectr, Villanova Univ, 59; asst prof educ, Beaver Col, 60-63; assoc prof art, West Chester State Col, 65-, chmn art dept, 73-74 & 77- *Awards:* Award in Drawing, Pa Acad Fine Arts, 39. *Mem:* Peale Club, Pa Acad Fine Arts; Nat Trust Hist Preserv; Am Asn Univ Profs; life mem Nat Educ Asn; Inst Study Art Educ. *Media:* Watercolor. *Publ:* Contribr, Course of study in art educ, Commonwealth Pa, 51. *Mailing Add:* 619 W Miner St West Chester PA 19380

HAXTON, DAVID
PHOTOGRAPHER, FILMMAKER
b Indianapolis, Ind, Jan 6, 43. *Study:* Univ South Fla, BA, 65; Univ Mich, MFA, 67. *Work:* Whitney Mus Am Art, New York; Denver Art Mus; Mus Mod Art, New York; Australian Mus Art. *Exhib:* Two-man show, Whitney Mus Am Art, New York, 78 & Biennial Exhib, 79; Cineprobe, Mus Mod Art, New York, 78; Photography in the 70's, Art Inst Chicago, 79; Attitudes, Santa Barbara Art Mus, Calif, 79; Concept Narrative Doc, Mus Contemp Art, Chicago, 79; one-man show, Sonnabend Gallery, New York, 79 & 83; Whitney Biennial Exhib, 81 & 83; Recent Color, San Francisco Mus Art, 83; and others. *Teaching:* Instr art, San Diego State Univ, 69-72; instr drawing & photog, William Paterson Col, Wayne, NJ, 74- *Awards:* NY State Coun on Arts grant, 77; Nat Endowment for the Arts Individual Artist's Grants, 78 & 79. *Bibliog:* Sally Euclaire (auth), The new color, Abbyville, 81; article, The art of photography, Time-Life, 81; David Shapiro (auth), Inner city, Camera Arts, 1-2/82. *Dealer:* Sonnabend Gallery 420 W Broadway New York NY 10012. *Mailing Add:* 139 Spring St New York NY 10012

HAY, DICK
SCULPTOR, CERAMIST
b Cincinnati, Ohio, Nov 19, 42. *Study:* Ohio Univ, BFA; NY State Col Ceramics, Alfred Univ, MFA. *Work:* Speed Art Mus, Louisville, Ky; Butler Inst Am Art, Youngstown, Ohio; Evansville Mus Arts & Sci, Ind; Sea of Japan, Kanazawa-shi, Japan; Edinboro Col, Pa; and others. *Exhib:* Sensible Cup Int Exhib, Sea of Japan Expos, 73; Ceramics USA-Circa 1975, Playhouse Sq Gallery, Cleveland, Ohio, 74; Nat Funk Exhib, Habitat Gallery, Dearborn, Mich, 75; Contemp Ceramic Sculpture, Univ NC, Chapel Hill, 77; Viewpoint Ceramics, Grossmont Col, El Cajon, Calif, 79; plus others. *Pos:* Guest lectr, Univ Iowa, 69, Alfred Univ, 72 & 74, Univ Del, 72, Ariz State Univ, 73, Sheridan Col Appl Arts, Toronto, Ont, 74, La State Univ, 76, Univ Miami, 76, Can Santa Fe, 77, Princeton Univ, 79, Ill State Univ, 82 & Ga State Univ, 83; and others; plus others. *Teaching:* Prof art & ceramics, Ind State Univ, Terre Haute, 66- *Awards:* Nat Coun Educ Ceramic Arts Fel. *Mem:* Nat Coun Educ Ceramic Arts (pres, 78-80). *Mailing Add:* Dept of Art Ind State Univ Terre Haute IN 47809

HAY, GEORGE AUSTIN
PAINTER, FILMMAKER
b Johnstown, Pa, Dec 25, 15. *Study:* Pa Acad Fine Arts; Art Students League; Nat Acad; Univ Rochester; Univ Pittsburgh, BS & MLitt; Columbia Univ, MA; also with Robert Brackman & Dong Kingman. *Work:* Pub Libr, Metrop Mus Art, New York; Dept Army; Libr Cong, Washington, DC; numerous pvt collections. *Exhib:* Manufacturers Hanover Trust, 73; Bicentennial Exhib of Am Painters in Paris, 76; Chevy Chase Gallery, Washington, DC, 79; Watergate Gallery, 81; Salon des Nations, Paris, 83. *Mem:* Am Artists Prof League; Fed Design Coun; Allied Artists Am. *Media:* Oil, Watercolor. *Publ:* Auth & illusr, Seven Hops to Australia, 45; auth & illusr, The Performing Arts

Experience, 69; auth & dir, Visit to the Museum of Modern Art (film), 72; dir, Highways of History (film), 76. *Dealer:* Arts Club Galleries 2017 Eye St NW Washington DC 20006. *Mailing Add:* 2022 Columbia Rd NW Washington DC 20009

HAY, IKE
SCULPTOR, EDUCATOR
b Atlanta, Ga, Apr 28, 44. *Study:* Univ Ga, BFA & MFA. *Work:* Indianapolis Mus Art; New Orleans Mus Art; Mint Mus Art, Charlotte, NC; Lancaster Co Courthouse, Pa; High Steel Corp, Lancaster; and others. *Comn:* Archit sculpture, Mansfield State Col, Pa, 79; Gestetner Corp, Philadelphia, 80; Pepsi-Cola, Philadelphia, 82; Hines Industrial Develop Corp, Tulsa, 83; Hiland Mt Correctional Ctr, Anchorage, 83. *Exhib:* High Mus Art, 69; one-man shows, New Orleans Mus Art, 69 & Franklin & Marshall Col, 81; Nat Sculpture 73 Traveling Show, 73; Penn Mem Mus, Harrisburg, Pa, 79; and others. *Pos:* Nat Endowment artist in residence, Decatur, 74-75. *Teaching:* Asst prof sculpture, Purdue Univ, West Lafayette, 69-74; asst prof sculpture, Millersville State Col, Pa, 75-81, assoc prof, 81- *Awards:* Rosenblatt Scholarship, Univ Ga, 68; Grant in Aid, Arts Festival Atlanta, 68; Fac Grant, Purdue Univ, 70. *Bibliog:* John Spofforth (auth), The Ike Hay workshop, Ala-Arts, Ala State Arts Coun, 74. *Mem:* Am Asn Univ Prof. *Media:* Steel, Bronze. *Dealer:* Architectural Arts Coalition Dallas TX. *Mailing Add:* 3200 Blue Rock Rd Lancaster PA 17603

HAYASHI, MASUMI
PHOTOGRAPHER, EDUCATOR
b Rivers, Ariz, Sept 3, 45. *Study:* Fla State Univ, BA, 75, MFA, 77. *Work:* St Petersburg Fine Arts Mus, Fla; Jacksonville Fine Arts Mus, Fla; George Eastman House, Rochester, NY; Cleveland Inst Art, Ohio. *Exhib:* Southeastern Graphics Invitational, Mint Mus Art, 82; Women's Art, Miles Apart, Berman Gallery, New York, 82; Collage and Assemblage, Miss Mus Art, Jackson, 82; Unrestricted Color, Handwerter Gallery, Ithaca, NY, 83; History of Stereo Photography, Boston Mus Sci, 83; Color, On the Edge, Mather Gallery, Cleveland, 84. *Pos:* Gallery cur, Univ Central Fla, 81-82; gallery dir, Miami-Dade Community Col, summer 82. *Teaching:* Adj instr photog, Univ Central Fla, 80-82; vis instr, Loyola Marymount Univ, 83; asst prof, Cleveland State Univ, 82- *Awards:* Individual Artist Fel, Fla Fine Arts Coun, 80; Product Grant, Nimslo Corp, 83; Res & Creative Activities Grant, Cleveland State Univ, 83. *Mem:* Los Angeles Ctr Photog Studies; Image Resource Ctr, Cleveland; Soc Photog Educ. *Publ:* Contribr, Photo Images in Art: Design, Process and Materials, 79 & Creative Photography, 83, Davis. *Dealer:* Virginia Miller Galleries Commodore Plaza 3112 Miami FL 33133. *Mailing Add:* Terminal Tower PO Box 13001 Cleveland OH 44113

HAYDON, HAROLD (EMERSON)
PAINTER, EDUCATOR
b Ft William, Ont, Apr 22, 09; US citizen. *Study:* Univ Chicago, PhB, 30, MA, 31; Sch Art Inst Chicago, 32-33. *Work:* Pickering Col, Newmarket, Ont. *Comn:* Wool ark cover, Temple Beth Am, Chicago, Ill, 58, now in Temple Sholom, Chicago; glass mosaic murals, Beth El, Gary, Ind, 59-60, now in Beth Israel, Hammond, Ind; St Cletus Roman Cath Church, La Grange, Ill, 63, Temple Beth Am, Chicago, 68; mosaic & stained glass murals, Sonia Shankman Orthogenic Sch, Univ Chicago, 66-77; porcelain enamel on steel mural, 77; stained glass windows, Rockefeller Mem Chapel and Surgery Brain Res Inst, Univ Chicago, 72-79; wool Ark curtain, Niles Township Jewish Congregation, Skokie, Ill, 76. *Exhib:* Seven Exhibs Artists Chicago & Vicinity, 37-67 &58th Ann Am Painting--Abstr & Surrealist Art, 47, Art Inst Chicago; Options, Mus Contemp Art, Chicago, 68. *Pos:* Pres, Renaissance Soc Univ Chicago, 56-65 & 74-75; art critic, Chicago Sun-Times, 63- *Teaching:* From instr art to asst prof, George Williams Col, 34-44; from instr art to prof, Univ Chicago, 44-75; emer prof, 75-; vis lectr murals, Sch of Art Inst of Chicago, 75-81; adj prof fine arts, Ind Univ NW, 76- *Mem:* Artists Equity Asn, Chicago Chap (pres, 50-52, 55-57); Chicago Soc Artists (pres, 59-61); Nat Soc Mural Painters; hon life mem Artists Guild Chicago. *Media:* Oil, Mosaic, Porcelain Enamel, Stained Glass. *Publ:* Auth, Great Art Treasures in America's Small Museums, 67. *Mailing Add:* 5009 Greenwood Ave Chicago IL 60615

HAYES, BARTLETT HARDING, JR
ADMINISTRATOR, WRITER
b Andover, Mass, Aug 5, 04. *Study:* Phillips Acad, grad, 22; Harvard Col, AB, 26; studied art in US, 27-29; study in Europe, 27-33. *Pos:* Asst cur, Addison Gallery Am Art, 34-40, dir, 40-69; trustee, Am Fedn Arts, 40-70, Mus Fine Arts, Boston, 49-71, St Gaudens Mem, 67-72 & 74-, Amon Carter Mus, Ft Worth, 68-76, Inst Contemp Art, Boston, 69-70 & 74-81; dir, Am Acad Rome, 69-73. *Teaching:* Instr art, Phillips Acad, 33-69; lectr, Salzburg Sem, Austria, 60 & 71, Harvard Univ, 64-68, Honolulu Acad Fine Arts, 69-70, Nat Humanities Faculty, 69-70, Lowell Lectures, Boston, 75; fac, Grad Sch Educ, Lesley Col, Cambridge, Mass, 76. *Mem:* Col Art Asn Am (secy, 59-64); fel Am Acad Arts & Sci; Colonial Soc Mass. *Publ:* Auth, Intent of Art (TV series), NET; auth, American Drawings (Drawings of the Masters Set), Little, 75; Tradition Becomes Innovation--Modern Religious Architecture in America, Pilgrim Press, 83; and others. *Mailing Add:* Phillips St Andover MA 01810

HAYES, DAVID VINCENT
SCULPTOR
b Hartford, Conn, Mar 15, 31. *Study:* Univ Notre Dame, AB; Ind Univ, sculpture with David Smith, MFA. *Work:* Mus Mod Art, Brooklyn Mus, Guggenheim Mus, New York; Mus Arts Decoratif, Paris; Mus Fine Arts, Houston. *Comn:* Ceramics, walls, De Porceleyne Fles, Delft, Holland, 67, Lee Kolker, Stanfordville, NY, 70 & Elmira Col, 71, mural, Great Southwest

Corp, Atlanta, Ga, 68 & relief, comn by David Anderson, Ardsley, NY, 69. *Exhib:* Salon Mai, Mus Art Mod, Paris, 66; Jewelry 71, Art Gallery Ont, 71; State Univ NY, Albany, 78, Dartmouth Col, NH, 78, Amherst Col, Mass, 79, Nassau Co Mus, Port Washington, NY, 79 & Univ Conn, Storrs, 79; and others. *Teaching:* Vis artist, Carpenter Art Ctr, Harvard Univ, 72. *Awards:* Fulbright Res Grant, 61; Guggenheim Found Fel, 61; Nat Inst Arts & Lett Award, 64. *Media:* Metal, Ceramics. *Dealer:* David Anderson Gallery 521 West 57th St New York NY 10019. *Mailing Add:* PO Box 109 Coventry CT 06238

HAYES, GERALD
PAINTER, PHOTOGRAPHER
b Los Angeles, Calif, April 9, 40. *Study:* Auburn Univ, BVA, 62; Univ Ill, MFA, 66. *Exhib:* Elements of Art, Mus Fine Art, Boston, 71; Dark-Light, Univ Calif Art Mus, Santa Barbara, 80; Abstract Painting, New York City, Hofstra Univ Gallery, 81; Art Abstrait, Univ Laval, Que, 82; Tondos & Squares, Harm Bouckaert Gallery, New York, 82; Newcastle Salutes New York, Polytechnic Art Gallery, England, 83. *Teaching:* Asst prof grad art, Pratt Inst, 70-83, chmn painting & drawing, 83-; vis prof painting, Parsons Sch Design, 81-83. *Bibliog:* Virginia Gunter (auth), Gerald Hayes: The creativity of the psychological eye, Artforum, 5/73; Robert Pincus-Witten (auth), Entries: Styles of artists and critics, 11/79 & Craig Fisher (auth), Gerald Hayes hybrid investigations, 5/80, Arts Mag. *Mailing Add:* 126 Chambers St New York NY 10007

HAYES, LAURA M
DEALER, HISTORIAN
b Birmingham, Ala, Nov 28, 27. *Study:* Univ Wyo. *Pos:* Head photog section, Wyo State Art Gallery, 65-74, art registrar, 67-71, curator art, 71-79; owner, Wild Goose Gallery, Cheyenne, Wyo. *Mem:* Wyo Press Women; Wyo Prof Photog; Wyo Artist Asn; Nat Fedn Press Women; and others. *Media:* Watercolor. *Mailing Add:* 211 W 18th St Cheyenne WY 82001

HAYES, RANDY (RANDOLPH ALAN)
PAINTER
b Jackson, Miss, June 11, 44. *Study:* Southwestern at Memphis, Tenn, 62-65; Memphis Acad Arts, BFA(Ford Found Grant), 68; Univ Ore, Eugene, 68. *Work:* Laguna Beach Mus Art, Calif; Seattle Art Mus; City Seattle One Percent for Art; Wash State One Percent for Art, Olympia. *Comn:* Murals, Seattle Ctr, 83 & State of Wash, Monroe, 83. *Exhib:* Outside New York: Seattle, The New Mus, New York, 83 & Seattle Art Mus, 83; West Coast Realism, Laguna Beach Mus Art, Calif, 83; solo exhibs, Manolides Gallery, Seattle, 83 & Linda Farris Gallery, Seattle, 84. *Awards:* WGBH New TV Workshop Grant, Boston, 75. *Bibliog:* Suzanne Muchnic (auth), What's wrong with West Coast realism, Los Angeles Times, 6/22/83; Regina Hackett (auth), Seattle artists come home in New York show, Seattle Post-Intelligencer, 10/20/83; Lynn Smallwood (auth), Seattle art from New York City, The Weekly, 10/26/83. *Media:* Pastel; Plexiglass. *Dealer:* Linda Farris Gallery 322 Second Ave S Seattle WA 98104. *Mailing Add:* 85 Yesler Way Seattle WA 98104

HAYES, TUA
PAINTER
b Anniston, Ala. *Study:* Converse Col, BA; Columbia Univ Teacher's Col; also with Henry Lee McFee. *Work:* Del Art Mus, Wilmington; Wilmington Trust Co; Univ Del; Chester Co Art Asn, Pa; Converse Col, Spartanburg, SC; and others. *Exhib:* Philadelphia Pro-Show, Pa, 67; Nat Acad Design, New York, 70; Baltimore Mus Regional Show, Md; Am Drawings 1976, Portsmouth, Va; Distinguished Mid-Atlantic Artists, Univ Del, 80; Del Ctr Contemp Art, 83; and others. *Awards:* First Prize for Drawing, Del Art Mus, 67; Second Prize, Asn Community Art Ctrs, Philadelphia, 82; First Prize, Hercules Expo, 82. *Mem:* Philadelphia Art Alliance; Studio Group, Inc (pres, 54-56); Del Art Mus (bd dirs, 62-80); Hilton Head Art League. *Media:* Oil, Watercolor. *Dealer:* Carspecken-Scott Gallery 1707 N Lincoln St Wilmington DE 19806. *Mailing Add:* 115 Bellant Circle Wilmington DE 19807

HAY-MESSICK, VELMA
PAINTER
b Bloomington, Ill. *Study:* Watercolor with Dong Kingman, 44; Chouinard Art Inst, 47, 48 & 50; Otis Art Inst, 49. *Work:* Seton Hall Univ, Newark, NJ; City of Hope, Duarte, Calif; Grumbacher Artists' Palettes, New York. *Exhib:* Nat League Am Pen Women Southwest Regional, Albuquerque, NMex, 71; Long Beach Community Theatre Gallery, 75; Exhibs, Nat League Am Pen Women, 76 & 77; Messick-Hay Studio Gallery, Apple Valley, Calif, currently; Scottish Cult, Scotland & Colonial Scots Immigrants, 17th century, Guild St Margaret of Scotland, 80; and others. *Pos:* Dir, Messick-Hay Studio Gallery, 52- *Awards:* Key Award, Seton Hall Univ, 58; Second Oils, Calif State Exhib, Nat League Am Pen Women, 71. *Bibliog:* John Oglesby (auth), Lively arts, Sacramento Bee, 57; Vera Williams (auth), Art is a way of life, Southland Mag, 66; Geraldine H Wheeler (ed), Profile, Ben Messick & Velma Hay-Messick, Athelings Mag, 75. *Mem:* Nat League Am Pen Women. *Media:* Oil. *Publ:* Auth, Art spirit in XVII century America, Pen Woman, 6/73; auth, XVII century art, Guild St Margaret of Scotland Mag, 78. *Dealer:* Messick-Hay Studio Gallery 20930 Lone Eagle Rd Apple Valley CA 92307. *Mailing Add:* c/o Messick-Hay Studio Gallery 20930 Lone Eagle Rd Apple Valley CA 92307

HAYNES, DOUGLAS H
PAINTER, EDUCATOR
b Regina, Sask, Jan 1, 36. *Study:* Provincial Inst Technol & Art, Calgary, Alta, with R Spickett; Royal Acad Fine & Appl Arts, The Hague, Holland. *Work:* Edmonton Art Gallery, Alta; Confederation Art Gallery, Charlottetown, PEI; London Pub Mus & Art Gallery, Ont; Univ Calgary, Alta. *Exhib:* Fifth Biennial Exhib Can Art, London, Eng & Ottawa, Can, 63 & Sixth Biennial Exhib, Ottawa, 65; All Alberta '70, Edmonton, 70; West '71 Exhib, Edmonton, 71; Royal Can Acad Arts 91st Ann, Montreal, 71. *Pos:* Art adv, Govt Alta, 67-70. *Teaching:* From assoc prof to prof art & design & chair dept, Univ Alta, 70- *Awards:* Govt of Neth Scholar, 60; All Alta First Prize, Jacox Gallery, 65; Can Coun Sr Award, Can Govt, 67. *Bibliog:* N Yates (auth), Three from Edmonton, Arts Can, 10/69; K Wilkin (auth), Western Canada, a survey, Art in Am, 5-6/72. *Mem:* Assoc Royal Can Acad Arts; Univ Art Asn Can. *Media:* Acrylic, Mixed. *Dealer:* Terry Burrell 207-5210 122nd St Edmonton AB Can. *Mailing Add:* 14312 Ravine Dr Edmonton AB T5N 3M3 Canada

HAYNES, GEORGE EDWARD
PAINTER, ILLUSTRATOR
b Hinton, WVa, Apr 29, 10. *Study:* Phoenix Art Inst, New York; Lockwood Sch Art, Kalamazoo, Mich; Art Inst Pittsburgh. *Work:* United Va Bank, Richmond; Country Club of Va, Richmond; Media General, Richmond; Northminster Baptist Church, Richmond. *Comn:* First Day Docking in America & First Clipper Built in United States Shipyard, Officers Mess, Norfolk Naval Shipyard, 60; mural, Merrimac Restaurant, Portsmouth, 65. *Exhib:* Irene Leach Mem, 64, Norfolk Mus, Tidewater Artists Ann, 65; Hunter Gallery Ann, Chattanooga, Tenn, 64; Va Mus Fine Art, 65; Watercolor USA, Springfield Art Mus, Mo, 72. *Pos:* Dir-owner, Portsmouth Artists Guild, Va, 38-66. *Awards:* Grumbacher Award, Norfolk Mus, 65; Best in Show, Portsmouth Jaycees, 66; Purchase Prizes, Petersburg Arts Festival, 72-74. *Mem:* Tidewater Artist Asn, Norfolk (pres, 63-64); James River Art League, Richmond (gallery dir, 68-). *Media:* Oil, Watercolor. *Dealer:* Art Cove 9030 W Broad St Richmond VA 23229. *Mailing Add:* 1521 Avondale Ave Richmond VA 23227

HAYNES, R (RICHARD THOMAS)
PAINTER, ILLUSTRATOR
b Rome, Ga, Feb 17, 34. *Study:* Auburn Univ, BS, 56; painting with James Harmon, 60; watercolor with Zoltan Szabo, 75. *Work:* Univ Pac, Stockton, Calif; Colby Col, Waterville, Maine; Mo Hist Soc Print Collection, St Louis. *Exhib:* NMex Int, Portales, 76; St Louis Artists Guild, Webster Groves, 77; Southern Watercolor Soc, Columbus Art Mus, Ga, 78; Pittsburgh Aqueous 78, Pa; Ark Wildlife Fedn, Pine Bluff, 78 & 79; and others. *Awards:* First Place, St Louis Co Div Parks, 75; Second Place, NMex Int, 76. *Bibliog:* Member of the issue, North Light Mag, 81. *Mem:* Southern Watercolor Soc; Acad Professional Artists. *Media:* Egg Tempera, Watercolor. *Dealer:* Aldridge Fine Arts I & II 104 Romero NW Albuquerque NM 87104. *Mailing Add:* 22 Orchard Ln Kirkwood MO 63122

HAYNIE, HUGH
CARTOONIST
b Reedville, Va, Feb 6, 27. *Study:* Col William & Mary, AB, 50; Univ Louisville, LHD, 68. *Pos:* Cartoonist, Richmond Times/Dispatch, Va, 50-53, Greensboro Daily News, NC, 53-55 & 56-58, Atlanta J, 55-56, with Louisville Courier J, 58-; ed cartoonist, Syndicated Los Angeles Times. *Awards:* Headliner Award, 66; Freedoms Found Award, 66-70. *Mem:* Soc Alumni Col William & Mary (past dir). *Publ:* Hugh Haynie: Perspective, 74. *Mailing Add:* Courier-Journal 525 W Broadway Louisville KY 40202

HAYWARD, JAMES
PAINTER
b San Francisco, Calif, Sept 22, 43. *Study:* San Diego State Univ, BA; Univ Calif, Los Angeles; Univ Wash, Seattle, MFA. *Work:* Los Angeles Co Mus Art. *Exhib:* New Abstract Painting in Los Angeles, Los Angeles Co Mus Art, 76; Less is More, Sidney Janis Gallery, New York, 77; three-person exhib, Los Angeles Inst Contemp Art, 79; Contemporary Los Angeles Artists, Nagoya City Mus, Japan, 82; Changing Trends--Content & Style, Laguna Beach Mus Art, 82 & Los Angeles Inst Contemp Art, 83; Black on Black, Santa Barbara Contemp Arts Forum, 83; Young Talent 1963-1983, Los Angeles Co Mus Art, 83. *Teaching:* Instr painting, Univ Calif, Berkeley, 83. *Awards:* New Talent, Los Angeles Co Mus Art, 77; Japan-US Friendship Comn Fel, 81-82; Guggenheim Fel, 83-84. *Media:* Acrylic, Oil. *Dealer:* Modernism 236 Eighth St San Francisco CA 94103; Mizuno Gallery 454 N Robertson Los Angeles CA. *Mailing Add:* 12241 Broadway Rd Moorpark CA 93021

HAYWARD, JANE
HISTORIAN, CURATOR
b Orange, Conn, Aug 13, 18. *Study:* Pa Acad Fine Arts, Philadelphia, 36-42; Cresson scholar, 40, 42; Sch Fine Arts, Univ Pa, BFA, 52, MA, 54; Yale Univ, fel 57-58, PhD, 58. *Collections Arranged:* Medieval Art from Private Collections (with catalog), 68-69; The Year 1200 (with catalog), 70; Ecclesiastical Vestments of the Middle Ages, 70; Stained Glass Windows of the Middle Ages & the Renaissance, 71-72; Cloisters Apocalypse Exhib, 73; The Secular Spirit: Life & Art at the End of the Middle Ages, 75. *Pos:* Tech illusr, Am Viscose Corp, Philadelphia, 45-54; res asst, Art Gallery, Yale Univ, 58-61; cur, Lyman Allyn Mus, New London, 61-65; cur, The Cloisters, Metrop Mus Art, New York, 69- *Teaching:* Lectr art hist, Yale Univ, 61; asst prof art hist, Conn Col, New London, 64-67; adj assoc prof art hist, Columbia Univ, 71- *Awards:* Am Coun Learned Socs Fel, 66-67. *Mem:* Col Art Asn; Int Ctr Medieval Art; Soc Francaise d'Archeologie. *Res:* Medieval stained glass. *Publ:* Contribr, History of stained glass, Encycl Americana, 73; auth, Cistercian glazed windows, Gesta, Vol XII, 73. *Mailing Add:* The Cloisters Ft Tryon Park New York NY 10040

HAYWARD, PETER
PAINTER, SCULPTOR
b Keene, NH, Nov 8, 1905. *Study:* Middlebury Col, 21-23. *Work:* USN Combat Art Collection, Washington, DC; State Found Cult & Arts, Hawaii; and others. *Comn:* Destroyers on Maneuvers, San Diego to Pearl Harbor, 60, Proteus, Guam, 66, Apollo 8 Splashdown & Recovery, 68 & Apollo 15 Splashdown & Recovery, Navy Art Coop & Liaison Comt, 72; Reader's Digest covers, Jan & Apr, 78. *Exhib:* Washington Sq Outdoor Art Show (Hors de Concours), New York, 56-63; Salmagundi Fall Show, New York, 60-70; Four Easter Art Festivals, Honolulu, Hawaii, 63-71; Nat Acad Design Shows, New York, 66, 68 & 70; Artists of Hawaii, Honolulu Acad, 68-70. *Teaching:* Instr sculpture, Riverdale Country Sch for Girls, 46-56; instr oil painting, pvt studio, New York summers & Honolulu winters, 62-67. *Awards:* Proctor Prize in Portrait Sculpture, Nat Acad Design, 48-49; Grand Prize All Media, Washington Sq Outdoor Art Show, 56-58. *Mem:* Salmagundi Club; Asn Honolulu Artists; Windward Artists Guild (pres, 69-70); Lahaina Art Asn. *Media:* Oil, Bronze, Clay. *Dealer:* Grand Central Galleries 40 Vanderbilt Ave New York NY 10017; Royal Hawaiian Gallery 2259 Kalakaua Ave Honolulu HI 96815. *Mailing Add:* 53-033 Kamehameha Hwy Hauula HI 96717

HAZEN, JOSEPH H
COLLECTOR
b Kingston, NY. *Mem:* Int Coun Mus Mod Art; Vis Comt Fogg Art Mus; Metrop Mus Art; Acquisitions Comt Nat Gallery; Chmn Emeritus Am Friends Israel Mus. *Collection:* Late nineteenth and early twentieth century paintings. *Mailing Add:* 645 Madison Ave New York NY 10022

HAZLEHURST, FRANKLIN HAMILTON
HISTORIAN, EDUCATOR
b Spartanburg, SC, Nov 6, 25. *Study:* Princeton Univ, BA, 49, MFA, 52, PhD, 56. *Teaching:* Instr art hist, Princeton Univ, 54-56; lectr art hist, Frick Collection, New York, 56-57; from asst to assoc prof, Univ Ga, 57-63; prof & chmn dept fine arts, Vanderbilt Univ, 67- *Awards:* Fulbright Fel, 53-54; Am Coun Learned Soc Grant in Aid, 67; Madison Sarratt Prize, Vanderbilt Univ, 70. *Mem:* Am Archaeol Soc; Col Art Asn Am; Southeastern Col Art Asn (pres, 73-74); French Soc Hist Art; Soc Archit Historians. *Res:* Seventeenth and 18th century French art, especially landscape architecture. *Publ:* Auth, Artistic origins of David's oath of the Horatii, Art Bulletin, 60; auth, Jacques Boyceau and the French Formal Garden, 66; auth, Additional sources for the Medici Cycle, Bulletin Musees Royal Beaux Arts Belg, 67; ed, French Formal Garden, Third Colloquium Landscape Archit, Dumbarton Oaks, 74; auth, Gardens of Illusion: The Genius of Andre Le Nostre, 80; and others. *Mailing Add:* 4430 Shepard Pl Nashville TN 37205

HAZLITT, DON
PAINTER
b Stockton, Calif, Jan 6, 48. *Study:* San Joaquin Delta Col, AA, 69; Sonoma State Col, BA(art), 71; Calif State Univ, Sacramento, MA(art), 73. *Work:* Univ Pac Art Dept; Musee de Toulon, France; Chase Manhattan Collection. *Exhib:* Crocker-Kingsley Art Ann, Crocker Art Mus, Sacramento, Calif, 73-74; Whitney Biennial Contemp Art, New York, 75; Contemp Reflections, Aldrich Mus Contemp Art, Ridgefield, Conn, 75; 15 Contemp New York Artists, Univ Denver, 75; one-man shows, Barbara Gladstone Gallery, New York, 80-81, Musee de Toulon, France, 82 & Rosa Esman Gallery, New York, 83. *Teaching:* Instr, Corpus Christi State Univ, Tex, 81 & Columbia Univ, New York, 82-83. *Awards:* Gold Key Award Art, Scholastic Mag, 67; August Ben-Day Award Art, Alpha Rho Tau, Delta Col, 69; Int Achievement Award, Stockton Arts Comn, 82. *Bibliog:* John Fitzgibbons (auth), article in Arts Mag, 2/80; Susan Larsen (auth), Artists to watch, Artnews, 5/81; Gerrit Henry (auth), article, Art Am, 83. *Media:* Mixed. *Dealer:* Rosa Esman Gallery 121 Spring St New York NY 10012; Galerie Farideh Cadot 77 Rue des Archives Paris France 75013. *Mailing Add:* 114 W 14th St Apt 3W New York NY 10011

HEAD, GEORGE BRUCE
PAINTER, DESIGNER
b St Boniface, Man, Feb 14, 31. *Study:* Univ Man, Dipl(fine art), 53. *Work:* Nat Gallery Can; Pub Libr, Art Mus, London; Montreal Mus Art; Can Coun Art Bank. *Comn:* Oil on panels, Manitoba Teachers Col, 59; cast concrete sculpture, City of Winnipeg Underground Concourse, 78. *Exhib:* Nat Gallery, Australian Art Tour, 67-68; Tenth Winnipeg Art Gallery Biennial, 70; Montreal Spring Exhib; Nat Gallery Can Biennial; one-man show, Winnipeg Art Gallery, 73. *Pos:* Graphic designer, Can Broadcasting Corp, 56- *Awards:* Purchase Prizes, Winnipeg Show, Winnipeg Art Gallery & 20th Western Ont Exhib; Benson & Hedges Art Wall Design Award, 72. *Bibliog:* H Ochi (auth), article, Ideas Mag; W Hertig (auth), Graphics Annual, Graphic Press; article, Art Director Ann; and others. *Mem:* Royal Can Acad. *Media:* Acrylic. *Mailing Add:* c/o 61 Gertie St Winnipeg MB R3A 1B5 Canada

HEAD, ROBERT WILLIAM
PAINTER, EDUCATOR
b Springfield, Ill, Aug 6, 41. *Study:* MacMurray Col, BA(art educ), 63, with Sidman & Foresterling; Kent State Univ, MFA, 65, with Shock, Morrow, Petersham & Short; Colo Outward Bound Sch, 71. *Work:* J B Speed Art Mus, Louisville, Ky; Mint Mus, Charlotte, NC; Del Mar Col, Corpus Christi, Tex; MacMurray Col, Jacksonville, Ill; Massillon Mus, Ohio. *Exhib:* Ball State Univ Nat Drawing Show, Muncie, Ind; Bucknell Nat Drawing Exhib, Lewisburg, Pa; Mainstreams Int Painting Exhib, Marietta, Ohio; Brooks Mem Gallery Show, Memphis, Tenn; Weatherspoon Ann Drawing Exhib, Univ NC. *Teaching:* Chairperson & prof drawing, painting & design, Murray State Univ, 65-; assoc prof drawing & introd art, World Campus Afloat, Chapman

Col, spring 70 & 72. *Awards:* Merit Award for Excellence in Teaching, Murray State Univ, 70; Purchase Award, Mid-States Exhib, Evansville Mus; Distinguished Professor, Murray State Univ. *Mem:* Col Art Asn; Ky Art Educ Asn; Nat Audubon Soc; Ky Ornith Soc. *Media:* Mixed media. *Mailing Add:* Murray State Univ Dept Art Box 2438 Univ Sta Murray KY 42071

HEADLEY, DAVID ALLEN
PAINTER
b Washington, Pa, Dec 11, 46. *Study:* Washington & Jefferson Col, BA, 68. *Work:* Corcoran Gallery Am Art, Washington, DC. *Exhib:* Eastern Mich Univ, Ypsilanti, Mich, 67; Butler Inst Art, Youngstown, Ohio, 67 & 68; Detroit Inst Art, 72; Corcoran Gallery, Washington, DC, 76 & 77; Health, Educ & Welfare Bldg, Washington, DC, 79-80; Manhattan Ctr Gallery, New York, 83; Pratt Inst Gallery, New York, 83; and others. *Awards:* First Prizes, Washington & Jefferson Arts Festival, 65 & 66 & Morgantown Art Asn, WVa, 66 & 67. *Bibliog:* John Deckert (auth), David Headley, Arts Mag, 9/81. *Mailing Add:* 158 Franklin St New York NY 10013

HEALY, ANNE LAURA
SCULPTOR, EDUCATOR
b New York, NY, Oct 1, 39. *Study:* Queens Col, New York, BA, 62. *Work:* Chemical Bank, NY; New York Cult Ctr; Allen Art Mus, Oberlin, Ohio; City Univ Grad Ctr, New York; Mich State Univ, East Lansing; and others. *Exhib:* Contemp Women: Consciousness & Content, Brooklyn Mus, NY, 77; individual exhib, Alfred Univ, 79; group exhib, South East Tex Mus, Corpus Christi, 77, Baruch Col, New York, 78, Candidates for Grants, Am Acad & Inst of Arts & Letters, 79 & Hofstra Univ, Hempstead, NY, 80; plus many others. *Teaching:* Instr sculpture, St Ann's Sch, Brooklyn; vis artist, Mich State Univ, East Lansing, 73 & Broward Col, Ft Lauderdale, Fla, 76; vis artist-in-residence, Univ Cincinnati, 76; adj asst prof, Baruch Col, City Univ New York, 76-; guest lectr, Sch Visual Arts, New York, 77, Bard Col & Univ Iowa, 78 & Univ Northern Iowa, 79; vis prof sculpture, Univ Iowa, Iowa City, 79, Univ Calif, Berkeley, 81- *Awards:* Award for Sculpture, Asn Am Univ Women, 76-77; Am Acad & Inst Arts & Letters, 79-80; Macdowell Colony, 80. *Bibliog:* Ellen Lubbell (auth), Healy's double header, Soho Weekly News, 10/18/78; Corinne Robins (auth), Anne Healey: ten years of temporal sculpture, arts, 10/78; The great goddess, Heresies 5th Issue, spring 78. *Mem:* Col Art Asn; Women's Caucus Art Asn. *Media:* Sculpture. *Dealer:* AIR Gallery 63 Crosby St New York NY 10012. *Mailing Add:* Dept Art Kroeber Hall Univ Calif Berkeley CA 94720

HEALY, DEBORAH ANN
ILLUSTRATOR, EDUCATOR
b Newark, NJ. *Study:* Col New Rochelle, BA; Montclair State Col, MA, 76; Syracuse Univ, with Isadore Selzer, James McMullen, Doug Johnson, Murray Tinkleman & others, MFA, 79. *Work:* Danish Pub Television; Swedish Pub Television; Italian Pub Television; Vanderbilt Univ; US Army. *Comn:* Six Sillies (film segments), Maureen Selwood, New York, 73; films, Owl & Pussycat, 80 & Three Love Poems, 82, Texture Films, New York; and others. *Exhib:* Film Festival, Morris Mus Arts & Sci, Morristown, NJ, 76; Artist in Am Series, Fairleigh Dickenson Col, Madison, NJ, 76; Annecy Int Film Festival, Paris, France, 77; Zagreb Int Animation Festival, Yugoslavia, 78; Sinking Creek Winners' Invitational, Chicago Art Inst, 78; Invitational, Montclair Art Mus, NJ, 79; and others. *Teaching:* Instr design & illus, Montclair State Col, 76-; lectr, Parsons Sch Design, 82- *Awards:* First Prize/Best in Show, Stockton State Spring Film Festival, NJ, 78; Grant, Alumni Asn, Montclair State Col, 80; Film grant, NJ State Coun Arts, 81-82; and others. *Mem:* NJ Women's Caucus Art (rec/corresp secy & ed, 78-79); Asn Int Film Animation; Col Art Asn; Graphic Artists Guild; Soc Illustrators; and others. *Media:* Film. *Dealer:* Art Direction Gallery. *Mailing Add:* 72 Watchung Ave Upper Montclair NJ 07043

HEALY, JULIA SCHMITT
PAINTER, EDUCATOR
b Elmhurst, Ill, Mar 28, 47. *Study:* Univ Chicago, 66-70; Yale Univ Summer Sch, 69, with Mel Bochner, Bob Mangold & Bob Moskowitz; Art Inst of Chicago, BFA, 70, MFA, 72. *Work:* Can Coun Art Bank, Ottawa, Ont; NS Art Bank, Halifax; Confederation Art Gallery, Charlottetown, PEI; Mount St Vincent Univ Art Gallery, Halifax; Dept of Educ, Prov of NS, Halifax. *Comn:* Halifax Diary (print), Dept Pub Works, NS, 75. *Exhib:* Art Inst Chicago, 72 & 76; solo exhibs, Owens Art Gallery, Mt Allison Univ, Sackville, NB, 77 & Susan Whitney Gallery, Regina, Sask, 81 & 83; Young Contemporaries (travelling exhib), London Art Gallery, Ont, 76-78; Atlantic Jour (travelling exhib), Nat Gallery of Can, 76-77; Drawing Centre, New York, 80 & 82; and others. *Collections Arranged:* Intercourse (co-cur with Ray Johnson), Wabash Transit Gallery, Chicago, 71; Grassroots-Nova Scotian Folk Art, Eye Level Gallery, Halifax, 75. *Pos:* Dir, Eye Level Gallery, 75-76. *Teaching:* Instr visual art, Ocean Co Col, Toms River, NJ, 79-82. *Awards:* Purchase Award, Graphics Atlantic, Mount St Vincent Univ, 76; Can Coun Arts grant, 76-77 & 77-78. *Bibliog:* Ron Shuebrook (auth), The Atlantic Provinces: Letter, Artscanada, 3/75; Marilyn Smith (auth), Some Nova Scotian Women Artists, 12/75 & Ron Shuebrook (auth), Some Major Nova Scotian Painters, 10-11/76, Art Mag. *Mem:* Col Art Asn; Found Commun of Artists. *Media:* Mixed Media. *Publ:* Ed, Recent Work: Julia Schmitt Healy, Dalhousie Art Gallery, 76. *Dealer:* Phyllis Kind Gallery 226 E Ontario Chicago IL 60611; Susan Whitney Gallery 1627 Victoria Regina SK. *Mailing Add:* 22 Marion Ave Staten Island NY 10304

HEANY, DAVID CAMERON
SCULPTOR
b Pittsburgh, Pa, Jan 19, 51. *Study:* Skowhegan Sch Painting & Sculpture, Maine, 71; Atlanta Col Art, Ga, BFA, 72. *Work:* Peachtree Walk Park, Atlanta, Ga. *Comn:* Steel sculpture, City Atlanta, Ga, 75; Broken Fall (sculpture), Midtown Bus Asn, Atlanta, Ga, 81. *Exhib:* High Mus Art, Atlanta, 72, 74 & 77; Miss Mus Art, Jackson, 78 & 79; solo exhib, Southeastern Ctr Contemp Art, Winston-Salem, NC, 79; Atlanta Art Workers Coalition Gallery, Ga, 81. *Awards:* Grants, Nat Endowment Arts, 74 & 81; Grant, Cent Atlanta Prog & Ford Found, 81. *Bibliog:* Dan Talley (auth), Conversations with artists, Atlanta Art Papers, 78; Brigid Panter (producer), David Heany/Sculptor (film), Ga Pub TV, 81. *Mem:* Atlanta Art Workers Coalition, Ga. *Media:* Welded Steel. *Publ:* Coauth & ed, Hire an artist, Atlanta Art Workers, 81. *Dealer:* Eve Mannes Gallery East Paces Ferry Rd Atlanta GA 30305. *Mailing Add:* 541 Edgewood Ave SE Atlanta GA 30312

HEARN, M F (MILLARD FILLMORE), JR
ADMINISTRATOR, HISTORIAN
b Lincoln, Ala, Aug 18, 38. *Study:* Auburn Univ, Ala, BA, 60; Ind Univ, MA(hist), 64, MA(art hist), 66, PhD, 69; Univ Calif, Berkeley, study with Jean Bony, 65-66; Courtauld Inst Art, 66-67. *Teaching:* From instr to prof medieval art & archit, Univ Pittsburgh, 67-, actg chmn fine arts dept, 73-74, chmn, 74-78, dir archit studies prog, 81- *Res:* Romanesque and Gothic architecture of England and France; Romanesque and Gothic sculpture of France and Italy. *Publ:* Auth, The Rectangular Ambulatory in English Medieval Architecture, J Soc Archit Historians, Vol 30, 71; auth, On the Original Nave of Ripon Cathedral, J Brit Archaeol Asn, Vol 35, 72; auth, Romsey Abbey: A Progenitor of the English National Tradition in Medieval Architecture, GESTA, Vol 14, 75; auth, Romanesque Sculpture: The Revival of Monumental Stone Sculpture in the Eleventh and Twelfth Centuries, Ithaca and Oxford, 81; auth, Ripon Minster: The Beginning of the Gothic Style in Northern England, Philadelphia Book Co, 83. *Mailing Add:* Univ of Pittsburgh 104 Frick Fine Arts Bldg Pittsburgh PA 15260

HEATH, DAVID C
DEALER
b Atlanta, Ga, June 6, 40. *Study:* Vanderbilt Univ; Univ Vienna; Columbia Univ. *Pos:* Pres, Heath Gallery, currently. *Specialty:* 20th century American, particularly of the '60's and '70's. *Mailing Add:* 416 East Paces Ferry Rd NE Atlanta GA 30305

HEATH, DAVID MARTIN
EDUCATOR, PHOTOGRAPHER
b Philadelphia, Pa, June 27, 31. *Study:* Philadelphia Col Art, 54-55; New Sch, with W Eugene Smith, 59 & 61. *Work:* Nat Gallery Can, Ottawa; Nat Film Bd Can; Mus Mod Art, New York; Int Mus Photog, George Eastman House, Rochester, NY; Philadelphia Mus Art. *Exhib:* A Dialogue with Solitude, Eastman House, Rochester & Art Inst Chicago, 64; Nat Gallery Can, 67, 74 & 81; Beyond the Gates of Eden, Peale Galleries Fine Art, Philadelphia, 70; Photography in America, Whitney Mus Art, New York, 74; Mirrors & Windows: Am Photog since 1960, Mus of Mod Art, New York, 78; Songs of Innocence, Harbourfront Gallery, Toronto, 81. *Pos:* Artist in residence, Univ Minn, Minneapolis, 65 & Int Ctr Photog, NY, 78. *Teaching:* Instr photog, Sch Dayton Art Inst, 65-67; asst prof photog, Moore Col Art, Philadelphia, 67-70; prof photog, Ryerson Polytech Inst, 70-; adj fac, Visual Studies Workshop, 76-77. *Awards:* Guggenheim Found Fel, 63 & 64. *Bibliog:* Charles Hagen (auth), Le grand ALBUM ordinaire, Afterimage Visual Studies Workshop, 2/74; James Borcoman (auth), David Heath: a dialogue with solitude, J 34, Nat Gallery of Can, 10/79. *Mem:* Soc Photog Educ. *Media:* Slide/Sound, Chromogenic Print. *Publ:* Contribr, Contemporary Photographer, Vol 5 No 1; auth, A Dialogue with Solitude, Community Press, 65; contribr, Photography in the 20th Century, 67; contribr, Photography in America, 75; contribr, Mirrors and Windows, 78. *Mailing Add:* 120 Wolfrey Ave Toronto ON M4K 1L3 Canada

HEATON, MAURICE
DESIGNER, CRAFTSMAN
b Neuchatel, Switz, Apr 2, 1900. US citizen. *Study:* Ethical Cult Schs, 15-19; Stevens Inst Technol, 20-21. *Work:* Metrop Mus Art, Cooper Union Mus Art & Mus Contemp Crafts, New York; Newark Mus Art, NJ; Corning Mus Glass, NY; Hudson River Mus, Yonkers, NY. *Comn:* Glass mural, Polygraphic Co Am; glass mobile, Valley Cottage Free Libr, NY; stained glass windows, glass murals & lighting fixtures for pvt comns, 23- *Exhib:* One-man & group shows in more than thirty mus & galleries in US & Can, and traveling exhibs. *Teaching:* Lectr glass, Renwick Gallery & Smithsonian Inst, Washington, DC. *Awards:* Medal, Boston Soc Arts & Crafts, 56; First Prize for Glass, Wichita Art Asn, 60. *Mem:* Artist-Craftsmen New York; Am Craft Coun; Rockland Ctr for Arts; Boston Soc Arts & Crafts. *Mailing Add:* 347 Old Mill Rd Valley Cottage NY 10989

HEBALD, MILTON ELTING
SCULPTOR, PRINTMAKER
b New York, NY, May 24, 17. *Study:* Art Students League, with Ann Goldwaithe, 27-28; Nat Acad Design, with Gordon Samstag, 31-32; Master Inst United Art, 31-34; Beaux-Arts Inst Design, 32-35. *Work:* Whitney Mus Am Art; Philadelphia Mus Art; Tel-Aviv Mus, Israel; Va Mus Fine Arts; Joyce Mus, Dublin, Ireland; and many others. *Comn:* Bronze frieze, Pan-Am Terminal, Kennedy Airport, NY; Ackland Mem, Univ NC; James Joyce Monument, Zurich, Switz, 66; Marshall Field Mem, Sun Times Bldg, Chicago, Ill, 66; Tempest Group Bronze, Central Park, New York, 72; and many others. *Exhib:* Va Mus Fine Arts, 67; solo exhibs, Yares Gallery,

Scottsdale, 76-78, Harmon Gallery, naples, Fla, 78, Randall Galleries, New York, 78, Byck Gallerry, Louisville, Ky, 78 & Cheekwood, Nashville, 78; and others. *Teaching:* Instr, Brooklyn Mus Sch Art, 46-51; instr, Cooper Union, 46-53; instr, Univ Minn, 49; instr, Skowhegan Sch Painting & Sculpture, summers 50-52; instr, Long Beach State Univ, Calif, summer 68. *Awards:* Second Prize, Pa Acad Fine Arts, 51; First Prize New York City Dept Pub Works, for E Bronx TB Hosp, 52; Prix de Rome, 55-58; and others. *Bibliog:* Martha C Cheney (auth), Modern Art in America, McGraw-Hill, 39; C Ludwig Brumme (auth), Contemporary American Sculpture, Crown, 48; Frank Getlein (auth), Milton Hebald, Viking, 71. *Mem:* Fel Am Acad in Rome; An Am Group. *Media:* Bronze, Wood; Lithography. *Mailing Add:* Via Santo Celso 22 Bracciano 00062 Italy

HEBERLING, GLEN AUSTIN
PAINTER, ILLUSTRATOR
b Ambridge, Pa, Nov 18, 15. *Study:* Ad Art Studio Sch, Pittsburgh, Pa, 36; Art Inst Pittsburgh, scholar, 36-38; Art Students League, New York, 46-48 & 51. *Work:* Old Economy Hist Mus, Ambridge, Pa; Ladycliff Col, Highland Falls, NY. *Comn:* World War II Mem Mural, Highland Falls High Sch, 50; five paintings, Marine Midland Bank, Highland Falls, 67; and many pvt comns. *Exhib:* Assoc Artists Pittsburgh, Carnegie Mus, 38-47; Am Watercolor Soc, Nat Acad Galleries, NY, 44-46; Butler Inst Am Art, Youngstown, Ohio, 45; US Army Arts Contest Nat, Nat Gallery Art, Washington, DC, 45; ACA Gallery, New York, 46; Boston Mus Fine Arts, 49; Kennedy Gallery, New York, 50; Artists of the Upper Hudson, Albany Inst Art & Hist, NY, 47; and others. *Pos:* Illusr, US Mil Acad, West Point, NY, 58-71. *Teaching:* Instr & lectr, Ladycliff Col, 61-71, Garrison Art Ctr, NY, 76, Mt St Mary Col, Newburgh, NY, 76 & Rec Serv, West Point, NY, 58-71. *Awards:* Orange Co Watercolor Soc Awards, 79-82; Newburgh, NY Art Show Ann Awards, 80 & 81; Arts Coun Orange Co, NY Awards, 81 & 83. *Mem:* Orange Co Watercolor Soc, NY. *Media:* All. *Publ:* Illusr, Handbook on Physical Education, 44; illusr, En Busco de Oro Negro, 59; illusr, Assembly, Asn Grads, West Point, 66; illusr, Kepler & Discovery of His Planetary Laws, 69; illusr, Engineering Fundamentals, 70. *Mailing Add:* 58 Church St Highland Falls NY 10928

HECHT, MARY
SCULPTOR
b New York, NY, June 23, 31; US & Can citizen. *Study:* Art Student's League, with Frank Riley & Reginald Marsh, 48 & 52; Columbia Univ, with David Fredenthal, 50; Univ Cincinnati, BA, 52; State Univ Iowa, MA, 57; Camberwell Sch Art, London. *Work:* Indianapolis Mus Art; Hamilton Art Gallery, Ont; Fairfield Univ, Conn; Ramapo Col, NY; Reconstructionist Rabinical Col, Philadelphia. *Comn:* Sculpture, comn by Kaiser Aluminum for Prime Minister Nehru, India, 63; The Jesse Tree (bronze relief), Kaiser Aluminum, Calif, 64; Flowers (bronze relief), Mt Sinai Hosp, New York, 64; Torah adornments (silver, with Paul Mayer), Temple Beth Shalom, Peabody, Mass, 81; Reconstructionist Synagogue Toronto, Ont, 82. *Exhib:* Interfaith Exhib Liturgical Art & Archit, Boston & Chicago, 76 & 81; Am Soc Contemp Artists, New York, 78-82; Catherine Lorillard Wolfe Exhib, New York; solo show, Hyde Collection, Glen Falls, NY, 81; Sculptors Soc Can, Toronto & traveling, 82; and others. *Teaching:* Tutor, York Univ, 77-; instr sculpture, Mohawk Community Col, 73-78; teacher, Inner City Angels, Toronto, 73- *Awards:* Artist in School Award, Ont Arts Coun, 75 & 79; Excalibur Bronze Work Award, Excalibur Foundry, 83. *Bibliog:* Antonio de Franco (auth), Art ego and consumer, Univ Waterloo, 2/73; James Purdie (auth), Hecht's art, Globe & Mail, 10/75; James Kettlewell (auth), Introduction to Mary Hecht, Ramapo Col/Hyde Collection, 1/81. *Mem:* Sculptors Soc Can; Am Soc Contemp Artists. *Media:* Bronze, Wood. *Publ:* Ed & illusr, Middle East Focus, Can Acad Found Peace Mid-East, 78-; illusr, Wagner notes, Wagner Soc New York, 79- *Dealer:* Gustafsson Galleries 107 Scollard Ave Toronto ON Can. *Mailing Add:* 267 St George St Toronto ON M5R 2P9 Canada

HECKSCHER, MORRISON HARRIS
CURATOR, HISTORIAN
b Harrisburg, Pa, Dec 12, 40. *Study:* Wesleyan Univ, BA; Univ Del, MA(early Am cult); 18th century English archit studied with Rudolf Wittkower, Columbia Univ. *Collections Arranged:* The Easy Chair in Am, 71 & An Architect & His Client: Frank Lloyd Wright & Francis W Little, 73, Metrop Mus of Art, New York. *Pos:* Chester Dale fel, Print Dept, Metrop Mus of Art, New York, 66-68; asst cur to cur, Am Wing, 68-78; cur, Am Decorative Arts, 78. *Teaching:* Lectr Am archit, Columbia Univ, 74-75. *Mem:* Soc of Archit Historians (dir, 73-76, pres, NY chap, 73-75); Furniture Hist Soc. *Res:* Eighteenth century American architecture and decorative arts, especially furniture; Eighteenth century English architecture and furniture. *Publ:* Auth, Form and Frame: New Thoughts on the American Easy Chair, 71 & The New York Serpentine Card Table, 73, Antiques Mag; contrib, The Chase, The Capture: Collecting at the Metropolitan, Metrop Mus, 75; auth, Lock and Copland: catalogue of the engraved works, Furniture History, 79; auth, John Townsends's block and shell furniture, Antiques Mag, 82. *Mailing Add:* 176 W 87th St New York NY 10024

HECKSCHER, WILLIAM SEBASTIAN
HISTORIAN
b Hamburg, Ger, Dec 14, 04; Can citizen. *Study:* Univ Hamburg, PhD, 35; NY Univ; Oxford Univ; McGill Univ, Montreal, DLett, 81. *Work:* Drawings, Kunsthalle, Hamburg, Ger. *Exhib:* One-man show, Allied Arts Gallery, Durham, NC, 67. *Pos:* Consult, Dept Rare Bks, Princeton Univ Libr, 76- *Teaching:* Univ Man, Sask, State Univ Iowa, 47-55; chmn & dir, Iconological Inst, Univ Utrecht, 55-66; chmn dept art, Duke Univ, 66-69, Benjamen N Duke prof & dir, Art Mus, 70-; Samuel H Kress prof in residence, Nat Gallery

Art, Washington, DC, 79-80; lectr, Col de France, Paris, 80-81. *Awards:* Festschrift, Netherlands Yearbook Hist Art, 64. *Bibliog:* Eric Koch (auth), Deemed Suspect, Toronto, Ont, 80; and others. *Mem:* Fel Folger Shakespeare Libr; Benjamin Franklin Fel Royal Soc Arts, London; corresp mem Soc Indexers London; Inst Advan Study, Princeton, NJ; res fel Herzog August Bibliothek, Wolfenbuttel, Ger, 81. *Publ:* Auth, books, exhibition catalogues, articles in the field of art history, iconology, history of anatomy, index making & emblematics; illusr books. *Mailing Add:* 32 Wilton St Princeton NJ 08540

HEDBERG, GREGORY SCOTT
CURATOR, HISTORIAN
b Minneapolis, Minn, May 2, 46. *Study:* Princeton Univ, BA, 68; Inst Fine Arts, NY Univ, MA, 71, PhD, 80. *Collections Arranged:* Barbizon School, Minneapolis Inst Arts, 75; Picasso, Braque, Leger (coauth, catalog), 75; Charles Biederman: A Retrospective (auth, catalog), 76; Millet's Gleaners (auth, catalog), 78; Victorian High Renaissance (auth, catalog), Manchester City Art Galleries, Minneapolis Inst Arts & Brooklyn Mus, 78-79; Leger's Le Grand Dejewner (auth, catalog), 80; German Realism of the Twenties: The Artist as Social Critic (auth, catalog), Minneapolis & Chicago, 80; The Tremaine Collection (auth, catalog), Hartford, 84. *Pos:* Lectr, Frick Collection, New York, 71-74; cur paintings, Minneapolis Inst Arts, 74-81; chief cur, Wadsworth Atheneum, Hartford, 81- *Res:* Fifteenth century painting in Rome. *Publ:* Auth, The Farnese Courtyard Windows and the Porta Pia: Michelangelo's creative process, Marsyas, 71; auth, The Jerome Hill bequest: Delacroix's Fanatics of Tangiers and Corot's Silenus, 76 & In favor of Nicola di Maestro Antonio d'Ancona, 77, Minneapolis Inst Arts Bulletin. *Mailing Add:* 125 Westerly Terrace Hartford CT 06105

HEDDEN-SELLMAN, ZELDA
PAINTER, INSTRUCTOR
b Farmington, Ill. *Study:* Bradley Univ, BS & MA; Ohio Univ; Harvard Univ; Western Reserve Univ; also with Ben Shahn, Arnold Blanch & Gladys Rockmore Davis. *Work:* Manias Manor, Peoria, Ill; Expos Bldg, Springfield, Ill; Spoon River Col, Canton, Ill. *Exhib:* Old Northwest Territory Show, Springfield, 52; Ohio Valley Watercolor Show, Athens, 53; Ill State Mus, Springfield, 59; three-man show, Kottler Gallery, New York, 72; one-man show, Western Ill Univ, 79 & 81. *Pos:* Dir, Peoria Art Ctr Sch, 54-56. *Teaching:* Instr art, Ind State Univ, Terre Haute, 53-54; insr art, Ill Cent Col, Peoria, 69-71; instr art, Spoon River Col, 66-74; instr, Bradley Univ, 76- *Awards:* Cent Ill Artists Award. *Media:* Acrylic, Watercolor. *Publ:* Auth, Treasures in the Snow, 64. *Dealer:* Upstairs Gallery Lakeview Ctr for Arts & Sci 1125 W Lake Ave Peoria IL 61614. *Mailing Add:* 241 Timberland Metamora IL 61548

HEDIN, DONALD MONROE
PAINTER, DIRECTOR
b Bridgeport, Conn, Nov 5, 20. *Study:* Pratt Inst, cert, 41; Art Students League, 45. *Work:* Favell Mus (five pieces), Klamath Falls, Ore. *Comn:* Christmas Stamp, US Postal Serv, DC, 75 & Savings & Loan Commemorative Stamp, 80. *Exhib:* The Decoy, Soc Illustrators Ann Exhib, New York, 70, The Bucket, 71, Bronte Homestead, 72, The Brown Cupboard, 73 & The Anvil, 80. *Pos:* Assoc art ed, Readers Dig, Pleasantville, NY, 48- *Awards:* William Church Osborne Award, Am Watercolor Soc, 54; Cert of Excellence, Soc Illustrators, 68; First Prize, Conn Festival Art, 70. *Bibliog:* Wendon Blake (auth), Complete Guide to Acrylic Painting, Watson-Guptill, 71; Henry C Pitz (auth), Inventing new challenges, Am Artist Mag, 10/72; Diane Finegold (auth), Artist as historian, storyteller and master craftsman, Southwest Art Mag, 8/77. *Mem:* Soc Illustrators (secy); Am Watercolor Soc. *Media:* Watercolor and Acrylic. *Mailing Add:* Heritage Hills 46-C Somers NY 10589

HEDMAN, TERI JO
PRINTMAKER, PAINTER
b St Paul, Minn, Oct 10, 44. *Study:* Univ Minn, BS(design); also with Paul Hapke, Toshi Yoshido, Pat Austin & Marge Horton. *Exhib:* All Alaska Exhib, 72, 74, 75 & 78; one-man show, Univ Minn, 67 & Artique Ltd, 73-80. *Pos:* Designer-draftsman, Minneapolis Housing Authority, 68-70; interior designer, Tiptons Interiors, Anchorage, 70-71. *Teaching:* Traveling instr printmaking, Naknek, Bethel & Nome, Alaska, 73. *Awards:* Print Award, All Alaska Juried Exhib, 78; Purchase Award, State Art Bank, State Print Competition, 79. *Mem:* Alaska Artists Guild (prof chmn, 72, funding chmn, 73, vpres, 74, pres, 75, mem bd, 76, vpres, 80); Anchorage Arts Coun (visual arts adv comt, 75). *Dealer:* The Gathering 28 Creek St Ketchikan AK 99901; Artique 314 G St Anchorage AK 99501. *Mailing Add:* 2219 St Elias Dr Anchorage AK 99503

HEDRICK, WALLY BILL
PAINTER, SCULPTOR
b Pasadena, Calif, July 21, 28. *Study:* Otis Art Inst; Calif Sch Fine Arts, BFA, 55; Calif Col Arts & Crafts; San Francisco State Col. *Work:* Mus Mod Art, New York; Aldridge Mus Contemp Art, Ridgefield, Conn; Oakland Mus Art; Los Angeles Mus Art; San Francisco Art Comn. *Exhib:* 16 Americans, Mus Mod Art, New York, 59; Places, San Francisco Mus Art, 62; Balboa Pavilion Gallery, Newport, Calif, 67; one-man show, Sonoma State Col Gallery, 68 & Gallery Paule Anglim, San Francisco, 82; Poets of the Cities, Dallas Mus Art, 74; Directions in Bay Area Painting, Univ Calif, Davis, 83; The Urban Milieu, Gallery Paule Anglim, San Francisco, 83. *Teaching:* Instr painting & drawing, San Francisco Art Inst, 60-70; instr painting & drawing, San Jose State Col, 72-74; instr painting & sculpture, Indian Valley Col, 75- *Awards:* Purchase Award, Los Angeles Co Mus, Los Angeles, 53; Purchase Award, San Francisco Art Comn, 58 & 76 & San Francisco Mus Mod Art, 76; Nat Endowment Arts Grant, 68 & 82. *Bibliog:* William Morehouse (auth), Funk

Daddy (catalog), Sonoma State Col, 68; Wayne Andersen (auth), American Sculpture in Process: 1930/1970, NY Graphic Soc, 75; Dan Tooker (auth), interview in Art Int, Vol 19 (Oct, 1975). *Media:* Oil, Welded Metal. *Mailing Add:* 2569 Whitaker Bluff Rd Fallon CA 94932

HEE, HON-CHEW
PAINTER, INSTRUCTOR

b Kahului, Hawaii, Jan 24, 06. *Study:* Calif Sch Fine Arts, dipl, 32; Art Students League, 48-49; Andre L'hote & Fernand Leger, Paris, 49-51. *Work:* Honolulu Acad Arts; Tennent Art Found Art Gallery, Honolulu; State of Hawaii Found Cult & Arts. *Comn:* Concrete mural, Hawaiian Holiday Bldg, Honolulu, 62; carved redwood mural, Honolulu Community Church, 65; enamel on metal murals, Manoa Libr, 78, Enchanted Lake Elem Sch, 79 & Kauai Community Col, 80. *Exhib:* 140th Ann Exhib, Nat Acad Design, New York, 65; 11th Ann Exhib, Artist Hawaii, Honolulu, 66; Nat Ann Exhib, El Paso Mus Art, Tex, 72; Taiwan Nat Hist Mus, 73; one-man show, Honolulu Acad Arts. *Collections Arranged:* Int show, Solon de l'Art Libre, Paris, 50. *Pos:* Dir, Tennent Art Found Gallery, 67- *Teaching:* Lectr watercolor, Univ Hawaii, Honolulu, 60-70; prof watercolor, Taiwan Normal Univ, Taipei, 71-72, prof serigraph, 72-73. *Awards:* Serigraphy for Text Book, Dr Sun Yet Sen Grant, Taiwan, 71; Artist of the Year, Hawaii Sertoma Club, 81; Gold Plaque for Serigrapher of Taiwan, 83. *Bibliog:* Demonstration of watercolor, Pau Hana Year, Univ TV Sta, 73; Haar & Neogy (auths), Artists of Hawaii, Univ Hawaii, 74. *Mem:* Hawaii Watercolor Soc (founder & pres, 61). *Publ:* Ed, Serigraphy Text, 71; auth, Thirty Serigraphs, 73; auth, Water Color, 75; ed & illusr, White Serpent, 78; auth, Yin Yang, 82. *Mailing Add:* 45-650 Kapunahala Rd Kaneohe HI 96744

HEFLIN, TOM PAT
PAINTER, DESIGNER

b Monticello, Ark, July 18, 34. *Study:* Northeast La State Col; Chicago Art Inst. *Work:* Marietta Col; Burpee Art Mus, First Nat Bank, & First Fed Savings, Rockford, Ill; Hill, Sherman, Meroni, Gross & Simpson Law Off, Chicago. *Exhib:* Chicago Art Inst, 71-73; House of Cong, Washington, DC, 72; Butler Inst Am Art, Youngstown, Ohio, 73; New Horizons in Art, Chicago, 75; Am Watercolor Soc, New York, 75. *Teaching:* Instr painting, Burpee Art Mus, 69-71 & Rock Valley Col, 70- *Awards:* First Prize Medal, Nat Soc Painters Casein & Acrylic; First Prize, Ark Nationwide Bicentennial Medal Design, Franklin Mint; First Prize in Painting, Mainstreams 72, Ohio. *Bibliog:* Article, Famous Artists Mag, 70. *Mem:* Nat Soc Painters in Casein & Acrylic; Rockford Art Asn; Fishy Whale Litho Workshop, Milwaukee. *Media:* Oil, Acrylic. *Publ:* Auth, Quiet Places, 77. *Dealer:* Overland Trail Gallery Main St Scottsdale AZ 85251; Call of The Wild Gallery Dallas TX. *Mailing Add:* 1162 S Weldon Rd Rockford IL 61102

HEFNER, HARRY SIMON
PAINTER, EDUCATOR

b Kalamazoo, Mich, Nov 20, 11. *Study:* Western Mich Univ, BA, 36; Columbia Univ, MA, 39. *Work:* Kalamazoo Col; South Bend Art Ctr; Albion Col; Western Mich Univ. *Exhib:* Detroit Inst Arts, 63-64; Kalamazoo Inst Arts, 63-66; Grand Rapids Inst Arts, Mich, 64-65; South Bend Inst Arts, Ind, 64-66; Battle Creek Inst Arts, 66; plus others. *Teaching:* Instr, Muskegon Pub Schs, Mich, 37-38, Cranbrook Boys Sch, summers 37-39 & Skidmore Col, 39; mem fac, Western Mich Univ, 40-77, prof watercolor & design, 56-77, head dept art, 63-66, emer prof, 77-; teacher, Harvard Univ, summer 41 & Univ Vt, summers 54-56; retired. *Mem:* Mich Watercolor Soc. *Mailing Add:* 3012 Bristol Court Bronson Woods Kalamazoo MI 49008

HEIDEL, FREDERICK (H)
PAINTER, EDUCATOR

b Corvallis, Ore, Dec 29, 15. *Study:* Univ Ore, with Andrew Vincent, David McCosh & Lance Hart, BS; Art Inst Chicago, with Boris Anisfeld & Francis Chapin, BFA & MFA(Anna Louise Raymond Foreign Traveling Fel). *Work:* World Bk Art Collection, Chicago; Portland Art Mus, Ore; Hazeltine Collection, Mus Art, Eugene, Ore; Eastern Ore Col, La Grande, Ore; Kaiser Found, Portland. *Comn:* Mural, Lane Co Comn, Lane Co Courthouse, Eugene, 58; fused glass wall, comn by Sally Stafford, Eugene, 70; fused glass panel, Brock Dixon House, Forest Grove, Ore, 70; laminated glass construction, Portland State Univ, Sci I Bldg, 71; laminated glass window, comn by Mr & Mrs Marvin Witt, Portland. *Exhib:* Drawing & Watercolor Exhib, Metrop Mus Art, New York, 51; Sao Paulo 3rd Biennial, Brazil, 56; 2nd Pac Coast Biennial, WCoast, 57; Vancouver, BC, 58; The West: 80 Contemporaries, 67. *Teaching:* Instr painting, Long Beach City Col, 46-49; instr painting, Univ Ore, 49-53; prof painting, Portland State Univ, 51-, head dept art & archit, 55-82, emer prof, 82. *Awards:* Painting Award, San Francisco Mus Art, 48; Chapelbrook Found Fel, 67. *Bibliog:* Rachel Griffin (auth), Painting & Sculpture of the Pacific Northwest, Portland Art Mus, 59; Nancy McCauley (auth), article, Artweek, Vol 13, No 15. *Mem:* Portland Art Asn; Col Art Asn Am; Art Ore. *Mailing Add:* Dept of Art Portland State Univ Portland OR 97207

HEIFERMAN, MARVIN
DEALER

b New York, NY, 1948. *Study:* Brooklyn Col, BA, 68; Columbia Univ: Sch Arts, Film Div; Sch Visual Arts, New York; Brooklyn Mus Art Sch. *Collections Arranged:* All Photographic Exhibitions, Castelli Graphics Inc, 74-; Some Color Photographs (auth, catalog), Castelli Graphics & Independent Curators Inc, 77-81; Picture Books, Franklin Furnace, NY, 78; Pictures of People, Soho Ctr for Visual Arts, 78. *Pos:* Asst dir, Light Gallery, New York, 72-74; dir photog, Castelli Graphics, New York, 75- *Specialty:* Contemporary photography. *Mailing Add:* Castelli Graphics Inc 44 E 77th St New York NY 10021

HEILOMS, MAY
PAINTER

US citizen. *Study:* Hunter Col; Art Students League. *Work:* Philadelphia Mus, Pa; Norfolk Mus, Va; Samuel Fleisher Art Found, Philadelphia; Bat Yam Mus, Israel; Kenny Int Art Found. *Exhib:* Pa Acad Fine Arts, Philadelphia; Denver Mus, Colo; Corcoran Gallery, Washington, DC; Okla Mus, Oklahoma City; Butler Inst Am Art, Youngstown, Ohio; one-man shows, Bennett Col, 61, Silvermine Guild, Conn, Cent State Mus, Okla, Cortland Art Ctr, New York, Hudson Gallery, New York & Mus Fine Arts, Mexico City; also in Portugal, Italy, Greece, Belgium, Israel, Can, Mex & Arg. *Pos:* Vpres, Nat Asn Women Artists, 60. *Teaching:* Instr fine art, City Col New York, 60-62; instr indust & fine art, Fashion Inst Technol, 63-65. *Awards:* Ann Prizes for Oil, Painters & Sculptors Soc NJ, 50-75; Elizabeth Morse Genios Mem Watercolor Prize, Nat Asn Women Artists, 60; Prize for Oil, Nat Arts, 76; and others. *Bibliog:* Archives Am Art, Smithsonian Inst. *Mem:* Painters & Sculptors Soc NJ (hon life pres); Audubon Artists (vpres, 56-58); Nat Soc Painters Casein & Acrylic (dir, 65-); NY Soc Women Artists (dir & chmn mem comt, 72-75); Am Soc Contemp Artists (mem comt). *Mailing Add:* 340 W 28th St New York NY 10001

HEIMDAL, GEORG
PAINTER, INSTRUCTOR

b Pocatello, Idaho, Aug 6, 43. *Study:* San Francisco State Univ, BA, 66; Univ Calif Davis, MA, 68; Claremont Grad Sch, res fel, 78-79; Wash State Univ, MFA, 80. *Work:* Eastern Wash State Hist Soc, Spokane; Ohio State Univ, Columbus. *Exhib:* Nat Drawing Ann, San Francisco Mus Art, 70; Northwest Ann, Seattle Mus Art, 75; one-man shows, Wash State Univ, 80, 81 & 83, Western Wash Univ, 80 & Traver-Sutton Gallery, 82; Northwest Eccentric Art, Nat Traveling Exhib, 76; Painters from the Other Side, Western Wash Univ, 77; Downtown Dog Show, M H De Young Mus Art, San Francisco, 78; and others. *Teaching:* Instr drawing, Spokane Falls Community Col, Wash, 69-80; assoc prof, Ohio State Univ, Columbus, 80- *Awards:* Painting Award, Spokane Ann, Fremont Lane S, 73; Juror's Award, Nat Art Roundup, 79; Nat Endowment Humanities/Mellon Found Grant, 79; and others. *Bibliog:* Allegra Berrian (auth), Bringing art to life, Spokesman-Rev, 74; Ron Glowan (auth), Painters from the other side, Artweek, 77. *Media:* Multimedia. *Mailing Add:* 492 Kenbrook Dr 2140 Bush St Suite 6 Worthington OH 43085

HEIN, MAX
GRAPHIC ARTIST, EDUCATOR

b Lincoln, Nebr, Dec 27, 43. *Study:* San Diego State Univ, AB, 66; Univ Calif, Los Angeles, MA, 68, MFA, 69. *Work:* Int Mus Photog, George Eastman House, Rochester, NY; Frederick S Wight Galleries, Univ Calif, Los Angeles; Newport Harbor Mus Art, Calif; Bradford City Art Gallery, Yorkshire, Eng; DeAnza Col Art Gallery, Calif; plus others. *Exhib:* Four Printmakers: Benson, Foote, Hein & Quandt, San Francisco Mus Art, 71; 3rd Brit Int Print Biennale, Bradford City Art Gallery, Yorkshire, Eng, 72; Recent Photog, NS Col Art & Design, Halifax, 72; San Francisco Bay Area Printmakers, Cincinnati Art Mus, Ohio, 73; 8th Nat Print & Drawing Competition, Dulin Gallery Art, Knoxville, Tenn, 74-75; Smithsonian Traveling Exhib, Nat Collection Fine Art, Washington DC. *Teaching:* Instr silkscreen printmaking, Univ Calif, Los Angeles Exten, 68-69; instr art, Santa Rose Jr Col, Calif, 69-; vis artist silkscreen printmaking, Visual Studies Workshop, Rochester, NY, summer 75. *Awards:* Guest Ed Award, 6th Ann Los Angeles Printmaking Soc Exhib, 69; Purchase Award, 3rd Brit Int Print Biennale, 72 & Bay Area Print Exhib, DeAnza Col Gallery, 75. *Bibliog:* Alfred Frankenstein (auth), Photo Image in Printmaking, San Francisco Chronicle, 11/71; Carole Schuck (auth), Max Hein Prints, 9/72 & Gerry Payne (auth), Geometric Dynamics, 11/75, Art Week. *Mem:* The Graphics Soc. *Media:* Silkscreen, Mixed Media. *Publ:* Illusr, Half a Century, Nat Football League, 70. *Dealer:* Allrich Gallery 251 Post St San Francisco CA 94108. *Mailing Add:* 2690 Bristol Rd Kenwood CA 95452

HEINE, HARRY
PAINTER

b Edmonton, Alta, Can, July 24, 28. *Work:* Wash State Arts Comn; Govt British Columbia; Captain Cook Mus, England; Nat Maritime Mus, Eng; Mystic Seaport Mus, Conn; and others. *Comn:* Facade-relief mural, Royal Can Legion, Edmonton, Alta, 68; murals, Syncrude, Can; Vegreville, Can; Ft Saskatchewan, Alta. *Exhib:* Royal Soc Marine Artists, Guildhall & Mall Galleries, London, England, 79-83; Fedn Can Artists, 79-83; Watercolor West Ann, Riverside, Calif, 80; Earls Court, London, England, 81-83; Mystic Int, 83 & Mystic Invitational, 83, Mystic Seaport Mus, Conn; and others. *Awards:* Shell Can Award, Fedn Can Artists, 78; Best in Show, Puget Sound Country, West Coast Paper Co, 80; Puchase Award, Mystic Seaport Mus, 83. *Bibliog:* Frances Dayee (auth), Five artists and the sea, Sea, 80; Carolyn Leier (ed), editorial, Arts West, 80; On the water's edge, Skyword Mag, 82; and others. *Mem:* Royal Soc Marine Artists; Fedn Can Artists; Northwest Watercolor Soc; Can Soc Marine Artists (vpres, currently). *Media:* Watercolor. *Publ:* Illusr, Sound Heritage, Prov Arch, BC, 78; illusr, Beautiful British Columbia, Govt BC, 78; illusr, Curve of time, 79 & Frances Barkley, 80, Grays Publ; illusr, Pacific salmon, Dept Fisheries & Oceans, Can, 79; and others. *Dealer:* Louise Matzke Gallery 1136 Poplar Pl S Seattle WA 98144; Mystic Seaport Mus Maritime Gallery Mystic CT 06355. *Mailing Add:* 7059 Brentwood Dr Brentwood Bay BC V0S 1A0 Canada

HEINECKEN, ROBERT FRIEDLI
PHOTOGRAPHER, EDUCATOR

b Denver, Colo, Oct 29, 31. *Study:* Univ Calif, MA, 60. *Work:* Mus Mod Art, New York; Int Mus Photog, Rochester, NY; Fogg Art Mus, Harvard Univ; Pasadena Art Mus; San Francisco Mus Art. *Exhib:* Persistence of Vision,

George Eastman House, Rochester, 67; one-man shows, Robert Heinecken, Witkin Gallery, New York, 70, Light Gallery, New York, 73 & Int Mus of Photog, George Eastman House, Rochester, NY, 76; Photography into Sculpture, Mus Mod Art, New York, 70; Photography in America, Whitney Mus, New York, 74. *Teaching:* Prof art & photog, Univ Calif, Los Angeles, 60-; vis prof art & photog, Art Inst Chicago, 70; vis prof art & photog, Harvard Univ, 72. *Awards:* Guggenheim Mem Fel, 75; Nat Endowment Arts Grants, 77 & 81. *Bibliog:* Carl Belz (auth), Robert Heinecken, Camera, Bucher Ltd, Luzerne, Switz, 1/68; Fred Parker (auth), Robert Heinecken, Untitled Number 5, Friends of Photog, 73; Andy Grundberg (auth), Robert Heinecken-Asking provocative questions, New York Times, 6/81; and others. *Mem:* Soc Photog Educ; Friends Photog. *Publ:* Contribr, Contemp Photogr, Vol 5, No 4; contribr, Untitled Number 7 & 8, Friends of Photog, 74. *Dealer:* Light Gallery 724 Fifth Ave New York NY 10019. *Mailing Add:* Univ Calif Los Angeles Dept of Art 405 Hilgard Ave Los Angeles CA 90024

HEINEMANN, PETER
PAINTER, INSTRUCTOR
b Denver, Colo, Apr 22, 31. *Study:* Black Mountain Col, 1 yr, with Joseph Albers, 48-49. *Comn:* Multi-figure oil mural, New York Coun Arts, 71-72. *Exhib:* Nat Inst Arts & Lett, New York, 60, 61 & biennially 70, 71 & 72; Heckscher Mus, Huntington, NY, 79; Nat Acad Design, 81 & 82; Gallery 120, New York, 83; Visual Arts Mus, 83; and others. *Teaching:* Instr painting & drawing, Sch Visual Arts, New York, 60- *Awards:* Creative Artists Pub Serv Grants, 71-72, 74-75 & 77-78; Childe Hassam Purchase Award, 72. *Media:* Oil. *Mailing Add:* 229 Grand St New York NY 10010

HEINZ, SUSAN
ADMINISTRATOR
b Rhode Island. *Study:* Brown Univ, BA; Harvard Univ, MA; Univ Calif, Los Angeles, MA(film hist & criticism). *Pos:* Educ coordr, Jr Arts Ctr, Los Angeles Munic Arts Dept, 68-73; mem, Los Angeles Munic Arts Comn, 73-78; exec dir, Palos Verdes Art Ctr & Mus, Rancho Palos Verdes, 74-78; mem, Mayor's Citizen's Adv Comt Arts, Los Angeles; dir, Bus Progs, The Asia Soc, New York, 78-; mem bd dirs, Cult Assistance Ctr, New York, 79- *Awards:* Am Film Inst Scholar, 72-73; Smithsonian Inst Grant res in India, 74. *Mem:* Am Asn Mus; Asian Studies Asn; Munic Art Soc New York. *Mailing Add:* 311 E 72nd St New York NY 10021

HEIPP, RICHARD CHRISTIAN
PAINTER, INSTRUCTOR
b Cleveland, Ohio, June 23, 52. *Study:* Ceveland Inst Art, BFA(Agnes Gund Scholar), 76; Univ Wash, Seattle, MFA, 79. *Work:* Univ Ky, Lexington; City Seattle; Miami Univ, Oxford, Ohio; Pratt Graphic, Exxon Collection, New York; Ohio Nat Bank, Columbus. *Comn:* Seattle City Fair Proj, 80. *Exhib:* May Show, Cleveland Mus Art, 75-77; Wash Open, Seattle Art Mus, 79; one-person exhib, Univ Puget Sound, 80; American Drawings III, 81-83 & IV, 83-84, Smithsonian Inst Nat Tour; 100 Years Cleveland Inst Art, 82; Intermont Nat, Intermont Col, 82; two-person exhib, Huntingdon Gallery, Montgomery, Ala, 83. *Teaching:* Vis instr drawing, Univ Puget Sound, 79-80; ast prof painting, Univ Fla, Gainesville, 80- *Awards:* Ford Found Traveling Grant, 80; State Fla Fel, 83. *Mem:* Utah State Studios Inc (pres, 79-80). *Media:* Airbrush. *Dealer:* Francine Seders Gallery 6701 Greenwood Ave N Seattle WA 98103. *Mailing Add:* 4420 NW 21st St Gainesville FL 32605

HEISE, MYRON ROBERT
PAINTER
b Bancroft, Nebr, June 30, 34. *Study:* Univ Omaha; Art Students League; Pratt Ctr Contemp Printmaking, New York; Acad Fine Arts, Florence, Italy; also with Arthur Lee, Robert Brackman & Marshall Glaisier. *Work:* Omaha Univ; Robert & Elizabeth Browning Soc, Florence, Italy; US Army Craft Serv, Ft Lewis, Wash. *Comn:* Portrait of John G Neihardt, J G Neihardt Found, Inc, Bancroft, 67; mural, Manhattan Laboratory Mus. *Exhib:* The New Realists, Gallery G, Wichita, Kans, 78; Street Painters, Ingber Gallery, New York, 78; Peekskill Mus, NY, 79 & Bronx Mus Art, 80; Realists, Country Art Gallery, Locust Valley, NY, 79; and others. *Pos:* Assoc art ed, Time Capsule Mag, currently. *Teaching:* Teacher painting & drawing, New Sch Social Res, 77-78, Educ Alliance Art Sch, 78- & Sch Body-Mind Centering, 78- *Awards:* Artist-in-residence, Neihardt Found, Bancroft, Nebr, 81-83. *Bibliog:* David L Shirey (auth), Fresh perceptions by realist painters, New York Times, 2/11/79; Roger Catlin (auth), Artist wants to come home again, Omaha World Herald, 9/80; Judy Johnson (auth), The New York street painter who also does Main Street, Mag Midlands, 11/83; and others. *Mem:* Figurative Artists Alliance (founding mem, 69-, chmn, 76-78); Artists Equity, New York; Audubon Artists, New York. *Media:* Oil, Etching. *Publ:* Auth, Introducing the street painters, Time Capsule, fall 81; and others. *Dealer:* Capricorn Gallery 4849 Rugby Ave Bethesda MD 20014. *Mailing Add:* 102 Forsyth St New York NY 10002

HEISKELL, DIANA
PAINTER
b Paris, France; US citizen. *Work:* Santa Barbara Mus Art, Calif; Slater Mus, Norwich, Conn. *Exhib:* Whitney Mus Am Art Ann, 2 yrs; Chicago Art Inst; Boston Arts Festival; De Cordova & Dana Mus, Lincoln, Mass; Southern Vt Art Ctr, Manchester; and others. *Awards:* Hon Mention, Berkshire Art Asn; Grumbacher Prize, Southern Vt Art Ctr. *Mem:* Southern Vt Art Asn (trustee); Berkshire Art Asn. *Mailing Add:* Marlboro VT 05344

HEIT, STEVEN ROBERT
DEALER
b Ellenville, NY, June 30, 43. *Study:* Univ Buffalo, BA; Baruch Col, MBA; Fashion Inst Technol, AA(art & photog). *Pos:* Owner, Heit Galleries, Phoenix, currently. *Mem:* Men's Art Coun. *Specialty:* Graphics, watercolors and photography. *Mailing Add:* Heit Galleries 1016 E Camelback Phoenix AZ 85014

HELANDER, BRUCE PAUL
PAINTER, DEALER
b Great Bend, Kans, Jan 27, 46. *Study:* RI Sch Design, Providence, BFA(illus), MFA(painting); Univ Kans, Lawrence, cert; RI Col, Providence. *Work:* Rochester Airport, Minn; RI Sch Design. *Comn:* Animated film, Perpetual Motion Pictures, New York, for Ohio Bell Systs, 71; Ann Exhib Poster, Exec Comt, RI State Coun Arts, 72. *Exhib:* First Cancelled Art Exhib, 152 Prince Street Gallery, New York, 73; Loeb Art Ctr, Harvard Univ, 73; Int Corresp Exhib, Minihan Gallery, Depere, Wis, 74; Watson Gallery, Wheaton Col, Norton, Mass, 76; Tyler Sch of Art, Temple Univ, 77 & 80; and others. *Pos:* Asst dir admis, RI Sch Design, 70-72, dir summer sessions & exten sch, 72-, actg assoc provost, 76, provost & vpres acad affairs, 77; spec asst to coordr, Fed Graphics Improv Prog, Nat Endowment Arts, Washington, DC, 73-; adv, Inst Am Indian Art, 75-; publ, Art Express Mag, 79-81; dir, Royal Palm Gallery, Palm Beach, Fla, 83- *Teaching:* Lectr design, RI Sch Design, 71-, mem, Fine Arts Workshop, summer 76; lectr painting, Inst Am Indian Art, Santa Fe, NMex, 75-; vis artist, Art Park, Lewiston, NY, 75- *Awards:* Purchase Prize, Providence Art Club, 71; Chmns Grant, 73 & Fel, 74, Nat Endowment Arts. *Bibliog:* Ray Johnson, Much ado about nothing (interview), Sunday New York Times, 10/75; Perfect pitchers, fancy frames, Provincetown J, 77; PM Mag, NBC, 80. *Mem:* Am Fedn Arts; Soc Preserv Indust Archit; Am Asn Univ Adminr; Col Art Asn Am; Provincetown Art Asn; and others. *Media:* Collage. *Publ:* Illusr, Growing Up with Education, Educ Develop Corp, Cambridge, Mass, 73; auth, Fantastic illustuation, Push Pin Mag, 79; auth, reviews, Art Express Mag, 80 & 81. *Mailing Add:* 151 Power St Providence RI 02906

HELBECK, DEWEES COCHRAN See Cochran, Dewees

HELCK, (CLARENCE) PETER
PAINTER, PRINTMAKER
b New York, NY, June 17, 1893. *Study:* Art Students League, with Frank Brangwyn, Harry Wickey & Lewis Daniel. *Work:* Metrop Mus Art, New York; Carnegie Inst, Pittsburgh; Mus Am Art, New Britain, Conn; Sheldon Swope Galleries, Terre Haute, Ind; Montagu Mus, Beaulieu, Eng. *Exhib:* Royal Acad, London, 23; Nat Acad Design Exhibs, 40-50; one-man shows, New York City, 24, 27, 30, 41, 54 & 61, Smithsonian Inst, 47 & Sheldon Swope Galleries, Lincoln, Nebr, 66. *Pos:* Art ed, Bulb Horn, Boston, 50-; assoc ed, Antique Automobile, Hershey, Pa, 50-; artist & auth, Automobile Quart, New York, 62-70. *Teaching:* Mem fac illus, Famous Artists Sch, Westport, Conn, 48-73. *Awards:* Pennell Medal, Philadelphia Acad, 28; five Medals, New York Art Dirs Asn, 31-51; Hall of Fame Gold Medal, Soc Illusr, 68. *Bibliog:* Y Inomoto (auth), Auto art, Automobile Illus, Tokyo, 71; Ken Browing (auth), Autographics, Ont, 77; Walter Reed (auth), 50 Great American Illustrators. *Mem:* Nat Acad Design; Am Watercolor Soc; Soc Illusr; Famous Artists Sch; Allied Artists Am. *Media:* Casein, Tempera. *Publ:* Illusr, Sat Eve Post, 33-55; illusr, Heavy Industry Advertising, 20-58; illusr, Esquire, 40-50; auth & illusr, The Checkered Flag, Scribner, 61; auth & illusr, Great Auto Races, Abrams, 76. *Mailing Add:* Boston Corners RD 2 Millerton NY 12546

HELD, AL
PAINTER
b New York, NY, Oct 12, 28. *Study:* Art Students League; Acad Grande Chaumiere, Paris. *Work:* Albright-Knox Gallery, Buffalo; High Mus, Atlanta; Hirshhorn Mus; Mus Mod Art, New York; San Francisco Mus Mod Art; and others. *Exhib:* Systemic Painting, Guggenheim Mus, 66; Documenta IV, Kassel, Ger, 68; one-man shows, San Francisco Mus Art, Corcoran Gallery Art, 68, Andre Emmerich Gallery, New York, 75, Donald Morris Gallery, Birmingham, Mich, 77, Inst Contemp Art, Boston, 78, Friedland Gallery, Toronto, 78 & Janus Gallery, Venice, Calif, 79; Retrospective, Whitney Mus Am Art, New York, 74 & Emmerich Gallery, Zurich, Switz, 77; and others. *Teaching:* Prof art, Yale Univ, 62-78, adj prof painting, 78- *Awards:* Logan Medal, Art Inst Chicago, 64; Guggenheim Found Fel, 66. *Bibliog:* Barbara Rose (auth), American Art Since 1900, a Critical History, Praeger, 67; Gregory Battcock (ed), Minimal Art: a Critical Anthology, Dutton, 68. *Dealer:* Donald Morris Gallery 20082 Livernois Detroit MI 48221. *Mailing Add:* c/o Andre Emmerich Gallery 41 E 57th St New York NY 10022

HELD, ALMA M
PAINTER
b Lemars, Iowa. *Study:* Univ Iowa, with Charles A Cumming, BA(cum laude) & MA; Nat Acad Design, New York, with Sydney Dickinson; Cape Cod Sch Art, Provincetown, Mass, with Charles Hawthorne & Richard Miller. *Work:* Waterloo Munic Galleries, Iowa; portrait & landscape paintings, Ft Dodge Pub Schs, Iowa; landscape, YWCA, Waterloo; Nat Bank Bldg Waterloo; Garwin Pub Libr, Iowa. *Comn:* Portrait of Jack Logan, Logan Jr High Sch, Waterloo, 62; portrait, Cedar Falls Woman's Club, Iowa, 71; Flight Into Egypt (painting), 71, portraits of Rev J Richmond Morgan & Rev Charles F Jacobs, 74, First Congregational Curch, Waterloo, Iowa. *Exhib:* Joslyn Mus Art, Omaha, Nebr, 35 & 46; 16th Ann Iowa Artists Exhib, Des Moines Art Ctr, Iowa, 64; Ithaca Collects, Ithaca Col Mus Art, NY, 69; 8th Ann Waterloo

Munic Galleries Show, 71; one-man retrospective, Waterloo Recreation & Arts Ctr, Iowa, 72. *Teaching:* Instr art & later assoc prof, Univ Iowa, formerly. *Awards:* Purchase Prize, First Iowa TV Art Show, Waterloo, 68 & 76; First Prize, Competitive Art Show Nat Cattle Cong, Waterloo, 68 & 74; First Prize in Oil, Nat Cattle Congress, Waterloo, 80. *Mem:* Waterloo Art Asn. *Media:* Oil, Watercolor. *Mailing Add:* 623 W Eighth St Waterloo IA 50702

HELD, (JON) JONATHAN, JR
LIBRARIAN, GRAPHIC ARTIST
b Brooklyn, NY, April 2, 47. *Study:* Utica Col, Syracuse Univ, BA, 69, Sch Info Sci, MLS, 71. *Work:* Jean Brown Arch, Tyringham, Mass; Hans Sohm Arch, Markgroningen, Ger; Munson-Williams-Proctor Inst, Utica, NY; Dallas Pub Libr. *Exhib:* Stampworks, Stempelplaats, Amsterdam, 76; Artists of Central New York, Munson-Williams-Proctor Inst, Utica, NY, 77 & 79; Rubber Stamp Art, Lightworks Gallery, Syracuse, NY, 80; Copycat Show, Franklin Furnace, New York, 81; Letters from Mohammed, Munson-Williams-Proctor Inst, Utica, NY, 81. *Collections Arranged:* Video Art, Munson-Williams-Proctor Inst, Utica, NY, 78; Their Indelible Mark: Rubber Stamps and Libraries, Dallas Pub Libr, 83; Mail Art About Mail Art, Richland Col, Dallas, 84. *Pos:* Video librn, Mid-York Libr System, Utica, NY, 76-81; art librn, Dallas Pub Libr, 81- *Teaching:* Mentor video art, Empire State Col, 80-81. *Bibliog:* Thompson & Miller (auths), The Rubber Stamp Album, Workman Publ, 78; News of the month, Wilson Libr Bulletin, 10/80; Catherine Egan (auth), Programming independent video, Sightlines, spring 83. *Mem:* Am Libr Asn; Nat Fedn Local Cable Programmers. *Media:* Rubber Stamps, Video. *Interests:* Video art; artists books. *Publ:* Contribr, Information science and the art of communication, Critical Assembling, 79. *Mailing Add:* c/o Mod Realism Gallery 1903 McMillan St #1 Dallas TX 75201

HELD, JULIUS S
EDUCATOR, WRITER
b Mosbach, Ger, Apr 15, 05; US citizen. *Study:* Univ Heidelberg, 23; Univ Berlin, 23-24, 27-28; Univ Vienna, 25-26, 29; Univ Freiburg, PhD, 30; Williams Col, DHL, 72; Columbia Univ, hon DLitt, 77; Dickson Col, DFA, 83. *Pos:* Asst, Staatliche Mus, Berlin, 31-33; mem ed bd, Art Bull, 42-; mem ed bd, Art Quart, 59-74; consult, Mus Arte Ponce, PR, 59-; mem, Inst Advan Study, Princeton Univ, 67. *Teaching:* Lectr, NY Univ, 35-41; lectr art, Barnard Col, Columbia Univ, 37-44, asst prof, 44-50, assoc prof, 50-54, prof, 54-70, chmn dept art hist, 67-70, emer prof, 70-; vis lectr, Bryn Mawr Col, 43-44; vis prof, New Sch Social Res, 46-47; vis prof, Yale Univ, 54 & 58; Robert Sterling Clark prof art, Williams Col, 69 & 74; Andrew W Mellon prof, Univ Pittsburgh, 72-73. *Awards:* Art Dealers Asn Am Award, 80; Medal of Distinction, Barnard Col, 80; Governor's Award, State of Vermont, 82. *Mem:* Col Art Asn Am (dir, 59-64, hon dir, 75, mem ed bd); Mediaeval Acad Am; Renaissance Soc Am; Soc Hist of Art Francaise; Deutscher Verein für Kunstwissenschaft. *Res:* Flemish and Dutch art. *Collection:* Old master paintings and drawings. *Publ:* Auth, Rubens, Selected Drawings, Phaidon, 59; auth, Rembrandt's Aristotle & Other Rembrandt Essays, Princeton, 69; co-auth, 17th & 18th century Art: Baroque & Rococo, 72, Abrams; auth, The Oil Sketches of Peter Paul Rubens, Princeton, 80; auth, Rubens and His Circle, Princeton, 82. *Mailing Add:* 81 Monument Ave Bennington VT 05201

HELD, PHILIP
PAINTER, PHOTOGRAPHER
b New York, NY, June 2, 20. *Study:* Art Students League, 38-42 & 46, with Kuniyoshi, Fiene, Blanch, Lee & Vytlacil; Sch Art Studies, New York, with Moses Soyer, 47-48; Columbia Univ Teachers Col, serigraphy with Arthur Young, 49. *Work:* Berkshire Mus, Pittsfield, Mass; Univ Mass, Amherst; Philadelphia Mus Lending Collection; Art Students League Collection; Ringling Mus, Sarasota Fla; and others. *Exhib:* Berkshire Mus, Pittsfield, Mass, 49-67; Mus Mod Art, New York, 57; Pa Acad Fine Arts, 62; Philadelphia Mus, 66; Univ Mass, Amherst, 66; Ringling Mus, Sarasota, Fla, 72; Harmon Gallery, Naples, Fla, 80; Fla Artists Group, 83; and others. *Pos:* Exhib juror, Manatee & Sarasota Co, 77- *Teaching:* Instr Fine Arts, Scarborough Sch, NY, 47-52; instr Fine Arts, Fieldston Sch, Riverdale, NY, 52-62, chmn dept, 62-71; instr & coordr Fine Arts Prog, Booker-Bay Haven Sch, Sarasota, Fla, 71-78; instr, Visual & Performing Arts Ctr, Sarasota Co, 79-83, retired. *Awards:* H Kleinert Found Grant, 66; Sarasota Art Asn Figure Exhib Award, 75; Realism Award, 77; Photo Award, 81; and others. *Bibliog:* Gordon Brown (auth), Art voices 1964-65, Art Voices, 65; article, St Petersburg Times, 3/12/82. *Mem:* Life mem Art Students League; Woodstock Artists Asn; Sarasota Art Asn; Fla Artists Group; Art League Manatee Co, Fla. *Media:* Oil, Photography. *Dealer:* Art Resource Inc 65 Bleeker St New York NY 10012. *Mailing Add:* 3035 Wood St Sarasota FL 33577

HELDT, CARL RANDALL
EDUCATOR, PAINTER
b Stanford, Ill, Sept 8, 25. *Study:* Wittenburg Col, Springfield, Ohio, 43-44; Univ Ill, Urbana, BFA, 53; Ariz State Univ, Tempe, 60-61. *Work:* Valley Nat Bank Collection & Phoenix Col, Ariz; Col Southwestern Utah. *Comn:* Murals, Kahler Hotel, Rochester, Minn, 54; watercolors, Ford Motor Co, Deerborn, Mich, 63; oil paintings, cards, toys, Hallmark Cards, Kansas City 68-73; mural, Campus Christian Ctr, Tucson, Ariz, 70; murals, New Libr Univ Ariz, Tucson, 74-75. *Exhib:* Southwestern Invitational, Yuma Art Ctr, Ariz, 67-75; Cedar City Invitational, Utah, 67-76; 5 Ariz Artists, Rocky Mountain, 68; 12th Nat Prints & Drawings, Oklahoma Art Ctr, 70; 4 Corners Biennial, Phoenix Mus, Ariz, 71; 22nd Ann NY Soc Illustrators; plus others. *Pos:* Med illusr, Univ Ill, Urbana, 49-53; art dir, Our Wonderful Encycl, Champaign, Ill, 53-55. *Teaching:* Instr graphic design, Univ Ill, Urbana, 55-60; prof graphic design, Univ Ariz, 61- *Awards:* Phoenix Art Dirs Club, 68; Purchase Award,

Cedar City Invitational; Col Southwestern Utah, 75. *Media:* Oil, Acrylic. *Publ:* Illusr, New York Times, 62; illusr, Ford Times Mag, 63; contribr, Arizona Alumnus, Univ Ariz, 65; contribr, Crown Ctr News, Hallmark Cards, 69; contribr, Star-Citizen, 79; and others. *Dealer:* Gekas-Nichols Gallery 6538 East Tanque Verde Rd Tucson AZ; Elaine Horwitch Gallery 4200 North Marshall Way Scottsdale AZ 85251. *Mailing Add:* 320 S Country Club Rd Tucson AZ 85716

HELFOND, RIVA
PAINTER, PRINTMAKER
b Brooklyn, NY. *Study:* Art Students League, with William Von Schlegell, Harry Sternberg, Yasuo Kuniyoshi, Morris Kantor & Alexander Brook; Sch Indust Arts, New York. *Work:* Mus Mod Art, New York; Libr Cong, Washington, DC; Los Angeles Mus; Newark Mus Fine Art; Springfield Mus Fine Art, Mass. *Exhib:* Carnegie Inst, Pittsburgh, 54; one-man show, Gallerie Collette Allendy, Paris, 57; Art USA, New York, 58 & 59; Corcoran Gallery Art, Washington, DC, 60; Newark Triennials, Newark Mus Fine Art, 64 & 67; Bethesda Art Gallery, Md, 83; and others. *Teaching:* Instr graphics, NY Univ, 65-67; instr painting & art appreciation, Union Col, Cranford, NJ. *Awards:* First Prize in Oil, Montclair Mus Art, 60-62 & 69; Prize in Oil, Monmouth Col Art Festival, 69; Prize in Painting, Audubon Artists, 83; and others. *Mem:* Audubon Artists; Soc Am Graphic Artists (mem coun bd); Assoc Artists NJ (pres, 66-70); Artists Equity Asn NY; Artists Equity Asn NJ (treas, 62-). *Media:* Oil; Etching, Lithography. *Dealer:* Frank Fidele Fine Arts 42 East 57th St New York NY 10022. *Mailing Add:* 919 Knollwood Ct Plainfield NJ 07062

HELIKER, JOHN EDWARD
PAINTER, EDUCATOR
b Yonkers, NY, 09. *Study:* Art Students League, 27-29; Colby Col, hon DFA. *Work:* Mus Mod Art, Whitney Mus Am Art, Metrop Mus Art, New York; Cleveland Mus Art, Ohio; Philadelphia Mus Art. *Exhib:* Am Painting Today, Metrop Mus Art, 50; Nature in Abstraction, 58, Art of the United States 1670-1966, Whitney Mus Am Art, 66; retrospective exhib, Whitney Mus Am Art, 68; one-man exhibs, Drew Univ, Madison, NJ, 71, Saint-Gaudens Nat Historical Site, Cornish, NH, 72 & Edmonton Art Gallery, Alta, 74; Windows and Doors, Heckscher Mus, Huntington, NY, 72; Centennial, Art Students League, 75; America 1976, US Dept Interior, 76. *Pos:* Vpres, Am Acad Arts & Lett, 72-74. *Teaching:* Prof painting, Columbia Univ, 47-74; instr, Art Students League, 75- & Parsons Sch Design, currently. *Awards:* First W A Clark Prize, Corcoran Gallery Art, 41; Prix de Rome, 48; Award of Merit Medal, Am Acad Arts & Lett, 67. *Bibliog:* J I H Baur (auth), New decade, 55 & L Goodrich (auth), John Heliker, 68, Whitney Mus Am Art; W Nordness (auth), Art USA now, Viking, 62. *Mem:* Nat Inst Arts & Lett. *Media:* Oil, Watercolor. *Dealer:* Kraushaar Galleries 1055 Madison Ave New York NY 10028. *Mailing Add:* Apt 3C 865 West End Ave New York NY 10025

HELIOFF, ANNE GRAILE (MRS BENJAMIN HIRSCHBERG)
PAINTER, COLLAGE ARTIST
b Liverpool, England; US citizen. *Study:* Art Students League; with Homer Boss & Kuniyoshi; Hans Hofmann Sch. *Exhib:* Pa Acad Fine Arts, Philadelphia; Dedication Exhibition, Nat Gallery Art, Washington, DC; Art USA Traveling Exhib; American Exhibition, Palazzo Uecchio, Florence, Italy & Mus Naples, Italy, 72; Bicentennial Expo Six Painters from New York, Annemasse & Cluses, France; Philadelphia Mus; Berkshire Mus; and many other group & one-man shows. *Pos:* Mem, US Deleg to 5th Cong, Int Asn Artists, Tokyo, 66. *Awards:* Oil Awards, Am Soc Contemp Artists, Riverside Mus, 62 & Berkshire Mus; Three Cert of Merit, Am Soc Contemp Artists, 70; and others. *Bibliog:* Dorothy Hall (auth), article, Park East, 11/76; C Offin (auth), article, Pictures on Exhib, 11/76; N Frachtman (auth), article, Arts Mag, 1/77; and others. *Mem:* Am Soc Contemp Artists; New York Soc Women Artists; life mem Woodstock Artists Asn. *Media:* Mixed. *Dealer:* Phoenix Gallery 939 Madison Ave New York NY 10021. *Mailing Add:* 340 W 28th St New York NY 10001

HELLER, BEN
DEALER, COLLECTOR
b New York, NY, Oct 16, 25. *Study:* Bard Col, BA. *Pos:* Benefactor, Metrop Mus Art, New York; past trustee or bd mem, Int Coun of Mus Mod Art, Friends of Whitney Mus Am Art & Jewish Mus. *Collection:* Contemporary American painting and ancient, Eastern and primitive arts. *Mailing Add:* 465 Park Ave New York NY 10022

HELLER, DOROTHY
PAINTER
b New York, NY. *Study:* With Hans Hofmann. *Work:* Univ Calif Art Mus, Berkeley; Allen Mem Art Mus, Oberlin, Ohio; Mus Mod Art, Haifa, Israel; Greenville Co Mus Art, SC. *Exhib:* Solo shows, Tibor de Nagy Gallery, 53, Galerie Facchetti, 55, Poindexter Gallery, 56 & Betty Parsons Gallery, 72, 76 & 78; Mus Mod Art Traveling Exhib, 63; Wadsworth Atheneum, Hartford, Conn, 64; Picadilly Gallery, London, England, 67; Albright-Knox Gallery, Buffalo, NY, 74; Otis Art Inst, Los Angeles, 79; and others. *Bibliog:* Archives of American Art, Smithsonian Inst, Washington, DC; and others. *Media:* Acrylic. *Mailing Add:* 8 W 13th St New York NY 10011

HELLER, GOLDIE (MRS EDWARD W GREENBERG)
COLLECTOR, CONSULTANT
b Salem, Mass. *Study:* Mass Col Art. *Mem:* Am Fedn of Art. *Collection:* Hans Hartung, Henry Botkin, Ralph Rosenborg, Byron Browne, Noel Rockmore, Andy Warhol, Francisco Larez, Jose de Creeft, Jean Marie Souverbie (School of Paris), John Ross, June Rogoff, Joseph Bolegard, Clare Romano, Erwin Wending, and others. *Mailing Add:* 440 E 56th St New York NY 10022

HELLER, JULES
PRINTMAKER, WRITER
b New York, NY, Nov 16, 19. *Study:* Ariz State Univ, BA, 39; Columbia Univ, MA, 40; Univ Southern Calif, PhD, 48. *Work:* Libr of Congress; Allan R Hite Inst, Univ Louisville; Tamarind Inst, Univ NMex; Toronto Dom Centre; Can Coun Art Bank, York Univ. *Exhib:* Soc Am Etchers, 50; 2nd Int Biennial Color Lithography, Cincinnati Art Mus, 52; First Nat Exhib Prints, DePauw Univ, 59; Pa Acad Fine Arts Ann, 59 & 63; Canada, Gallery Pascal, 75; Martha Jackson Gallery, New York, 76. *Pos:* Dir sch arts, Pa State Univ, University Park, 61-63, founding dean col arts & archit, 63-68; founding dean fac fine arts, York Univ, 68-72; dean, Col Fine Arts, Ariz State Univ, Tempe, 76- *Teaching:* Prof printmaking & art hist, Univ Southern Calif, 46-61; prof fine arts, York Univ, 72-76; prof papermaking, Ariz State Univ, 76- *Awards:* Can Coun Grant, 75. *Mem:* Col Art Asn Am; Int Coun of Fine Arts Deans; Authors League; Int Asn Paper Historians. *Media:* Graphics. *Publ:* Illusr, Canciones de Mexico, 48; contribr, Estampas de la revolucion Mexicana, 48; contribr, Prints by California Artists, 54; contribr, Dictionary of Art, McGraw, 69; auth, Printmaking Today, rev ed, 72; auth, Papermaking, 5/78. *Mailing Add:* 6838 E Cheney Rd Scottsdale AZ 85253

HELLER, REINHOLD AUGUST
HISTORIAN
b Fulda, Ger, July 22, 40; US citizen. *Study:* St Joseph's Col, Philadelphia, BS, 63; Ind Univ, Bloomington, MA, 66, PhD, 68, with Albert Elsen, John Jacobus & Sven Loevgren. *Pos:* Guest cur, Nat Gallery, Washington, DC, 78-79. *Teaching:* Prof art hist, Univ Pittsburgh, 68-78 & Univ Chicago, 78- *Awards:* Foreign Area Prog Fel, 66-68; Guggenheim Found Fel, 73-74; d'Harnoncourt Fel, Mus Mod Art, New York, 70. *Mem:* Col Art Asn; Mod Lang Asn. *Res:* Art criticism; symbolism; expressionism; German Romanticism; iconography of modern art. *Publ:* Auth, Art of Wilhelm Lehmbruck, Nat Gallery, Washington, DC, 72; auth, Munch: The Scream, Viking, 73; auth, Edvard Munch's Vision and the Symbolist Swan, Art Quart, 73; auth, Recent Scholarship on Vienna's Golden Age, Art Bulletin, 77; auth, Edvard Munch's Night, the content of biography and the aesthetics of decadence, Arts Mag, 78. *Mailing Add:* Art Dept Univ Chicago 5540 S Greenwood Chicago IL 60637

HELMAN, PHOEBE
SCULPTOR, PAINTER
b New New York, NY, Oct 29, 29. *Study:* Wash Univ, with Paul Burlin, BFA; Art Students League; also with Raphael Soyer. *Work:* Hampton Inst Mus, Va; Ciba-Geigy, Ardsley, NY; Fox, Flynn & Melamed, New York; Friedlich, Fearon & Strohmeier, New York; Guggenheim Mus, New York. *Comn:* Steel wall piece, comn by Milan Stoeger, New York, 73; steel wall piece, comn by Muriel Mannings, New York, 73; City of Raleigh, NC, 78. *Exhib:* One-woman shows, Sculpture Now Inc, New York, 78, Max Hutchinson Gallery, 78 & Wright State Univ Gallery, 79; Sculptors Drawings, Touchstone Gallery, New York, 79; Work on Paper--Four Artists, Upstairs Gallery, Ithica, 79. *Teaching:* Adj prof art, Pratt Inst, 72- *Awards:* Creative Artists Pub Serv Grant, 75-76; Guggenheim Fel, 79-80; Nat Endowment Arts Grant Visual Arts Prog, 83-84. *Bibliog:* E M Broner (auth), The art of falling down and standing up, New Women's Times, 8/79; Carol Spence (auth), Beyond the edges of the paper, Ithica Times, 10/79; C Robins (auth), American urban art triumphant; Cohn, Held, Helman, Stella, Arts, 5/82; and others. *Media:* Laminite & Wood; Steel. *Dealer:* Sculpture Now Inc & Max Hutchinson Gallery 142 Greene St New York NY 10012. *Mailing Add:* 217 E 23rd St New York NY 10010

HELSMOORTEL, ROBERT
SCULPTOR, PAINTER
b Antwerp, Belgium; US citizen. *Study:* Acad Royale Belgium, 46; Inst Superieur, Belgium, 48. *Work:* Chicago Art Inst, Ill; Yale Univ, New Haven, Conn; Royal Collection, Brussels, Belgium; Carnegie Mus, Pittsburgh, Pa. *Comn:* Sculpture (metal), Place Ville Marie, Montreal, 62; bas relief (metal), Alcan, London, Eng, 67; sculptures & bas relief, Forte Plaza, Miami, Fla, 73; sculpture, La Mer Bldg, Naples, Fla, 78; bas relief, Am Telephone & Telegraph Co, Ft Lauderdale, Fla, 79. *Exhib:* One-man shows, Palazzo Strozzi, Florence, Italy, 55, the Parrish Mus, Southampton, NY, 67 & The Nova-Scotia Mus Fine Arts, Halifax, Can, 69; Art in Architecture, Mus City London, Eng, 69; The Harmon Gallery, Naples, Fla, 80; The Antwerp Gallery, Belgium, 80. *Awards:* First Prize Painting & Prize Als Ickkan, Belgium State, 48. *Bibliog:* Louis G Redstone (auth), Art in Architectue, McGraw Hill, 68; Margaret O Robinette (auth), Outdoor Sculpture, Whitney Libr of Design, 76. *Mem:* Artists Equity Asn, Washington, DC; Artists Equity Asn, New York; P Bench Council Arts. *Media:* Oil; Steel, Bronze. *Mailing Add:* Irving Galleries Worth Avenue Palm Beach FL 33480

HELZER, RICHARD BRIAN
METALSMITH, EDUCATOR
b Hastings, Nebr, Aug 27, 43. *Study:* Kearney State Col, Nebr, BA, 65; Univ Kans, MFA, 69. *Work:* C M Russell Mus, Great Falls, Mont. *Comn:* Altar serv, St Elizabeth's Episcopal Church, Nebr, 69 & Hope Lutheran Church, Kans, 70; altar cross, Univ Kans Chapel, Lawrence, 70. *Exhib:* Hist of Gold & Silversmithing in Am, Lowe Art Mus, Univ Miami, Coral Gables, Fla, 75; NW Invitational Silversmiths, Seattle Art Mus, Wash, 76; US Off Info Goldsmiths Exhib, Melbourne, Australia, 76; NW Designer-Craftsman, Henry Gallery, Seattle, Wash, 77; 3rd Profile of US Jewelry, Tex Tech Univ, Lubbock, 77; Goldsmiths 77, Phoenix Art Mus, Ariz, 77; Metal-non Metal, Synopsis Gallery, Chicago, 80; North Am Goldsmiths European Exhib (traveling); and others. *Pos:* Guest Cur, Metalsmithing Invitational,

Yellowstone Art Ctr, Billings, Mont, 81. *Teaching:* Teaching asst, Univ Kans, Lawrence, 68-69, instr metalsmithing, 69-70; asst prof metalsmithing, Mont State Univ, Bozeman, 70-74, assoc prof metalsmithing, 75-; prof art & head metalsmithing, Mont State Univ, 80. *Awards:* Nat Endowment Arts Fel, 76; Runner-up, Western State Arts Found Fel, 77. *Bibliog:* Craft Horizons, 12/78; Jewelry Making, revised ed, Bavin Publ, 80. *Mem:* Soc NAm Goldsmiths; Am Crafts Coun. *Media:* Multi-Metals, Acrylics. *Dealer:* Synopsis Gallery 931 Linden Ave Winnetka Ill 60093. *Mailing Add:* 1612 W Olive 8 Bozeman MT 59715

HEMENWAY, NANCY (MRS ROBERT D BARTON)
TAPESTRY ARTIST
b Boothbay Harbor, Maine, June 19, 20. *Study:* Wheaton Col, 37-41; Europe, 54-56; Univ Madrid, 56; Art Students League, 57-61; Columbia Univ, MA, 66; Wheaton Col, Hon DFA, 83. *Work:* Seattle Art Mus, Wash; Art Inst Chicago; Woodmere Gallery, Philadelphia; Maine Savings Bank, Portland; Metrop Mus Art, New York; plus many works in pvt collections in Europe, Latin Am & USA. *Exhib:* Mus Fine Arts, Montgomery, Ala, 75; Bowdoin Col Mus Art, Brunswick, Maine, 77; Va Mus, Richmond, 77; Seattle Mus Art, Wash, 78; Textile Mus, Washington, DC, 78; one-person show, Watson Gallery, Wheaton Col, Mass, 79; Int Tapestry Exhib, Africa, 79-80; and many others. *Pos:* Founder, San Esteban Sch, Guadalajara, Mex, 70; pres, Hemenway Designs, Washington, DC, 72-79. *Teaching:* Lectr, Africa, 76 & 80 & Europe, 78; Mentor Prog, Wheaton Col, 79- *Bibliog:* Nancy Hemenway & Bayetage (film), produced by US Info Agency, 70; and various other newspaper and magazine articles. *Mem:* Art Students League; Maine Hist & Cult Soc; Maine Art Gallery; Maine Coast Artists; Textile Arts Found (vpres, 80-). *Interests:* Originator of Bayetage wall hangings. *Mailing Add:* Juniper Point West Boothbay Harbor ME 04575

HEMMERDINGER, WILLIAM JOHN, III
PAINTER, CRITIC
b Burbank, Calif, June 7, 51. *Study:* Col Desert, Calif, AA, 72; Univ Calif, Riverside, BA, 73; Claremont Grad Sch, MFA, 75, PhD, 79. *Work:* Smithsonian Inst; Tate Gallery, London; Barbara Hepworth Mus, Cornwall, Eng; Tate Gallery, London. *Exhib:* Calif Nat Watercolor Soc Ann, Laguna Beach Mus Art, 70-81; Act IV: Mixed-Media, Los Angeles Co Mus Art, 77; one-man shows, paintings & collages, Calif State Col, 78 & Libr Art Ctr, Newport, NH, 82; Act IV: Mixed-Media, Los Angeles Co Mus Art, Los Angeles, 77; Los Angeles Abstract Painting, Univ NMex, 79; Calif Collage, Baum-Silverman Gallery, Los Angeles, 79; Nagasaki Mus Art, Japan, 81; and others. *Pos:* Cur, Calif Mus Photog, Univ Calif, Riverside, 73-74. *Teaching:* Instr art, Col Desert, Calif, 74-; lectr, Calif State Univ, Long Beach, 79-80, Otis Art Inst, Parsons Sch Design, Los Angeles, 79-81, Univ Calif, Riverside, 82- *Bibliog:* Melinda Wortz (auth), Los Angeles Abstract Painting, Univ NMex & Univ Calif, 79; Suzanne Muchnic (auth), From flamboyant to deliberate, Los Angeles Times, 11/30/79; William Wilson (auth), The galleries downtown, Los Angeles Times, 10/29/82. *Mem:* Nat Watercolor Soc (4th vpres, 81-82); Col Art Asn; Southern Calif Art Writers Asn. *Media:* Watercolor, Acrylic. *Res:* Contemporary art, education, aesthetics and new materials. *Publ:* Auth, Ruth and Murray Gribin collection (catalog), LAICA J, 81; auth, Elaine Lustig Cohen/Raimund Girke, Arts Mag, 81; auth, The first show: Museum of Contemporary Art, Los Angeles, Artscene, 11/83. *Dealer:* Cirrus Ed Ltd 542 S Alameda St Los Angeles CA 90013. *Mailing Add:* 43-409 A Martini Court Palm Desert CA 92260

HEMPHILL, HERBERT WAIDE, JR
CURATOR, LECTURER
b Atlantic City, NJ, Jan 21, 29. *Collections Arranged:* Hunt for the Whale; Plenty of Pennsylvania; Occult; Tattoo!; Macrame: Hail to the Chief; Fabric of the State (with catalog), 73; Commerce in Wood; 20th Century American Folk Art, 74; Collector's Choice; America Expresses Herself, The Hemphill Collection, New Children's Mus, Indianapolis, Ind, 76; Missing Pieces-- George Folk Art, 76; Japan Celebrates America's Bicentennial--The Hemphill Collection, Tokyo & Osaka, Japan, 76. *Pos:* Founder, Mus Am Folk Art, 58, cur, 61-72; guest cur, Brooklyn Mus, 76-; guest cur, Abby Aldrich Folk Art Collection, 80. *Teaching:* Guest lectr, NY Univ, Smithsonian Inst, Univ Vt & Libr Cong. *Bibliog:* Robert Bishop, Mary Black, Tom Armstrong, Louis Jones, et al (auth), The H W Hemphill Collection of 18th, 19th & 20th Century American Folk Art, Heritage Plantation Mus; Michael Hall (auth), The Hemphill Collection of 20th Century American Folk Art, Contemp Arts Ctr, Cincinnati, 73. Interest: Gifts to various folk collections and museums; 18th, 19th & 20th century American folk art. *Publ:* Co-auth, Metal of the State, 74; coauth, with Julia Weissman, 20th Century American Folk Art & Artists, 74. *Mailing Add:* 108 E 30th St New York NY 10016

HEMPHILL, PAMELA
HISTORIAN
b Manchester, Eng, May 1, 27; US citizen. *Study:* Manchester Univ, BA; Univ Pa, PhD(classical archaeol). *Teaching:* Prof classical, medieval & modern art, Women's Studies, West Chester State Col, 70-, chairperson dept art, 79- *Awards:* Ital Govt Fel, 65; Fulbright Travel Grant, 65; Am Philos Soc Study Grant, 74. *Mem:* Am Inst Archaeol; Inst Studi Romani; Inst Field Archaeol. *Res:* Surface survey in Italy to find new pottery types and land usage in Italy from prehistoric to medieval times. *Publ:* Auth, Survey of the Hill Country North of Rome, Exped Mag, 70; auth, Notes to slide sets on Roman Forum, Palestine and Herculaneum, Am Inst Archaeol, 73; auth, Cassia--Claudia Survey, Papers of Brit Sch, Rome, Vol 43, 75. *Mailing Add:* Cheyney PA 19319

HEMPLER, ORVAL F
PAINTER, SCULPTOR
b Almena, Kans, Jan 9, 15. *Study:* Univ Colo, BFA, 38; Colorado Springs Arts Acad, 38; Frank Alva Parsons scholar, Paris, France, 38-39; Ital traveling & painting scholar, 39; Univ Iowa, with Jean Charlot, MA, 41. *Work:* Los Angeles Co Mus Mod Art & Litton Mus Visual Arts, Los Angeles; Univ Kans Mus Art, Manhattan; Colorado Springs Fine Arts Acad, Colo; Denver Mus Art. *Comn:* Tropical Jungle Cyclorama Mural, Baker Furniture Co, Chicago, 44. *Exhib:* New York Watercolor Soc, Mus Mod Art, New York, 42; print show, Wichita Mus Art, Kans, 43; invitational, Los Angeles Co Mus Mod Art, 50; serigraph show, Fine Arts Ctr, Sacramento, Calif, 78; watercolor show, Philadelphia Mus, 79; plus others. *Collections Arranged:* Sculptured Paintings (cataloged), St Johns Gallery, Santa Monica, Calif, 63. *Pos:* Designer, Carson Pirie Scott, Chicago, 42-45; artist designer, Lamps of Calif, Los Angeles, 46-65. *Teaching:* Instr watercolor, Univ NH, Durham, 40-42; instr, Los Angeles Unified Schs, 65-68. *Awards:* Sweepstakes, Kans State Fair Asn, 37; Best Am Painter in Europe, Paris, 38-39; Best of Show, Westwood Art Asn, 75. *Bibliog:* Art Seidenbaum (auth), Art and the market place, Los Angeles Times, 10/63; Caroll Heiss (auth), Artist returns to Colorado, Denver Post, 75; Michael Donohue (commentator), The art of Orval Hempler, videotape, 78. *Mem:* Delta Phi Delta (secy & publ); Univ Calif, Los Angeles Art Coun (jury bd). *Media:* Watercolor; Sculptured Paintings. *Publ:* Illusr, The Palette, Hayes, 38; auth, Designers West, Art Alliance Corp, 63; contribr, Kans Mag, Univ Kans, 75. *Dealer:* Mary Browne 401 E Maint St Norton KS 67654. *Mailing Add:* 2302 Second St Santa Monica CA 90405

HENDERSHOT, J L
PRINTMAKER, EDUCATOR
b Cleveland, Ohio, Nov 3, 41. *Study:* Cleveland Inst Art, with H C Cassill, Louis Bosa & Julian Stanczak; Syracuse Univ, NY, with George Vander Sluis & Donald Cortesse. *Work:* Rochester Mus Art, NY; Pennell Fund, Libr Cong. *Comn:* Drawing, Alumni Asn, St John's Univ, Collegeville, Minn, 73; drawing for gift, Spira Dance Co, Portland, Ore, 74; print, St Cloud State Col, 75; 50th Anniversary lithographs (50 ed), Minn Mus; lithographs ed, Assoc Am Artist. *Exhib:* One-man shows, RI Sch Design, Providence, 75, Assoc Am Artists Gallery, New York, 76, Red River Art Ctr Mus, Moorehead, Minn, 76 & Uptown Gallery, New York, 77; 7th Nat Biennial Drawing US Show, St Paul, Minn, 75; and others. *Pos:* Art gallery dir, St John's Univ, 75- *Teaching:* Asst instr drawing & printmaking, Syracuse Univ, 68-70; asst prof drawing & printmaking, St John's Univ, 71- *Awards:* Philadelphia Print Club Purchase Award, Philadelphia Mus Art, 68; Univ NDak Purchase Award, 15th Nat Print & Drawing Exhib, 72; Minn Mus Art Purchase Award, 7th Nat Biennial Drawing US Show, 75. *Mem:* Graphic Soc, Hollis, NH; Boston Printmakers; Pratt Graphics Print Club, New York. *Media:* Intaglio, Lithography. *Mailing Add:* St John's Univ Collegeville MN 56231

HENDERSON, JACK W
PAINTER, INSTRUCTOR
b Kenosha, Wis, Mar 12, 31. *Study:* Kansas City Art Inst, BFA & MFA, 47-52; Ecole des Beaux Arts, Paris, 52-53; Art Students League, 55-58; also with Edward Laning, Louis Bouche & Robert Beverly Hale. *Work:* Nat Acad Design, New York; Smithsonian Inst; Am Acad Rome, Italy; Nat Portrait Gallery, England; Curtis Inst Mus; and others. *Comn:* Murals in pvt collections, Rome & New York. *Exhib:* Pa Acad Fine Arts, 59 & 61; one-man shows, Nat Acad Design, 68 & Ranger Fund Exhib, 74; Am Watercolor Soc Ann, New York, 69-70; plus others. *Teaching:* Assoc prof drawing, Moore Col Art, 67-; instr life drawing & painting, Art Students League, 75- *Awards:* Pulitzer Traveling Fel, 55; Abbey Fel for Mural Painting, Am Acad Rome, 63-65; Ranger Fund Purchase Award, Nat Acad Design, 74; plus others. *Mem:* Nat Acad Design; Am Watercolor Soc; Nat Soc Mural Painters; Art Students League; Artists Equity. *Media:* All Media. *Mailing Add:* 118 Remsen St Brooklyn NY 11201

HENDERSON, LESTER KIERSTEAD
PHOTOGRAPHER
b Abington, Mass, May 9, 06. *Study:* Northeastern Univ, 27; self study. *Work:* Photog Hall of Fame, Santa Barbara, Calif. *Exhib:* Wichita Art Mus, Kans, 75; Marion Koogler McNay Art Inst, San Antonio, Tex, 76; Okla Mus Art, Oklahoma City, 77; Leigh Yawkey Woodson Art Mus, Wausau, Wis, 77; Houston Mus Natural Sci, 78. *Awards:* Binding Indust Am Product Excellence Award, 80; Bookbuilders West Book Show Cert Merit, 80; Nat Asn Printing Indust Am Award Excellence, 80. *Publ:* Auth & photog illusr, The Sublime Heritage of Martha Mood, Kierstead Publ, Vol 1, 80, Vol 2, 83. *Mailing Add:* PO Box 3195 Monterey CA 93942

HENDERSON, LINDA DALRYMPLE
HISTORIAN, EDUCATOR
b Warren, Pa, Jan 22, 48. *Study:* Dickinson Col, BA, 69; Yale Univ, MA, MPhil, 72, PhD, 75. *Pos:* Assoc cur mod art, Mus Fine Arts, Houston, 74-76, cur, 76-77. *Teaching:* Lectr, Univ St Thomas, Houston, 75-76; asst prof, Univ Tex, Austin, 78-84, assoc prof, 84- *Mem:* Col Art Asn. *Res:* Twentieth century European and American art, including its interaction with geometry, science and mysticism. *Publ:* Auth, A new facet of cubism: The fourth dimension and non-Euclidean geometry reinterpreted, Art Quart, 71; auth, The fourth dimension in Russia from Ouspensky to Malevich, Structurist, 75-76; auth, Italian futurism and the fourth dimension, Art J, 81; auth, Mabel Dodge, Gertrude Stein and Max Weber: A four-dimensional trio, Arts Mag, 82; auth, The Fourth Dimension and Non-Euclidean Geometry in Modern Art, Princeton Univ Press, 83. *Mailing Add:* Art Dept Univ Tex Austin TX 78712

HENDERSON, ROBBIN LEGERE
PAINTER, CURATOR
b Stockton, Calif, April 19, 42. *Study:* Reed Col, 59-61; Univ Calif, Berkeley, BA, 63; San Francisco Art Inst, 68-70. *Exhib:* Solo exhib, Mills Col Gallery, 76 & Southern Exposure Gallery, San Francisco, 78; 13 Artists from California, Bologna Festival, Italy, 77; Artists Soapbox Derby, 77 & Art for Giving & Collecting, 78, San Francisco Mus Mod Art; 14 Proposals for Battery Hill 129, Clorox World Hq, Oakland, 82; San Francisco Exchange Show, Fashion Moda, New York, 82. *Collections Arranged:* Alice Neel, Paintings from 1920-1974, Am Can Gallery, 74; Inside-Outside, Womens Bldg, Los Angeles, 77; Don't Call Me Sweetheart (auth, catalog), 78. *Pos:* Dir, Southern Exposure Gallery, San Francisco, 74-77; cur, Intersection Gallery, San Francisco, 77-79; cur & exec dir, Berkeley Art Ctr, 79- *Bibliog:* Thomas Albright (auth), The underground is looking up, San Francisco Chronicle, 4/18/78; Robert MacDonald (auth), Images of women, Artweek, 4/79. *Mem:* Northern Calif Gallery Asn; Briarcombe Found. *Media:* Oil on Canvas, Mixed Media. *Mailing Add:* 1275 Walnut St Berkeley CA 94709

HENDERSON, VICTOR (LANCE)
PAINTER, PHOTOGRAPHER
b Cuyahoga Falls, Ohio, Nov 30, 39. *Study:* San Francisco State Col, BA, 63. *Work:* Newport Harbor Mus, Newport Beach, Calif; Chicago Art Inst; M H De Young Mem Mus, San Francisco. *Comn:* Beverly Hills Sidhartha, Michael Huit, Los Angeles, 69-70; Venice in the Snow, Jerry Rosen, Los Angeles, 70; Isle of Calif, Jordy Hormel, Los Angeles, 70-72; Hippy Knowhow, French Govt, Paris, 71; Ghost Town, Ed Janss, Thousand Oaks, Calif, 72-73 (all the above murals were executed under the name Los Angeles Fine Arts Squad); Breakers Mural, comn by Arco Co, Santa Barbara, Calif, 78-79. *Exhib:* LA 8, Los Angeles Co Mus Art, Calif, 76; 100-plus, Los Angeles Inst Contemp Art, 77; Illusion & Reality, Australian Nat Gallery, Canbera, and six other Australian galleries & mus, 77; Victor Henderson Takes a Walk, Newport Harbour Art Mus, 78; one-person shows, Ulrike Cantor Gallery, Los Angeles, 81 & Los Angeles Co Mus, Calif, 83; Artists Space, New York, 83; and others. *Pos:* Co-founder, Los Angeles Fine Art Squad, Calif, 69-73. *Teaching:* Lectr drawing, Univ Calif, Los Angeles, 75-77; Otis Art Inst, Los Angeles, 80-83. *Awards:* Nat Endowment Arts Painting Fel, 83-84. *Bibliog:* T H Garver (auth), Artforum, Vol 9, 71; Peter Plagens (auth), Sunshine Muse, Praeger, NY, 73; Eva Cookcroft (auth), Towards a People Art, E P Dutton & Co, NY, 76. *Publ:* Auth, Mega Murals & Big Art, Running Press, Philadelphia, 77. *Mailing Add:* 52 Brooks Ave Venice CA 90291

HENDLER, RAYMOND
PAINTER, SCULPTOR
b Philadelphia, Pa, Feb 22, 23. *Study:* Acad Grande Chaumiere, Paris, France; Contemp Sch Art, Brooklyn, NY; Tyler Sch, Temple Univ; Pa Acad Fine Arts; Philadelphia Col Art; Graphic Sketch Club, Philadelphia. *Work:* NY Univ; Walker Art Ctr, Minneapolis; Birla Acad Mus, Calcutta, India; Univ Notre Dame; Geigy Chem Corp, New York; plus others. *Exhib:* One-man shows, Galerie Huit, Paris, 51, Rose Fried Gallery, New York, 62-, Minneapolis Inst Art, Minn, & others; exhibs at major mus, univs & galleries throughout US, Can & Europe. *Teaching:* Dir, Eve Art Sch Pratt Inst; dir, First Yr Prog Sch Visual Arts; head dept painting, Minneapolis Col Art; prof art, Univ Minn, Minneapolis, 68- *Awards:* Longview Found Purchase Award, 63. *Bibliog:* Orie (auth), Raymond Hendler, Quandrum XVII; Burton (auth), Hendler paintings, Art News, 5/67; Brown (auth), Hendler exhibition, Arts, 6/67. *Mem:* Artists Club, New York; Col Art Asn Am. *Media:* Acrylic, Polystyrene. *Mailing Add:* 2212 Seabury Ave S Minneapolis MN 55406

HENDRICKS, BARKLEY LEONNARD
PAINTER
b Philadelphia, Pa, Apr 16, 45. *Study:* Pa Acad Fine Arts, 63-67, William Cresson European Traveling scholar, 66; Yale Univ Sch Fine Art, 70-72. *Work:* Philadelphia Mus Art; Pa Acad Fine Arts, Philadelphia; Cornell Univ; Wichita State Univ, Kans; Nat Gallery, Washington, DC. *Exhib:* Fel Exhib, Pa Acad Fine Arts, 67-72; Nat Acad Design Ann, New York, 70-71 & 74-75; Contemp Black Artists, Whitney Mus Am Art, New York, 71; Childe Hassam Fund Exhib, Am Acad Arts & Lett, 71 & 75; Nat Inst Arts & Lett Ann, 71-72. *Teaching:* Instr painting & drawing, Pa Acad Fine Arts, 71-72; asst in painting, Yale Univ, 71-72; asst prof painting & drawing, Conn Col, 72-81, assoc prof, 81- *Awards:* Julius Hallgarten Second Prize, Nat Acad Design, 71; Richard & Hilda Rosenthal Award, Nat Inst Arts & Lett, 72. *Media:* Oil, Acrylic. *Dealer:* ACA Galleries 21 East 67th St New York NY 10021. *Mailing Add:* c/o Dept Art Conn Col New London CT 06320

HENDRICKS, DAVID CHARLES
PAINTER, VISUAL ARTIST
b Hammond, Ind, Mar 25, 48. *Study:* Skowhegan Summer Sch Painting & Sculpture, 69; Univ Ill, BFA, 70; Ox-Bow Summer Sch Painting, 70. *Work:* Hirshhorn Mus & Sculpture Garden, Washington, DC; NC Nat Bank, Davidson. *Exhib:* Childe Hassam Fund Show, Am Acad Arts & Lett, New York, 76; Monique Knowlton Gallery, New York, 76-78; Contemp Landscape: Image & Idea, Queensborough Community Col, NY, 77; Artists Salute Skowhegan, Kennedy Gallery, New York, 77; one-man show, Monique Knowlton Gallery, 77; and others. *Awards:* Purchase Award, Davidson Nat Print & Drawing Show, NC Nat Bank, 76; Visual Arts Fel, Nat Endowment Arts, 77. *Bibliog:* John Russell (auth), Invigorating breezes of the fall season, New York Times, Arts & Leisure, 10/2/76; Lenore Malen (auth), David Hendricks, Arts Mag, 2/77. *Media:* Pencil, Graphite; Oil. *Dealer:* Monique Knowlton Gallery Inc 19 E 71st St New York NY 10021. *Mailing Add:* 652 Broadway New York NY 10012

HENDRICKS, EDWARD LEE
SCULPTOR, KINETIC ARTIST
b Charleston, WVa, Nov 9, 52. *Study:* Birmingham Southern Col, BFA, 74; Univ NC, Chapel Hill, MFA, 76. *Work:* Hunter Mus Art, Chattanooga, Tenn; Mint Mus Art, Charlotte, NC; New Orleans Mus Art; Phoenix Art Mus, Ariz. *Comn:* Mobile, Birmingham Mus Art, 80; mobile, Am Republic Insurance, Des Moines, 81; sculpture, Birmingham Bd Educ, 76. *Exhib:* One-man shows, Southeastern Ctr Contemp Art, 80, Alexander F Milliken Inc, New York, 80, 82 & 84, Montgomery Mus Fine Arts, Ala, 81, Osuma Gallery, Washington, DC, 81 & 83, O K Harris West, Scottsdale, Ariz, 81, 83 & 84, Birmingham Mus Art, 81 & 84, Hunter Mus Art, 82 & Eric Makler Gallery, Philadelphia, 82 & 83. *Awards:* Second Award, Nat Sculpture, 75; Juror's Award, Birmingham Art Asn, 79; Southeast Artists Fel, Southeastern Ctr Contemp Art, 83. *Bibliog:* Bob Yoskowitz (auth), articles, Arts Mag, 80 & 81; Carol Donnel-Kotrozo, article, Art Express, 82. *Media:* Metal. *Dealer:* Alexander F Milliken Inc 98 Prince St New York NY 10012. *Mailing Add:* 2121 1/2 First Ave N Birmingham AL 35203

HENDRICKS, GEOFFREY
PAINTER, ENVIRONMENTAL ARTIST
b Littleton, NH, July 30, 31. *Study:* Amherst Col, BA, 53; Norfolk Art Sch, Yale Univ, scholar, summer 53; Cooper Union Art Sch, 53-56; Columbia Univ, MA, 62. *Work:* NJ State Mus, Trenton; Mus Mod Art & Metrop Mus Art, New York; Lehmbruck Mus, Duisburg, WGer; Mus Moderner Kunst, Vienna, Austria; and others. *Exhib:* Alternatives in Retrospect, New Mus, New York, 81; 1962 Wiesbaden Fluxus 1982, Mus, Wiesbaden, Ger; Fluxus, Etc, Neuberger Mus, Purchase, NY, 83; NJ State Mus, Trenton, 84; Neue Galerie-Samlung Ludwig, Aachen, Ger, 84; and many other group & one-man shows. *Teaching:* From assoc prof art, Douglass Col, Rutgers Univ to prof art & grad dir, Mason Gross Sch Arts, Rutgers Univ, 56-; instr art, New York Fine Arts Winter Term Prog of Earlham Col, Richmond, Ind, 65-69. *Awards:* MacDowell Colony Fel, 55; Individual Fel, Nat Endowment Arts, 76-77; Deutscher Akad Austauschdienst, Berliner Kunstler Prog, 83. *Bibliog:* Ichiro Haryu (ed), Art as action & concept, Art Now, 72; Gerd Winkler (auth), Wolken und Gitarren, Kunstforum Int, 2/74; Geoffrey Hendricks, Flash Art, 2/76; and others. *Mem:* Col Art Asn Am; Am Asn Univ Prof; Fluxus. *Media:* Acrylic, Intermedia. *Publ:* Auth, Ring Piece, Something Else Press, 73; auth, Between Two Points/Fra Due Poli, Edizioni Pari & Dispari, 75; auth, A Sheep's Skeleton & Rocks, Unpublished Ed, New York, 77; Five Found Photos, Printed Ed, 79; La Capra, Edizioni Morra, Napoli, 79; and others. *Dealer:* Galerie Baecker St Apern Strasse 21 D5000 Koln 1 West Germany. *Mailing Add:* 486 Greenwich St New York NY 10013

HENDRICKS, JAMES (POWELL)
PAINTER, SCULPTOR
b Little Rock, Ark, Aug 7, 38. *Study:* Univ Ark, Fayetteville, BA, 63; Univ Iowa, MFA, 64. *Work:* Univ Mass, Amherst; Smithsonian Inst, Washington, DC; Nat Portrait Gallery, Washington, DC; Hudson River Mus, Yonkers, NY; Nat Gallery Art, Washington, DC. *Comn:* Painting, Apollo 14 Launch, Nat Gallery Art & NASA, 71; painting (cover), Time Mag, 8/9/71. *Exhib:* One-man shows, Smithsonian Inst Nat Air & Space Mus, 69, Hudson River Mus, Yonkers, 70 & Tyler Art Mus, 83; Lamont Gallery, Phillips Exeter Acad, NH, 76; Helen Shlien Gallery, Boston, 80 & 82; IV Int Bien de Arte Medellin, Columbia, South Am, 81. *Teaching:* Grad instr drawing, State Univ Iowa, 63-64; instr art, Mt Holyoke Col, 64-65; from asst prof to assoc prof painting & drawing, Univ Mass, Amherst, 72-79, dir grad progs in art, 72-, prof art, 79- *Awards:* Painting Awards, Soc Four Arts, 68 & Silvermine Guild Artists, 69; Ark Traveler Award, 71. *Bibliog:* Robert Ackermann (auth), article, Arts Mag, 9-10/74 & Art in Am, 3-4/76; Nancy Stapen (auth), article, Artforum, 1/83; and others. *Media:* Acrylic, Mixed Media; Bronze, Wood. *Publ:* Illusr cover, Time, 71. *Dealer:* Helen Shlien Gallery 14 Newbury St Boston MA 02116. *Mailing Add:* Dept of Art Univ of Mass Amherst MA 01003

HENDRIX, CONNIE (CONNIE SANDAGE MANUS)
PAINTER, INSTRUCTOR
b Mt Ayr, Iowa, May 30, 42. *Study:* Drake Univ, Des Moines, BFA, 64; Memphis State Univ; special study with Jason Williamson, Irving Shapiro, Murray Wentworth, Larry Webster & Lee Weiss. *Work:* Foothills Art Ctr, Golden, Colo; Ponca City Fine Arts Ctr, Okla; Tenn Arts Comn, State of Tenn, Nashville; State of Iowa, Wallace Agriculture Bldg, Des Moines; Nat Bank Commerce, Memphis, Tenn. *Comn:* Six watercolors of vegetables (with Julie Wells), United Foods, Bells, Tenn, 76; three watercolors of Olympics for limited ed wall covering (with Tom Welsh), Welsh Forest Products, Memphis, Tenn, 79-80. *Exhib:* Southern Watercolor Soc, NTex State Univ Art Gallery, Denton, Columbus Mus Arts & Sci & Cheekwood Fine Arts Ctr, Nashville, Tenn, 76-79; Allied Artists Am Ann Exhib, Nat Arts Club, New York, 81. *Collections Arranged:* Nat Bank Commerce (auth, catalog), Commerce Sq Invitational, Memphis, Tenn, 73; Bicentennial Salute to Memphis, Nat Bank Commerce Salutes, 76. *Pos:* Artist, Look Mag, Des Moines, Iowa, 60-64; sr art designer, Ward Archer & Assocs Advert, Memphis, 69-79; designer & illusr, Connie Hendrix & Assocs, Memphis, 79- *Teaching:* Memphis City Sch System, Tenn, 66-69; instr Watercolor, Univ Tenn Student Alumni Educ Ctr, Adult Educ Prog, 73-; instr watercolor, Memphis State Univ Continuing Educ, 75- *Awards:* First Place Purchase Award, 11th Tenn All-State, First Am Nat Bank, 71; Top Cash Award, Watercolor Div, 8th Cent South Art Exhib, Commerce Union Bank, 73; Nat Bank of Commerce Award, Tenn Watercolor Soc Ann, 73, 74, 78 & 81. *Mem:* Tenn Watercolor Soc (regional dir, 71-73, corresp secy, 72, vpres, 74 & pres, 75-76); Am Watercolor Soc; Assoc Allied Artists Am; Art Dirs' Club Memphis (secy, 70 & 71, vpres, 72 & pres, 73); Memphis Watercolor Soc. *Media:* Watercolor. *Publ:* Auth,

Bicentennail Salute to Memphis (film), Cablecom/Educ TV, 76. *Dealer:* Gallery One, 306 Howard St Petrosky MI 49770; Forest Hill Art Gallery, 9076 Old Poplar Pike Germantown, TN 38138. *Mailing Add:* 1408 Flamingo St Memphis TN 38117

HENES, DONNA
ENVIRONMENTAL ARTIST, SCULPTOR
b Cleveland, Ohio, Sept 19, 45. *Study:* Ohio State Univ; City Col New York, BS, 70, MS, 72. *Comn:* Pub participatory event, Bicentennial Comn, New York, 76; Vernal Equinox Celebration, Port Authority NY & NJ, New York, 80; web installation, Indianapolis Mus, 83; installation, Maine Monument, New York Cult Affairs Dept, 83; seasonal pub celebrations, Lower Manhattan Cult Coun, 83. *Exhib:* Women in American Architecture, Brooklyn Mus & traveling, 77; Hilosphia, Spain, 82; Sculpture Tricentennial, Philadelphia Arts Alliance, 82; solo shows, Washington Proj Arts, 82 & Indianapolis Mus Art, 83; At Home, Newport Harbor Mus, Calif, 83; Artist Books Biennial, Ctr Arte & Communicacion, Buenos Aires, 83. *Bibliog:* Lucy Lippard (auth), Overlay, Pantheon Books, 82; Eggs on end, New Yorker, 83; Moira Roth (auth), The amazing decade, Astro Art, 83. *Mem:* Founding mem Ctr Celebration (bd dirs, 80-). *Media:* Ritual Celebration, Environmental Transformation. *Publ:* Contribr, The Politics of Women's Spirituality, Doubleday, 81; auth, Dressing Our Wounds in Warm Clothes, Astro Artz, 82. *Mailing Add:* 351 Jay St Brooklyn NY 11201

HENKLE, JAMES LEE
SCULPTOR, DESIGNER
b Cedar Rapids, Iowa, Mar 13, 27. *Study:* Univ Nebr, BA; Pratt Inst, cert(indust design). *Work:* Univ Okla Art Mus, Norman; Okla State Art Collection, Okla Arts & Humanities Coun, Oklahoma City. *Comn:* Sculpture & fountain, First Fed Savings & Loan Bldg, Ft Smith, Ark, 61; sculpture mural, Numerical Anal Res Ctr, Norman, 63; sculpture mural, Tulsa Pub Libr, Tulsa Hist Soc, Okla, 65; sculpture, Norman Pub Libr, 75th Anniversary Comt, 66; wall sculpture, Dale Hall, Univ Okla, Chi Omega Sorority, 69. *Exhib:* Eight State Art Exhib, Oklahoma City Art Ctr, 61; one-man sculpture exhib, Univ Okla Mus Art, 68 & Philbrook Art Ctr, Tulsa, 70; Okla State Univ, 79; Okla Designer Craftsman Exhibs, 76-81. *Pos:* Designer, Dave Chapman Design Firm, 52-53. *Teaching:* Prof art, Univ Okla, 53- *Awards:* Purchase Prize Sculpture, Okla Art Ctr, 65; Purchase Prize Painting, Springfield Art Mus; Purchase Award Crafts, Eighth Ann Print, Drawing & Crafts Exhib, Ark Arts Ctr, 75. *Mailing Add:* Sch of Art Univ of Okla Norman OK 73069

HENLE, FRITZ
PHOTOGRAPHER, FILMMAKER
b Dormund, Ger, June, 09; US citizen. *Study:* Univ Heidelberg, 30; Univ Munich, 30; Sch Photog, Munich, Ger, dipl(photog), 31. *Work:* Mus Mod Art, Int Ctr Photog, New York; Ctr Creative Photog, Tucson; George Eastman House, Rochester, NY; Univ Tex Photog Collection; and many others. *Exhib:* 20th Anniversary Exhib, APA Int Tokyo, 78; Color Photographs, Trinity Univ, San Antonio, 79; retrospective, Witkin Gallery, New York, 80; Body Electric: Color, Squibb Inst, Princeton, 80; Germany: The New Vision, Fraenkel Gallery, San Francisco, 81; and many others. *Pos:* Photogr, Life, 37-42, Harpers Bazaar, 45-52, City Serv Oil Co, 52-59 & free-lance, 60- *Awards:* Merit Award Photog, Popular Photog, eight times, 48-60; VI Coun Arts Grants; Nat Endowment Arts Photogr Fel. *Bibliog:* Article, Foto Mag, Munich, 3/80; Grace Glueck (auth), Art: Fritz Henle, Witkin Gallery, New York Times, 5/2/80; Grace Naismith (auth), Who, what, where, Overseas Press Club Bulletin, 5/15/80. *Mem:* Life mem VI Acad Arts & Lett; founding mem Am Soc Mag Photogr; Overseas Press Club Am. *Publ:* Illusr, Holiday in Europe, 63; illusr, A New Guide to Rollei Photography, 65; illusr, The American Virgin Islands, 71; illusr, Casals, 75; illusr, The Rolliflex SL66 and SLX Way, 75; and others. *Dealer:* Witkin Gallery 41 E 57th St New York NY 10022; Benteler Galleries 2409 Rice Blvd Houston TX 77005. *Mailing Add:* PO Box 723 Christiansted St Croix VI 00820

HENNESSEY, WILLIAM JOHN
MUSEUM DIRECTOR
b Summit, NJ, July 15, 48. *Study:* Wesleyan Univ, BA, 70; Ford Found fel, Worcester Art Mus, 71-73; Columbia Univ, PhD, 78. *Collections Arranged:* The American Portrait: From Stuart to Sargent (auth, catalog), Worcester Art Mus, 73; Artists Look at Art (auth, catalog), 78 & Permanent Collection, 78, Spencer Art Mus, Univ Kans. *Pos:* Res assoc, Solomon R Guggenheim Mus, 73-74; cur, Spencer Art Mus, Univ Knas, 75-79; dir, Vassar Col Art Gallery, 79-82; dir, Univ Ky Art Mus, currently. *Teaching:* Instr, Brooklyn Col & Sch Visual Arts, 73-75; asst prof, Univ Kans, 75-79; asst prof, Vassar Col, 79-82. *Mem:* Col Art Asn; Soc Archit Historians. *Res:* Victorian English art and architecture; contemporary American art and architecture. *Publ:* Auth, A Handbook of the Worcester Art Museum, 73; auth, Friedrich Overbeck's Drawing of Elijah, Regist Spencer Mus, spring 77; auth, Frank Lloyd Wright and the design of the Guggenheim Museum, Arts Mag, 4/78. *Mailing Add:* Art Museum Univ Ky Lexington KY 40506

HENNESY, GERALD CRAFT
PAINTER
b Washington, DC, June 11, 21. *Study:* Corcoran Sch Art; George Washington Univ; Am Univ; Univ Md; also with C Gordon Harris. *Work:* Nat Hq Am Legion, Nat Hq Daughters Am Revolution, Washington, DC; Md State Exec Mansion, Annapolis; US House Rep Off Bldg, Washington, DC. *Comn:* Paintings, Gibson Bldg, Fairfax, Va, 74; paintings, United Va Bank, Richmond, 75; painting, Hq Blue Cross & Blue Shield Asn, Washington, DC, 82; painting, Nat Hq Fed Deposit Insurance Corp, Washington, DC, 83.

Exhib: Corcoran Gallery Art, Washington, DC; Am Art League, Smithsonian Inst, Washington, DC, 62 & 64; Baltimore Mus Art Regional, 63; New York World's Fair, 65; Allied Artists of Am, New York, 75 & 76; one-man show, Pla Gallery, McLean, Va, 67; and many others. *Pos:* Advertising artist, Washington Times Herald, Washington, DC, 41-42. *Awards:* First Prize, Gilham Show, 66; Watercolor Medal, Landscape Club, 74. *Mem:* Landscape Club Washington (treas, 73-77); Potomac Valley Watercolorists; Artists Equity Asn; Fairfax Co Coun Arts. *Media:* Oil, Watercolor. *Dealer:* Tolley Galleries 821 15th St NW Washington DC 20005. *Mailing Add:* 6811 White Rock Rd Clifton VA 22024

HENNING, EDWARD BURK
CURATOR, HISTORIAN
b Cleveland, Ohio, Oct 23, 22. *Study:* Cleveland Inst Art, cert(painting); Western Reserve Univ, BS, MA; Acad Julian, Paris. *Collections Arranged:* Paths of Abstract Art (with catalog), 60; Fifty Years of Modern Art: 1916-1966 (with catalog), 66; Landscapes Interior and Exterior: Avery, Rothko and Schueler (with catalog), 75; The Spirit of Surrealism (with catalog), 79; and others. *Pos:* Asst cur educ, Cleveland Mus Art, 55-56, assoc cur educ, 56-59, asst to dir, 59-70, cur mod art, 63- *Teaching:* Adj prof mod art, Case Western Reserve Univ, 68- *Mem:* Col Art Asn; Am Asn Mus; Am Soc Aesthetics; Int Coun Mus. *Res:* Impressionism to present, especially Cezanne, cubism, dadaism and surrealism; abstract-expressionism, color-field painting and conceptualism. *Publ:* Auth, Patronage and Style in the Arts: A Suggestion Concerning Their Relations, 60; contribr, On Understanding Art Museums, 75. *Mailing Add:* 3325 Fairmount Blvd Cleveland Heights OH 44118

HENRICH, BIFF
PHOTOGRAPHER
b Erie, Pa, Oct 2, 53. *Study:* Hiram Col, BA, 75; Visual Studies Workshop, 76; State Univ NY, Buffalo, MFA, 78. *Work:* Albright-Knox Art Gallery; Ft Worth Mus Art. *Exhib:* Syracuse Show, Everson Mus Art, 79; Altered Images, PS1, New York, 79; In Western NY, Albright-Knox Art Gallery, 79, 81 & 83; New Photography, Contemp Art Mus, Houston, 81; Surface in Contemporary Art, Laguna Gloria Mus, Austin, Tex, 83; Artpark Installation, Lewiston, NY, 83; Grand Galop, Artist Space, New York, 83. *Pos:* Dir, CEPA Gallery, Buffalo, 78-82, pres bd dirs, 78- *Teaching:* Tutor & mentor photog, Empire State Col, 78-80; vis lectr, State Univ NY, Buffalo, 80 & 83. *Awards:* Nat Endowment Arts Fel, 79; NY State Coun Arts Sponsored Proj, 83. *Dealer:* Tex Gallery 2012 Peden Houston TX 77019. *Mailing Add:* PO 111 Buffalo NY 14222

HENRICKSON, PAUL ROBERT
PAINTER, WRITER
b Boston, Mass. *Study:* RI Sch Design, BFA; Boston State Col, ME; Univ Minn, PhD; Clark Univ; Statens Kunst Akademiet, Oslo; Statens Kunst Industriskole, Oslo. *Work:* La Jolla Art Ctr, Calif; Mus of NMex, Santa Fe; Statens Kunst Industriskole. *Comn:* Crash (canvas panel), in pvt collection, NDak; four part canvas panel, pvt collection, New York. *Exhib:* One-man exhibs, Am & Mex Mus. *Pos:* Exec dir, Insular Arts Coun, Gov Guam, 65-68; free lance art critic, Santa Fe Reporter, NMex & Art Voices/South, Palm Beach, Fla. *Teaching:* Prof & head div fine arts, Univ Gaum, 64-68; prof res art, Univ Northern Iowa, 68-72. *Res:* Psychology of art. *Publ:* Auth, Two Primitive Micronesian Art Forms, 68; Lying, Dogmatic and Creative Persons, 70; The Perceptive and Silenced Minorities, 72; auth, The Word for Cross is Cryptic, 77. *Mailing Add:* 428 Camino de las Animas Santa Fe NM 87501

HENRY, DALE
PAINTER
b Anniston, Ala, Feb 8, 31. *Work:* Calif Palace Legion Hon; Mills Col Art Gallery; Adirondack Planning Comn. *Comn:* Site installations (paintings), Brutten-Herrick Collection, Clocktower, New York, 75, Inst Art & Urban Resources, PS1, 76, Ben Shahn Gallery, William Paterson Col, 80 & Sarah Lawrence Col, 84. *Exhib:* Dallas Mus Contemp Art, 60; Calif Palace Legion Hon Ann, 60-65; one-man show, Calif Palace Legion Hon, 61, Fischbach Gallery, 71, Toselli Gallery, 72 & John Weber Gallery, 72, 73, 76, 77 & 79; Richmond Mus Art, 62; Works and Projects of the Seventies, Inst Art & Urban Resources & traveling, 77-80; and others. *Collections Arranged:* Collectors of the Seventies, Clocktower, New York, 75; A Collection in Progress, Moore Col Art, 77; Selections From the Collection: Drs Brutten-Herrick, Ben Shahn Gallery, William Paterson Col, 80. *Teaching:* Instr fine arts, Sch Visual Arts, New York, 70- *Awards:* Bd Mem Award, Calif Palace Legion Hon, 61; Painting Grants, Creative Arts Pub Serv, 81 & Nat Endowment Arts, 82. *Media:* All. *Publ:* Contribr, Inscriptions, 1977, Mollet-Vieville & Najar, 77; contribr, Sol Lewitt Wall Drawings, Wadsworth-Atheneum, Yale Press, 81. *Mailing Add:* PO Box 88 Bullville NY 10915

HENRY, GERRIT VAN KEUREN
CRITIC
b Baldwin, NY, May 30, 50. *Study:* Columbia Col, Columbia Univ, BA, 72. *Collections Arranged:* Work by Joe Brainard, Sch Visual Arts, 72. *Pos:* New York corresp, Art Int, 70-72; art critic, New Republic, 73-74; assoc ed, Artnews, New York, 73-75; sr ed, Print Collector's Newsletter, 79- *Teaching:* Adj asst prof art hist, C W Post Col, Greenvale, NY, 72-74. *Awards:* Art Critics' Fel, Nat Endowment Arts. *Bibliog:* Lawrence Alloway (auth), The renewal of realist criticism, Art in Am, 81. *Res:* Mid-20th century American painterly realism. *Publ:* Auth, two articles, In: Super Realism, Dutton, 75; auth, Interview with Jack Levine, Artnews, 79; auth, Painterly realism and the modern landscape, Art in Am, 81. *Mailing Add:* 265 W 90th St #7 New York NY 10024

HENRY, JEAN
PAINTER, INSTRUCTOR
b Oakland, Calif. *Study:* Art Acad, Amsterdam, Holland; Am Univ Berlin; Md Inst, Baltimore; Western Reserve Univ. *Work:* Triton Mus Art, San Jose, Calif; Chamber of Commerce, San Francisco; Schwartz Hall, Presidio, Calif; Kaiser Hosp, San Francisco; Letterman Hosp, San Francisco. *Comn:* Portrait of Sen Graham, Capitol Bldg, Frankfurt, Ky, 72; portrait, Dr Arthur Sammis, 80; portrait, Eubie Blake (famous jazz pianist & composer), 80; Turk Murphy (famous jazz musician), 80. *Exhib:* Soc Western Artists, De Young Mus, 68; De Saisset Gallery, Santa Clara, Calif, 69; one-man show, Triton Mus Art, 70; Marin Art & Garden Show, 71; Rosicrucian Mus Invitational Show, 71. *Pos:* Owner, art gallery, Burlingame, Calif, currently. *Teaching:* Instr portrait painting, Md Inst, Johns Hopkins Univ, 58-60; owner & instr painting, Jean Henry Sch Art, San Francisco, 69- *Awards:* First Award, De Young Mus, 68; First Award, Antioch Outdoor Festival, 69; First Award for Portrait, De Saisset Gallery Ann, 70. *Mem:* Soc Western Artists. *Media:* Oil, Acrylic. *Mailing Add:* 5340 Geary Blvd San Francisco CA 94121

HENRY, JOHN RAYMOND
SCULPTOR
b Lexington, Ky, Aug 11, 43. *Study:* Univ Ky; Univ Wash; Art Inst Chicago, Edward L Reyerson fel, 69. *Work:* City of Rockford, Ill; Ill State Mus, Springfield; British Mus; Smithsonian Inst, Washington, DC; Ft Worth Art Mus, Tex. *Comn:* Sculpture, Nat Endowment Arts, Works of Art in Pub Places, Govs State Univ, South Park Forest, Ill; Sun Target, Nat Endowment Arts, Mich Mus, Charlotte, NC, 75; Sculpture for City of Sioux City, Iowa, Nat Endowment Arts Matching Grant. *Exhib:* Art Inst Chicago, 68; Eight Am Sculptors, Chicago, 68; Sculpture Potsdam, 77, Potsdam State Univ, NY, 77; one-man shows, Riverside Park, New York, 75, Laguna Gloria Mus Art, Austin, Tex, 76 & Springfield Mus Art, Mo, 77; and others. *Pos:* Vpres, Chicago Creative Arts Found, 69- *Teaching:* Artist in residence, Univ Wis-Green Bay, 69-70. *Mem:* Sculptor's Group Inc, Chicago. *Media:* Metals. *Dealer:* Dorsky Galleries Ltd 111 Fourth Ave New York NY 10003. *Mailing Add:* c/o Richard Gray Gallery 620 N Michigan Ave Chicago IL 60611

HENRY, ROBERT
PAINTER, EDUCATOR
b Brooklyn, NY, Aug 3, 33. *Study:* Hans Hofmann Sch Fine Art, New York & Provincetown, Mass; Brooklyn Col, with Ad Reinhardt & Kurt Seligmann, BA. *Exhib:* Hudson River Mus, Yonkers, NY, 71; Contemporary Figurative Painting, Suffolk Co Mus, Stony Brook, NY, 71; one-man show, Green Mountain Gallery, New York. *Teaching:* From asst prof to prof art, Brooklyn Col, 60- *Bibliog:* L Campbell (auth), Stop, look & look & look, Art News, 2/72. *Media:* Oil. *Publ:* Auth, Horizontally oriented rotating kinetic painting, Leonardo, 69. *Dealer:* Blue Mountain Gallery 121 Wooster St New York NY 10012. *Mailing Add:* 803 Greenwich St New York NY 10014

HENRY, SARA LYNN
HISTORIAN, CRITIC
b Teaneck, NJ, Sept 24, 42. *Study:* Denison Univ, BFA; NY Univ, with Robert Goldwater, BA(art hist); Univ Calif, Berkeley, with Peter Selz & Herschel B Chipp, PhD. *Teaching:* Lectr art hist, Goucher Col, Towson, Md, 70-71; vis instr, Ohio State Univ, Columbus, 71-72; instr, Carnegie-Mellon Univ, Pittsburgh, 73-76; assoc prof, Drew Univ, 76- *Mem:* Col Art Asn; Women's Caucus for Art. *Res:* Paul Klee; abstract expressionism; contemporary art. *Publ:* Contribr, New Catholic Encyclopedia, McGraw-Hill, 66; contribr, Selection 1968, Univ Art Mus, Univ Calif, Berkeley, 68-69; coauth, The Political Art of Duncan MacPherson, Can Dimension, 3-4/70; auth, Form-creating energies: Paul Klee & physics, Arts Mag, 9/77; auth, Klee's Kleinwelt & creation, Print Rev, fall 77. *Mailing Add:* 17 Madison Ave Madison NJ 07940

HENSCHE, ADA RAYNER See Rayner, Ada

HENSCHE, HENRY
PAINTER, INSTRUCTOR
b Chicago, Ill, Feb 20, 01. *Study:* Charles W Hawthorne's Cape Cod Sch Art; Art Inst Chicago; Nat Acad Design; Art Students League; Beaux Arts Inst Design New York. *Work:* Fort Wayne Art Inst, Ind; Chrysler Collection, Norfolk; Mint Mus, NC; Harvard Club, New York; Oklahoma City Mus. *Exhib:* Pittsburgh Int, Nat Acad Design, New York, Chicago Am, Philadelphia Ann & Corcoran Biennial, Washington, DC, 22-33. *Teaching:* Instr oils & watercolors, Cape Cod Sch Art, 28- *Awards:* Hallgarten Prize, Nat Acad Design, 30. *Mem:* Boston Guild Artist; Provincetown Art Asn. *Media:* Oil. *Dealer:* Grand Central Art Gallery 27 W 57th New York NY 10019. *Mailing Add:* Provincetown MA 02657

HENSELMANN, CASPAR
SCULPTOR
b Mannheim, Ger, Mar 13, 33; US citizen. *Study:* Art Inst Chicago, BFA; Univ Ill Col Med, MMed-Art; Northwestern Univ; Columbia Univ. *Comn:* Lobby sculpture (glass, steel, oil, air), Technicon Corp, Tarrytown, NY, 68-69; multiple turbine (aluminum & stainless), Southridge Shopping Ctr, Milwaukee, Wis, 69-71; wave piece (stainless), A Clayburgh, Byram, Conn, 71; glass lobby piece (oil, air), Marshall-Ilsley Bank, Milwaukee, 71; Union Bank Switzerland, New York, 83. *Exhib:* Weatherspoon Gallery, Univ NC, 74; Marika Malcorda, Geneva, Switz, 76; Indoor/Outdoor Sculpture Show, Inst Art & Urban Resources, PS 1, New York, 78; Cult Coun Found, NY, 79; one-man show, Sculpture Now, New York, 79; and others. *Teaching:* Instr, St Cloud State Col, 75; asst prof, C W Post Ctr, Long Island Univ, 76-77; Univ NC, Chapel Hill, 83. *Awards:* Tiffany Award; Ford Found Artist in Residence, Am Fedn Arts; Nat Endowment Arts Award, 79. *Bibliog:* Articles in: The Village Voice, 74 & 79 & The Soho News, 76, 77, 78 & 79. *Mailing Add:* 21 Bond St New York NY 10012

HERA
SCULPTOR, ENVIRONMENTAL ARTIST
b New Orleans, La, Sept 28, 40. *Study:* Mt Holyoke Col; Sch Art Inst Chicago; Univ Dallas, Tex, BA, 70; Southern Methodist Univ, MFA, 74. *Work:* Okla Arts Ctr, Oklahoma City; New Orleans Mus; Longview Mus, Tex; Lafayette Natural Hist Mus, La; Rose Art Mus, Brandeis Univ, Waltham, Mass. *Comn:* Snail Shell Maze, Tri-Town Coun, Boxford, Mass, 79; Floribunda, Creedmoor Hosp, Queens, NY, 80; Stormflower, Univ New Orleans, 80. *Exhib:* One-woman shows, Lifeways, Inst Contemp Art, Boston, 76, Butcher Shop, Brooks Jackson Gallery Iolas, New York, 79; Family Room, Contemp Art Ctr, New Orleans, La & Nexus Gallery, Philadelphia, 81; Dream Feast, Alternative Mus, New York, 81; Niagara-Knossos-Carranza Connector, Artpark, 82. *Pos:* Procession designer, First Night, Inc, Boston, 77-78; consult, Women's Slide Arch, Schlesinger Libr Hist Women Am, Radcliffe Col, 77-80; vis artist, Sch Mus Fine Arts, Boston, 78; artist-in-residence, Palisades Interstate Park Com, Bear Mountain, NY, 81; major project artist, Artpark, 82. *Teaching:* Artist-in-residence painting, drawing & sculpture, Fed Correctional Inst, Nat Endowment for Arts Pilot Prog, Tallahassee, Fla, 75-76; instr, Framingham State Col, Mass, 77-78. *Awards:* Mass Coun Arts Award, 79; Dept Cult Affairs New York Award, 83; NY State Coun Arts Award, 83. *Bibliog:* E M Hatton (auth), The Tent Book, Houghton Mifflin, 79; Ronald Fleming & Renata Von Tscharner (auths), Placemakers, Hastings House, NY, 81; Lucy Lippard (auth), Overlay, Pantheon, 83. *Mem:* Col Art Asn; Women's Caucus Art. *Media:* Plants, Plastic; Fabric, Steel. *Mailing Add:* 32 W 20th St New York NY 10011

HERARD, MARVIN T
SCULPTOR, EDUCATOR
b Puyallup, Wash, July 4, 29. *Study:* Burnley Sch Art, Seattle; Seattle Univ; Univ Wash, BA; Cranbrook Acad Art, MFA; Acad Fine Arts, Florence, Italy; Fonderia Artistica Florentina, Italy. *Comn:* Sculpture, Renton Pub Libr; Lemieux Libr, Seattle Univ. *Exhib:* Palazzo Venezia, Rome, 62; Seattle Art Mus, 65-67; Gov Exhib, State Capitol Mus, 67-69; Henry Gallery, Univ Wash, 68; Cheney Cowles Mus, Spokane, Wash, 69; and others. *Teaching:* Instr, Seattle Pub Schs, 56-58; teaching fel sculpture, Cranbrook Acad Arts, 59-60; from assoc prof to prof art & chmn fine arts dept, Seattle Univ, 60-; instr painting, Pius XII Inst Art, Florence, Italy, 62. *Awards:* Am Craftsmen Award, Henry Gallery, 61 & 65; Spokane Pac Northwest Exhib, 63, 64 & 66; Seattle Art Mus, 65; and others. *Mem:* Nat Art Educ Asn; Am Asn Univ Prof. *Mailing Add:* 1131 23rd Ave E Seattle WA 98112

HERBERT, JAMES ARTHUR
PAINTER, FILMMAKER
b Boston, Mass, Feb 13, 38. *Study:* Dartmouth Col, AB(art hist, magna cum laude); Univ Colo, MFA; also with Clyfford Still, Kenzo Okada & Stan Brakhage. *Work:* Whitney Mus Am Art, New York; Mus Mod Art, New York; Walker Art Ctr; Royal Film Arch Belgium; Centre Beaubourg, Paris, France. *Comn:* Film. Kennedy Ctr Performing Arts, 81; film, Libr Congress, 83. *Exhib:* One-man shows, Walker Art Ctr, 73 & 82, High Mus Art, 75 & Mus Mod Art, 81; Cineprobe: An Evening with James Herbert, Mus Mod Art, 70-77, Kennedy Ctr, 81; Whitney Mus Am Art, 74, 75 & 83; Am Film Festival, New York, 74, 76 & 83; 5th Int Exp Film Competition, Knokke-Heist, Belgium, 75; PS 1, New York, 79; Libr Congress, 83; Monique Knowton Gallery, 83; and others. *Teaching:* Resident artist, Yale Summer Sch Art & Music, Norfolk, Conn, 65; prof painting, Univ Ga, 62- *Awards:* Guggenheim Mem Found Fel, 71; Nat Endowment Arts Grant, 75, 78, 81 & 82; Louis Comfort Tiffany Found Award, 80. *Bibliog:* David Curtis (auth), The informal vision, in Experimental Cinema, Dell, 71; Roger Greenspun (auth), Quick-who are David Rimmer & James Herbert?, NY Times Sunday Edition, 10/8/72; Larry Kardish (auth), Of Light and Texture, Andrew Noren/James Herbert, Mus Mod Art, 81. *Media:* Acrylic, Watercolor; 16mm Film. *Mailing Add:* 243 Dearing St Athens GA 30605

HERBERT, ROBERT L
HISTORIAN, EDUCATOR
b Worcester, Mass, Apr 21, 29. *Study:* Wesleyan Univ, BA, 51; Inst Art & Archeol & Ecole du Louvre, Paris, Fulbright Scholar, 51-52; Yale Univ, MA, 54, PhD, 57; Am Coun Learned Soc Grant, 60; Morse fel, London, Eng, 60-61; sr fac fel, Paris, 68-69; Guggenheim fel, Paris & New Haven, Conn, 71-72. *Collections Arranged:* Barbizon Revisited (auth, catalog), Mus Fine Arts, Boston, 62-63; Neo-Impressionists & Nabis in the collection of Arthur G Altschul (auth, catalog), Yale Univ Art Gallery, 65; Neo-Impressionism (auth, catalog), Solomon R Guggenheim Mus, New York, 68; Retrospective, J F Millet (auth, catalog), Mus Nat, Paris & Arts Coun, London, 75-76; Leger's Le Grand Dejeuner (auth, catalog), Inst Arts, Minneapolis. *Teaching:* Asst instr hist of art, Yale Univ, 54-55, actg instr, 55-56, instr & mem comt hist, arts & lett, 56-60, from asst prof to prof hist art, 60-74, Robert Lehman prof hist of art, 74-, dir undergrad studies, 62-64, interim dir grad studies, 65 & 66, actg chmn, 65-66, chmn, 66-68; Slade prof, Oxford Univ, 78. *Awards:* Frank Jewett Mather Award for Barbizon Revisited, Col Art Asn, 63; Chevalier dans l'Ordre des Arts et des Lettres, French government, 76; Distinguished Teaching of Art History Award, Col Art Asn, 82. *Res:* 19th and 20th century French art. *Publ:* Auth, Seurat's Drawings, Shorewood, 63; auth, The Art Criticism of John Ruskin, Doubleday, 64; auth, David, Voltaire, Brutus and the French Revolution, Penguin, London & Viking, New York, 72; coed, The Societe Anonyme, Yale Univ Press, 84. *Mailing Add:* Yale Univ Dept Hist Art 56 High St New Haven CT 06520

HERFIELD, PHYLLIS
PAINTER, PRINTMAKER
b Dec 6, 47. *Study:* Art Students League, with Ernest Fiene, 65; Rome, Italy, 67-68; Tyler Sch Art, Temple Univ, BFA, 69; Nat Acad Design, with Harvey Dinnerstein, 79-80. *Comn:* Etchings, Kornblee Gallery, New York, 76; multimedia canvas, 112 Greenstreet Gallery, New York, 77; etchings, Orion Gallery, New York, 78. *Exhib:* Mus Mod Art, Paris, 75; Kathryn Markell Gallery, New York, 76; Inst Contemp Art, Philadelphia, 77; Spectrum Gallery, New York, 77 & 78; Nat Arts Club, 80; Nat Acad Design, 81; and other group and solo exhibs. *Awards:* Julius Hallgarten Prize, Nat Acad Design, 81. *Bibliog:* Reviews, Print Collectors Newsletter, 5-6/77 & 5-6/78; Hilton Kramer (auth), review, New York Times, 3/5/81; review, Christian Sci Monitor, 3/81. *Media:* Watercolor, Oil; Etching. *Publ:* Illusr, New York Times, Esquire, New York Mag, Psychology Today, Nat Lampoon, Atlantic Monthly and others. *Dealer:* Orion Gallery 835 Madison Ave New York NY; William Soghor 1569 Third Ave New York NY 10028. *Mailing Add:* 172 East 90th St New York NY 10028

HERIC, JOHN F
SCULPTOR
b Reno, Nev, Feb 28, 42. *Study:* Ariz State Univ, with Ben Goo, BFA; Southern Ill Univ, Carbondale, with Milt Sullivan, MFA, 65. *Work:* City of Scottsdale, Ariz; Grossmont Col; Ariz State Univ; Mus Northern Ariz, Flagstaff; Mesa Community Col, Ariz. *Comn:* Steel sculpture, Ridgewood High Sch, 64; courtyard, Sopori Sch, Sahaurita Sch Dist, Ariz, 71. *Exhib:* St Paul Mus Art, Minn, 65; one-man shows, Univ Wis-Milwaukee, 66, Grossmont Col, 69 & Elaine Horwitch Gallery, Scottsdale, 74; Southwestern Invitational, Yuma, Ariz, 69-74. *Pos:* Vis artist, Grossmont Col, 74-75. *Teaching:* Instr sculpture, Wis State Univ-Platteville, 65-67; vis lectr sculpture, Ariz State Univ, 67-69; from lectr sculpture to assoc prof art, Univ Ariz, 69- *Awards:* Best of Show, Ariz Designer Craftsmen, 68; First Award Sculpture, Ariz Ann, 68; Purchase Award, Southwestern Invitational, 71, 72 & 74. *Media:* Stone, Plastics. *Dealer:* Elaine Horwitch Gallery 4200 N Marshall Way Scottsdale AZ 85251. *Mailing Add:* Dept of Art Univ of Ariz Tucson AZ 85721

HERMAN, ALAN DAVID
DESIGNER, GRAPHIC ARTIST
b Kew Gardens, NY, Mar 8, 47. *Study:* Pratt Inst Sch Art & Design, Ida D Haskell scholarship & BFA(cum laude), 69. *Comn:* Consumer advert promotion, Carrier Air Conditioning Co, Southern Calif, 73-; med insurance commun & marketing prog, Johnson & Higgins, Los Angeles, 76-; international design programs, Xerox Corp, 80- *Exhib:* 1972 Exhibit of Best Advertising & Editorial Art in the West, 72; IAM Graphics Exhib, New York, 74; Indust Graphics Int, San Jose, Calif, 77; AIGA Packaging Exhib, Chicago, 80; Creativity 80 Show, New York. *Pos:* Pres & creative dir, Alan Herman & Assoc, Inc, Los Angeles, 70- *Awards:* Top Package of the Yr, Print Mag, 76; IGI Distinctive Merit, 77; AIGA Graphic Design USA Award, 79. *Mem:* Art Dir Club Los Angeles; Los Angeles Co Mus Art. *Mailing Add:* 3601 Chevy Chase Dr Glendale CA 91206

HERMAN, LLOYD ELDRED
MUSEUM DIRECTOR
b Corvallis, Ore, Mar 19, 36. *Study:* Ore State Univ; Univ Ore; Am Univ, BA. *Pos:* Prog mgr, Off of Dir-Gen of Mus, Smithsonian Inst, 66-71, dir, Renwick Gallery, 71- *Awards:* William A Jump Mem Found Award, 72; Potomac Chap Am Soc Interior Designers Award, 79; Decoration, Order of Leopold II by King of Belgians, 80. *Mem:* Am Crafts Coun; hon mem Am Soc Interior Designers; Nat Trust Hist Preserv. *Interests:* Twentieth century crafts and industrial design. *Publ:* Auth, Form and Fire: Natzler Ceramics 1939-1972, 73; auth, A Modern Consciousness: D J De Pree and Florence Knoll, 75; auth, Paint on Wood: Decorated American Furniture Since the 17th Century, Smithsonian Inst, 77; auth, American Porcelain: New Expressions in an Ancient Art, 80; auth, Good as Gold: Alternative Materials in American Jewelry, 81. *Mailing Add:* Smithsonian Inst Washington DC 20560

HERMAN, VIC
PAINTER, WRITER
b Fall River, Mass. *Study:* Yale Puppeteers, Los Angeles, Calif, with Harry Burnett; Art Students League, with George Bridgeman; New York Com Illus Sch, with Lu Kimmel; Columbia Univ, with Ed Johnson; with Dr Samuel Penchansky. *Work:* Four US White House Presidential Collections; Syracuse Univ, NY; Columbia Univ, New York; Rutgers Univ, New Brunswick, NJ; Mus Cartoon Art, Port Chester, NY; and others. *Exhib:* Many Faces of Mexico Int Traveling Exhib, co-sponsored by US Info Serv & Govt Mexico, 60-; one-man show, San Francisco Int Art Expo, 81; San Diego COMBO Exhibs, 80-84; Ohio State Univ Festival Cartoon Art, 83; Collector's Choice Fine Arts Gallery, Del Mar, Calif, 83; and many others. *Pos:* Asst art dir, Warner Bros Studios, New York, 40-43; artist-field corresp, Yank Mag & Stars and Stripes, 43-46; pres & prod chief, Vic Herman Prod, 47-60; staff illusr & corresp, Hearst Features, New York Times, Readers Digest, Holt, Rinehart & Winston & Golden Books, New York & Mex, 50- *Teaching:* Bd Educ Los Angeles & San Diego, 65- *Awards:* Children's Book Coun Showcase Award, 76; Best Children's Book of the Year Award, Printing Industries Am, 78 & Independence Star, Mo, 80; Pres Lett Commendation, 82; and others. *Bibliog:* Sally Cass (auth), US artist portrays the Mexican feeling, Mexico City News, 68; Frederic Whitaker (auth), Vic Herman, ambassador with a brush, Am Artist Mag, 74; Herbert Johnson (auth), Vic Herman goes where the action is, Los Angeles Examiner, 79. *Mem:* Soc Illusr New York; Am Soc Training Dirs; Soc Children's Book Writers Calif; Nat Cartoonists Soc; Am Soc Mag Cartoonists; and others. *Media:* Mixed Media.

Publ: Auth & illusr, Winnie the Wac, McKay, 45; auth & illusr, My Days Are Made of Butterflies, 70 & auth & illusr, Sunday in Zamora Park, 72, Holt, Rinehart & Winston; illusr, God and Mr Gomez, Readers Digest Condensed Books, 75; auth & illusr, Juanito's Railroad in the Sky, Golden Books, 76; auth of over 52 books; cartoons & paintings in numerous national magazines. *Mailing Add:* 25 South Lane Del Mar CA 92014

HERMANN, M(ILDRED) L
PAINTER, COLLAGE ARTIST
b Brooklyn, NY. *Study:* Artists in Am Sch Painting, with Leo Manso & Jerry Okimoto, 68-74. *Work:* Norton Gallery & Mus, West Palm Beach, Fla. *Exhib:* Childe Hassam Purchase Fund Exhib, Am Acad & Inst Arts & Lett, New York, 78; Berkshire Art Asn Ann, Berkshire Mus, Pittsfield, Mass, 81; 39th Ann Exhib, Audubon Artists, New York, 81; Collage and Assemblage, Miss Mus Art, Jackson, 81 & Tampa Mus, Fla, 82. *Awards:* Childe Hassam Purchase Award, 78; Dr S Gelband Mem Award, Nat Asn Women Artists, 81; Ralph Fabri Award Oil, Audubon Artists, 81. *Bibliog:* Addison Parks (auth), Free style--Viridian, Arts Mag, 5/80; Helen A Harrison (auth), Library art exhibits, New York Times, 9/26/82; Malcolm Preston (auth), Large in quantity & quality, Newsday, 10/4/83. *Mem:* Nat Asn Women Artists; Audubon Artists; Artists Involvement Art; Artists Guild, Norton Gallery & Sch Art. *Media:* Collage. *Dealer:* Viridian Gallery 52 W 57 St New York NY 10019. *Mailing Add:* 55 Salem Rd Roslyn Heights NY 11577

HERNANDEZ, ANTHONY LOUIS
PHOTOGRAPHER
b Los Angeles, Calif, July 7, 47. *Study:* E Los Angeles Col, 66-70; Ctr Eye, Aspen, Colo, 69, with Lee Friedlander. *Work:* Univ Calif, Davis; Mus Mod Art, New York; Bibliot Nat, Paris, France; Int Mus Photog, George Eastman House, Rochester, NY. *Comn:* Photographs, Corcoran Gallery Art, Washington, DC, 76. *Exhib:* Calif Photogr, Pasadena Art Mus & Oakland Mus Art, Calif, 70; The Crowded Vacancy, Pasadena Art Mus & San Francisco Mus Art, Calif, 71; The Nation's Capital in Photographs, Corcoran Gallery of Art, 76; Unposed Portrait, Whitney Mus Am Art, New York, 77; Contemp Am Photog Works, Mus Fine Arts, Houston, Tex, 77. *Awards:* Ferguston Grant, Friends Photog, Carmel, Calif, 72; Nat Endowment Arts Photog Fel, 75 & 78. *Bibliog:* Douglas Davis (auth), Sweeping Up American, Newsweek, 7/12/76. *Mailing Add:* 255 1/2 S Carondelet Los Angeles CA 90057

HERNANDEZ, JO FARB
MUSEUM DIRECTOR, CURATOR
b Chicago, Ill, Nov 20, 52. *Study:* Univ Wis-Madison, BA, 74; Univ Calif, Los Angeles, MA, 75; Univ Calif, Berkeley; Mus Mgt Inst, 81. *Collections Arranged:* Miniatures 82; Made in Japan: Noritake Art Deco Porcelains, 82; Mexican Indian Dance Masks (auth, catalog), 82; Art of the Cuna, 82; Jewish Marriage Contracts, 83; Harriet Estel Berman: A Family of Appliances You Can Believe In (auth, catalog), 83; Ashanti Gold Weights, 83; New York/New Looks, 83; and many others. *Pos:* Curatorial asst, Mus Cult Hist, Los Angeles, 74-75; cur/educ asst, Dallas Mus Fine Arts, 76-77; dir, Triton Mus Art, Santa Clara, Calif, 77- *Teaching:* adj prof, ETex State Univ, 77, John F Kennedy Univ, 79 & San Jose State Univ, 79-80. *Awards:* Trewartha Award, Univ Wis, 74; Ralph C Altman Award, Mus Cult Hist, 75; Rockefeller Fel, 76-77. *Mem:* Non-Profit Gallery Asn (vpres); Am Asn Mus; Am Folklore Soc; Calif Folklore Soc. *Publ:* Coauth, Day of the Dead: Tradition and Change in Contemporary Mexico, 79; auth, Robot Sculptures/A Robot Builders Manual: Metal Works by Clayton Bailey, 81; auth, Crime and Punishment, Triton Mus Art, 84. *Mailing Add:* 54 S 14th St San Jose CA 95112

HERNANDEZ, SAM (SAMUEL RUDOLPH)
SCULPTOR, EDUCATOR
b Hayward, Calif, Jan 23, 48. *Study:* Calif State Univ, Hayward, BA, 70; Ariz State Univ; Univ Wis-Madison, MFA, 74; Univ Sonora, Hermosillo, Mex, Hon Degree, 72. *Work:* New Orleans Mus Art, La; Oakland Mus, Calif. *Exhib:* Tarrant Exhib, Ft Worth Art Mus, Tex, 76; La Chinche Galeria, Mexico City, 79; San Francisco Mus Mod Art, Galif, 79; Biennial Invitational, Contemp Arts Ctr, New Orleans, 79; de Saisset Mus, Univ Santa Clara, 81; and others. *Collections Arranged:* The Day of the Dead: Tradition and Change in Contemporary Mexico (coauth, catalog), Triton Mus Art, 79. *Teaching:* Asst prof sculpture, ETex State Univ, Commerce, 74-77; assoc prof sculpture, Univ Santa Clara, Calif, 77-, chmn art dept, 80-; vis prof sculpture, Univ Wis-Madison, summer 80. *Awards:* Mobil Found Grant, 76; First Place, Ft Worth Art Mus, 76; James D Phelan Found Award, San Francisco, 78-80. *Bibliog:* L Price Amerson (auth), Artists Working in Wood, Univ Calif, Davis, 78; Frank Cebulski (auth), Processes and forms in repetition, Artweek, 1/80; Thomas Albright (auth), Tangible sculpture from a pair of local winners, San Francisco Chronicle, 1/25/80. *Mem:* Nat/Int Sculpture Asn; Nat Coun Educ Ceramic Arts; Col Art Asn. *Media:* Wood. *Publ:* Auth, Mexican Indian Dance Masks, African Arts, 5/81. *Mailing Add:* 54 S 14th St San Jose CA 95112

HERNANDEZ-CRUZ, LUIS
PAINTER, SCULPTOR
b San Juan, PR. *Study:* Univ PR, BA; Am Univ, MA, with Ben Summerford. *Work:* Chase Manhattan Bank, New York; Ponce Mus Art, PR; Mus Am, Madrid, Spain; Univ PR Mus; Inst PR Cult Mus; and others. *Comn:* Murals, PR Med Ctr, 64 & 65; glass walls, Fine Arts Ctr, Santurce, PR, 80-81; and others. *Exhib:* Arte Actual de America y Espana, Madrid, Spain, 63; Esso Salon of Young Artists, Washington, DC, 64; 2nd Biennial, Coltejer-Medellin, Colombia, 70; III Int Triennial Graphic Art, Jyvaskyla, Finland, 81; Artspace Gallery, Miami, 83; and others. *Teaching:* Prof painting, Univ PR, Rio Piedras, 68, assoc dir dept fine arts, 68-75, dir dept fine arts, 75-78. *Awards:*

First Prize in Painting, Inst PR Cult, 63; First Prize, Esso Art Contest, 64; Nat Prize, 2nd Biennial Latin Am Prints, 72. *Bibliog:* Efrain Perez Chanis (auth), El arte abstracto de Luis Hernandez-Cruz, Ed Artisticas de PR, 67; Marta Traba (auth), El abstracto que se salva, Artes Visuales, 71; plus others. *Mem:* Ateneo Puertorriqueno (dir plastic arts sect, 67-71). *Media:* Oil, Silkscreen; Marble, Wood. *Mailing Add:* Dept of Art Univ of PR Rio Piedras PR 00931

HERO, PETER DECOURCY
ADMINISTRATOR, HISTORIAN
b Washington, DC, Sept 10, 42. *Study:* Williams Col, Williamstown, Mass, with George Heard Hamilton, BA, 64, MA(art hist), 75; Stanford Univ, Calif, MBA, 66. *Collections Arranged:* The Elegant Academics (contribr, catalog), Clark Art Inst, Williamstown, Mass & Wadsworth Atheneum, Hartford, Conn, 75; Folk Art of the Oregon Country, Univ Ore Art Mus, Ore Hist Soc, Renwick Gallery, 80; and others. *Pos:* Exec dir, Ore Arts Comn, 75-; ed, Ore Arts Newsletter, 75-; contribr, articles, NW Arts, 76-81. *Teaching:* Arts adminr, Lewis & Clark Col, Portland, Ore, 82. *Awards:* Kress Found Fel, 6/75. *Mem:* Western States Arts Found; Western Asn Art Mus (bd dirs, 79-81); Nat Assembly State Arts Agencies (bd dirs, 77-81, chmn bd, 79-81); Nat Endowment Arts. *Res:* Influence of Japanese prints upon evolution of perspective and space in Edgar Degas' work. *Publ:* Contribr, For Art: New legislation can integrate art and architecture, Western States Arts Found, 76; contribr, Marketing the arts, Study Ctr Cult Policy & Arts, Univ Calif Los Angeles, 78. *Mailing Add:* 835 Summer St Salem OR 97301

HERPST, MARTHA JANE
PAINTER
b Titusville, Pa. *Study:* Pa Acad Fine Arts, 32; Grand Cent Sch Art, New York, with Wayman Adams, Edmund Greacen, Harvey Dunn & Georg Lober; also with Guy Pene Du Bois. *Work:* Nat Arts Club, New York; Titusville Woman's Club; Univ Pittsburgh, Titusville; Gannon Col, Erie, Pa; Titusville Masonic Lodge. *Comn:* Portrait, Titusville Masonic Lodge, 43; porttaits, Titusville Recreation Ctr, 54; portrait, Gannon Col, 58. *Exhib:* Nat Arts Club, New York, 33-72; Butler Inst Am Art, Youngstown, Ohio, 38 & 45; Am Artists Prof League Grand Nat, New York, 46-70; Ogunquit Art Asn, Maine, 51-61; Catharine Lorillard Wolfe Art Club, New York, 54-62. *Teaching:* Instr art, St Joseph Acad High Sch, Titusville, 55-69; pvt instr painting, 70- *Awards:* Grand Cent Sch Art Medal, 33. *Mem:* Nat Arts Club; Am Artists Prof League. *Media:* Oil, Watercolor. *Mailing Add:* 118 W Main St Titusville PA 16354

HERR, RICHARD JOSEPH
SCULPTOR, INSTRUCTOR
b Sheboygan, Wis, Jan 17, 37. *Study:* Layton Sch Art, Milwaukee; Marquette Univ; Univ Wis-Milwaukee; also with Oscar Binder, Stuttgart, Ger. *Work:* Borg-Warner Collection, Chicago; Univ Wis-LaCrosse; Univ Wis-Parkside, Kenosha; Prairie Sch, Racine, Wis. *Comn:* Relief sculpture, Northern Precision Casting, Lake Geneva, Wis, 73; door, Nafziger & Assocs, Lake Geneva, 75. *Exhib:* Critic's Choice Show, Chicago Art Inst, 72; one-man shows, Wustum Mus, Racine, 73 & Ozaukee Art Ctr, Cedarburg, Wis, 78; First Chicago Sculpture Invitational, Fed Bldg, 74; Milwaukee Art Ctr, 77. *Pos:* Owner-dir, Art Independent Gallery, Lake Geneva, 68-; Johnson Wax Found grant sculptor in residence, Prairie Sch, 70-71. *Teaching:* Instr art & chmn dept, Col Racine, 71-72; instr art, Prairie Sch, 71-; instr 3-D design, Univ Wis-Parkside, 73-74. *Awards:* Award for Sculpture, Va Beach Invitational, 71; Chicago Tribune Duo Critic's Award, Chicago Art Inst, 72; Award for Sculpture, Old Orchard Invitational, Chicago, 73. *Mem:* Southern Asn Sculptors; Am Int Sculptors; Wis Art Educ Asn (bd mem). *Media:* Aluminum, Resin. *Publ:* Contribr, Sculpture Casting, 72, Collage and Assemblage, 73 & Soft Sculpture and Related Soft Art, 75, Crown; contribr, Playboy, 74. *Dealer:* Carson-Sapiro Gallery 1411 Market St Denver CO 80202. *Mailing Add:* c/o Art Independent Gallery 222 Broad St Lake Geneva WI 53147

HERRERA, CARMEN
PAINTER
b Havana, Cuba, May 31, 15; US citizen. *Study:* Studio Federico Edelman, Havana; Marymount Col; Paris, France; Sch Archit, Havana; Art Students League. *Work:* Havana Mus; Cintas Collection. *Exhib:* Art Cubain Contemporain, Mus Mod Art, Paris, 51; Geometric Classic & Romantic Painting, Jerrold Morris Gallery, Toronto, 62; Trabia Gallery, 63; Ctr Interam Rels, 68 & 75; Inst Int Educ, 80-81; Buecker & Harpsichords, 83; and others. *Awards:* Cintas Found Fel, 66 & 68; Creative Artists Pub Serv, 77-78. *Mem:* Women in Arts. *Mailing Add:* 37 E 19th St New York NY 10003

HERRERA, RAUL OTHON
PAINTER
b Mexico City, Mex, Jan 16, 41. *Study:* Univ Nacional Autonoma de Mex, BA(polit sci, archit, philos); Iberoamerican Univ, Mex, with Matias Goertiz. *Work:* Mus Brussels, Belg; Mus Mod Art, Mex; Mus Nottingham, Eng; Casa de las Campanas, Cuernavaca. *Exhib:* Latin American Art, Mod Art Mus, Paris, 64; Biennial, Paris, 66; Mexican Art, Mus Tokyo, 67; IV-India's Triennal, New Delhi, 78; 1st Iberoam Biennal, Museo Carillo Gallery, 78; one-man show, Palacio Nacional de Bellas Artes, Mexico City, 67, Mus Mod Art, Mexico City, 75 & Museo Carillo Gallery, 79. *Collections Arranged:* Mexican Art, Montreal, Ont, 67; Latin American Art, Mus Nottingham, Eng, 67 & Mus Hemel, Hempstead, Eng, 67. *Awards:* Acquisition Prize, 1st Salon Nacional de Pintura, Museo de Bellas Artes, 78. *Bibliog:* Jorge A Manrique (auth), Raul Herrera, Revista de la Univ Nat de Mexico, 66; Luis Cardoza y Aragon (auth), Nuevos Pintores, Arte Contemp Mex, 74; Gioconda Tomassi

(auth), Raul Herrera the Painter (film), Subsecretaria de Radiodifusion, Gov Mex, 75. *Media:* Collage, Acrylic on Canvas. *Publ:* Illusr, Histories of the Hermit Abdala, Comic Book, Prometeo Libre, Mex, 75 & 76. *Mailing Add:* Sierra Guadarrama Mexico DF 10 Mexico

HERRING, JAN (JANET MANTEL)
PAINTER, WRITER
b Havre, Mont, May 17, 23. *Study:* Northern State Teachers Col; also painting with Frederic Taubes. *Work:* Grumbacher Collection, New York; Lubbock Art Ctr, Tex; Univ Idaho, Pocatello; Roswell Mus, NMex. *Exhib:* One-woman shows, El Paso Mus Art, Santa Fe Mus Art, Tulsa Art Ctr, Roswell Mus & Brigham Young Univ. *Teaching:* Pvt instr. *Bibliog:* F Taubes (auth), article, Am Artist Mag, 55; articles, La Rev Mod, 61 & House Beautiful, 64. *Publ:* Auth, The Painters Composition Handbook, 71 & The Painter's Complete Portrait and Figure Handbook, 77, Poor-Henry Publ Co. *Mailing Add:* Box 156 Clint TX 79836

HERSCHLER, DAVID ELIJAH
SCULPTOR, PAINTER
b Brooklyn, NY, Mar 1, 40. *Study:* Acad Belli Arte, Perugia, Italy, 60; Univ Rome, 60; Cornell Univ, BArch, 62; Claremont Grad Sch, MFA, 67. *Work:* Joseph H Hirshhorn Found, Washington, DC; La Jolla Mus Art, Calif; Storm King Art Ctr, Mountainville, NY; Palm Springs Mus, Calif; Israel Mus, Jerusalem. *Comn:* Sculptures, comn by Mr & Mrs N S Walbridge, La Jolla, 70, Sigmund Edelstone, Chicago, 71, Mr & Mrs J W Constance, Santa Barbara, 72, Mr & Mrs Marvin Smalley, Beverly Hills, 72 & Storm King Art Ctr, 72. *Teaching:* Instr art, San Jocquil Delta Col, Stockton, Calif, 67-69. *Media:* Stainless Steel, Gold. *Mailing Add:* PO Box 5859 Aspen CO 81612

HERSEY, GEORGE LEONARD
HISTORIAN, EDUCATOR
b Cambridge, Mass, Aug 30, 27. *Study:* Harvard Univ, BA, 51; Yale Univ, MFA, 54, MA, 61, PhD, 64; Fulbright scholar & Am Philos Soc fel, Italy, 62. *Pos:* Co-ed, Architectura, 71-; ed, Yale Publ in Hist of Art, 74-; mem, Conn State Comn Capitol Restoration, 77-79; contribr, Pre-Raphaelite Review, 81- *Teaching:* Instr art, Bucknell Univ, Lewisburg, Pa, 54-55, asst prof, 54-59, actg chmn dept, 58-59; instr hist art, Yale Univ, New Haven, Conn, 63-65, asst prof 65-68, assoc prof, 68-74, prof, 74- *Awards:* Morse Fel, 68; Schepp Fel & Vogelstein Fel, Florence, Italy, 72 & 80. *Mem:* Soc Archit Historians (dir, 71-73); Renaissance Soc Am; Col Art Asn; Victorian Soc US & Gt Brit. *Publ:* Auth, The Aragonese Architecture at Naples, 1443-1475, 73; auth, Pythagorean Palaces: Magic and Architecture in the Italian Renaissance, 75; auth, Architecture, Poetry and Number in The Royal Palace at Caserta, 83; contribr, Storia dell'Arte Italiana, 83; auth, Sinking Below the Verge: The Pre-Raphaelite Fallen Woman, 84. *Mailing Add:* Dept Hist of Art Yale Univ 180 York St New Haven CT 06520

HERSHBERG, ISRAEL
PAINTER, INSTRUCTOR
b Linz, Austria, Nov 7, 48. *Study:* Brooklyn Mus Art Sch, 66-68; Pratt Inst, BFA, 72; State Univ NY Albany, MA, 73. *Exhib:* One-man shows, Prince Street Gallery, New York, 70 & 71 & Jacobs Ladder Gallery, Washington, DC; A Sense of Place: The Artist and the American Land, Joslyn Art Mus, Omaha, Sheldon Mem Art Gallery, Lincoln, Nebr & Arts Alliance, 73; Current Trends in Contemporary American Art, Washington Co Mus Fine Arts, Hagerstown, Md, 74. *Teaching:* Instr painting & drawing, Md Inst Col Art, 73- *Media:* Oil. *Mailing Add:* Md Inst Col Art Baltimore MD 21217

HERSHEY, NONA
PRINTMAKER
b New York, NY, Oct 31, 46. *Study:* Tyler Sch Art, BFA, 67; Tyler Sch Art in Rome, MFA, 69; Instituto Statale d'Arte di Urbino, dipl, 79. *Work:* Libr Congress, DC; Mus Munic de Artes Graficas, Venezuela; Minn Mus Art, St Paul; Mus Contemp Art, Skopje, Yugoslavia; and others. *Exhib:* New Talent in Printmaking, Asn Am Artists, New York, 75; 14th Int Biennial Graphic Art, Ljubljana, Yugoslavia; Prints USA 82, Pratt Graphics Ctr, New York, 82; one-man shows, Galleria Il Ponte, Rome, 82 & Mary Ryan Gallery, New York, 83; and many others. *Teaching:* Asst prof printmaking, Daemen Col, Buffalo, NY, 72-73 & Temple Abroad, Rome, Italy, 79- *Awards:* Special Purchase Award, Davidson Nat Print Competition, Davidson Col, NC, 73 & 75; J R Marsh Mem, 17th Nat Print Exhib, Hunterdon Art Ctr, 73; Special Purchase Award, 13th Lario Int Exhib, Cadorago, Italy; and others. *Bibliog:* Miller Williams (auth), Nona Hershey, Laboratorio Artevisive, 79; Marisa Volpi Orlandini (auth), Nona Hershey, Galleria Temple, 81; Italo Mussa (auth), Nona Hershey, Galleria Il Ponte, 82. *Mem:* Print Club; Printmaking Coun NJ. *Dealer:* Assoc Am Artists 663 Fifth Ave New York NY 10022; Mary Ryan Gallery 452 Columbus Ave New York NY 10024. *Mailing Add:* Via Quattro Novembre 96 Rome 00187 Italy

HERSHMAN, LYNN LESTER
SCULPTOR
b June 17, 41. *Study:* Case Western Reserve Univ, BS, 63; Calif State Univ, San Francisco, MA, 72; Calif Col Arts & Crafts, Univ Calif, Los Angeles; Ohio Univ; Otis Art Inst; Cleveland Inst Art. *Work:* Nat Collection Fine Arts, Smithsonian Inst; Cleveland Inst Art; City of San Francisco Collection Art; Calif State Cols Collection Art; Richmond Art Ctr; plus other pub & pvt collections. *Comn:* Art poster, San Francisco Mus, 69; cover for Robopaths, Penguin Books, 72. *Exhib:* Butler Inst Am Art, Youngstown, Ohio; Ball State Univ Painting Exhib; Nat Sculpture Exhib, San Diego Mus Art, 72; Nat Gallery, Adelaide, Australia, 77; Contemp Art Mus, Houston, 78; Musee National d'Art Moderne, Centre National d'Art et de Culture George

Pompidou, Paris, 79; San Francisco Mus Mod Art, 80; one-man shows, Stefanotty Gallery, New York, 75 & Circus Circus, Las Vegas, Nev, 75; and many others. *Pos:* Corresp ed, Artweek, 71-73; coordr, Insights, San Francisco Mus Art, 72-74; gallery curator, Walnut Creek Civic Art Ctr, Calif, 74-76; assoc coordr, Christo's Running Fence Project, 74-76; invited artist, Int Inst Experimental Printmaking, Santa Cruz, Calif, 75. *Teaching:* Instr, Cleveland Mus Art, 62-63; vis asst prof drawing, Calif Col Arts & Crafts, 72-73, assoc prof, 74; instr, Melville Col, Scotland, 73. *Awards:* Bates & Springer Award, 62; Purchase Prize, San Francisco Art Festival, 69; Purchase Prize, Olive Hyde Drawing Competition, 72. *Bibliog:* Peter Selz (auth), Six artists in search of a definition of San Francisco, Art News, 6/73 & Art in Am, 3/74; Jan Butterfield (auth), Pacific Sun, 4/74; Alfred Frankenstein (auth), Macabre roome of wax ladies, San Francisco Chronicle, 10/13/74; plus many others. *Publ:* Auth, Harold Paris, the Berkeley Years, Artweek, Vol 3, No 21; auth, Edinburgh as Oz, Vol 186, No 959 & Interview with Dennis Oppenheim, 11/73, Studio Int; co-auth, Toward light and space, City Mag, Vol 1, No 7; auth, Forming a Sculptured/Drama in Manhattan, Marginal Arts & Stefanotty Gallery, 75; plus others. *Mailing Add:* San Francisco CA

HERTZBERG, ROSE
PAINTER, COLLAGE ARTIST
b Passaic, NJ, Dec 17, 12. *Study:* With Ben Benn; Hans Hofmann Art Sch; Art Students League, with Vaclav Vytlacil & Will Barnet; New York Graphics Workshop; Rockland Community Col; Fairleigh Dickinson Univ Art Seminars. *Work:* Edward Williams Col, Hackensack, NJ; Rockland Community Col, Suffern, NY; Bloomfield Col; Broadway Bank & Trust Co, Paterson, NJ; Hackensack Pub Libr & Ramsey Pub Libr, NJ; plus numerous pvt collections. *Comn:* Numerous pvt commissions. *Exhib:* Painters & Sculptors Soc NJ, Jersey City, 69-79; Nat Asn Women Artists, 71-79; one-woman shows, Bergen Community Mus, NJ; Womanart Gallery, New York & Centro des Artes, Mijas, Spain; and others. *Teaching:* Instr, Fairlawn, NJ, 60-63, Mahwah, 63. *Awards:* Putnam Mem Awards, 71 & 77, Medal of Honor, 79 & Bertha P Greenblatt Mem Award, 82; Awards, Painters & Sculptors Soc, 71 & 76; plus others. *Mem:* Life mem Art Students League; Nat Asn Women Artists; Mod Artists Guild; Painters & Sculptors Soc NJ; Artist Affil NJ. *Media:* Oil, Watercolor; Collage; Paper. *Mailing Add:* 27 Buckingham Dr Ramsey NJ 07446

HERTZMAN, GAY MAHAFFY
ADMINISTRATOR, HISTORIAN
b West Liberty, Iowa, Jan 22, 31. *Study:* Univ Iowa, Iowa City, BA, 60; Univ NC, Chapel Hill, MS(libr sci), 65, MA(art hist), 69. *Pos:* Registr-librn, NC Mus Art, Raleigh, 61-64; actg cur, Wm Hayes Ackland Art Ctr, Univ NC, Chapel Hill, 67-69; asst cur & cur European painting, NC Mus Art, 71-75, head collections res & publ, 75-79, chief cur, 80-81, asst dir, 81- *Res:* Western European art. *Mailing Add:* 1615 Ambleside Dr Raleigh NC 27605

HERZBERG, THOMAS
PRINTMAKER, ILLUSTRATOR
b Chicago, Ill. *Study:* Northeastern Ill Univ, BA, 75; Art Inst Chicago, 76-77; Northern Ill Univ, MFA, 79. *Work:* Van Straaten Gallery, Chicago; De Cordova Mus, Lincoln, Mass; Terrance Gallery, Palenville, NY; Metrop Mus & Art Ctr, Coral Gables, Fla; Silvermine Guild Artists. *Exhib:* Works on Paper, Art Inst Chicago, 78; Boston Printmakers, De Cordova Mus, Lincoln, Mass, 78, 79 & 82; Int Mini Print Show, Pratt Graphic Ctr, New York, 79, 81 & 83; 13th Nat Print Exhib, Silvermine Guild Artists, New Canaan, Conn, 80; Miami Int Print Biennial, Metrop Mus & Art Ctr, Coral Gables, Fla, 80 & 82; 26th Nat Print Exhib, Hunterdon Art Ctr, Clinton, NJ, 82; Eighth Nat Print Invitational, Univ Dallas, 83. *Teaching:* Instr photog, Oak Park River Forest High Sch, 76-77; asst printmaking, Northern Ill Univ, 78-79; instr, Northeastern Ill Univ, 81-82. *Awards:* Best of Show, Third Ann Ill Regional Print Show, 80 & Award Excellence, New Horizons in Art, 80-82, North Shore Art League; Weston Press & Gallery Award, Eighth Int Miniature Print Exhib, Pratt Graphic Ctr, 81. *Mem:* Soc Boston Printmakers; Chicago Artists Coalition. *Media:* Etching, Wood Engraving. *Publ:* Illusr, Chicago Mag, 81-, Advertising Age, 81- & Success Mag, 83- *Dealer:* Chicago Ctr Print Ltd 1509 W Fullerton Ave Chicago IL 60614. *Mailing Add:* 4128 W Eddy St Chicago IL 60641

HERZBRUN, HELENE MCKINSEY
PAINTER, EDUCATOR
b Chicago, Ill. *Study:* Univ Chicago, BA; Art Inst of Chicago; Am Univ, Washington, DC, with Jack Tworkov. *Work:* Nat Collection of Fine Arts, Washington, DC; Watkins Gallery, Am Univ; Univ Va Mus, Charlottesville; Phillips Gallery, Washington, DC. *Comn:* Tapestry (with Gloria Finn), Harcourt-Brace Publ Co, New York, 63. *Exhib:* Biennial Exhib, Corcoran Gallery of Art, Washington, DC, 53; Washington Room/Helene Herzbrun, Corcoran Gallery Art, 76; Jack Rasmussen Gallery, Washington, DC, 78 & 80; Crapo Gallery, Swain Sch Art, 78; US Info Agency (Europ traveling show), 60-65; Washington/20 Yrs, Baltimore Mus of Art, Md, 70; Ann Pa Acad of Art, Philadelphia, Art in Embassies Prog (US State Dept traveling exhib), 72-; American Paintings of Fifties, Gallery K, DC, 79; 10x10x10 (30 Washington Artists), Corcoran Gallery, 82. *Teaching:* Prof painting, Am Univ, 59-, chmn art dept, 76-80. *Media:* Oil, acrylic. *Mailing Add:* 3539 Quebec St NW Washington DC 20016

HESKETH
SCULPTOR
b Maine. *Study:* Wellesley Col, BA; also with John Flannagan & Ahron Ben-Schmuel. *Work:* San Francisco Mus Art; Addison Gallery Am Art, Andover, Mass; Atlanta Mus Art, Ga. *Exhib:* Detroit Inst Art; Whitney Mus

Am Art, New York; Art Inst Chicago; Carnegie Inst, Pittsburgh; Pa Acad Fine Arts, Philadelphia; one-man shows, San Francisco Mus Art & Seattle Art Mus; and others. *Mem:* Artists Equity Asn. *Mailing Add:* Bluehills Studio RD 1 Kempton PA 19529

HESS, EMIL JOHN
PAINTER, SCULPTOR
b Willock, Pa, Sept 25, 13. *Study:* Duquesne Univ, 38-39; Art Inst Pittsburgh, 39-41; Art Students League, 46-49; Brooklyn Mus Art Sch, 50-51; NY Univ, 59. *Work:* Smithsonian Inst, Washington, DC; Pa State Mus, Harrisburg; Rockefeller Found, New York; Montclair Art Mus, NJ; Phillip Johnson Collection, NY. *Exhib:* Nat Acad Design, New York, 50; one-man show, Betty Parsons Gallery, 51, 52, 68 & 70; Metrop Mus Art, New York, 53; Stable Gallery, New York, 53 & 55; Mus Mod Art Traveling Exhibs, 59. *Bibliog:* New means for moderns, Life, 54; Emily Genauer (auth), Beatnik sculp in big museum show, New York Herald Tribune, 59; Sounds of Hess sculpture, WBAI, New York, 70. *Mem:* Life mem Art Students League; Am Fedn Arts. *Media:* Oil, Metal. *Dealer:* Betty Parsons Galleries 24 W 57th St New York NY 10019. *Mailing Add:* 130 W Tenth St New York NY 10014

HESS, JOYCE
LIBRARIAN
b Shreveport, La. *Study:* Tex Christian Univ, Ft Worth, BA, 66; Univ Tex, Austin, MLS, 69. *Pos:* Art libr, Univ Tex, Austin, 67- *Mem:* Art Libr Soc NAm. *Interests:* Painting. *Mailing Add:* 908 Red Bud Trail Austin TX 78746

HESS, STANLEY WILLIAM
LIBRARIAN
b Bremerton, Wash, July 9, 39. *Study:* Olympic Community Col, 58-60; Univ Wash, BA, 64 & grad work, 67-71; Case Western Reserve Univ, MSLS, 76. *Pos:* Supvr, Photog & Slide Libr, Seattle Art Mus, Wash, 64-73; assoc librn photographs & slides, Cleveland Mus Art, 73-80; head librn, Spencer Art Reference Libr, Nelson Gallery, Atkins Mus, Kansas City, 80- *Mem:* Art Libr Soc NAm; Col Art Asn Am; Am Mus Asn; Spec Libr Asn (picture div, pres elect & pres, 78-79); Kansas City Metrop Libr Network . *Interests:* Publishing, lecturing and teaching about the visual resources in the fine arts. *Publ:* Auth, Annotated Bibliography of Slide Library Literature, Sch Info Studies, Syracuse Univ, 2/78; co-auth, with A Hoffberg, et al, Directory of Art Libraries, Neal/Schuman Publ, 5/78; contribr, Picture Librarianship, Libr Asn, London, 81; and others. *Mailing Add:* 6101 Oak St Kansas City MO 64113

HESSING, VALJEAN MCCARTY
PAINTER
b Tulsa, Okla, Aug 30, 34. *Study:* Philbrook Art Ctr, Tulsa, 45-47; Mary Hardin-Baylor Col, 52-54; Univ Tulsa, 54-55. *Work:* Philbrook Art Ctr; Heard Mus, Phoenix, Ariz; Wheelwright Mus, Santa Fe, NMex; Five Civilized Tribes Mus, Muskogee, Okla; Bur Indian Affairs, Washington, DC. *Exhib:* Philbrook Art Ctr, Tulsa, Okla; Heard Mus, Phoenix, Ariz; Tsa-La-Gi, Cherokee Heritage Ctr, Tahlequah, Okla; Smithsonian Inst; Five Civilized Tribes Mus, Muskogee, Okla; and others. *Awards:* Pierce Avery Award, Heard Mus, Phoenix, 80; Grand Award, Tsa-La-Gi, Tahlequah, Okla, 83; First Award, Santa Fe Indian Market, NMex, 83. *Bibliog:* Patricia Broder (auth), American Indian Painting and Sculpture, 81; Charlotte Rubinstein (auth), American Women Artists, 82. *Media:* Watercolor, Gouache. *Mailing Add:* 201 Delnor Ave St Charles IL 60174

HESTON, JOAN
PAINTER, INSTRUCTOR
b Hartford, Conn. *Study:* Pratt Inst, three yr cert; Art Students League, with Robert Brackman; Stamford Mus, I; Silvermine Guild Art, 73-74; Studio II, 75-76; with Charles Reid, 76-78. *Exhib:* Conn Acad Fine Arts, Wadsworth Antheneum, Hartford, 75, 76, 77 & 79; Audubon Artists Inc, Nat Acad Design & Nat Arts Club, New York, 77-83; Allied Artists Am Inc, Nat Acad Design & Nat Arts Club, New York, 76-83; Allied Artists Am 67th Ann Exhib, Am Acad & Inst Arts & Letters, New York, 80; 155th Ann Exhib, Nat Acad Design, New York, 80; Am Watercolor Soc Traveling Exhib, 81-82; and many others. *Teaching:* Instr oils & watercolor, Professional Workshops, Darien Arts Council, Conn, 79-81. *Awards:* Gold Medal, Catharine Lorillard Wolfe Art Club, 81 & 83; Silver Medal, Nat Arts Club, 81; Emily Lowe Award, Audubon Artists, 81; and many others. *Bibliog:* Jolene Goldenthal (auth), Show at Atheneum, The Hartford Courant, 6/29/75; Muriel Brooks (auth), Art scene, New York Sunday News, 12/26/76; Public interest, Channel 13, 12/81 & 12/82. *Mem:* Allied Artists Am; Silvermine Guild Artists; Audubon Artists; Nat Arts Club; Catharine Lorillard Wolfe Art Club (bd mem, 82). *Media:* Oil, Watercolor. *Publ:* Contribr, Painting Flowers with Watercolor, North Light, 80. *Mailing Add:* 29 Hemlock Drive Stamford CT 06902

HEUSSER, ELEANORE ELIZABETH (ELEANOR H FERHOLT)
PAINTER
b North Haledon, NJ. *Study:* Cooper Union, dipl; Columbia Univ Sch Painting & Sculpture, fel, 45-46; Innsbruck Univ, Fulbright Fel, 52-55. *Work:* Newark Mus; Lending Libr Mus Mod Art, New York. *Exhib:* Kunsthistorisches Inst, Innsbruck, Austria, 54; Konzerthaus Gallery, Vienna, Austria, 54; Fulbright Grantees Show, Duveen-Graham Gallery & mus throughout US, 57-58; Pa Acad Fine Arts Ann, Philadelphia, 59 & 65; NJ Artists Biennial, NJ State Mus, Trenton, 72 & 79. *Teaching:* Instr fundamentals art, Columbia Univ Sch Painting & Sculpture, 46-52; instr drawing, City Col New York, 60-62; pvt instr painting, New York, 60-72 & North Haledon, NJ, 72- *Awards:* Private Grant Study in Mex, provided by George Grebe, 43. *Bibliog:* M Finkelstein (auth), Artist in the Alps, Inst Educ News Bulletin, 6/55; article, Revue Mod, 10/72. *Media:* Ink, Oil. *Mailing Add:* 60 Roosevelt Ave Paterson NJ 07508

HEWITT, DUNCAN ADAMS
SCULPTOR, EDUCATOR
b New York, NY, April 5, 49. *Study:* Colby Col, BA, 71; Univ Pa, MFA, 75. *Exhib:* Philadelphia Mus Art, 72; Inst Contemp Art, Philadelphia, 73-75; Payson Gallery Art, Portland, Maine, 81; Maine Artists Invitational, Bowdoin Col Mus Art, 83; Painting & Sculpture Exhib, Maine Coast Artists, Rockport, 83; New England Sculpture Invitational, Barn Gallery, Ogunquit, Maine, 83. *Teaching:* Asst prof art, Univ Southern Maine, 76-82, assoc prof, 82-, chairperson dept, 82-; vis artist, Colby Col, fall 82 & Portland Sch Art, spring 83. *Media:* Steel, Wood. *Mailing Add:* 127 Pleasant Hill Rd Hollis Center ME 04042

HEWITT, FRANCIS RAY
PAINTER, EDUCATOR
b Rutland, Vt, May 12, 36. *Study:* Carnegie-Mellon Univ, with Balcomb Greene, BFA; Oberlin Col, with Wolfgang Strechow & Charles Parkhurst, MA; Case Western Reserve Univ, with Thomas Munro. *Work:* Cleveland Mus Art; Lodz Mus Fine Art, Poland; Caracas Mus Mod Art, Venezuela. *Exhib:* Movement II, Denise Rene Gallery, Paris, 64; Responsive Eye, Mus Mod Art, New York, 65; One Plus One Equals Three, Univ Tex, 65; Plus & Minus, a Review of Constructivism, Albright-Knox Mus, Buffalo, 67; The Square in Painting, Am Fedn Arts Traveling Exhib, 68. *Teaching:* Instr painting, Cleveland Inst Art, 60-64; lectr design, Bath Acad Art, Corsham, Eng, 64-65; assoc prof drawing & design, Cooper Union, 65-70; assoc prof, Univ Vt, 70- *Media:* Acrylic. *Mailing Add:* Flanders Brook Rd East Corinth VT 05040

HEYMAN, LAWRENCE MURRAY
PAINTER, PRINTMAKER
b Washington, DC, June 30, 32. *Study:* Tyler Sch Fine Arts, Temple Univ, BFA, 54, BS(educ), 55; Atelier 17, Paris, experimental printmaking with S W Hayter, 60-63, 69-70; Am Univ, MFA, 72. *Work:* Brooklyn Mus; Bibliotheque Nat, Paris, France; Brooks Mem Mus, Memphis, Tenn; Portland Art Mus, Ore; Free Libr Philadelphia. *Comn:* Print eds, Assoc Am Artists, New York, 64, 68 & 69 & Antares Eds d'Art, Paris, France, 70, 71 & 72; cover painting for History of American West, US Info Agency, for Vent d'Ouest Book Collection, Paris, France, 65; prints, Judith Selkowitz Fine Arts, New York, 78. *Exhib:* Northwest Printmakers Int, Seattle Mus Fine Arts, 62-65; Audubon Artists Ann, Nat Acad Design, New York, 76; Realites Nouvelles, Parc Floral, Paris, 76 & 78; Le Trait, Cite des Arts, Paris, 77; World Print Competition '77, San Francisco Art Mus, 77; Atelier 17 Retrospective, Brooklyn Art Mus, 77-78 & Elvehjem Art Ctr, Minn, 77-78; L'Estampe Aujourd hui 73/78, Bibliotheque Nat, Paris, 79; and others. *Pos:* Critic/Evaluator printmaking books, Choice Mag, Middletown, Conn, 77-79. *Teaching:* Instr printmaking, RI Sch Design, 67-69, asst prof, 72-79 & dir print prog, 76-79; lectr printmaking, Am Univ, Washington DC, 71-72. *Awards:* Providence Art Club prizes, Open Print Show, 74 & 76; Purchase Award, Le Trait, Bibliotheque Nat, Paris, 77. *Bibliog:* Dale Jacquette (auth), Lawrence Heyman's paintings of street life, RI Rev, 1/81. *Mem:* Col Art Asn Am. *Media:* Oils, Watercolor; Intaglio. *Mailing Add:* 182 Raleigh Ave Pawtucket RI 02860

HEYMAN, THERESE THAU
CURATOR, HISTORIAN
b New York, NY. *Study:* Smith Col, BA; Yale Univ, MA(art hist), 58. *Collections Arranged:* California Prints, Prints of Calif; Monotypes in California, 72-73; Mirror of California (auth, catalog), Daquerrotypes in Calif, 72-74; Looking at Lange Today, Dorothea Lange Collection, 77-78. *Pos:* Cur catalog, Yale Univ Art Gallery, summers 56 & 57, cur Am prints & catalog, 61-62; educ asst Am art, Smithsonian Inst, 58-59; sr cur, Oakland Mus, Calif, 69- *Mem:* Col Art Asn; Women's Caucus Arts; Alameda Art Comn. *Res:* Prints and photographs in art and history of the West; American graphics. *Publ:* Auth, An American Exodus, Yale Press, 69; auth, Celebrating Collections, Sites, 78; auth, New California Views, Landweber Artists, 79. *Mailing Add:* 785 San Luis Rd Berkeley CA 94707

HEYWOOD, J C
PRINTMAKER
b Toronto, Ont, June 6, 41. *Study:* Ont Col Art, assoc degree, 63; Atelier 17, Paris, France, with Hayter, 67-69. *Work:* Nat Gallery Can; Victoria & Albert Mus, London; Mus Mod Art, Paris; Royal Libr Belg; Brooklyn Mus; and many others. *Exhib:* Brit Int Print Biennale, Bradford, Eng, 68-; Int Print Biennale, Krakow, Poland, 70-; Biennale Graphic Art, Ljubljana, Yugoslavia, 71-; Royal Can Acad; and many others including 43 one-man shows in three countries. *Teaching:* Prof drawing & painting, Univ Guelph, 73-74; prof printmaking & painting, Queen's Univ, 74- *Awards:* Graphex Award, Art Gallery of Brantford, 75, 78, 79 & 81; Second Prize, Norweg Int Print Biennale, 78; Prize, Int Print Biennale, Krakow, 80; and 8 others in USA and Can. *Mem:* Royal Can Acad; Ont Soc Artists; Print & Drawing Coun of Can. *Media:* Etching, Silkscreen. *Dealer:* Mira Godard Gallery 22 Hazelton Ave Toronto ON Can. *Mailing Add:* Dept of Art Queen's Univ Kingston ON K7L 3N6 Canada

HIATT, MARGARET SMITH
PAINTER, INSTRUCTOR
b Salem, Ohio, Sept 24, 10. *Study:* Randolph Macon Women's Col, Lynchburg, Va, 29-30; Martinet Sch Art, Baltimore, 30-31; Sch Design, Philadelphia, with Sophie Parsons, 36; with Richard Redd, 67-68; Art Students League, New York, with Mario Cooper, 73-74. *Work:* First Valley Bank, Bethlehem, Pa; City Hall, Atlantic City, NJ; First Nat Bank, Toms River, NJ; Las Cruces Libr Mus, NMex. *Comn:* Paintings, Anchor Savings

& Loan, Atlantic City, NJ, 75; paintings, Arsenal on the Green, New Castle, Del, 76. *Exhib:* One-woman show, Kemerer Mus, Bethlehem, Pa, 72; Am Artists Prof League, Lever House, New York, 73, 74 & 76; Atlantic City Art Ctr, NJ, 76-78; Ariz Watercolor Asn, Minell Gallery, Scottsdale, 80; Ariz Watercolor Asn, Kerr Cult Ctr, Scottsdale, 82; and others. *Teaching:* Instr hist art, Palm Beach Pvt Sch, 31-32; pvt lessons, painting & drawing, 58-; instr drawing, YWCA, Bethlehem, Pa, 60. *Awards:* Purchase Award, Founders Day Exhib, Moravian Col, 68; First National Bank Silver Award, Lehigh Art Alliance, 69; Best of Show, Atlantic City Art Ctr, 76. *Bibliog:* William D Gorman (auth), The New Jersey theme, Artforum, 11/12/79; and others. *Mem:* Fel Am Artists Prof League; assoc mem Am Watercolor Soc; Ariz Watercolor Asn; Ariz Artists Guild; Prof Artists South Jersey. *Media:* Oil, Watercolor. *Dealer:* Sidney Rothman Gallery Barnegat Light NJ 08006. *Mailing Add:* 15823 N 22nd Way Phoenix AZ 85022

HIBBARD, HOWARD
HISTORIAN, WRITER
b Madison, Wis, May 23, 28. *Study:* Univ Wis, BA & MA; Columbia Univ; Harvard Univ, PhD; Oxford Univ, England, hon MA. *Collections Arranged:* Florentine Baroque Art from American Collections, with participation of Columbia Univ (catalog with Joan Nissman), Metrop Mus Art, New York, 69. *Pos:* Bk rev ed, Art Bull, 61-65, assoc ed, 73-74, ed in chief, 74-78. *Teaching:* Prof art hist, Columbia Univ, 59-; Slade prof, Univ Oxford, 76-77. *Awards:* Am Coun Learned Soc Fel, 62-63; Guggenheim Fels, 65-66 & 72-73; Nat Endowment Humanities Fels, 67 & 79-80. *Mem:* Col Art Asn; fel Am Acad Arts & Sci; Soc Archit Historians (dir, 63-65); Renaissance Soc Am; Am Asn Univ Prof. *Res:* Renaissance and Baroque art and architecture in Italy. *Publ:* Auth, Bernini, 65; auth, Carlo Maderno and Roman Architecture 1580-1630, 72; auth, Michelangelo, 75; auth, The Metropolitan Museum of Art, 80; auth, Caravaggio, 83; and others. *Mailing Add:* 176 Brewster Rd Scarsdale NY 10583

HIBEL, EDNA
PAINTER, LITHOGRAPHER
b Boston, Mass, Jan 13, 17. *Study:* With Gregory Michael, 30-34; Boston Mus Fine Arts Sch, with Alexander Jacovleff & Karl Zerbe, Ruth B Sturtevant Traveling Fel, 35-39; also with Eliot O'Hara, 35-36. *Work:* Mus Fine Arts, Boston; Philatelic Mus, Palais Nations, Geneva, Switz; Columbus Mus Arts & Crafts, Ga; Harvard Univ; Hibel Mus of Art, Palm Beach. *Comn:* Mother Earth (oil on cameo paper), Ltd Ed Art Print & UN First Day Cover, World Fedn UN Asn, 83. *Exhib:* Nat Mus Fine Arts, Rio de Janeiro, 76; Monaco Fine Arts Gallery, 79; Castle Meinem, Constance, WGer, 80; Castle Borluut, Ghent, Belgium, 82; Hebrew Univ, Jerusalem, 83; plus others. *Pos:* Dir art & design, Edna Hibel Studios, 72- *Teaching:* Pvt masterclasses, Brookline, Mass, 60-63. *Awards:* Medal of Honor & Citation, Pope John Paul II, 83. *Bibliog:* Paintings of Edna Hibel, 74; Hibel Lithographs, 76 & Edna Hibel: The World I Love (film), 76, JAR Publ. *Mem:* Fel Royal Soc Arts, London. *Media:* Oil, Gold Leaf. *Publ:* Auth, Edna Hibel Demonstrates the Art of Lithography, 72; Hibel on Porcelain, 78 & The Sundial Ticking, 78, JAR Publ; Hibel Museum of Art Date Book, Hibel Mus Art, 81; Fay Burg's Lake Kezar Cookbook with a Gallery of Paintings by Edna Hibel, JAR Publ, 82. *Dealer:* Jar Publishers Box 9967 Riviera Beach FL 33404. *Mailing Add:* Box 9967 Riviera Beach FL 33404

HICKEN, PHILIP BURNHAM
PAINTER, PRINTMAKER
b Lynn, Mass, June 27, 10. *Study:* Mass Col Art. *Work:* Metrop Mus Art, New York; Philadelphia Mus Fine Art; Brooklyn Mus; Libr Cong. *Comn:* Mural, Fed Art Proj, Fort Warren, Mass, 41; combat art, European Theatre, US Army, 42-45; combat art assignment, US Dept Mil Hist, 70. *Exhib:* Brooklyn Mus, 59; Eastern States Expos, Springfield, Mass, 60; Boston Soc Watercolors, 60-72; DeCordova Mus, 71; Exhib, Am Painters in Paris, 76. *Teaching:* Instr painting, Harvard Univ Grad Sch Design, 50-53; instr painting, Boston Univ, 56-57; chmn dept fine arts, Art Inst Boston, 57- *Awards:* Brooklyn Mus Purchase Award, 58; Boston Soc Watercolor Painters Award, 60; Yankee Mag Award, Copley Galleries, 69. *Bibliog:* Patricia Wilson (auth), article, Christian Sci Monitor, 66; Charles Movalli (auth), article, Am Artist, 82. *Mem:* Boston Soc Watercolor Painters; Boston Printmakers; fel Royal Soc Art; Nantucket Art Asn. *Media:* Acrylic. *Dealer:* Savage Galleries Scottsdale AZ & Dallas TX. *Mailing Add:* 23 Pine St Nantucket MA 02554

HICKEY, ROSE VAN VRANKEN See Van Vranken, Rose

HICKMAN, JESSE LUTHER
SCULPTOR
b Chicago, Ill, June 18, 55. *Study:* Inst Design, Chicago, with Arthur Siegel, Elmer Ray Pearson & Ken Biasco, 74-77. *Exhib:* Univ Tex, Dallas, 78; Art Inst Chicago, 78; solo exhibs, Northern Ill Univ, DeKalb, 79, One Ctr, Chicago, 80 & Young Hoffman Gallery, 81; Newport Harbour Art Mus, Newport Beach, Calif, 80; Mus Contemp Art, Chicago, 81; Walker Art Ctr, Minneapolis, 81. *Media:* Wood. *Dealer:* Jay Johnson Gallery 1044 Madison Ave New York NY 10021; Rhonda Hoffman Gallery 215 W Superior Chicago IL 60610. *Mailing Add:* 486 11th St Brooklyn NY 11215

HICKS, LEON NATHANIEL
PRINTMAKER
b Deerfield, Fla, Dec 25, 33. *Study:* Kans State Univ, BS; State Univ Iowa, with Mauricio Lasansky, MA & MFA; Stanford Univ, study with Albert Elsen; La Romita Sch Art, Italy; Atlanta Univ, Ga. *Work:* Charleston Art Gallery at Sunrise, WVa; Tuskegee Inst, Ala; Oakland Art Mus, Calif; Libr Cong; Albrecht Art Mus, St Joseph, Mo. *Exhib:* St Mary's Col, Notre Dame, Ind, 80; The Studio Mus In Harlem: Impressions/Expressions: Black American Graphics, Washington DC, 80; Smithsonian Inst: Black Am Graphics Traveling Exhib, 80-83; Midwest Mus Am Art Exhib: Black Expression, Elkhart, Ind, 81. *Pos:* Chmn bd & exec vpres, Hicks Etchprint, Inc, Philadelphia, Pa. *Teaching:* Instr art, Concord Col, Athens, WVa, 65-67; asst prof art, Lincoln Univ, Jefferson City, Mo, 67; asst prof printmaking, drawing & hist, Lehigh Univ, Bethlehem, Pa, 70-74; assoc prof printmaking, drawing & hist, Webster Col, St Louis, Mo, 74- *Awards:* Second Prize, Atlanta Univ, 65; First Prize, Tuskegee Inst, Ninth Ann Beaux Arts Guild Exhib, 68; Arts and Humanities Commission winner, St Louis Edition Portfolio, 81. *Bibliog:* Black Artists on Art, Samella S Lewis & Ruth G Waddy, 70; Directions in Afro-American Art, Herbert F Johnson Mus Art, Cornell Univ, Ithaca, NY, 74; Art: African-American, Samella Lewis, 78. *Mem:* Assoc Brandywine Graphic Workshop, Philadelphia, Pa. *Media:* Drawing; engraving; etching; photo-etching. *Dealer:* Smith Mason Art Gallery 1207 Rhode Island NW Washington DC 20005. *Mailing Add:* Georgetown Apts A-2 844 Ravensridge Rd St Louis MO 63119

HICKS, SHEILA
TAPESTRY ARTIST, PUBLISHER
b Hastings, Nebr, July 24, 34. *Study:* Yale Univ, BFA, 57, MFA, 59. *Work:* Mus Mod Art, New York; Stedelijk Mus, Amsterdam; Mus des Arts Decoratifs, Paris; Victoria & Albert Mus, London; Mus Art Mod, Tokyo & Kyoto, Japan. *Comn:* Linen mural, Rothschild Bank, Paris, 69; 7 wall rugs, Mecca, Saudia Arabia, 71; stage curtain, Fiat Tour, Paris, 74; auditorium tapestry, Dresdner Bank, Frankfurt, 79; Embarcadero Ctr, San Francisco, 81; and others. *Exhib:* One-person show, Art Inst Chicago, 62 & Stedelijk Mus, 74; Bienalle de Tapisserie, Lausanne, Switz, 71-79; Nat Gal, Rabat, Morocco, 72; Kunsthal Lund, Sweden, 78; Grand Palais, Paris, 78 & 79; and others. *Pos:* Trustee, The Textile Mus, Washington, DC, currently. *Teaching:* Instr, The Hague, 78, Middlebury Col, Vt, 79 & Fontainbleau, 81-83; Middlebury Col, Vt, 79. *Awards:* Gold Medal for Craftsmanship, Am Inst Architects, 74; Hon fel Royal Acad Art, Hague, 75; Fel, Am Crafts Coun, 83. *Bibliog:* M Levi-Strauss, Sheila Hicks & P Horay, Paris, 73 & Studio Vista, London, 74; B Diamondstein (auth), Handmade in America, Abrams, NY, 83; article, Cimaise, Paris, No 158. *Publ:* contrib, American Fabrics & Fashions, 80-83. *Dealer:* Carmen Martinez Gallery 12 Rue Roi de Sicile 75001 Paris France; Cora de Vries Kaizergracht 516 1017 Amsterdam The Netherlands. *Mailing Add:* 3 Bis Cour de Rohan 75006 Paris France

HIGA (YOSHIHARU)
PRINTMAKER, PHOTOGRAPHER
b Okinawa, Japan, Jan 15, 38. *Study:* Tama Art Univ, Tokyo, BFA; Art Students League; Pratt Graphic Ctr, New York. *Work:* Mus Mod Art, New York; Brooklyn Mus; Philadelphia Mus; Los Angeles Co Mus; and others. *Exhib:* Contemp Japanese Art Exhib, Mus Tokyo, 64; 50th Ann Exhib, Soc Am Graphic Artists, 69; New Talent Printmaker, Assoc Am Artists, New York, 70; Int Engraving Biennial, Buenos Aires, Arg, 70; Am Graphics Artists traveling show to tour the East, US Info Agency, 70. *Teaching:* Asst prof fine arts, Southampton Col, Long Island Univ, currently. *Awards:* Best Print in Show, 50th Ann Exhib, Soc Am Graphic Artists, 69; Mus Purchase Awards, Int Print Exhib, Seattle Art Mus, Wash, 70 & Nat Print Exhib, Boston. *Bibliog:* Original art, hot off the presses, Life, 6/23/70; Famous Artist Annual, A Treasury of Contemporary Art, Famous Art Sch, 70. *Mailing Add:* 75 E Second St New York NY 10003

HIGBY, (DONALD) WAYNE
PAINTER, SCULPTOR
b Colorado Springs, Colo, May 12, 43. *Study:* Univ Colo, BFA, 66; Univ Mich, MFA, 68. *Work:* Philadelphia Mus Art; Mus Contemp Crafts, New York; Metrop Mus Art, New York; Minneapolis Mus Art, Wis; Everson Mus Art, Syracuse. *Exhib:* Objects USA, Smithsonian Inst, DC, 69; one-man shows, Joslyn Art Mus, 69 & Mus Contemp Crafts, 73; Int Ceramics, Victoria & Albert Mus, London, 72; 1st World Craft Exhib, Ont Sci Ctr, Toronto, 74; Am Crafts '76, Mus Contemp Art, Chicago, 76; Craft Art & Relig, Vatican Mus, Rome, 78. *Pos:* Chmn, Visual Arts Panel, NY State Coun Arts, 76-78; juror, Young Am: Clay/Glass, Am Crafts Coun, 78; adv, Task Force Individual Artist, New York State Coun Arts, 80-82. *Teaching:* Asst prof ceramic art, RI Sch Design, 70-73; prof ceramic art, NY State Col Ceramics, Alfred Univ, 73- *Awards:* Nat Merit Awards, Am Crafts Coun 66; Nat Endowment Arts Fels, 73 & 77; Nat Park Serv fel, 76. *Bibliog:* Julie Hall (auth), Tradition and Change: New American Craftsmen, E P Dutton, 77; Susan Wechsler (auth), Low Fire Ceramics, Watson-Guptill, New York, 81; B Diamonstein (auth), Handmade in American, H Abrams, 83. *Mem:* Am Crafts Coun; Empire State Craftsmen; NCECA. *Media:* Clay, Glaze, Fire. *Publ:* Contrib, Craft Horizons, ed by Rose Slivka, Am Crafts Coun, 70; contribr, Creative Landscape Containers, by Jane Holtz Kay, Christian Sci Monitor, 73; contribr, High Crafts (collecting boom), by Monica Meenan, Town & Country, 77; contribr, Ceramic Art, Comment and Review, 78 & Century of Ceramics In The United States, 79, by Garth Clark, E P Dutton; Ann Jarmusch (auth), Feature article, Am Craft, 4/81. *Dealer:* Helen Drutt Gallery Philadelphia PA 19106; Helen Pruitt Gallery 1625 Spruce St Philadelphia PA 19103. *Mailing Add:* Belmont Rd Alfred Station NY 14803

HIGGINS, DICK
DESIGNER, PRINTMAKER
b Cambridge, England, Mar 15, 38; US citizen. *Study:* Yale Univ, 55-57; Columbia Univ, 57-60; NY Univ, AM(Eng), 77; additional study with John Cage & Henry Cowell. *Exhib:* One-man shows, La Mamelle, San Francisco,

Calif, 77, Studio Morra, Naples, Italy, 77, Galerie Inge Baecker, Bochum, WGer, 78, Micro Gallery, Sacremento, 79, Franklin Furnace & C Space, New York, 79; Bookworks, Mus Mod Art, New York, 77; plus numerous other one-man & group shows. *Teaching:* Prof, Graphics Workshop, Calif Inst Arts, 70-71; dir, Vis Artists Prog & instr, Univ Wis, Milwaukee, 77; research assoc, State Univ NY, Purchase, 83- *Awards:* Deutscher Akadamischer Austauschdienst Fel, 81-82. *Bibliog:* Michael Nyman (auth), Experimental Music: Cage and Beyond, Studio Vista, London, 74; Richard Kostelanetz (auth), The End of Intelligent Writing, Sheed & Ward, New York, 75; and others. *Media:* Photo Silkscreen; Offset Camera. *Publ:* Auth, Towards the 1970's, 69; auth, Computers for the Arts, 70; coauth, Fantastic Architecture, 71; auth, Variations on a Natural Theme, 81; auth, Horizons: The Theory and Poetics of the Intermedia, Southern Ill Univ Press, 83; and 32 other bks. *Mailing Add:* Station Hill Rd PO Box 27 Barrytown NY 12507

HIGGINS, (GEORGE) EDWARD
SCULPTOR
b Gaffney, SC, Nov 13, 30. *Study:* Univ NC, BA, 54. *Work:* Mus Mod Art, Guggenheim Mus, Whitney Mus Am Art, New York; Albright-Knox Art Gallery, Buffalo, NY; Dallas Mus Fine Arts; and others. *Comn:* Sculpture, Cameron Bldg, New York, 62 & NY State Theatre, Lincoln Ctr for Performing Arts, New York, 64. *Exhib:* New York World's Fair, 64-65; Contemporary American Sculpture, Selection 1, Whitney Mus Am Art, 66; Flint Inst Art, Mich, 66; Documenta IV, Kassel, Ger, 68; Duke Univ, 69. *Teaching:* Instr sculpture, Parsons Sch Design, 61-62; Philadelphia Mus Sch, 63. *Awards:* Louis C Tiffany Grant, 62; Purchase Prize, Flint Inst Art, 66. *Bibliog:* Harriet Janis & Rubi Blesh (auth), Collage: Personalities--Concepts--Techniques, Chilton, 62; Sam Hunter (ed), New Art Around the World: Painting & Sculpture, Abrams, 66; Eduard Trier (auth), Form & Space: Sculpture in the 20th Century, Praeger, 68. *Mailing Add:* Box 345 RFD 4 Easton PA 18042

HIGGINS, EDWARD FERDINAND III See Doo Da Post

HIGGINS, EDWARD KOELLING
CERAMIST, JEWELER
b Milwaukee, Wis, Apr 30, 26. *Study:* Univ Wis, Milwaukee, BS(art educ), MS(ceramics); Univ Wis-La Crosse; Northwestern Univ. *Work:* Mus of Contemp Crafts, New York; Theo Portney Gallery, New York; many pvt collections. *Exhib:* Mississippi River Art Festival, Jackson, Miss, 67-; Southern Tier Art & Craft Exhib, Corning Mus, NY, 69-; Crafts-1970, Inst of Contemp Art, Boston, 70; Appalachian Corridors Exhib, Charleston Art Gallery, WVa, 70-; Harrisburg Festival of the Arts, Harrisburg Art Gallery, Pa, 70; Cooperstown NY Festival of the Arts, 70. *Collections Arranged:* Fantasy in Silver, Akron Art Inst, Ohio; Jewelers, USA, Calif State Col at Fullerton; Am Evolution in Art, Chambers Gallery, Pa State Univ; Box Exhib, Kohler Art Ctr; Celebration 20, Mus of Contemp Crafts, New York; Forms in Metal, Montgomery Mus of Fine Arts, Fine Arts Mus at Mobile, Ala, Philbrook Art Ctr, Tulsa, Okla, Va Mus of Fine Arts, Richmond & Huntsville Mus of Art, Ala; 100 Artists Celebrate 200 Yrs, Fairtree Gallery, New York; Xerox-Fun & Fantasy Exhib, Xerox Hall, Rochester, NY. *Teaching:* Asst prof jewelry, Mansfield State Col, Pa, 69-70; assoc prof jewelry, ceramics & photog, Mercyhurst Col, 71-82. *Awards:* Sculpture Award & Merit Award for Metal, Mississippi River Art Festival, Jackson Art Gallery; Silver Award, Appalachian Corridors Exhib, Charlestown Art Gallery. *Bibliog:* Dona Meilach (auth), Box Art Assemblages, Crown, 76; Jewelry: The Fine Art of Adornment Fabrication Method & Jewelry: The Fine Art of Adornment Casting Method (filmstrips), Warner Educ Productions; Casting, Bovin Publ. *Media:* Silver & clay. *Publ:* Contribr, Body Jewelry, Regnery, 73; contribr, Inventive Fiber Crafts, Prentice Hall, 75; contribr, Box Art Assemblages, 76, A New Look at Crochet, 76 & Career Opportunities in Crafts, 77, Crown. *Dealer:* Sol Del Rio 1020 Townsend San Antonio TX 78209. *Mailing Add:* Farrington Post Box 166 Pittsboro NC 27316

HIGGINS, MARY LOU
CERAMIST, WEAVER
b Milwaukee, Wis, June 27, 26. *Study:* Univ Wis-Milwaukee, BS(art educ), MS(weaving). *Work:* Slides of work in many mus such as Los Angeles Co Mus Art, Milwaukee Art Ctr, Mus Contemp Crafts, Art Now Series, Univ Galleries, New York. *Exhib:* Furs & Feathers, Mus Contemp Crafts, 70; Fun & Fantasy, Xerox Sq Galleries, Rochester & Fairtree, New York, 73; Angels-Whitte Mus, San Antonio, Tex; one-woman shows, Sol Del Rio, San Antonio, Tex, 77, 78, 79 & 80, Verzyl Gallery, Northport, NY, 81; Somerhill Gallery, Durham, NC, 84; and others. *Teaching:* Instr art educ & fiber & fabrics, Mansfield State Col, 69-71; asst prof ceramics, fiber & fabrics & art educ, Mercyhurst Col, 71-74. *Awards:* Wisconsin Designers & Craftsman Award, Milwaukee Art Ctr, 65; Textile Award, Cooperstown, NY, 70; Textile Award, 25th Pa Craftsman Award, 72. *Media:* Weaving, Ceramics. *Publ:* Contribr, Basketry, 44, A New Look at Crochet, 75 & Wearable Crafts, 76, Crown; auth, Inventive Fiber Crafts, Prentice-Hall, 77; auth, Career Opportunities in Crafts, Crown, 77. *Dealer:* Somerhill Gallery 5504 Chapel Hill Blvd Durham NC 27707; Shelia Nussbaum Gallery 358 Millburn Ave Millburn NJ 07041. *Mailing Add:* Farrington Post Box 166 Pittsboro NC 27312

HIGH, TIMOTHY GRIFFIN
PRINTMAKER, EDUCATOR
b Memphis, Tenn, Mar 10, 49. *Study:* Tex Tech Univ, BFA(printmaking), 73; Univ Wis-Madison, MA(printmaking), 75, MFA(printmaking), 76. *Work:* Chicago Art Inst; Elvehjem Art Ctr, Madison, Wis; De Cordova Mus, Lincoln, Mass; Col of Siskiyous, Weed, Calif; Fla Tech Univ, Orlando. *Comn:*

Point of Departure (portfolio), Univ Wis, 84. *Exhib:* 4th-10th Ann Colorprint USA Nat Competition, Tex Tech Univ, Lubbock, 73-83; First Colorblend, Nat Traveling Exhib, 78-80; Seventh & Eighth Brit Biennale, 79 & 82; solo exhibs, Chosy Seuferer Gallery, Madison, Wis, 82 & Soho Gallery, Austin, Tex, 83; and others. *Teaching:* Vis artist & lectr, Univ Tex, Austin, 76, asst prof serigraphy & printmaking, 76-80. *Awards:* Marshall S Mayer Award, 1st Nat Exhib, Col of Siskiyous, Weed, Calif, 75; Jurors' Purchase Award, 5th Int Matmedia Exhib, Dickenson State Col, NDak, 75 & Boston Printmakers 29th Nat, De Cordova Mus, 77. *Mem:* Philadelphia Print Club; Los Angeles Printmaking Soc; Boston Printmakers; Texas Print Alliance; Southern Graphics Coun. *Media:* Pencil, Ink. *Publ:* Contribr, New American Graphics--1975, Univ Wis-Madison, 75. *Mailing Add:* c/o Dept of Art Univ of Tex Austin TX 78712

HIGHTOWER, JOHN B
ADMINISTRATOR, MUSEUM DIRECTOR
b Atlanta, Ga, May 23, 33. *Study:* Yale Univ, BA, 55; Calif Col Arts & Crafts, hon DFA, 75. *Pos:* Asst to pub, Am Heritage Publ Co, 61-63; exec asst, NY State Coun on the Arts, 63-64, exec dir, 64-70, mem, 70-76; cult adv, Rockefeller Mission to Latin Am, 69; Am rep, United Nations Educ, Sci & Cult Orgn Conf on Performing Arts, Canberra, Australia, 69; dir, Mus Mod Art, New York, 70-72; pres, Assoc Councils of the Arts, 72-74; founder & chmn, Advocates for the Arts, 74-77; pres, S St Seaport, 77-83; dir & vchmn, Urban art Corps, 83- *Teaching:* Instr arts mgt, Wharton Sch of Bus, New Sch, Yale Grad Sch Drama, 75-77. *Awards:* NY State Award, 70. *Mem:* Century Asn; Buffalo Acad Fine Arts; Inst for Art & Urban Resources; Int Dance Coun (pres); and others. *Mailing Add:* 304 W 88th St 2B New York NY 10024

HIGH-WASIKHONGO, FREIDA
PRINTMAKER, EDUCATOR
b Starkville, Miss, Oct 21, 46. *Study:* Graceland Col, Lamoni, Iowa, AA, 66; Northern Ill Univ, De Kalb, BS, 68; Univ Wis, Madison, with Ray Gloeckler & Robert Grilley, MA, 70, MFA, 71. *Work:* Grad Sch, Univ Wis, Madison; Du Sable Mus of African & Afro-Am Art, Chicago; S Side Community Art Ctr, Chicago; Afro-Am Ctr, Univ Wis. *Comn:* Mixed-media drawing, Afro-Am Arts Inst, Univ Ind, Bloomington, 76; prints & drawings, Wis Arts Bd, 78. *Exhib:* Sixth Concours Int de la Palme d'Or des Beaux Arts, Palmares, Monte Carlo, France, 74; Prints & Drawings, MAMA Gallery, Madison, Wis, 76; Beloit Vicinity Ann Exhib, Wright Art Ctr, Wis, 76; 15th Nat Print Exhib, Art Gallery, Bradley Univ, Peoria, Ill, 76; Midwestern Black Artist, Performing Arts Ctr, Milwaukee, Wis, 76. *Pos:* Artist-in-residence, Univ Wis, Madison, 71-72. *Teaching:* Asst prof African/Afro-Am art, Univ Wis, Madison, 72-77, assoc prof African/Afro-Am art, 77- *Awards:* Wis Arts Bd Art Grant, 77; City Arts Grant, Prints & Drawings, Off of the Mayor, Madison, 77. *Bibliog:* Interest in African art is on the increase in US, Capital Times, 7/75; James Auer (auth), PAC surveys midwestern Black art, Milwaukee J, 2/76; Shirley Carley (auth), Starkville native making name in field of art, Starkville Daily News 3/76. *Mem:* Wis Women in the Arts; Nat Conf of Artists (regional coordr, 74); Nat Coun for Black Studies. *Media:* Woodcut. *Publ:* Illusr (cover), Ba Shiru, Univ Wis, 71 & 76-77; contribr, Center debut: A Black artist's view, Milwaukee J, 11/75. *Dealer:* Assoc Am Artist 663 Fifth Ave New York NY 10022. *Mailing Add:* c/o Univ Wisc Madison WI 53706

HIGHWATER, JAMAKE
CRITIC, LECTURER
b Glacier Co, Mont, Feb 14, 42. *Study:* Spec study in comparative lit, music, cult anthrop & art hist. *Pos:* Consult, NY State Coun Arts; mem art task panel, Pres Carter's Comn on Mental Health, 77-79; pres cult coun, Am Indian Community House, New York, 77-79; writer & narrator, Native Americans (8 part series), PBS, The Primal Mind, PBS; moderator, Aspen Inst Seminar, Indian America: Past, Present and Future, 81. *Teaching:* Lectr for Fox Chase Agency, New York; appointed lectr, NY Univ, Liberal Art, Continuing Educ, 76-81. *Awards:* Newbery Honor Award for Bk ANPAO, Am Libr Asn, 77; Ainsfield-Wolf Award for Song from the Earth, 81; Virginia McCormick Scully Literary Award, 83. *Mem:* Author's Guild; Dramatists Guild; PEN Int; Indian Arts & Crafts Found, NMex. *Res:* Concerned with all aspects of American Indian art, crafts and culture. *Publ:* Auth, The Sweet Grass Lives On: 50 Contemporary North American Indian Artists, Lippincott/Crowell Publ, 80; auth, The Primal Mind, Harper & Row, 81; auth, Moonsong Lullaby, William Morrow, 81; auth, Arts of the Indian Americas, Harper & Row, 83; auth, Legend Days, Harper & Row, 84. *Mailing Add:* c/o Fox Chase Agency 419 E 57th St New York NY 10022

HILDEBRAND, JUNE MARY ANN
PRINTMAKER, ILLUSTRATOR
b Eureka, Calif, Nov 2, 30. *Study:* Calif Col Arts & Crafts; Art Students League, scholar; Queens Col, BFA; Hochschule Bildende Kunste Berlin; Hunter Col, MA; Pratt Graphic Ctr. *Work:* Philadelphia Mus Art, Pa; Univ Wis-Madison; New York Pub Libr; Everson Mus Art; Univ Minn; plus others. *Exhib:* Pratt Int Miniature Print Exhib, 66 & 68; Oneonta State Univ, 67; Montclair State Col, 68; Gotham Bk Mart, New York, 69; Pratt Inst, 79; and others. *Mem:* Am Colorprint Print Soc. *Media:* Linoleum, Silkscreen. *Publ:* Contribr graphics, Artists Proof Mag; Wild Fruits & Flowers, Claremount Press, 80; A Book of Flowers, Claremount Press, 82; and others. *Dealer:* Associated American Artists 663 5th Ave New York NY 10022. *Mailing Add:* PO Box 177 Cooper Station New York NY 10003

HILDEBRANDT, WILLIAM ALBERT
PAINTER, ADMINISTRATOR

b Philadelphia, Pa, Oct 1, 17. *Study:* Tyler Sch Art, Temple Univ, BFA, BSEd & MFA; Philadelphia Col Art, cert advert design. *Work:* Glen-Croft Baptist Church, Folcroft, Pa. *Exhib:* Nat Drawing Soc Eastern Cent Regional Drawing Exhib, Philadelphia Mus Art, 65 & 70; Am Drawing Biennial, Norfolk Mus Arts & Sci, Va, 67; Avanti Gallery, New York, 69; Pennsylvania 71, William Penn Mem Mus, Harrisburg, 71; West '79/The Law, traveling, Minn Mus Art, St Paul, 79; Expressions, Philadelphia Civic Ctr Mus, 79; and others. *Teaching:* Supvr art educ, Philadelphia Pub Schs, 54- *Awards:* Best Ann Award, Philadelphia Art Teachers Asn, 70; Philadelphia Sketch Club Medal, 113th Ann Exhib Oil Painting, 76; Four Chaplains Legion of Honor Citation, 77. *Mem:* Philadelphia Art Teachers Asn; Temple Univ Gen Alumni Asn; Tyler Sch Art Alumni Asn; Woodmere Art Gallery; Philadelphia Asn Sch Adminr. *Media:* Oil; Miscellaneous Media. *Publ:* Illusr, The Keystone State, Arthur Graef (auth), 53 & illusr, Minnesota's Government, Joseph Kise (auth), 53, Winston; illusr, Humanities Curriculum, 68 & illusr, Echoes from Mount Olympus, 70, auth, Art in the Middle Years, 80, Off Curric & Instr, Sch Dist Philadelphia. *Mailing Add:* 417 Turner Rd Media PA 19063

HILDRETH, JOSEPH ALAN
PRINTMAKER, PAINTER

b Bowling Green, Ky, Sept 2, 47. *Study:* Western Ky Univ, BFA, 69; Pratt Inst, with Walter Rogalski, MFA, 71. *Work:* Mint Mus, Charlotte, NC; Erie Fine Arts Ctr, Pa; State Univ NY Col, Potsdam. *Exhib:* Eight Upstate, Artists' Space Gallery, New York, NY, 74; Nat Print Exhib, Second St Gallery, Charlottesville, Va, 76; 16th Bradley Nat Print Exhib, Bradley Univ, Peoria, Ill, 77; New York Landscape, Plaza Gallery, Albany, 81; 11th Nat Print & Drawing Exhib, Minot State Col, NDak, 82; and many others. *Teaching:* Assoc prof printmaking, State Univ NY Col Potsdam, 71- *Awards:* Carnegie Found Grant, 81; NY State Coun Arts Grant, 82. *Media:* Mixed. *Publ:* Auth, Contemporary Realism (catalog essay), 82. *Mailing Add:* Pierpoint Ave Dept Art State Univ Potsdam Potsdam NY 13676

HILL, CLINTON J
PAINTER, EDUCATOR

b Payette, Idaho, Mar 8, 22. *Study:* Univ Ore, BS, 47; Brooklyn Mus Art Sch, 49-51; Acad Grande Chaumiere, Paris, 51; Inst Arte Statale, Florence, Italy, 51-52. *Work:* Mus Mod Art, New York; Philadelphia Mus Art; Metrop Mus, New York; Albright-Knox Gallery, Buffalo, NY; Corcoran Gallery Art, Washington, DC; plus others. *Exhib:* Drawing USA, Mus Mod Art, New York, 56; Two Decades of American Prints, Brooklyn Mus, 68; one-man exhibs, Zabriskie Gallery, New York, 55-75, Gallerie Darthea Speyer, Paris, 73-75, Marilyn Pearl Gallery, 79-80 & Montclair Art Mus, NJ, 81; With Paper About Paper, Albright-Knox Art Gallery, Buffalo, NY, 80. *Teaching:* Prof, Queens Col, City Univ New York, 68- *Awards:* Caps Grant, 74-75; Fac Res Grant, City Univ New York, 75 & 79; Nat Endowment Arts, 76-77 & 80-81. *Bibliog:* Harriet Janis & Rudi Blesh (auth), Collage: Personalities, Concepts, Techniques, Chilton, 62; Leo Steinberg (auth), Other Criteria, Oxford Univ, 72; Jeremy Gilbert-Rolfe (auth), article, Artforum, 12/73 & 9/79; Gerrit Henry (auth), The permitting medium, Art Int, summer 74. *Media:* Handmade Paper, Acrylic. *Dealer:* Marilyn Pearl Gallery 29 W 57th St New York NY 10019. *Mailing Add:* 178 Prince St New York NY 10012

HILL, DALE LOGAN
PAINTER, INSTRUCTOR

b Boise, Idaho, July 23, 09. *Study:* Minneapolis Inst Art, scholar; Am Acad Art, Chicago; Frederick Mizen Sch Art; also with Pruett Carter, Stanley Parkhouse, Harry Timmins, Haddon Sundlom & others. *Comn:* Many pvt comns. *Exhib:* Village Gallery, Taos, NMex; Jamison Gallery, Santa Fe, NMex; Desert Southwest Gallery, Palm Desert, Calif; Desert Art Mus, Palm Springs, Calif; Laguna Art Asn Gallery, Laguna Beach, Calif; and others. *Pos:* Owner, dir & instr, South Coast Acad Art, Santa Ana & Newport Beach, Calif; former owner, D Logan Hill Fine Art Gallery, Carmel, Calif. *Teaching:* Instr art, Orange Co Art Inst; pvt instr art. *Mem:* Am Inst Fine Arts; Allied Artists Am; Los Angeles Art Dir Club. *Media:* Oil. *Mailing Add:* 23222 Caminito Andreta Laguna Hills CA 92653

HILL, DOROTHY KENT
MUSEUM CURATOR

b New York, NY, Feb 3, 07. *Study:* Vassar Col, AB; Johns Hopkins Univ, PhD; Wilson Col, LHD. *Pos:* Res assoc, Walters Art Gallery, Baltimore, Md, 34-37, assoc cur ancient art, 37-40, cur ancient art, 40-69, cur Greek & Roman art, 70-77; ed, Walters Art Gallery Bulletin, 48-71; ed, bk rev, Old World, Am J Archaeol, 58-73. *Teaching:* Instr, Johns Hopkins Univ, 78-82, asst prof 83- *Mem:* Archaeol Inst Am; Am Oriental Soc; corresp mem Deutsches Archäologisches Inst; Inst di Studi Etruschi ed Italici. *Publ:* Auth, Catalog of Classical Bronze Sculpture, Walters Art Gallery, 49; auth, articles in Am J Archaeol, Hesperia & others. *Mailing Add:* 249 W 31st St Baltimore MD 21211

HILL, DRAPER
EDITORIAL CARTOONIST, HISTORIAN

b Boston, Mass, July 1, 35. *Study:* Harvard Col, BA(magna cum laude), 57; Slade Sch Fine Arts, London, Eng, 60-63. *Work:* Wiggin Gallery, Boston Pub Libr; Univ Va; Lyndon B Johnson Libr, Austin; Nat Gallery Can, Ottawa; Worcester Art Mus, Mass. *Exhib:* Int Salon de Caricature, Montreal, PQ, 66-81; Editorial Art of Draper Hill, Brooks Mem Art Gallery, Memphis, 75; Image of America in Caricature and Cartoon, Amon Carter Mus, Ft Worth, 75; American Presidency in Political Cartoons, Univ Art Mus, Berkeley, 75-76. *Collections Arranged:* Cartoon and Caricature from Hogarth to Hoffnung, 62 & James Gillray 1756-1815, 67, Arts Coun Gt Brit; exhib on hist caricature, Boston Pub Libr, 64, 66 & 70. *Pos:* Ed cartoonist, Worcester Telegram, Mass, 64-71, Com Appeal, Memphis, Tenn, 71-76 & Detroit News, 76-. *Teaching:* Instr life drawing, Sch Worcester Art Mus, 67-71. *Bibliog:* Lydel Sims (auth), article, Cartoonist Profiles, 3/75; Guy Northrop (auth), The Editorial Art of Draper Hill, Brooks Gallery, Memphis, 75; Alan Westin (auth), Getting Angry Six Times a Week, Beacon Press, Boston, 79. *Mem:* Asn Am Ed Cartoonists (vpres & dir, 70-75, pres, 75-76). *Collection:* Caricature and cartooning, with particular emphasis on eighteenth and nineteenth century English satire. *Publ:* Auth, Mr Gillray, The Caricaturist, London, 65; auth, Illingworth on Target, 70; co-illusr, The Decline and Fall of the Gibbon, 74; auth, The Satirical Etchings of James Gillray, 76; auth, Cartoons and Caricatures, Vol III, Time-Life Encycl of Collectibles, 78. *Mailing Add:* Detroit News 615 W Lafayette Blvd Detroit MI 48231

HILL, ED
DEALER, COLLECTOR

b El Paso, Tex, June 23, 37. *Study:* Univ Tex, El Paso, BA(Eng lit), 62. *Pos:* Dir, Hill Gallery, Univ Houston, currently. *Specialty:* Original prints of Fritz Scholder. *Collection:* One of largest collections of Fritz Scholder prints. *Mailing Add:* Dept Art Univ Houston 4800 Calhoun Houston TX 77004

HILL, J TWEED
PAINTER, GRAPHIC ARTIST

b Boston, Mass. *Study:* Taubes Pierce Sch Art, Provincetown, Mass, 59-60; with Steven Trefonides, Boston, Marguerite Pearson & Wayne Morrell, Rockport, Mass & Roger Curtis, Gloucester, Mass. *Exhib:* North Shore Arts Asn, Gloucester, 66-81; Jordan Marsh Annual Exhibit of New England Artists, 67; Newburyport Art Asn Show, 71-77; Butler Art Inst Show, Youngstown, Ohio, 72; Grand National Show, Am Artists Prof League, New York, 75-76 & 79-81; Cayuga Mus Hist & Art, 81-82. *Pos:* Dir & owner, Pigeon Cove Gallery, Rockport, Mass, 68-71; mem & co-operator, Harbor Gallery, Rockport, 73- *Awards:* Third Prize for Oils, Newburyport Art Asn, 75 & First Prize, 77; Kiwanis Club Silver Bowl Award for Most Popular Painting, 76 & 77, Best in Show, 78. *Mem:* North Shore Arts Asn (mem bd dir, 73-); Newburyport Art Asn; Salmagundi Club; Am Artists Prof League. *Media:* Oil, Pen & Ink. *Dealer:* Harbor Gallery Main St Rockport MA 01966. *Mailing Add:* J Tweed Hill Studio Rockport MA 01966

HILL, JAMES BERRY
DEALER

b New York, NY, June 24, 45. *Study:* Cornell Univ, AB, 67. *Collections Arranged:* Coggins Collection, Selections from the Robert P Coggins Collection of American Painting, 76. *Pos:* Co-dir, Berry-Hill Galleries, Inc, 67- *Mem:* Nat Arts Club; Appraisers Asn Am; Artists Fel. *Specialty:* American art of the nineteenth and early twentieth century; China trade paintings. *Mailing Add:* Berry-Hill Galleries 743 Fifth Ave New York NY 10022

HILL, JOAN (CHEA-SE-QUAH)
PAINTER, ILLUSTRATOR

b Muskogee, Okla. *Study:* Northeastern State Col, BA, 52; Famous Artists Course, 53-; spec study Indian art, with Dick West, 58-63; pvt study with int artists, 58-72; extensive air-travel-study on T H Hewitt Painting Workshops, 65-78, with Dong Kingman, Millard Sheets, Robert E Wood, Rex Brandt & George Post. *Work:* Heard Mus, Phoenix; Mus Am Indian, Heye Found, New York; Fine Arts Mus NMex, Santa Fe; Philbrook Art Ctr Mus, Tulsa, Okla. *Comn:* Mural-type oil paintings of Cherokee Nation through Dept Interior, Tahlequah, Okla, 67; portrait (gouache) for book, Sam Houston with the Cherokees, comn by Rennard Strickland & Jack Gregory Collection, Tulsa, 67; portrait & illus for book poetry, Five Civilized Tribes Mus, Muskogee, 68; oil painting, USA Ctr Mil Hist for Bicentennial Collection, Washington, DC, 75; mural, Seattle Ann Comn, 77. *Exhib:* Five Ann Center Arts Indian America, Dept Interior, 64, 67-70; American Embassies Overseas, Dept Interior Traveling Exhib, 65-66; America Discovers Indian Art, Smithsonian Inst, Washington, DC, 67; Outstanding Indian Painters & Sculptors Hon Exhib, Princeton Univ, 70; Am for Indian Opportunity Hon Exhib, Washington Gallery of Art, 71; and others. *Pos:* Career day art consult, Am Asn Univ Women, 62-63. *Teaching:* Instr art, Tulsa Secondary Pub Schs, 52-56; instr art & adult art educ, Muskogee Art Guild, 59-60. *Awards:* First Award, Philbrook Art Ctr Mus, 66, 68, 71 & 75; Walter Bimson Grand Award, Scottsdale Nat Indian Arts Exhib, Ariz, 68; Grand Spec Award, All Am Indian Art Exhib, Sheridan, Wyo, 71; and many others. *Bibliog:* Joan Buckley Hale (auth), A critic views Indian art in general and painting in particular, New Dimensions in Indian Art, 65; Marion Gridley (auth), Indians of Today, Indian Coun Fire Publ, 71; Jamake Highwater (auth), Song From the Earth--American Indian Painting, NY Graphic Soc, 76. *Mem:* Nat League Am Pen Women; Southwestern Art Asn; Muskogee Art Students Guild (art dir & publicity dir, 58-64); Intercontinental Biog Asn. *Media:* Oil, Gouache; Collage, Acrylic. *Publ:* Illusr, Life en Espanol, Time-Life Int, Mex, 69; contribr, Look to the Mountain Top, 72; contribr & illusr, The American Way, Am Airlines, 72; illusr, The Cherokee People, Indian Tribal Series, Phoenix, 73; illusr, Fire & the Spirits, Univ Okla Press, 75. *Mailing Add:* Rte 6 Box 98 Harris Rd Muskogee OK 74401

HILL, JOHN ALEXANDER
COLLECTOR

b Shawnee, Okla, Feb 24, 07. *Study:* Univ Denver, AB, 28, LLD, 62. *Pos:* Trustee, Cheekwood Mus Art, 73-, chmn acquisitions comt, 75- *Interests:* American traditional. *Collection:* All media Western Americana, 1850 to present. *Mailing Add:* 105 Leake Ave Nashville TN 37205

HILL, JOHN CONNER
DESIGNER, PUBLISHER
b Philadelphia, Pa, Feb 17, 45. *Study:* Pratt Inst, BID, 68; Cosanti Found, Paradise Valley, Ariz, with Paolo Soleri, 72-76. *Exhib:* Ariz Photog Biennial, Phoenix Art Mus, 69; Southwest Biennial, Int Folk Art Mus, Santa Fe, NMex, 70, NMex Biennial, 71; Tucson Festival Crafts Exhib, Tucson Mus, Ariz, 77; Ariz Textile Exhib, Matthews Ctr, Ariz State Univ, Tempe, 77. *Pos:* Bronze sculpture casting, Cosanti Found, 74-76; publ-owner, Kokopelli Press, Phoenix, 76- *Teaching:* Instr art, Rough Rock Demonstration Sch, Navajo Nation, Ariz, 68-70. *Awards:* Third Award, Ariz Textile Exhib, Scottsdale Ctr for the Arts, 76. *Dealer:* Hand & Spirit Gallery 4200 N Marshall Way Scottsdale AZ 85251. *Mailing Add:* Box 33666 Phoenix AZ 85067

HILL, MEGAN LLOYD
PAINTER, DEALER
b Chicago, Ill, Sept 22, 42. *Study:* Ind Univ, BA, 65; Univ Chicago, with Max Kuhn; Univ NMex, with Charles Mattox, MA, 69. *Work:* Univ NMex Fine Arts Mus, Albuquerque; Mus NMex, Santa Fe. *Exhib:* Intrinsic Art, Friends Contemp Art, 71, Denver; Fall Invitational, Roswell Mus & Art Ctr, NMex, 72; one-man show, Lerner Heller Gallery, New York, 72; Fine Arts Mus NMex, Biennial, 73; Seven Artists, Francis McCray Gallery, Western NMex Univ; and others. *Pos:* Owner, Hill's Gallery, Santa Fe, currently. *Awards:* Southwest Biennial, Mus NMex, 72. *Bibliog:* Donna Meilach (auth), Leather Book, 71; article, Art in Am, 8/72; article, Southwest Art Gallery Mag, 12/72. *Mem:* Mus NMex Found. *Specialty:* Contemporary New Mexico fine arts and crafts. *Publ:* Contribr, Craft Horizons, 12/71; auth, Aiming at the creative environment, Southwest Art Gallery Mag, 11/71 & 1/73. *Mailing Add:* 1469 Canyon Rd Santa Fe NM 87501

HILL, PETER
PAINTER, EDUCATOR
b Detroit, Mich, Nov 29, 33. *Study:* Albion Col, AB, 56; Cranbrook Acad Art, Bloomfield Hills, Mich, MFA, 58. *Work:* Joslyn Art Mus, Omaha, Nebr; Sheldon Mem Gallery, Lincoln, Nebr; Springfield Art Mus, Mo; Sioux City Art Ctr, Iowa; Spiva Art Gallery, Joplin, Mo. *Exhib:* Springfield Art Mus Ann, Mo, 70 & 74; Midwest Biennial, Joslyn Art Mus, 72 & 74; Colo/Nebr Exchange Exhib, Denver, 73; one-man show, Sheldon Mem Art Gallery, Lincoln, Nebr, 78; American Art, The Pillsbury Co, Minneapolis, 81; and others. *Teaching:* From instr to chmn dept, Univ Nebr, Omaha, 58- *Awards:* Ann Exhib Purchase Awards, Springfield Art Mus, 63 & 74; Best Painting, Joslyn Mus, 78 & 82. *Media:* Acrylic, Oil. *Dealer:* Gallery 72 37th & Leavenworth Omaha NE 68102. *Mailing Add:* 11734 Shirley St Omaha NE 68144

HILL, POLLY KNIPP
ETCHER, PAINTER
b Ithaca, NY, Apr 2, 1900. *Study:* Univ Ill; Syracuse Univ, BP; Acad Colarossi, Paris; also painting with George Snow Hill, Paris. *Work:* Syracuse Mus Fine Arts, NY; Pub Libr, Metrop Mus Art, New York; J B Speed Mem Mus, Louisville, Ky. *Comn:* Gift print for Printmakers Soc Calif, 62. *Exhib:* Soc Am Graphic Artists; Chicago Soc Etchers; Libr Cong; one-man show, Smithsonian Inst; St Petersburg Main Pub Libr, Fla, 77; and many other one-man shows. *Awards:* Nathan I Bijur Award, Brooklyn Soc Etchers, 29; Purchase Prize, Libr Cong, 41; Purchase Prize, Soc Am Etchers, 47; and others. *Bibliog:* Fine Prints of the Year, 30, 32 & 33; Contemporary American Prints, 31; Albert Reese (auth), Prize Prints of the Twentieth Century, 49. *Mem:* Soc Am Graphic Artists. *Publ:* Illusr, Woodpile Poems, 36, Bible Chillun, 39, Dark Windows, 42 & Rainbow Through the Web, 44. *Dealer:* Wits End Highlands NC 28741; Hodgell Galleries Sarasota FL. *Mailing Add:* 2233 Green Way S St Petersburg FL 33712

HILL, RICHARD WAYNE
PAINTER, PHOTOGRAPHER
b Buffalo, NY, Aug 7, 50. *Study:* Art Inst of Chicago, 68-71; State Univ NY, Buffalo, 77-80. *Work:* Native Am Ctr for the Living Arts, Niagara Falls, NY; Arts & Crafts Bd, Dept of Interior, Washington, DC; Woodland Indian Cult & Educ Ctr, Brantford, Ont; Int Ctr of Photog, New York. *Comn:* Watercolor series, Farmer's Mus, Cooperstown, NY, 71; photog, Everson Mus, Syracuse, 72; drawings series, Buffalo Courier Express, NY, 74; photog, Smithsonian Inst, Washington, DC, 75-76. *Exhib:* Iroquois Confederacy Arts & Crafts Exhib, Everson Mus, Syracuse, NY, 72; one-man show, Paintings by Richard Hill, Buffalo Mus of Sci, NY, 73; Exhib of Iroquois Art, Dortmund, Ger, 76; 32nd Am Indian Artists Exhib, Philbrook Art Ctr, Tulsa, Okla, 77; Spirit of the Earth, Castilani Gallery, New York, 80; John F Kennedy Ctr, 82; and others. *Pos:* Photogr, Woodland Indian Cult & Educ Ctr, Brantford, Ont, 72-73; res asst, Buffalo & Erie Co Hist Soc, Buffalo, 73-76; treas, Native Am Ctr for the Living Arts, Niagara Falls, 75-; mem bd, Int Native-Am Coun of Arts, 75-77; mem expansion arts adv panel, Nat Endowment for the Arts, 77; mus adv panel, Nat Endowment Humanities. *Teaching:* Instr art & photog, Buffalo NAm Indian Cult Ctr, 74-76; lectr Indian art, State Univ NY, Buffalo, 75- *Awards:* Am the Beautiful Fund grant, NY, 74; Creative Artist Pub Serv grant, NY, 76. *Bibliog:* Susan Greenwood (auth), Indian mind, 74, Rebecca Irving (auth), Indian art, 75, Niagara Falls Gazette; Anthony Bannon (auth), CAPS winners, Buffalo Evening News, 77. *Media:* Watercolor, Graphite; Black & White Photog. *Publ:* Illusr (series on local hist), Buffalo Courier Express, 74; illusr, 1975 Festival of American Folklife, Smithsonian Inst Prog, 75; auth, On returning cultural objects, Mus News, 77. *Mailing Add:* 2235 Mt Hope Rd Sanborn NY 14132

HILL, WILLIAM MANSFIELD
HISTORIAN, MUSEUM DIRECTOR
b Middlesbrough, England, Dec 4, 25. *Study:* Calif State Univ, San Jose, BA, 49; Univ Calif, Berkeley, MA; Univ Calif, Los Angeles, post grad study with Walter Horn & James Ackerman. *Collections Arranged:* Southern California Regional Print & Drawing Annuals, 73-78 & Four Santa Monica Artists: Stanton MacDonald Wright, John Altoon, Sam Francis, Richard Diebenkorn, 75, Santa Monica Col; and others. *Pos:* Sr cur, Los Angeles Co Mus of Art, Los Angeles, 64-65; assoc dir arts & humanities, Univ Exten, Univ of Calif, Los Angeles, 68-71; dir, Art Gallery, Santa Monica Col, Calif, 73- *Teaching:* Lectr art hist, Otis Art Inst, Los Angeles, 58-71; chmn dept of art & assoc prof art hist, Calif State Univ, Northridge, 65-68. *Awards:* Four Creative Prog Awards, Nat Univ Exten Asn, 68-69. *Bibliog:* Walter W Horn (auth), Medieval origins of the bay system, Soc of Archit Hist J, 58. *Mem:* Western Asn of Art Mus; Col Art Asn. *Res:* Architecture of Constantine; Cathedral of St Pierre; Angouleme; history of 19th and 20th century art history and city planning. *Publ:* Contribr, Handbook, Los Angeles Co Mus of Art, 64. *Mailing Add:* 1900 W Pico Blvd Santa Monica CA 90405

HILLER, BETTY R
CURATOR, CONSULTANT
b El Paso, Tex, Sept 25, 25. *Study:* Univ Tex, El Paso; Univ NMex; Univ Southern Calif, BFA, 45; Univ Nebr, Omaha; Creighton Univ. *Collections Arranged:* Ralston Crawford Exhib, Creighton Univ Gallery, Omaha, Nebr, 69; Julian Brody Collection of African Art, Univ Nebr, Omaha, 76; Festival of Biblical art & archeol, Jewish Community Ctr, Omaha, 78. *Pos:* Original developer, Children's Mus, Des Moines Art Ctr, 52-58; gallery owner & dealer, Lubetkin Gallery, Des Moines, Iowa, 62-64; ed arts, Spectrum Page, Sun Newspaper, 68-69; gallery dir, Creighton Univ, Omaha, 68-70; original developer, Children's Mus of Omaha, 75, first mus pres, 77-78; gallery dir, Univ Nebr, Omaha, 76; dir & mgr gallery, Univ Nebr, Omaha, 76-78. *Bibliog:* George Shane (auth), Lubetkin Gallery, Des Moines Register, 62; Elizabeth Flynn (auth), Betty Hiller, painter and gallery director, 76, Omaha World Herald; and others. *Mem:* trustee San Diego Mus Art; Am Soc Appraisers; Int Soc Appraisers; and others. *Media:* Acrylic. *Specialty:* Ethnic arts both ancient and modern, and 20th century American arts. *Collection:* American, Middle Eastern & pre-conquest antiquities & 20th century art. *Mailing Add:* 11937 Bajada Rd San Diego CA 92128

HILLES, SUSAN MORSE
COLLECTOR, PATRON
b Simsbury, Conn, July 4, 05. *Study:* Mus Fine Arts Sch, Boston, 24-25; Sacker Sch Design, Boston, 26-29; Univ Kings Col, DCL, 58; Wheaton Col, LittD, 67. *Pos:* Trustee, Yale Art Gallery Governor, 57-; hon trustee, Mus Fine Arts Boston, 68-; trustee, Whitney Mus Am Art, 70, hon trustee, 79; hon trustee, Wadsworth Atheneum, 71; trustee, Boston Athenaeum. *Collection:* Contemporary sculpture and painting. *Mailing Add:* c/o D Rosenthal PO Box 1890 Boston MA 02105

HILLIGOSS, MARTHA M
LIBRARIAN
b St Louis, Mo, Oct 28, 28. *Study:* Washington Univ, St Louis, BS; Univ Ill, Champaigne, MSLS. *Pos:* Chief art dept, St Louis Pub Libr, 65- *Mem:* Art Libr Soc NAm (Kans-Mo Chap); Am Inst Architects (hon assoc mem St Louis Chap). *Publ:* Auth, Steedman Architectural Library Catalogue, 73. *Mailing Add:* 1301 Olive St St Louis MO 63105

HILLMAN, ARTHUR STANLEY
GRAPHIC ARTIST, INSTRUCTOR
b Brooklyn, NY, Feb 21, 45. *Study:* Philadelphia Col Art, with Jerome Kaplan & Benton Spruance, BFA; Univ Mass, Amherst, MFA. *Exhib:* Twenty-first & 22nd Nat Exhib, Libr Cong, Washington, DC, 69 & 71; Prize Winning Am Prints, 69 & 4th Int Miniature Print Exhib, 71; Pratt Graphics Ctr, New York; one-man show, Philadelphia Art Alliance, 70 & Williams Col Mus Art, 76; 16th NDak Ann Print & Drawing Exhib, Univ NDak, 73; and others. *Teaching:* Instr printmaking & chmn dept, Mass Col Art, Boston, 68-74; instr graphic arts, drawing, design & photog, Simon's Rock, Bard Col, Mass, 74-, chmn arts div, 81- *Awards:* Univ Mass Fel, 67; Pennell Fund Purchase Award, Libr Cong, 69; Northern Ill Univ Purchase Award, 70. *Mem:* Col Art Asn Am; Philadelphia Print Club. *Mailing Add:* PO Box 545 Great Barrington MA 01230

HILLS, LEO HIMMELFARB
DEALER, APPRAISER
b Brno, Czech, Sept 7, 14; US citizen. *Collections Arranged:* Beniamino Bufano, San Francisco Airport, 78. *Pos:* Dealer, Continental Art Gallery, currently. *Teaching:* Lectr art as an investment in conjunction with Beniamino Bufano, 64-69. *Mem:* Am Soc Appraisers. *Specialty:* Beniamino Buffano, Cucaro. *Mailing Add:* Continental Art Gallery 545 Sutter St San Francisco CA 94102

HILLS, PATRICIA
HISTORIAN, CURATOR
b Baraboo, Wis, Jan 31, 36. *Study:* Stanford Univ, BA, 57; Hunter Col, City Univ New York, MA, 68; NY Univ Inst Fine Arts, PhD, 73. *Collections Arranged:* Eastman Johnson (auth, catalog), Clarkson-Potter, 72; The American Frontier: Images and Myths (auth, catalog), 73, Turn-of-the-Century America: Paintings, Photographs (auth, catalog), 77 & The Figurative Tradition and the Whitney Museum (coauth, catalog), 80, Whitney Mus Am Art; The Painter's America: Rural and Urban Life, 1810-1910 (cur, auth, catalog), Praeger, 74. *Pos:* Assoc cur, Whitney Mus Am Art, 72-74, cur,

74- *Teaching:* Assoc prof, York Col, City Univ New York, 74-78; assoc prof Am painting, Boston Univ, 78-82. *Mem:* Col Art Asn; Women's Caucus for Art; Inst Res Hist; Arch Am Art. *Res:* American painting from Civil War to present, particularly figurative painting. *Mailing Add:* 36 Harrison St Brookline MA 02146

HILLSMITH, FANNIE
PAINTER, ASSEMBLAGE ARTIST

b Boston, Mass, Mar 13, 11. *Study:* Boston Mus Fine Arts Sch; Art Students League, with Alexander Brook, Kuniyoshi, Zorach & Sloan; Atelier 17, with Stanley Hayter. *Work:* Mus Mod Art, New York; Boston Mus Fine Arts; Currier Gallery Art, Manchester, NH; Fogg Mus Art, Cambridge, Mass; Metrop Mus Art, New York; and others. *Exhib:* Boston Arts Festival, 50-54 & 56-61; Cornell Univ, 64; one-man retrospective, Brockton Mus, Mass, 71 & Bristol Mus, RI, 72; Brattleboro Mus, 74; plus many others. *Teaching:* Vis critic, Cornell Univ, 63-64. *Awards:* Alumni Traveling Scholar, Boston Mus Fine Arts Sch, 58; Tour Gallery Award, 64; Berkshire Mus Award, 64; and others. *Publ:* Auth & illusr, The Ups and Downs of Needlepoint, Barnes, 76. *Mailing Add:* 915 Second Ave New York NY 10017

HILSON, DOUGLAS
PAINTER, EDUCATOR

b Flint, Mich, Dec 7, 41. *Study:* Cranbrook Acad Art, Bloomfield Hills, Mich, BFA; Univ Wash, MFA. *Work:* Indianapolis Mus Art; Ill Art Mus, Springfield, DeWaters Art Inst, Flint, Mich; Decatur Art Mus, Ill; Western Mich Univ Art Mus, Kalamazoo. *Exhib:* 76th Chicago Exhib, Chicago Art Inst, 76; Ann, 55 Mercer Gallery, New York, 82; From NY to Newcastle Traveling Exhib, 83-84; Art in New York Traveling Exhib, 83; one-person show, Bernice Steinbaum Gallery, New York, 83; and others. *Teaching:* Prof painting & dir grad painting prog, Univ Ill, Champaign, 65-; vis prof, Pratt Inst, 81-83. *Awards:* First Prize, Nat Works Art on Paper, 76; Purchase Award, 29th Ill Invitational, Ill Art Mus Permanent Collection, 76; Ctr Advanced Study, 73-74. *Media:* Oil, Acrylic; Graphite. *Dealer:* Bernice Steinbaum Gallery 903 Madison Ave New York NY 10021; Marianne Deson Gallery Chicago IL. *Mailing Add:* 407 Greewich St 226 East Ontario New York NY 10013

HILTON, JOSEPH
PAINTER

b Washington, DC, Jan 1, 46. *Study:* Md Inst, BFA(summa cum laude), 75; Art Inst Chicago, MFA(Fred J Forester Traveling Fel), 77. *Exhib:* Md Biennial, Baltimore Mus, 74; Traveling Fel Exhib, Art Inst Chicago, 77; Art for the 80s, Galleria Durban, Caracas, Venezuela, 80; Seven Artists, Mus Contemp Art, Chicago, 81; solo exhibs, Navy Pier, Chicago, 81, Chicago Now, Brentwood Gallery, Chicago, 82 & Four Imagists, Montpeleir Cult Arts Ctr, Md, 82; New Work, Monique Knowlton Gallery, New York, 83. *Mailing Add:* c/o Monique Knowlton Gallery 153 Mercer St New York NY 10012

HILTS, ALVIN
SCULPTOR

b Newmarket, Ont, Apr 2, 08. *Study:* In Mex & Can. *Work:* Churches, Kirkland Lake, Welland & Newmarket; also in schs. *Comn:* Memorial, Newmarket, 36; Univ Guelph, 61; Univ Lennoxville, 70; also pvt comn, Vancouver, Toronto, Ottawa, Oshawa & St Louis. *Exhib:* Sculpture Soc, 31-72; Royal Can Acad; Ont Soc Artists. *Mem:* Sculpture Soc Can (pres, 57, 58 & 61). *Media:* Wood, Stone. *Mailing Add:* 605 Oshawa Blvd N Oshawa ON L1G 5T8 Canada

HILTY, THOMAS R
GRAPHIC ARTIST, PAINTER

b Gary, Ind, May 29, 43. *Study:* Ind Univ; Western State Col, Colo, BFA, 65; Univ NMex; Bowling Green State Univ, MFA, 68. *Work:* Dayton Art Inst, Ohio; Toledo Mus Art, Ohio; Colgate-Sloane Found, Bowling Green, Ohio; IBM Corp; Toledo Trust Corp. *Comn:* Drawings, Bowling Green State Univ Business Admin Bldg, 72, Prog Liberated Death and Dying, WBGU TV, 78, Frames of Reference, Boston New TV Workshop, 79-80, Moore Musical Arts Ctr, 80 & J Barrett Galleries, Toledo, 82. *Exhib:* One-man shows, Chautauqua Inst, NY, 78 & Gallery Yolanda, Chicago, 79; Ohio Selection, Dayton Art Inst, 79; Ankrum Gallery, Los Angeles; J Rosenthal Gallery, Chicago; and others. *Teaching:* Prof art, drawing & painting, Bowling Green State Univ, 68- *Awards:* Purchase Awards, All Ohio Exhib, Ohio Arts Coun, 72, All Ohio Exhib, Dayton Art Inst, 76, 80 & 81 & Toledo Area Artists Exhib, Toledo Mus, 80, 81 & 82. *Bibliog:* Louise Bruner (auth), Thomas Hilty, Am Artist, 80. *Media:* Graphite, Charcoal, Pastels. *Publ:* Auth, article, Art News, 6/83. *Dealer:* J Barrett Galleries 3154 Markway Dr Toledo OH 43606. *Mailing Add:* 21 Parkwood Dr Bowling Green OH 43402

HIMMELFARB, JOHN DAVID
PAINTER

b Chicago, Ill, June 3, 46. *Study:* Harvard Univ, BA, 68, MAT, 70. *Work:* Art Inst Chicago; Nat Mus Am Art, Smithsonian Inst, Washington, DC; Fogg Mus Art, Cambridge, Mass; Baltimore Mus Art, Md; Brooklyn Mus. *Exhib:* Printmakers Mid-West Show, Walker Art Ctr, Minneapolis, 73; Brooklyn Mus, 74 & 80; Three Lithographers, Sheldon Mem Art Gallery, 75; 19th Ann, Okla Art Ctr, Oklahoma City, 77; Art Inst of Chicago, 78, 79 & 81; Gallery 72, Omaha, 79; Hull Gallery, Washington, DC, 80; Fountain Gallery, Portland, Ore, 80; Brooklyn Mus, 80. *Media:* Oil, Pen & Ink. *Dealer:* Terry Dintenfass 50 West 57th St New York NY; Balkin Fine Arts 425 North Clark Chicago Il. *Mailing Add:* 908 West 19th St Chicago IL 60608

HINDES, CHUCK (CHARLES AUSTIN)
CERAMIST, EDUCATOR

b Muskegon, Mich, May 30, 42. *Study:* Univ Ill, Urbana-Champaign, BFA(crafts), 66; RI Sch Design, MFA(ceramics), 68. *Work:* St Louis Mus Art; Everson Mus Art. *Exhib:* 27th Ceramic Nat, Everson Mus Art, 72; 31st Ann Scripps Invitational, Claremont Gallery, 75; Marietta Craft Nat, Marietta Col, 75; one-man show, Rochester Art Ctr, 76; A Century of Ceramics in the US 1878-1978, Everson Mus Art, 79; Nat Wood Fired Ceramics Exhib, Pittsburgh Ctr Arts, 81; Vessels Aesthetic, Taft Col Gallery, 81; four-person show, Departure Gallery, New York, 83. *Teaching:* Instr ceramics, Univ Fla, Gainesville, 69-72; adj prof, RI Sch Design, 72-73; from asst to assoc prof, Univ Iowa, Iowa City, 73- *Awards:* Purchase Award, Nat Exhib Ceramic Sculpture & Jewelry, Brigham Young Univ, 76; First Prize Ceramics, 32nd Ann Iowa Artists Exhib, Des Moines Art Ctr, 80. *Mem:* Nat Coun Educ Ceramic Arts. *Media:* Ceramics. *Publ:* Auth, Saggar firing, Studio Potter, 79. *Mailing Add:* 728 E Fairchild Iowa City IA 52240

HINES, RICHARD G
ART DEALER, COLLECTOR

b San Francisco, Calif, Mar 24, 49. *Study:* Univ Wash; Ariz State Univ; Univ Americas. *Specialty:* Major premier exhibitions of contemporary American masters. *Mailing Add:* Richard Hines Gallery 2030 Fifth Ave Seattle WA 98121

HINKHOUSE, FOREST MELICK
CONSULTANT

b West Liberty, Iowa, July 7, 25. *Study:* Coe Col, AB; Univ Mex; Fogg Art Mus, Harvard Univ; NY Univ Inst Fine Arts, MA; Univ Madrid, PhD; Eureka Col, DHL, 83. *Collections Arranged:* Industrial Gouaches of John Hultberg, 57; Paintings & Portraits by Frank Mason, 58; Contemporary Arizona Painting, 58; Festival of Arts, 58; One Hundred Years of French Painting 1860-1960, 61; English Landscape Painting, 61. *Pos:* Pub relations, Int House Asn, New York; art critic, Buffalo Eve News, Ariz Repub & Phoenix Gazette; founding dir, Phoenix Art Mus & Phoenix Fine Arts Asn, 57-67; co-founder, Hinkhouse Gallery, Coe Col, 65; consult & adv, Phoenix Art Mus, 67-; consult, Calif Art Comn, 68-; co-founder, Hinkhouse Collection, Melick Libr, Eureka Col, 69; mem bd trustees, Coe Col, Cedar Rapids, Iowa; founder, Hinkhouse Gallery Art, Stephens Col, Columbia, Mo. *Teaching:* Asst prof art, Albright Art Sch, Univ Buffalo, 56-57; guest lectr, Prudential Lines, 77. *Mem:* Claustro Extraordinario, Madrid; Col Art Asn Am; Am Asn Mus. *Publ:* Auth, Catalogue of the Collections of the Phoenix Art Museum; contribr, articles in Oregonian, 75- *Mailing Add:* 1815 Jones St Russian Hill San Francisco CA 94109

HINMAN, CHARLES B
PAINTER, SCULPTOR

b Syracuse, NY, Dec 29, 32. *Study:* Syracuse Univ, BFA, 55; Art Students League, with Morris Kantor. *Work:* Mus Mod Art, New York; Larry Aldrich Mus Contemp Art, Conn; Los Angeles Co Mus; Detroit Inst Art; Mus Mod Art, Nagaoka, Japan; and many others. *Exhib:* Solo exhibs, Galerie Denise Rene, Paris, 71, New York, 72, 73 & 75, Hokin Gallery, Chicago, 76 & 79, Palm Beach Fla, 77, Irving Galleries, Milwaukee, 76 & Donald Morris Gallery, Birmingham, Mich, 79; and others. *Media:* Acrylic. *Mailing Add:* 231 Bowery New York NY 10002

HINSON, TOM EVERETT
CURATOR, HISTORIAN

b Henderson, Tex, Oct 25, 44. *Study:* Univ Tex, Austin, BA(art hist), BS(archit studies); Case Western Reserve Univ, Cleveland, Ohio, MA(art hist). *Pos:* Mus fel, Toledo Mus Art, Ohio, 70-71; Asst cur, Dept Mod Art, Cleveland Mus Art, Ohio, 73-77, assoc cur, 78-81, cur contemp art, 82- *Mem:* Am Asn Mus. *Res:* Contemporary art; 19th and 20th century photography; 20th century architecture. *Mailing Add:* 2330 Euclid Heights Blvd 309 Cleveland Heights OH 44106

HIOS, THEO
PAINTER, GRAPHIC ARTIST

b Sparta, Greece, Feb 2, 08; US citizen. *Study:* Am Artists Sch; Art Students League; Pratt Inst; Nat Univ Athens. *Work:* Carnegie Inst, Pittsburgh; Nat Collection Fine Art, Washington, DC; Guild Hall Mus, Easthampton, NY; Parrish Art Mus, Southampton, NY; Nat Pinokothiki Mus, Athens, Greece; plus others. *Exhib:* Brooklyn Mus, 58; Carnegie Inst Int, 61; one-man retrospective, Harpur Col, 61; Nat Exhib, Pa Acad Fine Arts, 62; 27 one-man shows in mus & galleries; and others. *Teaching:* Instr painting & drawing, City Col New York, 58-61; instr painting & drawing, Dalton Sch, 62-73; instr painting & drawing, New Sch Social Res, 62- *Awards:* First Prize, New Eng Exhib, Silvermine Guild Artists, 48; Purchase Awards, Guild Hall Mus, 69 & Parish Art Mus, 70; Adolph & Esther Gottlieb Found Grant $10,000, 81; and others. *Bibliog:* article, Greek Daily, 81; Ikons, television film, 9/81; article, Art News Mag, 5/83; and others. *Mem:* Fedn Mod Painters & Sculptors (vpres, 57-62 & 66-75); Audubon Artists. *Media:* Oil, Acrylic; Pastel, Watercolor. *Mailing Add:* 136 W 95th St New York NY 10025

HIRSCH, GILAH YELIN
PAINTER, EDUCATOR

b Montreal, PQ, Aug 24, 44. *Study:* McGill Univ; Hebrew Univ; Sir George Williams Univ; Boston Univ; San Francisco State Univ; Univ Calif, Berkeley, BA, 67; Univ Calif, Los Angeles, MFA, 70. *Work:* Security Pac Banks, Los Angeles. *Exhib:* Solo exhibs, Los Angeles Co Mus Art, 69, Woman's Bldg, Los Angeles, 78, Space Gallery, Los Angeles, 81 & others; Whitney Mus Ann, New York, 73; Univ NMex, 79; Univ Calif, Irvine Gallery, 82; and others.

Collections Arranged: Metamajic (auth, catalog), Calif State Univ, Dominguez Hills, 78. *Teaching:* Prof art, Calif State Univ, Dominguez Hills, 73-; fac tutors, Int Col, 80- *Awards:* Artist in Residence Fel, Tamarind Lithography Workshop, 73 & Dorland Mountain Colony, 81 & 83; Dorland Mountain Colony Fel, 81 & 83. *Bibliog:* Article, New York Times; article, Los Angeles Times; article, Art News. *Mem:* Artists Equity. *Media:* Oil, Acrylic. *Publ:* Auth, Joan of art seminars, Artweek, 72; auth, Emily Carr, Feminist Art J, 76; auth, The Pararational, Visionary and Mystical Perspective, Calif State Univ, Dominguez Hills, 77; auth, Emily Carr, Women's Studies, 78. *Mailing Add:* 2412 Oakwood Ave Venice CA 90291

HIRSCH, WILLARD NEWMAN
SCULPTOR
b Charleston, SC, Nov 19, 05. *Study:* Nat Acad Design; Beaux Arts Inst Design. *Work:* Gibbes Art Gallery, Charleston; State Art Collection, Mus Art, Columbia, SC; Florence Mus Art, SC; IBM Corp. *Comn:* Stainless steel works, Clemson Univ, 49-55 & Charleston Co Libr, 61; pulpit sculpture, Woodsdale Temple, Wheeling, WVa, 65; steel & brass sculpture, Porter Gaud Sch, Charleston, 66; bronze fountain figure, Home Fed Savings & Loan, Charleston, 70; aluminum sculptures, Newberry Col, 73. *Exhib:* Nat Acad Design, New York, 35-42; Pa Acad Fine Art, Philadelphia, 42; Syracuse Mus Art, NY, 48; Fairmont Park 3rd Int, Philadelphia, 49; Whitney Mus Am Art, New York, 50; one-man show, Gibbes Art Gallery, 79. *Bibliog:* Article, Art Voices South, 11-12/79. *Mem:* Charleston Artists Guild; SC Artists Guild. *Mailing Add:* 2 Queen St Charleston SC 29401

HIRSCHFELD, ALBERT
GRAPHIC ARTIST
b St Louis, Mo, June 21, 03. *Study:* Nat Acad Design, New York; Julien's, Paris; London Co Coun; Art Students League; Hartford Univ, hon DFA. *Work:* Whitney Mus Am Art, New York; Mus Mod Art, New York; Metrop Mus Art, New York; Brooklyn Mus Art, NY; William Hayes Fogg Mus, Boston. *Comn:* History of Cinema, Fifth Ave Playhouse, New York, 45; Personalities, Eden Roc Hotel, Miami, Fla, 55; American Theatre, Brussels World's Fair, 59; Opening Night, Playbill Room, Manhattan Hotel, NY, 60. *Exhib:* One-man shows, Staten Island Mus, NY, 61, Hammer Gallery, New York, 67, Mus Performing Arts, Lincoln Ctr, New York, 68, Margo Feiden Gallery, New York, 72-74 & Seibu Gallery, Tokyo, Japan, 75; Gallery 18, London, Eng, 77; Fogg Mus & Posey Libr, Harvard Univ, Cambridge, Mass, 83; Gracie Mansion, New York, 83. *Pos:* Theatre caricaturist, New York Times, 23- *Awards:* Specialist Grant, US State Dept; Special Tony Award. *Media:* Ink. *Publ:* Auth, The World of Hirschfeld, Abrams, 71; auth, Rhythm, Touchstone, 70; auth, Kabuki, Goodstadt, 76; auth, The Entertainers, Elm Tree, London, 77; auth, Hirschfeld by Hirschfeld, Dodd, Mead, 79. *Mailing Add:* 122 E 95th St New York NY 10028

HITCH, JEAN LEASON
PAINTER
b Sydney, Australia, Oct 18, 18; US citizen. *Study:* Melbourne Tech Art Training Sch, Australia; Leason Sch Painting; Wayman Adams Sch Painting, Adirondacks, NY. *Exhib:* Allied Artists Am, Am Artist Prof League & Catharine Lorillard Wolfe Art Club, New York; Hudson Valley Art Asn, White Plains, NY; Audubon Artists, New York. *Pos:* Art cur, Staten Island Inst Arts & Sci, 45-51; dir, Educ Dept, Cape Cod Art Asn, currently. *Teaching:* Instr painting, Cape Cod Art Asn, currently. *Awards:* Kathleen Grumbacher Award, 66; Anna Hyatt Huntington Horse-Head Award, 72; Bronze Medal, Cape Cod Art Asn, 77. *Mem:* Cape Cod Art Asn; Allied Artists Am; Catharine Lorillard Wolfe Art Club ; Hudson Valley Art Asn; Am Artist Prof League. *Media:* Oil. *Mailing Add:* 51 Gordon Lane Yarmouth Port MA 02675

HITCH, ROBERT A
PAINTER
b Brooklyn, NY, May 12, 20. *Study:* Art Career Sch, New York; also painting with Wilford S Conrow, Percy Leason, Douglas Grant & Marshall Joyce. *Work:* Hickory Art Mus, NC; Tamassee DAR Sch, SC. *Exhib:* Allied Artists Am & Am Artists Prof League, New York; Hudson Valley Art Asn, White Plains, NY; Staten Island Mus Arts & Sci, NY; Nat Arts Club, New York. *Teaching:* Instr painting, Cape Cod Art Asn. *Awards:* Henry Ward Ranger Prize, Nat Acad Design, 54; Grand Nat Award, Am Artists Prof League, 54; Best Cape Cod Scene, Cape Cod Art Asn. *Mem:* Allied Artists Am (pub rels, 69-); Cape Cod Art Asn; Copley Soc of Boston; Hudson Valley Art Asn; Am Artists Prof League. *Media:* Oil. *Mailing Add:* 51 Gordon Lane Yarmouth Port MA 02675

HITCH, STEWART
PAINTER
b Lincoln, Neb, Feb 26, 40. *Study:* Univ Neb, BFA, 64, MFA, 68. *Work:* Aldrich Mus Contemp Art, Ridgefield, Conn; Ewing Mus Art, Normal, Ill. *Exhib:* Aldrich Mus, Ridgefield, Conn, 73; New Acquisitions, Ewing Mus, Normal, Ill, 74; American Painting: The 80's, Grey Gallery, NY Univ, 79, Am Ctr, Paris, 80 & Mus Contemp Art, Houston, 80; Painting Up Front, Cornell Univ Mus, Ithaca, NY, 81; Surface & Texture, Mus Mod Art, New York, 81. *Teaching:* Artist in residence, Fla Int Univ, Miami, 73; vis artist, Syracuse Univ, 83. *Bibliog:* Anita Feldman (auth), Space & subjectivity, Art Forum, 10/79; Hilton Kramer (auth), Neo-Modernists, New York Times, 10/23/79; Ted Bonin (auth), Stewart Hitch: New paintings, Arts Mag, 2/83. *Media:* Oil, Acrylic. *Mailing Add:* 187 E Broadway New York NY 10002

HITCHCOCK, HENRY RUSSELL
HISTORIAN, CRITIC
b Boston, Mass, June 3, 03. *Study:* Harvard Univ, AB, 24, MA, 27; NY Univ, Hon DFA; Glasgow Univ, Scotland, LHD; Univ Pa, DHL. *Teaching:* Asst prof art, Vassar Col, 27-28; asst prof, Wesleyan Univ, 29-41, assoc prof, 41-47, prof, 47-48; instr, Conn Col, 34-42; lectr, Mass Inst Technol, 46-48; prof, Smith Col, 48-61, dir, Mus Art, 49-55, Sophia Smith prof, 61-68; vis lectr, Yale Univ, 52-53, 59-60 & 69; Cambridge Univ, 62, Harvard Univ, 65 & Columbia Univ, 71; prof art, Univ Mass, Amherst, 68; adj prof, Inst Fine Arts, NY Univ, 69- *Awards:* Soc Archit Historians Book Award, 55; Col Art Asn Book Award, 58; Am Coun Learned Soc Prize, 61; and others. *Mem:* Franklin Fel Royal Soc Arts; Soc Archit Historians (dir & pres NY chap, 70-); Victorian Soc Am (pres, 69-); Col Art Asn Am; Royal Inst Brit Architects. *Publ:* Auth, In the Nature of Materials, the Buildings of Frank Lloyd Wright, 42 & 69; auth, Architecture: 19th and 20th Century, 58, 69, 72 & 77; auth, Rococo Architecture in Southern Germany, 69; co-auth, with W Seale, Temples of Democracy, 76; auth, German Renaissance Architecture, 82; and others. *Mailing Add:* 152 E 62nd St New York NY 10021

HLAVINA, RASTISLAV See Rasto

HNIZDOVSKY, JACQUES
PAINTER, PRINTMAKER
b Pylypcze, Ukraine, Jan 27, 15; US citizen. *Study:* Acad Fine Arts, Warsaw; Acad Fine Arts, Zagreb, Yugoslavia. *Work:* Boston Mus Fine Arts; Philadelphia Mus Art; Cleveland Mus; Nelson Rockefeller Collection. *Exhib:* Boston Printmakers Ann, Boston Mus Fine Arts, 61-; Triennale Int dellaxilogratia Contemporanea, Carpi, Italy; Contemporary US Printmakers, Tokyo, Japan, 67; one-man shows, Lumley-Cazalet, London, Eng, 69 & 72; one-man retrospective, Ten Years of Woodcuts, Assoc Am Artists, New York, 71; Long Beach Mus Art, Calif, 77; Yale Univ, 77; and others. *Awards:* First Prize for Woodcut, Boston Mus Fine Arts, 62; MacDowell Colony Fel, 63; YADDO, 78. *Bibliog:* Slavko Nowytski (auth), Sheep in Wood (film), Am Film Festival, New York, 71; Yearbook of the American Society of Bookplate Collectors and Designers, 81/82. *Mem:* Soc Am Graphic Artists; Audubon Artists; Boston Printmakers. *Media:* Oil; Woodcut. *Publ:* Illusr woodcuts, Poems of John Keats, 64 & Poems of Samuel Taylor Coleridge, 67, Crowell-Collier; illusr, Poems of Thomas Hardy, Folio Soc, London, 79; illusr, The Poetry of Robert Frost, Franklin Libr, 81; illusr, Modern Poems, Delacorte, 82; and others. *Dealer:* Assoc Am Artists 663 Fifth Ave New York NY 10017. *Mailing Add:* 5270 Post Rd Riverdale NY 10471

HO, FRANCIS T
PHOTOGRAPHER, EDUCATOR
b Honolulu, Hawaii, Aug 29, 38. *Study:* Yale Univ, BFA, 61; Rochester Inst Technol, MFA, 67. *Work:* Nikon Camera Co, New York; Canon Photo Gallery, Amsterdam; Photo Gallery Int, Tokyo; Silver Image Gallery, Seattle. *Comn:* Photograph, Seattle Arts Comn, 83. *Exhib:* The Oriental Eye, Focus Gallery, San Francisco, 73; A Temporary Possession: The Human Image in 20th Century Photography, Washington State Univ Mus Art, 76; solo exhibs, Canon Photo Gallery, Amsterdam, 77 & Photo Gallery Int, Tokyo, 80; Fantastic Photography in the USA, Mus Fundacio Miro, Barcelona, 78, Hall Palais Beaux Arts, Brussels, 78 & Mus Mod Art, Mexico City, 79. *Teaching:* Prof photog & graphic design, Washington State Univ, 67-; exchange prof graphic design, Nihon Univ, Tokyo, 79-80. *Awards:* Cert Excellence, Exhib Communication Graphics, Am Inst Graphic Arts, 74-75; Merit Award, The One Show, New York Art Dirs Club, 75; Award Excellence, 16th Ann Exhib, Communication Arts Mag, 75. *Bibliog:* Attilio Columbo (auth), Fantastic Photographs, Random House & Gordon Fraser, 79; Yaomi Yoshikawa (auth), article, Commercial Photo, Japan, 80; Tokumi Sawamoto (auth), article, Camera Mainichi, Tokyo, 2/80. *Mem:* Friends Photog. *Mailing Add:* PO Box 2472 Col Sta Pullman WA 99164

HOARE, TYLER JAMES
SCULPTOR, PRINTMAKER
b Joplin, Mo, June 5, 40. *Study:* Univ Colo; Sculpture Ctr, New York; Univ Kans, BFA, 63; Calif Col Arts & Crafts, Oakland; Univ Arti, Italia, Hon Dipl Merit. *Work:* US Info Agency, Washington, DC; State Univ NY Albany; Oakland Mus, Calif; Calif Col Arts & Crafts; and many pvt collections. *Exhib:* One-man shows, John Bolles Gallery, San Francisco, Calif, 69, 71 & 74, Camberwell Sch Art, London, Eng, 71 & Cent Sch Art & Design, London, 74; 4th Int Print Exhib, Pratt Graphics Ctr, New York, 71; 22nd Nat Print Exhib, Libr Cong, Washington, DC, 71; Calif Palace Legion Honor; Xerographic Art, Xerox Corp, New York; plus many others. *Teaching:* Guest lectr, San Francisco Art Inst, 72 & San Francisco State Univ, 72-74; guest lectr, San Francisco State Univ, 72-74; instr, Univ Calif, Berkeley, 73-74; guest lectr, Oakland Mus, Calif, 74; guest lectr, Oakland Mus, Calif, 74, Calif State Univ, Hayward, 74, Mo Southern State Col, 79, Univ Wyo, 79 & Colo State Univ, 79. *Awards:* Merit Award, 22nd Ann San Francisco Art Festival, San Francisco Art Comn, 68; 2nd Ann Graphic Exhib, Olive Hyde Art Ctr, 72; Focuserie Award, Nat Photog Exhib, Erie, Pa, 74; plus others. *Bibliog:* Thomas Albright (auth), Funk refinement, San Francisco Chronicle, 3/69; New American Sculpture, US Info Agency, 71; Robert Cartmell (auth), Xerox is okay-but will it last?, Albany Times Union, 2/72. *Mem:* Los Angeles Printmaking Soc; Nat Soc Lit & Arts; Metal Arts Guild, San Francisco; Richmond Art Ctr, Calif. *Media:* Wood, Metal. *Mailing Add:* 30 Menlo Pl Berkeley CA 94707

HOBBIE, LUCILLE
PAINTER, LITHOGRAPHER
b Boonton, NJ, June 14, 15. *Study:* Self-taught. *Work:* Montclair Art Mus, NJ; Newark Pub Libr, NJ; Colonial Williamsburg, Va; Seeing Eye, Morristown, NJ; Prudential Life, Newark; and others. *Comn:* Drawings of bicentennial historic sites, Jersey Cent Power & Light Co; portfolio of drawings, Koehler Estate, 82-83. *Exhib:* NJ State Ann, 50-72; NJ Watercolor Soc Ann, 50-72; Audubon Soc Ann, 53-72; Am Watercolor Soc Ann, Nat Acad Design Gallery, 56; 50 Artists, NJ State Mus, Trenton, 56. *Pos:* Admin asst, Newark Sch Fine & Indust Art, 63-75. *Awards:* First Prize Award for Lithography, NJ State Exhib, 51, Award for Watercolor, 52 & 62; Agnes Noyes Award, NJ Watercolor Soc, 56 & 63. *Mem:* NJ Watercolor Soc (pres, 50-52, mem bd, 81-83); Asn Artists NJ (bd dirs, 70-72); NJ Printmaking Coun; and others. *Media:* Watercolor, Acrylic. *Publ:* Illusr, A Calendar for Dinah, 69; illusr, Eclipteces, 70; illusr, Mansion Magic, 79. *Dealer:* Grand Central Galleries 40 Vanderbilt Ave New York NY 10017; Thomas Vokes Gallery Morristown NJ 07960. *Mailing Add:* Talmadge Rd Mendham NJ 07945

HOBBS, (CARL) FREDRIC
SCULPTOR, FILMMAKER
b Philadelphia, Pa, Dec 30, 31. *Study:* Cornell Univ, BA; Acad San Fernando Belles Artes, Madrid, Spain. *Work:* Mus Mod Art, New York; Metrop Mus Art, New York; Finch Col Mus, New York; San Francisco Mus Mod Art; Oakland Mus Art; plus others. *Exhib:* Biennial Exhib Am Art, Pa Acad Fine Arts, Philadelphia, 64; Nat Fine Arts Collection, Smithsonian Inst, Washington, DC, 64; The Highway Traveling Exhib, Inst Contemp Art, Philadelphia, 70; one-man shows, Calif Palace Legion of Honor, San Francisco & Mus Sci & Indust, Los Angeles, 76; San Francisco Mus of Mod Art, 80. *Pos:* Chmn bd, CED, Virginia City Restoration Corp. *Bibliog:* John W McCoubrey (auth), Art & the road, Highway, 70; Thomas Albright (auth), Visuals, Rolling Stone Mag, 71; plus others. *Media:* Steel Supported Fiberglass, Latex Acrylic. *Publ:* Coauth, The Richest Place on Earth, Houghton-Mifflin, 78; auth, An American Paradise, Calif Living Bks, 80 & 82; auth, Eat your house: ART ECO guide to self sufficiency, Mayfield, 80; auth feature articles, City Mag, San Francisco Mag; writer, dir & producer, 5 feature films & 2 TV-Expo short features. *Dealer:* Heritage Gallery 718 N La Cienega Blvd Los Angeles CA 90069; Braunstein Gallery 254 Sutter St San Francisco CA. *Mailing Add:* PO Box 221691 Carmel CA 93922

HOBBS, GERALD S
DEALER, PUBLISHER
b New York, NY, Nov 5, 41. *Pos:* Publ, Am Artist Mag, 73, The Artist Mag, 76, Art & Antiques: The Am Mag for Connoisseurs & Collectors, 78-, Interiors Mag, 78, Residential Interiors Mag, 78 & Int Soc Artists. *Mem:* Nat Arts Club; Salmagundi Club; Nat Art Material Trade Asn; Artists' Fel. *Specialty:* Publisher of The American Artist Collection (unlimited edition prints). *Mailing Add:* 33 Thornburg Rd Scarsdale NY 10583

HOBBS, JACK ARTHUR
EDUCATOR, WRITER
b Lincoln, Nebr, Dec 26, 30. *Study:* Univ Iowa, BA, 52, MA, 56, PhD, 71. *Exhib:* 14th & 17th Nat Exhibs Prints, Libr Cong, Washington, DC, 56 & 59 & Invitational Traveling Show, 59-61. *Pos:* Dir, Aesthetic Educ Learning Ctr, Ill State Univ, in conjunction with Cent Midwest Regional Educ Lab, St Louis, Mo, 77-79. *Teaching:* Prof art appreciation & aesthetic educ, Ill State Univ, 70- *Bibliog:* Robert Hiedemann (auth), bk rev in Art Educ J, Vol 29, 1/76; Howard Conant (auth), bk rev in Leonardo, spring 77. *Mem:* Nat Art Educ Asn; Ill Art Educ Asn; Am Educ Res Asn; Caucus Social Theory & Art Educ. *Res:* The perception and interpretation of subjects' responses to works of art. *Publ:* Auth, An Aesthetic Model for Art Education, Univ Mich, Ann Arbor Microfilms, 71; ed, Viewpoints: Dialogue in Art Education, Vol I, 73 & Vol V, 78, Art Dept, Ill State Univ; auth, Art in Context, Harcourt Brace Jovanovich, 75, 2nd ed, 80. *Mailing Add:* 811 Highpoint Rd Normal IL 61761

HOBBS, JOE FERRELL
ADMINISTRATOR, SCULPTOR
b Deport, Tex, June 30, 34. *Study:* Univ Tex, BFA, 57; Univ Southern Calif, MFA, 60. *Work:* Mus Fine Arts, Houston, Tex; Ft Worth Art Ctr Mus, Tex; Mus Fine Arts, Dallas, Tex. *Comn:* With John Alberty, belt buckle, Ft Worth Art Ctr Mus, 75 & brand, Art Park, Lewiston, NY, 77. *Exhib:* Ft Worth Art Ctr Mus, 75; Art Park, NY, 77. *Pos:* Dir, Sch Art, Univ Okla, Norman, 66- *Teaching:* From instr to prof art, Univ Okla, Norman, 66- *Bibliog:* Jan Butterfield (auth), article, Arts Mag, 75; Don Lipski (auth), article, Crisscross Art Commun, 76; article, Currant Mag, 76. *Mailing Add:* 719 Schulze Dr Norman OK 73071

HOBBS, ROBERT CARLETON
MUSEUM DIRECTOR, HISTORIAN
b Brookings, SDak, Dec 6, 46. *Study:* Univ Tenn, Knoxville, BA, 69; Nat Defense Educ Act grant fel, 71-74; Samual H Kress fel, 74-75; Helena Rubinstein fel, 75; Univ NC, Chapel Hill, PhD, 75. *Pos:* Cur, Mint Mus Art, 69-71; adj cur, Cornell Univ, Herbert F Johnson Mus, 76-; sr cur & chmn curatorial div, Tehran Mus Contemp Art, 78; dir, Univ Iowa Mus Art, currently. *Teaching:* Lectr mod art, Yale Univ, 75-76; assoc prof mod art, Cornell Univ, Ithaca, NY, 76-83. *Mem:* Am Asn Mus; Col Art Asn; Int Asn Art Critics. *Res:* Currently under contract to edit writings of Robert Motherwell for documents of 20th century art series. *Publ:* Auth, Elliott Daingerfield Retrospective Catalogue, Mint Mus, 71; coauth, Abstract Expressionism: The Formative Years, Whitney Mus & Cornell Univ Press, 78; auth, Robert Motherwell, Stadtische Kunsthalle, Dusseldorf, 76; auth, Michelle Stuart, Comt Visual Arts, MIT, 77; auth, Robert Smithson: Sculpture, Col Art J, fall 82; auth, Tony Smith, Pace Gallery, 83; and others. *Mailing Add:* Art Mus Univ Iowa Riverside Drive IA 52242

HOBBS, ROBERT DEAN
ADMINISTRATOR, PRINTMAKER
b Merkel, Tex, Apr 21, 28. *Study:* WTex State Univ, Canyon, with Emillio Caballero, BA; Northern Colo State Univ, Greeley, with Richard Ellinger, MA; Pa State Univ, State Col, with Will Barnett, DEd. *Work:* WTex State Univ, Canyon; Colo State Col, Greeley; Viktor Lowenfiel Mem Collection, Pa State Univ, State College; Smithsonian Inst, Washington, DC. *Exhib:* Solo exhibs, John Sloan Gallery, Lock Haven State Col, Pa, 78 & 80, Nat Art Educ Bldg, Reston, Va, 78, W Broadway Gallery, New York, 80 & Haas Gallery, Bloomsburg State Col, Pa, 81. *Teaching:* Art teacher in pub sch, Midland, Tex, 54-58; instr art, WTex State Univ, 58-63, assoc prof art, 67-71; grad asst, Pa State Univ, 65-67; prof art & chmn art dept, Clarion State Col, Pa, 71- *Mem:* Nat Art Educ Asn; Pa Art Teacher Asn, Harrisburg. *Media:* Silkscreen. *Dealer:* Westbroadway Gallery 431 W Broadway New York NY 10012. *Mailing Add:* PO Box 605 Clarion PA 16214

HOCHHAUSER, MARILYN HELSENROTT
PAINTER, EDUCATOR
b Chicago, Ill, April 18, 28. *Study:* C W Post Ctr, Long Island Univ, BA(art educ; magna cum laude), 73, MA(painting; scholar), 75; Educ Alliance Art Sch, New York. *Work:* Language Plus, Alma, Que. *Exhib:* Sixth Ann Exhib, Aldrich Mus Contemp Art, 77; Royal Acad, Stockholm, 78; one-person exhib, Pleiades Gallery, New York, 80 & 83, Jersey City State Col, 81 & Salle Tremble, Language Plus, Alma, Que, 82. *Teaching:* Instr art, Adult Educ, Roslyn & Merrick, NY, 71-79; prof, Trenton State Col, 80- *Bibliog:* Barbara Coller (auth), article, Womanart Mag, spring 78; Jeanne Paris (auth), article, 4/4/79 & Malcolm Preston (auth), article, 4/26/79, Newsday. *Mem:* Col Art Asn; Am Asn Univ Prof; Women in Arts. *Mailing Add:* 752 E 19th St New York NY 11230

HOCHSTETLER, T MAX
PAINTER, EDUCATOR
b Terre Haute, Ind, May 13, 41. *Study:* Univ Evansville, BA, 64; Southern Ill Univ, MFA, 67. *Work:* Tenn State Mus & Cheekwood Fine Arts Ctr, Nashville. *Comn:* First Am Tapestries, First Am Nat Bank, Nashville, 75; Nashville murals, 76-77 & Centennial murals, 80-81, Opryland Hotel, NLT Corp, Nashville; Cheatham County Paintings, Ashland City Bank & Trust, 82; Public Square Clarksville (mural), Northern Bank Tenn, 83. *Exhib:* Ind Artists Exhib, Evansville Mus, 75; Tenn Bicentennial Exhib, State Mus, Nashville, 76; Mid-Am Art Exhib, Owensboro Mus Art, Ky, 79; Tenn Artists, Doyle Fine Arts Ctr, Western Ky Univ, Bowling Green, 79; Choice Painting Invitational, Ctr Contemp Art, Univ Ky, 82; Eleventh Ann Midstates Exhib, Evansville Mus Arts & Sci, 83. *Teaching:* Prof painting & drawing, Austin Peay State Univ, 67- *Awards:* Second Place Award, City of Owensboro, 74; Patrons Purchase Award, Evansville Mus, 75; Mus Purchase Award, Owensboro Mus, 79. *Mem:* Tenn Watercolor Soc; Col Art Asn; Southeastern Col Art Asn; Nashville Artists Guild. *Media:* Acrylics; Watercolor. *Mailing Add:* 444 Winding Way Rd Clarksville TN 37040

HODEL, DIANE CAROL
PAINTER, PRINTMAKER
b Sturgis, SDak, Mar 29, 39. *Study:* Univ Colo, BFA, 74. *Work:* Empire Savings, Johns-Manville, Mountain Bell Telephone Co & Piton Found, Denver; Idaho 1st Nat Bank, Boise. *Exhib:* Denver Art Mus Regional, 71, 72 & 76; Watercolor USA, Springfield Art Mus, Mo, 71, 73 & 77; Rocky Mountain Nat Watermedia Exhib, Foothills Art Ctr, Golden, Colo, 74-76, 79 & 80; San Diego Watercolor Soc Nat, 78 & 79; Am Watercolor Soc 112th Ann, New York, 79; 44th & 45th Ann Mid-Yr, Butler Inst Am Art, Youngstown, Ohio, 80 & 81. *Awards:* 1st Prize, Boulder Art Asn Regional, 75; Merit Award, Colo Coun Arts & Humanities, 75; Traveling Award, Am Watercolor Soc 112th Ann, 79. *Bibliog:* James Mills (auth), Seven Coloradans exhibit in New York, Denver Post, 79; Katharine Smith Chafee (auth), Notes on the exhibition, Colo Women Arts, 79; Barbara Whipple (auth), On tour in Denver, Am Artist Mag, 79. *Mem:* Fine Art Assoc, Boulder; Rocky Mountain Nat Watermedia Asn. *Media:* Acrylic; Silkscreen. *Dealer:* Ledoux Gallery One Ledoux St Taos NM 87571; Carson Sapiro Gallery 1411 Market St Denver CO 80202. *Mailing Add:* 369 Arapahoe Boulder CO 80302

HODES, BARNEY
ADMINISTRATOR
b Mar 11, 43. *Study:* Columbia Col, AB, 64; Brooklyn Mus Art Sch, 64-66; Univ NC, MFA, 68. *Exhib:* NC Mus Art; Brooklyn Mus, Brooklyn Mus Art Sch; one-man show, Weatherspoon Gallery; Artists & Friends, First St Gallery, 81; Numeroff Gallery; and others. *Pos:* Co-dir, New York Acad Art, currently. *Teaching:* Lectr, Fairleigh Dickinson Univ, Teaneck, NJ, 70-72; instr, Brooklyn Mus Sch Art, 70-81; instr, Brooklyn Col, 73-76; assoc prof, St John's Univ, 77- *Mailing Add:* 980 Ocean Ave Brooklyn NY 11226

HODGE, R GAREY
PAINTER, INSTRUCTOR
b Moweaqua, Ill, July 27, 37. *Study:* Eastern Ill Univ, BS, 61, MA(painting), 73; Harvard Univ Summer Sch, with William Georgenes. *Exhib:* Tri-State Exhib, Evansville Mus, Ind, 59; Miss Valley Exhib, Ill State Mus, Springfield, 64; Ill Bell Tel Exhib, Chicago, 67; River Roads Exhib, St Louis, 69, 70 & 72; 5th Int Biennial Sport Fine Arts, La Pinacoteca, Barcelona, Spain, 75; Western Ill Univ, 78. *Teaching:* Instr painting, graphics & design, Lanphier High Sch, Springfield, 62- *Awards:* Runner Up, New York World's Fair Sculpture Design, Int Fair Consults, 63; Second in Painting, Northside Art Asn, St Louis, 69; Grand Prize, US Hockey Hall of Fame, 76. *Mem:* Artists Equity; Ill State Mus Soc; Springfield Art Asn; Visual Artists & Gallery Asn; Lahonton Valley Art Asn, Nev (vpres, 61-62). *Media:* Acrylic, Graphite. *Mailing Add:* 1133 N 14th St Springfield IL 62702

HODGE, SCOTTIE
DEALER, ADMINISTRATOR

b Darlington, SC, Oct 21, 40. *Study:* Winthrop Col, Rock Hill, SC, BA, 62; Furman Univ, Greenville, SC, MA, 73; Greenville Co Mus Art Sch, 74-75. *Exhib:* Guild of SC Artists Exhib, 79, 80 & 81; Charlotte Open Exhib, 80 & 81; Tempo Gallery, 80 & 83; Curators Choice Exhib, Greenville Mus, 81; Francis Marion Col, SC, 83. *Pos:* Founder & dir, Tempo Gallery (coop), 75- *Awards:* Curator's Choice Award, Greenville Mus, 80; Third Place, Greenville Artists Guild, 82. *Mem:* Greenville Artist Guild (secy-treas, 76-77, pres, 78-79); Guild of SC Artists; Greenville Art Asn (bd mem, 78-79); co-founder SC Watercolor Soc (bd mem, 81-); Greenville Metrop Arts Council. *Media:* Paper; Wood. *Specialty:* Works by regional and national artists in all media. *Mailing Add:* c/o Tempo Gallery 125 W Stone Ave Greenville SC 29609

HODGELL, ROBERT OVERMAN
PRINTMAKER, SCULPTOR

b Mankato, Kans, July 14, 22. *Study:* Univ Wis, BS & MA; Dartmouth Col; Univ Iowa; Univ Ill; Univ Michoacana, Mex; also with John Steuart Curry. *Work:* Joslyn Art Mus; Dartmouth Col; Libr Cong, Washington, DC; Ringling Mus Art, Sarasota, Fla; Metrop Mus Art; and others. *Pos:* Asst art dir & illus, Our Wonderful World, Champaign, Ill, 53-56; art dir, ed & commun serv, Exten Div, Univ Wis-Madison, 57-59; bk illusr for UNESCO in Pakistan, 60; co-owner, Joan Modgel Gallery, Sarasota, Fla, 77- *Teaching:* Artist in residence & instr, Des Moines Art Ctr, 49-53; assoc prof art, Eckerd Col, 61-67, artist in residence, 67-77, adj art instr, 81-; instr, Ringling Sch of Art, 77-; art instr, New Col, Univ SFla, Sarasota, 80. *Mem:* Nat Acad Design; Boston Printmakers; Soc Am Graphic Artists. *Mailing Add:* 4809 Featherbed Lane Sarasota FL 33581

HODGKINS, ROSALIND SELMA
PAINTER

b Farmington, Maine, May 25, 42. *Study:* Univ SFla; Pratt Inst, BFA; Art Students League. *Work:* Southern Ill Univ, Carbondale; Bronx Mus Fine Arts, NY; Hewitt Sch, New York. *Exhib:* One-woman shows, Warren Benedek Gallery, New York 72 & 73 & James Yu Gallery, New York, 76; Kensington Arts Asn, Toronto, Ont, 75; PS 1 Pattern Painting Show, New York, 77; O1A Art in Pub Places Show, New York, 77; and others. *Media:* Oil. *Mailing Add:* 325 W 16th St New York NY 10011

HODGSON, JAMES STANLEY
LIBRARIAN

b Detroit, Mich, Apr 26, 42. *Study:* Brown Univ, AB, 64; Simmons Col, MS, 67. *Pos:* Chief librn, Grad Sch Design, Harvard Univ, 68- *Mem:* Art Libr Soc North Am. *Mailing Add:* 710 County St New Bedford MA 02740

HODLEY, JANE See Dixon, Jenny

HOENER, ARTHUR
PAINTER

b Brooklyn, NY, June 4, 29. *Study:* Cooper Union, New York, cert, 53; Yale Univ, BFA, 56, MFA, 58. *Work:* Art for Embassies Prog, Smithsonian Inst, Washington, DC; Invest Wellington Collection, DeCordova Mus, Lincoln, Mass; Arthur D Little Corp, Cambridge, Mass. *Comn:* Poly dimensional painted wall hanging, Gen Cinema Corp, Boston, 68. *Exhib:* Twenty-Ninth Biennial, Corcoran Art Mus, DC, 59; Wood Sculpture, Soc Arts & Crafts, Boston, 63; Good Design, Mus Fine Arts, Boston, 64; Multiplicity, Inst Contemp Art, Boston, 66; Structured Art, 69 & 77 & New England Drawing Competition, 79, De Cordova Mus, Lincoln, Mass; Mass Open, 81 & Illusions of Light, 81, Worcester Art Mus, Mass. *Collections Arranged:* New England Art Today, Paintings & Sculpture, Northeastern Univ, Boston, 63 & 65. *Pos:* Moderator & producer, Studio Talks, WGBH-FM, Boston, 63-67. *Teaching:* Prof graphic design, Mass Col Art, Boston, 60-70; prof art & design, Hampshire Col, Amherst, Mass, 70- *Awards:* First Prize Drawing, Springfield Art League, George Walter Vincent Smith Art Mus, Springfield, Mass, 77; Drawing Prize, Mass Open, Worcester Art Mus, Mass, 77; Outstanding Achievement, Wistariahurst Mus, Holyoke, Mass, 81; and others. *Bibliog:* Bernard Chaet (auth), Artists at Work, Webb Bks, 60; Thelma Newman (auth), Plastics as an Art Form, Chilton Co, 64. *Mem:* New England Contemp Artists Inc (chmn, 63-67). *Mailing Add:* 289 Elm St Northampton MA 01060

HOEVELER, MARY-GRIFFIN SMITH See Smith, Griffin

HOFER, EVELYN
PHOTOGRAPHER

b Marburg, Ger; Brit citizen. *Study:* Switz. *Work:* Metrop Mus Art, New York; Smith Col Mus Art, Northampton, Mass; Univ Colo Libr, Boulder. *Exhib:* Manhattan Now, New York Hist Soc, 74; Witkin Gallery, 77. *Awards:* Art Dir Club, 76. *Media:* Four by Five Camera. *Publ:* Coauth, The Stones of Florence, 59, London Perceived, 63, The Presence of Spain, 64 & New York Proclaimed, 65, Harcourt, Brace, Jovanovich; coauth, Dublin, A Portrait, Harper & Row, 67. *Dealer:* Witkin Gallery 41 E 57th St New York NY 10022. *Mailing Add:* 55 Bethune St New York NY 10014

HOFER, INGRID (INGEBORG)
PAINTER, INSTRUCTOR

b New York, NY. *Study:* Meisterschule Fuer Mode, Hamburg, Ger, BA, 48; Univ Hamburg; Traphagen Sch Design, New York, 51; with A Odefey, Goettingen, Ger, Albert Bross, Jr, Pauline Lorentz, John R Grabach, Adolf Konrad & Nicholas Reale. *Work:* Fairleigh Dickinson Univ. *Comn:* Many pvt comns in Ger, Switz & US, 56-79. *Exhib:* Hudson Valley Art Asn, White Plains, NY, 70 & 71; Catharine Lorillard Wolfe Art Club, Nat Acad Design, New York, 70, 71 & 77; Am Artist Prof League Grand Nat, Lever House, New York, 70-75 & 78-81; Am Watercolor Soc, 73; Rocky Mountain Nat Watercolor Exhib, Colo, 75; Scarab Club, Detroit, 75-78; Tweed Mus; Mich Art Inst, Founders Gallery, 73-76; Union League, Chicago, 81. *Teaching:* Sr instr mixed media, YWCA Adult Educ, Summitt, NJ, 67-73; instr mixed media, Acad Artists, Trailside Mus, Mountainside, NJ, 68-70; instr, Grosse Pointe War Mem, Mich, 74-78, Country Side Art Ctr, Arlington Heights, Ill, 81-83 & Toledo Artists Club, 83- *Awards:* Award for Lily Lever House, Am Artists Prof League, 72; Am Watercolor Soc Traveling Show Award, 73; Purchase Award, Union League, Ill, 81; and others. *Mem:* Fel Am Artists Prof League; Catharine Lorillard Wolfe Art Club; Midwest Watercolor Soc; NJ Watercolor Soc; assoc Am Watercolor Soc. *Media:* Watercolor, Graphics. *Dealer:* Nathans Art Gallery West Paterson NJ 07013; Galleria Luisa E Grand Rapids MI 49506. *Mailing Add:* 9775 Carnoustie Rd Perrysburg OH 43551

HOFF, MARGO
PAINTER, COLLAGE ARTIST

b Tulsa, Okla. *Study:* Tulsa Univ; Art Inst Chicago; Pratt Graphics Ctr; St Marys Col, Notre Dame, hon DFA, 69. *Work:* Whitney Mus Am Art, New York; Brooklyn Mus, NY; Art Inst Chicago; Krannert Mus, Univ Ill, Champaign; Rosenwald Found Collection; plus others. *Comn:* Wall design, Home Fed Bank, Chicago, 66; Mirror to Man (mural), Mayo Clinic, Rochester, Minn, 68; stage set & costumes for Murray Louis Dance Co, 69; portrait of S Madeleva, St Marys Col, Notre Dame, 70; two murals, New Govt Bldg, Plattsburgh, NY, 77-79. *Exhib:* One-man shows, Banfer Gallery, New York, 64, 66 & 68, Fairweather Hardin Gallery, 64-79, Bednarz Gallery, Los Angeles, 67 & Babcock Gallery, New York, 74; Hadler Rodriguez Galleries, 78 & 79; and others. *Teaching:* Teacher, Am Univ, Beirut, 56-57; artist in residence, Univ Southern Ill, 66-67; artist in residence, St Marys Col, Notre Dame, 69-70 & 78; teaching grant, Goretti Sch, Fort Portal, Uganda, E Africa, 71; Col St Maria, Sao Paulo, Brasil; instr, Drew Univ, NJ, 77-78, New York. *Publ:* Illusr, Christmas House, Coachhouse, 65; illusr, 4 Seasons & 5 Senses, 66 & Christmas Cupboard, 67, Funk & Wagnall. *Dealer:* Babcock Gallery 20 E 67 St New York NY 10021. *Mailing Add:* c/o Fairweather Hardin Gallery 101 E Ontario St Chicago IL 60611

HOFFBERG, JUDITH A
PUBLISHER, CONSULTANT

b Hartford, Conn, May 19, 34. *Study:* Univ Calif, Los Angeles, BA(cum laude polit sci), MA(Ital lang & lit), MLS; Ital Govt grant, study of Leonardo da Vinci. *Pos:* Intern, Libr Cong, 65-66, cataloger, Prints & Photographs Div, 66-67; fine arts librn, Univ Pa, 67-69; bibliog in art, lit & lang, Univ Calif, San Diego, 69-71; librn, Brand Art Ctr Libr, Glendale, Calif, 71-73; ed newsletter, Art Libr Soc NAm 72-77; ed & dir, Umbrella Assoc, 78-; bd dir, Franklin Furnace 76-77; exec dir, Assoc Art Publ, 78-79; ed & publ, Umbrella, 78-; cur, Umbrella Show, Univ Calif, Riverside, 79; co-cur, Traction Gallery, Los Angeles, 81. *Awards:* Italian Govt Grant, 60-61; Kress Found Grant, 72; Nat Endowment Arts Grant, 79-80; Dutch Govt Grant, 82; Fulbright Grant, New Zealand, 84. *Mem:* Women's Caucus Art; Int Fedn Libr Asn (secy, Art Libr Round Table, 77-78); Col Art Asn Am (bd dirs, 75-78); Soc Archit Historians (mem bd dirs, 79-82); Int Coun Mus; and others. *Publ:* Auth, Libros de artistas Mexicanos en Artworks, Artes Visuales, 81; auth, Len Rivkin's drawings, Images & Issues, spring 81; news ed, Art Express, 5/81; auth, Interview: Henryk Gajewski, J Los Angeles Inst Contemp art, winter 83; auth, Interview: Jeff Gordon, High Performance, 83. *Mailing Add:* Po Box 40100 Pasadena CA 91104

HOFFMAN, ANDREA See Andrea, I

HOFFMAN, CAROL MAREE

b Denver, Colo, Sept 5, 44. *Study:* Cornell Univ, Ithaca, NY, BA, 66; Columbia Univ, New York, 67; Community Col Denver, assoc degree, 78. *Work:* Mus Folk Art, Santa Fe, NMex. *Comn:* Wallpiece, Mountain Bell, Denver, Colo, 78; Marietta Nat Crafts/Sculpture Show, Ohio, 77; Threads Unlimited, Foothills Art Ctr, Golden, Colo, 77; Object '79, W Colo Ctr Arts, Grand Junction, 79. *Pos:* Publ mag & exec dir, Craft Range, 74-80; publ, New Denver Arts Publ. *Mem:* Colo Artist Craftsmen (bd mem, 74-80); Am Crafts Coun; Metrop Denver Arts Alliance (mem bd dirs, 81-84). *Media:* Assemblage; Found objects. *Mailing Add:* 6800 W Oregon Dr Denver CO 80226

HOFFMAN, EDWARD FENNO, III
SCULPTOR

b Philadelphia, Pa, Oct 20, 16. *Study:* Pa Acad Fine Arts. *Work:* Philadelphia Art Mus; Pa Acad Fine Arts; Brookgreen Gardens, SC; Huntington Galleries, WVa; Grand Cent Art Galleries, New York. *Comn:* Girl with Basin (bronze), Philadelphia Col of Physicians, 60; bronze figures, Weightlifters Hall of Fame, York, Pa, 60-72; portrait heads, Am Col Life Underwriters, Bryn Mawr, Pa, 65-70; Winnie the Pooh, Children's Libr, Hanover, Pa, 66; Fawn, Newlin Mill Park, Lima, Pa, 72; and others. *Exhib:* Allied Artists Am Ann, New York, 71; Mainstreams 72, Marietta Col, 72; Nat Sculpture Soc Ann, New York, 72; Am Artists Prof League Ann, 72; Nat Acad Design Ann, New York, 72. *Awards:* Gold Medal of Honor, Am Artists Prof League, 72; Silver Medal, Nat Sculpture Soc, 73; Proctor Prize, Nat Acad Design Ann, 82. *Bibliog:* Proske (auth), Brookgreen Gardens Sculpture, Brookgreen Gardens. *Mem:* Nat Acad Design; Nat Sculpture Soc (1st vpres, 73-76); Am Artists Prof League; Allied Artists Am. *Media:* Bronze. *Dealer:* Grand Cent Art Galleries 50 East 50th St New York NY 10022; Fisher Galleries 1509 11 Connecticut Ave NW Washington DC 20036. *Mailing Add:* 353 Oak Terr Wayne PA 19087

HOFFMAN, ELAINE JANET
PAINTER

b Oak Park, Ill. *Study:* Averett Col; Portland Art Mus; Northwest Watercolor Sch, with Irving Shapiro; Maryhurst Educ Ctr, BA, 78; also with Charles Mulvey, Perry Acker, George Hamilton & Phil Austin. *Exhib:* Artists of Oregon, Portland Art Mus, 70; Am Artists Prof League, New York, 71; George Fox Col Invitational, Newberg, Ore, 72-75; Prof Ore Artists Invitational Exhib, Coos Bay Mus, Ore, 72-74; one man shows, Courtyard Gallery, 79 & Art Adventures, 80 & 81, Portland. *Pos:* Bd dirs, Lake Oswego Art Guild, Ore, 65-68. *Teaching:* Pvt classes in watercolor landscapes, 65-; instr, Portland Community Col, 75-81. *Awards:* Spec Merit Award, Watercolor Soc Ore, 69 & 70; Purchase Award, Coos Bay Mus, 73; First Award, Lake Oswego Art Festival, Ore, 78 & 82; and others. *Mem:* Fel Am Artists Prof League; Ore Watercolor Soc; Lake Area Artists (pres, 67-68, 71-72 & 75-76); Ore Soc Artists. *Media:* Watercolor. *Dealer:* Byron Pickering Gallery Lincoln City OR 97367; Michael's Gallery One Main St Portland OR. *Mailing Add:* 16695 Glenwood Ct Lake Oswego OR 97034

HOFFMAN, HELEN BACON
PAINTER

b San Antonio, Tex, July 14, 30. *Study:* Ogontz Col, Philadelphia; Parsons Sch Design. *Work:* NAm-Mex Inst Cult Relations, Mexico City, Mex. *Exhib:* One-man shows, North Star Gallery, San Antonio, Tex, 66-80, Grand Cent Art Galleries, New York, 69-80 & Veerhoff Galleries, Washington, DC, 64, 74 & 78; Pritchard Galleries, San Antonio, 81 & 82 & Houston, 82 & 83. *Awards:* First Place Award, Catherine Lorillard Wolfe Art Club Show, 73; First Place Painting, Salmagundi Club, 72; Kalikow Award Excellence, Pastel Soc Am, 82. *Mem:* Artists Equity Asn; Soc Wash Artists; Pastel Soc Am; Nat Arts Club; Catherine Lorillard Wolfe Art Club; and others. *Media:* Pastel, Oil. *Dealer:* Veerhoff Galleries 1512 Connecticut Ave Washington DC 20036; Pritchard Galleries San Antonio TX & Houston TX. *Mailing Add:* 6015 Lamont Court Springfield VA 22152

HOFFMAN, LARRY GENE
MUSEUM DIRECTOR

b Paola, Kans, Mar 12, 33. *Study:* Drake Univ, BFA; Des Moines Art Ctr, with Thomas S Tibbs. *Collections Arranged:* Arthur S Dayton Collection, 69; Grant Wood, 72; Neiswanger Haitian Art, 74; Roy W Carver Collection, 75; Deux Nouveaux Haitien, 78; John Steuart Curry, 79; L'Esprit Noir, 80; and others. *Pos:* Consult art, Des Moines Pub Sch Syst, 60-62; consult art, WVa Arts & Humanities Coun; collaborator, Walter Gropius Mus Bldg Addition, Huntington, WVa, 67-69; dir, Huntington Galleries, 67-71; dir, Davenport Munic Art Gallery, 71- *Teaching:* Instr & adminr, Des Moines Art Ctr, 52-67; instr art, Des Moines Pub Sch Syst, 55-60. *Awards:* Model jr mus, Saint Louis Conf, Am Asn Mus, 67. *Mem:* Am Asn Mus; Asn Am Mus Dirs; Delta Phi Delta (past pres). *Publ:* Contribr, Sch Arts & Mus News; auth, exhib catalogs. *Mailing Add:* Davenport Munic Art Gallery 1737 W 12th St Davenport IA 52804

HOFFMAN, MARILYN FRIEDMAN
MUSEUM DIRECTOR

Study: Brown Univ, Providence, RI, BA(hon; art hist), 67, MA(art hist), 71. *Pos:* Cur asst, Educ Dept, Mus Art, RI Sch Design, 67-68; gallery asst, Adelson Galleries, Inc, Boston, 68-69 & 70-71; grad asst, Educ Dept, Metrop Mus Art, New York, 69; adj lectr, Dept Pub Educ, Mus Fine Arts, Boston, 70-71; cur, Brockton Art Mus-Fuller Mem, Mass, 71-73, actg dir, 73-74, dir, 74-84. *Teaching:* Teaching asst, Brown Univ, 69-70. *Mem:* Am Asn Mus; Col Art Asn Am; Mass Cult Alliance Mus Dirs Group; New Eng Mus Asn (secy, treas). *Publ:* Auth, American Still Life Painting, 1860-1900 (catalog), Adelson Galleries, Inc, 68; auth, Pssst, Airbrush Painting (catalog), 72, The Good Things in Life/19th Century American Still Life (catalog), 73 & Unstretched Paintings (catalog), 73, Brockton Art Ctr-Fuller Mem; auth, Museum Loans at Brockton, Art J, Vol 32 (1973). *Mailing Add:* Brockton Art Mus Oak St Brockton MA 02401

HOFFMAN, MARTIN (JOSEPH)
PAINTER, ILLUSTRATOR

b St Augustine, Fla, Nov 1, 35. *Work:* Miami Mus Mod Art; Va Mus Fine Arts, Richmond; Indianapolis Mus Art; J B Speed Mus, Louisville, Ky. *Comn:* numerous paintings & illus, Playboy Mag, 66-83; cover, Art Direction Mag, 4/72; Ashleys, New York, 75; US Steel Corp, 82; NASA Space Shuttle Program, 82-83. *Exhib:* Mus Mod Art, New York, 64 & 67; Realism Now, New York Cult Ctr, 72; New American Landscape, Vassar Col, 73; O K Harris Gallery, New York, 73, 75 & 79; Our Land, Our Sky, Our Water, Int Expos, Spokane, Wash, 74; Air & Space Mus, Smithsonian Inst, 82-83; Johnson Space Ctr, Univ Houston, 83. *Pos:* Art dir, numerous Miami advert agencies, 57-70; designer-illusr, Graphic Arts, Inc, 60-70. *Teaching:* Instr grad painting & drawing, Univ Miami, 69-71. *Awards:* Art Dir Awards, Miami Art Dirs Club, 59-70; Illus Awards, Chicago Advert Club, 71-79; Elegance for the Eighties, Best Serv Illusr, Playboy, 79. *Bibliog:* Doris Reno (auth), var rev, 57-65 & article, 8/23/70, Miami Herald; Griffin Smith (auth), article in Tropic Mag, 9/71. *Publ:* Illusr, Playboy, 67-83; illusr, Art Direction, 4/72; illusr, New York Times & Artforum, 74; illusr, Fortune, 74; and others. *Dealer:* OK Harris Gallery 383 W Broadway New York NY 10012; Advert Rep: Frank & Jeff Lavaty 45 E 51st St New York NY 10022. *Mailing Add:* 300 Mercer St New York NY 10003

HOFFMAN, MICHAEL E
EDITOR, CURATOR

b New York, NY, July 5, 42. *Study:* St Lawrence Univ, BA, 64; also with Minor White. *Collections Arranged:* Paul Strand: Retrospective, Clarence

John Laughlin: The Personal Eye & French Primitive Photography, Philadelphia Mus Art; August Sander: Photographs of an Epoch; The Face of China; Tibet: The Sacred Realm; Minor White: Retrospective; 25 exhibs at Philadelphia Mus Art, with many traveling in US, Canada & abroad, 69- *Pos:* Ed & publ, Aperture Inc, 64-; exec dir, Paul Strand Found, New York & Silver Mountain Found, Millerton, NY, currently; dir, Alfred Stieglitz Ctr, Philadelphia Mus Art, currently. *Mem:* Soc Photog Educ. *Publ:* Editor of over 80 publications in fine arts photography, 64- *Mailing Add:* A Stieglitz Ctr Philadelphia Mus Art PO Box 7646 Philadelphia PA 19101

HOFFMAN, NANCY
DEALER

b New York, NY, Feb 23, 44. *Study:* Wellesley Col, 62-64; Barnard Col, Columbia Univ, BA(art hist), 66. *Pos:* Asst registrar, Asia House Gallery, New York, 64-69; dir, Fr & Co Contemp Gallery, New York, 69-72 & Nancy Hoffman Gallery, New York, 72- *Specialty:* Contemporary art: paintings, drawings, sculpture and graphics. *Mailing Add:* 429 W Broadway New York NY 10012

HOFFMAN, NEIL JAMES
ADMINISTRATOR, EDUCATOR

b Buffalo, NY, Sept 2, 38. *Study:* State Univ NY Buffalo, BS, 60, MS, 67. *Pos:* Dir, Prog Artisanry, Boston Univ, 74-79; dean & chief admin officer, Otis Art Inst Parsons Sch Design, 79-83; pres, Sch Art Inst Chicago, 83- *Teaching:* Art & chmn unified art dept, Grand Island Pub Schs, NY, 61-68; assoc prof design & art educ & assoc dean col fine & appl arts, Rochester Inst Technol, 68-74. *Mailing Add:* School of Art Institute of Chicago Columbus & Jackson Dr Chicago IL 60603

HOFFMAN, RICHARD PETER
PAINTER

b Allentown, Pa, Jan 10, 11. *Study:* Mercersburg Acad, grad, 29; Parsons Sch Design, grad, 33. *Work:* Butler Inst Am Art, Youngstown, Ohio; Maravian Col, Bethlehem, Pa; Pa Power & Light Co, Allentown; Call-Chronicle Newspapers, Allentown; Liberty High Sch, Bethlehem, Pa. *Exhib:* one-man shows, Allentown Art Mus, Pa, 72-77, Kemmerer Mus, Bethlehem, Pa, 73, Meirhans Art Gallery, Quakertown, Pa, 74, Woodmere Art Gallery, Philadelphia, 74 & New Britain Mus Am Art, Conn, 75; and many others. *Awards:* Gertrude Rowan Capolino Prize, Woodmere Artists Club, Philadelphia, 52; Grumbacher Prize for Casein, Knickerbocker Artists, 55; Com Mus Civic Ctr Award, Philadelphia, 65. *Mem:* Philadelphia Watercolor Soc; Lehigh Art Alliance. *Publ:* Auth, articles, Am Artist, 11/48 & La Rev Mod, 3/53. *Mailing Add:* 1035 N 30th St Allentown PA 18104

HOFFMAN, WILLIAM MCKINLEY, JR
PAINTER, EDUCATOR

b Blairsville, Pa, Jan 25, 34. *Study:* Pa Acad Fine Arts & Univ Pa, BFA, 62; Tyler Sch Art, Temple Univ, MFA, 67. *Work:* NJ State Mus, Trenton; Stedman Art Gallery, Rutgers Univ, Camden, NJ; Camden Co Cult & Heritage, NJ; Thomas Jefferson Univ, Philadelphia; City Camden, NJ. *Exhib:* 139th Ann Exhib, Nat Acad Design, New York, 64; Eastern Regional Drawing Soc Show, Philadelphia Mus Art, 65; 55th Ann, Allied Artists Am, Nat Acad Design, New York, 66; 164th Ann, Pa Acad Fine Arts, Philadelphia, 69; 34th & 35th Ann, Butler Institute Am Art, Youngstown, Ohio, 69 & 70; Earth Art 1 & 2, Philadelphia Civic Ctr Mus, 73 & 79; Art from NJ 9 & 10, NJ State Mus, Trenton, 74 & 75; Visual Arts Fel Winners Exhib, NJ State Mus, Trenton, 80; Peale House Gallery, Pa Acad Fine Arts, Philadelphia, 83. *Teaching:* From instr to assoc prof, Rutgers Univ, Camden Col Arts & Sci, NJ, 67-, chmn, Dept Art, 67-76 & 79-82. *Awards:* Gov Purchase Award, Art from NJ 10, NJ State Mus, 75; Purchase Award, Earth Art 3, Touche, Ross & Co, Philadelphia, 79; Artists Fel, NJ State Coun Arts, 80. *Bibliog:* Piri Halasz (auth), State artists display skills, New York Times, 7/6/75; Robert Baxter (auth), Romantic realist, Courier Post, NJ, 10/30/81. *Mem:* Artists Equity Asn; fel Pa Acad Fine Arts; Col Art Asn. *Media:* All. *Mailing Add:* 167 Elm Ave Camden NJ 08107

HOFFMANN, ARNOLD, JR
PAINTER, DIRECTOR

b New York, NY, Jan 16, 15. *Study:* Nat Acad Design; Art Students League. *Work:* Chrysler Mus, Provincetown; Corcoran Art Gallery, Washington, DC; 20th Century Fund; Honeywell Corp; Butler Inst Am Art, Youngstown, Ohio; and others. *Exhib:* Allied Artists Am; Am Watercolor Soc; Parish Art Mus, Southampton, NY, 77; one-man shows, Guild Hall, 80, Artists Proof Gallery, 81 & Bologna Landi Gallery, 83, East Hampton, NY. *Pos:* Art dir, New York Times Mag, 43-; dir silk screen fine art workshop, East Hampton, 72- *Mailing Add:* 924 Fireplace Rd East Hampton NY 11937

HOFMANN, DOUGLAS WILLIAM
PAINTER, PRINTMAKER

b Baltimore, Md, Feb 13, 45. *Study:* Md Inst Col Art, BFA(cum laude), studied with Joseph Sheppard, 64-68. *Work:* Del Art Mus, Wilmington; Joslyn Art Mus, Omaha; Marquette Univ Fine Art Collection, Milwaukee; Frederick P Winner Collection, Baltimore. *Comn:* Painted stained glass panels, Baltimore City Schs, Md, 70. *Exhib:* Peale Mus, Baltimore, 70; Md Biennial, Baltimore Mus Art, 71 & 73; Realism in Maryland, Washington Co Mus, Hagerstown, Md, 72; Allied Artists Am, 74 & Audubon Artists Ann, 76, Nat Acad, New York; Ann Mid-Yr Exhib, Butler Inst, Youngstown, Ohio, 74-75; Easton Acad Art, Md, 78; Cherry Creek Gallery, Denver, 78; one-man show, Jack Gallery, New York, 79 & 81. *Teaching:* Instr painting, Md Inst, Baltimore, 74-75. *Awards:* Best Traditional Painting, Md Biennial, Baltimore Mus, 71; Best in Show, Realism in Maryland, Washington Co Mus,

72; Grant, Stacey Scholar Fund, 75. *Bibliog:* Jack Solomon (auth), Douglas Hofmann, Circle Fine Art Corp, 81; Will Grant (auth), Old and established, Artspeak, 6/2/81; Jerry Tallmer (auth), Mr Vermeer say hello to this here Mr Hofmann, New York Post, 10/31/81. *Media:* Oil; Lithography. *Dealer:* Jack Gallery 138 Prince St New York NY 10012. *Mailing Add:* 8602 Saxon Circle Baltimore MD 21236

HOFSTED, JOLYON GENE
SCULPTOR, EDUCATOR
b San Antonio, Tex, Oct 21, 42. *Study:* Calif Col Arts & Crafts, Oakland; Brooklyn Mus Art Sch, NY. *Work:* Mus Mod Art, Kyoto, Japan; Brooklyn Mus & Mus Contemp Crafts, New York; Queens Mus, NY; Sea of Japan Expos Secretariat, Kanazawa-shi; Newark Mus, NJ. *Exhib:* Attitudes, Brooklyn Mus, NY, 70; Cloud Gallery, New York, 75; Clay 77, Goddard-Riverside Ctr, New York, 77; Land, Kohler Arts Ctr, Sheboygan, Wis, 77; Clay Attitudes, Queens Mus, New York, 79-80; 8th Chunichi Int Exhib Ceramics Arts, Nagoya, Japan, 80. *Pos:* Dir, Brooklyn Mus Art Sch, 70-73. *Teaching:* Instr art, Brooklyn Mus Art Sch, 63-71; asst prof art, Queens Col, City Univ New York, 66-; instr ceramics, Haystack Mountain Sch Crafts, Maine, 66 & 68. *Awards:* Alfred Harvey Parker Ceramics Award, Brooklyn Mus, 64; Craftsmen Nat Award; Del Art Mus, 66. *Mem:* Ulster Co Coun for Arts (vchmn). *Publ:* Auth, Ceramics, Western Publ Co, 67; auth, Pottery, Pan Bks, London, 74; contribr, Craft Encyclopedia, Time-Life Publ, 75; auth movie, Textures, Clay Works, 78; contribr, Encyclopedia of Crafts, Scribners, New York, 80. *Mailing Add:* Box 66 Shady NY 12479

HOGARTH, BURNE
CARTOONIST, ILLUSTRATOR
b Chicago, Ill, Dec 25, 11. *Study:* Art Inst Chicago, 25-27; Chicago Acad Fine Arts, 26-29; studio classes with Todros Geller, 27-31; Crane Col, 28-30; Univ Chicago, 30-32; Northwestern Univ, 31-32 & 37-38; Columbia Univ, 56-57. *Work:* Mus Bandes Dessinees, Paris, France; Pavilion Humour, Terre des Hommes, Montreal, Can; Graham Gallery, Inc, New York; Escola Pan-Am de Arte, Sao Paulo, Brazil; Mus Cartoon Art, Portchester, NY. *Exhib:* Four Masters of Narrative Art, Graham Gallery, Inc, New York, 77; V-Muestra Int, Gijon Mus Comics, Spain, 78; San Diego Comic Conv, Calif, 78; one-man show, Mus Cartoon Art, Portchester, NY, 78; and many others. *Pos:* Illusr, Tarzan Sunday comic page, 37-50; bd mem, Mus Cartoon Art, Portchester, NY, 77-79. *Teaching:* Founder, vpres, coordr curriculum & instr, Sch Visual Arts, Inc, New York, 47-70; instr anat, Parsons Sch Design, New York, 76-81. *Awards:* Best Illus Cartoonist, Nat Cartoonists Soc, 74, 75 & 76; Cartoonist of Yr, Pavilion Humour, Montreal, Can, 75; Premio Emilio Freixas, V-Muestra Int, Gijon, Spain, 78. *Bibliog:* Francis Lacassin (auth), Tarzan, ou le Chevalier Crispe, Union Gen Ed, Paris, 71; Walter James Miller (auth), Burne Hogarth and the art of pictorial fiction, In: Jungle Tales of Tarzan, Watson-Guptill, 76; Maurice Horn (auth), World Encyclopedia of Comics, Chelsea House, New York, 76; and others. *Mem:* Nat Art Educ Asn; Am Soc Aesthet; Nat Cartoonists Soc (pres, 77-79). *Media:* Watercolor, Oil. *Publ:* Auth-illusr, Dynamic Anatomy, 58, Dynamic Figure Drawing, 65, Drawing the Human Head, 68, Drawing Dynamic Hands, 77 & Dynamic Light and Shade, 81, Watson-Guptill, New York. *Dealer:* Richard Pryor Collector's Press Box 1009 Carmel Valley CA 93924; Graham Gallery 79th St & Madison Ave New York NY 10038. *Mailing Add:* 451 N Cliffwood Ave Los Angeles CA 90049

HOGBIN, STEPHEN JAMES
SCULPTOR
b Tolworth Surrey, United Kingdom. *Study:* Kingston Col Art, United Kingdom, NDD; Royal Col Art, United Kingdom, Des RCA. *Work:* Art Bank Can Coun, Ottawa, Ont; Australia Coun, Sydney; Melbourne State Col, Australia; Ont Crafts Coun, Toronto, Ont; Can Crafts Coun, Ottawa, Ont; and others. *Comn:* Wood sculpture, Melbourne State Col, Australia, 75; wood wall screen, Metrop Toronto Libr Can, 77; murals, Queens Park, 80 & CIL Int, Toronto, 81. *Exhib:* One-man shows, York Univ, Toronto, 75, Australian Design Centre, Melbourne, 76 & Parnham House Gallery, Dorset, United Kingdom, 77; Chairs, Art Gallery Ont, Toronto, 75; Language of Wood, State Univ NY Col, Buffalo, 75; Art of Woodworking, Am Craft Mus, New York, 83. *Pos:* Craftsman-in-residence, Melbourne State Col, Australia Coun, 75-76. *Teaching:* Instr wood, Sheridan Sch Design, Port Credit, Ont, Can, 68-71; instr wood, Col Educ, Univ Toronto, 71-72. *Awards:* Best Contemp Design, One Nation Exhib, Jordan Wines Ltd, 73; Sculpture Award, Tom Thomson Gallery, 80 & 81. *Bibliog:* D L McKinley (auth), The forms of Stephen Hogbin, Craft Horizons, 4/74; Tony Perryman (producer), Craftsman (film), pvt produced, 75; Peter Drummond (producer), Woodcraftsman Stephen Hogbin (film), Crafts Coun Australia, 76. *Mem:* Ont Crafts Coun (dir, 77-); Can Crafts Coun (vpres, 73-74); Can Artists Representation; Visual Arts Ont. *Media:* Wood. *Publ:* Auth, The purpose of making, 78 & Turing full circle, 79, Fine Woodworking; auth, Wood Turning, Van Nostrand Reinhold, 80; auth, Hogbin's Remarks, 82 & Critical Process, 83, Craftnews; and others. *Dealer:* Aggregation Gallery 83 Front St Toronto ON Can. *Mailing Add:* RR3 Owen Sound ON N4K 5N5 Canada

HOGE, ROBERT WILSON
MUSEUM DIRECTOR, EDUCATOR
b Wilmington, Del, Jan 5, 47. *Study:* Univ Colo, BA(anthrop); Univ Colo & Univ Chicago. *Collections Arranged:* Tatangka Wotin Ni Sa: the Buffalo People (Plains Indian cultures), Spring 76, First Hundred Yrs (Am Hist-Bicentennial), Fall 76, Children of the Blizzard (Inuit culture), Spring 77, Interweave (materials, techniques & hist of textiles), Fall 77, Suprising saurians (interpretation of the dinasaurs), Spring 78, SPQR: The Romans (life in Imperial Rome), Fall 78 & Hunters of the Valley: Iowa's First People (interpretation of Iowa's earliest dated archaeol site) Spring 79, Sanford Mus

& Planetarium. *Pos:* Asst dir, Sanford Mus & Planetarium, Cherokee, Iowa, 76, actg dir, 76 & dir, 76-; instr anthrop, Buena Vista Col, Storm Lake, Iowa, Fall 76. *Res:* American archaeology, historical studies; Old World archaeology; numismatics. *Publ:* Ed, Northwest Chapter Newsletter, Iowa Archaeol Soc, Sanford Mus. *Mailing Add:* Am Numismatic Asn PO Box 2366 Colorado Springs CO 80901

HOGLE, ANN MEILSTRUP
PAINTER
b San Francisco, Calif, Sept 23, 27. *Study:* Univ Ore; Portland Mus Sch; Calif Col Arts & Crafts, BFA; MFA, 79. *Work:* Neuberger Collection, New York; Kemper Group, Long Grove, Ill; St Francis Mem Hosp & Security Pac Bank, San Francisco; Int Bus Machines; Merril Lynch; and others. *Exhib:* Artists of Oregon, Portland Mus, 63 & 70; Phelan Awards, Calif Palace Legion Hon, San Francisco, 65; solo exhibs, Stanford Univ, Calif, 66, Janus Gallery, Los Angeles, 75, Ritz Gallery, Point Reyes, Calif, 79 & William Sawyer Gallery, San Francisco, 80; and others. *Bibliog:* Helga Epstein (auth), Ann Hogle: Painting toward consciousness, Am Artist, 79. *Media:* Oil. *Dealer:* William Sawyer Gallery 3045 Clay St San Francisco CA. *Mailing Add:* 45 Meadow Rd Woodside CA 94062

HOGUE, ALEXANDRE
PAINTER, LITHOGRAPHER
b Memphis, Mo, Feb 22, 98. *Work:* Mus Nat Art Mod, Paris; Nat Mus Am Art, Washington, DC; Dallas Mus Fine Arts, Tex; Okla Art Ctr, Oklahoma City; Univ Ariz Mus Art. *Exhib:* Int Exhib, Jeu de Paume, Paris, 38; Carnegie Inst Int Exhibs, 38 & 39; Tate Gallery, London, Eng, 46; Whitney Mus Am Art, New York; Wilderness, Corcoran Gallery Art, DC, 71; Hayward Gallery Art, London, 77; Berlin and Hamburg Museums, 81; Haus Der Kunst, WGer, 83. *Teaching:* Instr life drawing & painting, Tex State Col Women, summers 31-42; prof art & head dept, Univ Tulsa, 45-68, emer prof, 69- *Awards:* Purchase Award, 9th Southwest Prints & Drawings, Dallas Mus Fine Arts, 59; Grand Awards, Philbrook Art Ctr, Tulsa, Okla, 61 & 75; Purchase Award, Springfield Mus Art, Mo, 65. *Bibliog:* John Bauer (auth), Revolution & Tradition in Modern American Art, 51; Nouvelles acquisitions, La Revue Du Louvre, 61; Ralph K Andrist (ed), History of the 20's and 30's, Am Heritage, 70. *Media:* Oil, Watercolor; Lithography. *Mailing Add:* 4052 E 23rd St Tulsa OK 74114

HOIE, CLAUS
PAINTER, ETCHER
b Stavanger, Norway, Nov 3, 11; US citizen. *Study:* Pratt Inst; Art Students League; Ecole Beaux Arts, Paris. *Work:* Brooklyn Mus, NY; Norfolk Mus, Va; Butler Inst Am Art, Youngstown, Ohio; Okla Mus Art; Guild Hall Mus, East Hampton, NY. *Exhib:* Am Watercolor Soc Ann, New York, 60-80; Brooklyn Mus Watercolor Biennial, 63; Mus Watercolor Painting, Mexico City, Mex, 68; Pa Acad Fine Arts Ann, 69; Childe Hassam Award Exhib, Nat Inst Arts & Lett, 73; one-man show, Akershus Castle Mus, Oslo, Norway, 82; and others. *Awards:* Gold Medal of Honor, Am Watercolor Soc, 62; Award for Painting, Nat Inst Arts & Lett, 75; Award of Merit, Nat Acad Design, 81; and others. *Mem:* Nat Acad Design; Am Watercolor Soc (vpres, 60-62). *Media:* Watercolor, Graphics. *Publ:* Auth, Technique of watercolor, Am Artist Mag, 57; auth, My views on watercolor painting, North Light Mag, 70. *Mailing Add:* 20 W 12th St New York NY 10011

HOIE, HELEN HUNT
PAINTER, COLLAGE ARTIST
b Leetsdale, Pa. *Study:* Carnegie-Mellon Univ, BA; Univ Vt, with Kenneth Shopen, 45; New School of Social Research, with Henry Pearson, 69. *Exhib:* Parrish Mus Art, Southampton, NY; Guild Hall Mus, East Hampton, 72, 73 & 75; one-man shows, Babcock Galleries, New York, 74-77 & 80 & New York Univ, 76; Women Artists, Brooklyn Mus, NY, 75; Ann Exhib, Butler Inst Am Art, Youngstown, Ohio, 75; Ranger Fund Exhib, Nat Acad Design, New York, 78; Selections from the East Hampton Guild Hall Collection, Ft Lauderdale, Pensacola & Miss Mus, 79; and others. *Awards:* Elizabeth Erlanger Award, 76 & Gold Medal-First Prize, 78, Nat Soc Painters Casein & Acrylic; Individual Exhib Award for Ten Yr Retrospective, Parrish Mus Art, 77. *Mem:* Women Artists; Artists Equity. *Media:* Acrylic on Canvas. *Dealer:* Babcock Galleries 20 E 67th St New York NY 10021. *Mailing Add:* 20 W 12th St New York NY 10011

HOLABIRD, JEAN
PAINTER, PRINTMAKER
b Boston, Mass, Dec 3, 46. *Study:* Art Students League, New York, 65-69; Inst Allende, Mexico, summers 65-69; Bennington Col, Vt, BA, 69. *Work:* Prudential Life Insurance Co, Newark, NJ; First Nat City Bank, Chicago; Staatmuseum, West Berlin, Ger; Ragdale Found, Lake Forest, Ill; Metrop Mus Art, New York. *Comn:* Drawings, Bennington Rev, Vt, 69-70; cover illus, The World Mag, New York, 80; cover, Hanging Loose Mag, New York, 81; and others. *Exhib:* Camden Coun Arts, London, England, 73; Christmas Invitational, Wendy Glass Gallery, New York, 78; Two Painters, Saray Y Rentschler Gallery, New York, 78; one-woman show, Nathan A Bernstein Ltd, New York, 80; Hand-colored Etchings, Sarah Y Rentschler Gallery, New York, 82; and others. *Teaching:* Instr painting, Inst Allende, San Miguel Allende, Mexico, summer 68; guest lectr, Parsons Sch Design, Pratt Inst, Cooper Union, New York, 75 & Sch Visual Arts, 79; artist-in-residence, Ragdale Found, 81. *Awards:* Cert Merit, Vt Coun Arts, 69; and others. *Bibliog:* Barry Yourgrau (auth), Jean Holabird at Nathan Bernstein, Arts Mag, 5/81; Palmer Hasty (auth), A collaboration, Villager, 3/82. *Mem:* Artists Equity Asn. *Media:* Watercolor; Etching. *Mailing Add:* 81 Warren St New York NY 10007

HOLBROOK, ELIZABETH BRADFORD
SCULPTOR
b Hamilton, Ont, Nov 7, 13. *Study:* Hamilton Tech Inst; Ont Col Art, Toronto; Royal Col Art, London; also with Emanuel Hahn, Carl Milles & Ivan Mestrovic. *Work:* Nat Gallery Can, Ottawa, Ont; Art Gallery Ont; Anshe Sholom Temple, Hamilton, Ont; McMaster Univ; Nat Portrait Gallery, Washington, DC, 81. *Comn:* Bronze portrait bust of the Hon John G Diefenbaker, 79; medal commemorating Albert Einstein & solar energy, Fedn Int des Editeurs Medailles 79 Congress, Portugal, 79; sterling silver jewelry, Art Gallery Hamilton, 79; struck medal, Kenneth D Taylor, Can Ambassador Iran, 80; woodcarving, St Mark's Church, Vancouver, BC, 81; and others. *Exhib:* Int Fedn Medallists, Cologne, Ger, 71; Helsinki, Finland, 73 & Cracow, Poland, 75; retrospective, Art Gallery Hamilton, 74; one-man show of recent bronzes, Art Gallery, McMaster Univ, Hamilton, Ont, 79; plus others. *Teaching:* Instr sculpture, Dundas Valley Sch Art, 65-70. *Awards:* Lt Gov Medal, Ont Col Art & Govt Ont, 36; Gold Medal Award, Nat Sculpture Soc New York, 69. *Bibliog:* E Wyn Wood (auth), Canadian Sculpture, 48; Charles Comfort (auth), Observations on a decade 1938-48, Royal Archit Inst Can J; John Bryden (auth), Art, Hamilton Spectator, 70, 71 & 72. *Mem:* Royal Can Acad Art; Ont Soc Artists; Sculptor's Soc Can; life mem Art Gallery Hamilton (benefactor, 45-); life mem Art Gallery Ont. *Media:* Multimedia. *Mailing Add:* 1177 Mineral Springs Rd RR 3 Dundas ON L9H 5E3 Canada

HOLBROOK, HOLLIS HOWARD
MURALIST, PAINTER
b Natick, Mass, Feb 7, 09. *Study:* Mass Sch Art, dipl, 34; Yale Univ, BFA, 36; Univ Michoacan, Morelia, Mex, 50-51. *Work:* Norfolk Mus Arts & Sci, Va; Southern Col Fla; Sheldon Swope Art Gallery, Terre Haute, Ind; Canton Art Inst, Ohio; Clemson Univ, SC. *Comn:* Frescoes, Morelia Libr, Michoacan, Mex, 51; History of Florida (egg tempera), Univ Fla Libr, 53; Life in the World (collage panels), RI Col, 59; Ocala Industries (collage panels), US Post Off, Ocala, 61; John Eliot and Indians (mural), Natick, Mass Pub Libr, 72. *Exhib:* Contemporary Painting and Sculpture, Univ Ill Biennial, 61; Pa Acad Fine Arts Painting & Sculpture Ann, 64; 29th Biennial Contemp Am Painting, Corcoran Gallery Art, 65; 21st Am Drawing Biennial, Norfolk Mus Arts & Sci, 65; Norton Gallery, W Palm Beach, FL, 71; one-man show, Daytona Art Mus, 80; American Drawing, Brooklyn Mus Art, 81; and others. *Pos:* Designer-illusr, Dennison Mfg Co, Framingham, Mass, 29-30; designer-illusr, Assoc Press, New York, 41; designer, Warren Telechron Co, Ashland, Mass, 42. *Teaching:* Prof art, Univ Fla, 38-78. *Awards:* Top Award for Figure with Blue Patch, 22nd Southeastern Ann, High Mus Art, 67; Honor Award, Mainstreams, Marietta, Ohio, 76; First Award, Fla Artists, Daytona, 79. *Bibliog:* Jacqueline Barnitz (auth), Holbrook exhibit, New York City, Arts Mag, 12/65. *Mem:* Nat Soc Mural Painters. *Media:* Acrylic, Oils. *Publ:* Auth, Fresco painting, Design Mag, summer 51; auth, A media laboratory, Am Artist Mag, 9/60; auth, Development of the Plastic Arts of Central America, Univ Fla, 61; auth, Painting for non-majors, Art J, summer 70. *Mailing Add:* 1710 SW 35th Pl Gainesville FL 32601

HOLBROOK, PETER GREENE
PAINTER, PRINTMAKER
b New York, NY, Apr 13, 40. *Study:* Dartmouth Col, BA(Marcus Herman Award), 61; Brooklyn Mus, with Reuben Tam, cert(Beckman fel), 63. *Work:* Nat Collection Fine Arts, Washington, DC; Brooklyn Mus, NY; Art Inst Chicago; Springfield Art Mus, Mo; Mus of Southwest, Midland, Tex. *Exhib:* Chicago and Vicinity, Art Inst Chicago, 65 & 67-69; solo exhib, Indianapolis Mus Art, 70; Koffler Found Collection, Smithsonian Inst, 79; Realism, Walnut Creek Civic Arts Gallery, Calif, 80; Watercolor USA, Springfield Art Mus, Mo, 82; Contemporary American Watercolor, Univ Wis-Madison, 82; Davidson Collection, Pa Acad Fine Arts, Philadelphia, 82; Invitational Watercolor Exhib, Hamline Univ, St Paul, Minn, 83. *Teaching:* Lectr painting, Univ Ill, Chicago Circle, 68-70 & Calif State Univ, Hayward, 70-71. *Awards:* Wild, Bartels & Clark Prizes, Chicago and Vicinity, Art Inst Chicago, 65, 67 & 68; Walter H Stevens Award, Watercolor USA, Springfield Art Mus, 81. *Bibliog:* Robert McDonald (auth), article, Artweek, 1/77 & 12/78; Stephen Doherty (auth), Ten contemporary painters, Am Artist Mag, 2/83; Barbara Whipple (auth), article, Am Artist Mag, 3/84. *Media:* Watercolor, Acrylic; Miscellaneous. *Publ:* Auth, article, 11/67 & The Chicago saga of Carolee Schneemann, 3/68, Art Scene Mag. *Dealer:* Frunkin & Struve Gallery 309 W Superior St Chicago IL 60610; Kauffman Galleries Houston TX. *Mailing Add:* Star Route Redway CA 95560

HOLBROOK, VIVIAN NICHOLAS
PAINTER, ADMINISTRATOR
b Mount Vernon, NY, Mar 31, 13. *Study:* Yale Univ, BFA. *Work:* Univ Ga. *Exhib:* Butler Inst Am Art Ann, Youngstown, Ohio, 52; Ball State Univ Ann, 72; Ten Yr Retrospective, Fla Southern Col, Lakeland, 76; Prof Women Artists of Fla, Lowe Art Mus, Univ Miami & Women's Hemispheric Cong, 76; four-man show, Ctr of Mod Art, Micanopy, Fla, 77; West 80, Art and the Law, Minn Mus Art, 80-81; American Drawings III, Va Arts Ctr, Portsmouth, 81; 27th Ann Drawing & Sculpture Show, Ball State Univ, Ind, 81; and others. *Pos:* Dir, Ctr Mod Art, Micanopy, Fla, 69-; designer exhibs, Fla State Mus, summer 70. *Teaching:* Instr painting & drawing, Colby Jr Col, New London, NH, 36-39; interim instr painting & drawing, Univ Fla, 42-44; instr painting, Ctr Mod Art, Micanopy, Fla, 69-70. *Awards:* Second Award, Harry Rich Competition, Miami, 57; Top Award, Soc Four Arts, 58, Atwater Kent Award, 66. *Media:* Oil, Ink. *Mailing Add:* 1710 SW 35th Pl Gainesville FL 32608

HOLCOMB, ADELE MANSFIELD
HISTORIAN
b Scranton, Pa, June 25, 30. *Study:* Univ Utah; Univ Calif, Los Angeles, BA, PhD. *Teaching:* Asst prof, Hamline Univ, St Paul, Minn, 66-68; asst prof, State Univ NY Col, Brockport, 68-71; asst & assoc vis prof, Univ Guelph, Ont, Can, 75-77; assoc prof & chairperson, Bishop's Univ, Lennoxville, Que, 77-82; prof & chairperson, 82- *Awards:* Am Coun Learned Soc One-Yr Res Fel, 71-72; Res Grants, Bishop's Univ, 79 & 80; Social Scis & Humanities Res Coun Can Grant, 83; and others. *Mem:* Women's Caucus for Art (nat bd mem, 74-77); Col Art Asn; Univ Art Asn of Can; Walpole Soc; Can Women's Studies Asn. *Res:* Romantic landscape painting; history of art history and criticism, including contributions of women, the work of Anna Jameson. *Publ:* Auth, A-F Rio, Anna Jameson & the second volume of modern painters, Gazette des Beaux-Arts, 78; auth, John Sell Cotman, Brit Mus Publ, 78; co-ed (with M Y Ashcroft), John Sell Cotman in the Cholmeley Archive, Co Rec Off, Northallerton, Yorkshire, Eng, 80; ed & auth, Women as Interpreters of the Visual Arts, 1820-1979, Greenwood Press, 81; auth, Anna Jameson: The first professional English art historian, Art Hist, 83; and others. *Mailing Add:* 70A Downs Lennoxville PQ J1M 1Y1 Canada

HOLCOMBE, R GORDON, JR
COLLECTOR, PATRON
b Lake Charles, La, Oct 28, 13. *Study:* Vanderbilt Univ; Tulane Univ, BS, Sch Med, MD, *Pos:* Past pres, Art Assocs Lake Charles. *Collection:* Paintings, including works by Bernard, Derain, Buffet, Levier & Courbet; early 19th century American paintings. *Mailing Add:* 3624 Lake Lake Charles LA 70605

HOLDEN, DONALD (WENDON BLAKE)
EDITOR, WRITER
b Los Angeles, Calif, Apr 22, 31. *Study:* Parsons Sch Design, New York, 46-47; Art Students League, 48; Columbia Univ, BA, 51; Ohio State Univ, MA, 52. *Pos:* Dir pub rel, Philadelphia Col Art, 53-55; dir pub rel & personnel, Henry Dreyfuss, New York, 56-60; assoc mgr pub rel, Metrop Mus Art, New York, 60-61; art consult, Fortune Mag, 62; ed dir, Watson-Guptill Publ, 63-79, ed consult, 79-; ed dir, Am Artist Mag, 71-75. *Mem:* Authors Guild; Nat Art Educ Asn; New York Artists Equity Asn; Ages Man Fel; Century Asn. *Publ:* Auth, Whistler Landscapes and Seascapes, 69; auth (under pseudonym), Complete Guide to Landscape Painting in Oil, 81 & Creative Color for the Oil Painter, 83; and articles in Am Artist, New York Times, Penthouse, Am Inst Graphic Arts J, Intellectual Digest & Arts; and others. *Mailing Add:* 128 Deertrack Ln Irvington NY 10533

HOLDEN, RAYMOND JAMES
PAINTER, ILLUSTRATOR
b Wrentham, Mass, May 2, 01. *Study:* RI Sch Design, 23. *Work:* Children's Mus, West Hartford, Conn; Mus Am Art, New Britain, Conn; Slater Mem Mus, Norwich, Conn. *Exhib:* Jones Libr, Amherst, Mass, 69; Providence Pub Libr, RI, 70; Slater Mus, Norwich, Conn, 80. *Mem:* Providence Watercolor Club. *Publ:* Illusr, Thoreau's Cape Cod, 69; illusr, The Fenwick Story, Conn Hist Soc, 74; illusr, Thoreau's A Week on the Concord & Merrimack Rivers, Limited Editions Club, 75. *Mailing Add:* RFD Box 130 Sterling CT 06377

HOLDEN, RUTH EGRI See Egri, Ruth

HOLDER, KENNETH ALLEN
PAINTER, EDUCATOR
b Heald, Tex, Sept 11, 36. *Study:* Tex Christian Univ, BFA(com art), 59; Art Inst Chicago, MFA(painting), 65. *Work:* Ill State Mus, Springfield; Purdue Univ, West Lafayette; Ill State Univ, Normal; Quincy Art Asn, Ill; Western Ill Univ. *Comn:* Fresno City Col, Calif, 73; Va Commonwealth Univ, 73; Cent Mich Univ, 75; all in collab with Harold Gregor. *Exhib:* Made in Macomb, Hyde Park Art Ctr, Chicago, 69; Chicago Vicinity Show, Art Inst Chicago, 73; 118 Gallery, Minneapolis, 74; one-man shows, Nancy Lurie Gallery, Chicago, 75 & Zolla/Lieberman Gallery, Chicago, 82; Drawings USA, Minn Mus St Paul, 75. *Teaching:* Asst prof drawing & painting, Western Ill Univ, 65-69; assoc prof drawing & painting, Ill State Univ, 69- *Awards:* Purchase Award, Purdue Univ, 73; Third Prize for Painting, Grand Galleria, Seattle; Purchase Award, Ill State Mus, Springfield. *Bibliog:* Henry Glover (auth), Artist (video), Ill State Univ, 72. *Media:* Acrylic; Mixed Media. *Mailing Add:* 104 Kreitzer Bloomington IL 61701

HOLDER, TOM
PAINTER
b Kansas City, Mo, Jan 21, 40. *Study:* San Diego State Univ, BA; Univ Wash, MFA. *Work:* Metromedia Collection, Los Angeles; ITT, Los Angeles, Calif; San Diego Fine Arts Gallery, Calif; Valley Bank, Las Vegas & Reno, Nev; Las Vegas Art Mus, Nev. *Comn:* Mural, Seattle-Tacoma Int Airport, 73; exterior wall mural, Seattle Steam Corp Plant, Seattle Arts Comn, 75; exterior wall mural, CETA Bldg, Las Vegas, Nev, 79; painting, State Capitol Bldg, Nev, 81. *Teaching:* Instr painting, Univ Wash, 67-69; assoc prof painting, Univ Nev, Las Vegas, 71- *Dealer:* Foster-White Gallery 211 1/2 Occidental S Seattle WA 98104. *Mailing Add:* PO Box 19423 Las Vegas NV 89119

HOLEN, NORMAN DEAN
SCULPTOR, EDUCATOR
b Cavalier, NDak, Sept 16, 37. *Study:* Concordia Col, BA, 59; State Univ Iowa, MFA, 62; Univ Minn, Minneapolis, 72. *Work:* 3M Co, Minneapolis, Minn; Univ Lutheran Church of Hope, Minneapolis; Deaconess Hospital, Minneapolis; Civic Plaza, Richfield, Minn; and others. *Comn:* Sheet steel bas relief, Augsburg Col Libr, 66; welded steel sculpture, Nativity Lutheran, Minneapolis, 69; welded steel figure, Trinity Evangelical Lutheran Church,

Clear Lake, SDak, 67; half life size bronze figure, St Bridget's Catholic Church, Cavalier, NDak, 74; brazed steel bas relief, Luther Theological Seminary, St Paul, Minn, 77. *Exhib:* Drawing & Small Sculpture, Muncie, Ind, 65, 71, 74, 76, 77, 80 & 81; one-man show, Minneapolis Inst Art, 68; Nat Gallery, Washington, DC, 69; Mainstreams, Marietta, Ohio, 69, 71, 73, 74, 76, 77, 78 & 79; Allied Artists Am, New York, 80; and others. *Pos:* Art consult, Richfield High Sch, 73. *Teaching:* Instr art, Northwestern Col, Orange City, Iowa, 62-63 & Concordia Col, Moorhead, Minn, 63-64. *Awards:* Rachel Leah Armour Award, Allied Artists Am, 80 & 82; Bronze Medal, 80 & Joel Meisner Award, 83, Nat Sculpture Soc; and others. *Bibliog:* Chris Spotted Eagle (auth), Holen: His art and his tools, Educ Television, 80; Sharon Schmickle (auth), Richfield's family sculpture, Minneapolis Star, 8/81; Bob Ball (auth), City's plaza sculpture, Richfield Sun, 8/81; and others. *Mem:* Allied Artists Am; Nat Sculpture Soc; Minn Sculptors Soc. *Media:* Welded Steel, Terra Cotta. *Publ:* Auth, Upper midwest art: Minnesota, North Dakota, South Dakota, Rev of the Arts, 77; auth, A pressing need for clay, Today's Art, 78; auth, Preserving your self expression, Artists Market, 79; and others. *Mailing Add:* 7332 12th Ave S Minneapolis MN 55423

HOLGATE, JEANNE
PAINTER, ILLUSTRATOR

b London, Eng, Mar 11, 20. *Study:* Self-taught. *Work:* Queen Elizabeth, the Queen Mother, Brit Mus & Royal Horticultural Soc, London; Hunt Inst for Botanical Documentation, Pittsburgh; Franklin Mint, Pa. *Exhib:* One-man shows, Tryon Gallery, London, Los Angeles Co Mus, 66, Incurable Collector, New York, 70, Hunt Inst for Botanical Documentation, 73, Gertrude Posel Gallery, 73, Schiele Mus of Natural Hist, 77 & Mus of Natural Hist, Raleigh, NC, 77; Flowers of the World from East to West, British Mus, London, 79. *Teaching:* Instr flower illus, Longwood Gardens, Kennett Square, Pa, 67-70. *Awards:* Royal Horticultural Soc Gold Medals, London, 63, 64 & 79; Silver Trophy for Best Educ Exhib, 5th World Orchid Conf, Long Beach, Calif, 66; Silver Trophy, Del Orchid Soc, 69. *Bibliog:* John Dorsey (auth), Someone who cared fired her, Sunpapers, Baltimore, 73; Jeanne Holgate (film), Franklin Mint, 73; State Flowers, Hodge Podge Lodge, WPBS-TV, 75. *Mem:* Nat Arts Club, New York; Md Fedn Art. *Media:* Watercolor, Oil. *Publ:* Contribr, Royal Horticultural Soc Orchid J, 54-66; contribr, Proc Third World Orchid Conf, 60; illusr, Limited edition folio of orchid hybrids, 63; illusr, Flowers of America (limited ed folio), 74; illusr, Can the world feed its people?, Nat Geog Mag, 75. *Dealer:* Tryon Gallery London, Eng; Bendann Art Gallery Towson MD 21204. *Mailing Add:* 125 Country Ridge Rd Hendersonville NC 28739

HOLLADAY, HARLAN H
HISTORIAN, PAINTER

b Greenville, Mo, Dec 10, 25. *Study:* SE Mo State Col, BS(educ); Wash Univ, St Louis Mo; State Univ Iowa, MA; Cornell Univ, PhD. *Work:* Munson-Williams-Proctor Inst, Utica, NY; St Lawrence Univ Collection, Canton, NY; Des Moines Art Ctr, Iowa; SE Mo State Univ Collection; Springfield Art Mus, Mo. *Exhib:* Corcoran Gallery Art Biennial, Washington, DC, 51; Whitney Mus Am Art, New York, 52; Pa Acad Fine Arts, Philadelphia, 52, 53 & 59; 61st Nat Watercolor Ann, Washington, DC, 58; and others. *Teaching:* Art teacher, Poplar Bluff Pub Schs, Mo, 51-53 & Des Moines, Iowa, 53-55; from instr to asst prof drawing & painting, Univ Nev, Reno, 55-58; prof fine arts, St Lawrence Univ, 61-, head dept, 65-71, L M & G L Flint Prof, 67-; prof art & artist in residence, Am Col Switz, 68-69. *Awards:* Hon Mention, 61st Nat Watercolor Ann, Washington, DC, 58; Reynolds Awards, Cooperstown Art Asn, 67; First Prize Painting, NY State Fair, Syracuse, 74; plus others. *Mem:* Col Art Asn Am; Soc Archit Historians; Am Asn Univ Prof; Cooperstown Art Asn; St Lawrence Co Hist Asn. *Media:* Oil, Acrylic. *Res:* 15th century art, especially Northern European painters and sculptors. *Publ:* Auth, Art in the liberal arts curriculum, 64 & auth, The value of a teaching collection, 70, St Lawrence Bull; auth, Catalogue for the McGinnis Collection, St Lawrence Univ, 70. *Mailing Add:* Dept of Fine Arts St Lawrence Univ Canton NY 13617

HOLLADAY, WILHELMINA COLE
COLLECTOR, PATRON

b Elmira, NY. *Study:* Elmira Col, BA, 44; Univ Paris; Univ Va . *Pos:* Dir, Holladay Corp, Interior Design, Washington DC, 72-84; pres, The Holladay Found, Washington DC, 80-84; chmn, Nat Mus Women's Art, 81-84. *Mem:* Corcoran Gallery, Washington DC (trustee); Am Asn Mus; Am Federation Art; Mus Mod Art; Women's Caucus Art. *Interests:* Established archival library of periodicals and books on women's art for research purposes; donor of art to 3 major mus. *Collection:* Women's art from the Renaissance on to show the contribution of women to the history of art. *Mailing Add:* 3215 R Street NW Washington DC 20007

HOLLAND, HARRY CHARLES
PAINTER, EDUCATOR

b Childress, Tex, Jan 2, 37. *Study:* Univ Tex, Austin, 55-57; Sch of Art Inst Chicago, BFA, 62; Carnegie Inst Technol, MFA, 63. *Work:* Dravo Corp Collection, Pittsburgh. *Comn:* Mural, Urban Design Asn Bldg, Pa Coun Arts, Pittsburgh, 76; interior mural, Plaza, Reiber Construction, Pittsburgh, 80. *Exhib:* Westmoreland Co Mus Art, Greensburg, Pa, 64-81; one-man exhibs, Kipp Gallery, Ind Univ Pa, 75, Carnegie Inst Mus Art, Pittsburgh, 76 & Crandall Gallery, Mt Union Col, Alliance, Ohio, 78; Southern Alleghenies Mus Art, Loretto, Pa, 77-78; Sordoni Gallery, Wilkes Col, Wilkes-Barre, Pa, 79; and others. *Teaching:* Prof painting, Carnegie-Mellon Univ, Pittsburgh, 63- *Awards:* Allegheny Found & Purchase Award, Assoc Artists, 76. *Mem:* Pittsburgh Plan Art; Assoc Artists Pittsburgh. *Media:* Acrylic. *Publ:* Auth, Is Alechinsky Worth $50,000?, Pittsburgh Mag, 10/77. *Dealer:* PPA Gallery 407 Craig St Pittsburgh PA 15213. *Mailing Add:* 1140 Murray Hill Ave Pittsburgh PA 15217

HOLLAND, TOM
PAINTER

b Seattle, Wash, 1936. *Study:* Willamette Univ, 54-56; Univ Calif, Santa Barbara & Berkeley, 57-59. *Work:* Whitney Mus Am Art, New York; St Louis City Mus; San Francisco Mus Art; Mus Mod Art, New York; Art Inst Chicago; plus many others. *Exhib:* Kid Stuff, Albright-Knox Art Gallery, Buffalo, NY, 71, Working in Calif, 72; New Options in Painting, Walker Art Ctr, Minneapolis, 72; California Prints, Mus Mod Art, New York, 72; Calif Printmakers, Whitney Mus Am Art, 73, New Aquisitions, 78; Corcoran Biennial, Washington, DC, 75; Nat Collection Fine Arts, Washington, DC, 77; one-man shows, San Francisco Art Inst, 79, Blum-Helman Gallery, New York, 79 & Watson-De Nagy, Houston, 79; Felicity Samuel Gallery, London, 80; James Corcoran Gallery, Los Angeles, Calif, 80; Charles Cowles Gallery, New York, 81; and others. *Teaching:* Instr art, San Francisco Art Inst, 61-68 & 72-80, Univ Calif, Berkeley, 78-79 & Cornish Inst, Seattle, 78. *Awards:* Fulbright Grant, Santiago, Chile, 59-60; Nat Endowment Arts Sculpture Grant, 75-76. *Mailing Add:* 227 Tunnel Rd Berkeley CA 94705

HOLLEN-BOLMGREN, DONNA
ASSEMBLAGE ARTIST, PAINTER

b Willmar, Minn, May 28, 35. *Study:* Univ Minn, BS(art educ), 57; Univ Pittsburgh, 58; Carnegie-Mellon Univ, 59. *Work:* Blount Inc; Westinghouse; Alcoa; McDonalds; pvt collections. *Exhib:* Assoc Artists of Pittsburgh, Carnegie Mus, 68-; Gallery Upstairs, Arts & Crafts Ctr of Pittsburgh, 70, 76 & 82; William Penn Mus, Harrisburg, Pa, 71-73; Ogleby Mus, Wheeling, WVa, 72; Butler Mid-Year Nat, Ohio, 73 & 81. *Teaching:* Instr design, Arts & Crafts Ctr, 70-, instr painting, 73- *Awards:* Pittsburgh Soc Artists Award, 68, 69 & 71; Harrisburg Arts Festival Award, 73; Carnegie-Mellon Fiber Award, 80. *Mem:* Assoc Artists of Pittsburgh (pres, 74-); Craftsmen's Guild; Artists Equity. *Media:* Oil, Acylic; Handmade Paper Pulp. *Dealer:* Gallery G 408 Blvd of Allies Pittsburgh PA 15219; Artsouth Montgomery AL. *Mailing Add:* 5703 Kentucky Ave Pittsburgh PA 15232

HOLLERBACH, SERGE
PAINTER, INSTRUCTOR

b Pushkin, Russia, Nov 1, 23; US citizen. *Study:* Acad Fine Arts, Munich, Ger, 46-49; Art Students League, with Ernst Fiene, 50; Am Art Sch, with Gordon Samstag, 51. *Work:* St Paul Gallery Art, Minn; Bridgeport Mus Art, Sci & Indust, Conn; Ga Mus Art, Athens; Seton Hall Univ Art Gallery; Norfolk Mus Art & Scis, Va. *Exhib:* Am Watercolor Soc Ann Exhib; Nat Acad Design Ann Exhib; Drawings USA, St Paul, Minn; 200 Years of Watercolor Painting in America, Metrop Mus Art, New York; Am Acad Arts & Lett, New York. *Teaching:* Instr painting, Nat Acad Sch Fine Arts, New York. *Awards:* Adolph & Clara Obrig Prize, Nat Acad Design, 71, 75 & 81; Gold Medal, Allied Artists Am, 76; Gold Medal, Am Watercolor Soc, 83. *Bibliog:* Aleksis Rannit (auth), Arts Mag, 1/81; Scott Elliot (auth), Portrait of an artist (film). *Mem:* Am Watercolor Soc (vpres, 79); Audubon Artists; Allied Artists; Nat Soc Painters in Casein & Acrylics; Nat Acad Design. *Media:* Acrylic, Watercolor. *Dealer:* Newman & Saunders Galleries Wayne PA. *Mailing Add:* 304 W 75th St New York NY 10023

HOLLIDAY, JUDITH
LIBRARIAN

b Butler, Pa, Mar 16, 38. *Study:* Col Wooster, BA, 60; Columbia Univ, MSLS, 61. *Pos:* Head librn, Fine Arts Libr, Cornell Univ, 70-; pub ed, Soc Arch Hist Newletter, 79- *Mem:* Art Libr Soc NAm; Soc Archit Historians. *Interests:* Nineteenth century American architectural periodicals. *Mailing Add:* DeWitt Park Apts Box 13 Ithaca NY 14850

HOLLINGER, HELEN WETHERBEE
PAINTER, LECTURER

b Indianapolis, Ind. *Study:* Herron Sch Art, dipl fine arts; also with Donald Mattison, Henrik Mayer & Emile Gruppe. *Work:* First Fed Savings & Loan Asn, Miami, Fla; Herron Sch Art; Hialeah, Miami Springs Realty Bd. *Exhib:* Am Artists Prof League, New York, 69-75; Nat Biennial Art Exhib, Nat League Am Pen Women, Salt Lake City, Utah, 70; Miami Shores Community Ctr, 73 & 75; Mus Sci Fine Art Show, Miami, Fla, 75 & 76; Patrons Fine Art Show, Mus Sci, Miami, Fla, 79. *Teaching:* Instr art, Miami Shores Community Ctr, Fla, 71-72 & 75. *Awards:* First Place Art Achievement Award, Wometco Enterprises, Miami, 71; Poinciana Art Exhib Best in Show, Burdine's, Miami, 72; Landscape Award, Fla State Conf, 79; and others. *Mem:* Am Artists Prof League (pres, Miami Chap, 69-70, dir, 71-73); Nat League Am Pen Women (art chmn, Fla State Orgn, 66-68, nat art bd, 72-74); Miami Art League (pres, 66-67, dir 71 & 75). *Media:* Oil, Pastel. *Mailing Add:* 80 NE 97th St Miami Shores FL 33138

HOLLINGSWORTH, ALVIN CARL
PAINTER, INSTRUCTOR

b New York, NY, Feb 25, 30. *Study:* City Univ New York, BA, 56, MA, 59; Art Students League, with Kunioshi, Ralph Fabri & Dr Bernard Myers, 50-52. *Work:* Chase Manhattan Bank, New York; Brooklyn Mus Permanent Collection, NY; IBM Collection, White Plains, NY; Williams Col Art Collection; Johnson Publ Permanent Art Collection, Chicago; plus others. *Comn:* Don Quixote limited ed lithographs, Orig Lithographs Inc, 67; Don Quixote murals, Don Quixote Apts, Bronx, NY, 69; mural, Rutgers Univ, New Brunswick, NJ, 70. *Exhib:* Emily Lowe Award Exhib, 63; Traveling Exhib Black Painters America, Univ Calif, Los Angeles, 66; 15 New Voices, Hallmark Gallery, New York & traveling, 69; Am Black Painters, Whitney Mus Am Art, New York, 71; one-person shows, The Women, Interfaith Coun of Churches, 78, Reflections of the Prophet, Pa State Univ, 78 & others. *Pos:* Consult art & art coordr, Harlem Freedom Sch, Off Econ Opportunity, 66-67;

dir, Lincoln Inst Gallery, Lincoln Inst Psycho-Ther, 66-68; supvr art, Proj Turn-On, New York, 68-69. *Teaching:* Instr graphics, High Sch Art & Design, 61-70; instr painting, Art Students League, 69-75; asst prof painting, Hostos Community Col, 71-77, assoc prof, 77-, prof visual & performing arts, currently. *Awards:* Emily Lowe Art Competition Award, 63; Whitney Found Award, 64; Award of Distinction, Smith Mason Gallery, 71. *Bibliog:* Cedric Dover (auth), American Negro Art, 61; Samella Lewis (auth), Black Artist on Art, pvt publ, 71. *Media:* Acrylic, Collage. *Res:* Aesthetic use of fluorescent materials in the fine arts. *Publ:* Auth & illusr, I'd like the Goo-gen-heim, Regnery, 69; coauth, Art of Acrylic Painting, Grumbacher, 69; illusr, The Sniper, McGraw, 69; illusr, Black Out Loud, Macmillan, 70; illusr, Journey, Scholastic, 70. *Dealer:* Lee Nordness Gallery 252 W 38th St New York NY 10021; Harbor Gallery 43 Main St Cold Spring Harbor NY 11724. *Mailing Add:* Hostos Community Col City Univ of New York New York NY 10021

HOLLISTER, PAUL
PAINTER, WRITER
b New York, NY. *Study:* Harvard Col, BS. *Work:* Boston Mus Fine Arts; Mont Mus, Helena. *Exhib:* Seventeen solo exhibits. *Mem:* Nat Early Am Glass Club; Glass Circle, London; Int Asn Hist Glass, Liege, Belg. *Publ:* Auth, The glazing of the Crystal Palace, Corning J Glass Studies, 74; auth, Glass Paperweights an Old Craft Revived, Culross & Son, Ltd, 75; auth, Flowers Which Clothe the Meadows, Corning Mus Glass, 78; auth, The rebirth of Millefiori circa 1500, Eighth Glass Cong, AIHV, London, 79; auth, Muranese Millefiori revival of the nineteenth century, Corning J Glass Studies, 83; and many others. *Mailing Add:* c/o Clarkson N Potter Inc One Park Ave New York NY 10016

HOLLISTER, VALERIE (DUTTON)
PAINTER
b Oakland, Calif, Dec 29, 39. *Study:* Stanford Univ, AB, 61 & MA, 65; San Francisco Art Inst, 63; Col Art Study Abroad, Paris, 64-65. *Exhib:* Biennial Contemp Am Painting & Area Show, Corcoran Gallery Art, Washington, DC, 67; Whitney Mus Ann Contemp Am Painting, 67-68; one-woman shows, Madison Art Ctr, Wis, 68, Swarthmore Col, Pa, 72, 77 & 82, Westbroadway Gallery, New York, 73 & Selected Paintings Since 1965, Washington Proj for the Arts, Washington, DC, 78; and other one-woman & group shows. *Publ:* Coauth, Toward A History of Women's Traditional Arts, Heresies, winter 78. *Mailing Add:* 1 Whittier Pl Swarthmore PA 19081

HOLM, BILL
HISTORIAN, CURATOR
b Roundup, Mont, Mar 24, 25. *Study:* Univ Wash, BA, 49, MFA, 51. *Collections Arranged:* Arts of the Raven (with Doris Shadbolt, Bill Reid & Wilson Duff), Vancouver Art Gallery, 67; Northwest Coast Indian Life, Pac Sci Ctr, Seattle, 71-; Crooked Beak of Heaven, Henry Art Gallery, Univ Wash, Seattle; Smoky-Top (auth, catalog), Pac Sci Ctr, 83; The Bos of Daylight (auth, catalog), Seattle Art Mus, 83. *Pos:* Cur, Northwest Coast Indian art, Thomas Burke Mem Wash State Mus, Univ Wash, Seattle, 68- *Teaching:* Prof Northwest Coast Indian art, Univ Wash, Seattle, 68- *Awards:* Governor's Art Award, 76; Governor's Writers Award, 77 & 81. *Res:* All aspects of Northwest Coast Indian art, with concentration on form and style and relation to ceremonialism. *Publ:* Auth, Northwest Coast Indian Art: An Analysis of Form, 65; auth, Crooked Beak of Heaven, 72, Univ Wash Press; coauth (with Bill Reid), Indian Art of the Northwest Coast, Univ Wash Press, 76; Second Times of Willie Seaweed, Univ Wash Press, 83; Northwest Coast Indian Art, Seattle Art Mus, 83. *Mailing Add:* 1027 NW 190th St Seattle WA 98177

HOLM, MILTON W
PAINTER
b Rochester, NY. *Study:* With Edward S Siebert, Rochester. *Work:* Mem Art Gallery, Rochester; Rochester Inst Technol; Univ Rochester; Greenville Pub Libr, SC. *Exhib:* Mem Art Gallery, 24-82; Nat Acad Design Ann, New York, 35-73; Allied Artists Am, New York, 38-71 & 77; Currier Art Gallery, Manchester, NH, 40; Cincinnati Art Gallery, Ohio, 45. *Awards:* Ranger Purchase Award, Nat Acad Design, 40; James Hogarth Dennis Award, Mem Art Gallery, 58-62; Rochester Art Club Award, 69-82. *Bibliog:* C Movalli (auth), article in Am Artist, 11/78. *Mem:* Allied Artists Am; Rochester Art Club (pres, 57-59); Genesee Group (pres); Rockport Art Asn, Mass. *Media:* Oil. *Dealer:* Oxford Gallery 267 Oxford St Rochester NY 14607. *Mailing Add:* 30 Hathaway Rd Rochester NY 14617

HOLMAN, ARTHUR (STEARNS)
PAINTER
b Bartlesville, Okla, Oct 25, 26. *Study:* Univ NMex, BFA, 51; Hans Hofmann Sch Art, Provincetown, Mass, 51; Calif Sch Fine Arts, San Francisco, 53. *Work:* San Francisco Mus Art; Oakland Mus, Calif; Achenbach Collection, Fine Arts Mus San Francisco; Eureka Col. *Exhib:* One-man shows, Esther Robles Gallery, Los Angeles, 60, M H De Young Mem Mus, San Francisco, 63, William Sawyer Gallery, San Francisco, 71, 73, 74 & 76 & David Cole Gallery, Inverness, Calif, 80; Fifty California Artists, Whitney Mus Am Art, New York, 62; Calif Painting & Sculpture: The Mod Era, San Francisco Mus, 76; Smithsonian Inst, Washington, DC, 77. *Awards:* Purchase Award, Invitational Show, Stanford Univ, 62; Public Vote Prize, Bay Area Art, First Savings Bank of San Francisco, 64. *Media:* Oil. *Mailing Add:* Box 72 Lagunitas CA 94938

HOLMAN, THOMAS S
CURATOR, HISTORIAN
b New York, NY, Apr 21, 53. *Study:* Inst der Kunstgeschichte, Univ Vienna, Austria, 74-75; Macalester Col, St Paul, Minn, BA(cum laude), 76; Univ Chicago, MA, 77, Mus Mgt Inst, Univ Calif, Berkeley, 83. *Collections Arranged:* Engravings by William Hogarth, 76 & Albrecht Dürer: Woodcuts and Engravings, 76, Minneapolis Inst Arts; American and European Waterscapes, Norton Gallery of Art, West Palm Beach, Fla, 79; American Style: Early Modernist Works in Minnesota Collections (auth, catalog), 81 & George Bellows: Lithographs, 82, Minn Mus Art. *Pos:* Cur asst, Minneapolis Inst Arts, 75-76; res asst, Metrop Mus Art, New York, 76; cur collections, Norton Gallery & Sch Art, 78-80; cur collections, Minn Mus Art, 80- *Teaching:* Lectr, Minneapolis Inst Arts, 75-76, Metrop Mus Art, New York, 76 & Norton Gallery Art, 78-80. *Mem:* Col Art Asn; Am Asn Mus; Cable Arts Consortium. *Res:* Northern European painting, Renaissance and Baroque; European portraiture, Hans Holbein the Younger; prints and drawings, 15th-18th centuries; 19th-20th century American and European art; Reginald Marsh, Paul Manship, and Georgia O'Keeffe. *Publ:* Coauth & ed, Catalogue of the Collection, Norton Gallery of Art, 79; contribr, J of Metrop Mus Art, New York, 80; and others. *Mailing Add:* Minn Mus Art St Peter at Kellogg & Landmark Ctr St Paul MN 55102

HOLMES, DAVID BRYAN
PAINTER, PRINTMAKER
b London, Eng, Aug 8, 36; Can citizen. *Study:* Twickenham Tech Col, Eng; Harrow Sch Art, London; Queen's Univ, Ont; Art Students League, New York, with Robert Beverley Hale; London Sch Art & Design, Eng. *Work:* Willistead Art Gallery, Windsor, Ont. *Comn:* Many pvt comn in Eng & NAm. *Exhib:* Country Scenes in Quebec, City of Montreal, PQ, 69; one-man shows, Galerie Gauvreau, Montreal, 69 & 70 & Wally F Findlay Galleries, Inc, New York, 74-75, 78, 80 & 82, Chicago, 77 & Palm Beach, Fla, 79; and others. *Teaching:* Art master, St Lawrence Col Appl Arts & Technol, Kingston, Ont, 68-74. *Awards:* Ann Nat Spring Exhib, Queen's Univ, Ont, 67, 69 & 71; Award for Country Scenes in Quebec, City of Montreal, 69. *Mem:* Int Soc Artists; Print & Drawing Coun Can; Soc Can Artists; Art Students League, New York. *Media:* Tempera; Oil; Etching. *Dealer:* Wally F Findlay Galleries Int 17 E 57th St New York NY 10022. *Mailing Add:* RR 3 Odessa ON K0H 2H0 Canada

HOLMES, DAVID VALENTINE
SCULPTOR, PAINTER
b Newark, NY, Nov 27, 45. *Study:* Temple Abroad Tyler Sch, Rome, Italy, 66-67; Tyler Sch Art, Temple Univ, Philadelphia, Pa, BFA(cum laude), 68; Univ Wis, Madison, MFA, 72. *Work:* Milwaukee Art Mus, Wis; Kohler Arts Ctr, Sheboygan, Wis; Madison Art Ctr, Wis; Kent State Univ. *Exhib:* Chicago & Vicinity, Chicago Art Inst, Ill, 75; one-man shows, Madison Art Ctr & Kohler Arts Ctr, Wis, 72 & 77; Harmonous Craft, Am Craft Mus, New York, 79; Harmonous Craft, Renwick Gallery, Smithsonian, Washington, DC, 79; Out of the Woods, Milwaukee Art Mus, Wis, 80; Animal Images, Renwick Gallery, Smithsonian, Washington, DC, 81; Renwick Souvenir Show, Smithsonian Inst, 82; Traveling one-man show, Ind State Univ, Kent State Univ & Northwestern Univ, 83. *Teaching:* Resident artist, Madison Public Schools, Wis, 72-74; asst prof drawing & design, Univ Wis, Milwaukee, 74-76; assoc prof drawing & design, Univ Wis, Parkside, Kenosha, 77- *Awards:* Nat Endowment Arts Fel, US Government, 76-77. *Mem:* Col Arts Asn Am. *Media:* Wood; Acrylic. *Mailing Add:* 1428 S Wisconsin Ave Racine WI 53403

HOLMES, PAUL JAMES & MARY E
COLLECTORS
Mr Holmes, b North Henderson, Ill, Jan 28, 1896; Mrs Holmes, b Chicago, Ill, Sept 12, 1900. *Study:* Mr Holmes, Univ Mich, BS; Univ Toulouse; Mrs Holmes, Art Inst Chicago; also with Sadie M Hess, Gary, Ind. *Collection:* Eighteenth century porcelains and figurines; miniatures; patch and snuff boxes; Russian enamels, porcelains and Faberge; Russian icons; rare items in porcelain, art glass and graphics; medieval and 18th century enamels of England and the Continent; wax portraits and groups; silhouettes; Verre de Nevers; mementos mori; Oriental porcelains and enamels. *Mailing Add:* 836 Du Shane Ct South Bend IN 46616

HOLMES, WENDY (DIANA H NOYES)
PHOTOGRAPHER
b New York, NY, Oct 21, 46. *Study:* Mass Inst Technol. *Work:* Bibliot Nat, Paris; NJ State Mus, Trenton; Addison Gallery Art, Andover, Mass; Clarence Kennedy Gallery, Polaroid Corp, Cambridge, Mass. *Exhib:* Peters Valley Exhib, Newark Mus, NJ, 80; NJ State Mus, Trenton, 80; Upstate Exhib, NY State Mus, Albany, 82; Southern Ill Univ, Edwardsville, 82; Paul Mellon Arts Ctr, Wallingford, Conn, 82. *Collections Arranged:* Seven Photographers: The Delaware Valley (auth, catalog), Peters Valley, NJ, NJ State Mus & Nexus, Atlanta, Ga, 76-78. *Pos:* Staff photogr, Wave Hill Environ Ctr, Bronx, NY, 70-73. *Teaching:* Instr photog, Peters Valley Photog Workshop, Layton, NJ, 75-83 & Int Ctr Photog, New York, 79-81. *Awards:* Survey Grant for Seven Photographers Exhib, Nat Endowment Arts, 76; Fel, NJ State Coun Arts, 79. *Bibliog:* Article, New York Times, 7/22/79. *Publ:* Auth & illusr, Hudson City: The Living River, Wave Hill Ctr, 72; coauth, Brother Can You Spare a Dime, Paddington Press, 75. *Mailing Add:* Route 1 Box 183 Chatham NY 12037

HOLOUN, HAROLD DEAN
PAINTER, SCULPTOR
b Ord, Nebr, Oct 16, 39. *Study:* Hastings Col, Nebr, BA, 61; Univ Wyo, Laramie, MA, 62. *Work:* Sheldon Mem Gallery, Univ Nebr, Lincoln; Nebr

Art, Kearney; Nebr Wesleyan Univ, Lincoln. *Comn:* Portrait, Baker Univ, Baldwin, Kans, 75; two portraits, Liberty Glass Corp, Sapulpa, Okla, 79; painting/sculpture, City of Grand Island, Nebr, 81. *Exhib:* Painting/Sculpture Today, Indianapolis Mus Art, Ind, 78; Visions 81, Mid-Am Arts Alliance Touring Exhib, Kansas City, 80-81; Sheldon Mem Gallery, Lincoln, Nebr, 81; Art and Artists in Nebraska, Sheldon Mem Gallery, Lincoln, Nebr, 82; Twelve Midwest Realists, Sioux City Art Ctr, Iowa, 82; Reflectons Exhib, Elder Gallery, Lincoln, Nebr, 83. *Awards:* Juror's Award, Reflections Exhib, Elder Gallery, 83. *Media:* Oil, Alkyd; Bronze, Enamelled Wood. *Mailing Add:* 219 East 17th St Grand Island NE 68801

HOLSCH, ROBERT FRED
SCULPTOR
b Rosebud, Tex, Aug 10, 52. *Study:* Univ Tex, Austin, BFA, 70; Tex A&I Univ, BFA, 75; North Tex State Univ, MFA, 78. *Work:* Renaissance Ctr, Detroit, Mich; Rockwell Enterprises, Dallas, Tex; and other pvt collections. *Comn:* Sculpture, EnCom Graphics, Houston, Tex, 80. *Exhib:* One-man shows, Adelle M Fine Art Gallery, Dallas, 80 & O'Kane Gallery, Houston, 81; Nat Small Sculpture & Drawing Exhib, Los Angeles, Calif, 81; Le Salon de Nation, Paris, 83; DuBose Gallery, Houston, 84; and others. *Teaching:* Asst instr sculpture, Tex A&I Univ, 74-75 & North Tex State Univ, 77-78. *Awards:* Honors Award, Tex A&I Univ, 75. *Bibliog:* Harry Reed (auth), Artist profile, Art Voices, 9/81. *Media:* Wood, Marble. *Dealer:* DuBose Gallery Houston TX 77098; Adelle M Fine Art 3317 McKinney Ave Dallas TX 75204. *Mailing Add:* 10015 Raritan Houston TX 77080

HOLSCHUH, (GEORGE) FRED
SCULPTOR
b Beerfelden, Ger, Nov 19, 02; US citizen. *Study:* Indust art & archit dipl; Pa Acad Fine Arts; Univ Pa; also with Bauhaus founder, Walter Gropius. *Work:* Süddeutsches Mus, Darmstadt, Ger; Addisson Gallery, New York; Brookgreen Garden, SC. *Comn:* St Francis Monument, Yugoslav Order of St Francis, Washington, DC, 36; Murrell Dobbins Mem, Bd Educ, Philadelphia, 38; bronze sculptures (collabr with Bass Studio, Philadelphia), Penn Mutual Life Insurance Bldg, 39; copper sculpture, Irene Edmond Mem, Tallahassee, Fla, 67 & 10th anniversary figure, Garden Le Moyne Art Found, 72. *Exhib:* Pa Acad Fine Arts, Philadelphia, 36; Nat Acad Design, New York, 37; Int Sculpture Outdoor Show, Parkway Mus, Philadelphia, 39; Regional Sculpture Show, Smithsonian Inst, Washington, DC, 40. *Teaching:* Prof design & art hist & head dept art, Cedar Crest Col, Allentown, 36-38; prof humanities & sculpture, Fla State Univ, 46-72, emer prof, 72- *Awards:* Stimson Prize in Sculpture, Pa Acad Fine Arts, 35 & Europ Traveling Scholars, 35 & 36; Regional First Prize, Southern Sculptors Nat Show, 66. *Mem:* Am Southern Sculptors (bd dirs, 63-65); Am Asn Univ Prof. *Media:* Wood, Copper. *Dealer:* Harmon Gallery 1258 Third St Naples FL 33940. *Mailing Add:* 2007 W Randolph Circle Tallahassee FL 32303

HOLSTE, THOMAS JAMES
PAINTER, EDUCATOR
b Evanston, Ill, Jan 12, 43. *Study:* Calif State Univ, Fullerton, study with Vic Smith, BA, 67, MA, 68; Claremont Grad Sch, study with Guy Williams & Mowry Baden, MFA, 70. *Work:* La Jolla Mus Contemp Art, Calif; Chase Manhattan Bank, New York; Solomon R Guggenheim Mus, New York; Security Pac Nat Bank; Int Tel & Tel, New York. *Exhib:* The Market St Prog, Los Angeles Co Mus Art, Los Angeles, 72; one-man show, Newspace Gallery, Los Angeles, 73-81; Aber, Buchanan, Holste, Newport Harbor Art Mus, Newport Beach, Calif, 76; Mind Set: An Ongoing Involvement with the Rational Tradition, John Weber Gallery, New York, 79; Four Artists, Otis Art Inst Parsons Sch Design, Los Angeles, 79; Emergent Americans, Guggenheim Mus, New York, 81; Alice Aycock, Tom Holste, Michael Singer, Fort Worth Art Mus, Tex, 81; Concepts in Construction: 1910-1980 Traveling Exhib, 83-; and others. *Teaching:* Prof painting, Calif State Univ, Fullerton, 69- *Awards:* Individual Artists Fel Grant, Nat Endowment Arts, 80. *Bibliog:* Peter Frank (auth), Review--Tom Holste, Artforum, 2/78 & Unslick in LA, Art in Am, 9-10/78. *Media:* Mixed. *Dealer:* Newspace Gallery 5241 Melrose Ave Los Angeles CA 90038. *Mailing Add:* Star Rte Box 796 Orange CA 92667

HOLT, CHARLOTTE SINCLAIR
MEDICAL ILLUSTRATOR, SCULPTOR
b Springfield, Mass, June 11, 14. *Study:* Boston Mus Fine Arts, 29-34; Child-Walker Sch Fine Arts & Crafts, Boston, 32-34, dipl; Boston Univ, 33-34, Col Med, 34-35; portrait painting with Bernard Keyes, Boston, 34; med photog with Laurence Toriello & Anthony Kuzma, 36-37 & 71-72; Sch Med Illus, cert, 37; Rush Med Col, med art with Willard C Shepard, 37-38; sculpture with Malvina Hoffman, New York, 39-66; watercolor with Elliot O'Hara, Maine, 41 & 45; plaster casting with John Pletinkx, 49-54; plastic carving with Joseph Krstolich, 52-70; Marquette Univ Med Col, PhD, 73; Akron Ohio Gen Med Ctr, hon PhD, 72. *Work:* Miracle of Growth, Mus Sci & Indust, Chicago. *Exhib:* Many national & international medical education exhibits, 37-70. *Pos:* Chief illusr & sculptor, Visual Medical Educ Prog, Univ Ill Col Med in coop with Ill State Dept Pub Health, 35-70; free lance med illusr, sculptor & graphic artist for advert agencies & pharmaceut co, 36-; instr, Sch Med Illus, 37-45; adv ed, J Am Med Illusr, 59-70, assoc ed, 70-72; med artist, Am Med Asn, 61-63; dir, Med Audio/Visual Communications, Akron Ohio Gen Med Ctr, 72-78. *Teaching:* Instr, Univ Ill Col Med, 37-55; instr, workshops and exhibits, currently. *Awards:* Distinguished Serv Awards, Asn Med Illusr, 66 & 70, Presidential Award, 71; Gold Medal for Stained Glass Design, C Connick Studio; and others. *Mem:* Asn Med Illusr (vpres, 60-61, bd gov, 61-66 & 71-76, corresp secy, 65-69, pres, 70-71); fel Med Artists Asn Gt Brit; Royal Photog Soc; founding and assoc mem Inst Med & Biol Illus; life mem Biological Photo Asn; and many others. *Media:* Watercolor, Pen & Ink;

Mixed. *Publ:* Coauth & illusr, Expectant Motherhood, 37; coauth & illusr, Obstetric and Gynecologic Nursing, Mosby, rev ed, 41; coauth & illusr, Atlas of Obstetric Complications, Lippincott, 62; illusr many jour & med bks. *Mailing Add:* 738 Keystone Ave River Forest IL 60305

HOLT, MARGARET MCCONNELL
PATRON, COLLECTOR
b Gastonia, NC, July 26, 09. *Study:* Univ NC-Greensboro, BS(music), 30; painting with Louis Bouche, New York, 40; Black Mountain Col, ceramics with Marguerita Wildenhain, Bernard Leach & Shoji Hamada, 53; watercolor with Eliot O'Hara, 55, 65 & 68; Queens Col, with Philip Moose, 65-66; Univ NC-Charlotte, Bach Creative Arts, 73. *Interests:* Proceeds from art work go towards collecting works by living American artists, providing art scholarships and sponsoring creativity in university art schools. *Collection:* Founder of the D E McConnell Collection of American Art which is housed at the Gaston-Lincoln Regional Library Headquarters, Gastonia, NC; founder of Holt Art Collection, Cannon Memorial Library, Concord, NC; established Holt Scholarship Fund for the Cabarrus Artists Guild. *Mailing Add:* 962 Cherokee Rd Charlotte NC 28207

HOLT, MARTHA A
PAINTER, CERAMIST
b Chatham, NJ, Apr, 15, 45. *Study:* Univ Miami, Fla, BS, 67; Norfolk Mus Sch, 67-68; Penland Sch Crafts, 68-69; Cranbrook Acad Art, MFA, 71. *Exhib:* Campbell Mus, Camden, NJ, 76; Mus Contemp Crafts, New York, 76; solo exhibs, Portnoy Gallery, New York, 77, 79, 80 & 82 & Erie Art Mus, Pa, 83; Bronx Mus, New York, 78; San Francisco Mus Art, 78. *Pos:* Dir, Allegheny Col Galleries, 76-83. *Awards:* Visual Arts Fel Grant, Pa Coun Arts, 80. *Bibliog:* Susan Wechsler (auth), Low-Fire Ceramics, Watson Guptill, 81; article, Ceramics Mo, 5/81; Sharon Dale (auth), article, Arts Mag, 2/82. *Media:* Clay. *Publ:* Coauth, New Relationships, private publ, 80. *Dealer:* Theo Portnoy 162 W 56th St New York NY 10019. *Mailing Add:* 232 Church St Cambridge Springs PA 16403

HOLT, NANCY LOUISE
SCULPTOR, FILMMAKER
b Worcester, Mass, Apr 5, 38. *Study:* Jackson Col; Tufts Univ, BS. *Comn:* Landscape sculptures, Artpark, Lewiston, NY, 74, Wellesley Col, Mass, 80, Laguna Gloria Art Mus, Austin, 81, Arlington Co, Va & Gallaudet Col, Washington, DC; Wellesley Col, Mass, 80; Laguna Gloria Art Mus, Austin, Tex, 81; and others. *Exhib:* Collectors Video, Los Angeles Co Mus, 74; Video '75, Corcoran Mus, Washington, DC; New Am Filmmaker's Series, Whitney Mus Am Art, New York, 75 & 77; Art in Landscape Traveling exhib, Independent Cur, Washington, DC, 76; Whitney Biennial, 77, 79 & 81; Probing the Earth: Contemp Land Proj, Hirshhorn Mus, Washington, DC, 77; 11th Int Sculpture Conference, Washington DC, 80; Architectural Sculpture, Los Angeles Inst Contemp Art, 80; Artists' Gardens and Parks, Hayden Gallery, Mass Inst Technol, 81; City Site Sculpture, Toronto, 82; Independent Artists Open Air Sculpture Exhib, Marlay Park, Dublin, Ireland, 83. *Awards:* Creative Artists Pub Serv Grant, 75 & 78; Guggenheim Fel, 78; Nat Endowment Arts Media Arts Grant, 83. *Bibliog:* Kate Linker (auth), Public sculpture, Artforum, 3/81; Ted Castle (auth), Nancy Holt, Siteseer, Art in Am, 3/82; John Beardsley (auth), Art in Pub Places, 82; and others. *Publ:* Auth, Pine barrens, Avalanche, summer 75; auth, Some notes on video works, In: Video Art, Harcourt Brace Jovanovich, 76; auth, Sun Tunnels, Artforum, 4/77; auth, Stone enclosure: rock rings, Arts, 6/79; auth, Ransacked, Printed Matter, 80; and others. *Mailing Add:* 799 Greenwich St New York NY 10014

HOLTZ, ITSHAK JACK
PAINTER, PRINTMAKER
b Skernewiz, Poland, Dec 14, 25; US citizen. *Study:* Bezalel Acad Art, Jerusalem; Art Students League; Nat Acad Design, New York. *Exhib:* Karlebach Gallery, Fair Lawn, NJ, 65-; Audubon Artists of New York, 66; Tyringham Galleries, Mass, 66-75; Allied Artists Am, New York, 72; Nat Acad Design, 77. *Awards:* Gold Medal, Academic of Italy; Gold Medal, Accademia Italia, 83. *Bibliog:* Articles in Art Rev Mag, 5/66 & La Rev Mod, 6/66. *Mem:* Art Students League; Academia Italia delle Arti. *Media:* Oil, Felt Pen & Ink; Lithography. *Mailing Add:* 118 E 28th St New York NY 10016

HOLVERSON, JOHN
MUSEUM DIRECTOR
b Marshfield, Wis, June 14, 46. *Study:* Univ Iowa, 65-66; MacMurray Col, Jacksonville, Ill, BA, 67; Univ Iowa, Iowa City, MA, 71; Attingham Summer Sch, 82. *Collections Arranged:* Images of Women Photog Exhib (auth, catalog), 77; The Revolutionary McLellans, 77; Miss Mary Cassatt: Impressionist from Pennsylvania, 79; James Brooks: Paintings and works on Paper 1946-1982, 83; Winslow Homer: The Charles Shipman Payson Collection, 83; Maine Light: Temperas by Andrew Wyeth, 83. *Pos:* Summer intern, Art Inst Chicago, 68-69; grad asst, Mus Art, Univ Iowa, 68-69, head grad asst, 69-70; cur, Portland Mus Art, Maine, 70-73, ed monthly bulletin, 70-, cur collections, 73-81, actg dir, 73-75, dir, 75- *Teaching:* Asst dept art, MacMurray Col, Jacksonville, Ill, 63-65 & 66-67. *Mem:* Am Asn Mus; Asn Art Mus Dirs; Soc Preserv New England Antiq; Nat Trust for State & Local Hist Soc; Col Art Asn. *Publ:* Auth, Rene Dubois and the cathedrals of the future, Greater Portland Landmarks Observer, fall 73; auth, Fire buckets and bags in Portland, 1783, Antiques, 3/74. *Mailing Add:* Portland Mus Art 7 Congress Sq Portland ME 04101

HOLVEY, SAMUEL BOYER
SCULPTOR, DESIGNER
b Wilkes Barre, Pa, July 20, 35. *Study:* Syracuse Univ, BFA, 57; Am Univ, MA, 69. *Comn:* Bas-relief mural, Wyo Valley Country Club, Wilkes Barre, 62. *Exhib:* Corcoran Gallery Area Show, Washington, DC, 68; Greater Washington Area Show, 72; 2nd Ann Washington Area Sculpture Show, 74; The Am Genius, Corcoran Gallery, 76. *Pos:* Designer, William Fertig Interiors, Kingston, Pa, 57-58, 63-64; art dir, WFM-TV, Eatontown, NJ, 60-61; designer display exhibs, The Displayers Inc, New York World's Fair Pavilions, 61-63; designer, Robert Kayton Assocs, New York, 62; designer, Warner Communications, US Chamber Commerce. *Teaching:* Assoc prof design & chmn graphic design, Corcoran Sch Art, DC, 65-80; asst prof design, Univ Md, College Park, 67-78. *Media:* Metal Direct Construction, Lumia. *Mailing Add:* 5100 Elm St Bethesda MD 20814

HOLZER, JENNY
CONCEPTUAL ARTIST
b Gallipolis, Ohio, July 29, 50. *Study:* Ohio Univ, BFA, 72; RI Sch Design, MFA, 77; Whitney Mus Independent Study Prog, fel, 77. *Work:* Van Abbe Mus, Eindhoven, Neth; Mus Contemp Art, Chicago; Tate Gallery, London; Mus Mod Art Lending Serv, New York. *Comn:* Project Grand Central, Remy Martin, New York, 80; posters, Nouveau Mus, Lyon, France, 82; sign, City Amsterdam, 82; spectacolor board, Pub Art Fund, New York, 82; Urban Art Works Proj, City Seattle, 83. *Exhib:* Westkunst--Heute, Köln, WGer, 81; Documenta 7, Fridericianum, Kassel, Ger, 82; 79th Americans Show, Art Inst Chicago, 82; Whitney Mus Biennial, 83; Van Abbe Mus, Eindhoven, Neth, 83; Currents, Inst Contemp Art, Boston, 83; solo exhib, Inst Contemp Art, London, 83 & Inst Contemp Art, Philadelphia, 83. *Awards:* Blair Award, 79th Americans Show, Art Inst Chicago, 82. *Bibliog:* Carter Radcliffe (auth), article, Print Collectors Newslett, 82; hal Foster (auth), article, Art in Am, 82; Diana Nemiroff (auth), Personae & politics, Jenny Holzer, Vanguard, 83. *Mem:* Collaborative Proj, New York. *Media:* Multi-Media. *Publ:* Coauth, Position papers, Art Forum, 80; contribr, Hotel, 80 & coauth, Eating Through Living, 81, Tanam Press; coauth, Eating Friends, Top Stories, 81; auth, Truisms and Essays, Press NS Col Art & Design, 83. *Dealer:* Barbara Gladstone Gallery 152 Wooster St New York NY 10012. *Mailing Add:* 245 Eldridge St New York NY 10002

HOMAR, LORENZO
PRINTMAKER, PAINTER
b Puerta de Tierra, PR, Sept 10, 13. *Study:* Pratt Inst, 40-42; Brooklyn Mus, with Peterdi, Tamayo & Osver, 46-50; Inter-Am Univ PR, hon DFA. *Work:* Libr Cong, Washington, DC; Mus Mod Art & Metrop Mus Art, New York; Klingspor Mus, Offenbach, WGer; Children Art Mus, Rutgers Univ, NJ. *Comn:* Tile murals of olympic swimming pool, Dept Parks, San Juan, 67-68; ceramic mural of pub sch, Dept Educ, San Juan, 71; portfolio, Blanco-Casals-Homar, Galeria Colibri, San Juan, 71; porfolio six Colombian artists, Mus de Arte Mod, Cali, Colombia, 75. *Exhib:* Poster Biennale, Warsaw, 70 & 74; Havana Exhib Prints, Cuba, 72; Norwegian Int Print Biennale, 74; Ljubljana, Yugoslavia Biennale; Comprehensive Exhib 1942-83, Princeton Univ, 83; and others. *Collections Arranged:* First San Juan Print Biennale; Retrospective Exhib, Mus Int PR Cult, San Juan, 70; retrospective--45 yrs as an artist, Mus de Arte de Ponce, PR. *Pos:* Jewelry designer, Cartier Inc, New York, 38-50; dir graphic workshop, Div Community Educ, 50-56; dir graphic workshop, Inst PR Cult, 58-72. *Teaching:* Master printing silk-screen, Inter-Am Univ PR, summer 72; instr, Cali, Colombia, 72; instr, Sch Plastic Arts, Inst PR Cult, presently. *Awards:* Guggenheim Fel, 57. *Bibliog:* Lorenzo Homar & Fritz Eichenberg (auth), Posters in Puerto Rico, Artist Proof, Vol 6, No 9-10; Jose Gomez Sicre (auth), Six Puerto Rican Artists (film), Pan-Am Union, 68; Marta Traba (auth), Proposed Polemics on Puerto Rican Art, Libr Int Rio Piedras, PR, 71. *Media:* Silk-Screen, Woodcut. *Mailing Add:* Miramar PR 00907

HOMER, WILLIAM INNES
HISTORIAN, EDUCATOR
b Merion, Pa, Nov 8, 29. *Study:* Princeton Univ, BA; Harvard Univ, MA & PhD. *Work:* Cur, Mus Art, Ogunquit, Maine, 55-58; actg asst dir, Princeton Univ Art Mus, 56-57. *Teaching:* Asst prof art & archaeol, Princeton Univ, 61-64; assoc prof hist art, Cornell Univ, 64-66; prof, Univ Del, 66- *Awards:* Am Coun Learned Soc Fel, 64-65; Guggenheim Fel, 72-73; Nat Endowment Humanities Fel, 80-81. *Mem:* Col Art Asn; Royal Photog Soc; Wilmington Soc Fine Arts; Nat Arts Club. *Publ:* Auth, Seurat and the Science of Painting, 64; auth, Robert Henri & His Circle, 69; auth, Alfred Stieglitz & the American Avant-Garde, 77; auth, The Photographs of Gertrude Käsebier, 79; auth, Alfred Stieglitz and the Photo-Secession, 83. *Mailing Add:* Dept of Art Hist Univ of Del Newark DE 19711

HOMITZKY, PETER
PAINTER
b Berlin, Ger, Dec 7, 42; US citizen. *Study:* Art Students League, with F Reilly, J Leberte, J Hirsh, 59-63; San Francisco Art Inst, 65-66. *Work:* Wichita Mus Art, Kans; San Francisco Mus Art; Prudential Ins Co, Newark, NJ; Newark Mus, NJ; NJ State Mus, Trenton, NJ. *Exhib:* One-man show, State Mus, Trenton, NJ, 76; Alonzo Galleries, New York, 76-77; Educ Testing Serv, Princeton, NJ, 82; Sid Deutsch Galley, New York, 83; Jersey City Mus, 84. *Awards:* NJ State Coun Arts, 81; Harry Devlin Visual Arts Award, NJ Soc Contemp Artists, 82. *Bibliog:* Diane Cochrane (auth), Industrial American landscapes of Peter Homitzky, Am Artist, 5/74; Susan Myer (ed), 20 Landscape Painters, Watson-Guptill, 77; Hilton Kramer (auth), article, New York Times, 12/9/77. *Media:* Oil, Pastel. *Publ:* Contribr, Arts Mag, 71; auth exhib catalogs, Maxwell Galleries, 65-67. *Dealer:* Sid Deutsch Gallerry 20 W 57th St New York NY. *Mailing Add:* 227 Grand St Hoboken NJ 07030

HOMPSON, DAVI DET (DAVID ELBRIDGE THOMPSON)
CONCEPTUAL ARTIST
b Sharon, Pa, Aug 7, 39. *Study:* Anderson Col, BA; Indiana Univ, MFA. *Exhib:* Art by Telephone Show, Chicago Mus Contemp Art, 69; one-man shows, Alexandre Iolas Gallery, New York, 70, Apple Gallery, New York, 71-73, La Mamelle Inc, San Francisco, Calif, 77; Ideas at the Idea Warehouse, New York, 75; Franklin Furnace, New York, 78; Alternatives in Retrospect, New Mus, New York, 81. *Teaching:* Asst prof vis commun, Herron Sch Art, Ind Univ, 67-69; guest artist sculpture, Va Commonwealth Univ, 72-74; guest artist graphic design, RI Sch Design, summers 75-79; guest artist found, Kansas City Art Inst, 79-80. *Bibliog:* Richard Kostelanetz (auth), Breakthrough Fictioneers, Something Else Press, 73; George Cruger (ed), Arts in Virginia, Va Mus Art, 74; Clive Phillpot (ed), article, Art J, 82. *Publ:* Auth, S553 Study Manual, 69; auth, Blue Light Containment, 69; coauth, Word and Image Equations, 75; auth, 15, Hook, 80. *Mailing Add:* PO Box 7035 Richmond VA 23221

HONIG, MERVIN
PAINTER, PAINTING CONSERVATOR
b New York, NY, Dec 25, 20. *Study:* Art with Francis Criss, 39-41, Amadee Ozenfant, 46 & Hans Hofmann, 47-50; Brooklyn Mus, conservation with Caroline & Sheldon Keck, 56-58, Brooklyn Col, BA, 73. *Work:* Okla Mus Art, Oklahoma City; Nat Acad Design, New York; Emily Lowe Gallery, Hofstra Univ; Siena Heights Col, 79; Metrop Mus Art, New York, 80. *Exhib:* Portrait of America, Metrop Mus Art, New York, 44 & Carnegie Inst Fine Arts, 45; Whitney Mus Am Art Artists Ann, 49; Brooklyn & Long Island Artists, Brooklyn Mus, 60; Wadsworth Atheneum Artists Ann, 65; one-man show, Nat Art Mus of Sport, Madison Square Garden, NY, 77; group show, Nat Acad Design, Ann Exhib, 78 & 79; Los Angeles County Mus; The Queens Mus; The William Rockhill Nelson Gallery; The Butler Inst Am Art; and others. *Pos:* Trustee, Nat Art Mus Sport, New Haven, Conn, currently; head conservator & mem adv bd, Nassau Co Mus Fine Art, currently. *Teaching:* Lectr conserv painting, Hofstra Univ, 72-; fac mem conserv painting, New Sch, currently. *Awards:* Gold Medal for Best in Show, Am Vet Soc Artists, 66; Award of Excellence, Mainstreams '70, Marietta Col, 70; Samuel Morton Mem Award, Audubon Artists, 83. *Bibliog:* Cover Story, Pallette Talk, 80; Amy Pett (auth), Beneath suburban exterior are two dedicated artists, Port Washington News, 70; demonstr, Conservation of Paintings, Channel 21-TV, 77. *Mem:* Audubon Artists; Nat Acad Design; assoc Int Inst Conserv Artistic & Hist Works; fel Am Inst Conserv Artistic & Hist Works; Allied Artists Am (vpres, currently). *Media:* Oil on Canvas. *Publ:* Polyurethane Foam in the Process of Transfer, 10/14/73 & The Problem of Fungus Infestation of a Framed Pastel Portrait, 71, Bulletin Am Group, Int Inst Conserv Hist & Artists Works. *Mailing Add:* 64 Jane Ct Westbury NY 11590

HOOD, DOROTHY
PAINTER
b Bryan, Tex. *Study:* RI Sch Design, grad; Art Students League. *Work:* Mus Mod Art, New York; Whitney Mus Am Art, New York; Brooklyn Mus, NY; San Francisco Mus of Mod Art, Calif; Everson Mus, Syracuse, NY; and others. *Exhib:* One-man shows, Retrospective, Everson Mus, 72, Mus Fine Art, Houston, 76 & Meredith Long Contemporaries, NY, 78 & 80; Exhib New Work in Clay, Edmonton Art Gallery, 78; A Sense of Spirit, Paolo Soleri-Arcosanti, 81; The American's: Collage, Contemp Arts Mus, Houston, 82; Rutgers Univ, 82; Salzburg Kuntsverein, Villach, Austria, 83; and others. *Pos:* Set designer, Houston Ballet, Allen's Landing, 75, Royal Ontario Mus and Toronto Truck Theater, Royal Hunt of the Sun, 76. *Awards:* Childe Hassam Purchase Award, Am Acad Arts & Lett, 74. *Bibliog:* Philippe de Montebello (auth), Dorothy Hood, Haiti, a surrealist abstraction, Mus Fine Arts Bull, 71. *Media:* Oil, Ink. *Publ:* Auth, Sighting the invisible frontier, Art J, summer 80. *Dealer:* Meredith Long Houston Galleries 2323 San Felipe Houston TX 77019. *Mailing Add:* 819 Highland Houston TX 77006

HOOD, GRAHAM STANLEY
MUSEUM DIRECTOR, WRITER
b Stratford-on-Avon, England, Nov 6, 36; US citizen. *Study:* Keble Col, Oxford Univ, MA(mod hist); Courtauld Inst Art, London Univ. *Work:* Detroit Inst Art; Colonial Williamsburg Found, Va. *Pos:* Cur Europ decorative arts, Wadsworth Atheneum, Hartford, Conn, 61-64; assoc cur, Garvan Collection, Yale Univ Art Gallery, New Haven, 64-68; cur Am art, Detroit Inst Art, 68-71; vpres & dir collections, Colonial Williamsburg Found, 71- *Teaching:* Adj prof hist art, Wayne State Univ, Col William & Mary, Williamsburg, Va, 74- *Publ:* Auth, American Silver, a History of Style, 1650-1900, Praeger Publ, 71; coauth, The Garvan Collection of American Silver at Yale, Yale Univ Art Gallery, 71; auth, Bonnin and Morris of Philadelphia: The First American Porcelain Factory, Univ NC Press, 72; co-auth, The Williamsburg Collection of Antique Furnishings, 73 & auth, Charles Bridges and William Dering: Two Virginia Painters, 1735-1750, 78, Colonial Williamsburg Found; and others. *Mailing Add:* Colonial Williamsburg Found Williamsburg VA 23185

HOOD, MARY BRYAN
MUSEUM DIRECTOR, ADMINISTRATOR
b Central City, Ky, July 5, 38. *Study:* Ky Wesleyan Col, dipl(theatre), 60, dipl(art & art hist), 74. *Collections Arranged:* The American Artist Looks at the American Soldier: 1915-1975, 80; Mid America Biennial (auth, catalog), 80 & 82; The Regionalists: Three Dimensional Forms (auth, catalog), 81 & 83; The Kentucky Tradition in American Landscape Painting (coauth, catalog), 83; Kentucky Expatriates: In Major American Museum Collections (auth, catalog), 84. *Pos:* Exec dir, Owensboro Arts Comn, Ky, 73-77; founding dir, Owensboro Mus Fine Art, Ky, 77- *Mem:* Ky Asn Mus (pres, 81-83);

Southeast Mus Conf; Ky Art Educ Asn (mem exec bd, 80); Ky Arts Comn (mem bd, 77-78); Am Asn Mus. *Res:* Regional art with emphasis on art and artists with Kentucky connections. *Mailing Add:* 432 Maple Ave Owensboro KY 42301

HOOD, (THOMAS) RICHARD
PRINTMAKER, DESIGNER

b Philadelphia, Pa. *Study:* Univ Pa Sch Fine Arts; Philadelphia Mus Sch Art, BFA, 53. *Work:* Philadelphia Mus Art; Yale Univ Mus; Mus Mod Art, New York; Nat Portrait Gallery, Libr Cong, Washington, DC. *Exhib:* New Horizons, Mus Mod Art, New York, 36; Am Art Today, New York World's Fair, 39; Art Dirs Ann, Philadelphia, 52-72; Fabulous Decade, Smithsonian Inst, 64; Color Prints of Americas, NJ State Mus, Trenton & tour to mus in Hawaii, Alaska & nine cities in Japan, 70. *Pos:* Assoc dir advert design, Philadelphia Col Art, 57-60; dir exhibs, 67-; design consult, 67- *Teaching:* From instr to prof, Philadelphia Col Art, 51-82. *Awards:* Franklin Gold Medal, Printing Industs Philadelphia, 59, 69 & 70; Nat Graphic Arts Design Award, 68 & 70; Andy Award of Merit, 73. *Bibliog:* Gertrude Benson (auth), Tradition versus innovation, Pa Traveler, 5/59; Sam Gamburg (auth), Professor Hood and award winning invitation, Centennial News, spring 71; Victoria Donohoe (auth), Dick Hood's timeless, abstract, balancing act, Philadelphia Inquirer, 2/25/72. *Mem:* Philadelphia Art Alliance (chmn, 77, bd dirs, 79); Print Club Philadelphia; Am Color Print Soc (pres, 56-); fel Int Inst Arts & Lett; Wisdom Hall of Fame. *Mailing Add:* 1452 E Cheltenham Ave Philadelphia PA 19124

HOOD, WALTER KELLY
HISTORIAN, PAINTER

b Catawba Co, NC, Aug 19, 28. *Study:* Antioch Col, 48-49; Pa Acad Fine Arts, 49-53; Am Acad Rome, 53-55; Univ Pa, BFA, 57; Univ Hawaii, MFA, 61; Northwestern Univ, PhD(art hist), 66; mural studies with George Harding & Jean Charlot. *Work:* Pa Acad Fine Arts, Philadelphia; Fred T Foard Sch, Vale, NC; Corriher-Linn-Black Libr, Salisbury, NC. *Comn:* Six egg tempera murals, Christ's Life, Death & Resurrection, St Peter's Episcopal Church, Glenside, Pa, 57-58; three frescoes, Bd Regist for Engrs, Architects & Land Surveyors, Honolulu, 61. *Exhib:* III Mostra di Pittura Americana, Bordighera, Italy, 55; one-man exhib of mural designs, Archit League New York, 56; 152nd Ann Exhib, Pa Acad Fine Arts, 57; 1974 Grand Nat Exhib, Am Artists Prof League, Lever House, New York, 74. *Awards:* Cresson European Traveling Award, Pa Acad Fine Arts, 52 & Schiedt Foreign Traveling Award, 53; Abbey Mural Fel, Am Acad Rome, 53-54. *Bibliog:* Frederick Williams (auth), To the Glory of God: Glimpse of a Man (biog film), 70. *Mem:* Nat Soc Mural Painters; Am Artists Prof League; fel Am Acad Rome. *Media:* Fresco, Egg Tempera. *Res:* Definitive study of the art life of George Harding. *Publ:* Auth, Seventeen Hundred Syllables, 83 & Images in Ink, 83, private publ. *Mailing Add:* 2508 W Innes St Salisbury NC 28144

HOOK, FRANCES A
PAINTER, ILLUSTRATOR

b Ambler, Pa, Dec 24, 12. *Study:* Pa Mus Sch Art, Philadelphia, with Thornton Oakley & Henry C Pitz. *Work:* Standard Publ, Cincinnati, Ohio; Child's World, Elgin, Ill; Concordia Publ, St Louis, Mo; Hallmark Cards, Kansas City, Mo; also pvt collections. *Comn:* Steinway Piano advert featuring children & Gen Electric advert, N W Ayer Advert, Philadelphia; illus, Northern Tissue com & article in Teens of our Times, Good Housekeeping Mag. *Awards:* Mead Paper Co Ann Award; NY Advert Ann Award. *Media:* Pastel, Watercolor. *Publ:* Illusr, Fall, Winter, Summer, Spring is Here, 75, My Quiet Book, 77 & My Wonder Book, 77, Child's World; illusr, My Book of Special Days, 77 & My Jesus Book (in four lang), 77, Standard Publ; and others. *Mailing Add:* Ocean Point Rd East Boothbay ME 04544

HOOK, WALTER
PAINTER, PRINTMAKER

b Missoula, Mont, Apr 25, 19. *Study:* Univ Mont, BA, 42; Univ NMex, MA, 50, with Kenneth Adams & Randall Davey. *Work:* Cheney Cowles Mem Mus, Spokane, Wash; Butler Inst Am Art, Youngstown, Ohio; Springfield Art Mus, Mo; Richmond Art Mus, Va; Yellowstone Art Ctr, Billings, Mont. *Comn:* Stations of Cross (sculptures), St Anthony's Parish, Missoula, Mont, 63, mosaic, 64; mosaic, St Vincent de Paul Parish, Fed Way, Washington, DC, 65; low relief, Newman Ctr, Missoula, 65; low relief, Missoula Vo-Tech Ctr. *Exhib:* Butler Inst Am Art Ann, 64, 67 & 68; Pac Northwest Watercolor Soc Ann, Seattle, 68-79; Nat Watercolor Soc Ann, Los Angeles, 68-77; Pa Acad Fine Arts Ann, Philadelphia, 69; Am Watercolor Soc Ann, New York, 71-78. *Pos:* Sci illusr, Western Elec AEC Prog, Albuquerque, NMex, 51-54; art dir, Gen Elec AEC Prog, Richland, Wash, 54-55. *Teaching:* Prof painting & drawing, Univ Mont, 55-77. *Awards:* Watercolor USA Purchase Award, Springfield Art Mus, 71; Fred Marshall Watercolor Award, Northwest Watercolor Soc, Seattle, 71; Western States Art Found Cash Grant, 76. *Mem:* Ala Watercolor Soc; Nat Watercolor Soc; Philadelphia Watercolor Soc; Artists Equity Asn; Assoc Nat Acad. *Media:* Watercolor, Oil; Lithography. *Mailing Add:* PO Box 3238 Missoula MT 59806

HOOKHAM, ELEANOR KING See King, Eleanor

HOOKS, CHARLES VERNON
DEALER, COLLECTOR

b Houston, Tex, Aug 8, 30. *Study:* Univ Tex, 48; Univ Houston, 51. *Pos:* Pres, Hooks-Epstein Galleries, Houston. *Mem:* Houston Art Dealers Asn (pres, founder). *Specialty:* Prints, drawings and sculpture of 20th century; publisher and distributor of original graphics. *Collection:* Works on paper of 20th century American and European masters and sculpture from the 1950s. *Mailing Add:* 1200 Bissonnet Houston TX 77005

HOOKS, EARL J
EDUCATOR, SCULPTOR

b Baltimore, Md, Aug 2, 27. *Study:* Howard Univ, BAE; Cath Univ; Rochester Inst of Technol, NY, cert. *Work:* DePauw Univ, Greencastle, Ind; Harmon Found, New York; City of Gary, Ind; State of Tenn Arts Comn. *Comn:* Ceramic sculpture, State Gift to Gov Ray Blanton, Tanzania, 77. *Exhib:* Howard Univ Invitational, 61; 21st Syracuse Biennial Traveling Exhib, Smithsonian Inst, 61-62; Int Minerals & Chemicals, Skokie, Ill, 66; three-man show, Art Inst Chicago, 67; Ball State Mus, Muncie, Ind, 69; Two Centuries of Black Am Art, Los Angeles Co Mus Art, 76; Dallas Mus Fine Arts, 77; High Mus, Atlanta, 77; Brooklyn Mus, 77. *Teaching:* Instr ceramics & drawing, Shaw Univ, Raleigh, NC, 53-54; instr & art consult, Gary Pub Schs, Ind, 59-68; instr ceramics & drawing, Ind Univ, Gary, 64-67; assoc prof sculpture & ceramics & chmn dept art, Fisk Univ, 68- *Awards:* Second Prize, Arts & Crafts, John Herron Art Sch, 59; Purchase Prize, Dedication of Art Bldg, Howard Univ, 60; Cert of Honor, Int Festival of Lagos, Nigerian Govt, 77. *Bibliog:* Cedric Dover (auth), American Negro Art, 60; Elton Fax (auth), Seventeen Black Artists, Dodd-Mead, 71; Bruno Bak (auth), The Rites of Color and Form, Fisk Univ, 74. *Media:* Ceramics. *Publ:* Coauth, Extended Services in Museum Science Training, 72 & Ben Jones (catalog), 77, Fisk Univ. *Mailing Add:* 935 18th Ave Nashville TN 37208

HOOKS, GERI (GERALDINE LEE)
DEALER, COLLECTOR

b Houston, Tex, Apr 24, 35. *Study:* Stephens Col, AA, 53; Tex Univ. *Mem:* Houston Art Dealers Asn (founder). *Specialty:* Prints, drawings and sculpture by 20th century European masters. *Collection:* Sculpture and works on paper. *Mailing Add:* Hooks-Epstein Galleries Inc 1200 Bissonnet Houston TX 77005

HOOPER, JACK MEREDITH
PAINTER, PRINTMAKER

b Los Angeles, Calif, Aug 26, 28. *Study:* Los Angeles City Col, AA(art), 51; Col Am, Mexico City, asst to Siqueiros, BA(art; cum laude), 52; Acad Julian, Paris, with Chaplin Midi & Pierre Jerome, 54; Univ Calif, Los Angeles, MA(art), 56. *Work:* Lannan Found, Fla; Stanford Univ Mus; Long Beach Mus; Univ Calif, Los Angeles & Santa Cruz. *Exhib:* The Artist's Environment--The West Coast, Oakland Art Mus, Amon Carter Mus, Ft Worth & Univ Calif, Los Angeles Galleries, 62; Fifty Calif Artists, Whitney Mus Am Art, Albright Art Gallery & Walker Art Ctr, 62-63; Art Across America, San Francisco Mus Mod Art & Knoedlers Galleries, New York, 65-66; retrospective, Smith & Cowell Gallery, Santa Cruz & Univ Santa Cruz, 75; Sixth Hawaii Nat Print Exhib, Honolulu Acad Art, 82. *Pos:* Dir, Sculptural Walls, Los Angeles, 62-66. *Teaching:* Asst prof art, Univ Calif, Los Angeles, 57-62; vis prof, Univ Colo, Boulder, 62; prof, chmn dept & dir art galleries, Mt St Marys Col, 63-69; prof, Univ Calif, Santa Cruz, 76. *Awards:* New Talent in America--Top 100 in Nation, Art in Am, 57; Los Angeles Ann Award Painting, 59; Purchase Award, Long Beach Mus Art, 65. *Bibliog:* Jack Hooper, Univ Calif, Santa Cruz, 75. *Mem:* World Print Coun. *Mailing Add:* c/o Vorpal Gallery 393 Grove St San Francisco CA 94102

HOOTON, BRUCE DUFF
EDITOR, PUBLISHER

b Waukegan, Ill, Dec 11, 28. *Study:* Southwestern Col, 46-50; Memphis Acad Arts, 48-50; Harvard Univ, scholar, 51-52. *Collections Arranged:* Sculptors Guild Bryant Park Exhibition, in association with New York Cultural Affairs, 67; Niezvestny (modern Russian sculpture), Sculptors Guild, New York, 68; Drawing Society Regional Drawing Exhib (8 museums), Am Fedn Arts, 70-72; Venice Biennale, Castelli Gallery, 73; Benito Retrospective, New York Cult Ctr, 74. *Pos:* Ed & auth, Drawing Mag, 57-60; art critic, ed & reviewer, New York Herald Tribune, 62-65; head New York off, Archives Am Art, 65-66; ed, Art News, 68-69; assoc, Lee Ault & Co, 71-; ed & pub, Art World Newspaper, New York. *Mem:* Drawing Soc (vpres, 75); NY State Coun Arts. *Specialty:* Twentieth century paintings, sculpture and drawings; French and European masters; South American masters; young masters. *Publ:* Ed, Drawings of Edwin Dickinson, Yale Univ, 60; ed, Mother & Child in Modern Art, Duell, Sloan & Pearce, 64; ed, American Paintings in Reynolda House, Reynolda House, 70. *Mailing Add:* Art World 1295 Madison Ave New York NY 10028

HOOVER, FRANCIS LOUIS
COLLECTOR, APPRAISER

b Sherman, Tex, Mar 12, 13. *Study:* NTex State Univ, BS, 33; Columbia Univ, MA, 35; Art Students League, 40-41; New Sch Social Res, 40-41; NY Univ, DEd, 41. *Pos:* Dir, LaSalle Art Gallery, 33-36; ed, Arts & Activities Mag, 52-67; dir, Fairway Gallery, 62-67. *Teaching:* Asst prof art, NTex State Univ, 36-40; asst prof art, Eastern Ill State Univ, 41-44; prof art, Ill State Univ, 44-73, dir, Univ Mus, 72-73. *Awards:* Award of Merit for Ed Excellence, Indust Mkt 6th Ann, 54. *Mem:* Appraisers Asn Am; Am Soc Appraisers; Int Platform Asn. *Collection:* Art of the Cuna Indians; pre-Columbian ceramics and jade; primitive arts of Africa and Oceania; folk arts of Middle America; works are in permanent collections of Philadelphia Museum of Art, Cleveland Museum of Art, Art Institute of Chicago, Field Museum of Natural History, Peabody Museum, Smithsonian Inst and others. *Publ:* Auth, Art Activities for the Very Young, 62; auth, Young Printmakers I, 63; auth, Young Printmakers II, 64; auth, Young Sculptors, 67; auth, African Art, 74; and others. *Mailing Add:* 1770 Avenida del Mundo #1405 Coronado CA 92118

HOOVER, JOHN JAY
SCULPTOR, PAINTER
b Cordova, Alaska, Oct 13, 19. *Study:* Derbyshire Sch of Fine Arts, Seattle, Wash. *Work:* Bur Indian Affairs, Washington, DC; Seattle Art Mus, Wash; Gulf Paper Co; Heard Mus, Phoenix, Ariz; King Co & Seattle Art Comm. *Comn:* Mural, Tyonck Tribe, Anchorage, Alaska, 64; mobile, James Bialac, Ariz, 76; mural, City Light Co, Seattle, 77. *Exhib:* Sculpture I & Sculpture II, Heard Mus, Phoenix, Ariz, 73 & 74; one-man shows, Whatcom Co Mus, Bellingham, Wash & Mus of Plains Indians, Browning, Mont, 75; Sculpture Invitational, Heard Mus, Phoenix, Ariz, 77. *Teaching:* Artist-in-residence sculpture, Inst of Am Indian Art, Santa Fe, NMex, 72 & DOD Sch Syst, Japan, Taiwan & the Philippines, 74; instr, Northern Ariz Univ, Flagstaff, 79. *Awards:* First Prize/Sculpture, Cent Wash State Col, 73; Philbrook Art Ctr, Tulsa, Okla, 74 & Heard Mus, Phoenix, Ariz, 75. *Dealer:* Sacred Circle Gallery Am Indian Art 2223 4th Ave Seattle WA 98121; Stonington Gallery 2030 1st Ave Seattle WA. *Mailing Add:* 841 W Stadium Grapeview WA 98546

HOOWIJ, JAN
PAINTER
b Hengelo, Holland, Sept 13, 07. *Study:* Acad Fine Arts, The Hague, Holland, BA; Acad Grande Chaumiere, Paris; also painting with Henk Meyer, Holland. *Work:* Brooklyn Mus; Joslyn Mem Mus, Omaha; Art Ctr, Tulsa, Okla; Honolulu Acad Art. *Comn:* Portrait of Mayor Wagner, New York, 55; portrait of Gov Allred, Fed Courthouse, Corpus Christi, Tex, 59; mosaic mural, Ardmore Develop Co, Phoenix, 61 & Hollywood, 62; portrait of Neil Jacoby, Sch Bus Admin, Univ Calif, Los Angeles, 71. *Exhib:* Rijksmuseum Nat Show, Amsterdam, Holland, 35; Brooklyn Mus Regional Show, 42; Int Marine Art Show, Palais Chaillot, Paris, 46; Carnegie Inst Nat Ann, Pittsburgh, 47; Los Angeles Co Art Mus Regional Ann, 56. *Teaching:* Instr figure, Acad Fine Arts, The Hague, 31-34; pvt instr painting, 52-57. *Awards:* Royal Subsidy for Artists, Holland, 31-34; Therese Van Duyl Schwartz Prize for Best Portrait in Holland, 36; Purchase Prize, Witte Mem Mus, 59. *Bibliog:* Janice Lovoos (auth), The paintings of Jan Hoowij, Am Artist Mag, 8/65. *Media:* Oil, Acrylic. *Dealer:* Emerson Gallery 18676 Ventura Blvd Los Angeles CA 91356; Serisawa Gallery 8320 Melrose Ave Los Angeles CA 90069. *Mailing Add:* 16614 Chaplin Ave Encino CA 91436

HOPKINS, BENJAMIN
LIBRARIAN, ADMINISTRATOR
b Manchester, NH, Apr 20, 36. *Study:* New Eng Conserv of Music; Univ NH, BA; Univ RI, MLS. *Pos:* Librn, Mass Col Art, Boston, 67- *Mem:* Art Librn Soc NAm. *Res:* Design education. *Mailing Add:* 694 Windwood Dr Tiverton RI 02878

HOPKINS, BUDD
PAINTER
b Wheeling, WVa, June 15, 31. *Study:* Oberlin Col, BA, 53; Columbia Univ, with Meyer Schapiro, 53-54. *Work:* Whitney Mus Am Art, Guggenheim Mus Art, New York; San Francisco Mus Art; Corcoran Gallery Art, Hirshhorn Mus, Washington, DC. *Comn:* Oil painting, WVa State Humanities Coun, 72. *Exhib:* Solo exhibs, Lerner-Heller Gallery, New York, 77, 78 & 80, Middlebury Col, 78; Longpoint Gallery, Provincetown, 78 & 80, Colburn Gallery, Univ Vt, 80 & Frank Fedele Fine Arts, New York, 81; and many others. *Teaching:* Docent, Mus Mod Art, summers 55-56; docent, Whitney Mus Am Art, 57-60; instr, Pratt Inst, Provincetown, summer 75; instr, RI Sch Design, Provincetown, summer 75. *Awards:* Guggenheim Fcl, 75; Nat Endowment Arts Award, 79. *Bibliog:* Brian O'Doherty (auth), Budd Hopkins, master of a movement manque, Object & Idea, 67; April Kingsley (auth), Energy and order--the paintings of Budd Hopkins, Art Int, 4/73; Peter Frank (auth), Budd Hopkins: The works on paper, Kresge Art Ctr Bull, 4/74. *Mem:* Provincetown Art Asn (hon vpres, 68-70 & 77-79). *Media:* Oil, Acrylic. *Publ:* Auth, First person singular, Art Gallery Mag, 4/72; coauth, Concept vs art object, Arts Mag, 4/72; auth, Budd Hopkins on Budd Hopkins, Art in Am, 7-8/73; contribr, Roundtable on painting, 9/75, Richard Diebenkorn & Franz Kline, 79, Artforum; and others. *Dealer:* William Zierler Gallery 956 Madison Ave New York NY 10021. *Mailing Add:* 246 W 16th St New York NY 10011

HOPKINS, HENRY TYLER
MUSEUM DIRECTOR, EDUCATOR
b Idaho Falls, Idaho, Aug 14, 28. *Study:* Art Inst Chicago, BAE & MAE; Univ Calif, Los Angeles. *Collections Arranged:* 30 California Artists, 61; Reuben Nakian, 62; Josef Albers: White Line Squares (with catalog), 66; Robert Rauschenberg: Selections, 69; Milton Resnick: Large Paintings (with catalog), 71; Irwin-Wheeler, 72; Joe Goode: Work Until Now (with catalog), 73; Clyfford Still (with catalog), 75; Painting & Sculpture in California: The Modern Era (with catalog), 76; Philip Guston (with catalog), 80. *Pos:* Head educ, Los Angeles Co Mus Art, Los Angeles, 61-65; cur exhib, 65-68; dir, Ft Worth Art Mus, Tex, 68-74; dir, San Francisco Mus Mod Art, 74- *Teaching:* Instr art hist & theory, Univ Calif, Los Angeles Exten, 58-68; instr art hist, Tex Christian Univ, 68-73. *Awards:* Order of Leopold II, Knight. *Mem:* Asn Art Mus Dirs; Col Art Asn; Am Asn Mus; Western Asn Art Mus (pres, 77-78). *Res:* Twentieth century art of California; modern art. *Publ:* Contribr, Art in Am, Art News & Artforum Mag, 61-75. *Mailing Add:* San Francisco Mus Art Van Ness Ave at McAllister St San Francisco CA 94102

HOPKINS, KENDAL COLES
PAINTER
b Haddonfield, NJ, Jan 6, 08. *Study:* Pa Acad Fine Arts; Acad Grande Chaumiere, Paris. *Work:* Woodmere Art Gallery, Philadelphia; plus many pvt collections. *Comn:* Many pvt portrait & landscape comns. *Exhib:* Pa Acad Fine Arts Ann, Philadelphia; Philadelphia Mus Art, Pa; Nat Acad Design, New York; Ivan Spence Gallery, Ibiza, Spain; one-man show, Farnsworth Mus, Rockland, Maine; plus 15 other one-man shows. *Teaching:* Instr painting, Bryn Mawr Col, Pa; head dept art, Baldwin Sch, Bryn Mawr, Pa; instr art, Fieldston Sch, New York. *Mem:* Pa Acad Fine Arts; Philadelphia Mus; Peal Club, Philadelphia. *Dealer:* Hahn Gallery 8439 Germantown Ave Philadelphia PA 19118. *Mailing Add:* Maisfield Rd Phoenixville PA 19460

HOPKINS, KENNETH R
MUSEUM DIRECTOR
b Springfield, Mass, Aug 24, 22. *Study:* Pratt Inst; Univ Vt; Parsons Sch of Design; NY Univ, BS; Univ Wis, MS. *Pos:* Art dir, Univ Wis, Madison, 48-50; cur exhib, State Hist Soc Wis, Madison, 50-52; art dir, Old Sturbridge Village, Mass, 52-56; cur, Buffalo & Erie Co Hist Co, Buffalo, NY, 56-60; hist preservationist, Bethelehm Steel Co, Pa, 60-62; dir, Explorers Hall, Nat Geog Soc, Washington, DC, 62-65; dir, State Capitol Mus, 65-82; retired; woodcarver and restorer, currently. *Mailing Add:* 3001 Monte Vista Olympia WA 98501

HOPKINS, PETER
PAINTER, WRITER
b New York, NY, Dec 18, 11. *Study:* Art Students League. *Work:* Mus City of New York. *Comn:* Landscapes, Theatre Guild, New York, 49; portraits, 50; mural, comn by Stewart Chaney, New York, 54; mural, comn by Gino di Grandi, 55; illus, RCA Victor Corp, New York, 56. *Exhib:* Artists Equity, Whitney Mus Am Art, 51, Contemp Painting, 52; Ward Eggleston Galleries, New York, 58-65; Jr League of Buffalo, NY, 60; Women's Club of Westport, NY, 61; Am Mural Painters Asn, 76; Distinguished Mid-Atlantic Artists, Univ Del, 80; and many others. *Pos:* Supvr libr, NY Univ, 53; asst dir, Mortimer Brandt Gallery, 53-58; art consult, Nabisco Co, 76; dir, Peter Hopkins Workshop, 76- *Teaching:* Instr drawing & painting, Moore Inst Art, Sci & Indust, 49-50; instr, Newark Acad Art, 50; instr, Cartoonists & Illusr Sch, New York, 51; instr art, New York-Phoenix Schs Design, 61-77; chmn dept fine art & dean of men; asst prof art hist, Pratt Inst, 75-77; lectr perspective, Art Students League, 75- *Awards:* Art Grant, Am Acad Arts & Lett, 50; Art Grant, Nat Inst Arts & Lett, 50. *Bibliog:* The artist & the Copa girls, See, 53; C B (auth), Art exhibition notes, New York Herald Tribune, 1/25/58; History of Union Square (film), 78. *Mem:* Life mem Art Students League. *Media:* Oil, Chinese Ink. *Publ:* and others. *Dealer:* Grand Central Art Galleries 50 E 50th St New York NY 10022. *Mailing Add:* 36 Horatio St New York NY 10014

HOPKINSON, HAROLD I
PAINTER, COLLECTOR
b Salt Lake City, Utah, Aug 8, 18. *Study:* Univ Wyo, BA & MA; Art Ctr Sch, Los Angeles; Brigham Young Univ; also with Paul Bransom, O Conrad Schwiering & Robert W Meyers. *Work:* Church of Jesus Christ of Latter Day Saints, Historical Ctr, Salt Lake City; USAF Acad, Colorado Springs, Colo; Marriott Hotel, Salt Lake City; Hotel Utah, Salt Lake; Cult Ctr Am Embassy Prague. *Comn:* Mural & four paintings, Col Bus Admin, Ariz State Univ, 71; painting, Frontier Airlines, 76; mural, Blue Cross & Blue Shield, 81; paintings, Husky Oil Co, Can, 81; murals, Cody Latter Day Saints Visitors Ctr, Wyo, 82. *Exhib:* Whitney Gallery Western Art, 72; C M Russell Gallery & Mus, Great Falls, 73-74. *Pos:* Contribr & illusr, Nat Fedn State High Sch Asn, 63-70. *Awards:* Gold Medal Award, First Place Oil Painting, Western Artists Asn MGM Grand, Reno, Nev, 80 & 82-83; Gold Medal Classic, Nat Western & Wildlife, Cody, Wyo, 79; Silver Medal for Oil Painting, St George Art Festival, 80. *Bibliog:* Lucille N Patrick (auth), Hopkinson, Wyoming Artist, Western Horseman, 68; Royal B Hassrick (auth), Western Painting Today, Watson-Guptill, 75; South West Art Mag, 76. *Mem:* Life mem Nat Cowboy Hall of Fame & Western Heritage Ctr. *Media:* Oil. *Collection:* Paintings by Ken Riley, Robert Meyers, Harley Brown, Edward Grigware, James Bama, Ron Crook, Newman Myrah and others; historical paintings and studies of river life during 1840's on Mississippi from St Paul to St Louis. *Publ:* Contribr, Western Horseman, 68-74, Wyoming the Proud Land, 70 & Westerner, 74; illusr, Wyoming, Wild & Wooley, 83. *Mailing Add:* Box 175 Byron WY 82412

HOPPER, FRANK J
PAINTER, MURALIST
b Evansville, Ind, Oct 15, 24. *Study:* Ind Univ, BFA; Art Inst Chicago; Am Acad Art, Chicago. *Work:* Famous Am Series, Historic Mus, Washington, *Comn:* 200 paintings, Archdiocese of Chicago, 67; mural & 14 stations of the cross, St Mary Star of the Sea Catholic Church, Longboat Key, Fla, 78; mag covers, Yachting; portrait, Pres Reagan, now in White House; The Story of Israel, Technion; and others. *Media:* Acrylic, Watercolor. *Publ:* Illusr, co-auth, ed or contribr to various publ including Chicago publs & newspapers, Western Publ Co, Chicago Tribune, Art Inst Chicago & books for Chicago Area Sch TV. *Mailing Add:* PO Box 1806 Sarasota FL 33578

HOPPER, MARIANNE SEWARD
PAINTER
b Rochester, NY, June 10, 04. *Study:* Cleveland Sch Art; RI Sch Design; Montclair Art Mus, with Michael Lenson, also portraits with Douglas Prizer, acrylics with Tom Vincent, watercolors with Avery Johnson & sculpture with Ulric Ellerhausen. *Work:* Pvt collections in NJ, NMex, Calif, Fla, Ohio & Ill. *Comn:* Paintings for private individuals and businesses, 64-75. *Exhib:* Nat Miniature Art Show, Bellair, Fla, 75; Nat Am Artists Prof League Lever House Show, New York, 75; Am Artists Prof League, World Trade Ctr, 80; Nat Miniature Show, Nutley, NJ, 81; Int Miniature Show, Clearwater, Fla, 81; and others. *Awards:* Best in Show, Garden State Plaza, Paramus, NJ, 64; Purchase Awards, McBride Agency, Franklin Lakes, NJ, 71 & 72; ITT Space

Award, Int Tel & Tel Defense Space Group, Nutley, NJ, 73. *Bibliog:* Mary Clemens (auth), article, Herald News, Passaic, NJ, 65; Michael Lenson (auth), article, Newark Eve News, 68; article, NJ Music & Arts Mag, 73. *Mem:* Am Artists Prof League; Miniature Art Socs of NJ & Fla; Nutley Art Group, NJ. *Media:* Acrylic, Oil. *Mailing Add:* 121A Edinburgh Lane Lakewood NJ 08701

HOPPES, LOWELL E
CARTOONIST
b Alliance, Ohio, July 1, 13. *Pos:* Freelance cartooning for 50 yrs. *Publ:* Created over 36,000 cartoons in Colliers, Post, American, Esquire, New Yorker, Farm Jour, Parade, Family Weekly, King Features Syndicate, New Woman & others worldwide; cartoons for advertisers in numerous fields. *Mailing Add:* 642 Calle del Otono Sarasota FL 33581

HOPTNER, RICHARD
SCULPTOR
b Philadelphia, Pa, Apr 3, 21. *Study:* Univ Pa, 51-57; Cranbrook Acad Art, scholar, 60. *Work:* Philadelphia Civic Ctr Mus. *Exhib:* Philadelphia Mus Art, 61; Pa Acad Fine Arts, 69; Haverford Col, 74; Gallerie Illien, Atlanta, Ga; one-man show, Greenville Co Mus Art, Greenville, SC, 79; Allentown Mus Fine Arts, Pa, 83. *Teaching:* Instr 3-D design, Univ Pa, 68-70. *Awards:* Sculpture Grant, Louis Comfort Tiffany Found, 64. *Bibliog:* New forms-new materials (film), Pa Acad Fine Arts, 69; Sculpture at St Joseph College, WCAU TV, 69. *Media:* Teakwood, Rare Woods. *Publ:* Auth, Anti-art/anti-life, Great Speckled Bird, Atlanta, Ga, 70. *Dealer:* Judith Anne Munroe 714 W 3rd St Lansdale PA 19446. *Mailing Add:* 5000 Knox St Philadelphia PA 19144

HOREIS, WILLIAM RICHARD, SR
PHOTOGRAPHER, PRINTMAKER
b New York, NY, Oct 11, 45. *Work:* Jane Corkin Gallery, Art Gallery Ont, Ont Arts Coun, Toronto; Nat Film Bd Can, Ottawa; Bibliot Nat, Paris. *Exhib:* Exposure, 75 & Focal Point, 77, Art Gallery Ont; Arte Fiera 77, Bologna, Italy, 77; Art 77, Basel, Switz, 77; three-person exhib, Nat Film Bd Can Traveling Exhib, 79-84; Opening Exhib, 79 & Salon D'Ete, 80, Jane Corkin Gallery, Toronto. *Teaching:* Guest lectr, York Univ, Toronto, 75; Ont Col Art, Toronto, 75 & 79 & Ctr Creative Studies, Detroit, 76. *Awards:* Grants, Ont Arts Coun, 75 & 78 & Can Coun, 76. *Bibliog:* A Freedman (auth), Photogrpahy as an art form and as an investment, 9/75 & The frozen image: Renaissance, 5/77, Toronto Life Mag. *Media:* Carbro Process. *Publ:* Auth, Carbon-Carbro, A history and the method, 76 & coauth, Carbon images, 76, Camera, Can. *Dealer:* Jane Corkin Gallery 144 Front St W Suite 620 Toronto ON M5J 1G2. *Mailing Add:* 86 Beresford Ave Toronto ON M6S 3B1 Canada

HORN, BRUCE
PRINTMAKER, EDUCATOR
b Circleville, Ohio, June 30, 46. *Study:* Miami Univ, BFA; Ohio State Univ, with Sidney Chafetz, David Driesbach & Andrew Rush, MFA. *Work:* Kalamazoo Inst Art, Mich; Tyler Sch Art, Philadelphia; Philadelphia Mus Art; Univ Ariz; Drake Univ, Des Moines, Iowa; and others. *Exhib:* Mid-Am Exhib: Mid-Am 4, St Louis Art Mus, Mo, 72; Fifth Hawaii Nat Print Exhib, Honolulu Acad Arts, 79; Colorprint USA, Tex Tech Univ, Lubbock; Norwegian Int Print Biennale, Fredrikstad, 80; British Int Print Biennale, Bradford, 82; Prints: USA, Pratt Graphics Ctr, New York, 82; one-man show, Univ Ariz, 82; and others; Colorprint USA, Tex Tech Univ, Lubbock; Norwegian Int Print Biennale, Fredrikstad, Norway, 80; plus many others. *Pos:* Package designer, Diamond Nat Paper Co, Middletown, Ohio, summer 68; art dir, Eighth Ann Flagstaff Summer Festival, Ariz, 74. *Teaching:* Assoc prof printmaking, Blackburn Col, Carlinville, Ill, 70-72 & Northern Ariz Univ, 72- *Awards:* Purchase Awards, Trenton State Col, NJ, 80; Honolulu Academy of Arts, Hawaii, 80; Purchase Award, Int Exhib Prints, Wesleyan Col, Macon, 83. *Mem:* Am Color Print Soc; Los Angeles Printmaking Soc; World Print Council; The Print Club; Col Art Assoc Am. *Media:* Color Intaglio & Lithography. *Dealer:* Associated American Artists 663 5th Ave New York NY 10022. *Mailing Add:* 1625 N Sunset Dr Flagstaff AZ 86001

HORN, MILTON
SCULPTOR, WRITER
b Russia, Sept 1, 06; US citizen. *Study:* With Henry H Kitson, Boston; Beaux Arts Inst Design, New York; Olivet Col, Mich, Hon DFA, 76. *Work:* Brookgreen Gardens, SC; Nat Mus Fine Arts, Washington, DC; Olivet Col; Smithsonian Inst Div Numismatics; Nat Acad Design, New York. *Comn:* Three symbolic bronze groups hq bldg, Nat Cong Parents & Teachers, Chicago, 53-54; eight marble reliefs, WVa Univ Med Ctr, 54-59; symbolic bronze on facade & holy ark in sanctuary, B'nai Israel Temple, Charleston, WVa, 59-60; Hymn to Water (bronze), Central Water Filtration Plant, Chicago, 65; bronze, Nat Bank Commerce, Charleston, WVa, 68-69. *Exhib:* American Art Today, New York World's Fair, 39 & 40; Third Int Exhib Sculpture, Philadelphia Mus Fine Arts, 49; American Sculpture--1951, Metrop Mus, New York, 51; Chicago & Vicinity Exhib, Art Inst Chicago, 52; Nat Inst Arts & Lett, New York, 53, 55 & 77. *Teaching:* Artist in residence & prof art, Olivet Col, 39-49. *Awards:* Award Excellence, Chicago chap Am Inst Archit, 55; Nat Citation Honor, Nat Conf, Am Inst Architects, Washington, DC, 57; Henry Hering Mem Medal, Nat Sculpture Soc, New York, 72. *Bibliog:* Avram Kampf (auth), Contemporary Synagogue Art, Union Am Hebrew Congregations, 61; Cecil Roth (ed), History of Jewish Art, 61 & 71 & Louis Redstone (auth), Art in Architecture, 68, McGraw-Hill. *Mem:* Founding mem Sculptors Guild; nat academician Col Art Asn Am; fel Nat Sculpture Soc. *Media:* Bronze, Wood. *Publ:* Contribr, Proceedings of Teachers Seminar, Col Schs Archit, Aspen, Colo, 57; contribr, The Christian Century, 2/59; contribr, New City-Men in Metropolis, 64; contribr, Indland Architect, 65; contribr, Nat Sculpture Rev, 72. *Mailing Add:* 1932 N Lincoln Ave Chicago IL 60614

HORNADAY, RICHARD HOYT
PAINTER, EDUCATOR
b Joplin, Mo, Aug 15, 27. *Study:* State Univ Iowa, BFA & MFA; Art Inst Chicago. *Work:* State Univ Iowa Collection, Iowa City; Turner Print Gallery, Calif State Univ, Chico; Shasta Col Collection, Redding, Calif. *Exhib:* Recent Painting, USA, The Figure (catalog), Mus Mod Art, New York, 65; 23rd Am Drawing Biennial, Norfolk Mus, Va, 69; Nat Small Painting Exhib, Univ of the Pac, Stockton, 70; Fifty Years of Crocker-Kingsley (retrospective, catalog), Crocker Art Gallery, Sacramento, 75; Nat Drawing & Painting Exhib, Southeastern Mass Univ, 81; 30-Year Retrospective Survey, Redding Mus & Art Ctr, Calif, 83; and others. *Teaching:* Instr drawing-painting, Shasta Col, 56-63; grad adv, Calif State Univ, Chico, 68-72, prof, Grad Studios, 68-, chmn dept art, 72-80. *Awards:* Kingsley Exhib & Nat Coun Arts Exhib, Sacramento. *Bibliog:* Alfred Frankenstein (auth), Ruthermore Gallery--Richard Hornaday, San Francisco Chronicle, 62. *Media:* Watercolor. *Dealer:* The Watercolor Gallery 1959 Addison Berkeley CA 94704. *Mailing Add:* Dept of Art Calif State Univ Chico CA 95929

HORNAK, IAN JOHN
PAINTER
b Philadelphia, Pa, Jan 9, 44. *Study:* Univ Mich; Wayne State Univ, BFA, MFA. *Work:* Corcoran Gallery Art, Washington, DC; Indianapolis Mus Art, Ind; Canton Art Inst, Ohio; Owens Corning Fiberglas Corp, Toledo, Ohio; Albrecht Art Mus, St Joseph, Mo. *Exhib:* The Realist Revival, Am Fedn Arts Traveling Exhib, 72-75; one-man shows, Gertrude Kasle Gallery, Detroit, 74, Fischbach Gallery, New York, 77, 79 & 81, A J Wood Gallery, Philadelphia, 79 & Marie Selby Mus Art, Sarasota, Fla, 80; and others. *Teaching:* Instr drawing, Wayne State Univ, Detroit, Mich, 65-67 Henry Ford Col, Dearborn, Mich, 66-; A J Wood Gallery, Philadelphia, 79. *Media:* Acrylic. *Dealer:* Fischbach Gallery 29 W 57th St New York NY 10022. *Mailing Add:* Box 1371 East Hampton NY 11937

HORNE, (ARTHUR EDWARD) CLEEVE
PAINTER, SCULPTOR
b Jamaica, BWI, Jan 9, 12. *Study:* Ont Col Art, AOCA; also with D Dick, Eng & Europe. *Work:* Nat Gallery Can. *Comn:* Alexander Bell Mem, Brantford, Ont; War Mem, Law Soc Upper Can; Shakespeare Mem; Stratford, Ont; and others. *Exhib:* Nat Gallery Can; Royal Can Acad Arts, 28-; Ont Soc Artists, 39; Sculptors' Soc Can, 35- *Pos:* Art adv, Ont Hydro-Elec Power Comn, St Lawrence Seaway Power House Proj, 57-58; art consult, Imperial Oil Bldg, Toronto; art consult, Can Imperial Bank Com, 61-63; mem art consult comt, York Univ, 63-; art consult, Queen's Park Proj, Ont Govt, 66-69. *Awards:* Allied Arts Medals, Royal Archit Inst Can, 63, Royal Can Acad of Arts & Silver Jubilee. *Mem:* Ont Soc Artists; Arts & Lett Club (pres, 55-57); Royal Can Acad Arts. *Mailing Add:* 181 Balmoral Ave Toronto ON M4V 1J8 Canada

HORNUNG, CLARENCE PEARSON
DESIGNER, WRITER
b New York, NY, June 12, 1899. *Study:* Cooper Union, Baccalaureate Award; Art Students League; City Col New York, BS(Townsend Harris Medal), 20. *Work:* New York Pub Libr; Springfield Mus, Mass; Newark Pub Libr, NJ; NY State Mus, Albany; Nat Gallery Art, Washington, DC. *Mem:* Am Inst Graphic Artists; Typophiles. *Publ:* Auth, Background Patterns & Textures, Dover Publ, 76; auth, The Way It Was: New York, 1850-1890, Schocken Bks, 77; auth, The American Eagle in Art and Design, Dover Publ, 78; auth, The Way It Was in the USA, Abbeville Press, 78; auth, Italian Sketchbook, David R Godine Inc, 84; and many others. *Mailing Add:* 12 Glen Rd West Hempstead NY 11552

HORNUNG, GERTRUDE SEYMOUR
LECTURER, COLLECTOR
b Boston, Mass. *Study:* Wellesley Col, AB; Case Western Reserve Univ, MA & PhD(visual arts), 49. *Pos:* Founder & chmn, Jr Coun, Cleveland, 41-42; deleg, White House Conf Educ, Washington, DC, 55; pres, Adult Educ Coun Greater Cleveland, 56-58; founder & chmn, Greater Cleveland Educ TV Comt, 58-60; trustee, Cleveland Area Arts Coun, 75-79; consult to dir-gen, Mus Iran, 75; deleg, Int Coun Mus Cont, USSR, 77 & London, Eng, 83. *Teaching:* Lectr art hist, Cleveland Mus Art, 37-45, supvr, 45-60; free lance writer & lectr, 60-; lectr, John Carroll Univ, 72-81, Dublin, Ireland, Rome, Italy & Tehran, Iran, 74-75, Honolulu, 74-83 & Bangkok, Thailand, 78. *Awards:* Ital Ministry Foreign Affairs Res Grant, 62. *Mem:* Cleveland Mus Art; Asia Soc; Japan Soc; Am Arts Coun; Honolulu Acad Arts. *Res:* History of Italian art; art of the South Seas, especially Polynesia & Melanesia; contemporary American art; interrelations arts of East and West; art of Ancient Iran. *Collection:* Contemporary Italian, Japanese and American paintings, prints and ceramics. *Publ:* Auth & ed, Cultural Directory of Greater Cleveland, 47; contribr, articles on art history and education in art museums, var mags & journals, 50-83. *Mailing Add:* 2240 Elandon Dr Cleveland OH 44106

HOROWITZ, BENJAMIN
ADMINISTRATOR, DEALER
b New York, NY, Mar 13, 12. *Study:* Jamaica Teachers Col, cert; City Col New York, BA; NY Univ. *Pos:* Pres, Art Dealers Asn Southern Calif, 70-80; chmn appraisal comt; dir, Heritage Gallery. *Mem:* Los Angeles Co Mus Print Coun; Univ Calif, Los Angeles Print Coun; Calif Confederation Arts. *Res:* American art. *Specialty:* American artists; international prints. *Publ:* Images of Dignity-Drawings of Charles White, 67. *Mailing Add:* 718 N La Cienega Blvd Los Angeles CA 90069

HOROWITZ, NADJA
PAINTER, INSTRUCTOR
b Warsaw, Poland; US citizen. *Study:* Warsaw Acad Fine Art, with Pruszkowski & Schultz; Acad Grande Chaumiere, Paris, with L Lefevre; Ecole Superieure Art Graphiques, Belg, with Paul Van Maas & Tilla Vandervelde; Rheiman Sch, Berlin, Ger; silver sculpture with Sliwniak. *Comn:* Colina painting, comn by Dr Harrison-Pollock for Gerard Croisset, Holand, 68; Colina painting, comn by Vincent Lopez, 69; oil painting, comn by M Elkin for Tel Aviv Mus; Fly Me to the Moon (Colina painting), for Astronaut Neil Armstrong; plus murals in pvt houses in Fr Riviera, Israel, US & Holland. *Exhib:* One-man shows, New York Jewish Mus, New York Anthrop Soc Am, Herzl Gallery, New York, 81 & others; Haitian Mus, Port-o-Prince; Club Med Village, Haiti; and many others. *Pos:* Art exhib dir, Israeli 20th Anniversary Traveling Exhib, 68. *Teaching:* Asst instr art, Adam Rychtarski Art Sch, 37-38; instr pvt studio, 52-; spec teaching art therapy, Club Med Village, Haiti, 82 & 83. *Awards:* First Prize, Polish Art Asn, 57; Gelden Medal & Hon Acad, Italia della Arti Lavoro, Parma, Italy. *Bibliog:* J Lefevre (auth), article, 32 & A Werner (auth), article, 67, Grande Chaumiere; B Murphy (auth), article in E S Sentinel, Art Mag, 66. *Mem:* Nat Soc Lit & Arts, Washington, DC; Polish Am Artists Asn (vpres, 77); Artist Equity Asn New York; Nat Asn Women Artists; Artist 72 Group 8. *Mailing Add:* Apt 6 E 205 W 89th St New York NY 10024

HOROWITZ, (MR & MRS) RAYMOND J
COLLECTOR
b US citizen. *Study:* Mr Horowitz, Columbia Univ, AB, 36 & LLB, 39; Mrs Horowitz, NY Univ, AB, 36; Columbia Univ, MA, 37. *Bibliog:* John K Howat & Dianne H Pilgrim (auth), American Impressionist and Realist Paintings and Drawings from the Collection of Mr and Mrs Raymond J Horowitz, Metrop Mus Art, 4-6/73. *Collection:* American turn of the century Realist and Impressionist paintings, watercolors and drawings. *Mailing Add:* 930 Fifth Ave New York NY 10021

HORTON, CAROLYN
CONSERVATOR
b Buffalo, NY, July 13, 09. *Study:* Wellesley Col, 27-29; Univ Vienna, 29-30; apprentice bookbinder with Albert Oldach, Philadelphia; bookbinding also at Wiener Frauen Adademine. *Pos:* Conservator, Am Philosophical Soc, 35-39; conservator, Yale Univ Libr, 39-41; freelance work for numerous collections. *Mem:* Fel Int Inst Conserv; fel Am Inst Conserv; Guild Bookworkers; Grolier Club. *Publ:* Auth, Treating water-soaked books, Int Inst Conserv, Vol 2, 64; contribr, Encyclopedia Am, 67; auth, Saving the libraries of Florence, Wilson Libr Bulletin, 6/67; auth, Cleaning and preserving books and related materials, Am Libr Asn, 69. *Mailing Add:* c/o Carolyn Horton & Assoc Inc 430 W 22nd St New York NY 10011

HORVITZ, SUZANNE JOAN
PAINTER, PRINTMAKER
b Philadelphia, Pa. *Study:* Philadelphia Col Art, BFA, MA, 72; Columbia Univ, doctorate, 77. *Work:* Jean Brown Archives, Shaker Seed House, Tyringham, Mass; Deshong Mus, Widner Univ, Chester, Pa; Va Commonwealth Univ, Richmond; Pittsburgh Ctr Arts. *Exhib:* one-woman exhibs, Nexus Found Today's Art, Philadelphia, 77-80, Univ City Sci Ctr, Philadelphia, 80, ABF Gallery, Hamburg, Ger, 80 & Asinelli Gallery, Bologna, Italy, 81; Southern Alleghenies Mus, Loretto, Pa, 79; Unpainted Portrait, Kohler Art Found, Sheboygan, Wis, 79; and others. *Collections Arranged:* Toronto Philadelphia Exchange, ACT Gallery, Toronto, 78; 800 Miles From Home, Name Gallery, Chicago, 79; Xerox Art, Univ City Sci Ctr, Philadelphia, 80; Sexus at Nexus, Found Today's Art, 80; Words and Images (auth, catalog), Philadelphia Art Alliance, traveling, 81. *Pos:* Chmn & trustee, Found Today's Art/Nexus, Philadelphia, 75-; co-dir & pres, Synapse, Visual Art Press, Philadelphia, 80- *Teaching:* Instr, Corcoran Art Sch, Washington, DC, 61-64; instr, Fleisher Art Mem/Philadelphia Art Mus, 67-79; instr, Pa Acad Fine Arts, 80-81. *Awards:* Advan Painting Award, 69 & Samuel Heller Award, 70, Fleisher Art Mem, Philadelphia; Blumenthal Award, Cheltenham Art Ctr Ann, Pa, 77. *Bibliog:* Joel Colton (auth), Hot water review, New York, 77; Patrick Firpo (auth), Copyart, Richard Marek, New York, 78; Burton Wasserman (auth), In touch with tomorrow, Sch Arts Mag, 12/79. *Mem:* Philadelphia Art Alliance (vpres, 79-); Artists Equity Asn; Women's Caucus Arts. *Media:* Acrylic, Watercolor; Electrography. *Publ:* Auth, Graffetti and boxed assemblages, Sch Art Mag, 74; auth, Xerox art: Counterpoint, Philadelphia Print Club, 80; auth, Rope Trick, 80, auth, Thou Hast Ravished My Heart, 81 & auth, Sick of Love, 81, Synapse Press. *Dealer:* Benjamin Mangel Gallery 1604 Locust St Philadelphia PA 19103. *Mailing Add:* Philadelphian Suite 1A5 2401 Pa Ave Philadelphia PA 19130

HORWITT, WILL
SCULPTOR
b New York, NY, Jan 8, 34. *Study:* Art Inst Chicago, 52-54. *Work:* Boston Mus Fine Arts; Wadsworth Atheneum, Hartford, Conn; Hirshhorn Mus & Sculpture Garden, New York; Albright-Knox Art Gallery, Buffalo, NY; Guggenheim Mus; and others. *Exhib:* One-man shows, Stephen Radich Gallery, New York, 63, 65 & 67, Lee Ault & Co, 72-79, Summer Home of Boston Symphony Orchestra, Tanglewood, Mass, 74 & Vanderwoude Tanenbaum, NY, 83; Sculpture Ann, 68 & Biennial of Contemp Am Painting & Sculpture, 73, Whitney Mus Am Art, New York; Neuberger Mus, State Univ NY Col, Purchase, 76; Painting & Sculpture Today, Indianapolis Mus Art, Ind, 76; and others. *Awards:* Guggenheim Fel, 65; Louis Comfort Tiffany Found Purchase Grant, 68-69; Hereward Lester Cooke Found Grant, 79. *Mailing Add:* 60 Beach St New York NY 10013

HOTVEDT, KRIS J
PRINTMAKER
b Wautoma, Wis, 1943. *Study:* Layton Sch Art, Milwaukee, Wis, 61-64; San Francisco Art Inst, BFA, 65; Inst Allende, Mex, with D Kortlang, MFA, 67. *Work:* Mus NMex; Univ Sonora, Mex; Huntington Art Alliance, Calif; Ariz State Univ Mem Union Collection; Westat Inc, Rockville, Md; and others. *Exhib:* One-woman exhib, Ore Univ Mus, 74-76; Los Llanos Gallery, Santa Fe, NMex, 80; Ledoux Gallery, Taos, NMex, 81; Fields Gallery, Santa Fe, NMex, 82; La Bodega, Santa Fe, 83; and others. *Pos:* Art ed, Pembroke Mag, 72- *Teaching:* Instr painting & printmaking, Pembroke State Univ, 67-69; substitute art instr, St Johns Col, NMex, 69-80. *Awards:* NMex Arts Comn Grant, Art in Pub Places, 77-78. *Bibliog:* Article, Art Voices South, 7-8/80. *Media:* Woodcut, Serigraphs. *Publ:* Southwest Art, 74; Society for Common Insights, 77 & 78; Int Grafik, 77; Katapult-Pembroke, 77; and others. *Dealer:* Ledoux Gallery Taos NM 87571; La Bodega 667 Canyon Rd Santa Fe NM 87501. *Mailing Add:* 125 Spruce St Santa Fe NM 87501

HOUGH, JENNINE
PAINTER
b Charlotte, NC, Mar 17, 48. *Study:* Univ NC, Chapel Hill, BA, 70; Univ NC, Greensboro, MFA with cert, 73; Skowhegan Sch Painting & Sculpture, Maine, summer 74. *Work:* High Mus Art & Ga Arts Coun, Atlanta; Columbus Mus Art, Ga; Miss Mus Art, Jackson; Gibbes Art Mus, Charleston, SC; and others. *Exhib:* One-man show, Columbus Mus Fine Arts, Ga, 77; Southeastern Competition, Southeastern Ctr Contemp Arts, Winston-Salem, NC, 77 & 79 & Realist Ann-Landscape, 79; Southern Realism, Miss Mus Art, 79; Ga Artists 20th Century, Madison-Morgan Cult Arts Ctr, Madison, Ga, 79; New in New York, Monique Knowlton Gallery, 81; and others. *Teaching:* Eve prog, Emory Univ, 79- *Awards:* Fel, MacDowell Colony, Peterborough, NH, 76; Best of Show, LaGrange Nat III & IV, LaGrange, Ga, 77 & 80; Nat Endowment Arts & Southeastern Ctr Contemp Arts Fel Grant, 80. *Bibliog:* Southern realism reviewed, Art Voices Southeast, 12/79; Southern Realism, Art in Am, 12/80. *Media:* Oil, Watercolor. *Dealer:* Monique Knowlton Gallery 153 Mercer St New York NY 10012; Fay Gold Gallery Cains Hill Place Atlanta GA 30305. *Mailing Add:* 4012 Peachtree Dunwoody Rd NE Atlanta GA 30342

HOUGHTON, ARTHUR A, JR
ADMINISTRATOR
b Corning, NY, Dec 12, 06. *Study:* Harvard Univ, 25-29; 14 honorary doctorates. *Pos:* Dir, Corning Glass Works, 30-; pres, Steuben Glass, 33-72, chmn, 73-82; emer trustee, Pierpont Morgan Libr; emer trustee, past chmn & past pres, Metrop Mus Art; hon trustee & past chmn, Parsons Sch Design; trustee & emer chmn, Cooper Union; hon cur, Keats Collection, Harvard Univ; hon trustee, Inst Contemp Art, Boston; hon trustee, Baltimore Mus of Art. *Awards:* Comdr, l'Ordre des Arts et Lett; Michael Friedsam Medal in Indust Art; Gertrude Vanderbilt Whitney Award, Skowhegan Sch Painting & Sculpture; and others. *Mem:* Fel Royal Col Art; Royal Soc Arts. *Mailing Add:* Wye Plantation Queenstown MD 21658

HOUK, PAMELA P
CURATOR
b Dayton, Ohio, Jan 8, 35. *Study:* Skowhegan Sch Painting & Sculpture, Maine, 54; Sch Dayton Art Inst, Ohio, 55-65; Cincinnati Art Acad, Ohio, 61-63; Wright State Univ, Dayton, Ohio, BS, 71, MA, 81. *Work:* Bradford Col, Haverhill, Mass, Cincinnati Mus Art, Ohio. *Collections Arranged:* Bookforms (auth, catalog), Artists' Books, 78; Patterns Plus (auth, catalog), Patterns and Systems, 79; Japanese House (auth, catalog), Household Objects of Edo Period, 79; Woodworks II (auth, catalog), Folk Traditions in Ohio and Kentucky (auth, catalog), 81; Cloth Forms (auth, catalog), Fabric Constructions, 82; Inside Self, Someone Else (auth, catalog), The Alter Ego as Self Portrait, 83; Lines of Art Nouveau (auth, catalog), Aspects and Sources of International Art Nouveau Movement, 83-84. *Pos:* Dir, Living Arts Ctr Gallery, Dayton, Ohio, 72-76; cur, Experiencenter Gallery, Dayton Art Inst, Ohio, 76- *Mem:* Am Asn Mus; Ohio Mus Asn. *Mailing Add:* 310 W Schantz Ave Dayton OH 45409

HOULE, ROBERT JAMES
PAINTER, CONSULTANT
b St Boniface, Man, Mar 28, 47. *Study:* Univ Man, Winnipeg, BA(art hist), 72; Int Summer Acad Fine Arts, Salzburg, Austria, 72; McGill Univ, Montreal, BEd(art), 75. *Work:* Art Gallery Hamilton, Ont; Nat Mus Man, Ottawa; Owens Art Gallery, Sackville, NB; Royal Ont Mus, Toronto. *Comn:* Mural, McGill Univ, Montreal, 73; poster, Assembly First Nations, Regina, 81. *Exhib:* Works on Paper, Galerie Sarah McCutcheon, Montreal, 81; New Work by a New Generation, Norman Mackenzie Art Gallery, Regina, Sask, 82; New Growth from Ancestral Roots, Koffler Gallery, Toronto, 83; Contemporary Native American Art, Okla State Univ, Stillwater, 83; Innovations: New Expressions in Native American Painting, Heard Mus, Phoenix, 83. *Collections Arranged:* New Work by a New Generation, 82. *Pos:* Cur contemp Indian art, Nat Mus Man, Ottawa, 77-80; art consult, Indian & Northern Affairs, Ottawa, 80-81 & Assembly First Nations, Regina, Sask, 82. *Teaching:* Specialist art, James Lyng High Sch, Montreal, 74 & Verdun Cath High Sch, Montreal, 75-76. *Bibliog:* Carol Phillips (auth), New Work by a New Generation, Artscanada, 11/82; Nancy Baele (auth), Indian adds to Mondrian, Ottawa Citizen, 6/4/83. *Media:* Acrylic, Watercolour. *Res:* Contemporary native art in Canada. *Publ:* Auth, Search for identity, Tawow, Vol 1, No 3, 70; auth, Alex Janvier: 20th century native symbols and images, 78 & Odjig: An artist's transition, 78, Native Perspective; auth, A firm statement on the demoralization of Indian people, Gazette, 79. *Dealer:* Mitzi Bidner & Assoc 250A Lyon St Ottawa ON K1R 5W2. *Mailing Add:* 197 Wellsley St E Apt 4 Toronto ON M4X 1E9 Canada

HOUSE, JAMES CHARLES, JR
SCULPTOR

b Benton Harbor, Mich, Jan 19, 02. *Study:* Univ Mich, 19-21, Law Sch, 21-23; Pa Acad Fine Arts, 23-27; Univ Pa, BSEd, 41, MA, 72. *Work:* Whitney Mus Am Art; Woodmere Art Gallery, Germantown, Pa. *Comn:* Mem tryptich (birch wood), Swarthmore Presby Church, Pa, 56-57; large head of John Dewey (oak), Penniman Libr, Univ Pa, 56-57; St Christopher & Jesus (oak lunette), St Clements Episcopal Church, Philadelphia, Pa, 58; med emblem, Norfolk Med Tower, Va, 60; teak wall relief, Philadelphia Br Libr, Bustleton, Pa, 65-66. *Exhib:* Whitney Mus Am Art Sculpture Biennials, 34 & 36; Kansas City Art Inst, 35; Int Sculpture Shows, Philadelphia Mus Art, 40 & 50; Artists for Victory, Metrop Mus Art, 42; Nineteen Cities, Mus Mod Art, New York, 47. *Pos:* Free lance caricaturist, New York Eve Post, Philadelphia Pub-Ledger, New Yorker & others, 25-32; caricaturist, Philadelphia Eve Bull, 47-54. *Teaching:* Assoc prof sculpture & drawing, Univ Pa Grad Sch Fine Arts, 27-72, emer assoc prof, 72-75, vis critic, 76, 77 & 79; assoc prof, Philadelphia Mus Art Eve Class, 49-50; assoc prof, San Diego State Col, summer 56; vis sculpture critic, Univ Pa, 75-76; retired. *Awards:* John Frederick Lewis First Prize for Caricature, Pa Acad Fine Arts, 27. *Bibliog:* Dorothy Grafly (auth), article, Am Artist, 55. *Media:* Wood. *Publ:* Illusr, Fifty Drawings, 30. *Mailing Add:* 810 Crum Creek Rd Media PA 19063

HOUSE, SUDA KAY
PHOTOGRAPHER, EDUCATOR

b Du Quoin, Ill, Jan 31, 51. *Study:* Univ Southern Calif, BFA, 73; Calif State Univ, Fullerton, MA, 76. *Work:* Polaroid Corp, Boston; Los Angeles Co Mus Art; Mus Photog Arts, San Diego; Creative Ctr Photog, Univ Ariz; Minneapolis Inst Arts. *Exhib:* Attitudes: Photography in the 1970s, Santa Barbara Mus Art, 79; Uniquely Photographic, Honolulu Acad Art, 79; Electro Works, George Eastman House, Rochester, NY, 81; Photographer as Printmaker, Arts Coun Gt Brit, London, 82; Eight from San Diego, San Diego Mus Art, 82; Polaroid: The Big Picture, Mus Photog Arts, San Diego, 83. *Teaching:* Guest instr photog, Univ Calif, Los Angeles Exten, 77; instr, East Los Angeles Col, 78-79; prof, Grossmont Col, 79- *Awards:* Nat Endowment Arts Emerging Photogr Fel, 80. *Mem:* Los Angeles Ctr Photog Studies (trustee, 74-81, pres, 75-78); Soc Photog Educ (chmn western region, 81-82). *Publ:* Auth, Artistic photographic processes, Amphoto, 81. *Dealer:* BC Space 425 Forest Ave Laguna Beach CA. *Mailing Add:* 3887 Central Ave San Diego CA 92105

HOUSER, ALLAN C
SCULPTOR, PAINTER

b Apache, Okla, June 30, 14. *Study:* Chilocco Indian Sch, Okla; Santa Fe Indian Sch, NMex, spec study with Dorothy Dunn; mural techniques with Olle Nordmark, Okla; Utah State Univ, Logan; St Michael's Col, Santa Fe. *Work:* Heard Mus, Phoenix, Ariz; Philbrook Art Ctr, Tulsa, Okla; Mus Northern Ariz, Flagstaff; Denver Art Mus, Colo; Univ of Okla, Oklahoma City; and others. *Comn:* Murals, Dept of Interior, Washington, DC; dioramas, Southern Plains Indian Mus, Anadarko, Okla; medals, Soc Medalists; portrait of Stewart Udall, Dept Interior, Washington, DC. *Exhib:* Contemp Indian Painters, Nat Gallery Art, Washington, DC, 53; Art Inst Chicago, 53; Gov's Gallery, State Capital, Santa Fe, 77; Jamison Gallery, Santa Fe, 77; Sacred Circles Art Exhib, Kansas City, Mo, 77; Am Indian & Cowboy Exhib, San Dimas, Calif, 78; Wagner Gallery, Austin, Tex, 78. *Teaching:* Instr art, Intermountain Indian Sch, Brigham City, Utah; head, Dept Sculpture, Inst of Am Indian Arts, Santa Fe; slide lect, Lake Forest Col, Chicago, Ill, 78; slide lect & sem, Thomas Burke Mem State Mus, Univ of Wash, Seattle, 78; artist-in-residence, Dartmouth Col, Hanover, NH, 79. *Awards:* Gold Medal in Bronze, Silver Medal in Stone & Silver Medal in Other Metal, Heard Mus Sculpture I Show, 73; Best of Show & First Place in Sculpture, Am Indian & Cowboy Show, San Dimas, Calif, 78. *Bibliog:* Allan Houser, Working Sculptor (film), In: Am Indian Artists 1976 (TV series), Pub Broadcasting System, KAET TV, 76. *Mailing Add:* 1020 Camino Carlos Rey Santa Fe NM 87501

HOUSER, CAROLINE MAE
HISTORIAN

b Walla Walla, Wash. *Study:* Mills Col, BA; San Francisco Art Inst; Harvard Univ, AM, PhD; Am Sch Classical Studies, Athens, Greece. *Teaching:* Asst prof art hist, Univ Tex, Austin, 75-78; Mellon Fel art hist, Harvard Univ, Cambridge, Mass, 78-79; asst prof art hist, Smith Col, Mass, 79- *Awards:* Andrew W Mellon Fel. *Mem:* Archaeol Inst of Am; Col Art Asn; Am Sch Classical Studies (managing comt). *Res:* Greek sculpture, especially monumental work in bronze. *Publ:* Auth, Is it from the Parthenon, Am J Archaeol, 72; auth, Dionysos and his circle, 79; auth, The Riace Marina bronze statues, classical or classicizing?, Source, 82; auth, Greek Monumental Bronze Sculpture, Vendome, 83. *Mailing Add:* Art Dept Smith Col Northampton MA 01063

HOUSER, JIM
PAINTER, EDUCATOR

b Dade City, Fla, Nov 12, 28. *Study:* Ringling Sch Art; Fla Southern Col, BS; Art Inst Chicago; Univ Fla, MFA; Johns Hopkins Univ. *Work:* Univ Notre Dame; Cornell Univ; NY Univ; Soc Four Arts Collection, Palm Beach, Fla; Syracuse Univ Art Collection; and others. *Exhib:* Soc Four Arts, Palm Beach, Fla, 64-80; one-man shows, Grand Cent Mod, New York, 67 & Lehigh Univ, Bethlehem, 68; Mainstreams USA, Ohio, 68; David Findlay Galleries, New York, 76-; and others. *Teaching:* Asst prof painting, Ky Wesleyan Col, 54-60; instr painting, Palm Beach Jr Col, 60-, chmn dept, 64-70. *Awards:* Akston Award, Soc Four Arts, 77; Merit Award, 16th Hortt Competition, Ft Lauderdale Mus Arts, 74; Philip Hulitar Award, Soc Four Arts, Palm Beach, 82; and others. *Bibliog:* Article, Arts Mag, 81. *Media:* Acrylic. *Publ:* Auth,

Color for the Artist, Palm Beach Jr Col, 75. *Dealer:* Gallery Camino Real 399 Camino Gardans Blvd Boca Raton FL 33432; Sherry French Gallery 41 W 57th New York NY 10019. *Mailing Add:* 693 Jog Rd West Palm Beach FL 33406

HOUSKEEPER, BARBARA
SCULPTOR, PAINTER

b Ft Wayne, Ind, Aug 25, 22. *Study:* Knox Col, Ill; RI Sch Design; Art Inst Chicago; workshops with Marcia Tucker & Alan Kaprous. *Work:* Ill Bell & Tel, Chicago; Gould Found, Rolling Meadows, Ill; Kemper Ins Co, Long Grove; Phillips Corp, New York. *Comn:* Large sculpture, Exec Off Condecor Mfg, Mundelein, Ill, 72; sculpture, Kemper Ins Co, Long Grove, Ill, 74, painting, 80; Mem Sculpture, Am Bar Asn, Chicago, 75; Michael Reese Hosp, 81. *Exhib:* One-artist shows, Zaks Gallery, Chicago, 78, Artemesia Coop Gallery, Chicago, 79, Name Gallery, Chicago, 79, Kohler Art Ctr, Sheybogan, Wis, 80 & Montalvo Ctr Arts, Saratoga, Calif, 82; San Jose State Univ Gallery, Calif, 81. *Teaching:* Oxbow Summer Sch Art, Saugatuck, Mich, 72-75, dir, 73-74; teacher advan critique, North Shore Art League, Winnetka, Ill, 73-; instr, Columbia Col, Chicago, 77-79; vis artist, Countryside Art Ctr, Arlington Heights, Ill, 80; vis artist, Fine Arts Ctr, Highland Park, Ill, 81; instr, private studio, El Granada, Calif, 81-82. *Bibliog:* Jane Allen & Derek Guthrie (auth), From Brave New World to Village Smithy, Chicago Tribune, 4/23/72; Dorothy Andries (auth), She Gives Opportunity to Others, Pioneer, 74. *Mem:* Arts Club Chicago; Womens Caucus Arts. *Dealer:* Zaks Gallery 620 Michigan Ave Chicago IL. *Mailing Add:* Box 1148 El Granada CA 94018

HOUSMAN, RUSSELL F
PAINTER, INSTRUCTOR

b Buffalo, NY, Jan 13, 28. *Study:* Albright Art Sch, Buffalo, dipl; State Univ NY Col Buffalo, BS; NY Univ, MA & PhD; also with Hale Woodruff & Revington Arthur. *Work:* Human Resources Ctr Collection; NY Univ; State Univ NY, Albany; Butler Art Inst; Decatur City Art Ctr. *Comn:* Mural, USA, Kans Munic Auditorium, 52; painting, L Goodyear Collection, 57; Discovery Ctr, Human Resources Ctr, 72. *Exhib:* State Univ NY; Tri-State Exhib, Chautauqua, NY; one-man show, Silvermine Guild Art, Albany Inst Hist & Art & Wellons Gallery, New York; plus others. *Pos:* Dir, Decatur City Art Ctr, 59-61; art consult, Human Resources Ctr, Albertson, NY, 61-, Mind Inc, currently, Planners Industry & Educ, currently, Aging in America, currently. *Teaching:* Prof art, Adelphi Univ, 56-59; prof art & chmn dept, Milliken Univ, 59-61; prof art, Nassau Community Col, 63-, dir, Firehouse Gallery, 63-70. *Awards:* Purchase Award, State Univ NY, 68; Prizes, Silvermine Art Guild & Chautauqua Art Ctr. *Bibliog:* Viscardi (auth), The School, Eriksson, 64; 21 Paint in Hyplar, Grumbacher, 68; Watson (auth), The Artist as a Cook, Country Art Gallery, 72. *Mem:* Am Fedn Art; Silvermine Art Guild; NY State Art Teachers (ed, 69); Long Island Art Teachers. *Publ:* Auth, Psychological Warfare Capabilities & Vulnerabilities as Found in Soviet Art, 54; The Design of an Art Room, 55; Utilization of Artist Personnel in Psychological Warfare, 63; Telephone Assisted Teaching Devices, 69; Core Humanities Curriculum for Disabled Children, 70. *Mailing Add:* 38 Hampshire Rd Great Neck NY 11023

HOUSSER, YVONNE MCKAGUE
EDUCATOR, ENVIRONMENTAL ARTIST

b Toronto, Ont, Aug 4, 1898. *Study:* Ont Col Art, scholar; Acad Grande Chaumiere & Acad Ranson, with Prinet, 21-22 & 24; Univ Vienna; also with Hans Hofmann & Emile Bistram. *Work:* Nat Gallery Can; Art Gallery Ont; London Art Gallery, Ont; Robert McMichael Collection Art; Univ Toronto; and many others. *Comn:* Mural, The Canadian, Can Pac Railway. *Exhib:* Royal Can Ann, Ont Soc Artists; Can Group of Painters, Nat Gallery Can; Contemporanea, Rio de Janeiro; Century of Can Art, Tate Gallery, London, Eng; and many others. *Teaching:* Instr art, Ont Col Art, 20-41; instr, Doon Sch Fine Art & Ryerson Inst, formerly. *Awards:* Can Nat Purchase Award; Baxter Award, Ont Soc Artists, 65. *Mem:* Royal Can Acad; Ont Soc Artists; Can Group of Painters; Heliconian Club. *Media:* Mixed. *Mailing Add:* Mont Soudan No 1002 700 Mount Pleasant Rd Toronto ON M4S 2N7 Canada

HOUSTON, BRUCE
SCULPTOR, ASSEMBLAGE ARTIST

b Iowa City, Iowa, Jan 23, 37. *Study:* Univ Nebr, Lincoln, BA, 59; Art Ctr Col Design, Los Angeles, 61-62; Univ Calif Los Angeles, MA(graphic design), 65; Univ Iowa, MFA(painting), 74. *Work:* Univ Art Mus, Albuquerque. *Exhib:* Humor in Art, Los Angeles Inst Contemp Art, 81; Collage & Assemblage, Miss Mus Art, Jackson, 81; one-man shows, Allan Stone Galleries, New York, 82 & Claremont Grad Sch, Calif, 82; 20 Year Retrospective, Municipal Art Gallery, Los Angeles, 83; and many others. *Teaching:* Slide lectr in many cols & univs throughout Calif, 79- *Awards:* Best in Show, Davenport Art Mus, 72. *Bibliog:* Suzanne Muchnic (auth), Bruce Houston Assemblages, Art Voices S, 1/80. *Dealer:* Molly Barnes Gallery 750 N La Cienaga Los Angeles CA 90069; Allan Stone Galleries 48 E 86th St New York NY. *Mailing Add:* 600 Moulton Ave # 300 Los Angeles CA 90031

HOUSTON, JOHN STEWART See Stewart, John

HOVING, THOMAS
CONSULTANT, EDITOR

b New York, NY, Jan 15, 31. *Study:* Princeton Univ, BA(summa cum laude), 53, Grad Sch Art & Archaeol, Nat Coun Humanities Fel, 55, Grad Sch Fine Arts, MFA(Kienbusch & Haring Fel), 58, PhD(art hist), 59; five honorary doctorates. *Collections Arranged:* Initiated and developed series of art exchanges between museums of France, Soviet Union and the US; arranged Tutankhamun Tour of US, 76-79. *Pos:* Curatorial asst, Dept Medieval Art &

The Cloisters, Metrop Mus Art, 59-60, asst cur, 60-63, assoc cur, 63-65, cur, 65-66, dir, 67-; admin, Recreation & Cult Affairs, New York, 66-67; ed-in-chief, Connoisseur Mag. *Awards:* Distinguished Achievement Award, Advert Club Am, 66; NY Univ Creative Leadership in Educ Award, 75; Woodrow Wilson Award, Princeton Univ, 77. *Mem:* Int Ctr Medieval Art (mem bd dir). *Publ:* Auth, The Bury St Edmunds Cross, 64; auth, Italian Romanesque Sculpture, 65; auth, Branch out, Mus News, 68; auth, Tutankhamun, The Untold Story, 78; auth, King of the Confessors, 81. *Mailing Add:* 150 E 73rd St New York NY 10021

HOVSEPIAN, LEON
PAINTER, DESIGNER
b Bloomsburg, Pa, Nov 20, 15. *Study:* Worcester Art Mus Sch, cert; Yale Univ, Alice Kimball traveling fel, BFA, 42; Fogg Mus. *Work:* Worcester Art Mus, Mass; Fitchburg Art Mus, Mass; Fine Arts Collection, Washington, DC; Springfield Mus, Mass; Mus Mod Art, Yerevan, Armenia, USSR. *Comn:* Mosaics, Oblate Fathers Retreat House, Willimantic, 61; stained glass, Holy Cross Col, Worcester, 65; portraits, Leiceister Jr Col, Mass, 68-69; fresco mural, Church of the Annunciation, Washington, DC, 74; portrait, Judge Morris N Gould, Worcester, Mass; and others. *Exhib:* Art Inst Chicago, 41; Albright Art Gallery, 46; Nat Gallery Art, 47; RI Sch Design, 48; Worcester Art Mus Am Biennial, 48; By the People For the People--New Eng, De Cordova Mus, Lincoln, Mass, 77; and others. *Pos:* Dir, Boylston Summer Art Sch, Mass, 41-; fac, Clark Univ Sch Worcester Art Mus, formerly. *Teaching:* Instr art, Bancroft Sch, 36-38; prof, Woman's Col, New Haven, 38-40; instr, Worcester Art Mus Sch, 40-, instr, Pub Educ Div, 41-56. *Awards:* St Wulstan Soc Art Award, 38-40; Painting Prize, Fitchburg Art Mus; Ford Found Grant to exhib in Armenia, USSR. *Bibliog:* Adlow (auth), Stuart gallery, Christian Sci Monitor, 46; Sandrof (auth), Artist in his studio, Feature Parade, 53; Browne (auth), Leon Hovsepian, Art News, 11/66. *Publ:* Illusr, Worcester Fedral, Past--Present--Future, 52; illusr, Androck, 58. *Dealer:* Triart Studios 90 Pocasset Ave Worcester MA 01606. *Mailing Add:* 96 Squantum St Worcester MA 01606

HOWARD, (HELEN) BARBARA
PAINTER, PRINTMAKER
b Long Branch, Ont, Mar 10, 26. *Study:* Western Tech & Commun Sch, Toronto; Ont Col Art, Toronot, AOCA, 51; St Martins Sch Art, London, 54. *Work:* Nat Gallery Can; Art Gallery Ont; Brit Mus, London; Bodleian Libr, Oxford, England; Libr Cong. *Exhib:* Solo exhib, Wells Gallery, Ottawa, 66 & 82 & Prince Arthur Galleries, Toronto, 80 & 82; Can Soc Graphic Arts, 58-60 & 63; Can Watercolours, Drawings and Prints, Nat Gallery Can, 66; Douglas Duncan Collection, Windsor, London, Hamilton, 67; Drawings and Sculpture, Art Gallery Ont, 76. *Bibliog:* Passionate Spirits; A History of the Royal Canadian Academy of Arts, 1880-1980, Clarke, Irwin, Toronto, 80; Hubert de Santana (auth), Profile of Barbara Howard, Today Mag, 11/80. *Mem:* Royal Can Acad Arts (mem coun, 80-82). *Media:* Oil; Wood Engraving, Black and White Graphic. *Publ:* Illusr, Turns and Other Poems, Anson-Cartwright Ed, 75; illusr, Arbor, Gauntlet, 76; illusr, The Bass Saxophone, Anson-Cartwright Ed, 77; illusr, Whale Sound, Dreadnought Press, 77; illusr, The Promise of Light, Anson-Cartwright Ed, 80. *Dealer:* Yaneff Gallery 19 Hazelton Ave Toronto ON M5R 2E1. *Mailing Add:* 226 Roslin Ave Toronto ON M4N 1Z6 Canada

HOWARD, CECIL RAY
PAINTER, SCULPTOR
b Wichita, Kans, Jan 25, 37. *Study:* Kans State Teachers Col, BS; Wichita State Univ, MFA. *Work:* Amarillo Col Gallery, Tex; Wichita State Univ; Glendale Community Col, Ariz; Emporia Kans State Col. *Comn:* Collage mural, Western NMex Univ, 69; tympanum ceramic sculpture, Church Good Shepherd, Silver City, 71. *Exhib:* One-man shows, Marion Koogier McNay Gallery, San Antonio, Tex, 60 & Wichita Art Mus, 67; Mid-America Show, Nelson Gallery, Atkins Mus, Kansas City, Mo, 62; Mainstreams '68 Int Exhib, Marietta, Ohio, 68; Int Designer-Craftsmen Exhib, El Paso Art Mus, Tex, 69; Installations '78, Mus NMex, Santa Fe; Armory Sculpture Show, Santa Fe, 79; Santa Fe Mus Int Folk Art; Tucson Art Mus, Ariz. *Pos:* Dir, McCray Gallery, Western NMex Univ, 63- *Teaching:* Assoc prof painting & sculpture, Western NMex Univ, 63- *Awards:* Purchase Awards, Wichita Art Mus, 60 & 62; Juror's Award for Distinction, Mainstreams '68 Int Exhib, 68; First Place Award in Ceramics, El Paso Art Mus, 69. *Mem:* NMex Potters' Asn. *Media:* Collage, Assemblage. *Publ:* Illusr, Voyage to America, Univ Nebr, 67; contribr, Donna Meilach's Collage on Construction, Crown. *Dealer:* Mariposa Gallery Old Town Albuquerque NM 87104. *Mailing Add:* Rte 10 Box 138 Glenwood NM 88039

HOWARD, DAN F
PAINTER, EDUCATOR
b Iowa City, Iowa, Aug 4, 31. *Study:* Univ Iowa, BA, 53, MFA, 58. *Work:* Joe & Emily Lowe Art Mus, Univ Miami, Fla; Blanden Mem Art Gallery, Ft Dodge, Iowa; Ark Arts Ctr, Little Rock; Sioux City Art Ctr, Iowa; Sheldon Mem Art Gallery, Univ Nebr, Lincoln. *Exhib:* Contemporary Americans, Ark Arts Ctr, 67; Ark Pavilion, Hemis-Fair '68, San Antonio, Tex, 68; Chautauqua Nat Exhib Am Art, NY, 78, 80 & 83; West '79/The Law Nat Exhib, Minn Mus Art, St Paul, 79; Int Exhib, New Orleans Int Trade Mart, La, 80; Marietta Nat, Marietta Col, Ohio, 81; Nat Painting & Sculpture Exhib, Okla Art Ctr, Okla City, 81; Tex Fine Arts Nat Exhib, Laguna Gloria Art Mus, Austin, 82 & 83; traveling retrospective, 83-84. *Teaching:* From instr to assoc prof painting & drawing, Ark State Univ, 58-71, chmn div art, 65-71, dir art gallery, 67-71; prof painting & drawing & head dept art, Kans State Univ, 71-74; prof art, Univ Nebr, Lincoln, 74-, chmn dept, 74-83. *Awards:* Patron Award, Mid-Four Exhib, Kansas City, 82; Second Prize, Tex Nat Exhib,

Austin, 82 & 83; Baker Mem Award, Chautauqua Exhib, NY, 83. *Bibliog:* In View of the Law, West Publishing Co, St Paul, Minn, 79. *Mem:* Col Art Asn Am; Am Fedn Arts; Mid-Am Col Art Asn (vpres, 75, pres, 76, bd dir, 79); Nebr Art Asn (bd trustees, 74-83). *Dealer:* Carson-Sapiro Gallery 2601 Blake St Denver CO 80205; Joy Horwich Gallery 226 E Ontario Chicago IL 60611. *Mailing Add:* 6803 Hawkins Bend Lincoln NE 68516

HOWARD, DAVID
PHOTOGRAPHER, PAINTER
b Brooklyn, NY. *Study:* Ohio Univ; San Francisco Art Inst, MFA; additional study with Ansel Adams, Duane Michaels & Jerry Ulesman. *Work:* Mus Mod Art, New York; San Francisco Mus Mod Art; Oakland Mus, Calif; City San Francisco; de Saisset Art Gallery & Mus, Santa Clara, Calif. *Exhib:* 10th & 13th Int Festivals of Contemp Art, Royan, France, 73 & 76; Ultra Films, Oakland Mus, Calif, 74; 34th Int Salon of Japan, Tokyo, 74; Rainbow Show, De Young Mus, San Francisco, 75; Hansen Fuller Gallery, San Francisco, 75; Haml Baum Gallery, San Francisco, 83; and others. *Pos:* Vis artist art hist, San Francisco City Col, 73; dir photog, San Francisco Ctr of Visual Studies, 74- *Awards:* Purchase Award, 27th San Francisco Art Festival, City of San Francisco, 73. *Bibliog:* Alfred Frenkenstein (auth), Beauty & elegance, San Francisco Chronicle, 74; F McDonald (auth), Center page, Village Voice, 76; Joan Murry (auth), Realities, Artweek, 76. *Publ:* Illusr, Artweek, 73; illusr, Wester D Kemp (auth), Photography for Visual Communicators, Prentice-Hall, 73; illusr, San Francisco Chronicle, 75; auth & illusr, Realities, 76 & Perspectives, 77, San Francisco Ctr for Visual Studies. *Mailing Add:* c/o San Francisco Ctr 49 Rivoli San Francisco CA 94117

HOWARD, HUMBERT L
PAINTER
b Philadelphia, Pa, July 12, 15. *Study:* Univ Pa; Howard Univ Sch Fine Arts; Int Acad Arts & Lett, Rome, Italy, hon degree. *Work:* Howard Univ; Civic Ctr Mus, Pa Acad Fine Arts, Philadelphia; Libr Cong; Stanley Bernstein Collection; and other pub & pvt collections. *Exhib:* Grabar Gallery, 68; Howard Univ; Int Acad Arts & Lett, 70; William Penn Mem Mus Exhib, 71 & 77; Gross McCleaf Gallery, Philadelphia, 77 & 79; and others. *Teaching:* Fac mem, Allens Lane Art Ctr, Philadelphia, formerly. *Awards:* Silver Medal for Painting, Int Acad Arts & Lett, Rome, 70. *Mem:* Pyramid Club; Artists Equity Asn; Peale Club; Philadelphia Art Alliance; Pa Coun Arts. *Mailing Add:* 3411 Hamilton St Philadelphia PA 19104

HOWARD, LINDA
SCULPTOR
b Evanston, Ill, Oct, 22, 34. *Study:* Univ Colo; Northwestern Univ; Chicago Art Inst, 53-55; Univ Denver, BA, 57; Hunter Col, New York, MA, 71. *Work:* Maya (aluminum sculpture), 1980 Winter Olympics, Lake Placid, NY, 80; Pac Lumber Co, San Francisco; K & B Plaza, Virlane Found, New Orleans, La; City of Chicago; Allstate Insurance Corp, Bush Corporate Ctr, Columbus, Ohio; and others. *Exhib:* Park Sculpture, Hudson River Mus, Yonkers, NY, 74; Aldrich Mus Contemp Art, 75; Colorado Springs Fine Arts Mus, 76; Am Artists, A Celebration, McNay Art Inst, New York, 76; Sculpture Potsdam 77, State Univ NY Col, Potsdam, 77; one-person show, Sculpture Now Gallery, New York, 78; 100 years, 100 artists, Art Inst Chicago, Ill, 80; New Dimensions in Drawing, Aldrich Mus, Conn, 81. *Teaching:* Asst prof sculpture, Hunter Col, New York, 69-72 & Lehman Col, New York, 73-76; assoc prof, Hunter Col, New York, 76-82. *Awards:* Creative Artists Pub Serv Grant, NY State, 75; City Univ New York Fac Res Grant, 75. *Bibliog:* Doc films, Linda Howard, Sculpture, 76, Constructions Sculpture, 76 & 500 Mile Sculpture Garden, 76, Nebr Educ TV; and others. *Dealer:* Max Hutchinson c/o Sculpture Now Gallery 142 Greene St New York NY 10012. *Mailing Add:* 11 Worth St New York NY 10013

HOWARD, ROBERT A
SCULPTOR, EDUCATOR
b Sapulpa, Okla, Apr 5, 22. *Study:* Phillips Univ; Univ Tulsa; with Ossip Zadkine, Paris, France. *Work:* NC Mus Art, Raleigh; Ackland Art Ctr & NC Nat Bank, Chapel Hill, NC. *Comn:* Monumental sculpture, Fed Bldg, Louisville, Ky, 76. *Exhib:* 153rd Ann Exhib, Pa Acad Fine Arts, Philadelphia, 58; Art 65--Young American Sculpture, New York World's Fair, 65; Sculpture of the Sixties, Los Angeles Co Mus, 67; Ann Contemp Sculpture, Whitney Mus Art, New York, 68; Contemp Am Painting & Sculpture, Univ Ill, 69. *Teaching:* Prof sculpture, Univ NC, 51-72 & 74-; prof sculpture, Univ Southern Calif, 72-73. *Awards:* Coop Prog in Humanities, Duke Univ, Univ NC & Ford Found, 65 & Univ NC, 71; Nat Endowment for the Arts, 72. *Media:* Multimedia. *Publ:* Auth, Space as form, Col Art J, 51. *Mailing Add:* 1201 Hillview Rd Chapel Hill NC 27514

HOWARTH, SHIRLEY REIFF
PUBLISHER, HISTORIAN
b Ft Benning, Ga, Oct 1, 44. *Study:* Dickinson Col, Carlisle, Pa, BA(art hist); Pa State Univ, University Park, MA(art hist). *Collections Arranged:* Recent Sculpture: Steven Urry & Hackley Art Mus, Muskegon, Mich, 76; C Paul Jennewein (auth, catalog), Tampa Mus, Fla. *Pos:* Asst cur, William Penn Mem Mus, Harrisburg, Pa, 69-74; cur prints, Pa Collection Fine Arts, 74-75; dir, Hackley Art Mus, Muskegon, Mich, 75-79; dir, Tampa Mus, Fla, 79-80; publ, dir & ed, Int Art Alliance, Largo, Fla, 80-; dir & ed, Traveling Exhibition Information Service, Largo, FL, 80- *Teaching:* Adj prof, St Leo Col, Fla, 80- *Mem:* Am Asn Mus; Col Art Asn; Int Platform Asn; Southeast Museums Conference. *Res:* Primarily in fields of Medieval and Northern Renaissance art; history of prints and photography. *Publ:* Auth, Care of Works of Art on Paper and Care, Display and Storage of Photographs, Pa Hist & Mus Comn, 73; auth, European Paintings, Hackley Art Mus, 81; ed, Directory of Corporate Art Collections, Int Art Alliance, 82; auth, Marcel Breuer: Concrete and The Cross, Hackley Art Mus, 79. *Mailing Add:* 100 Bluff View Dr Apt 606C Belleair Bluffs FL 33540

HOWAT, JOHN KEITH
CURATOR, HISTORIAN

b Denver, Colo, Apr 12, 37. *Study:* Harvard Univ, BA, 59, MA, 62. *Collections Arranged:* David Smith, Hyde Collection, 64; John F Kensett (with catalog), Am Fedn Art, 68; 19th Century America: Paintings & Sculpture (with catalog), 70, American Paintings & Sculpture, 71, Heritage of American Art: Paintings from the Collection, 75 & A Bicentennial Treasury: American Masterpieces from the Metropolitan, 76, Am Wing, Metrop Mus Art, 80. *Pos:* Cur, Hyde Collection, 62-64; asst cur Am painting, Metrop Mus Art, 67-68, assoc cur, 68-70, cur Am painting & sculpture, 70-81, chmn, Dept Am Art, 81. *Awards:* Ford Found Fel, 65; Chester Dale Fel, Metrop Mus Art, 65-67. *Mem:* Arch Am Art. *Res:* American paintings of 18th and 19th centuries, especially the Hudson River School. *Publ:* Auth, Hudson River & Its Painters, 72. *Mailing Add:* 1100 Park Ave New York NY 10028

HOWE, NELSON S
DESIGNER, ASSEMBLAGE ARTIST

b Lansing, Mich, Nov 5, 35. *Study:* Univ Mich, BA, 57, MA, 61. *Work:* New Orleans Mus Fine Arts, La; Libr Collections, Mus Mod Art, Finch Col Mus Art & Chase Manhattan Bank Collection, New York; Univ Calif, Berkeley; and others. *Comn:* Wall I (fabric wall), comn by Mr & Mrs Keith Waldrop, Providence, RI, 68; Fur Music (installation unit), Mus Contemp Crafts, New York, 71; Fur Score (fur wall), New Orleans Mus Fine Arts, 72. *Exhib:* One-man show, Little Gallery, Minneapolis Inst Art, Minn, 67; Fur & Feathers Show, Mus Contemp Crafts, 71; Experimental Sound, ICES Festival, London, Eng, 72; Mus Mod Art, New York; and other group & one-man shows. *Pos:* Pres & founding artist mem, bd dirs, Participation Proj Found, 73- *Awards:* 50 Best Books of the Yr Award, Am Inst Graphic Arts, 69; Intermedia Found Grant for Lab Serv, 72. *Bibliog:* Rose De Neve (auth), Art - notation - art, Print Mag, Vol 25, No 1; Source: Music Avant Garde, No 9, 72; and others. *Publ:* Illusr, To the Sincere Reader, 68 & Body Image, 70 & co-auth, Job Art, 71, Wittenborn; illusr & auth, Daily translating systems, Circle Press (London), 71; contribr, Harpers' Mag Wraparound Sect, 5/73; and others. *Mailing Add:* Box 587 Van Brunt Sta Brooklyn NY 11215

HOWE, OSCAR
PAINTER, EDUCATOR

b Joe Creek, SDak, May 13, 15. *Study:* Dakota Wesleyan Univ, BA, 52; Univ Okla, MFA, 54. *Work:* Denver Art Mus; Joslyn Art Mus, Omaha, Nebr; Mus NMex, Santa Fe; Philbrook Art Ctr, Tulsa, Okla; Smithsonian Inst, New York Br; and others. *Comn:* Murals, Mitchell Libr, SDak, 40, Nebraska City, Nebr, City of Mobridge, SDak & Hillside, Ill, 56. *Exhib:* Mus Mod Art, New York, 36; Collectors Choice Exhib, Denver Art Mus, 63; one-man shows, Philbrook Art Ctr, Tulsa, 64; Joslyn Art Mus, 67 & Heard Mus, Phoenix, 71. *Pos:* Dir art, Pierre High Sch, SDak, 53-57. *Teaching:* Artist in residence, Dak Wesleyan Univ, 48-52; from prof art to prof emer & artist in residence, Univ SDak, 57-82; US State Dept lectr, SAsia & Near East, 71. *Awards:* Dorothy Field Award, Denver Art Mus, 52; Mary Benjamin Rogers Award, Mus NMex, 58; Waite Phillips Trophy, Philbrook Art Ctr, Tulsa, 66. *Bibliog:* Robert Pennington (auth), Oscar Howe, Artist of the Sioux, Dakota Territory Cent Co, 61; Panorama for Pakistan, US Info Serv, 71; John Milton (auth), Oscar Howe, The Story of an American Indian, Dillon, 72. *Mem:* Delta Phi Delta; fel Int Inst Arts & Lett. *Media:* Casein. *Mailing Add:* 128 Walker Vermillion SD 57069

HOWELL, CLAUDE FLYNN
PAINTER, EDUCATOR

b Wilmington, NC, Mar 17, 15. *Study:* With Charles Rosen, Woodstock, NY, Bernard Karfiol & Jon Corbino; Wake Forest Univ, DHL, 75. *Work:* Weatherspoon Gallery, Univ NC; NC Nat Bank, Charlotte; Wake Forest Univ; IBM Corp, New York; and others. *Comn:* Illus, John F Blair Publ Co, Winston-Salem, 58; mosaics, NC Dept Arch & Hist, Mus Old Brunswick, 65 & State Ports Maritime Bldg, Wilmington, 66. *Exhib:* Am Watercolors 1952, Metrop Mus Art, New York; Fifth Ann Painting Yr, Atlanta Art Asn Galleries, Ga, 59; Piedmont Purchase Award Show, Mint Mus Art, Charlotte, 63; Art on Paper, Weatherspoon Gallery, 67; retrospective, NC Mus Art, 75; St John's Mus Art, 81. *Teaching:* Assoc prof painting & art hist & chmn dept art, Univ NC, Wilmington, 58-80. *Awards:* Rosenwald Found Fel, 48; Purchase Awards, NC Mus Art, 64 & NC Col Durham, 68. *Bibliog:* Senta Bier (auth), Notes on a North Carolina artist, Longview J, 71; and others. *Mem:* NC Art Soc. *Publ:* Illusr, Hatterasman, 58, Exploring the Seacoast of North Carolina, 70 & Beachcombers Handbook of Seafood Cookery, 71; auth, A Balkan Sketchbook, 77; auth, The Tessie C Price, 79. *Mailing Add:* Univ of NC 601 S College Rd Wilmington NC 28406

HOWELL, DOUGLASS (MORSE)
PAINTER, HISTORIAN

b New York, NY, Nov 30, 06. *Study:* Study in Europe & tutorials. *Work:* Victoria & Albert Mus, London; Brooklyn Mus; New York Pub Libr; Boston Mus Fine Arts; Fogg Mus; and others. *Exhib:* Phillips Exeter Acad; Huntington Mus, Long Island, NY; Univ Tex, Austin, 61; NY State Art Teachers Asn Conv, Corning, NY, 61; Univ Western Ont, London & Sheridan Col, Oakville, 72; and others. *Pos:* Dir, Handmade Paper Workshop Fine Arts & Handpress of Douglass Howell, 46- *Teaching:* Lectr, Off Cult Develop, Nassau Co Pub Schs, 71 & 72; resident artist, C W Post Col, Long Island Univ, 72; resident artist, Nassau Co, 73-74. *Awards:* Ford Found Fel Res Papers, 61; Awards, Int Paper Co, 78-80. *Bibliog:* Helmut Becker (auth), Handmade papermaking for the Fine Arts, Artmag, Can, 3-4/77; John B Myers (auth), article in Arts, 5/77; The paper revolution, Am Artist, 8/77; article, Am Craft Mag, 2-3/81; and others. *Mem:* Int Inst Conserv Hist & Artistic Works,

London; New York Acad Sci; Hand Engravers NAm (pres, 54). *Interests:* A correct metrology for research in the fine arts aesthetics. *Publ:* Contribr, Fritz Eichenberg, auth, The Art of the Print, Abrams, 76; coauth, with Calvin Thomas, article, New Yorker, 6/76; auth, Eishiro Abe, national treasure of Japan, Craft Horizons, 10/76. *Mailing Add:* Educ Ctr-Fine Arts 1014 Woodcrest Ave Riverhead NY 11901

HOWELL, ELIZABETH ANN (MITCH)
PAINTER, GALLERY OWNER

b Hartselle, Ala, Feb 27, 32. *Study:* Birmingham Southern Col, BA; Famous Artists Sch; also with Edgar Whitney, Zoltan Szabo & Charles Reid. *Work:* Birmingham Mus Art, Ala; Montclaire Gallery, Birmingham; Firt Nat Bank, Decatur, Ala; Citizens Bank, Hartselle, Ala; Hartselle Med Ctr, Ala. *Comn:* Children's portraits, Mr & Mrs Thomas Caddell, Decatur, Ala, 70; children's portraits, Dr & Mrs William Sims, Decatur, 71; illus & cover for cook bk, Decatur Jr Serv League, Inc, 72. *Exhib:* Williamsburg Art Exhib, Va, 70; Charleston Art Exhib, SC, 70; Int Platform Asn Art Exhib, Washington, DC, 71; Am Watercolor Soc Nat Exhib, 80; and others. *Pos:* Dept head, Hubert Mitchell Industs, Inc, Hartselle, 49-55; owner, Howell-Baxter Gallery, Hartselle, Ala, 83- *Teaching:* Head dept fine art, Morgan Co High Sch, 64-66. *Awards:* Hannah Elliott Award, Lovemans of Birmingham, 69. *Bibliog:* France-Amerique, Courrier Etats-Unis, New York, 69; Huida G Lawrence (auth), article, Park East News, New York, 69; article, Aufbau, New York, 69. *Mem:* Life mem Kappa Pi (pres col chap, 53-54); founding mem Decatur Arts Coun; Decatur Art Guild (founder, actg pres, publ chmn & vpres, 67-); Ala Watercolor Soc; Birmingham Art Asn. *Media:* Watercolor, Acrylic. *Publ:* Illusr, Emmanuel-God With Us, 67 & Cotton Country Cooking, 72. *Dealer:* Allee Studios 14 S Church St Fairhope AL 36532. *Mailing Add:* PO Box 585 Hartselle AL 35640

HOWELL, HANNAH JOHNSON
LIBRARIAN

b Oskaloosa, Iowa, June 22, 05. *Study:* Penn Col, Oskaloosa; Univ Chicago, PhB; Columbia Univ Sch Libr Serv, BLS. *Pos:* Head librn, Frick Art Ref Libr, New York, 47-70, consult librn, 70- *Mailing Add:* 151 E 83rd St New York NY 10028

HOWETT, JOHN
HISTORIAN, CRITIC

b Kokomo, Ind, Aug 7, 26. *Study:* John Herron Inst, BFA; Univ Chicago, MA, 62, PhD, 68. *Collections Arranged:* Kress Study Collection Notre Dame (auth, catalog), 62; Renaissance Illuminations (auth, catalog), High Mus Art, Atlanta, 74; Twelve in Atlanta (auth, catalog), 79. *Teaching:* Asst prof & cur collections, Univ Notre Dame, 61-66; assoc prof Renaissance & Mod art, Emory Univ, 66-80, prof, 80-, chairperson dept hist art, 73- *Mem:* Col Art Asn; Southeastern Art Conf. *Res:* Italian and Northern Renaissance painting and sculpture; contemporary art and culture. *Publ:* Auth, Two panels by the master of the St George Codex in the Cloisters, Metrop Mus J, Vol 11, 85-102; auth, Edward Ross, High Mus Art, 77; auth, Boondocks Bohemias: A case for the regional avant-garde, Contemp Art/SE, Vol 1, 77; coauth, Martin Emanuel, High Mus Art, 80; coauth, Carl Andre, Heath Gallery Art, 83; and others. *Mailing Add:* 325 Hertford Circle Decatur GA 30030

HOWLAND, RICHARD HUBBARD
ARCHITECTURAL HISTORIAN

b Providence, RI, Aug 23, 10. *Study:* Brown Univ, AB, 31; Harvard Univ, AM, 33; Johns Hopkins Univ, PhD, 46; Brown Univ, Hon DArts, 62. *Pos:* Fel Agora Athens, Greece, 36-38; chief pictorial rec sect, OSS, 43-44; pres, Nat Trust Hist Preserv, 56-60; chmn dept civil hist, Smithsonian Inst, 60-67, spec asst to secy, 68-; founding mem, Am Comt Int Comn Hist Sites & Monuments; trustee, L A W Fund, Sotterley Fund & Evergreen Found. *Teaching:* Instr, Wellesley Col, 39-42; organizer dept hist art, Johns Hopkins Univ, 47, chmn dept, 47-56. *Mem:* Fel US Int Coun Monuments & Sites; Soc Archit Historians; Irish Georgian Soc (trustee); Archaeol Inst Am (trustee); Am Sch Classical Studies, Athens (trustee). *Publ:* Coauth, Architecture of Baltimore, 54; auth, Greek Lamps & Their Survivals, 58 & 66. *Mailing Add:* Smithsonian Inst Washington DC 20560

HOWLETT, CAROLYN SVRLUGA
EDUCATOR, PAINTER

b Berwyn, Ill, Jan 13, 14. *Study:* Art Inst Chicago, BAE, 37, MAE, 52; Northwestern Univ, MA, 53. *Comn:* Stained glass windows, State Ill Host House, Chicago World's Fair, 33. *Exhib:* Art Inst Chicago Ann, 45, 46, 52 & 55; Am Fedn Arts Print Show, 48; Arts Club of Chicago Annual Exhibitions, 53-81; Assoc Am Artists Galleries, Chicago, 50; two-man shows, Chicago Press Club, 66, 68 & 73; Retrospective Exhib, Morton Col, 83. *Pos:* Head dept art educ & Jr Sch, Art Inst Chicago, 43-63, assoc dean & educ consult, 63-68; dir, Gallery Studio, Coonley Estate, 70- *Teaching:* Instr art educ, Oak Park & Libertyville Pub Schs, 34-37; instr design & crafts, Art Inst Chicago, 37-70, prof art educ, 52-70, emer prof, 70-; tech consult, Arts & Skills Prog, Am Red Cross, 42-45; lectr fine art & crafts, Univ Ill Exten, 67-73; lectr, Travel Dept, Chicago Council on Foreign Relations, 74-78. *Awards:* Gen Excellence Award, Art Inst Chicago, 32 & Conf Club Pres Award, 33 & 34; Outstanding Serv Award, Ill Art Educ Asn, 76; Special Recognition Award, Nat Art Educ Asn, 81. *Mem:* Arts Club Chicago; Nat Art Educ Asn; Ill Art Educ Asn (pres, 62-63); Around Chicago Art Group (pres, 38-39). *Publ:* Contribr, Arts & Activities, Sch Arts, House Beautiful & Design, 42-70; auth, The need for art, Related Arts Serv Bull, 49; contribr, World Bk Encycl & Childcraft Encycl, 49-59; auth, Art in Craftmaking, Van Nostrand Reinhold, 74. *Mailing Add:* Gallery Studio 336 Coonley Rd Riverside IL 60546

HOWZE, JAMES DEAN
EDUCATOR, DRAFTSMAN
b Lubbock, Tex, Apr 8, 30. *Study:* Austin Col, BA; Art Ctr Col Design; Univ Mich, MS. *Work:* Del Mar Col, Corpus Christi; Hobbs Pub Schs, NMex; San Antonio Col. *Exhib:* Colorprint USA, Tex Tech Univ, 74; one-man exhib, Del Mar Col, 76; Smithsonian Inst Traveling Exhib, US and Can, 79-82; Nat Drawing & Small Sculpture Show, Ball State Univ, 79-80; American Drawing II & III, Portsmouth, Va, 79 & 81; National Small Works Exhibition, Schoharie Col, New York, 83; and others. *Teaching:* Assoc prof, dept archit & allied arts, Tex Tech Univ, 58-68, prof studio art, dept art, 68-, dir core curric, 79- *Awards:* Cash Awards, Nat Drawing & Small Sculpture Exhib, Del Mar Col, 70, 74, 78 & 81; Best in Exhib, Nat Mensa Mem Exhib, 71; Silver Award, Wichita Art Dir Club, 76. *Mem:* Hon mem Dallas-Ft Worth Soc Visual Commun; Am Asn Univ Prof; Tex Asn Col Teachers; Tex Asn Schs Art. *Publ:* Contribr, cartoons & humorous verse, Sports Car Graphic, 65-66; designer & illusr, var advert publ; auth & illusr, Images from the High Plains, Staked Plains Press, Canyon, Tex, 79; drawing, Design Concepts and Applications, Cheatham, Cheatham & Haler, Prentice Hall, 83. *Mailing Add:* 2503 45th St Lubbock TX 79413

HOYT, DOROTHY (DOROTHY HOYT DILLINGHAM)
PAINTER
b East Orange, NJ, Aug 11, 09. *Study:* Cornell Univ, BS & MA; Art Students League; New Sch Social Res; Graphic Arts Workshop, Pratt Inst. *Exhib:* Whitney Mus Am Art, New York; Nat Asn Women Artists, Kyoto, Japan; Pa Acad Fine Arts, Philadelphia; one-woman shows, Riverside Mus, New York & Manila, Philippines; Johnson Mus of Art, Cornell Univ, 76; and many other group & one-man shows. *Awards:* Medal of Honor for Graphics, Nat Asn Women Artists, 58; First Prize, Cent Adirondack Art Asn, 66; Jane Peterson Award for Oils, NJ Soc Painters & Sculptors. *Media:* Oil, Watercolor. *Mailing Add:* 92 Myers Rd Lansing NY 14882

HOYT, ELLEN
PAINTER
b Brooklyn, NY, Nov 8, 33. *Study:* Pratt Inst, 53; Brooklyn Mus & Mus Nat Hist, 65-75 & 83; with Ed Whitney, Frank Webb, Jankowski DeStefano & Ernest Crichlow. *Work:* Gateway Nat Recreation Area, New York. *Comn:* Painting, Sierra Club for Gateway Nat Park, New York, 82. *Exhib:* Metrop Mus Art, New York, 79; Brooklyn Mus, NY, 80; Nat Watercolor Show, Salmagundi Club, New York, 80, Nat Arts Club, New York, 81 & 82 & Knickerbocker Club, New York, 82; Stuhr Mus, Grand Island, Nebr, 83. *Teaching:* Instr art, Kingsway Acad, 70-75 & Studio Dragonette, 77-80. *Awards:* Best in Show, Brooklyn Mus, 80; Travel Award, Washington Sq Outdoor Art Exhib, 81. *Bibliog:* Emanuel Stromm (auth), Profile of an artist, Courier, 82; Eve Wilen (auth), New Exciting Approach, NY Artists Equity, 82. *Mem:* Artists Equity, New York; Visual Individualist; Brooklyn Watercolor Soc (secy, 79-83). *Media:* Watercolor. *Publ:* Auth, Bulletin, 65 & Mariner, 75, Flare Printing; auth, Mariner, Flare Printing, 75; auth, Never on Sunday Cookbook, Peerless Press, 70. *Mailing Add:* 1551 E 29th St Brooklyn NY 11229

HSIAO, CHIN
PAINTER, SCULPTOR
b Shanghai, China, 35. *Study:* Taipei Normal Col, BA; with Li Chun-Sen, Taipei, Taiwan. *Work:* Mus Mod Art & Metrop Mus Art, New York; Nat Gallery Mod Art, Rome, Italy; Philadelphia Mus Art; Detroit Inst Art. *Comn:* Mural, Mr S Marchetta, Messina, Sicily, 71. *Exhib:* Carnegie Int, Pittsburgh, 61; Int Malerei 1960/61, W Eschenbach, 61; Art Contemporain, Grand Palais Paris, 63; 7th Biennial Sao Paulo, Brazil, 63; 4th Salon Galeries-Pilotes, Lausanne, Switz & Paris, 70. *Teaching:* Instr art, Southampton Col, Long Island Univ, 69; prof visual commun, Inst Europeo Design, Milan, Italy, 71-72; vis artist, La State Univ, Baton Rouge, 72- *Awards:* City of Capo d'Orlando, Italy Prize, 70. *Bibliog:* K Leonhard (auth), Hsiao Chin, 63 & Hsiao Chin, 65, V Scheiwiller; W Schonenberger (auth), Hsiao, Prearo, 72; La Via Di Hsiao, Nuova Foglio, 78, Hsiao, Vanessa, 79. *Media:* Metal Constructions; Acrylic, Ink. *Dealer:* Giorgio Marconi 15 Via Tadino Milan Italy. *Mailing Add:* Via G Modena 35 Milano 20129 Italy

HU, CHI CHUNG
PAINTER
b Chekiang, China, Jan 27, 27. *Study:* Self-taught. *Work:* City Hall Art Mus, Hong Kong; Nat Mus Hist, Taipei, Taiwan & China Acad. *Exhib:* Fifth Moon Group Exhib, Fine Arts Gallery, San Diego, 73 & Arts Club of Chicago, 74; Contemp Chinese Paintings & Prints, Denver Art Mus, 73; Pittsburgh Int Exhib, Mus Art, Carnegie Inst, Pa, 67; Now Current Show, Smithsonian Mus, DC, 68; and others. *Collections Arranged:* A Collectors Exhibition, S B Nitikman Winnipeg Art Gallery, Can, 68. *Awards:* First Prize for Oil Painting, First Armed Forces Art Exhib, 52; Second Prize in Oil Painting, Young Chinese Artists Exhib, US Info Agency, 60; China Acad Fel, 69. *Bibliog:* The Imagery of Hu, Chi-Chung, Heritage Press, 62; Hu, Paintings by the Contemporary Artist, Nat Taiwan Arts Ctr, 67; Five Chinese Artists, Nat Mus Hist, 70. *Media:* Oil. *Dealer:* Zantman Art Gallery Box 5818 Carmel CA 93921; Naples Art Gallery 275 Broad Ave S Naples FL 33940. *Mailing Add:* PO Box 1039 Carmel CA 93921

HU, MARY LEE
EDUCATOR, JEWELER
b Lakewood, Ohio, Apr 13, 43. *Study:* Miami Univ, Oxford, Ohio, 61-63; Sch for Am Craftsmen, Rochester Inst Technol, with Hans Christensen; Cranbrook Acad Art, Bloomfield Hills, Mich, BFA, 65, with Richard Thomas; Southern Ill Univ, MFA, 67, with Brent Kington. *Work:* Goldsmith Hall, London, Eng; Mus Contemp Crafts, New York; Columbus Mus Fine Arts, Ohio; Ill State Univ, Normal; Ind Univ, Bloomington. *Exhib:* Goldsmith, Renwick Gallery, Smithsonian Inst, Washington, DC, 74; Contemp Jewelry Exhib, Design Ctr Philippines, 77; AM Crafts at the Vatican Mus, 78; Rings & Rattlesnakes, Goldsmiths Hall, London, 78; 4th Int Jewelry Art Exhib, Mikimoto, Tokyo, 79; Goldsmith '78, Schmuck Mus, Pfortzheim, Ger & touring 8 Europ countries, 79-80; Silver in Am Life, Carnegie Inst, Pittsburgh & touring US, 79-81; and many others. *Teaching:* Vis artist metalsmithing, Univ Iowa, Iowa City, fall 75; lectr, Univ Wis, Madison, 76-77; asst prof, Mich State Univ, East Lansing, 77-80; assoc prof metalsmithing, Univ Wash, Seattle, 80- *Awards:* Nat Endowment Arts Craftmen's Fel, 76; Purchase Award, Beaux Arts Designer/Crafts, 75; Merit Award, The Metalsmith, 77. *Bibliog:* Elizabeth Breckenridge (auth), Mary Lee Hu: high on the wire, Craft Horizons, 4/77. *Mem:* Soc North Am Goldsmiths (vpres, 76-77, pres, 77-80); Am Crafts Coun (craftsman trustee, 80-); World Crafts Coun; Northwest Designer Craftsmen. *Media:* Silver, Gold Wire. *Publ:* Contribr, Body Jewelry--International Perspectives, Henry Regnery, 73; contribr, Wire Art, Crown, 75; contribr, Textile Techniques in Metal, Van Nostrand Reinhold, 75; contribr, Jewelry Techniques, Doubleday, 78. *Mailing Add:* Dept of Art Mich State Univ East Lansing MI 48824

HUBBARD, JOHN
PAINTER
b Ridgefield, Conn, Feb 26, 31. *Study:* Harvard Univ, Cambridge, Mass, AB, 53; Art Students League, New York, study with Morris Kantor, 56-58; study painting with Hans Hofmann, Provincetown, Mass. *Work:* Tate Gallery, London, England; Scottish Nat Gallery of Mod Art, Edinborough; Arts Coun of Great Brit, London; Arts Coun of Northern Ireland, Belfast; Australian Nat Gallery, Melbourne; and others. *Comn:* Midsummer, Royal Opera House, Covent Garden, London, 83. *Exhib:* From Brit 75, Taidemuseo & Alvar Aalto Mus, Helsinki, 75; Brit Colour (S Am tour), Brit Coun, 78-79; one-man shows, Newlyn Gallery, Eng, 78, Fischer Fine Art, London, 79 & 81 & Warwick Arts Trust, London, 81; and others. *Pos:* Member, Coun of Mgt, SPACE/AIR, London, 71-75; collaborator, Mark Rothko Mem Portfolio, London, 73; chmn, Art Panel, Southwest Arts, Exeter, Devon, 73-75; mem, Arts Panel, Arts Coun of Great Brit, London, 73-78; consult, J Sainsbury Ltd, 79-81. *Teaching:* Vis painting instr, Camberwell Sch Art, London, 63-65. *Bibliog:* Hubbard's Search, Art Int, 78-79; article, Times, London, 2/81; Jeff Dunlop (dir), film, London Weekend Television, 3/81. *Dealer:* Fischer Fine Art 30 King St London SW1 Eng. *Mailing Add:* Chilcombe Near Bridport Dorset England United Kingdom

HUBBARD, ROBERT HAMILTON
HISTORIAN
b Hamilton, Ont, June 17, 16. *Study:* McMaster Univ, BA; Univ Wis, MA & PhD; Univ Paris, cert; Mt Allison Univ, Hon LLD, 62. *Exhib:* Can Painting, Tate Gallery, London, 64; 300 Yrs Can Art, 67 & Scottish Painting, 68, Nat Gallery Can; and many others. *Pos:* Cur Can art, Nat Gallery Can, 47-54, chief cur, 54-75; cult adv, Gov Gen of Can, Ottawa, 75-81, hon hist, 81- *Teaching:* Lectr hist art, Univ Toronto, 45-46. *Awards:* Jules & Gabrielle Leger Fel, 81-82. *Mem:* Fel Royal Soc Can; Officer Order Can; Can Hist Soc; Can Mus Asn; Royal Can Geog Soc. *Res:* History of Canadian art. *Publ:* Auth, National Gallery of Canada Catalog, Univ Toronto, Vols I-III, 56-60; auth, Development of Canadian Art, Queen's Printer, 63; auth, Rideau Hall, a History of Government House, 77; auth, Thomas Davies, Oberon, 72. *Mailing Add:* Govt House Ottawa ON K1A 0A1 Canada

HUBENTHAL, KARL SAMUEL
CARTOONIST, PAINTER
b Beemer, Nebr, May 1, 17. *Study:* Chouinard Art Inst, Los Angeles. *Work:* State Hist Soc Wis; Syracuse Univ; Truman Mem Libr; Eisenhower Mem Libr; Lyndon B Johnson Libr. *Exhib:* Am Ed Cartoonists Traveling Exhib, US, Mexico, Can & Eng, 62-77; Los Angeles Co Mus, 69 & 73; Madison Sq Garden Gallery Sport, 71; Univ Southern Calif, 75; Calif State Univ, Northridge, 77; private galleries, Washington, DC, NY, Los Angeles, San Francisco, 78-81; and others. *Pos:* Political cartoonist, Hearst Newspapers, 55-83. *Awards:* Nation's Best Ed Cartoonist, Nat Cartoonists Soc, 62, 67, 70 & 72; Helms Athletic Found Medal Contrib Sport in Art, 64; Nation's Best Sports Cartoonist, Nat Cartoonists Soc, 71, 79, 80 & 82. *Bibliog:* Articles, Cartoonist Profiles, 11/76 & 9/82. *Mem:* Marine Corps Newsmens Asn; Nat Cartoonists Soc (dir, 63-69); Los Angeles Soc Illusr (pres, 58-59); Asn Am Ed Cartoonists (pres, 63-64). *Publ:* Contribr, Comic Art in America, Simon & Schuster; contribr, The World Encyclopedia of Cartoons, Chelsea House; contribr, How to Draw: Tips from the Top Cartoonists, Donnor Publishing; contribr, Cartooning, Regnery; contrib, The 70's: Best Political Cartoons of the Decade, McGraw-Hill. *Mailing Add:* 5536A Via La Mesa Laguna Hills CA 92653

HUBERT, EDGAR F & ANNE M
CURATORS, COLLECTORS
US citizens. *Study:* Mr Hubert, Northeastern Univ, Boston, BS; Mrs Hubert, Boston Mus Fine Art, spec studies, with Claude Croney & King Coffin. *Exhib:* James Fitzgerald 1898-1971, Hopkins Ctr, Dartmouth Col, Hanover, NJ, 75, Mead Gallery, Amherst Col, Mass, 76, Ctr Visual Arts, Antioch Col, Columbia, Md, 77, Danforth Mus, Framingham, Mass, 77 & Monterey Peninsula Mus Art, Calif, 79. *Pos:* Curators, James Fitzgerald Collection, James Fitzgerald Mem Studio, Monhegan, Maine, 71- *Mem:* Danforth Mus (coun mems, 78-); Portland Mus Art; Boston Mus Fine Arts; Farnsworth Libr & Art Mus. *Interests:* Working on biography of James Fitzgerald. *Collection:* Twentieth century watercolors, oils and prints. *Publ:* Auth, Legacy of beauty, Kent Collector, 76; auth, Recollections of the Artist, Fitzgerald Mem Studio, 77. *Mailing Add:* One Rocky Brook Rd Dover MA 02030

HUBLER, JULIUS
PRINTMAKER, PAINTER
b Granite City, Ill, Dec 11, 19. *Study:* SE Mo State Univ, BS, 42; Columbia Univ, MA, EdD, 51; also studied with Hans A Mueller & Arthur Young. *Work:* B Spruance Collection, Philadelphia Mus Art, Pa; Nat Acad Design & Adolph Dehn Collection, New York Public Libr, New York; J Von Wicht Collection, Brooklyn Mus Art; Everson Mus Art, Syracuse, NY. *Exhib:* Nat Acad Design, New York, 56-83; Libr Cong, Washington, DC, 58-; US Print Exhib, Smithsonian Inst, Washington, DC, 62; US Info Agency Print Exhib, traveling, 65-68; traveling exhib, 67, 50 Years Am Prints, Asn Am Artists Gallery, New York, 69 & Nat Traveling Exhib, 77-79, Soc Am Graphic Artists. *Teaching:* Instr, City Col New York, 46-48; prof, State Univ NY Buffalo, 48-82. *Awards:* Warren Mack Mem Award, Soc Am Graphic Artists, 62; Samuel F B Morse Medal, 152nd Ann Exhib, Nat Acad Design, 77; anonymous prize, 155th Ann Exhib, Nat Acad Design, 80. *Mem:* Soc Am Graphic Artists; Nat Acad Design. *Media:* Collage, Relief. *Mailing Add:* 94 Danbury Lane Buffalo NY 14217

HUCHEL, FREDERICK M
MUSEUM DIRECTOR, GALLERY DIRECTOR
b Brigham City, Utah, Aug 28, 47. *Study:* Brigham Young Univ, Provo, Utah. *Work:* Brigham City Mus-Gallery, Utah; religious art, Minerva Teichert, 79. *Collections Arranged:* Minerva Kohlhepp Teichert, Brigham City Mus-Gallery, 77 & 79. *Pos:* Dir, Brigham City Mus-Gallery, 77- *Mem:* Western Asn Art Mus; Utah Mus Asn; Utah State Hist Soc. *Res:* Study of Utah and Mormon art and artists. *Specialty:* Varied types of mostly representational art. *Mailing Add:* PO Box 583 Brigham City UT 84302

HUCHTHAUSEN, DAVID RICHARD
SCULPTOR, EDUCATOR
b Wisconsin Rapids, Wis. *Study:* Univ Wis, BS, study with Harvey K Littleton; Ill State Univ, MFA, study with Joel Philip Myers; Vienna Univ of Applied Arts (Fulbright scholar). *Work:* Chrysler Mus of Art, Norfolk, Va; Smithsonian Inst; Metrop Mus Art, New York; Musee du Verre, Liege, Belg; Art Mus, Dusseldorf, Ger; and others. *Exhib:* Lake Superior Int Crafts Exhib, Tweed Mus, Duluth, Minn, 75-77; Mod Glass & Porcelain of Austria, Lugano Mus, Switz, 78; New Glass, Corning Mus Traveling Exhib, 79-81; Glass of Vienna, Mus, Zurich, Frankfurt & Ger; Glass from America, Glass Mus, Ger Tour, 79-80; Glass in the Mus, Ala, 81; Morris Mus, Morristown, NJ, 82; and others. *Pos:* Consult, Leigh Yawkey Woodson Art Mus, Wausau, Wis, 76-; vis artist, J & L Lobmeyr, Vienna, 77-78; design dir, Milropa Studios, New York, 79-80. *Teaching:* Instr glass, Ill State Univ, Normal, 76-77; lectr glass, Royal Col Art, London, formerly; prof, Tenn Tech Univ, 80- *Awards:* Newberry Award, Univ Wis, 73; Stein Fel, Ill State Univ, 76; Nat Endowment Arts Grant, 82. *Bibliog:* Cover article, Neues Glas, Eng/Ger ed, 9/83. *Media:* Glass. *Publ:* Auth, Americans in Glass, Marathon Press, 81. *Mailing Add:* c/o Heller Gallery 71 Greene St New York NY 10012

HUDSON, JACQUELINE
PAINTER, GRAPHIC ARTIST
b Cambridge, Mass. *Study:* Sch Nat Acad; Art Students League, with Jean Liberte, Will Barnet & Michael Ponce de Leon; Columbia Univ. *Work:* Libr Cong (Pennell Purchase), Washington, DC. *Exhib:* Nat Acad, New York; Pa Acad Fine Arts, Philadelphia; Am Watercolor Soc, New York; Allentown Art Mus, Pa, 74; Bowdoin Col Mus Art, Brunswick, Maine, 75; one-man shows, Maine Art Gallery, Wiscasset, 77 & Moulton Union, Bowdoin Col, Brunswick, Maine, 79. *Awards:* Nat Asn Women Artists Ann, 68 & Helen Turner Prize for Penobscot Bay (intaglio), 74, Donna Miller Mem Prize, 80; and others. *Mem:* Nat Asn Women Artists; Rockport Art Asn; Monhegan Assocs Inc, Maine (trustee, 60-63, chmn Monhegan Mus comt, 62-65). *Media:* Oil, Watercolor; Lithography, Etching. *Mailing Add:* Monhegan ME 04852

HUDSON, JON BARLOW
SCULPTOR
b Billings, Mont, Dec 17, 45. *Study:* Calif Inst Arts, with Allen Raprow, Paul Brach & Lloyd Harnroll, BFA, 71, MFA, 72; Stuttgart State Art Acad, West Germany, with Rudolph Hoflehner, 69; Dayton Art Inst, with Charles Ginnever, Bob Koepnick & Ann Tabatchnick, BFA, 75. *Work:* Univ Nebr, Lincoln; Petro-Lewis Corp, Denver; New York Grand Hyatt Hotel; Mead World Hq, Dayton; Case Western Reserve Univ, Cleveland. *Comn:* Polaris (sculpture), Public Libr, Homestead, Fla, 79; Vortex V (sculpture), Municipal Court Bldg, Toledo, Ohio, 79; Shiva: Shiwana (sculpture), Nat Radio Astronomy Observatory, Socorro, NMex, 80; Eidola (sculpture), Prestige Place, Midstates Develop Co, Dayton, 81; Dust Devil (sculpture), Eastern Pacific Corp, Santa Ana, Calif, 81. *Exhib:* Dayton Art Inst Mus, 66, 67, 78, 79 & 83; eight State Sculpture Ann, J B Speed Art Mus, 75 & 79; one-man shows, Galerie Foerster, Munster, West Germany, 79 & Galerie Regio, Freiburg, West Germany, 79 & 80; Recent Sculpture, Taft Mus, Cincinnati, 80; Mather Gallery, Case Western Reserve Univ, Cleveland. *Teaching:* Vis sculptor, Stephens Col, Columbia, Mo, 75-76; adj instr sculpture, Wright State Univ, Dayton, Ohio, 76-77; asst prof sculpture, Antioch Univ, Yellow Springs, Ohio, 80. *Awards:* State Artist Award, Nat Exhib, Marietta Col Art Dept, 76; First Place, Cash Award, Tex Fine Arts Asn, 77; Lusk Mem Fel Italy, 82-83. *Bibliog:* Jeff Kelley (auth), Time and the object, Art Week, 6/17/78; Johan DeRoey (auth), Geometry of mysticism, KNACK, Brussels, Belgium, 2/80; B Lealman & E Robinson (auths), Exploration into Experience, Knowing and Unknowing, Manchester Col, 81. *Mem:* Artists Equity; Ctr Visual Arts. *Media:* Stainless Steel, Marble. *Publ:* Auth, Pluralistic Vocabulary of Spiritual Unity, Studia Mystica, Calif State Univ, Sacramento, 80. *Dealer:* Condeso/Lawler Gallery New York NY; Tamara B Thomas Fine Arts Los Angeles CA. *Mailing Add:* 210B W Whiteman Yellow Springs OH 45387

HUDSON, RALPH MAGEE
HISTORIAN, EDUCATOR
b Fields, Ohio, Dec 18, 07. *Study:* Ohio State Univ, BA & BS, 30, MA, 31; Univ Ala, EdD, 65. *Work:* Univ Ark, Fayetteville; Mus Fine Arts, Little Rock, Ark. *Exhib:* Ark Watercolor Soc, 37-40; Grumbacher Aquarelle Travel Exhib, 38; one-man show, Hendrix Col, Conway, Ark, 40-41; Meridian Mus Art Asn, Miss, 46-50; Miss State Col Women, Columbus, 46-68. *Teaching:* Instr art & actg head dept, Morehead State Col, 31-36; head dept art, Univ Ark, Fayetteville, 36-46; prof art & chmn dept, Miss State Col Women, 46-69; prof art & chmn dept, Univ Ala, Huntsville, 69-73, lectr, 74- *Awards:* Univ Ala & Nat Endowment Humanities Res Grants Afro-Am Art; Distinguished Serv Award, Southeastern Col Art Conf, 74. *Mem:* Southeastern Col Art Conf (pres, 66-67, treas, 71-73); Nat Art Educ Asn; Kappa Pi (int historian, 48-74, int vpres, 74-); Ala Art Educ Asn. *Media:* Watercolor, Photography. *Res:* Nineteenth century American art, architecture and furnishings; Afro-American art. *Publ:* Ed, Ida Kohlmeyer, 68; auth, Afro-American art: A bibliography, Nat Art Educ Asn, 70; auth, Afro-American Art (slide sets with lecture scripts), Nat Endowment Humanities, 72-75; auth, Black Artists/ South (exhib catalog), Huntsville Mus Art, 79; coauth, African American arts and the ancestral African heritage, Art Teacher, 4/80. *Mailing Add:* 7102 Criner Rd SE Huntsville AL 35802

HUDSON, ROBERT H
PAINTER, SCULPTOR
b Salt Lake City, Utah, Sept 8, 38. *Study:* San Francisco Art Inst, BFA, 62, MFA, 63. *Work:* Los Angeles Co Mus; San Francisco Mus Art; Stedelijk Mus, Neth; Oakland Mus Art, Calif. *Exhib:* Five Whitney Mus Am Art Ann, New York, 64-72; Los Angeles Co Mus Art, 67; Philadelphia Mus Art, 67; Art Inst Chicago, 67; Walker Art Ctr, Minneapolis, 69; Retrospective, Moore Col of Art, 77. *Teaching:* Instr, San Francisco Art Inst, 64-65, chmn sculpture & ceramic dept, 65-66; asst prof art, Univ Calif, Berkeley, 66-73; asst prof art, San Francisco Art Inst, 76- *Awards:* Purchase Prize, San Jose State Col, 64; Nealie Sullivan Award, San Francisco, 65; Guggenheim Found Fel, 76; plus others. *Bibliog:* Peter Selz (auth), Funk, Univ Calif, 67; Maurice Tuchman (auth), American Sculpture of the Sixties, Los Angeles Co Mus Art, 67. *Dealer:* Allan Frumkin Gallery 41 E 57th St New York NY 10022; Hansen-Fuller Gallery 228 Grant Ave San Francisco CA. *Mailing Add:* 392 Eucalyptus Ave Cotati CA 94928

HUEBLER, DOUGLAS
CONCEPTUAL ARTIST
b Ann Arbor, Mich, 1924. *Study:* Univ Mich, Ann Arbor, MFA; Cleveland Sch Art, Ohio; Acad Julian, Paris, France. *Work:* Nat Gallery, Australia, Canberra; Van Abbemuseum, Eindhoven, The Neth; Nat Gallery of Can, Ottawa; Mus Mod Art, New York; Stedelijk Mus, Amsterdam, Neth. *Exhib:* One-man shows, Galerie Francoise, Lambert, Milan, 75, Galeria Akumulatory II, Poznan, Poland, 76, Leo Castelli Gallery, 78 & Van Abbemuseum, Eindhoven, 79; and others. *Pos:* Dean, Calarts Sch Art & Design, Calif Inst Arts, formerly. *Teaching:* Instr, Harvard Univ, Cambridge, Mass, formerly; instr studio art & printmaking, Calif Inst Arts, currently. *Bibliog:* Lynda Morris (auth), article, Studio Int, London, 2/73; I Leeber (auth), article, Chroniques Art Vivant, Paris, France, 4/73; J Gilbert-Rolfe (auth), article, Artforum, 2/74. *Publ:* Auth, Untitled, Xerox-Book, New York, 68; auth, Durata/Duration, Turin, 70; auth, Statements plus Location Pieces 1, 2, VH 101/3, Paris, autumn 70; auth, Trois Travaux, VH 101/6, Paris, 72. *Dealer:* Leo Castelli Gallery 420 W Broadway New York NY 10013. *Mailing Add:* c/o Calif Inst Arts Los Angeles CA 91355

HUEMER, CHRISTINA GERTRUDE
LIBRARIAN
b Orange, NJ, May 24, 47. *Study:* Mt Holyoke Col, BA, 69; Columbia Univ, MS, 70; Cornell Univ, MA, 75. *Pos:* Asst art librn, Cornell Univ, Ithaca, NY, 70-75; indexer, Art Index, H W Wilson Co, Bronx, NY, 75-76; art librn, Oberlin Col, 76-80; deputy librn, Avery Library, Columbia Univ, 80- *Teaching:* Instr, Sch Libr Serv, Columbia Univ, New York, 83. *Mem:* Art Libr Soc NAm. *Res:* Piranesi's Vedute de Roma. *Publ:* Contribr, articles, Art Libr Soc NAm Newsletter, 76- *Mailing Add:* Avery Library Columbia Univ New York NY 10027

HUETER, JAMES WARREN
SCULPTOR, PAINTER
b San Francisco, Calif, 1925. *Study:* Pomona Col, BA; Claremont Grad Sch, MFA, with Henry Lee McFee, Albert Stewart & Millard Sheets. *Work:* Scripps Col, Claremont, Calif; Nat Orange Show, San Bernardino, Calif; Long Beach State Col; Pomona Col, Claremont, Calif. *Exhib:* San Gabriel Valley Artists, Pasadena Art Mus, 50-56 & 58; Artists Los Angeles & Vicinity, Los Angeles Co Mus, 52 & 54-59; Denver Mus Art Ann, 54 & 59; Butler Inst Am Art Midyear Ann, 55, 57-59 & 62; Long Beach Mus Art Drawing Exhib, 60; Southern Calif 100, Laguna Beach Mus, 77; one-man shows, Pasadena Art Mus, 55 & Mt San Antonio Col, Walnut, Calif, 77; 38th Corcoran Biennial Am Painting, Washington, DC, 83. *Teaching:* Instr sculpture, Pomona Col, 59-60; instr drawing, Claremont Grad Sch, summer 63; lectr art, Pitzer Col, 72. *Awards:* First Prize for Sculpture, Los Angeles Co Mus, 55; First Prize for Painting, Frye Mus, Seattle, 57; Nat Design Award Drawing, Boulder Ctr Visual Arts, Colo, 82. *Bibliog:* A Segunda (auth), Reviews, Vol 1, No 8 & Delores Yonker (auth), James Hueter, Vol 2, No 2, Artforum. *Media:* Wood, Oil. *Mailing Add:* 190 E Radcliffe Dr Claremont CA 91711

HUFF, HOWARD LEE
EDUCATOR, PHOTOGRAPHER
b Kansas City, Mo, July 18, 41. *Study:* Col Idaho, BA; Univ Idaho, MFA. *Work:* J R Simplot Co, Boise; Boise Cascade Co, Boise; State of Ore Permanent Collection, Salem; Boise Gallery Art. *Comn:* Photographs (five 16in x 20in), Boise Cascade Corp, 71; photomurals (three 6ft x 12ft), Simplot Co, 76-78; six photographs, Boise City Hall Permanent Collection, 79; six photographs, Ore-Ida Permanent Collection, 79. *Exhib:* La Grange Nat Competition III, Ga, 77; Photog 78, Colby, Kans, 78; 4th Ann Coos Bay Regional Photo Competition, Ore, 78; two-man show, Univ Mo, Columbia, 78; Photospiva, Joplin, Mo, 81. *Teaching:* Prof photog, Boise State Univ, 65- *Awards:* Judges Merit Award, 41st Ann Exhib for Idaho Arts, Boise Art Asn, 76; Best of Show, Image 2000; Honorable Mention, Photospiva, Joplin, Mo, 81. *Media:* Photography. *Mailing Add:* 3319 Mountain View Boise ID 83704

HUFF, LAURA WEAVER
PRINTMAKER, ILLUSTRATOR
b Mt Vernon, NY, Dec 24, 30. *Study:* Syracuse Univ, New York; Univ Del, Newark, BA, 64; painting with James Twitty, Corcoran Sch Art, 65-67; George Washington Univ, Washington, DC, MFA, 68. *Exhib:* Masks for Unmasking, Anne Hathaway Gallery, Folger Libr, Washington, DC, 79; Prints & Sculpture, Salve Regina Gallery, Catholic Univ, Washington, DC, 80; US Photage, touring exhib, Student Union Gallery, Univ Md, College Park, 81; Prints by Printmakers, Wash Women's Art Ctr, Atheneum, Alexandria, Va, 81; Southern Graphics Traveling Show, 83. *Pos:* Illusr, Project LIFE, Washington, DC, 71-73; graphics specialist, Hazeltine Corp, McLean, Va, 79-80. *Teaching:* Lectr painting, Howard Community Col, Columbia, Md, 70-71; instr silkscreening, Graphics Workshop, Glen Echo Park, Md, 74-76; lectr silkscreening, NVa Community Col, Alexandria, 76. *Awards:* First Prize in Graphics, Md State Art Show, Nat League Am Pen Women, 72; Equal Award of Excellence, Art League Gallery, Alexandria, Va, 82. *Mem:* Artists Equity; DC Slide Registry Artists; Art League NVa. *Media:* Silkscreen; Collage; Pen & Ink, Wash. *Publ:* Illusr, Copycat Sam, Human Sci Press, New York, 82. *Mailing Add:* 11636 Brandy Hall Ln Gaithersburg MD 20878

HUGGINS, VICTOR, JR
PAINTER, PRINTMAKER
b Durham, NC, July 23, 36. *Study:* Univ NC, Chapel Hill, AB & MA. *Work:* Ackland Art Ctr, Univ NC, Chapel Hill; B Carroll Reece Mus, ETenn State Univ; Brooks Mem Gallery Art, Memphis, Tenn; Vanderbilt Univ; Weatherspoon Art Gallery, Univ NC, Greensboro. *Exhib:* One-man shows, Jane Haslem Gallery, Washington, DC, 71, 20th Century Gallery, Williamsburg, Va, 71 & B Carroll Reece Mus, Johnson City, Tenn, 72; group show, Gallery Contemp Art, Winston-Salem, NC, 71; Far Gallery, New York, 78 & 79. *Teaching:* Asst prof art, Vanderbilt Univ, 68-69; assoc prof painting & art educ, Va Polytech Inst & State Univ, 69-, head art dept, currently. *Awards:* First Purchase Awards, NC Nat Bank, 67; Springs Art Contest, Springs Mills, 67 & Ann Southern Contemp Painting Exhib, 68. *Media:* Acrylic. *Dealer:* Far Gallery 22 E 80th New York NY 10024. *Mailing Add:* Dept of Art Va Polytech Inst & State Univ Blacksburg VA 24060

HUGHES, EDWARD JOHN
PAINTER
b North Vancouver, BC, Feb 17, 13. *Study:* Vancouver Sch Art. *Work:* Nat Gallery Can, Ottawa; Art Gallery Ont, Toronto; Vancouver Art Gallery; Montreal Mus Fine Art; Gtr Victoria Art Gallery. *Exhib:* Retrospective, Vancouver Art Gallery, 67 & Surrey Art Gallery, 83; Art Gallery of Greater Victoria, 83; Edmonton Art Gallery, 83; Nat Gallery Can, 83; Glenbow Mus Calgary, 83; and others. *Pos:* War artist, Can Army, 40-42, off war artist, 42-46. *Awards:* Emily Carr Scholar, Lawren Harris, 47; Can Coun Fels & Awards, 58, 63 & 67, Short Term Grant, 70. *Bibliog:* Doris Shadbolt (auth), E J Hughes, Can Art Mag, spring 53; Anthony Robertson (auth), E J Hughes, Vanguard Mag, 12/81; Patricia Salmon & Leslie Black (auths), E J Hughes, Raincoast Chronicles Mag, 10/83. *Mem:* Royal Can Acad Art. *Media:* Oil. *Dealer:* Dr Max Stern 1438 Sherbrooke St W Montreal PQ Can. *Mailing Add:* 2449 Heather St Duncan BC V9L 2Z6 Canada

HUGHES, JOSEPH (FREDERICK)
PAINTER
b Moundsville, WVa, June 28, 41. *Study:* Univ London, cert, 64; Marshall Univ, BA, 64, MA, 67. *Work:* Staten Island Mus; Huntington Galleries, WVa; Appalachian Regional Collection, Huntington, WVa; Univ Ill, Chicago; C G Jung Inst, San Francisco. *Comn:* Paintings, Campus Christian Ctr, Marshall Univ, 63 & St Johns Unitarian Church, Cincinnati, 66; sculpture, Marshall Univ, 67; painting ser, Kasin, Gutman Assoc, San Francisco, 68 & Malrite Broadcasting, KNEW, Oakland, 81. *Exhib:* Solo exhibs, Oglebay Inst, Wheeling, WVa, 66 & Huntington Galleries, WVa, 67; Allied Artists WVa, Sunrise Gallery, Charleston, 67; 15th Ann, Downey Mus, Calif, 72; Contemp Ann, Nev Art Gallery, Reno, 73; Holiday Ann, San Francisco Mus Mod Art, 73. *Teaching:* Instr painting, San Francisco Mus Mod Art, 69-79. *Awards:* First Prize Sculpture, WVa Religious Arts Festival, 64; Second Prize Sculpture, Allied Artists WVa, 67; Third Prize Sculpture, Huntington Galleries, 67. *Bibliog:* Paul Allman (auth), article, San Francisco Phoenix, 9/13/72; Thomas Albright (auth), article, Artnews, 1/76; Frank Cebulski (auth), Color as perception, Artweek, 1/22/83. *Media:* Acrylic, Oil. *Publ:* Contribr & illusr, In the Late, Gnat Light and Other Poems, Art Asn Cincinnati, 65; auth, New spaces, Scene Mag, 81. *Dealer:* Bluxome Gallery 173 Bluxome St San Francisco CA 94107. *Mailing Add:* 4149 26th St San Francisco CA 94131

HUGHES, PAUL LUCIEN
DEALER, CONSULTANT
b New York, NY, Apr 8, 38. *Study:* NY Univ, BA, 67; Sch Visual Art, 68-69. *Collections Arranged:* Harry Bertoia Retrospective (guest cur), Colorado Springs Fine Arts Mus, 80; Vance Kirkland retrospective, 28-81; Geo Rickey, 84. *Mem:* Alliance for Contemp Art. *Specialty:* Contemporary abstract art. *Collection:* Bertoia, Anuszkiewicz, Henry Moore, Herbert Bayer, Vance Kirkland, Dave Yust, Sandra Dragul, Lee Simpson, Clayton Pond, J M W Turner and many others. *Mailing Add:* c/o Inkfish Gallery 1810 Market St Denver CO 80202

HUGHES, ROBERT S F
CRITIC, LECTURER
b Sydney, Australia, July 28, 38. *Study:* Sydney Univ, four yrs. *Pos:* Art critic & sr writer, Time Mag, 70- *Publ:* Auth, The Art of Australia, Penguin, 66; auth, Heaven & Hell in Western Art, Weidenfeld & Nicholson, 68; auth, The Shock of the New (8-part TV series on 20th century art), Brit Broadcasting Corp & Pub Broadcasting Corp. *Mailing Add:* c/o Time Mag Rockefeller Ctr New York NY 10020

HUGHTO, DARRYL LEO
PAINTER
b Watertown, NY, June 10, 43. *Study:* State Univ NY, Col Buffalo, BS(art educ), 65; Cranbrook Acad Art, MFA(painting), 69. *Work:* Edmonton Art Gallery, Alta; Everson Mus Art; Boston Mus Fine Arts; Mus Fine Arts, Houston; Guggenheim Mus. *Comn:* Mural (acrylic on canvas), Charlestown Savings Bank, Boston, 77. *Exhib:* Albright-Knox Mus, 66; one-man show, Everson Mus Art, 73; Corcoran Gallery, 77; New Abstract Art, Edmonton Art Gallery, Alta, 77; Theodoran Award Show, Guggenheim Mus, 77; 20th Century Painting & Sculpture, Metrop Mus Art, New York, 79; The New Generation: A Curator's Choice Traveling Exhib, 81. *Pos:* Instr painting & drawing, State Univ NY, Buffalo, 66; teaching asst painting, Cranbrook Acad Art, 68-69; asst prof, Syracuse Univ, 71-79. *Awards:* Theodoran Award, Guggenheim Found, 77. *Bibliog:* Ken Carpenter (auth), Third generation abstraction: Darryl Hughto, Arts Mag, 2/75; Kenworth Moffett (auth), The New Generation, Rhineburgh Press, 80. *Mem:* Visual Artists & Galleries Asn Inc. *Media:* Acrylic on Canvas. *Dealer:* Salander-O'Reilly Galleries 22 E 80 St New York NY 10021. *Mailing Add:* Canastota NY

HUGHTO, MARGIE A
CERAMIST, CURATOR
b Endicott, NY, March 29, 44. *Study:* State Univ NY, Buffalo, BS(art educ), 65; Cranbrook Acad Art, Bloomfield Hills, Mich, MFA(ceramics), 71; with Richard DeVore. *Work:* Boston Mus Fine Arts, Mass; Albright-Knox Art Gallery, Buffalo, NY; Everson Mus Art, Syracuse, NY; Cranbrook Acad Art Mus, Bloomfield Hills, Mich. *Comn:* Ceramic wall pieces, Marina Casino, NJ, 80; ceramic wall pieces, United Energy Resources, Houston, Tex, 81; ceramic wall pieces, Presbyterian Hospital, Philadelphia, Pa, 81. *Exhib:* Language of Clay, Birchfield Ctr, Buffalo, NY, 79-80; Century of Ceramics US, Everson Mus Art, Syracuse, NY, 79-81; Women Artists, Suzanne Brown Gallery, Scottsdale, Ariz, 80; Scripps Invitational, Scripps Col Mus, Claremont, Calif, 81. *Collections Arranged:* New Works in Clay by Contemp Painters & Sculptors (auth, catalog), Am Ceramics, 76, 78 & 81; A Century of Ceramics in the US 1878-1978 (auth, catalog), Am Ceramics, 78. *Pos:* Cur of Ceramics, Everson Mus Art, Syracuse, NY, 73-81; dir, Syracuse Clay Institute, NY, 75-81. *Teaching:* Prof ceramics, Syracuse Univ Sch Art, NY, 71-81. *Bibliog:* Sherry Chayat (auth), The Ceramic Fans of Margie Hughto, Ceramics Monthly, 5/80; Earth, Fire & Water (film), Philip Morris Corporation, 78. *Mem:* Inst Ceramic History. *Media:* Ceramic, Handmade Cotton Paper Pulp. *Res:* Contemporary American ceramics. *Dealer:* Andre Emmerich Gallery 41 East 57th St New York NY 10022. *Mailing Add:* 212 Boise Drive Syracuse NY 13210

HUGO, JOAN (DOWEY)
WRITER, INSTRUCTOR
b Weehawken, NJ, Jan 12, 30. *Study:* Studied performance with Rachel Rosenthal, 80-81 & Rudy Perez, 81-82. *Comn:* Simmons Col, Boston, Mass, BLS. *Collections Arranged:* Artworks & Bookworks Traveling Exhib, Los Angeles Inst Contemp Arts, Calif, 78. *Pos:* Cataloger, Brooklyn Mus Libr, 52-53; librn, Am Libr Paris, Left Bank Br, 53-54; art librn, Otis Art Inst Los Angeles Co, 57; Southern Calif ed, Artweek, 79- *Teaching:* Instr artist & the book, Otis Art Inst, 77-80; instr, Univ Calif, Los Angeles Extension, 82. *Mem:* Col Art Asn; Art Libr Soc of North Am. *Res:* History of artists' books; history of visual communications; also, the concept of the future and the arts; history of performance. *Interests:* Contemporary art, especially the relationships between the arts and social history; the concept of future and the arts; history of performance. *Publ:* Contribr, Art & Cinema, Visual Resources, 73-; contribr, spec issue on artists' bks, Dumb Ox, 77; ed, A Guide to Art Resources in Los Angeles, Art Libr Soc North Am, 77; ed, Artworks & Bookworks: A Set of Artists' Postcards, 77; contribr, Gutenberg in the gallery: A review of artists' books & bk objects at University of California, San Diego, Artweek. *Mailing Add:* 2601 Waverly Dr Los Angeles CA 90039

HUGUNIN, JAMES RICHARD
CRITIC
b Milwaukee, Wis, May 20, 47. *Study:* Art Ctr Col Design, Los Angeles, 71; Calif State Univ, Northridge, BA, 73; Univ Calif, Los Angeles, MFA, 75. *Exhib:* Language & Image, Santa Barbara Mus Art, 77; Narrative Art: 1967-1976, Contemp Arts Mus, Houston, 77; Book Exhib, Art Ctr, Sonja Henie-- Neils Onstand Found, Hovikodden, Norway, 78; Los Angeles Invitational, Fisher Gallery, Univ Southern Calif, 79; Object, Illusion & Reality,

Muckenthaler Gallery, Calif State Univ, Fullerton, 79; Kunstenaarsboeken, Stedelijk Mus, Schiedam, Neth, 81. *Pos:* Founder, ed & publ, Dumb Ox & U-Turn Art Mags, 76-80 & 82-; contrib ed, Obscura Mag, 79- *Teaching:* Prof art, Calif Lutheran Col, 77-; lectr, Chaffey Col, 82 & Art Ctr Col Design, 83. *Awards:* First Place, Calif Col Photog Exhib, Calif Stte Univ, Northridge, 74; Purchase Award, Light II, Calif State Univ, Humbolt, 76; David & Reva Logan Grant New Critical Writing, 83. *Bibliog:* Howardina Pindell (auth), article, Print Collectors Newslett, 9-10/77; Marcia Corbino (auth), Contemporary art criticism, Am Art, 10/83. *Mem:* Int Art Critics Asn. *Publ:* Auth, Apocryphal conversations, Afterimage, 6/81; auth, Photography: A bourgeois success story, J Los Angeles Inst Contemp Art, 5-6/82; auth, Joe Deal's optical democracy, Reading into Photog, Univ NMex, 82; auth, Meditations on an uranian Easter egg, Vies, Photog Resource Ctr, 83. *Mailing Add:* 901 1/2 S Berendo St Los Angeles CA 90006

HUI, HELENE
PAINTER, FILMMAKER
b New York, NY, June 24, 35. *Study:* Brooklyn Mus Art Sch, 57-60. *Work:* Hampton Col Mus, WVa. *Exhib:* 13 Women Artists, New York, 72; NY Women Artists, State Univ NY Albany, 72; Bard Col, Annandale on Hudson, NY, 73; 3rd Ann Contemp Reflections 1973-74, Aldrich Mus Contemp Art, Ridgefield, Conn, 74; Landmark Gallery, New York, 75-78; 55 Mercer St Gallery, New York, 79-80. *Awards:* Nat Endowment Arts Grant, 77-78. *Mailing Add:* 136 E 26th St New York NY 10010

HULDAH (HULDAH CHERRY JEFFE)
PAINTER
b Dallas, Tex. *Study:* Grand Cent Sch Art; Art Students League; also with Robert Brackman, New York. *Work:* Ga Mus Fine Arts; Columbia Mus Art; Norfolk Mus Art; Sheldon Swope Mus Art; Cornell Univ Med Club. *Exhib:* Salon des Artistes Francaise; Wally Findlay Galleries, New York, Chicago, Beverly Hills & Palm Beach. *Pos:* Artist, Hallmark Cards, formerly; ceramist, W Goechet & Co, Bavaria, Ger, formerly. *Mailing Add:* 680 S Country Rd Palm Beach FL 33480

HULDERMANN, PAUL F
ART DEALER, LECTURER
b Hamburg, WGer, June 29, 02; US citizen. *Pos:* Founder & pres, Scottsdale Nat Indian Art Coun, 62-72; founding mem & first chmn, Scottsdale Fine Arts Comn, 68-76; founder & bd mem, Scottsdale Ctr for the Arts Asn; Men's League of Scottsdale Ctr for Arts Asn (founder, first chmn, 78-80). *Mem:* Scottsdale Ctr for the Arts Asn; League Scottsdale Ctr Arts. *Specialty:* Indian art, including historic, prehistoric and contemporary. *Mailing Add:* 7051 Fifth Ave Scottsdale AZ 85251

HULETT, SIMONNE R
PAINTER, PRINTMAKER
b Blenne, Switzerland. *Study:* Okla State Univ, Stillwater, 46-48; Central State Univ, Edmond, Okla, BA, 71; with Virginia Cobb, Robert E Wood, Fredric Taubes, Charles Reid, Joseph Mugnani, Robert Kaupelis & Douglas Walton. *Work:* Amerax Oil Co, Baptist Hospital & Okla Childrens Hospital, Oklahoma City; Edmond Public Libr & Edmond Hospital, Okla. *Exhib:* Ann Southern Nat Watercolor, La Tech Art Gallery, Rustin, 81; Ann Print & Drawing & Craft Show, Ark Arts Ctr, Little Rock; Southwestern Watercolor, Brookhaven Col, Dallas, Tex, 82-83; Ann Southern Nat Watercolor, Columbia Mus Arts, SC, 80; Fifth Ann Exhib, Burpee Mus, Rockford, Ill, 81; and others. *Awards:* Bronze Award, Tri-state Show, Grumbacher Art, Colo, 79; Ruston Bank Award, Southern Watercolor, 81 & 82; Binney & Smith, Mid-West Watercolor, Binney & Smith Liqutex, 81. *Bibliog:* Martha Stermel (auth), Pen & ink drawings--high light Hulett art, Wichita Falls Times, Tex, 77. *Mem:* Kappi Pi; Individual Artists Okla; Southern Watercolor Soc; Midwest Watercolor Soc. *Media:* Watercolor, Oil. *Dealer:* Arts Place II 115 Park Place Oklahoma City OK 73103. *Mailing Add:* 2429 NW 59th Oklahoma City OK 73112

HULL, GREGORY STEWART
PAINTER
b Okmulgee, Okla, Sept 2, 50. *Study:* Univ Utah, BFA, 73, MFA, 77, studied with Alvin Gittins. *Work:* State Utah Inst Fine Arts, Salt Lake City. *Exhib:* 7th Intermountain Biennial, Salt Lake Art Ctr, Utah, 75; 52nd Ann, Springville Mus Art, Utah, 76; Utah Mus Fine Arts, Salt Lake City, 76; Munic Art Gallery, Los Angeles, 78; Butler Inst Am Art, Youngstown, Ohio, 81; and others. *Awards:* Best Show/Purchase, Utah Painting & Sculpture, 76; 1st Prize, Davis Co Art Ctr, Utah, 76. *Bibliog:* Stewart Bayle (auth), Art transcending cliches, Utah Holiday Mag, 8/6/76; Suzanne Muchnic (auth), Many called, few chosen for Barnsdall, Los Angeles Times, 5/22/78. *Media:* Oil. *Dealer:* Wally Findlay Galleries Int 814 N Mich Ave Chicago IL 60611. *Mailing Add:* 2114 N Deer Crossing Rd Flagstaff AZ 86001

HULMER, ERIC CLAUS
CURATOR, CONSERVATOR
b Heidelberg, Ger, Aug 4, 15. *Study:* Yale Univ, BA, 38; Univ Pittsburgh, PhD, 55; Harvard Univ; Kunst Acad, Oslo, Norway. *Pos:* Curator-conservator, George R Hann Collection, Sewickley Heights, Pa, currently, Westmoreland Co Mus Art, Greensburg, Pa, currently, Butler Inst Am Art, Youngstown, Ohio, currently & Pa State Univ Mus Art, currently. *Mem:* Fel Am Conserv Orgn. *Res:* Preservation materials and methods. *Mailing Add:* RD 1 Harmony PA 16037

HULTBERG, JOHN
PAINTER
b Berkeley, Calif, Feb 8, 22. *Study:* Fresno State Col, BA, 43; Calif Sch Fine Arts, 47-49; Art Students League, 49-51. *Work:* Metrop Mus Art, Mus Mod Art & Guggenheim Mus Art, New York; Albright-Knox Mus, Buffalo, NY; Stedelijk Mus, Eindhoven; and many others. *Comn:* Paintings of Newport News Shipyard, Fortune Mag, 57. *Exhib:* One-man shows, Martha Jackson Gallery, New York, 55-72, Corcoran Gallery Art, Washington, DC, 56, ICA Gallery, London, 56, Galerie Dragon, Paris, 56-71 & Oakland Mus, Calif, 60; and many others. *Teaching:* Instr painting, Art Students League, summer 60; instr painting, San Francisco Art Inst, 63-64; artist in residence, Honolulu Art Acad, 66-67. *Awards:* First Prize, Corcoran Biennial, Washington, DC, 55; Benjamin Altman Prize for Landscape, Nat Acad Design, 72; Nat Endowment Arts Grant, 81; and others. *Bibliog:* Emily Genauer (auth), article in New York Herald Tribune Mag, 55; article in Int Studio, London, 66. *Mem:* Nat Acad Design. *Media:* Oil. *Mailing Add:* Monhegan ME 04852

HUMMEL, CHARLES FREDERICK
ADMINISTRATOR
b Brooklyn, NY, Sept 16, 32. *Study:* City Col New York, BA(magna cum laude), 53; Univ Del, MA, 55. *Pos:* Curatorial asst, H F du Pont Winterthur Mus, Del, 55-58, asst cur, 58-60, assoc cur, 60-67, cur, 67-79, deputy dir for collections, 79- *Teaching:* Adj assoc prof art hist, Univ Del, 64- *Mem:* Nat Inst Conserv Cult Property; Early Am Indust Asn (dir, 64-); Int Rug Soc (dir, 71); Hajji Baba Soc, New York; Am Inst Conserv Hist & Artistic Objects. *Publ:* Auth, With Hammer in Hand, Univ Press Va, 68, 73, 77 & 83; contribr, Furniture to 1790, Britannica Encycl of Am Art, Encycl Brit Inc, 73; auth, A Winterthur Guide to American Chippendale Furniture: Middle Atlantic & Southern Colonies, Crown/Rutledge, 76; auth, Floor coverings in 18th century America, Irene Emery Textile Roundtable, 1975, Textile Mus, 77; coauth, The Pennsylvania Germans: A Celebration of Their Arts, Philadelphia Mus Art, 82. *Mailing Add:* c/o H F du Pont Winterthur Mus Winterthur DE 19735

HUMPHREY, DONALD GRAY
CURATOR
b Hutchinson, Kans, May 3, 20. *Study:* Univ Kans, BFA; State Univ Iowa, MFA & PhD. *Collections Arranged:* French & American Impressionism, 67; American Sense of Reality, Contemporary Latin American Painting, 69; Texas Collects 20th Century American Art, 71; American Folk Art from the Ozarks to the Rockies, 75. *Pos:* Dir, Philbrook Art Ctr, 59-75, Stark Mus Art, 76-77; chief cur, Mus Fine Arts, Mus NMex, Santa Fe, 79- *Teaching:* Instr art hist, State Univ Iowa, 50-51; asst prof, Okla Univ, 51-57; instr, State Univ Iowa, 57-58; adj prof, Tulsa Univ, 67-72. *Mem:* NMex Mus Asn; Southwestern Art Asn (pres, 72-74); Am Asn Mus; Am Fedn Arts; Asn Art Mus Dirs. *Mailing Add:* 2125 Calle Tecolote Santa Fe NM 87501

HUMPHREY, JUDY LUCILLE
GRAPHIC ARTIST, PRINTMAKER
b Columbia, SC, April 6, 49. *Study:* Univ Ga, BFA(art educ), 71, MFA(printmaking), 73. *Work:* Asheville Art Mus, NC; Ctr Art Gallery, Salisbury, NC; R J Reynolds Collection, Winston-Salem, NC; Springs Mills Collection, Fort Mill, SC; Equitable Life Collection, New York. *Exhib:* 24th Ann Nat Exhib Prints & Drawings, Okla Art Ctr, 82; 25th Chautauqua Nat Exhib Am Art, CAA Gallery Art, NY, 82; 44th Ann Exhib Contemp Am Paintings, Soc Four Arts, Palm Beach, Fla, 82; NMex Int, CAC Gallery, Clovis, 83; 59th Ann Nat April Salon, Springville Mus Art, Utah, 83; Fall Group, Terrain Gallery, New York, 83. *Teaching:* Assoc prof printmaking & photog, Appalachian State Univ, 73- *Awards:* Best in Show Award, Ann Nat Exhib, Shelby Gallery, NC, 79 & 80; Merit Award Graphics, 22nd Ann Springs Show, Springs Mills, SC, 80. *Media:* Pencil, Gouache; Etching. *Mailing Add:* 504 Grand Blvd Boone NC 28607

HUMPHREY, NENE
SCULPTOR, INSTRUCTOR
b Portage, Wis, Mar 18, 47. *Study:* St Mary's Col, Notre Dame, Ind, BFA, 69; Goddard Col, Boston, MA, 72; York Univ, Toronto, Can, MFA, 78. *Work:* York Univ, Toronto, Ont; Hofstra Univ; Best Products, Va. *Comn:* Four Mountains for a Grove of Trees (sculpture), Artists Representing Environmental Art, New York, 80; Enclosed Garden/Landscape (sculpture), Artpark, Lewiston, NY, 80; Meadow Passage/Forest House (sculpture), Morris Mus, Morristown, NJ, 81; Roadrise/Resting Space, Creative Time, New York, 83; Atlanta Road, Atlanta Arts Festival, 84. *Exhib:* Medieval Landscape, 55 Mercer Gallery, New York, 81; Paper Works, Frank Marino Gallery, New York, 81-82; Ambiance/Stimuli, Alternative Mus, New York, 81-82; Sculpture, Greene Space Gallery, New York, 82; Unending Roads, Hofstra Univ, 83; and others. *Pos:* Consult, Art in Public Places, Seattle Arts Commission, 81- *Teaching:* Vis artist, Ill State Univ, Normal, 82, Nova Scotia Col Art & Design, 82. *Awards:* Individual Artist Grant, Conn Commission Arts, 76; Macdowell Fel, Macdowell Colony, 78; Nat Endowment Arts Grant, 83. *Bibliog:* Janet Heit (auth), Nene Humphrey/medieval landscape, Arts Mag, 6/81; John Caldwell (auth), Modernism in Morristown, NY Times, 8/81; Grace Glueck (auth), Engaging experiments transform a sandy site, New York Times, 7/31/83. *Mem:* Col Art Asn; fel mem MacDowell Colony. *Publ:* Illusr & contribr, Three stories, Criss-Cross Communications Mag, Colo, 81. *Mailing Add:* 325 West 37th St New York NY 10018

HUMPHREY, RALPH
PAINTER
b Youngstown, Ohio, 1932. *Study:* Youngstown Univ, 51-52 & 54-56. *Work:* Bennington Col; Rose Art Mus, Brandeis Univ; Wadsworth Atheneum,

Hartford, Conn; Mus Mod Art, New York; Univ NC. *Exhib:* Abstract Expressionists and Imagists, 61 & Systemic Painting, 66, Solomon R Guggenheim Mus, New York; Focus on Light, NJ State Mus, Trenton, 67; Romantic Minimalism, Univ Pa, 67; The Art of the Real, Mus of Mod Art, 68; Whitney Mus of Am Art, 69 & The Structure of Color, 71; Color and Field: 1890-1970, Albright-Knox Art Gallery, Buffalo, NY, 70; one-man shows, Tibor de Nagy Gallery, 59 & 60; Emmerich Gallery, New York, 71 & Tex Gallery, 73; Butler Inst Am Art, 81. *Teaching:* Instr, Art Students League, New York; Harley House, New York, 59-60; Bennington Col, 61-63; New Sch Social Res & Hunter Col, New York, formerly. *Mailing Add:* c/o Willard Gallery 29 E 72nd St New York NY 10010

HUMPHREY, S L
PAINTER, ILLUSTRATOR

b Silver City, NMex, Nov 18, 41. *Study:* Western NMex Univ, BA. *Work:* Glendon E Johnson, Am Nat Ins Co, Galveston, Tex; Gerald I Freeman (corp collection), San Jose, Calif; Sen Benny Altamirano, Silver City, NMex; in pvt collection of Dennis Weaver, Calif. *Comn:* Cover for Frontier Days Publ, 73-75; paintings of Rio Grande Valley & settlement of Santa Fe between 1890 & 1900, comn by Clive Edgar, Colo, 75; background painting depicting uses of tools & Western paraphernalia, C O Crum Tool Mus, Henderson, Nev, 75; painting of hist stage line in Southwest Ariz, comn by Juel L Bell, San Diego, Calif, 75. *Exhib:* Women Artists Am West, Saddleback Western Gallery, Santa Ana, Calif, 74-75; George Phippen Mem Show, Prescott, Ariz, 75; Death Valley Exhib, Furnace Creek, Calif, 75; Nat Small Paintings Show, Albuquerque, NMex, 75; NMex State Fair, Albuquerque, 75; and numerous one-woman shows. *Teaching:* Instr painting, Lordsburg Pub Schs, NMex, 63-66. *Awards:* First & Second Place, Southwestern NMex State Fair, 74; First & Second Place, 74 & Second Place, 75, Women Artists Am Western Art Show. *Bibliog:* Mares, mules & mountain bells, Western Horseman Mag, 73; The 32nd El Paso art show, Sundial Sect, El Paso Times, 74; Regina Cooks (auth), article, Southwest Art Mag, 74. *Mem:* NMex Art League; Women Artists Am West; Grant Co Art Guild; Nat League Am Pen Women. *Media:* Oil, Watercolor. *Mailing Add:* 1 Western Heritage Silver City NM 80061

HUNDLEY, DAVID HOLLADAY
DESIGNER, EDUCATOR

b Phoenix, Ariz, Dec 25, 46. *Study:* Manchester Col Art & Design, Eng, dipl art & design, 69, with Keith Murgatroyd; Allgemeine Gewerbeschule, Basel, Switz, 70, with Armin Hofmann; Brigham Young Univ, Provo, Utah, BFA, 71, MA, 72. *Comn:* Graphic design for UN Declaration of Human Rights Plaque, Manchester City Hall, Eng, 70. *Pos:* Art critic, Ariz Daily Star, Tucson, 73-74; design consult, Ariz Inn, Tucson, 73-74; art dir, Tuesday Publ, Chicago, 74-75; graphic designer, Health & Hospital Gov Comn Cook Co, Chicago, 75-76; art dealer, Burles-Hundley Design Consults, Pasadena, Calif, 79- *Teaching:* Instr drawing & design, Brigham Young Univ, 72-73; guest lectr Bauhaus design, Chicago Educ Insts, Ill, 74-76; instr graphic design, Art Ctr Col Design, Pasadena, 77- *Publ:* Auth, The Influence of the Bauhaus on Contemporary Swiss Graphic Design, Brigham Young Univ Press, 72; and others. *Mailing Add:* 414 S Arroyo Blvd Pasadena CA 91105

HUNGERFORD, CONSTANCE CAIN
EDUCATOR, HISTORIAN

b Chicago, Ill, Apr 26, 48. *Study:* Wellesley Col, BA, 70; Univ Calif, Berkeley, MA, 72, PhD, 77. *Teaching:* From instr to assoc prof hist art, Swarthmore Col, Pa, 75-, chmn dept art, 81- *Awards:* Am Coun Learned Soc, 78; Am Philos Soc, 80; Am Assn Univ Women, 82-83. *Mem:* Col Art Asn. *Res:* Nineteenth century French painting, specifically Ernest Meissonier (1815-1891). *Publ:* Auth, Meissonier's Souvenir de Guerre Civile, Art Bulletin, 79; auth, Meissonier's first military paintings, Parts I & II, Arts Mag, 80. *Mailing Add:* Dept Art Swarthmore Col Swarthmore PA 19081

HUNISAK, JOHN MICHAEL
HISTORIAN, EDUCATOR

b Troy, NY, June 28, 44. *Study:* Williams Col, BA; NY Univ, MA, PhD. *Teaching:* Instr art hist, Middlebury Col, 70-75, asst prof Baroque & Mod art, 75-78, assoc prof, 79-, dept chmn, 81- *Mem:* Col Art Asn. *Res:* Later 19th century French sculpture. *Publ:* Auth, The Sculptor Jules Dalou: Studies in His Style & Imagery, Garland, 77; coauth, Romantics to Rodin (exhib catalog), 80; auth, Dalou's Triumph of the Republic: A study of private and public meanings, Acts 24th Int Cong Hist Art, 82; auth, Rodin, Dalou, and the monument to labor, In: Art the Ape of Nature, Abrams, 81; and others. *Mailing Add:* 4 Benedict Lane Middlebury VT 05753

HUNKLER, DENNIS FRANCIS
PAINTER, PRINTMAKER

b Oakland, Calif, Mar 3, 43. *Study:* New Sch Art, Toronto, 65-70; with Jack Bush, 69-70; San Francisco Art Inst, BFA, 72. *Work:* Oakland Mus, Calif. *Comn:* Walks US of A (set design), Oakland Theater of Dance, 74. *Exhib:* One-man shows, Humboldt Galleries, San Francisco, and others; Polly Friedlander Gallery, Seattle, Wash, 74; California Printmakers, Printmakers Coun Gt Brit, London, 75; 2nd Int Text-Sound-Image Festival, Antwerp, Belg, 78; Mercer Union, Toronto, 81. *Pos:* Asst dir, Artists Resource Ctr, Oakland, 73. *Bibliog:* Alexander Fried (auth), The fantasy of three artists, San Francisco Examr, 12/6/74; Thomas Albright (auth), Unique visions of nature, San Francisco Chronicle, 12/11/74; R F Stepan (auth), Dennis Hunkler's private world, Artweek, Vol 6 No 26. *Media:* Acrylic, Felt Pen. *Dealer:* S Alberts No 47 West 13th St New York NY. *Mailing Add:* 184 MacDonell Ave Toronto ON M6R 2A7 Canada

HUNT, BRYAN
SCULPTOR

b Terre Haute, Ind, June 7, 47. *Study:* Otis Art Inst, 69-72. *Work:* Solomon R Guggenheim Mus, Mus Mod Art & Whitney Mus Am Art, New York; Yale Art Gallery, New Haven, Conn; Stedelijk Mus, Amsterdam, Neth; and many others. *Exhib:* Young Am Artists, Guggenheim Mus, New York, 78; Made by Sculptors, Stedelijk Mus, Amsterdam, 78; Biennial, Whitney Mus Am Art, New York, 79 & 81; Contemp Sculpture, Mus Mod Art, New York, 79; Mus Mod Art, New York, 82; Whitney Mus Am Art, 82; Guggenheim Mus, 82; Houston Mus Fine Arts, 83; San Francisco Mus Mod Art, 83; one-man show, Los Angles Co Mus Art, 83; and others; and others. *Bibliog:* Melinda Wortz (auth), The LA/NY shift: For some artists, the fast land heads east, Art News, 1/83; Grace Glueck (auth), 2-Gallery shows are catching on, New York Times, 4/83; William Wilson, The galleries: La Cienega area, Los Angeles Times, 5/83; and others. *Media:* Construction, Bronze. *Publ:* Auth, Conversations with Nature, Mus Mod Art, New York, 82. *Dealer:* Blum-Helman Gallery 20 West 57th St New York NY 10021. *Mailing Add:* 31 Great Jones St New York NY 10012

HUNT, COURTENAY
PAINTER, INSTRUCTOR

b Jacksonville, Fla, Sept 17, 17. *Study:* Ringling Sch Art; Farnsworth Sch Painting. *Comn:* Univ Fla; Jacksonville Univ; City Hall, Duval Co Ct House, Jacksonville, Fla; Duval Co Ct House, Jacksonville; Shrine Mem, Washington, DC. *Exhib:* Allied Artists Am; Sarasota Art Asn, Fla; Audubon Artists Am; Soc Four Arts, Palm Beach, Fla; Fla Artist Group Inc, Norton Gallery, Palm Beach. *Mem:* St Augustine Art Asn. *Media:* Oil, Pastel. *Mailing Add:* 2587 Windwood Lane Orange Park FL 32073

HUNT, DAVID CURTIS
MUSEUM DIRECTOR, CURATOR

b Oswego, Kans, Dec 7, 35. *Study:* Univ Tulsa, BA(com design), 58, with Alexandre Hogue, MA(art hist), 68. *Exhib:* Okla Artists Ann, Philbrook Art Ctr, Tulsa, 62-65. *Pos:* Ed, Am Scene Quart, Gilcrease Mus, 65-72, cur art, Gilcrease Inst, Tulsa, Okla, 67-72; cur collections, Stark Mus, Orange, Tex, 72-76; dir, Missoula Mus of the Arts, Mont, 77-80; cur art, Ctr Western Studies, Joslyn Art Mus, Omaha, 80- *Teaching:* Instr mus practices, Univ Tulsa, 70-72. *Awards:* Margaret C Hewgley Award, Okla Artists Ann, 62; Wrangler Award, Western Heritage Ctr, 72. *Mem:* Am Assn Mus. *Res:* 19th & 20th century American western artists and works. *Publ:* Coauth, The Art of the Old West, Knopf, 71; contribr, Encyclopedia of the American West, Crowell, 76; coauth, The West as Romantic Horizon, Joslyn Art Mus & Univ Nebr Press, 80; auth, Guide to Oklahoma Mus, Univ Okla Press, 81; auth, Legacy of the West, Joslyn Art Mus and Univ Nebr Press, 82. *Mailing Add:* c/o Joplyn Art Mus 2200 Dodge St Omaha NE 68102

HUNT, RICHARD HOWARD
SCULPTOR

b Chicago, Ill, Sept 12, 35. *Study:* Art Inst Chicago, BAE. *Work:* Mus Mod Art, Metrop Mus Art, New York; Cleveland Mus Art, Ohio; Art Inst Chicago; Hirshhorn Mus; Mus 20th Century, Vienna, Austria. *Comn:* The Richmond Cycle (welded bronze), Social Security Ctr, Richmond, Calif, 76; Sentimental Scale and Wedge (welded bronze), Justice Ctr, Cleveland, Ohio, 77; A Bridge Across and Beyond (welded bronze), Howard Univ, 78. *Exhib:* Solo exhib, Dorsky Gallery, 68-, Columbia Univ, 81, Westbeth Art Gallery, 81, Fordham Univ, 81 & Brooklyn Artists Cult Asn, 82; retrospective, Mus Mod Art, New York, 71 & Chicago Art Inst, 71; and others. *Teaching:* Vis artist, Yale Univ, 64; Northwestern Univ, 68-69 & Washington Univ, 77-78. *Mem:* Nat Coun Arts; Am Coun Arts (bd dirs, 74-); Col Art Asn Am (bd dirs, 72-76); Am Acad Rome (bd trustees, 80-). *Media:* Metal. *Dealer:* B C Holland Gallery Inc 224 E Ontario Chicago IL 60611. *Mailing Add:* 1017 W Lill Ave Chicago IL 60614

HUNT, ROBERT JAMES
ADMINISTRATOR, EDUCATOR

b Fargo, NDak, Apr 5, 21. *Study:* Univ Iowa, BA, 47, MFA, 50. *Work:* Univ Iowa; Mulvane Art Mus; Des Moines Art Ctr; Friends of Art, Nelson Gallery; Wichita Art Mus. *Exhib:* Wichita Art Mus; Mid-America Artists; Kansas Free Fair; Am Fedn Arts; Colorado Springs Fine Arts Ctr; plus others. *Pos:* Dir, Mulvane Art Ctr, Washburn Univ, 64- *Teaching:* Prof art, Washburn Univ, 50- *Awards:* Purchase Prizes, Wichita Art Mus & Kans State Univ; Mid-Am, Nelson Gallery, 51. *Mem:* Mid-West Col Art Asn; Col Art Asn Am. *Mailing Add:* Dept Art Washburn Univ Topeka KS 66621

HUNTER, DEBORA
PHOTOGRAPHER, EDUCATOR

b Chicago, Ill, June 16, 50. *Study:* Northwestern Univ, BA, 72; RI Sch Design, MFA(photog), 76. *Work:* Yale Univ Art Mus; Wesleyan Univ Art Mus; Dallas Mus Fine Arts; RI Sch Design, Providence. *Exhib:* Dallas Mus Fine Arts, 79; The New Season, Witkin Gallery, New York; Second Sight, Carpenter Ctr Arts, Harvard, 81; Invisible Light Traveling Exhib, Smithsonian Inst, 80; one-person shows, Delahunty Gallery, Dallas, 80 & The Light Factory, Charlotte, NC, 81; Directions 1981, Hirshhorn Mus, 81; and others. *Teaching:* Instr, Swain Sch Design, New Bedford, Mass, 75-76; asst prof photog, Southern Methodist Univ, Dallas, 76- *Awards:* Boston Ctr for the Arts Award, Photovisions, 75; First Prize in Photog, Tarrant Co Ann, Ft Worth Art Mus, 76. *Bibliog:* Lucy Lippard (auth), From the Center: Feminist Essays on Women's Art, Dutton, 76; David Dillon (auth), From the lighthouse, D Mag, Dallas, 78; article, Artforum, 4/81. *Media:* Black & White. *Publ:* Contribr, Camera, 8-9/75; contribr, Women See Women, Crowell, 76; contribr, Ishmael, Brown, RI Sch Design Lit Arts Mag, 76; contribr, A Ten

Year Salute, Addison House, 79; contribr, Popular Photog, 8/80. *Dealer:* Witkin Gallery 41 E 57th St New York NY. 10022; Delahunty Gallery 2611 Cedar Spring Dallas TX 75201. *Mailing Add:* Dept of Art Southern Methodist Univ Dallas TX 75275

HUNTER, GRAHAM
CARTOONIST

b La Grange, Ill. *Study:* Landon Sch Cartooning, Cleveland, Ohio; Art Inst Chicago; Art Instr, Inc, Minneapolis, Minn. *Work:* Ed cartoons in permanent J Edgar Hoover FBI Collection; Peter Mayo Editorial Cartoon Collection, State Hist Soc, Columbia, Mo. *Exhib:* Editorial Cartoon Exhib, Wayne State Univ, Detroit, 64. *Pos:* Cartoonist, Nat Asn Mfrs, 49-, Milk Marketer Inc, 71- & Tobacco Inst, 77- *Awards:* Distinguished Serv Citation, US Treas; George Washington Honor Medal, Freedoms Found, 59 & 62; Hon Cert Awards for Cartoon, Freedoms Found, 60, 61, 75 & 76. *Publ:* Auth, Creating the Busy Scene Cartoon (cartoon course lesson), Art Instr, Inc. *Mailing Add:* Lindenshade 42 Clonavor Rd West Orange NJ 07052

HUNTER, JOHN H
PAINTER, PRINTMAKER

b Pa, Sept 26, 34. *Study:* Pomona Col, BA, 56; Claremont Grad Sch, MFA, 58. *Work:* Mus Mod Art, New York; Los Angeles Co Mus; Pasadena Art Mus, Calif; Amon-Carter Mus, Ft Worth, Tex; Nat Gallery Art, Washington, DC; and others. *Comn:* Poster for Tamarind Exhib, Mus Mod Art, Tamarind Lithography Workshop, Los Angeles, 69. *Exhib:* Western Painters Under 35, Univ Calif, Los Angeles, 58; Fulbright Artists Show, US Info Serv, Florence, Italy, 65; Cannes Film Festival, 66; Painters Behind Painters, Calif Palace of Legion of Honor, San Francisco, 67; Drawings, Ft Worth Art Ctr Mus, 69; Decade of Accomplishment, Ill Bell Tel Co, Chicago, 70. *Teaching:* Instr fine art, Ohio State Univ, 60-63; guest artist, Ind Univ, Bloomington, summer 63; prof art, Calif State Univ, San Jose, 65-; guest artist, Tamarind Lithography Workshop, 69 & Lakeside Studios, 79. *Awards:* Fulbright Fel Painting, Florence, 63-64, Renewal Grantee, 64-65. *Bibliog:* Peter Plagens (auth), Possibilities of drawing, Artforum, 10/69; articles, New York Times, Los Angeles Times, Rome Daily Am, Art News & others. *Mem:* Artists Equity Asn. *Media:* Multimedia. *Mailing Add:* Dept of Art Calif State Univ San Jose CA 95114

HUNTER, LEONARD LEGRANDE, III
SCULPTOR, EDUCATOR

b Washington, DC, July 3, 40. *Study:* Univ Miami, BA; Grad Sch Archit, Univ Pa; Univ Calif, Berkeley, MFA. *Work:* Hopkins Ctr, Dartmouth Col. *Comn:* Environmental outdoor hydraulic/kinetic sculpture, Crossroads Plaza, Lexington, Ky, 74. *Exhib:* one-man show, Univ Art Mus, Berkeley, 72; Biennial, New Orleans Mus Art, 73; Annual, Whitney Mus Am Art, 75; Film Festival of the Americas, Virgin Islands, 77; and others. *Pos:* Asst dir, Visual Arts Prog, Nat Educ Asn, 80-81, actg dir, 81-82. *Teaching:* Assoc prof art, Univ Ky, 72-80, chmn dept art, 78-80; prof art, San Francisco State Univ, 83- *Awards:* teaching fels, Univ Ky, 73-74; Golden Venus Medallion, Film Festival of the Americas, 77; and others. *Mem:* Col Art Asn; Nat Asn Artists Orgn. *Mailing Add:* 2105 Cactus Court Walnut Creek CA 94595

HUNTER, MEL
PRINTMAKER, PAINTER

b Oak Park, Ill, July 27, 27. *Study:* Northwestern Univ. *Work:* Japan Trade Bank; Am Heart Asn; Gen Re-Ins Corp; plus others. *Comn:* Several thousand illus comn by publ such as Life, Colliers, Nat Geog, Newsweek & Time-Life Bks, 53-68; 6 major murals, Transp Bldg, New York World's Fair, 64; 12 paintings, Gen Motors Corp, Detroit, 74; 110 editions orig hand-drawn lithographs, 71-83. *Pos:* Dir, Gallery North Star, Atelier N Star & Mel Hunter Graphics, Grafton, Vt, 75- & Pegasus Fine Art Publ, 82- *Bibliog:* Susan Ellis (auth), Drawing color separations on surfaced Mylar, Tamarind Tech Papers, 3/74; William G Cotner (auth), Mylar lithography: What it means to you, Decor Mag, 2/81. *Specialty:* Contemporary realism. *Publ:* Auth, Making pre-separation effective, Bk Production Indust Mag, 72; auth, Revolution in hand-drawn lithography, Am Artist Mag, 10/77; coauth & publ, The Mylar Method Manifesto, Atelier North Star, 80; auth, The New Lithography: A Complete Guide for Artists and Printers in the Use of Modern Translucent Materials for the Creation of Hand-Drawn Original Fine-Art Lithographic Prints, Van Nostrand Reinhold, 83. *Dealer:* Pegasus Fine Art Box 2 Grafton VT 05146. *Mailing Add:* Gallery North Star Box 2 Grafton VT 05146

HUNTER, MERIDITH
ART DEALER, SCULPTOR

b New York, NY, Nov 26, 27. *Study:* Univ Calif, Los Angeles; pvt study with Calvin Goodman; sculpture with Robert Ortlieb; Inst de Marmo, Carara, Italy, cert stonecarving. *Pos:* Art dealer, Santa Fe, NMex; consult art, var bus & insts. *Mem:* Artists Equity Asn; Santa Fe Art Dealers Asn. *Media:* Terra Cotta; Bronze. *Specialty:* Paintings, fiberwork, batiks, sculpture, Western art, photomontage and original prints. *Mailing Add:* Rte 4 Box 50 C Santa Fe NM 87501

HUNTER, MIRIAM EILEEN
EDUCATOR, PAINTER

b Cincinnati, Ohio, June 6, 29. *Study:* Ball State Univ, spec study with I Rice Perera & Margules, BS(art), 50, MA(art educ), 56; Wheaton Col, MA(Christian educ), 57; Art Inst Chicago, 60; Nova Univ, EdD, 79. *Work:* Burris Lab Sch, Ball State Univ, Muncie, Ind. *Comn:* Catalog cover design, 59 & centennial mural, 60, Wheaton Col; design consult, Glen Ellyn Baptist Church, Chicago, 61. *Exhib:* Prize-winning Entries, Carnegie Inst Int, 46-47; Fac Fine Arts Gallery, Art Inst Chicago, 60-; Ball State Univ Alumni Show,

63. *Pos:* Free lance design consult, Chicago, 52-72; chmn art dept, Wheaton Col, 69 & 75-79; art columnist, Record, Wheaton, Ill, 79. *Teaching:* Instr art & Eng, Hoagland Consolidated Sch, 51-52; fel instr art, Wheaton Col, 52-56, assoc prof art, 56-; guest instr art & art educ, Teacher Training Cols, Kenya, Africa, summer 63. *Awards:* First Place State of Ind, Nat Scholastic Art Exhib, Carnegie Inst Int, 47; Bronze Medal Award, DuPage Sesqui Centennial Design, Mayor's Off, Wheaton, 69; Outstanding Alumnus Award for Excellence in Educ, Ball State Univ, 75. *Mem:* Int Soc Lit & Arts; Nat Asn Advan Christian Scholar; Nat Art Educ Asn; Am Asn Univ Prof. *Media:* Oil combined with Textural Material; Clay for Stoneware. *Res:* Curriculum, education, policies, college governance, learning theory (Gestalt psychology and art). *Publ:* Auth, Color in the library, Christian Librn, Minneapolis, 59; illusr, Kenneth Taylor, auth, African Inland Mission, 63; illusr (booklet), Ensign for This Hour, Peru, Ind, 64. *Mailing Add:* 530 Aurora Way Wheaton IL 60187

HUNTER, ROBERT DOUGLAS
PAINTER, INSTRUCTOR

b Boston, Mass, Mar 17, 28. *Study:* Cape Sch Art, Provincetown, Mass, with Henry Hensche; Vesper George Sch Art, Boston; also with R H Ives Gammell, Boston. *Work:* Northeastern Univ, Boston; Tufts Univ; Boston Univ Med Ctr; Mass Inst Technol; Wheaton Col. *Comn:* Epiphany mural, Church St Mary of the Harbor, Provincetown, 56; altar frontal, Emmanuel Church, West Roxbury, Mass, 62. *Exhib:* Acad Artists Show, Springfield, Mass, 61; Am Artist Prof League Show, New York, 66, 67 & 70; New Eng Artists Exhib, Boston, 70 & 74. *Teaching:* Instr fine arts, Vesper George Sch Art, 55- & Worcester Art Mus, 70-79 & Mt Ida Jr Col, Newton, 78-79. *Awards:* 15 Richard Milton Gold Medals, New Eng Artists Exhib, 54-70; Newington Prize, 66 & 67, Am Artists Prof League; Frederick Thompson Found Award, 76. *Bibliog:* Richard Goets (auth), Sight sized method, Am Artist, 70. *Mem:* Guild Boston Artists (vpres, 68-73, pres, 73-78); Am Artists Prof League (dir, 60-70); Acad Artists Asn; Copley Soc Boston. *Media:* Oil. *Dealer:* Grand Central Art Gallery 40 Vanderbilt Ave New York NY 10017; Blair Gallery Santa Fe NM 87501. *Mailing Add:* 250 Beacon St Boston MA 02116

HUNTER, ROBERT HOWARD
PAINTER

b Auburn, Wash, May 17, 29. *Study:* Ore State Univ, 47-49; Univ Ore, BS & MFA, 49-53; Univ SC, 55-56. *Work:* Ackland Art Ctr, Univ NC, Chapel Hill; Duke Univ, Durham, NC; Greenville Co Mus Art, SC; SC Arts Collection; Lee Gallery, Clemson Univ, SC. *Exhib:* 159th Ann Painters & Sculptors, Philadelphia, 64; 7th Nat Show Art, Brockton, Mass, 64; Art on Paper, Weatherspoon Art Gallery, NC, 65; 16th Ann Drawing & Small Sculpture Show, Ball State Univ, 70; one-man show, Ackland Art Ctr, Univ NC, Chapel Hill, 68. *Pos:* Gallery dir, Rudolph Lee Gallery, Clemson Univ, 58-68; Ford Found fel, Univ NC, Chapel Hill, 66-67. *Teaching:* Instr figure drawing, Univ Ore, 52-53; prof printmaking, painting & basic design, Clemson Univ, 56-, head dept visual studies, 67-71. *Awards:* Guild of SC Artists Awards, 56-63; Springs Art Contest, SC, 61 & 77; 8th Ann Painting of Yr, Atlanta Art Asn, 62. *Mem:* Col Art Asn Am; SC Arts Comn (subcomt state art collection, 69-71, subcomt environ art, 71-73). *Media:* Mixed Media, Acrylic. *Publ:* Auth, Twenty Lithographs by Robert Hunter, 61; auth, The Shape of R Hunter, 66; illusr, The Binnacle, R Peterson, 67; contribr, Contemporary Artists of South Carolina, 70. *Dealer:* McDonald Gallery 715 Providence Rd Charlotte NC 28207. *Mailing Add:* Five N Gate Trace Greenville SC 29609

HUNTER, SAM
HISTORIAN

b Springfield, Mass, Jan 5, 23. *Study:* Williams Col, AB; Univ Florence, cert. *Collections Arranged:* Many exhibs at Mus Mod Art, New York, Minneapolis Inst Arts, Rose Art Mus, Jewish Mus, New York & Princeton Art Mus; American Art from the Commodities Collection (catalog), circulating exhib to six Am Mus, 81-82; Aspects of Post-Modernism: Decorative and New Image Art, E R Squibb & Sons Art Galleries, Princeton, NJ, 81. *Pos:* Art critic, New York Times, 47-49; cur, Mus Mod Art, 56-58; dir, Minneapolis Inst Arts, 58-60; dir, Rose Art Mus, Brandeis Univ, 60-65; dir, Jewish Mus, 65-68; consult ed, Harry N Abrams, Inc, 68-; fac cur mod art, Princeton Art Mus, 69-; Consult, Commodities Corp, Princeton, NJ, 80- *Teaching:* Former instr, Harvard Univ, Univ Calif, Los Angeles, Barnard Col, Columbia Univ, Cornell Univ & Brandeis Univ; prof art hist, Princeton Univ, 69-; Robert Sterling Clark vis prof, Williams Col, 76. *Awards:* Hubbard Hutchinson Fel Critical Studies, Williams Col, 49-52; Guggenheim Fel, 70-71. *Mem:* Col Art Asn Am. *Publ:* Auth, Masters of Twentieth Century Art, Abbeville Press, 80; contribr, Phaidon World Encyclopedia of Art, London, 81; auth, The Apocalyptic Vision: Four New Imagists (exhib catalog), Bellman Gallery, 83; auth, New Image/Pattern & Decoration from the Morton G Neumann Family Collection (exhib catalog), Kalamazoo Inst Arts, 83; auth, George Segal, Rizzoli, 84; auth, The Museum of Modern Art, New York, 84. *Mailing Add:* 146 Mercer St Princeton NJ 08540

HUNTER-STIEBEL, PENELOPE
CURATOR

b Washington, DC. *Study:* Barnard Col, BA; Inst Fine Art, NY Univ, MA. *Collections Arranged:* Twentieth Century Decorative Arts Gallery, 71-74 & 78-83, The Grand Gallery Int Exhib (ed, catalog), 74 & New Glass Exhib, 80, Metrop Mus Art, New York; New Glass Exhib, Metrop Mus Art, 80; The Fine Art of the Furniture Maker (coauth, catalog), Mem Art Gallery, Rochester, 81. *Pos:* Asst cur, Metrop Mus Art, 75-80, assoc cur, 80-; contrib cur, Philbrook Art Ctr, Tulsa, 82-; guest cur, Detroit Inst Arts, 83- *Res:* Twentieth century decorative arts; eighteenth century French furniture;

European ceramics, sixteenth through eighteenth century. *Publ:* Auth, Contemporary art glass, Art News, summer 81; auth, William Harper: Talismans for our time, Am Craft, 8-9/81; auth, Gustav Serrurier-Bovy, a forgotten master of art nouveau, Connoisseur, 11/82; auth, Renaissance on Wilshire Boulevard, Gentlemen's Quart, 10/83; and others. *Mailing Add:* 32 E 57th St New York NY 10022

HUNTINGTON, JIM
SCULPTOR
b Elkhart, Ind, Jan 13, 41. *Study:* Ind Univ, Bloomington, 58-59; El Camino Col, 59-60. *Work:* Addison Gallery Am Art, Andover, Mass; Rose Art Mus, Brandeis Univ; Smith Col Mus, Holyoke, Mass; Whitney Mus Am Art, New York; Oakland Mus, Calif; and others. *Exhib:* Corcoran Gallery Art Biennial, Washington, DC & Traveling Exhib, 65 & 67; Whitney Mus Am Art Painting Ann, 68 & Sculpture Ann, 69; one-man shows, Hayden Gallery, Mass Inst Technol, 68, Max Hutchinson Gallery, New York, 71 & Parker St 470, 72; David McKee Gallery, New York, 76 & 80; Seven Sculptors, Laguna Gloria Mus, Austin, Tex, 77-78; plus many others. *Awards:* Grand Prize Award, Sheraton-Boston Competition & Blanche Colman Award, Boston, 65; Nat Endowment Arts Fel, 80-81. *Media:* Stone, Metal, Wood. *Mailing Add:* 715 Driggs Ave Brooklyn NY 11211

HUNTLEY, DAVID C
PAINTER, ADMINISTRATOR
b Lenoir, NC, Oct 17, 30. *Study:* Univ NC, AB & MA. *Exhib:* City Art Mus St Louis, Mo, 66; Raymond Ducan Gallery, Paris, 66; Ligoa Duncan Gallery, New York, 67; Peoria Art Ctr, 68; Wesleyan Col, Macon, Ga, 69; and many other group & one-man shows. *Pos:* Dir, Univ Mus, Southern Ill Univ, Edwardsville, currently. *Teaching:* Instr children's art, Univ NC; instr hist art, design & art, Limestone Col; prof art, Ala Col, Montevallo; prof & chmn art & design dept, Southern Ill Univ, Edwardsville, formerly. *Awards:* Johnson Award, Birmingham Mus Art, 58; NC Mus Award, Raleigh, 60; Soc Independent Artists St Louis, 66; and others. *Mem:* Col Art Asn Am; Ill Art Asn; Ala Watercolor Soc; Nat Conf Art Admin; Am Asn Univ Prof; and others. *Mailing Add:* Off of Cult Arts & Univ Mus Southern Ill Univ Box 150 Edwardsville IL 62026

HUOT, ROBERT
PAINTER, FILMMAKER
b Staten Island, NY, Sept 16, 35. *Study:* Wagner Col, Staten Island, 53-57, BSc, 57; Hunter Col, grad art, New York, 61-62. *Work:* Frank Stella, NY; Paula Cooper, New York; William Rubin Collection, New York; Doberman Collection, Munster, Ger; Mus of Mod Art, New York, NY. *Exhib:* Systematic Painting, Guggenheim Mus, New York, 66; The Art of the Real Traveling Exhib, 68 & Recent Acquisitions, 78, Mus Mod Art, New York; Whitney Painting Ann, Whitney Mus, New York, 67 & 69; New Art USA, Mod Mus of Art, Minchem, WGer, 68; 557087, Seattle Art Mus, Wash, 69; Modular Painting, Albright-Knox Gallery, Buffalo, NY, 70; one-man shows, Paula Cooper Gallery, New York, 69-74, Millennium, New York, 75 & 79 & State Univ of NY, Albany, 76; Utica Col, 79-80; Hetzler Galerie, WGer, 80-81. *Pos:* Pigment chemist, Sun Chemical Co, Staten Island, 57-58 & 60-62; plant mgr, Neti Art Color, New York, 62-63. *Teaching:* Assoc prof painting, drawing & filmmaking, Hunter Col, New York, 63-81. *Awards:* Nat Coun Arts Grant, New York, 66 & with Twyla Harp Dance Co, 77. *Bibliog:* S MacDonald (auth), article, 4/79 & An interview with Robert Huot, 2/80, Afterimage. *Media:* Unstretched Canvas; Film. *Dealer:* Filmmakers Coop 175 Lexington Ave New York NY 10016; Max Hetzler Stuttgart WGer. *Mailing Add:* RD 1 New Berlin NY 13411

HUPP, FREDERICK DUIS
PAINTER, EDUCATOR
b Streator, Ill, Dec 21, 38. *Study:* Univ Ariz, BFA, 62, MFA, 66. *Work:* Tucson Mus Art, Ariz. *Exhib:* Univ Man, Winnipeg, 76; SW Biennial, Mus NMex, Santa Fe, 76; Eight State West Biennial, Grand Junction, Colo, 76; Four Corners Biennial, Phoenix, Ariz, 77; Univ Ariz Art Mus, Tucson, 79; and others. *Pos:* Cur, Univ Ariz Art Mus, 60-61 & Mus Fine Arts, Santa Fe, 62; instr, Fenster Ranch Sch, Tucson, 64-65. *Teaching:* Instr design, Univ Ariz, 68-79; asst prof drawing & painting, Tucson Mus Sch, 68-80, dir educ, 68-70; instr design & drawing, Pima Col, Tucson, 77- *Awards:* Eight West State Biennial Cash Award, Grand Junction, Colo, 74; Four Corners Biennial Cash Award, Phoenix, Ariz, 75; Cash Award, Cedar City Nat, Utah, 76. *Media:* Acrylic, Mixed Media. *Mailing Add:* 743 N Tenth Ave Tucson AZ 85705

HURD, PETER
PAINTER, WRITER
b Roswell, NMex, Feb 22, 04. *Study:* US Mill Acad, 21-23; Haverford Col, 23-24; Pa Acad Fine Arts, 24-26 with N C Wyeth; Tex Tech Univ, DFA; NMex State Univ, LLD, 68. *Work:* Metrop Mus Art, New York; Nat Gallery, Edinburgh, Scotland; Delaware Art Mus, Wilmington; Dallas Art Mus, Tex; Roswell Mus, NMex; and many others. *Comn:* 16 fresco panels, Tex Tech Univ Mus; fresco murals, Big Spring Post Off Bldg, Tex; mural panel, Prudential Insurance Co Bldg, Houston; portrait of Pres Johnson, White House Hist Asn (now in Nat Portrait Gallery); murals, Alamogordo Post Off Bldg, NMex; and others. *Exhib:* Retrospectives, Amon Carter Mus Art, Ft Worth, Tex, 64 & Calif Palace Legion Honor, 65; and many others. *Pos:* War corresp, Life Mag & USAAF, 42-45. *Awards:* Wilmington Soc Fine Arts, 41 & 45; Pa Acad Fine Arts Medal, 45; Isaac Maynard Prize, Nat Acad Design, 54. *Mem:* Nat Fine Arts Comn; Academician Nat Acad Design; Wilmington Soc Fine Arts; Am Watercolor Soc; Century Asn. *Publ:* Illusr, Last of the Mohicans, 26, Great Stories of the Sea & Ships, 33 & Habit of Empire, 38; auth, Count-down at Canaveral, Art in Am, 63; auth, Peter Hurd--The Lithographs, Baker Gallery, 69; auth, Sketch Book, Swallow, 71. *Mailing Add:* Sentinel Ranch San Patricio NM 88348

HURLEY, WILSON
PAINTER
b Tulsa, Okla, Apr 11, 24. *Study:* US Mil Acad, BS, 45; George Washington Univ Law Sch, LLB, 51. *Work:* Fairchild Hall, US Air Force Acad; US Air Force Mus, Wright-Patterson AFB, Ohio. *Exhib:* Nat Acad Western Art, Oklahoma City, 73-81; solo exhibs, Nat Cowboy Hall Fame, 77 & Thomas Gilcrease Mus, Tulsa, 83; Western Heritage, Houston, 79-81; Artists of America, Denver, 81-83. *Awards:* Silver Medal, 73 & 80 & Gold Medal, 77 & 78, Nat Acad Western Art. *Bibliog:* Mary C Nelson (auth), Wilson Hurley, Landscapist, In: American Artist, Watson-Guptill, 73 & Wilson Hurley, Lowell Press, 77. *Mem:* Nat Acad Western Art (exec comt, 75-81). *Media:* Oil. *Publ:* Illusr, Without Noise of Arms, Briggs, Northland, 75. *Dealer:* Lloyd M Taggart PO Drawer 42999 Las Vegas NV 89104; Fenn Gallery Santa Fe NM. *Mailing Add:* 237 Spring Creek Ct NE Albuquerque NM 87122

HURLSTONE, ROBERT WILLIAM
GLASS ARTIST, EDUCATOR
b Chicago, Ill, June 3, 52. *Study:* Ill State Univ, BS, 74; Southern Ill Univ, MFA, 78. *Work:* Corning Mus Glass, NY; Am Crafts Mus, NY; Rahr-West Mus & Civic Ctr, Manitowoc, Wis; Ind Univ Art Mus, Bloomington. *Exhib:* New Glass Traveling Exhib, 78-; Art for Use, Olympics Exhib, Lake Placid & Am Crafts Mus, NY, 80; Small group, Sales Gallery Show, Smithsonian Inst, Washington DC, 80; Ohio Glass Artists, Massillon Mus, Ohio, 80; one-man show, New Works, Habatat Gallery, Mich, 81; American Glass Now, III, touring Japan, 81- *Teaching:* Asst prof glass, 3-D design, Bowling Green State Univ, 78- *Awards:* Mus Dirs Award, Evansville Mus, 77; Third Place Award, Toledo Mus, 81. *Bibliog:* Terri Sharp (auth), Artist profile, Art Craft Mag; Portfolio Section, Am Craft Mag; Photograph of work, Village Voice. *Mem:* Glass Art Soc; Ohio Designer Craftman. *Media:* Glass. *Mailing Add:* 33 Indiancreek Dr Arlington Woods Rudolph OH 42462

HURSON, MICHAEL
DRAFTSMAN, PAINTER
b Youngstown, Ohio, 41. *Study:* Art Inst Chicago, BFA, 63; Oxbow Summer Sch Painting, Saugatuck, Mich, 60 & 61; Yale Univ, Norfolk, Conn, 62. *Work:* Art Inst Chicago; Guggenheim Mus, Whitney Mus Am Art & Metrop Mus Art, New York; Nat Gallery Australia, Canberra. *Exhib:* Chicago & Vicinity, Art Inst Chicago, 61, 63, 64 & 73, Small Scale in Contemp Art, Soc for Contemp Art, 75 & Drawings of the 70's, 77; one-man shows, Mus Contemp Art, Chicago, 72 & Mus Mod Art, New York, 74; Recent Acquisitions, Metrop Mus Art, New York, 74 & 20th Century Recent Acquisitions, 79; Nine Artists: Theodoron Awards, S R Guggenheim Mus, New York, 77; Am Art Since 1950, Whitney Mus Am Art, New York, 78, Art About Art, 78, New Image Painting, 78, Archit Analogues, 78 & Artists by Artists, 79; Summer Light, Mus Mod Art, New York, 81; New Dimensions in Drawing, Aldrich Mus, 81; and others. *Awards:* Nat Endowment Arts Grant, 74-75; Theodoron Award, Guggenheim Mus, 77; Vaklova Purchase Award, Mus Contemp Art, Chicago, 80. *Bibliog:* David Salle (auth), New image painting, Flash Art, 3-4/79; Reagen Upshaw (auth), Chicago: Michael Hurson at Dart, Art Am, 9/81; Edward L Saxe (auth), On the margin of society, Am Artists, 9/81. *Mailing Add:* c/o Paula Cooper Gallery 155 Wooster St New York NY 10012

HURST, RALPH N
SCULPTOR, EDUCATOR
b Decatur, Ind, Sept 4, 18. *Study:* Ind Univ, Bloomington, BS & MFA; Ogunquit Sch Painting & Sculpture, Maine, with Robert Laurent. *Work:* Evansville Mus Arts & Sci, Ind; Columbus Mus Arts & Crafts, Ga; Mobile Art Asn Gallery, Ala; Gulf Life Ins Co, Jacksonville, Fla; LeMoyne Art Found Gallery, Tallahassee, Fla. *Comn:* Relief sculpture, Fla State Univ Col Educ, 57; wall relief sculptures, Fla State Univ Union Bldg, Tallahassee, 63; sculpture-Madonna, St Thomas More Cath Church, Tallahassee, 71. *Exhib:* American Sculpture 1951, Metrop Mus Art, New York, 51; Contemporary Sculptors Drawings, Ohio State Univ, 54; Art USA, Madison Sq Garden, New York, 58; Nat Liturgical Art Exhib, San Francisco, 60; Southeastern Art Exhib, High Mus, 67. *Teaching:* Prof art educ & constructive design, Fla State Univ, 53-79, emer prof, 79- *Awards:* Ball Gallery Award, Nat Small Sculpture Exhib, Ball State Univ, 60; Community Purchase Award, Mobile Art Gallery, Ala, 71; Second Award, Maj Fla Artists, Harmon Gallery, Naples, Fla, 79. *Mem:* Artists Equity Asn; Nat Art Educ Asn; Int Sculpture Ctr, Washington, DC. *Media:* Alabaster, Wood. *Dealer:* Harmon Galleries Sarasota FL; Mickelson Gallery Washington DC. *Mailing Add:* 1801 Skyland Dr Tallahassee FL 32303

HURT, SUSANNE M
PAINTER
b New York, NY. *Study:* Duke Univ; Art Students League, with Frank V Dumond & Kenneth Hayes Miller; Corcoran Sch Art; also with Wayman Adams & A Ginsburg. *Work:* In pvt collections. *Exhib:* One-man show, Grist Mill Gallery, Chester, Vt, 76; Catharine Lorillard Wolfe Art Club, Nat Acad Design, New York, 71; Mus Fine Arts, Springfield, Mass; Hammond Mus, North Salem, NY; Nat Arts Club; and others. *Teaching:* Pvt classes & demonstrations. *Awards:* First Prize, Nat Biennial, 23; Grand Prize, Dept Parks & Recreation, New York, 78; Katherine A Lovell Mem Award, 81. *Mem:* Catharine Lorillard Wolfe Art Club (corresp secy, 71-74); Am Artists Prof League; Hudson Valley Art Asn; Composers, Authors & Artists Am (nat rec secy, 71-71-75); Royal Soc Arts; Nat League Am Pen Women. *Media:* Oil. *Mailing Add:* 299 Riverside Dr New York NY 10025

HURTADO DUHART, RODOLFO
PAINTER, ENGRAVER
b Mexico City, Mexico, Feb 23, 40. *Study:* Escuela Nacional de Arquitectura, Mexico City, 58-62; Atelier Paul Colin, Paris, France, 69-71; Atelier 17, Paris, 70-71. *Work:* Graphic Mus, Sophia, Bulgary; Salon de la Plastica Mexicana, Mexico City; Museo de Arte Moderno, Mexico City; General Motors Collection, Tex. *Exhib:* One-man show, Museo de Arte Moderno, Mexico City, 66; Solar Exposition, Museo de Bellas Artes, Mexico City, 68; Presence of Mexican Plastic Show, Museo de Bellas Artes, 68; Foreign Artist Show, United Nations Educ, Sci & Cult Orgn, Paris, 70; Mexican Painting & Sculpture Show, San Antonio, Houston, Ft Worth & Dallas, 72-73. *Awards:* First Prize, Third Ann Painting show, Univ Mexico, 62; Honorary Award, Ann Show, Mus Mod Art, Brussels, Belgium, 64; Honorary Award, Septentrion Group, Bondues, France, 71. *Bibliog:* Alfonso de Neuvillate (auth), Mexico actual painting 66, Artes de Mexico, 66. *Mem:* Sociedad Mexicana de Artistas Plasticos. *Dealer:* Galeria Proteus Estocolmo 16 Mexico City Mexico; Salon de la Plastica Mexicana Havre 7 Mexico City Mexico. *Mailing Add:* Marti 154-104 Col Escandon Del M Hidalgo 11800 Mexico DF Mexico

HURTIG, MARTIN RUSSELL
PAINTER, SCULPTOR
b Chicago, Ill, Aug 11, 29. *Study:* Inst Design Chicago, BS, 52, MS, 57; Atelier 17, Paris, 55. *Work:* Bibliot Nat, Paris; Philadelphia Free Libr; Carroll Reese Mus, Johnson City, Tenn; Honolulu Acad Art; Mus Contemp Art, Chicago. *Comn:* Stained glass windows & mural wall, Union Church, Lake Bluff, Ill, 63; outdoor court sculpture, Waukegan Pub Libr, Ill, 64; lobby relief sculpture, Midwest Iron Works, Chicago, 67. *Exhib:* Nat Print Exhib, Brooklyn Mus, 58 & 68; one-man shows, Flint Inst Arts, 61 & 68, Alonzo Gallery, 66 & 67 & Ecole Spec Archit, Paris, 69; 6th Am Artists Traveling Show, Paris & 12 French cities, 69-70; Jan Cicero Gallery, Chicago, 80, 81 & 83. *Teaching:* Asst prof drawing & design, Mich State Univ, 57-62; prof painting & printmaking, Univ Ill, Chicago Circle, 62-; dir, Sch Art & Design, Univ Ill, Chicago, currently. *Awards:* Purchase Awards, Carroll Reese Mus, 67 & Honolulu Acad Arts, 71. *Bibliog:* F Schulze (auth), Art news in Chicago, Art News, 11/71; A Goldin (auth), Vitality vs greasy kids stuff, Art Gallery Mag, 4/72; D Guthrie & J Allen (auth), Waging polemical warfare, Chicago Tribune, 4/30/72. *Dealer:* Jan Cicero Gallery 221 W Erie Chicago IL 60610. *Mailing Add:* 1727 Wesley St Evanston IL 60201

HURTUBISE, JACQUES
PAINTER
b Montreal, Que, Feb 28, 39. *Study:* Beaux Art Sch, Montreal. *Work:* Mass Inst Technol; Peter Stuyvesant Art Found, Amsterdam; Galerie Nat Can, Ont; Art Gallery Ont, Toronto; Vancouver Art Gallery; and others. *Comn:* Murals, Ottawa Univ, 69, Place Radio Can, Montreal, 72 & Ministry of Defense, Ottawa, 72. *Exhib:* 300 Ans d'Art Canadien, Galerie Nat Can, Ottawa, 67; Canada Art d'Aujourd'hui, Paris, France, Rome, Italy & Lausanne, Switz, 68; Seven Canadians, Mass Inst Technol & Gallery Mod Art, Washington, DC, 68; Edinburgh Festival, Scotland, 68; plus many one-man & group exhibs. *Pos:* Resident artist, Dartmouth Col, 67. *Awards:* First Prize, Concours Artistique Quebec, Que Govt, 65; Prize, Expos Hadassah, 68; Can Coun Arts Grant, 70; and others. *Bibliog:* Laurent Lamy (auth), Hurtubise, Lidec, 71. *Mem:* Royal Can Acad Art. *Dealer:* Moos Gallery Toronto & Calgary Can. *Mailing Add:* 1226 Rue St Louis Terrebonne PQ J6W 1K4 Canada

HURWITZ, SIDNEY J
PAINTER, PRINTMAKER
b Worcester, Mass, Aug 22, 32. *Study:* Sch Worcester Art Mus; Brandeis Univ, BA; Boston Univ, MFA. *Work:* Libr Cong; Mus Mod Art, New York; DeCordova Mus, Lincoln, Mass; Minneapolis Mus; Victoria & Albert Mus, London; and others. *Comn:* Mosaic mural, Skowhegan Sch Art, Maine, 64; ed of woodcuts, Wellesley Col, Mass, 67; six paintings of London, Japan Int Bank, London, 73; ten etchings, Bldg Design & Construction Mag, Chicago. *Exhib:* Am Drawing, Mus Mod Art, New York, 56; Print Biennial, Libr Cong, 62; Pa Acad, Philadelphia, 64; New Eng Artists, Boston, 71; Martin Sumers Gallery, New York. *Teaching:* Prof art, Boston Univ, 62- *Awards:* Louis Comfort Tiffany Award, 66; Artist Award, Am Inst Arts & Lett, 69; Mass Found Arts Fel, 76; and others. *Mem:* Col Art Asn Am; Boston Printmakers Soc. *Publ:* Auth, Etchings of Sigmund Abeles, 66 & auth, My woodcut technique, 67, Am Artist. *Mailing Add:* 202 Homer St Newton MA 02159

HUSEBYE, TERRY L
PHOTOGRAPHER
b El Paso, Tex, Mar 16, 45. *Study:* Univ Wis, Madison, BA, 68, MA, 73, MFA, 79; Univ NM, 73 & 78; studied with Van Deren Coke & Beaumont Newhall. *Work:* Boston Mus Fine Arts; Chicago Art Inst; Int Mus Photog; Mus Mod Art, New York; Corcoran Gallery Art. *Exhib:* Solo exhibs, Arco Ctr Visual Art, Los Angeles, 82 & NM Mus Fine Arts, Santa Fe, 82; Summer Light, Light Gallery, New York, 82; Four Color Photographers, Friends Photog, Carmel, Calif, 82; Twentieth Century Photographs from the Museum of Modern Art, Seibu Mus, Tokyo, 82; Color as Form: A History of Color Photography, Corcoran Gallery Art & George Eastman House, Rochester, NY, 82; Contemporary Photography from the Museum Collection, Mus Fine Arts, Houston, 83; Landscapes: Wolf Von Dem Bussche, Terry Husebye, Bernard Plossu, Phoenix Art Mus, 83. *Pos:* Photog coordr, Madison Art Ctr, Wis, 71-72. *Teaching:* Vis lectr, Univ Wis, Madison, 79. *Awards:* Nat Endowment Arts Fel, 81; Guggenheim Fel, 83. *Bibliog:* Contribr, Camera, Lucerne, Switz, 8/74; Dana Asbury (auth), Terry Husebye: Ocotillo Flat, Artspace, fall 82. *Mem:* Soc Photog Educ; Friends Photog. *Dealer:* Etherton Gallery Tucson AZ; Grapestake Gallery San Francisco CA. *Mailing Add:* 203 Alamo Dr Santa Fe NM 87501

HUSHLAK, GERALD
COMPUTER ARTIST, PAINTER
b Edmonton, Alta, Feb 15, 45. *Study:* Univ Alta; Univ Calgary, Alta; Univ Calif; Royal Col Art, London, Eng, MFA. *Work:* Can Coun Art Bank, Ottawa, Ont; San Francisco Mus Mod Art, Calif; Vancouver Art Gallery, BC; Smithsonian Inst, Washington, DC; Alta Art Found. *Exhib:* Glenbow Mus, Calgary; Burneby Art Gallery, Vancouver; Gallery Royal, Vancouver; Univ Manitoba Gallery, Winnipeg; Southern Alberta Art Gallery; and others. *Teaching:* Assoc prof painting, Univ Calgary, Alta, 75- *Awards:* Purchase Award, World Print Competition, San Francisco Mus Mod Art, 77. *Bibliog:* Articles, Vanguard Mag, 80, Arts Can, 80 & Arts Mag, 81. *Mem:* Col Art Asn; Can Artists Representation; Royal Canadian Acad. *Media:* Computers; Acrylic. *Dealer:* Bau-Xi Gallery Vancouver AB Can & Toronto ON Can. *Mailing Add:* 202 11th Ave Calgary AB T2M 0B8 Canada

HUSTON, PERRY CLARK
CONSERVATOR
b Mo, Jan 4, 33. *Study:* Univ Mo, AB, 55, Medical Sch, 55-57; Nelson Art Gallery, with James Roth, 63-70; special study with Sheldon & Caroline Keck, 68. *Pos:* Assoc conservator, Nelson Art Gallery, 66-70; chief conservator, Kimbell Art Mus, 71- *Teaching:* Supervisor internships, Conserv Grad Progs, Cooperstown & Oberlin Grad Conserv Progs, 72-, teaching consult, 75-77. *Mem:* Fel Am Inst for Conserv Hist & Artistic Works (vpres, 78-79, pres, 80-); fel Inst for Conserv Hist & Artistic Works . *Mailing Add:* Kimbell Art Mus PO Box 9440 Will Rogers Rd W Ft Worth TX 76107

HUTCHINGS, LA VERE
PAINTER, INSTRUCTOR
b Idaho Falls, Idaho, Sept 18, 18. *Study:* Brigham Young Univ, 40; Idaho State Col, AA, 41; Chouinard Art Inst, 54-55; Art Students League, 70; John Pike Watercolor Sch, 70; also studied with Sergei Bongart, Jo Rebert & E Hayward Veal. *Work:* Fashion Inst, Los Angeles; Brigham Young Univ Collection; Las Vegas Mus; Laguna Beach Mus. *Comn:* Watercolor, Caldwell Libr Bd, Idaho, 77. *Exhib:* Riverside Mus, Calif, 74 & 76 & 82; Cent Fed Power Plaza Gallery, San Diego, 77; Springville Mus Art, Utah, 77 & 78; Foothills Art Ctr, Golden, Colo, 80; solo exhib, Brigham Young Univ, 83; and others. *Teaching:* Instr, US Armed Forces Inst, Manila, 45-46; Ricks Col, Rexburg, Idaho, 68-69 & Hutchings Watercolor Sch, Jamestown, Calif, currently. *Awards:* Purchase Award, Elliot Block Co, San Bernardino, 71; Asn Award, Okla Watercolor Asn, 81; Best Landscape, Whisky Painters Am Int Show, Akron, 82. *Bibliog:* George Hoeper (auth), Gallery features Mother Lode art, Stockton Record, Calif, 8/31/79; Leo Stutzin (auth), A bird to crow about, Modesto Bee, Calif, 11/22/81; Leo Stutzin (auth), Lode watercolorist wins as author too, Modesto Bee, 1/83. *Mem:* Nat Watercolor Soc; Watercolor West (vpres, 78-79); Whiskey Painters Am; Soc Western Artists; Midwest Watercolor Soc. *Media:* Watercolor. *Publ:* Illusr, It's Fun to Paint Old Shacks and Barns, Walter Foster Art Co, 77; illusr, Palette talk, M Grumbacher Inc, 12/81; illusr, Reproductions, Haddads Fine Arts Inc, 81-82; illusr, It's Fun to Paint Roads and Rivers, Walter Foster Art Co, 82; La Vere Hutchings paints the mother lode, Southwest Art Mag, 1/83. *Mailing Add:* PO Box 249 Jamestown CA 95327

HUTCHINSON, JANET L
MUSEUM DIRECTOR, COLLECTOR
b Washington DC, May 2, 17. *Collections Arranged:* William Grant Sherry, Gene Klebe, Carmen Z Simpkins, Kan Man Shu (Diana Kan), Richard Tucker, and many others. *Pos:* Owner-dir, Broadlawn Gallery, Camden, Maine, 57-64; cur, Old Merchants House, New York, 61-62; dir, Martin Co Hist Soc; Elliott Mus & House of Refuge, 65- *Mem:* Salmagundi Club. *Mailing Add:* Elliott Mus 825 NE Ocean Blvd Stuart FL 33494

HUTCHINSON, MAX
DEALER
b Melbourne, Australia, Aug 25, 25. *Study:* Royal Melbourne Inst Technol. *Pos:* Dir, Max Hutchinson Gallery, New York, currently. *Specialty:* Contemporary painting and sculpture. *Mailing Add:* Max Hutchinson Gallery Inc 138 Greene St New York NY 10012

HUTCHINSON, PETER ARTHUR
CONCEPTUAL ARTIST
b London, Eng, Mar 4, 30. *Study:* Univ Ill, BFA, 60. *Work:* Mus Mod Art, New York; Munchengladbach Mus, WGer; Krefeld Mus, WGer; Rose Mus, Boston, Mass; Chrysler Mus, Norfolk, Va. *Exhib:* Paricutin Project, John Gibson Gallery, 70; Images: 2 Ocean Projects, 69 & Information, 70, Mus Mod Art; Nature & Art, Krefeld Mus, Haus Lange, WGer, 72; Stedelijk Mus, Amsterdam, 74; Venice Biennale, Am Pavilion, 79; and others. *Awards:* Outstanding Grad Painter, Univ Ill, 60; and others. *Bibliog:* Scheldahl (auth), Breadworks as earth works, NY Times, 69; Back to nature, Time, 6/70; James Collins (auth), Story art, New York Mag, 10/74. *Media:* Mixed Media, Film. *Publ:* Auth, Earth in upheaval, arts, 68; auth, Science fiction: an aesthetic for science, Art Int, 68; auth, Is there life on earth, 68 & Foraging: being an account of a hike through the snow-mass wilderness as a work of art, 72, Art Am; auth, Alphabet Cottage Book, OONA Press, WGer, 80; and others. *Mailing Add:* 10 Holway Ave Provincetown MA 02657

HUTCHISON, ELIZABETH S
PAINTER
Study: Otis Art Inst; and with Joseph Mugnaini & Aimee Bourdieu. *Work:* Rice Univ Permanent Collection; Utah State Univ Permanent Collection; Riverside Art Mus Collection, Calif; Am Fedn Social Settlements Permanent Collection, New York; and many others in pvt collections in US & foreign

countries. *Exhib:* Nat Watercolor Soc Ann, 66-75; Southern Calif Expo, Del Mar, 69-75; Old Bergen Art Guild, 70-75; Nat Acad Design, New York, 70-72; Nat Watercolor Soc tour of Sweden, 73-74; and many other group & one-man shows. *Awards:* Purchase Award, Watercolor USA, 69, 73 & 74; First Prize in Acrylic, Southern Calif Art for 75, Del Mar; Claire Falkenstein Awards, 73, 78 & 80; and many others. *Mem:* Nat Watercolor Soc (bd mem, 4 yrs, pres, 71-72, juror, 72-73); Women Painters West (juror, 69-72, bd mem, 8 yrs, pres, 73-75). *Media:* Watercolor, Mixed Media. *Dealer:* Albert J Kramer Gallery 3459 Meier St Los Angeles CA 90066. *Mailing Add:* 26320 Rim Rd Hemet CA 92343

HUTCHISON, JANE CAMPBELL
EDUCATOR, HISTORIAN

b Washington, DC. *Study:* Western Md Col, BA(cum laude), 54; Oberlin Col, MA, 58; Kunsthist Inst, Utrecht, with J G van Gelder, 60-61; Univ Wis, with James S Watrous, PhD, 64. *Exhib:* US Nat Printmakers, Libr Cong, 56. *Collections Arranged:* Dutch & Flemish Paintings from Private Collections, 74 & Graphic Art in the Age of Martin Luther, 83, Elvehjem Mus, Univ Wis, Madison. *Pos:* Libr asst, Toledo Mus Art, Ohio, 58-59. *Teaching:* Instr art hist, Univ Wis, Madison, 63-64, asst prof, 64-69, assoc prof, 69-75, prof, 75-, dept chmn, 77-80; vis asst prof, Tyler Sch Art, Temple Univ, summer 67. *Mem:* Col Art Asn; Medieval Acad Am; Midwest Art Hist Soc (secy-treas 81-83, pres 83-). *Res:* Late fifteenth and early sixteenth century Dutch and German engravings. *Publ:* Auth, The Master of the Housebook, Collectors Editions, 72; auth, Dutch and Flemish Paintings of the 17th Century, Elvehjem Mus, Univ Wis, 74; auth, The housebook master and the Mainz Marienleben, In: A Tribute to Wolfgang Stechow, 76; ed, Early German Artists: The Illustrated Bartsch, Vol 8 & 9, Abaris, 80 & 81; auth, Graphic Art in the Age of Martin Luther, Elvehjem Mus, Univ Wis, 83. *Mailing Add:* Elvehjem Mus Art Univ Wis 800 University Ave Madison WI 53706

HUTSALIUK, LUBO
PAINTER

b Lvov, Ukraine, Apr 2, 23; US citizen. *Study:* Cooper Union Art Sch, 54. *Work:* Palm Springs Desert Mus, Calif; Vt Art Ctr, Manchester; Bibliotheque Nat, Paris, France. *Exhib:* One-man shows, Galerie Norval, Paris, France, 59, Angle du Faubourg, Paris, 63 & Hilde Gerst Gallery, New York, 66; Galerie Royale, Paris, 76; 25 yrs retrospective, USOM Gallery, New York, 80; and others. *Bibliog:* P Imbourg (auth), Art d'Hutsaliuk, J Amateur Art, 64; J Hess Michel (auth), Vibrant paintings of Hutsaliuk, Am Artist, 69. *Mem:* Audubon Artists. *Media:* Oil; Watercolor. *Dealer:* Rolly-Michaux Gallery 943 Madison Ave New York NY 10021. *Mailing Add:* 260 Riverside Dr New York NY 10025

HUTTON, DOROTHY WACKERMAN
DESIGNER, PRINTMAKER

b Cleveland, Ohio, Feb 9, 1899. *Study:* Minneapolis Sch Art, cert; Univ Minn, with Vytlacil, Earl Horter & Hobson Pittman; Acad Andre L'Hote, Paris. *Work:* Smithsonian Inst, Washington, DC; Harvard Univ; and others. *Exhib:* Five Pennell Exhibs, Libr Cong, Washington, DC; Corcoran Gallery Art, Washington, DC; Philadelphia Print Club, Pa; Carnegie Exhib, Pittsburgh; Grand Cent Art Gallery, New York. *Mem:* Philadelphia Art Alliance; Am Colorprint Soc (corresp secy, 65-80); Philadelphia Watercolor Club (dir, 65 & 68); Plastic Art Club Women. *Mailing Add:* 203 N Essex Ave Narberth PA 19072

HUTTON, LEONARD
DEALER

Pos: Owner & dir, Leonard Hutton Galleries, currently. *Specialty:* German Expressionism and Russian Avant-Garde art. *Mailing Add:* 33 E 74th St New York NY 10021

HUTTON, WILLIAM
MUSEUM CURATOR

b New York, NY, Oct 2, 26. *Study:* Williams Col, BA, 50; Harvard Univ, MA, 52. *Pos:* Asst cur, Toledo Mus Art, 52-65, sr cur, 71-; dir, Currier Gallery Art, 65-68; res staff, Victoria & Albert Mus, London, Eng, 68-71. *Res:* Eighteenth century Meissen porcelain. *Publ:* Ed, Toledo Museum of Art American Paintings, 79. *Mailing Add:* Toledo Mus of Art Box 1013 Toledo OH 43697

HUXTABLE, ADA LOUISE
CRITIC

b New York, NY. *Study:* Hunter Col, AB(magna cum laude); NY Univ; Nine Hon doctorates. *Pos:* Asst cur archit & design, Mus Mod Art, New York, 46-50; contrib ed, Progressive Archit Art in Am, 50-63; archit critic, New York Times, 63-83, mem ed bd, 73-82. *Awards:* Elsie de Wolfe Award, Am Inst Interior Designers, 69; Pulitzer Prize for Distinguished Criticism, 70; Nat Arts Club Lit Award, 71; Macarthur Fel, 82; and others. *Mem:* Am Soc Archit Historians. *Publ:* Auth, Pier Luigi Nervi, Braziller, 60; auth, Classic New York, 64; auth, Will They Ever Finish Bruckner Boulevard?, Macmillan, 70; auth, Kicked A Building Lately?, 76. *Mailing Add:* 969 Park Ave New York NY 10028

HYDE, SCOTT
PHOTOGRAPHER, PRINTMAKER

b Montevideo, Minn, Oct 10, 26. *Study:* Art Ctr Sch, Los Angeles; Columbia Univ, with Ralph Mayer; Art Students League. *Work:* Mus Mod Art, Metrop Mus Art, Int Ctr Photog, New York; Int Mus Photog, Rochester, NY; Bibliot Nat, Paris. *Exhib:* Photo-Graphics, Int Mus Photog, George Eastman House, Rochester, NY, 71; Photog Invitational, Ark Arts Ctr, Little Rock, 71; Photo into Art, Scottish Arts Coun Gallery, Edinburgh, 73; Synthetic Color,

Southern Ill Univ, Carbondale, 74; Mirrors & Windows: Am Photog Since 1960, 78. *Teaching:* Adj prof photog, Cooper Union, 68-70, New York Univ Exten, 71-72 & Manhattanville Col, 72-75. *Awards:* Guggenheim Fel, 65; Creative Artists Pub Serv Prog Grants, 72 & 75. *Bibliog:* Syl Labrot (auth), Scott Hyde photographs, Aperture, 70; Thomas Dugan (auth), Photography between covers, Light Impressions, 75. *Media:* Offset Lithography. *Publ:* Auth, Dust Map, 79; auth, The Real Great Society Album, 79. *Mailing Add:* 430 E 6th St New York NY 10003

HYLAND, DOUGLAS K S
MUSEUM DIRECTOR

b Salem, Mass, Oct 7, 49. *Study:* Univ Pa, BA, 70; Univ Del, MA, 76, PhD, 80. *Pos:* Cur painting & sculpture, Spencer Mus Art, Univ Kans, 79-82; dir, Memphis Brooks Mus Art, 82- *Teaching:* Asst prof art hist, Univ Kans, 79-82; vis prof, Southwestern Univ, Memphis, 83- *Awards:* Fels, Kress Found, 78 & Smithsonian Inst, 78-79. *Mem:* Col Art Asn; Asn Art Mus; AAMD; SEMC. *Res:* American and European painting and sculpture of the 19th and 20th centuries. *Publ:* Agnes Ernst Meyer and the avant garde in America, Am Art J, 79; Thomas Hart Benton, 80, Sculpture Catalog, 81 & Marius deZayas: Conjurer of Souls, 81, Spencer Mus Art, Univ Kans; Adelheid Roosevelt: American cubist, J Arch Am Art, 82. *Mailing Add:* c/o Memphis Brooks Mus Art Overton Park Memphis TN 38112

HYMAN, ISABELLE
HISTORIAN, EDUCATOR

b New York, NY, April 19, 30. *Study:* Vassar Col, BA, 51; Columbia Univ, MA, 55; Inst Fine Arts, NY Univ, MA, 66, PhD, 68. *Teaching:* From instr to assoc prof, NY Univ, 63-79, prof hist art, 79- *Mem:* Col Art Asn; Soc Archit Historians; Renaissance Soc Am. *Res:* Art and architecture in Renaissance Florence. *Publ:* Ed, Brunelleschi in Perspective, Prentice-Hall, 74; auth, Fifteenth Century Florentine Studies, Garland, 77; articles relating to Italian Renaissance art in scholarly journals. *Mailing Add:* Fine Arts Dept 303 Main Bldg NY Univ New York NY 10003

HYMAN, LINDA
DEALER, HISTORIAN

b Buffalo, NY, June 11, 40. *Study:* Vassar Col, 58-60; Columbia Univ, with Barbara Novak, BA, 61, MA, 63; City Univ New York Grad Ctr, with Milton Brown, PhD, 78. *Collections Arranged:* New York Crystal Palace, City Univ New York Grad Ctr, 74; Gertrude Greene (auth, catalog), 81, Ernest Fiene (auth, catalog), 81 & Social Art in America 1930-1945 (auth, catalog), 81, ACA Galleries, New York. *Pos:* Historian, Metrop Mus Mod Art, 67-71; staff, ACA Galleries, 78-82; pvt art dealer & consult, 82- *Teaching:* Asst prof art hist, City Univ New York, Richmond Col, Staten Island, 73-76; asst prof art hist, Emory Univ, Atlanta, Ga, 76-78. *Specialty:* American paintings. *Publ:* Auth, Winslow Homer: America's Old Master, Doubleday, 73; auth, Hiram Powers' Greek slave: High art as popular culture, Art J, 75. *Mailing Add:* 172 W 79th St 21 E 67th St New York NY 10024

HYSON, JEAN
PAINTER

b Alvarado, Tex, Mar 4, 33. *Study:* NY Univ with William Baziotes, 52; Art Students League with Yasuo Kuniyoshi, George Grosz & Harry Sternberg, 52-56. *Work:* Walter Barriese Collection, New York; Oakland Art Mus, Calif; Int Banking Ctr, San Francisco, Calif; City of San Francisco; Levi-Strauss, San Francisco. *Exhib:* One-person shows, San Francisco Mus Art, 67, Calif Palace of the Legion of Honor, 69, William Sawyer Gallery, San Francisco, 72 & Richmond Art Mus, Calif, 77; Fine Arts Contemp Exhib, Northern Ill Univ, 69; Mus Mod Art Rental & Sales Gallery, New York, 71; California Artists, Western Art Mus Asn, 70. *Media:* Oil and Acrylic. *Mailing Add:* 950 Franklin San Francisco CA 94109

I

IACURTO, FRANCESCO
PAINTER, INSTRUCTOR

b Montreal, Que, Sept 1, 08. *Study:* Fine Arts Sch Montreal; Grande Chaumiere Colarossi, Paris, France, govt scholar; and with Charles Maillard, Ed Dyonnet, John Y Johnstone & others. *Work:* Prov Mus Que; Can House, London, Eng; House of Senate, Ottawa; Rideau Hall, Gov Gen Can; Lt Gov, Que. *Comn:* Fall landscapes, Bank Montreal, London, 71; painting, Janin Construction, PQ, 71; pastel, Can Govt, Ottawa, 71; portraits, Louis Albert Vachan, Quebec Seminary & Larkin Kerwin, Laval Univ; and others. *Exhib:* Royal Can Acad, Toronto, Ont, 48 & 51 & Montreal, 60; Spring Exhib, Montreal Mus Art, 52 & 53. *Teaching:* Instr drawing, Cath Sch Comn, 29-33 & Art & Trades Montreal, 29-38; instr painting, Libr Ste Foy, Que, 66- *Awards:* First Medal for Art, 28 & Scholar to Europe, 29, Govt Que; Silver Medal, Ministry Exterior, France, 29. *Mem:* Royal Can Acad Arts; Soc Artists Prof Que; Independent Art Asn. *Dealer:* Michel de Kerdour Quebec City PQ Can; Arts & Styles 896 Sherbrooke St W Montreal PQ Can. *Mailing Add:* 1232 La Vigerie Quebec PQ G1W 3W7 Canada

IANNETTI, PASQUALE FRANCESCO PAOLO
DEALER, COLLECTOR

b Florence, Italy, Apr 10, 40; US citizen. *Study:* Univ Florence; Acad di Belle Arti, Florence; Univ Minn, Minneapolis. *Pos:* Pres, Pasquale Iannetti Inc Galleries, San Francisco & Carmel, Calif. *Mem:* Int Am Soc of Appraisers;

Graphic Art Coun, Los Angeles Co Mus & Achenbach Found, San Francisco. *Specialty:* Fine original prints, drawings and other unique works form the sixteenth century through the twentieth century. *Collection:* Contemporary prints and drawings, Pre-Columbian and African art. *Mailing Add:* 575 Sutter St San Francisco CA 94102

IDAHERMA (IDAHERMA WILLIAMS)
PRINTMAKER, PAINTER
b Bronx, NY. *Study:* Philadelphia Col Art, BFA, 59; Pa Acad Fine Art, 60-63; Univ Pa, MFA, 63. *Comn:* Symbol (dragonfly design), Churchville Nature Ctr, Pa, 66. *Exhib:* Philadelphia Art Festivals, Philadelphia Mus Art, 55 & 59; Fel Ann Exhib, Pa Acad Fine Arts, 66; Art From NJ, NJ State Mus, Trenton, 69 & 71; solo exhib, NJ State Mus, Trenton, 75 & Western Electric Corp, Hopewell, NJ, 83; Peale House, Pa Acad Fine Arts, 82; Printmaking Coun NJ, Northbranch, 83; Philadelphia Watercolor Club, Plaza Hotel, 83. *Pos:* Contribr, Del Valley Advance, 66-67. *Teaching:* Instr painting & drawing, Fleisher Art Mem, Philadelphia, 60- *Awards:* Harrison S Morris Mem Fel Watercolor, Pa Acad Fine Arts, 66. *Bibliog:* Linda Holt (auth), Watercolor show a joy, Trentonian, 7/1/75. *Mem:* Printmaking Coun NJ; Artists Equity; Am Color Print Soc; Philadelphia Watercolor Club; Trenton Artists Workshop Asn. *Media:* Woodcut; Watercolor Collage. *Publ:* Auth, Old building transformed, Sch Arts Mag, 11/72; auth, Precautions for elementary and secondary art teachers, Art Hazards News, 9/79. *Dealer:* Assoc Am Artist Gallery Latimer St Philadelphia PA. *Mailing Add:* Coppermine Rd RD 1 Princeton NJ 08540

IDEN, SHELDON
PAINTER, EDUCATOR
b Detroit, Mich, Sept 29, 33. *Study:* Art Inst Chicago; Wayne State Univ, BFA; Cranbrook Acad Art, with Zoltan Sepeshy, MFA. *Work:* Cranbrook Acad Art, Bloomfield Hills, Mich; Ball State Univ, Muncie, Ind; Wayne State Univ, Detroit; Macomb Community Col, Warren, Mich. *Exhib:* Second Biennial, Pa Acad Fine Arts & Detroit Mus Art, 60; Mich Artists Ann, 60-70 & 72 & Other Ideas, 69, Detroit Inst Arts; Drawing & Sculpture Ann, Ball State Univ, 62; All Mich Show, Flint Mus Art, 72. *Pos:* Artist in residence, Mich Coun Arts, 69. *Teaching:* Instr drawing & painting, Wayne State Univ, 63-68; asst prof drawing & painting, Eastern Mich Univ, 68- *Awards:* Fulbright Fel to India, 62; Mus Purchase Award, 70 & Gertrude Kasle Award for Painting, 71, Detroit Inst Arts. *Bibliog:* Hakanson (auth), Made in Detroit, Art Scene, 67 & article, Detroit News, 71; Tall (auth), article, Detroit Free Press, 71. *Media:* Oil, Charcoal. *Mailing Add:* Dept of Art Eastern Mich Univ Ypsilanti MI 48197

IGLEHART, ROBERT L
EDUCATOR, WRITER
b Baltimore, Md, Feb 2, 12. *Study:* Md Inst Art, scholar for European study; Johns Hopkins Univ; Columbia Univ, BS Educ; New Sch Social Res. *Pos:* Writer & art critic, 78- *Teaching:* Instr sch art, Univ Wash, 38-41; chmn dept art educ, NY Univ, 46-55; prof art, Univ Mich, 55-77, emer prof, 77- chmn dept, 55-71. *Awards:* Nat Gallery Art Medal for Distinguished Serv to Art Educ, 66. *Mem:* Fel Royal Soc Arts; John Dewey Soc; Col Art Asn Am; Nat Art Educ Asn. *Publ:* Auth, numerous articles for prof mag. *Mailing Add:* 117 Dixboro Rd Ann Arbor MI 48105

IHARA, MICHIO
SCULPTOR
b Paris, France, Nov 17, 28; Japanese citizen. *Study:* Tokyo Univ Fine Arts, BFA, 53; Mass Inst Technol, Fulbright Fel; also with Gyorgy Kepes, 61. *Work:* Wind, Wind, Wind, Kanagawa Mus Mod Art, Kamakura, Japan. *Comn:* Metal screen, Rockefeller Ctr, 78; suspended sculpture, Neiman-Marcus, Beverly Hills, 79; suspended sculpture, Pavillion Hotel, Singapore, 82; suspended sculpture, AT&T Long Lines, Atlanta, 82; plaza sculpture, New World Ctr, Hong Kong, 82; and others. *Exhib:* Selection 64, Inst Contemp Art, Boston, 64 & Boston Celebrations, 75; Trends Contemporary Art, Kyoto Mus Mod Art, 68; Ann Exhib, Nat Inst Arts & Lett & Am Acad Arts & Lett, 73; Japanese Artists in America, Tokyo Mus Mod Art & Kyoto Mus Mod Art, 73-74; one-man show, Staempfli Gallery, New York, 77, 80 & 84. *Pos:* Fel, Ctr Advan Visual Studies, Mass Inst Technol, 70-75. *Teaching:* Instr basic design, Musashino Fine Arts Univ, Tokyo, 66-68. *Awards:* Graham Found Fel, 64; Ann Award, Am Acad Arts & Lett & Nat Inst Arts & Lett, 73; First Prize, Fitchburg Libr Art Competition, Mass Coun Arts & Humanities, 74. *Mem:* Japanese Artists Asn. *Media:* Stainless Steel, Brass. *Dealer:* Staempfli Gallery 47 E 77th St New York NY 10021. *Mailing Add:* 63 Wood St Concord MA 01742

IHLE, JOHN LIVINGSTON
PRINTMAKER, EDUCATOR
b Chicago, Ill, Feb 1, 25. *Study:* Univ Iowa, 49, with Maurice Lasansky; Ill Wesleyan Univ, Bloomington, BFA, 50; Bradley Univ, Peoria, Ill, MA, 51, with Ernest Freed; San Francisco State Univ, 54. *Work:* Libr of Cong, Washington, DC; Chicago Art Inst; New York Pub Libr; Achenbach Found for Graphic Arts, Calif Palace of Legion of Honor, San Francisco; Nat Gallery of Art, Washington, DC. *Comn:* Prints (210 each ed), Int Graphic Art Soc, New York, 57, 60 & 61; print, Roten Galleries, Baltimore, Md, 67; print, San Francisco Hosp Comn, San Francisco Art Comn, 73. *Exhib:* One-man shows, San Francisco Mus Art, 60, 66 & 77; Nat Print Exhib, Libr of Cong, Soc Am Graphic Artist, New York & Brooklyn Mus, NY; Nat Print Invitationals, Univ Ky, 61, State Univ NY, Albany, 68, Univ Ill, 70 & Cincinnati Art Mus, Ohio, 73. *Collections Arranged:* Prints of John Ihle (auth, catalogue), Achenbach Found of Graphic Art, 49-62; Ihle: Survey of Work, Univ NDak Art Galleries, 57-76; Traveling Exhibits, Univ NDak, Minot State Col, NDak,

Univ Mont, Univ Alta, Calgary & San Francisco Mus Art, 76-77; plus others. *Pos:* Chmn bd, San Francisco Tapestry Workshop, 78- *Teaching:* Prof art & printmaking, San Francisco State Univ, 55-; vis prof printmaking, Univ Alta, Edmonton, 68-69; vis artist printmaking, The Sch Art Inst Chicago, 80. *Mem:* Calif Soc Printmakers (former pres); Color Print Soc. *Dealer:* Fountain Gallery of Art 117 NW 21st Ave Portland OR 97965. *Mailing Add:* 49 Shell Road Mill Valley CA 94941

IIMURA, TAKA
FILMMAKER, VIDEO ARTIST
b Tokyo, Japan, Feb 20, 37. *Study:* Keio Univ, Tokyo, BA(political sci), 59. *Work:* Anthology Film Arch, New York; Centre Beaubourg des Art Plastiques, Paris; Everson Mus, Syracuse, NY; Royal Film Arch, Brussels, Belg; Neuer Berliner Kunstverein, Berlin. *Exhib:* Japanese Experimental Films, Mus Mod Art, New York, 66; one-man shows, Apple, New York, 72, Kitchen, New York, 72, Mus Mod Art, New York, 75, Centre Beaubourg des Art Plastique, Paris, 77, Anthology Film Arch, New York, 77 & Int Cult Ctr, Antwerp, Belg, 77; and many other group and one-man shows. *Teaching:* Vis tutor film, Schiller Col, Berlin, 73, Univ NMex, 75-76; vis asst prof film, Kent State Univ, 76. *Awards:* Spec Prize (for film Onan), 3rd Int Experimental Film Festival, Knokke, Belg, 63; Artist-in-residence Grant, Deutscher Akademischer Austamschdienst, Berlin, 73-74; Creative Artist Pub Serv Grant in Film, 75-76. *Mem:* Filmmakers Cooperative, New York; Univ Film Asn; Canyon Cinema Cooperative, San Francisco; and others. *Mailing Add:* 127 Second Ave Apt 15 New York NY 10003

IKEDA, YOSHIRO
CERAMIST, EDUCATOR
b Kushikino-City, Kagoshima, Japan, Apr 10, 47; US citizen. *Study:* Portland State Univ, Ore, BS(painting & drawing), 70; Kyoto City Univ Fine Art, Japan, cert, 73; Univ Calif, Santa Barbara, MFA, 77. *Work:* Japanese Govt Ministry Educ, Tokyo; Kyoto City Univ Fine Art, Japan; Utah State Univ, Logan; Calif Polytech State Univ, San Luis Obispo; Topeka Pub Libr, Kans. *Exhib:* El Paso Mus, Tex, 79; Foothills Art Ctr, Denver, 79; Cooperstown Art Asn, NY, 81; Purdue Univ Gallery, West Lafayette, Ind, 81; War Mem Mus, Aukland, NZ, 81; Wichita Mus, Kans, 81; and others. *Teaching:* Instr ceramics, Utah State Univ, 73-74; instr ceramics, Ventura Col, 77-78; asst prof ceramics, Kans State Univ, 78-, area head, 81- *Awards:* First Place Award, Austin Art Asn, 78; Juror's Award, Calif Polytech State Univ, 78; Merit Award, Fletcher Brownbuilt Pottery Guild, 81. *Mem:* Nat Coun Educ Ceramic Arts; Kans Artist Craftsman Asn; Kans Designer Craftsman Asn. *Media:* Clay. *Publ:* Auth, Asymmetrical thrown form, Ceramic Monthly, 6/78. *Dealer:* Marcia Rodell Gallery 11714 San Vicente Blvd Los Angeles CA 90049. *Mailing Add:* 2213 Todd Rd Manhattan KS 66502

IKEGAWA, SHIRO
PRINTMAKER
b Tokyo, Japan, July 15, 33; US citizen. *Study:* Tokyo Univ Arts; Otis Art Inst Los Angeles Co, MFA, 61. *Work:* Seattle Art Mus; Brooklyn Mus Art; Metrop Mus Art, New York; Libr Cong & Smithsonian Inst, Washington DC; and many others. *Comn:* Ed etchings, James B Lancer Corp, 68; three-dimensional print, comn by Mrs Martha Jackson, New York, 69; two ed etchings, Los Angeles Co Mus Art, Graphic Art Coun, 73; prints comn for Int Multiple Exhib, Nomura Display Co, Tokyo, 73; Tale of Genji (color etching), Los Angeles Times, 73; and others. *Exhib:* Sixty-seventh Western Ann, Denver Art Mus, 61; 16th Ann Exhib, Newport Harbor Art Ctr, 61; Int Print Show, Seattle Art Mus, 63-65 & 67-68; Nat Print Exhib, Brooklyn Art Mus, 64 & 66; Calif Soc Etchers Int Show, Calif Palace Legion Hon, 64; Pacific Heritage, DeYoung Mem Mus & others, 65; Ann Exhib Watercolors, Prints & Drawings, Pa Acad Fine Arts, 65; CSE Nat Print Exhib, San Francisco Mus Art, 65; Nat Print & Drawing Competition, Dulin Gallery Art, Tenn, 65; Okla Art Ctr, 65 & 67; Ann Exhib Sculpture & Print, Whitney Mus Am Art, 66; 20th Nat Exhib Prints, Libr Cong, 66; Smithsonian Inst Traveling Exhib, 70-73; Prints: New Points of View Traveling Exhib, Western Asn Art Mus, 80; Printmaking: Process/Innovation, Mus Asn NGrange Co, Fullerton, Calif, 80; Drawing 80, Col St Rose, Albany, NY; Los Angeles Print 1883-1980, Los Angeles Co Mus Art, 80-81; Otis Art Inst Alumni Show, Pac Design Ctr, Los Angeles, 80; one-person exhib, Los Angeles Inst Contemp Art, 80; and many others. *Teaching:* Asst prof art, Pasadena City Col, 61-67 & Calif State Univ, Los Angeles, 67-76; guest prof, Otis Art Inst Los Angeles Co, 67, prof art & chmn printmaking dept, 76-78; guest prof, Calif Inst Arts, Chouinard Art Sch, 68-71, Calif State Univ, San Francisco, 72, Univ Calif, Berkeley, summer 73, Vancouver Sch Art, BC, summer 74 & Univ Calif, Irvine, 74-75; prof art, Otis Art Inst, Parsons Sch Design, 79- *Awards:* Nat Endowment Arts Fel for Printmaking, 74; Ford Found Fac Enrichment Grants, 77 & 80; Nat Endowment Arts Fel for Conceptual Art & Performance Art, 81. *Bibliog:* Leonard Edmondson (auth), Etchings, Van Nostrand Reinhold, 73; article, Southwest Art Gallery Mag, 72; Interview (monograph), Asian Am Studies Ctr, Univ Calif, Los Angeles, 73; and others. *Media:* All. *Dealer:* Martha Jackson Gallery 521 W 57th St New York NY 10019; Comsky Gallery 9777 Wilshire Blvd Suite 815 Beverly Hills CA. *Mailing Add:* 323 E Altadena Drive Altadena CA 91001

ILOWITZ, THEODORA
PAINTER, PRINTMAKER
b New York, NY, Mar 15, 21. *Study:* Art Students League. *Work:* Bergen Community Mus, Paramus, NJ; Art Ctr Northern NJ, Tenafly. *Exhib:* Invitational, Newark Mus, NJ, 79; New England Silvermine Exhib, Silvermine Guild, New Canaan, Conn, 79; Invitational Exhib, Morris Mus, Morristown, NJ, 80; Invitational, Taiwan Cult Ctr, China, 80; Summit Art Ctr, NJ, 81; and others. *Awards:* Painting Award, Bergen Community Mus,

Painters & Sculptors Soc NJ, 79; Graphics Award, Nat Art Club, 79; Painting Award, Summit Art Ctr, Newark Mus, 81. *Bibliog:* Eileen Watkins (auth), Jersey art corner, Newark Star Ledger, 4/15/79; David Shirey (auth), Art, New York Times, 4/29/79; Diedre Sykes (auth), Profile, North Jersey Suburbanite, 11/28/79. *Mem:* Artist Equity New York; Women's Caucus Art. *Media:* Acrylic, Collage. *Dealer:* Art Couple Gallery 74 Broadway Nyack NY 10960. *Mailing Add:* 15 Central Ave Demarest NJ 07627

IMANA, JORGE GARRON
PAINTER, MURALIST
b Sucre, Bolivia, Sept 20, 30; US citizen. *Study:* Univ San Francisco Xavier, Sucre, MA. *Work:* Nat Mus, La Paz, Bolivia; Univ San Francisco Xavier Mus, Sucre; Nat Mus, Bogota, Colombia; Casa de la Cult, Quito, Ecuador; Bolivian Embassy, Moscow. *Comn:* Hist mural, Bolivian Govt, Junin Col, Sucre, 58; History of Education in Bolivia (mural), comn by Bolivian Govt, Padilla Col, Sucre, 59; Social History in Peru (mural), Constructors Union, Lima, Peru, 61; Ciudad de Dios Sch (mural), comn by students' parents, Lima, 62. *Exhib:* Nat Salon, La Paz, 62; Latin Am Show, Fine Arts Gallery, San Diego, 64; Bolivian Paintings, Mus of Mod Art, Paris, France, 73 & Nat Gallery, Warsaw, Poland, 75; House of Friendship of the Peoples, Moscow, 75; Gallery IDB, Washington, DC, 76; plus 70 one-man shows. *Pos:* Owner, The Artist's Showroom, San Diego. *Teaching:* Prof drawing, Univ San Francisco Xavier, Sucre, 54-60; prof drawing & watercolor, Nat Acad, La Paz, 60-62; dir art dept, Inst Normal Superior, La Paz, 60-62. *Awards:* Nat Award, Nat Show, La Paz, Bolivian Govt, 62; Watercolor Award, Nat Watercolor Show, Lima, Peru, Watercolor Soc, 62; Purchase Awards Oil & Watercolor, Ann Show, San Diego Art Inst, 64. *Mailing Add:* 3357 Caminito Gandara La Jolla CA 92037

INDIANA, ROBERT
PAINTER, SCULPTOR
b New Castle, Ind, Sept 13, 28. *Study:* John Herron Sch Art; Munson-Williams-Proctor Inst; Art Inst Chicago, BFA; Skowhegan Sch Painting & Sculpture; Univ Edinburgh & Edinburgh Col Art, Scotland; Franklin & Marshall Col, Lancaster, Pa, Hon DFA, 70; Ind Univ, Bloomington, Hon DFA, 77; Colby Col, Waterville, Maine, Hon DFA, 81. *Work:* Mus Mod Art, Whitney Mus Am Art, New York; Carnegie Inst Arts, Pittsburgh; Stedelijk Mus, Amsterdam, Neth; Detroit Inst Arts, Mich. *Comn:* Electric mural, New York World's Fair, 64-65. *Exhib:* Mus Mod Art, New York, 61, 63-64; Dunn Int, Tate Gallery, London, 63; Whitney Mus Am Art, New York, 63-67, 69 & 74; Va Mus Fine Arts, Richmond, 74; Hirshhorn Mus, Washington, DC, 74; Corcoran Gallery Art, Washington, DC, 75; 20th Nat Print Exhib, Brooklyn Mus, 77; Art Inst Chicago, 79; Whitney Mus Am Art, 80; and others. *Bibliog:* Brattinga (auth), Robert Indiana, Gebrauchsgraphik, 64; Swenson (auth), Horizons of Robert Indiana, Art News, 66; McCoubrey (auth), Robert Indiana, Univ Pa, 68. *Mem:* Royal Soc Arts. *Media:* Oil; Steel. *Publ:* Illusr, Numbers, 68. *Dealer:* Marian Goodman Gallery 38 East 57th St New York NY 10022. *Mailing Add:* c/o Star of Hope Vinalhaven ME 94863

INDICK, JANET
SCULPTOR
b Bronx, NY, Mar 3, 32. *Study:* Hunter Col, with Robert Motherwell & Dong Kingman, BA(art), 53; The New Sch, with Gregorio Prestopino & Richard Pousette-Dart, 61. *Work:* Bergen Community Mus Art & Sci, Paramus, NJ; NJ Col Medicine & Dentistry, Newark. *Comn:* Steel sculpture, The Jewish Ctr, Teaneck, NJ, 74; steel menorah, Wyckoff Public Sch, NJ, 80; wall sculpture (brass), Tree of Life Temple Beth Rishon, Wyckoff, NJ, 81; menorah (wood), Temple Beth Rishon, Wyckoff, NJ, 83. *Exhib:* 16 Sculptors, Morris Mus Art, Morristown, NJ, 79; 25 Artists, Bergen Mus, Paramus, NJ, 81; On & Off the Wall, Newark Mus, 82; Fellowship Exhib, Jersey City Mus, 83; Sculpture Exhib, Morris Mus, 83; and others. *Pos:* Mem, Teaneck Adv Bd on the Arts, NJ, 80. *Awards:* Sculpture Prize, Nat Asn Women Artists, 74; Sculpture Prize, Nat Asn Painters & Sculptors, 78 & 80; Fel Grant, NJ State Council Arts, 80-81. *Mem:* Nat Asn Women Artists (juror 80-81); Sculptors Asn Inc; New York Soc Women Artists; Nat Asn Painters & Sculptors of NJ; Mod Artists Guild (juror 80-81); and others. *Media:* Welded Steel, Mixed Media. *Dealer:* Opper-Nacht Assocs 256 Van Nostrand Avenue Englewood NJ. *Mailing Add:* 428 Sagamore Avenue Teaneck NJ 07666

INDIVIGLIA, SALVATORE JOSEPH
PAINTER, INSTRUCTOR
b New York, NY, Nov 16, 19. *Study:* Leonardo da Vinci Art Sch; Sch Indust Arts; Pratt Inst, BA; fresco & mural painting with Alfred D Crimi; also with Buck Ulrick, Nicholas Volpe, Earl Winslow & George Harrington, Jr. *Work:* USN Combat Art Collection, Washington, DC; Grumbacher & Sons Collection, New York; Mutual Benefit Life Insurance Co, NJ; Annin Flag Co & Morris Davis Collection, Emily Lowe Found, New York. *Comn:* Assisted Alfred D Crimi with hist mural for Northampton, Mass, 40, Gen Anthony Wayne Mural for Wayne, Pa, 41 & Bowery Mission Mural for Bowery Mission, New York, 42. *Exhib:* Am Watercolor Soc Ann, New York, 53-83; Audubon Artists Ann, New York, 53-83; Joe & Emily Lowe Found Show, 55 & 60; Operations Palette, USN Combat Art, Smithsonian Inst, Washington, DC, 65; Nat Acad Design, New York, 65-75. *Pos:* Off comdr, USN combat artist, 61-; art dir, acct exec & vpres, Pringle & Booth Inc, currently. *Teaching:* Asst & instr, City Col New York, 46-69; private classes, 46-72; instr watercolor, East Williston Libr, New York, 60-72; instr fine & appl arts, Mechanics Inst, New York, 62-66. *Awards:* Pauline Law Award in Oil, Knickerbocker Artists, 74; Gold Medal Watercolor, 75 & Jane Peterson Award in Oil, 76, Allied Artists Am. *Mem:* Artists Fel (pres, 60-63); Am Watercolor Soc (dir, chmn, 53-72); Allied Artists Am (secy, 59-62); Knickerbocker Artists (vpres, 57-59); Audubon Artists. *Media:* Watercolor,

Oil. *Publ:* Contribr, Direction, Int Rels Div, Off Info, 66; contribr, Watch, USNR, 67; contribr, Naval Aviation News, 68; contribr, All Hands, Bur Naval Personnel, 69; auth, Watercolor page, Am Artist Mag, 71. *Mailing Add:* 974 Lorraine Dr Franklin Square NY 11010

INGALLS, EVE
INSTRUCTOR, PAINTER
b Cleveland, Ohio, Sept 29, 36. *Study:* Skowhegan Sch Art; Smith Col, BA, 58; Yale Univ Sch Art, BFA, 60, MFA, 62. *Exhib:* Butler Inst Am Art, 66; Vassar Col Art Gallery, 70; Yale-Norfolk, Conn, 72; Art & Archit Gallery, Yale Univ, 77; Contemporary Reflections, Aldrich Mus, 77; Cleveland Mus, 77 & 80; Connecticut Painting, Sculpture and Drawing Traveling Exhib, 78; SoHo 20 Gallery, New York, 80, 81 & 84. *Teaching:* Instr painting & drawing, Silvermine Guild Sch Arts, 72- *Bibliog:* Katherine Nahum (auth), article, Art New Eng, 80; Virginia Mann (auth), article, 80 & Martha Scott (auth), article, 84, Arts Mag. *Media:* Mixed. *Dealer:* SoHo 20 Gallery 469 Broome St New York NY 10014. *Mailing Add:* 9 Tower Parkway New Haven CT 06511

INGBER, BARBARA
DEALER, COLLECTOR
b New York, NY, Apr 18, 32. *Study:* NY Univ; Feigan Dramatic Sch. *Pos:* Dir, Ingber Gallery Ltd, 72- *Mem:* Mus Mod Art; Whitney Mus Am Art; Guggenheim Mus; Metrop Mus. *Specialty:* 20th century American art. *Collection:* Paintings, drawings, sculpture and photographs by contemporary American artists. *Mailing Add:* Ingber Gallery Ltd 460 W Broadway New York NY 10012

INGLE, JOHN S
PAINTER, EDUCATOR
b Evansville, Ind, Sept 18, 33. *Study:* Univ Ariz, BFA, 64, MFA, 66. *Work:* Metrop Mus Art, New York; St Louis Art Mus, Springfield Art Mus, Mo; Evansville Mus Arts & Sci, Ind. *Exhib:* Contemporary American Realism Since 1960, 81 & Works on Paper From the Collection of Jalene and Richard Davidson, 82, Pa Acad Fine Art; Every Object Rightly Seen, Univ Va Art Mus, Charlottesville, 82; 20th Century American Watercolors Traveling Exhib, Gallery Asn NY State, 83; Contemporary Images Watercolor, Univ Wis, Oshkosh, 83; Realist Watercolor, Univ Conn, Hartford, 83 & Fla Int Univ, 83. *Teaching:* Prof painting, drawing & design, Univ Minn, Morris, 66- *Bibliog:* Hilton Kramer (auth), Critics choice, New York Times, 1/18/81; James Cooper (auth), article, News World, 1/18/81; John Driscoll (auth), Paradigms of reality, Am Artist, 3/82. *Media:* Watercolor. *Mailing Add:* c/o Tatischeff & Co 50 W 57th St 8th Floor New York NY 10019

INGRAHAM, JOHN DOUGLAS
DEALER, PUBLISHER
b Bristol, Conn, June, 28, 55. *Study:* Johns Hopkins Univ, Baltimore, BA, 77; private study with P J Pierce, 77-81. *Collections Arranged:* 58 Fine Boston Painters (auth, catalog), Concourse Gallery, Boston, 75; Boston Painters--Past & Present (auth, catalog), Pierce Galleries, Inc, Hingham, 76; The Watercolor World of J W S Cox (ed, catalog), 81; W S Barrett Retrospective (auth, catalog), Schenectady Mus, NY, 78; The Surreal World of Samuel Rose (auth, catalog), Pierce Galleries, Inc, 79. *Pos:* Pres, Pierce Galleries Publishing, Inc, Hingham, Mass, 79-; assoc dir, Pierce Galleries, Inc, 79- *Mem:* Mus Fine Arts; Arch Am; Friend Fogg. *Res:* The life & works of James A M Whistler; specialize in 19th & early 20th century american artists; American marine painters. *Specialty:* Edmund C Tarbell, J J Enneking, Frank Benson, Sam Rose (contemp), Robert Reid, Jane Peterson and others. *Publ:* Ed, Edmund C Tarbell & The Boston School of Painting, 80. *Mailing Add:* Pierce Galleries Inc 721 Main Rt 228 Hingham MA 02043

INGRAM, JERRY CLEMAN
PAINTER, DESIGNER
b Battiest, Okla, Dec 13, 41. *Study:* Inst Am Indian Arts; Okla State Univ Sch Tech Training, BA, 66. *Work:* Nat Gallery Art, Washington, DC; Heard Mus, Phoenix, Ariz; R C Gorman Navajo Gallery, Taos, NMex; also in collections of Jerry Bregman, New York & Dr Byron Butler, Phoenix. *Comn:* Mural of dancers, Okla State Univ Sch Tech Training, Okmulgee, 65. *Exhib:* Philbrook Art Ctr Indian Art Ann, Tulsa, Okla, 66 & 77; two-man show, 70, Indian Art Ann, 71 & one-man show, 72, Heard Mus, Phoenix, Ariz; Scottsdale Indian Art Ann, Ariz, 71 & 72; Charles W Bowers Mem Mus, Santa Ana, Calif, 72; Gallup Ceremonial & NMex State Fair, 72. *Awards:* Spec Award for Buffalo Dancer, Scottsdale Indian Art Ann, 72; First Prize for Buffalo Woman Dancing, Gallup Ceremonial, 72; Wolf Robe Hunt Award, 33rd Ann Am Indian Artists Exhib, Philbrook Art Ctr, Tulsa, Okla, 77; and others. *Bibliog:* Tom Bahti (auth), Southwest Indian ceremonials, K C Publ, 70; Doris Monthan (auth), Indian Individualists, Northland; Broder (auth), American Indian Painting & Sculpture, Abbeville. *Media:* Watercolor, Acrylic; Bronze, Beadwork. *Mailing Add:* PO Box 428 Corrales NM 87048

INGRAM, JUDITH
PAPERMAKER
b Philadelphia, Pa, Oct 12, 26. *Study:* Philadelphia Col Art; printmaking with Carol Summers. *Work:* Del Mus Ann; Philadelphia Mus Art; RCA Corp, Eastern US & PR; Emperor Japan; Int Paper Co, Hercules Inc. *Exhib:* Florence Duhl Gallery, New York, 79; Soc of Graphic Artists Ann Exhib; Hooks/Epstein Galleries, Houston, Tex, 79 & 81; Rosenfeld Gallery, Philadelphia, 80 & 82; Sutton Gallery, New York, 81; and others. *Teaching:* Handmade paper workshops, Univ Del, Univ Pa, Philadelphia Mus of Art & Arrowmont Sch of Crafts, Gatlinburg, Tenn; Haystack Mountain Sch Crafts, Deer Isle, Maine. *Mem:* Am Color Print Soc; Artists Equity Asn. *Mailing Add:* 5 Kenny Circle Broomall PA 19008

INJEYAN, SETA L (SETA LEONIE CHUTJIAN)
PAINTER
b Aleppo, Syria, May 3, 46; US citizen. *Study:* Beirut Univ Col, Lebanon, 69; Art Ctr Col Design, Pasadena, Calif, with Richard Diebenkorn, Lorser Feitelson, Llyn Foulkes, Ann McKoy & Peter Alexander, BFA, 75. *Work:* Kaloust Gulbenkian Found, Lisbon, Portugal; Wells Fargo Bank, Los Angeles; Eastern State Hosp, Medical Lake, Wash. *Exhib:* Los Angeles Co Mus Art, 80; Palos Verdes Art Ctr, Rancho Palos Verdes, Calif, 82; Santa Barbara Mus Art, Calif, 82; F Benjamin Gallery, Bakersfield, Calif, 82; Los Angeles Artcore Gallery, 82; Mona Lisa Gallery, Chiba Ken, Japan, 83; and others. *Awards:* First Place, Armenian Allied Arts Coun, 75; Best Show, Soc Art Ctr Alumni, Art Ctr Col Design, 76; Three Purchases Prizes, Wash State Arts Comn, 83. *Bibliog:* David G Gardner (publ) Contemporary hand-colored photography, Picture Mag, 80; Photography Year, Time-Life, 82; Contemporary photography as phantasy, Am Photogr, 9/83. *Mem:* Artists Equity Asn; Los Angeles Inst Contemp Art. *Media:* Mixed Media. *Mailing Add:* 5610 Pinecone Rd La Crescenta CA 91214

INMAN, PAULINE WINCHESTER
PRINTMAKER, ILLUSTRATOR
b Chicago, Ill, Mar 3, 04. *Study:* Smith Col, AB; and with Allen Lewis. *Work:* Carnegie Inst, Pittsburgh, Pa; Libr Cong, Washington, DC; Metrop Mus Art, New York; Montclair Art Mus, NJ; Boston Pub Libr, Mass. *Exhib:* Nat & int exhibs incl Exchange Ital Exhib, Contemp Print Exhib, Tokyo, Japan & London, Eng. *Mem:* Boston Printmakers; Soc Am Graphic Artists; Acad Artists Asn. *Media:* Wood. *Publ:* contribr, articles in, Antiques, 60, 69 & Artists Proof, 64; auth, Down East Reader, 62, Lippincott; illusr, Antiques Guide to Decorative Arts in America, Dutton, 72; and others. *Mailing Add:* 4 Currituck Rd Newtown CT 06470

INOUE, KAZUKO
PAINTER, LECTURER
b Fukuoka City, Japan, Jan 14, 46; US citizen. *Study:* Mich State Univ, BFA & MFA. *Work:* Wichita State Univ Mus Fine Arts, Kans; Mich State Univ. *Exhib:* Flint Inst Art, Mich, 73; one-woman show, Razor Gallery, New York, 74 & O K Harris Gallery, 77; Soho Ctr for Visual Artists, 78; Aldrich Mus Contemp Art, Conn, 79; and others. *Teaching:* Vis artist painting & drawing, Mich State Univ, 73; lectr drawing, Eastern Mich Univ, fall 74. *Awards:* Awards, Chautauqua Art Ctr, 70 & Detroit Inst Arts, 72. *Bibliog:* David Shirley (auth), article, New York Times, 69; article, Art News, 72; Joseph Dreiss (auth), article, Arts Mag, 74. *Mem:* Col Art Asn Am. *Media:* Acrylic, Mixed Media. *Dealer:* Allan Stone Gallery 48 E 86th St New York NY. *Mailing Add:* 543 Broadway New York NY 10012

INSEL, PAULA
DEALER, ADMINISTRATOR
b Paris, France, Jan 13, 03; US citizen. *Study:* City Col New York, cert, 54; NY Univ, cert, 55; New York Sch Interior Design, cert, 57. *Pos:* Dir, Artravelrama, NY State 20 Shows in Tex, 58; dir, Stuyvesant Outdoor Art Festival, Union Square Savings Bank, New York, 59; dir, Galerie Paula Insel, New York, 60-; founder, PR Gallery Mus, Ponce. *Awards:* Grumbacher Art Co Award of Merit for Var Nat Exhibs, 57; Citation for Original Art Exhibs, Murray Hills, New York, 57; Citation, State Mus City of New York by Police Athletic League Comnr, 59. *Mem:* Am Fedn Art. *Specialty:* Mostly contemporary. *Publ:* Auth column in Art World, 54-55; auth, New York galleries, Arts Mag, 4/71. *Mailing Add:* Galerie Paula Insel 987 Third Ave New York NY 10022

INSLEY, WILL
PAINTER, DRAFTSMAN
b Indianapolis, Ind, Oct 15, 29. *Study:* Amherst Col, BA; Harvard Univ Grad Sch Design, MA(archit). *Comn:* Great Southwest Indust Park, Atlanta, Ga, 68. *Exhib:* One-man shows, Walker Art Ctr, Minneapolis, 68, Albright-Knox Art Gallery, Buffalo, NY, 68, Mus Mod Art, New York, 71, Hause Lange Mus, Krefeld, WGer, 73, Fischbach Gallery, New York, 73, Wurttembergischer Kunstverein, Stuttgart, WGer, 74, Mus Contemp Art, Chicago, 76 & Max Protech Gallery, New York, 82. *Pos:* Artist in residence, Oberlin Col, 66; art critic, Univ NC, 67-68; art critic, Cornell Univ, 69. *Teaching:* Instr art, Sch Visual Arts, 69-84; art critic, Univ NC, 67-68; art critic, Cornell Univ, 69; instr art, Sch Visual Art, 69-84. *Awards:* Nat Found Arts & Humanities Award, 66; Guggenheim Fel, 69. *Bibliog:* The greater context, Tracks, Vol 1 (Nov, 1974); Alison Sky & Michelle Stone (auth), Unbuilt America, McGraw-Hill, 76; Abstract Space--The architectural space --The empty building, Tracks, Vol 3, spring, 77. *Dealer:* Max Protech 37 West 57th St New York NY 10019; Annemarie Verna Rontgenstrasse 44 8005 Zurich Switzerland. *Mailing Add:* 231 Bowery New York NY 10002

INUKAI, KYOHEI
PAINTER, SCULPTOR
b Chicago, Ill, July 13, 13. *Study:* Art Inst Chicago; Nat Acad Design; Art Students League. *Work:* Brandeis Univ Mus Fine Art, New York; Portland Mus, Maine; Wichita Univ Mus Art, Kans; Atlantic Richfield Collection, New York; Chase Manhattan Bank Collection, New York; plus many others. *Comn:* Sculptures for shopping malls, Knoxville, Tenn, Monmouth, NJ & North Riverside, Ill. *Exhib:* White House Rotating Exhib; Screenprints 1970, Int Silk Screen Asn, 70; Dixon White Art Ctr, Cornell Univ, 70; ann print exhib, Brooklyn Mus, NY, 71; Am Fedn Arts Traveling Print Show; Wichita Art Asn, Kans, 81; and others. *Media:* Multimedia. *Mailing Add:* 884 West End Ave New York NY 10025

INVERARITY, ROBERT BRUCE
DESIGNER, MUSEUM DIRECTOR
b Seattle, Wash, July 5, 09. *Study:* Univ Wash, BA, 46; Fremont Univ, MFA, 47, PhD, 48; and with Kazue Yamagishi, Blanding Sloan & Mark Tobey. *Work:* Univ Wash; US Naval Collection, Washington, DC; also in pvt collections. *Comn:* Two mosaics, Univ Wash, 40; cut aluminum decorations, US Naval Airstation, Seattle, 40; six panels, Wash State Mus. *Exhib:* One-man shows & numerous group exhibs, US & Can, 29-39. *Pos:* State dir, Works Progress Admin Art Proj, Seattle, 37-41; off war artist, USN, 43-45; art dir, Boeing Aircraft Co, Seattle, 46-47; dir, Mus Int Folk Art, 49-54; dir, Adirondack Mus, 54-65; dir, Philadelphia Maritime Mus, 69-76. *Teaching:* Dir sch creative art, Vancouver, Can, 31-33; instr, Univ Wash, 33-37; asst dir, Fred Archer Sch Photography, 47-49; assoc, Sch Am Res, 49-54; res asst, Yale Univ, 51-53. *Awards:* Meritorious Civilian Serv Award, USN, 45; Wenner-Gren Found Grant for Anthrop Res, 51. *Publ:* Ed, Winslow Homer in the Adirondacks, 59; auth & illusr, Visual Files Coding Index, 60; auth, Accessioning & Cataloguing, 65; coauth, Early Chinese Art & Its Possible Influence in the Pacific Basin, 72; auth, Catalogue of the Inverarity Collection in the British Museum, 78; and others. *Mailing Add:* 2610 Torrey Pines Rd C22 La Jolla CA 92037

IPCAR, DAHLOV
PAINTER, ILLUSTRATOR
b Windsor, Vt, Nov 12, 17. *Study:* Univ Maine, LHD, 78; Colby Col, DFA, 80. *Work:* Metrop Mus Art & Whitney Mus Am Art, New York; Newark Mus, NJ; Brooklyn Mus, NY; Univ Maine, Orono & Portland-Gorham. *Comn:* US Post Off Murals, Yukon, Okla, comn by US Treas Dept, Washington, DC, 39; murals, Patten Free Libr, Bath, Maine, 78, Sun Savings & Loan Asn, Auburn, Maine, 79; and others. *Exhib:* Corcoran Biennial, 37; two-man show, Colby Col Art Mus, 74; one-woman shows, Frost Gully Gallery, Portland, Maine, 77, William A Farnsworth Libr & Art Mus, 79-80 & Hobe Sound Galleries, 79; and many others. *Awards:* Maine State Award, Maine Comn Arts & Humanities, 72; Deborah Morton Award, Westbrook Col, 78. *Bibliog:* Lee Bennett Hopkins (auth), Books Are By People, Citation Press, 69; Margaret Hammel (auth), Dahlov Ipcar's Peaceable Kingdom, Down East Mag, Camden, Maine, 4/74; John Clayton (producer), Vision Series Number 47, (doc film), US Info Agency, 75. *Media:* Oil, Watercolor. *Publ:* Auth & illusr, Calico Jungle, 65 & Bright Barnyard, 66, Knopf; auth & illusr, The Land of Flowers, Viking, 74; auth & illusr, Hard Scrabble, 76 & Lost and Found, 80, Doubleday; and others. *Mailing Add:* Star Rte 2 Bath ME 04530

IPPOLITO, ANGELO
PAINTER, EDUCATOR
b St Arsenio, Italy, Nov 9, 22; US citizen. *Study:* Ozenfant Sch Fine Arts, New York; Brooklyn Mus Art Sch, with Ferren; Meschini Inst, Rome, Italy; also with Afro, Rome. *Work:* Whitney Mus Am Art, New York; Munson-Williams-Proctor Inst, Utica, NY; Phillips Gallery, Washington, DC; Norfolk Mus Arts & Sci, Va; Milwaukee Mus, Wis; and many others. *Comn:* Mural (oil painting), comn by Singer & Sons, now in collection of Montreal Trust Co, Que, 67. *Exhib:* Young America, Whitney Mus Am Art, 57; Abstract Impressionism, Arts Coun, London, 58; Sao Paulo Bienal, Brazil, 61; American Collages, Mus Mod Art, New York & Beuningen Mus, Rotterdam, 66; Retrospective, State Univ NY Binghamton, 75; one-man shows, Borgenicht Gallery, New York, 75 & 77; plus others. *Teaching:* Instr painting, Cooper Union, 56-66; artist in residence, Mich State Univ, 66-71; assoc prof art, State Univ NY Binghamton, 71-76, prof art, 76-. *Awards:* Fulbright Fel to Florence, Italy, 58; Ford Found Artist in Residence to Arnot Gallery, 65; Tiffany grant, 79; and others. *Bibliog:* Dore Ashton (auth), Arte Americana contemporanea, Commentari, Lionello Venturi Rome, 55; Irving Sandler (auth), Angelo Ippolito Landscapes, Provincetown Advocate, 7/4/57; Alfred Frankenstein (auth), Professors tell a story at Bolles, San Francisco Chronicle, 10/1/61; and others. *Media:* Oil. *Publ:* Contribr, Italy Rediscovered (catalog), Munson-Williams-Proctor Inst, 55; contribr, It Is, spring 58; contribr, Nature in Abstraction, Whitney Mus Am Art, 58; and others. *Dealer:* Grace Borgenicht Gallery 1018 Madison Ave New York NY 10021. *Mailing Add:* Friendsville Stage Binghamton NY 13903

IPSEN, KENT FORREST
GLASSWORKER, CRAFTSMAN
b Milwaukee, Wis, Jan 4, 33. *Study:* Univ Wis-Milwaukee, BS; Univ Wis-Madison, MS & MFA; also with Harvey K Littleton. *Work:* Milwaukee Art Ctr, Wis; Toledo Mus Art, Ohio; Corning Glass Mus, NY; Chrysler Mus, Norfolk, Va; Chicago Art Inst; and others. *Comn:* First Gov Awards for the Arts, State of Va, 79. *Exhib:* Vidrios, Estudio Actual, Caracas, Venezuela, 74; Wis Directions, Milwaukee Art Ctr, 75; Looking Forward, Fairtree Gallery, New York, 75; Relig & Art, Vatican Mus, 78; New Glass, Int Competition Corning Mus, 79; and others. *Teaching:* Asst prof glassworking, Mankato State Col, Minn, 65-68; assoc prof glassworking, Chicago Art Inst, 68-72; assoc prof glassworking & chmn dept crafts, Va Commonwealth Univ, 73-76, prof, 76-. *Awards:* Nat Endowment Arts, US Govt, 72 & 75. *Bibliog:* Lee Nordness (auth), Objects USA, Viking, 71; Ray Grover (auth), Contemporary Art Glass, Crown, 75. *Mem:* Am Craft Coun; Ill Craft Coun (pres, 70-72); Nat Coun Educ in Ceramic Arts; Nat Coun Art Adminr. *Media:* Glass. *Dealer:* Habatat Galleries 28235 Southfield Rd Lathrup Village MI 48076; Heller Gallery 965 Madison Ave New York NY 10021. *Mailing Add:* 11761 Bollingbrook Dr Richmond VA 23235

IRVIN, FRED MADDOX
ILLUSTRATOR, PAINTER
b Chillicothe, Mo, Nov 19, 14. *Study:* Kansas City Art Inst; Chicago Acad Fine Arts; Art Students League, New York. *Pos:* Illusr, New York City, Mag Covers & Stories, Advertising Art, 46-56; children's books illusr, approx 50 books, 60-80; animation layout & character design, Hanna Barbera, Ruby Spears Productions, Hollywood, Calif, 78-82; treas, Santa Barbara Art Asn, 74-75, bd dirs, 79-81. *Teaching:* Artist-in-residence, Fine Arts Fair, Chillicothe Fine Arts Coun, Mo State Coun Arts, Nat Endowment Arts, 75. *Mem:* Soc Illusr, Los Angeles; Artists Equity Asn. *Media:* Pencil with Watercolor; Acrylic with Brush & Palette Knife. *Publ:* Illusr, Sea Lion Island, Creative Educ Soc, 72; illusr, Hit the Bike Trail, Albert Whitman Co, 74; illusr, Dictionary for Children, Macmillan, 75; illusr, Hurry Up Christmas, Garrard, 76; illusr, Hurry Home, Addison-Wesley, 76. *Mailing Add:* 1702 Hillcrest Rd Santa Barbara CA 93103

IRVINE, BETTY JO
LIBRARIAN, INSTRUCTOR
b Indianapolis, Ind, July 13, 43. *Study:* Ind Univ, AB, 66, MLS, 69, PhD, 82. *Pos:* Fine arts slide librn, Dept of Fine Arts, Ind Univ, Bloomington, 66-68; asst fine arts librn, 68-69, fine arts librn, 69- *Teaching:* Instr art bibliog, Dept of Fine Arts, Ind Univ, Bloomington, 69- *Awards:* Officer's Grant, Coun of Libr Resources, Washington, DC, 71. *Mem:* Art Libr Soc NAm (co-founder Ill-Ind chap, 74); Col Art Asn; Am Libr Asn (vchmn/chmn-elect art sect, 78-79); Midwest Art Hist Soc (session chmn, 76). *Res:* Organization and management of slide libraries, art library planning & design. *Interests:* Library management, slide and photograph preservation. *Publ:* Auth, Slide Classification, Col & Res Libr, Vol 32, 1/71; auth, Slide Libraries, Colo Libr Unltd, 74, 2nd ed, 79; auth, Organization and management of art slide collections, Libr Trends, 1/75; coauth (with W Freitag), Slides, In: Non-print Media in Academic Libraries, Am Libr Asn, 75; coauth (with L Korenic), Survey of periodical use in an academic art library, In: Art Documentation, Bulletin Art Libr Soc/NAm, 10/82. *Mailing Add:* c/o Fine Arts Libr Ind Univ Bloomington IN 47401

IRVING, DONALD J
ADMINISTRATOR, WRITER
b Arlington, Mass, May 3, 33. *Study:* Mass Col Art, BA, 55; Columbia Univ Teachers Col, MA, 56, EdD, 63. *Pos:* Chmn dept art & dir, Peabody Mus Art, George Peabody Col Teachers, Nashville, Tenn, 67-69; dir sch, Sch of the Art Inst Chicago, 69-83; dean, fac fine arts, Univ Ariz, Tucson, 83- *Teaching:* Teacher art, White Plains High Sch, NY, 58-60; instr art, State Univ NY Col Oneonta, 58-60; prof art & dean, Moore Col Art, Philadelphia, 63-67. *Mem:* Nat Asn Schs Art (treas & mem bd dirs, 72-75); Union Independent Cols Art (bd dirs, 72-, chmn bd, 79-); Nat Coun Art Adminr (bd dirs, 73-); Fedn Independent Ill Cols & Univs (bd dirs, 74-). *Res:* Application of industrial materials and techniques to contemporary sculpture. *Publ:* Auth Sculpture: Material and Process, Van Nostrand Reinhold, 70. *Mailing Add:* Fac Fine Arts Univ Ariz Tucson AZ 85721

IRVING, JOAN
PAINTER, SCULPTOR
b Riverside, Calif, Mar 12, 16. *Study:* Riverside City Col, with Richard Allman, 33-35; Art Ctr Sch, Los Angeles, with Barse Miller & Edward Kaminski, 35-37. *Work:* Metrop Mus Art, New York; Newport Harbor Sch Collection, Calif; Crain Collection, Laguna Beach, Calif; Helen Hand Zillgitt Collection. *Comn:* Tile mural, Harbor View Sch, Newport Beach, Calif, 49; bronze fountain, comn by E Gene Crain, Laguna Beach, Calif, 72. *Exhib:* Am Watercolor Soc, Nat Acad, New York; Calif Watercolor Soc, Los Angeles Co Mus Art, Calif, 50, 51, 52, 53 & 55; The First 100 Years of the Am Watercolor Soc, Metrop Mus Art, New York, 66; and others. *Pos:* Co-dir, Brandt Painting Workshops, 46-; chmn, Newport Beach Arts Commission, 50-61; dir, Newport Harbor Art Mus, 60-62. *Awards:* Calif Watercolor Soc Award, 51; James D Phelan Award, 52; Watercolor West Award, 75. *Bibliog:* David W Scott (auth), The Brandts at blue sky, Country Beautiful, 7/63; Calif White Paper Painters, Art Gallery, Univ Calif, Fullerton, 76; Janice Lovoos (auth), The California school, Southwest Art, 1/82. *Mem:* Am Watercolor Soc; life fel Royal Soc Arts; hon life mem Laguna Beach Art Asn; hon life mem Watercolor West; hon life mem San Diego Watercolor Soc. *Media:* Watercolor, Oil; Terra-cotta, Wood. *Mailing Add:* 405 Goldenrod Corona Del Mar CA 92625

IRWIN, GEORGE M
PATRON, COLLECTOR
b Quincy, Ill, May 2, 21. *Study:* Univ Mich, BA, 43; Culver-Stockton Col, Hon DFA, 73. *Pos:* Chmn bd, Assoc Coun Arts, 62-72; chmn bd, Ill Arts Coun, 63-71; former mem bd, Ill State Mus & Mus Contemp Art, Chicago; pres, Quincy Soc Fine Arts, 48-78. *Awards:* Distinguished Service Award, Southern Ill Univ, Edwardsville, 81. *Mem:* Life mem Art Inst Chicago; Am Fedn Arts; Nat Trust Hist Preserv; and others. *Collection:* Twentieth century American artists. *Mailing Add:* 126 N Eighth St Quincy IL 62301

IRWIN, LANI HELENA
PAINTER
b Annapolis, Md, Oct 27, 47. *Study:* Am Univ, Washington, DC, BFA, 69, MFA, 74. *Exhib:* Md Biennial, Baltimore Mus, 74; 19th Area Exhib, Corcoran Gallery Art, Washington, DC, 74; solo exhibs, Washington Proj Arts, 76 & Gallery K, 81 & 83, Washington, DC; Graham Gallery, New York, 77; Areawide Painting Exhib & Realism and Representation: New Work by 25 Artists, Arlington Art Ctr, Va, 80; Bernice Steinbaum Gallery Ltd, New York, 84. *Bibliog:* Benjamin Forgey (auth), Irwin: A world of apparent serenity, Washington Star, 5/8/81; Jo Ann Lewis (auth), Views from inside, Washington Post, 5/9/81; Jill Wechsler (auth), Lani Irwin, Am Artist, 6/83. *Media:* Oil. *Dealer:* Gallery K 2032 P St Washington DC 20036. *Mailing Add:* Rte 1 Box 344 Hughesville MD 20637

IRWIN, LISA DRU
PHOTOGRAPHER, PAINTER
b Norfolk, Va, July 27, 53. *Study:* Univ Ga, 71-74; Atlanta Col Art, photography with Ben Davis, 76; San Francisco Art Inst, with Linda Connor, BFA, 77. *Work:* High Mus Art, Atlanta Arts Festival & Nexus Inc, Atlanta, Ga. *Comn:* Photo Mural, Atlanta Hist Soc, 81. *Exhib:* Fogg Art Mus, Harvard Univ, Cambridge, Mass, 80; High Mus Art, Atlanta, 81; solo show, Foto Gallery, New York, 81; Southeastern Ctr Contemp Art, Winston-Salem, NC, 81; Macon Mus Art & Sci, Ga, 81; and others. *Pos:* Com printer, Gamma Photo Lab, San Francisco, 78; photog asst & stylist, Atlanta & San Francisco, 79-81; freelance photogr, Atlanta, 79- *Awards:* 1st Place, North Beach Photog Fair, Columbus Camera, 78; Purchase Award, Arts Festival Atlanta, 80. *Bibliog:* Ben Davis (auth), Watersports, Atlanta Art Papers, 12/80; Judy Henson (auth), Lisa Irwin (review), Art Papers, 11/81. *Media:* Oil; Silkscreen. *Publ:* Contribr, Contemporary Arts Southeast, David Heath, 79; contribr, article, Atlanta Mag, 80; contribr, Brown's Guide to Georgia, 81; contribr, article, Atlanta J, 80-81. *Dealer:* Nexus Galleries Inc 360 Fortune St Atlanta GA 30312. *Mailing Add:* 4650 Papermill Rd Marietta GA 30067

IRWIN, ROBERT
ENVIRONMENTAL ARTIST, SCULPTOR
b Long Beach, Calif, 28. *Study:* Otis Art Inst, 48-50; Jepson Art Inst, Los Angeles, 51; Chouinard's Art Inst, Los Angeles, 51-53; San Francisco Col Art, Hon Dr. *Work:* Art Inst Chicago; San Francisco Mus; Mus of Mod Art, New York; Whitney Mus, New York; Walker Art Ctr, Minneapolis; plus others. *Exhib:* One-man shows, Jewish Mus, New York, 68, Mus Mod Art, New York, 70, Chicago Mus Contemp Art, 76, Walker Art Ctr, Minneapolis, 76; retrospective, Whitney Mus of Am Art, New York, 77. *Teaching:* Instr, Chouinard Art Inst, 57-58; instr, Univ Calif, Los Angeles, 62; instr, Univ Calif, Irvine, 68-69. *Bibliog:* Jan Butterfield (auth), article, Arts Mag; Lawrence Weschler (auth), Seeing is Forgetting the Name of the Things One Sees, Univ Calif Press. *Mailing Add:* 10966 Strathmore Dr Los Angeles CA 90024

ISAACS, AVROM
DEALER, PUBLISHER
b Winnipeg, Can, 26. *Study:* Univ Toronto, BA (polit sci & econ). *Pos:* Dir & owner, Isaacs Gallery, 56-; owner, Innuit Gallery of Eskimo Art, 70-; assoc fel, Calumet Col, York Univ, 70- *Specialty:* (Isaacs Gallery), Contemporary Canadian art; (Innuit Gallery) art of the Eskimo. *Mailing Add:* 832 Yonge St Toronto ON M4W 2H1 Canada

ISAACS, CLAIRE NAOMI
ADMINISTRATOR
b San Francisco, Calif, Feb 12, 33. *Study:* Pomona Col, BA, 54; Ohio State Univ, 54-55; Univ Calif, Berkeley, 62-64; Univ Southern Calif, 71; Claremont Grad Sch, MA(20th century art hist), 75; Harvard Univ, cert art mgt, 77, Coro fel pub affairs for arts mgr, 79. *Collections Arranged:* Children's Book Illustrators (artmobile exhib), 67; Art of the African (traveling exhib), 69; Children's Art From Three Countries: Japan, Iran, USSR, 76; Int Child Art Collection, 1978-83 (auth, catalog), 83. *Pos:* Asst, Art Gallery, Univ Calif, Berkeley, 61-63; educ supvr, San Francisco Mus Mod Art, 63-66; asst dir & coordr, Visual Art Proj, PACE (Proj to Advance Creativity in Educ), San Bernardino, Inyo & Mono Co Sch, 66-69; dir, Jr Arts Ctr, Munic Arts Dept, Los Angeles, 70-80, Burnsdall Art Ctr, Los Angeles Affairs Dept, 80-83; dir cult affairs, City & Co, San Francisco Arts Comm, 83- *Teaching:* Lectr art for deaf, Univ Calif Exten, Los Angeles, 72. *Awards:* Golden Grate Award, Western Asn Art Mus, 78. *Mem:* Am Asn Mus; Am Asn Youth Mus; Nat Art Educ Asn. *Publ:* Auth, Paul Klee and Galka Scheyer, Artforum, 62; auth, The Art of Borrowing and Distributing Art for the Small Community, Visual Arts Proj, 70; ed, Proceedings of the Conference on Art for the Deaf, Jr League Los Angeles, 75; contribr, The Museum and the Visitor Experience, Western Regional Conf Am Asn Mus, 77. *Mailing Add:* 429 Grand View San Francisco CA 94114

ISAACS, RON
PAINTER, INSTRUCTOR
b Cincinnati, Ohio, Oct 14, 41. *Study:* Berea Col, BA, 63; Ind Univ, MFA, 65. *Work:* Berea Col, Ky; Col of Mount St Joseph, Cincinnati, Ohio; AT&T Collection, New York; Chase Manhattan Bank Collection, New York; Kemper Ins Co Collection, Chicago, Ill. *Exhib:* Univ Southern Calif, 79; Honolulu Acad Art, 80; Oakland Mus, 80; Univ Tex, Austin, 80; Cornell Univ, 80; Toledo Mus Art, Ohio, 81; Nat Mus Am Art, Washington, DC, 81; Renwick Gallery, Smithsonian Inst, Washington, DC, 81; Heckscher Mus, Huntington, NY, 81; and many others. *Teaching:* Instr fine arts, Sue Bennett Col, London, Ky, 65-69; prof painting & drawing, Eastern Ky Univ, Richmond, 69- *Awards:* John Y Brown Award, Regional Fine Arts Biennial, J B Speed Art Mus, 71; First Purchase Awards, Preview 73, Col of Mount St Joseph, Cincinnati, Ohio, 72 & Fifth Berea Drawing Biennial, Berea Col, Ky, 73. *Bibliog:* Harold Olejarz (auth), Ron Isaacs, Arts Mag, 10/78; Madeleine Burnside (auth), Ron Isaacs (rev), Art News, 11/78; Dona Z Meilach (auth), Woodworking: The New Wave, Crown Publ, New York, 81. *Mem:* Am Crafts Coun; Nat Art Educ Asn. *Media:* Acrylic. *Dealer:* Monique Knowlton Gallery 153 Mercer St New York NY 10021. *Mailing Add:* 110 Millstone Dr Richmond KY 40475

ISAACSON, GENE LESTER
COLLECTOR, HISTORIAN
b Rugby, NDak, June 14, 36. *Study:* Concordia Col, Moorhead, Minn, BA, 58; Univ Northern Colo, MFA, 62; Univ Salzburg Orff Inst, Austria, 63-64. *Pos:* Consult art & aesthet, City of Garden Grove, Calif, 68- *Teaching:* Chmn dept art, Willamette Univ, 62-63; chmn art dept, Santa Ana Col, Calif, 64-; vis assoc prof art hist, Chapman Col, World Campus Afloat, 69-71. *Bibliog:* Richard E Ellinger (auth), Design and Color Structure, Int Press, 65. *Mem:* Southern Calif Art Asn. *Res:* Prehistoric and primitive art; African art; oceanic art; art collecting. *Collection:* Extensive survey of West African tribal sculpture; oceanic art, American Indian; United States and European modern painting and graphics. *Publ:* Coauth, Col Exhib Catalogs, Willamette Univ & Santa Ana Col, 62, 68, 72 & 77; auth, Monuments of African Sculpture, Santa Ana Col, 72. *Dealer:* Africa Afar Gallery 4900 E Chapman Ave Suite 73 Orange CA 92669. *Mailing Add:* PO Box 6157 Huntington Beach CA 92646

ISAACSON, MARCIA JEAN
DRAFTSMAN, EDUCATOR
b Atlanta, Ga, Sept 25, 45. *Study:* Univ Ga, Athens, BFA & MFA. *Work:* Minn Mus Art, St Paul; High Mus Art, Atlanta, Ga; Southeastern Ctr Contemp Art, Winston-Salem, NC; Fla House Rep, Tallahassee; Davidson Col, NC; and others. *Exhib:* Drawings USA, Minn Mus Art, St Paul, 71 & 73; 35 Artists in the SE Traveling Exhib, High Mus Art; Southeast 7, Nat Endowment for the Arts & Southeastern Ctr Contemp Art Fel Recipients, Winston-Salem, NC, 76; Southeastern Graphics Invitational: Drawing, Mint Mus Art, Charolotte, NC, 79; West '79/The Law, Minn Mus Art, St Paul, 79; Drawing: A Florida Perspective, Valencia Community Col, Orlando, 81; Drawing Show, Southeastern Ctr Contemp Arts, Winston-Salem, NC, 82; Kipnis Gallery, Atlanta, 82; Paper, Fibers and Drawing Invitational, Fla State Univ Gallery, Tallahassee, 83. *Pos:* Selections panel, Nat Endowment Arts Fel Grants, 80-81. *Teaching:* Instr printmaking & drawing, Wesleyan Col, Macon, Ga, 70-73; asst prof drawing, Univ Fla, Gainesville, 73-81, assoc prof, 81- *Awards:* MacDowell Colony Fel, Peterborough, NH, 77; Fla Fine Arts Coun Fel, 79; Fla House of Rep Art Purchase Award, 79; and others. *Media:* Pencil, Chalk. *Mailing Add:* Dept of Art Univ of Fla Gainesville FL 32611

ISAACSON, PHILIP MARSHAL
CRITIC, WRITER
b Lewiston, Maine, June 16, 24. *Study:* Bates Col, BA, 47; Harvard Law Sch, LLB, 50; Bowdoin Col, DFA, 83. *Pos:* Art critic, Maine Sunday Telegram, Portland, 68; mem fed-state adv panel, Nat Endowment for the Arts, 77-; second vpres & mem bd dir, Nat Assembly of State Arts Agencies, 77- *Mem:* Maine State Comn Arts & Humanities (chmn, 75-). *Res:* The American eagle as a decorative device; architecture of Maine since 1920. *Publ:* Auth, The American Eagle, NY Graphic Soc, 75; contrib, Marine Forms of American Architecture, Colby Col, 76; contrib, New Architecture, Marine Traditions, Westbrook Col, 83. *Mailing Add:* 2 Benson St Lewiston ME 04240

ISAAK, NICHOLAS, JR
PAINTER, CONSERVATOR
b Manchester, NH, July 5, 44. *Study:* Boston Univ, BFA, 67, MFA, 69; spec study with Walter Murch, Robert Gwathmey & Karl Fortess. *Work:* Va Mus Fine Arts, Richmond; Western Ill Univ, Macomb; Fitchburg Mus Art, Mass; Northern Ill Univ, DeKalb; Bradley Univ, Peoria, Ill; and others. *Exhib:* Pa Acad Fine Arts 164th Ann, 69; one-man shows, Robinson Gallery, Va Mus Fine Arts, 71 & Maxwell Davidson Gallery, New York, 81; Chrysler Mus Art, Norfolk, Va, 72; Print Invitational, Pratt Grahics Ctr, New York, 73; Mod Printmakers, Rochester Inst Technol, NY, 74; 2nd Graphics Biennial, Metrop Mus, Miami, Fla, 75; Fitchburg Mus Art, Mass, 76; Regional Selections, Dartmouth Col Mus, Hanover, NH, 79. *Pos:* Conservator, 79- *Teaching:* Instr printmaking, Norfolk State Col, Va, 69-72; asst prof painting, Boston Univ, Mass, 72-77; assoc prof printmaking & chmn dept, Keene State Col, NH, 77-81. *Awards:* Nat Teaching fel, Dept Health, Educ & Welfare, 69; Cert of Distinction, Va Artists Biennial, Va Mus Art, 71; Rosenthal Found Award, Am Acad & Inst of Arts & Letters, 79. *Media:* Oil, Etching. *Dealer:* Maxwell Davidson Gallery 43 E 78th St New York NY 10021. *Mailing Add:* Rte 63 Box 375 Westmoreland NH 03467

ISELIN, LEWIS
SCULPTOR
b New Rochelle, NY, June 22, 13. *Study:* Art Students League, 34-38, with Mahonri Young, John Stuart, Curry, George Bridgman & Gleb Derujunshy; Guggenheim Fel, 52. *Work:* Columbus Gallery Fine Arts, Ohio; Fogg Art Mus, Cambridge, Mass; Colby Col Mus, Waterville, Maine; Yale Univ; William A Farnsworth Libr & Art Mus, Rockland, Maine; Univ Main at Orono. *Comn:* Sculpture, US Mil Cemetery, Suresnes, France, 50; portraits of John Wanamaker & Marshall Field, Merchandise Mart, 54; figure of Gen Nathaniel Greene, City of Philadelphia, 60; figure of St Vincent de Paul, Vincent Astor Found, 65; sculpture mural, Midland Mutual Life Ins, 71. *Exhib:* Metrop Mus Art, 45; Pa Acad Fine Arts, 40-60; Whitney Mus Am Art, 40-60. *Awards:* Helen Foster Badnet Prize, Nat Acad Design, 38. *Media:* Bronze. *Mailing Add:* Belfast Rd PO Box 838 Camden ME 04843

ISENBURGER, ERIC
PAINTER
b Frankfurt am Main, Ger, May 17, 02; US citizen. *Study:* Frankfurt Art Sch. *Work:* Mus Mod Art, New York; Corcoran Gallery Art, Washington, DC; Pa Acad Fine Arts, Philadelphia, Pa; M H De Young Mem Mus, San Francisco, Calif; Wadsworth Atheneum, Hartford, Conn; and others. *Exhib:* Art of Today, 1951, Metrop Mus Art, New York; Pa Acad Fine Arts, Philadelphia; Art Inst Chicago, Ill; Carnegie Inst, Pittsburgh, Pa; eight one-man shows,

Knoedler's, New York. *Teaching:* Instr painting, Nat Acad Sch Fine Arts, 59-80. *Awards:* Edwin Palmer Mem Prize, Nat Acad Design, 57 & 70 & Henry Ward Ranger Purchase, Nat Acad, 57 & 80; Florence Breevort Eickemeyer Award, Columbia Univ, 80. *Mem:* Academician Nat Acad Design; Audubon Artists. *Media:* Oil. *Publ:* Auth, article, Am Artist, 48. *Mailing Add:* 140 E 56th St New York NY 10022

ISHAM, SHEILA EATON
PAINTER, GRAPHIC ARTIST
b New York, NY, Dec 19, 27. *Study:* Bryn Mawr Col, BA(cum laude), 50; Hochschule Bildende Künste, Berlin, Ger, 50-54. *Work:* Mus Mod Art, New York; Nat Collection Fine Arts, Washington, DC; Corcoran Gallery Art, DC; Albright-Knox Gallery, Buffalo; Hirshhorn Mus, New York; and others. *Exhib:* One-man shows, Jefferson Place Gallery, 68-70, French & Co Gallery, New York, 70 & Brockton Art Ctr, Mass, 72; Am Cult Ctr, Paris, 73; Corcoran Gallery, Washington, DC, 74; Albright-Knox Gallery, NY, 74 & 81; and many others. *Teaching:* Instr art hist & graphics, Chinese Univ, Hong Kong, 63-65. *Awards:* Print Award, Corcoran Gallery Art, 58; Print Award, Libr Cong, Pennell Comt, Wash Soc Printmakers, 60 & 61. *Bibliog:* New images, Art Mag, summer 70; Sidra Stich (auth), Five new Washington artists, Art Int, 12/71; Edward Fry (auth), article, Arts Int, 76. *Publ:* Coauth, I Ching (portfolio of eight lithographs with poems); Marakech (portfolio of four lithographs). *Mailing Add:* 1601 19th St NW Washington DC 20009

ISHIKAWA, JOSEPH
MUSEUM DIRECTOR, CONSULTANT
b Los Angeles, Calif, July 29, 19. *Study:* Univ Calif, Los Angeles, AB, 42; Univ Nebr. *Collections Arranged:* Jan Saudek: Photographs, 78; Edward S Curtis: Collotypes & Orotones, 78; Ceremonial Art of West Africa: The Victor DuBois Collection, 78; Esther Gentle Rattner: Sculptures & Watercolors, 79; Irwin Kremen: Collages, 79; Karen Massaro: Clay Paintings & Sculpture, 80; Robert Hansen: Paintings & Constructions, 80; Carl Toth: Photographs, 80; Canada: John Mars & Gary Nixon: Paingings, 80; Dominick Labino: Glass, 81; Ralf Henricksen Retrospective: Paintings & Drawings, 81; Jiri Anderle, Intaglios & Vladimir Gazovic: Lithographs, 81; 500 Years of German Printmaking, 82; George Bellows Centennial, 82; A Rift in the Curtain: Woodcuts by Tzuu-Hang Chen, 83; Libby Kowalski: Fibers, 84; and others. *Pos:* From asst cur to cur, Univ Nebr Art Galleries, 43-51; chief cur and asst dir, Des Moines Art Ctr, 51-58; dir, Sioux City Art Ctr, 58-61; dir, Wright Art Ctr, Beloit Col, 61-74; consult, Sheboygan Arts Found, 66 & Sloan Galleries, Valparaiso Univ, 79; dir, Kresge Art Gallery, Mich State Univ, 74- *Awards:* Scandinavian Sem, Am Asn Mus & Fulbright Fels, 65; Beloit Col & Ford Found Humanities Grant, 69; All Univ Res Grant, Mich State Univ, 82. *Mem:* Int Coun Mus; Am Asn Mus; Midwest Mus Conf (vpres, 70, pres, 73-74); Wis Fedn Mus (chmn, 70). *Res:* Influence of Puvis de Chavannes on 20th century painting. *Publ:* Auth, University as tastemaker, Palette, 58; auth, Puvis de Chavannes: Moderne Malgre Lui, Art J, 68. *Mailing Add:* Kresge Art Gallery Mich State Univ East Lansing MI 48824

ISKOWITZ, GERSHON
PAINTER
b Kelce, Poland, Nov, 1921; Can citizen. *Study:* Munich Acad Fine Arts; also with Oscar Kokschka. *Work:* Art Gallery Ont, Toronto; Nat Gallery Can, Ottawa; Ft Lauderdale Art Mus; Simon Fraser Univ; also in pvt collection of Joseph H Hirshhorn, Greenwich, Conn. *Exhib:* 36th Venice Biennale, Italy, 72; one-man retrospective, Glenbow-Alberta Art Inst, Calgary, 75; Nat Gallery Can, Ottawa, 73; Mus d'Arte Contemporani, Montreal, 74; Retrospective, Art Gallery Ont, 82, traveling throughout Can & London, Eng, 83. *Awards:* Senior Arts Grant, Can Coun, Ottawa, 74. *Bibliog:* Peter Mellen (auth), article, Arts Can, 71 & Standing Apart (film from 36th Venice Biennale), 72; Gershon Iskowitz (film), Can TV; Adel E Freedman (auth), Gershon Iskowitz, Merrit Publishing, Toronto, 82. *Mem:* Royal Soc Can Artists. *Media:* Oil, Watercolor. *Mailing Add:* c/o Gallery Moos 136 Yorkville Ave Toronto ON M5R 1C2 Canada

ISRAEL, MARVIN
DESIGNER, PAINTER
b Syracuse, NY, July 3, 24. *Study:* Syracuse Univ, BFA, 50; Yale Univ, MFA(graphic design), 55. *Work:* Whitney Mus Art, Mus Mod Art, New York; Art Inst Chicago; Galerie Ostergren, Sweden; J L Hudson, Detroit. *Exhib:* One-man shows, Cordier & Ekstrom, New York, 66, 69, 71 & 74; Staatliche Kunsthalle, Baden-Baden, Ger, 67; Brusberg Gallery, Hanover, Ger, 71 & Richard Feigen, Chicago, 72; Baltimore Mus Art, 68; Whitney Mus Art, 69; Pasadena Mus Art, Calif, 69; Indianapolis Mus Art, Ind, 70 & 72. *Pos:* Art dir, Seventeen Mag, 57-59 & Harper's Bazaar, 60-62. *Teaching:* Instr design & painting, Parsons Sch Design, 59-64, Sch Visual Arts, 65-67 & Cooper Union, 68-69. *Media:* Acrylic, Pastel; Charcoal. *Mailing Add:* c/o Cordier & Ekstrom Gallery 417 E 75th St New York NY 10021

ISSERSTEDT, DOROTHEA CARUS
DEALER, HISTORIAN
Study: Univ Munich; Univ Freiburg, PhD(art hist); Wheaton Col. *Pos:* Dir, Carus Gallery, currently. *Mem:* Art Dealers Asn Am. *Res:* Medieval art, mainly twelfth and thirteenth century sculpture. *Specialty:* Art of the German Expressionists and art of the twenties; focus on Russian Avant-Garde art 1913-1930. *Mailing Add:* Carus Gallery 872 Madison Ave New York NY 10021

ITALIANO, JOAN
SCULPTOR, EDUCATOR

b Worcester, Mass. *Study:* Siena Heights Col, PhB, Studio Angelico, MFA; Barry Col, Fla; Nino Caruso, Rome, Italy; Pietrasanta, Italy. *Work:* Siena Heights Col, Adrian, Mich; Anna Maria Col, Paxton, Mass; Barry Col, Miami, Fla; Int Ctr for Ceramics, Rome, Italy; and pvt collections in US & Can. *Comn:* Stations of the Cross, Navy Base, Chapel, Key West, Fla, 57; Our Mother of Joy Fountain, comn by John Cardinal Wright, St Vincent Hosp, Worcester, Mass, 59; Stations of the Cross, comn by architect, Our Lady of Lourdes Church, Milbury, Mass, 62; Last Supper Mural, Passionist Monastery, Shrewsbury, Mass, 64; Tree of Life Fountain, Mary Manning Walsh Home, New York, 71. *Exhib:* Dartmouth Col, 79 & 81; one-man shows, Anna Maria Col, Mass, 81, Fitchburg State Col, Mass, 82 & Pindar Gallery, New York, 83; Galerie Triangle, Washington, DC, 82. *Pos:* Dir, Art Gallery, Barry Col, 56-58; consult liturgical art, Dick Bros Archit Interiors, 62-72. *Teaching:* Instr sculpture, Barry Col, Miami, Fla, 56-58; assoc prof sculpture & ceramics, Col of the Holy Cross, 69, chmn fine arts dept, 77-80. *Awards:* First Prize in Sculpture, Palm Beach Art League Ann, 55 & 56; Batchelor Ford Fel, 76; Twentieth Nat Fall River, 80; and others. *Bibliog:* Leah Lamson (auth), Joan Italiano--She currently concentrates on modular sculpture, Evening Gazette, Worcester, Mass, 12/5/80; James Reil (auth), article, Worcester Mag, 5/20/81; George French (auth), Sculptor Joan Italiano's new direction is right on course, Evening Gazette, Worcester, Mass, 10/22/82. *Mem:* New Eng Sculptors Asn; Int Sculpture Ctr; Copley Soc Boston. *Media:* Mixed. *Dealer:* Artworks Gallery 51 Union Place Worcester MA; Pindar Gallery 127 Greene St New York NY. *Mailing Add:* Box 175 West Boylston MA 01583

ITATANI, MICHIKO
PAINTER

b Osaka, Japan, May 8, 48. *Study:* Art Inst Chicago, MFA, 76. *Work:* Art Inst Chicago, Mus Contemp Art & Kemper Collection, Chicago. *Exhib:* NAME Gallery, Chicago, 79; solo exhib, Marianne Deson Gallery, Chicago, 80 & 82; Ukrainian Inst Mod Art, Chicago, 81; Ill State Mus, Springfield, 80; Art Inst Chicago, 81; Ill Arts Coun Gallery, 82; Muskegon Mus, 82. *Pos:* Bd dirs, NAME Gallery, 76- *Teaching:* Asst prof painting & drawing, Art Inst Chicago, 79- *Awards:* Proj Completion Grants, Ill Arts Coun, 79 & 81; Fel, Nat Endowment Art, 80-81. *Bibliog:* Carry Ricky (auth), Special report: Chicago, 7-8/79 & Regan Upshaw (auth), Michiko Itatani at Deson, 11/80, Art Am; C L Morrison (auth), Michiko Itatani: NAME Gallery, Art Forum, 10/79. *Media:* Oil, Silverpoint. *Dealer:* Marianne Deson Gallery 340 W Huron Chicago IL 60610. *Mailing Add:* 2038 N Oakley Chicago IL 60647

ITCHKAWICH, DAVID MICHAEL
PRINTMAKER, ILLUSTRATOR

b Westerly, RI, Aug 18, 37. *Study:* RI Sch Design, BFA. *Work:* John Sloane Study Collection, Univ Del; Charles Dana Mus, Colgate Univ; New York Pub Libr; Munson, Proctor, Williams Inst, Utica, NY; Metrop Mus Art, New York. *Exhib:* Nat Print Exhib, Brooklyn Mus, NY, 70 & 72; Davidson Nat Print Show, Davidson Univ, 73-75; one-man shows, Munson, Proctor, Williams Inst, Utica, NY, 76, Newport Art Asn, RI, 78; Martin Sumers Graphics, 76; Nat Exhib, New York Soc Illusr, 78; and others. *Bibliog:* The visions of David Itchkawich, Intellectual Dig, 2/72; John Mattingly (auth), When Men Were Animals and Animals Were Men: A Study of the Graphic Work of David Itchkawich, Angelica Press, NY, 76; Suzanne Boorsch (auth), The pleasure of creation: The work of David Itchkawich, Print Collector's Newslett, 9-10/78. *Dealer:* Horizon Gallery 45 Christopher St New York NY 10014. *Mailing Add:* 223 E 85th New York NY 10028

IVERSEN, EARL HARVEY
PHOTOGRAPHER, EDUCATOR

b Chicago, Ill, Jan 26, 43. *Study:* Univ Ill, Chicago Circle, BA, 70; RI Sch Design, MFA, 73. *Work:* Mus Mod Art, New York; Univ Colo Art Mus, Boulder; Sheldon Gallery, Univ Nebr, Lincoln; Spencer Art Mus, Univ Kans, Lawrence; Sioux City Art Ctr, Iowa. *Exhib:* The Great West, Denver Art Mus, 77; solo exhib, Mass Col Art, 78; Metropolitan Col, Denver, 78, Kresge Gallery, Mich State Univ, Ann Arbor, 80 & Sioux City Art Ctr, 82; An Open Land, Chicago Art Inst, 83; two-person exhib, Spencer Art Mus, Lawrence, Kans, 83. *Teaching:* Instr photog, Mass Col Art, 73-74; assoc prof design & photog, Univ Kans, Lawrence, 74-; photogr, Univ Theater, 81- *Awards:* Excellence Award Photog, Univ & Col Designers Asn, 76; grant, 76 & fel, 83, Nat Endowment Arts. *Publ:* Illusr, Photo Art Mag, #12 & #14, 81; illusr, Erotic Photography, Demarais Press, 81; illusr, Kansas in Color, Regents Press Kans, 82. *Mailing Add:* 125 E 19th Lawrence KS 66044

IVES, ELAINE CAROLINE
PAINTER

b New York, NY, Oct 20, 22. *Study:* Jacksonville Art Sch, with Paul Toleffson & William Pachner; Inst de Allende, with Jim Pinto. *Exhib:* Sarasota Art Asn, 67-71; Butler Inst Am Art, Youngstown, Ohio, 69; Fla Artist Group, 72-74 & 76; Loch Haven Art Ctr, Orlando, 74 & 77; Tampa Bay Art Ctr, Fla, 75-77; Retrospective, Winter Haven Cult Art Ctr, Fla, 76; and others. *Teaching:* Pvt lessons. *Awards:* Best in Show for Causway Gale, Fla Fedn Art, 64; Second Prize for Wipe Out, Sarasota Art Asn, 70; Best in Show for Transition, Latin Quarter Gallery, 74; and others. *Bibliog:* Currier and Ives, then & now, Nationwide Ins Mag, 65; plus others. *Mem:* Fla Artist Group; Ridge Art Asn (pres). *Media:* Multimedia. *Dealer:* Ringling Art Rental & Sales Gallery PO Box 1838 Sarasota FL 33578; Arts on the Park Lakeland FL. *Mailing Add:* 2115 18th St NW Winter Haven FL 33880

IVEY, JAMES BURNETT
CARTOONIST, COLLECTOR

b Chattanooga, Tenn, Apr 19, 25. *Study:* Univ Louisville; George Washington Univ; Nat Art Sch. *Work:* Libr Cong, Washington, DC; Syracuse Univ, NY; Albert T Reid Collection, Univ Kans; Mo State Hist Soc; State Hist Soc Wis, Madison. *Collections Arranged:* Cartoons from Gillray to Goldberg, San Francisco Mus Art, 62; Cartoon Museum, Madeira Beach, Fla, 67-68; Cartoon from Hogarth to Herblock, Lock Haven Art Ctr, Orlando, Fla, 71. *Pos:* Political cartoonist, Washington Star, DC, 50-53, St Petersburg Times, 53-59, San Francisco Examr, 59-66, Rothco Syndicate, 63- & Orlando Sentinel, 67-77; cur & dir, Cartoon Mus, Madeira Beach, Fla, 67-68 & Orlando, Fla, 75-; ed & publ, Cartoon, 71-. *Teaching:* Adj prof cartooning, Univ Central Fla, 78- *Awards:* Reid Found Fel, 59; Silver T-Square, Nat Cartoonist Soc, 80. *Bibliog:* John Chase (auth), Today's Cartoon, Haiser Press, 63; Maurice Horn (auth), World Encyclopedia of Cartoons, Chelsea House, 80. *Mem:* Nat Cartoonist Soc (chmn Fla chap, 72-); Am Asn Ed Cartoonists. *Media:* Ink. *Collection:* Original cartoon art, approximately 2000 cartoons representing entire history of the art in twenty countries. *Publ:* Contrib, Freedom & Union: European Cartoonists, 61; contrib, Cartoonist Profiles, 70; contrib, Cartoon: Pen Mightier than Suit, 71; US History in Cartoon, Int Media, 79; Wash Tubbs, First Adventure Comic Strip, Luna Press, 74. *Mailing Add:* 561 Obispo Ave Orlando FL 32807

IVY, GREGORY DOWLER
PAINTER

b Clarksburg, Mo, May 7, 04. *Study:* Cent Mo State Col, BS; St Louis Sch Fine Arts, Wash Univ; Columbia Univ, MA; NY Univ. *Exhib:* Art Inst Chicago; Brooklyn Mus; Metrop Mus Art, New York; High Mus Art, Atlanta; Mint Mus Art, Charlotte, NC; and others. *Pos:* Bd dirs & exec comt, NC Mus Art, 56-58; mem policy comt, Col Art Asn Am, 56-58; vpres, Southeastern Col Artists Conf, 57-58; mem exec comt, Assoc Artists NC, 59-60; bd mem, NC State Artists Soc, 60-62. *Teaching:* Instr art, State Teachers Col, Indiana, Pa, 32-35; prof art & head dept, Woman's Col, Univ NC, Greensboro, 35-61, dir, Burnsville Sch Fine Arts, 52 & 53; dir summer session fine arts, Beaufort, NC, 54; chmn dept art, Calif State Univ, Fullerton, 65-67, prof, 65-71. *Mailing Add:* 2522 Brentwood Ave Springfield MO 65804

IWAMASA, KEN
EDUCATOR, PRINTMAKER

b Manzanar, Calif, Apr 28, 43. *Study:* Calif state Univ, Long Beach, BA, 66, MA, 72. *Work:* El Camino Col; City of Los Angeles; Rio Hondo Col. *Exhib:* One-man shows, Rio Hondo Col, 76 & Old Dominion Univ, 77; World Print Competition, San Francisco Mus Mod Art, Calif, 77; Detroit Nat Print Symposium, Cranbrook Acad Art, 80; Fantastic Art, Castle San Giorgo, Italy, 81; Works on Paper, Cheney-Cowles Mem Mus, Spokane, 81; Artist as Social Critic, Mich State Univ, Ann Arbor, 81; and others. *Teaching:* Asst prof drawing & printmaking, Univ Colo, Boulder, 72- *Awards:* Grants & Purchase Awards from Scott Found, Japan Found & Univ Colo. *Media:* Screen, Lithography. *Dealer:* Miriam Perlman Gallery 505 N Lake Shore Dr Chicago IL 60611; Sebastian Moore Gallery 1411 Market St Denver CO. *Mailing Add:* Dept of Fine Arts Univ Colo Boulder CO 80306

IWAMOTO, RALPH SHIGETO
PAINTER

b Honolulu, Hawaii, Sept 13, 27. *Study:* Community Col, New York, 49-51; Art Students League, 48-49 & 51-53. *Work:* Butler Inst Am Art, Youngstown, Ohio; Sheldon Swope Art Gallery, Terre Haute, Ind; Herbert F Johnson Art Mus, Cornell Univ; State Found on Cult & Arts, Honolulu; Wadsworth Atheneum, Hartford, Conn. *Exhib:* Pa Acad, Philadelphia, 58; Whitney Mus Ann, New York, 58; Paterson Col, NJ, 77; Betty Parsons Gallery, New York, 79; Arte Fiera, Bologna, Italy, 78; Bergen Co Mus, NJ, 83; Neward Mus, NJ, 83; and others. *Awards:* Purchase Prize, Butler Inst Am Art, 57; Fel, John Hay Whitney Found, 58. *Bibliog:* James Mellow (auth), Art rev, New York Times, 2/17/73; K Ichida (auth), article in Ichimai Art Mag, Tokyo, 12/80; Eileen F Watkins (auth), article, Newark Star-Ledger, 10/20/83. *Media:* Acrylic. *Mailing Add:* 463 West St A-1110 New York NY 10014

IZUKA, KUNIO
SCULPTOR

b Tokyo, Japan, Mar 2, 39. *Study:* Otis Art Inst, Los Angeles Co; Art Students League. *Work:* Mus Mod Art Tokyo, Japan; Mus Mod Art Kyoto, Japan. *Comn:* Monumental sculpture, Warner Commun, Los Angeles, 72. *Exhib:* First Int Exhib Mod Sculpture, Hakone Open-Air Mus, Japan, 69; Exhib Contemp Japanese Art, Mus Mod Art Rio de Janeiro, 71 & Milan, Italy, 72. *Teaching:* Asst instr sculpture, Art Students League, 68-69. *Awards:* Purchase Prize, 50th Anniversary Show, Otis Art Inst Los Angeles Co, 68; Second Prize, Exhib Contemp Japanese Art, New York, 72. *Mem:* Sculptors Guild; Japanese Artist Asn New York. *Media:* Metal. *Mailing Add:* 80 Amsterdam Ave 4-B New York NY 10023

IZUMI, KIYOSHI
ARCHITECT, EDUCATOR

b Vancouver, BC, Mar 24, 21. *Study:* Univ Man, BArch; Mass Inst Technol, MCP. *Pos:* Mem, Sask Arts Bd, 60; mem bd trustees, Nat Mus Can, Govt Can, 68-74; chmn vis comt, Nat Art Gallery Can, Ottawa, 70-74. *Teaching:* Mem fac environ studies, Univ Waterloo, currently. *Mem:* Academician Royal Can Acad Arts. *Publ:* Auth, Some considerations on the art of architecture and art in architecture, Structurist, Univ Sask, Modern Press, No 2, 61-62. *Mailing Add:* Sch Urban & Regional Plan Univ of Waterloo Waterloo ON N2L 3G1 Canada

J

JACHNA, JOSEPH DAVID
PHOTOGRAPHER, EDUCATOR
b Chicago, Ill, Sept 12, 35. *Study:* Univ Mo Photo-Jour Workshop, 57; Ill Inst Technol Inst Design, with Aaron Siskind, Harry Callahan & Frederick Sommer, BS(art educ), 58, MS(photog), 61. *Work:* George Eastman House, Int Mus Photog, Rochester, NY; Art Inst Chicago; Photog Collection, Exchange Nat Bank of Chicago; Mass Inst Technol; Mus Mod Art, New York. *Exhib:* Solo exhibs, Art Inst Chicago, 61, Nikon Salon, Tokyo, 74, Visual Studies Workshop Gallery, Rochester, NY, 79, Chicago Ctr Contemp Photog, 80, Focus Gallery, San Francisco, 81 & Perihelion Gallery, Milwaukii, 81; Photog in the 20th Century, Nat Gallery Can, 67; Photog: Midwest Invitational, Walker Art Ctr, Minneapolis, 73; Photographers and the City, Mus Contemp Art, Chicago, 77; The Target Collection of American Photography, Mus Fine Arts, Houston, 77; Second Sight, Carpenter Ctr Visual Arts, Harvard Univ, 81; and others. *Teaching:* From instr to asst prof photog, Inst Design, Ill Inst Technol, 61-69; from asst prof to prof photog, Univ Ill, Chicago Circle Campus, 69-82; workshops, Peninsula Sch Art, Door Co, Wis, summers 69-71. *Awards:* Fac Grant Color Photog, Univ Ill, Chicago Circle Campus, 72; Ferguson Grant, Friends of Photog, Carmel, Calif, 73; John Simon Guggenheim Mem Found Fel, 80. *Bibliog:* Landscape illusions, In: Photography Year 1974, Time/Life Bks, 74; John B Turner (auth), Joseph D Jachna, Photo-Forum, Auckland, NZ, 75. *Mem:* Soc Photog Educ; assoc George Eastman House-Int Mus Photog. *Publ:* Contribr, Aperture, 61; contribr, Art in America, New Talent Issue, 62; contribr, Photography in the 20th Century (catalog), Eastman House, 67; contribr, Camera Mainichi '74-9, 74. *Dealer:* Jeffrey Fuller 2108 Spruce St Philadelphia PA 19103. *Mailing Add:* 5707 W 89th Pl Oak Lawn IL 60453

JACKARD, JERALD WAYNE See Jacquard

JACKSON, A B
EDUCATOR, PAINTER
b New Haven, Conn, Apr 18, 25. *Study:* Yale Norfolk Summer Fel, with Josef Albers, Nicholas Marsicano & Gabor Peterdi, 52; Yale Univ Sch Art & Archit, BFA, 53, MFA, 55. *Work:* Yale Univ, New Haven, Conn; Dartmouth Col, Hanover, NH; Univ Mass, Amherst. *Exhib:* Int Figure Painting Traveling Show, 69-70; Smithsonian American Drawing Traveling Show, 69-72; Black Artists in Review, Cleveland State Univ, 72; Va Mus Traveling Exhibs. *Pos:* Artist in residence, Living Arts Ctr, Dayton, Ohio, summer 69; artist in residence, Dartmouth Col, Spring 71; vis artist, Humanities Ctr, Richmond, Va, 71; vis artist, Roanoke Fine Arts Ctr, Va, spring 72; owner, A B Jackson Sch Art, currently. *Teaching:* Instr art, Southern Univ, 55-56; asst prof art, Norfolk State Col, 56-67; prof art, Old Dominion Univ, formerly. *Awards:* Purchase Award, Va Biennial, Va Mus Fine Arts, 64; Purchase Award, Graphics Ann, Mint Mus, Charlotte, 67; Purchase Award, Am Drawing Exhib, Chrysler Mus, Norfolk, 71. *Bibliog:* Sidney Hurwitz (auth), A B Jackson: his porch people, Am Artist, 2/68. *Publ:* Illusr several issues of Red Clay Reader, 65-70; illusr, Randolph Bourne, Legend & Reality, 66. *Dealer:* Eric Schindler Gallery 2305 E Broad St Richmond VA 23223. *Mailing Add:* 324 London Blvd Norfolk VA 23503

JACKSON, BILLY MORROW
PAINTER, EDUCATOR
b Kansas City, Mo, Feb 23, 26. *Study:* Washington Univ, BFA; Univ Ill, Urbana, MFA. *Work:* Metrop Mus Art, New York; Calif Palace Legion of Honor, San Francisco, Calif; Nat Collection, Smithsonian Inst & Nat Gallery Art, Washington, DC; and others. *Exhib:* McClung Mus, Univ Tenn, 65-67; Fine Arts Gallery San Diego, Calif, 66; Lehigh Univ, Bethlehem, Pa, 66; Decatur Art Ctr, Ill, 66; 4 Arts Gallery Evanston, Ill, 67; and others. *Teaching:* Prof art, Univ Ill, Urbana, currently. *Awards:* Purchase Prize, Evansville Mus Arts & Sci, 66; Union League Club, Chicago, 67; and others. *Media:* Oil, Watercolor. *Dealer:* Jane Haslem Gallery 2121 P St NW Washington DC 20037. *Mailing Add:* Dept of Art Univ of Ill Urbana IL 61801

JACKSON, EVERETT GEE
PAINTER, ILLUSTRATOR
b Mexia, Tex, Oct 8, 1900. *Study:* Tex A&M Univ; Art Inst Chicago; San Diego State Col, BA; Univ Southern Calif, MA; also study in Mex. *Work:* Houston Mus Art, Tex; Fine Arts Gallery, San Diego, Calif; Los Angeles Co Mus Art; Pa Acad Fine Arts, Philadelphia. *Exhib:* Am Painting Exhib, Art Inst Chicago, Ill, 27; Whitney Mus Am Art, New York; Pa Acad Fine Arts, Philadelphia; Los Angeles Co Mus Art; San Francisco Mus Art; Retrospective Exhib, Inst Nacional de Bellas Artes & Inst Nacional de Arqueologia y Historia, Mexico City, 79; plus others. *Pos:* Bd trustees, Fine Arts Soc, San Diego, 35-80, chmn Latin-Am arts comt, 65-70, acquisitions comt; mem adv bd, Calif State Univ, San Diego, 63-70. *Teaching:* Prof art, Calif State Univ, San Diego, 30-63; prof art, Univ Costa Rica, 62. *Awards:* First Anne Bremer Prize, San Francisco Art Asn, 29; First Prize, 30 & Leisser Farnham Prize, 30, Fine Arts Gallery, San Diego; Los Angeles Co Mus Art Award, 34. *Mem:* San Diego Art Guild; Am Asn Univ Prof. *Media:* Oil. *Res:* Maya sculpture. *Publ:* Illusr, Wonderful adventure of Paul Bunyon, Ugly Duckling, Popol Vuh, Ramona & American Indian Legends, Limited Ed Club & Heritage. *Mailing Add:* 1234 Franciscan Way San Diego CA 92116

JACKSON, HARRY ANDREW
PAINTER, SCULPTOR
b Chicago, Ill, Apr 18, 24. *Study:* Art Inst Chicago, 31-38; with Ed Grigware, Cody, Wyo, 38-42; Brooklyn Mus Art Sch, with Hans Hofmann, 46-48. *Work:* Whitney Gallery Western Art, Cody; Vatican Mus; Minn Inst Arts; Woolarac Mus, Bartlesville, Okla; Am Mus Gt Brit, Bath, Eng. *Comn:* Stampede, 60 & Range Burial, 66 (oil murals), Whitney Gallery Western Art; Sor Capanna (monument), Piazza dei Mercanti, Rome, 62; painted sculpture of John Wayne (for cover), Time Mag, 8/8/69; Sacagawea, Buffalo Bill Historical Ctr, Cody, Wyo; Official Monument to John Wayne (heroic bronze), Beverly Hills, Calif, 84. *Exhib:* Nat Collection Fine Arts, Washington, DC, 64; Nat Acad Design, New York, 64, 65, 67, 68 & 70; Nat Cowboy Hall of Fame, Oklahoma City, 66 & 70-72; Gilcrease Mus, Tulsa, Okla, 80; retrospective, Buffalo Bill Historical Ctr, Cody, Wyo, 81; Palm Springs Desert Mus, Calif, 81; Minneapolis Inst Arts, Minn, 82. *Pos:* Off combat artist, USMC, 44-45. *Awards:* Interstate Gold Medal, Pennational Artists Ann, 67; Samuel Finley Breese Morse Gold Medal, Nat Acad Design, 68; Silver Medal, Nat Cowboy Hall of Fame, 71. *Bibliog:* M Amaya (auth), article, Connoisseur, 79; L Pointer & D Goddard (auth), Harry Jackson, Abrams Publ, 81; and others. *Mem:* USMC Combat Corresp Asn; Nat Sculpture Soc; Bohemian Club; fel Am Artists Prof League; assoc mem Nat Acad Design. *Media:* Oil; Bronze. *Publ:* Contribr monograph catalog, Kennedy Galleries, 69; auth, Lost Wax Bronze Casting, Northland Press, 72 & Van Nostrand Reinhold, 79. *Mailing Add:* PO Box 2836 Cody WY 82414

JACKSON, HAZEL BRILL
SCULPTOR
b Philadelphia, Pa. *Study:* Boston Mus Fine Arts; Scuola Rosatti, Florence, Italy; also with Angelo Zanelli, Rome & with Bela Pratt & Charles Grafly. *Work:* Concord Art Mus; Wellesley Col; Vassar Col; Dartmouth Col; Calgary Mus, Can. *Exhib:* Nat Acad Design; Nat Acad Rome; Nat Acad, Firenze, Italy; one-man shows, Boston Guild Artists & Corcoran Gallery Art, Washington, DC. *Mem:* Fel Nat Sculpture Soc. *Mailing Add:* Twin Oaks 83 Balmville Rd Newburgh NY 12550

JACKSON, HERB
PAINTER, PRINTMAKER
b Raleigh, NC, Aug 16, 45. *Study:* Davidson Col, BA; Philips Univ, Marburg, WGer; Univ NC, MFA. *Work:* Brit Mus, London; Libr Cong, Washington, DC; Brooklyn Mus Art, NY; Baltimore Mus Art, Md; Whitney Mus Am Art, New York. *Exhib:* One-person exhibs, Mint Mus Art, Charlotte, NC, Springfield Art Mus, Mo & Fundacao Calouste Gulbenkian, Lisbon, Portugal; Piedmont Graphics Exhib, Mint Mus, Charlotte, NC, 68 & 70-71; 35 Artists of the Southeast, High Mus, Atlanta, Ga, 76; 30 Yrs of Am Printmaking, Brooklyn Mus, NY, 77; XV Int Sao Paulo Bienal, Brazil, 79; Childe Hassam Purchase Fund Exhib, Am Acad & Inst Arts & Letters, New York, 81; Southeastern Ctr Contemp Art, 81; and many others. *Teaching:* From assoc prof to prof studio art, Davidson Col, 69-. *Awards:* Southeastern Ctr Contemp Art Grant, 81. *Bibliog:* Dr Pamela Allara (auth), Herb Jackson: Drawings, The Shape of Experience (exhib catalog), Mint Mus; Dr Roger Lipsey (auth), Herb Jackson Drawings at the Mint Museum, Arts, 6/83. *Mem:* Col Art Asn Am; Southeastern Col Art Conf. *Media:* Acrylic, Graphics. *Dealer:* Phyllis Weil & Co 1065 Park Ave New York NY 10028. *Mailing Add:* Box 2495 Davidson NC 28036

JACKSON, LEE
PAINTER
b New York, NY, Feb 2, 09. *Study:* NY Univ, 1 yr; Art Students League; also with John Sloan & George Luks. *Work:* Metrop Mus Art, New York; Corcoran Gallery Art; Walker Art Ctr, Minneapolis, Minn; Nebr Art Asn, Lincoln; Los Angeles Co Mus Art, Calif. *Exhib:* 56th Ann Paintings, Art Inst Chicago, 46; Whitney Mus Am Art, New York, 49-50; Am Painting Today 1950, Metrop Mus Am, 50; 23rd Biennial, Corcoran Gallery Art, 53; 140th Ann, Nat Acad Design, New York, 65; and many others. *Teaching:* Instr painting & drawing, Sch Art Studies, 47-48; instr painting & drawing, City Col New York, 48-54. *Awards:* Guggenheim Fel, 41; Univ Nebr Art Gallery Purchase Prize, 43; Thomas B Clarke Prize, Nat Acad Design, 51. *Mem:* Art Students League; Audubon Artists Am; Am Watercolor Soc; Artists Equity Asn; Nat Soc Painters in Casein. *Media:* Oil. *Publ:* Contribr, Drawings by American Artists, 47; contribr, Am Artist Mag, 9/53. *Mailing Add:* Strong's Lane Water Mill NY 11976

JACKSON, OLIVER LEE
PAINTER
b St Louis, Mo, 35. *Study:* Ill Wesleyan Univ, BFA, 58; Univ Iowa, MFA, 63. *Work:* San Francisco Mus Mod Art; Oakland Mus; Seattle Art Mus; Sheldon Mem Art Gallery, Lincoln, Neb. *Exhib:* Solo exhib, Seattle Art Mus, 82; Fresh Paint: 15 Calif Artists, San Francisco Mus Mod Art, 82; From the Sunny Side, Oakland Mus, 82; Biennial Exhib, Whitney Mus, 83. *Pos:* Visiting artist, Art Inst Chicago, 69; artist in residence, Wake Forest Univ, SE Ctr Contemp Art, 80 & NC Sch Arts, Winston-Salem, 80. *Teaching:* Instr, Southern Ill Univ, East St Louis, 67-69; Oberlin Col, 69-70 & Calif State Univ, Sacramento, 71- *Awards:* Award in Painting, Nat Endowment Arts, 80. *Bibliog:* Regina Hackett (auth), Oliver Lee Jackson: Forms that feelings take, Artforum, summer 79; Regina Hackett (auth), Oliver Lee Jackson (catalog), SE Ctr Contemp Art, 80. *Media:* Oils. *Dealer:* Quay Gallery 254 Sutter St San Francisco CA 94108; Alan Stone Gallery 48 E 86th St New York NY 10028. *Mailing Add:* c/o Anne Kohs & Assocs 251 Post St, Suite 300 San Francisco CA 94108

JACKSON, RUTH AMELIA
CURATOR

b Paterson, NJ; Can citizen. *Study:* Parsons Sch, Ridgewood, NJ; Holton Arms, Washington, DC; Maret French Sch, Washington, DC; Miss Spauldings, Queensgate, London, Eng. *Collections Arranged:* Auguste Rodin, 63, Mains et Merveilles, 72, Gold for the Gods, 77, The Decorative Scene--Montreal, 1860-1914, 77, Treasures of London, 77 & Spider Woman and the Navajo, 78, Montreal Mus Fine Arts. *Pos:* Dir, Can Guild of Crafts, 72-; cur dec arts, Montreal Mus Fine Arts, 72-79; hon councillor & arch consult, Montreal Mus Fine Arts, 80. *Publ:* Auth, Galerie Hosmer-Pillow-Vaughan, 69 & Clutch of Curiosities, 70, Can Collector; auth, Mobel, Silber und Keramik aus Quebec, Weltkunst, 74; auth, Canada's Heritage of Silver, Antique Monthly, 76; auth, Traditional Furniture from the Province of Quebec, Apollo, 76. *Mailing Add:* 202-400 Stewart St Ottawa ON K1N 6L2 Canada

JACKSON, SARAH
SCULPTOR, GRAPHIC ARTIST

b Detroit, Mich, Nov 13, 24. *Study:* Wayne State Univ, BA, 46, MA, 48. *Work:* Joseph H Hirshhorn Collection, Washington, DC; Nat Gallery Can, Ottawa; Montreal Mus Fine Arts; Montreal Mus Contemp Arts; Fine Arts Collection, Smithsonian Inst, Washington, DC. *Comn:* Dancer (bronze), Cloverdale Shopping Ctr, Toronto, 66; Metamorphosis (bronzes) & Mindscape (bronze hanging), Student Union Bldg, Dalhousie Univ; plastic & bronze sculpture, Mt Sinai Hosp, Toronto. *Exhib:* St Lawrence Centre, Toronto, 78; Win Gallery, Toronto, 79; one-person shows, Pa State Univ, 78 & NS Tech Col Art Gallery, 79; Mount St Vincent Univ, 81; plus many others. *Pos:* Artist-in-residence, Tech Univ NS. *Teaching:* Lectr, Mexico City Col, 48, London Univ, 54-55, Tate Gallery, London, 54-55, Thomas More Inst, 56, Nat Gallery, Ottawa, 57, Toronto Univ, 60-61, YMCA Adult Educ, Toronto, 62, St Mary's Univ, 63, Nova Scotia Col Art, 70, Dartmouth Adult Educ Div, 72-73 & Univ BC, 79. *Awards:* Sculpture Award, Winnipeg Art Gallery; Ontario Arts Coun Grant, 74. *Bibliog:* Brian Charent (auth), An interview with Sarah Jackson, Art Mag, winter 74; Guy Robert (auth), Eros et humour chez Sarah Jackson, Vie Des Arts, spring 75; article in Art Mag, Toronto, 12/79. *Mem:* Can Artists Rep. *Media:* Bronze, Plastic; Xerography. *Dealer:* Gadatsy Gallery 112 Yorkville Toronto ON Can. *Mailing Add:* 1411 Edward St Halifax NS B3H 3H5 Canada

JACKSON, SUZANNE FITZALLEN
PAINTER, WRITER

b St Louis, Mo, Jan 30, 44. *Study:* San Francisco State Col, BA; Otis Art Inst, Los Angeles, with Charles White. *Work:* Hirshhorn Mus; Palm Springs Desert Mus, Calif; Crenshaw Wall & New Health Ctr, Los Angeles, Calif; Daniel, Mann, Johnson & Mendenhall, Co, Los Angeles. *Comn:* Peace Bird, Secy State Edmund G Brown, Jr, Sacramento, 72; Stephen Chase, Arthur Elrod & Assoc, Palm Springs, 74; Artful Living, William Chidester Co, Pac Design Ctr, Los Angeles, 75. *Exhib:* Joseph Hirshhorn Collection, Palm Springs Desert Mus, 70; Black Untitled II/Dimensions of the Figure, Oakland Mus, 71; Blacks: USA: Now, New York Cult Ctr, 73; Directions in Afro-American Art, Herbert F Johnson Mus Art, Cornell Univ, 74; Pioneer Mus, Haggin Art Galleries, Stockton, Calif, 75; plus others. *Pos:* Owner-dir, Gallery 32, Los Angeles, 68-70; artist/coordr, CETA Prof Artists Pub Art Prog, Brockman Gallery Productions, 77-78. *Teaching:* Art instr, St Stephens Sch, San Francisco, 65-66; guest educ aide, Black Arts Coun Exhib, Los Angeles Pub Schs, 69-70; instr dance & crafts, Watts Towers Art Ctr, 70; lectr art, Stanford Univ, summer 72; lectr, Univ of the Pac, 72, 73 & 75, Scripps Col, 74, Calif Inst Women, 74 & San Diego Fine Arts Soc, 75. *Awards:* Univ of the Pac & Pioneer Mus Artists Merit Award, 75; Grand Prize, Int Fine Arts Billboard Competition, Eyes & Ears Found, 79. *Bibliog:* Gordon Hazlitt (auth), Creating her own world, Art News, 11/74. *Media:* Acrylic Wash. *Publ:* Contribr, Black Artists on Art, Vol 2, 71; auth & illusr, What I Love, Contemp Crafts, 72; contribr, Contextures, Just Above Midtown Gallery, 77; auth & illusr, Animal, 78. *Mailing Add:* 3013 Edward Ave Los Angeles CA 90065

JACKSON, VAUGHN L
PAINTER, ILLUSTRATOR

b Raymond, Ohio, Jan 7, 20. *Study:* Am Univ, AA, BA, 69; Corcoran Sch Art, with Richard Lahey, 47-50; Ohio State Univ, 42-43; Columbus Art Sch, 39-40; with Hans Hofmann, Provincetown, summer 55; also with Eliot O'Hara. *Work:* Many in pvt collections. *Comn:* Over 1100 free lance designs and illustrations in advertising, technical and military publications; displays and visual presentations for art studios, advertising agencies, government and commercial accounts. *Exhib:* Am Artists Prof League, 50-52 & 57; Washington Watercolor Club Ann Nat Exhibs, 54-58; Am Art League, 58; Soc Tech Writers & Publ Ann, 71; one-man show, Washington, DC, 56 & 58; and others. *Pos:* Advert artist, Kal, Ehrlich & Merrick Advert Agency, 47-52; artist-illusr, Opers Res Off, Johns Hopkins Univ, 52-55, asst art dir, 55-63; publ art dir, Res Anal Corp, 63-67, visual & graphics mgr, 67-72; visual & graphics mgr, Gen Res Corp, 72, tech publ dir, 72-76; visual dir, System Planning Corp, 76- *Awards:* Silver Medal, Landscape Club Washington, DC, 55; Award for Outstanding Achievement in Tech Commun, Soc Tech Writers & Publs, 71. *Mem:* Soc Tech Commun; Am Inst Graphic Arts; charter mem Art Dirs Club Metrop Washington; Washington Watercolor Asn. *Media:* Watercolor, Acrylic; Ink. *Publ:* Work in Ed & Publ, Printers Ink, Aviation Age, Electronics Mag, Agr Chemicals, Washington Post, Eve Star & other newspapers; also annual reports, point of sale and direct mail campaigns. *Mailing Add:* Ten Penny Studio PO Box 54 Fairfax Station VA 22039

JACKSON, WARD
PAINTER, EDITOR

b Petersburg, Va, Sept 10, 28. *Study:* Richmond Prof Inst, Col William & Mary, BFA & MFA; Hans Hofmann Sch Fine Arts, scholar, 52. *Work:* Nat Mus Am Art, Smithsonian Inst, Washington, DC; Riverside Mus Collection, Rose Art Mus, Brandeis Univ; Elvehjem Art Ctr, Univ Wis-Madison, Va Mus Fine Arts, Richmond; NY Univ Art Collection, New York; and others. *Exhib:* One-man show, Va Mus Fine Arts, Richond, 71; Inst Contemp Art, Richmond, 80; Schenectady Mus, New York, 81; Abstraction in Action, City Gallery, New York, 82; Weatherspoon Art Gallery, Univ NC, Greensboro; Moody Art Gallery, Univ Ala, 83; and others. *Pos:* Co-ed, Folio, 49-51; co-ed, Art Now: New York, 69-72, adv ed, Art Now Gallery Guide, 69-; archivist & head viewing prog, Solomon R Guggenheim Mus, New York, 55- *Teaching:* Instr art hist, Rollins Col, Winter Park, Fla, 54-55. *Awards:* Fel, Va Mus Fine Arts, 48 & 49; First Prize for painting, New York Ctr Gallery, 56; Nat Endowment Arts Artists Fel, 75-76. *Bibliog:* Ward Jackson Watercolors, Davidson Col, 75; Circular 24/25, Zeitschrift für Kunst und Gestaltung, Bonn, Ger, 78; The Vertical Image, New Gallery, Russell Sage Col, 81; and others. *Mem:* Am Abstract Artists; Col Art Asn Am. *Publ:* Auth, Art in glass (works of Art by Louis Comfort Tiffany), Rollins Col Lit Mag, 55; auth, George L K Morris: forty years of abstract art, Art J, 72; auth intro, George L K Morris, The Years 1945-1975, Hirschl & Adler Galleries, New York, 78. *Dealer:* Buecker & Harpsichords 465 W Broadway New York NY 10012. *Mailing Add:* 152 Forsyth St Apt 13 New York NY 10002

JACKSON, WILLIAM DAVIS
SCULPTOR, DESIGNER

b Philadelphia, Pa, Feb 1, 46. *Study:* Shop asst to J C McLauchlin, cabinetmaker, 61-63; Univ NH, BA(painting & graphic arts; Gladys & Charles Edgecomb Found Grant Music & Art), 68; Ind Univ, MFA(sculpture; fel), 72. *Exhib:* Copper, Brass & Bronze Exhib, Univ Ariz Mus Art, Tucson, 77; Nat Drawing Exhib, State Univ NY, Potsdam, 77; Outdoor Sculpture of the Berkshires, Chesterwood Mus, Stockbridge, Mass, 78; Four Sculptors, Rensselaer Polytechnic Inst, Troy, NY, 82; Art and Energy, Hartford Art Sch, Univ Hartford, Conn, 82; and many others. *Pos:* Shop asst, George Rickey, East Chatham, NY, 71-72. *Teaching:* Instr painting, drawing & graphics, The Phillips Exeter Acad, Exeter, NH, 68-70; instr sculpture, painting & drawing, Simon's Rock of Bard Col, Great Barrington, Mass, 72- *Media:* Mixed. *Mailing Add:* 125 Main St Stephentown NY 12168

JACOB, MARY JANE
CURATOR, HISTORIAN

b Queens, NY, Jan 5, 52. *Study:* Fla State Univ Study Ctr, Florence, Italy, 72; Univ Fla, Gainesville, BFA, 73; Univ Mich, Ann Arbor, 76. *Collections Arranged:* A Decade of Women's Performance Art, Contemp Arts Ctr, New Orleans & traveling, 80. *Pos:* Cur, Mich Artrain, Detroit, 74-75; curatorial asst, Detroit Inst Arts, 76-77, asst cur mod art, 77-78, assoc cur mod art, 78-82; chief cur, Mus Contemp Art, Chicago, currently. *Awards:* Nat Endowment Humanities Fel, 73-74; Nat Endowment Humanities Fel, 80-81. *Mem:* Nat Women's Caucus Art (adv bd, 79-80); Mich Coun Arts. *Res:* 20th century art with emphasis on American art of the 1920's and 1930's and contemporary American and European art. *Publ:* Auth, Germaine Keller, Arts Mag, Vol 50, No 8; auth, Michele Oka Doner, Detroit Inst Arts, 78; auth, Chicago: The city and its artists, 1945-1978, Arts Mag, Vol 53, No 1; coauth, An Interview with Keith Aoki, Nancy Pletos/Keith Aoki: Works in Progress VI, Detroit Inst Arts, 79. *Mailing Add:* Mus Contemp Art 237 E Ontario St Chicago IL 60611

JACOB, NED
PAINTER, SCULPTOR

b Elizabethton, Tenn, Nov 15, 38. *Study:* Pvt studies with Robert Gilbert, Robert Lougheed & Bettina Steinke. *Work:* Denver Art Mus; Indianapolis Mus of Art; Whitney Gallery of Western Art, Cody, Wyo; Albrecht Art Mus, St Joseph, Mo; Pac NW Indian Ctr, Spokane, Wash. *Exhib:* One-man shows, Nat Cowboy Hall of Fame & Western Heritage Ctr, Oklahoma City, 66, Colo Coun on Arts & Humanities, Colo Gov's Mansion, Denver, 74, Boise Gallery of Art, Idaho, 75, Birger Sandzen Mem Gallery, Lindsborg, Kans, 76 & Whitney Gallery of Western Art, 76; and others. *Awards:* John F & Anna Lee Stacy Fel, 74. *Bibliog:* Cover story, Am Artist Mag, 8/75; Royal B Hassrick (auth), Western Painting Today, Watson-Guptill, 75; James K Howard (auth), Ten Years with the Cowboy Artists of America, Northland Press, 76. *Mem:* Salmagundi Club, New York. *Mailing Add:* 206 McKenzie #1 Santa Fe NM 87501

JACOBOWITZ, ELLEN SUE
CURATOR, HISTORIAN

b Detroit, Mich, Feb 21, 48. *Study:* Univ Mich, BA, 69, MA, 70; Courtauld Inst Art, 70-71; Bryn Mawr Col, PhD. *Collections Arranged:* American Graphics: 1860-1940 (auth, catalog), Rijkmuseum & Philadelphia Mus Art, 82; The Prints of Lucas van Leyden and His Contemporaries (auth, catalog), Nat Gallery Art & Boston Mus Fine Arts, 83. *Pos:* Cur, Philadelphia Mus Art, 72- *Mem:* Print Coun Am (bd mem, 80-83); Print Club Philadelphia (bd mem, 78-); Illustrated Bartsch; Neth-Am Amity Trust (bd mem, 81-). *Res:* Early 16th century Netherlandish printmaking; American printmaking since the late 19th century. *Publ:* Auth, Three Centuries of Chiaroscuro Woodcuts, Pa Acad Fine Arts, 73; contribr, Philadelphia: Three Centuries of American Art, Philadelphia Mus Art, 76; coauth, The Illustrated Bartsch--Lucas van Leyden, Abaris, 81. *Mailing Add:* 1820 Spruce St Philadelphia PA 19103

JACOBS, DAVID (THEODORE)
SCULPTOR, EDUCATOR
b Niagara Falls, NY, Mar 1, 32. *Study:* Orange Coast Col, AA; Los Angeles State Col, AB & MA. *Work:* Guggenheim Mus & Assyrian Embassy, New York; Mus Art, Richmond, Va; Otterbein Col, Ohio; Valley Mall, Hagerstown, Md. *Comn:* Cloud Fountain (sculptured fountain), Valley Mall Assoc, Hagerstown, Md, 74; bronze relief, Paul Radin Mem, Hofstra Univ Libr, 74; Raingate (sculptured fountain), A Dworkin, Westbury, NY, 75; Ventura High, Deer Park High Sch, NY, 76; Rainframe (sculptured screen), Dawn-Joy Corp, New York, 76. *Exhib:* The Art of Assemblage, Mus Mod Art, New York, 61; 68th Am Exhib, Art Inst Chicago, 66; Sound, Light, Silence, Art That Performs, W R Nelson Gallery, Atkins Mus, Kansas City, 66; Inflatable Sculpture, Jewish Mus, New York, 69; Sound Sculpture, Vancouver Art Gallery, 73; plus many one-man shows, 61-81. *Teaching:* Prof sculpture, Hofstra Univ, 62-; vis critic sculpture, Cornell Univ, New York Prog, 69 & 70, Baruch Col, City Col New York, 77-79. *Awards:* Res grant, Hofstra Univ, 68; Creative Artists Pub Serv grant, 73 & 76. *Bibliog:* D J Irving (auth), Sculpture: Materials & Processes, Van Nostrand Reinhold, 68; Wayne Craven (auth), Sculpture in America, Crowell, 68; Chichura & Stevens (auths), Super Sculpture: Using Science, Technology and Natural Phenomena in Sculpture, Van Nostrand Reinhold, 74. *Media:* Aluminum, Rubber. *Mailing Add:* Dept of Fine Arts Hofstra Univ Hempstead NY 11550

JACOBS, HAROLD
PAINTER, SCULPTOR
b New York, NY, Oct 29, 32. *Study:* Cooper Union, 53; NY Univ; New Sch Social Res; Sorbonne, Fulbright scholar, 61. *Work:* Whitney Mus Am Art, New York; Portland Art Mus, Ore; Kalamazoo Art Ctr; Philadelphia Mus Art; Pa Acad Fine Arts. *Teaching:* Prof painting, Moore Col Art, 66- *Awards:* Nat Endowment Arts Collaboration Grant Visual & Performing Arts, 75; Distinguished Artist Award, Moore Col Art, 83. *Media:* Mixed; Inflatable Structures. *Mailing Add:* 632 South St Philadelphia PA 19147

JACOBS, HELEN NICHOLS
PAINTER
b Kent, Conn, Feb 16, 24. *Study:* With Spencer B Nichols & Arthur Maynard. *Exhib:* Nat Arts Club, 74-75; Audubon Artists, 75 & 77; Kent Art Asn, Conn, 75, 77 & 79; Catharine Lorillard Wolfe Art Club, 80-81; Am Artists Prof League, New York & NJ, 81. *Teaching:* Instr oil painting, Ridgewood Adult Sch, NJ, 68-72 & Ridgewood Art Inst, 71- *Awards:* Catharine Lorillard Wolfe Art Club Award, 79; Salmagundi Club Award, 81-82; Am Artists Prof League Award, 82. *Mem:* Am Artists Prof League; Catharine Lorillard Wolfe Art Club; Kent Art Asn; Hudson Valley Art Asn. *Media:* Oil. *Mailing Add:* 684 Terrace Dr Paramus NJ 07652

JACOBS, JIM
PAINTER, PRINTMAKER
b New York, NY, May 26, 45. *Study:* Boston Univ, BA; Bryn Mawr Col, study with Richmond Lattimore; Harvard Univ; Boston Mus of Fine Arts. *Work:* Rose Art Mus, Brandeis Univ, Waltham, Mass; Chase Manhattan Bank; Arman; Smith Mus. *Exhib:* Expressions of the Seventies, New York, 77; Elizabeth Weiner Gallery, New York, 79 & 80; Danforth Mus, Framingham, Mass, 81; Smith Mus, Springfield, Mass, 81; Gallery Yves Arman, 81 & 82; and others. *Pos:* Archivist, Leo Castelli Gallery, 67-68. *Teaching:* Instr vase painting, Boston Univ, 65, Harvard Univ, 66, Bryn Mawr Col, 67; lectr, Boston Mus Fine Arts, Mus Sch, Boston, Harvard Univ; instr vase painting, Bryn Mawr Col, 67. *Awards:* Creative Artists Public Service Program Grant, 81-82. *Bibliog:* Article, Art News, 6/80; article, Arts Mag, 5/81; article, Art Am, 2/83. *Media:* Lacquer, Board. *Dealer:* Yves Arman 817 Madison Avenue New York NY 10021. *Mailing Add:* 26 W 20th St New York NY 10011

JACOBS, PETER ALAN
ADMINISTRATOR, SCULPTOR
b New York, NY, Jan 31, 39. *Study:* State Univ NY Col New Paltz, with Ilya Bolotowsky, BS(art educ), 60, MA(art), 62; Vanderbuilt Univ-George Peabody Col, EdD(fine arts), 65. *Work:* Bloomsburg State Col, Pa; Col of the Mainland, Texas City, Tex; Muskingum Col, New Concord, Ohio; George Peabody Mus, Nashville, Tenn; Mus Satire & Humor, Bulgaria. *Exhib:* New Directions in Art, Beloit Mus, Wis; Wis Designer-Craftsman, Milwaukee Art Ctr & Wis Painters & Sculptors, 68 & 69; Southwest Invitational, Yuma, Ariz, 73 & 74; one-man shows, Work on Tour by Ariz Arts & Humanities Comn, Ariz, Tex, Ohio & Wis, 74-75 & Univ Ohio, Univ Colo, Grand Canyon Art Ctr & Univ Wyo Art Mus. *Collections Arranged:* Ilya Bolotowsky Retrospective, Crossman Gallery, Univ Wis-Whitewater, 68 & Northern Ariz Univ Mus, 73; Andy Warhol, 81, Robert Rauschenberg, 81, Roy Lichtenstein, 82, James Rosenquist, 82, Sam Francis, 83 & William de Kooning, 84, Colo State Univ. *Teaching:* Chmn dept art, Univ Wis-Whitewater, 65-70; chmn dept art, Northern Ariz Univ, 70-74; chmn dept art, Cent Mich Univ, 74-76; chmn art dept, Colo State Univ, 76- *Mem:* Nat Coun Art Adminr (founder & chmn bd dirs, 72-77); Col Art Asn Am; Mich Soc Arts, Lett & Sci (chmn fine arts div, 75); Nat Art Educ Asn; Coun Art Dept Chmn State Wis (pres, 65-70). *Res:* Contemporary Indian art. *Publ:* Auth, Visual Arts in the Ninth Decade, Nat Coun Art Adminr, 80. *Mailing Add:* 2643 Silver Creek Dr Ft Collins CO 80525

JACOBS, RALPH, JR
PAINTER
b El Centro, Calif, May 22, 40. *Study:* With Evelyn Nadeau, Frederic Taubes & Abel G Warshawsky. *Work:* Beirut Art Mus, Lebanon; Continental Telephone Co, Ga. *Comn:* Many pvt collections in Canada, Japan, Australia and SAmerica. *Exhib:* Rosicrucian Mus, San Jose, Calif, 63, 67 & 71; Coun Am Artists Soc Nat Exhib, New York, 64; Nat Exhib, Springville Mus Art, Utah, 65; Soc Western Artists Ann Exhibs, de Young Mus, San Francisco, 65 & 69; Armenian Allied Arts Ann, Los Angeles, 66. *Awards:* State Ann Exhib First Awards, Art League Galleries, Santa Cruz, 63 & 64; Soc Western Artists Ann Second Award for Silhouette in Morning Light, 64; Klumpkey Mem Award for Classic Nude, de Young Mus, San Francisco, 65. *Media:* Oil. *Mailing Add:* PO Box 5906 Carmel CA 93921

JACOBS, TED SETH
GRAPHIC ARTIST, MURALIST
b Newark, NJ, June 11, 27. *Study:* Art Students League, 43-47. *Work:* Mus Mod Art & Finch Col Mus, New York. *Comn:* Portraits in oil, Dr Theodor Reik, 62, Jane Fonda, 64 & Mrs Mary Ellen Fahs, 71; portrait drawing, Thomas Hoving, 66; mural, Le Restaurant/Regency Hotel, New York, 78; and over 200 portrait comns & many murals. *Exhib:* One-man shows, Drawing & Painting Exhib, Adelson Galleries, Boston, 67 & 68, Coe Kerr Gallery, New York, 77 & 81 & Galerie Mouffe, Paris, 77; Reyn Galleries, New York, 72; Pac Lutheran Univ, Tacoma, Wash, 81. *Teaching:* Instr, Art Students League, 77- *Awards:* Bridgeman Prize, Art Students League New York, 44; First Prize, John F & Anna Lee Stacey Award, 52. *Media:* Oil, Lithography; Acrylic Murals. *Dealer:* Coe Kerr Gallery 49 E 82nd St New York NY 10021. *Mailing Add:* 523 E 83rd St New York NY 10028

JACOBSEN, MICHAEL A
HISTORIAN, EDUCATOR
b Pasadena, Calif, June 4, 42. *Study:* Univ Calif, Santa Barbara, BA, 65, MA, 70; Columbia Univ, PhD, 76. *Teaching:* Asst prof Renaissance art, Cleveland State Univ, Ohio, 73-77; asst prof Renaissance art, Univ Ore, 77-79; assoc prof art, Univ Ga, 79- *Mem:* Col Art Asn; Mid-West Art Hist Asn; SE Col Art Conference. *Res:* Renaissance art history, Italian 15th century. *Publ:* Auth, A Phimister Proctor, Apelles, 80; auth, Hercules and Antaeus, Source, 81; auth, Mantegna's battle of sea monsters, Art Bulletin, 12/82; auth, Perspective in Mantegna's early panels, Arte veneta, 83; auth, Dolphins in Renaissance art, Studies in Iconocgraphy, fall 83. *Mailing Add:* Dept of Art Univ of Ga Athens GA 30602

JACOBSHAGEN, N KEITH, II
PAINTER, PHOTOGRAPHER
b Wichita, Kans, Sept 8, 41. *Study:* Kansas City Art Inst, Mo, BFA; Art Ctr Col Design, Los Angeles; Univ Kans, MFA. *Work:* Sheldon Mem Gallery, Lincoln, Nebr; Univ Kans Mus Art, Lawrence; Mus Art Okla Univ; Oakland Mus, Calif; Pasadena Art Mus, Calif. *Exhib:* A Sense of Place: The Artist & the American Land, Sheldon Mem Art Galelry, Lincoln, Nebr, 74; Southern Ark Univ, Magnolia & Westark Community Col, Ft Smith, Ark, 78; In Respect of Space, Swan River Mus, Paola, Kans, 79; Group, Volga-Consalvo Gallery, Boston, Mass, 79; Corp Exhib, auspices of Minneapolis Art Inst, 79 & NAm Casualty Exhib, 79; and others. *Teaching:* Assoc prof art, Univ Nebr-Lincoln, 68-80. *Awards:* Owen H Kenan Award, 34th Ann Contemp Am Painting, 72; Frank Woods Fel, Univ Nebr, 75. *Bibliog:* Alan Gussow (auth), A Sense of Place: the Artist and the American Land (film), Nebr Educ TV, 74. *Media:* Oil. *Publ:* Contribr, Twelve Photographers: A Contemporary Mid-America Document, Mid-Am Arts Alliance, 78; contribr, Special report: Midwest art, Art in Am, 7-8/79; contribr, Artists work range through human emotions, Kansas City Star, 8/12/79; contribr, Cottonwood Rev, fall 79; contribr, In respect of space, Forum/Kansas City Artists Coalition, 12/79; and others. *Dealer:* Dorry Gates PO Box 7264 Kansas City MO 64113; Charles Campbell Gallery 647 Chestnut St San Francisco CA 94133. *Mailing Add:* 1945 E St Lincoln NE 68510

JACOBSON, ARTHUR ROBERT
PAINTER, PRINTMAKER
b Chicago, Ill, Jan 10, 24. *Study:* Univ Wis, BS, MS(art); Madrid Print Workshop, Spain; London, Eng, 72. *Work:* Mus NMex, Santa Fe; Ariz State Univ, Tempe; Hastings Col, Nebr. *Comn:* Exterior mural in marblecrete, Phoenix Jewish Community Ctr, Ariz, 62. *Exhib:* Corcoran Biennial of Painting, Corcoran Gallery Art, Washington, DC, 57; Libr Cong Print Exhib, Washington, DC, 65; Minn Mus Art Exhib Drawings, St Paul, 71; Graphics USA, Clarke Col, Iowa, 71; Drawings USA, Minn Mus Art, 75; Watercolor USA, Springfield Mus, Mo, 79. *Teaching:* Prof painting & drawing, Ariz State Univ, 56-; guest prof painting, Univ Wis, 67-68. *Awards:* Purchase awards, Pa Acad Fine Arts & Dallas Mus Art, 65; First Prize for Painting, Phoenix Art Mus, 71. *Media:* Oil. *Mailing Add:* Dept Art Ariz State Univ Tempe AZ 85281

JACOBSON, URSULA MERCEDES
PAINTER, SCULPTOR
b Milwaukee, Wis, Mar 26, 27. *Study:* Univ Wis-Milwaukee, BS, 48; Western Reserve Univ; Cleveland Mus & Sch of Art; Univ Wis-Madison, MS, 50, grad study, 50-51. *Exhib:* 7th & 10th Southwest Prints & Drawings, Dallas Mus, 57 & 59; 154th Ann, Pa Acad, 59; Four Corners Biennial, Phoenix Art Mus, 73 & 75; Palace of the Legion of Honor, San Francisco; Weatherspoon Gallery, NC; Northern Ariz Univ, Flagstaff; Scottsdale Ctr for Arts, Ariz; plus many others. *Mailing Add:* 5618 E Montecito Phoenix AZ 85018

JACOBSON, YOLANDE (MRS J CRAIG SHEPPARD)
SCULPTOR
b Norman, Okla, May 28, 21. *Study:* Univ Okla, BFA; also study in Norway, France & Mex. *Work:* Gilcrease Mus Art, Tulsa, Okla; Jacobsen Mus Art, Norman; State Hist Soc, Reno, Nev; Hist Mus, Carson City, Nev. *Comn:* Sen Patrick McCarran (bronze statue), Statuary Hall, Washington, DC, 61;

president's portrait bust, Univ Nev, Reno, 62; bronze sculpture, Gov Mansion, Carson City, 65; bronze portrait sculpture, Makey Sch Mines, Univ Nev, 73; Walter Clark Mem Bronze Portrait, Univ Nev, 81. *Exhib:* Denver Mus Art, 41; Okla Ann, Tulsa, 42-45; Mid-West Ann, Kansas City, 51; Oakland Mus Art, 56; Silver Centennial, Virginia City, Nev, 61; Mem Exhib, Sheppard Gallery, Univ Nev, 79. *Pos:* Asst ed & bk designer, Univ Nev Press, 63-66. *Awards:* Mid-West Ann, Kansas City, 41; Denver Mus Art, 41; Silver Centennial, Virginia City, 61. *Media:* Bronze, Wood. *Mailing Add:* 1000 Primrose St Reno NV 89502

JACOBUS, JOHN M
EDUCATOR, HISTORIAN
b Poughkeepsie, NY, Sept 15, 27. *Study:* Hamilton Col, AB, 52; Yale Univ, MA, 54, PhD, 56. *Teaching:* From instr to asst prof, Princeton Univ, 56-60; from asst prof to assoc prof, Univ Calif, Berkeley, 60-63; assoc prof to prof, Ind Univ, Bloomington, 63-69; prof, Dartmouth Col, 69- *Res:* Nineteenth & twentieth century art, both architecture & painting. *Collection:* Prints & graphic arts from 18th century to present. *Publ:* Auth, Philip Johnson, Braziller, 62; auth, Twentieth Century Architecture: The Middle Years, Praeger, 66; auth, Matisse, Abrams, 73. *Mailing Add:* Art Dept Dartmouth Col Hanover NH 03755

JACQUARD (JERALD WAYNE JACKARD)
SCULPTOR, EDUCATOR
b Lansing, Mich, Feb 1, 37. *Study:* Mich State Univ, BA & MA. *Work:* Mus Am Art, Andover, Mass; Detroit Inst Arts, Mich; Kresge Mus, Mich State Univ, East Lansing; Kalamazoo Inst Art, Mich. *Comn:* Sculpture, Chicago Transit Authority, 74. *Exhib:* One-man shows, Detroit Inst Art, 65, Ill Inst Technol, 69, Univ Chicago, 70 & Indianapolis Mus, 75; Bicentennial Sculpture for a New Era, Chicago, 75. *Teaching:* Assoc prof sculpture, Univ Ill, Chicago Circle Campus, 66-75; prof sculpture, Ind Univ, Bloomington, 75- *Awards:* Fulbright Scholar, 63; Guggenheim Fel, 73; Nat Endowment Arts, 80; and others. *Media:* Steel. *Mailing Add:* Dept Art Ind Univ Bloomington IN 47405

JACQUEMON, PIERRE
PAINTER
b Lyon, France, Aug 6, 35; US citizen. *Study:* Self-taught. *Work:* Gotesborg Mus, Sweden; Magdalene Col, Cambridge, Eng; Mus d'Art Mod, Paris, France; St Paul Sch, NH; Ika-Shika Nat Univ, Tokyo, Japan. *Exhib:* one-man shows, Temple Gallery, London, 62, Bianchini Gallery, New York, 63, Weeden Gallery, Boston, 68, Berkshire Mus, Mass, 69 & Atrium Gallery, Geneva, Switz, 74; Inst Contemp Art, Boston, 70. *Media:* Oil. *Dealer:* Phoenix Gallery 30 W 57th St New York NY 10019. *Mailing Add:* 62 E Seventh St New York NY 10003

JACQUES, MICHAEL LOUIS
PRINTMAKER, EDUCATOR
b Barre, Vt, Apr 12, 45. *Study:* Boston Univ, BFA, 67; Univ Hartford Art Sch, MFA, 71; and with David Aronson, Walter Murch & Paul Zimmerman. *Work:* Nat Collection Fine Arts, Smithsonian Mus, Washington, DC; Mus Am Art, Washington, DC; Philadelphia Mus Art; Chrysler Mus, Va; Mus Fine Arts, Boston. *Exhib:* Silvermine Nat, 80; All on Paper, 80; Acad Artists Asn Exhib, 80 & 81; Audubon Artists Exhib, 80 & 82; Boston Printmakers Exhib, 80-82; Am Artists Prof League Exhib, 82; and many others. *Pos:* Artist in residence, ABT Assoc, Cambridge, Mass, 80-81 & Va Mus, 81-82. *Teaching:* Instr art, Emmanuel Col, Boston, 71-73, assoc prof art, 73-, chmn dept, 75-77. *Awards:* First Prize, Cooperstown Art Asn, 77; Charlotte Printmakers Purchase Award, 79; Am Artist Prof League Prize, 82. *Mem:* Audubon Artists Asn; Boston Visual Artists Union; Conn Acad Fine Arts; Boston Printmakers; Copley Soc. *Publ:* Auth & illus, Images of Age, ABT Books, 81. *Dealer:* Pucker Safrai Gallery 171 Newbury St Boston MA 02116. *Mailing Add:* 10 Wyman Ct Winchester MA 01890

JACQUES, RUSSELL KENNETH
SCULPTOR
b Springfield, Mass, Feb 19, 43. *Study:* Boston Univ, BFA, 66. *Work:* DeCordova Mus, Lincoln, Mass; Abilene Fine Arts Mus, Tex; Mead Mus, Amherst, Mass. *Comn:* Kinetic wood sculpture, Nat Ballet Can, Toronto, 81; stainless steel sculpture, Boston Univ, 82; bronze & stainless steel sculpture, Tex Commerce Bank, Dallas, 82; bronze & stainless steel floor sculpture, First Bank Boston, 83; stainless steel sculpture, Hammerson Can Inc, Toronto, 83. *Exhib:* Counterpoint at the Quadrangle, Springfield Fine Arts, Mass, 82; Boston Mus Fine Arts, 83; Interim I, Chesterwood Outdoor Invitational, Stockbridge, Mass, 83; Abilene Christian Univ, Tex, 83; Stewart Gallery, Dallas, 83; ISOA Gallery, Greenwich, Conn, 83; and others. *Teaching:* Instr basic drawing, Holyoke Community Col, 75, instr advan design & compos, 76. *Awards:* Second Place, Best in Show, 71 & Award of Excellence, 78, Springfield Art League, George Walter Vincent Smith Mus. *Bibliog:* Nancy Norcross (dir), The Emerging Artist (film), Mass Arts & Humanities Coun, 80; Nancy Goebel (auth), article, Art Voices, 8/81; Claudia Elferdink (dir), Art in Common: Russell Jacques--Sculptor (film), Continental Cablevision Channel 57, Springfield, 83. *Media:* All. *Mailing Add:* c/o Stewart Gallery 12610 Coit Rd Dallas TX 75251

JACQUETTE, YVONNE H (YVONNE HELEN BURCKHARDT)
PAINTER, PRINTMAKER
b Pittsburgh, Pa, Dec 15, 34. *Study:* RI Sch Design, 52-56, with John Frazier & Robert Hamilton; also with Herman Cherry & Robert Roche. *Work:* Weatherspoon Gallery, NC; Metrop Mus Art, Mus Mod Art, Whitney Mus Am Art, New York; Colby Col Mus. *Comn:* Five panel painting in oil, NCent

Bronx Hosp, NY, 73; five color lithograph, Horace Mann Sch, Riverdale, NY, 74; mural installation for Fed Bldg & Post Off, Gen Serv Admin, Bangor, Maine, 79-82. *Exhib:* Skying, Rutgers Univ Art Gallery, 72; Whitney Painting Ann, Whitney Mus Am Art, 72; Women Choose Women, New York Cult Ctr & US Traveling Show, 72-73; New Image in Painting, Int Biennial, Tokyo, Japan, 74; Small Scale in Contemporary Art, Art Inst Chicago, 75; Recent Acquisitions, Drawings, Mus Mod Art, New York, 81; New Work on Paper, Mus Mod Art, New York, 81-82; Brook Alexander Inc, New York, 82. *Teaching:* Instr, Moore Col Art, Philadelphia, 72; Vis artist & instr painting, Univ Pa, 72-76 & 79-82; vis artist, Nova Scotia Col Art, 74; instr, Parsons Sch of Design, 75-78. *Bibliog:* Susan Fillin (auth), article, Arts Mag, 79; Carter Ratcliff (auth), Yvonne Jacquette, American visionary, The Print Collectors Newsletter, 7-8/81; John Ashberg (auth), The pleasures of paperwork, Newsweek, 3/16/81; plus others. *Mem:* Artists Equity Asn. *Media:* Oil, Pastel; Miscellaneous. *Publ:* Illusr, Country Rush, Adventures in Poetry, 72; illusr, Aerial, Eyelight Press, 81. *Dealer:* Brooke Alexander Gallery 20 W 57th St New York NY 10019. *Mailing Add:* 50 W 29th St New York NY 10001

JAE
SCULPTOR
b Brooklyn, NY, Jan 9, 47. *Study:* Pace Univ, BA; also with Bruno Lucchesi, Jacques Lipchitz, Evangelous Moustakis & Manola. *Comn:* Garden sculpture, comn by Charles Nissen, London. *Exhib:* Am Hellenic Soc, Athens, Greece, 73; Brooklyn Visits the Met, Metrop Mus Art, New York, 76; Nat Arts Club, New York, 76; Black History Month, US Naval Acad, Annapolis, Md, 77; Brooklyn Mus Art, 77; Salmagundi Club, New York, 77; Int Art Show, Pietiasanta, Itlay, 80; and others. *Teaching:* Instr sculpture, privately, 74-75. *Bibliog:* Guerneri (dir), The World of Jae (film), 83. *Mem:* Artists Equity; Salmagundi Club; Int Asn Art. *Media:* Bronze, Gold. *Mailing Add:* 48 W 73rd St New York NY 10023

JAEGER, BRENDA KAY
PAINTER, CRAFTSMAN
b Fairbanks, Alaska, July 20, 50. *Study:* Eastern Wash Univ, Spokane, BA, 72; Whitworth Col, Spokane, MAT, 75. *Work:* Alaskan State Coun Contemp Art Bank, Alyeska Pipeline Serv Co & Anchorage Hist & Fine Arts Mus, Anchorage; Gonzaga Univ Contemp Art Collection, Spokane; Ketchikan Pioneer Home, Alaska. *Exhib:* Alaskan Representational Art Exhib, Anchorage Hist & Fine Arts Mus, 78; Handmade Paperworks, Anchorage Hist & Fine Arts Mus, 79; Int Hand Papermakers Conf, Boston Sch Artisanry, Mass, 80; Works of Paper, Nev Mus Art, Reno, 81; Mixed Media Paintings & Handmade Paperworks, The Gallery, Anchorage, 81; and others. *Pos:* Artist with studio, Brenda Jaeger Studio, formerly, Cold Mountain Visual Arts, Anchorage, 78 & Wash, 79- *Teaching:* Instr art, Whitworth Col, 74-75, Spokane Art Sch, 74-75, Columbia Basin Col, 76-77 & Walla Walla Community Col, 76-77; vis artist, Wash State Cult Enrichment Prog, 76-78; instr art, Univ Alaska, Anchorage, 78- *Awards:* First Award, Arts Expose Asn, 79; First Award, All Alaska Watercolor Show, The Gallery, 79 & 81; Second Award, 8th Nev Ann: Contemp Works of Paper, Sierra Nev Mus, 81. *Bibliog:* Schiller (auth), The revolution in paper, Am Artist, 77; Beverly Plummer (auth), How does your garden grow, Fiberarts, 78. *Mem:* Artists Equity Asn; Visual Artists & Galleries Asn; Nat Watercolor Soc; World Print Coun; Provincetown Art Asn & Mus. *Media:* Watercolor, Oil; Oriental & Western Paper. *Publ:* Book covers & logo, Intertext, Anchorage, 81. *Dealer:* Artique Ltd Anchorage AK; Gallery West Portland OR. *Mailing Add:* Box 2152 Longview WA 98632

JAFFE, IRMA B
HISTORIAN, EDUCATOR
b New Orleans, La. *Study:* Columbia Univ, BS, MA, PhD. *Pos:* Res cur, Whitney Mus Am Art, New York, 64-65; ed bd, Am Art Jour, currently. *Teaching:* Prof art hist & chmn dept, Fordham Univ, 66-77. *Awards:* Nat Endowment Humanities Fel, 73-74; Am Coun Learned Soc, 73 & 82. *Mem:* Col Art Asn Am; Am Studies Asn; Am Soc Eighteenth Century Studies. *Res:* American art. *Publ:* Auth, Joseph Stella, Harvard Univ Press, 70; auth, John Trumbull: Patriot-Artist of the American Revolution, NY Graphic Soc, 75; auth, Trumbull: The Declaration of Independence, Viking-Penguin, 76; auth, Copley's Watson and the Shark, Am Art J, spring 77; auth, The Sculpture of Leonard Baskin, Viking-Penguin, 80; contribr, Am Art J, Art Bulletin, Burlington & Gazette Beaux-Arts. *Mailing Add:* Dept of Fine Arts Fordham Univ Bronx NY 10458

JAFFE, NORA
PAINTER, SCULPTOR
b Urbana, Ohio, Feb 25, 28. *Study:* Dayton Art Inst, Ohio; also with Samuel Adler & David Hare, New York. *Work:* Brooklyn Mus, NY; Pa Acad Fine Arts, Philadelphia; Univ Art Mus, Berkeley, Calif; MacDowell Colony, Peterborough, NH. *Exhib:* Mus Mod Art, New York, 61; Baltimore Mus Art, Md, 63 & 68; Pa Acad Fine Arts, 63-67; Finch Col Mus, New York, 67-71; New Sch Art Ctr, New York, 69-73; Va Mus Fine Arts, Richmond, 70; Gallery Lasson, London, Eng, 70; ArnolFini Art Ctr, Rhinebeck, NY, 78; Vassar Col, Poughkeepsie, NY, 79; Pastoral Gallery, East Hampton, NY, 83; and others. *Awards:* Second Prize, Gymnasium Show I, New York, 64; MacDowell Colony Residency, 69-70. *Media:* Oil; Plaster, Wood. *Publ:* Illusr, Caterpillar 13, Caterpillar, 70; illusr, Realignment, 74 & The Name Encanyoned River, 78, Treacle Press; illusr, Sulfur 4, 82 & Sulfur 5, 83, Calif Inst Technol Press. *Mailing Add:* 285 Central Park W New York NY 10024

JAGGER, GILLIAN
PAINTER, SCULPTOR

b London, Eng, Oct 27, 30. *Study:* Carnegie Inst Technol, BFA; Colorado Springs Fine Arts Ctr, with Vytlacil, scholar, 52; Univ Buffalo; Columbia Univ; NY Univ, MA. *Work:* Finch Col Mus, New York; Brompton's, Montreal, Que; Carnegie Inst, Pittsburgh. *Comn:* Portrait comns, 47-51. *Exhib:* Two-man & group shows, Loft Gallery, 55-57; one-man shows, Ruth White Gallery, New York, 61, 63 & 64; Finch Col Mus, 64; Lerner-Heller Gallery, 71, 73, 75 & 77; The Horse: Light & Motion, Lerner-Heller Gallery, New York, 75. *Pos:* Textile designer, Wamsutta Mills, Fruit of the Loom, 55-57. *Teaching:* Lectr art, Radio Free Europe, cols & prof art schs; instr painting, NY Univ, Post Col & New Rochelle Acad, formerly. *Awards:* Guggenheim Fel, 83. *Mailing Add:* 418 Central Park W New York NY 10025

JAGMAN, ED
PAINTER

b Chicago, Ill, Nov 29, 36. *Study:* Am Acad Art, Chicago; Community Col, Denver, Colo; Rocky Mountain Sch Art, Denver, Colo. *Work:* Johns-Manville Corp, Colo; United Bank Denver; Nat City Bank Denver; Pub Serv & Mt Bell of Colo; Energy Ctr, Denver, Colo, 81; and others. *Exhib:* One-man show, Chicago Pub Libr, 66; Painters & Sculptors NJ 28th Ann, 69; Am Watercolor Soc 102nd Ann, 69; Mainstreams 74, 75 & 76, Marietta, Ohio; Baker Gallery, Lubbock, Tex, 81; and others. *Awards:* Spec Purchase Award, Colo Coun Arts & Humanities, 73; Purchase Award, Pratt Col, Kans, 80; and others. *Media:* Watercolor. *Publ:* Illusr, Compact Mag, 4/69; auth & illusr, Up Date Mag, 10/71; auth, Watercolor page, Am Artist Mag, 12/75. *Dealer:* Arnould Gallery Marblehead MA 01945; Colorado Artists Register PO Drawer H Boulder CO 80306. *Mailing Add:* 1300 Fairfax Denver CO 80220

JAIDINGER, JUDITH C (JUDITH CLARANN SZESKO)
PRINTMAKER, PAINTER

b Chicago, Ill, Apr 10, 41. *Study:* Art Inst Chicago, BFA. *Work:* Minot State Col, NDak; Washington & Jefferson Col, Washington, Pa; Ill State Mus, Springfield; Brand Libr, Glendale, Calif; Kemper Group, Long Grove, Ill. *Exhib:* Nat Acad Design Ann, New York, 67, 68, 70, 73-75 & 77; 8 State Ann, J B Speed Art Mus, Louisville, Ky, 81; 57th Ann Int Competition, The Print Club, Philadelphia, 81; 33rd Nat Exhib, Boston Printmakers, Mass, 82; Rockford Int, Rockford Col, Ill, 83. *Teaching:* Instr wood engraving, Office Field & Continuing Educ, Northeastern Ill Univ, 80- *Awards:* Graphics Award, Mercyhurst Col, Erie, Pa, 70; Smithsonian Traveling Exhib, Contemp Am Drawings V, Norfolk Mus Arts & Sci, 71-74; Graphics Award, Okla Mus Art, 75. *Mem:* Print Club, Philadelphia. *Media:* Wood Engraving; Opaque Watercolor, Mixed Media. *Mailing Add:* 6110 N Newburg Ave Chicago IL 60631

JAKSTAS, ALFRED JOHN
MUSEUM CONSERVATOR

b Boston, Mass, Oct 30, 16. *Study:* Harvard Col, AB, 38; Fogg Mus Dept Conservation, with George Stout, Murray Pease & Richard Buck. *Pos:* Conservator, Isabella Stewart Gardner Mus, Boston, Mass, 41-61; conservator, Art Inst Chicago, 61-81; consult in conservation, 82- *Mem:* Int & Am Insts Conserv Artistic Objects. *Res:* Study of materials and techniques of painting of various periods. *Publ:* Auth, Problems of Museum Conservation, 63. *Mailing Add:* 10737 Welk Dr Sun City AZ 85373

JAMEIKIS, BRONE ALEKSANDRA
STAINED GLASS ARTIST, DESIGNER

b Vilnius, Lithuania; US citizen. *Study:* Univ Vilnius, dipl; Ecole Arts et Metiers, Freiburg, Ger, dipl; Art Inst Chicago, BFA & MFA; Univ Hawaii, MA. *Comn:* Leaded stained glass, St Philomena Church, Chicago, 60; mosaic & faceted slab glass, Holy Cross Church, Dayton, Ohio, 64; faceted slab glass windows, Springdale Mausoleum, Peoria, Ill, 66; leaded & faceted slab glass, O'Hare Int Airport, Chicago, 68; faceted slab glass, St Peter's Episcopal Church, Honolulu, 79-81. *Exhib:* Artists of Lithuania, Windsor Mus, Can, 57; Artists of United States, Denver Mus Art, 57; Nat Biennial Relig Art Exhib, Cranbrook Acad, Detroit, Mich, 60-69; Artists of Hawaii, Honolulu Acad Arts, 61 & 72; Ecumenical Art Show, St Benet Gallery, Chicago, 65; Univ Hawaii, 77; Ciurlionis Gallery, Chicago, 80; stained glass exhib, Honolulu, 80-81. *Pos:* Art dir, Valeska Art Studios, Chicago, 51-58 & 62-71; keeper, AV educ, Honolulu Acad Arts, 71- *Teaching:* Instr art, Univ Hawaii, 58-61. *Awards:* Award for Leaded Stained Glass, Relig Art Exhib, Chicago, 56; Award for Stained & Slab Glass, Am Inst Designers, 60; Award for Faceted Slab Glass, Madonna Theme in Art Exhib, Honolulu, 61. *Bibliog:* David Asherman (auth), Rare gift from Europe to Hawaiian art, Honolulu Advertiser, 60; J Dainauskas (auth), Brone Jameikis-stained glass artist, Aidai-Echoes, Brooklyn, NY, 69; D J Anderson (auth), An artist brings light to dark corners, Vol 9, No 4, Chicago. *Mem:* Inst Lithuanian Artists; Hawaiian Artists League; Stained Glass Asn of Hawaii. *Mailing Add:* PO Box 4212 Honolulu HI 96813

JAMES, A EVERETTE, JR
COLLECTOR, LECTURER

b Oxford NC, Aug 22, 38. *Study:* Univ NC, AB, 59; Duke Univ Sch Medicine, MD, 63; Harvard Medical Sch; 66-69; Johns Hopkins Sch Hygiene, 69-71; Harvard Business Sch, 79. *Collections Arranged:* The Ahls: An American Art Family (auth, catalog), 81; Collector's Exhib, Angus Whyte Gallery, Washington, DC, 81; Spectrum of Portraiture, Centennial Club, Nashville, Tenn, 82; James Collection, 83; Jeannett Cross Collection, 83 & The American Scene, 83, University Club, Nashville. *Teaching:* Lectr Am impressionism, Womans Club, Centennial Club & Dixon Gallery, Memphis,

Tenn, 81. *Bibliog:* Minton & James (auth), Cowan collection, Antiques, 9/80; James (auth), Uncovering Works of Art, Diagnostic Imaging, 81. *Mem:* Nat Trust Historic Preserv; Soc Preservation Tenn Antiquities; Explorer's Club; Cosmos Club. *Res:* Use of imaging techniques to evaluate paintings; visual physiology and art. *Collection:* American impressionism; American landscape. *Publ:* Coauth, Digital Radiography; A Focus on Clinical Unity, 82; coauth, Certain radiographic techniques to evaluate paintings, Am J Roentgenology, 83; coauth, Digital radiography in the analysis of paintings, a new and promising technique, J Am Inst Consev, 83; auth, An introduction to Eugene Healan Thomason: The 'Ashcan Artist' who cames to the mountains, Appalachian J, 83; auth, Investing in American Impressionism, MD Mag, 83; and others. *Dealer:* Vose Gallery Newbury St Boston MA. *Mailing Add:* 519 Belle Meade Blvd Nashville TN 37205

JAMES, CATTI
SCULPTOR, CONSULTANT

b Mount Vernon, NY, Oct 8, 40. *Study:* Boston Univ, BFA; Columbia Univ, MA. *Work:* Harlem Art Collection; Indianapolis Mus Art; NY State Art Collection; Govt Ctr, Plattsburgh, NY; Primary Indust, New York. *Comn:* Mural, Sepia Enterprises, Toledo, 72; costume design, Harry Belafonte Tour, 74 & Walter Nicks Dance Theater & Repertory Co, 74; cover design & book layout, Nat Bd, YWCA, 77; cover design, Girls Clubs Am, 78; cover design & book layout, Nat Bd, YWCA, 79. *Exhib:* Contemporary Black Artists in America, 71 & Whitney Ann, Whitney Mus Am Art, 72; Wild Art Show, PS1, New York, 82; Ritual & Rhythm, Kenkeleba House Gallery, New York, 82; Collage & Assemblage, Gallery Hastings, Hastings-on-Hudson, 83; Exchange of Sources: Expanding Powers, Calif State Stanisleus, Turlock, 83; Artists of the 80s, Los Angeles Co Fair, Pomona, 83. *Teaching:* Art consult, Wiltwyck Sch Boys, 68-70 & Graham Sch, currently; instr anat, Col New Rochelle, 72; lectr African art & workshops on African design. *Awards:* Creative Artists Coun Grant in Painting, NY State Coun Arts, 71. *Bibliog:* Black artists in America (slides), Univ SAla & H Kress Found; Robert Doty (auth), Contemporary Black Artists in America. *Mem:* Am Crafts Coun. *Media:* Wood, Plexiglas. *Publ:* Auth, three articles in Arts & Activities Mag, 67-70; auth, A Black perspective on art, Black Enterprise Mag, 75. *Dealer:* Allan Stone Gallery 48 E 86th St New York NY 10028; Merton D Simpson Gallery 1063 Madison Ave New York NY 10028. *Mailing Add:* 6 Fulton St Hastings-on-Hudson NY 10706

JAMES, CHRISTOPHER P
PHOTOGRAPHER

b Boston, Mass, May 8, 47. *Study:* Cummington Community Arts, 68; Mass Col Art, BFA, 69; RI Sch of Design, MAT, 71. *Work:* Mus Mod Art, New York; Int Mus Photog, George Eastman House, Rochester, NY; Metrop Mus Art, New York; Boston Mus Fine Arts, Mass; Minneapolis Inst Arts Mus; and others. *Comn:* Subway steel enamel panels, Cambridge Arts Coun, 80. *Exhib:* One-man shows, Minneapolis Inst Arts, 77, Int Mus Photog, George Eastman House, 77, Centre d'Art Contemporain, Geneva, 79 & Univ Ore Mus Art, 80; Mirrors and Windows, Mus Mod Art, New York, 78; Metrop Mus Art, New York, 82; Worcester Art Mus, Mass, 80; and other one-man shows. *Teaching:* Asst prof photog & design, Greenfield Community Col, 71-78; artist in residence, Keene State Col, 77-78; lectr, Mass Inst Technol, Philadelphia Col Art, Univ Ore, Parsons Sch Design & RI Sch Design; prof, Harvard Univ, 78- *Awards:* Daguerre, Niepce Medal, Phot-Univers USA/USSR, Minister of Foreign Affairs, Paris, 76; Mass Arts Found Fel, 78. *Bibliog:* Hilton Kramer (auth), New York Review, Esman, New York Times, 9/23/77; David Bourdon (auth), New York Review, Esman, Village Voice, 10/10/77; John Russell (auth), New York Review, Witkin, New York Times, 10/21/83. *Mem:* Soc Photog Educ. *Media:* Photography. *Publ:* Contribr, Alternative Photographic Process, Morgan & Morgan, 78; contribr, portfolio, Popular Photography, NY, 79; contribr, portfolio, American Photographer, NY, 79; contribr, cover & portfolio, Camera, Suisse, 4/79. *Mailing Add:* Box 399 Dublin NH 03444

JAMES, FREDERIC
PAINTER

b Kansas City, Mo, Sept 28, 15. *Study:* Col Archit, Univ Mich, BDes; Cranbrook Acad Art. *Work:* Nelson-Atkins Gallery Art, Kansas City, Mo; Denver Art Mus; Univ Mo, Columbia; Cranbrook Acad Art, Bloomfield Hills, Mich. *Comn:* Murals, Trinity Lutheran Church, Missiion, Kans & Overland Park State BAnk, Kans; Wildflowers in America, New York Botanical Garden; Kans City Life Insurance Co Collection; Business Men's Assurance Co; Sante Fe Trail Collection, Kansas City, Mo; and others. *Exhib:* Milch Gallery, New York; Nelson Gallery Art; Mid-Am Ann; Maynard Walker Gallery, New York; plus others. *Teaching:* Instr, Kansas City Art Inst, 46-50. *Awards:* Prizes, Denver Art Mus & Nelson Gallery Art. *Mem:* Am Watercolor Soc; Kans City Municipal Art Comn. *Media:* Watercolor, Oil. *Dealer:* Graham Gallery 1014 Madison Ave New York NY 10021; Wichita Gallery Fine Art Fourth Financial Ctr Wichita KS 67202. *Mailing Add:* 850 W 52nd St Kansas City MO 64112

JAMESON, DEMETRIOS GEORGE
PAINTER, PRINTMAKER

b St Louis, Mo, Nov 22, 19. *Study:* Corcoran Sch Art, Washington, DC, 46; Washington Univ Sch Fine Arts, BFA, 49; Univ Ill Sch Fine & Appl Arts, Urbana, MFA, 50. *Work:* Portland Art Mus, Ore; Seattle Art Mus, Wash; Denver Art Mus, Colo; Victoria & Albert Mus, London, Eng; Am Embassy, Athens, Greece; and others in pub & pvt collections. *Exhib:* Younger Am Painters, Guggenheim Mus, New York, 54; Northwestern Art Today, Seattle World's Fair, Wash, 62; Corcoran Mus, Washington, DC; San Francisco Mus; Oakland Art Mus, Calif; Tacoma Art Mus, Wash; Butler Inst Am Art,

Youngstown, Ohio; Seattle Art Mus; Portland Art Denver Art Mus; New Forms Gallery, Athens, Greece; and many others. *Teaching:* Prof art, Ore State Univ, 50-82, prof emer, 82- *Awards:* J T Millican foreign Travel Award, Washington Univ, 50; Awards, Coos Art Mus, Ore & City Art Mus, St Louis, Mo; and many others. *Mem:* Portland Art Asn (pres, 57-58); Artists Equity Asn; Salem Art Asn; Portland Ctr Visual Arts; Corvallis Art Ctr. *Media:* Oil, Watercolor; Lithography. *Mailing Add:* 725 NW 28th St Corvallis OR 97330

JAMESON, PHILIP ALEXANDER
CERAMIST, PAINTER

b Corvallis, Ore, Feb 24, 52. *Study:* Ore State Univ, BFA, 77; Syracuse Univ, MFA, 81. *Comn:* Interior reliefs, State Wash, Battleground, 83 & Cronin & Caplan Realtors, Portland, Ore, 83. *Exhib:* Residency Exhib, Contemp Crafts Gallery, Portland, Ore, 82; 34th Spokane Ann, Cheney Cowles Mus, Wash, 82; Architectural Ceramics, A Documentation, Interart Ctr, New York, 82; Am Nat Ceramics Exhib, Downey Mus Art, Calif, 83; Portland Ctr Visual Arts, 83; Clay for Walls, Renwick Gallery, 83-84. *Teaching:* Instr, Mt Hood Community Col, 83- *Awards:* Purchase Award, Ore State Univ, 77; Ford Found Grants, 79 & 80; Residency Award, Contemp Crafts Asn, 81. *Bibliog:* Cheryl McLean (auth), Installations by Philip Jameson, Ceramics Mo, 83; Raylene Decatur (auth), Clay on the wall, Nat Coun Educ Ceramic Art J, 83. *Mem:* Col Art Asn; Nat Coun Educ Ceramic Art; Contemp Crafts Asn; Northwest Artist Workshop. *Media:* Ceramics. *Mailing Add:* 1301 NW Glisan St Portland OR 97209

JAMISON, PHILIP
PAINTER

b Philadelphia, Pa, July 3, 25. *Study:* Philadelphia Mus Sch Art, grad. *Work:* Pa Acad Fine Arts, Philadelphia; Wilmington Soc Fine Arts, Del; Nat Acad Design, New York; Flint Inst Art, Mich; Frye Art Mus, Seattle, Wash. *Exhib:* 200 Yrs of Watercolor Painting in Am, Metrop Mus Art, New York, 67; one-man shows, Hirschl & Adler Galleries, New York, 59-80,, Janet Fleisher Gallery, Philadelphia, 77, Grand Gallery, Wilmington, 77 & Whistler's Daughter Art Gallery, Basking Ridge, NJ, 81; and others. *Work:* Artist, Apollo Soyuz Space Launch, Kennedy Space Ctr, Fla, Nat Aeronautics & Space Admin, 75. *Teaching:* Instr watercolor, Philadelphia Col Art, 61-63. *Awards:* Dana Medal, Pa Acad Fine Arts, 61; Gold Medal of Honor, Allied Artists Am, 64; Nat Acad Design Prize, 67. *Mem:* Nat Acad Design; Am Watercolor Soc; Philadelphia Watercolor Club; Wilmington Soc Fine Arts. *Media:* Watercolor. *Publ:* Contribr, Am Artist Mag, 62; auth, Capturing Nature in Watercolor, 80. *Dealer:* Whistler's Daughter Art Gallery Basking Ridge NJ 07920; Newman Galleries 1625 Walnut St Philadelphia, PA 19103. *Mailing Add:* 104 Price St West Chester PA 19380

JAMPOL, GLENN D
PAINTER

b Los Angeles, Calif, July 3, 50. *Study:* Univ Calif, Berkeley, BA, 72, MA, 74, MFA, 75. *Work:* Oakland Mus; San Francisco Mus Mod Art; Mobil Oil Corp, New York. *Exhib:* San Francisco Art Inst Ann, 78; solo exhib, San Francisco Art Inst, 79, 80 Langton St, San Francisco, 80 & Baruch Col, City Univ New York, 83; Fresh Paint, San Francisco Mus Mod Art, 82; Klein Gallery, Chicago, 83. *Awards:* Soc Encouragement Contemp Art Award, San Francisco Mus Mod Art, 77; Nat Endowment Arts Grant, 82. *Bibliog:* J Perrone (auth), MFA candidates--Berkeley, 75 & J Dickson (auth), Glenn Jampol, 80, Art Forum; A Artner (auth), Glenn Jampol, Chicago Tribune, 83. *Dealer:* Klein Gallery 356 W Huron Chicago IL 60610; Modernism Gallery 276 Eighth St San Francisco CA 94103. *Mailing Add:* 178 Franklin New York NY 10013

JANDENI (JEAN-DENIS CRUCHET)
SCULPTOR, PAINTER

b Lausanne, Switz, Feb 26, 39. *Study:* Sch Fine Arts, Geneva, Switz, 57-60; Scuola Di Brera (Studio Marino Marini), 60-61. *Work:* Mus Fine Arts, Lausanne, Switz; Smith Col Mus Art, Northampton, Mass; Hopkins Ctr, Dartmouth Col, Hanover, NH; Mus del Ayuntamiento, Barcelona, Spain; Currier Gallery Art, Manchester, NH. *Comn:* Walnut bas-relief, Unitarian Church, Concord, NH, 77; stained glass windows, Denges Church, Switz, 73; bronze high relief, Duindam, Lausanne, 74. *Exhib:* Int Sculpture, Centro Int, Seravezza, Italy, 75; Latin-Am Artists, Mus de la Emporda, Figueras, Spain, 76; one-man show, Marion Koogler McNay, San Antonio, Tex, 78; Biennial, Mus Fine Arts, Santa Fe, 78; Sculptors on Sculpture, Philbrook Art Ctr, Tulsa, Okla, 78; plus others. *Bibliog:* Leonard Brooks (auth), Painting & Understanding Abstract Art, Van Nostrand Reinhold, NY, 64; M S Lehner, Cruchet, Wetter Zurich, 73. *Media:* Miscellaneous. *Dealer:* Shidony Gallery Tesuque NM 87574; Sally Knudson 2626 Westheimer Rd #201 Houston TX 77098. *Mailing Add:* RFD 2 Box 273 Concord NH 03301

JANELSINS, VERONICA
ILLUSTRATOR, PAINTER

b Riga, Latvia, May 20, 10; US citizen. *Study:* State Acad Fine Arts, Riga, grad, 40. *Work:* State Hist Mus Riga; State Art Mus Riga; Baumgarten-Schuler Collection, Stuttgart, WGer; Vitols Collection, Venezuela, Caracas. *Exhib:* Latvian State Art Mus, 40; Expos des Artistes en Exile, Paris, 49; Madonna Festival, Los Angeles, Calif, 55; Los Angeles Co Mus, 56; one-man show, Stockholm, 70; plus many others. *Awards:* Madonna Festival Awards, 53 & 55. *Media:* Oil. *Publ:* Many book covers and illus for Gramatu Draugs, Brooklyn. *Mailing Add:* 1298 Monument St Pacific Palisades CA 90272

JANIS, CONRAD
DEALER, COLLECTOR

b New York, NY, Feb 11, 28. *Collections Arranged:* Participated in arranging all exhibitions at Sidney Janis Gallery from New Realism, 62 through Sharp Focus Realism, 72; and others. *Pos:* Co-dir, Sidney Janis Gallery. *Specialty:* All historic movements in 20th century art to the present. *Collection:* Contemporary American art. *Mailing Add:* Sidney Janis Gallery 110 W 57th St New York NY 10019

JANIS, SIDNEY
DEALER, WRITER

b Buffalo, NY, July 8, 1896. *Collections Arranged:* Les Fauves, 50; Dada, 52; Futurism, 54; Analytical Cubism, 56; New Realists (Pop Art), 62; Sharp Focus Realism, 72; and many one-man shows, including Henri Rousseau, Delaunay, Leger, Kandinsky, Mondrian, deKooning, Pollock, Rothko, Kline & many others. *Pos:* Owner, Sidney Janis Gallery. *Teaching:* Lectr, Am Folk Art Mus, 79, Nassau Co Mus, 80 & Guggenheim Mus, 81. *Bibliog:* Interview, Dick Cavett Show, 81. *Mem:* Art Dealers Asn Am (bd dir, 69-71). *Specialty:* Presentation of work by four generations in 20th century art from cubism, surrealism, abstract expressionism, pop art, minimal painting and more recently photography. *Collection:* Sidney and Harriet Janis Collection of 20th century art given to Museum of Modern Art, New York, 67. *Publ:* Auth, School of Paris comes to US, Decision, 11-12/41; auth, They Taught Themselves, XXth Century American Primitive Painting, Dial Press, 42; auth, Abstract & Surrealist Art in America, Reynal Hitchcock, 44; co-auth, Picasso: the War Years 1939-46, Doubleday, 46; auth, Aims of the Janis Gallery, Arts Mag, 4/71; plus others, 40-75. *Mailing Add:* 110 W 57th St New York NY 10019

JANNEY, CHRISTOPHER DRAPER
ENVIRONMENTAL ARTIST, SOUND ARTIST

b Washington, DC, Mar 14, 50. *Study:* Princeton Univ, with Michael Graves & James Seawright, BA(archit, visual arts), 73; Mass Inst Techol, with O Piene, MS(environ art), 78. *Comn:* Soundstair on Tour, Three Rivers Art Festival, Pittsburgh, Pa, 79; Soundstair Bonds, Bonds Int, New York, 80; Reach!, Sonic Sports, Fourth Spiel und Klangstrasse Essen, Ger, 82; Heartbeats, 18th St Dance Found, New York, 82. *Exhib:* Soundstair, Boston Mus Fine Arts, 79, Walker Art Ctr, 80, Nat Gallery Art, 80, Corcoran Gallery Art, 80, Second Int Electronic Music Conf, Brussels, Belg, 81 & Santa Barbara Mus Art, Calif, 82; Sonic Pass, Miss Mus Art, Jackson, 81; Wall-to-Wall John Cage, Symphony Space, New York, 82; Inside Rhythms, Inst Contemp Art, Boston, 83. *Pos:* Res fel, Ctr Advan Visual Studies, Mass Inst Technol, 78- *Awards:* City Edges Prog Grant, Nat Endowment Arts, 73; Buhl Found Grant, Three Rivers Festival, 79; 18th St Dance Found Grant for Inside Rhythms, WBZ-TV, 83. *Bibliog:* Ron Blau (auth), Christopher Janney (film), Sound Sculptor, WCVB-TV, Boston, 4/82. *Media:* Sound, Electronics. *Mailing Add:* 40 Massachusetts Ave Cambridge MA 02139

JANSCHKA, FRITZ
PAINTER, GRAPHIC ARTIST

b Vienna, Austria, Apr 21, 19. *Study:* Acad Fine Arts, Vienna, with A Paris Guetersloh. *Work:* Albertina, Vienna; Mus XXth Century, Vienna; Philadelphia Mus Art, Pa; Grafische Sammlung, Zurich, Switz. *Exhib:* Pa Acad Fine Arts, Philadelphia, 51-54; Print Club, Philadelphia, 56; Graphische Sammlungen, Zurich, 72; Fantastic Realists, Wiener Schule, Near East & Far East countries, 72-74; Die Wiener Schule des Phantastischen Realismus, Mus Am Ostwall, Dortmund, Ger, 79; XXth Century, Art Club Oesterreich Mus, Vienna, 81. *Teaching:* Artist in residence in graphics & painting, Bryn Mawr Col, Pa. *Bibliog:* J Norton-Smith (auth), A Tribute to James Joyce's Ulysses, Reading Univ, Eng, 73; Johan Muschik (auth), Janschka Monograph & Vienna school of fantastic realism, Jugend & Volk, Vienna/Munich, 74; Otto Breicha (auth), Der Art Club, Oesterreichs, J & V, Vienna, 81. *Media:* Oil, Watercolor. *Publ:* Auth, 26 etchings to James Joyce's Ulysses, Rizet, 72; contribr, After Surrealism, 72, auth, Ulysses Alphabet, 73 & contribr, After Clacicism, 73, Propylaen. *Mailing Add:* 1013 Wyndon Ave Bryn Mawr PA 19010

JANSEN, ANGELA BING
PRINTMAKER, PHOTOGRAPHER

b New York, NY, Aug 17, 29. *Study:* Brooklyn Col, BA; NY Univ, MA; Atelier 17, New York, with S W Hayter; Brooklyn Mus Art Sch. *Work:* Metrop Mus Art, Mus Mod Art, New York; Philadelphia Mus Art; Art Inst Chicago; Tate Gallery, London, Eng; Worcester Mus, Mass. *Exhib:* Brooklyn Mus Nat Print Exhib, 50, 70 & 76; Nat Exhib of Prints, Libr of Cong, Washington, DC, 69 & 71; Ljubljana Int Print Biennale, Yugoslavia, 71-77; Venice Biennale, Italy, 72; Biennale of Graphic Art, Vienna, 72 & 77; Lang of Print, Pratt Ctr, New York, 73; Individual Exhib, Gimpel & Weitzenhoffer, New York, 74; Five Printmakers, Martha Jackson Gallery, New York, 75. *Teaching:* New York high schs, 55- *Awards:* Assoc Am Artists Gallery Award, Int Miniature Print Exhib, 71; George Roth Prize, Philadelphia Print Club, 71 & 74; Grant for Printmaking, Nat Endowment Arts, 74-75. *Bibliog:* Article, The Print Collector's Newsletter, 7-8/73; Judith Goldman (auth), The language of print, Review #1, Art Forum, summer 79. *Media:* Etching. *Dealer:* Gimpel & Weitzenhoffer 1040 Madison Ave New York NY 10021. *Mailing Add:* 1646 First Ave New York NY 10028

JANSEN, CATHERINE SANDRA
PHOTOGRAPHER, EDUCATOR

b New York, NY, Dec 14, 45. *Study:* Cranbrook Acad of Art, Bloomfield Hills, Mich, BFA, 68; Acad di Belle Arti, cert, 69; Temple Univ, MFA, 73. *Work:* Philadelphia Mus of Art. *Exhib:* Unique Photographs: Multiple

Sculpture, Mus of Mod Art, New York, 73; Photo Transfer, Akron Art Inst, Ohio, 73; Three Centuries of American Art, Philadelphia Mus Art, Pa, 76; Soft Sculpture, Living Arts Ctr, Dayton, Ohio, 76; Am Family Portraits, Philadelphia Mus of Art, 76; Breath of Vision, Smithsonian Inst Traveling Exhib, 76-77; and others. *Teaching:* Instr photog, Bucks Co Community Col, Newtown, Pa, 73- *Publ:* Illusr, Frontiers in Photography, Time Life, 73; illusr, Photography, Upton & Upton, 76; illusr, Design Through Discovery, Holt Rinehart & Winston, 77; illusr, Photography Catalogue, Harper & Row, 77. *Mailing Add:* c/o Dept Art/Bucks Co Community Col Swamp Rd Newton PA 18940

JANSON, AGNES
PAINTER, GRAPHIC ARTIST
b London, England; US citizen. *Study:* Art Sch, Berlin, Ger; Art Students League, New York; Silvermine Graphic Workshop; Rudolf Baranik Workshop. *Work:* Houbigant Co, Ridgefield, Conn & New York; Canaan Col, NH; Greenburgh Libr, Westchester, NY; Ardsley Methodist Church, NY. *Exhib:* Solo shows, Mari Gallery, Mamaroneck, NY, 69 & 82 & Pindar Gallery, New York, 79, 81, 83 & 84; Hudson River Mus, Yonkers, NY, 73-76 & 79; Lever House, New York, 74; Silvermine Guild Artists, 75 & 78-81; Lehigh Univ, Bethlehem, Pa; and others. *Teaching:* Adult educ, Ardsley High Sch, 74-77; and pvt classes. *Bibliog:* Article, Arts Mag, 9/83. *Mem:* Silvermine Guild Artists; Hudson River Contemp Artists; New York Artists Equity. *Media:* Plywood; Acrylic, Oil. *Dealer:* Pindar Gallery 127 Greene St Soho NY 10012; Bell Gallery Stamford CT. *Mailing Add:* PO Box 312 69 Mustato Rd Katonah NY 10536

JANSON, ANTHONY FREDRICK
CURATOR, HISTORIAN
b St Louis, Mo, Mar 30, 43. *Study:* Columbia Univ, BA; Inst Fine Arts, NY Univ, MA; Fogg Mus, Harvard Univ, PhD. *Pos:* Sr cur, Indianapolis Mus Art, 78-83; cur paintings, Ringling Mus Art, Sarasota, 83- *Teaching:* Asst prof, State Univ NY, Buffalo, 73-75; asst prof, Col Charleston, SC, 75-78. *Res:* Dutch 17th century and American 19th century painting. *Publ:* Auth, Instructor's Manual to H W Janson's History of Art, Prentice-Hall, 78; auth, Corot: Tradition and the muse, Art Quart, 78; reviser, A Basic History of Art, Abrams, 80; auth, 100 Masterpieces of Painting in the Indianapolis Museum of Art, Indianapolis Mus Art, 80; auth, The source of David's Anacreon paintings, Sources, 83. *Mailing Add:* 4726 N Park Indianapolis IN 46205

JAQUE, LOUIS
PAINTER
b Montreal, PQ, May 1, 19. *Study:* Inst Appl Arts, Montreal. *Work:* Nat Gallery Can, Ottawa; Montreal Mus Fine Arts; Mus Quebec; Mus d'Art Contemporain, Montreal; Societe Publicite Editoriale Collection, Milan, Italy. *Comn:* Mural, Quebec Pavilion, Expo 70, Osaka, Japan, 70; mural, Maison de Radio-Canada, Montreal, 72; mural, Place de la Bourse, Montreal, 74. *Exhib:* Europa 72, 3rd Int Exhib Painting, Milan, 72; Salon Int d'Art Contemp, Paris, 74 & 75. *Awards:* Jessie Dow Award, Montreal Mus Fine Arts, 60; Can Art Coun Grant to Artist, 64 & 72; Europa 72 Bronze Medal, City of Milan, 72. *Mem:* Founder Soc Prof Artists Que (pres, 64-65). *Media:* Oil, Tempera. *Dealer:* Galerie Bernard Desroches 1444 Sherbrooke St W Montreal PQ H3G 1K4 Can. *Mailing Add:* 1760 Ducharme Ave Outremont PQ H2V 1H3 Canada

JARAMILLO, VIRGINIA
PAINTER
b El Paso, Tex, Mar 21, 39. *Study:* Otis Art Inst, 58-61. *Work:* Long Beach Mus Art, Calif; Pasadena Art Mus, Calif; Aldrich Mus Contemp Art, Ridgefield, Conn; Schenectady Mus, NY. *Exhib:* Whitney Mus Am Art Ann, New York, 72; Contemporary Reflections 1971-72, Aldrich Mus Contemp Art, Ridgefield, 72; group exhib, Douglas Drake Gallery, Kansas City, Kans, 75 & one-man show, 76; plus others. *Pos:* Assoc dir & aesthet adv, Hybrid Inc, 72-74. *Awards:* Ford Found Grant, 62; Nat Endowment Arts, 72-73; Creative Artists Pub Serv Prog Grant, 75. *Bibliog:* F Bowling (auth), Outside the galleries: Four artists, Arts Mag, 11/70; Deluxe show, Houston Chronicle, 8/71; C Ratcliff (auth), The Whitney Annual, Part I, Artforum, 4/72. *Mem:* Nat Soc Lit & Arts. *Media:* Acrylic, Oil. *Res:* Religious architecture throughout Europe. *Publ:* Auth, Post-minimal artists, Arts Mag, 9/75. *Mailing Add:* 109 Spring New York NY 10012

JARDINE, DONALD LEROY
EDITOR, EDUCATOR
b Idaho Falls, Idaho, July 7, 26. *Study:* Weber Col, Ogden, Utah, CA, 48, Assoc Sci, 49; Univ Utah, BS, 50 & MS, 62; Univ Minn, Minneapolis, PhD, 75; studied with Farrell R Collett, Alvin Gittens, Arnold Friberg, Walter Wilwerding, Peter Busa & Reid Hastie. *Work:* Salt Lake Art Barn; Univ Utah; Weber State Col; Univ Minn. *Exhib:* Utah Artists' Invitational, Ogden, 54-58 & 61; Instructor's Exhib, Salt Lake Art Ctr, 57-60; Asn Prof Artists Ann, Minneapolis, 64-66; People-to-People Exhib, Santiago, Chile, 66; Studio Arts Fac Show, Univ Minn, 68 & 70. *Pos:* Pres, Utah Art Educ Asn, 58-60; ed, The Illustrator, 65- *Teaching:* Art teacher, Bountiful Sr High Sch, Utah, 51-62; assoc dir art educ, Westminster Col, Salt Lake City, 58-60; assoc educ dir art, Art Instr Sch, Minneapolis, 62-; assoc prof career art, Univ Minn, 68- *Awards:* Distinguished Art Award, Weber State Col. *Mem:* Asn Prof Artists (dir, 65-67); Art Instr Schs (vpres, 77); Art Dir Club; Nat Art Educ Asn (lectr, 74-75). *Publ:* Illusr, The Children's Friend, 55-62; illusr, Tell Me a Story, 60; contribr, Art Instruction School's Textbooks, 62-75; auth, How to Sell Your Artwork, 63; auth, Richard Lack's Atelier, Am Artist, 71. *Dealer:* Treehouse Art Gallery Farmington UT 84025. *Mailing Add:* 2390 Wisconsin Ave N Golden Valley MN 55427

JARVIS, DONALD
PAINTER, INSTRUCTOR
b Vancouver, BC, 23. *Study:* Vancouver Sch Art, with hon, 48; also with Hans Hofmann, New York, 48 & 49. *Work:* Nat Gallery Can, Ottawa, Ont; Art Gallery Greater Victoria, BC; Vancouver Art Gallery; London Pub Libr & Art Mus; Can Coun Art Bank, Ottawa; and others. *Exhib:* Nat Gallery of Can, 55-65 & 69; Some Painters of the BC Mainland, Art Gallery of Greater Victoria, 65; Int Exhib of Drawings & Prints, Lugano, Switz, 66; one-man show, Vancouver Art Gallery, 49, 55 & 77; Coasts, The Sea and Canadian Art, Stratford, Ont, 79; and others. *Teaching:* Instr painting & drawing, Emily Carr Col of Art, 51- *Awards:* Emily Carr Scholar, Vancouver Sch Art, 48; Sr Arts Fel, Can Coun, 61. *Mem:* Royal Can Acad Arts. *Media:* Mixed Media. *Mailing Add:* c/o Bau-Xi Gallery 3045 Granville St Vancouver BC V6H 3J9 Canada

JARVIS, JOHN BRENT
PAINTER
b American Fork, Utah, Nov 28, 46. *Study:* Snow Col, AS, 65; Utah State Univ, BS, 71; Brigham Young Univ. *Work:* Brigham City Mus, Utah. *Exhib:* Salt Lake Art Ctr Regional Show, 76; Am Watercolor Soc, New York, 76; one-man shows, Brigham Young Univ, Provo, Brigham City Mus, Bertha Eacles Gallery, Ogden, Utah & Trivoli Gallery, Salt Lake City. *Awards:* Merit Award, Utah Painting & Sculpture, Utah Inst Fine Arts, 74; Ann Noye Watercolor, Salt Lake Art Ctr Intermountain, 76; Merit Award, Mormon Art Show, Brigham Young Univ, 77. *Media:* Multimedia. *Mailing Add:* 1355 E 250 N Pleasant Grove UT 84062

JARVIS, LUCY
CONSULTANT, FILMMAKER
b New York, NY, June 23, 27. *Study:* Cornell Univ; Columbia Univ; New Sch Social Res, New York. *Pos:* Exec producer, Nat Broadcasting Corp, New York, 60-76; pres, Creative Proj Inc, 76- *Awards:* Emmys for The Kremlin & The Louvre (films); Nat Asn Television Arts & Sci, 63; Golden Mike Award for Kremlin Film, Am Women in Radio & TV, 64; Chevalier l'Ordre Arts & Lettres, Fr Govt, 69. *Mailing Add:* c/o Creative Proj Inc 45 Rockefeller Pl New York NY 10020

JAUDON, VALERIE
PAINTER
b Greenville, Miss, Aug 6, 45. *Study:* Miss State Col Women, Columbus; Univ Am, Mexico City; St Martin's Sch Art, London, Eng; Memphis Acad Art, Tenn. *Work:* Hirshhorn Mus, Washington, DC; Aldrich Mus Contemp Art, Ridgefield, Conn. *Comn:* Tile work (with Romaldo Giurgola, architect), State Off Complex, Harrisburg, Pa, 76; entrance courtyard (with Giurgola), Salk Inst, La Jolla, Calif, 76; ceiling mural, Insurance Co NAm, Philadelphia, 77. *Exhib:* Aldrich Mus Contemp Art, Ridgefield, 75; Mus Mod Art, New York, 75; Albright-Knox Art Gallery, Buffalo, NY, 76; Selections 1977, Aldrich Mus Contemp Art, 77; Recent Acquisitions, Hirshhorn Mus & Sculpture Garden, 77; one-man exhibs, Pa Acad Fine Arts, 77, Galerie Hans Strelow, Dusseldorf, 80 & Sidney Janis Gallery, 83; Pattern Painting, PS 1, Queens, NY, 77; Boston Mus Fine Arts, 82; and others. *Teaching:* Sch Visual Arts, New York, currently. *Awards:* Creative Artist Pub Serv Grant, NY, 80; Art Award, Miss Inst Arts & Letters, 81. *Bibliog:* Kay Larson (auth), Freezing Expressionism, New York Mag, 4/25/83; Richard Armstrong (auth), article, Artforum, 9/83; John Perreault (auth), Allusive depths: Valerie Jaudon, Art Am, 10/83. *Dealer:* Sidney Janis Gallery 100 W 57th St New York NY 10019. *Mailing Add:* 139 Bowery New York NY 10002

JAUSS, ANNE MARIE
PAINTER, ILLUSTRATOR
b Munich, Ger, Feb 3, 07; US citizen. *Study:* Art Sch State Munich. *Work:* New York Pub Libr Print Rm, NY. *Exhib:* Group shows, Ger, before 32; one-man & group shows, Lisbon, Portugal, 38-45; one-man shows, Portraits of Pets, Portraits Inc, New York, 47, Old Custom House, Philadelphia, Pa, 51, graphics, Netherwood Arts, Hyde Park, NY, 71 & watercolors, Larcada Gallery, New York, 74. *Awards:* Author's Award for Pasture, NJ Asn Teachers Eng, 68. *Bibliog:* R C (auth), Anne Marie Jauss, Panorama, 42; Eugen Guerster (auth), Anne Marie Jauss, Am-Ger Rev, 6/51; Bruno Werner (auth), Anne Marie Jauss, Die Kunst, 1/52. *Media:* Oil, Watercolor; Linoleum, Dry Point. *Publ:* Auth, Legends of Saints & Beasts, 54, Discovering Nature the Year Round, 55, River's Journey, 57, Under a Green Roof, 60 & Pasture, 68; co-auth, Little Horse of Seven Colors & other Portuguese folk tales, 70; illusr of over 60 bks, mostly for children. *Mailing Add:* 312 Stockholm Vernon Rd Stockholm NJ 07460

JAWORSKA, TAMARA
TAPESTRY ARTIST
b Archangelsk, Russia; Can citizen. *Study:* State Acad Fine Arts, Poland, BFA, Fac Art Weaving, MFA; Royal Can Acad Arts, fel academician. *Work:* Nat Mus, Warsaw, Poland; Molsons Brewery, Toronto; York-Hanover Corp, Toronto; JDS Investment Corp, Toronto; pvt collections. *Comn:* Tapestries-Gobelin, Olympia & York Co, Place Bell Can, Ottawa, 71 & Bank Montreal, Toronto, 75, Metrop Life Ins Co, Ottawa, 77, JDS Finch 1000, Toronto, 76 & var pvt collections in US, Can, Switz, Eng & Sweden. *Exhib:* Rothmans Art Gallery, Stratford, Can, 71; one-person shows, Art Gallery Hamilton, 80 & Nienkamper Art Gallery, Toronto, 80; Travelling exhibs, Nat Mus & State Art Galleries, Spain; Can Cult Ctr, Art Gallery, Paris, 81; Ctr Nat de la Tapisserie D'Aubusson, Galerie Inard, Paris, traveling abroad, 81-82; and others in Poland, Italy, Switz, WGer, Holland, Mex, Can & Iran. *Pos:* Artistic dir, Artist Guild Lab, Warsaw, 54-59, Lab for Design of Linen Indust, Poland, 59-63 & Polish Guild Arts & Crafts, Warsaw, 63-68; dir pvt

design-weaving art studio, Toronto, currently. *Awards:* Gold Medal, Trienale de Milano, Italy, Int Exhib Interior Design & Archit, 57; Award for Excellence, Wool Gathering, Can Guild Crafts, Montreal, 73. *Bibliog:* Tapestries by Tamara Jaworska (film), CBS Toronto, 70 & Tamara's Tapestry World, CBS Arts & Sci Prog in Film, Toronto, 75; Tad Jaworski (auth), film, Tapestries by Tamara, New Collection, CBC Arts Film, Toronto, 80. *Mem:* Royal Can Acad Arts; Acad Italia del Arti a del Lovoro. *Media:* Handspun Wool, Artificial Materials. *Dealer:* Centre Nationale de la Tapisserie D'Aubusson Galerie Inard 179 Boulevard St Germain Paris France. *Mailing Add:* 49 Don River Blvd Willowdale ON M2N 2M8 Canada

JAY, BILL
PHOTOGRAPHIC HISTORIAN, CRITIC
b Maidenhead, Berkshire, England, Aug 12, 40. *Study:* Berkshire Col Art, dipl; Univ NMex, MA & MFA; spec study with prof Van Deren Coke & prof Beaumont Newhall. *Work:* Int Mus Photog, Rochester, NY; Bibliotheque Nat, Paris, France; Art Mus, Univ NMex, Albuquerque; plus many pvt collections. *Exhib:* Mod Art, var locations in Brit & Europe, 67; Art Mus, Univ NMex, 76; one-man shows, Micro-Gallery, Phoenix, Ariz & Northlight Gallery, Tempe, Ariz, 77. *Collections Arranged:* Brit Documentary Photog 1850-1970, Brit Coun, 71; The English Scene, Tony Ray-Jones & Sir Benjamin Stone 1864-1914, 71, The Inst for Contemp Arts, London; plus others. *Pos:* Ed/dir, Album Mag, London, Eng, 69-71; dir photog, Inst Contemp Arts, London, Eng, 69-71. *Teaching:* From asst prof to assoc prof art hist, 19th century & 20th century photog, Ariz State Univ, Tempe, Ariz, 74- *Mem:* Soc for Photog Educ (mem bd dirs, 74-78); Royal Photog Soc Gt Brit (mem Royal comn, 72). *Res:* Photography of the 19th and 20th centuries, especially British topographical work of the wet-plate era. *Publ:* Auth, Robert Demachy: Photographs and Essays, 74, Acad Ed; auth, Victorian Cameraman: Francis Frith 1822-1898, 73 & Victorian Candid Camera: Paul Martin 1864-1944, 73, David & Charles; Negative/Positive: A Philosophy of Photography, Kendall-Hunt, 79; Addison House and Photography: Current Perspectives, Light Impressions, 79. *Mailing Add:* Dept of Art Ariz State Univ Tempe AZ 85281

JAY, NORMA JOYCE
PAINTER
b Wichita, Kans. *Study:* Wichita State Univ; Art Inst Chicago; Calif State Univ, Long Beach. *Exhib:* World Trade Ctr, New York, 78; Am Soc Marine Artists Ann, 78-82; Grand Central Galleries, New York, 79, 80 & 82; Peabody Mus, Salem, Mass, 81; Mystic Seaport Mus Gallery, Conn, 82; and others. *Awards:* Best Show, Ford Nat Competition, 61; Artists Award, Chriswood Galleries, 73; First Place, Traditional Artists 10th Ann, 76. *Bibliog:* Diane Cirincione (auth), Art: Enjoy, decorate or invest?, Bay Views, 10/78; Peter Rogers (auth), review, Sea History, winter, 80-81; article, Antiques & Arts Weekly, 12/82. *Mem:* Am Soc Marine Artists. *Media:* Oil. *Dealer:* Back Door Gallery 1406 South Coast Hwy Laguna Beach CA 92657. *Mailing Add:* 29501 Vista Plaza Laguna Niguel CA 92677

JEAN-LOUIS, DON (DONALD CHARLES)
SCULPTOR, CONCEPTUAL ARTIST
b Ottawa, Ont, May 17, 37. *Work:* Nat Gallery Can; Montreal Mus Fine Arts; Art Gallery Ont; Can Coun Art Bank; Bakken Mus, Minneapolis. *Comn:* Signage (light sculpture), Coca Cola Can Ltd, Toronto, 77; installation (neon & argon), Fed Govt Can, Toronto, 78; neon sculpture & installation, Can Indust Ltd, Toronto, 80. *Exhib:* Art, Basle, Switz, 74 & Rotterdamse Kunststichting, Holland, 75; From Electrica Fires, Vancouver Art Gallery, 77; Pulse and Process, York Univ, Toronto, 79; Light 4 Play, Harbourfront Art Gallery, Toronto, 79. *Teaching:* Instr photo-electric arts, Ont Col Art, Toronto, summer 78. *Bibliog:* Parkins-Boyle (auth), Art and Architecture, Visual Arts Ont, 82. *Mem:* Royal Can Acad Arts. *Media:* Light. *Dealer:* Electric Gallery 226 Steelcase Rd W Toronto ON. *Mailing Add:* 4 Chambers Ave Toronto ON M6N 3L9 Canada

JECT-KEY, ELSIE
PAINTER
b Koege, Denmark; US citizen. *Study:* Art Students League, with Bridgman; Nat Acad Art Sch, with Olinsky; Beaux Arts Inst. *Work:* Butler Inst Am Art, Youngstown, Ohio; Norfolk Mus, Va. *Exhib:* Butler Inst Am Art, 71; Nat Acad Design Ann, 71; Am Watercolor Soc Ann, 72; Charles & Emma Frye Mus, Seattle, Wash, 73; Panhandle Plains Mus, Canyon, Tex, 74; and others. *Awards:* William Church Osborne Mem Award, Am Watercolor Soc, 72; Frank Monaghan Mem Award, Nat Soc Painters Casein & Acrylic, 73; Medal Honor, 71 & 75 & Bicentennial Medal, 75, Knickerbocker Artists. *Mem:* Nat Asn Women Artists (first vpres, 67-69); Audubon Artists Am; Knickerbocker Artists (corresp secy, dir, 70, rec secy, 74-); Am Watercolor Soc (treas, 70); Nat Soc Painters Casein & Acrylic (treas, 74-76, dir, 76-78). *Media:* Oil, Watercolor. *Mailing Add:* 333 E 41st St New York NY 10017

JEFFE, HULDAH CHERRY See Huldah

JEFFERS, WENDY JANE
PAINTER, CURATOR
b Providence, RI, Sept 5, 48. *Study:* Univ Mass, BFA, 71; Pratt Inst, MFA(painting), 74. *Work:* Port Authority of NY & NJ; Chase Manhattan Bank, New York; Nelson A Rockefeller; Continental Group, Stamford, Conn. *Exhib:* Concepts in Small Formats, Veydras Ltd, New York, 79; The Icarus Odyssey, Guadalajara & Mexico City, 79; Wash Square East Galleries, New York Univ, 80; Paperworks 80, Hudson River Mus, Yonkers, New York, 80; AIR Gallery, New York, 82; and others. *Collections Arranged:* First Nat City Bank Art Collection, New York, 73-74; Seven Decades at the Colony (auth,

catalog), New York, 76; A Curators Choice: A Tribute to Dorothy C Miller, Rosa Esman Gallery, New York, 82. *Pos:* Art cur, Citibank, New York, 73-74; asst to Dorothy C Miller, 74-83. *Awards:* Max Beckman Fel, Brooklyn Mus, 72; MacDowell Fel, 77; Artist-in-residence, RI Creative Arts Ctr, 80-83. *Bibliog:* Article, Providence J, 7/1/80. *Mem:* Col Art Asn. *Media:* Oil, Graphite. *Dealer:* Veydras Ltd 215 E 79th St New York NY 10021; Corporate Art Directions 41 E 57th St New York NY 10019. *Mailing Add:* PO Box 419 Canal St Sta New York NY 10013

JELINEK, HANS
PRINTMAKER, EDUCATOR
b Vienna, Austria, US citizen. *Study:* Acad Appl Arts, Vienna; Univ Vienna. *Work:* Metrop Mus Art, New York; Victoria & Albert Mus, London, Eng; Libr Cong, Washington, DC; Philadelphia Mus Art, Pa; Boston Mus Fine Arts, Mass. *Comn:* Prints in color, Int Graphic Art Soc, 53 & 61 & Soc Am Graphic Artists, 56. *Exhib:* Am Watercolors, Drawings & Prints, Metrop Mus Art, New York, 52; First Int Exhib Woodcuts Xylon, Kunsthaus Zurich, Switz, 53; First Expos Int Gravure, Gallery Mod Art, Ljubljana, Yugoslavia, 55; Art from the US, De Beyerd Cult Ctr, Breda, Holland, 57; Contemp Am Prints, Tokyo, Japan, 67. *Teaching:* Prof graphic art, City Col New York, 48-79, emer prof, 79-; instr graphic art, New Sch Social Res, 45-50 & Nat Acad Sch Fine Arts, 73- *Awards:* First Prize for Woodcut, Artists for Victory, Nat Graphic Art Exhib, 43; Pennell Prize, Third Nat Exhib Current Am Prints, Libr Cong, 45; Paul J Sachs Prize, 15th Ann Exhib, Boston Printmakers, 62; and others. *Bibliog:* A Reese (auth), American prize prints of the 20th century, Assoc Am Artists; H C Pitz (auth), A Treasury of American Book Illustration; Lynd Ward (auth), Hans Jelinek, Soc Am Graphic Artists, 56. *Mem:* Academician Nat Acad Design; Benjamin Franklin fel Royal Soc Arts, London; Soc Am Graphic Artists; Audubon Artists. *Publ:* Auth, Dürer's etching the desperate man: Discovery of a date and some thoughts about an old controversy, Print Rev, No 4, 75. *Mailing Add:* 675 West End Ave New York NY 10025

JELLICO, JOHN ANTHONY
DIRECTOR, PAINTER
b Koehler, NMex, June 26, 14. *Study:* Art Inst Pittsburgh, dipl; Univ Pittsburgh, teaching cert; Phoenix Sch Design; Grand Cent Sch Art, New York. *Comn:* Seven relig murals, St Patricks Cath Church, Raton, NMex, 37; 62 chapel murals, Third Air Force, Tampa, Fla, 43-45. *Exhib:* Raton Ann Art Show, NMex, 37; Phoenix Art Inst Ann, New York, 38; Art Inst Pittsburgh Exhib, Pa, 40; Taos Art Colony Ann Show, NMex, 41; Gallery Santa Fe, NMex. *Pos:* Asst dir & head illusr, Art Inst Pittsburgh, 46-56; dir, Colo Inst Art, 56-62, pres, 62-72; contrib ed, Am Artist Mag, 68-81; assoc ed, Southwestern Art Mag, 74- *Teaching:* Dir drawing, Colo Inst Art, 56- *Mem:* Hon mem Eugene Fields Soc; Mark Twain Soc. *Publ:* Auth, textbks, Int Correspondence Schs, 59-60; auth, articles in Am Artist Mag, 59-68 & Westerner Mag, 72; contrib & writer, Artists of the Old West & Persimmon Hill, mags; and others. *Mailing Add:* 291 W Belleview Englewood CO 80110

JELLICO, NANCY R
PAINTER, SCULPTOR
b LaGrange, Ga, Sept 22, 39. *Study:* Colo Inst Art, Denver, with John Jellico & Charlie Dye, 60; Univ Denver, with John Witaschek, 81. *Comn:* Birds of Colo, Cherry Hills Elem Sch, Colo, 78-81; flag design, Pro Rodeo Hall Champions & Mus Am Cowboy, Colorado Springs, 83; The Good Things Don't Change (four paintings), 83 & Bunch Quitter (sculpture), 84, Upjohn Co, TUCO Div, Kalamazoo, Mich. *Exhib:* Third, Fourth & Sixth Western Art Rendezvous, Littleton, Colo, 80-81 & 83; Pastel Soc Am, Lever House Gallery, New York, 82; Western Regional Art Show, Old West Mus, Cheyenne, Wyo, 83; Nat Western Small Painting Show, Bosque Farms, NMex, 83; Pastel Soc SW Ann Mem Exhib, Dallas, Tex, 83. *Pos:* Registrar, Colo Inst Art, Denver, 61-64. *Teaching:* Instr figure drawing & anatomy, Colo Inst Art, 64-65. *Awards:* First Place, Western Regional Art Show, Cheyenne, 83; First Place, Western All Media Nat Small Painting Show, 83; Men of the West Award, Western Art Rendezvous, 83. *Bibliog:* Jo Cole (auth), In the arts, The Villager-Village Squire, 12/23/82. *Mem:* Pastel Soc Am; Pastel Soc SW; Nat Soc Painters Casein & Acrylic; Colo Fedn Arts; Am Portrait Soc. *Media:* All. *Publ:* Illusr of five art textbooks, Int Correspondence Schs, 60-65; illusr, Portrait of Franklin Booth for feature article, Am Artist Mag, 66; illusr, Portrait of Pawel Kontny for feature article, Artists Rockies & Golden West Mag, 81. *Dealer:* La Porta Art Gallery 3422 S Broadway Englewood CO 80110. *Mailing Add:* 1 Martin Ln Englewood CO 80110

JENKINS, DONALD JOHN
MUSEUM DIRECTOR, HISTORIAN
b Longview, Wash, May 3, 31. *Study:* Univ Chicago, BA & MA. *Collections Arranged:* The Woodcut in Japan, 1700-1969, Portland Art Mus, Ore, 69; Ukiyo-e Prints & Paintings, The Primitive Period, 1680-1745 (auth, catalog), Art Inst Chicago, 71; Louis V Ledoux, Collecting of Ukiyo-e Master Prints (auth, catalog), Japan House Gallery, New York, 73; Masterworks in Wood: China and Japan (auth, catalog), Portland Art Mus & Asia House Gallery, New York, 76; Japanese Folk Art and Ukiyo-e Prints, Portland Art Mus, 83; Images of a Changing World: Japanese Prints of the Twentieth Century (auth, catalog), St Louis Art Mus, Los Angeles Co Mus Art, Carnegie Inst Mus Art & Portland Art Mus, 83. *Pos:* Asst cur, Portland Art Mus, 66-68, dir, 80-; assoc cur Oriental art, Art Inst Chicago, 69-74; cur, Portland Art Mus, 74-75, dir, Portland Art Asn, 75- *Teaching:* Instr art hist, Mus Art Sch, Portland, Ore, 63-65; lectr hist art, Univ Mich, Ann Arbor, 74; vis instr, Dept Art, Univ Chicago, 74. *Mem:* Asn Art Mus Dir; Int Hajji Baba Soc; Soc Japanese Arts & Crafts; Am Asn Mus. *Res:* Japanese prints and paintings of the Ukiyo-e School. *Publ:* Coauth, Near Eastern Art in Chicago Collections (catalog), Art

Inst Chicago, 74; auth, Handbook of the Asian Collection of the Portland Art Mus, 81; auth, Two Utamaro Prints, Sawers, 82; auth, Ukiyo-e, Kodansha Encycl, Japan, Vol 8, 83. *Mailing Add:* Portland Art Mus 1219 SW Park Portland OR 97205

JENKINS, MARY ANNE KEEL
PAINTER, MURALIST
b Pitt Co, NC, Nov 20, 29. *Study:* Ferree Sch Art, Raleigh, dipl fine arts, with Donald Nolan; NC State Univ Sch Design, with Joseph H Cox; San Carlos Art Sch, Mexico City. *Work:* NC Mus Art, Raleigh; Minn Mus Art, St Paul; R J Reynolds World Hq; Weatherspoon Art Mus; Philip Morris Inc; plus others. *Comn:* Interior mural, Radio Station WPTF, Raleigh, 71; Philip Morris, 82; interior mural, MKH Asn, 83; portrait collection, NC Mus Hist, 83. *Exhib:* 24th Nat Acad Galleries Ann, New York, 77; Prints & Drawings 1978, Miami Univ, Oxford, Ohio; 19th Dixie Ann, Montgomery Mus Art, Ala; 19th Red River Ann, Plains Art Mus, Minn; Danville Art Mus, 82; and others. *Teaching:* Instr painting, Dullen Art's Ctr, Raleigh, NC. *Awards:* Third James River Art Exhib First Patron Award, Mariners Mus, Newport News, Va, 69; Drawings USA Purchase Award, Minn Mus Art, St Paul, 71; Purchase Award & Hon Mention, Piedmont Exhib, Mint Mus, Charlotte, NC, 77. *Mem:* Artists Equity. *Media:* All painting media. *Dealer:* Somerhill Gallery 5504 Chapel Hill Blvd Durham NC 27707. *Mailing Add:* PO Box 6548 Raleigh NC 27628

JENKINS, PAUL
PAINTER
b Kansas City, Mo, July 12, 23. *Study:* Kansas City Art Inst & Sch Design, 38-41; Art Students League, 48-52, DH, 73. *Work:* Mus Mod Art, Whitney Mus Am Art & Solomon R Guggenheim Mus, New York; Tate Gallery, London, Eng; Mus Art Mod, Paris; Stedelijk Mus, Amsterdam, Holland; Mus Western Art, Tokyo, Japan; and others. *Exhib:* Art Inst Chicago; Carnegie Inst, Pittsburgh; Corcoran Gallery Art, Washington, DC & watercolor traveling show; Arthur Tooth Gallery, London; Tokyo Gallery; Tate Gallery, London, Eng; Smithsonian Inst, Washington, DC; Inst Contemp Art, Boston; Whitney Mus Am Art, New York; Retrospective, San Francisco Mus Art, Calif, 72; and others. *Awards:* Golden Eagle Award for Ivory Knife (film), 67; Officier des Arts et Lettres Award, France, 80; Commandeur Arts & Lettres, France, 83. *Bibliog:* Gerald Nordland (auth), Paul Jenkins, Universe Bks, 71; Albert Elsen (auth), Paul Jenkins, Abrams, New York, 73; Alain Bosquet (auth), Paul Jenkins, Editions Georges, Paris, fall 82. *Publ:* Coed, Observations of Michel Tapie, Wittenborn, 56; coauth, Anatomy of a Cloud, Abrams, 83. *Dealer:* Gimpel-Weitzenhoffer Gallery 1040 Madison Ave New York NY 10021; Karl Flinker Gallery 25 rue de Tournon 75006 Paris France. *Mailing Add:* 831 Broadway New York NY 10003

JENKINSON, GEOFFREY
PAINTER
b Leeds, Eng, Aug 31, 25; US citizen. *Study:* Yorkshire Art Class, Eng, 41-48. *Work:* Leeds City Art Gallery; also pvt collections. *Exhib:* Royal Acad, London, 47-49 & 55; Hutchinson's Headrow Gallery, Leeds, 71-; Woodrow Wilson Fine Arts, Santa Fe, NMex; Tucson Mus Art, Ariz; Liberty Picture Gallery, London, Eng; and others. *Awards:* Saxton Barton Prize, Royal Cambrian Acad Art, 47. *Media:* Multimedia. *Publ:* Contribr oil painting reproduction, Western Painting Today; contribr watercolor reproduction, Royal Acad Illus, 49. *Mailing Add:* Gen Delivery Tubac AZ 85640

JENNERJAHN, W P
EDUCATOR, PAINTER
b Milwaukee, Wis, June 15, 22. *Study:* Univ Wis, Milwaukee, BS, 46; Univ Wis, Madison, MS, 47; Black Mountain Col, with Josef Albers, 48-50; Acad Grande Chaumiere, Paris, 50; Acad Julian, Paris, 50-51; also with Gerald Wagner, Dornach, Switz, 78 & 81. *Work:* NY Univ; Dulin Gallery Art, Tenn; Univ Mass, Amherst; Adelphi Univ; Nassau Community Col. *Comn:* Stained glass panel, Long Island Jewish Hosp, NY; stained glass mural, comn by Dr Fredrick Lane, Great Neck, NY; stained glass mural, with John Urbain, JFK Airport Int Hotel; murals for eight ships, with Elizabeth Jennerjahn for Mil Sea Transport Serv; painting, Avis World Hq, Garden City, NY. *Exhib:* Exhib Momentum, Chicago; Milwaukee Ann, Univ Wis, Milwaukee; Birmingham Ann, Ala; Dulin Ann, Tenn; Black Mountain Col Invitational, Johnson City, Tenn. *Teaching:* Art teacher, Black Mountain Col, NC, 49-50, Cooper Union, 52-54 & Hunter Col, 53; prof art, Adelphi Univ, 54- *Awards:* Tiffany Found Grant, 52; Adelphi Univ Humanities Grants, 62 & 68. *Mem:* Nat Drawing Asn. *Media:* Oil, Watercolor. *Publ:* Illusr, Respect for Life, 74; contribr (with Geo K Russell), Laboratory Investigations in Human Physiology, Macmillan, 78. *Dealer:* Peter Rose Gallery 200 E 58th St New York NY 10022 *Mailing Add:* 120 Brixton Rd Garden City NY 11530

JENNINGS, FRANCIS
SCULPTOR, PAINTER
b Wilmington, Del, Feb 27, 10. *Study:* Wilmington Acad Art; Fleischer Mem Sch Art. *Work:* Mural, Del Indust Sch Boys. *Exhib:* Brandt Gallery, New York, 62; Whitney Mus Am Art, New York, 62; Baltimore Mus Art, Md, 63; four shows, Makler Gallery, Philadelphia & Rose Fried Gallery, New York, 60-66; Tenth St Anniversary, Ward Nasse Gallery, New York, 77; Landmark Gallery, New York, 77; and others. *Teaching:* Lectr, Nat Art Teachers Asn Conv, 4/69. *Publ:* Contribr, The Artist in New York (radio series), 67; contribr, You and the Artist (TV series), 69. *Mailing Add:* 55 Greene St New York NY 10013

JENNINGS, JAN
WRITER
b Chicago, Ill, Apr 4, 43. *Study:* Northwestern Univ, Evanston, BSJ; Univ Mo-Columbia, grad studies jour & art. *Pos:* Art writer, San Diego Tribune, Calif, 71- *Mem:* San Diego Mus Art. *Publ:* Free-lance writer with contributing features to Southwest Art Mag & Am Artist. *Mailing Add:* 350 Camino de la Reina PO Box 191 San Diego CA 92112

JENNINGS, THOMAS
PAINTER, PRINTMAKER
b Superior, Wis, Feb 7, 14. *Study:* Los Angeles City Col, AA; Chouinard Art Inst; Univ Calif, Los Angeles, EdB; Univ Calif, Berkeley, MA. *Work:* Cult Arts Found, Honolulu, Hawaii. *Exhib:* Sixth National Drawing & Print, Dulin Gallery, Knoxville; 55th National Orange Show, San Bernardino; one-man shows, Roberts Gallery, Santa Monica, Calif, 71; Sunset Recreation Ctr, 72, Wetzler Weiss Gallery, Encino, Calif, 77 & Howards Gallery, Honolulu, 79; The Foundry Gallery, Honolulu, Hawaii, 71 & 72. *Pos:* Tech illusr, NAm Aviation, 42-43; visual aids specialist, Lockheed Aircraft, 43-44; animation designer, United Productions Am, 44-46. *Teaching:* Instr art, Kann Inst Art, Beverly Hills, Calif, 46-53 & Chouinard Art Inst, 53; prof graphic design, Univ Calif, Los Angeles, 53- *Awards:* Creative Arts Inst Appointment, 72 & Regents Fac fel creative arts, 77, Univ Calif; Univ Calif, Los Angeles, Council Award, 83. *Bibliog:* C W Anderson (auth), Art Critic, Honolulu Advertiser, 8/71 & 9/72; Judy Owyang (auth), Art Critic, Santa Monica Outlook, 1/71. *Mem:* Art Dir Club Los Angeles (secy, 63). *Media:* Mixed Media. *Publ:* Auth, The Female Figure in Movement, Watson-Guptill, 71. *Mailing Add:* 21267 Entrada Rd Topanga CA 90290

JENRETTE, PAMELA ANNE
PAINTER, COSTUME DESIGNER
b Ft Bragg, NC, Aug 24, 47. *Study:* Univ Tex, BFA, 69. *Exhib:* Clean, Well-lighted Place (two-artist show), Austin, Tex, 71; Whitney Biennial, New York, 75; Cologne Art Festival, Ger, 75; one-artist show, Artists Space, New York, NY, 75. *Pos:* Studio asst, Lawrence Poons, New York, 71-75. *Awards:* Competition Award, Conde Nast, 69. *Bibliog:* Martha Utterback (auth), Texas, Artforum, 1/71. *Media:* Acrylic, Watercolor. *Mailing Add:* 300 Mercer St New York NY 10003

JENSEN, BILL
PAINTER
b Minneapolis, Minn, Nov 26, 45. *Study:* Univ Minn, BFA, 68, MFA, 70. *Work:* Whitney Mus Am Art & Metrop Mus Art, New York; Worcester Mus Art, Mass. *Exhib:* Brooklyn Mus, NY, 71 & 74; Drawing NYC 1978, Inst Contemp Art, Tokyo, 78; The 1970s: New American Painting, traveling in Eastern Europe, New Mus, 79-81 & Whitney Biennial, Whitney Mus, 81, New York. *Teaching:* Instr, Univ Minn, 65-70; instr, Brooklyn Mus Art Sch, 71-75; instr, York Col, Queens, NY, 72-73. *Bibliog:* Roberta Smith (auth), Bill Jenson's abstractions, Art Am, 11/80; John Perreault (auth), Ryder on the storm, Soho News, 11/81; Addison Parks (auth), Bill Jensen and the sound and light beneath the lid, Arts, 11/81. *Media:* Oil, Gouache. *Mailing Add:* 42 E 57th St New York NY 10022

JENSEN, DEAN N
WRITER, CRITIC
b Milwaukee, Wis, Oct 9, 38. *Study:* Univ Wis, BA; Roosevelt Univ, Chicago; Univ Chicago. *Collections Arranged:* Center Ring: The Artist (auth, catalog), Milwaukee Art Mus, Columbus Mus Art, NY State Mus, Albany & Corcoran Gallery Art, 81. *Pos:* Art ed & critic, Milwaukee Sentinel, Wis, 67- *Res:* Ashcan School; circus as a theme in art. *Publ:* Auth, The Biggest, The Smallest, The Longest, The Shortest, Wis House, 75; auth, Reunion in Hell: The Drawings of Paul Caster, Perimeter Press, 82; contribr Art News, Arts, Midwest-Art & others. *Mailing Add:* 1638 N Marshall St Milwaukee WI 53202

JENSEN, GARY
PAINTER
b Great Falls, Mont, Mar 27, 47. *Study:* Mont State Univ; Col of Great Falls, Mont; Calif Col of Arts & Crafts, BFA & MFA, 71. *Work:* Mont State Univ; San Jose Mus of Art. *Exhib:* Water Works, Berkeley Art Ctr, Calif, 75; Realism in Painting & Ceramics, De Anza Col, Calif, 75; Oakland Mus Collectors Gallery Invitational, Calif, 77; one-man shows, Mont Hist Soc Mus, 77, C M Russell Mus, Great Falls, Mont, 78 & many others. *Teaching:* Vis lectr, Calif Col Arts & Crafts, 79. *Dealer:* Lonny Gans 8225 1/2 Santa Monica Blvd Los Angeles CA 90046. *Mailing Add:* 5813 Fremont St Oakland CA 94608

JENSEN, HANK
SCULPTOR
b Pittsburgh, Pa, Apr 29, 30. *Study:* Carnegie Mellon Univ; Pratt Inst, BID; additional study with Hans Hofmann. *Work:* Hirshhorn Mus, Washington, DC; Provincetown Mus of Art, Mass; Roswell Mus & Art Ctr, NMex. *Comn:* Stage construct for dance theater piece Sanctum, Nikolais Dance Co, Henry St Playhouse, New York, 64; Cor Ten steel sculpture, Lyndon State Col, Lyndonville, Vt, 69; two fiberglassed plywood sculptures, Roswell Mus, 72; pressure-treated wood sculpture, Goddard Col, Plainfield, Vt, 76. *Exhib:* One-person shows, Lyndon State Col, 69 & Roswell Mus, 72. *Pos:* Artist in residence, Roswell Mus & Art Ctr, 72-73 & Goddard Col, 76. *Teaching:* Goddard Exp Prog in Further Educ, Goddard Col, 69-71 & 73, vis artist, 74. *Awards:* Fulbright Grant to Florence, 64-65; Two Grants in Aid to Ind Artists, Vt Arts Coun, 74-76; CETA Grant, Goddard Col, 76; and others. *Media:* Steel, Wood. *Mailing Add:* Five Pageant St Bennington VT 05201

JENSEN, LEO (VERNON)
SCULPTOR, PAINTER
b Montevideo, Minn, July 10, 26. *Study:* Walker Art Ctr, scholar, 46-48. *Work:* Conn Savings Bank; New Britain Mus Am Art, Conn; Phillip Morris, New York; US Info Agency, Washington, DC; Brown Univ; and others. *Comn:* Sculpture, Sheraton Hotels, Minneapolis, 63; bronze musicians, United Artists Corp, New York, 67; construction, Macmillan Publ Co, New York, 68; polychrome relief, Gulf & Western Corp, New York, 69; polychrome relief, Med World News, New York, 70. *Exhib:* One-man shows, Young & Rubicam, New York, 66; New Britain Mus Am Art, Conn, 67; Far Gallery, New York, 73, Arras Gallery, New York, 76, A Book Gallery, San Francisco, 78 & Frank Fedele Gallery, New York, 81; Butler Inst Am Art, Ohio, 53; Mus Mod Art Lending Collection, New York, 64-65; Milwaukee Art Ctr, 65; Fourth Int Biennial Sport Art, Madrid, 73; Nat Portrait Gallery, 81; Am Mus Nat History, New York, 82; Baseball Hall Fame, 83; and others. *Bibliog:* L Lippard (auth), Pop Art, Praeger, 66; M B Scott (auth), The Art & the Sportsman, Renaissance, 68; D Z Meiloch (auth), Contemporary Art With Wood, Crown, 68. *Media:* Bronze, Wood; Acrylic, Watercolor. *Mailing Add:* PO Box 264 Ivoryton CT 06442

JENSEN, MARIT
PAINTER, SERIGRAPHER
b Buffalo, NY. *Study:* Carnegie Inst Technol Sch Painting; Hans Hofmann Sch Fine Art, Provincetown. *Work:* Pittsburgh Bd Pub Educ; Univ of the South; Cult Div, US Info Agency; Provincetown Heritage Mus. *Exhib:* Butler Art Int Youngstown, Ohio, 43-46 & 59; DeYoung Mus, San Francisco, 45; Houston Mus, Tex, 45; Corcoran Gallery Art, Washington, DC, 47; Pa Acad of Fine Arts, 52; Brooklyn Mus, 54; Serigraph Int, Riverside Mus, 59; Int Cult Ctr, New Delhi, 67; Nat Print & Drawing Exhib, Provincetown Art Asn & Mus, 75, 76 & 77; Gallerie Dubini, Locarno, Switz, 74; and others. *Awards:* Carnegie Inst Prize, 45; Purchase Prize, Va Mus Fine Arts, 47; Grumbacher Prize, Nat Asn Women Artists, 60. *Bibliog:* Frances Walker (auth), Artist paints space about us, 5/7/56 & Jeannette Jena (auth), Marit Jensen's recent work, 5/9/56, Pittsburgh Post Gazette; Eleanor Meldahl (auth), One man show opens in Provincetown, Cape Cod Standard Times, 6/28/69. *Mem:* Provincetown Art Asn (trustee, 75-77 & hon vpres, 71-74); Provincetown Group Inc (bd dir, 74-77). *Media:* Oil. *Dealer:* Provincetown Group Gallery 286 Bradford Provincetown MA 02657. *Mailing Add:* 7 Anthony St Provincetown MA 02657

JERGENS, ROBERT JOSEPH
PAINTER, EDUCATOR
b Cleveland, Ohio, Mar 18, 38. *Study:* Cleveland Inst Art; Skowhegan Sch Painting & Sculpture; Yale Univ, BFA & MFA; Am Acad in Rome. *Work:* Cleveland Mus Art; NAm Col, Rome, Italy; Newman Relig Art Gallery; Skowhegan Sch Painting & Sculpture; Brooklyn Art Mus; and others. *Exhib:* Cleveland Mus Art, 57-64; Exhib by US Info Agency; Mus Mod Art, New York; Corcoran Gallery Art, Washington, DC; Mostra Univ, Rome; and others. *Teaching:* Instr design, Cooper Union, formerly; instr drawing, Sch Art & Archit, Yale Univ, formerly; instr design, Cleveland Inst Art, currently. *Awards:* Mary C Page Grant, 61; Johnson Award for Printmaking, 61; Prize, Cleveland Mus Art, 61; and others. *Mailing Add:* 5356 Regency Dr Parma OH 44129

JERRY, MICHAEL JOHN
EDUCATOR, CRAFTSMAN
b Grand Rapids, Mich, Aug 18, 37. *Study:* Sch Am Craftsman, Rochester Inst Technol, AAS & BFA, 60, MFA, 63; Cranbrook Acad Art, 60-62. *Work:* Wustum Mus Fine Art, Racine, Wis; Mus Contemp Crafts, New York; Metrop Mus of Art, New York. *Exhib:* Objects USA, 69; Int Trade Fair Jewelry Exhib, Munich, Ger, 71; The 6th Goldsmiths Expos, Kersnikova, Yugoslavia, 72; Goldsmiths, Renwick Gallery, Washington, DC, 74; Contemporary Crafts of the Americas, Colo State Univ, 75. *Teaching:* Assoc prof metalsmithing, Wis State Univ, Menomonie, 63-70; prof metalsmithing, Syracuse Univ, 70- *Mem:* Am Crafts Coun; Soc NAm Goldsmiths. *Media:* Metal. *Publ:* Contribr, American jewelry, Design Quart, 59; contribr, Philip Morton, Contemporary Jewelry, Holt, 69; contribr, Objects: USA, Viking, 70; contribr, Contemporary Crafts of the Americas: 1975; contribr, The Craftsman in America, Nat Geog Soc, 75. *Mailing Add:* 208 Dewitt Rd Syracuse NY 13214

JERVISS, JOY
PRINTMAKER
b Palmerton, Pa, Feb 14, 41. *Study:* C W Post Col, also with Ruth Leaf. *Work:* Colgate Univ Libr, Hamilton, NY; Bibliot Nat, Paris; Syracuse Univ Art Collection, NY; Ariz State Univ, Tempe; Princeton Univ Art Mus, NJ. *Exhib:* Okla Printmakers Nat Travel Exhib, 65; Port Washington Pub Libr Group, 65; Huntington Twp Art League, 72. *Pos:* Art exhib dir, Winston Must Corp, New York, 66-73; pres, Joy J Indust Graphic Supplies, Northport, 68-; sponsor, Washington Square Outdoor Art Exhib, NY, 70-72; founder & dir, Northport Art League, 71- *Teaching:* Asst instr printmaking, North Shore Community Arts Ctr, Great Neck, NY, 66-68; instr printmaking, Union Free Sch Dist 4, Northport, NY, 70-72. *Awards:* Purchase Award, Talens & Son Corp, 66; First Prize Award, NY Bank for Savings, 67. *Mem:* North Shore Community Arts Ctr; Silvermine Guild Artists; Huntington Twp Art League. *Media:* Etching. *Mailing Add:* c/o Bermond Art Ltd 3000 Marcus Ave Lake Success NY 11040

JESS (JESS COLLINS)
PAINTER, COLLAGE ARTIST
b Long Beach, Calif, Aug 6, 23. *Study:* Calif Sch Fine Arts, with Clyfford Still, Edward Corbett, David Park, Elmer Bischoff & Hassel Smith. *Work:* Metrop Mus & Mus Mod Art, New York; Art Inst Chicago; Dallas Mus Fine Arts; Philadelphia Mus Art. *Exhib:* Assemblage, Mus Mod Art, New York, 61; Pop Art USA, Oakland Art Mus, 63; one-man shows, Mus Mod Art, San Francisco, 68, Mus Contemp Arts, Chicago, 72, Mus Mod Art, New York, 74, Dallas Mus Fine Arts, 77, Arts Blub, Chicago, 81, Venice Bienale, 82 & Ringling Mus, Sarasota, Fla, 83; 70th & 71st Ann, Art Inst Chicago, 72 & 74; Extraordinary Realities, Whitney Mus Am Art, New York, 73; Poets of the Cities, Dallas Mus Fine Arts, 74; Matrix Two, Wadsworth Atheneum, 75; Calif Painting & Sculpture, Mus Mod Art, San Francisco, 76; 8 Artists, Philadelphia Mus Art, 78; Four Seasons, Matrix, Univ Calif, Berkeley, 80; American Accents, Rothman's The Gallery, Stratford, Ont, 83; Comic Art Show, Whitney Mus, 83; and many others. *Awards:* Individual Artist Fed Grant, Nat Endowment Arts, 73. *Publ:* Illusr, Caesar's Gate, Divers Press, Mallorca, 55; illusr, Ballads, Acadia Press, 64; illusr, A Book of Resemblances, Henry Wenning, 66; illusr, The Cat and the Blackbird, White Rabbit Press, 67; illusr & translr, Gallowsongs, auth, Christian Morgenstern, Black Sparrow Press, 70. *Dealer:* Federico Quadrani c/o Odyssia Gallery New York NY. *Mailing Add:* 3267 20th St San Francisco CA 94110

JESSEN, SHIRLEY AGNES
PAINTER
b Brooklyn, NY, Jan 23, 21. *Study:* New York Sch Applied Design Women, scholar, cert, 39; Fashion Art Inst, Rockefeller Ctr, 40; also with Lou Eisele, Frederick Lehman, Paul Wood & Norman Nodell, 60-79. *Exhib:* Salmagundi Club, New York, 78; Long Beach Mus, NY, 79; Roslyn Mus Fine Arts, 79; Adelphi Univ, 80; Molloy Col, 84; and many others. *Pos:* Illusr, Wantagh Parent Teachers Asn, 50-65; illusr, United Cerebral Palsy, 59-75; illusr, Nassau Co Med Soc, 59- *Awards:* Finalist Nat, Am Artist Mag, Grumbacher, 78 & Int Soc Artists, 79; First Prize, South Shore Art League, 81. *Mem:* Nat Soc Painters Casein & Acrylic; South Shore Art League (secy-treas, 80-81); New York Artists Equity Asn; Audubon Artists; Suburban Art League. *Media:* Oils, Acrylics. *Mailing Add:* 90 Fifth St Garden City NY 11530

JESWALD, JOSEPH
ADMINISTRATOR, PAINTER
b Leetonia, Ohio, May 17, 27. *Study:* Acad Julian, Paris; with Fernand Leger, Paris; Columbia Univ. *Pos:* Dir, Montserrat Sch Visual Art, Beverly, Mass, 70- *Mailing Add:* 41 Front Beverly MA 01915

JETER, RANDY JOE
DRAWER, EDUCATOR
b Longview, Tex, Dec 25, 37. *Study:* Univ Tex, Austin; Stephen F Austin Univ, BA & MA; spec study with Robert J Martin. *Work:* Ark Art Ctr, Little Rock; Bank of Austin, Tex; Fellowship Church, Baton Rouge, La; Hudson Printing Co, Longview, Tex. *Exhib:* Marymount Col Nat Christmas Exhib, Union Carbide Bldg, New York, 67; 12th Nat Exhib Prints & Drawings, Okla Art Ctr, Oklahoma City, 69; 15th Mid-South Exhib, Brooks Mem Art Gallery, Memphis, Tenn, 70; one artist exhibs, Southwestern Univ, Georgetown, Tex, 73, Univ Tex Med Sch, San Antonio, 73, Ouachita Univ, Arkadelphia, Ark, 76, Longview Mus & Arts Ctr, Tex, 76 & Univ Cent Ark, Conway, 77. *Teaching:* Instr art, Gladewater, Tex Pub Schs, 65-72; instr drawing, Longview Mus & Arts Ctr, Tex, 73-75; instr art, Univ Cent Ark, Conway, 75-77; instr art, Coleman Pub Schs, Tex, 77- *Awards:* Mus Dirs Award, Beaumont Art Mus, Tex, 69; Award, 4th Nat Drawing & Small Sculpture Show, Del Mar Col, Corpus Christi, 69; Juror's Choice, Tex Fine Arts Asn Ann Fall Invitationals, 69 & 71. *Mem:* Longview Mus & Fine Arts Ctr; Tex Fine Arts Asn (mem bd dirs, Region 8, 70-72); Nat Asn Educators in Art. *Media:* Pen & Ink, Silverpoint. *Dealer:* L&L Gallery 216 N Fredonia Longview TX 75601. *Mailing Add:* 2517 Tryon Rd Longview TX 75601

JEWELL, JOYCE
PAINTER, PRINTMAKER
b Washington, DC, Oct 11, 45. *Study:* Montgomery Col, Md, AA, 65; Am Univ, Washington, DC, BA, 67; George Washington Univ, MFA, 72; Tamarind Inst Lithography, NMex, 74. *Work:* Montgomery County Contemporary Print Collection, Md; Owensboro Federal Savings & Loan Asn, Ky. *Exhib:* 19th Area Exhib, Corcoran Gallery Art, Washington, DC, 74; Irene Leache Mem Art Exhib, Chrysler Mus, Va, 78, 80; Va Printmakers, 1979, Va Mus Fine Arts, 79; 17th Bradley Nat Print & Drawing Exhib, Lakeview Mus, 79; Mid-Am Nat Art Exhib, Owensboro Mus Fine Art, Ky, 80; 22nd Area Exhib: Works on Paper, Corcoran Gallery Art, 80; Collage & Assemblage: A Nat Invitational Traveling Exhib, Miss Mus Art, Jackson, 81-83; Maryland Biennial: Works on Paper, Baltimore Mus Art, 83. *Pos:* Graphic designer, John Hoskins & Assocs, Arlington, Va, 67-71. *Teaching:* Prof design, drawing, etching & lithography, Montgomery Col, Md, 71- *Awards:* Printmaking Award, Montgomery Co Juried Art Show, 78; Mid-Am Volunteers Purchase Award, Owensboro Mus Fine Art, 80; Owensboro Federal Savings & Loan Purchase Award, Mid-Am Nat Art Exhib, 80. *Bibliog:* Article, Gargoyle Mag, No 17/18, 81. *Mailing Add:* 7424 Buffalo Ave Takoma Park MD 20912

JEWELL, WILLIAM M
EDUCATOR, PAINTER
b Lawrence, Mass, Dec 9, 04. *Study:* Harvard Col, AB, 27, Archit Sch, 27-29. *Work:* Fogg Mus, Cambridge, Mass; Farnsworth Mus, Rockland, Maine; DeCordova Mus, Lincoln, Mass. *Comn:* Ralph Taylor, dean (portrait), Dean's Off, Boston Univ, 55; Col Israel Putnam (portrait), Putnam Mason

Lodge, Conn, 58; Gov Milliken (portrait), State of Maine, Augusta, 62. *Exhib:* One-man shows, Doll & Richards, Boston, 53-59, Guild of Boston Artists, 42-73 & Currier Gallery Art, Manchester, 42; Boston Watercolor Soc, 36-; Am Watercolor Soc, 40- *Pos:* Archit designer, ETP Graham, Boston, 29-31; trustee, Boston Arts Festival, 55-62; asst ed, Speculum, 56-62. *Teaching:* Prof, Col Lib Arts, Boston Univ, 34-72, chmn fine arts dept, 55-68, emer prof fine arts, 72-; instr, Harvard Univ Exten, 58-75. *Awards:* Mitton Gold Medal & Cash Award, North East Artists, 41, 46, 47 & 62; Am Coun Learned Socs grant-in-aid, 60. *Mem:* Am Asn Univ Profs; fel Am Acad Arts & Sci; Am Watercolor Soc; NE Watercolor Soc (auditor, 40-70); Guild of Boston Artists (treas, 50-57). *Media:* Watercolor, Oil. *Res:* History of American landscape; all aspects of American art. *Publ:* Auth, Modern Architecture, Frontier Press, 60; auth, Lucia Fairchild Fuller, In: Biog of Notable Am Women, 1607-1950, 67; auth, A note on artistic interdependence, In: Festschrift in Honor of Samuel Montefiore Waxman, 65, Radcliffe Col, Boston Univ Press, 68; auth, George DeForest Brush, 70 & auth, Helen Gardner, Art Historian, 73, Dict Am Biog. *Dealer:* Guild of Boston Artists 162 Newbury St Boston MA 02116. *Mailing Add:* 37 Dana St Cambridge MA 02138

JILG, MICHAEL FLORIAN
PAINTER, PRINTMAKER
b Albert, Kans, June 28, 47. *Study:* Fort Hays State Univ, BA, 69 & MA, 70; Kent State Blossom Festival, with Jack Twarkok, Alex Katz & James Melchert, 70; Wichita State Univ, with John Fincher, MFA, 72. *Work:* Joslyn Art Mus, Omaha, Nebr; Wichita Art Mus, Kans Arts Commission, Wichita State Univ & Fort Hays State Univ. *Comn:* George Washington Mural Project, Ellis Bicentenial Comt, Kans, 76; St Ann (painting), St Ann Parish, Olmitz, Kans, 81; St Anthony (mural), St Anthony Hospital, Hays, Kans, 82. *Exhib:* Midwest Biennial, Joslyn Art Mus, Omaha, Nebr, 70; Nat Exhib Contemp Art, Soc Four Arts, Palm Beach, Fla, 73; Mid-Am V, Nelson Gallery Art, Kansas City, Mo, 74; Mainstreams 74, Herman Fine Art Ctr, Marietta, Ohio, 74; Selected Kansas Artists, Kans State Capital, Topeka, 77; Allied Artists Am, Nat Acad Galleries, New York, 77-78; 1st Kans Artists Competition, Judicial Bldg, Topeka, 81. *Teaching:* Asst prof painting, Ft Hays State Univ, 81- *Awards:* Junior League Omaha Purchase, 70; Purchase Award, Kans Arts Commission, 80; Cash Award, Kans Arts Commission, 81. *Bibliog:* Articles in Wichitian Mag & Kans Mag, 80; featured, Rush Co News & Hays Daily, 80-82. *Mem:* Kansas City Artists' Coalition; High Plains Printmakers; Hays Arts Coun (mem bd dirs, currently); Boston Printmakers; Kans Watercolor Soc. *Media:* Oil, Acrylic; Intaglio. *Mailing Add:* 317 W 20th Hays KS 67601

JIMENEZ, LUIS ALFONSO, JR
SCULPTOR, DRAFTSMAN
b El Paso, Tex, July 30, 40. *Study:* Univ Tex, Austin, BS(art), 64; asst to Semore Lipton, 66; Ciudad Univ Mexico City, 64. *Work:* Long Beach Mus, Calif; New Orleans Mus, La; Roswell Mus & Art Ctr, NMex; Plains Mus, Fargo, NDak; Nat Collection Fine Arts, DC. *Comn:* Southwest Monument, D Anderson & Roswell Mus, 71-75; glass goggles, Sea-Girl, Steuben, New York, 71; City Houston, Tex & Nat Endowment Arts, 81; City Fargo, NDak & Nat Endowment Arts, 82. *Exhib:* Human Concern Personal Torment, Whitney Mus, New York, 69; Recent Figure Sculpture, Fogg Art Mus, 71; Whitney Mus Biennial, New York, 71; Richard Brown Baker Collects, Yale Univ Art Mus, Hartford, Conn, 75; Jimenez Retrospective, Contemp Arts Mus, Houston, Tex, 75; Amon Carter Mus Western Art, Ft Worth, Tex, 77; Western States Biennal, Nat Collection Fine Arts, DC, 79; Centre Culturale Americaine, Paris, France, 79; San Diego Mus Art, 83; one-man show, Yares Gallery, Scottsdale, 83; and others. *Teaching:* Assoc prof sculpture, Univ Ariz, 76. *Awards:* nat Endowment Arts Grant, 77. *Bibliog:* Quirarte (auth), Mexican American Artists in the US, Univ Tex, 73; Hunter-Jacobus (auth), American Art of 20th Century, Abrams, 73; featured in Newsweek, 8/79, Washington Post, 6/79 & Smithsonian, 4/79. *Media:* Fiberglass Sculpture With a Jazzy Metal-Flake Epoxy Finish & Neon & Lights; Colored Pencil Drawings, Lithographs. *Dealer:* Phyllis Kind Gallery 136 Green St New York NY 10012; Yares Gallery 3625 Bishop Ln Scottsdale AZ. *Mailing Add:* 1415 E Nevada El Paso TX 79902

J J (JEAN-JACQUES DE LA VERRIERE)
GOLDSMITH, SCULPTOR
b Paris, France, Mar 8, 32; US citizen. *Study:* Ecole Nat Art Decoratif, BPh, Paris, France, 49; Escuela de Artes Suntuarias, Barcelona, Spain, 51; London Cent Col, Eng, 57; Pratt Inst, with Prof Albert, MFA, 75; Hunter Col, MA(art hist), 79. *Work:* Cooper Mus, New York; Nat Mus Design; Contemp Crafts Mus; Metrop Mus, New York; Mus Mod Art, New York. *Comn:* Monstrance, Eglise du Gesu, Montreal, 59; Masonic Jewelry, 68, ritual pieces, 70 & commemoration medals, 75, var Masonic Lodges, New York. *Exhib:* Jewelry Int, Plattsburg, NY, 63; solo exhib, Pellicone Gallery, Sothampton, NY, 82; Caroline Corre Gallery, Paris, 83; Small Works, NY Univ, 83; B Fendrick Gallery, Washington, DC, 83. *Teaching:* Instr enameling, Haystack Sch Art, 68; asst prof sculpture & electroforming, Pratt Inst, 72-75. *Awards:* First Prize Jewelry, Greenwich Village Outdoor Show, 61 & New York Craftsmen, 63. *Mem:* New York Craftsmen; Am Crafts Coun; Am Goldsmith Asn. *Media:* Gold, Precious and Semi-Precious Stones; Wood, Ivory. *Publ:* Auth, Electroforming for Jewelry & Sculpture, 70. *Mailing Add:* 99 MacDougall St #18 New York NY 10012

JOCDA (JOSEPH CHARLES DAILEY)
PAINTER
b Reynoldsville, Pa, Mar 4, 26. *Study:* Youngstown Univ, AB, with Margaret Evans, David P Skeggs, John Naberezny & Robert Elwell. *Work:* Youngstown Col; Westmar Col; Sioux City Art Ctr; Mo Synod; Des Moines Art Ctr; plus

others. *Exhib:* Butler Inst Am Art, 52 & 53; Siouxland Watercolor Exhib, 55-57; Six State Exhib, 55-58; Life of Christ Show, Iowa, 57 & 58; Laas-George Gallery, San Francisco, 61; plus others. *Pos:* Designer, Crest Johnson Studios, Youngstown, Ohio, 53; staff artist, Warren, Ohio, 54; asst dir, Sioux City Art Ctr, 55-61, instr & actg dir, 57-59; arts & crafts coordr, Cent Community Ctr, Columbus, 64-68. *Awards:* Awards, Trumble Co, 50 & Mahoning Co, 51; Youngstown Col Purchase Award, 52; 11th Iowa Artist Ann Purchase Award, 59. *Mem:* Midwest Mus Conf; fel Inst Arts & Lett; Nat Soc Lit & Arts. *Media:* Mixed. *Mailing Add:* 366 Lincoln Ave East Columbus OH 43214

JOFFE, BERTHA
DESIGNER
b Leningrad, Russia; US citizen. *Study:* New York-Phoenix Sch Design; City Col New York, BS; Teachers Col, Columbia Univ, MA; NY Univ Inst Fine Arts; Art Students League; studied with William Zorach, Winold Reiss & Oronzio Maldarelli. *Work:* Drapery designs in leading hotels; design on drapery fabric, UN Staff Dining Rm. *Exhib:* Provincetown Art Asn, Mass, 40; Artists for Victory, Metrop Mus Art, New York, 42; Art in Business Exhib, New York, 42; Int Textile Exhib, Weatherspoon Art Gallery, Univ NC, 44; and others. *Pos:* Free lance textile designer, 42- *Teaching:* Instr textile & costume design, City Col New York, 40-43; docent art hist, Metrop Mus Art, 41. *Mailing Add:* 77 Parker Ave Maplewood NJ 07040

JOHANNINGMEIER, ROBERT ALAN
PAINTER, WRITER
b St Louis, Mo, Aug 29, 46. *Study:* Kansas City Art Inst, BFA, 68. *Exhib:* Sun Carnival, Mus Fine Art, El Paso, Tex, 67; Allied Artists Am, New York, 80; Audubon Artists Ann Exhib, New York, 80; Grand Nat Exhib, New York, 80 & 81. *Awards:* First Place, Tri-State Art Exhib, Carlsbad Area Art Asn, NMex, 68. *Bibliog:* Flo Wilks (auth), Radiating harmony, SW Art, 82; Arejas Vitkauskas (auth), American scene, Worldwide News Bur, 83; Trish Garrigus (auth), Art of investing/collecting, Ctr Econ Revitalization, 83. *Mem:* Am Artists Prof League. *Media:* Oil. *Res:* Artistic styles and painting techniques from 1400 to the present; topics of special interest to collectors. *Publ:* Auth, The protection of works of art, 79, Art as investment, 79, Artline, 79 & Will your art investment retain its full market value?, 80, Art & Commun; auth & illusr, The Art of Investing While Collecting, Art & Commun, 83. *Dealer:* O'Brien's Art Emporium 7122 Stetson Dr Scottsdale AZ 85251. *Mailing Add:* 812 N Edwards Carlsbad NM 88220

JOHANSEN, ROBERT
PAINTER
b Kenosha, Wis, Mar 30, 23. *Study:* Layton Sch Art, Milwaukee, Wis. *Work:* Wustum Mus & Johnson's Wax, Racine, Wis; Univ Wis, LaCrosse; Continental Bank of Chicago; NY CTA Chem, Brooklyn. *Exhib:* Am Watercolor Soc Show & Traveling Exhib, New York, 72; Mainstreams '74, Marietta, Ohio; Watercolor USA, Springfield, Mo, 75; Nat Acad Design 150th Ann Exhib, New York, 75; Salmagundi Club, New York; Rocky Mountain Nat Watercolor Show, Colo; and several one-man shows. *Pos:* Aquarellist & advert artist, Eisenberg Studios, Milwaukee, Wis, 53- *Teaching:* Instr painting, Wustum Mus Fine Arts, 70-73. *Awards:* Top Award, Watercolor Wisconsin, 72; Best of Show, Springfield, Ill Exhib, 74; Kentucky Watercolor Soc; and others. *Bibliog:* Stephan Bellgraph, Watercolor Wisconsin (film), George Richards, 73; 40 Watercolorists and How They Work, Watson-Guptill. *Mem:* Signature mem Rocky Mountain Nat Watercolor Soc. *Publ:* Contribr, Watercolor Page, Am Artist, 3/75; contribr, Palette Talk, Grumbacher, 83. *Mailing Add:* 3017 Taylor Ave Racine WI 53405

JOHANSON, GEORGE E
PAINTER, PRINTMAKER
b Seattle, Wash, Nov 1, 28. *Study:* Portland Mus Sch, Ore; Atelier 17, New York. *Work:* Nat Collection, Washington, DC; Chicago Art Inst; New York Pub Libr; Victoria & Albert Mus, London, Eng; Oldham Co Coun, Eng; and many others. *Exhib:* Denver Art Mus; Calif Palace Legion Hon, San Francisco; Am Embassy, London, Eng; Seattle Art Mus; Portland Art Mus, Ore; Univ Ariz, Tucson; Univ Ill; Western NMex Univ; and others. *Teaching:* Instr painting & printmaking, Portland Mus Art Sch, 55- *Awards:* Artists of Ore Award, Corvallis Art Ctr, Ore, 75; First Ed Award, Ore Arts Comn, 76; Award, Ore State Fair, Salem, 77; and others. *Publ:* Creator, Etching and Color Intaglio (film), 73 & Printmaker (film), 76. *Mailing Add:* 2237 SW Market St Portland OR 97201

JOHANSON, PATRICIA
SCULPTOR, ARCHITECT
b New York, NY, Sept 8, 40. *Study:* Brooklyn Mus Art Sch; Art Students League; Bennington Col, BA, 62; Hunter Col, MA, 64; City Col Sch Archit, BS & BArch, 77. *Work:* Mus Mod Art, New York; Detroit Inst Arts; Storm King Art Ctr, Mountainville, NY; Metrop Mus Art, New York; Allen Memorial Art Mus, Oberlin, Ohio. *Comn:* Stephen Long (sculpture), Buskirk, NY, 68; Ixion's Wheel, State Univ NY Albany, 69; gardens, House & Garden Mag, 69; Cyrus Field (landscape sculpture park), Buskirk, 70-75; Mitchell/Giurgola Assoc Architects, 72-75. *Exhib:* One-man shows, Tibor de Nagy Gallery, New York, 66-68, Rosa Esman Gallery, New York, 78, 79, 81 & 83 & Dallas Mus Fine Arts, 82; Art of the Real, Mus Mod Art, New York, 68-69; Work of Venturi & Rauch & Mitchell/Giurgola Assocs, Pa Acad Fine Arts, 75; Women in Am Archit, Brooklyn Mus, NY, 77; Recent Acquisitions, Mus Mod Art, New York, 79; American Drawings in Black & White, Brooklyn Mus, 80; Contemp Art, Chicago, 81; Recent Acquisitions, Metrop Mus Art, 82; and many others. *Pos:* Design consult, Consolidated Edison Corp, NY, 72,

Yale Univ, 72 & Bartholomew Consolidated Sch Corp, Columbus, Ind, 73, Int Year Child Comm, 79, Corning Park, 82 & Fair Park, Dallas, 81-83. *Teaching:* Vis prof art, State Univ NY Albany, 69; vis artist, Mass Inst Technol, 74, Oberlin Col, 74 & Alfred Univ, 74; lectr, Colby Col, Maine, 81. *Awards:* Guggenheim Fel, 70 & 80; First Prize, Environ Design Competition, Montclair State Col, 74; Artist's Fel, Nat Endowment Arts, 75; plus others. *Bibliog:* Colin Naylor (ed), Contemporary Artists, St Martin's Press, NY, 77; Piri Halasz (auth), Patricia Johanson, Arts, 6/78; Eleanor Munro (auth), Originals: American Women Artists, Simon & Shuster, 79. *Dealer:* Rosa Esman Gallery 121 Spring St New York NY 10012. *Mailing Add:* RFD 1 Buskirk NY 12028

JOHNS, JASPER
PAINTER
b Augusta, Ga, 1930. *Study:* Univ SC. *Work:* Victoria & Albert Mus, London; Mus Mod Art & Whitney Mus Am Art, New York; Albright-Knox Art Gallery, Buffalo, NY; Wadsworth Atheneum, Hartford, Conn; Mus Mod Art, Paris. *Exhib:* Retrospective, San Francisco Mus Mod Art, 78; one-man show, Mus Mod Art, New York, 68, 70 & 72; Mus Contemp Art, Chicago, 71-72; Seattle Art Mus, Wash, 73; Art Inst Chicago, 74; Walker Art Ctr, Minneapolis, 74; Saidye Bronfman Ctr, Montreal, 80; Pace Gallery, New York, 80; Whitney Mus Am Art, New York, 80; Hirshhorn Mus, Washington, DC, 80; Stedelijk Mus, Netherlands, 80; Margo Leavin Gallery, Los Angeles, 81; Leo Castelli Gallery, New York, 81; and others. *Bibliog:* C Kelder (auth), Prints: Jasper Johns at Hofstra, Art in Am, 3/73; D Ward (auth), Jasper Johns drawings, Arts Rev, 9/74; J Reichardt (auth), The rendering is the content, Archit Design, 12/74. *Mailing Add:* 225 E Houston St New York NY 10002

JOHNSEN, MAY ANNE
PAINTER
b Port Chester, NY. *Study:* With John Carroll. *Work:* St Mary's Church, Hudson, NY; also in pvt collection of Philip Schyler, Albany, NY. *Comn:* Fire Equipment 1890's (painting), Tsaawassa Fire Dept, Brainard, NY, 53. *Exhib:* Bertrand Russel Int Peace Found Exhib, Nottingham, Eng; Women Artists in Am from 18th Century to Present; A Heritage, Nat Soc Marine Painters Nat Show, Plantation Gallery, Sandwich, Mass; Drawing International, Barcelona, Spain; Knickerbocker Nat Exhib, New York. *Awards:* Silvermine Guild Marine Award, 59; First Prize, Columbia Co Fair, 59; Ohio Marine Award, Ohio Miniature Soc, 69; and others. *Bibliog:* Article in La Rev Mod, 68. *Mem:* Assoc mem Miniature Painters, Sculptors & Gravers Soc of Washington, DC; Miniature Art Soc NJ; Am Soc Marine Painters. *Media:* Mixed. *Dealer:* Squillaci Gallery 524 Summit Ave Schenectady NY 12307. *Mailing Add:* Box 5 Brainard NY 12024

JOHNSON, AVERY FISCHER
PAINTER
b Wheaton, Ill, Apr 3, 06. *Study:* Wheaton Col, BA, 28; Art Inst Chicago, grad, 33. *Work:* Newark Mus, NJ; Montclair Art Mus, NJ; Philbrook Mus, Tulsa, Okla; Holyoke Mus, Mass; Libr of Cong, Washington, DC. *Comn:* Post Off murals, Catonsville, Md, Lake Village, Ark, Liberty, Ind, and others; The Lamp (painting), comn by Standard Oil Co-NJ; The Humble Way (painting), comn by Humble Oil & Refining Co, 49-50. *Exhib:* 200 Years of Watercolor Painting in America, Metrop Mus Art, New York, 67; Mus Aquarelle, Mexico City, 68; also numerous ann exhibs, Am Watercolor Soc, New York, Montclair Art Mus, NJ & NJ Watercolor Soc. *Pos:* Childrens bk illusr, Random House, Longmans Green, Abingdon Press, E P Dutton & Thomas Nelson, 39-61. *Teaching:* Instr painting, Montclair Art Mus, 40-70; instr painting, Newark Sch Fine & Indust Arts, 47-60. *Awards:* First Watercolor Award, Montclair Art Mus, 60; Sen George Hammond Watercolor Award, Mus Fine Arts, Springfield, Mass, 64; Winsor-Newton Award, Am Watercolor Soc, 65. *Mem:* Assoc Nat Acad Design; Am Watercolor Soc; Audubon Artists; NJ Watercolor Soc. *Media:* Watercolor. *Publ:* Auth, Suburban life (art column), NJ, 66-68; auth, Watercolor page, Am Artist, 10/67; illusr, Factory & Mod Mfg, 67-71. *Mailing Add:* 38 Cooper Rd RFD Denville NJ 07834

JOHNSON, BRENT
PAINTER
b Tyler, Tex, Aug 25, 41. *Study:* Cent State Univ, BFA, 67; Univ Okla; Univ Md. *Exhib:* Watercolor USA, Springfield Art Mus, Mo, 75; Am Watercolor Soc, Nat Acad Design, New York, 75-81; La Ann, La Mus Art, Shreveport, 76; Delta Art Asn, Ark Art Ctr, Little Rock, 76; San Diego Nat Watercolor Exhib, Cent Fed Tower, 77; Rocky Mountain Nat Watermedia Exhib, Foothills Art Ctr, Golden, Colo, 77; and others. *Pos:* Bd dirs, Oklahoma City Arts Coun, 79-80. *Awards:* Mercantile Bank Award, Watercolor USA, 75; Bus Community Award, Rocky Mountain Nat Watermedia Exhib, 77; John Young Hunter Mem Award, Am Watercolor Soc, 81. *Bibliog:* Lynn Martin (auth), Today's art, Syndicate Mag Inc, 74; Dean G Graham (auth), Outdoor Oklahoma, Okla Dept Wildlife, 1/76; Marcia Lionberger (auth), Oklahoma Art Gallery, Wall & Wall Publ Co Inc, fall 81. *Mem:* Prof Artist Asn Okla (pres, 77-78); Whiskey Painters Am. *Media:* Watercolor, Acrylic. *Dealer:* Temple Art Gallery 1102 S 31st St Temple TX 76501; American Legacy Gallery 5911 Main St Kansas City MO 64113. *Mailing Add:* 513 Sweetgum Oklahoma City OK 73127

JOHNSON, BRUCE (JAMES)
PAINTER, INSTRUCTOR
b Riverside, Calif, May 6, 44. *Study:* Univ Hawaii, Honolulu, BFA, 66; El Camino Col, Gardena, Calif; Calif Col Arts & Crafts, Oakland, MFA, 70. *Exhib:* James D Phelen Awards Exhib, Calif Palace of Legion of Honor, San Francisco, 69; Western Wash State Nat Drawing & Small Sculpture Exhib,

Western Wash State Univ, Bellingham, 70; San Francisco Art Inst Centennial Exhib, 71 & Work on Paper, 73, San Francisco Mus Mod Art; Grids, Inst Contemp Art, Univ Pa, Philadelphia, 72; Eighteen Bay Area Artists, Los Angeles Inst Contemp Art, 76 & Univ Calif, Berkeley Art Mus, 77; Art Hawaii Ann, Honolulu Acad Arts, 78, 79 & 83; Artists Hawaii Cult Exchange Exhib, Ohio & Manila, 80-81. *Teaching:* Instr art, Santa Rosa Jr Col, Calif, 72-76; lectr drawing, Univ Hawaii, Honolulu, 78-79; instr, Honolulu Acad Arts, 81. *Awards:* MacDowell Colony Fel, 71; Young Artist Award, Contemp Art Comt of Oakland Mus Art Guild, 73. *Bibliog:* Judith L Dunham (auth), Johnson and Linhares, Artweek, 3/73; Alfred Frankenstein (auth), She's somebody to watch, San Francisco Chronicle, 4/3/73. *Media:* Acrylic, Paste. *Mailing Add:* 1662 Lewalani Dr #103 Honolulu HI 96822

JOHNSON, BUFFIE
PAINTER, LECTURER
b New York, NY, Feb 20, 12. *Study:* Art Students League, 27-28; Univ Calif, Los Angeles, BA, 36; Acad Julien, Paris, 38; S W Hayter Atelier, with Francis Picabia, 38-39. *Work:* Boston Mus Fine Arts; Yale Univ Art Gallery; Nat Collection Fine Arts, Washington, DC; Whitney Mus Am Art, New York; Walker Art Ctr, Minneapolis; and many others. *Comn:* Murals, Astor Theatre, New York, 59. *Exhib:* Contemp Am Art Biennial Exhib, Whitney Mus Am Art, 73; one-woman shows, Howard Putzel's 67 Gallery, New Sch Social Res, Betty Parsons Gallery, Max Hutchinson Gallery, New York, 73 & Stamford Mus, Conn, 77; retrospective, Landmark Gallery, New York, 81; and others. *Teaching:* Instr, Parsons Sch Design, 46-50. *Awards:* Yaddo Fel; Bollingen Found Award; Edward Albee Found Fel; and others. *Bibliog:* Parker Tyler (auth), On Buffie Johnson: The city as cosmic mural, 10/60 & Horace Gregory (auth), The transcendentalism of Buffie Johnson, 11/65, Art Int; Ellen Lubell (auth), Arts reviews: Buffie Johnson at Palm Beach, 5/75; and others. *Mem:* Group Espace, Paris; Women in the Arts, New York. *Media:* Oil. *Dealer:* Max Hutchinson Gallery 138-142 Greene St New York NY 10012. *Mailing Add:* 102 Greene St New York NY 10012

JOHNSON, CECILE RYDEN
PAINTER, PUBLISHER
b Jamestown, NY. *Study:* Augustana Col, AB; Pa Acad Fine Arts; Art Inst Chicago; Am Acad Fine Arts; Univ Colo; Univ Wis. *Work:* Chicago Mus Sci & Indust; Davenport Munic Mus; Macalester Col; General Mills; Minn Mining. *Comn:* Ford Motor Co; Trans World Airlines; Rockefeller Resorts; Jamaican Govt; CBS/World Tennis; and many others. *Exhib:* Am Watercolor Soc; Washington Watercolor Soc; US Info Agency & State Dept Traveling Exhib to Europe, Asia, Africa & South Am; one-man shows, Davenport Munic Mus & Hudson River Mus; US Tennis Open, Nat Stadium, 83; and others. *Teaching:* Instr workshops, Ghost Ranch, Abiquiu, 82, Bermuda, 83. *Awards:* Catharine Lorillard Wolfe Art Club Gold Medal; Prizes, Am Watercolor Soc, Knickerbocker Artists & others. *Bibliog:* Feature article, Am Artist, 1/83; Kent (auth), 100 Watercolorists; Creating in Watercolor (film), Crystal Productions. *Mem:* Am Watercolor Soc; Nat Arts Club; Soc Illusr; hon mem Nat League Pen Women. *Media:* Watercolor, Acrylic. *Dealer:* Kimball Art Ctr Park City; Newman Gallery 1625 Walnut St Philadelphia PA 19103. *Mailing Add:* Des Artistes One W 67th St New York NY 10023

JOHNSON, CHARLES W, JR
HISTORIAN, EDUCATOR
b New York, NY, Apr 7, 38. *Study:* Westminster Col, BMEd; Union Theol Seminary, MSM; Ohio Univ, PhD, 70. *Teaching:* Asst prof, State Univ NY Col New Paltz, summer 66; asst prof art hist, Univ Richmond, 67-70, assoc prof art hist, 70-81, chmn dept fine arts, 67-, prof, 82- *Mem:* Col Art Asn Am. *Mailing Add:* Modlin Fine Arts Ctr Univ of Richmond Richmond VA 23173

JOHNSON, D'ELAINE A HERARD See d'Elaine

JOHNSON, DIANE CHALMERS
HISTORIAN, EDUCATOR
b Dubuque, Iowa, Jan 3, 43. *Study:* Harvard Univ, Radcliffe Col, BA(fine arts), 65; Univ Kans, MA(art hist), 67, PhD(art hist), 70. *Teaching:* Asst prof, Col Charleston, 70-75, assoc prof, 75-80, chmn dept art, 70-78, prof fine arts, 80- *Awards:* Nat Endowment Humanities Res Fel, 81-82. *Mem:* Col Art Asn Am; Historians Am Art Asn. *Res:* Nineteenth and 20th century European and American art; nouveau and symbolist art. *Publ:* Co-auth, Art as confrontation: the Black man in the art of Gericault, Mass Rev, 69; auth, The studio: a contribution to the nineties, Apollo Mag, 70; auth, Art Nouveau in America: three posters by Will H Bradley, Register Mus Art, Univ Kans, 71; auth, Odilon Redon's apocalypse de Saint-Jean, Arts Va, 72; auth, American Art Nouveau, Harry N Abrams Publ, 79. *Mailing Add:* 59 Smith St Charleston SC 29401

JOHNSON, DONALD MARVIN
CRAFTSMAN, SILVERSMITH
b Billings, Mont, Jan 24, 47. *Study:* SDak State Univ, Brookings, BS(fine arts); Mont State Univ, Bozeman, MA(jewelry & metalsmithing). *Work:* C M Russell Gallery, Great Falls, Mont; Renwick Gallery, Smithsonian Inst, Washington, DC. *Exhib:* Renwick Gallery, Smithsonian Inst, Washington, DC, 75 & 76; Contemp Crafts Exhib 1976, Del Art Mus, Wilmington, 76; Goldsmith 77, Phoenix Art Mus, Ariz, 77; Lake Superior 77, Tweed Mus Art, Duluth, Minn, 77; Third Profile of US Jewelry 1977, Art Mus, Tex Tech Univ, 77; Copper, Brass, Bronze Competition, Univ Ariz, 77. *Teaching:* Instr film, SPICE Prog fed grant, SDak State Univ, 69-70; instr metalsmithing, Dept Art, State Univ Col Oneonta, NY, 73- *Awards:* Purchase Awards, Crafts & Craftsmen, C M Russell Gallery, 73 & Craft Multiples, Lloyd E Herman, 75;

Juror's Award, Craft Forms, Brockton Art Ctr, 76. *Mem:* Soc North Am Goldsmiths; NY State Craftsman; Am Crafts Coun; Col Art Asn Am. *Media:* Miscellaneous Media. *Publ:* Auth, Stretched texture, 70 & Canteen forms adapted from stones, 71, Ceramics Monthly; auth, Non-soldering techniques for the metalsmithing craftsman, Casting & Jewelry Craft, 76. *Mailing Add:* 6531 Canyon Ferry Rd State Univ Col-Oneonta Helena MT 59601

JOHNSON, DONALD RAY
HISTORIAN, PRINTMAKER
b Poteau, Okla, Jan 14, 42. *Study:* Northeast Okla State Col, BA, 63; Univ Okla, MFA, 70 & MA, 71. *Comn:* Lithograph, Kans Cult Arts, 73. *Exhib:* Lithography 1969, Fla State Univ, 69; Images on Paper, Jackson, Miss, 71; Graphics 71, Western NMex Univ, 71; Santa Fe Trail Ctr, Larned, Kans, 81; Ft Hays State Univ, Kans, 81; and others. *Teaching:* Assoc prof art hist, Emporia Kans State Univ, 70- *Awards:* Emporia Kans State Univ Grants, 73, 75, 76, 78, 80-82; Wenner-Gren Found Grant, 83. *Mem:* Col Art Asn. *Res:* American West during the 19th century; Santa Fe Trail through Kansas; mound builders in eastern Oklahoma. *Mailing Add:* 901 Congress Emporia KS 66801

JOHNSON, DORIS MILLER
PAINTER
b Oakland, Calif, Dec 8, 09. *Study:* Calif Col Arts & Crafts, 32-33; Univ Calif, Berkeley, BA, 34, 34-36. *Work:* Piedmont High Sch Art Gallery, Calif. *Exhib:* Portland Art Mus Invitational, Ore, 40; Carnegie Traveling Show from San Francisco Mus Art, 40-41; Nat Drawing Exhib, San Francisco Mus Art, 70; San Francisco Women Artists Ann Show, One Market Plaza, San Francisco, 79; one-person show, Lucien Labaudt Art Gallery, San Francisco, 73; Crown Zellerbach, San Francisco, 81; Richmond Art Ctr, Calif, 81; San Francisco Women Artists' Opening Gallery, 83; and others. *Pos:* Founder children's art classes, Art League East Bay, 39; dir, Oakland Art Mus, 39-52, chmn art rental gallery, 56-59; chmn acquisitions comt of activities bd, San Francisco Mus Art, 57-64; mem bd trustees, Calif Col Arts & Crafts, 70-78. *Teaching:* Instr art, Oakland Art Mus, 39-52. *Awards:* 13th Ann San Francisco Women Artists Pres Purchase Prize, San Francisco Mus Art, 38; San Francisco Art Asn Ann Artists Fund Prize, 40; Merit Award, San Francisco Women Artists Painting Show, Zellerbach Plaza Gallery, 82; and others. *Mem:* San Francisco Women Artists (pres, 46-48); hon life mem Art League East Bay. *Media:* Mixed. *Mailing Add:* 329 Hampton Rd Piedmont CA 94611

JOHNSON, DOUGLAS WALTER
PAINTER, PRINTMAKER
b Portland, Ore, July 8, 46. *Study:* Self-taught. *Work:* Permanent Collection, Mus NMex, Santa Fe; Am Nat Collection, Am Nat Ins Co, Galveston, Tex; Univ NMex, Albuquerque; De Vries Insurance Agency, St Joseph, Mich. *Exhib:* Eight From Santa Fe, 71, Mus NMex, Santa Fe; Obsidian Mountain, 77; two-man show, Colo Springs Fine Arts Ctr, 79; New Paintings and Prints, Return Gallery, Taos, NMex, 81 & 83; one-man show, Krasl Art Ctr, St Joseph, Mich, 82. *Awards:* Jurors Award, NMex Biennial, Mus NMex, 73; Second Prize Award, Watercolor NMex, NMex Watercolor Soc, 74; Santa Fe Opera Poster, NMex, 81. *Bibliog:* Douglas Johnson, painter, Santa Fean Mag, 2/74; Richard Polese (auth), Douglas Johnson's Mesa Poled, El Palacio Mag, fall 79; Douglas Johnson, Four Winds Mag, summer 82; Douglas Johnson, artist, Santa Fean Mag, 10/83; and others. *Media:* Casein on Paper. *Dealer:* Elaine Horwitch Gallery Santa Fe NM & Scottsdale AZ; Return Gallery Taos NM 87501. *Mailing Add:* General Delivery Coyote NM 87012

JOHNSON, EDVARD ARTHUR
PAINTER, EDUCATOR
b Chicago, Ill, Dec 18, 11. *Study:* Chicago Acad Fine Arts; Art Inst Chicago; Univ Ga, BFA; Inst Design, Ill Inst Technol, with L Moholy-Nagy & Alexander Archipenko. *Work:* Nat Mus, Vaxio, Sweden; Ga Mus Art, Univ Ga, Athens; Univ Rochester Mem Art Mus, NY; Heublein Collection, Farmington, Conn. *Comn:* Paintings, Farrell Lines, 80. *Exhib:* Watercolor USA, Springfield, Mo, 66; Nat Acad Design, New York, 70; Southbury Libr Gallery, Conn, 77; one-man show, Silvermine Gallery, New Canaan, Conn, 73 & Little Studio Ltd, New York. *Pos:* Art dir for mags, Holt, Rinehart & Winston, New York, 53-58. *Teaching:* Asst prof advan design, illus & drawing, Univ Ga, 47-51; instr visual fundamentals, Inst Design, Ill Inst Technol, 52; instr painting & drawing, Famous Artists Schs, 60-73 & Heritage Village, Southbury, Conn, 73-78. *Awards:* Nat Swed-Am Art Asn Purchase Award, 41; Miss Art Asn Watercolor Prize, 50; Rockefeller Fel, 51-52. *Mem:* Conn Watercolor Soc; Silvermine Guild Ctr Arts; Wash Art Asn. *Publ:* Designer, American Sculptor Series, Univ Ga Press, 49; designer, Israel Revisited, Ralph McGill, 50. *Mailing Add:* 755A Heritage Village Southbury CT 06488

JOHNSON, ELLEN HULDA
HISTORIAN, CRITIC
b Warren, Pa, Nov 25, 10. *Study:* Oberlin Col, BA & MA; post-grad studies at Harvard Univ, Sorbonne, Uppsala & Stockholm Univs. *Collections Arranged:* Three Young Americans, Allen Art Mus, Oberlin Col, 63, 65, & 68; India Triennale of Contemporary World Art, American Collection, New Delhi, 68. *Pos:* Mus staff mem, Toledo Mus Art, Ohio, 36-39; art librn, Oberlin Col, 39-45; hon cur modern art, Allen Art Mus, 73- *Teaching:* From instr to prof modern & contemp art & Scandinavian art, Oberlin Col, 45-77; vis prof, Univ Wis-Madison, 49-50; vis prof, Uppsala Univ, 60. *Awards:* Sr Fel, Nat Endowment Humanities, 73; Guggenheim Fel, 75; Distinguished Teacher of Art Hist, Col Art Asn of Am, 78. *Bibliog:* Lawrence Alloway (auth), Art, The Nation, 3/29/75; Jay Gorney (auth), Oberlin's Tribute to Ellen Johnson, Art News, 4/75; Richard Morphet (auth), rev of Modern Art

and the Object, Studio Int, 3-4/77. *Mem:* Col Art Asn Am (bd dirs, 77-81). *Res:* Art since World War II. *Publ:* Auth, Cezanne, The Masters Series, London, 67; auth, Claes Oldenburg, Penguin Bks, Ltd, London, 71; auth, Modern Art and the Object, Thames & Hudson, Ltd, London, Harper & Row, Inc, New York, 76; auth numerous articles in Artforum, Art News, Art Int, Arts Mag, Studio Int, Art & Artists, etc; auth, American Artists on Art from 1940 to 1980, Harper & Row, New York, 82. *Mailing Add:* Dept of Art Oberlin Col Oberlin OH 44074

JOHNSON, ERNEST (MELVIN)
PAINTER, INSTRUCTOR
b Hampton, Va, April 18, 24. *Study:* Pratt Inst, cert(illus), 46-49; watercolor workshops with Georg Shook, 75, Edward Betts, 77 & Carl Schmalz, 80. *Work:* Chrysler Mus, Norfolk, Va; Roanoke Mus Fine Arts, Va; Phillip Morris USA, Richmond, Va; Barclays Am, Charlotte, NC. *Exhib:* Irene Leach Mem, Norfolk Mus, Va, 48 & 68; 17th Ann Exhib, Winston-Salem Gallery Fine Arts, NC, 64; Piedmont Graphics Exhib, Mint Mus, 64 & 66; 22nd Am Drawing Biennial, Norfolk Mus, Va, 67; Watercolor USA, Springfield Art Mus, Mo, 71 & 77; Watercolor Soc Ala Ann Exhib, Birmingham Mus Art, 78; Aqueous 82, J B Speed Art Mus, 82; Sixth Ann Southern Watercolor Soc Exhib, Pensacola Mus Art, Fla, 82. *Teaching:* Instr watercolor, WVa Craft Ctr, Ripley, 79, Roanoke Col, 79-81 & Longwood Col, Farmville, Va, 82. *Awards:* Purchase Awards, Irene Leach Mem, Norfolk Mus, Va, 68 & Watercolor USA, Citizens Bank, Springfield, Mo, 71; Potomac Valley Watercolorists Award, Ann Southern Watercolor Soc Exhib, 79. *Bibliog:* Stevens (auth), Expositions diverses, Rev Mod Arts Vie, 11/67; Shae Avery (auth), Ernest Johnson--portrait of a private person, Roanoker, 5-6/80; Janet Shaffer (auth), Paint-outs, Country Mag, 6/83. *Mem:* Va Watercolor Soc (pres, 80-81); Watercolor Soc, Southern & Am. *Media:* Watercolor. *Publ:* Illusr, Adventures in Handwriting, Macmillan Co, 71. *Mailing Add:* 7595 Mt Chestnut Rd Salem VA 24153

JOHNSON, EUGENE JOSEPH
HISTORIAN
b Memphis, Tenn, May 22, 37. *Study:* Williams Col, BA, 59; NY Univ, MA, 63, PhD, 70. *Teaching:* Prof art, Williams Col, Williamstown, Mass, 65-, chmn art dept, 78-80. *Publ:* Auth, S Andrea in Mantua, the Building History, 75. *Mailing Add:* Dept of Art Williams Col Williamstown MA 01267

JOHNSON, EVERT ALFRED
MUSEOLOGIST, LECTURER
b Sioux City, Iowa, Mar 2, 29. *Study:* Morningside Col, BA, 53; Univ Iowa, MA, 54. *Collections Arranged:* National Drawing Invitational, 71 & WPA Revisited, 72, Southern Ill Univ, Carbondale; Iron, Solid Wrought/USA 1776-1976 (with catalogue), 76. *Pos:* Dir, Sioux City Art Ctr, 61-65; dir, Col Mus, Hampton Inst, 65-66; cur, Univ Galleries, Southern Ill Univ, Carbondale, 66-, cur art & exhib, Univ Mus, 75- *Teaching:* Asst prof art & head dept, Westmar Col, 56-61; instr painting, Hampton Inst, 65-66; lectr hist & mus technol, Southern Ill Univ, Carbondale, 66- *Publ:* Auth, Animal sculpture, Sch Arts Mag, 59; auth, Unfired clay, Craft Horizons Mag, 70. *Mailing Add:* Univ Mus Southern Ill Univ Carbondale IL 62901

JOHNSON, FRIDOLF LESTER
DESIGNER, WRITER
b Chicago, Ill, Feb 24, 05. *Study:* Art Inst Chicago, 23-25. *Work:* Victoria & Albert Mus, London; New York Pub Libr; Fine Arts Gallery, San Diego; and others. *Exhib:* Pvt Press Shows, Int Inst Graphic Arts, 59 & 62; Pvt Press Printing: A Fine Art, Fine Arts Gallery, San Diego, 60. *Pos:* Art dir, Frankel-Rose Co, Chicago, 25-34; owner, Contempo Art Serv, Hollywood, Calif, 48-50 & Mermaid Press, 58-; exec ed, Am Artist Mag, New York, 62-70. *Bibliog:* John Ryder (auth), Miniature Folio of Private Presses, Ryder, London, 60; Roderick Cave (auth), The Private Press, Faber & Faber/Watson-Guptill, 71. *Mem:* The Typophiles, New York (vpres, 71-72). *Res:* Graphic arts; calligraphy; printing. *Publ:* Auth, Ornamentation & Illustrations for the Kelmscott Chaucer, Dover, 73; coauth, 200 Years of American Graphic Art, Braziller, 75; illusr, Mythical Beasts Coloring Book, Dover, 76; auth, A Treasury of Bookplates from the Renaissance to the Present, Dover, 77; auth, Treasury of American Pen-and-Ink Illustration 1881 to 1938, Dover, 82; auth & ed, Rockwell Kent: An Anthology of His Works, Knopf, 82. *Mailing Add:* 34 Whitney Dr Woodstock NY 12498

JOHNSON, GREGORY
PAINTER, PHOTOGRAPHER
b Chicago, Ill, Jan 30, 55. *Study:* Art Inst Chicago; Bowling Green State Univ; Ill State Univ, BA & MA, 80. *Work:* Ill State Mus, Springfield; Albany Mus, Ga; Columbus Mus, Ga; Butler Inst Fine Art, Youngstown, Ohio; Food Assoc, Inc, Statesboro, Ga. *Exhib:* 43rd Ann Midyear Show, Butler Inst Art, Youngstown, Ohio, 79; 31st Midstate Exhib, Evansville Mus Art, Ind, 79; Dittmar Mem Mus, Evanston, Ill, 80; Six Midwestern Artist, Millikin Univ, 80; About Faces, S Ohio Mus, Portsmouth, 81; The Contemporary Human Form, Chicago Art Guild, Ill, 81; Mid-America Biennial, Owensboro Mus Art, Owens, Ky, 82. *Teaching:* Grad asst art, Ill State Univ, Normal, 79-80. *Awards:* Best of Show, Ill State Mus Prof Show, 79. *Bibliog:* Mark Mosely (auth), Brown's guide to Georgia, 82; Linda Evans (auth), Presbyterian Survey, 83. *Media:* Oil on Birch Panel. *Dealer:* Stanley & Schenck Gallery Atlanta GA. *Mailing Add:* 6640 Akers Mill Rd NW 35-A3 Atlanta GA 30339

JOHNSON, HARVEY WILLIAM
PAINTER
b New York, NY, Apr 9, 21. *Study:* Art Students League, 46-49; with Howard Trafton & Robert Johnson; also with Annetta St Gaudens, Cornish, NH.

Work: Favell Mus, Klamath, Ore; Pac Northwest Indian Ctr, Spokane, Wash; Boatmen's Nat Bank, St Louis; Cowboy Artists Am Mus, Kerrville, Tex; Mus Fur Trade, Chadron, Nebr. *Exhib:* Cowboy Artists of America, Oklahoma City, 66-72, Phoenix, Ariz, 73-83; Haley Mem Libr Western Art Show, Midland, Tex, 80-82; Biltmore Celebrity Art Show, Los Angeles, 81-83; Western Heritage Sale, Houston, Tex, 82-83. *Teaching:* Instr com art, Famous Artists Sch, Inc, 53-72, Cowboy Artists Am Mus, 83. *Awards:* Silver Medal in Oil Painting, 13th & 14th Ann Cowboy Artists of Am, 78 & 79. *Bibliog:* James K Howard (auth), Ten Years With the Cowboy Artists of America, Northland Press, 76; Don Dedera (auth), Visions West, The Story of the Cowboy Artists Museum, 83. *Mem:* Cowboy Artists of Am (vpres, 75-76 & pres, 76-77). *Media:* Oil. *Publ:* Auth, Western art is fine, SW Art Mag, 80; auth, The sagebrush artist, Horse & Rider, 83; auth, It's that sense of achievement, Art W, 84. *Mailing Add:* PO Box 5733 Santa Fe NM 87502

JOHNSON, HOMER
EDUCATOR, PAINTER
b Buffalo, NY, Dec 24, 25. *Study:* Pa Acad Fine Arts with Julius Bloch & Hobson Pittman, 46-52. *Work:* Butler Inst Am Art, Youngstown, Ohio; Smith, Kline & French Labs, Philadelphia; Pa Acad Fine Arts. *Exhib:* Pa Acad Fine Arts Regional, 64; Mus Fine Arts, Springfield, Mass; Pa 71, Harrisburg, 71; one-man show, Philadelphia Art Alliance, 71; Philadelphia Earth Show, Philadelphia Civic Ctr, 73; Am Watercolor Soc Ann Traveling Exhib, 75-76; Univ Del Regional Art Exhib, 77 & 78. *Teaching:* Instr, Pa Acad Fine Arts & Fleisher Art Mem. *Awards:* Cresson Europ Scholar, Pa Acad Fine Arts, 61; Purchase Prize, Am Watercolor Soc, 72; First Prize Aqueous Media, Philadelphia Watercolor Club, 79. *Mem:* Am Watercolor Soc; Artists Equity. *Media:* Watercolor, Acrylic. *Dealer:* Pearl Fox Gallery 103 Windsor Ave Melrose Park PA 19126. *Mailing Add:* 2120 Spring St Philadelphia PA 19103

JOHNSON, IVAN EARL
EDUCATOR, CRAFTSMAN
b Denton, Tex, Sept 23, 11. *Study:* NTex State Univ, BA; Columbia Univ, MA; NY Univ, PhD. *Teaching:* Dir art, Ind Sch Dist, Dallas, Tex, 46-52; prof art educ, Fla State Univ, 52- *Awards:* Fla State Univ Grant for Study in Denmark, 71; Distinguished Service Awards, Southeastern Arts Asn, 80 & Fla Art Educators Asn, 80. *Mem:* Nat Art Educ Asn; Fla Art Educ Asn (mem bd, 60-61); Fla Coun Arts; Am Inst Designers. *Media:* Fabrics, Wood. *Res:* Investigation of evaluation instruments on basic color knowledge. *Publ:* Coauth, Design for Living, Laidlaw, 52; auth, Preparation of Art Teachers, Report of Commission on Art in Education, Nat Art Educ Asn, 69; auth, Relevance in art education, J Art Educ, 71. *Mailing Add:* Arts Educ Dept Fla State Univ Tallahassee FL 32304

JOHNSON, J SEWARD, JR
SCULPTOR, ADMINISTRATOR
b New York, NY, Apr 16, 30. *Study:* Univ Maine, 51; Harvard Univ, 66. *Work:* Vancouver Mus, Queen Elizabeth Park, BC; Morse Col, Yale Univ; Morris Mus, NJ; Hilton Head Island Inst Arts, SC; Exxon Park, Rockefeller Ctr, New York. *Comn:* The Awakening, Int Sculpture Conf, Washington, DC, 80; The Consultation, Univ Pa Hosp, Philadelphia, 82; four-piece installation, Richard Hughes Justice Complex, Trenton, NJ, 82; Taxi (life-sized bronze), Chemical Bank World Hq, New York, 83. *Exhib:* Mile of Sculpture Exhib, Chicago Arts Fair, 81; Bronze 82, Cheltenham Arts Coun, Pa, 82; 12th Int Sculpture Conf, Oakland, Calif, 83; Bronze Sculpture, Wave Hill Sculpture Park, New York, 83; Bronze at Washington Square, Washington, DC, 83-84; and others. *Pos:* Founder & pres, Johnson Atelier Inst, 74-; pres, Int Sculpture Ctr, 78. *Awards:* First Place, Design in Steel, US Steel Corp, 69, City Sculpture, Greenwich Art Coun, 82 & Citywide Survey, Washingtonian Mag, 83. *Bibliog:* Steven Brown (auth), article, Life Mag, 80; Steven DiLauro (auth), The foundry that makes sculptors dreams come true, Smithsonian Mag, 82; The Awakening: A narrative in bronze, Pub TV documentary, NJ Network, 82. *Mem:* Artists Equity. *Media:* Cast Metals. *Mailing Add:* c/o Sculpture Placement Suite 304 2828 Pennsylvania Ave Box 9709 Washington DC 20016

JOHNSON, J STEWART
CURATOR
b Baltimore, Md, Aug 31, 25. *Study:* Swarthmore Col, BA; Univ Del, Winterthur Prog in Early Am Cult, MA. *Pos:* Cur decorative arts, Newark Mus, 64-68; cur decorative arts, Brooklyn Mus, 68-73, vice dir collections, 70-72; consult contemp glass, Corning Mus Glass, 73-74; cur decorative arts, Cooper-Hewitt Mus Design, 75-76; cur design, Mus Mod Art, New York, 76- *Mem:* Victorian Soc Am (pres, 66-69); Am Friends of Attingham Park; Lockwood-Mathews Mansion, Norwalk, Conn. *Publ:* Auth, Eileen Gray: Designer, 79; auth, The Modern American Poster, 83. *Mailing Add:* Mus of Mod Art 11 W 53rd St New York NY 10019

JOHNSON, JAMES ALAN
PAINTER, EDUCATOR
b Malden, Mass, Apr 2, 45. *Study:* Mass Col Art, Boston, BFA, 67; Wash State Univ, Pullman, MFA, 70. *Work:* Denver Art Mus, Colo; Nebr Wesleyan Univ, Lincoln; Otis Art Inst Arch, Calif; Franklin Furnace Arch, New York; Tweed Mus, Univ Minn, Duluth. *Exhib:* One-man show, Nebr Wesleyan Univ, 75; Fifth Colo Ann, Denver Art Mus, 78; Artwords & Bookworks, Los Angeles Inst Contemp Art, Calif, 78; Univ Colo, Boulder, 80; Artists' Publications, Tweed Mus Art, Univ Minn, Duluth, 81; Artists' Books, Metronom Ctr de Documentacio d'Art Actual, Barcelona, Spain, 81; Showdown, Alternative Mus, New York, 83. *Teaching:* Asst prof painting & drawing, Univ Colo, Boulder, 70-78, assoc prof, 78- instr graphics, Dept of Archit, Wash State Univ, Pullman, 70. *Bibliog:* John Fisher (auth), James

Johnson at University of Colorado Art Galleries, Artspace, summer 81. *Media:* Mixed. *Publ:* Auth, Squares root two rectangles--matinal muses, Criss-Cross Art Commun, Vol 1 (1976); auth, Acrostics, Boulder, 79; auth, As Pretty as a Picture, Boulder, 80. *Mailing Add:* Fine Arts Dept Univ Colo Campus Bos 318 Boulder CO 80309

JOHNSON, JAMES EDWIN & SANDRA KAY
GRAPHIC DESIGNERS
James E, b Minneapolis, Minn, Feb 18, 42. Sandra K, b Minneapolis, Minn, Mar 3, 44. *Study:* James E, Col St Thomas, Minneapolis; Minn Col Art & Design, with Robroy Kelly & Joe Luca, BFA. Sandra K, Minneapolis Col Art & Design; Fed Regional Design Assembly Western States, Denver. *Work:* Minneapolis Col Art & Design; Nat Gallery Fine Arts. *Comn:* Bicentennial pinwheel (outdoor graphic wind piece), Ft Worth Art Mus, Tex, 76; commemorable collage, Dayton-Hudson Found. *Exhib:* James E, Making the City Observable, Int Design Conf, Aspen, Colo, 72; World Crafts Coun, Oaxtepec, Mex, 76; Images of an Era: The Am Poster 1945-1975 Int Traveling Exhib, 76; Exhib of Design Process, Clara M Eagle Gallery, Murray State Univ, 77. Sandra K, Alumni Exhib, Minneapolis Col Art & Design, 74. *Pos:* James E, graphic designer, Gen Mills & IBM Corp, 66-70; head graphic design dept, Walker Art Ctr, Minn, 70-78; James E & Sandra K, partners, Johnson plus Johnson Graphic Design, 78- *Teaching:* James E, Instr graphic design, Minneapolis Col Art & Design, 71-79; instr, Hamlin Univ, 74; vis lectr, St Cloud Univ, Univ Minn, Duluth, Bemidje Univ & Moorhead Univ. Sandra K, asst to chmn graphic design, Minneapolis Col Art & Design, 76-78. *Awards:* Cert Distinction, Creativity Eighty, 81; Oliver Award Merit, 81; Champion Papers Award, 82. *Bibliog:* Article, Design Quart 94/95, 75; The show awards exhib, Format Mag, 76; Publication design awards 1977, Soc Publ Designers, 77. *Mem:* Minn Graphic Designers Asn (James E, mem coun, 77); Am Inst Graphic Arts; James E, Soc Publ Designers; Fed Design Registry. *Publ:* James E, Designer, American Indian Art: Form and Tradition, Walker Art Ctr, 72; designers, The Great American Rodeo, Ft Worth Art Mus, 75. *Mailing Add:* 1800 Emerson Ave S Minneapolis MN 55403

JOHNSON, JAMES RALPH
PAINTER, WRITER
b Ft Payne, Ala, May 20, 22. *Study:* Howard Col, BS. *Exhib:* Death Valley Invitational, Calif, 73-81; one-man shows, NMex State Fair Fine Arts Gallery, Albuquerque, 73, 74 & 75; Art Barn Gallery, Ft Worth, Tex, 74; Saddleback Inn Roundup of Cowboy Art, Santa Ana, Calif, 74-82. *Awards:* Award of Merit, Prof Div, NMex State Fair, 73; Gov Purchase Prize, 75 & 77. *Bibliog:* Marian Love (auth), James Ralph Johnson, artist & author, Santa Fean Mag, 4-5/75; Royal Hassrick (auth), Western Painting Today, Watson-Guptill, 75; Peggy and Harold Samuels (auths), Contemporary Western Artists, 82. *Mem:* Artists Equity Asn (vpres, Santa Fe, 73); Am Indian & Cowboy Artists Soc; Grand Cent Art Galleries; Nat Western Artists; Sante Fe Soc Artists. *Media:* Acrylic, Oil. *Publ:* Auth & illusr, The Last Passenger, Macmillan, 56; auth & illusr, Utah Lion, Follett, 62; auth & illusr, Camels West, McKay, 64; auth & illusr, Animal Paradise, 69; auth & illusr, The Southern Swamps, 70; plus many others. *Mailing Add:* Box 5295 Santa Fe NM 87501

JOHNSON, JOYCE
SCULPTOR, INSTRUCTOR
b Newton, Mass, July 12, 29. *Study:* Escuela de Artes Oficios y Tecnicos, Madrid, Spain, study with Don Ramon Mateu, cert; Sch of Mus Fine Arts, Boston, study with Harold Tovish & Oscar Jespers, cert. *Work:* Cushing Acad, Ashburnham, Mass; Cape Cod Conserv, Barnstable, Mass; Provincetown Art Asn & Mus. *Exhib:* One-woman exhib, Annhurst Col, South Woodstock, Conn, 74; 20-Year Retrospective, Wellfleet Art Gallery, Mass, 77; Art in Transition--A Century of the Mus School, Mus Fine Arts, Boston, 77; Cape Cod Conserv, 83. *Pos:* Asst dir, Beaupre Arts Ctr, Stockbridge, Mass, 59-62; dir/founder, Nauset Sch Sculpture, North Eastham, Mass, 68-71; dir/co-founder, Truro Ctr for the Arts, Mass, 72-82, trustee 72-83, hon trustee, 83- *Teaching:* Instr sculpture from life, Cape Cod Conserv, Barnstable, Mass, 73-, Truro Ctr for the Arts, Truro, Mass, 74-82 & Provincetown Mus Sch, 83- *Bibliog:* Articles, Cape Arts, Vol 1, No 1, Cape Codder, 83 & Cape Cod Times, 83. *Mem:* Provincetown Art Asn (trustee, 76-78); Lower Cape Arts Coalition. *Media:* Mixed. *Mailing Add:* Box 201 Truro MA 02666

JOHNSON, KATE CHAMNESS See O'Meallie, Kitty

JOHNSON, KATHERINE KING
ADMINISTRATOR, PAINTER
b Lincoln, Nebr. *Study:* Univ Nebr Col Fine Arts, with Dwight Kirsh; Univ Vt, with Francis Colburn; also with Darwin Dunkin & Marshel Merritt, southern Calif. *Work:* Lyndon B Johnson Mem Libr, Austin, Tex; Bennington Mus Art & Hist, Vt; Fleming Mus, Burlington, Vt; Southern Vt Art Ctr, Manchester; Rutland Hosp Mem Collection, Vt. *Exhib:* Art to Live With Traveling Exhib, Southern Vt Art Asn, 49-50; Lyndon Baines Johnson Visitors Ctr, Stonewall, Tex, 67-68; Nat League Am Pen Women Nat Exhib, Vacardi Gallery, Miami, 74; Retrospective: Forty Years in the Creative Fields, 1940-1980, Rutland Area Art Asn, 80; solo exhib, Chaffee Art Gallery, Rutland, 83; and others. *Collections Arranged:* Humor in Art, commemorating 75th yr of the comicstrip & Honduras Art Loan Exhibit, 71; Gottlob Briem Mem Exhib, 72; Indian Art from Coast to Coast, 73; Living Arts from Africa, 74; Frederick Chaffee Mem Stamp Collection, 74. *Pos:* Founder, Rutland Area Art Asn Inc, 61, pres & exec dir, 61-74, chmn bd, 77-80, trustee, 82-; trustee, Chaffee Art Ctr, Rutland, 61-; designer, real estate develop, 61- *Awards:* President's Citation for Quality of Serv Rendered, Nat

League Am Pen Women, 74; Recognition Award/Art & Bus, Am Asn Univ Women, 77; Award of Merit, Vt Coun Arts, 77. *Mem:* Nat League Am Pen Women (br pres & state art chmn, 65, state pres, 73-74); Rutland Area Art Asn Inc, Vt; Southern Vt Artists Asn Inc; Vt Coun Arts. *Media:* Oil. *Mailing Add:* 40 Piedmont Pkwy Rutland VT 05701

JOHNSON, LEE
PAINTER, EDUCATOR
b Albion, Nebr, Nov 9, 35. *Study:* Minneapolis Col Art & Design, BFA; Skowhegan Sch Painting & Sculpture, with Alex Katz; Univ NMex, MA. *Work:* Denver Art Mus, Colo; Roswell Mus & Art Ctr, Roswell, NMex; Mus of NMex, Fine Arts, Santa Fe; Jonson Gallery, Univ NMex, Albuquerque, NMex; and others. *Exhib:* Watercolor USA, Springfield, Mo, 64; 1st Ann Painting Invitational, Mus of NMex, 68; Masterpieces from the Mus of NMex, McNay Art Inst, San Antonio, Tex, 70; Rocky Mountain Coun on Arts Traveling Exhib, Eight Western States, 72; 8 West Biennial, Grand Junction, Colo, 72-74. *Pos:* Asst dir-cur, Roswell Mus & Art Ctr, NMex, 62-68; dir, Gunnison Coun on Arts & Humanities, Colo, 73-75. *Teaching:* Instr drawing & painting, Eastern NMex Univ, Roswell, 62-67; asst prof drawing & painting, Western State Col, Gunnison, Colo, 68-81, assoc prof, 81- *Awards:* Five Artists from Colo Traveling Exhib, Rocky Mountain Coun on Arts, 71-72; First Prize Painting, 8 West Biennial, W Co Art Ctr, 74; Artist in Residence Grant, Roswell Mus & Art Ctr, 75. *Media:* Acrylic, Watercolor. *Dealer:* Carrie Kunzman Old Town Rd Albuquerque NM 87104. *Mailing Add:* 310 S Wisconsin Gunnison CO 81230

JOHNSON, LESTER F
PAINTER, EDUCATOR
b Minneapolis, Minn, Jan 27, 19. *Exhib:* Carnegie Int, Pittsburgh, 64, 68 & 72; Rosc '67, Dublin, Ireland; L'Art Vivant aux Etats-Unis Fondation, Maeght, France, 71; 10 Independents, Guggenheim Mus, New York, 72; Chicago Biennial, 72; 70th Am Exhib, Art Inst Chicago, 72; Minn Mus Art, 73; Whitney Mus Am Art, 73; Nat Acad Design, 74. *Teaching:* Prof painting & dir grad painting, Yale Univ, 65- *Awards:* Guggenheim Fel, 72. *Mailing Add:* c/o Gimpel & Weitzenhoffer 1040 Madison Ave New York NY 10021

JOHNSON, LESTER L
PAINTER, EDUCATOR
b Detroit, Mich, Sept 28, 37. *Study:* Wayne State Univ; Univ Mich, BFA, 73, MFA, 74. *Work:* Detroit Inst Arts; Osaka Univ Arts, Japan; Johnson Publ Co, Chicago; Sonnenblick-Goldman Corp, New York; City Hope Med Ctr, Los Angeles; and others. *Comn:* Urban Wall Mural, New Detroit, Living With Art Comt, 74; Detroit Workshop of Fine Prints, 74 & 76; Renaissance Ctr, Detroit Westin, 78; New Detroit Receiving Hosp, 80; Martin Luther King Community Ctr, Detroit, 82. *Exhib:* Whitney Mus Am Art, 71-73; Nat Afro-Am Exhib, Carnegie Inst, Pittsburgh, Pa, 71-72; one-man show, Flint Inst Arts, Mich, 72; Mich Focus, Detroit Inst Arts, 74-75; Midwest Black Artists Invitational, Milwaukee Performing Arts Ctr, 76; Source Detroit, Cranbrook Mus Art, 76; Henry Ward Ranger Nat Invitational, Nat Acad Design, New York, 77; Afro-Am Exhib, Detroit Inst Arts, 78; Black Artists in Mich, Detroit Hist Mus, 80; and others. *Teaching:* Instr drawing, Charles Stewart Mott Community Col, Flint, Mich, 71-73; assoc prof drawing & painting, Ctr Creative Studies, Col Art & Design, Detroit, 75- *Awards:* John S Newberry Purchase Prize, 54th Exhib Mich Artists, Detroit Inst Arts, 64; First Prize Painting, 69 & 73, Mich State Fair; Gallery Purchase Award, Harlem Gallery Sq, 72. *Mem:* Founders Soc, Detroit Inst Arts; hon mem Laguna Beach Art Asn. *Publ:* Contribr, Seven Black Artists, 69 & Misalliance, 69, Detroit Artists Mkt; contribr, Black Reflections, Flint Community Schs, 69-70; contribr, Gil Silverman Selects, Detroit Focus Gallery, 83. *Mailing Add:* Ctr Creative Studies/Col Art & Design 245 E Kirby St Detroit MI 48202

JOHNSON, LINCOLN FERNANDO
EDUCATOR, WRITER
b Lynn, Mass, May 21, 20. *Study:* Bowdoin Col, AB, 42; Harvard Univ, MA, 47, PhD, 56. *Pos:* Mem bd trustees, Md Inst Col of Art, Baltimore, 56-; mem, Munic Arts Comn, Baltimore, 60-61 & 77-; mem visual arts panel, Md Arts Coun, Baltimore, 69-; weekly art columnist, Baltimore Sun, 71-79; surveyor art in fed bldgs, US Gen Serv Admin, 72. *Teaching:* Vis prof art hist, Wellesley Col, 49-50; prof art hist, Goucher Col, 50-, chmn fine arts dept, 60-71 & 78- *Awards:* Bacon Fel, Harvard Univ, 48-49; Fulbright Scholar, 62; Award Merit, Artists Equity Asn, 76. *Mem:* Col Art Asn Am; Artists Equity; Univ Film Asn; Baltimore Film Forum. *Res:* International art, 1885-1910; history of film; 20th century art. *Publ:* Auth catalogs, Four Paris Painters, 62 & Art in 1914, 64, Baltimore Mus; auth, Amelie Rothschild Drawings, Goucher Col, 68; auth, Film: Space, Time, Light, Sound, Holt, Rinehart & Winston, 74. *Mailing Add:* c/o Dept Art Gowcher Col Towson MD 21204

JOHNSON, LOIS MARLENE
PRINTMAKER, EDUCATOR
b Grand Forks, NDak, Nov 1, 42. *Study:* Univ NDak, BS, 64; Univ Wis-Madison, MFA, 66. *Work:* Philadelphia Mus Art; Elvehjem Art Ctr, Madison; McCray Gallery, Univ NMex, Albuquerque; Univ NDak, Grand Forks; Adolph Behn Mem Collection, New York. *Comn:* Poster, Philadelphia Mus Art, 72. *Exhib:* Soc Am Graphic Artists, New York, 65-67, 70 & 71; Northwest Printmakers Int, Seattle, 68; Am Color Print Soc, 68-72; Silk Screen, Philadelphia Mus Art, 72; 18th Biennial Exhib, Brooklyn Mus, NY, 72; and others. *Teaching:* From asst prof to assoc prof printmaking & chmn dept, Philadelphia Col Art, 67- *Awards:* Abraham Hankins Award, Am Color Print Soc, 68; Award, Prints in Pa, 69; Eyre Medal, Philadelphia Watercolor Club, 71. *Mem:* Print Club; Am Color Print Soc (coun, 68-72); Philadelphia Watercolor Club (bd dirs, 72); Soc Am Graphic Artists; Philadelphia Art

Alliance. *Media:* Intaglio, Silkscreen. *Publ:* Contribr, Artist proof, Pratt Graphic Ctr, 67. *Dealer:* The Print Club 1614 Latimer St Philadelphia PA 19102. *Mailing Add:* Philadelphia Col Art Broad & Spruce Sts Philadelphia PA 19102

JOHNSON, (LEONARD) LUCAS
PAINTER, INSTRUCTOR
b Hartford, Conn, Oct 24, 40. *Study:* Univ Calif Los Angeles; Univ Hawaii. *Work:* Mus Mod Art, San Francisco; Mus Mod Art, Tel-Aviv, Israel; Brooklyn Mus; Inst Mex-Norteamericano, Mex; Smithsonian Inst. *Comn:* Four color lithographs, Masonite Co, Fibracel SA, Mexico City, Mex, 72. *Exhib:* Solo exhib, Univ Houston, 77; Image of Mexico Traveling Exhib, Gen Motors Permanent Collection; Pratt Inst Lithography Collection, traveling; Fire, Contemp Arts Mus, Houston, 79; Fac Show, Alfred C Glassell Sch Art, Houston, 80. *Teaching:* Instr watercolor, Alfred C Glassell Jr Sch of Art, Mus Fine Arts, Houston, 79- *Bibliog:* Tom Cranfield (auth), article in Tex Quart, 70; Ann Holmes (auth), Fantastic artists, Southwest Arts Mag, 72. *Media:* Oil, Watercolor. *Publ:* Illusr, Loss of Rivers, Azazel, 67; illusr, Moonshots, 67 & Pablo Neruda-early poems, 69, New Rivers; illusr, Master of Knives, Harmon, 70; illusr var works, Antaeus. *Mailing Add:* c/o Moody Gallery 2015J West Gray Houston TX 77019

JOHNSON, M L J
PAINTER, EDUCATOR
b Washington, DC, Oct 27, 47. *Study:* NY Univ Sch Art League, cert, 69; Brooklyn Col, BAMS, 76; City Univ, MFA, 78. *Work:* UN Univ, Los Angeles; Trenton State Mus, NJ; African Am Mus, Dallas; Bedford Stuyvesant Restoration Corp, New York. *Comn:* Mural, Bedstuy Restoration Art & Cult, Brooklyn, 75; Four Faces of St Joseph, comn by Brother Peter Russell, Montvale, NJ, 78. *Exhib:* Educator Exhib, Trenton State Mus, NJ, 77; Black & Hispanic Arts Festival I, Bedford Stuyvesant Restoration, Brooklyn, 80; Brooklyn 80, Brooklyn Mus, 80; Nat Conf Artists, African Am Mus, Dallas, 81; Ambience Stimuli, Alternative Mus, New York, 82; and others. *Teaching:* Art chmn, St Joseph Regional High Sch, 76-; artist in residence, Bedford Stuyvesant Art & Cult Ctr, 80. *Bibliog:* J W Watt (auth), Art briefs, Phoenix, 10/78; Harold Olejarz (auth), article, Arts Mag, 11/78; Che Baraka (auth), The executives, Daily Challenge, 2/80. *Mem:* Nat Conf Artists; Col Art Asn; Orgn Independent Artists. *Media:* Construction Relief. *Publ:* Illusr, Black Aesthetics, Donald Allen Publ, 75; contribr, Phoenix letters to downtown, Phoenix, 76; illusr, Ambience by Benny Andrews, Time Capsule, 81; contribr, New American art, Amsterdam News, 83; contribr, Festival group, Daily News, 83. *Mailing Add:* c/o Bedstuy Restoration Skylite Gallery 1368 Fulton St Brooklyn NY 11233

JOHNSON, MARGARET KENNARD
PRINTMAKER, EDUCATOR
b Madison, Wis, Feb 3, 18. *Study:* Col Wooster, Ohio, 36-38; Pratt Inst, Brooklyn, BFA, 41; Univ Mich, Master(design), 43. *Work:* Princeton Univ Graphics Collection, NJ; Minn Mus, Minneapolis; Am Embassy, Tokyo; Tochigi Prefectural Mus, Utsunomiya, Japan. *Comn:* Collage and Construction (with Victor D'Amico), Mus Mod Art, New York, 63; The Magic Muse, NJ State Mus, Trenton, 68; Portfolio I, II & III, Queenston Press, Princeton, NJ, 76-78. *Exhib:* NJ State Mus, Trenton, 66-69, 71 & 72; Newark Mus, NJ, 68; Int Print Soc, traveling, Brazil, Ger & Greece, 73 & 74; Sao Paulo Mus, Brazil, 73; and many others. *Teaching:* Acting asst prof, Drake Univ, Des Moines, 43-45; asst prof art, Tex State Col Women, Denton, 45-46; instr, Pratt Univ, Brooklyn, 46-49; instr, Mus Mod Art, New York, 46-71; instr, Princeton Adult Sch, NJ, 58-73; instr, Princeton Art Asn, NJ, 58-75; instr & lectr, Am Club, Tokyo, 81-82. *Awards:* Purchase Awards, NJ State Mus, 69 & Mercer Co Artists, 72 & 75. *Mem:* World Print Coun, San Franciso; Pratt Graphics Ctr, New York. *Media:* Intaglio. *Publ:* Contribr, Art for the family, Mus Mod Art, 60; contribr, printmaking article, Hangwa Geijutsu Quart, Tokyo, 78; coauth, Japanese Prints Today, Tradition with Innovation, Shufunotomo Publ, 80. *Dealer:* AAA Gallery 663 5th Ave New York NY 10021; Franell Gallery Okura Hotel Tokyo Japan. *Mailing Add:* Azabu Heights 711 1-5-10 Roppongi Minato-Ku Tokyo 106 08540 Japan

JOHNSON, MARIAN WILLARD
DEALER
b New York, NY, Apr 20, 04. *Pos:* Founder, East River Gallery, 36-38; assoc, Neumann-Willard Gallery, 38-40; owner & dir, Willard Gallery, 40-; chmn ad comt, Mus Mod Art, New York, 44-46, bd trustees & acquisitions comt, 44-46; chmn, Asia House Gallery, 59-, trustee, 61-, exec comt, 63-67; vpres, Mus Am Folk Art, 62-69, trustee, 62- & hon trustee, 74, secy, 71-73; bd overseers, Rose Art Gallery, Brandeis Univ, 65-69. *Specialty:* Contemporary American art. *Mailing Add:* Willard Gallery 29 E 72nd St New York NY 10021

JOHNSON, MARTIN BRIAN
PAINTER, SCULPTOR
b Elmer, NJ, May 2, 51. *Study:* Va Polytechnic Inst; Va State Univ, BArchit, 74; Univ NC, Chapel Hill, MFA, 77. *Work:* Ball State Univ, Muncie, Ind. *Exhib:* Icon Logos: The Word as Image, Alternative Mus, New York, 81; New York, Fine Arts Gallery, Fla State Univ, Tallahassee, 82; 20th Ann Exhib Vogel Collection, Brainard Art Gallery, State Univ NY, Potsdam, 82; Univ Northern Iowa, Cedar Rapids, 82; PS...PS1, 1701 E Main Gallery, Richmond, Va, 82. *Bibliog:* Allan Schwartzman (auth), article, Arts Mag, 1/80; Susan A Harris (auth), article, Arts Mag, 4/83; Donald B Kuspit (auth), article, Art Am, 9/83. *Media:* Mixed. *Dealer:* Phyllis Kind 136 Green St New York NY. *Mailing Add:* 118 West 83rd St New York NY 10024

JOHNSON, MIANI (MARIANNE) GUTHRIE
DEALER
b New York, NY, July 14, 48. *Study:* Barnard Col. *Pos:* Dir, Willard Gallery, currently. *Specialty:* Contemporary painting and sculpture. *Mailing Add:* 31 E 72nd St New York NY 10021

JOHNSON, NOTA
PRINTMAKER, PAINTER
b Maryville, Mo, Nov 20, 23. *Study:* Okla State Univ, with Doel Reed, BA, 45; Cincinnati Art Acad, cert(scholar), 46; Univ Tulsa, with Alexandre Hogue, MA, 73. *Work:* Furman Univ, Greenville, SC; Univ Miss, Oxford; Univ Tulsa; Cincinnati Art Acad; Okla State Univ, Stillwater. *Comn:* Carved oak altar gates, 81 & mural, 82, Greek Orthodox Church, Tulsa. *Exhib:* Audubon Artists Ann, 76-84; Nat Acad Design, New York, 77-81; World Art Expos, Hynes Auditorium, Boston, 79; US/USSR Mus, traveling, 79-82; Nat Asn Women Artists Ann, 79-84; First Ann Nat Greek Art Exhib, Springfield, Mass, 83; and others. *Teaching:* Art, Mem High Sch, Tulsa, 68-70; instr art, Tulsa Jr Col, 70- *Awards:* Graphics Award, 18th Ann, Mus Okla, 79; Hortense Ferne Mem Prize, 80 & Alice P Shafer Mem Prize, 82, Nat Asn Women Artists. *Mem:* Life mem Nat Asn Women Artists; life mem Audubon Artists; Visual Arts Comt Tulsa (comt mem, 76-81); Arts & Humanities Coun Tulsa (bd mem, 76-81); Southern Graphics Coun (vpres, 80-82). *Media:* Aquatint, Drypoint; Oil. *Dealer:* Mickelson Gallery 717 G St NW DC 20001. *Mailing Add:* 1500 S Frisco Tulsa OK 74119

JOHNSON, PHILIP CORTELYOU
COLLECTOR, ARCHITECT
b Cleveland, Ohio, July 8, 06. *Study:* Harvard Univ, AB, 30, Grad Sch Design, BA(archit), 43. *Comn:* Design of Mus Mod Art Annex & Sculpture Ct, NY State Theatre, Lincoln Ctr, New York, Glass House, New Canaan, Conn & Plaza of Seagram Bldg; and many others. *Pos:* Dir dept archit & design, Mus Mod Art, 30-36 & 46-54, trustee, 58- *Teaching:* Design critic, Cornell Univ & Yale Univ; instr, Pratt Inst; vis comt, Sch Design, Harvard Univ, 50-51; coun comt, Sch Art & Archit, Yale Univ, 59- *Awards:* Elsie DeWolfe Award, NY Chap, Am Inst Interior Designers, 65; Bronze Medallion, City New York, 79; Pritzker Prize, 79. *Mem:* Nat Inst Arts & Lett. *Collection:* Young Americans. *Publ:* Auth, Machine Art, 34; auth, Mies Van Der Rohe, rev ed 53; auth, Architecture, 1949-1965, 66; coauth, The International Style, rev ed 66. *Mailing Add:* 375 Park Ave New York NY 10022

JOHNSON, RAY
PAINTER
b Detroit, Mich, Oct 16, 27. *Study:* Art Students League; Black Mountain Col, with Josef Albers, Robert Motherwell, Mary Callery & Ossip Zadkine, 45-48. *Work:* Art Inst Chicago; Dulin Gallery; Houston Mus Fine Arts; De Cordova Mus, Lincoln, Mass; Mus Mod Art, New York. *Exhib:* Solo exhibs, Whitney Mus Am Art, New York, 70, Art Inst Chicago, 72, Gertrude Kasle Gallery, 75, Massimo Valsecchi Gallery, Milan, 75, NC Mus Art, Raleigh, 76, Sid Deutsch Gallery, New York, 76 & Brooks Jackson Gallery Iolas, New York, 78; Mus Fine Arts, Dallas, 74. *Pos:* Founder, New York Corresp Sch Art, 62- *Awards:* Nat Inst Arts & Lett Award, 66; Nat Endowment Arts Grant, 76; Creative Artists Pub Serv Prog Grant, 77. *Bibliog:* Becker et al (auth), Happenings, Fluxus, Pop, Nouveau Realism, Rowohlt Verlag GMBH, 65; Al Hansen (auth), A Primer of Happenings and Time/Space Art, Something Else Press, 65; John Russell & Suzi Gablik (auths), Pop Art Redefined, Praeger, 69. *Publ:* Auth, The Paper Snake, 65. *Mailing Add:* 44 W Seventh St Locust Valley NY 11560

JOHNSON, RICHARD A
PAINTER, EDUCATOR
b Minneapolis, Minn, Feb 26, 42. *Study:* Minneapolis Col Art & Design, BFA, 65; Washington Univ, St Louis, Mo, MFA, 67; Am Acad in Rome, fel, painting, Prix de Rome, Italy, 68. *Work:* Longview Mus Art, Tex; R J Reynolds Indus, Winston-Salem; Phillip Morris, New York; Pan Am Life, New Orleans; Katz & Bestoff Inc, New Orleans. *Exhib:* Walker Biennial, Walker Art Ctr, Minneapolis, 66; Tex Painting & Sculpture, Dallas Mus Fine Arts, 71; Photo Realism & Abstract Illusionism, Pittsburgh Arts & Crafts Ctr, 78; Operation Update 1979, Longview Mus, Tex, 79; Reality of Illusion, Denver Mus Art, 79; Illusion, Southeastern Ctr Contemp Art, Winston-Salem, NC, 83. *Teaching:* Chmn, Dept Fine Arts, Univ New Orleans, 79-, instr painting, 80, assoc prof painting, drawing & design, currently. *Awards:* Rockefeller Artist in Residence Grant, Southeastern Ctr Contemp Art, Winston-Salem, NC, 80. *Bibliog:* Mary King (auth), Two artists on display, St Louis Post-Dispatch, Mo, 5/74; Ted Calas (auth), Art scene, Figaro Newspaper, New Orleans, 10/79; Harry Schwalb (auth), Trick and treat, Pittsburgher Mag, Vol 2, No 8, 79. *Mem:* Artists' Equity Asn La (vpres, 76-78). *Media:* Mixed. *Dealer:* Galerie Simonne Stern 2727 Prytania St New Orleans LA 70130; Watson-DeNagy 1106 Berthea Houston Tex. *Mailing Add:* Fine Arts Dept Univ New Orleans New Orleans LA 70148

JOHNSON, ROBERT FLYNN
CURATOR, HISTORIAN
b Jersey City, NJ, Mar 20, 48. *Pos:* Cur asst, Worcester Art Mus, Mass, summer 72; asst cur prints & drawings, Baltimore Mus Art, 73-75; cur in chg, Achenbach Found Graphic Arts, Fine Arts Mus San Francisco, 75- *Awards:* Nat Endowment Arts Fel, 75. *Mem:* Print Coun Am; Print & Drawing Soc of Baltimore Mus Art (vpres, 74-75); Bay Area Graphic Arts Coun. *Res:* American prints of the 19th and 20th century; 19th century French drawings. *Publ:* Auth, American Prints, 1870-1950, Univ Chicago Press, 76. *Mailing Add:* Achenbach Found Graphic Arts Lincoln Park San Francisco CA 94121

JOHNSON, ROBERT JAY
DEALER, COLLECTOR
b Battlecreek, Mich, June 26, 51. *Pos:* Lectr, Long Island Hist Soc & Abigail Adams Smith Mus, 79. *Bibliog:* Film: Handel Film Corp, Art in Am Ser, 79. *Mem:* Mus Am Folk Art; Nat Hist Trust; Mus City New York; Am Mus, Bath, Eng. *Res:* American decorative arts specializing in folk art. *Specialty:* American folk art. *Collection:* Early American folk paintings, Shaker furniture, painted furniture and articles. *Mailing Add:* Jay Johnson Am Folk Heritage Gallery 1044 Madison Ave New York NY 10021

JOHNSON, RODELL C
PAINTER, ANIMATOR
b Spring Valley, Minn, July 29, 13. *Study:* Stanford Univ, with Edward Farmer & Daniel Mendelowitz, BA, 37; Walt Disney Prods Sch, with Don Graham, Rico Lebrun, Eugene Fleury & Homer Shoppee, 37-41; also with Joseph Rossi & Nicholas Reale, 74-75. *Exhib:* NJ Watercolor Soc, 72, 73, 76, 77 & 80-83; Salmagundi Club Open, New York, 78; Frye Mus, Seattle, 78; Anchorage Mus, 78; Purdue Univ, 79; NJ State Sr Art Exhib, State Mus NJ, Trenton, 82 & 83; and others. *Pos:* Animator, Walt Disney Prods, Burbank, Calif, 37-41 & Famous Studios, New York, 47-49; chief animation branch, US Army Signal Corp Photog Ctr, 41-46; dir & animator, five animated commercial, educ & entertainment motion picture studios, New York, 50-78. *Teaching:* Instr watercolor & drawing, Adult Sch, Chatham, NJ, 74-78; private instr watercolor, Bay Head, NJ, 78-83. *Awards:* John Bermingham Award, NJ Watercolor Soc Ann Open Exhib, 76; NJ Sr Art Exhib Watercolor Award, State Mus NJ, 82. *Bibliog:* Nancy Kingman (auth), article, Madison, NJ Eagle, 4/24/75; Sanne Young (auth), article, Asbury, NJ, Press, 8/26/82; Kathy Ferris (auth), article, Point Pleasant, NJ, Leader, 8/4/83. *Mem:* NJ Watercolor Soc (vpres, 80 & 81); Guild Creative Arts, Shrewsbury, NJ; Ocean Co Artists Guild, NJ. *Media:* Watercolor. *Mailing Add:* 348 East Ave Bay Head NJ 08742

JOHNSON, RONALD W
HISTORIAN, EDUCATOR
b Rockford, Ill, July, 29, 37. *Study:* Calif State Univ, San Diego, BA, 59 & MA, 63; Univ Calif, Berkeley, MA(hist art), 65 & PhD(hist art), 71. *Teaching:* Asst prof hist art, Univ Iowa, Iowa City, 70-73; prof hist art, Humboldt State Univ, Arcata, Calif, 73 ; vis instr hist art, Univ Calif, San Diego, 76; vis instr hist art, Univ Calif, Berkeley, 81. *Mem:* Col Art Asn Am. *Res:* Picasso and late 19th century art; emphasizing conceptual relationships between art and poetry. *Publ:* Auth, Picasso's old guitarist and the symbolist sensibility, Artforum, 12/74; auth, Dante Rossetti's Beata Beatridx and the new life, Art Bulletin, 12/75; auth, Poetic pathways to Dada: Marcel Duchamp & Jules Laforgue, 5/76, auth, Vincent van Gogh and the vernacular: His southern accent, 6/78 & auth, Picasso's Demoiselles d'Avignon and the theatre of the absurd, 10/80, Arts. *Mailing Add:* 1717 H Street Arcata CA 95521

JOHNSON, RUBIDOUX EARLY See Rubidoux

JOHNSON, SELINA (TETZLAFF)
MUSEOLOGIST, HISTORIAN
b New York, NY. *Study:* Hunter Col, AB(cum laude); City Col New York, MS(educ); Ctr Human Relations Studies, NY Univ, PhD(museology). *Work:* Bergen Community Mus Art & Sci, Paramus, NJ; Mus Natural Sci, Nantucket Island, Mass. *Comn:* Mem plaque for Hans Christian Andersen Madison, Bergen Mall, 59; Report on Museum Needs & Resources, 68 & Tricentennial History of Bergen County, NJ, 83, Bd Chosen Freeholders. *Exhib:* Fine Arts in Com Art, 3rd Ann Exhib, Freedom House, New York, 59; Painting & Sculpture Ann, Bergen Co Artists' Guild, 60; Photographic Art of Selina Johnson & Louis Davidson, Art Asn, Nantucket Island, Mass, 61; Books Illustrated by NJ Artists, Johnson Libr, Hackensack, NJ, 69; 25th Anniv Exhib, Bergen Community Mus, 81. *Pos:* Founder, dir & first pres, Bergen Community Mus, 56-70; dir, Mus Natural Sci, Nantucket Island, Mass, 59-65; Bergen Co Cult & Heritage Comnr, NJ, 72-83; cur, Greater Light, Nantucket Island, 73-; biol & med illusr, City Col New York & Harvard Univ, formerly. *Teaching:* Instr kinesiology & phys educ, Hunter Col, formerly; instr comp anat & biol, NY Univ & City Col New York, formerly; guest lectr landscape archit, Columbia Univ, formerly. *Awards:* First Prize Art, 51 & First Prize Photog, 65, 67 & 69, NJ State Fedn Women's Clubs. *Bibliog:* Clifford Mische (auth), Museum in Overpeck Park, Bergen Co Park Comn, 56; Georgianne Ensign (auth), The Hunt for the Mastodon, Watts, 71; Barbara Dexter (auth), History of Bergen Community Museum, 83. *Mem:* Life mem New York Acad Sci; life mem Caduceus Soc; life mem Maria Mitchell Asn; life mem Bergen Community Mus. *Publ:* Auth, Creating a Community Museum, 54; ed, Greater Light on Nantucket, Hill House, 73; auth & illusr, Bergen County, NJ--History: The Land and Its First Inhabitants, Vol I, Bd Chosen Freeholders, 83. *Mailing Add:* 24 Hawthorne Terr Leonia NJ 07605

JOHNSON, UNA E
CURATOR, WRITER
b Dayton, Iowa. *Study:* Univ Chicago, PhD, 28; Western Reserve Univ, MA, 37. *Collections Arranged:* All exhibs of prints & drawings, Brooklyn Mus, 41-68. *Pos:* Cur prints & drawings, Brooklyn Mus, 41-68, emer cur. *Awards:* Rockefeller Found Award, 52. *Publ:* Auth, Ambroise Vollard, 44 & rev ed, 77; auth, American Prints, 1660, 50; auth, What is a Modern Print, 56; auth, Twentieth Century Drawings, 1900-, 2 Vols, 64; auth, American Prints and Printmakers, 1900-, 80; and numerous monogr on mod artists including Bonnard, Rouault, Louise Nevelson & others. *Mailing Add:* 341 W 24th St New York NY 10011

JOHNSTON, BARRY WOODS
SCULPTOR

b Florence, Ala. *Study:* Ga Inst Technol, BS, 69; Art Students League, with Joseph De Creeft; Pa Acad Fine Arts, with Walker Hancock, Harry Rosen & Tony Greenwood; Nat Acad Fine Arts, with Michael Lantz; also studied in Italy, with Enzo Cardini & Madame Simi. *Comn:* Medal, Ann Letelier Moffitt Award, Inst Policy Studies, Washington, DC; Journey to Jerusalem, US Citizens Cong, Washington, DC; lobby centerpiece, Fentress Cancer Ctr, Hillside Methodist Hosp, Waco, Tex; Sen Sparkman bust, C of C, Hartsell, Ala; Wedlock (sculpture), Lafayette Ctr, Washington, DC. *Exhib:* One-man shows, St John's Church, 75, George Washington Univ Libr, 76 & Folger Shakespeare Libr, 79, Washington, DC; Four Realists, Foundry, Georgetown, 76; Nat Sculpture Soc Ann Group Show, New York, 80-83; Martin Luther King Libr, 83. *Awards:* Stewardson Award, Pa Acad Fine Arts, 66; Second Prize for Figurative Sculpture, Ga Marble Fest, 83. *Mem:* Nat Sculpture Soc; Founder, Art For Humanity Found (pres, 78-81). *Media:* Clay, Bronze. *Mailing Add:* 1622 Que St NW Washington DC 20009

JOHNSTON, HELEN HEAD
DEALER

b Atlanta, Ga. *Study:* Univ Ga, AB. *Collections Arranged:* Mounted more than 250 photog exhibs, Focus Gallery, San Francisco, 66-81. *Pos:* Dir publicity, M H DeYoung Mem Mus, Golden Gate Park, San Francisco, 53-65; dir, Focus Gallery, 66- *Awards:* Award for outstanding contribution to photography in Calif, Prof Photogr Northern Calif, 68; Second Ann Dorothea Lange Award, Oakland Mus, 72. *Mem:* Western Asn Art Mus; Asn Int Photog Art Dealers. *Specialty:* Photographs. *Mailing Add:* Focus Gallery 2146 Union St San Francisco CA 94123

JOHNSTON, JUNE FRAZIER
PAINTER, COLLAGE ARTIST

b Tarpon Springs, Fla, Jan 5, 27. *Study:* Ga State Univ, BA, 55; Fla State Univ, MA, 56; with Dong Kingman, Edward Betts, William Dunlap, Anton Weiss & Christopher Schink. *Work:* State Ga, Atlanta; Univ Ga, Athens; Nat Asn Co, Washington, DC; Brown & Williamson Tobacco Corp, Louisville, Ky. *Comn:* Watercolor collage (tryptich), Citicorp, Atlanta, 81; watercolor (abstract dyptich), IBM Corp, Charlotte, NC, 82; watercolor collages, Nissan Corp, Smyrna, Tenn, 83 & Guaranty Nat Bank, Tulsa, 83. *Exhib:* Butler Inst Am Art Midyear Show, 79; solo exhib, Asheville Mus, NC, 80 & Quinlan Art Ctr, Gainesville, Ga, 81; Nat Watercolor Soc, Laguna Mus, Calif, 81 & Palm Desert Mus, Calif, 84; Ky Watercolor Soc, J B Speed Mus, 83; Ga Watercolor Soc, High Mus Art, 83; Sea Grant Collection, Fla State Mus, Gainesville, 84. *Awards:* Merit Award, Ky Aqueous, 82; Third Prize, Southern Watercolor Soc, 83; 63 Ann Exhib Award, San Diego Watercolor Soc, 83. *Mem:* Nat Watercolor Soc; Artists Equity; Southern Watercolor Soc; Ga Watercolor Soc; NMex Watercolor Soc. *Media:* Watercolor, Collage. *Mailing Add:* 355 Wildwood Dr Watkinsville GA 30677

JOHNSTON, PHILLIP M
CURATOR

b Texarkana, Tex, July 24, 44. *Study:* Baylor Univ, BA(cum laude), 66; Southern Methodist Univ, MA, 68; Univ Del, MA, 74. *Collections Arranged:* Mark Twain in Hartford, 74, Victorian Furnishings from Armsmear and the James Goodwin House, 75, American Indian Baskets in the Wadsworth Atheneum, 76, Ancient Art of Peru: the Etherington Collection, 76, Glass from Six Centuries, 76 & Art in Seventeenth Century New England (auth, catalog), 77, Wadsworth Atheneum; Gerrit Thomas Rietveld, Designer (auth, catalog), 80. *Pos:* Assoc cur dept decorative arts, Wadsworth Atheneum, Hartford, Conn, 73-75; cur decorative arts, 75-78, chief cur & cur decorative arts, 78-82; cur decorative arts & head antiquities, Oriental & decorative art, Mus Art, Carnegie Inst, Pittsburgh, Pa, 82- *Teaching:* Instr dept English, Hannibal-LaGrange Col, Mo, 67-68 & Southern Methodist Univ, 68-71. *Res:* Wallace Nutting and related collections of 17th and early 18th century American furniture in the Wadsworth Atheneum. *Publ:* Auth, A discovery of Thomas Chippendale chairs in America, Connoisseur, 73; ed, English Silver: The Elizabeth B Miles Collection, Wadsworth Atheneum, 76; auth, Eighteenth and nineteenth century American furniture in the Wadsworth Atheneum, Antiques, 79. *Mailing Add:* Carnegie Inst Mus Art 4400 Forbes Ave Pittsburgh PA 15213

JOHNSTON, RICHARD M
SCULPTOR, EDUCATOR

b Kankakee, Ill, Sept 22, 42. *Study:* El Camino Jr Col; Calif State Col, Long Beach, BA; Cranbrook Acad Art, MFA. *Work:* Weber State Col; Salt Lake Co Bar Asn; Cranbrook Acad of Art. *Comn:* Steel wall sculpture, Western Airlines, Los Angeles, 69; bronze wall sculpture, Telemation Inc, Salt Lake City, Utah, 71; gold leaf/steel sculpture, Sun Valley Ski Corp, Idaho, 71; Temple Kol Ami, Salt Lake Int Ctr. *Exhib:* Craftsman USA, Los Angeles Co Mus Art, 66; Nat Crafts Exhib, Univ NMex, 68; Inter-Mountain Biennial, Salt Lake Art Ctr, 70; 73rd Western Ann, Denver Art Mus, 71; Nat Small Sculpture & Drawing Show, San Diego State Col, 72; one-man show, Salt Lake Art Ctr, 80. *Teaching:* Prof, Univ Utah, 68- *Awards:* First Prize, Sterling Silversmiths, 68; Purchase Award, Utah Mus Fine Art, 69; Purchase Award, Salt Lake Art Ctr, 70. *Media:* Metal. *Mailing Add:* Dept of Art Univ of Utah Col Fine Arts Salt Lake City UT 84112

JOHNSTON, ROBERT HAROLD
ADMINISTRATOR, CRAFTSMAN

b Reading, Pa, July 1, 28. *Study:* Kutztown State Col, BS(art educ), 51; Columbia Univ, MA(fine arts & fine arts educ), 54; Pa State Univ, PhD(ceramic archaeol), 70. *Pos:* Art ed, Biblical Archaeologist, 72-; sr conserv officer, Semetic Mus, Harvard Univ; res consult, Dominican Repub, 83. *Teaching:* Vis lectr art, Grad Sch, Rutgers Univ, 54-58; asst prof art, Lock Haven State Col, Pa, 58-65, chmn & head dept, 58-70, assoc prof, 64-70; prof ceramics, Sch for Am Craftsmen, Rochester Inst Technol, 70-, dean, Col Fine & Applied Arts, 70-, dean, Inst, 82-83. *Awards:* Grant-in-aid res, Am Schs Oriental Res, 73; affil Fulbright scholar, Afghanistan, 73-74; John D Rockefeller Third Found Ceramic & Glass res grant, Afghanistan, 74. *Mem:* World Crafts Coun; Am Crafts Coun; Nat Asn Schs Art; fel Am Anthrop Asn; Am Asn Univ Profs. *Res:* Ceramic archaeology; glass and clay technology. *Publ:* Auth, The aborigines of Cawichnowane, Lock Haven Bulletin, Ser 1(2); auth, The aborigines of Cawichnowane II, Pa Archaeologist, 12/61; auth, A statistical approach to archaeology, New World Antiquity, Vol 11(11-12), Markham House Press Ltd, London, Eng; auth, A statistical analysis of 1113 weapon points from the area related to Cawichnowane, Lock Haven Bulletin, Ser 1(4); auth, The School for American Craftsmen, Handweaver & Craftsman, 3-4/72; and many others. *Mailing Add:* 61 Lime Rock Lane Rochester NY 14610

JOHNSTON, ROBERT PORTER
EDUCATOR, SCULPTOR

b Philadelphia, Pa, Oct 25, 24. *Study:* Pa State Univ, BA & MA; Pa Acad Fine Arts; Philadelphia Print Club Workshop; Graphic Sketch Club, Philadelphia; Univ Wyo, MA; Univ Pa; Mich State Univ; also with Francis Speight, Walker Hancock, Harold Dickson & Francis Hyslop. *Comn:* Christ the King (bronze), Martin Luther Chapel, East Lansing, Mich, 64; Dr Dwight Rich (two bronzes), Lansing Community Col & D Rich Jr High Sch, Mich, 66; Drs Dunbar, Friedmann & Knauss (bronze), Western Mich Univ, Kalamazoo, 72 & Dr James W Miller, 74; Wacky Olson (bronze), Olson Hockey Arena, Marquette, Mich, 75; Dorothy U Dalton (bronze), Dalton Ctr, Western Mich Univ, 83. *Exhib:* One-man shows, Beadsley Art Gallery, Omaha, Nebr, 60, King Gallery, Kalamazoo, 75 & Gallery 2, Western Mich Univ, 81; Small Sculpture & Drawing Ann, Ball State Univ, Ind, 63; 5th Minn Artists' Biennial, Minneapolis Inst Arts, 67; Kalamazoo Art Inst, 75 & 78; and others. *Teaching:* Instr art, Northwood Sch, Lake Placid, NY, 48-49; asst prof, Hastings Col, Nebr, 58-63; instr, Lansing Community Col, Mich, 64-66; asst prof, Mankato State Univ, Minn, 66-67; assoc prof, Western Mich Univ, 67-79, prof, 79-; vis prof, Kalamazoo Col, 71 & St Mary's Col, Notre Dame, Ind, 74-75. *Awards:* Hon Mention, All-Nebr Exhib, Univ Nebr, 59; Recommended for Purchase, Springfield Art Mus, Mo, 62; Ford Foundation Grant, 77. *Mem:* Col Art Asn Am; Nat Asn Schs Art & Design; fel Pa Acad Fine Arts; Mich Acad Sci, Arts & Lett (treas fine arts sect, 70-74). *Res:* American and Afro-American art. *Publ:* Auth, articles and reviews in Mich Academician, Art, 71, Art Journal, 71, 73 & 79, and Minority Voices, 77, 78 & 79; Mich League of Handweavers, Newsletter, summer 80. *Mailing Add:* Dept of Art Western Mich Univ Kalamazoo MI 49008

JOHNSTON, THOMAS ALIX
PRINTMAKER, PAINTER

b Oklahoma City, Okla, June 4, 41. *Study:* San Diego State Col, BA, 65; Univ Calif, Santa Barbara, MFA, 65; Atelier 17, Paris, 80. *Work:* Henry Art Gallery, Univ Wash, Seattle; Portland Art Mus; Seattle Art Mus, Wash; Mod Art Mus, Kobe, Japan; Cheney Cowles Mus, Spokane, Wash; and others. *Exhib:* One-man show, Whatcom Mus, Bellingham, Wash, 71; 52nd Biennial, Libr Cong, Washington, DC; NW Ann, Seattle Art Mus, Wash, 72; W Coast Prints, Univ Calgary, Alta, 75; Rochester Inst Technol, 78; Evergreen State Col, Wash, 80; Traver Gallery, Seattle, 80; Black and White Drawings by 150 Americans 1970-1980, Brooklyn Mus, 80. *Pos:* Vis artist, Univ Lethbridge, Can, 70, Univ Calgary, Alta, 75 & Evergreen State Col, 80; vis prof, Intercambio Cult, Guadalajara, Mex, spring 76. *Teaching:* Prof art, Western Wash Univ. *Awards:* Purchase Award, 18th NW Printmakers Ann, Henry Gallery, Univ Wash, 67; First Place/Graphics, 14th Northern Calif Ann, Calif State Univ, Chico, 70; Purchase Award, 57th NW Ann, Seattle Art Mus, Wash, 72. *Bibliog:* William Ritchie (video interview), Thomas Johnston, Univ Wash, 70; L Hanson (auth), Seven from Washington, Wash State Arts Comn, 71; and others. *Media:* Intaglio. *Publ:* Illusr, Concerning Poetry, Western Wash Univ, 73 & 80; illusr, The Ventriloquist, R Huff, Univ Press Va, 77; Beyond the veil: the etching of Helen Loggie, Whatcom Mus, 79. *Mailing Add:* 1514 Bellevue Ave 711 Seattle WA 98122

JOHNSTON, WILLIAM MEDFORD
PAINTER, EDUCATOR

b Atlanta, Ga, Mar 2, 41. *Study:* Ga State Univ, BA, 65; Fla State Univ, MFA, 67. *Work:* High Mus Art, Atlanta, Ga; Chase Manhattan Bank, New York; Ft Worth Nat Bank, Tex; Mus Fine Art, Houston, Tex; Omni Int Hotel, Atlanta, Ga & Miami, Fla. *Comn:* Three panel paintings (4ft x 8ft each), 77 & 350 graphics, 77, Omni Int Hotel, Miami, Fla. *Exhib:* High Mus Art, Atlanta, Ga, 68, 75 & 79; Biennial Piedmont Painting & Sculpture, Mint Mus, Charlotte, NC; 18th Ann Drawing & Small Sculpture Show, Ball State Univ, Muncie, Ind, 72; Tex Fine Arts Asn Ann, Laguna Gloria Art Mus, Austin, 75 & 80; LaGrange Nat Competition, LaGrange Col, Ga, 74, 75 & 77; three-man show, Ga State Univ, Atlanta, 76; From Allan to Zucker, Tex Gallery, Houston, 79; Portland Ctr Visual Arts, Ore, 80; and others. *Teaching:* Prof painting, Ga State Univ, 67- *Awards:* Purchase Award, 10th Hunter Ann, Chattanooga Art Asn, 69; Soc of Four Arts Award, 32nd Ann Exhib of Contemp Am Painting, 70; Arts Festival Atlanta, 80. *Bibliog:* Clyde Burnett (auth), var rev in The Atlanta J, 72-78; John Howett (auth), Medford Johnston, Art Voices S, 1/78; John Howett (auth), The Avant-Garde: 12 in Atlanta, 79. *Media:* Acrylic. *Mailing Add:* 145 15th St NE Apt 828 Atlanta GA 30361

JOHNSTON, WILLIAM RALPH
HISTORIAN, ADMINISTRATOR
b Toronto, Ont, Feb 15, 36. *Study:* Univ Toronto Trinity Col, Hon BA, 59; NY Univ Inst Fine Arts, MA, 66. *Collections Arranged:* Anatomy of a Chair: Regional Variations in 18th Century Furniture Styles, Metrop Mus, New York, 62; J W Morrice (with catalog), Montreal Mus Fine Arts, Nat Gallery Can, 68; William & Henry Walters, Collectors & Patrons, Walters Art Gallery, 74-75. *Pos:* Cur, Robert Lehman Collection, New York, 64-66; gen cur, Montreal Mus Fine Arts, 66-68; asst dir, Walters Art Gallery, 68- *Awards:* Fel, Am Wing, Metrop Mus Art, 63-64. *Mem:* Am Ceramic Circle; Victorian Soc Am; Am Fedn Arts. *Res:* 18th and 19th century painting and decorative arts. *Publ:* Auth, W H Stewart, the American patron of Mariano Fortuny, Gazette des Beaux-Arts, 71; coauth, Japonisme, Cleveland Mus; auth, The Nineteenth Century Paintings in The Walters Art Gallery, Baltimore, 82; coauth, Alfred jacob Miller, Artist on the Oregon Trail, Fort Worth, 82. *Mailing Add:* Walters Art Gallery 600 N Charles St Baltimore MD 21201

JOHNSTON, YNEZ
PAINTER, PRINTMAKER
b Berkeley, Calif, May 12, 20. *Study:* Univ Calif, Berkeley, MFA, 46. *Work:* Mus Mod Art, Whitney Mus Am Art, Metrop Mus Art, New York; Hirshhorn Mus and Sculpture Garden, Washington, DC; Milwaukee Art Ctr, Wis; plus others. *Comn:* Etchings, Int Graphic Arts Soc, New York; drawings, Washington Gallery Mod Art, Washington, DC, 65; etchings, Roten Galleries, Baltimore, Md, 66-67; etching, Los Angeles Co Mus, 81. *Exhib:* One-man retrospective, San Francisco Mus Art, 67; Four Printmakers, Calif Inst Technol, 69; Wiener Gallery, New York, 77; Mitsukoshi Galleries, Tokyo, Japan, 77; Mekler Gallery, Los Angeles, 72, 74, 77 & 82; Worthington Gallery, Chicago, 83; and others. *Teaching:* Instr etching, Colorado Springs Fine Arts Ctr, 54-56 & Univ Judaism, 67; instr painting, Calif State Univ, Los Angeles, 66-67, 69 & 72-73; instr, Otis Art Inst of Parsons Sch of Design, Los Angeles, 78-81; artist in residence, Fullerton Col, 82. *Awards:* Tiffany Award in Painting & Graphics, 55 & 56; Tamarind Wookshop Grant, Ford Found; Nat Endowment for Arts, 76. *Bibliog:* Jules Langsner (auth), Ynez Johnston, Arts & Archit, 51; Gerald Nordland (auth), West Coast in review, Arts Mag, 61; John Berry (auth), View from the wind palace, Mankind Mag, 75. *Media:* Oil, Watercolor; Etching. *Dealer:* Mekler Gallery 651 N La Cienega Los Angeles CA 90069; Worthington Gallery 233 E Ontario St Chicago IL 60611. *Mailing Add:* 579 Crane Blvd Los Angeles CA 90065

JOHNSTONE, MARK (DAVID)
CRITIC, EDUCATOR
b St Louis, Mo, 1953. *Study:* Colo Col, BA, 75; Univ Southern Calif, MFA, 82. *Work:* Calif Mus Photog, Univ Calif, Riverside; Crocker Art Mus, Sacramento, Calif; Centro Documentazioni Arti Visive E Archivo/Rosamilia, San Giorgio, Italy. *Exhib:* One-man show, Vista: Some Landscape Observations, Calif Mus Photog, Riverside, 81. *Pos:* Contrib ed, Artweek, 77-; Los Angeles corresp, Afterimage, 81-; series content adv, The Photographic Vision, KOCE-TV, Huntington Beach, Calif, 83-84. *Teaching:* Instr photog, Univ Southern Calif, Los Angeles, 77-80; vis prof photog, Colo Col, Colorado Springs, summers 79-; lectr hist photog, Calif State Univ, Fullerton, 81- *Mem:* Soc Photog Educ. *Res:* Contemporary photography. *Publ:* Auth, Art in corporate places, Afterimage/Visual Studies Workshop, 11/80; auth, Landscape: Perceiving the land as image intro, New Landscapes, Friends of Photog, 81; auth, John Divola: Facts of the imagination, Exposure & Camera, 7-8/81. *Mailing Add:* PO Box 1279 Inglewood CA 90308

JOLLES, ARNOLD H
MUSEUM DIRECTOR, CONSERVATOR
b US, Jan 9, 40. *Study:* Univ Chicago, BA(hist of art); Art Inst Chicago, 6 yr apprenticeship in conservation of paintings with Alfred Jakstas. *Pos:* Asst conservator, Art Inst Chicago, 67-68; conservator, Minneapolis Inst of Arts, 68-74; asst dir for art, Philadelphia Mus Art, 74-77, actg dir, 77-79; dir, Seattle Art Mus, 79- *Mailing Add:* Seattle Art Mus Volunteer Park Seattle WA 98112

JOLLEY, DONAL CLARK
PAINTER
b Zion Nat Park, Utah, Oct 20, 33. *Study:* Brigham Young Univ, BS, 59; with Robert E Wood, Millard Sheets, William Smith, Virginia Cobb, R H Meltzer & Mort Solberg, 77. *Work:* First Nat Bank Nev, Reno; Santa Fe Fed Savings & Loan, Rialto, Calif; Aerospace Corp, El Segundo, Calif. *Exhib:* Watercolor West Ann, Riverside Art Ctr Mus, Calif, 75-81; one-man shows, Brigham Young Univ, 75 & 81 & Univ Nev, Reno, 78; Traditional Artists, San Bernardino Co Mus, Redlands, 76-79 & Fine Arts Inst, 78-79; and others. *Pos:* Jr illusr, Space Technol Lab, Redondo, Calif, 60-61; sr illusr, Aerospace Corp, El Segundo, Calif, 61-71. *Teaching:* Instr painting, San Bernardino Valley Col, 73-81. *Awards:* First Place, San Bernardino Fine Arts Inst, 78-81; Brand XII Award, 83; Riverside Centennial Award, 83. *Bibliog:* Rosemary Hite (auth), Donal Jolley, Southwest Art, 3/80; Fred Kiemel (auth), Making a presentation brochure self-promotion, Camera Life Mag, 5/80; Peggy & Harold Samuels (auths), Contemporary Western Artists, 82. *Mem:* Nat Watercolor Soc; Watercolor West (vpres, 78 & 79); San Bernardino Fine Arts Inst (bd mem, 78 & 79); Whiskey Painters Am. *Media:* Watercolor, Acrylic. *Dealer:* In The Spirit Gallery 1911A West 45th Ave Kansas City KS 66103. *Mailing Add:* 26375 Apache Trail Rimforest CA 92378

JOLLEY, GERALDINE H (JERRY)
PAINTER, SCULPTOR
b Geneva, NY, June 14, 11. *Study:* Rochester Inst Technol, with Margaret Weston & Ehrich; Rochester Mem Art Mus, with Francis Denny; Univ Wash;

also with Cora Scofield Johnson, New York, Richard Yip & Eliot O'Hara. *Work:* Rochester Inst Technol; Smithsonian Inst. *Exhib:* Rochester Mem Mus NY State Sculpture Show, 39; Western Painters Show, Oakland Art Mus, 54, Alameda Art Asn 11th Ann, 55; Henry Gallery, Univ Wash, 55; New York Int Art Exhib, Zantman Galleries, Carmel, 79 & Bannan Gallery, Burlingame, 83, Calif. *Awards:* Award for Tribulation (sculpture), Rochester Mem Art Mus, 33; Alameda Art Asn 11th Ann Award, Oakland Art Mus, 54, Award for Carriage Ride in Central Park (painting), 55. *Bibliog:* A J Bloomfield (auth), Art previews in San Francisco, News-Call Bull, 60; Felice T Ross (auth), Gallery previews in New York, Pictures Exhib, 67; Interesting Personalities, WROC-TV, Rochester, 6/67. *Mem:* Artists Equity Asn (mem bd Northern Chap, 70); Marin Soc Artists Ross Calif; Soc Western Artists; Eight Women Watercolorists of West (pres, 53-57). *Media:* Oil. *Publ:* Auth, Palette Knife Painting Instruction (rec), 68. *Mailing Add:* 1009 Ripple Ave Pacific Grove CA 93950

JONAITIS, ALDONA
HISTORIAN
b New York, NY, Nov 27, 48. *Study:* State Univ NY, Stony Brook, BA, 69; Columbia Univ, with Douglas Fraser, MA, 72, PhD, 77. *Pos:* Res assoc, Am Mus Natural Hist. *Teaching:* Assoc prof & chmn dept art, State Univ NY, Stony Brook, 81- *Res:* Northwest Coast Indian art, particularly of the Tlingit Indians. *Publ:* Auth, The devilfish in Tlingit sacred art, Am Indian Art Mag, 80; auth, Tlingit Halibut Hooks, Am Mus Natural Hist, 81; auth, Creations of mystics and philosophers, Am Indian Cult & Res J, 81; co-ed (with Zena Mathews), Native American Art History: Selected Readings, Peek Publ, 82; auth, Style and meaning in northern northwest coast Jhamanic art, In: Box of Daylight, Seattle Art Mus, 83. *Mailing Add:* Dept Art State Univ NY Stony Brook NY 11794

JONAS, JOAN
VIDEO ARTIST, CONCEPTUAL ARTIST
b New York, NY, July 13, 36. *Study:* Mount Holyoke Col, Mass; Boston Mus Sch, Mass; Columbia Univ, New York, MFA. *Work:* Mus Mod Art, New York. *Exhib:* The Video Show, Serpentine Gallery, London, 75; Van Abbe Mus, Eindhoven, 75; Mus Mod Art, New York, 75; Assoc Students, Univ Calif, Los Angeles, 75; one-woman shows, Walker Art Ctr, Minneapolis, Minn, 74, Anthology Film Archives, New York, 75 & Inst Contemp Arts, Los Angeles, 75; Mus Fine Arts, Montreal, 80; and others. *Awards:* Creative Artists Pub Serv Prog, 72, 73 & 75; Nat Endowment Arts Grant, 73 & 75. *Bibliog:* Laurie Anderson (auth), Joan Jonas, Art Press, Paris, 11-12/73; Wulf Herzgenrath (auth), Video Ein Neue Medium in der Bildenden Kunst, Mag Kunst, Mainz, 7/74; Marcus Guterich (auth), Art Presented According to the Evolution Principle, Kunst Kunst Kunst, Cologne, WGer, 74. *Media:* Mirrors; Videotape. *Publ:* Auth, Organic Honey's visual telepathy, Drama Rev, New York, 72; coauth, Show Me Your Dance, Art & Artists, London, 10/73. *Dealer:* Leo Castelli Gallery 420 W Broadway New York NY 10013. *Mailing Add:* 112 Mercer St New York NY 10012

JONES, AMY (AMY JONES FRISBIE)
PAINTER, INSTRUCTOR
b Buffalo, NY, Apr 4, 1899. *Study:* Pratt Inst, scholar; also with Peppino Mangrarite, Xavier Gonzales, Ippolito, Carlus Dyer & Roger Prince. *Work:* New Britain Mus Am Art, Conn; Chrysler Mus, Norfolk, Va; 35 works, New York Hosp; Hudson River Mus; two watercolors & oil, PepsiCo; and others. *Comn:* Murals, Winsted, Conn, 39, Painted Post, NY, 40 & Scotia, NY, 41, Fine Arts Sect, US Treas Dept. *Exhib:* Many one-man shows, incl Venice, 58, 72 & 74, New York, Philadelphia Art Alliance, New Brit Mus Am Art & Chrysler Mus; and others. *Teaching:* Instr art, Bedford Art Ctr, 62-; instr printmaking, Col New Rochelle, summer 72; pvt studio instr, Mt Kisco, NY & Venice, Italy, currently. *Awards:* Purchase Prize, Philadelphia Watercolor Club; Ranger Fund Watercolor Prize, Nat Acad Art; First Prize, Western NY Artists; and others. *Bibliog:* Norman Kent (auth), article, Am Artist Mag, 54; Norman Kent (auth), Amy Jones, Watson-Guptill, 56. *Mem:* Silvermine Guild Artists; Philadelphia Watercolor Club; The Print Club, Philadelphia; Audubon Artists; San Diego Print Club. *Media:* Oil, Watercolor. *Mailing Add:* Byram Lake Rd Mt Kisco NY 10549

JONES, BEN
PAINTER, SCULPTOR
b Paterson, NJ, May 26, 42. *Study:* Sch Visual Arts; NY Univ, MA; Pratt Inst; Univ Sci & Technol, Kumasi, Ghana. *Work:* Newark Mus, NJ; Howard Univ; Studio Mus, New York, NY; Johnson Publ, Chicago. *Exhib:* Mus Mod Art; Studio Mus in Harlem; Black World Arts Festival, Lagos, Nigeria; Newark Mus, 77; Fisk Univ, 77; Ala A&M Univ, 78; Bishop Col, Dallas, Tex, 78; and others. *Pos:* Art dir, Urban League Essex Co Exhib, 72. *Teaching:* Assoc prof fine arts, Jersey City State Col, 68- *Awards:* Nat Endowment Arts Grant, 74-75; NJ Arts Coun Grant, 77-78. *Bibliog:* Articles, Art Am, 71; articles, New York Times, 72. *Res:* African art and culture in WAfrica and Paris, France. *Mailing Add:* 117 Kensington Ave Jersey City NJ 07304

JONES, CALVIN B(ELL)
PAINTER, MURALIST
b Chicago, Ill, Jan 7, 34. *Study:* Art Inst Chicago; Univ Chicago. *Work:* Inst Positive Educ, Southside Community Art Ctr & Kermit Coleman Community Health Ctr, Chicago; Motorola Corp, Scottsdale, Ariz & Chicago, Ill. *Comn:* In Defense of Ignorance, Nat Endowment Arts, Nat Art Coun, Chicago, 77; Another Times Voice, Chicago Art Coun, 79; Ceremonies of Heritage Now, Nat Endowment Fine Arts, Chicago, 80; Builders of the Cultural Present, Chicago Coun Fine Arts, 81; and others. *Exhib:* Spokane World Fair, Black Arts Pavillion, Spokane, 75; Int Festac, Western Zone Pavilion, Lago,

Nigeria, 77; Black Esthetics, Mus Sci & Indust, Chicago, 78; Nat Conf Artists, Martin L King Libr, Washington, DC, 80. *Awards:* Builders Award, Third World Press, 78; Arron Douglas Muralist Award, Nat Conf Artists, 79 & 83. *Mem:* Nat Conf Artists. *Media:* Oil, Mixed Media. *Mailing Add:* 833 N Orleans Chicago IL 60610

JONES, CARTER R(UTHVEN)
SCULPTOR
b Mount Kisco, NY, Mar 6, 45. *Study:* Sch Visual Arts, with Edward Giobbi, 64-65; Boston Mus Sch, dipl, 69. *Exhib:* 47th & 48th Ann, Equitable Gallery, New York, 80 & 82. *Teaching:* Instr human & animal anatomy, Sch Visual Arts, New York, currently. *Awards:* Art Dirs Award, Art Dirs Am, 79; Youth Award, Nat Sculpture Soc, 80; and others. *Mem:* Nat Sculpture Soc; Soc Artists Anatomists; Am Medallic Sculpture Asn (pres, currently). *Media:* Clay, Plaster. *Dealer:* Portraits Inc 41 East 57th St New York NY 10022. *Mailing Add:* 215 East 80th St New York NY 10021

JONES, CHARLOTT ANN
EDUCATOR, GALLERY DIRECTOR
b Jonesboro, Ark, May 27, 27. *Study:* Col St Scholastica, BA, 62; NTex State Univ, MS, 70; Pa State Univ, PhD, 78. *Collections Arranged:* Anuskiewicz Silkscreen Prints, 83, Rauschenberg Purina Chow Prints, 83 & Anuskiewicz, Judd, Marisol Prints, 83, Stephens Collection; The Figure and Other Paintings, 83; Paintings and Ceramics, 83. *Pos:* Dir, Mus & Galleries, Ark State Univ, 83- *Teaching:* Dir childrens art, Charlott Jones Sch Art, Jonesboro, Ark, 72-; asst prof art, Ark State Univ, Jonesboro, 75- *Mem:* Nat Art Educ Asn; Ark Art Educ; Asn Col & Univ Mus & Galleries; Southeastern Mus Conf; Ark Mus Asn. *Res:* Free will in art making. *Publ:* Auth, A sister considers chastity, Am, 65; contribr, American Catholics, Am Press, 66; auth, The wellspring of Dylan, English J, 66; auth, Women and art, Delta Kappa Gamma Bulletin, 82; contribr, Gifted and Talented in Art Education (monogr), Nat Art Educ Asn, 83. *Mailing Add:* 217 E Cherry Ave Jonesboro AR 72401

JONES, CLAIRE (DEANN BURTCHAELL)
PAINTER, PRINTMAKER
b Oakland, Calif. *Study:* Stanford Univ, AB; Otis Art Inst; Univ Calif, Irvine; Laguna Beach Sch Art; San Diego Acad Fine Arts, Calif; also with Dong Kingman, Mario Cooper, Rex Brandt. *Work:* Hunt Wesson, Fullerton, Calif; Copley Found, San Diego; Home Savings & Loan, Fallbrook, Calif; HEAR Found, Pasadena, Calif; Sun Savings & Loan, San Diego, Calif. *Comn:* Many pvt comns. *Exhib:* Southern Calif Expos, Del Mar, 69-72; Death Valley Invitational, Furnace Creek, Calif, 71-79; Watercolor West, Riverside, Calif, 72-75; Cedar City Invitational, Utah, 74; West Coast Americana Realists, Fullerton. *Teaching:* Teacher dry brush watercolor, Jade Fon Watercolor Workshop, 75 & 76; teacher dry brush watercolor, Merced Col Watercolor Workshop, 8/75. *Awards:* First Award Watercolor, Southern Calif Expos, 69; Best of Show, Hillcrest Invitational, 74; Hon Mention, Hallmark/North Light Competition, 81. *Bibliog:* Arte unica, Life en Espanol, 11/3/69; R P Spencer (auth), Dramatis Personnae, Aesthetic Enterprises, 11/72; Fielding Greaves (auth), Nostalgia and old country houses, Southwest Art, 6/75. *Mem:* Watercolor West (scholar comt, bd mem, ed, 71-); Asn Western Artists; San Diego Art Inst (secy); Art Guild of San Diego Art Mus; San Diego Watercolor Soc. *Publ:* Illusr, Leanin' Tree, 72 & 76; illusr, Pictorial Publ; illusr (cover), SW Art, 9/76. *Mailing Add:* c/o Riggs Galleries Fifth Ave Financial Ctr Suite 167 San Diego CA 92103

JONES, DAVID LEE
PAINTER, SCULPTOR
b Columbus, Ohio, Feb 26, 48. *Study:* Kansas City Art Inst, BFA, 70; Univ Calif, Berkeley, Marion Davies Fel, 72, MFA, 73; studio asst to Peter Voulkos, 70-72. *Work:* San Francisco Mus Art; Univ Art Mus, Berkeley; DeSaisset Mus & Art Gallery, Univ Santa Clara, Calif. *Exhib:* Recent Acquisitions, Univ Mus, Berkeley, 73; Market St Prog, Pasadena Mus Mod Art, Calif, 73; Whitney Biennial Am Painting & Sculpture, Whitney Mus Art, New York, 75; Calif Painting & Sculpture--the Mod Era, San Francisco Mus of Art & Nat Collection of Fine Arts, Washington, DC, 76-77; one-man shows, Soc Encouragement Contemp Art, San Francisco Mus Art, 74 & Michael Walls Gallery, New York, 75; Braunstein Gallery, San Francisco, 84. *Awards:* Soc Encouragement Contemp Art Grant, 74; Individual Artists Grant, Nat Endowment Arts, 74. *Bibliog:* Ellen Lubell (auth), David Jones, Art Mag, 6/74; Al Frankenstein (auth), numerous reviews in San Francisco Chronicle & Examr. *Media:* 20th Century Media. *Dealer:* Branstein Gallery 254 Sutter St San Francisco CA. *Mailing Add:* 71 Haight St San Francisco CA 94102

JONES, (CHARLES) DEXTER (WEATHERBEE), III
SCULPTOR, DESIGNER
b Ardmore, Pa, Dec 17, 26. *Study:* Pa Acad Fine Arts, Philadelphia, 47-49; Charles Rudy & Walker Hancock, 51-52; Accad della Belle Arti, Florence, Italy, 55-56. *Work:* Nat Acad Design, New York; Pa Acad Fine Arts & Temple Univ, Philadelphia; Woodmore Gallery Art, Chestnut Hill, Pa; Smithsonian Inst, Washington, DC; and many others. *Comn:* Bronze coat of arms, City Philadelphia, 67; Welcoming Christ (bronze), St Paul's Lutheran Church, Warren, Ohio, 68; Charity (bas-relief group), Philadelphia Psychiatric Hosp, 68; trachodon (bronze), Philadelphia Zoological Soc, 69; McChesney Martin Tablet (portrait) plaque, Fed Reserve Bd, Washington, DC, 73; and others. *Exhib:* Pa Acad Fine Arts, Philadelphia; Nat Acad Design, New York, 50-54, 58-60, 67-71 & 73-81; Philadelphia Art League, 51, 58, 62, 64-65, 70 & 81; Nat Sculpture Soc, New York, 58-62, 67-70 & 73-81; Philadelphia Mus Art, 59-62 & 64; Archit League, New York, 59-62

& 64-67; Allied Artists Am, New York, 59-63, 65-66 & 73-81; Nat Arts Club, New York, 61, 63-65, 72 & 81; and others. *Awards:* Helen Foster Barnett Prize, Nat Acad Design, 60; Hexler Award, Allied Artists Am, 81; John Spring Founders Award, Nat Sculpture Soc, 83. *Bibliog:* Jack Bookbinder (film), Dexter Jones, sculptor: his work, KYW-TV, 51, Lighting in sculpture, WFIL-TV, 60 & Profiles in art, WHYY-TV, 65, Philadelphia. *Mem:* Nat Acad Design; Nat Sculpture Soc; Pa Acad Fine Arts; Allied Artists Am. *Media:* Bronze, Stone. *Publ:* Contribr, Dexter Jones' story book characters in bas-relief in Today Magazine, Philadelphia Inquirer, 69; contribr, American Council Arts, Nat Sculpture Rev, 76; contribr, Dinosaurs, clowns get Dexter Jones' touch, Philadelphia Bulletin, 80; and others. *Mailing Add:* 2112 Chancellor St Philadelphia PA 19103

JONES, DOUG (DOUGLAS MCKEE)
PAINTER, DEALER
b Sewell, Chile, Oct 16, 29; US citizen. *Study:* San Diego Fine Arts & Crafts; San Diego State Col; Los Angeles Art Ctr Col Design, grad; also with Lorser Feitelson, Audubon Tyler, Leon Franks & Sergei Bongart. *Comn:* Portraits, Mayor Charles Dail, San Diego & Mayor Kiyoshi Nakarai, Yokahama, San Diego Chap, Am Inst Architects, 63; 43 portraits, Int Aerospace Hall Fame, San Diego, 64-72; portrait, Gen Claire Chenault, Flying Tigers Asn, 71; portrait, Marie Winzer, Scripps Hosp; and others. *Pos:* Owner & dir, The Jones Gallery, 64- *Awards:* Merit Award, New York Portrait Club, 79. *Mem:* Int Soc Appraisers; Am Soc Appraisers. *Media:* Oil, Pastel. *Specialty:* Paintings, sculpture and ceramics by distinguished 19th and 20th century American artists. *Mailing Add:* The Jones Gallery 1264 Prospect St La Jolla CA 92037

JONES, EDWARD POWIS
PAINTER, SCULPTOR
b New York, NY, Jan 8, 19. *Study:* Harvard Univ; Art Students League; Acad Ranson, Paris. *Work:* Metrop Mus Art, Mus Mod Art, New York; Corcoran Gallery, Washington, DC; Philadelphia Mus Art; Brooklyn Mus; and others. *Exhib:* Libr Cong; Modern Religious Prints, Mus Mod Art Circulating Exhib, 63; Tokyo Print Bienale, Japan, 68; New York World Trade Ctr, 75; Vassar Col, 78; PS1, 81; Bks & Co, 83; Mead Mus, 83; and others. *Teaching:* Instr art, Loyola Sch, New York, 70-72. *Mem:* Philadelphia Print Club; Century Asn; Munic Art Soc; Artists Equity Asn; Fels Pierpont Morgan Libr (chmn coun, 72). *Media:* Oil, Watercolor; Bronze. *Mailing Add:* 925 Park Ave New York NY 10028

JONES, ELIZABETH A B
SCULPTOR, MEDALIST
b Montclair, NJ, May 31, 35. *Study:* Vassar Col, BA, 57; Art Students League, 58-60; Scuola Arte Medaglia, The Mint, Rome, Italy, 62-64; Acad Brasileira Belas Artes, Rio de Janeiro, hon dipl, 67. *Comn:* Fifty bronze busts, Revlon Co Res Labs, 83; Bronze & gilt tabernacle, St Paul's Anglican-Episcopal Church, Rome, 77; H E Sheikh of Dubai, United Arab Emirates, for Sheraton Hotels, 78; Ambassador Mahdi al-Tajir, London, 78; gold portrait medallion, Pope John Paul II, gift of State by Italy to the Pope, 79; Nobel Prize winners commemorative medal, A B Sporrong, Stockholm, Sweden, 79; and many others. *Exhib:* Tiffany & Co, New York, Houston, Los Angeles, Chicago & San Francisco, 66-68; Montclair Art Mus, NJ, 67; many int medallic art shows, Rome, Madrid, Paris, Athens, Prague, Cologne & Helsinki; Smithsonian Inst & Nat Sculpture Soc, New York, 72 & 78; USIS Consulate, Rome, Italy, 73; USA Exhib, FIDEM Show, Gulbenkian Mus, Lisbon, 79; retrospective, Vassar Col, 82. *Pos:* Chief sculptor/engraver, US Mint, Philadelphia, currently. *Awards:* Outstanding Sculptor of the Year, Am Numismatic Asn, Colorado Springs, Colo, 72; Louis Bennet Award, Nat Sculpture Soc, 78; Pres medal award, Vassar Col, 82 & 83. *Bibliog:* Mario Valeriana (auth), Medalists in Italy, Editalia, Rome, 72; and articles in New York Times, Coin World & other mags & newspapers in the US & Italy. *Mem:* Nat Sculpture Soc; Am Numismatic Asn; Fedn Int Medaille; Ital Soc Medalists; Am Medallic Sculpture Asn. *Media:* Wax, Plaster; Metals. *Mailing Add:* 1810 Rittenhouse Sq Apt 1110 Philadelphia PA 19103

JONES, ELIZABETH ORTON
ILLUSTRATOR, WRITER
b Highland Park, Ill, June 25, 10. *Study:* Univ Chicago, PhB, 32; Ecole Beaux Arts, Paris, dipl, 32; Art Inst Chicago, 32; Wheaton Col, Hon MA, 55. *Comn:* Murals, Crotched Mountain Ctr, Greenfield, NH; panel, Univ NH Libr. *Exhib:* O'Brien Galleries, Chicago; Smithsonian Inst. *Awards:* Charles Muller Prize, Chicago Soc Etchers, 39; Caldecott Medal for Illus, 44; Lewis Carroll Shelf Award, Univ Wis, 58. *Mailing Add:* Hillsboro NH 03244

JONES, FRANCES FOLLIN
CURATOR
b New York, NY, Sept 8, 13. *Study:* Bryn Mawr Col, AB, 34, MA, 36, PhD, 52; Am Sch Class Studies at Athens, 37-38. *Pos:* Secy & asst cur class art, Art Mus, Princeton Univ, 43-46, asst to dir & cur class art, 46-60, chief cur & cur class art, 60-71, cur collections & cur class art, 71- *Publ:* Contribr to prof journals & publ. *Mailing Add:* Art Mus Princeton Univ Princeton NJ 08544

JONES, FRANKLIN REED
PAINTER, WRITER
b Needham, Mass, May 18, 21. *Work:* Mus Art, Sci & Indust, Bridgeport, Conn; Conn Audubon Soc, Fairfield. *Exhib:* Univ of Utah Invitational Exhib, 76; Am Watercolor Soc, New York, 77; De Cordova Mus, Lincoln, Mass, 77; Berkshire Mus, Pittsfield, Mass, 77; Ellsworth Nat Exhib, Simsbury, Conn, 77; and others. *Pos:* Asst to dir, Famous Artists Sch, 58-74. *Teaching:* Instr painting, Famous Artists Sch, Westport, Conn, 53-58. *Awards:* Gold Medal

of Hon, Am Watercolor Soc, 75; Award of Excellence, Ellsworth Gallery, Simsbury Cult Comt, 77; Privet Prize, Adirondack Nat Exhib, 83. *Bibliog:* Fred Whitaker (auth), The Paintings of Franklin Jones, Am Artist Mag, 66. *Mem:* Am Watercolor Soc, Dolphin Fel. *Media:* Acrylic, Watercolor. *Publ:* Contribr, Acrylic Watercolor Painting, 70 & Complete Guide to Acrylic Painting, 71, Watson-Guptill; auth, The Pleasure of Painting, North Light, 75; illusr, Gray's Sporting J, 77; auth, Painting nature: solving landscape problems, North Light, 78. *Mailing Add:* RFD 1 West Stockbridge MA 01266

JONES, FREDERICK GEORGE
PRINTMAKER, EDUCATOR
b Llanymymech, Wales, Mar 6, 40. *Study:* Cardiff Col Art, Wales; Univ Pittsburgh; Univ Wis-Madison; print workshop, London & Atelier 17, Paris. *Work:* Lakeview Ctr for Arts, Peoria, Ill; Brit Mus, London; Victoria & Albert Mus, London; Krannert Mus, Univ Ill; Southern Ill Univ, Carbondale. *Exhib:* Int Print Biennale, Seoul, Korea, 71; Mid-Am Exhib, Montreal, Can, 71; Nat Image on Paper Show, Springfield, Ill, 72; Nat Print & Drawing Show, Macomb, 75; Gov Invitational, Gov Mansion, Springfield, 75. *Teaching:* Lectr design drawing, Chester Col Art, Eng, 66-68; prof printmaking, Western Ill Univ, 68-, gallery dir, 69-71. *Awards:* Painting Award, Container Corp Am, 70; Best of Show, Tri-State Exhib, Muscatine, Iowa, 73; Purchase Award, Ill State Mus, 74. *Mem:* Royal Cambrian Acad, Wales; Col Art Asn Am; NH Print Soc. *Media:* Mixed. *Dealer:* Van Stratten 646 N Michigan Ave Chicago IL 60611; Prairie Gallery Springfield IL. *Mailing Add:* RR 4 Macomb IL 61455

JONES, HAROLD HENRY
ADMINISTRATOR, PHOTOGRAPHER
b Morristown, NJ, Sept 29, 40. *Study:* Newark Sch Fine & Indust Arts, dipl, 63; Md Inst Art, BFA, 65; Univ NMex, MFA, 72. *Work:* George Eastman House, Rochester, NY; Univ Art Mus, Univ NMex. *Exhib:* Mus Mod Art, New York, 70; An Exhib: About Self Portraits, Northlight Gallery, Ariz State Univ, 78; The Hand Colored Photog, Philadelphia Col Art, 79; Document Competition, Calif Inst Arts, 79; Attitudes: Photog in the 1970's, Santa Barbara Mus Art, 79; Views of Am, Mus Mod Art, New York, 79; The West Show, Joseph Gross Gallery, Univ Ariz, 79; and many other group & one-man exhibs. *Pos:* Assoc cur, George Eastman House, 70-71; founding dir, Light Gallery, 71-75; founding dir, Ctr Creative Photog, Univ Ariz, 75-77; coordr photog prog, Univ Ariz, Tucson, 77. *Teaching:* Assoc prof art hist, Queens Col, 74-75; Univ Ariz, 77-83. *Awards:* Nat Endowment for the Arts Photogr Fel, 77. *Mem:* Soc Photog Educ (bd mem, 71-75). *Res:* Aspects of the history of photography. *Collection:* Contemporary photography and related material. *Publ:* Contribr photog, Artweek, 1/78 & 8/78, Contemp Calif Photog, 78, Am Photogr, 8/78 & House & Garden, 1/79. *Mailing Add:* Ctr for Creative Photog Univ of Ariz Tucson AZ 85721

JONES, HERB (LEON HERBERT), JR
PAINTER, PRINTMAKER
b Norfolk, Va, Mar 25, 23. *Study:* William & Mary Col; Univ delle Arti, Dipl Di Merito, 81. *Work:* Univ Va, Charlottesville; NC Nat Bank, Raleigh; Cong Off of William G Whitehurst, Washington, DC; Chrysler Mus at Norfolk; State Univ NY, Buffalo; and others. *Comn:* 3 major paintings, Noland Co, Chesapeake, Va, 79; prints ward room, USS Dwight D Eisenhower & USS John F Kennedy, 79; and others. *Exhib:* Chesapeake Maritime Mus, St Michaels, Md, 80; Fine Arts Pavilion, World's Fair, Knoxville, Tenn, 82; Art Buyers Caravan Exhib, Atlanta, Ga, 82; Harborfest, Norfolk, Va, 82; one-man show, Virginia Beach Maritime Hist Mus, 83; Mobile Mus, Ala & traveling, 83; Colonial Wildfowl Festival, Williamsburg, Va, 83; and other group and one-man shows. *Awards:* Three Best of Show Awards, Art Buyers Conventions, 79; Gold Medal, 80 & Gold Centaur, 83, Academie delle Arti. *Bibliog:* Barclay Sheaks (auth), Drawing & Painting the Natural Environment, Davis Publ, 74; conservation & art film, WTVZ-TV, 79; articles, Tidewater Virginian, Pace Mag, Lifestyle Mag, Metro Mag and others. *Mem:* Tidewater Artist Asn; Nat Soc of Arts & Lit. *Media:* Egg Tempera, Watercolor. *Publ:* Illusr (covers), Va Wildlife Mag, 64-68; and others. *Mailing Add:* 238 Beck St Norfolk VA 23503

JONES, HOWARD WILLIAM
PAINTER, SCULPTOR
b Ilion, NY, June 20, 22. *Study:* Toledo Univ; Columbia Univ; Syracuse Univ, BFA; Cranbrook Acad Art. *Work:* Jewish Mus, New York; Walker Art Ctr; Albright-Knox Mus; Milwaukee Art Inst; St Louis Art Mus. *Comn:* Time Columns: The Sound of Light (wall of light & sound), Whitney Mus Am Art, 68; Retinal Bypass I (sound environment), NJ State Mus, Trenton, 75; Retinal Bypass II (sound environment), Brooks Mem Art Gallery, 77. *Exhib:* Light, Motion, Space, Walker Art Ctr, 67 & Mus Contemp Art, Chicago, 68; Magic Theater, Nelson-Atkins Mus, Automation House, New York & others, 68-70; Moon Show, Mass Inst Technol & Newark Mus Fine Arts, NJ, 69 & 70; Art of the 60s, Princeton Univ, 70; Kinetic Art, Rockefeller Univ, Arts Coun Gt Brit & Hayward Gallery, London, 70; solo exhibs, Electric Gallery, Toronto, 71, St Louis Art Mus, 73, Nelson-Atkins Mus, 73, Wadsworth Atheneum, 74 & Forbes Found Mus, 76; Multiples, Philadelphia Mus Art, 71; Responsive Environment, NJ State Mus, Trenton, 72; Recent Media--Ten Years, Brooks Mem Art Gallery, 77; Art of the Space Era, Huntsville Mus Art, von Braun Civic Ctr, 78. *Teaching:* Instr painting & design, Tulane Univ, 51-54; asst prof, Fla State Univ, 54-57; prof multi-media, Wash Univ, 57- *Awards:* Graham Found Fel & Grant, 66-67; New Talent: USA, Art in Am, 66-67; Nat Endowment Arts Fel & Grant, 77. *Bibliog:* Ralph Coe (auth), Post pop possibilities: Howard Jones, Art Int, 1/66 & Breaking the sound barrier, Art News Mag, summer 71; Nat Endowment Arts (producer), Artist in America: Howard Jones (film), KETC-TV, 71. *Media:* Sound, Light. *Mailing Add:* 12 N Newstead St St Louis MO 63108

JONES, JAMES EDWARD
PAINTER, PRINTMAKER
b Paducah, Ky, Jan 27, 37. *Study:* Philadelphia Col Art, with Henry Pitz & Benton Spruance, dipl(illus) 60, fel, 56-61, BFA, 61; Univ Pa, with Barnett Newman, Angelo Seveili, David Smith, Richard Stankiewicz & Adja Yunkers, MFA, 62. *Work:* Morgan State Univ; McDonosh Sch, Md; Dennison Univ; Smith Mason Gallery; Univ Md, Eastern Shore. *Exhib:* 16th & 18th Area Exhib, Baltimore Mus Art, 63-64; Corcoran Mus Art, 64; Baltimore Co Campus, Univ Md, 79; Smith Mason Gallery, Washington, DC, 79, 80 & 82; Morgan State Univ, 79; Univ Md, Eastern Shore, 83; Morgan State Univ, 83. *Teaching:* From assoc prof to prof art educ, painting & printmaking, Morgan State Univ, 62-; instr, Dundalk Community Col, 77-78. *Awards:* Stewart Art Award, NJ State, 56; Univ Pa Fel & Thorton Oakley Creative Achievement Award, 62; Morgan State Univ Grant, 63-68. *Media:* Oil, Encaustic; Engraving, Lithography. *Mailing Add:* 2930 Silver Hill Ave Baltimore MD 21207

JONES, JERRY
SCULPTOR, PAINTER
b Pineville, Ky, Apr 9, 47. *Study:* Cooper Sch Art, cert fine art; Cleveland Inst Art, BFA. *Work:* El Paso Mus Art, Tex; Allen Mem Mus Art, Oberlin, Ohio; Mus Contemp Art, Sao Paulo, Brazil; Ga Mus Art, Athens. *Exhib:* Biennial Contemp Am Art, Whitney Mus Art, New York, 75; one-man shows, Cult Ctr, Washington, DC, 75-76 & Holly Solomon Gallery, 76, 78 & 80; Deconstruction/Reconstruction, New Mus, New York, 80; Grand Central Station: The Waiting Room, Grand Cent Station, 80; Projects at the Precinct, First Precinct Bldg, New York, 81; and many others. *Awards:* Painting grant, Creative Artists Pub Serv (CAPS), 78; Nat Endowment Arts fel, 80. *Bibliog:* Museums, New Yorker, 2/17/75; J Russell (auth), rev in NY Times, 12/15/78; D Davis (auth), Post Post-Art, Village Voice, 6/25/79; Kathi Norklin (auth), Galleries, Washington Market Rev, 80; Kay Lawson (auth), Art, Village Voice, 80; Tom Lawson (auth), New York Reviews, Artforum, 80; and others. *Media:* Mixed. *Mailing Add:* PO Box 98 New York NY 10013

JONES, JOHN PAUL
PAINTER, PRINTMAKER
b Indianola, Iowa, Nov 18, 24. *Study:* State Univ Iowa, with Mauricio Lasansky, BFA, 49, MFA, 51. *Work:* Mus Mod Art, New York; Brooklyn Mus; Nat Gallery Art, Libr Cong, Washington, DC; Los Angeles Co Mus Art. *Exhib:* Art of America in Spain, Madrid, 63; Pittsburgh Int, Carnegie Inst, 64-67; American Painting, Va Mus Arts & Sci, Richmond, 66-70; Tamarind: Homage to Lithography, Mus Mod Art, New York, 69; The New Vein-- Europe, Smithsonian Inst, touring in Europe, 69-70; one-man exhibs, Graphics Gallery, 73, Jodi Scully Gallery, 73 & 75, Charles Campbell Gallery, 74 & Univ Calif, Riverside, 75. *Teaching:* Asst prof prints, Univ Calif, Los Angeles, 53-63; prof prints & drawings, Univ Calif, Irvine, 70-82, prof studio art, currently. *Awards:* Graphics Award, Tiffany Found, 51; Creative Printmaking Award, Guggenheim Found, 60. *Bibliog:* Una Johnson (auth), John Paul Jones, Prints & Drawings 1948-1963 (monogr), Brooklyn Mus, 63; Henry Hopkins (auth), John Paul Jones, Painting & Sculpture 1955-1965 (monogr), Los Angeles Co Mus Art, 65; Eugene Anderson (auth), John Paul Jones (monogr), Felix Landau Gallery, Los Angeles, 67. *Dealer:* Mekler Gallery 651 N La Cienega Blvd Los Angeles 90069. *Mailing Add:* 22370 Third Ave South Laguna CA 92677

JONES, LOIS MAILOU (MRS V PIERRE-NOEL)
PAINTER, DESIGNER
b Boston, Mass, 1905. *Study:* Boston Mus Sch Fine Arts, scholar, 4 yrs; Boston Normal Art Sch; Designers Art Sch; Harvard Univ; Columbia Univ; Howard Univ, AB; Acad Julien, Paris, with Berges, Montezin, Maury & Adler; Acad Grand Chaumiere, Paris; Colo State Christian Col, Hon PhD, 73; Suffolk Univ, Boston, LHD, 81. *Work:* Brooklyn Mus; Metropolitan Mus Art; Hirshhorn Mus; Corcoran Gallery Art, Washington, DC; Mus Fine Arts, Boston; and others. *Comn:* Designed AKA Commemorative Stained Glass Window, Andrew Rankin Chapel, Howard Univ, 78; mural, The Light, Cook Hall, Howard Univ. *Exhib:* Nat Acad Design, New York; Rhodes Nat Gallery, SRhodesia; Trenton Mus, NJ; San Francisco Mus Art; Salon Artistes Francais, Grand Palais Champs-Elysees, Paris; and 50 one-man shows & numerous other group shows. *Teaching:* Emer prof design & watercolor painting, Howard Univ, 30- *Awards:* Chevalier, Nat Order Merit of Honor, Govt Haiti, 55; First Hon Mention Oil Painting, Salon Artistes Francais, Paris, 66; Alumni Award, Howard Univ, 78; plus others. *Bibliog:* Karen Peterson & J J Wilson (auths), Women Artists, Harper & Row, 76; Dr Samella Lewis (auth), Art: African American, Harcourt Brace Jovanovitch, 78; Charlotte Rubenstein (auth), American Women Artists, Avon Books & G K Hall, 82. *Mem:* Fel Royal Soc Arts; Artists Equity Asn; Soc Washington Artists; Washington Watercolor Asn; Nat Conf Artists. *Media:* Oil, Acrylic. *Publ:* Auth, Lois Mailou Jones peintures--1937-1951, Georges Frere, Tourcoing, France, 52. *Mailing Add:* 4706 17th St NW Washington DC 20011

JONES, LOIS SWAN
EDUCATOR, HISTORIAN
b Dallas, Tex, July 3, 27. *Study:* Univ Chicago, PhB, 47, BS, 48, MS, 54; NTex State Univ, PhD, 72; Ctr Univ d'Ete des Pyrenees, Univ Toulouse, summer 75. *Pos:* Conductor, Le Petite Cercle d'Art, Dallas, 52-75; narrator & photogr, Five Nights in Europe, Dallas Country Club, 63-75. *Teaching:* Lectr art hist, Univ Tex, Arlington, 69-70; from asst prof to assoc prof art hist, NTex State Univ, Denton, 72- *Mem:* Art Libr Soc NAm; Col Art Asn; Am Asn Mus; Nat Art Educ Asn; Midwest Art Hist Soc. *Res:* Art museum educational programs; art library research; medieval art. *Publ:* Auth, Art Research

Methods and Resources, Kendall/Hunt, 78, rev 84; auth, Pompeii in Dallas, 79; auth, Supplementing Your Art Library, 79; producer multi-media show, Ice Age Art Exhib, Dallas Health & Sci Mus, 80; auth, Self study guides for school age students, Mus Studies J, 83. *Mailing Add:* 3801 Normandy Dallas TX 75205

JONES, LOU (MARY LOUISE HUMPTON)
PAINTER, SCULPTOR
b West Chester, Pa. *Study:* Pa State Univ, BA(Eng lit), 49; with Gene Davis, 68-72; George Mason Univ, Fairfax, Va, BA(art hist), 77; Corcoran Sch Abroad, Leeds Univ, Eng. *Work:* Phillips Collection, DC; Northern Va Community Col, Alexandria; Am Embassy, Damascus, Syria; Am Embassy, Bern, Switz; Am Embassy, Bamako, Mali; and others. *Exhib:* 19th Area Show, Corcoran Mus, DC, 74; Va Artists, Va Mus, Richmond, 77 & 79; Works on Paper, Arlington Arts Ctr, Va, 79; 11th Int Sculpture Conference, Washington DC, 80; Catholic Univ Art Col, 81; Work on Paper, Mt Vernon Col, 83; Enclosures, Foundry Gallery, Washington, DC; and others. *Pos:* Panelist, Women Visual Arts, Women's Ctr, DC, 75; Artists Survival, Univ Md, 78 & Am Univ, DC, 79; art consult, Am Corrections, DC, 77-80; panelist, Corcoran Sch Art, Washington DC; panelist, Md Inst Art, Baltimore. *Teaching:* Instr drawing/mixed media children, Corcoran Gallery, DC, 75-80; instr drawing, Northern Va Community Col, Alexandria, 78-; vis prof, Univ Md, 81. *Awards:* Purchase Award, Northern Va Community Col, 75; Fel, Va Ctr Creative Arts, Sweet Briar, 81. *Bibliog:* Paul Richard (auth), Review of show, 77-79 & Joan Lewis (auth), Review of show, 78, Washington Post; Ben Forgey (auth), Review of show, Washington Star, 77-79; Joann Lewis (auth), Cheap Thrills, Washington Post, 81; Letty Bonnell (auth), New Art Examiner, 1/82; Jan Allen (auth), Washington Times, 10/83. *Media:* Paper, Collage. *Dealer:* Foundry Gallery 641 Indiana Ave NW Washington DC 20004; Marsha Mateyka Bethesda MD 20812. *Mailing Add:* 329 Maple Ave Falls Church VA 22046

JONES, LOUIS C
MUSEUM DIRECTOR
b Albany, NY, June 28, 08. *Study:* Hamilton Col, AB, 30; Columbia Univ, AM, 31, PhD, 41; Hamilton Col, LHD, 62. *Pos:* Ed, NY Folklore Quarterly, 45-50; exec dir, NY State Hist Asn & Farmers Mus, 46-72, emer dir, 72-82; ed, NY Hist, 47-52; mem NY State Coun Arts, 60-72; chmn, NY State Hist Trust, 66-72; state liaison off, Nat Regist Hist Places, formerly. *Teaching:* Assoc prof, State Univ NY Albany, 34-46; from instr to adj prof, Cooperstown Grad Prog, State Univ NY, 73-82; retired. *Awards:* Guggenheim Fel, 46; Award of Distinction, Am Asn State & Local Hist, 69; Rochester Mus Fel; and others. *Mem:* Fel Am Folklore Soc; Am Asn Mus; Am Asn State & Local Hist; NY Folklore Soc (co-founder); and others. *Interests:* American folk art, folklore and folk life. *Publ:* Ed, Growing Up in the Cooper Country, 65; coauth, Queena Stovall, Artist of the Blue Ridge Piedmont, 75; auth, Three Eyes on The Past, 82, Murder at Cherry Hill, 82 & Cooperstown, rev ed 83. *Mailing Add:* 11 Main St Box 351 Cooperstown NY 13326

JONES, MARVIN HAROLD
PRINTMAKER, PAINTER
b Flora, Ill, May 19, 40. *Study:* Univ Ill, Urbana; Roosevelt Univ, Chicago; Anderson Col, Ind, BA; Univ Calif, Davis, MA, with Roy DeForest, William Wiley & Peter Saul. *Work:* Libr of Cong, Washington, DC; Confederation Art Gallery, Charlottetown, PEI, Can; Osaka Univ of Arts, Japan; Edmonton Art Gallery, Alta; Univ Dallas, Irving, Tex. *Exhib:* Royal Can Acad of Art Ann Exhib, Montreal Mus of Fine Arts, 71; Brit Int Print Biennale, Bradford City Art Gallery, 72, 76 & 82; Drawings/USA, Minn Mus of Art, St Paul, 73, 75 & 77; Nat Print Invitational, Brooklyn Mus, NY, 74; Perth Int Drawing Exhib, Western Australian Art Gallery, 75; Miami Int Print Biennial, Miami Art Ctr, Fla, 75; Biennial Int Print Exhib, Print Club of Philadelphia, 77; Int Biennial Graphic Art, Mod Gallery, Ljubljana, Yugoslavia, 79 & 81; and others. *Teaching:* Asst prof printmaking, Univ Alta, Edmonton, 70-72, Karl Marx Univ, Leipzig, Ger, 81; assoc prof printmaking, Cleveland State Univ, 76- *Awards:* Purchase Award, Miami Univ Nat Print & Drawing Exhib, 77; Ohio Arts Council Grant, 78 & 80; Monntalvo Ctr for the Arts, 79. *Bibliog:* Derek M Besant (auth), Satirical graphics by Marvin Jones & John Will, Art Mag, 10/75; Claire Kelly (auth), West coast drawings, Artweek, 3/77; Art in the western reserve, The New Art Examiner, 10/79. *Mem:* Am Color Print Soc. *Media:* Print (intaglio and relief); acrylic. *Dealer:* Graphics Gallery 3 Embarcadero Ctr San Francisco CA 94111. *Mailing Add:* 12040 Lake 4 Lakewood OH 44107

JONES, NORMA L
PAINTER
b Morrisonville, Ill. *Study:* Univ Houston, Clear Lake City, 75-76; Univ NMex; Univ Mo; Tex Univ; Washington Univ, St Louis; also studied with Rex Brandt, George Post, Robert Wood, Mario Cooper & Edward Betts. *Work:* Banco Brazilia, Pondereille; Tex Instruments Co, Tenneco; AMOCO, Houston; Milestone Petroleum, Colo; First City Bank Albuquerque. *Exhib:* Own Your Own, Denver Mus; Am Watercolor Soc, Nat Acad, New York; Watercolor USA, Springfield Mus, Mo; Baytown Ann, Tex; Watercolor Art Soc Houston; NMex Watercolor Soc; and others. *Awards:* 2nd Place, Watercolor Art Soc Houston, 76; Purchase Award, NMex Watercolor Soc, 82; Merit Award, Western Fedn Watercolor Soc, 83. *Mem:* NMex Watercolor Soc; Watercolor Art Soc Houston; Southwestern Fedn Watercolorists; Am PEN Women. *Media:* Watercolor, Acrylic. *Dealer:* Fine Art Consult SW 1744 Norfolk Houston TX 77098; Vladimir Fine Arts Ansbach WGer. *Mailing Add:* 9312 Las Calabazillas NE Albuquerque NM 87111

JONES, PATTY SUE
PAINTER, CURATOR
b New Orleans, La, Aug 18, 49. *Study:* Auburn Univ, 67-69 & 74; Univ Calif, Los Angeles, photog with Robert Heinecken, BA, 72, MA, 74; Univ Wash, with Jack Lenor Larsen, summer 75. *Work:* Yuma Fine Arts Ctr, Ariz. *Comn:* Paintings, Regent Hotels Int, Beverly Hills, Calif, 74; tapestry, Fluor Corp, Irvine, Calif, 78; tapestry, Security Pac Bank, Topanga Canyon, Calif, 79. *Exhib:* Tucson Mus Art, Ariz, 75; Ariz State Univ, Tempe, 79; Security Pac Hq, Los Angeles, 81; Occidental Col, Los Angeles, 81; Los Angeles Inst Contemp Art, 81; and many others. *Collections Arranged:* Robert Delgado, Mural Making: The Process, 80, The Mask: Object and Image, 80, Paper: Cast/Torn/Formed, 80 & California Dada, 80, Old Venice Jail Gallery, Venice, Calif. *Pos:* Dir's coun mem, Yuma Fine Art Ctr, Ariz, 76-77; cur exhibs, Old Venice Jail Gallery, Venice, Calif, 79-81. *Teaching:* Teaching asst, Univ Calif, Los Angeles, 73-74; instr, Ariz Western Col, Yuma, 74-77; instr, Ariz State Univ, Tempe, 75-76; instr, Mt St Mary's Col, Los Angeles, 82. *Awards:* Purchase Award, 10th Ann Southwestern, 75. *Bibliog:* Laurel Meinig (auth), Artists-in-residence (catalog), Yuma Art Ctr, Ariz, 76; William Wilson (auth), Lint drawings (review), Los Angeles Times, 80. *Media:* Acrylic. *Publ:* Contribr, Spectrum: New directions in color photography, Univ Hawaii, 79. *Mailing Add:* 443 S San Pedro Los Angeles CA 90013

JONES, PIRKLE
PHOTOGRAPHER, EDITOR
b Shreveport, La, Jan 2, 14. *Study:* Calif Sch Fine Arts, cert, 49. *Work:* San Francisco Mus Mod Art; Art Inst Chicago; Ctr Creative Photog, Univ Ariz; Yokohama Mus, Japan; Mus Mod Art, New York. *Comn:* Commemorative UN Portfolio, Bank Am, San Francisco, 55; The Story of a Winery, Paul Masson, John Bolles, San Francisco, 59; Courthouses, Bicentennial Proj, Joseph E Seagram Inc, New York, 75. *Exhib:* Photography in the Twentieth Century, Nat Gallery Can, 67; A Photographic Essay on the Black Panthers, De Young Mus Art, 68, Studio Mus Harlem, 70, Hopkins Ctr, Dartmouth Col, 70 & Univ Calif, Santa Cruz, 70; Octive of Prayer, Mass Inst Technol, 72; The Land, 20th Century Landscapes, Victoria & Albert Mus, 75; Courthouse, Photographs from the Seagrams Collection, Mus Mod Art, New York, 78; Messages From West Coast, Photo Gallery Int, Tokyo, 79; Curator's Choice: By John Humphery, San Francisco Mus Mod Art, 80; Master Photographers: A Sentimental Celebration, Focus Gallery, San Francisco, 81; Awards of Honor, A Documentary Exhibition, San Francisco Arts Commission, Gallery, Bank Am, World Hq, San Francisco, 83; Photography in California: Pushing the Boundaries 1945-1980, San Francisco Mus Mod Art, 84; and others. *Teaching:* Instr photog, Calif Sch Fine Arts, 52-58, Ansel Adams Workshops, Yosemite Nat Park, 66-70 & San Francisco Art Inst, 70- *Awards:* Award Hon Photog, A Documentary Exhib, San Francisco Arts Comn, 83. *Bibliog:* Ansel Adams (auth), article, US Camera Mag, 10/52; Nancy Newhall (auth), article, Aperture Mag, 56; Robert Holmes (auth), article, Brit J Photog, 10/80. *Publ:* Auth, Portfolio One, Commemoration Signing United Nations Charter, private publ, 55; coauth, Death of a valley, Aperture Mag, 60; coauth, The Vanguard, A Photographic Essay on the Black Panthers, Beacon Press, 70. *Mailing Add:* 663 Lovell Ave Mill Valley CA 94941

JONES, RONALD LEE, JR
EDUCATOR, WRITER
b Beckley, WVa, Dec 4, 42. *Study:* Concord Col, BS, 64; Ariz State Univ, MA, 68; Univ Md, PhD, 75. *Pos:* Contrib ed, Art Voices/S, Palm Beach, Fla, 78-; chmn, WVa Arts & Humanities Comn, Capitol Complex, Charleston, 78- *Teaching:* Prof art & chmn dept, Shepherd Col, Shepherdstown, WVa, 69- *Mem:* Nat Art Educ Asn; Nat Coun Policy Study Art Educ; Col Art Asn, WVa (pres, 71, 72 & 75); Nat Asn Arts Adminr; Nat Asn State Art Agencies; and others. *Res:* Researching aesthetic response and writing art criticism for art journals. *Publ:* Auth, A reexamination of Mittler's Efforts toward art attitude modern, Studies in Art Educ, 75; contribr, Artists in Schools: Analysis and Criticism, Univ Ill Bur Educ Res, 78; auth, Phenomenological analysis effects on aspective perception: a review, Rev Res in Visual Arts, 78; auth, Critical reviews of artists, Art Voices/S 78-80; auth, Phenomenological balance and the aesthetic response, J Aesthetic Educ, 79. *Mailing Add:* PO Box 389 Shepherdstown WV 25443

JONES, RONALD WARREN
ARTIST, CRITIC
b Ft Belvoir, Va, July 8, 52. *Study:* Huntington Col, BA, 74; Univ SC, MFA, 76; Ohio Univ, PhD(art hist), 81. *Work:* Mus Mod Art, New York; Centrol Documentazione Artein, Rome, Italy. *Exhib:* One-person exhib, Theories of Art Criticism, Atlanta Art Workers Coalition, GA, 82 & Achievement is Myth, Centro Documentazione Artein, Rome, 83; Arteder 82, Muestra Int Arte Grafico, Bilbao, Spain; Artist's Dilemma, Orgn Independent Artists, New York, 82; A Likely Story, Artists Space, New York, 82 & NAME Gallery, Chicago, 82; Preparing for War, Brooklyn Army Terminal, NY, 83; 10 on 8, New York, 84. *Collections Arranged:* Ken Friedman Fluxus Events, Retrospective, 81. *Pos:* Mem bd dirs, Nat Sculpture Exhib, 79-82; contrib ed, Art Papers, Atlanta, Ga, 80-; mem bd dir, Southeastern Col Art Conf, 83. *Teaching:* Instr art & art hist, Univ S, Tenn, 79- *Awards:* Mellon Found Stipend, 83; Univ Res Grant, Univ S, Tenn, 83; Nat Endowment Arts Visual Artists Fel Grant, 84. *Bibliog:* Arteder 82 Muestra International de Obra Grafica: Fotografia, Feria Int de Muestras de Bilbao, 82; Gerald Mazorati (auth), Art Picks, Soho News, 3/82; Laura Lieberman, Editorial Introduction, Art Papers, 7-8/83. *Mem:* Kappa Pi (pres sigma chapter 72-74); Southeastern Col Art Conf (bd dir, currently); Col Art Asn; Int Asn Art Critics; Southern Asn Sculptors. *Publ:* Auth, Acts of faith without trust: Notes on recent European painting, 1-2/82, Artists projects and artist statements, 5-6/83 & Say, I've got an idea…, 9-10/83, Art Papers. *Mailing Add:* Univ South Sewanee TN 37375

JONES, RUTHE BLALOCK
PAINTER, EDUCATOR

b Claremore, Okla, June 8, 39. *Study:* Bacone Col, with Dick West, AA; Univ Tulsa, with Carl Coker, BFA. *Work:* Mus Am Indian, Heye Found, New York; Indian Arts & Crafts Bd, US Dept Interior, Washington, DC; Heard Mus, Phoenix; Philbrook Art Ctr, Tulsa; Five Civilized Tribes Mus, Muskogee, Okla. *Exhib:* One-man show, Southern Plains Indian Mus, Anadarko, Okla, 81; Turtle Show, Niagra, NY, 82; Night of the First Americans, Kennedy Ctr, Washington, DC, 82; Contemporary North American Indian Painting, Mus Natural Hist, Smithsonian Inst, Washington, DC, 82; American Indian Community House, New York, 82. *Teaching:* Instr art, Bacone Col, Muskogee, Okla, 79- *Awards:* First for Traditional Indian Painting, Philbrook Mus, 68; Spec Award, US Dept Interior, Okla State Soc; Second for Watercolor Painting, Scottsdale Nat Indian Art Exhib, 72. *Bibliog:* J Snodgrass (auth), Handbook American Indian Artists, Mus Am Indian, 67; Forum, Christian Sci Monitor, 6/67; Ruth B Jones--something a bit different, Ariz Repub, 7/67. *Media:* Watercolor, Acrylic, Graphics. *Publ:* Illusr, Nimrod (Am Indian issue), Univ Tulsa J, spring 72. *Dealer:* Linda Greever Art Market 4955J S Memorial Tulsa OK 74145; Don Humphrey Touring Print Exhibits Santa Fe NM. *Mailing Add:* 517 S Woodlawn St Okmulgee OK 74447

JONES, THEODORE JOSEPH
SCULPTOR, PRINTMAKER

b New Orleans, La, Sept 14, 38. *Study:* Xavier Univ, BA; Mich State Univ, MA; Univ Mont, MFA; Fla A&M Univ, cert; Fisk Univ, cert. *Work:* Johnson Publ Co, Chicago; Mus African Art, Washington, DC; First Am Nat Bank, Nashville. *Exhib:* One-man exhibs, Ala A&M Univ, Normal, 75, Tenn State Mus, 75 & Creatadrama Art Gallery, Bloomington, Ind, 75; 17th Tenn All-State Artists Exhib, Centennial Park Galleries, Nashville, 75; From These Roots Exhib, Tenn State Mus, Nashville, 77; Smith-Mason Galleries, Washington, DC, 77; and many others. *Pos:* Touring artist, Tenn Arts Comn, 70-; art consult, Claiborne Ave Design Team Symp, New Orleans, La, 74- *Teaching:* Instr art, Fla A&M Univ, 65-68; from assoc to prof art, Tenn State Univ, 68- *Awards:* Tenn State Univ Grant, 70; Third Place Sculpture, Tenn Art League, 74; Lyzon Galleries Award Graphics, Cent South Exhib, 75. *Bibliog:* Clara Hieronymus (auth), Ted Jones Exhibition, Tennessean Newspaper, 75; Kenneth Weedman (auth), article, Sculpture Quart, 75. *Mem:* Tenn Lit Arts Asn; Southern Independent Artists Asn; Southern Asn Sculptors; Southeastern Graphics Coun; Tennessee Art League. *Publ:* Contribr, Galaxy III Communication Arts Seminar Basic Holography, 74; ed, Faculty exhibition catalogs & brochures, Tenn State Univ, 74-75; auth, Thoughts and Verses (poetry and prints), 75 & Masonite-Printing: A New Approach in Relief Printing, 77, New Dimension Studio, Nashville. *Mailing Add:* 3872 Augusta Dr Nashville TN 37207

JONES, THOMAS WILLIAM
PAINTER

b Lakewood, Ohio, Aug 13, 42. *Study:* Cleveland Inst Art, dipl, 64. *Work:* City of Seattle Selects II (For Pub Collection of Seattle City Light, Wash); Rainier Bank Collection, Pacific Northwest Bell Collection, Seattle, 80. *Comn:* 25 landscape paintings, Gen Tel Co of the Northwest, Everett, Wash, 68; paintings of Old Holland, Western Int Design Serv, St Francis Hotel, San Francisco, 72; paintings for bd dirs, Seattle First Nat Bank, 74; four seasonal landscapes & 60th anniversary catalog cover, Eddie Bauer Inc, Seattle, 75, 80 & 82. *Exhib:* One-man show, Frye Art Mus, Seattle, 73; 154th Nat Acad Design, New York, 79; Northwest Art Today, 75, Works on Paper, 75 & Wash Open, 79, Seattle Art Mus; Artists of America, Denver, 81, 82 & 83; Nat Acad of Western Art, Oklahoma City, 80, 81 & 83; E R Squibb Invitational, Squibb Gallery, Princeton, NJ, 82. *Awards:* Ted Kautzky Mem Award, Am Watercolor Soc, 75 & Bronze Medal of Honor, 79; First Place, Water Media, Rocky Mountain Nat, 76. *Bibliog:* Sylva Coppock (auth), Watercolors that work: Thomas William Jones tradition, View Northwest, Murray Publ, 7/77; Tom Stockley (auth), Painter in the great American tradition, Seattle Times, 11/79; Barbara Dell (auth), feature article in Artists of the Rockies & Golden West, 12/79. *Mem:* Northwest Watercolor Soc (vpres, 74); West Coast Watercolor Soc; Am Acad of Taos, NMex; hon mem Fed Can Artists; Nat Acad Western Art. *Media:* Watercolor. *Publ:* Auth, Watercolor page, Am Artist, 9/79. *Dealer:* Foster/White Gallery 311 Occidental Ave S Seattle WA 98104. *Mailing Add:* 1420 W Lake Sammamish Pkwy NE Bellevue WA 98008

JONES, W LOUIS
PAINTER, SCULPTOR

b Durham, NC, Feb 22, 43. *Study:* Pa Acad Fine Arts; E Carolina Univ, BS; Cranbrook Acad Art, MFA. *Work:* Kalamazoo Inst Art, Mich; Flint Inst Art, Mich. *Exhib:* Butler Inst Am Art, 67; Nat Realists Exhib, Gallery Contemp Art, Winston-Salem, NC, 71; New Realism, Jacksonville Art Mus, Fla, 77; Photo Realist Painters, traveling show to three states; Univ Nebr-Lincoln, 78; Okla Art Ctr, 79; Springfield Art Mus, 79; and others. *Teaching:* Instr painting, Atlanta Sch Art, Ga, summer 65; instr painting, Univ Idaho, 67-69; asst prof drawing & painting, Skidmore Col, 69-74; asst prof grad painting, Russell Sage Col, Troy, NY, 75-77. *Awards:* Purchase Awards, NC Mus Art, 63, Butler Inst Am Art, 67 & Mint Mus Art. *Mem:* Nat Soc Painters in Casein; Am Asn Univ Prof. *Media:* Acrylic; Wood. *Dealer:* Arwin Galleries 222 Grand River W Detroit MI 48226; Kornblee Gallery 20 W 57th St New York NY. *Mailing Add:* Rte 4 Box 91-B Asheboro NC 27203

JONYNAS, VYTAUTAS K
SCULPTOR, PAINTER

b Alytus, Lithuania, Mar 16, 07. *Study:* Nat Art Col, Kaunas, Lithuania; Conservatoire Nat Arts et Metiers & Ecole Boulle, Paris. *Work:* Nat Mus in Lithuania, Latvia, Estonia, Weimar & Hamburg, Ger, Antwerp, Belg; Amsterdam City Mus; Metrop Mus Art, New York; Libr Cong, Washington, DC; Brooklyn Mus Art; and others. *Comn:* Mosaics in Chapel, Nat Shrine of the Immaculate Conception, Washington, DC; decorator bas-relief sculptures, Chapel of Our Lady of Vilnius, St Peter's Basilica, Rome; sculpture, Brooklyn Col, 72; monument, Sidney, Australia, 73; mosaic murals, City of New York, 74-75; and others. *Exhib:* Int Art Gallery, Cleveland, 64; USA Traveling Exhib, South Am; USA Int Traveling Exhib by Xylon, Europe; Kunst Geboide, Mus Tubingen, Ger; one-man show, Art Mus, Vilnius, Lithuania & Art Mus, Kaunas, 79; and others. *Teaching:* Instr drawing, painting & graphic arts, cols & insts in Europe, 35-51; instr, Catan-Rose Inst Fine Arts, 52-57; asst prof, Fordham Univ, 56-73. *Awards:* Print & Drawing Prize, Conn Acad Fine Arts, 59; Purchase Prize, Calif Soc Etchers, 61; Winner, Int Stained Glass Window Competition, Wilton, Conn; and many others. *Publ:* Contribr, illus in Das Kunstwerk, 47, 50 & 57 & Am Artist Mag, 52. *Mailing Add:* c/o Jonynas Studio Art 182-37 Jamaica Ave Hollis NY 11423

JOOST-GAUGIER, CHRISTIANE L
ADMINISTRATOR, HISTORIAN

b Ste Maxime, France; US citizen. *Study:* Radcliffe Col, BA(hon) & MA; Harvard Univ, PhD; Univ Munich. *Teaching:* Asst prof Renaissance art, Tufts Univ, 69-75; Prof Renaissance art, NMex State Univ, 75-, head art dept, 75-81. *Awards:* Fulbright Fel; Delmas Found Grant; Am Asn Univ Women Fel, Italy. *Mem:* Col Art Asn (bd dirs, 81); Nat Coun Arts Administrators (bd dirs); Renaissance Soc Am (coun); Women's Caucus Art (adv bd, currently); Mid Am Col Art Asn; and others. *Res:* Venetian drawings, series of famous men and women; Quattrocento art in Florence and Venice. *Publ:* Auth of var articles in Gazette des Beaux Arts, Art Bull, Zeitschrift für Kunstgeschichte, Commentari, Antichita Viva & Acta Historiae Artium; auth, The Selected Drawings of Jacopo Bellini. *Mailing Add:* Dept of Art NMex State Univ Las Cruces NM 88003

JORDAN, BARBARA SCHWINN
PAINTER

b Glen Ridge, NJ. *Study:* Parsons Sch Design, Paris; Grand Cent Art Sch; Art Students League, with Frank DuMond, Luigi Lucioni & others; Grande Chaumiere & Acad Julian, Paris, France; Columbia Univ; Nat Acad Design. *Work:* Holbrook Collection; Ga Mus Art Collection; numerous pvt collections. *Comn:* Portraits, incl Queen Sirikit, Princess Margaret & Princess Grace. *Exhib:* Guild Hall, 69, 79 & 81; one-man shows, Duquesne Univ, 73 & Bodley Gallery, 73 & 80 ; Summit Art Ctr, 81; 100 Years of Still Life Painting, Meredith Long Gallery, Houston, 83. *Pos:* Founder & chmn art comt, UNICEF, 50-61. *Teaching:* Lectr illus & portrait painting, instr illus, Parsons Sch Design, 52-54. *Awards:* Prizes, Guild Hall & Art Dirs Club. *Mem:* Cosmopolitan Club, New York; Soc Illustrators. *Media:* Oil. *Publ:* Auth, The technique of Barbara Schwinn, 56 & World of fashion art, Art Instr Schs, 68; contribr, Ladies Home J, Good Housekeeping, Colliers, Cosmopolitan, McCalls, Saturday Eve Post & French, Brit, Ger, Belg, Danish & Swed mag & other publ, 40-60. *Dealer:* Meredith Long Houston TX. *Mailing Add:* RFD 550 Mecox Rd Water Mill NY 11976

JORDAN, GEORGE EDWIN
CRITIC, HISTORIAN

b Ky, Oct 29, 40. *Study:* Univ Ky; Ringling Sch Art, Sarasota, Fla, BFA; ETenn State Univ. *Pos:* Cur, Reece Mus, Johnson City, Tenn, 66-69; cur Am art & registrar, New Orleans Mus Art, La, 69-72; art critic, New Orleans Times-Picayune, La, 74-77, ed World of Art column, 77-79; free-lance art writer, lectr, appraiser & consult, 79-; contrib ed, Art & Auction, 81-; co-ed, New Orleans Art Rev, 82-; auth, Critics Choice monthly column, Go Mag, 83- *Teaching:* Guest instr hist contemp painting, Adult Educ, Tulane Univ, 76- *Res:* Artists who worked in New Orleans and the Southeast, late 18th, 19th and early 20th centuries. *Publ:* Contribr, Works of John Vanderlyn, Univ Art Gallery, Binghamton, NY, 70; contribr, Louisiana Paintings 19th Century, The William Groves Collection, Groves Press, 71; contribr, Two Centuries of Black American Art, Los Angeles Co Mus Art & Alfred A Knopf, 76; contribr & coauth, Louisiana portraits, Colonial Dames of Am in La, 76; auth, Louisiana Artists 19th Century, WYES-Educ Television, New Orleans, 72-73. *Mailing Add:* 519 St Ann New Orleans LA 70116

JORDAN, JACK
ADMINISTRATOR, SCULPTOR

b July 29, 27; US citizen. *Study:* Langston Univ, BA; Univ Iowa, MA; Ind Univ, MS; State Univ Iowa, MFA; Okla Univ; Ind Univ, DEd. *Work:* State Univ Iowa Mus, Iowa City; Atlanta Univ Art Mus, Ga; Okla Art Ctr, Oklahoma City; Golden State Ins Co, Calif; Afro-Am Cult Heritage Ctr. *Comn:* Come Ye Children (sculpture), Bethany United Methodist Church, New Orleans, 71; Mural, Bell Baptist Church, 80; mural, Second Hwy Baptist Church, 81; mural, Guiding Light Baptist Church, 81; Contribution of Blacks to Lousiana History (mural), Southern Univ, 75. *Exhib:* New York Archit League & Nat Sculpture Soc; Nat Competitive Art Show, Walker Art Ctr, Minneapolis & El Mira Art Gallery, Pismo Beach, Calif; Nat Art Show, Carnegie Inst Int, Pittsburgh, Pa; Atlanta Art Gallery; Sculpture 81, Counterpoint Guild Nat Exhib of 16 Selected Black Sculptors, New York, 81. *Collections Arranged:* Emancipation Centennial Nat Art Exhib, 63; New Orleans Bicentennial Art Exhib, Bicentennial Comn New Orleans, 74; Black Family Bicentennial Art Show, 75. *Teaching:* Head art dept, Claflin Univ, Orangeburg, SC, 49-50; Allen Univ, Columbia, SC, 52-55 & Langston Univ,

Okla, 57-61; prof & head art dept, Southern Univ New Orleans, 61- *Awards:* Sculpture Awards, Joslyn Art Mus, Omaha, Nebr & Walker Art Ctr, Minneapolis; nine Nat Sculpture Awards, Atlanta Art Gallery, 50-73; and others. *Bibliog:* Cedric Dover (auth), American Negro Art, New York Graphic Soc, 60; Kaye Teall (auth), Black History of Oklahoma, Okla Pub Sch Title III, Elem & Sec Educ Act, 71; Judith W Chase (auth), Afro-American Arts & Crafts, Van Nostrand Reinhold, 71. *Mem:* Okla Art Asn; Nat Conf Artists (vpres, 65, pres, 66-67); Creatadrama Soc; Nat Conf Artists (chmn bd trustees, 83-); New Orleans Ctr Creative Arts (treas, 83-). *Mailing Add:* Southern Univ New Orleans Dept of Art 6400 Press Dr New Orleans LA 70126

JORDAN, JIM
CRITIC, PAINTER
b Memphis, Tenn, Nov 27, 40. *Study:* Univ Tex, with George Bogart & C Forsyth, BFA(summa cum laude), 63; Univ Ill, with Peter Bodnar, Lee Chesney & M Franciscono, MFA, 65, MA(art hist), 65; Harvard Univ, with F Deknatel, Michael Fried & James Ackerman, fel, 65-66; Saybrook Inst, PhD, 83. *Work:* Univ Tex, Austin; Univ Tex, Arlington; Ft Worth Mus Fine Arts; Univ Ill; Dayton Art Inst, Ohio. *Exhib:* All-Ohio Painting & Graphics, Dayton Art Inst, 67, 70 & 74; Ohio Drawings, Columbus Gallery of Fine Arts, 70; Antioch Arts, Contemp Art Ctr, Cincinnati, Ohio, 72; Noyes Gallery, Antioch Col, 79-81; SDak Artists Invitational, 81-82; and others. *Collections Arranged:* Robert Whitmore, American Impressionist Retrospective (auth, catalogue), 74 & Sid Chafetz, Thirty Years in Ohio Retrospective 1948-1978 (auth, catalogue), 78, Noyes Gallery Art, Antioch Col, Yellow Springs, Ohio; Art in a Public Place, SDak, 81-82. *Pos:* Chmn art dept, Antioch Col, 66-77; dir, Noyes Gallery Art, 73; vis artist, Univ Southern Calif, Los Angeles, 75; bk rev ed, Antioch Rev, Antioch Col, 78; chmn arts area, Antioch, 79-81; head dept visual art, SDak State Univ, Brookings, 81-; independent critic. *Teaching:* Prof art hist, painting & drawing, Antioch Col, 66-81. *Awards:* Ford Fel, 67-70; Nat Endowment Humanities, 78-79; Nat Endowment Arts, 79, 81-83. *Mem:* Midwestern Col Art Asn Am; Nat Coun Art Administr; Int Asn Art Critics; Am Asn Advan Sci. *Media:* Oil, Pastel. *Res:* Nineteenth century French painting and contemporary American art; art criticism. *Publ:* Ed, Bibliography of Victoriana, 65 & auth, Edouard Manet's Paintings Prior to 1870, Univ Ill, 68; critical writings in Dialogue & New Art Examiner; auth, The New Teachers, Josey-Bass, 70. *Mailing Add:* Dept of Art Solberg Hall SDak State Univ Brookings SD 57007

JORDAN, ROBERT
PAINTER, EDUCATOR
b Floral Park, NY, Sept 22, 25. *Study:* Dartmouth Col, BA; Columbia Univ, MA. *Work:* Addison Gallery of Am Art, Andover, Mass; Nat Air & Space Mus, Washington, DC; St Louis Art Mus; Boston Pub Libr; Washington Univ Art Gallery, St Louis, Mo. *Exhib:* Seven Decades, Addison Gallery, 69; one-man shows, Far Gallery, New York, 74, 76 & 77; Am 1976 (traveling exhib), US Dept Interior Bicentennial, 76; Butler Inst Am Art Ann, Youngstown, Ohio, 77; Creiger Sesen Gallery, Boston, 80; Capricorn Gallery, Bethesda, Md, 80; Sherry French Gallery, New York, 83; and others. *Teaching:* Prof painting & Am art hist, Washington Univ. *Media:* Oil, Pastel. *Dealer:* Sherry French Gallery 41 W 57th St New York NY 10019. *Mailing Add:* RFD Box 18 Center Conway NH 03813

JORDAN, WILLIAM B
MUSEUM DIRECTOR, HISTORIAN
b Nashville, Tenn, May 8, 40. *Study:* Washington & Lee Univ, BA, 62; NY Univ, MA, 64, PhD, 67. *Pos:* Chmn div fine arts, Meadows Sch of the Arts, Southern Methodist Univ, 67-73, dir, Meadows Mus, 67-81; deputy dir, Kimbell Art Mus, 81- *Teaching:* Assoc prof Span art hist, Southern Methodist Univ, 68-75, prof Span art hist, 75-81. *Mem:* Am Soc of Hispanic Art Hist Studies (pres, 76-78); Hispanic Soc of Am. *Publ:* Auth, Murillo's Jacob laying the peeled rods before the flocks of Laban, Art News, 68; auth, A museum of Spanish painting in Texas, 68 & The Meadows School of the Arts at Southern Methodist University: Progress..., 70, Art J; auth, The Meadows Museum: A Visitor's Guide to the Collection, Meadows Mus, 74; auth, El Greco of Toledo (catalog), Toledo Mus Art, 82. *Mailing Add:* c/o Kimbell Art Mus PO Box 9440 Ft Worth TX 76107

JORGENSEN, FLEMMING
PAINTER
b Aalborg, Denmark, May 29, 34; Can citizen. *Study:* Art Sch Denmark. *Work:* Nat Gallery Can, Ottawa, Ont; Can Coun, Ottawa; McGill Univ; Univ Victoria; Winnipeg Art Gallery, Man. *Exhib:* 2nd Biennial Int Prints, Paris, France, 70; one-man shows, Marlborough-Godard, Montreal, Que, 72, Gallery Allen, Vancouver, 74, Bau-Xi Gallery, Victoria, 75 & Gallery Mira Godard, Toronto, 76; Kyle's Gallery, 79-83. *Teaching:* Instr, Univ Victoria, BC, Lester B Pearson Col, currently. *Awards:* Can Coun Arts Bursary, 69 & 71. *Dealer:* Gallery Mira Godard 22 Hazelton Ave Toronto ON Can. *Mailing Add:* 2759 Seaview Rd 1545 Fort St Victoria BC V8N 1K7 Canada

JORGENSEN, SANDRA
PAINTER, EDUCATOR
b Evanston, Ill, Apr 21, 34. *Study:* Lake Forest Col, BA, 57; Akademie der Bildenden Kunste, Vienna, 58; Art Inst Chicago, MFA, 64. *Exhib:* Richard Gray Gallery, Chicago, 74 & 77 & Renaissance Soc, Univ Chicago, 74; Nancy Lurie Gallery, Chicago, 78; NAME Gallery, Chicago, 78; Art Inst Chicago, 78 & 80; ARC Gallery, Chicago, 79; and others. *Teaching:* Prof art, Elmhurst Col, 66- *Media:* Oil. *Mailing Add:* 245 Elm Park Elmhurst IL 60126

JORGENSON, DALE ALFRED
EDUCATOR, ADMINISTRATOR
b Litchfield, Nebr, Mar 20, 26. *Study:* Harding Col, Ark, philos with J D Bales, BMus, 48; George Peabody Col, Tenn, MA, 50; Ind Univ, aesthetics with John Mueller, PhD, 57; Harvard Univ, cert arts admin, 72. *Teaching:* Prof aesthetics, Bethany Col WVa, 59-62; dir fine arts, Milligan Col, Tenn, 62-63; head fine arts div & teacher aesthetics, Northeast Mo State Univ, 63- *Mem:* Am Soc Aesthetics; Midwest Col Art Asn. *Res:* Aesthetics and elementary aesthetics for contemporary students. *Publ:* Auth, Toward a biblical aesthetic, Christianity Today, 60; auth, The campus and the arts, Proceedings of the Nat Asn Sch Music, 70; auth, Preparing the educator for related arts, Music Educr J, 5/70; auth, The French lieutenant's woman, or to forego manipulation, Christianity Today, 5/11/73. *Mailing Add:* 1512 S Cottage Grove Kirksville MO 63501

JOSEPHSON, KENNETH BRADLEY
PHOTOGRAPHER, ASSEMBLAGE ARTIST
b Detroit, Mich, July 1, 32. *Study:* Rochester Inst Technol, BFA, 57; Inst Design, Ill Inst Technol, MS, 60. *Work:* Mus Mod Art, New York; Art Inst Chicago; Ctr Creative Photog, Univ Ariz; Mus Contemp Art, Chicago; Bibliot Nat, Paris. *Comn:* Great Ideas Series (assemblage), Container Corp Am, Chicago, 81. *Exhib:* The Photographers Eye, Mus Mod Art, New York 64; solo exhib, Art Inst Chicago, 71, Mus Art, Univ Iowa, Iowa City, 74, Fotoforum, Kassel, Ger, 78 & Mus Contemp Art, Chicago, 83; Painting in the Age of Photography, Kunsthaus, Zurich, 77; Mirrors and Windows, Mus Mod Art, New York, 78; American Photographs of the Seventies, Art Inst Chicago, 79. *Teaching:* Prof photog, Art Inst Chicago, 60-; exchange teacher, Konstfackskolan Stockholm, Sweden, 66-67; assoc prof, Univ Hawaii, Honolulu, 67-68; vis prof, Univ Calif, Los Angeles, 81-82. *Awards:* Fels, Guggenheim Mem Found, 72 & Nat Endowment Arts, 75 & 79; Ruttenberg Arts Found Grant, 83. *Bibliog:* Alex Sweetman (auth), Reading the bread book--a ten page note, Afterimage, 3/74; Floris M Neussüs (auth), Kenneth Josephson: The illusion of the picture, Fotoforum, Kassel, Ger, 78. *Publ:* Auth, The Bread Book, private publ, 73; contribr, New American imagery, Camera, Switz, Vol 53, No 5, 74; contribr, The Photographers Choice, Addison House, 75; contribr, Nude: Theory, Lustrum Press, 79. *Dealer:* Rhona Hoffman 215 W Superior St Chicago IL 60610. *Mailing Add:* Art Inst Chicago Columbus Dr at Jackson Blvd Chicago IL 60603

JOSIMOVICH, GEORGE
PAINTER, DESIGNER
b Mitrovica-Srem, Yugoslavia, May 2, 1894; US citizen. *Study:* Art Inst Chicago, 14-19; also with George Bellows, Randall Davey & Herman Sachs, 19-20. *Work:* Joslyn Art Mus, Omaha, Nebr. *Exhib:* One-man show, Galerie d'Art Contemporain, Paris, 27; 28th Int Exhib, Carnegie Inst, Pittsburgh, 29; Selected Paintings by Contemp Am Artists, Toledo Mus Art, 30; nine ann exhibs, Artists of Chicago & Vicinty, Art Inst Chicago, 33-49; Three Rivers Art Festival, Pittsburgh, 68 & 70. *Pos:* Vpres, Chicago Soc Artists, 42-43, pres, 43-44. *Teaching:* Supvr craft shop, Dayton Mus Art, 21; instr parents' ceramic class, Pine Grove Pre-Sch, Chicago, 53-55. *Awards:* Silver Medal, Chicago Soc Artists, 29. *Bibliog:* J Z Jacobson (auth), The Chicago independent, The Arts, 6/31 & Art of Today, L M Stein, 33; C J Bulliet (auth), Six Chicagoans, Art Digest, 5/50. *Media:* Oil, Acrylic. *Mailing Add:* 1800 Walker Ave Apt-A Irvington NJ 07111

JOUKHADAR, KRISTINA
DEALER, COLLECTOR
b New York, NY, Feb 9, 52. *Pos:* Dir, Joukhadar Gallery, 78- *Specialty:* Contemporary and naive art. *Collection:* Haitian and American art. *Mailing Add:* Joukhadar Gallery 440 E 85th St New York NY 10028

JOUKHADAR, MOUMTAZ
DEALER, PAINTER
b Damas, Syria, Apr 29, 40; US citizen. *Study:* Accademia di Belle Arti, Rome, Italy, MS, with Mario Mafai; Art Students League, 69-72. *Work:* Damascus Mus. *Exhib:* Group Exhib for Foreign Artists, Rome, Italy, 68; Joukhadar Gallery, New York; one-man shows, Nat Mus Damascus, Syria, 64, Nader Art Gallery, New York, 74 & Joukhadar Gallery, 76 & Retrospect, 79. *Pos:* Art dir, Adalia Anstalt, Rome, Italy, 64-68, Medical and Science, New York, 70-73, Media Properties, New York, 73-75 & Physics Today, New York, 75- *Teaching:* Prof fine art, Pub Sch Syst, Homs, Syria, 60-62. *Awards:* Biennial Venezia, Int Exhib, 66; Medal of the City of Rome, Group Exhib for Foreign Artists, Italy, 68. *Media:* Oil. *Res:* History of the Islamic architecture in Spain and the Alhambra of Granada. *Mailing Add:* 440 E 85th St New York NY 10028

JOVINE, MARCEL
MEDALIST, SCULPTOR
b Naples, Italy, July 26, 21; US citizen. *Study:* Univ Naples, Italy, BS; Royal Acad Turin, Italy, BS, 41; also studied with Brunetto Buracchini, Siena, Italy. *Work:* Horse Mus Ky, Lexington; Mus Racing, Saratoga, NY. *Comn:* Medal, Freedom Train Comn, Chicago, 76; US Bicentennial Soc & Time-Life, 76; Winter Olympic medal, Switz, 80; Myrtlewood (portrait), Spendthrift Farms, Lexington, Ky, 80; Thoroughbred Racing Asn, 82; and others. *Exhib:* Nat Sculpture Soc, Equitable Life Ann, New York, 77-81; Cult Ctr, Sch Art, Demarest, NJ, 80-81. *Pos:* Bd dirs, Cult Ctr, Sch Art, Demarest, NJ. *Awards:* Lindsey-Morris Mem Award, 77 & M H Lamson Prize, 83, Nat Sculpture Soc; Winner, Medal Competition, Am Numismatic Soc, 83. *Mem:* Nat Sculpture Soc; Fedn Int Medaille. *Media:* Mixed Metals. *Mailing Add:* 270 Harrington Ave Closter NJ 07624

JOYAUX, ALAIN GEORGES
MUSEUM DIRECTOR
b Lansing, Mich, Oct 28, 50. *Study:* Mich State Univ, BFA(studio), 75, MFA(studio), 77, MA(art hist), 78. *Collections Arranged:* European Tools From the 17th Century to the 19th Century (auth, catalog), 81; American Naive Painting: The Edgar William and Bernice Chrysler Garbish Collection (auth, catalog), Boston Flint Inst Arts, 82; The Elisabeth Ball Collection of Paintings, Drawings and Watercolors: The George and Frances Ball Foundation (auth, catalog), 83. *Pos:* Asst dir, Flint Inst Arts, Mich, 78-83; dir, Ball State Univ Art Gallery, 83- *Mem:* Am Asn Museums. *Res:* Late 19th century European art; Degas. *Mailing Add:* Art Gallery Ball State Univ Muncie IN 47306

JOYCE, J DAVID
PHOTOGRAPHER, SCULPTOR
b Kindersley, Sask, Jan 7, 46. *Study:* Carleton Univ, Ottawa, BA, 69; Univ Ore, Eugene, MA, 72, MFA, 75. *Work:* Seattle Arts Comn Portable Works Collection. *Comn:* Photosculpture, Ore Repertory Theatre, Eugene, 80; photosculpture theatre sets, Eugene Ballet Co, 82; photosculptures, Univ Ore Mus Art, Eugene, 82, Hult Ctr Performing Arts, Eugene, 83 & Mid-Valley Arts Coun, Salem, Ore, 83. *Exhib:* Solo exhib, Triton Mus Art, Santa Clara, Calif, 83; Alternative Image II, Kohler Art Ctr, Sheboygan, Wis, 83; Segmentations, Friends Photog, Carmel, Calif, 83; Theatre of Geture, Los Angeles Ctr Photog Studies, 83; Electrostatics Int, Cleveland State Univ, 84. *Teaching:* Asst prof film, Loyola Univ, Montreal, 75-76; instr mass communication & design, Lane Community Col, Ore, 78- *Awards:* Second Prize, Anacortes Arts Coun Festival, 81. *Bibliog:* Lee Evans (auth), David Joyce: A portrait, Denali Mag, Lane Community Col, 82. *Mem:* Artists Union Visual Arts Coop (pres, 82-); Northwest Media Proj; Lane Regional Arts Coun. *Media:* Life size photographic and photocopy sculpture. *Mailing Add:* 364 E Broadway #1 Eugene OR 97401

JOYCE, MARSHALL WOODSIDE
PAINTER, INSTRUCTOR
b Medford, Mass, Mar 12, 12. *Study:* Sch Practical Art, Boston. *Work:* Mus Fine Arts South, Mobile, Ala; Cranberry World & Plymouth Plantation, Mass; Peabody Mus, Salem; Mus Fine Arts, Anchorage; and others. *Comn:* Painting & carving, Plymouth Home Nat Bank, 65; painting, Plymouth Pub Libr, 67; calendar series, Davis Standard Co, Pawcatuck, Conn; painting, Kingston Pub Libr, Mass; Sears Tower, Chicago; and others. *Exhib:* Marine Painting Nat Competition, Franklin Mint, Philadelphia, 74; Rockport Art Asn, Mass, 74; NShore Art Asn, Gloucester; Cape Cod Art Asn, Barnstable, Mass; Am Soc Marine Artists, New York, 80; Guild Boston Artists, Boston, 80; and others. *Pos:* Demonstrator, workshops, Key West, Fla, Anchorage, Alaska, Mus Fine Arts, Mobile, Ala & Jackson, NH; free lance artist & illusr, Boston, 36-60; art dir, Gunnar Myrbeck, Quincy, Mass, 61-64. *Teaching:* Instr design illus, Butera Sch Art, Boston, 61-70. *Awards:* Marine Painting Prize, Franklin Mint, 74; Gold Medal of Honor, Rockport Art Asn, 74; 1st Prize, New Eng Watercolor Soc, 80. *Mem:* Rockport Art Asn, Mass; Am Soc Marine Artists; Cape Cod Art Asn; New Eng Watercolor Asn; Guild Boston Artists. *Media:* Oil, Watercolor. *Publ:* Illusr, Skipper Mag, 67; illusr calendars, Davis-Standard Co, Pawcatuck, Conn, 56-57. *Dealer:* Annapolis Marine Art Gallery 10 Dock St Annapolis MD 21401; Guild of Boston Artists Newbury St Boston MA. *Mailing Add:* 5 River St Kingston MA 02364

JU, I-HSIUNG
PAINTER, EDUCATOR
b Kiangyin, China, Sept 15, 23. *Study:* Nat Univ Amoy, China, AB(Chinese art), 47; Univ Santo Tomas, Manila, BFA, 55, MA(hist), 68. *Work:* Philippine Cult Ctr, Manila; Nat Mus Hist, Taipei, Taiwan; Int Ctr, Univ Conn; DuPont Art Gallery, Washington & Lee Univ; F&M Ctr, Richmond, Va; and others. *Comn:* 14 paintings, Gulf States Paper Corp Nat Hq, Tuscaloosa, Ala, 70-71; and others. *Exhib:* South-East Asian Art Contest, Manila, 57; Asian Arts Festival, Univ Philippines, Manila, 65; Philippine & Japan Joint Art Exhib, Nat Mus Hist, Taipei, 66; 10th Japan Nan-ga-in Exhib, Tokyo, Kyoto & Osaka Mus, 70; Nat Painting & Calligraph Exhib, Nat Gallery, Taipei, 70 & 74. *Teaching:* Lectr Chinese arts, Univ Maine, Univ NH, Univ Vt, Univ Conn, 68-69 & Va Mus Fine Arts, Richmond, 69-71; prof art, Univ Va & Washington & Lee Univ, 69- *Awards:* Ring-Tum-Phi Award, Washington & Lee Univ, 71; Art Educator of the Year, Taiwan, 74; Spec Award for Contrib to the Arts, Nat Mus of Hist, Taipai, 78. *Mem:* Col Art Asn Am. *Media:* Ink, Acrylic. *Publ:* Illusr, The Children of Light, 56; auth, About Art, 59; auth, Book of Bamboo, Book of Orchids & A Collection of Recent Landscape Paintings by Ju, Nat Mus of Hist, Taipei, 76. *Mailing Add:* Dept of Fine Arts Washington & Lee Univ Lexington VA 24450

JUAREZ, ROBERTO
PAINTER
b Chicago, Ill, 1952. *Study:* San Francisco Art Inst, BFA; Univ Calif, Los Angeles, 78-79. *Work:* Newark Mus, NJ. *Exhib:* New Wave, New York, Inst Art & Urban Resources, PS1, New York, 81; New Visions, Aldrich Mus, 81; New Directions ..., Mus Art, Ft Lauderdale, Fla, 82; Back to the USA, Kunstmuseum, Luzern, Theinisches Landesmuseum, Bonn & Württembergischer Kunstverein, Stuttgart, 83 & 84; American Artist as Printmaker, Brooklyn Mus, 83-84. *Bibliog:* Roberta Smith (auth), article, Village Voice, 12/81; Grace Glueck (auth), article, New York Times, 1/28/83; Susan Hapgood (auth), article, Flash Art, 3/83. *Media:* Oil, Acrylic. *Dealer:* Robert Miller Gallery 724 Fifth Ave New York NY 10019. *Mailing Add:* 137 E Houston New York NY 10002

JUDD, DE FORREST HALE
PAINTER, EDUCATOR
b Hartsgrove, Ohio, Apr 4, 16. *Study:* Cleveland Inst Art, grad, 38, post grad scholar, 39; Colorado Springs Fine Arts Ctr, with Boardman Robinson, 39-42. *Work:* Cleveland Mus Art, Ohio; Dallas Mus Fine Arts, Tex; Beaumont Mus Art, Tex; Univ Tex, Austin; Southern Methodist Univ. *Exhib:* American Painting Today, Metrop Mus Art, 50; Texas Contemporary Artists, Knoedler Gallery, New York, 52; New Accessions, USA, Colorado Springs Fine Arts Ctr, 52; Ten Texas Painters, Frank Perls Gollery, Beverly Hills, Calif, 53; Texas Painting & Sculpture, 20th Century, Southern Methodist Univ, 71. *Teaching:* Prof painting, Southern Methodist Univ, 46-82, prof emer, 82. *Awards:* First Prize, Cleveland Mus Art, 41; E M Dealey Purchase Award, Tex Painters & Sculptors Exhib, 50; First Prize, 2nd Ann Exhib, Beaumont Mus Art, 53. *Media:* Oil, Acrylic. *Mailing Add:* 11039 Tibbs St Dallas TX 75230

JUDD, DONALD CLARENCE
SCULPTOR
b Excelsior Springs, Mo, June 3, 28. *Study:* Art Students League, 47-53; Columbia Univ, BS(philos), 53, grad study, 58-61. *Work:* Mus Mod Art, New York; Whitney Mus Art, New York; Walker Art Ctr, Minneapolis, Minn; Los Angeles Co Mus; Albright-Knox Art Gallery, Buffalo; and others. *Comn:* Art Gallery SAustralia, 74, Northern Ky Univ, 77, Linz, Austria, 77 & Muenster, WGer, 77. *Exhib:* One-man shows, Whitney Mus Am Art, 68, Pasadena Art Mus, Calif, 70, Kunsthalle, Bern, 76,, Mus STex, Corpus Christi, 77 & Watari Gallery, Tokyo, Japan, 78; New York Painting & Sculpture: 1940-1970, Metrop Mus Art, New York, 69-70; retrospective, Nat Gallery Can, Ottawa, 75; Kunstmuseum Basel, Switzerland; Leo Castelli Gallery, New York, all years; Knight Gallery, Charlotte, NC, 83; and others. *Pos:* Contrib ed, Arts Mag, 59-65. *Awards:* US Govt grants, 67 & 76; Guggenheim Grant, 68. *Bibliog:* William Agee (auth), Don Judd, Whitney Mus Am Art, 68; John Coplans (auth), Don Judd, Pasadena Art Mus, 71; Brydon Smith (auth), article, Nat Gallery Can, Ottawa. *Media:* Metal, Plywood. *Dealer:* Leo Castelli 420 W Broadway New York NY 10013. *Mailing Add:* 101 Spring Rd New York NY 10012

JUDGE, MARY FRANCES
PAINTER
b Minneapolis, Minn, July 31, 35. *Study:* Col New Rochelle, NY, BA(art), 61; Webster Col, St Louis, Mo; Univ Notre Dame, Ind, MFA(painting), 71. *Work:* Carnegie Inst, Pittsburgh, Pa; Springfield Col Gallery, Ill; Nobles Co Art Ctr, Worthington, Minn. *Exhib:* Midwest Biennial, Joslyn Mus, Omaha, Nebr, 72; Ann Exhib, Springfield Mus, Mo, 70; Ann Mid-States Exhib, Evansville Mus, Ind, 71; Am Women Artists, Mus Contemp Art, Sao Paulo, Brazil, 80. *Pos:* Mem bd, Women's Art Ctr, St Louis Women Artists, Mo, 72-74; mem bd, Artist Equity, Dallas, Tex, 74-78; mem bd, Dallas Mus Fine Arts, Tex, 76-77. *Awards:* Strathmore Nat Art Award, Scholastic Art Awards, Strathmore Papers, 50. *Bibliog:* Hedy O'Beil (auth), article, Arts Mag, 10/78; Terry Trucco (auth), article, Art News, 5/79; Marian Courtney (auth), article, New York Times, 6/26/83. *Media:* Mixed. *Dealer:* Dolly Fiterman Art Gallery 238 Plymouth Bldg 12 South Sixth St Minneapolis MN 55402. *Mailing Add:* 265 East 162nd St Bronx NY 10451

JUDKINS, SYLVIA
PAINTER
b New York, NY. *Study:* Pratt Inst; Sch Visual Arts, New York; China Inst, New York; also painting tours with Edgar Whitney & Barse Miller; Nat Acad Fine Arts, scholar, 68-70. *Exhib:* Am Artists Prof League Grand Nat Exhib, Lever House, New York, 67 & 70; Parrish Mus Ann Exhib, Southampton, NY, 70; Nat Art League Spring Exhib, Adelphi Univ, 71 & 77; Am Watercolor Soc Ann, Nat Acad Design, New York, 73-75; Painters & Sculptors Soc NJ, Nat Arts Club, 75; and others. *Pos:* Display artist, 50-60; tech illusr, 60-65. *Awards:* High Winds Award, Am Watercolor Soc, 75; First Prize for Watercolor, State Univ NY Col, Westbury, 77; Best in Show, Manhasset Art Asn, 81; and others. *Mem:* Am Artists Prof League; Island Art Guild (vpres, prog chmn, 74-75); Am Watercolor Soc; Manhasset Art Asn. *Media:* Watercolor, Acrylic. *Mailing Add:* 35-36 76th St Jackson Heights NY 11372

JUDSON, JEANNETTE ALEXANDER
PAINTER
b New York, NY, Feb 23, 12. *Study:* Nat Acad Design, with Robert Phillip & Leon Kroll; Art Students League, with Vaclav Vytlacil, Charles Alston, Carl Holty & Sidney Gross. *Work:* NY Univ Collection; Brandeis Univ; Brooklyn Mus; Columbia Univ, New York, NY; US Embassies, Stockholm, Sweden & Pretoria, S Africa; and many other pub & pvt collections. *Exhib:* One-man shows, Pa State Univ, 69, NY Univ, 69, Syracuse Univ House, New York, 75 & Am Standard Gallery, 80; Key Gallery, New York, 80-83; and others. *Awards:* D Feigen Mem Award, Am Soc Contemp Artists, 77; Am Soc Contemp Artists Award, 78; Nat Asn Women Artists Award, 79. *Mem:* Nat Asn Women Artists; Am Soc Contemp Artists; Artists Equity New York. *Media:* Oil, Acrylic. *Dealer:* Key Gallery 130 Greene St New York NY 10012. *Mailing Add:* 1130 Park Ave New York NY 10028

JUDSON, WILLIAM D
CURATOR, HISTORIAN
b New London, Conn, Dec 10, 39. *Study:* Williams Col, BA, 60; Oberlin Col, MA, 68; Yale Univ. *Collections Arranged:* 73 var vis artist presentations, 75- *Pos:* Cur film & video, Mus Art, Carnegie Inst, Pittsburgh; panelist media arts, Nat Endowment Arts, 78-; bd mem, Pittsburgh Filmmakers Inc, 74- *Teaching:* Adj inst film hist, Univ Pittsburgh, 73- *Mem:* Col Art Asn; Ohio

Valley Regional Media Arts Coalition (pres, 80-); Am Film Inst; Am Fedn Arts (film adv bd, 78-). *Res:* Early film history; documentary film; experimental film; 20th century art. *Mailing Add:* 4623 Friendship Ave Pittsburgh PA 15224

JULES, MERVIN
PAINTER, EDUCATOR
b Baltimore, Md, Mar 21, 12. *Study:* Baltimore City Col; Md Inst Fine & Appl Arts; Art Students League. *Work:* Metrop Mus Art, New York; Art Inst Chicago; Mus Fine Arts, Boston; Portland Art Mus; Libr Cong, Washington, DC; plus many other pub & pvt collections. *Exhib:* Carnegie Inst Int, Pittsburgh; San Francisco World's Fair; Artists for Victory, sent to England; Corcoran Gallery Art; Whitney Mus Am Art; plus many others. *Teaching:* Vis artist, Smith Col, 45-46, assoc prof, 46-63, prof, 64-69; prof art & chmn dept, City Col New York, 69-80. *Awards:* Asian-African Study Prog Grant to Japan, 67; Alfred Vance Churchill Found Grant, 67; City Col New York Medal, 73; plus others. *Mem:* Audubon Artists; Soc Am Graphic Artists; Boston Printmakers; fel Royal Soc Arts. *Publ:* Auth, many articles in nat art publ. *Mailing Add:* 720 Burns St Flushing NY 11375

JULIAN, JUNE
PAINTER, SCULPTOR
b Wilmington, Del, Mar 8, 47. *Study:* Kutztown State Col, Pa, BS(art educ), 68; Pa State Univ, MEd(art educ), 72. *Comn:* Outdoor sculpture, Boulder Ctr Visual Arts, Colo, 80. *Exhib:* Southwest Biennial, NMex State Univ Gallery, Las Cruces, 77; Festival 9, Scottsdale Ctr Art, Ariz, 78; 8-West Biennial, West Colo Ctr Arts, Grand Junction, 80; Front Range, Arc Gallery, Chicago, Ill, 81; Front Range, Plains Art Mus, Moorhead, Minn, 81; 3 Artists, Boulder Ctr Arts, Colo, 81. *Pos:* Graphic artist, Div Instructional Media, Pa State Univ, 69-70; book illusr, Fairchild Publ Inc, New York, 71-75; graphic artist, Bureau of Educ Media, Univ Colo, 74-75. *Teaching:* Art, Public Schs in Pa, Colo & NMex, 64-77; art instr figure drawing, Community Col, Denver, Colo, 78-80; vis lectr, Univ Quebec, Montreal, 80. *Awards:* Cash Award, Festival 9, Scottsdale Ctr Visual Art, 78; Special Project Award, Unrelated Acts, St Charles on Wazee, Denver, Colo, 80. *Bibliog:* Lindy Lyman (auth), June Julian, Artspace, SW Arts Quarterly, 81; Irene Clurman (auth), Center goes for Baroque, Rocky Mountain News, 81. *Mem:* Front Range Women in Visual Arts. *Media:* Mixed Media, Performance. *Publ:* Auth, All Colorado women artists juried exhibition, 79 & auth, Front range--going through the changes, 80, Artspace; auth, Like a Kid with a Backyard Circus, Westword, 81. *Dealer:* Spark Gallery 3300 Osage St Denver CO 80211. *Mailing Add:* 845 Monroe Golden CO 80401

JULIAN, LAZARO
PAINTER, DESIGNER
b Guadalajara, Mex, Mar 12, 45. *Work:* Mus del Estado de Jalisco. *Exhib:* One-man show, Constructions, Rhoda Sande Gallery, New York, 76 & 77; Iman New York, Mod Art Mus, Ponce de Leon, PR, 76 & Ctr Inter-Am Relations, New York, 76; Primera Muestra de la Plastica Jalisciense, Guadalajara, 77; Artists 77 Int Exhib, Union Carbide Bldg, New York, 77. *Pos:* Dir graphic design dept, Departamento de Bellas Artes del Gobierno del Estado de Jalisco, Mex, 72-73. *Bibliog:* Diana Loercher (auth), Art posing a riddle, Christian Sci Monitor, 3/8/76; Abraham Kein (auth), Conceptual constructions, The Eastsider, New York, 5/26/77; Howard Katzander (auth), Mexican art, Archit Digest, 1/78. *Media:* Acrylic, Cardboard. *Mailing Add:* c/o Rhoda Sande 220 E 60th St New York NY 10022

JULIO, PAT T
EDUCATOR, CRAFTSMAN
b Youngstown, Ohio, Mar 1, 23. *Study:* Wittenberg Col, BFA, with Ralston Thompson; Univ NMex, MA, with Raymond Jonson & Lex Haas; Univ Colo, with Robert Lister; Ohio State Univ, with Edgar Littlefield; Tex Western Col, with Wiltz Harrison. *Comn:* Stained glass windows, Episcopal Good Samaritan Church, Community Church & pvt collections. *Exhib:* Denver Art Mus, 50 & 63; Pueblo Art Mus, 60; Pueblo Col, 60 & 69; one-man shows, Pueblo Art Mus, 64 & Western State Art Gallery, 69. *Teaching:* Prof art, Western State Col, 71- *Mem:* Col Art Asn Am; Western Art Asn; Am Ceramic Soc; Am Crafts Coun; Inst Indian Studies; and others. *Mailing Add:* Dept of Art Western State Col Gunnison CO 81230

JUNG, KWAN YEE
PAINTER
b Toysun, China, Nov 25, 32; US citizen. *Study:* Chinese Univ Hong Kong New Asia Col, BA(painting), 61; San Diego State Univ, postgrad studies, 68. *Work:* Springville Mus Art, Utah; Utah State Univ Galleries, Logan; IBM Corp, Austin, Tex; Southern Utah State Col, Cedar. *Exhib:* Calif Nat Watercolor Soc Ann, 72-79; Watercolor USA, 72 & 75; Am Watercolor Soc Ann Exhib, 73-78; Nat Acad Design Ann, 74; one-man shows, Univ Hong Kong, 75 & Edward Dean Mus, Calif, 77. *Awards:* Nat Watercolor Soc Award, Watercolor West Soc, 75; Edgar Whitney Award, 78; Best of Show, Sumi-E Soc Am, 79. *Bibliog:* Interview, Spectrum-TV 10, San Diego, 82; interview, Artist-TV 51, San Diego, 83; article, SW Art Mag, 1/83. *Mem:* Nat Watercolor Soc; Am Watercolor Soc; Watercolor West Transparent Soc; San Diego Watercolor Soc (dir, 70-71). *Media:* Watercolor. *Mailing Add:* 5468 Bloch St San Diego CA 92122

JUNG, YEE WAH
PAINTER
b Canton, China, Sept 4, 36; US citizen. *Study:* Chung Man Art Sch, WuHun, China, 56-57; Chinese Univ Hong Kong New Asia Col, 59-62. *Comn:* The Tours of Confucius (mosaic painting), Facade of Ambassador Hotel, 59 & The Sacred Text (mosaic painting), Facade of Tai Sing Mid Sch, Kowloon, Hong Kong, 65, both with Chiu Fung Poon. *Exhib:* Calif Nat Watercolor Soc, 73-74; Watercolor USA, 73-75; Nat Acad Design, 74; Butler Inst Am Art, 74; Am Watercolor Soc, 74-75. *Awards:* First Place, Southern Calif Expo Art, Del Mar, 71; Calif Nat Watercolor Soc Award, Watercolor USA, 73; Watercolor USA Award, Calif Nat Watercolor Soc, 74. *Bibliog:* Interview, Spectrum-TV 10, San Diego, 82; article, SW Art Mag, 1/83. *Mem:* Nat Watercolor Soc; Watercolor West Soc; San Diego Watercolor Soc. *Media:* Oil, Watercolor. *Mailing Add:* 5468 Bloch St San Diego CA 92122

JUNGWIRTH, I(RENE) GAYAS
PAINTER, DESIGNER
b McKees Rocks, Pa. *Study:* Cass Tech, Detroit; Marygrove Col, BA(art & philos); Wayne State Univ; Mich State Univ; also studied abroad. *Work:* Detroit Inst Arts; Marquette Univ Art Collection; Marygrove Col Art Collection; CSSP Seminary Collection, Ann Arbor. *Comn:* Stations of Cross (with Leonard D Jungwirth), Churches, Detroit, 55-62; crown in gold, topaz & diamonds, St Mary's Church, Detroit, 57-58; crucifixion (with Leonard D Jungwirth), St John's Church, East Lansing, 60; stained glass windows, YMCA-Children's Chapel, Baptist Church, 60-63; mural painting, Dept Hort, Mich State Univ, 67. *Exhib:* Michigan Artists, Detroit Art Inst, 43-63; two-person exhib, Flint Art Inst, 51; Int Ecclesiastical Show, 55-62; Butler Inst Am Art, Youngstown, Ohio; Art 76, Int Armory, Washington, DC; retrospective, East Lansing Peoples Church, Mich State Univ Art Dept, 80-82. *Awards:* Painting of Child, Detroit Inst Arts, 43; Whitcomb Prize, Spring Nocturne, Butler Art Inst, 52; Purchase Award for Nocturne with Figure & Peacocks, Detroit Inst Arts, 57. *Media:* Mixed. *Mailing Add:* 1872 Fulmer St Ann Arbor MI 48103

JURSEVSKIS, ZIGFRIDS
SCULPTOR
b Ceresy, Poland, Mar 11, 10; Can citizen. *Study:* Sch Fine Arts & Crafts, Latvia, cert, 30; Art Sch, Liepaja, Latvia, cert, 36. *Work:* Rodman Hall Gallery Collection, St Catharine's, Ontario. *Comn:* Geese (bronze sculpture), Vitols Tool & Machine Corp, Philadelphia, 78. *Exhib:* Salone Int Del Ceramica, Vicenza, Italy, 60; Art Gallery Hamilton, Ontario, 63 & 66; Winnipeg Art Gallery, BC, 64; First Can Place Exhib, Toronto, 76; MacDonald Gallery Traveling Show, 78; McMichael Exhib Gallery, Kleinburg, Ont, 80; and others. *Pos:* Head ceramics studio, Zigfrid's Art Pottery, Toronto, 77- *Teaching:* Head ceramics dept, Art Sch, Liepaja, Latvia, 36-44. *Awards:* First Prize, World Latvia Art Exhib, Cleveland, 73; Mem Award, Sculpture 80's, Mary Arthur Huper, 80; Award, Multicultural Art Exhib, Toronto, 83; and others. *Bibliog:* Suzanne Morrison (auth), Latvian won Canadian handicraft prize at Canadian National Exhibit, Toronto Daily Star, 9/2/65; Velta Toma (auth), Zigfrids Jursevskis, Labietis Mag, No 38, Chicago, 69. *Mem:* Sculptors Soc Can; Colour & Form Soc; Latvis Soc Artists (treas, 62-75, vpres, 75-); Am Latvian Artists Asn. *Media:* Bronze, Stone. *Mailing Add:* 1425A Bloor St W Toronto ON M6P 3L6 Canada

JUSZCZYK, JAMES JOSEPH
PAINTER
b Chicago, Ill, Jan 30, 43. *Study:* Univ Ill, 60-62; Cleveland Inst Art, BFA(Ford Found Grant), 66; Univ Pa, MFA(fel), 69. *Work:* Chase Manhattan Bank, Lehman Brothers, Harry Abrams Inc, Swiss Bank Corp, Citicorp, New York. *Exhib:* Eight Abstract Painters, Inst Contemp Art, Univ Pa, 78; Geometric Abstraction: A New Generation, Inst Contemp Art, Boston, 81; one-man shows, Rosa Esman Gallery, New York, 74, 75, 77, 78; Gimpel Hanover Galerie, Zurich, Switz, 75-77 & 82, Jan Cicero Gallery, Chicago, 80 & 83 & Galerie Knostruktiv Tendens, Stockholm, 82. *Pos:* Guest artist-in-residence, Ill State Univ, 79. *Bibliog:* Lenore Malen (auth), article, Arts Mag, 2/78. *Mem:* Am Abstract Artists. *Media:* Acrylic on Canvas. *Dealer:* Jan Cicero 437 N Clark St Chicago IL 60610; Gimpel Hanover & Emmerich Galeryien Todi Str 40 Zurich Switzerland. *Mailing Add:* 130 W 17th St New York NY 10011

K

KABAK, ROBERT
PAINTER, EDUCATOR
b Bronx, NY, Feb 15, 30. *Study:* Brooklyn Col, BA(cum laude), 52; Yale Univ, MFA(painting), 54. *Work:* Mus Mod Art, New York; NMex Mus Fine Arts, Santa Fe; Helene Wurlitzer Found, Taos, NMex; also collections of John D Rockefeller III and John Rewald, New York. *Exhib:* New Talent, 56 & Recent Acquisitions, 57, Mus Mod Art, New York; Painting Ann, Whitney Mus Am Art, New York, 56 & 58; Carnegie Int, Carnegie Mus Art, Pittsburgh, 67; A New Look at an Ancient Land, NMex Mus Fine Arts, Santa Fe, 77; and over 30 one-man shows. *Teaching:* Instr art, Brooklyn Col, 60-62; asst prof design, Univ Calif, Berkeley, 62-67; assoc prof painting, Northern Ill Univ, 68-74; prof design, Univ Mo, Columbia, 74- *Awards:* Painting grants, MacDowell Colony, 56-68, Inst for Creative Arts, Univ Calif, 65-66 & Wurlitzer Found, Taos, NMex, 69-72 & 76. *Bibliog:* James Smith Pierce (auth), Robert Kabak's big landscapes, Art Int, 69. *Media:* Oil on canvas. *Mailing Add:* 142C Stanley Hall Univ of Mo Columbia MO 65211

KABOTIE, FRED
PAINTER, DESIGNER
b Shongopavy Village, Second Mesa, Ariz, Feb 20, 1900. *Study:* Alfred Univ, New York; Col Ganado, Ariz, DFA, 79. *Comn:* Hopi Indian legendary designs, Fred Harvey Co, Watch Tower, Grand Canyon, Ariz, 34; Hopi Social Dances, Fred Harvey Co, Painted Desert Inn, Ariz, 39; Reproduction of Pre-Columbian Kiva Murals, Indian Arts & Crafts Bd, Washington, DC, 40; Indian & Tourists, Fred Harvey Co, Bright Lodge, Grand Canyon, 56. *Exhib:* San Francisco World's Fair, 39; Mus Mod Art, New York, 40; Ariz State Fair in Fine Art, Phoenix, 49; Chicago Art Inst, 49; Inter-Tribal Indian Ceremonial, Gallup, NMex. 50. *Pos:* Mgr, Hopi Arts & Crafts, Silver Coop Guild, Second Mesa, 37-59; arts & crafts specialist, Under Indian Arts & Crafts Bd, Washington, DC, 60-71; pres, Hopi Cult Ctr, Second Mesa, 71- *Teaching:* Fine art, graphic art, silversmithing, High Sch, Oraibi, Ariz, 37-59; teacher silversmithing & art, Univ Southern Calif, 75. *Awards:* Cert Appreciation, Univ Southern Calif, 76; Festival Artist Year, Tucson Festival, 76; Medallion, Hopi Arts & Crafts Guild, 83. *Mem:* Assoc Sci & Art Asn, Mus Northern Ariz; assoc Inter-Tribal Indian Ceremonial; Louis Comfort Tiffany Found (trustee); Indian Arts & Crafts Asn (bd dir, currently)). *Media:* Earth Color & Oil; Acrylic. *Publ:* Auth, Designs with my interpretations from Mimbrennos; illusr, many books of the Southwest Indians. *Mailing Add:* PO Box 4 Second Mesa AZ 86043

KACERE, JOHN C
PAINTER
b Walker, Iowa, June 23, 20. *Study:* Mizen Acad Art, Chicago, Ill, 38-42; State Univ of Iowa, Ames, 46-51, BFA, 49 & MFA, 51. *Work:* Stedelijk Mus, Amsterdam; Wadsworth Atheneum, Hartford, Conn; Mt Holyoke Col, Mass; Yale Univ, New Haven, Conn; Brandeis Univ, Waltham, Mass. *Exhib:* Walker Art Ctr (traveling), Minneapolis, Minn, 49; Corcoran Gallery, Washington, DC, 63; The Realist Revival, Mus Mod Art, New York, 72; Relativierend Realismus, Stedelijk van Abbemuseum, Eindhoven, Holland, 72; Super-realist Vision, DeCordova Mus, Lincoln, Mass, 73; Hyperrealistes Americaans Fotorealisme, Grafick, Hendendaagse Kunst, Utrecht & Palais van Schone Kunst, Brussels, Belg; Art Inst Chicago; one-man shows, Univ of Fla, Gainesville, 53 & 57, La State Univ, Baton Rouge, 57, Allan Stone Gallery, New York, 63 & Harris Gallery, New York, 73; O K Harris Gallery, New York, 75; O K Harris Works of Art, New York, 78 & 80; and others. *Teaching:* Asst, State Univ Iowa, 49-50; instr, Univ Manitoba, 50-53 & Univ Fla, Gainesville, 53-65; instr, Cooper Union, Parsons Sch Design & Univ NMex, formerly. *Bibliog:* I Narp (auth), Rent is the only Reality or the Hotel instead of the Hymn, Arts, New York, 12/71; P Sager (auth), Relativierend Realismus, Kunstwerk (Baden-Baden), 3/72. *Publ:* Auth, The End is Art, Oui, Paris, 5/74. *Mailing Add:* 152 Wooster St New York NY 10012

KACHADOORIAN, ZUBEL
PAINTER, EDUCATOR
b Detroit, Mich, Feb 7, 24. *Study:* Meinzinger Art Sch Detroit, 43-44; Saugatuck Summer Art Sch, Mich, 44-45; Skowhegan Sch Painting & Sculpture, Maine, 46; Colorado Springs Fine Arts Ctr, summer 47. *Work:* Detroit Inst Art; Art Inst Chicago; Worcester Mus, Mass; Smithsonian Inst, Washington, DC; William Rockhill Nelson Gallery, Kansas City; and others. *Comn:* Gold leaf & oil altar painting, St John's Amenian Church Greater Detroit, 67. *Exhib:* Univ Ill, Urbana, 61; Am Ann, Art Inst Chicago, 61; Art USA Now, Johnson Wax Collection, 62; Butler Inst Am Art Ann, Youngstown, Ohio, 64; Ball State univ, 73, 74 & 78-81; American Drawing II, Portsmouth, Va, 80. *Pos:* Adv, Common Grounds Detroit, 65-66; art dir, Detroit Repertory Theatre, 70-76; artist-in-the-school, Mich Coun for Arts, 79-82. *Teaching:* Artist in residence, Sch Art Inst Chicago, 60-61; instr painting & drawing, Skowhegan Sch Painting & Sculpture, summer 60, 61, 64, 68 & 69; prof drawing, Wayne State Univ, 67-73. *Awards:* Prix-de-Rome, Am Acad Rome, 56-59; Richard & Hinda Rosenthal Award, Nat Inst Arts & Lett, 61; Creative Artist Grant, Mich Coun Arts, 83-84. *Bibliog:* A S Weller (auth), Art USA Now, C J Bucher, 62. *Mem:* Fel Am Acad Rome. *Media:* Oil, Charcoal. *Mailing Add:* 1214 Beaubien Detroit MI 48226

KACHEL, HAROLD STANLEY
MUSEUM DIRECTOR, EDUCATOR
b Elmwood, Okla, Jan 25, 28. *Study:* Panhandle State Univ, Goodwell, Okla, BS; Okla State Univ, Stillwater, MS; Univ Northern Colo, EdD. *Collections Arranged:* Arrangement & cataloging of a minimum of nine exhibs annually. *Pos:* Asst cur, No Man's Land Hist Mus, Goodwell, Okla, 66-68, cur & mus dir, 68- *Teaching:* Instr crafts, Yarbrough Sch, Eva, Okla, 52-57; prof copper tooling & head, Indust Arts Dept, Panhandle State Univ, Goodwell, Okla, 57- *Awards:* Distinguished Serv Award, Area Artists Studio, Amarillo, Tex, 76; Teacher of Yr at Panhandle State Univ, Okla Educ Asn, 76; Palette Ward, Artists Studio NW, 82. *Bibliog:* Lee Tucker (auth), A Salute to No Man's Land Hist Mus, Old Timer's News, Keyes, Okla, 6/76. *Mailing Add:* PO Box 307 Goodwell OK 73939

KAEP, LOUIS JOSEPH
PAINTER
b Dubuque, Iowa, Mar 19, 03. *Study:* Loras Col; Art Inst Chicago; Julian Acad, Paris. *Work:* Loras Col; City of Chicago; Kalamazoo Inst Arts; Soc New York Hosps; Am Acad Arts & Lett, New York. *Exhib:* Royal Watercolor Soc, London, 62; 200 Years of Watercolor Painting in America, Metrop Mus, New York, 66; Am Watercolor Soc 100th Ann, New York, 67; 50 Am Watercolor Soc Watercolors, Mus Aquarelle, Mexico City, Mex, 68; Nat Acad Design 147th Ann, New York, 72. *Pos:* Vpres, Vogue Wright Studios, New York, 52-56, pres, 56-65; pres, Electrographic Corp, New York, 65-71, vchmn, 71- *Teaching:* Instr painting, Art Inst Chicago, 24-26; instr watercolors, Chicago Acad Fine Arts, 36-42. *Awards:* Olsen Award for Sampans & Junks, Hong Kong, Am Watercolor Soc 95th Ann, 62; Assoc Mem Award for the Old Quarry, Allied Artists Am, 69; Gold Medal for Fiesta, Toledo, Spain, Hudson Valley Art Asn, 70. *Bibliog:* Developing Paintings From Sketches (film), 71. *Mem:* Am Watercolor Soc (first vpres, 62); Salmagundi Club (bd dirs, 65); Artists & Writers Asn; Nat Acad Design; Allied Artists Am. *Media:* Watercolor. *Publ:* Contribr, Fairfield watercolor group, Am Artists Mag, 7/72. *Mailing Add:* 14 Anderson Rd Greenwich CT 06803

KAERICHER, JOHN CONRAD
PRINTMAKER, EDUCATOR
b Springfield, Ill, June 6, 36. *Study:* Millikin Univ with David Driesbach, BFA, 59; Univ Iowa, with Mauricio Lasansky, Stuart Edie, James Lechay & Robert Knipschild, MFA, 63. *Work:* Univ Iowa; Millikin Univ; Dordt Col; Northwestern Col Iowa; plus pvt collections. *Comn:* Medal, Northwestern Col, 66. *Exhib:* Cent Ill Ann, Decatur Art Ctr, 61-; Gov Off, State Capitol, Des Moines, Iowa, 71; Paper Works, 9th Ann, Waterloo Munic Gallery, 73; Kottler Galleries, New York, 73; Va Polytech Inst Ann, 74; Benjamin Galleries, Chicago, 76; and many others. *Pos:* Gallery dir, Northwestern Col, 63-79, chmn fine arts coun, 68-, coordr permanent collection. *Teaching:* Assoc prof printmaking & drawing & chmn art dept, Northwestern Col Iowa, 63- *Awards:* Creative Prod Grants, Northwestern Col Iowa, 66, 68, 75, 77 & 81. *Bibliog:* Rev of NY exhib in Park East Periodical, 10/25/73. *Mem:* Mid-Am Col Art Asn; Cols Mid-Am Art Fac Group; Iowa Print Group; Northwestern Printmakers. *Media:* Intaglio, Drawing. *Mailing Add:* 615 Arizona SW Orange City IA 51041

KAGAN, ANDREW AARON
HISTORIAN, CRITIC
b St Louis, Mo, Sept 22, 47. *Study:* Washington Univ, AB, 69; Harvard Univ, MA, 71, PhD, 77. *Pos:* Contributing ed, Arts Mag, New York; critic art & architecture, St Louis Globe-Democrat, Mo. *Teaching:* Critic in residence, Bennington Col, Vt, 72-73; vis prof art hist, Washington Univ, St Louis, Mo, 80-81. *Res:* Paul Klee studies; theory of absolute art; 18th & 20th century art hist, theory, criticism; 19th & 20th century architectural history & criticism. *Publ:* Auth, A Classical Source for David's Oath of the Tennis Court, Burlington Mag, 74; auth, Paul Klee's Ad Parnassum, 77, auth, Absolute art, 78 & auth, Louis Sullivan as classical visionary, 81, Arts Mag; auth, Paul Klee, Art and Music, Cornell Univ Press, 82. *Mailing Add:* 3434 Shenandoah St Louis MO 63104

KAGLE, JOSEPH L, JR
PAINTER, MUSEUM DIRECTOR
b Pittsburgh, Pa, May 2, 32. *Study:* Carnegie Mus Sch Art, 38-51; Dartmouth Col, AB, 55; Univ Colo, MFA, 58. *Work:* Southeast Ark Arts & Sci Ctr, Pine Bluff; Alcoa Collection, Pittsburgh; Nat Mus Taiwan, Taipei; Kimon Friar Collection, Athens, Greece; Sanford Besser Collection, Little Rock, Ark. *Comn:* Concrete mural, Hafa Adai Theatre, Agana, Guam, 72-73; mosaic mural, State Arts Coun, Univ Guam, 74; concrete mural, Nat Endowment for Arts, Agana, Guam, 75; acrylic painting, Bank of Guam, Agana, Guam, 75; sculptures, comn by lawyer in Guam, 75. *Exhib:* One-man show, US Info Serv Lincoln Ctr, Taipei, Taiwan, 75; Image of the South Pacific, Nat Mus Taiwan, Taipei, 76; NY State Ann, Arnot Mus, 77; Lakeview Series, Southeast Ark Arts & Sci Ctr, Pine Bluff, 79; retrospective, Hopkins Ctr, Dartmouth Col, Hanover, NH, 80. *Collections Arranged:* Buddhist Hell Scrolls (auth, catalog), travel exhib throughout South, 80; John Howard and Friends, group show of minority art, 80; Southeast Ark Arts & Sci Ctr Permanent Collection, 80; Wildlife Collection Ann Exhib, 80; Arkansas Annual, 80. *Pos:* Exec dir, Southeast Ark Arts & Sci Ctr, 78- *Teaching:* Assoc prof art & chmn dept, Keuka Col, Keuka Park, NY, 64-68; assoc prof & artist-in-residence, Wash State Univ, 65-66; assoc prof art, World Campus Afloat, 68-69; prof art & chmn dept, Univ Guam, 70-76. *Awards:* First Award in Painting, Cheney Cowles Mus, 66; Pac Artist of Yr, Am Inst Architects, Pac Chap, 77. *Bibliog:* State Council on the Arts Artists of Guam, Nat Endowment for Arts, 74; Getting better all the time, PB Com (Paul Greenberg), 78; Work by J Kagle, Dartmouth Col, 80. *Mem:* Col Art Asn; Am Mus Asn; Southeast Mus Asn; Mid-Southern Watercolorists; Ward-Nassee Gallery Asn. *Media:* Acrylic, Watercolor. *Collection:* Oriental and modern American art. *Publ:* Auth, The Twenty-Four Hour Day, China Press, 75; auth, Osiik is Dead, Glimpses, Guam, 76; contribr, The Future is Now, Com Press, 80; auth, Long walks at twilight and dawn, Islands Mag, 80; auth, The good old boy of art, Art Consortium, 80. *Dealer:* Ward-Nasse Gallery 178 Prince St New York NY 10012. *Mailing Add:* Rte 11 Box 2300 Pine Bluff AR 71603

KAGY, SHEFFIELD HAROLD
PAINTER, PRINTMAKER
b Cleveland, Ohio, Oct 22, 07. *Study:* Cleveland Sch Art; John Huntington Sch Art; Corcoran Sch Art; also with Oley Nordmark, Robert Laurant & Ernest Fiene. *Work:* Cleveland Mus Art. *Comn:* Agriculture & Industry, Walterboro Post Off, SC & Luray 1840, Luray Post Off, Va, 40, Sect Fine Arts, US Treasury Dept. *Exhib:* Int Watercolor Exhib, Art Inst Chicago, 34; Int Painting Competition, Greenbriar Hotel, WVa, 36; Libr Cong Pennell Show, 43; Venice Bicentennial, 44; US State Dept, 66. *Pos:* Exhib officer & designer, Agency Int Develop, US State Dept, 59-73. *Teaching:* Prof fine arts & printmaking, Abbott Art Sch, 36-37; head art dept, Chevy Chase Jr Col, 40-43; prof fine arts, Nat Art Sch, 46-56. *Mem:* Artists Guild Washington (vpres, 44); Soc Washington Artists (pres, 49-51); Landscape Club Washington (pres, 52-54); Washington Watercolor Asn; Arts Club Washington. *Media:* Oil, Watercolor; Mixed. *Mailing Add:* 5515 Carolina Pl NW Washington DC 20016

KAHAN, ALEXANDER
DEALER

Study: State Univ NY. *Pos:* Owner, Alexander Kahan Fine Arts Ltd, New York, currently. *Mem:* Appraisers Asn Am. *Specialty:* Paintings and graphics of 19th and 20th century. *Collection:* Appel, Matta, Dubuffet, De Chirico, Riopelle, Calder, Dufy, Jenkins, Miro, Francis, Chagall, Picasso, Renoir, Lautrec, Marini & Stella. *Mailing Add:* 565 West End Avenue New York NY 10024

KAHAN, LEONARD
DEALER, PAINTER

b Bronx, NY, Jan 21, 35. *Study:* Pratt Inst, BFA, 57; Brooklyn Col, MFA, 64. *Pos:* Owner, L Kahan Gallery, Inc, currently. *Mem:* Appraisers Asn Am. *Media:* Acrylic, Collage. *Specialty:* African art. *Mailing Add:* L Kahan Gallery Inc 48 E 57th St New York NY 10022

KAHAN, MITCHELL DOUGLAS
CURATOR, HISTORIAN

b Richmond, Va, May 1, 51. *Study:* Univ Va, BA, 73; Columbia Univ, univ fel, 73, MA, 75; City Univ New York Grad Sch, univ fel, 75-76, MPhil, 79, PhD, 83; Whitney Mus Am Art, Helena Rubinstein fel, 76; Nat Collection Fine Arts & Hirshhorn Mus, Smithsonian fel, 76-78. *Collections Arranged:* Art Inc: American Paintings from Corporate Collections (coauth & ed, catalog), Montgomery Mus & Brandywine Press, 79; American Paintings of the Sixties and Seventies: Selections from the Whitney Museum of American Art (auth, catalog), Montgomery Mus, 80 & Roger Brown (coauth, catalog), 80; Nicholas Africano (auth, catalog), NC Mus, 83. *Pos:* Cur painting & sculpture, Montgomery Mus Fine Arts, Ala, 78-82; cur Am & contemp art, NC Mus Art, 82- *Res:* American painting, sculpture, photography and architecture. *Mailing Add:* NC Mus Art 2110 Blue Ridge Blvd Raleigh NC 27607

KAHANE, MELANIE (MELANIE KAHANE GRAUER)
DESIGNER

b New York, NY, Nov 26, 10. *Study:* Parsons Sch Design, grad, 31; Paris, 32; Hon DFA, 82. *Comn:* Designer, Reid Hall, Paris, 48, Children's Mus, Ft Worth, Tex, 55, Gov Shriver's Mansion, Austin, Tex, 57, Playbill Restaurant, New York, 58 & Ziegfield Theatre, New York, 63; 15 Shubert Theatres, New York, Chicago, Boston and others. *Pos:* Illusr, Tobias Green Advert Co, 31-32; designer, Lord & Taylor, 33-34; founder & pres, Melanie Kahane, Inc, 35-; founder & pres, Melanie Kahane Assocs, Interior & Indust Design, 52-; designer, Charles of Ritz Beauty Salons throughout US, 57-; dir styling & design, Sprague & Carleton Furniture Co, 62- *Teaching:* Lectr, Parsons Sch Design, 50- *Awards:* Decorator of the Year Award, 53; Eleanor Roosevelt Humanities Award, 81; Today's Woman Award, United Cerebral Palsy, 81; and others. *Mem:* Fel Am Inst Interior Designers (past nat secy, bd dirs, past pres, NY Chap, nat treas, 71-75); Munic Art Soc; Decorator's Club New York (pres, 82-84); Inter-Soc Color Coun; Inst Practicing Designers, Eng; and others. *Publ:* Producer, Decorating, a Way of Life (doc film), 49; auth, There's a Decorator in Your Doll House, 68; also contribr to bks & encycl. *Mailing Add:* 29 E 63rd St New York NY 10022

KAHLENBERG, MARY HUNT
DEALER, CONSULTANT

b Wallingford, Conn, Oct 19, 40. *Study:* Boston Univ; Art Inst Chicago. *Pos:* Asst cur, Textile Mus, Washington, DC, 67-68; vis prof hist textiles, Univ Calif, Los Angeles, 75; cur, Los Angeles Co Mus Art, 68-78; pres, Textile Arts Inc, 79- *Teaching:* Instr hist textiles, Calif State Univ. *Awards:* Prof Travel Grant & Grant for Mus Storage Facil, Nat Endowment Arts, 74. *Mem:* Costume Soc Am; Am Mus Asn. *Res:* Islamic textiles; fabrics from West Malaysia & Indonesia; Japanese textiles; European textiles. *Publ:* Auth, A 17th century Indian figurative velvet, Burlington Mag, 12/73; auth, An Indian floral velvet, Los Angeles Co Mus Art Bulletin, 73; auth, Islamic textiles, Apollo Mag, 8/75; auth, Walk in beauty--the Navajo and their blankets, New York Graphic Soc; Textile Traditions of Sumatra, Atlantic Richfield Co, 81; and others. *Mailing Add:* 1424 N Ogden Dr Los Angeles CA 90046

KAHN, A MICHAEL
PAINTER, DESIGNER

b Russia, July 4, 17; US citizen. *Study:* Pratt Inst, Brooklyn, MFA; Art Students League, cert; Univ Mex, dipl; Univ Lima Bellas Artes, dipl; also with Robert Brackman, Ogden Pleisner & Chaves Morado; fresco in Mexico. *Work:* Judah L Magnes Mus, Berkeley, Calif; Los Angeles Mus; Matson Navig Co Collection, San Francisco; Peruvian Cult Ctr, Lima; Pomeroy Collection; also in pvt collections around the world. *Comn:* Graphics for Europe & Far East, Off of Surgeon Gen, Washington, DC. *Exhib:* One-man shows, US Info Serv Cult Ctr, US Info Serv, Lima, Peru, 51 & On Israel, Pomeroy Gallery, San Francisco, 68; Judah L Magnes Mus, Berkeley, 57 & Art of Israel, 70; US Info Serv Hellenic Am Exhib, Athens, Greece. *Bibliog:* E M Polley (auth), Sacred Cows, Art & Artist Mag, San Francisco, 69; Alexander Fried (auth), A Michael Kahn, Lively Arts-San Francisco Examr, 70; Allen Gadol (auth), A Michael Kahn, Directions in Art, Miami, 72. *Mem:* Am Artists Group, New York; Artists Club of San Francisco; Art Dirs Club San Francisco; Nat Writers Club. *Media:* Oil, Acrylic. *Mailing Add:* 1940 Biarritz Dr Miami Beach FL 33141

KAHN, ANNELIES RUTH
CERAMIST, CRAFTSMAN

b Dresden, Ger, Aug 17, 27; US citizen. *Study:* RI Sch Design, BFA; Tex Woman's Univ, MA. *Exhib:* Seventh Int Exhib Ceramic Art, Smithsonian Inst, Washington, DC, 58; Ann Area Competition, Corcoran Gallery, Washington, DC, 59; 22nd Ceramic Nat Traveling Show, Everson Mus, Syracuse, 62 & 68; Am Craftsmen's Coun Exhib, Oakland, Calif, 63; Form and Quality, Int Exhib, Munich, Ger, 64-69. *Pos:* Designer & glaze analyst, Calif Art Tile Co, Richmond, 51-52; asst to dir, Gump's Gallery, San Francisco, 52-53 & Fine Art Gallery, Dallas, 64-66. *Teaching:* Instr ceramics, Md Art Inst, Baltimore, 57-59 & Southern Methodist Univ, 64-69; instr ceramics & sculpture, Mountain View Col, Tex, 70-74. *Awards:* Craft Horizons Award, Smithsonian Inst, 58; First Prize, Corcoran Gallery, 59; 16th Tex Crafts Exhib Top Award, Dallas Mus Fine Arts, 74; and others. *Bibliog:* Creation in Clay (film), KERA TV, 68. *Mem:* Tex Designer Craftsmen (secy, 71, vpres, 74-75); Dallas Craft Guild; World Crafts Coun; Am Craftsmen Coun. *Dealer:* Contemporary Gallery 2800 Routh St Dallas TX 75201. *Mailing Add:* 10808 Snow White Dr Dallas TX 75229

KAHN, PETER
PAINTER, DESIGNER

b Leipzig, Ger, July 5, 21; US citizen. *Study:* With Hans Hofmann, 47-49; NY Univ, BS & MA. *Work:* Utica Mus; Va Mus; White Mus; Cornell Univ; Univ Notre Dame Gallery. *Exhib:* Art USA 1954, Va Mus, 54; New Graphic Art Traveling Show, Holland, 65; Natural Vision, Columbia Univ, 68; retrospective, Hobart Col. *Teaching:* Asst prof, La State Univ, Baton Rouge, 51-53; assoc prof & chmn dept, Hampton Inst, Va, 53-57; prof graphics & paintings, Cornell Univ, 57-68, prof art hist, 72-; Mellon prof, Calif Inst Technol, 78. *Awards:* Gov Award, Va Mus, 56; First Prize for Graphics, Binghamton Mus, 58; First Prize, Utica Mus, 59 & 60. *Media:* Graphics. *Publ:* Auth, The golden section fallacy, Leonardo, Paris, fall 80. *Mailing Add:* Dept of Art Hist Cornell Univ Ithaca NY 14853

KAHN, RALPH H
DEALER, LECTURER

b Trier, Ger, Aug 17, 20; US citizen. *Study:* Spec study with W Baumeister. *Collections Arranged:* Ten exhibs annually, Contemp Gallery, 65- *Pos:* Dir, Contemp Gallery, Dallas, 65- *Teaching:* Guest lectr 20th century art, art collecting & art processes, for mus, cols & pvt art groups. *Bibliog:* American Printmaking in the '70's, Oklahoma City TV. *Mem:* Terra Linda Art Asn (asst dir, 63); Tex Fine Arts Asn (pres, 72 & 75); Am Soc Appraisers; Appraiser's Asn Am; Assoc Art Gallery Dir, Dallas. *Res:* W Baumeister and other 20th century contemporary artists. *Specialty:* Twentieth century contemporary paintings, prints and sculpture. *Collection:* Baumeister, Braque, Chagall, Dine, Jenkins, Klee, Miro & Picasso. *Mailing Add:* Contemporary Gallery 5100 Belt Line Rd 544 Dallas TX 75240

KAHN, SUSAN B
PAINTER

b New York, NY, Aug 26, 24. *Study:* Parsons Sch Design; also with Moses Soyer. *Work:* Albrecht Gallery Mus, St Joseph, Mo; Montclair Mus, NJ; Butler Inst Am Art, Youngstown, Ohio; Reading Mus, Pa; Joslyn Art Mus, Omaha. *Exhib:* One-person shows, ACA Galleries, New York, 64, 68, 71, 76 & 80, Albrecht Art Mus, St Joseph, Mo, 74 & New York Cult Ctr, 74; Nat Acad Design, 70; Butler Inst Am Art, 73; St Peter's Col Art Gallery, Jersey City, NJ, 78; and others. *Awards:* Nat Arts Club Award, 67; Famous Artists Sch Award, Nat Asn Women Artists, 67; Anne Barnette Mem Prize, Nat Asn Women Artists, 81. *Bibliog:* Marshall Matusow (auth), Art Collectors Almanac, Jerome E Treisman, 65; Lincoln Rothschild (auth), Susan Swan, Asn Univ Presses Inc, 80. *Mem:* Artists Equity Asn; Nat Asn Women Artists; Knickerbocker Artists. *Media:* Oil. *Publ:* Contribr, How to Paint a Prize Winner, 65. *Dealer:* ACA Gallery 21 E 67th St New York NY 10021. *Mailing Add:* 870 United Nations Plaza New York NY 10017

KAHN, WOLF
PAINTER

b Stuttgart, Ger, Oct 4, 27. *Study:* New Sch Social Res, with Stuart Davis; Hans Hofmann Sch; Univ Chicago, BA. *Work:* Whitney Mus Am Art, Mus Mod Art, Metrop Mus Art, New York; Houston Mus Fine Arts; Los Angeles Co Mus Art, Los Angeles. *Exhib:* Ann, Whitney Mus Am Art, 58 & 59, Young America, 61; Univ Ill Biennial, 58-60; Bloedel Bequest, Whitney Mus Am Art, 77; one-man shows, RI Sch Design, Providence, 79 & Landscapes, San Diego Mus, Calif, 84; Chicago Arts Club, 81; Mint Mus, Charlotte, NC, 81; Fine Arts Ctr, Nashville, 81; Recent Acquisitions from the Metropolitan Museum, Queens Mus, New York. *Teaching:* Vis assoc prof painting, Univ Calif, Berkeley, 60-61; adj assoc prof painting, Cooper Union Art Sch, 60-77; artist in residence, Dartmouth Col, 84. *Awards:* Fulbright scholar to Italy, 63-65; Guggenheim fel, 66; Hassam Fund Purchase Award, Am Acad Arts & Lett, 79. *Bibliog:* L Campbell (auth), In the mist of life, Art News, 2/69; Gussow (auth), Sense of place, Friends of the Earth, 72; D Cochrane (auth), Updating landscape painting, Am Artist, 11/74; M Sawin (auth), W Kahn's Landscape Paintings, Arts Mag, 4/77; and others. *Mem:* Nat Acad Design. *Media:* Oil, Pastel. *Publ:* Auth, Uses of painting today, Daedalus Mag, 69; auth, Subject matter of new realism, Am Artist, 11/79; auth, Hans Hofmann's good example, Art J, 82; auth, Pastel Light, Station Hill Press, 83; auth, Milton Avery's good example, Art J, 83. *Dealer:* Grace Borgenicht 1018 Madison Ave New York NY 10021; Meredith Long Gallery 2323 San Felipe Houston TX 77019. *Mailing Add:* 813 Broadway New York NY 10003

KAINEN, JACOB
PAINTER, PRINTMAKER

b Waterbury, Conn, Dec 7, 09. *Study:* Art Students League, with Nicolaides; NY Univ Eve Sch Archit; Pratt Inst, grad. *Work:* Whitney Mus Am Art, Metrop Mus Art & Mus Mod Art, New York; Art Inst Chicago; Phillips Collection, Washington, DC; and numerous others. *Exhib:* Corcoran Gallery Art Painting Biennial, 57; one-man shows, Roko Gallery, New York, 64-66,

Pratt Manhattan Ctr, New York, 72, Lunn Gallery, Washington DC, 76-79 & 81-82; Print Retrospective 1938-1978, Assoc Am Artists, New York, 78; Jacob Kainen, Five Decades as Painter, Nat Collection Fine Arts, 79. *Bibliog:* Jacob Kainen (film), Nat Mus Art, Smithsonian Inst, 82. *Media:* Oil. *Mailing Add:* 27 W Irving St Chevy Chase MD 20815

KAISER, BENJAMIN
SCULPTOR, DESIGNER
b Tel Aviv, Israel, July 2, 43; US citizen. *Study:* San Jose State Univ, BA, 77, MFA, 79. *Work:* Mus Contemp Art in Glass, Valencia, Spain; City Palo Alto, City San Jose, Calif. *Comn:* Fountain, Villa Monterey Country Club, Phoenix, 82; glass panels, Rolm Corp, San Jose, Calif, 83. *Exhib:* New Glass Int Exhib, Corning Mus Art, 79; Contemporary Glass--Australia, Canada, USA and Japan, Nat Mus Mod Art, Kyoto & Tokyo, Japan, 81; International Directions in Glass Art, Art Gallery Western Australia, Perth, 82; Sculptural Glass, Tucson Mus Art, 83; Vicointer 83, Mus Contemp Art in Glass, Valencia, Spain, 83. *Teaching:* Instr glass-blowing, Bezalel Acad Art & Design, Jerusalem, 72-74. *Media:* Glass, Stainless Steel. *Dealer:* foster Goldstrom Fine Arts 2722 Fairmount St Dallas TX 75201. *Mailing Add:* PO Box 126 San Jose CA 95103

KAISER, CHARLES JAMES
PAINTER, GRAPHIC ARTIST
b Milwaukee, Wis, Mar 10, 39. *Study:* Layton Sch Art, Milwaukee; Univ Wis-Milwaukee, BFA, MS & MFA; painting with John Colt & Robert Burkert. *Work:* Wustum Mus, Racine, Wis; Union Art Gallery, Univ Wis-Milwaukee; Civic Art Collection, Munic Bldg, Springfield, Ill; Marquette Univ, Milwaukee; Miller Brewing Co Corp, Milwaukee. *Exhib:* Five shows, Watercolor USA, Springfield, Mo, 62-72; Northwest Miss Valley Artists Invitational, Ill State Mus, Springfield, 66; Calif Nat Watercolor Soc, Laguna Beach, 70 & 72-73; Exhib Contemp Am Painting, Palm Beach, Fla, 70; Chicago & Vicinity, Chicago Art Inst, 71; Wis Directions, 75 & 78, Wis Artists Make Toys, 79 & Drawing: The Fundamental Art, 81, Milwaukee Art Mus. *Teaching:* Assoc prof art, Mount Mary Col, currently. *Awards:* Calif Nat Watercolor Soc Purchase Award, Butrijamp Found, 70; Madison Salon Graphic Art Drawings & Prints Award, Wis State J & others, 70; Wis Watercolor Soc Award for Excellence, 71. *Mem:* Calif Nat Watercolor Soc; Wis Watercolor Soc; Wis Painters & Sculptors. *Media:* Watercolor; Prismacolor Pencil. *Dealer:* Bradley Galleries 2565 N Downer Ave Milwaukee WI 53211; Cudahy Gallery Wis Art Milwaukee Art Mus. *Mailing Add:* 5028 N Diversey Blvd Milwaukee WI 53217

KAISER, DIANE
SCULPTOR, EDUCATOR
b Brooklyn, NY, May 27, 46. *Study:* Brandeis Univ, BA(hon scholar); Columbia Univ, MFA; additional study with Peter Grippe & Sahl Swarz. *Exhib:* Rose Art Mus, Waltham, Mass, 74; Contemporary Reflections, Aldrich Mus Contemp Art, Ridgefield, Conn, 75; Women Artists Series, Douglass Col, 75 & 81; Flint Inst Art, Mich, 76; Art Feminine, Univ Mass, 79 & 80; two-person show, Mus Fine Arts, Springfield, Mass, 81; and others. *Collections Arranged:* Drawings & Prints, Independent Exhib Prog, Cont Visual Arts Inc, New York, 77. *Teaching:* Chmn & instr art dept, Chapin Sch, New York, 70-79; vis artist, Dwight-Englewood Sch, NJ, 76; instr, Northfield-Mount Hermon Sch, Northfield, Mass, 79-80; lectr art dept, Smith Col, Northampton, Mass, 80-83; chmn & instr art dept, St Hilda's & St Hugh's Sch, New York, currently. *Awards:* MacDowell Colony Fel, 73. *Mem:* Found Community Artists. *Media:* Multimedia. *Mailing Add:* 225 W 106th St New York NY 10025

KAISER, VITUS J
PAINTER, INSTRUCTOR
b Erie, Pa, May 3, 29. *Study:* NC State Col; Veterans Sch, Erie, with Joseph Plavcan; Univ Pittsburgh. *Work:* Erie Pub Libr. *Exhib:* Am Drawing Biennial, Norfolk Mus, Va, 71; Albright-Knox Art Gallery, Mem Gallery, Buffalo, 72; Butler Inst Am Art, 73; American Drawings III, Portsmouth, Va, 80; American Drawings, Smithsonian Inst traveling exhib, 81; and others. *Teaching:* Instr art, Tech Mem High Sch, 70- *Mem:* Erie Art Ctr; Soc Watercolor Painters Pa; and others. *Media:* Multimedia. *Mailing Add:* 551 W 26th St Erie PA 16508

KAISH, LUISE
SCULPTOR, EDUCATOR
b Atlanta, Ga. *Study:* Syracuse Univ, with Ivan Mestrovic, BFA & MFA; Escuela Pintura y Escultura, Mexico City, Mex; Taller Grafico. *Work:* Whitney Mus Am Art, New York; Jewish Mus, New York; Rochester Mem Art Gallery, NY; Continental Grain Co, NY; Metrop Mus Art, New York. *Comn:* Ark of Revelations (bronze), Temple B'rith Kodesh, Rochester; Great Ideas of Western Man & Walter Paepke Award Sculpture, Container Corp Am; Christ in Glory (bronze), Holy Trinity Mission Sem, Silver Spring, Md; ark doors, menorahs, eternal light (bronze), Temple Beth Shalom, Wilmington, Del; Wall of Martyrs (bronze), Beth El Synagogue Ctr, New Rochelle, NY. *Exhib:* Sculpture USA, Metrop Mus Art, New York; Recent Sculpture USA, Mus Mod Art, New York; Albright-Knox Mus, Buffalo; Hopkins Ctr, Dartmouth, NH; Whitney Biennials, Whitney Mus Am Art, New York; one-man shows, Minn Mus Art, Staempfll Gallery, New York, Rochester Mem Art Gallery & Jewish Mus, New York; plus others. *Pos:* Artist in residence, Hopkins Ctr, Dartmouth Col; vis artist, Univ Wash, Seattle. *Teaching:* Prof sculpture & chmn div painting & sculpture, Columbia Univ, New York, 80- *Awards:* Guggenheim Fel Creative Sculpture; Louis Comfort Tiffany Grant Creative Sculpture; Rome Prize Fel in Sculpture, Am Acad, Rome. *Mem:* Sculptors Guild. *Dealer:* Staempfll Gallery 47 E 77th St New York NY 10021. *Mailing Add:* 610 West End Ave New York NY 10024

KAISH, MORTON
PAINTER, EDUCATOR
b Newark, NJ, Jan 8, 27. *Study:* Syracuse Univ, BFA; Acad de la Grande Chaumiere, Paris; Ist d'Arte, Florence; Accad delle Belle Arti, Rome. *Work:* Brooklyn Mus, NY; Syracuse Univ; Whitney Mus Am Art; Atlantic Richfield Corp, New York; J C Penney Co, New York. *Comn:* Poster, Dartmouth Col, 74. *Exhib:* Young American Printmakers, Mus Mod Art, New York, 53; one-man shows, Staempfli Gallery, New York, 64-79 & New Sch Social Res, 74; Biennial of American Painting, Krannert Art Mus, Univ Ill, 65 & 67; Whitney Mus Ann of Am Painting, 66; Am Inst Arts & Lett, 66, 73 & 74. *Pos:* Artist in residence, Dartmouth Col, 74. *Teaching:* From instr to asst prof painting & drawing, Fashion Inst Technol, State Univ NY, 73-; instr, New Sch Social Res, 74-77 & Art Students League, 74-80; vis prof, Queens Col, 79 & Univ Wash, Seattle, 79. *Awards:* H H Sullivan Award, Everson Mus Art, Syracuse, NY, 50; Jurors Show Award, Rochester Mem Art Gallery, 52; artist in residence, Dartmouth Col, 74. *Bibliog:* Wendon Blake (auth), Complete Guide to Acrylic Painting, Watson-Guptill, 71; Z M Pike (auth), Roman light, Roman ladies, Art Int, 4/73; M L Kelly (auth), Kaishes find Dartmouth fruitful, Christian Sci Monitor, 8/23/74. *Mem:* Assoc Nat Acad Design. *Media:* Oil, Acrylic. *Dealer:* Staempfli Gallery 47 E 77th St New York NY 10021. *Mailing Add:* 610 West End Ave New York NY 10024

KAKAS, CHRISTOPHER A
PRINTMAKER, PAINTER
b Dayton, Ohio, Dec 11, 41. *Study:* Miami Univ, Ohio, BFA, 66; Univ Iowa, MA, 68, MFA, 69. *Work:* Minneapolis Inst Art; Sheldon Mem Art Gallery, Univ Nebr, Lincoln; Mus Art & Archit, Univ Mo, Columbia; Cleveland Mus Art, Ohio; Rockford Col, Ill; and others. *Exhib:* Metrop Mus, Coral Gables, Fla, 80; Univ SDak, Vermillion, 80; one-man show, Iliestand Art Gallery, Miami Univ, Oxford, Ohio, 80 & Mongomery Mus Fine Arts, Ala, 82; Rockford Int, Rockford Col, 83. *Teaching:* Asst prof, Syracuse Univ, NY, 75-76; asst prof art, Western Ky Univ, Bowling Green, 76-78; asst prof printmaking, Univ Ala, Tuscaloosa, 78- *Awards:* Purchase Awards, 1st Ann Nat Print Exhib, San Diego State Univ, 68 & 2nd Ann Nat Print Exhib, Ga Comn Arts, 71; Award, Rockford Int, 83. *Mem:* Col Art Asn; Los Angeles Printmaking Soc; Southern Graphics Coun. *Media:* Intaglio, Lithograph; Gouache, Acrylic. *Dealer:* Miriam Perlman Inc Lake Point Tower Suite 1902 505 N Lake Shore Dr Chicago IL 60611. *Mailing Add:* 10 Hickory Lane Tuscaloosa AL 35404

KALB, MARTY JOEL
PAINTER, EDUCATOR
b Brooklyn, NY, Apr 13, 41. *Study:* Mich State Univ, BA, 63; Yale Univ, BFA, 64; Univ Calif, Berkeley, MA, 66. *Work:* J B Speed Mus, Louisville, Ky; Univ Mass; Ohio Wesleyan Univ. *Exhib:* One-man show, Akron Art Inst, 75 & Canton Art Inst, 81; Wright State Univ, Ohio, 82; Denison Univ, Ohio, 82; Columbus Mus Art, Ohio, 82; and others. *Teaching:* Instr, Univ Ky, 66-67; assoc prof painting, Ohio Wesleyan Univ, 67-81, prof, 81- *Awards:* Ohio Arts Coun grant, 79-80. *Bibliog:* Articles, New York Times, 10/12/80, Art Speak, 10/80, Dialogue, 6 & 7/81, 4/82 & 12/82. *Mem:* Col Art Asn Am. *Media:* Acrylic. *Dealer:* Allan Stone Gallery 48 E 86th St New York NY 10028. *Mailing Add:* 165 Griswold St Delaware OH 43015

KALI (HANKA WEYNEROWSKI)
PAINTER
b Warsaw, Poland; US citizen. *Study:* Warsaw Acad Fine Arts, grad, 35-39; Acad Royale des Beaux Arts, Brussels, Belgium, grad, 45-47. *Exhib:* One-man shows, Palais Des Beaux Arts, Brussels, Belgium, 47, Calif Palace Legion Honor, 55 & DeYoung Mem Mus, San Francisco, 62. *Awards:* First Prize, Western Ont Exhib, London. *Mem:* Hon mem Artists Equity Asn. *Mailing Add:* 191 Robinhood Drive San Francisco CA 94127

KALINA, RICHARD
PAINTER
b New York, NY, May 21, 46. *Study:* Univ Pa, BA, 66. *Work:* Indianapolis Mus Art; Norton Gallery Art, Palm Beach, Fla; NY Univ; Lehman Brothers Kuhn Loeb, Inc; Amstar Corp; and others. *Exhib:* Inst Contemp Art, Boston, 70; Albright-Knox Gallery, 70 & 79; Aldrich Mus, Ridgefield, Conn, 70 & 80; Walker Art Mus, Minneapolis, 74; Mus Mod Art, New York, 75; one-man shows, Tibor de Nagy Gallery, 79, 80 & 82; Madison Art Ctr, Wis, 83; Univ Chicago, 83; Flint Inst Arts, Mich, 83; Univ Rochester, NY, 83; and others. *Media:* Oil on Canvas. *Mailing Add:* 139 Bowery New York NY 10002

KALISCHER, CLEMENS
PHOTOGRAPHER, GALLERY DIRECTOR
b Hoyren, Bavaria, Mar 30, 21; US citizen. *Study:* Cooper Union, New York; New Sch Social Res, New York, with Bernice Abbott. *Work:* Libr Cong, Washington, DC; Metrop Mus Art, New York; Williams Col, Lawrence Art Mus; Brooklyn Mus. *Exhib:* In and Out of Focus & Family of Man, Mus Mod Art, New York; Camera as a Witness, Expo 67, Montreal, Que, 67; Photog in the Arts, Metrop Mus Art, New York; Beacon Hill, Boston 200, 76; Portrait of Am Traveling Show, Smithsonian Inst, Washington, DC, 76-79; NE Photovision, Cycloram, Boston, 75; Photo-League Traveling Exhib, 78-79. *Pos:* Pres, Millay Art Colony, Austerlitz, NY, 76-; mem visual arts adv, Mass Coun for the Arts; dir, Image Gallery, Stockbridge, Mass, formerly. *Teaching:* Vis lectr art photog, Williams Col, Williamstown, Mass, 74-77; instr photog, Berkshire Community Col, Pittsfield, Mass, 73-82; vis instr print collecting, Simon's Rock Col, Great Barrington, Mass, 78. *Specialty:* Contemporary art. *Mailing Add:* Main St Stockbridge MA 01262

KALISHER, SIMPSON
PHOTOGRAPHER
b New York, NY, July 27, 26. *Study:* Ind Univ, BA, 48. *Work:* Mus Mod Art, New York; Art Inst Chicago; George Eastman House, Rochester, NY. *Exhib:* Photography at Mid-Century, George Eastman House, Rochester, NY, 58 & travelling; Four Directions in Photography, Albright-Knox Art Gallery, 64; History of the Picture Story, Mus Mod Art, New York, 67; 12 Photographers of the Social Landscape, Poses Inst, Waltham, Mass, 68; Harlem on My Mind, Metropolitan Mus Art, New York, 68; Photography in America, Whitney Mus, 75; Photography as Social Literture, Farmingham Valley Arts Ctr, Avon, Conn, 78; Mirrors and Windows, Mus Mod Art, New York, 78 & travelling, 78-80; Discovering America, Art Inst Chicago, 78; solo exhib, Voltaire Gallery, New Milford, Conn, 80. *Teaching:* Instr photog, Sch Visual Arts, New York, 80- *Bibliog:* Hugh Edwards (auth), Railroad Men, Infinity, 3/62; Thomas H Garver (auth), 12 Photographers of the American Social Landscape, 67; Robert Doty (ed), article, Photography in America, 74. *Mem:* Am Soc Mag Photogr. *Publ:* Auth, Railroad Men: Photographs and Collected Stories, Clarke & Wag, 61; auth, Propaganda and Other Photographs, Addison House, 76; illusr, Clinical Sociology, 79. *Dealer:* Witkin Gallery 41 E 57th St New York NY 10022. *Mailing Add:* Roxbury CT 06783

KALLEM, HENRY
PAINTER
b Philadelphia, Pa, May 2, 12. *Study:* Graphic Sketch Club, Philadelphia, Pa; Nat Acad Art, New York; Hans Hoffmann Sch. *Work:* Corcoran Gallery Art, Washington, DC; Newark Mus, NJ; Chrysler Mus Norfolk, Va; Colby Col Mus; Matatuck Mus Art, Waterbury, Conn. *Exhib:* Carnegie Inst Int, Pittsburgh, Pa, 51; Pa Acad Design, Philadelphia, 51 & 57; Nat Acad Design, New York, 56; Audubon Artists, New York, 74; Int Watercolor Soc, Brooklyn Mus, NY, 60; New York World's Fair, 65; Corcoran Biennial, Washington, DC, 65; Affect/Effect Exhib, La Jolla Mus of Art, Calif, 70; New York Work Progress Admin Artists, Then & Now, Parsons Sch of Design, New York, 77. *Teaching:* Instr painting, Craft Students League, YWCA, New York & Springfield Art Mus, Mo. *Awards:* First Prize, Pepsi Cola Paintings of the Yr, 47; Third Prize, Hallmark Exhib, 54 & 56; Hon Mention, Casein Soc Ann, 59. *Mem:* Audubon Soc. *Media:* Oil painting. *Mailing Add:* 209 W 97th St New York NY 10025

KALLER, ROBERT JAMESON
DEALER
US citizen. *Study:* Columbia Univ; Harvard Univ; NY Univ. *Pos:* Pres, Galerie de Tours, San Francisco, Carmel, Beverly Hills & Pebble Beach, Calif, 60-; pres, Arts & Humanities Coun, Monterey, Calif, 63-64. *Mem:* Am Soc Appraisers; Am Asn Appraisers. *Specialty:* Nineteenth and twentieth century American art; German expressionists; French impressionists; seventeenth century Dutch art. *Mailing Add:* PO Box 413 Pebble Beach CA 93953

KALLIR, JANE KATHERINE
DEALER, WRITER
b New York, NY, July 30, 54. *Study:* Brown Univ, Providence, RI, AB, 76. *Pos:* Dir, Galerie St Etienne, New York, 79- *Mem:* Art Dealers Asn Am. *Res:* Austrian & German expressionism; international naive art, especially in its relationship to modernism. *Specialty:* Klimt, Schiele, Kokoschka, Kubin, Kollwitz, Grandma Moses. *Publ:* Auth, Grandma Moses: A legend lives on, Southwest Art, 79; auth, Gustav Klimt/Egon Schiele, Crown, 80; auth, Austria's Expressionism, Rizzoli, 81; auth, The Folk Art Tradition, Viking, 82; auth, Grandma Moses: The Artist Behind the Myth, Clarkson N Potter, 82. *Mailing Add:* c/o Galerie St Etienne 24 West 57th St New York NY 10019

KAMEN, GLORIA
ILLUSTRATOR, GRAPHIC ARTIST
b New York, NY, Apr 9, 23. *Study:* Pratt Inst, New York; Art Students League, with Robert Brackman, Will Barnett & Kuniyoshi. *Work:* Kerlan Collection, Univ Minn; de Grummond Collection, Univ Southern Miss. *Awards:* Ed Press Award for Publ Art, Outstanding Covers, Syracuse Univ, NY, 69 & 74; Ohio State Award, Best Educ Television for Children, 75-77. *Mem:* Children's Bk Guild of Washington, DC (pres, 75-76); Artist Equity Asn; Washington Watercolor Soc. *Media:* Watercolor. *Publ:* Illusr, The Contest Kid Strikes Again, Abingdon Press, 80; illusr, Lisa & Her Soundless World, Human Sci Press, 74; illusr, The Children of Mt Vernon, Doubleday, 80; auth & illusr, Fiorello, His Honor, The Little Flower, Atheneum, 81; auth & illusr, Charles Chaplin, Atheneum, 82; and others. *Mailing Add:* 8912 Seneca Lane Bethesda MD 20817

KAMEN, REBECCA
EDUCATOR, SCULPTOR
b Philadelphia, Pa, July 8, 50. *Study:* Pa State Univ, BS, 72; Univ Ill, MA, 73; RI Sch Design, MFA, 78. *Work:* Uniweave Co Showroom, Chicago; Desanto-Morris Co Inc, Vienna, Va. *Comn:* Welded steel sculpture, Lynhaven Career & Vocational Ctr, Columbia, SC, 75; welded steel sculpture, Lancaster High Sch, Lancaster, SC, 75; laminated wood wall relief, Pa State Univ, 76. *Exhib:* Works on Paper, 80; Collage on Paper, 81; Corcoran Gallery Art; Collage and Assemblage, Miss Mus Art, Jackson, 81; Artscape, Baltimore, 83; Alexandria Sculpture Festival, Va, 83; Fresh Paint, Pleiades Gallery, New York, 83; Summer Sculpture, Gallery K, Washington, DC, 83. *Pos:* Artist in residence, SC Arts Comn, 74. *Teaching:* Asst prof sculpture, Northern Va Community Col, Alexandria, 78- *Awards:* Award, Artscape, 83; Citicorp Financial Inc, 83; award, Alexandria Sculpture Fest, Alexandria, Va, 83. *Bibliog:* Clarissa K Wittenberg (auth), Washington, DC, Art Voices, 80; Jack Perlmutter (auth), Collage on paper at Corcoran Gallery of Art, Art Voices, 81; Nancy G Heller, Washington, DC, Arts Mag, 83. *Mem:* Int Sculpture Ctr. *Media:* Wood, Steel. *Dealer:* Meredith Contemp Art 805 N Charles St Baltimore MD 21201. *Mailing Add:* 2224 N Pollard St Arlington VA 22207

KAMIHIRA, BEN
PAINTER
b Yakima, Wash, Mar 16, 25. *Study:* Art Inst Pittsburgh; Pa Acad Fine Arts, 48-52, J Henry Schiedt traveling scholar, 52. *Work:* Whitney Mus Am Art, New York; Pa Acad Fine Arts, Philadelphia; Ringling Mus, Sarasota, Fla; Colorado Springs Fine Arts Ctr, Colo; Dallas Mus Fine Arts; and others. *Exhib:* One-man exhibs, Forum Gallery, New York, 66, 73 & 76, Galleria La Medusa, Rome, Italy & touring throughout Italy, 78; Nat Acad Design; Pa Acad Fine Arts; Corcoran Gallery Art, Washington, DC; Butler Inst Am Art, Youngstown, Ohio; Mus Mod Art, New York; and many others. *Teaching:* Instr drawing & painting, Pa Acad Fine Arts & Pa State Univ, formerly; artist in residence, Rice Univ, Houston, Tex, formerly. *Awards:* First Altman Prize, Nat Acad Design, 62; First Prize, Chatauqua Nat Exhib, 62; Nat Acad Design, 75. *Mem:* Fel Pa Acad Fine Arts; academician Nat Acad Design. *Mailing Add:* Peale House 1811 Chestnut Philadelphia PA 19123

KAMINSKY, JACK ALLAN
PHOTOGRAPHER, PRINTMAKER
b New Brunswick, NJ, Sept 8, 49. *Study:* Brooklyn Mus Art Sch, 71; Brooklyn Col, with Walter Rosenblum, Phillip Pearlstein & Lucas Samaras, BS, 72, MFA(fel), 75; Pratt Inst, with Marvin Hoshino, 73. *Work:* LaGrange Col, Ga; Arch Am Art, Smithsonian Inst, Washington, DC. *Comn:* Graphic designs, Off of Neighborhood Govt & New York Mass Transit Authority for Eastern Pkway Subway Sta, 74. *Exhib:* Post Card Size Art, Arte Fiera 78, Bologna, Italy, 78; Brooklyn Scenes by Brooklyn Artists, Brooklyn Mus Community Gallery, 79; Summer Exhib, Salmagundi Club, New York, 79; Doors & Chairs & Windows, Snug Harbor Cult Ctr, Staten Island, NY, 79; Never Fail Imagery Show, Sch Mus Fine Arts, Boston, 80; Invitational, Henry Hicks Gallery Ltd, Brooklyn, NY, 81; and others. *Pos:* Photogr, Aunt Len's Doll & Toy Mus, 74- & Mus Archaeol, Staten Island, NY, 76; gallery asst, Ann Kendall Richards Inc, New York, 81- *Teaching:* Instr photog, Midwood Adolescent Proj, Brooklyn, NY, 73-76; head graphics & photog dept, Brooklyn Mus Art Sch, 73- *Mem:* US Coast Guard Artists; Salmagundi Club. *Mailing Add:* 855 E 19th St Brooklyn NY 11230

KAMMERER, HERBERT LEWIS
SCULPTOR
b New York, NY, July 11, 15. *Study:* Apprentice to Charles Keck & C Paul Jennewein; asst to Paul Manship; Nat Acad Design; Art Students League; New Yale Univ, BFA, 41; Am Acad Rome, 49-52. *Work:* Va Mil Inst; Eisenhower Collection; pvt collection of Queen Elizabeth, Eng. *Comn:* Many medals, portraits & archit sculpture. *Exhib:* Pa Acad Design Ann, 41, 48 & 52-; Fairmont Int Show, 49; Nat Acad Design, 49, 51 & 52; Palazzo Venezia Int, 50 & 51; plus many others. *Teaching:* Prof sculpture, State Univ NY Col New Paltz, 62- *Awards:* Prix d'Rome, Am Acad Rome, 49; Grant in Sculpture, Nat Inst Arts & Lett, 52; Proctor Portrait Prize. *Mem:* Fel Nat Sculpture Soc (pres, 63-65); Century Asn. *Media:* Mixed. *Mailing Add:* 64 Plains Rd New Paltz NY 12561

KAMROWSKI, GEROME
PAINTER, EDUCATOR
b Warren, Minn, Jan 29, 14. *Study:* St Paul Sch Art; Art Students League; New Bauhaus; Hans Hofmann Sch, New York. *Work:* Mus Mod Art, Whitney Mus Am Art & Metrop Mus, New York; Detroit Inst Art; Phillips Mem Gallery; plus others. *Exhib:* Surrealism Reviewer, Heywood Gallery, London; Surrealism, Rutgers Univ; one-man shows, Betty Parsons, New York, 42, Galerie Creuze, Paris, 51 & Monique Knowlton Gallery, New York, 78; Surrealism, Rutgers Univ Mus of Art, 77; Am Abstract Artists, Univ NMex Mus of Art, 77; plus many others. *Teaching:* Heller Distinguished prof art, Univ Mich, Ann Arbor, 46- *Awards:* Founders Prize, Detroit Inst Art; Guggenheim Fel, 37; Racknam Fel, 72. *Bibliog:* Andre Breton (auth), Surrealisme et la Peinture, Brentano's; Evan M Maurer & Jennifer L Bayles (coauth), Gerome Kamrowski--A Retrospective Exhibition, Univ Mich Mus. *Mailing Add:* 1501 Beechwood Dr Ann Arbor MI 48103

KAMYS, WALTER
PAINTER, EDUCATOR
b Chicago, Ill, June 8, 17. *Study:* Art Inst Chicago, 43, with Hubert Ropp & Boris Anisfeld; also with Gordon Onslow-Ford, Mex, 44. *Work:* Yale Univ; Mt Holyoke Col; Smith Col; Fogg Art Mus; Regional Contemp Art Collection, Fargo, ND; plus others. *Exhib:* One-man shows, Bertha Schaefer Gallery, New York, 55, 57 & 60, New Vision Centre Gallery, London, Eng, 60 & East Hampton Gallery, NY, 70; Recent Drawings, USA, Mus Mod Art, 56; 22nd Int Watercolor Biennial, Brooklyn Mus, 63; Inst Contemp Art, Boston, 66; Smithsonian Inst, 68; plus others. *Teaching:* Instr art, Putney Sch, Vt, 45; instr art, G W V Smith Art Mus, Springfield, Mass, 47-60; prof painting & drawing, Univ Mass, 60-, dir, Art Acquisition Prog, 62-74. *Awards:* Boston Art Festival Award, 55; Award, Drawing & Small Sculpture Shows, Ball State Teachers' Col, Art Gallery, Muncie, Ind, 61-62; Westfield State Col Purchase Prize, 68; plus others. *Bibliog:* Harriet Janis & Rudi Blesh (auth), Collage: Personalities, Concepts, Techniques, Chilton, 62; Morris Risenhoover & Robert T Blackburn (auths), Artists as Professors, Converstions with Musicians, Painters, Sculptors, Univ Ill Press, 76. *Mailing Add:* N Main St Sunderland MA 01375

KAN, DIANA
PAINTER, LECTURER
b Hong Kong, Mar 3, 26; US citizen. *Study:* With Chang Dai Chien, China, 46; Art Students League, with Robert Johnson & Robert B Hale, 49-51; Ecole Beaux Arts, Paris, with Paul Lavelle, 52-54. *Work:* Nat Acad Design, Metrop Mus Art, New York; Philadelphia Mus Art; Nelson Gallery, Atkins Mus,

Kansas City, Mo; Nat Hist Mus, Taiwan. *Comn:* Lotus painting, Nat Hist Mus, Taiwan, 71. *Exhib:* Royal Acad Arts, London, Eng, 64; Royal Soc Painters, London, 64; Nat Acad Design, New York, 67-82; one-man shows, Elliott Mus, 67 & 74, Nat Hist Mus, Taiwan, 71 & New York Cult Ctr, 72; Hobe Sound Galleries, Fla, 76; Nat Arts Club, 79; and others. *Awards:* Ralph Fabric Mem Award, Allied Artists Am, 75; Marthe T McKinnon Award, Am Watercolor Soc, 78; Sadie & Max Tesser Award, Audubon Artists, 79. *Bibliog:* Robert Harris (auth), Pictures by a Chinese artist, London Times, 64; Barbara Wright (auth), Diana Kan, Arts Rev, London, 64; Daniel Su (auth), Chinese paintings, Cosmorama Pictorial, 72. *Mem:* Am Watercolor Soc (dir, 75-77); Allied Artists Am (corresp secy, 75-78); Pen & Brush Club (dir, 68-70, 72-77); Audubon Artists (vpres, 83); assoc mem Nat Acad Design. *Media:* Watercolor. *Publ:* Auth, How and Why of Chinese Painting, 74; auth, article, Am Artists Mag, 74. *Dealer:* Grand Central Art Galleries 40 Vanderbilt Ave New York NY 10017; Hobe Sound Galleries 739 Bridge Rd Hobe Sound FL 33455. *Mailing Add:* 26 W Ninth St New York NY 10011

KAN, MICHAEL
HISTORIAN, ADMINISTRATOR
b Shanghai, China, July 17, 33; US citizen. *Study:* Columbia Col, BA(art hist & archeol), 53; State Univ NY Agr & Tech Col Alfred, MFA(ceramics & sculpture), 57; Columbia Univ, MA(art hist), 69, MPhil, 74. *Collections Arranged:* African Art & Simpson Collection, Brooklyn Mus, 70; guest cur, Ancient Art of West Mexico, Los Angeles Co Mus Art, 70; curatorial consult, African Art Tribal Art from West Africa, Portland Mus, 71; curatorial consult, Pre-Columbian Art in the Collection of Jay C Leff, Allentown Mus, 72; Detroit Collects African Art, 77; Treasures of Ancient Nigeria: Legacy of 2000 Years, 79. *Pos:* Assoc cur primitive art, Brooklyn Mus, 68-70, cur, 70-73, chief cur, 73-76; cur African, Oceanic & New World cult, Detroit Inst of the Arts, 77- *Teaching:* Lectr art hist, Univ Calif, Berkeley, 64-66; lectr art Eastern Asia, Finch Col, 66-67; lectr African art, NY Univ, 70- *Mem:* Mus Collaborative Inc (trustee, 75); Am Asn Mus. *Res:* The art of early cultures of pre-Columbian Peru and pre-Columbian Mexico; African art education. *Publ:* Contribr, Early Chinese Art and the Pacific Basin, 68; auth, African Sculpture, 70; coauth, Ancient Art of West Mexico, 70. *Mailing Add:* Detroit Inst of the Arts 5200 Woodward Ave Detroit MI 48202

KANE, BILL (WILLIAM DAVID)
ASSEMBLAGE ARTIST, PHOTOGRAPHER
b Holden, Mass, Feb 18, 51. *Study:* Univ Mass, Amherst, BA, 73; San Francisco State Univ, MA, 78. *Work:* San Francisco Mus Mod Art; Oakland Mus; Stanford Univ, Palo Alto, Calif; Crocker Art Mus, Sacramento. *Comn:* Photo/neon billboard, Eyes & Ears Found, San Francisco, 79; neon/Plexiglas installation, Washington Proj Arts, Washington, DC, 81; neon installation, Foster Goldstrom Gallery, Dallas, 83. *Exhib:* Altered Images, Ctr Creative Photog, Tucson, 81; Nat Mus Art, Kyoto & Tokyo, Japan, 81; Art Gallery Western Australia, Perth, traveling, 82-; and others. *Awards:* Photog Fel, Nat Endowment Arts, 80. *Bibliog:* Robert Atkins (auth), Bill Kane, Arts Mag, 1/81; Mark Levy (auth), Bill Kane, Art Voices, 1/82. *Media:* Neon, Plexiglas. *Dealer:* Foster Goldstrom Fine Arts 228 Grant St San Francisco CA 94108 & 2722 Fairmount St Dallas TX 75201. *Mailing Add:* 130 Dore Alley San Francisco CA 94103

KANE, BOB PAUL
PAINTER
b Cleveland, Ohio, July 11, 37. *Study:* Cornell Univ; Art Students League, with Will Barnet; Pratt Inst. *Work:* Cincinnati Art Mus; Mus Munic St Paul de Vence, France; Joseph H Hirshhorn Collection; Palm Springs Desert Mus; Pa Acad Fine Arts. *Exhib:* Collector's Choice, Okla Art Ctr, 68; Biennial of the Painters of the Mediterranean, Nice, France, 73; Biennial of Menton, France, 73; Bertha Schaefer Gallery, New York, 68, 70, 72 & 74; Galerie Marcel Bernheim, Paris, 70; Albright-Knox Mus, 73; Ankrum Gallery, Los Angeles, 69, 74, 79 & 81; plus many others. *Teaching:* Instr painting & art hist, Mt Clair Col, 69-70; instr painting & art hist, NY Univ, 69-70. *Bibliog:* Richard Boyle (auth), Bob Kane, Mus Munic St Paul de Vence, 72. *Media:* Oil. *Dealer:* Bertha Schaefer Gallery 41 E 57th St New York NY 10022; Ankrum Gallery 657 N La Cienega Blvd Los Angeles CA 90069. *Mailing Add:* 125 Riverside Dr New York NY 10024

KANE, MARGARET BRASSLER
SCULPTOR
b East Orange, NJ, May 25, 09. *Study:* Syracuse Univ; Art Students League; also with John Hovannes; Colo State Christian Col, Hon PhD, 73. *Work:* US Maritime Comn; Limited Ed Lamp Co; and pvt collections. *Comn:* Plaque for Burro Monument, Fairplay, Colo. *Exhib:* Lever House, New York, 59-79; Chicago Art Inst; New York Metrop Mus; Whitney Mus Am Art, New York; Philadelphia Mus Int Sculpture Exhibs; Pa Acad Fine Arts; plus others. *Pos:* Juror, Am Mach & Foundry Co, 57. *Teaching:* Lectr, Creative Approach to Sculpture. *Awards:* First Anna Hyatt Huntington Prize, 42 & Medal of Hon for Sculpture, 51, Nat Asn Women Artists; Henry O Avery Prize, NY Archit League, 44; plus others. *Mem:* Charter mem Sculptors Guild (past pres); Nat Asn Women Artists; Greenwich Art Soc; Silvermine Guild Artists; fel Int Inst Arts & Lett. *Media:* Wood, Marble. *Publ:* Contribr ann reproductions, Greenwich Time Publ, 50-77; auth, article, Am Artists, 1/70; reproductions, In: Contemporary Stone Sculpture, Crown, 71; reproductions of wood carvings used by McGraw-Hill, 73. *Mailing Add:* 30 Strickland Rd Cos Cob CT 06807

KANEGIS, SIDNEY S
DEALER
b Winthrop, Mass, Sept 6, 22. *Study:* Boston Mus Fine Art Sch. *Pos:* Owner & dir, Kanegis Gallery, Boston, 50- *Specialty:* Modern master graphics. *Mailing Add:* 244 Newbury St Boston MA 02116

KANEMITSU, MATSUMI
PAINTER, LECTURER
b Ogden, Utah, May 28, 22. *Study:* Painting with Fernand Leger, Paris, France; Art Students League; also sculpture with Karl Metzler, Baltimore. *Work:* Galleria Civica Arte Mod, Turin, Italy; Honolulu Acad Arts, Hawaii; Mus Mod Art, New York; San Francisco Mus Art; Corcoran Gallery Art; and many others. *Comn:* Watercolor, Shinwa Bowl, Kawasaki City, Japan, 72. *Exhib:* In Memory of My Feelings, Mus Mod Art, New York, 67, Tamarind: An Homage to Lithography, 69; Trends in 20th Century Art, Univ Calif, Santa Barbara, 70; Black & White Drawings & Watercolors, San Francisco Mus Art, 71; one-man show, Michael Smith Gallery, Los An Art, Chouinard Art Sch, 65-72; Los Angeles Municipal Art Gallery, 78. *Pos:* Artist in residence, Univ Calif, Berkeley, 66; artist in residence, Honolulu Acad Arts, 67-68. *Teaching:* Instr, Calif State Col, Los Angeles, 69; Art Ctr Col Design, Los Angeles, 70; Univ Calif, Berkeley, 70-71; Otis Art Inst, 71; Calif Inst Arts, Valencia, 71-72. *Awards:* Ford Found Awards, 61 & 64; Japan Cult Forum Award, 4th Int Young Artists Exhib, 67; Award, Nat Soc Literature & Art, 74. *Media:* Oil, Duco, Painting. *Dealer:* Janus Gallery 21 Market St Venice CA 90291. *Mailing Add:* 854 S Berendo St Los Angeles CA 90005

KANGAS, GENE
SCULPTOR, WRITER
b Painesville, Ohio, May 22, 44. *Study:* Miami Univ, BFA, Bowling Green Univ, MFA; Univ Ky, sculpture sem. *Work:* Butler Inst Am Art, Ohio; Univ NC, Chapel Hill; City of Upper Arlington, Ohio; Case Western Reserve Univ, Cleveland, Ohio. *Comn:* Sculptures, Cuyahoga Co Justice Ctr, Cleveland, Ohio, 77, Frank J Lausche State Off Bldg, Cleveland, 80, Case Western Reserve Univ, Cleveland, 81, Dade Co, Miami, Fla, 83, Coral Springs, Fla, 84. *Exhib:* Sculpture Invitational, Art Acad Cincinnati, 80; City of Upper Arlington Sculpture Invitational, Columbus, Ohio, 82; Art Assemblage, Columbus, Ohio, 82; Invitational Sculptor Exhib, Case Western Reserve Univ, 83; and numerous group and one-man exhibs. *Teaching:* Instr sculpture, Univ NC, 68-71; asst prof sculpture, Cleveland State Univ, 71-75, assoc prof, 75-84, prof, 84- *Awards:* Fulbright-Hays Scholar, 68; Univ Res Grant, Univ NC, 68-70; First Prize in Sculpture, Cleveland Mus Art, 75. *Bibliog:* Hollander (auth), Plastics for Artists and Craftsmen; Campen (auth), Outdoor sculpture in Ohio; McClelland (dir), Public Sculpture of Cleveland (film), 82. *Publ:* Coauth, Decoys; A North American Survey, Hillcrest Publ, 83. *Mailing Add:* PO Box 175 Painesville OH 44077

KANIDINC, SALAHATTIN
DESIGNER, CALLIGRAPHER
b Istanbul, Turkey, Aug 12, 27. *Study:* Defenbaugh Sch Lettering, under Roger I Defenbaugh; Zanerian Col Penmanship, text lettering under John P Turner; State Univ Iowa, cert lettering, under Prof Meyer; Univ Minn, cert lettering; Univ Calif, cert advert. *Work:* The White House, Washington, DC; Independence Hall, Philadelphia; Franklin Mint Mus Medallic Art, Franklin Center, Pa; Peabody Inst Libr, Baltimore, Md. *Comn:* Monogram design, Tiffany & Co, New York, 70; Genius of Michelangelo Medals, Franklin Mint, 71; medal design, Fedr Turkish-Am Socs, New York, 73; Christmas Card Design, UNICEF, New York, 73; postage stamp design, United Nations, 78; and others. *Exhib:* 1000 Yrs of Calligraphy & Illumination, Baltimore, 59; Bertrand Russell Centenary Int Art Exhib, London, 72-73. *Pos:* Chief calligrapher, Deniz Basimevi MD, Istanbul, Turkey, 50-61; lettering artist, Buzza-Cardozo, Anaheim, Calif, 62-64; asst art dir, Rust Craft Publ, Dedham, Mass, 64; lettering specialist-designer, Tiffany & Co, New York, 64-72; owner-creative dir, Kanidinc Int, New York, 72- *Awards:* First Prize, Ann McKay Christmas Card Contest, 74. *Mem:* Int Asn Master Penmen & Teachers Handwriting; Int Ctr Typographic Arts; Queens Coun Arts; Soc Scribes & Illuminators; Nat Soc Lit & Arts. *Media:* Ink, Gouache. *Publ:* Contribr, Alphabet Thesaurus, Vol II, III, 65-71; contribr, Turkish-Am Encycl Dig. *Mailing Add:* 62-34 99th St Rego Park NY 11374

KANOVITZ, HOWARD
PAINTER
b Fall River, Mass, Feb 9, 29. *Study:* Providence Col, BS, 49; RI Sch Design, 49-51; with Franz Kline, 51-52; Inst Fine Arts, NY Univ, 59-61. *Work:* Whitney Mus Am Art, New York; Wallraf-Richartz Mus, Cologne, Ger; Hirshhorn Mus & Sculpture Garden; Mus Boymans-Van Beuningen, Rotterdam, Holland; Los Angeles Co Mus, Calif; and others. *Comn:* The Opening, 180 Beacon Corp, Boston, 67; A Death in Treme, Florists Transworld Delivery Collection, Detroit, 71; Collector's Wall, F K Johnssen, Essen, Ger, 71. *Exhib:* Whitney Mus Am Art Ann, New York, 72; Dokumenta 6, Kassel, Ger, 77; Guild Hall, Easthampton, 78; Hamburg Kunstverein, Hamburg, Ger, 79; Akad der Kunste, Berlin, Ger, 79; Kestner-Gesellschaft, Hannover, 79. *Teaching:* Instr painting & design, Brooklyn Col, 61-64; instr 2-D design, Pratt Inst, 64-66; prof painting, Southampton Col, 77-78; Sch Visual Arts, New York, currently. *Awards:* Berlin Deutscher Akademischer Austauschdienst Fel, 79-80. *Bibliog:* Peter Sager (auth), Neve Formen des Realismus, Mag Kunst, 71; Sam Hunter (auth), Howard Kanovitz's new paintings, 4/75 & Michael Florescu (auth), Kanovitz, the new work, 2/79, Arts Mag. *Mem:* Fund Artists' Colonies (bd mem, currently). *Media:* Acrylic. *Mailing Add:* 237 E 18th St New York NY 10003

KAO, RUTH (YU-HSIN) LEE
FIBER ARTIST, EDUCATOR
b Peking, Repub of China; US citizen. *Study:* Univ Northern Iowa, Cedar Falls, BA & MA; Univ Kans, Lawrence; Haystack Mountain Sch of Crafts; also with Philip Evergood & Chunghi Choo. *Comn:* Weaving, Univ Northern Iowa Libr, Cedar Falls, 77. *Exhib:* Marietta Col Crafts Nat, Ohio, 75; InnerSpace, Mano Galleries, Chicago, 77; Ruth Kao Weavings & Paintings,

Bradley Galleries, Milwaukee, 77; Focus on Crafts, Univ Minn, St Paul, 77; Lake Superior 77, Tweed Mus Art, Duluth, 77; Fibers, Hadler Galleries, New York, 77; Currents 77, Mid Tenn State Univ, Murfreesboro, 77; Fiber Arts, Paul Waggoner Gallery, Chicago, 77. *Pos:* Juror, 4th Biennial Int Crafts Exhib, Tweed Mus Art, 77 & 5th Wis Union Crafts, Univ Wis, 77. *Teaching:* Instr fibers, Univ N Iowa, 70-74; from asst prof to assoc prof fibers, Univ Wis, Milwaukee, 74- *Awards:* Craftsmen's Fel, Nat Endowment Arts, 74; res grant, Grad Sch, Univ Wis, Milwaukee, 75. *Bibliog:* James Auer (auth), Her artistry looms large, Milwaukee J, 3/13/77; Joan Zyda (auth), A show of Ravioli, Chicago-Tribune, 12/18/77; Sonia Katz (auth), Eighteen fiber artists, New Art Examr, Chicago, 1/78. *Mem:* Am Crafts Coun; Surface Design Asn. *Media:* Weaving, Fiber Contruction. *Dealer:* Hadler Galleries 35-37 E 20th St New York NY 10003. *Mailing Add:* 2906 N Downer Ave Milwaukee WI 53211

KAPLAN, JACQUES
COLLECTOR, DEALER
b Paris, France, Oct 22, 24. *Study:* Sorbonne Univ, France, PhD. *Awards:* Croix de Guerre. *Bibliog:* Articles in New York Times, 66, Life Mag, 68, Time & Newsweek. *Collection:* Contemporary American art, 19th century European art and the Old Masters. *Mailing Add:* 222 E 61st St New York NY 10021

KAPLAN, JEROME EUGENE
PRINTMAKER
b Philadelphia, Pa, 1920. *Study:* Philadelphia Col Art, dipl; also with Paul Froelich & Benton Spruance. *Work:* Libr Cong, Washington, DC; Philadelphia Mus Art; Nat Gallery Art, Washington, DC; New York Pub Libr. *Comn:* Portfolio, White House Etchings, for President Jimmy Carter, 80. *Exhib:* 4th Int Prints, Ljubjana, Yugoslavia, 61; Am Prints Today, Print Coun Am, 62; First Biennial Int l'Estampe, Epinal, France, 71; 25th Nat Exhib, Washington, DC, 77; 57th Nat, Soc Am Graphic Artists, New York, 79; and 19 one-man exhibs. *Teaching:* Prof printmaking, Philadelphia Col Art, 48-, chmn dept, 80- *Awards:* Guggenheim Fel, 61; Fel, Tamarind Lithography Workshop, 62. *Mem:* Print Club Philadelphia; Artists Equity Asn; Soc Am Graphic Artists. *Media:* Intaglio, Lithography. *Publ:* Illusr, The Bucket Rider, 72; illusr, From a Housewife's Diary, 78; illusr, Charlie in the House of Rue, 80. *Dealer:* Rosenfeld Gallery 113 Arch St Philadelphia PA 19106; Assoc Am Artists 1614 Latimer St Philadelphia PA 19103. *Mailing Add:* 7029 Clearview St Philadelphia PA 19119

KAPLAN, JULIUS DAVID
HISTORIAN
b Nashville, Tenn, July 22, 41. *Study:* Wesleyan Univ, Middletown, Conn, BA; Columbia Univ, MA & PhD. *Collections Arranged:* Symbolism, Europe and America at the End of the 19th Century, 80, Gaston Lachaise, Sculpture and Drawings, 80 & Kate Steinitz, Art and Collection, Avant-Garde Art in Germany in the 1920's and 1930's, 82, Art Gallery, Calif State Col, San Bernardino; Gaston Lachaise, Sculpture and Drawings, Calif State Col, San Bernardino, 10/80-11/80. *Teaching:* Lectr, Colby Col, Waterville, Maine, 66; asst prof, Univ Calif, Los Angeles, 69-77; assoc prof art hist, Calif State Col, San Bernardino, 77-, chmn dept, 78-82, prof, 82- *Awards:* Grant-in-aid, Am Coun Learned Socs, 77; Nat Endowment Arts Grant, 81; Calif Art Coun Grant, 81, 82 & 83. *Mem:* Col Art Asn; Art Historians Southern Calif. *Res:* Academic and official art in France, 1850-1900. *Publ:* Auth, The religious subjects of James Ensor 1877-1900, Revue Belge d'Archaeol d'Hist l'Art, 66; auth, Gustave Moreau, Los Angeles Co Mus Art, 74; auth, Gustave Moreau, UMI Res Press, 82. *Mailing Add:* 3414 Troy Dr Los Angeles CA 90068

KAPLAN, LEO
ASSEMBLAGE ARTIST, COLLAGE ARTIST
b Binghamton, NY, Jan 21, 12. *Study:* Rochester Inst Technol, 32. *Work:* Chase Manhattan Bank, New York; Everson Gallery, Syracuse; McNey Mus, San Antonio, Tex; Skidmore Col, Saratoga Springs, NY; and others. *Comn:* The Humanities, Monroe Community Col, Rochester, NY, 66; History Assemblage, AMF Inc, White Plains, NY, 78; Kodak Centennial, Lincoln First, Rochester, 79; Regents Publ, New York, 83. *Exhib:* One-man show, Two Rivers Gallery, Binghamton, NY, 68; Miss Mus Art, Jackson, 81; Hunter Mus, Chatanooga, 82; Roanoke Mus Fine Art, 82; Mus Art, Ft Lauderdale, 82 & 83; Tampa Mus, 83; and others. *Awards:* Best of show, Brockport State Univ, 66; Ida Abrams Award, Mem Art Gallery, Finger Lakes, 71. *Dealer:* Alan Brown Gallery Hartsdale NY 10530; Oxford Gallery Rochester NY 14607. *Mailing Add:* 5310 Buttonwood Ct Tamarac FL 33319

KAPLAN, LEONARD
PAINTER, DEALER
b New York, NY, Jan 15, 22. *Study:* Art Students League. *Work:* Los Angeles Co Mus Art, Los Angeles; Laguna Beach Mus Art, Calif; James S Copley Libr, La Jolla, Calif. *Comn:* Mural, Goldwater's, Scottsdale, Ariz; mural, Stix-Baer-Fuller, St Louis; sculpture, Beverly Hilton, Beverly Hills. *Exhib:* Retrospectives, Univ Ariz Art Gallery, Tucson, 67; Edward Dean Mus, Cherry Valley, Calif, 72; Laguna Beach Mus Art, 74. *Pos:* Co-dir, Ancient Art, Laguna Beach, currently. *Teaching:* Lectr life drawing, Laguna Beach Sch Art, 74-; lectr life drawing, Univ Calif, Irvine, 75; vis artist-in-residence, Calif State Univ, Fullerton, 76-77. *Awards:* Los Angeles Co Purchase Award, 56. *Media:* Conte, Charcoal. *Specialty:* Oriental and pre-Columbian. *Mailing Add:* 860 Glenneyre Laguna Beach CA 92651

KAPLAN, MARILYN FLASHENBERG
PAINTER
b Brooklyn, NY. *Study:* Syracuse Univ, BFA; Columbia Univ Teachers Col, MA, 54. *Work:* New York Port Authority; US Army Corps Engr, Saudi Arabia; Nat Collection of Fine Arts, Smithsonian Inst, Washington, DC; Lanvin-Charles of the Ritz Collection, New York; Johnson & Johnson Collection, New Brunswick, NJ. *Comn:* Poster, No More War by Personality Posters, New York for Nat Peace Movement, 69. *Exhib:* Allied Artists Am, New York, 69; Heckscher Mus Ann, Huntington, 69-72 & 75; Nat Acad Design, New York, 70, 72 & 75; New Eng Ann Exhib, Silvermine, Conn, 72-73; Images of an Era: The Am Poster 1945-1975, Smithsonian Inst Bicentennial Art Traveling Exhib, 76-78; Palazzo Delle Esposizioni, Rome, Italy; and others. *Teaching:* Art coordr elem & jr high sch art, Croton-Harmon Schs, NY, 54-56. *Awards:* Award, Invitational Show, Hofstra Univ, 66; Second Prize Oils, Hecksher Mus, 72; Benjamin Altman Landscape Prize for Painting, Nat Acad Design, 75; and many others. *Bibliog:* Gary Yanker (auth), Prop Art; Images of an Era: The American Poster 1945-1975 (catalogue), Nat Collection of Fine Arts, Smithsonian Inst; Phyliss Braff (auth), Celebrating land and sea, New York Times, 5/5/83. *Mem:* Artists Equity Asn; Prof Artists Guild (treas, 73-76). *Media:* Oil on Canvas. *Dealer:* Madison Avenue Gallery 985 Madison Ave New York NY 10021; Isis Gallery 326 Main St Port Washington NY. *Mailing Add:* 26 Birchwood Park Dr Jericho NY 11753

KAPLAN, SANDRA
PAINTER, PRINTMAKER
b Cincinnati, Ohio, May 23, 43. *Study:* Art Acad Cincinnati, with Julian Stanczak, 60-61; Pratt Inst, BFA(with hons), 65; City Univ New York, with Richard Lindner, Stephen Greene & Jacob Landau, 68-70. *Work:* John Mansville Corp, Chicago; Midland Fed Savings Bank, Denver, Colo; Ideal Basic Industries Denver; US Plywood Corp, New York; plus numerous pvt collections. *Exhib:* Inkfish Gallery, Denver, 79, 80 & 82; Invitational Watermedia Exhib, Colo Women's Col, Denver, 79; State Invitational, Okla Art Ctr, Oklahoma City, 79; Artists with Small Works, Arras Gallery, New York, 79; All Colo Women's Exhib, Arvada Ctr, Colo, 79; Janus Gallery, Santa Fe, 81; and others. *Teaching:* Instr painting & design, Arapahoe Community Col, 74-75; instr oil painting, Emily Griffith Opportunity Sch, 74-76; art instr, Metro State Col, 77-78; guest art instr, Denver Univ, 78-79. *Awards:* Deans Medal in Graphic Arts, Pratt Inst, 75; Best of Show, Jefferson Unitarian Church, Golden, Colo, 75; Rocky Mountain Nat Watermedia Award, 79. *Bibliog:* Irene Clureman (auth), article, Rocky Mountain News, 12/3/78; Vicki Thomas (auth), article, Westword Mag, 12/8/78; Lucy Lippard (auth), article, Art in Am, 12/79. *Media:* Watercolor; Silkscreen, Lithography. *Publ:* Illusr, Rationale, 65; contrib, Art Work, No Commercial Value, Grossman, 71. *Dealer:* Janus Gallery 110 Gallisteo Santa Fe NM 87501. *Mailing Add:* Inkfish Gallery 1810 Market St Denver CO 80202

KAPLAN, STANLEY
PRINTMAKER, MURALIST
b Brooklyn, NY, Sept 4, 25. *Study:* Cooper Union Sch of Art, cert fine arts, 49; NY Univ, BS, 52; Pratt Inst, New York, MS, 68. *Work:* Metrop Mus of Art, New York; Brooklyn Mus, New York Pub Libr; Columbia Univ; Philadelphia Mus Art. *Comn:* Murals, Int Tel & Tel Community Develop Corp, New York & Fla, 73, 74 & 75; mural, Manuche's Restaurant, New York, 62. *Exhib:* One-man show, Shelter Rock Libr, Albertson, NY, 80; Libr of Cong, Washington, DC, 51, Audubon Artists, 66, Nat Acad of Design, New York, 71, Kennedy Gallery, 71 & Assoc Am Artists Gallery, 72; and others. *Pos:* Mgr, Tortoise Press, 78- *Teaching:* Art teacher, Levittown Pub Schs, NY, 54-59; prof art, Nassau Community Col, Garden City, 66- *Awards:* Award, Sixth Ann Competition, Port Washington Pub Libr, 71; Purchase Award, Soc Am Graphic Artists 55th Nat Print Exhib, 77. *Mem:* Soc Am Graphic Artists (vpres, 72-74, pres, 76-78). *Mailing Add:* 47 Trapper Lane Levittown NY 11756

KAPLINSKI, BUFFALO
PAINTER
b Chicago, Ill, May 25, 43. *Study:* Art Inst Chicago; Am Acad Art. *Work:* Denver Pub Libr, Johns-Manville, United Bank & Petro-Lewis, Denver. *Exhib:* 98th Ann, Am Watercolor Soc, New York; 162nd Ann, Pa Acad Fine Arts, Philadelphia; 27th Exhib, Audubon Artists, New York; 15th-18th Ann, Nat Soc Painters in Casein; High Country in Art, Boulder Pub Libr, 79; Wilderness and Wildlife--Nature Conservancy, Aspen, Colorado Springs & Denver, 79; plus many others. *Awards:* 15th Ann Exhib Hon Mention, Nat Soc Painters in Casein; Southwestern Watercolor Soc Purchase Award, Southern Methodist Univ Fine Arts Ctr; Southwestern Biennial Hon Mention, NMex Arts Mus, Santa Fe. *Bibliog:* Article in Am Artist Mag, 8/72; article, Artists Rockies, 9/77 & 10/83; Harold & Peggy Samuels, Contemp Western Artists, 11/82. *Media:* Acrylic, Watercolor. *Dealer:* Deer Dancer Gallery 1475 Lawrence Denver CO 80202; American Legacy Gallery 5911 Main St Kansas City MO 64113. *Mailing Add:* PO Box 44 Elizabeth CO 80107

KAPPEL, R ROSE (MRS IRVING GOULD)
PRINTMAKER
b Hartford, Conn, Sept 23, 10. *Study:* Pratt Inst, New York, 30; NY Univ, BS, 47, MA, 50, EdD, 54; Wash Univ; Univ Wis; Yale Univ. *Work:* Metrop Mus Art, New York; Cleveland Mus Art, Ohio; New Britain Mus Fine Arts, Conn; Mt Holyoke Mus, Mass; Fogg Mus, Cambridge; and others. *Comn:* Murals on educ, Cult & Health Sch, Brooklyn, 50. *Exhib:* Nat Acad of Art, 60-67; Washington Art Asn; 12 one-man shows in New York. *Pos:* Art dir, Great

Detective Mag, 35-40. *Teaching:* Art specialist, Bur for Educ of Phys Handicapped Children, New York, 31-75. *Awards:* Beth Creedy Hamm Prize/Watercolor, Nat Acad, 69; Watercolor Award, Nat Asn Women Artists, 62 & Nat Acad, 61. *Mem:* Am Asn Univ Women; Queens Pres Coun (gen vpres, 68-); Am Fedn Art; Municipal Art Soc. *Publ:* Illusr, Ships & Sails, 47. *Mailing Add:* 35-36 76th St Jackson Heights NY 11372

KAPROV, SUSAN
PAINTER, PRINTMAKER

b New York, NY, Aug 11, 46. *Study:* City Col New York, BA, 67; Dartmouth Col, Hanover, NH, MA, 68. *Work:* Mus Mod Art & Metrop Mus Art, New York; Corcoran Gallery Art, Washington, DC; Nat Mus Am Art, Washington, DC; Brooklyn Mus. *Comn:* Western Union, NJ, 78; Reeves Communication Corp, NY, 81; NASA, Washington, DC, 81; Prudential Insurance Co, 82; Hexcel Corp, 83; and others. *Exhib:* Prints: Acquisitions 1973-76, Mus Mod Art, New York, 77; one-man show, Hayden Planetarium, New York, 78 & Brooklyn Mus, 81; Recent Acquisitions, Nat Mus Am Art, Washington, DC, 78; Art/Technol, Philadelphia Print Club, 79; Alternative Imaging Systems, Everson Mus, Syracuse, NY, 79; installation, Granite Gallery, Nat Mus Am Art, 83-84. *Awards:* MacDowell Colony Fel, 71 & 73; Ossabaw Island Proj Fel, 73; Creative Artists Pub Serv fel, NY State Coun on Arts, 79-80. *Bibliog:* Donald Saff (auth), History of American Printmaking, Holt, Rinehart, Winston, 77; Ellen Lubell (auth), article, Art in Am, 81; V Butera (auth), article, Arts Mag, 81. *Mem:* Nat Soc Mural Painters. *Media:* Oil; Encaustic, Color Xerox on Aluminum. *Mailing Add:* 149 Willow St Brooklyn Heights NY 11201

KAPSALIS, THOMAS HARRY
PAINTER, SCULPTOR

b Chicago, Ill, May 31, 25. *Study:* Sch Art Inst Chicago, BAE, 49, MAE, 57; Fulbright Grant, Ger, 53-54. *Work:* Main Bank, Chicago, Ill; Elmhurst Col, Ill; Art Inst Chicago, Ill; Ill State Mus, Springfield. *Exhib:* Pa Acad Fine Arts Ann Watercolor & Print Exhib, Philadelphia, 46; Chicago & Vicinity Exhib, 12 times, 50-81 & Contemp Drawings From 12 Countries, 52, Art Inst Chicago; 27th Biennial Exhib Contemp Painting, Corcoran Gallery Art, Washington, DC, 61; Visions/Painting & Sculpture: Distinguished Alumni 1945 to Present, Art Inst of Chicago, 76; two-person exhib, Art Inst Chicago, 79; Sixth Ann Baer Art Competition, Beverly Art Ctr, Chicago, 82; Morton Col Art Gallery, Ill, 82; Chicago: Some Other Traditions, Madison Art Ctr, Wis, 83; Fans, 83 & Artists Choose Artists, 83, Hyde Park Art Ctr, Chicago. *Teaching:* Assoc prof drawing & painting, Art Inst Chicago. 54-; lectr painting, Northwestern Univ, Chicago & Evanston, 58-71. *Awards:* Huntington Hartford Found Grant, 56 & 59; Pualine Palmer Prize, 60 & Jule F Brower Prize, 69, Art Inst Chicago. *Bibliog:* Meilach & Seiden (auth), Direct Metal Sculpture, Crown, 66; Meilach & Hinz (auth), How to Create Your Own Designs, Doubleday, 75. *Media:* Oil, Watercolor; Bronze. *Mailing Add:* 5204 N Virginia Ave Chicago IL 60625

KARAWINA, ERICA (MRS SIDNEY C HSIAO)
PAINTER, STAINED GLASS ARTIST

b Ger; US citizen. *Study:* Study in Europe; also with Frederick W Allen & Charles J Connick, Boston. *Work:* Metrop Mus Art, New York; Mus Mod Art, New York; Boston Mus Fine Arts; Libr Cong, Washington, DC; Honolulu Acad Arts. *Comn:* Crux Gemmata (glass in concrete), Manoa Valley Church, Honolulu, 67; six windows of sculptured glass, St Anthony's Church, Kailua, Oahu, Hawaii, 68; This Earth is Ours (sculptured glass), News Bldg Foyer, Honolulu Advertiser, 72; translucent glass mosaic murals, Hawaii State Off Bldg, Honolulu, 75; The Sanctuary Windows, St Anthony Church, Wailuku, Maui; plus others. *Exhib:* Dance Int, Rockefeller Ctr, New York, 37; Competition of State of Mass, New York's Fair, 39; Protestant Orthodox Ctr, New York World's Fair, 64; one-man shows, China Int Inst, Taipei, Taiwan, 56 & Contemp Arts Ctr, Honolulu, 77; Ryan Gallery, Kailua, 81; plus others. *Pos:* Draftsman stained glass, Connick Studios, Boston, 30-33; designer stained glass, Burnham Studios, Boston, 35-38. *Awards:* John Poole Mem Prize, Honolulu Acad Arts, 52; James C Castle Award, Narcissus Art Festival, Honolulu, 61. *Bibliog:* Jean Charlot (auth), Exhibition of stained glass, 5/53; Joanne Shaw (auth), Echoes of universality, Vol 72, No 9, Paradise of Pac; Francis Haar & Murray Turnbull (ed), Artists of Hawaii, Vol II, 77. *Mem:* Honolulu Print Makers; Honolulu Acad of Arts; Hawaii Artists League; fel Int Inst Arts. *Media:* Stained Glass. *Publ:* Contribr, From Maui to Mainz, 56-57 & From Hawaii to Holland, 63, Stained Glass. *Mailing Add:* 3529 Akaka Pl Honolulu HI 96822

KARDON, JANET
MUSEUM DIRECTOR, CURATOR

b Philadelphia, Pa. *Study:* Temple Univ, BS(educ); Univ Pa, MA(art hist). *Collections Arranged:* Line (cataloged), Sch of Visual Arts, New York, 76; Seventies Painting (cataloged), Philadelphia Col Art, 78, Siah Armajani (cataloged), 78, Alice Aycock (cataloged), 78 & Point (cataloged), 78; Masks Tents Vessels Talismans (cataloged), Inst Contemp Art & Urban Encounters: Art Architecture Audience (cataloged), 80; Drawings: The Pluralist Decade (cataloged), Venice Biennial, 80; Machineworks: Acconci, Aycock, Oppenheim (cataloged), 80-81; Robert Zakanitch (cataloged), 81. *Pos:* Dir exhib, Philadelphia Col of Art, 76-78; dir, Inst Contemp Art, Univ Pa, 79- *Teaching:* Lectr Am art & 20th century art, Philadelphia Col of Art, 68- *Awards:* Nat Endowment Arts Res Grant, 78. *Mem:* Col Art Asn; Pa Coun Arts; Am Asn Mus; Asn Art Mus Dirs. *Res:* Twentieth century; post-World War II; earthworks performance sculpture. *Publ:* Auth, Janet Kardon interviews some modern maze makers, Arts Int, 4-5/76. *Mailing Add:* 56 Crosby Brown Rd Gladwyne PA 19035

KARLEN, PETER H
EDUCATOR, WRITER

US citizen. *Study:* Univ Calif, Berkeley, BA(hist), 71; Univ Calif, Hastings Col Law, JD, 74; Univ Denver Col Law, MS, 76. *Pos:* Art attorney, self-employed, 78-; writer, syndicated Artlaw column, 79-; contrib ed & columnist, Artweek, 79- *Teaching:* Lectr law & the arts, Univ Warwick Sch Law, 76-78; adj prof, Univ San Diego Sch Law, 79-; adj prof, Western State Univ Col Law, 80. *Mem:* Artists Equity; Am Soc Aesthetics; British Soc Aesthetics; Volunteer Lawyers Arts, NY; Bay Area Lawyers Arts, San Francisco. *Res:* Property rights in aesthetic creations. *Publ:* Auth, What is art? A sketch for a legal definition, Law Quart Rev, 78; auth, Legal aesthetics, British J Aesthetics, 79; auth, The preservation of art in California, J Media Law & Practice, 81; auth, Moral rights in California, Univ San Diego Law Rev, 82; auth, Aesthetic quality and art preservation, J Aesthetics & Art Criticism, 83. *Mailing Add:* 7730 Herschel Ave Suite A La Jolla CA 92037

KARLSEN, ANNE-MARIE
PAINTER, PRINTMAKER

b Detroit, Mich, Sept 16, 52. *Study:* Mich State Univ, BFA, 74; Univ Wis, MA, 77, MFA, 79. *Work:* Brooklyn Mus; Mus Art, Carnegie Inst, Pittsburgh; Univ Calif, Los Angeles; Tex Tech Univ, Lubbock; Univ Wis, Madison. *Exhib:* Brooklyn Mus, 78; Los Angeles Print Soc, 79; Boston Printmakers, 80; Honolulu Acad Arts, 80; Philadelphia Print Club, 81; Newspace Gallery, Los Angeles, 82 & 84; and others. *Teaching:* Lectr, Univ Calif, Los Angeles, 79-; asst prof fine arts, Calif State Univ, Northridge, 80. *Awards:* Purchase Awards, Colorprint USA, Tex Tech Univ, 79 & Univ SDak, Vermillion, 79; Award Excellence, Dittmar Gallery, Northwestern Univ, 79. *Mem:* Col Art Asn. *Media:* Acrylic, Gouache; Lithography, Etching. *Dealer:* Newspace 5241 Melrose Los Angeles CA 90038. *Mailing Add:* 13816 Bora Bora Way Apt 333A Venice CA 90292

KARLSTROM, PAUL JOHNSON
HISTORIAN, ADMINISTRATOR

b Seattle, Wash, Jan 22, 41. *Study:* Stanford Univ, BA(Eng lit), 64; Univ Calif, Los Angeles, MA(art), PhD, 73. *Collections Arranged:* Venice Panorama (auth, catalog), Grunwald Ctr for Graphic Arts, Univ Calif, Los Angeles, 69; Archives of American Art, California Collecting, (auth, catalog), Oakland Mus, Calif, 77; Louis M Eilshemius in the Hirshhorn Museum Traveling Exhib (auth, catalog), 78; Impressionism and American Painting (catalog introd), San Jose Mus Art, Calif, 79; Clande Buck (auth, catalog), Glastonbury Gallery, San Francisco, 83. *Pos:* Asst cur, Grunwald Ctr for the Graphic Arts, Univ Calif, Los Angeles, 67-70; guest cur, Smithsonian Inst Traveling Exhib Serv, Washington, DC, 77; dir, West Coast Area Ctr, Arch Am Art, Smithsonian Inst, San Francisco, 73-; mem adv bd, Ctr Mus Studies, San Francisco. *Teaching:* Instr Renaissance to mod art, Calif State Univ, Northridge, 72-73; vis instr mus practices, Calif Col Arts & Crafts, Oakland, 76. *Awards:* Samuel H Kress Fel, Nat Gallery Art, Washington, DC, 70-71; Acad Distinction, Col Fine Arts, Univ Calif, Los Angeles, 74. *Mem:* Col Art Asn Am. *Res:* American art history, 19th and 20th century. *Publ:* Auth, Americans Abroad: Painters of the Victorian Era, San Jose Mus Art, Calif, 75; Louis Michel Eilshemius, Harry N Abrams, 78. *Mailing Add:* c/o Arch of Am Art de Young Mus Golden Gate Park San Francisco CA 94118

KARN, GLORIA STOLL
PAINTER, INSTRUCTOR

b New York, NY, Nov 13, 23. *Study:* Art Students League; also with Eliot O'Hara & Samuel Rosenberg. *Work:* Yale Univ; Brooklyn Mus; Pittsburgh Pub Schs. *Exhib:* Assoc Artists Pittsburgh Ann, 49-; Butler Inst Am Art Ann, 61; one-man shows, Pittsburgh Plan for Art, 65; Carnegie Inst Mus, 66 & North Hills Art Ctr, 78 & 83; Sacred Arts Show, St Stephens, Pittsburgh, 66. *Teaching:* Instr painting & collage, North Hills Art Ctr, 65-; instr, Community Col Allegheny Co, 73-79. *Awards:* Carnegie Inst Purchase Prize, 60; Westinghouse Purchase Prize, 66; North Hills Art Ctr Achievement Award, 83. *Mem:* Assoc Artists Pittsburgh; Group A, Pittsburgh (pres, 66-70); Arts & Crafts Ctr, Pittsburgh (bd mem, 69-72); North Hills Art Ctr (bd mem, 70-72 & 78-80, pres, 80-81). *Media:* Oil. *Mailing Add:* 151 Louise Rd Pittsburgh PA 15237

KARNES, KAREN
CERAMIST, CRAFTSMAN

b New York, NY, Nov 17, 25. *Study:* Brooklyn Col, BA, 46; NY State Col Ceramics, Alfred Univ, 51. *Work:* Baltimore Mus Art, Md; Everson Mus, Syracuse, NY; Mus Contemp Craft & Hadler Rodriguez Gallery, New York; Del Mus Art, Wilmington; and others. *Comn:* Fireplace, sink & garden seats, comn by Jack Lenor Larsen, Easthampton, NY, 62. *Exhib:* 13th Trienale de Milano, Milan, Italy, 64; Am Studio Pottery, Victoria & Albert Mus, London, Eng, 68 & Int Ceramics, 72; Objects USA, Smithsonian Inst, DC, 69; Salt Glazed Ceramics, Mus Contemp Crafts, New York, 72; 100 Yrs of Ceramics Art, Everson Mus, 79. *Collections Arranged:* Salt Glazed Ceramics, Hadler Rodriguez Gallery, 77. *Awards:* Am Crafts Coun Fel, 76; Nat Endowment Arts Fel, 76; Nat Coun Ceramic Fel, 80; and others. *Bibliog:* Dido Smith (auth), Karen Karnes, Craft Horizons, 7/67; Soenaid Robertson (auth), Karen Karnes, Ceramic Rev, Brit, 79. *Dealer:* Hadler Rodriguez Gallery 38 E 57th St New York NY 10003. *Mailing Add:* West Danville VT 05873

KARNIOL, EUGENE
DEALER, COLLECTOR

b Hungary, Feb 11, 09; Can citizen. *Pos:* Art dir, Kar Gallery Fine Art, Toronto, Ont, Can, 67- *Mem:* Prof Art Dealers Asn Can; Arts & Letters Club. *Specialty:* Master graphics; modern figurative art; Canadian Indian art. *Mailing Add:* 10 Tangreen Ct Willowdale ON M2M 4B9 Canada

KARNIOL, HILDA
PAINTER
b Vienna, Austria, Apr 28, 10; US citizen. *Study:* With Olga Konetzny-Maly & A F Seligman, Vienna, 25-28; Acad for Women, 26-30. *Work:* Lincoln Sch, Honesdale, Pa; US Dept Health, Educ & Welfare; Lewisburg Art Coun, Pa; Lycoming Col, Williamsport, Pa; State Col, Bloomsburg, Pa. *Exhib:* Pa State Mus, Harrisburg, 54; Adha Artzt Gallery, New York, 60; Drexel Inst Technol, 60; La Salle Col, 64; La State Univ, New Orleans, 71; over 100 solo exhibs. *Teaching:* Instr painting, Susquehanna Univ, 58-75. *Awards:* First Prize in Portraiture, Berwick Art Ctr, Pa, 65; Artist in residence, Fed Govt Cult Enrichment Prog, 67; First Merit & Purchase Prize, Lewisburg Art Asn, 75 & 78. *Bibliog:* L E L (auth), Art & artists, gallery guide, New York-J Am, 11/60; Sigmund Stoler (auth), Upstate artist's 14th show, Harrisburg Patriot, 67; Michael Lenson (auth), The realm of art, culture mirror, Newark Sun News, 11 /67. *Mem:* Midstate Artists; Nat Forum Prof Artists; Art Alliance Cent Pa; Pa Soc Watercolor Painters; L'Alliance Francaise, Tampa, Fla. *Media:* Oil, Watercolor. *Publ:* Illusr, Melusine & illusr, The Nose, 29, Adolf Synek; auth, From the Sketchbook of Hilda Karniol, Standard, 70. *Mailing Add:* 960 Race St Sunbury PA 17801

KARP, AARON S
PAINTER
b Altoona, Pa, Dec 7, 47. *Study:* State Univ NY Col Buffalo, BA, 69; Ind Univ, MFA, 73. *Work:* Guggenheim Mus, New York; Southeastern Ctr Contemp Art, Winston-Salem, NC; Albuquerque Mus & Univ NMex Art Mus, Albuquerque; Ackland Art Ctr, Chapel Hill, NC; Roswell Mus, NMex. *Exhib:* Chrysler Mus, Norfolk, Va, 78; Six Painters, Southeastern Ctr Contemp Art, Winston-Salem, NC, 79; Systems, NC Mus Art, Raleigh, 79; Mint Mus Art, Charlotte, NC, 79; Roswell Mus, NMex, 80; Recent Acquisitions, Albuquerque Mus, 81; New Perspectives in American Art, 1983 Exxon Nat Exhibition, Guggenheim Mus, 83. *Pos:* Oper supervisor, Guggenheim Mus, 74-75; dir, E Carolina Univ Gallery, Greenville, NC, 77-79. *Teaching:* Asst prof, Univ NMex, Albuquerque, 79- *Awards:* Grand Award, R J Reynolds Corp NC Artists, 78; Atwater Kent Award, Soc Four Arts, 79; Artist-in-Residence Grant, Roswell Mus, 81-82. *Bibliog:* Dana Asbury (auth), Aaron Karp, Artspace, winter 81; Kathleen Shields & Steve Shipp (authors), article, Ariz Arts & Lifestyles, winter, 1982. *Media:* Acrylic. *Dealer:* Davis McClain Gallery 2818 Kirby Dr Houston TX 77098. *Mailing Add:* 214 Headingly Albuquerque NM 87107

KARP, RICHARD GORDON
PAINTER, LECTURER
b Brooklyn, NY, May 17, 33. *Study:* City Col New York, BBA(advert) & MA(fine art); Brooklyn Mus Art Sch, with John Bageris. *Work:* Aankoop Gemete, Stedlijk Mus, Amsterdam, Neth; Northern Ill Univ, DeKalb. *Exhib:* Stedlijk Mus, Amsterdam, 70; RAI Exhib, Amsterdam, 70; Heckscher Mus, Huntington, NY, 74; Viridian Gallery, New York, 77; Parrish Mus, South Hampton, NY, 78. *Bibliog:* Julie Attkiss (auth), Karp, riding his intuition, Holland Herald, 3/69. *Mem:* Visual Artist & Gallery Asn; Artists Equity. *Media:* Oil & Mixed Media. *Dealer:* Ronald Hunnings Inc 139 Spring St New York NY 10012; Kunsthandel K 276 Keizersgracht 276 Amsterdam Netherlands. *Mailing Add:* 8 E 12th St New York NY 10003

KARPEL, ELI
SCULPTOR
b New York, NY, Oct 25, 16. *Study:* City Col New York, BA; Univ Calif, Los Angeles, MA; Univ Southern Calif; Ohio State Univ; with Chaim Gross. *Work:* Palm Springs Desert Mus; Hirshhorn Mus, Washington, DC; Storm King Mountain Mus, Mountainville, NY; Skirball Mus, Los Angeles. *Exhib:* One-man shows, Ankrum Gallery, 72, 78 & 80, Pierce Col, 73 & 82 & Gumps Gallery, San Francisco, 79 & 82. *Teaching:* Lectr art, Univ Calif, Los Angeles, 50-53; prof art, Pierce Col, Los Angeles, 58-82. *Media:* Bronze & other materials. *Dealer:* Ankrum Gallery 657 N La Cienega Los Angeles CA 90069; Gump's Art Gallery 250 Post St San Francisco CA 94108. *Mailing Add:* 689 Brooktree Santa Monica CA 90402

KARPOWICZ, TERRENCE EDWARD
SCULPTOR, KINETIC ARTIST
b East St Louis, Ill, May 11, 48. *Study:* Albion Col, BA, 70; Univ Ill, Champaign, MFA(Fulbright Hays Fel), 75. *Work:* Northern Ill Univ; Gov State Univ, Ill; Kemper Collection, Chicago. *Comn:* Per Cent for Arts, State Ill, Northeastern Ill Univ, 82. *Exhib:* Chicago & Vicinity, Art Inst Chicago, 74; Sixth Dollhouse Invitational, Corcoran Gallery Art, 80; 33rd Ill Invitational, Ill State Mus, Springfield, 81; Int Mile of Sculpture, Navy Pier, Chicago, 82-83. *Teaching:* Instr sculpture, Art Inst Chicago, 79-81 & Univ Ill, Chicago Circle, 83- *Awards:* Frank Logan Medal & Prize, Chicago & Vicinity, Art Inst Chicago, 74; Nat Endowment Arts Fel, 80 & 82. *Bibliog:* Alan Artner (auth), Mystery dogs freewheeling show, Chicago Tribune, 80; Ann Morgon (auth), article, Art Int, 82; Paul Richards (auth), It's a dream--sculptors on paper, Washington Post, 83. *Media:* Wood. *Dealer:* Zolla-Lieberman Gallery 356 W Huron Chicago IL 60606. *Mailing Add:* 555 W Adams Chicago IL 60606

KARSH, YOUSUF
PHOTOGRAPHER
b Armenia, Dec 23, 08; Can citizen. *Study:* With John H Garo, Boston; hon degrees from twelve univs. *Work:* Metrop Mus Art, New York; Mus Mod Art, New York; Nat Portrait Gallery, London, Eng; St Louis Art Mus, Mo; Nat Gallery Can, Ottawa, Ont. *Exhib:* One-man shows, Boston Mus Fine Arts, 68, Corcoran Gallery Art, 69, Seattle Art Mus, 70, Mus Mod Art, Tokyo, 71-81, Mus Sci & Industry, Chicago, 77-79, Mus Photogr & Film, Bradford, Eng, Int Ctr Photogr NY, 83 & Nat Portrait Gallery, London, 83; plus many others, including Nat Gallery of Australia & Prov Alta, Can. *Pos:* Photog adv, Expo 70, Osaka, Japan, 69-70; trustee, Photog Arts & Sci Found, 65-72. *Teaching:* Vis prof photog & fine arts, Ohio Univ, 68-70; vis prof photog & fine arts, Emerson Col, 72-73. *Awards:* Can Coun Medal, 65; Order of Can, Can Govt, 68; Rochester Sci Mus Fel, 72. *Bibliog:* Forsee (auth), In: Five Famous Photographers, 70; featured article, Reader's Digest, 2/77; featured on Sixty Minutes, Columbia Broadcasting Syst, 5/77. *Mem:* Hon fel Royal Photog Soc; Dutch Treat Club, New York; Rideau Club, Ottawa; Royal Can Acad Arts; Prof Photog Asn Can; Century Club; hon fel Prof Photog Am. *Publ:* Auth, Karsh Portfolio, 67; auth, Faces of Our Time, 71; auth, Karsh Portraits, 76; Karsh Canadians, 78; auth, Karsh, A Fifty Year Retrospective, 83; and others. *Mailing Add:* Karsh Photog Studio 6th Floor Chateau Laurier Ottawa ON K1N 8S7 Canada

KARWELIS, DONALD CHARLES
PAINTER, INSTRUCTOR
b Rockford, Ill, Sept 19, 34. *Study:* Univ Calif, Irvine, with Robert Irwin, BA, 69, with Robert Morris, MFA, 71. *Work:* Long Beach Mus Art, Calif; Paul Schorr III, Lincoln, Nebr; Flour Corp, Irvine, Calif; Coopers & Lybrand, Houston, Tex; Baker Int Corp, Orange, Calif. *Exhib:* Saddleback Col, 79; Newport Harbor Art Mus, 79; Abraxas Gallery, Calif, 81; Pasadena City Col, 81; Orange Co Ctr Contemp Art, 81; and many others. *Teaching:* Lectr sculpture, Univ Calif, Irvine, 69-71; lectr drawing & painting, Riverside City Col, 71-72. *Awards:* Nat Defense Educ Act Res Grant, 70; Nat Endowment Arts Grant, 76. *Bibliog:* Robert Ewing (auth), Geometry, mystery and the sea, Artweek, 10/31/81; Melinda Wortz (auth), article, Artnews, 4/83; Christine Fryman Schwable (auth), article, Images & Issues, 9-10/83. *Media:* Acrylic, Multimedia. *Publ:* Contribr, Los Angeles Artists' Publ, 73; auth, Color, 75. *Dealer:* Ocean Works Ltd Ed Lithographs 2811 Villa Way Newport Beach CA 92663; Hunsaker/Schlesinger 812 N La Cienega Blvd Los Angeles CA 90069. *Mailing Add:* 202-K E Stevens Santa Ana CA 92707

KARWOSKI, RICHARD CHARLES
PAINTER, EDUCATOR
b Brooklyn, NY, Oct 3, 38. *Study:* Pratt Inst, with Richard Lindner & Jacob Landau, BFA, 61; Columbia Univ, MFA, 63. *Work:* Okla Art Ctr, Oklahoma City; Everson Mus, Syracuse, NY; Wichita Mus, Kans; Detroit Art Inst, Mich; Butler Inst Am Art, Youngstown, Ohio. *Exhib:* Manscape: 77 & Cityscape: 78, Okla Art Ctr, Oklahoma City; Heckscher Mus, 78 & 81; Watercolor USA, Springfield Mus, Mo, 80; 44th & 45th Midyear Ann, Butler Inst Am Art, Youngstown, Ohio, 80 & 81; Winterscape, Guild Hall Mus, East Hampton, NY, 81-82; Pittsburgh Watercolor Soc Ann, 81-83; Watercolor USA, Springfield, Mo, 80; Perham Arts Ctr, NY, 83; and others. *Pos:* Dir, Grace Gallery, New York City Tech Col, Brooklyn, 70-82, assoc dir, 82; adv comn mem, Art & Design High Sch, New York, 77- *Teaching:* Prof painting & design, New York City Tech Col, 69- *Awards:* Materials Award, Pa Soc Watercolor Painters, 81; First Prize, Adelphi Univ, Garden City, NY, 82; Purchase Award, Prints: USA, New York, 82. *Bibliog:* Chauncey Howell (reporter), NBC News, 74; John Perrault (ed, critic), article, SoHo Weekly News, 11/27/75; Helen A Harrison (auth), article, New York Times, 2/3/80. *Mem:* Soc Am Graphic Artists; Pa Soc Watercolor Painters; Audubon Soc of Artists; Nat Arts Club; NY Artists Equity (bd dirs, 82-84). *Media:* Watercolor, Oil. *Publ:* Contribr, Art in Society, The Arts Academe, Univ Wis, 76; auth, Am Artist Mag Watercolor page, Bill Publs, 3/79; contribr, Footwear, Van Nostrand, 79; illusr, The Intimate Hour (bk jacket), Avery, 79; contribr, Pratt Reports, Pratt Inst, spring, 81. *Dealer:* Gallery East 257 Montauk Hwy E Hampton NY 11937. *Mailing Add:* 28 E 4th St New York NY 10003

KASAK, NIKOLAI (KAZAK)
PAINTER, SCULPTOR
b Lushtcha, Russia; US citizen. *Study:* City Col Arts, Warsaw, BFA; Acad Fine Art, Vienna, MFA; Acad Fine Art Sch Advan Study, Rome, dipl. *Work:* Mus Fine Art, Baranowicze & Minsk; McCrory Collection, New York; Smithsonian Inst Arch Am Art, Washington, DC; Denis Rene Gallery, Paris. *Comn:* Sgraffito, City Hall Warsaw; mural, City Hall Baranowicze. *Exhib:* Guggenhiem Mus, New York; Mus Mod Art, Buenos Aires & Denis Rene Gallery, Paris, 61; NC Mus of Art, Raleigh, 69; Albright-Knox Art Gallery, Buffalo, NY, 79; Seattle Art Mus, Wash, 80; San Francisco Mus Mod Art, Calif, 80; Mus Art, Carnegie Inst, Pittsburgh, 81; Detroit Inst Arts, Mich, 81; Milwaukee Art Ctr, Wis, 81; Mus Fine Arts, Kansas City, Mo, 81; and others. *Awards:* First Prize for Warsaw Emblem, City Hall Warsaw; First Prize for Mural, City Hall Baranowicze; Prize for Painting-Construct, Art Club Rome. *Bibliog:* Robert Kramer (ed), Constructivism and the Geometric Tradition, McCrory, 79; Silvia Conforto (auth), Due Tempi, Una Storia, Rome, 79; John E Bowlt (auth), Physical art of Nikolai Kasak: 1945-1980 (monogr), New York, 82. *Mem:* Am Abstr Artists. *Publ:* Auth, Physical art--Action of positive & negative space, 46-47; auth, Storia de Pitture Contemporanee, Domani, Rome, 48; auth, Arte fisico-constructivo, arte Madi, Buenos Aires, 52; auth, Kasak on Art and Other Related Matters, 1945-1980, John E Bowlt, New York, 82. *Mailing Add:* 5648 Delafield Ave Riverdale NY 10471

KASHDIN, GLADYS SHAFRAN
PAINTER, EDUCATOR
b Pittsburgh, Pa, Dec 15, 21. *Study:* Art Students League, with Stefan Hirsch; Univ Miami, BA(magna cum laude), 60; Fla State Univ, with Karl Zerbe, MA, 62, PhD(humanities), 65. *Work:* Tex Tech Mus, Lubbock; Tampa Pub Libr; Columbus Mus Arts & Sci, Ga; Pensacola Art Ctr, Fla; Futan Univ, Shanghai, China. *Comn:* Silkscreen eds, LeMoyne Art Found, Tallahassee, Fla, 70, 71 & 73. *Exhib:* 28th Ann Brooklyn Mus, 44; one-woman shows, 2nd & 3rd

Southeastern Ann, High Mus, Atlanta, 47, Palm Beach Art League, Norton Gallery, West Palm, 48-63 LeMoyne Art Found, Tallahassee, 66-74, Columbus Mus Arts & Sci, Ga, 73, 76 & 83, Univ SFla, 75 & 81 & Tex Tech Mus, 78. *Pos:* Photogr, Shafran Co, NY & Fla, 38-60. *Teaching:* Instr & dir oil painting, Adult Educ, Palm Beach Co, Fla, 56-60; instr watercolor, Thomasville Art Guild, Ga, 61-62; prof humanities, Univ SFla, Tampa, 65-, Humanities Visual Arts Workshops, 66-71. *Awards:* Award Merit, Palm Beach Art League, 58, 60 & 63; Gold Medal, Univ Miami, 60. *Bibliog:* Dr Hans Juergensen (auth), Kashdin's Everglades series, 73 & Herb Allen (auth), Local rivers series theme, 75, Tampa Tribune; Pam Renner (auth), Gladys Kashdin: An artist in her sun-lit years, Bay Life, 79. *Media:* Watercolor, Acrylic. *Publ:* Auth, A new approach to a humanities-visual arts workshop, Humanities J, fall 70; auth, Life long education for women--general & liberal studies...from their point of view, Perspectives, winter 74; auth, Women artists and the institution of feminism in America, SEASA, 79. *Mailing Add:* 441 Biltmore Ave Temple Terrace FL 33617

KASKEY, RAYMOND JOHN
SCULPTOR, ARCHITECT
b Pittsburgh, Pa, Feb 22, 43. *Study:* Carnegie Mellon Univ, BA(archit), 67; Yale Univ, Sch Art & Archit, also sculpture with Erwin Haver, 69. *Work:* Mus Mod Art, New York. *Comn:* Sculpture, Sch Archit, Univ Md, Col Park, 72. *Exhib:* Salon des Realites Nouvelles, Parc Floral Mus, Paris, 72; Nat Sculpture Soc Ann, Equitable Gallery, New York, 80 & 81. *Teaching:* Asst prof arch & design, Univ Md, College Park, 69-76; vis critic, Yale Univ, New Haven, Conn, spring 77 & Kans State Univ, Manhattan, spring 78. *Awards:* Traveling fel, Pittsburgh Plate Glass Co, 65-66; Creative & Performing Arts Award, Univ Md, 70 & 72. *Mem:* Nat Sculpture Soc. *Media:* Bronze. *Mailing Add:* 2221 Hall Pl NW Washington DC 20007

KASLE, GERTRUDE
CONSULTANT, COLLECTOR
b New York, NY, Dec 2, 17. *Study:* Art Students League, with John Barber; NY Univ; Univ Mich; Ctr Creative Studies, Detroit; Wayne State Univ, BS(art educ). *Pos:* Assoc dir & partner, Franklin Siden Gallery, 64-65; pres, Gertrude Kasle Gallery, 65-77; mem comt visual arts & mus, Mich Coun Arts, 71; adj cur art, Marie Selby Mus of Botany & Art, 79-80; trustee Mich Found Arts. *Awards:* Distinguished Alumni Award, Wayne State Univ, 68; President's Cabinet Award, Univ Detroit, 77. *Mem:* Patron Detroit Inst Arts (Founders' Soc); Nat Soc Lit & Arts; Artists Equity Asn. *Mailing Add:* 26705 Irving Franklin MI 48025

KASS, JACOB JAMES
PAINTER
b Brooklyn, NY, Jan 24, 10. *Study:* Self-taught. *Work:* Lowe Mus Art, Univ Miami, Coral Gables; Va Polytech Inst & State Univ. *Exhib:* Solo exhib, Lowe Mus Art, Univ Miami, Coral Gables, 82, Brevard Art Ctr & Mus, Melbourne, Fla, 83 & Va Polytech Inst & State Univ, 83; Eccentrics, Southeastern Ctr Contemp Art, Winston-Salem, 83; Paris Art Fair, Grand Palais, France, 83. *Awards:* Nat Endowment Arts Fel, 81. *Bibliog:* John Yau (auth), Jacob Kass at Allan Stone, Art in Am, summer 81; Theodore Wolff (auth), The many masks of modern art, Christian Sci Monitor, 6/9/83. *Media:* Oil and Magna on Steel Saw Blades. *Dealer:* Allan Stone Gallery 48 E 86th St New York NY. *Mailing Add:* 1005 Imperial Palm Dr Largo FL 33541

KASS, RAY
PAINTER
b Rockville Centre, NY, Jan 25, 44. *Study:* Univ NC, BA, 67, MFA(painting), 69; also painting with Keith Crown. *Work:* Addison Gallery Am Art, Andover, Mass; Smith Col Mus, Northampton; Boston Pub Libr; Griffith Art Ctr, St Lawrence Univ, Canton, NY; Tufts Univ Med Ctr, Boston. *Exhib:* One-man shows, Calif State Univ, Humboldt, 70, Allan Stone Gallery, New York, 72, 75, 77 & 81, Addison Gallery Am Art, 74, Osuna Gallery, Washington, DC, 79 & Southeastern Ctr Contemp Art, NC, 80; 4 Artists Sponsored by Inst Contemp Art, Boston City Hall, 72. *Pos:* Guest cur, Phillips Collection, Washington, DC, 80-83. *Teaching:* Asst prof painting, Calif State Univ, Humboldt, 69-71; guest lectr, Landscape Workshop, Univ NH, Durham, summer 73; asst prof painting, Va Polytechnic Inst, Blacksburg, Va, 76-81, assoc prof, 81- *Awards:* Norfolk Biennial Painting Prize, Norfolk Mus, Va, 68; Blanche E Colman Found Award, 73-74; Individual Artists Grant, Nat Endowment Arts, 81; and others. *Bibliog:* John Canaday (auth), Ray Kass at Allan Stone Gallery, New York Times, 6/3/72; John Yau (auth), Ray Kass, article, Art Am, summer 81. *Mem:* Col Art Asn Am. *Media:* Watercolor, Oil. *Dealer:* Allan Stone Gallery 48 E 86th St New York NY 10028. *Mailing Add:* Rte 2 Box 725 Christiansburg VA 24073

KASSMAN, SHIRLEY
COLLAGE ARTIST, EDUCATOR
b Hamburg, NY, July 29, 29. *Study:* Albright Art Sch, Buffalo, NY, with Seymour Drumlevitch in painting, cert, 50; State Univ Col Buffalo, NY, BS(art educ), 51, MS(art educ), 58. *Work:* Penny Collection, Rochester Mem Art Gallery; Ithaca Col, NY; Springfield Col, Mass. *Exhib:* Women are Many Faces, Everson Mus, Syracuse, NY, 74; Albright-Knox Art Gallery, 75, 78 & 79; 55th & 56th Erie Art Ctr Ann, Pa, 78 & 79; one-person show, False Quilts & Other Collages, Chautauqua Art Asn, NY, 79. *Collections Arranged:* Patteran Artists Traveling Exhib, Burchfield Ctr, Buffalo, 75-77. *Teaching:* Prof design & women in art, State Univ Buffalo, 58-80. *Awards:* State Univ NY Grants, 74 & 75; Elizabeth M Reeb Mem, 75; Silver Medal Patron Award, Buffalo Soc Artists, 79. *Bibliog:* Dr Judith Herman (auth), Shirley Kassman: Feminist artist, Spree Mag, 79. *Mem:* Buffalo Soc Artists (vpres, 77-78, pres, 78-79); Patteran Artists; Western NY Women's Art Registry; Women's Caucus for Art; Coalition of Womens Art Orgn. *Dealer:* More-Rubin Gallery 470 Franklin St Buffalo NY 14204. *Mailing Add:* 231 Anderson Pl Buffalo NY 14222

KASSOY, BERNARD
PAINTER, PRINTMAKER
b New York, NY, Oct 23, 14. *Study:* City Col New York, BSS(cum laude), MSE(fine arts); Cooper Union Art Sch, grad, 37; also with John Ferren, Isaac Soyer & Arthur Osver. *Work:* Workmans Circle Community House, Bronx, NY; Butler Inst Am Art, Youngstown, Ohio; Slater Mem Mus, Norwich, Conn; Arch Am Art; pvt collections, Ceylon, England, Italy, US & Sicily. *Comn:* Birdiness (film photog & editing), Bd Educ, High Sch Music & Art, New York, 57. *Exhib:* Nat Acad Design, New York, 68 & 75; Showcase, Bronx Coun Arts, New York, 68 & 69; 28 Contemporaries, Bronx Mus Arts, New York, 71; Int Sculpture Exhib, Pietrasanta, Italy, 76 & Forte dei Marmi, Italy, 76; one-man shows, Ward-Nasse Gallery, New York, 79 & Mid-Hudson Art & Sci Ctr, Poughkeepsie, NY, 79; plus others. *Teaching:* Instr fine arts, High Sch Music & Art, 39-72; instr lithography, City Col New York, 66-67; instr lithography, Nat Acad Design, 68; instr painting & mem fac, Harriet FeBland Advan Painters Workshop, New Rochelle, NY, 74- *Awards:* Merit Award, 58th Ann, Art Dirs Club, 79; Award Merit, Pastel Soc Am, 81. *Mem:* Artists Equity Asn New York (bd dirs, 62-, secy, 75-78); Contemp Artists Guild; Am Soc Contemp Artists (vpres, 83-85); Pastel Soc Am. *Media:* Oil, Watercolor; Woodcut, Lithography. *Publ:* Illusr, ed drawings, NY Teacher News, 50-60; illusr, Therapeutic Dance/Movement, Human Sci Press, 79. *Dealer:* Ward-Nasse Gallery 178 Prince New York NY 10012. *Mailing Add:* 130 Gale Pl Bronx NY 10463

KASSOY, HORTENSE
SCULPTOR, PAINTER
b Brooklyn, NY, Feb 14, 17. *Study:* Pratt Inst, grad; Columbia Univ Teachers Col, with Oronzo Maldarelli, BS & MA; Am Artists Sch, with Chaim Gross. *Work:* Slater Mem Mus, Norwich, Conn; Bocour Artists Colors, Inc. *Comn:* Maternal Force (marble sculpture), Amalgamated Housing Coop Towers, Bronx, NY, 71. *Exhib:* Nat Acad Design, New York, 71; 28 Contemporaries, Bronx Mus Art, 71, Ann, 72, Year of the Woman, 75; Brooklyn Mus, Contemp Artists Guild, 74; 150th Ann, Nat Acad Design, 75; Int Sculpture Exhib, Forte dei Marmi, Italy, 76 & Pietrasanta, Italy, 76; one-man show, Caravan House Gallery, New York, 75; plus others. *Pos:* Chmn visual arts, Bronx Coun Arts, 73-76; corresp secy, Int Asn Art (UNESCO). *Teaching:* Instr sculpture, painting & 3D design, Evander Childs High Sch, Bronx, 61-72; instr sculpture, Harriet FeBland Advan Workshop, 75- *Awards:* Grumbacher First Prize in Watercolor, Painters Day at World's Fair, 40; Erlanger Award in Sculpture, Am Soc Contemp Artists, 80. *Bibliog:* J L Collins (auth), Women Artists in America II, 75. *Mem:* Artists Equity Asn, New York (bd dir, 71-75 & 79-, vpres, 75-79); Contemp Artists Guild; Am Soc Contemp Artists; Am Soc Contemp Artists. *Media:* Wood, Marble; Watercolor, Batik. *Mailing Add:* 130 Gale Pl Bronx NY 10463

KASTEN, KARL ALBERT
PAINTER, PRINTMAKER
b San Francisco, Calif, Mar 5, 16. *Study:* Marin Col; Univ Calif, AB & MA; Univ Iowa, with Lasansky; Hans Hofmann Sch Art. *Work:* Victoria & Albert Mus, London, Eng; Mus Mod Art, New York; Auckland City Mus, New Zealand; Mus Beaux-Arts, Rennes, France; Los Angeles Co Art Mus. *Exhib:* Fifth Contemporary Printmakers, Univ Ill, Champaign, 56; Art Inst Chicago Am Painting Ann, 60; Contemporary American Painting & Sculpture, Univ Ill, 69; Achenbach Found Graphic Arts, San Francisco, 75; World Print III Traveling Exhib, 80-81; and others. *Teaching:* Instr painting & drawing, Univ Mich, 46-47; asst prof painting & drawing, San Francisco State Col, 47-50; prof painting & graphics, Univ Calif, Berkeley, 50-82, emer prof art, 82- *Awards:* Oakland Art Mus Women's Bd Purchase Prize, Western Painters Exhib, 54; Creative Arts Inst Fel, 64 & 71; Tamarind Lithography Fel, 68; plus others. *Bibliog:* L Edmondson (auth), Etching, Van Nostrand Reinhold, 73; Meilach & Ten Hoor (auth), Assemblage & Collage, Crown, 73; A Kurasaki (auth), Modern Woodcut Techniques, Kyoto, Japan, 78; and others. *Mem:* Calif Soc Printmakers (coun mem, 72-76). *Dealer:* Rorick Gallery 637 Mason St San Francisco CA 94108; Running Ridge Gallery 640 Canton Rd Santa Fe NM 87501. *Mailing Add:* 1884 San Lorenzo Ave Berkeley CA 94707

KASTEN, SHERRY ZVARES
PAINTER
b Washington, DC, Oct 18, 37. *Study:* George Washington Univ, BA, 59; Am Univ, MFA, 74. *Work:* Phillips Collection, Washington, DC; Phillip Morris Co, Richmond, Va; Frostburg State Col, Md; First Nat Bank Boston, Mass; Columbia Hospital for Women, Washington, DC. *Exhib:* Solo exhib, Phillips Collection, Washington, DC, 80; 22nd Area Exhib: Works on Paper, Corcoran Gallery, 80; Washington Light, Armory, Washington, DC, 80; 25 Washington Artists: Realism & Representation, Foundry Gallery, Washington, DC, 80; Works on Paper, Hood Col, Fredrick, Md, 81; New Purchases, Frostburg State Col, Md, 81; Empty Rooms, Empty Places, 81 & Sanctuaries, 83, Baumgartner Gallery, Washington, DC. *Bibliog:* Paul Richard (auth), A sense of hush, a sense of the holy, Washington Post, 11/4/80; Lee Fleming (auth), article, New Art Examiner, 4/81; Benjamin Forgey (auth), Kasten's impressive sanctuaries, Washington Post, 3/3/83. *Mem:* Artist Equity; Washington Womens Arts Ctr. *Media:* Acrylic. *Dealer:* Baumgartner Galleries 2016 R St NW Washington DC 20009. *Mailing Add:* 111 Grafton St Chevy Chase MD 20815

KASUBA, ALEKSANDRA
ENVIRONMENTAL ARTIST
b Lithuania, Jan 10, 23; US citizen. *Study:* Art Inst Kaunas, Lithuania, 41-42; Acad Fine Rrts, Vilnius, Lithuania, 42. *Work:* Atlanta Univ Collection; Delgado Mus Art, New Orleans; Mus Contemp Crafts, New York; Johnson's Wax Collection; Bank Calif; and others. *Comn:* White marble wall, Container

Corp Am, Chicago, 69; 20th Century Environment, Carborundum Mus Ceramics, Niagara Falls, 73; Int Furnit Exhib, Paris, 80; Brick Relief, 560 Lexington Ave, New York, 81; Old Post Office Plaza Pavement, Pa Ave, Washington DC, 81; and others. *Exhib:* One-man show, Waddell Gallery, New York, 66; Experiments in Art & Technology, Brooklyn Mus Art, 68; Contemplative Environments, Mus Contemp Crafts, New York, 70; Space Shelters for Senses, New York, 71-72; Spectral Passage, DeYoung Mem Mus, San Francisco, 75; Cranbrook Acad Art Mus, 76; Women in Am Archit, Brooklyn Mus, 77; Art in Science, Philadelphia Art Alliance, 78; Transformations in Modern Architecture, Mus Mod Art, 79; and others. *Pos:* Consult, Nat Endowment Arts, 80. *Teaching:* Instr creative processes & elements art in archit scale, Sch Visual Arts, 71-72; instr stretched fiber structures, Cranbrook Acad Art, 76. *Awards:* Am Inst Archit Citation, Artist-Archit Collab, 71; Citation for Innovative Space Treatment, Women's Archit Auxiliary & New York Chap Am Inst Archit, 72; Nat Endowment Arts Fel, 83. *Bibliog:* Rita Reif (auth), article, New York Times, 5/11/71; James D Morgan (auth), article, Archit Rec, 8/71; Ronald Najman (auth), Saturday Revue, 8/12/72; and others. *Publ:* Contribr, Report on Art & Technology Program of the Los Angeles County Museum of Art, 71; contribr, Underground Interiors, Quadrangle, 72; contribr, Women in American Architecture & Design, Whitney Publ, 77. *Mailing Add:* 43 W 90th St New York NY 10024

KATANO, MARC
PAINTER
b July 17, 52. *Study:* Calif Col Arts & Crafts, Oakland, BFA(with distinction), 75. *Exhib:* Calif Palace Legion Honor, San Francisco, 74; Sun Gallery, Hayward, Calif, 77; Calif Col Arts & Crafts, Oakland, 78; Berkeley Arts Ctr, 80; E B Crocker Art Mus, Sacramento, 81; Mus Mod Art, San Francisco, 81; Calif State Univ, Hayward, 82; and others. *Awards:* KQED Award, Crown Zellerbach Inc, 80; Soc Encouragement Contemp Art, 81. *Bibliog:* Mark Katano (review), Images & Issues Mag, fall, 80; Suzaan Boettger (auth), SECA awards, Artweek, 8/29/81; Knute Stiles (auth), Marc Katano, Art Am, 11/83. *Media:* Oil. *Mailing Add:* c/o Stephen Wirtz Gallery 345 Sutter St San Francisco CA 94108

KATAYAMA, TOSHIHIRO
PAINTER, DESIGNER
b Osaka, Japan, July 17, 28. *Study:* Self-taught. *Work:* Mus Mod Art, New York; Seibu Mus Mod Art, Tokyo, Japan; Mus Mod Art, Oita, Japan; Rose Art Mus, Brandeis Univ, Waltham, Mass; Tokyo Munic Mus; and others. *Comn:* Two murals, Alaska Bldg, 74; mural, Metrop Boston Transit Authority, State St Sta, 76; Super Graphic Mural, Rensselaer Polytech Inst, NY, 79; marble floor design, NS Bldg, Tokyo, 82; relief mural with stainless steel pipes, Akasaka Prince Hotel, Tokyo, 83. *Exhib:* Graphic Image, Cent Mus Mod Art, Tokyo & Kyoto Nat Mus, Japan, 73 & 74; Identity, Seibu Mus Mod Art, Tokyo, 76; one-man shows, Gallery Art Asia, Cambridge, Mass, 76, Kunstler Haus, Wine, Austria, 77 & Nantenshi Gallery, Tokyo, 78 & 80; and others. *Pos:* Art dir, Nippon Design Ctr, Tokyo, 60-63; graphic designer, Geigy, Basel, Switz, 63-66. *Teaching:* Sr lectr graphic design, Carpenter Ctr for Visual Arts, Harvard Univ, Cambridge, 66- *Bibliog:* George Kepes & Ivan Chermaeff (auth), Work by Toshi, Graphic Design, Number 50, 73; Shutaro Mukai, Susumu Shingu, Koji Taki & Tsunehisa Kimura (auth), World of Toshi Katayama, Design, Number 7, 74; The Work of Toshi Katayama, Kajima Inst Publ Co, 81. *Mem:* Alliance Graphique Int (head official, Zurich, 75); Am Inst Graphic Art, New York. *Media:* Mixed. *Publ:* Coauth, Twelve Persons in Graphic Design Today, Bijutsu Shuppan-Sha, 69; coauth, Three Notations, Rotations with Mr Octavio Paz, Harvard Univ, 74. *Dealer:* Nantenshi Gallery 3-6-5 Kyobashi Chuo-Ku Tokyo Japan. *Mailing Add:* 16 Mystic Bank Arlington MA 02174

KATO, KAY
CARTOONIST
b Budapest, Hungary. *Study:* Art Acad, Budapest; Pa Acad Fine Arts; also with Janos Vaszary. *Comn:* Cover, Am Tel & Tel Mag, 54; book jacket for The Television-Radio Audience and Religion, 55; cover, Today's Living, New York Herald-Tribune, 57; also covers for Christian Sci Monitor, Sat Eve Post & others. *Exhib:* One-woman shows at Pa Acad Fine Arts, Boston Pub Libr, Newark Pub Libr & Newark Mus, 80; At Man and His World, Int Salon of Cartoons, Montreal, Que, 75-81; two-woman show, NJ Blood Ctr, East Orange, 81; and others. *Teaching:* Instr, Cambridge Ctr Adult Educ, Mass, 44-47; instr, South Orange & Maplewood Adult Sch, 63. *Awards:* First Prize Award for Cartoons, NJ State Fedn Women's Clubs, 77 & 78; Cert of Merit, Excellent Prog on Cartooning, Belleville Pub Libr, NJ, 79; Plaque Award, Newark Mus Paleontology Prog, 79; and others. *Bibliog:* Essex Co Libr Prog, Channel 3, Cablevision TV, 79. *Mem:* Essex Watercolor Club; Overseas Press Club Am (chmn graphic arts comt, mem bull comt). *Publ:* Contribr, This Week, Nation's Bus, New York Times Mag, Am Weekly & others; contribr, Bicentennial July 4th souvenir ed, Philadelphia Bulletin, 76; contribr, Staten Island Advance, 77; auth, weekly cartoon column, Star Ledger, Newark. *Mailing Add:* 60 Chapman Pl PO Box 134 Glen Ridge NJ 07028

KATSIFF, BRUCE
PHOTOGRAPHER, EDUCATOR
b Philadelphia, Pa, Dec 10, 45. *Study:* Philadelphia Col Art, 64-65; Rochester Inst Technol, BFA, 68; Pratt Inst, MFA, 73. *Work:* George Eastman House, Rochester, NY; Am Arts Doc Ctr, Exeter, England; Allentown Art Mus, Pa. *Exhib:* Photog as Printmaking, Mus Mod Art, New York, 68; Ann Printmaking & Drawing, Pa Acad Fine Arts, 69; Philadelphia Mus Art, 70; Underground Gallery, New York, 70; Lumberville, Peale House Gallery, Pa Acad of Fine Arts, 73; Pennsylvania Photographers, 83. *Collections*

Arranged: Vision & Expression, George Eastman House, 69; Past & Present, Bucks Co Community Col, 83. *Pos:* Asst producer, Darcey Assoc, 67-69. *Teaching:* Prof art, Bucks Co Community Col, 69-, chmn, Fine Arts, 73-; prof art, Thomas Edison Col, 76-78. *Bibliog:* Gene Thorton (auth), Photography Review, New York Times, 70; A D Coleman (auth), article, Village Voice, 71. *Mem:* Col Art Asn; Soc Photographic Educators. *Mailing Add:* River Rd Lumberville PA 18933

KATZ, ALEX
PAINTER
b New York, NY, July 24, 27. *Study:* Cooper Union; Skowhegan Sch, Maine. *Work:* Mus Mod Art, New York; Art Inst Chicago; Whitney Mus Am Art, New York; Hirshhorn Mus; Tate Gallery, London; and others. *Exhib:* Twenty Years of American Painting, Mus Mod Art, New York, 66; Figures and Environments, Walker Art Ctr, Minneapolis, 70; Retrospective Exhib, Wadsworth Atheneum, 71, Whitney Mus & Va Mus, 74-75; 32nd Biennial Exhib Contemp Am Painting, Corcoran Gallery Art, Washington, DC, 71; American Collage, Mus Mod Art, New York; Fresno Arts Ctr, 77-78; Portland Ctr Visual Arts, 81; Queens Mus, Flushing, New York, 80; Recent Drawings, Mus Mod Art, New York, 81. *Teaching:* Adj prof, New York Univ, 83-84. *Awards:* Guggenheim Fel, 72; St Gaudens Medal, 80; Cooper Union Skowhegan Award, 80. *Bibliog:* Sam Hunter (auth), American Art Since 1945, 69 & Irving Sandler (auth), Alex Katz, 79, Abrams; Irving Sandler & William Berkson (ed), Alex Katz, Praeger, 71. *Media:* Oil on Canvas. *Mailing Add:* c/o Marlborough Gallery 40 W 57th St New York NY 10019

KATZ, EUNICE
PAINTER, SCULPTOR
US citizen. *Study:* Art Students League, with Harry Sternberg; Sculpture Ctr, with Dorothea Denslow; also with Angelo di Benedetto, Frederick Taubes, Donald Pierce & Edgar Britton. *Work:* US State Dept Art Embassies Prog, Washington, DC; Temple Emanuel Collection, Denver, Colo; Denver US Nat Bank; Hillel House, Boulder; Children's Hosp, Pittsburgh, Pa. *Comn:* Stained glass window, BMH Congregation, Denver, 67 & 13' walnut & bronze tablet, 75; stained glass window, East Denver Orthodox Congregation, 68; four figure sculpture (bronze), Beth Israel Hosp, 70; two stained glass windows, Hebrew Congregation, Wichita, Kans, 72. *Exhib:* Allied Artists Am, Nat Acad, 49-66; Nat Soc Painters & Sculptors, NJ, 64; NAm Sculpture Exhib, Golden, Colo, 79; one-man shows, Pietrantonio Gallery, New York, 65 & La Salle Univ, Philadelphia, 65. *Teaching:* Instr drawing & painting, Studio Classes, 57-65. *Awards:* Award of Merit, Rocky Mountain Liturgical Arts, 58; Patron's Award, Art Mus NMex Biennial, 66; First Place Award, Am Asn Univ Women, 66. *Bibliog:* KRMA TV Fine Artist Series, Educ TV, 66; Woman artists of the Southwest, Artist Mag, 73. *Mem:* Allied Sculptors Colo; Artists Equity (secy, Denver Chap, 63-64); Rocky Mountain Liturgical Arts; Greater Denver Coun Arts & Humanities; Am Fedn Arts. *Media:* Oil; Bronze. *Dealer:* Saks Galleries 3019 E Second Ave Denver CO 80206. *Mailing Add:* 3131 E Alameda Ave Denver CO 80209

KATZ, HILDA (HULDA WEBER)
PAINTER, PRINTMAKER
b June 2, 09; US citizen. *Study:* Nat Acad Design; New Sch Social Res, scholar, 40 & 41; Accad Sci, Lett & Arts, Milan, Italy, Hon Dr, 74. *Work:* Baltimore Mus Art; Fogg Mus; also in spec collections of Metrop Mus Art, New York, Brooklyn Mus Art & Nat Collection Fine Arts; and many others. *Exhib:* Venice Biennial, US Pavilion, Italy, 40; Corcoran Gallery Art Biennial, Washington, DC; Boston Pub Libr Invitations to Turin, Venice, Florence & Naples, Italy & France & Israel; US Info Agency Exhib to Europe, Asia, MidE & Africa; Soc Am Graphic Artists-Japan & Ecuador Invitational Exchanges; Pa Acad Fine Arts; Brooklyn Mus, NY; and many others. *Teaching:* Lectures & demonstrations in painting & graphics for art associations until 1951. *Awards:* Six Purchase Awards, Libr Cong; Prize, Soc Am Graphic Artists; Honor Award Plaque, Exec & Prof Hall of Fame, 66; plus others. *Bibliog:* Report & studies in history of art, Nat Gallery Art, 67-69; article, Nat Air & Space Catalog, 71; America in the War (catalog), Libr Cong, 83. *Mem:* Soc Am Graphic Artists; Nat Asn Women Artists; fel Metrop Mus Art; hon mem Acad Sci, Lett & Arts, Milano, Italy; plus others. *Media:* Oil, Watercolor. *Mailing Add:* 915 West End Ave Apt 5D New York NY 10025

KATZ, JOSEPH M
COLLECTOR, PATRON
b July 7, 13. *Study:* Univ Pittsburgh, 31-34. *Collection:* Nineteenth and twentieth century paintings and sculpture; gold and enamel snuff boxes of seventeenth, eighteenth and nineteenth centuries; Chinese snuff bottles; antiquities; ancient glass of the Roman era; French and English porcelain; eighteenth century French furniture. *Mailing Add:* Gateway Towers Pittsburgh PA 15222

KATZ, LEANDRO
ASSEMBLAGE ARTIST, FILMMAKER
b Buenos Aires, Arg, June 6, 38; US citizen. *Study:* Univ Nac Buenos Aires, BA, 61; Pratt Graphic Arts Ctr, 65-67. *Exhib:* Structure, John Gibson Gallery, New York, 78; Cineprobe, Mus Mod Art, New York, 79; The Lunas Alphabet, Clocktower, New York, 80; Metropotamia, PS1, Long Island City, 81; The Judas Window, Whitney Mus Am Art, 82; Orpheus Beheaded, RI Sch Design Mus, 83. *Pos:* Guest cur, PS1, 79- *Teaching:* Fac mem pre-Columbian art, Sch Visual Arts, New York, 71-; fac mem semiotics & cinema, Brown Univ, 81- *Awards:* Fels, Nat Endowment Arts, 79 & Guggenheim Found, 80. *Bibliog:* Ted Castle (auth), Verbal art speaks up, Flash Art, 11/80; Lucy Lippard (auth), Overlay, Pantheon Books, 83. *Publ:* Auth, Es Una Ola, Ed Sudamericana, 68; auth, Self Hipnosis, TVRT Press, 75. *Mailing Add:* 25 E Fourth St New York NY 10003

KATZ, MORRIS
PAINTER
Study: Ulm, WGer & Gunsburg; with Hans Facler; Art Students League. *Work:* Evansville Mus Arts & Sci, Ind; Jr Col Albany, NY; Butler Inst Am Art, Youngstown, Ohio; St Lawrence Univ Gifffiths Art Ctr, Canton, NY; Univ Art Gallery, State Univ NY Binghamton. *Exhib:* Instant Art Shows, more than 5500 throughout the world. *Mem:* Am Guild of Variety Artists; Int Platform Asn; Artists Equity Asn; Int Arts Guild Monaco. *Media:* Oil, Pencil. *Mailing Add:* 406 Sixth Ave New York NY 10011

KATZ, THEODORE (HARRY)
PAINTER, LECTURER
b Philadelphia, Pa, July 29, 37. *Study:* Franklin & Marshall Col, AB, 59; Philadelphia Col Art, 59-60; Art Students League, 61-65; Acad Grande Chaumiere, Paris, 64-65; Boston Mus Sch Arts, 68-71; Carpenter Ctr, Harvard Univ, 69, Grad Sch Educ, 68-70, EdM, 69, EdD, 72. *Exhib:* The Reading Room: an Exhibition of Artists' Books, Pa Coun Arts, Philadelphia; Re: Pages, New Eng Found Arts, Univ RI; Words and Images: A Contemporary Survey of Artists' Books, Pittsburgh Ctr Arts, Philadelphia Art Alliance & Southern Alleghenies Mus Art, Loretto, PA; Philadelphia Books 1982, Moore Col Art, Philadelphia; and others. *Pos:* Field reader, Off Educ, Arts & Humanities, Dept Health, Educ & Welfare, 67-71; res asst proj, Grad Sch Educ, Harvard Univ, 69-71; consult, Northwest Regional Educ Lab, Portland, Ore, 71-74; dir, Ford Found Proj, Inst Am Indian Arts, Santa Fe, NMex, 72-74; dir, Outreach Prog, Appalachian Regional Libr, North Wilkesboro, NC, 76; chief educ div, Philadelphia Mus Art, Pa, 77- *Teaching:* Master instr & curric developer, NC Advan Sch, Winston-Salem, 65-67 & Skidmore Col, 67; dir commun prog, Pa Advan Sch, Philadelphia, 67-68; lectr & consult classroom Renaissance arts, Humanities Leadership Inst, State of NJ, 68-70; lectr, Philadelphia Col Art, 78- *Awards:* Purchase Award, John F Kennedy Ctr, Washington, DC. *Bibliog:* Feature portfolio, Arts J, Vol III, No 1; Ted Katz: Reaching out to meet the challenge of artistic growth, Arts J, Vol IV, No 5; Featured artist: Ted Katz, Freelance Monitor, No 1, 80. *Mem:* Nat Art Educ Asn; Am Asn Mus; Archives of Am Art; Asn for Supv & Curric Develop. *Media:* Oil, Watercolor; Pen and Ink. *Publ:* Auth, Poetry and drawings, Sunstone Rev, Vol II, No 4; auth, Art, education and people: The need for common denominators, Prism, winter 80; auth, Art as a reflection of human concerns and other common denominators, In: Museums, Adults and the Humanities: A Guide for Educational Programming, Am Asn Mus, Washington, DC, 81; auth, Educating family audiences: Philadelphia family photos, Roundtable Reports, J Mus Educ, Vol VII, No 1; auth, Children, teenagers and adults in museums: A developmental perspective, Mus News, 5-6/82. *Dealer:* Rosenfeld Gallery Philadelphia PA; Susan Montezinos Gallery Philadelphia PA. *Mailing Add:* 350 Balligomingo Rd Conshohocken PA 19428

KATZEN, HAL ZACHERY
DEALER
b Baltimore, Md, July 16, 54. *Study:* San Francisco Col Art; Johns Hopkins Univ; Md Inst Col Art, BFA, 76. *Pos:* Asst dir, B R Kornblatt Gallery, Baltimore, Md, 76-78; assoc dir, Transworld Art, Alex Rosenberg Gallery, 78- *Specialty:* Contemporary art, American painting and sculpture. *Mailing Add:* c/o Transworld Art 20 W 57th St New York NY 10019

KATZEN, LILA (PELL)
SCULPTOR, EDUCATOR
b New York, NY. *Study:* Art Students League; Cooper Union; also with Hans Hofmann, New York & Provincetown, Mass. *Work:* Nat Mus Am Art, Smithsonian Inst, Washington, DC; Town of Greenwich, Conn; Norton Art Gallery, Palm Beach, Fla; Nat Gallery of Art, Washington, DC; Fordham Univ, Lincoln Ctr; and others. *Comn:* Bilevel Symphony (sculpture), comn by Dept Housing & Urban Develop, Miami, Fla, 79; Floten Escort (sculpture), comn by Gen Serv Agency, Rodino Bldg, Newark, NJ, 82; Royal Naval Airport, Jidda & Jubail, Saudi Arabia; Royal Guest House, Al-Batan, Saudi Arabia; Wand of Inquiry (sculpture), Brandeis Univ, Waltham, Mass, 83; and others. *Exhib:* Biennial of Contemporary Painting and Sculpture, Whitney Mus Am Art, New York, 73; Sculpture and Site '75, Everson Mus, Syracuse, NY & Baltimore Mus, 75; Fordham Univ, Lincoln Ctr, 78; Fan/Ribbon and Plate Works, Univ NC, Chapel Hill, 79; Mus Fine Arts, St Petersburg, Fla, 80; Metrop Mus Art Ctr, Coral Gables, Fla, 80; plus others. *Teaching:* Instr 2-D design-media, sculpture, art & perception, Md Inst Col Art, 62-80. *Awards:* Nat Endowment Grant, 73; Goodyear Fel, 74; Creative Arts Award, Am Asn Univ Women, 74; and others. *Bibliog:* Eleanor Munro (auth), Originals: American Women Artists, Simon & Schuster, 79. *Mem:* Archit League, New York; College Art Asn; Municipal Art Soc, New York. *Media:* Various Metals, Concrete. *Mailing Add:* 345 W Broadway New York NY 10013

KATZENBERG, DENA S
CONSULTANT, CURATOR
b Baltimore, Md. *Study:* McCoy Col of Johns Hopkins Univ; New York Sch of Interior Design. *Collections Arranged:* Great Am Cover-Up: Counterpanes of the 18th & 19th Century (auth, catalog), 71, Contemp Egyptian Folk Tapestries, 73, Blue Traditions: Indigo Dyed Textiles & Related Cobalt Glazed Ceramics from the 17th Century through the 19th Century (auth, catalog), 73-74, And Eagles Sweep Across the Sky: Indian Textiles of the North American West (auth, catalog), 77, Quilts (auth catalog), 81-82, Imperial Costume from the Manchu Dynasty, 82, Baltimore Mus of Art. *Pos:* Consult & cur, Baltimore Mus Art, currently. *Mem:* Centre Int d'Etude des Textiles Anciens, Lyon, France; Needle & Bobbin Club, New York. *Res:* History of Indigo dye, Irish textile printing and manufacturing; North American Indian weaving; Baltimore album quilting. *Collection:* Textiles. *Publ:* Auth, Copper plate-printed Irish textile, Antiques, 4/77. *Mailing Add:* Baltimore Mus of Art Art Mus Dr Baltimore MD 21218

KATZIVE, DAVID H
ADMINISTRATOR
b San Francisco, Calif, Mar 23, 42. *Study:* Brown Univ, BA; Univ Chicago, MA. *Pos:* Chief educ div, Philadelphia Mus of Art, 70-76; consult, Art Park, Lewiston, NY, 74-; asst dir, Brooklyn Mus, 76-81; dir, DeCordova Mus, 81- *Teaching:* Instr art hist, Univ Chicago Exten, 66-68 & Ill Inst Technol, Chicago, 68-70. *Mem:* Am Asn Mus; Col Art Asn; Art Mus Asn; Asn Art Mus Dirs. *Mailing Add:* c/o DeCordova & Dana Mus Sandy Pond Rd Lincoln MA 01773

KATZMAN, HERBERT
PAINTER, INSTRUCTOR
b Chicago, Ill, Jan 8, 23. *Study:* Art Inst Chicago, cert. *Work:* Mus Mod Art & Whitney Mus Am Art, New York; Art Inst Chicago; Hirshhorn Mus, Washington, DC; Crocker Art Mus, Sacramento, Calif. *Exhib:* Fifteen Americans, Mus Mod Art, New York, 52; New Decade, Whitney Mus, 54; Venice Biennial, Italy, 57; Carnegie Biennial, Pa Acad Fine Arts. *Teaching:* Instr painting & drawing, Sch Visual Arts, New York, 69- *Awards:* Grants, Nat Coun Arts & Humanities, 66, Guggenheim, 68 & New York Coun Arts, 76. *Bibliog:* Art USA, Viking, 63; Eric Protter (auth), Painters on Painting, Dunlap, 63. *Media:* Oil. *Dealer:* Dintenfass Gallery 50 W 57th St New York NY 10021. *Mailing Add:* 463 West St Apt 919C New York NY 10014

KAUFFMAN, (CAMILLE) ANDRENE
PAINTER, MURALIST
b Chicago, Ill, Apr 19, 05. *Study:* Art Inst Chicago, BFA; Univ Chicago, MFA; Ill Inst Technol; Univ Ill, Chicago; also with Andre Lhote, Paris. *Work:* Art Inst Chicago; Vanderpoel Gallery, Beverly Art Ctr, Chicago; Rockford Col; Mt Mary Col, Wis; Elmhurst Art Mus, 80. *Comn:* Murals (oil on canvas), Works Progress Admin & US Treas Dept, Burbank & Hirsch High Sch, Cook Co Hosp, Ida Grove & Iowa Post Off Bldgs, 34-42; bas reliefs (wood or stone), Works Progress Admin, schs & field houses, Oak Park & Evanston, Ill, 34-42; murals (ceramic tile), Winnebago Medical Ctr, Rockford, Ill, 51-52; murals (ceramic) & stained glass window, Third Unitarian Church Chicago, 55-69; mural (acrylic), Forest Park Pub Libr, Ill, 72. *Exhib:* One-woman shows, San Diego Mus, 50, La Jolla Fine Arts Gallery, Calif, 50, Bernard Gallery, Chicago, early 60's, Vanderpoel Gallery, 70, Univ Club Chicago, 74 & Elmhurst Col, 77; one-woman retrospective, Third Unitarian Church Chicago, 67. *Teaching:* Prof, Art Inst Chicago, 27-67, chmn div fine arts, 63-66, emer prof, 67- *Awards:* John Quincy Adams Fel Europe, Art Inst Chicago, 27; Second Prize Block Print Calendar, Chicago Soc Artists, 72; Achievement Award, Women's Caucus Art, 83. *Bibliog:* Robert B Jonson (auth), Sermon results in murals, Unitarian Register, 1/59; Prof John Hayward (narrator), Third Church Trilogy (TV prog), Channel 11, Chicago, 8/59; Donald Key (auth), Kauffmann show rich in color, Milwaukee J, 9/17/61. *Mem:* Arts Club Chicago; Nat Soc Mural Painters; Chicago Soc Artists. *Media:* Acrylics, Ceramic Glaze; Oil, Watercolor. *Dealer:* Art Rental & Sales Gallery Art Inst Chicago Michigan Blvd at Adams St Chicago IL 60603. *Mailing Add:* 411 N West Ave Elmhurst IL 60126

KAUFFMAN, RICHARD JOEL
DEALER
b Houston, Tex, Jan 20, 50. *Study:* Stanford Univ, BA, 72; Acad Hispano-Am, San Miguel de Allende, Mex; Found for Res on Nature Man, Durham. *Collections Arranged:* Weingarten Realty Company, Corp Hq, 79; Coca Cola Company, Foods Division, Corp Hq, 79-80; Colonial Savings and Loan, Corp Hq, 80; Exxon Chemical Co Technol Ctr, 81; Int Bus Machines Corp Hq, Houston, 81. *Pos:* Art dealer & corp consult, Kauffman Fine Art, Houston, 76- *Mem:* Cult Arts Coun Houston; Am Inst Architects. *Specialty:* Consultant to corporations for business environments; handling prints, paintings, tapestries and sculpture. *Mailing Add:* P O Box 56143 Houston TX 77027

KAUFFMAN, ROBERT CRAIG
PAINTER, SCULPTOR
b Los Angeles, Calif, Mar 31, 32. *Study:* Univ Southern Calif Sch Archit, 50-52; Univ Calif, Los Angeles, MA, 56. *Work:* Whitney Mus Am Art, New York; Tate Gallery Art, London, Eng; Art Inst Chicago; Los Angeles Co Mus Art; Pasadena Art Mus, Calif; and others. *Exhib:* The 1960's, Mus Mod Art, New York, 67; California Prints, Mus Mod Art, New York, 72; Corcoran Biennial, 73; 71st Am Exhib, Art Inst Chicago, 74; Whitney Downtown, 74; Univ Ill, 74; Inst Contemp Arts, Los Angeles, Calif, 75; Fullerton Art Gallery, Calif State Univ, 79; Whitney Mus Am Art, 80; Va Commonwealth Univ, Richmond, 81; Asher/Faure, Los Angeles, Calif, 81; La Jolla Mus, Calif, 81; and others. *Teaching:* Assoc prof painting & sculpture, Univ Calif, Irvine, 67-72; instr painting & sculpture, Univ Calif, Berkeley, 69 & Sch Visual Arts, New York, 70-71. *Awards:* US Govt Fel for the Arts, 67; 69th Am Exhib First Prize, Art Inst Chicago, 70. *Bibliog:* Jane Livingston (auth), Recent works by Craig Kauffman, 69 & Review of Kauffman show, 70, Artforum. *Media:* Acrylic, Plastic. *Publ:* Coauth, Transparency, Reflection, Light, Space, 71. *Dealer:* Pace Gallery 32 E 57th St New York NY 10022. *Mailing Add:* 31-33 Mercer St 5B New York NY 10013

KAUFMAN, IRVING
PAINTER, EDUCATOR
b New York, NY, Oct 4, 20. *Study:* Art Students League; NY Univ, BA & MA. *Work:* Univ Mich Mus Art; Saginaw Mus Art; Ohio State Univ; Parke-Davis Co; Columbia Univ Law Libr. *Exhib:* Various group shows and one-man exhibs. *Teaching:* Assoc prof art, Univ Mich, Ann Arbor, 56-64; prof art, City Col New York, 64- *Awards:* Manual Barkan Award, Nat Art Educ Asn, 81. *Mem:* Inst Study Art in Educ (pres, 72); Col Art Asn Am; Univ Coun Art Educ. *Media:* Oil. *Publ:* Auth, Art & Education in Contemporary Culture, 66;

contribr, Concepts in Art Education, 70; contribr, New Ideas in Art Education, 72; ed, Arts Issue, Curriculum Theory, Network, 74; contribr, Arts in Society, 75; and others. *Dealer:* Rehn Gallery 655 Madison Ave New York NY 10021. *Mailing Add:* Three Perigee Path East Hampton NY 11937

KAUFMAN, JANE
PAINTER, LECTURER
b New York, NY, May 26, 38. *Study:* Cornell Univ, 56-58; NY Univ, BA, 60; Hunter Col, MA, 65. *Work:* Whitney Mus Am Art, New York; Wooster Mus Fine Arts, Mass; Mus Mod Art S Australia, Canberra; Brooklyn Mus, NY; Aldrich Mus Contemp Art, Ridgefield, Conn; and others. *Exhib:* One Man's Choice, Dallas Mus Fine Arts, Tex, 69; Highlights of 1970 Season, Aldrich Mus Contemp Art, Ridgefield, Conn, 70; one-person show, Whitney Mus Am Art, New York, 71; Lyrical Abstraction, 71, The Struct of Color, 71 & Ann, 73, Whitney Mus Am Art; Corcoran Gallery Art, 72 & 73; Critic's Choice, Lowe Art Gallery, Syracuse Univ, NY & Munson-Williams-Proctor Inst Mus Art, Utica, 77; Decorative Art: Recent Works, Douglas Col Gallery, New Brunswick, NJ, 78; Intricate Struct-Repeated Images, Tyler Sch Art, Philadelphia; and many others. *Teaching:* Teacher fine arts, New York Pub High Schs, 60-69; instr fine arts, Lehman Col, Bronx, NY, 69-70; Bard Col, Annandale-on-Hudson, NY, 71-73 & Brooklyn Mus Art Sch, 72-73; lectr, Queens Col, 73-74; vis artist, workshops & lect, var cols & univs, US & Can, 74-; instr fine arts, Cooper Union Sch Art, New York, 81- *Awards:* Guggenheim Fel, 74; Nat Endowment for Arts Fels, 79; Creative Artists Pub Serv Prog Grant for sculpture, 81. *Mailing Add:* 151 W 18th St New York NY 10011

KAUFMAN, JOE
ILLUSTRATOR, WRITER
b Bridgeport, Conn, May 21, 11. *Study:* Lab Sch Indust Design; also with Herbert Bayer. *Exhib:* Art Dirs Club, 43-60; Soc Illustrators, 45; one-man shows, Fleisher Art Mem, Philadelphia, 50 & Parsons Sch of Design, New York, 78. *Mem:* Soc Illustrators. *Publ:* Illusr, I Spy With My Little Eye, McGraw, 70; auth & illusr, Busy People, 73; auth & illusr, How We Born, How We Grow, Work, Learn, 75; auth & illusr, About the Big Sky, High Hills, Rich Earth, Deep Sea, 78; auth & illusr, Wings, Paws, Hoofs and Flippers, 81; and many others. *Mailing Add:* 18 W 70th St New York NY 10023

KAUFMAN, MICO
SCULPTOR
b Romania, Jan 3, 24; US citizen. *Study:* Acad Fine Arts, Rome & Florence, Italy, 47-51. *Work:* Bas relief, Rivier Col, Nashua, NH; Andover Gallery Fine Arts, Mass; Kiski Acad, Saltburg, Pa; Weltman, Weltman Conserv Music, Malden, Mass. *Comn:* Official Ford VPres Commemorative Medal; Official Ford Pres Commemorative Medal Obverse; 200 Bicentennial Medals, Danbury Mint; Official NC Bicentennial Medal; 12 Legendary Americans, Am Sculpture Soc; and many others. *Exhib:* Rockport Artists Asn, 67; Prudential Art Festival, New Eng Sculpture Soc, 69; Nat Sculpture Soc, New York, 70-71; Audubon Artists, 71; Allied Artists Am, 71. *Teaching:* Instr sculpture, Boston Ctr Adult Educ, 59-62, New Eng Sch Art, Boston, 69-70 & Nashua Arts & Sci, 70-71. *Awards:* Alma & Ulysses Ricci Award for Best Conservative Sculpture or Painting, 67, R V T Steeves Award for Most Outstanding Work in Sculpture, 69 & 72, Rockport Artists Asn; Bronze Medal of Honor, Concord Art Asn, 69. *Bibliog:* Ann Schecter (auth), Vivid sculptural works, 11/19/67 & Perlinax (auth), Maggie Walker Medal, 11/11/71, Lowell Sun, Mass; Brenda Badolato (auth), The sculpture of Mico Kaufman, Lawrence Eagle Tribune, Mass, 6/18/68. *Mem:* Nat Sculpture Soc; New Eng Sculpture Asn; Cambridge Art Asn; Rockport Artists Asn. *Media:* Bronze, Stainless Steel. *Publ:* Auth, The Making of Mold Block and Case, 60; auth, Your most penetrating portrait ever, Nat Sculpture Rev, 72. *Mailing Add:* 23 Marion Dr Tewksbury MA 01876

KAUFMAN, NANCY
CONSULTANT, WRITER
b Woonsocket, RI. *Study:* Boston Univ, AB(art hist), 60; Univ Calif, Berkeley, art & archit hist. *Collections Arranged:* Halahmy & Howard, Manhattan, summer 75; West Side Sculpture Show, 76; Coop City Sculpture Show, summer 77. *Pos:* Dir visual arts referral serv, Creative Artists Pub Serv prog, 74-79; bd dirs, Ctr for Arts Info, 78; partner, Kaufman Randolph Tate, Fine Art Services, 79-; pres, Nancy Kaufman Fine Art Servs, 83- *Mem:* Art Table. *Mailing Add:* 305 W 86th St New York NY 10024

KAUFMANN, ROBERT CARL
ART LIBRARIAN
b Birmingham, Ala, Apr 27, 37. *Study:* Birmingham Southern Col, Ala, BS(Fr & hist), 61; Sch Libr Serv, Columbia Univ, New York, MSLS, 65, MA candidate in art hist, 65-69. *Pos:* Asst librn, Fine Arts Libr, Columbia Univ, New York, 64-68, fine arts librn, 68-69; librn, Cooper-Hewitt Mus, Smithsonian Inst, New York, 65-; art libr, Div Art, Donnell Br, New York Pub Libr, 69; art & archit librn, Yale Univ, New Haven, Conn, 71-74. *Awards:* Joe Delmore Langston Award, Ala Libr Asn, 63; Comt to Rescue Italian Art Res Fel, Bibliot Naz Centrale, Florence, Italy, 69-71. *Mem:* Victorian Soc Am; Art Libr Soc NAm. *Res:* Nineteenth century furniture and decorative arts; subject headings for twentieth century decorative arts. *Mailing Add:* 220 W 93rd St Apt 11-A New York NY 10025

KAULITZ, GARRY CHARLES
PAINTER, PRINTMAKER
b Rapid City, SDak, Oct 6, 42. *Study:* Rochester Inst Technol, BFA & MFA. *Work:* Gallery Today Collection, Indianapolis, Ind; State of Ky; City of Louisville, Ky; Art Inst Chicago. *Exhib:* One-man shows, J B Speed Art Mus, Louisville, 71, Bellarmine Col, Ky, 76 & Brookhaven Col, Tex, 79; Print Club of Philadelphia, 79-80; Freichen International Print Exhib, 80; Crackow Biannual, 80; and others. *Teaching:* Prof printmaking, Louisville Sch Art, 68-; vis artist, Brookhaven Col, Tex, 79 & Southern Ill Univ, 79; guest speaker, Detroit Print Symposium, 80. *Awards:* Brockport State Col Purchase Award, 67; Evansville Mus Ann Exhib Award, 68; Arthur D Allen Mem Award, Regional Fine Arts Biennial, 71. *Bibliog:* Sarah Lansdell (auth), Review of work, 2/71 & Linda Bousch (auth), A printmakers excursion into fact & fantasy, 2/75, Courier-J & Times. *Media:* Acrylic, Serigraphy. *Publ:* Auth, A Portfolio of Prints & Poems, pvt publ, 73. *Mailing Add:* 154 N Ewing Louisville KY 40206

KAUPELIS, ROBERT JOHN
PAINTER, EDUCATOR
b Amsterdam, NY, Feb 23, 28. *Study:* State Univ NY Col Buffalo, BS; Albright Art Sch, cert; Teachers Col, Columbia Univ, MA & DEd. *Work:* Duke Univ Mus; Oleonta State Univ; Atlanta Art Inst; NY Univ Art Collection; Mich State Univ; and others. *Exhib:* Over 30 one-man shows incl Image South Gallery, Atlanta, 77-79, 82, Bell Gallery Greenwich, Conn, 79 & 80, The Schenectady Mus, 80, Marino Gallery, New York, 81 & Hudson River Mus, 83; and others. *Teaching:* Prof art, NY Univ, 56- *Awards:* Prize for Sculpture, New Eng Ann, 69; Painting Prize, Silvermine New Eng Ann, 73, First Prize, 79 & 80; plus others. *Bibliog:* Herbert Livesey (auth), The Professors, Charterhouse, 75; Gerald M Monroe (auth), Teaching drawing: The personal approaches of Robert Kaupelis, Drawing, 5-6/79 & American Artist, 8/81; Ruth Bass (auth), article, Arts, 9/83. *Mem:* Nat Art Educ Asn; NY State Art Teachers Asn; Silvermine Guild Artists; Univ Coun on the Arts; Inst Study Art & Educ. *Media:* Acrylic, Oil. *Publ:* Auth, Learning to Draw, 66 & Experimental Drawing, 80, Watson-Guptill. *Dealer:* Bell Gallery 202 Field Point Rd Greenwich CT 06830; Image South Gallery 1931 Peach Tree Rd NE Atlanta GA 30309. *Mailing Add:* 988 Barberry Rd Yorktown Heights NY 10598

KAWA, FLORENCE KATHRYN
PAINTER
b Weyerhaeuser, Wis, Feb 24, 12. *Study:* Minneapolis Sch Art, 30-34; Univ Wis, Milwaukee, BS, 40; La State Univ, Baton Rouge, MA, 44; summers, Black Mountain Col, 44, Columbia Univ, 46-48, Cranbrook Acad Art, 51, Mass Inst Technol, 56 & Leeds Col Art, England, 70. *Work:* Univ Wis, Madison; La Art Comn, Baton Rouge; US Info Agency for Am Embassies; Pub Bldgs Admin for Marine Hosps. *Exhib:* Int Watercolor Biennial, Brooklyn Mus, 51, 55, 57, 59 & 61; Ann Exhib Contemp Am Sculpture, Watercolor & Drawings, Whitney Mus Art, New York, 53; Nat Competition Watercolors, Drawings & Prints, Metrop Mus Art, New York, 53; Contemp Watercolor in the US, sponsored by US Embassy Cult Div, France, 53; 20th Century American graphic arts, US Info Agency Touring Foreign Mus, 56-57; one-man show, Des Moines Art Ctr, 76. *Teaching:* Asst prof painting & design, Fla State Univ, 46-62; prof painting & design, Drake Univ, 64-78, emer prof, 78- *Awards:* Edmundson Award for Best Work in Any Medium, Des Moines Art Ctr, 70; Esther & Edith Younker Award, 77; 13th Midwest Biennial Purchase Award & Best in Show, Joslyn Mus, Omaha, 74; plus others. *Media:* Oil, Watercolor. *Mailing Add:* 46 Andrews Pl Roswell NM 88201

KAWABATA, MINORU
PAINTER, INSTRUCTOR
b Tokyo, Japan, May 22, 11. *Study:* Tokyo Acad Fine Art, grad, 34; also study in Paris & Italy, 37-39. *Work:* Albright-Knox Art Gallery, Buffalo, NY; Everson Mus Art, Syracuse, NY; Guggenheim Mus; Mus Mod Art, Sao Paulo, Brazil; Mus Mod Art, Tokyo. *Exhib:* Guggenheim Int, New York, 59 & 64; Betty Parsons Gallery, NY, 60-; Venice Biennial, 62; Everson Mus Art, 74; Mus Mod Art, Kamakura, Kamakurashi, Japan, 75; Juda Rowan Gallery, London, 80. *Teaching:* Prof painting, Tama Univ Art, Japan, 50-58; prof painting, drawing & compos, New Sch Social Res, 60- *Awards:* Rhythm of Brown, Guggenheim Mus, 59; Work, Mus Mod Art, Sao Paulo, 60; Work B, Mus Mod Art, Kamakura, 61. *Bibliog:* Kramer (auth), article, 11/23/74, Raynor (auth), article, 3/7/80 & John Russell (auth), article, 10/16/81, New York Times. *Dealer:* Jack Tilton Gallery 24 W 57th St New York NY 10019. *Mailing Add:* 463 West St New York NY 10014

KAWASHIMA, TAKESHI
PAINTER, SCULPTOR
b Takamatsu City, Japan, Jan 13, 30. *Study:* Musashino Univ Art, 51-56; Art Students League New York, 66. *Work:* Mus Mod Art, New York; State Univ Col, Potsdam, NY; Housatonic Mus Art, Stratford, Conn; Tokyo Nat Mus Mod Art; Kyoto Nat Mus Mod Art. *Comn:* Daito Press Co, Tokyo, 71; Nisho Press Co, Tokyo, 73; Mitsui Trust Banking Co, New York, 74; Yamashita Hosp, Takamatsu, Japan, 76; Miki-cho Town Hall, Kagawa, Japan, 83; and others. *Exhib:* New Eye Show, Chrysler Art Mus, Mass, 64; Mus Mod Art, New York, 65-67; Aldrich Mus Contemp Art, Ridgefield, Conn, 67; Krannert Art Mus, Univ Ill, Champaign, 69; Kagowa Cult Mus, Takamatsu, Japan, 71; Nat Mus Mod Art, Kyoto, 73-74; Nat Mus Art, Osaka, Japan, 77. *Collections Arranged:* Hosetsu Ohtsuka Calligraphy (auth, catalog), 82. *Awards:* Silvermine Prize, 18th Ann New Eng Exhib, New Canaan, Conn, 67. *Bibliog:* Udo Kulterman (auth), The new painting, Frederick A Praeger, 69; Joseph Love (auth), Art Int, 71; John Canaday, New York Times, 72. *Publ:* Auth, Art now in New York, Gendai Bijutsu Sha, 65; contribr, New image of eroticism, Bijutsu Shuppan, 69; contribr, Decoration art, 72 & contribr, The base of sculpture, 78, Shicho-sha; New York for twelve years, Shikoku Shinbun, 76. *Dealer:* Nantenshi Gallery 3-6-5 Kyobashi Chuo-ku Tokyo Japan. *Mailing Add:* 135 Wooster St New York NY 10012

KAWECKI, JEAN MARY
SCULPTOR, GALLERY DIRECTOR
b Liverpool, England, June 24, 26; US citizen. *Study:* Liverpool Col Art, Eng; Art Career Sch, New York; also with Douglas Prizer. *Comn:* Wall sculpture, First Montclair Housing Corp, 83. *Exhib:* Nat Miniature Soc, Nutley, NJ, 75; Audubon Artists, Nat Acad Design, New York, 78; Newark Mus, 78; Nabisco World Hq, 79; solo show, NJ Inst Technol, 80-; Bergen Mus, 81; and others. *Pos:* Free lance illusr mag, London, Eng, 46-51; Sol Vogel & Am-Mitchell Publ, New York, 51-53, Tobias Meyer & Nebenzahl, New York, 58-66; co-founder & dir, Doubletree Coop Art Gallery, Upper Montclair, 74- *Awards:* Art Ctr Combined Award, Tri-State Ann, Art Ctr NJ, 74; Patrons Award, Hudson Artists at the Bergen Mus, 76; First Prize, St John's Ann Juried Show, Newark, 79. *Bibliog:* Anne Betty Weinshenker (auth), M & A on Art, NJ Music & Arts, 12/76. *Mem:* Artists Equity Asn NJ & NY; Doubletree Coop Gallery (dir & chmn hanging comt & spec shows, 74-). *Media:* Found Stone, Metal & Epoxy. *Dealer:* Doubletree Art Gallery 76 Church St Montclair NJ 07043 *Mailing Add:* 28 Mountainside Park Terr Upper Montclair NJ 07043

KAY, REED
EDUCATOR, PAINTER
b Boston, Mass, Mar 29, 25. *Study:* Sch Mus Fine Arts, Boston, dipl, 49, with Karl Zerbe; also with Oskar Kokoschka. *Exhib:* New Eng Regional Drawing, Smith Col Mus Art, 65; Am Fedn Arts Nat Exhib, 66; Urban Aesthetics, Queens Mus, New York, 76; A Selection of Am Art, Inst Contemp Art, Boston, 76; Art in Transition, Mus Fine Arts, Boston, 77; one-man exhib, Alpha Gallery, Boston, 78 & 83. *Teaching:* Instr painting, Sch of Mus Fine Arts, Boston, 51-56; instr painting techniques, Skowhegan Sch Painting, Maine, 52-60; prof painting, Boston Univ, 56- *Awards:* Artist Fel Grant for painting, Nat Endowment Arts, 81-82. *Media:* Oil, Gouache. *Res:* Effects of painter's materials and media on aesthetic qualities of pictures and on way they change with age. *Publ:* Auth, The Painter's Companion, Webb Bks, 61; auth, The Painter's Guide to Studio Methods & Materials, Doubleday, 72 & rev ed, Prentice-Hall, 83; contribr, World Bk Encycl, 71-77. *Dealer:* Alpha Gallery 121 Newbury St Boston MA 02116. *Mailing Add:* 109 Rawson Rd Brookline MA 02146

KAYE, DAVID HAIGH
TEXTILE ARTIST, DESIGNER
b Kingston, Ont, 1947. *Study:* Ont Col Art, Toronto, AOCA; Univ Guelph, BA; Cranbrook Acad Art, Bloomfield Hills, Mich, MFA. *Work:* Jean A Chalmers Collection of Contemp Can Crafts, Ont Crafts Coun, Toronto; Permanent Collection of Dept of External Affairs, Ottawa; Nat Mus Mod Art, Kyoto, Japan; Massey Found Collection, Ottawa. *Comn:* Linen & Jute (tapestry), comn by P Farlinger, Glouchester News, Toronto, 74; Relief Illusion (tapestry), comn by L Gladstone, Videogenic Corp, Toronto, 81; Relief Illusion Number Two (tapestry), comn by Helena Hernmarck & Niels Diffrient, Ridgefield, Conn, 82. *Exhib:* 100 Yrs: Evolution of the Ontario College of Art, Art Gallery Ont, Toronto, 76; Fiberworks, Cleveland Mus Art, Ohio, 77; Fiber Works: Americas & Japan, Nat Mus Mod Art, Kyoto & Tokyo, Japan, 77 & 78; Fibre Structures & Fabric Surfaces, Sarnia Art Gallery, 81; Contemporary Canadian Tapestries, Barbican Ctr, London, Eng, 82; Tapices Canadienses Contemporaneos, Palacio de Cristal, Madrid, Spain, 83; Canada Mikrokosma, Textilmuseum, Krefeld, WGer, 83; and others. *Awards:* Lt-Gov's Medal, Grad Medal, Ont Col of Art, 72; Can Coun Short-Term Grant, Ottawa, 75 & 78; F Javier Sauza Arts Award, 80. *Bibliog:* M E Bevlin (auth), Design Through Discovery, Holt, Rinehart & Winston, 77; S W Keene (auth), Toronto artist seeks integrity of idea, materials, technique, Weaving & Fiber News, Homer, NY, 80; J Parkin (auth), Art in Architecture, Visual Arts, Ont, 82. *Mem:* Ontario Soc Arts. *Media:* Natural Fibers, Mixed Media. *Mailing Add:* 585 Bloor St W Apt 4 Toronto ON M6G 1K5 Canada

KAYE, GEORGE
PAINTER, INSTRUCTOR
b Malden, Mass, Nov 21, 11. *Study:* Swain Sch Design; Brooklyn Mus Art Sch; Brooklyn Col, BA; City Col New York Grad Sch; NY Univ, MA. *Work:* Philathea Col Mus, London, Ont; Dept Educ Film Libr, Mus Mod Art, New York. *Exhib:* One-man show, Nena's Choice Gallery, 77 & Wave Hill, New York, 79; Clayman Gallery, Nyack, NY, 80 & 81; Images Art Gallery, Briarcliff Manor, NY, 81; Trisdonn Contemp Gallery, Nyack, NY; and others. *Pos:* Asst dir art, Bd Educ, New York, 59-68, mem coun dirs, 60-73, dir art, 68-73; consult art, Mayor's Off, New York, 65-66, Dept Pub Events, 66-73; cult dir, Coun Supt & Adminr, 75- *Teaching:* Instr art, New York City Pub Schs, 34-53; chmn dept art, High Sch Music & Art, New York, 53-59; lectr art educ, NY Univ, 60-62; lectr hist art, Pratt Inst, 65-66 & Bronx Community Col, 67-68. *Awards:* Cert Appreciation, New York City Soc Osteopathic Physicians & Surgeons, 70; Citation, NY State Educ Dept, 72; New York Pub Schs, 82. *Bibliog:* J M McCormick (auth), Gallery reviews in New York, Pictures on Exhib, 3/66; J Gollin (auth), Reviews & previews, Art News, 3/66. *Mem:* Nat Art Educ Asn (local chmn, 72); NY State Art Teachers Asn (New York City liaison, 59-72); NY State Coun Adminr Art Educ (vpres, 63-72); New York Sch Art League, NY (trustee, 60-); NY Soc Exp Study Educ (chmn art sect, 63-72). *Media:* Mixed. *Publ:* Contribr, Color in education, Color Eng, 64; ed, Art & the Young Child, 68; ed, Creative Crafts for Today, 70; coauth, A Child's Story of Vincent Van Gogh, 70; auth, Pastels, 74. *Mailing Add:* 3333-F Henry Hudson Pkwy Bronx NY 10463

KAYE, MILDRED ELAINE
PRINTMAKER, INSTRUCTOR
b New York, NY, Sept 24, 29. *Study:* Ind Univ, PA, 51; Montclair State Col, MA, 77. *Work:* John Herron Inst, Indianapolis; Leonard Bocour Co

Collection, Garnerville, NY; Ind Univ Permanent Collection, Bloomington; Montclair State Col Permanent Collection, Upper Montclair, NJ; Am Cult Ctr, Taipei, China. *Comn:* Logos & corp images, Metrop Area Rep, New York, 81, Tradco Int, Saddle Brook, NJ, 81, METCO USA Inc, Paramus, NJ, 82 & SGE Marketing Corp. *Exhib:* Ann Graphics Exhib, Hunterdon Art Ctr & traveling, 77 & 81; Knickerbocker Ann, 79 & Audubon Ann, 81, Nat Art Club, New York; Art Expo, Washington, DC, 80; Cult Exchange Exhib, traveling Taiwan, 80-81; Nat Asn Jewish Women, Fairleigh Dickinson Univ, Teaneck, NJ, 81; and others. *Pos:* Art ed, Am Book Co, 52-56; graphic designer, Guy-Mar Printing, 65-72. *Teaching:* Instr graphic arts, Bergen City Vocational-Technol High Sch, 72- *Awards:* Best in Show, Cork Gallery, Lincoln Ctr, 78; Judges Choice, Women in Arts, Leonia Libr Asn, 81 & Lever House, 83. *Bibliog:* Segment on exhibit (film), NJ Nightly News, 11/81; Henry Doren (auth), The face of the coin, NJ Artform, 12/81; Art in Orange County, 83. *Mem:* Women in Arts (secy, 80-); NJ Craftsman's Coun (secy, 80-); Art Ctr Northern NJ (exec comt, 81-); Printmakers Coun NJ. *Media:* Mixed. *Publ:* Auth, The want ad, 10/80, auth, The other side of the coin, 12/80, auth, The layout and paste-up, self taught, 8/81, auth, Introduction to typography, 10/81 & auth, Introduction to copyfitting, 2/82, NJ Artforms. *Dealer:* Mari Gallery 133 E Prospect Ave Mamaroneck NY 10543. *Mailing Add:* 87 Kern Pl Saddle Brook NJ 07662

KAYSER, THOMAS ARTHUR
MUSEUM DIRECTOR
b Milwaukee, Wis, Oct 4, 35. *Study:* Layton Sch Art, 58; Cranbrook Acad Art, 59; Mus Mgt Inst, Berkeley, 80. *Collections Arranged:* The American Indian/The American Flag, 76; The Art of Haute Couture, 78; German Expressionism from Western Michigan, 80-81; Kalamazoo Collects Photography, 80; Super Realism from the Morton G Neumann Collection, 81; New Image/Pattern & Decoration from the Morton G Neumann Collection, 83. *Pos:* Asst dir, Flint Inst Arts, Mich, 65-78; exec dir, Kalamazoo Inst Arts, Mich, 78- *Mem:* Am Asn Mus; Art Mus Asn; Mich Mus Asn; Mich Coun Arts. *Mailing Add:* 314 S Park St Kalamazoo MI 49007

KAZ (LAWRENCE KATZMAN)
DESIGNER, CARTOONIST
b Ogdensburg, NY, June 14, 22. *Study:* Univ Pa, BS; Art Students League, with Reginald Marsh. *Pos:* Pres & chmn bd, Kaz Mfg Co, 47-; bus mgr, Cartoonist; chmn, Int Cong Comics. *Awards:* Silver Cup of City of Bordighera, Italy, 59; Palma d'Oro, 66; Silver T-Square, Nat Cartoonists Soc. *Mem:* Art Students League; Nat Cartoonists Soc; Cartoonists Guild. *Publ:* Auth & illusr, Nellie the Nurse, 58, Calling Nurse Nellie, 61 & Nellie's Laff-In, 68; auth & illusr, For Doctors Only, Eng, 60; auth & illusr, Prima y Dopo i Pasti, Italy, 60; and other bks & cartoons in mags & newspapers throughout the world; illusr, greeting cards & bks, Gibson-Buzza. *Mailing Add:* 101 Central Park W New York NY 10023

KAZ, NATHANIEL
SCULPTOR, INSTRUCTOR
b New York, NY, Mar 9, 17. *Study:* Art Students League, with George Bridgman, Samuel Cashwan & William Zorach. *Work:* Brooklyn Mus; Whitney Mus Am Art, Metrop Mus Art, New York; also in pvt collections. *Comn:* Limestone carving, Fine St Temple, Nashville, Tenn; bronze sculpture, Pub Sch 59, Brooklyn; two colored aluminum reliefs to Thespians Tragedy & Comedy, Jr High Sch 164, Queens; sculpture, Temple Beth Emeth, Albany, NY, 65; and others. *Exhib:* Whitney Mus Am Art, New York; Metrop Mus Art, New York; Mus Mod Art, New York; Art Inst Chicago; Philadelphia Mus Fine Arts; and others. *Teaching:* Instr sculpture, Art Students League of NY, currently. *Awards:* Prize, 47, Medal of Hon, 60 & Silver Medal, 81, Audubon Artists; Brooklyn Soc Artists Award, 48 & 52; and others. *Mailing Add:* 160 W 73rd St New York NY 10023

KAZOR, VIRGINIA ERNST
CURATOR
b Detroit, Mich, Sept 28, 40. *Study:* Univ Southern Calif, BA, MA. *Collections Arranged:* Separate Realities (catalog), 73; 24 From Los Angeles (with catalog), 74; Peter Krasnow (with catalog), 75; Ron Davis/Tom Holland: Works from the Collection of Mr & Mrs Robert Rowan (with catalog), 75; Dreams for Sale: The Great Work of Hollywood Still Photographers 1927-1949, 76; Greene and Greene: Architecture and Related Design of Charles Sumner Greene and Henry Mather Greene, 1894-1934 (with catalog), 77; The Barnsdall Projects: Drawings by Frank Lloyd Wright, 80. *Pos:* Curatorial asst mod art, Los Angeles Co Mus Art, 65-68; cur, Los Angeles Munic Art Gallery, 70-78; cur, Frank Lloyd Wright's Hollyhock House, 78- *Mem:* Los Angeles Bicentennial Orgn (chmn mus comt, 74-); Soc Archit Hist, Southern Calif Chap (pres, 81-83). *Mailing Add:* Hollyhock House 4808 Hollywood Blvd Los Angeles CA 90027

KEANE, BIL
CARTOONIST
b Philadelphia, Pa, Oct 5, 22. *Work:* Bil Keane Original Cartoon Collection, Syracuse Univ; Mus Cartoon Art, Greenwich, Conn. *Pos:* Staff artist, Philadelphia Eve Bull, 45-59; creator & nat syndicated cartoonist, The Family Circus & Channel Chuckles. *Awards:* Best Syndicated Panel Cartoonist, Nat Cartoonists Soc, 69, 71 & 74. *Mem:* Nat Cartoonists Soc; Newspaper Comics Coun; Cartoonists Guild. *Media:* Pen and Ink. *Publ:* Auth, Pasghetti & Meat Bulbs, 81, Can I Have a Cookie, 82, Jeffy's Lookin at Me, 82 & Go To Your Room, 82, Fawcett; auth, That Family Circus Feeling, Andrews & McMeel, 82; and many others. *Mailing Add:* 5815 E Joshua Tree Lane Paradise Valley AZ 85253

KEANE, LUCINA MABEL
PAINTER, PRINTMAKER
b Gros, Nebr, 04. *Study:* Ashland Col; Ohio State Univ, BS(educ); Teachers Col, Columbia Univ, MA; Pa State Univ; Temple Univ; NY Univ. *Exhib:* Allied Artists WVa; Clarksburg Art Ctr, WVa; Centennial Exhib, Huntington Art Gallery, WVa. *Pos:* Pres bd & mem steering comt, Charleston Art Gallery, 63-66. *Teaching:* Instr art, Univ NDak, 26-29; instr art, Ill State Univ, 30-31; assoc prof art & head dept, Morris Harvey Col, 36-72. *Awards:* Five Prizes, Allied Artists WVa, 36-59. *Mem:* Col Art Asn Am; Tri-State Art Asn; Allied Artists WVa; Pen Women Am. *Mailing Add:* 2908 Noyes Ave Charleston WV 25304

KEARL, STANLEY BRANDON
SCULPTOR
b Waterbury, Conn, Dec 22, 13. *Study:* Yale Univ, BFA, 41, MFA, 42; Univ Iowa, PhD, 48; study in Rome, Italy, 9 yrs. *Work:* Iowa State Univ; Univ Minn, Duluth; Naz Galeria, Rome, Italy; Nat Mus, Stockholm, Sweden; Mus Goteborgs, Sweden; plus others. *Exhib:* Penthouse Exhib, 60 & Art Lending Libr Exhib, 65, Mus Mod Art, New York; Whitney Mus Am Art Ann, New York, 62; Grand Cent Mod, New York, 65 & 68; Art in Am Embassies Abroad, selected by Mus Mod Art, New York, 68; Art in Embassies Prog, US State Dept, 79; one-man shows, Gallery of Mod Art, Basel, Switz, 51, Hudson River Mus, Yonkers, 64, Benson Gallery, Bridgehampton, NY, 76 & 82 & Guild Hall Mus, East Hampton, NY, 82. *Pos:* Fulbright exchange prof to Univ Rome, Italy, 49-50. *Teaching:* Lectr, Univ Minn, Duluth, 47-48; lectr, Pratt Inst, 67. *Awards:* Hudson River Mus Sculpture Award, 63; Silvermine Guild Asn Ann Award, 67; Sculpture Award, Ludwig Vogelstein Found Inc, 82-83; and others. *Bibliog:* Torsten Bergmark (auth), Paletten, Swed Art J, 52; Michel Seuphor (auth), The Sculpture of This Century, Dictionary of Modern Sculpture, A Swemmer, Ltd, London, 59. *Mem:* Col Art Asn Am. *Media:* Cast Bronze. *Dealer:* Ingber Gallery 3 E 78th St New York NY 10021. *Mailing Add:* 344 Sprain Rd Scarsdale NY 10583

KEARNEY, JOHN (W)
SCULPTOR, ADMINISTRATOR
b Omaha, Nebr, Aug 31, 24. *Study:* Cranbrook Acad Art, Bloomfield Hills, Mich, 45-48; Univ Stranieri, Perugia, Fulbright Grant Italy & Ital Govt Grant Sculpture, 63-64. *Work:* Norfolk Art Mus, Va; Detroit Children's Mus; Minn Mus, St Paul; Edwin A Ulrich Mus of Art, Wichita, Kans; New Sch Soc Research; plus others. *Comn:* Large outdoor sculptures, Wichita State Univ, City Chicago, Chicago Park Dist, Wichita Coliseum, Springfield Art Asn, Ill & Lincoln Park Zoo, Chicago, 82. *Exhib:* Corcoran Biennial, Washington, DC, 55; Am Fulbright Artists, Palazzo Venezia, Rome, 64; Painting & Sculpture Today, John Herron Mus, Indianapolis, 65; Soc Contemp Am Art Exhib, Art Inst Chicago, 66; one-man shows, ACA Galleries Biennial, New York, 65-, Ill Inst of Technol, 76, Ulrich Mus of Art, Wichita, 76 & Contemp Art Workshop, Chicago, 81; two-man show, Art Inst of Chicago, 77. *Pos:* Dir, Contemp Art Workshop, Chicago, 51-; mem adv bd, Art Inst Art Rental & Sales Gallery, Art Inst of Chicago. *Teaching:* Instr sculpture, Contemp Art Workshop, Chicago, 50-70 & Mundelein Col, 70-71. *Awards:* Ringling Mus Award, 60; Man of Year, Adult Educ Coun Chicago, 62; Fulbright Award, 63-64. *Mem:* Provincetown Art Asn & Mus (vpres, 62-70); Fine Arts Work Ctr, Provincetown (adv bd); Arts Club Chicago. *Media:* Bronze, Steel. *Dealer:* ACA Gallery 21 E 67th St New York NY 10021; Contemporary Art Workshop Chicago. *Mailing Add:* 830 Castlewood Terr Chicago IL 60640

KEARNS, JAMES JOSEPH
SCULPTOR, PAINTER
b Scranton, Pa, Aug 7, 24. *Study:* Art Inst Chicago, BFA, 51. *Work:* Mus Mod Art & Whitney Mus Am Art, New York; Newark Mus Art; NJ State Mus, Trenton; Nat Collection Fine Arts, Smithsonian Inst & Hirshhorn Mus, Washington, DC; Hirshhorn Mus, Washington, DC. *Exhib:* Nat Inst Arts & Lett, 59; Whitney Mus Am Art Ann, 59-61; Johnson Wax Collection, World Tour, 62-67; Pa Acad Fine Arts, Philadelphia, 64-65; The Figurative Tradition, Whitney Mus Am Art, 80. *Pos:* Mem bd gov, Skowhegan Sch Painting & Sculpture, 64-70. *Teaching:* Instr drawing, painting & sculpture, Sch Visual Arts, 60-; instr sculpture, Fairleigh-Dickinson Univ, 62-63; instr painting & sculpture, Skowhegan Sch Painting & Sculpture, summers 62-65. *Awards:* Nat Inst Arts & Lett Grant, 59. *Bibliog:* Selden Rodman (auth), Conversations with Artists, Devin Adair, 57 & The Insiders, La State Univ, 60; Lee Nordness (auth), Art USA Now, Viking, 63. *Media:* Bronze, Fiberglass. *Publ:* Illusr, Can these bones live, New Directions, 60; illusr, The Heart of Beethoven, Shorewood Press, 62. *Dealer:* Grippi Gallery 315 E 62nd St New York NY 10021. *Mailing Add:* 452 Rockaway Rd Dover NJ 07801

KEATS, EZRA JACK
ILLUSTRATOR, WRITER
b Brooklyn, NY, Mar 11, 16. *Exhib:* Assoc Am Artists Gallery, New York, 50-54. *Pos:* Mag advert illusr, Sch Visual Arts, 47-48 & Workshop Sch, New York, 55-57. *Awards:* Newberry-Caldecott Medal, 63; Boston Globe-Horn Book Award, 70. *Mem:* PEN; Authors Guild; Soc Illusr. *Publ:* Auth & illusr, The Snowy Day, 62, Hi, Cat, 70, Pet Show, 72 & Skates, 73; ed & illusr, Regards to the Man in the Moon, 81; and others. *Mailing Add:* 444 E 82nd St New York NY 10028

KEAVENEY, SYDNEY STARR
LIBRARIAN, LECTURER
b Grand Rapids, Mich, Nov 12, 39. *Study:* Wellesley Col, BA(art hist), 61; Simmons Col, MS(libr sci), 64; Rutgers Univ, PhD(libr & info sci); S L A Plenum Scholar), 83. *Pos:* Fine arts librn, Boston Pub Libr, Mass, 62-66. *Teaching:* Prof art & archit dept, Pratt Inst Libr, 66-; teacher & lectr art info resources & picture resources, Pratt Inst Grad Sch Libr & Info, Brooklyn, 68-. *Mem:* Special Libr Asn (pres, NY chap, 73-74); Art Librn Soc NAm; Art Librn Soc NY (chmn, 77). *Res:* Research methods in art and architecture. *Interests:* Modern art, architecture and American art. *Publ:* Auth, American Painting: An Information Guide, 74 & ed, Art and Architecture Information Guide Series, 74-80, Detroit, 14 vols. *Mailing Add:* Pratt Inst Libr Brooklyn NY 11205

KECK, SHELDON WAUGH
EDUCATOR, CONSERVATOR
b Utica, NY, May 30, 10. *Study:* Harvard Univ, BA, 32; Fogg Art Mus, apprentice in restoration, 32-33; Hamilton Col, DFA, 76. *Pos:* Conservator, Brooklyn Mus, 34-61; private consult & lectr painting conservation. *Teaching:* Dir art conserv, NY Univ Conserv Ctr, 61-65, prof fine arts, 64-66; prof art conserv, Cooperstown Grad Progs, State Univ NY Col Oneonta, 69-81. *Awards:* Fulbright Fel, 59; Guggenheim Fel, 59-60. *Mem:* Cooperstown Art Asn; Int Inst Conserv Hist & Artistic Works (mem coun, pres, 74-80); Int Coun Mus; Am Inst Conserv Hist & Artistic Works (pres, 72-74). *Publ:* Auth, numerous articles in prof jour & art periodicals on exam & conserv of paintings. *Mailing Add:* 31 River St Cooperstown NY 13326

KEELER, DAVID BOUGHTON
ADMINISTRATOR, PAINTER
b Cleveland, Ohio, Feb 11, 31. *Study:* Cleveland Inst Art, dipl; Case Western Reserve Univ, Cleveland. *Work:* Cleveland Inst Art, Ohio; Cleveland Art Asn; Nat Collection of Fine Arts, Washington, DC. *Exhib:* Cleveland Mus Art Regional, 60-63, 65, 67, 74 & 76; Butler Inst Am Art Nat, Youngstown, Ohio, 60 & 62; Corcoran Gallery of Art, Washington, DC, 65 & 69; one-man shows, 323 Gallery, Alexandria, Va, 65; Studio Gallery, Alexandria, 66; Barbara Fielder Gallery, Washington, DC, 76; Wolfe St Gallery, Alexandria, 77. *Pos:* Preparor & exhib designer, Cleveland Mus Art, 61-64; tech asst to cur, Nat Collection Fine Arts, Washington, DC, 66-71 & chief exhib & design, 72- *Bibliog:* Andrew Hudson (auth), article, Washington Post, 10/65 & 10/66; Ben Forgey (auth), article, Washington Evening Star, 4/76. *Dealer:* Barbara Fiedler Gallery 1621 21st St NW Wasington DC 20009. *Mailing Add:* 1308 Namassin Rd Alexandria VA 22308

KEELING, HENRY CORNELIOUS
PAINTER, EDUCATOR
b St Albans, WVa, Sept 4, 23. *Study:* Pratt Inst, BFA(interior design); NY Univ; Hans Hofmann Sch Fine Art, New York; Art Students League; Marshall Univ, MA(fine art); also with Bernard Klonis, Reuben Tam, Leo Manso & Victor Kandell. *Work:* Parkersburg Art Ctr, Parkersburg, WVa; Charleston Art Gallery of Sunrise, WVa; WVa Arts & Humanities Coun, Charleston; Herbert M Rothchild Collection, New York; WVa State Col. *Comn:* Three paintings & mural, Consolidated Gas Corp, Clarksburg, WVa, 67; two paintings, Roanoke Indust Savings & Loan Corp, Va, 68; mural, New River Bank & Trust Co, Oak Hill, WVa, 80. *Exhib:* Brooklyn Mus Art Sch Ann, 54 & 55; Invitational, Parkersburg Art Ctr, 76-77; Invitational Relig Show, WVa State Col, 77; one-man shows, Gallery 4, Charleston, WVa, 78, 80 & 81, Morris Harvey Col, 78 & Ghent Gallery, Norfolk, Va, 80. *Teaching:* Assoc prof art & head dept, Univ Charleston, 73- *Awards:* Purchase Awards for Graphics, Charleston Art Gallery, 71 & WVa Arts & Humanities, 71; Merit Award, Parkersburg Art Ctr, 77. *Mem:* Provincetown Art Asn; WVa Allied Artists. *Media:* Watercolor, Collage. *Mailing Add:* 406 Park St St Albans WV 25177

KEEN, HELEN BOYD
PAINTER
b Tacoma, Wash. *Study:* Calif Sch Fine Arts; with Mark Tobey, 8 yrs; Art Students League, with Cobino, Hale & Vytlacil, 4 yrs. *Work:* Seattle Art Mus; Addison Gallery Am Art, Andover, Mass; Art Gallery Greater Victoria, BC; Tacoma Art Mus; Archives Am Art, Smithsonian Inst, Washington, DC. *Exhib:* US State Dept Show (selected by Mus Mod Art), France, 56-57; Pa Acad Fine Arts, 57; Brooklyn Mus, 57; Norfolk Mus Arts & Sci, 63; Avanti Gallery, New York, 72; Nat Arts Club Graphics Show, Gramercy Park, NY, 76; plus others. *Awards:* First Award, Tacoma Art Mus, 45. *Mem:* Art Students League; Art Gallery of Greater Victoria, Smithsonian Inst. *Media:* Oil. *Collection:* Mark Tobey, Pehr, Vytlacil, John Ford, Mario Bambagini, Judith Rothschild, Toko Shinoda & Ethel Schwabacher. *Dealer:* Avanti Galleries 145 E 72nd St New York NY 10021. *Mailing Add:* 201 E 79th St New York NY 10021

KEENA, JANET LAYBOURN
PAINTER
b St Joseph, Mo, Sept 11, 28. *Study:* William Woods Col; Univ Kans; Univ Calif, Los Angeles; Am Acad Art, Chicago. *Work:* Albrecht Mus, St Joseph, Mo; Park Col, Parkville, Mo; Dart Drug Hq, Los Angeles. *Comn:* Painting, Weight Watchers Hq, Kansas City, Mo, 74; Designs for Miniature Gallery, Hallmark Cards, Kansas City, 74. *Exhib:* Nelson Art Gallery, Kansas City, 70; Albrecht Art Mus, 72; Ft Smith Art Ctr, Ark, 72; Int Traveling Show Americana, Am Art by Mid-West Artists, 72; Richmond Mus, Va, 79. *Pos:* Free-lance artist, Hallmark Cards, Kansas City, 74. *Teaching:* Teacher, Kansas City Art Guild & Studio Delaware, Mo, 70-74; artist in residence, William Jewell Col, 73. *Awards:* First Publ Award, Fine Arts Discovery Mag, 70; First Prize, Kans State Fair, 54, Mo State Fair, 71 & 72 & Northern Va Community Col, 75. *Bibliog:* Donald Hoffmann (auth), Art in Mid-America, Kansas City Star, 5/69 & 5/74; Jean Trusty (auth), Art, Kansas City Squire Mag, 4/71; R C Seine (ed), Contemporary American Artists, La Rev Mod, Paris, 11/71. *Mem:* Alexandria Art League; Wash Watercolor Asn; Washington Womens Art Assoc. *Media:* Oil, Watercolor. *Dealer:* Atlantic Gallery 1055 Thomas Jefferson St NW Washington DC 20007; Art League 105 N Union St Alexandria Va. *Mailing Add:* 7501 Range Rd Alexandria VA 22306

KEENE, PAUL
PAINTER
b Philadelphia, Pa, Aug 24, 20. *Study:* Philadelphia Mus Sch & Univ Pa, 39-41; Tyler Sch Art, Temple Univ, 45-48; Acad Julien, Paris, 49-51; Whitney Fel, 52-54. *Work:* Pa Acad Fine Arts, Philadelphia; Philadelphia Mus; Howard Univ; Morgan State Col; Bowdoin Col. *Comn:* History of University (mural), Johnson C Smith Univ; medal for Am Negro Commemorative Soc, Philadelphia. *Exhib:* Pa Acad Fine Arts, 52-53 & 68-69; Lagos Mus, Nigeria, 61; Master Series, Carnegie Libr, Pittsburgh, 70; one-man show, Festac-Lagos, Nigeria, 79; Painting Show, Morgan State Univ, Baltimore, Md, 80; Alfred Deshong Mus, Widener Univ, 81. *Teaching:* Prof painting, Centre D'Art, Port-au-Prince, Haiti, 52-53; assoc prof drawing & painting, Philadelphia Col Art, 54-68, chmn basic art prog, 63-66; prof drawing & design, Bucks Co Community Col, Newton, 68- *Bibliog:* Briskin (auth), New talent art in America, Art in Am, 54; Lewis/Waddy (auth), Black artists on art, Contemp Crafts, 71. *Media:* Mixed. *Mailing Add:* c/o Bucks Co Community Col Swamp Rd Newton PA 18940

KEENER, ANNA ELIZABETH
PAINTER, PRINTMAKER
b Flagler, Colo, Oct 16, 1895. *Study:* Bethany Col (Kans), BFA & BA; Art Inst Chicago; Kansas City Art Inst; Univ NMex, MA; also graphics with George Miyasake & mural painting with James Pinto. *Work:* Rare Bk Sect, NMex State Libr; Mus NMex Fine Arts; Birger Sandzen Mem Gallery, Lindsborg, Kans; US Nat Monument, Los Alamos, NMex; Sul Ross State Univ, Alpine, Tex. *Comn:* Zuni Pottery Making (mural), McKinley Co Courthouse, Gallup, NMex; Baptistry, Bd Dirs, Baptist Church, Portales. *Exhib:* Southwestern Art Festival, Tucson, Ariz, 70; 47th Ann, Springville, Utah, 71; 5 State Exhib, Port Arthur, Tex, 71; Tex Fine Arts Ann, 72; Ex Patriots Exhib, Kansas City Art Inst, 73. *Teaching:* Supvr art, Ariz Pub Schs, Globe, formerly; instr art, Kansas City High Sch, formerly; head dept art, Eastern NMex Univ, formerly. *Awards:* Bronze Medal for Barn on the Hill, Kansas City Art Inst; Poorbough Press Award for Giraffes, 56; award for collagraph, Mus NMex Fine Art, 62. *Mem:* Artists Equity Asn. *Media:* Acrylic. *Mailing Add:* 312 Cadiz Rd Santa Fe NM 87501

KEENEY, ALLEN LLOYD
EDUCATOR, MUSEUM DIRECTOR
b Salt Lake City, Utah, July 19, 33. *Study:* Colo Inst Art; Univ Wyo, BA; studied design with Robert Russin. *Comn:* Three hist landscapes, Sweetwater Co Mus, Green River, Wyo, 70; Western design, Antler Hotel, Newcastle, Wyo, 60. *Exhib:* One-man shows, Wyo Artists's Asn, 60 & Community Fine Arts Ctr, 67. *Collections Arranged:* 256 original art works owned by Sch Dist Number One, Sweetwater Co, Wyo. *Pos:* Asst dir, Community Fine Arts Ctr, 66-69, dir, 70- *Teaching:* Instr art, Weston Co Pub Schs, 57-60; chmn dept art, Sch Dist Number One, Sweetwater Co, Wyo, 60- *Mem:* Wyo Art Educ Asn (vpres, 68-69, pres, 69-70); Nat Art Educ Asn; Colo & Wyo Mus Asn; Wyo Artist's Asn. *Media:* Oil; sculpture. *Collection:* North American art 1900-1950. *Mailing Add:* 400 C St Rock Springs WY 82901

KEHLMANN, ROBERT
GLASS ARTIST, CRITIC
b Brooklyn, NY, March 9, 42. *Study:* Antioch Col, Ohio, BA, 63; Univ Calif, Berkeley, MA, 66. *Work:* Corning Mus Glass, NY; Leigh Yawkey Woodson Art Mus, Wausau, Wis; Hessisches Landes Mus, WGer; Tucson Mus Art, Ariz; Hokkaido Mus Mod Art, Sapporo, Japan. *Exhib:* Americans in Glass, Leigh Yawkey Woodson Art Mus, Wausau Wis, 78 & 81; New Stained Glass, Mus Contemp Crafts, New York, 78; New Glass, Corning Mus Glass, NY, 79; International Directions in Glass Art, Art Gallery Western Australia, Perth, 82; Sculptural Glass, Tucson Mus Art, Ariz, 83. *Collections Arranged:* Current Trends in Glass (auth, catalog), Walnut Creek Civic Art Gallery, Calif, 80; Emerging Artists in Glass (auth, catalog), Calif Crafts Mus, Palo Alto, 81. *Pos:* Contributing ed, Glass Art Mag, Oakland, Calif, 75-76; ed, Glass Art Soc J, Berkeley Calif, 81- *Teaching:* Instr glass design, Calif Col Arts & Crafts, Oakland, 78-80; instr glass design, Pilchuck Glass Ctr, Stanwood, Wash, 78-80. *Awards:* Craftsman's Fel Grant, Nat Endowment Arts, 77; Art Critic's Fel Grant, Nat Endowment Arts, 79. *Bibliog:* Grace Glueck (auth), Art people, The New York Times, 2/10/78; Lindsay Stamm Shapiro (auth), American stained glass now, Craft Horizons, 2/78; Johannes Schreiter (auth), Die Glasbilder von Robert Kehlmann, Neues Glas, 3/81. *Mem:* Glass Art Soc (jour ed, 80-); Stained Glass Asn Am. *Media:* Glass. *Res:* Twentieth century stained glass. *Publ:* Auth, Duane Hanson's sculpture, Artweek, 77; auth, Schaffrath: Stained glass and mosaic, Craft Horizons, 2/78; auth, Stained glass in the USA today, Canada Crafts, 10-11/78; auth, Glasfenster der siebziger jahre, Kunst Und Kirche, Linz, Austria, 4/79. *Dealer:* William Sawyer Gallery 3045 Clay Street San Francisco CA 94115. *Mailing Add:* 2207 Rose St Berkeley CA 94709

KEISTER, STEVE (STEPHEN LEE)
SCULPTOR
b Lancaster, Pa, Aug 22, 49. *Study:* Tyler Sch Art, Philadelphia & Rome, BFA, 70, MFA, 72. *Work:* Whitney Mus Am Art; Mus Contemp Art, Chicago; Dallas Mus Fine Arts; Lannan Found, West Palm Beach, Fla. *Exhib:* New Work-New York, New Mus, 78; Eight Sculptors, Albright-Knox Gallery, Buffalo, 79; solo exhib, Options, Mus Contemp Art, Chicago, 80; Biennial, 81, Selected Painting & Sculpture Acquired Since 1978, 82 & Minimalism to Expressionism, 83, Whitney Mus Am Art; Beelden-Sculpture 1983, Rotterdam Arts Coun, Neth, 83; Language, Drama, Source & Vision, New Mus, New York, 83. *Bibliog:* Peggy Kutzen (auth), article, Arts Mag, 5/81; Prudence Carlson (auth), Otherworldly geometrics, Art in Am, 10/81; Jeanne Silverthorne (auth), article, Artforum, 1/83. *Media:* Plywood, Miscellaneous Media. *Dealer:* Blum Helman Gallery 20 W 57 St New York NY 10019. *Mailing Add:* 46 Laight St New York NY 10013

KEITH, EROS
ILLUSTRATOR, PAINTER
b Fulton, Mo, June 24, 42. *Study:* Art Inst Chicago; Denver Univ; Univ Chicago, BA & BFA. *Exhib:* Shepard Gallery, New York, 69; one-man show (paintings & drawings), K&F Studio, Evergreen, Colo. *Publ:* Auth & illusr, A Small Lot, 68, auth, The King's Falcon, 69 & auth & illusr, Rrra-ah, 69, Bradbury; auth & illusr, Nancy's Backyard, Harper & Row, 73; auth & illusr, The Biggest Noise, Doubleday, 78. *Mailing Add:* 105 W 73rd St New York NY 10023

KELDER, DIANE M
HISTORIAN, CRITIC
b New York, NY, May 23, 34. *Study:* Queens Col, AB, 55; Univ Chicago, MA, 57; Bryn Mawr Col, PhD, 66. *Collections Arranged:* Drawings by the Bibiena Family, Philadelphia Mus Art, 68 & Finch Col Mus, 68; Five Centuries of Stage Design, Finch Col Mus, 71. *Pos:* Asst cur prints & drawings, Philadelphia Mus Art, 66-67; ed, Art J, currently. *Teaching:* Instr art hist, Queens Col, 60- & Finch Col, 67-71; prof art hist, Col Staten Island, 71- *Awards:* Fanny Workman Fel, Am Asn Univ Women, 62-63; Jr Humanist Fel, Nat Endowment Humanities, 71; Ingram Merrill Found Award, 72. *Mem:* Int Art Critics Asn; Col Art Asn. *Interests:* Baroque stage design; late 18th century painting; graphic art from the 16th through the 20th centuries. *Publ:* Auth, Rembrandt, McGraw-Hill, 70; auth, The French Impressionists and Their Century, 70 & ed, Stuart Davis, 71, Praeger; contribr, Ferdinando Galli Bibiena's Architettura Civile, Blom, 71; The Great Book of French Impressionism, Abbeville, 80; and others. *Mailing Add:* c/o Col of Staten Island 130 Stuyvesant Pl Staten Island NY 10301

KELEMEN, PAL
HISTORIAN
b Budapest, Hungary, Apr 24, 1894; US citizen. *Study:* Univ Ariz, DHL; Univ Budapest; Univ Munich; Univ Paris; mus res in Budapest, Vienna, Florence, London, Madrid & Seville. *Pos:* Survey trips, US Dept State, Mex, Cent Am & Europe, 33-; mem comn for protection & salvage of artistic & hist monuments in war areas, World War II. *Teaching:* Lectr, Nat Gallery Art, Metrop Mus Art & other mus & univs; spec lect tour, US Dept State, Europe & the Near East. *Awards:* Comdr, Order of Merit, Ecuador. *Bibliog:* Pal Kelemen (auth), SMRC, Ariz State Mus, 81. *Mem:* Fel Royal Anthrop Inst; mem var sci socs in US, Latin Am & Europe. *Res:* Early Christian art; pre-Columbian and colonial art in Latin America. *Publ:* Auth, Ancient, Colonial Art of the Americas, Dutch, 62, Ger, 64, Fr, 65, Span, 67, Port, 69; auth, Art of the Americas, 69 & 70, Hungarian, 80; auth, Peruvian Colonial Painting, 71; contribr, Folk Baroque in Mexico, 74, Vanishing Art of the Americas, 77 & Stepchild of the Humanities, 79, Encycl Britannica, Stauffacher's World Art History & others. *Mailing Add:* Box 447 Norfolk CT 06058

KELLEHER, PATRICK JOSEPH
HISTORIAN, MUSEOLOGIST
b Colorado Springs, Colo, July 26, 17. *Study:* Colo Col, AB, 39; Princeton Univ, MFA, 42 & PhD, 47; Am Acad Rome, fel, 47-49; fine arts specialist off, Ger, 45-46. *Collections Arranged:* Art Mus, Princeton (new bldg), 66 & numerous spec exhibs, incl European & American Painting & Sculpture in Princeton Alumni Collections, 72. *Pos:* Chief cur art, Los Angeles Co Mus, 49; cur collections, Albright-Knox Art Gallery, 50-54; cur European art, Nelson Gallery-Atkins Mus, 54-59; dir, Art Mus, Princeton Univ, 60-73. *Teaching:* Lectr art hist, Univ Buffalo, 50-51; res prof art hist, Univ Mo, 56-59; prof art hist, Princeton Univ, 60-73. *Publ:* Auth, The holy crown of Hungary, Am Acad Rome, 50; auth, Expressionism in American art, Albright-Knox Art Gallery, 53; co-auth, The century of Mozart, Nelson Gallery, 56; auth, Living with Modern Sculpture, Princeton Univ Press, 82. *Mailing Add:* 176 Parkside Dr Princeton NJ 08540

KELLER, DEANE
EDUCATOR, PAINTER
b New Haven, Conn, Dec 14, 01. *Study:* Art Students League, with George Bridgman; Yale Univ Sch Fine Arts, with Eugene F Savage & E C Taylor; Am Acad Rome, 26. *Work:* Hq, US Post Off, Washington, DC; Portrait of Sen Robert Taft, Senate Reception Chamber, Capitol Bldg, Washington, DC; Conn Ct Errors, Hartford; Yale Univ, New Haven; New York Hosp, Cornell Univ. *Comn:* Two murals, Shriver Hall, Johns Hopkins Univ, Baltimore, Md, 57; mural (with Bauncel La Farge), Pub Libr, New Haven. *Exhib:* Portraits, Inc, New York, 60's; Yale Univ; Hartford, Conn; Harrisburg, Pa; plus others. *Pos:* Chief fine arts sect, Fifth Army, Italy, 43-46. *Teaching:* Prof art, Yale Univ Sch Art & Archit, 30-70; prof art, Paier Col Art. *Mem:* New Haven Paint & Clay Club (pres, 36-39). *Media:* Oil. *Dealer:* Portraits Inc 41 E 57th St New York NY 10022. *Mailing Add:* 18 Brookhaven Rd Hamden CT 06517

KELLER, FRANK S
PAINTER
b Minneapolis, Minn, Aug 31, 51. *Study:* Creighton Univ, Nebr, 69-70; Univ Minn, Minneapolis, BA, BFA, 74; Pratt Inst, MFA, 77. *Work:* Phillips Collection; Mus Art, Carnegie Inst, Pittsburgh; Mus Fine Arts, Houston; Edwin A Ulrich Mus Art, Wichita, Kans; Andrew Crispo Gallery, New York. *Exhib:* Minnesota Artists, Rochester Art Ctr, 72 & 74; Baltimore Mus Art, 75; solo exhibs, Andrew Crispo Gallery, New York, 77, 79 & 81; Ariz Nat Painting Exhib, Scottsdale Ctr Arts, 78; Art in Embassies, Dept State, Am Embassy, Bonn, WGer, 79-; American Works on Paper: 100 Years of American Art History Traveling Exhib, 83-85. *Awards:* Purchase Award, Baltimore Mus Art, 75. *Bibliog:* Ann Sargent Wooster (auth), article, Art News, 5/77; Peter Frank (auth), article, Village Voice, 1/2/78; Christa Lancaster (auth), Frank Keller: Tending the formal tradition, Arts Mag, 11/81. *Mem:* Visual Artists & Galleries Asn. *Dealer:* Andrew Crispo Gallery 41 E 57th St New York NY 10022. *Mailing Add:* 57 Thompson St 6A New York NY 10012

KELLEY, CHAPMAN
PAINTER, DEALER

b San Antonio, Tex, Aug 26, 32. *Study:* Hugo D Pohl Art Sch, San Antonio; Trinity Univ; Pa Acad Fine Arts, with Franklin Watkins, Hobson Pittman, Walter Steumpfig, Abraham Rattner, Morris Blackburn, Julius Bloch, Harry Rosin, Francis Speight & Roswell Weidner. *Work:* Mulvane Art Ctr, Topeka, Kans; Witte Mem Mus, San Antonio; Dallas Mus Fine Arts; Tex Instruments, Inc, Dallas; Colorado Springs Fine Arts Ctr. *Exhib:* Southwestern Art Exhib, Dallas Mus Fine Arts, circulated nationally by Am Fedn Art, 57; 157th Ann Am Painting & Sculpture, Pa Acad Fine Arts, Philadelphia, 62; Childe Hassam Fund Exhib, Am Acad Arts & Lett, New York, 63; Butler Inst Am Art Midyear Shows, 64 & 66-67; 11th Midwest Biennial, Joslyn Mus, Omaha, Nebr, 70; Artists Southeast & Tex Biennial, Delgado Mus, New Orleans, 71; and many other group & one-man shows. *Teaching:* Pvt instr, Dallas, 57-68; instr painting & drawing, Dallas Mus Fine Arts, 59-67; sem instr, Northern Ill Univ, 71. *Awards:* Top Purchase Award, Okla Art Ctr, 65; El Paso Mus Art Purchase Prize, Sun Carnival Nat, 69. *Bibliog:* Sold out art, Life Mag, 9/20/63; article, Burlington Mag, 64. *Media:* Oil, Pastel. *Specialty:* Contemporary, major twentieth century and impressionist works. *Collection:* Twentieth century and contemporary works. *Mailing Add:* 2526 Fairmount St Dallas TX 75201

KELLEY, DONALD CASTELL
GALLERY DIRECTOR, LIBRARIAN

b Boston, Mass. *Study:* Sch of Mus Fine Arts, Boston, dipl; Yale Univ, BFA & MFA. *Pos:* Art librn & gallery dir, Boston Atheneum, 68- *Interests:* Work of nineteenth century American contemporary artists and photographers. *Mailing Add:* Boston Atheneum 10 1/2 Beacon St Boston MA 02108

KELLEY, DONALD WILLIAM
PRINTMAKER, SCULPTOR

b Tulsa, Okla, July 20, 39. *Study:* Univ Tulsa, with Alexandre Hogue & Duayne Hatchett, BA, 62; Claremont Grad Sch, MFA, 66; Univ NMex with Garo Antreasian, 66; Tamarind Lithography Workshop, Los Angeles, 66-69. *Work:* Art Inst Chicago; Cincinnati Art Mus; Los Angeles Co Mus Art, Los Angeles; Mus Mod Art, New York; Pasadena Art Mus. *Exhib:* One-man shows, Not in New York Gallery, Cincinnati, 75, Antioch Col, 75 & Cincinnati Invitational Awards Exhib, Cincinnati Art Mus, 75; Alternative Landscape, Contemp Art Ctr, Cincinnati, 72; Environ Sculpture--Proposals for Sawyer Point Park, Contemp Arts Ctr, Cincinnati, Ohio, 77. *Teaching:* Assoc prof printmaking & sculpture, Univ Cincinnati, 69-75, chmn, currently; vis artist lithography, Antioch Col, 75. *Bibliog:* Jules Engel & Ivan Dryer (auth), Look of a lithographer (film), Tamarind Lithography Workshop, 69; Kristin L Spangenberg (auth), Cincinnati Invitational Awards Exhibition: Drawings and Prints, Midwest Art, 3/75. *Mem:* Cincinnati Graphic Arts Forum. *Media:* Lithography. *Mailing Add:* 3168 Pond Run Rd New Richmond OH 45157

KELLEY, RAMON
PAINTER

b Cheyenne, Wyo, Feb 12, 39. *Study:* Colo Inst Art. *Work:* Santa Fe Art Mus, NMex; Marietta Col, Ohio; Mus Native Am Cult, Spokane, Wash; Tex Tech Univ Mus, Lubbock; Charles & Emma Frye Mus Fine Art. *Exhib:* Ann Exhib, Am Watercolor Soc, 71-77; Mainstreams, Marietta, Ohio, 72, 75 & 76; Allied Artists Am, 72, 73 & 74; Nat Arts Club Pastel Exhib, 74; Pastel Soc Am, 75-79; and others. *Awards:* Artists & Dealers Award, Mus Native Am Cult, 79; Mem Award Portrait, Pastel Soc Am, 79; Best of Show Medal, Kalispell Art Show & Auction, 79; and others. *Mem:* Pastel Soc Am (juror, 78). Nat Arts Club; Am Watercolor Soc (nat juror); Allied Artists Am; Pastel Soc Am. *Media:* Oil, Watercolor. *Publ:* Contribr, Am Artist Mag, 3/69 & 12/72 & Southwest Art Mag, 11/73; contribr, Joe Singer's How to Paint Figures in Pastel, Watson-Guptill, 76; coauth, Ramon Kelley Paints Portraits & Figures, Watson-Guptill, 77. *Dealer:* Canyon Rd Art Gallery 710 Canyon Rd Santa Fe NM 87501. *Mailing Add:* 180 Franklin St Denver CO 80218

KELLOGG, MAURICE DALE
PAINTER, LECTURER

b Wellington, Kans, Dec 15, 19. *Study:* Univ Kans, AB; Harvard Univ, MA. *Work:* W H Over Dakota Mus, Vermilion, SDak; Southeast Arts & Sci Ctr, Pine Bluff, Ark; SArk Arts Mus, El Dorado; Secy of State, State Capitol, Little Rock; Dept Parks & Tourism, State Capitol, Little Rock. *Comn:* Paintings, comn by Mrs Jeanette Rockefeller, Little Rock, Ark, 69; First Nat Bank, Little Rock, 71; Mickey Rooney, Ft Lauderdale, Fla, 73; Winthrop Paul Rockefeller, Petit Jean, Ark, 74; Johnny Cash, 77 & Gregory Peck, 77; and others. *Exhib:* Mid-South Exhib, Memphis, 72; Shreveport Nat, La, 73; Delta Exhib, Little Rock, 74; one-man show, Univ Tenn, Memphis, 74; Univ Ark Purchase Invitational, Little Rock, 74. *Pos:* Assoc dir, Graphics & Design Div, Ginn & Co, Boston, 49-67. *Teaching:* Lectr painting, Univ Ark, Little Rock, 74-; instr painting, Southeast Ark Arts & Sci Ctr, 74- *Awards:* Best of Show Contemporary Painting, Ark Festival Arts, Ark Arts Ctr, Little Rock, 75; Senate Resolution of Commendation, 77; Gold Medal, Accademia Italia delle Arti e del Lavoro, 81; and others. *Mem:* Academician Accademia Italia delle Arti e del Lavoro. *Media:* Acrylic. *Dealer:* Konrad Toch Corp 1734 W Shady Grove Rd Irving TX 75060. *Mailing Add:* 5804 Scenic Dr Little Rock AR 72207

KELLY, ARLEEN P See Schloss, Arleen P

KELLY, ELLSWORTH
PAINTER, SCULPTOR

b Newburgh, NY, May 31, 23. *Study:* Pratt Inst, 41-42; Boston Mus Sch, 46-48; Ecole Des Beaux-Arts, Paris, 48-49. *Work:* Metrop Mus Art; Mus Mod Art; Guggenheim Mus; Whitney Mus Am Art, New York; Tate Gallery, London. *Comn:* Sculpture, Penn Ctr Transp Bldg Lobby, Philadelphia, 56; wall sculpture, comn by Philip Johnson, New York World's Fair, New York Pavilion, 64; mural, UNESCO, Paris, 69; mural, Central Trust Co, Cincinnati, Ohio, 79; sculpture, Friends of the Park, Chicago, Ill, 81. *Exhib:* 16 Americans, 59 & Art of the Real, 68, Mus Mod Art, New York; Paintings, Sculpture & Drawings by Ellsworth Kelly, Washington Gallery Mod Art, 63; Documenta III, IV & VI, Kassel, Ger, 64, 68 & 77; Venice Biennale Int Art, 66; New York Painting & Sculpture, 1940-1970, Metrop Mus Art, 69; Paintings & Sculpture, Metrop Mus Art, New York, 79; Recent Painting & Sculpture, Stedelijk Mus, Amsterdam, 79-80; retrospective, Mus Mod Art, New York, 73. *Awards:* Carnegie Int Prizes, 62 & 64; Brandeis Creative Arts Award, 63; Tokyo Int Educ Ministry Award, 63. *Bibliog:* Eugene Goossen (auth), Derriere le miroir, Paris, Maeght Ed, 58 & (auth), Ellsworth Kelly, Mus of Mod Art, New York, 73; Diane Waldman (auth), Ellsworth Kelly drawings, collages, prints, New York Graphic Soc, 71; John Coplans (auth), Ellsworth Kelly, Abrams, 72. *Mem:* Nat Inst Arts & Lett. *Mailing Add:* RD PO Box 170B Chatham NY 12037

KELLY, ISAAC PERRY
PHOTOGRAPHER, EDUCATOR

b Orlando, Fla, June 2, 25. *Study:* Univ Hawaii; Univ Fla, BD, 53, MEd, 55; Peabody Col, EdD, 65. *Comn:* Tapestry (woven), comn by Mrs Ed Buerk, Delray Beach, Fla, 75; tapestry (woven), comn by Dr William Chovan, Cullowhee, NC, 75. *Pos:* State supvr art, Dept Pub Instr, Raleigh, NC, 63-68; bd dirs, Campbell Folk Sch. *Teaching:* Assoc prof art educ & weaving & dir exhib, Western Carolina Univ, 68- *Mem:* Assoc Artists NC (pres, 73-75); NC Art Educ Asn (pres, 77-79); Handweavers Guild Am; Int Soc Educ Arts; NC Crafts Asn; and others. *Media:* Weaving, Pottery. *Publ:* Auth, Art Education in North Carolina, 65. *Mailing Add:* Box 755 Cullowhee NC 28723

KELLY, JAMES
PAINTER

b Philadelphia, Pa, Dec 19, 13. *Study:* Pa Acad Fine Arts, Philadelphia; Barnes Found, Merion, Pa; Calif Sch Fine Arts, San Francisco. *Work:* San Francisco Mus Art; Mus Mod Art, New York; Los Angeles Mus Art; Univ Mass, Boston; Westinghouse Corp, Salem, NC & Pittsburgh, Pa. *Exhib:* San Francisco Mus Art Painting Ann, 55-58; Minneapolis Inst Art, Minn, 57; Los Angeles Co Mus Art, 68; Huntsville Mus of Art, Ala, 77; one-man shows, Albright Col, Reading, Pa, 66, Long Island Univ, Brooklyn, NY, 68, East Hampton Gallery, New York, NY, 69 & Westbeth Galleries, New York, 71-72; and others. *Teaching:* Lectr painting, Univ Calif, Berkeley, summer 56. *Awards:* Ford Found grant lithography, 63; Nat Endowment Arts grant painting, 77-78. *Mailing Add:* 463 West St New York NY 10014

KELLY, LEE
SCULPTOR

b McCall, Idaho, May 24, 32. *Study:* Mus Art Sch, Portland, Ore. *Work:* Univ Houston; Portland Art Mus; Univ Ore Mus, Eugene. *Comn:* Welded steel play piece, Unthanr Park, Portland, 68; welded steel fountain, Milwaukee Ore Libr, 69; welded stainless steel wall piece, Pac Northwest Bell, Portland, 71; welded stainless steel water piece, Univ Houston, 72; welded steel gateway, Candlestick Park, San Francisco, 72. *Exhib:* Ore Centennial Invitational, 60; Denver Mus Ann Invitational, 61 & 71; Pacific Profile, Pasadena Mus, Calif, 62; West Coast Now, Portland Art Mus, 68. *Teaching:* Instr art, Mt Angel Col, 68-71; prof art, Reed Col, 76-80. *Awards:* Seattle Art Mus Purchase Award, 60-61; Ford Found Purchase Award, 63; Art Advocates Proj Award, 70. *Media:* Metal. *Dealer:* Foster/White Gallery Seattle WA. *Mailing Add:* 13099 S Warnock Rd Oregon City OR 97045

KELLY, LEON
PAINTER

b Perpignan, France, Oct 21, 01; US citizen. *Study:* Pa Acad Fine Arts, traveling scholar, 24; Acad Grande Chaumiere, Paris; also with Jean Auguste Adolphe, Alexandre Portinoff, Arthur Carles & Earl Horter. *Work:* Mus Mod Art, Whitney Mus Am Art & Metrop Mus Art, New York; Wadsworth Atheneum, Conn; Tel Aviv Mus, Israel; and many others. *Exhib:* Retrospective 1920-65, Int Gallery, Baltimore, Md, 65; Pa Acad Fine Arts, 57; Long Beach Found, NJ, 68; Richard Feigen Gallery, Chicago, 68 & 70; Newark Mus, NJ, 69; and many other one-man & group shows. *Teaching:* Instr, Pa Acad Fine Arts & Brooklyn Mus Sch, formerly. *Awards:* William & Nora Copley Award, 58. *Media:* Oil. *Mailing Add:* c/o Washburn Gallery 42 E 57th St New York NY 10022

KELLY, MARY
EDUCATOR

b Albert Lea, Minn, June 7, 41. *Study:* Col St Teresa, Minn, BA, 63; Pius XII Inst, Florence, Italy, MA, 65; St Martins Sch Art, London, 68-70. *Work:* Zurich Mus, Switz; Australian Nat Gallery, Canberra; Arts Coun Gr Brit; Victoria & Albert Mus. *Exhib:* Solo exhib, Mus Mod Art, Oxford, England, 77; Un Certain Art Anglais, Mus Mod Art, Paris, 79; Europa 79, Hetzler, Muller & Schurr, Stuttgart, Ger, 79; Fourth Biennale Sydney, Gallery New South Wales, Australia, 82; Difference, Grey Art Gallery, New York, 84; Yale Ctr Brit Art, New Haven, Conn, 84. *Teaching:* Lectr fine art, Goldsmiths Col, London Univ, England, 78- *Awards:* Visual Arts Award, Arts Coun Gr Brit, 77; Lina Garnade Mem Found Award, West Surrey Col Art & Design, 78; Visual Arts Award, Greater London Arts Asn, 80. *Bibliog:* R Parker & G Pollock (auths), Old Mistresses, Routledge & Kegan Paul, 81; M Iverson (auth), Reading Mary Kelly's post-partum document Discourse, Berkeley J Theoretical Studies, winter 81; J Isaak (auth), Our mother tongue, Vanguard, 4/11/82. *Mem:* Artists Union Gr Brit. *Publ:* Auth, On femininity, Control

Mag, No 11, 79; auth, Sexual politics, In: Art & Politics, Winchester Sch Art Press, 80; auth, Re-viewing modernist criticism, Screen, Vol 22, No 23, 81; coauth, Feminist practice in art, Studio Int, Vol 195, No 991, 81; auth, Post-Partum Document, Routledge & Kegan Paul, 83. *Mailing Add:* 105 Balfour Rd London N5 2HE England United Kingdom

KELLY, WILLIAM JOSEPH
DRAFTSMAN, PAINTER
b Buffalo, NY, May 4, 43. *Study:* Philadelphia Col Art, BFA; Prahran Col Adv Educ; Nat Gallery Sch, Australia, MA. *Work:* Victorian Trades Hall Council, Mebourne, Australia; Lehigh Univ; Accademia de Belle Art, Perugia, Italy; Australian Nat Gallery, Canberra; Victorian Arts Ctr; and many others. *Exhib:* Ann Exhib, Albright-Knox Art Gallery, Buffalo, 63; one-man shows, Prince St Gallery, New York, 74, Accad de Belle Arti, Perugia, Italy, 75 & William Kelly: Realism in Transition, Butler Inst Am Art, 82; Tapestry & the Australian Painter, Nat Gallery, Melbourne, 79; Australian Printmaking, Brown Univ, 80; Invitational, New York Studio Sch Galleries, 80; and others in Canada, Sweden, Denmark & Gr Brit. *Pos:* Dean sch art, Victorian Col Arts, Melbourne, 75- *Awards:* S M Egnal Painting Award, Philadelphia Col of Art, 68; Fulbright Grant, 68-69; Fulbright Fel, 69-70; British Council Grant, 77. *Bibliog:* Robert Godfrey (auth), Towards Human Intent, Westminster Col, 80; Walter Brayman & Myron Brody (auths), Conversation with William Kelly, Forum Mag, 3/80; and others; Dr Louis Zona (auth), William Kelly: Realism in Transition, Butler Inst Am Art; and others. *Media:* Acrylic; Charcoal. *Publ:* Auth, Two Who Responded, Art & Artists, London, 4/76; auth, Robert Godfrey, Arts Mag, New York, 3/80; auth, Drawing Now, Artist's Choice Mus Newslett, New York, 4/80; auth, Photomontage of a painting, Leonardo, winter 80; auth, Imaged art: The subjectified aspect in the age of new figuration, Artists Choice Mus J, New York, fall 82. *Mailing Add:* PO Box 368 Prahran (Melbourne) 3004 Australia

KELPE, PAUL
PAINTER
b Minden, Ger, 1902; US citizen. *Study:* Univ Chicago, MA & PhD. *Work:* Whitney Mus Am Art & Mus Mod Art, New York; Nat Collection Fine Arts, Washington, DC; Univ NMex Art Mus; Kresge Art Ctr, Mich State Univ; Detroit Inst Arts; and others. *Exhib:* Geometric Abstraction of 1930s, Zabriskie Gallery, New York, 72; The Emergence of Modernism in Illinois 1914-1940, Ill State Mus, Springfield, 76; Am Abstract Artists, Univ NMex Art Mus, Albuquerque, 77; one-man show, Paul Kelpe: American Abstract Artist, Long Beach Mus Art, Calif, 80; and many others. *Bibliog:* Jacobson (auth), Art of Today, Stein Publ, 33; M Candler Cheney (auth), Modern Art in America, McGraw, 39; American abstract artists, Art J, fall 77. *Mem:* Am Abstr Artists. *Media:* Oil, Watercolor. *Mailing Add:* 705 Texas Ave Austin TX 78705

KELSEY, MURIEL CHAMBERLIN
SCULPTOR
b Milford, NH. *Study:* Univ NH, BS, 19; Univ Vt, 21; Teachers Col, Columbia Univ, 33; New Sch Social Res, 34; Sculpture Ctr New York, with Dorothea Denslow. *Comn:* Dancing Pickaninny (bronze statuette), Brookgreen Gardens Mus, SC, 37; plus many others in pvt comns. *Exhib:* Sculpture Ctr New York, 34-; Audubon Artists, New York, 58-62; Nat Acad Design, New York, 59-62; Harmon Gallery, Naples, Fla, 64-; 3rd Sculpture Int, Fairmount Park Art Asn, Philadelphia. *Teaching:* Asst zool lab, Univ NH, 20; asst zool lab, Univ Vt, 21. *Awards:* Sarasota Festival Arts, 53; Art League Manatee Co, 59; First Prize, Longboat Key Art Ctr, 65. *Mem:* Sculpture Ctr New York. *Media:* Stone. *Mailing Add:* c/o Oehischlaeger Galleries 107 E Oak St Chicago IL 60611

KEMBLE, RICHARD
PRINTMAKER, SCULPTOR
b Erie, Pa, Nov 7, 32. *Study:* Trenton State Col, NJ, BA; Pratt Graphics Art Ctr, study with Carol Summers. *Work:* Newark Mus, NJ; NJ State Mus, Trenton; Kresge Art Ctr, Mich State Univ; Allentown Art Mus, Pa; Firestone Libr, Princeton Univ; and others. *Comn:* Sculpture, Mercer Hosp, Trenton, NJ; altarpiece & vestments, St Andrews Church, Yardley, Pa, 72; cake, Mus Contemp Crafts, New York, 73; Circle F Industry, Trenton, 73; sculpture, Gloucester Co Col, NJ, 75. *Exhib:* Albright Knox Art Gallery, Buffalo; Pratt Graphics Ctr, New York; Exposicao de Cinco Gravados Contempores Americanos, Brazil, 73; Pratt on Paper, Phoenix Gallery, New York, 75; Suzuki Gallery, New York, 77-78; Sornbol Gallery, Guatamala City, 79; and others. *Teaching:* Instr printmaking, Pratt Inst, 67-78, Long Beach Island Found Arts & Sci, Loveladies, NJ, 73; artist in residence, North Country Sch, 73 & NJ State Coun Arts, 74-75. *Awards:* Purchase Award, NJ State Mus, 70; Printmaker's Fel, Nat Endowment Arts, 74-75; NJ State Coun Arts Grant, 78. *Bibliog:* Mary Midura (auth), Renaissance man leads the good life, Trentonian, 12/71; Burton Wasserman (auth), Kemble's woodcuts, Camden Courier Post, 10/73; Experimente mit dem Druckstock, Frankfurt Allgemeine Zeitung, Ger, 76. *Mem:* Pratt Graphic Arts Ctr; Soc Am Graphic Artists; Am Color Print Soc. *Dealer:* Suzuki Gallery 38 E 57th St New York NY 10022; Int Print Soc New Hope PA 18938. *Mailing Add:* c/o Forager House Studio Box 82 Washington Crossing PA 18977

KEMENYFFY, STEVEN
CERAMIST, EDUCATOR
b Budapest, Hungary, Aug 18, 43; US citizen. *Study:* Augustana Col, Rock Island, Ill, BA, 65; Univ Iowa, Iowa City, MA, 66, MFA, 67. *Work:* Mus Contemp Crafts, New York; State Univ NY, Geneseo; Butler Inst Am Art, Youngstown, Ohio; Blount Collection, Montgomery, Ala; Erie Art Mus, Pa. *Comn:* Ceramic wall murals (with Susan Kemenyffy), 41st Int Eucharistic

Cong Exhib Liturgical Arts, Philadelphia, Pa, 76 & Fairtree Gallery, 76. *Exhib:* Int Pottery Competition, Nagoya, Japan, 73; This Plastic Earth, John Michael Kohler Art Ctr, Sheboygan, Wis, 73; Baroque 74, Mus of Contemp Crafts, 74; Ceramic Invitational, Philadelphia Mus of Art, 77 & Pratt Sch of Art, 77; National Clay Invitational, Univ Hartford, Conn, 81; and others. *Teaching:* Prof ceramics, Edinboro State Col, Pa, 69-; lecturer at numerous universities and art associations. *Awards:* Cash Ceramic Award, Cleveland May Show, Cleveland Mus Art, 72; Nat Endowment Arts Grant, 77; Erie Spring Show Award, Pa, 83. *Mem:* Nat Coun Educ Ceramic Arts; Pittsburgh Craftsman Guild; Pa Guild Craftsmen. *Media:* Clay. *Dealer:* Contemp Artisans San Francisco CA; Mindscape Chicago IL. *Mailing Add:* 4570 Old State Rd McKean PA 16426

KEMENYFFY, SUSAN B HALE
CERAMIST
b Springfield, Mass, Oct 4, 41. *Study:* Syracuse Univ, New York, BFA, 63, study with Robert Marks; Univ Iowa, Iowa City, MA, 66, study with Mauricio Lasansky, MFA(with hons), 67. *Work:* Butler Inst Am Art, Youngstown; Chrysler Art Mus, Provincetown, Mass; Marietta Col, Ohio; Blount Collection, Montgomery, Ala; Erie Art Mus, Pa. *Comn:* Ceramic wall murals (with Steven Kemenyffy), 41st Int Eucharist Cong Exhib Liturgical Arts, Philadelphia, 76; Centennial Invitational, Fairtree Gallery, New York, 76; Lincoln Nat Life Ins Co, Ft Wayne, Ind, 79; Anshe Hesed Temple, Erie, 79. *Exhib:* The Am Hand, Raku Exhib, Washington, DC, 78; Ceramics Invitational, Pratt Inst, Brooklyn, 78; Westwood Clay Nat, Otis Art Inst, Los Angeles, 80; A Woman's Place, Sheboygan, Wis, 81; Nat Clay Invitational, Univ Hartford, Conn, 81; and others. *Teaching:* Instr, Vancouver Sch Art, BC, Can, 78 & Haystack Mountain Sch Crafts, Deer Isle Maine, 80; lecturer at numerous universities and art associations, 78- *Awards:* Nat Endowment Arts Grant, 77; Assoc Artist's Pittsburgh Award, Carnegie-Mellon Mus, 81 & 83; Ann Ceramic & Small Sculpture Show Award, Butler Mus Art, Youngstown, Ohio, 82. *Dealer:* Contemp Artisans San Francisco CA; Rodell/Retreat Los Angeles CA. *Mailing Add:* 4570 Old State Rd McKean PA 16426

KEMP, PAUL ZANE
PAINTER
b Apache Creek, NMex, Nov 6, 28. *Study:* NMex Highlands Univ, BA, 50, MA, 54; Cranbrook Acad Art, MFA, 60. *Exhib:* Third Ann Prints, Drawings & Crafts, Ark Arts Ctr, Little Rock, 69; Am Graphics 69, Col of the Pac, 69; Nat Graphic Arts & Drawing Show, Wichita Art Asn, Kans, 69; Northwest Printmaker's Int, Seattle, 69; Tex Fine Arts Asn Ann Citation Show, Austin, 69 & 70. *Teaching:* Asst prof art, Baylor Univ, 61-64, assoc prof, 64-69, prof, 69- *Awards:* Jurors Choice, Tex Fine Arts Asn Citation Show, 69 & 70; Purchase Entry, Ark Art Ctr, 69; Cash Award, 8th Baytown Ann, 74. *Mem:* Tex Designer-Craftsmen; Am Asn Univ Prog; Am Crafts Coun. *Publ:* Contribr & illusr, Tex Trends Art Educ, spring 69. *Mailing Add:* Dept of Art Baylor Univ Waco TX 76706

KEMPER, JOHN GARNER
PAINTER, GRAPHIC ARTIST
b Muncie, Ind, June 3, 09. *Study:* Ohio State Univ, BFA; Columbia Univ, MA; Chicago Acad Fine Arts. *Exhib:* Ann Exhibs Mich Artists, 44 & 46 & Relig Christmas Card Competition, 55, Detroit Inst Arts; 11th Ann Yr Show, Butler Inst Am Art, Youngstown, Ohio, 46; Ogunquit Art Ctr, Maine, 58-62; retrospective, Gallery II, Western Mich Univ, 82. *Pos:* Designer, Ohio Wax Paper Co, 34-36; designer, Dell Publ Co, 36-41; graphic designer, Western Mich Univ, 70-77. *Teaching:* Prof art, Western Mich Univ, 42-70, prof emer, 70- *Awards:* Awards, for Three Houses (serigraph), Friends Am Art, Grand Rapids, 46 & The Experiment Station (oil), Ohio Valley Oil & Water Show, 54; Report of Pres, Am Col Pub Rel Asn, 69. *Bibliog:* Kemper donates art collection to WMU, Western Herald, 3/22/82; Kemper designs live on at Western, Westerner, 6/83. *Media:* Graphic Design, Oil. *Publ:* Illusr, var articles and covers, Design Mag, 31-33; auth & illusr, A portable marionette stage, Indust Arts & Vocational Educ Mag, 43; auth & illusr, Marionettes, Sch Arts Mag, 46; co-auth, Art consciousness comes to Kalamazoo, Design Mag, 47. *Mailing Add:* 605 W Lovell St Kalamazoo MI 49007

KEMPNER, HELEN HILL
COLLECTOR, PATRON
b Houston, Tex, Jan 30, 38. *Pos:* Bd trustees, Contemp Arts Mus, Houston, 77-, vpres, 77-78, secy, 78-79, pres, 79- *Collection:* Contemporary paintings and sculpture; primitive, mostly African art. *Mailing Add:* 3811 Del Monte Dr Houston TX 77019

KEMPTON, GRETA
PAINTER
b Vienna, Austria, Mar 22, 03. *Study:* Nat Acad Design; Art Students League. *Work:* The White House, The Pentagon, US Treas Dept, US Supreme Court, Nat Portrait Gallery, Apostolic Delegation & Georgetown Univ, Washington, DC; and many other mus & pvt collections in US & abroad. *Comn:* Official portraits of President & Mrs Truman, White House. *Exhib:* One-woman shows, Corcoran Gallery Art, Washington, DC, Canton Art Inst, Ohio, Col Wooster, Ohio, Art Asn Harrisburg, Pa, Akron Art League, Ohio, Circle Gallery, Cleveland, Ohio & Adelphi Univ; and many others. *Mem:* Fel Royal Soc Arts; life mem Corcoran Gallery; Salmagundi Club; Truman Mus. *Mailing Add:* 14 E 75th St New York NY 10021

KENDA, JUANITA ECHEVERRIA
PAINTER, WRITER
b Tarentum, Pa, Nov 12, 23. *Study:* Stephens Col; Art Students League; Temple Univ, BFA; Univ Hawaii; also with Jon Corbino, Sam Hershey, Boris

Blai, Raphael Sabatini, Jean Charlot, George Bridgman & others. *Comn:* Murals, Straub Clinic & Children's Hosp, Honolulu. *Exhib:* Honolulu Painters & Sculptors, 60 & 61; Moorestown Friends Sch, 61; Univ Hawaii, 65; Galeria Santiago, San Juan, PR, 67; Downtown Gallery, 79; and many others. *Collections Arranged:* Art of Hawaii Children, circulated by Smithsonian Inst, 60-64. *Pos:* chmn sch art exhib, Honolulu Acad Arts, 50-, head creative art sect, 49-63; state prog spec, State Dept Educ, Honolulu, 63-64; community relations officer, East-West Ctr, 68-70; pres, Downtown Gallery Ltd, 69-82. *Teaching:* Instr workshop, Hawaii Summer Sch, 51; instr, Univ Hawaii Sch Educ, 65-66. *Awards:* Hon Consul of Mex in Hawaii. *Mem:* Hawaii Painters & Sculptors League; Asn Art Mus; Pac Art Asn; Nat Art Educ Asn; Int Comt Mus; and others. *Publ:* Auth & illusr, Art and art education in Hawaii & Art guide for Hawaii, Sch Arts Mag; auth & illustr, Curriculum outline--elementary art and curriculum outline--secondary art, Dept Educ, State of Hawaii; contribr to Paradise of the Pacific; auth, Art guide for pre-school and kindergarten, San Diego Schs, Calif, 71; and others. *Mailing Add:* 3708 Lurline Dr Honolulu HI 96816

KENDALL, THOMAS LYLE
CERAMIST, EDUCATOR
b St Louis, Mo, Apr 30, 49. *Study:* Ill State Univ, BS, 71, MS, 73. *Work:* Ill State Univ, Normal; Kalamazoo Inst Arts, Mich; Mich Arts Coun, Lansing. *Exhib:* Columbus Mus Art, Ohio, 75 & 79; Marietta Col, Ohio, 78; Raku V-Nat, Peters Valley, NJ, 79; solo exhib, Craft Alliance Gallery, St Louis, Mo, 81; Mich Ceramics, 83; and others. *Collections Arranged:* Contemporary Ceramics: The Artist's Viewpoint (auth, catalog), 77. *Teaching:* Chmn, Dept Ceramics, Kalamazoo Inst Arts, Mich, 73-81. *Awards:* First Place, Battle Creek Craft Biennial, 79; Purchase Award, Kalamazoo Art Competition, 83; Cash Award, Mich Ceramics, 83. *Mem:* Nat Conf Educ Ceramic Arts; Am Crafts Coun; Kalamazoo Area Ceramists Asn. *Publ:* Auth, Computerized glass calculation, Ceramics Monthly, 12/83. *Mailing Add:* 10936 Three Mile Rd Plainwell MI 49080

KENNEDY, GENE (EUGENE MURRAY)
PHOTOGRAPHER, EDUCATOR
b San Diego, Calif, Mar 13, 46. *Study:* San Diego State Univ, BA, 69, MA, 76. *Work:* Mus Mod Art, New York; Central Washington Univ; San Diego Natural Hist Mus. *Exhib:* One-man shows, San Diego Natural Hist Mus, 83 & Moore Col Art, 83; Central Washington Univ, Ellensburg, 83; San Francisco Camerawork, 83; Moore Col Art, 83; and others. *Collections Arranged:* Robert Bechtle: Reference and Realism in Four Modes, 78, Fletcher Benton Sculpture, 79 & Helen Levitt: Color Photographs, 80, Tom Holland: Works from 1969-1979, 80, Manuel Neri: Twenty Years, 81 & Helen Shirk: Metalwork, 81, Grossmont Col Gallery, El Cajon, Calif. *Pos:* Dir, Art Gallery Grossmont Col, 73-81. *Teaching:* Instr photog, San Diego State Univ, 70-73; Grossmont Col, El Cajon, Calif, 72-, Univ Calif, San Diego, 82-83, Maine Photographic Workshops, 82. *Awards:* Award of Excellence, Potlatch Corp, 79; Special Award of Excellence, Moore Col Art, 83. *Mem:* Soc Photographic Educ. *Publ:* Ed, Gerry Winogrand, 76, ed & illusr, Carol Shaw-Sutton: Crossing Over, 78, er & illusr, Viewpoint: Ceramics 1978, 78, ed & illusr, Viewpoint: Ceramics 1979, 79 & ed, Helen Levitt: Color Photographs, 80, Grossmont Col Pub. *Dealer:* The Photographic Gallery 7468 Girard Ave La Jolla CA 92037; Ledel Gallery 168 Mercer St New York NY 10012. *Mailing Add:* 8997 Moisan Way La Mesa CA 92065

KENNEDY, J WILLIAM
PAINTER
b Cincinnati, Ohio, Aug 17, 03. *Study:* Art Acad Cincinnati; Carnegie Inst Technol, AB; Univ Ill, MFA. *Work:* Portraits, Ind Univ, Bloomington & Univ Ill, Champaign; A E Staley Co, Decatur, Ill; Withrow High Sch, Cincinnati. *Comn:* Portraits, Pres Herman B Wells, 62, VPres Joseph Franklin, 63 & Dean Edmundson, 64, Ind Univ, Bloomington & Dean Carl Brandley, 67 & Col Leslie A Bryan, 69, Univ Ill, Champaign. *Exhib:* 1st, 2nd & 3rd Nat Exhibs, Rockefeller Ctr, New York; San Francisco World's Fair; Corcoran Biennial; two Pa Acad Fine Arts Ann; Richmond Biennial, Va. *Teaching:* Prof art, Univ Ill, Champaign, 26-70. *Awards:* Award of Merit, Fla Gulf Coast Art Ctr, 72; hon mention, Milwaukee Art Gallery; First Prize in painting, Decatur Art Ctr. *Mem:* Provincetown Art Asn; Fla Gulf Coast Art Ctr. *Media:* Vinyl. *Dealer:* Galerie Macler Sarasota FL 33578. *Mailing Add:* 1414 Monte Carlo Dr Clearwater FL 33516

KENNEDY, JAMES EDWARD
PAINTER, SCULPTOR
b Jackson, Miss, Sept 30, 33. *Study:* Ala State Univ, BS; Ind Univ, MAT(painting); Spring Hill Col. *Work:* Johnson Publ Co Collection, Chicago. *Exhib:* Atlanta Univ Nat Exhib, 60-64; Eastern Shore Art Gallery, 67; Birmingham, Ala Festival Arts Centennial Exhib, 72; Ala State Univ, 72; Univ WFla, 73. *Teaching:* Prof art hist & painting, Univ S Ala, Mobile, 68-, chmn dept art, currently; guest instr Afro-Am art, Morehead State Univ, Minn, summer 72. *Awards:* Afro-Am Art Slide Grant, 69 & Ethnic-Am Minority Art Slide Libr Grant, 71, Samuel H Kress Found. *Bibliog:* Afro-American Artists, Boston Pub Libr, 73. *Mem:* Nat Conf Artists; Col Art Asn Am. *Publ:* Coauth, An Afro-American Slide Project, Art J, 70-71 & An Afro-American Art and Artist's Finders Index, Am Revolution Bicentennial Comn, Washington, DC, 73. *Mailing Add:* 2073 Tucker St Mobile AL 36617

KENNEY, ESTELLE KOVAL
ART THERAPIST, PAINTER
b Chicago, Ill, Feb 15, 28. *Study:* Sch Art Inst Chicago, with Joshua Kind & Park Chambers, BFA, 76, MFA, 78; registered art therapist, ATR; Chicago Inst Psychoanalysis, TEP grad, 78; Loyola Univ Chicago, 82- *Work:* Ill State

Mus, Springfield; Union League Club Chicago. *Exhib:* The Chicago Connection, traveling, 76-77; Contemp Issues--Works on Paper by Women, Woman's Bldg, Los Angeles, plus others, 77-78; solo show, Renaissance Soc, Bergman Gallery, Univ Chicago, 80; Navy Pier, Chicago, 80; Artists Urban Gateways, 81; and others. *Pos:* Art therapist, Grove Sch Handicapped, Lake Forest, Ill, 72-77, New Triar E & C, Spec Educ, Winnetka, Ill, 77-78, Cove Sch Learning Disabled, Evanston, Ill, 79-81 & North Shore Inst Therapy through Arts, Winnetka, Ill, 79-81; contrib ed, Format Mag, 78- *Teaching:* Art therapy lectr, Univ Ill Circle Campus, Chicago, 77 & Nat Col Educ, Evanston, Ill, 77; dir art therapy prog, Loyola Univ Chicago, 81- *Awards:* First Purchase Prize, Union League Club of Chicago, 74 & Ill State Mus, Springfield, 75. *Mem:* Ill Art Educ Asn; Nat Art Educ Asn; Am Art Therapy Asn; Ill Art Therapy Asn (pres). *Media:* Enamel, Watercolor. *Publ:* Auth, Joshua Kind: Naive painting in Illinois, Format Mag. *Dealer:* Sonia Zaks Gallery 620 North Michigan Ave Chicago IL 60611. *Mailing Add:* 3830 North Clark St Chicago IL 60613

KENOJUAK (ASHEVAK)
PRINTMAKER, SCULPTOR
b Ikerasak, Baffin Island, NT, Can, Dec 25, 33. *Work:* Nat Gallery Can, Ottawa, Ont; Mus Man, Ottawa; Toronto Dominion Bank, Ont. *Comn:* Metal plaque, Alcan Can, 64; mural, Expo 67, Montreal, Expo 70, Osaka, Japan. *Awards:* Order of Can, Govt Can. *Mem:* Royal Can Acad of Arts. *Media:* Lithography, Engraving; Stonecut. *Publ:* Auth, Kenojuak, Nat Film Bd, 61. *Dealer:* West Baffin Eskimo Coop Ltd Cape Dorset NT X0A 0C0 Can. *Mailing Add:* Cape Dorset NT X0A 0C0 Canada

KENT, H LATHAM
GALLERY DIRECTOR, PAINTER
b Mass, June 20, 30. *Study:* Vesper George Sch Art, Boston, Mass; study with Artie McKenzie, Fla. *Exhib:* Beaux Arts, Lowe Art Gallery, Miami, Fla; Artists Unlimited Gallery, Key West, Fla; Coral Gables Art Gallery, Coral Gables, Fla; Int Boat Show Art Exhibs, Miami Beach, Fla; Gingerbread Sq Gallery, Key West, Fla; and others. *Pos:* Artist, Steve Hannagan, New York 51-54 & Bronzini of New York, 54-57; owner, Dodge House Art Gallery, Chatham, Mass, 68- *Mem:* Copley Soc, Boston, Mass; Soc Marine Painters, Fla; Am Artists Prof League, SFla (pres, 78-83). *Media:* Oil. *Mailing Add:* 5800 SW 51st St Miami FL 33155

KENT, JACK
ILLUSTRATOR
b Burlington, Iowa, Mar 10, 20. *Work:* Kerlan Collection, Univ of Minn. *Exhib:* Children's Book Art, Contemp Arts Mus, Houston, Tex, 75; Original Children's Book Illustration, Master Eagle Gallery, New York, 81-82. *Pos:* Free-lance cartoonist for various mag, 34-50; comic strip artist for King Aroo, 50-65. *Awards:* Top Honor Book, 22nd Ann Exhib, Chicago Book Clinic, 71; one of the New York Times Outstanding Picture Bks of the Yr, 76; Tex Inst Letters Award, 83. *Mem:* Nat Cartoonist Soc; Am Inst Graphic Arts; Author's Guild; Author's League Am. *Media:* Ink, Watercolor. *Publ:* Over 60 children's books, 68- *Mailing Add:* 103 W Johnson St San Antonio TX 78204

KENYON, COLLEEN FRANCES
PHOTOGRAPHER, ADMINISTRATOR
b Dunkirk, NY, Aug 6, 51. *Study:* Skidmore Col, Saratoga Springs, NY, BS, 73; Ind Univ, Bloomington, with Henry Holmes Smith in photog, MFA, 76. *Work:* Mus Mod Art, New York; Int Mus Photog, George Eastman House, Rochester, NY; Ind Univ, Bloomington. *Exhib:* Mirrors & Windows: Am Photog Since 1960, Mus Mod Art, New York, 78; one-person show, Foto Gallery, New York, 80, Camerawork Gallery, San Francisco, 80, Sacred Childern, ARCO Ctr Visual Art, Los Angeles, Calif, 80, Color & Hand-Colored Photographs, Silver Image Gallery, 81 & Catskill Ctr Photog, Spring 82. *Collections Arranged:* Correspondents, Catskill Ctr for Photog, Woodstock, NY, 78 & Color in Question, 79. *Pos:* Dir educ, Catskill Ctr for Photog, Woodstock, NY, 78-80, dir, 81- *Teaching:* Instr photog, Slippery Rock State Col, Pa, Jan-May, 77; instr photog, Bard Col, Annandale, NY, winter 79. *Bibliog:* Lawrence Audette (auth), Ulster Arts, Ulster Co Coun on Arts, 79; Portfolio, (interview & photogs), Darkroom Mag, 5-6/80. *Mem:* Soc for Photog Educ; Women's Caucus for Art. *Media:* Photography; Painting. *Publ:* Contribr (work featured), Alternative Photographic Processes, Morgan & Morgan, 78, Self-Portrayal, Friends of Photog, 79, Popular Photography Annual 1979, Popular Photog, 79 & Ulster Arts, Ulster Co Coun on Arts, 79; auth, Portfolio (interview & photographs), Darkroom Mag, 80. *Dealer:* Photofind Woodstock NY. *Mailing Add:* Box 77 Rte 212 Shady NY 12479

KEPALAS (ELENA KEPALAITE)
SCULPTOR, PAINTER
b Vilnius, Lithuania; US citizen. *Study:* Ont Col Art, Toronto; Brooklyn Mus Sch Art. *Work:* Pa Acad Fine Arts, Philadelphia; Univ Mass Art Gallery, Amherst; Libr & Mus of Performing Arts, Lincoln Ctr, NY; Lithuanian Mus, Adelaide, Australia; Mus Mod Art Lending Serv, New York. *Comn:* Bronze bust, Mr Louis Horst, New York, 62; bronze bust, Mrs Gunilla Kessler, New York, 71. *Exhib:* Pa Acad Fine Arts, Philadelphia, 68; Silvermine Guild Artists Ann, New Canaan, Conn, 69; Jersey City Mus, NJ, 69-71; Phoenix Gallery, New York, 70, 72, 74, 76 & 78-81. *Awards:* 1970 Sculpture House Award, Jersey City Mus, 70; Am Soc Contemp Artists First Prize Award, Union Carbide, New York, 74; First Prize, Coun Advan Lithuanian Cult, Chicago, Ill, 78. *Mem:* Am Soc Contemp Artists; Southern Asn Sculptors Inc. *Media:* Metal, Wax. *Mailing Add:* c/o Phoenix Gallery 84-25 109th St Jamaica NY 11418

KEPES, GYORGY
PAINTER, EDUCATOR
b Selyp, Hungary, Oct 4, 06. *Study:* Royal Acad Fine Arts, Budapest, MFA, 28; RI Sch Design, Hon PhD, 81. *Work:* Univ Ill; Dallas Mus Fine Arts; Albright-Knox Art Gallery, Buffalo, NY; Mus Mod Art & Whitney Mus Am Art, New York; and many others. *Comn:* Murals, Grad Ctr, Harvard Univ, Travelers Ins Co, Los Angeles, Sheraton Hotel, Dallas & Chicago, Children's Libr, Fitchburg, Mass & Church of Redeemer, Baltimore; and many others. *Exhib:* Art Inst Chicago; San Francisco Mus Art; Mus Fine Arts, Houston; Nat Collection Fine Arts, Washington, DC; Whitney Mus Am Art, New York; one-man shows, Dartmouth Col, 77, Prakapas Gallery, New York, 77, Hayden Gallery, Mass Inst Technol, 78 & Alpha Gallery, Boston, 80, 81 & 83; and many others. *Collections Arranged:* Designed exhib, Arts of the United Nations, Art Inst Chicago, 64; designer sect of Triennale de Milano, 68. *Pos:* Head light dept, Chicago Inst Design, 37. *Teaching:* Head light & color dept, New Bauhaus, 37-38; instr, Chicago Inst Design, 38-43; prof visual design, Mass Inst Technol, 46-80, dir, Ctr Advan Visual Studies, 67-74, Inst prof emer, 71-; vis prof, Harvard Univ, 64-66 & 79; artist in residence, Am Acad Rome, 74-75. *Awards:* Guggenheim Fel, 60-61; Medaglia d'Oro, Convengo Int Artisti Critici e Studiosi d'Arte, 66; Fine Arts Award, Am Inst Architects, 68. *Mem:* Nat Inst Arts & Lett; fel Am Acad Arts & Sci. *Publ:* Auth, Language of Vision, 44 & The New Landscape, 56, Paul Theobald & Co; ed, Visual Arts Today, 60; ed, Vols I-VII, In: Vision & Value Series, Braziller, 65, 66 & 72. *Mailing Add:* Mass Inst Technol 160 Memorial Dr Cambridge MA 02142

KEPETS, HUGH MICHAEL
PAINTER, PRINTMAKER
b Cleveland, Ohio, Feb 6, 46. *Study:* Carnegie-Mellon Univ, BFA, 68; Ohio Univ, MFA, 72. *Work:* Metrop Mus Art, New York; Philadelphia Mus Fine Arts; Cleveland Mus Art; Libr Cong, Washington, DC; Yale Univ Art Gallery. *Comn:* Cover, Paris Rev 65, spring 76; City Walls Inc, New York, 76. *Exhib:* Cleveland Mus Art, 68-81; Brooklyn Mus, NY, 72 & 76; 35th Midyear Show, Butler Inst Am Art, 72; Works on Paper, Va Mus Fine Arts, Richmond, 74; West '79/The Law, Minn Mus Art, St Paul, 79; Am Acad Arts & Lett, New York, 78 & 80; One-man shows, Galerie Ninety-Nine, Bay Harbor, Fla, 81, Marcus/Gordon Assoc, Pittsburgh, 81 & Michael Berger Gallery, Pittsburgh, 82. *Awards:* Nat Endowment Arts Grant, 76; Cleveland Arts Prize, 79; Creative Artists Pub Serv Grant, 80. *Dealer:* Orion Ed 835 Madison Ave New York NY 10021. *Mailing Add:* 35 Gramercy Park N New York NY 10010

KEPNER, RITA M
SCULPTOR, WRITER
b Binghamton, NY, Nov 15, 44. *Study:* Elmira Col, NY, 62-63; Harpur Col, State Univ NY, Binghamton, BA, 63-66; Univ Wash, Seattle, 74-75 & 80; Univ Art, Terme Italy, dipl merit, 82. *Work:* Valley Mus Northwest Art, La Conner, Wash; Warsaw Contemp Art Mus, Poland; Outdoor Mus, Znin, Poland; Seattle Art Comn & King Co Art Comn, Seattle, Wash. *Comn:* Unity (wood), Polonia Soc, Warsaw, Poland, 76; Game of Life (bronze), Children's Hospital, Seattle, Wash, 77; Almost Free (wood), Arts Commission, Zalaegerszeg, Hungary, 77; Rough to Smooth (granite), Seattle Public Libr, Wash, 78; Trumpet (wood), Kenmore Public Libr, Wash. *Exhib:* Artist in the City, Seattle Art Mus, Wash, 75; Master Works in Wood, Portland Art Mus, Ore, 76; A Show of Hands, Manawath Art Gallery, Palmerstown, New Zealand; Int Sculpture, Zalaegerszeg City Mus, Hungary, 77; Hajnowka Int, Bialystok Mus, Poland, 77; one-woman show, Zoliborg Mus, Warsaw, Poland, 81. *Pos:* Cultural ambassador informal, Polonia Soc & Ministry of Culture, Warsaw, Poland, 76- *Teaching:* Instr life sculpture, Experimental Col, Univ Wash, Seattle, 74-75; master sculptor sculpture, Evergreen State Col, 75 & 77-78. *Awards:* First Prize, City Waterbury, Conn, 67; Bronze Medal, Int Sculpture, Zalaegerszeg, Hungary, 77; Jury's Choice, Hajnowka 77, Bialystok Mus, Poland, 77. *Bibliog:* David Miller (auth), The Kepner Way (video), 81. *Mem:* Accad Italia Pelle Art E Del Lavaro; Int Asn Art; Int Artists Coop; Artists Equity Asn; Polonia Cult Soc. *Media:* Wood, Stone. *Publ:* Contribr, We are all cousins in the arts, Poland Mag, Interpress, Warsaw, 76; contribr, Artist on Travel Grant, Hearst Publ, 76; contribr, My sculpture made from polyester resin and bones, Leonardo, 77; contribr, An interview with Henry Moore, 77 & Art not neglected in Poland, 81, Northwest Arts. *Mailing Add:* 6681 Flagler Rd Nordland WA 98358

KERMES, CONSTANTINE JOHN
PAINTER, PRINTMAKER
b Pittsburgh, Pa, Dec 6, 23. *Study:* Carnegie-Mellon Univ, BFA; also with Victor Candell, Leo Manso & Frank Lloyd Wright. *Work:* Storm King Art Ctr; Notre Dame Art Mus, South Bend, Ind; Stockmanshove Mus, Damme, Belgium; Pa State Univ, University Park; Hershey Med Ctr, Pa. *Comn:* Murals, Pa Hist & Mus Comn, Cornwall Mus, 68; Fontrier Found, Paris; assemblage murals, Sperry Rand Corp, Pa & Brussels, Belg; Farm & Indust Equip Inst, Wrigley Bldg, Chicago. *Exhib:* Butler Inst Am Art Ann, Youngstown, Ohio, 64; Design Rev, Smithsonian Inst, Washington, DC, 69; one-man show, Grimaldis Gallery, Baltimore, 79 & Reading Mus, 80; Pa Watercolor Soc, 79 & 80; Art 81, Washington, DC; and many others. *Awards:* Ann Design Rev Awards, Indust Design Mag, 62, 64, 68 & 72; Design Awards, Am Iron & Steel Inst, 65, 69, 73 & 75; Traveling Exhib Painting Prize, Petrol Indusits, 71. *Bibliog:* Festival printmaker, Nat Geog, 4/73; Morse (auth), Shakers & Worlds People, Dodd Mead, 80; Horgan (auth), Shaker Holy Land, Harvard Press, 82. *Media:* Oil, Acrylic; Woodcut, Lithography. *Publ:* Auth, Shaker Architecture, 70; auth & illusr, American Icons, 75; Folk images of rural Pennsylvania, Pa Folklife, 6/75 & 6/81. *Dealer:* Jacques Seligmann Gallery 5 E 57th St New York NY 10022. *Mailing Add:* 981 Landis Valley Rd Lancaster PA 17601

KERN, ARTHUR (EDWARD)
EDUCATOR, SCULPTOR
b New Orleans, La, Oct 27, 31. *Study:* Tulane Univ La, BA, 53, MFA, 55. *Exhib:* One-man shows, Ariz State Univ, 74 & Int Sculpture Conf, Tulane Univ, 76; South Houston Gallery, New York, 75. *Teaching:* Asst prof drawing, Univ Southwestern La, 67-69; assoc prof painting & sculpture, Tulane Univ La, 69-, assoc chmn dept art, 72- *Mailing Add:* 1730 Pine St New Orleans LA 70118

KERNS, ED (JOHNSON), JR
PAINTER
b Richmond, Va, Feb 22, 45. *Study:* Va Commonwealth Univ, BFA; Md Inst Col Art, Baltimore, with Grace Hartigan, MFA. *Work:* Aldrich Mus Art, Ridgefield, Conn; Chase Manhattan Bank, New York; Edward Albee Found, New York; Citicorp, New York; Corcoran Gallery, Washington, DC. *Exhib:* Albright-Knox Art Gallery, Buffalo, NY, 71 & 72; one-man shows, A M Sachs Gallery, 72 & 74 & Rosa Esman Gallery, 76-83; Brooklyn Mus, NY, 74; Grey Art Gallery, New York Univ, NY, 77; Dayton Art Inst, Ohio, 77; Ctr Arts, Muhlenberg Col, Allentown, Pa, 77 & 81; San Francisco Mus Mod Art, 78; Pa Acad Fine Arts, 82; and others. *Teaching:* Prof art & dept head, Lafayette Col, Easton, Pa, 80- *Awards:* Art Achievement Key, Va Commonwealth Univ, 67; Artist of the Year, Larry Aldrich Assoc, New York, 71. *Bibliog:* Articles, Art News, 12/78; Arts Mag, 1/79 & Artforum, 1/80. *Mem:* Col Art Asn. *Media:* Acrylic, Collage. *Mailing Add:* c/o Rosa Esman Gallery 29 West 57th St New York NY 10019

KERR, JAMES WILFRID
PAINTER, CONCEPTUAL ARTIST
b New York, NY, Aug 7, 1897. *Study:* Poppenhusen Inst, College Point, NY, 14; New York Sch Fine & Appl Art, 20-22, Social Res, 33-34; study with Howard Giles & Camilio Egas, Ecuador, Jacques Maroger, Louvre, Paris. *Work:* Mus City New York; Joslyn Art Mus, Omaha; Newark Mus, NJ; NMex State Fair Permanent Art Collection, Albuquerque; Albuquerque Mus; and others. *Exhib:* Painting in the United States, Carnegie Inst, Pittsburgh, 49; Art USA, Madison Sq Garden, New York, 58; Allied Artists Am Ann, New York, 61, 62 & 63; Albuquerque Exhib, Mus NMex, Santa Fe, 61; 47th Ann Nat Art Exhib, Mus Art, Springville, Utah, 71. *Pos:* Founder & owner, Fairbairn Publ, New York, 25-40; art dir, Harry Doehla Co, Fitchburg, Mass, 45-50. *Teaching:* Asst instr art, NY Sch Fine & Appl Art, summer 21; dir art educ, Kerr Summer Sch Art, Detroit, summers 23-24; spec lectr art educ, Syracuse Univ, summer 32. *Awards:* First Altman Prize, Nat Acad Design, New York, 45; Purchase Prize, NMex State Fair, Albuquerque, 63; Silver Medal, Am Vet Soc Artists, New York, 63. *Mem:* Salmagundi Club; Allied Artists Am; Am Vet Soc Artists; Artists Equity Asn; Presidents Club, Western Mich Univ, Kalamazoo. *Media:* Oil. *Publ:* Contribr, Art recovery, Sch Arts Mag, 33; coauth, Historic design for modern use, 38; auth, Modern lettering, 39. *Dealer:* Grand Central Art Galleries 24 W 57th St New York NY 10017. *Mailing Add:* 7017 Bellrose Ave NE Albuquerque NM 87110

KERRIGAN, MAURIE
SCULPTOR
b Jersey City, NJ, Apr 28, 51. *Study:* Moore Col Art, Philadelphia, Pa, BFA, 73; Art Inst Chicago, MFA, 77; Whitney Mus Am Art, 77. *Work:* Philadelphia Mus Art & Please Touch Mus, Philadelphia, Pa; Lanon Found, Palm Beach, Fla; Phillips Collection, Smithsonian Inst, Washington, DC; Nat Womens Mus, Washington, DC; Best Corp Collection, NC. *Comn:* Candy Corns Visit Chicago, Pippers Alley, Chicago, Ill, 76. *Exhib:* Chicago & Vicinity, Art Inst Chicago, Ill, 77; Contemp Drawings, Philadelphia Mus Art, Pa, 79; Morris Gallery Summer Exhib, Acad Fine Art, Philadelphia, Pa, 79; Projects IV, Inst Contemp Art, Philadelphia, Pa, 80; Awards in the Visual Arts I, Nat Mus Am Art, Washington, DC, 82-83; De Moines Art Ctr, 82-83; Denver Art Museum, 82-83. *Awards:* Visual Arts, Equitable Life Insurance, Nat Endowment for the Arts. 81; Artist Fel, Pa Coun for the Arts, 82; Penn's Landing Sculpture Award, Philadelphia, 83. *Bibliog:* Richard Flood (auth), Philadelphia, Art Forum, 10/79; Jean Silverthorne (auth), Maurie Kerrigan, Arts, 12/79; Ann-Sargent Wooster (auth), Maurie Kerrigan at Touchstone, Art in Am, 12/81. *Mem:* Womens Caucus Art; Int Sculpture Ctr. *Media:* Portable Frescoes, Wood. *Dealer:* Max Hutchinson Gallery 138 Green St New York NY 10012; Jeffrey Fuller Fine Art 2108 Spruce St Philadelphia PA 19146. *Mailing Add:* 422 B South 21st St Philadelphia PA 19146

KERSLAKE, KENNETH ALVIN
PRINTMAKER, EDUCATOR
b Mt Vernon, NY, Mar 8, 30. *Study:* Pratt Inst, 50-53, with Calvin Alberts & Philip Guston; Univ Ill, Urbana, with Lee Chesney, BFA, 55 & MFA, 57; Tamarind Lithography Workshop with Garo Antreasian, 64. *Work:* Libr Cong, Washington, DC; Brooklyn Mus, NY; Nat Gallery Art, Washington, DC; High Mus, Atlanta; Boston Mus Fine Arts; plus others. *Exhib:* 30 Years of Am Printmaking, 20th Ann Exhib of Prints, Brooklyn Mus, NY; Art Under Pressure: Printmaking, Southeastern Ctr Contemp Art, Winston-Salem, NC; In Celebration of Prints, Print Club, Philadelphia; one-man show, Oxford Gallery, Eng; Am Prints & Printmaking, Pratt Graphic Ctr, New York; Graphics Invitational, Mint Mus, Charlotte, NC, 81; 30 American Printmakers, Ohio State Univ, Columbus; and others. *Teaching:* Prof art & printmaking, Univ Fla, Gainesville, 58-; artist in residence, Univ Mo, Columbia, summer, 81; prof art, Univ Ga Studies Abroad Prog, Cortona, Italy, summer, 82. *Awards:* Assoc Am Artists Gallery Award, Soc Am Graphic Artists Nat Print Exhib, 79; Distinguished Fac Award, Univ Fla, 79. *Bibliog:* H Williams (auth), Notes for a Young Painter, Prentice-Hall, 63; R Fichter

(auth), Three Florida artists using photography, Fla Arts, 5/78; portfolio, Art Visions, Winter Park, Fla. *Mem:* Nat Print Council (bd dirs); Boston Printmakers; Print Club, Philadelphia; Los Angeles Printmakers Soc; Soc Am Graphic Artists. *Media:* Intaglio and Photo Intaglio. *Dealer:* Assoc Am Artist Gallery 663 Fifth Ave New York NY 10022; Lumley-Cazalet Ltd 24 Davies St London WIY ILH Eng. *Mailing Add:* 1114 NW 36th Dr Gainesville FL 32605

KERSTETTER-BAILEY, BARBARA ANN
PAINTER, INSTRUCTOR
b Kokomo, Ind, Mar 20, 28. *Study:* Art Inst Pittsburgh; Univ Hawaii; Univ Pittsburgh, BA(cum laude); Seton Hill Col, with Frank Webb. *Work:* Air Force Mus Art Collection, Dayton, Ohio. *Exhib:* Three Rivers Art Festival, 72, 75 & 83; Hoosier Salon Indianapolis, 72; Am Artists Prof League Exhib, New York, 74 & 75; Washington & Jefferson Nat Painting Exhib, Washington, Pa, 75 & 81; one-person show, Clarion State Col, Pa, 75 & Pa State Univ, 83; Mus Show Assoc Artists, Butler Inst Am Art, Youngstown, Ohio, 79; Aqueous Open Nat Show, 80 & 82-83. *Teaching:* Instr oil painting, Boyce Community Col, Riverview High Sch Campus, 69- & Westmoreland Community Col, 80- *Awards:* Best of Show Award, Indiana Co Fair Art Exhib, Pa, 73; Mus Award, Greensburg Art Asn, Pa, 73. *Mem:* Am Artists Prof League; Indiana Art Asn, Pa; E Suburban Artists League, Pittsburgh; Assoc Artists Pittsburgh. *Media:* Oil, Pastel. *Publ:* Auth, Painting on black velvet, Today's Art, 7/66. *Mailing Add:* 111 Marion Ave Pittsburgh PA 15221

KERSWILL, J W ROY
PAINTER
b Bigbury, Eng, Jan 17, 25; US citizen. *Study:* Plymouth Col Art, Eng; Bristol Col Art, scholar. *Work:* Wyo State Art Gallery; Mus Mountain Man; Grand Teton Natural Hist Asn Nat Park, Wyo; Jefferson Nat Expansion Mem, St Louis, Mo; Dept Interior Nat Collection, Washington, DC. *Comn:* Hist murals, Alpenhof Teton Village, Wyo, First Nat Bank, Englewood, Colo & Cheyenne Nat Bank, Wyo. *Exhib:* Am Artists Prof League Ann, New York, 50- *Mem:* Am Artists Prof League; Artist Equity Asn. *Media:* Watercolor, Oil. *Dealer:* May Gallery PO Box 1972 Jackson WY 83001. *Mailing Add:* Box 2440 Jackson Hole WY 83001

KERZIE, TED L
PAINTER
b Tacoma, Wash, May 10, 43. *Study:* Wash State Univ, Pullman, BA, 65; Claremont Grad Sch, Calif, MFA, 72. *Work:* Power Mus, Sydney, Australia; Wayne Anderson Collection, Boston; Luigiani Rossi Collection, Milan, Italy; Arco Collection Visual Arts, Los Angeles; Reader's Digest Collection, New York. *Exhib:* Solo show, Cirrus Gallery, Los Angeles, 80; Arco Collection Visual Arts, Los Angeles, 81; M M Shinno Gallery, Los Angeles, 81; Nagasaki Prefecture Mus, Japan, 81; Tengin Salon Gallery, Fukuoka, Japan, 81; and others. *Collections Arranged:* Los Angeles Abstract Painting (catalog), Univ Calif, Riverside, 80. *Teaching:* Asst prof fine arts, Scripps Col, Claremont, Calif, 73-76; assoc prof fine arts, Calif State Col, Bakersfield, 76- *Bibliog:* William Wilson (auth), article, 8/80 & Suzanne Munchnic (auth), article, 8/81, Los Angeles Times; Melinda Wortz (auth), article, Art News, 80 & 83. *Media:* Acrylic. *Dealer:* Cirrus Gallery 542 S Alameda Los Angeles CA. *Mailing Add:* 320 Oleander Bakersfield CA 93304

KESSLER, ALAN
PAINTER, SCULPTOR
b Philadelphia, Pa, Oct 15, 45. *Study:* Philadelphia Col Art, BFA; Yale Univ Summer Sch, Norfolk, Conn, Yale fel, 66; Md Inst Col Art, Baltimore, Hoffberger fel painting, MFA, 69. *Work:* Am Fedn Arts, New York; NY Univ Collection; Brockton Art Mus, Mass; Rose Art Mus, Brandeis Univ; State Univ NY Col Cortland. *Exhib:* One-man shows, Brown Univ, 77, O K Harris Gallery, New York, 77, 79 & 80, Everson Mus Arts, Syracuse, NY, 78 & Morgan Gallery, Kansas City, Mo, 78; Directions, Hirschhorn Mus, Washington, DC, 79; Real, Really Real, Super Real, Directions in Contemporary American Realism, 81 & 82; and others. *Teaching:* Instr painting & drawing, Md Inst Col Art, 68-69; instr, Hudson River Mus, 74; asst prof art, Brown Univ, 77-82. *Awards:* First Prize in Painting, Acad Arts, Easton, Md, 68; Elizabeth T Greenshields Mem Found Grant in Painting, Montreal, 74; Artist in Residence Grant, Nat Endowment Arts, Del State Arts Coun, 75-76. *Bibliog:* Gregory Battcock (auth), Super Realism, a Critical Anthology, Dutton, 75; Vivian Radnor (auth), Art: While waiting for tomorrow, New York Times, 10/23/77; Kim Levin (auth), Preview exhibition wood sculpture, O K Harris Gallery, Arts Mag, 10/77. *Media:* Polychrome, Wood. *Dealer:* O K Harris Gallery 383 W Broadway New York NY 10021. *Mailing Add:* 45 Bond St New York NY 10012

KESSLER, EDNA LEVENTHAL
PAINTER, PRINTMAKER
b Kingston, NY. *Study:* Parsons Sch Design, teaching cert; NY Univ; Columbia Univ; Queens Col; Inst San Miguel, Mex; also with Joseph Margulies, Paul Puzinas, Edgar A Whitney, Charles Kinghan, Dong Kingman, Victor D'Amico & George Post. *Work:* In pvt collections in Eng, Can & throughout US. *Exhib:* Dallas Mus of Fine Arts, 62; Smithsonian Inst, Washington, DC, 63; Travel Show, USA, Am Watercolor Soc-Nat Acad Design, New York, 65; Am Artists Prof League Grand Nat, New York & Dallas, 62-69; Fine Arts Festival, Parrish Mus, Southampton, NY, 65-69; La Biennale Int, Vichy & Clermont-Ferrand, France, 66-68; Metrop Mus & Art Ctr, Miami, Fla, 75, 76 & 77; plus 16 one-artist shows. *Pos:* Pres, Edna L Kessler-Interior Designs, NY, 46-69, Fla, 69-83; free lance artist, New York & Miami Beach, Fla, 58-83. *Teaching:* Instr costume design & illus, Parsons

Sch Design, 29-31; instr oils & watercolors, Temple Sholom, Glen Oaks, NY, 60-69; instr pvt classes, Hallandale & Hollywood, Fla, 69- *Awards:* Miami Watercolor Soc, 76, 80 & 83; Medaglia D'Oro, Acad Italia; and others. *Mem:* Fla Watercolor Soc; Miami Watercolor Soc; Women's Caucus for Art; Artists Equity Asn; Allied Arts North Miami (dir, 71-81). *Media:* Oil, Watercolor. *Publ:* Auth, Prize Winning Art, 65, 66 & 67; contribr, Enciclopedia Internazionale Degli Artisti, 70-71; contribr, Artists USA, 72-73; contribr, Artisti Contemporanei, 82; contribr, Premio Centauro Doro, 82; and others. *Dealer:* Deligny Art Galleries 709 E Las Olas Blvd Ft Lauderdale FL 33301. *Mailing Add:* 1050 93rd St Bay Harbor Islands FL 33154

KESSLER, HERBERT LEON
EDUCATOR
b Chicago, Ill, July 20, 41. *Study:* Univ Chicago, BA, 61; Princeton Univ, MFA, 63, PhD, 65. *Teaching:* From asst prof to prof hist art, Univ Chicago, 65-76; prof & chmn dept, Johns Hopkins Univ, 76- *Mem:* Medieval Acad Am; Col Art Asn; sr fel Dumbarton Oaks. *Res:* Medieval art, especially manuscript illumination. *Publ:* Ed, Studies in Classical and Byzantine Manuscript Illumination, Univ Chicago Press, 71; auth, Illustrated Bibles from Tours, 77 & The Cotton Genesis (in press), Princeton Univ Press. *Mailing Add:* Dept Hist Art Johns Hopkins Univ Baltimore MD 21218

KESSLER, JANE Q
CURATOR, CRITIC
b Charlotte, NC, June 14, 46. *Study:* ECarolina Univ, BS, 69; Yale Univ Printroom, with Richard Field, 82; Boston Pub Libr Printroom, with Sinclair Hitchings, 83. *Collections Arranged:* Harvey Littleton: Glass, 78; Southeastern Graphics Invitational (auth, catalog), 79-82; Southeastern Contemporary Metalsmiths (auth, catalog), 80 & 81; Contemporary American Prints from the Permanent Collection of the Mint Museum (auth, catalog), 83; Ida Kohlmeyer: Thirty Years (auth, catalog), 83. *Pos:* Mgt, 501 Gallery, Mint Mus, 72-78, asst cur exhibs, 78-82, asst cur art, 82- *Mem:* NCarolina Print & Drawing Soc (pres bd, 83); Southeastern Col Arts Conf (bd dirs, 82-85); Southern Graphics Coun; World Print Coun; Am Crafts Coun Southeastern Assembly. *Res:* Regional exhibitions of prints, drawings and crafts; history of American prints and print workshops. *Publ:* Auth, Profile: Rod MacKillop, 82 & Clemson National Print and Drawing Competition, 83, Art Papers; auth, North Carolina Artist Fellowship Exhibition, Arts J, 83; auth, Towards a new iron age, Metalsmith, 83; ed, Ida Kohlmeyer: Thirty Years, Mint Mus, 84. *Mailing Add:* Mint Mus 501 Hempstead Pl Charlotte NC 28207

KESSLER, LEONARD H
ILLUSTRATOR
b Akron, Ohio, Oct 23, 21. *Study:* Carnegie Inst of Tech, BFA(painting & design), 49. *Awards:* New York Times 10 Best Illus Children's Books, 54, 55 & 57. *Mem:* Soc of Illusr; Graphic Artists Guild; Author's League; Authors Guild. *Media:* Pen and Ink, Watercolor, Gouache. *Publ:* Auth & illusr, Ghosts and Crows and Things with O's, Scholastic Books, 76; auth & illusr, Superbowl, 80, Old Turtle's Baseball Stories, 82, The Big Mile Race, 83 & Old Turtle's Winter Games, 83, Greenwillow Books. *Mailing Add:* 6 Stoneham Ln New City NY

KESSLER, SHIRLEY
PAINTER
b New York, NY. *Study:* Art Students League. *Work:* Iowa State Mus, Iowa City; Nashville Mus Art, Tenn; Asheville Mus Art, NC; Norfolk Mus Art, Va; Bulter Inst Am Art. *Exhib:* Museo Nacional Bellas Artes, Buenos Aires, 63; Am Watercolor Soc Ann, 64 & Audubon Artists, 65, Nat Acad Design, New York; 1st Int Exhib Women Painters, Cult Ctr, Cannes, France, 66; Int Peinture de Saint Germaine-des-Pres, Paris, 70. *Awards:* Palmes d'Or Promotion Queen Fabiola, Belg, 75; Grand Prix Humanitaire de France & Medaille d'Argent with Laureate Dipl, Int Arts Festival, De Saint Germain-des-Pres, France, 75; Medal of Merit, Nat Soc Painters Casein & Acrylic, 83. *Bibliog:* Archives of American art, Smithsonian Inst, 70. *Mem:* Nat Asn Women Artists (pres, 67-70, permanent adv bd, 71-); Nat Soc Painters Casein & Acrylic (bd dirs, 70-); Soc D'Encouragement au Progress (USA permanent officer, 70-); Audubon Artists (bd dirs, 80-). *Media:* Acrylic, Watercolor. *Mailing Add:* Apt 23L 185 E 85th St New York NY 10028

KESTER, LENARD
PAINTER
b New York, NY, May 10, 17. *Work:* Brooklyn Mus, NY; Toledo Mus, Ohio; Denver Mus, Colo; Boston Mus Fine Arts, Mass; Everson Mus Art, Syracuse, NY. *Comn:* First Nowell (painting), Life, 47; Pictorial Record of Pacific Northwest, Louis Comfort Tiffany Found, 49; Man's Musical Heritage (mural), Mayo Clin, Rochester, Minn, 53; stained glass windows, Billy Rose Mausoleum, NY, 67. *Exhib:* Five exhibs, Los Angeles Mus, 43-55; Art Inst Chicago, 47; Carnegie Inst, Pittsburgh, 47-49; six exhibs, Nat Acad Design, New York, 51-66; Corcoran Gallery Art, Washington, DC, 57. *Teaching:* Pvt instr & pub lect. *Awards:* First Prize, Storm in the Canyon, Los Angeles Mus, 43; Saltus Gold Medal for Merit, November 7th, Nat Acad Design, 58; First Prize, Venice Reflections, Calif State Expos, 71; plus many others. *Bibliog:* Janice Lovoos (auth), The art of Lenard Kester, Am Artist, 2/59. *Mem:* Assoc Nat Acad Design; Am Watercolor Soc. *Style & Technique:* Representational realism. *Media:* Oil, Watercolor, Gouache. *Mailing Add:* 1117 N Genesee Ave Los Angeles CA 90046

KESTNBAUM, GERTRUDE DANA
COLLECTOR
b Boston, Mass. *Study:* Wellesley Col, BA, 16; Simmons Col, BS, 19. *Collection:* Contemporary painting and sculpture; antique silver, porcelain and furniture; Chinese and Japanese porcelain, jade. *Mailing Add:* 209 E Lake Shore Dr Chicago IL 60611

KETCHAM, HANK (HENRY KING)
CARTOONIST
b Seattle, Wash, Mar 14, 20. *Study:* Univ Wash, 38. *Work:* Albert T Reid Collection; William Allen White Found, Univ Kans; Achenbach Found for Graphic Arts, Calif Palace Legion Hon; Boston Univ Libr. *Pos:* Animator, Walter Lantz Prod, 38-39, Walt Disney Prod, 39-42; co-designer, Dennis the Menace Playground, Monterey, Calif, founder, Playart Found, 69. *Awards:* Billy De Beck Award as outstanding cartoonist, 52; Cert for Best Comic Mag, Boys' Club Am, 56. *Mem:* Nat Cartoonists' Soc. *Interests:* Donor, Hank Ketcham Collection to Boston University Libraries. *Publ:* Auth & illusr, Dennis the Menace ann bk collection, 54-; auth & illusr, daily syndicated cartoon, Dennis the Menace, US & foreign newspapers, 51-; contribr, cartoons to nat newspapers; auth, I Wanna Go Home, McGraw-Hill, 65. *Mailing Add:* PO Box 800 Pebble Beach CA 93953

KETCHAM, RAY WINFRED, JR
DEALER, DESIGNER
b Hartford, Ala, Dec 4, 22. *Study:* Ringling Sch Art, Fla, 46-48. *Comn:* Home Calendar, Coca-Cola Company, 55-67; mural, Delta Airlines, 66. *Pos:* Owner, Ray Ketcham Gallery, 66- *Awards:* Freelance Artist of the Year, Professional Artists Asn Atlanta Inc, 65. *Specialty:* Nineteenth & early twentieth century American & European paintings. *Mailing Add:* 540 Forestdale Drive NE Atlanta GA 30342

KETCHUM, ROBERT GLENN
PHOTOGRAPHER, CURATOR
b Los Angeles, Calif, Dec 1, 47. *Study:* Univ Calif, Los Angeles, with Heinecken & Teske in photog, BA(design, cum laude), 70; Brooks Inst, 71; Calif Inst Arts, MFA(photog), 74. *Work:* Mus Mod Art, New York; Los Angeles Co Mus Art, Los Angeles; Fogg Art Mus, Harvard Univ; Ctr Creative Photog, Univ Ariz, Tucson; Corcoran Gallery Art, Washington, DC. *Comn:* Print ed, comn by William Lund, Nat Park Found, DC, 76; color portfolio, Los Amigos de Pueblo Los Angeles, 76-77; four murals, Fluor Corp, Newport, Calif, 76-77; book, comn by Harry N Abrams, Int Ocean Inst, New York, 77; portfolio, Reader's Digest, 82-84. *Exhib:* White House, Washington, DC, 79; Smithsonian Traveling Exhib Service, 80-84; American Photography and the National Parks Traveling Exhib, 81-83; Hunter Mus Art, Chattanooga, Tenn, 83; Los Angeles Municipal Art Gallery, 83; Lyndon Johnson Library, Austin, Tex, 84; one-man exhib, Sheldon Mem Art Gallery, Lincoln, Nebr, 84; and others. *Pos:* Cur, Nat Park Found, DC, 78-; bd trustees, Los Angeles Ctr Photog Studies, 75-81, pres & exec dir, 79. *Teaching:* Founder & teacher photog workshop, Sun Valley Ctr Arts & Humanities, 71-73; instr photog, Calif Inst Arts, 75. *Awards:* Nat Park Found Award, 78 & 79; Mat Res Award, Ciba-Geigy, 79; Pentax Corp Award, 83. *Bibliog:* William Wilson (auth), Photography: the state of the art, Los Angeles Times, 1/28/79; Suzanne Muchnic (auth), Ketchum, Evert at Municipal, Los Angeles Times, 6/14/83; Katherine Livingston (auth), Order from chaos, Am Photogr, 10/83. *Mem:* Friends Photog. *Media:* Cibachrome Color Prints, Books. *Publ:* Coauth, Outerbridge, Los Angeles Ctr Photog Studies, 76; auth, Photographic Directions: Los Angeles 1979, Security Pac Bank, 79; auth, Landscape Photographers and America's National Parks, Nat Park Found, 79. *Mailing Add:* 696 Stone Canyon Rd Los Angeles CA 90077

KETTNER, DAVID ALLEN
ARTIST, EDUCATOR
b Sunman, Ind, Oct 19, 43. *Study:* Skowhegan Sch Painting and Sculpture, 64; Cleveland Inst Art, BFA, 66; Ind Univ, MFA, 68. *Work:* Pa Acad Fine Arts; Philadelphia Mus Art, Pa; Rutgers Univ, Col Arts & Sci, Camden, NJ. *Exhib:* Six Self-Portraits 1975 Series, Whitney Mus Am Art, New York, 76; 41st Int Eucharistic Congress Liturgical Arts Exhib, Civic Ctr, Philadelphia, 76; Philadelphia Houston Exchange, Inst Contemp Art, Philadelphia, 76; Recent Acquisitions, Philadelphia Mus Art, 77; Am Drawing Show, Fine Arts Gallery, San Diego, Calif, 77; Contemp Drawing, 78 & A Bach Transcription, 81, Pa Acad Fine Arts. *Teaching:* Assoc prof painting & drawing, Philadelphia Col Art, 68- *Bibliog:* Victoria Donohue (auth), article, Philadelphia Inquirer, 10/9/81. *Mailing Add:* c/o Philadelphia College Art Broad and Spruce Philadelphia PA 19102

KEVESON, FLORENCE
PAINTER, ILLUSTRATOR
b New York, NY. *Study:* Cooper Union Art Sch, art degree; Art Students League, Ford Found Scholar; also with Sidney Gross & Leo Manso. *Exhib:* Albany Inst Hist Art Ann, 68-72; solo exhib, Silvermine Guild Artists, 69 & Marist Col, 72; Wadsworth Atheneum Mus Ann, 69-77; Berkshire Mus Ann, Pittsfield, Mass, 70-80; Painters & Sculptors NJ, Bergen Mus, Paramus, NJ, 70-83; Butler Inst Ann, 72. *Pos:* Illusr, Conde Nast Publ, 49-52; free-lance illusr, 52- *Awards:* Shandoff Award, Berkshire Ann, 70; G Paley Award, Nat Asn Women Artists Ann; Michael M Engel Award, Am Soc Contemp Artists. *Media:* Oil. *Publ:* Illus in Vogue, McCalls & Good Housekeeping. *Dealer:* Rudolph Galleries 24 Mill Hill Rd Woodstock NY 12498. *Mailing Add:* 314 E 201 St Bronx NY 10458

KEVORKIAN, RICHARD
PAINTER
b Dearborn, Mich, Aug 24, 37. *Study:* Pa Acad of Fine Arts, Philadelphia, 58; Richmond Prof Inst, BFA(painting), 61; Calif Col of Arts & Crafts, Oakland, MFA(painting), 62. *Work:* Philip Morris, USA, Richmond, Va; Walter Rawls Mus, Courtland, Va; Southeastern Ctr for Contemp Art, Winston-Salem, NC; First & Merchants Nat Bank, Richmond; Bank & Trust of Wachovia, NC. *Exhib:* The 15th Irene Leach Mem Exhib, Chrysler Mus at Norfolk, Va, 70; Drawing Exhib, Mint Mus Art, Charlotte, NC, 70; Va Biennial, Va Mus Fine Arts, Richmond, 73; 35 Southeastern Artists, High Mus, Atlanta, Ga, 76; Southeast 7, Southeastern Ctr Contemp Art, Winston-Salem, 77. *Teaching:* Instr painting, Richard Bland Col, Petersburg, Va, 61-64; prof & chmn dept of painting & printmaking, Va Commonwealth Univ, Richmond, 64- *Awards:* Nat Endowment Arts, Individual Sr Artists Grant (painting), 72 & Southeastern Contemp Arts Grant (painting), 76; Guggenheim Fel Painting, 78. *Mem:* Nat Coun of Art Adminr. *Media:* Oil, acrylic. *Mailing Add:* 325 N Harrison St Richmond VA 23220

KEY, TED
CARTOONIST
b Fresno, Calif. *Study:* Univ Calif, Berkeley. *Pos:* Creator, Hazel, daily panel syndicated by King Features; auth, Gus, Walt Disney Prod; auth, So'M I. *Awards:* Best Syndicated Panel, Nat Cartoonists Soc, 77. *Publ:* Auth & illusr, 18 Hazel bks, The Biggest Dog in the World, Phyllis, Many Happy Returns & Squirrels in the Feeding Station; auth, Cat From Outer Space; auth, Million Dollar Duck, Walt Disney Prod. *Mailing Add:* 1694 Glenhardie Rd Wayne PA 19087

KEYSER, ROBERT G
PAINTER
b Philadelphia, Pa, July 24, 27. *Study:* Studied with Fernand Leger, Paris, 49-51. *Work:* Philadelphia Mus Art; Philips Gallery, Washington, DC; Munson-Williams-Proctor Inst, Utica, NY; Pa Acad Fine Arts; Col William & Mary. *Exhib:* Solo exhibs, Yale Univ Art Gallery, 62, Galleria Temple Univ, Rome, 77 & Col William & Mary, 78. *Teaching:* Prof painting & drawing, Philadelphia Col Art, 58- *Media:* Oil, Watercolor. *Dealer:* Marian Locks Gallery 1524 Walnut St Philadelphia PA 19102. *Mailing Add:* Box 328 RD 4 Quakertown PA 18951

KEYSER, WILLIAM ALPHONSE, JR
CRAFTSMAN, EDUCATOR
b Pittsburgh, Pa, July 30, 36. *Study:* Carnegie-Mellon Univ, Pittsburgh, BS, 58; Sch for Am Craftsman, Rochester Inst of Tech, MFA(furniture design), 61. *Work:* Univ Collection, Univ of Nebr, Lincoln; Am Crafts Coun, New York; Interfaith Chapel, Univ of Rochester; State Univ of NY, Brockport; Sybron-Ritter Corp, Rochester, NY. *Comn:* Window Screen sculpture (20ft x 14ft), 68 & sculpture wall shelf, 78, Rochester Inst of Tech; complete office comn by Mr J Kevin Mahoney, 75; altar, lecturn, chair & cross, St John Evangalist, 77; altar, lecturn & cross, Risen Christ Lutheran, 77, Rochester; sculptural subway benches, Mass Bay Transportation Authority, 83. *Exhib:* Mus of Contemp Crafts, New York, 69 & 79; Bed & Board, DeCordova Mus, Lincoln, Mass, 75; Contemp Works by Master Craftsman, Mus of Fine Arts, Boston, 78; Hayden Gallery, Mass Inst Technol, 80; Colony Sq, Atlanta, Ga, 80; Ancient Inspirations/Contemporary Interpretations, Roberson Ctr, Binghampton, NY, 83. *Teaching:* Instr, industrial design, Ohio Univ, Athens, 61-62; prof furniture design, Sch for Am Craftsman, Rochester Inst of Technol, 62-, chmn crafts, 81- *Awards:* Young Americans Award, Am Crafts Coun, 62; Gertrude H Moore, Rochester Finger Lakes, 72; Craftsmen's Fel, Nat Endowment for the Arts, 75. *Bibliog:* Dona Z Meilach (auth), Creating Mod Furniture: Trends, Techniques, Application, Crown Publ, 75; Dona Z Meilach (auth), Woodworking: The New Wave, Crown Publ, 81; Jonathan L Fairbanks & Elizabeth Bidwell Bates (co-auth), American Furniture 1620 to the Present, 81; and others. *Mem:* Am Crafts Coun; Empire State Crafts Alliance. *Media:* Wood. *Publ:* Auth, Steam Bending--Heat and Moisture Plasticize Wood, 77 & auth, Portfolio: W A Keyser, The Challenge of Churches, 79, Fine Woodworking Taunton Press. *Dealer:* Pritam & Eames East Hampton NY. *Mailing Add:* 6543 Rush-Lima Rd Honeoye Falls NY 14472

KHENDRY, JANAK KUMAR
GALLERY DIRECTOR, SCULPTOR
b Amritsar, India, Sept 26, 35. US citizen. *Study:* Col Fine Arts, Hyderabad, India, dipl, 61; Ohio State Univ, MA(sculpture), 63. *Exhib:* One-man shows, Ohio State Univ, 63, Va Mus 67 & Philbrook Art Ctr, Tulsa, Olka, 75. *Pos:* Owner/dir, Glass Art Gallery, 65-; guest cur, Allentown Mus Art, Pa, 78. *Media:* Wax, Bronze. *Res:* Indian art. *Mailing Add:* 21 Hazelton Ave Toronto ON M5R 2E1 Canada

KHOURI, GRETA MATSON See Matson, Greta

KIAH, VIRGINIA JACKSON
PAINTER, MUSEUM DIRECTOR
b East St Louis, Ill, June 3, 11. *Study:* Philadelphia Mus & Sch Art, 27-31, dipl; Art Students League, 29-32, study with Louis Bouche, Robert Brackman & Vincent Dumonde; Columbia Univ, AB, 49 & MA, 50. *Comn:* Portrait of Finley Wilson, Elks, Washington, DC, 40; portrait of Judge Thomas L Griffith, comn by self, Los Angeles, Calif, 41; two portraits of Mrs Thomas Dyett, comn by Thomas Dyett, New York, 52; portrait of Rev Harry Hoosier, Washington Delaware Conf, Methodist Church Retreat, Gulfside, Miss, 54; portrait of Vpres, Ga State Univ, Urban Life Bldg, 79. *Exhib:* Philadelphia Mus & Sch Art Ann Exhib, 30; Baltimore Mus Art Ann Md Artists Show, 35;

Nat Columbia Motion Pictures Portrait Painting Contest Prizewinners Exhib, Eggleston Galleries, New York, 37; Art Students League Ann Show, 37; Southern Regional Art Show, Williamsburg, Va, 69. *Collections Arranged:* Marie Dressler Exhib, Kiah Mus, Savannah, Ga; African Art & William H Johnson Pastel & Print Collection, Found, New York. *Pos:* Founder & dir, Kiah Mus, Savannah, Ga, 59-; chmn, Comt for the Ga United Nations Arts, 74-75; founder & dir, Lillie Carroll Jackson Mus, Baltimore, Md, 74-79. *Teaching:* Instr art & chmn dept, Cuyler, Beach & Scott Jr High Schs, 51-62. *Awards:* Nat Conf of Artists Distinctive Merit, 60-62, 68 & 70-72. *Bibliog:* Dr K B Raut (auth), Mrs Virginia Kiah--artist, Kiah Mus, Savannah Mag, Joseph Chauhan Publ, 1/71; Burchart, Denilov, Naeve & Taylor (auths), Treasures of America, Reader's Digest Asn, 74; Helen C Smith (auth), She couldn't go to museums so she started one, Atlanta Constitution Newspaper, 11/9/74. *Mem:* Nat Conf Artists; Savannah Ga 36th St Improv Asn; Ga Coastal Mus Asn; and others. *Media:* Oil. *Publ:* Auth, Gone fishing, Afro-Am Newspaper Mag, 55; auth, Black artists, Savannah Mag, 72; auth, Ulysses Davis: Folk Sculptor, Southern Folklore Quart, Univ Fla, 78. *Mailing Add:* 505 W 36th St Savannah GA 31401

KIDD, STEVEN R
ILLUSTRATOR, INSTRUCTOR
b Chicago, Ill, June 27, 11. *Study:* George Bridgman Scholar, Art Students League; Art Inst Chicago with Henry Varnum Poor; Grand Cent Sch Art, New York, with Harvey Dunn; additional study with Dean Cornwell; graphics at Pratt Inst. *Work:* Baseball Hall Fame, Cooperstown, NY; US Army Hist Sect, Pentagon Bldg, US Army Art Mus, USAF Mus, Washington, DC. *Exhib:* US Army Hist War Art Traveling Exhib, 46-; USAF Hist War Art, USAF Mus & Smithsonian Inst, Washington, DC; Art Students League Yearly Prof Exhib, 62-; Retrospective Show, Soc Illusrs, New York, 63; 200 Yrs of Am Illus Bicentennial Show, New York Hist Mus, 76. *Pos:* Illusr, New York Sunday News-Chicago Tribune Syndicate, 31-69; court reporting artist, Famous Hines Trial, New York Daily News, 38 & Watergate Verdict for Assoc Press, 76. *Teaching:* Instr illus, Newark Sch Fine & Indust Art, 47-50; Art Students League, 62- *Awards:* Gold Medal of Honor, Hudson Valley Art Asn, 60; Second Prize, New York Sports Show, Abercrombie & Fitch, New York, 66; Theodore Croslin Award, Warwick Murals, 68. *Bibliog:* Articles in Life Mag, 51 & Am Artist, summer 67; Henry Pitz (auth), The Brandywine Tradition. *Publ:* Contrib, Bob Crozier's Two Hundred Years of American Illustrations, Random, 77; contrib, Walter Reed's The Illustrator in America, 73; contrib, History of American Breweries Collectors' Series, 78-; contrib, Illustrators XXI, Ann Am Illust, 79/80 ed. *Mailing Add:* c/o Art Students League 215 W 57th St New York NY 10019

KIEFERNDORF, FREDERICK GEORGE
PAINTER, EDUCATOR
b Milwaukee, Wis, May 12, 21. *Study:* Univ Wis, BA & MS. *Work:* Springfield Art Mus, Mo; Mo State Hist Soc Permanent Collection (painting requested 75); Wis Salon Art, Madison; Sch Ozarks, Point Lookout, Mo; Pittsburgh State Col, Kans. *Exhib:* Watercolor USA, Springfield, Mo, 67, 68, 71 & 79; Ann Delta Show, Little Rock, 67 & 74; Ten Painters of Missouri, Traveling Exhib, Mo State Coun Arts, 68; Springfield Art Mus Midwest Exhib, 72; retrospective exhib, Park Central Gallery, 81. *Teaching:* Prof art, Southwest Mo State Univ, 53-81. *Awards:* Purchase Award, Springfield Art Mus, 56 & 65 & Award of Merit, 67; Purchase Award, Sch Ozarks, 70 & Award of Merit, 81. *Bibliog:* Edgar A Albin (auth), article in Art Voices/South, 7-8/78. *Media:* Polymer, Vinyl Cement. *Mailing Add:* 1748 Madaline Springfield MO 65804

KIELKOPF, JAMES ROBERT
PAINTER
b St Paul, Minn, July 13, 39. *Study:* Minneapolis Sch Art, BFA, 65; Grand Marias Art Colony, summer 63; Skowhegan Sch Painting, summer 64. *Work:* Walker Art Ctr. *Exhib:* Walker Art Ctr Biennial, 64 & 66; Minneapolis Inst Art Biennial, 67; Interchange, Dallas Mus Fine Arts, Tex, 72; Landmark Ctr, St Paul, 79. *Media:* Oil, Graphite. *Dealer:* Eye Corp 214 S Clinton St Chicago IL 60606; Barry Richard Gallery 102 Lumber Exchange Bldg 10 South 5th St Minneapolis MN 55401. *Mailing Add:* 1963 Ashland St Paul MN 55104

KIENHOLZ, LYN
PATRON, ADMINISTRATOR
b Chicago, Ill. *Study:* Sullins Col; Md Col Women. *Collections Arranged:* Echange Entre Artisttes (auth, catalog), Mus Art Mod, Paris, 82; California Sculpture (auth, catalog), Fisher Gallery, Univ Southern Calif, 84. *Pos:* Asst to artist Edward Kienholz, 66-74; exec dir, Beaubourg Found, Ctr Pompidou, Paris, 77-81; founder & pres, Calif-Int Arts Found, Los Angeles, 81- *Bibliog:* Hunter Drohojowska (auth), Carrying a torch for Olympic artists, Los Angeles Herald Examiner, 7/31/83. *Mem:* Artists Equity. *Interests:* All forms of contemporary art. *Mailing Add:* 2737 Outpost Dr Los Angeles CA 90068

KIKER, EVELYN COALSON
PAINTER, INSTRUCTOR
b Belzoni, Miss, May 17, 32. *Study:* Delta State Col, BS(educ), 69; Univ Miss, MA, 71, PhD, 81. *Work:* Miss State Univ, Starkville; Miss Univ Women, Columbus. *Exhib:* Mid-South Exhib, Brooks Mem Art Gallery, Memphis, Tenn, 64 & 65; Arts & Crafts Show, Miss Art Festival, Jackson, 65 & 66; Belzoni Group, Ahda Artzt Gallery, New York, 67 & Meridian Mus Art, Miss, 72; Jr Col Art Teachers, Jackson Municipal Art Gallery, Miss, 70. *Teaching:* Miss Delta Jr Col, Moorhead, 69- *Awards:* Best in Show, Miss Collegiate Exhib, 67; Purchase Award, Miss Art Colony, Commercial Nat Bank, Laurel, Miss, 78; Second Prize, Laurel Art in the Park Comt, 79. *Bibliog:* R Stephens (auth), L'Art a L'Etranger: Expositions diverses, La

Revue Moderne, 11/65; C N White (auth), Reviews & previews, Art News, 2/67; O C McDavid (auth), O C McDavids gallery talk, Clarion-Ledger/Jackson Daily News, 10/29/72. *Media:* Oil, Acrylic. *Mailing Add:* PO Box 651 Belzoni MS 39038

KIKUCHI-YNGOJO, ALAN
PHOTOGRAPHER, COLLAGE ARTIST
b San Francisco, Calif, Feb 6, 49. *Study:* Diablo Valley Col, 67-69; Univ Calif, Davis, BA, 71, MFA, 75. *Work:* Metrop Mus Art, Alternative Mus, New York; Clarence Kennedy Gallery, Polaroid Corp, Cambridge, Mass; Cleveland Mus Art; Erie Art Ctr, Pa. *Exhib:* Contemporary Icons, San Francisco Mus Mod Art, 75; Beyond Photography, Alternative Mus, New York, 80; US Art Now, Gotesborgs Konstforening, Sweden, 81; Painting and Sculpture Today, Indianapolis Mus Art, 82; Counterparts, Metrop Mus Art, New York, 82; solo exhib, Triton Mus Art, Santa Clara, Calif, 82; Recent Acquisitions, Clarence Kennedy Gallery, Polaroid Corp, Cambridge, Mass, 83; Seven American Artists, Cleveland Mus Art, 83. *Awards:* Nat Endowment Arts Fel, 81. *Bibliog:* Grace Glueck (auth), article, New York Times, 1/15/82; Lynn Zelevansky (auth), article, Art News, 4/82; Christopher French (auth), Redefining figures, Art Week, 7/3/82. *Dealer:* Hal Bromm Gallery 90 W Broadway New York NY 10013. *Mailing Add:* 284 Lafayette St 5D New York NY 10012

KILGORE, AL
CARTOONIST
b Newark, NJ, Dec 19, 27. *Study:* Art Career Sch, New York, grad, 51. *Pos:* Illusr children's books, Pageant Press, 52-55; gag cartoons for weekly trade paper, 52-62; auth & illusr, Bullwinkle comic strip, Bell McClure Syndicate, 62-65; advert comics, Quaker Oats Co, 65; Storyboards for Underdog, TV show, 66-67; weekly caricature puzzle feature, TV Star-Screen, 69-; co-producer, dir, auth & lyrics, animated cartoon, World of Hans Christian Andersen, 70-71. *Mem:* Nat Cartoonists Soc. *Publ:* Auth, Bullwinkle Comic Books, Western Publ Co, 60-62; illusr, Pink Panther Books, Lion Press, 68. *Mailing Add:* 216-55 113th Dr Queens Village NY 11429

KILIAN, AUSTIN FARLAND
PAINTER, EDUCATOR
b Lyons, SDak, Sept 19, 20. *Study:* Augustana Col, SDak, BA, 42; Univ Iowa, MFA, 49; Acad Montmartre, Paris, with Fernand Leger, 51; Mexico City Col, 52; Ohio State Univ, 55; Univ Calif, Los Angeles, 66. *Work:* D D Feldman Collection, Dallas; Univ Iowa Galleries, Iowa City. *Exhib:* Laguna Gloria Mus Citation Regional, Austin, Tex, 58; Art Asn New Orleans, Delgado Mus, 59; Made in Tex by Texans, Dallas Mus Contemp Arts, 59; San Diego Art Instr Show, Art Ctr La Jolla, Calif, 61; Inland Empire Country Club Fac Exhib, San Bernardino, 81; and others. *Collections Arranged:* Waco Art Forum Mus Regional Shows, 59; San Diego Art Guild Shows, Fine Arts Gallery, 61; Art In All Media, Southern Calif Expos, Del Mar, 63-70; Col of the Desert Shows, 70- *Teaching:* Instr photog, Univ Idaho, 49-50; head dept art, Dillard Univ, 50-53; asst prof, Baylor Univ, 53-59; chmn dept art, Calif Western Univ, 59-64; assoc prof, Col Desert, Calif, 70- *Awards:* Art Asn New Orleans Third Award, Delgado Mus, 52; Sons of Herman Award, San Antonio, Tex, 55; Purchase Award, D D Feldman Exhib, 68. *Bibliog:* Henry Burnett & Orville Voigt, Today Painting (film), Col Desert, 80; William Hemmerdinger (auth), Collectors, Palm Springs Life Mag, 12/81. *Mem:* Art Hist Southern Calif; Palm Springs Desert Mus; Col Art Asn Am; Am Fedn of Arts. *Media:* Collage, Oil. *Publ:* Auth, Catalog loan exhibition of notable works from the Metropolitan, 52; auth, Culture makes a face, KABC-TV, Hollywood, 62; auth, The two Californias (catalog), 63; auth, Southern California Exposition, Art in All Media (catalogs), 63-70; auth, article, San Diego Eve Tribune, 6/14/64. *Mailing Add:* 3720 Wawona Dr San Diego CA 92107

KILLEEN, MELISSA HELEN
DEALER, GALLERY DIRECTOR
b Binghamton, NY, Oct 28, 55. *Study:* Syracuse Univ, NY, BFA(cum laude), 76; Johnson Atelier Tech Sch Sculpture, NJ, cert, 78. *Collections Arranged:* Wood Biennial (twelve wood designer-craftsmen; auth, catalog), 78, 80 & 82; Monumental Sculpture Traveling Exhib, 79 & 82; Monumental Weaving, 83. *Pos:* Craft coordinator, By Hand Crafts Gallery, NJ, 76-77; mgr, Richard Kagan Gallery, Pa, 78-79; dir & owner, The Gallery at 401, Magnolia, NJ, 79-; owner & dir, Landsman Gallery, 82-; vpres, ArtMarkit Inc, 82- *Teaching:* Asst dept chairperson ceramic shell & plastics, Johnson Atelier, NJ, 76-79. *Specialty:* Contemp fine art, monumental sculpture and graphic art. *Mailing Add:* Landsman Gallery Atrium Centre 706 Haddonfield Rd Cherry Hill NJ 08002

KILLMASTER, JOHN H
PAINTER, ENAMELIST
b Allegan, Mich, Dec 2, 34. *Study:* Soc Arts & Crafts, Detroit, Mich; Hope Col, BA; Univ Guanajuato, Mex, Cranbrook Acad Art, MFA. *Work:* Boise Cascade World Hq Collection Fine Art, Idaho; Northwestern Col, Orange City, Iowa; Idaho First Nat Bank; Sunshine Mining; Gulf Oil Corp; and others. *Exhib:* 31st Ann Northwest Watercolor, Seattle Art Mus, 71; San Francisco Mus Mod Art, Calif, 79-80; Nat Mus Am Art, Smithsonian Inst, 79-80; Newport Harbor Mus, Calif, 80; Denver Art Mus, 80; Art from Idaho, Nat Mus Am Art, 83; Vitrous Enamel Nat Show, San Diego, Calif, 83. *Pos:* Illusr & designer, Ladriere Art Studio, Detroit, 58-61. *Teaching:* Asst prof painting, Ferris State Col, 69-70; prof art, Boise State Univ, 70- *Awards:* Purchase Awards, Idaho Artists Ann, Boise Art Mus, 70, 74, 76 & 77; Western States Art Found fel & grant, 74; Governors Award for Excellence in the Arts, 78. *Bibliog:* Idaho landscape painter (film), Idaho Arts Comn, 72; Crafts in Architecture, West States Arts Found, 81-82; Enamel Work, Am

Crafts Mag, 83. *Mem:* NW Designer Craftsman Asn; Idaho Art Asn; Nat Enamelist Guild, Washington, DC. *Publ:* Illusr, Gen Motors Stockholders Publ, 59 & Ford Times Mag, 78; Enamel, Enameling, Enamelists, Chilton Book Pub, 83. *Dealer:* Gallery West 4836 SW Scholls Ferry Rd Portland OR 97225; Spring Street Enamels Gallery New York NY. *Mailing Add:* 220 Cotterell Dr Boise ID 83709

KILMER, NICHOLAS JOHN
ADMINISTRATOR, PAINTER
b Washington, DC, Dec 3, 41. *Study:* Georgetown Univ, AB, 62; Harvard Univ, AM, 63. *Work:* Bristol Community Col, Fall River, Mass. *Exhib:* Wadsworth Atheneum, Hartford, Conn, 74 & 79; solo exhib, Fayetteville Mus Art, NC, 82. *Pos:* Dean, Swain Sch Design, New Bedford, Mass, 79- *Teaching:* Assoc prof liberal arts & dean, Swain Sch Design, Mass, 79- *Mem:* Col Art Asn. *Media:* Oil. *Publ:* Contribr, F C Frieseke 1874-1974 (catalog), Telfair Acad, Savannah, Ga, 74; auth & illusr, Poems of Pierre de Ronsard, Univ Calif Press, 79; auth, Francis Petrarch: Songs and Sonnets, North Point Press, 81; auth, F C Frieseke: A retrospective (catalog), Maxwell Galleries, San Francisco, 82. *Mailing Add:* c/o Swain Sch Design 19 Hawthorn St New Bedford MA 02740

KIM, BONGTAE
PAINTER, PRINTMAKER
b Pusan, Korea, July 23, 37; US citizen. *Study:* Col Fine Arts; Seoul Nat Univ, BFA; Otis Art Inst, Los Angeles, BFA & MFA. *Work:* French Govt, Univ Southern Calif; Chase Manhattan Bank; Contemp Mus of Art, Seoul, Korea; Seoul Nat Univ Gallery. *Comn:* Geometric image murals, Lathem & Watkins, 70; Paul Hastings, Janofsky & Walker, 71, Allison Co, 72, Baker, Ancel & Redmond, 72 & K T Color Lab, 77, Los Angeles. *Exhib:* The Reality of Illusion, Denver Art Mus, 79; Space Expose II, Los Angeles Co Mus Art, 79; West Meets East, Azuma Gallery, New York, 79; Nat Mus Mod Art, 80; one-man shows, Dong Sanbang Gallery, Seoul, 80 & Am Cult Ctr, Pusan, 80; and many other group and one-man exhibs. *Pos:* Co-dir & co-founder, Triad Graphic Workshop, 67- *Teaching:* Senior lectr printmaking, Univ Southern Calif, 71-80; instr, Otis/Parson Sch Design, 79- *Awards:* Purchase awards, 4th & 5th Ann Print Show, San Diego State Col, 71, 72 & Ink & Clay Show, Calif State Politech Univ, 75; cash award, 3rd Nat Print Show, Univ of Southern Calif, 75. *Bibliog:* Innovative Printmakers (article) Southwest Art Mag, 72; Leonard Edmondson (auth), Etching, Van Nostrand Reinholt Co, 73; Thelma R Newman (auth), Innovative Printmaking, Crown Publ, 77. *Mem:* Los Angeles Printmaking Soc (pres, 72). *Mailing Add:* 6518 Greenbush Ave Van Nuys CA 91401

KIM, PO (HYUN)
PAINTER
b Korea; US citizen. *Study:* Univ Ill, MFA, 57. *Work:* Chicago Art Inst, Ill; Solomon R Guggenheim Mus, New York; Okla Art Ctr; Tenn Fine Art Ctr. *Exhib:* Painting & Sculpture Today, Indianapolis Mus Art, Ind, 78; one-man shows, Squibb Gallery, Princeton, NJ, 79, Gallery Mod Art Int, Munich, West Germany, 80 & Art Alliance, Philadelphia, Pa, 80; Korean Drawing Now, Brooklyn Mus, NY, 81; A Feast for the Eyes, Heckscher Mus, Huntington, NY, 81. *Teaching:* Instr, New York Univ. *Media:* Oil, Pencil. *Mailing Add:* 417 Lafayette St New York NY 10003

KIMBALL, WILFORD WAYNE, JR
LITHOGRAPHER, DRAFTSMAN
b Salt Lake City, Utah, July 15, 43. *Study:* Southern Utah State Col, BA, 68; Univ Ariz, MFA, 70; Tamarind Inst, Albuquerque, NMex, fel printmaking, 70-71, Master Printer, 71. *Work:* Tamarind Collection, Albuquerque, NMex; Brooklyn Mus; Libr Cong, Washington, DC; Lessing J Rosenwald Collection, The Philadelphia Mus of Art & Nat Gallery Fine Arts, Washington, DC. *Comn:* Lithographs, Madison Print Club, Wis, 76. *Exhib:* Brooklyn Mus Biennial Print Exhib, New York, 78; 56th Ann Philadelphia Competition, The Print Club, 80; Colorprint USA, Texas Tech Univ, Lubbock, Tex, 80; Tenth Anniversary Exhib, Tyler Mus Art, Tex, 81; one-man shows, Phoenix Art Mus, Ariz, 81, Art Mus STex, 81 & Thirty Am Printmakers Invitational, Univ Gallery Fine Art, Ohio State Univ, 82; Seventh British Int Print Biennale, Cartwright Hall, Bradford, W Yorkshire, Eng, 82; and others. *Pos:* Artist in residence, Roswell Mus & Art Ctr, NMex, 72; co-dir, Print Research Facility, Ariz State Univ, Tempe, 79- *Teaching:* Lectr lithography, Univ NMex, fall 71; vis lectr lithography & drawing, Univ Wis, Madison, 72-73 & summers 73 & 74; asst prof lithography & drawing, San Diego State Univ, 73-74; asst prof lithography, Calif State Univ, Long Beach, 74-75; asst prof lithography & drawing, Univ Tex San Antonio, 75-77; lectr lithography & serigraphy, San Diego State Univ, 77-78; prof lithography & drawing, Ariz State Univ, Tempe, 78- *Awards:* William H Walker Purchase Award, 55th Philadelphia Am, 79; Purchase Awards, 17th Bradley Nat Print & Drawing Exhib, 79 & Vermillion '79 Nat Print & Drawing Competition, 79. *Media:* Lithography. *Dealer:* Rubicon Gallery 398 Main St Los Altos CA 94022; Assoc Am Artists 663 Fifth Ave New York NY 10022. *Mailing Add:* 1328 E Harvest St Mesa AZ 85203

KIMBRELL, LEONARD BUELL
HISTORIAN
b Archibald, La, Aug 3, 22. *Study:* Northwestern State Univ, La, BA, 42; Univ Ore, MS, 50, MFA, 54; Univ Iowa, PhD, 65. *Work:* Univ Ore, Eugene. *Pos:* Contrib ed, Artweek, 71-; art critic, NW Mag, 81- *Teaching:* Prof art, Eastern Ore Col, 54-61; prof art, Portland State Univ, 61-, head dept art & archit, 76- *Awards:* Purchase Award, Portland Art Mus, 53. *Mem:* Col Art Asn; Soc Archit Historians. *Res:* Cranach's nudes in the light of Luther's ethics; Alexander Pope as failed painter; guide to art in the Pacific Northwest; Rodins at Maryhill. *Publ:* Auth, Some new light on Astoria Column, Festshrift: Marion Ross, Soc Archit Historians, 76. *Mailing Add:* 1785 SW Montgomery Dr Portland OR 97201

KIMBROUGH, SARA DODGE
PAINTER
b New York, NY. *Study:* Cooper Union; Grand Cent Art Sch, scholar; also with William DeLeftwich Dodge, Henry Lee McFee, Jerry Farnsworth & Frederick MacMonnies. *Work:* Phoenix Pub Libr, Ariz; Leflore Co Courthouse, Greenwood, Miss; US Sen Pat Harrison Libr, Univ Miss; Mem Rm, Davison Speech Sch, Atlanta, Ga; Beauvoir, Jefferson Davis Shrine, Biloxi, Miss. *Comn:* Many portrait commissions of prominent persons, 30-78. *Exhib:* Nat Gallery Art, Washington, DC; Ariz State Fair, Phoenix; Nat Asn Women Painters & Sculptors; solo shows, Phoenix Art Ctr & Wright Art Gallery, Cleveland, Miss; and many others. *Awards:* League Am Pen Women, 36; Grand Nat Finalist, Am Artists Prof League, 53; Award, Ill Valley Art Exhib, 60. *Mem:* Miss Art Asn; Gulf Coast Arts Coun; regional mem Portraits, Inc; Nat Soc Lit & Arts; Miss Inst Arts & Lett. *Media:* Oil, Watercolor. *Publ:* Auth, Drawn From Life, Univ Miss Press, Jackson, 76. *Mailing Add:* 806 North Beach Bay St Louis MS 39520

KIMMEL-COHN, ROBERTA
DEALER, DESIGNER
b Milwaukee, Wis, Feb 1, 37. *Study:* Sophie Newcomb Col, with George Rickey; Univ Wis; Boston Univ Sch Fine & Appl Arts, BFA. *Pos:* Art dir, McGraw-Hill Publ Co, New York, 61-62, Macmillan & Co, 64-65 & Walker & Co, 65-67; pres, Roberta Kimmel Advert, New York, 67-; partner, Kimmel/Cohn Photog Arts, New York, 74- *Bibliog:* Surrealism in advertising, Art Dir Mag, 70; article in Art Dir Ann, 72; People in the news, New York Times, 74. *Specialty:* Photography; Man Ray; nineteenth and twentieth century art. *Publ:* Auth, Erste Landung, portfolio of photographs by George Grosz, 77; Man Ray: Vintage Photographs, Rayographs and Solarizations, 77. *Mailing Add:* 41 Central Park W New York NY 10023

KIMMELMAN, HAROLD
SCULPTOR
b Philadelphia, Pa, Feb 20, 23. *Study:* Cape Sch Art, Provincetown, Mass; Pa Acad Fine Art, Philadelphia. *Comn:* Helios Flame, Sun Oil Corp Hq, Radnor, Pa, 76; Burst of Joy, The Gallery, Philadelphia, 77; Marino Monument, Casa Enrico Fermi Corp, Philadelphia, Pa, 77; Man Helping Man, Am Col Cardiology, Bethesda, Md, 79; Holocaust Mem, Cooper River Pkwy, Pennsauken, NJ, 81; and others. *Exhib:* Pa Acad Fine Arts, 68; Philadelphia Civic Ctr Show, 71. *Awards:* Braverman Karp Prize for sculpting, 68; May Audubon Prize for sculpting, 69. *Bibliog:* Sculpture of a City, Walker Publ Co, 74. *Mem:* Artists Equity Asn (pres, Philadelphia Chap, 72); fel Pa Acad Fine Arts. *Media:* Stainless Steel, Bronze. *Mailing Add:* 538 W Carpenter Lane Philadelphia PA 19119

KIMURA, RIISABURO
PAINTER, PRINTMAKER
b Yokosuka, Japan, Oct 13, 24. *Study:* Yokohama Univ, 47; Hosei Univ, Tokyo, 54. *Work:* Mus Mod Art, New York; Nat Mus Mod Art, Kyoto, Japan; US Info Agency; City of Hamburg, WGer. *Comn:* Print ed, Brooklyn Mus, 75. *Exhib:* USA Pavillion Expo 70, Osaka, Japan; two-man show, Gimpel Gallery, New York, 71; Japanese Artists in the Americas, Nat Mus Mod Art, Kyoto, Japan, 74; one-man shows, Michido Gallery, Tokyo, Osaka & Nagoya, Japan, 74 & Gallery Mod Art, Munich, WGer, 77; Frank Fedele Fine Arts, New York. *Awards:* Int Biennal Print Award, Tokyo, 70. *Mailing Add:* 463 West St New York NY 10014

KIMURA, SUEKO M
PAINTER
b Hawaii. *Study:* Univ Hawaii, BA & MFA; Chouinard Art Inst; Columbia Univ; Brooklyn Mus Sch Art; Art Students League. *Work:* State Found Cult & Arts; Contemp Arts Ctr; State Dept Educ Artmobile; Int Savings & Loan; Kaiser Hawaii-Kai Develop Co; Bilger Hall, Univ Hawaii; Honolulu Acad Art. *Exhib:* One-man shows, George Hall Gallery, Contemp Arts Ctr & Crossroads Gallery; Brooklyn Mus; San Diego Art Mus; Bibliot Am, Bucharest; Kyoto Mus Mod Art. *Teaching:* Emer prof art, Univ Hawaii, 52- *Awards:* Honolulu Printmakers, 62; Easter Art Show, 62, 65 & 68; Purchase Prizes, State Found Cult & Arts, 68, 69 & 72; plus others. *Mem:* Hawaii Painters & Sculptors League; Honolulu Printmakers. *Publ:* Illusr, cover design & drawings, Philosophy and Culture, East & West, 62. *Mailing Add:* 2567B Henry St Honolulu HI 96817

KIMURA, WILLIAM YUSABURO
PAINTER, PRINTMAKER
b Seattle, Wash, June 28, 20. *Study:* Hollywood Art Ctr, 39; Cornish Sch Art, Seattle, 40; also with Adolph Kronengold, Danny Pierce, Junichiro Sekino, Bill Richie & Evan Phoutrides. *Work:* Fine Art Mus, Alaska Methodist Univ, Color Ctr Gallery, Anchorage. *Comn:* Homage to Salmon (aluminum welded sculpture), Anchorage CofC, 79; Stainless Steel Welded Sculptural Fountain, Balanced Arcs, Anchorage, 81. *Exhib:* Smithsonian Traveling Exhib, USA & Europe, Washington, DC, 62; one-man shows, Anchorage Fine Art Mus, 71, prints, The Gallery, Anchorage, 77 & Painting & Prints, Anchorage Fine Arts Mus, 78; Ann All Alaska Exhib Artists & Craftsmen, 65-72; Wenatchee Apple Blossom Festival, Wash, 71. *Teaching:* Instr painting, Anchorage Community Ctr, 59-60 & Anchorage Community Col, 61-63; artist in residence, Alaska Methodist Univ, 66, assoc prof art, 73; artist in residence, Visual Arts Ctr of Alaska, 77. *Awards:* Mel Kohler Award in Painting, Ann All Alaska Exhib, 66; Prints Alaska Award, Alaska Coun Arts, 76; First Award in Prints, All-Alaska Juried Art Exhib, 76 & 77. *Bibliog:* Paintings & Prints, Alaska Methodist Univ, 63; Woodcuts & Prints, Mel Kohler Gallery, 64; Paintings & Prints, Anchorage Fine Art Mus, 71. *Mem:* Life mem Alaska Artist Guild (pres, 63-65). *Dealer:* Artique Ltd 314 G St Anchorage AK 99501. *Mailing Add:* 1025 W 11th Ave Anchorage AK 99501

KINCADE, ARTHUR WARREN
COLLECTOR, PATRON
b Chillicothe, Mo, Aug 14, 1896. *Collection:* About 100 paintings from 16th century Italian Baroque to artists of the southwest; Henri, etc. *Mailing Add:* 255 N Roosevelt Wichita KS 67208

KIND, JOSHUA B
EDUCATOR, CRITIC
b Philadelphia, Pa, Nov 5, 33. *Study:* Univ Pa, Philadelphia, BA, 55; Columbia Univ, PhD, 67. *Pos:* Chicago ed, Art News, New York, 64-70; dir, Oxbow Summer Sch Art, Saugatuck, Mich, 67-68; contrib ed, New Art Examr, Chicago, 75- *Teaching:* Instr art hist, Northwestern Univ, Evanston, Ill, 59-62; instr humanities, Univ Chicago, 62-65; vis prof art hist, Sch of Art Inst Chicago, 64-76; asst prof art hist & humanities, Ill Inst Technol, Chicago, 65-69; prof art hist, Northern Ill Univ, DeKalb, 69- *Awards:* Nat Endowment for the Arts Critics Fel, 77. *Mem:* Col Art Asn; Soc Architectural Historians. *Res:* Modernism; creativity and the avant-garde; Renaissance inconography; modern architecture. *Publ:* Auth, Rouault, 69; auth, Art and the Corps of Women, New Art Examr, 3/78; auth, The corruption of Norman Rockwell, New Art Examr, 1/79; contribr, World Bk Year Book, 70-; contribr, Encyclopedia Brit Year Book, 70- *Mailing Add:* 5619 Dunham Rd Downers Grove IL 60515

KIND, PHYLLIS
ART DEALER
b New York NY. *Study:* Univ Pa, AB; Univ Chicago, MA. *Pos:* Dir, Phyllis Kind Gallery. *Specialty:* Representing major Chicago artists; acquiring prints and drawings by modern and old masters; introducing exhibitions and selected works by other major contemporary American artists. *Mailing Add:* 226 E Ontario Chicago IL 60611

KINDERMANN, HELMMO
PHOTOGRAPHER
b Lancaster, Pa, Oct 11, 47. *Study:* Tyler Sch Fine Art, Temple Univ, BFA, 69; study of photog, Visual Studies Workshop, Rochester, NY, 71-73; State Univ NY Buffalo, MFA, 73. *Work:* Miss Art Asn, Jackson; Visual Studies Workshop, Rochester, NY; St Lawrence Univ, Canton, New York; Alternative Mus, New York. *Exhib:* Images, Dimensional, Movable, Transferable, Akron Art Inst, Ohio, 73; New Approaches, Ctr for Exploratory and Perceptual Arts, Buffalo, NY, 75; New Photographics/76, Cent Wash State Col, Ellensburgh, 76; Photo/Synthesis, Herbert F Johnson Mus of Art, Ithaca, NY, 76; Auto as Icon, Int Mus Photog, George Eastman House, Rochester, NY, 79; and others. *Pos:* Cur, US Eye Photo Exhib, Nat Fine Arts Comt, XIII Olympic Winter Games, Lake Placid, NY, 78- *Teaching:* Asst prof photog, Lake Placid Sch Art, Ctr for Music, Drama & Art, NY, 73-81. *Awards:* Purchase Prize, Images on Paper, Miss Art Asn, 71. *Mem:* Soc for Photog Educ; Col Art Asn Am; Photog Instr Asn; Friends of Photog. *Media:* Miscellaneous. *Publ:* New Photographics/76, Cent Wash Col, 76; contribr, Works and Process, CMDA Publ Co, 76; contribr, Photo/Synthesis, Herbert F Johnson Mus Art, 76; contribr, The Photograph Collectors Guide, Lee Witkin & Barbara London, NY Graphic Soc; contribr, Uniquely Photographic, Quiver No 5, Honolulu Acad Arts; and others. *Mailing Add:* Wardner Rd Rainbow Lake NY 12976

KING, ELAINE A
CURATOR, HISTORIAN
b Oak Park, Ill, Apr 12, 47. *Study:* Northern Ill Univ BA(20th century art hist), MA with Robert Bonnhuetter, Jan Swenson & Joshua Kind; Columbia Col, Chicago, photog hist with Arthur Siegel; intern, George Eastman House, summer 77; Northwestern Univ, with Howard Baker, Donald Kuspit, Leland Roloff & Charles Kleinhaus. *Collections Arranged:* Photographs James Newberry 1963-1977, 6/77, Dittmar Mem Gallery, Northwestern Univ; Focus on Chicago, 11/77, David Avison & Annie Noggle-Photographs, 3/78; Ill Wesleyan Univ; 70's Wide View Photographs, Northwestern Univ, 78; Retrospective Douglas Heubler's work, 80; Notley Maddox (auth, catalog), 81; Jo Mielziner/Sketches, from the collection of Jules Fisher (auth, catalog), 83; New York Painting-Today (auth, catalog), 83; Ed Paschke: New Paintings (auth, catalog), 83; Mary Beth Edelson: New Works (auth, catalog), 83; and others. *Pos:* Craft studio supvr, Northwestern Univ, 74-75; dir, Artemisia Photo Gallery, Artemisia Gallery/Fund, Chicago, 76-77; cur, Dittmar Mem Gallery, Northwestern Univ, 77-81 & guest cur & consul, Ill Wesleyan Univ, Bloomington, 77-79; dir, Hewlett Art Gallery, Carnegie-Mellon Univ, 81- *Teaching:* Lectr art dept, Northwestern Univ, 75-81; asst prof art hist, Carnegie-Mellon Univ, 81- *Awards:* Chicago Art Award & Richare Hunt Art Award, 5/77; Pa Coun Arts Grant. *Mem:* Soc for Photog Educ; Col Art Asn; Art Table. *Publ:* Auth, Bernice Abbott, Midwest Art, 10/76; auth, Elaine A King talks with Alice Adam at the Frumkin Gallery, Exposure, winter 76; auth, Five Chicago Photojournalists, Afterimage, 6/77; auth, Carnegie International 1982: The way we were, New Art Examiner, 12/82; auth, Art into the eighties, NY Painting Today, 6/83. *Mailing Add:* 5604 Fair Oaks St Pittsburgh PA 15217

KING, ELEANOR (ELEANOR KING HOOKHAM)
PAINTER, PRINTMAKER
b Marlow, Okla, April 5, 09. *Study:* Okla City Col, with Martha Avey, 23; Acad Cult France, Dr Hon Causa, 80. *Work:* Mus Nat Art Mod, Paris; Mus Ville Paris; Cantigny War Mus, Wheaton, Ill; Univ Ind Art Mus, Bloomington; Ill Wesleyan Univ Mus Art. *Exhib:* Int Feminine, Mus Art Ville Paris, 68; Int Art Feminine, Mus Athens, Greece, 68; Int Expo, City Hall, Nice, France, 71; Woman Artists, Palais Goblein, Paris, 72; Int Exposition Art, Bruxelles, Belg, 73-75; Int Artists, Sony Art Mus, Osaka, Japan, 79-83.

Teaching: Privately, 26-80. *Awards:* Medaille Vermeil, Galerie Marcel Bernheim, Repub Francaise Encouragement Progress; Medaille D'Or, Galerie Marcel Bernheim, Accad Ital, Parma, 79; Medaille Vermeil, Grand Prix Humanitaire France, 83. *Bibliog:* Elmhurst (producer), film, Continental Cable Vision, 82; John Knudson (producer), film, Cable Vision, Harper Col, 82. *Mem:* Elmhurst Artists Guild (pres, 51-52 & 71-73); Elmhurst Fine Arts & Civic Ctr Found (pres, 75-); Acad Arts, Sci & Lett, France. *Media:* Watercolor, Oil; Etching, Lithography. *Dealer:* Galerie Marcel Bernheim 18 Ave Matignon Paris France 75008. *Mailing Add:* 289 Adelia St Elmhurst IL 60126

KING, LYNDEL IRENE SAUNDERS
DIRECTOR, ADMINISTRATOR
b Enid, Okla, June 10, 43. *Study:* Univ Kans, BA, 65; Univ Minn, MA, 71, PhD, 82. *Pos:* Asst dir, Art Mus, Univ Minn, 76-78, dir, 78-; dir, Exhibs & Mus Relations, Control Data Corp, 79-81; exhib coordr, Nat Gallery Art, 80. *Mem:* Art Mus Asn (bd secy, 83); Asn Art Mus Dirs; Am Asn Mus; Asn Col & Univ Mus & Galleries. *Res:* Nineteenth century England, especially interaction of arts and society. *Publ:* Auth, Exhibition diplomacy, Mus News, 79; auth, Museums and special exhibitions, Art J, 80. *Mailing Add:* 110 Northrop Auditorium Univ Minn Minneapolis MN 55455

KING, MYRON LYZON
DEALER
b Hampton Bays, NY, Oct 22, 21. *Study:* David Lipscomb Col, Peabody Col, BA. *Pos:* Lyzon Pictures & Frames, Inc, Nashville. *Specialty:* Contemporary American art; Sterling Strauser and Paul Lancaster. *Mailing Add:* 411 Thompson Lane Nashville TN 37211

KING, WILLIAM DICKEY
SCULPTOR
b Jacksonville, Fla, Feb 25, 25. *Study:* Univ Fla, 42-44; Cooper Union Art Sch, 45-48; Brooklyn Mus Art Sch, 49; Skowhegan Sch Painting & Sculpture, 48; also in Rome. *Work:* Univ Calif; Cornell Univ, Ithaca, NY; Univ NC; Syracuse Univ, NY; Addison Gallery Am Art, Andover, Mass. *Comn:* Murals, SS United States, 52, Bankers Trust Co, New York, 60, Miami-Dade, 72, State Univ NY, Potsdam, 73-74, Detroit Med Ctr, 79 & Madison Art & Civic Ctr, Wis, 79. *Exhib:* Whitney Mus Am Art, Mus Mod Art & Guggenheim Mus, New York; Philadelphia Mus Art; Los Angeles Co Mus Art; Retrospective, San Francisco Mus Art, Calif, 70 & 74; Am Acad Arts & Lett, 70 & 74; New Sch Social Res, New York, 72; Harvard Univ, 72; 2nd Int Biennial Small Sculptures Exhib, Art Gallery of Budapest, Hungary, 73; Cranbrook Acad Art, Bloomfield Hills, Mich, 74; one-man show, Univ Conn, 79; and others. *Teaching:* Instr sculpture, Brooklyn Mus Sch Art, 53-59; lectr sculpture, Univ Calif, Berkeley, 65-66; instr sculpture, Art Students League, 68-69, Univ Pa, 72-73 & State Univ NY, 74-75. *Awards:* Fulbright Fel, 49; St Gaudens Medal, Cooper Union, 64; Creative Artists Pub Serv Proj Grant, 74. *Bibliog:* S Schwartz (auth), New York letter: William King, Art Int, 11/72; John Sanders (auth), Photography Year Book 1973, London, 72; Hilton Kramer (auth), The Age of the Avant-Garde, London, 74. *Dealer:* Terry Dintenfass Inc 18 E 67th St New York NY 10021. *Mailing Add:* 17 E 96th St New York NY 10028

KINGHAN, CHARLES ROSS
PAINTER
b Anthony, Kans, Jan 18, 1895. *Study:* Am Acad Art; Art Inst Chicago. *Work:* Philadelphia Mus Art, Pa; Nat Acad Design, New York; Smithsonian Inst, Washington, DC. *Exhib:* Wichita Art Asn, Kans, 56; Allied Artists Am, New York, 57-; Am Watercolor Soc, 57-; Nat Acad Design, New York, 57- *Pos:* Sketch man, Maxon Advert Agency, New York, 51-53; sketch man, Batton Barton Durstin Advert Co, New York, 53-62. *Teaching:* Instr art, Am Acad Art; instr watercolor, pvt classes, 37-; instr oil & watercolor, Huguenot Sch Art, 45-51. *Awards:* Gold Medal, Am Watercolor Soc, 56; Gold Medal, Hudson Valley Art Asn, 60; Gold Medal for portrait, Allied Artists, 64. *Bibliog:* Rendering techniques, 58 & Ted Kautzky, Master of Pencil and Watercolor, 59, Reinhold. *Mem:* Academician Nat Acad Design; Am Watercolor Soc; Hudson Valley Art Asn; Allied Artists Am. *Media:* Acrylic, Oil, Watercolor. *Dealer:* Huney Gallery 3746 Sixth Ave San Diego CA 92103. *Mailing Add:* Forest Hill Manor 551 Gibson Ave Pacific Grove CA 93950

KINGMAN, DONG M
PAINTER, ILLUSTRATOR
b Oakland, Calif, Mar 31, 11. *Study:* Lingnan Sch, Hong Kong, with Sze-To-Wai, 26; Fox & Morgan Art Sch, Oakland. *Work:* Metrop Mus Art, Mus Mod Art & Whitney Mus Am Art, New York; Boston Mus Fine Arts, Mass; M H De Young Mus, San Francisco. *Comn:* Murals, Hilton Hotel, New York, 63, mosaic, Pres Hotel, Hong Kong, 64, Bank Calif, San Francisco, 68 & Boca Raton Hotel, 70; tapestry designed for Ambassador Hotel, Hong Kong, 74; and others. *Exhib:* Am Watercolor Soc; San Francisco Art Asn; Metrop Mus Art Watercolor Exhib; Whitney Mus Am Art Ann; Columbus Mus Arts & Crafts, Ga. *Teaching:* Instr art, Columbia Univ, 46-54; instr watercolor & hist Chinese art, Hunter Col, 48-53; fac mem, Famous Artists Sch, Westport, Conn, 54- *Awards:* Prizes at San Francisco Art Asn Ann Exhib, 36, Metrop Mus Art Watercolor Exhib & Am Watercolor Soc Ann. *Bibliog:* James Wong Howe (dir), Dong Kingman (film), 54; Alan D Gruskin (auth), The Watercolors of Dong Kingman, Crowell Co, 58. *Mem:* Am Watercolor Soc; West Coast Watercolor Soc; Dutch Treat Club. *Media:* Watercolor, Lacquer. *Publ:* Illusr, China's Story, 46; illusr, Johnny Hong in Chinatown, 52; illusr, City on the Golden Hill, 67; illusr, The Effect of Gamma Rays on Man-in-the-moon Marigolds, 71; dir, Hongkong Dong (film), 75. *Dealer:* Hammer Gallery 33 W 57th St New York NY 10019. *Mailing Add:* 21 W 58th St New York NY 10019

KINGREY, KENNETH
DESIGNER, EDUCATOR
b Santa Ana, Calif, Dec 23, 13. *Study:* Univ Calif, Los Angeles, BE & MA. *Exhib:* 50 Best Books, Am Inst Graphic Arts, 58; Traveling Exhib, US, Europe, Cent Am & Russia; Univ Hawaii; Honolulu Acad Arts; plus others. *Teaching:* Prof advert art, Univ Calif, Los Angeles, 40-53; prof art, Univ Hawaii, 50-51 & 53-80, retired. *Awards:* 50 Best Bk Awards, Am Inst Graphic Arts, 58 & 61; Western Bk Awards, 58-63. *Mem:* Los Angeles Art Dirs Club; Hawaii Artists League; Nat Art Dirs Club. *Publ:* Ed, Design Quart, Walker Art Ctr, 60; contribr, Idea, 61; contribr, Graphic design, Eur-Asian Graphics. *Mailing Add:* 5959 Kalanianaole Hwy Honolulu HI 96821

KINGSLEY, APRIL
CRITIC, LECTURER
b New York, NY, Feb 16, 41. *Study:* NY Univ, BA(art hist) & MA. *Pos:* Asst cur, Mus Mod Art, New York, 70-71; assoc cur, Pasadena Art Mus, Calif, 71-72; regular critic, Soho Weekly News, NY, 75-77 & Village Voice, 77-79, Newsweek, 79; dir, Sculpture Ctr, New York, 80-; assoc ed, ArtexPress Mag, 81-82. *Teaching:* Instr ideas in art, Sch Visual Arts, 73-, RI Sch Design, 83. *Mem:* Int Art Critics Asn. *Res:* Conceptual art. *Publ:* Auth, James Brooks dialogue & critique, Arts Mag, 75; auth, Six women at work in the landscape, 77 & Carol Haerer, 83, Arts Mag; auth, Balthus, 79 & Philip Austin, 82, Horizon. *Mailing Add:* 246 W 16th St New York NY 10011

KINGSTON, EMILY FULLER See Fuller, Emily

KINGTON, L(OUIS) BRENT
SCULPTOR, EDUCATOR
b Topeka, Kans, July 26, 34. *Study:* Univ Kans, BFA, 57; Cranbrook Acad Art, MFA, 61. *Work:* Mus Contemp Crafts, New York; Johnson Collection, Racine, Wis; St Paul Art Ctr, Minn; Krannert Art Mus, Univ Ill, Urbana; Univ Wis-Milwaukee; and others. *Exhib:* North American Goldsmiths, Renwick Gallery, Smithsonian, Washington, DC, 74; Reprise, Cranbrook Mus Art, Bloomfield Hills, Mich, 75; American Crafts, 1976, Mus Contemp Art, Chicago, 76; Wind and Weathervanes, Craft & Folk Mus, Los Angeles, 76; American Crafts for the Vatican Museum, Rome, 78; Towards a New Iron Age, Victoria & Albert Mus, London, 82; and others. *Teaching:* Prof metal smithing, Southern Ill Univ, Carbondale, 61- *Awards:* Design in Steel Award for Excellence, Am Iron & Steel Inst, 71; Grand Prize, 3rd Creative Arts Festival, Cincinnati, 73; Award Excellence, 36th Ann Wabash Valley Exhib, Swope Art Gallery, 80. *Mem:* Soc NAm Goldsmiths (pres, 70-74); Am Crafts Coun (trustee, 76-80); Artists-Blacksmiths Asn NAm (dir, 75-79). *Media:* Metals. *Dealer:* Theo Portnoy Gallery 56 W 57th St New York NY 10019; Gilman Galleries 277 E Ontario St Chicago IL 60611. *Mailing Add:* Sch of Art Southern Ill Univ Carbondale IL 62901

KINIGSTEIN, JONAH
PAINTER, DESIGNER
b New York, NY, June 26, 23. *Study:* Cooper Union Art Sch, 41-43; Grande Chaumiere, Paris, 47-51; Belle Arte, Rome, Fulbright Fel, 53-54. *Work:* Mus Mod Art, New York; Albright-Knox Art Gallery, Buffalo, NY; Nelson Gallery Art; Washington Mus; Ain Herod Mus, Tel-Aviv, Israel; also in pvt collections. *Exhib:* Butler Inst Am Art, Youngstown, Ohio, 56; Young Americans, Whitney Mus Am Art, New York, 57; Nat Acad Arts & Lett, 68; one-man shows, ACA Gallery, 68 & Rittenhouse Gallery, Philadelphia, 75; Washington Irving Gallery, New York, 82; Art & the Law, Landmark Ctr, St Paul, Minn, 82; Rittenhouse Gallery, Philadelphia, 82; and others. *Teaching:* Brooklyn Mus Art Sch, 70. *Awards:* First Prize, Silvermine Guild, 59; Louis Comfort Tiffany Found Award, 62; Perkins-Elmer Prize, 62; and others. *Mailing Add:* 105 E Ninth St New York NY 10003

KINNAIRD, RICHARD WILLIAM
PAINTER, EDUCATOR
b Buenos Aires, Arg, Nov 19, 31; US citizen. *Study:* Univ Mich, Ann Arbor, 49-51; Carleton Col, Northfield, Minn, BA, 53; Art Inst Chicago, 52; Univ Ill, with Lee Chesney, MFA, 58. *Work:* Seattle Mus of Art; NC Mus of Art, Raleigh; Hanes Knitting Corp & R J Reynolds Corp, Winston-Salem, NC. *Comn:* Thomas Wolfe Mem Sculpture, class gift to Univ NC-Chapel Hill, 66; pediment sculpture, Mint Mus of Art, Charlotte, NC, 72. *Exhib:* Award Winners Exhib of Chicago No-Jury Show, Art Inst of Chicago, 57; Southeastern Ann Painting & Sculpture, High Mus, Atlanta, Ga, 66; Experimental Media, Corcoran Gallery of Contemp Art, Washington, DC, 70; Painting & Sculpture Exhib, Mint Mus of Art, 71; Third Ann Contemp Reflections, Aldrich Mus of Contemp Art, 73; solo exhibs, Sandhurst Art Coun, Aberdeen, NC, 78 & Rowan Art Ctr, Salisbury, NC, 79; Selections from the Collection, Aldrich Mus Contemp Art, Ridgefield, Conn, 78; Patron Art Patron, Southeastern Ctr Contemp Art, 79; Exhib of Works by Tenn Valley States Artists, Tenn Valley Auth Washington Visitors Ctr, DC, 79. *Collections Arranged:* Univ Evansville Fine Arts Exhib, Ind, 73. *Teaching:* Instr printmaking & etching, Auburn Univ, Ala, 60-64; from instr to assoc prof painting, Univ NC, 64-76, prof painting, 76- *Awards:* Purchase Award, Third Ann Contemp Reflections, Aldrich Mus of Contemp Art, 74; First Painting Award, Spring Mill Ann Art Exhib, Spring Mills Corp, Lancaster, SC, 76; First Award, 40th Ann NC Artists, NC Mus of Fine Art, Raleigh, 77. *Media:* Acrylic and oil. *Mailing Add:* 403-B Smith Ave Chapel Hill NC 27514

KINNEE, SANDY
PRINTMAKER
b Port Huron, Mich, Mar 30, 47. *Study:* Univ Mich, Ann Arbor, BFA(printmaking), 69; Wayne State Univ, Detroit, MFA(printmaking), 76. *Work:* Metrop Mus Art, New York; Mus NMex, Santa Fe; Evergreen State Col; Portland Art Mus; Allen Art Mus, Oberlin, Ohio. *Exhib:* Works on Handmade Paper, Mus Mod Art, New York, 76; Paper as Medium, Smithsonian, traveling, 78-81; one-man shows, Philadelphia Art Alliance, 81 & Creighton Univ, Omaha, 81; Mather Gallery, Case Western Univ, 82; New American Graphics II Travelling Exhib, 82-83; and others. *Awards:* Major Award, Four Corners States Biennial, Phoenix Art Mus, 77; SW Biennial Purchase Award, Mus NMex, 78; Printmakers Fel, Western States Arts Found, 79. *Bibliog:* Jules Heller (auth), Papermaking, Watson-Guptill, 78; Virginia Butera (auth), Sandy Kinnee, Arts Mag, 6/81; Suzanne M Singletary (auth), Sandy Kinnee, Fans and Kimonos, Artspace, 1/82. *Media:* Screenprinting, Handcolored Intaglio on Handmade Paper. *Publ:* Papermaking (film), Crystal Productions, Aspen, Colo, 80; auth, Fans, bridges, kimonos and the role paper plays in my work, Print Club, Philadelphia, 81; Printmaking (film), Crystal Prod, Aspen, Colo, 83. *Dealer:* Orion Editions 835 Madison Ave New York NY 10021; Robischon Gallery 1122 E 17th Ave Denver CO 80218. *Mailing Add:* 1202 N Institute Colorado Springs CO 80903

KINNEY, GILBERT HART
COLLECTOR, ADMINISTRATOR
b New York, NY, May 11, 31. *Study:* Yale Univ, BA, 53 & MA, 54; John F Kennedy Sch, MPA, 73. *Pos:* Trustee, 74-77, 78- & chief exec officer, 77-78, Corcoran Gallery of Art, Washington, DC; trustee, Archs Am Art, 74-, pres, 78-82; trustee, Am Federation of the Arts, 78. *Collection:* Major emphasis post-war American painting and sculpture, also European 20th century painting and sculpture and Far Eastern ceramics and sculpture. *Mailing Add:* 1231 31st St NW Washington DC 20007

KINOSHITA, GENE
ARCHITECT
b Vancouver, BC, Jan 18, 35. *Study:* Univ BC, BArch (honors), 59; Yale Univ, MArch, 62. *Comn:* Detention Ctr, Ont Govt, 74; Humber Col Master Planning, 75; Ont Col of Art expansion & renovations, 77-; High Park Libr, Toronto, 77; Environ Studies Bldg, Univ Waterloo, 79; and others. *Exhib:* Travelling Exhib Can Art Mus, Royal Can Acad Arts, 67; Can Unit Masonry Awards Prog Travelling Exhib Can, 72; Ont Masons Rels Coun, Travelling Prov Exhib, 73; Am Inst Arch & Am Correctional Asn Traveling Show, 80. *Pos:* Partner design, Moffat-Kinoshita Partnership Architects, 65- *Awards:* Leather Medals Award for Great W Beef Co Restaurant & Lounge, Waterloo, Ont, 76; Metro Toronto Detention Centre, Award of Excellence from Ont Asn of Architects Design Awards, 77 & Award of Excellence from Ont Masons' Rels Coun, 77; and others. *Mem:* Can Conf Arts; life mem Royal Ont Mus; fel Royal Archit Inst Can; Ont Asn Archit; academician Royal Can Acad Arts; and others. *Publ:* Auth, The ROM: A new lease on life, Canadian Collector, 7-8/82; auth, Museums are for people, the evolution of a design concept, Rotunda Mag, Vol 15, No 2, 82. *Mailing Add:* 278 Sheldrake Blvd Toronto ON M4P 2B6 Canada

KINSEL, MICHAEL LESLIE
MUSEUM DIRECTOR
b Council Bluffs, Iowa, May 5, 47. *Study:* Augustana Col, Rock Island, Ill, BA, 69; Univ Chicago, MBA, 73; Lutheran Sch Theology, Master Divinity, 73, DD, 75. *Pos:* Asst dir, Lutheran Sch Theology, Chicago, 70-73; vpres, Knophurst Co, Chicago, 73-74; proj dir, Western Heritage Soc, Omaha, 74-78; dir, Western Heritage Mus, Omaha, 78- *Teaching:* Instr, Western Heritage Mus, Omaha, 76- & Creighton Univ, 82. *Mem:* Am Asn Mus Dirs; Mountain Plains Mus Conf. *Mailing Add:* c/o Western Heritage Mus 801 South Tenth St Omaha NE 68108

KINSMAN, ROBERT DONALD
GALLERY DIRECTOR, HISTORIAN
b Bridgeport, Conn, Sept 13, 29. *Study:* Columbia Univ, BS, 58, MA(art hist), 66. *Collections Arranged:* Jimmy Ernst Retrospective (auth, catalog), 63 & Lyonel Feininger: The Formative Years (auth, catalog), 64, Detroit Inst Arts; The Sculpture of Primitive Peoples (auth, catalog), Mary Washington Col, Univ Va, 66; Leroy Lamis Retrospective (auth, catalog), 79 & Julius Schmidt Retrospective (auth, catalog), 80, Sheldon Swope Art Gallery, Terre Haute, Ind. *Pos:* Asst cur, Nat Gallery Art, Washington, DC, 61-62; cur contemp art, Detroit Inst Arts, 63-65; mus dir, Mary Washington Col, Univ Va, Fredericksburg, 66-68; dir, Sheldon Swope Art Gallery, Terre Haute, Ind, 78-; bd dirs, Arts Illiana Inc, 81- *Teaching:* Instr art hist, Mary Washington Col, Univ Va, Fredericksburg, 62-63, asst prof, 66-68; asst prof, State Univ NY, Albany, 68-77. *Mem:* Am Asn Mus; Col Art Asn Am; Am Asn Univ Prof. *Res:* American and European painting and sculpture since 1850. *Mailing Add:* 4951 Dixie Bee Rd Apt 65 Apt 65 Terre Haute IN 47802

KINSTLER, EVERETT RAYMOND
PAINTER, INSTRUCTOR
b New York, NY, Aug 5, 26. *Study:* Nat Acad Design, New York; Art Students League, with DuMond; also with Wayman Adams, John Johansen & Jas Montgomery Flagg; Rollins Col, Hon DFA, 83. *Work:* Metrop Mus Art, New York; Carnegie Inst, Pittsburgh; Brooklyn Mus; Smithsonian Inst, Washington, DC; Mus City New York; and others. *Comn:* Portraits of Astronaut Scott Carpenter, 63, Astronaut Alan Shepard, 65 & Gov John Connally, 75; official White House Portrait of Pres Gerald R Ford & Pres Richard M Nixon; and others. *Exhib:* One-man shows, Grand Cent Art Galleries, New York, 58 & 82, Lotos Club, New York, 72, Luisa Gallery, Mich, 81, Artists of Am, Denver, 81 & 83 & Rollins Col, Fla, 82. *Teaching:* Instr painting & drawing, Art Students League, 70-75. *Awards:* Purchase Prize, Ranger Fund, Nat Acad Design, 71; Gold Medals, Lotos Club, New York, 72 & Knickerbocker Artists, 80. *Bibliog:* Wendon Blake (auth),

Acrylics, Am Artist Mag, 1/72; article, Southwest Art, 3/82; Artists of the Rockies, summer 83. *Mem:* Nat Acad Design; Am Watercolor Soc; Nat Arts Club; Pastel Soc Am; Audubon Artists; and others. *Publ:* Illusr, Opera Companion, Dodd, 61 & Verdi, 63; auth, Painting Portraits, Watson-Guptill, 71; auth, Painting Faces, Figures & Landscapes, Watson-Guptill, 81. *Mailing Add:* 15 Gramercy Park New York NY 10003

KIPNISS, ROBERT
PAINTER, LITHOGRAPHER
b New York, NY, Feb 1, 31. *Study:* Art Students League; Wittenberg Col; Univ Iowa, BA & MFA; Wittenberg Univ, hon PhD, 79. *Work:* Whitney Mus Am Art, New York; Chicago Art Inst; Yale Univ Art Gallery; Libr Cong, Washington, DC; Albright-Knox Mus, Buffalo, NY; Nat Collection of Fine Arts, Smithsonian Inst, Washington, DC; Cleveland Mus Ohio. *Exhib:* One-man shows, Allen R Hite Inst, Univ Louisville, 65, Museo de Arte Moderno La Tertulia, Colombia, 75 & Hirschl & Adler Galleries, New York, NY, 77; Recent Acquisitions, Whitney Mus Am Art, 72; Int Exhib of Original Drawings, Mus of Mod Art, Rijeka-Dolac, Yugoslavia, 76; III Bienal Americana de Artes Graficas, Museo La Tertulia, Cali, Colombia, 76; Retrospective, Assoc Am Artists, New York, NY, 77. *Awards:* Medal Honor, Audubon Artists, 82; Prize, Nat Acad of Design, 76, 80 & 81. *Bibliog:* Robert Kipniss: The Graphic Works, Abaris Books, 80. *Mem:* Audubon Artists (dir graphics); Nat Acad Design; Soc Am Graphic Artists; Charlotte Printmakers; Boston Printmakers. *Media:* Oil; Lithography. *Publ:* Illusr, Poems of Emily Dickinson, Thomas Y Crowell, 64; illusr, Collected Poems of Robert Graves, Anchor Doubleday, 66; illusr, Poems of Rilke, Limited Ed Club, 81. *Dealer:* Merrill Chase Galleries 620 N Michigan Ave Chicago IL 60611; Weisberg Payson 822 Madison Ave New York NY. *Mailing Add:* 26 E 33rd St New York NY 10016

KIPP, LYMAN
SCULPTOR
b Dobbs Ferry, NY, Dec 24, 29. *Study:* Pratt Inst, 50-52; Cranbrook Acad Art, 52-54. *Work:* Whitney Mus Am Art, New York; Albright-Knox Art Gallery, Buffalo; High Mus of Art, Atlanta, Ga; Univ Ala, Huntsville; State NY Albany Mall. *Comn:* Sculpture for Post Off & Fed Off Bldg, Van Nuys, Calif; sculpture, Village Lake Placid, NY; Grosse Pointe Libr, Mich. *Exhib:* Four Whitney Mus Am Art Sculpture Ann, 64-70; Sculpture in Environment, New York, 67; Cool Art, 68 & Highlights of the Season, 68, Larry Aldrich Mus, Conn; Art of the Real, Mus Mod Art, New York & London, 68, Paris & Berlin, 69; Change of View, Larry Aldrich Mus, 75; Sculpture in the Constructivist Tradition, Hamilton Gallery, NY, 77; Urban Structures/ Monumental Sculpture, Nat Endowment Arts Traveling Exhib originated in Akron, Ohio, 77-79; Art in Public Places, Ferris State Col, Mich, 79; and many others. *Teaching:* Instr sculpture, Bennington Col, 60-63; asst prof sculpture, Hunter Col, 63-66, prof & chmn dept, 75-; prof sculpture & chmn dept, Lehman Col, 66-75. *Awards:* Guggenheim Fel, 66; Fulbright Grant, 66; City Univ Fac Res Awards, 70 & 75. *Mailing Add:* Route 100 Somers NY 10589

KIPP, ORVAL
PAINTER, EDUCATOR
b Hyndman, Pa, May 21, 04. *Study:* Carnegie Inst, AB(with hon); Teachers Col, Columbia Univ, AM; Univ Pittsburgh, PhD. *Work:* Latrobe High Sch, Aspinwall High Sch, Greensburg Pub Schs, IUP Mus & Uniontown High Sch, Pa. *Exhib:* Provincetown Art Asn; Assoc Artists Pittsburgh; Am Fedn Arts Traveling Exhib; Am Artists Prof League Grand Nat, 72; Three Rivers Arts Festival, Pittsburgh; and others. *Teaching:* Instr art, Indiana Univ Pa, 36-41, dir art dept, 41-60, chmn, 60-64, prof, 60-69, prof emer, 69-; artist-in-residence, Kiski Sch, 64-69; instr, Ivy Sch of Prof Art, 64-69; lectr, Trick or Treat in Art Education, Ind State Art Teachers, Indianapolis; lectr & demonstrations, The Mystery of The Masters. *Awards:* Prizes, Indiana Art Asn, 47-57; Spec Jury Award, Pittsburgh Soc Art, 68. *Mem:* Eastern Art Asn; Assoc Artists Pittsburgh; Indiana Art Asn; Pa Art Educ Asn; Pittsburgh Watercolor Soc; and others. *Media:* Watercolor, Oil. *Mailing Add:* 635 Church St Indiana PA 15701

KIRBY, KENT BRUCE
PRINTMAKER, PHOTOGRAPHER
b Fargo, NDak, Dec 31, 34. *Study:* Carleton Col, with Albert Elsen, BA, 56; Univ NDak, with Robert Nelson, MA, 59; Univ Mich, with Emil Weddige, MFA, 70. *Work:* Art Inst Chicago; Metrop Mus Art, Guggenheim Mus, New York; Philadelphia Mus Art; Grand Rapids Art Mus, Mich. *Comn:* Prints, comn by Joseph Kinnebrew, Carl Toth, Irwin Hollander, Phil Davis & Brian Blount. *Exhib:* Mich Arts Biennial, Detroit Art Inst, 69; Hunterdon Nat Print Exhib, Clinton, NJ, 75; NDak Ann, 77; Mid-Western Print and Drawing Ann, Philbrook Art Ctr, Tulsa, Okla, 80; Nat Invitational Print Show, Southeast Mo State Univ, 81. *Teaching:* Instr drawing & painting, Muskingum Col, 59-61; instr, Wilkes Col, 61-62; prof printmaking & photog & chmn dept art, Alma Col, 62-76, chmn fine arts div, 73-74, Charles A Dana prof art, 76-. *Awards:* Newberry Libr Res Fel, 74; Mich Coun Arts Grants, 75, 79 & 81; Nat Endowment Arts Grant, 76. *Bibliog:* Richard Lyons (auth), Kent Kirby, Minn Rev, 60; Joyce Macrorie (auth), Collotype, Print Rev 6, winter 77. *Mem:* Nat Coun Art Adminr; Col Art Asn Am; Artists Equity; Mich Coun Arts. *Res:* Light print press to revive collotype technique; publishing works by American artists. *Publ:* Auth, Art, technology & the liberal arts college, Art J, spring 70; auth, The collotype printing process: A proposal for its revival, In: Leonardo, Vol 9, Pergamon Press, 76. *Dealer:* Miriam Perlman Gallery Chicago IL. *Mailing Add:* 4100 Riverview Alma MI 48801

KIRK, JEROME
SCULPTOR
b Detroit, Mich, Apr 3, 23. *Study:* Mass Inst Technol, BS. *Work:* San Francisco Mus Mod Art; Sheldon Art Gallery, Univ Nebr; Phoenix Art Mus, Ariz; Storm King Art Ctr, Mountainville, NY; and others. *Comn:* Sixteen maj sculpture comn in pub places; Phoenix Bird Ascending & Tiered Orbits, Civic Plaza, Phoenix, 71; Silver Orbit, Storm King Art Ctr, 73; Waves, Monterey Conf Ctr, Calif, 77; Solar Semaphore, Lincoln, Nebr, 79; Standing Waves, Univ Calif, Berkeley, 80; and others. *Exhib:* De Young Mus Collectors Show, 65; Contemporary American Painting & Sculpture, Krannert Art Mus, Champaign, Ill, 67; Santa Barbara Mus, 69; Storm King Art Ctr, 73; Painting & Sculpture Today, Indianapolis Mus Art, 76; Sculpture Potsdam, NY, 77; Sheldon Art Gallery, Univ Nebr; 22 solo exhibs. *Bibliog:* Selleck (auth), Principles of Design, 75; Robinette (auth), Outdoor Sculpture, 76; Brommer & Horn (auths), Art in Your World, 77. *Media:* Multimedia. *Mailing Add:* 874 41st St Oakland CA 94608

KIRK, MICHAEL
PRINTMAKER, INSTRUCTOR
b New York, NY, Oct 31, 47. *Study:* Rutgers Univ, NJ, BA(art hist), 69; Pratt Inst, MFA(printmaking), 73. *Work:* Philadelphia Mus of Art; Boston Mus of Fine Arts; Nat Collection of Fine Arts, Washington, DC; Brooklyn Mus; Libr of Cong, Washington, DC. *Exhib:* The 18th & 19th Nat Print Exhib, Brooklyn Mus, 72 & 73; A New York Album, Brooklyn Mus, 79; Prints in Sequence, State Mus of NJ, Trenton, 77; Primera Bienal del Grabado de America, Maracaibo, Venezuela, 78; One-man exhibs, Ctr Music, Drama & Art, Lake Placid, 82, Murisori Williams Proctor Mus, Utica, 82 & Kiva Gallery, New York, 83; and others. *Teaching:* Instr printmaking, Parsons Sch of Design, Manhattan, 73-, Rutgers Univ, 83- *Mem:* Soc Am Graphic Artists. *Mailing Add:* 309 Canal St New York NY 10013

KIRKLAND, VANCE HALL
PAINTER, COLLECTOR
b Convoy, Ohio, Nov 3, 1904. *Study:* Cleveland Sch Art, BEA; Cleveland Col Educ, Western Reserve Univ, with Henry Keller, Frank Wilcox, William Joseph Eastman & Albert Olson; also study in Europe, Africa, SAm & Asia. *Work:* Denver Art Mus; Art Inst Chicago; Nelson Gallery Art, Kansas City, Mo; Columbus Gallery Fine Arts, Ohio; Norton Gallery Fine Arts, West Palm Beach, Fla. *Exhib:* International Watercolors, Art Inst Chicag, 30-46; Contemporary American Painting, Univ Ill, 52; Artists West of Mississippi, Colorado Springs Fine Arts Ctr, 65; 73rd Western Ann, Denver Art Mus, 71; Color Exp Space Retrospective, 73 & 50 Year Retrospective, 78, Denver Art Mus; First Western States Biennial Exhib, 79-80. *Teaching:* Prof art & dir sch art, Univ Denver, 29-32 & 46-69. *Mailing Add:* 817 Pearl St Denver CO 80203

KIRKPATRICK, DIANE
HISTORIAN
b Grand Rapids, Mich, June 28, 33. *Study:* Vassar Col, BA, 55; Cranbrook Acad Art, MFA, 57; Univ Mich, Ann Arbor, MA, 65, PhD, 69. *Collections Arranged:* Chicago: The City and Its Artists, Univ Mich Art Mus, Ann Arbor, 78. *Pos:* Manuscript & layout ed, Fideler Publ Co, Grand Rapids, Mich, 57-58; dir children's educ, Grand Rapids Art Mus, Mich, 60-62; dir film & video studies, Univ Mich, 77-78. *Teaching:* Instr, Univ Mich, 69-70, asst prof, 72-74, assoc prof, 74-82, prof, 82- *Awards:* Spec Exhib, Nat Endowment Arts, 67-68; Meadows Distinguised Professor of Art History, Southern Methodist Univ, 82. *Mem:* Col Art Asn Am. *Res:* Contemporary art, including photography, film, video and computers. *Publ:* Auth, Record, Icon, and Idea: The Muses of Photography and the other Visual Arts, Nat Arts Guide, 80; auth, Modern British Sculpture at the Univ of Mich, Univ Mich Mus Art Bull, 80 & 81; auth, Generative systems in contemporary visual art, Generative Lit & Generative Art, 82; auth, On the trail of time with Sonia Landy Sheridan, Lightworks, 82; auth, Religious photography in the Victorian age, Mich Quart Rev, 83. *Mailing Add:* 1306 Wells Ann Arbor MI 48104

KIRKWOOD, LARRY THOMAS
PHOTOGRAPHER, PRINTMAKER
b Knoxville, Iowa, Oct 4, 43. *Study:* Univ Iowa; Univ Mo, BA; Univ Kans. *Work:* City Hall, Kansas City, Kans; Simpson Col, Indianola, Iowa. *Comn:* Patrons print, Jewish Community Ctr, Kansas City, Mo, 73; 1000 prints for Ocho Rios Jamaica Hotel, Playboy Enterprises, Jacklyn Interiors, Miami, Fla, 74. *Exhib:* 17th Ann Nat Print & Drawing Exhib, Oklahoma Art Ctr, 75; 6th Greater New Orleans Int Exhib, 76; 20th Nat Print Exhib, Hunterdon Art Ctr, Clinton, NJ, 76; 3rd Ann Nat Exhib, Ga Tech Univ, 76; 19th Ann Nat Print & Drawing Exhib, Oklahoma Art Ctr, 77; Arena 77 4th Ann Art Open, Binghamton, NY, 77; mem exhib, Norton Mus, 78; and others. *Teaching:* Norton Gallery & Sch Art, 78- *Awards:* First Place, Winter Arts Exhib, 74; Third Place, Rock Springs Art Ctr, 77; Fla Fine Arts Coun Grant, 78. *Mem:* Am Graphics Soc. *Media:* Serigraph, Acrylic. *Mailing Add:* Box 1471 Lake Worth FL 33460

KIRKWOOD, MARY BURNETTE
PAINTER
b Hillsboro, Ore, Dec 21, 04. *Study:* Univ Mont, BA; Univ Ore, MFA; Harvard Univ Sch Fine Arts, art hist with Prof Paul J Sachs; Royal Art Sch, Stockholm, Sweden, with Prof Otte Skold; Art Students League, with Reginald Marsh; also with Joseph Stefanelli & Robert Goldwater, Paris. *Work:* Cheney Cowles Mus, Spokane, Wash; Boise Art Gallery, Idaho; IBM Corp; Bank of Idaho; Boise Cascade Corp. *Comn:* Murals for agr sci bldg, 48 & libr, 52, Univ Idaho. *Exhib:* West Coast Juried, Seattle Art Mus, 62; West of the Mississippi Exhib, Colorado Springs, 63; Intermountain Exhib, Salt

Lake City Art Ctr, 63 & 65; Fifty States Exhib, Burpee Art Mus, Rockford, Ill, 66; Western States Exhib, Denver Art Mus, 71; plus others. *Teaching:* Prof art, Univ Idaho, 30-70. *Awards:* Third Prize for Miercoles Santo, Pac Coast Ann, Wenatchee, Wash, 63; Best of Show for El Cristo de la Columna, 63 & Second Prize for Trampoline, 66, Cheney Cowles Mus, Spokane, Wash. *Mem:* Portland Art Asn; Idaho Art Asn; Boise Art Asn. *Media:* Oil. *Mailing Add:* 812 Apple Lane Moscow ID 83843

KIRSCHENBAUM, BERNARD EDWIN
SCULPTOR
b New York, NY, Sept 3, 24. *Study:* Cornell Univ; Inst Design, Chicago, BA. *Work:* Storm King Art Ctr, Mountainville, NY. *Comn:* Sculptures, Spectrum II, Mass Inst Technol, Cambridge, 68 & Walkthrough, J Patrick Lannan Found, Palm Beach, Fla, 69. *Exhib:* Sculpture in Environment, Cent Park, New York, 67; Cool Art: Abstraction Today, Newark Mus, NJ, 68; Painting & Sculpture Today, Indianapolis Mus Art, 70; Three New York Artists, Corcoran Gallery Art, Washington, DC, 73; Sculpture in the Fields, Storm King Art Ctr, 74. *Awards:* Guggenheim Fel Sculpture, 72. *Dealer:* Sculpture Now Inc Max Hutchinson 142 Greene St New York NY 10012. *Mailing Add:* 180 Park Row New York NY 10038

KIRSCHENBAUM, JULES
PAINTER, EDUCATOR
b New York, NY, Mar 25, 30. *Study:* Brooklyn Mus Art Sch. *Work:* Butler Inst Am Art, Youngstown, Ohio; Whitney Mus Am Art, New York; Weatherspoon Art Gallery; Des Moines Art Ctr, Iowa; Everhardt Mus, Scranton, Pa. *Comn:* Hist of Iowa, Cent Nat Bank, Des Moines, 64. *Exhib:* Drawings USA, Mus Mod Art, New York, 34; Whitney Mus Am Art Ann, 55; Painting USA: The Figure, Mus Mod Art, New York, 63; Artists Abroad, Paintings from Whitney Collection, 69; Gov Exhib Nine Iowa Artists, 71. *Teaching:* Artist in residence, Des Moines Art Ctr, 63-67; prof painting, Drake Univ, 67-; vis prof art, Temple Univ, 72-73. *Awards:* Fulbright Fel, 56; First Prize for Figure Painting, Nat Acad Design, 57; First Prize for Oils, Butler Inst Am Art, 60. *Bibliog:* The figure, Time, 62. *Media:* Acrylic. *Dealer:* Forum Gallery 1018 Madison Ave New York NY 10021. *Mailing Add:* 2829 Forest Dr Des Moines IA 50312

KIRSTEN-DAIENSAI, RICHARD CHARLES
PAINTER, PRINTMAKER
b Chicago, Ill, Apr 16, 20. *Study:* Art Inst Chicago; Univ Wash; also study in Japan, 58-83. *Work:* Seattle Art Mus; Bell Tel Co; Libr of Cong, Washington, DC; Metrop Mus Art, New York; Tokyo Mus Mod Art, Japan. *Exhib:* Seattle Art Mus, numerous shows, 45-69; Frye Mus, Seattle, 60-65 & 69; Gov Invitational, 67; Collector's Gallery, Bellevue, Wash, 67; Richard White Gallery, Seattle, 68; Kirsten Gallery, Seattle, 75-83; plus many others. *Awards:* Purchase Prize, Univ Ore, 68; Purchase Prize, Seattle First Nat Bank, 69; plus others. *Mem:* Northwest Watercolor Soc (pres, 68 & 69); Artists Equity (pres, Seattle Chap, 52-56). *Media:* Watercolor, Acrylic; Mixed Media. *Dealer:* Kirsten Gallery WA. *Mailing Add:* 900 N 102nd St Seattle WA 98133

KISCH, GLORIA
SCULPTOR
b New York, NY, Nov 14, 41. *Study:* Sarah Lawrence Col, BA, 63; Boston Mus Sch, 64-65; Otis Art Inst, Los Angeles, BFA & MFA, 69. *Work:* Mildura Art, Victoria, Australia; Milwaukee Art Mus; Newport Harbor Art Mus, Calif; Denver Art Mus; Palm Spring Art Mus. *Exhib:* Recent Int Forms in Art, Biennale of Sydney Art Gallery, Australia, 76; one-woman shows, Los Angeles Inst Contemp Art, 78, Touchstone Gallery, New York, 79 & Inst of Art & Urban Resources, P S 1, New York, 80; Milwaukee Art Mus, 81; and others. *Mailing Add:* 620 Broadway New York NY 10012

KISELEWSKI, JOSEPH
SCULPTOR
b Browerville, Minn, Feb 16, 01. *Study:* Minneapolis Sch Art, 18-21; Nat Acad Design, 21-23; Beaux-Arts Inst Design, 23-25; Am Acad in Rome; Acad Julian, Paris, France. *Comn:* Harold Vanderbilt (statue), Nashville, Tenn, 65; Moses (statue), Law Col, Syracuse Univ, 66; Sylvanus Thayer bronze bust for Hall of Fame for Great Americans, NY Univ, 66; groups, Bronx Co Ct House, NY; fountain, Huntington Mus, SC; and others. *Awards:* Beaux Arts Paris Prize, 25-26; Prix de Rome, 26-29; Elizabeth N Watrous Gold Medal, 37; and others. *Mem:* Nat Acad Design; assoc fel Am Acad Rome; fel Nat Sculpture Soc; Archit League New York. *Mailing Add:* Browerville MN 56438

KISH, MAURICE
PAINTER
b Russia; US citizen. *Work:* Brooklyn Mus, NY; Ein Horod Mus, Israel; City New York Mus; Smithsonian Inst, Washington, DC; Springville Mus, Utah; and others. *Exhib:* Nat Acad Design, since 32; Corcoran Gallery Art, 37; Pa Acad Fine Arts, 38; Carnegie Inst Fine Arts, 41; Detroit Inst Fine Arts, 59. *Awards:* Minnie R Stern Medal for Street of Forgotten Men, Audubon Artists, 64; Emily Lowe Cash Award for Painting (The Great Eclipse), 75; Cash Prize, Painters & Sculptors Soc, 76; and many others. *Mem:* Allied Artists Am; Audubon Artists; Painters & Sculptors Soc NJ; Conn Acad Fine Arts; Am Vet Soc Artists. *Media:* Oil. *Publ:* Auth, The World is My Song, Ykuf, 68. *Mailing Add:* 417 Brightwater Ct Brooklyn NY 11235

KISKADDEN, ROBERT MORGAN
PAINTER, EDUCATOR
b Tulsa, Okla, Dec 6, 18. *Study:* Univ Kans, BFA; Ohio Wesleyan Univ, MA. *Work:* Wichita Art Mus, Kans; Birger Sandzen Mem Gallery, Lindsborg,

Kans; Bloomfield Collection, Wichita State Univ; Univ Tex, El Paso Gallery; Kans State Univ Gallery, Manhattan; also in other pub & pvt collections. *Exhib:* Many local, regional and nat exhibs. *Teaching:* Prof painting, Wichita State Univ, 49-84, asst dean, Col Fine Arts, 70-84, retired. *Media:* Oil, Watercolor. *Mailing Add:* 301 N Old Manor Rd Wichita KS 67208

KISSEL, WILLIAM THORN, JR
SCULPTOR
b New York, NY, Feb 6, 20. *Study:* Harvard Univ, BA, 44; Pa Acad Fine Arts, 51-53; Barnes Found, Merion, Pa, grad, 53; Rinehart Grad Sch Sculpture, with Sidney Waugh, Cecil Howard & Bruce Moore, grad, 58. *Comn:* Granite Mem, Montclair, NJ, 56; many bronze animal sculptures, eastern US, 65-70. *Exhib:* Mass Sculptor's Exhib, Beverly, Mass, 58; Am Artists Prof League Grand Nat, Lever House, New York, 64 & 66; Nat Acad Design Exhibs, New York, 65-68 & 71; Nat Sculpture Soc Exhibs, Lever House, 67 & 70; Md Arts Coun Exhib & State Tour, 71 & 72. *Awards:* Speyer Awards, Nat Acad Design, 66 & 68; Am Artists Prof League Award, 66. *Bibliog:* Articles, Am Art Stone, 59 & La Rev Mod, Paris, 66. *Mem:* Nat Sculpture Soc; fel Am Artists Prof League; fel Pa Acad Fine Arts; Munic Art Soc New York. *Media:* Bronze, Marble. *Mailing Add:* Owings Mills MD 21117

KITAJ, R B
PAINTER, PRINTMAKER
Cleveland, Ohio, 32. *Study:* Ruskin Sch, Univ Oxford, dipl, 60; Royal Col Art, grad, 62; Univ Col, Univ London, 82. *Work:* Mus in the US & Europe. *Exhib:* One-man shows, Los Angeles Co Mus Art, 65; Stedelijk Mus, Amsterdam, 67; Cleveland Mus, 67 & 81; Gemeente Mus, Hague, 68 & Univ Calif, Berkeley, 68; Hirshhorn Mus, Washington, DC, 81; Kunsthalle, Dusseldorf, 82; and others. *Teaching:* Vis lectr, Slade Sch, Univ London; vis prof, Univ Calif, Berkeley & Univ Calif, Los Angeles. *Awards:* Cooper Union Citation, New York, 82. *Bibliog:* Retrospective (catalog), Hirshhorn Mus, Washington, DC, 81. *Mem:* Inst Arts & Letters, New York. *Mailing Add:* c/o Marlborough Fine Arts Ltd 6 Albermarle St London W1 England United Kingdom

KITAO, T KAORI
HISTORIAN, EDUCATOR
b Jan 30, 33; US citizen. *Study:* Univ Calif, Berkeley, AB(archit), 58, MA(art hist), 61; Harvard Univ, PhD(art hist), 66. *Pos:* Asst prof hist archit, RI Sch Design, 63-66; asst prof art hist, Swarthmore Col, 66-68, assoc prof, 68-75, prof & chair, 75- *Mem:* Col Art Asn; Soc Archit Historians; Soc Cinema Studies; Semiotic Soc Am; Int Soc Comparative Study Civilizations (vpres, 80-). *Res:* Philadelphia row houses; comparative semiotics, east and west; Bernini and Baroque Rome. *Publ:* Auth, Circle and Oval in the Square of St Peter's, NY Univ Press, 74; contribr, La prospettiva rinascimentale, Centro Di, Florence, 80. *Mailing Add:* Dept Art Swarthmore Col Swarthmore PA 19081

KITNER, HAROLD
PAINTER, EDUCATOR
b May 18, 21; US citizen. *Exhib:* Simultaneous one-man shows, retrospective, Kent State Univ; recent works, Canton Art Inst, 79, Kuban Galleries, 83 & 84. *Pos:* Art critic, Akron Beacon J, 48-61; dir, Blossom-Kent Art Prog, 67- *Teaching:* Prof painting & drawing, Kent State Univ, 47-79, chmn painting & sculpture dept, 50-67, chmn sch art, 64-65, prof emer, 79- *Mailing Add:* Sch Art Div Painting & Sculpture Kent State Univ Kent OH 44242

KITTA, GEORGE EDWARD
PRINTMAKER, PAINTER
b Omaha, Nebr, Jan 1, 53. *Study:* Kansas City Art Inst, BFA; Art Inst Chicago, MFA. *Work:* Springfield Art Asn, Ill. *Exhib:* Strange Sensibilities, Stowe Gallery, Davidson, NC, 75; Spokane Nat Drawing Competition, Chaney Cowles Mus, Wash, 76; Drawing Missouri, Albrecht & Springfield Art Mus, Mo, 76; and others. *Teaching:* Instr, printmaking & drawing, Univ Mo, Kansas City, 76-82. *Awards:* Purchase Prize, Mid-America Five, Nelson/Atkins Mus, 74; Purchase Awards, Davidson Nat, Davidson Col, 74 & 17th NDak Ann, Univ NDak, 74. *Bibliog:* Benjamin Forgey (auth), A printmakers print show, Art News, 9/76; Special report: Midwest art, Art Am, 7-8/79. *Media:* Oil, Stone Lithography. *Dealer:* Dorry Gates 5321 Belleview Kansas City Mo 64110. *Mailing Add:* 1108 W Barry Ave Chicago IL 60657

KITTREDGE, NANCY (ELIZABETH)
PAINTER
b Ellsworth, Maine, Nov 12, 38. *Study:* Vesper George Sch Art, Boston, 56-57; Univ NH, Durham, 57-59; Univ Maine, Orono, BA, 61; Univ Miami, Coral Gables, Fla, MA, 63. *Work:* Household Corp, Chicago; R L Kotrozo Inc, Scottsdale, Ariz; Indust Metals South Inc, New Orleans; Dow Theory Lett Inc, La Jolla, Calif; Klineman & Saltzman, Empire State Bldg, New York. *Comn:* Portrait, Univ Maine Theatre Dept, Orono, 76. *Exhib:* Yokohama-San Diego, Women's Jr Col Arts, Yokohama, Japan, 79; solo exhib, San Diego Mus Art, 81; Women's Invitational Exhib, John Douglas Cline Gallery, Phoenix, 81; Art Guild All-Media, San Diego Mus Art, 81; Ankrum Gallery Invitational, Los Angeles, 82; and others. *Awards:* First Prize, San Diego Art Inst Exhib, 69; Artists Equity Asn. *Mem:* San Diego Art Guild (mem bd, 76-77 & 82-83). *Media:* Oil, Mixed Media. *Dealer:* Suzanne Brown Gallery 7156 Main St Scottsdale AZ 85251. *Mailing Add:* 13646 Mira Montana Dr Del Mar CA 92014

KITZINGER, ERNST
HISTORIAN
b Munich, Ger, Dec 27, 12; US citizen. *Study:* Univ Rome, 31-32; Univ Munich, PhD, 34; Swarthmore Col, DHL, 69. *Pos:* Asst, Brit Mus, London, Eng, 35-40; with Dumbarton Oaks Ctr for Byzantine Studies, Washington, DC, 41-67; mem, Inst Advan Study, Princeton Univ, 66-67, 80 & 82. *Teaching:* A Kingsley Porter univ emer prof, Harvard Univ. *Mem:* Medieval Acad Am; Col Art Asn Am; Archeol Inst Am; Ger Archaeol Inst; Am Philos Soc; plus others. *Res:* Early Christian, Byzantine and medieval art. *Publ:* Auth, Early Medieval Art in the British Museum, third ed, 83; auth, The Mosaics of Monreale, 60; auth, The Art of Byzantium and the Medieval West, Selected Studies, 76; auth, Byzantine Art in the Making, 77. *Mailing Add:* 14 Richmond Rd Oxford OX1 2JJ England United Kingdom

KIVA, LLOYD See New, Lloyd H

KJARGAARD, JOHN INGVARD
PAINTER, COLLAGE ARTIST
b Denmark, Sept 13, 02; US citizen. *Study:* Cooper Union; Calif Sch Fine Arts, San Francisco; Univ Calif, Berkeley; Univ Hawaii, with Joseph Albers. *Work:* Mint Mus Art, Charlotte, NC; Honolulu Acad Arts, Hawaii; Libr of Cong, Washington, DC; Hawaii State Found Cult & Arts. *Comn:* Glass mosaic mural, Honolulu Int Airport, Hawaii State Dept Transportation, 72. *Exhib:* One-man shows, 58, 69, 74, 76 & 77 & Hawaii Nat Print Exhibs, 71, 73 & 75, Honolulu Acad Arts, Hawaii; print exhib, Rochester, NY, 62; Mex-Hawaii Exchange Exhib, 68; Pac Cities Loan Exhib, Auckland City Art Gallery, NZ, 71; Contemp Art of Hawaii, Bucharest, Romania, 77. *Awards:* Watumull Found Purchase Award, 58; Elsie Das Mem Award, 63; Honolulu Printmakers, 66. *Mem:* Hawaii Painters & Sculptors League; Honolulu Printmakers; Honolulu Acad Arts. *Media:* Acrylic; Collage. *Publ:* Contribr, The technique of collage, 68, New Ways in Collage, Mayer & Webb, 73, Artists of Hawaii, Haar & Neogy, 74 & The Art of Collage, Brommer, 78. *Dealer:* Downtown Gallery 125 Merchant St Honolulu HI 96813. *Mailing Add:* 2080 Mauna Pl Honolulu HI 96822

KLABUNDE, CHARLES SPENCER
PRINTMAKER, PAINTER
b Omaha, Nebr, Oct 1, 35. *Study:* Univ Nebr, Omaha, BFA, 58; Univ Iowa, Iowa City, MFA, 62; also studied with Mauricio Lasansky. *Work:* Mus Mod Art, Metrop Mus Art & Whitney Mus Am Art, New York; Art Inst of Chicago; Philadelphia Mus of Art. *Comn:* Prints, Assocs Am Artist, New York, 71, 72 & 74. *Exhib:* Five Printmakers, Whitney Mus, 70; one-man shows, Sheldon Mem Art Gallery, Nebr, 72, Philadelphia Art Alliance, 73, Assoc Am Artists, New York, 75, Van Straaten Gallery, Chicago, 76 & Franz Badger Gallery, Washington, DC, 76; and others. *Teaching:* Asst prof printmaking, The Cooper Union, New York, 68-75. *Awards:* Guggenheim Fel, 71-72; Purchase Awards, Davidson Nat Print and Drawing Competition, 73 & The Print Club, Philadelphia, 75. *Media:* Copper; Oil. *Publ:* Illusr, The Lost Ones, 83. *Dealer:* Assoc American Artists 663 Fifth Ave New York NY 10022. *Mailing Add:* 68 W Third St New York NY 10012

KLARIN, WINIFRED ERLICK
PAINTER, JEWELER
b Portland, Maine, Dec 8, 12. *Study:* Portland Mus Fine Art, Hayloft scholar, 30; Vesper George Sch Art, grad, 33; Soc Arts & Crafts, Detroit, 58-60; Wayne State Univ, 58-62; Cranbrook Grad Sch Art, 63. *Work:* US Libr, State Dept, Washington, DC; Owens-Corning Fiberglass Corp, Toledo, Ohio; Steel Case Corp, Grand Rapids, Mich; First Fed Savings & Loan, Detroit; Masco Corp, Ypsilanti, Mich. *Exhib:* One-woman shows, J B Speed Art Mus, Louisville, Ky, 69 & Long Boat Key Art Ctr, Fla, 78; Showcase Gallery, Southfield, Mich; three person show, Eckerd Col, 82; Art Ctr Show, 83; Temple Beth El Art Show, 83. *Pos:* Vis artist, Eckerd Col, St Petersburg, 74-75. *Awards:* Awards, Art Ctr, St Petersburg, 78 & 81; Award, Suntan Art Show, 82. *Bibliog:* Jean Paul Susser (auth), Art in review, Ann Arbor News, 4/7/67; Jeanette Crane (auth), St Petersburg Independent, 4/10/75; Darcy Arpke (auth), The Islander, Long Boat Key, 1/5/78. *Media:* Multimedia. *Mailing Add:* 5950 Pelican Bay Plaza #203 Gulfport FL 33707

KLAVANS, MINNIE
PAINTER, SCULPTOR
b Garrett Park, Md, May 10, 15. *Study:* Wilson Teachers Col, BSEd, 35; with pvt instr in silversmithing, 51-55; painting with Laura Douglas, 58-60; Am Univ, 60-64; with Luciano Penay, 65-70; Corcoran Gallery Art, plastics with Ed McGowin, 70-71. *Work:* Nat Collection Fine Arts, Smithsonian Inst, White House, Corcoran Gallery Art & Nat Endowment Arts, Washington, DC; Mus Contemp Art, Madrid, Spain. *Exhib:* Corcoran Gallery Art, 65 & 67; Baltimore Mus Art, Md, 67 & 72; Cisneros Gallery, New York, 67; Mus Mod Art, Bilbao, Spain, 69; Chrysler Mus Art, Norfolk, Va, 72. *Awards:* First Prize for silversmithing, Smithsonian Inst, 53 & 55; Spec Award, Baltimore Mus Art, 67. *Mem:* Artists Equity Asn. *Dealer:* Mickelson Gallery 707 G St NW Washington DC 20001; Plum Gallery Kensington MD 20795. *Mailing Add:* 2134 Bancroft Pl NW Washington DC 20008

KLAVEN, MARVIN L
PAINTER, EDUCATOR
b Alton, Ill, Apr 8, 31. *Study:* State Univ Iowa, BA & MFA. *Work:* Univ Iowa; Millikin Univ; Mayer Collection, Gilman Collection & Ill Bell, Chicago. *Exhib:* 24 Illinois Artists, 67; Chicago Sun Times Exhib, 68; 21st NMiss Valley Art Exhib, 68; Artists Who Teach, 69; Contemp Am Painting & Sculpture, 69. *Pos:* Dir, Decatur Art Ctr, Ill, 61-69; dir, Kirkland Art Gallery, 69- *Teaching:* Asst prof drawing, Northern Ill Univ, 59-61; chmn art dept, Millikin Univ, 61- *Awards:* Tiffany Found Grant, 64. *Media:* Acrylic, Silk Screen. *Dealer:* Gilman Gallery 201 E Ohio St Chicago IL 60611. *Mailing Add:* Art Dept Millikin Univ Decatur IL 62522

KLEBE, GENE (CHARLES EUGENE)
PAINTER, WRITER
b Philadelphia, Pa, Sept 18, 05. *Study:* Philadelphia Col Art; Univ Pa. *Work:* US Navy & Marine Art Gallery, Washington, DC; Farnsworth Mus, Rockland, Maine; Nat Acad Design, New York; Univ Maine, Orono; Maine Nat Bank, Portland. *Comn:* Combat art, US Navy, 59-77; Maine State series, Maine Nat Bank, Portland, 60-72; Expo '67 mural, State of Maine, 67; sesquicentennial seal, Maine Sesquicentennial Comn, 70. *Exhib:* Salmagundi Club, 45-77; Am Watercolor Soc, 50-76; Allied Artists Am, 50-74; Acad Artists Asn, 64-76; Nat Acad Design, 69-76. *Pos:* Pres, Pemaquid Group Artists, 55-82; mem, Gov Coun Art & Cult, 65-69; chmn, Maine State Art Comn, 66-71; retired. *Awards:* Wu-Ject-Key Award, Am Watercolor Soc, 69; Salmagundi Club Award, 71; Franklin Mint Gold Medal, 74. *Bibliog:* Lew Deitz (auth), Gene Klebe--Maine artist, Down East Mag, 69. *Mem:* Acad Artists Asn; Am Watercolor Soc; Allied Artists Am; Salmagundi Club; Nat Acad Design. *Media:* Watercolor. *Publ:* Coauth, Penguin Family, 64; contribr, Maine Through the Eyes of Her Artists, 65; contribr, US Navy combat art, 63-77; auth, Gene Klebe watercolor page, Am Artists Mag, 3/72. *Mailing Add:* Pemaquid Rd Bristol ME 04539

KLECKNER, SUSAN
PHOTOGRAPHER, FILMMAKER
b New York, NY, July 5, 41. *Study:* Art Students League, with Landes Lewitin; City Univ New York; Pratt Inst. *Comn:* Birth Film, Women's Interart Ctr & NY State Coun Arts, New York, 72; Another Look, Teleprompter & Women's Video Service, NY, 72; Desert Piece, Women Artist Filmakers, 82; media, Feast or Famine, Interart Theatre, 83. *Exhib:* Brooklyn Mus, NY, 72; film Festival, Whitney Mus Am Art, New York, 73 & Mod Mus, Paris, France, 74; Wild Art Show, Project Studio One, New York, 82; AIR Gallery, 82; Moonmade Space, 83; West 22nd St Show, 83. *Pos:* Dir photog workshop, Community Resource Ctr, NY, 68-70; co-dir, Women's Liberation Cinema, 70-71; founding coordr, Women's Interart Ctr, New York, 70-71; video ed, Women's Video News Service, 72-73; artist-in-residence, Cummington Sch Arts, 74 & Women's Interart Ctr, 82; co-dir, Workshops for Women, 80-83. *Teaching:* Asst chmn photog, Pratt Inst, New York, 70-74; consult writing, City Univ New York, 72-73; dir, Fresh Film Ctr Photog, NY Univ Undergrad Film Sch, New York, 73-74; instr, NY Inst Photog, 78-80, Int Ctr Photog, 82-, New York Univ/Int Ctr Photog grad prog, 83 & New York Univ performance studies, 83. *Awards:* Grant, Whitney Mus, NY State Coun Arts, 72. *Bibliog:* Gazzette, Ms Mag, 73; Rochelle Ratner (auth), Beyond the limits, Soho Weekly News, 80; Carrie Rickey (auth), Third wave, Village Voice, 81. *Mem:* Women Artists in Revolution; Feminists in the Arts; Womens Caucus Art; Peacock Brigade; Professional Women Photogr. *Media:* Video, Xerography; Pastel, Watercolor. *Publ:* Auth, A personal decade, Heresies, No 16, 83. *Dealer:* New Yorker Films 43 West 61st St New York NY 10011. *Mailing Add:* 3 York St New York NY 10013

KLEEMANN, RON
PAINTER
b Bay City, Mich, July 37. *Study:* Univ Mich, BS(design), 61. *Work:* Guggenheim Mus, Mus Mod Art, New York; Hirschhorn Mus, Washington, DC; Indianapolis Mus Art; Univ Va Art Mus; and others. *Exhib:* Ann Sculpture & Painting Show, San Francisco Mus Art, 61; Mus Contemp Art, Chicago, 71; Aldrich Mus Contemp Art, Ridgefield, Conn, 72; Addison Gallery Am Art, Andover, Mass, 74; Butler Inst Am Art, Youngstown, Ohio, 74; Wadsworth Atheneum, Hartford, Conn, 74; Brooks Mem Art Gallery, Memphis, Tenn, 74; Wichita Mus, Wichita State Univ, Kans, 75; New Acquisitions, Mus Mod Art, New York, 77; Flint Inst Fine Arts, 78; Louis K Meisel Gallery, New York, 79. *Pos:* Official Artist, Indianapolis 500, 77- *Bibliog:* Andrea Mikotajok (auth), American Realists at Louis K Meisel, Arts Mag, 1/75; articles, Indianapolis News, 4/77 & Chicago Tribune, 10/77. *Mailing Add:* c/o Louis K Meisel Gallery 141 Prince St New York NY 10012

KLEIDON, DENNIS ARTHUR
EDUCATOR, DESIGNER
b Chicago, Ill, Sept 20, 42. *Study:* Bradley Univ, Peoria, Ill, 60-61; Univ Ill, Champaign, 61-64; Ill Wesleyan Univ, Bloomington, BFA(com art), 66; Ill State Univ, Normal, MS(sculpture), 67. *Work:* Massillon Mus, Ohio; Northern Ill Univ, DeKalb; Ill State Univ; Numa Ltd, Akron. *Comn:* Commemorative sculpture wall piece (wood, assemblage), Akron Nat Bank & Trust, Tuchman, Canute, Ryan & Wyatt, Architects, Rolling Acres Shopping Ctr, 76; promotional design, Scheeser & Buckley, Inc, Akron, 76; illustration, Hesselbart & Mitten Advert, Akron, 75 & Alsides, Inc, Akron, 75. *Exhib:* All-Ohio Exhib, Canton Art Inst, 71 & 72; Images, Nat Drawing Competition, Baldwin Wallace Col, Berea, Ohio, 72; Cleveland Invitational Exhib, Cooper Sch of Art, 72 & Lake Erie Col, 73; one-man show, Akron Art Inst, 76; and others. *Pos:* Designer/deliniator, Wight & Assoc, Downers Grove, Ill, 65-66 & Richard R Cramer, Architects, Hinsdale, Ill, 67; pres, Kleidon & Assoc, 75- *Teaching:* Instr drawing, Univ Ill, Champaign, 67-69; From assoc prof to prof graphic design, Univ Akron, 69- *Awards:* Res grants, Univ Akron, 70 & 77; First Place/Painting, All-Ohio Exhib, Canton Art Inst, 71; Merit Award/Design, Nat Univ & Col Designers Asn Design Competition, 75. *Bibliog:* Tex Tech Univ, Color Print USA (filmstrip), 71; Packaging education: The case for cooperation, Boxboard Container Mag, 11/79. *Media:* Acrylic, Vinyl. *Dealer:* Gallery 200 200 W Mound Columbus OH 43223. *Mailing Add:* 26 Waterside Dr Medina OH 44256

KLEIMAN, ALAN
PAINTER, SCULPTOR
b Brooklyn, NY, Feb 20, 38. *Study:* Richmond Prof Inst, BFA; Cranbrook Acad Art, MFA; study with Oscar Kokoschka, Salzburg, Austria. *Work:* Mus

Mod Art, Whitney Mus Am Art, Metrop Mus Art, New York; Carnegie Mus, Pittsburgh, Pa; Boston Mus Fine Art, Mass. *Comn:* Abstract fresco, Richmond City Fathers, Va, 57; rubber paint pool mural, comn by Mr & Mrs Pechenik, York, Pa, 60; abstract painted wall, Detroit Archit League, Mich, 65; abstract painted wall, City Walls, New York, 72. *Exhib:* Biennale, Sao Paulo, Brazil, 68; Silvermine, Conn, 70; Carnegie Inst Int, Pittsburgh, 71; In The Realm of the Monocramatic, Chicago & New York, 79; Painting About Painting, Paterson Col, NJ, 81; and others. *Pos:* Asst publicity dir, Artist Tenents Asn, 60-67; vpres, Grand St Artist Group, 70-75; chmn, Soho Artifacts, 71-75. *Awards:* First Prize for Print, Boston Arts Festival, 59; Creative Artists Pub Serv fel & CETA grant, 78. *Bibliog:* Hans Van Deljen (auth), Alan Kleiman paints Europe, Frie Folkes, Amsterdam, 56. *Media:* Watercolor, Oil. *Publ:* Auth, Painting Provincetown water, The Beacon, 61; auth, Investigations into the light of red color, Arts, 76; auth, Light dazzle and glow, The Soho Artist. *Dealer:* Area Code Gallery 31 Wooster St New York NY 10013 *Mailing Add:* 70 Grand St New York NY 10013

KLEIN, CECELIA F
HISTORIAN, EDUCATOR
b Pittsburgh, Pa, June 5, 38. *Study:* Oberlin Col, BA, 60, MA, 67; Columbia Univ, PhD with Douglas Fraser, 72. *Collections Arranged:* Art of Pre-Columbian Am, Meadow Brook Art Gallery, Oakland Univ, Rochester, Mich, 76; Mother, Worker, Ruler, Witch: Cross-Cultural Images of Women, Mus Cult Hist, Univ Calif, Los Angeles, 80. *Teaching:* Asst prof art hist, Oakland Univ, Rochester, 72-76; assoc prof art hist, Univ Calif, Los Angeles, 76- *Mem:* Col Art Asn; Asn Latin Am Art. *Res:* Pre-Columbian art history, with emphasis on Aztec art/iconography. *Publ:* Contribr, Death and the Afterlife in Pre-Columbian America, Dumbarton Oaks, 75; auth, The Face of the Earth: Frontality in Two-Dimensional Mesoamerican Art, Garland, 76; contribr, The Identity of the central deity on the Aztec calendar, Art Bull, 76; contribr, Who Was Tlaloc?, J Latin Am Lore, 80. *Mailing Add:* 4237 Sunnyslope Ave Sherman Oaks CA 91423

KLEIN, DORIS
PAINTER
b New York, NY, Nov 10, 18. *Study:* Art Students League, with Sidney Gross; Works Progress Admin Sch, with James Leschay & Anton Refregier; also sculpture with Maurice Glickman. *Work:* Univ Maine Permanent Collection; New Sch Permanent Collection, New York, NY. *Exhib:* Mus Belles Artes, Arg, 63; Maxwell Gallery, San Francisco, 67; Audubon Artists, 68; Roko Gallery, New York, 68-72; and many others. *Awards:* Best of Show, Jersey City Mus, 63-66; Marion K Haldenstein Mem Prize, Nat Asn Women Artists, 68; Grumbacher Award, Mamaroneck Artists Guild, 69. *Bibliog:* Hilton Kramer (auth), Rev of Roko show, New York Times, 68; Betty Chamberlain (auth), Philharmonic Hall program, 72. *Mem:* Nat Asn Women Artists. *Media:* Oil, Watercolor. *Dealer:* Phoenix Gallery 30 W 57th St New York NY 10019. *Mailing Add:* 235 W 76th St New York NY 10023

KLEIN, ELLEN LEE
PAINTER, WRITER
b New York, NY. *Study:* City Col New York, BA, 70; Pratt Inst, MFA, 72. *Work:* Thirteen Collection, New York. *Exhib:* Solo exhib, Maples Gallery, Fairleigh Dickinson Univ, 74; Hudson River Mus Ann, Yonkers, NY, 77; Terrance Gallery Nat All On Paper Show, Palenville, NY, 83; Sotheby's Thirteen Collection, Channel 13 Auction, New York, 83; 15th Ann Art Show, Fairleigh Dickinson Univ, 83. *Pos:* Adminr, Sch Fine Arts, New Acad Design, New York, 81-; reviewer & writer, Arts Mag, New York 82- *Teaching:* Instr drawing & art hist, High Sch Music & Art, New York, 72-73; adj prof contemp art, Jersey City State Col, 74; instr painting, Usdan Ctr Creative & Performing Arts, Wyandanch, NY, 80. *Awards:* Second Prize Graphics, Flushing Merchants Asn Spring Art Exhib, 70. *Bibliog:* Lawrence Campbell (auth), article, Art News, 9/73; Klein at Phoenix, Park East, 3/76; Nina French-Frazier (auth), Gallery guide, Westsider, 4/27/78. *Mem:* Col Art Asn; Artists Equity; Womens Caucus Art. *Media:* Oil, Paper Collage. *Publ:* Auth, In the spirit with artists toys, 83, The magic of Leopoldo Maler, 83, Lynn Isaacson, 83, The language of David Shapiro, 83 & Bill Spira, 83, Arts Mag. *Mailing Add:* 139-12 84th Dr Jamaica NY 11435

KLEIN, ESTHER M
PATRON, COLLECTOR
b Philadelphia, Pa, Nov 3, 07. *Study:* Temple Univ, BS; Univ London; Temple Univ, Hon Dr Humanities, 80. *Pos:* Ed, Philadelphia Art Alliance Bull; art critic, WPEN daily radio prog; founding dir, Long Beach Island Found Arts & Sci, NJ. *Awards:* Gimbel Award, 75; Art Alliance Award of Merit, given jointly to Esther & Philip Klein, 75. *Mem:* Life mem Pa Acad Fine Arts; life mem Philadelphia Print Club; Philadelphia Art Alliance (comt mem). *Interests:* Donor of annual prizes to Print Club and Clothesline Exhibit to encourage young Philadelphia artists. *Collection:* Philadelphia artists. *Mailing Add:* 135 S 18th Street Philadelphia PA 19103

KLEIN, GWENDA J
DEALER, WRITER
b San Francisco, Calif, Nov 10, 49. *Study:* Colo Col, BA, 71, MAT, 72. *Collections Arranged:* Contemporary Mexican Prints Travelling Exhib, Art Mus Asn Am, 80-83 & Burpee Art Mus, Rockford, Ill, 83. *Pos:* Arts columnist, Peninsula Mag, 78-80; interviewer & scriptwriter, Kaleidoscope, KTEH-TV, San Jose, Calif, 78-81; dir & owner, Klein Gallery, Chicago, 81- *Mem:* Young Women Arts. *Specialty:* Contemporary American painting and sculpture. *Publ:* Auth, Francisco Zuniga, Oakland Mus, 77; auth, Behind the paintings on the walls, Peninsula Mag, 79; auth, article, New Art Examiner, 80. *Mailing Add:* 356 W Huron Chicago IL 60610

KLEIN, LYNN (ELLEN)
PRINTMAKER, PHOTOGRAPHER
b San Francisco, Calif, April 14, 50. *Study:* Univ Minn, BA, 74, MA, 76. *Work:* Minneapolis Inst Arts; Philadelphia Mus Art; Atlantic Richfield Co, Los Angeles; Am Tel & Tel, New York. *Comn:* Mural, Mayo Clinic, Rochester, Minn, 77. *Exhib:* West 81, Art & Law, Minn Mus Art, St Paul, 81; solo exhib, Diffusion Thru Sequent Impressions, Allrich Gallery, San Francisco, 82; Phelan Award Exhib Printmaking, World Print Coun, San Francisco, 83; Photograms & Photographs, Los Angeles Ctr Photog Studies, 83; Photog Invitational, Tweed Mus Art, 83; Lensless Photography, Franklin Inst, Philadelphia, 83; Printed by Women, Port Hist Mus, Philadelphia, 83. *Teaching:* Instr design, Univ Minn, 74- *Awards:* Minn State Arts Bd Grant, 78; Photog Fel, Film in the Cities Gallery, 83; James P Phelan Art Award, World Print Coun, 83. *Bibliog:* Chuck Nicholson (auth), Coexistent realities, 3/26/83 & Frank Cebulski (auth), The Phelan Awards, 8/27/83, Artweek. *Dealer:* Allrich Gallery 251 Post St San Francisco CA 94108. *Mailing Add:* 1523 Elliot Ave Minneapolis MN 55404

KLEIN, MEDARD
PAINTER
b Appleton, Wis, Jan 6, 05. *Study:* Var art schs, Chicago. *Exhib:* Int Watercolor Show, Art Inst Chicago; Salon Realities Nouvelles, Paris; Joslyn Mem Mus, Omaha, Nebr; San Francisco Mus Art; Ill State Mus, Springfield; Oakland Art Gallery; Libr Congress; Pa Acad Fine Arts; Brooklyn Mus; Carnegie Inst, Walker Art Ctr, Minneapolis, Minn; and others. *Media:* Oil, Watercolor. *Mailing Add:* 807 North Wabash Apt 14 Chicago IL 60611

KLEIN, MICHAEL EUGENE
HISTORIAN, WRITER
b Philadelphia, Pa, July 30, 40. *Study:* Rutgers Col, New Brunswick, NJ, BA, 62; Columbia Univ, New York, MA, 65, PhD, 71. *Collections Arranged:* John Covert, 1882-1960 (auth, bk), Smithsonian Inst Press, 76. *Pos:* Vis cur, Hirshhorn Mus, 76. *Teaching:* Asst prof art hist, State Univ NY Brockport, 71-73; asst prof, Univ SC, 73-77; asst prof, Western Ky Univ, 77-80, assoc prof, 81- *Mem:* Col Art Asn Am; Southeastern Col Art Conf; Turner Soc. *Res:* American modernism of early 20th century, especially John Covert; political iconography of J M W Turner. *Publ:* Auth, John Covert's time: Cubism, Duchamp, Einstein, a quasi scientific fantasy, summer 74 & auth, John Covert's studios in 1916 and 1923, fall 79, Art J; auth, Scotese collection at the Columbia Museum of Art, Southeastern Col Art Conf J, fall 74; auth, John Covert and the Arensberg circle, Arts Mag, 5/77. *Mailing Add:* Dept of Art Western Ky Univ Bowling Green KY 42101

KLEIN, PATRICIA WINDROW See Windrow, Patricia

KLEIN, PAUL R
DEALER, GALLERY DIRECTOR
b New York, NY, Dec 30, 46. *Study:* Colo Col, BA, 69, MAT, 70. *Collections Arranged:* Emil Carlson (auth, catalog), Nat tour to mus & galleries, 75; Francisco Zuniga Lithographs (auth, catalog), Oakland Mus, 77; Contemporary Mexican Prints (auth, catalog), Western Asn Art Mus Tour, 80. *Pos:* Dir, Rubicon Gallery, Los Altos, Calif, 73-81, Mex Mus, San Francisco, 80-81 & Klein Gallery, Chicago, 81- *Mem:* Am Soc Appraisers; Fine Arts Club, Chicago, Ill; Chicago Art Dealers Asn. *Specialty:* Contemporary American and Mexican art. *Mailing Add:* 356 W Huron Chicago IL 60657

KLEIN, SANDOR C
PAINTER, SCULPTOR
b New York, NY, Oct 27, 12. *Study:* Nat Acad Design; Acad Julien, Paris; Beaux-Arts, Paris; Acad Fine Arts, Vienna; Royal Acad Art, Budapest; Am Acad Rome, fel, 31. *Work:* Smithsonian Inst Mus Am Art, Washington, DC; Albany State Mus, NY; Luxembourg Mus; Fine Arts Mus of South, Mobile, Ala; Pentagon, Washington, DC. *Comn:* Portraits of Hon Schuyler Otis Bland, Chmn Maritime & Fisheries Comn, 46, Gen Nathan F Twining, Chmn Joint Chiefs of Staff, 61 & Gen Curtis E LeMay, USAF Chief of Staff, 62, comn by US Govt; Eleanor Roosevelt, comn by Am Cancer Soc, 63; Armand Hammer, Occidental Co, 67. *Exhib:* Paris Salon; Carnegie Inst Int; plus others in the US & abroad. *Teaching:* Instr painting, Nat Acad, New York, Beaux Arts & Acad Julien, Paris. *Awards:* Pulitzer Prize for Painting, 31; Silver Medal, Paris Salon; medal, Int Biennale, Venice, 32. *Media:* Oil. *Mailing Add:* 33 W 67th St New York NY 10023

KLEINBAUER, W EUGENE
HISTORIAN, EDITOR
b Los Angeles, Calif, June 15, 37. *Study:* Univ Calif, Berkeley, with Walter Horn, BA & MA, 59; Princeton Univ, with Richard Krautheimer & Kurt Weitzmann, PhD, 67. *Pos:* Chmn visual arts adv panel, Ind State Art Comn, 75-76; bd dir, Midwest Art History Soc, 80-82. *Teaching:* Asst prof hist art, Univ Calif, Los Angeles, 65-72; chmn dept fine arts, Ind Univ, 73-76, chmn arts admin prog, 73-75 & fall 78, prof hist art, 77-; Sam & Ayala Zacks vis prof hist of art, Hebrew Univ, Jerusalem, 78. *Awards:* Nat Endowment Humanities Fel, 76-77. *Mem:* Col Art Asn Am; Int Ctr Medieval Art (mem bd dir, 70-73, 74-77 & 81-83, ed, GESTA, 80-83); Medieval Acad Am; US Nat Comt Byzantine Studies; Soc Armenian Studies; Cent Ind Soc, Archeol Inst Am (pres, 77-80). *Res:* Specialist in late antique and Byzantine art and architecture; historiography of Western art. *Publ:* Ed, Modern Perspectives in Western Art History, Holt Rinehart, 71; ed, E Kitzinger, Art of Byzantium & Medieval West, Ind Univ, 76; auth, Research Guide to the History of Western Art, Am Libr Asn, 82. *Mailing Add:* Sch of Fine Arts Ind Univ Bloomington IN 47405

KLEINHOLZ, FRANK
PAINTER, WRITER
b Brooklyn, NY, Feb 17, 01. *Study:* Fordham Univ, LLB, 23; also with Alexander Dobkin, Yasuo Kuniyoshi & Sol Wilson; Colby Col, Hon DFA. *Work:* Metrop Mus Art, New York; Brooklyn Mus, NY; Marquette Univ, Milwaukee, Wis; Mus Mod Art, Tel-Aviv, Israel; Fine Arts Mus, Moscow. *Comn:* Outdoor mural, Blankman Found, Sands Point, NY, 58. *Exhib:* Directions in American Painting, Carnegie Inst, Pittsburgh, 41; Artists for Victory, Metrop Mus Art, 42; one-man shows, Assoc Am Artists, New York, 42 & ACA Gallery, Rome, Italy, 65; American Painting Today, Metrop Mus Art, 50. *Awards:* Sixth Purchase Prize for Back Street, Hearn Fund, Metrop Mus Art, 42; First Prize for Bright Lights, Manhasset Art Asn, 53; First Prize for Prints for Sunflower, YMHA, Miami, 72. *Bibliog:* Edwin Alden Jewell (auth), Frank Kleinholz holds art show, New York Times, 42; Donald Bear (auth), Contemporary American painting, In: Encycl Britannica, 46; August L Freundlich (auth), Frank Kleinholz, the Outsider, Univ Miami, 69. *Media:* Oil. *Publ:* Auth, Frank Kleinholz, a Self Portrait, Shorewood Press, 64; auth, Abstract art is dead, Am Dialog, 7/64; auth & illusr, Ile de Brehat--the Flowering Rock, Univ Miami, 71. *Dealer:* ACA Galleries 25 E 73rd St New York NY 10021. *Mailing Add:* 21 Second Ave Port Washington NY 11050

KLEINMAN, ALYCE CHAIKIN See Chaikin, Alyce

KLEINMAN, SUE
PAINTER, LECTURER
b New York, NY. *Study:* Pratt Inst, Brooklyn, BFA; Caton-Rose Inst Fine Arts; New Sch Social Res, New York; Mus Mod Art, New York, with Zoltan Hecht & Donald Stacey; also with Raphael Soyer & Anthony Toney. *Work:* Brown Univ, RI; Fairleigh Dickinson Univ, Rutherford, NJ; Maimonides Hosp, Brooklyn. *Exhib:* Knickerbocker Art, 59 & Audubon Art, 60, Weiner Gallery, New York; one-woman shows, Lord & Taylor Gallery, New York, 76; Pompano Recreation Ctr, Pompano Beach, Fla, 80; Contextual Galleries, Ft Lauderdale, Fla, 80 & Pompano Beach Pub Libr, 83. *Pos:* Lectr & docent, Ft Lauderdale Mus Art, 74-81. *Awards:* Bronze Medal, Village Art Ctr, 58; Silver Medal, Trade Bank New York. *Bibliog:* Jane Jaffe (auth), article, Manhattan E, 65; Dorothy Hall (auth), article, Park E, 69; Saint-Evermond (auth), article, France-Amerique, 69. *Mem:* Artists Equity Asn; Nat Women's Art Asn; Broward Art Guild; Boca Raton Art Ctr. *Media:* Oil and Palette Knife. *Dealer:* Contextual Gallery 813 E Los Olas Blvd Ft Lauderdale FL 33301. *Mailing Add:* 405 N Ocean Blvd Pompano Beach FL 33062

KLEINSMITH, BRUCE JOHN See Nutzle, Futzie

KLEINSMITH, GENE (EUGENE DENNIS)
CERAMIST, WRITER
b Madison, Wis, Feb 22, 41. *Study:* Augustana Col, SDak, with Palmer Eide & Ogden Dalyrymple, BA(art), 63; Northern Ariz Univ, Flagstaff, with Dr Donald Bendel & Dr Peter Jacobs, MA(art), 69; Univ Nev, Las Vegas, with Dr Mark Beals, 70. *Work:* Ariz Western Col & Yuma Art Ctr, Yuma, Ariz; Walker Art Ctr, Minneapolis; Los Angeles Co Mus, Los Angeles; Mus Int delle Ceramiche, Faenza, Italy; Calif Designer-Craftsman. *Comn:* Facade for new church, Ascension Lutheran Church, Ft Collins, Colo, 63; ceramic sculptures, Univ Wis-Madison, 66, Long Beach State Col, Calif, 74 & IBM Corp, La Crosse, Wis, 79-80. *Exhib:* Am Bicentennial Exhib, Paris, France, 76; West Coast Clay, San Francisco Art Mus, 77; Nat Endowment Traveling Exhib, southern Calif, 70 & 80; Clay as Art, Ariz Comn Arts & Humanities, Flagstaff, 80, 81 & 83; Kaleidoscope USA, Gallery II, 82; Art USA, Charlottesville, Va, 83. *Collections Arranged:* The Arizona Annual, works of Ariz artists, 70; The Lip People, works of Peter Jacobs, 78. *Teaching:* Instr ceramics & sculpture, San Bernardino Valley Col, Calif, 67-71; art dept chmn & instr ceramics & sculpture, Victor Valley Col, Victorville, Calif, 71- *Awards:* Victor Valley Col Fac Fel Art, 74; Lutheran Brotherhood Corp Nat Exhib Award, 79. *Bibliog:* Don Bendel (auth), The Great American Potters on Australian Tour, 81; Kleinsmith Finds that Clay's the Way, Rampage Newspaper, 81; Richard Notkin (auth), The Artist as Social Critic, 82. *Mem:* Nat Coun on Educ Ceramic Arts; Am Crafts Coun; Nat Coun Art Adminr; Inst for Ceramic Hist; Southern Calif Designer/Craftsmen. *Media:* Stoneware, Porcelain. *Res:* Aesthetic or technical information to sustain an interchange of dialogue and consequence. *Publ:* Auth, Earth, Fire and Water, 76 & Clay's the Way, 78, 2nd ed, 81, Victor Valley Col Press; auth, Rudy Autio, 80 & Artist as Innovator, 9/83, Ceramics Monthly; auth, William C Alexander, Nat Coun Educ Ceramic Arts J, 10/83. *Dealer:* Gallery II 218 W Main St Charlottesville VA. *Mailing Add:* 13925 Kiowa Rd Apple Valley CA 92307

KLEMENT, VERA
PAINTER, EDUCATOR
b Danzig, Poland, Dec 14, 29; US citizen. *Study:* Cooper Union Sch Art & Archit, grad, 50. *Work:* Mus Mod Art, New York; Philadelphia Mus Art; Ill State Mus, Springfield; Univ Tex; Continental Bank, Chicago. *Comn:* Ed of etchings, NY Hilton/Rockefeller Ctr, 61; 27 & 1/2 ft painting, Kemper Ins Co, Long Grove, Ill, 75. *Exhib:* Modern Art in US, Mus Mod Art Traveling Exhib, New York, 56; NC Mus Art, Raleigh, 60; Print Club, Philadelphia, 62; Art Inst Chicago, 67; Ill State Mus, 74; Walker Art Ctr Invitational, Minneapolis, Minn, 76; Jewish Mus, New York, 82. *Teaching:* Instr painting, Univ Ill, 68-69; asst prof art, Univ Chicago, 69-78, assoc prof, 78- *Awards:* Louis Comfort Tiffany Found Award, 54; Illinois Arts Council Grant, 81; Guggenheim fel, 81-82. *Bibliog:* William S Lieberman (auth), Printmaking & the American woodcut today, Perspectives USA, 53; Amy Goldin (auth), Vitality vs greasy kid stuff, Art Gallery Mag 4/72; article in Artists' Writings,

publ by NAME, 77. *Mem:* Chicago Network. *Media:* Encaustic. *Dealer:* Roy Boyd Gallery Chicago IL; CDS Gallery 13 E 75 St New York NY 10021. *Mailing Add:* 727 S Dearborn Chicago IL 60605

KLINDT, STEVEN
ADMINISTRATOR
b Davenport, Iowa, Dec 18, 47. *Study:* Sch of Art, Univ Iowa, BA(studio art), 70, MA(photog), 74. *Work:* Art Inst Chicago; Ill State Mus, Springfield; Knox Col, Galesburg, Ill; Monmouth Col, Ill. *Exhib:* City of Man, Univ Chicago, 70; Contemp Photog, Sheldon Art Gallery, Univ Nebr, Lincoln, 72; Third Ann Photog, Kansas City Art Inst, 73; Ill Photogr 75, Ill State Mus, 75; Photographs by Steven Klindt & Gretchen Garner, St Xavier Col Gallery, Chicago, 76; and other group & one-man shows. *Collections Arranged:* Photograph Invitational, Galesburg Civic Art Ctr, Ill, 76; Proposals for Lake Sculpture, Evanston Art Ctr, Ill, 77; New American Photography (auth, catalog), Columbia Col, 82. *Pos:* Dir, Galesburg Civic Art Ctr, 74-76; dir, Evanston Art Ctr, 76-79; dir, Chicago Ctr Contemp Photog, Columbia Galleries, Columbia Col, 79-83; dir, Mus Contemp Photog, Columbia Col, Chicago, 83- *Teaching:* Mus studies MA program, Columbia Col, Chicago, currently. *Mem:* Col Art Asn; Am Asn Mus; Art Mus Asn. *Publ:* Ed, Jerry N Uelsmann, Photographs from 1975-1979, Columbia Col, Chicago, 80; ed, Light Touching Silver-Photographs, Columbia Col, Chicago, 80; and others. *Mailing Add:* Chicago Ctr Contemp Photog Columbia Col 600 S Michigan Ave Chicago IL 60605

KLINE, ALMA
SCULPTOR
b Nyack, NY. *Study:* Radcliffe Col, AB; also sculpture with Jose De Creeft. *Work:* Cronkhite Grad Ctr, Cambridge, Mass; Chrysler Mus Arts & Sci, Va; St Lawrence Univ, NY. *Exhib:* One-man shows, Travel Art Guild, 64 (ten shows), Thomson Gallery, New York, 69 & Caravan House Gallery, New York, 76; Soc Animal Artists, Natural Hist Mus, Smithsonian Inst, 71; Acad Natural Sci Philadelphia, 81; and others. *Awards:* Grumbacher Purchase Award, Audubon Artists, 60; Medal of Honor, Knickerbocker Artists, 64; Patrons of Art Award, Painters & Sculptors Asn NJ, 69. *Bibliog:* Nat Wildlife, 67; Nat Sculpture Rev, 69; The Arthur & Elizabeth Schlesinger Library on the History of Women in America, Cambridge, 74. *Mem:* Hon life mem Audubon Artists; Nat Asn Women Artists; Soc Animal Artists (treas, 73); Knickerbocker Artists; NY Artists Equity Asn. *Media:* Stone, Wood. *Mailing Add:* 225 E 74th St New York NY 10021

KLINE, HARRIET
PAINTER, PRINTMAKER
b New York, NY, Sept 25, 16. *Study:* Hunter Col, BA; also with Isaac Soyer; Art Students League, with Robert Philipp & Morris Kantor; China Inst, NY, with Prof Y C Wang, 45-59. *Work:* Art Collection, NY Univ; State Art Collection, Dresden, EGer; State Univ NY Col Oswego; Western New Eng Col. *Exhib:* Silvermine Nat Exhib, Silvermine Guild, New Canaan, Conn, 59; Nat Asn Women Artists, Nat Acad, New York, 59-; solo exhibs, Selected Artists Gallery, New York, 60-75 & Paper Work, Katonah Gallery, NY, 80; 38th Ann, Butler Inst Am Art, 74; First Exhib American Graphics, Albertinum Mus, Dresden, 80; First Nat Asn Women Artists, traveling show, Israel, 80 & Egypt, 82; and other group & one-man shows. *Teaching:* Instr, pvt classes, 59-68. *Awards:* Donor's Prize, Greenwich Art Soc, 80 & 81; Citation Color Award, Stamford Art Asn, 81; and others. *Mem:* Nat Asn Women Artists; Silvermine Guild Artists; Am Soc Contemp Artists; Greenwich Art Soc; life mem Art Students League; and others. *Media:* Oil, Watercolor; Etching, Cast Paper. *Mailing Add:* 390 Heathcote Rd Scarsdale NY 10583

KLINE, RICHARD R
PAINTER, SCULPTOR
b Three Rivers, Mich. *Study:* Mich State Univ, MFA, 64; Ox Bow Sch Art; Art Inst Chicago, with Abraham Rattner. *Work:* Emerson Mus Art, Syracuse, NY; Richard DeMarco Gallery, Edinburgh, Scotland. *Exhib:* Everson Mus Art, Syracuse, NY, 74; Henri Gallery, Washington, DC, 74; Colgate Univ, Hamilton, NY, 76; Edinburgh Art Festival, Scotland, 80; and others. *Teaching:* Prof, Cent Mich Univ, Mt Pleasant, 64-, chmn, Dept Art, 79- *Bibliog:* Film event (review), Village Voice, 72; 55 Mercer Street (review), Art News, 72. *Mem:* Col Art Asn; Nat Coun Art Admnr. *Media:* Pastel; Paper. *Mailing Add:* Art Dept Cent Mich Univ Mt Pleasant MI 48858

KLINGHOFFER, SHIRLEY
SCULPTOR
b NJ, Aug 22, 42. *Study:* Univ Miami, BEd(magna cum lauda), 63; Sch Visual Arts, 64-65; Univ Md, with Ken Campbell, 80. *Work:* Morris Mus Arts & Sci, Morristown, NJ. *Comn:* Sculpture (marplex & bronze), Southwst Gas Corp, Las Vegas, 82. *Exhib:* Surface and Form, Bergen Mus, Paramus, NJ, 80; Nat Asn Women Artists Traveling Exhib, Israel & Egypt, 81; Allied Artists Exhib, Nat Arts Club, New York, 82; Artists in Residence, Brandeis Univ, 82; Solid Directions, Morris Mus Arts & Sci, Morristown, NJ, 83-84. *Awards:* Patron Arts Award, Painters & Sculptors Soc, 79 & 80; First Prize Sculpture, Summit Art Ctr, 82 & 83. *Bibliog:* Maryanne Gabowsky (auth), Shirley Klinghoffer: The artist, NJ Art Forum, 82; Eileen Watkins (auth), Sculptor sees through stone, Newark Star Ledger, 83. *Mem:* Sculptors League; Nat Asn Women Artists; Sculptors Asn NJ; NJ Coun Arts; Painters & Sculptors Soc NJ. *Media:* Stone. *Mailing Add:* 21 Rodman Lane Westfield NJ 07090

KLIPPER, STUART DAVID
PHOTOGRAPHER
b Bronx, NY, Aug 27, 41. *Study:* Univ Mich, Col Lit, Sci & Arts, BA, 62, Col Archit & Design, 62-63. *Work:* Minneapolis Inst Art; Walker Art Ctr, Minneapolis; Art Inst Chicago; Mus Art, Univ Kans, Lawrence; Gallery, Fermi Nat Accelerator Lab, Batavia, Ill; and others. *Comn:* Anasazi Plates, Univ Mich; Cray I Computer, Cray Res Inc; The World in a Few States, First Bank Systems, Minneapolis. *Exhib:* One-man shows, Color & Black & White Photographs, 1971-74, O K Harris Works of Art, New York, 75, Multiple Strip Images, Walker Art Ctr, Minneapolis, 78, Recent Work, Minn Mus Art, Minneapolis, 80, Art Inst Chicago, 80 & Douglas Kenyon Gallery, 80 & Three Photog Groups, 1978-79, Minn Mus Art, 80; 20th Century Am Photogr, Atkins Mus Fine Art, Kansas City, 74; Am Photog in the 70's, Art Inst Chicago, 79; Duluth Photogrs, Tweed Mus; George Eastman House, Rochester, 82; Minn Mus Art, 82; and others. *Collections Arranged:* Seven Photogr (guest-cur), Art Gallery, Macalester Col, St Paul, Minn, 78. *Teaching:* Instr photog, Minneapolis Col Art & Design, 70-71, vis prof, 74-75 & 78; vis prof photog, Colo Col, Colorado Springs, 78, 79, 80. *Awards:* Nat Endowment Arts Photogr Fel, 79; J S Guggenheim Mem Found Photogr Fel, 79-80; Bush Found Visual Arts Fel, 80-81; and others. *Mem:* Minn Artists' Exhib Prog. *Publ:* Contribr, Midwest Invitational Catalogue, Walker Art Ctr, 74; auth, The History of Photography in Limericks, privately publ, 77; contribr, Minnesota Survey: Six Photographers Catalogue, Minneapolis Inst Art, 78; auth, The Art of the Twin Cities, Portfolio Mag, summer 80. *Mailing Add:* 614 W 27th St Minneapolis MN 55408

KLITZKE, THEODORE ELMER
EDUCATOR, HISTORIAN
b Chicago, Ill, Nov 4, 15. *Study:* Art Inst Chicago, BFA, 40; Univ Chicago, BA, 41, PhD, 53; Kansas City Art Inst, Hon DFA, 80. *Teaching:* Instr art hist, Univ Chicago, 46-47; asst prof art hist, State Univ NY Col Ceramics, Alfred Univ, 53-59; prof art hist & chmn dept art, Univ Ala, Tuscaloosa, 59-68. *Mem:* Am Studies Asn; Col Art Asn Am; Soc Archit Historians; fel Nat Asn Sch Art. *Res:* Social history of American art; 19th century French art; German expressionism; history of prints and drawings. *Publ:* Contribr, reviews in Col Art J & Art Bull, 59-; contribr, Alexis de Tocqueville and the Arts in America, Festschrift Ulrich Middeldorf, 68; auth, Melville Price Retrospective: 1920-1970, Frame House Gallery, 70; contribr, Hermann Wilhelm (catalog), 72. *Mailing Add:* 1300 Mt Royal Ave Baltimore MD 21217

KLONIS, STEWART
PAINTER, DIRECTOR
b Naugatuck, Conn, Dec 24, 01. *Study:* Art Students League. *Work:* IBM Collection & many pub & pvt collections. *Exhib:* Am Watercolor Soc; Century Asn; Nat Acad Design. *Teaching:* Instr, Queens Col, 40-45; exec dir, Art Students League, 46-80. *Awards:* Gari Melchers Award, Artists Fellowships Inc, 75. *Mem:* Nat Arts Mus Sports; Benjamin Franklin fel Royal Soc Arts; MacDowell Colony; Inst Int Educ; assoc mem Nat Acad Design. *Media:* Watercolor. *Mailing Add:* 19 Upper Commons Woodbury CT 06798

KLOPFENSTEIN, PHILIP ARTHUR
PAINTER, MUSEUM DIRECTOR
b Lake Odessa, Mich, Apr 28, 37. *Study:* Mich State Univ, with Abraham Ratner & Linsey Decker, BFA; Western Mich Univ, with Harry Hefner, MFA; Harvard Univ, Arts Admin Cert. *Exhib:* State Ark Educ Dept Traveling Exhib, 76-; Mid Southern Watercolor Soc Ann, 72-74. *Collections Arranged:* John Henry Byrd (1840-1880), Southeast Ark Arts & Sci Ctr, Pine Bluff, 70; Ernest Trova One-Man Exhib, 71; Art Inc II (Am paintings from Am corp collections), 80. *Pos:* TV writer & teacher, Ark Educ TV, Conway, 68-69; dir, Southeast Ark Arts & Sci Ctr, 70-76; exec dir, Augusta Richmond Co Mus, Ga, 77-79; dir, Montgomery Mus Fine Arts, Ala, 79-82; vice pres, Res and Reclamation, 83. *Teaching:* Instr, Paw Paw Pub Sch, Mich, 63-65; instr painting, watercolor & art educ, Little Rock Univ, 65-68. *Mem:* Am Asn Mus; Southeastern Mus Conf (regional rep, 74-75); Am Asn Mus; Am Asn Art Mus Dirs; Rotary Int; and others. *Media:* Watercolor, Acrylic. *Res:* John Henry Byrd. *Publ:* Auth, John Henry Byrd (1840-1880), 71. *Mailing Add:* 2155 Kingsbury Dr Montgomery AL 36106

KLOSS, GENE (ALICE GENEVA GLASIER)
ETCHER, PAINTER
b Oakland, Calif, July 27, 03. *Study:* Univ Calif, Berkeley, AB(hon in art), 24; Calif Sch Fine Arts, 24-25; Calif Sch Arts & Crafts. *Work:* Metrop Mus Art, New York; Smithsonian Inst, Washington, San Francisco Art Mus; Mus Tokyo, Japan. *Comn:* Prints, Soc Print Connoisseurs, New York, 49; prints, Print Club Albany, NY, 52; prints, Soc Am Graphic Artists, New York, 53; prints, Print Makers Calif, Los Angeles, 56. *Exhib:* Three Centuries of Art in United States (in collab with Mus Mod Art, New York), Paris, 38; Nat Acad Design Ann, New York, 50-; Three Am Regionalist Printmakers, Pratt Graphic Ctr, NY, 76; one-man shows, Muckenthaler Cult Ctr, Fullerton, Calif, 80, Roswell Mus, 82 & WTex Mus, 84. *Awards:* Purchase Award, Libr Cong, 53; Fower Prize, 60 & Purchase Prize, 61, Print Club Albany; anonymous prize, Nat Acad Design, 61. *Bibliog:* Mary Carrol Nelson (auth), Intaglios by Gene Kloss, Am Artist, 2/78. *Mem:* Academician Nat Acad Design; Soc Am Graphic Artists; Philadelphia Watercolor Club; Albany Print Club. *Media:* Oil, Watercolor, Etchings. *Publ:* Illusr, The Great Kiva, 80 & illusr, Gene Kloss Etchings, 81, Sunstone Press; illusr, Gene Kloss Etchings (incl cat raisonne), Sunstone Press, 81. *Mailing Add:* Box 33 Taos NM 87571

KLOTZ-REILLY, SUZANNE RUTH
PAINTER, SCULPTOR
b Shawno, Wis, Oct 15, 44. *Study:* Washington Univ, St Louis, 62-64; Kansas City Art Inst, 64-66, BFA, 66; Univ Mo, Kansas City, 66-67; Tex Tech Univ, 70-72, MFA, 72. *Work:* Nat Mus, Smithsonian Inst; Spencer Art Mus, Lawrence, Kans; Scripps Col, Claremont, Calif; Ariz State Univ, Tempe; Fred Marer Collection Contemp Ceramics; and others. *Exhib:* Drawings, Dallas Mus Fine Arts, Tex, 73; one-person exhibs, Scottsdale Ctr Arts, 78, Phoenix Art Mus, 81, Spencer Art Mus, Lawrence, Kans, 82 & Mus STex, Corpus Christi, 83; Invitational, Miss Mus Art, 82; and many others. *Teaching:* Instr painting, drawing & design, Angelo State Univ, San Angelo, Tex, 72-75; asst prof drawing & design, Scripps Col, Claremont, Calif, 76-78. *Awards:* Craftsman Fels, 76 & 78 & Performance Grant, 83, Nat Endowment Arts; and others. *Bibliog:* Hubert Crehan (auth), Dream houses & fanciful creatures of Suzanne Klotz, St Louis Post Dispatch, Mo, 74; Berman & Pinto (auths), Creative Exploration Series, Merrick, 75; and many articles in various magazines. *Media:* Mixed. *Publ:* Coauth, Everything's the Same, Country Western Press, 77; coauth, Everything's Different, 78. *Dealer:* Elaine Horwitch Gallery 4211 N Marshall Way Scottsdale AZ 85251; Jeremy Stone Gallery 126 Post St San Francisco CA 94108. *Mailing Add:* 2113 E Concorda Dr Tempe AZ 85282

KLUVER, BILLY (JOHAN WILHEM)
ADMINISTRATOR
b Monaco, Nov 13, 27; Swedish citizen. *Study:* Royal Inst Technol, Stockholm, EE; Univ Calif, Berkeley, PhD. *Work:* Mus Mod Art, New York; Kunsthaus, Zurich, Switz; Centre George Pompidou, Paris, France; Mus Ludwig, Cologne, WGer; and others. *Collections Arranged:* Four Americans, Mod Museet, Stockholm, 62; Art 1963--A New Vocabulary (cur), Arts Coun YMHA, Philadelphia, 62; American Pop-Art, Mod Museet, Stockholm, 64; Some More Beginnings (cur), Brooklyn Mus, NY, 68; The New York Collection for Stockholm, Mod Museet Stockholm, 73; What Are You Working On Now? 1960-1970, PS 1, New York, 83. *Pos:* Mem tech staff, Bell Tel Lab, Murray Hill, NJ, 58-68; co-founder & pres, Experiments in Art and Technol, 66- *Awards:* Royal Order of Vasa, New York Collection for Stockholm, Govt Sweden, 74. *Bibliog:* Jill Johnston (auth), Marmelade Me, E P Dutton, 71; Douglas Davis (auth), Art and The Future, Praeger, 73; Calvin Tomkins (auth), The Scene, Viking Press, 76. *Publ:* Contribr, The Machine, Mus Mod Art, New York, 68; contribr, Scienza Tecnica 71, In: Enciclopedia Della Scienze E Della Tecnica, 72; contribr & ed, Pavilion, Dutton, 72; ed, Experiments in Art and Technology Bibliog 1965-1980, 80; auth, What Are You Working on Now: A Pictorial Memoir of the '60's, Experiments Art & Technol, 83. *Mailing Add:* 49 E 68th St New York NY 10021

KNAPP, SADIE MAGNET
PAINTER, SCULPTOR
b New York, NY, July 18, 09. *Study:* NY Training Sch Teachers, lic; City Col New York; Brooklyn Mus Art Sch; Atelier 17; Sculpture Ctr. *Work:* Ga Mus Art, Athens; Norfolk Mus Art, Va; Riverside Mus, New York. *Exhib:* Corcoran Gallery Art, Washington, DC; Baltimore Mus; Pa Acad Fine Arts, Philadelphia; Butler Inst Art, Youngstown, Ohio; and others in Can, Eng, France, Switz, Arg, Mex, Japan, India, Scotland & Italy. *Collections Arranged:* Exchange exhibits arranged for women artists of Japan, 60 & artists of Argentina, 65 & Nat Asn Women Artists--both exhibs shown in var foreign & domestic mus. *Teaching:* Instr enamels, Worcester Crafts Ctr, 63. *Awards:* Grumbacher Award for Painting, Nat Acad Design, 68; Awards (two), Am Heritage Art Exhib, 77; Cramer Prize, 80; and others. *Mem:* Nat Asn Women Artists (vpres, 61-65, pres, 65-67); Nat Soc Painters in Casein & Acrylics; Artists Equity Asn; and others. *Mailing Add:* 162 Somerset H West Palm Beach FL 33409

KNAPP, TOM
SCULPTOR, PAINTER
b Gillette, Wyo, Sept 28, 25. *Study:* Santa Rosa Jr Col, Calif; Calif Col Arts & Crafts, Oakland; Art Ctr Sch, Los Angeles. *Work:* Whitney Gallery Western Art, Cody, Wyo; Indianapolis Mus Art; Heritage Libr, Bank of Alaska, Anchorage; Mescelero Tribe, Mescalero Indian Reservation, NMex; Midland Nat Bank Collection, Tex. *Comn:* Paul Stock Mem, Stock Found, Cody, Wyo, 72; Bronze Plaque of Sen Quinn, Quinn Mem Auditorium, Mass, 73; Larry Mahan, Oil City Brass Works, Beaumont, Tex, 74. *Pos:* Owner, Buckhorn Bronze Foundry, Ruidoso Downs, NMex, 71- *Teaching:* Instr painting, Carrizo Lodge Workshop, Ruidoso, NMex, 72-74, instr sculpture, 73-75; instr, Las Cruces Art Asn Sculpture Workshop, NMex, 73. *Awards:* Best of Show Bronze, Sacramento Indian Art Show, 74; First Place Indian Art, Great Western Exhib Ctr, Los Angeles, 74; First Place Bronze, San Diego Indian Art Show, 74. *Bibliog:* Barbara Funkhouser (auth), A sculptor casts his bronzes, El Paso Sun Dial Mag, 74; Marilyn Watson (auth), Pouring in the Hondo Valley, NMex Mag, 2/78; Kay Mayer (auth), Dancers of Ruidoso, Art West Mag, 3/82. *Media:* Bronze; Drawing. *Mailing Add:* Box 510 Ruidoso Downs NM 88346

KNAUB, DONALD E
MUSEUM DIRECTOR
b York, Pa, Dec 18, 36. *Study:* Elizabethtown Col, Pa, BA, 59; Boston Univ, Sch Fine & Appl Arts, MFA, 62; summer sch, Harvard Arts Adminr Inst, cert, 75. *Collections Arranged:* Contemporary Painting in Alabama (auth, catalog), 80, Nall: Image & Symbol (auth, catalog), 81, Five Figurative Painters (auth), 81 & Southern Furniture 1740-1820 (auth, catalog), 81, Huntsville Mus Art, Ala. *Pos:* Info asst, Libr Mus, Lincoln Ctr, 62-69; civic arts dir, Davis, Calif, 77-78; dir, Muchenthaler Cult Ctr, 78-79; dir, Huntsville Mus Art, 79- *Mem:* Int Coun Mus; Am Asn Mus; SEastern Mus Conf; Art Mus Asn; Asn Art Mus Dirs. *Mailing Add:* 700 Monroe St Huntsville AL 35801

KNAUB, RAYMOND L
PAINTER, INSTRUCTOR
b Gering, Nebr, July 6, 40. *Study:* Baylor Univ, 58-60; Univ Nebr, Lincoln, BFA, 63; Univ Colo, Boulder; also with Frederick Mizen, David Seyler & Frank Sampson. *Work:* United Bank of Colo; Dixon Paper Co; Empire Savings & Loan, Denver, Colo; WTex Mus Asn Collection; Atlantic Oil Co; and others. *Exhib:* Denver Art Mus, 72 & 73; 20th Nat Soc Painters Acrylic & Casein, New York, 73; 61st Allied Artists Am, New York, 74; Rocky Mountain Nat Watermedia Exhib, Golden, Colo, 75; Colo Exhib, Arvada Cult Ctr, Colo, 77; Spring Panorama Art, Baker Gallery Fine Art, 81. *Teaching:* Instr art, Jefferson Co Schs, Lakewood, Colo, 68-; instr art, Community Col Denver, 71-73. *Bibliog:* Feature article in Southwest Art Mag, 9/78. *Media:* Oil. *Mailing Add:* 859 S Miller Ct Lakewood CO 80226

KNECHT, JOHN
FILMMAKER
b Iron Ridge, Wis, Mar 5, 47. *Study:* Univ Wis, Oshkosh, BS, 72; Idaho State Univ, MFA, 74. *Exhib:* Solo shows, Millennium, 79 & Collective for Living Cinema, 80, New York; Frames, Hunter Gallery, New York, 80; Film as Installation, Clocktower Gallery, New York, 80; Int Forum des Jungen Films, Berlin, WGer, 81; Edinburgh Film Fest, Edinburgh, Scotland, 81; and others. *Teaching:* Asst prof, Univ Okla Sch Art, 74-79; asst prof, Colgate Univ Fine Arts, 81-; vis lectr, Brown Univ, spring 81. *Awards:* Golden Athena Best Experimental Film, Athens Films Festival, 78; Independent Filmmakers Grant, Jerome Found, 79; Lightworks Grant, 83. *Bibliog:* Adam Brooks (auth), review, New York Rocker, 12/81; Vivien Raynor (auth), article, New York Times, 6/18/82; Mick Eaton (auth), Continuing the adventures of Adrian Block, Film Bulletin, London, 2/83; and others. *Mem:* Collective Living Cinema. *Mailing Add:* Box 83 Hamilton NY 13346

KNERR, SALLIE FROST
PAINTER, PRINTMAKER
b Plattsburg, Mo, Apr 7, 14. *Study:* Univ Mo; Cincinnati Acad Com Art; Corcoran Sch Art; Canal Zone Jr Col; Nat Acad Design; Am Univ; George Washington Univ, BA, 64; Univ Ga, scholarship for travel-study in Mex & Guatamala, 67, MFA, 68; Studies Abroad Prog in Italy, Univ Ga, summer 78. *Work:* Gibbes Gallery Art, Univ Miss; Biblioteca Nac, Panama; George Washington Univ; Florence Mus, SC. *Exhib:* Contemporary Artists of South Carolina, Greenville Co Mus Art & Gibbes Gallery Art, Charleston, SC, 70; 13th Dixie Ann Montgomery Mus Fine Arts, Ala, 72; Prints from the Persian Suite (travelling exhib, including Iran), Iran-Am Soc, 77; Old Masters & Contemp Printmakers, Huntsville Mus of Art, Ala, 77; A Sense of Pattern, City Gallery, Charleston, SC, 83. *Teaching:* Asst prof art, Baptist Col Charleston, 68-70; instr art appreciation, painting, drawing & printmaking, Gibbes Gallery Sch, 68-70. *Awards:* First in watercolor, Marshall Award Show, Art League Northern Va, 62; hon mention for woodcut, SC Guild Artists Show, Greenville, 65; Award of Merit, Coastal Carolina Fair, 70. *Bibliog:* Jack Morris & Robert Smeltzer (auths), Contemporary artists of South Carolina, Greenville Co Mus Art, 70; Louise & Paul Trescott (auths), Sallie Frost Knerr, printmaker, Sandlapper Mag, 2/70; article, Art Voices South, 3-4/80. *Mem:* Carolina Art Asn; SC Guild Artists; Southern Graphics Coun. *Media:* All. *Publ:* Illusr, The student pilot's training primer, Knerr, 41. *Mailing Add:* Box 335 Isle of Palms SC 29451

KNIEF, HELEN JEANETTE
PAINTER
b Brooklyn, NY, July 16, 09. *Study:* Art Students League, with Bridgeman, I'Olinsky & S Dickinson; Brooklyn Mus Art Sch, with Victor Candell, David Stone Martin; Nat Acad Sch, with Robert Phillip; Phoenix Sch Design; Pratt Inst. *Work:* Work in over 200 private collections. *Comn:* Portraits, pres of Flushing Savings Bank, NY, 54; police comnr, Nassau Co Police Dept, 55, seven grandchildren, comn by Mrs John Ryan, Baldwin, NY, 64-74; Phillip Chasin, shown in his honor at Waldorf Astoria Dinner, 74 & Mr B C Cobb, comn by Mrs Carl Miller, New York, 74. *Exhib:* Brooklyn Mus, NY, 57; Long Beach Arts Asn, NY, 69-70; Nat Acad Gallery, New York, 70-71; Lever House, Union Carbide, NY, 71-72; Garden City Galleries, Kans, 75; plus several one-man shows. *Teaching:* Pvt adult classes, 68-72. *Awards:* Numerous, including First Prize, Kathy, Malverne Artists Long Island, 68; First Prize, Walled Garden & Second Prize, The Garden, Long Beach Art Asn, 70. *Bibliog:* Catharine L Wolfe (auth), Jeanne Paris, Long Island Press, 71. *Mem:* Catharine Lorillard Wolfe Art Club; Malverne Artist Long Island; Art League Nassau Co; Long Beach Art Asn (bd dirs). *Media:* Oil, Pastel. *Publ:* Articles in Long Island Press, 58, Long Island New Owl, 58-75, Malverne Herald, 68, Long Island Entertainer & Nassau Star & Independent, 71. *Dealer:* Mrs Harry Glosner 345 E 81st St New York NY 10028. *Mailing Add:* 154 Fonda Rd Rockville Centre NY 11570

KNIFFIN, RALPH GUS
GRAPHIC ARTIST
b San Carlos Reservation, Ariz, Nov 21, 46. *Study:* Inst Am Indian Art, Santa Fe, NMex, dipl; study with Allan Houser, Charles Loloma, Otellie Loloma & Fritz Scholder. *Work:* Gila Co Court House, Globe, Ariz; Sentry Ctr, Scottsdale, Ariz; San Carlos Indian Hosp, Ariz; Gallo Winery, Modesto, Calif; United Bank, Tempe & Phoenix, Ariz. *Exhib:* All Indian Art Show, Gallery La Luz, Alamagordo, NMex, 74; Scottsdale Nat Indian Art Exhib, Scottsdale, Ariz, 75 & 76; Nat Indian Art Show, Heard Mus, Phoenix, Ariz, 76; Invitational in Drawing, Heard Mus, Phoenix, Ariz, 77. *Awards:* Best of Show, Gallery La Luz, Alamagordo, NMex, 74; First Place, Scottsdale Nat Art Exhib, Ariz, 76; First Place Spec in Graphics, Heard Mus, Phoenix, Ariz, 76. *Bibliog:* Articles in Carefree Enterprise, 74 & Phoenix Cent News, 75; Maggie Wilson (auth), New Artist Stunned by Limelight Status, Ariz Repub, 76. *Media:* Pen & Ink. *Mailing Add:* c/o Gallery 3 3819 N Third St Phoenix AZ 85012

KNIGHT, CHRISTOPHER ALLEN
CRITIC, ADMINISTRATOR
b Westfield, Mass, Nov 23, 50. *Study:* Hartwick Col, NY, with Prof Bruce Kurtz, BA, 72; State Univ NY, Binghamton, with Dr Albert Boime, MA, 76. *Collections Arranged:* The Modern Chair (cataloged), Origins & Evolution, 1840-1940, 77; The Angel of Mercy (cataloged), Eleanor Antin Installation, 77. *Pos:* Cur, La Jolla Mus Contemp Art, Calif, 76-79; asst pub info dir, Los Angeles Co Mus Art, Calif, 79-80; Southern Calif art critic, Artforum Mag, New York, 79-; art critic, Los Angeles Herald Examiner, 80- *Teaching:* Vis lectr renaissance & mod art, State Univ NY at Binghamton, 76; vis instr mod art, Hartwick Col, Oneonta, NY, 76. *Awards:* Nat Endowment Arts Fel, 73-74; Manufacturers Hanover Trust--Art World Award, 82. *Mem:* Col Art Asn; Int Asn Art Critics. *Res:* Early 20th century concepts of American modernism; post-1960 American art and media. *Publ:* Auth, Some recent art and an architectural analogue, Los Angeles Inst Contemp Art J, 78; auth, DeWain Valentine: New Work, Los Angeles Co Mus Art, 79; auth, The Elusive Image: Eight Artists, Michael C McMillen, Walker Art Ctr, 79; contribr, The Word Made Flesh: L A Pop Revisited, 81 & Art in Los Angeles: 17 Artists in the Sixties, Los Angeles Co Mus Art, 81. *Mailing Add:* 11047 Sarah St North Hollywood CA 91602

KNIGHT, HILARY
ILLUSTRATOR, WRITER
Study: Art Students League. *Publ:* Auth & illusr, Where's Wallace, Harper & Row, 64; auth, Mother Goose, Western, 73; illusr, The Golden Picture Dictionary, Western/Golden, 76; auth & illusr, The Circus is Coming, Western/Golden, 78; auth & illusr, Cinderella, Random House, 79; and others. *Mailing Add:* 300 E 51st St New York NY 10022

KNIGHT, JACOB JASKOVIAK
PAINTER, ILLUSTRATOR
b Worcester, Mass, Feb 26, 38. *Study:* Self-taught. *Work:* West Point Pepperell, New York; General Electric Co; Rockefeller Collection, New York; Hugh Heffner Collection; Exxon, New York. *Comn:* Historical painting (mural), Salem Cross Inn, West Brookfield Mass, 83, Hodgkins Sch, East Brookfield, Mass, 83 & Ye Olde Tavern, Mass, 83; James Beard Regional American Calendar, Workman, 83; historical mural, Quaboag Plantation, 83. *Exhib:* One-man shows, Art Dir Club, New York, 74, Main St Gallery, Nantucket, Mass, 75, Hubris Galley, New York, 78, Adam L Gimbel Gallery, New York, 83 & Saks 5th Ave, New York, 83-84. *Bibliog:* Fred Karden (auth), The artist as his own man, Worcester Telegram & Gazette, Mass, 69; Leslie Powell (auth), Art: Primative, Villager, Greenwich Village, 70; Valerie Brooks (auth), Love & magic: The naive style in illustrations, Print Mag, 74. *Media:* Oil and Acrylic. *Publ:* Illusr, What's gone right with the United Nations, Vista, UN Mag, 73; illusr, All things bright and beautiful, McCalls, 74; illusr, We must decide which species will go on forever, Smithsonian, 76; illusr, A very quiet horror, Playboy, 77. *Mailing Add:* Wigwam Hill West Brookfield MA 01585

KNIGHT, JOHN
CONCEPTUAL ARTIST
b Los Angeles, Calif, Mar 26, 45. *Study:* Univ Calif, Los Angeles, BA, 70; Univ Calif, Irvine, MFA, 73. *Work:* Stedelijk Stadtisches Van Afbemuseum, Eindhoven, NL. *Exhib:* Documenta 5, Fredericivum Kusthalle, Kassel, West Germany, 72; Attitudes 72/Southern Calif, Pasadena Mus Art, 72; Southland Video Anthology, Long Beach Mus Art, Calif, 75; 74th American Exhib, Art Inst Chicago, Ill, 82; Documenta 7, Fredericivum Kunsthalle, Kassel, West Germany, 82. *Teaching:* Instr studio, Nova Scotia Col Art & Design, formerly, Otis Art Inst, Los Angeles, 76-77; instr studio, Southern Calif Inst Archit, 76- *Mailing Add:* 2930 Colorado C-3 Santa Monica CA 90404

KNIGHT, TOM (THOMAS LINCOLN), JR
EDUCATOR, PHOTOGRAPHER
b Oakland, Calif, June 17, 25. *Study:* Humboldt State Univ, BA, 50, MA(art educ), 56. *Exhib:* One-man show photog, Col of the Redwoods Gallery, Eureka, Calif, 79 & Museo Regional Michoacano, Morelia, Mex, 79; Univ Glasgow Art Mus, Scotland, 82; Humboldt Cult Ctr, Eureka, 83; Rufino Tamayo Gallery, Mexico, 84; and others. *Teaching:* Prof photog & art, Humboldt State Univ, 56-; vis instr photog, Univ Nev, Reno, summers 68 & 69, Grand Valley State Col, summer 71. *Publ:* Photog, Anza's bones in Arizona, J West, Vol VII, No 3; photog (back cover), Imogene Cunningham & Margery Mann's Imogene Cunningham-Photographs, Univ Wash, 70; photog, Sunset Bks, 74; photog, British Photogr J, 76; photogr, Photo Metro, 83. *Dealer:* Focus Gallery 2146 Union St San Francisco CA 94123. *Mailing Add:* 76 California St Arcata CA 95521

KNIGIN, MICHAEL JAY
PAINTER, PRINTMAKER
b Brooklyn, NY, Dec 9, 42. *Study:* Tyler Sch Art, BFA. *Work:* Whitney Mus Art, New York; Nat Collection Fine Arts, Washington, DC; Copper Hewitt Mus, NY; Albright-Knox Art Gallery, Buffalo; Portland Mus Fine Arts, Ore. *Exhib:* Smithsonian Inst, Washington, DC, 69; Albright-Knox Art Gallery, 70; Mus Mod Art Lending Serv, New York, 71; Recent Acquisitions, Whitney Mus Am Art, New York, 71; Sch Worcester Art Mus, Mass, 72; Israel Mus, Jerusalem, 76; Taiwan Mus, 77; Mus Mod Art, New York, 78; Nat Soc Illusr Show, 78-79; US Dept of State, Washington, DC, 79; Foreign Corresp Club, Tokyo, 79; and many exhibs in US and abroad. *Teaching:* Assoc prof, Pratt Inst, currently. *Awards:* Ford Found Grant, Tamarind Lithography Workshop, 64; Mod Lang Asn-Am Libr Asn Lithographic Tech Inst Award, 69; John B Turner Mem Award, Soc Am Graphic Artists, 79. *Bibliog:* Benjamin Forgey (auth), article, Washington Star, 12/10/78; Elizabeth

Stevens (auth), article, Baltimore Sun, 1/21/79; Jane Rees (auth), article, Asahi Evening News, Japan, 10/17/79. *Publ:* Coauth, The Technique of Fine Art Lithography, 70; auth, Local Choice, Pratt Graphics Ctr, 72. *Dealer:* Circle Fine Art Corp 345 Park Ave S New York NY. *Mailing Add:* 832 Broadway New York NY 10003

KNIPPERS, EDWARD CADE, JR
PAINTER, PRINTMAKER
b Oklahoma City, Okla, Sept 7, 46. *Study:* Pa Acad Fine Arts, 67; Sorbonne, Paris, 68; Asbury Col, Wilmore, Ky, BA, 69; Int Summer Acad Fine Arts, Salzburg, Austria, with Zao Wou-ki, 70, with Otto Elgau & Wolfgang Zeiszner, 76; Univ Tenn, Knoxville, MFA, 73; S W Hayter's Atelier 17, Paris, fel, 80. *Work:* Int Summer Acad Fine Arts, Salzburg, Austria; Tenn Fine Arts Ctr, Cheekwood, Nashville; Vanderbilt Univ, Nashville; Asbury Col, Wilmore, Ky; Messiah Col, Grantham, Pa. *Exhib:* Solo exhibs, Tenn Fine Arts Ctr, Cheekwood, Nashville, 74, Patmos Gallery, Toronto, 75, Univ Ky, Lexington, 82, Foxhall Gallery, Washington, DC, 82 & Wheaton Col, Ill, 83; J B Speed Mus, Louisville, Ky, 77; Fresh Paint Traveling Exhib, 77-79; and many others. *Teaching:* Instr, Transylvania Univ, Lexington, Ky, 73-75; asst prof, Asbury Col, Wilmore, Ky, 75-81. *Awards:* Salzburg Prize, Int Summer Acad Fine Arts, Austria, 76. *Bibliog:* Cynthia Djuita Vetters (auth), Edward Knippers: Profile, Art Voices, 5-6/81. *Mem:* Christians Visual Arts (bd dirs, 80-). *Media:* Oil, Watercolor; Intaglio. *Publ:* Coauth, Artists log in studio, Contemp Art/SE, Vol II No VI, 81. *Mailing Add:* Arlington Arts Ctr 3550 Wilson Blvd Arlington VA 22201

KNIPSCHER, GERARD ALLEN
PAINTER, GRAPHIC ARTIST
b New York, NY, July 9, 35. *Study:* Calif Col Arts & Crafts, BFA (with hon); Acad Art, San Francisco; Sch Fine Art, San Francisco; Sch Visual Arts, New York; also with Richard Diebenkorn. *Work:* Calif Col Arts & Crafts, Oakland, Calif; NACAL Operation Palette, US Navy Combat Art Collection, DC; M H de Young Mem Mus, San Francisco. *Comn:* Launch US second moon shot, Apollo XII, Cape Kennedy, Fla, comn by US Naval Combat Art, 69; US Navy Amphibious Exercise Operation Exotic Dancer, Onslow Beach, NC, 74; portrait & drawings of Lt Al Cisnernos, first pilot of Mex-Am heritage to fly with US Navy Blue Angels flight demonstration team, Pensacola, Fla, 75; portraits Mario, Gala & Ronnie Broeders, comn by Mr Mario Broeders, Buenos Aires, Arg, 75. *Exhib:* Nat Acad Design Ann Exhib, New York, 67 & 71; 60th Ann Exhib Allied Artists Am, Inc, New York, 73; Nat Arts Club Open Oil Exhib, New York, 75; Am Artists Prof League, Lever House, NY, 75; Am Fortnight Exhib, Hong Kong, 75. *Teaching:* Instr figure painting, Salmagundi Club, currently. *Awards:* Allied Artists Am Award, 73; Macown Tuttle Mem Prize, Salmagundi Club, 74; Sara Boal Mem Award, Am Artists Prof League, Grand Nat Exhib, 79. *Mem:* Salmagundi Club; Artists Fellowship (vpres, 73-75); Navy League US; Hudson Valley Art Asn; Am Artists Prof League. *Media:* Oil, Graphite Pencil. *Dealer:* North Light Studio PO Box 454 Berwick NS B0P 1E0 Can. *Mailing Add:* PO Box 45 Glen Cove NY 11542

KNIPSCHILD, ROBERT
PAINTER, EDUCATOR
b Freeport, Ill, Aug 17, 27. *Study:* Univ Wis, BA, 49; Cranbrook Acad Art, MFA, 51. *Work:* Pa Acad Fine Arts, Philadelphia; Baltimore Mus Art, Md; Phillips Gallery & Hirshhorn Mus, Washington, DC; Cranbrook Mus, Bloomfield Hills, Mich. *Exhib:* American Painting Today, Metrop Mus Art, New York, 51; Pa Acad Fine Arts Ann, 51; Carnegie Inst Int, Pittsburgh, 52; Container Corp Am, 63; 50 Artists from 50 States, Am Fedn Arts, 65. *Teaching:* Vis artist, Am Univ, 52; instr painting, Univ Conn, 54-56; asst prof, Univ Wis-Madison, 56-60; assoc prof, Univ Iowa, 60-66; prof painting, Univ Cincinnati, 66-. *Awards:* Purchase Awards, Libr Cong, 51, Pa Acad Fine Arts, 51 & Am Fedn Arts, 63. *Bibliog:* Patricia Boyd (auth), Exhibition of Robert Knipschild, Christian Sci Monitor, 11/3/69. *Mem:* Mid Am Col Art Asn; Nat Asn Schs Art. *Media:* Oil. *Dealer:* Yares Gallery 3625 Bishop Lane Scottsdale AZ 85252; Gallery K 2032 P St NW Washington DC 20036. *Mailing Add:* Sch of Art Univ Cincinnati Cincinnati OH 45221

KNOBLER, LOIS JEAN
PAINTER
b New York, NY, Feb 2, 29. *Study:* Syracuse Univ Col Fine Arts, BFA; Fla State Univ, MA. *Work:* Worcester Mus, Mass; Fla State Univ Mus. *Exhib:* Art for US Embassies, Inst Contemp Art, Boston, 66; one-woman show, Jorgensen Gallery, 70 & Atrium Gallery, 83, Univ Conn, Storrs, 70; St Lawrence Univ Acquisition Exhib, NY, 74; William Benton Mus, Univ Conn, Storrs, 75; two-person show, Hillyer Gallery, Smith Col, Northamton, Mass, 76. *Awards:* Greater Hartford Civic Arts Festival Award, 72. *Mailing Add:* 2041 Wallace St Philadelphia PA 19130

KNOBLER, NATHAN
SCULPTOR, EDUCATOR
b Brooklyn, NY, Mar 13, 26. *Study:* Newark Sch Fine & Indust Art; Ohio State Univ; Syracuse Univ, BFA, 50; Fla State Univ, MA, 51. *Work:* US Info Agency; Smith Col Mus, Northampton, Mass; Munson-Williams-Proctor Mus, Utica, NY; Fla State Univ; Slater Mus, Norwich, Conn. *Comn:* Silver Award Sculpture, Int Silver Co, Meriden, Conn; Bronze Award Sculpture, G Fox & Co, Hartford, Conn. *Exhib:* Pa Acad Fine Arts Nat Print Show, Philadelphia; Brooklyn Mus Nat Print Show, NY; Drawing Soc Traveling Nat; Selection 1964, Inst Contemp Art, Boston; Surreal Images, De Cordova Mus, Lincoln, Mass & Smith Col. *Teaching:* Dean fac & prof art, Philadelphia Col Art. *Mem:* Col Art Asn Am; Am Soc Aesthetic. *Media:* Multimedia. *Res:* Art appreciation; drawing. *Publ:* Auth, The Visual Dialogue, rev ed 76; auth, El Dialogo Visual, 70, rev ed, 80. *Mailing Add:* Philadelphia Col of Art Broad & Spruce Sts Philadelphia PA 19102

KNOEBEL, DAVID JON
SCULPTOR
b Elysburg, Pa, July 19, 49. *Study:* Yale Univ, with William Bailey, BA, 72; Skowhegan Sch, with William Stankiewicz, 72; also with George Sugarman, 79-82. *Work:* Indianapolis Mus Art. *Exhib:* Nat Sculpture Competition, Univ SC, Columbia, 78; Nat Small Works Competition, NY Univ, 79; Nat Sculpture Show, Md Inst Art, Baltimore, 80; Pool Proj, Artist's Space, New York, 80; Painting & Sculpture Today, Indianapolis Mus Art, 80; one-man show, Baruch Col, State Univ NY, 82; Gold Show, Mus Mod Art, New York, 82. *Bibliog:* Kay Larson (auth), Voice choices, Village Voice, 1/28/80; Tiffany Bell (auth), article, Arts Mag, 3/80; Helen Harrison (auth), Four forms of light, New York Times, 6/13/82. *Media:* Metal, Miscellaneous. *Publ:* Auth, Coal tipples: Photographs by the Bechers, Shamokin News Item, Pa, 12/20/75; contribr catalog statement, Painting & Sculpture Today, Indianapolis Mus, 80; auth catalog statement, Light, Islip Art Mus, 82. *Mailing Add:* 56 Lispenard St New York NY 10013

KNOLL, ISABEL A GIAMPIETRO See Giampietro, Isabel

KNORR, JEANNE BOARDMAN
PAINTER, EDUCATOR
b Chambersburg, Pa. *Study:* Indiana Univ Pa, BS; Columbia Univ Teachers Col, MA; Art Students League, scholar; Ohio State Univ, PhD(painting). *Work:* Dallas Theol Sem, Tex; Lakeview Ctr Arts, Peoria, Ill; Ohio State Univ Mus Collections, Columbus; First & Merchants Bank Collection, Richmond, Va. *Comn:* Fabric wall hanging, St Paul's Episcopal Cathedral, Peoria, 69; fabric wall, Computer Ctr, Norfolk & Western Railroad, Roanoke, Va, 78; and many fabric wall hangings in pvt collections in Ill, NY & Va. *Exhib:* One-man exhibs, Robinson House, Va Mus, Richmond, 72, Peninsula Art Asn, 80; Crafts Invitational, Bank of Va, Norfolk, 77; Artists Invitational, Hermitage Found, Norfolk, Va, 77; Fiber Invitational, Portsmouth Art Ctr, Va, 81; and others. *Teaching:* Assoc prof art, Norfolk State Col, 69- *Awards:* Artist of Distinction in crafts, 70 & in sculpture, 71, Va Mus; Third & Fourth Ann Crafts Fabric Award, Norfolk, Va, 73 & 74. *Bibliog:* Dona Meilach (auth), Creative stitchery, 8/71 & Soft sculpture, 74, Craft Horizon Mag; Cornelia Justice (auth), rev of exhibs at Studio Gallery, 4/66; Elyse & Mike Sommer (auth), A new look at crochet, 75; and others. *Mem:* Am Craftsmen Coun; Tidewater Artists Asn. *Publ:* Contribr, Directions, Ill Art Educ Asn, 70. *Mailing Add:* 730 Maury Ave Norfolk VA 23517

KNOWLES, ALISON
PERFORMANCE ARTIST, PRINTMAKER
b New York, NY, Apr 29, 33. *Study:* Middlebury Col, Vt, 52-54; Pratt Inst, 54-57, BFA(hon); Manhattan Sch of Printing, 62; Pratt Inst, Hon BFA. *Work:* Mus of Mod Art Bk Collection, New York; Oakland Mus, Calif; Jean Brown Archives, Tyringham, Mass. *Comn:* The Identical Lunch (two self-portraits), comn by Alberto Zopellari, 77; Leone D'oro (silkscreen edition), comn by Francesco Conz, 78. *Exhib:* The Big Book, Mus of Contemp Art, Chicago, 67; The Identical Lunch solo exhib, Galerie Inge Baecker, Bochum, Ger, 73; Collections from the Full Moon, Galerie Rene Block, Berlin, De Appel, Amsterdam, 74; SumTime, Everson Mus, Syracuse, NY, 74; 03 23 03, Mus of Fine Art, Montreal, Can, 77; Walker Art Ctr performance, exhib, Univ Minn, 80; and others. *Teaching:* Dir graphics lab, Calif Inst of the Arts, Valencia, 70-72. *Awards:* Guggenheim Fel, 68; Nat Endowment Arts, 81; Travel Grant, Deutscher Acad, WGer, 83. *Bibliog:* William Wilson (auth), The Big Book, Art in Am, 7-8/68; Women in Communications, The Big Book, 68; Tom Johnson (auth), Shoes, Shoestrings & Gertrude Stein, Village Voice, 78. *Mem:* Printed Ed; The Performance Workshop. *Publ:* Coauth (with James Tenney), The House of Dust, Gerb Konig Verlag, 69; auth, More By Alison Knowles, Unpublished Ed, 76; auth, Gem Duck, Pari & Dispari, 78; auth, A Bean Concordance, Printed Eds, 83. *Mailing Add:* 122 Spring St New York NY 10012

KNOWLES, RICHARD H
PAINTER, WRITER
b Evanston, Ill, June 29, 34. *Study:* Grinnell Col; Northwestern Univ, Evanston, BA, 56; Ind Univ, MA, 61. *Work:* Ind Univ, Bloomington; Ark State Univ; State of Tenn Collection, Reece Mus, Nashville; Brooks Mem Art Gallery, Memphis, Tenn. *Exhib:* Six Americans, Ark Art Ctr, Little Rock, 64; 50 States Exhib & Tour, Rockford Art Asn & Am Fedn Arts, 65-67; 40 Tenn Artists Exhib & Tour, 68-69; Am Painters & Sculptors, Colgate Univ, 75; Edinburgh Arts Festival, Scotland, 80; plus other group & one-man shows. *Pos:* Publ, Untitled (art jour), currently. *Teaching:* Asst prof art, Univ Ark, 61-65; prof art, Memphis State Univ, 66- *Awards:* Best Entry for Ark Artist, Delta Ann, 61 & 62; Painting Prize, Mid-South Exhib, 72. *Media:* Acrylic. *Mailing Add:* 7034 Rose Trail Dr Memphis TN 38134

KNOWLTON, DANIEL GIBSON
BOOKBINDER, CONSERVATOR
b Washington, DC, Nov 14, 22. *Study:* With Marian U M Lane, Washington, DC; Boston Arts & Crafts, grad. *Work:* Univ Chicago Libr; Brown Univ Libr, Providence, RI; Dumbarton Oaks Libr, Washington, DC; Harvard Univ Libr; Cornell Univ Libr. *Comn:* Epistle (gold & leather binding), Grace Church, Providence, 56; The Anguish of the Jews (gold & leather binding), comn by Ciro Scotti, Vatican Libr, 68. *Exhib:* Hand bookbinding exhibs, Corcoran Gallery Art, 58; one-man shows, Bristol Hist Soc RI, 69, RI Sch Design, 71 & 75 & Ctr Bk Arts, New York, 75; Rockefeller Libr, Brown Univ, 81; Providence Hist Soc, 81; and others. *Pos:* Bookbinder, Providence, 56-; owner & bookbinder, Daniel G Knowlton Co, Bristol, RI, 74- *Teaching:* Instr bookbinding, Daniel G Knowlton Co Home Bindery, 74- *Bibliog:* Yankee

Damon (auth), article, Yankee Mag, 62; Ann Banks (auth), article, Brown Alumni Monthly, 71. *Mem:* Miniature Painters, Sculptors & Gravers Soc Washington, DC; Guild Book Workers New York. *Mailing Add:* 1202 Hope St Bristol RI 02809

KNOWLTON, GRACE FARRAR
SCULPTOR, PHOTOGRAPHER
b Buffalo, NY, Mar 15, 32. *Study:* Smith Col, BA; Columbia Univ Teachers Col, MA. *Work:* J Patrick Lannan Mus, Palm Beach, Fla; Metrop Mus Art, New York; Newark Mus, NJ; Corcoran Gallery Art; Houston Mus Fine Arts; and others. *Comn:* Pottery prototypes for Appalachian Workshops, Am Fedn Arts, New York, 71. *Exhib:* One-man shows, Henri Gallery, Washington, DC, 73, Razor Gallery, New York, 74, Parsons-Dreyfuss Gallery, New York, 79, Aaron Berman Gallery, 81 & Susan Harder Gallery, 83. *Pos:* Asst to cur graphic arts dept, Nat Gallery Art, Washington, DC, 54-57. *Teaching:* Instr art, Arlington Co Pub Schs, 57-60. *Media:* Film. *Dealer:* Suan Harder Gallery 37 W 57th St New York NY 10019. *Mailing Add:* Sneden's Landing Palisades NY 10964

KNOWLTON, JONATHAN
PAINTER, EDUCATOR
b New York, NY, Feb 22, 37. *Study:* Yale Univ, BA; Univ Calif, Berkeley, MA. *Work:* Mus Mod Art, New York; Victoria & Albert Mus, London; Univ Calif Art Mus, Berkeley; La Jolla Mus Fine Art, Calif. *Exhib:* Survey '68, Montreal Mus Fine Arts, 68; 17th Nat Print Exhib, Brooklyn Mus, 70; Edmonton Art Gallery, 72; John Bolles Gallery, San Francisco, 73; Latitude 53, Edmonton, 75. *Teaching:* Assoc prof drawing & painting, Univ Alta, 66- *Awards:* Purchase Award, Los Angeles Co Mus Art, 61; Fulbright Grant, 64-65; Can Coun Grant, 68-69. *Media:* Oil. *Dealer:* Downstairs Gallery Edmonton AB Can. *Mailing Add:* c/o Dept Art & Design Univ Alta Edmonton AB T6G 2E1 Canada

KNOWLTON, MONIQUE
DEALER, COLLECTOR
b Karlsruhe, Ger, May 24, 37; French citizen. *Study:* Ecole Polyglotte, Montreaux, Switz, dipl; NY Univ, cert(decorative arts), 65-69. *Pos:* Dir & pres, Monique Knowlton Gallery, New York, 75- *Specialty:* Twentieth century and contemporary American painting and sculpture. *Collection:* Willem de Kooning, Robert Beauchamp, Oscar Bluemner, Alexandra Exter, Tom Wesselmann, Frank Faulkner, Betye Saar, Tommasi Ferroni, Gaylen Hansen, Phyllis Bramson, Joseph Piccillo, Edward Kienholz, Frank Holmes, Robert Lostutter, Robert Smithson, Helen Oji, Robert Donley, Helen Miranda Wilson, Richard Thompson, Ed Larson, Ed Paschke, Jim Nutt, Carl Wirsum, Ida Apple-Broog, Gregory Amenoff, Cindy Sherman & Tom Butter. *Mailing Add:* c/o Monique Knowlton Gallery 19 E 71st St New York NY 10021

KNOX, GEORGE
HISTORIAN, WRITER
b London, Eng, Jan 1, 22. *Study:* Courtauld Inst Art, Univ London, BA, MA & PhD. *Collections Arranged:* Tiepolo Bicentenary Exhib, Fogg Art Mus, Cambridge, Mass, 70; Tiepolo Drawings, Staatsgalerie, Stuttgart, 70; Tiepolo: Tecnica e Immaginazione, Palazzo Ducale, Venice, 79; Piazzetta: Disegni, Incisioni, Libri, Manoscritti, Fondazione Giorgio Cini, Venice, 83; Piazzetta, A Tercentenary Exhibition, Nat Gallery Art, Washington, DC, 83. *Teaching:* Instr, Slade Sch Art, Univ London, 50-52; instr, King's Col, Newcastle, Univ Durham, 52-58; instr, Queen's Univ, Ont, 69-70; prof fine arts & head dept, Univ BC, 70- *Interests:* Venetian 18th century art, particularly the drawings of the Tiepolo family. *Publ:* Auth, Catalogue of the Tiepolo Drawings in the Victoria & Albert Museum, 60; auth, Domenico Tiepolo: Raccolta di Teste, Udine, 70; auth, Giambattista & Domenico Tiepolo ... The Chalk Drawings, Oxford, 80. *Mailing Add:* Dept of Fine Arts Univ Brit Columbia Vancouver BC V6T 1W5 Canada

KNOX, SEYMOUR H
PATRON
b Buffalo, NY, Sept 1, 98. *Study:* Yale Univ, BA, 20; Univ Buffalo, hon DFA, 62; Syracuse Univ, hon LHD, 66; St Lawrence Univ, hon DFA, 67. *Pos:* Chmn, NY State Coun on the Arts; pres bd dir, Buffalo Fine Arts Acad; fel Rochester Mus & Sci Ctr. *Awards:* Buffalo & Erie Co Hist Soc Red Jacket Medal, 62; Buffalo Club Medal, 62; Michael Friedsam Archit Award, 66; Yale Medal. *Mailing Add:* 57 Oakland Pl Buffalo NY 14222

KNUDSEN, CHRISTIAN
PAINTER, PRINTMAKER
b June 3, 45; Danish citizen. *Study:* Sir George Williams Univ, BFA, 69. *Work:* Mus Fine Arts & Musee D'Art Contemporain, Montreal; Art Gallery Ont, Toronto; Vancouver Art Gallery, BC; Can Coun Art Bank, Ottawa. *Comn:* Painting, Govt Can Post Off, Quebec, 78. *Exhib:* Concordia Univ, Montreal, 74; Vancouver Art Gallery, 78; Montreal Mus, Que, 79; Glenbow Mus, Calgary, 80; Agnes Etherington Art Ctr, Kingston, Ont, 81. *Bibliog:* David Burnett (auth), Knudsen at Godard, Art Am, 1/78; David Burnett (auth), Christian Knudsen, Parachute No 11, summer, 78; Robert Swain (auth), Christian Knudsen, Agnes Etherington Art Ctr, Kingston, Ont, 81. *Media:* Mixed Media; Silkscreen. *Dealer:* Mira Godard Gallery 22 Hazelton Toronto ON M5R 2E2 Can. *Mailing Add:* 3827 Drolet Montreal PQ H2W 2L3 Canada

KNUDSON, ROBERT LEROY
PAINTER
b Wadena, Minn, Nov 16, 29. *Study:* Minneapolis Art Inst Sch Art, 50. *Work:* William Penn Mem Mus, Harrisburg, Pa; Tex Tech Univ, Lubbock; Mus Northern Ariz, Flagstaff; Orme Ranch Sch, Mayer, Ariz. *Exhib:* Panhandle Plains Mus-WTex State Univ, Canyon, 68; William Penn Mem Mus, 69; Northern Ariz Univ, Flagstaff, 69 & 70; The West--Artists & Illusrs, Tucson Art Ctr, 71; 3rd Ann Phippen Mem, Prescott, Ariz, 77; and others. *Teaching:* Instr oil painting, Kachina Sch Art, Phoenix, 63-65; instr oil & acrylic painting, Sedona Arts Ctr, Ariz, 67-68. *Awards:* Purchase Award, 3rd Southwestern, Valley Nat Bank, 68; Purchase Award, 6th Southwestern, Ariz Pub Serv, 71. *Bibliog:* Jean Micuda (auth), Knudson, 72 & Magnetic--Rishell & Knudson at Troy's, 73, Ariz Living. *Media:* Multimedia. *Publ:* Contribr, They Came to Jerome, Jerome Hist Soc, 72; contribr, Ariz Hwy Mag, 7/72, 9/73 & 6/75; contribr cover painting, Southwest Art Mag, 10/74. *Dealer:* Main Trail Galleries 7169 Main St Scottsdale AZ 85251 & PO Box 1253 Jackson WY 83001. *Mailing Add:* PO Box 37675 Phoenix AZ 85069

KO, ANTHONY
PRINTMAKER, EDUCATOR
b Hong Kong, Dec 8, 34; US citizen. *Study:* Nat Taiwan Univ, BA; Univ Nev, with James McCormick, Charles Ross & Craig Sheppard; Univ Calif, Davis, MA, with Ralph Johnson, Roland Petersen & William Wiley; Univ NMex & Tamarind Lithography Workshop, with Garo Antreasian. *Work:* Mus Mod Art, New York; Art Inst Chicago; Los Angeles Co Mus Art; Achenbach Found for Graphic Arts, San Francisco; Hong Kong City Mus Art Gallery. *Comn:* Six Impressions (suite of six lithographs), Univ Nev, Reno, 68; Return to Harmony (edition of 50 multicolor lithographs), Erie Art Ctr, 69. *Exhib:* Nat Lithography Exhib, Fla State Univ, Tallahassee, 69; Brooklyn Mus 17th Ann Print Exhib, New York, 70; Color Print USA, Tex Tech Univ, Lubbock, 70 & 71; Soc Am Graphic Artists, Kennedy Gallery, New York, 71; 20 American Printmakers, State Univ NY Col Oneonta, 72. *Teaching:* From asst prof to assoc prof printmaking, Edinboro State Col, 68- *Awards:* Ford Found Fel, Tamarind Lithography Workshop, 66. *Mem:* Col Art Asn Am; Pittsburgh Print Group. *Media:* Lithography. *Mailing Add:* RD 2 Box 620 Edinboro PA 16412

KOBAYASHI, KATSUMI PETER
PAINTER, LECTURER
b Hiroshima, Japan, Feb 5, 35. *Study:* Univ Hawaii, BFA, 64, MFA, 66. *Comn:* Oil paintings, Cent Pac Bank, Honolulu, 71 & Manoa, C S Wo & Sons, Honolulu, 71. *Exhib:* Two-man show, Libr Hawaii, 65; Artist Hawaii Exhib Acad Arts, Honolulu, 65, 66, 69 & 71; one-man shows, Gateway House, Honolulu, 66 & Advertiser Contemp Arts Ctr, Hawaii, 72; Hawaii Painters & Sculptors Exhib, 69-72. *Pos:* Visual Aid Media Specialist, Univ Hawaii, 66- *Teaching:* Instr oil painting, Adult Educ, Farrington High Sch, Honolulu, 64-71 & Unitarian Church, Honolulu, 66. *Awards:* Found Cult & Arts Purchase Award, State of Hawaii, 70-72, Dept Educ Award, 71-72; Purchase Award, Honolulu Advertiser, 72. *Mem:* Hawaii Painters & Sculptors League (vpres, 70-72, pres, 73-74); Hawaii Art Educ Asn. *Media:* Oil, Watercolor, Pastel. *Dealer:* Downtown Gallery 125 Merchant St Honolulu HI 96813. *Mailing Add:* 5304 Malu Pl Honolulu HI 96816

KOBER, ALFRED JOHN
EDUCATOR, SCULPTOR
b Great Bend, Kans, June 3, 37. *Study:* Dodge City Col, AA, 58; Ft Hays State Col, BS(art), 60 & MS(art), 66. *Work:* Boise Gallery Art, Idaho; Ft Hays State Col. *Comn:* Two outdoor sculptures, Boise State Univ, 71 & 72; stainless steel sculpture, Bank of Idaho, Boise, 72; welded steel sculpture, Boise Cascade World Hq, Boise, 74; sculpture for Veterans Park, Boise, comn by Idaho Veterans, 76; stainless steel sculpture, Atlantic Richfield, Denver, 78. *Exhib:* Ann Exhib Northwest Artists, Seattle, Wash, 69-74; Mainstreams, 72 & 77; LaGrange Nat Competition II, Ga, 75; 21st Ann Drawing & Small Sculpture Show, Ball State Univ, 75. *Teaching:* Instr art, Hutchinson Community Jr Col, Kans, 66-68; assoc prof sculpture, Boise State Univ, 68-78, assoc prof, 78, prof, 79. *Awards:* Purchase Award, Grover M Hermann Fine Arts Ctr, Marietta, 72; Award of Excellence, Marietta Col, 72; Award, Ball State Univ, 75. *Mem:* Boise Art Asn. *Media:* Mixed. *Mailing Add:* 2024 Crystal Way Boise ID 83706

KOCH, ARTHUR ROBERT
PAINTER, EDUCATOR
b Meriden, Conn, Feb 26, 34. *Study:* Wesleyan Univ; RI Sch Design, with John Frazier, BFA, 57; Univ Wash, MFA, 61. *Exhib:* Art: USA: 59, New York; US Info Agency Painting Show, Europe, 62-66; Tex Painting & Sculpture of the 20th Century, 70-71. *Teaching:* Instr studio, Univ NH, 57-59; instr studio, El Centro Col, Dallas, 66-70; head dept studio art, Meadows Sch Arts, Southern Methodist Univ, 70-, assoc prof design & painting, 78- *Awards:* Ft Worth Art Ctr Award, 70. *Mem:* Dallas Area Artists Equity Asn (pres, 70-71); Artists Equity Asn (vpres, 71); Blue Bonnets Anonymous (chmn, 71-72); Tex Asn Schs Art. *Dealer:* Contemp Fine Arts Gallery 2425 Cedar Springs Dallas TX 75201. *Mailing Add:* 11149 Lanewood Circle Dallas TX 75218

KOCH, EDWIN E
SCULPTOR, PAINTER
b New York, NY, Feb 21, 15. *Study:* Mus Mod Art Sch; also with E Kramer. *Work:* Butler Inst of Am Art, Youngstown, Ohio. *Exhib:* Am Watercolors, Drawings & Prints, Metrop Mus Art, 52; Int Exhib Watercolors, Prints, Drawing, Pa Acad Design, 52; Int Watercolor Exhib, Brooklyn Mus, 53; Nat Acad Design, 58-75; var one-man shows. *Awards:* Framemakers Award,

Silvermine Guild Artists, 62; Medals of Honor for Watercolor, 70 & Oils, 72, Painters & Sculpture Soc NJ; Grumbacher Award, Audubon Artists, 79. *Bibliog:* Brian O'Doherty (auth), One-man show, 62 & John Canady (auth), One-man show, 66, New York Times. *Mem:* Audubon Artists; Nat Soc Painters in Casein & Acrylic (bd dirs, 75-); Knickerbocker Artists (vpres, 77-78); Painters & Sculptors Soc NJ (vpres, 74-); Am Vet Soc Artists (treas, 70-75). *Media:* Oil, Casein. *Mailing Add:* RD-1 Box 76 Hoagberg Hill Rd Wallkill NY 12589

KOCH, GERD (HERMAN)
PAINTER, EDUCATOR
b Detroit, Mich, Jan 30, 29. *Study:* Wayne State Univ, BFA; Univ Calif, Los Angeles; Univ Calif, Santa Barbara, MFA. *Work:* La Jolla Art Mus; Pasadena Art Mus; Univ NC; Santa Barbara Art Mus. *Comn:* Design of Ash Grove (folk music cabaret), 58. *Exhib:* Los Angeles Co Mus Art Ann, 59; La Jolla Art Mus Ann, 60-62; three man traveling show, Western Asn Mus, 62-65; Calif State Fair, 63; Art or Anti Art, Occidental Col, 65; Univ NC, 66; Butler Inst Am Art, Youngstown, Ohio, 66; Calif Palace of Legion of Honor, San Francisco, 67; Calif Arts Festival, 68. *Teaching:* Prof painting & drawing, Ventura Col, 60-61 & 67-; instr, Univ Calif Exten, 66- *Awards:* Purchase & First Award, Los Angeles Co Mus Art, 59; Calif State Fair First Award, 63; Calif Nat Watercolor Soc Purchase Award, 67. *Mem:* Calif Nat Watercolor Soc; Ventura Art Asn. *Media:* Oil, Acrylic. *Mailing Add:* 444 Aliso Ventura CA 93001

KOCH, PHILIP
PAINTER, INSTRUCTOR
b Rochester, NY, Mar 30, 48. *Study:* Oberlin Col, BA, 70; Ind Univ, MFA, 72. *Work:* Minn Mus Art, St Paul; Ind Univ Fine Arts Mus, Bloomington. *Exhib:* Md Biennial, Baltimore Mus Art, 75; Drawings USA-77, Minn Mus Art, St Paul, 77; one-person shows, C Grimaldis Gallery, Baltimore, 80 & Gross McCleaf Gallery, Philadelphia, 81; Gross McCleaf Gallery, Philadelphia, 81 & 82; C Grimaldis Gallery, Baltimore, 81 & 83; Meredith Long & Co, Houston, 84; and others. *Teaching:* Instr painting, Cent Wash State Col, 72-73 & Md Inst Col Art, 73- *Awards:* Purchase Prize, Minn Mus Art, 75; Union Independent Cols Art Inst Teaching Fel, 76; Ford Found Fac Enrichment Grant, Md Inst, 79. *Media:* Oil, Charcoal. *Publ:* Auth, Direct painting outdoors, Am Artist, 4/82. *Dealer:* Meredith Long & Co 2323 San Felipe Houston TX 77019; C Grimaldis Gallery 928 N Charles Baltimore MD 21201. *Mailing Add:* 4823 Hawksbury Rd Baltimore MD 21208

KOCH, ROBERT
HISTORIAN, WRITER
b New York, NY, Apr 7, 18. *Study:* Harvard Univ, AB, 39; NY Univ, MA, 53; Yale Univ, PhD, 57. *Teaching:* Prof art hist, Southern Conn State Univ, 56-79, prof emer, 79- *Awards:* Fac Scholar Award, Southern Conn State Univ, 74. *Res:* Art nouveau in France, Spain, Latin America and the US. *Publ:* Auth, articles in Art in Am, 62, 64 & 65 & Antiques, 74; auth, Louis C Tiffany, Revel in Glass, 64; contribr, Artistic America, Tiffany Glass and Art Nouveau, 70; auth, Louis C Tiffany's Glass-Bronzes-Lamps, 71; auth, Louis C Tiffany's Art Glass, 77. *Mailing Add:* 143 Hoyt St Stamford CT 06905

KOCH, VIRGINIA See Greenleaf, Virginia

KOCH, WILLIAM EMERY
DEALER, COLLECTOR
b Brooklyn, NY, Jan 7, 22. *Pos:* Owner-dir, Koch Galleries. *Specialty:* Graphics, all periods; paintings, including American and 20th century, also continental; American impressionist. *Collection:* American impressionist; Cubist School of Paris, Barbizon artists; 20th century French and English. *Mailing Add:* Koch Galleries 162 S Lawrence St Mobile AL 36602

KOCHER, ROBERT LEE
PAINTER, EDUCATOR
b Jefferson City, Mo, Dec 19, 29. *Study:* Univ Mo-Columbia, AB & MA; also with Fred Shane & Paul Brach. *Comn:* Religious Feasts, Culver-Stockton Col Dining Hall, 57; outdoor sculpture, Duane Arnold Residence, Cedar Rapids, Iowa. *Exhib:* Mid-Am Ann, Kansas City, Mo, 60; All Iowa Artists, Des Moines Art Ctr Ann, 63-75; Miss Corridor Competition, Renwick Gallery, Washington, DC, 80; 26 one-person exhibs, Nat Surface Design Competition. *Teaching:* Prof art, Coe Col, 59- *Awards:* First Prize Painting, All Iowa Artists, Des Moines Art Ctr, 69; Yonkers Award. *Mem:* Cedar Rapids Art Ctr (bd dirs, 61-81); Cedar Rapids Marion Coun Arts. *Media:* Dye. *Mailing Add:* 1955 Park Ave SE Cedar Rapids IA 52403

KOCHERTHALER, MINA
PAINTER
b Munich, Ger; US citizen. *Study:* Columbia Univ; Art Students League, with Mario Cooper; Nat Acad Design Sch Fine Art, with Ralph Fabri. *Work:* Norfolk Mus Arts & Sci; also in many pvt collections. *Exhib:* Royal Soc Painters Watercolours, London, 62; 200 Yrs Watercolor Painting Am, Metrop Mus Art, New York, 66-67; Mus Acuarela, Mexico City, 68; Butler Inst Am Art, 70; Can Soc Painters Watercolour, 71-72. *Pos:* Deleg, US Comt Int Asn Arts, New York, 60-62. *Awards:* John J Karpick Mem Medal, Audubon Artists, 62; seven prizes, Nat Soc Painters Casein & Acrylic, 58-77; Grumbacher Polymer Award, Catharine Lorillard Wolfe Art Club, 71. *Mem:* Am Watercolor Soc (rec secy & coordr chmn, 62-82, dir, 82-); Audubon Artists; Nat Soc Painters Casein & Acrylic (vpres, 62-); Allied Artists Am (rec secy, 74-78, mem coordr, 78-); Catharine Lorillard Wolfe Art Club. *Media:* Acrylic. *Mailing Add:* 124 W 79th St New York NY 10024

KOEBBEMAN, SKIP
EDUCATOR, SCULPTOR
b Cleveland, Ohio, Nov 11, 43. *Study:* Northern Ill Univ, 61-64; Univ Ill, Champaign, BFA(indust design), 67, with Frank Gallo, MFA(sculpture), 71. *Exhib:* J B Speed Art Mus, Louisville, Ky, 72; one-man shows, Floyd Co Mus, New Albany, Ind, 79 & Nonson Gallery, New York, 80; Mid-States Exhib, Evansville Mus Art, Ind, 74 & 75; 22nd Ann Drawing & Small Sculpture Show, Ball State Univ, Muncie, Ind, 76; Dayton Collection 77, Ohio; Light, Mass and Color, Hallwalls, Buffalo, NY, 81; and others. *Teaching:* Asst prof art & chmn dept sculpture, Louisville Sch Art, 71-81, prof, 81- *Bibliog:* Article, Artforum Mag, 10/79. *Mailing Add:* 2011 Ben Ali Rd Louisville KY 40223

KOEHLER, HENRY
PAINTER
b Louisville, Ky, Feb 2, 27. *Study:* Yale Univ, BA, 50. *Work:* Calif Palace of Legion of Honor, San Francisco; Speed Mus Art, Louisville, Ky; Parrish Art Mus, Southampton, NY. *Comn:* Baseball murals, NY Mets, Shea Stadium, 64. *Exhib:* One-man shows, Calif Palace Legion Honor, 66 & Speed Art Mus, 67; Wildenstein, London, 71, 73, 76 & 78; The Horse in Art, Santa Barbara Mus Art, Calif, 74; Aiken Racing Hall Fame, 78; Ackermann, London, 82; Gallerie La Cymaise, Paris, 82; and others. *Pos:* Trustee, Parrish Mus of Art, Southampton, NY. *Media:* Oil. *Dealer:* Arthur Ackermann & Son 50 E 57 St New York NY 10022; Sportsman's Edge 136 East 74th St New York NY 10021. *Mailing Add:* PO Box 1776 Southampton NY 11968

KOENIG, CATHERINE CATANZARO
PAINTER
b Buffalo, NY, Aug 25, 21. *Study:* Buffalo Fine Arts Acad; Albright Art Sch, with Philip Elliot, Isaac Soyer, Ralston Crawford & Charles Burchfield, dipl, 43. *Work:* Albright-Knox Art Gallery; Burchfield Art Ctr, Buffalo, NY; Libr Cong. *Exhib:* Brooklyn Mus Print Ann, 48; Nat Watercolor Show, Pa Acad Fine Arts, 51, 53 & 57; Int Watercolor Show, Brooklyn Mus, 53; Butler Inst Am Art Midyear Painting Show, 54, 72 & 75; Nat Drawing Show, Okla Art Ctr, 73, 76, 77 & 80; Nat Print & Drawing Exhib, Dulin Gallery Art, 77 & 80; solo exhib, Albright-Knox Art Gallery, 80 & Ball State Univ Art Gallery, 81. *Teaching:* Instr watercolor, Art Inst Buffalo, 46-56; lectr figure drawing, Millard Fillmore Col, State Univ NY, Buffalo, 61-79; instr, Niagara Co Community Col, 78-81. *Awards:* Award Distinction Painting, Mainstreams, Herman Fine Arts Ctr, 77; Purchase Awards, 22nd Nat Drawing Show, Okla Art Ctr, 80 & 26th Nat Drawing & Sculpture Show, Ball State Univ Gallery, 80. *Mem:* Buffalo Soc Artists. *Media:* Egg Tempera, Pastel. *Dealer:* Lillian Heidenberg Gallery 50 W 57th St New York NY 10019. *Mailing Add:* 18 E Girard Blvd Kenmore NY 14217

KOENIG, ELIZABETH
SCULPTOR
b New York, NY, Apr 20, 37. *Study:* Sorbonne, Paris, 57; Wellesley Col, BA, 58; Yale Univ, MD, 62; Art Students League, New York, with John Hovannes, 63-64; Corcoran Mus Sch Art, with Heinz Warnecke & John Rood, 64-67. *Work:* Curator's Collection, Eugene O'Neill Mem Theater Found, Waterford, Conn; Art Students League, New York. *Comn:* Tenn marble carving, Washington Hebrew Cong, Washington, DC, 78; monumental bronze sculpture for front of Admin Bldg, George Meany Ctr Labor Studies, Silver Spring, Md, 82. *Exhib:* Ten Sculptors, Washington Womens Arts Ctr, Washington, DC, 77; retrospective 1963-1978, Lyman Allyn Mus, New London, Conn, 78 & Rotunda, Pan-Am Health Orgn, Washington, DC, 78; Finalist Exhib, Outdoor Sculpture Competition, Rockville Munic Gallery, Md, 78; 11th Ann Sculpture Conf, Meridian House Int, Washington, DC, 80; Sculpture & Prints, Cath Univ Am, 80. *Awards:* First Prize for Sculpture, 70 & Second & Third Prizes for Sculpture, 71, Tri-State Regional Sculpture Exhib, Montgomery Co Art Asn. *Bibliog:* Patricia Raymer (auth), From iron to gold, Washington's metal artists, Washingtonian Mag, 75; Robert Spring (auth), New projects: Sculpture for the George Meany Center, In: The Artists Foundry for Practicing Sculptors, Vol 5, No 1, 82. *Mem:* Artists Equity Asn, Washington, DC (vpres, 77-83); life mem Art Students League, New York; Int Sculpture Ctr; Washington Womens Arts Ctr. *Publ:* Coauth, Ten Sculptors, Washington Womens Arts Ctr, 77; auth, Sculpture--Elizabeth Koenig, Retrospective Exhibition 1963-1978, Lee Douglas Assoc, 78; auth, Report on membership, 78 & Monumental torso, 81, Washington Artists News. *Dealer:* Mickelson Gallery 707 G St NW Washington DC 20001. *Mailing Add:* 9014 Charred Oak Dr Bethesda MD 20817

KOENIG, JOHN FRANKLIN
PAINTER
b Seattle, Wash, Oct 24, 24. *Study:* US Army Univ, France, 45; Univ Wash, grad, 48. *Work:* Mus Art Mod, Paris, France; Ctr Nat Art Contemp, Paris; Mus Western Art, Tokyo; Seattle Art Mus; Mus Art Contemp, Montreal. *Comn:* Mural & glass windows (with Wogenscky), CHU Hosp, St Antoine, Paris, 65. *Exhib:* Galerie Arnaud, 52-74; Carnegie Inst Int, Pittsburgh, 64; Retrospective, Seattle Art Mus, Wash, 70; one-person exhibs, Paris Art Ctr, 82, Galerie Erval, Paris, 82, Galerie Treize, Montreal, 83, Galerie Kutter, Luxemburg & Greg Kucera Gallery, Seattle, 83; Recent Paintings, Foster/White Gallery, Seattle. *Awards:* Student Show Prize, Univ Wash, 48; Third Prix Artistes Etrangers, Mus Art Mod, Paris, 59; Prix Critiques Art de Presse Parisienne, 1st Biennale Paris, 59. *Bibliog:* Pierre Restany (auth), John Franklin Koenig, Galerie Arnaud, Paris, 60; Michel Ryon (auth), John Franklin Koenig, Galerie Arnand, Paris, 69; Liliane Thorn-Petit (auth), John Franklin Koenig, Radio-Television Luxem, Bourgeoise, 75. *Media:* Oil, Acrylic. *Publ:* Coauth, John Franklin Koenig, 65 & 70; ed, La Danse Contemporaine, Fayard, Paris, 80. *Mailing Add:* 400 18th Ave E Seattle WA 98112

KOENIG, ROBERT J
MUSEUM DIRECTOR
b Jersey City, NJ, June 6, 35. *Study:* Pratt Inst, BS(art educ), 57; Yale Univ, BFA, 59, MFA, 61. *Collections Arranged:* Paintings by Robert Slutsky, Montclair Art Mus, NJ, 77, Collage: American Masters (auth, catalog), 79, Anne Ryan: a Tribute, 79, Robert Rauschenberg: Two Serial Works, 80, Adolf Konrad Retrospective (auth, catalog), 80, Clinton Hill: Paintings and Paperworks (auth, catalog), 81, Josef Albers: His Art and His Influence (auth, catalog), 81. *Pos:* Exhib designer, Newark Mus, NJ, 61-63; asst dir, Morris Mus Arts & Sci, 69-76; from asst dir to assoc dir, Montclair Art Mus, NJ, 76-80, dir, 80- *Teaching:* Instr art, Pub Schs, Union City, NJ, 63-69. *Mem:* Am Asn Mus; Northeast Mus Conf; Mus Coun NJ; Asn Mus Dirs. *Mailing Add:* Montclair Art Mus PO Box X Montclair NJ 07042

KOEPNICK, ROBERT CHARLES
SCULPTOR, EDUCATOR
b Dayton, Ohio, July 8, 07. *Study:* Dayton Art Inst, dipl; Cranbrook Acad Art; also with Carl Milles. *Comn:* Soaring Spirits (bronze sculpture), Woodland Cemetery, Dayton, Ohio, 81; Jesse Phillips (bronze portrait), Phillips Indust, 82; aluminum relief sculpture, Washington & Jefferson Univ, Pa, 82; Ralph Stolle (aluminum relief portrait), Stolle Corp, Sidney, Ohio, 83; bronze sculpture, St Stephen Church, Dayton, Ohio, 83; and many others. *Exhib:* Pa Acad Fine Arts, Philadelphia; Art Inst Chicago; Metrop Mus Art, New York; Nat Acad Design, New York; Syracuse Mus Fine Arts, NY; two-man show, Shillito-Rikes Art Gallery, 83; and others. *Pos:* Tech adv, Ohio Art Coun, 68- *Teaching:* From instr to prof sculpture, Dayton Art Inst, 36-41 & 46-74, emer prof, 74-; vis sculptor, Mt St Joseph Col, 51-55; vis sculptor, Antioch Col, 53-54. *Mem:* Dayton Soc Painters & Sculptors; Cincinnati Liturgical Art Group. *Mailing Add:* 1134 E Lower Springboro Rd Lebanon OH 45036

KOERNER, HENRY
PAINTER, LECTURER
b Vienna, Austria, Aug 28, 15; US citizen. *Study:* Acad Appl Art, Vienna; also with Victor Theodore Slama, Vienna. *Work:* Whitney Mus Am Art; Mus Mod Art; Art Inst Chicago; Munson-Williams-Proctor Inst, Utica, NY; Metrop Mus Art; and others. *Comn:* 65 Time Mag cover portraits. *Exhib:* Nat Cancer Poster Competition, 39; Nat War Poster Competition, Mus Mod Art, 42; Philadelphia Mus Art, 50; Artist of Yr, Pittsburgh, 63; Westmoreland Co Mus Art, Greensburg, Pa; retrospective, Carnegie Inst, 83. *Pos:* Head graphic div, Off Mil Govt, Berlin, Ger, 45-47; artist-in-residence, Chatham Col, 52-53. *Teaching:* Instr art, Munson-Williams-Proctor Inst, 47-48; instr art & head dept, Washington Univ, 56, Art Inst Pittsburgh, 78- *Awards:* First Prize, Nat Cancer Asn, 39 & First & Second Prize, Nat War Poster Competition, 42, Mus Mod Art; Temple Award, Art Inst Philadelphia, 50. *Bibliog:* His own tragedy spurs artist to paint moving post war paintings, Life, 48; Alexander Eliot (auth), Story teller, 3/27/50 & 300 years of American painting, 59, Time. *Mem:* Nat Acad Design. *Media:* Ink, Watercolor. *Publ:* Illusr, Tracy's tiger, 49, A sense of purpose, Col Art J, 51; The Living God, Jewish Commentary, 59 & CBS Yearbook, 59; auth & illusr, University of Pittsburgh in Drawings, 65; and others. *Mailing Add:* 1055 S Negley Ave Pittsburgh PA 15217

KOESTNER, DON
PAINTER
b St Paul, Minn, Nov 28, 23. *Study:* Minneapolis Sch Art, four yrs. *Comn:* Mural, St Olaf's Church, Minneapolis, 50; diorama-mural, Goodhue Co Hist Soc, Red Wing, Minn, 69. *Exhib:* Am Artists Prof League, 68; Classical Realism Show, Springville Mus Art, Utah, 82; Amarillo Art Ctr, Tex, 83; Maryhill Mus Art, Goldendale, Wash, 83; The Painters of Light, Dallas, Tex, 83; and others. *Teaching:* Instr painting, Art Instr Schs, Minneapolis, 60-69; instr oil painting & drawing, Minn Mus Art Sch, 70-75 & Atelier Lack, Minneapolis, 75- *Awards:* Grumbacher Award, Ogunquit Art Ctr Nat Exhib, 64; First Prize for oil painting, Minn State Fair, 66; Award, Am Artists Prof League, 68. *Media:* Oil. *Mailing Add:* 9501 123rd St E Hastings MN 55033

KOGA, MARY
PHOTOGRAPHER
b Sacramento, Calif, Aug 10, 20. *Study:* Art Inst Chicago, MFA; Univ Chicago, MA; Univ Calif, Berkeley, BA. *Work:* Ill Art Coun, Chicago; San Francisco Mus of Mod Art; Exchange Nat Bank, Chicago; J P Seagram Collection, New York; Kimberley Clark, Wis. *Exhib:* One-man shows, Art Inst Chicago, 71, Evanston Art Ctr, 72, Shado Gallery, Ore, 77, Utah State Univ, 79 & Pittsburgh Film-Makers Gallery, 83; Art Inst Chicago, 73; San Francisco Mus Mod Art, 78; Women of Photography, San Francisco Mus Art, 75; Los Angeles Co Mus Nat Hist, 80; Wellesley Col Mus, Univ Wis & others, 75; Los Angeles Co Mus Nat Hist, 80; Sch Mus Fine Art, Boston, 80; Field Mus Nat Hist, Chicago, 83. *Teaching:* Asst prof, Univ Chicago, 59-69; mem fac, Columbia Col, 73. *Awards:* Nine Women Photogrs, Ill Art Coun, 75; Proj Completion Grant, Ill Arts Coun, 79; Nat Endowment Arts, 82. *Bibliog:* Chicago: The City and its Artists, 1945-78, Univ Mich, 78; Family of Children, Grosset & Dunlap, 77; and others; The Human Condition, Temple Univ, 80; and others. *Mem:* Soc Photog Educ; Friends Photog; Photographic Soc, Art Inst Chicago. *Dealer:* Douglas Kenyon Gallery 155 E Ohio St Chicago IL 60611. *Mailing Add:* 1254 Elmdale Ave Chicago IL 60660

KOGAN, DEBORAH (DEBORAH RAY)
PAINTER, ILLUSTRATOR
b Philadelphia, Pa, Aug 31, 40. *Study:* Philadelphia Col Art; Pa Acad Fine Arts, 58-62; Univ Pa, Albert C Barnes Found, 62-64. *Work:* Drexel Univ, Philadelphia, Pa; Libr Cong, Washington, DC; Univ Minn, Minneapolis; Free Libr Philadelphia; Montgomery Co Col, Center Square, Pa. *Comn:* Graphic murals, Chase Manhattan Bank, 69. *Exhib:* Pa Acad Fine Arts Bienniel, 67 & 69; Philadelphia Artists, Philadelphia Mus Art, 73, 74 & 79; 110th Exhib Am Watercolor Soc, Nat Acad of Design, New York, 77; American Women in Fine Arts, Moore Col Art, Philadelphia, 77; Mus Philadelphia Civic Ctr, 78; US-Israeli Exchange Exhib, Tel Aviv, 78; Albright Col, 80; Rosenfeld Gallery, Philadelphia, 80 & 81; also many one-woman shows. *Teaching:* Lectr, Col William & Mary, formerly. *Awards:* Am Inst of Graphic Arts Award for Illustration, 76; Moore Col Art, Philadelphia, 77; Purchase Award, Millersville State Col. *Bibliog:* Paul West (auth), Children's books, New York Times, 77; Books Books Books, Philadelphia Col Art, 77; 21 Women Artists, Muse, 79; and others. *Mem:* Artists Equity Asn (mem bd dir, 77-79); Women's Caucus for Art; Muse: Woman's Collab (mem bd dirs, 77-80). *Media:* Acrylic; Mixed. *Publ:* Illusr, The Train, 72, Pantheon; illusr, I Have a Sister, My Sister is Deaf, 77, illusr, That is That, 79 & illusr, Through Grandpa's Eyes, 80, Harper & Row; auth & illusr, Sunday Morning We Went to the Zoo, Harper & Row, 81; and others. *Mailing Add:* 223 E Gowen Ave Philadelphia PA 19119

KOGER, IRA MCKISSICK
COLLECTOR, PATRON
b Charleston, SC, Dec 5, 12. *Study:* Col Charleston, BS, 33; Univ SC Law Sch; Rollins Col, hon DFA; Univ SC, LLD. *Collections Arranged:* Celebration of the Art of the Oriental Potter (cataloged), Jacksonville Art Mus, 73. *Pos:* Hon trustee, Jacksonville Art Mus, Fla; trustee, Ringling Mus, currently; trustee, Rollins Col. *Interests:* Oriental porcelain. *Collection:* American paintings; French 19th century paintings; Oriental and English ceramics. *Mailing Add:* 3986 Boulevard Ctr Dr Jacksonville FL 32207

KOHL, BARBARA
PRINTMAKER, PAINTER
b Milwaukee, Wis, Feb 10, 40. *Study:* Univ Wis Madison, BS(art hist); Univ Wis Milwaukee. *Work:* Milwaukee Art Ctr. *Comn:* Painting, comn by Golda Meier, 77. *Exhib:* Wis Painters & Sculptors, Milwaukee Art Ctr, 65; Washington Art, Washington Armory, DC, 77 & 78; New York Show, Allen Park Gallery, 77; Janus Gallery, Washington, DC, 78; Alex Rosenberg Gallery, 78-79; Voices of Past, Women in Jewish Art, Jewish Community Ctr, Washington, DC, 79. *Teaching:* Asst trainer of docents in art hist, Milwaukee Art Ctr, 78- *Awards:* Pub Television Auction Award for Best in Show, 77. *Media:* Color and Fabric on Paper. *Collection:* Milton Avery oils, Morris Lewis, Dubuffet, Hockney, Ralph Fasanella, Wayne Thiebold, Hepworth, Suttman, Saul Steinberg. *Mailing Add:* c/o Judith L Posner & Assoc 7641 North Pt Wash Rd Milwaukee WI 53217

KOHLER, RUTH DEYOUNG
MUSEUM DIRECTOR, CURATOR
b Chicago, Ill, 41. *Study:* Smith Col, Northhampton, Mass, BA; Univ Hamburg, Ger; Kunsthochschule, Hamburg, Ger; Banff Sch of Fine Arts; Univ Wis, Madison. *Pos:* Dir & mem, Kohler Found, Inc, Wis, 60-; asst dir, John Michael Kohler Arts Ctr, Sheboygan, Wis, 68-72, dir, 72-; mem, Wis Arts Bd, Madison, 73- & chmn, 74-77; mem, Wis Am Revolution Bicentennial Commission, Madison, 74-77; mem crafts panel, Nat Endowment Arts, Washington, DC, 75-, mem mus panel, 76-78. *Teaching:* Instr printmaking, Univ Alta, Calgary, Can, 64-66. *Mailing Add:* 608 New York Ave Sheboygan WI 53081

KOHLHEPP, NORMAN
PAINTER, CONSERVATOR
b Louisville, Ky. *Study:* Univ Cincinnati; Grande Chaumiere, Paris; Acad Colorossi; Andre L'Hote Acad, Paris. *Work:* J B Speed Art Mus; Univ Louisville; Seagram Collection; Nat Mus Am Art, Smithsonian Inst; Howard Steamboat Mus; and others. *Exhib:* Mid-States Exhib, 65-67; Cincinnati Mus, Ohio, 67; J B Speed Art Mus, 68; Pa Acad Fine Arts, 66; Latin-Am Festival, 69; Liberty Bank Gallery, 76; Jr League of Louisville, 78; 50 Years in the Arts, Speed Art Mus, 79; and others. *Awards:* Va-Intermont Exhib, 58; First Prize, Ky State Fair, 67 & 68; Corporate Purchase, Eight State Ann, 77; plus others. *Mem:* Louisville Art Ctr Asn. *Mailing Add:* 2116 Lauderdale Rd Louisville KY 40205

KOHLMEYER, IDA (R)
PAINTER, PRINTMAKER
b New Orleans, La, Nov 3, 12. *Study:* Newcomb Col, BA, 33, MFA, 56; also with Hans Hofmann, 56. *Work:* Mus Fine Arts, Houston, Tex; High Mus Art, Atlanta, Ga; Corcoran Gallery Art & Nat Collection, Smithsonian Inst, Washington, DC; Brooklyn Mus; plus many others. *Exhib:* Biennial Contemp Am Painting, Corcoran Gallery Art, Washington, DC, 63 & 67; An Anthology of Modern American Painting, from collections of High Mus, Atlanta & Whitney Mus Am Art, New York, 66; Painting in the South: 1564-1980, Va Mus; American Women: 20th Century, Lakeview Ctr Arts & Sci, Peoria, Ill, 72; North, East, West, South & Middle, Moore Col Art, Philadelphia, 75; plus many other group & one-man shows. *Teaching:* Instr drawing & painting, Newcomb Col, 56-64; assoc prof painting, Univ New Orleans, 73-75. *Awards:* Ford Found Purchase Award, 28th Corcoran Biennial Am Art, 63; Mus Purchase Award, High Mus, Atlanta, 63 & 66; Artists of SE & Tex Biennial Award, New Orleans Mus Art, 75; Outstanding Achievement in Visual Arts Award, Nat Women's Caucus for the Arts, 81; plus many others. *Bibliog:* Ida Kohlmeyer: New dimensions, Arts Mag, 4/82; Ida Kohlmeyer, Times Picayunne, 4/83. *Media:* Oil. *Dealer:* Gimpei & Weitzenhoffer 1040 Madison Ave New York NY 10021; Gimpel Fils 30 Davies St London England WIYILG. *Mailing Add:* 11 Pelham Ave Metairie LA 70005

KOHN, BERNARD A
PRINTMAKER

b Philadelphia, Pa, Nov 21, 05. *Study:* Univ Pa, 22-24; studied with Morris Blackburn, 41-45. *Work:* Bibliot Nat, Paris; Israel Mus, Jerusalem; Philadelphia Mus At; Art Inst Chicago; Reading Pub Mus, Pa. *Comn:* Two silkscreen prints, Temple Univ Med Bldg, 83. *Exhib:* Am Color Print Soc Ann Exhib, Philadelphia Art Alliance, 51-81; A Decade of American Printmaking, Philadelphia Mus Art, 52; Accent on the Orient, East Side Gallery, New York, 67; 164th Ann Exhib, Pa Acad Fine Arts, 69; Drawing Soc Regional Drawing Exhib, Philadelphia Mus Art, 70; Estampe Centemporain, Bibliot Nat, Paris, 73; solo exhib, Reading Mus, 74; Hahn Gallery, 78 & 81. *Pos:* Illusr covers, Elkan-Vogel Co, 50-72. *Teaching:* Instr painting, Cheltenham Township Adult Sch, Wyncote, Pa, 48-63. *Awards:* Paul Revere Awards, Music Publ Asn US, 50-70. *Mem:* Artists Equity Asn (secy & treas Philadelphia chap, 53-55); Am Color Print Soc (treas, 66-); Music Publ Asn US (pres, 62-65). *Media:* Wood Engraving, Monotype. *Dealer:* Hahn Gallery 8439 Germantown Ave Philadelphia PA 19118. *Mailing Add:* 8115 Cedar Rd Elkins Park PA 19117

KOHN, EDMOND
PAINTER, INSTRUCTOR

b Philadelphia, Pa. *Work:* Houston Mus Art, Tex; City of Los Angeles Collection, Calif. *Exhib:* Corcoran Gallery Art, Washington, DC, 49; Am Painting Today (catalog), Metrop Mus Art, New York, 50; Contemp Painting in the US (catalog), Los Angeles Co Mus Art, Calif, 51; American Watercolors (catalog), Metrop Mus Art, New York, 52; The Southwest Painting & Sculpture, Houston Mus Fine Art, Tex, 63; and 16 one-man shows. *Pos:* Illusr & Designer, Paramount Studios, 38-43 & 45-46. *Teaching:* Instr oil painting, Chovinard Art Inst, 49-52 & 59-62. *Awards:* The Hallmark Art Award, Corcoran Gallery Art, 49; NY Soc Illusr, NY Soc of Ill, 59; Ford Found Purchase, 63. *Bibliog:* Robert Coughanan (auth), The Private World of William Faulkner, Harper & Brothers, 54; Homage to Jewish Artists of LA, Jewish Federation Council, 81. *Media:* Oils, Acrylics. *Collection:* Realism to non-objective. *Publ:* Contemporary Painting in the US, Los Angeles Co Mus, 51; Homage to Jewish Artist of LA, Jewish Fedn Coun, 81. *Mailing Add:* 12020 Vanowen North Hollywood CA 19605

KOHN, MISCH
PAINTER, PRINTMAKER

b Kokomo, Ind, Mar 26, 16. *Study:* John Herron Art Inst, BFA, 39; also with Jose Clemente Orozco & Leopoldo Mendez, Mexico City, 43. *Work:* Bibliot Nat, Paris; Victoria Mus, Melbourne, Australia; Whitney Mus Am Art, Mus Mod Art, Metrop Mus Art, New York; and others. *Exhib:* Art Inst Chicago, 51, 60 & 70; Los Angeles Co Mus Art, 61; Mus Nat Art Mod & Bibliot Nat, Paris, 59; retrospective, Ford Found & Am Fedn Arts, 61; one-man exhibs, David Stuart Gallery, 63-66 & Zabriskie Gallery, New York, 72-77; and many others. *Teaching:* Assoc prof art, Ill Inst Technol, 53-65, prof art, 65-70; prof, Calif State Univ, Hayward, 72-80. *Awards:* Guggenheim Fel, 67; Philadelphia Print Club, 69; Mark Rothko Found Grant, 71; and others. *Bibliog:* Gabor Peterdi (auth), Printmaking: Methods Old and New, Macmillan, 59; S W Hayter (auth), About Prints, Oxford Univ Press, 62. *Mem:* Print Coun Am; Nat Acad Design; and others. *Mailing Add:* 1860 Grove Way Castro Valley CA 94546

KOHN, WILLIAM ROTH
PAINTER, EDUCATOR

b St Louis, Mo, Aug 23, 31. *Study:* Wash Univ, BFA, 49; Atelier 17, Paris, with S W Hayter, 54; Mills Col, MA, 60. *Work:* Springfield Art Mus, Mo; St Louis Art Mus; Carlton Col, Minn; Dalhousie Art Gallery, Halifax; Chase Manhattan Bank. *Comn:* Mural, Am Automobile Asn, Mo, 78; Mayor's Award for the Arts (print), Arts & Humanities Comn, St Louis, 81. *Exhib:* Seventy-Ninth & eighty-first Ann Painting & Sculpture Show, San Francisco Mus, 60 & 62; Mid Am Show, Nelson Gallery, Kansas City & St Louis Art Mus, 65-67; one-man shows, Loretto Hilton Gallery, Webster Col, 70, Mobile Art Gallery, Ala, 73, Terry Moore Gallery, St Louis, 76 & Ex Convento Del Carmen, Guadalajara, Mex, 79; Int Exhib Graphic Art, Mus Art, Ljubljana, Yugoslavia, 71; Midwest Invitational, Krannert Mus, Univ Ill, 76; Salon de Octubre, Casa de la Cultura, Guadalajara, Mex, 79 & 82; Currents 7, St Louis Art Mus, 80. *Teaching:* Prof painting & design, Wash Univ, 63- *Awards:* Fulbright Hays Grant to India, 65; Mo State Coun Arts Grant, 77; 1st Prize, St Louis Posters, First St Forum, 82. *Mem:* Art Coord Coun (chmn St Louis Area, 75-76). *Media:* Acrylics, Watercolor. *Dealer:* Timothy Burns 343 N Euclid St Louis Mo 63108; Jan Cicero 437 N Clark Chicago IL 61610. *Mailing Add:* 6100 Kingsbury St Louis MO 63112

KOHUT, LORENE
PAINTER

b La Port, Tex, Nov 16, 29. *Study:* With Coulton Waugh & John Gould. *Work:* Court Gen Sessions, Washington, DC; Pa State Univ; Fred Clark Mus, Carversville, Pa; Del State Col; Wesley Col. *Exhib:* Ogunquit Arts Ctr 49th Nat, Maine, 69; Hudson Valley Art Asn, 42nd & 43rd Nat, White Plains, NY, 69-70; Nat Acad Design, NY, 70; Catharine Lorillard Wolfe Nat, New York, 80; Am Artist Prof League Grand Nat Exhib, 81. *Awards:* Gold Medal Oils, Hudson Valley Art Asn, 69; Gold Medal, watercolor, Catharine Lorillard Wolfe Nat, 80; Gold Medal, oil, Am Artist Prof League Grand Nat Exhib, 81. *Mem:* Artists Equity Asn; Philadelphia Art Alliance; Am Artist Prof League. *Media:* Mixed Media, Acrylic. *Dealer:* McBride Gallery Annapolis MD. *Mailing Add:* Rte 3 Andrews Lake Felton DE 19943

KOLBERT, FRANK L
DEALER

b Detroit, Mich, Oct 17, 48. *Study:* Yale Univ, BA, 70. *Pos:* Cur asst, Detroit Inst Arts, 70-72; assoc dir, Inst Art & Urban Resources, 73-74; dir, Bykert Gallery, 74-76; pres, Droll/Kolbert Gallery Inc, New York, 76-81, private dealer, 81- *Specialty:* Twentieth century painting and sculpture, especially post-war Americans; publisher prints and multiples. *Mailing Add:* 30 West 15th Street New York NY 10011

KOLISNYK, PETER
PAINTER, SCULPTOR

b Toronto, Ont, Can, Nov 30, 34. *Study:* Western Tech Sch Toronto, Ont, with Fred Fraser, Julius Griffith & Margaret Aitken, 51-54. *Work:* Art Gallery Ont, Toronto; Art Bank, Can Coun, Ottawa; Winnipeg Art Gallery, Man; Queen's Silver Jubilee Art Collection, Govt Ont, Toronto; Ukrainian Inst Mod Art, Chicago. *Exhib:* One-man exhibs, Art Gallery Ont, 77-78; Mercer Union, Toronto, 83 & Art Gallery Lindsay, 83; Montreal Mus Fine Arts, 60, 62, 67 & 69; Fourth Biennial Exhib Can Art, Nat Gallery Can, Ottawa, 61; Art Gallery Ont, Toronto, 67, 69, 70, 72 & 77; Albright-Knox Art Gallery, 68; A Plastic Presence, San Francisco Mus Art, and others, 69-70; 49th Parallels--New Canadian Art, Mus Contemp Art, Chicago, and others, 71; Contemporary Outdoor Sculpture, Guildwood Hall, Toronto, 82; Rational Alternatives, Harbourfront Art Gallery, Toronto, 83; Works on Paper, Ukrainian Inst Mod Art, Chicago, 83; and many others. *Pos:* Cur, Cobourg Art Gallery, 64-69; trustee, Art Gallery Ont, 82- *Teaching:* Dir & lectr art, Glendon Col, York Univ, Toronto, 75-; instr, Prison Arts Found, Kingston, Ont, 78 & Emily Carr Col Art, Vancouver, 82- *Awards:* Sculpture Award, Ont Soc Artists, 72; Can Coun Sr Arts Grant, 75-76; Ont Arts Coun Grants, 75, 77-79 & 81-83. *Bibliog:* Clara Hargittay (auth), article, Art Mag, 5-7/82; David Nasby & Fern Bayer (coauth), Art for Architecture, Govt Ont, 82. *Mem:* Can Artists Representation Ont; Can Soc Painters Watercolour; Ont Soc Artists; Royal Can Acad Arts. *Media:* Watercolor; Miscellaneous. *Mailing Add:* 247 King St E PO Box 971 Cobourg ON K9A 4W4 Canada

KOLLIKER, WILLIAM AUGUSTIN
PAINTER, PRINTMAKER

b Bern, Switz, Oct 12, 05; US citizen. *Study:* Berner Secundar Schule, Bern; Nat Acad Design, Md Inst; Boston Sch Art, Grand Cent Art Sch; Art Students League; Univ Tex, El Paso. *Work:* El Paso Mus Art, Tex; Univ Tex, El Paso; Grumbacher Col, New York; El Paso Nat Bank; Johnson Libr, Austin. *Comn:* Mosaic mural, El Fed Savings & Loan, El Paso, 64; design of bronze eagles, Amistad Dam, Del Rio, Tex, 68; gold medal, 69 & bronze plaques, 70, Chamisal Settlement. *Exhib:* Dept Interior, Washington, DC, 75; one-man shows, Santa Fe Mus Art, NMex State Univ, Las Cruces Art Ctr & El Paso Mus Art; and many others. *Pos:* Dir art, Cunningham & Walsh Advert Agency, New York, 52-54; dir art, White & Shuford, El Paso, 54-65. *Teaching:* Instr com art, Univ Tex, El Paso, 60-63; mem fac staff, El Paso Mus Art, 73-75. *Mem:* Watercolor Soc El Paso. *Media:* Watercolor. *Collection:* Pre-Columbia artifacts and graphic collection. *Publ:* Illusr, Aesop's Fables, 40; illusr, Adventures in Puddle Muddle, 41. *Dealer:* Jinx Galleries 6513 N Mesa El Paso TX 79912. *Mailing Add:* 3812 Hillcrest Dr El Paso TX 79902

KOLODNER, NATHAN K
DEALER

b Baltimore, Md, Sept 10, 50. *Study:* Brandeis Univ, BA; NY Univ, MA; Inst Fine Arts, NY Univ. *Specialty:* Modern and contemporary painting and sculpture. *Mailing Add:* Andre Emmerich Gallery 41 E 57th St New York NY 10022

KOLTUN, FRANCES LANG
COLLECTOR, LECTURER

b New York, NY. *Study:* Brooklyn Col, BA; Columbia Univ, MA. *Pos:* Ed, writer & broadcaster, NBC & Syndicated Radio on Collecting, 70- *Mem:* Drawing Soc. *Collection:* Nineteenth and twentieth century drawings and etchings. *Publ:* Numerous articles on art. *Mailing Add:* 45 E 66th St New York NY 10021

KOMODORE, BILL
PAINTER

b Athens, Greece, Oct 23, 32; US citizen. *Study:* Tulane Univ La, BA, 55 & MFA, 57; Hans Hofmann Sch, Provincetown; also with George Rickey, Mark Rothko & David Smith. *Work:* Whitney Mus Am Art; Des Moines Art Ctr, Iowa; Nat Gallery Art; Walker Art Ctr; Milwaukee Mus Art. *Exhib:* Albright-Knox Art Gallery, Buffalo, NY, 65 & 68; Whitney Mus Am Art, New York; Marcia Tucker's The Art of the Invisible, Visual Arts Gallery, New York, 70; one-man shows, Haydon Calhoun Gallery, Dallas, 61, Automation House, New York, 73 & D W Gallery, Dallas, 81; retrospective show, Mary Washington Col, 75; Made in Texas, Univ Tex, Austin, 79; 12 Artists from North Texas, Dallas Mus Fine Arts, 79. *Teaching:* Vis artist, Mary Washington Col, 73-76, Richland Col, Arts Magnet High Sch, Dallas, 77-78, Brookhaven Col, Dallas, 81-, Dallas Theatre Ctr, 81- & Univ Tex, Dallas, 82- *Awards:* Bausch & Lomb Sci Award, 50; Houston Mus Award, Dallas Mus of Fine Arts, 60; Tex Comn on Arts Grant, 79-80. *Bibliog:* Robert Trout (interviewer), Op art, CBS News, 64; Cyril Barrett (auth), An introduction to optical art, Studio Vista, 71. *Media:* Oil, Watercolor. *Publ:* Illusr, Fishes of Lake Pontchartrain, Tulane Univ Press, 54; contribr, Contemporary American Painting and Sculpture, Univ Ill Press, 65; contribr, Young America, 1965, Whitney Mus Am Art, 65; Ballad of a Sweet Dream of Peace: A Charade for Easter, Press Works, Dallas, 81. *Mailing Add:* 5946 Oram Dallas TX 75206

KOMOR, MATHIAS
DEALER

b Jan 24, 09; US citizen. *Study:* Univ Grenoble, Dr Univ, 29. *Pos:* Dir, Mathias Komor Works of Art, currently. *Specialty:* Antiquities, Greek, Egyptian, Far East and others. *Mailing Add:* 19 E 71st St New York NY 10021

KONI, NICOLAUS
SCULPTOR, LECTURER

b Hungary, May 6, 11; US citizen. *Study:* Acad Fine Art, Vienna, Austria, dipl anat fine art; Masters Sch, Paris; Masters Sch, Florence, Italy. *Work:* Bronze sculptures, Fountain of the Night, Okla Art Ctr, Oklahoma City; bust of J V Forrestal, Forrestal Bldg; bust of Marian Anderson, Metrop Opera at Lincoln Ctr, New York & Kennedy Ctr Performing Art, Washington, DC; The Freedom of Man, Sen Margaret Chase Smith Libr, Washington DC; and others. *Comn:* Bronze sculpture of C Walter Nichols, NY Univ Bus Admin Sch. *Exhib:* Whitney Mus Am Art, New York; Birmingham Mus Fine Art, Ala; Parrish Art Mus, South Hampton, NY; Milch Galleries, New York; Int Expos of Sculpture (sponsored by Smithsonian Inst), Paris. *Teaching:* Instr sculpture, Graham-Eckes Sch, Palm Beach, formerly; lectr, Univ Bridgeport, formerly; instr fine art, Univ Mo, Columbia, formerly. *Awards:* First Prize in Art, Eighth Ann Art Festival, Parrish Art Mus. *Bibliog:* Nicolaus Koni, A Sculptor Bringing Out the Spirit Asleep in Matter (film), New York Fine Arts Coun. *Mem:* Nat Sculpture Soc; Quilleis Art Soc. *Media:* Wood, Marble. *Dealer:* Studio & Sculpture Garden East Gate Montauk Highway Westhampton Long Island NY 11977; Studio & Gallery 146 Australian Avenue Palm Beach FL 33480. *Mailing Add:* 146 Australian Ave Palm Beach FL 33480

KONOPKA, JOSEPH
PAINTER

b Philadelphia, Pa, Oct 6, 32. *Study:* Cooper Union, grad, 54; Columbia Univ, 55. *Work:* Nat Mus Am Art; Montclair Art Mus, NJ; Butler Inst Am Art, Youngstown, Ohio; Cooper Hewitt Mus; Nat Mus of Design, Smithsonian Inst, New York; and others. *Exhib:* Butler Inst Am Art, 74, 77, 79 & 82; Brooklyn Mus, 76, 78 & 81; Hunterdon Art Ctr, Clinton, NJ, 78-81; Recent Acquisitions, 81 & Drawings from Permanent Collections, 82, Montclair Art Mus, NJ; New Jersey Artists, Newark Mus, 81; New Jersey Artists, NJ State Mus, 83; and others. *Awards:* Purchase Awards, Newark Mus, 68 & NJ State Mus, 70; Medal of Honor, NJ Painters & Sculptors Soc, 71. *Bibliog:* Sunday New York Times, 76 & Newark Star-Ledger, 10/79 & 1/82; article, NJ Art Form Mag, 3-4/81. *Mem:* Assoc Artists NJ (vpres); NJ Painters & Sculptors Soc; United Scenic Artists, NY. *Dealer:* Capricorn Gallery 8004 Norfolk Ave Bethesda MD 20014. *Mailing Add:* 26 Snowden Pl Glen Ridge NJ 07028

KONRAD, ADOLF FERDINAND
PAINTER

b Bremen, Ger; US citizen. *Study:* Newark Sch Fine & Indust Art, NJ; Cummington Sch, Mass; Newark State Col, Hon DFA. *Work:* Newark Mus; Springfield Mus Fine Art, Mass; Montclair Art Mus, NJ; Nat Acad Design, New York; NJ State Mus, Trenton. *Exhib:* Am Painting Today, Metrop Mus Art, 50 & Whitney Mus Am Art Ann, 52, New York; Butler Inst Am Art, Youngstown, Ohio, 56; Pa Acad Fine Arts Painting Exhib, 64; Mainstream 70, Marietta Col, Ohio, 70; Mus Fine Arts, Springfield, Mass, 73; retrospective exhibs, Montclair Art Mus, NJ & State Mus, Trenton, 80. *Teaching:* Adj instr painting, Newark State Col, 72; artist in residence, Somerset Co Col, NJ, 76-80. *Awards:* Tiffany Found Fel Creative Painting, 61; Andrew Carnegie Prize, Nat Acad Design, 67; NJ Symphony Ann Arts Award, 69. *Bibliog:* An artist looks at Newark, Newark Mus, 66; Henry Gasser (auth), Adolf Konrad, painter of the American scene, Am Artist, 11/68. *Mem:* Nat Acad Design; Artists Equity Asn; Assoc Artists NJ. *Media:* Oil. *Mailing Add:* Asbury NJ 08802

KONRAD, TONY (ANTON JOSEPH)
CONSERVATOR, RESTORER

b Neckarsteinach, Ger, Mar 12, 17; US citizen. *Study:* Arts & Crafts Sch, Prof Sch for Painters & training in conserv, Ger, 33-39; NY Univ Conserv Ctr, with Caroline & Sheldon Keck, Master Conservator, 61. *Work:* Art Inst Chicago; Brooklyn Mus; Mus Mod Art, New York; Nat Collection of Fine Arts-Nat Portrait Gallery, Smithsonian Inst, DC; Ponce Mus Art, PR. *Pos:* From asst to actg conservator, Art Inst Chicago, 58-63; conservator sculpture & consult, Mus Mod Art, New York, 64-70; head conserv dept, Nat Collection of Fine Arts-Nat Portrait Gallery, 70-74; conserv, Smithsonian Inst, 74-76; head conserv dept, Ponce Mus Art, PR, 77-82. *Teaching:* Dir, Ponce Mus Art Conserv Prog, formerly. *Mem:* Fel Int Inst Conserv Hist & Artistic Works; Am Inst Conserv Hist & Artistic Works. *Mailing Add:* Bucare Six Punta las Marias Santurce PR 00913

KONZAL, JOSEPH
SCULPTOR

b Milwaukee, Wis, Nov 5, 05. *Study:* Beaux-Arts Inst Design, New York; Art Students League, with Max Weber & Robert Laurent, 26-31. *Work:* Tate Gallery Art, London; Whitney Mus Am Art & New Sch Social Res, New York; Canton Art Inst, Ohio; Storm King Art Ctr, Mountainville, NY. *Comn:* Sculpture, Blossom Music Ctr, Cuyahoga Falls, Ohio, 72; Outdoor Sculpture, Gen Servs Admin, Art & Archit Prog, Fed Off Bldg, Dayton, Ohio, 77. *Exhib:* Six Ann Shows, 48-68 & Geometric Abstraction in America, 62, Whitney Mus Am Art; Recent Sculpture, Mus Mod Art, New York, 58; NJ State Mus Ann, 65-71; May Show for Ohio Artists, Cleveland Mus Art, 72 & 75; one-man exhibs, Canton Art Inst, Ohio, 74 & Andre Zarre Gallery, New York, 78 & 80; Boston Mus Fine Arts; Larry Aldrich Mus, Conn; Am Acad & Inst

Arts & Lett, 81, 82 & 83. *Teaching:* Instr, Newark Sch for Fine & Indust Arts, Queens Col, New York, Adelphi Univ, Malloy Col, Brooklyn Mus Art Sch & Kent State Univ, formerly. *Awards:* Guggenheim Fel for Creative Work in Sculpture, 65-66; Sculpture Competition Prize for Nassau Co Ct House, John F Kennedy Mem Cult Ctr, 68; Adolph & Ester Gottlieb Found Grant, 82. *Mem:* Sculptor's Guild. *Media:* Metal, Wood. *Publ:* Auth, Who are the tastemakers, spring 69; auth, A reply, Art J, winter 70-71. *Mailing Add:* 160 E Third St New York NY 10009

KOOCHIN, WILLIAM
SCULPTOR, EDUCATOR

b Brilliant, BC, Dec 15, 27. *Study:* Vancouver Sch Art; Sevres Ceramics, Paris. *Work:* Vancouver Art Gallery; Univ Ore Mus; High Park, Toronto, Ont. *Comn:* Welded steel mural and free standing pieces, Can Govt, Brussels World's Fair, 57; wood carving wall hanging & crucifix, Redemptorist Col, 59; wood carved mace, Vancouver Int Arts Festival, 61; cast bronze trophy, Vancouver Maritime Festival, 62; carved granite fountain, Pacific Press Bldg, 66. *Exhib:* One-man shows, Agnes Lefort Gallery, Montreal, 57, Gallery Contemp Art, Toronto, 58, Vancouver Art Gallery, 59, Victoria Art Gallery, 61 & Burnaby Art Gallery, 80; BC Sculptors, Mido Gallery, Vancouver, 75. *Teaching:* Instr sculpture, Vancouver Sch Art, 64-80. *Bibliog:* Arla Sarre (auth), Sculpture Koochin (film), Can Broadcasting Corp, 64. *Mem:* BC Sculpture Soc; Royal Can Acad Arts. *Media:* Carved Stone & Wood, Cast Bronze. *Mailing Add:* 4814 Fernglen Burnaby BC V5G 3V8 Canada

KOONS, DARELL J
PAINTER, EDUCATOR

b Albion, Mich, Dec 18, 24. *Study:* Bob Jones Univ, BS, 51; Western Mich Univ, MA, 55; Eastern Mich Univ. *Work:* Butler Inst Am Art, Youngstown, Ohio; Mint Mus Art, Charlotte, Gov Mansion, Columbia, SC State Art Collection Mus Art, SC. *Comn:* Hist mural of Homer, Mich, for Homer Community Schs, 55. *Exhib:* Southeastern Exhibs, Atlanta, Ga, 63-65; Acquavella Galleries, New York, 64 & 66; Springfield Mus Art Nat, Mass, 65; Soc Four Arts Nat, Palm Beach, Fla, 67; Chico State Col Invitational, Calif, 72. *Teaching:* Instr art, Homer Community Schs, 52-54; instr art, Bob Jones Univ, 55- *Awards:* Purchase Awards, Guild SC Artists, 63, Davis Assocs, Chattanooga, Tenn, 65 & Wake Forest Univ Gallery Contemp Art, 65. *Bibliog:* Steve Yates (auth), Greenville's noted barn painter, Sandlapper, 3/68. *Mem:* Greenville Art Asn & Guild; Guild SC Artists. *Media:* Watercolor, Acrylic. *Mailing Add:* 6 Yancy Dr Greenville SC 29615

KOPPELMAN, CHAIM
PRINTMAKER, EDUCATOR

b New York, NY, Nov 17, 20. *Study:* Am Artists Sch; Art Col Western Eng, Bristol; Ozenfant Sch Fine Arts; also with Eli Siegel. *Work:* Victoria & Albert Mus, London; Mus Fine Arts, Caracas, Venezuela; Metrop Mus Art & Whitney Mus Am Art, New York; and many others. *Exhib:* 2nd Nat Print Invitational, Purdue Univ, 72; 2nd Ann Print Int, Utah State Univ, 72; one-man show, Assoc Am Artists Gallery, 73; Warwick Gallery, Eng, 75; Terrain Gallery, 83, New York; and many others. *Pos:* Consult, Aesthet Realism Consultations, 71- *Teaching:* NY Univ, 47-55, Brooklyn Col, 50-60, State Univ NY New Paltz, 52-58 & Sch Visual Arts, 59- *Awards:* Soc Am Graphic Artists Prize, 66; 3rd Int Miniature Print Exhib Prize, 68; Creative Artists Pub Serv Grant, 76; plus others. *Bibliog:* Barry Schwartz (auth), The New Humanism, Praeger, 74; Una Johnson (auth), American Prints and Printmakers, Doubleday; Fritz Eichenberg (auth), The Art of the Print, Abrams, 76. *Mem:* Assoc Nat Acad Design; Soc Aesthet Realism; Soc Am Graphic Artists (former pres). *Publ:* Contribr, Liberation Mag, 69; co-auth, Aesthetic Realism: We Have Been There, 69; auth, This Is the Way I See Aesthetic Realism, 69; illusr, Damned Welcome, Definition, 72. *Mailing Add:* 498 Broome St New York NY 10012

KOPPELMAN, DOROTHY
PAINTER, GALLERY DIRECTOR

b New York, NY, June 13, 20. *Study:* Brooklyn Col; Am Artists Sch; Art Students League; also with Eli Siegel. *Work:* Yale Univ, New Haven, Conn; Hampton Inst, Va. *Exhib:* Mus Mod Art, New York, 62; San Francisco Mus Art, Calif; Pratt Graphics Traveling Exhib, 62-63; two-man show, Terrain Gallery, 69; three-man exhib, The Kindest Art, 70; plus many others. *Pos:* Dir, Terrain Gallery, 55- & Visual Arts Gallery, 63-64; pres, Aesthetic Realism Found Inc, 73- *Teaching:* Instr art, Adult Educ, Brooklyn Col, 52; consult aesthetic realism, 71- *Awards:* First Prize for Painting, City Ctr Gallery, 57; Prize Painting, Brooklyn Soc Artists, 60; Tiffany Found Grant, 65-66. *Mem:* Soc Aesthet Realism. *Media:* Oil. *Publ:* Coauth, Aesthetic Realism: We Have Been There, 69; illusr, Children's Guide to Parents & Other Matters, 71. *Mailing Add:* 498 Broome St New York NY 10012

KOPRIVA, SHARON ORTMAN
PAINTER, EDUCATOR

b Houston, Tex, Feb 11, 48. *Study:* Univ Houston, with J Alexander & J Surls, BS, 70, MFA(teaching fel), 81; Houston Mus Arts, with Dorothy Hood & P Renteria, 79; Art Students League New York, with B Dorfmann, 79. *Work:* United Energy Resources & Monsanto Chemical Co, Houston; Brazosport Mus Fine Arts, Lake Jackson, Tex; Dow Chemical Co, Freeport, Tex. *Comn:* Painting, Dow Chemical Co, Plaquemine, La, 79; 3-D construction, City Houston, Tex, 80; mural, Morgan Construction Co, Houston, 80. *Exhib:* Laguna Gloria Art Mus, Austin, 79; Nat Arts Club, New York, 79; Mus Great Plains, Lawton, Okla, 80; Main Houston Pub Libr, 80; Arteder Int, Bilbao, Spain, 82; and others. *Awards:* First Place, Art League Houston, 78; Best Show, Houston Art Educ Asn, 78 & 80 & Brazosport Art Mus, 79 & 80. *Bibliog:* Local painters, Houston Chronicle, 74; J Vanderlea (auth), article,

Artspace, 82; B Long (auth), Mainstreet, Houston Art Scene, 80. *Mem:* Nat Art Educ Asn; Artists Equity Asn; Women's Caucus Arts. *Media:* Oil, Pencil. *Dealer:* Fine Art Consult SW Houston TX 77096. *Mailing Add:* 5611 Arncliffe Houston TX 77088

KORAS, GEORGE
SCULPTOR
b Florina, Greece; US citizen. *Study:* Sch Fine Arts, Athens, Greece, dipl, 55; study in Paris & Rome, 55; Art Students League, 57; with Jacques Lipchitz, 55-59. *Work:* W P Chrysler Collection; Provincetown Mus, Mass; Norfolk Mus, Va; Nat Mus Athens, Greece, 78. *Comn:* Cast bronze sculptures, Bd Educ, Queens, NY, 71 & Bd Educ, Bronx, 72 & 74. *Exhib:* Panhellenios Zapeion, Athens, Greece, 49; Brooklyn Mus, NY, 60; Pa Acad Fine Arts, Philadelphia, 64; Silvermine Guild Artists, New Canaan, Conn, 67; Consulate General of Greece, 79. *Teaching:* Prof art, State Univ NY, Stony Brook, 66- *Awards:* Brooklyn Mus, 60, Pa Acad Fine Arts, 64 & Hofstra Univ, 65. *Bibliog:* Radio interview, produced on Voice of Am, New York, 72; G Koras Sculptor (TV film), produced by NY State Coun Arts, 72; Nat Radio-Television of Greece, 79. *Mem:* Audubon Artists. *Media:* Bronze. *Mailing Add:* 43-44 149th St Flushing NY 11355

KOREN, EDWARD B
CARTOONIST, ILLUSTRATOR
b New York, NY, Dec 13, 35. *Study:* Columbia Univ, BA, 57; Atelier 17, Paris, with S W Hayter; Pratt Inst, MFA, 64. *Work:* Fogg Mus, Cambridge, Mass; Princeton Univ Mus; RI Sch Design Mus; US Info Agency; Libr Congress; and others. *Exhib:* Exposition Dessins d'Humeur, Soc Protectrice d'Humeur, Avignon, France, 73; Art from the New York Times, Soc Illusr, New York, 73; Art from the New Yorker, Grolier Club, 75; Terry Dintinfass Gallery, New York, 75-77 & 79; Koren: Prints and Drawings 1954-1981 Traveling Exhib, 82-83; and others. *Teaching:* Adj prof art, Brown Univ, 64- *Awards:* Third Prize, Biennale Illusr, Bratislava, Czech, 73; Ten Best Childrens Books of the Year, New York Times, 76; Prix d'Humour, Soc Protectrice d'Humour, Avignon, France, 76. *Mem:* Authors Guild; Soc Am Graphic Artists. *Media:* Pen & Ink. *Publ:* Illusr, Noodles Galore, Basic Bks, 77 & Dragons Hate to Be Discrete, 78; illusr, How to Eat Like a Child, 78 & Teenage Romance, 81, Viking; auth, Well, There's Your Problem, 80 & Small Ensembles, 83, Pantheon; and others. *Mailing Add:* c/o The New Yorker 25 W 43rd St New York NY 10036

KORJUS, VERONICA MARIA ELISABETH
PAINTER, LECTURER
b Tallinn, Estonia; US citizen. *Study:* Prof Women's Col, Higher State Acad Art, Estonia, dipl, 42; Univ Stockholm, 43-45; Columbia Univ, MA, 52; Phoenix Sch Art, 53-56; Nat Acad Design, New York, 60-61; La Grande Chaumiere, Paris, 61 & 69-70; also pvt studies in Mus Louvre, Mus Jeu Paume & others. *Work:* Yasuda Art Collection; World Coun Churches; Ky Wesleyan Col. *Comn:* Portraits, Dr Richard Fafara, 69, Susan Bell, 70, Countess Maria Therese Perez de Cavanillas, 70; Ingrid Bergman, 72; three comn portraits, World Coun Churches. *Exhib:* Int Art Gallery, Toronto, 64-66; one-man shows, IBM Country Club, Poughkeepsie, NY, 64 & 69 & Las Mimosas, Tangier, Morocco, 66; Barnard Col Art Asn, New York, 69. *Teaching:* Lectr & demonstr portraits, IBM Country Club, 64, Riverside Arts, New York, 65-67, Mus Louvre & Mus Jeu Paume, 70 & Cape Coral Art League, Fla, 72. *Mem:* Am Artists Prof League; Fraternitas Artis; Int Platform Asn. *Media:* Oil, Pastel. *Mailing Add:* 5350 Del Monte Ct Cape Coral FL 33904

KORMAN, BARBARA
SCULPTOR, ASSEMBLAGE ARTIST
b New York, NY, Apr 8, 38. *Study:* Art Students League; NY State Col Ceramics; Alfred Univ, BFA(cum laude), 59, MFA(Grad Fel) 60. *Work:* In many pvt collections throughout the world. *Exhib:* Rochester Mem Art Gallery, NY, 59; Albright-Knox Art Gallery, Buffalo, NY, 60; Hartford Mus Gallery Shop, Conn, 61; Hudson River Mus, Yonkers, NY, 73, 74 & 76; Nat Acad Design, New York, 73-77; Metrop Mus of Art, New York, 76; Bronx Mus, NY, 77; Queens Mus, NY, 81. *Teaching:* Fel painting & basic 2-D design, NY State Col Ceramics, 59-60; teacher & dir ceramics, Ceramic Workshop, Berkshires, summer 59; teacher sculpture, New York Bd Educ, 61- *Awards:* Int Women's Yr Award, 75-76; House Heydenryk Prize Sculpture, 74. *Mem:* Nat Asn Women Artists; Bronx Coun Arts; Hudson River Artists Comt; Int Soc Artists. *Dealer:* Creative Concepts in Art New York NY 10017. *Mailing Add:* 357 E 201st St New York NY 10458

KORMAN, HARRIET R
PAINTER
b Bridgeport, Conn, Dec 10, 47. *Study:* Skowhegan Sch Painting & Sculpture, summer 68; Queens Col (NY), BA, 69. *Work:* Weatherspoon Art Gallery, Univ NC, Greensboro; Solomon R Guggenheim Mus. *Exhib:* Solomon R Guggenheim Mus, 71; Whitney Ann Exhib Painting, Whitney Mus Am Art, New York, 72 & 73; one-person shows, Copley Gallery, Los Angeles, 74, 112 Greene St Gallery, New York, 75 & Daniel Weinberg Gallery, San Francisco, 76 & 78; Willard Gallery, New York, 76 & 80. *Awards:* Theodoron Found Award, 71; Nat Endowment for the Arts Fel Grant, 74. *Bibliog:* Jeanne Siegel (auth), article in Art News, 72; Roberta Smith (auth), article in Artforum, 75; Hilton Kramer (auth), rev, NY Times, Jan 18, 80. *Dealer:* Willard Gallery 29 E 72nd St New York NY 10021. *Mailing Add:* 349 Greenwich St New York NY 10013

KORNBLATT, BARBARA RODBELL
DEALER
b Baltimore, Md, Jan 25, 31. *Study:* Community Col Baltimore, AA; Goucher Col, with Hilton Brown, BA. *Pos:* Dir, B R Kornblatt Gallery, Washington, DC. *Bibliog:* Articles in Sun, 5/26/76, News Am, 9/23/79 & Baltimore News Am, 11/2/80. *Specialty:* Contemporary American sculpture, prints and painting. *Mailing Add:* 406 Seventh St NW Washington DC 20004

KORNBLAU, GERALD
DEALER, CONSULTANT
b New York, NY, Aug 12, 28. *Specialty:* American 19th century folk art; paintings, sculpture, pottery and decorated furniture; weathervanes, quilts. *Mailing Add:* 305 E 61st St New York NY 10021

KORNBLUM, MYRTLE
PAINTER, PRINTMAKER
b Chicago, Ill, Aug 18, 09. *Study:* Washington Univ, St Louis; Univ Miami, Coral Gables, studied with Hans Hoffman. *Exhib:* City Art Mus, St Louis, Mo, 60-62; Print Club New York, 60; Art USA, Madison Sq Garden, New York, 60; Libr Cong, Washington, DC, 63; Silvermine Printmakers, New Canaan, Conn, 65; Atkins Mus Fine Art, Kansas City, Mo; Joslyn Mus, Omaha, Nebr; one-woman shows, St Louis Artists Guild, 70-81 & Norton Gallery, St Louis, Chicago, Kansas City, Madrid & Haifa; and others. *Awards:* First Prize, New Testament Show, Temple Israel, St Louis Co, Mo, 70; Second Prize, 70 & First Energy Prize, 75, St Louis Artists Guild. *Mem:* St Louis Artists Guild; Acad Prof Artists; Community Women Artists. *Media:* Collagraph, Woodcut. *Mailing Add:* 550 Coeur De Royal Dr St Louis MO 63141

KORNETCHUK, ELENA
DEALER, HISTORIAN
b Ger, June 10, 48; US citizen. *Study:* Univ Md, College Park, BA, 70; Univ Iowa, MA, 72; Georgetown Univ, DC, 80. *Collections Arranged:* The Graphics of Estonia, Latvia and Lithuania, Russian Images Ltd, 78, Contemporary Russian Painting, 78 & Kaplan's Lithographs, 79; Retrospective of Anatolii Kaplan, Russian Images Ltd, Pittsburgh, 79. *Pos:* Partner, Masterworks Int, Chicago, 76-77; pres, Russian Images Ltd, Pittsburgh, 77-; mem bd adv, Tamburitzans Nat Folk Arts Inst, 80- *Teaching:* Instr Russian lang, lit & cult, Univ Iowa, 70-72 & Unvi Md, College Park, 73-75. *Specialty:* Contemporary art from Russia, Latvia, Estonia, Bulgaria and other countries of eastern Europe. *Collection:* Contemporary art from the USSR, Japanese wood engravings. *Publ:* Auth, The politics of Soviet art, Bull of Atomic Scientists, 77; auth, Contemporary Russian printmaking: an overview, 79, Contemporary Russian printmaking: national diversity, 80 & Demian Utenkov: a young Moscow printmaker, 80, Graphics. *Mailing Add:* Russian Images Ltd 307 Fourth Ave Pittsburgh PA 15222

KORNMAYER, J GARY (JOHN)
PAINTER, PHOTOGRAPHER
b Omaha, Nebr, July 10, 34. *Study:* San Diego State Univ, 59-61; Nat Univ, San Diego, BA, 70, MA(audio-visual commun), 74. *Work:* Riverside Art Mus, Calif. *Comn:* Tex Hist, Nat Univ, San Diego, 73 & Am Hist of Slavery, 74. *Exhib:* Noho Gallery, New York, 75-78; Calif-Hawaii Biennial, Fine Arts Gallery San Diego, 76; Ann Small Image Art Show, Span Village Art Ctr, San Diego, 76-78; one-man shows, Inst Mex NAm Relaciones Cult, Mexico City, & Inst Allende, San Miguel Allende, Mexico, 80; and many others. *Pos:* Photogr, Gen Dynamics Corp, San Diego, 58-60, sr audio-visual commun, 60-69. *Awards:* Distinctive Merit, San Diego Art Director's Soc, 65; Second Place, Fine Arts Gallery San Diego, 68; First Place Purchase Award, Riverside Art Mus, 70. *Bibliog:* Hedy O'Beil (auth), J Gary Kornmayer, artist, Arts Mag, 10/77; Hal Gray (auth), Horizons, Channel 39, 12/77; In the Public Interest, City of San Diego, Channel 2, 1/78. *Mem:* San Diego Fine Arts Soc-Art Guild (mem bd dirs, 68-70); Span Village Art Asn (mem bd dir, 72-74, pres, 74-78). *Dealer:* Knowles Gallery 7420 Girard Ave La Jolla CA 92037. *Mailing Add:* 3436 Park W Lane San Diego CA 92117

KOROT, BERYL
PAINTER, VIDEO ARTIST
b New York, NY, Sept 17, 45. *Study:* Univ Wis, 63-65; Queens Col, BA, 67. *Exhib:* Solo exhibs, Everson Mus, Syracuse, 75 & 79, Castelli Gallery, New York, 77 & Whitney Mus, 80; Documenta 6, Kassel, Ger, 77; Yesterday and After, Musee des Beaux Arts, Montreal, 80; Burden, Kos, Korot, San Francisco Art Inst, 81; and others. *Awards:* Creative Artists Pub Serv Grant, 72 & 75; Nat Endowment for the Arts Grant, 75, 77 & 79; NYSCA grant, 78. *Bibliog:* Jeff Paerrone (auth), Text and Commentary (rev), Art Forum, 75; Grace Glueck (auth), New York Times, 6/75, 3/18/77 & 12/5/80. *Publ:* Ed, Radical software, Vol I & Vol II, Gordon & Breach Sci Publ, 72-74; ed, Video Art, Harcourt, Brace, Jovanovich (in press). *Dealer:* Castelli/Sonnabend Film/Video Distribution Inc 420 W Broadway New York NY 10012. *Mailing Add:* 258 Broadway Apt 7E New York NY 10007

KORSHAK, YVONNE
HISTORIAN, EDUCATOR
b Chicago, Ill. *Study:* Radcliffe Col, BA, 58; Univ Calif, Berkeley, with D A Amyx, H Chipp, J K Anderson & J Bony, MA(classical archaeol), 66, PhD(art hist), 73. *Collections Arranged:* Selections from the Adelphi Univ Art Collection (co-ed, catalog), 79. *Teaching:* Assoc prof, Adelphi Univ, 75-, chairperson dept art & art hist, 79-82, dir mus studies prog, 79- *Awards:* Bella K Zellerbach Fel, 68-69; Samuel H Kress Res Grant, 70-71. *Mem:* Charter mem Long Island Art Historians Asn; Col Art Asn Am; Archaeol Inst Am; Asn Ancient Historians; Found Art Theory & Educ. *Res:* Nineteenth century

French painting; iconography and hidden imagery; Greek classical painting. *Publ:* Auth, Suffering in western art, J Dharma, 7/77; auth, Der Peleusmaler und sein Gefahrte, der Hektormaler, Antike Kunst 23, 80; auth, Courbet's Burial at Ornans, the passion of an idea, Pantheon XL, 82; coauth, Selections from the Permanent Collection of the Arkansas Arts Center, 83; auth, The three-quarter view face in classical painting, XII Cong Int Archaeol Classique, Athens, 84. *Mailing Add:* 1025 Fifth Ave New York NY 10028

KORTENHAUS, LYNNE M
DEALER, CONSULTANT
b Long Branch, NJ, Jan 11, 51. *Study:* RI Sch Design, Providence, BFA, 73, MFA, 75; Florence, Italy, independent study, 74. *Work:* Norwich Savings Bank, Conn; Cent Jersey Bank & Trust Co, Marlboro, NJ. *Pos:* Asst dir, Arvest Galleries, Boston, Mass, 75-78; art consult, pvt/corp insts in Boston, 78-79; New Eng Rep, Phillips Fine Art Auctioneers & Appraisers, 79-82; fine arts consult, Haley & Steele Gallery, 83- *Teaching:* Instr lithography, RI Sch Design Printmaking Workshop, 73-75; language instr Eng, Inst Americano, Florence, Italy, 74. *Awards:* Europ Hons, RI Sch Design, 75. *Mem:* Inst Contemp Art; Newbury St League; English Speaking Union. *Specialty:* American and European paintings, furniture, silver, Oriental works of art, antiques. *Dealer:* Phillips New Eng 6 Faneuil Hall Marketplace Boston MA 02109. *Mailing Add:* 6 Mt Vernon Ave Charlestown MA 02129

KORTHEUER, DAYRELL
PAINTER, CONSERVATOR
b New York, NY, July 25, 06. *Study:* Art Students League, with Frank DuMond, George Bridgman & John Carroll; Nat Acad Design, with Charles Hawthorne. *Work:* Portraits, Landscapes Merchant's Asn, New York; Mint Mus Art; Emory Univ; Univ NC; Hickory Mus Art, NC, 81; and others. *Exhib:* Blowing Rock Art Asn, 55; Statesville, NC, 57 & 64; Hickory, NC, 58; Carson-McKenna Gallery, Charlotte, NC, 69; Mint Mus Art, 74; Betty Graham Gallery, Charlotte, NC, 80. *Awards:* Nat Arts Club Prizes, 28; Mint Mus Art Awards, 41 & 42; Gold Medal, Blowing Rock Art Asn, 54 & Award, 55. *Mem:* Portraits, Inc; fel Am Inst Conserv Hist & Artistic Works; NC State Art Soc; Mint Mus Art. *Mailing Add:* 1924 Sharon Lane Charlotte NC 28211

KORTLANDER, WILLIAM
PAINTER
b Grand Rapids, Mich, Feb 9, 25. *Study:* Mich State Univ, BA; Univ Iowa, MA & PhD. *Work:* Columbus Mus Art, Ohio; Schumacher Gallery, Capitol Univ, Columbus, Ohio; Zanesville Art Inst, Ohio; Huntington Galleries, WVa; WVa State Col. *Exhib:* Dallas Mus Fine Arts, Tex, 58, 59 & 61; Pa Acad Fine Arts, Philadelphia, 65; Wadsworth Atheneum, Hartford, Conn, 65; Corcoran Gallery, Washington, DC, 68; Baltimore Mus, Md, 68; A M Sachs Gallery, New York, 79; one-man show, Haber/Theodore Gallery, New York, 80, 82 & 84; Nat Mus Am Art, Smithsonian Inst, Washington, DC, 81; Contemporary Landscape, Haber/Theodore Gallery, New York, 81; Parrish Art Mus, Southhampton, NY, 83; and many others. *Teaching:* Instr art hist, Lawrence Univ, 54-56; asst prof art hist, Univ Tex, Austin, 56-61; vis asst prof art hist, Mich State Univ, summer 61; prof painting, Ohio Univ, 61- *Awards:* Painting of Year, Mead Corp, 65; Baker Award, Ohio Univ, 67. *Media:* Multimedia. *Publ:* Auth, Painting with Acrylics, Van Nostrand Reinhold, 73. *Dealer:* Haber/Theodore Gallery 24 West 57th St New York NY 10019. *Mailing Add:* Angel Ridge Rte 4 Athens OH 45701

KORZENIK, DIANA
EDUCATOR
b New York, NY, Mar 15, 41. *Study:* Vassar Col, Oberlin Col, with Linda Nochlin, Wolfgang Letz & Wolfgang Stechow, BA; Yale Art Sch, Norfolk, Conn; Harvard Univ, with Rudolph Arnheim, EdD. *Teaching:* Chairperson, Dept Art Educ, Mass Col Art, Boston, 72- *Awards:* Fel, Yale Art Sch, Norfolk, 59; Fel, Woodrow Wilson/Ford Found, 62; Award, NY State Prof Women, 68. *Bibliog:* David Perkins (auth), Project Zero, J Aesthetic Educ; Howard Gardner (auth), Artful Scribbles, Basic Books Inc. *Mem:* Nat Art Educ; Caucus Social Theory & Art Educ; Mus Fine Arts; Ephemera Soc Am. *Publ:* Auth, Recognizing one's rationale, Art Teacher, 79; auth, Drawing and socialization, 79 & auth, Child art: Historical perspective, 81, Art Educ. *Mailing Add:* Mass Col Art 364 Brookline Ave Boston MA 02215

KOS, PAUL JOSEPH
SCULPTOR, EDUCATOR
b Rock Springs, Wyo, Dec 23, 42. *Study:* San Francisco Art Inst, BFA, 65, MFA, 67. *Work:* Ft Worth Art Mus, Tex; Mus Mod Art, Mus Conceptual Art, San Francisco; Inst Contemp Art, Univ Pa; Austrian Govt, Ganz, Austria. *Comn:* Floating (sculpture), Winery Lake, Napa, Calif, 68, Wind (sculpture), 69 & Performance (sculpture), 70. *Exhib:* One-man show, M H De Young Mem Mus, San Francisco; Bienal Sao Paulo, Brazil, 73 & 75; Trigon 74, Neue Galerie am Landesmuseum Joanneum, Ganz, Austria, 74; Art Now '74, John F Kennedy Ctr Performing Arts, Washington, DC, 74; Whitney Biennial, Whitney Mus Am Art, New York, 75; Paris Biennial, 77; Univ Mus, Berkeley, Calif, 80. *Teaching:* San Francisco Art Inst, 78- *Awards:* Nat Endowment Fel, 74 & 76. *Mailing Add:* 920 Natoma San Francisco CA 94103

KOSCIANSKI, LEONARD J
PAINTER, EDUCATOR
b Cleveland, Ohio, April 20, 52. *Study:* Cleveland Inst Art, BFA, 77; Univ Calif, Davis, MFA, 79. *Work:* Metrop Mus Art, New York; Philadelphia Mus Art; Cleveland Mus Art; Chase Manhattan Bank. *Exhib:* Beast: Animal Imagery in Recent Painting, PS 1, New York, 82; Ann Print & Drawing Show, Weatherspoon Art Gallery, Greensboro, SC, 82; Grace Borgenicht Gallery Invitational, New York, 83; Chicago Int Art Exposition, Navy Pier, 83; one-

man show, Phyllis Kind Gallery, New York, 83 & Newport Harbor Mus, Calif, 84; New Narrative Paintings, Metrop Mus Art, New York, 83. *Teaching:* Asst prof art, Univ Tenn, Knoxville, 80- *Awards:* Fels, Awards Visual Arts, 83 & Nat Endowment Arts--Southeastern Ctr Contemp Arts, 83. *Bibliog:* Grace Glueck (auth), Art view, New York Times, 1/14/82; Susan Harris (auth), Dialect, dialectic, Arts, 3/83; Susan Larsen (auth), article, Art Forum, 5/83. *Media:* Oil on Canvas, Pastel on Paper. *Dealer:* Phyllis Kind Gallery Greene St New York NY; Karl Bornstein Gallery Santa Monica CA. *Mailing Add:* 114 Busbee Rd Knoxville TN 37920

KOSCIELNY, MARGARET
SCULPTOR, PAINTER
b Tallahassee, Fla, Aug 13, 40. *Study:* Tex Woman's Univ, with Toni Lasalle; Univ Ga, BA(art hist) & MFA, with Irving Marantz, Joseph Schwarz & Charles Morgan. *Comn:* Omni, Norfolk, Va, 75; Hyatt Hotel, Washville, 76; Fla Senate, 78; Atlanta Airport, 80; ATT, Jacksonville, 83; and others. *Exhib:* Two-man exhib, Contemp Gallery, St Petersburg, 75; Four Jacksonville Artists, Cummer Gallery, Fla, 76; one-person shows, Vanderbilt Univ, Nashville, Tenn, 77 & Univ Conn, 81; Flight Patterns, Third Floor Gallery, Atlanta, 80; and many others. *Pos:* Asst to dir, Cummer Gallery Art, 69-74. *Teaching:* Instr printmaking, Jacksonville Art Mus, 68; Jacksonville Univ, 67. *Awards:* Nat Endowment Arts Grant, 76; Nat Competition, Atlanta Airport Comn, 79. *Bibliog:* Photos & Essays, Kalliope, 79. *Mem:* Artists Equity. *Media:* Plexiglass, Assemblage. *Mailing Add:* 1254 Belvedere Ave Jacksonville FL 32205

KOSHALEK, RICHARD
MUSEUM DIRECTOR
b Wausau, Wis, Sept 20, 41. *Study:* Univ Wis, Madison; Univ Minn, Minneapolis, BA(archit), MA(art hist). *Collections Arranged:* 9 Artists/9 Spaces (auth, catalog), 70; Stephen Antonakos: Outdoor Neons, 75; Dan Flavin: Drawings, Diagrams & Spaces, 75; Larry Bell: The Iceberg & It's Shadow, 75; Robert Irwin: Continuing Responses, 75-76; The Great American Rodeo (auth, catalog), 76 & 77; Ronald Bladen: Outdoor Sculpture Proposals, 78; Warburton Ave: The Architecture of a Neighborhood, 78; John Mason: Installations From the Hudson River Series, 78; Richard Serra: Elevator 80; and many others. *Pos:* Cur, Walker Art Ctr, Minneapolis, 67-72; asst dir, Nat Endowment Arts, 72-73; dir, Ft Worth Art Mus, 74-76; dir, The Hudson River Mus, 76-80; deputy dir, Mus Contemp Art, Los Angeles, 80- *Awards:* IBM Int Fel; Nat Endowment Arts Fel. *Publ:* Auth, Midwest Photographers, Walker Art Ctr, 72. *Mailing Add:* 11011 Strathmore Drive Los Angeles CA 90024

KOSS, GENE H
SCULPTOR, EDUCATOR
b La Crosse, Wis, Nov 17, 47. *Study:* Univ Wis, River Falls, BS; Tyler Sch Art, Temple Univ, Philadelphia, MFA. *Work:* The Lannan Found, Palm Beach, Fla; Univ Wis, La Crosse; Tyler Sch Art, Temple Univ, Philadelphia; One Canal Place, New Orleans. *Comn:* Ceramic sculpture, Schie Eye Inst, Philadelphia, 76. *Exhib:* Third Biennial Lake Superior Int Craft Exhibit, Tweed Mus Art, Minn, 75-77; Marietta Col Crafts Nat, Ohio, 76; 55th Am Exhib, Meadows Mus Art, Shreveport, La, 77; one-man shows, Univ Southwestern La, Lafayette, 76 & Newcomb Art Sch, Tulane Univ, New Orleans, La, 77; two-man show, Glass & Ceramic Sculpture, Circle Gallery, New Orleans, La, 78; and others. *Collections Arranged:* Louisiana Craftsmen Show, 77-78 & Glass & Ceramics Student Show, 77-78, Newcomb Art Sch, Tulane Univ, New Orleans. *Teaching:* Instr glass, Tyler Sch Art, Temple Univ, Philadelphia, summer 76; asst prof ceramics & glass, Newcomb Art Sch, Tulane Univ, New Orleans, 76- *Awards:* Best of Show, Five State Ceramic Exhib, Minn Clay Co, 74; Sculpture Award, Marietta Col Crafts Nat, 77; Award of Excellence, La Craftsmen Show, La Craft Coun, 77. *Bibliog:* Joel Myers (auth), New American glass, Craft Horizons, 8/76; Fred Adams (auth), Glass, Glass Mag, 6/77; Michael Flaherty (auth), Ceramic activities, Ceramics Mo, 9/77. *Mem:* Glass Art Soc; Am Crafts Coun; Nat Coun on Educ in Ceramic Arts; Contemp Art Ctr; La Crafts Coun (mem standards comt bd, 77-78). *Media:* Glass, Ceramics. *Publ:* Auth, The techniques of manufacture, In: Vasilike Ware: An Early Bronze Age Pottery Style in Crete, Paul Astroms Forlag, Sweden, 77. *Dealer:* Perception Galleries Glass Art Houston TX; Arthur Roger Galleries New Orleans LA. *Mailing Add:* 7710 Sycamore St New Orleans LA 70118

KOSTA, ANGELA (ANGELA KOSTA DRIESSEN)
ASSEMBLAGE ARTIST, DRAFTSMAN
US citizen. *Study:* Art Inst Chicago, 76-78; primarily self-taught. *Exhib:* Art Inst Chicago, 62 & 77; Main St Art Gallery, Chicago, 65; Chicago Cult Ctr, 78; Gallery 8, La Jolla, 81; A R T Beasely Gallery, San Diego, 82; solo show, Spectrum Gallery, San Diego, 83. *Awards:* First Prize, Hyde Park Art Ctr, Chicago, 63; Purchase Award, New Horizons Art, North Shore Art League, 77. *Bibliog:* Hale (auth), article, San Diego Evening Tribune, 5/21/82; Miller (auth), article, Los Angeles Times, 6/2/82; Lewinson (auth), article, San Diego Union, 4/7/83. *Mem:* Artists Equity Asn; Am Crafts Coun; San Diego Artists Guild. *Media:* Mixed Media; Collage, Drawing. *Publ:* Auth, California fibers, Fiberarts Mag, 11-12/83. *Dealer:* Spectrum Gallery 726 Seventh Ave San Diego CA 92101. *Mailing Add:* 3151 Mooney St San Diego CA 92117

KOSTECKA, GLORIA
PAINTER
b Bloomfield, NJ, Dec 7. *Study:* Am Art Sch, New York; Traphagen Sch Fashion, New York. *Exhib:* Federated Art Asn Exhib, NJ State Mus Cultural Ctr, Trenton, 77; Nat Soc Painters Casein & Acrylic 24th Exhib & Nat Audubon Soc Exhib, Nat Acad Galleries, New York, 77 & 78; Am Artists

Professional League, Bergen Co Mus, NJ, 80; Nat Soc Painters Casein & Acrylic 28th Ann Exhib, Nat Arts Club, New York, 81. *Awards:* Travel Awards, Nat Soc Painters Casein & Acrylic, 81-84 & Wash Square Outdoor Art Exhib, 81-82. *Mem:* Nat Soc Painters Casein & Acrylic; Am Portrait Soc. *Media:* Acrylic, Pencil. *Mailing Add:* 23 Elmwood Dr Clifton NJ 07013

KOSTER, MARJORY JEAN
PRINTMAKER
b Grand Rapids, Mich, Feb 9, 26. *Study:* Univ Mich Exten Night Sch, 47-64; Pratt Graphic Workshop, New York, summer 64. *Work:* Metrop Mus Art, New York; Brooklyn Mus Art, NY; Art Inst Chicago; Detroit Art Inst, Mich; Grand Rapids Art Mus, Mich; and others. *Exhib:* Ann Exhib Prints & Drawings, Oklahoma Art Ctr, 67; 7th Ann Mercyhurst Col Nat Graphics Exhib, Erie, Pa, 67; 3rd Nat Print & Drawing Exhib, Western Mich Univ, Kalamazoo, 68; 16th Nat Print Exhib, Brooklyn Mus, 68; 1st Nat Print Exhib, Honolulu, 71. *Mem:* Nat Inst Arts & Lett. *Media:* Woodcut. *Mailing Add:* 940 Maynard NW Grand Rapids MI 49504

KOSTIUK, MICHAEL MARION, JR
ASSEMBLAGE ARTIST, BOOK ARTIST
b Paris, Tex, Dec 9, 44. *Study:* Univ Tex, Austin, 63-66; Md Inst Art, Baltimore, 69; Visual Studies Workshop, Rochester, NY, 73. *Work:* Mus Fine Arts, Boston; Dallas Mus Fine Arts; New Orleans Mus Art; Whitte Mus, San Antonio Mus Asn, Tex; Humanities Res Ctr, Univ Tex, Austin. *Exhib:* San Francisco Mus Mod Art, 75 & 76; Philadelphia-Houston Exchange, Univ Pa Inst Contemp Art, Philadelphia, 76 & 77; Young Tex Artist Ser, Amarillo Art Ctr, 77; Four Texans: About Photog, Whitte Mus, San Antonio Mus Asn, 77; Bookworks, Dayton Art Inst, Ohio, 78 & 79; Attitudes: Photog in the 1970's, Santa Barbara Mus Art, 79; Smithsonian Inst, traveling, 81; Walker Art Ctr, Minneapolis, Minn, 81; and others. *Pos:* Proj dir, Bookworks: 1982 Conf, Philadelphia, 81-83. *Bibliog:* Dave Simpson (auth), Four Texans: About Photography, San Antonio Mus Asn, 77; Jon Holmes (auth), Deep in the heart of Texas, Camera, 8/77; Tom Livesay (auth), Young Texas Artist Ser, Artspace, fall 77. *Publ:* Contribr, Darkroom Dynamics: a Guide to Creative Darkroom Techniques, Van Nostrand, Reinhold, Curtin & London, 79; co-auth, Two by two, Houston City Mag, Tex, 79. *Dealer:* Books & Bookart 15 Gramercy Park New York NY 10003. *Mailing Add:* 1140 N 63 St Philadelphia PA 19151

KOSTYNIUK, RONALD P
SCULPTOR, EDUCATOR
b Sask, Can, July 8, 41. *Study:* Univ Sask, BSc & BEd; Univ Alta, BFA; Univ Wis, MS & MFA. *Work:* Edmonton Art Gallery, Alta; Saskatoon Art Gallery, Sask; Kresge Art Found, Detroit, Mich; Can Coun Art Bank, Ottawa, Ont; Dalhousie Univ, Halifax, NS. *Comn:* Relief mural, exec off Paul Albertsen Ltd, Winnipeg. *Exhib:* One-man shows, Mem Univ, St John's, Nfld, 73, Sarnia Art Gallery, Ont, 74, Univ Moncton, NB, 74, Mt St Vincent Univ, Halifax, NS, 75 & Univ Calgary, Alta, 78. *Teaching:* Prof design & sculpture, Univ Calgary, Alta, 71-, head grad studies, Dept Art. *Awards:* Can Council Arts Bursary, 69; Foreign Exchange Scholar, External Affairs Govt Can, 78; Killam Resident Fel, Univ Calgary, 79. *Bibliog:* Jan Van der Marck (auth), Relief sculpture, 69; John Stocking (auth), Relief sculptures, Arts Mag, 75; John Graham (auth), Kostyniuks reliefs, Vie des Arts, 75. *Mem:* Royal Can Acad Art; Univ Art Asn; Can Conf of the Arts. *Mailing Add:* 4907 Viceroy Dr Calgary AB T3A 0V2 Canada

KOSUTH, JOSEPH
CONCEPTUAL ARTIST
b Toledo, Ohio, Jan 31, 45. *Study:* Toledo Mus Sch of Design, 55-62; Cleveland Art Inst, 63-64; Sch of Visual Arts, New York, 65-67. *Work:* Mus of Mod Art, New York; Nat Gallery of Can, Ottawa, Ont; Tate Gallery, London, Eng; Solomon Guggenheim Mus, New York; Whitney Mus of Am Art, New York. *Exhib:* One-man shows, Pasadena Art Mus, Calif, 70, Aarhus Kunstmuseum, Denmark, 70, Kunstmuseum Luzern, Switz, 73 & Mus van Hedendaagse Kunst, Gent, Belg, 77; Practice Praktijk Pratique, Int Cult Ctr, Antwerp, Belg, 75; Art Now, John F Kennedy Ctr for Performing Arts, Washington, DC, 74; Mus Mod Art, Oxford, 78; and others. *Pos:* Rev critic, Arts Mag, New York, 67; Am ed, Art-Lang J, New York, 69-73. *Teaching:* Fac mem, Sch Visual Arts, New York, 68-; lectr, Univ Chile, Santiago, 71. *Bibliog:* Catherine Millet (auth), Joseph Kosuth, Flash Art, 2-3/71; Elizabeth Baker (auth), JK: Information Please, Art News, 2/73; Bruce Boice (auth), Kosuth: two shows, Artforum, Vol 11 (1973). *Publ:* Coauth, Germano Celant, ed, Function, Ed Sperone, 70; auth, Art after philosophy, Art Press, 72; coauth, Art & Language, DuMont Int, 72; auth, Dopo la filosofia l'arte, Data, 72; auth, Un Texte de Joseph Kosuth, Art Press, 74. *Dealer:* Caremn Lamanna Gallery 840 Yonge Street Toronto Ontario Can M4W 2H1. *Mailing Add:* c/o Carmen Lamann Gallery 840 Yonge St Toronto ON M4W 2H1 Canada

KOTALA, STANISLAW WACLAW
PAINTER, LIBRARIAN
b Boleslawiec, Poland, Sept 27, 09; US citizen. *Study:* Inst Design, Poland, dipl, 37; Acad Fine Arts, Cracow, Poland, with K Sichulski & P Dadlez, 38-39; Acad Fine Arts, Dusseldorf, Ger, with T Champion & W Heuser, BA, 49; Rutgers Univ, New Brunswick, MLS, 65. *Work:* Dom Wojska Polskiego, Warszawa, Poland; Mus Slaskie, Katowice, Poland. *Exhib:* Int Festival, Polish Arts Exhib, Edinburgh, Gt Brit, 47; Polish-Am Artist Exib, Kosciuszko Found, New York, 50; Nat Exhib Paintings by Am Artists of Polish Descent, Alliance Col, Cambridge Springs, Pa, 51; Plastyka za Drutami, Warszawa, 63; one-man show, Samuel Fleisher Art Mem, Philadelphia, 60. *Pos:* Artist-painter, Cordey China Art Studio, Philadelphia, 52-59; art ref librn, Free Libr Philadelphia, 59- *Teaching:* Dir art hist, Inst Art Teachers, Dossel,

Ger, 43-44; instr com art, Com High Sch, Lippstadt, Ger, 46-47. *Awards:* First Award, Off Club, 45; First Prize, Acad Fine Arts, Dusseldorf, 48. *Bibliog:* W Borzecki (auth), W zwierciadle sztuki, Nowy Swiat, 10/15/50; W Denkowski (auth), S W Kotala lecture, Gwiazda, 2/6/69. *Mem:* Am Libr Asn. *Media:* Watercolor, Oil. *Publ:* Illusr, Nasz Plomyczek, 46; illusr, Wiadomosci, 46. *Mailing Add:* 8147 Revere St Philadelphia PA 19152

KOTIK, CHARLOTTA
CURATOR, HISTORIAN
b Prague, Czech, Dec 13, 40; US citizen. *Study:* Kunsthistorisches Inst, Univ Wien, 65; Charles Univ, Prague, BA(art hist), 66, MA(art hist), 68. *Collections Arranged:* Jiri Kolar: Transformations (auth, catalog), 78, With Paper, About Paper (auth, catalog), 80, Jennifer Bartlett (auth, catalog), 80, Figures: Forms and Expressions (auth, catalog), 81 & Fernand Leger (auth, catalog), 81, Albright-Knox Art Gallery, Buffalo, NY. *Pos:* Cur asst, Jewish Mus, Prague, Czech, 58-61; cur asst, Nat Gallery, Prague, Czech, 61-64; assoc & asst cur, Nat Trust, Prague, Czech, 67-70; cur, Albright-Knox Art Gallery, Buffalo, NY, 70-83; cur, Brooklyn Mus, 83- *Teaching:* Tutor fine arts, Empire State Col, Buffalo, NY, 76-83; adj asst prof, State Univ NY Buffalo, 79-83. *Res:* Contemporary American art and architectural history. *Publ:* Coauth, Contemporary Art 1942-72, Collection Albright-Knox, 72; co-auth, Albright-Knox Art Gallery, Paintings and Sculpture from Antiquity to 1942, 78; co-auth, Fernand Leger, Abbeville Press, 81. *Mailing Add:* Dept Prints & Drawings Brooklyn Mus Brooklyn NY 11238

KOTOSKE, ROGER ALLEN
SCULPTOR, EDUCATOR
b South Bend, Ind, Jan 4, 33. *Study:* Univ Notre Dame, Ind, 50-52; Univ Denver, Colo, BFA, 54, MA, 56. *Work:* Rockhill Nelson Gallery, Kansas City, Mo; State Univ NY Col Oswego; Denver Art Mus; Franklin Mint, Philadelphia. *Comn:* Large outdoor sculpture, City of Denver, 68. *Exhib:* Artist Teacher Today USA, State Univ NY Col Oswego, 68; one-man shows, Pollock Gallery, Southern Methodist Univ, Dallas, 69 & James Y Gallery, New York, 76; Report from Soho, Grey Gallery, New York, 76; Contemp Am Painting & Sculpture, Indianapolis Mus Art, 78; Ill Painters III Traveling Exhib, 81-81; and others. *Teaching:* Prof art, Univ Denver, 58-68; prof art, Univ Ill, Urbana, 68- *Awards:* Purchase Awards, Nelson-Atkins Mus, 59 & State Univ New York Col Oswego, 68. *Bibliog:* Meilach & Kowal (coauth), Sculpture Casting, Crown Publ, 72; Meilach (auth), The Artist Eye, Regnery Press, 72; Verhelst (auth), Sculpture: Tools, Materials and Techniques, Prentice-Hall, 73. *Media:* Acrylic, Wood. *Dealer:* Brena Gallery 313 Detroit Denver CO 80222. *Mailing Add:* 1611 W White St Champaign IL 61820

KOTROZO, CAROL DONNELL
HISTORIAN, CRITIC
b St Louis, Mo, Oct 7, 45. *Study:* Pomona Col, BA, 67; Univ Calif, Los Angeles, MA, 68, PhD, 72. *Teaching:* Assoc prof art & aesthet, Ariz State Univ, 72- *Mem:* Am Soc Aesthet. *Res:* Aesthetics; modern art. *Publ:* Auth, Representation versus expression in the art of Gauguin 3/75 & The purloined paradigm: Critical evaluation of art and language group, 3/77, Art Inst; auth, The problem of post-impressionist art, Brit J Aesthet, 7/75; auth, Synaesthesia and aesthetic education, 7/77 & Cezanne, cubism, and the destination theory of style, 10/79, J Aesthet Educ. *Mailing Add:* 6144 Camelback Manor Dr Paradise Valley AZ 85253

KOTT, ETHEL FISHER See Fisher, Ethel

KOTTEMANN, GEORGE & NORMA
COLLECTORS
Dr Kottemann, b St Louis, Mo, Aug 17, 31; Mrs Kottemann, b Springfield, Ill, Jan 1, 32. *Collection:* Contemporary paintings, prints and sculpture. *Mailing Add:* 3300 N Bigelow Peoria IL 61604

KOTTLER, HOWARD WILLIAM
SCULPTOR, EDUCATOR
b Cleveland, Ohio, Mar 5, 30. *Study:* Ohio State Univ, BA, 52, MA, 56, PhD, 64; Cranbrook Acad of Art, Bloomfield Hills, Mich, MFA, 57. *Work:* Victoria & Albert Mus, London, Eng; Nat Mus of Mod Art, Kyoto, Japan; Cleveland Mus of Art; Mus of Contemp Crafts, New York; Detroit Inst of Art, Mich. *Exhib:* A Decade of Ceramic Art, 1962-72, San Francisco Mus Art, 72; Sensible Cup Int Exhib, Kanazawa-shi, Japan, 73; Illusionistic-Realism Defined in Contemp Ceramic Sculpture, Long Beach Mus, Calif, 77; A Century of Ceramics in the USA: 1878-1978, Everson Mus Art, Syracuse, 79; The Reality of Illusion, Denver Art Mus, Colo, 79; Another Side of Art: Ceramic Sculpture of Northwest: 1959-1979, Pavilion, Seattle Art Mus, Wash, 79; plus others. *Teaching:* Instr art hist, Ohio State Univ, 61-64; prof ceramics, Univ of Wash, 64- *Awards:* US Govt Fulbright Grant, 57; Arts-Craftsman's fel, Nat Endowment Arts, 75; Japan-US Friendship Comn Travel Grant, 78; and others. *Bibliog:* Nancy McCauley (auth), Artist explores six concepts, Sunday Oregonian, 67; Sally Hayman (auth), Crafts enter 20th century, Seattle Post-Intelligencer, 68; C E Licka (auth), A prima facie clay sampler, Current Mag, 75. *Mem:* Am Craftsman's Coun. *Media:* Clay. *Mailing Add:* Sch of Art Univ of Wash Seattle WA 98195

KOTTLER, LYNN
DEALER
b New York, NY. *Study:* Columbia Univ; NY Univ; City Col New York; New Sch Social Res. *Pos:* Founder, Acad Galleries, 40-44; founder, Portrait Painters Guild, 45-48; dir, Lynn Kottler Galleries, 49- *Specialty:* Paintings, sculpture and all media by leading contemporary artists, both American and foreign. *Mailing Add:* 3 E 65th St New York NY 10021

KOTUN, HENRY PAUL
MUSEUM DIRECTOR
b Uniontown, Pa, July 31, 31. *Study:* Mus Art Sch, Hagerstown; Syracuse Univ; Corcoran Sch Art, Washington, DC; George Washington Univ, MA, 66. *Comn:* Stage sets for hist pageant, Rogers Co, Ohio, 62-63. *Exhib:* Cumberland Valley Exhib, Co Mus, Hagerstown, Md, 56-68; Md Craft Coun Traveling Exhib, 65; Land of Pleasant Living, WCBM Gallery, Baltimore, Md, 69; Easton Acad Fine Arts, Md, 69. *Collections Arranged:* 200 yrs Am Interiors, 76; Art in Bloom, 78; Antique Laces, 79; Three Views thru Six Eyes, 80; Contemp English Landscapes, 81; Paintings by James Voshell, 81; and others. *Pos:* Color designer & consult, Jurica Bros Biol & Zool Charts, Chicago, 50-52; dir, The Gallery, Hagerstown, 66-70; dir, Washington Co Mus Fine Arts, 70- *Teaching:* Instr, Washington Co Bd Educ, Md, 55-70; instr ceramics & sculpture, Mus Art Sch, Hagerstown, 66-68; instr art appreciation, ceramics & sculpture, Hagerstown Jr Col, 66-69; instr crafts, Shepherd Col, 67-68. *Awards:* Mus, Award Sculpture, Washington Co Mus Fine Arts, 68. *Mem:* Am Asn Mus; Washington Co Arts Coun (pres, 67-70); Nat Art Educ Asn. *Mailing Add:* 428 N Potomac Hagerstown MD 21740

KOTZKY, ALEX SYLVESTER
CARTOONIST
b New York, NY, Sept 11, 23. *Study:* Art Students League, 41. *Pos:* Free-lance commercial artist, 46-57; cartoonist syndicate strip Duke Hand, 58-59, syndicate strip Apt 3-G, Field Enterprises, 61- *Mem:* Nat Cartoonists Soc. *Mailing Add:* 203-17 56th Ave Bayside NY 11364

KOURSAROS, HARRY G
PAINTER
b Reading, Pa, Feb 14, 28. *Study:* Albright Col, Reading, Pa, BA, 50; George Washington Univ Law Sch, Washington, DC, 50-53; Am Univ, Washington, DC, MFA, 56. *Work:* Birmingham Mus, Ala; Reading Mus, Pa; Neuberger Mus, Purchase, NY; Prudential Insurance Co, Newark, NJ; Newark Mus, NJ. *Comn:* Blue Archangel (silkscreen), Reading Mus, Pa, 74; four-panel painting, Pa State Univ, Wyomissing, Pa, 79. *Exhib:* Perspective 1976, Freedman Gallery, Reading, Pa, 76; Persistent Patterns, Andre Zarre Gallery, New York, 79; New York Pattern Painting, Ill Wesleyan Univ, Bloomington, 80; Islamic Allusions, Alternative Mus, New York, 80; retrospective, Freedman Gallery, Reading, Pa, 81; Art on Paper, Weatherspoon Art Gallery 17th Ann, Greensboro, NC, 81. *Teaching:* From assoc prof to prof painting, Albright Col, Reading, Pa, 64- *Awards:* Fulbright Fel, 56; Fulbright Grant Award, 57; Pa Arts Coun Grant, 83. *Bibliog:* Robert Browning (auth), article, Arts Mag, New York, 11/81 & 5/83; Theodore Wolff (auth), Decorative--It can be a misleading word in art, Christian Sci Monitor, Boston, 11/10/81; John Yau (auth), article, Art Am, 10/83. *Media:* Oil, Acrylic. *Dealer:* Haber-Theodore Gallery 24 W 57th St New York NY 10019; Ana Sklar Gallery 1019 Kane Concourse Bay Harbor Islands FL 33154. *Mailing Add:* 362 W Broadway New York NY 10013

KOUWENHOVEN, JOHN A
WRITER, EDUCATOR
b Yonkers, NY, Dec 13, 09. *Study:* Wesleyan Univ, AB; Columbia Univ, AM & PhD. *Collections Arranged:* Backgrounds of Modern Design, for Modern Living Exhib, Detroit Inst Arts, 49; Art Out of the Attic Exhib, Vt Coun Arts, Johnson Art Ctr, Middlebury, Vt, 70. *Pos:* Trustee, Vt Coun Arts, Montpelier; mem adv bd, Arch Am Art, Smithsonian Inst; trustee, Park-McCullough House Assocs. *Teaching:* Prof vernacular in Am arts of design, Barnard Col, Columbia Univ, 46-75, emer prof, 75- *Awards:* Governor's Award for Excellence in the Arts, Vt, 82. *Publ:* Auth, Made in America: The Arts in Modern Civilization, 48; auth, The Columbia Historical Portrait of New York, 53; auth, The Beer Can by the Highway: Essays on What's American about America, 61; auth, Half a Truth Is Better Than None: Some Unsystematic Conjectures on Art, Disorder, and American Experience, Chicago, 82. *Mailing Add:* Dorset VT 05251

KOVATCH, JAK
PRINTMAKER, EDUCATOR
b Los Angeles, Calif, Jan 17, 29. *Study:* Univ Calif, Los Angeles, 46; Chouinard Art Inst, Los Angeles, 47-49; Calif Sch of Art, Los Angeles, 49-50; Univ Southern Calif, Los Angeles, 51; Los Angeles City Col, 55-56; Art Students League, spec study with Michael Ponce de Leon, 72 & 75. *Work:* Fogg Mus Art, Harvard Univ; Libr Congress; Joseph Hirshhorn Collection; Fairfield Art Collection, Town Hall, Conn; John Slade Ely House Collection, New Haven. *Exhib:* Los Angeles Co Mus Art, 49, 54 & 55; Boston Mus Fine Arts, 54; Libr Congress, 54; Butler Inst Am Art, 54; M H de Young Mem Mus, San Francisco, Calif, 54; Mus Mod Art, New York, 56; Wadsworth Antheneum, Hartford, Conn, 58 & 72-76 & 79; Audubon Artists Inc, Nat Acad Galleries, New York, 73-78; Nat Acad Design Exhib, 77 & 80; Boston Ctr Arts, 76; Honolulu Acad Arts, Hawaii, 77; Print Club, Philadelphia, Pa, 78; and over 250 others. *Pos:* Student asst, Lynton Kistler Lithography Studio, Los Angeles, 52-53; animation dept, Walt Disney Prod Inc, Burbank, Calif, 53-54. *Teaching:* Instr, Famous Artists Schs Inc, Westport, Conn, 57-59, New York City Col Exten Div, 59-60; assoc prof, Univ Bridgeport, Conn, 62- *Awards:* Mellon Found Fel, 79-83; Zinn Ltd Award, Audubon Artists, Nat Arts Club, New York, 81; Conn Comn Arts Grant, 84-85; and others. *Mem:* Audubon Artists; Artists Equity; Westport-Weston Arts Coun, Conn; Los Angeles Printmaking Soc; Silvermine Ctr Arts; and others. *Media:* Multimedia. *Dealer:* Silvermine Ctr for Arts Inc 1037 Silvermine Rd New Canaan CT 06880. *Mailing Add:* 34 Sasco Creek Rd Westport CT 06880

KOVINICK, PHILIP PETER
WRITER, HISTORIAN
b Detroit, Mich, July 4, 24. *Study:* Calif State Univ, Chico, BA & MA. *Mem:* Collegium Western Art (pres). *Res:* Art and artists of the American West, 1819 to present. *Publ:* Auth, South Dakota's other Borglum, SDak Hist, 71; auth, The Woman Artist in the American West, 1860-1970 (catalog), 76; coauth, Women artists: The American frontier, Art News, 12/76. *Mailing Add:* 4735 Don Ricardo Dr Los Angeles CA 90008

KOVNER, SAUL
PAINTER, PRINTMAKER
b Russia, Jan 13, 04; US citizen. *Study:* Nat Acad Design, with Ivan Olinski, Charles W Hawthorne & William Auerbach-Levy, 20-28. *Work:* Libr Cong, Washington, DC; Metrop Mus Art, New York; Montpelier Mus Art, Vt; Tel-Aviv Mus Art, Israel; State Teachers Col, Indiana, Pa. *Comn:* Mural, Evavder High Sch, Bronx, NY, 38. *Exhib:* Pa Acad Fine Arts, Philadelphia, 32; Art Inst Chicago, 38; Whitney Mus Art, New York, 38; Corcoran Gallery, Washington, DC, 41; Am Printmakers, Downtown Gallery, New York; and many others. *Awards:* Pa Acad Fine Arts Award for Child With Instrument, 32; Soc Am Etchers Award for Picnic; Art Inst Chicago Award for Day of Rest, 39. *Bibliog:* Walter Gutman (auth), article, Art in Am, 31; Janice Lovoos (auth), Art of Saul Kovner, Am Artist, 68. *Mem:* Am Watercolorists (first pres, 38); Soc Am Etchers & Lithographers. *Media:* Oil, Watercolor; Lithograph. *Mailing Add:* 11733 La Maida St North Hollywood CA 91607

KOWAL, DENNIS J
SCULPTOR, WRITER
b Chicago, Ill, Sept 9, 37. *Study:* Art Inst Chicago; Univ Ill, Chicago Circle; Southern Ill Univ, BA, 61, MFA, 62. *Work:* Gillette Corp, Boston; Lakeforest Col, Ill; Inst Contemp Art, Boston; Babson Col, Wellesley, Mass; Boston Univ, Mass; and many others. *Comn:* Monuments, Milton Acad, Mass, 78, Newsweb Corp, Chicago, 78, Bally Design Assocs, Pittsburgh, 80, Nat Fire Protection Asn, Batterymarch Park, Mass, 80 & 81, Federal Reserve Bank, Boston, 82 & many others. *Exhib:* Dorsky Gallery Ltd, New York, 74; Robert Freidus Gallery, New York, 77; Worthington Gallery, Chicago, 77-78; Mead Art Mus, Amherst Col, Mass, 78; NC Mus Art, 78; Gilbert Gallery Ltd, Chicago, 79; and many others. *Teaching:* Prof sculpture, Columbus Col Art, Ohio, 63-64, Univ Ill, Champaign, 66-70 & Mass Col Art, Boston, 71-72; vis lectr, Univ Ga, 73. *Awards:* Numerous awards, 70- *Bibliog:* Eva Jacob (auth), The real paper, Boston, 3/77; article, Portrait of the artist-The Boston art market and sculptor Dennis Kowal, 77; Rituals of celebrations, Dennis Kowal, Decade Mag, 79; and numerous others. *Mem:* Boston Visual Artists Union; New Eng Sculptors Asn, Boston; and others. *Media:* Multimedia. *Publ:* Contribr, Contemporary Wood Sculpture, 68, contribr, Contemporary Stone Sculpture, 69 & auth, Casting Sculpture, 72, Crown; auth, Artists speak, NY Graphic Soc, 76. *Mailing Add:* 602 Jerusalem Rd Cohasset MA 02025

KOWALEK, JON W
MUSEUM DIRECTOR, LECTURER
b Swarthmore, Pa, Dec 11, 34. *Study:* Kutztown State Col, BS; Pa State Univ, MArtEd; Cranbrook Acad Art, MFA; Kunstgewerbe Mus, Zurich, Switz; also studies in Eng, France & Italy. *Collections Arranged:* Major exhibs of Phillip Pearlstein, 68, Mark Tobey, 71, Video Tape as Fine Art, 71, Morris Graves, 72; Wood Sculpture of the Northwest, 73 & Japanese Imari, 74; Imperial Robes of China, 78; The American Eight (auth, catalog), 79. *Pos:* Asst dir, Flint Inst Arts, Mich, 63-65; dir, Ft Lauderdale Mus Art, Fla, 66-67; dir, Art Galleries, Univ South Fla, 68-69; dir, Tacoma Art Mus, Wash, 69-; mem, Gov Adv Comn on the Arts, 78- *Awards:* 1974 Award Excellence in the Arts, City of Tacoma Arts Comn, 74. *Mem:* Int Comn Mus; Am Asn Mus; Asn Art Mus Dirs; Western Asn Art Mus (vpres, 70); Wash Arts Consortium (vpres, 77, pres, 78). *Publ:* Auth, Carl Lander, Lunar Landings, 72; auth, Mark Tobey, 72; auth, Video Tape as Fine Art, 73; auth, Arts of China, 81; auth, China Revisited, 82; and others. *Mailing Add:* 818 N Tenth Tacoma WA 98403

KOWALKE, RONALD LEROY
PAINTER, PRINTMAKER
b Chicago, Ill, Nov 8, 36. *Study:* Univ Chicago, 54-56; Art Inst Chicago, 54-56; Rockford Col, BA, 59; Cranbrook Acad Art, MFA, 60. *Work:* Mus Mod Art & Metrop Mus Art, New York; Libr Cong & Nat Gallery, Washington, Dc; Rockford Col, Ill. *Exhib:* Nat Print Exhib, Calif Soc Etchers, San Francisco Mus Art, 65; 15th Ann Print Exhib, Brooklyn Mus, 66; New Directions 1982, Hawaii Artist League, Amfac Plaza Gallery, 82; Hawaii '82-Works on Paper, Univ Hawaii, Hilo, 82; Hawaii Craftsman '82, Amfac Plaza Gallery, 82; two-man exhib, Structures, Art Loft Gallery, Hawaii, 83; Easter Arts Festival, Ala Moana Art Ctr, Hawaii, 83. *Teaching:* Instr design, Northern Ill Univ, 60-61; instr drawing, design & printmaking, Swain Sch Design, New Bedford, Mass, 61-64; assoc prof art, Univ Hawaii, 69-72, prof, 72- *Awards:* Purchase Awards, Honolulu Acad Arts, 69 & 71; Faculty Res Grant, Univ Hawaii, 69 & 70; Faculty Travel Grants, Univ Hawaii, 79 & 82. *Bibliog:* Dantes Inferno: A Portfolio of Ten Etchings, Impressions Workshop, Boston, 70; Gentle Words and Gentle People: A Portfolio of Ten Etchings, Univ Hawaii, Honolulu, 71; Artists of Hawaii, Vol 11, Univ Hawaii Press, 77. *Mem:* Honolulu Printmakers. *Dealer:* Associated American Artists Inc 663 Fifth Ave New York NY 10022; Ferdinand Roten Inc 123 W Mulberry Baltimore MD 21201. *Mailing Add:* Univ of Hawaii 1801 University Ave Honolulu HI 96844

KOWALSKI, DENNIS ALLEN
SCULPTOR, EDUCATOR
b Chicago, Ill, May 14, 38. *Study:* Univ of Ill, Chicago (archit), 55-57; Sch Art Inst Chicago, BFA(sculpture), 62; Sch Art Inst Chicago, MFA(sculpture), 66. *Work:* Gov State Univ; Ill State Univ; Art Inst Chicago. *Comn:* Outdoor sculpture, Univ of Chicago, 75. *Exhib:* Art Inst Chicago, 65-66, 75 & 80; Artpark, Lewiston, NY, 78; Indianapolis Mus of Art, 78; one-man shows, NAME Gallery, 76 & 80 & Marianne Deson Gallery, 78, 81 & 83, Chicago; Wards Island, New York, 79-83; Semaphore Gallery, New York, 83; and others. *Teaching:* Assoc prof sculpture, Univ of Ill, Chicago, 70- *Awards:* Fel-Grant, Nat Endowment Arts, 75; Grant, Ill Arts Coun, 80, Fel, 80. *Bibliog:* Holliday T Day (auth), article, Art in Am, 9-10/78; Holly Day (auth), The syntax of shelter, New Art Examiner, 3/80; Alan Artner (auth), article, Chicago Tribune, 10/7/83; and others. *Media:* Mixed. *Dealer:* Marianne Deson Gallery 226 E Ontario Chicago IL 60611. *Mailing Add:* 4134 N Damen Ave Chicago IL 60618

KOWALSKI, RAYMOND ALOIS
PAINTER
b Erie, Pa, June 21, 33. *Study:* Pa State Teachers Col, Edinboro; Cleveland Inst Art, BFA, 77. *Work:* State of Pa Educ Syst. *Exhib:* May Show, Cleveland Mus Art, 69-71; one-man show, Bluffton Col, Ohio, 70; Preview 71, Mt St Joseph's Col, Cincinnati, 71; Butler Mus Show, Youngstown, Ohio; one-man show, Green Mansion Gallery, Cleveland, 79; Ohio State Fair, 79; Willoughby Fine Arts Ctr, Ohio, 79; May Show, Cleveland Mus Art, 83; and others. *Pos:* Designer, Am Greetings Corp, Cleveland, 59-65, art dir, 65-, managing art dir, 73-, dir, Creative Planning, 81, dir design, 83. *Teaching:* Instr design, Cooper Sch Art, Cleveland, 69-70; instr painting for local art groups, 70- *Awards:* Award, Jewish Community Ctr Ann, Cleveland Heights, 79; Award, Erie Art Ctr Ann, Penn, 79; Ohio State Fair, 81; and others. *Bibliog:* Helen Borsick (auth), article in Cleveland Plain Dealer Suppl, 68; Ray Kowalski--painter of houses, Wonderful World Ohio, 10/69; Ray Kowalski-House Painter, WKYC-TV, Cleveland. *Media:* Acrylic, Collage. *Mailing Add:* 2780 Berkshire Rd Cleveland Heights OH 44106

KOZLOFF, JOYCE
PAINTER, ENVIRONMENTAL ARTIST
b Somerville, NJ, Dec 14, 42. *Study:* Carnegie Inst Technol, BFA, 64; Columbia Univ, MFA, 67. *Work:* Brooklyn Mus, Metropolitan Mus Art, Mus Mod Art, New York; Nat Gallery Art, Washington, DC; Neue Galerie Sammlung Ludwig, Aachen, WGer; and many others. *Exhib:* Painting Ann, 72 & Whitney Biennial, 79, Whitney Mus Am Art; one-woman exhibs, Everson Mus, 79, Mint Mus, 80, Renwick, Smithsonian Inst, 80-81, Joslyn Mus, 82, Inst Contemp Art, Philadelphia, 83 & Del Mus, Wilmington, 84; Drawings: A Pluralist Decade, 39th Venice Biennale, Am Pavilion, 80; Arts on the Line, Hayden Gallery, Mass Inst Technol, 80; Printed Art: A View of Two Decades, Mus Mod Art, New York, 80; A Private Vision: Contemporary Art from the Graham Gund Collection, Mus Fine Arts, Boston, 82; Soft as Silk, Wadsworth Atheneum, 82; Back to the USA, Lucerne Mus, Switz, 83; and others. *Teaching:* Instr ACE prog, Queens Col, Flushing, NY, 71-72; instr, Sch Visual Arts, 73-74, Art Inst Chicago, 75, Syracuse Univ, 77 & Univ NMex, 78. *Awards:* Creative Artists Pub Serv Grant, NY State Coun Arts, 73 & 75; Am Asn Univ Women Grant, 75; Nat Endowment Arts Grant, 77. *Bibliog:* Jeff Perrone (auth), Joyce Kozloff, Artforum, 11/79; Robin White (auth), Joyce Kozloff, In: View, Crown Point Press, 81; Robert Jensen & Patricia Conway (auths), Ornamentalism, Clarkson N Potter, 82. *Mem:* Heresies Collective. *Media:* Acrylic; Ceramic Tiles. *Publ:* Auth, Thoughts on my art, In: Name Book I, Name Gallery, Chicago, 77; coauth (with Valerie Jaudon), Art hysterical notions of progress and culture, Heresies IV, winter 78; auth, Frida Kahlo at the Neuberger Museum, Art in Am, 5-6/79. *Mailing Add:* 152 Wooster St New York NY 10012

KOZLOFF, MAX
PHOTOGRAPHER
b Chicago, Ill, June 21, 33. *Study:* Univ Chicago, BA, 53, MA, 58; Inst Fine Arts, NY Univ; Fulbright scholar, France, 62-63. *Pos:* Art critic, The Nation, 61-69; NY corresp, Art Int, 62-64; contrib ed, Artforum, 63-74, exec ed, 74-76; photogr, one-man shows, Holly Solomon Gallery, New York, 77 & 79. *Teaching:* Cooper Union, 60-61; Wash Sq Col, NY Univ, 61-62; Calif Inst Arts, 70-71; Yale Univ, 74. *Awards:* Pulitzer Fel in Critical Writing, 62-63; Frank Jewett Mather Award in Art Criticism, 66; Guggenheim Fel, 68-69. *Publ:* Auth, Renderings: Essays on a Century of Modern Art, 68; auth, Jasper Johns, 69 & new text, 72; auth, Cubism/Futurism, 74; auth, Photography and Fascination, 79; contribr art & photography criticism to major journals. *Mailing Add:* 152 Wooster St New York NY 10012

KOZLOW, RICHARD
PAINTER
b Detroit, Mich, May 5, 26. *Study:* Cass Tech, Detroit; Detroit Soc Arts & Crafts. *Work:* Art Gallery Windsor, Ont; Akron Art Mus, Ohio; Ohio Univ Mus Art, Athens; Detroit Inst Arts; Butler Art Mus. *Comn:* Four Seasons (four-part mural), Am Savings & Loan, Detroit, 60; Sky Series (three paintings), Ford Motor Co, NAAO Bldg, Dearborn, Mich, 80; The Opera's Not Over (painting), Yaffe-Berline Inc, Southfield, Mich, 81; Great Ideas of Western Man Series, Container Corp Am. *Exhib:* Mich Artists Exhib, Detroit Inst Arts, 50, 53, 58 & 63; Regional Ann, Butler Inst Am Art, 52; 20th Century Am Art, San Diego Art Mus, 68; Lithographs from Mourlot Graphics, Hudson River Mus, New York, 70; solo exhibs, Art Gallery of Windsor, Ont, 77, Ohio Univ, Athens, 82 & Am Embassy, Madrid, Spain, 84; and others. *Teaching:* Instr & dept head, Detroit Soc Arts & Crafts, 50-60;

instr special workshops, Birmingham-Bloomfield Art Asn, Mich, 70-79; artist in residence, Inst Allende, San Miguel Allende, Gto, Mexico, formerly; instr special travel workshops, Costa Rica, 81, Smokey Mountains, 81 & Mexico, 82. *Awards:* Founders Award, Mich Artist Exhib, Detroit Inst Arts, 63. *Bibliog:* Louise Brunner (auth), Landscape painting of Richard Kozlow, Am Artist Mag, 56; Wendon Blake (auth), Complete Guide to Acrylic Painting, Watson-Guptill. *Media:* Acrylic. *Publ:* Auth & illusr, Of Man's Inhumanity to Man, Lark Press, 65. *Dealer:* Schweyer-Galdo Gallery Birmingham MI; El Presidio Gallery Tucson AZ. *Mailing Add:* 176 Suffield Birmingham MI 48009

KOZLOW, SIGMUND
PAINTER, INSTRUCTOR
b New York, NY, Dec 7, 13. *Study:* Nat Acad Design; Fontainbleau Sch Fine Arts, France. *Work:* Indiana Univ Pa; Munson-Williams-Proctor Inst, Utica, NY; Univ Ga; Mus Fine Arts, Springfield, Mass. *Exhib:* Rockport Art Asn Ann, Mass, 72-79; Springfield Mus Nat Ann, Mass; Hunterdon Art Ctr, Clinton, NJ, 77; Phillips Mill Ann, New Hope, Pa; one-man show, Rockport Art Asn, Mass, 77 & 79; and others. *Pos:* Pres, Delaware Valley Artists Asn, 52-60; trustee, Hunterdon Art Ctr, Clinton, NJ, 71. *Teaching:* Instr painting, Summit Art Ctr; instr painting, Annie S Kemmerer Mus, Bethlehem, Pa, 79. *Awards:* Pulitzer Prize, Nat Acad Design, 36-37; S J Wallace Truman Award, 45; Marine Award, Silvermine Guild Artists, Conn, 60. *Mem:* Audubon Artists; Allied Artists Am; Rockport Art Asn; Acad Artists Asn; Allied Artists NJ. *Media:* Oil, Pastel. *Dealer:* Grand Central Art Galleries 40 Vanderbilt Ave New York NY 10017; Kozlow Gallery Bearskin Neck Rockport MA 01966. *Mailing Add:* RD 1 Box 125 Phillipsburg NJ 08865

KOZLOWSKI, EDWARD C
PAINTER, DESIGNER
b Bridgeport, Conn, Mar 11, 27. *Study:* Butera Sch Fine Art, 47; Whitney Sch Art, portrait with Simka Simkovitch, dipl, 51; Yale Sch Design, color with Josef Albers, BFA, 54. *Work:* Yale Univ, New Haven, Conn. *Exhib:* Connecticut Yale Artists, Yale AA Gallery, New Haven, 76; 2nd Ann Int Soc Arts, Foothills Art Ctr, Golden, Colo, 79; 27th Ann Nat Soc Painters Casein & Acrylic, Nat Arts Club, New York, 80; 3rd Ann, Salmagundi Club, New York, 80; 156th Ann, Nat Acad Design, New York, 81. *Pos:* Staff artist, Bridgeport Post, Conn, 47-54; advert designer, Int Silver Co, Meriden, Conn, 54-56; dir packaging develop, Warner Packaging, Bridgeport, Conn, 56-64; owner, Edward C Kozlowski Design Inc, New York, 64- *Teaching:* Instr design, Pratt Inst, Brooklyn, 65-69. *Awards:* Best Show, 20th Ann, Barnum Festival Soc, 80; Best Acrylics, 20th Ann, Barnum Festival Soc, 80; Frederick Lowey Award, Salmagundi Club, 81. *Mem:* Salmagundi Club; Conn Classical Arts; Am Inst Graphic Arts; Advertising Club Fairfield Co (pres, 64-65). *Media:* Acrylic, Watercolor; Conte Pencil, Lithograph. *Publ:* Coauth, The package designer looks at packaging materials, Packaging Design, 64; contribr, Changing times, Indust Design, 75; auth, Job sheet: A better link between packager and marketer, Product Mgt, 76. *Dealer:* Art/Place 400 Center St Southport CT. *Mailing Add:* 74 Columbine Dr Trumbull CT 06611

KRAEFT, JUNE K & NORMAN
DEALER, COLLECTOR
June, b Chippewa Co, Wis, Feb 23, 28, Norman, b St Louis, Mo, Sept 5, 19. *Study:* June, Univ Wis, Eau Claire; Iowa State Univ; Norman, Univ Ill, Urbana, BA, 41. *Pos:* Co-dirs, June 1 Gallery, Washington, DC, 71-75 & Bethlehem, Conn, 75- *Specialty:* American prints, 1900-1950. *Publ:* Coauths, Armin Landeck: The Catalog Raisonne of His Prints, June 1 Gallery, 77; coauths, four articles on American prints, Graphics Mag, 79; coauths, American Architectural Etchers: The Traditionalists (exhib catalog), 80; coauths, Great American Prints: 1900-1950, Dover Publ (in prep). *Mailing Add:* June 1 Gallery Bellamy Lane & Lake Dr Bethlehem CT 06751

KRAKOW, BARBARA L
DEALER
b Boston, Mass, June 9, 36. *Study:* Boston Univ, BA, 58. *Pos:* Owner & dir, Barbara Krakow Gallery, Boston, currently; art adv panel, Internal Revenue Service, 80- *Specialty:* American art 1945 to present, paintings, sculpture, drawings and prints. *Mailing Add:* Barbara Krakow Gallery 10 Newbury St Boston MA 02116

KRAMER, BURTON
DESIGNER, GRAPHIC ARTIST
b New York, NY, June 25, 32. *Study:* Inst Design, Ill Inst Technol, BSc(visual design), 54; Yale Univ Sch Fine Arts, MFA(design), 57; also with Josef Albers & Paul Rand. *Exhib:* Biennial Graphic Design, Brno, Czech, 70, 74 & 78; Can Graphic Design, Tokyo, Japan, 75; Spectrum Can, Montreal, 76; VI Poster Biennale, Warsaw, Poland, 76; RCA Designers 78, Toronto, 78. *Pos:* Chief designer, Halpern Advert, Zurich, Switz, 62-65; dir corp graphics, Clairtone Sound Corp, 66-67; pres, Burton Kramer Assocs, Ltd, Graphic Design Consult. *Teaching:* Mem design fac, Ont Col Art, 77- *Awards:* Gold Medal Award, Int Typographic Composition Asn, 71; Gold Medal Award, Art Dir Club, 73. *Mem:* Royal Can Acad Art; fel Graphic Designers Can (pres, 75-77); Alliance Graphique Int; Am Inst Graphic Arts; Allgemein Schweizer Grafiker. *Publ:* Auth, Typographic eye, New York, 74; auth & contribr, Top trademarks and symbols of the world, Milan, 74; auth & ed, Idea Mag, Tokyo, 75; auth, Canadian Interiors, Toronto, 75. *Mailing Add:* Burton Kramer Assocs Ltd 20 Prince Arthur Ave Suite 1E Toronto ON M5R 1B1 Canada

KRAMER, GERTRUDE M
DEALER
b Germany; US citizen. *Pos:* Vpres & asst dir, Arras Gallery, Ltd, New York, 71- *Specialty:* Contemporary art. *Mailing Add:* Arras Gallery Ltd 29 W 57th St New York NY 10019

KRAMER, HILTON
CRITIC
b Gloucester, Mass, Mar 25, 28. *Study:* Syracuse Univ, BA; Columbia Univ; New Sch Social Res; Harvard Univ; Ind Univ. *Pos:* Assoc ed & feature ed, Arts Digest, 54-55; managing ed, Arts Mag, 55-58, ed, 58-61; chief art critic & art news ed, New York Times, formerly. *Teaching:* Lectr art today. *Publ:* Auth, The Age of the Avant-Garde, Farrar, Straus & Giroux, 74; contribr, Arts Mag, Partisan Rev, Commentary, New Repub, New York Rev Bks, Encounter, Art in Am, Artforum, The Hudson Rev, Artscanada & others. *Mailing Add:* New York Times 229 W 43rd St New York NY 10036

KRAMER, JACK N
PAINTER, EDUCATOR
b Lynn, Mass, Feb 24, 23. *Study:* Sch Mus Fine Arts, Boston, with Karl Zerbe, dipl(Albert H Whittin Traveling Fel), 49; Univ Reading, with J Anthony Betts, 50; with Oskar Kokoschka, London, 50; RI Sch Design, BFA, 54. *Work:* Addison Gallery Am Art; Phillips Acad, Andover, Mass; William Gurlitt Mus, Linz, Austria. *Exhib:* Boston Psychoanalytic Soc & Inst, Mass, 77; Cambridge Art Asn, Mass, 78; Gallery of World Art, Newton, Mass, 79; Attleboro Mus, Mass, 81; Kingston Gallery, Mass, 81; Wenniger Graphics Gallery, Boston, 81; and others. *Pos:* Pres, Artists Studio Co-op, Fenway Studios Inc, 82. *Teaching:* Instr, Sch Vision, Salzburg, Austria, 55-58; prof art, Boston Univ, 57- *Awards:* Thomas B Clarke Award, 157 Ann, Nat Acad Design, 82. *Bibliog:* Portfolio of drawings, Audience Mag, 61; Portfolio of drawings, Liberal Context, 65. *Mem:* Copley Soc Boston. *Media:* Oil. *Publ:* Auth, Human Anatomy & Figure Drawing, 72. *Mailing Add:* Fenway Studios 30 Ipswich St Boston MA 02215

KRAMER, JAMES
PAINTER
b Columbus, Ohio, Oct 24, 27. *Study:* Cleveland Sch Art; Western Reserve Univ; Ohio State Univ; studied painting with Carl Gaertner & Frank Wilcox. *Work:* Monterey Peninsula Mus Art, Calif; Georgetown Hist Soc, Colo; United Bank Denver; Univ Nevada, Reno; Colo Heritage Ctr Mus, Denver. *Exhib:* Mainstreams 74, Marietta Col, Ohio, 74; Nat Acad Western Art, Cowboy Hall Fame, Okla City, 77-81; Western Heritage Sale & Auction, Houston, Tex, 81; Contemp Western Art Exhib, Haley Mem Libr, Midland, Tex, 81; Artists of America, Mus Colo Heritage Ctr, Denver, 81; and many others. *Teaching:* Watercolor workshop, Mont Art Educ Asn, Great Falls, 74; watercolor workshop, Soc Western Artists, Fresno, Calif, 75 & Ghost Ranch, Abiquiu, NMex, 80. *Awards:* Robert Wolfe Mem Prize, Columbus Gallery Fine Art, 49; Best of Show, Mother Lode Art Asn, 72; Gold Medal, Calif Art Club, 73. *Mem:* Nat Acad Western Art. *Media:* Watercolor. *Publ:* Contribr, The Watercolor Page, Am Artist Mag, 73; contribr, 40 Watercolorists & How They Work, 76 & Executive Diary, 76, Watson-Guptill; contribr, Paint has a soul, Southwest Art, 82. *Dealer:* Wadle Galleries Santa Fe NM; Carson Gallery Western Am Art Denver CO. *Mailing Add:* 631 Calle de Valdes Santa Fe NM 87501

KRAMER, MARJORIE ANNE
PAINTER
b Engelwood, NJ, Apr 21, 43. *Study:* Cooper Union, BFA, 66; New York Studio Sch, with M Matter & C Cajori. *Exhib:* New Images in American Figurative Painting, Queens Mus, NY, 74-75; Report from Soho, NY Univ Grey Art Gallery, New York, 76; Acquisition Show, Randolph-Macon Women's Col, 76; In Praise of Space Am Landscape Painting, Parsons Sch Design, 76; Johnson State Col, Dibden Ctr, 79; Artists Choice, Tibor de Nagy Gallery, New York, 80; and others. *Pos:* Ed, Women & Art Quart, New York, 71-72. *Teaching:* Instr, Artists Environment, Delaware Water Gap, 77. *Bibliog:* Larry Campbell (auth), article, Art News Mag, 71; Joyce Kozloff (ed), Interviews with 10 women artists, Sch Visual Arts, 74; Bob Sievert (auth), Majorie Kramer, WomanArt Mag, summer 77. *Mem:* Alliance Figurative Artists. *Media:* Oil, Watercolor. *Mailing Add:* RR 1 Box 92A Lowell VT 05847

KRAMER, REUBEN
SCULPTOR
b Baltimore, Md, Oct 9, 09. *Study:* Rinehart Sch Sculpture, Europ traveling scholar, 31 & 33; Am Acad Rome; Acad Grand Chaumiere. *Work:* Baltimore Mus Art, Md; Corcoran Gallery Art, Washington, DC; Peale Mus, Baltimore; Harvard Univ Law Libr; Univ WVa Dental Hall. *Comn:* Statue of Supreme Court Justice Thurgood Marshall, 80. *Exhib:* Prix Rome Exhib, 36; Nat Art Week, IBM Corp, Md, 41; Int Sculpture Show, Philadelphia, 49; Nat Inst Arts & Lett, 64; 35 Years of Sculpture & Drawings, Retrospective Exhib, Jewish Community Ctr, Baltimore, Md, 74; 50-Yr Retrospective of Reuben Kramer's Art, Baltimore Mus Art, 78. *Teaching:* Pvt instr sculpture, 39-; instr sculpture, Adult Educ, Baltimore City Col & Polytech Inst; head dept sculpture, Am Univ, 51-52. *Awards:* Prix de Rome, Am Acad Rome, 34; Nat Inst Arts & Lett Grant, 64; Statue Award, nat competition, 77. *Bibliog:* Alton Balder (auth), Six Maryland Artists, Balboa Publ, 55; Man the Maker (film), WMAR-TV, Baltimore, 61; Theodore L Low (auth), The Art of Reuben Kramer, Walters Art Gallery, 63. *Mem:* Artists Equity Asn (vpres, 68). *Media:* Bronze. *Mailing Add:* 121 Mosher St Baltimore MD 21217

KRAMRISCH, STELLA
CURATOR, EDUCATOR
b Vienna, Austria; US citizen. *Study:* Univ Vienna, PhD; three hon doctorates. *Collections Arranged:* Art of Nepal (auth, catalog), Asia House, New York, 64; Unkown India: Tribal & Ritual Art (auth, catalog), Philadelphia Mus Art, 68; Manifestations of Shiva (auth, catalog), Philadelphia Mus Art, 81. *Pos:* Ed, J Indian Soc Oriental Art, 32-50; emer cur Indian & Himalayan art,

Philadelphia Mus Art, 54-; ed, Artibus Asiae, 60- *Teaching:* Prof Indian art, Univ Calcutta, 23-50; lectr Indian art, Courtauld Inst, Univ London, 37-40; prof SAsian art, Univ Pa, 50-69; prof Indian art, Inst Fine Arts, NY Univ, 64- *Awards:* Bollingen Found Fel; Austrian Cross of Honor for Sci & Art; Padma Bhushan Award, India, 82. *Bibliog:* Joseph Dye (auth), Marsyao, Vol 17, 75; B S Miller (auth), Exploring India's Sacred Art, Univ Pa Press, 83. *Publ:* Auth, Indian Sculpture, 32 & 81; auth, The Hindu Temple, 46 & 76. *Mailing Add:* Philadelphia Mus of Art PO Box 7646 Philadelphia PA 19101

KRANE, SUSAN
CURATOR, HISTORIAN
b Gary, Ind, June 8, 54. *Study:* Carleton Col, BA(magna cum laude), 76; Columbia Univ, MA, 78. *Collections Arranged:* Figures: Forms & Expressions (auth, catalog), 81; Surfacing Images: The Paintings of Joe Zucker (auth, catalog), 82; Judy Pfaff (auth, catalog), 82; Jan Kotik: The Painterly Object (auth, catalog), 84; Mario Merz (auth, catalog), 84. *Pos:* Rockefeller Found Intern, Walker Art Ctr, Minneapolis, 78-79; asst cur, Albright-Knox Art Gallery, Buffalo, NY, 79-82, assoc cur 83, cur 83- *Teaching:* Adj prof art hist, State Univ NY, Buffalo, 80- *Publ:* Contribr, Sonia Delaunay, 80, coauth, Made for Buffalo, 80 & auth, Jim Pomeroy: 3D Photos, 81, Albright-Knox Art Gallery. *Mailing Add:* c/o Albright-Knox Art Gallery 1285 Elmwood Ave Buffalo NY 14222

KRANKING, MARGARET GRAHAM
PAINTER, INSTRUCTOR
b Florence, SC, Dec 21, 30. *Study:* Am Univ, Washington, DC, BA(summa cum laude, Clendenin Fellow in Art Hist), 52; pvt study with Edith McCartney, Sister Irenita Ecklin & Ralph Smith. *Work:* Fed Nat Mortgage Asn, United Nuclear Corp & Wall St J, Washington, DC; Triton Investment Co Inc; Philip Morris USA; and others. *Comn:* Portrait, Rear Admiral Harold C Train & Vice Admiral Harry D Train II, comn by Mrs Harold C Train, Washington, DC, 71; portrait, Dr Cecile Bolton Finley, Univ Va, Mrs Joseph V Marcoux, Alexandria, Va, 79; Charles H Jones, Water Pollution Control Fed, Washington, DC, 83. *Exhib:* 7th Ann Area Show, Corcoran Gallery of Art, Washinton, DC, 52; Maryland Biennial, Baltimore Mus of Art, 74 & 76; 37th Ann Exhib, Watersolor Soc of Ala, Birmingham Mus of Art, 77; 54th Ann Nat April Exhib, Springville Mus of Art, Utah, 78; one-man shows, Dunbarton Col Art Gallery, Washington, DC, 72; Spectrum Gallery Inc, 74, 76, 78, 79, 81 & 83 & Gallery Kormendy, Alexandria, Va, 79; The Fascinating Cat, Mid-Am Arts Alliance, Kansas City, Mo, 80-81; Philip Morris USA, Richmond, Va, 82 & 83; and others. *Pos:* Asst to head of publications, The Nat Gallery of Art, 52-53. *Awards:* Second Place, Watercolor Okla, Oklahoma City, 78; Purchase Award, WTex Watercolor Soc, 79; Mobay Purchase Award, Pittsburgh Watercolor Soc, 82; and others. *Mem:* Artists Equity; Potomac Valley Watercolorists (pres, 81-83); Acad Artists Asn; Southern Watercolor Soc. *Media:* Watercolor, Pastel. *Dealer:* Spectrum Gallery Inc 3033 M St Washington DC 20007; Capricorn Galleries 4849 Rugby Ave Bethesda MD 20814. *Mailing Add:* 3504 Taylor St Chevy Chase MD 20815

KRANTZ, LES (LESLIE J)
EDITOR, PUBLISHER
b St Louis, Mo, Dec 20, 45. *Study:* Univ Mo, BA, 68. *Pos:* Publ, The Krantz Co, Chicago, currently; ed, The Chicago Art Review, 77-, The New York Art Review, 78-, The Washington DC Art Review, 80-, The California Art Review, 81-, The Texas Art Review, 82- & The Southwest Art Review, 83-, Krantz Co. *Bibliog:* John Greenwater (dir), Literary Critic (film), PBS, 80; Jo Ann Lewis (auth), article, Washington Post, 81; Allen Artner (auth), article, Chicago Tribune, 81. *Mem:* Chicago Artists Coalition; Art Inst Chicago; Mus Contemp Art, Chicago. *Mailing Add:* 2210 N Burling Chicago IL 60614

KRASHES, BARBARA
PAINTER, DIRECTOR
b New York, NY. *Study:* Art Students League, with Reginald Marsh, Julian Levi & Vaclav Vytlacil; NY Univ, BS; Hunter Col, NY; Educ Alliance, with Chaim Gross; New Sch Social Res, New York. *Work:* Ulrich Mus Art, Wichita, Kans; St Lawrence Univ Mus, Canton, NY; Am Can Co, New York; The Katz Agency, Inc, Chicago; Dartmouth Col Mus, Hanover, NH. *Exhib:* Art: 1965, Am Express Pavilion, New York World's Fair; Am Abstract Artists, Riverside Mus, NY, 68; Fordham Univ at Lincoln Ctr, New York, 80; NY Univ, 80; Hyde Collection, Glens Falls, NY, 78. *Pos:* Arts dir, Adult Educ Ctr, New York. *Awards:* George B Bridgman Mem Scholar, Art Students League. *Bibliog:* Art World Problems (tape), Today's World, Fordham Univ, 73; *Mem:* Int Asn Art, US Comt; Fedn Mod Painters & Sculptors, Inc (pres, 70-74); Art Students League; NY Artists Equity Asn. *Media:* Mixed-Media. *Publ:* Contribr, Art '65 Lesser Known & Unknown Painters, Young Am Sculpture-East to West, 65; contribr, The New York Arts Calendar (spec issue) for New York World's Fair Am Express Show, 65; contribr, The Art Gallery, 66; contribr, Feigin Memorial Collection (catalog), St Lawrence Univ, 71. *Mailing Add:* 77 W 85th St New York NY 10024

KRASNER, LEE
PAINTER
b Brooklyn, NY, 1908. *Study:* Woman's Art Sch, Cooper Union, 26-29; Nat Acad Design, 29-32; City Col New York, 33; also with Hans Hofmann, 38-40. *Work:* Philadelphia Mus Art; Whitney Mus Am Art, New York; Nat Gallery Australia; also in pvt collections. *Exhib:* Mus Mod Art, New York, 69; one-man shows, Whitney Mus, New York, 73-74; Traveling Exhib, Corcoran Gallery, Washington, DC, 75; Mus Mod Art, New York, 78; Centre Culturel Americain, Paris, France, 79; Metrop Mus Art, New York, 79; Guggenheim Mus, New York, 79; Heckscher Mus, Huntington, NY, 79; Hirshhorn Mus, DC, 80; Saidye Bronfman Ctr, Montreal, 80; Wildenstein Gallery, London, England, 80; and others. *Awards:* Lowe Fel Distinction, Barnard Col, 74. *Mailing Add:* The Springs East Hampton NY 11937

KRATINA, K GEORGE
SCULPTOR

b New York, NY, Feb 12, 10. *Study:* Syracuse Univ, BS & MS; Yale Univ, BFA. *Comn:* Ceramic relief, St Bonaventure Univ, NY; wood statues, St Paul Cathedral, Los Angeles; sanctuary mosaic sculptures, Fac Chapel, Fr Judge Sem, Va; steel sculpture, Adath Israel Temple, Merion, Pa; Uncle Sam heroic monument, Troy, NY, 80; and many others. *Teaching:* Prof design, Sch Archit, Rensselaer Polytech Inst, 63-77, emer prof archit & art, 77-; prof, Div Art & Archit, Cooper Union, formerly. *Awards:* Prix de Rome, 38; Nat Prize for Sculpture Competition for Cath Welfare Bldg, Washington, DC, 40; Awards for Collaboration Excellence, Am Inst Architects, 41, 58 & 60. *Mem:* Fel Nat Sculpture Soc. *Mailing Add:* RD Box 76 Pitts Rd RR 1 Old Chatham NY 12136

KRATZ, MILDRED SANDS
PAINTER

b Pottstown, Pa. *Study:* With Edgar Whitney & Paul C Burns, Portugal. *Work:* Mint Mus; Gen Mills; Goodyear Inc; Fitchburg Mus; Motorola; and others. *Exhib:* Nat Acad Design, New York, 73-80; 45 one-woman shows incl, Fitchburg Art Mus, Mass, 75; Wistariahurst Mus, Holyoke, Mass, 79; Dyer-York Mus, Saco, Maine, 80; Canton Art Inst, 80. *Teaching:* Artist-instr, Queen Elizabeth II, New York to Eng, 75. *Awards:* Pa Senatorial Citation, 77; Grumbacher Award, Watercolor USA, 82; Gold Medal, Watercolor Soc Ohio, 83. *Bibliog:* Mildred Sands Kratz-Contemporary Artist, PBS Show. *Mem:* Am Watercolor Soc; Am Artists Prof League; Pottstown Area Artists Guild (co-founder & pres, 66); Philadelphia Water Color Club; Ohio Watercolor Soc. *Media:* Watercolor. *Publ:* Illusr, Nat Antiques Rev, 71; illusr, Stories of French Creek, 73; auth, Watercolor page, Am Artist Mag, 73; illusr, Prints, 83; illusr, Stitchery, 83. *Dealer:* Gallery II Exton PA 19341; Gallery Madison 90 New York. *Mailing Add:* 2988 Silverview Dr 1305 Lisa Ann Dr Stow OH 44224

KRAUS, (ERSILIA) ZILI
SCULPTOR, PAINTER

b Sat Chinez, Timisoara, Romania; US citizen. *Study:* Graphic Sketch Club, Philadelphia, Pa, 28-30; Nat Acad Design with Leon Kroll, 30-32; Barnes Found, Pa, 33-35; Samuel S Fleisher Art Mem with Frank Gasparro, 62-74; Inst Allende, San Miguel de Allende with Enrique Lopez, 72-81. *Work:* Cinnaminson Town Hall, NJ; Burlington Co Libr, Westhampton, NJ. *Comn:* Resurrection (mural), Calvin Presbyterian Church, Pa, 35; Yearbook (cover illustration), Columbia Univ Sch Health & Admin, New York, 67. *Exhib:* Puppeteer, Painting, Philadelphia Acad Fine Arts, Pa, 35; Earth Edge, Painting, Montreal Mus Fine Art, Quebec, 56; Sculptures, Regional Coun Community Art Ctrs, Philadelphia, Pa, 71, 75, 77, 79 & 81; Thru the Snow, sculpture, Philadelphia Mus Art, Pa, 75. *Collections Arranged:* Philadelphia Area Artists, Art Crafts Studio Gallery, 35-37; Membership Show, Cinnaminson Art Centre, 66-67; Triboro Artists, Burlington Co Libr, 69. *Pos:* Textile designer, Shapiro & Co, New York, 45-48. *Teaching:* Instr painting, Art League Long Island, Queens, NY, 50-51; instr painting, Northern Burlington City Region High School, Columbus, NJ, 64-65; instr beginning & advanced painting, Cinnaminson High Sch, NJ, 65-76. *Awards:* First Prize, Cheltenham Art Ctr, 77; First Prize, DaVinci Art Alliance, Henry Coscia, 79; First Prize, Woodmere Art Gallery, 80. *Mem:* Int Soc Artists, New York. *Media:* Oil, Pastel; Wood, Plaster. *Mailing Add:* 503 Wayne Drive Cinnaminson NJ 08077

KRAUSE, GEORGE
PHOTOGRAPHER, EDUCATOR

b Philadelphia, Pa, Jan 24, 37. *Study:* Philadelphia Col Art. *Work:* Mus Mod Art, New York; Bibliot Nat, Paris; Libr Cong, Washington, DC; Philadelphia Mus Art; George Eastman House, Rochester, NY. *Exhib:* Five Unrelated Photographers, Mus Mod Art, New York, 63; one-man shows, George Eastman House, Rochester, NY, 72, Philadelphia Print Club, 75, Mus Bellas Artes, Caracas, Venezuela, 76, Witkin Gallery, New York, 78, Houston Mus Fine Art, 78, Am Acad Rome, 79 & Pa Acad Fine Art, Philadelphia, 82. *Teaching:* Assoc prof photog, Bucks Co Community Col, Newtown, Pa, 73-75; prof photog, Univ Houston, 75-82, prof art, currently; dir photog workshops, Venice Photog Biennale, Italy, summer 79; artist in residence, Am Acad Rome, 79-80. *Awards:* Grants, Guggenheim Found, 76 & 77. *Bibliog:* Mark Power (auth), George Krause I, Monog Toll & Armstrong, 72; Nancy Hellebrand (auth), I Nudi/George Krause, Photo Rev, 80; Arno Minkkinen (auth), article, Contemp Photogr, 81. *Mem:* Am Acad Rome. *Publ:* Illusr, The photographer's eye, 66 & illusr, Looking at pictures, 73, Mus Mod Art; auth, I Nudi (catalog), Mancini, 80. *Dealer:* Mancini Gallery 5020 Montrose Houston TX 77006. *Mailing Add:* 420 E 25th St Houston TX 77008

KRAUSE, LAVERNE ERICKSON
PAINTER, PRINTMAKER

b Portland, Ore, July 21, 24. *Study:* Univ Ore, BS, 46; Mus Art Sch, Portland, 52-58; Pratt Graphic Ctr, New York, summer 66. *Work:* Seattle Art Mus; Portland Art Mus; Salt Lake Art Ctr, Utah; La State Univ Union, Baton Rouge; Deichmanske Bibliot, Oslo, Norway; plus others. *Exhib:* One-person shows, Deichmanske Bibliot, Oslo, 74, Rockford Col, Ill, 74 & Delta State Univ, 78; Artists of Oregon, Portland Art Mus Ann, 49-; six shows, Int Printmakers, Seattle Art Mus, 60-71; West Coast Graphics, Univ Ky, circulated by Smithsonian Inst, 71-72; Atelier Nord Exhib, Oslo, 75 & 82; and many others. *Teaching:* Vis artist, Mt Angel Col, Ore, summer 65; from asst prof to prof painting & printmaking, Univ Ore, 66-; vis assoc prof, La State Univ, Baton Rouge, summer 70. *Awards:* Ford Found Purchase Prize for Painting, 64; Governor's Arts Award, 80; Wurlitzer Found Grant, 81. *Mem:* Artists Equity Asn (nat pres, 69-70); Col Art Asn Am; Portland Art Asn; NW

Print Coun. *Media:* Oil, Acrylic; Etching, Monoprint. *Publ:* Illusr, Clouded Sea (etchings), 71, Deady & Villard (etchings), 74 & Portraits, Friends, Artists (etchings & woodcuts), 79, Press 22. *Dealer:* Fountain Gallery Art 117 NW 21st Ave Portland OR 97210; The Fountain Fine Arts 810 Madison St Seattle WA 98104. *Mailing Add:* 3295 W 16th Ave Eugene OR 97402

KRAUSHAAR, ANTOINETTE M
DEALER

b New York, NY, Dec 25, 02. *Pos:* Dir, Kraushaar Galleries, currently. *Specialty:* Twentieth century American art. *Mailing Add:* 724 Fifth Ave New York NY 10019

KRAUSS, ROSALIND E
CRITIC, HISTORIAN

b Washington, DC, Nov 30, 40. *Study:* Wellesley Col, BA, 62; Harvard Univ, PhD, 69. *Collections Arranged:* Joan Miro: Magnetic Fields, Guggenheim Mus, 71; 200 Years of American Sculpture, Whitney Mus Am Art, 76; Richard Serra, Mus Mod Art, New York, 85. *Pos:* Assoc ed, Artforum, 71-76; ed, October Mag, 76- *Teaching:* Assoc prof art hist, Mass Inst Technol, 65-71; lectr, Princeton Univ, 72-74; prof, Hunter Col, 75- *Awards:* Guggenheim Found Fel, 71; Mather Award Criticism, Col Art Asn, 72. *Res:* Theory and criticism of modernist art; history of photography. *Publ:* Auth, Terminal Iron Works: Sculpture of David Smith, MIT Press, 71; auth, Passages in Modern Sculpture, Viking Press, 77; auth, Sculpture of David Smith: Catalog Raisonne, Garland Press, 78; auth, The Originality of the Avant-Garde and Other Modernist Myths, MIT Press, 84. *Mailing Add:* 12 Greene St New York NY 10013

KRAUTH, HARALD
PAINTER

b Eberbach, Ger, June 29, 23; US citizen. *Study:* Paedagogium, Bad-Godesberg, Ger, Abitur, 42; studied with Keh Haber, 46-52; Dartmouth Col, with Hannes Beckmann, 70-74; Goddard Col, MA, 73; Union Grad Sch, PhD, 78. *Exhib:* Painters of Bonn, Mus City Bonn, Ger, 51; Vt Invitational, Norwich Univ, 69, 70 & 72-; solo exhibs, Goddard Col, 73 & Dartmouth Col, 74; Vt Artists, Fleming Mus, 76. *Teaching:* Assoc prof & chmn dept philos, religion & fine arts, Norwich Univ, 68- *Bibliog:* Richard Wolkomir (auth), A Vermont artist & designer, Christian Sci Monitor, 75. *Mem:* Col Art Asn Am; Copley Soc Boston. *Media:* Tempera, Oil. *Publ:* Auth, The Weston Priory, Liturgical Arts, 70; auth, Artistic Photography, Methods & Techniques, Amphoto, 76. *Dealer:* Charles Fenton Gallery Woodstock VT 05091. *Mailing Add:* Turkey Hill Northfield VT 05663

KRAVIS, JANIS
DESIGNER, ARCHITECT

b Riga Latvia, Oct 20, 35; Can citizen. *Study:* Sch Archit, Univ Toronot. *Exhib:* Royal Can Acad Arts, Nat Gallery Can, Ottawa, 70. *Awards:* Ont Tourist Accommodation Award, 67; Ont Eedee Design Award, 67. *Mem:* Ont Asn Architects; Asn Can Indust Designers; Royal Can Acad Art; Royal Archit Inst Can. *Mailing Add:* 38 Cedarbank Cres Toronto ON M3B 3A4 Canada

KRAVITZ, WALTER
SCULPTOR, PAINTER

b Chicago, Ill, Oct 25, 38. *Study:* Art Inst Chicago, BFA(fel), 64; Syracuse Univ, MFA, 67. *Comn:* Suspended sculptures, comn by Mary Swift, Washington, DC, 82 & George Mason Univ, 83; pyramid with lights & sound, Artpark, New York, 83; stairwell installation, Washington Proj Arts, 83. *Exhib:* Installations, Washington Proj Arts, 81; Ten From DC, Lawndale Ctr, Univ Houston, 82; PS1, New York, 82. *Teaching:* Prof design, Philadelphia Col Art, 69-74; prof painting & drawing, George Mason Univ, 76- *Mailing Add:* 1017 Independence Ave SE Washington DC 20003

KREBS, ROCKNE
SCULPTOR

b Kansas City, Mo, Dec 24, 38. *Study:* Kans Univ, Lawrence, BFA, 61. *Work:* Phillips Collection, Smithsonian Inst, Corcoran Gallery Art, Hirshhorn Mus & Sculpture Garden, Washington, DC; Philadelphia Mus Art, Pa. *Comn:* Rite Da Passage (5 color laser pieces), New Orleans Mus Art, La, 71; Sky Bridge Green (laser structure), Philadelphia Mus Art, Pa, 73; The Laser, City St Petersburg, Fla, 75; The White Tornado (solar environmental sculpture), GSA New Federal Bldg, Topeka, Kans, 79; Still Green (laser environment), Disneyland Hotel, Anaheim, Calif, 79. *Exhib:* Seventh Area Exhib, Corcoran Gallery Art, Washington, DC, 65; Ann Sculpture, Whitney Mus Am Art, New York, 66; Gilliam, Krebs, McGowin, Corcoran Gallery Art, Washington, DC, 69; 69th Am Exhib, Art Inst Chicago, Ill, 70; Rockne Krebs Laser, Albright-Knox, Buffalo, NY, 71; Art & Technol, Los Angeles Co Mus Art, Calif, 71; Works for New Spaces, Walker Art Ctr, Minneapolis, Minn, 71; Projected Images, Walker Art Ctr, Minneapolis, Minn, 74; Sculpture Am Directions, Nat Mus Am Art, Washington, DC, 75; Laser Sculpture, Ft Worth Art Mus, Tex, 78. *Pos:* Bd dir, Washington Project Arts, 80- *Awards:* First Prize, Sculpture, Corcoran Gallery Art, 65; Individual Artist Fel Grant, Nat Endowment Arts, 70; J S Guggenheim Fel, 72. *Bibliog:* Paul Richard (auth), The city at night is light, Washington Post & News Serv, 73; Nina Felshin (auth), article, Art Int, 5/74. *Publ:* Coauth, Rockne Krebs, Artist on Their Art, 68 & Walter Hopps, and Nina Felshin, Three Washington Artists, 70, Art Int; coauth, Jane Livingston, Art & Technol Catalog, Los Angeles Co Mus, 71; coauth, Nina Felshin, Projected Images (catalog), Walker Art Ctr, 74; coauth, Sam Hunter, American Art, Abrams, 79. *Dealer:* Diana Brown Gallery 406 P St NW Washington DC 20036. *Mailing Add:* Box 6508 Washington DC 20009

KREEGER, DAVID LLOYD
PATRON, COLLECTOR
b New York, NY, Jan 4, 09. *Study:* Rutgers Univ, AB; Harvard Law Sch, LLB; numerous hon doctorates. *Mem:* Corcoran Gallery Art (pres bd trustees); Nat Mus Am Art Comn. *Interests:* Donor of Kreeger Ann Purchase Awards at Corcoran Gallery Biennial and area shows, Kreeger Ann Art Prize at Am Univ and prizes in painting, sculpture and art hist at George Washington Univ. *Collection:* Painting and sculptures, especially from mid-nineteenth century to the contemporary period. *Mailing Add:* 2401 Foxhall Rd NW Washington DC 20007

KREILICK, MARJORIE E
MOSAIC ARTIST, EDUCATOR
b Oak Harbor, Ohio, Nov 8, 25. *Study:* Ohio State Univ, BA, 46, MA, 47; Cranbrook Acad Art, MFA, 52; apprentice to Gulio Giovanette, Rome, 56; Am Acad in Rome, FAAR, 63. *Work:* Joslyn Mus, Omaha, Nebr; Col Mus Art. *Comn:* Marble pebble mural, Wonderland Shopping Ctr, Livonia, Mich, 59; ten marble murals, State Off Bldg, Milwaukee, 63; mosaic Foucault pendulum, Augustana Univ, Sioux Falls, SDak, 67; marble mosaic mural, Mayo Clinic, Rochester, Minn, 69; marble mosaic pool, Telfair Acad Arts & Sci, Savannah, Ga, 73. *Exhib:* Palace of Expos, Rome; Minn Mus Art, St Paul; solo show, Archit League, New York; Fairweather Hardin Gallery, Chicago. *Teaching:* Instr-docent design, Toledo Mus Art, 48-51; from instr to prof design-sculpture, Univ Wis-Madison, 53- *Awards:* Univ Wis Grant, 60; Prix de Rome, Am Acad in Rome, 61. *Mem:* Nat Soc Mural Painters; Int Asn Contemp Mosaicists, Ravenna, Italy. *Media:* Marble Mosaic. *Publ:* Contribr, Art in Architecture, 69. *Dealer:* Fairweather Hardin 101 E Ontario Chicago IL 60611. *Mailing Add:* 2713 Chamberlain Ave Madison WI 53705

KREITZER, DAVID MARTIN
PAINTER
b Ord, Nebr, Oct 23, 42. *Study:* Concordia Teachers Col, BS, 65; San Jose State Col, MA, 67. *Work:* Santa Barbara Mus, Calif; San Diego Mus, Calif; Joseph Hirshhorn Found, Washington, DC; Sheldon Gallery, Univ Nebr. *Comn:* Woman's Place & US Army Corps of Engrs, covers for Atlantic Mag, 70; California & the War, cover for Motorland Mag, 70; Tristan und Isolde (opera posters), Seattle, 81. *Exhib:* One-man shows, American Art Since 1850, 68, Maxwell Gallery, San Francisco; Ankrum Gallery, Los Angeles, 71, 75, 77 & 79-81; Gumps Gallery, San Francisco, 81; Benedictine Art Awards, New York, 69; 6th Mobile Ann, Ala, 71; Adelle Mus Fine Arts, Dallas, 83. *Teaching:* Instr painting, San Jose State Col, 68; instr life drawing, Poly State Univ, San Luis Obispo, Calif, 83. *Awards:* Ciba-Geigy Award, 71. *Bibliog:* Am Artist, 4/82. *Media:* Watercolor, Oil. *Mailing Add:* 1442 12th St 657 N La Cienega Los Osos CA 93402

KRENECK, LYNWOOD
PRINTMAKER
b Kenedy, Tex, June 11, 36. *Study:* Univ Tex, BFA, 58, MFA, 65. *Work:* Fine Arts Gallery San Diego, Calif; Wichita Art Asn Galleries, Kans; Print Collection, Philadelphia Mus Art; Springfield Art Mus, Mo; Art in Embassies Prog, US State Dept. *Exhib:* Libr of Cong Nat Print Show, 75; Minot Print & Drawing Competition, NDak, 78; Dulin Nat Print Exhib, Tenn, 79; 30 American Printmakers, Ohio State Univ, 81-82; British Biennial, 82; New American Graphics III, 83; and many others. *Teaching:* Prof printmaking, Tex Tech Univ, 65- *Awards:* Purchase Awards, Univ SDak Art Cnt Print & Drawing Ann, 81 & Univ SDak Print Show, 79, 83. *Mem:* Tex Watercolor Soc (dir-at-lg, 72-73); Boston Printmakers; Philadelphia Print Club; Los Angeles Print Soc; Soc Am Graphic Artists. *Media:* Serigraph. *Mailing Add:* 5224 14th St Lubbock TX 79416

KRENTZIN, EARL
SCULPTOR, SILVERSMITH
b Detroit, Mich, Dec 28, 29. *Study:* Wayne State Univ, BFA, 52; Cranbrook Acad Art, MFA, 54; Royal Col Art, London, Fulbright Fel, 57-58. *Work:* Detroit Inst Art, Mich; Cranbrook Galleries, Bloomfield Hills, Mich; St Paul Art Ctr, Minn; Jewish Mus, New York; Mus Contemp Crafts, New York. *Comn:* Enamel plaque, Gloria Dei Lutheran Church, Detroit, 54; Menorah, Temple Israel, Detroit, 63; metal sculpture, Westland Shopping Ctr, Detroit, 65; plus many pvt comn of silver sculptures. *Exhib:* Mus Contemp Crafts, New York, 63 & 65; NJ State Mus, Trenton, 70; one-man shows, Kennedy Galleries, New York, 68-75 & Detroit Inst of Art, 78, Oshkosh Mus, 82. *Teaching:* Instr art, Univ Wis-Madison, 56-60; vis prof silversmithing, Univ Kans, 65-66; vis prof metalwork, Fla State Univ, 69. *Awards:* Tiffany Grant, 66; Nat Decorative Arts Exhib, Wichita Art Ctr, Kans, 66. *Bibliog:* Article, Am Mag, 11-12/82. *Media:* Silver and Related Materials. *Publ:* Auth, Centrifugal casting, Craft Horizons Mag, 11/54. *Dealer:* Donna Jacobs Gallery Birmingham MI 48011. *Mailing Add:* 412 Hillcrest Grosse Pointe MI 48236

KRETSINGER, MARY AMELIA
GOLDSMITH, DESIGNER
b Emporia, Kans, Sept 29, 15. *Study:* Univ Kans, Lawrence, AB, 37; State Univ Iowa, Iowa City, MA, 41; grad study, Columbia Univ, New York & Ind Univ, Bloomington. *Work:* Johnson Wax Co Collection Contemp Am Art, Racine, Wis; Goldsmith's Hall, London; Mus Contemp Crafts, New York; Wichita Art Asn Galleries; Rochester Mem Gallery, NY. *Comn:* Gold & enamel box for pres award, Beech Air Corp, Wichita, 66; tabernacle and wall cross, St Peter's Church, Southwest Harbor, Maine, 70; crucifix & candleholders, Brandeis Univ Catholic Chapel, Waltham, Mass, 70; processional cross & font, Our Lady of Perpetual Help, North Windham, Maine, 71; baptismal font cover, St Andrew's Church, Emporia, Kans, 79.

Exhib: Philadelphia Art Alliance, 57-60; State Dept Europe, 60; Int Exhib Mod Jewelry, Goldsmiths Hall, London, 61; Int Handicrafts Exhib, Stuttgardt, WGer, 67; Objects USA, Lee Nordness Gallery, New York, 70; Art Gallery Ont, 71; Art of Cloisonne, Lowe Mus, Univ Miami, Fla, 72; Art of Enamels, Gallery State Col New York & Metrop Mus, New Paltz, 73; Exhib Liturgical Arts, 41st Int Eucharistic Cong, Philadelphia Civic Ctr, 76. *Teaching:* Assoc prof metalsmithing design, Emporia State Univ, Kans, 49-63; instr enameling, Brookfield Craft Ctr, Conn, 59 & 66; instr enameling, Worcester Craft Ctr, Mass, 63 & 65; instr cloisonne enameling, Young Women's Christian Asn, Dallas, 65; instr silversmithing & enameling, Wichita Art Asn, 69-71. *Awards:* Best in Show, Mid West Designer Craftsman, 59; Purchase Awards, Mus Contemp Crafts, 68, Wichita Art Asn, 69, Goldsmith's Hall, London, 69, Johnson Wax Co, 71 & Univ Neb, 76. *Bibliog:* Phillip Morton (auth), Contemporary jewelry, Holt, Rinehart & Winston, 2nd ed, 76; Thelma Newman & J H Newman (auths), The Container Book, Crown Publ, New York, 77; Lee Nordness (auth), Objects USA, Viking Publ, New York, 77. *Media:* Gold, Enamel. *Mailing Add:* 911 Market St Emporia KS 66801

KREZNAR, RICHARD J
SCULPTOR, PAINTER
b Milwaukee, Wis, May 1, 40. *Study:* Univ Wis, BFA; Brooklyn Col, MFA; Inst Allende, Mex. *Work:* Walker Art Ctr, Minneapolis; Milwaukee Art Mus, Wis; Univ Wis-Madison; Colgate Univ, Hamilton, NY; Sidney Lewis Best Co; and others. *Exhib:* Pa Acad Fine Arts, 63; Butler Inst Am Art, Youngstown, Ohio, 65; Milwaukee Art Ctr, 66; Wis Directions, Milwaukee Art Ctr, 75; Brooklyn Col Art Dept Past & Present, Robert Schoelkopf Gallery, New York, 77; The Mat Dominant--Some Current Artists & Their Media, Pa State Univ, University Park, 77; Small is Beautiful (traveling show), Freedman Gallery, Albright Col; one-man shows, Paley & Lowe Inc, New York, 72 & O K Harris Gallery, New York, 74, 76 & 83; Transparent Structures, Thorpe Intmedia Gallery, Sparkill, NY, 83; and others. *Teaching:* Instr studio art courses, Brooklyn Col, 64-73; asst prof, 74-79; instr, Parsons Sch of Design, 78; instr sculpture, Skowhegan Sch Painting & Sculpture, 78; instr sculpture, Philadelphia Col Art, 80-82; vis artist, Univ Wis-Milwaukee, 84. *Awards:* Ford Found Purchase Award, 62 & 64; Prizes, Milwaukee Art Ctr, 62, Wis Salon of Art, 63 & Walker Art Ctr, 64. *Dealer:* O K Harris Gallery 383 West Broadway New York NY 10012. *Mailing Add:* 284 Lafayette St New York NY 10012

KRIEGER, RUTH M
PAINTER, PRINTMAKER
b Newark, NJ, May 17, 22. *Study:* With Stuart Davis, 41; Moses Soyer, 42; Newark State Col, BA, 43. *Work:* State Mus, Trenton, NJ; Miss Art Asn, Jackson; Rosenberg Libr, Galveston, Tex; Burndy Engineering Co, Norwalk, Conn; Montclair State Col, NJ. *Exhib:* Conn Acad, Hartford Atheneum, Conn, 71; Audubon Artists, Nat Acad Gallery, New York, 71; Boston Printmakers, Boston Mus Fine Arts, Mass, 72; Ann Small Sculpture & Prints, Butler Inst, Youngstown, Ohio, 72; Assoc Artists of NJ, Montclair Art Mus, NJ, 74; Drawing Invitational, Hunterdon Co Art Ctr, Clinton, NJ, 81; Assoc Artists of NJ, Nabisco Galleries, Parsippany, NJ, 81. *Awards:* Clyde L Carnahan Award, 70 & 72; Second in Oils, Nat Acad New York, 70 & Conn Acad Ann, 71. *Mem:* Assoc Artists of NJ (pres 78-80, bd mem 74-); Artists Equity Asn of NJ. *Media:* Oils, Acrylic; Seriagraph, Cliche Verre. *Dealer:* Witchcraft Gallery Vose Ave South Orange NJ 07079. *Mailing Add:* 33 Winding Way West Orange NJ 07052

KRIENKE, DOUGLAS ELLIOT
DEALER, COLLECTOR
b Summit, NJ, Mar 31, 47. *Study:* Wilkes Col, BA, 73. *Pos:* Dealer-dir-owner, Whistler's Daughter Gallery Inc, Basking Ridge, NJ, 74- *Bibliog:* Marion Filler (auth), Ridge Gallery explores contemporary realism, Morristown Daily Record, 4/80; David Shirey (auth), The art sampler, New York Times, 6/80; Eye on the arts (film), NJ Pub Television, 11/81. *Specialty:* Eighteenth, nineteenth and twentieth century fine American paintings, including Philip Jamison, Ken Davies, Don Stone, Ray Ellis, Daivd Armstrong, Gary Erbe, Robert Vickery, Dan and Pauline Campanelli, Andrew Wyeth, J F Murphy, A T Britcher and A H Wyant. *Collection:* 19th and 20th century American and European painting. *Mailing Add:* Whistler's Daughter Gallery Inc 88 S Finley Ave Basking Ridge NJ 07920

KRIENKE, KENDRA-JEAN CLIVER See Cliver, Kendra-Jean

KRIENSKY, (MORRIS E)
PAINTER
b Glasgow, Scotland, July 27, 17; US citizen. *Study:* Boston Mus Fine Arts, 36-40, with Alma O LeBrecht; Art Students League, 48-49; Escuela Tech Mex, 50-51. *Work:* Pushkin Mus, Moscow; Alfred Khouri Mem Collection, Norfolk Mus, Va; Lincoln Ellsworth Collection; also in many pvt collections, US, China, USSR & Mex. *Exhib:* Am Watercolor Soc; Nat Acad Design; Inst Mex-Norte Am Relac Cult; one-man shows, Knoedler Gallery, White House, Washington, DC, Art Inst Chicago, Frick Art Libr, Univ Conn (15 yr retrospective) & many others. *Awards:* First Prize, Inst Mex-Norte Am Relac Cult, 50; and others. *Mem:* Visual Artists & Galleries Asn; Artist's Equity. *Media:* Oil, Pen & Ink. *Publ:* Auth, The Way is Peace, The Road is Love (drawings, paintings & poems), Gibson, 73; auth, The art of Art (painting & prose--formerly titles Visions of Hope & Faith), 76. *Dealer:* Gregory Bloch Honolulu HI. *Mailing Add:* 463 West St New York NY 10014

KRIESBERG, IRVING
PAINTER
b Chicago, Ill, Mar 13, 19. *Study:* Art Inst Chicago, BFA, 41; Escuela de Artes Plasticas, Esmeralda, Mexico City; NY Univ, MA, 72. *Work:* Mus Mod Art, Whitney Mus Am Art, Chase Manhattan Bank, New York; Corcoran Gallery; Detroit Inst Art. *Exhib:* One-man shows, St Louis Mus Art, Mo, 53, Everson Mus, 80, Rose Mus, Boston, 81 & Washington Univ Art Gallery, St Louis, 82; 16 Americans, Mus Mod Art, New York, 54; 10 Independents, Guggenheim Mus, New York, 71. *Teaching:* Prof painting, Yale Grad Sch, 62-70 & State Univ NY, 71-76. *Awards:* Ford Purchase Fund, 64; Guggenheim Mem, 76; Nat Endowment Arts, 81. *Media:* Oil. *Publ:* Auth, Looking at Pictures, Ford Found, 56; auth, Art, The Visual Experience, Pitman, 65; auth, Working with Color, Van Nostrand Reinhold, 84. *Dealer:* Terry Dintenfass 50 W 57th St New York NY 10013. *Mailing Add:* 210 Spring St New York NY 10012

KRIGSTEIN, BERNARD
PAINTER, ILLUSTRATOR
b New York, NY, Mar 22, 19. *Exhib:* Anchorage Mus, Alaska; Knickerbocker Artists Annuals; Audubon Artists Annuals; WPA Art: Then & Now, New York, 77; one-man show, Adirondack Ctr Mus, Elizabethtown, NY, 79; plus many other group & one-man shows. *Teaching:* Instr painting & drawing, High Sch Art & Design, New York, 62-70 & 71-81; asst prof fine art, Fashion Inst Technol, State Univ NY, 70-71. *Awards:* 40th Anniversary Award, Audubon Artists; Grumbacher Gold Medal, Allied Artists Am; Ralph Mayer Memorial Award, Am Soc Contemp Artists; and others. *Bibliog:* Jerry West, publ & John Benson, ed, Squa Tront 6, Special Issue: Bernard Krigstein, Cambridge, Mass, 75. *Mem:* Painters & Sculptors Soc NJ; Pastel Soc Am (bd dirs); WPA Artists; Artists Equity Asn of NY (mem bd dirs, 77, 78 & 79); Audubon Artists; and others. *Media:* Multimedia. *Publ:* Illusr, Manchurian Candidate, McGraw; illusr, Various Fables from Various Places, Capricorn-Putnam; illusr, Buccaneers & Pirates of Our Coasts, Random; illusr, Boy's Life Mag, Harpers Mag, Saturday Evening Post & many others; Comic Art Show, Whitney Mus. *Mailing Add:* 140-21 Burden Crescent Jamaica NY 11435

KRIMS, LESLIE ROBERT
PHOTOGRAPHER, CONCEPTUAL ARTIST
b New York, NY, Aug 16, 42. *Study:* Cooper Union, New York, BFA; Pratt Inst, Brooklyn, MFA. *Work:* Mus Mod Art, New York; Nat Gallery Can, Ottawa; Musee Nat d'Art Moderne, Centre Georges Pompidou, Paris; George Eastman House, Rochester, NY; Bibliot Nat, Paris. *Exhib:* One-man shows, George Eastman House, 69 & 71, Galerie Delpire, Paris, 74 & Fictcryptokrimsographs, Light Gallery, New York, 75; two-man show, Witkin Gallery, New York, 69 & 72; Photographs of Women, Mus Mod Art, 71; and others. *Teaching:* Lectr art, State Univ NY Col, Buffalo, 69-81, prof, 81- *Awards:* State Univ NY Res Found Grant & Grant-in-Aid, 70 & 71; Nat Endowment Arts Fel, 71, 72 & 76; NY State Coun Arts Grant, 71, 73 & 75. *Bibliog:* Article, Photo Image, Japan, 70, Camera, Switz, 71 & Zoom, France, 82. *Mem:* Soc Photog Educ. *Publ:* Auth & illusr, The Incredible Case of the Stack O'Wheats Murders, 72; auth & illusr, The Little People of America 1971, 72; auth & illusr, Making Chicken Soup, 72; auth & illusr, Fictcryptokrimsographs, 75; auth & illusr, Idiosyncratic Pictures, 80. *Dealer:* Robert Freidus Gallery 158 Lafayette St New York NY. *Mailing Add:* 187 Linwood Ave Buffalo NY 14213

KRINSKY, CAROL HERSELLE
HISTORIAN, EDUCATOR
b Brooklyn, NY, June 2, 37. *Study:* Smith Col, BA, 57; NY Univ, MA, 60, PhD, 65. *Teaching:* Prof fine arts, NY Univ, 65- *Mem:* Soc Archit Historians (NY chap pres, 79-81, first vpres, 82-); Col Art Asn; Planning Hist Group. *Res:* Renaissance Vitruvius studies; architecture in New York and Chicago; European synagogue architecture. *Publ:* Auth, Seventy-eight Vitruvius manuscripts, J Warburg & Courtauld Inst, Univ London, 67; auth, Vitruvius De Architectura, Wilhelm Fink Verlag, 69; auth, Rockefeller Center, Oxford Univ Press, 78; auth, St Petersburg on the Hudson: The Albany Mall, In: Art the Ape of Nature: Festschrift for HW Janson, Abrams, Prentice-Hall, 81; auth, Synagogues of Europe: Architecture and History, Archit Hist Found, Mass Inst Technol, 84. *Mailing Add:* 370 First Ave New York NY 10010

KRISTENSEN, GAIL MARIE
CERAMIST, SCULPTOR
b Miltown, Wis, Mar 3, 24. *Study:* Univ Minn, Minneapolis, 42-43 & 51-54; Iowa State Univ, Ames, 43-45; Drake Univ, Des Moines, 45-47. *Work:* Walker Art Ctr, Minneapolis; Minn Mus Art, St Paul; Denver Fine Arts Ctr; Greenville Fine Arts Mus, SC. *Comn:* Wall relief, Univac Corp, St Paul, Minn, 72; ct yard fountain, Unity Church, St Paul, 73; ceramic wall relief, Pacemaker Inc, St Paul, 77; ceramic wall relief, Production Credit Asn, River Falls, Wis, 78; ceramic wall relief, Pentair Corp, St Paul, 79. *Exhib:* Nat Ceramic Competition, Mus Mod Art, New York, 68; Kristensen Ceramics, Minn Mus Art, St Paul, 68 & 73; Nat Ceramic Expo, Milwaukee Art Ctr, Wis, 69; Exhib '70, Columbus Gallery Fine Arts, Ohio, 70 & Exhib '79, 79; Kristensen Ceramics, Minneapolis Inst Art, Minn, 74; Am Crafts, Gallery of Art Asn, Springfield, Ill, 80; Int Acad Ceramics Expo, Kyoto Mus, Japan, 80; and others. *Pos:* Com artist, Meredity Publ Co, Des Moines, Iowa, 56-57; guest Am artist-in-residence, Wurkunst Sch, Weisbaden, Ger, 62-64. *Teaching:* Resource instr, Univ Minn & numerous local cols & univs, 65-67; adj asst prof art, Macalester Col, 68- *Awards:* Nat Merit Awards, Am Craft Coun, 66 & 70; Purchase Award, Brooks Mem Gallery, 71. *Bibliog:* P Roghenberg (auth), Enamels on Metal, 69 & Complete Book of Ceramic Art, 72, Crown Publ Co; B Young (auth), Ceramics by Kristensen, 72. *Mem:* Artists' Equity Asn (local vpres, 76-79); Am Craft Coun; hon mem Int Acad

Ceramics, Switz; Minn Sculptors Soc. *Media:* Clay, Glass. *Publ:* Auth, articles, Ceramic Mo Mag, 4/67, 1/68 & 11/68. *Dealer:* Int Design Ctr 100 Second Ave N Minneapolis MN 55401. *Mailing Add:* 1775 Hillcrest Ave St Paul MN 55116

KROLIK, OLGA See Sheirr, Olga

KRONENGOLD, ERIC A
PHOTOGRAPHER, EDUCATOR
b Long Island, NY, June 29, 35. *Study:* San Francisco State Univ, BA, 66, MA, 70. *Work:* Bibliot Nat, Paris, France; Ctr Creative Photog, Univ Ariz; Chicago Art Inst; Ariz Comn Arts; Hayden Gallery, Mass Inst Technol. *Exhib:* Octave Prayer, Hayden Gallery, 72; Attitudes: Photog in the 70's, Santa Barbara Mus Art, Calif, 79; Am Vision, Washington Square E Gallery, New York, 79 & NY Univ, 80; Arboretum, Boulder Ctr Visual Arts; Shwayder Gallery, Univ Denver; Auraria Higher Educ Complex, Denver; and others. *Teaching:* Prof art photog, Ariz State Univ, Tempe, 70- *Bibliog:* Article, New Orleans Time, 4/79; and others. *Mem:* Soc Photog Educ. *Media:* Black & White Film, Color Film. *Publ:* Contribr, Young Photographers, Univ NMex Press, 68; contribr, Modern Photography, Vol 34, No 9, 70; contribr, Octave of Prayer, Aperture One, MIT Press, 72; contribr, Object and Image, Prentice-Hall, 2nd ed; auth, New America, A Review, Vol 3, No 1, Univ NMex Press. *Mailing Add:* 1136 W Tenth St Tempe AZ 85281

KRONSNOBLE, JEFFREY MICHAEL
PAINTER, EDUCATOR
b Milwaukee, Wis, Feb 9, 39. *Study:* Univ Wis-Milwaukee, BS, 61; Univ Mich, Ann Arbor, MFA, 63. *Work:* Mus Fine Arts, St Petersburg, Fla; Addison Gallery Am Art, Andover, Mass; Daytona Beach Mus Art; Fla Capitol Bldg; New Orleans Mus Art; and others. *Exhib:* Chicago & Vicinity Exhib, Art Inst Chicago, 61-63; one-man shows, New Orleans Mus Art, 67, Univ Fla, Gainesville, 75 & ACA Galleries, New York, 79 & 81. *Teaching:* Prof art, Univ SFla, 63- *Awards:* Thomas B Clarke Prize, Nat Acad Design, New York, 80; William A Paton Prize, Nat Acad Design, New York, 81. *Bibliog:* Barbara Gallati (auth), Jefferey Kronsnoble, Arts, 12/81. *Media:* Drybrush Oil, Charcoal. *Dealer:* ACA Galleries 21 E 67th St New York NY 10021. *Mailing Add:* 908 S Dakota Ave Tampa FL 33606

KROPF, JOAN R
CURATOR, LECTURER
b Cleveland, Ohio, Aug 4, 49. *Study:* Cleveland Art Inst; Cooper Sch Art; Cuyahoga Community Col; St Petersburg Jr Col. *Collections Arranged:* Worked with others to assemble and arrange, Important Writings of Dali, 74, Cancelled Graphic Plates, 75, Hiram College Graphics Show, 76, Erotic Art by Dali, 76, Dali's Anamorphoses, 77, Dali/Hasman Photography Exhib, 78, Important Dali Statements & Surrealist Documents, 79, Homage to Gala, 82, Secret Life Drawings, 82 & Flor Dali, 83, Salvador Dali Mus. *Pos:* Asst dir, Salvador Dali Mus, Cleveland, 71-76, dir, 76-82. *Mem:* Am Asn Mus. *Publ:* Auth, Secret Life Drawings, 82 & Flor Dali (photographs), 83, Salvador Dali Mus. *Mailing Add:* 1000 Third St S St Petersburg FL 23701

KRUEGER, LOTHAR DAVID
PAINTER, EDUCATOR
b Two Rivers, Wis, Sept 19, 19. *Study:* Milwaukee State Teachers Col, Wis, BS, 42; Univ Wis-Madison, MS, 47; Univ Iowa, with Mauricio Lassansky in printmaking, grad, 50; Ohio State Univ, Columbus, grad art hist, 53. *Work:* Wis Mem Union, Madison; Am Inst Architects, Ark Arts Ctr, First Nat Bank Little Rock & Pulaski Savings & Loan, Little Rock, Ark. *Exhib:* 6 Ann Exhibs Art, Springfield Art Mus, Mo, 48-67; 9 Midwestern Delta Exhibs, Ark Art Ctr, Little Rock, 60-75; St Paul Art Ctr, 63 & 64-65; 10th Midsouth Exhib, Brooks Mem Gallery, Memphis, Tenn, 65; Ann, Ark Arts Ctr, Little Rock, 80; 22nd Ann, Oklahoma Arts Ctr, 80; and others. *Collections Arranged:* Am Inst Architects Art Collection, Ark Artist Exhib, traveling since 66; Arts, Crafts & Design Fair, Ark Distinguished Artists Collectors Exhib, 74. *Pos:* Vpres, Ark Educ Asn, 65-66, pres, 66-68. *Teaching:* Instr painting & drawing & ed, Northern Iowa Univ, Cedar Falls, 47-51; prof painting & drawing, Univ Ark, Fayetteville, 53-81, prof emer, 81- *Awards:* First Place, Ark Artist Exhib, Am Inst Architects, 60-61 & 77; Honorable Mention, 12th Ann Delta Regional, Ark Arts Ctr, 69; Purchase Prize, Ark Arts Ctr, 80. *Bibliog:* Edgar A Albin (auth), An expert in abstract expressionism, Ark Democrat, 61 & The Arts, Sunday News & Leader, Springfield, Mo, 72. *Media:* Acrylic, Watercolor. *Mailing Add:* 720 E Skyline Dr Fayetteville AR 72701

KRUG, HARRY ELNO
PRINTMAKER, EDUCATOR
b Oshkosh, Wis, Aug 20, 30. *Study:* Univ Wis-Milwaukee, BFA; Univ Wis-Madison, MS; Nat Art Acad, Stuttgart, Ger, with Erich Monch. *Work:* Libr of Cong, Washington, DC; Nelson-Atkins Art Gallery, Kansas City, Mo; US Info Agency; Springfield Art Mus, Mo; Ohio Univ Galleries. *Exhib:* 22nd Am Color Print Exhib, Am Color Print Soc, 63; 6th Nat Print Exhib, Silvermine Guild Artists, New Canaan, Conn, 67; 19th Ann Exhib, Boston Mus Fine Arts, Mass, 68; Teacher-Artist Today, State Univ NY Col Oswego, 69; Hopman, Krug, Ecker, Galerie Feursee, Stuttgart, 70. *Pos:* Crafts dir, Spec Serv, Baumholder, Ger, 62-64 & Stuttgart, 68-71. *Teaching:* Prof & chmn printmaking, Pittsburg State Univ, currently. *Awards:* Mid-Am Ann Purchase Award, Nelson-Atkins Art Mus, Kansas City, 60; Sonia Watter Award, Am Color Print Soc, Pa, 62; Prize for Graphics, Jersey City Mus, NJ, 68. *Mem:* Boston Printmakers; Philadelphia Print Club. *Mailing Add:* Rte 3 Box 182 Pittsburg KS 66762

KRUGER, BARBARA
CONCEPTUAL ARTIST, FILM CRITIC
b Newark, NJ, Jan 26, 45. *Study:* Syracuse Univ; Parsons Sch Design; Sch Visual Arts. *Exhib:* Whitney Biennial of Contemp Am Art, 73; Audio Narratives, Los Angeles Inst of Contemp Art, 77; Kitchen, New York, 80; PS 1, New York, 82; Documenta 7, Kassel, Ger, 82; Venice Bienalle, 83; Whitney Bienniel, 83; Mary Boone Gallery, 83; and others. *Teaching:* Vis artist, Calif Inst Art, Art Inst Chicago & Univ Calif, Berkeley. *Awards:* Creative Artists Serv Progr Grant, 76-77; Nat Endowments Arts Grant, 83-84. *Media:* Mixed. *Publ:* Auth, Picture/Readings, 79; auth, No Progress in Pleasure, 82; contribr, film criticism, Artforum. *Mailing Add:* 55 Leonard St New York NY 10013

KRUGMAN, IRENE
SCULPTOR
b New York, NY. *Study:* Kansas City Art Inst; New York Univ; New Sch Social Res, with Yasuo Kuniyoshi. *Work:* Joan & Lester Avnet Collection, Great Neck, NY; Univ Notre Dame, Ind; Kresge Art Ctr, Mich State Univ, East Lansing; NJ State Mus, Trenton; Newark Mus, NJ. *Comn:* Sculptural installation, City Univ New York, 77 & site sculpture, Queensboro Community Col, Bayside, 78, Nat Endowment Arts & New York Coun Arts; Sculpture, Morris Mus, Morristown, NJ, 80. *Exhib:* Some More Beginnings, 68 & Works on Paper Women Artists, 75-76, Brooklyn Mus, NY; Contemporary Americans, Riverside Mus, New York, 70; one-women shows, Summit Art Ctr, NJ, 74, NJ State Mus, Trenton, 75-76 & Bertha Urdang Gallery, 80 & 55 Mercer, 81. *Bibliog:* Lenore Malen (auth), article, Arts Mag, 4/78; Judith Lopes Caroozo (auth), article, Artforum, 5/80. *Media:* Wire, Plaster. *Dealer:* Ivan Karp c/o O K Harris Gallery 383 W Broadway New York NY 10012. *Mailing Add:* 22 Washington Ave Morristown NJ 07960

KRUKOWSKI, LUCIAN
PAINTER, EDUCATOR
b Brooklyn, NY, Nov 22, 29. *Study:* Brooklyn Col, BA, 52; Yale Univ, BFA, 55; Pratt Inst, MS, 58, PhD, 77. *Work:* St Louis Art Mus, Mo. *Comn:* Outdoor wall painting, Nat Endowment Arts, St Louis, 72. *Exhib:* Staempfli Gallery, 58 & 62 & Cee-je Gallery, New York, 67; Loretto Hilton Gallery, 70, Moore Gallery, St Louis, 75 & 78 & Burns Gallery, St Louis, 81. *Teaching:* Prof art, Pratt Inst, 55-69, chmn dept fine arts, 67-69; prof art & dean, Sch Fine Arts, Washington Univ, 69- *Mem:* Am Soc Aesthetics; Col Art Asn. *Publ:* A basis for attributions of art, J Aesthetics Art Criticism, fall 80 & Artworks that end and objects that endure, winter 81; commentary on Beardsley's fiction as representation, Synthese 46, 81. *Mailing Add:* 24 Washington Terr St Louis MO 63112

KRUSHENICK, JOHN
PAINTER, MUSEUM DIRECTOR
b New York, NY, Mar 18, 27. *Study:* City Col New York; Art Students League, with Johnson, Hale, Browne & Vytlacil; Hans Hofmann Sch Fine Arts, New York; Univ Wis, BFA. *Work:* Mus Mod Art & Bank St Col Educ, New York; Weatherspoon Gallery, NC; Ft Wayne Mus Art, Ind. *Comn:* Playground Equipment, Crescent Ave Pre-School, Ft Wayne, Ind, 78. *Exhib:* Mus Mod Art, Tokyo, Hiroshima & Kyoto, 59; Martha Jackson Gallery, 71; New York Civil Liberties Show, Leo Castelli-Downtown, 72; 10th Street New York City, 77; Ft Wayne Mus Art, 78. *Pos:* Owner & dir, House of Brata Frames & Brata Gallery Coop, 57-64; dir & cur, Dorsky Gallery, 70-71; mem mus adv panel, Ind Arts Comn, 75-76; dir, Mus Art, Fort Wayne, Ind, 75-78; art critic, News-Sentinel, Ft Wayne, 78-79; assoc creative hangups, Resource-Corp Art Collections, NJ, 81. *Teaching:* Adj instr studio crafts & procedures, Cooper Union, 68-69; assoc prof mus & gallery procedures & dir, Fine Arts Gallery, Univ Wis-Milwaukee, 72-; instr adult educ art conserv, Pequannock, NJ, 82. *Media:* Oil. *Publ:* Contribr, Mus News, 6/73; contribr, Mid-West Art, 12/74; contribr catalogue, First International Mail Exhibition, Bway Galleries, Milwaukee, Wis, 3/77; auth transcript lecture, Collections Users View, Asn Ind Mus, 9/77; auth & designer catalogs, Ilya Bolotowsky & Western Artists of Taos, New Mexico, Ft Wayne Mus Art, 78. *Mailing Add:* 27 Caroline Ave Pompton Plains NJ 07444

KRUSHENICK, NICHOLAS
PAINTER
b New York, NY, May 31, 29. *Study:* Art Students League, 48-50; Hans Hofmann Sch, New York, 50-51. *Work:* Metrop Mus Art, Whitney Mus Am Art & Mus Mod Art, New York; Los Angeles Co Mus Art; Stedelijk Mus, Amsterdam, Holland. *Comn:* Large painting, State Univ NY Albany, 69. *Exhib:* Whitney Mus Am Art Ann, 63, 65 & 67, Biennial, 73; Systemic Painting, Guggenheim Mus, New York, 66; 1960 Mus Mod Art, 66; Documenta IV, Kassel, WGer, 68; Retrospectives, Walker Art Ctr, Minneapolis, 68 & Kestner-Gesellschaft, Hanover, WGer, 72; Aldrich Mus Contemp Art, Ridgefield, Conn, 71 & 75; one-man shows, Fishbach Gallery, New York, 65, Pace Gallery, 67, 69, 71 & Portland Ctr for Visual Arts, Ore, 74; plus others. *Pos:* Art critic, Yale Univ, 69-70. *Teaching:* Vis artist, Univ Wis, 69; artist in residence, Dartmouth Col, 69; artist, Cornell Univ, 70. *Awards:* Tamarind Lithography Award, 65; Guggenheim Found Fel, 67. *Mailing Add:* 140 Grand St New York NY 10013

KRUSKAMP, JANET
PAINTER, INSTRUCTOR
b Grants Pass, Ore, Dec 10, 34. *Study:* Chouinard Art Inst, Los Angeles. *Work:* Rosicrucian Egyptian Mus, San Jose & Triton Mus Art, Santa Clara, Calif; Springville Mus Art, Utah; Alexandria Mus Art, La; and others. *Exhib:* Soc Western Artists Ann, M H De Young Mus, San Francisco, 71; Soc Western Artists, Rosicrucian Egyptian Mus, 72; Mainstreams, Marietta Col, Ohio, 75; solo-show, Springville Mus Art, Utah, 78; San Jose Mus Art, Calif, 80; Redding Mus Art, Calif, 80; and others. *Awards:* Soc Western Artists Ann First Place Oils, 70; Trustees' Award & Andy Trophy, Grand Galleria Art Competition, Seattle, 72 & First Grand Prize, 73; and others. *Bibliog:* Janice Lovoos (auth), Janet Kruskamp's America, Southwest Art, 6/75; Reva Remy (auth), Le Solon Annuel National D'Art, La Rev Mod; Ted Bredt (auth), A romantic display, Calif Today, 76; and others. *Mem:* Fel Am Artists Prof League; Soc Western Artists; Los Gatos Art Asn (pres, 69). *Media:* Multimedia. *Publ:* Auth, Painting from your own photos, another view, North Light Mag. *Dealer:* Center Art Gallery Honolulu HI 96815; Gallery La Costa Rancho LaCosta CA. *Mailing Add:* 1627 Hyde Dr Los Gatos CA 95030

KUBLER, GEORGE ALEXANDER
HISTORIAN, WRITER
b Los Angeles, Calif, July 26, 12. *Study:* Yale Univ, BA, 34, MA, 36, PhD, 40. *Teaching:* Prof hist art, Yale Univ, 38- *Res:* Pre-Columbian and colonial Latin American art; art of Spain and Portugal. *Publ:* Auth, Religious Architecture of New Mexico, 40; auth, Mexican Architecture of the Sixteenth Century, 48; co-auth, Art & Architecture of Spain & Portugal, 59; auth, Art & Architecture of Ancient America, 62; auth, The Shape of Time, 62. *Mailing Add:* 56 High St New Haven CT 06520

KUBLY, DONALD R
DESIGNER, ADMINISTRATOR
b Los Angeles, Calif, Nov 14, 17. *Study:* Pasadena Jr Col, AA; Art Ctr Col Design, BPA. *Exhib:* NY Art Dirs Ann Exhib, 56 & 71. *Pos:* Sr art dir, N W Ayer & Son, Advert, 49-63; dir, Art Ctr Col Design, Los Angeles, 63-, pres, 65- *Awards:* Gold Medal, NY Art Dirs Ann Exhib, 56 & 71. *Mem:* Am Inst Graphic Arts (dir, 72); Los Angeles Art Asn; Soc Typograph Arts. *Publ:* Contribr, Graphics & Creative Arts, 56-71. *Mailing Add:* Art Ctr Col Design 1700 Lida St Pasadena CA 91103

KUBOTA, SHIGEKO
VIDEO CURATOR, VIDEO ARTIST
b Niigata, Japan, Aug 2, 37. *Study:* Univ Tokyo, BA(sculpture). *Exhib:* Video Sculpture: Duchamp's Grave, The Kitchen, New York, 75, Seattle, Wash, 75, Everson Mus, Syracuse, NY, 76 & Acad Kunste, Berlin, WGer, 76; Nude Descending a Staircase, Seattle, 76 & Dokumenta 6, Kassel, Ger, 77; Video Sculptures, Rene Block Gallery, New York, 77. *Pos:* Video cur, Anthology Film Archives, 74- *Teaching:* Mem video art fac, Sch of Visual Arts, New York, 78- *Awards:* Documentary video grant, Nat Endowment for the Arts, 76; grant, 3 video sculptures, Creative Artist Pub Serv, 76. *Bibliog:* Jonathan Price (auth), Video Visions: A Medium Discovers Itself, New Am Libr, 77; David Bourdon (auth), A critics diary, The New York Art Year, 7-8/77 & The young generation: A cross section, 9-10/77, Art Am. *Publ:* Auth, Marcel Duchamp & John Cage, Takeyoshi Miyazawa, 70. *Dealer:* Rene Block Gallery 1000 Berlin 5 Schaperstrabe 11 Berlin WGer. *Mailing Add:* PO Box 846 Canal St Sta New York NY 10012

KUCHAR, KATHLEEN ANN
PAINTER, EDUCATOR
b Meadow Grove, Nebr, Feb 4, 42. *Study:* Kearney State Col, BA, 63; Ft Hays Kans State Col, MS, 66; Brooklyn Mus Art Sch, Max Beckmann Mem scholar, 66-67, with Reuben Tam, 67; Wichita State Univ, MFA, 74. *Work:* Wichita State Univ Art Gallery; Ft Hays State Univ Art Gallery; Nebr Arts Collection. *Exhib:* Watercolor USA, Springfield Art Mus, Mo, 68 & 79; one-person show, Nat Design Ctr, New York, 68; Drawing & Small Sculpture Exhib, Ball State Univ, 72; Am Watercolor Soc Exhib, New York, 79; 1st & 2nd Tri-State Watercolor Exhibs, Wichita Art Mus, 79 & 81; and others. *Teaching:* Instr art, Minden Pub Schs, Nebr, 63-65; assoc prof painting-design, Ft Hays State Univ, 67-78, prof, 78- *Awards:* Best in Show, Tri-State Watercolor Exhib, Wichita Art Mus, 79 & 81; Purchase Award, Nat Watercolor Soc Exhib, 83; Purchase Award, San Diego Int Watercolor Soc Exhib, 83. *Bibliog:* Rev in Art News, 68 & Art Rev, 69; Female Artists, Past & Present, Women's Hist Res Ctr, Inc, 74. *Mem:* Kans Watercolor Soc; Nat Watercolor Soc. *Media:* Acrylic; Felt Markers. *Mailing Add:* 2202 Fort St Hays KS 67601

KUCHEL, KONRAD G
ADMINISTRATOR
b Salem, Mass, Aug 25, 37. *Study:* Bowdoin Col, AB, 60; Inst Fine Arts, New York Univ, MA, 63. *Pos:* Asst to dir & ed, Mus Bulletin, Mus Art, RI Sch Design, 63-64; coordr loans, Exhib Dept, Am Fedn Arts, 65-69 & 76-, dir exhibs, 69-75. *Mailing Add:* c/o Am Fedn of Arts 41 E 65th St New York NY 10021

KUCHTA, RONALD A
MUSEUM DIRECTOR, LECTURER
b Lackawanna, NY, June 23, 35. *Study:* Cape Cod Sch Art, Provincetown, Mass, 53-57; Kenyon Col, Gambier, Ohio, BA, 57; Western Reserve Univ, Cleveland, Ohio, MA(art hist), 62; Mgt Inst, Cornell Univ, 79. *Collections Arranged:* Modern Mexican Painting, 70; Tantra (with catalog), 70; Interior Vision, European Abstract Expressionism, 1945-1960 (with catalog), 70; Animals in African Art (with catalog), 73; 15 Abstract Artists--Los Angeles, 73; New Works in Clay, 76; Provincetown Painters, 77; Diversions of Keramos: American Clay Sculpture 1925-1950, 83. *Pos:* Cur, Chrysler Art Mus, 61-68; cur, Santa Barbara Mus Art, 68-74; dir, Everson Mus Art, 74- *Teaching:* Adj prof museology, Syracuse Univ, 74- *Awards:* Outstanding Serv Educ, Northeastern Baptist Asn, 83. *Mem:* Am Asn Mus; Am Asn Mus Dir; Int Coun Mus. *Publ:* Auth, Provincetown Painters, Everson Mus Art, 77; auth introd, A Century of Ceramics in the United States 1878-1978, E P Dutton & Everson Mus Art, 79; auth, Batuz: Works in Paper, Rizzoli Int, 81; auth, Inscapes: Real Estate Paintings of Mati Klarwein, Crown, 83; auth introd, The Diversions of Keramos: American Clay Sculpture 1925-1950, Everson Mus Art, 83. *Mailing Add:* Everson Mus Art Syracuse NY 13202

KUCZUN, ANN-MARIE
PRINTMAKER, PAINTER
b Springfield, Mass. *Study:* Bay Path Jr Col, AS; Univ Colo, Boulder. *Work:* Pratt Community Col, Kans; E F Hutton & Co, Colo. *Exhib:* San Diego Watercolor Soc Nat, 80; one-person shows, Women's Bank, Denver, 82 & Univ Northern Colo, 84; Buell Gallery, 83; and others. *Pos:* Bd dirs, publicity chmn & exhib chmn, Boulder Fine Arts Ctr, 72-73. *Bibliog:* Illus feature in Colorado Mag, 9-10/77; feature with color photos in Boulder Daily Camera, 9/16/77 & 6/17/79. *Media:* Watermedia, Pastel; Intaglio. *Publ:* Contribr, Collaging with Paper, 78 & Printworld Inc, 81. *Dealer:* The Art Collector 4151 Taylor St San Diego CA; Alpha Gallery 9618 E Arapahoe Rd Englewood CO. *Mailing Add:* 930 Miami Way Boulder CO 80303

KUEHN, EDMUND KARL
PAINTER, LECTURER
b Columbus, Ohio, Aug 18, 16. *Study:* Columbus Art Sch, cert, 38; Art Students League, cert, 39. *Work:* Columbus Gallery Fine Arts. *Collections Arranged:* Paintings from Columbus Homes, 63; Jean Crotti in Retrospect, 65; The Gordian Knot, 80; Works by David Blythe, 68. *Pos:* Cur, Columbus Gallery Fine Arts, 39-43, asst dir, 62-67, cur collections, 67-76. *Teaching:* Asst prof drawing & painting, Ohio State Univ, 46-47; assoc prof drawing & painting, Columbus Col Art & Design, 52-62. *Mem:* Columbus Art League; Am Asn Mus. *Mailing Add:* 828 City Park Ave Columbus OH 43206

KUEHN, FRANCES
PAINTER
b New York, NY, Feb 16, 43. *Study:* Douglass Col, Rutgers Univ, BA, Rutgers Univ, New Brunswick, MFA. *Work:* J B Speed Art Mus, Louisville, Ky; Weatherspoon Art Gallery, Univ NC; Power Inst, Univ Sydney, Australia; Allen Mem Art Mus, Oberlin, Ohio; New Jersey State Mus, Trenton; and others. *Comn:* Portrait for private collection, 72. *Exhib:* Whitney Mus Ann, 72 & Biennial, 73; one-woman shows, Douglass Col Libr, 73, Max Hutchinson Gallery, 73 & 74 & A M Sachs Gallery, New York, 78; Contemporary Portraits by Well-Known American Artists, Lowe Art Mus, Coral Gables, Fla, 74; Selections in Contemporary Realism, Akron Art Inst, Ohio, 74. *Teaching:* Artist-in-residence, Rice Univ, 80. *Awards:* NJ State Coun Arts Artist's Fel, 78-79; Nat Endowment Arts Artist's Fel, 82-83. *Bibliog:* Phyllis Derfner (auth), Frances Kuehn, Art Spectrum, 2/75; Lynn Miller & Sally Swenson (auths), Lives and Work, Talks with Women Artists, Scarecrow Press, 81. *Media:* Acrylic. *Mailing Add:* 880 W 181st St New York NY 10033

KUEHN, GARY
SCULPTOR, GRAPHIC ARTIST
b Plainfield, NJ, 1939. *Study:* Drew Univ, NJ, BA(art hist), 62; Rutgers Univ, NJ, MFA, 64. *Work:* NJ State Mus, Trenton; also in pvt collections of Richard P Kaplan, New York, Roy Lichtenstein, New York & Robert Scull, New York. *Exhib:* Cool Art Today, Larry Aldrich Mus Ridgefield, Conn, 68; Whitney Ann, New York, 68; When Attitudes Become Form (toured Krefeld, London), Kunsthalle Berne, Switz, 69; New Materials, Procedures in Sculpture, Austin Arts Ctr, Tex, 70; Sculptor's Drawings, Margo Leavin Gallery, Los Angeles, Calif, 73; one-man shows, Fischbach Gallery, New York, 69 & 74, Paley and Lowe Gallery, New York, 72 & Stefanotty Gallery, New York, 74; and others. *Teaching:* Instr, Fairleigh Dickinson Univ, NJ, 65, Drew Univ, NJ, 65-68, Sch of Visual Arts, New York, 68, Hochschule fur Bildende Kunst, Braunschweig, Ger, 70, Douglass Col & Rutgers Univ, 73. *Awards:* Nat Endowment Arts, 77; Tiffany Found Grant, 77; DAAD Fel, Berlin, 79. *Dealer:* Galerie Ricke Lindenstrasse 22 Cologne Germany. *Mailing Add:* Buffalo Hollow Rd Glen Gardner NJ 08821

KUEHNL, CLAUDIA ANN
GOLDSMITH
b Kenosha, Wis, Aug 11, 48. *Study:* Philadelphia Col Art, Pa, BFA, 70; State Univ NY Col, New Paltz, MFA, 74. *Exhib:* Contemp Am Gold-Silversmiths, Corcoran Gallery Art, Washington, DC, 72; Southern Tier Arts & Crafts Exhib, Corning Mus, NY, 74; Contemp Crafts of the Americas Int Exhib, Ft Collins, Colo, 75; Mex Exhib, Univ Mex, Mexico City, 75; Silver & Goldsmithing in Am Exhib, Lowe Art Mus, Univ Miami, Coral Gables, Fla, 76; NAm Goldsmiths Exhib, Phoenix Art Mus, Ariz, 77; Jewelry & Metal Objects from the Society of North American Goldsmiths (Europ traveling show). *Teaching:* Instr art appreciation, Suffolk Co Community Col, Selden, NY, 75-; asst prof jewelry, Southampton Col, NY, 76- *Awards:* Nat Endowment Arts Fel, Crafts, 75-76. *Mem:* Soc NAm Goldsmiths; Am Crafts Coun; NY State Craftsmen Inc. *Media:* Gold, Stone. *Dealer:* Works Gallery Jobs Lane Southampton NY 11968; Rosenfeld Gallery 113 Arch St Philadelphia PA 19106. *Mailing Add:* Quogue St Box 622 Quogue NY 11959

KUEKES, EDWARD D
CARTOONIST
b Pittsburgh, Pa, Feb 2, 01. *Study:* Baldwin-Wallace Col, Hon LHD, 57; Cleveland Inst Art; Chicago Acad Fine Arts. *Work:* Cartoon collection at Western Reserve Hist Soc, Cleveland, Ohio & Baldwin-Wallace Col, Berea, Ohio; five thousand original cartoons in collection at Syracuse Univ. *Pos:* Cartoonist, Cleveland Plain Dealer, 22-49, chief ed cartoonist, 49-66, cartoonist emer, 66-; cartoonist, Metro Newspapers, Inc, Cleveland, 68- *Teaching:* Lect, So you can't draw a straight line, either, art groups nationally. *Awards:* Pulitzer Prize, Cartoon Div, 53; three First Prize Awards, Freedom Found. *Mem:* Asn Am Ed Cartoonists; Nat Cartoonist Soc. *Publ:* Auth, Funny Fables, 38; coauth, Alice in Wonderland & Knurl the Gnome (cartoon features), United Features Syndicate; creator, All in the Week, Along the Road, Cartoonists Looks at the News & other featured cartoons. *Mailing Add:* 1280 Medfield Dr Rocky River OH 44116

KUEMMERLEIN, JANET
FIBER ARTIST
b Dearborn, Mich, Jan 10, 32. *Study:* Detroit Soc Arts & Crafts, 50-51; Cranbrook Acad Art, with Harry Osaki, 51-52. *Work:* Chicago Art Inst; Rochester Inst Technol; Ga Inst Technol; Smithsonian Inst Gallery Art; 3M Corp. *Comn:* Fiber relief sculpture, Gen Serv Admin, Richmond, Calif, 76; fiber mural, Williams Ctr, Tulsa, 80 & State Bar Calif, Sacramento, 80; fiber & sculpture, State Fed Savings, Tulsa, 82; fiber relief sculpture, Richardson-Vicks, Shelton, Calif, 83. *Exhib:* Five Fiber Artists, Sheldon Mem Gallery, Lincoln, Nebr, 63; Objects USA Travelling Exhib, US & Europe, 69; Forms in Fibre, Chicago Art Inst, 71; American Craft Exhib, Dallas Mus, 72; Craft Invitational, San Diego Mus Fine Art, 74; Art in Worship, Mus Contemp Crafts, New York, 74; Women, Fiber, Clay & Metal, Bronx Mus, 77; Fiberworks, Cleveland Mus, 78. *Collections Arranged:* Contemporary Crafts (auth, catalog), Rockhurst Col, 64. *Awards:* Awards, Univ Kans, 65-69 & Am Inst Archit, 69-71 & 75-79. *Bibliog:* Louise Schulteis (auth), Artist in fiber, Kansas City Star, 71; Irene Reynolds (auth), Fiber artist, Kansan Mag, 76. *Mem:* Mo Coun Arts; Am Craft Coun. *Media:* Fiber. *Publ:* Contribr, Textile Art in the Church, Abingdon Press, 71; contribr, Quilting, Patchwork, Applique, Trapunto, 74 & Soft Sculpture, 74, Crown; contribr, The Place of Art in the World of Architecture, Chelsea House, 80; contribr, Sewing Machine Craft Book, Van Nostrand Reinhold, 80. *Mailing Add:* 7701 Canterbury Prairie Village KS 66208

KUH, HOWARD
PAINTER
b New York, NY, 1899. *Study:* Art Students League; Marine painting with Jay Conaway, Maine; painting with S M Alder, New York. *Work:* Butler Inst Am Art, Youngstown, Ohio; Slater Mem Mus, Conn; Tweed Mus & Minneapolis Mus, Minn; Stratford Col, Va; Evansville Mus Arts & Sci. *Exhib:* Audubon Artists, Nat Acad of Design, New York; Riverside Mus; New Eng Ann, Silver Mine, Conn; Avery Mem Mus, Hartford, Conn; one-man shows, Roko Gallery & Bodley Gallery. *Mem:* Am Soc Contemp Artists; Artists Equity NY. *Mailing Add:* 45 Christopher St New York NY 10014

KUH, KATHARINE
CRITIC, CONSULTANT
b St Louis, Mo, July 15, 04. *Study:* Vassar Col, BA; Univ Chicago, MA(art hist); NY Univ; also five hon PhDs. *Pos:* Owner & dir, Katharine Kuh Gallery, Chicago, 36-42; cur mod art, Art Inst Chicago, 42-59; art ed, Sat Rev, 59-77; art consult, First Nat Bank Chicago, 68-79. *Publ:* Auth, Art Has Many Faces, 51, auth, The Artist's Voice, 61 & auth, The Open Eye, 70, Harper & Row; auth, Leger, Univ Ill, 58; auth, Break-Up: The Core of Modern Art, NY Graphic, 65. *Mailing Add:* 140 E 83rd St New York NY 10028

KUHLENSCHMIDT, RICHARD EDWARD
DEALER
b Cleveland, Ohio, Feb 27, 51. *Study:* Calif State Univ, Fullerton, BA, 75. *Pos:* Cur exhibs, Bowers Mus, Santa Ana, Calif, 77-79; owner & dir, Richard Kuhlenschmidt Gallery, Los Angeles, 80- *Bibliog:* Karen Back (auth), Best of Los Angeles, Los Angeles Weekly, 9/83. *Specialty:* Contemporary Los Angeles and New York artists. *Mailing Add:* 4121 Wilshire Blvd Los Angeles CA 90010

KUHLMAN, WALTER EGEL
PAINTER, EDUCATOR
b St Paul, Minn, Nov 16, 18. *Study:* St Paul Sch Art, with Cameron Booth; Univ Minn, BA; Calif Sch Fine Arts; Acad Grande Chaumiere. *Work:* Phillips Mem Gallery, Washington, DC; San Francisco Mus Art; Mus Mod Art, Sao Paulo, Brazil; Oakland Mus, Calif; Roswell Mus, NMex. *Exhib:* New York World's Fair, 40; Realities Nouvelles, Paris, 51; Art in 20th Century, San Francisco Mus Art, 55; Calif Palace Legion Honor, 67; Midyear Show 35, Butler Inst Am Art, 70; Contemporary ERA, San Francisco Mus Mod Art, 72; one-man shows, Walker Art Ctr, Minneapolis, Stanford Univ & Charles Campbell Gallery, 81 & 83; Twenty-Year Retrospective, de Saisset Mus, Univ Santa Clara. *Teaching:* Stanford Univ; Calif Sch Fine Arts; Univ NMex, 60-65; Univ Santa Clara, 66-69; prof painting & chmn dept art, Sonoma State Col, Calif, 69- *Awards:* Cummington Found Fel, 42; Graham Found Fel, 57; Calif Arts Coun Fel, 83. *Media:* Oil, Monoprints. *Mailing Add:* 27 Glen Ct Sausalito CA 94965

KUHN, BOB
DRAFTSMAN, PAINTER
b Buffalo, NY, Jan 28, 20. *Study:* Pratt Inst, 3 yrs; Art Students League. *Work:* Nat Cowboy Hall Fame, Oklahoma City; Genesee Country Mus, Rochester, NY; Wildlife World Mus, Monument, Colo. *Exhib:* One-man show, Abercrombie & Fitch, New York, 65 & two-man show, 67; one-man show, Tryon Gallery, Nairobi, Kenya, 73; Animals in Art, Royal Ont Mus, Toronto, 75. *Awards:* Gold Medal, Silver Medal, Nat Acad Western Art; Gold Medal, Nat Cowboy Hall Fame; Three Medals of Honor, Soc Animal Artists. *Mem:* Soc Animal Artists. *Media:* Acrylic on Masonite. *Publ:* Auth, Animal Art of Bob Kuhn, Watson-Guptill, 73; contribr, Classic African Animals, Winchester, 73. *Dealer:* Sportsman's Edge New York NY; Collector's Covey Dallas TX. *Mailing Add:* Good Hill Rd Roxbury CT 06783

KUHN, BRENDA
HISTORIAN
b New York, NY, June 13, 11. *Study:* Friends Sem, New York; also art estate mgt with Walt & Vera Kuhn. *Pos:* Co-mgr, Kuhn Estate, 49-56, mgr, 56-66; mgr, Collection of Brenda Kuhn, 66-75; pres, Kuhn Mem Corp, 68-75, third vpres, currently; historian, Kuhnhouse; founder, Walt Kuhn Gallery, Cape Neddick Park, Maine. *Mem:* Arch Am Art; Friends of Art of Colby; Portland Mus Art, Maine; Am Fedn Arts; York Art Asn. *Mailing Add:* Cape Neddick Park RFD 1 Box 7A Cape Neddick ME 03902

KUHN, MARYLOU
EDUCATOR, PAINTER
b South Bend, Ind, Oct 18, 23. *Study:* Layton Sch Art; Univ Wis; Art Inst Chicago; Ohio State Univ, univ fel, 53, BSc & PhD; Teachers Col, Columbia Univ, MA. *Exhib:* LeMoyne Art Found, 65-; Ind Univ, 74; Gulf Coast Jr Col, 75; Fla A&M Univ, 76. *Pos:* Ed, Fla Art News, 60-62; ed, Southeastern Arts Bulletin, 62-64; Regional ed, Art Educ J, 64-66, co-ed, Studies in Art Educ, 70-73, sr ed, 73-75; treas, Sem Res in Art Educ, 76-78. *Teaching:* Prof art educ, Fla State Univ, 51-, chmn dept art, currently; guest lectr art educ, Inst Educ, Univ London, 66-67; distinguished vis prof, Southern Ill Univ, Carbondale, 78. *Mem:* Int Soc Educ Through Art; Nat Art Educ Asn; Women's Caucus Art (pres, 78-79); Adult Educ Asn USA; Am Coun Arts; Am Fedn Arts. *Media:* Encaustic, Watercolor. *Res:* Community and adult art education, curriculum and teacher education in art, philosophy and theory. *Publ:* Auth, Standards and criteria, Adult & Exten Art Educ, 66; auth chap, In: Behavioral Emphasis in Art Education, 75; auth, Priorities for arts in everyday living and education, Registry Vol 16; auth, Philosophical base for lifelong learning, In: Life-Long Learning in Visual Arts, 80; auth, Women, work and cultural equality, In: Ninth Decade in Visual Arts, 80. *Dealer:* LeMoyne Art Found 125 N Gadsden St Tallahassee FL 32303. *Mailing Add:* Dept of Art Educ Fla State Univ Tallahassee FL 32306

KUJUNDZIC, ZELJKO D
CERAMIST, SCULPTOR
b Subotica, Yugoslavia, Oct 23, 20; Can citizen. *Study:* Royal Col Art, Budapest, Hungary, BA, 44; Inst Fine Arts, Budapest, MFA, 46, with Jeno Barchai. *Work:* Nat Mus, Geneva, Switzerland; Edinburgh Univ Col, Scotland; Pa State Univ, University Park & Fayette Campus; Univ BC, Vancouver; Kyoto City Mus, Japan; and others. *Comn:* Reverence (mural), Prov Hosp BC, Nelson, 68; Ceramic mural, First Fed Bank, Pittsburgh, Pa, 73; libr mural, Pa State Univ, Uniontown, 74; Ancestor (sculptor), Credit Union, Vernon, BC, 75; Holocaust Mem, B'nai B'rith, Uniontown, Pa, 81. *Exhib:* Seattle Int Sculpture, Pioneer Sq, 81; one-man exhib, Art Inst Pittsburgh Gallery, 81; Robson Media Ctr Gallery, Vancouver, 81; Int Ceramics, Maya Behis Gallery, Zurich, 83; Palazzo Medici-Riccardi, Florence, 83; and others. *Pos:* Pres, Okanagan Contemp Artists, 66-68; exec dir, Pioneer Crafts Coun, Mill Run, Pa, 70-71. *Teaching:* Assoc prof, Pa State Univ, Uniontown, 68-79, prof, 79-82, prof emer, 82-; sculpture workshop partic, Nat Univ Mex, 79; Raku Workshop, Wenatchee Valley Col, Wash, 81. *Awards:* Merit Awards, Expo 67 Can, Nat Crafts Coun Can, 67 & Int Ceramics, Nat Mus Art, Poland, 73; Purchase Award, Int Medalist Exhib, Nat Gallery Art, Poland, 76. *Bibliog:* Anne Payne (auth), Kujundzic, Arts West, 66; Ray Turner (auth), Art with Zeljko, CHBC-TV, 67-68; Philip R Shepherd (auth, feature), Z Kujundzic, Onion, Toronto, 77. *Mem:* Int Acad of Ceramics, Switz; Sculptors Soc of Can; Sculptors Soc of BC (regional rep). *Publ:* Auth (autobiog), Torn Canvas, Richard Patterson, 57, paperback ed, 64; auth, Paolo Soleri, Art & You, 73; auth, Experimental solar kilns, Ceramic Mo, 75; auth, Cuire au soleil, l'Atelier des Metiers d'Art, Paris, 76; auth, Les ceramistes americains, La Ceramique Moderne, 82. *Mailing Add:* PO Box 462 Entiat WA 98822

KULICKE, ROBERT M
PAINTER, CRAFTSMAN
b Philadelphia, Pa, Mar 9, 24. *Study:* Philadelphia Mus Sch Art; Tyler Sch Fine Arts, Temple Univ; Atelier Fernand Leger, 46-50. *Work:* Philadelphia Mus Art. *Exhib:* Silvermine Guild, 64; Art Inst Chicago; Dayton Art Inst, Ohio; 100 Years of American Realism, Am Fedn Arts, 65; Whitney Mus Am Art, New York, 69; Davis & Long Gallery, New York, 75-81. *Teaching:* Instr, Univ Calif, 64 & 70 & Kulicke-Stark Acad Jewelry Art, New York, 64-*Awards:* Int Design Award, Am Inst Interior Designers, 68. *Mailing Add:* c/o Davis & Langdale 29309 Second St Belvidere NJ 07823

KULTERMANN, UDO
HISTORIAN, EDUCATOR
b Stettin, Ger, Oct 14, 27. *Study:* Univ Greifswald, Ger, 47-50; Univ Munster, 50-53. Exhibitions Arranged: Monochrome Painting, Mus Leverkusen, 60, Ad Reinhardt-Lo Savio-Jef Verheyen, 61, Glass Chain, 62. *Pos:* Dir, City Art Mus, Leverkusen, Ger, 59-64; consult to art collectors, galleries and govt agencies. *Teaching:* Prof hist & theory archit, Washington Univ, 67- *Res:* History of art history; African culture; Third World architecture. *Publ:* Auth, Art Events & Happenings, Matthew, Miller & Dunbar, 71; Ernest Trova, Abrams, 78; I Contemporanei, Mondadori, 79; Architecture in the Seventies, Architectural Press, 80; Architects of the Third World, Dumont, 80; and others. *Mailing Add:* Washington Univ Campus Box 1079 St Louis MO 63130

KUMLER, KIPTON (CORNELIUS)
PHOTOGRAPHER, LECTURER
b Cleveland, Ohio, June 20, 40. *Study:* Cornell Univ, BEE, 63, MEE, 67; Mass Inst Technol, with Minor White, MBA, 69; spec study with Paul Caponigro, 70. *Work:* Mus Mod Art, Metrop Mus Art, New York; Mus Fine Arts, Boston; Victoria & Albert Mus, London; Int Mus Photog, George Eastman House, Rochester, NY. *Comn:* Essay on Danish Archit in Frederiksted, St Croix, Landmark Soc, 75-76; Photog Surv, Del Water Gap, Nat Endowment Arts, 76-77. *Exhib:* Recent Acquisitions, Boston Mus Fine Arts, 74; Addison Gallery Am Art, 74; solo exhibs, NJ Mus, Trenton, 78, Photog Place, Philadelphia, 79; Cronin Gallery, Houston, 80, Harcus Krakow Gallery, Boston, 80 & Worcester Art Mus, Mass, 80; and others. *Collections Arranged:* Traveling Exhib, Nat Endowment Arts Survey Work, NJ, 77-78. *Teaching:* Instr photog, Project Inc, Cambridge, Mass, 69-72; instr advan photog, Maine Photog Workshops, Rockport, 77-80. *Awards:* Nat

Endowment Arts Photog Survey Grants, Peters Valley, NJ, 76-77 & Boston Hist Survey, 80-81; Mass Coun Arts Photog Fel, 77. *Publ:* Contribr, Camera, Lausanne, Switz, 70; contribr, Popular Photography, 75; auth, Kipton Kumler: Photographs, 75 & Plant Leaves, 78, David Godine; contribr, Print Letter, Zurich, 77. *Dealer:* Marcuse Pfeifer Gallery 825 Madison Ave New York NY 10016; Harcus Krakow Gallery 7 Newbury Boston MA 02116. *Mailing Add:* 34 Grant St Lexington MA 02173

KUMM, MARGUERITE ELIZABETH
PAINTER, PRINTMAKER
b Redwood Falls, Minn. *Study:* Minneapolis Sch of Art, cert design & painting, with Cameron Booth & Anthony Angarola; Corcoran Sch Art, Washington, DC, painting & composition with Eugene Weisz & Richard Lahey. *Work:* Boston Mus Fine Arts; Calif State Libr, Sacramento; Libr Cong, Washington, DC; Metrop Mus Art, New York; Smithsonian Inst, Div Graphic Arts, Washington, DC; and others. *Exhib:* Artists for Victory, Metrop Mus Art, New York, 42; Nat Acad Design, New York, 42-44 & 49; three-person show, Three Va Artists, Va Mus Fine Arts, Richmond, 45; one-person shows, Smithsonian Inst, 50, Mint Mus, Charlotte, NC, 51, Isaac Delgado Mus, New Orleans, 52, Butler Art Inst, Youngstown, Ohio, 52, Calif State Libr, 53 & Witte Mem Mus, San Antonio, Tex, 53; and others. *Awards:* 25 Selected Miniature Prints Award, Soc Am Etchers, 40 & 45 & Henry B Shope Prize, 43; Pennell Fund Purchase Award, Libr of Cong, 51 & 53; and others. *Bibliog:* Albert Reese (auth), American Prize Prints of the 20th Century, Am Artists Group, New York, 49. *Media:* Oil, Acrylic; Aquatint, Etching. *Dealer:* Betty Minor Duffy Bethesda Art Gallery 7950 Norfolk Ave Bethesda MD 20014. *Mailing Add:* 212 Noland St Falls Church VA 22046

KUNSTLER, MORTON
PAINTER, ILLUSTRATOR
b New York, NY, Aug 28, 31. *Study:* Brooklyn Col; Univ Calif, Los Angeles; Pratt Inst, cert, 50. *Work:* USAF Mus, Boulder, Colo; San Mateo Co Historical Mus, Calif; Nat Art Mus Sport, New York; Lowie Mus Anthrop, Berkeley, Calif; Nassau Co Mus Fine Arts, Roslyn, NY; and others. *Comn:* Paintings, National Geographic, Washington, DC, 66-69; movie posters, MGM, 20th Century, Warner Bros, Hollywood, 64-77; six paintings, American Cyanamid, NJ, 71-76; four paintings, NY Bank for Savings, New York, 76; seven paintings, Rockwell Int, Pa, 80; and many others. *Exhib:* One-man shows, Hammer Galleries, New York, 77, 79 & 81-82, USN Mem Mus, Washington, DC, 79 & 82 & Pittsburgh Ctr Arts, Pa, 81; 200 Yrs of American Illustration, NY Hist Soc Mus, Oakland Mus, Mint Mus Art & Sewall Art Gallery, 78; Pictorial History USAF, Soc Illustrators, New York, 81; and others. *Bibliog:* Henry Steele Commager (auth), Mort Kunstler's 50 Epic Paintings of America, 79 & Walt Reed (auth), Great American Illustrators, 79, Abbeville Press; Rich Gigler (auth), Painting the sound and fury, Sunday Mag, Pittsburgh Press, 9/27/81. *Media:* Oil, Watercolor. *Publ:* Illusr, Ghost Dog, Saturday Evening Post, 57; illusr, San Francisco Bay, the westward gate, National Geographic, 11/69; illusr, Giant, Fawcett Crest, 70; illusr, Reach for tomorrow, Good Housekeeping, 8/75; illusr covers, Newsweek, 75-82; and many others. *Dealer:* Hammer Galleries 33 W 57th St New York NY 10019. *Mailing Add:* Cove Neck Oyster Bay NY 11771

KUOPUS, CLINTON
PAINTER, COLLECTOR
b Detroit, Mich, Dec 8, 42. *Study:* US Navy Photog Intelligence Sch, 63; Eastern Mich Univ, BFA(painting), 70, MA(painting), 75. *Work:* Mich Educ Asn Collection, Lansing; Hiram Col, Ohio; J Walter Thompson Advert Agency, Troy, Mich; Lake Erie Col Permanent Collection, Painesville, Ohio; Pub Collection, Cedar City, Utah. *Exhib:* Mich Art Train (traveling exhib), Mich Coun Arts, statewide, 73-74; Source Detroit Exhib, Cranbrook Mus Art, Bloomfield Hills, Mich, 76; May Show Exhibs, Cleveland Mus Art, Ohio, 76-78; 43rd Nat Mid-Yr Show, Butler Inst Am Art, Youngstown, Ohio 79; 38th Cedar City Nat, Cedar City Utah, 79; Pencil, Ft Wayne, Ind Mus Art, 79; one-person show, Ind Purdue Univ, Ft Wayne, 80. *Pos:* Photog interpreter, US Navy, 62-66; instr painting & design, Birmingham-Bloomfield Art Asn, 72-74. *Teaching:* Photog intelligence training petty off, US Navy, 64-66; instr visual art, Bloomfield Hills Schs, Mich, 70-75; asst prof art, Lake Erie Col, Painesville, Ohio, 75-80, 82-83; adj fac, Youngstown Univ, 80-82, Univ Akron, 81-82, Mt Union Col, 81-82. *Bibliog:* Art Editor (auth), article, Detroit Free Press, 73; Joy Hakinson-Colby (auth), Weekly art criticism, Detroit News, 73-74; Helen Cullinen (auth), article, Cleveland Plain Dealer, 76-78. *Mem:* Mich Watercolor Soc (bd dirs & dir exhibs, 72-74); Mich Art Educ Asn; Phi Kappa Phi Hon Soc; Am Asn Univ Profs. *Media:* Multimedia. *Mailing Add:* 162 E 91st 2A New York NY 10128

KUPFERMAN, MURRAY
PAINTER, SCULPTOR
b Brooklyn, NY. *Study:* Pratt Inst; Nat Acad Design. *Work:* St Vincent Col, Latrobe, Pa; Brooklyn Mus; New Rochelle Col, NY; Smithsonian Inst, Washington, DC; La Monte Dougherty Geol Observ; and others. *Comn:* Undersea murals, Caravelle Hotel, St Croix, VI & Hotel Bonaire, Dutch W Indies. *Exhib:* The White House, Washington DC; Wash Co Mus Fine Arts; Children's Mus, Brooklyn, NY; Maritime Col; Yonkers Mus, NY; plus others. *Teaching:* Instr art appreciation & painting, Brooklyn Tech; instr painting, Educ Alliance. *Awards:* Allied Artists; Audubon Artists. *Mem:* Am Watercolor Soc; Allied Artists Am; League of Present Day Artists; Audubon Artists; Nat Soc Painters in Casein; plus others. *Media:* Casein, Acrylic; Brass, Plastics. *Mailing Add:* 1270 E 19th St Brooklyn NY 11230

KURAHARA, TED
PAINTER, EDUCATOR
b Seattle, Wash, July 16, 25. *Study:* St Louis Sch Fine Arts, Washington Univ, with Paul Burlin, BFA, 51; Bradley Univ, Peoria, Ill, with Leon Engers, MA, 52. *Work:* NY Univ, New York; Hofstra Univ, Hempstead, NY; Springfield Art Ctr, Ill; Univ Sidney, Australia. *Exhib:* Amaganset Drawings, Pratt Inst, Brooklyn, NY, 77; Occidental Col, Los Angeles, Calif, 80; Woodside/Braseth Gallery, Seattle, Wash, 80; Galleriet, Lund, Sweden, 81; Black Paintings, Pratt Manhattan Ctr, New York, 81; and many others. *Pos:* Dir, Emily Lowe Gallery, Hofstra Univ, 67-70. *Teaching:* Asst prof, Hofstra Univ, 67-70; assoc prof art, Pratt Inst, Brooklyn, 70-, chairperson painting & drawing dept, 80-83. *Awards:* First Prize for Painting, Des Moines Ann, Iowa, 58; Purchase Prize, Des Moines Art Ctr, 59. *Bibliog:* John Watts (auth), Kurahara Exhibition, Manhattan E, 65; Wallace Barker (auth), Second Kurahara show, St Louis Post-Dispatch, 65. *Media:* Mixed. *Dealer:* Oil and Steel Gallery New York NY; Woodside Braseth Seattle WA. *Mailing Add:* 78 Greene St New York NY 10012

KURHAJEC, JOSEPH A
SCULPTOR
b Racine, Wis, Oct 13, 38. *Study:* Univ Wis, BS, 60, MFA, 62. *Work:* New Sch Social Res, New York; Espanol Mus Contemp Art, Madrid; Mus Mod Art, New York; Chicago Art Inst; Walker Art Ctr, Minneapolis, Minn. *Comn:* Bronze cone, Allan Stone, Purchase, NY, 71; bronze sculpture, Norman Shaifer, Brooklyn Heights, NY, 71. *Exhib:* Am Fedn Art Traveling Exhib, 64; Sculpture Ann, Whitney Mus Am Art, New York, 64, Young America, 65; Espanol Mus Contemp Art, 69; Ten Independents, Guggenheim Mus, New York, 72; Basel Art, 76. *Teaching:* Asst prof, Cornell Univ, 65-66; asst prof, Newark Sch Indust & Fine Art, 67-69; asst prof, Univ Wis-Stout, 71-73, State Univ NY, New Paltz, 73-74, Lo Studiolo, Rome, 74-83. *Awards:* Int Fur Designers Award, 83. *Mailing Add:* c/o Allan Stone Gallery 48 E 86th St New York NY 10028

KURKA, DONALD FRANK
PAINTER, ADMINISTRATOR
b Chicago, Ill, July 29, 30. *Study:* Syracuse Univ, BFA, 52; Art Inst Chicago, MFA, 56; NY Univ, PhD, 68. *Exhib:* Contemporary Prints, Libr Cong, 55; Art Inst Chicago, 55-56; New Directions, Parrish Mus, Southampton, NY, 63; Long Island Artists, Heckscher Mus, Huntington, NY, 73; solo exhib, McClung Mus, Univ Tenn, Knoxville, 78 & Hunter Mus, Chattanooga, Tenn, 81; Southern Realism, Miss Mus Art, Jackson, 80 & Montgomery Mus Art, 80. *Teaching:* Prof painting, Southampton Ctr, Long Island Univ, 69-77, dir, Div Fine Arts, 73-77; prof & head dept art, Univ Tenn, Knoxville, 77- *Awards:* Vandergrift Award, Art Inst Chicago, 55; Founders Day Award, NY Univ, 68; Best in Show, Long Island Painters, Hecksher Mus, 73. *Mem:* Nat Coun Art Adminr; Nat Asn Schs Art & Design; Col Art Asn. *Media:* Acrylic, Oil. *Dealer:* Norman Worrell Assoc 2328 Gulf Lane Nashville TN. *Mailing Add:* 819 Cherokee Blvd Knoxville TN 37919

KURZ, DIANA
PAINTER, EDUCATOR
b Vienna, Austria; US citizen. *Study:* Brandeis Univ, BA(fine arts, cum laude); Columbia Univ, MFA(painting). *Work:* Corcoran Gallery Art, Washington, DC. *Exhib:* Brooklyn Mus, 75; Alex Rosenberg Gallery, New York, 82; solo exhibs, Snug Harbor Cult Ctr, 82, Rider Col, 84 & Alex Rosenberg Gallery, New York, 84; A M Sachs Gallery, New York, 83; and others. *Teaching:* Lectr drawing, Philadelphia Col Art, 68-73; adj lectr art, Queens Col, NY, 71-76; vis prof art, Pratt Inst, 73; vis asst prof, Univ Colo, 78; vis asst prof art, State Univ NY Stony Brook, 79; vis artist painting, Va Commonwealth Univ, 80; vis artist painting, Cleveland Inst Art, 80-81. *Awards:* Yaddo Fels, 68 & 69; Creative Artists Pub Serv Grant, 77; MacDowell Fel, 77. *Mem:* Women's Caucus Art; Col Art Asn. *Media:* Oil, Watercolor. *Dealer:* Alex Rosenberg Gallery 20 W 57th St New York NY 10019. *Mailing Add:* 152 Wooster St New York NY 10012

KUSAMA, YAYOI
SCULPTOR, PAINTER
b Tokyo, Japan, Mar 22, 41; US citizen. *Study:* Kyoto Arts & Crafts Sch, Japan, 59. *Work:* Chrysler Mus, Provincetown, Mass; Stedelijk Mus, Amsterdam. *Exhib:* DeCordova Mus, Boston, 60; Stadt Mus, Schloss Morsbroish Leverkusen, Ger, 61; Whitney Mus, 62; Inst Contemp Art, 64; Chrysler Mus, 65; one-man shows, Ginza, Tokyo, 75 & 76; plus numerous other group and one-man shows. *Mailing Add:* 1008 Ushigome Heim Shinjuku-Ku 30-2 Chome Haramachi Tokyo Japan

KUSHNER, DOROTHY BROWDY
PAINTER, PRINTMAKER
b Kansas City, Mo. *Study:* Kansas City Teachers Col, BS, 37; Columbia Univ, MA, 38; Art Students League; Art Inst Chicago; Kansas City Art Inst. *Work:* Pasadena Art Mus; Univ Ill; Va Mus Fine Arts; Los Angeles Cedars-Sinai Collection; Palmcrest House, Long Beach. *Exhib:* Libr of Cong, 60; Boston Mus Fine Arts, 65; Calif State Fair, 69; Nat Acad Design, 71; Nat Watercolor Soc, 72-83. *Teaching:* Instr art, Kansas City Pub Schs; instr art, Grover Cleveland High Sch, New York, 40-46; instr art, Pasadena City Col, 69- *Awards:* Laguna Beach Art Asn, 69, Nat Watercolor Soc, 70 & 79 & Pasadena Soc Artists Awards, 70. *Mem:* Am Color Print Soc; Nat Watercolor Soc; Los Angeles Art Asn; Laguna Beach Art Asn; Pasadena Soc Artists. *Media:* Acrylic, Watercolor. *Mailing Add:* 316 San Vincente Blvd #105 Santa Monica CA 90402

KUSHNER, ROBERT ELLIS
PAINTER, PERFORMANCE ARTIST
b Pasadena, Calif, Aug 19, 49. *Study:* Univ Calif, San Diego, BA. *Exhib:* All Calif Exhib, Laguna Beach Art Asn, 69; Biennial, Whitney Mus, New York, 75; New York Hat Line, Mus Mod Art, 78; The Decorative Impulse, Philadelphia Inst Contemp Art, 79; one-man shows, Mayor Gallery, London, 78 & Galerie Daniel Templon, Paris, 79; Venice Biennial, 81; Whitney Ann, Whitney Mus Am Art, 81; Sentimental Fables, Mus Mod Art, New York, 81; Traveling, Inst Contemp Art, Boston, 83; and others. *Bibliog:* Vicky Alliata (auth), Da New York la moda erotica e assurda di Bob Kushner, Luomo, 4/74; Amy Goldin (auth), The new Whitney Biennial: Pattern emerging?, Art in Am, 5/75. *Media:* Acrylic, Found Materials. *Publ:* Contribr, Dimensions of Black, 70; contribr, Unnatural Acts 5, Unnatural Acts Press, 74; The Wonnerful World of Food, Sweet 16 Press, 78; The New York Hat Line, Bozeaux of London Press, 79 & Persian Poems, 81; and others. *Dealer:* Holly Solomon Gallery 724 Fifth Ave New York NY 10019. *Mailing Add:* c/o Holly Solomon Gallery 724 Fifth Ave New York NY 10019

KUSNERZ, PEGGY ANN F
LIBRARIAN, ADMINISTRATOR
b Detroit, Mich, Jan 12, 47. *Study:* Univ Mich, BA(art hist), 71, MLS, 71, MA(Am cult), 82. *Collections Arranged:* Images of Old Age 1790 to Present (coauth, catalog), SITES Exhib, 79. *Pos:* Head libr exten serv & mus libr, Univ Mich, 72-80, head art & archit libr, 80- *Mem:* Art Libr Soc NAm. *Res:* History of photography; art libraries; art bibliography. *Interests:* History of photography. *Publ:* Auth, Selection and acquisition of slides in special libraries, Picturescope, 72; auth, Elsa Fuller: Perceptions of another era, Chronicle, Mich, 74; auth, Oral history, 79 & Collection evaluation techniques in academic art library, 83, Drexel Libr Quart. *Mailing Add:* PO Box 7585 Ann Arbor MI 48107

KUSPIT, DONALD BURTON
HISTORIAN, CRITIC
b New York, NY, Mar 26, 35. *Study:* Columbia Univ, BA; Yale Univ, MA(philos); Univ Frankfurt, PhD; Pa State Univ, MA(art); Univ Mich, PhD(art hist). *Pos:* Contrib ed, Art in Am, Art Voices/SW & Contemp Art/SE; ed, Art Criticism, currently. *Teaching:* Prof art & chmn dept, State Univ NY Stony Brook, 78- *Awards:* Can Coun Leave Fel, 68-69; Nat Endowment for Humanities Younger Humanist Fel, 73-74; Guggenheim Mem fel, 77-78. *Mem:* Col Art Asn Am; Am Soc Aesthet. *Res:* Northern Renaissance art, Dürer in particular; modern art and contemporary criticism. *Publ:* Auth, Art criticism and ideology, Art in Am, summer 81; auth, Civil war: Artist contra critic, 1/81 & auth, The new expressionism: Art as damaged goods, 11/81, Artforum; auth, Clement Greenberg, Art Critic, Univ Wis, 79; The Critic is Artist, UMI Res Press, 82. *Mailing Add:* Dept of Art State Univ NY Stony Brook NY 11794

KUTKA, ANNE (MRS DAVID MCCOSH)
PAINTER
b Danbury, Conn. *Study:* Art Students League, with Kenneth Hays Miller, Kimon Nicolaides & Eugene Fitsch. *Work:* Portland Art Mus, Ore; Am Red Cross, Washington, DC. *Exhib:* New York World's Fair, 39; Seattle Art Mus, 45; Exhib of Watercolors, Drawings & Prints, Metrop Mus Art, New York, 52; Portland Art Mus, 70, 72 & 73; Pac Northwest Art Ann, Eugene, Ore, 72; Earthworks-Artworks, Kerns Art Ctr, Eugene, 77; Mus of Art, Univ Ore, 77. *Teaching:* Instr painting & drawing, M I Kerns Art Ctr, Eugene, 60- *Awards:* Tiffany Fel, 30; G R D Traveling Scholar, 34. *Mem:* Art Students League; Portland Art Mus; Mus Art, Eugene. *Media:* Oil. *Mailing Add:* 1870 Fairmount Blvd Eugene OR 97403

KUVSHINOFF, BERTHA HORNE
PAINTER, SCULPTOR
b Wash. *Work:* Tacoma Art Mus, Wash; Phoenix Art Mus, Ariz; Evansville Art Mus, Ind; Eureka Col Mus, Ill; Miami Art Mus, Fla. *Exhib:* Seattle Russian Ctr, 66; Cath Ctr Gallery, Baltimore, Md, 67; Edmonds Art Gallery, Wash, 70; Eureka Col Gallery, Ill, 71; Int Depeinture, Paris. *Awards:* Silver Medal, 70 & Gold Medal, 71, Acad Int Tommasso Companelia, Rome, Italy. *Bibliog:* Visual Arts, Seattle Times, 7/30/70; article in Roanoke Rev, 9/23/71; Hartland of Nebraska Living, Grand Island Independent, 4/1/72; plus others. *Media:* Oil. *Mailing Add:* 121 1/2 Yale Ave N Seattle WA 98109

KUVSHINOFF, NICOLAI
PAINTER, SCULPTOR
b Siberia. *Work:* Seattle Art Mus, Wash; Atlanta Art Mus, Ga; Omaha Art Mus, Nebr; Santa Fe Art Mus, NMex; Tacoma Art Mus, Wash. *Exhib:* Novikoff Found Fine Arts, Seattle, 61-72; Hutzler's Westview Exhib Hall, Baltimore, Md, 65 & 67; Tacoma Allied Arts, Wash, 66; Seattle Russian Ctr, 66; Stuhr Mus, Grand Island, Nebr, 72; Tacoma Art Mus, Wash; Lima Mus Mod Art, Peru. *Awards:* Silver Medal, 70 & Gold Medal, 72, Acad Int Tommasso Campanelia, Rome, Italy. *Bibliog:* Articles in New York Herald Tribune, Paris, France, 57; articles in Monde, Paris, 57; articles in Art News, New York, 60; plus others. *Media:* Oil on Canvas. *Publ:* Auth, Art Book, Libr Cong, Washington, DC, 59; auth, Drawings, 66. *Mailing Add:* 121 1/2 Yale Ave N Seattle WA 98109

KUWAYAMA, GEORGE
CURATOR, HISTORIAN
b New York, NY, Feb 25, 25. *Study:* Williams Col, BA; Inst Fine Arts, NY Univ; Univ Mich, MA. *Collections Arranged:* Arts Treasures from Japan (auth, catalog), 65; Contemporary Japanese Prints (auth, catalog), 72; Ceramics of Southeast Asia (auth, catalog), 72; Ancient Ritual Bronzes of

China (auth, catalog); Chinese Jade from Southern California Collections (auth, catalog); Chinese Ceramics: The Heeramaneck Collection (auth, catalog); The Joy of Collecting: Far Eastern Art from the Lidow Collection (auth, catalog); The Bizarre Imagery of Yoshitoshi (auth, catalog); Far Eastern Lacquer (auth, catalog). *Pos:* Cur Oriental art, Los Angeles Co Mus Art, 59-63; sr cur Far Eastern art, 63- *Teaching:* Instr Chinese painting, Univ Calif, Los Angeles, 62; instr Far Eastern painting, Univ Southern Calif, 63. *Awards:* Freer Fel, Univ Mich, 55; Hackney Fel, Am Oriental Soc, 56; Inter-Univ Fel, Ford Found, 57. *Mem:* Asn Asian Studies; Chinese Art Soc; Japan Soc; Int House Japan; Col Art Asn. *Res:* Far Eastern art and archaeology. *Publ:* Auth, Sung lacquers, In: Acad Sinica, Proc Int Conf Sinology, Taipei, 82; auth, The Korean celadon, Vol 3, No 3 & Korean art in Western collections: The collection of Robert Moore, Vol 4, No 1, Korean Culture; auth, Object of the month: Chinese carved lacquer tray in the Los Angeles County Museum of Art, Orientations, Vol 14, No 7; auth, The Great Bronze Age of China: A Symposium, Los Angeles Co Mus Art, 83. *Mailing Add:* Los Angeles County Mus Art 5905 Wilshire Blvd Los Angeles CA 90036

KUWAYAMA, TADAAKI
PAINTER
b Nagoya, Japan, Mar 4, 32. *Study:* Tokyo Univ Art, BFA, 56. *Work:* Albright-Knox Art Gallery, Buffalo, NY; Worcester Art Mus, Mass; Wadsworth Atheneum, Hartford, Conn; Larry Aldrich Mus, Ridgefield, Conn; Herron Art Mus, Indianapolis. *Exhib:* Carnegie Int, Pittsburgh, 61-67; Formalist Show, Washington Gallery Mod Art, Washington, DC, 63; Systemic Show, Guggenheim Mus, New York, 66; New Forms & Shapes of Color, Stedelijk Mus, Amsterdam, 67; Plus by Minus, Today's Half-Century, Albright-Knox Art Gallery, 68. *Awards:* Nat Coun Arts Grant, 69. *Media:* Acrylic. *Mailing Add:* 136 W 24th St New York NY 10011

KWIECINSKI, CHESTER MARTIN
EDUCATOR, PAINTER
b Youngstown, Ohio, July 7, 24. *Study:* Kansas City Art Inst, BFA & MFA; Kansas City Univ; Youngstown Univ. *Work:* Butler Inst Am Art, Youngstown, Ohio; El Paso Mus of Art, Tex. *Comn:* Historical murals, McSorley Colonial, Pittsburgh, Pa, 54; murals (with Bill Rakocy), Colonial House and Congo Rm, Youngstown, Ohio, 60 & Alberini Restaurant, Niles, Ohio, 65. *Exhib:* Mo State Fair, 49 & 50; Albright-Knox Gallery Art, Buffalo, NY, 52; El Paso Regional Show, 76; one-man show, Butler Inst Art, Youngstown Ohio, 62. *Pos:* Mus dir, Abilene Fine Arts Mus, Tex, 73-80. *Teaching:* Instr, Warren City Schs, Ohio, 54-66; assoc prof painting, Col of Artesia, NMex, 67-71. *Awards:* Best Local Art, New Year Show, Butler Inst Am Art, 42; Purchase Award, Carlsbad Art Asn, NMex, 68; Purchase Award, Hobbs-LLano Estacado, Hobbs Art Asn, NMex, 69. *Mem:* Am Asn Mus; Tex Asn Mus; Permian Basin Mus Asn, 78. *Media:* Watercolor, Oil. *Publ:* Guest art ed, Abilene Reporter News, 74; auth, articles, Pigment & Form, 64. *Mailing Add:* 4010 Potomac Abilene TX 79605

L

LAATSCH, GARY
SCULPTOR
b Saginaw, Mich, June 13, 56. *Study:* Cranbrook Acad Art, BFA(sculpture), 78; Art Inst Chicago, MFA(sculpture), 81. *Exhib:* 78th Exhibit by Artists of Chicago and Vicinity, Art Inst Chicago, 81; Michigan Artists, Detroit Inst Art, 82; 12th Biennial Michiana Regional Exhibition, Art Ctr Inc, South Bend, Ind, 82; solo exhib, Saginaw Art Mus, Mich, 82 & Pontiac Art Ctr, Mich, 83; A Sense of Humor, Visual Arts Ctr Alaska, Anchorage, 83; 25th Mid-Michigan Exhibition, Midland Ctr Arts, 83; 47th Flint Art Exhib, Flint Inst Arts, Mich, 83. *Teaching:* Artist in residence, Millet Learning Ctr, Bridgeport, Mich, 83; instr design & sculpture, Saginaw Valley State Col, 83-84. *Awards:* First Prize, 21st Mid-Michigan Exhibition, Midland Coun Arts, 80; Purchase Award, 78th Exhibition by Artists of Chicago and Vicinity, Peat, Marwick, Mitchell & Co, 81; Award Merit, 47th Flint Art Exhib, J L Hudson Co, 83. *Bibliog:* Marsha Miro (auth), Exhibit proves too much is too much, Detroit Free Press, 3/21/82; Barron M Hirsch (auth), Laatsch in progress, Saginaw News, 8/21/82; James E Harvey (auth), Area show focuses on simple, direct, Flint J, 9/30/83. *Dealer:* Robert Kidd Assoc 107 Townsend St Birmingham MI 48011; Gallery 106 106 W Third St Perrysburg OH 43551. *Mailing Add:* 2680 Midland Rd Saginaw MI 48603

LABINO, DOMINICK
GLASS BLOWER, SCULPTOR
b Fairmount City, Pa, Dec 4, 10. *Study:* Carnegie Inst Technol, 29-32; Toledo Mus Art Sch Design, 47-49; Bowling Green State Univ, hon DFA, 70; Univ Toledo, hon DFA, 79. *Work:* Smithsonian Inst, Washington, DC; Pilkington Mus Glass, St Helens, Eng; Victoria & Albert Mus, London. *Comn:* Entrance to Glass Gallery, Toledo Mus Art, 69; Long Chain Molecules, Johns-Manville Corp, Denver, 73; Pyradon, State Off Tower, Columbus, Ohio, 75; Icosahedron, Bowling Green State Univ, 76; Ionic Struct of Glass (circular window), Corning Mus Glass, 80; and others. *Exhib:* Toledo Glass Nat & Traveling Exhib, 66, 68 & 70; 20th-24th Ceramic & Sculpture Show, Butler Inst Am Art, Youngstown, Ohio; Dominick Labino--A Retrospective Exhib, Corning Mus Glass, 69; one-man exhib, Columbus Gallery Fine Arts, Ohio, 70 & 71; Dominick Labino--A Decade of Glass Craftsmanship, 1964-74, Pilkington Mus Glass, Victoria & Albert Mus & Toledo Mus Art, 74-75. *Pos:* Hon cur glass, Toledo Mus Art, 68-; retired vpres, Johns-Manville Corp,

res consult glass fibers, 74-75. *Teaching:* Instr hot glass, Toledo Mus Art, 66 & 67; vis prof hot glass, Bowling Green State Univ, 72-73. *Awards:* First Award for Glass, Toledo Mus Art, 66, 68 & 70; Ohio Arts Coun Award for Glass, 71; Toledo Glass & Ceramic Award, Am Ceramic Soc, 72. *Mem:* Fel Am Ceramic Soc; fel Am Crafts Coun; Toledo Fedn Art Soc; Craft Club Toledo; Int Inst Arts & Lett. *Media:* Molten glass. *Res:* Technical and creative aspects of glass-making in earliest times; technique of Eighteenth Dynasty Egyptian hollow glass vessels; glass fibers. *Publ:* Auth, The Egyptian sand-core vessels, Corning J Glass Studies, 66; auth, Visual Art in Glass, W C Brown, 68. *Mailing Add:* 23271 Kellogg Rd Grand Rapids OH 43522

LABLE, ELIOT
PAINTER, SCULPTOR
Study: Brooklyn Mus Art Sch, 72-73. *Exhib:* Reflections Ann, Aldrich Mus Contemp Art, 76; Whitney Counterweight, New York, 79 & 81; solo exhib, Frank Marino Gallery, New York, 79-81; Alternative Mus, New York, 81; Constructed Paintings, Allan Frumkin Gallery, New York, 83. *Teaching:* Mem fac, Brooklyn Mus Art Sch, 78- *Awards:* Comt Visual Arts Grant, 78; New York Found Arts Grant, 82; Nat Endowment Arts Artist in Residence Grant, 83. *Bibliog:* Palmer Pordner (auth), article, Art Speak, 4/80; Robert Harding (auth), article, Arts Mag, 4/81; Barnaby Ruhe (auth), Falling show, Art World, 3/83. *Mailing Add:* 152 W 25th St New York NY 10001

LABRIE, ROSE
PAINTER, WRITER
b Boston, Mass, Aug 31, 16. *Study:* Univ NH, 44-45; with Robert Grant & Carroll Towle, 54-56; Univ Wis, 58-59. *Work:* Strawbery Banke Colonial Preserv Mus, Portsmouth, NH; Mus Am Folk Art, New York; Univ NH Colonial Heritage Film Ser, Durham; John F Barker Collection, Cambridge, Eng; Elliot Mus, Stuart, Fla; and others. *Comn:* Mural, USS Thresher, comn by George Bergeron Collection, New Market, NH; Elliott Mus, Stuart, Fla; Mus Am Folk Art, New York; Strawberry Banke Mus, Portsmouth, NH. *Exhib:* Shayne Gallery, Montreal, Can, 76; Palm Beach Galleries, Fla, 76; Greenwich Workshop Gallery, Fairfield, Conn, 79; Harold Anderson's Shop, Palm Beach, Fla, 80; Nassau Co Mus Fine Arts, Roslyn Harbor, New York, 80-81; one-man exhib, Chape Art Ctr, St Anselm's Col, Manchester, NH, 83; and others. *Awards:* First Prize for Mem Painting of USS Thresher; Works Being Reproduced for Needlepoint Kits, Early Am Soc; Diploma of Merit, Univ Arts, Salsomaggiore Terme, Italy, 80; and others. *Bibliog:* Vermont Life, 79; Robert Bishop (auth), Folk Artists in America, Dutton, 79; Jay Johnson & William C Ketcham Jr (auths), American Artists of the Twentieth Century, Rizzoli Int Publ; Henry Niemann (auth), A Collector's Guide to American Folk Art, Chanticleer Press. *Mem:* Copley Soc; York Art Asn; Seacoast Writers Asn; and others. *Media:* Oil. *Publ:* Contribr, Yankee, NH Profiles, 58-68 & Nat Antiques Rev, 71; contrib cover artist, Early Am Life, 73; auth & illusr, King the Leprechaun Pony, 78; auth, Dancer's Image, 81; auth, Randy the Rooster, 83; and others. *Dealer:* Jay Johnson America's Folk Heritage Gallery 1044 Madison Ave New York NY 10001. *Mailing Add:* 45 Washington Rd Rye NH 03870

LACHAPELLE, JOSEPH ROBERT
SCULPTOR, EDUCATOR
b Little Fall, Minn, July 12, 43. *Study:* Wayne State Univ, Detroit, Mich, BS, 67; Ohio State Univ, Columbus, MFA, 70, PhD, 77. *Exhib:* Va Artists, Richmond Mus, 72; Nat Invitational, Madison Art Ctr, 72; Artists in Wood, Ohio State Univ & Univ Ky, 74; Columbus Mus Art, Ohio, 74, 75 & 76; one-man show, Centro de Arte y Comunicacion, Buenos Aires, 82; Hudson River Mus, 82. *Pos:* Asst gallery dir, Ohio State Univ, 75-76. *Teaching:* Instr sculpture, Western Ill Univ, 70-71; instr sculpture, Hampton Inst, Va, 71-74; asst prof sculpture, New York Univ, 77- *Awards:* Purchase Award, Western Ill Univ, 71. *Mem:* Col Art Asn. *Media:* Wood, Light. *Publ:* Auth, Conflict between research and practice, 82 & auth, Creativity research: Its sociological and educational limitations, 83, Studies Art Educ. *Mailing Add:* 63 Inwood Dr Bardonia NY 10954

LACHER, JOHANNES
PAINTER
b Marburg, Ger, Dec 26, 40. *Study:* Acad Fine Arts, Munich, cert, 68; Univ Ga, MFA, 70. *Work:* Downey Mus Art, Calif; Albuquerque Mus; Tamarind Inst, Univ NM Art Mus, Albuquerque. *Exhib:* Systems, ECarolina Univ, 77; Fall Invitational, Roswell Mus & Art Ctr, NM, 77; Patterns, Downey Mus Art, Calif, 80; Spring in Show, Los Angeles Co Mus Rental Gallery, 81; Quiet Commitment, Fisher Gallery, Univ Southern Calif, 82. *Teaching:* Asst prof painting, Univ NM, Albuquerque, 73-77 & Univ Southern Calif, 78-82. *Awards:* Ford Found Travel Grant, 75; Nat Endowment Arts Visual Artists Fel, 81. *Bibliog:* Van Deren Coke (auth), Perfections of line, Art News, 11/74; William Peterson (auth), article, Artspace, 7/78; Betty Brown (auth), article, Arts Mag, 5/83. *Media:* Acrylic, Oil. *Mailing Add:* c/o Kirk de Gooyer Gallery 1308 Factory Pl Los Angeles CA 90013

LACK, RICHARD FREDERICK
PAINTER, INSTRUCTOR
b Minneapolis, Minn, Mar 26, 28. *Study:* Minneapolis Sch Art; R H Ives Gammell Studios, Boston. *Work:* Maryhill Mus Fine Arts, Washington; Elizabeth T Greenshields Mem Found Collection, Montreal, Que; Springville Mus Art, Utah. *Comn:* Six portraits of Joseph P Kennedy, Jr, comn by Ambassador Kennedy & Kennedy Found, New York. *Exhib:* Allied Artists Am, 53; Boston Arts Festival, 53 & 54; Nat Acad Design Ann, 55; Twin City Biennial, Minneapolis Inst Arts, 62; Am Artists Prof League Nat, 67-73. *Teaching:* Dir & instr painting & drawing, Atelier Lack, Minneapolis, 69- *Awards:* First Prize, Copley Soc, Boston, 62; Gold Medal, Am Artists Prof

League, 67 & 73 & Margaret Fernald Dole Prize for Best Portrait, 72; and others. *Bibliog:* D Jardine (auth), Richard Lack's atelier system of training painters, Am Artist Mag, 6/71. *Mem:* Am Artists Prof League. *Media:* Oil. *Publ:* Auth, On the Training of Painters and Notes on the Atelier Program, 79 & Classical Realism, The Other Twentieth Century, 82, Atelier Lack Inc. *Mailing Add:* 5827 Louis Ave Minnetonka MN 55343

LACKTMAN, MICHAEL
CRAFTSMAN, JEWELER
b Philadelphia, Pa, Mar 1, 38. *Study:* Pa State Col, 57-61; Cranbrook Acad of Art, Bloomfield Hills, Mich, 61-63; Kunsthaandverskolen, Copenhagen, Denmark, 65-66. *Work:* Pa State Col, Millersville, Pa; Cranbrook Acad Art, Bloomfield Hills, Mich. *Comn:* Liturgical metalry, Redeemer Lutheran Church, Livermore, Calif, 71; Kiddusch cup, Brandeis Univ, Waltham, Mass, 63. *Exhib:* Calif Design VI, Crocker Art Mus, Sacramento, Calif, 69; Calif Design XI, Pasadena Art Mus, Calif, 71; Metal Experience, Oakland Art Mus, Calif, 71; Fourth Int Jewelry Exhib, Schmuckmuseum, Pzorheim, Ger, 72; Diamond Today: Int Jewelry Exhib, New York, 75. *Teaching:* Asst prof design, Univ Calif, Berkeley, 66-73, Univ Chile, Santiago, 72-73; prof jewelry & metalsmithing, Univ Wis-Milwaukee, 73- *Awards:* Louis Comfort Tiffany Grant, 63; Ford Found Grant, 72-73; Nat Endowment Humanities Grant, 75. *Bibliog:* Articles & photographs of work, Art & Archit, 71 & Playboy Mag, 75. *Mem:* Am Craftsman Coun; San Francisco Bay Asn; Sterling - Silversmiths Guild Am; Scand-Am Found; Col Art Asn. *Media:* Jewelry, Metals. *Mailing Add:* Dept of Art Univ of Wis Milwaukee WI 53201

LACROIX, FLORA LUISA
PAINTER
b Mexico City, Mex; nat US. *Study:* Acad Jerome, Paris, 29-30; Ecole Nat Superior Beaux Arts, Paris, with Morrisset, 30-31; Ecole Nat Arts Decoratifs, Nice, with Paul Audra, 32-33; Inst Tecnol Sonora, Hon Dipl Fine Arts, 82. *Work:* State Capitol Bldg, Phoenix; Centennial Mus, El Paso, Tex. *Exhib:* Solo exhibs, El Kiosco Artes, Hermosillo, Mex, 76, Centennial Mus, El Paso, Tex, 77, Las Vegas Art Mus, 79 & Inst Tecnol Sonora, Mex, 82; Silver City Art Mus, NMex, 76. *Pos:* Archit student, Indian Hill Land Co, Tucson, 55-60 & Lusk Corp, Tucson, 62-64. *Teaching:* Instr fine arts, Canyon Oro Adult Educ, Tucson, 71-73, Lacroix Studio, 73-81 & Inst Tecnol Sonora, Mex, 82. *Awards:* Third Prize, Salon Tuilleries Regional Ann, 33. *Bibliog:* Edna Gundersen (auth), Kino misssions immortalized, El Paso Times, 6/12/77; Laurence W Cheek (auth), Flora Lacroix has a mission in life, Tucson Citizen, 12/8/78. *Mem:* Salmagundi Club; Am Artists Prof League; Am Soc Prof Consult. *Media:* Oil, Charcoal. *Res:* Imaginative thinking. *Mailing Add:* 2600 Skyline Dr #10 Tucson AZ 85718

LACROIX, RICHARD
PAINTER, PRINTMAKER
b Montreal, Que, July 14, 39. *Study:* Montreal Inst Graphic Arts, dipl; Atelier 17, Paris; Montreal Sch Fine Art, cert pedagog. *Work:* Montreal Mus Fine Arts; Nat Gallery Can; Cabinet Estampes, Paris; Mus Mod Art, New York; Victoria & Albert Mus, London. *Comn:* Several print albums, Montreal Graphic Guild, 66-72; kinetic sculptures, Can Pavilion & Youth Pavilion, Expo 67 & Montreal Int Airport, 68; murals, Montreal Sch Bd, 71. *Exhib:* Color Prints Am, 70; 2nd Int Bienal Engraving, Paris, 70; Quebec Pavilion, Osaka, Japan, 70; 4th Am Bienal Engraving, Chile, 70; 2nd Brit Int Print Bienal, 70. *Pos:* Co-founder, Fusion Arts. *Teaching:* Instr etching, Montreal Sch Fine Art, 60-61; vis instr art hist, Univ Quebec, 69-70. *Awards:* Can Graphic Asn Prize, 64; Prize, Int Biennal, Lugano, Switz, 64; Prize for Painting, Montreal Hadassah, 65. *Bibliog:* Lacroix, 65 & S Raphael (auth), Richard Lacroix, 71, Vie Arts; Deroussan (auth), Richard Lacroix, Lidec, 66. *Mem:* Soc Prof Artists Quebec; Graphic Guild (pres, 66-75); Atelier Libre Recherches Graphiques (dir, 64-75). *Media:* Acrylic. *Mailing Add:* 9 St Paul Ouest Montreal PQ H2Y 1Y6 Canada

LACY, ROBERT EUGENE
PAINTER
b St James, Mo, Aug 29, 43. *Study:* Pvt study with Earl Strebeck. *Exhib:* Sixty-first Ann Exhib, Birmingham Art Mus, Ala, 68; Mid-America I, Nelson-Atkins Art Mus, Kansas City & City Art Mus of St Louis, 68; Tulsa Regional Art Exhib, Arts Coun of Tulsa, 68; Okla Touring Exhib, Arts Coun of Tulsa, 69; March Ann Exhib, William A Fransworth Art Mus, Rockland, Maine, 69; 34th Ann Midyear Show, Butler Inst Am Art, Youngstown, Ohio, 69; 60th Anniversary Exhib, Wadsworth Atheneum, Hartford, Conn, 70. *Awards:* Second Ann Tulsa Award for Painting, Inc, 68. *Media:* Oil, Pencil. *Dealer:* Midtown Galleries 11 E 57th St New York NY 10022. *Mailing Add:* 517 N Charles Ave St James MO 65559

LACY, SUZANNE
CONCEPTUAL ARTIST, EDUCATOR
b Wasco, Calif, Oct 21, 45. *Study:* Univ Calif, Santa Barbara, BA; Fresno State Col; Calif Inst Arts, MFA; study with Judy Chicago, Sheila de Bretteville & Allan Kaprow. *Comn:* Three Weeks in May (sociological performance structure), Los Angeles, 77; International Dinner Party (honoring Judy Chicago), San Francisco, 79; Making it Safe: A Project on Violence Against Women in Ocean Park, Ocean Park Proj, 79; Women's Caucus Arts Conf Design, New Orleans, 80; Freeze Frame, San Francisco, 82. *Exhib:* performances, Mus Contemp Art, Bologna, Italy, 77, Col Art Asn Conf, Los Angeles Hilton, Calif, 77, De Young Downtown Ctr, San Francisco, 77, Floating Mus, San Francisco, 77, and/or Gallery, Seattle, 80 & Inst Contemp Art, London, 80. *Teaching:* Mem fac performance & feminist educ, Feminist Studio Workshop, Los Angeles, 74-77; mem fac critical studies, San Francisco

Art Inst, 75-77; lectr performance, Univ Calif, San Diego, 76-79. *Awards:* Nat Endowment Arts Grants, 79 & 81. *Bibliog:* Martha Rosler (auth), The private & the public, 9/77 & Moira Roth (auth), Visions, 10/80, Artforum; Moira Roth (auth), article, Village Voice, 9/82. *Mem:* Los Angeles Inst Contemp Art; The Woman's Bldg (mem bd, 74-79); Women's Caucus Arts (nat bd, 80-82). *Media:* Theatrical and non-theatrical performance; conceptual photography, books and video. *Publ:* Auth, Rape Is, 76 & Falling Apart, 76, pvt publ. *Mailing Add:* 812 Traction Ave Los Angeles CA 90013

LADEN, FRIEDA SAVITZ See Savitz, Frieda

LADER, MELVIN PAUL
HISTORIAN, EDUCATOR
b Auburn, NY, Jan 30, 47. *Study:* State Univ NY, Albany, BA, 69, MA, 72; Univ Del, PhD, 81. *Teaching:* Asst prof art hist, George Washington Univ, 78- *Awards:* Mus Fel, Smithsonian Inst, 77-78; Fel, Rockefeller Found, 78. *Mem:* Col Art Asn; Arch Am Art. *Res:* Abstract expressionism; twentieth century American art; modern art patronage. *Publ:* Contribr, Avant-Garde Painting and Sculpture in America, Del Art Mus, 75; auth, Graham, Gorky, DeKooning and the Ingres revival in America, 78 & Howard Putzel: Proponent of surrealism and abstract expressionism in America, 82, Arts Mag; auth, Charles Seliger (exhib catalog), Andrew Crispo Gallery, 83; auth, Arshile Gorky's The artist and his mother, Arts Mag, 1/84. *Mailing Add:* Dept Art George Washington Univ Washington DC 20052

LADERMAN, GABRIEL
PAINTER, EDUCATOR
b Brooklyn, NY, Dec 26, 29. *Study:* Brooklyn Mus Sch; Brooklyn Col, BA; Hans Hofmann Sch Fine Arts; Cornell Univ, MFA; Atelier 17, fel, 52. *Work:* Cleveland Mus; Boston Mus; plus others. *Exhib:* Milwaukee Art Ctr, 69; Corcoran Gallery of Art, 69; Milwaukee Art Ctr, Wis, 69; Whitney Mus Am Art, New York, 70; NJ State Mus, Trenton, 70; De Cordova Mus, Lincoln, Mass, 71; Am Acad Arts & Lett, 72; Joslyn Mus Art, Omaha, Nebr, 73; Arts Club of Chicago, 73; Mus Fine Arts, Boston, 74; plus others. *Pos:* Founding dir, Godwin Ternbach Mus, Queens Col. *Teaching:* Asst, Cornell Univ, 55-57; asst prof, State Univ NY New Paltz, 57-59; asst prof, Pratt Inst, 59-69; prof art & chmn art dept, Queens Col, 69-82; prof, Yale Univ, 83-84. *Awards:* Fulbright Fel to Italy, 62-63; Nat Endowment Arts Sr Fel, 82-83; Ingram Merrill Found, 75-77 & 84. *Bibliog:* L Campbell (auth), Gabriel Laderman: a world inside itself, Art News, 10/72. *Publ:* Articles in Col Art J, 65 & 82, Art News, 67 & 70 & Art Forum, 70-73. *Dealer:* Schoelkopf Gallery 825 Madison Ave New York NY 10021; Harkus Gallery Boston MA. *Mailing Add:* 760 West End Ave New York NY 10025

LAEMMLE, CHERYL
PAINTER
b Minneapolis, Minn, Aug 11, 47. *Study:* Humboldt State Univ, BA, 74; Washington State Univ, MFA, 78. *Exhib:* New New York, Fla State Univ, Tallahassee, 82 & Metropolitan Mus & Art Ctr, Coral Gables, 82; Agitated Figures: The New Emotionalism, HallWalls, Buffalo, NY, 82 & Hal Bromm Gallery, New York, 82; By the Sea, Barbara Toll Fine Arts Gallery, New York, 82; New Mus, New York, 82; Self Image, Sharpe Gallery, New York, 83; solo exhib, Barbara Toll Fine Arts, New York, 83. *Awards:* First Place Painting, Pac NW Arts, 77; Creative Artists Pub Serv Prog Fel, 80. *Bibliog:* Lisa Peters (auth), article, Arts Mag, 5/83; Richard Armstrong (auth), article, Art Forum, summer 83; Ronny Cohen (auth), article, Art News, summer 83. *Mailing Add:* 123 W 20th St New York NY 10015

LAESSIG, ROBERT
PAINTER, ILLUSTRATOR
b NJ, 20. *Study:* Art Students League; also study in Ger. *Work:* Cleveland Mus Fine Arts, Ohio; Butler Inst Am Art, Ohio; Norfolk Mus, Va; Springfield Inst Fine Arts, Ohio; Akron Art Inst, Ohio. *Comn:* Official White House Christmas card, comn by President & Mrs Johnson, 64-68. *Exhib:* Philadelphia Watercolor Soc, 64-70; Allied Artists, New York, 70-72; Pittsburgh Watercolor Show, 78; Ohio Watercolor Show, 78-79; Am Watercolor Show, 79. *Pos:* Pres, Robert Laessig Fine Arts Co, West Richfield, Ohio, 69- *Awards:* Prizes, Am Watercolor Soc, 70 & 71, Wichita Centennial, 70 & Pittsburgh Watercolor, 80. *Mem:* Nat Acad Design; Am Watercolor Soc; Ohio Watercolor Soc. *Mailing Add:* 5026 Hawkins Rd Richfield OH 44286

LAFAYE, NELL MURRAY
PAINTER, EDUCATOR
b Columbia, SC, Nov 9, 37. *Study:* Sullins Col, with Alvin Sella; Cranbrook Acad Art, BFA, 58, with Fred Mitchell, MFA, 59; with Zolton Sepeshy & Marianne Strengall. *Work:* SC State Collection; Univ SC. *Exhib:* Spring Mills Traveling Art Show, Lancaster, SC, 61-69; Crafts Exhib, 65 & Painting Exhib, 66 & 67, Mint Mus Art; Mainstreams Int, Marietta, Ohio, 68 & 69; Gardens Art Festival, Pine Mountain, Ga, 72. *Teaching:* Asst prof art, Univ SC, 68-75, assoc prof art, 75-, dir undergrad studies, 76-80, asst head, 80- *Awards:* First Prize, Spring Mills, 68; First Prize, SC State Fair, 83. *Bibliog:* Jack Morris (auth), Contemporary South Carolina artists, SC Tricentennial Comn, 70. *Mem:* SC Art Educ Asn (pres, 67-69); Nat Art Educ Asn; Am Craftsmen Coun; SC Artist Guild. *Media:* Oil, Acrylic. *Mailing Add:* 2630 Stratford Rd Columbia SC 29204

LAFON, DEE J
PAINTER, SCULPTOR
b Ogden, Utah, Apr 23, 29. *Study:* Weber State Col; Univ Utah, BFA, 60, MFA, 62; also with Francis de Erdley, Phil Paradise & Marquerite Wildenhain. *Work:* Utah State Fine Art Collection, Salt Lake City; Okla Art

Ctr, Oklahoma City; Philbrook Art Mus, Tulsa, Okla; Univ Okla, Norman; Dillard Collection, Univ NC, Greensboro. *Comn:* Wood sculpture, Univ Okla, 72. *Exhib:* Am Drawing Bienniale, Norfolk, Va, 69; Int Miniature Prints Show, Pratt Graphic Ctr, New York, 70; Midwest Bienniale, Omaha, Nebr, 72; one-man shows, Springfield Art Mus, Mo, 78 & Goddard Art Ctr, Ardmore, Ore, 78. *Teaching:* Instr ceramics & drawing, Weber State Col, 62-64; assoc prof painting & drawing, ECent State Col, 64-, chmn dept art, 79- *Awards:* Eight State Exhib Purchase Award, 70; Hon Mention, Midwest Bienniale, 72; Tulsa Regional Painting & Drawing Award, 72. *Mem:* Okla Designer Craftsman. *Media:* Oil, Multi-media. *Dealer:* Oklahoma Art Ctr 3113 General Pershing Blvd Oklahoma City OK 73118; Ben Pickard Gallery 541 NW 39th St Oklahoma City OK 73118. *Mailing Add:* 2127 Woodland Dr Ada OK 74820

LA FON, JULIA ANNA
PAINTER, CRAFTSMAN
b New Salem, Pa, Nov 24, 19. *Study:* George Washington Univ; Univ NMex. *Work:* Santa Fe Fine Arts Mus, NMex; NMex Bank, Hobbs; Albuquerque Nat Bank, NMex; Jonson Gallery, Univ NMex; Mus Albuquerque, NMex. *Exhib:* Colorado Springs Fine Art Ctr, 75; Four Corners Biennial, Phoenix Art Mus, Ariz, 77; Recent Acquisitions, 77 & In the Pub Interest, 78, Santa Fe Fine Arts Mus; Santa Fe Festival Arts, NMex, 79; Women in the Southwest, Albuquerque, NMex, 79. *Awards:* First & Second Prizes, Contemp Crafts Exhib, Albuquerque, 71; First Prize, Carlsbad Regional Art Exhib, NMex, 73. *Bibliog:* Article, La Rev Mod, Paris, 72; Steve Edwards (auth), The Art of Working with Leather, Chilton, 75. *Dealer:* Thompson Gallery 815 N Central Phoenix AZ 85004; Meridian Gallery 220 Central Ave SW Albuquerque NM 87102. *Mailing Add:* 803 Martingale SE Albuquerque NM 87123

LAGER, FANNIE
SCULPTOR, COLLECTOR
b New York, NY, Nov 14, 11. *Study:* Brooklyn Col, painting with Nancy Ranson, 39-41; Brooklyn Mus Art Sch, painting with Isaac Soyer, 42-70 & sculpture with Toshio Odate, Barney Hodes & Lee Ackerman, 74-81; Sculpture Ctr, sculpture with Shulamith Brumer, 71-73. *Exhib:* Second Ann Open Juried--Non Members, Salmagundi Club, New York, 79; one-woman shows, Atlantic Gallery, Brooklyn & Soho, NY, 79 & 81; Knickerbocker Artists 29th Ann, Nat Arts Club, New York, 79; Brooklyn 1980, Community Gallery, Brooklyn Mus, NY, 80; First open show for sculpture, Salmagundi Club, 82. *Bibliog:* Sheila H Jacobs (ed), Retirees--Aetna Life & Casualty, Aetna Circle, 3-4/81; Denise Bibro (auth), 3 Dimensions by 3, Artspeak, 6/81; Kevin Flood (auth), Second Career Fills Her Retirement Years, Aetna Circle, 9-10/82. *Mem:* Assoc mem Audubon Artists; New York Artists Equity Asn Inc; Salmagundi Club. *Media:* Wood, Stone. *Collection:* American contemporary impressionism. *Dealer:* Dorsey's Art Gallery 533 Rodgers Ave Brooklyn NY 11225. *Mailing Add:* 2215 Newkirk Ave Brooklyn NY 11226

LAGORIO, IRENE R
CRITIC, PRINTMAKER
b Oakland, Calif, May 2, 21. *Study:* Calif Col Arts & Crafts, Oakland, 38-39; Univ Calif, Berkeley, AB & MA, 42; Columbia Univ, 45. *Work:* Monterey Art Comn Conf Ctr Collection, Calif; Monterey Peninsula Mus of Art Collection; Northern Calif Savings & Loan Collection; Germanischen Mus & Libr Collection, Nuremberg, Ger; Sunset Cult Ctr Collection, Carmel, Calif. *Comn:* Mosaic murals, SS President Roosevelt, Am Pres Lines, 61 & Soc Nat Bank, Cleveland, Ohio, 69; jewel painted mural, Lloyd Ctr, Portland, Ore, 60 & metal sculpture mural, Seaside, Ore, US Bancarp, 64; mosaic mural design, Episcopal Condominium, Los Gatos, Calif, 70. *Exhib:* Metrop Mus Art Watercolor Exhib, 53; Am Color Print Soc Ann, Philadelphia, 72; US Info Serv Traveling Color Print Exhib, throughout Europe, 72; one-man shows, Onstage and Backstage at Sunset Ctr, Marjorie Evans Gallery, Sunset Ctr, Carmel, Calif, 79 & Fluoro Paint & Printers Ink, Monterey Peninsula Mus Art, Calif, 80. *Pos:* Cur educ dept, Calif Palace of Legion of Honor, 50, dir, Achenbach Found Graphic Arts, 51-55; art critic, Monterey Peninsula Herald, currently & artist, Weekend Mag, 75- *Teaching:* Spec lectr, Univ Calif Exten Courses, 60- *Awards:* Chapelbrook Found Grand for Graphic Proj, Boston, 69; Best in Show, Monterey Peninsula Mus Art 7th Competitive, 71. *Bibliog:* E Loran (auth), The San Francisco scene, Art News, 53; G Dorfles (auth), Modern painters in USA, Domus Mag, 54; Exposition de San Francisco, La Rev Mod, 60. *Mem:* Carmel Art Asn (pres, 72-); Ars Assoc Found (dir, 61-). *Publ:* Illusr, This Open Zoo-A Bestiary, Salamander, 71. *Mailing Add:* First & Mission Sts Box 153 Carmel CA 93921

LAGUNA, MARIELLE
PAINTER, INSTRUCTOR
b New York, NY. *Study:* NY Univ (archit); New Sch; Brooklyn Mus Art Sch, with Reuben Tam & Manfred Scwartz; Adelphi Univ; Pratt Graphic Ctr. *Work:* Rockefeller Family; Brooklyn Col; also in many pvt & indust collections. *Exhib:* Pa Acad Fine Arts, Philadelphia, 64; Allied Artists Am Ann, 64; Nat Acad Design Ann, 64; Salvatora Rosa, Naples, Italy, 72; Pallazzo Vechio, Florence, Italy, 72; and others. *Pos:* Colorist, Lawrence Laguna Architect, 60-; interior designer (free lance). *Teaching:* Instr art, Baldwin, Oceanside, Rockville Centre Pub Schs continuing educ workshops, 57- *Awards:* Gold Medal (First Prize), Hofstra Univ, 61; 11 Resident Fels including Yaddo & The Edward MacDowell Colony, 65, 69, 73, 75 & 77; Medal of Honor, Nat Asn Women Artists, 67. *Bibliog:* Newspaper interviews, Taos, Long Island Press, News Day, and others. *Mem:* Artist Equity of New York, Inc; Nat Asn Women Artists, Inc; New York Soc Women Artists; Contemp Artists. *Media:* Oil, Acrylic. *Mailing Add:* 324 Christopher St Oceanside NY 11572

LA HOTAN, ROBERT L
PAINTER
b Cleveland, Ohio, 1927. *Study:* Columbia Univ, Brevoort-Eickmeyer fel, 50-53. *Work:* Lehigh Univ, Bethlehem, Pa; Northern Trust Co, Kansas City, Mo; Univ NC; Hirshhorn Collection. *Exhib:* Corcoran Biennial, 56; Dallas Mus Contemp Art, 58; Rochester Mem Art Gallery, 66; one-man show, Lehigh Univ, 69; Kraushaar Galleries, 69, 72, 75, 78 & 81; Hull Gallery, Washington, DC, 79 & 82. *Awards:* Fulbright Fel to Ger, 53-55; Purchase Awards, Am Acad Inst Arts & Letters, 73-77. *Media:* Oil, Watercolor. *Dealer:* Kraushaar Galleries 724 Fifth Ave New York NY 10028. *Mailing Add:* 865 West End Ave New York NY 10025

LAHR, J(OHN) STEPHEN
PAINTER, EDUCATOR
b Lincoln, Nebr, Aug 5, 43. *Study:* Univ Nebr, Lincoln, BFA, 68, with James Eisentrager, MEd, 72, EdD, 79. *Work:* Univ Nebr, Omaha; Pub Libr, Lincoln, Nebr; Joslyn Art Mus. *Exhib:* Paper in Particular, Columbia Col Gallery, Mo, 81, 82 & 83; Mid-Four Regional Competition, Nelson Gallery Art, Atkins Mus, Kansas City, Mo, 81 & 82; Winter Art/Manhattan, Strecker Gallery, Manhattan, Kans, 83; Watercolor Missouri, William Woods Col, Fulton, 83; two-person exhib, Joslyn Art Mus, Omaha, 83. *Collections Arranged:* Missouri Folk: Their Creative Images, Folk Arts Exhib, 82. *Pos:* State art dir, Nebr Dept Educ, Lincoln, 74-79. *Teaching:* Instr art, Lincoln Pub Sch, Nebr, 69-72 & Univ Nebr, Lincoln, 72-73; asst prof art educ & studio, Univ Nebr, Omaha, 78-80; asst prof art educ & painting, Univ Mo, Columbia, 80- *Awards:* Purchase Awards, Joslyn Art Mus, 80 & Univ Nebr, Omaha, 82; Second Place, Watercolor Missouri, William Woods Col, 83. *Mem:* Nat Art Educ Asn; Nat Asn State Dir Art Educ (secy-treas, 74-79). *Media:* Watercolor, Acrylics. *Publ:* Auth, Handbook for Art Education, Nebr Dept Educ, 78; contribr, Who teaches art: Report of recent surveys, In: Studies in Art Educ, Nat Art Educ Asn, 83-84. *Mailing Add:* 302 Longfellow Lane Columbia MO 65201

LAI, WAIHANG
PAINTER, INSTRUCTOR
b Hong Kong, Jan 7, 39. *Study:* Chinese Univ Hong Kong, BA, 64; Claremont Grad Sch & Univ Ctr, MA, 67. *Comn:* Painting of McBryde Mill, A&B, Inc, 75 & 77. *Exhib:* Watercolor USA, Springfield Art Mus, Mo, 69; The Best in the West, Edward-Dean Mus, Calif, 70; Philadelphia Watercolor Club Exhib, Philadelphia Civic Ctr Mus, 72; one-man shows, Phoenix Art Mus, Ariz, 67, Kauai Mus, Hawaii, 71 & 72 & Kahana Kii Fine Art Gallery, 82. *Teaching:* Vis prof art, Ariz State Univ, Tempe, summer 67; asst prof art, Maunaolu Col, Maui, Hawaii, 68-70; instr art, Kauai Community Col, 70- *Awards:* Hon Mention, Hong Kong Art Exhib, Univ Hong Kong, 59-61; First Award for Watercolor, 1st Ann Spring Festival Fine Arts, Rowland Heights, Calif, 68; First Place for Watercolor, Maui Co Creative Arts Exhib, Hawaii, 68. *Mem:* Am Watercolor Soc; Philadelphia Watercolor Club; Kauai Watercolor Soc (pres); Kauai Oriental Art Soc (pres, currently). *Media:* Watercolor, Acrylic. *Publ:* Auth, The Chinese Landscape paintings of Waihang Lai, 66; auth, The Watercolors of Waihang Lai, 67; auth, Waihang Lai, Watercolor Calendar, 78. *Mailing Add:* PO Box 363 Lihue HI 96766

LAING, RICHARD HARLOW
ADMINISTRATOR, ARTIST
b Ypsilanti, Mich, Apr 19, 32. *Study:* Eastern Mich Univ, BS(art); Wayne State Univ, MA(printmaking, sculpture); Pa State Univ, DEd(art educ). *Comn:* Fountain (bronze & stainless), comn by Paul Vortman, Denton, Tex, 62; wall sculpture, comn by Blazier Comn for Civic Ctr, Denton, Tex, 66; three stainless steel sculptures, Pa State Univ, University Park, 67-68; bronze sculpture fountain, Ewing-Miller Assoc, Terre Haute, Ind, 68; 10 piece stained glass design & construction, Elizabeth's Restaurant, Meadville, Pa, 77. *Exhib:* Am Inst of Architects Exhib, Rice Univ, Houston, 67; 16th Ann Nat Drawing & Small Sculpture, Muncie, Ind, 70; Wabash Valley Regional Exhib, Terre Haute, Ind, 71; Allegheny Col Galleries, Pa, 78; Theil Col Galleries, Grove City, Pa, 78; Butler Mus Art, Youngstown, Ohio, 79. *Pos:* Develop specialist cult affairs, ECarolina Univ, Greenville, 83- *Teaching:* Instr design shop, Col Art & Design, Univ Mich, 54-55; instr studio art & humanities, Edsel Ford High Sch, 55-60; asst prof studio art & art educ, NTex State Univ, 60-68; art dept head & assoc prof, Ball State Univ, Muncie, Ind, 68-71; prof & chair, Edinboro State Col, Pa, 71-79; dean & prof, ECarolina, Greenville, NC, 79- *Awards:* First Cash Prize/Painting, Eastern Ind Artist Exhib, Muncie Art Asn, 69 & 71; Community Arts Award, Greenville, NC, 80. *Mem:* Col Art Asn. *Media:* Mixed. *Mailing Add:* 204 Pineview Dr Greenville NC 27834

LAIRD, E RUTH
SCULPTOR
b Houston, Tex, Mar 21, 21. *Study:* Cranbrook Acad Art, Bloomfield Hills, Mich, with Maija Grotell, summer 51 & 53-55. *Work:* Mus Contemp Crafts, New York; Everson Mus & Iroquois China Collection, Syracuse, NY; Children's Mus, Detroit; Cranbrook Mus, Mich. *Comn:* Altar Sculpture, Meditation Chapel, Rice Univ, Houston, 63 & Mem Sculpture, 75; Fountain, New Harmony, Ind, 65; Baptismal Fountain, St Basil Church, Angelton, Tex, 65. *Exhib:* One-woman shows, Univ Houston, 57, NMex Highlands Univ, 59, Laguna Gloria Mus, Austin, Tex, 65 & Mus Fine Arts, Houston, 67; Syracuse Int Traveling Exhib, New York, 57. *Teaching:* Instr ceramic sculpture, St Thomas, Houston, 55-57 & Univ Houston, 55-58; asst dean & instr ceramic sculpture, Mus Fine Arts Sch, Houston, 58-68. *Awards:* Tex Swed Cult Found Summer Study-Travel Grant, Int Designers' Conf, 55; Iroquois China Award, Int Exhib, Everson Mus, 57; Woman of Year Outstanding Contrib Fine Arts, Theta Sigma Phi, Houston, 68. *Bibliog:* Dr William Pryor (dir), The Arts in

Houston (TV show), 60; Campbell Geeslin (auth), Emerging reputations, Am Artist, 62; The American Ceramist, Craft Horizon, 62. *Media:* Clay, Stone. *Dealer:* Handmakers The Galleria 5015 Westheimer Rd Houston TX 77027. *Mailing Add:* 205 South Orange St Fredericksburg TX 78624

LAKE, JERRY LEE
PHOTOGRAPHER, EDUCATOR
b Manhattan, Kans, Apr 1, 41. *Study:* Va Commonwealth Univ, Richmond Professional Inst, BFA, 66; Ohio Univ, Athens, MFA, 68. *Exhib:* One-man shows, Sign of Jonah Gallery, Washington, DC, 69 & Northern Va Community Col, 69; Fac Exhib, Corcoran Gallery Art, 68-70; Corcoran Gallery Art, 69; Unpeopled Spaces Traveling Exhib, Va Mus, 81; Biennial Exhib, Va Mus, 81; In Celebration: Art at George Washington University, The Art Barn, Washington, DC, 82; Fac Show, Dimock Gallery, Washington, DC, 83; The Ritz, Washington DC Proj Arts, 83; 1734 Gallery, 83; Best of Kathleen Ewings Gallery, 83. *Teaching:* Dir photog prog, Corcoran Sch Art, 68-71; head photog section, George Washington Univ, 71- *Bibliog:* Benjamin Forgey (auth), Designed for design, Washington Post, 83; Jo Ann Lewis (auth), Professorial pictures, Washington Post, 83. *Mem:* Soc Photog Educ; Int Photog Soc; Am Asn Col Prof. *Publ:* Contribr photog, Horizon Mag, 75-76 & America Mag, 76; contribr cover photog, Environmental Action, 12/77. *Mailing Add:* Rt 2 Box 82 Lovettsville VA 22080

LAKE, RANDALL
PAINTER, PRINTMAKER
b Long Beach, Calif, Aug 2, 47. *Study:* Acad Julian, Paris, 67; Univ Colo, BA, 69; Ecole Superieure Beaux Arts, Paris, 72; Atelier 17, Paris, 72-73; Univ Utah, MFA, 77. *Work:* Springville Mus Art, Utah; Am Embassy, Am Libr, Paris. *Comn:* Oil paintings of Jerusalem, Mormon Church, Salt Lake City, 79; portrait Willard Eccles, Weber State Col, 81; portrait Nellie Tayloe Ross, Wyo State Capitol, Cheyenne, 82; portrait Dr Leonard W Jarcho, Univ Utah Med Sch, 83. *Exhib:* Salon D'Automne, Grand Palais, Paris, 70 & 72; Salon De Mai, Musee D'Art Mod, Paris, 72; Utah Painting & Sculpture, Mus Fine Arts, Univ Utah, Salt Lake City, 75-76; Intermountain Biennial, Salt Lake Art Ctr, 76; Assoc Utah Artists Bicentennial Exhib, Salt Palace, Salt Lake City, 76. *Pos:* Assoc dir, Guthrie Inst Fine Arts, 73-78, painter in residence, 80- *Teaching:* Assoc instr, Univ Utah, 76-78. *Awards:* First Place, Assoc Utah Artists Bicentennial Exhib, 76; Purchase Award, Deseret News Show, 78; Gold Medal, April Salon, Springville Mus Art, 81. *Bibliog:* Genevieve Breerette (auth), A travers les galeries, Monde, 71; Lois Collins (auth), Painters of the Guthrie, Expression Mag, 81; Diane Casella Hines (auth), Randall Lake--traditional realist, Am Artist Mag, 2/3/84. *Media:* Oil, Pastel; Gouache. *Dealer:* Randall Lake Studio 158 E 200 South St Salt Lake City UT 84108; New Masters Gallery PO Box 7009 Carmel CA 93921. *Mailing Add:* 1749 Cornell Circle Salt Lake City UT 84108

LALLY, JAMES JOSEPH
DEALER
b Mt Vernon, NY, Apr 18, 45. *Study:* Harvard Univ, BA, 67; Columbia Univ, MBA, 68, MIA, 70. *Pos:* Dir, Chinese Works of Art Dept, Sotheby Parke Bernet NY, Inc, 74-, dir, Sotheby Parke Bernet Hong Kong, Ltd, 75- *Specialty:* Chinese works of art (ceramics, archaic bronzes, jades, sculpture, paintings and the minor arts). *Mailing Add:* Sotheby's 1334 York Ave New York NY 10021

LAM, JENNETT (BRINSMADE)
PAINTER, EDUCATOR
b Ansonia, Conn, May 2, 11. *Study:* Yale Univ, with Josef Albers, BFA & MFA. *Work:* Mus Mod Art, Whitney Mus Am Art, New York; Brooklyn Mus, NY; Philadelphia Mus Fine Arts, Pa; Yale Art Gallery. *Exhib:* Carnegie Inst Int, 64; Painting Ann, 65 & Women in Permanent Collection, 71, Whitney Mus Am Art; USA Group 67, US Embassy, Paris & Mus France, 67; Selections from Chase Manhattan Collection, Finch Col Mus, 71. *Teaching:* Emer prof art, Univ Bridgeport, 72- *Awards:* MacDowell Colony Fel, 60 & 61. *Media:* Oil. *Dealer:* Harmon Gallery 1258 Third St S Naples Fla 33940; Le Point Cardinal 3 Rue Jacob Paris 6 France. *Mailing Add:* 27238 Elwood Dr SE Bonita Springs FL 33923

LA MALFA, JAMES THOMAS
SCULPTOR, EDUCATOR
b Milwaukee, Wis, Nov 30, 37. *Study:* Univ Wis, Madison, BS, 60, MS, 61 & MFA, 62; studied sculpture with Leo Steppat & printmaking with Alfred Sessler. *Work:* Memphis Acad Art; Univ Wis, La Crosse; Neville Art Mus, Green Bay, Wis. *Comn:* Relief sculpture, Phillips Hall, Univ Wis, Eau Claire, 66; sacred sculpture, Wittenberg Univ, Ohio, 68. *Exhib:* The States First Ann, Neville Pub Mus, Green Bay, Wis, 65; Springfield Art Ctr, Ohio, 67; Print & Drawing Nat, Minot State Teachers Col, NDak, 70; 29th Northeastern Wis Art Ann, Green Bay, 70; 23rd Ohio Ceramic & Sculpture Ann, Butler Inst Art, 71. *Teaching:* Instr visual arts, Univ Wis-Eau Claire, 63-66 & Wittenberg Univ, 66-69; asst prof, Univ Wis, Green Bay, 69-72; assoc prof, Univ Wis Ctr, Marinette, 72- *Bibliog:* J J (auth), article, Art News, 4/64; Pierre Mornand (auth), Expositions diverses review, Rev Mod, 11/71. *Media:* Multimedia. *Mailing Add:* Univ Wis Ctr-Marinette Bay Shore Rd Marinette WI 54143

LAMANNA, CARMEN
DEALER, RESTORER
b Monteleone, Avellino, Italy, May 19, 27; Can citizen. *Study:* Accad di Belle Art e Liceo Artistico, Napoli, Italy, 47. *Collections Arranged:* Carmen Lamanna Gallery at Third Int Pioneer Galleries Exhib, Musee Cantonal, Lausanne, Switzerland & Musee des Beaux Arts, Paris, 70; Boucherville, Montreal, Toronto, London, Touring Exhibit, Nat Gallery Can, 73; Carmen Lamanna at Owens Art Gallery (auth, catalog), Mt Allison Univ, Sackville, NB, Can, 75; 37th Venice Biennial, Italy, 78; Paterson Ewen Recent Work, 78; Kanadische Künstler, at Kuntshalle, Basel, Switzerland, 78; Fiction Touring Exhib, Art Gallery Ont, 82; Murray Favro: A Retrospective Touring Show, Art Gallery Ont, 83-84. *Pos:* Dir, Carmen Lamanna Gallery, 66- *Teaching:* Instr woodcarving, Central Tech Sch, Toronto, 51-52. *Awards:* Can Coun Grant, 3e Int Salon de Galeries Pilotes, Lausanne, Switzerland, 70; Queen's Silver Jubilee Medal, 77; Can Coun Grant, Kanadische Künstler, Basel, Switzerland, 78. *Bibliog:* Gail Dexter (auth), Man from Montelone, Toronto Star, 9/28/68; Time ed staff, The arts: in search of innovation, Time mag, 12/7/70; Adele Freedman (auth), Art: Guarding the case for the avante-garde: the case for Carmen Lamanna, Toronto Life, 12/77. *Mem:* Professional Art Dealers Asn, Toronto, Ont, Can. *Specialty:* Experimental art including minimalist sculpture, installations, painting, narrative art, earthworks, environmental art (nature systems), inventions, art-language, video, films, audio, body art, poetry, performances, record art. *Publ:* Contribr, Le 3e Salon International de Galleries-Pilotes, Musee Cantonal des Beaux Arts, Lausanna, Switzerland, 70; contribr, The Canadian cultural revolution--looking ahead, Artscanada, Toronto, 75; auth, Carmen Lamanna Gallery 1974, Queen St mag, spring/winter 76-77. *Mailing Add:* 840 Yonge St Toronto ON M4W 2H1 Canada

LAMANTIA, JAMES
EDUCATOR, COLLECTOR
b New Orleans, La, Sept 22, 23. *Study:* Tulane Univ La, BSArch, 43; Harvard Univ Grad Sch Design, BArch, 47; Skowhegan Sch, 47. *Pos:* Prof archit, Tulane Univ, currently. *Awards:* Prix de Rome, 48-49; Fulbright fel, Italy, 49-50; Fulbright prof archit, Univ Jordan, Amman, 78-79. *Bibliog:* Equal arts of James Lamantia, Archit Forum, 52. *Media:* Oil. *Collection:* English drawings and paintings of the 19th century; architectural drawings; Piranesi prints. *Mailing Add:* 539 Bienville St New Orleans LA 70130

LAMANTIA, PAUL (CHRISTOPHER)
PAINTER
b Chicago, Ill, Jan 20, 38. *Study:* Art Inst Chicago, BFA, 66, MFA, 68. *Work:* Koffler Found Collection, Nat Collection Fine Arts, Smithsonian Inst; Jean Dubuffet Collection, Paris; Dennis Arian Collection, Mus Contemp Art, Chicago. *Exhib:* Violence in Recent American Art, Mus Contemp Art, Chicago, 68; What They're Up To In Chicago Traveling Exhib, Nat Gallery Can, Ottawa, 72-73; North, East, South & Middle: An Exhibition on Contemporary American Drawing, Corcoran Gallery Art & Ft Worth Art Mus, 75-76; The Chicago Connection Traveling Exhib, E B Crocker Art Gallery, Sacramento, 76-77; Works on Paper, Art Inst Chicago, 77; Chicago Currents, Koffler Found Collection, Nat Collection Fine Arts, Smithsonian Inst, 79-80; Selections from the Dennis Adrian Collection, Mus Contemp Art, Chicago, 82; retrospective, Hyde Park Art Ctr, Chicago, 82; Chicago--Some Other Traditions Traveling Exhib, Madison Art Ctr, Wis, 83-85. *Bibliog:* Peter Frank (auth), Hunting the emergent American: On the trail of the Exxon National, Nat Art Guide, 1/81; David Elliott (auth), Cunning painter of the smart set, Chicago Sun-Times, 3/29/81. *Media:* Oil. *Dealer:* Sonia Zaks Gallery 620 N Michigan Chicago IL. *Mailing Add:* 315 W Concord Pl Chicago IL 60614

LAMARCA, HOWARD J
DESIGNER, EDUCATOR
b Teaneck, NJ, July 11, 34. *Study:* Cooper Union Art Sch, scholar, 52-56, cert graphic arts, 56; Columbia Univ, BFA, 60; Syracuse Univ, grad asst, 60-62, MFA, 62. *Collections Arranged:* James Gordon Irving-Painter, 71; Grant Reynard-Painter, 71; Charles Shedden, Sculptor-Ralph Didriksen, Painter, 71; Anita Friend, Paintings-Rush Cowell, Gravestone Rubbings, 71; New Jersey Designer-Craftsmen, 71; George Fish, Painting-Shirley Yudkin, Paintings, 72; Marion Lane, Painting Retrospective, 72; Arts in Parts, 72; Paul Burns, Painting Retrospective, 72; Arnoldo Miccoli-Painter, 73; Solomon Rothman-Sculptor, 73; Mod Artists Guild, 73; Lillian Marzell-Painter, 73; Paul Sisko-Sculptor, 73; Nat Asn Women Artists, 74; Sam Weinik-Painter, 74; Erna Weill-Sculptor, 74; Eleanor Smoler-Painter, 74; Elaine Hyman-Sculptor, 74; Esther Rosen-Painter, 74; Batiks--Giovanna Bellia La Marca, Co Col Morris, 76; Best of the World, 76; Art Director's Club of New Jersey, 78. *Pos:* Advert art dir, Givalldan Advert, New York, 57-; dir, Bergen Community Mus, 71-74; sem dir Europ advert, Paris, France, Dusseldorf & Frankfurt, WGer, Zurich, Switz & Milan, Italy, 78-84. *Teaching:* Asst prof art, Trenton State Col, 74-80; assoc prof art, Co Col of Morris, 74; adj asst prof, Parsons Sch Design, 79-81; assoc prof art, C W Post Ctr, Long Island Univ, 80- *Awards:* Graphics Design Award, New York, 79 & 81. *Mem:* Soc Scribes; Art Dir Club NY & NJ; Col Art Asn Am; Am Inst Graphic Arts. *Media:* Graphics, Calligraphy. *Publ:* Auth, An analysis of Gauguin's-What Are We? Where Do We Come From? Where Are We Going?, Artist Mag, London, 3/62; auth, An analysis of the facade of San Marco, Eleven Mag, spring 72; auth, Some Thoughts on Design, City Univ New York, 74; auth, Ethics & aesthetics, Focus, 76. *Mailing Add:* 3 Crescent Ave Cliffside Park NJ 07010

LAMB, ADRIAN
PAINTER
b New York, NY. Mar 22, 01. *Study:* Art Students League; Julian Sch, Paris, with Frank V Dumond & George Bridgeman. *Work:* Nat Portrait Gallery & Capitol Bldg, Washington, DC; Harvard Law Sch; Supreme Court, Tallahassee, Fla; Rockefeller Found, New York; Nat Headquarters Cincinnati Soc, Washington DC. *Comn:* Portraits of Stillmans, Chauncey Stillman, Stillman Mem, Brownsville, Tex, 58; portrait of Charles Merrill, Merrill Lynch, Fenner & Smith, Wall St, New York, 60; founder of Buford Col, Carnation Co, Buford, SC, 65; portrait of Mr Duke, Duke Endowment, New

York, 68; portrait of Gheen, father & son, Mrs Richard Hill, Baptist Sem, Louisville, Ky, 72. *Exhib:* Westchester, White Plains, NY; Salmagundi Club, New York; Sculpin Gallery, Edgartown, Mass; New Canaan Libr, Conn. *Teaching:* Adult class, Stamford High Sch, Conn. *Awards:* Ann Award portrature, Hudson Valley Art Asn. *Mem:* Salmagundi Club; Nat Arts Club; Art Students League. *Media:* Oil. *Dealer:* Portraits Inc 985 Park Ave New York NY 10028; Hershel Adler Galleries 21 E 70th St New York NY 10021. *Mailing Add:* Des Artists Hotel 1 W 67th St New York NY 10023

LAMB, ALBERTA CARMELLA See Cifolelli, Alberta

LAMBERT, ED
PRINTMAKER, PAINTER
b Atlanta, Tex, Jan 27, 49. *Study:* Tex Tech Univ, BFA & MFA. *Exhib:* Sixth and 7th Ann Nat Drawing & Small Sculpture Show, Del Mar Col, 72 & 73; Pratt Graphic Ctr Int Miniture Print Exhib, 75; Mach I Int Print Exhib, Metrop Mus Art, Miami, Fla, 75; 19th Ann Nat Print & Drawing Exhib, Okla Art Ctr, 77; one-man show, M E's Gallery, Houston, 83. *Teaching:* Asst prof printmaking, Del Mar Col, Corpus Christi, Tex, 74-, chmn art dept, 80-. *Bibliog:* Joseph A Cain (auth), Profile, Art Voices South, 7-8/80. *Media:* Etching & Serigraph. *Mailing Add:* 607 Del Mar Corpus Christi TX 78404

LAMBERT, NANCY S
LIBRARIAN
b Southbend, Ind, June 29, 32. *Study:* Univ of Mich, MALS, 69, MA(art hist), 71. *Pos:* Art librn, Univ Rochester, NY, 71-73 & State Univ NY Binghamton, 73-75; librn, Art & Archit Libr, Yale Univ, New Haven, Conn, 75- *Mem:* Col Art Asn; Art Libr Soc North Am. *Interests:* Bibliography and graphic arts. *Mailing Add:* 1206 Forest Rd New Haven CT 06515

LAMBERT, PHYLLIS
ARCHITECT, COLLECTOR
b Montreal, Que, Jan 24, 27. *Study:* Vassar Col, BA, 48; Ill Inst Archit, with Myron Goldsmith & Fazlur Khan, MS(archit), 63. *Comn:* Saidye Bronfman Ctr, with Webb, Zerafa & Menkes, YWHA, Montreal, 63-68; Jane Tate House Renovation, with Arcop Assoc, Phyllis Lambert off & residence, Montreal, 74-76; Small Cinema, with Arcop Assoc, pvt house, Montreal, 75-76; Biltmore Hotel Renovation, with Gene Summers, Los Angeles, Calif, 76-77. *Exhib:* Sculpture, Royal Can Acad of Arts, Toronto & Montreal, 40-44; two-person show, Perspectives: Archit Heritage of Montreal, Paintings & Photographs, McCord Mus Exhib, 75. *Collections Arranged:* Joseph E Seagram & Sons Inc Collection, 54-; Can Indian Exhib, 69 & Aaron Siskind Exhib, 70, Saidye Bronfman Centre, Montreal; Seagram Plaza: Its Design & Use, Seagram Bldg, New York, 77. *Pos:* Dir planning, Seagram Bldg, New York, 54-58; dir, Seagram Bicentennial Proj, Co Courthouse in the US, 74-; founder/dir, Can Ctr for Archit, 79; Commissioner, Int Confederation Archit Mus, 79. *Awards:* Robinson's Design Award, Renovation of Biltmore Hotel, Los Angeles, 77; Medaille de Merite, Ordre des Architectes du Que, Montreal, 81; Nat Preservation Honor Award, Nat Trust Historic Preservation, 81. *Bibliog:* Peter Blake (auth), Neat showcase for the arts, Archit Forum, 5/69; D Gerin-Lajoie (auth), Attention ne detruisez pas notre entite, Archit Concept, 11-12/74; Claude R Lussier (auth), L'apport des femmes a l'architecture et au design, Decormag, 1/77. *Mem:* Royal Can Acad Arts; Soc du Patrimoine Urbain de Montreal (pres, 79). *Collection:* Architectural drawings from the 16th century to the 20th century; photographs of the 19th and 20th century; manuscripts and books on architecture. *Publ:* Contribr, Exploring Montreal, Montreal Soc Archit, 74; coauth, Dossier 25--Inventair des batiments du Vieux Montreal, Ministry of Cult Affairs, Que 77; contribr, Mount Royal Montreal, McCord Mus, 77; contribr, Court House, Horizon Press, spring 78. *Mailing Add:* 2e etage 1440 Ouest Ste-Catherine Montreal PQ H3G 1R8 Canada

LAMELL, ROBERT (C)
PAINTER, DESIGNER
b Oradea, Romania, Nov 21, 13; US citizen. *Study:* Hindenburg Polytech, Oldenburg, Ger, 35; Royal Hungarian Polytech Univ, Budapest, dipl, 41. *Comn:* Murals, restaurants, Carynthia, Austria, 46-47; murals, St Anthony Hosp, Denver, 57; mural, Okla Tile Co, Oklahoma City, 60; mural, Utica Bank & Trust Co, Tulsa, 75. *Exhib:* One-man shows, Kleinmayr Galleries, Klagenfurt, Austria, 48 & Ashville Mus Art, NC, 53; Okla Art Ctr, Oklahoma City, 60; Arts Place II, Okla Art Ctr, Oklahoma City, 82; Mabel-Gerrer Art Mus, Shawnee, Okla, 83. *Pos:* Deliniator & designer, C L Monnot Jr & Assoc, archit, Oklahoma City, 55- *Awards:* Best Show, Fidelity Bank, 81; Strathmore Award, Watercolor Oklahoma, 82; Dick Blick Award, Tri-State Exhib Kans Watercolor Soc, 83. *Mem:* Okla Art Guild; Okla Watercolor Asn; Am Inst Archit. *Media:* Acrylic, Oil; Watercolor. *Dealer:* Gallery West Inc PO Box 1589 Taos NM 87571. *Mailing Add:* 2640 Wilshire Blvd Oklahoma City OK 73116

LAMIS, LEROY
SCULPTOR, EDUCATOR
b Eddyville, Iowa, Sept 27, 25. *Study:* NMex Highlands Univ, BA, 53; Columbia Univ Teachers Col, MA, 56. *Work:* Albright-Knox Mus; Des Moines Art Ctr; Whitney Mus Am Art; Joseph H Hirshhorn Collection, Washington, DC; Larry Aldrich Mus. *Exhib:* Whitney Mus Am Art Sculpture Ann, New York, 64, 66 & 68; Responsive Eye, Mus Mod Art, New York, 65; Art Today, Albright-Knox Art Gallery, Buffalo, 65; one-man shows, Staempfli Gallery, New York, 66, 69 & 73 & Traveling Show, 69, J B Speed Mus, Louisville, John Herron Mus, Indianapolis, La Jolla Mus Art, Calif; Neuberger Collection, Smithsonian Inst & RI Sch of Design, 68; Am

Sculpture, Univ Nebr, Lincoln, 70; Artists at Dartmouth, New City Hall, Boston, Mass, 71. *Pos:* Pres, PC Art Inc, currently. *Teaching:* Asst prof, Cornell Col, 56-60; prof sculpture, Ind State Univ, Terre Haute, 61-; artist in residence, Dartmouth Col, 70. *Awards:* NY State Coun Arts Award, 70. *Mem:* Am Abstract Artists. *Media:* Plastics. *Mailing Add:* 3101 Oak Terre Haute IN 47803

LAMPITOC, ROL PONCE
PAINTER, PRINTMAKER
b Laoag City, Philippines; Can citizen. *Study:* Univ Philippines Sch Fine Arts, 52; Univ Windsor, 74; Nat Art Seminars, with John Howard Sanden, cert, 80. *Work:* Malacanang Palace & US Embassy, Manila, Philippines; St Claire Col Art Collections, Windsor, Ont. *Exhib:* SEast Asian Art Conference, Art Asn Philippines, Manila, 57; Art Gallery, Windsor, Ont, 74; Pastel Soc Am, Nat Arts Club, New York, 74, 76, 77 & 79; 6th Int Art Friendship, Int Friendship Asn Japan, Tokyo, 81; Pilipino Artist North Am, Nat Archives, Ottawa, Ont, 81. *Pos:* Asst art dir, Piercell Merchandising, Windsor, Ont, 73-80. *Teaching:* Instr painting, St Clair Col Continuing Educ, 73-74; instr painting, Windsor Art Gallery, 74. *Awards:* Silver Medal, Art Asn Philippines, 57; Bronze Medal, Art Asn Philippines, 58; First Prize, Art Asn Philippines, 72. *Bibliog:* Dorothy Hall (auth), Art & artists, Park East, 1/10/77; Barbara Gesicki (auth), Agincourt artist, Scarborough Mirror, 8/7/81; Barbara Scott (auth), Artist paints famous face, Toronto Star, 12/22/81; and others. *Mem:* Canadian Art Asn; Pastel Soc Am; Portrait Club New York; Pilipino Artists North Am. *Media:* Oil, Pastel; Serigraphy. *Dealer:* Morley Hall 15 United Sq Scarborough Can. *Mailing Add:* 25 Tunmead Sq Agincourt ON M1B 1X1 Canada

LANCASTER, MARK
PAINTER
b Yorkshire, Eng, May 14, 38. *Study:* Dept of Fine Art, Newcastle Univ, Eng, 61-65. *Work:* Victoria & Albert Mus & Tate Gallery, London; Arts Coun of Northern Ireland, Belfast; Allen Art Mus, Oberlin, Ohio; Art Gallery of S Australia, Adelaide; Mus of Mod Art, New York. *Exhib:* British Drawings: The New Generation, Mus Mod Art, New York, 67; Six Artists (toured Britain), Victoria & Albert Mus, London, 67; Young British Artist (traveling), Mus Mod Art, New York, 68; British Painting, Hayward Gallery, London, 75; one-man shows, Walker Art Gallery, Liverpool, Eng, 73 & Multiples, New York, 75; Tate 79, Tate Gallery, London, 79; Am Painting: the 80's, Grey Art Gallery, New York, 79. *Pos:* Artist-in-Residence, King's Col, Cambridge, Eng, 68-70; designer, Merce Cunningham Dance Co, New York, 74-80, artistic adv, 80- *Teaching:* Instr, Dept of Fine Art, Newcastle Univ, Eng, 65-66; Bath Acad of Art, Corsham, Wiltshire, Eng, 66. *Awards:* Purchase Prize, British Int Print Biennale, Bradford, 70. *Bibliog:* Mark Lancaster, Betty Parsons Gallery, article in New York Times, 10/74; John Russell (auth), Lancaster sets the stage for Cunningham, Art Am, 7-8/79; Richard Shone (auth), Mark Lancaster, Burlington Mag, 7/80; and others. *Dealer:* Rowan Gallery 31 A Bruton Pl London WIX 7AB England; Betty Parsons Gallery 24 W 57 St New York NY. *Mailing Add:* 225 E Houston St New York NY 10002

LAND, ERNEST ALBERT
PAINTER, DESIGNER
b Hamilton, Ont, Sept 21, 18; US citizen. *Work:* NASA Space Mus, Washington, DC; Grumbacher Collection Fine Art; IBM Collection Fine Art, New York; Marietta Col, Ohio; Butler Inst Am Art, Youngstown, Ohio. *Comn:* Mural, USA Corps Engrs, Seattle World's Fair, 60; nine murals on hist solid propellants, USN Mus, Indian Head, Md, 62-63; mural, Work of Dr Leakey, Olduvai Gorge, Africa (with Robert Widder & Ken Hopkins), Nat Geog Explorers Hall, 63-64. *Exhib:* Butler Inst Am Art Ann, Youngstown, Ohio, 70; Mainstreams Int, Marietta Col, Ohio, 70 & 72; Allied Artists Am 58th Ann, Nat Acad Design Galleries, 71; Am Artists Prof League Grand Nat, 71. *Pos:* Dir art & designer scenics, US Info Agency TV & Film Serv, Washington, DC. *Teaching:* Lectr, Chase Manhattan Bank, New York, 54-55; lectr, Am Tel & Tel, New York, 55-62. *Awards:* John J McDonough Award, Butler Inst Am Art, 72; Best in Show & First Prize, Mainstreams, Marietta Col, 77; Lester Cook Mem Prize, 77. *Bibliog:* Joseph Grumbacher (auth), Twenty-one paint in polymer, M Grumbacher, 65; Gutierrez & Roukes (auth), Painting with Acrylics, Watson-Guptill, 65; Joseph Giacalone (auth), Leonardo would have us use polymer, Syndicate Mag, 66. *Mem:* Life fel Royal Soc Art, London; fel Am Artists Prof League; Art League Northern Va. *Media:* Oil. *Publ:* Illusr, US Senate Comt Aeronaut & Space Sci, US Govt Printing Off, 63. *Dealer:* Capricorn Galleries 4849 Rugby Ave Bethesda MD 20014. *Mailing Add:* 412 Lincoln Ave Falls Church VA 22046

LAND, SARAH AGNES RILEY See Riley-Land, Sarah

LANDAU, JACOB
PAINTER, PRINTMAKER
b Philadelphia, Pa, Dec 17, 17. *Study:* Philadelphia Col Art, with Earl Horter & Franklin Watkins, cert, 38; New Sch Social Res, with Erich Fromm, Rudolf Arnheim & Eugene O'Neill, Jr, 48-49 & 52-53. *Work:* Mus Mod Art, New York; Whitney Mus Am Art; Metrop Mus Art; Libr of Cong; Philadelphia Mus Art; and others. *Comn:* Ten stained glass windows, Keneseth Israel Synagogue, Philadelphia, 71; Meditation on Love & Death (lithograph), NJ State Arts Coun, 75; and others. *Exhib:* The Figure, Recent Paintings USA, 62 & Tamarind--Homage to Lithography, 69, Mus Mod Art, New York; Human Concern/Personal Torment, Whitney Mus Am Art, 69; one-man shows, Jorgenson Auditorium, Univ Conn, 71, Hopkins Hall, Ohio State Univ, 73 & ACA Gallery, New York, 76; Am Acad Arts & Lett, 73 & 74;

Graphic Retrospective, NJ State Mus, 81; and other group & one-man shows. *Teaching:* From instr to assoc prof, Pratt Inst, 57-68, prof graphic art, 68-83, founder, Univ-Without-Walls Proj, prof emer, 83- *Awards:* Nat Arts Endowment Sabbatical Grant, 66; Guggenheim Found Fel, 68; Ford Found Travel-Study Grant, 75; and others. *Bibliog:* H C Pitz (auth), Jacob Landau, Am Artist, 10/56; Jacob Landau, Current Biog, 12/64; Barry Schwartz (auth), Tiger of wrath--Jacob Landau, Arts Soc, spring-summer 71; and others. *Mem:* Soc Am Graphic Artists; Visual Artists & Galleries Asn; academician Nat Acad Design. *Media:* Watercolor; Woodcut, Lithography. *Publ:* Auth, Charades, Tamarind Lithography Workshop, 65; auth, Yes-no, art-technology, Wilson Libr Bulletin, 9/66; auth, Holocaust, Assoc Am Artists, 68; illusr, Out of the whirlwind, Union Am Hebrew Congregations, 68; illusr, Selected Writings of Hoffmann, Univ Chicago, 69; and others. *Dealer:* Assoc Am Artists 663 Fifth Ave New York NY 10022. *Mailing Add:* 2 Pine Dr Roosevelt NJ 08555

LANDAU, MITZI
DEALER, CURATOR
b New York, NY, Sept 18, 25. *Study:* NY Univ, BA, 45. *Collections Arranged:* Gaston Lachaise sculptures & drawings; Edward Muybridge, Picasso Vollard Suite, Margaret Bourke-White & Joseph Albers photographs & prints. *Pos:* Cur, Gaston Lachaise Found, 67-; founder, Circulating Exhib Serv; lectr Gaston Lachaise & mod sculpture, var mus, pub groups & docents; bd dirs, Los Angeles Munic Art Gallery Assocs, currently. *Mem:* Col Art Asn; Asn Am Mus. *Specialty:* Art of the 20th century, both European and American sculpture & photography. *Mailing Add:* 1625 Thayer Ave Los Angeles CA 90024

LANDAU, MYRA
PAINTER, MURALIST
b Bucarest, Rumania; Mex citizen. *Study:* Studied with Oswaldo Goeldi, Authodactic engraving on metal in painting. *Work:* Mus, Mexico; Pinocoteca del Estado, Sao Paulo, Brazil; Casa de Las Americas, Habana, Cuba; Univ Vera Cruzana, Xalapa, Mexico; Casas de Cultura, Mexico; and others. *Exhib:* Mus Mod Art, Mexico City, 75; Mus Mod Art, Salvador, Brazil, 78; Casa de La Cultura, Reafe-Pe, Brazil, 78; Gallery Arte Global, Sao Paulo, Brazil, 78; Centro de Estudios del Mundo, Mexico City, 77; Mus Carrillo, Mexico City, 79; Univ Metrop Mexico City, 80; Ctr Cult Mexique, Paris, 83. *Pos:* Docente, Facultad de Artes Plasticas, 74-75; investigadora, Inst de Investigaciones; tiempo completo, Esteticas, 75. *Mem:* Foro de Arte Contemporaneo, Mexico City. *Media:* Linen, Pastels. *Publ:* Se Sabes Ver, Univ Mex, 76. *Dealer:* Lourdes Chumacero Galeria Calle Estocolmo Mexico City Mex. *Mailing Add:* Alfaro 6 Xalapa Veracruz Mexico

LANDECK, ARMIN
PAINTER, ENGRAVER
b Crandon, Wis, June 4, 05. *Study:* Columbia Univ, BArch, 27. *Work:* Mus Mod Art, Metrop Mus Art & New York Pub Libr, New York; Toledo Mus Art, Ohio; Libr Cong, Washington, DC; Swedish Nat Mus, Stockholm; Kaiser Friedrich Mus, Berlin, Ger; plus others. *Exhib:* Libr Cong; Soc Am Graphic Arts; Nat Acad Design; Pa Acad Fine Arts; Int Graphic Exhib, Yugoslavia. *Awards:* S F B Morse Gold Medal, Nat Acad Design, 62; Wiggin Award, Boston Printmakers, 69; Purchase Prize, Soc Am Graphic Arts, 69. *Mem:* Soc Am Graphic Arts; Am Inst Arts & Lett; Nat Acad Design; fel Int Inst Arts & Lett. *Publ:* Norman & June Kraeft (auths), Armin Landeck: Catalogue Raissone, June Gallery, Bethlehem, Conn, 77. *Mailing Add:* RD 1 Litchfield CT 06759

LANDERS, BERTHA
PAINTER, PRINTMAKER
b Winnsboro, Tex. *Study:* Sul Ross Col, BSArt; Colorado Springs Fine Arts Ctr, Colo, grad study with Arnold Blanch, Adolf Dehn, Boardman Robinson & Henry Varnum Poor; Art Students League, grad study with Reginal Marsh. *Work:* Dallas Mus Art; Denver Mus Art; Libr Cong, Washington, DC; Witte Mem Mus, San Antonio, Tex; Ft Worth Art Ctr, Tex. *Exhib:* Dallas Allied Arts Show Ann, 36-45; Nat Print Ann, New York, 42-57; Nat Acad Design, New York, 43-44; Corpus Christi Nat Exhib, Tex, 45; Nat Gallery, Washington, DC, 46; Brooklyn Art Mus Exhib, 53; and others. *Pos:* Cur & cataloguer, Mrs A A Zonnie Print Collection, 42-49; pres, Tex Women Printmakers, 44-46; art librn, Dallas Pub Libr, 46-49; art librn, Kansas City Pub Libr, Mo, 50-58. *Awards:* Painting Purchase, Corpus Christi Nat Exhib, 45; Print Purchase, Libr Cong, 45; Painting Purchase, Denver Art Mus, 47. *Bibliog:* Albert Reese (auth), American Prize Winning Prints of the 20th Century, 49. *Mem:* San Diego Print Club. *Media:* Printing, Etching, Aquatinting & Lithography; Oil, Watercolor. *Dealer:* S/R Gallery 337 S Robertson Blvd Beverly Hills CA 90211; Kennedy Galleries 20 E 56th St New York NY 10022. *Mailing Add:* 13622 Fairlane Rd Villa Twelve Oaks Valley Center CA 92082

LANDFIELD, RONNIE (RONALD T)
PAINTER
b Bronx, NY, Jan 9, 47. *Study:* Art Students League, 62-63; Kansas City Art Inst, Mo, 63; San Francisco Art Inst, 64-65. *Work:* Mus Mod Art, New York; Whitney Mus of Am Art, New York; Hirshhorn Mus of Art, Washington, DC; RI Sch of Design Mus, Providence; Walker Art Ctr, Minneapolis, Minn. *Comn:* Mural (painting 11 ft x 20 ft), Westinghouse Corp & I Chermayoff, Pittsburgh, Pa, 70. *Exhib:* Whitney Ann & Biennial Exhib of Am Painting, New York, 67, 69 & 73; Lyrical Abstraction, Whitney Mus of Am Art, 71 & Aldrich Mus of Contemp Art, Ridgefield, Conn, 71; Art for Your Collection, RI Sch of Design, Providence, 71; Recent Acquisitions, Mus of Mod Art, New York, 72; one-man shows, Linda Farris, Seattle, Wash, 78 & 79, Sarah

Rentschler Gallery, New York, 78 & 79 & Medici-Berensen, Miami, Fla, 79; Charles Cowles Gallery, New York, 80, 82 & 83; and others. *Teaching:* Instr fine arts, Sch of Visual Arts, New York, 75- *Awards:* Gold Medal, San Francisco Art Inst, Calif, 65; Cassandra Found grant for painting, 68; nat Endowment Arts, 83. *Bibliog:* Whee Kim (auth), A personal definition of pictorial space, Arts Mag, 11/74; Noel Frackman (auth), article, Arts, Vol 50, No 1, 9/75; Phyllis Tuchman (auth), article, Art News, Vol 77, No 3, 3/78. *Media:* Acrylic, Watercolor. *Dealer:* Charles Cowles Gallery 420 W Broadway New York NY 10013. *Mailing Add:* 31 Desbrosses St New York NY 10013

LANDIS, ELLEN JAMIE
CURATOR, HISTORIAN
b Chicago, Ill, May 6, 41. *Study:* Univ Calif, Berkeley, BA; Univ Vienna, 60-61; NY Univ, Inst Fine Arts, MA. *Collections Arranged:* Homage to Rodin (coauth, catalog), Los Angeles Co Mus Art, Los Angeles, 67; Rodin Bronzes from the Collection of B Gerald Cantor, Am Fedn Art, 70; Vincent Van Gogh, Baltimore Mus Art, 70; Four Americans in Paris: The Collections of Gertrude Stein and Her Family, Baltimore Mus Art, 71; Early 20th Century European Masterpainters (coauth, catalog), 77, Indian Art Today (auth, catalog), 77, Metro Youth Art (auth, catalog), 77 & Albuquerque Artists I (auth, catalog), 77, Mus of Albuquerque; Reflections of Realism (auth, catalog), Albuquerque Mus, 79; Katachi: Form and Spirit in Japanese Art, Albuquerque Mus, 80; Here and Now, 35 Artists in New Mexico (auth, catalog), 81, West/Southwest (auth, catalog), 82, In Place, 82, Eve Laramee, 83 & Hiroshige, 83, Albuquerque Mus. *Pos:* Cur, B Gerald Cantor Art Found, Beverly Hills, Calif, 68-70; actg cur, Robert Gore Rifkind Collection, Beverly Hills, Calif, 70 & 71-72; cur art, Mus Albuquerque, NMex, 77- *Teaching:* Lectr introd to art, Yuba Col, Marysville, Calif, 76-77. *Awards:* The Chris Award, Homage to Rodin, Film Coun Greater Columbus, 69. *Mem:* Col Art Asn; Am Asn Mus. *Res:* Centralized research in areas of 19th century and 20th century art. *Publ:* Co-auth, The David E Bright Collection, Los Angeles Co Mus Art, Los Angeles, 67; co-auth, Matisse in Baltimore, Television Spec, 71. *Mailing Add:* 9509 Dona Rowena NE Albuquerque NM 87111

LANDIS, LILY
SCULPTOR
b New York, NY. *Study:* Sorbonne, France; sculpture with De Creeft; Art Students League. *Work:* Lobby, Merck, Sharpe & Dohme Bldg, New York. *Exhib:* Art Inst Chicago; Mus Mod Art, New York; Pa Acad Fine Arts; Whitney Mus Am Art; Corcoran Gallery Art. *Awards:* Peabody Award, 68; Tiffany Grant. *Media:* Multimedia. *Dealer:* Miriam Redein 343 E 30th St New York NY 10016. *Mailing Add:* 400 E 57th St New York NY 10022

LANDON, EDWARD AUGUST
PRINTMAKER, PAINTER
b Hartford, Conn, Mar 13, 11. *Study:* Hartford Art Sch; Art Students League; also with Carlos Merida, Mex. *Work:* Bibliot Nat, Paris; Mus Mod Art & Metrop Mus Art, New York; San Francisco Mus; Nat Mus, Stockholm. *Exhib:* Am Color Print Soc Ann, 45-65; Northwest Printmakers Ann, 50-60; Boston Printmakers Ann, 55-70; Univ Maine, Orono, 70; Duxbury Art Ctr, 80; and others. *Pos:* Pres, Artists Union Western Mass, 34-38; pres, Nat Serigraph Soc, 52-53. *Awards:* First Prize for Prints, Springfield Art League, 45; Purchase Prize, Boston Printmakers, '54; First Prize, Nat Serigraph Soc, 59; plus others. *Bibliog:* Making a Serigraph (film), Harmon Found, 47. *Mem:* Am Color Print Soc; Southern Vt Artists; Boston Printmakers; Print Coun Am; Philadelphia Print Club; and others. *Dealer:* Gallery 2 Woodstock VT 05091; North Star Gallery Grafton VT 05146. *Mailing Add:* Lawrence Hill Rd Weston VT 05161

LANDREAU, ANTHONY NORMAN
ADMINISTRATOR
b Washington, DC, Apr 2, 30. *Study:* Cath Univ Am, with Kenneth Noland; Black Mountain Col, NC, with Kline, Fiore & Rice, BA, 54. *Collections Arranged:* Smithsonian Travelling Exhib Serv, 69-71; Carnegie Inst, 78-79; Textile Mus, 83-85. *Pos:* Exec dir, Textile Mus, Washington, DC, 67-75; cur educ, Carnegie Inst Mus Art, Pittsburgh, 75-81; pres, Int Collection Inc, 81- *Teaching:* Instr weaving-design, Black Mountain Col, 54-56; lectr hist of textiles, Univ Md, 75. *Awards:* Near E Res Ctr Grant, rug studies in Turkey, 73; Nat Endowment Arts Prof Fels, study in Turkey, 73 & study in USSR, 75; Turkish res proj, Nat Endowment Humanities, 80. *Mem:* Am Asn Mus; Archaeol Inst Am; Col Art Asn; Am-Turkish Asn (bd mem, 74-); Iran-Am Soc (bd mem, 74-). *Res:* Folk weaving, particularly in the Middle East. *Publ:* auth, Yoruk, The Nomadic Weaving Tradition in the Middle East, Carnegie Inst, 78; auth, Carpets and rugs, Encycl Americana, 80; Flowers of the Yayla, Textile Mus, 83. *Mailing Add:* 1101 Heberton Pittsburgh PA 15206

LANDRY, ALBERT
DEALER
b New York, NY, Oct 9, 19. *Study:* Columbia Univ, MA(art hist); Nat Acad Design; Atelier Leger, Paris, France. *Pos:* Dir, Galerie Villand-Galanis, Paris, 50-54; dir, Assoc Am Artists, 54-58; dir, Albert Landry Galleries, New York, 58-64; dir, J L Hudson Co Art Gallery, Detroit, 64; vpres, Marlborough-Gerson Gallery, 69; former dir, Landry-Bonino Gallery; dir, New York Art '73; pvt dealer for corp art collections, presently. *Specialty:* Contemporary American and European art. *Mailing Add:* 22 E 36th St New York NY 10016

LANDRY, RICHARD MILES
PHOTOGRAPHER, VIDEO ARTIST
b Cecilia, La, Nov 16, 38. *Study:* Univ Southwestern La, with Calvin Harlan, BME. *Exhib:* Whitney Mus Biennial, 72; Brazil Biennial, 73; Xerox Art in

Evolution, 73; Los Angeles Co Mus, 74; ICA Gallery, Philadelphia, 75. *Awards:* Creative Artists Award, 74; Creative Artists Pub Serv Award for Mixed Media, 74; Nat Endowment Arts Grant for Video, 75. *Dealer:* Leo Castelli Gallery 420 W Broadway New York NY 10021. *Mailing Add:* PO Box 64 Cecilia LA 70521

LANDSMAN, STANLEY
SCULPTOR
b New York, NY, Jan 23, 30. *Study:* Univ NMex, with Randall Davey, Adja Yunkers & Agnes Martin, BFA, 55. *Work:* Mus Mod Art, Whitney Mus Am Art, New York; Larry Aldrich Mus, Ridgefield, Conn; Mus Mod Arte, Paris, France; Walker Art Ctr, Minneapolis, Minn; and others. *Exhib:* Whitney Mus Am Art Sculpture Ann & Light, Object and Image, 68; one-man shows, Univ Wis, Madison, 69 & Contemp Art Mus, Houston, 70; Electric Art, Univ Calif, Los Angeles, 69; Univ Ill, Urbana, 69; Automation House, New York, 70; plus other group & one-man shows. *Teaching:* Instr sculpture, Adelphi Col, Sch Visual Arts & Pratt Inst, formerly; artist in residence, Aspen Inst & Univ Wis, formerly. *Dealer:* Leo Castelli Gallery 4 E 77th St New York NY 10021. *Mailing Add:* 45 Downing St New York NY 10014

LAND-WEBER, ELLEN E
PHOTOGRAPHER, EDUCATOR
b Rochester, NY, Mar 16, 43. *Study:* Univ Iowa, Iowa City, BA(art hist), MA & MFA(creative photog). *Work:* Int Mus of Photog, George Eastman House, Rochester, NY; San Francisco Mus Mod Art, Calif; New Orleans Mus Art; Libr Cong, Washington, DC. *Comn:* Bicentennial Doc Proj on Archit of Courthouses in US (in collab with 23 other photogrs with assigned geog areas), Seagrams's Inc, New York, 75-76. *Exhib:* One-person shows, San Francisco Mus Mod Art, 78, Bard Col, Annandale on Hudson, NY, 79, Focus Gallery, San Francisco, 80 & Shada Gallery, Tokyo, 83; Women of Photog, San Francisco Mus Mod Art, traveling, 75-76; Photog Synthesis Nat, Herbert Johnson Mus, Cornell Univ, Ithaca, NY, 76; Electroworks, George Eastman House, Rochester, NY, 79. *Teaching:* Instr photog, Univ Calif, Los Angeles, 70-74; asst prof photog, Humboldt State Univ, Arcata, Calif, 74-79, assoc prof, 79-83, prof, 83- *Awards:* Nat Endowment Arts Photographer's Fel, 74, 79 & 82. *Mem:* Soc for Photog Educ (nat treas, 79-81, nat secy, 81-83). *Publ:* Illusr, Vision & Expression, Horizon Press, 69; illusr, Women of photography: an historical survey, San Francisco Mus of Mod Art, 75; Translations, Herbert F Johnson Mus, Ithaca, NY, 79; illusr, Courthouse, a photographic Document, Horizon Press, 79; The Passionate Collector, photographs by Ellen Land-Weber, Simon & Schuster, 80. *Mailing Add:* 620 Park Ave Arcata CA 95521

LANDWEHR, WILLIAM CHARLES
MUSEUM DIRECTOR
b Milwaukee, Wis, Sept 19, 41. *Study:* Univ Wis-Stevens Point, BS, 63; Univ NDak, MA, 68. *Collections Arranged:* Barry Le Va: Six Blown Lines (Accumulation Drift), Art Ctr Gallery, Univ Wis-Menomonie, 69; Richard Hunt: Small Sculpture/Drawings/Lithographs, Quincy Art Ctr, Ill, 72; Realism in North Carolina, Mint Mus Art, Charlotte, NC, 74; Watercolor USA, Springfield Art Mus, Mo, 77-83 & The Lithographs & Etchings of Philip Pearlstein (auth, catalog), 78; 21st Ann Eight State Exhib Painting & Sculpture, Okla Art Ctr, Oklahoma City, 79; Transitional Light: Facing Death With Dignity--Photographs by Leslie Brown and Alan Brown, Springfield Art Mus, Mo, 83. *Pos:* Cur, Art Ctr Gallery, Univ Wis-Menomonie, 68-69; dir, SDak Mem Art Ctr, 69-71; artist & dir, Quincy Art Ctr, 71-73; cur exhib, Mint Mus Art, Charlotte, 73-76; dir, Springfield Art Mus, 76- *Teaching:* Instr art, SDak State Univ, 69-71; lectr art, Western Ill Univ, 72-73; instr art, Cent Piedmont Community Col, Charlotte, 73-75. *Mem:* Am Asn Mus; Art Mus Asn; Mo Mus Assoc. *Publ:* Auth, Melvin F Spinar: figure & fantasy, SDak Mem Art Ctr, 71; auth, Richard Hunt: small sculpture/drawings/lithographs, 72, Quincy Art Ctr; auth, The villain as hero, Southwest Art, 6/75; ed, Selections from the Permanent Collection of the Springfield Art Mus, 80. *Mailing Add:* c/o Springfield Art Mus 1111 E Brookside Dr Springfield MO 65807

LANE, ALVIN SEYMOUR
COLLECTOR
b Englewood, NJ, June 17, 18. *Study:* Univ Wis, PhB; Harvard Univ Law Sch, LLB; New Sch Social Res, with Seymour Lipton. *Pos:* Chmn comt on art, New York Bar Asn, 63-65; mem bd overseers fine arts, Brandeis Univ, 66-70; mem adv bd to NY Atty Gen on Art Legis, 66-71; secy, Aldrich Mus Contemp Art, 68-76, dir & vpres, 79; Soho Ctr for Visual Artists Inc, 76; bd dirs, Artists Equity Asn, New York, 81-83. *Collection:* Contemporary sculpture and sculptors' drawings. *Publ:* Auth, How the bar can assist the art community, New York Bar Asn, 65; auth, The case of the careless collector, Art in Am, 65; auth, Disclosure on disclosure, Print Collector Newslett, 74. *Mailing Add:* 60 E 42nd St New York NY 10017

LANE, H PALMER
DEALER
b Jacksonville, Fla, Oct 11, 51. *Study:* Sweet Briar Col, BA, 73; Tulane Univ, MA, 75. *Pos:* Co-owner, Middendorf/Lane Gallery, Washington, DC, currently. *Specialty:* Twentieth century American prints and paintings. *Mailing Add:* c/o Middendorf/Lane Gallery 2009 Columbia Rd NW Washington DC 20009

LANE, JOHN RODGER
MUSEUM DIRECTOR, HISTORIAN
b Chicago, Ill, Feb 28, 44. *Study:* Williams Col, BA, 66; Univ Chicago, MBA, 71; Harvard Univ, AM, 73, PhD, 76. *Collections Arranged:* Stuart Davis: Art

and Art Theory, Brooklyn Mus & Fogg Art Mus, 78; Modernist Art from the Edith and Milton Lowenthal Collection, Brooklyn Mus, 81; Robert Bourdan: Auto Rex, Carnegie Inst, 82; The Groups: Paintings by Archie Rand, Carnegie Inst, 83; Abstract Painting and Sculpture in America, Carnegie Inst, San Francisco Mus Mod Art, Minneapolis Inst Art & Whitney Mus, 83-84. *Pos:* Asst dir, Fogg Art Mus, 74; exec asst to dir, Brooklyn Mus, 75-78, adminr curatorial affairs, 79, asst dir curatorial affairs, 80; dir, Mus Art, Carnegie Inst, 80- *Teaching:* Teaching fel art hist, Harvard Univ, 73-75. *Mem:* Col Art Asn; Am Asn Mus; Int Coun Mus; Asn Art Mus Dirs; Pa Coun Arts. *Res:* 20th century American art. *Publ:* Auth, Maxim Karolik, benefactor to Museum of Fine Arts, Boston, Am Art Rev, 1-2/75; auth, The sources of Max Weber's Cubism, Art J, spring 76; auth, Stuart Davis and the issue of content in New York school painting, 2/78 & auth, Archie Rand: the consistency of choice, 11/79, Arts Mag; auth, Ilya Bolotowsky's abstraction 1936-1937, Carnegie Mag, summer 81. *Mailing Add:* c/o Carnegie Inst Mus Art 4400 Forbes Ave Pittsburgh PA 15213

LANE, LOIS
PAINTER, PRINTMAKER
b Philadelphia, Pa, Jan 6, 48. *Study:* Yale Summer Sch Music & Art, 68; Philadelphia Col Art, BFA, 69; Yale Univ Sch Art & Archit, MFA, 71. *Work:* Whitney Mus Am Art, & Mus Mod Art, New York; Albright-Knox Gallery, Buffalo, NY; Des Moines Art Ctr, Iowa; Mus Fine Art, Houston. *Exhib:* One-person exhibs, Willard Gallery, New York, 77, 79, 80 & 83, Akron Mus Art, Ohio, 80 & Nigel Greenwood Gallery, London; New Image Painting, 78-79 & Biennial, 79, Whitney Mus Am Art; Ten Artists/Artists Space, Neuberger Mus, Purchase, NY, 79; Painting & Sculpture Today, Indianapolis Mus Art, 80; A New Bestiary: Animal Imagery in Contemp Art, Va Mus, 81; Back to the USA, traveling to var Ger mus, 83; Recent Acquisitions, Mus Mod Art, New York, 83. *Awards:* NY State Coun Arts Creative Artists Pub Serv Prog grant, 77; Nat Endowment for Arts fel painting, 78. *Bibliog:* Jeanne Siegal (auth), Arts, 11/80; Brian Wallis (auth), Arts, 1/81; Carolyn Kinder Carr (auth), introd to The Image in American Photography & Sculpture 1950-1980, Akron Art Mus. *Media:* Oil; Etching. *Publ:* Contribr, New Image Painting, Whitney Mus, 78; contribr, American Painting: the Eighties, Barbara Rose/Vista Press, 79. *Mailing Add:* Willard Gallery 29 E 72nd St New York NY 10021

LANE, MARION JEAN ARRONS
PAINTER, INSTRUCTOR
b Brooklyn, NY. *Study:* Brooklyn Mus Art Sch, with Manifred Schwartz & Reuben Tam; Pratt Inst, NY; Art Students League, with Morris Kantor; William Paterson Col, NJ, BA; Rutgers Univ, MFA. *Work:* Bloomfield Col, NJ. *Exhib:* Brooklyn Mus Alumni Exhib, 58; Work by New Jersey Artists, Newark Mus Triennial, 61; Art from New Jersey, NJ State Mus, Trenton, 68; Lincoln Ctr, Philharmonic Hall, New York, 68; New Talent, Kraushaar Gallery, New York, 75; Pleiades Gallery, New York, 76 & 77. *Teaching:* Instr, art appreciation & drawing, Bergen Community Col, 80-81. *Awards:* Essex Award, Painters & Sculptors Soc, Jersey City Mus, 65; NJ State Council Arts Fel Grant, 82; Edward Albee Found Fel, 83. *Bibliog:* Hedy Obeil Pazz (auth), article, Arts Mag, 10/77; Deborah Jerome (auth), article, Record, 82. *Mem:* Life mem Art Students League. *Media:* Acrylic, Sheetmetal. *Mailing Add:* 441 Hawthorne Pl Ridgewood NJ 07450

LANG, AVIS
CURATOR, WRITER
b Chicago, Ill, Jan 18, 44. *Study:* Univ Mich, Ann Arbor, BA, 65, MA(art hist), 68. *Collections Arranged:* Pork Roasts: 250 Feminist Cartoons Traveling Exhib, US, Can & Europe, 81-; Mirrorings: Women Artists of the Atlantic Provinces Traveling Exhib, Can, 82-83. *Teaching:* Lectr, Univ BC, Vancouver, 68-78, Banff Ctr, Alta, 80 & NSCAD, Halifax, formerly; asst prof, Simon Fraser Univ, Burnaby, BC, 83. *Res:* Women artists of the past; feminist concerns; cartoons; contemporary Canadian art. *Publ:* Auth, Toby MacLennan: Writings and rituals, 9/75 & auth, Women artists and the Canadian art world: A survey, fall 78, Criteria; auth, Nancy Holt: Stone enclosure/rock rings, 2/79 & auth, Liz Magor: Working sculpture, 12/80, Vanguard. *Mailing Add:* 202 W 78th St 3E New York NY 10024

LANG, DANIEL S
PAINTER
b Tulsa, Okla, Mar 17, 35. *Study:* Northwestern Univ, Evanston; Univ Tulsa, BFA, with Alexander Hogue; Univ Iowa, MFA, 59, with Mauricio Lasansky. *Work:* Mus Mod Art, New York; Art Inst Chicago; Libr Cong, Washington, DC; Nelson-Atkins Mus Fine Art, Kansas City; Victoria & Albert Mus, London; and others. *Comn:* Beneficial Management Group, NJ, 82. *Exhib:* Boston Mus Fine Arts, 61; Gimpel & Weitzenhoffer, New York, 75; Fischbach Gallery, New York, 77, 79 & 80; Graphik Int, Stutgart, WGer, 79; David Findlay Gallery, New York, 81; Sherry French Gallery, New York, 84; and others. *Teaching:* Asst prof painting, Art Inst Chicago, 62-64, Wash Univ, 64-65; vis artist, Ohio State Univ, 68-69, Univ SFla, fall 72, Univ Utah, spring 84. *Media:* Multimedia. *Dealer:* Sherry French Gallery New York NY. *Mailing Add:* 46 MacDougal St New York NY 10012

LANG, J T
PRINTMAKER, EDUCATOR
b Maple Shade, NJ, Dec 24, 31. *Study:* Philadelphia Col Art, Cert; Tyler Sch Art, BFA, BS(educ) & MFA; Barnes Found, with Violette De Mazia; also with Toshi Yoshida, Hirooyuki Tajima & Yuji Abe, Tokyo. *Work:* Philadelphia Mus Art; Cincinnati Mus Art; Birmingham Mus Art; State Dept, Washington, DC; Philadelphia Libr Collection. *Comn:* Large ed/woodcut, Print Club Philadelphia, 65; Exodus (litho ser), Pearl Fox Gallery of Elkins

Park, 71; color litho ed, La Salle Col, Philadelphia, 74; John Baptist de La Salle, La Salle Col, Philadelphia, 81. *Exhib:* Japan Print Soc Ann, Tokyo, 62, 63, 65 & 66; one-man print shows, Yoseido Gallery, Tokyo, 65 & Birmingham Mus, Ala, 74; USA Print Workshop Exhib, Cincinnati, 67; Am Color Print Soc Ann, Philadelphia, 68-81. *Teaching:* Asst prof Western cult, Aoyama G Univ, Tokyo, 63-67; vis lectr printmaking, Tyler Sch Art, Philadelphia, 68-70; asst prof printmaking & Asian art hist, LaSalle Col, Phildelphia, currently. *Awards:* Purchase Award, Cincinnati Mus Art, 67; Purchase Award, Pa Acad Fine Arts, 69; Outstanding Printmaker Award, Philadelphia Bd Educ, 73. *Bibliog:* Dorothy Grafly (auth), Summer print show, Sun Bulletin, Philadelphia, 7/30/67; Richard L Bell (auth), Prints of J T Lang (video tape), Springfield High Sch, 4/71; Sally Ann Harper (auth), Lang/printmakers, La Salle Collegian, 3/27/73. *Mem:* Am Color Print Soc (coun mem, 72-); Philadelphia Print Club; Col Art Teacher's Asn. *Dealer:* Pearl Fox Gallery 104 Windsor Ave Melrose Park Philadelphia PA 19126. *Mailing Add:* 251 W Somerville Ave Philadelphia PA 19120

LANG, MARGO TERZIAN
PAINTER

b Fresno, Calif. *Study:* Stanford Univ; Fresno State Univ; Ariz State Univ; Prado Mus, Madrid, Spain; also spec study with Edgar Whitney, Dong Kingman, Rex Brandt, George Post and others. *Work:* Over 50 paintings in US Embassies worldwide; and many others. *Comn:* Sunrise Tomorrow (cross superimposed on desert sunrise) comn by J Parker Nicholson, Glass & Garden Church, Scottsdale, Ariz, 71; Arizona Scenes, Pepsi Cola Bldg. *Exhib:* Int Platform Asn, Washington, DC, 70-75; Phoenix Art Mus, 70 & 71; one-person shows, Grand Cent Galleries, New York, 68 & 69; Corcoran Mus, 74 & Hammer Galleries, New York, 77; and others. *Awards:* Ann Competition Award, Grand Cent Galleries, 68 & 69; Best of Show Award, 70 & Silver Medal of Excellence, 71, Int Platform Asn. *Mem:* Nat Soc Arts & Lett; Nat Soc Lit & Arts; Am Artists Prof League; Ariz Watercolor Asn. *Media:* Oil, Watercolor. *Dealer:* Hammer Galleries 525 Park Ave New York NY 10021. *Mailing Add:* 6127 Calle del Paisano Scottsdale AZ 85251

LANG, RODGER ALAN
CERAMIST, EDUCATOR

b Chicago, Ill, Feb 9, 42. *Study:* Cornell Col, BA(art); Univ Wis-Madison, with Don Reitz & Harvey Littleton, MA(art) & MFA. *Work:* Brooks Mem Art Gallery, Memphis, Tenn; Mesa Col, Grand Junction, Colo. *Comn:* Ceramic tile wall mural, Mountain Bell, 78; ceramic tile wall mural, State of Colorado, 80. *Exhib:* Objects: USA The Johnson Collection of Contemporary Crafts, Traveling Exhib, 69; Clayworks: 20 Americans, Mus Contemp Crafts, New York, 71; Phases of New Realism, Lowe Art Gallery, Coral Gables, Fla, 72; Contemporary Crafts of the Americas, Colo State Univ & Orgn Am States, 75; Civilizations, Kohler Arts Ctr, Sheboygan, Wis, 77; 20 Colo Artists, Denver Art Mus, 77. *Teaching:* Instr, Cleveland Inst Art, 66-70; assoc prof, Metrop State Col, 70-77, prof, 77- *Bibliog:* Rose Slivka (auth), Laugh-in in clay, Craft Horizons, 10/71. *Media:* Ceramics, Wood. *Mailing Add:* 1655 Hoyt St Lakewood CO 80215

LANG, WENDY F
ADMINISTRATOR, PHOTOGRAPHER

b Cleveland, Ohio, Feb 15, 38. *Study:* Antioch Col, BA(design), 61; Stanford Grad Sch, MA, 63. *Work:* Nara Mus, Japan. *Exhib:* Butler Inst Am Art, Youngstown, Ohio, 78; Canton Inst Art, Ohio, 78; Friends Photog, 78; Downey Mus Art, Los Angeles Ctr Photog Studies, 78; Tenth Ann Int Photog Meet, Arles, France, 79; and many others. *Pos:* Bd dirs, Cameravision, Los Angeles, 76-80; mem bd trustees, Los Angeles Ctr Photog Studies, 78-; coordr, Photog Mus, Los Angeles, 79-80. *Teaching:* Instr, Los Angeles City Col, 79- *Mem:* Soc Photog Educators; and others. *Publ:* Contribr, Communication Arts, London Records, 74; contribr, Rufus, 78 & contribr, Shards, 79, Small Press; co-illus, Ballet Box, RCA Records, 79; contribr & coauth, Sequences: Baptism of Eros II, Peterson's Photog, 6/79. *Mailing Add:* 1231 Kipling Ave Los Angeles CA 90041

LANGER, SANDRA LOIS
HISTORIAN, CRITIC

b Woodridge, NY, Dec 18, 41. *Study:* Univ Miami, BA, 67, MA, 69; NY Univ, PhD, 74. *Pos:* Freelance art critic & contrib critic, Art Papers, 74-79. *Teaching:* Asst prof mod/contemp art, Fla Int Univ, 73-78; asst prof to assoc prof mod/contemp art hist/criticism, Univ SC, Columbia, 78- *Mem:* Col Art Asn; Women's Caucus for Art (adv bd, 75-77, 79-); Nat Women's Studies Asn; Southeast Women's Caucus for Art (state coordr, SC, 79-81); Southeastern Col Art Conf. *Res:* John F Kensett: a critical study of his life and art. *Publ:* Auth, Feminism and art history, Art Criticism, State Univ NY, Stony Brook, winter 80; auth, The aesthetics of democracy, Col Art J, winter 80; auth, The Rising South (catalog), Southeastern Ctr Contemp Art, Winston-Salem, NC, 80; auth, Against the grain, Int J Women's Studies, 82; auth, American Realist & Impressionist Paintings: Tashjian Col, 84. *Mailing Add:* 3300 Heyward St Columbia SC 29205

LANGFORD, JAMES
PAINTER

b Feb 14, 48. *Study:* Atlanta Sch Art, with Dorothy Berge, 69-71; Ga State Univ, with Medford Johnson, 72-73. *Work:* Loch Haven Mus & Valencia Col, Orlando, Fla. *Comn:* Abstract art, Kilpatrick Cody McCarthy, 73 & 3445 Corp, 74, Atlanta; three abstract works, Burdine's Inc, Orlando, 75; Polonaise in Clay (with Deanette Kühn), Crealde Art Ctr, Winter Park, Fla, 76; cast paper construction, Rich's Inc, Atlanta, 80. *Exhib:* 64th Nat Painting Exhib, Wadsworth Atheneum, 74; 36th Ann Exhib Contemp Painting, Soc Four Arts, Palm Beach, Fla, 74; Artists in Ga, High Mus, 74; La Grange Nat II,

La Grange Col, 75; Dimensions 76, Loch Haven Mus, Orlando, 76; Spectrum, Hunter Mus, 79; Paperworks 80 Southeast, Loyola Univ & traveling, 80; 11th Ann Works on Paper, Tex State Univ, San Marcos, 81. *Teaching:* Instr drawing & painting, Loch Haven Mus, Orlando, 76-77. *Awards:* Best in Show, Decatur Sesquicentennial, Decatur Fed Savings & Loan, 73; Merit Awards, Arts Festival Atlanta, 73 & 74; Purchase Award, Spectrum Exhib, Hunter Mus, 79. *Mem:* charter mem Fine Arts Guild; Am Craft Coun; Am Fedn Arts; Artists Equity Asn. *Media:* Acrylic, Oil. *Dealer:* Image South Gallery 1931 Peachtree St Atlanta GA 30309. *Mailing Add:* PO Box 934 Darien GA 31305

LANGLAND, HAROLD REED
SCULPTOR, EDUCATOR

b Minneapolis, Minn, Oct 6, 39. *Study:* Univ Minn, BA(art), 61, MFA(sculpture), 64. *Work:* Univ Minn Gallery, Minneapolis; Ind Univ, South Bend; Midwest Mus Am Art, Elkhart, Ind; St Paul Acad & Summit Sch, Minn. *Comn:* Standing Christ (bronze), House of Hope Presby Church, St Paul, Minn, 69; Ring Ribbons II (corten), Ind Univ, South Bend, 74; Christ Teaching (bronze), Univ Notre Dame, Ind; Violin Woman (bronze), South Bend, Ind, 82; Polymnia (bronze), Ft Wayne, Ind, 84. *Exhib:* one-man shows, Kalamazoo Inst Art, Mich, 77, St Catherine's Col Gallery, St Paul, Minn, 77, Small Bronzes, traveling, Eng, 77-78, Tweed Mus, Duluth, Minn, 78, Reflections, South Bend Art Ctr, Ind, 80 & Mid-W Mus Am Art, Elkhart, Ind, 84; and others in US & Eng. *Teaching:* Asst lectr sculpture, Carlisle & Sheffield Cols of Art, Eng, 64-67; assoc prof sculpture, Murray State Univ, 67-71; assoc prof & chmn dept fine arts, Ind Univ, South Bend, 71-82; vis lectr, Stoke-on-Trent, Eng, 77-78; prof, Ind Univ, South Bend, 82- *Awards:* 1st Prize, Midwest Mus Am Art, 79; Outstanding Sculpture, Hoosier Salon, 80 & 82; Best of Show, Northern Ind Arts Asn, 83. *Mem:* Artists Equity. *Media:* Bronze. *Dealer:* Poole Fine Art London; Poole-Wills Gallery New York NY. *Mailing Add:* 12632 Anderson Rd Granger IN 46530

LANGMAN, RICHARD THEODORE
GALLERY DIRECTOR

b Philadelphia, Pa, June 9, 37. *Study:* Cornell Univ, 54-55; Univ Calif, Berkeley, BA(urban design), 60. *Collections Arranged:* Alice Neel, Paintings, 74; Clayton Pond, Paintings & Graphics, 74; Graphics of the 70's (Int Graphics Show), 75 & Craft Art (Nat), 77, Langman Gallery; Bruce Evans, Paintings, SICA, 78 & 80, Constructions, 80; Andy Warhol, Paintings & Graphics, 83. *Pos:* Dir, Langman Gallery, Jenkintown, Pa. *Specialty:* Contemporary painting and sculpture. *Mailing Add:* 218 Old York Rd Jenkintown PA 19046

LANGNER, NOLA
ILLUSTRATOR, WRITER

b New York, NY, Sept 24, 30. *Study:* Bennington Col, graphics with Daniel Shapiro & painting with Paul Feeley; Summer Art Sch, graphics with Gabor Peterdi, scholar. *Pos:* Illusr & retoucher, Videocrafts Television Art Studio, New York, 54-55. *Awards:* Outstanding Book Award, New York Times Juvenile Bk Sect, 69; Boston Globe, Horn Book Award, 75. *Mem:* Author's Guild; PEN Club; Artists Equity Assoc, New York. *Media:* Pencil, Watercolor. *Publ:* Illusr, Scram, Kid, 74 & auth & illusr, Rafiki, 77, Viking Press; auth & illusr, Dusty, Coward, McCann & Geoghegan, 76; illusr, Half a Kingdom, Warne & Co, 77 & Ms Mag, anniversary ed, 77. *Dealer:* Marilyn Marlow c/o Curtis Brown Ltd 575 Madison Ave New York, NY 10012. *Mailing Add:* 353 Amsterdam Ave New York NY 10024

LA NOUE, TERENCE DAVID
PAINTER, EDUCATOR

b Hammond, Ind, Dec 4, 41. *Study:* Ohio Wesleyan Univ, BFA; Hochschule für Bildende Künste, West Berlin, Fulbright Scholar; Cornell Univ, MFA. *Work:* Roy Neuberger Mus, Purchase, NY; Corcoran Gallery Art, Washington, DC; Indianapolis Mus Art; Carnegie Inst; Whitney Mus Am Art; and others. *Exhib:* Philadelphia Mus Art; Albright-Knox Gallery, 71; Indianapolis Mus Art, 72; one-man shows, Nancy Hoffman Gallery, 74-78 & 80, Galerie Farideh Cadot, Paris, 77 & 78 & 80, Arts Club Chicago, 83 & Siegel Contemp Art, New York, 83; 9th Paris Biennial Am Art, 75; Philadelphia Mus Art, 77; 34th Corcoran Biennial of Am Painting; Iran-Am Soc, 78; and others. *Teaching:* Asst prof art, Trinity Col, 67-72; assoc prof art & head dept, La Guardia Col, 72- *Awards:* Nat Endowment Arts Grant, 72-73 & 83-84; Guggenheim Fel, 82-83. *Bibliog:* Ted Wolff (auth), article, Christian Sci Monitor, 82; Article, Art in Am, 82 & Arts Mag, 83; articles in Arts Mag, 76, 80 & 81, Art Int, 80. *Media:* Rhoplex, Acrylic on Canvas. *Mailing Add:* 36 Cooper Sq New York NY 10003

LANSDON, GAY BRANDT
PAINTER, PRINTMAKER

b San Antonio, Tex, Dec 6, 31. *Study:* Univ Houston, Tex, BFA, 65; Mus of Fine Arts Sch, Houston, 66-68; Sam Houston State Univ, MFA, 75. *Work:* Univ Houston, Univ Ctr; Sam Houston State Univ; Shell Oil Co; Xerox Corp; Price Waterhouse; and others. *Comn:* 16 paintings, comn by Dr Robert Stewart, Houston, 67; serigraph, comn by Jean Geeslin, Huntsville, Tex, 69; three printed fiber panels, Bellville State Bank, Tex, 72. *Exhib:* SW Crafts Biennial, Mus Santa Fe, NMex, 71; 15th Ann Tex Craftsman, Dallas Mus Fine Arts, 71; Colorprint USA, Lubbock, Tex, 75; Third Nat Print Exhib, Univ Southern Calif, Los Angeles, 75; 14th Midwest Biennial, Joslyn Art Mus, Omaha, Nebr, 75; Purdue Univ Small Print Exhib, 76; and others. *Teaching:* Instr art, Houston Mus of Fine Arts, Tex, 69-71; art dept fac, Univ Houston, Cent Campus, 71-82, coordr printmaking, 76-82; mem fac continuing educ, Univ Tex, Austin, currently. *Awards:* Jurors' Merit Awards, SW Graphics Invitational, 72 & Dimension X, 76, Houston Art League; First Prize, Baytown Ann, 78. *Bibliog:* Kit Van Cleave (auth), Gay Lansdon: Mixed-media printmaking, Today's Art, 2/77. *Media:* Mixed. *Dealer:* Dubose Gallery 2950 Kirby Houston TX 77098. *Mailing Add:* 11631 River Oaks Trail Austin TX 78753

LANSDOWNE, JAMES FENWICK
PAINTER
b Hong Kong, Aug 8, 37. *Work:* Ulster Mus, Belfast; Montreal Mus Fine Arts; Art Gallery of Greater Victoria; Beaverbrook Found; Audubon House, New York. *Exhib:* Lab Ornithol, Cornell Univ, 68; Nat Mus Natural Hist, Smithsonian Inst, Washington, DC, 69; Animals in Art, Royal Ont Mus, Toronto, 75; retrospective, Vancouver Art Gallery, 81; Scripps Inst Oceanography, La Jolla, Calif, 81; and others. *Mem:* Royal Can Acad Arts. *Media:* Gouache. *Publ:* Coauth, Birds of Northern Forest, 66; coauth, Birds of Eastern Forest, Part I, 68 & Part II, 70; auth, Birds of the West Coast, Part I, 76 & Part II, 80; illusr, Rails of the World, 76. *Dealer:* M F Feheley Arts Co 5 Drumsnab Rd Toronto ON Can. *Mailing Add:* 941 Victoria Ave Victoria BC V8S 4N6 Canada

LANSNER, FAY
PAINTER, TAPESTRY ARTIST
b Philadelphia, Pa. *Study:* Tyler Sch Fine Art, 45-47; Art Students League, 47-48; Hans Hofmann Sch, 48-50; also with Leger & L'Hote, Paris, 50-51. *Work:* Weatherspoon Art Mus, Greensboro, NC; NY Univ Art Collection; Corcoran Gallery Art, Washington, DC; Newsweek, Metrop Mus, New York; Neuberger Mus, State Univ NY Col, Purchase; and others. *Exhib:* Corcoran Gallery, Washington, DC, 67; Albright-Knox Art Gallery, Buffalo, NY, 67; Mus Mod Art, New York, 68, 69 & 71; 17th Brooklyn Mus Print Ann, NY, 70; Women in the Arts, Stamford Mus, Conn, 72; Women Choose Women, New York, 72; Hofmann Students, Metrop Mus Art, New York, 78; Poets & Painters, 79; one-person exhib, Denver Mus, Ingber Gallery, New York, 80. *Bibliog:* Harold Rosenberg (auth), Hofmann students, Art News Ann, 63; Doris Reno (auth), Lansner paintings show, Times Herald Post, 66; Fay Lansner (monograph), Essay 13, Guest Conversation, I Sandler, 77. *Publ:* Auth, Barbara Riboud, Craft Horizons Mag, 4/72. *Dealer:* Marlborough Graphics 40 W 57th St New York NY 10022; Arras Gallery 29 W 57th St New York NY 10019. *Mailing Add:* 317 W 80th St New York NY 10024

LANTZ, MICHAEL
SCULPTOR
b New Rochelle, NY, Apr 6, 08. *Study:* Nat Acad Design, 24-26; also with Lee Lawrie, 26-35; Beaux Arts Inst Design, 28-31. *Work:* Pan Am World Health Ctr; Architects Bldg, Albany, NY; Lynchburg Courthouse, Va; Nat Guard Mem Bldg, Washington, DC. *Comn:* Sculptural Outlines, Architect's Bldg, Albany, NY, 68; Thomas Jefferson Bicentennial Medal, US Mint, 76; New Rochelle Bicentennial Medal, 76; bronze eagle, Peoples Bank for Savings, 77; Brookgreen Gardens Anniversary Medal, 78; and others. *Exhib:* Philadelphia Mus Art, Pa, 40 & 48; Silver Medal Int Exhib, Madrid, Spain, 59; many exhibs, Nat Sculpture Soc, Nat Acad Design & Lever House, New York. *Pos:* Ed, Nat Sculpture Rev, 50-55, ed adv, 69- *Teaching:* Prof sculpture adult educ, New Rochelle, 36-38; instr, Nat Acad Design, 65- & Old Lyme Acad Fine Arts, 77- *Awards:* Medal of the City of New York, 48; J Sanford Saltus Medal, 69; Elizabeth Watrous Gold Medal, Nat Acad Design, 70 & 75. *Bibliog:* Sculpture by Michael Lantz, Am Artist Mag, 57; article, Nat Sculpture Rev, 72. *Mem:* Nat Sculpture Soc (pres, 70-73); Nat Acad Design; Am Acad Achievement; Fine Arts Fedn New York (vpres, 70). *Media:* Miscellaneous. *Publ:* Auth, articles in Nat Sculpture Rev. *Mailing Add:* 979 Webster Ave New Rochelle NY 10804

LANYON, ELLEN
PAINTER, PRINTMAKER
b Chicago, Ill, Dec 21, 26. *Study:* Art Inst Chicago, with Joseph Hirsch, BFA, 48; State Univ Iowa, with M Lasansky, MFA, 50; Courtauld Inst, Univ London, with Helmut Reuhman. *Work:* Art Inst of Chicago; Walker Art Ctr, Minneapolis; Nat Collection, Smithsonian, Metrop Mus Art, New York; McNay Art Inst, San Antonio, Tex. *Comn:* Painting, Florists' Tel Delivery Asn Traveling Exhib, 70; Container Corp Am: Great Ideas, US Dept Interior Bicentennial Exhib; Workingmans Coop Bank, Boston, 81; State Ill Bldg, Chicago, 83. *Exhib:* Art Inst Chicago, 46-81; Young Printmakers, Metrop Mus Art, 53; Recent Painting USA: The Figure, Mus Mod Art, New York, 62; solo exhibs, Richard Gray Gallery, 68-83, Susan Caldwell Inc, New York, 82-83 & Name Gallery, Chicago, 83; Landscape, Whitney Mus; 20th Century Am Watercolor Traveling Exhib, 83; The Artist and the Quilt Traveling Exhib, McNay Art Inst, 83; 52 one-women shows. *Teaching:* Instr painting & dir, Ox Bow Summer Sch of Painting, Saugatuck, Mich, 60-; vis artist-lectr, Stanford Univ, 73 & Univ Calif, Davis, 73 & 80; vis artist & fel, Inst Arts & Humanistic Studies, Pa State Univ, 74; vis artist, State Univ Iowa; instr painting, State Univ NY Col, Purchase, 78-, Parsons Sch Design, 79-80 & Sch Visual Arts, 80-; instr painting, Cooper Union, 79-82, adj assoc prof, 83- *Awards:* Nat Endowment Arts Award, 74; Yaddo Fel, 74-75 & 76; Hereward Lester Cooke Found, 81. *Bibliog:* John Friedman (auth), article, 11/80 & Martica Sawin (auth), article, 3/83, Arts Mag; Lucy Lippard (auth), article, Art in am, 5/83. *Mem:* Col Art Asn (bd dir, 77-). *Media:* Acrylic, Prismacolor; Lithography. *Publ:* Illusr, Jataka Tales, Houghton Mifflin, 75; auth, Transformations, Printed Matter, 77; auth, Mirabai Versions, 80 & The Managed World, 80, Redozier Press; auth, Transformations II, Chicago Books, 83. *Dealer:* Richard Gray 620 N Michigan Ave Chicago IL 60611; Susan Caldwell Inc 383 W Broadway New York NY 10012. *Mailing Add:* 412 N Clark St Chicago IL 60610

LA PELLE, RODGER
PAINTER, DEALER
b Philadelphia, Pa, July 31, 36. *Study:* Univ Pa; Pa Acad Fine Arts. *Work:* Free Libr Philadelphia, Pa; Munson-Williams Proctor Mus, Utica, NY; Mus Mod Art, New York. *Exhib:* Nat Exhib, Pa Acad Fine Art, Philadelphia, 58, Calif Palace of Legion Honor, San Francisco, 62 & San Francisco Art Mus, Calif, 63. *Pos:* Owner, Roger La Pelle Galleries. *Awards:* First Prize, Graflex Photog, 51; Silver Medal, Cologne, Germany, 56; Cresson Traveling Scholarship, Pa Acad Fine Art, 61. *Media:* Oil. *Specialty:* Contemporary painting, sculpture and graphics. *Mailing Add:* 2002 Rittenhouse Square Philadelphia PA 19103

LAPENA, FRANK RAYMOND
PAINTER, EDUCATOR
b San Francisco, Calif, Oct 5, 37. *Study:* Chico State Univ, AB(art); San Francisco State Univ, life credential educ(art); also with tribal elders and medicine men/traditionalists; Sacramento State Univ, MA. *Work:* Indian Arts & Crafts Bd, Washington, DC; Southern Plains Indian Mus, Anadarko, Okla; Crocker Mus, Sacramento, Calif. *Comn:* There is Remembering (chap heading-painting, In: The Human Condition), Scott, Foresman & Co, 73. *Exhib:* One-man show, Calif Indian Days, Calif Expos, Sacramento, 77; Fetishes, San Francisco Mus Art, 75; Am Indian Art Heritage, Art Inst of Chicago, 77; Indian Images (travelling exhib), Univ NDak, Grand Forks, 77; Am Indian Art Now, Wheelwright Mus, Santa Fe, NMex, 78; The Real People, Am Indian, group show, Havana, Cuba, 79; Philbrook Art Ctr, Tulsa, Okla; and others. *Pos:* Alternate mem art, Calif Comn Teacher Preparation & Licensing, State Calif, 72; bd mem, Ctr Arts of Indian Am, Washington, DC, 74- *Teaching:* Instr art & photog, Shasta Community Col, Redding, Calif, 69-71; assoc prof art hist, Calif State Univ, Sacramento, 71-; vis prof Indian Art hist, Lethbridge Univ, Alta, Can, summer 74. *Awards:* Best Painting Award, October Art Festival, Davis, 80; Purchase Award, 57th Ann Crocker-Kingsley Exhib, 82; First Place & Purchase Award, St John's Ann Religious Art Festival, Sacramento, 82; and others. *Bibliog:* Jamake Highwater (auth), The Sweet Grass Lives On, Lippincott & Crowell, 80; Wade & Strickland (auths), Magic Images: Contemporary Native American Art, Univ Okla Press, 81 & Four Winds, spring 82. *Mem:* Native Am Indian Artists; Native North Am Indian Artists; Int Soc Preserv Black & White Photog; Int Native Coun Arts, New York. *Media:* Mixed Media, Oil. *Res:* Culture and arts of the traditional and evolving arts and crafts of California tribal people. *Publ:* Contribr, Wintu Indian, In: Handbook of North American Indian, 20 vols, Smithsonian, 76; auth, Legends of the Yosemite Miwok, Yosemite Natural Hist Asn, 82; auth, A native American's view of rock art, Ancient Images on Stone: Rock Art of the Californias, UCLA Press, 82. *Mailing Add:* 5859 Woodleigh Dr Carmichael CA 95608

LA PIERRE, THOMAS
PAINTER, PRINTMAKER
b Toronto, Ont, Dec 28, 30. *Study:* Ont Col Art, AA; Ecole Beaux Arts; Atelier 17. *Work:* Montreal Mus Fine Art, PQ; Sir George Williams Univ; Art Gallery, Hamilton, Ont. *Exhib:* Sao Paulo Biennial, 63; Focus on Drawing, Art Gallery Ont, 65; Price Fine Art Awards Exhib, 70; Atlantic Provinces, 74; W Coast traveling exhib, Burnaby Art Gallery. *Teaching:* Instr drawing & painting, Ont Col Art, 58- *Awards:* Ont Soc Artists Award, 68; Price Fine Art Award, 70; Can Soc Painters in Watercolour Honour Award, 78, 79 & 80. *Bibliog:* William McElcheran (auth), Dialogue with demons, Arts Can, 70; Robert Percival (auth), 20th Century mystic, Art Mag, 75; Paul Duval (auth), article in Art Mag, 76 & 77. *Mem:* Can Soc Graphic Art; Can Soc Painters in Watercolour; Royal Can Acad Arts. *Media:* Oil, Watercolor. *Mailing Add:* 2067 Proverbs Dr Mississauga ON L4X 1G3 Canada

LAPINSKI, TADEUSZ (A)
PRINTMAKER, EDUCATOR
b Rawa Mazowiecka, Poland, June 20, 28; US citizen. *Study:* Acad Fine Arts, Warsaw, Poland, MFA, 55. *Work:* Mus Mod Art, New York; Nat Collection Fine Arts & Nat Gallery, Washington, DC; Mus Mod Art, Tokyo; Albertina Mus, Vienna; plus others. *Comn:* Washington Portfolio, Washington DC Print Club & Soc of Graphic Arts, 74. *Exhib:* Am Print in Venice, 77; one-man exhibs, Baak Gallery, Cambridge, Mass, 79, Bacardi Art Gallery, 79, Forum Gallery, Zagreb, Yugoslavia & Klevit Gallery, Washington, DC. *Teaching:* Assoc prof lithography, Univ Md, 72-82, prof, 83- *Awards:* First Prize, Int Print Festival Vienna, 78; Second Prize, World Print, Paris, 80; Outstanding Achievement Award, Univ Md, 81; and others. *Bibliog:* Fritz Eichenberg (auth), The Art of the Prints, Abrams, 77; Jane Haslem (ed), American Paintings and Graphics, Washington, DC; Lillian Dobbs (auth), Lapinski prints are unique, hard to find, Miami News, 11/16/79. *Mem:* Soc Am Graphic Artists; Painters Sculptors Soc of NJ (vpres, 72-76); Washington Printmakers Soc; Soc Graphic Arts, New York. *Dealer:* F Bader Gallery 2124 Pennsylvania Ave NW Washington DC 20037. *Mailing Add:* 10413 Eastwood Ave Silver Spring MD 20901

LAPLANTZ, DAVID
JEWELER, EDUCATOR
b Toledo, Ohio, June 12, 44. *Study:* Bowling Green State Univ, with Hal Hasselschwert, BS(art), 66; Cranbrook Acad Art, with Richard Thomas, MFA, 69; Southern Ill Univ, with Alex Bealer, 70. *Work:* St Paul Art Ctr, Minn; Colo State Univ; Bowling Green State Univ; Am Craft Mus; Schmuck Mus, Pforzheim, Ger. *Comn:* Commemorative (scale model of house), Civil Rights Group, Detroit, 67. *Exhib:* Exhib of Eight American Metalsmiths & Jewelers, Sheffield Polytech Sch Art & Design, Sheffield, Eng & Richard Demarco Gallery, Edinburgh, Scotland, 74; The Goldsmith, Renwick Gallery, Smithsonian Inst, Washington, DC, 74; Blacksmith as Artist & Craftsman 1776-1976, Mus Contemp Crafts, New York & Renwick Gallery, Smithsonian Inst, Washington, DC, 76-77; NAm Goldsmith Biennial Exhib, Phoenix Art Mus, Ariz, 77; Copper, Bronze & Brass Competition, Univ Ariz Mus Art, Tucson, 77; 3rd Profile of US Jewelry, Tex Tech Univ, Lubbock, 77; For the Table Top, Am Craft Mus, traveling show, 80-83; Gold as Gold-Alternative Materials in American Jewelry, Renwick Gallery, Smithsonian

Inst, Washington, DC, 81-84; and many others. *Teaching:* Instr, Inst Am Indian Arts, Santa Fe, NMex, 67-68, Kent State Univ, 67-68, Colo State Univ, 69-70, San Diego State Col, 70-71 & Humboldt State Univ, 71- *Awards:* Second Place, Nat Sterling Silver Design Competition, Sterling Silversmiths Guild Am, 69; St Paul Art Ctr Purchase Award, 70; Merit Award, NAm Goldsmith Biennial Exhib, Phoenix Art Mus, 77. *Bibliog:* Articles in Crafts Horizons, 69-70 & 75, Goldsmith J, 80 & Art Craft Mag, 80; article, Ornament Mag, Vol 5, No 4, 82. *Mem:* Am Craftsman's Coun; Friends of Calif Design; Soc NAm Goldsmiths. *Media:* All Media. *Publ:* Contrib, Body Jewelry-International Perspective, 73; contrib, Contemporary Jewelry, rev ed, 76; contribr, Jewelry Concepts & Technology, 82; and others. *Mailing Add:* 899 Bayside Cutoff Bayside CA 95524

LAPLANTZ, SHEREEN
WEAVER, INSTRUCTOR
b Glendale, Calif, Feb 9, 47. *Study:* Los Angeles State Univ, BA, 68; Cranbrook Acad Art, 69. *Work:* Mendocino Art Ctr, Calif; Murray St Univ. *Exhib:* Virginia Beach Arts Ctr, Va, 82; Eve Mannes Gallery, Atlanta, 82; Seattle Ctr, 83; one-person show, Murray St Univ, Ky, 83; Gallery 8, La Jolla, 83; and others. *Pos:* Publ, Press de LaPlantz, Bayside, Calif, 81- *Teaching:* Instr fiberarts, Col Redwoods, Eureka, Calif, 74-77. *Awards:* Textiles Awards, Spring Show, Redwood Art Asn, 73 & 75; Cash Award, Calif Crafts IX, Crocker Art Gallery, 75. *Bibliog:* Dona Meilach (auth), Basketry Today, Crown, 79; Fiberarts Design Book, Hastings House, 80; Fiberarts Design Book II, Hastings House, 83. *Mem:* Handweavers Guild Am; Am Crafts Coun. *Media:* Fiber, Reed. *Publ:* Auth, Baskets and curls, Shuttle, Spindle & Dyepot, 81; auth & ed, Plaited Basketry-The Woven Form, Press de LaPlantz, 82; contrib ed, ARC, 82; auth, Handwoven, Basketry Materials Guide, 83; auth, The artist in business, Humboldt Bay Sheep & Wool Newsletter, 83; and others. *Mailing Add:* 899 Bayside Cutoff Bayside CA 95524

LAPOINTE, FRANK
PAINTER, PRINTMAKER
b Port Rexton, Nfld, May 11, 42. *Study:* Ont Col of Art, AOCA, 66. *Work:* Can Coun Art Bank, Fed Dept of Pub Works, Ottawa, Ont; Univ Ore, Corvallis; Simon Fraser Univ, Burnaby, BC; Confederation Centre for the Arts, Charlottetown, PEI. *Comn:* Nfld postcard ser: What do you think of Jack?, Mem Univ Art Gallery Jubilee Portfolio, St John's, Nfld, 75; stainless steel & aluminum mirror sculpture, Fed Bldg, Grand Falls, Nfld, 79; lithograph portfolio, Can Saltfish Corp, 81. *Exhib:* Aspects of Can Printmaking, Nat Touring Show, Mira Godard Gallery, Toronto, 79-80; Survival-Atlantic Style, Nat Touring Show, Mt St Vincent Art Gallery, Halifax, 79-80; Hudson's Bay Exhib, Art CORE Consult, Vancouver, 79; Island Interlude, Mem Univ Nfld Art Gallery, St John's, 81; Elements, Nat Film Board Gallery, Ottawa, 81; and many others. *Pos:* Asst cur & art specialist, Art Gallery, Mem Univ, St John's, Nfld, 70-72, cur, 72-73. *Teaching:* Instr painting & printmaking, Dundas Valley Sch of Art, Dundas, Ont, 69-70. *Awards:* Silver Medal, 67 & Bronze Medal, 68, Nfld Arts & Lett, Govt Nfld; Can Coun Grant, 77. *Bibliog:* Joe Bodolai (auth), Visit to Newfoundland, 75-76 & Peter Bell (auth), Frank Lapointe/Gerald Squires, 76-77, Artscanada; Peter Bell (auth), Oberheide, Wright, Lapointe, Vie des Arts, Montreal, winter 76. *Mem:* Can Soc of Painters in Watercolor. *Media:* Watercolor, Acrylic; Lithography, Etching. *Dealer:* Mira Godard Gallery 22 Hazelton Ave Toronto ON Can. *Mailing Add:* Tors Cove Southern Shore NF A0A 4A0 Canada

LAPOSKY, BEN FRANCIS
DESIGNER, VIDEO ARTIST
b Cherokee, Iowa, Sept 30, 14. *Work:* Sanford Mus, Cherokee, Iowa; Univ Okla, Norman; Mus Sci & Technol, Tel Aviv, Israel. *Exhib:* Light as a Creative Medium, Carpenter Ctr, Harvard Univ, 66; Cybernetic Serendipity, Inst Contemp Art, London, 68; On the Eve of Tomorrow, Computer Art, Hannover, Ger, 69; Computer Graphics Art Exhib, Rhinelander Gallery, New York, 76; Computer Art Exhib, Univ Waterloo Galleries, Can, 77; Cybernetic Symbiosis, computer art exhib, Univ Calif, Berkeley, 79; plus others. *Awards:* Art Dirs Club Medal, New York, 57. *Bibliog:* Electronic Gayety, Fortune Mag, 12/56; H Franke (auth), Computer Graphics-Computer Art, Phaidon, London, 71; Andrew Kagan (auth), Ben F Laposky: Midwestern pioneer of absolute light form, Arts Mag, 6/80. *Media:* Kinetic Light Assemblages, Photography. *Publ:* Auth, Electronic abstracts: Art for space age, Proc Iowa Acad Sci, 58; auth, Oscillographic design, Perspective Mag, London, 60; auth, Oscillons: electronic abstractions, Leonardo Mag, Oxford, 69 & Kinetic Art, 74; contrib, Ruth Leavitt, ed, Electronic Abstractions in Artist & Computer, Harmony Bks, 76; auth, Magic squares: A design source, Leonardo Mag, Eng, 78. *Mailing Add:* 301 S Sixth St Cherokee IA 51012

LARCADA, RICHARD KENNETH
DEALER
b Brooklyn, NY, Sept 11, 35. *Study:* NY Univ, BA, 56. *Pos:* Assoc dir, Maynard Walker Gallery, New York, 61-65; dir, Larcada Gallery, New York, 65-77; dir, One Art Serv, New York, 77-; Am rep, Ketterer Auction, Munich, Ger. *Specialty:* Neo-Romantics; artists of the twenties and thirties. *Mailing Add:* 790 Madison Ave New York NY 10021

LARIAR, LAWRENCE
CARTOONIST, WRITER
b Brooklyn, NY, Dec 25, 08. *Study:* New York Sch Fine & Appl Arts, 26-29; Acad Julien, Paris; Art Students League. *Pos:* Com advert artist, 30-33; illusr & polit cartoonist, 33-; cartoon ed, Liberty Mag, 41-48; ed, Best Cartoons of Year, 42-; cartoon ed, Parade Mag, 57- *Teaching:* Dir, Prof Sch Cartooning.

Mem: Author's League Am. *Publ:* Auth, You've Got Me From 9 to 5; auth, You've Got Me on the Rocks, 56; auth, The Real Lowdown, 56; auth, Girl Running, 56; auth, Boat & Be Damned, 57; contribr cartoons in leading nat mags & New York daily newspapers; also auth & ed many other bks. *Mailing Add:* 399 F Heritage Village Southbury CT 06488

LARK, RAYMOND
PAINTER, DRAFTSMAN
b Philadelphia, Pa, June 16, 39. *Study:* Philadelphia Mus Sch Art; Dobbins Voc, Philadelphia; Temple Univ, BS; Los Angeles Tech Col. *Work:* Libr Cong; Mus African & African-Am Art & Antiquities, Buffalo, NY; and many others. *Comn:* Universal City Studios, Calif, 65; Movie Land Wax Mus & Palace of Living Arts, Buena Park, Calif, 65; Blue Cross Ins Co, 67 & CBS-TV Studios, Los Angeles, 73; and others. *Exhib:* Smithsonian Inst, 71; NJ State Mus, Trenton, 71; Libr Cong, 73; Guggenheim Mus, 75; Honolulu Acad Arts, Hawaii, 75; Metrop Mus Art, New York, 76; Portsmouth Mus, Va, 79; Univ Calif Ctr Afro-Am Studies, Los Angeles, 83; Salon Nations Centre Int D'Art Contemporain, Paris, 83; and many others. *Collections Arranged:* Black Sculpturing Exhibition, Charles W Bowers Mem Mus (auth, catalog), Santa Ana, Calif, 69; Five Black Artists Exhibit, Florenz's Art Gallery, Hollywood, 69; Nine American Artists Exhibit (auth, catalog), Emerald Gallery, Hollywood Beach, Fla, 70; and others. *Pos:* Pres, Art West Assoc Inc, Calif, 68-70. *Teaching:* Lectr, Compton Col, Calif, 72, Los Angeles Trade Tech Col, 73, Univ Calif, Los Angeles, 83, Calif Mus Afro-Am Hist & Cult, 83 & others. *Awards:* Proclamations, President Nixon, 72, President Ford, 75 & President Carter, 77; plus others. *Bibliog:* Robert J Rhodes (auth), Raymond Lark: A study in determination, Southwest Art, 3/82; Fred Anderson (dir), Raymond Lark: From rags to riches (film), ABC-TV Calif, 2/2/83; Melody Jackson (dir), Raymond Lark: Good Day Los Angeles (film), KTTV-TV Calif, 2/19/83; and others. *Mem:* Artists Equity Asn; Int Platform Asn; plus others. *Media:* Oil, Pencil. *Rcs:* Graphic art masters. *Publ:* Contribr, Drawings and paintings by an Afro-American artist, Leonardo, 82; and others. *Mailing Add:* PO Box 8990 Los Angeles CA 90008

LARK, SYLVIA
PAINTER, PRINTMAKER
b Buffalo, NY, Nov 8, 47. *Study:* State Univ New York Col, Buffalo, BA, 69; Univ Siena, Italy, 67-68; Mills Col, Calif, 69-70; Univ Wis, Madison, MA, 70, MFA, 72. *Work:* Metrop Mus Art, New York; Mus Contemp Art, Chicago; Oakland Mus; Crocker Mus, Sacramento; Munic Mus Graphic Art, Maracaibo, Venezuela. *Exhib:* San Francisco Mus Mod Art, 75; Oakland Mus, 78; Pratt Graphics Ctr, New York, 80; American Colorist Prints, World Print Gallery, San Francisco, 81; Allan Stone Gallery, New York, 82; Galerie Akmak, Berlin, 83; Jeremy Stone Gallery, San Francisco, 83. *Pos:* Nat adv bd mem, Women's Causus Art, 78- *Teaching:* Assoc prof art, Calif State Univ, Sacramento, 72-77; assoc prof art, Univ Calif, Berkeley, 77- *Awards:* Fulbright-Hays Grant, 77. *Bibliog:* Joanna Frueh (auth), Chicago: Kathe Keller & Sylvia Lark, Art Am, 1-2/79; Roberta Loach (auth), Sylvia Lark, Visual Dialogue, 1-2/79; Suzanne Boettger (auth), Decoration and Transcendence, Artwk, vol 12, 1/21/81; Cynthia Nadelman (auth), Sylvia Lark, Artnews, 10/82. *Mem:* World Print Coun. *Media:* Oil, Pastel; Monotype. *Dealer:* Allan Stone Gallery 48 E 86th St New York NY 10028; Jeremy Stone Gallery 126 Post St San Francisco CA 94108. *Mailing Add:* Art Dept Kroeber Hall Univ Calif Berkeley CA 94720

LARKIN, EUGENE
DESIGNER, EDUCATOR
b Minneapolis, Minn, June 27, 21. *Study:* Univ Minn, BA & MA. *Work:* Mus Mod Art, New York; Nat Gallery Art & Libr Cong, Washington, DC; Art Inst Chicago; Addison Gallery Am Art, Andover, Mass; Nat Collection of Fine Arts, Smithsonian Inst, Washington, DC; and others. *Comn:* Int Graphic Arts Soc; Gen Mills Corp; Bus Wk; Minneapolis Soc Fine Arts; US Info Agency. *Exhib:* US Info Agency Traveling Exhib to Iran, Italy, France, Spain & Ger; one-man shows, Minneapolis Inst Art, 68 & Hamline Univ, 68; State Univ NY Albany, 69; Univ Calif, Long Beach, 69; Univ Minn, 74 & 78; plus others. *Teaching:* Instr, Kans State Col, Pittsburg, 48-54; head printmaking dept & chmn fine arts div, Minneapolis Sch Art, 54-69; prof, Design Dept, Univ Minn, Minneapolis, 69- *Awards:* Walker Art Ctr, 60 & Washington Watercolor & Print Exhib, 63; plus many others. *Mem:* Am Asn Univ Prof; Col Art Asn Am. *Media:* Woodcuts, Lithographs, Oil. *Mailing Add:* 64 Groveland Terr Minneapolis MN 55403

LARKIN, JOHN E, JR
COLLECTOR, PATRON
b St Paul, Minn, Nov 8, 30. *Study:* Univ Minn, BS & MD; Harvard Univ. *Pos:* Trustee, Minn Mus Art; benefactor, Minneapolis Inst Art; trustee, Minneapolis Soc Fine Arts. *Collection:* American art. *Mailing Add:* 7 Yellow Birch Rd Dellwood White Bear Lake MN 55110

LARMER, OSCAR VANCE
PAINTER, EDUCATOR
b Wichita, Kans, July 11, 24. *Study:* Minneapolis Sch of Fine Arts, cert painting; Univ Kans, BFA; Wichita State Univ, MFA. *Work:* Nelson Gallery of Art, Kansas City, Mo; Kans State Univ, Manhattan; Wichita State Univ, Kans; Wichita Art Asn Gallery; and others. *Comn:* Medallion, Kans State Col Centennial, Manhattan, 61; President's Medallion, Kans State Univ, 74; painting, Kans 4-H Found, Kans State Univ, 77. *Exhib:* Mid-Am Exhib, Nelson Gallery of Art, Kansas City, Mo, 52-70; Watercolor USA, Springfield Art Mus, Mo, 57 & 68; Rocky Mountain Exhib, Denver Art Mus, Colo, 65; 45th Ann 17-State Exhib, Springfield, Mo, 75; Nat Watercolor Exhib, La Watercolor Soc, 76; Works of Art on Paper, Nat-Western Ann,

Western Ill Univ, Galesburg, 76; Summer Invitational, Nelson Gallery of Art, Kansas City, Mo, 77, 79 & 81. *Pos:* Asst dir, Wichita Art Mus, Kans, 53-55. *Teaching:* Prof drawing & painting, Kans State Univ, Manhattan, 56-, head art dept, 67-71. *Awards:* Purchase Awards, Smoky Hills Art, Hadley Med Ctr, 77, Kans Watercolor Soc, United Bank & Trust, 77 & Prairie Exhib, 83. *Bibliog:* V W Bell (auth), The Kansas Art Reader, Univ Kans Press, 76. *Mem:* Nat Col Art Asn; Mid-Am Col Art Asn; Kans Watercolor Soc; Kans Fedn of Art. *Media:* Watercolor, Oil. *Publ:* Coauth, A Foundation for Expressive Drawing, Burgess Publishing, 83. *Mailing Add:* 2441 Hobbs Dr Manhattan KS 66502

LARRAZ, JULIO F
PAINTER

b La Habana, Cuba, Mar 12, 44. *Study:* Drawing and painting with Burton Silverman. *Work:* Westmoreland Co Mus Art, Greensburg, Pa. *Exhib:* Artists & Space, Nat Gallery, Washington, DC, 70; one-man show of drawings, New Sch Social Res, New York, 72; Childe Hassam Fund Purchase, Am Acad Arts & Lett, New York, 74; 39th Ann Midyear Show, Butler Inst Am Art, Youngstown, Ohio, 75; Art in the Kitchen, Westmoreland Co Mus Art, 75. *Awards:* Cintas Found Fel, Inst Int Educ, 75; Am Acad Arts & Lett Award, 76. *Bibliog:* David L Shirey (auth), Julio Fernandez, New York Times, 72; Doreen Mangan (auth), Julio Fernandez and his rogues gallery, Am Artist, 74. *Media:* Oil, Watercolor. *Publ:* Contrib, The Eye Witness to Space, Abrams, 70; illusr, The Perfect Wagnerite, Time-Life Bks, 72; illusr, The Whitehouse Enemies, New Am Libr, 73; contribr, Still the flypaper of politics, New York Times Mag, 74; contribr, New York Mag. *Dealer:* Hall Gallery 4719 Camp Bowie Blvd Ft Worth TX 76107; Nohra Haime Gallerie 1000 Madison Ave New York NY 10021. *Mailing Add:* 31 River Rd Nyack NY 10960

LARSEN, D DANE
CERAMIST, SCULPTOR

b Oct 21, 50. *Study:* Harvard Univ, BA, study with William Reimann, Rudolf Arnheim & Buckminster Fuller; Univ Calif, Study with Ron Nagle; San Francisco State Univ, MA, study with Charles McKee, Hayward King, Dale Roush, Daniel Rhodes & Paul Soldner. *Work:* San Francisco State Univ Ceramics Collection; Carpenter Ctr for the Visual Arts, Harvard Univ, Cambridge, Mass; Oakland Mus, Calif; Prieto Gallery, Mills Col, Oakland. *Exhib:* Calif Ceramics & Glass, Oakland Mus; The Calif Craftsman, Monterey Peninsula Mus Art, Monterey, Calif; Marietta Col Crafts Nat, Grover M Hermann Fine Arts Ctr, Marietta, Ohio; Designer-Craftsman Nat, Richmond Art Ctr, Calif; Calif Crafts X, E B Crocker Gallery & Mus, Sacramento; Nat Cone Box Show, Kans Univ Union Gallery, Lawrence. *Pos:* Consult & dir of ceramics prog, San Rafael City Recreation Dept, 77- *Teaching:* Instr ceramics, Col of Marin, Kentfield, Calif, 76- & Columbia Jr Col, Calif, summer 77; Art Acad, San Francisco, Calif, 80. *Awards:* Cash Awards, Calif Craftsman, 76, San Jose Mus Art, 76 & 76 & Civic Arts Gallery, 77. *Mem:* San Francisco Potters Asn; Am Crafts Coun; Col Art Asn. *Media:* Clay, Wood. *Dealer:* Meyer, Breir & Weiss Fort Mason Ctr San Francisco CA 94123. *Mailing Add:* PO Box 973 San Rafael CA 94901

LARSEN, ERIK
CONSULTANT, EDUCATOR

b Vienna, Austria, Oct 10, 11; US citizen. *Study:* Inst Superieur Hist Art & Archeol, Brussels, Belg, BA; Cath Univ Louvain, MA & PhD; restoration with Jef Lammens, Ghent & Jules Defort, Brussels. *Pos:* Dir & ed-in-chief, Pictura; Belg Govt Cult Mission in Brazil, 46-47; Am ed, Artis. *Teaching:* Lectr, Belg; res prof art, Manhattanville Col Sacred Heart, 47-55; instr, Sch Gen Studies Exten Div, City Col New York, 48-55; from lectr to vis prof, Georgetown Univ, 55-58, assoc prof fine arts, 58-63, prof fine arts, 63-67, head dept fine arts, 60-67; prof hist art, Univ Kans, 67-80, dir, Ctr Flemish Art & Cult, 70-80, prof emer art hist, 80- *Awards:* Knight's Cross, Order of Leopold & Order of the Crown, Belg; Laureate, Inst France, Prix Thorlet, 62; mem, Jury Taras Shevshenko Mem, Washington, DC. *Mem:* Appraisers Asn Am; Am Asn Univ Prof; Asn Dipl Hist Art & Archeol, Cath Univ Louvain. *Res:* History of northern baroque and northern renaissance art. *Publ:* Auth, Les Primitifs Flamands au Musee Metropolitain de New York, 60; auth, Frans Post, Interprete du Bresil, 62; auth, Van Dyck, Lekturama, Rotterdam, 80; auth, Anton Van Dyck, Rizzoli, Milan, 81; auth, Anton Van Dyck, Ullstein, Frankfort, 80; and others. *Mailing Add:* Dept Art Univ Kans Lawrence KS 66045

LARSEN, JACK LENOR
DESIGNER, WEAVER

b Seattle, Wash, Aug 5, 27. *Study:* Univ Wash, BFA, 50; Cranbrook Acad Art, MFA, 51. *Work:* Mus Mod Art, New York, NY; Victoria & Albert Mus, London, Eng; Stedelijk Mus, Amsterdam, Holland; Cooper-Hewitt Mus Decorative Arts & Design, New York; and others. *Comn:* Theatre curtain, comn by Charles Luchman Assocs for Phoenix Civic Plaza, Concert Hall, Ariz, 72. *Exhib:* One-man show, Mus Decorative Art, Copenhagen, Denmark, 76; retrospectives, Stedelijk Mus, Amsterdam, 68, Mus Fine Arts, Boston, Mass, 71, Renwick Gallery, Washington, DC, 72 & Fashion Inst Technol, New York, 78; 30 Yrs of Creative Textiles, Mus des Arts Decoratifs, Pavillon de Marsan, Louvre, Paris, 81. *Collections Arranged:* Co-dir, Wall Hangings, Mus Mod Art, New York, 70. *Teaching:* Dir fabric design dept, Philadelphia Col Art, 61-63; artist in residence, Royal Col Art, London, 75; affiliate prof, Univ Wash. *Awards:* Gold Medal for design dir US Pavilion, Triennale, Milan, Italy, 57; Elsie DeWolfe Award, Am Inst Interior Designers, 71; Gold Medal, Am Inst Archits, 74. *Mem:* Am Crafts Coun (bd trustees, 54-, pres, 81); Royal Soc Art, London; hon fel Am Inst Interior Designers. *Publ:* Coauth, Elements of Weaving, Doubleday, 67; coauth, Beyond Craft: the Art Fabric, Van Nostrand; coauth, Fabrics for Interiors, 75; auth, The Dyer's Art, 76; coauth, The Art Fabric: Mainstream, Van Nostrand, 81. *Mailing Add:* 41 E 11th St New York NY 10003

LARSEN, JOHN CHRISTIAN
EDUCATOR, LIBRARIAN

b Menominee, Mich. *Study:* Univ Mich, BDes, 50, MA(art hist), 51, MALS, 55, PhD, 67. *Pos:* Reference librn, Fine Arts Dept, Detroit Pub Libr, Mich, 54-57; head art div, Mich State Univ, Lansing, 57-61. *Teaching:* Instr bibliog fine arts, Sch Libr Sci, Univ Mich, Ann Arbor, 65-68; asst prof bibliog visual arts, Col Libr Sci, Univ Ky, Lexington, 68-71; asst prof lit fine arts, Sch Libr Serv, Columbia Univ, New York, 71-77; assoc prof bibliog visual arts, Sch Libr Sci, Northern Ill Univ, De Kalb, 77- *Mem:* Art Libr Soc NAm; Am Libr Asn; Asn Col & Res Libr; Spec Libr Asn; Victorian Soc Am (bd mem, 75-76). *Res:* Use of information resources in visual arts. *Interests:* Evaluation of reference materials treating visual arts; education of art librarians. *Publ:* Auth, A seminar in fine arts bibliography, J Educ Librarianship, 70; auth, The use of art reference sources in museum libraries, Spec Libr, 71; auth, The education of fine arts/music librarians, Libr Trends, 75. *Mailing Add:* Sch of Libr Sci Northern Ill Univ De Kalb IL 60115

LARSEN, MERNET RUTH
PAINTER, EDUCATOR

b Houghton, Mich, June 2, 40. *Study:* San Francisco Art Inst, with Nathan Olivera, 60; Univ Fla, with Hiram Williams, BFA, 62; Univ Ill, 62-63; Ind Univ, with James McGarrell & William Bailey, MFA, 65. *Work:* Univ Okla; Okla Art Ctr; Fla House of Rep; Tampa Electric Co; Ind Univ. *Exhib:* Thirteen Young Artists You Should Collect, Okla Art Ctr, 65; Mid-Am Ann, Nelson Gallery, Kansas City, Mo, 66; Realism & Figuration, Fla State Univ Mus, Tallahassee, 71; All Fla Painters, St Petersburg Mus, 76; one-person show, Mont State Art Gallery, Bozeman, 77; Realism & Metaphor, Jacksonville Mus and others, 80; Artists Choice, Swain Sch Design, 82. *Teaching:* Vis instr, Univ Okla, Norman, 65-67; prof painting & drawing, Univ SFla, 67-; instr, Cath Univ Milan, Rome, Italy, summer 70; vis artist painting, Ridgewood Sch Art, NJ, 73-74 & Mont State Univ, Bozeman, winter, 77; vis asst prof drawing, Yale Univ, fall 76. *Media:* Oils. *Mailing Add:* 13710 N 20th St Tampa FL 33612

LARSEN, OLE
PAINTER, ILLUSTRATOR

b Manistee, Mich. *Study:* Chicago Acad Fine Arts; Art Inst Chicago; Am Acad Art; also landscapes with Edward Timmons. *Work:* Michigan City Pub Libr, Ind; Riveredge Found, Calgary, Alta; Am Saddle Horse Mus, Lexington, Ky. *Exhib:* West Suburban Artists Guild, Hillside, 72; Naperville Woman's Club Art Fair, 72 & 74; Hinsdale Fine Arts Festival, 74; Lyon's Club Ann Horse Show & Art Exhib, Oak Brook, 74; DuPage Hosp Auxillary Ann Art & Crafts Fair, Glen Ellyn, Ill, 75; and others. *Awards:* For Sir Dudly, Ky State Fair Animal Artists Exhib, 37 & Early Days of a Thoroughbred, Ill State Fair, 56. *Bibliog:* Articles in Globe Dem Tempo Mag, 51, Chicago Tribune, 51 & 52 & State J Regist, 67. *Mem:* Soc Animal Artists; Hinsdale Community Artists. *Media:* Oil, Pastel. *Dealer:* Findlay Galleries 814 N Michigan Ave Chicago IL 60611; O'Brien's Art Emporium Inc 7122 Stetson Dr Scottsdale AZ 85261. *Mailing Add:* 90 S 6th Ave La Grange IL 60525

LARSEN, PATRICK HEFFNER
PAINTER, SCULPTOR

b Port Arthur, Tex, July 11, 45. *Study:* Lamar Univ, BBA, 68; Sam Houston State Univ, teacher cert, 69; Stephen F Austin State Univ, MA, 70, MFA, 73. *Work:* Stephen F Austin State Univ, Nacogdoches, Tex; First Nat Bank of Ark, Little Rock; Univ Cent Ark, Conway. *Exhib:* Okla Art Ctr, Oklahoma City, 70 & 72; 16th & 17th Ann Delta Exhib, Ark Art Ctr, Little Rock, 73 & 74; one-man shows, Ft Smith Art Ctr, Ark, 75 & SArk Art Ctr, El Dorado, 76; 54th Ann Exhib, Meadows Mus of Art, Shreveport, La, 76; Rocky Mountain Ann Watercolor Exhib, Foothills Art Ctr, Golden, Colo, 77; Ariz Nat Painting Exhib, Scottsdale Art Ctr, Ariz, 77. *Teaching:* Asst prof painting, drawing, sculpture, watercolor & design, Univ Cent Ark, Conway, 70-80, assoc prof, 80- *Awards:* First Place & Purchase Award, Fifth Ann Ark Artist Exhib, Southeastern Ark Art Ctr, 72; First Place in 19th Invitational Exhib of Ann Ark State Festival, 76; Top Award, 18th Ann Ark Oil Painting Exhib, 77. *Mem:* Nat Art Educ Asn; Ark Art Educ Asn. *Media:* Acrylic, Watercolor; Wood. *Mailing Add:* Univ Cent Ark Box U1724 Conway AR 72032

LARSEN, ROBERT WESLEY
PAINTER

b Aurora, Ill, Nov 22, 23. *Study:* Kansas City Inst Art, 46-47; Detroit Sch Arts & Crafts, 47-50; Ringling Sch Art, 50-51. *Work:* High Mus; Polk Mus Art, Lakeland, Fla. *Exhib:* Tenth Southeast Exhib, High Mus, 55; Gulf Caribbean Exhib, Houston Mus Fine Arts, 56; Art in Embassies Prog, US Dept State, 66; solo exhib, Columbia Mus Art, SC, 67, Columbus Mus Art, Ga, 68 & Hodgell Hartman Gallery, 80; Polk Mus Exhib, Lakeland, Fla, 79. *Teaching:* Instr painting, Ringling Sch Art & Design, Fla, 66- *Awards:* First Prize, Tenth Southeast Exhib, High Mus, 55 & Fla Festival Art, Lauderdale Lakes Asn, 64; Spec Award, Soc Four Arts, Ft Lauderdale, Fla, 67. *Bibliog:* Jeanette Crane (auth), Robert Larsen at Hodgell Hartman, 78; Robert Larsen artist, Sarasota Town & Country Mag, 11-12/78. *Media:* Oil. *Dealer:* Hodgell Hartman Gallery 46 S Palm Ave Sarasota FL 33577. *Mailing Add:* 1393 40th St Sarasota FL 33580

LARSEN, SUSAN C
HISTORIAN, CRITIC

b Chicago, Ill, Oct 3, 46. *Study:* Knox Col, Galesburg, Ill, 64-66; Northwestern Univ, BA, 68, MA, 72, PhD, 75; Graves Found Fel, 80. *Collections Arranged:* The Montages of Charles Shaw, Washburn Gallery, New York, 77; Wallworks, Univ Southern Calif Gallery, 81; Abstract Painting and Sculpture in America 1927-44 (auth, catalog), Mus Art, Carnegie Inst, Pittsburgh, Pa, 83. *Pos:* Reviewer, Choice, 75-; guest lectr, series of lectures on Richard Diebenkorn, Los Angeles Co Mus Art, Los Angeles, 77; mem, Advisory Bd, Archives Am Art. *Teaching:* Asst prof hist of art, Carleton Col, Northfield, Minn, 74-75; assoc prof hist of art, Univ Southern Calif, Los Angeles, 75- *Mem:* Col Art Asn Am; Am Studies Asn; Southern Calif Art Historians Asn. *Res:* Abstract art of the 1930's; WPA in New York City; contemporary art in California; American folk art. *Publ:* Coauth, A Conversation with Richard Diebenkorn, J Los Angeles Inst Contemp Art, summer 77; auth exhib catalogue, Vija Celmins, Newport Art Mus, 12/79; auth, Richard Tuttle, Baxter Art Gallery, 79; auth, C Y Twombly, Newport Art Mus, 10/81; auth, Selections from 8 Collections (catalog), Mus Contemp Art, Los Angeles, 83; regular contribr, Art News Mag, Artweek & Artforum. *Mailing Add:* Dept of Fine Arts Watt Hall Univ of Southern Calif Los Angeles CA 90007

LARSON, BLAINE (GLEDHILL)
PAINTER, INSTRUCTOR
b Salt Lake City, Utah, July 13, 37. *Work:* Corcoran Gallery Art, Washington, DC; Rochester Art Mus, NY; Nat Collection Fine Arts, DC. *Exhib:* Seven one-man shows, Jefferson Place Gallery, Washington, DC & Diane Brown Gallery, 77 & 78; Ten Washington Artists, Edmonton Art Mus, 70; Int Art Wash Exhib, 77 & 78; Gesture on Paper, Corcoran Mus, 80; Jack Rasmussen Gallery, 81; On Going Dialogue, Andrew Hudson & Blaine Larson, Corcoran Gallery Art, 81; and others. *Teaching:* Chmn painting, Corcoran Sch Art, 70- *Bibliog:* Ben Forgey (auth), articles in Washington Star & Art News; Jack Perlmutter (auth), article, Art Voices South, 5-6/80. *Media:* Acrylic. *Mailing Add:* Box 54 Point of Rocks MD 21777

LARSON, JANE (WARREN)
CERAMIST, WRITER
b San Francisco, Calif, June 2, 22. *Study:* Mem Art Gallery, Rochester Inst of Technol, NY; Swarthmore Col; Univ Rochester, BA(Eng, cum laude); Univ Calif, Los Angeles, sculpture with Anna Mahler; Antioch Univ, Visual Arts Ctr, MFA(ceramics). *Work:* Wash Co Mus of Art, Hagerstown, Md; Oak Ridge Community Art Ctr, Tenn. *Comn:* Outdoor mural Oak Ridge Community Art Ctr, Tenn, 65; four tile murals & 30 vases, Germaine's Restaurant, Washington, DC, 78; 28 vases, East Wind Restaurant, Alexandria, Va, 80. *Exhib:* Natural Themes & Ancient Glazes, McLean Gallery, Va, 74; Natural Themes & Glazes II, The Am Spirit Gallery, The Watergate, Les Champs, Washington, DC, 76; Stoneware, Hagerstown Co Mus of Art, 77; Nature's Reflections, Am Spirit Gallery, 79; Four Views of Three Dimensions, Maryland Fedn of Art Gallery, Anapolis, Md, 81. *Teaching:* Instr ceramics, Oak Ridge Community Art Ctr, Tenn, 63-66; workshops, slab construction, Kiln Club of Washington, DC, 81; Potter's Guild, Annapolis, Md, 81. *Awards:* Purchase Award, Objects 73, Western Colo Ctr for the Arts, 73. *Bibliog:* Gretchen Larson & Joyce Inderbitzin (auths), Ceramics at the torpedo factory, Ceramics Mo, 9/76; Libbie Powell (auth), Crafts reach fine arts realm as shown at museum this month, Daily Mail, Hagerstown, Md, 10/77; C Stapleton (auth), Tomorrow's Antiques, The Washingtonian, 5/79. *Mem:* Artists Equity; Kiln Club Washington, DC; Va Art League. *Media:* Reduction Stoneware. *Publ:* Auth, A Tennessee mural, 6/68, Ceramics at Expo 70, 6/70, Hamada legacy, 10/70 & Collecting ceramics, 5/72, Ceramics Mo; auth, Can we consider beauty?, Crafts Horizons, 6/73. *Dealer:* Full Circle GAllery 317 Cameron St Alexandria VA 22314. *Mailing Add:* 6514 Bradley Blvd Bethesda MD 20034

LARSON, KAY L
CRITIC, WRITER
b Cedar Rapids, Iowa, Sept 18, 46. *Study:* Pomona Col, Claremont, Calif, with Mowry Baden, BA(philos, art practice), 69. *Pos:* Art critic/writer, Real Paper, Cambridge, Mass, 72-75; contribr, Art News Mag, New York, 73- assoc ed, 75-78; art critic/writer, Village Voice, 79-80; art critic, New York Mag, 80- *Awards:* Nat Endowment Arts Critic Grants, 78 & 80. *Mem:* Int Art Critics Asn. *Mailing Add:* c/o New York Magazine 755 Second Ave New York NY 10017

LARSON, ORLAND
GOLDSMITH, EDUCATOR
b Shaunavon, Saskatchewan, Can, Mar 6, 31. *Study:* Sask Teachers Col, 50-51; Univ Wis, BSc, 59, MFA, 60; Columbia Univ, fel, 63-64; Sch Am Craftsmen, 65; Tyler Univ, 66-67. *Work:* NS Art Bank, Halifax, 77; NS Designer Craftsmen, Halifax; Ont Craft Coun, Toronto; Govt of Can Craft Collection, Ottawa; Univ of Wis, Madison. *Comn:* Presentation Ladle (silver), Dalhousie Art Gallery, Halifax, NS, 74; plaque, Eastern Provincial Airways, Halifax, 75; Int Fencing Awards with Herbert Hatt, NS Fencing Asn, Halifax, 75; Presentation Medal, Sch Bus Admin, Dalhousie Univ, 76; and numerous pvt comn. *Exhib:* Soc of NAm Goldsmiths, Humber Col, Toronto, 74; Crafts of the Americas, Univ of Colo, 75; Crafts at the Olympics, Montreal, Que, 76; Cartwright Gallery, Vancouver, 80; Can Jewelry Exhib, Israel, 82; and others. *Collections Arranged:* Crafts Seventy-Eight Traveling Exhib, 78; Artisan 78 Traveling Exhib, 78; Massey Col Nat, 79; Can Jewellers Abroad, Toronto, 81; Transition, Saskatoon, 82. *Pos:* Art supervisor, Govt NT, 61-63; ed, NS Designer Craftsman Newsletter, Halifax, 74-76; Artisan, 77-80; Ont Crafts, 79 & Alloy/Alliage, 83-84. *Teaching:* Instr, Northwest Territories & Sask, 51-56; lectr art educ, Ottawa Teachers Col, summers 62-64; assoc prof jewelry, NS Col Art & Design, Halifax, 68-77; vis instr, Sask Arts Bd, Ft Qu'Appelle, summers, 71-77; instr, Electrum Design Studio, Ottawa, 77-80; head jewelry dept, Alta Col Art, 80-; instr, workshops across Can, US & abroad, 74- *Awards:* Five Can Coun Travel Grants, 76-83; Inst PR Medal, 83; Alta Cult Travel Grant, PR, 83; and others. *Bibliog:* Marilyn MacDonald, (auth), Take

Thirty: NS Goldsmith, CBC Documentary (film), 74; Charles Atkinson (auth), Craft as Work, CBC (film series), 75; Pat Lotz (auth), International sabbatical farm, Atlantic Insight, 83; and others. *Mem:* Can Crafts Coun (provincial dir, 74-76 & pres, 76-79); Can Conf Arts (dir, 75-77); Soc NAm Goldsmiths (vpres, 71-73); World Crafts Coun (vpres North Am, 81-84); Alta Crafts Coun (pres, 80-82). *Publ:* Auth, Craftsmen and the Government of Nova Scotia, 76; auth, Report from the President, 77; auth, The Massey's Collect, 78; auth, article, Profile, 81; auth, Contemporary Canadian metal, In: New Can Encycl, 83. *Mailing Add:* 205 33rd Ave SW Calgary AB T2S 0S7 Canada

LARSON, PHILIP SEELY
SCULPTOR, EDUCATOR
b Ventura, Calif, July 21, 44. *Study:* Univ Minn, Minneapolis, BA, 66; Columbia Univ, PhD, 71. *Comn:* Interior design & installation, Collection of Keyboard Instruments, Schubert Club, Landmark Ctr, St Paul, 79. *Exhib:* Hanson-Cowles Gallery, Minneapolis, 77; Glen Hanson Gallery, Minneapolis, 79 & 81; Emergent Americans, Guggenheim Mus, New York, 81; Mus Art, RI Sch Design, 83; Thomson Gallery, Minneapolis, 83; and others. *Collections Arranged:* Burgoyne Diller, 71; DeKooning: Drawings & Sculptures (auth, catalog), 74; Naives/Visionaries (auth, catalog), 74; World Architecture in Minnesota, 78; Prairie School Architecture in Minnesota, Iowa and Wisconsin (auth, catalog), 82. *Pos:* Cur, Walker Art Ctr, Minneapolis, 70-75; frequent contribr, Print Collector's Newsletter. *Teaching:* Prof, Minneapolis Col Art & Design, 75- *Awards:* Artist's Fel, Nat Endowment Arts, 79 & 81. *Media:* Cast Bronze, Cast Iron. *Mailing Add:* Minneapolis Col Art & Design 133 E 25th St Minneapolis MN 55404

LARSON, SIDNEY
PAINTER, CONSERVATOR
b Sterling, Colo, June 16, 23. *Study:* Univ Mo, AB & MA; Univ Okla; also with Thomas Hart Benton & Fred Shane. *Work:* State Hist Soc, Mo. *Comn:* Life Along the Missouri River (murals), Mo State Training Sch Boys, Boonville, 50; Social History of Phelps Co, Rolla Daily News, Mo, 52; Social History of Insurance, Shelter Ins Co, Columbia, Mo, 59; Social History of Ceramics & Metal, Riback Industs, Columbia, 67; Historical Architecture, First Bank Com, Columbia, 71. *Pos:* Mus cur, State Hist Soc, Mo, 61- *Teaching:* Instr, Oklahoma City Univ, 50-51; instr, Univ Mo-Columbia, summers; dir art, Columbia Col, 51- *Awards:* Huntington Hartford Found, 62. *Mem:* Nat Soc Mural Painters; Am Asn Mus; Int Inst Conserv Hist Artistic Works; Am Inst Conserv Hist Artistic Works. *Res:* Private, federal, state and municipal restorations. *Publ:* Auth, Introduction to Fred Shane Drawings, 64; auth articles on Thomas Hart Benton, 69, 74 & 75 & auth, Conservation of a Bingham, 72, Mo Hist Rev. *Mailing Add:* 2025 Crestridge Dr Columbia MO 65201

LARSON, THERESA GAIL See Farris-Larson, Gail

LARSON, WILLIAM G
PHOTOGRAPHER, EDUCATOR
b North Tonawanda, NY, Oct 14, 42. *Study:* State Univ NY, Buffalo, BS(art), 64; Inst Design, Ill Inst Technol, Chicago, MS(photog), with Aaron Siskind & Wynn Bullock, 67. *Work:* Mus Mod Art, New York; Philadelphia Mus Art; New Orleans Mus Art; Smithsonian Inst, Washington, DC; Nat Gallery Art, Sidney, Australia. *Exhib:* Portraits in Photog, Mus of Mod Art, New York, 69; The Expanded Photograph, Philadelphia Mus of Art, 72; Sewn, Stitched & Stuffed, 73, Mus of Contemp Crafts, New York; Unique Photographs, Sculpture Multiples, Mus of Mod Art, New York, 73; Light & Lens, Hudson River Mus, Yonkers, NY, 73; Three Centuries of Am Art, Philadelphia Mus of Art, 76; Locations in Time, Int Mus of Photog, Rochester, 77; Electroworks, Int Mus Photography, Rochester, 79; American Color Photography, Gallerie Rudolf Kicken, Koln, Ger, 80; Whitney Biennial, Whitney Mus Am Art, New York, 81; The Still Life, Mus Mod Art, New York, 81; and others. *Collections Arranged:* Moholy-Nagy Photographs (75 photographs with monogr picture ed), Claremont Col, 75. *Teaching:* Prof & dept chmn photog, Tyler Sch of Art, Temple Univ, Philadelphia, 67- *Awards:* Nat Endowment Arts, 71 & 79; Guggenheim Fel, 82. *Bibliog:* Rourke & Davis (auths), New Frontiers in Color, Newsweek, 4/76; Skip Atwater (auth), William Larson--Time & Structure, Afterimage, Rochester, 12/76; David Featherstone (auth), Tension through color, Artweek, San Francisco. *Publ:* Contribr, Three Centuries American Art, Philadelphia Mus Art, 76; auth, Fire Flies, Gravity Press, 76; ed, Quiver, Temple Univ, 77; contribr, One of a kind, Polaroid Corp, 79; auth, Big Pictures, Little Pictures, Gravity Press, 80; and others. *Dealer:* Light Gallery 724 Fifth Ave New York NY 10019. *Mailing Add:* 152 Heacock Lane Wyncote PA 19095

LASANSKY, LEONARDO
DRAFTSMAN, PRINTMAKER
b Iowa City, Iowa, Mar 29, 46. *Study:* Univ Iowa, BGS, 71, MA, 72 & MFA, 72; also with Byron Burford & Stuart Edie. *Work:* Brooklyn Mus, New York; Princeton Univ Mus; Philadelphia Mus Art; Achenback Collection, San Francisco; Nat Mus, Krakow, Poland; and many others. *Exhib:* Minneapolis Inst Art, Minn, 77; Am Drawing 1927-1977, Minn Mus Art, St Paul, 77; Hassam Fund Purchase Exhib, Am Acad Inst Arts & Letters, New York, 79; 21st Nat Print Exhib, Brooklyn Mus, New York, 79; Int Print Biennale, Krakow, Poland, 80; Am Drawing in Black & White, Brooklyn Mus, New York, 80-81; Int Book Design Exhib, Mus Kunsthandwerks, Leipzig, Ger, 82; 7th Nat Print Exhib, Univ Calif, Los Angeles, 82; one-man show, Dartmouth Col, 82; and many others. *Teaching:* Assoc prof art, Hamline Univ, 72-, chmn fine arts div, 80-84; artist in residence, Dartmouth Col, 82. *Awards:* Purchase Award, 5th Nat Hawaii Print Exhib, Honolulu, 80; Purchase Award, 4th

Miami Int Print Exhib, Fla, 80; Distinguished Alumni Award, Univ Iowa, 81; and others. *Bibliog:* Lane Stiles (auth), article, Projekt Mag, Warsaw, Poland, 3/81. *Media:* Intaglio. *Mailing Add:* 1536 Hewitt Hamline Univ Print Dept St Paul MN 55104

LASANSKY, MAURICIO L
PRINTMAKER, DRAFTSMAN
b Buenos Aires, Arg, 1914; US citizen. *Study:* Superior Sch Fine Arts, Arg; Iowa Wesleyan Col, Hon DA, 59; Pac Lutheran Univ, Hon DFA, 69; Carleton Col, Northfield, Minn, Hon DA, 79. *Work:* Art Inst Chicago; Seattle Mus, Wash; Libr Cong, Washington, DC; Uffizi Gallery, Florence, Italy; Mus Arte Contemp, Madrid, Spain; and over 100 univs & galleries, US & abroad. *Exhib:* One-man shows, Mauricio Lasansky: Selections from 30 Years of Printmaking, The Nazi Drawings, Palace Fine Arts, Mexico City, 69; Dickinson Col, Carlisle, Pa, 72 & 74 & Third Int Biennial Mexico, 80; Whitney Mus Am Art, New York, 71; and others. *Teaching:* Dir, Free Fine Arts Sch, Villa Maria Cordoba, Arg, 36 & Taller Manualidades, Cordoba, 39; vis lectr, Univ Iowa, 45, asst prof art, 46, assoc prof, 47, prof, 48-, res prof, 65-67, Virgil M Hancher Distinguished Prof, 67-71, res prof, 71-72; Lucas lectr, Carleton Col, 65. *Awards:* Bertha von Moschzisker Prize, Philadelphia Print Club Ann, 71; Dickinson Col Arts Award, 74-75; Distinguished Teaching of Art Award, Col Art Asn, 80; and many others. *Bibliog:* L Edmondson (auth), Etching, Van Nostrand Reinhold, 72; Barry Schwartz (auth), Humanism in 20th Century Art, Praeger, 72; Jules Heller (auth), Printmaking Today, Holt, 72; and many others. *Mem:* Col Art Asn Am (bd dirs, 70-); life mem Nat Acad Design. *Mailing Add:* Print Dept Univ Iowa Sch Art & Art Hist Iowa City IA 52242

LASCH, PAT
SCULPTOR
b New York, NY, Nov 20, 44. *Study:* Queens Col, City Univ New York, BA. *Work:* Queens Col, City Univ New York; Mus Mod Art, New York. *Comn:* Hommage: 1929-1979 (sculpture), Mus Mod Art, New York, 79. *Exhib:* One-woman exhibs, AIR Gallery, New York, 73, 77, 79 & 80, Galerie Ahlner, Stockholm, Sweden, Gallerie Lund, Sweden, 80 & Lerner-Heller Gallery, New York, 81; Out of House, Whitney Mus Am Art, New York, 78; traveling exhibs, Walker Art Ctr, Minneapolis, 73, Inst of Contemp Art, Boston, 73, Wadsworth Atheneum, Hartford, Conn, 73; Art 1981, Chicago Navy Pier, Ill, 81; and many others. *Pos:* Guest panelist, Soho Ctr Visual Arts, New York, 77. *Teaching:* Parson's Sch Design. *Awards:* Creative Artists Pub Serv Prog, 80; Nat Endowment Arts, 80; Rome Prize, 82-83. *Bibliog:* article, New York Times, 11/15/79; April Kingsley, article, Arts Mag, 81; Ralph Hermans (auth), Varfog New York, Forlags, A B Wiken, Sweden, 82; and many others. *Media:* Mixed. *Dealer:* Kathryn Markel Gallery 50 W 57th St New York NY. *Mailing Add:* 463 West St 228G New York NY 10014

LASH, KENNETH
EDUCATOR, WRITER
b New Britain, Conn, July 27, 18. *Study:* Yale Univ, BA, 39; Univ NMex, MA, 48; Univ Lille, France, Fulbright schol, 51. *Pos:* Chief planner & adminr, Carnegie Corp grant for teaching the humanities in art sch, 64-67; consult art & humanities progs, formerly; lectr changing concepts of cult, Conf Arts & Human Needs, Univ Wis-Madison, 75; mem, Role of the Arts Task Force, President's Comn on Mental Health, 77-78; contrib ed, North American Review, formerly. *Teaching:* Lectr art hist, San Francisco Art Inst, 59-64, chmn dept humanities, 64-70; head art dept, Univ Northern Iowa, 70-76, dir humanities prog, 76-83; retired. *Awards:* Rockefeller Found Travel Grant in Arts, Latin Am, 54-55. *Mem:* Nat Coun Art Adminr; Nat Art Educ Asn. *Res:* Researching, planning, consulting and working on art programs based on changing concepts in culture. *Publ:* Auth, Notes toward a new curriculum in art, NY State Coun Arts, 71; auth, The Elitist, the Populist and Mr Phillips, Leonardo, 73; auth, Art: Saved by the infantry?, Arts Soc, 75; auth, TV: The ultimate drug, Vision, London, 78; auth, A Lot for the Money: Stories, Poems, Essays, 83. *Mailing Add:* 789 Lumberts Mill Rd Marstons Mills MA 02648

LASKE, LYLE F
SCULPTOR, EDUCATOR
b Green Bay, Wis, May 10, 37. *Study:* Univ Wis, Platteville, BS, 59; Univ Wis, Madison, MS, 61 & MFA, 65; Univ Minn, 68. *Work:* Plains Art Mus, Moorhead, Minn. *Exhib:* One-man show, Walker Art Ctr, Minneapolis, Minn, 66; Artists of Central NY, Everson Mus Art, Syracuse, 71; Draw and Small Sculpture Show, Ball State Univ, Ind, 74; Miss River Crafts Show, Memphis, Tenn, 77; Am Woodcarvers, Craft Ctr, Worchester, Mass, 78; New Handmade Furniture, Am Craft Mus, New York, 79. *Teaching:* Instr, Wis State Univ, Platteville, 62-64; prof sculpture, Moorhead State Univ, Minn, 65-; assoc prof, New York State Univ Col Oneonta, 70-71. *Media:* Wood, Bronze. *Publ:* American woodcarvers, Craft Horizons, 4/78; Air-powered tools, Fine Woodworking, 1-2/79; Some abrasive facts, Fine Woodworking, 3-4/80; Woodworking: The New Wave, Crown Publ, 81; Fine Woodworking Techniques 3, The Taunton Press, 81. *Mailing Add:* Art Dept Moorhead State Univ Moorhead MN 56560

LASKER, JOE (JOSEPH L)
PAINTER, ILLUSTRATOR
b Brooklyn, NY, June 26, 19. *Study:* Cooper Union Art Sch, cert, 39. *Work:* Whitney Mus Am Art, New York; Philadelphia Mus Art; Springfield Mus, Mass; Joseph H Hirshhorn Collection, Washington, DC; Calif Palace of Legion of Honor, San Francisco. *Comn:* Murals, US Pub Works Admin, Post Off, Calumet, Mich, 41, Milbury, Mass, 42 & Henry St Settlement Playhouse, New York, 48. *Exhib:* Pa Acad Fine Arts Ann, 47-53; Whitney Mus Am Art Ann, 47-58 & Nat Acad Design Ann, New York, 47-82; plus many others.

Teaching: Assoc prof painting, Univ Ill, 52-53. *Awards:* Prix de Rome Fel, Am Acad Rome, 50 & 51; Guggenheim Fel, 54; Nat Inst Arts & Lett Grant, 68. *Bibliog:* 19 Young Americans, Life, 3/20/50; American art of our century, Praeger, NY, 61; Figurative Tradition, Whitney Mus Am Art, New York, 61. *Mem:* Nat Acad Design. *Media:* Oil. *Dealer:* Kraushaar Galleries 724 Fifth Ave New York NY 10019. *Mailing Add:* 20 Dock Rd Norwalk CT 06854

LASKIN, MYRON, JR
CURATOR, HISTORIAN
b Milwaukee, Wis, Apr 7, 30. *Study:* Harvard Univ, AB, 52, AM, 54; Inst Fine Arts, NY Univ, PhD, 64. *Collections Arranged:* Fountainebleau, Nat Gallery Can, 72. *Pos:* Cur Europ art, Nat Gallery Can, 68. *Teaching:* Asst prof art hist, Washington Univ, 61-66. *Awards:* Italian Govt Grant, NY Univ, 59-60; Villa I Tatti Fel, 65-67, Kress Fel, 66-67, Harvard Univ. *Res:* Italian 16th and 17th century painting. *Publ:* Contribr, Burlington Mag, Art Bulletin, Arte Illustrata & others. *Mailing Add:* Nat Gallery of Can Ottawa ON K1A 0M8 Canada

LASLO, PATRICIA LOUISE (LASLO-NEUKRANZ)
SCULPTOR
b Park Ridge, Ill, Feb 22, 30. *Study:* De Paul Univ; Univ Ill, BFA; Univ Wis; Northern Ill Univ, MA. *Comn:* Sculpture, Landsmiths, Co, 72. *Exhib:* 51st Ann Show Wis Artists, Milwaukee Art Ctr, 68; woman artists show, Young Auditorium, Sturgis, Mich, 78 & 79; two-person shows, Battlecreek Art Ctr, 80; one-person shows, Prajna Gallery, 81, Art Emporium, 81, Mich; Kalamazoo Inst Arts, 81; and others. *Teaching:* Instr sculpture & painting, Countryside Art Ctr, 66-70, gallery dir, 67-68; instr life drawing & 3D design, Chicago Acad Fine Art, 68-70; instr art, Maine N High Sch, 70-75. *Awards:* Award for War God, Milwaukee Art Ctr, 68 & for Cyrano, Evanston Art Ctr, 69; 1st Place, Kalamazoo Inst Arts, 81; and others. *Bibliog:* D Anderson (auth), article, Chicago Today, 72; F Schultz (auth), article, Chicago Daily News, 72; article, New Art Examr, 75; and others. *Mem:* Kalamazoo Art League; and others. *Media:* Multimedia. *Dealer:* Prajna Gallery Saugatuck MI; Troy Gallery Troy MI. *Mailing Add:* 26693 72nd Ave Lawton MI 49065

LASSAW, IBRAM
SCULPTOR
b Alexandria, Egypt, May 4, 13; US citizen. *Study:* Sculpture Ctr, 26-30; Beaux Arts Inst Design, 30-31; City Col New York. *Work:* Albright-Knox Art Gallery, Buffalo; Baltimore Mus Art; Whitney Mus Am Art & Mus Mod Art, New York; Mus Mod Art, Rio de Janeiro, Brazil; plus many others. *Comn:* Sculpture, comn by Percival Goodman for Beth El Temple, Springfield, Mass; Baldachin & altar screen, House of Theology of Franciscan Fathers, Centerville, Ohio; hanging sculpture for lobby, Hilton Hotel, New York; sculpture for Beth El Temple, Providence, RI, Temple of Aaron, St Paul, Minn & Temple Anshe Chesed, Cleveland, Ohio, plus others. *Exhib:* Recent Acquisitions, Whitney Mus Am Art, New York; Two Hundred Years of American Sculpture, Whitney Mus Am Art, New York, 76; Five Distinguished Alumni, Hirschhorn Mus, 82; solo exhib, Lafayette Col, Pa, 83; Abstract Painting and Sculpture in American, Mus Art, Carnegie Inst, 83, San Francisco Mus Mod Art, 84 & Whitney Mus Am Art, 84; and many others. *Pos:* Fed Arts Proj, Pub Works Admin, 33-42. *Teaching:* Instr sculpture, YMHA, 92nd St, New York, 35-36; instr sculpture, Am Univ, 50; artist in residence, Duke Univ, 62-63; vis artist, Univ Calif, Berkeley, 65-66; adj fac, Southampton Col, 66-; vis prof, Brandeis Univ, Waltham, NY, 72 & Mt Holyoke Col, 78; also pvt classes in studio. *Mem:* Founder Am Abstract Artists (pres, 46-49); Artists Club. *Dealer:* Zabriskie Gallery 29 W 57th St New York NY 10019. *Mailing Add:* PO Box 487 East Hampton NY 11937

LASUCHIN, MICHAEL
PRINTMAKER, PAINTER
b Kramatorsk, USSR, July 24, 23; US citizen. *Study:* Rostow Col Art, Russia, 40-41; Philadelphia Col Art, BFA; Tyler Sch Art, Temple Univ, MFA. *Work:* Libr Cong, Washington, DC; Philadelphia Mus Art; Nat Libr Print Collection, Paris; Mus Mod Art, Barcelona; Brooklyn Mus Art; and others. *Comn:* Print, Print Club Philadelphia, 74; print, Pratt Graphics Ctr, New York, 80. *Exhib:* Nat Exhib Prints, Libr Cong, 73 & 75; New American Graphics, Univ Wis-Madison, 75; 11th Int Exhib Graphic Arts, Mus Mod Art, Ljubljana, Yugoslavia, 75; 3rd Int Drawing Biennale, Cleveland, Eng, 77; 4th Hawaii Nat Print Exhib, Honolulu Acad of Art, 77; Watercolor USA, Springfield Art Mus, Mo, 77; 21st Nat Print Exhib, Brooklyn Mus, 78. *Teaching:* Asst prof printmaking, Philadelphia Col Art, 72- *Awards:* Purchase Award, Sharlotte Printmaking Soc, 79; Philip & Ester Klein Award, Am Color Print Soc, 79; Medal of Honor, Audubon Artists, 80; Grumbahcer Gold Medal Award, Nat Watercolor Soc, 81. *Bibliog:* Cynthia B Frost (auth), Paintings suggest..., Daily Pennsylvanian, 11/20/74; Bill Southwell (auth), Exhibiting new talent, Drummer, 4/22/75; Dorothy Grafly (auth), Art contrasts, Art in Focus, 4/75. *Mem:* Boston Printmakers; Audubon Artists; Nat Watercolor Soc; Artists Equity Asn; Am Color Print Soc; and others. *Media:* Printmaking, Watercolor. *Publ:* Contribr, Folio '76. *Dealer:* Venable-Neslage Gallery 1742 Connecticut Ave NW Washington DC 20009; Assoc American Artists Gallery 1614 Latimer St Philadelphia PA 19103. *Mailing Add:* 120 E Cliveden St Philadelphia PA 19119

LATHAM, BARBARA
PAINTER, ILLUSTRATOR
b Walpole, Mass, June 6, 1896. *Study:* Norwich Art Sch, Conn; Pratt Inst; Art Students League; also with Andrew Dasburg. *Work:* Metrop Mus Art Print Collection; Libr of Cong, Washington, DC; Santa Fe Mus; Philadelphia Mus; var Tex mus. *Exhib:* Three Whitney Mus Am Art Ann; Brooklyn Mus Watercolor Int, 40; Prints, Carnegie Inst, 44; Prints, Nat Acad Design, 46, 48

& 49; Chicago Mus Watercolor Int; Gov's Gallery, Capitol Bldg, Santa Fe, NMex, 77; plus others. *Awards:* Several Purchase Prizes. *Media:* Oil. *Publ:* Illusr, Pedro, Nina & Perrito, Harper & Row, 39; illusr, Calling South America, Ginn, 45; illusr, Perrito's Pup, Knopf, 46; illusr, Tales of Old Time Texas, Little, 55; illusr, Flying Horseshoe Ranch, Viking Press, 55; illusr, nine books for Holiday House & one for Chilton Books. *Dealer:* Allied Artists Gallery A Taos NM 87571; Canyon Rd Gallery Santa Fe NM 87501. *Mailing Add:* 250 E Alameda Apt 137 Santa Fe NM 87501

LATHROP, CHURCHILL PIERCE
HISTORIAN
b New York, NY, Aug 26, 1900. *Study:* Rutgers Univ, with John C Van Dyck, LittB, 22; Princeton Univ, with Rufus Morey, AM, 22; Dartmouth Col, hon AM, 37. *Pos:* Dir art galleries, Dartmouth Col, 40-66, dir emer, 66-, actg dir, 73-74; art consult, Dartmouth Col, 68. *Teaching:* Prof Medieval, Renaissance & Mod Art, Dartmouth Col, 28-70, chmn dept art, 37-47 & 64-68. *Mem:* Am Asn Mus; Mus Mod Art, New York; Am Asn Univ Prof. *Publ:* Coauth, The Individual & the World, 42; auth, Paul Sample, 48; auth, The Story of Art at Dartmouth, 51; coauth, The Orozeo Murals at Dartmouth, Montgomery Found, 81. *Mailing Add:* 7 Sargent St Hanover NH 03755

LATHROP, GERTRUDE K
SCULPTOR
b Albany, NY, Dec 24, 1896. *Study:* Art Students League; Sch Am Sculpture; also with Solon Borglum & Charles Grafly. *Work·* Houston Pub Libr, Tex; Albany Pub Libr, NY; NY State Teachers Col; Smithsonian Inst, Washington, DC; Brookgreen Gardens, SC. *Comn:* Medals, Garden Club Am, 42 & 50, Hispanic Soc Am, 50, Mariners' Mus, 54, NY State Univ Hall of Fame, 62 & 66 & Nat Steeplechase & Hunt Asn, 64; and others. *Exhib:* One-man shows, Albany Inst Hist & Art, 57 & 66 & Woodmere Art Gallery, Philadelphia, 63. *Awards:* Medal of Honor, Allied Artists Am, 64; Silver Medal, Pen & Brush Club, 67; Saltus Gold Medal for Merit, Nat Acad Design, 70; plus others. *Mem:* Nat Acad Design; Nat Inst Arts & Lett; Nat Sculpture Soc; Soc Medalists; Am Numismatic Soc. *Mailing Add:* Under Mountain Rd Falls Village CT 06031

LATTANZIO, FRANCES
PHOTOGRAPHER, EDUCATOR
b Detroit, Mich, Oct 2, 49. *Study:* Univ Mich, BFA, 71, MFA, 73. *Work:* Bank of Ind & Vincennes Univ, Ind; Madison Plaza Corp & Hyatt Int Corp, Chicago; Ind State Univ, Terre Haute. *Exhib:* Womanworks, Union Gallery, Ann Arbor, Mich, 77; Tri-State Invitational, Vincennes Univ, 80; Midwest Photog Invitational, Univ Wis, Green Bay, 80; Paper in Particular, Columbia Col, Mo, 81; Ind Artists Show, Indianapolis Mus Art, 81; and others. *Teaching:* Asst prof photog, Ind State Univ, Terre Haute, 75-; adj asst prof photog, St Mary of the Woods Col, Ind, 80. *Awards:* Engraph Award, Engraph Inc, 81. *Bibliog:* Cheryl Bopp (auth), article, Arts Insight, 3/80. *Mem:* Col Art Asn; Soc Photog Educ; Friends of Photog. *Dealer:* Balkin Fine Arts 425 N Clark Chicago IL 60610. *Mailing Add:* c/o Balkin Fine Arts 425 N Clark Chicago IL 60610

LAUB-NOVAK, KAREN
PAINTER, PRINTMAKER
b Minneapolis, Minn, Aug 25, 37. *Study:* Carleton Col, Northfield, Minn, BA; State Univ Iowa, with Mauricio Lasansky, MFA; Sch Vision, Salzburg, Austria, with Oskar Kokoschka. *Work:* Carleton Col; Yale Univ; St Vincent's Archabbey; Continental Bank, Chicago; Pac Sch Relig; and others. *Comn:* 12-ft bronze tribute to Norman Borlaug, 1971 Nobel Peace Prize Winner, Cresco, Iowa. *Exhib:* One-woman shows, Rochester Art Ctr, Minn, 70, Rockefeller Found, 74, Univ Tenn, 74, Pac Sch Relig, 74 & Yale Univ, 75; and others. *Pos:* Free lance illusr, Books, Mag & Newspapers. *Teaching:* Instr drawing, Carleton Col, 61-62; lectr, Georgetown Univ, Stanford Univ, Syracuse Univ, Mt Vernon & Univ Calif, Riverside. *Awards:* Kokoschka Award, Salzburg, Austria. *Bibliog:* L P Ruotolo (auth), A new apocalypse, Motive Mag, 66. *Publ:* Illusr, Skunk Named Zorrie (children's bk), 72; auth & illusr, Art & Mysticism are a Journey, 73; auth & illusr, The art of interpretation, Anima, 78; contribr, New Rev Bks, Catholic World, Parabola Mag & Catholicism in Crisis; auth, Art Creativity and the Sacred, Crossroads Bks, 83. *Mailing Add:* 3211 Northhampton St NW Washington DC 20015

LAUCK, ANTHONY JOSEPH
SCULPTOR, EDUCATOR
b Indianapolis, Ind, Dec 30, 08. *Study:* John Herron Art Sch, Indianapolis, dipl prof grade in sculpture; Corcoran Sch Art, Washington, DC, cert advan study in sculpture & painting; also with Oronzio Maldarelli, Ivan Mestrovic, Carl Milles, Hugo Robus & Heinz Warneke. *Work:* Pa Acad Fine Arts, Philadelphia; Corcoran Gallery Art, Washington, DC; Butler Inst Fine Arts, Youngstown, Ohio; Indianapolis Mus Art; Gary Art Ctr, Ind. *Comn:* Set of facet windows, Congregation of Holy Cross, 48 Prov, Moreau Sem Chapel, Univ Notre Dame, 53; limestone image of Our Lady of the Univ, Univ Notre Dame, 63; 12 stained glass windows, Ursuline Motherhouse, Chatham, Ont, Can, 64. *Exhib:* Fairmount Park Art Asn Int Exhib, Philadelphia, 48; Nat Exhib Art, Pa Acad Fine Arts, 49 & 53; Ind Artists' Exhib, Indianapolis Mus Art, 50, 51, 54 & 56; Audubon Artists, Nat Acad Arts, NY, 52-75. *Collections Arranged:* The Work of John B Flannagan, Art Gallery, Univ Notre Dame, 61, The German Impressionists, 67 & The Graphic Work of Georges Rouault (with introd), 72. *Pos:* Conf planning comt, Mid-Am Col Art Asn, 67-72. *Teaching:* Prof drawing & sculpture in var media, Univ Notre Dame, 50-73. *Awards:* For St John Beside the Cross (carved walnut), Fairmount Park Art Asn, 48; Monk at Prayer (limestone), Pa Acad Art, 53; The Wife of Lot (terra cotta), Indianapolis Mus Art, 54. *Bibliog:* Dean A Porter (auth), Anthony Lauck: Sculptor, 70 & Edward Fischer (auth), The many facets of Anthony Lauck, 73; Univ Notre Dame Art Gallery Publ. *Media:* Wood, Stone. *Dealer:* Bodley Gallery 1063 Madison Ave New York NY 10022. *Mailing Add:* Notre Dame Univ Notre Dame IN 46556

LAUFFER, ALICE A
PAINTER, PRINTMAKER
b Mokena, Ill, Oct 25, 19. *Study:* Chicago Acad Fine Art, cert; Art Inst Chicago; also with Paul Weighardt. *Work:* Art Inst Chicago; Minn Mus Art, St Paul; Mus Contemp Art, Chicago. *Exhib:* Drawings USA, Minn Art Mus, St Paul, 68, Traveling Exhib, 73-75; Contemporary American Drawings V, Smithsonian Traveling Exhib, 72-74; Nat Collection Fine Arts, Washington, DC & Smithsonian Traveling Exhib, 73-75; one-person shows, Ill Arts Coun, Chicago, 75 & Artemisia S Gallery, Chicago, 77; Hyde Park Art Ctr, Chicago, 78; one-person show, Art Inst Chicago, Alonzo Mather Hall, 78; 6 x 9 invitational, NAME Gallery, 79; Paper in Particular, Columbia Col, Mo, 83; and others. *Awards:* James Broadus Clarke Award, Art Inst Chicago, 69; Drawings USA Purchase Award, Minn Mus Art, 73. *Bibliog:* Role and Impact, Chicago Soc Artists, 79. *Mem:* Arts Club Chicago; Women's Caucus Art (vpres 82 & pres, 83). *Media:* Acrylic, Watercolor, Lithography. *Mailing Add:* 123 North Jefferson St Chicago IL 60606

LAUFMAN, SIDNEY
PAINTER
b Cleveland, Ohio, Oct 29, 1891. *Study:* Cleveland Sch Art; Art Inst Chicago; Art Students League. *Work:* Metrop Mus Art, Mus Mod Art & Whitney Mus Am Art, New York; Art Inst Chicago; Corcoran Gallery Art, Washington, DC; plus others. *Exhib:* One-man show, De Haucke Gallery, New York, 31; Retrospective, Forum Gallery, New York, 62; George Peabody Col, Nashville, Tenn, 63; Lowe Gallery, Univ Miami, Fla, 64 & Ft Lauderdale Mus, Fla, 64; plus many others. *Teaching:* Instr painting, Art Students League, 38-50; vis lectr painting, Brandeis Univ, 59-60. *Awards:* Mr & Mrs Frank G Logan Prize, Art Inst Chicago, 32; Third Prize, Carnegie Int, 34; First Altman Prize, Nat Acad Design, 37; and many others. *Mem:* Nat Acad Design; Woodstock Artists Asn. *Media:* Oil. *Dealer:* Sid Deutsch Gallery 20 W 57 St New York NY 10019. *Mailing Add:* 1038 S Osprey Ave Sarasota FL 33577

LAUGHLIN, MORTIMER
PAINTER
b San Francisco, Calif, July 24, 18. *Study:* Hollywood Art Ctr, Calif, 41; Abbott Art Sch, Washington, DC, 45; Art Students League, New York, 46. *Exhib:* Mus Mod Art, New York; Stamford Mus, Conn; San Francisco Mus Art, Calif; Newport Art Asn, RI; Silvermine Art Asn, Conn; Albany Inst Hist Art, NY; Art USA, New York; one-man shows, bartholet Gallery, 80-84. *Media:* Mixed Media. *Dealer:* Bartholet Gallery 55 East 76th St New York NY 10021. *Mailing Add:* Rd 1 Box 8 Susquehanna PA 18847

LAURENT, JOHN LOUIS
PAINTER, EDUCATOR
b Brooklyn, NY, Nov 27, 21. *Study:* With Walt Kuhn, 46-48; Syracuse Univ, BFA, 48; Acad Grande Chaumiere, Paris, 48-49; Ind Univ, MAT, 54. *Work:* Univ Ill; First Nat Bank, Boston; De Cordova & Dana Mus, Lincoln, Mass; Addison Gallery Am Art, Andover, Mass. *Comn:* Great Bay Area Mural, Univ NH; Dove & Fish (two panels), St George's Church, York, Maine, 64. *Exhib:* One-man show, Addison Gallery Am Art, Andover, Mass, 72; Frost Gully Gallery, Portland, Maine, 77; St Paul's Sch, Concord, NH, 78; Art in Embassies Prog, Dept of State, Washington, DC, 79-82; Barridoff Galelries, Portland, Maine, 82; Payson-Weisberg Gallery, New York, 83. *Teaching:* Asst dir drawing & painting, Ogunquit Sch Painting & Sculpture, summers 46-60; asst prof drawing & painting, Va Polytech Inst, 50-53; prof drawing & painting, Univ NH, 54- *Awards:* Louis Comfort Tiffany Found Grant, 62; Nat Coun Arts Award, 66-67; City of Manchester Prize, Currier Gallery, NH, 70. *Bibliog:* Peter Cox (auth), A talk with John Laurent, 69 & The best of Maine at Frost Gallery, 69, Maine Times; Edward Betts (auth), Creative Seascape Photog & Creative Landscape Photog, Watson-Guptill Publ. *Mem:* Barn Gallery (bd dirs, 68-71); York & NH Art Asns. *Media:* Acrylic, Oil. *Dealer:* Hobe Sound Galleries 739 Bridge Rd Hobe Sound FL 33455; Payson-Weisberg Gallery 822 Madison Ave New York NY 10021. *Mailing Add:* Mill Lane Rd York ME 03909

LAURER, ROBERT A
EDUCATOR, MUSEUM DIRECTOR
b Rochester, NY, Mar 10, 21. *Study:* Univ Rochester, BA; Harvard Univ, MA. *Pos:* Asst dir, Mus Contemp Crafts, 56-60, assoc dir, 60-62. *Teaching:* Asst prof art, Univ Colo, 49-53, Univ Ark, 54-55 & Skidmore Col, 55-56; asst prof & actg chmn dept art, Fairleigh Dickinson Univ, 62-68, assoc prof art, 68-75, chmn dept fine arts, 72-82, prof, 75- *Mailing Add:* Fine Arts Dept Fairleigh Dickinson Univ Rutherford NJ 07070

LAVATELLI, CARLA
SCULPTOR, WEAVER
b Rome, Italy, Aug 21, 28; US citizen. *Work:* Nat Gallery, Rome; Phillips Collection, Washington, DC; Stanford Univ Law Bldg; H E Leone, Pres Repub Italy; Freidburgh Univ, Ger. *Comn:* Lobby Spingold Theater, Brandeis Univ, 69; New Bldg Upjohn Pharmaceuticals, Kalamazoo, Mich, 70; portrait group of S A S Ranier, III Prince of Monaco & his family, 71; Shah of Iran, 68-76. *Exhib:* Spoleto, Palazzo Collicola, Italy, 66; Palazzo della Quadriennale, 67; one-man shows, Hakone Mus, Japan, 72-73 & Phillips Collection, Washington, DC, 74; San Francisco Mus Art, 75-76. *Bibliog:* Lorenza Trucchi (auth), Lavatelli at Carpine, Momento Sera, 65; Ruggero Orlando (auth), Contemporary Art From NY (film), Rai Italian TV, 74; Gene Baro (auth), Carla Lavatelli Ritmi Spaziali, Washington Post, 74. *Media:* Stone, Paper. *Mailing Add:* 140 Thompson St New York NY 10012

LAVENSON, ALMA (ALMA LAVENSON WAHRHAFTIG)
PHOTOGRAPHER

b San Francisco, Calif, May 20, 1897. *Study:* Self-taught photographer; Univ Calif, Berkeley, BA, 19. *Work:* Oakland Mus, Calif; Calif Ctr Photog, Riverside; San Francisco Mus Mod Art, Calif; Metrop Mus, New York; Bancroft Libr, Univ Calif, Berkeley. *Exhib:* F 64 Show, M H DeYoung Mem Mus, San Francisco, Calif, 32; Brooklyn Inst Art, NY, 33; one-woman show, San Francisco Mus Art, Calif, 42 & Focus Gallery, San Francisco, Calif, 81; Calif Mother Lode, San Francisco Mus Art, Calif, 48; Photographs of a Vanishing Life, San Francisco Mus Art, Calif, 60; Three Photographers and the Place, 80 & Recent Photographs, 81, Focus Gallery, San Francisco; Retrospectives, Calif Mus Photog, Riverside, 79, Oakland Mus, Calif, 79 & Univ Art Mus, Albuquerque, NMex, 79; 50 Years of Photography, Univ Calif Press Gallery, 83. *Awards:* Dorothea Lange Award, Oakland Mus, 79. *Bibliog:* Alma Lavenson, Calif Mus Photog, 79. *Mailing Add:* 58 Wildwood Gardens Piedmont CA 94611

LAVENTHOL, HANK
PAINTER, PRINTMAKER

b Philadelphia, Pa, Dec 22, 27. *Study:* Yale Univ, with Robert Georges Eberhard, BA(sculpture); Acad Belli Arti, Florence, Italy. *Work:* Yale Univ Art Mus, New Haven, Conn; Rosenwald Collection, Nat Gallery Fine Arts, Washington, DC; Print Collection, New York Pub Libr; Lowe Mus Art, Univ Miami, Coral Gables, Fla; Duke Univ Mus; and others. *Comn:* Image du Rose (etching), 72, Assoc Am Artists, New York; Ruth (four-color etching), Commentary Bk Soc, New York, 71; seven color etchings, George Visat, Paris, 72; 9 ed (color etching), New York Graphic Soc, Greenwich, Conn, 72-78; 12 ed (color etching), Original Print Collectors Group, New York, 75-80. *Exhib:* Philadelphia Mus Art, 68; Atheneum of Philadelphia, 73; Mickelson Gallery, Washington, DC, 73; Nat Arts Club, New York, 75; Best Prints, 73-78, Bibliot Nat, Paris; Frank Fedele Fine Arts, New York, 79, 80 & 81; and many other group & one-man shows in US & Europe. *Mem:* Artists Equity Asn New York; Visual Arts & Galleries Asn; Circulo Bellas Artes, Palma de Mallorca. *Publ:* Le Miroir aux alouettes', Ed Georges Visat, Paris, 72; Les Crises, Reves D'Enfant, Eyedeas, portfolios etchings, Hanover Atelier, 80. *Dealer:* Frank Fedele Fine Arts 42 E 57th St New York NY 10022. *Mailing Add:* RFD 1 Hanover St Yorktown Heights NY 10598

LAVIN, IRVING
HISTORIAN

b St Louis, Mo, Dec 14, 27. *Study:* Cambridge Univ, Eng, 48-49; Washington Univ, BA, 49; NY Univ, MA, 52; Harvard Univ, MA, 52, PhD(Sheldon Fel), 55. *Teaching:* Lectr hist art, Vassar Col, 59-62; from assoc prof to prof, NY Univ, 63-73; prof, Sch Hist Studies, Inst for Adv Study, 73- *Awards:* Fulbright Fel, 61-63; Am Coun Learned Soc Fel, 65-66; Guggenheim Found Grant, 68-69. *Mem:* Fel Am Acad Arts & Sci; Corpus Ancient Mosaics Tunisia (mem steering comt, 69-); Nat Comt for the Hist of Art; Comite int d'histoire de l'art. *Res:* Art of late antiquity; Renaissance and Baroque sculpture. *Publ:* Auth, Bernini and the Crossing of Saint Peter's, Arts, Archaeol Inst Am & Col Art Asn Am, 68; auth, Five new youthful sculptures by Gianlorenzo Bernini and a revised chronology of his early works, 68, Bernini's death, 72 & Divine inspiration in Caravaggio's two St Matthews, 74, Art Bull; auth, Bernini and the Unity of the Visual Arts, Oxford Univ Press, 80; auth, Drawings by Gianlorenzo Bernini from the Museum der bildenden Künste, Princeton Univ Press, 81. *Mailing Add:* Sch Hist Studies Inst for Adv Study Princeton NJ 08540

LAVIN, MARILYN ARONBERG
EDUCATOR, HISTORIAN

b St Louis, Mo, Oct 27, 25. *Study:* Washington Univ, BA, 47, MA, 49; Univ Rome, cert, 52; Inst Fine Arts, NY Univ, PhD, 73. *Teaching:* Prof hist art, Princeton Univ, 75-; vis prof, Yale Univ, 78 & Univ Md, 79-80. *Awards:* Carles Rufus Morey Book Award, Col Art Asn, 77. *Mem:* Col Art Asn Am (mem bd dirs, 79-83); Renaissance Soc. *Res:* Italian Renaissance painting with special interest in work of Piero della Francesca and history of fresco painting. *Publ:* Auth, The Corpus Domini Altarpiece of Urbino, Art Bulletin, 67; auth, Piero Della Francesca: The Flagellation, Penguin, Viking, 72; auth, 17th Century Barberini Documents & Inventories of Art, NY Univ Press, 75; auth, Piero della Francesca's Baptism of Christ, Yale Univ Press, 81; auth, The Eye of the Tiger: Department of Art & Architecture, Princeton University, Princeton Univ Press, 83. *Mailing Add:* 56 Maxwell Lane Princeton NJ 08540

LAVOY, WALTER JOSEPH
JEWELER, EDUCATOR

b Glens Falls, NY. *Study:* State Univ NY Buffalo, BA(art educ); Albright Art Sch, cert; Columbia Univ, MFA; Pa State Univ, DEd. *Comn:* 18K gold & diamond engagement ring, comn by Bruce Edgerton, Plainville, Conn, 73; 14K gold & diamond engagement ring, comn by Joseph Roberts, New Britain, Conn, 74; sterling silver & filled gold constructed necklace with pirite nuggets, comn by Mr Bertram N Carvalho, Jr, Ft Lauderdale, Fla, 74; sterling silver forged & fused pendant, comn by Mrs Reba M Hille, Ft Lauderdale, 75; sculptured sterling silver dinner ring (with large fragment of rare Tiffany glass), Mrs Celeste LeWitt, West Hartford, Conn, 77. *Exhib:* Conn Watercolor Asn 36th & 37th Ann Show, Wadsworth Atheneum, Hartford, 74 & 75. *Pos:* Supvr art, K-12 Chappaqua Pub Sch Syst, NY, 48-52 & Clarkstown Pub Sch Syst, NY, 54-56. *Teaching:* Instr, State Univ NY Plattsburg, 52-54; instr home arts, Pa State Univ, 56-57; prof jewelry, Cent Conn State Univ, 57-, chmn dept art, 67-80, prof emer, 80- *Mem:* Am Crafts Coun; Conn Watercolor Soc (bd mem, treas, currently); Nat Art Educ Asn; Conn Art Educ Asn. *Media:* Sterling Silver, Gold. *Mailing Add:* 1941 SE 19th Ave Bel Air Isle Pompano Beach FL 33061

LAW, C ANTHONY
PAINTER

b London, Eng, Oct 15, 16; Can citizen. *Study:* With Franklin Brownell, Ottawa, Frederick Varley, Percyval Tudor-Hart, Quebec & expeditions with Frank Hennessey, Ottawa; St Mary's Univ, Halifax, NS, Hon DLitt, 81. *Work:* Nat War Mus, Ottawa; Can House, London, Eng; Dalhousie Univ Art Gallery, Halifax, NS; Univ NB Art Gallery, Fredricton; Heritage Mus, Dartmouth, NS. *Comn:* Two paintings, New Court House, NS, 75. *Exhib:* Royal Can Acad, 39-71; Nat Art Gallery, London, Eng, 44; Nat Gallery Can, 46; Biennal 1970, Atlantic Provinces Art Circuit; Can Soc Watercolour; Retrospective, Centennial Art Gallery, NS Mus Fine Art, 68; one-man show, Amall Galleries, London, 79. *Pos:* Artist-in-residence, St Marys Univ, Halifax, NS; retired; vchmn bd dir, Art Gallery, NS, 75-78, chmn bd dir, 78-; dir bd, Talent Trust NS, 75- *Awards:* Jessier Dow Award, Montreal Mus of Fine Arts, 39-50. *Mem:* NS Soc Artists. *Media:* Oil, Watercolor. *Dealer:* Duke of Argyle Gallery 1572 Argyle St Halifax NS B3J 2B3 Can; Kastel Gallery 1366 Greene Montreal PQ H3Z 2B1 Can. *Mailing Add:* 8 Halls Rd Boulderwood Halifax NS B3P 1P3 Canada

LAW, PAULINE ELIZABETH
PAINTER

b Wilmington, Del, Feb 22, 03. *Study:* Art Students League; Grand Cent Art Sch; with John F Carlson, Henry Snell, Margery Ryerson, Aldro Hibbard, John Pike, Wayman Adams, John Conaway & George Bridgman. *Work:* Norfolk Mus Arts & Sci, Va; Mus Athens, Greece; Ringwood Mus, NJ; Lyndon B Johnson Collection, Tex. *Comn:* Amon Carter Peak, Big Bend Nat Park, Tex, 61. *Exhib:* Allied Artists Am, 72; Nat Asn Women Artists, 72; Nat Arts Club, 72; Am Artists Prof League, 72; Knickerbocker Artists, 72. *Awards:* Allied Artists Am Prize, 60; Southern Vt Art Asn Prize, 62; First Prize, Catharine Lorillard Wolfe Art Club, 75. *Mem:* Pen & Brush Club; Nat Asn Women Artists (first vpres, 55-57); Nat Arts Club; Catharine Lorillard Wolfe Art Club; Salmagundi Club. *Media:* Oil, Watercolor. *Mailing Add:* 15 Gramercy Park New York NY 10003

LAWALL, DAVID BARNARD
HISTORIAN, CURATOR

b Detroit, Mich, Aug 27, 35. *Study:* Oberlin Col, BA, 56; Princeton Univ, MFA, 59 & PhD, 66. *Collections Arranged:* A B Durand 1796-1886 (auth, catalog), Montclair Art Mus, 71; Small Paintings Toward a Renewal of Classicism, 74-79, Anton Refregier (auth, catalog), 77, Image of Post-Modern Man, 79 & Ernest Fiene/Leon Kroll (auth, catalog), Univ Va Art Mus. *Pos:* Cur, Univ Va Art Mus, 71- *Teaching:* Instr, Univ Mo, Columbia, 60-61; instr, Ohio State Univ, Columbus, 61-64, asst prof, 64-68; assoc prof, Univ Va, Charlottesville, 69- *Awards:* Fel, Nat Endowment Humanities, 69. *Publ:* Auth, Asher Durand: Art and Art Theory, 77 & auth, Asher Durand: Catalog of Paintings, Garland, 78. *Mailing Add:* 108 Bollingwood Rd Charlottesville VA 22903

LAWLESS, BILLIE (WILLIAM B)
SCULPTOR, CRAFTSMAN

b Boston, Mass, July 16, 50. *Study:* Univ Notre Dame, with Konstantine Milonadis, 70-72; Rutgers Col, New Brunswick, NJ, BFA, 74; State Univ NY, Buffalo, with Duayne Hatchett, MFA, 82. *Work:* Elm-Oak Corridor & State Univ NY, Buffalo; Univ Pa, Philadelphia. *Exhib:* Albright-Knox Art Gallery, Buffalo, NY, 78, 80 & 83; Toys to the Third Power, Montclair Art Mus, NJ, 79; Drawing & Small Sculpture, Ball State Univ, 82; Outdoor Sculpture in Rittenhouse Sq, Philadelphia Art Alliance, 82; Roswell Art Mus, NMex, 82; Hallwalls Inc, Buffalo, NY, 83. *Collections Arranged:* Outdoor Sculpture, Aquarium of Niagara Falls, NY, 81. *Mem:* Col Art Asn, New York. *Media:* Mixed. *Mailing Add:* 324 Highgate Ave Buffalo NY 14215

LAWRENCE, HOWARD RAY
DESIGNER, EDUCATOR

b San Francisco, Calif, Mar 21, 36. *Study:* Univ Calif, Berkeley, BA(archit), 62, MA(sculpture), 64. *Exhib:* Light, Pa State Univ, 74, Space, 74, Systems, 75, Movement, 75 & Structure, 75. *Pos:* Archit apprenticeship to var architects, Calif, 65-69. *Teaching:* Asst prof archit, San Francisco City Col, 69-70, Hampton Inst, Va, 70-71, Univ Kans, 71-72 & Pa State Univ, 72- *Awards:* Harry Lord Ford Sculpture Prize, Univ Calif, 64. *Mem:* Asn Col Sch Archit. *Media:* Wood, Metal. *Res:* Basic design process and visual communication products; color theory. *Publ:* Auth, Basic Design Process & Visual Communication Products, 74. *Mailing Add:* Architecture University Park PA 16802

LAWRENCE, JACOB
PAINTER, EDUCATOR

b Atlantic City, NJ, Sept 7, 17. *Study:* Harlem Art Workshop, 34-39; Am Artists Sch, 38; Denison Univ, Hon DFA, 70; Pratt Inst, Hon DFA, 72. *Work:* Mus Mod Art, Am Acad Arts & Lett, Whitney Mus Am Art, Metrop Mus Art, New York; Phillips Mem Gallery, Washington, DC. *Comn:* Three paintings, Fortune Mag, 8/48; painting, Container Corp Am, 53; lithograph, Benrus Watch Co, 67; portrait of Jesse Jackson for cover, Time Mag, 4/70; Olympic poster, Ed Olympia 1972, Munich, Ger, 72; plus others. *Exhib:* Migration Series, Mus Mod Art, New York, 44; John Brown Series, Am Fedn Art Traveling Exhib, 47; retrospective, Brooklyn Mus, 61 & Whitney Mus Am Art, 74; one-man shows, Brandeis Univ, 65, Seattle Art Mus, 74, Birmingham Mus Art, 74, St Louis Art Mus, 74 & New Orleans Mus Art, 75; Toussaint L'Overture Series, Fisk Univ, 68. *Pos:* Mem, Wash State Arts Comn, 74 & 77; mem app by pres, Nat Endowment for the Arts Coun, 77- *Teaching:* Instr painting, Black Mountain Col, summer 47; instr painting, Pratt Inst, 56-71; prof painting, Univ Wash, 71- *Awards:* Guggenheim Fel, 46;

Nat Inst Arts & Lett Grant, 53; Brooklyn Art Bks Children Citation for Harriet and the Promised Land, 73. *Bibliog:* Alain Locke (auth), And the migrants kept coming, Fortune Mag, 41; Aline B Saarinen (auth), Jacob Lawrence, Am Fedn Arts, 60; Bearden & Henderson (auth), 6 Black Masters of American Art, Zenith, 72. *Mem:* Artists Equity Asn New York (past pres); Nat Inst Arts & Lett; Black Acad Arts & Lett. *Media:* Multimedia. *Publ:* Illusr, One Way Ticket, 49; illusr, Harriet and the Promised Land, 68; illusr, Aesops Fables, 70. *Dealer:* Terry Dintenfass Gallery 50 West 57th St New York NY 10019. *Mailing Add:* 4316 37th Ave NE Seattle WA 98105

LAWRENCE, JAMES A
PAINTER, PHOTOGRAPHER

b San Mateo, Calif, May 23, 10. *Study:* Univ Calif, Davis, grad, 33; Art Ctr, Los Angeles, art & photog, with Barse Miller, Will Connell & Charles Kerlee, 35-37; Chouinard Art Inst, Los Angeles, with Phil Paradise & Ricco Lebrun, 38; Art Students League, 40; New York Sch Mod Photog; also with illusr Louis J Rogers, San Francisco, 34. *Work:* Ford Collection, Dearborn, Mich. *Exhib:* One-man shows, Reed Galleries, New York, 41; Gump Galleries, San Francisco, 43 & Univ Nev, 53; Golden Gate Int Exhib, San Francisco; Art Inst Chicago; Metrop Mus Art, New York; Los Angeles Co Mus Art. *Pos:* Tech photogr, Pagano Inc, New York, 40-41; mem, Nev State Coun Arts, 67-71. *Teaching:* Guest instr watercolor, Stanford Univ, spring 48; also pvt students in watercolor at var periods. *Awards:* Cert Merit & Gold & Silver Medals, Golden Gate Int Exhib, 40-41; Am Artists Prof League, 42; Terry Art Inst Award; and others. *Mem:* Nat Watercolor Soc. *Media:* Watercolor. *Publ:* Contribr, Ford Times, Sunset Mag, US Camera & Carson Valley-Historical Sketches; and others. *Mailing Add:* Rock Creek Ranch Rt 1 Box 201 Gardnerville NV 89410

LAWRENCE, JAYE A
SCULPTOR, CRAFTSMAN

b Chicago, Ill, Jan 8, 39. *Study:* Univ Ariz, BFA, 60; Ariz State Univ, MFA, 75. *Work:* Ariz State Univ Collection, Tempe; Pac Lutheran Univ Collection, Tacoma, Wash; Yuma Fine Arts Asn Collection, Ariz. *Exhib:* Americana, 76 & Gifts That Artists Give, 76, Mus Mod Art, San Francisco, Calif; three-person exhib, Celebrations Gallery, San Diego; Leather Art, Yuma Fine Arts Asn, The Depot, Ariz, 79; Leather Forms: Functional to Fantastic, Grossmont Col, El Cajon, Calif, 81; Spectrum Gallery, San Diego, Calif, 81; 32nd Allied Craftsmen Exhib, San Diego Mus Art, Calif, 81; and many others. *Teaching:* Instr leather art, Grossmont Col, El Cajon, Calif, 81. *Awards:* Best of Show, 3rd Ann Phoenix Jewish Community Ctr Show, 69; Purchase Award, 4th Ann SWestern, 69; 12th Ariz Ann Award, 69. *Bibliog:* Marilyn Hagberg (auth), Jaye & Les Lawrence, 10/73 & Erik Gronborg (auth), Jaye Lawrence, 8/74, Craft Horizons; Kathlyn Russell (auth), Rope forms sculpture, Daily Times Advocate, 4/28/74. *Mem:* Am Crafts Coun; Allied Craftsmen San Diego (corresp secy, 74). *Media:* Rawhide, Hog Casing; Dog Hair. *Dealer:* Spectrum Gallery 4011 Goldfinch San Diego CA 92103; Gallery Eight La Jolla 7464 Girard Ave La Jolla CA. *Mailing Add:* 2097 Valley View Blvd El Cajon CA 92021

LAWRENCE, LES
CERAMIST, SCULPTOR

b Corpus Christi, Tex, Dec 17, 40. *Study:* Southwestern State Col, Okla, BA, 62; Tex Tech Univ; Ariz State Univ, MFA(ceramics), 70. *Work:* Whitty Mus, San Antonio; Phoenix Art Mus, Ariz; E B Crocker Art Gallery, Sacramento, Calif; Pac Lutheran Univ, Tacoma, Wash; Ariz State Univ Collection, Tempe; and others. *Exhib:* Southern Sculpture 67, Smithsonian Traveling Exhib, 68-70; Baroque 74, Mus Contemp Crafts, New York, 74; 28th Allied Craftsman Exhib, Fine Arts Gallery, San Diego, Calif, 76; Photo/Synthesis, Johnson Mus, Cornell Univ, Ithaca, NY, 76; Americana, San Francisco Mus Mod Art, Calif, 76; Ceramic Conjunction, Long Beach Mus Art, Calif, 77; Great Am Foot, Mus Contemp Crafts, New York, 78; and others. *Teaching:* Instr ceramics-sculpture, Hardin-Simmons Univ, Abilene, Tex, 66-68; instr ceramics, Grossmont Col, El Cajon, Calif, 70- *Awards:* Tex Watercolor Soc 16th Ann First Purchase Award, San Antonio Art League, 67; First Purchase Award, Region 20 Tex Fine Arts Asn, 68; Calif Crafts IX Purchase for E B Crocker Art Gallery, 75. *Bibliog:* Marilyn Hagberg (auth), Jaye & Les Lawrence, 10/73 & Erik Gronborg (auth), Les Lawrence, 6/75, Craft Horizons; Les Lawrence, Ceramics Monthly, 4/74. *Mem:* Am Crafts Coun; Allied Craftsmen San Diego (secy, 74). *Media:* Clay, Cast Metal. *Dealer:* Elaine Horwitch Gallery 4200 N Marshall Way Scottsdale AZ 85251. *Mailing Add:* 2097 Valley View Blvd El Cajon CA 92021

LAWSON, EDWARD PITT
ADMINISTRATOR

b Newton, Mass, Sept 12, 27. *Study:* Bowdoin Col, BA; Inst Fine Arts, NY Univ, AM. *Pos:* Curatorial asst, Toledo Mus Art, 56-57; supvr art educ, 57-59; asst cur, The Cloisters, 59-62; asst dir, Montreal Mus Fine Arts, 62-67; dir, Tucson Art Ctr, 67-69; admin asst, Int Exhibs Found, 69-70; asst dir, Am Asn Mus, 70-72; chief, dept educ, Hirshhorn Mus & Sculpture Garden, 73- *Teaching:* Instr, Toledo Mus Art Sch of Design, 54-56; vis lectr, Sir George Williams Univ, 63-67; lectr, Univ Ariz, 68-69; lectr, Northern Va Community Col, 73 & Smithsonian Assocs, 74-; spec vis lectr, George Washington Univ, 74- *Awards:* Belg-Am Summer Fel, 56; Metrop Mus Art Travel Grant, 61; Montreal Mus Travel Grant, 65. *Mem:* West Mus League (vpres, 68-69); Am Asn Mus; Can Mus Asn (coun mem, 63-67); PQ Mus Asn (vpres, 63-65, pres, 65-67). *Mailing Add:* 1216 Raymond Ave McLean VA 22101

LAWSON, THOMAS
PAINTER

b Glasgow, Scotland, 1951. *Study:* Univ St Andrews, MA, 73; Univ Edinburgh, MA, 75; Grad Sch City Univ New York. *Work:* Chase Manhattan Bank, New York. *Exhib:* Art and the Media, Renaissance Soc, Univ Chicago, 82; New Figuration in America, Milwaukee Art Ctr, 82; The Image Scavengers, Inst Contemp Art, Univ Pa, Philadelphia, 82; La Forme e L'Informe, Galleria d'Arte Mod, Bologna, Italy, 83; Sao Paulo Bienale, Brazil, 83; and others. *Awards:* Nat Endowment Arts Fel, 82-83. *Bibliog:* Joan Casademont (auth), article, Artforum, 81; D A Robbins (auth), article, Arts Mag, 83. *Media:* Oil. *Publ:* Auth, Making some distinctions, Flash Art, 79; auth, Going places, Real Life Mag, 80; auth, Silently, by means of a flashing light, October, 80; auth, Last exit: Painting, 81 & The dark side of the bright light, 82, Artforum. *Dealer:* Metro Pictures 150 Greene St New York NY 10012. *Mailing Add:* 171 Johnson St Brooklyn NY 11201

LAWTON, FLORIAN KENNETH
PAINTER, INSTRUCTOR

b Cleveland, Ohio, June 20, 21. *Study:* Cleveland Sch Art, 42 & 48-50; John Huntington Polytech Inst, 48-49; Cleveland Col, 48-49. *Work:* Johnson Rubber Co; Nat Engineering & Contracting Co; Miami Univ, Oxford, Ohio; Marietta Col, Ohio; in pvt collection of King Kahlid, Saudi Arabia. *Comn:* Paintings, McLeery-Cumins Co, Washington, Iowa, 75 & 79-80; historic landmarks, Soc Crippled Children, Cleveland, 77, Pre-Mix, Inc, Ashtabula, Ohio, 77-78 & Ohio Conserv Found, Cleveland, 78; Cleveland Citiscape, Ohio Bell Tel Co, 79. *Exhib:* May Show, Cleveland Mus Art, 77-78; Butler Mus Am Art Nat, Youngstown, Ohio, 77-79; Nat Watercolor Soc, All-West Traveling Exhib, Los Angeles, 77-80; Salmagundi Club, New York, 78-80; Ky Watercolor Soc, Owensboro Mus, 79; one-man show, Willoughby Fine Arts Ctr, Ohio, 79; and others. *Pos:* Art consult, Cleveland, Ohio, 72-; adv, Orange Arts Coun, Ohio, 77- *Teaching:* Instr painting & watercolor, Cleveland Inst Art, 81-; instr watercolor, Orange Arts Coun, Ohio, 77- *Awards:* Grand Buckeye Leaf Award, Nat Watercolor Soc, 81; Peoples Choice Award, Great Lakes Regional, 82; First Prize & Larry Quackenbush Award, Hudson Ann, 82. *Bibliog:* Modern art review, Revue Mod Desarts, Paris, France, 6/70; Amish Romance (doc film), Scripps-Howard TV, Hiram Col, 75. *Mem:* Ohio Watercolor Soc; Assoc Am Watercolor Soc; Audubon Artists Am; Ky Watercolor Soc; Midwest Watercolor Soc. *Media:* Mixed. *Publ:* Auth, Watercolor page, In: American Artist, Watson-Guptill, 70. *Dealer:* Bonofoey Co 1710 Euclid Ave Cleveland OH 44111; Bernhard Gallery 278 E Garfield Dr Aurora Ohio 44202. *Mailing Add:* 152 S Strawberry Lane Chagrin Falls OH 44022

LAWTON, JAMES L
SCULPTOR, EDUCATOR

b Louisville, Ky, July 28, 44. *Study:* Louisville Sch Art, Ky; Murray State Univ, Ky, BSc; Kent State Univ, Ohio, MFA. *Work:* Western Mich Univ, Kalamazoo; City Hartland, Mich. *Comn:* Three Trusses Plus (painted steel sculpture), Cass Park, City Detroit, 77-78. *Exhib:* Seven for 76, Seven State Exhib, Eastern Ill Univ, Charleston, 76; Nat Sculpture 76 (travelling exhib), Univ Ga, 76-77; Michigan Art Train Traveling Exhib, Renaissance Ctr, Detroit, 78; National Sculpture 1979, Univ Ga, Athens, 79; Invitational, Oakland Univ, 80; and others. *Pos:* Head dept sculpture, Mich State Univ, 79- *Teaching:* Assoc prof sculpture & ceramics, Kresge Art Ctr, East Lansing, 68- *Awards:* Third Place, Nat Metal Sculpture, Wis State Univ, 67; Mich State Univ Grants, 68- & 79; First Place, Mich State Fair, 74. *Mem:* Nat Asn Sculptors; Artists Equity. *Dealer:* Robert Kidd Gallery Birmingham MI 48011; Bay St Galley Northport MI. *Mailing Add:* 3485 Zimmer Rd Williamston MI 48895

LAX, DAVID
PAINTER

b Peekskill, NY, May 16, 10. *Study:* Ethical Cult Sch, with H R Kniffen, Victor D'Amico & Victor Frisch, CFA(scholar), 28; Archipenko Art Sch, with Alexander Archipenko. *Work:* Gallery Mod Art, New York; Clearwater Mus, Fla; Bevier Collection, Rochester Inst Technol; Pentagon War Art Collection; State Univ NY Collection; plus others. *Comn:* Several hundred genre paintings, Irving Mills Collection, 32-42; combat paintings, USA, Pentagon, 42-45; Denunciation (paintings), Grossman Mem, NY, 45-50; murals, Vet Admin Regional Off Bldg, New York, 50-52; paintings of New York in the 50's, comn by group of New Yorkers, Dutchess Community Col, 52-57. *Exhib:* Grand Cent Founders Show, New York, 39-46; Corcoran Gallery 18th Biennial, 43; Painting in the US, Carnegie Inst, Pittsburgh, 46; Nat Arts Club 20th Ann, New York, 70; 60th Anniversary Exhib, Tex Fine Arts Asn, 71, one-man tour, 74-75; West 80, Art & the Law; one-man show, Bevier Gallery, Rochester Inst Technol, 83. *Teaching:* Chmn dept art, Dutchess Community Col, 58-73, prof, 73-77; emer prof, State Univ NY, 77- *Awards:* Bronze Star Medal, War Art, 45; Silver Medal for Painting, Int Inst Arts & Lett, 60; Presidential Medallion, Rochester Inst Technol, 83. *Bibliog:* Valente (auth), 60 Paintings Since Denunciation, Hamilton Reproductions, 70; Brass (auth), Raunchy dogs of defeat, J Am Med Asn, 72; Brown & Ferri (auths), Paintings and Drawings, David Lax, Rochester Inst Technol Press, 83. *Mem:* Assoc Am Artists; Dutchess Co Art Asn; Int Inst Arts & Lett; Dutchess County Arts Coun. *Media:* Oil, Polymer. *Publ:* Coauth, Lax Paintings, TC in the Battle of Europe, 45, Denunciation, Paintings Concerning Man's Fate, 49, David Lax, Portraits, 51, David Lax, Paintings of New York in the Fifties, 72 & One Man Show, 75; and others. *Dealer:* Washington Irving Gallery 117 E 17th St New York NY 10003. *Mailing Add:* Box 94 Red Hook NY 12571

LAXSON, RUTH
CONCEPTUAL ARTIST

b Roanoke, Ala. *Study:* Auburn Univ; Atlanta Col Art. *Work:* Ga Council Arts, Atlanta; Tweed Mus Art, Univ Minn, Minneapolis; Sackner Collection, Miami; Mus Mod Art, New York; Emory Univ, Atlanta, Ga; and others. *Exhib:* Southeast Invitational, Mem Hall Gallery, Athens, Ga, 79; Paper Works/80, Quinlan Art Mus, Gainesville, Ga, 80; Artists' Bookworks, Zone, Springfield Mass, 81; New in 82, Ctr Bk Arts, New York, 82; Breaking the Bindings, Univ Wis, Madison, 83; and others. *Awards:* Nat Endowment Arts Grant, 80. *Bibliog:* Clyde Burnett (auth), Heath Exhibit, Atlanta J, 81; Cathrine Fox (auth), Form is the Content, Atlanta Constution, 81; Catherine Fox (auth), article, Profile, 83. *Mem:* Atlanta Col Art Alum. *Dealer:* Heath Gallery 416 E Paces Ferry Rd Atlanta GA 30305; Artworks 170 S La Brea Los Angeles CA. *Mailing Add:* PO Box 9731 Atlanta GA 30319

LAY, PATRICIA ANNE
SCULPTOR

b New Haven, Conn, Aug 14, 41. *Study:* Rochester Inst Technol, MFA; Pratt Inst, BS. *Work:* NJ State Mus, Trenton. *Exhib:* Twenty-fifth Ceramic Nat, Everson Mus Art, Syracuse, NY, 68-69; Warren Benedek Gallery, New York, 73; one-person show, NJ State Mus, 74; Contemporary Reflections, Aldrich Mus, Ridgefield, Conn, 75; Whitney Mus Am Art Biennial, 75. *Teaching:* Asst prof sculpture, State Univ NY Buffalo, 68-69; instr ceramics, Wagner Col, 69-71; lectr ceramics, Hunter Col, 71-72; asst prof ceramics, Montclair State Col, 72- *Bibliog:* Leon Nigrosh (auth), Claywork, 75 & Low Fire: Other Ways to Work in Clay, 80, Davis Publ. *Media:* Clay, Metal. *Mailing Add:* Dept of Art Montclair State Col Upper Montclair NJ 07043

LAYCOX, (WILLIAM) JACK
PAINTER, DESIGNER

b Auburn, Calif, Mar 11, 24. *Study:* Univ Calif, Berkeley; San Francisco State Univ, BA, 48; Inst Allende, Mex, 79; Art Students League, New York, 80. *Work:* Holy Names Col Gallery, Calif; Gen Tire Int Collection, Akron, Ohio; Naval Hosp Collection, Oakland; Latter Day Saints Collection, Salt Lake City; Rosicrucian Egyptian Art Mus, San Jose, Calif; plus others. *Comn:* Watercolor Series, Williamhouse-Regency, Van Nuys, Calif, 69-75; oil paintings, Delta Air Lines, Atlanta, Ga, 75-80; DeAnza Bicentennial (theme painting), City of Monterey, Calif, 76; paintings, Monterey Savings & Loan, 78-79; paintings, Robert Larsen Corp, Walnut Creek, Calif, 81. *Exhib:* Briand Galleries, Glendale, Calif, 77-80; Modesto Jr Col Gallery, Calif, 78-80; Kaiser Ctr Gallery, Oakland, 79 & 81; Crown Zellerbach Gallery, San Francisco, 79; Copenhagen Galleries, Solvang, Calif, 81; and many others. *Pos:* Tech illusr, AEC, Oak Ridge, Tenn, 43-46; art dir, Bacon Am Corp, Muncie, Ind, 49-56; designer, Mission-Regency Cards, Van Nuys, 66-78. *Teaching:* Instr watercolor, Jade Fon Watercolor Workshop, Asilomar, Calif, summers 71-73; instr advan oils, Sunset Ctr Studio 15, Carmel, Calif, 80-81. *Awards:* Best of Show, Diablo Pageant Arts, 61; Second Award for Watercolor, Soc Western Artists, 63; Second Award for Oils, Calif State Fair, 65. *Bibliog:* Robert Miskimon (auth), From engineer to artist, Carmel Pine Cone, 73; Bold themes of American artists, Eastern Daily Press, Holt, Eng, 10/17/75; Eugenia West (auth), The fine art of travel posters, Sky Mag, 6/76; Irene Lagorio, reviews, Monterey Peninsula Herald, 80 & 81; and others. *Mem:* Soc Western Artists; West Coast Watercolor Soc; Asn Honolulu Artists. *Media:* Oil, Watercolor. *Publ:* Auth, Dramatic Paintings From Familiar Scenes, Walter Foster Bks, 72. *Mailing Add:* PO Box 5054 Carmel CA 93921

LAYMON, CYNTHIA J
COLLAGE ARTIST, GRAPHIC ARTIST

b Gary, Ind, Feb 17, 48. *Study:* Ind Univ, Bloomington, BA, 70; Southern Ill Univ, MFA, 77. *Exhib:* A Common Ground, Alexandria Mus, La, 81; New American Graphics, Al Batha Mus, Am Cult Ctr, Am Embassy & Legation Mus, Morocco, 82-83; Paper/Fiber VI Nat Exhib, The Arts Ctr, Iowa City, 83; Craft Invitational, Southeast Ctr Contemp Art, Winston-Salem, NC, 83; Contemp American Fibers, Redding Mus, Calif, 83. *Teaching:* Asst prof studio art, Lake Erie Col, 77-79 & Univ NC, Greensboro, 79- *Awards:* Best in Show, Womensart, Columbus Inst Contemp Art, 78; Award & Merit Award, Survey Illinois Fibers, Handweavers Guild Am & Lakeview Mus, 78; Award of Excellence, NC/SC Fibers Competition, Charlotte Handweavers Guild, 80. *Bibliog:* Gilda Morina Syverson (auth), Cynthia Laymon: Fiber/paper constructions, Fiberarts Mag, 7-8/82. *Mem:* Col Art Asn; Am Craft Coun; NC Fiber Arts Asn (treas, 79-81, educ dir, 81-82); Tri-State Sculptors Guild; NC Print & Drawing Soc. *Media:* Mixed. *Publ:* Auth, Martha Matthews: Tapestry, 82, Ceremonial garments, 82, North/South Carolina fibers competition, 83 & The quilts of Patsy Allen, 83, Fiberarts Mag. *Mailing Add:* 5007 Korem Dr Greensboro NC 27409

LAYNOR, HAROLD ARTHUR
EDUCATOR, PAINTER

b New York, NY, Jan 10, 22. *Study:* Parsons Sch Design, New York, cert, 42; Art Students League, with Kuniyoshi, Barnot, Klonis & Baziotes; NY Univ, BA, 46, MA, 47; Tiffany Found fel, 52; Huntington Hartford fel, 56; State Univ NY Albany, EdD, 66. *Work:* Albany Inst Hist & Art, NY; IBM Collection, Poughkeepsie; Munson-Williams-Proctor Mus, Utica; Taylor Hall, Vassar Col, Poughkeepsie; Elmira Col Mus, NY. *Exhib:* Art in World War II, Mus Mod Art, New York, 42; Allied Artists Am, New York, 50; Audubon Artists, New York, 50; Albany Inst Hist & Art Ann, NY, 60; Schenectady Mus Ann, NY, 60; Munson-Williams-Proctor Mus, Utica, 60. *Teaching:* Art super, Poughkeepsie City Schs, NY, 47-56; supt art, NY State Dept Educ, Albany, 56-66; prof art, Millersville Univ, Pa, 66- *Awards:* Purchase Prize, Albany Inst Art, 58; George E Brown Award, NJ Soc Painters & Sculptors, 60. *Bibliog:* Painting in lacquer, Am Artist Mag, 58; Lois A

Goldblatt (auth), A Man and His Images (film), West Chester State Col, Pa, 78. *Mem:* Artists' Equity Asn; Pa Soc Watercolor Artists; Torch Int. *Media:* Watercolor; Stitchery and Acrylic. *Res:* Comparative analysis of creativity measures. *Publ:* Ed, Films and Filmstrips for Art Education, 63, Art in the Elementary Schools, 65 & Studio in Art for High School Students, 68, NY State Dept Educ. *Dealer:* Val Hall Gallery Lancaster PA. *Mailing Add:* 210 E Charlotte St Millersville PA 17551

LAYTON, RICHARD
PAINTER, DEALER

b Wilmington, Del, Apr 15, 29. *Study:* With Frank E Schoonover & Carolyn Wyeth; Philadelphia Mus Col Art. *Work:* In many bus and pvt collections in US and abroad. *Comn:* Ten murals, incl Univ Del & E I du Pont de Nemours & Co; designer of 1973 Am Revolution Bicentennial Comn Medal. *Exhib:* Corcoran Gallery Art, Washington, DC; Am Watercolor Soc; Audubon Artists; Pa Acad Fine Arts, Philadelphia; Del Art Mus; plus many others. *Collections Arranged:* Sixteen regional & nat exhibs incl N C Wyeth Exhib, Pa State Mus, Harrisburg, 65, Brandywine Heritage, 71 & N C Wyeth Exhib, 72, Brandywine River Mus. *Pos:* Former cur, Brandywine River Mus, Chadds Ford, Pa; pres, Del Arts Soc, currently; pres, Brandywine Editions, Ltd; bd dirs, Christian Sanderson Mus, Chadds Ford, Pa. *Bibliog:* Del Today Mag, 5/71. *Mem:* Nat Soc Mural Painters. *Specialty:* Brandywine & Wyeth art; illustrators of the Howard Pyle school. *Publ:* Auth, introd to N C Wyeth, Crown, 72. *Mailing Add:* 2600 W 19th St Wilmington DE 19806

LAZAROF, ELEANORE BERMAN
PAINTER, PRINTMAKER

b New York, NY, Sept 2, 28. *Study:* Black Mountain Col, with Albers & Zadkine, 45; Univ Calif Los Angeles, BA, 50; spec study with Manfred Schwartz, New York & Fernand Leger, Paris, 50-51. *Work:* Grunwald Ctr Graphic Arts, Los Angeles; Exxon Corp Original Print Collection, Darien, Conn; Portland Art Mus, Ore; Brooklyn Mus, NY; Los Angeles Co Mus Art; and others. *Exhib:* Nat Watercolor Soc Exhib, Brand Libr Galleries, Glendale, Calif, 76; Int Exchange Show, Seoul Mus Art, Korea, 77; one-woman shows, Paintings, Pastels, Prints, Riverside Mus Art, Calif, 78, Stuhr Mus, Grand Island, Nebr, 78 & Tweed Mus, Univ Minn, 79; Los Angeles Co Mus Art, 80; Kirk de Gooyer Gallery, Los Angeles, 81; and others. *Collections Arranged:* Graphic Arts Coun Mem Exhib, Calif Palace Legion Honor, 78. *Awards:* Purchase Prize, Los Angeles All City Exhib, Home Savings & Loan, 69; Purchase Award, Brand VI Graphics Exhib, 76. *Bibliog:* Robert McDonald (auth), Six years of work by Eleanore Lazarof, Art Week, 11/77; Los Angeles Prints (exhib catalog), Los Angeles Co Mus Art, 80; article, Archit Digest, 6/83. *Mem:* Los Angeles Printmaking Soc; Nat Watercolor Soc; Artists Equity Asn; World Print Coun; Artists Econ Action. *Media:* Oil, Pastel. *Dealer:* Kirk de Gooyer Gallery 1308 Factory Pl Los Angeles CA 90013. *Mailing Add:* 718 N Maple Dr Beverly Hills CA 90210

LAZARUS, DIANE GAIL
GALLERY DIRECTOR, CURATOR

b Windsor, Ont, Jan 6, 51; US citizen. *Study:* Univ Mich, BA(art hist), 73, MMP, 75. *Collections Arranged:* Western Art: Selections from the Harrison Eiteljorg Collection (auth, catalog), Indianapolis Mus Art, 76; 200 Years of Indiana Art (cataloged), Mirages of Memory, 77; Wilbur Peat, Portraits and Painters of the Governors of Indiana (co-auth, catalog), Ind Hist Soc, 79. *Pos:* Asst cur, Indianapolis Mus Art, 75-78; exec dir, Hunterdon Art Ctr, Clinton, NJ, formerly. *Mem:* Am Asn Mus; Col Art Asn; Nat Trust for Hist Preserv. *Res:* 19th and 20th centuries American art. *Publ:* Co-auth, A note on a sixteenth century drawing, Univ Mich Mus Art Bull, 73. *Mailing Add:* Evanston Art Ctr 2603 Sheridan Rd Evanston IL 60201

LAZARUS, FRED, IV
ADMINISTRATOR

b New York, NY, Jan 1, 42. *Study:* Claremont Men's Col, BA, 64; Harvard Univ, MBA, 66. *Pos:* Exec asst to chmn, Nat Endowment for Arts, 75-78; pres, Md Inst Col Art, 78- *Mem:* Baltimore Sch Arts (bd mem, currently); Md Art Place; Partners for Liveable Places; Alliance Independent Cols Art (chmn, 83); Md Independent Cols & Univs Asn. *Mailing Add:* Md Inst Col of Art 1300 W Mt Royal Ave Baltimore MD 21217

LEA, LAURIE JANE
SCULPTOR, PAINTER

b Atlanta, Ga, May 7, 48. *Study:* Newcomb Col, with Frank Boles, 66-67; Univ Colo, Boulder, with Gene Matthews & Frank Sampson, BFA, 70; Univ Ga, Athens, apprenticed with William Thompson, 78-79. *Work:* Ga Arts Coun, State Art Collection, Kilpatrick, Cody, Rogenstein, Rogers & McClatchey Law Off, First Nat Bank, Atlanta; Bank Cornelia, Ga; and others. *Comn:* Student Mem, Riverwood High Sch, Atlanta, 80. *Exhib:* Watercolor Exhib, Birmingham Mus Art, 73; American Drawings, Smithsonian Inst Exhib, Portsmouth, Va, 76; Nat Asn Art Sch Invitational, Univ Ga, Athens, 80; Southern Watercolor Soc Fourth Ann Exhib, Columbia Mus, SC, 80; Ga Watercolor Soc Third Exhib, Mus Arts & Sci, Macon, 81; Southern Watercolor Soc Sixth Ann Exhib, Pensacola Mus Art, Fla, 82; The Great Garden Sculpture Show, Sculptural Arts Mus, Atlanta, 82; and others. *Pos:* Recreational art therapist consult, Art Rehabilitation Program, Scottish Rite Hosp, Atlanta, 81-82. *Teaching:* Vis artist, Atlanta Pub Schs & Trinity Schs, 74-81. *Awards:* Purchase Award, Atlanta Arts Festival, 72; First Place Heritage Award, Ga Comn Nat Bicentennial Celebration, 76; Best of Show, Southern Watercolor Soc Sixth Ann Exhib, Pensacola Mus Art, 82. *Bibliog:* Creating an Artwork (videotape), WETV 30, PBS, 83. *Mem:* Watercolor Soc Ala; Southern Watercolor Soc; Ga Watercolor Soc; Southeastern Ctr Contemp Art. *Media:* Mixed. *Dealer:* Fay Gold Gallery 3221 Cains Hill Place NW Atlanta GA 30305. *Mailing Add:* 49 Ivy Ridge Ave Atlanta GA 30342

LEA, STANLEY E
PRINTMAKER, PAINTER

b Joplin, Mo, Apr 5, 30. *Study:* Pittsburg State Univ, BFA; Univ Ark, MFA. *Work:* Smithsonian Inst & Libr Cong, Washington, DC; Brit Mus, London; Inst Mex Norteamericano, Mexico City; Mus Fine Arts, Houston. *Comn:* Collagraphs, Hyatt Regency Hotel, Houston, 72; paintings, Ft Worth Nat Bank, 73, Citizens Bank, Richards, Tex, 74, Am Nat Bank, Austin, 74 & USAA Bldg, San Antonio, 74; City of Hanstville (mural), Bradford Hotel, Dallas, Tex. *Exhib:* 48th Ann Soc Am Graphic Artists, New York, 67; Mainstreams Int, Marietta, Ohio, 68; Watercolor USA, Springfield, Mo, 69; 148th Ann Nat Acad Design, New York, 73; Nat Color Print USA, Lubbock, Tex, 74. *Teaching:* Prof printmaking & painting, Sam Houston State Univ, Huntsville, Tex, 61-; vis prof, Mus Fine Arts, Houston, 68-71. *Awards:* Arts Nat, Tyler, Tex, 62; 4th Ann Print & Drawing, Ark Art Ctr, 70; Award, 68th Nat Texas Fine Arts, 79. *Bibliog:* Gerald F Brommer (auth), Art of Collage, Davis, Publ, Inc, 78. *Mem:* Col Art Asn; Southern Graphics Coun. *Media:* Collagraphs, Mixed Media Collage; Mixed Media. *Dealer:* Sol Del Rio 1020 Townsend San Antonio TX 78209; Valley House Gallery 6616 Spring Valley Rd Dallas TX 75240. *Mailing Add:* 2118 Pleasant Huntsville TX 77340

LEA, TOM
PAINTER, ILLUSTRATOR

b El Paso, Tex, July 11, 07. *Study:* Art Inst Chicago, 24-26; study in Italy, 30 & NMex, 33-35; Baylor Univ, hon LittD, 67; Southern Methodist Univ, hon LHD, 70. *Work:* Dallas Mus Fine Art, Tex; El Paso Mus Art, Tex; State Capitol, Austin, Tex; Pentagon War Art Collection; Humanities Res Ctr, Univ Tex, Austin; also in pvt collections. *Comn:* Murals, US Court House & Pub Libr, El Paso, US Post Off Bldgs, Pleasant Hill, Mo, Odessa, Tex & Washington, DC. *Exhib:* One-man shows, Ft Worth Art Ctr, Tex, 61 & El Paso Mus Art, 63 & 71; Inst Texan Cult, San Antonio, 69. *Pos:* Artist & war corresp, Life Mag, 41-46. *Publ:* Auth & illusr, The Wonderful Country, 52, The King Ranch, Vols I & II, 57, The Primal Yoke, 60, The Hands of Cantu, 64 & A Picture Gallery, 68, Little; and others. *Mailing Add:* 2401 Savannah St El Paso TX 79930

LEACH, FREDERICK DARWIN
PAINTER, HISTORIAN

b Arkansas City, Kans, Sept 19, 24. *Study:* James Millikin Univ, BA; Univ Wis, with Carlos Lopez; State Univ Iowa, MA, MFA & PhD. *Work:* State Univ Iowa; Ball State Univ; Minn Mus Art. *Exhib:* Old Northwest Territory, Springfield, Ill, 46-57; Ohio State Fair, Columbus, 56 & 57; Ball State Univ Drawing & Small Sculpture; Exhibition 180, Huntington, WVa, 56-62; Encounter, Minn Mus Art, St Paul. *Collections Arranged:* National Print & Drawing Exhibition: Ultimate Concerns, Ohio Univ, 60. *Teaching:* From instr to asst prof art hist, State Univ Iowa, 48-56, actg head dept, 55; prof art hist & drawing & dir, Sch Art, Ohio Univ, 56-68; prof art hist & drawing, Hamline Univ, 68-, actg head dept art, 71-72, chmn fine arts div, 72-73, chmn art dept, 75-81. *Awards:* Juror's Exhib Award, Huntington, WVa, 57; Drawing Prize, Ball State Univ, 63. *Mem:* Col Art Asn Am; Midwest Col Art Asn; Minn Art Historians. *Media:* Oil, Watercolor. *Publ:* Auth, Speculation on an artistic common denominator, Topic: 5, 63; auth, The Found Object, State Univ NY Col Buffalo, 65; auth, Review of Nathan Lyons', Photographers on Photography, Aperture, 67; auth, Paul Manship: An Intimate View (monogr), Minn Mus, 72; auth, The Ketuba: Variations within a consistent Jewish imagery, In: The Ketuba, Hamline Univ Press, 75. *Mailing Add:* Dept of Art Hamline Univ St Paul MN 55104

LEADER, GARNET ROSAMONDE
ADMINISTRATOR

b Bessemer, Ala. *Study:* Maryville Col, Tenn, AB; Columbia Univ, MA(fine arts); Peabody Col, Tenn; Univ Tenn; Art Students League, New York, with Reginald Marsh; Univ Ala, AA. *Exhib:* Birmingham Asn Art, Ala; Ala State Fair Art Exhib, Birmingham; Miss Univ for Women, Columbus. *Pos:* Pres, Bessemer Art Club; vpres, Kappa Pi Int Hon, 38-68, pres, 69- *Teaching:* Instr arts & crafts, Birmingham Pub Schs, 28-71. *Mem:* Birmingham Art Club; Watercolor Soc Ala; Nat Art Educ Asn; fel Royal Soc Arts, London. *Dealer:* Lassctter & Co Birmingham AL 35203. *Mailing Add:* 5117 Main St Bessemer AL 35020

LEAF, JUNE
PAINTER, SCULPTOR

b Chicago, Ill, 1929. *Study:* Inst Design, Chicago; Univ Ill; Roosevelt Univ, Chicago. *Work:* Mus Mod Art, New York; Art Inst Chicago & Mus Contemp Art, Chicago, Ill; Smithsonian Inst, Washington, DC; Madison Art Ctr, Wis; Col Cape Breton, Sydney, NS, Can. *Exhib:* Torment, Whitney Mus Am Art, New York, 70; Drawings by Contemp Am Artists, Cranbrook Acad Art Mus, Mich, 74; Contemp Drawings, Boston Univ Art Gallery, Mass, 75; A Retrospective Exhib, Mus Contemp Art, Chicago, Ill, 78; Alternative Realities in Contemp Am Art, Univ Minn, Katherine Nash Gallery, Minneapolis, 81; Col Cape Breton Art Gallery, Sydney, NS, 82; Dalhousie Art Gallery, Halifax, NS, 82; NDak Mus Art, 83. *Pos:* Instr painting & drawing, Art Inst Chicago, 54-58, Parson Sch Art & Design, New York, 66-68. *Awards:* Fulbright Grant to Paris, 58; Can Coun Arts Award, 78 & 82. *Bibliog:* Franz Schulze (auth), Fantastic Images; Lucy Lippard, article, Art Am, 76; Dennis Adrian (auth), June Leaf, Mus Contemp Art, Chicago, 78. *Media:* All Media. *Mailing Add:* RR 3 Mabou NS 60610 B0E 1X0 Canada

LEAF, RUTH
PRINTMAKER, INSTRUCTOR

b New York, NY. *Work:* NY Univ; US Info Agency; Bowdoin Col Mus Art; Colgate Univ. *Exhib:* Sala Exposiciones, Escuela Nac Artes Plasticas, 67; Boston Mus, 70; De Cordova Mus, Mass, 71; Soc Am Graphic Artists, New York, 71; Galerie Art & Gravure, Paris, 72. *Teaching:* Instr intaglio, NShore Community Art Ctr, 69- *Awards:* Purchase Awards, Libr Cong, 46, Hofstra Univ, 63 & Olivet Col, 67. *Bibliog:* Ron Perkins (auth), Artists at Work--Filmstrip 4, Jam Handy Sch Serv, 70. *Mem:* Soc Am Graphic Artists; Boston Printmakers; Silvermine Artists Guild; Print Club, Philadelphia; Am Color Print Soc. *Media:* Graphics. *Mailing Add:* c/o Bermond Art Ltd 3000 Marcus Ave Lake Success NY 11040

LEAKE, EUGENE W
PAINTER

b Jersey City, NJ, Aug 31, 11. *Study:* Yale Univ Sch Art & Archit; Art Students League. *Work:* Baltimore Mus Art; J B Speed Art Mus, Louisville, Ky; Wash Co Mus, Hagerstown, Md. *Dealer:* C Grimaldis Gallery 928 Charles St Baltimore MD 21239; Tatistcheff & Co 38 E 57th St New York NY. *Mailing Add:* Turner Rd Monkton MD 21111

LEATHERS, WINSTON LYLE
PAINTER, PRINTMAKER

b Miami, Man, Can, Dec 29, 32. *Study:* Univ Man, BFA, 56, Univ Mex, 57-58; Man Teachers Col, 60; Univ BC, 61. *Work:* Can Coun Collection; Winnipeg Art Gallery; Univ of Fife, Scotland; Edmonton Art Gallery. *Comn:* Environmental wall mural, Roghmans Ltd, Winnipeg, 73; low relief concrete wall mural, Porv of Man, Portage La Prarie, 77; mural, IKOY Archit Partnership, Winnipeg, Man, 77; low relief wall mural, BACM Co Ltd, Winnipeg, 78. *Exhib:* Paris Int Print Exhib, France, 72; Bermuda Biennial, 72; Brit Fedn Int, 73; Int Print Exhib, Zurich, Switz, 74; Manisphere Int, Moorehead, Minn, 75. *Collections Arranged:* Univ of Mex, Contemp Gallery of Art, Mexico City, 57; University of BC, 61; Western Canadian Art Circuit Traveling Exhib, Winnipeg Art Gallery, 66-67; British Fedn of Artist Gallery, London, Eng, 68; Winnipeg Art Gallery, 74. *Pos:* Man art curric revision comt, Prov of Man, 61-66; art adv, Libr Comn, City of Winnipeg, 76- *Teaching:* Assoc prof design & drawing, Univ of Man, 69- *Awards:* Sr Can Coun Grant for Printmaking, 67-68 & Proj Grant for Printmaking, 73, Can Coun; Purchase Award, Man Soc Artists, Winnipeg, 76. *Bibliog:* Prof Vann (auth), Perspective--Winston Leathers, Univ Man, 69; Philip Fry (auth), Manitoba Artists, Winnipeg Art Gallery, 72; Ann Davis (auth), Cosmic Variations--Winston Leathers, Winnipeg Art Gallery, Bulletin Mag, 6/75. *Mem:* Can Artists Representation (pres, 72); Royal Can Acad Arts; Brit Fedn of Artists, Eng; Can Soc of Printmakers; Can Soc of Graphic Artists. *Dealer:* Thomas Gallery Osborne St Winnipeg MB Can. *Mailing Add:* 55 Roslyn Crescent Winnipeg MB R3L 0H6 Canada

LEAVITT, THOMAS WHITTLESEY
MUSEUM DIRECTOR

b Boston, Mass, Jan 8, 30. *Study:* Middlebury Col, AB, 51; Boston Univ, MA, 52; Harvard Univ, PhD, 58. *Collections Arranged:* New Renaissance in Italy (with catalog), Pasadena, Calif, 58; Piet Mondrian (with catalog), Santa Barbara, Calif, 65; American Portraits in California Collections (with catalog), Santa Barbara, 66; Brücke (with catalog), Cornell Univ, 70, Georg Kolbe, 72; Seymour Lipton, 73; Directions in Afro-American Art, 74; Painting Up Front, 81; and others. *Pos:* Asst to dir, Fogg Art Mus, 54-56; exec dir, Fine Arts Comn, People to People Prog, 57; dir, Pasadena Art Mus, 57-63; dir, Santa Barbara Mus Art, 63-68; dir, Andrew Dickson White Mus Art, Cornell Univ, 68-72, dir mus prog, Nat Endowment for Arts, 71-72, mem mus adv panel, 72-75; trustee, Am Fedn Arts, 72-; dir, Herbert F Johnson Mus Art, Cornell Univ, 73-; mem mus pancl, NY State Coun Arts, 75-78 & 80-81. *Teaching:* Lectr Am art, Univ Calif, Santa Barbara, 64-65; prof hist art, Cornell Univ, 68- *Mem:* Col Art Asn Am; Am Asn Mus (coun mem, 76-79, vpres, 80-82, pres, 82-84); Asn Art Mus Dirs; Independent Sector (bd mem, 80-). *Res:* American 19th & 20th century painting. *Publ:* Auth, The Crisis in Museums, 71; auth, George Loring Brown (catalog), 73; auth, Let the dogs bark, George Loring Brown and the critics, Am Art Rev, 1-2/74; and others. *Mailing Add:* H F Johnson Mus of Art Cornell Univ Ithaca NY 14853

LEBECK, CAROL E
CERAMIST

b Spokane, Wash, Sept 8, 31. *Study:* Univ Calif, Los Angeles, MA(ceramics); Swed State Sch Design, Stockholm, Sweden, HKS(ceramics). *Work:* Los Angeles Co Cult Art Asn, Brand Libr, Los Angeles; Marietta Col, Ohio; Univ Ariz. *Exhib:* California Women in Crafts, Craft & Folk Art Mus, Los Angeles, 77; California Crafts X, Crocker Art Gallery, Sacramento, 77; Viewpoint: Ceramics, 1978, Grossmont Col Gallery, El Cajon, Calif; Celebrations Gallery Invitational: Dinner for Eight, San Diego, 79; West Coast Clay Spectrum, Security Pac Bank, Los Angeles, 79; and many others. *Teaching:* Instr ceramics, Grossmont Col, El Cajon, Calif, 62- *Awards:* Fel, Swed Am Found Grant, 58; Purchase Award, Marietta Crafts Nat, 75; Award of Merit, California Crafts X, 77. *Mem:* Am Crafts Coun; Allied Craftsmen of San Diego (corresp secy, 75). *Media:* Clay, Mixed Media. *Mailing Add:* 7108 Stanford Ave La Mesa CA 92041

LEBEDEV, VLADIMIR
PAINTER

b Moscow, Russia, June 17, 10; US citizen. *Study:* Tech Indust Art, grad; Acad Arts, Leningrad, with Bernstein & Filanov, grad; also with V Favorski & El Lisitski, Moscow. *Work:* Acad Arts, Leningrad; Kunstkabinett Keterer, Stuttgart, Ger; Berry Hill Gallery, New York; Far Gallery, New York; also mus in Moscow & Khazan, Russia. *Comn:* Interior decoration, USSR Bldg, New York World's Fair, 39. *Exhib:* Expos Artistes Exile, Paris, 48; Expos Stedelijk Mus, Amsterdam, 49; Expos Artistes, Mus Nat Belg, 49; one-man show, Charles Barzansky Gallery, New York, 57; Nat Acad Design, New

York, 65-66. *Awards:* First Prize, Art Exhib, Block Island, RI, 61. *Mem:* Artists Equity Asn; Am Fedn Arts; Int Inst Conserv. *Media:* Oil. *Dealer:* Far Gallery 746 Madison Ave New York NY 10021. *Mailing Add:* 144 E 36th St New York NY 10016

LEBER, ROBERTA (ROBERTA LEBER MCVEIGH)
CERAMIST, INSTRUCTOR
b Hoboken, NJ. *Study:* NY State Col Ceramics, Alfred Univ, BS; Columbia Univ. *Exhib:* Vision, George Jensen New York, 60; Environ Gallery, New York; Contemp Crafts, Worcester Mus, Mass; Rockland Ctr Arts-Craft Award Show, 72; Craftsmen of the West Hudson Highlands, 79-81; and others. *Pos:* Art coordr, Community Resources Pool-South Orangetown Cent Sch, 62 & 63. *Teaching:* Instr ceramics, NY Art Workshop, New York, 34-47; head dept ceramics, Craft Students League, 35-81; instr ceramics, Rockland Ctr Arts, West Nyack, NY, 57-; instr continuing educ, Rockland Community Col, 75-80. *Awards:* Ceramic Stoneware Vase Award of Merit, Rockland Ctr Arts, 72. *Mem:* Artist Craftsmen NY (bd dirs, 68-70, 72, 75-76 & 78, first vpres, 75-76); Rockland Ctr Arts (bd dirs, 68-69 & 71-74, chmn bd, 71 & 72, emer bd mem); Worlds Craft Coun. *Mailing Add:* 8200 14th St St Petersburg FL 33702

LECHAY, JAMES
PAINTER
b New York, NY, July 5, 07. *Work:* Art Inst Chicago; Nat Collection Fine Arts, Smithsonian Inst; Des Moines Art Ctr; Pa Acad Fine Arts, Philadelphia; Mus Art, Univ Iowa; plus others. *Exhib:* Metrop Mus Art, New York; Art Inst Chicago; Pa Acad Fine Arts; Carnegie Inst, Pittsburgh; Toledo Mus Art; Denver Art Mus; Palace of the Legion of Honor, San Francisco; Walker Art Ctr, Minneapolis. *Teaching:* Instr art, Stanford Univ, summer 51; instr art, Skowhegan Sch Painting & Sculpture, summer 63; prof art, Univ Iowa, 45-75; vis prof, Chinese Univ of Hong Kong, 76. *Awards:* Childe Hassam Fund Purchase Award, Am Acad Arts & Lett, 74; Ranger Fund Purchase Prize, Nat Acad Design, 79; Palmer Mem Award, Nat Acad Design, 81; plus others. *Mem:* Nat Acad Design. *Dealer:* Kraushaar Galleries 724 Fifth Ave New York NY 10019. *Mailing Add:* Box 195 Wellfleet MA 02667

LECHTZIN, STANLEY
GOLDSMITH, EDUCATOR
b Detroit, Mich, June 9, 36. *Study:* Wayne State Univ, BFA; Cranbrook Acad Art, Bloomfield Hills, Mich, MFA. *Work:* Mus Am Crafts, New York; Detroit Inst Arts; Schmuckmuseum Pforzheim, Ger; Philadelphia Mus Art; Goldsmiths Hall, London. *Comn:* Silver mace, Temple Univ, 66; Longwood Col, 74; paten, 41st Int Eucharistic Cong, Philadelphia, 76. *Exhib:* one-man shows, Mus Contemp Crafts, New York, 65, Lee Nordness Galleries, NY, 69, Int Jewelry Exhib, Tokyo, Japan, 73, Rand Show, Johannesburg, SAfrica, 75 & Goldsmiths Hall, London, 75; Philadelphia: Three Centuries of Am Art, Philadelphia Mus Art, Pa, 76; plus others. *Teaching:* Prof metalsmithing, Tyler Sch Art, Temple Univ, 62-, chmn dept crafts, 65-79. *Awards:* Founders Soc Prize, Detroit Mus Art, 66; Louis Comfort Tiffany Found Award in Crafts, 67; Nat Endowment Arts Craftsmen's Grant, 76. *Bibliog:* Graham Hughes (auth), The Art of Jewelry, Viking, 72; Karl Schollmayer (auth), Neuer Schmuck, Ernst Wasmuth-Verlag, Ger, 74; C E Licka (auth), Stanley Lechtzin: Technic and the organic paradigm, Metalsmith, summer 82. *Mem:* Soc NAm Goldsmiths (mem bd dirs, 70-75); Am Crafts Coun. *Media:* Metal, Plastic. *Publ:* Auth, Electrofabrication of metal, Craft Horizons, 64; contribr, Metal Techniques for Craftsmen, 68; auth, Museum of Contemporary Crafts (brochure), 69; contribr, Contemporary Jewelry, 70. *Mailing Add:* Temple Univ Tyler Sch Art Beech & Penrose Ave Elkins Park PA 19126

LECKY, SUSAN
PAINTER
b Los Angeles, Calif, July 19, 40. *Study:* Univ Southern Calif, BFA; also European travel. *Work:* Los Angeles Co Mus; Bloomington Fed Savings & Loan, Bloomington, Pontiac & Streator Br. *Exhib:* Joslyn Mus, Omaha, 72; Winter Invitational, Norris Cult Arts Ctr, St Charles, Ill, 83; four-person exhib, Operaworks Ltd Gallery, Champaign, Ill, 83; one-person exhib, Millikin Univ, Decatur, Ill, 83; Ill Artists: Works on Paper, Champaign, Ill, 83; Ill State Fair Prof Art Exhib, Springfield, Ill, 83. *Pos:* Restorer, Univ Ill Libr, 73-; art critic, New Art Examr, 76-78. *Media:* Acrylic, Watercolor. *Dealer:* Neville-Sargent Gallery Evanston IL. *Mailing Add:* 306 S Orchard St Urbana IL 61801

LE CLAIR, CHARLES
PAINTER, EDUCATOR
b Columbia, Mo, May 23, 14. *Study:* Univ Wis, BS & MS, 35; Acad Ranson, Paris, 36; Columbia Univ, 40-41. *Work:* Beaver Col; Temple Univ; Chatham Col; Albright-Knox Art Gallery; Provincetown Art Asn & Mus. *Exhib:* Butler Inst Am Art, Youngstown, Ohio, 51, 56 & 71; Whitney Mus Am Art, New York, 51-56; Int Watercolor Exhib, Brooklyn Mus, 59; Nat Acad Design Ann, 60; Pa Acad Fine Arts, Philadelphia, 63 & 65. *Teaching:* Assoc prof painting, Chatham Col, 46-52, chmn dept art, 46-60, prof painting, 52-60; dean, Tyler Sch Art, Temple Univ, 60-74, prof painting, 60-81, chmn dept painting & sculpture, 79-81, prof emeritus, 81- *Awards:* Ten Awards, Assoc Artists Pittsburgh, 46-; Ford Found Fel Advan Educ, 52-53; Pennell Mem Award, Pa Acad Fine Arts, 65. *Media:* Oil, Watercolor. *Publ:* Coauth, Integration of the Arts, Harper, 54; coauth, Meeting student needs through the humanities, In: Current Issues in Higher Education, Asn Higher Educ, Washington, DC, 55; auth, A Salute to William Pitt (catalog), Chatham Col, 58; auth, Humanities, In: Principles of Evaluation and Measurement for Higher Education, Rochester Inst Technol, 61; auth, Education of the artist, Alumni Rev, Temple Univ, 1/62. *Mailing Add:* 2052 Lombard St Philadelphia PA 19146

LEDERMAN, SHEYA NEWMAN See Sheya

LEDERMAN, STEPHANIE BRODY
PAINTER, COLLAGE ARTIST
b New York, NY, July 30, 39. *Study:* Univ Mich Sch Archit & Design, 57-59; Finch Col, BS(design), 61; C W Post Ctr, Long Island Univ, MA(studio art), 75. *Work:* Univ Sydney, Australia; Alternative Mus & City Univ New York, New York; State Univ NY, Cortland; Newark Mus, NJ. *Comn:* two-part painting, comn by Herman Warsh, Santa Barbara, Calif, 82; edition of 100 small artworks, Franklin Furnace, New York, 83. *Exhib:* American Narrative Story Art 67-77, Contemp Arts Mus, Houston, 77-79; Great Am Foot, Mus Contemp Crafts, New York, 78-80; Artists Postcards II, Cooper-Hewitt Mus, New York, 78-80; Words & Images, Philadelphia Col Art, 79; Penthouse Aviary, Mus Mod Art, New York, 80; Salon Du Livre, Grand Palais, Paris, 83; Breaking the Bindings, Univ Wis, Madison, 83. *Pos:* Docent, Queens Mus, 82- *Teaching:* Instr & tutor art, Empire State Col, 83-; vis artist, Hunter Sch Visual Arts, Long Island Univ, 77- *Awards:* Creative Artists Serv Prog Grant, NY State Coun Arts, 76; Nat Endowment Arts--NY State Coun Arts Grant, 84. *Bibliog:* Grace Glueck (auth), Visual diaries, New York Times, 2/80; Carrie Rickey (auth), Glitter, Artforum, 11/80; Cathy Courtney (auth), American artists books, Art Monthly, London, 10/83. *Mem:* Independent Studios One, Long Island City, NY. *Media:* Acrylic, Pastel; Collage. *Publ:* Auth & illusr, Chocolate Cake, 79 & He Doesn't Walk Funny-He Wore Corrective Shoes, 79, pvt publ; auth & illusr, Romantic couplet (the hustle) (portfolio), Paris Rev, 79; auth & illusr, Spring Chicken, Artifacts at End of Decade, 81; auth & illusr, The adventuress tries fantasy, Whitewalls, 83. *Dealer:* Kathryn Markel Gallery 50 W 57th St New York NY 10019. *Mailing Add:* 10 Fourth Rd Great Neck NY 11021

LEDYARD, WALTER WILLIAM
SCULPTOR, PRINTMAKER
b Rockford, Ill, Mar 6, 15. *Study:* Rockford Col, with Marquis Reitzel; Univ Ill, AB, Col Med, MD; Univ SC; also with Gil Petroff. *Work:* SC State Art Collection; Columbia Mus Art, SC. *Exhib:* SC Artists Guild Ann, 62-71; SC Invitational, 69; one-man shows, Columbia Mus Art, SC, 65 & 73, Newberry Col, SC, 76, Sumter Mus Art, SC, 77 & Columbia Col, 79; and others. *Awards:* SC State Art Comn Purchase Prize, 69. *Bibliog:* Adger Brown (auth), His is a Friendly Art Form, 65 & Dottie Ashley (auth), Scalpels and Chisels, 80, The Columbia Record, SC; Mary Terry (auth), Dr Ledyard's Carved Out His Future, The State, Columbia, SC, 75. *Mem:* SC Artists Guild; Southern Graphics Council. *Media:* Marble, Alabaster. *Collection:* Etchings and lithographs from 17th century to contemporary and contemporary sculpture. *Mailing Add:* 3900 MacGregor Dr Columbia SC 29206

LEE, AMY FREEMAN
PAINTER, LECTURER
b San Antonio, Tex, Oct 3, 14. *Study:* St Mary's Hall, San Antonio, grad, 31; Univ Tex, Austin, 31-34; Incarnate Word Col, 34-42, Hon LittD, 65. *Work:* D D Feldman Collection, Univ Tex Mus, Austin; Smith Col Mus Fine Arts, Mass; Ft Worth Art Ctr, Tex; Norfolk Mus Arts & Sci, Va; Nat Saltonstall Collection, Boston; and others. *Comn:* Camellia Award Painting, Joskes of Texas, San Antonio, 71. *Exhib:* Black & White Exhib, Silvermine Guild Artists, Ctr Arts, New Canaan, Conn, 80; Nat Watercolor Soc, Laguna Beach Mus Art, Calif, 80-81; Nat Soc Painters Casein & Acrylic, New York, 81; 32nd Ann Tex Watercolor Soc, McNay Art Inst, San Antonio, 81; Nat Watercolor Soc, Brand Libr Art Galleries, Calif, 81; and others. *Pos:* Art critic, San Antonio Express, 39-42; art critic, KONO Radio Sta, San Antonio, 47-52. *Teaching:* Lectr, Trinity Univ, 54-57, San Antonio Art Inst, 55-57 & Our Lady of Lake Col, 69- *Awards:* Ann Local Artists Exhib Frost Purchase Prize, 75, Drought Award, 77, Tex Watercolor Soc; M J Kaplan Award, Nat Soc Painters in Casein & Acrylic, 78. *Bibliog:* She's no queen of the May, San Antonio Mag, 74; Reality is becoming, Today's Art, 1/75. *Mem:* Founding mem Tex Watercolor Soc; Nat Watercolor Soc; Nat Soc Painters in Casein; Int Soc Educ Through Art; SW Watercolor Soc. *Media:* Watercolor. *Publ:* Auth, The Desert is Blooming, Tex Philos Soc Proc, 71; auth, Mary Smith, Tom Brown & Dow Jones, Incarnate Word Col, San Antonio, 76; auth, The taste of art is bittersweet, San Antonio Mag, 77; auth, A heavenly view, Dallas Times Herald, 79. *Dealer:* L & L Gallery 1107 N Fourth St Longview TX 75601; Sol Del Rio Art Gallery 1020 Townsend Ave San Antonio TX 78209. *Mailing Add:* 127 Canterbury Hill San Antonio TX 78209

LEE, BRIANT HAMOR
HISTORIAN, EDUCATOR
b New Haven, Conn, May 6, 38. *Study:* Carnegie-Mellon Univ; Adelphi Univ, BA; Acad de Belle Arti, Rome, Cert di Frequenza; Univ Italiana per Stranieri-Perugia; Ind Univ, MA; NY Univ; Mich State Univ, PhD. *Comn:* Over 100 theatrical productions, Scenographer, (in collaboration with staging dir); 25 theatrical productions, staging dir & scenographer, 64- *Pos:* Design engineer, Kliegl Lighting, New York, 63-64. *Teaching:* Instr scenography, US Int Univ, San Diego, Calif, 62-63; asst prof scenography, Bradley Univ, Peoria, Ill, 67-68; assoc prof theatre, Bowling Green State Univ, Ohio, 68- *Mem:* Am Theatre Asn; Speech Commun Asn; Am Soc for Theatre Res; Ohio Theatre Alliance; Ohio Community Theatre Asn. *Media:* Watercolor, Ink. *Res:* Late 18th century European theatre architecture and theatrical staging. *Publ:* Auth, Pierre Patte, Late 18th century lighting innovator, Theatre Survey, 76; auth, To the novice scenographer, In: The OCTA Manual, ACT, Inc, 76; auth, The origins of the box set in the late 18th century, Theatre Survey, 78; auth, Creative dramatics and the very young, In: The Year of the Child, Bowling Green State Univ, 79; auth, Corruagted Scenery, Oracle Press, 82. *Mailing Add:* 336 S Church St Bowling Green OH 43402

LEE, CAROLINE D
DEALER, CURATOR
b Dallas, Tex, Nov 27, 34. *Study:* Stephens Col, 52-53; Univ Ariz, 53-55; San Antonio Art Inst, 68-70; Trinity Univ, with Robert Tiemann, 70-71; Univ Tex, San Antonio, with Kazaya Sakai, 78-79. *Collections Arranged:* Craft as Art in Texas, Laguna Gloria Art Mus, Austin, Tex, 75; The Earthbound Object, Lufkin Hist & Creative Arts Ctr, Tex, 81; Shrines-Altars, Tex Christian Univ, Ft Worth, 82-83; Texas Clay, Southwest Tex State Univ & Univ Tex, San Antonio, 83. *Pos:* Dir, Southwest Craft Ctr Gallery, San Antonio, 71-75; owner & dir, Objects Gallery, San Antonio, 80- *Teaching:* Hon instr art, Trinity Univ, Tex, 70-71. *Awards:* Award Excellence, Houston Designer-Craftsmen Exhib, 79; Second Prize Mixed Media, Tex Women Artists, Nat Orgn Women, 80. *Bibliog:* Ginger Wright (auth), New directions in clay, Ultra Mag, 7/82; Ruth Fawcett (auth), No objections, San Antonio Monthly, 7/82; Jan Tips (auth), Texas clay and a survey of Texas ceramics, Artspace, fall 83. *Mem:* Am Craft Coun; San Antonio Artist Alliance. *Specialty:* Painting, clay, paper and sculpture. *Publ:* Auth, Texas: The future climate for crafts, Tex Crafts, 79; auth, The new decade: The emergent shape, Tex Designer Craftsmen, spring 80. *Mailing Add:* 4010 Broadway San Antonio TX 78209

LEE, DORA FUGH
PAINTER, SCULPTOR
b Peking, China, Aug 16, 30; US citizen. *Study:* With Prince Pu Ju, Chao Meng-chu & Yen Shao-Hsiang, Peking, China; additional study with sculptor, Pietro Lazzari, Washington, DC. *Work:* China Inst, New York; Pearl Buck Found, Philadelphia, Pa; Smithsonian Inst; National Cathedral, Washington, DC; Univ Va. *Exhib:* Watercolor USA, Springfield, Mo, 75; one-woman show, Franz Bader Gallery, Washington, DC, 76; Mainstreams, Marietta Col, Ohio, 76; Md Acad of Arts, Easton, 77; Northern Va Fine Arts Asn Traveling Exhib, 77. *Teaching:* Private lessons in Chinese traditional painting & calligraphy, Bethesda, Md, 70-; Chinese calligraphy, George Washington Univ. *Awards:* Best of Show, 68, First Prize/Watercolor, 71 & 72, Montgomery Co Art Asn. *Mem:* Washington Watercolor Asn; Potomac Valley Watercolorists; Montgomery Co Art Asn; Northern Va Fine Arts Asn. *Media:* Mixed. *Dealer:* Franz Bader Gallery 2001 Eye St Washington DC 20037; Gallery Madison 90 1248 Madison Ave New York NY 14305. *Mailing Add:* 6305 Orchid Dr Bethesda MD 20817

LEE, ELEANOR GAY
PAINTER
b Atlanta, Ga. *Study:* Nat Acad Design Sch Fine Art. *Work:* Mus City New York; Mus Fine Art, Hickory, NC; Mus Fine Art, Greenville, SC; River Edge Mus, Can; John St Methodist Church, New York; and others. *Exhib:* Guild Hall, East Hampton, NY, 63; Burr Galleries, New York, 71; Nat Biennial Composers, Authors & Artists Am, 71; Catharine Lorillard Wolfe Art Club Open, 71; Governor's Mansion, Jackson, Miss, 81; and others. *Pos:* Dir one-man shows, Burr Galleries, 57-64; attendant, Thompson Gallery, New York, 66-74. *Awards:* First Prize, 71 & Second Prize, 79, Composers, Authors & Artists Am; 4th Prize, 7th Regiment Armory, Company K, 80; and others. *Mem:* Burr Artists (founding pres, 71); Catharine Lorillard Wolfe Art Club (pres, 50-53); Composers, Authors & Artists Am (nat pres, 79-81); Nat League Am Pen Women, New York Br; hon mem Gotham Painters; and others. *Media:* Oil, Pastel. *Mailing Add:* Nat Arts Club 15 Gramercy Park S New York NY 10003

LEE, GERALDINE See Hooks, Geri

LEE, JANIE C
DEALER
b Shreveport, La, Apr 22, 37. *Study:* Sarah Lawrence Col, BA, 59. *Mem:* Art Dealers Asn Am (mem bd dirs, 80-82). *Specialty:* Modern American and European art from 1950 through 1980's, specializing in drawings. *Mailing Add:* 2304 Bissonnet Houston TX 77005

LEE, KATHARINE C
CURATOR
b Detroit, Mich, Dec 12, 41. *Study:* Vassar Col, BA(art hist, magna cum laude), 63; Fulbright Scholar, 63-64; Harvard Univ, MA, 66. *Collections Arranged:* Prairie School Furniture: Wright, Elmslie, Maher, 72, Art Deco: Trends in Design, 73, Collection of Contemporary Art of Mid-America Club, Chicago, 76-78, Artists View the Law of the 20th Century (auth, catalog), 77, Renaissance Soc & Smart Gallery, Univ Chicago; Some Recent Art from Chicago (auth, catalog), Ackland Art Mus, Univ NC, 80. *Pos:* Asst cur, Toledo Mus Art, Ohio, 68-70; dir exhib, Renaissance Soc, Univ Chicago, 71-73, cur collections, Smart Gallery, 73-; cur, Ackland Art Mus, Univ NC, Chapel Hill, 79-82; asst dir, Art Inst Chicago, currently. *Teaching:* Mus course in hist mus & collection inst, Univ Chicago, 78. *Awards:* Ford Found Grant in Mus Curatorial Training Internship, 66-68. *Mailing Add:* 201 E Chestnut St Chicago IL 60611

LEE, MARGARET F
PAINTER
b South St Paul, Minn, May 19, 22. *Study:* Rochester Art Ctr, with Adolph Dehn, Arnold Blanch & Robert Birmelin, 60-74; John Pike Watercolor Sch, Woodstock, NY, 72; watercolor with Zoltan Szabo, 74; Japanese woodblock with Toshi Yoshida, 74; Univ Minn, BA(art), 75. *Work:* YMCA-YWCA Permanent Collection, Rochester, Minn. *Exhib:* One-man show, Augsburg Col, Minneapolis, 73; 17th & 18th Int, Galerie Int, New York, 73-74; Mainstreams USA, Marietta Col, Ohio, 74; American Painters in Paris, French Ministry & Paris City Coun, 75; Arts of Asia Gallery, Rochester,

Minn, 75-77; and others. *Teaching:* Lectr Japanese Sumi-e, Winona Art Ctr, Minn, 74; instr Japanese painting, Rochester Art Ctr, 74. *Awards:* First Place, Northern Lights 75, St Paul, 75; Award of Excellence, Arts Omnibus, 76, St Paul; Award, Midwest Watercolor Soc Exhib, Minn Mus of Art, St Paul, 77. *Mem:* Minn Artists Asn; Sumi-e Soc Am, New York; Fine Arts Soc Dakota Co, St Paul. *Media:* Acrylic, Sumi Ink. *Dealer:* Sky Gallery 950 S Robert St Paul MN 55118. *Mailing Add:* 145 E Eighth St Zumbrota MN 55992

LEE, NELDA S
DEALER
b Gorman, Tex, July 3, 41. *Study:* Tarleton State Col, AA, 61; N Tex State Univ, BFA, 63; Tex Tech Univ, Lubbock, grad study, 65 & San Miguel de Allende Art Inst, Mex, 65. *Work:* Delgado Mus of Art, New Orleans, La; El Paso Mus of Art, Tex. *Comn:* Portrait of late Sam Jones, Supt Rising Star Pub Sch, comn by Student Coun, 66; designed terrazo marble floors, Sweetwater High Sch, Tex, comn by Balfour Co, 67 & Student Ctr, Tarleton State Univ, Stephenville, Tex, comn by Student Coun, 68. *Exhib:* Artist of SE in Tex, Delgado Mus Art, New Orleans, La, 64; Tex Fine Arts Asn Travelling Exhib, 64-67; Int Designer/Craftsmen Exhib, El Paso Mus, Tex, 65; Tex Watercolor Soc Exhib, Elizabeth Ney Mus, San Antonio, Tex, 67. *Collections Arranged:* President Carter's Inaugural Reception Exhibition, The Capitol, Washington, DC, 77. *Pos:* Partner, Pandoras, 68-69 & owner-operator, Nelda Lee's Painting & Jewelry, Odessa, 69-; owner-operator, Nelda Lee's Painting & Jewelry, Odessa, 69-, Nelda Lee Inc, 74- *Teaching:* Chairperson art dept, Ector High Sch, Odessa, Tex, 63-68. *Awards:* First Place/Sculpture, Artist of the SE in Tex, Delgado Mus of Art, 64; First Place/Design, Int Designer/Craftsmen Exhib, 65; First Place/Mixed-Media, Tex Fine Arts Exhib, 65. *Bibliog:* Scheryl Vannoy (auth), Texas art dealer stages exhibition at Capitol, San Angelo Standard Times, 77; article, SW Art Mag, 80; Carrie Steenson (auth), A rare work of art, Business Mag, 81. *Mem:* Am Soc of Appraisers; Tex Asn Art Dealers (pres, 79-81); Int Soc Appraisers; Appraisers Asn Am. *Specialty:* Eighteenth--twentieth century English and American masters. *Publ:* Auth, History of Art in Odessa, Texas, Permian Basin Hist Ann, 69; co-auth, Painter of a vanishing America, SW Art, 74. *Mailing Add:* 2610 E 21st St PO Box 6385 Odessa TX 79762

LEE, RENSSELAER WRIGHT
HISTORIAN, EDUCATOR
b Philadelphia, Pa, June 15, 1898. *Study:* Princeton Univ, AB, 20, PhD, 26; Northwestern Univ, LHD, 71; Princeton Univ, LHD, 82. *Teaching:* Prof hist art, Northwestern Univ, Evanston, 31-40, Smith Col, 41-48 & Columbia Univ, 48-54; prof, Inst Fine Arts, NY Univ, 54-55; prof hist art, Princeton Univ, 55-66. *Mem:* Renaissance Soc Am (pres, 77-78); Col Art Asn Am (pres, 44-46); Am Acad Rome (pres, 70-72). *Res:* Theory of art, especially in its relation to literature; influence of Italian Renaissance literature on painting. *Publ:* Auth, An English Gothic Embroidery in the Vatican, 30; auth, Ut Pictura Poesis: the Humanistic Theory of Painting, 40 & 67, Ital transl, 74; auth, Poetry into Painting: Tasso and Art, 70; auth, Names on Trees: Ariosto Into Art, Princeton Univ Press, 76. *Mailing Add:* 120 Mercer St Princeton NJ 08540

LEE, ROBERT J
PAINTER, EDUCATOR
b Oakland, Calif, Dec 26, 21. *Study:* Acad Art, San Francisco, with Richard Stephens, Hamilton Wolf & Richard Guy Walton. *Work:* US Air Force Hist Soc; Mt Holyoke Mus, Mass; Springfield Mus Fine Arts, Mass; Evanston Mus, Ill; Columbia Mus Art, SC. *Exhib:* Calif Palace Legion of Honor, San Francisco, 46; Art Inst Chicago, 47-49; Butler Inst Am Arts, Youngstown, Ohio; Conn Acad Fine Arts, Hartford; Smithsonian Inst, Washington, DC, 71; 200 Yrs Am Illus, New York Hist Soc, 77; 25 one-man shows in galleries. *Teaching:* Instr illus, Pratt Inst, 55-57; assoc prof painting & design, Marymount Col (NY), 62- *Awards:* First Prize Gold Medal of Honor, Allied Artists, 60; Award of Excellence, Soc Illusr, 67; First Prize Painting, Putnam Arts Coun, 81. *Publ:* Illusr, Old Devil Wind, 70 & Exploring Music, 71, Holt Rinehart & Winston; illusr ltd ed, Our Town, 76; illusr, A Fable, Franklin Press, 76; Poets on Pain and Sensation, A Colish Press, 80. *Dealer:* Charles A Pace 10202 Piping Rock Houston TX 77042. *Mailing Add:* c/o Marymount Col Dept Art Tarrytown NY 10591

LEE, ROGER
EDUCATOR, CURATOR
b Vancouver, BC, Dec 1, 42. *Study:* Inst Allende, San Miguel Allende, Mex, 63; Univ BC, BA, 64, MA(fel), 66; Alliance Francaise, 74; also with George Riviere, Paris, 73-74. *Collections Arranged:* Line in Chinese and Japanese Art, Norman Mackenzie Art Gallery, Univ Regina; Sculpture in Movement, Evelyn Roth; plus others. *Pos:* Cur, Norman Mackenzie Art Gallery, formerly. *Teaching:* Asst prof art hist, Univ Regina, 66- *Awards:* Grant for Exhib, Sask Arts Bd, 71. *Mem:* Univ Art Asn Can. *Res:* Contemporary international art trends; conceptual art. *Publ:* Auth, Jack Sures: Organic pottery, Arts Can, 68; auth, Hans Hofmann acquisition, 69 & China and Japan: A comparison, 70, Norman Mackenzie Art Gallery News Lett. *Mailing Add:* Dept Visual Arts Univ Regina Regina SK S4S 0A2 Canada

LEE, RUSSELL
PHOTOGRAPHER, EDUCATOR
b Ottawa, Ill, July 21, 03. *Study:* Lehigh Univ, ChE, 25; Calif Sch Fine Arts; Art Students League; study with John Sloan. *Work:* Yale Univ Art Gallery; Libr Cong & Nat Arch, Washington, DC; Univ Ariz Ctr Creative Photog, Tucson; Boston Mus Fine Arts. *Exhib:* Family of Man, 55, The Bitter Years, 62, Mus Mod Art, New York; Russell Lee Retrospective, Univ Tex, Austin, 65, Witte Mem Mus, San Antonio, 65 & Smithsonian Inst, 66; Just Before the

War, Newport Harbor Art Mus, Newport Beach, Calif & Libr of Cong, Washington, DC, 68; Salford 80, Salford, Eng, 80; The American Image, Nat Archives, 80. *Teaching:* Dir & mem staff, Univ Mo Photog Workshop, 49-76; lectr photog, Univ Tex, Austin, 65-73. *Bibliog:* Roy Stryker & Nancy Wood (coauths), In This Proud Land, New York Graphic Soc, 73; Hank O'Neal (auth), A Vision Shared, St Press, 76; Jack Hurley (auth), Russell Lee--Photographer, Morgan & Morgan, 78. *Media:* Black and white silver prints. *Publ:* Illusr, Image of Italy, Tex Quart, Univ Tex, 61. *Dealer:* Witkin Gallery 41 E 57th St New York NY 10022. *Mailing Add:* 3110 West Ave Austin TX 78705

LEE, SHERMAN EMERY
MUSEUM DIRECTOR
b Seattle, Wash, Apr 19, 18. *Study:* Am Univ, BA & MA; Case Western Reserve Univ, PhD. *Pos:* Cur Far Eastern art, Detroit Inst Art, 41-46; with dept arts & monuments div, Civil Info & Educ Sect, Gen Hq, Supreme Comdr, Allied Powers, Tokyo, 46-68; asst dir to assoc dir, Seattle Mus Art, 48-52; cur Oriental art, Cleveland Mus Art, 52-, asst dir, 57, assoc dir, 58, dir, 58-83; consult comt, Artibus Asiae. *Teaching:* Lectr art hist, Univ Wash, 48-52; lectr art hist, Case Western Reserve Univ, 58, prof art, 62-; adj prof, Univ NC, Chapel Hill, currently. *Awards:* Legion of Honor; Order of the North Star; Order of the Sacred Treasure, Third Class. *Mem:* Am Asn Mus; Asn Art Mus Dirs (past pres); Am Acad Arts & Sci; Asia Soc, NY (trustee). *Publ:* Auth, Japanese Decorative Style, 61; auth, History of Far Eastern Art, 64; co-auth, Chinese Art Under the Mongols, 68; auth, Reflections of Reality in Japanese Art, 83; auth, Past and Present: East and West, 83; and others. *Mailing Add:* 102 Dixie Dr Chapel Hill NC 27514

LEEBER, SHARON CORGAN
SCULPTOR
b St Johns, Mich, Oct 1, 40. *Study:* Univ Wyo; Cent Mich Univ; Nat Open Univ, Washington, DC; Trinity Univ. *Work:* Las Cumbres, Acapulco, Mex; Univ Tex, Dallas, Tex. *Comn:* Univ Tex, Arlington, 76; Arlington City Hall, Tex, 76; large welded male, Incarnate Word Col, San Antonio, Tex, 77. *Exhib:* Tex Fine Arts Nat, Austin, 69; one-man retrospective show, Elizabet Ney Mus, Austin, 71; Tex Sculpture & Painting, Dallas, 71; Dallas Art, City Hall, Dallas, Tex, 78; Big Name Artists Show, Dallas, 78 & 79. *Teaching:* Instr photog, El Centro Col, Tex, 72-82. *Awards:* Purchase Awards, Shreveport Mus, 69 & Dallas Mus Fine Arts, 78; Purchase Award, Dallas Mus Fine Arts, 78. *Bibliog:* J Kutner (auth), article, Art News, 4/77; Thelma Neuman (auth), The Mirror Book, 78; L Haacke (auth), Art is more comfortable, Dallas Times Herald, 3/30/78. *Mem:* Nat Sculptor's Asn; Artists Equity Asn (secy, Dallas Chap, 71-72); Engrs, Artists & Technologists; Tex Fine Arts Asn; Tex Soc Sculptors. *Media:* Welded Steel, Glass. *Dealer:* Contemporary Gallery 2800 Routh St The Quadrangle Dallas TX 75201. *Mailing Add:* 6410 Dykes Way Dallas TX 75230

LEECH, MERLE EUGENE
SCULPTOR, PRINTMAKER
Study: Kans State Col, BFA & MA; NY Univ; Pratt Inst. *Work:* Smithsonian Inst; Cooper Hewitt Mus, New York; New York Pub Libr Collection. *Exhib:* Twelfth Ann Nat Exhib Prints & Drawings, Oklahoma City, 70; 30 Yrs of Am Printmaking, Brooklyn Mus, NY; World Print Competition, San Francisco Mus Art, Calif; Soc Am Graphic Artist Traveling Exhib; NDak Nat Print & Drawing Exhib. *Teaching:* Prof printing, Sch Visual Arts, 70- *Awards:* Outstanding Printing Award, Metrop Printing Indust, New York, 74; Purchase Award, Soc Am Graphic Artist. *Dealer:* Peter Rose Gallery 200 E 58th St New York NY 10022. *Mailing Add:* Sch Visual Arts New York NY 10010

LEEDS, ANNETTE
PAINTER
b Boston, Mass. *Study:* Mass Col Art, grad; Art Students League; Brooklyn Mus, with Moses Soyer; also with Paul Puzinas & Howard Boesendahl. *Exhib:* Metrop Mus of Art, New York, 77; Union Carbide, 77; Cork & Arsenal Galleries, 78; Hansen Gallery, 79; Gov Mansion, Miss, 80; Queens Mus, St John's Univ, 81; plus others. *Teaching:* Pvt instr, 68- *Awards:* First Prizes, Assoc Artists, 77 & Artists Inc, 79; Second Prize, Nat Arts Club, 83. *Mem:* Catharine Lorillard Wolfe Art Club; Burr Artists; Nichibei Fukinkai; Alliance Queens Artists; Oi-Sumi-e Club. *Media:* Oil, Watercolor. *Mailing Add:* 116-17 Union Turnpike Forest Hills NY 11375

LEEPA, ALLEN
PAINTER, EDUCATOR
b New York, NY, Jan 9, 19. *Study:* Am Art Sch New York, scholar; Art Students League; New Bauhaus, Chicago, scholar; Columbia Univ, BS, MA & EdD(scholar, dean's fel); Sorbonne & Grande Chaumiere, Paris. *Work:* South Bend Mus Art, Ind; Royal Acad, Scotland; Grand Rapids Mus, Mich. *Exhib:* Mus Mod Art, New York, 53; Sao Paulo Biennale, Brazil, 63; one-man show, Galerie La Cour d'Ingres, Paris, 63; Mus Art Mod, Paris, 64 & 65; Retrospective, Hofstra Univ, 65; and many others. *Teaching:* Instr art, Hull Sch, Chicago, 37-38; instr art, Brooklyn Art Ctr, 39-41; instr art, Brooklyn Mus & Metrop Mus Art, 40-41; prof art, Mich State Univ, 45- *Awards:* Childe Hassam Painting Award, Am Acad Arts & Lett, 69; Ford Found Grant, 70; Statewide Mural Competition, Mich, 80; and others. *Bibliog:* Michael Seuphor (auth), Abstract Painting, 62 & Dictionary of Abstract Art, 63, Abrams. *Mem:* Am Asn Univ Prof; Mich Acad Arts, Sci & Lett. *Media:* Acrylic on Canvas. *Publ:* Auth, The Challenge of Modern Art, Barnes, 49 & 61; contrib, articles in Humanities in Contemp Life, 60, New Art, 66, Minimal Art, 68 & New Ideas in Art Educ, 73; auth, Abraham Rattner, Abrams, 74; and others. *Dealer:* Forsythe Galleries 201 Nickels Ann Arbor MI 48108. *Mailing Add:* 540 E South St Mason MI 48854

LEEPER, DORIS MARIE
PAINTER, SCULPTOR
b Charlotte, NC, Apr 4, 29. *Study:* Duke Univ, BA, 51. *Work:* Nat Mus Am Art, Washington, DC; Miss Mus Art, Jackson, Miss; Columbus Mus Art, Ohio; 180 Beacon Collection, Boston, Mass; Wadsworth Atheneum, Hartford, Conn. *Comn:* Fiberglass sculpture, Alpert Investment for Forum 303, Arlington, Tex, 71; 160 modular unit wall sculpture, Hunter Mus Art, Chattanooga, Tenn, 73-75; enamel painting, Int Bus Machines, Atlanta, Ga, 76; concrete sculpture, Regional Serv Ctr, Jacksonville, Fla, 78; stainless steel wall sculpture, Orlando Int Airport, Fla, 83. *Exhib:* Contemporary Women Artists, Nat Arts Club, New York, 70; Hunter Mus Art, Chattanooga, 75 & 79; one-person shows, High Mus Art, Atlanta, 75, Ringling Mus Art, Sarasota, Fla, 76 & Miss Mus Art, Jackson, 79; Southeastern Ctr Contemp Art, Winston-Salem, NC, 77; Norton Gallery Art, West Palm Beach, Fla, 79. *Awards:* Nat Endowment Arts Grant, 72; Artist-in-Residence Fel, Rockefeller Found, 77; Fine Arts Coun Fla Grant, 77. *Bibliog:* Edith Neely (auth), The world of Doris Leeper, Jacksonville Fine Arts Illus, 69; An interview with Doris Leeper, Enjoy, 73; The Floridian, St Petersburg Times, 76. *Media:* Oil; Mixed. *Dealer:* Art Sources Inc 1253 Southshore Dr Orange Park FL 32073. *Mailing Add:* PO Box 2093 New Smyrna Beach FL 32069

LEEPER, JOHN P
PAINTER
b Dandridge, Tenn, Apr 23, 09. *Study:* Otis Art Inst. *Work:* IBM Collection; Long Beach Mus; Calif State Fair Collection; Ahmanson Collection. *Comn:* Mural, Ariz State Univ. *Exhib:* Santa Barbara Mus Art; Long Beach Mus Art; Southern Calif 100, Laguna Beach Mus of Art, 77; one-man shows, Adele Bednarz Galleries, 66, 69, 71, 73 & 75 & Challis Galleries, 78; two-man show, Challis Galleries, 81; plus others. *Awards:* Los Angeles Co Mus, 56 & 58; Calif State Fair Purchase Prize, 64; Los Angeles Festival Arts Purchase Prize, 64. *Media:* Acrylic. *Dealer:* Challis Galleries 1390 S Coast Hwy Laguna Beach CA 92652. *Mailing Add:* 1721 Crisler Way Los Angeles CA 90069

LEEPER, JOHN PALMER
MUSEUM DIRECTOR
b Denison, Tex, Feb 4, 21. *Study:* Southern Methodist Univ, BS, 42; Harvard Univ, MA. *Pos:* Keeper, W A Clark Collection, Corcoran Gallery Art, 48-49, asst dir, 49-50; dir, Pasadena Art Mus, 50-53; dir, McNay Art Inst, 54- *Teaching:* Instr art hist, Dexter Sch, Boston, 46, Univ Southern Calif, 51, Pasadena Sch Fine Arts, 52 & Trinity Univ, 56-57. *Mem:* Am Asn Mus; Asn Art Mus Dirs. *Publ:* Auth, Everett Spruce, 59; auth, Otis Dozier, 60; ed, The autobiography of Jose Clemente Orozco, 62; auth, A Caribbean sketchbook by Jules Pascin, 64. *Mailing Add:* 6000 N New Braunfels San Antonio TX 78209

LEE-SISSOM, E (EVELYN JANELLE SISSOM)
PAINTER
b Oakland, Calif, Feb 11, 34. *Study:* Art Instruction, Inc; Watkins Inst; Univ Tenn. *Work:* Parthenon Galleries & Mus, Tenn State Mus & Opryland Hotel's Collection Tenn Art, Nashville; Sunkist Corp Off, Atlanta, Ga; Putnam Libr, Cookeville, Tenn. *Comn:* Painting, Cookeville General Hospital, Tenn, 81. *Exhib:* 26th Nat Soc Painters Casein & Acrylic, Am Acad & Inst Arts & Letters, NY, 79; 22nd Traveling, Nat Soc Painters Casein & Acrylic, 79-80; 2nd Ann Open, Salmagundi Club, New York, 79; Grand Nat, Am Artists Prof League, New York, 79 & 80; one-woman show, Parthenon Galleries, Nashville, Tenn, 79 & 81. *Awards:* Third Award, 17th Tenn All-State, 77; Grand Award, 13th Central S, 78; Lyzon Art Gallery, 16th Central South, 81. *Mem:* Assoc mem Nat Soc Painters Casein & Acrylic; Am Artists Prof League; Tenn Art League; Cumberland Arts Soc Cookeville Tenn (bd dirs, 75-80). *Media:* Acrylics. *Publ:* Contribr, Tennessee Conservationist, Tenn Dept Conserv, 78; contribr, Int Soc Artists Communicator, Billboard Publ, 81; illusr cover, Key: Nashville, Silversmith, 82; contribr, Nashville!, Advantage Publ, 83. *Dealer:* Pickering Galleries Inc 1810 Hayes St Nashville TN 37203. *Mailing Add:* Tenn Tech Univ Box 5005 Cookeville TN 38501

LEE-SMITH, HUGHIE
PAINTER, INSTRUCTOR
b Eustis, Fla, Sept 20, 15. *Study:* Art Sch Detroit Soc Arts & Crafts, Scholastic Mag Scholar; Cleveland Inst Art, cert, 38; Wayne State Univ, BS(art educ), 53; John Huntington Polytechnic Inst. *Work:* Detroit Inst Arts, Mich; Parrish Mus, Southampton, NY; Lagos Mus, Nigeria; USN Art Ctr, Washington, DC; Univ Mich, Ann Arbor; and many others. *Exhib:* Detroit Inst Arts Regional, 48-57; Nat Acad Design Nat, New York, 57-72; Boston Mus Nat, 70; An American Dream World: Romantic Realism 1930-1955, Whitney Mus, 75; Princeton Univ Mus, 75; and others. *Teaching:* Instr painting, Grosse Pointe War Mem, Mich, 56-66 & Vt Acad, summer 68; instr drawing & painting, Princeton Country Day Sch, NJ, 63-65; artist in residence, Howard Univ, 69-71; instr, Art Students League, 72- *Awards:* Allied Artists Am Prize, 58; Clarke Prize, Nat Acad Design, 58; Binney & Smith Award, Audubon Artists, 83. *Bibliog:* The metaphysical world of Hughie Lee-Smith, Am Artist, 10/78; article, Link, Cleveland Inst Art, 81; Art of Hughie Lee-Smith and Jacob Lawrence, Pub TV, 82. *Mem:* Nat Acad Design; Artists Equity Asn (mem bd dir, 82-); Audubon Artists; Artists Fel (mem trustee bd, 82-). *Media:* Multimedia. *Dealer:* Summit Gallery Ltd 101 West 57th St Suite 2D New York NY 10019. *Mailing Add:* 52-16 Garden View Terr Hightstown NJ 08520

LEET, RICHARD EUGENE
MUSEUM DIRECTOR, PAINTER
b Waterloo, Iowa, Sept 11, 36. *Study:* Univ Northern Iowa, BA, 58, MA, 65, with Ansei, Uchima, Ted Egri, Paul R Smith & John Page; Univ Iowa, 61-64,

with Stuart Edie & Robert Knipschild. *Work:* Mus Art, El Paso; Charles H MacNider Mus, Mason City, Iowa; Waterloo Munic Galleries, Iowa; Des Moines Art Ctr; Sioux City Art Ctr, Iowa. *Exhib:* Ann Iowa Artists Exhib, Des Moines Art Ctr, 58-80; Ann Midyear Show, Butler Inst Am Art, Youngstown, Ohio, 69, 75 & 77; Midwest Biennial, Joslyn Art Mus, Omaha, 72, 74 & 76; Spiva Art Ctr, Joplin, Mo, 77; Tweed Mus Art, Minn, 80; John Nelson Bergstrom Art Ctr, Neenah, Wis, 81; Pillsbury Corp, American Art: Challenge of the Land, Minn, 81; and others. *Pos:* Mus dir & founding dir, C H MacNider Mus, 65- *Teaching:* Instr art, Oelwein Community Schs, Iowa, 58-65; instr painting & drawing, C H MacNider Mus, Mason City, Iowa, 65- *Awards:* Purchase Award, Mus Art, El Paso, 71; Wallace Agr Bldg Purchase Award, State Iowa, 77; Esther & Edith C Younker Painting Award, Iowa Artist's Show, Des Moines Art Ctr, 78. *Bibliog:* Nick Baldwin (auth), Visual arts, Des Moines Register, 8/24/69, 2/17/74 & 3/28/76; article in Iowan Mag, summer 74; and others. *Mem:* Am Asn Mus (coun, 83-); Midwest Mus Conf; Iowa Arts Coun (mem coun, 70-76); Iowa Mus Asn (pres 78-80). *Media:* Watercolor, Oil. *Publ:* Auth, Monthly column, Mason City Globe Gazette, 68- *Mailing Add:* 1149 Manor Dr Mason City IA 50401

LEETE, WILLIAM WHITE
PAINTER
b Portsmouth, Ohio, June 12, 29. *Study:* Yale Univ, BA, 51, BFA, 55 & MFA, 57. *Work:* De Cordova Mus, Lincoln, Mass; Cleveland Mus, Ohio; Worcester Mus, Mass; Univ Mass. *Exhib:* New Eng Contemp Artists, Boston, 63 & 65; Silvermine Guild, Conn, 66; Art in Embassies, Inst Contemp Arts, Boston, 66; Structured Art, De Cordova Mus, 69; Young New England Painters, John & Mabel Ringling North Mus, Fla; Portland Mus & Currier Gallery, Manchester, 69. *Teaching:* Assoc prof art, Univ RI, 57-74, prof, 74- *Media:* Acrylic. *Dealer:* Lenore Grey 15 Meeting St Providence RI 02903; Ward-Nasse Gallery 178 Prince St New York NY 10013. *Mailing Add:* Univ RI Dept Art Kingston RI 02881

LEFCOURT, IRWIN
DEALER
b New York, NY, Jan 15, 10. *Study:* Nat Acad of Design, New York; Art Students League. *Pos:* Asst cur graphic art div, Smithsonian Inst, Washington, DC, 39-41; owner & dir, Art Fair Gallery, Larchmont, 57- *Mem:* Appraisers Asn of Am. *Specialty:* Modern and old master graphics; Japanese prints; Fin de Siecle posters. *Mailing Add:* 3 Washington Sq Larchmont NY 10538

LEFEBRE, JOHN
DEALER
b Berlin, Ger; US citizen. *Study:* Univ Berlin, with Deri. *Pos:* Dir, Lefebre Gallery. *Specialty:* Contemporary European artists. *Mailing Add:* 47 E 77th St New York NY 10021

LEFEBVRE D'ARGENCE, RENE-YVON
MUSEUM DIRECTOR, WRITER
b Plouescat, France, Aug 21, 28. *Study:* Col St Aspais, Fountainebleau; Lycee Albert Sarraut, Hanoi; Ecole Libre des Sci Polit; Sorbonne; Pembroke Col; Brevete de Ecol Nat Langues Orientales Vivantes, Licencie es Lettres. *Collections Arranged:* Avery Brundage Collection, 63-; Chang Dai-Chien (with catalog), 72; Hans Popper Collection (with catalog), 73; Exhib Archaeol Finds People's Repub China, 75; 5,000 Years of Korean Art (ed & coauth, catalog), 79; Treasures from the Shanghai Museum, 6,000 Years of Chinese Art (ed, catalog), 83. *Pos:* Cur, Musee Cernuschi, Paris, 53; mem, Ecole Francaise d'Extreme-Orient, 54; cur, Blanchard de la Brosse Mus, Saigon & Louis Finot Mus, Hanoi, 54-58; Quai d'Orsay grant, Taiwan, 59; cur, Asiatic Collections, M H De Young Mem Mus, San Francisco, 64; dir, Avery Brundage Collection, 65-68; dir & chief cur, Asian Art Mus San Francisco, 69-; bd mem, Asian Art Found; bd mem, Inst Sino-Am Studies; pres, Fr-Am Bilingual Sch; vpres, Chinese-Am Bilingual Sch, 81- *Teaching:* Prof art hist, Univ Calif, Berkeley, 62-65. *Awards:* Chevalier de l'ordre National de Merite, France, 70; Order Cult Merit, Korea, 80; Chavalier de la Legion d'Honneur, France, 83. *Publ:* Auth, Avery Brundage Collection, Chinese, Korean & Japanese Sculpture, 74; auth, Bronze Vessels of Ancient China in the Avery Brundage Collection, 77; ed & coauth, Museum & University Collections of Asian Art in the San Francisco Bay Area, 77; and others. *Mailing Add:* Asian Art Mus San Francisco Golden Gate Park San Francisco CA 94118

LE FEVRE, RICHARD JOHN
PAINTER, DESIGNER
b Rochester, NY, Feb 11, 31. *Study:* Rochester Inst Technol, BS, 55, MFA, 67. *Work:* State of Tenn, Nashville; Fall Creek Falls State Park, Tenn; E Tenn State Univ; Univ Tenn, Knoxville; Nat Bank NC, Charlotte. *Comn:* Oil, St Stephen's Church, Rochester, 60; acrylic on Plexiglas, Church of Epiphany, Rochester, 65; polymer, Marine Midland Bank, Rochester, 65; acrylic on Plexiglas, Capital Cadillac Corp, Atlanta, Ga, 70; acrylic on Plexiglas altarpiece, Tyson Episcopal Ctr, Knoxville, Tenn, 71. *Exhib:* Appalachian Corridors Exhib 1, Va, 68; Experiments in Art and Technology, High Mus, Atlanta, 69; Midsouth Competition, Parthenon Mus, Nashville, 70; Art USA 2, Univ Northern Ill, 71; Tenn Arts Comn, Dulin Gallery, Knoxville, 72. *Pos:* Designer, Todd Co, Rochester, 54-55; designer, S M Crossett, Rochester, 55-58; pres, Le Fevre Studios, Rochester, 58-65. *Teaching:* Dir arts & graphic arts, Rochester Inst Technol, 65-67; asst prof design & area coord, Univ Tenn, Knoxville, 67- *Awards:* Purchase Award, Carroll Reece Mus, 71; Purchase Award, Mint Mus, 71; First, Second & Third Prizes, Graphic Art Show, Knoxville, 79; and over 50 awards in design. *Media:* Acrylic, Watercolor. *Dealer:* The Class Act PO Box 281 Seymour TN 37865. *Mailing Add:* Rte 1 Lefevre/Heard Lane Seymour TN 37865

LEFF, JULIETTE
PAINTER, EDUCATOR
b New York, NY, Mar 20, 39. *Study:* City Col New York, BA(art, honors), 62; Hunter Col, with Rothko, Tony Smith & Eugene Goossen, MA, 76; Brooklyn Mus, NY, Max Beckmann Painting Fel; Pratt Graphic Ctr, Lowengrund Scholar. *Work:* Chase Manhattan Bank Collection, New York; US Info Agency Print Collection; Aubrey Cartwright Gallery, Cathedral Mus of Religious Art; also pvt collections. *Exhib:* Butler Inst of Am Art, Youngstown, Ohio, 70; two-person show, NY Univ, 71; Year of the Woman: Reprise, Bronx Mus of the Arts, NY, 76; What is Feminist Art? Writings of 200 Women Artists, Women's Bldg, Los Angeles, Calif, 77; Drawing Defined, Nat Arts Club, 80; Int Festival Women Artists, Copenhagen, Denmark, 80; and others. *Pos:* Art educ coordr, Bronx Mus Arts, 76-77. *Awards:* Nat Grant Painting, Louis Comfort Tiffany Found, 66-67; and many others. *Mem:* Col Art Asn; Women's Caucus Art. *Media:* Multimedia. *Mailing Add:* 98 Riverside Dr New York NY 10024

LEFF, RITA
PRINTMAKER, PAINTER
b New York, NY. *Study:* Art Students League; Brooklyn Mus; Parsons Sch Design; also with Abraham Rattner, Louis Shanker, Adja Yunkers, Worden Day & Louis Calapai. *Work:* Metrop Mus Art, New York; Libr Cong, Washington, DC; Brooklyn Mus; Pa Acad, Philadelphia; Dallas Mus. *Exhib:* Libr Cong Print Ann; Pa Acad Design Print & Watercolor Ann; one-man shows, Esterhazy Gallery, Palm Beach, 71, Gallery Cassell, Palm Beach, 73 & Lighthouse Gallery, Tequesta, Fla, 75; and others. *Awards:* Medals of Honor, Nat Asn Women Artists, 64, 66, 68 & 69; Grand Prix, Salon Int De Femme, Cannes, France, 69; First Prize Norton Gallery, Palm Beach, 71 & 72. *Mem:* Soc Am Graphic Artists (coun mem); Audubon Artists; Nat Asn Women Artists; Boston Printmakers. *Media:* Oil, Watercolor; Collage. *Mailing Add:* 1707 Consulate Pl West Palm Beach FL 33409

LEFRANC, MARGARET (MARGARET LEFRANC SCHOONOVER)
PAINTER, ILLUSTRATOR
b New York, NY. *Study:* Art Students League, NY; Kunstschule des Westerns, Berlin, Ger; Acad Grande Chaumiere, Paris, France; Acad Russe Paris; study with Andre l'Hote, Charles Bissiere, Antoine Bourdelle & Richard Merrick. *Work:* Hall of Fame, Oklahoma City; Univ Okla Press, Norman; Lowe Gallery, Univ Miami, Fla. *Exhib:* Pa Acad Fine Arts, Philadelphia, 36; New York World's Fair Fine Arts Exhib, 39; solo shows, Okla Art Ctr, 50 & Meridith Hunter Gallery, 81; Southwestern Ann, Tulsa, 52; Ann Exhib NMex Artists, Mus NMex, 56; Lowe Gallery Ann, Univ Miami, Fla, 62; and others. *Pos:* Founder & dir, Guild Art Gallery, New York, 35-37; designer, colorist & stylist, Gilman Fabrics, Inc, New York, 38-42; liaison secy to cur, Cooper Union Mus, New York, 43-45. *Teaching:* Metrop Mus & Art Ctr, Miami, 83. *Awards:* Illustration Award, 50 Best Bks of Yr, Libr Cong, Washington, DC, 48. *Mem:* Artists Equity Asn (mem bd dirs, 60-76, pres, 61-63 & 65-67); Fla Artists Group. *Media:* Oil, Watercolor; Line, Wash. *Res:* Pueblo pottery design for synoptic series of San Ildefonso pottery. *Publ:* Illusr, Maria, the Potter of San Ildefonso, Univ Okla Press, 48; illusr, Indians on Horseback, T Y Crowell, 48; illusr, Indians of the Four Corners, T Y Crowell, 52; ed, Songs of the Tewa, Sunstone Press, 76; illusr, Dance Around the Sun, T Y Crowell, 77. *Mailing Add:* 627 Camino de la Luz Santa Fe NM 87501

LEHMAN, ARNOLD L
MUSEUM DIRECTOR, HISTORIAN
b New York, NY, July 18, 44. *Study:* Johns Hopkins Univ, BA, 65, MA, 66; Yale Univ, MA, 68, PhD, 73. *Collections Arranged:* Archit of World Fairs (auth, catalog), Dallas Mus Fine Arts, Tex, 72; Boom or Bust, Am Painting from World War I through 1939, 74; Art Deco, 74; Judaica from Am Collections, 75; The Vanderbilts: Collectors, 75; Am Magic Realists (auth, catalog), 76; World of Haitian Printing, (auth, catalog), 77; 50 Years of Cuban Painting, 77. *Pos:* Chester Dale Fel, Metrop Mus Art, New York, 69-70; dir, Urban Improvements Prog, New York, 70-73; dir, Parks Coun, New York, 73-74; dir, Metrop Mus & Art Ctr, Miami, Fla, 74-79; dir, Baltimore Mus Art, Md, 79- *Teaching:* Lectr art hist, Cooper Union Sch Art & Archit, New York, 69-71; lectr art hist, Hunter Col, City Univ New York, 71-72. *Mem:* Soc Archit Historians; Col Art Asn; Am Asn Mus Dirs. *Res:* American architecture and urban planning; American painting, 20th century; late 19th century French painting. *Mailing Add:* Baltimore Mus Art Art Museum Dr Baltimore MD 21218

LEHMAN, IRVING
PAINTER, SCULPTOR
b Jan 1, 1900. *Study:* Cooper Union, 20-24; Nat Acad, 25-30. *Work:* St Edmund's Hall, Oxford Univ; Ein Harod, Israel; Nat Mus Bezalel, Israel; John H Vanderpoel Mem Collection, Chicago; Mus Art Populaire Juif, Paris; and others. *Exhib:* Albany Inst Hist & Art; Brooklyn Mus; Charleston Art Gallery; Art Inst Chicago; Cordy Gallery, New York, 77; one-man shows, Columbia Mus Art, SC & Philadelphia Art Alliance, Pa, and many others. *Teaching:* Instr, Brooklyn Col Adult Educ & New York Bd Educ, formerly; pvt instr, currently. *Awards:* Am Soc Contemp Artists 44th Ann Distinctive Merit Award, 61; Lafayette Nat Bank Award, Am Soc Contemp Artists 47th Ann, 64; Priscilla Ward Sculpture & Pincu Mem Awards, 78; plus others. *Bibliog:* Articles in Am Abstr Art, 36-66; articles in Univ Syracuse Libr Mss, Art News & Art Digest; articles in House & Garden Decorating Guide, fall-winter, 68-69; plus others. *Mem:* Am Abstr Artists; Am Soc Contemp Artists. *Mailing Add:* RD Box 122 East Chatham NY 12060

LEHMAN, LOUISE BRASELL
PAINTER
b Orwood, Miss, Oct 15, 1897. *Study:* Miss State Col Women; George Washington Univ; Corcoran Sch Art; Teachers Col, Columbia Univ, BS. *Work:* Nat Bank of Com; Montgomery Mus Fine Arts; Brooks Mem Art Gallery. *Exhib:* Southern Art Festival, 67; one-person show, Brooks Mem Art Gallery, 70; Miss Art Asn, 68; Tenn Art Comn Traveling Exhib, 68; Smithsonian Inst Traveling Exhib to Europe, 68; and others. *Awards:* Prizes, Brooks Mem Art Gallery, 68; Tenn All-State Art Exhib, Nashville, 68; Tenn Art Comn Purchase Prize, 68; and others. *Mailing Add:* 476 N Willett St Memphis TN 38112

LEHMAN, MARK AMMON
EDUCATOR, SCULPTOR
b Philadelphia, Pa, Apr 12, 30. *Study:* Philadelphia Col Art, BFA, 60; Tyler Sch Art, MFA, 62; Columbia Univ, 64- *Comn:* Head of J F Kennedy, Students of Trenton State Col, 65. *Exhib:* NJ State Mus Ann, 66 & 67; Columbia Univ, 66 & 77; Pa Guild Craftsmen Traveling Exhib, 67; NJ Designer Craftsmen, NJ State Mus, 68; Centenary Col, 76. *Teaching:* Asst prof art hist, ceramics & sculpture, Trenton State Col, 63- *Awards:* NJ Tercentenary Exhib Award, 64. *Mem:* NJ Designer Craftsmen. *Media:* Clay. *Publ:* Auth, Article pertaining to ceramic kiln burners, Studio Potter, 75. *Mailing Add:* 30 Wardman Ave Trenton NJ 08638

LEHR, HAROLD
SCULPTOR, KINETIC ARTIST
b Brookline, Mass, July 19, 45. *Study:* Univ Rochester, BA, 67; Mass Inst Technol Ctr Advan Visual Study, vis scholar, 70-72; RI Sch Design, MFA, 71. *Work:* City of Buffalo, NY; Dade Co, Fla; Nat Shopping Ctrs, Rochester, NY; Hughes Justice Ctr, Trenton, NJ; Living Hist Ctr, Independence Hall, Philadelphia. *Exhib:* One-man exhibs, South St Seaport Mus, New York, 71, Inst Contemp Art, Boston, 72 & Indianapolis Mus Art, 73; Art of the Space Era, Huntsville Mus Art, Ala, 78; Sky Clock-Calendar, Grad Ctr, City Univ New York, 78; Energy into Art, Mem Art Gallery, Rochester, NY, 78; Area Shoreline Exhib, Ward's Island, NY, 81; Soundings, Neuberger Mus, Purchase, NY, 81. *Media:* Metals. *Mailing Add:* 45 Lawton St New Rochelle NY 10801

LEHR, JANET
DEALER
b New York, NY, June 7, 37. *Study:* Brooklyn Law Sch, Doctorate of Law, 58. *Res:* Photographically illustrated books of the 19th century. *Specialty:* Fine vintage photographs of both the 19th and 20th century; the role of the photomechanical reproduction processes as used in book illustration; exceptional contemporary. *Publ:* Auth, Talbot's Role in the History of Photography, Antiquarian Bookman, J Chernofsky, 78; auth, John Thomson, History of Photography, 1/80. *Mailing Add:* PO Box 617 Gracie Sta New York NY 10028

LEHRER, LEONARD
PAINTER, LITHOGRAPHER
b Philadelphia, Pa, Mar 23, 35. *Study:* Philadelphia Col Art, BFA, 56; Univ Pa, MFA, 60. *Work:* Mus Mod Art, New York; Nat Gallery of Art, Washington, DC; Libr Cong, Washington, DC; Philadelphia Mus Art; Cleveland Mus Art; and others. *Exhib:* Brooklyn Mus Print Show, 72; one-man shows, Utah Mus Fine Arts, 73 & 82 & Marian Locks Gallery, Philadelphia, 77 & 84; Galerie Kuhl, Hannover, Ger, 79; 4th Miami Int Print Biennial, 80; 7th Int Print Biennial, Bradford, Eng, 82; and others. *Teaching:* Prof art & chmn dept, Univ NMex, 70-74; prof art, Univ Tex, San Antonio, 74-77; prof art & dir, Sch Art, Ariz State Univ, Tempe, 77- *Awards:* First Prize, Fourth Miami Int Print Biennial, 80; Heitland Found Prize, Celle, WGermany, 80; Gold Medal Award, Nat Soc Arts & Letters, 81; and others. *Bibliog:* V D Coke (auth), The Painter and the Photograph, Univ NMex Press, 72; Fritz Eichenberg (auth), The Art of the Print, Abrams, 76; Carol Kotrozo (auth), Leonard Lehrer, Art Int, 11-12/82. *Mem:* Col Art Asn Am. *Media:* Watercolor, Oil. *Dealer:* Marian Locks Gallery 1524 Walnut St Philadelphia PA 19102; Marilyn Butler Fine Art Scottsdale AZ. *Mailing Add:* 2105 E Golf Ave Tempe AZ 85282

LEIBER, GERSON AUGUST
PRINTMAKER
b Brooklyn, NY, Nov 12, 21. *Study:* Art Students League; Brooklyn Mus Art Sch. *Work:* Metrop Mus Art, New York; Whitney Mus Am Art, New York; Nat Gallery Art, Washington, DC; Libr Cong, Washington, DC; Boston Mus Fine Arts. *Comn:* Print eds, Assoc Am Artists & Int Graphic Arts Soc. *Exhib:* Am Prints Today, USA, New York, 59; Cincinnati Int Biennial, 60; American Prints, in Russia, Rome, Italy, Mexico City, Mex & Salzburg, Ger; Libr Cong Exhibs; and many others. *Teaching:* Instr graphics & illus, Newark Sch Fine & Indust Art, 61-68. *Awards:* Tiffany Fels, 57 & 60; Audubon Medals of Honor for Graphics, 63-65; Am Nat Print Exhib Prize, Assoc Am Artists Gallery. *Bibliog:* Frank Getlein (auth), Bite of the Print, Potter, 63; Hooten & Kaiden (auth), Mother and Child in Modern Art, Meredith Corp. *Mem:* Assoc of Nat Acad; Soc Am Graphic Artists (pres, 78-80); Soc Am Graphic Artists; Audubon Artists; Boston Printmakers. *Media:* Intaglio. *Publ:* Illusr, Crisis (poem), Oxhead Press, 69. *Mailing Add:* 20 E 35th St New York NY 10016

LEIBERT, PETER R
CERAMIST, SCULPTOR
b New York, NY, Mar 13, 41. *Study:* Buffalo State Univ, BS(art educ), 63; Indiana Univ, MS(art educ), 67, MFA(ceramics, with distinction), 67. *Exhib:* 25th Ceramic Nat, Everson Mus, Syracuse, 68; one-man shows, Portogallo Gallery, New York, 69, Cooper Union, New York, 71 & Kogei Gallery, Dobbs Ferry, NY, 74; Conn Artists Exhib, Slater Mus, Norwich, 69, 71 & 81; American Crafts Nat, Currier Gallery Art, Manchester, NH, 81. *Teaching:* Artist in residence, Haystack Mountain Sch Crafts, Deer Isle, Maine, 78; assoc prof ceramics, Conn Col, 67-, chmn dept art, 78- *Awards:* Purchase Prize, Rose Arts Festival, Norwich, Conn, 70-78 & 83; Best in Clay, 22nd Ann Exhib, 78 & First Prize for Sculpture, New Eng Regional Exhib, 83, Mystic Art Asn. *Mem:* Am Crafts Coun; Nat Coun Educ Ceramic Arts; Soc Conn Craftsmen. *Media:* Ceramics; Mixed. *Publ:* Illusr, Back to gum prints, Camera 35, 70 & A portfolio of photography, Pukka, 70; contribr, The artist as photographer, Conn Col Alumni News, 71. *Mailing Add:* RFD #6 Preston City Norwich CT 06360

LEICESTER, ANDREW JOHN
ENVIRONMENTAL ARTIST
b Birmingham, England, Mar 5, 48. *Study:* Portsmouth Polytechnic, England, BA, 69; Manchester Polytechnic, England, MA, 70; Univ Minn, Minneapolis, MFA, 72. *Work:* Walker Art Ctr; Sheldon Mem Art Gallery. *Comn:* Cloverleaf (interstate hwy), Nat Endowment Arts & State & Fed Hwy Dept, Minneapolis, 78-84; Floating Mesa, Stanley Marsh 3, Amarillo, Tex, 81; Octal (water labyrinth), Cray Res, Mendota, Minn, 82; Prospect V-III (coal mining mem), Md State Legislature, Frostburg, 82; Toth (mining monument), Rapid City Arts Coun & Nat Endowment Arts, SDak, 83. *Exhib:* Invitation, 75 & The River--Images of the Mississippi, 76, Walker Art Ctr; Proposals for Sawyer Point, Contemp Art Ctr, Cincinnati, 77; Artpark, Lewiston, NY, 78; Art on the Beach, Creative Time, Battery Park, New York, 80; Artists Gardens & Parks, Hayden Gallery, 81; Nature-Sculpture, Wurttembergischer, Kunstverein, Stuttgart, WGer, 81. *Pos:* Mem, Minneapolis Arts Comn, 80-84. *Teaching:* Instr sculpture & drawing, Carleton Col, Minn, 73-74; instr sculpture, Minneapolis Col Art & Design, 75-80. *Awards:* Fels, Minn Arts Bd, 80-81, Nat Endowment Arts, 81-82 & Bush Found, 83-84. *Bibliog:* Heinz Thiel (auth), Natur-Kunst: Erosion, Kunstforum Int, 82; John Beardsley (auth), Earthworks, Abbeville Press, 84. *Media:* Mixed. *Mailing Add:* 3029 Holmes Ave S Minneapolis MN 55408

LEIGH, HARRY E
SCULPTOR, PAINTER
b Buffalo, NY, Nov 7, 31. *Study:* Albright Art Sch, dipl, 52; State Univ New York, Buffalo, BA, 53; painting with Richard Pousette-Dart, 56-60; Columbia Univ, MA, 59. *Work:* Va Mus Fine Art, Richmond; Birchfield Collection, Buffalo. *Exhib:* Albright-Knox Art Gallery, Buffalo, NY, 52, 53 & 57; Everson Mus, Syracuse, 61; one-man shows, Brata Gallery, New York, 67 & 69, Berkshire Mus, Mass, 71 & OK Harris Gallery, New York, 74 & 78; Projected Artist at Work, Finch Col Mus, New York, 71; Rockland Ctr Arts, Nyack, NY, 82; and others. *Awards:* MacDowell Fel, artist-in-residence, 68-70, 72 & 74-75; Yaddo Fel, artist-in-residence, 72, 79 & 80; Creative Arts Prog Serv fel, 78-79. *Bibliog:* Martin Last (auth), rev, Art News, 1/69; Elizabeth Frank Perlmutter (auth), article, Art News, 9/74; Grace Glueck (auth), Harry Leigh & Keith Long, New York Times, 5/12/78. *Media:* Wood, Bricks. *Dealer:* OK Harris Gallery 383 W Broadway New York NY 10012. *Mailing Add:* 66 Haverstraw Rd Suffern NY 10901

LEIGH, JACK DAVID
PHOTOGRAPHER
b Savannah, Ga, Nov 8, 48. *Study:* Univ Ga, BA, 72; Maine Photog Workshop, with George Tice, Eva Rubinstein & Jill Freedman, 78 & 79. *Work:* NY Univ; Gibbes Art Gallery. *Exhib:* 48th Southeastern Competition, Southeastern Ctr Contemp Art, Winston-Salem, NC, 80; Southeastern Photog Competition, Greenville Co Mus Art, SC, 80; Artists in Ga, High Mus Art, 80; one-man shows, Simon Gallery Photog, Montclair, NJ, 81, Leeds Gallery, Earlham Col, 82, NY Univ Sch Arts, 82 & Gibbes Art Gallery, 83; and others. *Teaching:* Artist in residence photog, Savannah Co Day Sch, Ga, 82- & SC Arts Comn, 83- *Awards:* Best in Photog, Savannah Arts Festival, 77; Best in Show, Savannah Art Asn, 79. *Bibliog:* Elizabeth Leopard (reporter), Nat Pub Radio, 5/80; video doc, WJWJ-TV, SC, 5/80; Vivien Raynor (auth), article, New York Times, 2/82. *Mem:* Soc Photog Educ. *Publ:* Auth, Oystering: A Way of Life, Carolina Art Asn, 83. *Mailing Add:* 132 E Oglethorpe Ave Savannah GA 31401

LEIGHTON, DAVID S R
ADMINISTRATOR
b Regina, Sask, Feb 20, 28. *Pos:* Dir, Sch Fine Arts, Banff Ctr, 70- *Mailing Add:* 101 St Julien Rd Banff AB T0L 0C0 Canada

LEIN, MALCOLM EMIL
ADMINISTRATOR, DESIGNER
b Havre, Mont, July 19, 13. *Study:* Univ Minn, BArch. *Collections Arranged:* Fiber, Clay and Metal Biennial, 52-; Drawings USA, Biennial, 61-; Goldsmith, 70; The Introspective Italian, 71. *Pos:* Pres, Minn Mus Art, 47-82. *Mem:* Am Asn Mus. *Mailing Add:* 79 Western Ave St Paul MN 55102

LEIPZIG, ARTHUR
PHOTOGRAPHER
b Brooklyn, NY, Oct 25, 18. *Study:* Photo League, 42; Paul Strand Workshop, 46. *Work:* Mus Mod Art, New York; Brooklyn Mus; Nat Gallery Art, Ottawa; Art Inst Chicago; Eastman House, Rochester, NY. *Exhib:* New Faces, 46,

Xmas Sale of Photographs, 53, Family of Man, 55 & From the Museum Collection, 58, Mus Mod Art, New York; Photography as a Fine Art, Metropolitan Mus Art, New York, 61 & 62; Eastman House, Rochester, NY, 73; retrospective, Nassau Mus Fine Art, Roslyn, NY, 75; Photo League, Int Ctr Photog, New York, 78; Photographs of Jewish Life Around the World, Nassau & Queens Mus, NY, 82; Int Photog Art Exhibs, Beijing, China, 83. *Pos:* Staff photogr, PM Newspaper, 42-46 & Int News Photo, 46-47. *Teaching:* Dir photog & prof art, Long Island Univ, 68- *Awards:* Nat Urban League Award, 67; res grant, 80-81 & Trustees Award Scholarly Achievement, 82, Long Island Univ. *Bibliog:* Jacob Deschin (auth), Six great teachers, 35 M Photog, 74; Documentary Photography, Time Life Books, 83. *Mem:* Am Soc Mag Photogr. *Publ:* Contribr, US Camera Ann, 53, 54, 56 & 60; contribr, The Family of Man, Mus Mod Art, 55; contribr, Photography Yearbook, Fountain Press Ltd, 57, 59, 62 & 72; contribr, The Family of Children, Ridge Press, 77; auth, Photography & social change, Ventures in Res, 78. *Mailing Add:* 378 Glen Ave Sea Cliff NY 11579

LEITHAUSER, MARK ALAN
PRINTMAKER, DESIGNER
b Detroit, Mich, June 22, 50. *Study:* Wayne State Univ, BA, 72, MA, 73, MFA, 74. *Work:* Nat Gallery Art; Brooklyn Mus; Libr Cong. *Exhib:* Michigan Focus, Detroit Inst Arts, 74; Boston Printmakers Nat Show, DeCordova Mus, Lincoln, Mass, 76; 30 Years of American Printmaking, Brooklyn Mus, 76; Nat Printmakers Show, Libr Cong, 77; In Celebration of Prints, Philadelphia Art Alliance, 80; Nat Print & Drawing Competition, Dulin Gallery Art, Knoxville, Tenn, 81; American Perspective, Nat Mus Am Art, 81; Recent Acquisitions on Paper, Corcoran Gallery Art, 81. *Pos:* Exhib designer, Nat Gallery Art, 74- *Awards:* Purchase Award, Nat Print Show, Libr Cong, 75, Nat Printmakers Show, Nat Mus Am Art, 77 & Nat Print & Drawing Exhib, Dulin Gallery Art, 81. *Media:* Etching. *Dealer:* Hom Gallery 2103 O St NW Washington DC 20037. *Mailing Add:* 3614 Idaho Ave NW Washington DC 20016

LEITMAN, NORMAN
DEALER
b New York, NY, June 24, 33. *Study:* Cornell Univ, BA; NY Univ Inst Fine Arts, 54-57. *Collections Arranged:* Old Master Drawings, 60 Anonymous Drawings, The Neglected 19th Century & 17th Century Dutch Paintings, H Shickman Gallery. *Pos:* Dir, H Shickman Gallery, New York, 65-79 & LFAC Fine Arts Corp, Geneva, Switz, 79- *Mem:* Art Dealers Asn; Col Art Asn. *Specialty:* Old master and nineteenth century paintings and sculpture. *Mailing Add:* 3 Weech Rd London NW6 1DL England United Kingdom

LEJA, MICHAEL JOSEPH
CURATOR, CRITIC
b Woonsocket, RI, Dec 2, 51. *Study:* Swarthmore Col, BA(hist art); Tufts Univ, MA; independent study prog, Whitney Mus Am Art; Helena Rubenstein fel art hist & mus studies. *Collections Arranged:* Gaslight Phenomena Kinetic Light Works by Alejandro Sina, 77, New Boston Filmmakers, 77, Fred Wiseman Retrospective, 77 & Wit & Wisdom: Works by Baldessari, Hudson, Levine, Oppenheim, 78 & Narration, 78, Inst Contemp Art, Boston; Aspects of the 70's Mavericks, Rose Art Mus, Waltham, Mass, 80. *Pos:* Cur & film programmer, Inst Contemp Art, Boston, Mass, 76-78; cur, Rose Art Mus, Brandeis Univ, Waltham, Mass, 79- *Mailing Add:* 62 Dartmouth St Somerville MA 02145

LEKAKIS, MICHAEL NICHOLAS
SCULPTOR
b New York, NY, 1907. *Work:* Mus Mod Art, Whitney Mus Am Art & Guggenheim Mus, New York; Dayton Art Mus, Ohio; Portland Art Mus, Ore; and others. *Comn:* Sculpture & paintings, Nat Pinakothiki, Athens, Greece. *Exhib:* One-man show, Whitney Mus Am Art, New York, 53-54; Seven Sculptors, Guggenheim Mus, 58; Mus Mod Art, New York; Dayton Art Mus, Ohio; Sculpture Acquisition, Philadelphia Mus Art, 77; Drawing Collection Acquisition, Univ Lexington Mus, Ky; Weatherspoon Gallery, Univ NC Mus, Greensboro; Univ Nebr Mus, Lincoln; and others. *Awards:* Purchase Grant, Ford Found. *Mailing Add:* 345 West 29th St New York NY 10001

LEKBERG, BARBARA HULT
SCULPTOR
b Portland, Ore, Mar 19, 25. *Study:* Univ Iowa, BFA & MA, with Humbert Albrizio; Simpson Col, hon DFA, 64. *Work:* Montclair Mus Art, NJ; Des Moines Art Ctr, Iowa; Knoxville Art Ctr, Tenn; Whitney Mus Am Art. *Comn:* Three interior sculptures, Beldon-Stratford Hotel, Chicago, 53; three interior sculptures, Socony-Mobil Co, New York, 55; lobby relief, Riedl & Freede Advert, Clifton, NJ, 64; life-size figures, Bayfield Clark, Bermuda, 71 & 74; and others. *Exhib:* Five Pa Acad Fine Arts Ann, Philadelphia, 50-62; New Talent, Am Fedn Arts Traveling Show, 59-60; Recent Sculpture USA, Mus Mod Art, New York, 59; one-man shows, Sculpture Ctr, New York, 59, 65, 71, 75, 77 & 83; traveling solo show, Birmingham Mus Art, Ala & Columbia Mus Art, SC, 73; retrospective, Mt Holyoke Col Mus, Mass, 78. *Teaching:* Fac, Col New Rochelle, 80-; fac, Philadelphia Col Art, 81- *Awards:* Am Inst Arts & Lett Grant, 56; Guggenheim Found Fels, 57 & 59. *Bibliog:* Interview, Hudson Valley Cable TV, 81; The Figure (film), Nat Sculpture Soc, 83. *Mem:* Sculptors Guild; Nat Sculpture Soc; Nat Acad Design. *Media:* Bronze, Steel. *Dealer:* Sculpture Ctr 167 E 69th St New York NY 10021. *Mailing Add:* 911 Stuart Ave Mamaroneck NY 10543

LELAND, WHITNEY EDWARD
PAINTER, EDUCATOR
b Washington, DC, Apr 12, 45. *Study:* Memphis Acad Arts, BFA; Univ Tenn, Knoxville, MFA. *Work:* Tenn Arts Comn; Chase Manhattan Bank, New York; Hunter Mus Art, Chattanooga; Int Bus Machines, Tampa; and others. *Exhib:* NEA/SECCA II Traveling Exhib, 78-79; Dulin Gallery Art, Knoxville, 79; Western Asn Art Mus Traveling Exhib, 79-81; solo exhib, Am Gallery, Bern, Switzerland, 81; Southern Abstraction Five Painters Traveling Exhib, 83-84; and others. *Teaching:* Asst prof painting, Univ Tenn, Knoxville, 70-78, assoc prof art, 78- *Awards:* Nat Endowment Arts Grant; Purchase Award, Ford Found; Cash Award, Springfield Art Mus, Mo. *Bibliog:* Article, Contemp Art/SE, Vol 2, No 1; article, Art Voices/S, 11-12/78; article, Smithsonian, 1/79. *Media:* Acrylic, Watercolor. *Dealer:* Heath Gallery Atlanta GA. *Mailing Add:* Dept Art Univ Tenn 1715 Volunteer Blvd Knoxville TN 37916

LEM, RICHARD DOUGLAS
PAINTER
b Los Angeles, Calif, Nov 24, 33. *Study:* Univ Calif, Los Angeles, BA; Calif State Univ, Los Angeles, MA; Otis Art Inst; Calif Inst Arts; also with Rico LeBrun & Herbert Jepson. *Work:* San Diego Fine Arts Gallery. *Exhib:* 3rd Ariz Ann, Phoenix Art Mus, 61; Calif State Univ, Los Angeles, 65; California: South, San Diego Fine Arts Gallery, 65; two-man show, Palos Verdes Art Gallery, 68; Lynn Kottler Galleries, New York, 73; Galerie Mouffe, Paris, France, 76; plus others. *Awards.* Los Angeles Fine Arts Soc & Art Guild Award for Painting, 65. *Media:* Oil, Watercolor. *Mailing Add:* 1861 Webster Ave Los Angeles CA 90026

LEMBECK, JOHN EDGAR
PAINTER
b St Louis, Mo, Dec 25, 42. *Study:* Univ Kans, BFA, 66; Yale Univ, MFA(Univ Scholar, State Conn Scholar), MFA, 70. *Exhib:* One-man shows, Spectrum Gallery, New York, 72 & Louis K Meisel Gallery, New York, 75; Butler Inst Am Art, Youngstown, Ohio, 75; Taft Mus, Cincinnati, Ohio, 76; Indianapolis Mus Art, Ind, 76; State Univ NY Col, Potsdam, 77; and others. *Teaching:* Asst lectr art, St Louis Art Mus, 69, lectr art, 70; instr design & drawing, Yale Univ Sch Art & Archit, 70-80, instr drawing, Yale Summer Sch Music & Art, 71 & 72, dir, Gallery, 71. *Bibliog:* Article, Houston Chronicle, 9/77, Die Zeit, Ger, 12/77 & Art News, 1/77. *Mailing Add:* c/o L K Meisel Gallery 141 Prince St New York NY 10012

LEMER, ELLEN TERRY
DEALER, COLLECTOR
b Brooklyn, NY, Dec 27, 43. *Study:* Ithaca Col, 61-64; Hofstra Univ, BA, 65; NY Sch Interior Design, cert, 71. *Work:* Brooklyn Mus. *Collections Arranged:* Ideas '79, Resources Coun Show, 79. *Pos:* Art consult, Bass & Lemer, New York, 79- & MMT Sales Inc, New York, 80- *Bibliog:* O Gueft (ed), article, Interiors, 12/79. *Specialty:* Contemporary paintings, constructions, fiber objects and sculpture plus some ethnic art. *Collection:* Works by younger contemporary artists: Neda al Hilali, Leslie Goldberg, David Kraisler, Lee Milmon, Beth Ames Swartz and Jim Waid. *Mailing Add:* 242 E 72 New York NY 10021

LEMIEUX, IRENEE
PAINTER
b Quebec, Can, Aug 3, 31. *Study:* Laval Univ; Conserv de Musique de Quebec, Montreal; Fontainebleau, France. *Work:* La Minerve, Quebec. *Exhib:* Third Salon Int de la Riviera, Grasse, France; 3rd Salon Int de la Cote d'Azur, Chateau des Requiers; 2nd Salon Int du Carnaval de Nice; 2nd Salon Int de Baden-Baden, Allemagne, 73; 7th Grand Prix Int Painting & Sculpture, Antibes, 74; among others. *Awards:* First Prize with Gold Medal, 3rd Salon Int de la Cote d'Azur, 73; Spec First Prize with Gold Medal, Acad de Lutece, Paris, 73; Second Prize with Silver Medal, 7th Grand Prix Int Painting & Sculpture, 74; and others. *Bibliog:* Roland Laznikas (auth), article, 3/73 & Raymond Clermont (auth), article, 6/74, La Rev Mod, Paris; and others. *Mem:* Asn Beaux-Arts Cannes. *Media:* Acrylic. *Mailing Add:* 5 Ave du Pont Scott Quebec PQ G1N 3S3 Canada

LEMIEUX, JEAN PAUL
PAINTER
b Quebec, Que, Nov 18, 04. *Study:* Beaux-Arts, Montreal; Acad Colarossi, Paris; Laval Univ, Quebec, Hon Dr, 69. *Work:* Collection of Queen Elizabeth; Art Gallery Toronto, Ont; Mus Prov Quebec. *Exhib:* Warsaw, 62; Tate Gallery, London, Eng, 63; Mus Mod Art Traveling Exhib through Can, 63; Mus Galliera, Paris, 63. *Teaching:* Instr, Beaux-Arts Montreal, 33-34 & Ecole du Meuble, Montreal, 35-36; instr, Beaux-Arts, Quebec. *Awards:* Prize, Quebec Prov Painting; Govt Overseas Award, 54-55; Companion, Order of Can, 68. *Mem:* Royal Can Acad Arts. *Mailing Add:* 2008 Dickson Sillery PQ G1T 1C5 Canada

LEMMY, LEMMY
PAINTER, PRINTMAKER
b Ipoh, Perak, Malaysia, Jan 7, 40; US citizen. *Study:* Univ Ore, 56-59; San Francisco State Univ, BA, 64. *Work:* Mus Mod Art, San Francisco, Calif; Univ Calif Art Mus, Berkeley; Nat Gallery, Singapore; Mus Art & Hist, Geneva, Switz; Commonwealth Inst, London, Eng. *Comn:* Abegg Mus, Zurich, Switz, 74; Hess Holding Corps, Bern, Switz, 76; Rohm GMBH Corps, Darmstadt, Ger, 80. *Exhib:* Collector's Choice, Calif Palace Legion Honor, 76; one-man shows, Mus Fine Art, Lausanne, 81, Mus Contonal Beaux Arts, Lausanne, 82, Kunstverein, Ludwigshafen, 82, Mus Petit Palais, Geneva, 82 & 83, Ctr Int D'Art Contemp, Paris, 83; and others. *Pos:* Artist-in-residence,

Centre de Gravure Contemp, Geneva, 69-70, 74 & 76-77. *Bibliog:* Walter Blum (auth), Lemmy and his art, Calif Living Mag, 72; Thomas Albright (auth), Lemmy--retrospective, San Francisco Chronicle, 72; Patricia B Wilson (auth), Lemmy, Christian Sci Monitor, 78. *Mem:* Nat Soc Literature and the Arts; Associated Art Coun New York; Stanford Comt Art; Nat Adv Art Coun, Eureka Col, Ill; Archives Am Art. *Media:* Chemical Polyester; Acrylic, Plexiglas. *Res:* Chemical etching process on Plexiglas. *Dealer:* Hoover Gallery 1681 Folsome St San Francisco CA 94013. *Mailing Add:* PO Box 1083 Menlo Park CA 94026

LENGYEL, ALFONZ
HISTORIAN, WRITER
b Godollo, Hungary, Oct 21, 21; US citizen. *Study:* Univ Budapest, JD, 48, 48-50; San Jose State Col, BA(art hist), 58, MA(art hist), 59; Inst Art & Archaeol, Univ Paris, PhD(summa cum laude), 64; London Inst Applied Res, Hon JD, 75. *Pos:* Adj cur, Detroit Inst Arts, 68-72; *Teaching:* Asst prof, San Jose State Col, 61-63; mem fac, Univ Md Europ Div, Paris & Heidelberg, 63-68; prof art hist & classical archaeol, Wayne State Univ, 68-72; prof & dir archaeol prog, Northern Ky Univ, 72-77; dean & prof, Inst Mediterranean Art & Archaeol, 77-82; coordr art hist & museology prog, Rosemont Col, 82- *Awards:* Gold Medal, Brazil Acad Humanities, 75; Lilly Grant, 82; Connelly Grant, 83. *Mem:* Int Inst Archaeocivilization, Paris; Renaissance Soc Am; Am Asn Mus; Col Art Asn Am; Am Sch Oriental Res. *Publ:* Auth, Art and Life of A L Barye, Brown, 63; auth, Quattrocento, Kendall-Hunt, 72; coauth, L'Art et le Monde Moderne, Larousse, 72; coauth, Lexicon der Kristlichen Ikonographie, Herder Verlag, 73; ed & coauth, The Archaeology of Roman Pannonia, Ky Univ Press, 80. *Mailing Add:* Arts Div Rosemont Col Rosemont PA 19010

LENNEY, ANNIE
PAINTER
b Potsdam, NY. *Study:* Art Students League; Grand Cent Art Sch, New York; Syracuse Univ; Col St Elizabeth, BA. *Work:* Butler Inst Am Art, Youngstown, Ohio; Denver Art Mus, Colo; Newark Mus, NJ; Oklahoma City Art Ctr; Brook Mem Art Gallery, Memphis; plus many others. *Exhib:* Audubon Artists, Allied Artists & Nat Asn Women Artists, Nat Acad Design, New York; Assoc Artist Exhibs & Mus Ann, Montclair Mus, NJ; St Lawrence Univ, Canton, NY, 79; Col St Elizabeth, NJ, 80; and many others. *Teaching:* Instr art, Sch Fine & Indust Arts, Newark, 46-63; suprv, Sat Jr Art Sch, Newark, 53-55; instr art, Newton Pub Sch Syst, NJ, 63-71. *Awards:* Elizabethan Award for Distinguished Achievements in the Arts, Col of St Elizabeth, NJ, 74; Gene Alden Walker Prize for Oil, Pen & Brush Club, New York, 75; Ray A Jones Award, Hudson Artists NJ, 76; and others. *Bibliog:* Gerry Turner (auth), The magic of a home town, Design Mag, 1-2/60; M J R Arthur (auth), Blairstown's Annie Lenney is renowned artist, Family Forum, 3/30/71; and others. *Mem:* Audubon Artists (dir oils, 71, rec secy, 72-73); Allied Artists Am; Nat Asn Women Artists; Philadelphia Watercolor Club, 46-62. *Media:* Oil, Watercolor. *Publ:* Auth, American watercolor, Am Artist, 2/51. *Mailing Add:* 39 Pierrepont Ave Potsdam NY 13676

LENNIE, BEATRICE E C
SCULPTOR, DESIGNER
b BC. *Study:* Vancouver Sch Art; Calif Sch Fine Art; pvt study in Rome & Florence; also with Frederick H Varley, J W G Macdonald, Ralph Stackpole, Carlo Marega & Harry Taüber, Vienna. *Work:* Winnipeg Art Gallery; pvt collections, Can & USA. *Comn:* Vancouver Labor Temple, Dom Construct Stone; Shaughnessy Mil Hosp, Fed Govt, Mercer & Mercer; Ryerson Mem Ctr United Church Can, P Underwood; Acad Med Libr, BC Med Soc; St John's Mem Church, C Thornton Sharp; plus others. *Exhib:* Many shows, Royal Can Acad, Toronto, Ont & Montreal, Que, Can Nat Exhib, Sculptor's Soc Can & Seattle Art Mus, Wash; one-man show, Toronto Picture Loan, Queen's Univ; plus others. *Pos:* Dir, Child Art Ctr, Vancouver Art Gallery; broadcaster art subj, Can Broadcasting Corp Trans Can. *Teaching:* Head dept sculpture, BC Col Art, Vancouver; instr sculpture & theatre arts & creative puppetry, Univ BC; spec art lectr, Crofton House Sch, Vancouver. *Awards:* Award, Sculptor's Soc Can. *Bibliog:* Archit rev in Can Rev Mus & Art, Vancouver Prov, Toronto Sat Night & others. *Mem:* Life mem BC Soc Art; Sculptor's Soc Can. *Mailing Add:* 4011 Rose Crescent West Vancouver BC V7V 2N6 Canada

LENNON, TIMOTHY
PAINTING CONSERVATOR
b Chicago, Ill, Sept 18, 38. *Study:* Loras Col, BA; Univ Notre Dame, MA; Art Inst Chicago. *Pos:* Conservator, Art Inst Chicago, 80- *Mem:* Fel Am Inst Conserv Artistic & Hist Works; Int Inst Conserv Artistic & Hist Works. *Mailing Add:* 835 Forest Oak Park IL 60302

LENSSEN, HEIDI (MRS FRIDOLF JOHNSON)
PAINTER, LECTURER
b Frankfurt, Ger; US citizen. *Study:* Uffizi, Florence, Italy, copy degree, 25; Berlin State Acad Fine Arts, cert, 29; pvt study in Paris, France; also with Count Merveldt, Rome, 32-33; Acad Rossi, Florence; Ecole Arts et Metiers, Paris. *Work:* Berlin Mus; Kunsthalle, Mannheim. *Comn:* More than 100 comns, US & Europe. *Exhib:* Schoneman Gallery, 40; Audubon Artists, 44 & 45; one-man show, Lynn Kottler Gallery, 54 & 70 & Walt Kuhn Gallery, 83; Show of Pastels, Kingston, NY, 80; and others. *Teaching:* Instr art & co-dir, Am Sch Design, New York, 37-42; lectr art, City Col New York Adult Educ, 45-58; instr art & lectr, Hunter Col, 49-51; lectr art, Franklin Sch Prof Arts, 52-57. *Awards:* Arthur Brown Gold Medal Oil Painting, 54. *Bibliog:* Marthe Davidson (auth), article, Art News, 37; Emily Genauer (auth), article, World Telegram New York, 40. *Mem:* Woodstock Artists Asn; life mem Mark Twain Soc. *Media:* Oil, Pastel. *Publ:* Auth & illusr, Art and Anatomy, J J Augustin, Inc & Barnes & Noble, 44; auth, Hands in Nature and Art, Studio Publ. *Mailing Add:* 34 Whitney Dr Woodstock NY 12498

LENT, BLAIR
ILLUSTRATOR, WRITER
b Boston, Mass, Jan 22, 30. *Study:* Boston Mus Sch, Cummings Mem travel fel to Switz & Italy, 1 yr, Bartlett travel fel to USSR, grad(hons). *Work:* Boston Pub Libr; Kerlan Collection, Univ Minn. *Comn:* Why the Sun and the Moon Live in the Sky (animated film), ACI Films, New York, 71; Christmas card design, UNICEF. *Exhib:* Solo show, Wiggin Gallery, Boston, 70; Work by Five Major American Illustrators, Univ Art Gallery, Albany, NY, 72; Contemp Am Illusr Children's Bks, Rutgers Univ, 74-75; Brattleboro Mus, Vt, 80; Univ Conn, Storrs, 82. *Awards:* Silver Medal, Bienal Int Arte Grafice, Sao Paulo, Brazil, 65; Bronze Medal, Bienale Illustrators, Bratislava, Czech, 69; Caldecott Medal, Am Libr Asn, 73. *Bibliog:* Lee Hopkins (auth), Books Are By People, Citation, 69; Anne Commire (auth), Something About the Author, Gale, 72; and others. *Publ:* Auth & illusr, From King Boggen's Hall to Nothing-at-all, 67, Little; auth (pseud Ernest Small) & illusr, Baba Yaga, Houghton Mifflin, 66; illusr, The Funny Little Woman, Dutton, 72; auth & illusr, Bayberry Bluff, Houghton Mifflin, 84. *Mailing Add:* 10 Dana St Cambridge MA 02138

LEON, ANA (ANA M RODRIGUEZ-LEON)
PAINTER
Study: Rio Piedras, PR, painting with Fran Cervoni, 76; Univ PR, Rio Piedras, silkscreen with Myrna Baez, 80; Escuela Artes Plasticas, Inst Cult Puertorriquena, BFA, 80. *Comn:* Scale model (with Jose Maria Iranzo), Inst Cult Puertorriquena, San Juan, 78; mural paintings (with Joaquin Torres Feliciano & Esteban de Jesus), Proj Off Cult Affairs, Gov's Off, San Juan, PR, 79. *Exhib:* Torsos, Winfinsky Gallery, Salem State Col, Mass, 83; Boston: The Humane Condition, Bromfield Gallery, Boston, 83; NE Juried Exhib, Millhouse-Bundy Arts Ctr, Waitsfield, Vt, 83; Women's Perspective, Mill Gallery, Guilford, Conn, 83; Greater Boston Women Artists Exhib, Northeastern Univ, 83; and many others. *Pos:* Mus attendant, Fogg Art Mus & Busch-Reisinger Mus, Harvard Univ, 83- *Awards:* Special Painting Award, Pintura, Esso Standard Oil, 80; First Prize, Women's Perspective, Guilford Handcraft Ctr, 83. *Bibliog:* Ernesto J Ruiz de la Mata (auth), Ana Leon--De La Mujer, Caribbean Business, PR, 12/81; Samuel R Cherson (auth), El Desnudo Como Naturaleza Muerta, El Nuevo Dia, 1/82; Jose A Perez Ruiz (auth), Anatomia--De La Mujer, El Mundo Newspaper, PR, 1/82. *Mem:* Copley Soc Arts, Boston; Boston Visual Artists Union; Orgn Independent Artists, New York; Provincetown Art Asn, Mass. *Media:* Airbrush Acrylic. *Dealer:* Imprimatvr Ltd 451 First Ave N Minneapolis MN 55401. *Mailing Add:* 11 Danforth St Jamaica Plain MA 02130

LEON, DENNIS
SCULPTOR, EDUCATOR
b London, Eng, July 27, 33; US citizen. *Study:* Temple Univ, BSc(educ), 56; Tyler Sch Art, MFA, 57. *Exhib:* Pa Acad Fine Arts, 56, 64 & 68; Philadelphia Mus Art; James Willis Gallery, 73; Univ Calif, Davis, 74; JPL Fine Arts, London, Eng, 75; Am 76, San Francisco Mus Mod Art, 77; Hanson-Fuller Goldeen Gallery, San Francisco, 77, 79, 81 & 82; San Jose Mus Art, 81; and others. *Teaching:* Prof sculpture, Philadelphia Col Art, 60-72; prof sculpture, Calif Col Arts & Crafts, 72-; vis artist, Sheffield Polytech, Eng, 75 & 76. *Awards:* Nat Inst Arts & Lett Award, 67; MacDowell Fel, 81; Djerassi Found Fel, 83; and others. *Media:* Mixed Media. *Publ:* Auth, Paul Harris, 73. *Dealer:* Fuller Goldeen Gallery 228 Grant Ave San Francisco CA 94108. *Mailing Add:* 3143 Eton Ave Berkeley CA 94705

LEON, RALPH BERNARD
PAINTER, ILLUSTRATOR
b Atlantic City, NJ, Mar 10, 32. *Study:* Pratt Inst, BFA, 57; Ecole de Musique et Beaux Arts de Fontainebleau, Walter Damrosch Scholar, 58; La Grande Chaumiere, Paris, France, with Henri Goetz. *Work:* Found, State Univ NY Binghamton; Pentagon Art Collection, Washington, DC. *Exhib:* Butler Inst Am Art Ann, Youngstown, Ohio, 56, 73 & 74; one-man show, Somerset Art Asn, Bernardsville, NJ, 76; Santa Fe Six, Fenn Gallery, NMex, 77; Armory Show, Santa Fe, 77; Santa Fe Festival of Arts, 79 & 80; 30 Year Retrospective, Ernesto Mayans Gallery, Sante Fe, 82. *Pos:* Illusr & art dir, Airscoop (flight safety mag), USAFE, Wiesbaden, 59-69; illusr, US Bureau Land Mgt, 76- *Awards:* Benjamin Altman Prize & Ranger Fund Purchase Prize, Nat Acad, New York, 74; Leon Lehrer Mem Award, Allied Artists Am Ann Exhib, New York, 75. *Bibliog:* Maiariv, Tel Aviv Daily, 71. *Media:* Oil. *Dealer:* Ernesto Mayans Gallery 601 Canyon Rd Santa Fe NM 87501. *Mailing Add:* 1707 Callejon Zenaida Santa Fe NM 87501

LEONARD, JOANNE
PHOTOGRAPHER, EDUCATOR
b Los Angeles, Calif, 1940. *Study:* Univ Calif, Berkeley, BA, 62; San Francisco State Col, 63-64. *Work:* US State Dept; Am Arts Doc Ctr, Exeter, England; San Francisco Mus Art; Int Mus Photog, Rochester, NY; Stanford Univ Mus; and numerous private collections. *Exhib:* Focus Gallery, San Francisco, 67-74; one-person shows, M H De Young Mus, 68, San Francisco Art Inst, 74 & Laguna Gloria Art Mus, Austin, Tex, 80; George Eastman House, Rochester, NY, 69-70; San Francisco Mus Art, 71 & 75; Light Gallery, New York, 72; Baltimore Mus Art, 73; Seattle Art Mus, 76; two-person show, San Francisco Mus Mod Art, 81; and others. *Teaching:* Instr photog, San Francisco Art Inst, 73-75; Mills Col, Oakland, Calif, 75-77 & Univ Mich Sch Art, Ann Arbor, 78- *Awards:* Phelan Award, 71; Nat Endowment Arts Grant, 77; Josephine Nevins Keal Award, Univ Mich, 81. *Dealer:* Paule Anglim Gallery 14 Geary St San Francisco CA 94108. *Mailing Add:* Sch Art Univ Mich Ann Arbor MI 48109

LEONARDI, HECTOR
PAINTER, INSTRUCTOR
b Waterbury, Conn, Jan 18, 30. *Study:* RI Sch Design, BFA; Yale Univ, MFA. *Work:* Univ Notre Dame; Univ Bridgeport. *Exhib:* Albright-Knox Art Gallery, Buffalo, 66; Spectrum Gallery, New York, 72 & 73; Razor Gallery, New York, 74 & 75; Benson Gallery, Bridgehampton, NY, 76; Roy G Biv Gallery, New York, 78; Art Latitude Gallery, New York, 79; and others. *Teaching:* Instr color, design, drawing & painting, Univ Bridgeport, formerly; instr color, Parsons Sch Design, formerly. *Mailing Add:* 334 W 20th St New York NY 10003

LEONG, JAMES CHAN
PAINTER
b San Francisco, Calif, Nov 27, 29. *Study:* Calif Col Arts & Crafts, BFA & MFA; San Francisco State Col, MA; Univ Oslo. *Comn:* Mural, Chung Mei Home for Boys, El Cerrito, Calif, 51; mural, Ping Yuen Housing Proj, San Francisco, 52; mural, San Francisco State Col, 54; prologue sequence, John Huston's Movie Freud, 62. *Exhib:* Mus Mod Art, Whitney Mus Am Art & Nat Inst Arts & Lett, New York; Tate Gallery, London; Inverse Illusionism, Am Fedn Arts Traveling Exhib, 71-72; Istanbul, Izmir, Ankara, Turkey, 74; Larcada Gallery, New York, 75; US Info Serv Bicentennial Exhib, Oslo, Copenhagen, Helsinki, 76; and others. *Teaching:* Vis prof painting, Univ Ga, 71. *Bibliog:* Robert Craft & Igor Strawinsky (auth), Themes and Episodes, Doubleday. *Media:* Mixed Media. *Mailing Add:* Piazza del Biscione 95 Rome Italy

LEOPOLD, BARRY FRANCIS See Barry, Frank

LEOPOLD, MICHAEL CHRISTOPHER
CRITIC
b Wichita Falls, Tex, July 22, 29. *Study:* Univ Ariz. *Pos:* Dir pagina ingles, El Gran Mundo, Mex, 59-60; Los Angeles ed, Artnews, 71 & Artgallery Mag, 72-73; Los Angeles contribr, Art Int, Lugano, Switz, 73- *Awards:* Fel, Huntington Hartford Found, 50. *Res:* 20th century sculpture; Guerriero--his conscious, subconscious and unconsious, six-volume fiction work of psychological development of artist. *Publ:* Auth, Artists of Mexico, El Gran Mundo, Mex, 59; auth, Guerriero, Santa Barbara Mus Art, Calif, 69; auth, The Art of Henry Guerriero, Univ Southern Calif, 70. *Mailing Add:* 3036 Veteran Ave Los Angeles CA 90034

LEPPER, ROBERT LEWIS
EDUCATOR, SCULPTOR
b Aspinwall, Pa, Sept 10, 06. *Study:* Carnegie Inst Technol, BA; Harvard Univ Grad Sch Bus Admin, cert. *Work:* Butler Mus Am Art, Youngstown, Ohio; Carnegie Mus Art, Pittsburgh, Pa; Ind Univ, Bloomington; Mus Mod Art, New York, NY; Stedelijk Mus, Amsterdam, Holland. *Comn:* Mural, WVa Univ, Morgantown, 40 & Airport, Charleston, WVa, 50; sculpture, Pittsburgh Hilton Hotel, Pa, 59; windows, Convent Immaculate Conception, Washington, Pa, 61; sculpture, New York World's Fair, 64. *Exhib:* Pittsburgh Int, 61; Artist-Teacher Today-USA, State Univ NY Col Oswego, 69; Blossom, Kent Third Invitational, 70. *Teaching:* Prof design, Carnegie-Mellon Univ, 30-75. *Awards:* Medal, Pa Soc Architects, 61; Purchase Award, Carnegie Mus Art, 63; Honored Artist, Assoc Artists Pittsburgh, 70. *Bibliog:* Student projects, Indust Design, 2/57; T R Newman (auth), Plastics as an Art Form, Chilton, 64; N Roukes (auth), Sculpture in Plastics, Reinhold, 69. *Mem:* Assoc Artists Pittsburgh (mcm bd, 64). *Media:* Mixed Media. *Publ:* Auth, The problem of the creative artist in America today, Col Art J, 54; auth, Signs & symbols, Archit Record, 56; co-auth, Transit vehicle design & rider satisfaction, Urban & Social Change Rev, 70; co-auth, Ride on, Indust Design, 71. *Mailing Add:* 5732 Kentucky Ave Pittsburgh PA 15232

LERMAN, DORIS (HARRIET)
PAINTER, SCULPTOR
b Newark, NJ. *Study:* Inst Mod Art; Napeague Inst Art; also with Victor D'Amico & William Baziotes. *Work:* Guild Hall, East Hampton, NY. *Comn:* Poster, Guild Hall, Exhib, Mus Mod Art, 55. *Exhib:* One-man show, Gallery 84, New York, 71, 73, 75 , 78 & 81; Artists of the Spring, East Hampton, 73-83; Circulating Exhib, Suffolk Co Schs, 75; Invitationals, Guild Hall, East Hampton, 77-81; Benson Gallery, Bridgehampton, 77-80; and others. *Pos:* Mem bd dirs & pres, Victor D'Amico Inst Art, 73- *Awards:* Hon Mention, Guild Hall, 65 & 74; Best in Mixed Media, Guild Hall, 78. *Mem:* Metrop Painters & Sculptors; Guild Hall; NY Soc Women Artists. *Media:* Miscellaneous. *Dealer:* Gallery 84 30 W 57th St New York NY 10019. *Mailing Add:* 145 E 15th St New York NY 10003

LERMAN, LEO
WRITER, HISTORIAN
b New York, NY, May 23, 14. *Pos:* Feature ed, Vogue, 72-83; ed-in-chief, Vanity Fair, 83- *Teaching:* Lectr, TV & radio; lectr art of biog & writing of children's bks, NY Univ. *Awards:* Lotus Club Award for the Museum--100 Years of the Metropolitan Museum of Art, 69. *Res:* Italian Renaissance; international 19th century social history art, especially 1830-1914. *Publ:* Auth, Leonardo da Vinci: Artist & Scientist, Bobbs-Merrill, 40; auth, Michelangelo: A Renaissance Profile, Knopf, 41; auth, The Museum 100 Years of the Metropolitan Museum of Art, Viking, 69; contribr, Vogue, New York Times, Atlantic Monthly, Sat Rev & others. *Mailing Add:* 350 Madison Ave New York NY 10017

LERMAN, ORA
PAINTER, SCULPTOR
b Campbellsville, Ky, Mar 14, 38. *Study:* Antioch Col, BA; Pratt Inst, with Calvin Albert, MFA; Art Students League, with Theodoros Stamos; Brooklyn Mus, with Reuben Tam. *Work:* Nat Collection Fine Arts, Smithsonian Inst, Washington, DC. *Exhib:* One-woman shows, Prince St Gallery, 71, 72, 74 & 76; Contemporary Sculpture, Suffolk Mus, Stony Brook, NY, 74; 20 Fulbright Artists, Inst Int Educ, NY, 75; Works on Paper, Brooklyn Mus, 75; Sons & Others, Women See Men, Queens Mus, 75. *Teaching:* Mem fac sculpture, New Sch Social Res, 67-69; prof art, Suffolk Co Community Col, 71-82. *Awards:* MacDowell Colony fel; State Univ NY res grants; Ossabaw Found fel. *Bibliog:* Lawrence Campbell (auth), articles, Art News, 4/71 & 10/73; John Gruen (auth), article, Soho Weekly News, 10/75. *Mem:* Col Art Asn Am; Women in the Arts. *Media:* Oil, Watercolor; Wax, Clay. *Mailing Add:* 463 West St New York NY 10014

LERNER, ABE
BOOK DESIGNER
b New York, NY, Sept 14, 08. *Exhib:* Cooper Union (bk designs), 48; YMCA (photographs), Newburyport, Mass, 74-75; New York Community Col, 75. *Pos:* Asst prod mgr, Viking Press, 37-42; art dir & prod mgr, World Publ Co, Cleveland & New York, 42-50 & 54-64; chmn, Trade Bk Clin, Am Inst Graphic Arts, 53-54; chmn, 50 Bks of Yr Comt, 55; dir design & prod, The Macmillan Co, 64-71, ed art bks, 71-74; free lance designer, currently. *Teaching:* Lect series on design problems and their solution for young bk designers, Am Inst Graphic Arts; instr bk design & prod, Am Inst Graphic Arts, 41-42; instr bk design & prod, Columbia Univ, 53-54. *Awards:* Bks included in Fifty Books of the Year, eight yrs, 38-54; Trade Bk Clin monthly selections, 38- *Mem:* The Grolier Club; The Typophiles (vpres); Am Printing Hist Asn. *Publ:* Contribr, Fine Print, Publ Weekly & Bk Prod; auth, Assault on the Book, Bird & Bull Press, 79; auth, Form and Content, Angelica Press, 79. *Mailing Add:* 101 W 12th St New York NY 10011

LERNER, ABRAM
MUSEUM DIRECTOR
b New York, NY, Apr 11, 13. *Study:* NY Univ, BA; also var art schs, New York & Florence. *Exhib:* One-man exhib, Davis Gallery, New York; Brooklyn Mus; Pa Acad Fine Arts; ACA Gallery, New York; Peridot Gallery, New York. *Pos:* Asst dir, ACA Gallery, 45-55; asst dir, Artists Gallery, 55-56; cur, Hirshhorn Collection, 56-67, dir, Hirshhorn Mus & Sculpture Garden, Smithsonian Inst, 67- *Mem:* Arch Am Art (adv bd). *Publ:* Contribr mag & mus catalogs; auth, Gregory Gillespie, 77. *Mailing Add:* Hirshhorn Mus & Sculpture Garden Independence Ave & Eighth St SW Washington DC 20560

LERNER, ALEXANDRIA SANDRA
PAINTER, PUBLISHER
b Philadelphia, Pa. *Study:* Pa Acad Fine Arts, cert, 75; Philadelphia Col Art, BFA, 76. *Work:* Philadelphia Mus Art, Pa; Rutgers Univ, NJ; Art Inst Chicago, Ill; Houghton Libr, Harvard Univ; Franklin Furnace Archive, New York. *Exhib:* 25 Pa Women Artists, Southern Alleghenies Mus, 79; Artists Books, Tweed Mus, Minn, 80; Speaking Volumes, AIR Gallery, New York, 80; Small Works, Washington Square East Gallery, New York, 81; Three American Artists, ABF Gallery, Germany, 81; A Contemporary Survey Art Books, Southern Alleghenies Mus, Loretto, Pa, 81; Beyond the Garden Wall (solo exhib), Marian Locks Gallery, Philadelphia, 82. *Collections Arranged:* Erotic Art, Nexus Gallery, Philadelphia, 80; Bookworks (auth, catalog), Nexus Gallery, Philadelphia, 80; A Contemporary Survey Art Books (auth, catalog), Philadelphia Art Alliance, 81; Women in Art, William Penn Mus, Pa, 81. *Pos:* Co-dir, Artist Book Project, Nat Endowment Arts & Pa Council Grants, 80-; co-dir, Synapse: A Visual Art Press, Pa, 80- *Awards:* Stedman Fund Purchase Prize, Rutgers Univ, 76; Philadelphia Mus Purchase Prize, Cheltenham Art Ctr, 80; Purchase Award, Art Inst Chicago, 81. *Mem:* Found for Today's Art/Nexus (trustee 76-); Philadelphia Art Alliance (chmn 80-); Fel Pa Acad Fine Arts; Citizens Arts in Pa; Artists Equity. *Publ:* Auth, Ruffled Passions, Visual Art Press, 80. *Dealer:* Marian Locks Gallery 1542 Walnut St Philadelphia PA 19102. *Mailing Add:* 907 Pine St Philadelphia PA 19107

LERNER, MARTIN
CURATOR, HISTORIAN
b Brooklyn, NY, Nov 14, 36. *Study:* Brooklyn Col, BA, 59; Inst Fine Arts, New York, 62-65. *Collections Arranged:* Indian Miniatures from the Jeffrey Paley Collection (auth, catalog), Metrop Mus Art, New York, 74, Bronze Sculptures from Asia (auth, catalog), 75, Blue and White: Early Japanese Export Ware (auth, catalog), 76-77 & Along the Ancient Silk Routes, Cent Asian Art from Berlin, 82. *Pos:* Asst cur Oriental art, Cleveland Mus Art, 66-72; vchmn in charge of Far Eastern art, Metrop Mus Art, New York, 72-76 & cur, Indian & Southeast Asian art, 76- *Teaching:* Asst prof Oriental art, Univ Calif, Santa Barbara, 65-66 & Case-Western Univ, Cleveland, 68-71. *Res:* Indian and Southeast Asian art. *Publ:* Auth, Treasures of South Asian Sculpture, The Connoisseur, 76; Early Chola Bronzes at the Norton Simon Museum of Art, Chhavi-2, 81. *Mailing Add:* Metrop Mus of Art Fifth Ave at 82nd St New York NY 10028

LERNER, NATHAN BERNARD
PHOTOGRAPHER, PAINTER
b Chicago, Ill, Mar 30, 13. *Study:* Nat Acad Art, Chicago; Art Inst Chicago; New Bauhaus, Chicago; Sch Design Chicago, BA; also with Archipenko, Moholy-Nagy and G Kepes. *Work:* George Pompidou Ctr, Paris, France; Mus Mod Art, New York; Bauhaus-Archiv, Berlin, Ger; Nihon Univ, Tokyo, Japan; Art Inst Chicago. *Exhib:* Pentax Gallery, Tokyo, Japan, 75; Emergence of Modernism in Ill, 1914-1940, Ill State Mus, Springfield, 75; Photogr & the

City, Mus of Contemp Art, Chicago, 76; Lazlo Moholy-Nagy Exhib, Georges Pompidou Centre, Paris, 77; Recent Acquisitions, Int Mus of Photog, George Eastman House, Rochester, NY, 77. *Teaching:* Instr photogr, Sch Design, Chicago, 39-43; instr product design, Inst Design, Chicago, 45-49. *Bibliog:* Gerald Fromberg (auth), Nathan Lerner--The Bauhaus Years (film), Bradley Univ, Peoria, Ill, 74; Elaine A King (auth), Nathan Lerner--Photographer, Midwest Art, 76. *Mem:* Artists Guild of Chicago. *Publ:* Auth, Space in Your Pictures, Minican Photog, 42; coauth (with Gyorgy Kepes), Light as a medium of expression, Encyclopedia of Arts, 45. *Dealer:* Allen Frumkin Gallery 520 N Michigan Ave Chicago IL 60611. *Mailing Add:* 849 W Webster Chicago IL 60614

LERNER, SANDRA (SANDRA LERNER GROSS)
PAINTER, COLLAGE ARTIST
b New York, NY. *Study:* Brooklyn Col; Pratt Graphic Inst, Artists Am Art Sch; Hofstra Univ, BA. *Work:* Township of Wantagh, NY; Nassau Community Col. *Exhib:* Silvermine Guild of Artists, New Canaan, Conn, 70; Works on Paper, Women in Arts, Brooklyn Mus, 75; Contemp Reflections, 76, New Acquisitions & Loans, 78 & Acquisitions Plus, 81, Aldrich Mus Contemp Art, Ridgefield, Conn; Five Yr Retrospective, Nassau Co Mus Fine Arts, 76; solo shows, Elaine Benson Gallery, Bridgehampton, NY, 79 & Betty Parsons Gallery, New York, 81 & 82; NY Carlsberg Glyptothek Mus, Copenhagen, 80; Striped House Mus, Tokyo, 81; Fine Arts Mus, Long Island, 82; Mus Fine Arts, Houston, 82; and others. *Pos:* Artist in residence, Nassau Co Bd Coop Educ, 75; art coordr, Friends Sch, Old Westbury, NY, 75- *Teaching:* Lectr-demonstr, Nassau Co Pub Sch, NY, 73-75 & Nassau Co Art Mus, 74-75; art lectr, Brandeis Univ Womens Group, 73-75; art teacher, Children's Shelter, Mineola, NY, 74; lectr, Int Commun Agency, Japan, 81. *Awards:* Purchase Prize, Aldrich Mus, Silvermine Guild; Nat Endowment Arts Grant; Int Commun Agency Grant. *Bibliog:* Article, Art News, 4/82; Ferretti (auth), article, 6/12/82 & David Shirey (auth), article, 6/20/82, New York Times. *Mem:* Col Art Asn; Women's Caucus Arts; Nat Asn Women Artists. *Media:* Oil, Acrylic; Mixed Media. *Dealer:* Betty Parsons Gallery 24 W 57th St New York NY 10019; Kauffman Gallery 2701 W Alabama Houston TX 77098. *Mailing Add:* 10 E 18th St New York NY 10003

LERNER, SANDY R
PAINTER, LITHOGRAPHER
b Pa, May 13, 18. *Study:* Lafayette Col, BA; Pratt Inst, MFA; Art Students League; Nat Univ Mex; Washington Univ; also with Diego Rivera, Orozco, Fred Conway, Frank Reilly, Hans Hofmann & Zorach. *Work:* Smithsonian Inst & Navy Mus, Washington, DC; Brooklyn Navy Yard, NY; Tel Aviv Mus, Israel; Pratt Inst, Brooklyn; and others. *Exhib:* Nat Arts Club; Burr Artists; Audubon Artists; Salmagundi Artists; NJ Prof Artists; and others. *Pos:* Exec dir, Art Restoration Tech Inst; ed, Shrine Mag, currently. *Teaching:* Instr, Pratt Inst, Parsons Sch Design, New Sch Soc Res, currently. *Mem:* Salmagundi Club; Burr Artists; Col Art Asn Am (vpres, 69-70); Am Inst Art & Conserv; Int Inst Conserv Hist Works & Fine Arts; and others. *Media:* Oil, Mixed Media. *Mailing Add:* c/o Art Restoration Tech Inst 71 West 23rd New York NY 10010

LE ROY, HAROLD M
PAINTER, GRAPHIC ARTIST
b New York, NY, Dec 12, 05. *Study:* Columbia Univ, BA; Brooklyn Mus Art Sch; Art Students League; Hans Hofmann Art Sch. *Work:* Butler Inst Am Art, Youngstown, Ohio; Chrysler Mus at Norfolk, Va; Slater Mem Mus, Norwich, Conn; Smithsonian Inst, Washington, DC; Fine Arts Mus Lincoln, NY. *Exhib:* Societe de L'Ecole Francaise, Mus Artes Mod, Paris, France, 69 & 70; Audubon Artists Ann Exhibs, Nat Acad Galleries, New York, 70-77; Am Soc Contemp Artists 57th Ann, Lever House, 75; Artists Equity Exhib, Union Carbide Gallery, 75; Brooklyn Mus, 79 & 80. *Awards:* Heydenryk Award for Graphic Art, 77; Am Vet Award for Oil Painting, 79; Binney & Smith Award for Oil Painting, 81. *Bibliog:* Barbara Consolas (auth), Le Roy & the World of Art, Plotinus Press, 72; Robert S Orlove (auth), The Mind of Le Roy, W T M Publ, 73; E Flomenhaft (auth), The Unique Art of Harold Le Roy, Profile Press. *Mem:* Artists Equity Asn New York (bd dir, 67-80); Metrop Painters & Sculptors; Am Vet Soc Artists; Am Soc Contemp Artists (pres, 79-81). *Media:* Oil, Serigraph. *Dealer:* Randall Galleries 823 Madison Ave New York NY 10021. *Mailing Add:* 1916 Ave K Brooklyn NY 11230

LESCALLEET
PAINTER, PHOTOGRAPHER
b Baltimore, Md, Dec 5, 23. *Study:* Temple Univ, 58; Md Inst Col Art, BFA, 58, MFA, 63; with John C Pellew. *Work:* Center Club, Baltimore, Md. *Exhib:* Internaz Ai Frati Int, Italy, 71; Md Show, Easton Acad Fine Arts, 71; Laguna Gloria Mus Nat Competition, Austin, Tex, 72; Peale Mus, Baltimore, Md, 74; Bicentennial Exhib, Kennedy Ctr, Washington, DC, 75. *Teaching:* Instr basic drawing, Md Inst Col Art, 64-65. *Awards:* Robert F McCellan Award, Rehoboth Art League, 71; First Prize, League Am Pen Women, 75; Baltimore's Best Award, City Hall, 79. *Bibliog:* Otto Dekom (auth), Gallery Tour, Morning News, Wilmington, Del, 75; Harbor Art by Lescalleet, The Sunpapers-Sunday Sun, 79; Harriss (auth), Lively Arts, Baltimore News American, 79. *Mem:* Artist Equity; League Am Pen Women; assoc mem Rehoboth Art League; Baltimore Women's Art Commission. *Media:* Acrylics. *Publ:* Illusr, School zoo, Camera Mag, 50. *Mailing Add:* 239 W Lanvale St Baltimore MD 21217

LESCH, ALMA WALLACE
TAPESTRY ARTIST, EDUCATOR
b McCracken Co, Ky, 1917. *Study:* Murray State Univ, BS, 41; Louisville Sch Art, 59-61; Univ Louisville, MEd, 62. *Work:* Objects: USA, Johnson

Collection; J B Speed Art Mus, Louisville, Ky; Evansville Mus of Art, Ind; Mint Mus, Charlotte, NC; Flint Inst Art, Mich. *Comn:* Draperies, Bernheim Forest Nature Mus, Clermont, Ky, 62; wall hangings, First Nat Bank, Louisville, 67, First Presby Church, Columbus, Ind, 70 & Citizens Fidelity Bank, Louisville, 72; tapestry, Meldinger Tower, Louisville, 83. *Exhib:* Nat Decorative Arts Wichita, Kans, 62, 66 & 70; Fabric Collage, Mus Contemp Crafts, New York, 65; Fine Art of Collage, Kunstegewerbemus, Zurich, Switz, 68; Objects: USA, Smithsonian Inst, 70; 1st World Crafts Exhib, Toronto, Ont, 74; plus others. *Teaching:* Assoc prof textiles, Louisville Sch Art, 61-78; instr vegetable dyeing, Haystack Mountain Sch Crafts, Deer Isle, Maine, summers 66 & 70, Philadelphia Col Textiles, Memphis Acad Art, summer 67 & Indian Sch, Santa Fe, 72; instr, Arrowmont Sch Crafts, Gatlinburg, Tenn, 70-77; adj prof, Univ Louisville, 75- *Awards:* Merit & Craft Awards, J B Speed Art Mus, 68, 70 & 72; Nat Competition Award, Wichita, Kans, 72; Best of Show, Evansville Mus Art, 78. *Bibliog:* Rose Slivka (auth), Craftsmen of the Modern World, Horizon, 68; Lee Nordness (auth), Objects: USA, Viking, 70; Portraits without Faces (film), Ky Arts Comn, 77-78. *Mem:* World Crafts Coun; Am Crafts Coun; Ky Guild Artists & Craftsmen; Louisville Craftsmen Guild. *Media:* Textiles. *Publ:* Auth, Vegetable Dyeing, Watson-Guptill, 70. *Mailing Add:* PO Box 67 Shepherdsville KY 40165

LESH, RICHARD D
PAINTER, INSTRUCTOR
b Grand Island, Nebr, May 3, 27. *Study:* Univ Nebr; Univ Denver, BA & MA; Mexico City Col. *Exhib:* Midwest Biennial, 58; Nebraska Centennial, Joslyn Mus, Omaha, 67 & Sheldon Gallery, Lincoln, 68; Nebr Wesleyan Univ Painting Ann, Lincoln, 78. *Pos:* Pres, Nebr Art Coun, 68-69. *Teaching:* Instr painting & head dept art, Wayne State Col, 51- *Awards:* Second Prize for Painting, Midwest Biennial, Joslyn Mus, 55; First Prize for Painting, May Show, Sioux City Art Mus, 58. *Mem:* Col Art Asn Am; Nebr Art Teachers Asn; Kappa Pi. *Mailing Add:* 2631 Flintridge Pl Ft Collins CO 80521

LESHER, MARIE PALMISANO
SCULPTOR
b Reading, Pa, Sept 20, 19. *Study:* Art Students League; Berte Fashion Studio, Philadelphia, Pa; Mus of Fine Arts Sch & Univ, Houston, Tex. *Work:* Beaumont Art Mus, Tex; Laguna Gloria Art Mus, Austin, Tex; Carver Mus, Tuskegee, Ala; Reading Pub Mus, Pa; San Jacinto Col North, Houston, Tex. *Exhib:* Seventh Ann Eight State Exhib, Okla Art Ctr, Oklahoma City, 65; 28th Ann Nat Exhib, Jersey City Mus, NJ, 69; 22nd Ann, Butler Inst of Am Art, Youngstown, Ohio, 70; Catharine Lorillard Wolfe Art Club Ann, New York, 73, 79 & 81; Nat Sculpture Soc 40th & 41st Ann, New York, 73 & 74; Int Women's Arts Festival, New York, 76; 14th Biennial, Joslyn Mus of Art, Omaha, Nebr, 76; and many others. *Pos:* Advert mgr & art dir, Lowensteins, Memphis, Tenn, 45-46, Levy's, Houston, Tex, 46-50, Sakowitz, Houston, 50-52, Battelstein's, 59-60. *Teaching:* Instr sculpture, Sculptors Workshop, Houston, 72-73. *Awards:* First Award, Tex Fine Arts Asn, 73; First Purchase Award, Tri-State Exhib, Beaumont, Tex, Mobil Found, 75; Prix de Paris, 78; and others. *Bibliog:* Reva Remy (auth), L'Art a l'estranger, La Revue Mod, Paris, 6/68; Helen Anderson (auth), Objects: USA, The sculptress, Houston Post, 3/68; Marie David (auth), Please do touch!, Houston Chronicle, 6/69. *Mem:* Artists Equity, New York; Tex Soc Sculptors Int (dir, 73-); Artists Equity, Philadelphia; Fashion Group (secy-treas, 47-48); Knickerbocker Artists New York; and others. *Media:* Multimedia. *Dealer:* Sol Del Rio 1020 Townsend Ave San Antonio TX 78209. *Mailing Add:* 10130 Shady River Rd Houston TX 77042

LESKO, DIANE
HISTORIAN, EDUCATOR
US citizen. *Study:* State Univ NY, Binghamton, AB, 71, MA, 75, PhD, 81. *Teaching:* Asst prof art hist, Lycoming Col, 78- *Mem:* Col Art Asn; Womens Caucus Art. *Res:* Nineteenth and twentieth century European art, emphasis on French and Belgian painting. *Publ:* Auth, Cezanne's Bather and a found self-portrait, 76 & Ensor in his milieu, 77, Artforum; auth, From genre to allegory in Gustave Courbet's Les Demoiselles de Village, Art J, 79; auth, Il Faut Etre de Son Temps: Charles Negre as painter-photographer in mid-19th century France, Arts, 81; auth, James Ensor, the Creative Years, Princeton Univ Press (in prep). *Mailing Add:* 550 Woodland Ave Williamsport PA 17701

LESLIE, SEAVER
PAINTER, INSTRUCTOR
b Boston, Mass, Aug 22, 46. *Study:* RI Sch Design, BFA, 69 & MA, 70; with Peter Blake, London, Eng, 73-74. *Work:* Fogg Art Mus, Cambridge, Mass; The Continental Corp, Tatistcheff & Co & Simpson, Thatcher & Bartlett, New York. *Comn:* Art Park, Lewiston, NY, 75. *Exhib:* Nat Arts Club Invitational Drawing, New York, 80; Manhattan, Whitney Mus, New York, 82. *Teaching:* Instr painting, RI Sch Design, 71-81, Parsons Sch Design, 80-82, Wellesley Col, 83-84. *Awards:* Second Prize Painting, Providence Art Club, Hilton Kramer, 70. *Bibliog:* Addison Parks, (auth), Seaver Leslie, Arts Mag, 80; Edward Sozanski (auth), Seaver Leslie, Providence J, 82; Daniel Schulman (auth), Seaver Lesie, Arts Mag, 83. *Media:* Oil, Watercolor. *Publ:* West by East, RI Sch Design, 70; 12 Points--Putting the Case for Customary Weight and Measure, Am Customary Weight & Measure, 79. *Dealer:* Tatistcheff & Co 50 W 57th St New York NY 10019. *Mailing Add:* 50 W 57th St New York NY 10019

LESNICK, STEPHEN WILLIAM
PAINTER, INSTRUCTOR
b Bridgeport, Conn, Mar 22, 31. *Study:* Silvermine Col Art; Art Career Sch; also with Revington Arthur, Jon McCleand, Jack Wheat & Gail Symon.

Work: Boulder City Hosp Art Collection, Nev. *Comn:* Indust paintings, Burndy Libr Art & Sci, 59; portrait of Gov mansion, Gov Paul Laxalt, Carson City, 68; commemorative coin (Boulder Dam), Elks Lodge, Las Vegas, 71-78; medallion series, Nev State Mus, 77- *Exhib:* All New Eng Art Exhib, Conn, 55; Layout & Design Int Art Competition, Japan, 63; Ann Conn Relig Art Exhib, 63 & 64; Ann Am Watercolor Soc Show, 68; Helldorado Western Art Exhib, Nev, 68. *Pos:* Layout designer, Vacart Art Studio, Stamford, Conn, 60-65; art dir, Kelley & Reber Advert, Las Vegas, 65-66; illusr, E G & G, Inc, Las Vegas, 66-73; art ed, Las Vegas Sun, 70-; syndicated newspaper columnist, Art for Everyone. *Teaching:* Instr art, Desert Art League, Boulder City, 65-66; instr art, Las Vegas Art League & Artists & Craftsmans Guild, Nev, 65-68 & Clark Co Community Col; owner & instr, Lesnick Art Studio, Las Vegas, 65- *Awards:* Int Design Show, Japan, 63; Conn Relig Show, Hallmark Greeting Cards, 63 & 64; First Prize, Nev Bicentennial Commemorative Medallion, Franklin Mint, 72. *Bibliog:* Articles in Desert Scope, 69-71. *Mem:* Nev State Watercolor Soc. *Media:* All Media. *Interests:* Inventor and manufacturer of The Funny Brush. *Mailing Add:* 1127 Westminster Ave Las Vegas NV 89119

LETENDRE, RITA
PAINTER
b Drummondville, Que, Nov 1, 28. *Study:* Ecole Beaux Arts, Montreal; P E Borduas, Montreal. *Work:* Mus Art Contemporain, Montreal; Mus Beaux-Arts, Montreal; Long Beach Mus Fine Arts, Calif; Rose Art Mus, Brandeis Univ, Waltham, Mass; Mus Que. *Comn:* Wall painting, Calif State Col, Long Beach, 65; mural, Greenwin of Toronto, 71; wall painting, Benson & Hedges, Neil-Wyick Col, Toronto, 71; mural, J D S Investment, Sheridan Mall, Pickering, Ont, 72. *Exhib:* Internationalism des Arts, Mus Beaux-Arts, 60; 5 Festival di due Mondi, Spoleto, Italy, 62; IV Biennale Can Painting, Tate Gallery, London, Eng, 63; Can Pavilion Expo 67, Montreal, 67; Que Pavilion, World's Fair, Osaka, Japan, 70; and others. *Awards:* Le Prix de Peinture, Concours Artistique Que, 61; Que Bourse de Recherche, 67; Can Arts Coun Sr Grant Award, 71. *Bibliog:* C Delloye (auth), Rita Letendre, Art Aujourdhui, 62; D Travers (auth), Rita Letendre wall painting, Arts & Archit, 66; Jules Heller (auth), Printmaking Today, Holt, Rinehart & Winston, 71. *Mem:* Royal Can Acad Art. *Media:* Acrylic. *Mailing Add:* 288 Sherbourne St Toronto ON M5A 2S1 Canada

LEUTWYLER, BRUCE
PUBLISHER, PATRON
b Great Berd, Kans, 1957. *Study:* Rice Univ. *Pos:* Pres, Eidos Fine Art, Inc, Houston, Tex. *Specialty:* Publishers & distributors of original lithographs by Fernando Casas & Steve Adams. *Interests:* Art that runs counter to the conventional wisdom about contemporary art. *Collection:* Fernando Casas, Steve Adams & Jean Arp. *Mailing Add:* Eidos Fine Art, Inc 4906 Travis Houston TX 77002

LEVEE, JOHN H
PAINTER, SCULPTOR
b Los Angeles, Calif, Apr 10, 24. *Study:* Art Ctr Sch & Chenard Sch, Los Angeles; Univ Calif, Los Angeles, BA, 48; New Sch Social Res, with Stuart Davis, Abe Rattner & Kunyoshi, 48-49; Acad Julian, Paris, grand prix, 51. *Work:* Mus Mod Art, New York; Whitney Mus Am Art, New York; Guggenheim Mus, New York; Corcoran Gallery Art, Washington, DC; Mus Mod Art, Paris; plus many others in pub & pvt collections. *Comn:* Wall, Architects, Chateau Vaudreuil, Paris, 71-72; walls, Bank Credit Com, Paris, 72-73; floor design, Sch Marne-le-Vallee, Paris, 75; walls & banners, Prudential Life Insurance Co, Los Angeles, 77. *Exhib:* Corcoran Gallery Art, 56-58; New Acquisitions, Mus Mod Art, New York, 57, Young Am Painters, 57-58; Whitney Mus Am Art, 57, 58 & 66; Haifa Mus Art, Israel, 63; Phoenix Art Mus, Ariz, 64; Krannert Art Mus, Univ Ill, 65; Walker Art Ctr, Minneapolis, 65; Tel Aviv Mus, Israel, 69; Palm Springs Mus, Calif, 77; plus many others. *Teaching:* Vis prof art, Univ Ill, 64-65, Washington Univ, 67, NY Univ, 67-68 & Univ Southern Calif, 70. *Awards:* Ford Fel, Tamarind Workshop, 69; Woolmark Found Prix, 74. *Media:* Acrylic; Plexiglas. *Collection:* African, pre-Columbian and contemporary painting and sculpture. *Dealer:* Andre Emmerich Gallery 41 E 57th St New York NY 10022; Leavin Margo Gallery 812 N Robertson Blvd Los Angeles CA 90035. *Mailing Add:* 119 rue Notre Dame des Champs Paris France

LEVEN, ANN R
ADMINISTRATOR
b Canton, Ohio, Nov 1, 40. *Study:* Brown Univ, AB, 62; studio work at RI Sch of Design; Harvard Bus Sch, MBA, 64; Fogg Mus. *Pos:* Asst treas, 70-72 & treas, 72-79, Metrop Mus of Art, New York: Mus Aid Panel (mem), New York State Coun on the Arts, 77-79; adv comt, Art Dept, Brown Univ; trustee, Artist's Choice Mus; vpres, Chase Manhattan Bank, 79-; staff laison, Nat Endowment Arts, 81. *Teaching:* Adj prof, Grad Sch Business, Columbia Univ. *Mailing Add:* 1160 Third Ave New York NY 10021

LEVENTHAL, RUTH LEE
SCULPTOR, PAINTER
b New York, NY, Oct 5, 23. *Study:* Art Students League; Nat Acad Design; also with John Terken, Robert Tompkins, Maxim Bugester & Frank Eliscu. *Work:* Fedn Jewish Philanthropies, New York; Mus Mod Art, Israel; Tel Aviv Univ, Israel; Goldsmith's Hall, London, Eng; Riverside Mem Chapel, New York; and others. *Comn:* Three paintings, New York World's Fair, 64-65; sculptures, Riverside Mem Chapel, 70 & 72; portrait of Golda Meir, pvt comn, 72. *Exhib:* Parke Bernet Galleries; Nat Arts Club, New York; one-man shows, Kottler Galleries, New York, 70; Temple Sinai, Roslyn, Long Island, 71 & Chapman Sculpture Gallery, Sculptured Gold Jewelry, Bergdorf-Goodman,

New York, 72; and others. *Awards:* Gold Medal, Catharine Lorillard Wolfe Art Club, 70, 73 & 81; Salmagundi Award, 75, 76, 78, 79, 81 & 83; Award for Portraiture Sculpture, Nat Acad Design, 78; and others. *Mem:* Fel Royal Soc Arts; Nat Soc Arts & Lett (bd dir, 74-77); Catharine Lorillard Wolfe Art Club (bd dir, 74-77); Allied Artists Am; Salmagundi Club; and others. *Media:* All Media. *Publ:* Coauth, Take One of My Pills, 65 & Our Romance is Over, 66, New Recording; cover illusr, NATA Quart, fall-winter 70. *Mailing Add:* 425 E 58th St New York NY 10022

LEVERING, ROBERT K
PAINTER, ILLUSTRATOR
b Ypsilanti, Mich, May 22, 19. *Study:* Univ Ariz, AB; Art Inst Chicago; Brooklyn Mus Sch Art; Art Students League. *Work:* USAF Collection, Washington, DC; also in pvt collections. *Comn:* Portraits of Kennedy, Eisenhower, U Thant, Martin Luther King & Dag Hamerskjold. *Exhib:* Seven exhibs, New York City Ctr Gallery; Soc Illustrators Gallery, New York; Mikelson Gallery, Washington, DC, 68; Art Dirs Exhib, 69. *Teaching:* Guest lectr & critic, Parsons Sch Design, 65- *Awards:* Gold Medal, Sol Illusr, 69; Citation, NJ Art Dirs Club, 69; Soc Publ Designers Award, 69. *Mem:* Graphic Artists Guild. *Publ:* Illusr, leading nat mag, bks & newspapers. *Mailing Add:* 330 E 79th St New York NY 10021

LEVI, JOSEF
PAINTER
b New York, NY, Feb 17, 38. *Study:* Univ Conn, BA, 59; Columbia Univ, 60. *Work:* Mus Mod Art, New York; Albright-Knox Gallery, Buffalo; Aldrich Mus Contemp Art, Ridgefield, Conn; Krannert Art Mus, Univ Ill, Urbana; Des Moines Art Ctr. *Exhib:* Highlights of the 65-66 Art Season, Aldrich Mus Contemp Art, 66; Sound, Light, Silence, Art that Performs, Nelson Atkins Gallery, Kansas City, 67; Light, Motion, Space, Walker Art Ctr, Minneapolis, 67; Whitney Mus Am Art Ann, New York, 68; Smithsonian Inst Near East & SAsia Traveling Exhib, 71; Art About Art, Whitney Mus Am Art, NY, 78-79; Illusions of Light, Worcester Art Mus, Mass, 81. *Awards:* Purchase Award, Univ Ill, Urbana, 66; Selected for New Talent USA, Art in Am, 66. *Bibliog:* William Wilson (auth), In the eye of the beholder, Art News, 2/70; J Patrice Marandel (auth), Preface for Silkscreen Portfolio, Domberger, 71; Allen Ellenzweig (auth), Still life with art history: The collage paintings of Josef Levi, Arts Mag, 12/76. *Mailing Add:* 171 W 71st St New York NY 10023

LEVICK, (MR & MRS) IRVING
COLLECTORS
Collection: Contemporary American and European artists, including Gatch, Weber, Dove, Hartley, Rivers, Levine, Marin, Weinberg, King, Knaths, Shahn, Roth, Tam, Greene, Guerero, Avery, Dubuffet, Levee, Nikos, Nicolson, Sutherland, Marini, Fraser, Francis, Wiley, Buggiani, Kinley, Lawrence, Appel, Corneille, Severini, Kingstein, Katzman, Rouault, Graves, Brice, Heerup, Wols, Bauermeister, Jimmy Ernst, James Wines, Lynn Chadwick, Saul Steinberg, Davies, Seymour Drumlevitch, Harriet Grief and others. *Mailing Add:* 227 Nottingham Terr Buffalo NY 14216

LEVIN, GAIL
CURATOR, HISTORIAN
b Atlanta, Ga, Feb 19, 48. *Study:* Sorbonne, Paris, 68; Simmons Col, BA(art hist), 69; Tufts Univ, MA, 70; Rutgers Univ, PhD(art hist), 76. *Collections Arranged:* Morgan Russell: Synchromist Studies, 1910-1922, Mus Mod Art, New York, 76; Synchromism and Am Color Abstraction, 1910-1925, Whitney Mus Am Art, 78; Abstract Expressionism: The Formative Years, traveling exhib, 78; Edward Hopper: Prints and Illustrations, 79 & Edward Hopper: the Art and the Artist, traveling exhib, 80. *Pos:* Assoc cur, Edward Hopper Collection, Whitney Mus Am Art, 76- *Teaching:* Instr, New Sch for Social Res, 73-75; asst prof art hist, Conn Col, New London, 75-76; vis asst prof, Graduate Sch, City Univ New York, 79-80. *Awards:* Rutgers Univ grad fel, res award, 71-72; citation of excellence, Art Libr Soc of New York, 79. *Bibliog:* Ron Peck (auth), Edward Hopper (film, based on conversations with Gail Levin), Arts Council of Great Britain, 81. *Mem:* Am Asn Mus; PEN Freedom to Write; Col Art Asn Am. *Interests:* Modern American and European art. *Publ:* Auth, Edward Hopper: The Complete Prints, 79, Edward Hopper as Illustrator, 79 & Edward Hopper: The Art and the Artist, 80, Norton; auth & illusr, In the footsteps of Edward Hopper, Geographic Mag, 2/83. *Mailing Add:* Whitney Mus Am Art 945 Madison Ave New York NY 10021

LEVIN, HUGH LAUTER
PUBLISHER, DEALER
b Rye, NY, July 2, 51. *Study:* Univ Pa, BA, 73; Wharton Sch. *Pos:* Vpres, Harry N Abrams, Inc, 74-; dir, Abrams Original Editions, 74-83; pres, Hugh Lauter Levin Assoc Inc, 74- *Mem:* Fine Art Publs Asn (treas, 82-); Org Ind Artists. *Specialty:* Publication of contemporary prints and illustrated books. *Mailing Add:* 130 W 17th St New York NY 10011

LEVIN, JEANNE
PAINTER, COLLECTOR
b Cleveland, Ohio, Dec 13, 01. *Study:* Cleveland Sch Art; Wells Col, BA; Cranbrook Acad Art; Soc Arts & Crafts, Detroit; Norton Gallery & Sch Art; pvt study with Gerald Brockhurst, Ernest Fiene, Bruce Mitchell & Zubel Katchadoorian. *Work:* Hirshhorn Mus & Sculpture Garden, Washington, DC; Norton Gallery, West Palm Beach; and others. *Exhib:* Compass Gallery, Nantucket, Mass, 67; Artists of the Hamptons, Guild Hall, East Hampton, NY, 75; Artists of the Region, Ashwaugh Hall, East Hampton, 75-77; Fla Artists Group, Norton Gallery, 75; Lighthouse Gallery, 77; and others incl

many one-man shows. *Pos:* Assoc trustee, Detroit Int Arts, 58-63; founding mem, Gallery Contemp Art, Palm Beach, 63; trustee, New York Studio Sch, 65-69. *Awards:* Four Arts Award, Soc Four Arts, Palm Beach, 67; First Prize, Lighthouse Gallery, 77. *Mem:* Artists Equity; Nat Soc Arts & Lett; Fla Artists Group Inc. *Collection:* Post-impressionists paintings and sculpture; contemporary paintings and sculpture; primitive sculpture, Greek, African and pre-Columbian; the complete collection was exhibited at Cranbrook Academy of Art, Detroit Institute of Arts and Norton Gallery of Art. *Mailing Add:* 316 Garden Rd Palm Beach FL 33480

LEVIN, KIM (KIM PATEMAN)
CRITIC, PAINTER
US citizen. *Study:* Vassar Col, AB; Yale-Norfolk Summer Sch Art; Columbia Univ, MA. *Exhib:* One-woman shows, Suffolk Mus, Stony Brook, Long Island, 63, Poindexter Gallery, NY, 64 & 67 & Vassar Col Art Gallery, 65. *Pos:* Ed assoc, Art News, New York, 64-73; contrib ed, Arts Mag, 73-; NY corresp, Opus Int, 73-77; contribr, Village Voice, 80-; NY corresp, Flash Art, 80- *Teaching:* Lectr drawing, Philadelphia Col Art, 67-70; lectr drawing & painting, Parsons Sch Design, New York, 69-72. *Bibliog:* Jane Holtz Kay (auth), For art's sake, Mademoiselle, 68. *Publ:* Contribr, Am J Archaeol, 64; contribr, Light in Art, Collier, 69; contribr, Super Realism, 75 & contribr, New Artists Video, 78, Dutton; auth, Lucas Samaras, Abrams, 75. *Mailing Add:* 52 W 71st St New York NY 10023

LEVIN, MORTON D
PRINTMAKER, PAINTER
b New York, NY, Oct 7, 23. *Study:* City Univ New York, BS(art educ); studies in Paris, France; painting with Andre Lhote, sculpture with Ossip Zadkine, etching & engraving with Stanley W Hayter & etching with Federico Castellon; studied lithography, Pratt Graphic Arts Ctr, New York. *Work:* New York Pub Libr; Libr of Cong, Washington, DC; Hist of Med Div, Nat Libr Med, Md. *Exhib:* Northwest Printmakers 18th & 21st Ann, Seattle Art Mus, 46-49; 4th-7th Ann Nat Exhib of Prints, Libr of Cong, 46-49; Nat Acad Design & Soc Am Etchers, Gravers, Lithographers and Woodcutters, Inc, 46-48; 46th Ann Watercolor & Print Exhib, Pa Acad Fine Arts, 48; Salon de Mai, Musee D'Art Mod, Paris, France, 51; Biennale Int d'Arte Marinara, Pallazzo del Academia, Genoa, Italy, 51; one-man shows, Galerie Breteau, Paris, France, 52 & Winston Gallery, San Francisco, 77 & 79-81; and others. *Teaching:* Founder, dir & instr printmaking & painting, Morton Levin Graphics Workshop, San Francisco, Calif, 72- *Awards:* Hon Mention, 21st Ann Northwest Printmakers, Seattle Art Mus, 49; Bryan Mem Prize, The Villager Travel Exhib, New York, 64; Third Prize, Washington Sq Art Exhib, Inc, 64. *Media:* Etching, Woodcut; Watercolor, Oil. *Dealer:* Winston Gallery 780 Sutter St San Francisco CA 94109. *Mailing Add:* 1416 Broadway #6 San Francisco CA 94109

LEVINE, DAVID
CARTOONIST, PAINTER
b Brooklyn, NY, Dec. 26. *Study:* Tyler Sch Fine Arts; Hans Hoffman Sch. *Work:* Hirshhorn Mus & Sculpture Garden, Washington, DC; Cleveland Mus, Ohio; Brooklyn Mus, NY; Fogg Art Mus, Cambridge, Mass; Nat Portrait Gallery, Washington, DC. *Exhib:* Whitney Mus Am Art Sculpture & Drawing Ann, 60 & 63; David Levine & Aaron Shikler, Brooklyn Mus, 71; Butler Inst Am Art, 58, 60, 72; Satirical Drawings, Hirshhorn Mus, spring 76; Painting Art Exhib, Claud Bernard Gallery, Paris, France, 79; Caricature Show, Am Cult Ctr, Paris, 79; Philips Gallery, DC, 80; Caricatures Eng 19th century authors, Morgan Libr, 81. *Awards:* Tiffany Found Award, Julius Hallgarten Prize, 60; Thomas B Clarke Prize, Nat Acad Design, 62; Guggenheim Fel. *Bibliog:* P A Dreyfus (auth), The double image of David Levine, Am Artist, 71. *Media:* Ink; Watercolor. *Publ:* Illusr, The Man from MALICE, 66; illusr, Pins and Needles, 69; illusr, No Known Survivors, David Levine's Political Plank, 70; illusr, New York Rev Books; illusr, NY Mag. *Mailing Add:* 161 Henry St Brooklyn NY 11201

LEVINE, JACK
PAINTER
b Boston, Mass, Jan, 3, 15. *Study:* Study with Dr Denman W Ross, 29-31; also with Harold Zimmerman; Colby Col, Hon DFA, 46. *Work:* Metrop Mus Art, New York; Mus Mod Art, New York; Walker Art Ctr, Minneapolis; Art Inst Chicago; Whitney Mus Am Art, New York; plus others. *Exhib:* Retrospectives, Inst Contemp Art, Boston, 53, Whitney Mus Am Art, New York, 55 & Palacio Bellas Artes, Mexico City, Mex, 60; annually, Carnegie Inst, Pittsburgh & Art Inst Chicago; Corcoran Gallery Art, Washington, DC; Mus Mod Art, New York; Mus Fine Arts, Boston; Pa Acad Fine Arts; one-man show, DeCordova Mus, Lincoln, Mass, 68; plus many others. *Teaching:* Lectr, Art Inst Chicago, Skowhegan Sch Painting & Sculpture, Univ Ill, Pa Acad Fine Arts, Am Art Sch, New York & Cleveland Mus Art Sch. *Awards:* Guggenheim Fel, 45 & 46; Corcoran Gallery Art Award, 59; Altman Prize, Nat Acad Design, 75; plus others. *Mem:* Nat Inst Arts & Lett; Artists Equity Asn; Am Acad Arts & Sci; Nat Acad Arts & Lett; and others. *Dealer:* Kennedy Galleries 40 W 57th St New York NY 10019. *Mailing Add:* 68 Morton St New York NY 10014

LEVINE, LES
SCULPTOR, VIDEO ARTIST
b Dublin, Ireland, Oct 6, 35; US citizen. *Study:* Cent Sch Arts & Crafts, London, Eng. *Work:* Nat Gallery Can, Ottawa, Ont; Metrop Mus Art, New York; Whitney Mus Am Art, New York; Mus Mod Art, New York; Philadelphia Mus Art. *Comn:* Contact (sculpture), Gulf & Western Indust, 69. *Exhib:* One-man exhibs, Slipcover, Walker Art Ctr, 67, Star Garden, Mus Mod Art, New York, 67, Contact, Inst Contemp Art, Chicago, 69, I Am Not Blind, Wadsworth Atheneum, 76, Prayer Rug, Philadelphia Mus Art, 79 & We Are Not Afraid, Lower Manhattan Cult Coun, NY Subways, 81; Software Show, Jewish Mus, 70; Documenta, Kassel, WGer, 77; Gold, Mus Mod Art, 78; Everson Video Revue, Everson Mus, Syracuse, 80; San Francisco Int Video Festival, 83; and others. *Collections Arranged:* Open To New Ideas (organizer), Jimmy Carter Collection, Ga Mus Art, Athens, 77. *Pos:* Pres, Mus Mott Art, Inc, 71- *Teaching:* Artist in residence, Aspen Inst, Colo, 67 & 69; assoc prof commun, NY Univ, 72; assoc prof video art, William Paterson Col, 74-75. *Awards:* First Prize for The Star Machine, Sculpture Biennale, Art Gallery Ont, 68; Nat Endowment Arts Fel, 74 & 80; Video Award, New York State Coun Arts, 80; and others. *Bibliog:* David Bourdon (auth), Plastic art's biggest bubble, Life Mag, 8/69; Barbara Cavaliere (auth), Les Levine's ads---and more ads, Arts Mag, 3/81; Vivien Raynor (auth), Not Afraid in the Subway, New York Times, 5/21/82; and others. *Media:* Gold; Multimedia; Videotape. *Publ:* Auth, Cornflakes, The Image of Culture, Jean-Luc Daval (auth), 78; The poets' encyclopedia, Unmuzzled Ox, Vol 4, No 4, New York, 79; publ, Media: The Bio Tech Rehearsal for Leaving the Body, Alberta Col Art, 79; Biennale van de la Critique, Palais des Beaux Arts, Antwerpen Charleroi, 79; auth, Handmade Etchings by Les Levine, Artist Profusions, 81; and others. *Mailing Add:* 20 E 20th St New York NY 10003

LEVINE, MARILYN ANNE
SCULPTOR, EDUCATOR
b Medicine Hat, Alta, Dec 22, 35. *Study:* Univ Calif, Berkeley, MA, 70, MFA, 71. *Work:* Montreal Mus Fine Arts; Nat Mus Mod Art, Kyoto & Tokyo; San Francisco Mus Mod Art; Israel Mus, Jerusalem; Mus Mod Art, Bogota, Colombia; and others. *Exhib:* Fuller Goldeen Gallery, San Francisco, 71, 75, 80 & 83; one-man shows, O K Harris Gallery, New York, 74, 76, 79, 81 & 84; GalerieD; Canada Trajectories, Mus Art Mod, Paris, 73; Retrospectives, Norman McKenzie Art Gallery, Regina, 74 & Inst Contemp Art, Boston, 81; Illusion & Reality, Australian Nat Gallery; Galerie Alain Blondel, Paris, 81; and other group & one-man shows. *Teaching:* Asst prof sculpture & ceramics, Univ Utah, 73-76; vis lectr, Univ Calif, Berkeley, 75-80. *Awards:* Gold Medal, XXVII Concorso Int della Ceramica Arte, 69; Ceramics Int Medal, 73; Nat Endowment Arts Fel, 76 & 80; and others. *Bibliog:* Nancy Foote (ed), The photo realist--12 interviews, Art in Am, 11-12/72; Susan Peterson (auth), The ceramics of Marilyn Levine, Crafts Horizons, Vol 37, 2/77; Hiroshi Matsubara (auth), American west coast artist, Marilyn Levine, Contemp Sculpture, Tokyo, 6/78. *Media:* Clay. *Dealer:* O K Harris Gallery 383 W Broadway New York NY 10012; Fuller Goldeen Gallery 228 Grant Ave San Francisco CA 94108. *Mailing Add:* 950 61st St Oakland CA 94608

LEVINE, MARION LERNER
PAINTER, INSTRUCTOR
b London, Eng, Oct 31, 31; US citizen. *Study:* Art Inst of Chicago, BFA, 54, study with Paul Wieghardt, Max Kahn, Vera Berdich. *Work:* Citibank; Bank Am; Bellevue Hosp; Brooklyn Mus. *Exhib:* Contemp Reflections, Aldrich Mus, Ridgefield, Conn, 76; The New Am Still Life, Westmoreland Co Mus Art, Greensburg, Pa, 79; one-man show, Watercolors, Foundry Gallery, Washington, DC, 80 & Paul Klapper Libr, Queens Col, NY, 81; Nassau Co Mus, Roslyn, NY, 80; Albright-Knox Mus, Buffalo, NY, 81; Douglass Col, New Brunswick, NJ, 82; Andrews Gallery, Col William & Mary, 83; Springfield Art Mus, 83. *Pos:* Chmn, Exhib Momentum, Chicago, 52-53. *Teaching:* Lectr watercolor, Sch Gen Studies, Brooklyn Col, 76-80; instr drawing, Univ Calif, Los Angeles, 77; vis artist, Art Inst Chicago, 81; vis artist, Southwest Mo State Univ, Springfield, 81; instr painting, Col Staten Island, City Univ New York, 81-82. *Awards:* Yaddo Fel, 78, 79 & 83; Award, Am Acad Inst Arts & Letters, 80; Creative Artists Pub Serv Program Fel, 83; and others. *Bibliog:* Ruth Bass (auth), Art rev, Art News, 79; Anselm Hollo (auth), The Shelves of Paradise, Marion Lerner Levine's Watercolors, 79; June Cutler (auth), Marion Lerner Levine, Am Artist, 84; and others. *Mem:* Col Art Asn; Womens Caucus Art. *Media:* Oil, Watercolor. *Dealer:* Prince Street Gallery 121 Wooster St New York NY 10012. *Mailing Add:* 430 Third St Brooklyn NY 11215

LEVINE, MARTIN
PRINTMAKER
b New York, NY, May 14, 45. *Study:* Calif Col Arts & Crafts, MFA(printmaking); State Univ New York, Buffalo, BS(art educ). *Work:* Smithsonian Inst, Washington, DC; Brooklyn Mus; Mus Fine Arts, Boston; Art Inst Chicago, Ill; Carnegie Inst, Pittsburgh; and others. *Comn:* Two etchings of hist landmark (with ADI Gallery, San Francisco), Clorox Co, Oakland, Calif, 76; etchings, Union League Club, Chicago, 83. *Exhib:* 30 Years of American Printmaking, Brooklyn Mus, NY, 76; Seventh Int Print Biennale, Cracow, Poland, 78; XV Int Bienal, Sao Paulo, Brazil, 79; Int Grafik Biennale, Frechen, West Germany, 78, 80 & 82; Bienal Americana de Artes Graficas, Cali, Columbia, 81; Chicago & Vicinity, Art Inst Chicago, 81; Francis Kyle Gallery, London, 83; and many others. *Collections Arranged:* Calif Printmakers Exhib, Brit Printmakers Coun, Ely House, London, 75; Los Angeles Printmaking Socs 75 Foreign Exchange Exhib, Seoul, Korea, 75; Nat Invitational Drawing Exhib, Emporia State Univ, 77 & 78; West Coast Printmakers, RI Sch Design, 79; Archit in Contemp Prints, Pratt Graphics Ctr, 83. *Teaching:* Asst prof printmaking, Northwestern Univ, Evanston, currently. *Awards:* Spec Purchase Award, Davidson Nat Print & Drawing Competition, 73; Purchase Award, 24th Nat Exhib of Prints, Libr Cong, 75; Nat Endowment Arts Printmaking Fel Grant, 77; and others. *Bibliog:* Articles, Art Week, 76 & Bldg Design, London, 83; article & cover, Arts Rev, London, 83. *Mem:* Boston Printmakers; Calif Soc Printmakers; Audubon Artists; Soc Am Graphic Artists. *Media:* Intaglio, Lithography. *Dealer:* Assoc Am Artist 663 Fifth Ave New York NY 10022; Van Straaten Gallery 361 W Superior Chicago IL 60610. *Mailing Add:* Dept of Art, Northwestern Univ Kresge Hall 216 Evanston IL 60201

LEVINE, MELINDA (ESTHER)
CRITIC, EDITOR
b Buffalo, NY, Apr 18, 47. *Study:* State Univ NY, Buffalo, BA, 70; State Univ NY, Stony Brook, 70-71. *Pos:* Asst ed, Artweek, 80-81, managing ed, 81-82; cur, Art Gallery Notre Dame, Belmont, Calif, 82; art critic, San Francisco Mag, 82-83, Berkeley Gazette, 82-83 & San Francisco Focus, 83- *Mem:* Int Asn Art Critics; Media Alliance; Northern Calif Art Writers Guild. *Res:* West Coast contemporary art, particularly that of Northern California and the California clay movement. *Publ:* Articles in San Francisco Focus, San Francisco, Images & Issues, Am Craft & Artweek. *Mailing Add:* 456 61st St Oakland CA 94609

LEVINE, REEVA (ANNA) MILLER
PAINTER, INSTRUCTOR
b Los Angeles, Calif, Nov 23, 12. *Study:* With Emil Bistrom & Alexander Rosenfeld. *Work:* Temple Israel, Long Beach; E Madison YMCA, Seattle; Mt Zion Baptist Church, Seattle; Temple De Hirsch Sinai, Seattle; Providence Hosp, Seattle. *Comn:* Stained glass windows, Temple Beth Sholom, Santa Monica, 44; stained glass windows, Temple Sinai Wedding Chapel, Oakland, 49; ceiling of dome, Al Jolson Mem, Los Angeles, 51; relig arks, Temple Beth Israel, Aberdeen, Wash, 60; mosaic, Temple Beth Sholom, Anchorage, 66; and others. *Exhib:* Solo show, Jewish Community Ctr, Mercer Island, Wash, 79-84; Frederick & Nelson, 79; Temple De Hirsch Sinai, 81; Stillwater Gallery, Seattle, 82; and others. *Pos:* Art dir, Camp Ben Swig, Saratoga, Calif, 52-58. *Teaching:* Jewish Community Ctr, Mercer Island, Wash, 75-79; Bellevue Community Col, Wash, 77-80. *Awards:* First in Drawing, Santa Monica Art Asn, 47; Second in Watercolor, Calif Art Asn, 48; Artist of Year, Music & Art Found, Seattle, 70. *Mem:* Artists Equity Asn. *Media:* Miscellaneous. *Publ:* Illusr, Holy Mountain, 53; illusr, Wild Branch on the Olive Tree, 75. *Mailing Add:* 16 Skagit Key Bellevue WA 98006

LEVINE, SEYMOUR R
COLLECTOR
b Russia, May 28, 06. *Study:* Sch Law, Wash Square Col, NY Univ, JD. *Collection:* Includes works by de Creeft, Elkan, Rubin, Blum, Neujean and others. *Mailing Add:* Carhart Ave Peekskill NY 10566

LEVINE, SHEPARD
PAINTER, EDUCATOR
b New York, NY, June 21, 22. *Study:* Univ NMex, BA & MA; Univ Toulouse, France. *Work:* Parnassus Hall, Athens, Greece; Ore State Univ; Arkia Airlines, Israel. *Exhib:* Am Graphic Arts Asn; Brooklyn Mus; Henry Gallery, Univ Wash; San Francisco Mus Art; Portland Art Mus, Ore; Spokane Art Mus; and others. *Teaching:* Lectr to mus & pvt groups; prof art, Ore State Univ, currently. *Awards:* Purchase Award, Univ Ore. *Mailing Add:* Dept of Art Ore State Univ Corvallis OR 97331

LEVINSON, JOEL D
PHOTOGRAPHER
Study: Univ Calif, Berkeley, BA(communications), 75, MA(visual arts), 77. *Work:* Brandeis Inst; Minneapolis Inst Arts; Boston Mus Fine Arts; J B Speed Art Mus; Addison Gallery Am Art. *Exhib:* Solo exhib, Photographics Gallery, New Canaan, Conn, 77; Ctr Creative Photog, Tucson, 79; Midwest Mus Am Art, Ind, 81, J B Speed Art Mus, 82, O K Harris Gallery, New York, 82 & Art Mus STex, Corpus Christi, 83; Addison Gallery Am Art, 80; Minneapolis Inst Arts, 82; d. *Awards:* Eisner Award, Univ Calif, 78. *Publ:* Auth, article, Artweek, 3/79; auth, article, Photo Communique, 10/82. *Mailing Add:* 8352 Kent Dr El Cerrito CA 94530

LEVINSON, MIMI
PAINTER, LECTURER
b Kenosha, Wis, June 6, 40. *Study:* Carnegie-Mellon Univ, with Roger Anliker, BFA, 62; San Jose State Col, Frick Scholarship, 64. *Work:* Ga Railroad Bank Collection, Augusta; Mesa Vista Hospital, San Diego, Calif. *Comn:* Stained glass wall mosaic, Casselhoff's, Pittsburg, Pa, 62; Batiks, Medical Clinic, San Ysidro, Calif, 77; painted fabric mural, Kaiser-Permanente, San Diego, Calif, 78; silk batik panel, Rocco's Restaurant, San Diego, Calif, 79; batiks, Hillcrest Psychotherapy Ctr, San Diego, Calif, 80. *Exhib:* Craftman's Guild Shows, Arts & Crafts Ctr, Pittsburgh, Pa, 66-67; Art Guild All Media, San Diego Mus Art, Calif, 75 & 81; Fiber Show, Golden West Col, Huntington Beach, Calif, 76; Calif Crafts XI, E B Crocker Art Mus, Sacramento, 79; Exchange Exhib, Yokohama Art Ctr, Japan, 79. *Teaching:* Instr art, Sunnyside Sch, Pittsburgh, Pa, 62-67; workshop leader batik-weaving, Convergence 76, Pittsburgh, Pa, 76; instr cultural arts, Jewish Community Ctr, San Diego, Calif, 79-84. *Awards:* First Prize, Augusta Art Asn, 71; Purchase Prize, Ga Railroad Bank, 72; Third Prize, Weaver's Guild, 75. *Bibliog:* Dan Coyro (auth), Batik: How to turn wax and dye into art, The Sentinel, 75; Jan Jennings (auth), Natural history museum, San Diego Evening Tribune, 78; Elise Miller (auth), Womanism to surrealism, San Diego Mag, 79. *Mem:* Allied Craftsmen; Am Crafts Council; Artists Equity; Calif Fibers (chmn, 77); San Diego Mus Art Guild. *Media:* Batik, Mixed Media. *Publ:* Contribr, Crafts 1976, Southern Calif Designer Inc, 76; contribr, Exotic Needlework, Crown, 78. *Dealer:* Spectrum Gallery 726 Seventh Ave San Diego CA 92101. *Mailing Add:* 1730 Alta Vista Way San Diego CA 92109

LEVINSON, MON
SCULPTOR, PAINTER
b New York, NY, Jan 6, 26. *Work:* Whitney Mus Am Art, New York; Joseph H Hirshhorn Collection, Washington, DC; NY Univ Art Collection; Rose Art Gallery, Brandeis Univ; Columbia Broadcasting Syst, New York. *Comn:* Objects, Mus Mod Art, New York, 64, 66 & 69; sculpture, Pub Sch 166, New York, 67; mural-sculpture, Housing & Redevelop Bd, Demountable Vest Pocket Parks, New York, 69; and others. *Exhib:* Plus by Minus, Albright-Knox Gallery, Buffalo, 68, Paper about Paper, 80; A Plastic Presence, Milwaukee Art Ctr, Wis, New York & San Francisco, 69-70; Whitney Mus Am Art Sculpture Ann, 70 & 73; Storm King Arts Ctr, Mountainville, NY, 72 & 75; Hirshhorn Collection, 74; Rosa Esman Gallery, New York, 76 & 77; 55 Mercer St Gallery, 80; Getler Pall Gallery, New York, 81; Fine Arts Mus, Long Island, 81; and others. *Teaching:* Vis artist, C W Post Col, 70-72 & 76-77. *Awards:* Cassandra Found Award, 72; Creative Artists Pub Serv Prog Award, NY State Coun Arts, 74; Nat Endowment for the Arts fel, 76. *Mailing Add:* 309 W Broadway New York NY 10013

LEVIT, HERSCHEL
PHOTOGRAPHER, HISTORIAN
b Shenandoah, Pa, May 29, 12. *Study:* Pa Acad Fine Arts, Cresson traveling scholar, 33; Barnes Found. *Work:* Mus Mod Art, New York; Metrop Mus, New York. *Exhib:* Pa Acad Fine Arts, 66-69; Art Inst Chicago; Springfield Art Mus, Ill; Brooklyn Mus, NY; Metrop Mus Art & Whitney Mus Am Art, New York; Boston Mus Fine Arts; Columbia Univ, 78; one-man shows, Vassar Col, 79 & Drawings, New Sch, New York; plus others. *Teaching:* Emer prof art, Pratt Inst; vis scholar, City Col, New York, 78-79; instr medieval & renaissance, Parsons Sch, New York, currently. *Publ:* Auth & illusr, Just Point, 72; contribr (photographs), Great Historic Places of Europe, Horizon, 74; auth & photogr, Views of Rome--Then & Now, 76; auth & photogr, French Gothic Art and Architecture, in preparation; auth & photogr, Architecture of Renaissance Venice, in preparation; and others. *Mailing Add:* 220 W 93rd St New York NY 10025

LEVITINE, GEORGE
HISTORIAN
b Kharkoff, Russia, Mar 17, 16; US citizen. *Study:* Univ Paris, PCB, 38; Boston Univ, MA, 46; Harvard Univ, Edward R Bacon scholar & PhD, 52. *Pos:* Mem, Inst for Advanced Study, Princeton, NY, 77-78; ed bd, The Art Bull. *Teaching:* From instr to prof hist art, Boston Univ, 49-64; prof hist art, Harvard Univ Exten, 59-64; prof & head dept art, Univ Md, College Park, 64-78. *Awards:* Am Coun Learned Socs grant, 61; Am Philosophical Soc Grant, 74 & 78; Nat Endowment for the Arts, 77-78. *Mem:* Col Art Asn Am; Soc Hist Art Francais; Am Soc Eighteenth Century Studies. *Res:* European art of the eighteenth and nineteenth century, particularly romanticism. *Publ:* Auth, Some emblematic sources of Goya, J of Wartburg & Courtauld Inst, 59; auth, The 18th century rediscovery of Alexis Grimou and the emergence of the Proto-Bohemian Image of the French artist, Eighteenth Century Studies, Vol 21, No 1; auth, The sculpture of Falconet, New York Graphic Ltd, 72; The Dawn of Bohemianism: The Barbu Rebellion and Primitivism in Neoclassical France, Pa State Univ Press, 78; Girodet-Trioso: An Iconographical Study, Garland Press, 78. *Mailing Add:* Dept of Art Univ of Md College Park MD 20742

LEVITT, ALFRED
PAINTER, PREHISTORIAN
b New York, NY, Aug 15, 94. *Study:* Columbia Univ; Art Students League; Acad Grand Chaumiere, France; also with Hans Hofmann, New York. *Work:* Neveh-Sha'anan Mus, Haifa, Israel; plus many other pvt collections in Europe & US. *Exhib:* Butler Inst Am Art, Youngstown, Ohio, 46; Pa Acad Fine Arts, Philadelphia, 48; Brooklyn Mus Exhibs, 47-59; Whitney Mus Am Art, New York, 49, 53 & 55; one-man shows, Babcock Galleries, New York, 45 & 46, Art Alliance Philadelphia, 47 & Terry Dintenfass Galleries, 83; and many others. *Pos:* Coord chmn, Mod Artists Cape Ann, Mass, 47; founder, dir & instr, Ecole Mod de Provence, St Remy de Provence, France, 49-50 & 59-62. *Teaching:* Lectr cave art, NY Univ, Cooper Union, Archaeol Inst Am at Wagner Col, North Shore Soc Archaeol Inst Am, New York Pub Libr, Philadelphia Art Alliance & also in France; lectr mod art. *Awards:* Chevalier de L'ordre des Arts et Lettres for Outstanding Studies of Stone Age Cave Art, Fr Govt, 75. *Mem:* Archaeol Inst Am; Soc Prehistorique L'Ariege, France; life mem Archaeol Soc Staten Island. *Res:* Various researches of cave art and prehistory; extended visits and studies of the drawing, engraving, painting and sculpture of Stone Age artists in France, Spain and Italy; made extensive studies of prehistoric engravings on boulders in Valcamonica, Brescia, Italy, 80. *Mailing Add:* La Guardia Pl New York NY 10012

LEVITT, HELEN
PHOTOGRAPHER, FILMMAKER
b New York, NY, 1918. *Work:* Mus Modern Art, New York; Metropolitan Mus Art, New York; Boston Mus Fine Arts; Corcoran Gallery Art; Mus Fine Arts, Houston. *Exhib:* Solo exhibs, Mus Modern Art, 43 & 74, Nexus Gallery, Atlanta, 76, Sidney Janis Gallery, 80, Corcoran Gallery Art, 80 & Boston Mus Fine Arts, 83. *Awards:* Guggenheim Fel, 59, 60 & 80; Ford Found Fel, 64; Nat Endowment Arts fel, 76. *Bibliog:* Walker Evans (auth), Quality: Its image in the arts, Atheneum, 69; John Szarkowski (auth), Looking at Photographs, Mus Mod Art, New York, 73; Roberta Hellman & Marvin Hosking (auths), Color Photographs by Helen Levitt, Grossmont Col, 80. *Publ:* Coauth (with James Agee), A Way of Seeing, Horizon, 81. *Dealer:* Daniel Wolf Gallery 30 W 57 St New York NY; Jeff Fraenkel Gallery 55 Grant Ave San Francisco CA. *Mailing Add:* 4 E 12 St New York NY 10003

LEVY, BERNARD
DEALER
b New York, NY, Feb 10, 17. *Study:* NY Univ, BA, 37. *Pos:* Pres, Bernard & S Dean Levy Inc, 73- *Bibliog:* On Madison Avenue, Fortune Mag, 12/47; Rita Reif (auth), Antiques, New York Times, 10/76; Douglas Villiers (auth), Next Year in Jerusalem, Viking Press, 76. *Mem:* Art & Antique Dealers League Am (pres, five yrs). *Specialty:* American paintings; American antique furniture; silver; English and American ceramics. *Mailing Add:* 981 Madison Ave New York NY 10021

LEVY, DAVID CORCOS
PHOTOGRAPHER, EDUCATOR
b New York, NY, Apr 10, 38. *Study:* Columbia Col, BA, 60; NY Univ, MA, 67, PhD, 79. *Work:* Guggenheim Mus, New York. *Teaching:* Exec dean, Parsons Sch Design, New York, 70- *Mailing Add:* c/o Parsons Sch of Design 66 Fifth Ave New York NY 10011

LEVY, HILDA
PAINTER
b Pinsk, Russia. *Study:* Univ Calif, Berkeley, AB; Pasadena City Col; Jepson Art Inst; Univ Calif, Los Angeles; also with Adolph Gottlieb. *Exhib:* Nat Gallery Can, Ottawa, Ont; Libr of Cong, Washington, DC; Butler Inst Am Art, Youngstown, Ohio; San Francisco Mus Art & M H de Young Mem Mus, San Francisco; one-woman show, Calif Palace Legion Hon, Pasadena Mus & McNay Inst, Calif; and others. *Awards:* 40 local & nat awards. *Bibliog:* Edward Reep (auth), Content of Watercolor, Reinhold; Lawrence C Goldsmith (auth), Watercolor Bold & Free, Watson Guptill. *Mem:* Nat Watercolor Soc; Bay Printmakers. *Mailing Add:* 2411 Brigden Rd Pasadena CA 91104

LEVY, MARGARET WASSERMAN
SCULPTOR
b Dec 13, 1899; US citizen. *Study:* Wellesley Col, BA, 22; Bryn Mawr Col, 23; Philadelphia Sch Occupational Therapy, 23-24; Stella Elkins Tyler Sch Art; Pa Acad Art. *Work:* Pa Acad Fine Arts, Philadelphia; Philadelphia Mus Fine Arts, Pa; Drexel Univ, Pa; Woodmere Art Gallery, Philadelphia. *Comn:* Bronze sculpture, Julius Rosenwald II for Alverthorpe Park, Pa, 70; polyester & resin sculpture, Leon Berkowitz for Delaware Valley Col Agriculture, Pa, 76; bronze, Mossand Leatherbee Architects for Blackwell Mansions Park, Pa; Whale for playground, Re-development Authority City Philadelphia, Pa; Little Persian Goat Plicare, St Peters Sch, Pa, 77. *Exhib:* Ann Exhibs, Pa Acad Fine Arts, 50, 52, 60, 61, & 72; Third Philadelphia Arts Festival, Philadelphia Mus Art & Pa Acad Fine Arts, 62; Nat Acad Design, New York, 63 & 81; Artists Equity Exhib, Mus Civic Ctr, Philadelphia, 71 & 81; Bodley Gallery, New York, 83; and others. *Pos:* Bd mem, Woodmere Art Gallery, currently. *Awards:* Lloyd Van Sciver Mem Prize for best work, Ann Juried Exhib, 61; Honorable Mention, Woodmere Art Gallery, 62 & 63; Second Prize, Exhib by Soc Am Pen Women, Smithsonian Inst. *Mem:* Artists Equity, Philadelphia (bd mem); Philadelphia Art Alliance (sculpture comt). *Publ:* Article, Sculpture 73 Drexel Inst Mag, 64; contribr, Changing Sculpture Concepts, Wellesley Alumnae, 72. *Mailing Add:* 1016 Westview St Philadelphia PA 19119

LEVY, PHYLLIS HOUSER
PAINTER
b Brooklyn, NY, June 20, 27. *Study:* Cooper Union Art Sch, cert; San Francisco State, AB(art), MA(art educ). *Exhib:* 15th Ann Watercolor, San Francisco Mus Art, Calif, 51; 26th Ann Women, San Francisco Mus Art, Calif, 51; Am Watercolor Drawings & Prints, Metrop Mus, New York, 52; 2nd Ann Exhib, Richmond Art Ctr, Va, 53; NJ Artists, Newark Mus, 55; 71st Ann Exhib, Nat Collection Fine Arts, Washington, DC, 64. *Teaching:* Teacher art, Montgomery Co Public Sch, 69-78. *Awards:* San Francisco Art Asn Prize, 51. *Mem:* Artists Equity Asn. *Media:* Acrylic, Watercolor. *Mailing Add:* 9202 Friars Road Bethesda MD 20817

LEVY, S(TEPHEN) DEAN
DEALER, GALLERY DIRECTOR
b New York, NY, Nov 17, 42. *Study:* Yale Univ, BA, 64. *Pos:* Vpres, Bernard & S Dean Levy, Inc, 73- *Bibliog:* On Madison Avenue, Fortune Mag, 12/47; Rita Reif (auth), Antiques, New York Times, 10/76; Douglas Villiers (auth), Next Year in Jerusalem, Viking Press, 76. *Mem:* Art & Antique Dealers League. *Specialty:* American paintings, antique furniture, silver; English and American ceramics. *Mailing Add:* 981 Madison Ave New York NY 10021

LEVY, TIBBIE
PAINTER
b New York, NY, Oct 29, 08. *Study:* Cornell Univ, with Arshile Gorky, AB; Art Students League; Acad Grand Chaumiere & Acad Andre Lhote, Paris, France; NY Univ, JD. *Work:* Contemp Art Soc Gt Brit; Mus Mod Art, Madrid, Barcelona & Bilbao, Spain; Princeton Univ Mus; Cornell Univ Mus; plus 40 other mus. *Exhib:* Bodley Gallery, New York, 60-70; Galerie Ror Volmar, Paris, 61; Sala Nebli, Madrid, 62; Galeria Forum, Madrid, 63; Portal Gallery, London, Eng, 63 & 65; plus others. *Teaching:* Lectr art. *Media:* Oil. *Dealer:* Bodley Gallery 787 Madison Ave New York NY 10021. *Mailing Add:* 2 Sutton Pl S New York NY 10022

LEW, EILEEN
CURATOR
b San Francisco, Calif. *Study:* City Col San Francisco, AA, 71; San Francisco State Univ, BA, 73. *Collections Arranged:* The Prints of Peter Le Blanc and the Poets of the Beat Generation, M H De Young Mem Mus, 74 & The Food Show, 75; The Greatest Little Show on Earth, Fine Arts Mus San Francisco, Downtown Ctr, 76 & The Cover Story: An Exhibition of Ethnic Clothing Traditions, 77; and others. *Pos:* Cur, M H De Young Mem Mus Art Sch/Fine Arts San Francisco, formerly; chmn, Children's Classics, currently. *Bibliog:* Cooperative Interagency Arts, Arts & Handicapped/Educ Facilities Lab/Nat Endowment for Arts, 75; The Art Museum as Educator, Coun on Mus Educ in Visual Arts, 78. *Mailing Add:* 1289 Green St San Francisco CA 94109

LEW, WEYMAN
PAINTER, PRINTMAKER
b San Francisco, Calif, Feb 17, 35. *Study:* Univ Calif, Berkeley, BS, 57; San Francisco Art Inst, with Jay deFeo, 65-66. *Work:* M H de Young Mem Mus, San Francisco; Univ Calif Mus, Berkeley; Inst Arte Contemporaneo, Lima, Peru; Santa Barbara Mus Art, Calif; Oakland Art Mus, Calif; and others. *Comn:* Univ Calif Mus, Berkeley, 74. *Exhib:* One-man shows, M H de Young Mem Mus, 70, Art Gallery Greater Victoria, BC, Can, 72, Bonython Art Gallery, Sydney, Australia, 72-75, Wallnuts Gallery, Philadelphia, 72, 74, 77 & 80; and many others. *Pos:* Dir, Kelley Galleries, San Francisco, 68. *Teaching:* Guest instr painting, drawing & serigraphy, M H de Young Mem Mus Art Sch, 70-71. *Awards:* Merit Award, San Francisco Art Festival, 80. *Mem:* Calif Soc Printmakers. *Media:* Ink, Watercolor; Etching, Serigraph. *Publ:* Auth, Weyman Lew Sketches Away, Triton Assocs, 81. *Mailing Add:* 2810 Pacific Ave San Francisco CA 94115

LEWANDOWSKI, EDMUND D
PAINTER, ADMINISTRATOR
b Milwaukee, Wis, July 3, 14. *Study:* Layton Sch Art, 31-35. *Work:* Addison Gallery Am Art, Andover, Mass; Brooklyn Mus, NY; Boston Mus Fine Arts; Mus Mod Art, New York; Corcoran Gallery Art, Washington, DC; plus many others. *Comn:* Polanki Fountain, Milwaukee Civic Ctr, Wis, 70; mural, First Wis Ctr, Milwaukee, Wis, 73; Polish-American Bicentennial Graphics, Polish Nat Alliance, Chicago, Ill, 75; 4 mosaic murals, Vet Mem, Milwaukee War Mem, 76; mural, St Lukes Hosp, Milwaukee, Wis, 79. *Exhib:* Art Inst Chicago; Carnegie Inst, Pittsburgh; Corcoran Gallery Art, Washington, DC; Pa Acad Fine Arts, Philadelphia; Phillips Collection, Washington, DC; plus others. *Teaching:* Prof, Layton Sch Art, 45-49; prof painting, Fla State Univ, 49-54, head dept, 52-54; dir, Layton Sch Art; chmn dept art, Winthrop Col, Rock Hill, SC, 79- *Awards:* Merit Award, SC Bicentennial Comn, 76; Purchase Award, SC Art Comn, 76; Distinguished Achievement in the Field of Art Award, Am Coun Polish Cult Clubs, 79; plus many others. *Bibliog:* Andrew C Ritchie (auth), Abstract painting and sculpture in America, Mus Mod Art, 51; Nathaniel Pousette-Dart (ed), American Painting Today, Hastings House, 56; John I Baur (auth), Revolution and Tradition in Modern American Art, Harvard Univ, 59. *Mem:* Wis Painters & Sculptors; Polish-Am Artists; Chicago Fine Arts Club. *Publ:* Contribr, annual report cover, Falk Corp, 58; contribr, 10 Distinguished Am Artists, New York Times, 6/58; contribr, Ford Times, 10/61; contribr, cover, The Diplomat, 12/61; contribr, cover, Wis Architect, 11/63. *Dealer:* Sid Deutsch Gallery New York NY. *Mailing Add:* Dept of Art Winthrop Col Rock Hill SC 29733

LEWICKI, JAMES
ILLUSTRATOR, EDUCATOR
b Buffalo, NY, Dec 13, 17. *Study:* Albright Art Sch; Art Sch Detroit Soc Arts & Crafts, scholar; Pratt Inst, cert. *Exhib:* Audubon Artists Ann; Am Watercolor Soc Ann; Christmas Paintings, Dartmouth Col, 54; one-man show, Golden Bough Paintings, C W Post Col, Long Island Univ, 70; 200 Yrs of Am Illus, 77. *Teaching:* Instr art, Pratt Inst, 46-52; chmn dept art, C W Post Col, Long Island Univ, 63-69, prof art, 63-, chmn grad prog art, 69- *Awards:* Christmas Card Competition Second Prize, Am Artists, 43; New Masters Award for Sunflowers (painting), Audubon Artists 25th Anniversary Exhib, 67. *Bibliog:* Articles, Am Artist Mag, 62 & North Light Mag, 71; 200 Years of American Illustration, 77. *Mem:* Am Watercolor Soc; Audubon Artists. *Publ:* Ed & illus, Christmas Tales, Golden, 56; ed & illus, Life Treasury of American Folklore, 61; illus, Tales of Old Russia, Garrard, 64; illus, Little Christmas, Houghton Mifflin, 64; illus, The Golden Bough, Vols I & II, 68 & 69. *Mailing Add:* 5 Hawthorne Ct Centerport NY 11721

LEWIN, BERNARD
DEALER, COLLECTOR
b Ger; US citizen. *Study:* With Kurt Wagner, Berlin. *Pos:* Art dir, B Lewin Galleries, Beverly Hills, 60- *Awards:* Twenty-fifth Anniversary of Mexican Masters, City of Los Angeles. *Mem:* Art Dealers Asn. *Specialty:* Mexican masters, Tamayo, Siqueiros, Merida, R Martinez, R Coronel, Diego Rivera, Felipe Castenada, Gustavo Montoya and others. *Collection:* Mexican masters, American and European. *Mailing Add:* B Lewin Galleries 266 N Beverly Dr Beverly Hills CA 90210

LEWIS, DON S, SR
DEALER, PAINTER
b July 21, 19; US citizen. *Study:* Carnegie Mus, Pittsburgh; painting with Virginia Cuthbert. *Exhib:* One-man show, Gallerie Int, New York, 67. *Pos:* Pres, dir & lectr on investment art & conserv, Aushew Gallery, Norfolk, Va, 54- *Mem:* Nat Soc Lit & Arts; Am Asn Mus; Am Fedn Arts; Int Inst Conserv Hist & Artistic Works. *Media:* Metal, Acrylic. *Specialty:* Nineteenth and twentieth century American paintings. *Mailing Add:* 101 Granby St Norfolk VA 23510

LEWIS, DONALD SYKES, JR
DEALER
b Norfolk, Va, Dec 13, 47. *Study:* Randolph-Macon Col, Ashland, Va, BA(fine arts); Univ Va, MA(hist of art). *Pos:* Vpres, Auslew Gallery, Inc, Norfolk, 73-76, dir, 76-; adv comt, Chrysler Mus, currently. *Teaching:* Instr Am art, Hermitage Mus, Norfolk, 75, 78 & 79 & Old Dom Univ, 75-76. *Mem:* Archives of Am Art; Assoc Int Inst Conserv Hist & Artistic Works; Assoc Am Inst Conserv Hist & Artistic Works. *Res:* Cataloging works of Herman Ottomar Herzog and his son, Lewis E Herzog. *Specialty:* 19th & 20th century American art. *Publ:* Contribr, Herman Herzog (catalog), Chapellier Galleries,

New York, 73; auth, Emily Nichols Hatch (catalog), 74 & auth foreword, In: Carolyn Wyeth (catalog), 12/74, Auslew Gallery, Inc; auth, Herman Herzog, Southwest Art Rev, 75; contribr, Carolyn Wyeth Exhibition Catalogue, R W Norton Art Gallery, Shreveport, La, 1/76; auth, Herman Herzog (1831-1932), German landscapist in America, Am Art Rev, 7-8/76. *Mailing Add:* 5309 Argall Ave Norfolk VA 23508

LEWIS, DOUGLAS
HISTORIAN, CURATOR
b Centreville, Miss, Apr 30, 38. *Study:* Lawrenceville Sch, NJ, dipl, 56; Yale Col, BA, 59 & 60; Clare Col, Cambridge Univ, BA, 62, MA, 66; Yale Univ, MA, 63, PhD, 67; Am Acad Rome, Chester Dale fel, 64, dipl, 66. *Collections Arranged:* African Sculpture, 70, The Far North (American Eskimo and Indian Art), 73 & The Drawings of Andrea Pallido Traveling Exhib, 81, Nat Gallery Art. *Pos:* David E Finley fel Venetian art, Nat Gallery Art, Washington, DC, 65-68; cur sculpture, Nat Gallery Art, 68- *Teaching:* Asst prof baroque & romantic art, Bryn Mawr Col, 67-68; asst prof renaissance & baroque art, Univ Calif, Berkeley, spring 70; sem leader renaissance archit, Folger Inst, Renaissance Sem, Washington, DC, spring 72; adj prof, Renaissance & baroque art, Johns Hopkins Univ, 73-77; prof Renaissance art & archit, Univ Calif, Berkeley, fall 79; lectr, Iowa State Univ, Ames, 80, Georgetown Univ, 80- *Awards:* Copley Medal, Smithsonian Inst, 81. *Mem:* Fel Am Acad in Rome; Soc Archit Historians; Col Art Asn Am; Belg-Am Educ Found; Centro Palladiano, Vicenza; and others. *Res:* Art and architecture in Renaissance Venice; monographic studies on Michele Sanmicheli, Jacopo Sansovino, Andrea Palladio, Baldassare Longhena & Francisco Muttoni. *Publ:* Auth, The Late Baroque Churches of Venice, 67 & Garland, 79; auth, The Drawings of Andrea Palladio, Nat Gallery Art, 81. *Mailing Add:* Nat Gallery of Art Washington DC 20565

LEWIS, ELIZABETH See Sprang, Elizabeth

LEWIS, ELIZABETH MATTHEW
STAINED GLASS ARTIST, WRITER
b Charleston, SC. *Study:* Richmond Prof Inst, Va; Purdue Univ, Lafayette, Ind, BA; sculpture course at Barry I, Wales, Glamorgan Educational Comt; Univ London; Pratt Inst, MLS; Teachers Col, Columbia Univ, EdD; Inst Arts Admin, Harvard Univ, cert; Ctr Medieval & Renaissance Studies, Oxford, cert(stained glass). *Work:* Ball State Univ Art Gallery, Muncie, Ind; Miami Mus Mod Art. *Comn:* Bronze reliefs, George's Restaurant, Indianapolis, Ind, 51; mural, Loeb Playhouse, Mem Union, Purdue Univ, 52; mural, First Fed Savings & Loan, Lafayette, Ind, 58; ceramic relief, United Methodist Church, Lafayette, Ind, 61; mem stained glass window, Second Presby Church, Ft Lauderdale, 82. *Exhib:* Pa Ann, Univ Pa, Indiana, 55; Drawing & Print Show, Ball State Univ Art Gallery, Muncie, Ind, 55; one-man shows, Lafayette Art Ctr, Ind, Ft Wayne Union Bank, Ind, Miami Mus Mod Art, Fla & Ft Lauderdale Art Ctr, Fla, 64. *Collections Arranged:* Four Generations of Waughs: An American Family of Artists 1827-1970, 70, Illustrators of the American West, loan from the collection of George Goodstadt, 75, Drawings by Al Hirschfeld, 76 & Military Medicine and the Wound Man (with Gordon E Mestler), 76, US Military Acad. *Pos:* Co-partner, Lewis Workshop Studios, Kokomo, W Lafayette, Ind, 50-62; fine arts librn, US Military Acad, West Point, NY, 67-78; cur slides, Dept Art, City Col New York, 71; dir, Lyon Productions Ltd, Ft Lauderdale, Fla, 77- *Teaching:* Instr painting, Ind Univ Extension, Kokomo, 50-52; sr lectr, US Military Acad, 67-78. *Awards:* Patent, Graphics Retrieval Systems, 78; Sculpture Prize, Broward Art Guild, 80. *Mem:* Stained Glass Asn Am; Am Crafts Coun; Am Asn Univ Prof; Artists Equity. *Res:* Color in visual perception; design for transparent media; filming the making of antique glass. *Interests:* Research in medieval architecture and experimental models of contemporary cathedral glass set in aluminum. *Publ:* Auth, A Summer School in Wales, Art Educ, 66; auth, A Cost Study of Library Color in Microimage Storage and Retrieval, DC Col, 74; ed, Military Medicine and the Wound Man: A Graphic Display of the Wound Man Through History, US Military Acad, 76. *Mailing Add:* 1500 NE 18th Ave Ft Lauderdale FL 33304

LEWIS, ELMA INA
ADMINISTRATOR
b Boston, Mass, Sept 16, 21. *Study:* Emerson Col, BLI, 43; Boston Univ, MEd, 44; Emerson Col, Hon LHD, 68; Anna Maria Col, Hon LHD, 71; Boston Col, Hon LHD, 71; Colby Col, Hon DFA, 72; Harvard Univ, Hon ArtD, 72. *Pos:* Founder & dir, Elma Lewis Sch Fine Arts, Boston, 50- & Nat Ctr Afro-Am Artists, Boston, 68- *Awards:* Outstanding Woman's Award, Campfire Girls Am, 70; Mayor's Citation, City of Boston, 70; Henry O Tanner Award, Black Arts Coun Calif, 71; plus others. *Bibliog:* Margo Miller (auth), Black Boston's Miss Lewis: Art czarina with a needle, Boston Globe, 4/18/68; Caryl Rivers (auth), Black America's Barnum, Hurok & Guthrie, New York Times, 11/17/68; A century of New England news photos, Boston Globe Mag, 1/77. *Mem:* Fel Black Acad Arts & Lett; Gov Task Force on Arts & Humanities; Metrop Cult Alliance, Boston; Mass State Dept Educ Adv Bd. *Publ:* Contribr, Who Took the Weight, Little, 72; auth, At the crossroads: Doom or bloom, Forum Mag, 72; auth, Celebrating us little people, Boston Rev of Arts, 9/72. *Mailing Add:* Nat Ctr of Afro-Am Artists 122 Elm Hill Ave Dorchester MA 02121

LEWIS, GLENN ALUN See Flakey Rose Hip

LEWIS, GOLDA
ASSEMBLAGE ARTIST, PAPERMAKER
b New York, NY. *Study:* With Vaclav Vytacil, Hans Hofmann & Jack Tworkov; Papermaking with Douglass Howell. *Work:* Ciba-Geigy Chem Co,

Ardsley, NY; Madden Corp, New York; Hercules Powder Co, Wilmington, Del; Foundations of Paper Hist, Haarlem, Holland; Cheney Pulp & Paper Co, Franklin, Ohio; and others. *Exhib:* One-woman shows, Benedicta Arts Ctr Gallery, Col St Benedict, Minn, 74 & Museo de Arte Moderno Tertulia, Colombia, 82; Handmade Paper, Prints & Unique Works, Mus Mod Art, New York, 76; New Ways with Paper, Nat Collection Fine Arts, Smithsonian Inst, Washington, DC, 77-78; Retrospective, Gallery K, Washington, DC, 79; Gallery Beni, Kyoto, Japan, 83; Centro Cult Costarricense Norteamericano, San Jose, Costa Rica, 83; Paper as Image, Sunderland Arts Ctr, 83-84; and others. *Pos:* Built, equipped & consult, Papermaking Dept, Wildcliff Mus, New Rochelle, NY, 77. *Teaching:* Instr, Ballard Sch, New York, 61-71; lectr, Marymount Manhattan Col, 71; Am Fedn Arts rent an artist workshop on paper and artists working in paper, 74; lectr & workshops handpapermaking, Univ Mass, Amherst, 78. *Awards:* NY State Coun Arts Grant, 71; Award, Clayworks, 80. *Bibliog:* Innovative Printmaking, Crown, 78; Silvie Turner & Birgit Skiold (coauths), Handmade Paper Today; Bernard Toale (auth), The Art of Papermaking; and others. *Media:* Made Paper, Terra Cotta. *Publ:* Auth, 77 Hand Papermaker's Conf, Women Artists Newsletter, 1/78. *Mailing Add:* 31 Union Sq W New York NY 10003

LEWIS, HELEN NATALIE
GALLERY DIRECTOR, CURATOR
b St Louis, Mo, Oct 2, 46. *Study:* Calif State Univ, Los Angeles, BA, 72, MA, 74, mus prog cert, 78. *Collections Arranged:* Michael Asher, 75, Albuquerque, Arnoldi, Benglis, Castro and Steir, 76 & Artattack, 79, Otis Art Inst Gallery; Joe Goode (auth, catalog), Mt St Mary's Col Art Gallery, 77; Michael Asher, David Askevold, Richard Long (coauth, catalog), Los Angeles Inst Contemp Art, 77. *Pos:* Dir, 707 Gallery, 74; asst cur, Otis Art Inst Gallery, 74-79; asst dir, Otis/Parsons Gallery, 79-; dir, L A Louver Gallery, Venice, Calif, currently. *Specialty:* Painting and sculpture by leading American and European contemporary artists; also newly emerging talents. *Publ:* Ed, Richard Tuttle, Whitney Mus, 76; auth, On Kawara, Otis Art Inst, 77; ed, Wallace Berman Retrospective, Fels of Contemp Art, 78. *Mailing Add:* c/o L A Louver Gallery 55 N Venice Blvd Venice CA 90291

LEWIS, JOHN CHAPMAN
PAINTER, INSTRUCTOR
b Washington, DC, Sept 26, 20. *Study:* Corcoran Sch Art, 38-40. *Work:* Corcoran Gallery Art; Phillips Collection; High Mus Art, Atlanta, Ga; NC Mus Art, Raleigh; Nat Collection Fine Arts. *Exhib:* Corcoran Biennial, Corcoran Gallery Art, 49, 51, 55, 61 & 63 & one-man show, 64; Young Am Painters, Metrop Mus Art, New York, 50 & Am Painting Today, 50; one-man shows, NC Mus Art, Raleigh, 44 & Baltimore Mus Art, 53 & Phillips Collection, 73; Trends in Watercolor Today, Italy & the US, Brooklyn Mus, 57; Am Paintings from the Phillips Collection, White House, Washington, DC, 77-78. *Teaching:* Instr painting & drawing, Corcoran Sch Art, 49-50, 53-58; artist-in-residence studio art, Marymount Col Va, Arlington, 66- *Awards:* First Award in Painting, Golden Anniversary Exhib, Isaac Delgado Mus, New Orleans, 51; First Award in Painting, 16th Area Exhib, Corcoran Gallery Art, 63. *Bibliog:* Harriet Griffiths (auth), Painting with feeling, 1/24/60 & Benjamin Forgey (auth), Lewis' harmonious reveries, rev of Phillips Exhib, 5/30/73, Washington Star; Leslie Judd Ahlander (auth), Review of one-man show, Corcoran Gallery, Washington Post, 3/1/64. *Mailing Add:* Shenandoah North Rt 1 Box 899 Harpers Ferry WV 25425

LEWIS, JOHN CONARD
SCULPTOR, GLASSBLOWER
b Berkeley, Calif, Mar 13, 42. *Study:* Univ Calif, Berkeley, BA, 68, MA, 72, studied with Peter Voulkos, Marvin Lipofsky & Ron Nagle. *Work:* Ariz State Univ Art Mus, Tempe; Tacoma Art Mus, Wash; Univ Wis-Madison Mus Art. *Exhib:* Am Glass Now, Toledo Mus Art, Ohio, 73; Statements, Oakland Mus Art, Calif, 73; Collectors Exhib, Mus Contemp Crafts, New York, 74; Contemp Crafts of the Americas, Colo State Univ, Boulder, 76; Nat Glass Invitational III, Univ Wis-Madison, 76; and others. *Collections Arranged:* New American Glass Focus WVa, Huntington Art Gallery, WVa, 76. *Awards:* Purchase Awards, Corning Mus Glass, NY, 70, Designer-Craftsman Ann, Richmond Art Ctr, 70 & Blown Glass Invitational, Tacoma Art Mus, Wash, 71. *Mem:* Am Crafts Coun; Glass Art Soc. *Media:* Blown Glass, Cast Glass. *Mailing Add:* 1677 Eighth St Oakland CA 94607

LEWIS, MARCIA
JEWELER, INSTRUCTOR
b Washington, DC. *Study:* Corcoran Sch, Washington, DC; San Diego Univ, Calif; Calif State Univ, Long Beach. *Work:* Mus of Contemp Crafts, New York. *Exhib:* Int Handwerks Messe, Munich, Ger 71; Am Metalsmiths, DeCordova Mus, Lincoln, Mass, 73; Kunstindustri Mus, Copenhagen, Denmark, 73; Goldsmiths 74, Smithsonian Inst, Washington, DC, 74; Crafts of the NAmericas, Colo State Univ & Smithsonian Inst, 75; Calif Design 12, Los Angeles, 76. *Pos:* Apprentice goldsmith, Ingrid Hansen, Zurich, Switz, 71-72; asst silversmith, Tony Laws Studio Ltd, Londin, Eng, 72-73. *Teaching:* Instr metalsmithing & gen crafts, Univ Wis, Whitewater, 73-75 & San Jose State Univ, Calif, 75-76; assoc prof art, Long Beach City Col, Calif, 78- *Awards:* Sterling Silversmiths Award, Design Competition, Silversmiths Guild, 69; George C Marshall Mem Fel, Denmark-Amerika Fondet, 72; Nat Endowment Arts Award, Washington, DC, 76. *Bibliog:* Beverly Edna Johnson (auth), Biographical, Los Angeles Times Home Mag, 72; Thelma Newman (auth), Containers, Crown Publ, 77; Oppi Untracht (auth), Jewelry Techniques for Craftsmen, Doubleday, 75. *Mem:* Soc NAm Goldsmiths. *Media:* Metal. *Publ:* Auth, Wearable aluminum ornaments, Calif State Univ, Long Beach, 77. *Mailing Add:* 214 Covina Ave Long Beach CA 90803

LEWIS, MARY
SCULPTOR
b Portland, Ore, June 18, 26. *Study:* Univ Ore, 45-50, BS(sculpture), 49; Ore Div Am Asn Univ Women Mabel Merwin fel, 50, Syracuse Univ, with Ivan Mestrovic, tech asst to Mestrovic, 51-53, MFA, 53. *Comn:* Copper bird & marble skunk cabbage, Joseph Stein & Waterbury Club, Conn, 64; Madonna & Child, St Joseph's Church Chapel, Roseburg, Ore, 78; Mother & Son, St John's Hospital, Longview, Wash,.83. *Exhib:* Artists of Ore, Portland Mus Art, 51 & 69; 12th & 14th Ann New Eng Exhibs, Silvermine Guild Artists, New Canaan, Conn, 61 & 63; 62nd & 63rd Ann Exhib, New Haven Paint & Clay Club, John Slade Ely Ctr, New Haven, 63 & 64; Plaza Seven 3rd Ann Arts Festival Regional Exhib, Hartford Nat Bank & Trust Towers, 67; Retrospective, Fine Arts Gallery, Lower Columbia Col, Longview, Wash, 81. *Pos:* Staff artist, GAF Corp Photo Div, Portland, Ore, 70-76. *Teaching:* asst prof sculpture, Nat Col Arts, Pakistan, 58-60; pvt classes, 61-68. *Awards:* Tiffany Traveling Scholar, 53; Fulbright Lectr, 58 & 59. *Bibliog:* Texas Woman's Univ Libr Arch, Denton, 81. *Mem:* Liturgical Arts Resource Ctr. *Media:* Most Media. *Publ:* Coauth & illusr, The Little Yellow Dinosaur, 71, illusr, In the Beginning--the Bible Story of Creation, Adam & Eve, Cain & Abel, 72, illusr, Jesus Christ, His Youth, Disciples, Miracles, 75, GAF View-Master. *Mailing Add:* Rte 3 Box 3164 Rainier OR 97048

LEWIS, MICHAEL H
PAINTER, EDUCATOR
b Brooklyn, NY, Aug 10, 41. *Study:* State Univ NY Col, New Paltz, painting with Ben Bishop, George Wexler & Ilya Bolotowsky, BS, 63, MFA, 75; Mich State Univ, MA, 64. *Work:* Fogg Mus Art, Harvard Univ; Seiden & De Cuevas Corp, New York; Mich State Univ Art Dept Collection. *Comn:* Oil portrait, comn by Edmund S Muskie, 83. *Exhib:* 24th Ann Drawing & Small Sculpture Show, Ball State Univ, Muncie, Ind, 78; two-person show, Paintings on Paper, Fogg Art Mus, Harvard Univ, 79; one-man shows, Betsey Van Buren Gallery, Cambridge, Mass, 80, Uptown Gallery, New York, 80 & Van Buren, Brazecton, Cutting Gallery, Cambridge Mass, 80 & 83; and many others. *Pos:* Mem, Maine Comn Arts & Humanities, 72-78, visual arts adv panel, 79-81. *Teaching:* Instr art, Kingston City Pub Schs, NY, 64-66; prof painting & drawing, Univ Maine, Orono, 66-, chmn, Dept Art, 75-81, acting assoc dean col arts & sci, 81-83. *Awards:* Video Work of Art Grant, Maine State Arts Comn & Maine Pub Broadcasting Network, 83. *Bibliog:* Christine Temin (auth), Spiritual essences, Boston Globe, 5/19/83; Edgar Allen Beem (auth), An uncomfortable sermon, Maine Times, 5/20/83; Paul Grosswiler (auth), Cupid and psyche project, Bangor Daily News, 9/3/83. *Media:* Oil, Video. *Mailing Add:* 104 Bennoch Rd Orono ME 04473

LEWIS, NAT BRUSH
PAINTER, INSTRUCTOR
b Boston, Mass, Dec 17, 25. *Study:* Pembroke Col, Brown Univ & RI Sch Design, AB; Art Students League; watercolor with Mario Cooper; also with Henry Gasser & Ray Ellis. *Work:* Am Asn Univ Women, Somerset Hills, NJ; Bloomfield Art League, NJ; Bergen Community Mus. *Exhib:* NJ Watercolor Soc, Morris Mus, Morristown, NJ; Am Watercolor Soc, Nat Acad Design Galleries, 68 & 72 & Traveling Exhib, 72; Am Artists Prof League Grand Nat, 75-81; Salmagundi Club Exhib, 75-80; Hudson Valley Art Asn; and others. *Awards:* Solo Exhib Award, Salmagundi Club, 79; Best in Show, Art Ctr, NJ, 79 & 81; First place portrait, Am Artists Prof League, 79-82; and others. *Mem:* NJ Watercolor Soc (corresp secy, 69-71, vpres, 71-73, pres, 73-75); Am Artists Prof League; Hudson Valley Art Asn; Nat Asn Women Artists; and others. *Media:* Oil, Watercolor. *Mailing Add:* 51 Overlook Rd Caldwell NJ 07006

LEWIS, PHILLIP HAROLD
CURATOR
b Chicago, Ill, July 31, 22. *Study:* Art Inst Chicago, BFA, 47; Univ Chicago, MA, 53; Fulbright grant, Australian Nat Univ, 53-54; Univ Chicago, PhD, 66. *Collections Arranged:* Anthrop, geol & hist exhibs, Grout Hist Mus, Waterloo, Iowa, 55; What is Primitive Art, Field Mus Natural Hist, 58, estab Hall of Primitive Art, 61, with exhibs Primitive Artists Look at Civilization, The Human Image in Primitive Art & Australian Aboriginal Art: Arnhem Land, from collection of Louis A Allen, Palo Alto, Calif. *Pos:* Field res proj primitive art, New Ireland, 53-54, 70 & 81; asst cur primitive art, Field Mus Natural Hist, 57-59, assoc cur, 60, cur, 61-67, cur primitive art & Melanesian ethnol, 68- *Teaching:* Lectr anthrop, Univ Chicago, 67-71; lectr, Eve Div, Northwestern Univ, Chicago, 73. *Awards:* Chicago Natural Hist Mus Fel, 50-51, 54-55; Wenner-Gren Mus Res Fel, 68; Nat Sci Found Res Grant, 69-71. *Mem:* Fel Am Anthrop Asn; fel Royal Anthrop Inst Gt Brit & Ireland. *Publ:* Auth, A Definition of Primitive Art, Vol 36, 61 & The Social Context of Art in Northern New Ireland, Vol 58, 69, In: Fieldiana, Field Mus Nat Hist; auth, Changing memorial ceremonial in Northern New Ireland, J Polynesian Soc, Vol 182, No 2. *Mailing Add:* Field Mus Natural Hist Roosevelt Rd & Lake Shore Dr Chicago IL 60605

LEWIS, RONALD WALTER
PAINTER, INSTRUCTOR
b Atlanta, Ga, Jan 27, 45. *Study:* Ala Col, BS(art & bus), 67. *Work:* Birmingham Mus Art, Ala; Fayette Art Mus, Ala; Jefferson State Col, Birmingham; Sylacauga Civic Ctr, Ala. *Exhib:* Ala Watercolor Soc, Birmingham Mus Art, 71-77; Dixieland Watercolor & Drawing Show, Montgomery Mus Art, Ala, 73; Watercolor USA, Springfield Art Mus, Mo, 73-74; Rocky Mountain Nat Watercolor, Golden, Colo, 76; Mainstreams, Marietta Col, Ohio, 76-77; Southern Watercolor Soc, Nashville, Tenn, 77; and others. *Teaching:* Instr drawing, Birmingham Mus Art, 73-; instr watercolor & oil, Mountain Brook Community Sch, Ala, 76- *Awards:*

Seventy-five awards including Ala Watercolor Soc & Southern Watercolor Soc. *Bibliog:* Stevens (auth), Ronald Lewis Paintings, La Revue Mod, Paris, 9/73. *Mem:* Ala Watercolor Soc (vpres, 73-74); Birmingham Art Asn (mem bd, 76-); Southern Watercolor Soc; Am Watercolor Soc. *Media:* Miscellaneous Media. *Publ:* Illusr, My Country Roads & illusr, Pappa's Old Trunk, 11/81, Buck Publ Co; illusr, Birmingham Mag, 7/83; illusr, Southern Accents Mag, winter 83. *Dealer:* Little House on Linden 2915 Linden Ave Homewood AL 35209; Bryant Gallery 524 Royal St New Orleans LA. *Mailing Add:* 2728 Ossa Wintha Dr Birmingham AL 35243

LEWIS, SAMELLA SANDERS
PAINTER, HISTORIAN
b New Orleans, La, Feb 27, 24. *Study:* Hampton Inst, BS; Ohio State Univ, MA & PhD;. Tunghai Univ, Taiwan; Fulbright fel, 62; Univ Southern Calif, 64-66; NY Univ Inst Fine Arts, 65. *Work:* Oakland Mus, Calif; Baltimore Mus Fine Arts; Va Mus Fine Arts, Richmond; High Mus, Atlanta, Ga; Atlanta Univ Mus Contemp Art. *Comn:* Mural Fla hist, comn by pres, Fla A&M Univ, 55; paintings, comn by dean, Hampton Inst, 67. *Exhib:* Joseph Hirshhorn Collection, Palm Springs Mus, 69; Dimensions of Black, La Jolla Mus Art, 70; Two Generations of Black Artists, Calif State Univ, Los Angeles, 70. *Collections Arranged:* Five Black Artists, 70 & The Renaissance in Harlem, 71, Lang Art Gallery, Scripps Col; The Art of African Peoples, Ankrum Gallery, 73. *Pos:* Coordr educ, Los Angeles Co Mus Art, 69-70; pres, Contemp Crafts Publ, 69; owner, Multi-Cul Gallery, 71; art ed, Black Art Mag, 78. *Teaching:* Prof fine arts & head dept, Fla A&M Univ, 53-58; prof humanities & art hist, State Univ NY, 58-68; prof art hist, Scripps Col, 69. *Awards:* NY State-Ford Found Grant, 65; Ford Found Research Grant, 81-82. *Bibliog:* The Black Artists (film), Afrographics, 68; Focus, KNBC-TV, 68; article, Los Angeles Times, 70. *Mem:* Col Art Asn Am; Nat Conf Artists (co-chairperson, 70-73); Am Soc Aesthetics. *Res:* African, Asian and Afro-American art. *Collection:* Rare African works, including Bakuba in the 1890's; sand paintings of the American Indian; contemporary Asian and African-American works. *Publ:* Co-ed, Black Artists on Art, Vols I & II, 69 & 71; auth, Art: African American (textbk), Harcourt, 76. *Dealer:* Ankrum Gallery 657 N La Cienega Blvd Los Angeles CA 90069. *Mailing Add:* 259 W Radcliffe Dr Claremont CA 91711

LEWIS, STANLEY
SCULPTOR, PRINTMAKER
b Montreal, Que, Mar 28, 30. *Study:* Montreal Mus Fine Arts, 48-51; Inst Allende, San Miguel, Mex, scholars, 52-55; Elizabeth T Greenshields Mem Found grant, Florence, Italy, 56-59. *Work:* Nat Gallery Can, Ottawa; Montreal Mus Fine Arts; Jerusalem Mus, Israel; Samuel Zacks Collection; Primal Portraits (5 stone cut prints), Los Angeles Mus Natural Hist; and others. *Comn:* Sleeping Spirit (lava boulder), 53, Standing Nude (white marble), 53 & The Corngrinder (gray marble), 54, Inst Allende; late Samuel Bronfman, Can Jewish Cong, 66. *Exhib:* One-man shows, Montreal Mus Fine Arts, 52 & 59, Israel Art Auction Gallery, Tel Aviv, 65 & Nat Gallery Can, 71; Atelier J Lukacs, Montreal, 75, 76 & 78. *Teaching:* Instr sculpture, McGill Univ Sch Archit, 52, Montreal Mus Fine Arts, 61-63 & Saidye Bronfman Art Ctr, Montreal, 61-; lectr, The Eskimo Artist, Nat Film Bd, Montreal, 75. *Awards:* Prize, Concours Artistiques, Que, 59. *Bibliog:* Peter Olwyer (auth), article, Can Art, fall 55; Earle Birney (auth), article, Sat Night, 55; Folch (auth), article, Vie Arts, summer 59. *Mem:* Founding mem Que Sculptors' Asn; hon rep Int Acad Leonardo da Vinci. *Res:* Contributed original research on Michelangelo's childhood and marble carving techniques to writing of Irving Stone's The Agony and the Ecstasy. *Publ:* Auth, The Stone Speaks, 53; auth, Hands to Create Wonders, 61; auth, Space, Man and Stone, 69. *Mailing Add:* Apt 4 4131 Cote des Neiges Rd Montreal PQ H3H 1X1 Canada

LEWIS, VIRGINIA ELNORA
MUSEUM DIRECTOR, HISTORIAN
b Sault Ste Marie, Ont, Apr 7, 07; US citizen. *Study:* Wellesley Col, 26-28; Univ Pittsburgh, AB, 31, AM, 35; Carnegie Inst Technol, cert, 33; Harvard Univ; Brit Mus Dept Prints, with Arthur M Hind, summer 38. *Pos:* Actg head, Frick Fine Arts Dept, Univ Pittsburgh, 40-63, cur exhibs, 46-47; head librn, Frick Fine Arts Libr, 63-65; asst dir, Frick Fine Arts Bldg, 65-67; dir, Frick Art Mus, 70-; dir, Dennis Art Gallery, Raymond Moore Found, Mass, summer 53; consult dir, Westmoreland Co Mus Art, Woods Marchand Found, Greensburg, Pa, 54-56. *Teaching:* Prof fine arts, Univ Pittsburgh, 57-67, prof emer, 67- *Mem:* Am Asn Mus; Int Coun Mus; Col Art Asn Am; Soc Archit Hist; Nat Trust Hist Preservation. *Publ:* Auth, Russell Smith: Romantic Realist, Univ Pittsburgh Press, 57; ed, Walter Read Hovey, auth, The Arts in Changing Societies: Reflections Inspired by Works of Art in the Frick Art Museum, 72 & Treasures of the Frick Art Museum, 75, Frick Art Mus, Pittsburgh; auth, Firenze, In: The Pittsburgh Bibliophiles Pilgrimage to Italy, Pittsburgh Bibliophiles, 76. *Mailing Add:* Frick Art Mus 7227 Reynolds St Pittsburgh PA 15208

LEWIS, WILLIAM ARTHUR
PAINTER, ADMINISTRATOR
b Detroit, Mich, Mar 20, 18. *Study:* Col Archit & Design, Univ Mich, BDesign, 48. *Work:* Butler Inst Am Art, Youngstown; Grand Rapids Mus Art; Univ Mich Grad Sch; Grinnell Col; and others. *Comn:* Two groups of watercolors, Detroit Bank & Trust Co, Detroit & London, 63 & 69; watercolor series, Bohn Aluminum Co, Detroit, 70; oil painting, Grand Rapids City Hall, 71; acrylic painting, Soc Mfg Engrs, Dearborn, Mich, 71. *Exhib:* Five Ann Exhibs, Butler Inst Am Art, 54-65; Drawing USA, Mus Mod Art, 56; Corcoran Gallery Biennial, Washington, DC & Am Fedn Art Tour, 57; one-man show, The Last Year of the Civil War, Detroit Hist Soc, Mint Mus, Madison Col, Va, Eastern Mich Univ, Dearborn Hist Mus & others, 62-65;

Drawing USA, St Paul Art Ctr, 63 & 66. *Pos:* Assoc dean, Sch Art, Univ Mich, Ann Arbor, 66-75; dir, Comn Accreditation, Nat Asn Schs Art, 72-75; chief reader, Advanced Placement Studio Art, Col Bd-ETS, 78-81. *Teaching:* Prof art, Sch Art, Univ Mich, Ann Arbor, 64- *Awards:* Rackham Sch Grad Studies Fac Res Grants for Last Year of the Civil War, 60-62; Purchase Award, Drawing USA, St Paul Art Ctr, 63; J M W Turner, 64. *Bibliog:* Hazen Schumacher (auth), The Painting Professor, Univ Mich TV Studios, 62; Louise Bruner (auth), Feelings of an artist, Toledo Blade, 64. *Mem:* Col Art Asn Am; Mich Watercolor Soc. *Media:* Watercolor, Acrylics. *Publ:* Auth & illusr, The Civil War--A contemporary approach, Dimension, spring 62; illusr, cover & article, Limnos, summer 69. *Dealer:* DeGraaf-Forsythe Galleries 201 Nickels Arcade Ann Arbor MI 48104. *Mailing Add:* 1021 Barton Apt 101 Ann Arbor MI 48105

LEWIS, WILLIAM R
INSTRUCTOR, PAINTER
b Osceola, Iowa, Sept 23, 20. *Study:* Drake Univ, BFA, 49; Univ Wash; Ariz State Univ, MA, 52. *Work:* Ariz Western Col, Yuma; Glendale Community Col, Ariz; Scottsdale Civic Ctr, Ariz. *Exhib:* Ariz Ann, Phoenix Art Mus, 61-68; Butler Art Mus Ann Midyear Show, 62; Am Watercolor Soc Ann, 63-65; Southwestern Invitational, Yuma, 67-72; Watercolor USA Traveling Show, 68. *Teaching:* Chmn dept art, S Mountain High Sch, Phoenix, 64- *Awards:* Ariz Ann First in Watercolor, Phoenix Art Mus, 62. *Mem:* Ariz Watercolor Asn (pres, 63-64). *Media:* Watercolor. *Mailing Add:* 313 E 15th St Tempe AZ 85281

LEWISON, FLORENCE (MRS MAURICE GLICKMAN)
WRITER, ART DEALER
b Jersey City, NJ. *Study:* Sch Art Studies, 45-49, art hist & criticism with Maurice Glickman; also study in Eng, France & Italy, 56 & 61. *Collections Arranged:* Louis Eilshemius (1864-1941) Paintings and Drawings, (illus catalogue), NJ State Mus, Trenton, 79. *Pos:* Art critic, feature writer & art news ed, Design Mag, 49-51; founder & dir, Florence Lewison Gallery, 61- *Res:* Revival and reevaluation of 19th and early 20th century American artists. *Specialty:* A program of exhibitions devoted solely to the reintroduction and reevaluation of 19th and early 20th century American artists. *Publ:* Auth, Theodore Robinson: America's first impressionist, 2/63, The uniqueness of Albert Bierstadt, 9/64, John Frederick Kensett: a tribute to man and artists, 10/66 & G P A Healy: a success at home and abroad, 12/68, Am Artist Mag; auth, Theodore Robinson and Claude Monet, Apollo Mag, London, Eng, 9/63. *Mailing Add:* 30 E 60th St New York NY 10022

LE WITT, SOL
SCULPTOR
b Hartford, Conn, 1928. *Study:* Syracuse Univ, BFA, 49. *Work:* Stedelijk Mus, Amsterdam, Holland; Albright-Knox Art Gallery, Buffalo, NY; Art Gallery Ont, Toronto; Los Angeles Co Mus Art, Los Angeles, Calif; Mus Mod Art, New York; work also in Ger mus. *Exhib:* Sculpture Ann, Whitney Mus Am Art, New York, 67; Guggenheim Int, New York, 71; one-man shows, Guggenheim Mus, 71, Mus Mod Art, New York, 71 & Walker Art Ctr, 72; San Francisco Mus Art, 75; Retrospective travelling exhib, Mus Mod Art, New York, Mus Contemp Art, Montreal, Krannert Mus, Champaign, Mus Contemp Art, Chicago & La Jolla Mus, Calif, 78-79; Wall Drawings 1968-1981, Wadsworth Atheneum, Hartford, 81; Paula Cooper Gallery, New York, 81; and many other group & one-man shows. *Teaching:* Instr, Mus Mod Art Sch, 64-67 & Cooper Union, 67. *Bibliog:* E C Goosen (auth), The Art of the Real USA 1948-1968, Mus Mod Art, 68; Lucy R Lippard (auth), Minimal Art, Haags Gemeentemuseum, 68; Alicia Legg (ed), Sol Le Witt, Mus Mod Art, 78; and others. *Publ:* Auth, I am still alive: On Kawara, Studio Int, 7-8/70; auth, Sentences on conceptual art, 7/71 & Sol Le Witt, 6/73, Flash Art, Milan; auth, All wall drawings, Arts Mag, 2/72; auth, Sentences on conceptual art, Uber Kunst, Cologne, WGer, 74; and many others. *Mailing Add:* c/o John Weber Gallery 1452 Greene St New York NY 10012

LEWTON, JEAN LOUISE
CURATOR, EDITOR
b Niles, Mich, Sept 7, 39. *Study:* Pomona Col, BA(with honors), 61; Claremont Univ Col, 63; Catholic Univ, 65-69; Trinity Col, 70. *Collections Arranged:* Alice Barney, 79 & Edwin Scott, 79, Cosmos Club; 14 Washington Women Artists, Market V Gallery, Washington, DC, 79; Alice Pike Barney & Her Friends, Nat Mus Am Art, 80; Covers from Washington Review, Lansburg Art Ctr, Washington, DC, 81. *Pos:* Cur & registr, Alice Pike Barney Collection & Barney Studio House, Washington, DC, 64-80, Barney Studio House, 81-; producer & moderator, Washington Review of the Arts on the Air, 75-78; managing ed, Washington Review, 75-; admin dir, Capitol Hill Arts Workshop, 71-78. *Bibliog:* Sarah-Booth Conroy (auth), Barney Studio House, Washington Post, 2/22/81. *Res:* Art's politics and art criticism; Alice Pike Barney. *Mailing Add:* 404 10th St SE Washington DC 20003

LEWTON, VAL EDWIN
DESIGNER, PAINTER
b Santa Monica, Calif, May 23, 37. *Study:* Claremont Univ Col, Calif, MFA, 62. *Work:* Nat Mus Am Art, Washington, DC; Corcoran Gallery, DC; and others. *Exhib:* Eastern Regional Exhib, Nat Drawing Soc, Philadelphia, 65; Corcoran Area & Vicinity Exhib, Washington, DC, 66-68; one-man shows, Studio Gallery, 75-77, Washington New Realists, Middendorf-Lane, DC, 78, among others. *Collections Arranged:* Exhib designer for Nat Mus Am Art-Smithsonian Inst, Washington, DC & Mark Toby, 74; Robert Rauschenburg Retrospective, Nat Mus Am Art, 76, Decorative Designs of Frank Lloyd Wright, 77, Renwick Gallery, 77, Smithsonian Inst, Washington, DC;

Seymour Lipton Retrospective, Nat Mus Am Art & Jewish Mus, New York, 79; La Pintura de los Estados Unidos, 80; and others. *Pos:* Chief, Design Unit, Nat Mus Am Art-Smithsonian Inst, 63- *Teaching:* Lectr art, Univ Calif, Riverside, 62-63; lectr art, Georgetown Univ, Washington DC, 81- *Bibliog:* Harry Rand (auth), The watercolors of Val Lewton, Arts Mag, 5/80; and others. *Media:* Acrylic, Watercolor. *Publ:* Auth, Washington Review (column), 75- *Dealer:* Studio Gallery Box 50782 Washington DC 20004. *Mailing Add:* 404 Tenth St SE Washington DC 20003

LEYS, DALE DANIEL
EDUCATOR, DRAFTSMAN
b Sheboygan, Wis, Dec 10, 52. *Study:* Yale Univ, 73; Layton Sch Art, Milwaukee, BFA, 74; Univ Wis, Madison, MA, 75, MFA, 77. *Work:* Evansville Mus Arts & Sci, Ind; Austin Peay State Univ, Clarksville, Tenn; Northern Mich Univ, Marquette; Hospital Corp Am, Nashville, Tenn. *Exhib:* Evansville Mus Arts & Sci, Ind, 77, 78 & 80; Ball State Univ Art Gallery, Muncie, Ind, 78 & 83; Rutgers Univ, NJ, 80; Greenville Mus, SC, 81; Davenport Mus, Iowa, 81; J B Speed Art Mus, Louisville, Ky, 82; Cheekwood Fine Arts Ctr, Nashville, Tenn, 84. *Teaching:* Assoc prof drawing, Murray State Univ, 77- *Awards:* Drawing Award, State Univ NY, Potsdam, 77; Graphics Award, Mid States Exhib, Evansville Mus, 80; Purchase Award, Appalachian State Univ, Boone, NC, 83. *Bibliog:* Jerry Spieght (auth), Dale Leys: Ideas and his work, Sch Arts, 78 & Dale Leys, Art Voices S, 78. *Media:* Mixed Media. *Mailing Add:* 206 Woodlawn Murray KY 42071

LHOTKA, BONNY PIERCE
PAINTER
b La Grange, Ill, July 14, 42. *Study:* Bradley Univ, BFA, 64. *Work:* Petro Lewis, United Banks, Rocky Mountain Energy, Midland Savings & Loan, Denver; First Nat Bank, Boise. *Exhib:* Allied Artists Am, Nat Acad Design, New York, 74, 76 & 77; Nat Watercolor Soc, Palm Springs Desert Mus, Calif, 74-81; Am Watercolor Soc, Nat Acad Design, 77; Nat Acad Design Exhib, 77, 79 & 81; one-man show, Wyo State Art Gallery, Cheyenne, 79. *Teaching:* Instr abstract watermedia & acrylic, Colo Watercolor Soc, summer 77 & Colo Artist Workshops, summer 78. *Awards:* First Nat Top Ten, Am Artist Mag, 78; Strathmore Awards, Strathmore Paper Co, 79; Century Award of Merit, Rocky Mountain Watermedia Exhib, 81. *Mem:* Nat Watercolor Soc; Audubon Artists; Nat Soc Painters in Casein & Acrylics; Rocky Mountain Nat Watermedia Soc. *Media:* Watermedia; Acrylic. *Publ:* Contribr, Watercolor page, Am Artist Mag, 77; contribr, Watercolor, The Creative Experience by Nochis, North Light, 79; contribr, article, Southwest Art Mag, 3/81; contribr, Creative Seascape Painting, Watson Guptill. *Dealer:* Carson & Sapiro Gallery 1411 Market St Denver CO 80202. *Mailing Add:* 5011 Ellsworth Pl Boulder CO 80303

LI, CHU-TSING
HISTORIAN
b Canton, China, May 26, 20; US citizen. *Study:* Univ Nanking, China, BA (Eng lit), 43; Univ Iowa, MA(Eng), 49, PhD(art hist), 55; post-doctoral res, Harvard Univ, 59 & Princeton Univ, 60. *Pos:* Res cur, Nelson Gallery Art, Kansas City, 68-; fac cur, Spencer Mus Art, Lawrence, Kans, 66- *Teaching:* From instr to prof art hist, Univ Iowa, Iowa City, 54-66; prof Oriental art, Univ Kans, Lawrence, 66-, chmn, Dept Hist Art, 72-78, Judith Harris Murphy Distinguished prof art hist, 78- *Mem:* Col Art Asn; Midwest Art Hist Soc; Asia Soc. *Res:* Painting of the Yuan Dynasty in China (13th to 14th century) and of the modern period. *Publ:* Auth, The Autumn Colors on the Ch'iao and Hua Mountains, 65 & A Thousand Peaks and Myriad Ravines: Drenwatz Collection, 74, Artibus Asiae; auth, Liu Kuo-sung: Development of a Modern Chinese Artist, 69 & contribr, Five Chinese Painters: Fifth Moon Exhibition, 70, Nat Gallery Art, Taipei, Taiwan; auth, Trends in modern Chinese painting, Artibus Asiae, 79. *Mailing Add:* Dept of Art Hist Univ of Kans Lawrence KS 66045

LIAO (SHIOU-PING LIAO)
PAINTER, PRINTMAKER
b Taipei, Taiwan, Sept 2, 36. *Study:* Nat Taiwan Normal Univ, Taipei, BA, 59; Tokyo Univ Educ, Japan, MA, 64; Ecole Nat Superienredes Beaux Arts, Paris, 65-68. *Work:* Nat Mus Mod Art, Tokyo, Japan; Victoria & Albert Mus, London, Eng; Musee Municipal d'Art Mod, Paris, France; Cincinnati Art Mus, Ohio; New York Pub Libr. *Comn:* Mural, Cathy Hospital, Taipei, 76; mural, Howard Plaza Hotel, Taipei, 83. *Exhib:* Salon de Mai & Salon d'Antonne, Musee Municipal d'Art Mod, Paris, France, 68; Nat Print, Brooklyn Mus, New York, 70; one-man shows, Taft Mus, Cincinnati, 70 & Calif Palace Legion Honor, San Fransisco, 73; Int Print Biennial, Nat Mus Mod Art, Tokyo, Japan, 70; Oversize Print, Whitney Mus Am Art, New York, 71; Int Print Exchange Exhib, Mus Art, Soeul, Korea, 79; Five from the Orient, Bergen Co Mus, Paramus, NJ, 81. *Collections Arranged:* Paintings by Leading Overseas Artist (auth, catalog), Hong Kong Mus Art, 82; Contemporary Printmaking Asn (auth, catalog), Singapore, 82. *Teaching:* Vis prof printmaking, Tsukuba Univ, Japan, 77-79; vis prof printmaking, Daemen Col, Amherst, NY, 78; adj prof painting & printmaking, Seton Hall Univ, NJ, 79- *Awards:* Silver Medal, Salon des Artistes Francais, Paris, 65; De Cordova Mus Purchase Prize, Boston Printmaker Show, 71. *Mem:* Soc Am Graphic Artists; Chinese Graphic Soc Taipei (bd dir, 74). *Media:* Mixed Media; Watercolor, Oil. *Publ:* Auth, The Art of Printmaking, 74 & auth, Appreciation of Modern Prints, 76, Taipei Lion Art Book Co. *Mailing Add:* 284 Center Street Englewood Cliffs NJ 07632

LIBBY, GARY RUSSELL
MUSEUM DIRECTOR, EDUCATOR
b Boston, Mass, June 7, 44. *Study:* Univ Fla, studied with Jerry Uelsmann, AA, BA, studied with Philip Hultman, MA; Tulane Univ, studied with Leo Steinberg, MA. *Collections Arranged:* Masterpieces of Middle Am Art, Inst of Middle Am Studies, New Orleans Mus Art, 69; Audubon: Birds and Animals, 75, The Third Empire Porcelains and Silver, 77 & Artistic Taste in Pre-Castro Cuba, (auth, catalog), 77, Mus Arts & Sci, Daytona Beach, Fla; 400 Years of Prints, Eight Cuban Masters, Sampson Hall Gallery, Stetson Univ, Deland, Fla, 77. *Pos:* Dir, Mus Arts & Sci, Daytona Beach, Fla, 77-*Teaching:* Instr, Tulane Univ, New Orleans, La, 68-71; asst prof humanities-art hist, Stetson Univ, 72-73, asst prof art hist surv, 72-77. *Mem:* Southeast Col Art Conf; Col Art Conf; Col Art Asn. *Res:* Latin American: Cuban and Caribbean, 19th century English and American painting; Pre-Columbian ceramics. *Collection:* Pre-Columbian, etchings, engravings, 19th century painting. *Publ:* Auth, Pat Bannister: Mysterious world of women, 1/78, Mort Kunstler: Careful research..., 5/78, Cuban art, 6/78, Bruce Elliott Roberts, 1/79 & Perry Cosentino: An interview, 2/80, Southwest Art Mag. *Mailing Add:* c/o Mus Arts & Sci 1040 Museum Blvd Daytona Beach FL 32014

LIBBY, WILLIAM C
PAINTER, WRITER
b Pittsburgh, Pa. *Study:* Univ Pittsburgh; Carnegie-Mellon Univ, BA; Univ Tex; Colorado Springs Fine Arts Ctr; Acad Grande Chaumiere; Atelier 17, with Stanley W Hayter. *Work:* Pennell Collection, Libr Cong, Washington, DC; Carnegie Mus Art, Pittsburgh; Butler Inst Am Art, Youngstown, Ohio; Metrop Mus Art, New York. *Comn:* Presentation print, Print Club, Rochester, NY, 56; bicentennial dir cover, Bell Tel Co Pa, Pittsburgh, 57; commemorative hist painting, Pa RR, Pittsburgh, 58; History of Pittsburgh (hist illus), 60; altar piece, Carnegie-Mellon Chapel, Pittsburgh, 63. *Exhib:* Painting in the US, Carnegie Mus Art, 48; Nat Acad Design, New York, 51; US Info Agency Overseas Exhib Am Graphic Art, 61; 6th Int Graphics Exhib, Ljubljana, Yugoslavia, 65; 1st Biennial Graphic Art, Krakow, Poland, 68. *Teaching:* Prof drawing & painting, Carnegie-Mellon Univ, 45-, prof painting & design, currently. *Awards:* Purchase Award, Nat Print Exhib, Brooklyn Mus, 52; Jury Award of Distinction, Assoc Artists Pittsburgh, 66; Purchase Award, Nat Print Exhib, Kutztown, Pa, 66. *Bibliog:* Norman Kent (auth), William Libby, Am Artist Mag, 59. *Mem:* Soc Am Graphic Artists; Assoc Artists Pittsburgh (pres, 55-57); Nat Acad Design. *Media:* Oil. *Publ:* Auth, They know what they like, Eastern Arts Asn Bulletin, 59; auth, A look at printmaking, Carnegie Mag, 60; auth, Offset lithography as a fine art, 67 & auth, Marco de Marco, 70, Am Artist Mag; auth, Color and the Structural Sense, Prentice Hall, 74. *Mailing Add:* Box 135 Carnegie-Mellon Univ Pittsburgh PA 15213

LIBERI, DANTE
PAINTER, SCULPTOR
b New York, NY, Oct 15, 19. *Study:* Acad Fine Arts, Montecatini, Italy. *Exhib:* Knickerbocker Artists, New York, 52; one-man shows, Galleria Vannucci, Pistoia, Italy, 70, Galleria Ghelfi, Montecatini, Italy, 72, Bottega D'Arte, Quarrata & Galleria San Luca, Verona, Italy, 79; plus others. *Awards:* First Prize for Sculpture, Oper Democracy. *Media:* Oil. *Publ:* Illusr, New Yorker Mag, 43. *Dealer:* Country Art Gallery The Plaza Locust Valley NY 11560. *Mailing Add:* 15 Ardis Lane Plainview NY 11803

LIBERMAN, ALEXANDER
PAINTER, SCULPTOR
b Kiev, Russia, 1912; US citizen. *Study:* Painting with Andre L'Hote, Paris, France, 29-31; Ecole Special d'Archit with August Perret, 32-32; Ecole Beaux-Arts, Paris, 32-33; RI Sch Design, hon DFA, 80. *Work:* Mus Mod Art, New York; Albright-Knox Art Gallery, Buffalo; Art Inst Chicago; Tate Gallery, London, Eng; Nat Collection Fine Arts, Washington, DC; and many others. *Exhib:* One-man shows, Mus Mod Art, New York, 60, Vernissage, Rome, 78, Greenberg Gallery, St Louis, 79, Landau Alexander Gallery, Los Angeles, 79 & Arts Gallery Limited, Baltimore, 79; Mus Mod Art, New York, 62, 64, 65, 67, 68 & 69; Contemp Am Sculpture Ann, Whitney Mus Am Art, 69; Pure and Clear, Philadelphia Mus Art, 69; Retrospectives: Painting and Sculpture, Corcoran Gallery Art, Washington, DC & Mus Fine Arts, Houston, 70; Color As Language, Mus Mod Art, New York, 75; Black and White are Colors, Pomona Col, Calif, 79; and others. *Pos:* Ed dir, Conde Nast Publ, 62- *Awards:* Chevalier, Legion Honor, France. *Bibliog:* Barbara Rose (auth), Alexander Liberman (monogr), Abbeville Press, 81. *Publ:* Auth, The Artist in His Studio, 60 & Greece, Gods and Art, 68, Viking. *Dealer:* Andre Emmerich Gallery 41 E 57th St New York NY 10022. *Mailing Add:* 173 E 70th St New York NY 10021

LIBHART, MYLES LAROY
ADMINISTRATOR, WRITER
b Marietta, Pa, Mar 8, 31. *Study:* Brooklyn Mus Art Sch; pvt instr with Nicholas Marsicano. *Work:* Newark Mus, NJ. *Comn:* Painted enamel murals, Grace Shipping Lines, New York, 61. *Exhib:* Arts & Crafts Regional, Newark Mus, NJ, 59; Enamels, Mus of Contemp Crafts, New York, 60. *Collections Arranged:* Am Indian Art, US Pavilion, Int Expo, Montreal, Can, 67; Contemporary American Indian Arts, US Pavilion, Japan World Expo, Osaka, Japan, 70; Contemporary Sioux Painting (auth, catalog), 71, Contemporary Sioux Quillwork, 72 & The Inspiration of Oscar Howe, 83, Sioux Indian Mus, Rapid City, SDak; Contemporary Southern Plains Indian Painting (ed, catalog), 72 Painted Tipis by Contemporary Plains Indian Artists (coauth, catalog), 73 & Contemporary Eskimo Carvers of Gambell, 83, Southern Plains Indian Mus, Anadarko, Okla; Plains Indian Arts, Indian Mus Buffalo Bill Hist Ctr, Cody, Wyo, 79. *Pos:* Dir exhibs & publ, Brooklyn Mus, NY, 60-63; dir mus, exhibs & publ, Indian Arts & Crafts Bd, US Dept Interior, Washington, DC, 63- *Teaching:* Instr painted enamels, Brooklyn Mus Art Sch, NY, 61-63. *Bibliog:* David Cambell (auth), Art in Am, Vol 1, No 1, 60. *Mem:* Am Asn Mus. *Media:* Oil, Enamel. *Res:* Development of contemporary Native American arts of the United States. *Mailing Add:* Indian Arts & Crafts Bd Rm 4004 US Dept of the Interior Washington DC 20240

LICHACZ, SHEILA ENIT
PAINTER
b Monagrillo, Panama, Oct 9, 42; US & Panamanian citizen. *Study:* Our Lady of the Lake Univ, San Antonio, Tex, BS, 65; Inter-Am Univ, PR, MA(educ), 68. *Work:* Mus of Man, Panama City; Bank of Am, Panama City; Tocumen Int Airport, Panama; Bank of Tokyo, Panama City; Nat Inst Culture, Panama. *Exhib:* Miniatures, Galeria el Marco Mundial, 78; Red, White & Blue, Chase Manhattan Bank, 78; Summer's Paintings, US Ambassador's Residence, 79; Mus of Man, 79; Echoes of the Future, Banco Santander y Panama, 79. *Media:* Pastel. *Mailing Add:* 2001 Trevino Dr Austin TX 78746

LICHT, EVELYN M
PAINTER, SCULPTOR
b New York, NY, Mar 4, 05. *Study:* Art Students League, 24; Hunter Col, 20-24; Rutgers Univ, 27-32; Academia de Belle Arte, Perugia, Italy, 62-69; New Sch Social Research, 68-72. *Work:* Everson Mus & John Mayfield Libr, Syracuse, NY; Hinkhouse Collection, Eureka Col, Ill; Philadelphia Mus Art, Pa; Mus Cathedral of St John, New York. *Comn:* Homage Dal Vesuvio, Serrento Palace Hotel, Italy, 81. *Exhib:* Women Sculptors, Grammercy Arts Club, New York, 63; Contemp Religious Art, Community Church, New York, 64; Women Watercolorists, Lever Bldg, New York, 64; Casein Artists, Union Carbide Bldg, New York, 65; Contemp Landscapes, Katonah, New York, 65. *Pos:* Chmn, Kirbutz Scholarship Art, 64-70; dir art gallery, United Fedn New York, 66-70. *Teaching:* Instr art, Teaneck, NJ, 24-29; supervisor arts, District 18, Bronx, NY, 48-50; chmn art, Kieran Jr High, 50-60. *Bibliog:* Shea Tenenbaum (auth), Art of Evelyn Licht, Montreal Chronicle, 73. *Mem:* Artists Equity; Arts Int; Arts Interaction; Nat Art Club. *Media:* Oil, Watercolor; Bronze. *Dealer:* Glass Gallery 315 Central Park West New York NY 10025. *Mailing Add:* 90 La Salle St New York NY 10027

LICHT, JENNIFER MCCONNELL
CURATOR, HISTORIAN
b London, Eng, June 11, 40. *Study:* Columbia Univ, pres fel & MA(art hist), 77; MPh, 82. *Collections Arranged:* Dir var exhibs, Mus Mod Art, New York, 66-75. *Pos:* Assoc cur painting & sculpture, Mus Mod Art, New York, 68-76; bk rev ed, Art J, New York, 79. *Teaching:* Vis prof art hist, Sch Visual Arts, New York, 71. *Awards:* Guggenheim Mem Found Fel, 71; Chester Dale Fel, Nat Gallery Art, Washington, DC, 83-84. *Res:* Nineteenth and twentieth century painting and sculpture. *Publ:* Auth, various catalogs and articles on nineteenth and twentieth century art. *Mailing Add:* 47 E 87th St New York NY 10027

LICHTENBERG, MANES
PAINTER
b New York, NY. *Study:* Art Students League; with Fernand Leger, Paris; Acad Grande Chaumiere, Paris. *Exhib:* Philadelphia Acad Fine Arts; Nat Acad Design, New York; Mus Mod Art, Paris; Allied Artists Am, New York; Mus I'lle de France, Paris. *Awards:* Prix Othon Friesz, Paris, 61; Gold Medal of Honor, Allied Artists Am, 64; Prix Maurice Utrillo, Utrillo Found Int, Paris, 64. *Mem:* Allied Artists Am; Am Watercolor Soc. *Media:* Watercolor, Oil. *Mailing Add:* 835 Mix Ave Hamden CT 06514

LICHTENSTEIN, ROY
PAINTER, SCULPTOR
b New York, NY, Oct 27, 23. *Study:* Ohio State Univ, BFA, 46, MFA, 49. *Work:* Solomon R Guggenheim Mus, New York; Whitney Mus Am Art, New York; Mus Mod Art, New York; Stedelijk Mus, Amsterdam, Holland; Metrop Mus, New York; and many others. *Comn:* Outside wall for Circarama, NY State Pavilion, New York World's Fair, 63; painting, Expo 67, Montreal; Mermaid, Miami Beach Theatre Performing Arts, 79. *Exhib:* Print Biennial, Brooklyn Mus, 68; Solomon R Guggenheim Mus, 69; one-man show, Seattle Art Mus, Wash, 70, and others; Whitney Mus Am Art Ann, 70, 72 & 73, Am Pop Art, 74; Mus Fine Arts, Osaka, Japan, 70; Va Mus Art, Richmond, 70; Contemp Arts Ctr, Cincinnati, 70 & 74; Corcoran Biennial, Washington, DC, 71; Albright-Knox Art Gallery, Buffalo, NY, 71; Art Inst Chicago, 72 & 74; Detroit Inst of Arts, 73; Art Mus STex, Corpus Christi, 74; Mus Mod Art, New York, 74; Blum-Helman Gallery, New York, 81; and many others. *Teaching:* Instr, Ohio State Univ, 46-51; instr, State Univ NY Col Oswego, 57-60; instr, Douglass Col, Rutgers Univ, 60-63. *Bibliog:* John Coplans (ed), Roy Lichtenstein, 72; Jack Cowart (auth), Roy Lichtenstein 1970-1980, 81; Laurence Alloway (auth), Lichtenstein, 83; plus many others. *Dealer:* Leo Castelli Gallery 420 W Broadway New York NY 10012. *Mailing Add:* PO Box 1369 Southampton NY 11968

LICHTNER, SCHOMER FRANK
PAINTER, PRINTMAKER
b Peoria, Ill, Mar 18, 05. *Study:* Milwaukee State Teachers Col with Gustave Moeller, 24; Art Inst Chicago, 26; Art Students League with Boardman Robinson, 27; Univ Wis, Madison with Oscar Hagen, 29-30. *Work:* Milwaukee Art Mus, Wis; Univ Wis Union Gallery, Madison; Wustum Mus, Racine, Wis; Milwaukee Journal, Wis; White House (selected by Pres Roosevelt), Washington, DC. *Comn:* Murals, Walker Jr High, Milwaukee, Wis, 34; murals, Sheboygan Post Off, WPA Treas Dept, Wis, 38; mural,

Oconomowoc Canning Co, Wis, 52; mural, Northern & Marine Bank, Milwaukee, Wis, 55; sculpture screen (exterior), Masonic State Headquarters, Milwaukee, Wis, 56. *Exhib:* Two man show, Milwaukeee Art Mus, Wis, 62; Artists of Chicago & Vicinity, Art Inst Chicago, 63; Three Man Show, Art Inst Chicago; Davidson Nat Print & Drawing, Stowe Gallery, NC, 72; Wis Directions, Milwaukee Art Mus, 75; Wis Painters & Sculptors, Univ Wis Fine Arts Gallery, 80; Am Show, Art Inst Chicago; Carnegie Int, Carnegie Inst, Pittsburgh, Pa; Ballet Art, Performing Art Ctr, 83 & Bradley Galleries, 83, Milwaukee; Retrospective, Milwaukee Art Mus, 84. *Teaching:* Instr drawing & design, Univ Wis, 60-69. *Awards:* Award for Serigraph, Wis Salon, Madison, 50; Award for Painting, Mr & Mrs Jule E Brower, Chicago Artists & Vicinity, Art Inst Chicago, 64; Award for Painting, Wis Painters & Sculptors, 65. *Bibliog:* Richard Olney (auth), Schomer Lichtner Drawings, 64; Dennis Stone (auth), The Light Touch of Schomer Lichtner, Art Scene, 68. *Media:* Acrylic, Casein; Serigraph, Etching. *Publ:* Auth, Schomer Lichtner Drawings, Gallery Press, 64; auth, Schomer Lichtner Spotted Cow Drawings, 69 & auth, Schomer Lichtner Drawings from the Nude, 74, Spotted Cow; auth, Schomer Lichtner Alphabet Drawings, 73 & auth, Ballerinas' Holiday, 79, self pub. *Dealer:* Bradley Galleries 2565 N Downer Ave Milwaukee WI 53211; Seuferer Chosy Gallery 218 N Henry St Madison WI 53703. *Mailing Add:* 2626A N Maryland Ave Milwaukee WI 53211

LICHTY, GEORGE M
CARTOONIST
b Chicago, Ill, May 16, 05. *Study:* Art Inst Chicago; Univ Mich, BA. *Work:* Truman Libr, Independence, Mo; Presidential Mus, Austin, Tex; Mus Cartoon Art, Greenwich, Conn; Tate Gallery, London, Eng. *Pos:* Syndicate cartoonist, United Features Syndicate, 34-40 & Field Newspaper Syndicate, 40- *Awards:* Best Syndicate Panel Award, Nat Cartoonists Soc, 59, 63, 65 & 73. *Bibliog:* Greer William (auth), Does Lichty hate people, Saturday Eve Post, 52; news article in Time Mag, 56. *Mem:* Nat Cartoonists Soc. *Media:* Ink, Oil. *Mailing Add:* Field Newspaper Syndicate PO Box 19620 Irvine CA 92714

LIDDLE, NANCY HYATT
ADMINISTRATOR, GALLERY DIRECTOR
b Martinsville, Ind, Aug 27, 31. *Study:* Ind Univ, AB. *Collections Arranged:* The Sculpture of Richard Stankiewicz 1953-1979 (ed, catalog); International Exposition of Fine Arts (auth, catalog), Belgrade, Yugoslavia, 80; Edward Koren: Prints and Drawings (ed, catalog), 82; Thom O'Connor: Prints and Drawings (ed, catalog), 83. *Pos:* Vpres, 327 Gallery, Albany, NY, 59-63; art critic, Knickerbocker News, Albany, NY, 64-65; asst dir, Univ Art Gallery, State Univ NY, Albany, 66-67, dir, 77- *Teaching:* Lectr, State Univ NY, Albany, currently. *Awards:* Chancellors Award, State Univ NY, 80; Preservation Award, Hist Albany Found, 81. *Mem:* Albany Inst Hist & Art; Hist Albany Found; Am Asn Mus; Gallery Dirs Coun, State Univ NY. *Mailing Add:* 34 Willett St Albany NY 12210

LIDOV, ARTHUR HERSCHEL
PAINTER, SCULPTOR
b Chicago, Ill, June 24, 17. *Study:* Univ Chicago, BA, 36, study art hist, 38-39. *Comn:* Mural, Post Off, Chillicothe, Ill, 39 & J W Thompson, New York, 64; series of bio-medical paintings, Life Mag, 61-63. *Exhib:* One-man shows, Art Inst Chicago, 41, Pineapple Gallery, Brooklyn, 43 & J Walter Thompson Gallery, 64; Art Inst Chicago, 33 & 34; Nat Acad Art, 58; Mus Mod Art, 62; Numismatic Mus, New York, 83; and others. *Pos:* Creative consult & mem exec comt, Sudler & Hennessey Advert Agency, New York, 50-52; gen partner & prin exec officer, SWP3, New York, 72-79. *Awards:* Art Dirs Club Awards, 52, 53 & 59; Illusr Club New York Award, 63, 73 & 74; Am Inst Graphic Arts Award, 63. *Mailing Add:* Pleasant Ridge Rd Poughquag NY 12570

LIEBER, THOMAS ALAN
PAINTER
b St Louis, Mo, Nov 5, 49. *Study:* Florissant Valley Jr Col, 67-69; Univ Ill, BFA, 71, MFA, 74. *Work:* Guggenheim Mus, Mus Mod Art, New York; San Francisco Mus Mod Art; Los Angeles Mus Mod Art. *Exhib:* Mid-Am IV, St Louis Art Mus, 72; Bloomington Bi-Centennial, Bloomington Art Mus, Ill, 76; The Aesthetics of Grafitti, San Francisco Mus Mod Art, Calif, 78; The Controlled Gesture, Palo Alto Cultural Ctr, Calif, 80; Fresh Paint, San Francisco Mus Mod Art, 82; New Perspectives in American Painting, Guggenheim Mus, 83. *Awards:* Nat Endowment Arts, 75. *Bibliog:* Robert McDonald (auth), Physicaally finds its place, 76 & Tom Liebers environmental paintings, 77, Art Week; John Russell (auth), Younger Americans, New York Times, 83. *Media:* Acrylic, Watercolor. *Dealer:* John Berggruen 228 Grant San Francisco CA; Nancy Lurie Gallery 1632 N La Salle St Chicago IL. *Mailing Add:* 1229 Solano Ave Albany CA 94706

LIEBERMAN, LAURA CROWELL
EDITOR, CRITIC
b Oak Ridge, Tenn, Apr 7, 52. *Study:* Pomona Col,72; Swarthmore Col, BA, 74. *Collections Arranged:* Atlanta Women Artists: A Personal Survey, Atlanta Art Workers' Gallery, 78; 36 Women Artists (coed, catalog), Peachtree Ctr Gallery, Atlanta, 78; Nine Diverse Directions: Atlanta, Ga Southern Col, 83. *Pos:* Artist-in-residence, Ga Coun for Arts & Humanities, Atlanta, spring, 77; artist-in-residence, Atlanta Women's Art Collective, 77-78; ed-in-chief, Atlanta Art Workers' Coalition Newspaper, 78-80; ed-in-chief, Atlanta Art Papers, Inc, 80- & Words Art Inc, 82- *Bibliog:* Karen Wantuck (auth), Subjective (catalog), 78; Sherry Baker (auth), 36 women artists, Atlanta Gazette, 4/78; Clyde Burnett (auth), A personal survey, Atlanta J-Constitution, 7/78. *Mem:* Atlanta Women's Art Collective;

Southeastern Women's Caucus for Art (panelist, 79); Col Art Asn. *Res:* Contemporary art in Atlanta, Georgia and the Southeast. *Publ:* Co-ed, Other Harmonies, Atlanta Women's Poetry Workshop, 77; auth, Five Atlanta women artists, Southern Quart, Univ Southern Miss, 79; auth, Sensation, Atlantic Mag; ed, Contracts for Artists, 83; and others. *Mailing Add:* 28 16th St NW Atlanta GA 30309

LIEBERMAN, LOUIS (KARL)
SCULPTOR, DRAFTSMAN
b Brooklyn, NY, May 7, 44. *Study:* Brooklyn Mus Art Sch, with Isaac Soyer, cert, 64; Brooklyn Col, BA, 62; RI Sch Design, with Richard Merkin, BFA, 69. *Work:* Metrop Mus Art, New York; Staten Island Mus, Richmond, NY; Georgetown Col, Ky; Philadelphia Mus Art, Pa; Aldrich Mus, Ridgefield, Conn. *Comn:* Wall relief, Aldrich Mus Contemp Art, Ridgefield, Conn, 73; Wall relief, Kenan Ctr, NY State Coun on Arts, Lockport, NY, 73. *Exhib:* 2nd Ann Contemp Reflections, Aldrich Mus Contemp Art, Ridgefield, Conn, 73 & 10th Ann Exhib, 74; Clay Attitudes, Queens Mus, NY, 79; Handmade Paper, Visual Art Ctr, Beer-Sheva, Israel, 79; Graphics Plus, Herbert F Johnson Mus Art, Ithaca, Burchfield Ctr, Buffalo, Rochester Inst Technology, Rochester, New York, 80-81; and many others. *Pos:* Contribr art critic, New York Arts J, 78-79. *Teaching:* Adj lectr drawing, Brooklyn Col, NY, 71-78; adj lectr sculpture/design, Lehman Col, Bronx, 72-75; vis artist sculpture, Ill State Univ, Normal, 79; vis artist, Hamilton Col, Clinton, New York, 82. *Awards:* NY State Coun Arts Creative Artists Pub Serv Prog Grant, 72-73; Nat Endowment Arts Papermaking Grant, 79 & 80. *Bibliog:* Charles Bennet (dir/producer), Lieberman (film), 76; Kenneth Wahl, On abstract literalist works, Arts Mag, 4/77; Bernard Toale (auth), The Art of Papermaking, Davis Publ, 83. *Media:* Multimedia. *Mailing Add:* 16 Greene St New York NY 10013

LIEBERMAN, MEYER FRANK
PAINTER, PRINTMAKER
b New York, NY, Aug 28, 23. *Study:* Art Students League, with Reginald Marsh; Pratt Graphics Ctr, with Andrew Stasik. *Work:* Jewish Mus, New York; Flatbush Jewish Ctr, Brooklyn. *Exhib:* Coney Island, Mus City New York, 55; Drawing USA, Mus Mod Art, New York, 56; one-man shows, Bodley Gallery, 78; Night Gallery, 81; Terrance Gallery, 81; Vassar Col Ctr Gallery, 81 & others, New York. *Teaching:* Instr drawing, painting & composition, Art Life Craft Studios, New York, 64-68; instr drawing, collage painting & composition, Temple Emanu-El, Yonkers, NY, 66-74; instr drawing, painting & composition, Flatbush Jewish Ctr, Brooklyn, 67-78; instr, Temple Emanuel, Kingston, NY, 78-80. *Mem:* Woodstock Artists Asn; Artists Equity Asn. *Media:* Multimedia. *Mailing Add:* Box 421 Zena Rd Woodstock NY 12498

LIEBERMAN, VICKIE
TAPESTRY ARTIST, GALLERY DIRECTOR
b Philadelphia, Pa, July 11, 52. *Study:* Syracuse Univ Art Sch, BA(fine art), 70-74; Syracuse Univ Art Sch, Florence, Italy, BA(studio art), 73; Handweavers Guild Am, special study with Janet Taylor, 76. *Comn:* Tapestry, Mrs Paul's Frozen Foods, Philadelphia, 76; tapestry, Meditation Chapel, Methodist Church, NJ, 77; 6ft tapestry, Girard Bank, Philadelphia, 77; and others. *Exhib:* Philadelphia Weavers, Univ Mus, Pa, 76; one-woman show, Fifth St Gallery, Wilmington, Del, 77; Fiberwork, Del Art Mus, Wilmington, 78. *Pos:* Designer area rugs, Thor Enterprises, Boca Raton, Fla, 76-77; dir, Wadsworth Gallery, Bryn Mawr, Pa, 77-80. *Teaching:* Instr weaving, Chester Co Art Ctr, West Chester, Pa, 74-78 & Holy Family Col, 79. *Awards:* First Prize, Whitford Country Club, 76, Media City Coun, 76 & 77 & Cabrini Col, 77. *Bibliog:* Vera Kaminski (auth), Department head weaving, University Delaware, Fiber Arts mag, 80. *Mem:* Handweavers Guild Am; Am Crafts Coun. *Media:* Textiles, Weaving. *Specialty:* Contemporary painting, sculpture, graphics and craft. *Mailing Add:* c/o Wadsworth Gallery 826 W Lancaster Ave Bryn Mawr PA 19010

LIEBERMAN, WILLIAM S
ADMINISTRATOR
b Paris, France, Feb 14, 24. *Study:* Swarthmore Col, BA(hons), 43; Harvard Univ, with Paul J Sachs, 44-45. *Collections Arranged:* Max Ernst, 61; The New Japanese Painting & Sculpture, 66; Jackson Pollock, 67; Jean Dubuffet, 68; Julio Gonzalez, Kandinsky Watercolors, Tamarind: Homage to Lithography, George Grosz: Drawings & Watercolors, Archipenko: The Parisian Years & The Sculpture of Richard Hunt, 69-71; and others. *Pos:* Mem staff, Dept Exhibs & Publ, Mus Mod Art, New York, 43, asst to dir mus collections, 45-49, assoc cur prints & illus bks, 49-53, cur prints, 53-66, dir drawings & prints, 66-81, cur painting & sculpture, 67-71, chmn dept 20th century art, 79-81; chmn, Dept 20th Century Art, Metropolitan Mus Art, New York, currently. *Awards:* Chevalier de l'Ordre des Arts et des Lett, Repub France. *Mem:* Grolier Club; Am Fedn Arts; Cassandra Found; Drawing Soc; Int Graphic Arts Soc; and others. *Collection:* Eighteenth century silver boxes, Japanese prints of the Meiji ear. *Publ:* Auth, Picasso: Blue & Rose Periods, Abrams, 54; auth, Matisse: 50 Years of His Graphic Art, Braziller, 56; auth, Edvard Munch, Los Angeles Co Mus Art, 69; auth, Redon: Prints & Drawings & Jacques Villon, Mus Mod Art; and others. *Mailing Add:* Metropolitan Mus Art Fifth Ave at 82nd St New York NY 10028

LIEBLING, JEROME
PHOTOGRAPHER, FILMMAKER
b New York, NY, April 16, 24. *Study:* Brooklyn Col, with Walter Rosenblum, Milton Brown & Art Reinhardt; New Sch Social Res, with Lew Jacobs & Paul Falkander. *Work:* Mus Mod Art, New York; Corcoran Gallery Art; Boston Mus Fine Art; Libr Cong; Minneapolis Inst Art. *Exhib:* The Photo League,

Int Ctr Photog, New York, 78; Mirrors and Windows, Mus Mod Art, New York, 78; 14 Northeast Photographers, Boston Mus Fine Arts, 78; solo exhibs, Corcoran Gallery Art, 80, Fogg Art Mus, 82 & Portland Art Mus, Maine, 83; American Children, Mus Mod Art, New York, 81; Northeast Perambulations, Addison Gallery, 82. *Teaching:* Prof photog & film, Univ Minn, Minneapolis, 49-69 & Hampshire Col, 70-83; prof photog, Yale Univ, 76-77. *Awards:* Fels, Guggenheim Found, 77 & 81 & Nat Endowment Arts, 79. *Bibliog:* Estelle Jussim (auth), #15, Friends Photog, 77; Alan Trachtenberg (auth), Jerome Liebling--Photographs, Univ Mass Press, 82. *Mem:* Soc Photog Educ (trustee, 73-78); Univ Film Study Ctr (vpres, 75-77). *Publ:* Coauth, Face of Minneapolis, Dillon Press, 66; illusr, Photography Current Perspectives, Mass Rev, 77. *Dealer:* Vision Gallery 216 Newbury St Boston MA 02116. *Mailing Add:* 39 Dana St Amherst MA 01002

LIENAU, DANIEL CLIFFORD
DEALER, COLLECTOR
b Sturgeon Bay, Wis, May 30, 43. *Study:* Univ Wis-Madison, studied sculpture for four yrs; studied with Leo Steppat. *Pos:* Owner-dir, Annex Galleries, Santa Rosa, Calif, 70-; gallery dir, Santa Rosa Jr Col Gallery, Calif, 74-75, wholesale rep, The Roten Collection, Brentano. *Teaching:* Instr conserv framing, Riley St Annex, Santa Rosa, Calif, 77- *Awards:* Santa Rosa Civic Art Award, City of Santa Rosa, Calif, 74. *Specialty:* Prints & drawings, 17th through 20th centuries with an emphasis on American Prints 1890-1940; color woodcuts and California prints; selected photography, painting and sculpture. *Collection:* Prints and drawings: Marcoussis, Marquet, Carriere, G Baumann, H Hyde, B Lum, Tooker, American and European color woodcut, Cubist prints, California prints from 1890-1940. *Mailing Add:* 604 College Ave Santa Rosa CA 95404

LIGARE, DAVID H
PAINTER
b Oak Park, Ill, 1945. *Study:* Art Ctr Col Design. *Work:* Mus Mod Art, New York; Univ Kans Mus Art, Lawrence; Sara Roby Found Collection; Atlantic-Richfield Corp; Weatherspoon Art Gallery, Greensboro, NC. *Exhib:* Drawings USA & Traveling Exhib, Minn Mus Art, St Paul, 71-73; Mus Mod Art, New York, 77; Phoenix Art Mus, Ariz, 77; Mus Contemp Art, Chicago, 78; Andrew Crispo Gallery, 79; Reality of Illusion Traveling Exhib, Denver Art Mus, Colo & Univ Southern Calif, Los Angeles, 79-80; and many others. *Bibliog:* Article, Artforum, 4/77. *Mailing Add:* c/o Andrew Crispo Gallery 41 E 57th St New York NY 10022

LIJN, LILIANE
SCULPTOR, WRITER
b New York, NY, Dec 22, 39. *Study:* Ecole de Louvre, Paris, Sorbonne, Paris. *Work:* Tate Gallery, London, Eng; Mus de la Ville de Paris, France; Centre Nat d'Art Contemporain, Paris; Arts Coun Great Brit, London; Victoria & Albert Mus, London. *Comn:* Kinetic sculpture, Peter Stuyvescent Corp & Arts Coun Great Brit, Warwick Univ, Coventry, Eng, 72; Circle of Light, Milton Keynes Shopping Arcades, Eng, 79; Split Spiral Spin, Birchwood Sci Park, Warrington New Town, Eng, 79; Extrapolation, Norfolk & Norwich Triennial Festival, Norwich, 82. *Exhib:* Serpentine Gallery, London, 76; Mus d'Art Mod, Paris, 67; Prospect 68, Dusseldorf Mus, 68; Int Visuele Poezie, Rotterdam, 75; Art in the Sixties, Tate Gallery, London, 76; Haywood Ann, Haywood Gallery, London, 78; British Sculpture in the Twentieth Century, Part II, Whitechapel Art Gallery, London, 81; Electra, Mus d'Art Modern, Paris, 83; and others. *Awards:* Alecto Print Award, Bradford Print Biennale, 76; Publishing Award, Art Coun GB, 81; Award, Arts Coun Bursary Holography, 82. *Bibliog:* Cyril Barrett (auth), Art as research: the experiments of L Lijn, Studio Int, Vol 173 (June, 1967); Vera Lindsay (auth), Liliane Lijn in discussion with Vera Lindsay, Studio Int, Vol 177 (May, 1969); Joan Murray (auth), Beyond the image: Liliane Lijn, Fireweed 5 & 6, Woman & Language, Toronto, 80. *Media:* Kinetic Sculpture, Etching. *Publ:* auth, Inside & out: notes on anti-gravity koans, Flash Art, Milan, Italy, 2/71; auth, Reflections: Three Poems, Time Zone, Grosseteste Rev, 71; auth, What is art?, Ostrich No 9, Northumberland, 9/73; Six Throws of The Oracular Keys, Ed de la Nepe, Paris, 82; Crossing Map, Thames & Hudson, 83. *Mailing Add:* 28 Camden Sq London NW1 9XA England United Kingdom

LIKAN, GUSTAV
PAINTER, INSTRUCTOR
b Srb, Yugoslavia, May 1, 12; US citizen. *Study:* Akad der Bildenden Kunste, Munich, Ger; Franz Hals Mus, Haarlem; Louvre, Paris. *Work:* Moderna Galerija & Strossmayer Mus, Zagreb, Yugoslavia; Mestrovic Mus, Split, Yugoslavia; Kunstlerhaus Mus, Salzburg, Austria; Kunstmouseet, Copenhagen, Denmark. *Comn:* Murals of schs, comn by Eva Peron, Buenos Aires, 50, Cordoba, 51 & Mendoza, Arg, 51, mural of a hosp, comn by Eva Peron, 50 & mural of a church, Buenos Aires, 51. *Exhib:* Nat Mus Vienna, 41; one-man shows, Merrill Chase Galleries, Chicago, 64, Laguna Gloria Art Mus, Austin, Tex, 76, Abilene Fine Arts Mus, Tex, 76 & Am House, Heidelberg, WGer, 83; and others. *Teaching:* Prof fine art, Chicago Acad Fine Art, 60-67, Laguna Gloria Mus Fine Art, Austin, Tex, 69-78, Austin Community Col, 82- *Bibliog:* Article, Third Coast, 9/10/83. *Media:* Graphic & Acrylic Painting. *Publ:* Auth, Art Classes 2,5: Meaning, Method & Media, 72; auth, Likan Drawings, 73; also auth articles in bks & newspapers in Austria & Yugoslavia. *Dealer:* Merrill Chase Galleries Ltd 620 N Michigan Ave Chicago IL 60611. *Mailing Add:* 1407 Ridgecrest Dr Austin TX 78746

LI-LAN (LI-LAN GEE)
PAINTER
b New York, NY, Jan 28, 43. *Work:* Guild Hall Mus, E Hampton, NY; Sydney & Francis Lewis Found Collection, Richmond; Estee Lauder Inc,

New York; Seibu Art Mus, Tokyo; Mod Art Mus, Toyama, Japan. *Exhib:* Albright-Knox Art Gallery, 70; Late Twentieth Century Art Traveling Exhib, Sydney & Frances Lewis Found, 78-83; solo exhibs, Asher/Faure Gallery, Los Angeles, 80 & 82 & OK Harris Gallery, New York, 83; Sheldon Memorial Art Gallery, Univ Nebr, 81; Eye to Eye, Asian Arts Inst, New York, 83; Selections form the Permanent Collection, Guild Hall Mus, East Hampton, NY, 83; Prime Works by Representative OK Harris Artists, OK Harris West, Scottsdale, Ariz, 83; and many others. *Bibliog:* Susan Lewis (auth), Sydney & Francis Lewis Foundation, Va, 79; Judy Tannenbaum (auth), article, Arts Mag, 9/78; Kazuko Matsuoka (auth), Li-Lan's White, Watash Wa Onna, Tokyo, 7/77. *Publ:* Auth, Canvas with an Unpainted Part, An Autobiography, Asahi Newspaper Publishing, Tokyo, 76. *Dealer:* OK Harris Gallery 383 W Broadway New York NY 10012. *Mailing Add:* PO Box 1194 East Hampton NY 11937

LILES, RAEFORD BAILEY
PAINTER, SCULPTOR
b Birmingham, Ala, July 20, 23. *Study:* Birmingham-Southern Col; Auburn Univ, BSEE, 49; Atelier Fernand Leger, Paris, France, 49-51. *Work:* Musee d'Art Mod, Eliat, Israel; Andrew Dickson White Mus Art, Cornell Univ; Corcoran Gallery Art, Washington, DC; Amos Andersons Konstmuseum, Helsinky, Finland; Alfred Khouri Collection, Norfolk Mus, Va; and others. *Comn:* Silk screen series, East Hampton Gallery, NY, 67; also pvt collections. *Exhib:* Salon d'Art Independent & Art Libre, Paris, 51; Salon Nouvelle Reality, Mus Mod Art, Paris, 55; Mirco Salon d'Avril, Paris, 56; Carroll Reece Mus 11 Ann Purchase Exhib, Johnson City, Tenn, 68; Art for Peace, New York, 70; and others. *Awards:* Prize, Students of Leger, 51; First Prize, Alpine Gallery, 58. *Bibliog:* Turpin (auth), L'Orleanais Dans Les Art, 52; Orinese (auth), Tour D'Expositions Combat, 55; Brown (auth), Review of expositions, Art Mag, 68. *Mem:* Birmingham Art Asn; Ala Watercolor Soc. *Mailing Add:* 446 W 38th St New York NY 10018

LILJEGREN, FRANK
PAINTER, INSTRUCTOR
b New York, NY, Feb 23, 30. *Study:* Art Students League, with John Groth, Dean Cornwell & Frank J Reilly. *Work:* Manhattan Savings Bank, New York; Am Educ Publ Inst, New York; New Britain Mus Am Art, Conn. *Exhib:* Coun Am Artists Soc, Lever House, New York, 64 & 67; Salmagundi Club, New York, 64-68; Acad Artists Asn, Springfield Fine Arts Mus, Mass, 66-70; O S Ranch Exhib, Tex, 77-80; Fort Wayne Mus Art, Ind, 79; and others. *Teaching:* Instr painting, Westchester Co Art Workshop, White Plains, 66-77, Art Students League, 73-74, Wassenberg Art Ctr, Van Wert, Ohio, 77-80, Wright State Univ, 81- *Awards:* Allied Artists Am Awards; Frank V Dumond Award, Salmagundi Club, 65 & 67; Medal of Merit for Oil Painting, Today's Art Mag, 71. *Bibliog:* Jo Mary McCormick-De Guyton (auth), Frank Liljegren and his old friends, Am Artist Mag, 2/72; Ralph Fabri (auth), Medal of merit winner in 58th A A A annual, Today's Art Mag, 3/72. *Mem:* Allied Artists Am (corresp secy, 67, exhib chmn, 68-76, pres, 70-72, dir, 72-76); Artists Fellowship; Salmagundi Club; life mem Art Students League. *Media:* Oil, Pastels. *Mailing Add:* 203 S Cherry St Van Wert OH 45891

LILYQUIST, CHRISTINE
EGYPTOLOGIST, CURATOR
b Glendale, Calif, Aug 15, 40. *Study:* Pomona Col, BA, 62; NY Univ, MA, 65, PhD, 71. *Collections Arranged:* Dir, Dendur Temple Installation, Metrop Mus Art, New York, 72-78, dir, Egyptian Reinstallation, 72-83, consult, Renovation of the Cairo Mus, 75-77 & cur, Mus Consortium for the Exhib Treasures of Tutankhamun, 75-79. *Pos:* Asst cur Egyptian dept, Metrop Mus Art, New York, 70-72, assoc cur in charge, 72-74 & cur, 74-; consult, New York City Dept Park & Rec (Cleopatra's Needle), 78-80. *Mem:* Col Art Asn. *Res:* Egyptian gold, Middle Kingdom arts. *Publ:* Ed, Tutankhamun Exhib Publ, Metrop Mus Art, New York, 76; auth, Ancient Egyptian Mirrors: From the Earliest Times Through the Middle Kingdom, Munchner Aegyptologische Studien 27, 79. *Mailing Add:* Dept Egyptian Art Metrop Mus Art New York NY 10028

LI MARZI, JOSEPH
PAINTER, GRAPHIC ARTIST
b Chicago, Ill. *Study:* Art Inst Chicago. *Comn:* Historical, Fed Govt, Fed Bldg, Wapokeneta, Ohio, 37; mil hist of army co, Fed Govt, Staten Island, NY, 42; story of food, Royal Scarlet Foods, New York, 51; indust uses of Gen Cables, Inc, New York, 52. *Exhib:* Art Inst Chicago Nat; Brooklyn Mus Nat; Pa Acad Fine Arts Nat; one-man shows, Contemporary Arts, New York, Simon's Rock, Mass & Lehman Gallery, Red Rock, NY, 75; Cleveland Inst Art; Mus Mod Art, New York; Libr Arts Ctr, Newport, NH; Berkshire Mus, Pittsfield, Mass; Spencertown Acad, NY. *Teaching:* Instr painting, High Sch Art & Design, New York, 52-73. *Awards:* Hon Award, Mural Competition, Fed Govt, 37. *Mem:* Painters & Sculptors Soc NJ; Audubon Artists New York. *Media:* Oil, Graphics. *Dealer:* Ella Lerner Gallery 17 Franklin St Lenox MA 02140. *Mailing Add:* Box 144 East Chatham NY 12060

LIMONE, FRANK
SCULPTOR
b Brooklyn, NY, Aug 14, 38. *Study:* St Louis Univ, BA, 69; Tyler Sch Art, Philadelphia, MFA, 72. *Work:* Walker Art Ctr, Minneapolis; High Mus Art, Atlanta, Ga; Collection of Dial Finance & Collection of Am Rep Insurance Co, Des Moines & Scottsdale, Ariz; Meredith Corp, Des Moines & Kansas City, Mo; KCMO Broadcasting Co, Kansas City, Mo. *Exhib:* One-man shows, Walker Art Ctr, Minneapolis, 79; Douglas Drake Gallery, Kansas City, Mo, 79, 80 & 81; Creighton Univ, Omaha, Nebr, 79; Alternative Ctr for Int Arts, 4 Installations, New York, 79; Sheldon Mem Art Gallery, Lincoln, Nebr, 81;

Greenberg Gallery, Richard S Haw & Frank Limone, St Louis, Mo, 81. *Teaching:* Artist-in-residence, Des Moines Art Ctr, 74-78; asst prof painting & drawing, Drake Univ, 72-73. *Awards:* Mid-Career Sculpture Grant, Nat Endow for Arts, 81. *Bibliog:* Graham W J Beal (auth), Walker Art Ctr Arch, 79; Holliday T Day (auth), Frank Limone at Roy Boyd, Art in Am, 10/79; Victoria Melcher (auth), Frank Limone at Douglas Drake, Kansas City Star, 2/79, 10/81; Fade to Black (film), KCMO-TV, CBS, 11/81. *Media:* Mixed. *Dealer:* Douglas Drake Gallery 4500 State Line Kansas City KS 66103. *Mailing Add:* 6 Ogden Ave White Plains NY 10605

LIMONT, NAOMI CHARLES
PRINTMAKER, INSTRUCTOR
b Pottstown, Pa. *Study:* Pa Acad Fine Arts, BFA; Pratt Graphic Ctr, with Michael Ponce de Leon; Barnes Found; Univ Pa, BFA; Tyler Sch Art, with Romas Viesulas, MFA; also with Jerome Kaplan. *Work:* Philadelphia Mus Art & Pa Acad Fine Arts; Yale Univ; Eastern Mennonite Col, Va; Univ Southern Calif; Rutgers Univ, NJ. *Comn:* Mural, St Christopher's Children's Hosp, Philadelphia, 65; Creation (folio of prints), Philadelphia Print Club, 67; Folio '76 (bicentennial folio), Graphics Guild, Cheltenham, Pa, 75; Polio of Prints, The Centennial of Sun Printing Co, 80. *Exhib:* The Earth Art Show, Philadelphia, 75; Int Biannual Print Show, Print Club, 77; Eye on the Seventies, Philadelphia Mus Art, 79; Int Miniature Print Exhib, New York, 79; Nat Print Exhib, Cedar City, Utah, 78; and others. *Teaching:* Instr graphics, Cheltenham Art Ctr, 65-; artist residence, Lock Haven State Col, 81. *Awards:* Sun Oil Award, Earth Art Exhib, 75; Stella Drabkin Award & Bronze Medal, Am Color Print Soc, 76; Grumbacher Award, 81. *Bibliog:* Bagnell & Sosin (coordrs), The Tyler Show working women artists from Tyler School of Art, Samuel Paley Libr, Temple Univ, 73; review, Art News, 9/80; review, Art Voices, 3-4/81. *Mem:* Philadelphia Print Club; Philadelphia Art Alliance; Artists Equity Asn; Am Color Print Soc; Philadelphia Watercolor Club. *Dealer:* Richard Rosenfeld Gallery 113 Arch St Philadelphia PA 19106. *Mailing Add:* 137 Harvey St Philadelphia PA 19144

LINCOLN, RICHARD MATHER
CERAMIST, EDUCATOR
b Ann Arbor, Mich, Mar 1, 29. *Study:* Potters Guild, Ann Arbor, with Rhoda Le Blanc Lopez & J T Abernathy. *Work:* Dallas Mus Fine Arts; Witte Mus, San Antonio, Tex; Detroit Inst Arts; Davenport Art Ctr, Iowa. *Comn:* Mural, Apparel Mart, Dallas; mural, Ft Worth Children's Hosp, Tex; light fixtures, The Quadrangle, Dallas. *Exhib:* Eight Ceramic Nat & Int Exhibs, Everson Mus, Syracuse, NY, 54-68; Young Americans, New York, 56; Fiber, Clay & Metal, St Paul, Minn, 60; Miami Ceramic Nat, 60; five SCent Regional Exhibs, Santa Fe, NMex, 62-71. *Teaching:* Assoc prof ceramics, Tex Christian Univ, 63- *Awards:* Third Pottery Prize, Young Americans, 56; Purchase Award, Univ Mich Mus, 56; First Pottery Award, SCent Regional Exhib, 62. *Bibliog:* Texas potter--Richard Lincoln, Designers W, 11/70. *Mem:* Am Craftsmen Coun. *Mailing Add:* Sch Fine Arts Tex Christian Univ Ft Worth TX 76129

LINDEMANN, EDNA M
MUSEUM DIRECTOR, EDUCATOR
b Buffalo, NY. *Study:* Univ Buffalo, BS(art); Albright Art Sch; Northwestern Univ, MA(magna cum laude), 40; Cranbrook Acad Art; Columbia Univ, Augusta Larned fel, EdD, 41. *Collections Arranged:* Wallpapers, Charles E Burchfield Ctr, 73, George William Eggers Archive, 74 & Charles Burchfield Facets of the Artist's Expression, 74 & 79. *Pos:* Dir cult affairs, State Univ NY Col Buffalo, 65-68; dir, Charles Burchfield Ctr, 68-; chmn, Gallery, Asn NY State, 70-72; mem bd dirs, 72-77. *Teaching:* Instr art educ, NY Univ, 49-56; prof design, State Univ NY Col Buffalo, 56- *Awards:* Honorary, Creative Leadership Coun, Creative Educ Asn, 69; Focus Award for Outstanding Contribution to Cult Affairs, Western New York-Buffalo Courier Express, 76. *Mem:* Hon mem Patteran Artists, hon mem Buffalo Soc Artists; hon mem Assoc Artists; hon mem Creative Educ Asn. *Res:* Charles Burchfield, particularly his Buffalo years, 1921-1968. *Publ:* Auth, Our Legacy of Art in Western New York, 72; ed, Edwin Dickinson, 77; ed, Roycroft: Spirit for Today, 77; ed, The American Landscape: Paintings by Allen D'Arrangelo, 79. *Mailing Add:* 74 E Hazeline Ave Kenmore NY 14217

LINDERMAN, EARL WILLIAM
PAINTER
b Endicott, NY, Jan 1, 31. *Study:* Albright Art Sch, Buffalo, NY, BFA, 52; Pa State Univ, MA, 56, PhD, 60. *Work:* Phoenix Art Mus, Ariz; Plains Art Mus, Moorhead, Minn; Valley Nat Bank Art Collection, Phoenix; William C Brown Publ Co, Dubuque, Iowa. *Exhib:* One-man shows, Tally Richard's Gallery Contemp Art, Taos, NMex, 78-83; Heydt/Blair Gallery, Santa Fe, NMex, 80; Marilyn Butler Fine Art, Scottsdale, Ariz, 80-83; Aberbach Fine Art, New York, 82. *Teaching:* Prof painting & drawing, Ariz State Univ, Tempe, 66- *Awards:* Bronze Vessel Second Award, Plains Art Mus, Moorhead, Minn, 79. *Media:* Oil, Pastel. *Publ:* Auth, Invitation to Vision, 67, coauth, Developing Artistic and Perceptual Awareness, 4th ed, 79 & auth, Teaching secondary School Art, 2nd ed, 80, William C Brown; coauth, Crafts in the Classroom, Macmillan Publ Co, 77, 84. *Mailing Add:* c/o Dept Art Ariz State Univ Tempe AZ 85282

LINDGREN, BJORN FRANK
COLLECTOR, DEALER
b Falkenberg, Sweden, Oct 26, 43; US citizen. *Collections Arranged:* George Anthonisen, 81; Cesar Martinez-Serra, 82. *Pos:* Gallery owner, Bjorn Lindgren Gallery, New York, 81- *Specialty:* Sculpture & paintings; Chagall, Dali, John Taylor-Arms and Hogarth. *Mailing Add:* 500 E 77th New York NY 10022

LINDGREN, CHARLOTTE
SCULPTOR
b Toronto, Ont, Feb 1, 31. *Study:* Univ Mich, BS; with Jack Lenor Larsen; Can Coun studies in Finland, Sweden & Eng. *Work:* Can Dept External Affairs, Ottawa; York Univ; Winnipeg Art Gallery; Confederation Ctr Art Gallery, Charlottetown, PEI; McLaughlin Gallery, Oshawa. *Comn:* Ten Light Nets, Queen's Col, Nfld, 68; IBM Headquarters Conference Room, Toronto, 68; woven sculpture, Expo '70, Can Dept External Affairs, Osaka, Japan, 70; sculpture, CBC Bldg, Montreal, 74; wall sculpture, Fed Fisheries Bldg, 77. *Exhib:* Perspective Competition, Art Gallery Ont, Toronto, 67; Expo '67, Can Art Gallery Pavilion, Montreal, 67; Art Gallery of Ont, 74; Can House, London, 76; Can Cult Centre, Paris, France, 76; London Regional Art Gallery, 80; IV Triennale, Poland, 81; Barbican Centre, London, Eng, 82; and others. *Pos:* Juror arts bursaries, Can Coun, 70, mem adv arts panel, Can Coun; consult, Nat Capitol Commission, 78, Panguiring Tapestries, 78-81. *Teaching:* Mem fac, NS Col Art & Design, 78-79 & 81-82 & Banff Ctr Fine Arts, 79; vis prof, Royal Col Art, London, 83. *Awards:* Haystack Sch Scholar Award, 64; Can Coun Arts Award, 65; First Prize Award, Perspective Competition Centennial Comn, Govt Can, 67. *Bibliog:* C Fraser (auth), article, 6/66 & J Graham (auth), article, 7/71, Arts Can; L Rombout (auth), article, Vie Art, winter 67; J Murray (auth), article, Arts Atlantic, winter 80. *Mem:* Royal Can Acad Artists; Can Artists' Representation (NS rep). *Media:* Fibers. *Mailing Add:* 1557 Vernon St Halifax NS B3H 3M8 Canada

LINDMARK, ARNE
PAINTER, INSTRUCTOR
b Poughkeepsie, NY, Oct 26, 29. *Study:* Pratt Inst; also watercolor with Edgar Whitney. *Work:* Huntington Gallery, WVa. *Exhib:* Am Watercolor Soc Traveling Exhibs, 66-79; Nat Arts Club Ann, 69-71; Allied Artists Am, 71-72; Mainstreams 72, Marietta, Ohio, 72; Am Watercolor Soc Exchange Show, Sydney, Australia, 79. *Teaching:* Instr painting & watercolor, Huntington Gallery, summer 71; instr, SW Watercolor Soc, Dallas, 78-79 & Mid-W Watercolor Soc, Wis, 79, Houston Art Group, 80, Pocono Pines Workshops, Pa, 82 & 83, & Seven S St Workshops, Rockport, Mass, 83. *Awards:* Samuel J Bloomingdale Mem Award, 73 & Edgar A Whitney Award, 74, Am Watercolor Soc; Ranger Fund Purchase Award, Nat Acad Design, 79. *Bibliog:* Wendon Blake (auth), Acrylic Watercolor Painting, Watson-Guptill, 70; Margit Malstrom (auth), Arne Lindmark, master of the watercolor scene, Am Artist Mag, 1/71; Frank Webb (auth), Watercolor Energies, 83. *Mem:* Am Watercolor Soc; Allied Artists Am; Hudson River Art Asn, Duchess Co Art Asn; Nat Acad Design. *Media:* Watercolor. *Mailing Add:* 101 Forbus St Poughkeepsie NY 12603

LINDNER, ERNEST
PAINTER, CONCEPTUAL ARTIST
b Vienna, Austria, May 1, 1897; Can citizen. *Study:* Univ Sask, Hon LLD, 72. *Work:* Nat Gallery Can, Ottawa; Art Gallery Ont, Toronto; Winnipeg Art Gallery, Man; Mendel Art Gallery, Saskatoon; Beaver Brook Art Gallery, Fredericton, NB; and others. *Exhib:* One-man show, Banfer Gallery, New York, 64; 7th Biennial of Can Painting, Nat Gallery, Ottawa, 68. *Pos:* Dir dept art, Saskatoon Tech Inst, 31-62. *Bibliog:* Article, Time Mag, 7/19/68; Paul Duval (auth), High Realism in Canada, Clarke & Cougar Ltd, 74. *Mem:* Can Artists Representation. *Mailing Add:* 414 Ninth St E Saskatoon SK S7N 0A8 Canada

LINDQUIST, EVAN
PRINTMAKER, EDUCATOR
b Salina, Kans, May 23, 36. *Study:* Emporia Kans State Univ, BSE, 58; Univ Iowa, MFA, 63. *Work:* Whitney Mus Am Art, New York; Uffizzi, Florence, Italy; Albertina Mus, Vienna, Austria; Nelson-Atkins Art Mus, Kansas City; Art Inst Chicago. *Exhib:* Prints by Seven, Whitney Mus Am Art, New York, 71; Boston Printmakers Ann Exhib, 71-75; two-men circulating exhib, Ark Arts Coun, 79-81; Opera Bevilacqua La Masa, Venice, Italy, 77; Gallerie V Kunstverlag Wolfbrum, Vienna, Austria, 79; Ark Arts Ctr, Little Rock, 83; and others. *Teaching:* Prof art, Ark State Univ, Jonesboro, 63- *Awards:* More than 60 awards including Boston Printmakers, 71-74 & Potsdam Prints, NY State Univ Potsdam, 72. *Mem:* Visual Artists & Galleries Asn; Boston Printmakers; The Print Club, Philadelphia; World Print Coun; Southern Graphics Coun. *Dealer:* Jay Street Gallery New York. *Mailing Add:* Box 2782 State University AR 72467

LINDQUIST, MARK
SCULPTOR
b Oakland, Calif, May 16, 49. *Study:* New England Col, BA, 71; Pratt Inst. *Work:* Metrop Mus Art, New York; Greenville Co Art Mus, SC; Schenectady Mus, NY; Nat Mus Am Art, Washington, DC; Philadelphia Mus Art. *Exhib:* The Art of the Turned Bowl, Renwick Gallery, Smithsonian Inst, 78; 20th Century Decorative Art, Metrop Mus Art, 78-80; National Touring Exhib, Bowdoin Co Mus Art, 80-82; Featured Object May/June, Nat Mus Am Art, 82; Columbia Mus Art, SC, 82; Art Art of Wood Turning, Am Craft Mus, New York, 83; Masterworks, Jess Besser Mus, Mich, 83; and others. *Teaching:* Instr welding & three-dimensional design, New Eng Col, 70-71; head of woodworking, Craft Ctr, Worcester, Mass, 77-78. *Awards:* MacDowell Colony Fel, NH, 79. *Bibliog:* John Gonser (dir), Film: Consider the Good Life, Micah Prod, Switz, 79; Nanch Means Wright (auth), Mark Lindquist: The bowl is a performance, Am Craft Mag, 10/11/80. *Media:* Wood. *Publ:* Auth, Spalted Wood, 77 & Turning the Spalted Bowl, 78, Fine Woodworking Mag. *Mailing Add:* Patch Rd Henniker NH 03242

LINDROTH, LINDA
PHOTOGRAPHER, PRINTMAKER

b Miami, Fla, Sept 4, 46. *Study:* Douglass Col, BA(art), 68; Rutgers Univ, MFA(art), 79. *Work:* Mus Mod Art & Metrop Mus Art, New York; Bibliot Nat, Paris; New York City Mus; Polaroid Corp. *Exhib:* NJ State Mus, Trenton, 74; US Info Agency, traveling, Ger, 75; Int Triennial Photog, Mus Art Hist, Fribourg, Switz, 75; Rutgers Univ Art Mus, New Brunswick, NJ, 76; Photo/Synthesis, Cornell Univ Art Mus, Ithaca, NY, 76; Morris Mus Arts & Sci, Morristown, NJ, 78; Arboretum, Univ Colo, 83; and others. *Teaching:* Teaching asst, Douglass Col, New Brunswick, NJ, 77-79. *Awards:* Documentary Photog, NJ Photog, 74; photog fel, NJ State Coun Arts, 75; Mixed Media Fel, NJ State Coun Arts, 84. *Bibliog:* Thelma Newman (auth), Innovative Printmaking, Crown Publ, 77; Joyce T Cohen (auth), In/Sights: Self-Portraits of Women, David Godine, 78; James Hugunin (auth), Notions of presence and absence, Afterimage, 3/80. *Mem:* Soc Photog Educ. *Publ:* Contribr, New Jersey Photography, 74 & Photographic Process as Medium, 76, Rutgers Univ; contribr, Artists' Books USA, Independent Cur Inc, 78. *Mailing Add:* 95 Watchung Ave Chatham NJ 07928

LINDSAY, KENNETH C
HISTORIAN, WRITER

b Milwaukee, Wis, Dec 23, 19. *Study:* Univ Wis, PhB, 41, scholar, 47, MA, 48, PhD, 51; Ecole du Louvre, Fulbright fel, 49. *Collections Arranged:* Marshall Glasier, An Exhibition of Paintings & Drawings, 59; Jean Leppien, Paintings, Watercolors, Graphic Works, 64; Architectural Process, Works of James Mowry, 67; The Works of John Vandelyn, 70; Angello Ippolito, Retrospective, 75. *Pos:* Mem, NY State Comn Arts, 66-67; coun archit & urban design, Binghamton, 67-68. *Teaching:* Asst surv, Univ Wis, 47-49; instr, Williams Col, 50-51; prof, State Univ NY Binghamton, 51- *Awards:* NY State Res Found Grants, 67, 69 & 72. *Res:* Modern American painting. *Publ:* Co-auth, Method in Breughel's paintings, J Aesthet & Art Criticism, 15: 376-386; auth, Kandinsky in 1914 New York, Art News, 55: 32-33; auth, Kandinsky in Russia (catalog), Guggenheim Mus, 63; auth, Les themes de l'inconscient, XXe Siecle, 27: 46-52; auth, Millet's Winnower rediscovered, Burlington Mag, 74; plus others. *Mailing Add:* Dept of Art State Univ of NY Binghamton NY 13901

LINDSTROM, GAELL
PAINTER, EDUCATOR

b Salt Lake City, Utah, July 4, 19. *Study:* Univ Utah, BS; Calif Col Arts & Crafts, MFA; also with Roy Wilhelm, Gloucester, Mass. *Work:* Utah State Univ; Southern Utah State Col. *Comn:* Murals, Southern Utah State Col & Cedar City Pub Libr; mosaic mural, Utah State Univ Forestry Bldg, 61. *Exhib:* Am Watercolor Soc, 53 & 57; Calif Watercolor Soc, 57. *Collections Arranged:* Maynard Dixon Exhibition, Southern Utah State Col, 55; Nat Ceramic Exhibition, 57 & 58 & Nat Painting Exhibition, 58, Utah State Univ. *Teaching:* Prof art, Southern Utah State Col, 53-56; prof art, Utah State Inst Fine Arts, 57-61; prof art, Utah State Univ, 57- *Awards:* Prizes & Purchase Awards, Utah State Fair, 52-54; Utah State Art Inst, 54; Am Watercolor Soc, 57. *Mem:* Am Watercolor Soc; Nat Watercolor Soc. *Mailing Add:* c/o Dept of Art Utah State Univ Logan UT 84322

LINHARES, PHILIP E
CURATOR

b Visalia, Calif, Aug 8, 39. *Study:* Calif Col of Arts & Crafts, BFA, MFA, 66; post-grad study in Florence, Italy, 72. *Exhib:* San Francisco Mus of Art, Calif, 65; Nev Art Gallery, Reno, 77; La Mus, Copenhagen, Denmark, 77; one-man shows, Berkeley Gallery, San Francisco, 70, Lone Mountain Col, San Francisco, 77 & Oakland Mus, 79; and others. *Pos:* Curatorial asst, Oakland Mus of Art, Calif, 67; dir exhib, San Francisco Art Inst, Calif, 67-77; artist-in-residence, South of Market Cult Ctr, San Francisco, 77-; dir, Mills Col Art Gallery, 78- *Publ:* Auth, articles in Currant Mag, 75-76; auth, California Communication, Sydney Biennale Exhib catalogue, Australia, 76. *Mailing Add:* Mills Col Art Gallery 5000 MacArthur Blvd Oakland CA 94613

LINK, HOWARD ANTHONY
CURATOR

b Rochester, NY, Dec 18, 34. *Study:* Pa State Univ, BAppArts, MA(art hist); Univ Pittsburgh, PhD(art hist). *Collections Arranged:* Utamaro & Hiroshige (auth, catalog), 76-77 & The Theatrical Prints of the Torii Masters (auth, catalog), Japan, 77, Honolulu Acad of Arts. *Pos:* Assoc cur of Oriental art, Honolulu Acad of Arts, 71-74, keeper of Ukiyo-e Print Ctr, 71-, cur Asian art, 74- *Teaching:* Instr art hist, Sophia Univ, Tokyo, Japan, 66-67; asst prof art hist, 67-70; assoc prof art hist, Univ Hawaii, Hilo, 70-71. *Awards:* Nat Best Lect Series Award, Cherry Blossom Festival, Univ Hawaii, 71. *Mem:* Oriental Art Soc of Hawaii; Ukiyo-e Soc Japan; Ukiyo-e Soc Am. *Res:* Torii Sch of Ukiyo-e, Rimpa paintings and Nikuhitsu. *Publ:* Coauth, Japanese Prints in the Honolulu Academy of Arts--The Primitives, Univ Hawaii Press, 78; auth, The Art of Shibata Zeshin: The Mr and Mrs James E O'Brien Collection at the Honolulu Academy of Arts, Robert G Sawers Publ, 79; and many others. *Mailing Add:* Honolulu Acad Arts 900 S Beretania Honolulu HI 96814

LINK, LAWRENCE JOHN
PAINTER

b Oklahoma City, Okla, Sept 2, 42. *Study:* Univ Okla, BA, 65, with Joe Hobbs, MFA, 68. *Work:* San Francisco Mus Art; Smithsonian Inst; Osaka Univ Arts, Japan; Chase Manhattan Bank, New York; Ore State Univ Mus. *Exhib:* 11th Midwest Biennial, Joslyn Art Mus, Nebr, 70; 12 Ann Exhib Prints & Drawings, Okla Art Ctr, 70; 2nd Ann Hawaii Nat Prints Exhib, Honolulu Acad Arts, 73; World Print Competition 73, San Francisco Mus Art, 73; Nev State Mus, 75; Corcoran Gallery, Washington, DC, 75; one-man show, Fred

Jones Mem Mus, Okla, 78; Bold Statements: Painting, Southeastern Ctr Contemp Art, NC, 80; two-man show, Pontiac Art Ctr, Mich, 83. *Pos:* Mich ed, New Art Examiner, 83- *Teaching:* Asst prof painting, Southern Ill Univ, 68-77; prof painting, Western Mich Univ, 77 & 79, chmn, Dept Art, 77-; prof painting & head, Dept Art, Va Polytech Inst, 79-80. *Awards:* Purchase Award, World Print Competition, 73. *Mem:* Nat Asn Sch Art (nominating comt, 81-84). *Media:* Oil, Encaustic. *Publ:* Auth, Provincialism dominates selections from Neuman collection, 7/83, Power and coercion: A review, 10/83, Night thoughts and day dreams: A review, 10/83 & Betty's black: A review, 11/83, New Art Examiner. *Mailing Add:* 3382 Sandra Dr Kalamazoo MI 49004

LINK, VAL JAMES
JEWELER, EDUCATOR

b Shreveport, La, Apr 28, 40. *Study:* Cranbrook Acad Art, Bloomfield Hills, Mich, MFA; Univ Tex, Austin, BFA; Del Mar Jr Col, Corpus Christi, Tex, AA. *Work:* Ark Art Ctr Mus, Little Rock; Sarah Campbell Blaffer Gallery, Univ Houston; Mus Contemp Crafts Touring Exhib, NY; Denver Art Mus & Am Crafts Coun Touring Exhib. *Comn:* Sic Holloware & jewelry works, comn by Mr C A Harlan, Birmingham, Mich, 67-68; commemorative cup, comn by Univ Houston for Mrs Sarah Blaffer, 73; sculptural awards, Am Petrol Inst, Washington, DC, 73 & 74; seven major jewelry pieces, comn by Kenneth Helfand, Mill Run, Pa, 74-75; and others. *Exhib:* The Goldsmith 70 Exhibition, Minn Mus Art, St Paul; Inter-D III, Crafts 74 Int, McAllen Int Mus, Tex, 74; Reprise, Int Exhib Metalsmithing Work, Cranbrook Acad Art, 75; Contemp Metalcrafts, Clifford Gallery, Pittsburgh Arts & Crafts Ctr, Pa, 77; Soc NAm Goldsmiths Nat Metalsmith 77, Phoenix Art Mus, Ariz & Henry Gallery Fine Arts, Univ Wash, Seattle, 77; American Goldsmiths--Now, Soc NAm Goldsmiths, Steinberg Gallery, Washington Univ, 78; and others. *Teaching:* Instr jewelry & metal, Interlochen Arts Acad, Mich, 67-70; assoc prof & head jewelry & metal area, Univ Houston, 70- *Awards:* First Place, 15th Tex Crafts Exhib, Dallas Mus Fine Arts, 71; Ark Art Ctr Mus Purchase Award, 71-72. *Bibliog:* Lisa Hammel (auth), Thank technology, New York Times, 6/20/70; Murray Bovin (auth), Photographic representation of work, In: Silversmithing, Bovin Publ, 4th ed, 73. *Mem:* Soc NAm Goldsmiths; Sterling Silversmiths Guild Am; Am Contemp Arts & Crafts Slide Libr; Am Crafts Coun; Tex & Houston Designer Craftsmen. *Media:* Gold, Silver. *Mailing Add:* 5531 Darnell Houston TX 77096

LINKER, KATE PHILIPPA
CRITIC

b New York, NY, July 22, 52. *Study:* Radcliffe Col, BA(magna cum laude), 72; Columbia Univ, 73. *Pos:* Assoc ed, Tracks J, New York, 75-77. *Mem:* Int Asn Art Critics; Col Art Asn. *Publ:* Auth, An anti-architectural analogue, Flash Art, 1-2/80; auth, Meditations on a goldfish bowl: Autonomy and Analogy in Matisse, Artforum, 10/80; auth, Mystery and Meaning in the Works/Mac Adams, Ludwig Mus, 81; auth, Public sculpture, Parts I & II, Artforum, 3/81 & 6/81; auth, On Representation and sexuality, Parachute, 9-11/83; and others. *Mailing Add:* 30 W 15th St New York NY 10011

LINN, JOHN WILLIAM
ADMINISTRATOR, WRITER

b Shanghai, China, May 25, 36; US citizen. *Study:* Art Inst Chicago; San Diego State Univ, BA & MA; Univ Ga, PhD; worked with Edmund B Feldman and Albert Christ-Janer. *Work:* San Diego State Univ Gallery, Calif; Paul Sargent Gallery, Eastern Ill Univ, Charleston; First Nat Bank, Springfield, Ill. *Exhib:* San Diego Fine Arts Gallery, 66; Second Ann Nat Contemp Arts & Crafts Exhib, Fla, 75; Wabash Valley Exhib, 77; Ill State Fair Exhib, Springfield, 77; Provincetown Nat Print & Drawing Exhib, Mass, 77; plus others. *Collections Arranged:* Seven State Bicentennial Exhibition, Paul Sargent Gallery, Eastern Ill Univ, 9/77. *Pos:* Dir & owner, Art Cellar Gallery, San Diego, Calif, 65-67. *Teaching:* Assoc prof art hist, Eastern Ill Univ, 67-77, chmn dept art, 75-77; prof art hist & dean fine arts, Henderson State Univ, 77- *Awards:* Best in Show, All San Diego Co Collegiate Exhib, San Diego State Univ, 63 & Del Mar Southern Calif Exhib, Del Mar Co Fair, 67; First Place, San Diego Co Exhib, San Diego Art Guild, John Paul Jones, 66; and others. *Bibliog:* Naomi Baker (auth), John Linn, San Diego Union, 64; Charlotte Steen (auth), Art rev, Art Forum, 65; Donovan Mailey (auth), Art Cellar Gallery, San Diego Mag, 65. *Mem:* Nat Coun Art Adminrs; Am Coun Arts. *Media:* Multimedia. *Res:* Using the phenomenological method of art criticism in the analysis of art, particularly Chinese landscape painting. *Publ:* auth, In praise of brevity, Acad Forum, 83. *Mailing Add:* c/o Henderson State Univ Dept Art Arkadelphia AR 71923

LINN, STEVEN ALLEN
SCULPTOR

b Chicago, Ill, May 3, 43. *Study:* Univ Ill, BS(floricult & ornamental hort). *Work:* Indianapolis Mus Art; Milwaukee Art Mus; Univ Va. *Exhib:* Flint Inst Fine Arts, Mich, 78; Indianapolis Mus Art, 78; Whitney Mus Am Art, 79 & 80; Rochester Mem, 79; Newport Art Asn, 79; Shidoni Outdoor, 81; Milwaukee Art Mus, 81; Corcoran Gallery Art, 82; and others. *Pos:* Graphics designer, Counselector Mag, 75. *Teaching:* Lectr theatre design, Smith Col, Northampton, Mass, 68-69; tech instr sculpture, Univ Calif, Santa Cruz, 71-74. *Awards:* Ward Sculpture Prize, Berkshire Mus, 68; Rome Prize, Am Acad in Rome, 75; MacDowell Colony Fel, 80. *Bibliog:* Helene Zucker Seeman & Alanna Siegfried (coauths), Soho, Providence Sunday J, 8/19/79; Jennifer Stephens (auth), New from Kenworth, Overdrive Mag, 4/79; Marsha S Pels (auth), Steve Linn: Shadowboxing within narrative realism, Arts Mag, 3/81. *Media:* Bronze, Wood. *Dealer:* Louis K Meisel Gallery 141 Prince St New York NY 10012. *Mailing Add:* 101 Crosby St New York NY 10012

LINTAULT, ROGER PAUL
EDUCATOR, SCULPTOR

b New York, NY, June 13, 38. *Study:* State Univ NY New Paltz, BS(art) with distinction, 60; Southern Ill Univ, MFA(sculpture & ceramics), 62. *Work:* Honolulu Acad Arts, Hawaii; Mus Contemp Crafts, New York; Warner Brothers Records, Los Angeles, Calif; Calif State Col. *Exhib:* Craftsmen USA, Los Angeles Co Mus Art, Calif, 66; Looking West 1970, Joslyn Art Mus, Omaha, Nebr, 70; All Calif Art Exhib, Nat Orange Show, San Bernardino, 74, 75 & 77; one man show, Esther-Robles Gallery, Los Angeles, 75; Calif State Col, San Bernardino, 79; Janus Gallery, Los Angeles, 79. *Teaching:* Asst prof art, Univ Hawaii, Honolulu, 65-68; lectr art, Calif State Univ, Long Beach, 68-69; prof art, Calif State Col, San Bernardino, 69-, chmn dept, 72-77. *Awards:* First & Purchase Prizes, All Calif Art Exhib, Nat Orange Show, 74. *Bibliog:* Jim Rosen (auth), article, 10/5/74 & Don Woodford (auth), Truth, illusion and Roger Lintault, 4/26/75, Artweek; Louis William Fox (auth), article, Artweek, 1/13/79. *Media:* Various Media. *Mailing Add:* 787 W Edgehill Rd San Bernardino CA 92405

LIONNI, LEO
SCULPTOR, PAINTER

b Amsterdam, Holland, May 5, 10; US citizen. *Study:* Univ Genoa, Italy, PhD. *Work:* Philadelphia Mus Art; Mus Mod Art, Metrop Mus Art, New York. *Exhib:* Four American Graphic Artists, Mus Mod Art, New York, 53; Venice Biennale, 72; Klingspor Mus, Ger, 73; Baukunst Gallery, Cologne, Ger, 74; Staempfli Gallery, New York, 77 & 78; Verona Mus, 79; and others. *Pos:* Art dir, NW Ayer & Son, Philadelphia, 39-48; art dir, Fortune, 48-60. *Awards:* Art Dir of the Year, Nat Soc Art Dirs, 55. *Media:* Bronze; Oil. *Publ:* Auth & illusr, Little Blue & Little Yellow, 59, Swimmy, 63, Frederick, 66, Alexander & with Wind-Up Mouse, 69, Taccuino di Lionni, 72 & Parallel Botany, 77. *Mailing Add:* c/o Staempfli Gallery 47 East 77th St New York NY 10021

LIPINSKY DE ORLOV, LINO S
PAINTER, PRINTMAKER

b Rome, Italy, Jan 14, 08; US citizen. *Study:* Brit Acad Arts, Rome; Lipinsky Art Acad, Rome; Accad Belle Arti, Rome. *Work:* Metrop Mus Art, New York; New York Pub Libr; Detroit Inst Art; Galleria Naz Arte Mod, Rome; Libr Cong. *Comn:* The Grenadier (mosaic), Hq Second Battalion, Rome, 37; etchings, Libr of Cong, Washington, DC; diorama, Verrazzano's Landing in New York Bay in 1524, 57 & mural, New Amsterdam, 1660, 66, Mus City New York. *Exhib:* Int Biennale, Venice, Italy, 34-36; Libr of Cong, Washington, DC, 42-54; Cleveland Art Mus, 43; Nat Acad Design, New York, 43-49; Am Watercolors, Drawings & Prints, Metrop Mus Art, 52. *Pos:* Founder & dir, Garibaldi & Meucci Mem Mus, Staten Island, NY, 56; exhibs dir, Mus City New York, 59-67; admis comt, Huntington Hartford Found, 62-65; cur hist, John Jay Homestead, Katonah, NY, 67- *Teaching:* Prof graphic arts, Lipinsky Art Acad, 25-39. *Awards:* Gold Medal & Cert of Merit, Order Sons of Italy Am, 61; L L Huttleston Staff Award, State Coun Parks & Recreation, 74; Tomahawk Award, Westchester Co Hist Soc, 79. *Bibliog:* Elena Canino (auth), Clotilde tra due guerre, Longanesi & Co, Milan, Italy, 57; Nancy Rubin (auth), Jay Homestead: A curator's dream, New York Times, 9/18/77; to two young boys, it's home, New York Times, 9/22/70. *Mem:* Audubon Artists; Soc Am Graphic Artists; NY State Asn Mus; Bedford Hist Soc (bd dirs, 68-); Coun Arts Westchester. *Media:* Etching, Oil. *Publ:* Auth, Pocket Anatomy in Color for Artists, Int House Publ, 47; auth, Giovanni da Verrazzano, the Discoverer of New York Bay, 1524, 58; illusr, Roman People, Houghton Mifflin Co, 59; illusr, The Ghost of Peg-leg Peter, Vanguard, 65; contribr, Giovanni da Verrazzano, Yale Univ, 70. *Dealer:* James St L O'Toole 667 Madison Ave New York NY 10021. *Mailing Add:* John Jay Homestead PO Box AII Katonah NY 10536

LIPMAN, HOWARD W
COLLECTOR

b Albany, NY, July 11, 05. *Pos:* Trustee, Whitney Mus Am Art, 67-, pres, 74-77, chmn bd, 77- trustee, Arch Am Art, 56-, pres, 72-74; trustee, Phoenix Art Mus, 71- *Mem:* Smithsonian Inst; Guggenheim Found; Mus Mod Art, New York; Whitney Mus Am Art; Metrop Mus Art. *Collection:* Sculpture through the Howard and Jean Lipman Foundation for the Whitney Museum of American Art; sculpture of the 1960's with special accent on Alexander Calder and Louise Nevelson. *Mailing Add:* Box 893 Carefree AZ 85377

LIPMAN, STAN
SCULPTOR, INSTRUCTOR

b Lancaster, Pa, Mar 18, 31. *Study:* Temple Univ, Millersville State Col, BS(educ); Univ Southern Calif. *Work:* Nat B'nai B'rith Traveling Show & Smithsonian Fine Arts Gallery, Washington, DC; Los Angeles Co Art Mus; Sperry Rand Collection, Cincinnati, Ohio & Lancaster, Pa. *Comn:* Phoenix (large copper fountain sculpture), Park City Asn, Lancaster, 71; Abstract (aluminum pouring, mural), comn by Dr Kahn, Clinic, Cincinnati, 73; The Wall (steel blocks arranged to form wailing wall), Jewish Community Ctr, Lancaster, 74; Why Not (large outdoor metal sculpture), Baltimore, 81; Tree of Life and Burning Bush (large indoor brass mural), St Anns Church, Lancaster, Pa, 81. *Exhib:* Two-man show, Nat B'nai B'rith Gallery, Washington, DC, 69; Sculptured Small Table, New York Sch Design, 71 & 73; Los Angeles Co Art Mus Nat Exhib, 72; Philadelphia Mus Art Contemp Art Show, 73; Lancaster Open Nat, 74; one-man shows, Gallery See, New York, 81, Gallery II, Philadelphia, 81. *Teaching:* Instr spec educ, Manheim Twp High Sch, Lancaster, 62-75. *Awards:* Best over All, Lancaster C of C, Lancaster Open Nat, 74; Fun to look at nicest to touch Award, Summer Show, Paris, 82; First Place, Best of Show, New Port Summer Arts Festival, 83. *Bibliog:* Articles in Life Mag, 61, The Millstone, 74 & Nikon World, 75. *Media:* Steel, Bronze. *Mailing Add:* 2407 Helena Rd Lancaster PA 17603

LIPMAN-WULF, PETER
SCULPTOR, PRINTMAKER

b Berlin, Ger, Apr 27, 05; US citizen. *Study:* State Acad Fine Arts, Berlin, with Ludwig Gies. *Work:* Metrop Mus Art & Whitney Mus Am Art, New York; Nat Gallery Art, Washington, DC; Brit Mus, London; Nat Mus, Berlin. *Comn:* Bronze busts of Bruno Walter & Karl Bohm, Metrop Opera, New York, 58 & 72; St Andrew (ceramic), St Andrew Lutheran Church, Chicago, 67; Joy of Life (ceramic relief), Mill Lane High Sch, Farmingdale, Conn, 68; bronze bust of Pablo Casals, Corcoran Gallery Art, Washington, DC, 74; St Michael Chapel, Rutgers Univ, NJ. *Exhib:* Pa Acad Fine Arts Ann, 50-64; Whitney Mus Am Art Ann, 50-68; Jewish Mus, NY, 60; Goethe House, New York, 69 & 74; Guild Hall, East Hampton, NY, 79 & 80; Rutgers Univ, New Brunswick, NJ, 80; and others. *Teaching:* Prof sculpture, Adelphi Univ, 61-77, emer prof, 77- *Awards:* Guggenheim Fel, 49-50; Olivetti Award, Silvermine Guild Artists, 62; Widner Medal, Widener Univ. *Mem:* Guild Hall, East Hampton, NY; Silvermine Guild Artists. *Publ:* Auth, Wall and space, 71, Artist as teacher in America, 72, On teaching a fundamental course of sculpture, 73, On my illustrations of Goethe's Faust, 75 & Artist-in-residence in a Secondary Sch, 77, Leonardo Mag. *Dealer:* Kramoris Gallery Sag Harbor New York 11963; Rizzoli Int Galleries 712 Fifth Ave New York NY 10019. *Mailing Add:* Whitney Rd Sag Harbor NY 11963

LIPOFSKY, MARVIN B
SCULPTOR, GLASS ARTIST

b Barrington, Ill, Sept 1, 38. *Study:* Univ Ill, Urbana, BFA; Univ Wis-Madison, MS & MFA. *Work:* Kunstgewerbe Mus, Berlin; Mus Bellerive, Zurich, Switzerland; Nat Mus Mod Art, Kyoto, Japan; Corning Mus Glass, NY; Oakland Art Mus, Calif. *Comn:* Glass, plastic, metal twin panels, Metro Media Bldg, Los Angeles, 69; Frank Lloyd Wright, Calif Col Arts & Crafts Founders Award, 72. *Exhib:* One-man shows, Gallery Marronnier, Kyoto, Japan, 78, Florence Duhl Gallery, New York, 79, S M Galerie, Frankfurt, 81 & Galerie L, Hamburg, 81, Betsy Rosenfield Gallery, Chicago, 82. *Pos:* Ed, Glass Art Soc J, 76-80. *Teaching:* Asst prof design, Univ Calif, Berkeley, 64-72; prof & head glass dept, Calif Col Arts & Crafts, Oakland, 67-; vis prof, Rietveld Acad, Amsterdam, Holland, 70, Bazalel Acad Art, Jerusalem, Israel, 71, Univ Calif Los Angeles, 73, Pilchvck Sch Glass, Stanwood, Wash, 74, 77 & 81 & Colo Mountain Col, Summervail, 81 & 83. *Awards:* Purchase Awards, Toledo Mus Art, 68 & Northern Ill Univ, 69; Nat Endowment Arts Fels, 74 & 76; plus others. *Bibliog:* Judy Spurgin (auth), Marvin Lipovsky, Artcraft Mag, 4-5/80; Olivia Emery (auth), Craftsman Lifestyle, Gentle Revolution, Calif Design Publ. *Mem:* Int Comt Artists in Glass; Glass Art Soc (pres, 78-80). *Media:* Glass. *Mailing Add:* 1012 Pardee Berkeley CA 94710

LIPPARD, LUCY ROWLAND
WRITER

b New York, NY, Apr 14, 37. *Study:* Smith Col, BA, 58; NY Univ Inst Fine Arts, MA, 62; Moore Col Art, Hon DFA, 72. *Awards:* Guggenheim Fel, 68; Nat Endowment Arts Grant, 72-73 & 76-77. *Mem:* Ad Hoc Women Artists Comt; West-East Bag; Heresies Publ Collective; Printed Matter Inc; Political Art Documentation/Distribution. *Publ:* Ed, Dadas on Art, 71; ed, Surrealists on Art, 71; auth, Six Years: The Dematerialization of the Art Object, 73; auth, Eva Hesse, 76; coauth, Kathe Kollwitz, 81; and many others. *Mailing Add:* 138 Prince St New York NY 10012

LIPPINCOTT, JANET
PAINTER

b New York, NY, May 16, 18. *Study:* Colorado Springs Fine Art Ctr; Art Students League; San Francisco Art Inst; also with Emil Bisttram, Taos, NMex. *Work:* Utah Fine Arts Mus, Salt Lake City; Columbia Fine Arts Mus, SC; Denver Art Mus, Colo; Roswell Mus & Art Ctr, NMex; Albuquerque Mus, NMex. *Exhib:* Colo State Univ, Greeley, 61; Denver US Nat Ctr, Colo, 63; St John's Col, Santa Fe, 68 & 80; Britton Gallery, Denver, Colo, 80; Col Santa Fe, NMex, 81; and many others. *Pos:* Instr, Santa Fe Community Col, NMex, currently. *Awards:* Atwater Kent Award, Palm Beach, Fla, 63; Southwestern Biennial Award, Santa Fe, 66; Arts in Residence, Durango, Colo, 68. *Bibliog:* Artist of the month, Southwest Art Gallery Mag, 5/72. *Mem:* Friends of Art, Albuquerque, NMex. *Mailing Add:* 1270 Canyon Rd Santa Fe NM 87501

LIPPMAN, JUDITH
GALLERY DIRECTOR, EDUCATOR

b New York, NY, June 11, 29. *Study:* Syracuse Univ, BA, 49. *Collections Arranged:* Maryland Art in Legislative Spaces (auth, catalog), 80 & Maryland Art & Artists (auth, catalog), 81, Gen Assembly Md. *Pos:* Dir & cur 20th century Am art, Meredith Contemp Art/The Arts Gallery, Md, 77-; mem, Artistic Properties Comn, State of Md, 77-80; capitol arts coordr, Gen Assembly Md, 80- *Teaching:* Guest lectr, Col Notre Dame, Md, 74-76 & New Sch, New York, 80 & 81. *Mem:* Artist Equity Asn (exec bd, currently). *Specialty:* 20th century Am art. *Publ:* Coauth, Gene Davis, Ed Baynard, Dorothy Gillespie, 80, Arts Gallery. *Mailing Add:* Meredith Contemp Art/The Arts Gallery 805 N Charles St Baltimore MD 21201

LIPPMANN, JANET GURIAN
GALLERY DIRECTOR, PAINTER

b New York, NY, May 10, 36. *Study:* Brooklyn Col, with Ilya Bolotowsky, Ad Reinhardt, Kurt Seligman, John Russell, Mark Rothko & Burgoyne Diller, BA(art educ), 56, MA(art educ), 60; NY Univ, with Knox Martin. *Pos:* Founder, pres & dir, The River Gallery, Irvington-on-Hudson, NY, 74- *Teaching:* Instr art, Traphagen Elem Sch, Mt Vernon, 62-68; instr, Children's Art Series, Mt Vernon, 64-71; pvt instr, Adult Art Classes, Tarrytown, NY, 71-75. *Specialty:* Paintings, prints and sculpture by living American artists; also emphasis on Hudson River material, Japanese prints and other Oriental arts. *Mailing Add:* c/o The River Gallery 49 Main St Irvington NY 10533

LIPPOLD, RICHARD
SCULPTOR
b Milwaukee, Wis, May 3, 15. *Study:* Art Inst Chicago, BFA, 37; Univ Chicago; Univ Mich. *Work:* Metrop Mus Art, Mus Mod Art, New York; Detroit Art Inst; Wadsworth Atheneum; Whitney Mus. *Comn:* Retiring room, King of Saudi Arabia, Riyadh, 76; Ad Astra, Nat Air & Space Mus, Washington, DC, 76; seven sculptures, Iran, 77-78; atrium, Seagram Bldg, New York, 82; Shinto Temple, Kyoto, Japan, 82-83. *Exhib:* Fifteen Americans, Mus Mod Art, New York, 52; Salute to France, Mus Arte Mod, Paris, 55; The New Decade, Whitney Mus Am Art, New York, 55; Portraits of Speakers, Arts Club Chicago, 75; Post-War Am Sculptors, Nat Collection Fine Arts, Washington, DC, 75; Am Directions, Smithsonian Inst, Washington, DC, 75; 200 Yrs Am Sculpture, Whitney Mus Am Art, New York, 76; Art in Archit, Meadow Brook Art Gallery, Rochester, Mich, 77; Pvt Images: Photographs by Sculptors, Los Angeles Co Mus Art, Los Angeles, Calif, 78; 100 Artists 100 Years Centennial Exhibition, Art Inst Chicago, 79; A Tribute to Dorothy Miller's A Curator's Choice, New York, 82. *Teaching:* Head art dept, Trenton Jr Col, 47-52; prof art, Hunter Col, 52-65. *Awards:* Creative Arts Award, Brandeis Univ, 58; Silver Medal, Architects League New York, 60; Fine Arts Medal, Am Inst Architects, 70; and others. *Bibliog:* Brian O'Dougherty (producer), Richard Lippold (TV film), Boston Educ TV, 60; The sun and Richard Lippold (TV film), New York TV, 69. *Media:* Wire, Metal. *Mailing Add:* PO Box 248 Locust Valley NY 11560

LIPSCHULTZ, MAURICE A
COLLECTOR
b Chicago, Ill, Aug 5, 12. *Pos:* Mem bd gov, Mus of Contemp Art, Chicago; mem art vis comt, Smart Gallery, Univ Chicago; mem art bd, Spertus' Mus & D'Arcy Gallery, Loyola Univ; mem bd, Boca Raton Mus. *Collection:* Primarily contemporary; specializing in structurist art and large scale sculpture. *Mailing Add:* 214 S Clinton St Chicago IL 60606

LIPSCOMB, GUY FLEMING, JR
PAINTER, INSTRUCTOR
b Clemson, SC, Apr 11, 17. *Study:* Univ SC, BS, 38; 40 watercolor workshops, 67-83; Art Student League, New York, 75. *Exhib:* Southern Watercolor Soc Regional, 78-83; Am Watercolor Soc, New York, 79; Watercolor USA Nat, Springfield, Mo, 79; Rocky Mountain Nat, Golden, Colo, 80; Butler Inst Am Art, 80; Nat Arts Club, New York, 80; Allied Artists Nat, New York, 81; and many others. *Teaching:* Instr watercolor & painting, Columbia Mus Art workshops throughout the Southeast. *Awards:* Best of Show, Ky Nat Watercolor Soc, 82; Am Artists Prof League Award, New York, 82; Second Award, Guild SC Artists, 83. *Mem:* Southern Watercolor Soc (secy, 81-83); Salmagundi Club; Copley Soc Boston; Midwest Watercolor Soc. *Media:* Watercolor, Oil. *Publ:* Contribr, Art Voices, 82. *Mailing Add:* 1717 W Buchanan Columbia SC 29206

LIPSON, GOLDIE
SCULPTOR, PAINTER
b New York, NY, Nov 18, 05. *Study:* With Carl Nelson; fresco painting, Mex, 51. *Work:* Randolph-Macon Womens Col. *Comn:* Fresco murals, San Miguel Inst, Mex, 51; mural in oil, comn by Mr & Mrs Samuel Carson, Purchase, NY, 60; murals in tile, cement & oil, Orchid Spring, Winter Haven and Lake of the Hills, Fla, 68- *Exhib:* Metrop Mus Art, New York, 40; one-man shows, Charles Barzansky Gallery, New York, 46-47, 49, 53, 58, 64 & 67 & Ridge Art Asn, 75; retrospectives, County Ctr, White Plains, NY, 53, Barzansky Gallery, 67, Ridge Art Cult Art Ctr, Winter Haven, Fla, 70 & Melvin Gallery, Fla Southern Univ, 80; Nat Arts Women Artists Traveling Show, US & Europe, 67; and others. *Pos:* Dir art, YM-YWHA, Mt Vernon, NY, 51-55. *Teaching:* Dir art classes, YMCA, Bronx, NY, 40-41; dir & instr, Goldie Lipson Studio Workshop, 47-64; instr, Arnold Col, 51-52. *Awards:* First Prize, New Rochelle Art Asn, 48-50; Top Prize in Oil, 49 & Prize for Colored Print, 57, Westchester Co Ctr. *Bibliog:* Mae McKinley (ed), Many Faces of Goldie, pvt publ, 78. *Media:* All. *Publ:* Auth & illusr, Rejuvenation, 63, We, 65 & Beyond Yoga, rev ed 77; illusr, Yoga, Youth and Reincarnations, 65; auth, Rejuvenation through Yoga, rev ed 78. *Mailing Add:* 724 Master Piece Rd Lake of the Hills Lake Wales FL 33853

LIPTON, BARBARA B
WRITER, CURATOR
b Newark, NJ. *Study:* Univ Iowa, BA(art hist); Univ Mich, studied Oriental art with James Plummer, MA; Rutgers Univ, MLS. *Exhib:* One-woman photog exhib, Newark Mus, NJ, 78; Am Mus Nat Hist, New York, 81; Anchorage Mus, 81. *Collections Arranged:* Newark Long Ago (auth, catalog), 74, Whaling Days in New Jersey (auth, catalog), 75 & Survival: Life and Art of the Alaskan Eskimo (auth, catalog), 77-78, Newark Mus, NJ; Images of the Alaskan Eskimo, New England Found Arts, 80-82; Arctic Vision: Art of the Canadian Invitational Traveling Exhib (auth, catalog), Govt Canada, 84-86. *Pos:* Art libr dir, Newark Mus, NJ, 70-75, guest cur, 76-77, spec proj consult 77-; asst dir, Castle Gallery, Col New Rochelle, 83-; guest cur, New Eng Found Arts, 80-81. *Teaching:* Instr sch continuing ed, Pratt Univ, Brooklyn, NY, 79; instr eskimo art, Ctr Northern Studies, Wolcott, Vt, summer 84. *Mem:* Am Asn Mus. *Res:* Whaling history; life and art of the Alaskan and Canadian Eskimo; New Jersey history; archival Eskimo films. *Collection:* Eskimo art and artifacts. *Publ:* Coauth, Westerners in Tibet, Newark Mus, 73; auth, John Cotton Dana and the Newark Museum, 79; exec producer, Village of No River (film), 81. *Mailing Add:* 282 Scotland Rd South Orange NJ 07079

LIPTON, SEYMOUR
SCULPTOR
b New York, NY, Nov 6, 03. *Study:* City Col New York, 21-22; Columbia Univ, 23-27. *Work:* Whitney Mus Am Art, Mus Mod Art, Metrop Mus Art, New York; Brooklyn Mus, NY; Hirshhorn Mus, Washington, DC; Baltimore Mus, Md; plus many others. *Comn:* Lincoln Ctr Performing Arts, New York; Dulles Int Airport, Washington, DC; Milwaukee Ctr for Performing Arts, Wis, 69; City of Philadelphia, Pa; and others. *Exhib:* Whitney Mus Am Art Ann, Art Inst Chicago, 66; Mus Mod Art, New York, 68 & 69; Smithsonian Inst, Washington, DC, 68; one-man shows, Milwaukee Art Ctr, Wis, 70, Mass Inst Technol, 71, Va Mus Fine Arts, 72, Cornell Univ, 73 & Everson Mus, Syracuse, NY, 73; Jewish Mus, 80; and others. *Pos:* Vis art critic, Yale Univ, 56; sculptor chmn, Art Comn New York City, 67. *Teaching:* Instr sculpture, Cooper Union, 42-44; instr sculpture, New Sch Social Res, 40-64. *Awards:* Ford Found Grant, 62; Archit League Award, 63; Widener Gold Medal, Pa Acad Fine Arts, 68; and many others. *Bibliog:* Barbara Rose (auth), American Art Since 1900-A Critical History, Praeger, 67; Allen S Weller (auth), The Joys & Sorrows of Recent American Art, Univ Ill, 68; Albert E Elsen (auth), Seymour Lipton, Abrams, 69; and many others. *Dealer:* Marlborough Gallery 41 E 57th St New York NY 10022. *Mailing Add:* 302 W 98th St New York NY 10025

LIPTON, SONDRA (SAHLMAN)
PAINTER, SCULPTOR
b New York, NY. *Study:* NY Univ, sculpture with Vincent Glinsky. *Work:* Pres Lyndon B Johnson Libr & in private collections of Mrs Pierre du Pont II, Paul Mellon, Mrs Seward Mellon, Jacqueline Kennedy Onassis, Gov Winthrop Rockefeller. *Media:* Oil. *Mailing Add:* 501 E 87th St New York NY 10028

LIPZIN, JANIS CRYSTAL
FILMMAKER, PHOTOGRAPHER
b Colorado Springs, Colo, Nov 19, 45. *Study:* Ohio Univ, BFA; NY Univ; Univ Pittsburgh, MLS; San Francisco Art Inst, MFA; Pittsburgh Filmmakers Workshop. *Exhib:* Solo exhibs, Anthology Film Archives, 81 & 83, de Saisset Mus, 82 & Pasadena Film Forum, 82; Neuberger Mus, 81; NY Culture Ctr, 83. *Collections Arranged:* Founder/dir, Eye Music: Filmworks Series Inc, 75-; co-dir, Miami Valley Home Movie Festival (Ohio), 77. *Pos:* Media cur, Anne Bremer Mem Libr, San Francisco Art Inst, 74-76; bd dirs, Canyon Cinema Coop, 81-83; contribr ed, Artweek, 81-; bd dir, Found Art in Cinema, San Francisco, 83- *Teaching:* Asst prof art in film & photog, Antioch Col, 76-80; mem fac filmmaking, San Francisco Art Inst, 78-; vis artist, San Francisco State Univ, 81. *Awards:* Bellevue Film Festival Award, 76; Ohio Arts Coun Individual Artist Grant, 78; Nat Endowment Arts Individual Artist Grant, 83. *Bibliog:* Jeff Fraenkel (auth), Janis Crystal Lipzin: A filmmaker's retrospective, San Francisco Chronicle, 78; Margaret Ahwesh (auth), Janis Crystal Lipzin's The Bladderwort Document, Field of Vision, 79; Jim Jordan (auth), Points along the mainstream, Artweek, 81. *Mem:* Canyon Cinema Coop; Soc Photog Educ; Col Art Asn; Calif Confederation Arts. *Media:* Photography & Film. *Publ:* Auth, Talking with Joyce Wieland, Cinemanews, 78; auth, Performing performance, Artweek, 11/14/81; auth, Looking for gems, Artweek, 81; producer, Light Currents, Exploratorium, San Francisco, 83; auth, Addressing urban issues, Artweek, 83. *Dealer:* Canyon Cinema Coop 2325 Third St Suite 338 San Francisco CA 94107. *Mailing Add:* 633 San Bruno Ave San Francisco CA 94107

LIS, JANET CHAPMAN
PAINTER
b Cleveland, Ohio, Jan 9, 43. *Study:* Cleveland Inst Art, scholar, 57-61; Ohio Univ Sch Fine Arts, BFA, 65; also with David Driesbach & Gary Pettigrew. *Work:* Hollywood Mus Art, Fla; Int Inst Human Rights, Strasbourg, France; Nat Red Cross, Cleveland. *Exhib:* Scottsdale Watercolor Biennial, 80; Watercolor USA, 80 & 81; Watercolor Southeast, Fla Gulf Coast Art Ctr, 81; Ga Watercolor Soc Exhib, Columbus Mus Art, 81; Aqueous, Ky Watercolor Soc, 81; and others. *Awards:* Purchase Awards, Southeastern Ctr Contemp Art, 79; Eastman Mem Found, Lauren Rogers Mus, 79; Cash Awards, Watercolor USA, 80 & Arts Assembly of Jacksonville, 81. *Bibliog:* Shubert Jonas (auth), Color in Janet Lis' paintings impressive with boldness, Ft Lauderdale News, 9/28/75; Lorraine Huber (auth), The colorful world of Janet Lis, Fiesta Mag, 9/75; Mary Crowe Dorst (auth), article, Art Voices, 11-12/81. *Mem:* Southern Watercolor Soc. *Media:* Acrylic. *Publ:* Contribr, Miami Herald, 3/1/74, Tribune Publ, 10/14/76 & Ft Lauderdale News, 3/20/77; illusr cover, Hi-Riser, 1/30/75. *Dealer:* Capricorn Galleries 4849 Rugby Ave Bethesda MD 20014. *Mailing Add:* 12 Sunset Lane Pompano Beach FL 33062

LISKER, SARA
DESIGNER, CRAFTSMAN
b Odessa, Russia, July 31, 18; US citizen. *Study:* Pa Acad Fine Arts, 35-39; Univ Pa, 35-36; Philadelphia Col Art, with Jack Lenor Larsen, 61-64. *Work:* Del Art Mus, Wilmington. *Exhib:* Crafts 1970, Boston Mus Fine Arts, 70; Craftsmanship, Franklin Inst, Philadelphia, 70-71; Craftsman 73, Civic Ctr Mus, Philadelphia, 73; Clothing to Be Seen, Mus Contemp Crafts, New York, 74; Marianne Deson Gallery, Chicago, 80; Philadelphia Art Alliance, 81. *Awards:* Purchase Prize, Kentmere Mus, Wilmington Fine Arts Soc, 67; Cash Award, Harrisburg State Festival, 73. *Mem:* Charter mem Philadelphia Crafts Group (bd dirs, 75-, exhib chmn, 75-78); Am Crafts Coun; Surface Design Asn. *Media:* Fabric, Wax. *Publ:* Contribr, Clothing Decoration, Lane Publ, 77. *Dealer:* Gallery Five 5 Gallery Sq S Tequesta Dr Tequesta FL 33458. *Mailing Add:* 127 Fitzwater Philadelphia PA 19147

LIST, CLAIR Z
CURATOR

b Baltimore, Md, Dec 2, 53. *Study:* Univ Pa, BA & MA, 75; NY Univ Inst Fine Arts, MA, 80. *Collections Arranged:* Images of the 70's: 9 Washington Artists (auth, catalog), Corcoran Gallery Art, 80 & John Dickson/Ed Mayo (auth, catalog), 80; 22nd Area Exhib: Works on Paper, 80; Personal Narratives: Will Brunner/John Ryan, 80; Collage on Paper, 81; Corcoran After Hours, 81; Narrative Wood, 81; On-going Dialogue: Andrew Hudson/Blaine Larson, 81; Video, 82, 38th Corcoran Biennial Exhibition of American Painting, (cataloged), 83 & Watercolors Washington (cataloged), 84, Corcoran Gallery Art. *Pos:* Curatorial asst, Solomon R Guggenheim Mus, New York, 76-78, curatorial coordr, 78; assoc cur contemp art, Washington Region, Corcoran Gallery Art, DC, 79-81; assoc cur contemp art, Corcoran Gallery Art, 82- *Mem:* Col Art Asn. *Mailing Add:* Corcoran Gallery of Art 17th St & New York Ave NW Washington DC 20006

LIST, VERA G
PATRON, COLLECTOR

b Boston, Mass, Jan 6, 08. *Study:* Simmons Col; Jewish Theological Sem Am, LHD. *Pos:* Trustee & vpres, New Mus Contemp Art & New Sch Social Res, currently; trustee & vpres, New Mus Contemp Art, currently. *Awards:* Solomon Schechter Medal, Jewish Theol Sem Am, 59; Louise Waterman Wise Award, 64; NY State Coun on Arts Award to Albert A List Found for List Art Poster Prog, 69. *Interests:* Established List Art Poster Program; many gifts of art to New York museums and others. *Collection:* Contemporary sculpture and painting. *Mailing Add:* Byram Shore Rd Greenwich CT 06830

LISTER, ARDELE DIANE
VIDEO ARTIST

b Calgary, Alta, Jan 21, 50. *Study:* Univ BC, BA, 67. *Work:* Stedelijk Mus, Amsterdam; Donnell Libr, New York; Art Bank, Ottawa; Acad Kunst, Berlin. *Exhib:* Ithaca Video Festival, Long Beach Mus Art, Calif, 82; Tokyo Video Festival, Japan, 82; US Film & Video Festival, Park City, Utah, 83; O Kanada, Kunsthalle, Berlin, 83; New Narrative, Mus Mod Art, New York, 83. *Pos:* Ed, Criteria, 74-78. *Awards:* Selected Work, Tokyo Video Festival, 81 & 82; WSB Award, Atlanta Film & Video Festival, 82; NY State Coun Arts Grant, 83. *Bibliog:* Ann Sargent Wooster (auth), Video art?, Afterimage, 82 & Views by Women Artists, New York City, 82; Victor Ancona (auth), Video art, Videography, 3/83. *Media:* Video. *Publ:* Auth, article, Heresies, 77; coauth, Performance by Artists, Art Metropole, 79; auth, article, Independent, 79. *Dealer:* Castelli-Sonnabend Tapes & Films 142 Greene St New York NY 10012. *Mailing Add:* 80 Varick St #10C New York NY 10013

LITTELL, BIZ
GLASS BLOWER, MURALIST

b Denver, Colo, Nov 14, 43. *Study:* Univ Northern Colo, BA, 68 & MA, 69; Alfred Univ, MFA, 71. *Work:* Mem Art Gallery, Rochester, NY; Alfred Rossin Permanent Collection, Spring Valley, NY; Soc Arts & Crafts, Detroit Inst Art, Mich; Alfred Univ Permanent Collection, NY. *Comn:* Mural (ceramic), Nat Endowment, Denver, Colo, 75; mural (ceramic), Opus Found, Sedalia, Colo, 76; mural (ceramic), Tex A & M Univ, College Station, 77; mural (ceramic), Lutheran Church, Littleton, Colo, 81. *Exhib:* Am Potters Exhib, Asn Great Britain, Ltd, London, Eng, 70; Glass, Corning Mus, NY, 70; Am Craftsmen, Mem Art Gallery, Rochester, NY, 70; Crafts 1970, Inst Contemp Art, Boston, Mass, 70; Things 72, Brocton Art Ctr, Mass, 72; The Movement, The Soc, Detroit Inst Arts, Mich, 76; Glass & Ceramics, Houston Mus Art, Tex, 78; and others. *Pos:* Glass consult, Int Labor Off, United Nations Affiliate, 76; co-founder & dir, Opus Symposium Sch Arts, 76-78; consult product design, Grumbacher, New York, 83-84. *Teaching:* Adj prof ceramics, RI Sch Design, Providence, 71-73; div chmn glass, Soc Arts & Crafts, Detroit, Mich, 73-75; vis prof ceramics, Tex A & M Univ, College Station, 77-78. *Awards:* Purchase Award, Inst Contemp Art, Boston, Mass, 70; Permanent Collection, Corning Mus, 73; Best of Show & RCA Purchase Award, RCA, 75. *Bibliog:* Ceramic Reference Book, Wichita State Univ, 75; Jack Troy (auth), Salt Glazed Ceramics, Watson-Guptill, 77. *Mem:* Nat Coun Educ for the Ceramic Arts; Nat Educ Asn; Colo Artists-Craftsmen; Delta Phi Delta. *Media:* Multi-media. *Publ:* Auth, Biz Littell, contribr, Daniel Rhodes & contribr, Val Cushing Potter Handbook, 75, Opus Foundation. *Mailing Add:* 4310 S Kipling St Littleton CO 80123

LITTLE, JAMES
PAINTER

b Memphis, Tenn, July 21, 52. *Study:* Memphis Acad Arts, BFA, 74; Syracuse Univ, MFA(fels), 76. *Work:* Ark Arts Ctr, Little Rock; Everson Mus Art; Brooks Mus Art; Twentieth Century Fund, New York; Mrs RaFaella de Ussia Collection, Mexico DF. *Comn:* Oil painting, Stephen Mallory Assoc, New York, 77. *Exhib:* Solo exhib, Everon Mus, 76; Contemporary Abstractionists, Studio Mus Harlem, New York, 79; Memphis: Six Artists, Brooks Mus, 80; Afro-American Abstraction, PS1 Inst Art & Urban Res, New York, 80, Los Angeles Munic Art Gallery, 83 & Oakland Mus, 83; Works on Paper, Albright-Knox Art Gallery, 83; Contemporary Black Artists, Fine Arts Mus Long Island, 83. *Teaching:* Asst drawing, Syrcuse Univ, 74-76; instr drawing & painting, Memphis Acad Arts, 77-78. *Awards:* Creative Artists Pub Serv Grant, 81. *Media:* Oil on Linen or Canvas. *Mailing Add:* c/o Harold Hart 156 W 86th St New York NY 10021

LITTLE, JOHN
PAINTER, SCULPTOR

b Jones Mill, Ala, Mar 18, 07. *Study:* Buffalo Fine Arts Acad; Art Students League, with George Grosz; Hans Hofmann Sch Fine Arts, New York & Provincetown, Mass. *Work:* Metrop Mus; Guild Hall, East Hampton, NY; Berkeley Art Mus, Calif; Dillard Univ; Bruce Mus, Greenwich, Conn. *Exhib:* Major one-man shows, Calif Palace of Legion of Honor, San Francisco, 46, A M Sachs Gallery, New York, 71 & Tower Gallery, Southampton, NY, 77; Pittsburgh Int 61, Carnegie Inst, 61; Panorama Gallerie, Beyeler, Basle, Switzerland, 61; New Haven Contemp Paintings 1960-1961, Yale Univ Art Gallery, 61; Worth Ryder Gallery, Univ Calif, Berkeley, 63; John Little, Work of the 1970's, State Univ NY, Stony Brook, 81; John Little, A Retrospective 1934-1982, Guild Hall Mus, East Hampton, 83; and others. *Pos:* Founder & treas, Signa Gallery, East Hampton, NY, 57-61. *Teaching:* Lectr painting, Univ Calif, Berkeley, spring 63 & Long Island Univ, summer 67. *Awards:* Anne Bremer Mem Prize, San Francisco Mus Ann, 48; Purchase Prize, Longview Found, 62. *Bibliog:* Judith Wolfe (auth), John Little, 25 Artists, Univ Publs Am, 82. *Media:* Oil, Bronze. *Publ:* Auth, Statement of the artist, It Is, 59. *Mailing Add:* 367 3-Mile Harbor-Hog Creek Hwy East Hampton NY 11937

LITTLE, KEN DAWSON
SCULPTOR, EDUCATOR

b Canyon, Tex, April 8, 47. *Study:* Tex Tech Univ, BFA, 70; Univ Utah, MFA, 72. *Work:* Seattle Art Mus; Everson Mus; Phoenix Art Mus; Contemp Arts Found, Honolulu; Lannan Found, Palm Beach. *Exhib:* Southern Fictions, Contemp Arts Mus, Houston, 83; Shattered Portraits and Unlikely Heroes, J M Kohler Ars Ctr, Sheboygan, Wis, 83; solo traveling exhib, 83-84. *Teaching:* Instr art, Univ SFla, 72-74; assoc prof, Univ Mont, 74-80 & Univ Okla, 80- *Awards:* Western States Arts Found Fel, 77; Nat Endowment Arts Fel, 82-83. *Media:* Mixed. *Dealer:* Quay Gallery 254 Sutter San Francisco Calif; Susan Caldwell Gallery 383 W Broadway New York NY. *Mailing Add:* 1107 W Symmes Norman OK 73069

LITTLE, NINA FLETCHER
COLLECTOR, WRITER

b Brookline, Mass, Jan 25, 03. *Pos:* Trustee, consult & chmn curatorial comt, Old Sturbridge Village. *Awards:* Art Res Award, Hist Soc Early Am Decoration, 53; Crowninshield Award, Nat Trust for Hist Preserv, 64. *Res:* New England painting, architecture and decorative arts. *Collection:* American decorative arts, especially folk paintings and furniture. *Publ:* Auth, Abby Aldrich Rockefeller Folk Art Collection (catalog), 57, Maine's role in American art (1700-1865 sect), 63 & 72 & Country art in New England, 65; Country arts in early American homes, 75. *Mailing Add:* 305 Warren St Brookline MA 02146

LITTLE CHIEF, BARTHELL
PAINTER, SCULPTOR

b Lawton, Okla, Oct 14, 41. *Work:* Southwestern Mus Los Angeles, Calif; Southern Plains Mus, Anadarko, Okla; Morris Mus, Morristown, NJ; Mus Art, Univ Okla, Norman; Okla Historical Soc, Oklahoma City. *Comn:* Terra-cotta sculpture, US Dept Interior, Washington, DC, 69; tempera painting, US Dept Interior, Washington, DC, 81. *Exhib:* Am Indian Artist, Philbrook Art Mus, Tulsa, Okla, 78; Vestiges and Resurgence, Morris Mus, Morristown, NJ, 79; Am Contemp Paintings Traveling Exhib, SAm, 79; one-man show, Mus Art, Univ Okla, Norman, 79; Am Indian Art 1980's, Native Am Ctr Living Arts, Niagara Falls, NY, 81. *Media:* Tempera, Gouache; Terra-Cotta, Bronze. *Publ:* Auth, Kiowa Voices, Tex Christian Univ Press, 83. *Dealer:* The Galleria 1630 W Lindsey Norman OK 73069; Oklahoma Indian Art Gallery 2335 SW 44th Oklahoma City OK. *Mailing Add:* Rt 3 Box 109A Anadarko OK 73005

LITTLER, CHARLES ARMSTRONG See Rubylee

LITTLETON, HARVEY K
SCULPTOR, EDUCATOR

b Corning, NY, June 14, 22. *Study:* Univ Mich, BDesign; Brighton Sch Art, Eng; Cranbrook Acad Art, MFA; Philadelphia Col Arts, Hon DFA. *Work:* Toledo Mus Art, Ohio; Victoria & Albert Mus, London; Mus Mod Art, New York; Kunstmuseum, Dusseldorf, WGer; Metrop Mus Art, New York. *Exhib:* Objects USA, Johnson Wax Collection, 69-72; 15th Triennale Exhib Archit & Decorative Art, 74; New Glass, Corning Mus Glass, 79-81; Retrospective, Mint Mus Art, 79; Retrospective, Renwick Gallery, Smithsonian Inst, 84; and others. *Pos:* bd trustees, Pilchuck Sch, Wash, Penland Sch, NC, currently. *Teaching:* Instr ceramic art, Toledo Mus Art Sch Design, 49-51; prof art, Univ Wis-Madison, 51-77, emer prof, 77-, chmn dept art, 64-67 & 69-71, univ res grants, 54, 57, 62, 72 & 75. *Awards:* Louis Comfort Tiffany Found Grant, 70-71; Nat Endowment Art Fel, 78-79; Gold Medal, Am Crafts Coun, 83. *Bibliog:* Colescott (auth), Harvey Littleton, 59 & Dido Smith (auth), Off hand glassblowing, 64, Craft Horizons; Joan Falconer Byrd (auth), Pioneer in American studio glass, Am Craft, 2-3/80. *Mem:* Fel Am Crafts Coun (trustee, 57 & 59-64); hon mem Nat Coun Educ in Ceramic Arts; hon mem Glass Art Soc; Corning Mus Glass; NAm Assembly World Crafts Coun. *Media:* Glass. *Publ:* Auth, Erwin Eisch, 63 & auth, Glass in the Ozarks, 73, Craft Horizons; auth, Glassblowing--a Search for Form, Van Nostrand Reinhold, 72. *Dealer:* Heller Gallery 965 Madison Ave New York NY 10021. *Mailing Add:* Rte 1 Box 843 Spruce Pine NC 28777

LITTRELL, DORIS MARIE
DEALER

b Apache, Okla, April 30, 28. *Pos:* Owner, Okla Indian Art Gallery, currently. *Specialty:* Native American arts, with emphasis on Oklahoma Indian artists and craftsman. *Mailing Add:* 2335 SW 44th St Oklahoma City OK 73119

LIU, HO
COLLECTOR, PAINTER
b Canton, China, Mar 20, 17; US citizen. *Study:* Lingnan Univ, Canton, BA; George Washington Univ, MA. *Collection:* Chinese calligraphy and painting. *Mailing Add:* 1946 Hopewood Dr Falls Church VA 22043

LIU, KATHERINE CHANG
PAINTER, PRINTMAKER
b Kiang-si, China; US citizen. *Study:* Studied with Chun-bi Huang, Taiwan, 59-63; Univ Calif, Berkeley, MS, 66. *Work:* Va Mus Fine Arts; Roanoke Mus Art, Va; State Collection Baja, Calif, Mex. *Exhib:* Va Mus Fine Arts, 78; Rocky Mountain Nat Watermedia Exhib, Foothills Art Ctr, Golden, Colo, 78 & 80-83; solo show, Roanoke Mus, 78 & Utah State Univ Mus, 83; Nat Watercolor Soc, Laguna Beach Mus, 80 & 82; Knickerbocker Artists, Salmagundi Club, New York, 81; Nat Midyear Exhib, Butler Inst Am Art, 82. *Teaching:* Instr watercolor, Roanoke Mus Art, Va, 75-79, Conejo Valley Art Mus, 80-82 & watercolor groups, Colo, Tex, Tucson & Utah. *Awards:* Art Asn Awards, Rocky Mountain Nat Watermedia Ann, 78 & 80; Purchase Award, Nat Watercolor Soc, Utah State Univ, 79; Top Purchase Award, First City Acquisition Competition, City Thousand Oaks, 83. *Bibliog:* Ann Weinstein (auth), Four with paper, Art Voices, 3/80; Carol Dickinson (auth), Reverberation stunning at watercolor show, Transcript, 9/81; Ann H Wen-Chang (auth), Katherine Liu watercolors, China Times, 11/21/83. *Mem:* Nat Watercolor Soc (first vpres, 82-83, pres, 83-84); Rocky Mountain Nat Watermedia Soc. *Media:* Watercolor, Monotype; Mixed Media. *Publ:* Contribr, Watercolor in US, Crown Mag, 79; contribr, Watercolorist, North Light, 80; contribr, Art in Your World, Davis Publ (in prep); contribr, Painting the Spirit of Nature, Watson-Guptill (in prep). *Dealer:* Louis Newman Galleries Los Angeles CA; Fendrick Gallery Washington DC. *Mailing Add:* 2872 E Panamint Ct Westlake Village CA 91362

LIVESAY, THOMAS ANDREW
MUSEUM DIRECTOR
b Dallas, Tex, Feb 1, 45. *Study:* San Francisco Art Inst, 63-65; Univ Tex, Austin, BFA, 68, MFA, 72; Harvard Univ, 78. *Collections Arranged:* Five Austin Artists (with catalog), 74; The Amarillo Competition, 75 & 77; Charles Burchfield Selected Works (with catalog), 75; Henri Matisse Etchings, 75; American Masters, 75; Warren Davis Retrospective (with catalog), 75; American Images, 76, with Nat Endowment for the Humanities; Young Texas Artists Series, 76-78. *Pos:* Tech staff, Univ Tex Art Mus, Austin, 66-70; cur, Elisabet Ney Art Ctr, Austin, 70-73; dir, Longview Mus & Art Ctr, Tex, 73-75; cur, Amarillo Art Ctr, 75-77, dir, 77-80; asst dir admin, Dallas Mus Fine Arts, 80- *Awards:* Roy Crane Award Fine Arts, Univ Tex, Austin, 68. *Mem:* Am Asn Mus; Tex Asn Mus (pres, 83-85). *Res:* Twentieth century American art with particular emphasis on sculpture. *Publ:* Coauth, Larson/Walsh/Sculpture, 74; auth, Young Texas Artists Series, 78; American Images, 78; coauth, Made in Texas, 78; auth, Russell Lee, 79. *Mailing Add:* c/o Dallas Mus Fine Arts Fair Park Dallas TX 75226

LIVET, ANNE HODGE
ADMINISTRATOR, CRITIC
b Ft Worth, Tex, Jan 23, 41. *Study:* Wellesley Col, Mass, 59-61; Univ Tex at Austin, 61-62; Tex Christian Univ, Ft Worth, BA, 72, MA, 74. *Collections Arranged:* Brazos River: a Television Exhibition with Robert Rauschenberg, Viola Farber and David Tudor, Ft Worth Art Mus, 77, The Record as Artwork: from Futurism to Conceptual Art (ed & contribr, catalog), 77 & Stella Since 1970 (ed, catalog), 78; David McManaway: Works-Twenty Years (auth, catalog), Univ Gallery, Meadows Sch Arts, Southern Methodist Univ, Dallas, 79; The Works of Edward Ruscha (auth, catalog), San Francisco Mus Mod Art, Calif, 81. *Pos:* Dir performing arts, Ft Worth Art Mus, 74-78 & cur, 75-78; cofounder with Stephen Reichard, Livet Reichard Co Inc, 79- *Awards:* Nat Endowment for Arts fel for mus prof, 76; Inst for Art & Urban Resources Fel, New York, 78-79. *Mem:* Elmwood Found Arts & Humanities, Ft Worth; Performing Arts Jour; Contemp Art Southeast, Atlanta. *Publ:* Ed & contribr, Contemporary Dance, Abbeville Press, 78; ed & contribr, Contemporary Art Southeast, Vol II, No 2, 79. *Mailing Add:* c/o Livet Reichard Co Inc 87 Franklin New York NY 10013

LIVINGSTON, JANE S
CRITIC, CURATOR
b Upland, Calif, Feb 12, 44. *Study:* Pomona Col, BA(art hist), 65; Harvard Univ, MA(fine arts), 66. *Pos:* Cur mod art, Los Angeles Co Mus Art, 67-75; corresp ed, Art in Am, 70-; chief cur, Corcoran Gallery Art, 75-, assoc dir, 78-; mem mus adv panel, Nat Endowment for the Arts, 77- *Mem:* Asn Am Mus; Col Art Asn; Int Coun Mus (bd, 79-). *Publ:* Coauth, Art & Technology, Viking Press & Los Angeles Co Mus Art, 70; auth, Manuel Alvarez Bravo, Godine, 78. *Mailing Add:* Corcoran Gallery Art New York Ave & 17th St Washington DC 20006

LIVINGSTON, MARGARET GRESHAM
ADMINISTRATOR, PATRON
b Birmingham, Ala, Aug 16, 24. *Study:* Vassar Col, AB, 45; Univ Ala, MA, 46. *Pos:* Founder & pres, Mem Birmingham Mus, 71-72; chmn bd, Mus Art Educ Coun, Birmingham, Ala, 70-; art comt, Birmingham Civic Ctr Authority, 75-; bd, Greater Birmingham Art Alliance, 77-; chmn bd, Birmingham Mus Art, 78- *Awards:* Silver Bowl Award for Contrib Arts, Birmingham Festival Arts, 67. *Mem:* Am Asn Mus (ed comt & pub relations, 81); Am Fedn Arts; Ala Mus Asn (vpres, 78-79); Birmingham Festival Arts (vpres, 78-79); Birmingham Art Asn (vpres, 60-63); Int Coun Mus (ed comt, 81). *Interests:* Art history, education, board administration & organization and publication of museums. *Collection:* American graphics and drawings.

Publ: Co-ed, Bull Mem Birmingham Mus, 71-74 & Birmingham Festival Arts Bull, 71-77, Birmingham Mus; co-ed, Spain Rehabilitation Center Art Catalog, Spain Hosp, 74. *Mailing Add:* 12 Country Club Rd Birmingham AL 35213

LIVINGSTON, SIDNEE
PAINTER
b New York, NY. *Study:* Nat Acad Design. *Work:* Princeton Univ; Everhart Mus, Pa; Univ Miami, Fla; Univ Miss; Columbus Mus, Ga; and others. *Exhib:* Art Inst Chicago; Butler Art Inst; Philadelphia Acad Fine Arts; St Louis Mus, Mo; Libr of Cong, Washington, DC; three solo traveling shows (monotypes); and many others. *Awards:* Mildred Tommy Atkins Prize, Nat Asn Women Artists, 71, Award/Oil, 77; MacDowell Colony Fel; First Prize Watercolor, NJ Painters & Sculptors. *Mem:* Artists Equity Asn New York. *Media:* Oil, Watercolor. *Mailing Add:* 50 E 89th St New York NY 10128

LIVINGSTON, VIRGINIA (MRS HUDSON WARREN BUDD)
PAINTER, ILLUSTRATOR
b Baltimore, Md. *Study:* Md Inst Art; Cooper Union Art Sch; Art Students League; Nat Acad Design; Beaux Art Am, Fontainbleau, France; with Fernand Leger, Paris Acad, France; also with Brackman, Ryerson, Kroll, O'Hara & Phillip, New York. *Work:* Draped Figure, Home Fed Bank Bldg, Charleston, SC. *Exhib:* Salon de L'Arte Libre, Paris, 51; Miniature Painters, Sculptors & Gravers Soc, Smithsonian Inst, Washington, DC, 52; Am Watercolor Soc Ann & Allied Artists Am Ann, Nat Acad Art, New York, 54-60; Corcoran Gallery Art, Washington, DC, 55; one-man show, Mus City New York, 60; and others. *Awards:* First Prize, Ann Studio Club, YWCA, New York, 52; Medal of Honor, Ann Artists Prof League, New York, 56; and others. *Bibliog:* Article, La Rev Mod, Paris, 56. *Mem:* Copley Soc Boston; Carolina Art Asn; Charleston Artists Guild. *Media:* Watercolor. *Interests:* Organized new gallery, LaPetite Louve, to promote young artists. *Publ:* Illusr fashions & by-line, Chicago Tribune Synd, 24-26; illusr textbks, Scribners, 24-25; coauth & illusr ann calendar, Am Cyanamid Co, 59-60. *Dealer:* Blue Knight Gallery 82 Broad St Charleston SC 29401. *Mailing Add:* c/o Sherrill House 135 S Huntington Ave Boston MA 02130

LIVINGSTONE, BIGANESS
PAINTER, EDUCATOR
b Cambridge, Mass. *Study:* Mass Col Art, BFA; Univ Wis-Madison, MFA. *Work:* Chase Manhattan Bank Collection, New York; Merrimack Co Courthouse, NH; Radcliffe Col, Cambridge; Sheraton Hotel Corp, Boston. *Comn:* Mural, Pierce Chapel, Lenox, Mass, 66. *Exhib:* One-artist shows, Fitchburg Art Mus, Mass, 76, Bergstrom-Mahler Mus, Wis, 78, Univ Wis, Madison, 82 & Ann Conner Gallery, Wis, 83; Mus Mod Art, New York; Zolla/Lieberman Gallery, Chicago, Ill, 81-82. *Pos:* Regional dir, City Spirit Grant, NH Comn Arts, 75. *Teaching:* From asst prof to assoc prof & dept head, Univ Wis, Fox Valley, 76- *Awards:* Mary T Bunting Inst Grant, Radcliffe Col, Mass, 63-65; Purchase Award, Neville Pub Mus, Wis, 81; Wis Arts Bd Grant, 83. *Bibliog:* James Collins (auth), Women Artists in America, Vol 2 (1975); Bartlett Hayes (auth), Tradition Becomes Innovation, Pilgrim Press, 83; article, New Month Mag, Wis, 10/82. *Mem:* NH Art Asn (pres, 75). *Dealer:* Cudahy Gallery Wis Art Milwaukee Art Mus; Ann Conner Gallery Appleton WI 54911. *Mailing Add:* 1500 Palisades Dr Appleton WI 54911

LLORENTE, LUIS
PAINTER, DESIGNER
b Santander, Spain; US citizen. *Study:* Sch Indust Arts & Sch Visual Arts, Columbia Univ; also with Anthony Thieme & Umberto Romano. *Work:* USN Combat Art Collection, Washington, DC; Neighborhood Med Ctr, Bronx, NY; also in many pvt collections. *Comn:* Bathyscaph Trieste, San Diego Naval Base, USN, 61; atomic submarine, Rota Naval Base, Spain, 64; Gemini V Recovery, Aboard USS Lake Champlain, 65; USS New Jersey, Philadelphia Navy Yard, 68; US Marines Distributing candy to children, 69. *Exhib:* Audubon Artists, Nat Acad Design, 60-61 & Am Watercolor Soc, twelve times & seven travel awards, 60-79; Mus de la Marine, Paris, 63; Smithsonian Inst & Dept of State Exhib Hall, Washington, DC, 65; and others. *Awards:* Ford Times Award, Am Watercolor Soc, 75; Louis E Seley Award, Salmagundi Club, 78; Alicia Sutherland Award, Knickerbocker Artists, 79. *Bibliog:* John Smee (auth), Portrait of an artist, Chronicle, New York, 61; Mann Sierra (auth), American-Spaniard paints in Rota Naval Base, Alerta, Santander, Spain, 64. *Mem:* Artists Fellowship; Am Watercolor Soc (asst corresp secy, 71-); Knickerbocker Artists (1st vpres, 77-); Salmagundi Club; Am Vet Soc Artists. *Media:* Watercolor, Oil. *Mailing Add:* 245 Fort Washington Ave New York NY 10032

LLOYD, GARY MARCHAL
CONCEPTUAL ARTIST, EDUCATOR
b Los Angeles, Calif, Aug 27, 43. *Study:* Art Ctr Col Design, 63-65; Otis Art Inst Los Angeles Co, BFA & MFA, 70. *Work:* Los Angeles Co Mus Art, Los Angeles, Calif; Berkeley Mus Art; Mus Mod Art, Poland. *Comn:* Site work, Univ Southern Calif, 73; site work, Univ Calif, Irvine, 74. *Exhib:* Picture Phone, Long Beach Mus Art, 79; PS 1, 79; Real Time is the Only Time, Univ Art Mus, Berkeley, 80; one-man show, Ulpike Kantor, 82; Whitney Mus Am Art, New York; Long Beach Mus Art; and others. *Pos:* Dir, Nat Conf, Innerdependence Art & Sci, Calif State Univ, Los Angeles, 71-72; mem bd dirs, Los Angeles Inst Contemp Art, 74-75. *Teaching:* Asst prof intermedia sculpture, Otis Art Inst Los Angeles Co & Univ Calif, Los Angeles, 75-80. *Awards:* Nat Endowment Arts Individual fel, 80-81. *Bibliog:* Kay Larson (auth), Quips for the new decade, Village Voice, 10/15/79; interview, Today Show, Channel 4, NBC, 11/19/79; James Huginum (auth), An answer driving the problem, Los Angeles Inst Contemp Art J, 3/80; Peter Clothier (auth),

Gary Lloyd at Santa Monica Col, Art Am, 3/83; and others. *Media:* Mixed. *Res:* Realtime events, painting, sculptures & video. *Publ:* Coauth, Bob Went Home, Ellie Blankfort Gallery Publ, 72. *Mailing Add:* 112 N Center St Los Angeles CA 90012

LOAR, PEGGY A
MUSEUM DIRECTOR, ADMINISTRATOR
b Cincinnati, Ohio, May 14, 48. *Study:* Univ Cincinnati, BA(art hist), 70, MA, 71. *Collections Arranged:* Indiana Stoneware (auth, catalog), Indianapolis Mus Art, 72; Bulgarian Medieval Jewelry, Dunbarton Oaks, 81; American Impressionism, Petit Palais, Paris, 82; Master Drawings from the National Gallery of Ireland, 83; The Precious Legacy: Judaic Treasures from the Czechoslovak State Collections, 83; Jamaican Art: 1922-1982, 83. *Pos:* Cur educ, Indianapolis Mus Art, 72-, asst dir, 77-; proj dir, Learning Mus, Nat Endowment Humanities, Washington, DC, 75-, mem nat bd consult, 77-; prog dir, Inst Mus Serv, Washington, DC, 77-78, asst dir, 78-; dir, Smithsonian Inst Traveling Exhib Service, 81- *Teaching:* Lectr art hist, Indianapolis Mus Art, Ind Univ & Purdue Univ, 71-75 & numerous mus & conf, 71- *Awards:* Nat Endowment Arts Grants, Ind Pottery, 75 & Role of Humanities in Art Mus Educ, 76; Nat Endowment Humanities, Learning Mus Program, 81. *Bibliog:* Adele Silver (auth), Issues related to museum education: curators/directors and educators interface, Midwest Mus Conf, Vol 36, No 4; Priscilla Brouillette (auth), Loar adds new enthusiasm, Vision, Ind Comt Humanities, 77. *Mem:* Ind Comt Humanities; Am Asn Mus; Indianapolis Art League Found; Int Coun Mus; Soc Women Geographers. *Res:* Museum education; Indianapolis Museum of Art accessions and collections; humanities curriculum. *Publ:* Auth, Arts and the three Rs/43, Mus News, 9-10/76; auth, Issues, Midwest Mus Conf, Vol 36, No 4; auth, Sculpture Eleven, Vol 5, No 3, & A Maze of Opportunities, Vol 6, No 1, Ocular Mag; auth, Success through sharing: The team approach to cultural understanding, In: Education 10, Int Coun Mus, 82-83; coauth, General operating support for women: Problems in paradise, J Col & Univ Law, Vol 7, No 3-4e. *Mailing Add:* 1536 15th St NW Washington DC 20005

LOBDELL, FRANK
PAINTER
b Kansas City, Mo, 21. *Study:* St Paul Sch Fine Art, Minn, 38-39; Calif Sch Fine Art, 47-50; Acad Grande Chaumiere, Paris, 50-51. *Work:* Pasadena Art Mus, Los Angeles Co Mus, Stanford Mus, San Francisco Mus Art & Oakland Mus Art, Calif. *Exhib:* Salon du Mai, Paris, 50; 3rd Biennial of Sao Paulo, Brazil, 55; International Art of a New Era, Osaka, Japan, 58; Kompas 4, West Coast USA, Van Abbemuseum, Eindhoven, 70; 32nd Biennial Am Painting, Corcoran Gallery Art, Washington, DC, 71; Reed Col Art Gallery, Portland, Ore, 81. *Teaching:* Prof art, Stanford Univ, 66- *Awards:* Nealie Sullivan Award, San Francisco Mus Art, 60; Tamarind Fel, 66; Knight of Mark Twain, 71. *Bibliog:* Michel Tapie (auth), Frank Lobdell, David Anderson (Paris), 66; Walter Hoppe (auth), Frank Lobdell 1948-1965, Pasadena Art Mus, 66; Gerald Nordland (auth), Frank Lobdell, San Francisco Mus Art, 69. *Dealer:* Martha Jackson Gallery 32 E 69th St New York NY 10021. *Mailing Add:* 340 Palo Alto Ave Palo Alto CA 94301

LOBELLO, PETER
SCULPTOR, GRAPHIC ARTIST
b New Orleans, La, Nov 18, 35. *Study:* Sch Archit, Tulane Univ, 53-55, Newcomb Sch Art, 54-55. *Work:* Aldrich Mus Contemp Art; Geneva Mus Art, Switz; Phoenix Art Mus; Plains Art Mus, Moorhead, Minn; New Orleans Mus Art. *Comn:* Sculptures, Chateau Bellereve, Geneva, 74; Villa Savoia, Geneva, 76 & Hyatt Hotels Corp, New York, 80. *Exhib:* Contemporary Reflections 73, Aldrich Mus Contemp Art, 73; Selections from the Art Lending Service, Mus Mod Art Penthouse Gallery, New York, 78; Prospectus: 1970s, Aldrich Mus Contemp Art, 79; Robert Kidd Gallery, Detroit, 80; 21st Midwestern Invitational, Plains Art Mus, Moorhead, Minn, 80; Alexander Rosenberg Gallery, New York, 80; Inaugural Show, Alexander Carlson Gallery, New York, 80; Rutgers Univ, 83; and others. *Bibliog:* Paul Goldberger (auth), 42nd St: The Grand Hyatt, New York Times, 9/22/80; Isabel Forgang (auth), At home with sculptor Peter Lobello, New York Daily News Tonight, 10/15/80; Ada Louise Huxtable (auth), Architecture view: Two new triumphant hotels, New York Times, 10/19/80. *Mailing Add:* 71 Grand St New York NY 10013

LOBERG, ROBERT WARREN
PAINTER, INSTRUCTOR
b Chicago, Ill, Dec 1, 27. *Study:* City Col San Francisco, AA; Univ Calif, Berkeley, BA & MA; San Francisco State Univ; Hans Hofmann Sch Art, Provincetown, Mass. *Work:* Art Inst Chicago; San Francisco Art Comn; Henry Gallery, Univ Wash, Seattle; Oakland Art Mus, Calif; Gallery Mod Art, Washington, DC; plus others. *Exhib:* San Francisco Mus Art, ann, 55-; Henry Gallery, Univ Wash, 68; Calif Col Arts & Crafts, Oakland, 69; Both-Up Gallery, Berkeley, 69; Berkeley Art Ctr, 77; San Jose Art Mus, Calif, 78; San Francisco Mus Mod Art, 81; and others. *Teaching:* Art lectr; instr painting & drawing, Calif Col Arts & Crafts, 61-63; instr art, San Francisco Art Inst, 63-66; instr art, Univ Calif, Berkeley, 65; vis fac, Dept Art, Univ Wash, 67-68. *Awards:* Yaddo Found Scholar, 57; MacDowell Colony Scholar, 59 & 60; La Jolla Art Mus Prize, 62; Nat Endowment Arts Fel, 82; and others. *Mailing Add:* 2020 Vine St Berkeley CA 94709

LOCHNAN, KATHARINE A
CURATOR, LECTURER
b Aug 8, 46; Can citizen. *Study:* Univ Toronto, BA, 68, MA, 71; Courtauld Inst, Univ London, Eng, PhD, 82. *Pos:* Cur asst, Royal Ont Mus, 68-69; asst cur, Art Gallery Ont, 69-75; volunteer asst, Brit Mus, 75-76, cur prints &

drawings, 76- *Mem:* Print Coun Am (bd mem, 80-); NE Victorian Studies Asn; Univ Art Asn Can; London House Asn Can (chmn bd, 81-); William Morris Soc Can. *Res:* Whistler's etchings; 19th century French and English prints. *Publ:* Auth, Master Prints from the Presgrave Collection, 80, auth, The Department of Prints and Drawings at the National Galley of Canada: The First Hundred Years, 80 & coauth, The Arts of Italy in Toronto Collections, 81, Art Gallery Ont; auth, Whistler and the transfer lithograph, Print Collectors Newsletter, 81; auth, The Walker Papers: Reminiscences of Lavery and Holman Hunt, 82. *Mailing Add:* 21 Mackenzie Crescent Toronto ON M6J 1S9 Canada

LOCK, CHARLES L
PAINTER, ILLUSTRATOR
b Chiswick, London, England, June 15, 19. *Study:* Polytech Sch of Art, Chiswick, London, Eng; further studies with George Ayling & Kenneth Washburn. *Work:* Air Force Art Collection, Art & Mus Branch, Pentagon, Washington, DC; Naval Aviation Mus, Pensacola, Fla. *Pos:* Art dir, Aero-Marine Specialties, Washington, DC, 74-77; partner, LTD Fine Art Prints, Vienna, Va, 77- *Mem:* Guild of Aviation Artists; Royal Soc of Marine Artists; Soc of Illusr; Am Soc of Marine Artists. *Media:* Water Media, Pen and Ink; Pastel Oil. *Publ:* Illusr, Airways to Airlines--A 50 Year History of Commercial Aviation, John Meyers, 75; illusr, Fundamentals of meteorology, United Air Lines, 76; illusr, These were the ugliest airplanes, Aircraft Owners & Pilots Asn Mag, 77; illusr, The three musketeers, Am Aviation Hist Soc, 77; illusr, Allegheny Aircraft (ltd ed prints), Moore & Moore, 78. *Mailing Add:* c/o Ships Chandlery 1640 W Campbell Ave Campbell CA 95008

LOCK, EARL WAYNE
PAINTER, GALLERY DIRECTOR
b Rector, Ark, Mar 26, 48. *Study:* Ark State Univ, BFA, 70; Kans State Univ, Manhattan, MA, 76; Univ Nebr, Lincoln, MFA, 79. *Work:* Springfield Art Mus, Mo; Ark State Univ Gallery; Kans State Univ Art Gallery, Manhattan; Omaha Art Gallery, Univ Nebr. *Exhib:* Watercolor Biennial, Ctr Arts, Scottsdale, Ariz, 78; 54th Ann, Springville Mus Art, Utah, 78; Joslyn Art Mus, Omaha, Nebr, 80; Ann Nat, Laguan Gloria Art Mus, Austin, 80; Pillsbury Co, St Paul, Minn, 81; and others. *Collections Arranged:* Drawings: Jim Roche, Terry Allen, Harold Boyd, Fran Noel, Power Booth, Ann Karlsen (ed, catalog), 81, Eight Nebraska Sculptors (auth, catalog), 81, Four Potters Exhibit (ed, catalog) 81 & Uno Art Faculty Exhibit (ed, catalog), 81, Eppley Competitive Art Exhib (ed, catalog), 82 & Drawing from Chicago (ed, catalog), 82, Univ Nebr, Omaha Art Gallery. *Pos:* Dir, Paducah Art Gallery, Ky, 83- *Teaching:* Instr, Cent Tech Community Col, Hastings, Nebr, 79-80; vis instr, Univ Nebr, Omaha, 80-82, asst prof, 82-83. *Awards:* Chatauqua Inst Award, Exhib Am Art, 78; Juror's Award, Scottsdale Ctr Arts Watercolor Biennial, Ariz, 78. *Media:* Acrylic, Rhoplex. *Dealer:* Joslyn Art Mus Sales Gallery Dodge St Omaha NE 68132. *Mailing Add:* 4904 Chicago St Omaha NE 68132

LOCKE, CHARLES WHEELER
PAINTER, PRINTMAKER
b Cincinnati, Ohio, Aug 31, 1899. *Study:* Ohio Mechanics Inst; Cincinnati Art Acad; Art Students League, with Joseph Pennell; study in Paris, 28. *Work:* Metrop Mus Art, Whitney Mus Am Art, New York; Nat Gallery, London, Eng; Corcoran Gallery Art, Phillips Collection, Washington, DC; and other pub & pvt collections. *Teaching:* instr lithography, Art Students League, 22-37. *Awards:* Logan Award, 36; Am Acad Arts & Lett Grant; Ranger Fund Purchase Award, Nat Acad Design, 74; and others. *Mem:* Nat Acad Design; Century Club. *Publ:* Illusr, Tale of a Tub, Walden. *Mailing Add:* Old Post Rd Garrison NY 10524

LOCKE, MICHELLE WILSON
CURATOR, HISTORIAN
b Dallas, Tex, June 10, 47. *Study:* Trinity Univ, San Antonio, Tex; Univ Tex, Austin, BFA. *Pos:* Lectr-librn, Art Mus of STex, Corpus Christi, 72-76, cur, 76-79. *Mem:* Am Asn of Mus; Col Art Asn. *Res:* Fifteenth Century French illuminated manuscripts. *Mailing Add:* 207 Leming Corpus Christi TX 78404

LOCKE, RHEA G
PAINTER, DRAFTSMAN
b Hattiesburg Miss. *Study:* Univ Ala, BA, 31; Belhaven Col, cert(art), 32. *Work:* Northern Va Community Co, Annandale; Fairfax Co Coun Arts, Green Spring Farm, Alexandria, Va. *Exhib:* Nineteenth Area Exhib, Corcoran Gallery Art, Washington, DC, 74; one-woman shows, Fredericksburg Gallery Mod Art, Va, 77 & Carroll Reece Mus, Johnson City, Tenn, 77. *Teaching:* Head dept art hist, Mt Vernon High Sch, Fairfax Co, Va, 53-71. *Mem:* Artists Equity Asn, Washington, DC; Washington Womens Art Ctr; Art League; Springfield Art Guild. *Media:* Acrylics, Charcoal; Pen & Ink. *Mailing Add:* 7427 Little River Annandale VA 22003

LOCKS, MARIAN
GALLERY DIRECTOR, COLLECTOR
b Philadelphia, Pa, June 24, 15. *Pos:* Dir, Marian Locks Gallery, Philadelphia; bd dirs, Please Touch Mus, Samuel Yellin Found, Am Israel Cult Found, Citizens Arts Pa, Muse Gallery & Nexus Gallery, currently. *Mem:* Pa Acad Fine Arts; Inst Contemp Art, Univ Pa; assoc Philadelphia Mus Art; Art Table; Philadelphia Art Dealers Asn. *Specialty:* Contemporary Delaware Valley Art; development of local talent; gallery is internationally recognized as a showcase for Contemporary Philadelphia area artists as well as noted young talent from other areas. *Collection:* Largely Philadelphia art of the seventies and eighties; also special groups of works by Beauford Delaney; small works by European Masters. *Mailing Add:* 1524 Walnut St Philadelphia PA 19102

LOEB, JUDY
PAINTER, WRITER
b Bridgeton, NJ, Nov 10, 31. *Study:* Tyler Sch Art, Temple Univ, MFA, 68. *Work:* Wurlitzer Found, Taos, NMex; Eastern Mich Univ, Ypsilanti; Plaza Savings Asn, Kansas City, Kans; Careers, San Juan, PR. *Exhib:* Nat Ann, Pa Acad Fine Arts, Philadelphia, 54; one-man shows, Philadelphia Art Alliance, Pa, 68 & 76; Constructivists, Kresge Mus, East Lansing, Mich, 71; Philadelphia Civic Ctr Mus, Pa, 71, 76 & 79; Women's Caucus Art Show, Detroit Inst Art, Mich, 78; Source Detroit, Cranbrook Acad, Bloomfield Hills, Mich; Va Images, Roanoke Mus, 80-81. *Teaching:* Prof art, Eastern Mich Univ, 69- *Awards:* Teacher of the Year Award, Mich Art Asn, 76; Keal Fund Grant, 80; Artists Colony Residencies, Wurlitzer, Montalvo, Va Ctr, Ossabaw. *Bibliog:* Article, Ga Rev, winter 80, Woman's Art J, 80 & Nat Arts Gide, 5-6/81. *Mem:* Artists Equity Asn; Women's Caucus Art (mem bd, 76-79 & 81-83); Coalition Women's Art Organizations (mem bd, 78-85); Nat Women's Studies Asn. *Media:* Gouache, Acrylic. *Res:* Influence of the feminist art movement on women artists' imagery. *Publ:* Auth, Educating women in the visual arts, Visual Dialog, 77; ed, Women's Studies and the Arts, Women's Caucus Art, 78; ed, Feminist Collage, Columbia Univ Teachers Col Press, 79 & 81. *Dealer:* Nestor Assocs 9865 Edwards Dr Brighton MI 48116. *Mailing Add:* 3286 Alpine Dr Ann Arbor MI 48104

LOEFFLER, CARL EUGENE
EDITOR, VIDEO ARTIST
b Cleveland, Ohio, Nov 14, 46. *Work:* San Francisco Mus Mod Art; Mus Mod Art, New York; Tex Tech Univ, Lubbock. *Exhib:* La Mamelle Inc 1975-80, San Francisco Mus Mod Art, 80; Performance Art, Mus Contemp Art, Chicago, 80; Video Art: A History, Mus Mod Art, New York, 83. *Collections Arranged:* Performance Art, 80; Watching Television, 83. *Pos:* Founding dir, La Mamelle Inc, 75- & Contemp Art Press, 75-; ed, Art Com Mag, 81- *Teaching:* Instr performance studio, Acad Art Col, 76- *Awards:* Artist Space Grant, 77-83 & Critics Fel, 80, Nat Endowment Arts. *Media:* Telecommunications, Print. *Res:* Performance art; television art; telecommunications in the arts. *Publ:* Auth, Performance Anthology, Contemp Arts Press, 80. *Mailing Add:* Rincon Annex PO Box 3123 San Francisco CA 94119

LOEHLE, BETTY BARNES
PAINTER
b Montgomery, Ala, Mar 21, 23. *Study:* Auburn Univ, Ala, 40-42; Harris Sch Art, Nashville, Tenn, 42-46; Evanston Art Ctr, Ill, 63-67. *Work:* Ga Council Arts & Humanities, Atlanta; DeKalb Community Col, Clarkston, Ga; R J Reynolds Tobacco Co, Winston-Salem, NC; Coca-Cola Int, Atlanta. *Exhib:* Hunter Ann, Hunter Mus Art, Chattanooga, Tenn, 77; Piedmont Show, Mint Mus, Charlotte, NC, 77; Artists in Ga, High Mus, Atlanta, 78; Southern Watercolor Soc, 76-79 & 81-83; Ala Watercolor Soc, 79-81 & 83; Ga Watercolor Soc, 79 & 81-83; Ky Watercolor Soc, 81 & 83; Art in Ga, Albany Mus, Ga, 81. *Awards:* Purchase Award, Olin Mills Corp, Hunter Mus, 77; Hans Hofman Award, Southern Watercolor Soc, 79; Award, Southern Watercolor Soc, 80. *Bibliog:* Pat Hetzler (auth), Betty Barnes Loehle, Art Voices Mag, 5-6/81. *Mem:* Artists Assocs Inc (pres 78 & 79); Atlanta Artists Club; Southern Watercolor Soc; Ala & Ky Watercolor Socs; Ga Watercolor Soc (bd dir, 80-84). *Media:* Mixed. *Dealer:* Artists Associates Gallery 3261 Roswell Rd NE Atlanta GA 30305. *Mailing Add:* c/o Artists Asn Gallery 3261 Roswell Rd NE Atlanta GA 30305

LOEHLE, RICHARD E
PAINTER, ILLUSTRATOR
b Atlanta, Ga, Mar 9, 23. *Study:* Atlanta Col Art, 40; Harris Sch Art, grad cert, 48; Evanston Art Ctr, Ill, 67. *Work:* High Mus Art; Montgomery Mus Art, Ala; Ala Watercolor Soc, Birmingham; Ga Coun Arts & Humanities; Chicago Artists Guild. *Exhib:* Southeastern Ctr Contemp Arts Nat, Winston-Salem, 72,74 & 76; Ga Artists Show, High Mus, 74 & 76; Southern Watercolor Soc, Columbus Mus, 78 & 82; Ga Watercolor Soc, Macon Mus, 82; Ky Watercolor Soc, Owensboro Mus, 83; Southern Watercolor Soc, Asheville Mus, NC, 83; and others. *Awards:* Purchase Prize, Dixie Ann, Montgomery Mus Art, 72; Best in Show, Atlanta Arts Festival, 73 & Southern Watercolor Soc, 80 & 83. *Bibliog:* Edith Coogler (auth), Prize-winning artist, Atlanta Constitution, 6/28/70; Richard Vanleek (auth), Art in Ashville, Ashville Citizen-Times, 6/72; S Coleman & C Anderson (auths), article, Southern Watercolor Soc Newslett, 83. *Media:* Oil, Acrylic; Watercolor. *Publ:* Coauth, Great Am Depression Book of Fun, Harper & Row, 81. *Mailing Add:* c/o Evelyn Lagerquist Gallery Art 3235 Paces Ferry Pl Atlanta GA 30305

LOEHR, MAX
MUSEUM CURATOR, EDUCATOR
b Chemnitz, Ger, Dec 4, 03; US citizen. *Study:* Univ Berlin, 33-34; Univ Munich, PhD, 36; Harvard Univ, Hon MA. *Pos:* Asst cur, Mus Volkerkunde, 36-40, cur, 50-51; dir, Sino-Ger Inst, Peking, 41-45; ed, Sinologische Arbeiten, Peking, 43-45; hon res assoc, Freer Gallery Art, 52-60; Far Eastern ed, Arts Orientalis, 54-60; cur Oriental art, Fogg Art Mus, Harvard Univ, 60-74, emer cur Oriental art, 78-; co-ed, Harvard J Asian Studies, formerly. *Teaching:* Assoc prof, Tsinghua Univ, Peking, 47-48; lectr Far Eastern art, Univ Munich, 50-51; prof, Univ Mich, 51-60; Abby Aldrich Rockefeller prof Oriental art, Harvard Univ, 60-78, emer prof Oriental art, 78- *Awards:* Guggenheim Found Grant, 57-58. *Mem:* Fel Am Acad Arts & Sci; Am Oriental Soc; Chinese Art Soc Am. *Res:* Chinese art and archaeol. *Publ:* Auth, Chinese Bronze Age Weapons, 56; auth, Relics of Ancient China, 65; auth, Chinese Landscape Woodcuts, 68; auth, Ritual Vessels of Bronze Age China, 68; auth, Ancient Chinese Jades, 75; also contribr to Artibus Asiae, Ars Orientalis, Oriental Art, J Asian Studies & others. *Mailing Add:* 14 Loring Rd Lexington MA 02173

LOERKE, WILLIAM CARL
HISTORIAN, ADMINISTRATOR
b Toledo, Ohio, Aug 13, 20. *Study:* Oberlin Col, AB, 42; Princeton Univ, MFA, 48; PhD(Danforth Teacher Fel), 57. *Teaching:* From instr to asst prof art hist, Brown Univ, 49-59; assoc prof, Bryn Mawr Col, 59-64; prof, Univ Pittsburgh, 64-71, chmn, Frick Dept Fine Arts, 64-68; prof Byzantine art, Dumbarton Oaks, Harvard Univ, 71-, dir, Ctr Byzantine Studies, 71-77; vis prof hist of archit, Cath Univ Am, 78- *Awards:* Fulbright Res Fel to Am Acad, Rome, 52-53; A K Porter Prize, Col Art Asn, 61. *Mem:* Col Art Asn; Medieval Acad; Soc Fels Am Acad, Rome; Ctr Advan Study Visual Arts, Nat Gallery (chmn, 79-80, mem bd adv, 79-82). *Res:* Early Christian and Byzantine art; Roman architecture; relation between art and history of ideas. *Publ:* Auth, Byzantine art, New Cath Encycl, 67; auth, The monumental miniature, In: Book Illumination in Byzantine Art, Princeton Univ Press, 75; auth, Doxa in Rome and Sinai, Gesta, Vol XX, No 1, 81; auth, Georges Chedanne and the Pantheon, Modulus, 82; auth, Real presence in early Christian art, In: Monasticism and the Arts, Syracuse Univ Press, 83. *Mailing Add:* 1021 Independence Ave SE Washington DC 20003

LOEW, MICHAEL
PAINTER, EDUCATOR
b New York, NY, May 8, 07. *Study:* Art Students League, 26-29, with Richard Lahey & Boardman Robinson; Acad Scandinave, Paris, France, 29, with Orthon Friesze; Hans Hofmann Sch Fine Arts, New York, 46-49; Atelier Leger, Paris, 50. *Work:* Albright-Knox Art Gallery; Whitney Mus Am Art; Philadelphia Mus Art; Sheldon Mem Mus, Lincoln, Nebr; Hirshhorn Mus & Sculpture Garden; and many others. *Comn:* Evolution of Textile Making (mural), Works Progress Admin, Charles E Hughes High Sch, New York, 33; mural (with Wilhelm DeKooning), Hall of Pharm, New York World's Fair, 39; murals, comn by US Treas Dept Sect Fine Arts for Post Off Bldgs, Amherst, Ohio, 41 & Belle Vernon, Pa, 42. *Exhib:* Whitney Mus of Am Art, New York, 61, 62, 75 & 77; Hans Hofmann & His Students, Mus of Mod Art Travelling Show, 63; Art Inst Chicago, 64; Selections from the Permanent Collection, Hirshhorn Mus, Washington, DC, 76-77; New Deal Art, Gallery Asn of NY State Travelling Exhib, 77; Works on Paper, Neuberger Mus, NY, 77; solo exhibs, Marilyn Pearl Gallery, New York, 77, 79, 81 & 82; Geometric Abstraction and Related Works, Newark Mus, 78-79; Queens Mus, 81; and many other group & one-man shows. *Pos:* Pres & secy, Artists Union, New York, 34-35; mem, Mayor LaGuardia's Art Comt of 100, 35-36. *Teaching:* Sr instr painting, Sch Visual Arts, 58-, co-chmn dept fine arts, 62-70; vis prof painting, Univ Calif, Berkeley, 60-61, vis lectr painting, 65-66; vis lectr painting, New York Studio Sch, 83- *Awards:* Ford Found Purchase Award, Art Inst Chicago Exhib, 64; Nat Endowment for the Arts grant, 76-77; Guggenheim Mem Found Fel, 79-80. *Bibliog:* Hilton Kramer (critic), New York Times, 11/11/77; Deborah Rosenthal (critic), Arts Mag, 11/77; Susan C Larsen (auth), A painter's geometry: The art of Michael Loew, Arts Mag, 11/79; and others. *Mem:* Am Abstract Artists; Fedn Mod Painters & Sculptors. *Media:* Multimedia. *Publ:* Auth, statement in Realities Novelles, Paris, 50; auth, statement in It Is, autumn 58; contribr, Josef Albers, impersonalization in perfect form, 56 & Academy, 59, Art News; auth, Artists and critics, a letter, Arts Mag, 10/62. *Dealer:* Marilyn Pearl Gallery 29 W 57th St New York NY 10019. *Mailing Add:* 280 Ninth Ave New York NY 10001

LOEWER, HENRY PETER
ILLUSTRATOR, WRITER
b Buffalo, NY, Feb 13, 34. *Study:* Albright Art Sch, Univ Buffalo, with Lawrence Calcagno & Anne Coffin Hanson, BFA, 58. *Work:* Hunt Inst for Botanical Doc, Carnegie-Mellon Univ, Pittsburgh, Pa; Catskill Art Soc, Hurleyville, NY. *Exhib:* Int Exhib of Botanical Drawings, Hunterdon Art Ctr, Clinton, NJ, 77; 4th Int Exhib of Botanical Art, Carnegie-Mellon Univ, Pittsburgh, Pa, 77-78; one-man show, Horticultural Soc of New York, 77. *Awards:* First Place, Garden Writers Am, 81. *Media:* Pen and Ink, Watercolor. *Publ:* Auth & illusr, Seeds and Cuttings, 75 & Growing and Decorating with Grasses, 77, Walker; illusr, Wildflower Perennials for Your Garden, Hawthorn, 76; auth & illusr, Evergreens, Walker, 81; auth & illusr, Peter Loewer's Garden Almanac, Perigee, 83. *Mailing Add:* PO Box 43 Cochecton Center NY 12727

LOGAN, DAVID GEORGE
METALSMITH, EDUCATOR
b Milwaukee, Wis, June 14, 37. *Study:* Univ Wis-Madison, BS, 63, with Arthur Vierthaler, MFA, 68; Univ Ill-Urbana, with Robert von Neumann, Jr, MA, 67. *Comn:* Art in Worship (slide series), Am Crafts Coun. *Exhib:* Michiana Crafts Competition, Lafayette, Ind, 72; 37th Ann Nat Crafts Competition, Cedar City, Utah, 78; Nat Invitational Exhib, Northern Mich Univ, 79; Nat Print & Small Sculpture Exhib, Copus Christi, 81 & 83; Marietta Crafts Nat, Ohio, 82; and others. *Teaching:* Art teacher, Oregon Pub Schs, Wis, 63-66; asst prof art, Mich State Univ, 68-79; vis artist metalsmithing, Northern Mich Univ, summer 71 & 74; assoc prof art, ETenn State Univ, 79- *Awards:* Jewelry Award, Westchester Art Soc, NY, 70; Assention Lutheran Church Award for Liturgical Jewelry, East Lansing, 73; Haas Found Award, Nat Print & Small Sculpture Exhib, 83. *Mem:* Mich Art Educ Asn (pres, 71-72, ed newsletter, 73-74); Nat Art Educ Asn; Am Crafts Coun; Soc NAm Goldsmiths; Tenn Art Educ Asn (bd mem, 81-). *Media:* Non-ferrous Metals, Glass. *Mailing Add:* 1601 Seward Dr Johnson City TN 37601

LOGAN, FREDERICK MANNING
EDUCATOR, WRITER
b Racine, Wis, July 18, 09. *Study:* Milwaukee State Teachers Col, BE, 32; Art Inst Chicago, 33; Columbia Univ Teachers Col, MA, 39; Northern Mich Univ,

LLD, 74. *Teaching:* Head div art educ, Milwaukee State Teachers Col, 43-46; prof art, Univ Wis-Madison, 46-79, emer prof art & art educ, 79-; vis lectr, Sch Art Educ, Birmingham, Eng, 64. *Awards:* Distinguished Serv Awards, Nat Gallery Art, 66 & Nat Art Educ Asn, 75; Fine Arts Achievement Award, Miami Univ, 75; Barkan Award, Nat Art Educ Asn, 76. *Mem:* Inst Study Art Educ; Nat Art Educ Asn; Wis Acad Sci, Arts & Lett; Int Soc Educ Art. *Res:* Aesthetics of the environment; history of American art education. *Publ:* Auth, Growth of Art in American Schools, 55; contrib, Report of Commission on Art Education, 65; ed, A Report for Urban America, Educ Aesthetic Awareness Environ, 66; ed, Geography and psychology of urban cultural centers, Arts & Soc, 67; auth, A challenge to art education, J Nat Art Educ, 70. *Mailing Add:* 2913 Waunona Way Madison WI 53713

LOGAN, GENE ADAMS
SCULPTOR, PAINTER

b Kickapoo, Kans, June 14, 22. *Study:* Southwest Mo State Univ, BS, 49; Univ Southern Calif, PhD, 60; Univ Ore, 65; Univ Kans, MFA, 67; also with Elden Tefft & Jan Zach. *Work:* El Camino Col Sculpture Garden, Torrance, Calif; included in over 300 pvt collections. *Comn:* Sculpture, Chase Nat Ins Co, Springfield, Mo, 66, Westmont Industs, Santa Fe Springs, Calif, 75 & City of La Mirada, Calif. *Exhib:* one-man shows, Ankrum Gallery, Los Angeles, 70-72, 75, 78 & 82; Pioneer Mus & Haggin Galleries, Stockton, Calif, 78; Zantman Art Galleries, Carmel, Calif, 79; Townhouse Gallery, New Orleans, 80; Crowther of Syon Lodge, London, Eng, 80. *Teaching:* Prof art anat, Southwest Mo State Univ, Springfield, 67-69; prof life drawing, Pasadena Sch Fine Arts, Calif, 70. *Awards:* First Award Sculpture, All-Calif Exhib, Laguna Beach, 60 & 61; Sculpture Gold Medal Award, Calif State Fair & Expos, Sacramento, 62. *Bibliog:* Michael Leopold (auth), Beverly Hills Mag, 4-5/78; Irene Lagorio (auth), Art & artists, Monterey Peninsula Herald, 2/9/79; Sharon Apfelbaum (auth), Art, Palm Springs Life Mag, 2/80; and others. *Media:* Welded Cor-Ten Steel, Bronze; Acrylic. *Dealer:* Ankrum Gallery 657 N La Cienega Los Angeles CA 90069; Zantman Art Galleries Sixth & Mission Carmel CA 93921. *Mailing Add:* 1551 W 13th St Suite 215 Upland CA 91786

LOLOMA, CHARLES
JEWELER, SILVERSMITH

b Hotevilla, Hopi Reservation, Ariz, Jan 7, 21. *Study:* Sch Am Craftsmen, Alfred Univ, NY, journeyman cert; Univ Ariz, Tucson. *Work:* Mus Northern Ariz, Flagstaff; Heard Mus, Phoenix, Ariz; Denver Art Mus, Colo; US Dept of Interior Gallery, Washington, DC; Mus Int Folk Art, Santa Fe, NMex. *Exhib:* Nat Ceramics Show, Syracuse, NY, 48; Dept of Interior Show, Washington, DC, 65; Scottsdale Nat Indian Arts Exhib, Ariz, 65-75; Objects USA, Johnson Wax Collection Contemp Crafts Traveling Exhib, 69; Loloma, Mus Contemp Crafts, New York, 74. *Teaching:* Instr pottery, Ariz State Univ, summer 54-58; instr pottery & jewelry, Rockefeller Found on Indian Youth, Tucson, Ariz, 59-61; dir dept plastic arts, Inst Am Indian Arts, Santa Fe, NMex, 61-65. *Awards:* Whitney Found Fel, 49-51; Award, Objects USA, Johnson Wax Found, 69. *Mem:* Ariz Comn Arts & Humanities; fel Am Craftsman Coun; Ariz Designer Craftsman. *Media:* Gold, Silver. *Publ:* Illusr, Hopi Hoya, 39; illusr, Indians of the Southwest, 42; contrib, Objects: USA, 69; contribr, Indian Voices, 70. *Mailing Add:* PO Box 185 Hotevilla AZ 86030

LOMAHAFTEWA, LINDA (LINDA JOYCE SLOCK)
PAINTER, INSTRUCTOR

b Phoenix, Ariz, July 3, 47. *Study:* Inst Am Indian Arts, Santa Fe, NMex; San Francisco Art Inst, BFA & MFA. *Work:* Ctr Arts Indian Am, Washington, DC. *Exhib:* Riverside Mus, New York, 65; Mus NMex, Santa Fe, 65-66; Ctr Arts Indian Am, 67-68; San Francisco Art Inst Spring Show, 70-71; Scottsdale Nat Indian Art Exhib, Ariz, 70-71. *Teaching:* Asst drawing, San Francisco Art Inst, 70; painting instr, Assoc Am Indian Arts, San Francisco, summer 72; asst prof Native Am studies, Calif State Col, Sonoma, 72-; lectr, Native Am Studies, Univ Calif, Berkeley, 74-76; instr painting, Inst Am Indian Arts, Santa Fe, NMex, 76- *Awards:* Hon Mention for Oil Painting, Mus NMex, 65; First Place in Graphic Arts Purchase Award, Ctr Arts Indian Am, 67; Third Place in Drawing, Scottsdale Nat Indian Art Exhib, 70. *Bibliog:* Lloyd E Oxendine (auth), 23 contemporary Indian artists, Art in Am, 7-8/72. *Publ:* Illusr, Indian Mag, 71; illusr, Weewish Tree, Am Indian Historian Press, 71; contribr, Art in Am, 72. *Mailing Add:* Rt 11 Box 20 SP 59 Santa Fe NM 87501

LOMBARD, ANNETTE
PAINTER, INSTRUCTOR

b New York, NY, Jan 25, 29. *Study:* Art Students League, with Louis Bouche, 65-66, Daniel Green, 76-78 & David Leffel, 80-82. *Work:* Mt Calvary Fire Baptized Holiness Church, Brooklyn, NY; Pa State Univ, Hazelton; Calvary Hosp; US Navy, Pentagon, Washington, DC; and pvt collection of Willis R Casey, dir athletics, NC State Univ, Raleigh. *Exhib:* Vet Soc Am, Customs House Mus, World Trade Ctr, New York, 79 & 81; Chung-Cheng Cult Ctr, St John's Univ, Long Island, NY, 80; solo pastel exhib, Salmagundi Club, New York, 80; Pastel Exhib, Pen & Brush, New York, 81 & 82; Pastel Soc Am, Lever House, New York, 82. *Collections Arranged:* Fifth & Sixth Ann Non-Member Exhibs (with catalog), Salmagundi Club, 82 & 83. *Teaching:* Free lance instr still life, anat & portraits, 71- *Awards:* Gold Medal, Grand Nat Exhib, Am Artists Prof League, 77; Salmagundi Club Award, 82; Pen & Brush Award, Knickerbocker Artists, 83. *Mem:* Salmagundi Club; Am Artists Prof League; Pastel Soc Am; Artists Fel; US Navy Art Coop & Liaison Comn. *Media:* Mixed. *Mailing Add:* 47 Fifth Ave New York NY 10003

LOMBARDO, JOSEF VINCENT
HISTORIAN, WRITER

b New York, NY, Nov 6, 08. *Study:* Cooper Union, dipl; NY Univ, BA & BFA, Columbia Univ, MA & PhD; Univ Florence, LittD; with Mario Salmi & Erwin Panofsky; Princeton Univ Am Fel, Accad Belle Arti, Florence; Villanova Univ, Hon LLD. *Teaching:* Prof fine arts, Queens Col, New York, 38-73, emer prof, 73- *Awards:* Columbia Univ Res Grant Spec Study of Michelangelo, 68; Res Grants, Dartmouth Foundation; Univ Medal, Univ Florence. *Mem:* Renaissance Soc Am; Soc Archit Historians; Metrop Mus Art. *Publ:* Auth, Chaim Gross, Sculptor, Dalton House, 49; coauth, Italian Culture in the Twentieth Century, Columbia Univ, 52; auth, Michelangelo: the Pieta and Other Masterpieces, Simon & Schuster, 65; auth, Michelangelo: New Discoveries, Dartmouth Found, 76; auth, Michelangelo: The Beginnings--New Findings and Critical Analyses, 84. *Mailing Add:* 100-11 70th Ave Forest Hills NY 11375

LO MEDICO, THOMAS GAETANO
SCULPTOR, DESIGNER

b New York, NY, July 11, 04. *Study:* Beaux Arts Inst Design. *Work:* New York Pub Schs, 60; Deerfield Acad, 61; Seal for City of Rye, NY, 64; Alice Freeman Palmer Medal for Hall of Fame, NY, 64; Jr High Sch, Staten Island, NY, 64. *Comn:* Family Group, Metrop Life Ins Co, New York World's Fair, 39-40. *Exhib:* Metrop Mus Art; Whitney Mus Am Art; Pa Acad Art; Nat Acad Design; and many others. *Teaching:* Instr, Nat Acad Design Sch Fine Arts, New York. *Awards:* J Stanford Saltus Medal, Am Numismatic Soc, 56; Mrs Louis Bennet Prize & Lindsey Morris Mem Prize, Nat Sculpture Soc. *Mem:* Fel Nat Sculpture Soc (coun); fel Am Numismatic Soc; Archit League New York; Allied Artists Am; Nat Acad Design. *Mailing Add:* 61 Main St Tappan NY 10983

LONDON, ALEXANDER
COLLECTOR, ILLUSTRATOR

b Paris, France; US citizen. *Study:* Lycee Mantaigne, Paris; Univ Pa, MS; Columbia Univ. *Pos:* Pres, Marstin Printing Corp, 69-; publ, Electronic & Appliance Co, 70-; exec dir, Imprimerie Centrale Commerciale, Paris, 70- *Awards:* Ten typographical & printing design awards, 56-79; spec awards for illus in Kalevala, 54 & design of Holocaust catalog, 79. *Collection:* French Impressionists; French Montparnasse; American contemporary. *Publ:* Illusr, Kalevala, 54; contribr & illusr var catalogs & art mag. *Mailing Add:* 350 Central Park W New York NY 10025

LONDON, BARBARA
CURATOR

b Glen Cove, NY, July 3, 46. *Study:* Hiram Col, Ohio, BA, 68; Inst of Fine Arts, New York Univ, MA, 72. *Collections Arranged:* Projects: Video I-XXXII, 74-81, Loren Madsen, 75, Peter Campus, 76, Nam June Paik, 77, Bookworks, 77 (Sachs Gallery), Projects: Shigeko Kubota, 78, Video Viewpoints, 78-80, Laurie Anderson, 78, Donald Lipski, 79, Video from Tokyo to Fukui and Kyoto (auth, catalog), 79 & Sound Art, 79, Mus Mod Art, New York. *Pos:* Asst int prog, Mus Mod Art, New York, 71-73, curatorial asst dept of prints & illus bks, 73-77, cur video prog, 77- *Publ:* Auth, Video art in USA, Video, Mus d'Art Mod, Geneva, 77; auth, Video at the Museum of Modern Art, The New Television: A Public/Private Art, Mass Inst Technol Press, 77; auth, Independent video: A report for the Rockefeller Foundation and the Museum of Modern Art, Mus Mod Art, 78; Independent video: The first fifteen years & A chronology of video activity in the United States: 1965-1980, 9/80, Artforum; Video in the land that practically invented it, Art News, 9/81. *Mailing Add:* c/o Mus of Mod Art 11 W 53rd St New York NY 10019

LONDON, ELCA
DEALER

b St John, NB, Can, July 11, 30. *Study:* Dalhousie Univ, Halifax, NS, BA; McGill Univ, Montreal, Que, MS. *Pos:* Dir, Elca London Gallery, 61- *Mem:* Prof Art Dealers Asn of Can. *Specialty:* Contemporary Canadian art; separate Eskimo Gallery. *Mailing Add:* 1616 Sherbroome St West Montreal PQ H3H 1C9 Canada

LONDON, PETER
PAINTER, EDUCATOR

b New York, NY, June 27, 39. *Study:* Queens Col, BA, 61; Columbia Univ, MFA, 62; EdD, 68. *Work:* Columbia Univ; Concordia Univ; Queens Col. *Comn:* Stainless steel sculpture, John Bowne High Sch, New York, 69. *Pos:* Pres, Pub Arts Coun, Mass, 75-79; post doctoral fel, Lesley Col, Cambridge, Mass; art critic, New Bedford Mag. *Teaching:* Asst prof art & art educ, Concordia Univ, 67-71; prof art & art educ, Southeastern Mass Univ, 71- *Awards:* Traveling Fel to Israel, 83-84. *Mem:* Nat Art Educ Asn; Int Soc for Educ through Art; Int Art Educ Asn. *Media:* Charcoal, Pastel. *Publ:* Auth, Taming of the American Imagination, Nat Art Educ Asn J, 74; auth, Towards a New Philosophy of Art Education, Art for the Primary Level, 74; auth, Trust and Education, Southeastern Mass Union J, 75; Alternative Careers in Art, Careers in Art, 79. *Dealer:* Galarie Don Steward Sherbrook St W Montreal PQ Can. *Mailing Add:* 69 Green St Fairhaven MA 02719

LONEY, DORIS HOWARD
PAINTER, INSTRUCTOR

b Everett, Wash, Jan 24, 02. *Study:* Univ Wash, BA; Art Students League, with Robert Brackman & Yasuo Kuniyoshi; Farnsworth Sch Art; Scripps Grad Art Sch, with Henry McFee & Millard Sheets; watercolor with Dong Kingman. *Comn:* Portraits, three pres, Univ Wis-Superior, bd dirs, First Nat Bank, Superior, pres, Univ Ariz, Dr & Mrs Richard Harvill, Columbia Univ,

Dr Robert Terry; plus other outstanding persons. *Exhib:* One-man show, Rosequist Gallery, Tucson, 56 & 73; two-man show, Fine Arts Gallery, Univ Ariz, 60; three-man show, Tucson Art Ctr, 62; Nat League Am Pen Women Nat Biennial, 62, 64 & 70; Tucson Festival Six State Show, 62 & 70; and others. *Awards:* First for Figure Painting, Seattle Art Mus, 50; First Prize for Papago Today (portrait), Nat Biennial, Nat League Am Pen Women, 70; Third Prize, Nat League Am Pen Women, Flagstaff, Ariz, 77; and others. *Mem:* Life mem Art Students League; Nat League Am Pen Women; Tucson Palette & Brush. *Dealer:* Portraits Inc 41 E 57th St New York NY 10022. *Mailing Add:* 2727 E Elm St Tucson AZ 85716

LONG, FRANK WEATHERS
SCULPTOR, JEWELER
b Knoxville, Tenn, May 7, 06. *Study:* Art Inst Chicago, 25-27; Pa Acad Fine Art, 27-28; Acad Julien, Paris, 28-29. *Work:* Nat Collection, Smithsonian Inst, Washington, DC; Int Bus Machines Corp, New York; Berea Col, Ky; Univ NMex. *Comn:* One panel, Davidson Col, Libr, 35; one panel, US Post Office, Drumright, Okla, 36, one panel, US Post Office, Berea, Ky, 38, one panel, US Post Office, Morehead, Ky, 39 & one panel, US Post Office, Crawfordsville, Ind, 42, Treas Dept, Fed Govt. *Exhib:* Media 1966, Walnut Creek Mus, Calif, 66; Hemisfair Preview Exhib, San Antonio, Tex, 67; Nat Crafts Exhib, Univ NMex Gallery, 68; Jewelry Invitational Exhib, NMex Western Univ, 72; Crafts VII Exhib, 77 & One Space, Three Visions, 79, Mus of Albuquerque; and others. *Pos:* Dir, Alaska Off of Indian Arts & Crafts Bd, Juneau, 51-57; field rep, SW Off of Indian Arts & Crafts Bd, Gallup, NMex, 57-59, Albuquerque, 62-69. *Teaching:* Instr lapidary, Univ NMex. *Awards:* First Prize, NMex State Fair, 63, 65 & 67; First Prize, Southwest Biennial, 63; First Prize, NMex Crafts Biennial, 64 & 66. *Mem:* Albuquerque Chap NMex Designer-Craftsmen (pres, 69). *Media:* Gem Material; Metal. *Publ:* Auth & illusr, Herakles, The 12 Labors, Black Archer Press, 31; auth & illusr, The Creative Lapidary, 77 & Lapidary Carving, 82, Van Nostrand Reinhold. *Dealer:* Mariposa Gallery 113 Romero St NW Albuquerque NM 87104; Sunrise Shop La Fonda Hotel Santa Fe NM 87501. *Mailing Add:* 1836 Florida NE Albuquerque NM 87110

LONG, HUBERT
SCULPTOR
b Sydney, Australia, Feb 2, 07; US citizen. *Study:* Newark Sch Fine & Indust Art, NJ, 10 yrs. *Work:* Guild Hall Mus Collection, East Hampton, NY; Phoenix Art Mus, Ariz; pvt collection of Mr Samuel Miller; Otto Spaeth Collection; and many other pub & pvt collections. *Comn:* Cyclops, comn by Hugh Horner, Scottsdale, Ariz, 74. *Exhib:* One-man shows, Andrew Crispo Gallery, New York, 74 & 76 & Guild Hall, East Hampton, NY, 76; Painting & Sculpture Today, Indianapolis Mus & Taft Mus, Cincinnati, 74; Tower Gallery, Southampton, NY, 77; plus others. *Pos:* Art dir, Reynolds Corp, New York, until 39. *Awards:* First Prize, Membership Exhib, Guild Hall, East Hampton, 60. *Bibliog:* M L D'Otrnge Mastai (auth), Intellect & emotion in contemporary sculpture, Art Voices, 10/63. *Media:* Wood. *Dealer:* Andrew Crispo Gallery 41 E 57th St New York NY 10022. *Mailing Add:* Box 166 55 The Circle East Hampton NY 11937

LONG, MEREDITH J
DEALER
b Joplin, Mo, Sept 14, 28. *Study:* Univ Tex, BA, 50, Law Sch, 50-51, 53-54. *Pos:* Munic arts comnr, Houston; pres, Meredith Long & Co, Houston, 57- *Mem:* JFK Ctr Performing Arts (pres, adv bd); Contemp Arts Mus, Houston (bd trustees); Mus Fine Arts, Houston (bd trustees); Alley Theatre, Houston (mem bd); Houston Ballet Found (mem bd); and others. *Specialty:* 19th and 20th century American art. *Publ:* Ed, Americans at Home and Abroad Catalogue, 71; ed, Tradition and Innovation--American Paintings 1860-1870, 74; ed, Americans at work and play, 80. *Mailing Add:* 2323 San Felipe Houston TX 77019

LONG, ROSE-CAROL WASHTON
HISTORIAN, WRITER
b New London, Conn, Mar 1, 38. *Study:* Wellesley Col, BA, 59; Yale Univ, MA(hist art), 62, PhD(hist art), 68. *Collections Arranged:* Twentieth Century Prints, Godwin-Ternbach Mus, 83. *Teaching:* Lectr, Queens Col & Grad Ctr, City Univ New York, 67-69, asst prof, 69-78, assoc prof, 79-83, prof European art, 84- *Awards:* Nat Endowment Humanities Fel, 72-73; Am Coun Learned Soc Grant, 72-73 & 82-83; Guggenheim Fel, 83-84. *Mem:* Col Art Asn; Am Fedn Arts. *Res:* Pioneers of 20th century abstract painting; Kandinsky; German Expressionism. *Publ:* Auth, Kandinsky and abstraction: The role of the hidden image, Artforum, 6/72; auth, Kandinsky, The Development of an Abstract Style, Clarendon Press, 80; coauth, The Life of Vasilii Kandinsky in Russian Art: A Study of On the Spiritual in Art, Oriental Res Partners, 80; auth, Kandinsky's vision of utopia as a garden of love, Art J, spring 83; auth, Sources and Documents of German Expressionism, G K Hall (in prep). *Mailing Add:* 76 MacDougal St New York NY 10012

LONG, SCOTT
CARTOONIST
b Evanston, Ill, Feb 24, 17. *Study:* Harvard Univ, AB, 39. *Pos:* Reporter & cartoonist, Zanesville News, Ohio, 39; ed cartoonist, St Paul Pioneer Press, 41 & Minneapolis Tribune, 43-80; retired. *Awards:* Page One Awards, 50-54; Headliner Award, 54; Int Salon Cartoons Award, Montreal, 75. *Mem:* Asn Am Ed Cartoonists (pres, 62); Minneapolis Skylight Club; Minneapolis Press Club. *Publ:* Auth, Please Turn to Page Six, 67; auth, Hey! Hey! LBJ!, Sorenson Printing, 69. *Mailing Add:* 4501 Dupont Ave S Minneapolis MN 55409

LONG, WALTER KINSCELLA
MUSEUM DIRECTOR, PAINTER
b Auburn, NY, Feb 2, 04. *Study:* Syracuse Univ, BFA & MFA; also with Gutzon Borglum & Charles Hawthorne. *Work:* Syracuse Univ Collection Fine Arts; Univ Fla; Lansing Cent Sch; Shotwell Park, Skaneateles, NY. *Comn:* Church murals; portraits for pvt comns; City of Auburn Civic Award Medal; Syracuse Univ Sch Journalism. *Exhib:* Syracuse Mus Fine Arts; Rochester Mem Art Gallery; New York City Galleries. *Collections Arranged:* Homespun Art; Shoes Thru the Ages; Cayuga County Inventions; Helen Hayes Memorabilia; and others. *Pos:* Ed, Archaeol Soc Cent NY Bulletin, formerly; dir Cayuga Mus Hist & Art, currently. *Teaching:* Instr basic art & art appreciation, Auburn Community Col. *Awards:* Mus Asn Fel, Rochester Mus Arts & Sci; Citizen of the Year, 63; Honor Teacher of the Year, 64; and others. *Mem:* Fel Royal Soc Arts; fel Int Inst Arts & Lett; Nat Acad TV Arts & Sci; Int Platform Asn; and others. *Mailing Add:* Cayuga Mus of Hist & Art 203 Genesee St Auburn NY 13021

LONGAKER, JON DASU
EDUCATOR, WRITER
b Davos, Switz, Jan 5, 20; US citizen. *Study:* Univ Pa, BA(fine arts), 41; Barnes Found, Merion, Pa, 46-47; Cinquantenaire Mus, Brussels, Belg Am Educ Found, summer 51; Columbia Univ, 47-52. *Pos:* Art critic, Richmond Times-Dispatch, Va, 56-64, drama critic, 65-; columnist on arts, Commonwealth Mag, Richmond, 67-; mem, State Art Comn, Richmond, 70-74. *Teaching:* Instr art appreciation, Barnes Found, Merion, Pa, 50-51; prof art hist, Randolph-Macon Col, Ashland, Va, 53-; prof art hist, Inst Am Univs, Aix-en-Provence, France, 64-65. *Publ:* Auth, Painting in the South--a Double Portrait, Inst Southern Cult, Longwood Col, 61; auth, Strive and succeed, Arts in Va, 70; auth, Art, Style and History: A Selective History of Art, Scott, Foresman, 70. *Mailing Add:* 133 Beverly Rd Ashland VA 23005

LONGLEY, BERNIQUE
PAINTER, SCULPTOR
b Moline, Ill. *Study:* Art Inst Chicago, grad(Byron Lathrop traveling fel), 45; Inst de Allende, San Miguel de Allende, Mex, 71; Santa Fe Sch Arts & Crafts, 75. *Work:* Mus NMex, Santa Fe; Dallas Mus. *Comn:* Murals, comn by Alexander Girard, Santa Fe, 59; murals, La Fonda Del Sol, NY, 60. *Exhib:* Int Watercolor Show, Art Inst Chicago, 48; NMex Mus Fine Arts Invitational Show, 68; Kermezaar Festival, El Paso, Tex, 75; Santa Fe Festival Arts, 77-81; Margaret Jamison Presents, 79-80; one-woman show, Gov Gallery, NMex State Capital; retrospective, Santa Fe East Gallery, NMex, 82. *Awards:* Honorable Mention, Art Inst Chicago, 48; Honorable Mention, Denver Mus Art Regional Show Sculpture, 48; Purchase Prize, Mus NMex, 53, Honorable Mention, 65. *Mem:* Int Liaison Network Women Artists; Artists Equity Asn; Advocates for Arts. *Media:* Oil, Acrylic. *Publ:* Auth, Suite of Lithographs, Tamarind Inst, 72. *Mailing Add:* 427 Camino del Monte Sol Santa Fe NM 87501

LONGMAN, LESTER DUNCAN
HISTORIAN, EDUCATOR
b Harrison, Ohio, Aug 27, 05. *Study:* Oberlin Col, AB & MA; Princeton Univ, MFA(Carnegie Fel), 30, PhD(Am Coun Learned Soc Fel), 34; Iowa Wesleyan Col, LHD, 55; Simpson Col, Hon DFA, 61. *Pos:* Ed, Parnassus, 40 & 41. *Teaching:* Prof hist art, McMaster Univ, 33-36; prof art & head dept, Univ Iowa, 36-58; prof art, Univ Calif, Los Angeles, 58-, chmn dept, 58-63. *Awards:* Fulbright Fel, 52-53. *Mem:* Midwestern Col Art Conf (pres, 39, 49 & 58); Am Soc Aesthetics (pres, 53-55); Col Art Asn Am (mem bd dirs, 40-42). *Mailing Add:* 718 Enchanted Way Pacific Palisades CA 90272

LONGSTAFFE, JOHN RONALD
COLLECTOR
b Toronto, Ont, Apr 6, 34. *Pos:* Pres, Vancouver Art Gallery, 66-68; vchmn, Nat Mus Can, 68-69, dir, 75-79. *Awards:* Award of Merit, Canadian Mus Asn, 78. *Interests:* Aid to Vancouver Art Gallery's and National Gallery of Canada's Permanent Collection. *Collection:* Contemporary Canadian art; contemporary international graphics. *Mailing Add:* 4460 West Second Vancouver BC V6R 1K6 Canada

LONGSTREET, STEPHEN
PAINTER, HISTORIAN
b New York, NY, Apr 17, 07. *Study:* New York Sch Fine & Appl Art, 27; also with Matisse & Bonnard & sketching with Pascin, Grosz, Arp & Feitelson, Paris, 27-29 & 33-38. *Work:* San Francisco Mus; Yale Univ; Jazz Mus New Orleans; Los Angeles Art Asn; Mus Mod Art; Memphis Music Mus, Univ Wis; plus others. *Exhib:* Nu-World Shows, Balbac Gallery, Paris, 40-60; San Francisco Mus Show, 65; Santa Barbara Mus Show, 67; Southern Calif Ann, 70; Paideia Galleries, Los Angeles, 71; one-man shows, Brooks Mem Mus, Memphis, Tenn, 78 & Wolf Galleries, Munich, Ger, 80; plus others. *Pos:* Ed-in-chief, The Great Draftsmen (30 vols), 65-75; bd dir, Viewpoints Inst. *Teaching:* Lectr, Los Angeles Art Asn, 50-; prof art, Viewpoints Inst, 65-; lectr mod art, Univ Calif, Los Angeles, 69; lectr, Los Angeles Co Mus; instr at large, Univ Southern Calif, 73-78. *Awards:* Winader Found First Prize for Watercolor, 30; First Prize for Oils, Am Art Festival, 46; Second Prize for Drawings, Midwest Antiwar Soc, 69. *Mem:* Los Angeles Art Asn (pres, 72-75); Writers Guild Film Soc; co-founder Los Angeles Co Mus Art Graphic Soc; Paris-Am Arts. *Media:* Oil, Collage. *Collection:* Daumier prints; Rowlandson; Goya; Japanese prints. *Publ:* Auth, A Treasury of the World's Great Prints, 62 & rev ed, 78; auth, Burning Man (Picasso), 58; auth, Yoshiwara, 70; auth & illusr, We All Went to Paris, 72; auth, Geisha, Pocket Bks, rev ed, 77. *Mailing Add:* 1133 Miradero Rd Beverly Hills CA 90210

LONIDIER, FRED SPENCER
INSTRUCTOR, PHOTOGRAPHER
b Lakeview, Ore, Feb 19, 42. *Study:* San Francisco State Col, BA(sociol), 66; Univ Calif, San Diego, MFA; also with David Antin. *Work:* Long Beach Mus Art, Calif; Faith Flam, Studio City, Calif; Oakland Mus, Calif; Los Angeles Video Libr, Calif; Southern Calif Libr Social Studies & Research. *Exhib:* One-man shows, I Sent You a Rose, Ha, Ha, Oakland Mus, Calif, 73-74, Photo Text Works: Toward a New Social Realism, and/or Gallery, Seattle, 75, Whitney Mus Am Art, New York, 77, Alberta Col of Art Gallery, Calgary, 78 & Real Art Ways, Hartford, Conn, 79; San Francisco Art Inst, Calif, 77; Mus Folkwang, Essen, W Germany, 80-81; Orange Co Ctr Contemp Art, Calif, 81; S Wiener Int Beinnale, Austria, 81. *Teaching:* Lectr photog, Univ Calif, San Diego, 72-75, asst prof, 75- *Awards:* Regents Fel, Regents of the Univ Calif, 71-72. *Bibliog:* William Spurlock (auth), Dialogue/Discourse/Research, Santa Barbara Mus, 79; William Spurlock, Nat Arts Guide, 3-4/80; Hal Fischer, Artweek, 5/17/80. *Mem:* Los Angeles Inst Contemp Art; Col Art Asn Am. *Media:* Photo Prints, Slides & Video. *Publ:* Contribr, David Antin's eight artists, Studio Int, Vol 170, 70; contribr, Autobiography/history, Los Angeles Inst Contemp Art J, No 7, 75. *Mailing Add:* Dept Art Univ Calif PO Box 109 La Jolla CA 92037

LOONEY, NORMAN
PAINTER, EDUCATOR
b Seattle, Wash, Oct 31, 42. *Study:* East Los Angeles Col, Calif, AA; Calif State Univ, Long Beach, MFA(drawing & painting). *Comn:* Security Pacific Nat Bank, Calif; Calif State Univ, Long Beach; Environetics Int, Los Angeles; Innovax Methods Group, Los Angeles; Naples Prof Ctr, Long Beach. *Exhib:* Los Angeles Co Mus Art; NC Mus Art, Raleigh; Birmingham Mus Fine Art, Alabama; Montgomery Mus Art, Alabama; Hunter Mus Art, Tenn; 11th Dulin Nat Print & Drawing Competition, Knoxville, Tenn, 77; 11th Ann Nat Drawing & Small Sculpture Show, Corpus Christi, Tex, 77; 19th Ann Nat Exhib of Prints & Drawings, Okla Art Ctr, Oklahoma City, 77; The Texas Thirty, Nave Mus, Victoria, Tex, 77; and others. *Pos:* Artist in resident, City Long Beach, Calif, 79-80. *Teaching:* Instr two demensional art, univs in southern Calif & southwest Tex. *Awards:* Trask Found Fel, Yaddo, NY, 77; Project Grant, Robinson Gallery, Houston, 78; Ossabow Island Project Grant, Ga, 79. *Mem:* Col Art Asn. *Mailing Add:* 311 E Ocean Blvd Long Beach CA 90802

LOONEY, ROBERT FAIN
CURATOR, LIBRARIAN
b Rocky Mount, NC, July 20, 25. *Study:* Univ NC, BA, 53, MA, 55, MS, 60. *Pos:* Librn, Art Dept, Free Libr Philadelphia, 61-64, cur, Print Collection, 64- *Mem:* Mus Arts & Humanities Div & Picture Div, Spec Libr Asn (chmn, 72-73); Philadelphia Print Club (bd dirs, 76-). *Res:* Early American prints; modern prints. *Publ:* Auth, Old Philadelphia in Early Photographs, Dover, 76; ed, Philadelphia Printmaking: Prints Before 1860, Free Libr Philadelphia, 76. *Mailing Add:* 427 N 20th St Philadelphia PA 19130

LOPEZ, BEA (BEATRIZ LOPEZ-MEAD)
DESIGNER, FIBER ARTIST
b San Diego, Calif, June 22, 53. *Study:* Calif Col Arts & Crafts, BFA, 76. *Work:* San Jose Mus, Calif. *Exhib:* De Young Mem Mus, San Francisco, 76; Fifth Sun, Univ Art Mus, Berkeley, 77; one-woman show, San Jose Mus, Calif, 79; San Francisco Mus Mod Art, 79. *Pos:* Art consult, Calif Arts Coun, 77-78. *Awards:* Grant, Calif Arts Coun, 76. *Mem:* Artists Equity Asn; World Print Coun. *Media:* Cotton Fiber, Paint. *Publ:* Contribr, The Jaspe Process, Shuttle, Spindle & Dye Pot, 77; contribr, Fifth Son Artist, San Francisco Chronicle, 77. *Mailing Add:* PO Box 532 Forest Knolls CA 94933

LOPEZ, MICHAEL JOHN
CERAMIST
b Los Angeles, Calif, Oct 19, 37. *Study:* Los Angeles City Col, 56-60; Calif Col Arts & Crafts, BFA & MFA, 63. *Work:* Oakland Mus, Calif; E B Crocker Art Gallery, Sacramento, Calif. *Comn:* Leslie Ceramics Supply Co, Berkeley, Calif. *Exhib:* 18th Nat Decorative Arts & Ceramics Exhib, Wichita Art Asn, Kans, 64; 23rd & 24th Ceramic Nat, Everson Mus Art, Syracuse, NY, 64 & 65 & traveling show, 65; Media 72, a Western State Craft Competition, Civic Arts Gallery, Walnut Creek, Calif, 72; Calif Design 76, Pac Design Ctr, Los Angeles, 76. *Teaching:* Instr ceramics, Calif Col Arts & Crafts, 65-70; instr ceramics, Diablo Valley Col, 70- *Awards:* Am Craftsmen Coun Award of Merit, 2nd Biennial Calif Craftsman Exhib, Oakland Mus, 63; First Place Ceramics, Chicago Festival Art, 63; Asn San Francisco Potters Award, 71. *Bibliog:* Jacinto Quirarte (auth), Mexican American Artists, Univ Tex, 73. *Mem:* Asn San Francisco Potters. *Media:* Clay. *Mailing Add:* 1031 Walker Ave Oakland CA 94610

LOPEZ, RHODA LE BLANC
SCULPTOR, EDUCATOR
b Detroit, Mich, Mar 16, 12. *Study:* Detroit Art Acad, Wayne State Univ; Cranbrook Acad Art, with Maija Crotell; Scripps Col. *Work:* Detroit Inst Arts; Univ Wis-Madison; Scripps Col, Claremont, Calif; Juvenile Ct, City San Diego. *Comn:* Many banks & pvt & pub collections; baptismal fountain, University City Lutheran Church, 70; wall fountain, Med Ctr, Dr Larry Fine, 71; mem wall (9ft x 40ft), Unitarian Church, San Diego, 77-78; two 12ft x 7-1/2ft panels, Juv Ct Bldg, San Diego, 78; and others. *Exhib:* Syracuse Nat, 49-55; Mich Craftsmen Ann, Detroit, 49-58; five shows, Scripps Invitational, 53-66; Allied Craftsmen Ann, San Diego, 60-76; Design 8-11, Pasadena, 65, 68 & 71; and many maj shows. *Pos:* Med artist, Univ Mich Med Sch, 53-59; founder & dir, Clay Dimensions, San Diego, 69- *Teaching:* Instr ceramics, Ann Arbor Potters Guild, Mich, 50-59, La Jolla Mus Art Ctr, Calif, 60-65 &

Univ Calif Exten, San Diego, 65-78; lectr, Pac Arts Conf, 67; lectr series, San Diego Co Pub Schs, 72. *Bibliog:* Rhoda Le Blanc Lopez, Designers West, 71; Valerie Hatch (auth), article in Art West, 71; Marie Stanton (auth), A visit into Rhoda Lopez world of clay, San Diego Union, 1/72; and others. *Mem:* African Arts Soc. *Media:* Clay. *Mailing Add:* 1020 Pacific Beach Dr San Diego CA 92109

LOPEZ-REY, JOSE
HISTORIAN, EDUCATOR
b Madrid, Spain; US citizen. *Study:* Inst Cardinal Cisneros, Madrid, BA, 25; Univ Madrid, Licenciado Filosofia y Letras, 29, Dr Filosofia y Letras, 35; Southern Methodist Univ, Dr Humane Lett, 79. *Pos:* Tech adv fine arts, Ministry Educ, Madrid, 33-39; vpres, Int Found Art Res, New York, 70-74. *Teaching:* Asst prof hist art, Univ Madrid, 32-39; lectr, Smith Col, 42-45; from lectr to prof, Inst Fine Arts, NY Univ, 44-73, prof emer, 73-; vis prof, Scuola Normale Superiore, Pisa, Italy, 65. *Awards:* Guggenheim Fels, 47-48, 60-61 & 67-68. *Res:* History of Spanish and modern art. *Publ:* Auth, Goya's Caprichos: Beauty, Reason and Caricature, Princeton Univ Press, 53; auth, A Cycle of Goya's Drawings: The Expression of Truth and Liberty, 56 & Velazquez: A Catalogue Raisonne of his Oeuvre, 63, Faber & Faber, London; auth, Velazquez: The Artist as a Maker, Bibliot Arts, Paris, 79, Fr transl, 81. *Mailing Add:* Callejon de la Sierra 3 Santo Domingo Algete Madrid Spain

LOPINA, LOUISE CAROL
PAINTER
b Chicago, Ill, Nov 24, 36. *Study:* Chicago Art Inst; Purdue Univ, BS; study with Lawrence Harris & Don Dennis. *Work:* Miami Deposit Bank; Cincinnati Club. *Exhib:* Texas Relays Western & Wildlife Art, 81; Cincinnati Club, 81; Nature Interpreted, 82 & Wonderous Wildlife, 83, Cincinnati Mus Natural Hist; Soc Animal Artists Show, Denver Mus Natural Hist, 82; and others. *Teaching:* Instr drawing & painting, USAF Acad-Officer's Wives Club, 72-75. *Awards:* Best in Show, Nat Nature Art Exhib, 78, 79 & 82; and others. *Bibliog:* Al Rosen & Faith Every, dirs, Louise Lopinas Art on the Wild Side (feature program), television, 2/78; article, A sampling of assorted artists, Dayton Mag, 5-6/81. *Mem:* Nat Audubon Soc; Nature Conservancy; Soc of Animal Artists. *Media:* Oil, Watercolor. *Publ:* Illusr, A Cook's Tour of the Airforce Academy Vol II, AFA Officer's Wives Club, 72; illusr, The Complete Old English Sheepdog, Howell Book House, 76; illusr, Reptiles and Amphibians of Aullwood & Wild Flowers of Aullwood, Nat Audubon, 78; illusr, View form the top snow leopards, Color Print, 82. *Mailing Add:* 3132 Southfield Dr Village of Beavercreek Xenia OH 45385

LORAN, ERLE
PAINTER, WRITER
b Minneapolis, Minn, Oct 3, 05. *Study:* Univ Minn, 22-23; Minneapolis Sch Art, grad, 26; Chaloner Found Scholar Study Europe, 26-30; also with Hans Hofmann, New York, 54; Minneapolis Sch Art & Design, Hon MFA. *Work:* Univ Art Mus, Univ Calif, Berkeley; Smithsonian Inst, Washington, DC; San Francisco Mus Art; Denver Art Mus; and others. *Exhib:* Sixteen American Cities, Mus Mod Art, New York, 33; Five shows, Contemporary American Painting, Whitney Mus Am Art, New York, 37-52; American Painting & Sculpture, 38 & Int Exhibs Watercolors, 39-46, Art Inst Chicago; Carnegie Inst, Pittsburgh, 41; six shows, Krannert Art Mus, Univ Ill, 49-69; Recent Watercolors, Oakland Mus, 81. *Teaching:* Prof art, Univ Calif, Berkeley, 36-81, chmn dept art, 52-56, emer prof art, 81- *Awards:* Bronze Medal, Pepsi-Cola Nat, New York, 48; Artists' Coun Prize, San Francisco Mus Art, 56; Purchase Prize, Krannert Art Mus, 65; and others. *Bibliog:* Forbes Watson (auth), American Painting Today, Am Fedn Arts, 39; Allen S Weller (auth), Contemporary American Painting, Univ Ill, 49-69; Nathaniel Pousette-Dart (auth), American Painting Today, Hastings House, 56. *Media:* Acrylic, Oil. *Publ:* Auth, Cezanne, Les Peintres Celebres, Ed Art Lucien Mazenod, Geneva & Paris, 48; auth, Trial by juries, Art News, 12/52; auth, Cezanne in 1952, Art Inst Chicago Quart, 2/52; auth, Cezanne and Lichtenstein: Problems of transformation, Artforum, 9/63. *Mailing Add:* 10 Kenilworth Ct Berkeley CA 94707

LORBER, D MARTIN H B
CONSULTANT
b Macon, Ga, July 22, 43. *Study:* Univ NC, BA, 65. *Mem:* Nippon Bijutsu Token Hozon Kyokai; Oriental Ceramic Soc; Japan Soc, New York; Asia Soc, New York; Pres Coun. *Interests:* Korean, Sung ceramics; Impressionist & Post-Impressionist paintings. *Publ:* Auth, The Eugene W Kettering Collection of Japanese Metalwork, Dayton Art Inst, 75; auth, Japanese sword fittings, 5/77 & auth, Japanese Buddhist paintings, 7/78, Arts of Asia. *Mailing Add:* 71 E 71st St New York NY 10021

LORBER, RICHARD
CRITIC, ADMINISTRATOR
b New York, NY, Dec 9, 46. *Study:* Columbia Col, with Meyer Schapiro & Lionel Trilling, BA(lit & art hist), 67; Columbia Univ, with Meyer Schapiro & Linda Nochlin, MA(art hist), 70, EdD(art), 77. *Pos:* Ed, Dance Scope Mag, 74-; contrib ed, Arts Mag, 75-; community liaison, Mus of Mod Art, 76-77; critic & contribr, Artforum, Portfolio, 77-; adv panelist, NY State Coun on Arts, 78-; proj dir, Nat Video Clearinghouse, 79-; consult, Electronic Arts Intermix, 81; pres, Fox/Lorber Assoc Inc, 81- *Teaching:* Instr art hist, Parsons Sch of Design, 74-77; asst prof art & art educ, Grad Sch of Educ, NY Univ, 77-79. *Mem:* Dance Critics Asn. *Publ:* Coauth, The Gap, McGraw-Hill, 68; auth, articles in Arts in Soc & Filmmakers Newsletter, 77; contribr, Video Art, Dutton, 78; article, Videodance, Millenium Film J, 12/81. *Mailing Add:* 60 Gramercy Park N New York NY 10010

LORBER, STEPHEN NEIL
PAINTER, PRINTMAKER
b New York, NY, Aug 30, 43. *Study:* Pratt Inst, BFA; Brooklyn Col, MFA; Yale Univ, Stoekel fel, 64. *Work:* Okla Art Ctr, Oklahoma City; Western NMex Univ, Silver City; Roswell Mus & Art Ctr, NMex; Am Tel & Tel Co; Chase Manhatten Bank, New York; and others. *Exhib:* Albright-Knox Gallery, Buffalo, NY; Weatherspoon Art Gallery, Univ NC, Greensboro; Things Seen, Univ Nebr, Mulvane Art Ctr, 78; Museum Choice, Loch-Haven Art Ctr, Orlando, Fla, 78; Tyler Sch Art, Temple Univ, 78; Williams Proctor Mus, Utica, NY, 82; and others. *Awards:* Artist in Residence Grant, Roswell Mus & Art Ctr, NMex; Yaddo Fel, 71 & 75; Nat Endowment Arts Fel, 76-77. *Bibliog:* Hilton Kramer (auth), article, New York Times, 4/22/77; Allen Ellenzweig (auth), article, Arts Mag, 9/77. *Mailing Add:* RD 3 Box 198 Greenwich NY 12834

LORCINI, GINO
SCULPTOR, MURALIST
b Plymouth, Eng, July 7, 23; Can citizen. *Study:* Montreal Mus Sch Art. *Work:* Nat Gallery Can, Ottawa; Mus Art Contemporain, Montreal; Chase Manhattan Bank, New York; Art Gallery Ont, Toronto; Matsushita Corp, Tokyo; and others. *Comn:* Mural, Nat Arts Ctr, Ottawa, 68; mural, Montreal Forum, Que, 69; fountain sculpture, Ste Anne's Hosp, PQ, 70; sculpture, Nat Defence Bldg, Ottawa, 72; Ontario Prov Court House, London. *Exhib:* Op from Montreal, Fleming-Hull Mus, 66; Sculpture 67, Toronto, 67; Surv 68, Montreal, 68; one-man traveling exhib, Atlantic Provinces Mus, Can, 69; 3-D Into the 70's, Art Gallery Ont, Toronto, 70; Constructivist Heritage, Harbourfront Gallery, Toronto, 81; and other group & one-man shows. *Teaching:* Asst prof painting & sculpture, McGill Univ, 60-68; resident artist, Univ Western Ont, 69-72. *Awards:* Jessie Dow Award, Montreal Mus Fine Arts, 65; Arts Award, Can Coun, 68. *Bibliog:* M Gaulin (auth), Sculptor Lorcini, Time, 68; D Sanders (auth), Gino Lorcini, Bus Quart, 71. *Mem:* Assoc Royal Can Acad Arts. *Media:* Aluminum, Bronze. *Publ:* Coauth, Creative response, McGill J Educ, 67. *Mailing Add:* 67 Brock Rd London ON L9H 5H6 Canada

LORD, MICHAEL HARRY
DEALER, CURATOR
b Milwaukee, Wis, Nov 19, 54. *Study:* Univ Wis-Milwaukee. *Pos:* Asst to dir, Irving Galleries, 68-77; owner & dir, Michael H Lord Gallery, 78- *Mem:* Milwaukee Art Dealers Asn (pres, 81-); Wisconsin Coalition Arts & Human Needs (bd dirs, 83-). *Specialty:* Contemporary American art; masters in photography and sculpture. *Mailing Add:* 700 N Milwaukee St Milwaukee WI 53202

LORENTZ, PAULINE
PAINTER, INSTRUCTOR
b Newark, NJ. *Study:* Newark Sch Fine & Indust Arts, NJ, grad; Art Students League; also with John R Grabach. *Exhib:* Am Artists Prof League Grand Nat, New York, 65, 67-69; Expos Intercontinentale, Monaco & Dieppe, France, 67-68; 24th Am Drawing Biennial, Norfolk Mus Arts & Sci, Va, 71; Nat Exhib, Mus Fine Arts, Springfield, Mass, 71-73; Smithsonian Traveling Exhib, US, 71-73. *Teaching:* Instr, Summit Art Ctr, NJ, 62-; instr, Art Ctr NJ, Orange, 73-80. *Awards:* Gold Medals for Drawing, Catharine Lorillard Wolfe Art Club, 67, 69-70, 72 & 74-75; Am Artists Prof League Award, 67 & 70 & Arts Atlantic Award, Gloucester, Mass, 72; and many others. *Bibliog:* Philbrook Smith (auth), article, NJ Mus & Arts Mag, 2/64; article, Palette Talk, Vol 32, 77. *Mem:* Am Artists Prof League; Catharine Lorillard Wolfe Art Club; Hudson Valley Art Asn, NY; Acad Artists Asn, Mass; Rockport Art Asn, Mass. *Media:* Oil, Charcoal. *Mailing Add:* 20 Southview Dr Berkeley Heights NJ 07922

LORENZANI, ARTHUR EMANUELE
SCULPTOR
b Carrara, Italy, Feb 12, 86; US citizen. *Study:* Acad Belle Arti, Carrara, grad, 04; Rome Prize & three yr pension. *Work:* Acad Gallery, Carrara; Golden Age, Brookgreen Gardens; Young Mother; Kinney Direct, Kansas City, Mo. *Comn:* John F Kennedy (bronze portrait), M Labetti Post Vet Foreign Wars, Staten Island, 64. *Exhib:* Nat Acad Design, New York; Pa Acad Fine Arts, Philadelphia; Albright-Knox Gallery, Buffalo; Nat Sculpture Soc, New York. *Teaching:* Instr sculpture, Staten Island Mus, 51-53. *Awards:* First Prize, City of Parma, Italy; Honorable Mention, Garden Club Am, 29; Spec Silver Medal, Nat Sculpture Soc, 68. *Bibliog:* B G Proske (auth), Brookgreen Gardens Sculpture. *Mem:* Fel Nat Sculpture Soc; Allied Artists Am. *Media:* Bronze, Marble. *Publ:* Auth & illusr, article in Nat Sculpture Rev, summer 62. *Mailing Add:* 273 McClean Ave Staten Island NY 10305

LORING, JOHN
PAINTER, PRINTMAKER
b Chicago, Ill, Nov 23, 39. *Study:* Yale Univ, BA, 60; Ecole des Beaux Arts, Paris, 61-64; printmaking with Johnny Friedlaender, Paris, 62-64. *Work:* Metrop Mus Art, Whitney Mus Am Art, Mus Mod Art, New York; Art Inst Chicago; Boston Mus Fine Arts. *Comn:* Mural, US Customs Serv, Main Hall, US Customhouse, World Trade Ctr, New York, 74; three posters, New York Cult Ctr, 74; murals, Prudential Life Insurance Co, Eastern Home Off, Woodbridge, NJ, 76; outdoor mural proj, Nat Endowment Arts, Scranton, Pa, 77; murals, Nat Hq, Western Savings, Philadelphia, 79. *Exhib:* Silkscreen: History of a Medium, Philadelphia Mus Art, 71; Realism Now, New York Cult Ctr, 72; one-man shows, Baltimore Mus Art, 72 & Long Beach Mus Art, Calif, 75; Biennale of Graphic Art, Ljubljana, Yugoslavia, 73 & 77; Intergrafia 74 & 76, Krakow, Poland; Painting & Sculpture Today, Indianapolis Mus Art, 74; Silkscreen Prints, Chicago Art Inst, 75; Pace Editions, New York, 77. *Pos:* Art ed, Deleg World Bulletin, UN, 72; contribr, Print Collector's Newsletter, 73-75; assoc ed & contribr, Arts Mag, 73-; contrib ed, Archit Digest, 76-; contribr, Art in Am, 77-; Design dir & exec vpres, Tiffany & Co, 79- *Teaching:* Distinguished vis prof art, Univ Calif, Davis, 77. *Awards:* Fourth Prize, Intergrafia 74, Krakow. *Bibliog:* Ellen Lubell (auth), John Loring, 2/74 & Mario Amaya (auth), John Loring, 2/78, Arts Mag; Robert Hughes (auth), Murals without walls, 6/79. *Media:* Oil; Photo Silkscreens. *Publ:* Auth, Marisol Prints (catalog), New York Cult Ctr, 73; auth, David Hockney: Drawings (catalog), Dayton's Gallery 12, 74; coauth, Multiples, Neuen Berliner Kunstvereins, 74. *Dealer:* Pace Gallery 32 E 57th St New York NY 10022. *Mailing Add:* 143 Prince St New York NY 10012

LOTHROP, KRISTIN CURTIS
SCULPTOR
b Tucson, Ariz, Feb 8, 30. *Study:* Bennington Col, BA; also sculpture with George Demetrois, 4 yrs. *Exhib:* Nat Sculpture Soc, 67-71; Hudson Valley Art Asn, 68; Nat Acad Design, 68-71; Allied Artists Am, 69. *Awards:* Mrs Louis Bennett Award, Nat Sculpture Soc, 67; Thomas R Proctor Award, Nat Acad Design, 68, Daniel Chester French Award, 70. *Mem:* Nat Sculpture Soc. *Media:* Bronze, Wood, Stone. *Mailing Add:* Bridge St Manchester MA 01944

LOTTERMAN, HAL
PAINTER, EDUCATOR
b Chicago, Ill, Sept 29, 20. *Study:* Univ Ill, BFA, 45; Univ Iowa, MFA, 46. *Work:* Butler Inst Am Art, Youngstown, Ohio; Akron Art Inst; Ohio Univ; Ball State Univ; Mulvane Art Ctr, Topeka, Kans. *Exhib:* Metrop Mus Art, New York, 50; Carnegie Inst Int, Pittsburgh, 52; Pa Acad Fine Arts Am, Philadelphia, 53; Nat Acad Design Ann, New York, 54; Art USA 58, New York, 58. *Teaching:* Instr art, Univ Iowa, 47-50; instr art, Toledo Mus Art, 50-56; prof art, Univ Wis-Madison, 65- *Awards:* Tiffany Fund Painting Scholar, 51; Univ Iowa Purchase Award, 57. *Media:* Oil, Photography. *Mailing Add:* 2337 Atwood Ave Madison WI 53704

LOTTES, JOHN WILLIAM
EDUCATOR, ADMINISTRATOR
b Minneapolis, Minn, Apr 8, 34. *Study:* Concordia Jr Col, St Paul, Minn, AA, 53; Minneapolis Sch Art, BFA, 60; Hochschule Gestaltung, Ulm, Ger, 58-59; Univ Iowa, 67; Minneapolis Col Art & Design, Hon MFA, 73. *Pos:* Dean col & registr, Kansas City Art Inst, 66-68, pres, 70-83; dir planning & develop, Corcoran Gallery & Sch Art, Washington, DC, 68-69; asst to pres acad affairs, Calif Col Arts & Crafts, Oakland, 69-70; comnr, Munic Arts Comn, Kansas City, 79-; bd dirs, Kansas City Arts Coun, 79-, treas, 79-80, vpres, 80; pres, Minneapolis Soc Fine Arts, 83- *Teaching:* Chmn indust design, Minneapolis Sch Art, 62-63; asst prof indust design, Kansas City Art Inst, 64-66. *Mem:* Fel Nat Asn Sch Art (bd dirs, 72-83, pres, 79-81); Alliance Independent Cols Art (bd dirs, 70-83, chmn bd, 76-79). *Mailing Add:* 6108 Morningside Dr Kansas City MO 64113

LOTZ, STEVEN DARRYL
PAINTER, EDUCATOR
b Los Angeles, Calif, Dec 28, 38. *Study:* Univ Calif, Los Angeles, with Brice & Amato, BFA, 61; Univ Fla, Gainesville, with Hiram Williams, MFA, 63; Acad Fine Arts, Vienna, Austria, 65-66. *Work:* Jacksonville Art Mus, Fla; Orlando International Airport; His Royal Highness, Prince Phillip, London; Palace Hotel, Lake Buena Vista. *Exhib:* Solo exhibs, Jacksonville Art Mus, Fla, 70, Galerie Zeitgendssische Kunst, Hamburg, WGer, 73, Loch Haven Art Ctr, Orlando, Fla, 73 & traveling exhib, Ringling Mus Art, 74-76; Royal Scottish Acad Exhib, Edinburgh, Scotland, 81. *Teaching:* Asst prof drawing & painting, Jacksonville Univ, Fla, 66-68; chmn drawing, Univ Cent Fla, Orlando, 68-78, prof drawing, 68-; vis exchange instr, Edinburgh Col Art, 78-79 & 80-81. *Awards:* First Prize, Jacksonville Arts Festival, 65; First Prize, Ocala Arts Festival, Ocala Nat Bank, 69; State Fla Grant. *Bibliog:* Roger Ortmayer (dir), Space Cathedral (film), CBS TV, New York, 72; Frank Martin (auth), article, Art Voices South, 11-12/79; Egberclien Van Rossum (auth), article, Bres 99 Mag, 4/83. *Media:* Oil, Acrylic. *Dealer:* Louise Peterson Galleries Int 517 N Virginia Ave Winter Park FL 32789. *Mailing Add:* 1115 Ridgewood St Orlando FL 32803

LOUGHLIN, JOHN LEO
PAINTER
b Worcester, Mass, Apr 11, 31. *Study:* Worcester Art Mus Sch; Clark Univ, AB, 57; Bridgewater State Col, EdM, 64; also with Eliot O'Hara, Edgar Whitney & Barse Miller. *Work:* M & M Karolik Collection, Boston Mus Fine Art; Cumberland RI Housing for Elderly; Old Colony Savings Bank, Providence, RI; US Naval War Col, Newport, RI; Gen Elec Corp, Schenectady, NY. *Exhib:* Boston Arts Festival, 55; Acad Artists Show, Springfield, Mass, 59; Bristol Art Mus Show, RI, 70; Am Watercolor Soc, Nat Acad Design Galleries, New York, 71 & 83; Providence Art Club Open Watercolor Show, 72. *Pos:* Illusr cartogr, Nat Geog Mag, 58-59; head dept art, US Naval War Col, 61-68; art dir, WSBE-TV, Providence, 68- *Teaching:* Pvt instr, 69-; vis lectr watercolor, Providence Col, 70-72. *Awards:* Gold Medal, Providence Watercolor Club, 83; First Award, Int Soc Marine Painters, 83; Chas P Fonda Award, Rockport Art Asn, 83. *Bibliog:* Watercolor, WSBE-TV, 69. *Mem:* Assoc Am Watercolor Soc; Providence Art Club; Providence Watercolor Club (vpres, 70-72, pres, 72); artist mem Rockport Art Asn. *Media:* Watercolor, Oil. *Publ:* Illusr, Nat Geog Mag, 58; illusr, Mass Wildlife Mag, 59; contribr & illusr, Salt Water Sportsman Mag, 59; illusr, Naval Rev, 67; illusr, New Eng Sch Develop Coun Publ. *Dealer:* Limerock Studio/Gallery Lincoln RI 02865. *Mailing Add:* 124 Angell Rd Lincoln RI 02865

LOVATO, CHARLES FREDRIC
PRINTMAKER, CRAFTSMAN

b Santa Fe, NMex, May 23, 37. Work: Heard Mus, Phoenix; Philbrook Art Ctr, Tulsa, Okla. Comn: Two murals, Indian Pueblo Cult Ctr, Albuquerque, 78-79. Exhib: Scottsdale Nat, Ariz, 68; Heard Mus, Phoenix, 69; Washington, DC Biennial, 69; Gallup Inter-Tribal Ceremonial, NMex, 72. Awards: Most Outstanding Painting, Dr Avery, Pecos, Tex, 70 & 71; Best Artist-Best Painting, Philbrook Art Ctr, 71. Media: Acrylic. Publ: Auth & illusr, Life Under the Sun, Sunstone Press, 80. Mailing Add: Sile Star Rte 72 Pena Blanca NM 87041

LOVE, FRANCES TAYLOR
MUSEUM DIRECTOR, WRITER

b Salina, Kans, Apr 25, 26. Study: Univ Tex, BA(journalism & speech); studied television writing, Univ Houston; sem in Gt Brit & other Europ study, Smithsonian Inst. Collections Arranged: Steamboats Along the Louisiana Bayous (auth, catalog), 69, 19th Century Painters in Louisiana (auth, catalog), 72, Louisiana French Furnishings: 1750-1830 (ed, catalog), 74, Haitian Voodoo Art (auth, catalog), 76 & Victorian Decorative Arts in Louisiana (auth, catalog), 77, Art Ctr Southwestern La. Pos: Pub relations dir, Lafayette Art Asn, 60-63; dir, Art Ctr Southwestern La, Lafayette, 65- Res: Louisiana colonial decorative arts; Texas and Louisiana decorative art and architecture; Victorian decorative art. Publ: Auth & ed, My Home is Austin, Texas, 58 & Here is South Louisiana, 65, Tribune Press. Mailing Add: PO Box 51998 Lafayette LA 70505

LOVE, JIM
SCULPTOR

b Amarillo, Tex, 1927. Exhib: Dallas Mus Contemp Art; Mus Mod Art, New York; Mus Fine Arts, Houston; Whitney Mus Am Art, New York; Contemp Arts Mus, Houston; Rice Univ Mus, Houston; and others. Dealer: Janie C Lee Gallery 2304 Bissonnet Houston TX 77005. Mailing Add: 5009 Blossom Houston TX 77007

LOVE, PAUL VAN DERVEER
GALLERY DIRECTOR, HISTORIAN

b Long Branch, NJ, Aug 1, 08. Study: Princeton Univ, BA; Univ Pa, Am Inst Archit Scholar, 45; NY Univ, scholar, 48; Columbia Univ, PhD(fel), 50. Exhib: Ala Watercolor Soc, 53; Kresge Art Ctr Gallery, East Lansing, Mich, 71; 15th Nat Exhib, Fall River, Mass, 72; Butler Inst Art, Youngstown, Ohio, 72; Galeria San Miguel, Mex, 74-75; plus others. Collections Arranged: The Turn of the Century; American Nineteenth Century Painting, 66; Earl Kerkam: Paintings and Drawings, 72. Pos: Dir, Kresge Art Ctr Gallery, 63-74; ed, Kresge Art Ctr, Bull, 67-74. Teaching: Prof Am, mod & pre-Columbian art, Mich State Univ, 53-66, prof mus training, 70-74, emer prof, 74- Res: Study of the architecture, architectural ornament & retables in the municipality of San Miguel Allende, Mexico, 16th-19th century. Publ: Auth, Modern Dance Terminology, 53; co-auth, An Introduction to Literature and Fine Arts, 53; auth, Patterned Brickwork in Southern New Jersey, 55. Mailing Add: 2233 N 87th Way Scottsdale AZ 85257

LOVE, RICHARD HENRY
DEALER, HISTORIAN

b Schneider, Ind, Dec 27, 39. Study: Univ of Md, Europe; Bloom Col, Chicago Heights, Ill; Univ of Ill, Chicago; Northwestern Univ, Evanston, Ill; Villa Schifanoia, Florence, Italy; independent study in Europe. Comn: Murals, Flak Kaserne Bldg, US Army, Augsburg, Ger, 62 & Dorchester Club, Ramada Inn, Dolton, Ill, 65. Pos: Art critic, Star-Tribune Newspaper, Chicago Heights, Ill, formerly; art commentator, WNIB, WBBM & WEFM radio, Chicago, formerly; WCIU TV, Chicago, 78-; pres & owner, R H Love Galleries, Inc, Chicago, 67-; chmn bd, Haase-Mumm Publ Co, Chicago, 81- & Amart Book and Catalog Distributing Co, 81-; consult, Dallas Biblical Art Ctr, 83- Teaching: Prof art hist, Prairie State Col, Chicago Heights, Ill; commentator art hist, WCIU-TV Chicago, 78- Bibliog: Louise Morgan (auth), A Love story, Sunday J, Kankakee, Ill, 11/28/82; John Forwalter (auth), For the Love of art ... and quarter horses, Sunday Post-Tribune, Gary, Ind, 1/16/83. Mem: Friends Am Art, Yale Univ; Mid-W Ctr, Arch Am Art (adv bd); New England Hist Soc. Media: Oil. Res: 18th, 19th & 20th century American art, most particularly American impressionists, T E Butler, J J Cunningham; John Barber. Specialty: 18th, 19th & 20th century American paintings; American folk art. Publ: Auth, Harriet Randall Lumis: 1870-1953 (exhib catalog), 77, William Chadwick (1879-1962) (exhib catalog), 78, Walter Clark and Eliot Clark (exhib catalog), 80 & Cassatt: The Independent, 80, R H Love Galleries; auth, John Barber: The Artist, The Man, 81 & Theodore Earl Butler: Emergence from Monet's Shadow, 83, Haase-Mumm Publ. Mailing Add: c/o R H Love Galleries 100 E Ohio Chicago IL 60611

LOVEJOY, MARGOT R
PRINTMAKER, EDUCATOR

b Campbellton, NB, Oct 21, 30. Study: Mt Allison Univ, with Alex Colville & Lawren Harris, 47-49; St Martins Sch Art, London, cert(design & illus), 50; Pratt Graphics Ctr, with Ponce de Leon, Stasik & Zimilies, 66-71; also with Bob Strassman, Mervin Honig & David Attie. Work: NB Mus; Hudson River Mus, New York; NY Univ Print Collection; Bibliotheque Nat, Paris; Dresden Mus, Ger. Comn: Prints, John Barton Fine Arts, New York, 65-72; membership print, Pratt Graphics Ctr, 69; etchings, Nabis Fine Arts, New York, 73-74. Exhib: Copier Art, Hansen Gallery, New York, 78; Printmaking in Modern American Illustration, Pratt Manhattan Ctr, New York, 79; Int Biennial, Print Club, Philadelphia, 79; In Celebration of Prints, Print Club, Philadelphia, 80; Portfolio Project Travelling Show, WGer, 81; Electra, Mus

Art Mod, Paris, 83. Teaching: Instr, Pratt-Phoenix Schs Design, New York, 72-78, Pratt Grahics Ctr, New York, 72-79 & Parsons Sch Design, New York, 75-77; asst prof fine art, State Univ NY, Purchase, 78- Awards: Dr Paul Bradlow Award, Pratt Graphics Ctr, 69; Alice Buell Mem Award, Nat Asn Women Artists, 76; Soc Am Graphic Artists Purchase Award, 78. Bibliog: Patrick Firpo & Steve Ditler (auths), Copy Art, Richard Marek, 78; Nancy Howell Koehler (auth), Photo Art Processes, Davis Publ, 79. Mem: Soc Am Graphic Artists (vpres, 83); Nat Asn Women Artists. Media: Etching, Silkscreen. Publ: Auth, Printing inks for the fine art print I, 71 & II, 78, National experimental graphics workshop of Cuba, 79 & Innovation in American printmaking: 1956-1981, 81, Print Rev; auth, Silkscreen joins the mainstream, Print News, 83. Dealer: Orion Gallery 835 Madison Ave New York NY. Mailing Add: 166-04 81st Ave Jamaica NY 11432

LOVELESS, JIM
EDUCATOR, PAINTER

b Saginaw, Mich, Apr 24, 35. Study: DePauw Univ, AB, 57; Ind Univ, MFA, 60. Work: Munson-Williams-Proctor Inst, Utica, NY; Itaca Col Mus of Art, NY; Oneida Valley Nat Bank, Hamilton, NY; Chase Manhattan Bank, New York. Exhib: Munson-Williams-Proctor Inst Ann, Utica; Ithaca Col Mus of Art, NY, 68; one-man shows, Art Inst Pittsburgh, 76, Kalamazoo Col, Mich & Everson Mus, Syracuse, NY, 77; and others. Teaching: Asst prof studio & art hist, Hope Col, Holland, Mich, 60-64 & Univ Ky, Lexington, 64-66; prof studio & art hist, Colgate Univ, Hamilton, 66- Awards: Heffner Award, Grand Rapids Mus of Art Ann, 62; Yaddo Fel. Mem: Col Art Asn. Media: Watercolor, Acrylic. Mailing Add: 31 Madison St Hamilton NY 13346

LOVELL, MARGARETTA MARKLE
CURATOR, HISTORIAN

b Pittsburgh, Pa, Oct 30, 44. Study: Smith Col, BA, 66; Univ Del, MA, 75; Yale Univ, PhD, 80. Pos: Cur Am painting, San Francisco Mus, 81- Teaching: Actg instr, Am art, Yale Univ, 77-80, asst prof, 80-81; asst prof American art, Univ Calif, Berkeley, 81- Mailing Add: 405 Doe Libr Univ Calif Berkeley CA 94720

LOVELL, TOM
PAINTER, ILLUSTRATOR

b New York, NY, Feb 5, 09. Study: Syracuse Univ, BFA. Work: Explorers Club, New York; US Merchant Marine Acad, King's Point, NY; Nat Cowboy Hall Fame, Oklahoma City. Comn: Hist paintings, US Marine Corps, 45, Life Mag, 61, Nat Geog Soc, Washington, 65-68 & Abell-Hanger Found, Midland, Tex, 69-73. Exhib: Soc Illustrators, New York, 63; solo exhib, Syracuse Univ Centennial, Lubin House, 70; Nat Cowboy Hall Fame, 73-83. Awards: Prix West, Cowboy Hall Fame, 74; Gold Medals, Cowboy Artists Am, 75-77 & 80 & Nat Acad Western Art Show, 76-78 & 82-83. Bibliog: Norman Kent (auth), Tom Lovell & his work, Am Artists. Mem: Soc Illustrators; Cowboy Artists Am; Nat Acad Western Art. Media: Oil. Publ: Auth, Persimmon Hill, Nat Cowboy Hall Fame. Mailing Add: 3 Tano Rd RR 4 Santa Fe NM 87501

LOVING, RICHARD MARIS
PAINTER, EDUCATOR

b Vienna, Austria, Jan 27, 24. Study: Fieldston Sch, Riverdale, NY, 39-42; Bard Col, Annandale, NY, 43-44; New Sch Soc Res, 46. Work: Art Inst Chicago; Joslyn Art Mus, Omaha, Nebr; First Nat Bank Chicago; Kemper Art Collection, Chicago; Borg-Warner Corp, Chicago; and others. Comn: Enamel triptych, Concordia Col, River Forest, Ill, 67; enamel & stainless wire, Graver Water Conditioning, Union, NJ, 68; Vitreous enamel mural, Union Tank Car Corp, Chicago, 70. Exhib: Chicago & Vicinity Drawings & Prints, Art Inst Chicago, 68 & 69; Collector's Choice Exhib, Joslyn Art Mus, Omaha, Nebr, 68; Contemp Art in Midwest, Univ Notre Dame, 69; Karlsruhe/Chicago, Karlsruhe, WGer, 79; Chicago; Some Other Traditions, 83-85. Teaching: Prof painting & drawing, Sch Art Inst Chicago, 63- Awards: Nat Endowment Arts Fel. Media: Oil and Acrylic on Canvas or Wood Paneling. Dealer: Roy Boyd Gallery 215 W Superior St Chicago IL 60610. Mailing Add: 1857 W Armitage Chicago IL 60622

LOW, JOSEPH
PAINTER, PRINTMAKER

b Coraopolis, Pa, Aug 11, 11. Study: Univ Ill, 30-32; Art Students League, with George Grosz, 35. Work: Princeton Univ; Harvard Univ; Libr Cong; Va Mus Fine Arts; San Francisco Pub Libr; plus many others. Exhib: Boston Mus Fine Arts; New York Pub Libr; Metrop Mus Art, New York; Herron Inst Art, Indianapolis; Philadelphia Mus Art; and others. Media: Watercolor; Graphics. Mailing Add: Box 337 Cruz Bay St John VI 00830

LOWE, HARRY
ADMINISTRATOR, DESIGNER

b Opelika, Ala, Apr 9, 22. Study: Auburn Univ, BA, 43, MFA, 49; Cranbrook Acad Art, 51 & 53. Collections Arranged: Stuart Davis Memorial, Nat Collection Fine Arts, Washington, DC, Art Inst Chicago, Univ Calif Art Galleries, Los Angeles & Whitney Mus Am Art, New York, 65; The Charles Sheeler Exhibition, Philadelphia Mus Art & Whitney Mus Am Art, 69. Pos: Dir, Tenn Fine Arts Ctr, Nashville, 59-64; cur, Dept Exhib & Design, Nat Collection Fine Arts, 64-72, asst dir, 72-74, asst dir, 74-81, acting dir, 81-82, deputy dir, 82-83. Teaching: Prof art, Auburn Univ, 49-59; fac, Sem for Hist Adminrs, Williamsburg, Va, 65, 67-71. Mem: Am Asn Mus; Nat Trust Hist Preserv; Col Art Asn Am; Skowhegan Sch Painting & Sculpture (mem adv comt). Mailing Add: Nat Collection Fine Arts Eighth & G Sts Washington DC 20560

LOWE, J MICHAEL
SCULPTOR, EDUCATOR
b Cincinnati, Ohio, Aug 18, 42. *Study:* Ohio Univ, BFA; Cornell Univ, MFA. *Work:* State Univ NY Col Potsdam; Cornell Univ; St Lawrence Univ (NY). *Exhib:* Butler Inst Am Art Ann, 64, 71, 72 & 80; Artists of Central New York, Munson-Williams-Proctor Inst, Utica, NY, 65, 67-69, 71 & 79; Sculpture 75, Philadelphia, 75; Sculpture Now, Inc, New York, 78; Univ SC, 80; solo exhib, Ohio Northern Univ, 83; and others. *Teaching:* Instr fine arts, St Lawrence Univ, 66-67, asst prof, 67-72, chmn dept, 71-, assoc prof, 72-78, prof, 78- *Awards:* Purchase Awards, Tyler Mus Art, 70, Butler Inst Am Art, 72 & Clinton Co Govt Bldg, 76. *Mem:* Col Art Asn Am. *Media:* Welded Metal. *Mailing Add:* Dept of Fine Arts St Lawrence Univ Canton NY 13617

LOWE, MARVIN
PRINTMAKER, PAINTER
b Brooklyn, NY, May 19, 27. *Study:* Juilliard Sch; Brooklyn Col, BA, 54; Univ Iowa, MFA, 60. *Work:* Philadelphia Mus Art; Brooklyn Mus; British Mus; Libr Cong; Nat Collection Fine Arts, Smithsonian Inst; and 67 others. *Exhib:* Libr Cong, 60, 62 & 65; Mus Mod Art, New York, 65; Brooklyn Mus, 67; Philadelphia Mus Art, Nat Print Exhib, 68 & 72; two-person show, Am Embassy, Ankara, Turkey, 74; solo exhibs, Zriny Gallery, Chicago, 77-83, Sheldon Swope Gallery, Terre Haute, Ind, 79, Kit Basquin Gallery, Milwaukee, 82; Indianapolis Mus Art, 82 & 83; and others. *Teaching:* Prof printmaking, Ind Univ, Bloomington, 68- *Awards:* Fel, Nat Endowment Arts Artists Award, 75; Lessing J Rosenwald Purchase Prize, Philadelphia Print Club, 66; Ford Found Grant, 79; and others. *Bibliog:* Thelma Newman (auth), Innovative printmaking, Crown Publ, 75. *Mem:* Soc Am Graphic Artists. *Dealer:* Zriny Gallery 1963 N Halsted Chicago IL 60614. *Mailing Add:* Sch of Fine Arts Ind Univ Bloomington IN 47401

LOWINSKY, SIMON L
DEALER
b Black Mountain, NC, Nov 19, 45. *Pos:* Owner, Phoenix Gallery, San Francisco; partner, Lowsky & Arai; owner, Lowinsky Gallery, currently. *Specialty:* Nineteenth & twentieth century photography, prints, paintings and sculpture. *Mailing Add:* 228 Grant Ave 6th Floor San Francisco CA 94108

LOWNEY, BRUCE STARK
PAINTER, PRINTMAKER
b Los Angeles, Calif, Oct 16, 37. *Study:* NTex State Univ, BA; San Francisco State Univ, MA; Univ NMex, asst to Garo Antreasian; Tamarind Lithography Workshop. *Work:* Minneapolis Inst Art; Art Inst Chicago; Art Mus Univ NMex, Albuquerque; Oklahoma City Art Ctr; Libr Cong Collection, Washington, DC; and others. *Exhib:* Whitney Mus Am Art Print Exhib, New York, 70; one-man shows, Martha Jackson Gallery, New York, 71, Hills Gallery, Santa Fe, 73 & Univ NDak, Grand Forks, 74; 23rd Nat Exhib Prints, Libr Cong, 73; and others. *Teaching:* Instr, Minneapolis Col Art & Design, Fort Lewis Col & Univ Tex, Austin, formerly. *Awards:* Louis Comfort Tiffany Found Graphics Art Award, 69; Nat Endowment Arts Grant, 74; Western States Arts Found fel, 79; and others. *Media:* Oil, Lithography. *Dealer:* Elaine Horwitch Galleries Scottsdale AZ & Santa Fe NM. *Mailing Add:* 800 Oso Ridge Rt Grants NM 87020

LOWRY, BATES
HISTORIAN
b Cincinnati, Ohio, June 21, 23. *Study:* Univ Chicago, PhB, 44, MA, 53, PhD, 56. *Pos:* Ed, Monogr Series, Col Art Asn, 57-59 & 65-68; ed, Art Bulletin, 65-68; dir, Mus Mod Art, New York, 68-69; mem bd dirs, Comt for Nat Mus Building Arts, 78-80; dir, Nat Bldg Mus, Wash, 80- *Teaching:* Asst prof art, Univ Calif, Riverside, 54-57 & Inst Fine Arts, NY Univ, 57-59; asst prof art, Inst Fine Arts, NY Univ, 57-59; prof art & chmn dept, Pomona Col, 59-63; Brown Univ, 63-68 & Univ Mass, Boston, 71-80; mem, Inst Advan Study, 71. *Awards:* RI Gov's Award for Contribution to Arts, 67; Grand Off, Star of Solidarity, Italy, 68; Guggenheim Fel, 72. *Mem:* Soc Archit Historians (bd dirs, 59-61, 63-65); Art Historians Southern Calif (pres, 61-63); Comt to Rescue Italian Art (co-founder); Am Fedn Arts (trustee, 69-71); Dunlap Soc (pres, 74-). *Publ:* Auth, The Visual Experience, 61; auth, Renaissance Architecture, 62; auth, Architecture of Washington, DC, 77-79; auth, articles in Art Bull & Col Art J. *Mailing Add:* Essex NY 12936

LOY, JOHN SHERIDAN
PAINTER
b St Louis, Mo, Nov 4, 30. *Study:* Colorado Springs Fine Art Ctr, Colo; Wash Univ Sch Fine Arts, BFA, 54; Cranbrook Acad Art, Bloomfield Hills, Mich, MFA, 58. *Work:* Munson-Williams-Proctor Inst, Utica, NY; Utica Col, NY; Lincoln-Rochester Bank Collection, Rochester, NY; Hayes Nat Bank, Clinton, NY; Savings Bank Utica. *Exhib:* Mo Show, St Louis City Art Mus, 59; Artists Cent NY, Munson-Williams-Proctor Inst, 60-70; Albany Inst Hist & Art Regional, NY, 69; Everson Mus Regional, Syracuse, NY, 70; Cooperstown Art Asn Ann, NY, 71. *Pos:* Prog dir, Peoples Art Ctr, St Louis, 59; dir, Munson Williams Proctor Inst Gallery, Utica, NY, 78- *Teaching:* Instr drawing, Wash Univ, 59; instr drawing & painting, Munson-Williams-Proctor Inst, 60- *Awards:* First Painting Prize, Cooperstown Art Asn, 71, 74, 76 & 77; Best in Show Award, Arena 77 Exhib, Binghamton, NY; Grand Prize, Cooperstown Art Asn, 83. *Media:* Oil. *Mailing Add:* 602 Tracy St Utica NY 13502

LUBART, HENRIETTE D'ARLIN
EDUCATOR, SCULPTOR
b Beirut, Lebanon, Dec 3, 15; US citizen. *Study:* Columbia Univ, New York, MA, 42, PhD, 53; Art Students League, with William Zorach & Jose de Creeft. *Work:* Inst Study Man, New York; St Francis Col, Jersey City; Israel Art Collection, Jaffa; and many private collections in Europe and South Am; Mount Sinai Hosp; and others. *Exhib:* Nat Asn Women Artists, New York Soc Women Artists & Audubon Artists, New York; Silvermine Guild Artists, New Canaan, Conn; and other solo and group shows. *Teaching:* Asst instr, Columbia Univ, 42-44; asst prof, Vassar Col, 44-53; adj prof, New York Univ, 54-55. *Awards:* Gold Medals, Knickerbocker Artists, 62 & Artists Equity Asn. *Media:* Wood, Stone. *Publ:* and numerous articles. *Mailing Add:* 275 W 96 St Apt 27E New York NY 10025

LUBBERS, LELAND EUGENE
SCULPTOR, EDUCATOR
b Stoughton, Wis, June 6, 28. *Study:* St Louis Univ, AB, MA, PhL & STL; Univ Paris, Dde l'U Paris; Acad Grande Chaumiere, Paris. *Work:* Duchesne Col, Omaha, Nebr; Sheldon Gallery, Univ Nebr, Lincoln; Seattle Opera Asn, Wash; Art in Embassies Prog, US State Dept; Jacksonville Art Mus, Fla. *Comn:* Outdoor fountain, City Omaha, 69; sculptured constructions, Canisius Col, NY, 70; crucifix group (wrought iron), St John's Church, Omaha. *Exhib:* One-man shows, Automated Junk Sculpture Exhib, Sheldon Mem Art Gallery, 65, Jacksonville Art Mus, 67 & Frye Art Mus, Seattle, 68; Ward-Nasse Gallery, New York, 74 & 77; Sheldon Gallery, Lincoln, 74-77; SW State Univ, Marshall, Minn, 77. *Teaching:* Assoc prof fine arts, founder & head dept, Creighton Univ, 65-72. *Bibliog:* Robert Reilly (auth), Jesuit junkman, Critic Mag, 2-3/68; John Wain (auth), To Lee Lubbers in Omaha, In: Letters to Five Artists, Viking, 70; Larry Austin (auth), Caritas: Symphony of the gigantic hammered welded aluminum imitation earth volumes, Source, 11/70. *Mem:* Asn Int Dde l'U Paris; Nebr Art Educ Asn; Assoc Artists Omaha; Nebr Arts Coun (dir, 66-72). *Media:* Metals. *Publ:* Auth, L'image publicitaire actuelle et ses origines, Univ Paris, 63. *Dealer:* Artists Coop Omaha NE. *Mailing Add:* Fine Arts Dept Creighton Univ 2400 California St Omaha NE 68131

LUBELL, ELLEN
CRITIC, WRITER
b Brooklyn, NY, Apr 7, 50. *Study:* State Univ NY at Stony Brook, with Lawrence Alloway, BA, 71. *Pos:* Contrib ed, Arts Mag, 72-79; dir, Landmark Gallery, New York, 73-75; ed/publ, Womanart Mag, Brooklyn, 76-78; art critic, Soho Weekly News, New York, 77-79; free lance contribr, Art Am, 81- *Teaching:* Instr art criticism & art journalism, Sch Visual Arts, New York, 79-80. *Awards:* Art Critics Fel, Nat Endowment Arts, 78. *Bibliog:* Corinne Robins (auth), The women's art magazines, Art Criticism, Vol 1, No 2, 79; Cynthia Nadelman (auth), Women artists: Self-images, Art News, 82. *Mem:* Int Asn Art Critics. *Res:* To produce a cohesive body of needed information on women artists. *Publ:* Auth, Whatever happened to the women's artist movement, Womanart Mag, 77; auth, Can museums collect contemporary sculpture, Soho Weekly News, 79; auth, Systemic Patterning (catalog), Hansen Gallery, 80; auth, Park Slope: An Overview (catalog), Brooklyn Mus, 80; auth, Women Artists: Self-Images (catalog essay), Women's Caucus Art, 82. *Mailing Add:* 161 Prospect Park W Brooklyn NY 11215

LUCA, MARK
PRINTMAKER
b San Francisco, Calif, Oct 14, 18. *Study:* San Francisco State Univ, with John Gutmann, AB(hon), 40; Columbia Univ, MA(fine arts), 48; Univ Calif, Berkeley, PhD(mus educ), 58. *Work:* Achenbach Found, Calif Palace Legion Hon; Art Mus & Morrison Libr, Univ Calif, Berkeley; Oakland Mus; Mills Col Art Gallery. *Comn:* Mural, Fine Arts Dept, Columbia Univ, 48. *Exhib:* Albany Inst Arts Ann, 48; San Francisco Mus Print Ann, 49 & 57; Crocker Mus Ann, Sacramento, 56; Calif Palace Legion Hon Invitational, 61; Print, Painting & Sculpture Exhib, Richmond Art Ctr, Calif, 62, 63, 68 & 71; Oakland Mus Art Ann, 63 & 68; one-person exhib, Panoras Gallery, New York, 66 & US Cult Inst, Lima, Peru, 80. *Collections Arranged:* Elio Benvenuto, Survey (coauth, catalog), Mus Italo Am, San Francisco, 82. *Pos:* Cur, Mus Italo Am, San Francisco, 81-82. *Teaching:* Instr art, State Univ NY, Potsdam, 48-50 & Sacramento State Univ, 55-56; lectr art educ, Univ Calif, Berkeley, 58-78. *Awards:* First Prize, San Francisco State Univ Ann Painting Exhib, 40 & 41. *Bibliog:* Articles, Art Week, 8/21/71, Westart, 2/22/74 & Lima Times, Peru, 11/14/80. *Mem:* Calif Soc Printmakers; East Bay Art Asn (pres, 81-82); Ctr Visual Arts; Oakland Art Asn; Calif Art Educ Asn. *Media:* Collagraph, Lithography. *Publ:* Illusr, Back to the Cave, 56 & auth & illusr, San Francisco: Seven Stages, 58, Peregrine Press; coauth, Understanding Children's Art, Charles Merrill, 67; coauth, Art Education: Strategies ..., Prentice-Hall, 68; auth, The Museum as Educator, Museums, 73. *Dealer:* Ctr Visual Arts 1515 Webster Oakland CA 94612. *Mailing Add:* 6-E Captain Dr #439 Emeryville CA 94608

LUCCHESI, BRUNO
SCULPTOR
b Lucca, Italy, July 31, 26; US citizen. *Study:* Inst Arte, Lucca, MFA, 53. *Work:* Pa Acad Fine Arts, Philadelphia; Dallas Mus Fine Arts; Ringling Mus, Sarasota, Fla; Hirshhorn Mus, Washington, DC; Whitney Mus Am Art, New York. *Comn:* Sculpture, Trade Bank, New York; sculpture, Cornell Univ. *Exhib:* Whitney Mus Am Art, New York; Pa Acad Fine Arts; Corcoran Gallery Art, Washington, DC; Nat Inst Arts & Lett; Brooklyn Mus, NY; plus others. *Teaching:* Instr, Acad Fine Arts, Univ Florence, Italy, 52-57; instr, New Sch Social Res, 62- *Awards:* Watrous Gold Medal, Nat Acad Design, 61; Gold Medal, Nat Arts Club, 63; S F B Morse Medal, Nat Acad Design, 65; and others. *Mem:* Sculptors Guild; Artists Equity Asn; Nat Acad Design; Am Asn Univ Prof. *Dealer:* Forum Gallery 1018 Madison Ave New York NY 10021. *Mailing Add:* 14 Stuyvesant St New York NY 10003

LUCE, MOLLY (MOLLY LUCE BURROUGHS)
PAINTER
b Pittsburgh, Pa, Dec 18, 1896. *Study:* Wheaton Col, Norton, Mass, Assoc, 16; Art Students League, 16-18 & 19-22. *Work:* Metrop Mus Art & Whitney Mus Am Art, New York; Mus Art, Carnegie Inst, Pittsburgh. *Exhib:* Art Inst Chicago, 29, 31-32 & 36-37; Brooklyn Mus, 31; Nebr Art Asn, Lincoln, 33, 36 & 38-39; Mus Mod Art, New York, 33; Whitney Mus Am Art, New York, 34-41 & 43-50; Addison Gallery Am Art, Andover, Mass, 36; Pa Acad Fine Arts, Philadelphia, 37-43; Dallas Mus Fine Art, 37; Virginia Mus, Richmond, 38 & 40; Baltimore Mus Art, 38; Corcoran Gallery Art, Washington, DC, 39, 43 & 45; Carnegie Inst, Pittsburgh, 40, 43 & 45; Toledo Mus, 42; one-woman exhibs, Wheaton Col Mus, Norton, Mass, 37 & 66, Newport Art Asn, RI, 43 & RI Sch Design, Providence, 79; Eight Decades of the American Scene, Traveling Exhib, 80-; and many others. *Bibliog:* D Roger Howlett & Lloyd Goodrich (auth), Molly Luce: Eight Decades of the American Scene, Childs Gallery, Boston, 80. *Media:* Oil. *Mailing Add:* c/o Childs Gallery 169 Newbury St Boston MA 02116

LUCERO, MICHAEL (LEWIS)
SCULPTURE
b Tracy, Calif, Apr 1, 53. *Study:* Humboldt State Univ, Arcata, Calif, BA, 75; Univ Wash, Seattle, MFA, 78. *Exhib:* Seattle Art Mus, Wash, 78 & 79; Graphics Plus, Herbert F Johnson Mus Art, Cornell Univ, Ithaca, NY, 81; Bay Area Collects: A Diverse Sampling, San Francisco Mus Mod Art, 83; Self Portraits, Linda Farris Gallery, Seattle, 83; Sculpture Now: Recent Figurative Works, Inst Contemp Art, Va Mus Fine Arts, Richmond, 83; Ceramic Directions: A Contemporary Overview, State Univ NY, Stony Brook, 83; Contemp Clay Sculpture: Selections from the Daniel Jacobs Collection, Heckscher Mus, Huntington, NY, 83; Eight Visions, One Penn Plaza, New York, 83; The Raw Edge: Ceramics of the 80s, Hillwood Gallery, CW Post Col, Long Island Univ, 83. *Teaching:* Instr, New York Univ, 79-80 & Parsons Sch Design, 81-82; guest lectr, RI Sch Design, Providence, 79, Wake Forest Univ, Winston-Salem, NC, 80, Moore Col Art, Tyler Sch Art & Philadelphia Col Art, formerly. *Awards:* Nat Endowment Arts Fels, 79 & 82; Creative Artists Public Service Program Fel, 81; Nettie Marie Jones Fel, Ctr Music, Drama & Art, Lake Placid, NY, 83. *Bibliog:* William Zimmer (auth), A new figure on the horizon, Am Ceramics, winter issue; The figure; a celebration, Grand Forks Herald, 11/13/81; John Perreault (auth), Good for the figure, Soho News, 12/1/81. *Mailing Add:* 123 W 20th St New York NY 10011

LUCEY, JACK
PAINTER, EDUCATOR
b San Francisco, Calif, Feb 11, 29. *Study:* Acad Art Col, San Francisco, 55; San Francisco Art Inst, 59; San Francisco State Univ, BA, 76. *Work:* USAF Mus, Nellis, Nev; Naval Aviation Mus, Pensacola, Fla; Hall of Justice Bldg, San Francisco; Trans World Airlines, New York; Calif Hwy Patrol Collection, Sacramento, Calif. *Comn:* Murals of Alaska, Pac Orient Lines, San Francisco, 72; London Illus, Trans World Airlines, New York, 74; Irish Countryside Paintings; Irish Tourist Bd, Dublin, 75; US Coast Guard Aircraft Scene, US Coast Guard Air Sta, San Francisco, 77. *Exhib:* 29th Ann Soc Western Artists, M H De Young Mus, San Francisco, 71; San Francisco Art Festival, Civic Ctr, 76; Zellerbach Invitational, Zellerbach Plaza, San Francisco, 76; Industrial Graphics Int, San Jose, 77; Watercolor Technique, Marin Co Watercolor Soc, Mill Valley, Calif, 77; Third Falkirk Ann, Falkirk Cult Ctr, San Rafael, Calif, 78. *Collections Arranged:* Veterans Mem Mus, 79; one-man show, Sport's Art, Zellerbach Art Mus, 80 & Aviation Art, Bohemian Club, San Francisco, Calif, 81. *Pos:* Graphics artist, Shell Oil Co, San Francisco, 52-56; art dir, Independent J, San Rafael, Calif, 56- *Teaching:* Instr art, Acad Art Col, San Francisco, 76-77; instr illus, Col Marin, 75-; instr graphics, Indian Valley Col, Novato, Calif, 78- *Awards:* First Place Illus, San Jose State Univ, Calif, 77. *Bibliog:* Harry Callahan (auth), California Landmarks, Calif Publ, 77. *Mem:* Col Art Asn; Soc Western Artists; San Francisco Soc Commun Arts; Artists in Print; North Bay Advert Commun. *Media:* Oil, Watercolor. *Publ:* Illusr, The Alamo, Reader's Digest, 73; illusr San Francisco Giants, San Francisco Mag, 78; illusr, Chemical facts of life, Standard Oiler Mag, Standard Oil of Calif, 78. *Dealer:* Allport Assoc Gallery 1000 Magnolia Ave Larkspur CA 94939. *Mailing Add:* 84 Crestwood Dr San Rafael CA 94901

LUCHS, ALISON
HISTORIAN
b Washington, DC, Oct 5, 48. *Study:* Vassar Col, Poughkeepsie, NY, BA, 70; Johns Hopkins Univ, Baltimore, PhD, 76. *Pos:* Res asst, Ctr Advan Study Visual Arts, Washington, DC, 80-83, asst cur sculpture, 82- *Teaching:* Asst prof Swarthmore Col, Pa, 76-77; asst prof, Syracuse Univ, NY, 77-80. *Res:* Italian Renaissance, all media; local Washington, DC, architecture. *Publ:* Auth, A Relief by Benedetto da Rovezzano in the National Gallery of Art, Mitteilungen des Kunsthistorischen Inst, Florence, 74; auth, Cestello: A Cistercian Church of the Florentine Renaissance, Garland, New York, 77; auth, Michelangelo's Bologna Angel, Burlington Mag, 78; translr, Martin Wackernagel's The World of the Florentine Renaissance Artist, Princeton, 81; auth, A note on Raphael's Perugian patrons, Burlington Mag, 83. *Mailing Add:* c/o Ctr Advan Study Visual Arts Nat Gallery Art Washington DC 20565

LUCIER, MARY
VIDEO ARTIST, PHOTOGRAPHER
b Bucyrus, Ohio, Jan 25, 44. *Study:* Brandeis Univ, BA, 65. *Work:* Whitney Mus Am Art. *Comn:* Equinox (video installation), Grad Ctr, City Univ New York, 79; Planet (video installation), Hudson River Mus, 80; Winter Garden (video installation), Lower Manhattan Cult Coun, New York, 82. *Exhib:*

Everson Mus Art, 77; solo exhibs, Whitney Mus Am Art, 81 & Carnegie Inst, Pittsburgh, 83; Espace Lyonnais d'art Contemp, Lyons, France, 81; Biennial Exhib, Whitney Mus Am Art, 83; Long Beach Mus Art, Calif, 83; Walter Phillips Gallery, Banff, Alta, 83; Stedelijk Mus, Holland, 83; Mus Mod Art, New York, 83; Am Film Inst, Los Angeles, 83; and many others. *Pos:* Artist in residence, WNET Channel 13, New York, 82. *Teaching:* Instr video art, Sch Visual Arts, 79-; vis artist, Minneapolis Col Art & Design, 80 & Cleveland Inst Art, 82. *Awards:* Jerome Found Grant, 82; Media Arts Grant, Nat Endowment Arts, 83; Media Grant, NY State Coun Arts, 83; and others. *Bibliog:* Jane Bell (auth), article, Art News, summer 83; Calvin Tomkins (auth), article, New Yorker, 7/18/83; Ann Daly (auth), article, Pittsburgh Press, 8/4/83; and others. *Mem:* Media Alliance, NY (bd mem, 81-82); Parabola Arts Found Inc (bd mem & secy, currently). *Publ:* Contribr, Women's Work, Allison Knowles, 75; ed & contribr, Video Art, Harcourt Brace Jovanovich, 76; contribr, Scenarios, Assembling, 80. *Mailing Add:* 223 W 20th St New York NY 10011

LUCIONI, LUIGI
PAINTER, ETCHER
b Malnate, Italy, Nov 4, 1900; US citizen. *Study:* Cooper Union Eve Sch, 16-20; Nat Acad Design, 20-25; also with William Starkwether, 18-25. *Work:* Whitney Mus Am Art, Metrop Mus Art, New York; Pa Acad Fine Arts; Carnegie Inst. *Exhib:* Carnegie Inst Int; Art Inst Chicago; Venice Biennale, Italy; Pa Acad Fine Arts; Corcoran Gallery Art Biennial, Washington, DC; 75th Anniversary Exhib of Complete Etchings, Assoc Am Artists, New York, 76. *Teaching:* Instr portrait painting, Art Students League, 32-33. *Awards:* First Popular Prize, Carnegie Inst Int, 39; First Popular Prize, Corcoran Biennial, 47-48; Purchase Prize, Nat Acad Design, 57. *Bibliog:* The Art of Luigi Lucioni (film), Vt Educ TV, 68. *Dealer:* Hirschl & Adler Galleries 21 E 70th St New York NY 10021. *Mailing Add:* 33 W Tenth St New York NY 10011

LUCK, ROBERT
CURATOR, INSTRUCTOR
b Tonawanda, NY, Oct 31, 21. *Study:* Univ Buffalo, BFA, 47; Harvard Univ, MA, 49; Inst Meschini, Rome, Italy, cert painting, 50; Attingham Summer Sch, England, 62. *Pos:* Cur, Cincinnati Art Mus, 54-55; dir, Akron Art Inst, 55-56; dir, Telfair Acad Arts & Sci, Savannah, Ga, 56-57; asst dir, Am Fedn Arts, 58-72; cur, Contemp Wing, Finch Col Mus Art, 73-75; vis cur, Neuberger Mus, State Univ NY, Col Purchase, 78-79 & Cooper-Hewitt Mus, 80- *Teaching:* Instr, Toledo Mus Art, 52-54; instr art hist, Parsons Sch Design, 73-78; instr, Pratt Inst Sch Continuing Educ, New York, 78- *Mem:* Am Asn Mus; Col Art Asn Am. *Mailing Add:* 150 E 27th St New York NY 10016

LUCKNER, KURT T
CURATOR
b Stafford Springs, Conn, Dec 29, 45. *Study:* Georgetown Univ, AB(art hist); Stanford Univ, MA(art hist). *Collections Arranged:* Silver for the Gods: 800 Years of Greek and Roman Silver (int loaned exhib), Toledo Mus Art, Ohio, Nelson Gallery, Kansas City, Mo & Kimbell Mus Art, Ft Worth, Tex, 77-78. *Pos:* Asst cur ancient art, Stanford Univ Mus, summer 69; curatorial asst, Toledo Mus Art, Ohio, 69-70, asst cur, 70-73, cur ancient art, 73- *Mem:* Col Art Asn; Archaeol Inst Am (pres, Toledo Chap, 71-75). *Publ:* Auth, Art of Egypt-part I, Vol 14, No 1 & II, auth, Vol 15, No 3, auth, Greek vases: Shapes & uses, Vol 15, No 3, auth, African art, Vol 16, No 2 & auth, Greek gold jewelry, Vol 17, No 1, Toledo Mus News. *Mailing Add:* Toledo Mus Art 2445 Monroe St Toledo OH 43697

LUCZUN, ROBERT
SCULPTOR, PAINTER
b Passaic, NJ, Apr 6, 46. *Study:* William Paterson Col, BA, 72; Brooklyn Col, MFA, 75. *Work:* Bergen Community Mus, Paramus, NJ; Passaic Col High Sch, NJ; Espace Cardin, Paris, France. *Comn:* Mural, Collingwood High Sch, NJ, 73; bronze relief, City of Passaic, NJ, 73; Commemorative Bicentennial Envelope, US Postal Serv, 75; mural, Seton Hall Univ, 83; St Peter's Col, 83; and others. *Exhib:* Exit 154, Gregories Galleries, New York, 73; NJ Watercolor Nat, NJ Watercolor Soc, Trenton, 73; First Auction in Paris--A Flash of US Avant Garde, Espace Cardin, Paris, France, 73; Sunset Ctr Arts, Carmel, Calif, 78; Cent Wyo Mus Art, 79; and others. *Teaching:* Asst instr metal sculpture, Brooklyn Col, 73-74; instr art, Harrington Park Sch, 76- *Awards:* Nat Watercolor Soc Award, 72; First Prize, Podell Mem, 72; Academic Gold Medal of Italy, 80. *Bibliog:* Herbert C Bardes (auth), Bicentennial Metal, New York Sunday Times, 1/5/75. *Mem:* Audubon Artists; Nat Soc Painters Casein & Acrylic; Salmagundi Club; Nat Painters & Sculptors Soc; Mod Artists Guild. *Media:* Stainless Steel, Bronze; Acrylic. *Publ:* Illusr, Sculptor Luczun helps adorn village, Herald News, 10/5/72; illusr Exit 154 (cover), NJ Music & Arts Mag, 12/72; illusr, cover, New Engineering Mag, 12/72; illusr, Just between artists, Sunday Star Ledger Spectrum Mag, 9/17/72; illusr, L'Art et L'Automobile, Switz, 73. *Mailing Add:* 838 Paulison Ave Clifton NJ 07011

LUDMAN, JOAN HURWITZ
WRITER, DEALER
b Brooklyn, NY, Feb 1, 32. *Study:* Barnard Col, BA, 53; C. W. Post Col, Long Island Univ, MA, 71. *Pos:* Assoc, Mason Fine Prints, Glen Head, NY, 72-; pres, Highland House Publ Inc, Westbury, NY, 81. *Specialty:* American and European original prints. *Publ:* Coauth (with Lauris Mason), Print Reference Sources: A Select Bibliography 18th-20th Centuries, 75, 2nd ed, 79 & The Lithographs of George Bellows: A Catalogue Raisonne, 77, Kraus-Thomson Orgn Ltd; contribr, Cecile Shapiro, auth, Fine Prints: Collecting, Buying and Selling, Harper & Row, 76; co-ed (with Lauris Mason), Print Collector's

Quart: An Anthology of Essays on Eminent Printmakers of the World, 77, Kraus-Thomson Orgn Ltd; auth, Fairfield Porter: A Catalogue Raisonne of his Prints, Highland House Publ, Inc, 81. *Mailing Add:* 74 Hunters Lane Westbury NY 11590

LUDMER, JOYCE PELLERANO
LIBRARIAN, HISTORIAN

b New York, NY. *Study:* Hunter Col, BA; Univ Calif, Los Angeles, with Carlo Pedretti, MLS & MA(art hist). *Pos:* Humanities bibliographer, Calif State Univ, Northridge, 70-72; librn, Elmer Belt Libr Vinciana, Univ Calif, Los Angeles, 73-75; head librn, Art Libr, Univ Calif, Los Angeles, 75- *Mem:* Art Libr Soc NAm (vchmn & chmn elect, 78-79); Col Art Asn; Am Libr Asn; Asn Col & Res Libr. *Res:* Leonardo da Vinci studies; art bibliography. *Interests:* Renaissance, classical & baroque art history; art bibliography. *Mailing Add:* Art Libr Univ Calif 405 Hilgard Ave Los Angeles CA 90024

LUDTKE, LAWRENCE MONROE
SCULPTOR

b Houston, Tex, Oct 18, 29. *Study:* Univ Houston, BS; Coppini Acad Fine Art, San Antonio, with Waldine Tauch. *Comn:* Charging Bronze Rams, Johnson & Johnson Inc, San Angelo, Tex, 66; Dr Denton Cooley (bronze bust), St Lukes Hosp, Houston, 69; Eddie Wokecki (bronze bas relief), Rice Univ, Houston, 69; Pieta (bronze group), St Marys Sem, Houston, 74; Fiona O'Donnell (bronze bust), comn by Dr Manus O'Donnell, Houston, 74; and many others. *Mem:* Fel Nat Sculpture Soc. *Media:* Bronze, Marble. *Mailing Add:* 10127 Whiteside Houston TX 77043

LUDWIG, ALLAN I
PHOTOGRAPHER, HISTORIAN

b Yonkers, NY, June 9, 33. *Study:* Yale Univ, with Josef Albers, Charles Seymour, Jr & Erwin R Goodenough, BFA, 56, MA, 60, Bollingen Found fel, 60-63, PhD, 64. *Work:* Mus Mod Art, New York; Smithsonian Inst & Libr Cong; Yale Univ Art Gallery, New Haven, Conn; Walker Art Ctr; Polaroid Found Collection; and others. *Exhib:* One-man shows, Reflections out of Time, Metrop Mus & Art Ctr, Miami, Fla, 76, Photographs, Jorgenson Art Gallery, Univ Conn, Storrs, 76, Alternative Ctr for Int Arts, New York, 77, Alonzo Gallery, New York, 78, Watson Art Gallery, Wheaton Col, Norton, Mass, 78 & The City as Image, Art Gallery, RI Col, Providence, 78; Independent Am Photog, Int Show, Poland, 80; il Diaframma, Milan, Italy, 81; Newhouse Invitational, New York, 81; Simon Gallery, Mountclair, NJ, 83. *Pos:* Pres, Colonial Arts Found, 60-; chmn bd, Alternative Mus, New York, 78-83; dir, Ludwig Portfolios, 81- *Awards:* Am Philosophical Soc Fel, 66; Am Coun Learned Soc Fel, 67; H M Forbes Award, Asn Gravestone Studies, 81. *Mem:* Col Art Asn; Asn for Gravestone Studies. *Publ:* Auth, Graven Images, Wesleyan Univ Press, 66; auth, Philip Grausman sculptor, 11/76, Lawrence Fane: sculptor, 11/76 & Richard Lytle: paintings, 3/77, Arts Mag; auth, Holy Land USA, The Clarion, summer 79; auth, Beyond Photography I, II, Alternative Mus, 81 & 82. *Dealer:* Jack Alonzo Gallery 30 W 57th St New York NY 10019; Douglas Elliott Gallery San Francisco CA. *Mailing Add:* 141 Upper Mountain Ave Montclair NJ 07042

LUDWIG, EVA
SCULPTOR

b Berlin, Ger, May 25, 23; US citizen. *Study:* Greenwich House Pottery, with Lu Duble, 58-62; Sculptor's Workshop, with Harold Castor, 64; Craft Students League, wood sculpture with Domenico Facci, 68; Queens Col, sculpture with Richard Miller, 80-81. *Exhib:* Own Your Own, Denver Art Mus, 68; Cooperstown Art Asn Ann, NY, 71, 73 & 74; Nonmem Exhib, Nat Sculpture Soc, New York, 72; Ann, 81 & Artist of the Month, 82, Woodstock Guild Craftsmen; Pen & Brush Sculpture Exhib, 82; Catherine Lorillard Wolfe Art Club Exhib, 83. *Awards:* Best in Wood, 69 & Bert Wangler Mem Award, 72, Woodstock Guild Craftsmen; First Prize in Sculpture, Cooperstown Art Asn, 71. *Mem:* Woodstock Guild Craftsmen; Artists Equity Asn NY. *Media:* Wood, Clay. *Mailing Add:* 57-44 164th St Flushing NY 11365

LUECKING, STEPHEN JOSEPH
SCULPTOR, EDUCATOR

b Belleville, Ill, Aug 11, 48. *Study:* Quincy Col, Ill, BFA, 70; Bradley Univ, Peoria, Ill, grad study, 71; Miami Univ, Oxford, Ohio, MFA, 73. *Work:* Ill State Mus, Springfield. *Comn:* Miami Sun Reservoir (with Margaret Lanterman), Miami Univ & Nat Endowment Arts, Oxford, Ohio, 80. *Exhib:* Ill Arts Coun, traveling, 78; Fed Ctr Mus, Chicago, 78; Ill State Mus, Springfield, 78; Art Inst Chicago, 79; Contemp Arts Ctr, Cincinnati, 80; Chicago Cult Ctr, 81; and others. *Collections Arranged:* Seven Sculptors, 78 & Stuart Court Installations (auth, catalog), 81-82, DePaul Univ; Paul Caponigro & Charles Ross, Archaeoastronomy Am Conf, St John's Col, 79. *Teaching:* Asst prof, Purdue Univ, West Lafayette, Ind, 74-76; assoc prof, DePaul Univ, Chicago, 76-; vis artist, Sch Art Inst Chicago, 79. *Awards:* Clussman Prize, Art Inst Chicago, 78; project grants, Ill Arts Coun, 78, 80 & 81; Pougialis Award, Columbia Col, 81. *Bibliog:* Alan Artner (auth), The Nation: Chicago, Art News, summer, 77; Holliday T Day (auth), Chicago Invitational, Art Am, 11/78; Wendy Hoffman-Yuni, article, New Art Examiner, 3/79. *Media:* Steel, Concrete. *Dealer:* Roy Boyd 215 West Superior Chicago IL 60610. *Mailing Add:* 1837 West Roscoe Chicago IL 60657

LUEDERS, JIMMY C
PAINTER, INSTRUCTOR

b Jacksonville, Fla, July 4, 27. *Study:* Pa Acad Fine Arts, William Emlen Cresson Mem traveling scholar, 50, Henry Schiedt Mem scholar, 51. *Work:* Pa Acad Fine Arts; Philadelphia Mus Art; Sch Pharmacy & Tyler Sch Art,

Temple Univ; Moore Col Art, Philadelphia. *Exhib:* Butler Art Inst, Youngstown, Ohio; Am Fedn Art Traveling Exhib Art Schs, 56; Metrop Young Artist Show, Nat Arts Club, New York, 60; Nat Acad Design, New York, 60; Nat Inst Arts & Lett, New York, 69. *Teaching:* Instr painting, Pa Acad Fine Arts, 57- *Awards:* Third Hallgarten Prize, Nat Acad Design, New York, 60; Percy M Owens Mem Award for Distinguished Pa Artist, 80. *Media:* Acrylic. *Dealer:* Marian Locks Gallery 1524 Walnut St Philadelphia PA 19102. *Mailing Add:* c/o Pa Acad Fine Arts Broad & Cherry Sts Philadelphia PA 19102

LUISI, JERRY
SCULPTOR, INSTRUCTOR

b Minneapolis, Minn, Oct 7, 39. *Study:* Nat Acad Design, cert; Art Students League. *Work:* Agriculture Hall Fame, Kansas City, Mo; Nat Acad Design, New York. *Comn:* BASF Corp, Parsippany, NJ, 81. *Exhib:* Nat Acad Design, 70, 74 & 81; Allied Artists Am, 71, 72 & 75; Nat Sculpture Soc, 74-; Mus Fine Arts, Springfield, Mass, 77; Salmagundi Club, 80 & 81; and others. *Teaching:* Instr sculpture, Fine Arts Prog, Fashion Inst Technol, 72- & Nat Acad Design, 79- *Awards:* Greenshields Found Grant, 72 & 75; Anna Hyatt Huntington Award, Hudson Valley Art Asn, 80; John Gregory Award, Nat Sculpture Soc, 80; and others. *Bibliog:* Articles, Nat Sculpture Rev, fall 80. *Mem:* Nat Sculpture Soc; Acad Artists Asn; life mem Art Students League; Artists Equity Asn. *Media:* Multimedia. *Mailing Add:* 37 E 28th St New York NY 10016

LUITJENS, HELEN ANITA
INSTRUCTOR, PAINTER

b Bakersfield, Calif. *Study:* Univ Redlands, BA; Univ Southern Calif, MA; Univ Hawaii, scholar, 63; Univ Calif, Los Angeles; Inst Art San Miguel de Allenda. *Work:* Munic Art Dept, Los Angeles; Inst Mex Norteamericano de Relaciones Cult, Mexico City; Anderson Konstmuseum, Helsinki, Finland; Konst Salongen Kavaletten, Uppsala, Sweden; Union Bank, Los Angeles. *Exhib:* Inst Mexicano Norteamericano de Relaciones Cult, 69; Konst Salongen Kavaletten, 73; Nat Watercolor Soc, Laguna Beach, Calif, 74; Pac Cult Mus Pasadena, 74; Palos Verdes Art Mus, 75. *Teaching:* Chmn dept art, Paul Revere Jr High, Los Angeles, 55-72; teacher pvt classes, 72-79; lectr painting & drawing, Chapman Col World Campus Afloat; lectr art hist, E Mediterr, Black Sea, Panama Canal & Alaska Cruises, 75. *Awards:* 30 awards in art shows in Southern California, 65-75. *Mem:* Nat Watercolor Soc (mem bd, corresp secy, 75); Women Painters West; Arizona Artists Guild; Los Angeles Art Asn Watercolor West; Ariz Watercolor Asn. *Media:* Watercolor. *Publ:* Contribr, Mosaics, Drawing, Elegant Era, Los Angeles Times & Beter Homes & Gardens. *Dealer:* Challis Gallery Laguna Beach CA. *Mailing Add:* 9818 Lindgren Ave Sun City AZ 85373

LUKAS, DENNIS BRIAN
PAINTER, EDUCATOR

b Hamilton, Ont, Can, June 21, 47. *Study:* St Michael's Sch Cantorum, Toronto, Dipl(ancient music); Doon Sch Fine Art, Ont, with Henri Masson, Carl Schaefer & Tony Onley; McMaster Univ, with Tony Urquhart; Montreal Mus Sch Fine Art, with Arthur Lismer, grad dipl; Atelier 17, Paris, France, with Stanley Hayter. *Work:* Munson-Williams-Proctor Inst, Utica, NY; Art Gallery Hamilton, Ont; Bibliot Nat, Paris; Montreal Mus Fine Arts; Art Gallery Greater Victoria, BC; and many others. *Exhib:* One-man show, Stable Gallery, Montreal Mus Fine Arts, Can, 70; Retrospective Eleven Yrs, McKenzie Gallery, Trent Univ, Peterborough, Ont, 74; Peripheries, Mus d'Art Contemporain, Montreal, 74; Young Contemporaries, Art Gallery of London, Ont, 75; Forum 76, Montreal Mus Fine Arts, 76; On View Visual Arts Ont (touring 14 mus), 76-77; traveling exhib, Ctr Cult, Drummondville, Que, 80; Gallery 76, Ont Col Art, Toronto, 80; and others. *Teaching:* Instr drawing & painting, Montreal Mus Sch, Que, 71-74; lectr drawing & painting, Univ Toronto, Ont, 75-76; vis asst prof drawing & painting, Hamilton Col, Clinton, NY, 76-78. *Awards:* Can Coun Grants, 67, 68 & 72; Ontario Arts Coun Award, 74-76, 78 & 80; A J Casson Award, Seneca Col, Willowdale, Ont, 78. *Bibliog:* Catharine Bates (auth), article, Montreal Star, 73; Kim Todd (auth), article, The Grimsby Independent, 74; Andre Dupont & Henri Barras (coauth), Lukas, Ctr Cult, Drummondville, Que, 80. *Mem:* Niagara Artists Co. *Media:* All. *Dealer:* Flavio Belli PO Box 6395 Station A Toronto ON M5W 1X3; Le Groupe Somerville CP8 Victoria Sta Westmount PQ H3Z 1Q3 Can. *Mailing Add:* 51 Main St W Grimsby ON L3M 1R3 Canada

LUKASIEWICZ, RONALD JOSEPH
PRINTMAKER, SCULPTOR

b Pittsburgh, Pa, Apr 20, 43. *Study:* Carnegie-Mellon Univ, BFA; Univ Ga, MFA. *Work:* Pittsburgh Pub Schs, Pa; Dow Chemical Co, Midland, Mich; City of Athens, Ga; Bankers Trust Co, NC; and others. *Comn:* Suite of serigraphs, 73 & bound book of serigraphs, 73, Dow Chemical Co, Midland, Mich; modular sculpture, Scorpio Rising Workshop, Farmington, Ga, 73; modular sculpture, City of Athens, Ga, 77; suite of serigraphs, Thornet Furniture, Dallas, 81. *Exhib:* 10th Ann Piedmont Graphics Exhib, Mint Mus of Art, Charlotte, NC, 73; Assoc Artists Ann Show, Carnegie Mus, Pittsburgh, Pa, 73; Medals, Banners, Ribbons, Pittsburgh Arts & Crafts Ctr, Pa, 74; Ga Nat, Lyndon House Galleries, Athens, 76; Moving Parts & Captured Light, The Third Floor, Atlanta; Spectrum I, Lyndon House Art Ctr, Athens, Ga, 80; Western Carolina Univ, Cullowhee, NC, 81; and others. *Pos:* Dir cult activities, Athens, Ga, 74-76; preparator, Ga Mus of Art, Univ Ga, 76-; dir, Climax Press, 83- *Awards:* Purchase Award, Assoc Artists of Pittsburgh, Pittsburgh Pub Schs, 72; Award, Lyndon House Art Ctr, 81. *Bibliog:* D Miller (auth), Exhibit review, Pittsburgh Post Gazette, 74; J Chappell (producer), Scorpio Rising (16mm film doc), 74; Screen Printing Today, WGTV Television, 74. *Mem:* Col Arts Asn; Assoc Artist of Pittsburgh; Athens Art Asn. *Mailing Add:* 181 W Cloverhurst Ave Athens GA 30605

LUKIN, SVEN
PAINTER

b Riga, Latvia, Feb 14, 34. *Study:* Univ Pa. *Work:* Albright-Knox Art Gallery, Buffalo, NY; Los Angeles Co Mus Art; Larry Aldrich Mus, Ridgefield, Conn; Univ Tex, Austin; Whitney Mus Am Art, New York; and others. *Exhib:* Univ Ill, Urbana, 65; Torcuato di Tella, Buenos Aires, Arg, 65; New shapes of Color, Stedelijk Mus, Amsterdam, Holland, 66; Univ Colo, Denver, 67; Painting: Out From the Wall, Des Moines Art Ctr, Iowa, 68; New Work, Los Angeles Co Mus Art, 78; and others. *Awards:* Guggenheim Fel, 66. *Bibliog:* Sam Hunter (ed), New Art Around the World, Abrams, 66; Allen S Weller (auth), The Joys & Sorrows of Recent American Art, Univ Ill, 68; Gregory Battcock (ed), Minimal Art: a Critical Anthology, Dutton, 68. *Mailing Add:* 807 Ave of the Americas New York NY 10001

LUKOSIUS, RICHARD BENEDICT
PAINTER, EDUCATOR

b Waterbury, Conn, Oct 26, 18. *Study:* Yale Univ, with Josef Albers, BFA & MFA. *Exhib:* New Eng Artists, Slater Mus, Norwich, Conn, 68; Contemp Drawings, Univ Conn, Storrs, 71; Frascati Gallery, Stonington, Conn, 77; Sculpture & Drawings by Conn Artists, Slater Mus, Norwich, 79; Invitational Print Exhib, Mystic Art Gallery, Conn, 79; and many other group & one-man shows. *Teaching:* Prof painting, drawing & graphic design, Conn Col, 54- *Media:* Acrylic. *Mailing Add:* Dept of Art Conn Col New London CT 06320

LUMBARD, JEAN ASHMORE
DEALER

b Clinton, SC. *Study:* Columbia Univ. *Specialty:* Contemporary art; original prints, paintings on canvas, tapestries and sculpture by international artists with emphasis on American artists. *Mailing Add:* 38 E 57th St New York NY 10022

LUMBERS, JAMES RICHARD
PAINTER, DESIGNER

b Toronto, Ont, Can, Oct 8, 29. *Study:* Ont Col of Art, AOCA, 50; study with William Maltman, Toronto. *Exhib:* Ont Soc of Artists, Oshawa, 71; Nature Can, Nat Mus Can, 73, 76-78; Beckett Gallery, Hamilton, Ont, 75; Sportsman's Edge Gallery, New York, 78; one-man shows, Royal Ont Mus, Toronto, Can, 69, 73; Ont Sci Ctr, Toronto, 70; Kennedy Galleries Inc, New York, 72; Toronto Dominion Ctr, McMichael Can Collection, Kleinburg, Ont, 78; Le Moyne Art Found, Tallahassee, Fla, 78; and many others. *Pos:* Graphic designer, James Lumbers Graphics Ltd, Toronto, 62-; artist-in-residence, Edward Ball Wildlife Found, Tallahassee, Fla, 78. *Awards:* Two Silver Medals, Packing Asn of Can, 67. *Bibliog:* Anker Idum (auth), James Lumbers, Artist, Nature Can, 75; Prime Time Tu Show, WFSU, Public Broadcasting System, 78; Documented by Nat Gallery Can, Ottawa. *Mem:* Fel Explorers Club, New York; Soc Animal Artists, New York. *Media:* Acrylic, Tempra & Watercolor. *Publ:* Illusr, Encyclopedia Canadian, Grolier Soc, 58; illusr, The Firebirds, Queen's Printer, 74. *Dealer:* Westmount Gallery Ltd 3067 Bloor St W Toronto Can N8X 1C4. *Mailing Add:* Pointe Au Baril ON P0Q 1K0 Canada

LUMSDEN, IAN GORDON
DIRECTOR

b Montreal, Que, June 8, 45. *Study:* McGill Univ, Montreal, BA, 68. *Collections Arranged:* The First Decade (with catalog), Confedn Ctr Art Gallery & Mus, Charlottetown, PEI, 75; Wallace S Bird Mem Collection (with catalog), Beaverbrook Art Gallery, Fredericton, NB, 75; Bloomsbury Painters & Their Circle (US & Can traveling exhib), 76-78; The Queen Comes to New Brunswick: Paintings & Drawings by Molly Lamb Bobak (Can traveling exhib), 77-78; Drawings by Jack Weldon Humphrey (Can traveling exhib), 77-79; The Murray and Marguerite Vaughan Inuit Print Collection (Can traveling exhib), 81-82. *Pos:* Cur art dept, New Brunswick Mus, St John, NB, 69; cur & dir, Beaverbrook Art Gallery, 69-; dir, Arts Atlantic, 77-; dir, Can Cult Property Export Rev Bd, 82- *Mem:* Can Art Mus Dirs Orgn (pres, 83-); Can Mus Asn (secy-treas, 73-75); Atlantic Prov Art Gallery Asn (chmn, 70-72); Secondary Art Sub-Comt for NB Schs; Am Asn Mus. *Res:* 19th & 20th century Canadian art. *Publ:* Auth, Warkov, No 66 & Forrestall: de l'expressionnisme a l'hyperrealisme, No 67, Vie des Arts; auth, Artist in New Brunswick: George Neilson Smith, Can Antiques Collector, 5-6/75. *Mailing Add:* Beaverbrook Art Gallery PO Box 605 Fredericton NB E3B 5A6 Canada

LUNA, (ANTONIO RODRIGUEZ)
PAINTER

b Montoro, Spain, June 22, 10; Mex citizen. *Study:* Sch Fine Arts, Seville, 23-27; Royal Acad San Fernando, Madrid, 27-29. *Work:* Nat Mus Mod Art, Madrid; Fine Arts Gallery San Diego; Nat Mus Mod Art, Mexico City. *Exhib:* One-man shows, Venice Biennial, 34, Nat Mus Art, Washington, DC, 41, Fine Arts Gallery San Diego, 67 & Mus Mod Art, Mex, 74; Retrospective, Nat Palace Fine Arts, Mexico City, 59. *Teaching:* Prof painting, San Carlos Acad, Nat Univ Mex, 49-69. *Awards:* First Prize Painting, Nat Contest Painting & Design, Barcelona, 38; Guggenheim Fel, 41-43; First Prize Painting, Nat Inst Fine Arts Ann, Mex, 63. *Bibliog:* M Nelkin (auth), El expressionismo Mexicano, Inst Nac Bellas Artes, 64; Image of Mexico, Tex Quart, 69; Juan Rejano (auth), Antonio Rodriguez Luna, Nat Univ Mex, 71. *Media:* Oil. *Mailing Add:* c/o Wenger Gallery Box 3100 La Jolla CA 92038

LUND, DAVID
PAINTER, EDUCATOR

b New York, NY, Oct 16, 25. *Study:* Queens Col (NY), BA; New York Univ. *Work:* Toronto Art Gallery; Whitney Mus Am Art; Chase Manhattan Bank, NY; Baltimore Mus, Md; Corcoran Gallery Art, Washington, DC. *Exhib:* Whitney Mus Am Art, New York, 58, 60-62 & 77; eight one-man shows, Grace Borgenicht Gallery, NY, 60-83; Baltimore Mus, Md, 60; Albright-Knox Art Gallery, Buffalo, NY, 63; Everson Mus Art, Syracuse, NY, 63; Pa Acad Fine Arts, Philadelphia, 65, 66 & 69; Nat Collection Fine Arts, White House, 66-69; Am Acad Arts & Lett, 69-70, 76 & 77; Kent State Univ, Ohio, 69 & 71; Denver Art Mus, Colo, 70; Smithsonian Inst, Washington, DC, 70, 72 & 73; and many others. *Pos:* Consult, Creative Artists Pub Serv Program, 79-81. *Teaching:* Instr painting, Cooper Union Art Sch, 55-74; Parsons Sch Design, 63-69; asst prof painting, Columbia Univ, 69-; vis prof, Boston Univ, 75-76. *Awards:* Fulbright Grant Italy, 57-59; Ford Found Purchase Prize, Whitney Mus Am Art, 61; Childe Hassam Purchase Award, Am Acad Arts & Lett, 69. *Bibliog:* Bruce St John (auth), David Lund, Arts, 10/76; Diane Cochrane (auth), The psychological landscape of David Lund, Am Artist, 10/78; Barbara Rosecrance (auth), Landscape as metaphor: The recent work of David Lund, Arts, 84. *Dealer:* Borgenicht Gallery Inc 724 Fifth Ave New York NY 10019. *Mailing Add:* 470 West End Ave New York NY 10024

LUND, JANE
PAINTER, PRINTMAKER

Study: Pratt Inst, 56. *Work:* Nelson Gallery Found, Kansas City, Mo; de Saisset Mus, Santa Clara, Calif; De Cordova Mus, Lincoln, Mass. *Exhib:* New England Women 1975, De Cordova Mus, Mass, 75; Davidson Nat Print & Drawing Competition, NC; Worcester Mus, Mass; Women on Women, George W V Smith Art Mus, Springfield, Mass; one-person show, Pucker-Safrai Gallery, Boston, 79. *Teaching:* Instr drawing, Berkshire Community Col, Pittsfield, Mass, 72-81. *Awards:* Cini Found Summer Scholar, Venice, Italy, 66; First Prize Painting, Berkshire Art Asn, Berkshire Mus, 78; Rose Art Mus Art of the State Artists Found Grant, 79. *Bibliog:* Pastel paintings of Jane Lund, Mass Rev, spring 77; Eight women portrait artists, Mass Rev, summer 83. *Media:* Highly Finished Pastels & Lithographs; Hand Built Figure Ceramics. *Dealer:* Forum Gallery Inc 1018 Madison Avenue New York NY 10021. *Mailing Add:* Norton Hill Rd Ashfield MA 01330

LUNDE, KARL ROY
HISTORIAN, WRITER

b New York, NY, Nov 1, 31. *Study:* Columbia Univ, BA, MA & PhD. *Pos:* Dir, The Contemporaries, New York, 56-65. *Teaching:* Instr art hist, Sch Gen Studies, Columbia Univ, 58-70; prof art hist, William Paterson Col NJ, 70- *Res:* Italian Renaissance bronzes; 19th century romantic art in Scandinavia; 20th century American painting. *Publ:* Contribr, Art & Artists, 72; contribr, Arts Mag, 75-; auth, Isabel Bishop, 75 & auth, Richard Anuszkiewicz, 77, Abrams; auth, The Graphic Works of Robert Kipniss, Abaris Bks Inc, 80. *Mailing Add:* 440 Riverside Dr New York NY 10027

LUNDEBERG, HELEN (HELEN LUNDEBERG FEITELSON)
PAINTER

b Chicago, Ill, June 24, 08. *Study:* With Lorser Feitelson. *Work:* Los Angeles Co Mus Art, Calif; San Francisco Mus Art; Joseph H Hirshhorn Collection; La Jolla Mus Contemp Art; Nat Mus Am Art, Washington, DC. *Exhib:* Fantastic Art, Dada, Surrealism, Mus Mod Art, New York, 36-37; Whitney Mus Am Art, New York, 62, 65 & 67; Painting & Sculpture in Calif: The Mod Era, San Francisco Mus Mod Art & Nat Collection Fine Arts, Washington, DC, 76-77; First Western States Biennial Traveling Show, 79 & 80; Lorser Feitelson and Helen Lundeberg Retrospective Exhib, San Francisco Mus Mod Art, 80; Helen Lundeberg Since 1970, Palm Springs Desert Mus, 83; California Contemporary, Monterey Peninsula Mus, 83; and others. *Awards:* Award for Outstanding Achivements in the Visual Arts, Women's Caucus Art, 81. *Bibliog:* Diane Moran (auth), Helen Lundeberg: the sixties and seventies, Art Int, 5/79; Charlotte S Rubinstein (auth), American Women Artists, Hall & Co, 82; Prudence Carlson (auth), Deep space, Art Am, 2/83; and others. *Media:* Acrylic & Oil. *Mailing Add:* 8307 W Third St Los Angeles CA 90048

LUNDEEN, GEORGE WAYNE
SCULPTOR

b Holdrege, Nebr, Aug 26, 48. *Study:* Hastings Col, Nebr, BA, 71; Univ Ill, MFA(sculpture), 73; Accademia de Belle Arte, Italy, 74. *Work:* Nebr State Collection, Kearney; Peoples Republic China, Nat Gallery, Peking; Holdrege, Nebraska. *Exhib:* North Am Sculpture Exhib, Foot Hills Art Ctr, 79-81; Allied Artists Am Ann, New York, 80 & 81; Nat Sculpture Soc Ann, New York, 80 & 81; Nat Acad Design Ann, New York, 81; Am Western Art Exhib, Peking Arts Gallery, China, 81. *Pos:* Fulbright-Hays Scholar, Florence, Italy, 73-74; artist-in-residence, Texas A & M Univ, 78-79. *Awards:* Silver Medal, Nat Sculpture Soc, 82; Gold Medal, Nat Acad Design, 82; Art Castings of Colorado Award, NAm Sculpture Exhib, 83. *Bibliog:* John Jellico (auth), G W Lundeen, Artist of the Rockies & Golden West, spring 81; M Lantz & T Morgan (auths), The western art of 12 western sculptors, Nat Sculpture Review, fall, 80; Libby James (auth), George Lundeen, Southwest Art, 5/83. *Mem:* Nat Sculpture Soc; Allied Artists Am. *Media:* Bronze, Terra-cotta. *Mailing Add:* PO Box 432 Loveland CO 80539

LUNDIN, NORMAN K
PAINTER

b Los Angeles, Calif, 1938. *Study:* Sch Art Inst Chicago, BA, 61; Univ Chicago, 61; Univ Cincinnati, MFA, 63; Univ Oslo, Norway, 63. *Work:* Whitney Mus Am Art & Mus Mod Art, New York; Nat Collection Fine Arts, Washington, DC; San Francisco Mus Mod Art; Seattle Art Mus. *Exhib:* Barnsdale Gallery, Los Angeles Munic Mus; Seattle Art Mus; solo exhibs, Allan Stone Gallery, New York, Space Gallery, Los Angeles & Jack Rasmussen Gallery, Washington, DC. *Pos:* Vis artist, Hornsey Col Art, London, Eng, 69-70, Wash State Univ, Pullman, 73, Ohio State Univ,

Columbus, 75, San Diego State Univ, 78 & Brighton Col Art, Eng, 79. *Teaching:* Prof art, Univ Washington, Seattle, 64- *Awards:* Grants, Fulbright Found, 63-64, Ford Found, 78-79 & Nat Endowment Arts, 83. *Dealer:* Allan Stone Gallery 48 East 86th St New York NY 10028; Jack Rasmussen Gallery 313 G St NW Washington DC. *Mailing Add:* c/o Francine Seders Gallery 6701 Greenwood Ave N Seattle WA 98103

LUNN, HARRY, JR
DEALER
b Detroit, Mich, Apr 29, 33. *Pos:* Pres, Lunn Gallery/Graphics Int Ltd, currently. *Mem:* Art Dealers Asn Am; Royal Photographic Soc, Eng. *Specialty:* Nineteenth and twentieth century prints and drawings; rare photographs; the estates of Milton Avery and George Grosz. *Publ:* Auth, Milton Avery-Prints (catalog), 73. *Mailing Add:* 3242 P St NW Washington DC 20007

LUNSFORD, JOHN (CRAWFORD)
HISTORIAN, CURATOR
b Dallas, Tex, Apr 15, 33. *Study:* Harvard Univ, AB(Eng lit), 54; Columbia Univ, MA(pre-Columbian art hist & archaeol), 67. *Collections Arranged:* The Clark and Frances Stillman Collection of Congo Sculpture (with catalog), 69; Arts of Oceania (with catalog), 70; The Romantic Vision in America (with catalog), 71; African Art from Dallas Collections (with catalog), 72; The Gustave and Franyo Schindler Collection of African Sculpture (with catalog), 75; Nora and John Wise Collection of Pre-Columbian Art, 76. *Pos:* Curator, Dallas Mus Art, 68-80, sr cur, 80- *Teaching:* Adj prof art hist, Southern Methodist Univ, Dallas, 67- *Res:* The arts of pre-Columbian Mesoamerica and West and Central Africa; pre-Columbian Central and South America, Oceania. *Mailing Add:* Dallas Mus of Art 1717 N Harwood Dallas TX 75201

LUNTZ, IRVING
DEALER
b Milwaukee, Wis, Jan 9, 29. *Pos:* Pres & dir, Irving Galleries, Inc, Palm Beach, Fla, 59- *Mem:* Art Dealers Asn Am; Appraisers Asn Am. *Res:* Nineteenth and twentieth century American and European painting; sculpture and graphics. *Mailing Add:* 332 Worth Ave Palm Beach FL 33480

LUPORI, PETER JOHN
EDUCATOR, SCULPTOR
b Pittsburgh, Pa, Dec 12, 18. *Study:* Carnegie-Mellon Univ, BFA, 42; Univ of Minn, MS(educ), 47; studied with Joseph Bailey Ellis & John Rood. *Work:* The Walker Art Ctr, Minneapolis, Minn; Ball State Teachers Col Art Gallery, Muncie, Ind; North Hennepin Community Col Art Gallery, Fridley, Minn; Albert Lea Pub Libr, Minn; Minn Alumni Asn Art Gallery, IDS Ctr, Minneapolis. *Comn:* Crucifix & Madonna (aluminum), Stations (ceramic), Holy Childhood Church, St Paul, Minn, 56-58; ten stained glass windows, First Methodist Church, Monmouth, Ill, 61; Medicine Int (ceramic bas-releif), Fairview-Southdale Hosp, Edina, Minn, 65-67; 24 stained glass windows, Minnehaha United Methodist Church, Minneapolis, Minn, 66; Creation (ceramic bas-releif), Westminster Presbyterian Church, Minneapolis, 82. *Exhib:* Ann Assoc Artist of Pittsburgh, Carnegie Inst of Art, Pa, 40-62; Biennial Exhib of Paintings & Prints, Walker Art Ctr, Minneapolis, 47-49; 1st Biennial Exhib Prints & Drawing, Minneapolis Inst of Arts, 50, 52-54; Six-State Sculpture Exhib, Walker Art Ctr, 47, 51; Ann Local Artists Exhibs, Minneapolis Inst of Arts, 47-48, 50-52; 16th Ceramic Ann Nat Exhib, Syracuse, NY, 51; Fine Arts Exhib, Minn State Fair Art Gallery, St Paul, 46-; one-man show, St Paul Mus of Art, 52. *Teaching:* Instr sculpture, Univ of Minn, Minneapolis, 46-49; asst prof, sculpture, Col of St Thomas, St Paul, Minn, 49-51; prof sculpture, The Col of St Catherine, St Paul, 47- *Awards:* 2nd award in sculpture, Prix de Rome, NY, 41; Carnegie Inst Prize for Sculpture, Assoc Artists of Pittsburgh, 49; Emily Aylsenberg Award, Asn Artists Pittsburgh, 62. *Mem:* Artists Equity Asn; Soc Minn Sculptors; Minn Artists Asn; Pittsburgh Artists Asn. *Media:* Ceramic, Wood. *Mailing Add:* c/o Dept of Art 2004 Randolph Ave St Paul MN 55105

LUPPER, EDWARD
PAINTER
b NJ, Jan 4, 36. *Study:* With Wesley Lea, Frenchtown, NJ; Trenton Jr Col; Parsons Sch Design, New York; Calif Col Arts & Crafts, Oakland; San Francisco Art Inst; San Francisco State Col; M H de Young Mem Mus Sch, 78. *Work:* Works in pvt collections only. *Exhib:* Baltimore Mus Art, 55; Tucson Art Ctr, Ariz, 59; Fort Worth Art Ctr, 60; San Francisco Mus Art, 60; Am Embassy, Belg, 77-78. *Awards:* Huntington Hartford Found Fel, 64. *Bibliog:* Article, San Francisco Chronicle, 60, San Francisco Examr, 62 & 65 & Seattle Times, 71. *Media:* Casein, Oil. *Publ:* Auth, article, Playgirl, 74, Apartment Life, 9/74, Popular Gardening Indoors, 77, Eaton Paper Corp, 77 & 78 & Sunrise Publ, 79-80. *Dealer:* Phillips Galleries 2517 Fairmount Dallas TX 75201; Phillips Gallery 206 North Ave Palm Beach FL 33480. *Mailing Add:* 1255 Pacific San Francisco CA 94109

LURAY, J (J LURAY SCHAFFNER)
PRINTMAKER, DESIGNER
b Columbus, Ohio, Apr 14, 39. *Study:* Ohio State Univ; Columbus Col Art & Design, BFA(advert), 62. *Work:* Nat Educ Asn, Cleveland, Ohio; Prather, Seeger, Farmer & Doolittle, Washington, DC; Columbus Col Art & Design; Commun Satellite Corp, Washington, DC. *Exhib:* James River Contemp Art Exhib, Mariners Mus, Norfolk, Va, 72-73; Northern Va Fine Arts Asn Artists Exhib, Alexandria, 73-75, 77, 79 & 81; First Int Exhib of Monoprints, Oglethorpe Univ, Atlanta, Ga, 73; Ann Paper Works Show, Charlottesville, Va, 74-76; 19th Area Exhib, Corcoran Gallery Art, Washington, DC, 74. *Pos:* Advert designer, W P Simpson, Columbus, 60-62 & Paul L Devaney Studio,

Columbus, 62-69. *Awards:* First Prize Graphics (monoprint), J Carter Brown, Washington, DC, 72; First in Graphics (monoprint), Sigsbe Gilham Award, Art League, 73-76; Jane Livingston Graphics Award, Northern Va Fine Arts Asn, Alexandria, 75. *Bibliog:* Martin Sharter (auth), Art & singular images, Atlanta Mag, 73. *Mem:* Columbus Gallery Fine Art; Springfield Art Guild, Va; Art League Northern Va, Alexandria; St Louis Artist Guild. *Media:* Monoprints. *Dealer:* Foliograph Gallery Tyson's Corner Ctr McLean VA 22101. *Mailing Add:* 483 Hillbrook Dr St Louis MO 63011

LURIA, GLORIA
DEALER
b New York, NY. *Study:* Pratt Inst; Art Students League; Skidmore Col, BS. *Pos:* Owner-dir, Gloria Luria Gallery, Miami, Fla, currently. *Mem:* Art Dealers Asn SFla. *Specialty:* Contemporary paintings; sculpture; graphics; tapestries. *Mailing Add:* 1033 Kane Concourse Bay Harbor Island Miami Beach FL 33154

LUSKER, RON
PAINTER, DESIGNER
b Chicago, Ill, Jan 28, 37. *Study:* Sch Art Inst Chicago, 54-60; Univ Ill, Chicago Circle, Ill State Gen Assembly scholar, 57-62; Univ Chicago, 62-63; Southern Ill Univ, Carbondale, BA, 65, MFA, 66. *Work:* Univ NC; Price Waterhouse, Chicago; Chase Manhattan; Southern Ill Univ; Aldrich Mus Contemp Art. *Exhib:* 14th Ann Painting & Sculpture Exhib, Peoria Art Ctr, Ill, 66; 70th Ann Midwest Painting Exhib, Art Inst Chicago, 67; Convocation Arts, Sculpture, State Univ NY Albany, 68; 4th Ann Art Exhib Sculpture, Staten Island, 69; Eastern Seaboard Regional 3rd Ann Sculpture Exhib, 70; plus others. *Teaching:* Instr art, Southern Ill Univ, Carbondale, 65-67; asst prof art, State Univ NY Stony Brook, 68-72; assoc prof art, Kingsborough Community Col, 72-74. *Awards:* Grad Sch for Sculpture Fel & Grant in Aid, State Univ NY Stony Brook, 69 & 70. *Bibliog:* Malcolm Preston (auth), Assemblages display intellectual fantasy, Newsday, 5/21/69; Claire White (auth), Exhibition review, Craft Horizons, 6/70; Albert Boime (auth), Cosmic artifacts: The work in lucite of Ron Lusker, Art J, winter 72. *Mem:* Am Craftsmen Coun; Col Art Asn Am; Ctr Study Democratic Insts. *Media:* Acrylic, Oils. *Publ:* Auth, New York: The season in sculpture, 8/70, The green meadow school, 8/70, The jewelry of Marci Zelmanoff, 12/70 & Attitudes, Brooklyn Museum, 70, Craft Horizons Mag. *Mailing Add:* 85 Mercer St New York NY 10012

LUST, HERBERT
HISTORIAN, COLLECTOR
b Chicago, Ill, Oct 31, 26. *Study:* Univ Chicago, MA, 49. *Pos:* Bd trustees, Nova Realty, Falls Church, Va & Brt Real Estate Investment Trust, New York. *Awards:* Fulbright Scholar to France, 50. *Res:* Giacometti; surrealism; minimal art. *Collection:* Giacometti drawings; also Bellmer, Leaf, Baj & Calder; minimal art. *Publ:* Auth, The Twelve Principles of Art Investment, 69; auth, Giacometti: The Complete Graphics and Fifteen Drawings, Tudor, 71; auth, Enrico Baj, Dada Impressionist with Catalogue Raisonne, 72. *Mailing Add:* 54 Porchuck Rd Greenwich CT 06830

LUST, VIRGINIA
DEALER
b Chicago, Ill, July 23, 30. *Study:* Art Inst Chicago, 46; Mundelein Col, grad, 52. *Collections Arranged:* Paintings, Drawings, Early Prints (first Am show of Hans Bellmer); The Complete Graphics (first world show of Delvaux); The History of Surrealism, Drawings & Paintings, 72. *Pos:* Dir, Virginia Lust Gallery, New York; sales dir, Collectors Press. *Specialty:* Surrealism; Giacometti, paintings and drawings. *Mailing Add:* 54 Porchuck Rd Greenwich CT 06830

LUTZ, MARJORIE BRUNHOFF
SCULPTOR
b Cincinnati, Ohio, Jan 25, 33. *Study:* Art Students League, with Sidney Simon; Duke Univ. *Work:* Southern Vt Art Ctr, Manchester. *Comn:* Early Bird, Todd Hunter Develop Corp & welded steel abstract, Taft Steel Corp, New York, 81. *Exhib:* Ann Fall Show, Southern Vt Art Ctr, Manchester, 77-83; Energy Art, Foothills Art Ctr, Golden, Colo, 82; Lehman Libr, Fordham Univ, 82; Am Soc Contemp Artists Traveling Show, 84; solo show, Southern Vt Art Ctr, 84; and others. *Mem:* Am Soc Contemp Artists; Organization Independent Artists (dir, 81); Screen Dir Guild. *Media:* Wood, Stone. *Dealer:* Gallery in Williamstown Spring St Williamstown MA 01267. *Mailing Add:* 203 East 72nd St New York NY 10021

LUTZ, WINIFRED ANN
SCULPTOR, ENVIRONMENTAL ARTIST
b Brooklyn, NY, May 6, 42. *Study:* Cleveland Inst Art, BFA, 65; Atelier 17, with Stanley William Hayter, 65; Cranbrook Acad Art, MFA, 68. *Work:* Cleveland Mus Art; Albright-Knox Art Gallery; Chicago Art Inst; Desert Mus, Palm Springs, Calif; Crocker Gallery, Sacramento. *Exhib:* One-man show, Paper Reliefs, Am Craft Mus, New York, 75; Handmade Paper Objects, Santa Barbara Mus Art, Calif, 76; Handmade Paper, Prints & Unique Works, Mus Mod Art, New York, 76; Wood, Nassau Co Mus, Long Island, NY, 77; New Ways with Paper, Nat Collection Fine Art, DC, 78; Paper about Paper, Albright-Knox Art Gallery, Buffalo, New York, 80. *Teaching:* Asst prof sculpture, Yale Sch Art, 75-81, prof, 81-82. *Bibliog:* Jean Feinberg (auth), Findings of Winifred Lutz, Craft Horizons, 4/79; Jules Heller (auth), Papermaking, Watson-Guptill, 78; and others. *Mem:* Col Art Asn; Am Crafts Coun; Artists Equity. *Media:* Wood; Handmade Paper. *Publ:* Article, Felting, Am Crafts Mag, 8-9/80; Casting to Acknowledge the Nature of Paper, Int Conf Hand Papermakers, Carriage House Press, 81. *Dealer:* Marilyn Pearl Gallery 29 W 57th New York NY 10019. *Mailing Add:* 2316 Terwood Rd Huntingdon Valley PA 19006

LUTZE, (HILDEGARDE)
CONSULTANT, DEALER

b Wuppertal, Ger, 1937. *Study:* Art Sch Wuppertal; Univ Berlin, Ger, MFA. *Work:* Wilhelm Lehmbruck Mus, Duisberg, Ger; Berson Collection, Karlsruhe, Ger; Gallwitz Collection, Frankfurt, Ger; Fischer Collection, Baden-Baden, Ger. *Comn:* Marble sculpture, 65 & hydrant monument, 66, City WBerlin; 100 Kohl Koepfe, Kunstverein, Dusseldorf, 68; epoxy resin mural, Wuppertal, 70. *Exhib:* One-woman shows, Kunsthalle, Baden-Baden, 70, Hausam Luetzowplatz, Berlin, 70, Gallery Klang, Cologne, 70, Trinity Col, Hartford, Conn, 71; performance with Trisha Brown, 72; and others. *Pos:* Gallery dir, Onnasch Gallery, New York, 73-74; organizer, Soho in Berlin, Berlin Festival, 75-76; organizer, Berlin Now, Senat Berlin & Goethe Haus, New York, 77. *Teaching:* Assoc prof sculpture, Trinity Col, 70-71; adv art & poetry, Tombs, Men's House of Detention, New York, 71-75. *Awards:* Maison de France, Paris, 64; Ford Found Traveling Grant for US & Mex, 65; Villa Romana Prize, Florence, Italy, 68. *Bibliog:* Udo Kultermann (auth), German Sculptress, Das Kunstwerk, 62; R G Dienst (auth), Young German Artists, Du-Mont-Aktuell, 66; J Russel (auth), Soho in Berlin, NY Times, 76. *Mailing Add:* 207 Second Ave New York NY 10003

LUX, GLADYS MARIE
PAINTER

b Chapman, Nebr. *Study:* Kearney State Col, SS, 18; Univ Nebr, BFA, 25, AB, 33, MA, 35; Art Inst Chicago, SS, 29. *Work:* Peru State Col; Doane Col; Pub Schs, Kearney, Nebr; Artists Guild Collection, Lincoln, Nebr; Wesleyan Univ, Nebr. *Exhib:* Regional shows, Omaha, Minneapolis, Kansas City, Wichita & Topeka, 27-67; Art Inst Chicago, 36; Rockefeller Ctr, 36-38; New York World's Fair, 39; Joseph Pennell Mem Print Exhib; Art & Artists in Nebraska, Sheldon Mem Art Gallery, Univ Nebr, 82. *Teaching:* Instr art methods, Summer Schs, Univ Nebr, Lincoln, 23-25; instr art methods, Sioux City Pub High Sch, Iowa, 25-27; chmn dept art, Nebr Wesleyan Univ, 27-33 & 36-66, asst prof art, 36-50, assoc prof, 50-66, artist in residence, 66-67. *Awards:* Nebr Art Teachers Asn Serv Award, 69; Gov Arts Award, Nebr Arts Coun, 79; Distinguished Serv Award, Teachers Asn, 80. *Bibliog:* Article, Art Digest, 36-38; World's Fair exhibit, New Yorker, 39. *Mem:* Lincoln Artist Guild (past pres, secy); Nebr Art Teachers Asn (past pres, vpres). *Media:* Watercolor, Oil. *Publ:* Auth, Symbols of Good Neighbors, Christ of the Andes, Candle Beam, 43; auth, European arts seen internationalletiny, Western Arts Asn Bull, 55; auth, Students Exhibits, 59; illusr, In a Tall Land, 63; auth, The baby doll, an evolution, 72 & Our hobby with TLC, 74, In: United Federation Doll Clubs Book 5. *Mailing Add:* 5203 Garland St Lincoln NE 68504

LUX, GWEN (GWEN LUX CREIGHTON)
SCULPTOR

b Chicago, Ill. *Study:* Md Inst Arts; Boston Mus Fine Arts Sch; also study in Paris & with Ivan Mestrovic, Yugoslavia. *Work:* Detroit Mus; Hawaii State Found Cult & the Arts. *Comn:* Totem pole, bird pole (metal & wood), Northwood Shopping Ctr, Detroit, 52; chrome abstraction, Gen Motors Tech Ctr, Detroit, 56; stainless steel abstraction, Aviation Trades High Sch, New York, 58; bronze & concrete abstraction, KRON TV Bldg, San Francisco, 65; concrete abstraction, State Off Bldg, Kauai, Hawaii, 71. *Exhib:* Whitney Mus Am Art, New York, 35; Detroit Mus, 48; World House Galleries, New York, 62; Pomeroy Galleries, San Francisco, 68; Contemp Arts Ctr, Honolulu, 70; Downtown Gallery, Honolulu, 76; plus others. *Teaching:* Instr sculpture, Arts & Crafts Soc, Detroit, 45-48. *Awards:* Guggenheim Found Fel, 33; Detroit Inst Award, 45 & 46; Nat Indust Arts Coun Can Award, 65. *Bibliog:* C Ludwig Brumme (auth), Contemporary American Sculpture, Crown, 48. *Mem:* Hawaii Artists & Sculptors League. *Media:* Polyester Resin, Concrete, Metals. *Dealer:* Gregory Northrup 1418 Halekoa Dr Honolulu HI. *Mailing Add:* 4340 Pahoa Ave Honolulu HI 96816

LUZ, VIRGINIA
PAINTER

b Toronto, Ont, Oct 15, 11. *Study:* Cent Tech Sch. *Work:* Robert McLaughlin Gallery, Oshawa, Ont; Can Dept External Affairs; Can Embassies; J S McLean Collection; London Art Mus; also in many pvt collections. *Exhib:* Ont Soc Artists, 45-83; Can Women Artists Show (travelling exhib to New York & Can), 47-49; Can Soc Painters in Watercolour, 47-75; Can Tours; Can Group Painters; Tribute to Ten Women, Sisler Gallery, Toronto, Ont, 75; and others. *Teaching:* Instr illus, Cent Tech Sch, Toronto, 40-74, head dept art, 69-74. *Mem:* Ont Soc Artists; Royal Can Acad; Can Soc Painters in Watercolour. *Mailing Add:* 113 Delaware Ave Toronto ON M6H 2S9 Canada

LYFORD, CABOT
SCULPTOR, PAINTER

b Sayre, Pa, May 22, 25. *Study:* Skowhegan Sch Art, summer 47; Cornell Univ, BFA, 50; Sculpture Ctr, New York, 50-51. *Work:* Lamont Gallery, Exeter, NH; Addison Gallery Am Art, Andover, Mass; Wichita Mus, Kans; Colby Col, Waterville, Maine; New England Ctr Continuing Educ, Durham, NH; over 50 pvt collections. *Comn:* granite Christ head, Christ Church, Exeter, 69, candelabra, 70 & black granite & brass flower holder, 71; Harbor Sculpture (black granite), Portsmouth, NH, 75; black granite whale, Prescott Park, Portsmouth, NH, 79; and others. *Exhib:* Payson Mus, Portland, Maine; RI Festival, Providence; NH Art Asn, Manchester; Addison Gallery, Andover, Mass; Fitchburg Art Mus; plus others. *Teaching:* Instr sculpture, Phillips Exeter Acad, NH, 63- *Awards:* Prizes, City Manchester, 70 & NH Architects Asn, 71 & 74-77. *Media:* Stone, Metal; Watercolor. *Publ:* Contribr, Contemporary Stone Sculpture, 71. *Dealer:* Hobe Sound N Portland Maine; Hobe Sound Galeries Hobe Sound FL 33455. *Mailing Add:* 9 Center St Exeter NH 03833

LYLE, CHARLES THOMAS
ADMINISTRATOR

b Duluth, Minn, July 16, 46. *Study:* Univ Minn, James Wright Hunt scholar, 67-68, BA(cum laude), 68; Univ Del, Hagley fel, 68-70, MA(Am hist), 71. *Collections Arranged:* New Jersey Arts & Crafts: The Colonial Expression (with catalog), 72; American Crafts: The New Jersey Contribution, 75; American Folk Art, 75. *Pos:* Dir, Monmouth Co Hist Asn, Freehold, NJ, 71-78; dir mus, Nat Trust for Historic Preservation, 78-80; exec dir, Historical Soc Del, 80- *Teaching:* Vis instr, Mus Studies Dept, Univ Del; instr Am decor arts prior to 1900, Lincroft, NJ, 75-76. *Bibliog:* Buildings and furniture of the Monmouth Co Hist Asn, Antiques, 1/80. *Mem:* Am Asn Mus; NE Mus Conf; Am Asn State & Local Hist; Nat Trust for Hist Preservation; Victorian Soc Am. *Mailing Add:* c/o 505 Market St Mall Washington DC 19801

LYMAN, THOMAS WILLIAM
EDUCATOR, HISTORIAN

b Chicago, Ill, Apr 28, 26. *Study:* Univ Ill, BS, 49; Univ Chicago, PhD, 64. *Teaching:* Instr art hist, Art Inst Chicago, 60-65, dir admissions, 60-64; assoc prof, Southern Ill Univ, 65-67; from assoc prof to prof, Emory Univ, 62-, chmn, Art Hist Dept, 77-79 & 81-82. *Awards:* Nat Endowment Humanities Fel, 80-81. *Mem:* Col Art Asn; Medieval Acad Am. *Publ:* Auth, Architectural portraiture and Jan Van Eyck's Washington Annunciation, Gesta, 81; auth, Saint-Sernin de Toulouse: Que Faire du XIX siecle, Bulletin Monumental, 81; auth, Saint-Sernin, Vrollet-le-Duc et la Theorie de l'harmonie des proportions, Gazette Beaux-Arts, 81; auth, La table d'autel de Bernard Goldwin et son ambience orginelle, 82 & L'ornementation sculturale au seine de l'architecture romane du debut du XI siecle, 83, Cahiers de Saint-Michel de Cirxa. *Mailing Add:* Dept Art Hist Emory Univ Atlanta GA 30322

LYNCH, BETTY
PAINTER, INSTRUCTOR

b McAlester, Okla, June 25, 1917. *Study:* Univ Tex, BA, 38; workshops with Robert E Wood, 72-83; also with Leonard Brooks, Rex Brandt & Charles Reid. *Work:* Mus Southwest, Midland, Tex. *Exhib:* Tex Watercolor Soc, Witte Mem Mus, San Antonio, 67, 68, 75 & 82; Sun Carnival Art Exhib, El Paso, Tex, 67; Southwestern Print & Drawing Exhib, Dallas Mus Fine Arts, 69; Western Fedn Watercolor Soc, San Antonio, Tex, 79 & Phoenix, Ariz, 82; Am Watercolor Soc, Salmagundi Club, 83. *Teaching:* Workshop instr watercolor, NMex Watercolor Soc, Okla, Calif, Kans, England & Spain, 77-83; instr watercolor, La Romita Sch, Terni, Italy, 83. *Bibliog:* Florence Hutchinson Lonsford (auth), Spotlight on Kappa artists, The Key, 82. *Mem:* Tex Watercolor Soc; Midland Arts Asn; San Antonio Watercolor Group. *Publ:* Auth, Watercolor page, Am Artist Mag, 80. *Dealer:* Baker Gallery Fine Art 13th & Ave L Box 1920 Lubbock TX 79408. *Mailing Add:* 1500 Harvard Midland TX 79701

LYNCH, GERALD FRANCIS
SCULPTOR, DRAFTSMAN

b Philadelphia, Pa, Jan 26, 44. *Study:* Maryknoll Seminary Col, BA, 61-65; Philadelphia Col Art, 66 & 69; Nat Cathedral, 74. *Comn:* Wood carving, Don Quanella Ctr, Springfield, Pa, 80; life size marble carving, Cathedral St Peter & Paul, Philadelphia, Pa, 79; sculpture & stone carving, Nat Cathedral, Washington, DC, 82. *Exhib:* Allied Artists Am Annuals, Nat Acad Design, New York, 75, 77-78 & 80-83; Salmagundi Club, New York, 79 & 80; Knickerbocker Artists Am, Nat Arts Club, New York, 79; one-man show, House Rep, Cannon House Rotunda, Washington, DC, 82; Inaugural Show, Noyes Mus Fine Art, NJ, 83. *Teaching:* Asst instr stone & wood carving, Glen Echo Art Ctr, 75-76; instr drawing, Cape May Co Art League, NJ, 76-78 & 83; instr sculpture, Ocean City Art Ctr, NJ, 76-79. *Awards:* Gold Medal (sculpture), Allied Artists Am 62nd Ann Show, 75; Gold Medal, Ocean City Art Ctr Sixth Ann Show, 78. *Mem:* Allied Artists Am; Artists Equity; Ocean City Art Ctr. *Media:* Marble, Bronze; Chalk, Ink. *Dealer:* Mickelson Gallery 707 G St NW Washington DC. *Mailing Add:* 206 E New York Ave Villas NJ 08251

LYNCH, JAMES BURR, JR
HISTORIAN

b Miona, Va, Aug 23, 19. *Study:* Harvard Univ, AB, AM & PhD. *Teaching:* Assoc prof art hist, Boston Univ, 55-66; prof art hist, Univ Md, College Park, 66- *Mem:* Col Art Asn Am. *Res:* Latin American painting and architecture, especially Mexican and Cuban; Italian art of the sixteenth century. *Publ:* Auth, History of Raphael's small St George in the Louvre, 4/62 & G P Lomazzo's self-portrait in the Brera, 10/64, Gazette Beaux-Arts; auth, Lomazzo & the Accademia della Valle de Bregno, Art Bulletin, 6/66; auth, Siqueiros, Encycl World Art, Vol XIII; auth, An unsung artist of the Mexican renaissance, Americas, 6/70. *Mailing Add:* Dept of Art Univ of Md College Park MD 20742

LYNCH, MARY BRITTEN
PAINTER

b Pruden, Ky, Sept 30, 32. *Study:* Univ Tenn, Chattanooga, BA; Provincetown Workshop, Mass, studied with Leo Manso & Victor Candell; Univ Tenn, Knoxville, 65. *Work:* Anchorage Hist & Fine Arts Mus; Tenn State Mus, Nashville; Little Rock Fine Arts Ctr; Watkins Art Inst, Nashville; Univ Tenn. *Exhib:* Nat Asn Women Artists--Nat Acad Design, New York, 73-76; Tenn Painters, Cheekwood Mus, Nashville, 74; Okla Arts Ctr, Oklahoma City, 74; USA Oil Exhib, cols, mus & univs in US, 74-76; Watercolor USA, Springfield Art Mus, Mo, 76; solo traveling show, Southeast & West, 79-80; and others. *Pos:* Founder, Lenoir City Arts Festival, Tenn, 63. *Teaching:* Instr watercolor & acrylics, Hunter Mus Art, Chattanooga, 69-77, Watercolor Workshop, Univ Tenn, Chattanooga, 75 & Chattanooga Christian High Sch, 80- *Awards:*

Purchase Award, Tenn Watercolor Soc, 77; Top Purchase Award Oils, Tenn All State; Medal Hon, Nat Asn Women Artists, Nat Acad Design, New York. *Bibliog:* Southern Artisans (film for TV), 73; Featured artist, Am Artist, 12/83. *Mem:* Nat Asn Women Artists; founding mem Tenn Watercolor Soc (founder, 69, treas, 70, vpres, 71, pres, 72-); Nat Watercolor Soc. *Media:* Watercolor, Acrylic. *Dealer:* Art South Montgomery AL; Mainspace Houston TX. *Mailing Add:* 1505 Woodnymph Trail Lookout Mountain TN 37350

LYNCH, TOM (THOMAS MICHAEL)
INSTRUCTOR, PAINTER
b Chicago Ill, Feb 22, 50. *Work:* Neville Pub Mus, Wis; Burpee Art Mus, Rockford, Ill; Sagamon State Univ, Springfield, Ill; Standard Oil Corp, Chicago; and others. *Comn:* A Man and His City (paintings), Chicago Coun Fine Arts, 78; Portrait of a City (paintings), IBM Corp, Green Bay, Wis, 79 & Calumet City, Ill, 80; Chicago at Night & Chicago Harbors (paintings), Chicago Coun Fine Arts, 80; and others. *Pos:* Consulting dir, Am Int Art Ctr, Des Plaines, Ill, 81-; dir art, Ill Watercolor Soc, currently; consult, Hunt Speedball & Crescent Cardboard Co, currently. *Teaching:* Instr watercolor, Dillman's Sand Lake Lodge, Wis, 79-81, 82 & 83, Northwestern Ohio Watercolor Soc & Southwest Watercolor Soc, Dallas, 81, 82 & 83 & Southern Ariz Watercolor Soc, Tucson & Phoenix, 81, 82 & 83. *Awards:* Graphic Art Award, Chicago Artist Guild, 79; First Place, Int Soc Artists, 80; and others. *Bibliog:* Steve Fosdick (auth), Chicago at night, Herald, 5/81; Leona Toppel (auth), Profile, Downtown News, 12/81; Steve Doherty (auth), article, Am Artists, 5/81. *Media:* Watercolor. *Publ:* Auth & illusr, Watercolor lesson with Tom Lynch, Crafts & Things Mag, 81; auth, Watercolor page, Am Artist Mag, 81; illusr, Winter in Sleepy Hollow, Ford Times Mag, 81; contribr, Ford Times, 1/82, 4/82 & 12/82 & Readers Digest, 82. *Dealer:* Richard Jamiolkowski 151 Laurel Ct Wheeling IL 60090. *Mailing Add:* 605 N Chestnut Arlington Heights IL 60004

LYNDE, STAN
CARTOONIST, ILLUSTRATOR
b Billings, Mont, Sept 23, 31. *Study:* Univ Mont; Sch Visual Arts, New York, 56-57. *Exhib:* The Evolution of Rick O'Shay, Yellowstone Co Fine Arts Ctr, Billings, Mont, 63; The Paintings of Stan Lynde, Midland Nat Bank, Billings, 75. *Pos:* Creator, auth & artist comic strip, Rick O'Shay, Chicago Tribune-New York News Syndicate Inc, 58-77 & Latigo, Field Newspaper Syndicate, 79. *Awards:* Inkpot Award Achievement in Comic Arts, 77; Mont Gov Award Arts, 83. *Bibliog:* A History of the Comic Strip, 68; Comics of the American West, 77; articles, Cartoonist Profiles Mag, 69, 70, 79, & 81. *Media:* Pen & Ink; Oil. *Publ:* Auth, Rick O'Shay and Hipshot--The Great Sunday Pages, Tempo Bks, 76. *Mailing Add:* Rte 2 Box 123 Red Lodge MT 59068

LYNDS, C (CLYDE WILLIAM)
SCULPTOR, PAINTER
b Jersey City, NJ, June 22, 36. *Study:* Art Students League, 58-63; Frank J Reilly Sch, New York, 63-68. *Work:* NY Univ; McNay Art Inst, San Antonio; Baaken Mus, Minneapolis; Best Products Corp, Va; My Prospect Plaza, Chicago. *Comn:* Sculpture, Am Film Corp, Philadelphia, 74; sculpture, Art Public Space Inc, New York, 81; sculpture, Cermak Merchants' Asn, Chicago, 82; sculpture, Nat Shopping Ctrs Management Corp, Rye, NY, 82. *Exhib:* Solo exhibs, Babcock Galleries 69-71, 73 & 75 & Electric Gallery, 77 & 78; Corcoran Gallery Art, 73; Univ Rochester, 78; World Trade Ctr, New York, 83; Bruce Mus, Greenwich, Conn, 83; and others. *Awards:* First Prize, Monmouth Col, 68; First Prize & Medal of Honor, Jersey City Mus, 68; NJ State Coun Arts Fel, 83. *Media:* Mixed Media. *Dealer:* Art for Public Space Inc 150 Purchase St Rye NY; Electric Gallery 226 Steelcase Rd Markahm ON L3R 1B3 Can. *Mailing Add:* 237 Innes Rd Wood-Ridge NJ 07075

LYNES, RUSSELL
WRITER, CRITIC
b Great Barrington, Mass, Dec 2, 10. *Study:* Yale Univ, BA; Union Col, DFA; Md Inst Col Art, LHD, 73; NAdams State Col, DLitt, 77; City Univ NY, LHD, 80. *Pos:* Managing ed, Harper's Mag, 47-67, contrib ed, 67-; pres, Arch Am Art, 64-71, trustee, currently; pres bd dirs, MacDowell Colony, formerly, trustee, currently; trustee, New York Hist Soc; vchmn, New York Found Arts; vis comt, Costume Inst, Metrop Mus Art, formerly, vis comt, Am Dept, currently; mem, New York City Art Comn, formerly; writer-in-residence, Am Acad in Rome, 68 & 79, trustee, currently. *Publ:* Auth, The Domesticated Americans, 63; auth, Confessions of a Dilettante, 66; auth, The Art-makers of 19th Century America, 70 & auth, Good Old Modern, 73, Antheneum; auth, Russell Lynes Observes Column, Archit Digest; auth, More Than Meets the Eye, Cooper-Hewitt Mus, 80; also auth many articles for Harper's Mag, Life, Look, Yale Rev, Vogue & others. *Mailing Add:* 427 E 84th St New York NY 10028

LYON, HAYES PAXTON
PAINTER
b Athol, Kans, Feb 10, 09. *Study:* Univ Colo, BA, 31; Univ Denver, BFA, 37; also with Andrew Dasburg, Jozef G Bakos & Dr Raymond Stites. *Work:* Denver Art Mus; US Marine Hosp, Carville, La. *Comn:* Original Fort Lupton, Pioneer Man & Pioneer Woman, Lupton High Sch, 40. *Exhib:* Am Paintings & Sculpture Ann, Art Inst Chicago, 38; 133rd Ann Exhib, Pa Acad Fine Arts, 38; Am Art Today, New York Worlds Fair, 39-40; Artists West of Miss, Colorado Springs Fine Arts Ctr, 40, 41, 46 & 48; Exhib of 200 Water Colors, Nat Gallery Art, Washington, DC, 41. *Pos:* Tech illusr, Lowry Tech Training Ctr, Denver, 54-73. *Teaching:* Instr drawing, design, oil painting, watercolor, Univ Tex, Austin, 46-51. *Awards:* Yetter Mem Prize, 45th Ann Show, Denver Art Mus, 39; Purchase Prize, First Nat Water Color Competition, Washington, DC, 40. *Media:* Oil, Watercolor. *Mailing Add:* 10105 W 78th Ave Arvada CO 80005

LYONS, LISA
CURATOR, HISTORIAN
b Minneapolis, Minn, Dec 13, 50. *Study:* Northwestern Univ, Evanston, Ill, BA(art hist), 72; Columbia Univ, New York, MA(art hist), 73. *Collections Arranged:* Scale & Environment: 10 Sculptors (contribr, catalog), 77, Nicholas Africano, 78, Eight Artists: The Elusive Image (auth, catalog), 79, Close Portraits (auth, catalog), 80, Walker Art Ctr, Minneapolis. *Pos:* Fel, Toledo Mus Art, Ohio, 73-74; Rockefeller Found Fel, Walker Art Ctr, Minneapolis, 75-77, asst cur, 77-78, cur, 79- *Publ:* Auth, Henri Matisse: 1914-1917, Arts Mag, 5/75; auth, An interview with James Byrne, Studio Int, 5-6/76; contribr, The river: images of the Mississippi, Walker Art Ctr, 76. *Mailing Add:* c/o Walker Art Ctr Vineland Pl Minneapolis MN 55403

LYSUN, GREGORY
PAINTER, RESTORER
b Yonkers, NY, Oct 24, 24. *Study:* Art Students League, with Louis Bouche, Edwin Dickinson, John Groth, Robert Beverly Hale & Reginald Marsh, 47-53. *Work:* Art Students League; Berkshire Mus, Pittsfield, Mass; New Britain Mus Am Art, Conn; De Cordova Mus, Lincoln, Mass; Butler Inst Am Art, Youngstown, Ohio. *Comn:* Restoration work of the Whistle & Simon Stevens, comn by Mrs D E Kastner, Chatham, Mass, 71; portrait of Ruth Taylor, Westchester Community Serv Coun, Inc, White Plains, NY, 75; restoration work of 6 paintings by Edward Gay, comn by Mrs S Gay Linville, Scarsdale, NY, 81; restoration work of painting by John Steuart Curry, comn by Eugene Curry, Armonk, NY, 81; restoration of John Stewart Curry's Portrait of a Gypsy, Jefferson Co Hist Soc, Oskaloosa, Kans, 82. *Exhib:* 35 Years in Retrospect, 1936-1970, Butler Inst Am Art Midyear Show, 71; Conn Acad Fine Arts Exhib, New Brit Mus Am Art, 72; 67th Ann Exhib Conn Acad Fine Arts, Wadsworth Atheneum Mus, Hartford, Conn, 77; Art Teachers Juries Exhib, Neuberger Mus, State Univ NY, Col at Purchase, 77; From the 1920's to the present, works from the League's permanent collection, Art Students League, New York, 77; Directors Choice Exhib, selections from DeCordova Mus, Lincoln, Mass, 78; Ann Allied Arts Am, 81; and others. *Teaching:* Instr painting & drawing, Westchester Art Workshop, Co Ctr, White Plains, NY, 69-, Pelham Art Ctr, 78- & State Univ NY Col, Purchase, 82-; instr painting & drawing & chmn, Dept Art, Fairview-Greenburg Community Ctr, Greenburgh, NY, 72- *Awards:* Purchase Prize, 31st Ann Nat, Butler Inst Am Art, 66; Coun Am Art Socs Award, Miniature Painters & Sculptors Soc NJ Nat, 71; Allen H Newton Award, 67th Ann Exhib Conn Acad Fine Arts, 77; and others. *Bibliog:* Winifred B Bell (auth), Paintings by Gregory Lysun, Berkshire Eagle, 71; Helen Ganz Spiro (auth), Art students follow teacher's example, 82 & Painter takes students to a different world, 83, Gannett Westchester Newspapers. *Mem:* Life mem Art Students League; Allied Artists Am; life fel Am Artists Prof League; Conn Acad Fine Arts; Hudson Valley Art Asn. *Media:* Oil. *Publ:* Auth, The construction of a painting, Palette Talk, 79. *Mailing Add:* 481 Winding Rd N Ardsley NY 10502

LYTLE, RICHARD
PAINTER, EDUCATOR
b Albany, NY, Feb 14, 35. *Study:* Cooper Union; Yale Univ, BFA & MFA; also with Josef Albers. *Work:* Mus Mod Art, New York; Yale Art Gallery; Nat Collection Art, Washington, DC; Columbia Univ Int House; Cincinnati Art Mus. *Comn:* Concrete relief mural, Fairfield Univ, 65. *Exhib:* 16 Americans, Mus Mod Art, New York, 59; Seattle World's Fair, 62; Whitney Mus Am Art Ann, New York, 63; Art: USA: Now, SC Johnson Collection, World Tour, 63-; one-man show, De Cordova Mus, Lincoln, Mass, 74; plus others. *Teaching:* Instr art, Yale Univ, 60-63; dean, Silvermine Col Art, 63-66; assoc prof art, Yale Univ, 66-81, prof, 81-; actg dean, Yale Sch Art, 80-81. *Awards:* Fulbright Grant to Italy, 58; Prof Achievement Citation, Cooper Union. *Media:* Oil, Watercolor. *Dealer:* Marilyn Pearl Gallery 29 W 57th St New York NY 10019. *Mailing Add:* Sperry Rd Woodbridge CT 06525

M

MAASS, RICHARD ANDREW
MUSEUM DIRECTOR
b New York, NY, Apr 11, 46. *Study:* Univ Wis, Madison, BA(Am hist), 68; New Sch for Social Res, New York, MA, 72; Cooperstown Grad Prog, MA(mus admin), 73. *Collections Arranged:* Maynard Dixon--A Bicentennial Retrospective, 12/75; Calif-Texas Art Exchange, 3/76. *Pos:* Ecol supvr, Mus City New York, 70-71; asst prog dir, South St Seaport Mus, New York, 71-72; dir, Fresno Art Ctr, 73-80; exec dir, Tucson Mus of Art, 80- *Awards:* Fel, Sem for Hist Adminr, Colonial Williamsburg, 71; Fel, Harvard Bus Sch Arts Admin Sem, 73. *Mem:* Am Asn Mus; Am Asn State & Local Hist; Nat Soc Arts & Lett; Manuscript Soc; Advocates for Arts. *Mailing Add:* Tucson Mus Art 140 N Main Tucson AZ 85701

MABRY, JANE
PAINTER, DEALER
Study: Univ NMex, BFA; Art Students League; Corcoran Sch Art; also with Jerry Farnsworth; Grand Cent Sch Art; Critcher Sch Art, with Catherine Critcher. *Exhib:* NMex State Fair, 40-73; Smithsonian Inst, Washington, DC, 45; Mus NMex Biennial, 64; All Am Indian Exhibition, Indianapolis, Ind, 74. *Pos:* Co-owner, Galeria del Sol, currently. *Awards:* Numerous first place ribbons for pastels and oils. *Mem:* Pastel Soc Am. *Media:* Oil, Pastel. *Specialty:* Southwestern subjects, landscapes and portraits of Southwestern Indians, the New Mexico Pueblos and their people; sculptured tiles Indian designs. *Mailing Add:* c/o Galeria del Sol 206 1/2 San Felipe NW Albuquerque NM 87102

MCADOO, CAROL WESTBROOK
PAINTER, PRINTMAKER
b Colonial Heights, Va, Dec 28, 37. *Study:* Self taught. *Work:* Lauren Rogers Mus, Laurel, Miss; NCNB Art Collection, Charlotte, NC; P Hanes Collection, Winston-Salem, NC; AT&T Corp; Coca-Cola Corp. *Comn:* Mag cover, Brown's Guide to Georgia, Atlanta, 73. *Exhib:* Piedmont Painting & Sculpture, Mint Mus Art, Charlotte, NC, 71; 4th Realist Exhib, SEastern Ctr Contemp Art, Winston-Salem, NC, 72; Rogers Mus Exhib, Lauren Rogers Mus, Laurel, Miss, 72; one-woman exhibs, Mint Mus Art, Charlotte, NC, 73 & Wilson Arts Coun, NC, 75; Soc Four Arts, Palm Beach, Fla, 73; Catharine Lorillard Wolfe, Nat Arts Club, New York, 80. *Awards:* 3rd Place, Cape Coral Nat Exhibit, 71; Purchase Award, Lauren Rogers Mus, 72; 1st Place Painting, 23rd Ann Poplar Lawn Art Festival, 81. *Mem:* Nat Soc Painters Casein & Acrylic. *Media:* Acrylic; Serigraphs. *Publ:* Auth, Reflections of the Outer Banks, Island Publ House, 76. *Dealer:* Edward L Greene Box 265 Manteo NC 27954. *Mailing Add:* 5070 Sunset Trail NE Marietta GA 30067

MCADOO, DONALD ELDRIDGE
PAINTER, PRINTMAKER
b Chicago, Ill, Feb 8, 29. *Study:* Self-taught. *Work:* Va Mus Fine Arts; Columbia Mus Art, SC; Ga Mus Art; Mint Mus Art, NC; Springfield Mus Art, Mo; and others. *Exhib:* A Brush with Realism, one-man touring exhib, nine major southeastern mus, 72-74; Americana, Greenwich Workshop, Conn, 79. *Teaching:* Painting safaris & lectures to art groups. *Awards:* Numerous awards for paintings and graphics. *Mem:* Audubon Soc; Watercolor Soc La & Ala; Southeastern Ctr Contemp Art. *Media:* Watercolor, Acrylic Tempera; Woodcut. *Publ:* Coauth, Reflections of the Outer Banks, Island Publ House, 76. *Mailing Add:* 5070 Sunset Trail Marietta GA 30067

MACALISTER, PAUL RITTER
DESIGNER, COLLECTOR
b Camden, NJ, Oct 15, 01. *Study:* Pa Acad Fine Arts, Philadelphia; Sch Indust Design; Yale Univ Sch Archit; Ecole Beaux Arts, Fontainebleau, France, with Bourdelle & Carlu. *Work:* Astrasphere (celestial globe), Maritime Mus, Greenwich, Eng & White House Libr; Capellini Glassware, Mus Arts Decoratifs et Metiers, Paris, France. *Comn:* Co-designer, Trilogy of Time Instruments Kit, 76; Macet Astrolabe, 77; Macet Nocturnal, 79; Macet Graphometer, 83 & Macet Mariners Astrolabe, 83. *Exhib:* Miniature TV Room Settings, Art Inst Chicago, 50. *Pos:* Dir, Paul MacAlister, Inc, 26-42; designer & dir, Permanent Exhib Decorative Arts & Crafts, 33-40; comdr, USN Spec Devices Div & Navy Exhibs, 42-46; dir, Bureaus Indust & Interior Design, Montgomery Ward & Co, 46-48; dir & sr partner, Paul MacAlister & Assocs, Lake Bluff, Ill, 48-; dir, Americana Hayloft Mus, 50- *Awards:* Beaux Arts Medal, 24; Silver Medal, Indust Designers Inst, 56; Dorothy Dawes Award, Am Furniture Mart Press Ann, 55. *Bibliog:* Articles in House & Garden, 7/66 & Interior Design, 4/68, 10/68 & 9/72. *Mem:* Fel Indust Designers Soc Am (pres, 50 & 51, chmn design award prog, 50-60); fel Royal Soc Arts, London; Early Am Industs Asn; Midwest Tool Collectors Asn. *Collection:* American eagle in art form; early hand tools; early scientific instruments; rare books on perspective, architecture and the arts; collections exhibited Chicago Pub Libr, Lake Forest Libr, Lake Forest Acad Antiques Show & Art Inst Chicago. *Publ:* Auth, Display for Better Business, 54; auth, articles in Lake Forest Acad Antiques Show Catalog, 69-71. *Mailing Add:* Box 157 Lake Bluff IL 60044

MCANDREW, DENNIS ANTHONY
CURATOR, INSTRUCTOR
b Buffalo, NY, June 13, 45. *Study:* Harvard Univ, 66-70; St John Vianncy Seminary, East Aurora, NY, BA, 67, MA, 71. *Pos:* Specialist fine art, Art & Archit Comn, Diocese Buffalo, 71-77; assoc dir educ marketing, Buffalo Philharmonic Orchestra, 79; corp art consult, Joan Rothenmeyer Inc, Arlington, Va, 80; cur educ, Huntsville Mus Art, Ala, 81- *Teaching:* Lectr, Mt St Joseph Acad, Buffalo, 72-73 & State Univ NY, Buffalo, 74-76. *Mem:* Southeastern Mus Conf; Am Asn Mus; Am Fedn Arts; Am Art Educ Asn. *Mailing Add:* 700 Monroe St SW Huntsville AL 35801

MCANINCH, BETH
PAINTER
b Corn, Okla, Nov 23, 18. *Study:* Southwestern State Univ, grad; also with Jack Valle, Millard Sheets & others. *Work:* Okla Art Ctr, Southwest Christian Col, State of Okla Collection of Okla Art & Humanities Coun; Oklahoma City Arts Coun; Kerr Convention Ctr; and many others. *Exhib:* Okla Nat Printmakers & Watercolor Show, 61; Southwestern Watercolor Soc Regional & Open, Dallas, Tex, 67, 69 & 71; 8 State Exhib Painting & Sculpture Ann, Okla Art Ctr, 71; Watercolor USA, Springfield, Mo, 73 & 79; Okla Artists Ann, Philbrook, Tulsa, 61-72; Butler Inst Am Art, Youngstown, Ohio, 78; and many others. *Teaching:* Instr painting & drawing, pvt classes, 60-70; instr painting & drawing, Okla Sci & Art Found, 62-66. *Awards:* Southwestern Watercolor Soc Award, 67; First Painting Award, 7th Ann Artists Salon, Okla Mus Art, 68; First Award, 7th Ann Southwestern Watercolor Soc, 71. *Bibliog:* Numerous articles in newspapers. *Mem:* Southwestern Watercolor Soc. *Media:* Watercolor, Pencil. *Dealer:* Norman Wilks Interiors 3839 NW 63rd St Oklahoma City OK 73116; Okla Art Ctr 3113 General Pershing Oklahoma City OK 73107. *Mailing Add:* 1409 Dorchester Dr Oklahoma City OK 73114

MACARAY, LAWRENCE RICHARD
PAINTER, EDUCATOR
b Elsinore, Calif, May 8, 21. *Study:* Whittier Col, BA, 51; Calif State Univ, Long Beach, MA, 55. *Work:* Bowers Mus, Santa Ana, Calif; San Bernardino Co Mus Art; Bertrand Russell Peace Found, Nottingham, Eng; Spectrum Press, Orange, Calif; pvt collection of art critic, William Wilson, Los Angeles Times. *Comn:* Location oil paintings of Eng & Ireland, 75. *Exhib:* New Talent, New York, Los Angeles Co Mus Art, 71-72; Bertrand Russell Centenary Art Exhib, Nottingham, 73; Southern Calif Regional Print & Drawing Exhib, 73, 74 & 76; Long Beach Mus Art, 80; Joslyn Ctr Arts, Torrance, Calif, 82; Grants Pass Mus Art, Ore, 83; and others. *Pos:* Art & travel ed, Torrance Press-Herald, Calif, 63-70. *Teaching:* Prof drawing & painting, El Camino Col, 62- *Awards:* Prize for Art Unlimited, Downey Mus Art, Calif, 74; Southern Calif Exposition Prize, Del Mar, 74. *Media:* Oil. *Mailing Add:* 628 Buttonwood St Anaheim CA 92805

MACAULAY, DAVID ALEXANDER
DESIGNER, ILLUSTRATOR
b Burton on Trent, Eng, Dec 2, 46. *Study:* RI Sch Design, BArchit. *Work:* Cooper Hewitt Mus, New York. *Exhib:* Ann Int Exhib Children's Bk Illus, Bologna, Italy, 76 & 77; 200 Years Am Illus, Mus of Hist Soc, New York, 77; Buildingbooks, 77 & Drawing the Line, 78, Montclair Art Mus, NJ; Children's Book Art, Monterey Peninsula Mus Art, Calif & Triton Mus Art, Santa Clara, Calif, 78-79. *Teaching:* Asst prof of illus, RI Sch of Design, 74-79, head dept illus, 79. *Awards:* First runner-up, Caldecott Medal, Am Libr Asn, 74 & 78; Deutscher Jungenbuchpreis (Best non-fiction picture book), Ger, 75; Medal, Am Inst of Archit, 78. *Bibliog:* Paul Goldberger (auth), Schede/Libri, Abitare, Edtrice Segesta, Milan, 5/76 & How to Build a Castle, New York Times, 11/77; Stefan Kanfer (auth), Books, Time Mag, 11/77. *Media:* Pen & Ink. *Publ:* Auth & illusr, Cathedral, The Story of It's Construction, 73, City, A Story of Roman Planning and Construction, 74, Underground, 76, Great Moments in Architecture, 78 & Motel of the Mysteries, 79, Houghton Mifflin Co. *Mailing Add:* 27 Rhode Island Ave Providence RI 02906

MACBIRD, ROSEMARY
PAINTER
b St Joseph, Mo, Nov 19, 21. *Study:* Art Inst Chicago, 41-43; also with Robert Wood, 82, Zoltan Szabo, 82 & Charles Reid, 83. *Comn:* Watercolors, Santa Barbara Bank, Calif, 81, Off Lawrence Stewart, Phoenix, 82-83 & Norman G Oliverr, Hollywood, 83. *Exhib:* Brand Libr Gallery Ann, Glendale, Calif, 81; Nat Watercolor Soc Ann Exhib, Laguna Beach Mus, Calif, 82; Catharine Lorillard Wolfe Women Artists of America, 82-83 & Allied Artists Am Ann Exhib, 82-83, Nat Arts Club; Knickerbocker Artists Ann Exhib, Salmagundi Club, New York, 82-83. *Awards:* Richter Moore Award, Laguna Beach Mus Art Ann Exhib, 79; Santa Fe Fed Purchase Award, Watercolor West Ann Exhib, 80; Grumbacher Gold Medal, Knickerbocker Artists, 83. *Mem:* Nat Watercolor Soc; Knickerbocker Artists; Am Soc Marine Artists; San Diego Watercolor Soc. *Media:* Watercolor. *Dealer:* Watercolor Gallery 1415 South Coast Hwy Laguna Beach, CA 92651. *Mailing Add:* 3403 P Calle Azul Laguna Hills CA 92653

MCBRYDE, SARAH ELVA
PAINTER, PRINTMAKER
b Columbus, Ohio, July 2, 42. *Study:* Syracuse Univ; Washington Univ, St Louis, Mo, BFA, study with Fred Becker & Arthur Osver; Washington Univ scholar, Skohegan Sch Painting & Sculpture; Am Univ, Washington, DCA, MFA. *Work:* Many pvt collections. *Comn:* Mural on Hotel, San Blas Islands, Panama, Cent Am; paintings, Mrs & Mrs Harry B Willis, Panama City, Cent Am & Mrs Hestlene Martin, Washington, DC; mural, Transemantics, Inc, Washington, DC; and others. *Exhib:* Batik Exhib, Martin Luther King Libr; Washington, New Archit, Washington, DC, 83; Potomac Craftsmen Gallery, Torpedo Factory Art Ctr, 83; Greenspring Gallery, Alexandria, Va, 83; Nat Zoo: GAllery & Bookstore, 83; and others. *Pos:* Gallery asst, Stuttman Art Gallery, Washington, DC, formerly; art libr, Martin Luther King Mem Libr, currently. *Awards:* Design Award, Am Libr Asn, 82. *Bibliog:* Paul Richard, Art Review, Washington Post, 10/77. *Mem:* Artists Equity; Art Libr Soc NAm; Am Soc Picture Prof. *Media:* Egg Tempera, Acrylic; Woodcut, Batik. *Publ:* Illusr (covers), Nat Educ Asn Publ, Sci & Children's Mag; illusr (cover), Weekender Mag, Washington Star Newspaper, 72-74. *Mailing Add:* 2647 41st St NW 3 Washington DC 20007

MCCABE, CYNTHIA JAFFEE
CURATOR, HISTORIAN
b New York, NY, Feb 8, 43. *Study:* Cornell Univ, BA, 63; Columbia Univ, MA, 67. *Collections Arranged:* Sculptors and Their Drawings: Selections from the Hirshhorn Mus Collection (auth, catalog), Lyndon B Johnson Libr, Austin, Tex, 74; The Golden Door: Artist-Immigrants of America, 1876-1976 (auth, catalog), Hirshhorn Mus & Sculpture Garden, 76; Fernando Botero (auth, catalog), Hirshhorn Mus & Sculpture Garden, touring, 79-80; Hans Richter's Stalingrad (Victory in the East) (auth, catalog), Hirshhorn Mus & Sculpture Garden, 80-81; Nakian Exhib, Hirshhorn Mus & Sculpture Garden Collection, 80-81; and others; The American Artist-Immigrant Experience Since 1930, Balch Inst Ethnic Studies, Philadelphia & Smithsonian Inst Traveling Exhib Serv, 83-85. *Pos:* Art historian, Mus Mod Art, New York, Nakian Exhib, 66; art historian, Jewish Mus, New York, 66 & NY State Coun Arts, 67; cur painting & sculpture, Hirshhorn Mus & Sculpture Garden, 67-76, cur exhib, 76-; guest cur, Balch Inst Ethnic Studies, Philadelphia & Smithsonian Inst Traveling Exhib Serv, 83-85. *Teaching:* Asst prof lectr, Am civilization & art, George Washington Univ, Washington, DC, 75-76; lectr, Smithsonian Resident Assoc, 75-76; adj prof, Univ Md, College Park, 81. *Awards:* John J McCloy Fel Art, Am Coun on Art, 82-83. *Mem:* Am Asn Mus; Col Art Asn Am; Int Coun Mus; Int Asn Art Critics; Soc Archit Hist. *Res:* Twentieth century painting and sculpture; history of America's immigrant artists. *Publ:* Contribr, The Hirshhorn Mus and Sculpture Garden, 74; auth, Henry Moore at the Hirshhorn Museum & Sculpture Garden, 74; auth, Wanted by The Gestapo: Saved by America, Varian Fry and the Emergency Rescue Committee, In: The Muses Flee Hitler: Cultural Transfer and Adaptation 1930-1945, 83; plus others. *Mailing Add:* Hirshhorn Mus & Sculpture Garden Eighth & Independence SW Washington DC 20560

MCCABE, MAUREEN M
COLLAGE ARTIST
Study: RI Sch Design, Providence, BFA, 69; Cranbrook Acad Art, Bloomfield Hills, Mich, MFA, 71. *Work:* RI Sch Design; Wadsworth Atheneum, Hartford, Conn; Samuel Greenbaum & Kogod Collection, Washington, DC. *Exhib:* One-person shows, Gallery K, Washington, DC, 72, 75, 79, 82 & 84, Allan Stone Gallery, New York, 77 & Marianne Deson Gallery, Chicago, 84; Renwick Gallery, Smithsonian Inst, 81; Neuberger Mus, 82; Washington Project for the Arts, 83; Art Expo Chicago, 83; and others. *Teaching:* Asst prof studio art, Conn Col, New London, 71-81, assoc prof studio art, 81- *Awards:* Yaddo Fel, 75; Residence Grant, Cite des Arts, Paris, 77-78; Individual Artist Grant, Conn Comn Arts, 80. *Dealer:* Allan Stone Gallery 48 E 86th St New York NY 10028; Gallery K 2032 P St NW Washington DC 20024. *Mailing Add:* 50 Old Norwich Rd Quaker Hill CT 06375

MCCAFFERTY, JAY DAVID
VIDEO ARTIST, PAINTER
b San Pedro, Calif, Feb 21, 48. *Study:* Los Angeles State Col, BA; Univ Calif, Irvine, MFA. *Work:* Los Angeles Co Mus Art, Calif; Long Beach Mus Art. *Exhib:* Southland Video Anthology Traveling Show, Long Beach Mus Art, 75; one-man shows, Grapestake Gallery, San Francisco, 78 & Cirrus Gallery, Los Angeles, 79; Baudoin Lebon, Paris, France, 80; Los Angeles Co Mus Art, 81; and others. *Teaching:* Vis lectr art, World Campus Afloat, Chapman Col, 74; instr, Los Angeles Harbor Col, Wilmington, Calif, 76-; instr, Claremont Col Grad Sch Art, 78; vis lectr, Univ Calif, Irvine, 80. *Awards:* New Talent Award, Los Angeles Co Mus Art, 74; Nat Endowment for the Arts Fel, 76. *Bibliog:* Joseph Youth (auth), Los Angeles, Art Int, 1/75; article, Art News, 9/83. *Dealer:* Cirrus 542 S Alameda Los Angeles CA 90013; Galerie Krebs Bern Munstergasse 43 Bern Switzerland. *Mailing Add:* 1017 Beacon St San Pedro CA 90731

MCCALL, ANN
PAINTER, PRINTMAKER
b Toronto, Ont, Can, Dec 12, 41. *Study:* McGill Univ, Montreal, BA, 64; Univ Pittsburgh, 71-74; Concordia Univ, Montreal, BFA, 78. *Work:* DeCordova Mus, Lincoln, Mass; Vancouver Art Gallery, BC; Winnipeg Art Gallery, Man; Can Coun Art Bank, Ottawa. *Exhib:* Rockford Int, Ill, 79, 81 & 83; World Print III, San Francisco, 80; Norwegian Int Print Biennial, Frederikstad. Norway, 80 & 82; Biennale Graphic Art, Ljubljana, Yugoslavia, 81 & 83; Seventh British Int Print Biennial, Bradford, England, 82; and others. *Awards:* Purchase Award, Burnaby Biennale, BC, 77; Merit Awards, Boston Printmakers Exhib, 77 & 83. *Bibliog:* Diana Nemiroff (auth), article, Vie des Arts, 78; Giles Daigneault & Ginette Deslauriers (coauth), Ann McCall, In: La Gravure au Quebec 1940-1980, 80; Virginia Nixon (auth), article, The Montrealer, 82. *Mem:* Soc Can Artists; Boston Printmakers; Print & Drawing Coun Can; Visual Arts Ont; Royal Can Acad Arts. *Media:* Acrylic; Silkscreen. *Dealer:* Galerie Theo Waddington Inc 1504 Sherbrooke St W Montreal PQ; Waddington-Shiell Gallery 511 Hazleton Lanes Toronto ON. *Mailing Add:* 509 Argyle Ave Montreal PQ H3Y 3B6 Canada

MCCALL, ANTHONY
FILMMAKER
b London, Eng, Apr 14, 46. *Study:* Whitgift Sch, Croydon, Eng, 56-64; Ravensbourne Col of Art & Design Bromley, Kent, Eng, 64-68, BA(first class hons), 68. *Work:* Royal Belgium Film Arch, Brussels; Arts Coun of Gt Brit, London; Mus of Mod Art, New York. *Exhib:* Documenta, Kassel, Ger, 77; Film as Film, 1910 to the Present, Kunstverein, Cologne, 78; Int Film Theory Conf 5, Univ Wis-Milwaukee, 79; Edinburgh Int Film Festival, 80; Berlin Film Festival, 81; and others. *Teaching:* Instr, London Col Printing, 70-71; vis lectr avant-garde film theory, NY Univ Dept of Cinema Studies, 77. *Awards:* Marie-Josi Prize 5th Int Experimental Competition, Knokke, Belg, 75; Creative Artists Prog Serv Grant, 76; Film Production Grant, New York State Coun Arts, 81; and others. *Bibliog:* Annette Michelson & P Adams Sitney (auth), A on Knokke and the Independent Filmmaker, Artforum, 5/75; Jane Weinstock (auth), The subject of argument, Downtown Rev, Vol 1, No 1; E Ann Kaplan (auth), Feminist approaches to history, psychoanalysis and cinema in Sigmund Freud's Dora, Millennium Film J, fall/winter 81; and others. *Mailing Add:* 11 Jay St New York NY 10013

MCCALL, ROBERT THEODORE
PAINTER, ILLUSTRATOR
b Columbus, Ohio, Dec 23, 19. *Study:* Scholar, Columbus Fine Art Sch, Ohio, two yrs. *Work:* Phoenix Art Mus, Ariz; Art Mus Univ NMex, Albuquerque; Collection of US Air Force, Washington, DC. *Comn:* Four Paintings for the film 2001 A Space Odyssey, MGM Film Corp, now in Nat Air & Space Mus, Washington, 68; six commemorative stamps, US Postal Serv, 72-78; The Space Mural, A Cosmic View (2100 sq ft, in the Lobby), Smithsonian Inst for the Nat Air & Space Mus, Washington, DC, 76; Three Decades of Achievement (10 ft x 20 ft mural in visitors ctr), Nat Air & Space Admin, Hugh L Dryden Flight Res Ctr, Edwards, Calif, 77; Opening the Space Frontier--the Next Giant Step, mural, mus at Johnson Space Ctr, Houston, Tex, 78-79; The Prologue and the Promise (mural), Disneyworld, Fla. *Exhib:* Am Watercolor Soc, 65; Space Art, Nat Gallery Art, Washington, DC, 70; Air & Space, Grand Cent Art Galleries, New York, 78; one-man show, Space Artist Robert McCall, Phoenix Art Mus, Ariz, 71; retrospective, Scottsdale Ctr Arts, Ariz, 81; Exhib, Nat Air & Space Mus, Smithsonian Inst, 84; and many other one-man shows. *Pos:* Art dir, The Black Hole (motion picture), Walt Disney, 79; conceptual designer, Star Trek, the Motion Picture, Paramount Pictures, 79. *Bibliog:* Pat Dryfus (auth), Space Artist Robert McCall, Am Artist, 70; Joe Stacy (auth), Worlds Premier Aerospace Artist,

Ariz Highways Mag, 73. *Mem:* Soc Illusr, New York (Air Force art prog chmn, 63-64, secy, 66). *Media:* Oil, Acrylic; Watercolor, Ink. *Publ:* Illusr many articles & covers for Life, Saturday Evening Post, Nat Geographic Mag, Popular Sci, Newsweek, Readers Digest, Colliers & others, 56-75; co-auth (with Isaac Asimov), Our World in Space, NY Graphic Soc, 74; auth, A vision of the future: The art of Robert McCall, Harry Abrams, fall 82. *Mailing Add:* 4816 Moonlight Way Paradise Valley AZ 85253

MCCALLUM, CORRIE (MRS WILLIAM HALSEY)
PAINTER, PRINTMAKER
b Sumter, SC, Mar 14, 14. *Study:* Univ SC, cert fine arts, 36; Boston Mus Sch, with Karl Zerbe. *Work:* La State Univ, Baton Rouge; SC Arts Comn, State Collection; Columbia Mus Arts, SC; Ford Motor Co. *Exhib:* 1st South Carolina State Invitational, Columbia Mus Art, 69; Contemporary Artists of South Carolina, Greenville Mus, Columbia Mus Art, Gibbes Art Gallery & Florence Mus, 70; one-man show, Concourse Gallery, State St Bank, Boston, Mass, 71; Art in Transition, Boston Mus Fine Arts, 77. *Teaching:* Cur art educ for Charleston Co, Gibbes Art Gallery, 60-69; instr painting & drawing, Newberry Col, SC, 69-71; instr painting, drawing & printmaking, Col Charleston, 71-79. *Awards:* Purchase Prize for Drawing, Mint Mus Graphics Ann, 64; Painting Award, Guild SC Artists Ann, 65; Scientific Educ Found Grant for Travel & Study Around the World, 68. *Bibliog:* J A Morris, Jr (auth), Contemporary Artists of South Carolina, Greenville Co Mus Art, 70; Art in Transition, Boston Mus Fine Arts, 77. *Mem:* Guild SC Artists (pres, 61); Col Art Asn Am; Copley Soc, Boston. *Publ:* Illusr, Dutch Fork Farm Boy, & 50 Years Along the Way, Univ SC, 68; coauth, A Travel Sketchbook, R L Byran Co, 71. *Dealer:* Kunstsalon Wolfsberg Bederstrasse 109 Zurich Switzerland; Nancy's Gallery 38 Queen St Charleston SC 29401. *Mailing Add:* 26 Archdale St Charleston SC 29401

MCCANE, MALLORY (MALLORY ANN MCCANE-O'CONNOR)
PAINTER
b Decatur, Ill, Feb 15, 43. *Study:* Univ Calif, Davis, with Wayne Thiebaud & Bill Wiley, 61-63; Univ Calif, Santa Barbara, with William Dole, 63-64; Ohio Univ, Athens, with William Kortlander & Jim Leedy, BFA, 66 & with Gary Schwindler, MA, 68 & MFA, 70. *Exhib:* Book Int, Kansas City Art Inst, Mo, 72; Pictorial Hist Nat, Kansas City Art Inst, Mo, 75; Californians Show in Fla, Univ Fla, Gainesville, 76; Gallery K, Washington, DC, 77-80; Southern Exposure, Hanson Gallery, New Orleans, La, 80. *Pos:* Cur, Slide Collection Special, Santa Fe Community Col, Gainesville, Fla, 72-73; workshop & special exhib coordr, Thomas Ctr, Gainesville, Fla, 80. *Teaching:* Instr art hist, Ohio Univ, Athens, 68-69; instr art hist, Univ Fla, Gainesville, 72-78. *Awards:* Grants, Ulrich Bay Found, 79, Fla Fine Arts Coun, 80 & Southern Arts Fedn, 80. *Mem:* Col Art Asn Am; Women's Caucus Art; Southeastern Womens Caucus Art; Southwestern Asn Indian Affairs; Nat Trust Historic Preservation. *Media:* Pen & Ink, Watercolor. *Res:* Extensive research in native American art history with special emphasis on prehistoric sculpture of the southeastern United States. *Publ:* Auth, Design Motifs on Weeden Island and Fort Walton Cer, Temple Mound Mus, 79; auth, Prehistoric ceramics of the Florida/Georgia area, Am Indian Art Mag, 80; auth, Janice Billie: Seminole patchwork artist, Flying Needle Mag, 80; auth, Fort Walton ceramics of the North Florida Area, Southeastern Ctr Contemp Arts Review, 80; contribr, Native North American Art History, Peek Publ, 82. *Dealer:* Gallery K 2032 P Street Washington DC 20036. *Mailing Add:* c/o Gallery K 2032 P St Washington DC 20036

MCCANN, CECILE NELKEN
EDITOR, CRITIC
b New Orleans, La. *Study:* Vassar Col; Tulane Univ; San Jose State Univ, Calif, BA & MA; Univ Calif, Berkeley; also with Herbert Sanders, Robert Fritz, Shoji Hamada & Peter Voulkos. *Work:* City of San Francisco; San Jose City Col; San Jose State Univ; Mills Col, Oakland; State of Calif, Sacramento. *Exhib:* Everson Mus Art, Syracuse, 62 & 64; one-woman shows, Crocker Gallery, Sacrmento, 65 & Calif Col Arts & Crafts, Oakland, 66; Calif Design, Pasadena Mus Art, 65 & 68; Wichita Design Craftsmen, Kans, 66. *Pos:* Ed & publ, Artweek, Oakland, 69- *Awards:* Critic's Grant, Nat Endowment Arts, 75. *Mem:* Col Art Asn; Int Asn Art Critics; Art Table. *Publ:* Contribr, Craft Horizons, 71 & 73; contribr, William Wiley, Opus, France, 73; auth, Ken Friedman (catalog essay), Yugoslavia, 74. *Mailing Add:* 1305 Franklin St Oakland CA 94612

MCCANNEL, (MRS) MALCOLM A
COLLECTOR
b Minneapolis, Minn, Nov 20, 15. *Study:* Smith Col, BA; Minneapolis Sch Art. *Pos:* Bd mem, Walker Art Ctr, Minneapolis, currently. *Collection:* Contemporary American sculpture and painting. *Mailing Add:* 1520 Waverly Pl Minneapolis MN 55403

MCCARTHY, DENIS
PAINTER
b New York, NY, Feb 21, 35. *Study:* Cooper Union, 59-64; Yale Univ, BFA & MFA, 64-66. *Work:* Work in pvt collections only. *Exhib:* Painting Ann, 70 & Biennial Exhib, 73, Whitney Mus Am Art; Exhib, O K Harris, New York, 72; Spring Exhib, Aldrich Mus, Ridgefield, Conn, 73; Automation House, New York, 76; Hundred Acres Gallery, New York, 77; New York Acad Sci, 78; one-man show, 55 Mercer Gallery, New York, 78 & NY State Col, Old Westbury, NY, 80. *Teaching:* Instr drawing, Sch Visual Arts, New York, 67-72; instr painting & printmaking, Hunter Col, 71-; instr drawing, NY Univ, 76-77. *Mailing Add:* 147 Spring St New York NY 10012

MCCARTHY, DORIS JEAN
PAINTER, INSTRUCTOR

b Calgary, Alta, July 7, 10. *Study:* Ont Col Art, 30; Cent Sch Arts & Crafts, London, Eng. *Work:* Art Gallery Ont, Toronto; London Art Gallery, Ont; Imp Oil Collection; Ont Centennial Collection; Hudson Bay Oil; and others. *Comn:* Mural, Toronto Pub Libr, 33; mem bk, Malvern Col, Toronto, 48; creche figures, Church of St Aldan, Toronto, 48; fabric banner Trinity, St James Cathedral, Toronto, 75; wall hangings, St Aidan's Church, Cana Place, Toronto. *Exhib:* Ont Soc Artists Ann, 33-; Royal Can Acad Ann, 34-; Can Soc Painters Watercolor, 38-; solo shows, Aggregation Gallery, 82 & Wynick/Tuck Gallery, 83, Toronto; and others. *Teaching:* Instr drawing, painting & hist art, Central Tech Sch Toronto, 33-, asst head, 68-72. *Mem:* Royal Can Acad; Ont Soc Artists (pres, 65-68); Can Soc Painters in Watercolor (pres, 56-57); Fedn Can Artists; Prof Artists Can (chmn, 67-69). *Media:* Oil, Watercolor. *Dealer:* Aggregation Gallery 83 Front St E Toronto ON; Wynick/Tuck Gallery 80 Spadina Ave Fourth Floor Toronto ON Can M5V 2J3. *Mailing Add:* 1 Meadowcliff Dr Scarborough ON M6B 2X8 Canada

MCCARTIN, WILLIAM FRANCIS
PAINTER

b New York, NY, Dec 9, 05. *Study:* Art Students League, with Richard Lahey, five yrs; New Sch Social Res, one yr. *Exhib:* Gallery Contemp Arts, Pittsburgh; Maine Coast Artists; 7 from Monhegan, Phillips Exeter Acad, NH, 70; Joseph De Meers Ltd, Hilton Head, SC, 71; one-man show, Beaumont Art Mus, Tex, 71; and others. *Awards:* Tiffany Found Grant, 25; John Newman Medal, Casein Soc, 60; Nat Endowment Arts Fel, 77. *Media:* Acrylic. *Mailing Add:* 381 Bleeker St New York NY 10014

MCCARTY, LORRAINE CHAMBERS
PAINTER, INSTUCTOR

b Detroit, Mich. *Study:* Detroit Art Acad, Wayne State Univ, with G Alden Smith; Meinzinger Art Acad; Stephens Col, with Albert Christ-Janer, also with Glen Michaels, Emil Weddige, Robert Wilbert & Adolph Dehn. *Work:* Butler Mus Am Art, Youngstown, Ohio; Smithsonian Nat Air & Space Mus; Muskegon Mus Art, Mich; Northwood Inst, Midland, Mich; Stephens Col; and others. *Comn:* Painting, Bohn Copper & Brass, Detroit; painting, R L Polk Co Int Hq, Detroit, 73; painting, Wyandotte Paint Products, Troy, Mich, 74; mural, Int Women's Air & Space Mus, Dayton, Ohio, 77. *Exhib:* Butler Mus Am Art Ann, 67 & 70-74; Womanart, Saginaw Mus Arts, Mich, 74; Fed Aviation Admin, DC, 77; Dayton Art Inst, Ohio, 78; Battle Creek Art Ctr, Mich, 78; Smithsonian Air & Space Mus, DC, 80-82; Flint Inst Traveling Exhib, 83; and 43 solo exhibs. *Pos:* Mem, Arts Cult Coun, Oakland Co, Mich, 75- *Teaching:* Instr painting, Flint Inst Arts, 70-; instr, Grosse Pointe War Mem, Mich, 70-79; instr oil painting, Art Ctr, Pontiac, Mich, 75- *Awards:* Purchase Prize, Butler Mus, 67; Cooke Found Fel, 83; Mich Coun Arts Grant, 83. *Bibliog:* Joy Hakenson (auth), Abstract artists focus on a real world, Detroit News, 79; Corinne Abatt (auth), Flight's romance captured, Birmingham Eccentric, Mich, 79; Cheryl Beller (auth), Take off just beginning, Royal Oak Daily Tribune, 79. *Mem:* Mich Acad Arts, Sci & Lett; Mich Watercolour Soc; Detroit Soc Women Painters & Sculptors; Scarab Club, Detroit; Artists Equity; and others. *Media:* Acrylic, Oil. *Mailing Add:* 1112 Pinehurst Royal Oak MI 48073

MCCAULEY, GARDINER RAE
ADMINISTRATOR, PAINTER

b Oakland, Calif, Aug 8, 33. *Study:* Calif Col Arts & Crafts, studied with Hamilton Wolf, 48-51; Univ Calif, Berkeley, BA, 55, MA, 57, studied with Milton Resnick, David Park, Esteban Vicente, Erle Loran & Corrado Marca-Relli. *Exhib:* Ann Exhib of San Francisco Art Asn, San Francisco Mus Art, 55-57; Bay Area Invitational, Calif Palace of the Legion of Honor, San Francisco, 58; one-man shows, Berkeley Gallery, San Francisco, 64 & Columbia Art League Galleries, 81; Artists of Ore, 67, 70, 72 & Spectrum 70, Portland Art Mus, Ore; Stephens Faculty, Merril Chase Gallery, Chicago, 74; Marymount Manhattan Col, NY, 78; Area Painters, Art Gallery, Univ Mo-Columbia, 78; and others. *Pos:* Crafts dir, US Spec Serv, France & Ger, 59-62; exec dir, Montalvo Ctr Arts, Saratoga, 82- *Teaching:* Lectr drawing, Univ Calif, Berkeley, 62-65; lectr art, Univ Santa Clara, Calif, 64; asst prof painting & drawing, Lewis & Clark Col, Portland, Ore, 66-72; head dept art, painting & drawing, Stephens Col, Columbia, Mo, 72-82; vis artist, Barnfield Col, Eng, 80. *Awards:* Juror's Prize, San Francisco Art Asn Ann, San Francisco Mus Art, 63; James D Phelan Found Award, Calif Palace of Legion of Honor, San Francisco, 65; Firestone-Baars Found Grant, 80. *Bibliog:* Joanna Magloff (auth), From the Berkeley Gallery, 12/63, Elizabeth Polley (auth), San Francisco: Gardiner McCauley & Howard Margolis, 3/64, Artforum; Anita Ventura (auth), Pop, Photo & Paint, Arts Mag, 4/64. *Mem:* Nat Coun Art Adminrs; Col Art Asn Am; Mid-Am Col Art Asn; Am Asn Univ Profs. *Media:* Acrylic and oil. *Mailing Add:* Montalvo Ctr Arts PO Box 158 Saratoga CA 95071

MCCHESNEY, CLIFTON
PAINTER, EDUCATOR

b Gary, Ind, Feb 8, 29. *Study:* Am Acad Art, dipl; Ind Univ, with Jack Tworko, BS; Cranbrook Acad Art, with Zolton Sepeshy, MFA. *Work:* Detroit Inst Art; Cranbrook Acad Art, Bloomfield Hills, Mich; Univ Ryuukus, Okinawa, Japan; Biwako Mus, Otsu, Japan; Ginza Nova Gallery, Tokyo, Japan; and others. *Exhib:* 24 Ann, Soc Contemp Arts, Chicago Art Inst, 64; one-man shows, Benni Gallery, Kyoto, 67 & Ginza Nova Gallery, Tokyo, Japan, 75; Arwin Galleries, Detroit, 80; Freeman Gallery, East Lansing, Mich, 81 & 82; Western Mich Univ, 84; and others. *Pos:* Guest artist, Kalamazoo Art Ctr, Mich, summer 64; Vis artist, State Univ NY Albany, fall 65; instr, Leland summer workshop, 65, 66, 80-83. *Teaching:* Prof painting &

drawing, Mich State Univ, East Lansing, 60- *Awards:* Purchase Awards, Detroit Inst Arts, 61 & Purdue Univ, 70; Travel Grant to Japan, Ford Found, 74. *Bibliog:* Man and Humanity (film), Mich State Univ, 71; Spec American Issue, Arts Mag, Vol 39, No 7; article in, Geijutsu Seikatsu, No 4, 75. *Media:* Oil, Pencil. *Dealer:* Freeman Gallery East Lansing MI. *Mailing Add:* Kresge Art Ctr Mich State Univ East Lansing MI 48824

MCCHESNEY, MARY FULLER See Fuller, Mary

MCCHESNEY, ROBERT PEARSON
PAINTER, MURALIST

b Marshall, Mo, Jan 16, 13. *Study:* Washington Univ Art Sch, with Fred Conway; Otis Art Inst, Los Angeles. *Work:* Chicago Art Inst; Oakland Art Mus; Muskegon Mus Art, Mich; and others. *Comn:* Wall decoration, USS Monterey; mural, Social Serv Admin Bldg, San Francisco, Calif, 77. *Exhib:* Art Inst Chicago Ann, 47-61; Sao Paulo Third Biennial, 55; Corcoran Gallery Art, 57; Calif Palace Legion Hon, 62; Expo 70, Osaka, Japan, 70; Retrospective, San Francisco Art Comn Gallery, 74; 19 Yrs, Calif State Univ, Hayward, 77; and many others. *Awards:* Purchase Prizes, San Francisco Art Comn, 50 & 69; Purchase Prize, Whitney Mus Am Art, 55; Prize, San Francisco Mus Art, 60. *Mem:* San Francisco Art Inst. *Dealer:* Vorpal Gallery 393 Grove St San Francisco CA. *Mailing Add:* 2955 Sonoma Mountain Rd Petaluma CA 94952

MCCHRISTY, QUENTIN L
PAINTER, DESIGNER

b Cushing, Okla, Jan 24, 21. *Study:* Okla State Univ, with Doel Reed, BA; Cincinnati Acad Art, with Helwhig & Crawford. *Work:* Philbrook Art Ctr, Tulsa, Okla; Joslyn Mus Art, Omaha, Nebr; Butler Inst Am Art, Youngstown, Ohio; Pa State Univ, State College; Dean Weller, Col Fine Arts, Univ Ill, Urbana. *Comn:* Murals, Ft Worth Children's Mus & Wesley Found, Methodist Church, Stillwater, Okla; designed decorations glassware, Bartlett Collins, mfrs domestic & export glassware; plus others. *Exhib:* 26th Biennial, Corcoran Gallery, Washington, DC, 59; Contemporary American Art, Oklahoma City, 60; All City Arts Festival, Los Angeles, Calif, 60-; Audubon Artist Nat Galleries, New York, 62; Pa Acad Fine Arts, Philadelphia, 63; plus others. *Pos:* Art dir, Ft Worth Children's Mus, 50; Nat Artist Show judge, 65. *Teaching:* Instr drawing, Okla State Univ; instr art, Ft Worth Children's Mus. *Awards:* Purchase Award, 47, Prize, 48 & Ruskin Award, 62, Philbrook Art Ctr; Butler Mus Art Friends of Art Award, 60; Painting Exhib Awards, Wind River Valley Nat Show, Dubois, Wyo, 61 & 65; plus others. *Mem:* Int Platform Asn. *Media:* Transparent Watercolor, Oil; Ink. *Publ:* Four pen drawings, Am Artist Mag, 6-8/64. *Mailing Add:* 117 Parkville Ave Brooklyn NY 11230

MCCLAIN, MATTHEW
CURATOR, WRITER

b Des Moines, Iowa, Mar 26, 56. *Study:* Univ Mont Inst Intensive Humanitarian Study, cert, 75; Univ Cincinnati Col Design, Archit & Art, BA(art hist), 78; Whitney Mus Am Art, 78-79, Rubinstein fel, 78-79. *Exhib:* Symbolist Mood Around 1900 (auth, catalog), Whitney Mus Am Art, New York, 78, Indust Sights, 79 & Enclosure & Concealment (auth, catalog), 79; Urban Encounters (auth, catalog), Inst Contemp Art, Philadelphia, 80 & Made in Philadelphia III (auth, catalog), 80. *Collections Arranged:* Symbolist Mood Around 1900, Whitney Mus Am Art, New York, 78, Indust Sights, 79 & Enclosure & Concealment, 79; Urban Encounters, Inst Contemp Art, Philadelphia, 80 & Made in Philadelphia III, 80; John C Gregory: Recent Works, Grey Gallery, Philadelphia, Pa, 81; Maureen Garvin: Ruffles and Roses, Wallingford Art Ctr, Pa, 82; Susan Chyrsler White and Sam Karen Norgard, Kling Gallery, Philadelphia, 82. *Pos:* Pub Info Mgr, Contemp Arts Ctr, Cincinnati, 76-78; curatorial intern, Whitney Mus Am Art, 78-79; cur/adminr, Inst Contemp Art, Philadelphia, 79-80; columnist, Philadelphia City Paper. *Mem:* Col Art Asn Am. *Mailing Add:* 2102 Pine St Philadelphia PA 19103

MCCLANAHAN, JOHN D
PAINTER, EDUCATOR

b Saline, Kans. *Study:* Bethany Col, Lindsborg, Kans, BFA; Univ Iowa, Iowa City, MFA. *Work:* Art Mus, Univ Iowa, Iowa City; Weatherspoon Art Gallery, Univ NC, Greensboro; Mint Mus Art, Charlotte, NC; Second Street Gallery, Charlottesville, Va; Seguin Art Ctr, Tex. *Exhib:* Watercolor USA, Springfield Art Mus, Mo, 66-69, 72-75, 79 & 81; one-man exhib, Mint Mus Art, 71; 8th & 14th Hunter Painting Ann, Hunter Mus Art, Chattanooga, Tenn, 67 & 73; Mid-Am Art Exhib, Owensboro, Ky, 79 & 82; Baylor Univ, 81; 6th Biennial Five State Exhib, 81; Art Ann Two, Okla Art Ctr, Oklahoma City, 81; Biennial Nat Small Painting Exhib, Mullaly-Matisse Galleries, Birmingham, Mich; and many others. *Teaching:* Instr painting, Stephen F Austin State Univ, Nacogdoches, Tex, 64-67; from asst prof to assoc prof painting, Queens Col, Charlotte, NC, 67-76, chmn dept art, 75-76; assoc prof painting, Baylor Univ, Waco, Tex, 76- *Awards:* Purchase Prizes, Tex Painting & Sculpture Exhib, 77 & 82 & Fifth Biennial Five State Exhib, 79. *Mem:* Col Art Asn Am; Tex Fine Arts Asn. *Media:* Water Media, Collage. *Mailing Add:* Dept of Art Baylor Univ Waco TX 76798

MCCLEARY, MARY FIELDING
PAINTER, EDUCATOR

b Houston, Tex, Feb 27, 51. *Study:* Tex Christian Univ, Ft Worth, BFA, 72; Univ Okla, Norman, MFA, 75. *Work:* Miami Univ Mus, Oxford, Ohio; Gihon Found, Dallas, Tex; Western Ill Univ, Macomb; First Int Bank, Houston, Tex; State of Okla Art Collection, Oklahoma City. *Exhib:* Boston Printmakers 27th

Ann Nat Exhib, Boston Mus Fine Arts, 75; Works on Paper: Southwest 1978, Dallas Mus Fine Arts, 78; Paperworks, Witte Mus, San Antonio, Tex, 79; Made in Tex, Huntington Art Gallery, Univ Tex, Austin, 79; one-man show, Watson/de Nagy & Co Gallery, Houston, Tex, 79 & 83; Tyler Mus Art, Tyler, Tex, 82; Mattingley Baker Gallery, Dallas, Tex, 82, and others. *Pos:* Gallery dir, Stephen F Austin State Univ, 79-82. *Teaching:* Assoc prof art, Stephen F Austin State Univ, Nacogdoches, Tex, 75- *Awards:* First Place Award, Blaffer Gallery, Univ Houston, Tex, 77; Purchase Prize, Miami Univ, Oxford, Ohio, 78; Second Place Award, Assistance League of Houston, Tex, 78. *Bibliog:* Donna Tennant (auth), ref in Artspace, summer 79; Susie Kalil (auth), rev in Artweek, 7/79; Alexis Krasilorsky (dir), From the heart (film), Gihon Found, Dallas, 81-82. *Media:* Mixed media. *Dealer:* Watson/de Nagy & Co Gallery 1106 Berthea Houston TX 72006; Mattingley Baker Gallery 3000 McKinney Ave Dallas TX 75204. *Mailing Add:* 4005 Raguet Nacogdoches TX 75961

MCCLELLAN, DOUGLAS EUGENE
PAINTER
b Pasadena, Calif, Oct 10, 21. *Study:* Art Ctr Sch, Los Angeles, Calif; Colorado Springs Fine Arts Ctr, with Boardman Robinson & Jean Charlot; Claremont Grad Sch, MFA. *Work:* Los Angeles Co Mus Art; Los Angeles Co Fair Asn; Pasadena Art Mus. *Exhib:* Libr Cong, 48; San Francisco Mus Art, Calif, 49-52; Los Angeles Co Mus Art, 49-55; Metrop Mus Art, New York, 50; Pa Acad Fine Arts, Pa, 53; Corcoran Gallery Art, Washington, DC, 53; Pacific Coast Biennial, 55; Carnegie Inst of Technol, Pittsburgh, Pa, 55 & 57; Whitney Mus Am Art, New York, 57; one-man shows, Felix Landau Gallery, 53-59, Pasadena Art Mus, 54 & Univ Calif, Riverside, 55. *Teaching:* Instr, Chaffey Col, 50-59, Otis Art Inst, Los Angeles, Calif, 59-61; Scripps Col & Univ of Calif, Santa Cruz; prof art, Univ Calif, Santa Cruz, 70- *Awards:* Painting Prize, Los Angeles Co Mus Art, 50 & 53; Nat Orange Show, 54. *Mailing Add:* c/o Art Dept Univ of Calif Santa Cruz CA 95064

MCCLELLAND, JEANNE C
PRINTMAKER, PAINTER
b Edmeston, NY. *Study:* Albright-Knox Sch Fine Arts, Buffalo, dipl; State Univ NY Col Buffalo, BS(art educ); Munson-Williams-Proctor Inst, Utica, NY; Hartwick Col, Oneonta, NY; State Univ Col NY, Oneonta. *Work:* Mus Fine Arts, Springfield, Mass; St John Fisher Col (NY); Holyoke Mus, Mass; Munson-Williams-Proctor Inst, Utica, NY. *Exhib:* Cooperstown Art Asn, NY; Artists of Central New York, Munson-Williams-Proctor Inst; Academic Artists, Springfield Art Mus, Mass; Soc Am Graphic Artists, New York; Arena, Binghamton, NY; one-person show, State Univ NY Col, Oneonta; and others. *Mem:* Munson-Williams-Proctor Inst; Acad Artists; Cooperstown Art Asn; Roberson Ctr-Arts & Sci. *Mailing Add:* 17 Sharon St Sidney NY 13838

MCCLENDON, MAXINE (MAXINE MCCLENDON NICHOLS)
PAINTER, CRAFTSMAN
b Leesville, La, Oct 21, 31. *Study:* Univ Tex, Austin; Tex Women's Univ; Pan Am Univ. *Work:* Mus Int Folk Art, Santa Fe, NMex; IBM Collection; Lauren Rogers Mus Art, Laurel, Miss; Ark Arts Ctr, Little Rock; McAllen Int Mus, McAllen, Tex. *Comn:* Panels, Meridith Woodworth, Dallas, Tex, 77; Tex Instruments, Houston, 79; Union Bank of Switz, 80; Hyatt Regency Hotel, Ft Worth, Tex, 81; Continental Plaza, Ft Worth, Tex, 82; and others. *Exhib:* 16th Tex Crafts Exhib, Dallas Mus Fine Arts, 74; 8th & 9th Ann Southwestern Area Exhibs, Mus of the Southwest, Midland, Tex, 74 & 75; Fourth Nat Crafts Exhib, Marietta Col, 75; Invitational Biennial, Beaumont Art Mus, Tex, 76; 19th Nat, El Paso Mus Art, Tex, 76; McAllen Int Mus, 76; Southwest Craft Ctr, Tex Designer/Crafts Ctr, San Antonio, 78; and others. *Pos:* Cur Mex Folk Art, McAllen Int Mus, 74-80. *Awards:* Best in Exhib, 6th Ann Prints, Drawings & Crafts, Ark Art Ctr, 74; Award of Excellence, Houston Designer/Craftsman, 76; Judges Award, Fourth Marietta Nat, 75. *Mem:* Am Crafts Coun (state rep, 76-80); Tex Designer/Craftsmen (pres, 73-74). *Dealer:* Adelle M Fine Art 3317 McKinney Ave Dallas TX 75204. *Mailing Add:* 2018 Sharyland Rd Mission TX 78572

MCCLENNEY, CHERYL ILENE
ADMINISTRATOR
b Chicago, Ill, July 18, 48. *Study:* Art Inst Chicago, BFA, 69. *Work:* Solomon R Guggenheim Mus, New York. *Pos:* Cur coordr, Solomon R Guggenheim Mus, 70-74; asst prog dir, Mus Collab Inc, 74-76; asst comnr, New York City Dept Cult Affairs, 76-78; dir mus prog, Nat Endowment Humanities, 78-83; asst dir prog, Philadelphia Mus Art, currently. *Teaching:* Instr, Art Inst Chicago, 68-69. *Mem:* Am Asn Mus; Am Asn State & Local Hist; African-Am Mus Asn. *Mailing Add:* Philadelphia Mus Art Box 7646 26th & Parkway Philadelphia PA 19101

MACCLINTOCK, DORCAS
SCULPTOR
b New York, NY, July 16, 32. *Study:* Smith Col, AB; Univ Wyo, AM. *Exhib:* Birds, Beasts & Fish, Slater Mem Mus, 73 & 77; Fur-Feathers-Flora, Foot of Main Gallery, Essex, Conn, 76; Soc of Animal Artists, Sportsman Edge Ltd, NY, 78; A M Adler Galleries, New York, 81; Soc Animal Artists, Acad Nat Sciences, Philadelphia, 81. *Pos:* Res assoc, Calif Acad Sciences, San Francisco. *Mem:* Soc of Animal Artists Inc (mem exec bd & jury 76-). *Media:* Plastilene, Clay. *Publ:* Auth, A Natural History of Giraffes, 73, A Natural History of Zebras, 76, Horses as I See Them, 80, A Natural History of Raccoons, 81 & A Raccoon's First Year, 82, Scribners. *Mailing Add:* 33 Rogers Rd Hamden CT 06517

MCCLOSKEY, ROBERT
PAINTER, ILLUSTRATOR
b Hamilton, Ohio, Sept 15, 14. *Study:* Vesper George Sch Art, Boston; Nat Acad Design, New York; Miami Univ, LittD; Mt Holyoke Col, LittD. *Work:* May Massee Collection; William Allen White Libr, Emporia State Teachers Col, Kans. *Awards:* Caldecott Medal, Am Libr Asn, 42 & 58; Regina Award, Cath Libr Asn, 74. *Bibliog:* Marc Simont (auth), Robert McCloskey, Inventor, Horn Bk, 58; Robert McCloskey (film), Weston Woods Studio, 65. *Mem:* Fel Am Acad in Rome; Author's League; PEN. *Publ:* Auth & illusr, Make Way for Ducklings, 41, Homer Price, 42, Blueberries for Sal, 47, Time of Wonder, 57 & Burt Dow, Deep Water Man, 63. *Mailing Add:* Scott Islands Little Deer Isle ME 04650

MCCLURE, CONSTANCE
PAINTER, INSTRUCTOR
b Huntington, WVa, Feb 12, 34. *Study:* Ringling Sch of Art, Sarasota, Fla; Col of Mt St Joseph, BA; Univ Cincinnati, MFA. *Work:* Cincinnati Zoological Soc; Bell Telephone Co, Cincinnati; Cincinnati Art Mus; Federated Dept Stores, Cincinnati; Jewish Community Ctr, Cincinnati; and others. *Comn:* Portrait of conductor, Cincinnati Symphony Orchestra, 70; 18 ft canvas mural, Ohio Nat Bank, Columbus, 76; portrait of pres, Mt St Joseph Col, Ohio, 77. *Exhib:* Ohio Women Artists: Past & Present, Butler Inst of Am Art, Youngstown, Ohio, 76; 14 Cincinnati Artists, Tampa Bay Arts Ctr, Fla, Peachtree Ctr, Atlanta, Ga & Contemp Arts Ctr, Cincinnati, 76; Cincinnati Art Mus, 81; Daniel Brown's Collection, Middlebury Col, Vt, 81; and others. *Collections Arranged:* Drawing & Print Awards Exhib, Cincinnati Art Mus, 75; Regional Proj, Contemp Arts Ctr, Cincinnati, 73. *Teaching:* Instr painting, Art Acad of Cincinnati, 74-, portrait painting, 78. *Awards:* Best in Show, Cincinnati Zoo Arts Festival, 65-68 & 73; First Prize/Drawing, Exhib 180, Huntington Galleries, 66; Purchase Prize, Jewish Community Ctr Invitational, 68. *Bibliog:* Sally Webster (auth), Regional project, Cincinnati Post, 10/73; Daniel Brown (auth), Big money, big business and big art, Cincinnati Mag, 6/80; Monica Geran (auth), Balancing the scales, Interior Design, 12/80; and others. *Media:* Oil, Silverpoint. *Mailing Add:* 2356 Park Ave Cincinnati OH 45206

MCCLURE, THOMAS F
SCULPTOR, EDUCATOR
b Pawnee City, Nebr, Apr 17, 20. *Study:* Univ Nebr, BFA, 41; Wash State Col, 41; Cranbrook Acad Art, MFA, 47. *Work:* Seattle Art Mus; Syracuse Mus Fine Arts, NY; Detroit Inst Arts; Wright Mem Ctr, Beloit Col, Wis; DeWaters Art Mus, Flint, Mich. *Comn:* Welded bronze relief, Victor Gruen Assocs, Eastland Shopping Ctr, Detroit, 56; cast bronze relief, DeWaters Art Ctr, 58; welded bronze free standing sculpture, Albert Kahn Assocs, Univ Mich Undergrad Libr, Ann Arbor, 59; ten cast bronze relief sculptures, Congregation Shaarey Zedek, Detroit, 69; large cast bronze sculpture, Mich Blue Cross Bldg, Detroit, 74; and others. *Exhib:* Pa Acad Fine Arts Ann, Philadelphia & Detroit, 58; Contemporary Sculpture 1961, Cincinnati Art Mus & John Herron Art Inst, 61; Drawings USA, St Paul, Minn, 61; one-man exhibs, Gilman Galleries, Chicago, 68, 70 & 75, Arwin Gallery, Detroit, 76 & Flint Inst Art, 78. *Teaching:* Instr design, Sch for Am Craftsmen, Alfred, NY, 47-48; asst prof drawing & design, Univ Okla, 48-49; prof sculpture, Univ Mich, 49-79. *Awards:* First Prize for Painting, Northwest Artists Ann, Seattle, 43; Prize in Sculpture, 12th Nat Ceramics Ann, Syracuse, 47; Founders Prize in Sculpture, 45th Mich Artists Ann, Detroit, 54. *Media:* Metal. *Dealer:* Elaine Horwitch Galleries 4211 N Marshall Way Scottsdale AZ 85251; Ankrum Gallery 657 N Lacienega Blvd Los Angeles CA 90069. *Mailing Add:* 2406 Pine Cove Rd Prescott AZ 86301

MCCOLLEY, SUTHERLAND
CONSULTANT, DESIGNER
b Philadelphia, Pa, Oct 17, 37. *Study:* Westminster Choir Col, BMus, 60, MMus, 62; NY State Coun Arts Mus Training Prog, 70; Intermus Conserv Lab, 71; Harvard Univ Inst Arts Admin, 73; Int Mus Studies Prog, 74, Mus Exchange Prog, 76. *Pos:* Researcher, M Knoedler & Co, 67-69; cur art, Hudson River Mus, Yonkers, NY, 69-76; dir, Dulin Gallery Art, Knoxville, 78-80; arts adv, Tenn Valley Authority, Knoxville, 80-81; consult, Sutherrland Co, Easthampton, NY, 82- *Awards:* City Knoxville Mayor's Award, 81. *Publ:* Auth, The Works of James Renwick Brevoort, 72. *Mailing Add:* PO Box 155 Wainscott NY 11975

MCCONNELL, JAMES HOUSTON
PRINTMAKER
b Chicago, Ill, Oct 19, 14. *Study:* Denison Univ, BA, 36; State Univ Iowa, Iowa City, MFA, 38. *Work:* Brooklyn Mus; Mus Art & Indust, St Etienne, France; Smith Col; Univ Mich, Ann Arbor; Northwest Mich Col. *Comn:* Wall mural, City Lansing, Mich; frescoes, Univ Iowa, Iowa City. *Exhib:* Nat Acad Design Print Ann, 40-47; Am Color Print Soc Exhib, Philadelphia Mus Art, 42; Nat Serigraph Soc Ann, 46-61; Brooklyn Mus Ann, 47, 48 & 60; Serigraph Int, Nat Serigraphic Soc, 58; Miniature Art Show, NJ State Mus, 82-; Second Ann Pratt Graphics, Pratt Inst. *Teaching:* Instr art, Denison Univ, 36-37; grad asst printmaking, State Univ Iowa, Iowa City, 37-40; from instr to prof art, Mich State Univ, 45-82. *Awards:* Brooklyn Mus Ann Awards, 47, 48 & 60; Nat Serigraph Soc Awards, 58 & 60; Miniature Art Show Awards, 82. *Media:* Serigraphy. *Mailing Add:* 11600 Woodbury Rd Laingsburg MI 48848

MCCONNELL, MICHAEL PATRICK
SCULPTOR
b Troy, Ohio, Dec 4, 48. *Study:* Ohio Univ, Athens, BFA(sculpture), 70, MFA(sculpture), 74. *Work:* Butler Inst Am Art, Youngstown, Ohio; Laguna Gloria Art Mus, Austin, Tex; Currier Gallery Art, Manchester, NH;

Meadows Mus Art, Shreveport, La; Zanesville Art Ctr, Ohio. *Comn:* Sculpture, NH Comn Arts, 83. *Exhib:* Mainstreams, Marietta Col, Ohio, 75 & 76; Int Craft, Tweed Mus Art, Duluth, Minn,77; Drawing and Small Sculpture, Ball State Univ Art Gallery, Muncie, Ind, 77, 78, 79 & 81; Grand Prix Int d'Art Contemp de Monte-Carlo, Nat Mus Monaco, 80 & 82. *Teaching:* Assoc prof sculpture, Univ NH, 76- *Awards:* Sculpture Award, Marrietta Col, 76; Finalist, Int Competition, Johnson Atelier Inst, 79; Award of Merit, Saenger Nat, Univ Southern Miss, 78. *Media:* Welded Steel, Cast Bronze. *Mailing Add:* 25 Faculty Rd Durham NH 03824

MCCORISON, MARCUS ALLEN
LIBRARIAN
b Lancaster, Wis, July 17, 26. *Study:* Ripon Col, BA, 50; Univ Vt, MA, 51; Columbia Univ, MS, 54. *Collections Arranged:* A Society's Chief Joys (auth, catalog), Grolier Club, Newberry Libr, Univ Calif, Los Angeles, 68-70. *Pos:* Librn, Kellogg-Hubbard Libr, Montpelier, Vt, 54-55; chief rare bk, Dartmouth Col, Hanover, NH, 55-59; head spec collections, Univ Iowa, Iowa City, 55-60; librn & dir, Am Antiq Soc, Worcester, Mass, 60-; trustee, Fruitlands Mus, 79- & Old Sturbridge Village, 81- *Awards:* Pepys Medal, Ephemera Soc, London, 80. *Mem:* Bibliog Soc Am (pres, 80-84); Rare Bk Sect, Asn Col & Res Libr (chmn, 65); Independent Res Libr Asn (chmn, 72-73 & 78-80); Grolier Club (councillor, 80-), Century Asn. *Res:* History of American printing, publishing, book trades, including American prints. *Interests:* American prints in all media prior to year 1877. *Collection:* American prints of the 18th and 19th century. *Publ:* Auth, Vermont Imprints, 1777-1820, Am Antiq Soc, 63; auth, 1764 Catalogue of the Redwood Library, Yale Univ Press, 65; ed, The history of printing in America, Imprint Soc, 70. *Mailing Add:* Am Antiq Soc 185 Salisbury St Worcester MA 01609

MCCORMICK, JO MARY (JO MARY MCCORMICK-SAKURAI)
PAINTER, PHOTOGRAPHER
b New York, NY, Mar 6, 18. *Study:* Nat Acad Design, 47; Art Students League, scholar, 48; Columbia Univ, 47-55; Empire State Col, BS, 77; Hunter Col, 83. *Comn:* Series of pastel paintings, Grace Manney, 80-; Mus Mod Art; Yale Univ; Columbia Univ. *Exhib:* Burr Gallery, 62; Graphics Show, Nat Arts Club, 63; Brazansky Art Gallery, 65; New York Pub Libr, 72-74; Archives, Mus Mod Art, New York. *Pos:* Art critic, Pictures on Exhib Mag, 59-75; auth, Wings of Thought and Art Column, New York Column Newspaper, 71-72; writer & photogr, Cats Mag, 83- *Teaching:* Instr journalism, Newspaper Inst Am, 71. *Awards:* Cert Award, NBC-TV, 45. *Mem:* Life mem Art Students League. *Publ:* Illusr, Art: USA Now, 64; contribr, Am Artist Mag, 71. *Mailing Add:* 444 Second Ave 22A New York NY 10010

MCCOY, ANN
MURALIST, DRAFTSMAN
b Boulder, Colo, July 8, 46. *Study:* Univ Colo, BFA, 69; Univ Calif, Los Angeles, MA, 72. *Work:* Metrop Mus Art, Whitney Mus Am Art, New York; Hirshhorn Mus, Washington, DC; Los Angeles Co Art Mus; Art Inst Chicago. *Comn:* Mural in pencil, Harris Bank. *Exhib:* 10 Years of Contemporary Art Acquisitions, Los Angeles Co Art Mus, 73; Whitney Mus Am Art, New York, 73; Painting & Sculpture Today, Contemp Art Ctr, Cincinnati, 74; 71st Am Exhib, Art Inst Chicago, 74; one-person exhibs, Inst Contemp Art, Boston, 75, Arts Club Chicago, 79, Roy Boyd Gallery, Chicago, 79 & Margo Leavin Gallery, Los Angeles, 79; America 1976, Corcoran Gallery Art, Washington, DC, Wadsworth Atheneum, Hartford, Conn & Fogg Art Mus, Cambridge, Mass, 76; 31st Ann Exhib, Brooklyn Mus, 78; and many others. *Media:* Pencil. *Dealer:* Brooke Alexander 20 W 57th St New York NY 10019; Margo Leavin Gallery 812 N Robertson Los Angeles CA 90069. *Mailing Add:* 24 W 76th St New York NY 10023

MCCOY, JOHN W, (II)
PAINTER
b Pinole, Calif, May 11, 10. *Study:* Am Sch, Fontainebleau, France, 30-32; Cornell Univ, BFA, 33; also with N C Wyeth. *Work:* Pa Acad Fine Arts, Philadelphia; Farnsworth Mus, Rockland, Maine; Montclair Mus, NJ; Brandywine River Mus, Chadds Ford, Pa; Del Art Mus, Wilmington. *Comn:* Portrait of Gov Reed, State of Maine, State Capitol, Augusta, 70. *Exhib:* Pa Acad Fine Arts Ann, 40-68; Carnegie Int, 50; Metrop Mus; Whitney Mus Am Art; Nat Acad Design, 72. *Teaching:* Instr painting, Pa Acad Fine Arts, 47-70. *Awards:* Whitmer Prize, Am Watercolor Soc, 55; Philadelphia Watercolor Club Award, Pa Acad Fine Arts, 55; W F B Morse Medal, Nat Acad Design, 72. *Mem:* Philadelphia Watercolor Club (vpres, 50-58); Nat Acad Design; Am Watercolor Soc; Audubon Artists; Wilmington Soc Fine Arts (trustee, 45-, vpres, 60-68). *Media:* Mixed. *Dealer:* Coe Kerr Gallery 49 E 82nd St New York NY 10028. *Mailing Add:* RFD 1 Chadds Ford PA 19317

MCCOY, KATHERINE BRADEN
DESIGNER, EDUCATOR
b Decatur, Ill, Oct 12, 45. *Study:* Mich State Univ, BA, 67. *Comn:* Poster & catalog, Detroit Inst Arts, 73-76; archit signage & graphic design, Pontiac Silver Dome, Mich, 75-79; package design & signage, Tivoli Ltd, Birmingham, Mich, 77; environ design, Univ Mich, 78-79. *Exhib:* Commun Graphics Shows, Am Inst Graphic Arts Gallery, New York, 72, 76 & 79; Five Years of Posters, 79 & Covers Show, 79; Artists in Residence, Cranbrook Acad Art, Bloomfield Hills, Mich, 78; Station 100, Chicago, 78-81. *Collections Arranged:* Knoll and Herman Miller: The Development of Contemporary Furniture (auth, catalog), Cranbrook Acad Art, 75 & Design in Michigan (auth, catalog), 77; International Graphic Design Education, Icograda Chicago, 78. *Pos:* Designer, Unimark Int, Detroit, 67-68; sr designer, Chrysler Corp Identity Off, Detroit, 68-69; sr designer, Omnigraphics, Boston, 69-70; sr designer, Designers & Partners, Detroit, 70-71; partner, McCoy & McCoy,

Detroit, 71-; bd ed, Indust Design Mag, 76- *Teaching:* Co-chmn, Dept Design, Cranbrook Acad Art, 71- *Awards:* Industrial Design Excellence Award, 80; I Award, Interiors Mag, 80; Showroom of the Year Award, Inst Business Designers, 80. *Bibliog:* Articles, Graphic Design Educ, 81, Interiors Mag, 82 & Novum Grebrauschgraphik, 82. *Mem:* Indust Designers Soc Am (pres, 83-84); Am Inst Graphic Arts; Soc Typographic Arts. *Publ:* Auth & ed, Projects and Processes, Cranbrook Acad Art, 76; auth & ed, Design in Michigan, Wayne State Univ Press, 78. *Mailing Add:* 500 Lone Pine Rd Box 801 Bloomfield Hills MI 48013

MCCOY, MICHAEL DALE
DESIGNER, EDUCATOR
b Eaton Rapids, Mich, Sept 16, 44. *Study:* Mich State Univ, BA, 66; Wayne State Univ, MA, 68. *Work:* Am Inst of Graphic Art, New York; Cranbrook Acad Art Mus, Bloomfield Hills, Mich; Cooper Hewitt Mus, New York; Philips Design Ctr, Neth; JIDA, Tokyo. *Comn:* Archit graphics, Pontiac Silverdome, Mich, 76; furniture, Knoll Int, New York, 78; Experimental dealership design, Chrysler Corp, Detroit, 78; interior design, Univ Mich, 79; furniture, Interior Ctr, Tokyo. *Exhib:* Commun Graphics, Am Inst Graphic Arts, New York, 74, 76 & 79; Cranbrook Art Mus, 77, 78 & 83; Cooper-Hewitt Mus Design, New York, 81; Progressive Archit Furniture Exhib, 81. *Pos:* Partner, McCoy & McCoy Design Consult, Bloomfield Hills, Mich, 71- *Teaching:* Co-chmn design dept, Cranbrook Acad Art, Bloomfield Hills, Mich, 71- *Awards:* Ann Design Rev Awards, Indust Design Mag, 71-80; Print Casebooks Award, Print Mag, 76-78; Design Excellence Award, Industrial Designers Soc Am, 80. *Bibliog:* Cranbrook comes back, 9/82 & Office of the year, 5/83, Interiors Mag. *Mem:* Indust Design Soc Am. *Publ:* Coauth, Problem Solving in the Man-Made Environment, Cranbrook Acad Art, 74. *Mailing Add:* 500 Lone Pine Rd Box 801 Bloomfield Hills MI 48013

MCCOY, WIRTH VAUGHAN
PAINTER
b Duluth, Minn, Dec 16, 13. *Study:* Univ Minn, BA, 37; Univ Iowa, MFA, 48; Acad Grande Chaumiere, cert painting & design, 51; Calif Sch Fine Art, 49; Acad Montmartre, 50; also with James Lechay, Maurice Lasansky, Mark Rothko, Yasuo Kunioshi & others. *Work:* Portland Art Mus; Seattle Art Mus; Mineral Industs Mus, Pa State Univ; Univ Iowa; Wash State Univ. *Exhib:* Artists Ore, Portland, 54; Centennial Exhib, Kansas City Art Inst, 62; Spokane Int Art Exhib, 64; one man show, Mus Art, Pa State Univ, 79; retrospective, Zoller Gallery, Pa State Univ, 80. *Teaching:* Asst prof painting & drawing, Ore State Univ, 48-53; prof painting & drawing, resident artist & dir, Wash State Univ Ctr, 53-64; head dept art, Pa State Univ, 64-71, prof art, 71-79, emer prof, 79- *Mem:* Col Art Asn Am; Peale Club Philadelphia; Pa Acad Fine Arts; Art Alliances Cent Pa; Cent Pa Festival Arts (bd dirs). *Media:* Oil. *Mailing Add:* 932 E McCormick State College PA 16801

MCCRACKEN, HAROLD
ADMINISTRATOR, HISTORIAN
b Colorado Springs, Colo, Aug 31, 1894. *Study:* Hope Col, Hon DLit, 57; Univ Alaska, Hon DLit, 66; Colo State Univ, Hon LHD, 72; Univ Wyo, Hon LLD. *Pos:* Dir, Whitney Gallery Western Art & Buffalo Bill Hist Ctr, Cody, Wyo, 59-78, dir emer, 78-82. *Publ:* Auth, Frederic Remington-Artist of the Old West, 47; auth, The Charles M Russell Book, 57; auth, George Catlin and the Old Frontier, 59; auth, The Frederic Remington Book, 66; auth, The Frank Tenney Johnson Book, 74; and others. *Mailing Add:* Whitney Gallery Western Art Cody WY 82414

MCCRACKEN, JOHN HARVEY
SCULPTOR, PAINTER
b Berkeley, Calif, Dec 9, 34. *Study:* Calif Col Arts & Crafts, BFA, 62, grad work, 62-65. *Work:* Mus Mod Art, Whitney Mus Am Art & Guggenheim Mus, New York; Los Angeles Co Mus; Pasadena Art Mus, Calif. *Exhib:* Primary Structures, Jewish Mus, New York, 66; American Sculpture of the Sixties, Los Angeles Co Mus Art, 67; 5th Guggenheim Int Exhib, Guggenheim Mus, 67; Art of the Real, Mus Mod Art, New York, 69, Ways of Looking, 71; 69th Am Exhib, Art Inst Chicago, 70; Mus Contemp Arts, Chicago, 70; Documenta, Kassel, WGer, 72; and others. *Teaching:* Asst prof sculpture & painting, Univ Calif, Irvine & Los Angeles, 65-68; asst prof sculpture, Sch Visual Arts, New York, 68-69; asst prof sculpture & painting, Hunter Col, 71-82. *Awards:* Nat Endowment for the Arts Award, 68. *Media:* Fiberglas, Wood. *Mailing Add:* c/o Nicholas Wilder Gallery 8225 1/2 Santa Monica Blvd Los Angeles CA 90046

MCCRACKEN, PHILIP
SCULPTOR
b Bellingham, Wash, Nov 14, 28. *Study:* Univ Wash, BA; sculpture with Henry Moore, Eng, 54. *Work:* Detroit Inst Art; Mus Art, Victoria, BC; United Nations Asn, New York; St Louis Art Mus,Mo; Anchorage Mus Art, Alaska. *Comn:* Norton Bldg, Seattle, Wash, 79; Kankakee State Hosp, Ill, 61; Swinomish Indian Tribal Ctr, LaConner, Wash, 64; Fed Bldg, Gen Serv Admin, Seattle, Wash, 76; King County Home Dome, Seattle, Wash, 78. *Exhib:* One-man shows, Seattle Art Mus, 61, Victoria Mus, BC, 64, La Jolla Mus Art, Calif, 70 & Anchorage Mus Art, 70; Corcoran Gallery Art, 66; Rutgers Univ, 68; Grand Rapids Art Mus, 69; Whitney Mus Am Art, New York, 78; and many others. *Awards:* Norman Davis Award, 57; Artists of the Year, 64; Irene Wright Mem Award, Seattle Art Mus, 65. *Bibliog:* Dore Ashton (auth), Modern American Sculpture, Abrams, 67; James J Kelly (auth), The Sculptural Idea, Burgess Press, 70; Colin Graham (auth), Philip McCracken, Univ Wash Press, 80. *Dealer:* Kennedy Galleries 40 W 57th St New York NY 10019. *Mailing Add:* Guemes Island Anacortes WA 98221

MCCRAY, DOROTHY M
PRINTMAKER, PAINTER
b Madison, SDak, Oct 13, 15. *Study:* State Univ Iowa, BA, 37, MA, 39; Calif Col Arts & Crafts, MFA, 55; Tyler Sch Art, Temple Univ; Univ Florence; independent Europ study. *Exhib:* Exhibitor of paintings and prints in regional and national shows. *Teaching:* Assoc prof emer, Western NMex Univ, Silver City, currently. *Mailing Add:* 802 N Cheyenne St Silver City NM 88061

MCCREADY, ERIC SCOTT
MUSEUM DIRECTOR, HISTORIAN
b Vancouver, Wash, Mar 14, 41. *Study:* Univ Ore, BS, 63, BA, 65, MA, 68; Univ Pavia, Italy, BA, 65; Univ Del, PhD(art hist), 72; Wintherthur Summer Inst. *Teaching:* Asst prof art hist, Bowling Green State Univ, 72-75; Asst prof art hist, Univ Wis-Madison, 75-79; assoc prof art, Univ Tex, Austin, 79- *Mem:* Assoc Art Mus Dir; Soc Archit Historians (mem decorative arts chap); Mid-West Art Hist Soc; Victorian Soc Am. *Res:* American art. *Publ:* Auth, The Nebraska State Capitol: Its Design, Background and Influence, Nebr State Hist Soc, 74; auth, Tanner and Gilliam: Two American black painters, Negro Lit Forum, 74; auth, Richard Taliaferro: 18th Century Virginia Architect, Univ Ore Press, 77; auth, Bertram Goodhue: Master of many arts (rev), J Soc Archit Historians, 78. *Mailing Add:* c/o Huntington Art Gallery 23rd & San Jacinto Austin TX 78712

MCCREADY, KAREN
DEALER, WRITER
b Beaver Falls, Pa, May 2, 46. *Study:* Austin Col, Sherman Tex, BA, 68; Aspen Inst Humanistic Studies, with Alan Kaprow, 69; Parsons Sch Design, 71. *Pos:* Dir, Pare Editions, Inc, New York, 73- *Res:* Survey of porcelain and its use in the studio setting today. *Specialty:* Contemporary American prints. *Collection:* Contemporary English & American ceramics; antique English & Japanese ceramics. *Publ:* Auth, 8 for the 80's, Quay Gallery, 80; co-auth, Porcelain: Traditions and New Visions, Watson-Guptill, 81. *Mailing Add:* 39 Bond St New York NY 10012

MCCULLOCH, FRANK E
PAINTER, PRINTMAKER
b Gallup, NMex, Aug 24, 30. *Study:* Univ NMex, BA, 53; Princeton Univ, 53-54; NMex Highlands Univ, 55; Inst Allende, Mex, MFA, 65. *Work:* Amarillo Art Ctr, Tex; Mus Albuquerque; Roswell Mus & Art Ctr, NMex; Mus Fine Arts, Univ NMex, Albuquerque; Inst Allende, San Miguel, Mex. *Comn:* Don Quixote Proj, One Percent For Arts Prog, Albuquerque, 82; acrylic, Cent Bank Cooperatives, Denver, 83. *Exhib:* Southwest Biennial, Mus NMex, Santa Fe, 63, 67, 74 & 76; one-man exhib, Jonson Gallery, Univ MNex, Albuquerque, 75, 77, 78 & 81; Roswell Mus & Art Ctr, NMex, 79 & Governors Gallery, State Capitol, Santa Fe, 81; Here & Now, Mus Albuquerque, 80; 46th Ann Midyear Exhib, Butler Inst Am Art, 82; and others. *Teaching:* Mem fac art, pub schs, Albuquerque, 56-, Inst Allende, Mex, 63-65, Univ NMex, 70-73 & Southern Methodist Univ, 77. *Awards:* Second Award, Fiesta Biennial, Mus NMex, 59; First Award, Inst Allende Exhib, Mex, 64; Grumbacher Award & Fifth Award, Nat Sun Carnival Exhib, El Paso Mus, 68. *Bibliog:* William Ebie (auth), article, Roswell Mus Quart, 79; Frank Walker (auth), article, Artspace, 81; Larry Smith (dir), Four Plates, Ten Colors, (film), 83. *Mem:* Albuquerque United Artists (mem bd, 78-80); NMex Art Educr (mem bd, 72-74). *Media:* Acrylics on Canvas; Lithography. *Publ:* Auth, Raymond Jonson, Artspace, 81. *Dealer:* Munson Gallery 653 Canyon Rd Santa Fe NM 87501; Art Resources Denver CO. *Mailing Add:* 1025 Sandia Rd NW Albuquerque NM 87107

MCCULLOUGH, DAVID WILLIAM
PAINTER, SCULPTOR
b Springfield, Mass, Dec 28, 45. *Study:* Boston Inst of the Arts, Mass, 63-64; Aspen Sch of Contemp Art, Colo, summer 68, with Wilbur Neiwald & Doris Cross; Kansas City Art Inst, Mo, BFA(printmaking, painting), 70; Univ Mich, 69, with printmaker, Emil Weddige; Calif Inst of the Arts, 70, with Allan Kaprow & Dick Higgins. *Work:* Continental Insurance Co, New York; Sony Corp, Parkridge, NJ; Joslyn Art Mus, Omaha; Indianapolis Mus Art; Kemper Insurance Co, Chicago. *Comn:* Sculptural fountain, Am Petrofina Oil Co, Dallas, 74; three monumental sculptures, Tex Comn Arts & Humanities, 74. *Exhib:* Dallas Mus of Fine Arts Bicentennial, 71; Okla Art Mus, Oklahoma City, 71; South by SW Exhib, Ft Worth Art Mus, 72; two-man exhib, Tyler Mus of Art, 74; Beaumont Art Mus, Tex, 75; Joslyn Art Mus, Omaha, Nebr, 76; two-man exhib, Amarillo Art Ctr, 77; and others. *Teaching:* Artist in residence video-audio, Western Wash State Col, Bellingham, 76; artist in residence painting & sculpture, Santa Fe Contemp Art Sch, NMex, 76; lectr, Kansas City Art Inst, 82, Minneapolis Sch Art & Design. *Awards:* First Prize, Painting/Sculpture Biennial, Dallas Mus of Fine Arts; 71; First Prize, Univ Tex, Arlington, 76; Best of Show, Meadows Art Mus, Shreveport Art Guild, La, 77. *Bibliog:* Museum People, KERA-TV film, 74; Victoria Melcher (auth), David McCullough, Arts Mag, 1/76; Sarah Burns (auth), David McCullough, Arts Mag, 1/82. *Media:* Acrylic; Sand, Mixed Media. *Dealer:* Douglas Drake Gallery 4500 State Line Kansas City KS 66103; Jan Cicero Gallery 437 N Clark Chicago Ill 60610. *Mailing Add:* c/o Virginia Miller Galleries 3112 Commodore Plaza Coconut Grove FL 33133

MCCULLOUGH, JOSEPH
ADMINISTRATOR, PAINTER
b Pittsburgh, Pa, July 6, 22. *Study:* Cleveland Inst Art, dipl, 48; Yale Univ, with Lewis York, 49-50, BFA, 50, with Josef Albers, 50-51, MFA, 51; Univ Evansville, Ill, hon DFA, 80. *Work:* Cleveland Mus Art; Ohio Univ; Syracuse Univ; Youngstown Pub Schs, Ohio. *Comn:* Stained glass windows, St Edmund Roman Cath Church, Warren, Mich, 69. *Exhib:* Corcoran Biennial Exhib,

Washington, DC, 55; Audubon Artists Ann Exhib, New York, 56; Contemp Am Painting & Sculpture, Univ Ill, 57; All Ohio Painting & Sculpture Show, Dayton Art Inst, 67; Cleveland Arts Prize Exhib, 71. *Pos:* Pres, Cleveland Inst Art, 55-; secy, Cleveland Art Asn, 55-; pres, Nat Asn Schs Art, 62-65. *Awards:* Spec Award for Painting, Cleveland Mus Art, 58; Purchase Award for Painting, Dayton Art Inst, 67; Cleveland Arts Prize for Visual Arts, Women's City Club Cleveland, 71. *Mem:* Alliance Independent Col Art; Col Ceramics Adv Coun, Alfred Univ; hon trustee Osaka Univ Arts, Japan; Col Art Asn (bd dirs, 63-68). *Media:* Acrylic, Watercolor. *Publ:* Contribr, Art in Cleveland Architecture, AIA Handbook to Cleveland Architecture, Reinhold, 58; contribr, The Enamelist, Kenneth Bates, World, 66. *Mailing Add:* 2637 Wellington Rd Cleveland Heights OH 44118

MCDARRAH, FRED WILLIAM
PHOTOGRAPHER, CRITIC
b Brooklyn, NY, Nov 5, 26. *Study:* NY Univ, dipl(journalism), 54. *Work:* Albright-Knox Art Gallery, Buffalo. *Exhib:* Frank O'Hara, Poet Among Painters, Whitney Mus, 74; Poets of the Cities (1950-1965), Dallas Mus Fine Arts, 74, San Francisco Mus Art, 75 & Wadsworth Atheneum, 75; Surface, Edge & Color, Whitney Mus, 77; Westkunst Int Ausstellung, Koln, WGer, 81; Portraits of Artists 1959-1979, Lightworks Gallery, Syracuse Univ, 81; Art & the Law, Minn Mus Art, 81; Photographs of Candy Darling, Rolen Samuel Gallery Ltd, New York, 82; Provincetown 1959, Cape Cod Gallery, Mass, 82; Rauschenberg/Performances 1954-1979, Galleria di Franca Mancini, Pesaro, Italy, 83; and others. *Pos:* Writer, photogr & photog reviewer, Village Voice, 59-71, picture ed, 71- *Teaching:* Lectr, numerous photog orgn & schs, 64- *Awards:* Guggenheim Fel Photog, 72; Second Place News Photos, Edward Steichen Mem Awards, 76; Best Spot News Photo Page One Award, New York Newspaper Guild, 80; plus many others. *Bibliog:* Interviews with seven picture editors, 35MM Photog, winter 77; Hot shots, Darkroom Photog, Vol 3, No 2; Carol Holebein (auth), Focus '81: A Unique Workshop, Camera 35, 81. *Mem:* NY Press Club; Am Soc Picture Prof; Photog Soc Am; Author's Guild; NY Press Photogr Asn. *Publ:* Auth, Photography Marketplace, R R Bowker, 2d ed, 77; auth, Ted Cowell--photographer, Village Voice, 12/4/78; auth, A family affair--their favorite museums, Cue Mag, 12/22/78; auth, Museums in New York, Simon & Schuster, 4th ed, 83; auth, Kerouac & Friends: A Beat Generation Album, William Morrow & Co, 84; and others. *Mailing Add:* 505 LaGuardia Pl New York NY 10012

MCDERMOTT, GERALD
ILLUSTRATOR, DESIGNER
b Detroit, Mich, Jan 31, 41. *Study:* Pratt Inst, BFA, 64. *Exhib:* Film as Art, San Francisco Film Festival, 66; Best Short Films, Am Film Festival, New York, 69; Contemp Animated Films, Annecy Int Film Festival, France, 71; one-man shows, Illustrating Myth & Legend, Everson Mus, Syracuse, NY, 75 & Illustrating Picture Bks, Children's Mus, Indianapolis, 79; Best Am Animators, Whitney Mus, New York, 80. *Awards:* Blue Ribbon, Educ Film Libr Asn, 69; Silver Lion, Ital Govt, 70; Caldecott Award, Am Libr Asn, 75. *Bibliog:* M L Lasser & W J Dalton (auth), Teaching the myth of the hero, Independent Sch Bull, 74; C Stephens (auth), Gerald McDermott: animating myth and legend, Print Mag, 74; D White (auth), Mythic hero/trickster hero: The work of Gerald McDermott, Language Arts Mag, 3/82. *Media:* Animated Films; Illustrated Books. *Publ:* Auth & illusr, The Knight of the Lion, 79 & Sun Flight, 80, Four Winds Press; auth, Papagayo, Simon & Schuster, 80; illusr, The Adventures of Pinocchio, Four Winds Press, 81; illusr, The Wizard of Oz, Random House, 82. *Mailing Add:* PO Box 334 New Milford CT 06776

MACDONALD, COLIN SOMERLED
WRITER, PUBLISHER
b Ottawa, Ont, Mar 5, 25. *Study:* Self taught artist; also study with Mabel May & Carleton Col, eve, 47-49. *Exhib:* One-man show, Little Gallery, Photog Stores, Ottawa, Ont, 62; Ottawa Born Artists, Univ Ottawa, 67. *Pos:* Ed & publ, Dictionary Can Artists, 67-; pres-dir, Can Paperbacks Publ Ltd, 74- *Awards:* Exploration Program Research Award, Can Coun, 78; Visual Arts Research Award, Can Coun, 81; Publisher Award, Can Coun, 82; and others. *Bibliog:* W Q Ketchum (auth), Faces of Ottawa, Ottawa J, 3/70. *Media:* Oil. *Res:* Biographical information on living and dead Canadian visual artists with bibliography and critical comments. *Publ:* Auth, Dictionary of Canadian Artists, Vols I-VI, 67-81. *Mailing Add:* 17 Gwynne Ave Ottawa ON K1Y 1X1 Canada

MCDONALD, DOROTHY EISNER See Eisner, Dorothy

MACDONALD, GAYLE COLEMAN See Coleman, Gayle

MACDONALD, GRANT
PAINTER, ILLUSTRATOR
b Montreal, Que, June 27, 09. *Study:* Ont Col Art, Toronto; Art Students League; Heatherley's Art Sch, London; Queens Univ, Kingston, Ont, hon LLD, 74. *Work:* Redpath Libr, McGill Univ; Hart House, Univ Toronto; Art Gallery Toronto; Queen's Univ; Kingston Col Inst; also in galleries, schs, univs, libr & pvt collections, Can, USA & Eng. *Exhib:* Nine shows, Art Asn Montreal, 41-68; Art Asn Kingston, 48-55, 67 & 68; Royal Can Acad, 49, 51-55 & 67; Ont Soc Artists, 49, 51-55, 66 & 67; seven shows, Art Gallery Hamilton, 49-68; Retrospective, Agnes Etherington Art Centre, Kingston, 66; and others. *Teaching:* Instr figure drawing, Summer Sch, Queen's Univ, Kingston, 48, 52, 53, 64 & 65. *Awards:* Medal, Art Dirs Club, Toronto, 52; Kraft-Price Award, 65; Forster Award, Ont Soc Artists, 66. *Mem:* Royal Can

Acad. *Publ:* Illusr, Shakespeare for Young Players, 42, Haida, 46, Behind the Log, 47, Sunshine Sketches of a Little Town, 48 & A Masque of Aesop, 52; and others. *Mailing Add:* Tarquin 32 Lakeshore Rd Kingston ON K7M 4J6 Canada

MACDONALD, KEVIN JOHN
GRAPHIC ARTIST
b Washington, DC, July 2, 46. *Study:* Montgomery Jr Col, Takoma Park, Md, 64-66; George Washington Univ, BFA, 69; Corcoran Sch of Art, Washington, DC, 69. *Work:* Metrop Mus Art, New York; Corcoran Gallery Art, Washington, DC; Phillips Collection, Washington, DC; Hirshhorn Mus Art; Nat Mus Am Art, Washington DC; and others. *Exhib:* Nineteenth Area Show, 74 & Am Drawings, 76, Corcoran Gallery Art, Washington, DC; Fifth Davidson Nat, Davidson Col, NC, 76; Md Biennial, Baltimore Mus Art, 76, 78 & 80; Drawing Show, Phillips Collection, DC, 77; Images of the 70's (with catalog), Corcoran Gallery Art, 80. *Bibliog:* Martha Wright (auth), article, Art Int, 1/78; David Tannous (auth), article, Art in Am, 5/78; Charlotte Moser (auth), article, Art News, 10/81; and others. *Media:* Colored Pencil, Graphite. *Dealer:* Adamson Editions 406 7th St NW Washington DC 20004; Martin Gallery 3243 P St NW Washington DC 20007. *Mailing Add:* 8207 Georgia Ave 5 Silver Spring MD 20910

MCDONALD, ROBERT HERWICK
CURATOR, WRITER
b Philadelphia, Pa. *Study:* Univ Calif, Berkeley, BA & MA, Mus Mgt Inst. *Pos:* Dir, Daniel Weinberg Gallery, San Francisco, 74-76; admin asst dir, Univ Calif Art Mus, Berkeley, 77-79; chief cur, La Jolla Mus Contemp Art, Calif, 79-; dir, Art Mus Santa Cruz, Calif, 82- *Teaching:* Instr Europ cult hist, Univ Calif, Riverside, 67-71, & Calif State Univ, Hayward, 71, 72 & 74. *Awards:* San Diego Press Club Award, 82. *Bibliog:* Peter Karlen (auth), A conversation with Mr Robert McDonald, Community Arts Newsletter, San Diego Co, 10/81; Greg Gianas (auth), Appreciating modern art, San Diego Sentinel, 10/7/79; Isabelle Wasserman (auth), New curator, San Diego Union, 11/5/79. *Mem:* Col Art Asn; Am Asn Mus; Art Mus Asn. *Res:* Contemporary American art, California artists. *Publ:* Ed, Just a great thing to do: Selected works by Charles Garabedian, La Jolla Mus Contemp Art, 81; auth, Craig-Kauffman-A comprehensive Survey 1957-1980, Fels Contemp Art, Los Angeles, 81; auth, The Carolyn and Jack Ferris collection-Selected contemp works, La Jolla Mus Contemp Art, 82; auth, A Contemporary Collection-On Loan From the Rothschild Bank AG, Zurich, La Jolla Mus Contemp Art, 83; auth, Rooms and Stories: Recent work by Terry Allen, La Jolla Mus Contemp Art, 83. *Mailing Add:* Art Mus Santa Cruz County PO Box 8407 Santa Cruz CA 95061

MACDONALD, SCOTT
CRITIC, EDUCATOR
b Easton, Pa, Oct 10, 42. *Study:* DePauw Univ, BA, 64; Univ Fla, MA, 66, PhD, 70. *Teaching:* Asst prof humanities, Univ Fla, 69-70; from asst prof to prof film & Am lit, Utica Col, 71-, dir, Art Gallery, presently. *Res:* Researching, writing critical introductions to and interviewing Avant-Garde filmmakers. *Specialty:* Upstate New York artists whose work poses a challenge to the local Utica-Rome community. *Publ:* Auth, The Expanding Vision of Larry Gottheim's Films, 78; auth, Surprise, The films of Robert Huot, Quart Rev Film Studies, 80; auth, Interview with Taka Iimura, Part 1, Art & Cinema, 80; auth, Interview with Robert Huot, Afterimage, 80; and others. *Mailing Add:* 5 Sherman St New Hartford NY 13413

MCDONALD, SUSAN STRONG
PAINTER, EDITOR
b Rochester, NY, Aug 18, 43. *Study:* Sweet Briar Col, BA, 65; studied with Kathan Brown, 68-71; Yoshida Hanga Acad, 71-74. *Work:* Walker Art Ctr; Minneapolis Inst Art; Univ Minn Gallery, Minneapolis; Michael C Rockefeller Gallery, Fredonia, NY; Western Regional Post Off, San Francisco. *Comn:* Camden Logging Mural, Minneapolis Arts Comn & Nat Endowment Arts, 80. *Exhib:* Kingsley Art Club Award Exhib, Kingsley Mus Art, Sacramento, 71; Photoetchings from Crown Point Press, Ames Gallery, Berkeley, 71; Oakland Mus Art, 74; Japan Printmakers Asn Ann Exhib, Tokyo, 75; Portrait of an Artist, Minneapolis Inst Art, 81; Five Minneapolis Artists, Tweed Mus Art, 82. *Pos:* Ed, WARM J, 78- *Awards:* CUE Award, City Minneapolis, 82. *Mem:* Founding mem Womens Art Registry Minn. *Publ:* Auth, State: State of the art/art: Art of the state, Craft Connection, 75; auth, Harmony Hammond: A ten year retrospective, 81, In the studio, 83 & Fitting into the fifties, 83, WARM J. *Dealer:* Artbanque Inc Butler Sq Suite 114 Minneapolis MN 55403. *Mailing Add:* 1056 Thirteenth Ave SE Minneapolis MN 55414

MACDONALD, WILLIAM L
ARCHITECTURAL HISTORIAN
b Putnam, Conn, July 12, 21. *Study:* Harvard Col, AB, Harvard Univ, AM & PhD(Emerton Fel & Shaw Fel); Am Acad Rome, ACLS(Prize Fel & Morse Fel). *Pos:* Exec secy, Byzantine Inst, 50-54. *Teaching:* Prof art & archit, Yale Univ, 56-65; prof art & archit, Smith Col, Northampton, Mass, 65-81. *Awards:* Bryant Found Fel. *Mem:* Soc Prom Roman Studies, London; Soc Archit Historians (dir, 58-64); Soc Libyan Studies, London; Am Asn Archit Bibliogr; Am Inst Archaeol. *Res:* History of architecture; ancient, early Christian, Baroque & American architecture. *Publ:* Auth, The Architecture of the Roman Empire, Vol 1, rev ed 82, Vol 2, 84; auth, Northampton Massachusetts Architecture & Buildings, 75; auth, The Pantheon: Meaning and Progeny, 76; assoc ed, Princeton Encyclopedia of Classical Sites, 77; auth, Piranesi's Carceri: Sources of Invention, 79. *Mailing Add:* 3811 39th St NW Washington DC 20016

MACDONNELL, CAMERON
PAINTER, SCULPTOR
b Elmira, NY, May 29, 38. *Study:* State Univ NY Col Educ Buffalo, BS(art educ), studied with John Davidson, Mort Grossman, Larry Calcognio & Trevor Thomas; independent study, Santa Barbara, Calif. *Work:* IBM Collection, Oswego, NY; City of Santa Barbara, Calif. *Comn:* Backdrops for the Nutcracker Suite, Madam Helena Ballet Sch & New York Coun on the Arts, 66-79; Logo, Samuel L Clemens Performing Arts Ctr, Elmira, NY, 77; bust of Thomas Coughlin, III, NY State Comnr of Corrections, 79. *Exhib:* Regional, Albright Knox Art Gallery, NY, 60; Regional, Santa Barbara Mus Art, Calif; Our Town Gallery, Santa Barbara, 74; Goleta Galleria, Calif, 75; one-man show, 76, regional group show, 76-79, Arnot Art Mus, Elmira, NY; Artists Gallery, Elmira, NY, 79-81; and others. *Pos:* Art dir marketing develop, Art Frame Publ, Santa Barbara, Calif, 70-76; mgr Econoline advert, Asn Retarded Children, Elmira, NY, 77-81. *Awards:* Silver Medallions, Bicentennials, City of Santa Barbara & Co of Santa Barbara, 76; Artistic Serv Award, OMRDD, NY, 79. *Bibliog:* Trevor Thomas (auth), Views of Art, Buffalo Evening News, 60; Larry Griffis, Jr (auth), World of art, Buffalo Courier Express, 61; Lee Batten (auth), California Artists, Art Fame Publ, 75. *Mem:* Southern Tier Arts Asn (co-chmn, 79-80); Arts in the Park, Elmira, NY. *Media:* Watercolor, Oil; Resin. *Publ:* Illusr & contribr, Sethmaterial, Prentice Hall, 70; contribr, Reflections, 72 & illusr, Salvang, 75, Art Fame Publ. *Dealer:* Art Shop/Arnot Art Mus 235 Lake St Elmira NY 14901; Art & Frame Gallery Water St Elmira NY 14901. *Mailing Add:* 742 Dawn Dr Elmira NY 14904

MCDONNELL, JOSEPH ANTHONY
SCULPTOR, PAINTER
b Detroit, Mich, Oct 20, 36. *Study:* Univ Notre Dame, with Ivan Mestrovic, BFA & MFA; Acad Belli Arte, Florence, Italy. *Work:* Milwaukee Pub Mus. *Comn:* Mural, Chicago Bank Commerce, Standard Oil Bldg, 75; sculpture fountain, Citadel Mall, Charleston, SC, 81; relief sculpture, Tallyrand Bldg, Tarrytown, NY, 82; sculpture, Waterway Tower, Irving, Tex, 82; suspended kites, One Countryside Place, San Antonio, Tex, 83; Strouse-Greenberg Bldg, Philadelphia, 71; stainless steel fountain, Janesville Mall, Wis, 72; mural, Chicago Bank Commerce, Standard Oil Bldg, 75; Deptford Mall, NJ, 75; Citadel Mall, Charleston, SC, 81; and others. *Exhib:* one-man shows, McNay Art Inst, San Antonio, 64; Flint Art Inst, Mich, 64; John Wanamaker Fine Arts Gallery, Philadelphia, 70 & Katonah Gallery, NY, 79; Hastings on Hudson, Snite Mus, Univ Notre Dame, 80; and others. *Awards:* Dept of Housing & Urban Development Award, Nat Community Art Competition, 73; Award, New Eng Silvermine Exhib, 76 & 77. *Bibliog:* Article, Philadelphia Inquirer, 11/1/70; Harriet Schiff (auth), article, Detroit News, 9/17/71; Louis G Redstone (auth), New Directions in Shopping Centers and Stores, McGraw-Hill, 73; and others. *Media:* Multimedia. *Mailing Add:* 1110 Hardscrabble Rd Chappaqua NY 10514

MCDOUGAL, IVAN ELLIS
PAINTER, INSTRUCTOR
b Lometa, Tex, June 29, 27. *Study:* Schreiner Inst, Kerrville, 47; Trinity Univ, San Antonio, 48; Am Acad Art, Chicago, 49. *Work:* McNay Art Mus, San Antonio. *Exhib:* Western Fedn Watercolor Soc Ann, Albuquerque Art Mus, 76; San Antonio Art League, Koehler Cult Ctr, 78; Rocky Mountain Nat Watermedia Exhib, Foothills Art Ctr, Golden, Colo, 80; Southern Watercolor Soc, La Tech Univ Gallery, Ruston, 81; San Diego Watercolor Soc; and others. *Teaching:* Instr watercolor, Jewish Community Ctr, 78-81. *Awards:* Merit Award, Ky Watercolor Soc, 78; Aspen Studio Award, Rocky Mountain Nat Watermedia Exhib, 80; Juror's Award, San Diego Watercolor Soc. *Mem:* San Antonio Art League; Tex Watercolor Soc; Allied Artists; Southwestern Watercolor Soc; Tex Fine Arts Asn. *Media:* Watercolor, Acrylic. *Publ:* Contribr, The Texas hill country, interpretations of 13 artists, North Light Mag, Tex A&M Univ Press, 81; contribr, Pecos to Rio Grande, Tex A&M Univ Press, 83. *Dealer:* Sol Del Rio Art Gallery 1020 Townsend San Antonio TX 78209. *Mailing Add:* 6850 Oxford Trace San Antonio TX 78240

MACDOUGALL, ANNE (ANNE MACDOUGALL BALLOU)
PRINTMAKER, PAINTER
b Winchester, Mass, Apr 27, 44. *Study:* Abbot Acad; Randolph-Macon Woman's Col, AB(art); Syracuse Univ, grad study in art. *Work:* Boston Univ, Mus Fine Arts, Boston; Va Mus Fine Arts; De Cordova Mus, Lincoln, Mass; Indianapolis Mus. *Exhib:* Boston Printmaker's Nat, 74, 76 & 77; Nat Print, Trenton State, 79; Drawings, DeCordova Mus, 80; Nat Print & Drawing, NDak State, 81; Addison Gallery Am Art, 81. *Awards:* Va Ctr Fel, 78; MacDowell Fel, 80; Purchase Award, Berkshire Mus, 81. *Bibliog:* Robert Taylor (auth), article, Boston Globe, 9/21/72; Meryle Secrest (auth), article, Washington Post, 4/5/75; Paul Ciano (auth), article, Jewish Advocate, 2/8/78 & 6/81. *Mem:* Nat Asn Women Artists; Boston Printmakers; Boston Visual Artists Union; Cambridge Art Asn (vpres, 72-73). *Media:* Serigraphy. *Dealer:* Bernard Pucker c/o Pucker/Safrai Gallery 171 Newbury St Boston MA 02116. *Mailing Add:* 51A Red Spring Rd Andover MA 01810

MACDOUGALL, PETER STEVEN
CERAMIC ARTIST, EDUCATOR
b Willimantic, Conn, Oct 23, 51. *Study:* Northwestern Conn Community Col, 70-72; Alfred Univ, New York, BFA, 75; Wichita State Univ, Kans, MFA, 77. *Work:* Tyler Art Gallery, State Univ New York, Oswego; Elrich Mus, Wichita State Univ; Nelson Gallery, Alfred Univ, New York; and others. *Exhib:* Copperstown Ann, Copperstown Art Asn, New York, 79-80; Fingerlakes Show, Mem Art Gallery, Rochester, 80; Everson Mus, Syracuse, New York, 80; Artworks Gallery, Hartford, Conn, 81; Univ Dallas, Irving, Tex, 81; and others. *Teaching:* Instr ceramics, Wichita Art Asn, 76-78; asst

prof, State Univ New York, Oswego, 78-82. *Awards:* Craft Award, Northwestern Community Col, 72; Jury Award, Hartford Civic Art Show, 75; Third Place, Adironack Invitational, 81. *Mem:* Col Arts Asn; Nat Coun Educ Ceramic Arts; Am Craft Coun. *Media:* Clay. *Dealer:* Hanover Gallery New York NY. *Mailing Add:* c/o Am Hand Gallery 2904 M St NW Washington DC 20007

MCELCHERAN, WILLIAM HODD
DESIGNER, SCULPTOR
b Hamilton, Ont, July 9, 27. *Study:* Ont Col Art, Toronto. *Work:* Art Gallery Hamilton, Ont; Art Gallery London, Ont; York Univ; Univ Toronto Sch Archit. *Comn:* Archit design & sculpture, Divinity Col, McMaster Univ, 60; wood sculpture, Briar Cliff Col, 62; Stations of the Cross (mahogany), St Augustines Col, Scarboro, Ont, 66; plastic relief, Walkerton Fed Bldg, Ont, 70; sculpture, St Michael's Libr, Univ Toronto, 72. *Exhib:* Sculpture '67, Toronto, 67; one-man shows, Roberts Gallery, Toronto, 69 & Art Gallery Hamilton, 69; Fed Int Medaille, Cologne, Ger, 71; La Galerie de L'Esprit Montreal, 75; New Talent Exhib, Forum Gallery, New York, 75. *Pos:* Art dir & designer, Valley City Mfg Co, Dundas, 52-56; designer, Brown, Brisley & Brown, Architects, Toronto, 56-60. *Teaching:* Instr carving, Ont Col Art, 63-66; artist in residence, Sch Archit, Univ Toronto, 71-72. *Awards:* Medal, Lt Gov Ont, 49; Can Coun Sr Arts Award, 69; Aviva Sculpture Prize, Aviva Chap, Hadassah, 69. *Bibliog:* Paul Duval (auth), William McElcheran, The Hamilton Spectator, 11/69; Eric Freifeld (auth), William McElcheran, Artscan Mag, 4-5/71; Kay Kritzwizer (auth), article, Toronto Globe & Mail, 5/71. *Mem:* Royal Can Acad Arts; Sculptors Soc Can. *Publ:* Auth, The Revolution in Liturgical Art, Brief to the Bishops, Longmans Green, 65; illusr, By the Circus Sands, 67. *Dealer:* Roberts Gallery 641 Yonge St Toronto ON Can. *Mailing Add:* 191 Balsam Ave Toronto ON M4E 3G2 Canada

MCELROY, JACQUELYN ANN (J MCELROY-EDWARDS)
PRINTMAKER, EDUCATOR
b Rice Lake, Wis, June 28, 42. *Study:* Univ Minn; Univ Mont, BA, 65, MA, 66, MFA, 67. *Work:* Dulin Gallery Art, Knoxville, Tenn; Pillsbury Co, Minneapolis; Winnipeg Art Gallery, Man, Can; Plains Art Mus, Moorhead, Minn; Okla Art Ctr, Oklahoma City; and others. *Exhib:* Midwest Biennial Exhib, Joslyn Mus, Omaha, Nebr, 74; 2nd Miami Graphics Int, Coral Gables, Fla, 75; Artist as Social Critic, Miriam Perlman Inc, Chicago, Ill, 81; Art & the Law, Minn Mus & Western Publ Co, 81; Printed by Women, Women's Caucus Art, Philadelphia, 83; and others. *Teaching:* Prof art hist & printmaking, Univ NDak, Grand Forks, 68-, asst dean, 81- *Awards:* Purchase Awards, Art & the Law, Minn Mus & Western Publ Co, 80, Challenge of the Land, Pillsbury Co, 81 & Tempo Gallery, Appleton, Wis, 83. *Mem:* Print Club, Philadelphia; Grand Forks Art Asn. *Media:* Serigraphy. *Dealer:* Arteam 326 A St Boston MA 02210. *Mailing Add:* 917 Chestnut St Grand Forks ND 58201

MCEVILLEY, THOMAS
WRITER, CRITIC
b Cincinnati, Ohio, July 13, 39. *Study:* Univ Cincinnati, BA, 63, PhD, 68; Univ Wash, MA, 65. *Pos:* Contrib ed, Artforum, 82- *Teaching:* Instr, Rice Univ, 70- *Res:* Contemporary art; art and philosophy; iconography; art theory. *Publ:* Auth, James Lee Byars and the atmosphere of question, summer 81, Yves Klein: Messenger of the age of space, 1/82, Heads it's form, tails it's not content, 11/82, Diogenes of Sinope: Selected performance pieces, 3/83 & Art in the dark, summer 83, Artforum. *Mailing Add:* c/o Artforum 205 Mulberry New York NY 10012

MCEWEN, JEAN
PAINTER
b Montreal, Que, Dec 14, 23. *Work:* Mus Mod Art, New York; Walker Art Ctr, Minneapolis; Albright-Knox Art Gallery; Ottawa Mus; Toronto Mus; and others. *Comn:* Stained glass window, Sir George Williams Univ, 66; murals, Toronto Airport & Plase Arts, Montreal, 67. *Exhib:* One-man shows, Gallery Godart-Lefort, Montreal, four times, 62-69 & Gallery, Montreal, 63, Gallery Moos, Toronto, four times, 63-69 & Mayer Gallery, Paris, 64; Dunn Int Exhib, Tate Gallery, London, 63; and others. *Teaching:* Lectr painting, Univ NDak & Concordia Univ. *Awards:* Quebec Art Competition, 62; Jessie Dow Award, Montreal Spring Show, 64. *Mem:* Academician Royal Can Acad Arts. *Publ:* Illusr, La Pain Quotidien, 64; illusr, Les iles Reunies, 73. *Dealer:* Mira-Godard Ltd 22 Hazelton Toronto ON Can. *Mailing Add:* 3908 Parc Lafontaine Ru Montreal PQ H2L 3M6 Canada

MCFADDEN, DAVID REVERE
CURATOR
b Aug 28, 47. *Study:* Univ Minn, BA(magna cum laude), 72, MA, 78. *Collections Arranged:* The Education of the Craftsman: Silver, 75; Exotic Entrepreneurs: Trade with the Orient, 76; The Cooper-Hewitt Collections of Decorative Arts (auth, catalog), 78-84; Scandinavian Modern 1880-1980 (auth, catalog), 82; English Majolica, 82; Tiffany Studios Metalwork, 83. *Pos:* Cur, Minneapolis Inst Arts, 74-78 & Cooper-Hewitt Mus, 78- *Teaching:* Cooper-Hewitt/Parsons MA program, 82- *Mem:* Worshipful Co Goldsmiths; Decorative Arts Soc; Soc Silver Collectors; founder Decorative Arts Asn; Royal Oak Found. *Res:* Eighteenth century decorative arts, silver, ceramics and furniture, twentieth century design. *Collection:* Porcelain, 79, The Cooper-Hewitt Collection: Glass, 79 & The Cooper-Hewitt Collection: Furniture, 79. *Publ:* Auth, Recent Acquisitions in Silver: A Petrie and D Willaume, 75 & An Aldobrandini Tazza: A Preliminary Study, 77, Minneapolis Inst Bull. *Mailing Add:* 120 E 89th St New York NY 10028

MCFADDEN, MARY
COLLECTOR, DESIGNER
b New York, NY, Oct 1, 38. *Study:* Columbia Univ: Traphagen Sch of Design. *Work:* Lannan Found, Palm Beach, Fla; Metrop Mus Art Costume Inst, New York. *Collections Arranged:* Biet Giorgis Teust, Lannan Found. *Pos:* Ed, Vogue Mag, S Africa, 65-68, US, 71-74; contribr, Rand Daily Mail, 69-70; pres, Mary McFadden Inc, 74- & Mary McFadden Jewels, 78-; pres & cur, Lannan Found, Palm Beach, Fla, 74- *Teaching:* Instr fashion, Fashion Inst of Technol, New York, 76; instr chic, Hunter Col, 77 & instr style, Cooper-Hewitt Mus of Decorative Arts & Design, New York, 77. *Awards:* Legendary Women Award, Birmingham, Ala, 77; Coty Hall of Fame, 78; Gov Award, RI Sch Design, 78. *Media:* Silk. *Collection:* Ancient artifacts from Egypt, Greece and Madagascar; primitive sculpture from Africa and New Guinea; Oriental artifacts and furniture; contemporary American art, including painting by Tom Wudl, Clyfford Still, Jane di Braghenti and Robert Mangold, sculpture by Mark di Suvero, Kenneth Shores & Isamu Noguchi. *Publ:* Auth, var articles on Iran, Haiti, Usbzcistan-Tashken & Easter Island, Vogue USA, 71. *Mailing Add:* 264 W 35th St New York NY 10001

MCFARREN, GRACE
PAINTER, DEALER
b Philadelphia, Pa, Feb 6, 14. *Study:* Sch Design for Women; Graphic Sketch Club; Pierce Jr Col, Philadelphia; study with Clayton Bachtel, Peter Dubaniewicz & Joseph McCullough, Del Art Ctr, Wilmington, with Robert McKinney, 60; study with Edgar Whitney, New York, 69; also study with Marion Bryson & Doris Peters. *Work:* Univ Del; Hagley Mus; DuPont de Nemours & Co; Nelson Rockefeller Collection; three Wilmington Banks; and others. *Exhib:* Ann May Show, Cleveland Art Mus; Dayton Art Mus Lending Libr of Paintings; Smithsonian Inst, Washington, DC; Am Watercolor Soc Regional, Univ Del; Philadelphia Mus Art; Del Mus Art; and others. *Pos:* Founder, Wilmington Circulating Gallery of Paintings, dir, currently. *Teaching:* Lectr, Univ Del Days for Women Exten, four yrs. *Awards:* Three Purchase Prizes, Univ Del Ann Regional Shows; First, Second & Hon Mention, Chester Co Art Asn; Best in Show, Nat League Am Pen Women Nat Show & Rehoboth Art League; and others. *Mem:* Am Watercolor Soc; Del Mus Art Asn; Chester Co Art Asn. *Media:* Watercolor, Oil. *Mailing Add:* 3 Winterbury Circle Wilmington DE 19808

MCFEE, JUNE KING
EDUCATOR
b Seattle, Wash, June 3, 17. *Study:* Whitman Col, 35-37; Univ Wash, BA, 39; Cent Wash Col, MEd, 54; Stanford Univ, EdD, 57; Archipenko Sch Art; Cornish Sch Art; also with Amede Ozenfant; Eastern Mich Univ, Hon Dr, 82. *Exhib:* Seattle Art Mus; Seattle Artists Summer Shows; Wash State Invitational; Stanford Art Gallery Fac Exhibs. *Pos:* Ed, Studies in Art Educ. *Teaching:* From instr to asst prof art educ, Stanford Univ, 55-63; vis assoc prof, Ariz State Univ, 64-65; from assoc prof to prof art educ & dir, Inst Community Art Studies, Univ Ore, 65-77, head, Dept Art Educ, 77-83. *Awards:* Art Educr Yr, Miami Univ, 81; Nat Art Educ Asn Distinguished Serv Award, 83. *Mem:* Nat Art Educ Asn (pres, 67-69); Soc Res in Art Educ; Coun Policy Studies Art Educ. *Publ:* Auth, Preparation for Art, Wadsworth, 70; auth, Art for Academically Talented, Encycl Educ, Macmillan, 72; auth, Art, Culture & Environment, Kendall/Hunt, 80; auth, Cultural Influences on Aesthetic Experiences in Arts and Cultural Diversity, Holt Rinehart Winston, 80; auth, Art abilities, In: Int Encycl Educ, England (in prep). *Mailing Add:* Dept of Art Educ Univ Ore Sch Archit & Arts Eugene OR 97403

MCGAHEE, DOROTHY (DOROTHY MCGAHEE BRAUDY)
PAINTER, EDUCATOR
b Los Angeles, Calif. *Study:* Univ, Ky, BA; NY Univ, MA(art educ); pvt study with Richard Pousette-Dart; Art Students' League, with Stamos, Kantor & Glasier; Columbia Univ Teachers Col. *Work:* Fed Reserve Bank, Richmond, Va; Mason Co Mus, Maysville, Ky. *Comn:* Portrait, comn by David Brooks family, London, 74; portrait, comn by Richard Poirier, New York, 75; George Davis family, Calistoga, Calif, 79; John Irwin family, Baltim Baltimore, 80; William Chamness family, Aberdeen, Ohio. *Exhib:* One-person shows, Philosophy Hall, Columbia Univ, 76; Viridian Gallery, New York 77 & 78; B R Kornblatt Gallery, Baltimore, 79 & 81, Goucher Col, 82 & Mason Co Mus, Maysville, Ky, 82. *Teaching:* Prof art educ, Pratt Inst, New York, 71-77; prof art hist & drawing, Towson State Univ, Md, 78-79; prof visual arts, Goucher Col, Towson, Md, 79-83. *Bibliog:* Article, New York J Arts, 9-10/78; article, Baltimore Sun, 9/81 & 9/83; article, New Art Examiner, 10/81. *Mem:* Col Art Asn; Artists Equity. *Media:* Oils, Watercolor. *Mailing Add:* 2008 N Oxford Ave Los Angeles CA 90027

MCGARRELL, JAMES
PAINTER, EDUCATOR
b Indianapolis, Ind, Feb 22, 30. *Study:* Ind Univ, AB, 53; Skowhegan Sch Painting & Sculpture, 53; Univ Calif, Los Angeles, MA, 55; Stuttgard Acad Fine Arts, Ger, Fulbright fel, 56. *Work:* Whitney Mus Am Art, New York; Mus Mod Art, New York; Mus Mod Art, Paris; Mus Hambourg, Ger; Joseph Hirshhorn Mus, Washington, DC. *Exhib:* Dokumenta III, Kassel, Ger; Americans, Art Inst Chicago; Salons Galeries Pilotes, Lausanne, Switz; Carnegie Inst Int, 58 & 82; Venice Biennale, Italy, 68; Art About Art, Whitney Mus, 78; The Human Figure in Contemporary Art, Contemp Arts Ctr, New Orleans, 82. *Pos:* Bd gov, Skowhegan Sch, 81- *Teaching:* Vis artist, Reed Col, 56-59; prof fine arts, Ind Univ, 59-80; prof fine arts, Wash Univ, Sch Fine Arts, 81- *Awards:* Nat Inst Arts & Lett Citation & Grant, 63; Guggenheim Found Fel, 64; Nat Endowment Arts Award for Artists Who Teach, 66. *Bibliog:* Giovanni Testori (auth), McGarrell, Claude Bernard

(Paris), 67; Norman Geske (auth), Venice 34, the Figurative Tradition in Recent American Art, Smithsonian, 68; Edward Bryant (auth), James McGarrell, Recent Work, Univ NMex Art Mus, Albuquerque, 81; and others. *Mem:* Col Art Asn Am (bd dirs, 70-74). *Publ:* Auth, Towards an art of eloquence, Artists Choice Mus Newletter, spring 82. *Dealer:* Allan Frumkin Galleries 50 W 57th St New York NY 10022; Galerie Claude Bernard 5 Rue des Beaux Arts Paris France. *Mailing Add:* Sch Fine Arts Wash Univ St Louis MO 63130

MCGARRY, PATRICIA JOSEPHINE
INSTRUCTOR, SCULPTOR
b Chicago, Ill, May 23, 47. *Study:* Univ Ill, Urbana, BFA, 70; Sch Art Inst Chicago, MFA, 72. *Comn:* Mural, Echo Special Educ Cooperative, South Holland, Ill, 74. *Exhib:* Art Inst Chicago, 72; Milwaukee Lakefront Art Festival, Wis, 72, 75 & 76; Beaux-Arts Designer Craftsman, Columbus, Ohio, 73; Six on Six, NAME Gallery, Chicago, 80; two-person show, ARC Gallery, 82; Potters Exhib, Springfield Art Asn, Ill, 82; and others. *Teaching:* Prof art, Thornton Community Col, South Holland, Ill, 77-82. *Awards:* Midwest Crafts Award, Nat Home Fashions League, 71; Second Place, Greater Fall River Art Asn, 72. *Mem:* Chicago Artists Coalition; Am Craftsman Asn. *Media:* Clay. *Dealer:* ARC Gallery 6 West Hubbard Chicago IL. *Mailing Add:* 14108 S Tracy Riverdale IL 60627

MCGARRY, SUSAN HALLSTEN
EDITOR, WRITER
b Minneapolis, Minn, June 27, 48. *Study:* Univ Minn, BA, 74, MA(art hist), 78. *Pos:* Freelance arts writer & critic, 78-; ed, Southwest Art Mag, 79- *Res:* Artists living and working in the Western U S. *Mailing Add:* 3718 Grennoch Lane Houston TX 77025

MACGARVEY, BERNARD B
PAINTER
b San Francisco, Calif. *Study:* St Mary's Col, Calif, BA; NTex State Univ; Calif Arts & Crafts, Oakland. *Work:* Univ Calif Mus, Berkeley; Henry Gallery, Univ Wash, Seattle; Long Beach Mus, Calif; Victoria Mus, BC, Can; Dublin Mus, Ireland. *Comn:* Mural, Palmer Sch, Walnut Creek, Calif, 70. *Exhib:* One-man shows, Humboldt Galleries, San Francisco, 68, 71, 73 & New York, 75; Univ Calif, Berkeley, 72. *Bibliog:* Judith Dunham (auth), Exhibit Rev, Art Week, 5/73; S Tarshiss (auth), Exhibit Rev, Art News, 6/73; Summer Gallery, Archit Dig, 6/73. *Media:* Tempera, Oil. *Mailing Add:* 245 Front St Brooklyn NY 11201

MCGEE, OLIVIA JACKSON
PAINTER, ILLUSTRATOR
b SC, Nov 19, 15. *Study:* Limestone Col, BA; Clemson Univ Sch Visual Arts; Rex Brandt's Sch Painting, Europe & Corona del Mar, Calif; Art Students League; painting with Eliot O'Hara. *Work:* Chemstrand Corp, Empire State Bldg, New York; People's Nat Bank & Trust Co, Greenville, SC; Clemson Univ Alumni Ctr; Gov Mansion, Columbia, SC. *Exhib:* Guild SC Artists, Columbia; Greenville Arts Festival; Clemson Univ Union Gallery, 77; Pickens Co Art Mus, Pickens, SC, 77; Sumter Co Art Mus, Sumter, SC, 78; and others. *Pos:* Illusr, Clemson Univ Exten Serv, 50-56; state pres, Nat League Am Pen Women, 66-68; mem, Pickens Co Art Comn, 71-72. *Awards:* Merit Award, SC Watercolor Soc, 80, 82 & 83; and others. *Bibliog:* Jack Morris (auth), Contemporary Artists of South Carolina, Greenville Co Mus Art, 70; Charles M Israel (auth), Artist Olivia McGee, Sandlapper Mag, 71; Southern Living Mag, 84. *Mem:* SC & Southern Watercolor Socs; Greenville Co Artists Guild; Guild SC Artists. *Media:* Watercolor. *Mailing Add:* 221 Riggs Dr Clemson SC 29631

MCGEE, WINSTON EUGENE
PAINTER, EDUCATOR
b Salem, Ill, Sept 4, 24. *Study:* Univ Mo, BJ, 48 & MA, 49; Univ Wis; Ecole Superieure Beaux-Arts, 50-51; Atelier-M Jean Souverbie, French Nat Acad, 51; Fulbright Scholar to Paris, 51. *Work:* Whitney Mus Am Art, New York; Calif Palace of Legion of Honor, San Francisco; Philadelphia Mus Art; Smithsonian Inst, Washington, DC; Indianapolis Mus Art, Ind. *Comn:* Relief painting, Mo State Hist Soc, Columbia; mural, Trinity Cathedral, Cleveland, Ohio; mural, David Leach estate, Madison, Ohio; Sara Beck Mem, Lake Erie Col, 78; Mural, Turlock Centennial Foundation, Calif, 81. *Exhib:* One-man show, Mitchell Mus, Mt Vernon, Ill, 74; 50th Yr Anniversary Traveling Show, Cleveland Mus, 68; Lincoln Fine Arts Ctr Dedication Exhib, 70; Atelier II, La Defense, Paris, France, 78; Calif State Col-Stanislaus, Turlock, 78. *Pos:* Head, Dept Art, Lake Erie Col, 52-69; actg chmn art, Cleveland State Univ, 69-72, fac in painting, 72-76; prof & chmn art dept, Calif State Col, Stanislaus, 77- *Awards:* Cleveland Mus May Show Jury Award, 68; Annie McEntree Norton Award Painting & Graphic, Univ Mo. *Bibliog:* Articles, Graphic Artists, 72 & Mo State Hist Soc Bulletin, 9/75; article in Mo State Hist Soc Bulletin, 9/75. *Mem:* Cleveland Coun Arts; Cleveland Art Community; New Orgn for Visual Arts; fel Int Inst Arts & Lett (Switz). *Media:* Oil, Acrylic. *Mailing Add:* 800 Monte Vista Turlock CA 95380

MCGILL, FORREST
HISTORIAN, MUSEUM ADMINISTRATOR
b East Orange, NJ, Oct 25, 47. *Study:* Cornell Univ, BA, 69; Univ Mich, MA, 73, PhD(Fulbright-Hays res award), 77. *Pos:* Coordr pub prog, Univ Mich Mus Art, Ann Arbor, 77-78; asst dir, Archer M Huntington Art Gallery, Univ Tex, Austin, 80- *Teaching:* Vis instr Asian art, Oakland Univ, Mich, 78; vis asst prof, Univ Colo, Boulder, 79; adj asst prof, Univ Tex, Austin, 79- *Mem:* Col Art Asn; Am Asn Mus; Am Comt South Asian Art. *Res:* Buddhist art in Southeast Asia. *Publ:* Coauth, A Catalog of the Mr and Mrs Henry Jewett Greene Memorial Collection of Far Eastern Ceramics, Univ Mich Mus Art, 74. *Mailing Add:* 1206 Castle Hill Austin TX 78703

MACGILLIS, ROBERT DONALD
PAINTER, PRINTMAKER
b Bayonne, NJ, June 30, 36. *Study:* Mech Inst, New York; Newark Sch Fine Arts, NJ. *Work:* Grover M Hermann Fine Arts Ctr, Marietta Col; Bayonne Pub Libr; Caldwell Art Ctr, Caldwell Col; Univ Conn. *Exhib:* Allied Artists Am, New York; Acad Artists, Springfield, Mass; Conn Watercolor Soc, Hartford; Am Watercolor Soc, New York; and others. *Pos:* Indust artist, Gen Dynamics Elec Boat Div, Groton, Conn, 60-75. *Awards:* Over 65 awards for nat & regional juried exhibs; Gold Medal for graphics, Acad Artists, 78; Louis E Sealey Award, Salmagundi Club, 80; and others. *Mem:* Salmagundi Club; Am Artists Prof League; Artists Fel; Conn Watercolor Soc; Hudson Valley Artists. *Media:* Watercolor, Oils; Graphics. *Dealer:* Hearth Gallery Scottsdale AZ; Joseph Danley Gallery Cranford NJ. *Mailing Add:* 96 School St Groton CT 06340

MCGILVERY, LAURENCE
BOOK DEALER, PUBLISHER
b Los Angeles, Calif, May 21, 32. *Study:* Pomona Col, BA, 54. *Pos:* Mem adv bd, Artbibliographs Mod, Santa Barbara, 73 & Who's Who in Am Art & Am Art Dir, 78. *Mem:* Art Libr Soc of NAm; Antiquarian Booksellers Asn Am; San Diego Booksellers Asn (pres, currently). *Res:* Art periodical indexes and art bibliographies. *Publ:* Auth, Artforum, 1962-1968: A Cummulative Index to the First Six Volumes, McGilvery, 70. *Mailing Add:* PO Box 852 La Jolla CA 92038

MCGINNIS, CHRISTINE
PAINTER
b Philadelphia, Pa. *Study:* Pa Acad Fine Arts. *Work:* Mus Nat Sci, Philadelphia; Civic Ctr Mus, Philadelphia; Free Libr Philadelphia; Am Embassy, Dublin, Ireland; Pa Acad Fine Arts. *Exhib:* Pa Acad Fine Art Nat Ann, 59; Philadelphia Art Mus Regional Exhib, 64; Brooklyn Art Mus 14th Nat Exhib, New York, 65; Am Express Pavillion, New York World's Fair, 66; Libr Cong 20th Nat, Washington, DC, 67; Washington Art Mus, 77-80; Art Expo Traveling Show, 80-83; one-person show, Roger LaPelle Galleries, 82. *Awards:* William J Scttiedt Traveling Scholar, 61; Award, Albany Print Club, 68; First Prize, Pa Acad, 74. *Media:* Acrylic, Graphics. *Publ:* Illusr, Ctr City Mag, 63; illusr, Promenade Mag, 68; illusr, Audubon Mag, 70; illusr, Decor Mag, 78; illusr, Imfad Cat, 77-80. *Mailing Add:* c/o Rodger La Pelle Graphics 5929 Devon Pl Philadelphia PA 19138

MCGLAUCHLIN, TOM
GLASSBLOWER, INSTRUCTOR
b Beloit, Wis, Sept 14, 34. *Study:* Univ Wis, BS, 59, MS(art), 60; pottery with James McKinnell, Univ Iowa, 62; Oriental art hist, Univ Washington, 66-67. *Work:* Corning Mus Glass, NY; Toledo Mus Art, Ohio; Minn Art Mus, St Paul; Portland Mus Art, Ore; Mus Contemp Crafts, New York; and others. *Exhib:* Glass Aus USA, Glasmuseum Frauenau, WGer, 79; American Glass Now II, touring Japan, 80; Glass: Artist and Influence, Detroit Art Inst, 81; Nat Mus Mod Art, Kyoto, Japan, 81; and many others. *Pos:* Chmn art dept, Cornell Col, Mt Vernon, 68-71. *Teaching:* Prof art, Cornell Col, Mt Vernon, Iowa, 61-71; instr glass blowing, Toledo Mus Art, 71- *Awards:* Award for Glass, Miami Nat, Lowe Gallery, Univ Miami, Coral Gables, Fla, 65; First Jury Award, Toledo Glass Nat II, Toledo Mus of Art, 68; First Award Glass, 7th Beaux Arts, Pittsburgh Glass Co, Pa, 75. *Mem:* Glass Art Soc; Am Crafts Coun; Col Art Asn. *Media:* Hand-Blown Glass. *Mailing Add:* 2527 Cheltenham Toledo OH 43606

MCGOUGH, CHARLES E
PRINTMAKER, EDUCATOR
b Elmhurst, Ill, Aug 2, 27. *Study:* Southwestern Univ; Ray Vogue Commercial Art Sch, dipl; Univ Tulsa, BA & MA; NTex State Univ; also with Hardin Simmons. *Work:* Boston Mus; Philbrook Mus; Dallas Mus Fine Arts; Little Rock Mus Fine Arts. *Comn:* Genre mural, Southern Hills Country Club, Tulsa, Okla, 56; mural, ETex State Univ, Commerce, 63; mural, Goodfellow AFB, San Angelo, Tex, 64; several graphic works, First Nat Bank, Dallas, Tex, 65; several graphic works, Southwestern Life Ins Co, Dallas, 67. *Exhib:* Nat Serigraph Ann, Brooklyn Mus Art, 65; Drawing USA, Walker Art Ctr, 66; Nat Print Ann, Boston Mus Fine Arts, 67; Southwest Print & Drawing Ann, Dallas Mus Fine Arts, 67, 68 & 70; Nat Print & Drawing Ann, Okla Art Ctr, 69-72. *Pos:* Owner, McGough Advert Co, 45-50; art dir, Crane Advert, Tulsa, 50-52. *Teaching:* Instr art, N R Crogier Tech High Sch, Dallas, 52-56; prof & head art dept, ETex State Univ, 56- *Awards:* Graphic Purchase Award, Boston Univ Mus Show, 65; Southwest Print & Drawing Ann Award, Dallas Mus Fine Arts, 67; Graphic Purchase Award, Nat Print Ann, Okla Art Ctr, 71. *Mem:* Southwest Print & Drawing Soc; Tex Asn Schs Art. *Media:* Graphics. *Publ:* Auth, Print painting, Dallas Morning News, 67; auth, Serigraphy, Dallas Times Herald, 68; auth, Serigraph & the total image, Tex Trends Art Educ, 68. *Dealer:* Cushing Galleries 2723 Fairmount St Dallas TX 75201. *Mailing Add:* 1603 Walnut Commerce TX 75428

MCGOVERN, ROBERT F
PAINTER, SCULPTOR
b Philadelphia, Pa, Apr 1, 33. *Study:* Philadelphia Col Art, Pa, with Benton Spruance. *Work:* Mus Art, Free Libr, Philadelphia; Rare Bk Collection, Cornell Univ, Ithaca, NY. *Comn:* Portraits of Bishop Lorenz Grassel & Mathew Carey, Am Cath Hist Soc, Philadelphia, 76; carving of Bishop Neumann, Bishop Neumann High Sch, Philadelphia, 77; banner of St John Neumann, comn by Sister of St Francis for use at Canonization, Rome, Italy, 77; wood relief of St John Neumann for Daylesford Abbey, Paoli, Pa, 78. *Exhib:* Prints & Drawings, Philadelphia Art Alliance, 62; Print Club, Philadelphia, 63; Am Color Print Soc, Philadelphia, 73-77; Liturgical Arts,

41st Int Eucharistic Cong, 77. *Pos:* Co-chmn found prog, Philadelphia Col Art, 76- *Teaching:* Prof drawing design & anatomy, Philadelphia Col Art, 56-82, prof painting, currently. *Mem:* Philadelphia Print Club; Artists Equity (pres, Philadelphia Chap, 64-65); Am Color Print Soc. *Media:* Wood Carving, Woodcuts; Oil. *Publ:* Auth rev, Religious Art in 20th Century--An Understanding, Pax Romano, Fribourg, Switz, 65; coauth, Saturday Waiting, 60 Pen & Ink Drawings, Fortress Press, Philadelphia, 70; auth, A Re-emergence of religious art in the seventies, Dimension Mag, Philadelphia, 74; illusr, Uncommon Book of Prayer, Seabury Press, 78. *Mailing Add:* 120 Woodside Ave Narberth PA 19072

MCGOWAN, KENNETH
PHOTOGRAPHER
b Ogden, Utah, Dec 3, 40. *Study:* Univ Calif, Los Angeles, MA, 66. *Work:* Metrop Mus Art & Mus Mod Art, New York; Fogg Art Mus, Harvard Univ, Cambridge, Mass; Australian Nat Gallery, Sydney; Nat Archives, Washington, DC. *Exhib:* Views Over America, Mus Mod Art, New York, 79; Spectrum of Recent Photography, Milwaukee Art Ctr, Wis, 79; Urban/Suburban Photos, Addison Gallery Am Art, Andover, Mass, 80; Aspects of the 70's, DeCordova Mus, Lincoln, Mass, 80; Contemporary Photographs, Fogg Art Mus, Harvard Univ, Cambridge, Mass, 80; solo shows, Johnson Mus, Cornell Univ, 81 & Mus Fine Arts, Houston, 82; New Color, Int Ctr Photog, New York, 81. *Bibliog:* Carol Squiers (auth), Color photography, Artforum, 11/78; Sally Eauclaire (auth), The New Color, Abbeyville Press, 81. *Dealer:* Leo Castelli 4 East 77th St New York NY 10021. *Mailing Add:* 504 La Guardia Place New York NY 10012

MCGOWIN, ED
SCULPTOR, PAINTER
b Hattiesburg, Miss, June 2, 38. *Study:* Miss Southern Col, BS; Univ Ala, MA. *Work:* Corcoran Gallery Art, Nat Collection Fine Arts & Philips Collections, Washington, DC; Whitney Mus Am Art, New York; Guggenheim Mus; and others. *Comn:* Sculpture, Nat Endowment Arts, 76; sculpture, Gen Serv Admin, 78. *Exhib:* Whitney Ann Am Sculpture, 68; Gilliam Krebs McGowin, Corcoran Gallery, 69; one-man shows, Baltimore Mus Art, 72 & Corcoran Gallery Art, Washington, DC, 75; Narrative Art/Story Art, Contemp Mus Art, Houston, Tex, 77; From Self-Portrait to Autobiography, Neuberger Mus, Purchase, New York, 78; The Sense of Self, Nat Collection Fine Arts, 80; Southern Voice, Ft Worth Mus Art, 81; Harvard Univ, 83; and others. *Awards:* Nat Endowment Arts Grants, 67, 76 & 80; Award, Am Ctr Students & Artists, Paris, 74; Oscar for Painting, 9th Int Painting Exhib, Cagnes Sur-Mer, France, 77. *Bibliog:* Rose (auth), Gallery without walls, Art in Am, 68; Hopps & Osnos (auth), Three Washington artists Gilliam Krebs McGowin, Art Int, 70; Don W Thatcher (auth), Place of Art in the World of Architecture, Chelase House Publ, 80. *Media:* Multimedia. *Publ:* Don W Thatcher (auth), Place of Art in the World of Architecture, Chelsea House Publ, 80. *Mailing Add:* 96 Grand St New York NY 10013

MACGREGOR, GREGORY ALLEN
PHOTOGRAPHER
b La Crosse, Wis, Feb 13, 41. *Study:* Univ Calif, San Francisco, MA(photog), 71; with Jack Welpott & Don Worth. *Work:* San Francisco Mus Mod Art, Calif; Oakland Mus, Calif; Chicago Art Inst, Ill; Mus Mod Art & Whitney Mus, New York. *Exhib:* Deus Ex Machima, Friends of Photog, Carmel, Calif, 75; On the Go, Fine Arts Mus, San Francisco, Calif, 78; Attitudes in the 70's, Santa Barbara Mus Art, Calif, 79; Recent Work, O K Harris Works of Art, New York, 79; American Tractor, Foster Goldstrum Fine Arts, San Francisco, 82; and others. *Teaching:* Asst prof & chmn photog, Lone Mountain Col, San Francisco, Calif, 70-78; asst prof photog, Calif State Univ, Hayward, 80-84. *Bibliog:* Ted Hedypath (auth), The real as sureal, Artweek, 2/25/80; Jim Hughes (auth), Proofsheet, Popular Photog, 6/80; Mark Levy (auth), article, Images & Issues, 10/82. *Mem:* Soc Photog Educ. *Publ:* Illusr, Points of view, New West, 11/79; contribr, Darkroom Dynamics, Curtin-London, 79; auth, Explosions, Headlands Press, 80; auth, article, Art Comn, 6/83; illusr, Darkroom Mag, Vol 4, No 8, 82; and others. *Dealer:* O K Harris 383 W Broadway New York NY 10012; Equivalents Gallery 1822 Broadway Seattle WA. *Mailing Add:* 6481 Colby St Oakland CA 94618

MACGREGOR, JOHN BOYKO
PAINTER, ADMINISTRATOR
b Dorking, Eng, Jan 12, 44; Can citizen. *Study:* Cent Tech Sch, Toronto. *Work:* Nat Gallery Can; Art Gallery Ont; Owens Art Gallery, NB; Univ Western Ont; Winnipeg Art Gallery. *Comn:* Sculpture (with Paul Wilson), Gallery One, Toronto, 76. *Exhib:* Survey 70-Realism, Art Gallery Ont, Montreal Mus of Fine Arts, 70; Making Marks, Norman MacKenzie Art Gallery, Regina; Contemp Prints from Can, Ore State Univ, 76; one-man shows, Hart House, Univ of Toronto, 67, Isaacs Gallery, 68-77 & 79 & Gallery Graphics, Ottawa, 75; and many other group & one-man shows. *Pos:* Dir, New Sch Art, Toronto, 77- *Teaching:* Instr, Artist's Workshop, 67-77, Ont Col Art, 70-72 & 75, York Univ, 71-73, New Sch, 72-75 & Hart House, Univ Toronto, 76 & 77. *Awards:* Winnipeg Biennial Purchase Award, 70; Can Coun Grant, 78; Ont Arts Coun Grant, 78. *Bibliog:* Article, Art Mag, 6/80; article, Vanguard, 11/80. *Mem:* Can Artist Representation. *Media:* Multimedia. *Dealer:* Issacs Gallery Ltd 832 Yonge St Toronto M4W 2H1 Can. *Mailing Add:* c/o Isaacs Gallery 832 Yonge St Toronto ON M4W 2H1 Canada

MCGREW, BRUCE ELWIN
PAINTER
b Wichita, Kans, Oct 20, 37. *Study:* Wichita State Univ, Kans, BFA; Univ Ariz, MFA, 64. *Work:* Nat Park Serv, Three Rivers, Calif & Haleakala Nat Park, Maui, Hawaii; Univ Minn, Morris; Univ Kansai, Osaka, Japan; Univ Ariz, Law Sch. *Comn:* Oil landscape, Georgetown Leather, Washington, DC, 77; watercolor, Pennie Edmonds Law Firm, New York, 77. *Exhib:* Kiosko del Arte, Hermosillo, Mex, 78; Maggie Kress Gallery, Taos, NMex, 79; Marion Locks, Philadelphia, 81; Colorado Springs Fine Arts Ctr, Colo, 81; Univ Ark, Fayetteville, 81; and others. *Teaching:* Instr painting & drawing, Univ Minn, Morris, Univ Ariz, Tucson, 66-; artist-in-residence, Nat Park Serv, Sequoia & Kings Canyon Nat Park, Three Rivers, Calif, summer 75 & Haleakala Nat Park, Maui, Hawaii, summer 76; mem staff watercolor workshop, Summervail Art Workshop, Vail, Colo, summer 77; mem staff drawing & watercolor workshop, Univ Tex, El Paso, 4/78 & Guadalajara Summer Sch, Univ Ariz, 79. *Awards:* Fac Res Support in Humanities & Sociology, Univ Ariz, Tucson, 72-73; Purchase Awards, 13th Ann Cedar City Exhib, Utah, 74 & Ninth South Western Invitational Yuma Fine Arts Asn, Ariz, 75. *Media:* Watercolor, Oil. *Publ:* Contribr, Oracle: A Voluntary of Poems and Prints, Oracle Press, 74. *Dealer:* Marion Locks Gallery 1524 Walnut Philadelphia PA 19102. *Mailing Add:* Box E Oracle AZ 85623

MCGREW, RALPH BROWNELL
PAINTER, DRAFTSMAN
b Columbus, Ohio, Sept 6, 16. *Study:* Otis Art Inst, four years; studied with Edouard Vysekal, Ralph Holmes & E Roscoe Shrader; Concordia Col, Minn, Dr Lett, 81. *Work:* Cowboy Hall Fame, Oklahoma City; Mus Northern Ariz; Diamond M Mus, Snyder, Tex; Anschutz Collection, Denver; Nat Acad Western Art. *Exhib:* Cowboy Artists Am, Cowboy Hall Fame; Death Valley Invitational, Calif; All-Calif Invitational, Laguna Beach; Charles Russell Rendezvous Invitational, Helena, Mont, 72; Nat Acad Western Art. *Teaching:* Asst instr art, Otis Art Inst. *Awards:* Gold Medal Drawing, Cowboy Hall Fame, 72; Gold Medals, 73 & 74 & Silver Medal, 75, Nat Acad Western Art. *Bibliog:* Ed Ainsworth (auth), Painters of the Desert, Desert Mag Press, 60 & 61; Western Painting Today, Watson-Guptill, 75; McGrew, Lowell Press, 78. *Mem:* Fel Am Inst Fine Arts; Nat Acad Western Art; fel Soc Western Artists. *Media:* Oil; Charcoal. *Publ:* Auth, Artist on the Colorado, 61 & Tewa-quaptewa, Hopi Chief, 61, Desert Mag; auth, Water of life for God's red children, This Day Mag, 65; auth, The art of R Brownell McGrew, Ariz Hwys, 7/69 & 10/77. *Dealer:* O'Brien's Art Emporium 7122 Stetson Scottsdale AZ 85251; Trailside Galleries Jackson WY. *Mailing Add:* PO Box 2 Quemado NM 87829

MCGUIRE, MAUREEN
DESIGNER, STAINED GLASS ARTIST
b Flushing, NY, July 13, 41. *Study:* NY State Col Ceramics, Alfred Univ, BFA, 63; Pope Pius XII Inst, Florence, Italy (affil Rosary Col, Ill), Cardinal Spellman scholar & MA, 64; workshop, with Ludwig Schaffrath, Berkeley, Calif, 75. *Comn:* Design for large tapestry, La Casa De Cristo Lutheran Church, Paradise Valley, Ariz; leaded stained glass windows & laminated glass screen wall, St Matthew's United Methodist Church, Bowie, Md; faceted glass window, skylights, mosaic walls, exterior concrete bas relief sculptures, interior design, furniture design incorporating flower display system, St Francis Cemetery Resurrection Mausoleum; commercial installation: 15 faceted glass windows, Paradise Valley Mall, Paradise Valley, Ariz; residential installation: leaded glass window & light fixtures, Logan Van Sittert residence, Phoenix; and many others. *Pos:* Apprentice designer-craftsman, Glassart Studio, Scottsdale, Ariz, 64-69; independent artist-designer, Phoenix, 69- *Awards:* Honor Awards, Nat Conf Relig Archit, 68 & Interfaith Forum Relig, Art & Archit, 79. *Bibliog:* Ann Patterson (auth), Stained glass: The art, Ariz Repub, 9/30/79. *Mem:* Stained Glass Asn Am; Interfaith Forum Relig, Archit & Arts; Am Craft Coun; Ariz Stained Glass Asn. *Media:* Leaded and Faceted Stained Glass; Mosaics in Glass. *Publ:* Auth-illusr, The case for the independent designer, Stained Glass Quart, 4/80. *Mailing Add:* 924 E Bethany Home Rd Phoenix AZ 85014

MACHETANZ, FRED
PAINTER, LITHOGRAPHER
b Kenton, Ohio, Feb 20, 08. *Study:* Ohio State Univ, AB, 30, MA, 35; Chicago Art Inst, 30-32; Am Acad, Chicago, 30-32; Art Students League, 45; Univ Alaska, Hon DFA, 73; Alaska Pac Univ, LHD, 83. *Work:* Rasmuson Libr, Univ Alaska; Glenbow Found, Alta Mus, Calgary; Anchorage Hist & Fine Arts Mus; Northwest Indian Ctr, Gonzaga Univ; Frye Art Mus, Seattle. *Comn:* Scripps Inst Res Ship, Alpha Helix, 63; Dept Interior, Washington, DC, 69; Inst Arctic Biol, Univ Alaska, 71; The Tender Arctic, Frye Mus, Seattle, Wash, 73; Eben Hobson (portrait), N Slope Borough, Fairbanks, 81; and others. *Exhib:* One-man shows, Univ Alaska, 64 & 72, Anchorage Hist & Fine Arts Mus, 68, 74 & 80, Frye Mus, 72 & Tryon Gallery Ltd, London, 79. *Pos:* Distinguished assoc art, Univ Alaska, 64- *Awards:* Silver Medal, NAm Wild Animal Art Exhib, 79; Artist of Yr, Am Artist Mag, 81. *Bibliog:* Sara Machetanz (auth), The Oil Paintings of Fred Machetanz, F Lewis Publ, London, 80; Stephen Doherty (auth), '81 artist of the year, Am Artist, 81; Sara Machetanz (auth), The Fifty Stone Lithographs of Fred Machetanz, Mill Pond Press, 83. *Mem:* Soc Animal Artists; Explorers Club. *Media:* Oil; Lithography. *Publ:* Auth & illusr, Panuck, Eskimo Sled Dog, 39 & auth & illusr, On Arctic Ice, 41, Scribners. *Mailing Add:* PO Box 2589 Palmer AK 99645

MCHUGH, ADELIZA SORENSON
DEALER, COLLECTOR
b St George, Utah, Apr 29, 12. *Study:* Spec study with Robert Arneson, Roy De Forest, David Gilhooly, Nilsson, Jim Nutt & Maija Peeples. *Collections Arranged:* Roy De Forest Drawings, San Francisco Mus & Whitney Mus, New York. *Pos:* Dir, Candy Store Gallery, Folsom, Calif, 62- *Specialty:* Contemporary American art. *Collection:* Californian ceramic sculpture, American primitive drawings of today; California paintings. *Mailing Add:* 605 Sutter St Folsom CA 95630

MCILROY, CAROL J
PAINTER, DEALER
b Sandpoint, Idaho, Feb 21, 24. *Study:* Univ Colo, with John Pellew; Univ NMex, with Joe Morello, Arthur Sussman & Sam Smith. *Work:* Am Bank Com, Albuquerque NMex; NMex Jr Col. *Exhib:* Mainstreams, 69; Regional Art Exhib, Phoenix, 71; McAddo II Gallery, Prescott, Ariz, 73; Lubbock Tex Art Exhib, 74. *Pos:* Chmn standards comt, NMex Arts & Crafts Fair, 72-73; mem, Bicentennial Art Comt, 75; co-owner, Galeria del Sol. *Awards:* Grand Prize & Best of Show, Sky Country, Montrose Art Festival, Colo, 70; First Prize, RFD, NMex State Fair, 71; First Prize Landscape, 4th Regional Art Exhib, Phoenix, 71. *Mem:* Am Artists Prof League; Artists Equity (vpres, 71-72); NMex Art League. *Media:* Oil. *Mailing Add:* Galerie del Sol 206 1/2 San Felipe NW Albuquerque NM 87102

MCILVAIN, DOUGLAS LEE
EDUCATOR, SCULPTOR
b Mt Holly, NJ, July 26, 23. *Study:* Tyler Sch Fine Arts, Temple Univ, BFA & BS, Tyler Sch Fine Arts Rome; NY Univ, MA(art educ); also with Raphael Sabatini & Jose De Creeft. *Work:* Monmouth Col; Georgian Court Col; Tyler Sch Fine Arts Rome; Monmouth Mus, NJ; Morris Mus, NJ. *Comn:* Portrait, Stephenson Corp, 67; portrait, Hosp Picture Serv Co, 74; four portraits, Health Hall of Fame, 80; Bell Tel Labs, 82; Jack Leiner Archit Design, 83. *Exhib:* Detroit Inst Art, 59; Pa Acad Art, 60; Philadelphia Civic Ctr Mus, 72; Staten Island Children's Mus, 79-80; Monmouth Mus, NJ, 81; Morris Mus, NJ, 82; Art Expo, New York, 83. *Pos.* Art designer, Monmouth Mus, 78-79. *Teaching:* Assoc prof art, Georgian Court Col, 68- *Awards:* First Prize, Jersey City Mus, 61; First Prize, Red Bank Festival Arts, 61-62, 64-65, 67, 69-71 & 73; Two First Prizes, Guild Creative Art, 82. *Mem:* Sculpture Asn NJ; Guild Creative Arts; Art Alliance; Am Asn Univ Prof; Int Sculpture Ctr. *Media:* Bronze, Wood. *Mailing Add:* 40 Whitman Dr Red Bank NJ 07701

MCILVAIN, FRANCES H
PAINTER, INSTRUCTOR
b Newark, NJ, May 11, 25. *Study:* Tyler Sch Art, Temple Univ, BFA & BS, 47, Temple Univ Rome, with Charles LaClair, 65; Philadelphia Mus Sch Art, with W Emerton Heitland, 48. *Work:* Temple Univ, Philadelphia, Pa; Bell Laboratories, Holmdel, NJ; United Methodist Church, Red Bank, NJ; Monmouth Medical Ctr, Long Branch, NJ; Tinton Falls Sch, NJ. *Comn:* Mural of Noah's Ark, First Presbyterian Church, Red Bank, NJ, 60; paintings, Atchison Sch, Tinton Falls, NJ, 70 & 81; mural, Monmouth Mus, Lincroft, NJ, 80. *Exhib:* Monmouth Co Arts Coun Ann, Monmouth Mus, Lincroft, NJ, 80; Garden State Watercolor Soc, Princeton, NJ, 81; Nabisco Art Gallery, 82; Summit Gallery, NJ, 83; Art Expo, New York, 83. *Teaching:* Instr art, Rancocas Valley Regional High Sch, Mt Holly, NJ, 47-53; instr art, Tinton Falls Sch, NJ, 63- *Awards:* Best in Show, Methodist Church Red Bank, 64; Best in Show, Henry Luhrs Award, 80; Monmouth Arts First Prize, 83. *Mem:* Guild Creative Arts, (bd mem, 75-79); Monmouth Arts Found; Am Watercolor Soc; NJ Watercolor Soc (bd mem, 79-81); Art Educators NJ. *Media:* Watercolor. *Mailing Add:* 40 Whitman Dr Red Bank NJ 07701

MCINERNEY, GENE JOSEPH
PAINTER
b Easton, Pa, Jan 6, 30. *Work:* Miniature Art Soc of NJ, Nutley; Fred Clark Mus, Carversville, Pa; Meadowbrook Sch, Philadelphia, Pa. *Comn:* Bicentennial Calendar, Northampton Co, Pa, Bicentennial Comn, 75. *Exhib:* Miniature Art Soc, NJ, Nutley, 71-73; Painters & Sculptors Soc NJ, Jersey City Mus, 71, 72 & 74; Miniature Painters, Sculptors & Gravers Soc, Washington DC Arts Club, 72 & 73; Nat Soc Painters in Casein & Acrylic, Nat Acad, New York, 72-75; Mainstreams, Marietta, Ohio, 72 & 73. *Awards:* First Prize, Atlantic City Nat Boardwalk Show, 70; Mainstreams Award of Excellence, Marietta Col, 72; Presidents Prize, Painters & Sculptors Soc NJ, 74. *Bibliog:* Art, Gene McInerney, La Rev Mod, 11/72. *Mem:* Old Bergen Art Guild; Painters & Sculptors Soc NJ. *Media:* Acrylic, Watercolor. *Dealer:* Capricorn Gallery 4849 Rugby Ave Bethesda MD 20814; Bernard Picture Co New York NY. *Mailing Add:* Northlight Studio RD 4 Bangor PA 18013

MCINTOSH, HAROLD
PAINTER
b Galashiels, Scotland, Mar 1, 16; US citizen. *Study:* Winnipeg Sch Art; with L L Fitzgerald. *Work:* Berkshire Mus, Pittsfield, Mass; Sharon Hist Mus, Conn. *Comn:* Three paintings, Int Tel & Tel Grinnell, Providence, RI, 74. *Exhib:* Springfield Mus Fine Art, Mass, 62; one-man shows, Mus Hist & Art, Albany, NY, 64; Berkshire Mus, 68 & 74 & Butler Mus, Youngstown, Ohio, 71-73; Conn Acad Fine Arts, Wadsworth Atheneum, Hartford, 70-72. *Awards:* Best in Show, New Haven Festival Arts, 60, 64 & 69; Best in Show, Wash Art Asn, 74; Medal of Merit, Kent Art Asn, 74. *Mem:* Berkshire Art Asn; Wash Art Asn; Kent Art Asn (pres, 74-75). *Media:* Acrylic, Egg Tempera. *Mailing Add:* Cornwall Bridge Rd Sharon CT 06069

MCINTOSH, HARRISON EDWARD
CERAMIST, DESIGNER
b Vallejo, Calif, Sept 11, 14. *Study:* Art Ctr Sch, Los Angeles, 38; Univ Southern Calif study with Glen Lukens, 40; Claremont Grad Sch, Calif, 49-52; Mills Col with Bernard Leach, 50; also with Marguerite Wildenhain, 53. *Work:* Mus of Contemp Crafts, New York; Smithsonian Inst, Washington, DC; Mus Nat de la Ceramique de Severes, Paris; Belg Royal Collection, Ostend, Belg; Kiushu Mus, Japan. *Comn:* Cross, Kingman Chapel, Claremont, Calif, 63; Bank of Calif, Claremont, 72; sculpture series (ltd ed), Claremont Men's Col, 77. *Exhib:* Objects: USA, Traveling Exhib, Smithsonian Inst, 69-76; Media Survey 73, Fine Arts Gallery San Diego, Calif, 73; Oakland Mus, Calif, 74; Masters in Ceramic Art, Everson Mus & Alfred Univ, New York, 75; Philadelphia Mus Art, 77; Renwick Gallery, Washington, DC, 79; retrospective exhib, Chaffey Col, Calif, 79. *Teaching:* Instr ceramics, Otis Art Inst, Los Angeles, 56-57, summer session, 59. *Awards:* Purchase Award, Second Int Ceramic Festival, Ostend, Belg, 59; Purchase Award, 21st Ceramic Nat, Everson Mus of Art, Syracuse, 60; Cash Prize, Calif Ceramics & Glass, Oakland Mus, Calif, 74. *Bibliog:* Richard Petterson (auth), Harrison McIntosh, Ceramics Monthly Mag, 6/69; Maggy Loyau (auth), Harrison McIntosh, Potier de Californie, Cahiers de la Ceramique, Paris, 74; Catherine McIntosh (auth), Harrison McIntosh: Studio Potter, Ceramics Mo Mag, 10/79. *Mem:* Am Crafts Coun; World Crafts Coun; Am Ceramic Soc, Design Div. *Mailing Add:* c/o MiKapa 25 Enterprise Ave Secaucus NJ 07094

MACIVER, LOREN
PAINTER
b New York, NY, Feb 2, 09. *Study:* Art Students League, 19. *Work:* Whitney Mus Am Art, Metrop Mus Art, Mus Mod Art, New York; Corcoran Gallery Art, Washington, DC; Addison Gallery Am Art, Andover, Mass; and others. *Exhib:* Venice Biennale, 67; Tolouse Mus Fine Arts, 67; Mus Beaux Arts, Lyons, France, 68; Mus Art Mod Ville de Paris, 68; Mus Ponchettes, Nice, France, 68; Corcoran Gallery Art; Whitney Mus Am Art, New York; Mus Mod Art, New York; and others. *Awards:* Ford Found Grant, 60; First Prize, Art Inst Chicago, 61; Purchase Prize, Krannert Art Mus, Univ Ill, 63; and others. *Mem:* Nat Inst Arts & Lett. *Dealer:* Pierre Matisse Gallery 41 E 57th St New York NY 10022. *Mailing Add:* 61 Perry St New York NY 10014

MCIVOR, JOHN WILFRED
PRINTMAKER, PAINTER
b Henderson, Ky, July 17, 31. *Study:* Murray State Univ, 49-50; Univ Ill, BFA(summa cum laude), 57, fel, 57-59, MFA, 59. *Work:* Albright-Knox Art Gallery, Buffalo, NY; Am Fedn Arts, New York; Libr Cong, Washington, DC; State Univ NY Albany; Jacksonville Mus, Fla. *Comn:* Exterior (with David Hatchett), Buffalo Rehab Comn, 71. *Exhib:* 100th Anniversary Show of Land Grant Colleges, Kansas City Art Inst, 68; Master Drawings & Watercolors Since the 15th Century, Albright-Knox Art Gallery, 69; North of the Penn Line, traveling show to mus of Northeast, 69-71; Am Fedn Arts Traveling Exhib, 70-71; Watercolors Since 1900, Birmingham Mus Art, Ala, 72. *Pos:* Founder, Team Workshop, Buffalo. *Teaching:* Asst prof art, Auburn Univ, 59-63; prof art, State Univ NY Buffalo, 63-; vis prof, Southern Ill Univ, spring 70. *Awards:* Fac Fel, State Univ NY Res Found, 70 & 72. *Bibliog:* Edward Reep (auth), The Content of Watercolor, Reinhold, 69. *Mailing Add:* Dept of Art State Univ NY Buffalo NY 14214

MACK, CHARLES RANDALL
EDUCATOR, HISTORIAN
b Baltimore, Md, May 23, 40. *Study:* Univ NC, Chapel Hill, AB, PhD(hist art). *Collections Arranged:* Classical Art from Carolina Collections (auth catalog), Columbia Mus Art, SC & NC Mus Art, Raleigh, 74; H Robert Bonsack: Thirty-Eight Paintings and Drawings by the German Artist, Columbia Mus Art, 75; Art and Artifacts from Antiquity (auth catalog), Univ SC Mus, Columbia, 76. *Pos:* Intern asst, Supt of Galleries, Florence, Italy, 68-69. *Teaching:* Assoc prof Ancient & Renaissance art, Univ SC, Columbia, 70-; vis assoc prof Renaissance art, Univ NC, Chapel Hill, summer 1977. *Awards:* Comt to Rescue Italian Art Internship, Florence, 68-69; Kress Found Res Fel, Rome, Italy, 68-70, prof, 69-70. *Mem:* Col Art Asn; Soc Archit Historians; founding mem Int Survey of Jewish Monuments; Southeastern Renaissance Conf; Southeastern Col Art Conf (pres, 75-76, co-ed, Review, 73-75). *Res:* Archival investigation of fifteenth century Italian architecture; Renaissance art; Etruscan and Roman art. *Publ:* Auth, The building programme of the Cloister of S Miniato, Burlington Mag, 73; auth, The Rucellai Palace: some new proposals, Art Bulletin, 74; auth, Michelangelo's Doni Madonna: A recapitulation, SECAC Rev, 75; coauth, Art History for our Schools, 1976. *Mailing Add:* Dept of Art Univ SC Columbia SC 29208

MACK, RODGER ALLEN
SCULPTOR, EDUCATOR
b Barberton, Ohio, Nov 8, 38. *Study:* Cleveland Inst Art, BFA, 61; Cranbrook Acad Art, Bloomfield Hills, Mich, MFA, 63; Acad Belle Arti, Florence, Italy, Fulbright Grant, 63-64. *Work:* Albrecht Mus Art, St Joseph, Mo; Munson-Williams-Proctor Inst, Utica, NY; St Lawrence Univ; State Univ NY Col Fredonia; Hamline Univ. *Comn:* Plaza sculpture, Mkt Plaza, North Little Rock, 68; Syra cast bronze, Dellplain Hall, Syracuse Univ, 69. *Exhib:* One-man shows, Galleria Arte, Florence, 64; Krasner Gallery, New York, 70-81; Sid Deutsch Gallery, New York, 84 & Everson Mus, 84; Sculpture Invitational, Rochester Inst Technol, 75; and others. *Teaching:* Instr sculpture, Arks Sch Art/Drama, Little Rock, 64-68; assoc prof sculpture, Syracuse Univ, 68-77, prof, 77-81, dir, Sch Art, 82-; chmn, Triangle Trust Workshop, Pine Plains, NY, 83- *Awards:* Nat Endowment Arts Award, Nat Coun Arts, 67; CAPS Grant, NY State Coun Arts, 77-78; Ford Found Grant, 80-81. *Bibliog:* John Canaday (auth), article, New York Times, 1/70, 1/71 & 1/72. *Media:* Bronze, Stone. *Dealer:* Sid Deutsch Gallery 20 West 57th St New York NY 10019. *Mailing Add:* 2400 Euclid Ave Syracuse NY 13224

MCKAY, ARTHUR FORTESCUE
PAINTER, EDUCATOR
b Nipawin, Sask, Sept 11, 26. *Study:* Alta Col Art; Acad Grande Chaumiere, Paris; Columbia Univ; Barnes Found, Pa. *Work:* Nat Gallery, Ottawa, Ont; Art Gallery Ont, Toronto; Montreal Mus Fine Arts, Que; Vancouver Art Gallery, BC; Nat Gallery Can. *Exhib:* Five Printers from Regina, Nat Gallery Ottawa, 61; Post Painter Abstraction, Los Angeles Co Mus, 64; Religious Art Today, Regis Col, 65; Images of a Canadian Heritage, Vancouver Art Gallery,

67; retrospective exhib, Norman MacKinzie Art Gallery, 68; Nat Gallery of Can, 81. *Teaching:* Assoc prof art, Univ Regina, 51- *Awards:* Humanities Res Coun Grant, 57 & 58; Can Coun Sr Fel, 63. *Bibliog:* C Greenberg (auth), Art on the prairie, Arts Can Mag, 9/63; T Fenton (auth), Canada's Art McKay, Artforum, 12/68. *Media:* Watercolor, Oil. *Publ:* Auth, Emma Lake Artists Workshop, Arts Can, 64 & 82. *Mailing Add:* Dept Visual Art Univ of Regina Regina SK S4S 0A2 Canada

MACKAY, HUGH
DEALER
b New York, NY, July 4, 34. *Pos:* Pres, Nabis Fine Arts Inc, New York, 70-74; pres, HMK Fine Arts Inc, 74-83; pres, Lambic-HMK Fine Arts Inc, 83- *Mem:* Am Fedn Arts; Mus Mod Art. *Specialty:* International publisher of graphics; art consultants to architects, design groups, corporations and galleries in all media. *Mailing Add:* HMK Fine Arts 112 E 19th New York NY 10003

MCKAY, JOHN SANGSTER
EDUCATOR, ADMINISTRATOR
b Farmers City, Ill, May 30, 21. *Study:* Univ Ill, Urbana-Champaign, BFA, 47; Inst Design, Chicago, Ill, cert, 48; Univ Buffalo, 50. *Teaching:* Instr design, Albright Art Sch, Buffalo, 47-54; asst dean design, Sch Fine Arts, Wash Univ, 54-68; prof visual arts, Univ Kans, 68-, assoc dean Sch Fine Arts, 68-75, dir grad studies, Dept Design, 77-80, acting chmn, 80-82, assoc chmn, 83- *Mem:* Fel Nat Asn Schs Art (pres, 69-72); Am Coun Arts Educ (bd dirs, 69-72); Int Coun Fine Arts Deans; Lawrence Community Arts Coun (chmn, 73-74). *Publ:* Co-auth, Nat Asn Schs Art Bull, 72. *Mailing Add:* 742 Indiana Lawrence KS 66044

MCKAY, RENEE
PAINTER
b Montreal, Que; US citizen. *Study:* Inst Pedagogique, Montreal; McGill Univ, Montreal, BA, 41; studied with Ben Shahn, Morris Davidson & Joe Jones. *Work:* Slater Mem Mus, Norwich, Conn; Norfolk Mus, Va; Butler Inst Am Art, Youngstown, Ohio; Lydia Drake Libr, Pembroke, Mass. *Exhib:* Open Ann, Newark, NJ & Montclair, NJ; Nat Asn Women Artists Traveling Show, Butler Inst Am Art, Youngstown, Ohio; Nat Asn Women Artists Ann & Audubon Ann, Nat Acad Galleries, New York; Nat Asn Women Artists, Lever House & Union Carbide, New York; Weyhe Gallery, New York, 79. *Teaching:* Instr art, Peck Sch, Morristown, NJ, 55-57. *Awards:* Watercolor Award, 75 & Oil Award, 80, Audubon Artists; Acrylic Award, Nat Soc Painters Casein & Acrylic, 83; and others. *Mem:* Audubon Artists (pres, 79-80); Artists's Equity Asn (vpres, 79-81); Nat Asn Women Artists (adv bd, 74-76); Nat Soc Painters Casein & Acrylic; Nat Arts Club; and others. *Media:* Acrylic, Watercolor. *Mailing Add:* 200 E 66th St New York NY 10021

MCKEAN, HUGH FERGUSON
PAINTER, EDUCATOR
b Beaver Falls, Pa, July 28, 08. *Study:* Pa Acad Fine Arts; Art Students League; Ecole Beaux-Arts, Fontainebleau, France; Rollins Col, BA & DFA; Williams Col, MA; Stetson Univ, LHD; Brevard Col, DSpaceEd; Univ Tampa, LLD. *Work:* Toledo Mus Art; Univ Va. *Exhib:* Soc Four Arts, 48; Allied Artists Am, 49; Exhib, Atlanta, Ga, 49. *Pos:* Dir, Morse Gallery Art, Rollins Col & actg pres, Col, 51-52, pres, 52-69, chmn bd, 69-75; treas, Winter Park Land Co, 52-; trustee, Ringling Mus State of Fla; mem, Fla Arts Coun, 69-; trustee, Edyth Brush Charitable Found, 75-; pres, Charles Hosmer Morse Found (reorganization of the Morse Gallery of Art, removed from Rollins Col to Winter Park, Fla), 76- *Teaching:* Prof art, Rollins Col, 52-69. *Awards:* Prizes, Fla Fedn Art, 31 & 49; Cervantes Medal, Span Inst; Decoration of Honor, Rollins Col. *Mem:* Fla Fedn Art (pres, 51-52); Louis Comfort Tiffany Found (trustee); NH Art Asn; Orlando Art Asn; Am Fedn Arts; and others. *Publ:* Auth, The "Lost" Treasures of Louis Comfort Tiffany, Doubleday & Co, 80. *Mailing Add:* 930 Genius Dr Winter Park FL 32789

MCKEAN, JEANNETTE M See Genius, Jeannette

MCKEEBY, BYRON GORDON
PRINTMAKER, EDUCATOR
b Humboldt, Iowa, Feb 27, 36. *Study:* Coe Col, BA, 59; Art Inst Chicago, BFA, 63; Tulane Univ, MFA, 65; Univ NMex, with Garo Antresian, Tamarind Artist-Teacher Fel, summer 65. *Work:* Dallas Mus Fine Arts; Philadelphia Mus; Brooklyn Mus; Norfolk Mus Arts & Sci, Va; Ark Art Ctr, Little Rock. *Exhib:* Four exhibs, Northwest Printmakers, Seattle, 65-69; four exhibs, Okla Printmakers, Oklahoma City, 65-71; Potsdam Print Ann, State Univ NY Col Potsdam, 68 & 69; Print & Drawing Nat, Northern Ill Univ De Kalb, 68, 69 & 71; Nat Print Ann, Ga State Univ, Athens, 70 & 71. *Teaching:* Prof printmaking, Univ Tenn, Knoxville, 65- *Bibliog:* Edward Brohel (auth), New American Printmakers (TV prog), NY Educ TV, 66. *Media:* Lithography, Intaglio. *Dealer:* Assoc Am Artists Inc 663 Fifth at 52nd New York NY 10022. *Mailing Add:* Art Dept Univ of Tenn Knoxville TN 37916

MACKENDRICK, LILIAN
PAINTER
b New York, NY. *Study:* Sculpture with Louis Keila; drawing & painting with Dorothy Block; Art Students League; Washington Sq Col, NY Univ, BS. *Work:* Metrop Mus Art, New York; Brooklyn Mus, New York; Walker Art Ctr; Wadsworth Atheneum, Hartford, Conn; and others. *Exhib:* New York Dealers' Show, Witte Mus Art, San Antonio, Tex, 52; 3rd Biennial of American Painting, Bordighera, Italy, 55; Eleven Americans, touring Fr Mus, 56-57; 32 one-woman shows up to 1983. *Awards:* Honorable Mention, Brooklyn Soc Artists, 53; Gold Medal, 3rd Biennial American Painting, Bordighera, Italy, 55; Award for Public Service, Northside Ctr for Child

Develop, 61. *Bibliog:* Allene Talmey (auth), More art than money, Vogue, 12/59; Dian Buchman (auth), Last of the great lady painters, Show, 4/70; Omar Del Carlo & R I Hall (auth), Lilian MacKendrick, Connoisseur, 5/74; and others. *Mem:* Artists Equity Asn. *Media:* Oil, Pastel. *Publ:* Illusr, Cat in My Mind, Putnam, England, 58; illusr, cover mag sect, New York Herald Tribune, 2/9/59; illusr, cover, Reader's Digest, 8/81. *Mailing Add:* 230 Central Park S New York NY 10019

MCKENZIE, ALLAN DEAN
EDUCATOR, HISTORIAN
b Pendleton, Ore, Aug 17, 30. *Study:* San Jose State Univ, BA(com art), 52; Univ Calif, Berkeley, MA(art hist), 55; Inst Fine Arts, NY Univ, PhD(art hist; Fulbright Scholar), 65. *Teaching:* Instr medieval art, NY Univ, 57-64; asst prof medieval & classical art, Univ Wis, Milwaukee, 64-66; from assoc prof to prof medieval art & photog, Univ Ore, 66- *Awards:* Founders' Day Award, NY Univ, 66; Grant for Poland, Int Res Exchanges Bd, New York, 73. *Mem:* Col Art Asn; Archeol Inst Am (Eugene Chap pres & secy, formerly); Int Ctr Medieval Art; Medieval Acad Am. *Res:* Russian and Byzantine icons, fresco paintings; Medieval art. *Publ:* Auth, Greek & Russian Icons, Northwest, 65; auth, Russian Art: Old and New, Univ Ore, 68; auth, Provincial Byzantine painting in Attica, Cahiers Arch, 82; auth, Russian Icons in the Santa Barbara Museum of Art, 82 & auth, Windows to Heaven: The Icons of Russia, 82, Santa Barbara Mus Art. *Mailing Add:* Dept Art Hist Univ Ore Eugene OR 97403

MACKENZIE, DAVID, IV
PAINTER
b Los Angeles, Calif, Nov 8, 42. *Study:* Orange Coast Col, Costa Mesa, Calif, AA; San Francisco Art Inst, BFA & MFA; also with Ron Nagle & Tom Holland. *Work:* Oakland Mus Art, Calif. *Exhib:* One-man shows, San Francisco Art Inst, 73, Grapestake Gallery, San Francisco, 75, 76 & 80 & A Ten Year Survey, Bluxome Gallery, San Francisco, 83; 18 Bay Area Artists, Art Mus, Univ Calif, Berkeley, 75; Whitney Biennial, Whitney Mus Am Art, 77; Tough Stuff, San Francisco Mus Mod Art, 83. *Pos:* Guest cur, Los Angeles Inst Contemp Art, Los Angeles, 78 & San Francisco Art Inst, 78; guest organizer, San Francisco Art Inst, 83. *Awards:* Nat Endowment Arts Grant, 75. *Bibliog:* Peter Frank (auth), On the Trail of the Exxon National, Nat Arts Guide, Vol 3, No 1, 81. *Mem:* San Francisco Art Inst (artist comt, artist trustee). *Media:* Cast Rhoplex, Oil/Acrylic. *Dealer:* Bluxome Gallery 173 Bluxome St San Francisco CA 94107. *Mailing Add:* 442 Shotwell St San Francisco CA 94110

MACKENZIE, HUGH SEAFORTH
PAINTER
b Toronto, Ont, June 19, 29. *Study:* Ont Col Art; Mt Allison Univ, BFA. *Work:* Montreal Mus Fine Arts, PQ; Art Gallery Ont, Toronto; Univ Waterloo; London Art Gallery, Ont; House of Commons, Ottawa. *Comn:* Portrait of L B Pearson, Ottawa Dept State, 68. *Exhib:* One-man shows, Morris Gallery, Toronto, 63-77 & Univ Waterloo, 75; Art Gallery Ont, 58-59, 61, 68 & 70; Montreal Mus Fine Arts, Que, 64 & 70; Ann Exhib Contemp Can Artists, Art Gallery of Hamilton, 70-72; Lithographs in collabr with NS Col Art, Nat Gallery Can, 71; Bau-Xi Gallery, Toronto, 81, 82 & 83. *Teaching:* Instr art, Ont Col Art, 68- *Awards:* J W G Forster Award, Ont Soc Artists, 61; Can Coun Award, 70. *Bibliog:* Dauct (auth), article, Arts Can, spring 72; Hale (auth), article, Arts Mag, 2/70; Duval (auth), High Realism in Canada, Irwin Clarke & Co, Ltd, 74. *Mem:* Assoc Royal Can Acad. *Media:* Tempera, Etching. *Mailing Add:* Ontario Col Art 100 McCaul St Toronto ON M5T 1W1 Canada

MCKESSON, MALCOLM FORBES
PAINTER, SCULPTOR
b Monmouth Beach, NJ, July 24, 09. *Study:* Harvard Col, AB(art), 33; Art Career Sch, 51-53; Art Students League, 55; NY Univ, MA(art educ), 56; NY State Teachers Col, New Paltz. *Exhib:* Nat Arts Club, 65-69; Lynchburg Art Ctr, 69; Burke Rehabilitation Ctr, White Plains, NY, 80; Town of Greenburgh, NY, 81; Twilight Artist, Twilight Park, Haines Falls, NY; and others. *Pos:* Pres, Eleanor Gay Lee Gallery Found, New York, NY. *Teaching:* Instr art, New York Pub Schs, 56-60. *Awards:* Art Comt Award in Oil Painting, Nat Arts Club, 76. *Mem:* Composers, Authors & Artists Am; Burr Artists. *Media:* Watercolor, Oil; Wood. *Interests:* Architectural and landscape subjects; construction of 1 1/2 ton sailing model of English historic galleon of 1610. *Mailing Add:* 22 E 29th St New York NY 10016

MCKIE, TODD STODDARD
PAINTER
b Boston, Mass, Apr 25, 44. *Study:* RI Sch Design, BFA(painting), 66. *Work:* Philip Morris, USA; Mass Inst Technol; Fogg Mus, Cambridge, Mass; Wellington Mgt Co, Boston; Lincoln Ctr for the Performing Arts, New York. *Comn:* Mural (90ft x 40ft), City of Boston, 72. *Exhib:* Eat Art, Contemp Art Ctr, Cintinnati, Ohio, 72; Boston Collects Boston, Mus Fine Arts, Boston, 73; Works on Paper, Fogg Art Mus, Harvard Univ, Cambridge, Mass, 74; Biennial Exhib, Whitney Mus Am Art, New York, 75; Painted in Boston, Inst of Contemp Art, Boston, 75; Boston Watercolor Today, Mus Fine Arts, Boston, 76; Collectors Collect Contemporary, Inst Contemp Art, Boston, 77. *Awards:* Colman Award, Blanche E Colman Found, 72; Creative Artists Fel, Mass Arts & Humanities Found, 74. *Bibliog:* Carl Belz (auth), The grid and the buffet, Art in Am, 3/72; David Greenberg (auth), Big art, Running Press, Philadelphia, 77. *Media:* Oil, watercolor and silkscreen. *Dealer:* Acquavella Gallery 18 E 79th St New York NY 10021; Krakow Gallery 7 Newbury St Boston MA 02116. *Mailing Add:* 484 Broadway New York NY 10013

MCKIM, WILLIAM WIND
PRINTMAKER, PAINTER

b Independence, Mo, May 13, 16. *Study:* Kansas City Art Inst, with Thomas Hart Benton & John S DeMartelly. *Work:* William Rockhill Nelson Gallery; Kansas City Art Inst. *Comn:* Wildlife panorama, Kansas City Mus, 62; lithograph, Midamerica Art Asn. *Exhib:* Art of Two Cities, Kansas City & Minneapolis, 66; one-man show, Kansas City Art Inst & Albrecht Gallery, St Joseph, Mo, 67-68; 10 Missouri Painters Traveling Exhib, 68-69; Mid Am Artists Exhib, St Louis & Kansas City, 68 & 70; Printmakers Traveling Exhib, 69. *Teaching:* Instr drawing, Kansas City Art Inst, 45-48, instr lithography, 48-58, prof lithography, 58- *Awards:* D M Lighton Award, Midwestern Ann, Kansas City, 40; New York State Fair Award. *Media:* Tempera, Acrylic. *Mailing Add:* 8704 E 32nd St Kansas City MO 64129

MCKININ, LAWRENCE
EDUCATOR, PAINTER

b Yukon, Pa, Aug 24, 17. *Study:* Wayne State Univ, BS, 39; Soc Arts & Crafts, Detroit, Mich, with John Carroll, 39-40; Univ Wis, summer 41; Cranbrook Acad Art, with Zoltan Sepeshy, MFA, 48; Inst Design, Chicago, summer 49; Handy & Harman Silversmithing Workshop, Sch Am Craftsmen, Rochester, NY, summer 50. *Work:* Vera Mott Mem Collection, Mo Hist Soc & Columbia Art League, Columbia, Mo. *Comn:* Portrait of O M Stewart & H M Reese, Univ Mo Physics Dept, Columbia, 67. *Exhib:* Seven shows, Springfield Art Mus Ann, 50-76; Midwest Exhib, Joslyn Mus, Omaha, Nebr, 51 & 52; American Jewelry and Related Objects, circulated by Smithsonian Inst, 55-57; Ten Missouri Painters II, Mo Arts Coun Circulation Exhib, 68-69; Watercolor USA, 74. *Pos:* Art ed, Archaeol Mag, 53-54. *Teaching:* Instr art, Univ Mo-Columbia, 48-50, asst prof art, 50-55, assoc prof art & chmn dept, 55-59, prof art, 59-80, prof emer, 80- *Awards:* Purchase Prize, Mid-Am Exhib, Nelson Gallery, Kansas City, Mo, 50; Purchase Prize for painting White Lake, Springfield Art Mus, 50; Award for design of bk, Fred Shane Drawings, Chicago Bk Clinic 16th Ann Exhib, 65. *Mem:* Mid-Am Col Art Asn. *Media:* Oil, Acrylic. *Publ:* Designer & art ed, Fred Shane Drawings, 65. *Mailing Add:* 1005 Belleview Ct Columbia MO 65201

MCKINNEY, DONALD
DEALER

b New York, NY, May 2, 31. *Study:* Columbia Univ, 54-57; London Univ, 60-62. *Pos:* Pres, Marlborough Gallery, New York, 74-78; dir, Hirschl & Adler Mod Galleries, 81- *Specialty:* Fine post-war and contemporary art. *Publ:* Contribr, Jackson Pollack Catalogue Raisonne, Yale Univ Press, 78; coauth, Mark Rothko, Kunsthaus Zurich, 71. *Mailing Add:* c/o Hirschl & Adler Mod Galleries 851 Madison Ave New York NY 10021

MCKINNICKINNICK, MARGARET I
PAINTER, PRINTMAKER

b Marlboro, Mass, Feb 2, 24. *Study:* Silvermine Guild Sch Art; lithography with Hiroshima Morimoto. *Work:* Town Hall, Westport, Conn; City Hall, Norwalk, Conn; Norwalk Community Col; Silvermine Ctr Arts. *Comn:* Etching, Friends Silvermine Ctr Arts, 80. *Exhib:* On a Small Scale, Silvermine Ctr Arts, 80; Berkshire Mus, Pittsfield, Mass, 81; two-person exhib, Hampshire Col Gallery, Adelphi Univ, 81; one-person exhib, Silvermine Ctr Arts, 82; Prints & Drawings Spring Show, Prize Art Barn, Greenwich, Conn, 83; Trustees Choice, Aldrich Mus, 83; and others. *Teaching:* Instr art, Mus Mod Art, New York, 65-69; Calhoun Sch, New York, 70-75 & Sacred Heart Univ, 81-83. *Awards:* Print Award, Berkshire Mus, Pittsfield, Mass, 81. *Bibliog:* Russell Jinishian (auth), Artist lays it on the line, Bridgeport Sunday Post, 9/25/83. *Mem:* Silvermine Guild Ctr Arts (mem bd trustees, 78-81); Westport-Weston Coun Arts. *Mailing Add:* 42 Maple Lane Greens Farms CT 06436

MACKLIN, ANDERSON D
ADMINISTRATOR, POTTER

b Luther, Okla, Jan 17, 33. *Study:* Lincoln Univ, Mo, with J D Parks, BS, 54; Univ Mo, with D Hanson & B Shane, MA, 56; Pa State Univ, with K Beittel & D Dontigney, PhD, 69. *Work:* Oils, Lincoln Univ, Jefferson City, Mo. *Exhib:* Dallas Mus Fine Arts Ann, 59; Atlanta Univ Ann, 60-70; Va Mus Biennial, 71; Lincoln Univ, Jefferson City, 73; Carriage House Gallery, Richmond, Va, 77; one-man show, Pa State Univ, pottery show, 67. *Teaching:* Prof art & ceramics, Va State Univ, 62- *Awards:* First Place, Cole Co Ann, Mo, 58; Purchase Award, Atlanta Univ Ann, 68. *Mem:* Nat Conf Artists; Nat Art Educ Asn; Va Art Educ Asn (vpres, 72-74). *Media:* Stoneware, Acrylic. *Mailing Add:* 11200 Rosewood Lane Ettrick VA 23803

MCKNIGHT, THOMAS FREDERICK
PAINTER, PRINTMAKER

b Lawrence, Kans, Jan 13, 41. *Study:* Wesleyan Univ, Middletown, Conn, BA(art); Columbia Univ. *Work:* Davison Art Ctr, Wesleyan Univ; New York State Mus, Albany; Smithsonian Inst, Washington, DC. *Exhib:* One-man shows, Basel Art Fair, 75-77, Tomic Galerie, Dusseldorf, Ger, 76, Hartmann Gallery, Munich, Ger, 77 & Newport Art Asn, RI, 81; Graphic Biennial, Llubljana, Yugoslavia, 81; and others. *Media:* Casein; Serigraphy, Intaglio. *Dealer:* Chalk & Vermilion Fine Arts Ltd Five E 57th St New York NY 10022. *Mailing Add:* 322 W 57th St Apt 33-S New York NY 10019

MCKOY, VICTOR GRAINGER
SCULPTOR

b Fayetteville, NC, Apr 21, 47. *Study:* Clemson Univ, BS(biology), 70, Sch of Archit, two years. *Work:* Charleston Mus, SC; Ward Found Mus, Salisbury State Col, Md; Gibbes Art Gallery, Charleston, SC. *Exhib:* Expressions of Nature in Art, Greenville Mus Art, SC, 75 & Columbia Mus Art, SC, 75; Bird Sculpture Birmingham Mus Art, Ala, 76; The Artist and the Animal, High Mus Art, Atlanta, Ga, 77; Wild America, Kodak Gallery, New York, 78; one-man show, Hammer Galleries, New York, 76; Coe Kerr Gallery, NY, 81; and others. *Bibliog:* Anne Small (auth), Masters of Decorative Bird Carving, Winchester Press; Rodger Schroder (auth), Grainger McKoys carved birds, Fine Wood Working Mag; Pat Robertson (auth), Oyster House connection, Sporting Classics Mag, 9/83. *Media:* Wood and oil paint. *Dealer:* Coe Kerr Gallery New York NY. *Mailing Add:* Rte 1 Box 42 Wadmalaw Island SC 29487

MACLAGGER, RICHARD JOSEPH
DEALER, COLLECTOR

b Utica, NY, Aug 8, 47. *Study:* Sch Visual Arts, New York, cert, 71; New Sch Social Res, 72-74. *Pos:* Asst, Rosa Esman Gallery, New York, 72-75; coordr, Artist Rights Today, New York, 74-75; dir ed, Gallerie Denise Rene, New York, 75-78; dir, Neill Gallery, New York, 78-81; co-dir, Fred Dorfman Contemporary Art Publ, currently. *Specialty:* Contemporary painting and sculpture. *Collection:* Contemporary paintings, drawings and graphics. *Mailing Add:* 50 Grand St New York NY 10013

MCLANATHAN, RICHARD B K
CONSULTANT, WRITER

b Methuen, Mass, Mar 12, 16. *Study:* Harvard Univ, AB, 38, grad sch, 41-43, Soc fels, 43-46, PhD, 51. *Collections Arranged:* The M & M Karolik Collection of American Paintings, 1815-1865, Mus Fine Arts, Boston, 49; Art Across America, Munson-Williams-Proctor Inst, Utica, 60; Romantic Am, The Middle Decades of the 19th Century, Tampa Mus, Fla, 79. *Pos:* Secy mus, Mus Fine Arts, Boston, 52-56, ed publ, 52-57, cur decorative arts, 54-57; dir mus art, Munson-Williams-Proctor Inst, 57-61; cur art exhib, Am Nat Exhib, Moscow, 59; mem, NY State Coun Arts, 60-64; mem, NY State Comnr Comt Art & Mus Resources, 60-66; dir, Am Asn Mus, 76-78. *Awards:* Prix de Rome, Am Acad Rome, 48; Distinguished Serv Award, US Info Agency, 59; Sr Rockefeller Fel, Metrop Mus Art, 75. *Mem:* Am Asn Mus; Northeast Conf Am Mus Asn; NY State Mus Asn; Asn of Fels of Am Acad Rome. *Res:* Medieval art; renaissance art, especially Italian; American arts; modern art. *Publ:* A Guide to Civilisation, the Kenneth Clark Films on the Cultural Life of Western Man, 70; Art in America, A Brief History, 73; auth, The Art of Marguerita Stix, 77; East Building, National Gallery of Art: A Profile, 78; auth, World Art in American Mus, A Personal Guide, 83; and others. *Mailing Add:* The Stone Sch House Phippsburg ME 04562

MCLAREN, NORMAN
FILMMAKER

b Stirling, Scotland, Apr 11, 14; Can citizen. *Study:* Glasgow Sch Art, Scotland. *Work:* Nat Gallery Can, Ottawa. *Pos:* Film dir, Nat Film Bd Can, 41- *Awards:* Motion Picture Acad Oscar for Neighbors, 52; Award for Blinkity Blank, Grand Prix, Cannes, France, 55; Outstanding Achievement Award, Can Govt, 72. *Bibliog:* M E Cutler (auth), Unique genius of Norman McLaren, Can Art, 5-6/65; Laurence Elliott (auth), Norman McLaren, gentle genius of the screen, Reader's Digest, 8/71; Maynard Collins (auth), Norman McLaren, Can Film Inst, 76. *Mem:* Academician Royal Can Acad Art. *Publ:* Auth, Cameraless animation, 58; illusr, Six musical forms, Jeunesses Musicales, Montreal, 67; illusr, Interplay, Mutations, Graphic Guild, Montreal, 71; auth, The Drawings of Norman McLaren, Tundra Bks, Montreal, 75. *Mailing Add:* PO Box 730 Hudson PQ J0P 1H0 Canada

MCLARTY, WILLIAM JAMES (JACK)
PAINTER, PRINTMAKER

b Seattle, Wash, Apr 24, 19. *Study:* Mus Art Sch, Portland, Ore; Am Art Sch, NY; also with Anton Refregier & Joseph Solman. *Comn:* Murals, Collins-View Sch, Laurelhurst Sch, Riverdale Sch, Ridgewood Sch, Portland & Portland Civic Auditorium. *Exhib:* Recent Paintings: USA, Mus Mod Art, 62-63; 20 yr retrospective, Portland Art Mus, 63; 1st & 2nd Int Miniature Print Exhib, Pratt Graphic Art Ctr, NY, 64; Nat Drawing Soc Exhib, 70-72; Art of the Pacific Northwest, Smithsonian Inst, 74. *Teaching:* Instr advan woodcut & painting, drawing & compos, Portland Mus Art Sch, currently. *Awards:* Purchase Prize, Lewis & Clark Col Invitational, Portland, 65; Prize, Northwest Printmakers, Seattle, 66; Artists of Ore Award, 70. *Bibliog:* Jack McLarty, Painter as Poet, Stepping Out NW, summer, 82. *Publ:* Auth, Seventeen love poems, Image Gallery, 67; contribr, Prize-winning graphics, 67; Northwest review, 67; Of Wind and Pines, 77, Image Gallery & To his coy mistress, Marvell, 73. *Mailing Add:* 1525 NW 24th Portland OR 97210

MACLAY, DAVID (SEARS), JR
PHOTOGRAPHER, SCULPTOR

b Boston, Mass, June 27, 46. *Study:* Sch Mus Fine Arts, Boston, 64-67, dipl, 72; San Francisco Art Inst, BFA, 68. *Comn:* Sculpture, Bundy Gallery, Waitsfield, Vt, 78; Maze, New Gallery, Cleveland, Ohio, 80. *Exhib:* Eighteen Bay Area Artists, Los Angeles Inst Contemp Arts & Berkeley Mus, Calif, 76-77; Invented Landscape, New Mus, New York, 79. *Awards:* Furgeson Award, Friends of Photog, 79; Nat Endowment Arts, 80. *Dealer:* Grapestake Gallery 2876 California St San Francisco CA 94115. *Mailing Add:* 83 Converse St San Francisco CA 94103

MACLEAN, ARTHUR
PAINTER

b New York, NY. *Study:* Nat Acad Design, New York; Art Students League; Grand Cent Art Sch. *Exhib:* Nat Acad Design, 60-70 & 75; Allied Artists Am, 60-81; Hudson Valley Art Asn, 60-81; Knickerbocker Artists, 60-72; Acad Artists, 60-68 & 75-79; and others. *Awards:* William McKillop Prize, 74 & 77 & Helen C Nelson Award, 76, Kent Art Asn; Coun Am Artist Soc Award, Allied Artists Am, 75; Irene Rickenback Mem Award, Hudson Valley Art Asn, 77; and many others. *Mem:* Allied Artists; Hudson Valley Art Asn; Kent Art Asn; Acad Artists. *Mailing Add:* 84 South Ave New Canaan CT 06840

MCLEAN, JAMES ALBERT
EDUCATOR, PRINTMAKER
b Gibsland, La, Nov 25, 28. *Study:* Southwestern La Inst, AB, 50; Southern Methodist Univ, BD, 53; Tulane Univ, MFA with J L Steg, 61. *Work:* Seattle Mus Art, Wash; The High Mus, Atlanta, Ga; Brooklyn Mus, NY; Olivet Col, Mich; Minot State Col, ND. *Exhib:* 33rd, 35th, 36th & 38th Northwest Printmakers Int, Seattle Mus, Wash, 62, 64, 65 & 67; 14th, 15th, 19th & 20th Nat Print Exhibs, Brooklyn Mus, 64, 66, 74 & 76; Nat Print & Drawing Exhibs, Minot State Col, 73-76; Colorprint, USA, Tex Tech Univ, Lubbock, 74-76. *Teaching:* Assoc prof gen art, LaGrange Col, Ga, 63-66; prof printmaking, Ga State Univ, Atlanta, 66- *Awards:* Purchase Award, Northwest Printmakers Int, 64, Western NMex Univ Nat Print Exhib, 73 & Minot State Col Nat Print & Drawing Exhib, 76. *Bibliog:* Illus in: Fritz Eichenberg (auth), The Art of the Print, Abrams, 76, Gene Baro (auth), 30 Years of American Printmaking, Brooklyn Mus. *Media:* Photoengraving. *Dealer:* Heath Gallery 416 E Paces Ferry Atlanta GA 30305. *Mailing Add:* 3509 Cold Spring Lane Chamblee GA 30341

MCLEAN, RICHARD THORPE
PAINTER, EDUCATOR
b Hoquiam, Wash, Apr 12, 34. *Study:* Calif Col Arts & Crafts, BFA, 58; Mills Col, MFA, 62. *Work:* Guggenheim Mus, New York; Whitney Mus Am Art, New York; Va Mus Fine Arts, Richmond; Utrecht Mus, Holland; Mus Boymans-Van Beuningen, Rotterdam. *Exhib:* 22 Realists, Whitney Mus Am Art, 70; Sharp Focus Realism, Sidney Janis Gallery, New York, 72; Documenta 5, Kassel, Ger, 72; Working in Calif, Albright-Knox Art Gallery, Buffalo, NY, 72; Tokyo Biennale, 74; New/Photo Realism, Wadsworth Atheneum, Hartford, Conn, 74; Contemp Images in Watercolor, Akron Art Inst, Ohio, 76; Painting & Sculpture in Calif: The Mod Era, San Francisco Mus Mod Art & Smithsonian Inst, 76; Thirty Yrs of Am Art, 1945-1975, Whitney Mus Am Art, New York, 77; and many others. *Teaching:* Prof painting & drawing, San Francisco State Univ, 63- *Bibliog:* Alwynne Mackie (illus), New realism and the photographic look, Am Art Rev, 11/78; Christine Lindey (illus), Superrealist Painting & Sculpture, William Morrow & Co, 80; Louis K Meisel (auth), Photorealism, Harry N Abrams, 80. *Media:* Oil, Watercolor. *Dealer:* O K Harris Works of Art 383 W Broadway New York NY 10012. *Mailing Add:* 5840 Heron Dr Oakland CA 94618

MACLEAN-SMITH, ELIZABETH
SCULPTOR, LECTURER
b Springfield, Mass, Feb 18, 16. *Study:* Wellesley Col, AB; Belgian-Am Educ Found Traveling Fel, Belg, 37; Boston Mus Sch, with Frederick Warren Allen, Sturdivant Traveling Fel, Mex, 41. *Work:* Mus Fine Arts, Boston; Mus Fine Arts, Springfield, Mass; Williams Col, Williamstown, Mass. *Comn:* Polyester murals, Dini's Sea Grill, Boston, 62-70. *Exhib:* One-man shows, G W V Smith Mus, Springfield, 50, Tufts Col, Medford, Mass, 52, Crane Mus, Pittsfield, Mass, 56 & McIver-Ready Gallery, Boston, 68; New England Sculptor's Asn, Prudential Ctr, Boston, 68 & 70; and others. *Teaching:* Instr sculpture, Boston Mus Sch, 40-53; instr sculpture, Bradford Jr Col, 3 yrs. *Mem:* Fel Nat Sculpture Soc; New Eng Sculptor's Asn. *Media:* Stone, Clay. *Mailing Add:* 92 Russell St Charlestown MA 02129

MCMAHON, JAMES EDWARD
DEALER
b New York, NY, Jan 1, 37. *Study:* Hofstra Col, BA. *Pos:* Owner, Gallery Madison 90, currently. *Specialty:* American art of the 19th and 20th centuries; American illustrators. *Mailing Add:* Gallery Madison 90 1248 Madison Ave New York NY 10028

MCMANUS, JAMES WILLIAM
SCULPTOR, GALLERY DIRECTOR
b Glenwood Springs, Colo, Jan 1, 42. *Study:* Colo State Univ, BFA, 65; Univ Wash, MFA, 67. *Work:* Oakland Art Mus; San Diego Art Mus, Calif; Reading Art Ctr, Eng; Henry Art Mus, Univ Wash; 3M Corp, Chicago. *Comn:* Expo '74, Spokane, Wash; Admin Bldg, Wash State Hwy Comn, Olympia; Electro-Develop Corp, Seattle. *Exhib:* Six-man traveling exhib, Brit Art Coun, 73-75; Allrich Gallery, San Francisco, 77; Selected Works 1967-1977, de Saisset Mus, Univ Santa Clara, Calif, 77; Calif State Univ, Fresno, 77; Allrich Gallery, San Francisco, 79; Oakland Art Mus, 81. *Collections Arranged:* California Realism, 19th & 20th Century Comparison, 78; Mel Ramos, 79; Stanton Macdonald Wright, 80; Adja Yunkers, 80; Robin's Burghers of Calais, 81; Alice Hutchins Survey, 82. *Teaching:* Teaching asst, Univ Wash, 67, instr art, 67-68; prof art & gallery dir, Calif State Univ, Chico, 68-; vis prof art, High Wycombe Col Art, Eng, 71-72. *Awards:* Fac Res Grant, Calif State Univ, Chico, 69; Fulbright-Hays Grant, Eng, 72. *Bibliog:* John Marlowe (auth), article, Current Art Mag, 6/75; James W McManus (30 min video tape), Calif State Univ, Chico, 77; Kevin Star (auth), article, San Francisco Examiner, 11/18/79; and others. *Media:* Bronze, Steel, Aluminum. *Dealer:* Allrich Gallery 251 Post St San Francisco CA 94133. *Mailing Add:* 1734 Mangrove Chico CA 95926

MCMILLAN, CONSTANCE
PAINTER, ILLUSTRATOR
b Millinocket, Maine, Mar 10, 24. *Study:* Bennington Col, painting with Karl Knaths & sculpture with Simon Moselsio, BA, 46; Colorado Springs Fine Arts Ctr, with Boardman Robinson, 46; Mills Col, fel, 53-55, art hist with Alfred Neumeyer & ceramic sculpture with Antonio Prieto, MA, 55. *Exhib:* One-person shows, Morris Gallery, New York, New York, every two yrs, 59-74; Alternate Space Gallery at Westbroadway, 79-80; Slusser Gallery, Univ Mich, Ann Arbor, 80; West Broadway Gallery, New York, 80, 82 & 84; and others. *Teaching:* Instr painting, design & art hist, San

Luis Sch, Colorado Springs, 49-51; instr painting, design & art hist, Emma Willard Sch, Troy, NY, 52-53; instr painting & design, Angel Sch, Ann Arbor, 62-63. *Awards:* First Prize, Morris Gallery, 56; First & Hon Mention Awards, Mich Watercolor Soc Ann, 67 & 68. *Mem:* Am Fedn Arts; Ann Arbor Art Asn. *Media:* Oil, Gouache; Charcoal, Pastel. *Publ:* Illusr, Chikka, 62, Ponies for a King, 63, Reilly & Lee; illusr, Memory of a Large Christmas, Norton, 62; drawing reproduced record cover, Gateway Summer Sounds, Folkways Records. *Dealer:* Westbroadway Gallery 431 W Broadway New York NY 10012. *Mailing Add:* 2760 Heather Way Ann Arbor MI 48104

MCMILLAN, JERRY EDWARD
PHOTOGRAPHER, SCULPTOR
b Oklahoma City, Okla, Dec 7, 36. *Study:* Oklahoma City Univ; Chouinard Art Inst, Los Angeles, Calif. *Work:* Norton Simon Mus, Pasadena, Calif; Des Moines Art Mus, Iowa; Ft Worth Art Mus, Tex; San Francisco Mus Art, Calif; La Jolla Mus Contemp Art, Calif. *Exhib:* Photog into Sculpture, Mus Mod Art, New York, 70; Calif Painting & Sculpture: The Mod Era, 76; one-man shows, Norton Simon Mus, Pasadena, Des Moines Art Ctr, Ft Worth Art Mus, San Francisco Mus Art, La Jolla Mus Contemp Art & Newport Harbor Art Mus, Calif. *Teaching:* Instr photog, Calif State Univ, Northridge, 70-80 & Univ Calif, Los Angeles Exten, 70-80. *Media:* Miscellaneous. *Mailing Add:* 1024 1/4 N Western Ave Los Angeles CA 90029

MCMILLAN, ROBERT W
PAINTER, EDUCATOR
b Belleville, Ill, Jan 22, 15. *Study:* Southern Ill Univ, BEd, 37; Columbia Univ, MA, 40; Washington Univ, 48; Univ Iowa, PhD, 58. *Exhib:* Brooklyn Mus, 40; Joslyn Mem Mus, Omaha, Nebr, 44; St Louis City Mus, 47; Cincinnati Mus, 56; Des Moines Art Ctr, 64; and others. *Pos:* Dir, Schaeffer Gallery, Grinnell Col, 60-69. *Teaching:* Instr art, Univ Kansas City, 46-48; prof, Southern Ill Univ, Carbondale, 50-60; prof, Grinnell Col, 60-69, chmn dept art, 61-68; prof art, Univ Ariz, 69-, head dept, 69-76. *Mailing Add:* Dept Art Univ of Ariz Tucson AZ 85721

MCMILLAN, STEPHEN WALKER
PRINTMAKER, PHOTOGRAPHER
b Berkeley, Calif, Dec 21, 49. *Study:* Hornsey Col Art, London, Eng, 70-71; Univ Calif, Santa Cruz, AB, 72, BFA, 75. *Work:* Brooklyn Mus, NY; Achenbach Collection, San Francisco; Oakland Mus, Calif; Mem Mus, Petah-Tiqua, Israel; US Embassy, Tokyo, Japan; and others. *Exhib:* US Info Agency Two Yr Traveling Exhib in 8 Japanese Cities, US Embassy, Tokyo, 77-78; 21st Nat Print Exhib, Brooklyn Mus, 78; 17th Bradley Nat Print & Drawing Exhib, Lakeview Mus, Peoria, Ill, 79; 31st Ann Boston Printmakers Exhib, De Cordova Mus, Lincoln, Mass, 79; New Aquisitions, Achenbach Collection, San Francisco, 80; 4th Miami Int Print Biennial, Metrop Mus, Miami, Fla, 80. *Teaching:* Instr, Kala Inst, Berkeley, currently. *Awards:* Purchase Awards, San Francisco Art Comn, 78, Davidson Gallery, Seattle, Wash, 78 & Los Angeles Printmaking Soc, 78. *Mem:* Calif Soc Printmakers. *Media:* Etching, Lithograph. *Mailing Add:* 1814 Blake 3 Berkeley CA 94703

MCMILLEN, MICHAEL C(HALMERS)
ENVIRONMENTAL ARTIST, SCULPTOR
b Los Angeles, Calif, Apr 6, 46. *Study:* Calif State Univ, Northridge, BA; Univ Calif, Los Angeles, MA & MFA. *Work:* Australian Nat Gallery, Canberra; Art Gallery New South Wales, Australia; Los Angeles Co Mus Art; Oakland Mus, Calif; Guggenheim Mus, New York. *Exhib:* Eight Artists from Los Angeles, San Francisco Art Inst, Calif, 75; Sounds: Environments by Four Artists, Newport Harbor Art Mus, Newport Beach, Calif, 75; Biennial of Sydney, Art Gallery New South Wales, Australia, 76; Los Angeles in the 70s, Ft Worth Art Mus, Tex, 77; one-man shows, Inner City, Los Angeles Co Mus, Los Angeles, 77 & Whitney Mus Am Art, New York, 78; Eight Artists: The Elusive Image, Walker Art Ctr, Minneapolis, 79; Art in Los Angeles-The Museum as Site, Los Angeles Co Mus, 81; New Perspectives in American Art: Exxon Nat Exhib, Guggenheim Mus, 83; 38th Corcoran Biennial: Exhibition of American Painting, Corcoran Gallery Art, 83. *Teaching:* Lectr at var inst, 74- *Awards:* travel grant, Biennale of Sydney, Australia Coun, 76; Nat Endowment Arts Fel, 78; Young Talent Award, Los Angeles Co Mus Art, 78. *Bibliog:* Melinda Wortz (auth), Inner City of the Mind, Art News, 2/78; Christopher Knight (auth), Some recent art and archit analogue, Los Angeles Inst Contemp Art J, 2/78; Christopher Knight (auth), Michael C McMillen, Arts & Archit, Fall 83. *Publ:* Auth, True confessions, Los Angeles Inst Contemp Art J, 75; contribr, Choke, Choke Publ, 76; auth, Special effects breakdown, Los Angeles Inst Contemp Art J, 77. *Mailing Add:* 906 Princeton St Santa Monica CA 90403

MCNALLY, SHEILA JOHN
EDUCATOR, HISTORIAN
b New York, NY, Dec 10, 32. *Study:* Vassar Col, BA; Univ London; Univ Kiel; Univ Munich; Harvard Univ, PhD, 65. *Pos:* Prin investr, Excavations Diocletian's Palace, Split, Yugoslavia, 68-; dir, Excavations, Akhmim, Egypt, 78- *Teaching:* Prof art hist, Univ Minn, Minneapolis, currently. *Awards:* Fulbright Res Grants, Ger, 53-54 & Yugoslavia, 67-68. *Mem:* Col Art Asn (bd dirs, 75-79); Midwest Art Hist Soc; Archaeol Inst Am; Libyan Soc; Women's Archaeol Caucus. *Res:* Late Roman art. *Mailing Add:* Dept Art Hist 108 Jones Hall Univ Minn Minneapolis MN 55455

MCNAMARA, JOHN STEPHEN
PAINTER
b Cambridge, Mass, Feb 16, 50. *Study:* Mass Col Art, BFA(painting), 71, MFA(painting), 77. *Work:* Mus Fine Arts, Boston; Rose Art Mus, Brandeis Univ; De Cordova Mus, Lincoln, Mass; Mass Inst Technol; Fitchburg Mus,

Mass. *Exhib:* Epic Abstractionists, Fitchburg Art Mus, Mass, 81; Boston Now, Inst Contemp Art, Boston, 81-83; one-man show, Exhib Space, New York, 82, Stavaridis Gallery, Boston, 83 & Bess Cutler Gallery, New York, 84; Awards in the Visual Arts, Mus Contemp Art, Chicago, 83 & Mint Mus Contemp Art, Charlotte, NC, 83. *Teaching:* Instr, Mass Col Art, currently. *Awards:* Mass Arts & Humanities Grant, 80-83; Nat Endowment Arts Fel, 81; Awards in Visual Arts II Fel, 82. *Bibliog:* Bonnie Saulnier (auth), John McNamara's cathedrals, New Boston Rev, 6-7/80; Carl Belz (auth), John McNamara, Arts Mag, 11/82; Theodore Wolff (auth), The home forum, Christian Sci Monitor, 4/7/83. *Media:* Oil on Canvas. *Dealer:* Bess Cutler Gallery 164 Mercer St New York NY 10012; Stavaridis Gallery 73 Newbury St Boston MA 02116. *Mailing Add:* 16 Addington Rd Brookline MA 02116

MCNAMARA, MARY JO
HISTORIAN, EDUCATOR
b Troy, NY, Jan 23, 50. *Study:* Vassar Col, AB, 72; Stanford Univ, MA, 75. *Pos:* Cur, Vassar Col Art Gallery, 76-78. *Teaching:* Instr art hist, Vassar Col, Poughkeepsie, NY, 76-78; lectr, Univ Wis-Milwaukee, 78-79; instr, Oberlin Col, Ohio, 79-80; acting asst prof, Univ Calif, Irvine, 80- *Awards:* Cantor-Fitzgerald res grant, 75-76. *Mem:* Col Art Asn. *Res:* Modern Art. *Publ:* Coauth, Rodin's Burghers of Calais, The Cantor-Fitzgerald Group, Los Angeles, 77. *Mailing Add:* c/o Art Hist Dept Univ Calif Irvine CA 92717

MCNAMARA, WILLIAM PATRICK, JR
PAINTER, PRINTMAKER
b Shreveport, La, Sept 3, 46. *Study:* Centenary Col La, BA, 69; NMex Highlands Univ, MA, 72. *Work:* Centenary Col La; First Nat Banks, Shreveport, La, Idabel, Okla & Broken Bow, Okla; Forest Heritage Ctr, Beaver's Bend, Okla. *Exhib:* La Waatercolor Soc Ann Exhib, Baton Rouge, La, 80; Delta Art Exhib, Ark Arts Ctr, Little Rock, 80 & 81; Watercolor USA, Springfield Art Mus, Mo, 80, 82 & 83; Butler Inst Am Art, 82 & 83. *Teaching:* Instr drawing & composition, Centenary Col La, 73-76. *Awards:* Award Merit, Watercolor USA, Springfield Art Mus, Mo, 80. *Bibliog:* M Stephen Doherty (auth), Watercolor today: Ten contemporary artists, Am Artist, 2/83. *Media:* Watercolor. *Publ:* Auth, Watercolor page, Am Artist, 5/83. *Dealer:* Moulton Galleries 501 Garrison Ft Smith AR 72913; Capricorn Galleries 4849 Rugby Bethesda MD 20014. *Mailing Add:* Star Route 1 Pettigrew AR 72752

MCNARY, OSCAR L
PAINTER
b San Antonio, Tex, Mar 23, 44. *Study:* San Antonio Jr Col, Tex; Tex Southern Univ; Southern Methodist Univ; Warren Hunter's Sch Art. *Exhib:* One-man shows, Works on Paper & Canvas, Promenade Nat Bank, Richardson, Tex, 76, Resurgence Series, Phoenix Cultural Arts Ctr, Atlanta, Ga, 79 & Mis Media, Arthello's Gallery, Dallas, Tex, 80; 15th Joslyn Biennial, Joslyn Art Mus, Omaha, 78; First Int Art Exhib, Int Soc Artists, Nat Arts Club, New York, 78; Richardson Civic Art Soc Regional Juried Painting & Sculpture Show, 80; 37th Ann Nat Painting Competition, The Abilene Fine Arts Mus, Tex, 81. *Awards:* First Place Citation Award, Tex Fine Arts Asn Region II, 75; Purchase Award, 2nd Ann Black SW Art Exhib, SW Res Ctr & Mus, Bishop Col, 78; Best of Show Award, Art Community Ctr, Corpus Christy, 78. *Bibliog:* Article, Art Voices South, 9-10/80. *Mem:* Assoc Am Watercolor Soc; Artists Coalition of Tex ; Richardson Civic Art Soc; Phoenix Cult Art Ctr. *Mailing Add:* 1308 Timberlake Cir Richardson TX 75080

MCNEAR, EVERETT C
PAINTER, DESIGNER
b Minneapolis, Minn, Sept 30, 04. *Study:* Minneapolis Sch Art, with Cameron Booth; also with Edmund Kinzinger & Louis Marcoussis. *Comn:* Mosaic panels, Skiles Sch, Evanston, Ill, 59; mural, Perkins & Will Partnership. *Exhib:* Art Inst Chicago; Pa Acad Fine Arts; one-man shows, San Francisco Mus Art, 46; Walker Art Ctr, Minneapolis, 48; group show, 61, Painter, Designer, Collector, 75 & Drawings, 81, Univ Notre Dame Gallery; plus others. *Pos:* Design consult, Art Inst Chicago, 58-; consult mus design & installation of permanent collection, Snite Mus Art, 78-80. *Awards:* Medal, Art Dirs Club, Chicago, 50 & 55; Prizes, Art Guild, 51, 55, 57 & 58 & Ill State Mus, 60; plus others. *Mem:* Arts Club Chicago; 27 Designers; life trustee Art Inst Chicago. *Collection:* Manuscripts; primitive art; Cubist paintings and prints; Persian and Indian miniatures. *Publ:* Illusr, Many a Green Isle, 41 & Young Eye Seeing, 56; contribr, Bull Atomic Scientists & Am Artist Mag. *Mailing Add:* 1448 Lake Shore Dr Chicago IL 60610

MCNEIL, GEORGE J
PAINTER, PRINTMAKER
b New York, NY, Feb 22, 08. *Study:* Pratt Inst, Brooklyn, 27-29; Art Students League, 30-31 & 32-33; Hans Hofmann Sch Fine Art, 33-36; Teachers Col, Columbia Univ, MA, 43, EdD, 52. *Work:* Mus Mod Art, New York, Havana, Cuba; Newark Mus Art; Walker Art Ctr, Minneapolis; Whitney Mus Am Art; plus others. *Exhib:* Mus Mod Art, New York, 36, 51, 63-64 & 69; Whitney Mus Am Art Ann, 53, 57, 61 & 65, The 1930s, 68; US Info Agency Pan-Am Exhib, circulated Latin Am, 61-62; Pa Acad Fine Arts, 62; Wadsworth Atheneum, Hartford, Conn, 62; Art Inst Chicago, 63; plus many other group & one-man shows. *Awards:* Nat Coun Arts Award, 66; Guggenheim Fel, 69; Am Acad Arts & Lett Award, 82. *Mailing Add:* 195 Waverly Ave Brooklyn NY 11205

MACNELLY, JEFFREY KENNETH
CARTOONIST
b New York, NY, Sept 17, 47. *Study:* Univ NC. *Pos:* Mem staff, Richmond News Leader, 70-81; creator, comic strip Shoe, currently. *Awards:* Pulitzer Prize as Editorial Cartoonist, 72 & 78. *Media:* India Ink, Watercolor. *Publ:* Auth, MacNelly, The Pulitzer Prize Winning Cartoonist: a Specially Selected Collection, Westover, 72. *Mailing Add:* 333 E Grace St Richmond VA 23219

MCNICKLE, THOMAS GLEN
PAINTER
b New Castle, Pa, Oct 17, 44. *Study:* Edinboro State Col, BS(art), 66, MEd(studio), 72. *Work:* Butler Inst Am Art; Hoyt Inst Fine Art, New Castle, Pa. *Exhib:* Marietta Nat, Marietta Col, 80; Audubon Artists Ann, Nat Arts Club, New York, 80, 81 & 82; Nat Watercolor Soc Ann Exhib, Los Angeles, 81; San Diego Watercolor Soc Int, 81, 82 & 83; Views of Youngstown, Butler Inst Am Art, 82; Am Artists Prof League Grande Nat, New York, 82 & 83. *Collections Arranged:* Forty Watercolors (auth, catalog), from collection Butler Inst Am Art, 82; Hoyt Nat Painting Show (auth, catalog), 82 & 83. *Teaching:* Instr art, Weshannock Twp Schs, New Castle, Pa, 66-; instr painting, Hoyt Inst Fine Art, New Castle, Pa, 66-; private workshops watercolors, 79- *Awards:* Award Excellence, Black Forest Inst, Exhib, 82; Second Prize Watercolor, Terrance Gallery Nat Exhib, 82; Award Merit, Nat Arts Club Watercolor Ann, New York, 82. *Mem:* Nat Watercolor Soc; Pa Soc Watercolor Painters; Pittsburgh Watercolor Soc (bd dirs, 83); Knickerbocker Artists, New York. *Media:* Watercolor. *Mailing Add:* 3009 Fernwood Lane New Castle PA 16105

MCNULTY, KNEELAND
CURATOR, WRITER
b Soochow, Ku, China, Oct 25, 21; US citizen. *Study:* Princeton Univ, AB, 43; Harvard Univ Grad Sch; Columbia Univ, MLS, 52. *Collections Arranged:* The Lithographs of Jean DuBuffet (with catalog), 64; Master E S: Five Hundreth Anniversary (with catalog), 67; Mauricio Lansansky: The Nazi Drawings (with catalog), 67. *Pos:* Rare book cataloger, Houghton Libr, Harvard Univ, 46-47; apprentice in prints, Philadelphia Mus Art, 47-49; asst librarian, NY Pub Libr, 49-52; asst & assoc cur prints, Philadelphia Mus Art, 52-63, cur prints, drawings & photographs, 64-80; retired, 80. *Teaching:* Distinguished vis prof, Univ Tex, Austin, 78. *Mem:* Print Club Philadelphia. *Publ:* Auth, Ben Shahn: Graphic Work, 67; ed, Suzuki Harunobu, 70; auth, Foreigners in Japan: Yokohama and Related Woodcuts, 72; ed, The Theatrical World of Osaka Prints, 73; auth, Peter Milton: Complete Etchings, 77. *Mailing Add:* Star Route Box 555 Sandia Park NM 87047

MACNUTT, GLENN GORDON
PAINTER, ILLUSTRATOR
b London, Ont, Jan 21, 06; US citizen. *Study:* Sch Mus Fine Arts, Boston, 30-32; Mass Sch Art, Boston, 24-28. *Work:* Boston Mus Fine Arts; Mus Am Art, Hartford, Conn; Tufts Univ; Frye Mus, Seattle; Harvard Univ; and others. *Exhib:* One-man shows, Guild Boston Artists, 40-41, 43 & 75, Whistler House, 42, Wellesley Col, Doll & Richards Gallery, 47; Metrop Mus, 41-42; Pa Acad Fine Arts, 42-52; Los Angeles Pub Libr, 54. *Awards:* Ford Times Award, 72 & C R Kinghan Award, 73, Am Watercolor Soc; Frank Liljegren Award, Allied Artists Am, 72; and others. *Mem:* Boston Soc Watercolor Painters (vpres, secy-treas, 45-48); Guild Boston Artists (bd mgrs); Am Watercolor Soc; Nat Acad Design; Allied Artists Am. *Mailing Add:* 129 Minot St Dorchester MA 02122

MACOMBER, WILLIAM B
ADMINISTRATOR
b Rochester, NY, Mar 28, 21. *Study:* Yale Univ, AB, 43, MA, 47; Harvard Univ, LLB, 49; Univ Chicago, MA, 51. *Pos:* Pres, Metrop Mus Art, New York, 78- *Mailing Add:* Metrop Mus of Art 5th Ave at 82nd St New York NY 10028

MCPHERSON, BRUCE RICE
EDITOR, PUBLISHER
b Atlanta, Ga, Oct 12, 51. *Study:* Brown Univ, AB, 73; Annenberg Sch Commun, Univ Pa, 75. *Pos:* Ed & publ, McPherson & Co (Documentext, Treacle Press), 74- *Res:* Avant-Garde, 1958-present, principally United States, especially concerned with happenings, fluxus, performance art, and related areas. *Publ:* Ed, More than Meat Joy: Complete Performance Works and Selected Writings, by Carolee Schneemann, 79 & Something Else Press: An Annotated Bibliography, by Peter Frank, 82, Documentext. *Mailing Add:* PO Box 638 New Paltz NY 12561

MCPHERSON, LARRY E
PHOTOGRAPHER, EDUCATOR
b Newark, Ohio, May 1, 43. *Study:* Ohio State Univ, 61-65; Rochester Inst Technol, 65-66; Columbia Col, Chicago, BA, 76; Northern Ill Univ, MA, 78. *Work:* Mus Mod Art, New York; Art Inst Chicago & Exchange Nat Bank, Chicago, Ill; Int Mus Photog at George Eastman House, Rochester, NY; New Orleans Mus Art, La. *Exhib:* One-man shows, Art Inst Chicago, Ill, 69, 78 & 81; Vision and Expression, George Eastman House, Rochester, NY, 69; Mirrors & Windows, Mus Mod Art, New York, 78; Farbwerke, Kunsthaus Gallery, Zurich, Switzerland, 80; Contemp Am Color, Galerie Rudolf Kicken, Koln, Germany, 80; Color as Form: A History of Color Photography, Corcoran Gallery & George Eastman House, 82. *Teaching:* Asst prof photog, Memphis State Univ, Tenn, 78- *Awards:* Nat Endowment Arts Fel Photog, 75 & 79; Guggenheim Fel Photog, 80. *Bibliog:* Nathan Lyons (auth), Vision and Expression, Horizon Press, 69; Candida Finkel (auth), review, Afterimage, 10/78; Elaine King (auth), article, Camera Mag, 80. *Mem:* Soc Photog Educ. *Dealer:* Rhona Hoffman Gallery 215 West Superior Street Chicago IL 60610. *Mailing Add:* 4595 Buffer Drive Memphis TN 38128

MCQUILLAN, FRANCES
PAINTER, INSTRUCTOR
b Chicago, Ill. *Study:* New York Sch Fine & Appl Art, dipl; Caldwell Col, BA; Art Students League; Fairleigh Dickinson Univ; Montclair Art Mus Adult Sch. *Exhib:* Conn Acad Fine Arts; Allied Artists Am; Expos Intercontinental

Exhib, Dieppe, France & Monaco; Am Artists Prof League; Montclair Art Mus Exhib. *Pos:* Illusr, Peerless Fashions, New York, 32-37; freelance window display, New York, 38-39. *Teaching:* Instr drawing, watercolors, oils & acrylics, Montclair Art Mus, NJ, 50-; instr drawing, Montclair Adult Sch, 67-70; instr oil painting, Yard Sch Art, Montclair, 67-70 & 83. *Awards:* Silver Medal Oil Painting, Knickerbocker Artists, 53; First Prize Watercolors, Am Artists Prof League, 70; First Prize Oils, Art Ctr of NJ. *Mem:* NJ Watercolor Soc; Am Artists Prof League; Art Ctr of NJ. *Media:* All Media. *Mailing Add:* 3 Godfrey Rd Upper Montclair NJ 07043

MCREYNOLDS, (JOE) CLIFF
PAINTER, INSTRUCTOR
b Amarillo, Tex, Jan 26, 33. *Study:* San Diego State Univ, BA, 59, MA, 60. *Comn:* Portrait of pres, Mesa Col, San Diego, Calif, 75. *Exhib:* Drawing USA Traveling Exhib, Minn Mus Art, St Paul, 75; Alternative Realities, Mus Contemp Art, Chicago, Ill, 76; Mindscapes--5 Calif Artists, Oshkosh Mus, Wis, 76; Calif Painting & Sculpture--the Modern Era, San Francisco Mus Mod Art, 76; Juried Drawing Exhib, Chicago Art Inst, 77; Invitational Am Drawing Exhib, Fine Arts Gallery, San Diego, Calif, 77; Fourth Triennial-- India Traveling Exhib, New Delhi, 78 & Tokyo, Japan, 79; For God's Sake-- Cliff McReynolds, San Jose Mus Art, Calif, 83; and many others. *Pos:* Illusr, Psychol Today, 70-73, Esquire Mag, 73, Visions, 77 & OMNI Mag, 78-79. *Teaching:* Instr drawing, Mesa Col, San Diego, 69- *Awards:* Best in Show, Del Mar Exhib, 63; Best in Show, All Calif Exhib, 63 & First Prize, Calif-Hawaii Regional, 72, Fine Arts Gallery, San Diego. *Bibliog:* Marily Hagberg (auth), McReynolds--sharp satirist, San Diego Mag, 2/67; Jan Jennings (auth), One man show on view, San Diego Union, 12/71. *Media:* Oil, Pencil. *Publ:* Auth, All things new, Revelation Art, 80. *Mailing Add:* 6311 Dowling Dr La Jolla CA 92037

MCREYNOLDS, KIRK See St Maur, Kirk

MCSHEEHY, CORNELIA MARIE
PRINTMAKER, PAINTER
b Floral Park, New York, Aug 10, 47. *Study:* Mass Col Art, Boston, BFA, 69; State Univ NY, Albany, MA, 72. *Work:* Libr Cong, Washington, DC; Univ NDak, Grand Forks; State Univ NY, Potsdam; Minot State Col, NDak; Tex Tech Univ, Lubbock. *Exhib:* Boston Printmakers, De Cordova Mus, Lincoln, Mass, 73; 18th Print Exhib, Brooklyn Mus, 73; Calif Palace Legion Honor, San Francisco, 73; Print Exhib, Libr Cong, 75; Mus Fine Arts, Boston, 76; Mus Art, RI Sch Design, 79, 81 & 83; Mednarodini Graficini Bienale Int, Mod Gallery, Yugoslavia, 81; New American Graphics 2 & 3, Madison Art Ctr, Wis, 82 & 83; Printed by Women, Port Hist Mus, Philadelphia, 83. *Pos:* Contribr, Art Now, Inc, 76. *Teaching:* Instr printmaking, Mass Col Art, Boston, 72-75; asst prof, Brown Univ, 76-77; assoc prof, RI Sch Design, 77-, head printmaking prog, 79-81. *Awards:* Nat Endowment Arts Grant Printmaking, 75-76; Visual Artist Residency, MacDowell Colony, 83; numerous purchase awards in current national exhibitions. *Bibliog:* Ross Romano (auth), The Collograph, 80. *Mem:* Boston Printmakers; Col Art Asn; Women's Caucus Art; Boston Visual Artist's Union. *Media:* Multimedia. *Mailing Add:* 48 Mt Vernon St Boston MA 02108

MCSHINE, KYNASTON LEIGH
CURATOR
b Port of Spain, Trinidad, Feb 20, 35. *Study:* Dartmouth Col, AB, 58; Univ Mich, 58-59; Inst Fine Arts, NY Univ, 60-64. *Collections Arranged:* Marcel Duchamp (auth, catalog), 73, Robert Rauschenberg, 77, Jackie Winsor (auth, catalog), 79 & Joseph Cornell, (auth, catalog), 80, Mus Mod Art, New York; and others. *Pos:* Cur painting & sculpture, Jewish Mus, New York, 65-67, acting dir, 67-68; assoc cur painting & sculpture, Mus Mod Art, New York, 68-71, cur, 71-80, sr cur, 80- *Teaching:* Asst prof art hist, Hunter Col, New York, 68-69; lectr art hist, Sch Visual Arts, New York, 69-76. *Mem:* Trustee Am Fed Arts; Int Asn Art Critics; Col Art Asn; Am Asn Mus. *Publ:* Auth, Josef Albers: Homage to the Square, 64 & Information, 70, ed & contribr, Marcel Duchamp, 73 & The Natural Paradise: Painting in American 1800- 1950, 76, Mus Mod Art, New York; auth, Primary structures, Jewish Mus, 66. *Mailing Add:* c/o Mus of Mod Art 11 W 53rd St New York NY 10019

MCTWIGAN, MICHAEL
CRITIC, EDITOR
b Lincoln, Nebr, July 9, 48. *Study:* Lake Forest Col, Ill, BA(anthrop), 71; Columbia Univ, postgrad studies, 76-77. *Pos:* Ed asst, Craft Horizons Mag, New York, 72 & 74-78; asst ed, Art Quart, Metrop Mus, New York, 78-79; sr ed, Watson-Guptill Publ, New York, 79-81; ed, Indust Design, New York, 82-83; ed, Am Ceramics Mag, New York, 82- *Awards:* Art Critics Fel, Nat Endowment Arts, 80. *Mem:* Decorative Arts Soc of Soc Archit Historians; Col Art Asn. *Res:* Post-World War II sculpture in the new craft media of clay, glass and fiber; architecture, decorative arts and portraiture. *Publ:* Auth, Heroes and Clowns (sculpture of Robert Arneson exhib catalog), Allan Frumkin Gallery, 79; auth, William Daley: Duality in Clay, Am Craft, 80; auth, First things first, 82 & The fruitful mysteries of Graham Marks, 82, Am Ceramics; auth, An interior exchanged: Cynthia Carlson and Betty Woodman, Arts Mag, 82; authD. *Mailing Add:* 344 W 17th St New York NY 10011

MCVEIGH, MIRIAM TEMPERANCE
PAINTER, CONSULTANT
b Wabash, Ind. *Study:* Calif Col Arts & Crafts, BFA; Acad Goetz, Paris; also with Elmer Tafflinger, Clifton Wheeler & Eugen Neuhaus. *Work:* Mus Monbart, Dijon, France; Musee des Beaux Arts de Montbard, Paris. *Exhib:* Am Vet Soc Artists, New York, 61; one-man shows, St Petersburg Jr Col, Fla,

71 & Galerie Internationale, New York, 74; Artistes USA, Galeries Raymond Duncan, Paris, 72; Festival Int de Saint-Germain-des-pres, Paris, 73, 74 & 75. *Teaching:* Chmn, Fine Arts Dept, Shorecrest Sch, formerly; pvt classes, currently. *Media:* Oil, Acrylic. *Dealer:* Chimera 8200 14th St N St Petersburg FL 33702. *Mailing Add:* 8200 14th St N St Petersburg FL 33702

MCVEIGH, ROBERTA LEBER See Leber, Roberta

MCVEY, LEZA
CERAMIST, WEAVER
b Cleveland, Ohio, May 1, 07. *Study:* Cleveland Sch Art, dipl; Cranbrook Acad Art. *Work:* Craft Mus, New York; Smithsonian Inst, Washington, DC; Syracuse Mus, NY; Butler Inst Am Art, Youngstown, Ohio; Cleveland Mus Art. *Comn:* Ceramic mural (with William McVey), Fine Art Ctr, Flint, Mich, 61; tiles, Hicks Sch, Cleveland, 71. *Exhib:* Syracuse Mus & Nat Circuit, 45-69; Smithsonian Inst, 51-61; Int Cong Contemp Ceramics, Ostend, Belg, 60; one- man shows, Distinguished Alumni Art Show, Cleveland Inst Art, 65, Albright-Knox Art Gallery, 65 & Pa Acad, Pomona, Calif. *Awards:* Ceramic Form 33 Award, Harshaw Chem Co, 51; spec awards & group awards, Cleveland Mus Art, 54-67; Ceramic Form 39 Award, Grand Prix des Nations, Ostend, Belg, 60. *Bibliog:* Louis G Farber (auth), article, Ceramic Mo, 53; Meg Torbert (auth), article, Every Day Art Quart, 53. *Media:* Clay. *Mailing Add:* 18 Pepper Ridge Rd Cleveland OH 44124

MCVEY, WILLIAM M
SCULPTOR, EDUCATOR
b Boston, Mass, July 12, 05. *Study:* Rice Univ; Cleveland Inst Art; Acad Colarossi, Acad Grande Chaumiere & Acad Scandinave, Paris, 29-31; pupil of Despiau; John Carroll Univ, Ohio, Hon DFA, 83. *Work:* Heroic head of Winston Churchill, Smithsonian Inst, Washington, DC & Chartwell, Eng; Sister Ann (hollow built ceramic), Ariana Mus, Geneva, Switz; L'Ecrivain (bronze), Houston Mus, Tex; Rumination (Ga marble) & Waiting Woman, Cleveland Mus Art, Ohio; Beached Whale (cement fondu), Lincoln Ctr, Univ Ill, Urbana. *Comn:* Jan Hus, St Olga of Russia for Washington Cathedral; Entire Churchill Porch at Nat Cathedral; George Washington at Fed Bldg, Cleveland; J Edgar Hoover for FBI Acad, Quantico, Va; Senator Harry Flood Byrd (10ft statue), capital grounds, Richmond, Va, 77; and numerous others. *Exhib:* Grand Salon; Salon d'Automne; Pa Acad Fine Arts; Tex Ann; Nat Acad Design; Nat Sculpture Soc; and others. *Pos:* Chmn, Nat Fulbright Screening Comt, four yrs; mem, Fine Arts Advisory Comt, Cleveland, Ohio. *Teaching:* Instr, Cleveland Mus, 32; instr, Houston Mus, 36-38; asst prof, Univ Tex, 39-46; instr, Ohio State Univ, summer 46; instr, Cranbrook Acad Art, 46-53; head sculpture dept, Cleveland Inst Art, 53-68; guest prof, Sch Fine Arts, Ohio State Univ, 63-64. *Awards:* Nat Syracuse Ceramic Show Award, 54; Purchase Awards, Everson Mus, Syracuse, NY, 51 & 52 & Butler Inst Am Art, Youngstown, Ohio, 67. *Bibliog:* Helen Borsick (auth), Story of a statue (Winston Churchill at the British Embassy in Washington), Plain Dealer Mag, 66; Sculptor for today, Ohio Mag; Animals, animal sculpture and animal sculptors, Nat Sculpture Rev, 71. *Mem:* Col Art Asn Am; fel Nat Sculpture Soc; Int Platform Asn (bd gov); assoc Nat Acad Design. *Media:* Stone, Bronze. *Mailing Add:* 18 Pepper Ridge Rd Cleveland OH 44124

MCVICKER, CHARLES TAGGART
ILLUSTRATOR, INSTRUCTOR
b Canonsburg, Pa, Aug 31, 30. *Study:* Principia Col, BA, 52; Art Ctr, Col of Design, BPA, 57. *Work:* US Capitol, US Hist Soc & US Air Force, DC; Princeton Univ; Soc Illusr, New York. *Exhib:* NJ Artists, Newark Mus, 64; NJ Ann, NJ State Mus, Trenton, 70; Illusr Ann, Soc Illusr, New York; NJ Art Dirs Ann, Newark; Am Watercolor Soc Ann, Nat Acad, New York. *Teaching:* Assoc prof illus, Pratt/Phoenix, New York, 79- *Awards:* Best in Show, Alumni Exhib, Art Ctr, Col Design, 75. *Mem:* Soc Illusr (pres, 76-78); Graphic Artists Guild (vpres, 79-); Am Watercolor Soc; Princeton Art Asn (vpres, 64-65). *Media:* Oil, Acrylic. *Publ:* Illusr, Addie and the King of Hearts, Knopf Publ, 76; illusr, The Soccer Book, 76 & The Circus Book, 78, Random House; illusr, Guard of Honor, Franklin Libr, 78. *Mailing Add:* 4 Willow St Princeton NJ 08542

MCVICKER, J JAY
PAINTER, PRINTMAKER
b Vici, Okla, Oct 18, 11. *Study:* Okla State Univ, BA & MA. *Work:* Libr Cong, Washington, DC; Dallas Mus Fine Arts, Tex; Joslyn Art Mus, Omaha; Okla Art Ctr; Nat Mus Am Art, Washington DC. *Exhib:* Dallas Mus Fine Arts, 69; one-man show, Longview Mus & Arts Ctr, Tex, 77 & Exhib of Aquatints, Bethesda Art Gallery, Md, 79; retrospective exhibs, Bethesda Art Gallery, Md, 83 & Rachel W Davis Gallery, Houston, 83; Rockford International, Ill, 83. *Teaching:* Prof & chmn dept art, Okla State Univ, 41-77. *Awards:* Purchase Awards, Okla Art Ctr, 67, Dallas Mus Fine Arts, 69 & Longview Jr Serv League, Tex, 71. *Mem:* Audubon Artists; Soc Am Graphic Artists; Philadelphia Print Club. *Media:* Acrylic, Aquatint. *Dealer:* Bethesda Art Gallery 7950 Norfolk Ave Bethesda MD 20814. *Mailing Add:* 4212 N Washington Stillwater OK 74045

MCWHINNIE, HAROLD JAMES
PRINTMAKER, CERAMIST
b Chicago, Ill, July 15, 29. *Study:* Art Inst Chicago, BAE; Univ Chicago, MFA; Stamford Univ, EdD. *Work:* Los Angeles Mus Art, Calif; Pasadena Art Mus, Calif; Borg-Warner Collection, Chicago; Ohio State Univ Fine Arts. *Exhib:* Libr Cong Print Show, 55; Art League NVa, 78 & 79 & Md Fedn Arts, 78-79; Artbarn, Washington DC, 81; 409 Gallery, Baltimore, 81; Acad Arts, Easton, Md, 81; and many other group shows & one-man exhibs. *Teaching:*

Asst prof art educ, Ohio State Univ, 65-70; assoc prof ceramics, Univ Md, College Park, 70-; vis lectr, Maryland Inst Art, Baltimore, 82. *Awards:* Nat Endowment for Arts, 74; Hambidge Ctr Fel, 83; Nat Arts Handicapped Grant, 83-84. *Mem:* Nat Art Educ Asn; Am Crafts Coun; Md Crafts Coun; Md Alliance Arts; and others. *Publ:* Auth, Glaze Data Book, Bulletin Am Ceramics Soc, 80; Glaze Data Bank, Studio Potter, 81; A Revision of Seger glaze theory, J Nat Coun Educ Ceramic Arts, 82; and numerous glaze articles in Ceramics Monthly. *Mailing Add:* Thought Gallery 10111 Fredorrk Ave Kensington MD 20795

MAC WHINNIE, JOHN VINCENT
PAINTER, SCULPTOR
b Rockville Centre, NY, April 22, 45. *Study:* Southampton Col, NY, BA(magna cum laude), 71; studied with Fairfield Porter, Larry Rivers & Ilya Bolotowsky. *Work:* Guggenheim Mus; Brooklyn Mus; Phillips Collection; Walker Art Ctr; Parrish Art Mus. *Exhib:* Summer Loan Exhib, Metrop Mus Art, New York, 79; Art in America Since World War Two, Guggenheim Mus, 79; 24th Ann Contemp Am Painting Exhib, Lehigh Univ, 79; American Drawing in Black and White, Brooklyn Mus, 81; Am Acad & Inst Arts & Lett, New York, 81; Human Figure in Contemporary Art, New Orleans Mus Contemp Art, 82; Poets and Artists of the Region, Guild Hall, Easthampton, NY, 82. *Awards:* First Prize Painting, Parrish Mus, Southampton, NY, 71; Excellence in Painting, Heckscher Mus, Huntington, NY, 74. *Bibliog:* David Shapiro (auth), Transcending photography, Art Int, 76. *Media:* Oil, Encaustic. *Dealer:* Marlborough Gallery New York NY. *Mailing Add:* Deerfield Rd Water Mill NY 11976

MCWHORTER, ELSIE JEAN
PAINTER, SCULPTOR
b Laurel, Miss, Apr 5, 32. *Study:* Univ Ga, BFA, 54 & MFA, 56, with Lamar Dodd, Howard Thomas, Abbott Patterson, Joseph Di Martini, Ulfert Wilkie & Dan Lutz; Brooklyn Mus Art Sch, Max Beckmann scholar, 56-57, with Reuben Tam & Yonia Fain. *Work:* Gibbes Art Gallery, Charleston, SC; Brooks Art Gallery, Memphis, Tenn; Greenville Co Mus Art, SC; Arts Comn SC, Columbia; Miss Art Asn, State Coliseum, Jackson; and others. *Comn:* Seal for Sumter Co, SC, 65; welded bronze fountain, Tom Jenkins Realty Co, Columbia, 66; mural, US Post Off, Camden, SC, 67; mural, Baker Bldg, Southern Bell Tel Co, Columbia, 68; eight historic paintings, McDonald's Restaurant, Conway, SC, 76; bronze relief, Sen Rembert Dennis, Dennis Bldg, Capital Complex SC, 81; McNair Monument, SC State Capital Complex. *Exhib:* Mid-South Exhib, Memphis, Tenn, 62; Butler Inst Am Art Ann, Youngstown, Ohio, 63; Drawing USA, St Paul 2nd Biennial Competition, St Paul Art Ctr, Minn, 63; one-woman shows, Columbia Mus Art, SC & Art Gallery, Fine Arts Ctr, Univ Tenn, Chattanooga, 81. *Teaching:* Asst prof art, Morningside Col, 58-61; instr drawing, painting & sculpture, Richland Art Sch, Columbia Mus Art, 61-, supvr, 78-; instr sculpture & design, Univ SC, 66-67; vis prof, Newberry Col, 82. *Awards:* First Prize Painting, Spartanburg Art Asn Ann, SC, 74; First Prize, Dutch Fork Art Asn Exhib, Cola, SC, 74; First Prize Sculpture, Art of the Carolinas, Spring Mills Ann, Lancaster, SC, 75; and many others. *Bibliog:* Jack Morris (auth), article in Contemp SC Artist, 70. *Mem:* Guild SC Artist; Artist Guild Columbia; SC Craftmen. *Mailing Add:* 5419 Sylvan Dr Columbia SC 29206

MADDEN-WORK, BETTY I
HISTORIAN, PAINTER
b Chicago, Ill, Nov 15, 15. *Study:* Am Acad Art, Chicago; Northwestern Univ; Univ Ill, BFA; Inst Design, Chicago; with Herb Olson, Spain & Italy; John Pellew, Ireland & Eng; Tom Hill, Mex; Zornes, Vt. *Work:* Ill State Hist Libr, Springfield. *Exhib:* Springfield Artist Invitational, Lincoln Land Col, 79; one-man shows, Western Ill Univ, Macomb, 78 & Caterpillar Tractor Co, Peoria, 79, Midwest Watercolor Soc, 81, Ill Dept Transportation, 81. *Pos:* Com artist & illusr, Consolidated Bk Publ, Chicago, 44-46; com artist, Evans, Work & Costa Advert, Springfield, Ill, 55-59; fashion illusr, S A Barker Co, Springfield, 59-61; tech asst art dept, Ill State Mus, 61-63; cur art, 63-78; art teacher, Art Asn, Springfield, 78- *Mem:* Clayville Folk Arts Guild; Ill Art League; Springfield Art Asn. *Media:* Watercolor. *Publ:* Auth, Art, Crafts and Architecture in Early Illinois, Univ Ill Press, 64. *Mailing Add:* 1145 S First St Springfield IL 62704

MADDOX, JERALD CURTIS
CURATOR, HISTORIAN
b Decatur, Ind, June 9, 33. *Study:* Ind Univ, AB, 55 & MA, 60; Harvard Univ, 60-61. *Work:* Int Mus Photog, George Eastman House, Rochester, NY. *Collections Arranged:* American Photography: The Sixties, Univ Nebr Art Galleries, 66; Creative Photography 1869-1969, Libr Cong, Washington, DC. 70. *Pos:* Asst to dir, Univ Nebr Art Galleries, 63-66; head curatorial section, Prints & Photog Div, Libr Cong, 66-78, cur photog, 66-, collections planner & coordr, 78-; consult photog, Northern Va Community Col, 77. *Teaching:* Instr art hist, NY State Univ Col New Paltz, 62-63. *Awards:* Mus Prof Fel, Nat Endowment Arts, 74. *Mem:* Col Art Asn; Soc Photog Educ (treas, 68-73). *Res:* History and criticism of photography. *Publ:* Auth, Essay on a tintype, 1/69 & Creative photography, 1869-1969, 1/71, Quart J Libr Cong; auth, Photography in the first decade, Art Am, 7-8/73; auth, How much is a photograph worth, After Image, 2/75. *Mailing Add:* 4514 Highland Ave Bethesda MD 20814

MADDOX, JERROLD WARREN
EDUCATOR, PAINTER
b Ft Wayne, Ind, Mar 6, 32. *Study:* Ind Univ, BS, 54 & MFA, 59. *Exhib:* Recent Painting USA: The Figure, Mus Mod Art, New York, 62-63; Moods of Light, Am Fedn Art, 63-64. *Teaching:* Asst prof humanities, Monteith Col,

Wayne State Univ, Detroit, 60-63; lectr painting & drawing, Regional Col Art & Crafts, Hull, Eng, 64; asst prof painting & drawing, Univ Ky, Lexington, 64-66; asst prof drawing & painting, Amherst Col, Mass, 66-69; assoc prof drawing & painting, Reed Col, Portland, Ore, 69-70; assoc prof drawing & painting, Ind Univ, Bloomington, 70-74; head prof, Kans State Univ, Manhattan, 74-; dir, Pa State Univ, University Park, 80- *Mem:* Col Art Asn Am; Nat Coun Art Adminr (chmn, 82); Nat Asn Sch Art & Design. *Media:* Oil. *Publ:* Co-auth, Images and Imagination: an Introduction to Art, 65. *Mailing Add:* Pa State Univ University Park PA 16802

MADIGAN, MARY JEAN SMITH
EDITOR, WRITER
b Nanticoke, Pa. *Study:* Cornell Univ, BA; Am Univ, MA. *Collections Arranged:* Photography of Rudolf Eickemeyer (with catalog), 72; Eastlake-Influenced American Furniture (with catalog), 73; The Sculpture of Isidore Konti 1862-1938 (with catalog), 75. *Pos:* Cur Am decorative art & hist, Hudson River Mus, Yonkers, NY, 70-76, cur exhib & collections, 76-77, asst dir, 77-78; bk reviewer, Mus News, 75-; dir mus prog, Opportunity Resources Arts, 78; ed, Art & Antiques, 78-, publisher, 83- *Teaching:* Lectr Am antiques, Westchester Community Col, Valhalla, NY, 75. *Awards:* Harry M Grier Scholar, Asn Art Mus Dir, 75. *Mem:* Am Asn Mus; Am Soc Mag Ed; Author's Guild; Author's League Am. *Res:* American decorative arts. *Publ:* Auth, Steuben Glass, Harry N Abrams, 82; ed, 19th Century Furniture, 82, ed, Americana, 82, ed, Early American Furniture, 83 & ed, Prints & Photographs, 83, Watson-Guptill; auth, articles in Art & Antiques, Connoisseur, Ultra & Winterthur Portfolio; ed, Nineteenth Century Furniture, 82 & ed, Americana, 82, Watson-Guptill; auth, The Story of Steuben, Harry N Abrams, 82. *Mailing Add:* 565 Broadway 6I Hastings-on-Hudson NY 10706

MADIGAN, RICHARD ALLEN
MUSEUM DIRECTOR
b Corning, NY, Oct 29, 37. *Study:* Drew Univ, AB, 59; Univ Del; Am Univ. *Collections Arranged:* Contemporary Japanese Painting, 64; Australian Painters, 65-67; Contemporary Peruvian Painting & Sculpture, 67; Imagist Realism (with catalog), 74. *Exhibitions Organized:* Philip Evergood Retrospective, 77; Sculpture of Fumio Yoshimura, 78; The Art of Polly Hope, 79; City Images, 80; Masterpieces of Canadian Painting, 84. *Pos:* Dir, White Art Mus, Cornell Univ, 60-63; asst dir, Corcoran Gallery Art, Washington, DC, 63-67; dir, Mus Resources Coun, Ft Worth, Tex, 67; dir, Brooklyn Children's Mus, 68; exec dir, Wave Hill Ctr, New York, 69-74; dir, Norton Gallery & Sch Art, West Palm Beach, 74- *Teaching:* Instr mus studies, George Washington Univ, 64-67; instr Am art, Foreign Serv Inst, US Dept State, 65-67; instr mus studies, Lehman Col, 67-69. *Awards:* European Study Grant, NY State Coun Arts, 71. *Mem:* Am Asn Mus; Fla Art Mus Dir Asn (pres, 77-78 & 82-83); Int Coun Mus; Asn Art Mus Dirs. *Publ:* Contribr, Australian Painters, 71; auth, The Collection (catalog), Norton Gallery Art, 79; auth, Sculpture of Michael Schreck, 79. *Mailing Add:* c/o Norton Gallery Art 1451 S Olive Ave West Palm Beach FL 33401

MADONIA, ANN C
HISTORIAN, CURATOR
b New York, NY. *Study:* Hunter Col, City Univ New York, AB, 72, MA, 77; Hofstra Univ, cert(appraisal), 79. *Collections Arranged:* Prairie Visions and Circus Wonders: Complete Lithographic Suite by John Stewart Curry (auth, catalog), 80; American Profile: Drawings by Norman Rockwell (auth, catalog), 80; Selected Paintings from Charles August Ficke Collection (auth, catalog), 80; Byron Burford: Recent Paintings, 1960-1980 (auth, catalog), 81; Mexican Colonial Paintings in the Davenport Art Gallery, 83. *Pos:* Cur collections, Davenport Art Gallery, Iowa, 79- *Mem:* Am Inst Conservation Artistic & Hist Works; Am Asn Mus; Col Art Asn; Midwest Art Hist Soc. *Res:* American art, particularly 19th century painting and sculpture. *Publ:* Auth, Davenport: 1836-1936--The Centennial Mural, 80, Ralph Albert Blakelock--poet of the landscape, 80, Limners and likenesses, 81, Water works, 81 & The Mexican Colonial Collection, 83, Bulletin, Davenport Art Gallery. *Mailing Add:* 1315 E 39th St Davenport IA 52807

MADSEN, LOREN WAKEFIELD
SCULPTOR
b Oakland, Calif, Mar 29, 43. *Study:* Reed Col, Portland, Ore, 61-63; Univ Calif, Los Angeles, BA, 66, MA, 70. *Work:* Walker Art Ctr, Minneapolis, Minn; Mus Mod Art, New York; Georges Pompidou Ctr, Paris; Hirshhorn Mus, Washington, DC; Israel Mus, Jerusalem, . *Comn:* Broken Ring, Los Angeles Co Mus Art, Los Angeles, Calif, 77; 12in x 12in Timber Piece, Cedars-Sinai Med Ctr, Los Angeles, Calif, 77; untitled sculpture, First Bank Atrium, Minneapolis, 81; Suspended Sentence, Area Two Police Ctr, Chicago, 81; Bootstrap Variation, Veterans Asn Nursing Home, Hine, Ill, 83. *Exhib:* Los Angeles 6, 74 & New Selections, 76, Los Angeles Co Mus Art, Los Angeles, Calif; one man show, Mus Mod Art, New York, 75; Sculpture Made in Place, Walker Art Ctr, Minneapolis, Minn, 76; David McKee Gallery, New York, 76, 77 & 82; Wright State Univ, Dayton, Ohio, 80; Stacking, Rigging, Binding: 10 Contemporary Sculptors, Whiskey Painters Asn, Washington, DC, 80; Univ Mass, Amherst, 81; Shift LA/NY, Newport Harbor Art Asn, Newport Beach, Calif, 82; and others. *Awards:* New Talent Award, Mod & Contemp Art Coun, Los Angeles Co Mus Art, 75; Nat Endowment Arts Fel Grant, 76. *Media:* Brick and lumber. *Mailing Add:* 428 Broome St New York NY 10013

MADSEN, VIGGO HOLM
PRINTMAKER, CRAFTSMAN
b Kaas, Denmark, Apr 21, 25; US citizen. *Study:* Anderson Col, Syracuse Univ, BFA, 51, MFA, 52; NY Univ; Columbia Univ Teachers Col; Adelphi Univ; Inst Allende, San Miguel, Mex; Det Danske Selskab, Denmark. *Work:* Philadelphia Ctr Older People, Pa; Nassau Community Col, Garden City, NY; Anderson Col, Ind; C W Post Col, Brookville, NY; Nat Cintric Co, Danbury, Conn; and others. *Exhib:* Nat Acad Design Show, New York, 75; Surface Design Conf Exhib, Towson Univ, Md, 77; Drawing USA II, Smithsonian Inst, 79; Functional Forms, Ore State Univ, 79; Silvermine Guild Artists Print Show, 80; and others. *Pos:* Ed, Newsletter, Long Island Art Teachers Asn, 62-64, pres, Graphic Eye Gallery, 82-83. *Teaching:* Instr art, Roslyn High Sch, NY, 60-82; prof, adj staff, Nassau Community Col, 66-; instr, Crafts Workshops, Adelphi Univ, 74-78. *Awards:* Award of Excellence, Long Island Art Teachers Exhib, C W Post Col, 75; Best in Show Award, Long Island Art, 75; Cover design award, New York State Teacher's Asn, 81; and others. *Bibliog:* Jeanne Paris (auth), rev in Long Island Press, 7/71; Malcolm Preston (auth), rev in Newsday, 2/72; Dona Z Meilach (auth), chap in Creating Art with Textiles, Reilly & Lee; Helen Harrison (auth), rev, New York Times, 1/81. *Mem:* Long Island Craftsmen's Guild; lifetime mem NY State Art Teachers Asn; Am Crafts Coun; Long Island Art Teachers Asn; and others. *Media:* Multimedia. *Publ:* Contribr, Art in action, 61, J Nat Art Educ Asn, 63 & J Eastern Arts Asn, 64; auth & publ, three demonstration booklets: Batik, Silk screening & Woodcut prints, 70-72. *Dealer:* Graphic Eye Gallery Main St Port Washington NY 11050; Robley Gallery Roslyn NY 11576. *Mailing Add:* 5 Meldon Ave Albertson NY 11507

MADURA, JACK JOSEPH
PAINTER, INSTRUCTOR
b Chicago, Ill, Feb 6, 41. *Study:* Murray State Univ, BS(art), 64 & MA(art educ), 66; Northern Ill Univ, with Robert Kabak, MFA(painting), 70. *Work:* City Springfield Munic Collection, Ill; Temple B'rith Sholom, Springfield; Lincoln Land Community Col; Northern Ill Univ, DeKalb; Southern Ill Medical Sch, Springfield; and others. *Exhib:* Chicago State Univ Flat Show, 74; Rocky Mountain Nat Water Media Exhib, Golden, Colo, 74; Watercolor USA, Springfield Art Mus, Mo, 75, 77, 78, 80 & 81; Watercolorists of Ill, Charleston, 77; one-man show, Ill State Mus, 78; and others. *Teaching:* Instr drawing & painting, Somerset Community Col, Ky, 66-68; instr art, Lincoln Land Community Col, 70- *Awards:* Second Place for Watercolor, Ill State Fair Prof Show, 75, 76 & 77; Purchase Prize in Watercolor, 7 for 76 Seven State Regional Show, Paul Sargent Gallery, Charleston, Ill, 76; Merit Award, Springfield & Vicinity Show, Ill State Mus, 81; and others. *Mem:* Ala & Ky Watercolor Socs. *Media:* Watercolor. *Mailing Add:* 4 Long Bay Springfield IL 62707

MAESTRO, GIULIO MARCELLO
ILLUSTRATOR, PAINTER
b New York, NY, May 6, 42. *Study:* Cooper Union Art Sch, BFA; Pratt Graphics Ctr. *Awards:* Cert Excellence, Children's Book Show, Am Inst Graphic Arts, 74; Cert Merit, Art Dir Club, New York, 78 & 82 & Conn Illusr Show, 79. *Mem:* Am Inst Graphic Arts. *Media:* Pencil, Pen; Dyes, Gouache. *Publ:* Illusr, The Key to the Kingdom, Harcourt, 81; auth & illusr, Raft of Riddles, Dutton, 82; illusr, Big City Port, Four Winds, 83; auth & illusr, Halloween Howls, Dutton, 83; auth & illusr, Riddle Romp, Clarion, 83. *Mailing Add:* 702 Summer Hill Rd Madison CT 06443

MAGAFAN, ETHEL
PAINTER, MURALIST
b Chicago, Ill. *Study:* Colorado Springs Fine Arts Ctr, with Frank Mechau, Boardman Robinson & Peppino Mangravite. *Work:* Metrop Mus Art, New York; Munson-Williams-Proctor Inst, Utica, NY; Butler Inst Am Art, Youngstown, Ohio; Wichita Art Mus; Evansville Mus, Ind; and others. *Comn:* Prairie Fire, Post Off Lobby, Madill, Okla, 40; Mountains in Snow (with Jenne Magafan), Social Security Bldg, Washington, DC, 41; Horse Corral, Post Off Lobby, S Denver Br, Colo, 42; Battle of New Orleans, Recorder of Deeds Bldg, Washington, DC, 43; Grant in the Wilderness (mural), Vis Ctr, Fredericksburg Nat Mil Park, Va, 79. *Exhib:* American Painting Today, Metrop Mus Art, New York, 50; Pa Acad Design, Philadelphia, 61, 62, 64, & 69; Butler Inst Am Art, 63-66, 68-74, 78, 79 & 82; New England Exhib, Silvermine Guild Artists, 64, 78 & 79; Nat Acad Design, New York, 65-81; Munson, William, Proctor Inst, 69, 72, 77, 79 & 80; Mowhawk Regional, Albany & Schenectady, eight times, 70-; Cooperstown Ann Nat, 78, 82 & 83; and others. *Awards:* Benjamin Altman Prize, Nat Acad Design, 56, 64, 73 & 80; Childe Hassam Purchase Award, Am Acad Arts & Lett, 70; Andrew Carnegie Award, Nat Acad Design, 77. *Bibliog:* Edward Betts (auth), Creative landscape painting, 78; Howard Wooden (auth), Neglected Generation of American Realistic Painters, 81; Charlotte S Rubinstein (auth), American Women Artists, 82. *Mem:* Nat Acad Design (mem coun, 72-75); Am Watercolor Soc; Audubon Artists; Philadelphia Watercolor Club; Woodstock Artists Asn. *Media:* Egg Tempera, Woodcuts. *Dealer:* Midtown Galleries 11 E 57th St New York NY 10022. *Mailing Add:* RFD Box 284 Woodstock NY 12498

MAGALI, LARA
PAINTER
b Mexico, DF, Nov, 5, 56. *Study:* Escuela Nac de Artes Plasticas. *Work:* Gallery Nat Univ Mex & Collection Univ Mex, Mexico City. *Exhib:* Nuevas tendencias, Mus de Arte Moderno, Mexico City, 78; Nueva Acuarela, Palacio de Bellas Artes, Mexico City, 78; 35 Mexican Artists, Kunstlerhaus Bethanien, Berlin West, 81; No-Objectual, Museo de Arte Mod, Medellin, Colombia, 81; XVI Bienal de Sao Paulo, Fundaccion Bienal, Brasil, 81. *Pos:*

Dir cult dept, Nat Sch Fine Arts, Univ Nac Autonama Mexico, currently. *Bibliog:* Docs (auth), Visual Poetry, Julien Blaine, 80; Carmen Boullosa (auth), Lealtad, Martin Pescador, 81. *Publ:* Coauth, Dos Historias, Otros Editores, 81; ed & contribr, Tesis de Humor, 81 & auth, De la Ciudad, 81, Serie Textual. *Mailing Add:* Nicolas San Juan 1421 Mexico DF Mexico

MAGAZZINI, GENE
PAINTER
b New York, NY, Nov 5, 14. *Study:* Siena, Italy, with pvt tutors; Brooklyn Col; Art Students League, with Ivan Olinsky. *Work:* Sloan-Kettering Inst, New York. *Exhib:* Allied Artists Am, Nat Acad Design, New York; Palais Congres, Expos Intercontinentale, Monaco; Nat Arts Club & Salmagundi Club, New York; Burr Artists, Metrop Mus Art, New York, 77. *Awards:* First Prize, Salmagundi Club, 69; Best in Show & Purchase Prize, Salmagundi Club, 70; Best in Show & Gold Medal, Nat Art League, 71. *Mem:* Salmagundi Club; Artists' Fel; Nat Art League; Art Students League; Am Artists Prof League. *Media:* Oil. *Mailing Add:* 249 Euclid Ave Brooklyn NY 11208

MAGEE, ALAN ARTHUR
ILLUSTRATOR, PAINTER
b Newton, Pa, May 26, 47. *Study:* Tyler Sch Art, 65-66; Philadelphia Col Art, 67-69. *Work:* Palace Legion Honor, San Francisco; Mobil Oil Corp; Arco Corp; Ark Art Ctr; Playboy Inc, Chicago; and many others. *Comn:* Illus novels, Graham Greene, Pocket Books, New York, 74, Bernard Malamud, 74, Agatha Christie, 74-78 & Patrick White, Avon Books, New York, 75; mural for Am Hospital Supply Co, Chicago, 78. *Exhib:* Styles in 20th Century Drawing, Allport & Assoc Gallery, Larkspur, Calif, 79; Art of Drawing, Staempfli Gallery, New York, 80; one-man show, Staempfli Gallery, New York, 80; Am Acad Inst Arts & Letters (auth, catalog), New York, 81; The Art of Drawing II (auth, catalog), Ark Art Ctr, 81; and many others. *Awards:* Cert of Excellence, Chicago, 78; Richard & Hinda Rosenthal Award, Am Acad & Inst Arts & Letters, 81; American Book Awards, 82; and others. *Bibliog:* Theodore F Wolff (auth), The many masks of modern art, 3/80 & Drawing is back in style, 6/80, Christian Sci Monitor; John Canday (auth), A dazzling new realist painter, Saturday Rev Mag, 12/80. *Mem:* Soc Illusr, New York. *Media:* Acrylics, Watercolor. *Publ:* Illusr, The Alexandria Quartet, Lawrence Durrell, 74, Pocket Books, Inc; illusr, Good Night Sweet Prince, Playboy Mag, 77; illusr, The Computer Society (cover), 78 & illusr, How Gay is Gay? (cover), 79, Time Mag; illusr, I Herbert Boyer-geneticist (cover), Time Mag, 81; and others. *Dealer:* Staempfli Gallery 47 E 77th St New York NY 10021; Allport & Assoc Gallery 1000 Magnolia Ave Larkspur CA 94939. *Mailing Add:* Pleasant Point Rd Cushing ME 04563

MAGEE, ALDERSON
GRAPHIC ARTIST, PAINTER
b Hartford, Conn, Oct 5, 29. *Study:* Univ Conn, BS; West Hartford Art League; also with Estelle Coniff & Walter Korder. *Exhib:* Conn Acad Fine Arts, Wadsworth Atheneum, Hartford, 74; Hudson Valley Art Asn Exhib, White Plains, NY, 74, 75 & 78; Salmagundi Club Ann Graphics Exhib, New York, 76-77; Federal Duck Stamp Art, Peabody Mus, Salem, Mass, 77; Soc Animal Artists Exhib, Sportsman's Edge Gallery, New York, 78, Grand Nat Exhib, Am Artists Prof League, 78; and others. *Awards:* First Prize, Conn Acad Fine Arts, 74; Gold Medal, Hudson Valley Art Asn, 75 & Grand Nat Exhib, Am Artists Prof League, New York, 78. *Bibliog:* Russell A Fink (publ), Duck Stamp Prints, 76; Nelson Bryant (auth), Duck stamp art on sale, New York Times, 4/16/76; Stunning black & white engraving, Audubon Mag, 1/76. *Mem:* Salmagundi Club; Hudson Valley Art Asn; Soc Animal Artists; Am Artists Prof League. *Publ:* Illusr cover, Ducks Unlimited Mag, 75 & 77; illusr, Federal Duck Stamp Design, US Govt, 76; illusr cover, Field & Stream Mag, 1 & 4/79. *Dealer:* R A Fink Lorton VA; Sportsman's Edge New York NY. *Mailing Add:* Toad Hall Sharon CT 06069

MAGENTA, MURIEL
SCULPTOR, EDUCATOR
b New York, NY, Dec 4, 32. *Study:* Queens Col, BA, 53; Johns Hopkins Univ, MA(art hist), 62; Ariz State Univ, MFA, 65, PhD, 70. *Work:* Univ Art Collections, Ariz State Univ, Tempe; Valley Nat Bank, Phoenix. *Comn:* Environ sculpture, Ariz State Univ, 74, 76, 79 & 82-83, Phoenix Art Mus, 77 & Univ Ariz, 79. *Exhib:* Bride: Environment and Film, Univ Gallery, Univ Southern Calif, 78; Athens Int Film Festival, Ohio State Univ, Athens, 78; NY Women Artists Filmmakers, Anthology Film Arch, New York, 78; Art Words/Bookworks, Los Angeles Inst Contemp Art, 78; Four Artist Exhib, Univ Wis-Madison Gallery, 79; In Defense of A Hairdo, AIR Gallery, New York & Gammage Ctr Performing Arts, Ariz State Univ, 83. *Pos:* Exec ed & designer, Hue Points Women's Caucus for Art Newsmagazine, currently. *Teaching:* Prof inter-media art, Ariz State Univ, 69-; vis artist in residence studio art, Univ Wis, Madison, summer 79. *Bibliog:* L Wachtel (auth), Bride, Film News, 10/77; S Muchnic (auth), Here comes Magenta's bride, Los Angeles Times, 10/78; B Perlman (auth), Hiding from infinity, Artnews, 9/79. *Mem:* Mid-Am Col Art Asn (exec bd, 78-79); Coalition Women's Art Orgn (nat vpres, 78-80); Women's Caucus Art (nat pres 82-84). *Media:* Film, Video. *Publ:* Contribr, Women's view of art, In: Women Studies and the Arts, Whittenborn, 80; auth, Feminist art criticism: A political definition, J Theory & Criticism Visual Arts, 81. *Mailing Add:* 8322 E Virginia Scottsdale AZ 85257

MAGGS, ARNAUD (CYRIL BENVENUTI)
PHOTOGRAPHER, GRAPHIC ARTIST
b Montreal, Que, May 5, 26. *Study:* With Carl Dair, late 40s; Scuola Belle Arti Brera, Milan, 59; Three Schs, Toronto, 74. *Work:* Nat Gallery Can; Art Gallery Winnipeg; Edmonton Art Gallery; Nickle Arts Mus, Univ Calgary,

Alta; Can Coun Art Bank, Ottawa. *Comn:* Restaurant mural (photographs), Windsor Arms Hotel, Toronto, 67. *Exhib:* Sweet Immortality, Edmonton Art Gallery, 78; Persona, Nickle Arts Mus, Univ Calgary, Alta, 82; solo exhibs, Joseph Beuys, Optica, Montreal, 83 & Turning, Harbourfront Gallery, Toronto, 83; retrospective, Charles H Scott Gallery, Vancouver, 84 & Nickle Arts Mus, Univ Calgary, Alta, 84; and others. *Awards:* Gold Medal, Can Grahica Exhib, Montreal, 65; Can Coun Sr Arts Grants, 69 & 81. *Bibliog:* Martha Fleming (auth), Arnaud Maggs' downwind photographs, Afterimage, 1/82; Gail Fisher-Taylor (auth), Anatomy of a portrait, Photo Communique, 82. *Mailing Add:* 24 Noble St Toronto ON M6K 2C8 Canada

MAGISTRO, CHARLES JOHN
PAINTER, PRINTMAKER

b Cleveland, Ohio, June 27, 41. *Study:* Carnegie Inst Technol, BFA, 64; Ohio State Univ, MFA, 67. *Work:* Brooklyn Mus Art; Va Mus Fine Arts, Richmond; Mint Mus Art, Charlotte, NC; Reese Mus, Tenn; Mariners Mus, Newport News, Va. *Comn:* Triptych, Gen Reinsurance Corp, New York, 78; painting, Gould Corp, Chicago, 79. *Exhib:* Juried Show, Mint Mus Art, Charlotte, NC, 70; Va Mus Art Biennial, Richmond, 71; Extraordinary Realities, Whitney Mus Art, New York, 73; 19th Nat Print Exhib, Brooklyn Mus Art, 74; one-man shows, Tibor de Nagy, New York, 80 & 81, Nancy Lurie Gallery, Chicago, 80, John Davis Gallery, Akron, Ohio, 82-83, Passaic Co Col, 83 & Jr Col Albany, NY, 83. *Collections Arranged:* Works from the Tibor de Nagy Gallery, Tibor de Nagy, New York, 79; Current/New York (auth, catalog), Syracuse Univ, 80. *Pos:* Fac adv, Nat Student Mag, 77- *Teaching:* Asst prof design & printmaking, Va Commonwealth Univ, 67-79; asst prof design & drawing, William Patterson Col, NJ, 77. *Bibliog:* Peter Frank (auth), New trend in art, Village Voice, 79; Carl Lunde (auth), Chuck Magistro, Arts Mag, 5/81. *Publ:* Auth, Objects Altered, Kendall/Hunt, 72. *Dealer:* Tibor de Nagy Gallery 29 W 57th St New York NY 10019; John Davis Gallery Akron OH. *Mailing Add:* 52 White St New York NY 10013

MAGLEBY, FRANK (FRANCIS R)
PAINTER, EDUCATOR

b Idaho Falls, Idaho, Mar 22, 28. *Study:* Brigham Young Univ, BA & MA, 52; Art Students League; Am Art Sch, New York; Columbia Univ, EdD, 67. *Comn:* Historical paintings for various church bldgs, Mormon Church, Salt Lake City, Utah & New York, 58-59; Heleman (mural), Brigham Young Univ, 65. *Exhib:* One-man shows, Southern Vt Art Ctr, 55-59 & 71, Grand Cent Art Gallery, 57 & Brigham Young Univ, Utah, 68 & 78. *Pos:* Dir, B F Larson Gallery, Brigham Young Univ, 62-69. *Teaching:* Prof painting, Brigham Young Univ, 59- *Mem:* Am Fedn Arts; Southern Vt Art Ctr; Grand Cent Art Gallery; Western Asn Mus; Art Students League. *Media:* Oil. *Mailing Add:* 464 E 2200 N Provo UT 84601

MAGNAN, OSCAR GUSTAV
PAINTER, SCULPTOR

b Cienfuegos, Cuba, Dec 16, 37. *Study:* San Alejandro, Habana, Cuba, with Mateo Dela Torriente, MFA; Oxford Univ, Eng, Master in aribus; Sorbonne, with Dufrenne, PhD(aesthet). *Work:* Okla Art Ctr; Kansas City Art Inst; AVX Corp, NY; RCA Corp; NY Univ; and others. *Comn:* Three panel mural, Univ Autonoma, Dom Repub, 68; bronze statue, Haina, Dom Repub, 68. *Exhib:* Salzburg Int Biennial, 64; one-man shows, Palazzo Strozzi, Florence, Italy, 66 & Galerie Motte, Paris, 70; Int Fair, Basle, Switz, 72; Inter-Kunst-Infomaturien, Dusseldorf, Ger, 72; New Jersey Selects, Squibb Corp, Princeton, NJ. *Pos:* Dir art gallery, St Peter's Col, 72-, cur mus, 73- *Teaching:* Assoc prof aesthet/sculpture, St Peter's Col, Jersey City, NJ, 70-, chmn dept fine arts, 77- *Awards:* Can Coun Fel, 64; Cintas Found Inst Int Educ Fel, 66; Guggenheim Found Fel, 68. *Media:* Acrylic, Tempera; Aluminum, Bronze. *Dealer:* Barry Snyder Princeton Gallery Princeton NJ. *Mailing Add:* 2652 Kennedy Blvd Jersey City NJ 07306

MAGRIEL, PAUL
COLLECTOR

b Mar 12, 16. *Study:* Columbia Univ. *Pos:* Cur dance arch, Mus Mod Art, New York, 39-42. *Collection:* Sport in art; American still life paintings, numismatics, drawings, watercolors; Renaissance bronzes; has been exhibited in 84 American museums. *Mailing Add:* 85 East End Ave New York NY 10028

MAGUIRE, HENRY POWNALL
HISTORIAN, WRITER

b Bath, England, May 20, 43. *Study:* Kings Col, Cambridge, BA, 65; Harvard Univ, PhD, 73. *Teaching:* Asst prof medieval art, Harvard Univ, 73-76 & Dumbarton Oaks, 76-79; asst prof, Univ Ill, Urbana-Champaign, 79-82, assoc prof, 82- *Mem:* Col Art Asn; Archaeol Inst Am; Int Ctr Medieval Art. *Res:* Late Roman, early Christian and Byzantine art. *Publ:* Auth, Truth and convention in Byzantine descriptions of works of art, 74 & The depiction of sorrow in middle Byzantine art, 77, Dumbarton Oaks Papers; auth, Art and Eloquence in Byzantium, Princeton, 81. *Mailing Add:* Sch Art & Design Univ Ill 408 E Peabody Dr Champaign IL 61820

MAHAFFEY, MERRILL DEAN
PAINTER, INSTRUCTOR

b Albuquerque, NMex, Aug 12, 37. *Study:* Mesa Col, Colo; Calif Col Arts & Crafts; Sacramento State Col, BA; Ariz State Univ, MFA, 66. *Work:* Ariz State Univ; Phoenix Art Mus; Tucson Art Ctr; Mus Am Art; Colo Springs Fine Arts Ctr. *Exhib:* Joslyn Mus Biennial, Omaha, Nebr; Newport Art Mus, 79; Mus Am Art, Washington, DC, 79; San Francisco Mus Mod Art, 79; Sierra Nev Mus Art, 81; Fresno Art Ctr, 81; Tucson Art Mus, 82; Colo Springs Fine Arts Ctr, 83. *Teaching:* Instr painting & art hist, Phoenix Col, 67-83; lectr & writer art hist Am West. *Media:* Acrylic, Oil. *Publ:* Auth, Merrill Mahafley Monumental Landscapes, Northland Press, 79. *Mailing Add:* 8776 Streamcrest Dr 1202 W Thomas Rd Boulder CO 80302

MAHEY, JOHN A
GALLERY DIRECTOR

b Du Bois, Pa, Mar 30, 32. *Study:* Columbia Col, 50-52; Pa State Univ, BA & MA(art hist). *Collections Arranged:* Sarah Miriam Peale (with catalog), Peale Mus, Baltimore, Md, 68; Master Drawings from (with catalog), E B Crocker Art Gallery, Calif, 71; Painter of the Humble Truth, Philbrook, Tulsa, Okla, 81. *Pos:* Asst dir, Peale Mus, Baltimore, 64-69; dir, E B Crocker Art Gallery, Sacramento, 69-72; dir, Cummer Gallery Art, Jacksonville, 72-75; dir, Mem Art Gallery, 75-79; chief cur, Philbrook Art Ctr, Tulsa, 79- *Teaching:* Adj prof art hist, Univ Rochester, 75-79. *Res:* James McNeil Whistler & Rembrandt Peale. *Publ:* Auth, Letters of James McNeil Whistler to George Lucas, 67, The lithographs of Rembrandt Peale, 69 & The studio of Rembrandt Peale, 69. *Mailing Add:* 4160 S Rockford Pl Tulsa OK 74105

MAHLKE, ERNEST D
SCULPTOR, EDUCATOR

b Madison, Wis, Sept 15, 30. *Study:* Univ Wis, BS & MS; Inst Allende, Univ Guanajuato, Mex, MFA. *Work:* State Univ NY Oneonta; and many pvt collections. *Exhib:* Smithsonian Inst Traveling Exhibs, 55, 57 & 58; Smithsonian Inst, 55, 61 & 62; Cooperstown Art Asn Nat Ann, NY, 66-81; Artists of Cent NY Regional Ann, Munson-Williams-Proctor Inst, Utica, NY, 68-79; one-man shows, Two Rivers Gallery, Binghamton, NY, 72, The Art Ctr, Albany, NY, 76 & State Univ NY Oneonta, 80; Drawing & Small Sculpture Show, Ball State Univ Art Gallery, 75, 79 & 81; Sculpture 75 Nat, 75. *Pos:* Pres, Wis Designer Craftsmen, Milwaukee, 62; mem bd, Oneonta Art Ctr, NY, 77. *Teaching:* Assoc prof sculpture, State Univ NY Oneonta, 62-78, prof, 78- *Mem:* Am Craftsmen's Coun. *Media:* Wood, Metal. *Dealer:* Gallery 53 Cooperstown NY 13326. *Mailing Add:* 39 Spruce St Oneonta NY 13820

MAHLMANN, JOHN JAMES
PUBLISHER, ADMINISTRATOR

b Washington, DC, Jan 21, 42. *Study:* Boston Univ, BFA, 62, MFA, 63; Univ Notre Dame, summer 62; Pa State Univ, EdD, 70. *Pos:* Asst exec secy, Nat Art Educ Asn, Washington, DC, 69-71, exec dir, 71-; ed, Art Education, 81- & Art Teacher, 81- *Teaching:* Grad asst, Boston Univ, 62-63; grad asst & res asst, Pa State Univ, 63-64, instr, 66-67, dir gallery, Art Educ Dept, 66-67; asst prof, Tex Tech Col, 67-69. *Mem:* Nat Art Educ Asn. *Mailing Add:* c/o Nat Art Educ Asn 1916 Association Dr Reston VA 22091

MAHMOUD, BEN
PAINTER

b Charleston, WVa, Oct 6, 35. *Study:* Columbus Art Sch, prof cert; Ohio Univ, BFA & MFA. *Work:* Ill State Mus, Springfield, Ill; Krannart Mus, Univ Ill, Urbana; Art Inst Chicago; Columbus Gallery Fine Arts, Ohio; Brooklyn Mus, New York. *Exhib:* Art Today, Indianapolis Mus Art, Ind, 70; New Horizons in Painting, Chicago, 72; Zaks Gallery, Chicago, 78, 80 & 83; Nardin Gallery, New York, 80. *Pos:* Mem bd, Ill Arts Coun, 73-77. *Awards:* Purchase Award, Images on Paper '70, Miss, 70; Best of Show, New Horizons in Painting, Chicago, 72; Nat Endowment Arts Fel Painting, 75. *Bibliog:* Franz Schultze (auth), review, Chicago Daily New Panorama, 67; Joshua Kind (auth), review, Art News, 67; Kulterman (auth), New Painting, Praeger, 70. *Media:* Acrylic. *Publ:* Auth, article in Prize Winning Paintings, Allied Fla, 61 & 64; contribr, Chicago Omnibus, Chicago Midwest Art & Art Gallery Mag, 67; illusr, Motive Mag, 68. *Dealer:* Zaks Gallery 620 N Michigan Ave Chicago IL 60611. *Mailing Add:* Dept of Art Northern Ill Univ De Kalb IL 60115

MAHONEY, JAMES OWEN
PAINTER, EDUCATOR

b Dallas, Tex, Oct 16, 07. *Study:* Southern Methodist Univ, BA, 29; Yale Sch Fine Arts, BFA, 32; Am Acad Rome, Prix Rome, 32-35. *Comn:* Murals, Hall of Judiciary, Fed Bldg & Commun Bldg, New York World's Fair, 38, Pres Suite, Adolphus Hotel, Dallas, 50 & Shriver Hall, Johns Hopkins Univ, 57; altar piece, All Saints Episcopal Church, Chevy Chase, Md, 58; Fairmont Hotel, Atlanta, 74; Acad Med, Atlanta, 83. *Exhib:* Pa Acad Fine Arts; Grand Cent Art Gallery; Mace Gallery, Dallas; Archit League. *Teaching:* Prof art, Cornell Univ, 54-75, chmn dept, 63-68, emer prof, 75- *Mem:* Nat Soc Mural Painters; Century Asn. *Mailing Add:* 45 Twin Glens Rd Ithaca NY 14850

MAHONEY, MICHAEL R T
HISTORIAN, EDUCATOR

b Worcester, Mass, Jan 24, 35. *Study:* Phillips Acad, 53; Yale Univ, BA, 59; Courtauld Inst, Univ London, PhD, 65. *Pos:* Mus cur, Nat Gallery of Art, Washington, DC, 64-69, cur sculpture, 67, ed, 68-69. *Teaching:* Prof art hist, Trinity Col, Hartford, 69- *Res:* Seventeenth century art. *Publ:* Auth, Drawings of Salvator Rosa, Garland, 77. *Mailing Add:* Austin Arts Ctr Trinity Col Hartford CT 06106

MAIER, MARYANNE E
PAINTER

b Rochester, NY. *Study:* With Dana Gibson Noble, 75-77; Paier Col Art, dipl(fine arts), 77; with Charles Gruppe, 81. *Comn:* Seascapes, Condominiums, comn by J Kopstein, Tampa, Fla, 78; Sand Dune, Fagen's Restaurant, Stratford, Conn, 79; Scenes of Connecticut, Bull's Bridge Inn, Kent, 79; Harbors & Seascapes, Guenster Home Inc, Bridgeport, Conn, 82. *Exhib:* One-woman show, Milford Fine Arts Coun, Conn, 79; Audubon Artists, Nat Acad Galleries, New York, 79; Mus Art & Sci, Bridgeport, Conn, 80; Hudson Valley Art Asn, Westchester Co Ctr, White Plains, NY, 80; Seascapes of New England, Hartford State Capitol, Conn, 83. *Awards:* Salmagundi Club Prize, 79; Judge's Spec Award, Bridgeport Art League, 79; Best in Show, Conn Classic Arts, 80. *Bibliog:* Edward Meaney (auth), Family life, Lynn Item News, Mass, 76; Lynn Doherty (auth), In her eyes all the world is a canvas, Milford Citizen, 80. *Mem:* Nat League Am Pen Women; Conn Classic Arts; Milford Fine Arts; life mem Kent Art Asn; Salmagundi Club. *Media:* Oil. *Mailing Add:* 465 Gulf St Milford CT 06460

MAILMAN, CYNTHIA
PAINTER, MURALIST

b Bronx, NY, Dec 31, 42. *Study:* Pratt Inst, BS, 64; Art Students League; Brooklyn Mus Art Sch; Rutgers Univ, MFA, 78. *Work:* Everson Mus, Syracuse; Staten Island Mus; Rutgers Univ Art Gallery, New Brunswick; Prudential Life Ins Co, Newark, NJ; NJ State Mus, Trenton. *Comn:* Mural, Citywalls Pub Arts Coun, 77; mural, World Trade Ctr, Port Authority, New York. *Exhib:* One-person shows, Soho 20 Gallery, New York, 74, 76, 78, 80 & 83, Mabel Smith Douglass Libr, NJ, 76, Fox-Richmond Gallery, Keuka Col, NY, 77, Everson Mus, Syracuse, NY, 81 & Maurice M Pine Libr, NJ, 81; Contemporary Reflections, Aldrich Mus, Ridgefield, Conn, 75; NY State Mus, 81; and others. *Pos:* Lectr, 77- *Teaching:* Instr art, Queensborough Community Col, 80- *Awards:* Creative Artists Pub Serv Grant in Painting, 76-77. *Bibliog:* Peter Frank (auth), article, Art News, 10/78; David L Shirey (auth), article, New York Times, 11/1/81; Diana Morris (auth), article, Woman Artists News, summer 83. *Mem:* NY Womens Caucus Art. *Media:* Acrylic. *Mailing Add:* 49 Broad St Staten Island NY 10304

MAINARDI, PATRICIA M
PAINTER, WRITER

b Paterson, NJ, Nov 10, 42. *Study:* Vassar Col, AB, 63; Columbia Univ, 63-65; New York Studio Sch, 65-66; Brooklyn Col, City Univ New York, MFA, 76; Hunter Col, MA, 80; City Univ New York, MPhilos, 81. *Exhib:* The Representational Spirit, State Univ NY Albany Gallery, 70; Painterly Realism, Am Fedn Arts, 69-71; New Images: Figuration in American Painting, Queens Mus, 74; one-artist show, Green Mountain Gallery, New York, 71 & 74 & Ingber Gallery, 75, 78 & 81. *Pos:* Ed, Women & Art, 71-72; ed, Feminist Art J, 72-73; contrib ed, 73-74; contrib ed, Arts Mag, 79-; dir, Goddard MFA Visual Arts Prog, 78-81. *Teaching:* Vis lectr, Pratt Inst, Mass Col Art, 73 & 74, Brooklyn Col, 76-78, Sch Visual Arts, 77 & Goddard Col, 77- *Awards:* Chester Dale fel, Nat Gallery Art, 81-82. *Bibliog:* Articles, Art 10/74 & 1/76, Arts, 9/74 & 2/76 & Art Int, summer 74; and others. *Mem:* Col Art Asn; Int Asn Art Critics. *Dealer:* Ingber Gallery 460 West Broadway New York NY 10012. *Mailing Add:* 602 Carlton Ave Brooklyn NY 11238

MAIONE, ROBERT
PAINTER

b New York, NY, 1932. *Study:* Art Students League; also with Frank Dumond & Frank Mason. *Exhib:* Allied Artists Am, 65-; Nat Acad Design Ann, 65-; Audubon Artists, 65-; The Realistic Tradition, State Univ NY, Albany, 74. *Awards:* Art Students League, 51-53; Arthur T Hill Mem Prize, 60; Allied Artists Am Award, 74. *Mem:* Allied Artists Am; Salmagundi Club. *Media:* Oil. *Mailing Add:* c/o Harbor Gallery 43 Main St Cold Spring Harbor NY 11724

MAITIN, SAM (SAMUEL CALMAN)
PAINTER, SCULPTOR

b Philadelphia, Pa, Oct 26, 28. *Study:* Philadelphia Mus Sch Art, dipl, 49; Univ Pa, BA, 51; printmaking with Ezio Martinelli and painting with Paul Froelich. *Work:* Libr Cong & Nat Gallery Art, Washington, DC; Mus Mod Art, New York; Pa Acad Fine Arts; Currier Gallery, Manchester, NH; SmithKline Beckman Collection, Philadelphia; and others. *Comn:* 47 posters, Philadelphia YM/YWHA Arts Coun, 61-68; Standing Structures, Luther Brady, Acey Wolgin, Collectors, Philadelphia, 73; Philadelphia Mus Art, Print & Construction, 74; mural, Annenberg Sch Commun, Univ Pa, 75; tapestry, Adath Jeshurun Synagogue, Jenkintown, Pa, 76. *Exhib:* Yoseido Gallery, Tokyo, 67, 69 & 70; 3rd Int Graphic Biennale, Poland, 70; Samuel Fleisher Art Mem, 71; William Penn Mus, Harrisburg, Pa, 75; Bicentennial Exhib, Philadelphia Mus Art, 76; Curwen Artists, Tate Gallery, London, 77; Gallery 10, Aspen, Colo, 81; and others. *Teaching:* Instr design, Moore Col Art, 49-51; instr printmaking & drawing, Philadelphia Col Art, 49-59; head visual graphic commun, Annenberg Sch Commun, Univ Pa, 64-70; instr drawing & printmaking, Philadelphia Mus Art, 64-69. *Awards:* John Simon Guggenheim Found Fel graphics, 68; 50 Best Bks of Yr, Minor White, 70. *Bibliog:* Willard Randall (auth), Is Philadelphia ready for Sam Maitin?, Philadelphia Inquirer, Today Mag, 11/18/73; Walter Plata (auth), Typografen unserer Zeit, Samuel Maitin, Heft; Maryanne Conheim (auth), Of many things; a conversation with a master of human arts--Sam Maitin, Philadelphia Inquirer, 9/17/79. *Media:* Graphics, Acrylic. *Publ:* Designer, mirrors, messages, manifestations, work of Minor White, 69 & The Appalachian photographs of Doris Ulmann, 71, Aperture; illusr, Turning of the Year, 70, Holt, Rinehart & Winston; designer, Sculpture of a City: Philadelphia's Treasures in Bronze and Stone, FPAA, Walker Publ Co, 74; designer, A Rising People, Am Philos Soc, 75-76. *Mailing Add:* 704 Pine St Philadelphia PA 19106

MAJDRAKOFF, IVAN
PAINTER, ASSEMBLAGE ARTIST

b New York, NY, June 19, 27. *Study:* Cranbrook Acad Art, with Wallace Mitchell. *Work:* Univ Minn Gallery; Minneapolis Inst Art. *Comn:* Black & white photographic collage, Bronx State Hosp, NY, 71; Masonite outdoor mural, San Francisco Art Comn. *Exhib:* Pa Acad Art, Philadelphia; Detroit Art Inst, Mich; Walker Art Ctr, Minneapolis; San Francisco Mus Art; Drawing Exhib, Mus Mod Art, New York. *Pos:* Actg dir, Univ Art Gallery, Univ Minn, 52-55; dir, Stanford Univ Gallery, 62. *Teaching:* Instr drawing &

painting, San Francisco Art Inst, 57-; instr drawing, Stanford Univ, 57-58 & 68-69. *Bibliog:* Al Wong (auth), Portrait of Ivan (film), 68. *Media:* Acrylic, Ink. *Mailing Add:* Dept of Drawing/Painting 800 Chestnut St San Francisco CA 94133

MAJESKI, THOMAS H
PRINTMAKER, EDUCATOR

b Council Bluffs, Iowa, Sept 14, 33. *Study:* Univ Omaha, BFA, 60; Univ Iowa, with Mauricio Lasansky, MFA, 63. *Work:* Philadelphia Mus Art, Pa; Sheldon Mem Art Mus, Lincoln, Nebr; Joslyn Mus, Omaha, Nebr; Utah State Univ, Logan. *Exhib:* Prints, Watercolors & Drawings, Pa Acad Fine Arts, Philadelphia, 65; Brooklyn Mus, New York, 66; Philadelphia Print Club, Pa, 67; Northwest Printmakers Int Print Exhib, Seattle, Wash & Portland, Ore, 67; Art On Paper, Univ NC, Greensboro, 68; 17 State Exhib, Springfield Art Mus, Mo, 74; Colorprint USA, Tex Tech Univ, Lubbock, 74. *Teaching:* Prof printmaking, Univ Nebr Omaha, 63-82, prof art, currently. *Awards:* Purchase Awards, Philadelphia Print Club, 67, Nebr Centennial, 67 & Springfield Art Mus, 74. *Mem:* Philadelphia Print Club; Col Art Asn; Mid-Am Col Art Asn. *Media:* Intaglio, Lithography. *Mailing Add:* 1730 N 106 St Omaha NE 68114

MAKI, ROBERT RICHARD
SCULPTOR, LECTURER

b Walla Walla, Wash, Sept 15, 38. *Study:* Western Wash State Col, BA, 62; Univ Wash, MFA, 66; San Francisco Art Inst Summer Workshop, 67. *Work:* Washington Univ; State Hwy Admin Bldg, Olympia, Wash; Stanford Univ; Nat Collection of Fine Art, Washington, DC; Seattle Art Mus. *Comn:* Evergreen State Col, Olympia, Wash; Wake Forest Univ, Winston-Salem, NC; State Administration Bldg, Salem, Ore; and others. *Exhib:* West Coast Now, Seattle Art Mus Pavilion & De Young Mus, 68; Reality of Illusions, Herbert F Johnson Mus Art, Cornell Univ, 79; one-man shows, Seattle Art Mus Pavilion, Wash, 73, Portland Ctr Visual Arts, Ore, 74, Southeastern Ctr Contemp Art, Winston-Salem, NC, 78 & Richard Hines Gallery, Seattle, Wash, 79 & 81. *Pos:* Guest lectr at many schs & mus nationwide, 70- *Teaching:* Hon lectr, Univ Wash, Seattle, 66-68. *Awards:* Gen Serv Agency Sculpture Comn Award, 74; Rockefeller Found Artist-in-Residence, 78-79; Purchase Award, Wright Found, 80. *Bibliog:* Peter Selz & Tom Robbins (auth), West Coast report: The Pacific Northwest today, Art Am, 11-12/68; Jan Van de Marck (auth), Robert Maki at Center for Visual Arts, Art Am, 9-10/74; Bruce Guenther (auth), 50 NW Artists, 83; and others. *Mailing Add:* 8 Florentia Seattle WA 98109

MAKLER, HOPE WELSH
DEALER

b Philadelphia, Pa, Mar 24, 24. *Study:* Drexel Univ, BS; Bryn Mawr Col & Univ Pa, MA; Barnes Found. *Pos:* Owner & dir, Makler Gallery, Philadelphia, currently. *Specialty:* Twentieth century painting, sculpture and graphics; Indian and African art. *Mailing Add:* 1716 Locust St Philadelphia PA 19103

MALDJIAN, VARTAVAR B
PAINTER, WEAVER

b Marash, Cilicia, July 12, 1918; US citizen. *Study:* Maristes Brothers Col; Sch of Art, Paris, grad(fine painting). *Exhib:* Nat Aleppo for Carpet Picture, 50; Int Exhib, Damascus, Carpet Picture, 56; Nat Competition of Benedictine, New York, 66; Nat for Prof Artists, New York, 68; Davinci Int Open Art, New York Coliseum, 70; and many others. *Awards:* Silver Medal, Gustod of Terra Sancta (carpet picture), 50; Gold Medal for Carpet Picture, Int Exhib, Damascus, 56; Award for Original Oil, Davinci Int, New York, 70. *Bibliog:* Rev V Hovhanessian (auth), article on carpet picture, Massis, Beirut, 49; Abdallah J Hallack (auth), Ad-Dad, Monthly Art, 52; article about Pres Kennedy's carpet picture, Newark Eve News, 11/26/63. *Mem:* Am Fedn Art, New York. *Media:* Oil, Oriental Knots. *Collection:* V B Maljian Museum, original oils and carpet pictures. *Mailing Add:* 38 Oriental St Newark NJ 07104

MALDRE, MATI
PHOTOGRAPHER, EDUCATOR

b Geestacht, Ger, Apr 3, 47; US citizen. *Study:* Univ Ill, with Joseph Jachna, BA(design), 69; Inst Design, Ill Inst Technol, with Aaron Siskind, Arthur Siegel & Charles Swedlund, Encycl Britannica grant, 70-72, MS(photog), 72; also with Paul Caponagro, Jerry Uelsmann, Nathan Lyons & Les Krims. *Work:* Kalamazoo Art Ctr, Mich; Humboldt Arts Coun, Eureka, Calif; Pasadena Mus Art, Calif; Visual Studies Workshop, Rochester, NY. *Exhib:* Int Photo Show, Chicago, 74; First Light & Light II, Humboldt Arts Coun, 75; Ill Photogr Traveling Exhibs, Ill State Mus, Springfield, 78 & 82; Freshworks 79, Va Mus Fine Arts, Richmond; Friends of Photography, Carmel, Calif, 79 & 80; Univ Wis, Green Bay, 80; and others. *Pos:* Photogr & lab technician, Encycl Britannica, Chicago, 70-74; consult photog & graphics, Chicago Urban Corps, 72- *Teaching:* Asst prof photog, Chicago State Univ, 72-78, assoc prof, 78-; instr photog, Beverly Art Ctr, Ill, 73- *Awards:* Grand Award, Photo Images '76, Springfield; Merit Award, Radius '76, Burdee Mus, Rockford, Ill; Purchase Awards, Ill Photogr, Ill State Mus, 78 & 82. *Mem:* Soc Photo Educ; Int Mus Photo, George Eastman House; Friends of Photography. *Media:* Black and White, Cibachrome. *Publ:* Illusr, Encycl Britannica & Britannica Bk of Yr, 70-74; illusr, Comptons Encycl & Comptons Yr Bk, 70-74; illusr, Great Ideas Today, 70-74; illusr, Chicago: Metropolis of the Mid-Continent, Kendel/Hunt Co. *Mailing Add:* 1727 West Griffin 104th Pl Chicago IL 60643

MALENDA, JAMES WILLIAM
ENAMELIST, EDUCATOR

b Kingston, Pa, Sept 14, 46. *Study:* Miami Dade Community Col, 69; Kent State Univ, BFA, 71; State Univ NY, MFA, 75. *Work:* Roberson Ctr Arts & Sci, Binghamton, NY; Univ Ga, Athens. *Comn:* Advent Wreath, St Paul's Cathedral, Peoria, Ill, 80; Crucifix, Salem Lutheran, Peoria, Ill, 80. *Exhib:* Art for Use at XIII Olympics, Fine Arts Gallery, Lake Placid, NY, 80; Enamels 50/80, Manchester Inst Art, NH, 81; Email, Goldsmiths' Hall, London, Eng, 81; Int Exhib Enameling Art, Tokyo Central, Japan, 81; Material, Handwerkammer, Munich, Ger, 83. *Teaching:* Instr enamel & metal, Mohave Community Col, Kingman, Ariz, 75-76; asst prof, Bradley Univ, Peoria, Ill, 76- *Awards:* Enameling Award, Thomas C Thompson Co, 78; Table Piece Award, Scope Gallery, 78; Completion Grant, Ill Arts Coun, 80. *Mem:* Distinguished mem Soc NAm Goldsmiths. *Media:* Enamel, Metal. *Publ:* Contribr, Contemporary Practice of an Ancient Craft, Decade, 78; auth, Autobiography, Goldsmiths J, 79; contribr, Off the Body, Craft Range, 80; contribr, Off the Body, Metalsmith, 80. *Dealer:* Spring St Enamel Gallery 171 Spring St New York NY 10012. *Mailing Add:* 1630 W Ayres Ave Peoria IL 61606

MALLARY, ROBERT
SCULPTOR, EDUCATOR

b Toledo, Ohio, Dec 2, 17. *Study:* Escuela Artes Libro, Mexico City, 38-39; Tamarind Litho Workshop, 62. *Work:* Mus Mod Art, Whitney Mus Am Art, New York; Los Angeles Co Mus; Albright-Knox Art Gallery, Buffalo; Univ Calif, Berkeley. *Comn:* Glass and plastic mosaic (with Dale Owen), Beverly Hills Hotel, 54; NY State Pavilion, New York World's Fair, 64; welded steel mural, Albany Mall Proj, 67. *Exhib:* 16 Americans, 59 & The Art of Assemblage, 61, Mus Mod Art, New York; Carnegie Int, Pittsburgh, Pa, 62; Ten American Sculptors, Seventh Sao Paulo Biennial, Brazil, 63; Cybernetic Serendipity, Inst Contemp Art, London, 68. *Pos:* Dir, Arstecnica: Interdisciplinary Ctr for Art & Technol, Univ Mass, 72- *Teaching:* Asst prof art, Univ NMex, 55-59; adj prof, Pratt Inst, 59-67; prof sculpture, Univ Mass, Amherst, 67- *Awards:* Guggenheim Grant, 64. *Bibliog:* Art crashes through the junk pile, Life Mag, 51 & 60-64; Collage: personalities, concepts, techniques, Janis & Plesh, 62; Harris Rothenstein (auth), Ideologue in lotus land, Art News, 10/66. *Publ:* Auth, Self interview, Location, spring 63; auth, The air of art is poisoned, Art News, 10/63; coauth, interview, Artforum, 1/64; auth, Computer sculpture: Six levels of cybernetics, Artforum, 5/69; and others. *Dealer:* Allan Stone Gallery 86th St at Madison New York NY 10028. *Mailing Add:* PO Box 97 Conway MA 01341

MALLORY, MARGARET
COLLECTOR, FILMMAKER

b Brooklyn, NY, Oct 30, 11. *Pos:* Former pres, Falcon Films, Inc (doc art films); trustee, Santa Barbara Mus Art; trustee, Mystic Seaport, Conn; hon life dir, art affil, Univ Calif, Santa Barbara; adv bd, Women's Nat Mus Bd, Univ Calif, Santa Barbara; trustee mem Assoc Mus Asn; adv coun, Am Mus Britain. *Collection:* American and European paintings, drawings, sculpture, predominantly 19th & 20th century. *Mailing Add:* 305 Ortega Ridge Rd Santa Barbara CA 93108

MALLORY, NINA AYALA
EDUCATOR, HISTORIAN

b Madrid, Spain; US citizen. *Study:* Columbia Univ, BArchit, 56, MA, 62 & PhD, 65. *Teaching:* Instr art hist, Rutgers Univ, New Brunswick, NJ, 65-66; asst prof renaissance, The Cooper Union, New York, 66-68; assoc prof renaissance & baroque, State Univ New York, Stony Brook, 68- *Awards:* Fulbright Fel, US Govt, 63; Grant-in-Aid, Am Coun of Learned Socs, 67; Fac Rcs Fel, State Univ New York Res Found, 69-75 & 79. *Mem:* Col Art Asn; Am Soc for Hispanic Art Hist Studies. *Res:* Seventeenth-eighteenth century Spanish art. *Publ:* Auth, Narciso Tome's transparente in the Cathedral of Toledo, J Soc of Archit Hist, 70; auth, Notices on sculpture in 18th-century Rome Bollettino d'Arte, 74, 76 & 82; auth, Roman Rococo architecture from Clement XI to Benedict XIV, 1700-1758, Garland, 77; coauth, Painting in Spain 1650-1700, Princeton, 82; auth, Bartolome Esteban Murillo, Alianza, 83. *Mailing Add:* 4 Washington Sq Village New York NY 10012

MALLORY, RONALD
SCULPTOR

b Philadelphia, Pa, June 17, 35. *Study:* Univ Colo, BA, 51; Univ Fla, BArch, 52; Sch Fine Arts, Rio de Janeiro, with Roberto Burle Marx, 56; Acad Julian, Paris, 58. *Work:* Mus Mod Art, Whitney Mus Am Art, New York; Univ Mus, Berkeley, Calif; Inst Contemp Art, Boston; Inst Contemp Art, Philadelphia; and others. *Exhib:* Mus Mod Art, 66 & 68; Worcester Mus Art, Mass, 67; Univ Ill, 67 & 68; Larry Aldrich Mus, Ridgefield, Conn, 67 & 68; Torcuato di Tella, Buenos Aires, Arg, 69; Univ Calif, Los Angeles, 69; one-man exhibs, Galleria Bonino Ltd, New York, 69 & 73; Whitney Mus Am Art; and others. *Teaching:* Instr, Univ Calif, Berkeley, 72. *Mailing Add:* 353 W 12th St New York NY 10014

MALO, TERI (TERI A MALO-SPRAWKA)
PAINTER, PRINTMAKER

b Whitinsville, Mass, July 20, 54. *Study:* Emmanuel Col, with Michael Jacques, BA, 76; Univ Mass, Amherst, with John Townsend & Fred Becker, MFA, 78. *Work:* Philadelphia Mus Art; IBM Inc, John Hancock Insurance Co, Boston; Otis Elevator, Hartford, Conn; Holyoke Community Col. *Exhib:* Philadelphia Int Print Exhib, Philadelphia Mus Art, 79; solo exhib, Pucker-Safrai Gallery, Boston, 79, 80, 82 & 83 & Art Collectors Gallery, New York, 81; Miami Int Print Exhib, Fla, 80; Silvermine 13th Nat Print Exhib, 80; Prints, Heritage Mus, Sandwich, Mass, 82; Jerusalem to Boston, Mitchell Mus, Mt Vernon, Ill, 83. *Media:* Oil; Woodcut, Linocut. *Dealer:* Pucker-Safrai Gallery 171 Newbury St Boston MA 02116. *Mailing Add:* 518 Pleasant St Northampton MA 01060

MALONE, LEE H B
MUSEUM DIRECTOR

b Las Cruces, NMex, 28, 13. *Study:* Univ Sch, Cleveland, Ohio; Yale Sch Fine Arts, BA; also study in Switz. *Collections Arranged:* Art in Colonial Mexico, Columbus Gallery Fine Arts, Ohio, 52; Translucent and Transparent, 71 & Flowing Form, 72, Mus Fine Arts, St Petersburg, Fla, 72. *Pos:* Dir, Columbus Gallery Fine Arts, Ohio, 45-54; dir, Mus Fine Arts, Houston, Tex, 53-59; art consult, New York, 59-67; dir, Mus Fine Arts, St Petersburg, Fla, 68- *Teaching:* Instr hist art, Notre Dame Col, Staten Island, NY, 40-41; instr, Mus Fine Arts, St Petersburg, Fla, 68- *Awards:* W L Ehrich Mem Prize, Yale Univ, 39; Cavalier Ordine de Merito, Italy, 74. *Mem:* Am Asn Mus (secy, 73-75); Fine Arts Coun Fla; Southeastern Mus Conf. *Publ:* Auth, Spiritual Values in Art, Abrams Press, 53. *Mailing Add:* 701 15th Ave NE St Petersburg FL 33702

MALONE, ROBERT R
PAINTER, PRINTMAKER

b McColl, SC, Aug 8, 33. *Study:* Furman Univ; Univ NC, BA; Univ Chicago, MFA; State Univ Iowa. *Work:* New York Pub Libr; Calif Palace of Legion of Honor, San Francisco; Philadelphia Mus Art, Pa; Smithsonian Inst, Washington, DC; Libr of Cong, Washington, DC. *Comn:* Color etching, Int Graphic Arts Soc, New York, 66; several editions of intaglio & relief prints, Ferdinand Roten Galleries, Baltimore, Md, 66-69; two editions intaglio & relief prints, De Cinque Gallery, Hollywood, Fla, 67; color etching, Ill Arts Coun, 1st Print Comn, 73; several editions of lithographs, Lakeside Studio, Lakeside, Mich, 71-80. *Exhib:* 15th Nat Print Exhib, Brooklyn Mus Art, NY, 66; New Talent in Printmaking, AAA Gallery, New York, 68; Biennial Print Exhib, Calif State Col, Long Beach, 69; Bienniale Int L'Estampe 1970, Mus Mod Art, Paris, 70; 26th Ann Exhib Boston Printmakers, De Cordova Mus, 74. *Teaching:* Assoc prof painting & printmaking, Wesleyan Col, Macon, Ga, 61-68; assoc prof printmaking, WVa Univ, Morgantown, 68-70; assoc prof printmaking, Southern Ill Univ, Edwardsville, 70-75, prof, 75- *Awards:* Purchase Award, Colorprint USA, Tex Tech Univ, 71; Recent Am Graphics Purchase Award, Univ Wis-Madison, 75; Southern Ill Univ Sr Res Scholar Award, 75. *Mem:* Col Art Asn Am. *Media:* Oil; Lithography, Etching. *Dealer:* Lakeside Studio Lakeside MI. *Mailing Add:* 600 Chapman St Edwardsville IL 62025

MALPASS, MICHAEL ALLEN
SCULPTOR, EDUCATOR

b Yonkers, NY, Aug 18, 46. *Study:* Pratt Inst, BFA, 69, MFA, 73, MS, 77. *Work:* Mint Mus Art. *Comn:* Sculpture (iron & steel), New York City Fire Dept, 80; sculpture, TRW, Cleveland, 84. *Exhib:* Williamsburg Iron & Steel, Brooklyn Mus, 71; Iron Wrought, Univ Southern Ill, 76; solo exhib, Betty Parsons Gallery, New York, 76 & 78 & Andre Zarre Gallery, New York, 82; Albright-Knox Art Gallery, 77; Metro Mus Miami Int Print Exhib, 77; Great Atlanta & New York Sculpture Exchange, 79. *Pos:* Sculpture & welding technician, Pratt Inst, 65-70. *Teaching:* Instr sculpture, Pratt Inst, 72-77, asst prof, 77- *Bibliog:* Diane Clayton (auth), Body art, Washington Star, 10/17/76; Grace Glueck (auth), article, New York Times, 6/11/82. *Mem:* Blacksmiths NAm; Am Welding Soc; Artists Representing Environmental Art; Orgn Independent Artists; Sculptors Guild (exec bd, 83-). *Media:* Welded Iron and Steel. *Dealer:* Andre Zarre Gallery 41 E 57 St New York NY 10022. *Mailing Add:* 593 Parker Ave Brick NJ 08723

MALSCH, ELLEN L
PAINTER, INSTRUCTOR

b Copenhagen, Denmark; US citizen. *Study:* Art Inst Chicago. *Work:* Univ Wis-Madison; Luther Col, Decorah, Iowa; Univ Wis-La Crosse; Waukesha Co Tech Inst, Pewaukee, Wis; Univ Wis, Rockcount Campus, Janesville. *Exhib:* Wis Painters & Sculptors Show, Milwaukee Art Ctr, 62; three-man show, Wright Art Ctr, Beloit Col, Wis, 64; Drawings USA, Nat Biennial Show, St Paul, Minn, 66; Ill State Fair Prof Show, Springfield, Ill, 69; Watercolor USA, Springfield, Mo, 71; and others. *Teaching:* Pvt classes, 60-72; instr watercolor, Burpee Art Mus, Rockford, Ill, 67-70; lectr, watercolor techniques. *Awards:* Purchase Prize, Univ Wis-La Crosse, 69; Best of Show Award, Wis Festival Arts, 75; Purchase Prize, Burpee Mus Permanent Collection, 79. *Bibliog:* Article in La Rev Mod, 67. *Mem:* Wis Painters & Sculptors. *Media:* Watercolor. *Dealer:* Wustum Mus Fine Arts 2519 Northwestern Ave Racine WI 53404; Madison Art Ctr 720 E Gorham St Madison WI 53703. *Mailing Add:* Walker Rd Rte 1 Box 298 Beloit WI 53511

MALTA, VINCENT
INSTRUCTOR, PAINTER

b Brooklyn, NY, Apr 9, 22. *Study:* Art Students League. *Work:* Univ of Minn; Philadelphia Mus; Immaculate Heart Col; Birmingham Mus Art. *Exhib:* Brooklyn Mus Biennial Print Exhib, 52; Metrop Mus Nat Exhib of Watercolors, 52; Pa Acad Fine Arts, 53; Brooklyn Mus Int Watercolor Exhib, 53; Nat Acad of Design, 53. *Teaching:* Instr fine arts, painting, Art Students League, 66- *Awards:* Emily Lowe Award, 52; Tiffany Award, Louis Comfort Tiffany Found Award, 54; Betti Salzman Award, Nat Arts Club, 77. *Bibliog:* Marlene Schiller (auth), Return of the art spirit, Am Artist Mag, 3/78; Art Showcase, Manhattan Cable TV, 5/25/83 & 10/12/83. *Mem:* Artist Equity; Artists' Fel Inc, New York. *Media:* Mixed. *Mailing Add:* 1960 60th St Brooklyn NY 11204

MALTBY, HAZEL FARROW
WEAVER, DESIGNER

b San Francisco, Calif. *Study:* San Francisco State Univ; with Karen Melander, Ada Rominger & Berta Frey; Portland Sch Arts & Crafts, with Theo Moorman. *Work:* Triton Mus Art, San Jose, Menlo Park Civic Ctr &

Metrop Furniture, Ice House, San Francisco; First Fed Savings & Loan Asn, Rugby, NDak. *Comn:* Theme Piece (rug hanging), Northern Calif Handweavers Conf, 71; seven large tapestries, Episcopal Church, San Carlos, Calif, 77. *Exhib:* Calif Expo, Sacramento, 69-70; Las Vegas Art League Nat, 71; Festival '70, Livermore Cult Art Coun, Calif; Tex Fine Arts League Nat, Austin, 74; Handweavers Guild Am Nat Conf, San Francisco, 74; Int Weaving Exhib, Kouvola, Finland, 77. *Teaching:* Pvt art classes, 67-; lectr weaving, Foothill Community Col, 73-74; lectr painting warps, Nat Conf Handweavers Guild Am, 74. *Awards:* State of Calif Expo, 71; twelve awards, First or Second Place, Palo Alto Art Club, 71-75; Las Vegas Art League Nat Roundup, 71. *Mem:* Palo Alto Art Club; Handweavers Guild Am; Bay Area Arts & Crafts Guild; Trampornus Weaving Guild; Loom & Shuttle Weaving Guild. *Publ:* Auth, Painting Warps, 74. *Mailing Add:* 118 Plazoleta Los Gatos CA 95030

MALTZMAN, STANLEY
PRINTMAKER, PAINTER
b New York, NY, July 4, 21. *Study:* New York Phoenix Sch Design, degree, 48. *Work:* Schenectady Mus, New York; Readers Digest; Hudson River Mus, Yonkers, NY; Carnegie-Mellon Univ; Mus Fine Arts, Springfield, Mass. *Comn:* Steuben Glass, Corning, NY; Danbury Mint, Norwalk, Conn. *Exhib:* Am Acad Arts & Lett, 69 & Nat Acad Design, 70 & Int:, New York; Norfolk Mus Arts & Sci, Va, 71; Smithsonian Inst Traveling Exhib, 71-72; Acad Artists Asn, Mus Fine Arts, Springfield, Mass, 72; Albany Inst Hist & Art, NY, 81; Berkshire Mus, Pittsfield, Mass, 79; Am Watercolor Soc, NY, 80. *Awards:* First Prize, Conn Acad Fine Arts, 76; Ball State Univ Award, 81; Drawing Prize, Berkshire Mus, Pittsfield, Mass. *Mem:* Greene Co Coun Arts, Catskill, NY. *Media:* Charcoal, Graphics; Watercolor. *Publ:* Sounds of Mystery-Sounds of a Distant Drum, Rinehart & Winston Inc, 67; Botanical Arts & Illusration, Carnegie-Mellon Univ, 77-78; Printworld Directory, 82. *Dealer:* Weyhe Gallery 794 Lexington Ave New York NY 10021; Assoc Am Artists Gallery 663 Fifth Ave New York NY 10022. *Mailing Add:* Rte 1 Box 158 Freehold NY 12431

MANAREY, THELMA ALBERTA
PRINTMAKER, PAINTER
b Edmonton, Alta, May 2, 13. *Study:* Inst Technol & Art, Calgary; Univ Alta; Univ Wash Summer Workshops; Banff Sch Fine Arts, with Charles Stegeman; Univ Calgary, with Shane Weare & Andrew Stasik; also at Emma Lake, with John Ferren & Ken Noland. *Work:* Alta Found; Mem Union, Univ Ore; Edmonton Art Gallery; Mem Univ Art Gallery, Nfld; Alta House Eng. *Comn:* Portrait of Roberta MacAdams, Women of Alta, Prov Legis, 67; Lt Gov Walsh, 73. *Exhib:* 10th Winnipeg Show, 66; Can Graphics, 70; one-person shows, Edmonton Art Gallery, Alta, 70 & 72; Lefebvre Galleries, Greece, 77; Ports of Call, 78 & A Visit to Portugal, 79; Printmakers Showcase West, Ottawa, 74; and others. *Awards:* Centennial Visual Arts Award, 67; award, Pac Northwest Art Ann, 69; City of Edmonton Visual Arts Award, 73. *Mem:* Alta Soc Artists (prov vpres, 65, 67, 68 & 75); Print & Drawing Coun of Can. *Media:* Graphics. *Dealer:* John Arends Galleries Ltd 10238 123rd St Edmonton AB T5N 1N4 Can. *Mailing Add:* 12026 93rd St Edmonton AB T5G 1E8 Canada

MANCINI, JOHN
PAINTER, ILLUSTRATOR
b Comiso, Italy, Jan 9, 25; US citizen. *Study:* Scuola d'Arte, Comiso, Italy, dipl; Liceo & Accad di Belle Arti, Palermo, Italy, BA; Art Students League; Columbia Univ. *Work:* Galleria Della Accademi, Palermo, Italy; Bank Am, Bank of Wells Fargo, San Francisco; Mus Ital Art, Stone Park, Ill; Galeria de Colecionistas, Mexico City. *Exhib:* Premio Naz di Terni, Rome, 50; Premio Naz di Suzzara, Italy, 51; 68th Western Ann Denver Mus, Colo, 62; Crocker Mus Art, Sacramento, Calif, 67; Palace of Fine Art, San Francisco, 68. *Pos:* Art dir, Gridley Studio, New York, 51-58; art dir, Aerojet Gen Corp, Sacramento, Calif, 59-65; art dir, R W Graphics, Palo Alto, Calif, 66-70. *Teaching:* Art teacher painting, Scuola d'Arte, Comiso, Italy, 49-51. *Awards:* Second Premio Naz, La Soffitta, 50; Purchase Award Western Image 71, Frontier Savings, 71; Gold Medal, Italian-Am Artists in USA, 77. *Bibliog:* Robert Brabski (auth), Italienishe Maler Und Bildhauer, William Herzog-Wien VI, 50; E M Polley (auth), John Mancini, Artforum, 65; Thomas Albright (auth), John Mancini, San Francisco Chronicle, 73. *Media:* Oil. *Dealer:* Village Artistry PO Box 5493 Carmel CA 93921; Toni Danzie Source Gallery 1099 Folsom San Francisco CA 94103. *Mailing Add:* 604 Connie Ave San Mateo CA 94402

MANCUSO, LENI (LENI MANCUSO BARRETT)
PAINTER, INSTRUCTOR
b New York, NY. *Study:* Brooklyn Mus Art Sch; Art Students League; Pratt Inst, NY. *Work:* Newberry Collection, Detroit, Mich; First Nat Bank Boston; Portland Mus Art, Maine; Kresge Gallery, Ann Arbor, Mich; Mich Bell Tel. *Exhib:* Wadsworth Atheneum, Hartford, Conn; Masters of Watercolor, Lamont Gallery, Exeter, NH, 78; one-man shows, Currier Gallery Art, Manchester, NH, 78-81; Art Ctr Hargate, Concord, NH, 81 & Thorne-Sagendorph Gallery, Keene, NH, 81; Chapel Arts Ctr, St Anselm's Col, 84. *Teaching:* Instr painting & head art dept, Proctor Acad, Andover, NH, 55-60; instr painting & watercolor, Currier Gallery Art Sch, Manchester, NH, 62-70; instr painting & compos, St Paul's Sch, Concord, NH, 67-75. *Awards:* Watercolor Prize, Portland Mus Art, Maine, 61 & Currier Gallery Art, NH, 68 & 81. *Mem:* NH Art Asn; Boston Visual Artists Union; Deer Isle Artists' Asn; Col Art Asn. *Media:* Watercolor, Casein. *Dealer:* Arnold Klein Gallery 4520 N Woodward Royal Oak MI 48072; Frost Gully Gallery 92 Exchange St Portland ME 04111. *Mailing Add:* St Paul's Sta Concord NH 03301

MANDEL, HOWARD
PAINTER, SCULPTOR
b Bayside, NY, Feb 24, 17. *Study:* Pratt Inst, New York; New York Sculpture Ctr; Art Students League; Atelier Fernand Leger, Paris; Atelier Andre L Hote, Paris; Ecole Beax Arts, Sorbonne, France. *Work:* Whitney Mus Am Art, New York; Butler Inst Am Art, Youngstown, Ohio; Norfolk Mus Arts & Sci, Va; State Univ Teachers Col Mus, Oswego, NY; San Antonio Mus, Tex. *Comn:* Three-dimensional mural, Zenith Radio Corp, Woodstock, NY, 58. *Exhib:* Whitney Mus Am Art Ann, 48-59; American Painting Today 1950, Metrop Mus Art, New York, 50 & Am Watercolors, Drawings & Prints, Metrop Mus Art, New York; Nat Inst Arts & Lett, Acad Art Gallery, New York, 55 & 61; Fulbright Painters, Whitney Mus Am Art & Smithsonian Inst, Washington, DC, 59. *Pos:* Graphic artist, film design, CBS-TV Studio One, 54-57; graphic artist, film design, NBC-TV Amahl and the Night Visitors, 55; art dir, Heath de Rochemont, D C Heath & Co, Boston, 63-68; art dir, Roemer-Young Assocs, New York, 69; art dir, Film Group, Inc, Cambridge, Mass, 71. *Awards:* Louis Comfort Tiffany Fel, 39 & 49; Hallmark Int Awards, 49, 52 & 55; Fulbright Scholar to Paris, 51-52. *Bibliog:* Herdeg & Rosner (auth), article in Graphics Ann, 55; The Art Comics & Satires of A D Reinhardt, George Wittenborn; Archives of American Art, Smithsonian Inst, Washington, DC. *Mem:* Am Watercolor Soc; Nat Soc Mural Painters; Nat Soc Painters in Casein & Acrylic; Audubon Artists; Allied Artists Am; and others. *Media:* Multimedia. *Mailing Add:* 285 Central Park W New York NY 10024

MANDEL, JOHN
PAINTER
b New York, NY, Dec 6, 41. *Study:* Pratt Inst, BFA, 64. *Work:* Nat Gallery Australia; Pa State Univ. *Exhib:* Whitney Mus Am Art Painting Ann, 69 & 72; The Contemporary Figure, A New Realism, Suffolk Mus & Carriage House at Stony Brook, NY, 71; In Sharp Focus, Sidney Janis Gallery, New York, 72; Indianapolis Mus Ann, Ind, 72; one-man shows, Max Hutchinson Gallery, New York, 71-73, 75 & 79. *Pos:* Assoc dean, Sch Art & Design, Calif Inst Arts. *Teaching:* Instr painting, grad & undergrad sch, Pratt Inst, 71-76; instr painting, Calif Inst Arts, 72- *Awards:* Paul Mellon Fel, 79. *Bibliog:* John Canaday (auth), Art: The figure as defined by Mandel, 11/21/71 & Art: In Mandel's Art, superb control, 4/28/73, New York Times. *Mailing Add:* c/o Art Sch Calif Inst of Arts Valencia CA 91355

MANDEL, SAUL
ILLUSTRATOR, PAINTER
b New York, NY, Jan 1, 26. *Study:* Studied fine arts, figure study & painting at Pratt Inst. *Work:* Mus Am Illus, New York; Air Force Mus, Washington, DC. *Comn:* Five Postage Stamps, 79, One Postage Stamp, 81, US Postal Serv. *Exhib:* US Info Serv Am Designers Traveling Exhib, E Europe, 63-65; Children from Around the World, Allied Chemical Bldg, New York, 64; Sicherheit Lernen-Unfalle Vermeiden, Int Plakatwettbewerb, Essen, WGer, 81; Japan Design Found, Semba Ctr, Osaka, Japan, 82; one-man show, Mus Am Illus, New York, 83. *Teaching:* Assoc prof concept illus, Syracuse Univ, 82; assoc prof concept commun, Southampton Col, 82; guest lectr concept illus at numerous univ. *Awards:* Award of Excellence, Soc Illusrs, 63; Gold Medal, 35th Nat Outdoor Advert Competition, Inst Outdoor Advert, 71; Gold Medal for Best Illus, Conn Art Dir Club, 78. *Bibliog:* Articles in Graphis Mag, Idea Mag, Art Direction & Mod Publicity. *Mem:* Soc Illusrs; NY Art Dir Club; Am Inst Graphic Arts. *Media:* Mixed. *Publ:* Twenty Years of Award Winners, Hasting House, 81. *Mailing Add:* 163 Maytime Dr Jericho NY 11753

MANDELBAUM, LYN
PAINTER, PRINTMAKER
b New York, NY, Sept 7, 50. *Study:* Tyler Sch Art, Rome, 70-71, Philadelphia, BFA, 72, MFA, 74. *Work:* Philadelphia Mus Art; Otis Libr, Los Angeles; New York Libr; Jean Brown Arch, Tyringham, Mass. *Exhib:* Mus Mod Art, New York, 73; Images-Dimensional-Movable-Transferable, Akron Art Inst, Ohio, 73; Fed Reserve Bd, Washington, DC, 74; Pa State Univ Mus Art, 74; Photo-Synthesis, Johnson Mus Art, 76; two-person exhib, 14 Sculptors Gallery, New York, 80; solo exhib, Foundations Gallery, New York, 82. *Pos:* Founder & dir, Eastern Shore Press, Philadelphia, 74-76 & Street Ed Inc, New York, 79-; pres, Island Magic Inc, New York, 82- *Teaching:* Lectr printmaking, Philadelphia Col Art, 76-78; instr, Tyler Sch Art, 77-78. *Awards:* Purchase Award, Univ Del, Newark, 71. *Publ:* Auth, Moderate Expectations, 78 & Anita's Revenge, 78, pvt publ; auth, Consider Yourself Lucky, Street Ed Inc, 79; auth, Notes: Keep a Candle Burning, pvt publ, 80; auth, Say, Street Ed Inc, 82. *Mailing Add:* 20 Desbrosses St New York NY 10013

MANDELMAN, BEATRICE M
PAINTER
b Newark, NJ, Dec 31, 12. *Study:* Art Students League. *Work:* NMex Mus Fine Arts; Metrop Mus, New York; Baltimore Mus. *Exhib:* One-woman shows, Mus Fine Arts, Santa Fe, NMex & Stables Gallery, Taos, NMex; El Paso Mus, Tex; Denver Mus. *Teaching:* Teacher painting, Taos Valley Art Sch, 46-53. *Awards:* Oakes First Prize, Taos Art Asn Gallery, 62; Best Painting, Stables Art Gallery, 68; First Prize, Jury Show, 75. *Bibliog:* John Nichols (auth), article, NMex Mag, 72; Trisha Hurst (auth), article, Southwest Art, 74. *Mem:* Taos Art Asn. *Media:* Mixed. *Mailing Add:* Box 891 Taos NM 87571

MANDLE, EARL ROGER
MUSEUM DIRECTOR
b Hackensack, NJ, May 13, 41. *Study:* Williams Col, BA, 63; Art Students League; Inst Fine Arts, NY Univ, mus training cert & MA, 67; Metrop Mus Art; Victoria & Albert Mus; Univ Toledo, Hon DFA, 83. *Collections Arranged:* 30 Contemporary Black Artists, 68; Catalogue of European Paintings, Minneapolis Inst Arts, 70; Dutch Masterpieces from the 18th Century, 71-72. *Pos:* Cur, Inst Fine Arts Photog Arch, New York, 67; asst dir, Minneapolis Inst Arts, 67-71, assoc dir, 72-74; assoc dir, Toledo Mus Art, 74-77, dir, 77- *Teaching:* Instr art, Phillips Acad, Andover, Mass, 63-64; instr art, McBurney Sch, New York, 64-65; vis lectr, Univ Wis, 73; adj prof, Univ Toledo, currently. *Awards:* Ford Found Mus Fel, 66-67; Nat Educ Asn Mus Fel, 74; Ohio Govenors Award, 83. *Bibliog:* J Woelm (auth), Dutch Masterpieces from the 18th century (film), Woelm-Polister Prod, 72; J Canaday (auth), Dutch masterpieces from the 18th century, New York Times, 72. *Mem:* Am Asn Mus; Asn Art Mus Dirs; Col Art Asn; Nat Educ Asn; Art Mus Asn Am. *Res:* Eighteenth century Dutch art and nineteenth century English art. *Publ:* A ceiling design by Jacob de Wit, Toledo Mus Art News, 75; auth, Jacob de Wit's drawings of temperance, Register, Univ Kans, 2/77; Adriaen Coorte, a unique late seventeenth century Dutch still-life painter, Burlington Mag Publ Ltd; The Fine Arts and Human Values in Higher Education, Univ Toledo, 79; Lifelong Learning in the Humanities, Philadelphia, Pa, 12/79. *Mailing Add:* c/o 2445 Monroe St Box 1013 Toledo OH 43697

MANDZIUK, MICHAEL DENNIS
PAINTER, SERIGRAPHER
b Detroit, Mich, Jan 14, 42. *Work:* Minn Mus Art, St Paul; Borg Warner Corp, Chicago; Kemper Ins Collection, Long Grove, Ill; Art Ctr Collection, Park Forest, Ill; Springfield City Collection, Ill. *Exhib:* Minn Mus Art Drawing Biennial, St Paul, 73; Butler Inst Am Art, Youngstown, Ohio, 73-74; Ukrainian Inst Mod Art, Chicago, 75; Mitchell Art Mus, Mt Vernon, Ill, 75; Battle Creek Art Ctr, Mich, 76. *Pos:* Artist-craftsman juror, Ann Arbor St Art Fair, 71; graphic specialist, Ford Motor Co. *Awards:* Best of Show Award; Old Capt Art Fair Award, Springfield, Ill, 73-74. *Media:* Acrylic; Silk Screen. *Mailing Add:* 7191 Kolb St Allen Park MI 48101

MANES, BELLE
PAINTER
b New York, NY. *Study:* Cooper Union, BFA, 50. *Exhib:* Philadelphia Mus, 47; Ann Print Show, Brooklyn Mus, 49; Albright-Knox Gallery Ann, 54; Nat Asn Women Artists Ann, Nat Acad, Fed Bldg, New York, 62-83; Hudson River Mus Ann, New York, 75-78; Ann New England Show, Silvermine Gallery, Conn, 79 & 81; Art of the 80's, Westport Mus, Conn, 82; Branchville Soho Gallery 82-83; Trustees Choice, Larry Aldrich Mus, Conn, 83. *Teaching:* Instr art, Plainfield Community Ctr, NJ, 56-59 & privately, White Plains, NY, 62-64; mentor, Pratt Inst, 78. *Awards:* Medal Hon, Nat Asn Women Artists, 79; Top Silvermine Award, New England Show, 81. *Mem:* Nat Asn Women Artists; Hudson River Contemp Artists; Silvermine Guild. *Media:* Oil. *Dealer:* Branchville Soho Gallery RR Sta Rtes 7 & 102 Ridgefield CT 06829. *Mailing Add:* 1097 North St White Plains NY 10605

MANETTA, EDWARD J
ADMINISTRATOR, PAINTER
b Export, Pa, Dec 26, 25. *Study:* Carnegie-Mellon Univ, BA, 53; Univ Pittsburgh; Herron Sch of Art, Ind Univ, Indianapolis, MFA, 55; Fulbright Exchange fel, Gt Brit, 58-59; John Hay Humanities fel, Williams Col, Williamstown, Mass & Bennington Col, Vt, 61; NY Univ, EdD(creative arts), 65. *Work:* Ansty Col, Eng; Marygrove Col, Detroit; Ball State Art Mus, Muncie, Ind; South Bend Art Mus, Ind; HWA Kang Mus, Taipei, Taiwan; and others. *Comn:* Paintings, Ford Motor Co, Detroit, 63; paintings, St Vincent's Priory, New York, 70; paintings, RCA Corp, New York, 70; mural, Mule Plastics Corp, Haupague, NY, 73; mural, Electrical Union Cult Ctr, New York, 75. *Exhib:* Butler Inst Am Art, Youngstown, Ohio, 53; Pa Acad Fine Arts, Philadelphia, 53; Cincinnati Art Mus, Ohio, 55; Nat Acad Design, New York, 56; Royal Soc Galleries, Birmingham, Eng, 59; Herron Art Mus, Indianapolis, 60; Nat Hist Mus, Taipei, 77; HWA Kang Mus, Taipei, 77. *Teaching:* Instr, Herron Sch Art, 55-61; Fulbright lectr art, Ansty Col, Sutton Coldfield, Eng, 58-59; prof, Marygrove Col, Detroit, 61-63; prof fine arts, St John's Univ, Jamaica, NY, 63-67, chmn fine arts dept, 68-, Fulbright exchange prof, Nat Taiwan Normal Univ, Taipei, spring 78. *Awards:* Vis artist fel, Col Chinese Cult, Taipei, 76-77. *Mem:* Col Art Asn; Nat Coun Art Adminrs; Am Asn Univ Prof; Nat Soc Skull & Circle; Am Acad Art & Lett. *Media:* Oil, Acrylic. *Publ:* Contribr, Evolution of the City, 74 & illus, Education Textbook, 77, St John's Press; illus, Administrators Guide to New Programs for Faculty Management and Evaluation, Parker Publ Co, West Nyack, NY, 77. *Mailing Add:* 52 Glenmere Lane Coram NY 11727

MANGEL, BENJAMIN
DEALER
b Philadelphia, Pa, Jan 12, 25. *Pos:* Owner, Benjamin Mangel Gallery, Philadelphia, Pa. *Specialty:* Contemporary paintings and sculpture. *Mailing Add:* 1604 Locust St Philadelphia PA 19103

MANGIONE, PATRICIA ANTHONY
PAINTER, MURALIST
b Seattle, Wash. *Study:* Fleisher Art Mem, Philadelphia; Barnes Found, Merion, Pa. *Work:* Inst Contemp Art, Dallas; Fleisher Art Mem, Philadelphia; Fidelity Bank, Philadelphia; Westchester State Mus, Pa; Univ Pa. *Comn:* Acrylic on wood mural, Continental Bank & Trust Co, Philadelphia, 69. *Exhib:* One-man shows, Frank Rehn Gallery, 60-74 & Univ Pa, 64 & 80; Philadelphia Art Alliance, 75; Newman Galleries, Philadelphia, 78; More Gallery, Philadelphia, 82. *Pos:* Illusr, Sicilia, Ital Govt Quart, 66 & 68. *Awards:* Philadelphia Art Teachers Asn First Prize, 57 & 64; six Yaddo Resident Fels, 62-78; Artistic Contrib Philadelphia, Artists Equity Asn, 82. *Bibliog:* Burton Wasserman (auth), The Art of Patricia Mangione, Sims Press, 71; James R Mellow (auth), Mangione at Rehn Gallery, New York Times, 74; Victoria Donohoe (auth), Paintings by Pat Mangione, Philadelphia Inquirer, 82. *Mem:* Artists Equity Asn; Philadelphia Art Alliance; Women's Caucus for Art. *Media:* Oil, Acrylic. *Publ:* Auth, Some observations on the experience of painting, Parapsychology Found, 70; auth, Exercise in magic, Sunday Bulletin, Philadelphia, 71. *Dealer:* More Gallery 1630 Walnut St Philadelphia PA 19103. *Mailing Add:* 1901 Kennedy Blvd Apt 2404 Philadelphia PA 19103

MANGOLD, ROBERT PETER
PAINTER
b North Tonawanda, NY, Oct 12, 37. *Study:* Cleveland Inst Art, 56-59; Yale Univ, BFA, 63, MFA. *Work:* Solomon R Guggenheim Mus, Mus Mod Art & Whitney Mus Am Art, New York; Mus Fine Arts, Houston; La Jolla Mus Contemp Art, Calif; and others. *Exhib:* Artists Under Forty, 68 & Am Drawings: 1963-1973, 73, Whitney Mus Am Art; Albright-Knox Art Gallery, Buffalo, NY, 70; Solomon R Guggenheim Mus, 71; Documenta, Kassel, WGer, 72; La Jolla Mus Contemp Art, 74; Mus Contemp Arts, Chicago, 74; New York Cult Ctr, 74; Mus Mod Art, New York, 75; one-man exhibs, Protetch-McIntosh, Washington, DC, 78 & Bielefeld Kunsthalle, 80; and others. *Teaching:* Instr art, Sch Visual Arts, 63-, Hunter Col, 64-65, Skowhegan Summer Art Sch, 68, Yale-Norfolk Summer Art Sch, 69 & Cornell Univ, 70. *Awards:* Nat Coun on Arts Award, 66; Guggenheim Mem Grant, 69. *Bibliog:* Lucy R Lippard (auth), Silent art: Robert Mangold, In: Changing Essays in Art Criticism, Dutton, 71; Joseph Masheck (auth), A humanist geometry, Artforum, 3/74; and others. *Dealer:* John Weber Gallery 420 W Broadway New York NY 10012. *Mailing Add:* 90 Eldridge St New York NY 10002

MANGOLD, SYLVIA PLIMACK
PAINTER
b New York, NY, Sept 18, 38. *Study:* Cooper Union, cert, 59; Yale Univ Art Sch, BFA, 61. *Exhib:* One-person shows, Young Hoffman Gallery, Chicago, Ohio State Univ, Columbus, Droll/Kolbert Gallery, New York, 80, Contemp Arts Mus, Houston & Wadsworth Atheneum, Hartford, 81; American Painting in the 70's, Albright-Knox Gallery, Buffalo, 78-79; The Elusive Image, Walker Art Ctr, Minneapolis; Yale Univ Art Gallery, New Haven, 81; and many others. *Teaching:* Instr drawing, Sch Visual Arts, New York, 70, instr painting, 70-71 & 74- *Bibliog:* Barbara Cavaliere (auth), article, Arts Mag, 6/78; Jeff Perrone (auth), Sylvia Plimack Mangold: Droll/Kolbert, Artforum, summer 78; Peter Frank (auth), article, Art News, 10/78. *Media:* Acrylic, Oil. *Dealer:* Brooke Alexander Inc 20 W 57th St New York NY 10019. *Mailing Add:* MD 1 Bull Rd Washingtonville NY 10992

MANGUM, WILLIAM (GOODSON)
SCULPTOR, PAINTER
b Kinston, NC. *Study:* Corcoran Sch Art, Washington, DC; Art Students League; Univ NC, Chapel Hill, BA & MA. *Work:* Univ of NC, Chapel Hill; NC Mus Art, Raleigh; Salem Col, Winston-Salem, NC; Carl Sandburg Mem Mus, Flat Rock, NC. *Comn:* Lamp of Learning Monument, Dunning Industs, Greensboro, NC, 67; portrait bust of Carl Sandburg, Greensboro CofC, 68. *Exhib:* Bodley Gallery Nat, New York; Mass Mus Art, Springfield; Isaac Delgado Mus, New Orleans, La; Va Mus Fine Art Exhib; Southeastern Ctr Contemp Art, Winston-Salem, NC; and others. *Teaching:* Prof art hist & sculpture, Salem Col, currently. *Awards:* Cert of distinction, Va Mus Fine Art; Isaac Delgado Mus Award; NC Mus Art Award. *Publ:* Auth, Marino Marini as portraitist, 70. *Dealer:* Southeastern Ctr Contemporary Art Marguerite Dr Winston-Salem NC 27108. *Mailing Add:* Dept of Art Salem Col Winston-Salem NC 27108

MANHART, MARCIA Y
ADMINISTRATOR, CURATOR
b Wichita, Kans, Jan 14, 43. *Study:* Univ Ariz, Tucson, with Maurice Grossman, 62; Univ Tulsa, Okla, with Duayne Hatchett, Tom Manhart & Alexandre Hogue, BA, 65, MA, 71. *Work:* Okla State Art Collection, Okla Arts Ctr, Oklahoma City; Ark Arts Ctr, Little Rock; Fred Jones Mem Mus Art, Univ Okla, Norman; Philbrook Art Ctr, Tulsa; Univ Tulsa. *Exhib:* Southwestern Craftsmen Biennial, Mus Int Folk Art, Santa Fe, NMex, 65, 67, 71 & 75; Craftsmen USA '66, Dallas Mus Fine Arts, Tex, 66; Ceramic Nat, Everson Mus, Syracuse, NY, 68; Manharts, Fred Jones Mem Mus Art, Norman, Okla, 73; Ceramics Invitational, Little Gallery, Mus Contemp Crafts, New York, 74; Ann Print, Drawing & Crafts Exhib, Ark Arts Ctr, Little Rock, 74 & 76. *Collections Arranged:* Our Oklahoma Indian Heritage: The Old Ways, 76; Traders Cargo from the China Sea: The Gilleret Collection of Southeast Asian Ceramics, 78; Nature's Forms--Nature's Forces: The Work of Alexandre Hogue, 84. *Pos:* Dir, Alexandre Hogue Gallery, Univ Tulsa, Okla, 67-69; dir educ, Philbrook Art Ctr, Tulsa, 72-77, asst dir, 77-83, actg dir, 83- *Awards:* One-man Award, Southwestern Crafts Biennial, Mus Int Folk Art, 71. *Bibliog:* Garth Bethel (auth), Manharts, Garth Horizons, 74; Research and education, In: Your Portable Museum, Am Crafts Coun, 75; John Conrad (auth), Contemporary Ceramic Technique, Prentice-Hall, 79. *Mem:* Tulsa Designer Craftsmen (pres, 72); Okla Arts & Humanities Coun; Art Mus Asn; Nat Endowment Arts. *Media:* Clay, Porcelain. *Res:* Contemporary art in craft media. *Mailing Add:* Philbrook Art Ctr PO Box 52510 Tulsa OK 74152

MANHART, THOMAS ARTHUR
EDUCATOR, CERAMIST

b Canon City, Colo, July 16, 37. *Study:* Univ Hawaii; Univ Tulsa, BA & MA. *Work:* Ark Arts Ctr, Little Rock; Fred Jones Mem Art Mus, Univ Okla, Norman; Philbrook Art Ctr, Tulsa; Okla State Art Collection, Okla Art Ctr, Oklahoma City; Tulsa Performing Arts Ctr, Okla. *Exhib:* Nat Decorative Arts Exhib, Wichita, Kans, 61, 64 & 66; Southwestern Crafts Biennial, Santa Fe, NMex, 65, 72 & 75; Craftsmen USA, Dallas & New York, 66; Regional Prints, Drawings & Crafts Exhib, Little Rock, 67 & 75; Nat Craftsmen's Exhib, Wichita, 68, 70 & 72. *Teaching:* Instr ceramics, Univ Tulsa, 61-68, asst prof ceramics, 69-73, assoc prof ceramics, 74- *Awards:* Nat Decorative Arts Exhib Medal of Honor, Wichita Art Asn, 66; Nat Merit Award, Craftsmen USA, Am Crafts Coun, 66; Okla State Art Collection, Okla Arts & Humanities Coun, 73. *Bibliog:* Gar Bethel (auth), Manharts, Craft Horizons, 74; Okla Designer Craftsmen Exhibition, Ceramics Monthly, 75. *Mem:* Am Crafts Coun (state rep, 66); Okla Designer Craftsmen; Tulsa Designer Craftsmen (pres, 68). *Media:* Clay and Fibers. *Publ:* Contribr, Profile, Am Crafts Coun, 60; contribr, Craft Horizons, 66, 68 & 74-75, Cimarron Rev, 69, Tulsa Univ Alumni Mag, 69 & Ceramics Monthly, 75. *Mailing Add:* c/o Univ Tulsa 600 S College Tulsa OK 74104

MANHOLD, JOHN HENRY
SCULPTOR

b Rochester, NY, Aug 20, 19. *Study:* Univ Rochester, BA; Washington Univ, St Louis, MA; New Sch, with Chaim Gross & Manolo Pasqual; also with Ward Mount. *Work:* City of West Orange, NJ; Mem Sloan-Kettering Hosp, New York; Pyrofilm Corp, Whippany, NJ; A J Levera Assocs, Madison, NJ; Jacques Piccard Inst, Bern, Switz; and others. *Comn:* Bronze bust, Kallman Assocs, Jersey City, NJ; four bronze busts, Col Med & Dent NJ, Newark, 69, 70 & 78; bronze figure, Bernard Koven, 71; and others. *Exhib:* Allied Artists Am, 66; Audubon Artists Am, 67-69; Mainstreams '68 & '71, Grover M Hermann Fine Arts Ctr, Ohio, 68 & 71; Nat Sculpture Soc, 69; Am Artists Prof League, 70-72; and others. *Pos:* Dir sculpture, Ringwood Manor Asn Arts, 68-70, 1st vpres, 70-71. *Awards:* Medal of Honor for sculpture, State of NJ, 68; Second Prize Patrons Award, Painters & Sculptors Soc NJ, 71; John Subkis Award, Nat Arts Club, 71; and others. *Bibliog:* David Leis (auth), pictures in Life Mag, 69; Pierre Morand (auth), La section Americaine de la Salon del'arte Francaise, La Rev Mod, 70; Ruth Ann Williams (auth), Art of the oranges, NJ Music & Art, 72. *Mem:* Acad Artists Asn; Am Artists Prof League; Painters & Sculptors Soc NJ (vpres sculpture, 74-); Nat Arts Club; Knickerbocker Artists. *Media:* Marble, Bronze. *Mailing Add:* 352 Shunpike Rd Chatham NJ 07928

MANILLA, TESS (TESS MANILLA WEINER)
PAINTER, COLLAGE ARTIST

b Poland; US citizen. *Study:* Educ Alliance, New York, with Abbo Ostrowsky; Brooklyn Mus Art Sch, with Reuben Tam, Victor Candell, Manfred Schwartz & Louis Finkelstein; Art Students League, with Morris Kantor, Sidney Gross & Morris Davidson; Pratt Graphics Ctr, with Walter Ragolsky; Willimantic Teachers Col, Conn; Provincetown Workshop, with Leo Manzo. *Work:* Long Island Univ; Butler Inst, Youngstown, Ohio; and many private collections throughout the US. *Exhib:* Aames Gallery, 75; one yr travelling watercolor show, Nat Asn Women Artists, Va Mus & State of Va; Nat Acad NY, 75; one-person shows, Lincoln Savings Bank, 76 & Statesman's Club New York, 77. *Teaching:* Instr pvt classes, children & adults. *Awards:* Helen Hurzberger Scholar, Art Students League, 61; Nat Asn Women Artists Award, 72; Medal of Merit, League of Present Day Artists, 74. *Mem:* Nat Asn Women Artists (pub rels chmn, 73-75); Metrop Painters & Sculptors (pres, 68-83); Art Students League; League of Present Day Artists; New York Soc Women Artists. *Media:* Oil, Collage, Graphic. *Mailing Add:* 140 Ocean Pkwy Brooklyn NY 11218

MANILOW, LEWIS
COLLECTOR, PATRON

b Chicago, Ill, Aug 11, 27. *Pos:* Pres, Mus Contemp Art Chicago, 76-; mem of bd, Beaubourg Found, 78- *Collection:* Contemporary art, Mannerist prints and Turkish rugs. *Mailing Add:* 2450 N Lakeview Chicago IL 60614

MANKOWSKI, BRUNO
MEDALIST, SCULPTOR

b Ger, Oct 30, 02; US citizen. *Study:* Munic Art Sch & State Art Sch, Berlin; Beaux Arts Inst, New York. *Work:* Am Numis Soc, Metrop Mus Art, Nat Acad Design & Soc Medalists, New York; Smithsonian Inst Div Numis, Washington, DC; Brookgreen Gardens, SC. *Comn:* Sculptured panel, by US Govt-Soc Fine Arts, Chesterfield, SC, 39; mem plaque, Macombs Jr High Sch, NY, 49; carvings, architect of capitol, Washington, DC, 50 & 60; designs for Steuben Glass, Corning, NY, 54-55; medal-Asa Gray, Hall Fame Great Am, NY Univ, 72; and others. *Exhib:* Nat Acad Design Ann, 40-78; Pa Acad Fine Arts Ann, 47-54; Nat Sculpture Soc Ann, 47-78; Am Acad Arts & Lett, 49-50; Allied Artists Am Ann, 52-77. *Awards:* Daniel Chester French Award, Allied Artists Am, 78; Gold Medal, Bicentennial Exhib, Nat Sculpture Soc, 78; Gold Medal, Am Numismatic Asn, Colorado Springs, 80; and others. *Bibliog:* Articles, Am Artists Mag, 49-59; articles, Nat Sculpture Soc, 53-77. *Mem:* Nat Acad Design; fel Nat Sculpture Soc; life fel Am Numis Soc; Allied Artists Am. *Mailing Add:* 27 Columbine Trail De Bary FL 32713

MANN, KATINKA
PAINTER, PHOTOGRAPHER

b New York, NY, June 28, 25. *Study:* Univ Hartford Art Sch; Pratt Graphic Arts, New York. *Work:* Northport Veterans Hospital, NY; Publishers Clearinghouse, Port Washington, New York; Williamsburg Savings Bank & Russ Togs Inc, New York. *Exhib:* One-man shows, Cent Hall Gallery, 74-83, Hansen Gallery, New York, 76-79, Heckscher Mus, Huntington, NY, 77; Nassau Community Col, New York, 71, 78 & 79; Brooklyn Mus, 76; Aldrich Mus Contemp Art, 78; plus many others. *Awards:* Judith Leiber Co Purchase Award, Soc Am Graphic Artists, 69; Purchase Award, Nassau Community Col, 71. *Bibliog:* Art in the World, Rinehart Press, 75; article, Arts Mag, 78; article, New York Times, 83. *Mem:* Nat Asn Women Artists; Prof Artists Guild (vpres, 69-71, co-chmn & bd mem, 72-73); Artists Equity Asn; Prof Women Photogr. *Media:* Polymer. *Dealer:* Central Hall Gallery 386 West Broadway New York NY 10012. *Mailing Add:* 294 Pidgeon Hill Rd Huntington Station NY 11746

MANN, MAYBELLE
HISTORIAN, WRITER

b Joliet, Ill, May 27, 15. *Study:* Queens Col, City Univ New York, BA(hist; hon), 65; NY Univ, MA, 67, PhD, 72. *Collections Arranged:* Francis William Edmonds (auth, catalog), Stony Brook, NY, 75-76; The American Art Union (auth, catalog), Whitney Mus Am Art, 77-78; St Augustine Artists (auth, catalog), H M Flagler Mus, Palm Beach, 84-85; Walter Launt Palmer (auth, catalog), Albany Inst Hist & Art, 84-85. *Teaching:* Lectr Am art, NY Univ, 74-76. *Res:* Nineteenth and early twentieth century American art. *Publ:* Auth, Francis William Edmonds: Mammon and Art, Garland, 77; auth, The American Art Union, ALM Assoc, 77; auth, Walter Launt Palmer: Poetic Reality, Schiffer Publ, 84; and articles in Antiques, Art & Antiques & Am Art J. *Mailing Add:* 3264 Cove Rd Jupiter FL 33458

MANN, VIRGINIA
ADMINISTRATOR, CRITIC

b Troy, NY, Sept 2, 38. *Study:* Univ Calif, Riverside, BA, 66; Yale Univ, New Haven, Conn. *Collections Arranged:* The Pursuit of Happiness, Yale Ctr Brit Art, 77; Connecticut Painting, Sculpture and Drawing 1978 (auth, catalog), Carlson Art Gallery, New Brit Mus Am Art & Cummings Art Ctr, Art Resources, New Haven, 78; Silvermine Painting and Sculpture (auth, catalog), Corp/Yankelovich, Skelly & White, 79; Still Life and Beyond (auth, catalog), Silvermine Guild Ctr Arts, 81; Seven Artists (auth, catalog), Neuberger Mus, 80; and others. *Pos:* Registr, Yale Ctr Brit Art, New Haven, Conn, 73-77; exhib dir, Art Resources, New Haven, Conn, 77-79; dir, Silvermine Guild Ctr Arts, New Canaan, Conn, 79-83; sr registr, Fine Arts Mus San Francisco, currently. *Mem:* Am Asn Mus; New Eng Mus Asn (chmn ethics comt, 76-77); Col Art Asn; Int Coun Mus. *Publ:* Auth, Kenneth Morgan, 2/79, Connecticut & American impressionism, 11/80, All in line, 2/81, Carol Anthony, 11/83, Arts Mag; and others. *Mailing Add:* c/o Silvermine Guild Ctr Arts 1037 Silvermine Rd New Canaan CT 06840

MANN, WARD PALMER
PAINTER

b Detroit, Mich. *Study:* Detroit Inst Art, 33; Univ Mich, BS, 49. *Work:* Univ Rochester & Strong Mus, Rochester, NY. *Comn:* Cityscape, the New Buffalo, Marsh & McLennon, Inc, Buffalo, NY, 75; Birthplace of Xerography, Xerox Corp, Webster, NY, 80; oil paintings, Webster Optical Co, NY, 80. *Exhib:* Ann Shows, Salmagundi Club, New York, 75-82; Ann Nat Acad Artists, Greek Cultural Ctr, Springfield, Mass, 79-81; Foothills Art Ctr, Golden, Colo, 80; 31st Ann Knickerbocker Art, Salmagundi Club, New York, 81; Artists of New England, Cayuga Mus Hist & Art, Auburn, NY, 81. *Awards:* First Watercolor Award, Anco Wood Spec Found, 80; Frank Spradling Award, Hudson Valley Art Asn, 83; Chrislee Darrand Award, Rockport Art Asn, 83. *Bibliog:* Walt Reed (ed), Ward Mann, artist, North Light Mag, 11-12/77; Artists of Rockport, Rockport Art Asn 60th Anniv Ed, 80. *Mem:* Salmagundi Club; Rockport Art Asn; North Shore Arts Asn; Academic Artists Asn; Rochester Art Club (pres, 74-76). *Media:* Oil, Watercolor. *Dealer:* Kings Loa Gallery 50 State St Pittsford NY 14534. *Mailing Add:* 163 Stony Point Trial Webster NY 14580

MANNING, HILDA SCUDDER
SCULPTOR

b Boston, Mass. *Study:* Mass Sch Art, Boston, with Cyrus Dallin; also with Felix Benneteau, Paris. *Work:* Supreme Ct, Washington, DC; Gunston Hall, Lorton, Va; Smith Col Libr, Northampton, Mass; Tobey Hosp, Wareham, Mass. *Comn:* Portrait, Touro Infirmary, New Orleans; portrait, Vellore Christian Med Hosp, India; portrait, late Justice Harland Fisk Stone; portrait, Justice Van Devanter; bas reliefs, Benjamin Cardoso. *Exhib:* Paris Spring Salon; Corcoran Gallery, Washington, DC; solo exhibs, Delgado Mus, New Orleans, Boston Guild Artists & Wellesley Art Gallery, Mass; and others. *Awards:* Cash Award, Pen & Brush, 81 & 82; and others. *Mem:* Nat Sculpture Soc; Pen & Brush. *Media:* Bronze, Cast Stone. *Mailing Add:* One Oval Ct Bronxville NY 10708

MANNING, JO
PRINTMAKER

b Sidney, BC, Dec 11, 23. *Study:* Ont Col Art, Toronto, grad, 45, spec study printmaking, 60. *Work:* Nat Gallery Can, Ottawa; Montreal Mus Fine Art; London Libr & Art Mus, Ont; Willistead Gallery, Windsor; Univ Calgary, Alta. *Exhib:* Expos Int Dessins, Rijeka, Yugoslavia, 70 & 72; Venice Biennale, 72; one-man show, Earlscourt Gallery, Hamilton, 78; Prints, Gallery Pascal, 79; Earlscourt Gallery, Hamilton, 79; and others. *Teaching:* Assoc master printmaking, Sheridan Col, Brampton, Ont, 71- *Awards:* Purchase Award, Graphex 11, Brantford, 74; Kenneth Siddal Award, On View, 76; and others. *Mem:* Can Soc Graphic Arts (pres, 68-69); Can Soc Painter-Etchers & Engravers (exec, 63-65); Royal Canadian Acad (jury). *Publ:* Contribr, seven drawings, Canadian Catholic Conf, Sunday Missal, 76. *Mailing Add:* 61 Balmoral Ave Toronto ON M4V 1J5 Canada

MANNING, REG (REGINALD WEST)
CARTOONIST, DESIGNER

b Kansas City, Mo, Apr 8, 05. *Work:* Cartoon Collection, Syracuse Univ; Lyndon Johnson Libr, Austin, Tex; Presidential Mus, Odessa, Tex; Univ Southern Miss, Hattiesburg. *Exhib:* One-man shows, Phoenix Art Mus, 61 & 73. *Pos:* Ed cartoonist, Ariz Republic, 26-; cartoonist, McNaught Syndicate, NY, 48-71. *Awards:* Pulitzer Prize, Columbia Univ, 51; Abraham Lincoln Award, Freedoms Found, 70 & 71. *Bibliog:* Alan D Covey (auth), Southwestern authors, Ariz Librn, fall 66; Dean Smith (auth) & Barry Goldwater (auth, foreword), The Best of Reg, 80. *Mem:* Asn Am Ed Cartoonists; Nat Cartoonists Soc; Phoenix Fine Arts Asn. *Interests:* Copper wheel crystal engraver and designer. *Publ:* Auth & illusr, What Kinda Cactus Izzat?, 41, From Tee to Cup, 54, What is Arizona Really Like?, 68 & Desert in Crystal, 73. *Mailing Add:* 5724 E Cambridge Scottsdale AZ 85257

MANSARAM, P(ANCHAL)
COLLAGE ARTIST, PHOTOGRAPHER

b Mount Abu, India, Mar 4, 34. *Study:* Sir J J Sch Art, Bombay, India, 54-59; State Acad Fine Arts, Amsterdam, fel, 63; Ryerson Polytech, Toronto, Can, cert(motion picture prod), 70. *Work:* Gemeente Mus, The Hague; Nat Gallery Mod Art, New Delhi, India; Mem Univ Gallery, St Johns, Nfld; Cent Libr New York; Art Gallery Hamilton. *Exhib:* Int Original Drawing Show, Mus Mod Art, Rijeka, Yugoslavia, 74; New York Drawing Biennial, Bronx Mus Art, 76; Conceptual Mobile Miniature Show (with Bobby Jones, Los Angeles), Guggenheim Mus, New York, 77; Aqurius Gallery, Harrogate, Eng, 78; New India House, New York, 79; Surlington Cult Ctr, Ont, 80; plus many others. *Awards:* First Prize, Bombay State Art Exhib, 59; Colour & Form Soc Award, Toronto, 75. *Mem:* Int Asn Educ Through Art; Colour & Form Soc (pres, 78-79); Visual Arts Ont. *Media:* Collage; Films, Video. *Dealer:* Dhoomimal Gallery, New Delhi, India. *Mailing Add:* 298 Gardenview Burlington ON L7T 1K6 Canada

MANSFIELD, ROBERT ADAMS
SCULPTOR, EDUCATOR

b Chicago, Ill, May 4, 42. *Study:* Minneapolis Sch Art & Design, 61-62; St Cloud State Univ, BA, 68; Univ Mass, Amherst, MFA, 70. *Work:* Univ Mass, Amherst; Smith Col Mus Art, Mass; San Diego State Univ; St Cloud State Univ, Minn. *Exhib:* Abstract Painting of 70's, DeCordova Mus, Lincoln, Mass, 71; Nat Juried Exhib, Austin Mus Art, 79; 13th Ann, Marietta Col, Ohio, 80; North Am Sculpture Exhib, Golden Col Art Ctr, Colo, 80; Corpus Christi Col Mus, Tex, 81; and others. *Collections Arranged:* New Directions, Univ Mass, 69; Twombly & Diao, Hampshire Col, 71; Arthur Hoener, San Diego State Univ, 76; Jerome Liebling Photographs, San Diego State Univ, 78. *Teaching:* Instr art, Smith Col, 70-71; asst prof art, Hampshire Col, 71-79; assoc prof art & head sculpture dept, San Diego State Univ, 76- *Awards:* Second Prize, Southern Calif Expos, Del Mar, 77; Best of Show, Marietta Col, 80. *Bibliog:* Mary Vercauteren (auth), Robert Mansfield, Holyoke Transcript, 4/12/73; Edward Silver (auth), Elliptical construction, Advocate, 12/4/75; Susan Muchnic (auth), Sculpture is alive and well, Los Angeles Times, 1/22/79. *Mailing Add:* 5940 Zora St La Mesa CA 92041

MANSHIP, JOHN PAUL
PAINTER, SCULPTOR

b New York, NY, Jan 16, 27. *Study:* Harvard Univ, AB, 46; with George Demetrios; Brera Acad, Milan. *Work:* Nat Collection Fine Arts, Washington, DC; Louisville Art Mus, Ky; Long Beach Art Mus, Calif; New Britain Mus, Conn. *Comn:* Baptism of Christ, Baptistry, St John Martyr, New York, 63; Pentecost (fresco), Chapel Sisters of St Joseph, Pawtucket, RI, 65; stations of cross, St Clements Church, Warwick, RI, 66; Resurrection (with Margaret Cassidy), St Anthony's Church, Springfield, Mass, 71; portrait of Judge O'Connor, Worcester Co Courthouse, 72. *Teaching:* Instr drawing & painting, Marymount Col, New York, 63; instr, Minnetonka Art Ctr, 78. *Awards:* Ranger Fund Purchase Award, Nat Acad Design, 65; Gold Medal, Burckhardt Acad, Rome, 78; Rockport Art Asn, 83. *Mem:* Am Watercolor Soc; Nat Soc Mural Painters (secy, 72-75); Rockport Art Asn (pres, 81-); North Shore Art Asn (dir, 70-72); Artists Equity NY. *Media:* Oil, Gouache; Mosaics. *Publ:* Auth, Paul Claudel, Commonweal, 55; auth, Raphael, Cath Encycl Youth, 64. *Dealer:* Quarry Gallery Gloucester MA; Manship Gallery 20 Main St Rockport MA 01966. *Mailing Add:* 10 Leverett St Gloucester MA 01930

MANSO, LEO
PAINTER, EDUCATOR

b New York, NY, Apr 15, 14. *Study:* Nat Acad Design; New Sch Social Res. *Work:* Mus Mod Art & Whitney Mus Am Art, New York; Mus Fine Arts, Boston; Worcester Mus, Mass; Corcoran Gallery Art, Washington, DC. *Comn:* Mural, Lincoln Pub Libr, Nebr, 65. *Exhib:* Nat Inst Arts & Lett, 61 & 69; Mus Mod Art, New York, 61 & 65; Whitney Mus Am Art Ann, 47-66; Pa Acad Fine Arts, Philadelphia, 68; New Eng Arts Festival, 71; Am Masters of Collage, Mt Clair Mus, NJ, 79. *Teaching:* Co-founder, Provincetown Workshop, Mass, 59-; prof painting presently; artist-in-residence, Am Acad Rome, 79; prof painting & drawing, NY Univ, 50-; instr painting, Art Students League, NY, presently; artist-in-residence, Am Acad in Rome, 79. *Awards:* Childe Hassam Purchase Award for Juggernaut (construct), Am Acad Arts & Lett, 69; $5000 Award, Am Acad Inst Arts & Letters, 81; Guggenheim Fel Printmaking, 82; and others. *Mem:* Am Abstract Artists; Century Club; Nat Acad Design. *Media:* Multimedia. *Dealer:* Arras Gallery 29 W 57th St New York NY; Long Point Gallery Provincetown MA 02657. *Mailing Add:* 460 Riverside Dr New York NY 10027

MANTON, JOCK (ARCHIMEDES ARISTIDES GIACOMANTONIO)
SCULPTOR, ADMINISTRATOR

b Jersey City, NJ, Jan 17, 06. *Study:* Leonardo da Vinci Art Sch, New York; Royal Acad Fine Arts, Rome, Italy; also with Onorio Ruutolo & Vincenzo Gemito; Jersey City State Col, Hon DFA, 83. *Work:* Truman (sculpture), Fel Truman Libr, Independence, Mo; Vincenzo Gemito (sculpture), Galleria di Arte Moderna, Rome, Italy; Grandma (sculpture), Royal Palace, Rome; Mediterranean Flower (sculpture), Mus Capitoleum, Rome. *Comn:* Spanish American War Soldier (sculpture), Union City, 42; Eisenhower (sculpture), West Point Mil Acad, NY, 45; Wounded Soldier (sculpture), Lincoln High Sch, Jersey City, 46; Christopher Columbus (sculpture), Jersey City Columbus Mall, 50; bust of Milton Cross, Metrop Opera. *Exhib:* Montclair Art Mus, 38; Metrop Mus Art, New York, 43; Nat Acad Design; Allied Artists Am; Nat Sculpture Soc. *Pos:* Trustee, Mus Jersey City, NJ, 32-48; reviewer arts, Am Broadcasting Co, 51-71; exec dir, Sussex Co Arts Coun, Inc, 71-71. *Awards:* Maynard Prize, Nat Acad Design; Dr Martin Luther King-Therese Richard Mem Award for Religious Sculpture, 76 & Joel Meisner & Co Award, 77, Allied Artists Am; and others. *Bibliog:* Truman Poses for Giacomantonio (film), produced on ABC TV. *Mem:* Fel Nat Sculpture Soc; Lotos Club; assoc Nat Acad Design; Allied Artists Am; academician Accad Italia. *Media:* Bronze, Marble. *Mailing Add:* 42 W 67th St New York NY 10023

MANUELLA, FRANK R
DESIGNER, SCULPTOR

b New York, NY. *Study:* Cooper Union Advan Sci & Art, BFA; Pratt Inst, MSc. *Comn:* Graphic design, Am Airlines, New York, 71; mural, Weis, Voisin & Co, Ft Lee, NJ, 73; graphic design, E C Ernst, Inc, Washington, DC, 74; graphic design, Caprice, New York, 75; S B Thomas & Co, 81; and others. *Exhib:* Plastic Show, Jewish Mus, New York, 69; one-man shows, Avanti Galleries, New York, 70 & 72 & Young Collector, New York, 73; Director's Choice Show, Environment Gallery, New York, 71-81; MacAllen Int Mus, 83; and others. *Pos:* Pres, F R Manuella Associates, currently; vpres & creative dir, L D Armstrong & Co Inc, currently. *Teaching:* Asst prof light & color, Pratt Inst, 75-82; asst prof art, Pan Am Univ, 82- *Bibliog:* Carompsun, New York Time Mag, 12/1/68; Karen Fisher (auth), Five careers, Cosmopolitan Mag, 3/69; Reviews & previews, Art News, 1/71; plus many others. *Media:* Acrylic, Reinforced Polyester. *Dealer:* Environment Gallery 405 E 54 St New York NY 10022. *Mailing Add:* 9104 96th St Woodhaven NY 11421

MANUS, CONNIE SANDAGE See Hendrix, Connie

MANVILLE, ELSIE
PAINTER

b Philadelphia, Pa, May 11, 22. *Study:* Tyler Sch Fine Arts, Temple Univ, BFA, BS(educ). *Work:* Temple Univ, Philadelphia; Butler Inst Am Art; Guild Hall Permanent Collection, East Hampton, NY. *Exhib:* Butler Inst Am Art, 56; Walker Art Ctr, 58; one-man exhibs, Kraushaar Galleries, 58, 66, 69, 75, 78 & 82; Dallas Mus, 63; Nat Acad; 30 Year Retrospective Exhib, Snug Harbor Cultural Ctr, Staten Island, 83. *Teaching:* Adj instr, Fashion Inst Technol, currently. *Awards:* Cert of Merit, Nat Acad Design, 76; Purchase Award, Butler Inst Am Art, 78; Nat Endowment Arts Visual Artists Fel, 81; plus others. *Bibliog:* Paintings reproduced, Arts Mag, 6/75 & 4/78 & Art News, 10/78. *Media:* Oil, Pastel. *Mailing Add:* c/o Kraushaar Galleries 724 Fifth Ave New York NY 10019

MANZO, ANTHONY JOSEPH
PAINTER, INSTRUCTOR

b Saddle Brook, NJ. *Study:* Sch Fine Art, Nat Acad Design; Phoenix Sch Design, New York; also with Salvatore Lascari. *Work:* Losurdo Foods Collection, Hackensack, NJ. *Comn:* Landscape and still life portraits, comn by Mr & Mrs Losurdo, Saddle River, NJ, 68-79; still life portrait, Mr & Mrs Perlman, Elkins Park, Pa, 68 & 70; landscape portrait, Mr & Mrs J Lauren, New York, 74-79; portrait of Former Middleweight Champion Rocky Graziano, 78; still life, Don & Dona Casey, Dallas, Tex, 78. *Exhib:* Hudson Artists Inc 21st Ann, Jersey City Mus, 74; Salmagundi Club Summer Exhib, 75-77; Nat Miniature Art Show, 75; NJ Painter & Sculptor Soc, Nat Arts Club, 76; Hudson Valley Art Asn, 76; and others. *Teaching:* Instr life painting & drawing & oil painting composition, Renaissance Sch Art, Saddle Brook, NJ, 73- *Awards:* Oil Awards, Hudson Artist Inc, 73-74 & Am Artist Prof League, 74; Ray A Jones Mem Award, NJ Painter & Sculptor Soc, 76. *Bibliog:* Article, Southwest Art, 10/79. *Mem:* Salmagundi Club; Am Artists Prof League; Artist Fel. *Mailing Add:* c/o Collector's Gallery Box 2708 Taos NM 87571

MAPES, DORIS WILLIAMSON
PAINTER

b Russellville, Ark, June 25, 20. *Study:* Little Rock Jr Col; Hendrix Col, Ark; Ark Arts Ctr, Little Rock; Rex Brandt's Sch Painting, cert, Corona del Mar, Calif; also with George Post, Millard Sheets, John C Pellew, Louis Freund, Edgar A Whitney, Robert E Wood, John Pike & Robert Andrew Parker, 72. *Work:* Winthrop Rockefeller Gallery, Petit Jean, Ark; Ark Col Mus, Batesville; Am Found Life Ins Co, First Nat Bank & Ark Arts Ctr, Little Rock. *Exhib:* Mid-South Exhib, Brooks Mem Mus, Memphis, 68; Delta Exhib, Ark Arts Ctr, Little Rock, 69; Southwestern Watercolor Soc, Dallas, 68, 69, 71 & 73 & Albuquerque, 72; 107th Ann Am Watercolor Soc, New York, 74; Watercolor USA, Springfield, Mo, 75; Southern Watercolor Soc, Cheekwood Mus, Jackson, Miss, 77. *Awards:* Top of Show, Ark State Festival Arts, 68 & 75; First Award, Mid-Southern Watercolorists, 74; First Award,

Southern Artists Asn, 72; plus many others. *Mem:* Mid-Southern Watercolorists (pres, 70-72); Southwestern Watercolor Soc; Am League Penwomen (vpres, Little Rock Br, 66-70); assoc mem Am Watercolor Soc; Southern Artists Asn. *Media:* Watercolor, Acrylic. *Dealer:* Sketch Box Gallery 5606 R St Little Rock AR 72207. *Mailing Add:* 622 N Bryan Little Rock AR 72205

MAPPLETHORPE, ROBERT
PHOTOGRAPHER

b New York, NY, Nov 4, 46. *Study:* Pratt Inst, 70. *Work:* Mus Mod Art & Metrop Mus Art, New York; Mus Fine Arts, Boston, Mass; Victoria & Albert Mus, London, Eng; Mus Fine Arts, Houston, Tex. *Exhib:* Documenta, Kassel, West Germany, 77 & 82; Collection of San Wagstaff, Corcoran Gallery Art, Washington, DC, 77 & 78; Mirrors & Windows, Mus Mod Art, New York, 78; Artists by Artists, Whitney Mus Am Art, New York, 79; one-man show, Frankfurter Kunstverein, West Germany, 81; Whitney Biennial, Whitney Mus Am Art, New York, 81; Three New York Photographers, Kunsthalle Basel, Switzerland, 82; Robert Mappelthorpe, Inst Contemp Art, London, 83. *Pos:* Illusr, Interview Mag, Esquire Mag & Vogue Mag, 80-82. *Awards:* Creative Artists Public Service Program. *Bibliog:* Rein Von Der Fuhr (auth), Robert Mapplethorpe, Galerie Jurka, Amsterdam, 79; Samuel Wagstaff (auth), Robert Mapplethorpe, Kunsthalle Basel, 81; Bruce Chatwin (auth), Lady: Lisa Lyon, Viking Press, 83. *Publ:* Photogs, Interview, Vogue, Esquire, New York Mag, Geo, Italian Vogue & GQ, 80-; photog, Lady: Lisa Lyons, Viking Press, 83. *Dealer:* Robert Miller Gallery 724 Fifth Ave New York NY 10019. *Mailing Add:* 24 Bond St New York NY 10012

MARADIAGA, RALPH
GALLERY DIRECTOR, DESIGNER

b San Francisco, Calif, Oct 27, 34. *Study:* City Col San Francisco, AA(design), 65; San Francisco State Univ, BA, 71 & MA(printmaking), 75; Stanford Univ, MA(doc film making), 75. *Work:* Mus Mod Art, New York. *Comn:* Logo, Tecolote (community newspaper), San Francisco, 72; posters, San Francisco State Univ, 72 & 75; coloring bk, Galeria de la Raza, 73 & calendario, 73, 74 & 75; logo, Southwest Network, Hayward, Calif, 74. *Exhib:* San Francisco Art Festival, 70-75; San Francisco Mus Mod Art MIX Exhib, 73; Philadelphia Print Club, 73; Posters and Society, San Francisco Mus Art, 74-75. *Collections Arranged:* Santos Exhib, 73-74; Colors of the Guatemalan Indians, 74; Mola Exhib from the Cuna Indians of Panama, 74-75; Huichol Yarn Paintings, Part 1, 75. *Pos:* Co-dir, Galeria de la Raza, 70- *Teaching:* Instr printmaking, La Raza Art Workshop, San Francisco State Univ, 73-75 & Art Workshop, Jewish Community Ctr, summer 74. *Media:* Serigraphy, Film Making. *Mailing Add:* 2851 24th St San Francisco CA 94110

MARAIS (MARY RACHEL BROWN)
PAINTER

b New York, NY. *Study:* Self-taught. *Work:* J Aberbach Collection, Long Island, NY; Hugo Perls NY Collection; Dr Milton Reder NY; UNICEF Collection NY; Theodora Settele Collection, New York. *Exhib:* Galerie Chantepierre, Aubonne, Switz, 72; Galerie Internationale, New York, 75; Cafe de la PAIX Exhib, Paris, 79; Lincoln Bank Exhib, NY, 79; Public TV Channel 13, 79-80; and others. *Mem:* Visual Artists & Galleries Asn; Nat Soc Lit & Arts. *Mailing Add:* c/o Mary Rachel Brown 33 W 67th St New York NY 10023

MARAK, LOUIS BERNARD
CERAMIST, EDUCATOR

b Shawnee, Okla, Sept 9, 42. *Study:* Univ Ill, Champaign-Urbana, BFA, 65; Alfred Univ, MFA, 67. *Work:* Krannert Art Mus, Univ Ill, Urbana; Western Gallery, Western Wash State Col, Bellingham; Utah Mus Fine Arts, Univ Utah, Salt Lake City. *Exhib:* San Francisco Art Inst Centennial Exhib, M H De Young Mem Mus, 71; Calif Ceramics & Glass, Great Hall, Oakland Mus, 74; Crafts IX, E B Crocker Art Gallery, Sacramento, 75; Calif Design 76, Pac Design Ctr, Los Angeles, Calif, 76; Soup Tureens: 1976, Mus Contemp Crafts, New York, 76; Northern Calif Clay Routes: Sculpture Now, San Francisco Mus Mod Art; Contemporary Ceramics, Mus Philadelphia Civic Ctr, 80; American Porcelain: New Expressions in an Ancient Art, Renwick Gallery, Nat Collection Fine Arts, Washington, DC, 80; Soup, Soup, Beautiful Soup, Campbell Mus, Camden, NJ, 83; and others. *Teaching:* Instr art, Keuka Col, New York, 67-69; prof art, Humboldt State Univ, Arcata, 69- *Awards:* Purchase Award, Utah Mus Fine Arts, 71; Award, E B Crocker Art Gallery, 75; Nat Endowment Arts Craftsmen's Fel Grant, 75. *Media:* Earthenware, Porcelain. *Mailing Add:* 1110 Freshwater Rd Eureka CA 95501

MARASCO, ROSE
PHOTOGRAPHER, EDUCATOR

b Utica, NY, Dec 25, 48. *Study:* Syracuse Univ, BFA, 71; Goddard Col, with Todd Webb, MA, 81; Visual Studies Workshop, with Nathon Lyons & John Wood, 82 & 83. *Exhib:* Everson Mus Art Regional, 75; 41st Ann Artists Upstate NY, 78 & Realist Tradition in Central NY, 79, Munson-Williams-Proctor Inst, Utica, NY; solo exhib, Portland Sch Art, Maine, 82; two-person exhib, Alexander Hall Gallery, Portland, Maine, 83; Four Women Artists, Payson Gallery, Portland, Maine, 84. *Collections Arranged:* Todd Webb--Photographs, Univ Southern Maine Art Gallery, 81. *Teaching:* Instr & dept head photog, Munson-Williams-Proctor Inst, 74-79; adj prof photog & design, Univ Southern Maine, 79-; instr photog, Portland Sch Art, Maine, 81- *Awards:* Maine State Comn Arts & Humanities Grant, 83. *Bibliog:* George Bennington (auth), article, Views J, Vol 3, No 4, 82; Edgar A Beem (auth), article, Maine Times, 4/8/83; Bruce Kidman (auth), interview, Maine Sunday Tel, 4/83. *Mem:* Soc Photog Educ. *Publ:* Auth, A personal reflection based on the SPE Questionnaire: Teaching and learning, Exposure 20:1, 82. *Mailing Add:* 854 Methodist Rd Westbrook ME 04092

MARAZZI, WILLIAM C P
PAINTER, CERAMIST

b France, Oct 5, 47. *Work:* Palm Springs Desert Mus, Calif; Evansville Mus Arts, Ind; Huntsville Mus Art, Ala; Rutgers Univ Art Gallery; Metrop Mus Art, New York; and others. *Comn:* Altar, St Barnabas House Chapel, New York, 78; murals, Holman residence, New York, 81; Maitreya Buddha, Mandaraji Temple, New York, 81. *Exhib:* Greene Gallery, 74; Evansville Mus Arts, 75; one-man shows, Rowe House Gallery, Washington DC, 76, E W Ctr, NY, 78 & 79; Bodley Gallery, New York, 77; Wingspread Gallery, Northeast Harbor, Maine, 78; Anichini Gallery, 80 & 81; and many others. *Media:* Flo-paque, Pastel; Porcelain. *Mailing Add:* 2 E 82nd St New York NY 10028

MARBERGER, A ALADAR
DEALER, MUSEUM DIRECTOR

b Philadelphia, Pa, June 15, 47. *Study:* Carnegie-Mellon Univ, BFA. *Pos:* Consult, Carnegie-Mellon Col of Fine Art, 75-77; spec asst to dean, NY Studio Sch, 69-70; dir-partner, Fischbach Gallery Inc, 70- *Mem:* Art Dealers Asn Am Inc. *Specialty:* Contemporary art. *Publ:* Auth, Opinion: Corporate Collection, Carnegie-Mellon Ann, 77. *Mailing Add:* c/o Fischbach Gallery Inc 29 W 57th St New York NY 10019

MARCA-RELLI, CONRAD
PAINTER, COLLAGE ARTIST

b Boston, Mass, June 5, 13. *Work:* Mus Mod Art; Whitney Mus Am Art; Wadsworth Atheneum; Metrop Mus Art; Nat Collection Fine Arts, Washington, DC; and others. *Exhib:* Carnegie Inst; one-man retrospective, Whitney Mus Am Art, 67; Art Inst Chicago; Am Fedn Arts, 67-68; The New American Painting & Sculpture, Mus Mod Art, 69; New Sch Social Res, 69; Am Painting 1970, Va Mus Fine Arts, Richmond, 70; plus many other group & one-man shows. *Teaching:* Former vis critic, Yale Univ, Univ Calif, Berkeley & New Col, Sarasota, Fla. *Awards:* Logan Medal & Purchase Prize, Art Inst Chicago, 54, Kohnstamm Prize, 63; Ford Found Award, 59; Purchase Prize, Detroit Inst Art, 60. *Bibliog:* Parker Tyler (auth), Marca-Relli (monogr), 60; H Harvard Arnason (auth), Marca-Relli (monogr), Abrams, 62; Gerard Miracle & Harold Rosenberg (auth), Marca-Relli, Barcelona, Spain, 75; and others. *Mailing Add:* 7337 Point of Rocks Rd Sarasota FL 33581

MARCHESCHI, (LOUIS) CORK
SCULPTOR, EDUCATOR

b San Mateo, Calif, Apr 5, 45. *Study:* Col San Mateo, 63-66; Calif State Col, Hayward, 66-68; Calif Col Arts & Crafts, Oakland, MFA, 70; also with Mel Ramos & Paul Harris. *Comn:* Outdoor spark-gap, Walker Art Ctr, Minneapolis, 71 & 76; suspended neon sculpture, Can Broadcasting Co, Toronto, 74; fluorescent sculpture in barge in Lake Mich, Summerfest, Milwaukee, Wis, 75; environmental energy sculpture, Morgan Gallery, Kansas City, Kans, 75; fluorescent & spark relief, Ulrich Mus, Wichita, Kans, 75. *Exhib:* One-man shows, Kunsthalle Dusseldorf, Ger, 76, Milwaukee Art Ctr, Wis, 76, Hanson-Cowles Gallery, Minneapolis, Minn, 77, Tubingen Mus, Ger, 78, Van Abbe Mus, Endhoven, Holland, 78 & Nat Gallery, Berlin, Ger, 78; and others. *Teaching:* Assoc prof art & intermedia, Minneapolis Col Art & Design, 70- *Awards:* Minn State Arts Coun Grant, 75; Bush Found Grant, 78; DAAD Berlin Artist Prog Grant, 78. *Bibliog:* Paul Owen (auth), Energy works (16mm film), 71; Merike Weiler (auth), article, Art Can, 73; Heiner Hepper (auth), Cork Marcheschi (film), Ger Pub Broadcasting, 75. *Mem:* Twin Cities Arts Alliance. *Media:* Electricity, Found Objects. *Collection:* Art deco objects and architectural period writings. *Publ:* Auth, Objects for producing visual phenomena with high-voltage electricity, 73; auth, Heat, light and motion, 74; auth, Neon, 75. *Dealer:* Louis K Meisel Gallery 141 Prince St New York NY 10012. *Mailing Add:* 2418 Stevens Ave S Minneapolis MN 55404

MARCHESE, PATRICIA DAVIS
ADMINISTRATOR, CONSULTANT

b Johnstown, Pa, July 12, 43. *Study:* Univ SFla, BA, 64; Fla Atlantic Univ, 67; Univ Fla, 68; Morehead State Univ, 70-71; Univ Nev, Las Vegas, 72; Inst Arts Admin, Harvard Univ, 76. *Work:* Western Div Univ Student Traveling Exhib. *Exhib:* Midwest Univ Student Drawing & Print Exhib, Ill State Univ, 70; Regional Fine Arts Biennial, J B Speed Mus, Louisville, Ky, 71; Eastern Regional Fine Arts Exhib, Morehead, Ky, 72. *Pos:* Instr humanities, Alachua Co Bd Educ, Gainesville, Fla, 66-69; adminr, City of Las Vegas Cult Affairs Branch, 73-79, independant arts consult, 80-81; chmn, Nev Humanities Comt, 79-80. *Mem:* Assoc Coun Arts; Southern Nev Allied Arts Coun; Nev Alliance Arts; and others. *Media:* Serigraphy. *Publ:* Coauth, Soupcans to the Parthenon, Fla Schs, 69; coauth, Humanities Curriculum Outline, 70; auth, A home for the arts, Emphasis, 75; and others. *Mailing Add:* 624 S 9th St Las Vegas NV 89101

MARCHISOTTO, LINDA A
DEALER

b New York, NY. *Study:* Wells Col, BA(fine arts); Trinity Col, Rome, Italy. *Pos:* Curatorial intern, Solomon R Guggenheim Mus, New York, 75; gallery asst, Andre Emmerich Gallery, New York, 75-76; asst dir, Monique Knowlton Gallery, New York, currently. *Specialty:* Contemporary art with a few specialized shows on American Surrealists. *Mailing Add:* c/o Monique Knowlton Gallery 19 E 71st St New York NY 10021

MARCUS, ANGELO P
DEALER, COLLECTOR

b Apr 4, 44. *Study:* Cairo Univ, MA. *Pos:* Dealer, Eagle Art Gallery, currently. *Mem:* Nat Cowboy Hall Fame. *Specialty:* Western art. *Collection:* Olaf Wieghorst, Frank McCarthy, Robert Lougheed, William Whitaker, George Marks, John Clymer, Don Crowley, James Bama & Norman Rockwell. *Mailing Add:* c/o Eagle Art Gallery 1250 Prospect La Jolla CA 92037

MARCUS, IRVING E
PAINTER, EDUCATOR
b Minneapolis, Minn, May 17, 29. *Study:* Univ Minn, BA; Univ Iowa, MFA. *Work:* Minneapolis Inst Art; Allen Art Mus, Oberlin Col; Crocker Art Mus, Sacramento, Calif; Reed Col, Portland, Ore; Oakland Mus Art, Calif; also in many pvt collections. *Exhib:* One-man shows, Zara Gallery, San Francisco, 78 & 80, Artspace, Crocker Art Mus, 78, Vedra Gallery, San Jose, 78 & Southeastern Ctr Contemp Art, Winston-Salem, NC, 79; Faces, Artists Contemp Gallery, Sacramento, 78; Vollum Gallery, Portland, Ore; and others. *Teaching:* Instr art, Oberlin Col, 55-56; instr, Univ Hawaii, 56-57; instr, Blackburn Col, 57-59; prof painting & printmaking, Sacramento State Col, 59-, chmn dept art, 66-69; artist-in-residence, Wake Forest Univ, NC Sch Arts, Winston-Salem, 79. *Awards:* Prizes, Denver Mus Art, 52 & 58 & Crocker Art Mus, 63. *Bibliog:* Thomas Albright (auth), An extraordinary artist, San Francisco Chronicle, 2/11/73; Thomas Albright (auth), Bay area mythmakers, Art Gallery Mag, 11/74. *Dealer:* Candy Store Gallery Folsom CA 95630; Joseph Chowning Gallery 1717 17th St San Francisco CA. *Mailing Add:* 601 Shangri Lane Sacramento CA 95825

MARCUS, MARCIA
PAINTER, EDUCATOR
b New York, NY, Jan 11, 28. *Study:* NY Univ, BA, 47; Art Students League, 54, with Edwin Dickinson. *Work:* Whitney Mus Art, New York; Philadelphia Mus Art; Univ Colo, Boulder; Hirshhorn Mus; Neuberger Mus; and others. *Exhib:* Young Artists, Whitney Mus Art, 60; Four Women, Kansas City, 63; Carnegie Inst, Pittsburgh, 64; Woman Choose Women, New York Cult Ctr, 73; Everson Mus, Syracuse, 75; Canton Art Inst, 84. *Teaching:* Adj instr painting, Cooper Union Sch Art, New York, 70-71; assoc prof painting & drawing, La State Univ, Baton Rouge, spring 72; instr, Vassar Col, 73-74; vis artist, Cornell Univ, spring 75; vis artist, Syracuse Univ, 76, Purdue Univ, 77-78; asst prof, RI Sch Design; assoc prof, Univ Iowa, 79-80; adj assoc prof, Queens Col, 81 & Ohio State Univ, winter 83. *Awards:* Fulbright Fel to France, 62-63; Ingram Merrill Award, 64 & 77; artist in residence, RI Sch Design, Ford Found, 66. *Bibliog:* Paul Cummings (auth), Smithsonian Archives Interview, 75; Noel Frackman (auth), The Attic Mind of Marcia Marcus, Arts, 9/75. *Media:* Oil, Pastel. *Mailing Add:* 80 N Moore St New York NY 10013

MARCUS, STANLEY
COLLECTOR
b Dallas, Tex, Apr 20, 05. *Study:* Harvard Univ, BA, 25, Bus Sch, 26; Southern Methodist Univ, Hon HHD, 65; N Tex Univ, LHD, 82. *Pos:* Dir, Dallas Symphony Soc; adv dir, Ft Worth Art Asn; trustee, Eisenhower Exchange Fellowships; Bus Comt for the Arts; pres, Dallas Art Asn, formerly; emer chmn, Neiman-Marcus Co; consult, Carter, Hawley Hale Stores, Inc. *Collection:* Paintings, contemporary art; prehistoric American Indian pottery; pre-Columbian textiles and pottery. *Mailing Add:* 4800 Republic Nat Bank Tower Dallas TX 75201

MARDEN, BRICE
PAINTER, PRINTMAKER
b Bronxville, NY, Oct 15, 38. *Study:* Boston Univ, BFA, with Reed Kay, Arthur Hoener & Hugh Townley; Yale-Norfolk Summer Sch Music & Art, with Bernard Chaet & Jon Schueler; Sch Art & Archit, Yale Univ, MFA, with Esteban Vicente & Alex Katz. *Work:* Mus Mod Art, New York; Whitney Mus Am Art, New York; Walker Art Ctr, Minneapolis, Minn; Ft Worth Art Ctr, Tex; Stedelijk Mus, Amsterdam; and others. *Exhib:* Whitney Mus Am Art Ann, New York, 69, 77 & 83; Modular Painting, Albright-Knox Art Gallery, Buffalo, 70; Painting--New Options, Walker Art Ctr, 72; Documenta 5, Kassel, Ger, 72; 17th Guggenheim Mus, New York, 75; Brice Marden: Recent Paintings and Drawings, Pace Gallery, New York, 78; A New Spirit in Painting, Royal Acad Arts, London, 81; and others. *Media:* Oil. *Dealer:* Pace Gallery 32 E 57th St New York NY 10022. *Mailing Add:* 54 Bond St New York NY 10012

MARDER, DORIE
PAINTER, PRINTMAKER
b Poland; US citizen. *Study:* Sorbonne; Art Students League; New Sch Social Res; also with Harry Shoulberg & Morris Kantor. *Work:* Roberson Ctr Arts, NY; Butler Inst Am Art, Youngstown, Ohio; Seattle Art Mus; San Francisco Mus Art; Nat Acad Design; and others. *Exhib:* Hudson Guild Gallery, 81. *Awards:* Award for Oil Painting, Clendenen, 61; Award for Serigraph, Montag, 65; First Prize, Village Art Ctr. *Mem:* League Present Day Artists (dir, 71-72); Nat Asn Women Artists; Artists Equity, Asn New York; Nat Serigraph Soc; Nat Asn Women Artists (exec bd, 80-84); and others. *Mailing Add:* 223 W 21st St New York NY 10011

MARGO, BORIS
PAINTER, PRINTMAKER
b Wolotschisk, Russia, Nov 7, 02; US citizen. *Study:* Polytechnik Art, Odessa, USSR, cert; Futemas (workshop for art of the future), Moscow, USSR; Pavel Filonov Sch, Leningrad, USSR. *Work:* Metrop Mus Art & Mus Mod Art, New York; Nat Collection Fine Arts, Washington, DC; Art Inst Chicago; Sao Paulo Mus Art, Brazil. *Exhib:* Abstract and Surrealist Art in the United States, San Francisco Mus Art & others, 44; Carnegie Inst Pittsburgh, 52; Japan Print Asn 30th Anniversary Int, 62; Venice Biennales, 56 & 70; Honolulu Acad Art, 73; Rutgers Univ Art Gallery, 77. *Pos:* Res assoc (on the creative process), Psychiatric Inst, Univ Md, 57-58. *Teaching:* Vis artist, Am Univ, 46-48; vis prof painting, Art Inst Chicago, 57-59; vis prof printmaking & drawing, Sch Art, Syracuse Univ, 66-67; artist in residence, Acad Art, Honolulu, 72. *Awards:* Purchase Award for oil painting, Portland Mus Art, Maine, 60; six Purchase Awards, Brooklyn Mus Print Exhibs, 47-68; Award in printmaking, Nat Endowment Arts, 74. *Bibliog:* Laurence Schmeckebier (auth), Boris Margo, Graphic Work, 1932-1968, Syracuse Univ Press, 68. *Mem:* Provincetown Art Asn; MacDowell Colony Fels; Soc Am Graphic Artists. *Publ:* Auth, Boris Margo: my theories and techniques, Mag Art, 11/47; auth, Margo: is there an American school of art?, The Tiger's Eye, 12/47; auth, Surrealism and American Art, Jeffrey Wechsler, 77. *Mailing Add:* c/o Monique Knowlton 19 E 71st St New York NY 10021

MARGOLIES, ETHEL POLACHECK
PAINTER
b Milwaukee, Wis, Aug 1, 07. *Study:* Smith Col, AB, 29; Silvermine Guild Artists; Umberto Romano Sch, East Gloucester, Mass; Univ Vt Summer Sch. *Work:* Burndy Libr, Norwalk, Conn; Gen Time Corp, Stamford, Conn; Springfield Mus, Mass; Int Petroleum Corp; New Haven Paint & Clay Club, Conn. *Exhib:* Silvermine Guild Artists, New Eng Exhib, New Canaan, Conn, 54-57, 60-68 & 74-75; Int Petroleum Art Festival, Tulsa, Okla, 66; Conn Acad Fine Arts, Hartford; Conn Watercolor Soc, Hartford; Audubon Artists, New York. *Pos:* Gallery dir, Larry Aldrich Mus Contemp Art, 64-66; gallery dir, Silvermine Guild Artists, 54-72. *Awards:* Awards for indust painting, Silvermine Guild, 54, 57, 60 & 64; Purchase Award, Springfield Mus, Mass, 57; New Haven Paint & Clay Club Award, 75. *Mem:* Artists Equity Asn New York; Silvermine Guild Artists (bd trustees, 54-75); Conn Acad Fine Arts; Conn Watercolor Soc; New Haven Paint & Clay Club. *Media:* Multimedia. *Mailing Add:* 103 Jelliff Mill Rd New Canaan CT 06840

MARGOLIS, DAVID
PAINTER, SCULPTOR
b Voloshisk, USSR, Sept 3, 11; US citizen. *Study:* Acad Fine Arts, Odessa, USSR, BFA(equivalent), 27; Ecole de Beaux Art, Montreal, BFA(equivalent), 29; Nat Acad, New York. *Work:* Tel Aviv Mus, Israel. *Comn:* Progress of Man (mural), Rockefeller Ctr, New York, 33; Modern Communications (mural), Amalgamated Broadcasting, New York, 34; History of American Music (mural), Tilden High Sch & WPA, New York, 37; Materials for Relaxation (mural), Bellevue Hosp & WPA, New York, 41; Industrial Development (mural), Design for Living, New York, 43. *Exhib:* Contemporary Sculpture, Brooklyn Col Mus, New York, 69; solo exhib, NY Univ, 72; WPA Art, Then and Now, Parsons Sch Design, New York, 77; Alphabet as Art, Tragetto Gallery, Venice, Italy, 78 & Samuel Dorsky Gallery, New York, 80; Am Soc Contemp Artists, New York, 79 & 80; and others. *Awards:* Sculpture Award, 79, Award of Merit, 80 & Contemp Art Award, 81, Am Soc Contemp Artists. *Bibliog:* Francis V O'Connor (auth), American Art, Smithsonian Inst, 76; Emily Genauer (auth), New York City WPA Art, New York WPA Artists Inc, 77. *Mem:* Provincetown Art Asn; Am Soc Contemp Artists; New York WPA Artists Inc. *Media:* Mixed Media; Constructed Metal. *Mailing Add:* 39 W 14th St New York NY 10011

MARGOLIS, RICHARD M
PHOTOGRAPHER, EDUCATOR
b Lorain, Ohio, June 10, 43. *Study:* Kent State Univ, BS, 69; Visual Studies Workshop, 72; Rochester Inst Technol, MFA, 78. *Work:* Mus Mod Art, New York; Victoria & Albert Mus, London, Eng; Bibliotheque Nat, Paris, France; George Eastman House, Rochester, NY; Yale Univ Art Gallery, New Haven, Conn. *Exhib:* One-man shows, Foto, New York, 76 & George Eastman House, Rochester, NY, 79; St Lawrence Univ, Canton, NY, 77; Carpenter Ctr, Harvard Univ, Cambridge, Mass, 78; Creative Artists Pub Serv Prog Photog Show, Whitney Mus Am Art, New York, 78; Mem Art Gallery, Rochester, NY, 79; Englandish Landscapes, Camden Arts Ctr, London, Eng, 81; Foto, New York, 83. *Collections Arranged:* Personal Landscapes, Rochester Landscape in Various Media, Artworks Gallery, 80; Francis Murray & H Jones, Gallery 696, Rochester, 81; Photography-Art of the State (auth, catalog), State Univ NY, Brockport, 83 & NY State Mus, 83. *Teaching:* Instr photog, Penland Sch Crafts, 79-80; adj instr photog, Nazareth Col, Rochester, NY, 79-81; asst prof photog, State Univ NY, Brockport, 81-; vis artist, Chautauqua Inst, 83. *Awards:* New York State Coun Arts Grant, Creative Artists Public Service Program, 77-78. *Bibliog:* Owen Edwards (auth), Raveling the knot, Saturday Review, 4/28/79; Owen Edwards (auth), The complex complex, Am Photographer, 6/81. *Mem:* Soc Photog Educ (chmn, NE region, 83); United Univ Professors; Ctr Creative Photog. *Mailing Add:* 113 Cypress St Rochester NY 14620

MARGOULIES, BERTA (BERTA MARGOULIES O'HARE)
SCULPTOR, EDUCATOR
b Lovitz, Poland, Sept 7, 07; US citizen. *Study:* Hunter Col, BA; Art Students League; Acad Colarossi & Acad Julien, Paris, France. *Work:* Whitney Mus Am Art, New York; Nat Archives, Smithsonian Inst; Willamette Univ, Salem, Ore; Wyandotte Co Mus, Kans; Int Lithographers Union, Washington, DC. *Comn:* Colonial foot postman, comn by US Govt, Postmaster Gen Off, Washington, DC, 37; Woman & Deer, Garden Ct Fed Bldg, comn by US Govt, 39; Terra Cotta Reliefs, Post Office, Mena, Ark; Founding of Canton (relief), Post Office, Canton, NY. *Exhib:* Whitney Mus Am Art, New York; Metrop Mus Art, New York; Pa Fine Arts Acad, Philadelphia; Chicago Art Inst; Archit League of NY; Nat Acad Design, New York; Corcoran Gallery, Washington, DC; Int Sculpture Exhib, Arts Coun Paramus, NJ, 75. *Collections Arranged:* Sculptors' Guild First Outdoor Exhib, New York, 19. *Teaching:* Instr sculpture, Finch Col, New York, 36-43, Five Mus & Art, Long Island, NY, 44-53 & Somerset Art Asn, Bernardville, NJ, 70. *Awards:* Avery Prize for Sculpture, Archit League of NY, 37; Accomplishment in Sculpture, Am Acad Arts & Lett, 44; Guggenheim Fel, 46. *Bibliog:* Women Artists of America, Newark Mus, 65; Charlotte Rubinstein (auth), American Women Artists, G K Hall & Co, 82; Library Archives of Women Sculptors, Tex

Woman's Univ, 83. *Mem:* Founding mem Sculptors' Guild (exec secy, 38-46); founding mem Artists Equity; Assoc Artists NJ; Somerset Art Asn, NJ. *Media:* Miscellaneous Media. *Publ:* Contribr, Jack C Rich's Materials and Methods of Sculpture, Oxford Univ Press, 47; contribr, One Hundred American Jewish Artists, YKUF, 47; contribr, Contemporary American Sculpture, Crown, 48; contribr, Cecil Roth's Jewish Art--An Illustrated History, McGraw-Hill, 61. *Dealer:* Benedict Gallery 254 Main St Madison NJ 07940. *Mailing Add:* Tinc Rd Flanders NJ 07836

MARGULES, GABRIELE ELLA
ILLUSTRATOR, PAINTER
b Tachau, Czech, May 30, 27; US citizen. *Study:* Cambridge Sch Art, Eng, nat dipl fine arts; Royal Acad Schs, London; New York, studies with Hans Hofmann, Camilo Egas & Norman Carton. *Work:* Kerlan Collection, Univ Minn Res Ctr for Children's Books, Minneapolis. *Exhib:* 100 Best Children's Books, Am Inst Graphic Arts, 68 & 70; Sumi-e Soc New York, 70-73; New York Ctr; Sale Collection, Jr Coun, Mus Mod Art; Garrison Art Ctr, 79. *Awards:* Two-Year Grad Scholar, Cambridge Co Coun, Eng, 48; Silver Medal-First Prize for Life Drawing, Royal Acad, London, 49; Myers Art Scholar, New Sch Social Res, 61. *Mem:* Artists Equity New York (coun mem, 66-70); Dutchess Co Art Asn; Putnam Arts Coun; Putnam Co Hist Soc. *Media:* Sumi-e Ink, Watercolor. *Publ:* Illusr, Harper's Mag, 63; illusr, Out of the Ark, Atheneum, New York & Longman Young, London, 68; illusr, Bird Songs, Atheneum, 69. *Mailing Add:* 7 High St Cold Spring NY 10516

MARGULIES, HERMAN
PAINTER
b Boryslaw, Poland, Dec 7, 22; US citizen. *Study:* Royal Acad Fine Arts, Brussels, Belgium, 47-49. *Work:* Chosen Work, Yad Vashem Mus, Holocaust Mem, Jerusalem, Israel. *Exhib:* Pastel Soc Nat Ann, Nat Arts Club Gallery, New York, 82-83; Pastel Soc Am, Hermitage Found Mus, Norfolk, Va, 83; American Impressionists, A M Adler Fine Arts Gallery, New York, 83; Old Bergen Art Guild, Hickory Art Mus, NC & Cayuga Mus of Art & Hist, Auburn, NY, 83; Pastel & Drawing Ann Exhib, Salmagundi Club Gallery, New York, 83. *Awards:* Award for Pastel, Knickerbocker Artists Nat Ann, 82; Exceptional Merit, Pastel Soc Nat Ann, 83; First Award for Pastel, Salmagundi Pastel & Drawing, 83. *Bibliog:* Rhoda Sherbell (auth), Pastel Society Annual (film), Cultural Break, Channel 13 TV, 9/82; Eileen Watkins (auth), Pick of the crop, 1/30/83 & Full strength, 10/23/83, Star Ledger NJ. *Mem:* Pastel Soc Am, New York (bd dirs, 83-); Am Artists Professional League, New York; Salmagundi Club; Painters & Sculptors Soc NJ; Kent Art Asn, Conn. *Media:* Pastel. *Dealer:* A M Adler Fine Arts Gallery 21 East 67th St New York NY 10021. *Mailing Add:* 229 Audley St South Orange NJ 07079

MARGULIES, ISIDORE
SCULPTOR, KINETIC ARTIST
b Vienna, Austria, Apr 1, 21. *Study:* Cooper Union Art Sch, New York, 40-42; State Univ NY, Stony Brook, BA(liberal arts), 73; C W Post Col, MAA, 75; with Robert White, James Kleege & Alfred Van Loan. *Work:* Hall of Fame, State Univ NY Stony Brook; Brookgreen Gardens, Myrtle Beach, SC. *Exhib:* Nat Acad Design, New York, 75 & 81; Nat Sculpture Soc, 78-81; Joel Meisner Gallery, 77-81; R K Parker Gallery, Soho, NY, 80; Nelson Rockefeller Collection, 80-81. *Awards:* Coun Am Artists Award, Nat Sculpture Soc, 79; Gold Medal, Nat Sculpture Soc, 80; C Percival Dietsch Sculpture Prize, Nat Sculpture Soc, 83. *Mem:* Huntington Twp Art League (chmn, 76-78); Nat Sculpture Soc. *Media:* Mixed Media. *Mailing Add:* 650 Washington Ave Plainview NY 11803

MARGULIES, JOSEPH
PAINTER, PRINTMAKER
b Austria, July 7, 1896; US citizen. *Study:* Cooper Union; Nat Acad Design; with Maynard; Art Students League, with Joseph Pennell; also study abroad. *Work:* Nat Portrait Gallery, Smithsonian Inst, Libr Cong & Judiciary, House of Representatives, Washington, DC; Metrop Mus Art, New York; Cleveland Mus Art, Ohio. *Comn:* Portrait of John F Brosnan, regent & chancellor, Univ of State NY, 61; portrait of Sen Jacob K Javits, comn by Atty Gen, NY State Capitol, Albany; portrait of Congressman Emanuel Celler, comn by chmn Judiciary Staff, 63; portrait of Dr Bela Schick, Nat Portrait Gallery, 69; portrait of John Dewey, for Dewey Ctr, Carbondale, Ill. *Exhib:* Graphics, Univ Maine, Orono, 65; also yearly exhibs, Provincetown Art Asn, Audubon Artists, Allied Artists Am & Am Watercolor Soc. *Awards:* Gold Medal for Graphics, Acad Artists Asn, Springfield, Mass, 77; N Shore Art Asn Award, Gloucester, Mass, 77; Award, Hugh Botts Award & Seley Purchase Prize, Salmagundi Club. *Bibliog:* B F Morrow (auth), The Art of Aquatint, Putman, 35; Norman Kent (auth), 100 Watercolor Techniques, Watson-Guptill, 65. *Mem:* Audubon Artists; Allied Artists Am; Salmagundi Club; Am Watercolor Soc; Rockport Art Asn. *Media:* Oil, Watercolor; Graphics. *Publ:* Auth, Joseph Margulies paints a portrait in watercolor, Am Artist Mag, 60. *Dealer:* Assoc Am Artists 663 Fifth Ave New York NY 10022. *Mailing Add:* 27 W 67th St New York NY 10023

MARGULIS, MARTHA (BOYER)
PAINTER
b Jersey City, NJ, Jan 5, 28. *Study:* Syracuse Univ, NY, BFA, 49; Columbia Univ, New York, 50-51; with Rudolph Baranik, 58-61. *Work:* Herbert F Johnson Mus, Cornell Univ, Ithaca, NY; Syracuse Univ Art Collections, Lowe Gallery, Syracuse, NY; Everson Mus Art, Syracuse, NY; Smithsonian Inst; Pepsi Cola Corp, Valhalla, NY. *Comn:* Mural, F D Rich & Co, Inc, Stamford, Conn, 81; triptych, Bankers Trust Co, Inc, White Plains, NY, 81; mural, Summit Assocs, Edison, NJ, 82; triptych, Kramer & Levin Inc, New

York, 83. *Exhib:* Brook Artists, Riverside Mus, New York, 68; Works on Paper, Brooklyn Mus, NY, 75; NMex Int, Eastern NMex Univ, Clovis, 76; Hudson River Contemp Artists, Hudson River Mus, Yonkers, NY, 78; New Eng Exhib of Painting, Drawing & Sculpture, Silvermine Ctr Arts, New Canaan, Conn, 79, 81 & 83; Nat Acad Design Ann, New York, 80; 44th Ann Midyear Show, Butler Inst Am Art, Youngstown, Ohio, 80; Nat Asn Women Artists: Israel & Egypt traveling exhib, 81-82. *Awards:* Int Women's Year Award, Ford Found, 75 & 76; Jean Magid Leeman Mem, Nat Asn Women Artists, 79; Condec Corporation Award, New Eng Exhib, 81. *Bibliog:* Madeleine Burnside (auth), article, Art News Mag, 78; Robert Yoskowitz (auth), articles, Arts Mag, 12/79 & 12/81; Jacqueline Moss (auth), article, Arts Mag, 5/83. *Mem:* Artists Equity New York; Nat Asn Women Artists; Silvermine Guild of Art. *Media:* Acrylic, Crayon. *Dealer:* Payson-Weisberg Gallery 822 Madison Ave New York NY 10021. *Mailing Add:* Valley Ridge Road Harrison NY 10528

MARI (M EAGERTON)
CRAFTSMAN, PAINTER
US citizen. *Study:* Atlanta Sch Art, BFA; Butler Univ; Ga State Univ; Principia Col. *Work:* Mus Contemp Crafts, Slide Libr, New York; Vogue Fabrics Libr, Conde Nast, New York. *Comn:* Batik wallhanging, Emory Univ, Atlanta, Ga. *Exhib:* Midstates Painting Exhib, Evansville Mus Art, 72-74; American Fiber Art, Ball State Univ, 74; Fibers Invitational, Austin Peay State Univ, 74; Spoleto Festival, 77; The Dyers Art, Cincinnati, Ohio, 78. *Teaching:* Instr batik, silkscreen & fabric painting, Ind Univ, Indianapolis, 69-72; instr painting & drawing, 72-77; instr painting, Herron Sch Art, 77. *Awards:* Objects 71, Textile Award, IMA, 71; Purchase Award, Bardstown Invitational, Ky, 73; Southeastern Arts Festival Painting Award, Atlanta, Ga, 70. *Bibliog:* Dona Meilach (auth), Contemporary Batik & Tie Dying, Crown, 73; Joanifer Gibbs (auth), Batiks Unlimited, Watson-Guptill, 74. *Mem:* Surface Design Int; Am Crafts Coun. *Media:* Batik on Silk, Oil on Canvas. *Dealer:* Collector's Showroom 325 N Wells St Chicago IL 60654. *Mailing Add:* c/o Editions Ltd Gallery 919 E Westfield Blvd Indianapolis IN 46220

MARIANNE (M MARIANNE MILES)
PAINTER, DRAFTSMAN
b Austin, Tex, Aug 18, 41. *Study:* Laguna Gloria Art Mus, Austin, 52 & 53; Tex Southern Univ, with John Biggers; Fisk Univ, with Aaron Douglas, BA, 63; New York Univ, with Robert Kaupelis & John Opper, MA, 68. *Work:* First Am Nat Bank & Fisk Univ, Nashville. *Comn:* Cover illus, From these Roots (book), Austin, 70; mural, Golden Horn Music Industry, Nashville, 72. *Exhib:* Parthenon, Nashville, 69; one-woman show, Sam Rayburn Mem Ctr, East Tex State Univ, Commerce, 70, The Parthenon, Nashville, 70; and others. *Pos:* Designer, Golden Horn Production Co, 73-76; graphic designer, Huston-Tillotson Col, 77-80. *Teaching:* Instr art, Fisk Univ, 66-69; instr art, Austin Community Col, 81- *Bibliog:* James W Byrd (auth), Such is the South & Center shows artists work, Herald Banner, Greenville, Tex, 70; Clara Hieronymus (auth), Some gifts not wrapped, 12/18/70 & Art on deposit, 8/26/73, Tennessean. *Media:* Oil, Casein; Charcoal, Pencil. *Dealer:* The Home Gallery 1108 Chicon Austin TX 78702. *Mailing Add:* PO Box 6083 Austin TX 78762

MARIANO, KRISTINE
PAINTER
b Rochester, NY, Jan 16, 39. *Study:* Sch Fine Arts, Rochester Inst Technol, BFA; also at Mem Art Gallery, Univ Rochester. *Work:* Univ Mem Art Gallery, Univ Rochester, NY; Blue Cross/Blue Shield Corp, New York; Am Embassy Art Collection, Washington, DC; Eastman Kodak Co; Xerox Corp. *Comn:* 10 paintings, Kidder-Peabody Corp, New York & Los Angeles, 78. *Exhib:* Everson Mus Art, Syracuse, NY, 63; Provincetown Art Asn, Mass, 66-70; Chautauqua Nat Exhib Am Art, NY, 63 & 67; Albright-Knox Gallery, Buffalo, NY, 67; one-man shows, Kendall Art Gallery, Wellfleet, Mass, 67-76; Baracca Gallery, North Hatfield, Mass, 78. *Mem:* Boston Visual Artists Union. *Media:* Acrylic, Collage. *Dealer:* Kendall Art Gallery Inc Box 742 E Main St Wellfleet MA 02667; Hambleton Gallery Nantucket MA 02554. *Mailing Add:* 292 Winter St Weston MA 02193

MARIL, HERMAN
PAINTER, PRINTMAKER
b Baltimore, Md, Oct 13, 08. *Study:* Md Inst Fine Arts, grad. *Work:* Whitney Mus Am Art & Metrop Mus Art, New York; Baltimore Mus Art; Nat Collection Fine Arts, Smithsonian Inst, Washington, DC; plus others. *Comn:* Murals, West Scranton Post Off, Pa, Stamford & Alta Vista Post Off, Va, 40, Pub Bldgs Admin, US Treas Dept. *Exhib:* San Francisco Golden Gate Expos, 39; Carnegie Inst Int Ann, Pittsburgh, Pa, 40-45; retrospective, Baltimore Mus Art, 67; Pa Acad Fine Arts, Philadelphia; Corcoran Gallery Art Biennials, Washington, DC; Selected Works 1929-1977, Univ Md Art Gallery, Galleries, Dallas, Tex; Provincetown, A Painter's World, Everson Mus, Syracuse, NY, 77; plus others. *Teaching:* Instr painting, Philadelphia Mus Col Art, 55-56; prof painting, Univ Md, 47-77, emer prof, 78- *Awards:* Stefan Hirsch Mem Award, Audubon Artists, 72; Inst/Acad Arts & Lett, New York, 78. *Bibliog:* Eliot O'Hara (auth), Restraint (film), 61; Emery Grossman (auth), Art and tradition, Yoseloff, 67; Frank Getlein (auth), Herman Maril, Baltimore Mus Art, 67. *Mem:* Baltimore Mus Art (hon trustee, 72); Provincetown Art Asn; Col Art Asn Am; Artists Equity Asn; Assoc Nat Acad Design. *Media:* Oil, Acrylic; Casein. *Dealer:* Forum Gallery 1018 Madison Ave New York NY 10021. *Mailing Add:* 5602 Roxbury Pl Baltimore MD 21209

MARIN, AUGUSTO
PAINTER, EDUCATOR
b San Juan, PR, Nov 20, 21. *Study:* Art Students League, under Reginald Marsh, John Corbino, Ivan Olinsky & Harry Sternberg; Los Angeles Co Art Inst, under Jack Otterson; PR Inst Cult, stained glass under Arnold Maas. *Work:* Mus Mod Art, New York; Metrop Mus Art, New York; Ponce Art Mus, PR; San Juan Mus Art, PR; Mus Univ PR, Rio Piedras. *Comn:* Two murals, Juan R Jimenez Sch, Bayamon, 64; mural, Cruv Bldg, Rio Piedras, Govt of PR, 66; mural, Laguna Gardens Ctr, EHG Enterprises, 70, mural, Surfside Mansions, Atlantic Construct, 72 & mural, Fine Arts Ctr, San Juan, 81; and others. *Exhib:* Primer Bienal Int Painting & Engraving, Mexico City, Mex, 58; Eleven Puerto Rican Painters, Bonn, Ger, 73; one-man shows, Ponce Art Mus, PR, 61, Inst Cult Puertorriquena, San Juan, 61, 65 & 73 & Mus Univ PR, Rio Piedras, 67. *Pos:* Art dir, Badillo Advert, San Juan, PR, 46-48, 58 & 59, illusr, 60-64. *Teaching:* Prof painting & composition, Sch Plastic Arts, San Juan, PR, 66-; prof drawing, Univ PR, Rio Piedras, 71- *Awards:* Second Prize, Oil Painting, Ateneo Puertorriqueno, 57 & 62, First Prize, Oil Painting, 61. *Bibliog:* John Gruen (auth), Latin American artist, New York Herald Tribune, 4/21/63; E Fernandez (auth), Testigo de su Tiempo, Avance Mag, PR, 5/14/73; Reinhard Fuchs (auth), Exhibition in Bonn, Gen Reporter, Ger, 12/3/75. *Media:* Acrylic, Watercolor. *Mailing Add:* J7 25th St Jard Country Club Carolina PR 00630

MARINO, FRANK
DEALER
b Danbury, Conn, Aug 24, 42. *Study:* Parson's Sch Design, cert(environ design), 69; NY Univ, 69-70; Art Students League, 70-72. *Pos:* Owner & pres, Frank Marino Gallery, New York, currently. *Specialty:* Twenty century & contemporary painting, sculpture and photography. *Mailing Add:* 489 Broome St New York NY 10013

MARINSKY, HARRY
SCULPTOR, PAINTER
b London, Eng, May 8, 09; US citizen. *Study:* RI Sch Design; Pratt Inst. *Work:* Metrop Mus Art, New York; Lincoln Ctr, Fordham Univ; Syracuse Univ Art Mus; York Univ Mus; Hunt Botanical Libr, Carnegie-Mellon Univ; and others. *Comn:* Large bronze bird for scent & touch garden, Stamford Mus, Conn, 60; five bronze figures representing spirit of nationalism, Vet Mem Park, Norwalk, Conn, 66; St Francis, St James Episcopal Church, Danbury, Conn, 67; bronze figures, Harlequin Plaza, Denver, Colo, 81. *Exhib:* Mus Mod Art, New York; Art Inst Chicago, 47; Florence Art Gallery, Italy; Redfern Gallery, London, Eng; Hammer Galleries, New York; Shayne Galerie, Montreal; and others. *Awards:* Silvermine Guild Sculpture Award, 56. *Mem:* Nat Sculpture Soc, New York. *Media:* Bronze, Watercolor. *Dealer:* Hammer Galleries, New York. *Mailing Add:* Villa Capriglia Via Fornace 2 Capriglia 55045 Pietrasanta (Lucca) Italy

MARIONI, PAUL
SCULPTOR, GLASS BLOWER
b Cincinnati, Ohio, July 19, 41. *Study:* Univ Cincinnati, BA, 67. *Work:* Corning Mus Glass; Hessisches Landesmuseum, Darmstadt, WGer; Oakland Mus; Yamaha Corp, Tokyo; City Seattle Portable Works Collection. *Comn:* Leaded glass windows, Stanford Univ, 78; cast glass window, Seattle Arts Comn, 80; cast glass wall, Timberline Lodge, Mt Hood, Ore, 82; cast glass sculptures, Seattle Arts Comn, 83; leaded glass windows, Wash Arts Comn, Woodinville, 83. *Exhib:* Glass, Mus Contemp Crafts, New York, 78; New Glass, Corning Mus & traveling, 78-81; Contemporary Glass, Smithsonian Inst, 80; American Glass Now Traveling Exhib, Japan, 80-83; American Glass Traveling Exhib, Europe, 82-83; Pacific Glass 83, Govett-Brewster Mus, New Plymouth, NZ, 83; Vicointer 83, Cevider Mus, Valencia, Spain, 83. *Pos:* Dir, Canyon Cinema, San Francisco, 72-74; coordr glass prog, Summervail, Vail, Colo, 79- *Teaching:* Lectr art, San Francisco Art Inst, 73-75; asst prof, San Francisco State Univ, 74-78; guest artist, Pilchuck Sch, Stanwood, Wash, 74- *Awards:* Nat Endowment Arts Grants, 75-76 & 82; First Prize Archit, Fragile Art, 83. *Bibliog:* Otto Rigan (auth), New Glass, Simon & Schuster, 76; Narcissus Quagliata (auth), From Mind to Light, Mattole Press, 76; Julie Hall (auth), Tradition and Change, Dutton Press, 78. *Mem:* Glass Arts Soc; Northwest Glass Artists. *Media:* Glass. *Dealer:* Walter-White Gallery 7th & San Carlos PO Box 4834 Carmel CA 93921. *Mailing Add:* 4136 Meridian Ave Seattle WA 98103

MARIONI, TOM
MUSEUM DIRECTOR, ENVIRONMENTAL ARTIST
b Cincinnati, Ohio, May 21, 37. *Study:* Cincinnati Conserv Music, 54; Cincinnati Art Acad, 55-59. *Work:* Oakland Mus, Calif; Student Cult Ctr, Belgrade, Yugoslavia; City of San Francisco; Santa Barbara Mus Art, Calif. *Comn:* Free standing concrete wall (with Jacques Overhoff), Golden Gateway, San Francisco, 67; playground (with Jacques Overhoff), Fashion Island, Newport Beach, Calif, 67; Logo, Western Asn Art Mus, 69. *Exhib:* Sound Sculpture As, Mus Conceptual Art, 70; De Marco Gallery, Edinburgh, Scotland, 72; White Chapel, London, Eng, 72; Student Cult Ctr, Belgrade, Yugoslavia, 74; one-man show, Foksol Gallery, Warsaw, Poland, 75, Mod Art Gallery, Vienna, Austria, 79, Pellegrino Gallery, Bologna, Italy, 79, Kunst Mus, Bern, Switzerland, 80, Ctr G Pompidou Mus, Paris, 80. *Collections Arranged:* All Night Sculptures, Mus Conceptual Art, 73; Actions by Sculptors for the Home Audience, KQED TV, 74; Chinese Youth Alternative, Mus Conceptual Art, 74. *Pos:* Cur art, Richmond Art Ctr, 68-71; dir, Mus Conceptual Art, 70-; ed, Vision, Oakland, 75- *Awards:* Nat Endowment Arts, 76-79; J S Guggenheim Grant, 80. *Bibliog:* Cordelia Oliver (auth), Man of sound vision, Manchester Guardian, 6/5/72; P Juris (auth), The newer art, Studio Int, 6/72; Hilla Futterman (auth), Activity as sculpture, Art & Artists,

8/73. *Mem:* San Francisco Art Inst (bd dirs, 74-). *Publ:* Auth, Invisible Painting & Sculpture, 69; auth, The Return of Abstract Expressionism, 69; auth, The San Francisco Performance, 72; auth, Notes & Scores for Sounds, 72; auth, Vision (California), 75, Vision (Eastern Europe), Vision (New York City), Vision (Word of Mouth), 80 & Vision (Artist Photographs), 81. *Mailing Add:* 75 Third St San Francisco CA 94103

MARISOL, ESCOBAR
SCULPTOR
b Paris, France, 1930. *Study:* Ecole Beaux Arts, 49; Art Students League, 50; New Sch, 51-54; Hans Hofmann Sch; Moore Col Art, Philadelphia, Hon DFA, 70. *Work:* Mus Mod Art, New York; Whitney Mus Am Art, New York; Albright-Knox Art Gallery, Buffalo; Mus Bellas Artes, Caracas, Venezuela; Nat Portrait Gallery, Washington, DC. *Exhib:* One-man exhibs, Sidney Janis Gallery, New York, 66, 67, 73, 75 & 81 & Mus Contemp Art, Houston, 77; The Year of the Woman, Bronx Mus, 76; The Golden Door, Hirshhorn Mus, 76; Women Artists 1976, McNay Gallery, San Antonio, 77; Contemp Women, Brooklyn Mus, 77; The Opposite Sex, Univ Mo, 79. *Bibliog:* Barbara Gold (auth), Portrait of Marisol, Interplay, 1/68; Don Cyr (auth), A conversation with Marisol, Arts & Activities, Vol 63, No 1; Lawrence Campbell (auth), Marisol, Art News, 11/67; plus others. *Publ:* Contribr, The Art of Assemblage, Doubleday; contribr, Pop Art, Praeger; contribr, The New American Arts, Collier, 67; contribr, In Memory of My Feelings, Crafton Graphic Co, 67; contribr, Stamps Indelibly, Multiples, Inc, 67. *Mailing Add:* c/o Sidney Janis Gallery 6 W 57th St New York NY 10019

MARK, BENDOR
PAINTER
b New York, NY, June 5, 12. *Study:* Cooper Union. *Work:* Denver Art Mus, Colo; Nat Collection Fine Arts, Washington, DC; Butler Inst Am Art, Youngstown, Ohio; Ga Mus Art, Athens; Los Angeles Co Mus Art, Calif. *Exhib:* ACA Nat Competition, New York, 36; American Art Today, New York World's Fair, 39; Art Inst Chicago, 40; Am Fedn Art Traveling Show, 40-41; Pepsi Cola Nat Competition, Metrop Mus, New York, 45; Am as Art Bicentennial Exhib, Nat Collection Fine Arts, Washington, DC, 76; plus others. *Awards:* Second Prize, Cooper Union, 29; Second Prize, ACA Nat Competition, 36. *Mailing Add:* 5727 Chelsea Ave La Jolla CA 92037

MARK, ENID (EPSTEIN)
PRINTMAKER, PAINTER
b New York, NY, 32. *Study:* Art Students League; Smith Col, BA; West Chester State Col, lithography with Victor Lasuchin. *Work:* Smith Col Mus Art; Univ Pa; Univ Del; Philadelphia Mus Art; Free Libr Philadelphia. *Exhib:* Solo-exhibs, Swarthmore Col, Pa, 80, Shipley Sch, Bryn Mawr, Pa, 82; Artist's Bookworks, Albright-Knox Art Gallery, Buffalo, 82; Philadelphia Bookworks, Moore Col Art, 82; Books by Printmakers, Print Club, Philadelphia, 82; Women: Self-Image, Philadelphia Art Alliance, 83; plus others. *Pos:* Artist in residence, Springfield Sch Dist, Pa, 68-69. *Teaching:* Community Arts Ctr, Wallingford, Pa, 81- *Awards:* Beaver Col Purchase Award, 80; Del Art Mus Purchase Award, 81; Graphics Award, Cheltenham Arts Ctr, Pa, 83. *Mem:* Am Color Print Soc; Cheltenham Graphics Guild, Pa; Artists Equity Asn; Southern Graphics Coun; Women's Caucus Arts. *Media:* Acrylic; Silkscreen, Lithography. *Dealer:* Orion Editions 835 Madison Ave NY. *Mailing Add:* 210 Sykes Lane Wallingford PA 19086

MARK, MARILYN (SABETSKY)
PAINTER, DIRECTOR
b Brooklyn, NY. *Work:* Nat Art Mus Sport, Univ New Haven; Du Musee des Beaux Arts, Montbard, France; Stuhr Mus Prairie Pioneer, Grand Island, Nebr; Downstate Med Hosp, Brooklyn. *Comn:* Portraits of Ligoa Duncan & her dog Chi Chi, comn by Ligoa Duncan, Paris, 75; Leur Majeste Le Roi Baudouin Et La Reine Fabiola, comn by Mr Lebon, Asn Belgo-Hispanica, Belg, 77. *Exhib:* Mus Mod Art, Paris, 74; Mus du Luxembourg, Paris; Nat Arts Club, Metrop Mus Art, New York, 77; one-woman show, Long Island Univ, Brooklyn Ctr, 79; two-person show, Esta Robinson Gallery, New York, 82; Pa State Univ, University Park, 83; US Pro Indoor Tennis Championships Preview Exhib, 83 & 84. *Pos:* Founder & pres, Visual Individualists United. *Awards:* Gold Medal & Global Award, Acad de Ciencas Humanisticas y Relaciones & Asn Belgo-Hispanica, Belg, 77; Peter Paul Rubins Medal from Holland & Citation, 78; Cert Merit, 24th Ann Exhib, Mus Soc Illustrators, New York, 82. *Mem:* Nat League Am Pen Women Inc; Women in Arts Found; Burr Artists (mem bd, 74-); Artists Equity Asn New York, Inc. *Media:* Acrylic; Mixed Media on Paper. *Publ:* Contribr, Riverrun Mag, Brooklyn Col, 1/82. *Mailing Add:* 2261 Ocean Ave Brooklyn NY 11229

MARK, MARY ELLEN
PHOTOGRAPHER
b Philadelphia, Pa, Mar 20, 40. *Study:* Annenberg Sch, Univ Pa, BFA, 62, MA(communications), 64. *Work:* Bibliot Nat, Paris; Australian Nat Gallery. *Exhib:* Ward 81, Santa Barbara Mus, Calif, 77; American Images, Corcorn Gallery, 79; Portraits, Rheinschef Landes Mus, Bonn, Ger, 81; Color as Form, Corcoran Gallery, 82. *Awards:* Grants, NY State Coun Arts, 77 & Nat Endowment Arts, 77 & 80. *Bibliog:* Robert Hughes (auth), Pictures at an institution, Time Mag, 1/78; Douglas Davis (auth), A Glimpse of madness, Nesweek Mag, 1/78; Fred Richin (auth), Off camera on film, Camera Arts Mag, 3/83. *Publ:* Coauth, The Photojournalist, Thomas Crowell, 74; auth, Passport, Lustrum Press, 74; auth, Ward 81, Simon & Schuster, 79; auth, Falkland Road, Alfred A Knopf. *Dealer:* Castelli Graphics 4 E 77th St New York NY 10021. *Mailing Add:* 143 Prince St New York NY 10012

MARK, PHYLLIS
SCULPTOR

b New York, NY. *Study:* Ohio State Univ; New Sch Social Res, sculpture study with Seymour Lipton. *Work:* Dickerson-White Mus, Cornell Univ; Allentown Mus Art, Pa; Lowe Art Mus, Univ Miami, Coral Gables, Fla; Corcoran Gallery Art, Washington, DC; Ft Wayne Mus Art, Ind; and others. *Exhib:* Sculpture as Jewelry, Inst Contemp Art, Boston, 73; Albright-Knox Mus, Buffalo, NY, 75 & 76; Works on Paper by Women Artists, Brooklyn Mus, NY, 75; Art in the Space Age, Huntsville Mus, Ala, 78; Arteder, Mus Graphic Arts, Bilbao, Spain, 82; solo exhib, Friedberg Gallery, Long Boat Key, Fla, 82, Fontana Gallery, Bala Cynwyd, Pa, 82 & others; Works on Paper by Sculptors, Payson-Weisberg Gallery, New York, 82; Muscarelle Mus, Williamsburg, Va, 84; and many others. *Awards:* Ind Arts Comn & Nat Endowment Arts Grant, 79. *Bibliog:* Article, Sarasota Herald Tribune, Fla, 1/10/82; Kevin Dean (auth), article, Longboat Observer, Fla, 1/14/82; Phyllis Braff (auth), East Hampton Star, NY, 7/22/82. *Mem:* Artist Rep Environ Art; Womens Caucus for Art. *Dealer:* Theo Portnoy Gallery 56 W 57th St New York NY 10019. *Mailing Add:* 803 Greenwich St New York NY 10014

MARKEL, KATHRYN E
DEALER

b Richmond, Va, Oct 19, 46. *Pos:* Dir, Kathryn Markel Gallery, New York, currently. *Specialty:* Specialty work on paper by contemporary American artists; artists' books. *Mailing Add:* 50 W 57th St New York NY 10019

MARKELL, ISABELLA BANKS
PAINTER, GRAPHIC ARTIST

b Superior, Wis, Dec 17, 1891. *Study:* Fountainbleau, France, 30; Md Inst, 33-34; Pa Acad Fine Arts, 35; O'Hara Sch, 38; Brackman Sch, 42, 43 & 46; also with Farnsworth. *Work:* New York Pub Libr; NY Hist Soc; Mus City of New York; Northwest Printmakers; Metrop Mus Art; and others. *Exhib:* Newark Mus Art; Northwest Printmakers; Metrop Mus Art; Baltimore Mus Art; Birmingham Mus Art; and others. *Awards:* Prizes, Pen & Brush Club, 53, 55 & 64; Prizes, Nat Asn Women Artists, 56, 58-60 & 64; Three Gold Medals, Am Artists Prof League, 60, Prize, 64; and others. *Mem:* Soc Am Graphic Artists; Pen & Brush Club; Philadelphia Print Club; Washington Printmakers; Miami Art Asn; and others. *Mailing Add:* 10 Gracie Sq New York NY 10028

MARKER, MARISKA PUGSLEY
PAINTER

b San Francisco, Calif. *Study:* With Leon Berkowitz, Robert Newmann, Hank Harmon, Horace Day, Dwight Roberts, Daniel Green, and others. *Work:* Prime Minister Dominic Mintoff, Malta; Nat Mus Fine Arts, Valletta, Malta; Astronaut Allan Bean, Houston, Tex. *Exhib:* two-person show, Nat Mus Fine Arts, Valletta, Malta, 76; one-person shows, Charles Co Art League, La Plata, Md, 79, Fed Reserve Bd Govs, Washington, DC, 81, Art League, Alexandria, Va, 82, Virginia Beach Art Ctr, 83, and others; Continuum V, Dulin Gallery Art, Knoxville, Tenn, 84. *Bibliog:* The Markers at the Museum of Fine Arts, Times Malta, 10/20/76; Teresa Annas (auth), Energetic Marker creates art with depth, 9/4/83; John Levin (auth), Illuminating images, a unique technique, 9/8/83; and others. *Mem:* Art League Alexandria, Va (bd mem, 69-70); Artists Equity. *Media:* Miscellaneous. *Res:* Max Schallinger, a rediscovered artist. *Publ:* Auth, Korean arts have a great potential, Feel of Korea, Hollym Corp, 66; also feature articles in Kansas City Star and catalogs for Northern Va Fine Arts Asn. *Dealer:* Fine Arts Am Inc 404 W Franklin St Richmond VA 23220. *Mailing Add:* 300 Queen St Alexandria VA 22314

MARKER, RALPH E
PAINTER, COLLECTOR

b Salamanca, NY, Dec 7, 25. *Study:* Pvt study with Leon Berkowitz; Art League Northern Va, with Robert Newmann. *Work:* Nat Mus Fine Arts, Valletta, Malta. *Exhib:* Ann Regional Show, NVa Artists, NVa Fine Arts Asn, 70 & 71; 16th Nat Sun Carnival Show, El Paso Mus Art, 71; one-man show, Nat Mus Fine Arts, Valletta, Malta, 76; one-man shows, Federal Reserve, Washington, DC, 80 & Charles Co Community Col, 81. *Awards:* First Prize Watercolor, Gilham Award Show, Art League, Alexandria, Va, 69. *Bibliog:* The Markers at the Museum of Fine Arts, Times Malta, 10/20/76; E Fiorentino (auth), The Washington School at Valletta, Sunday Times, Malta, 10/24/76; Peter Mayo (auth), Minimal representation, Malta News, 10/28/76; and others. *Media:* Acrylic, Oil. *Collection:* Seventeenth and eighteenth century English painting; contemporary American and American Indian paintings. *Mailing Add:* 300 Queen St Alexandria VA 22314

MARKLE, JACK M
DEALER, SCULPTOR

b Winnipeg, Man, July 9, 39. *Study:* With Jack Markel; Ont Col Art. *Work:* Art Bank, Fed Govt, Ottawa, Ont. *Comn:* Neon chandelier, Mr & Mrs Sommerville, Toronto, Ont, 75. *Exhib:* Basel Art Fair, Switz, 73-75; IKI Art Fair, Dusseldorf & Cologne, Ger, 73-75; Art Gallery Ont, Toronto, 74; Rotterdam Cult Ctr, Holland, 75. *Pos:* The Electric Gallery, Toronto, Ont. *Awards:* Autumn Festival of the Arts, Toronto, Kiwanis Club, 70. *Mem:* Prof Art Dealers Asn Can; IKI, Ger. *Specialty:* Electric art. *Mailing Add:* c/o Electric Gallery 226 Steelcase W Markham ON L3R 1B3 Canada

MARKLE, SAM
DEALER, SCULPTOR

b Winnipeg, Man, 1933. *Study:* Self-taught. *Work:* Nat Art Bank, Ottawa; McLaughlin Mus, Oshawa. *Comn:* Neon installations (with Jack Markle), Alcan Aluminum, Head Off, Toronto, 70; United Trust, Head Off, Toronto,

72, Famous Players Theatre, Four Seasons Hotel, Toronto, 73, Sunoco Bldg, Toronto, 73 & Concourse & Plaza, Hudson Bay Co, 73, Toronto, 74. *Exhib:* One-man shows, Pop Sign Art, Gallery Pascal, Toronto, 64, Alpha 64, Four Seasons Hotel, Toronto, 64 & Flower & Garden Show, Electric Gallery, Toronto, 71; New Media, Art Gallery Ont, 71; Espace V Gallery, Montreal, 74. *Pos:* Dir, Electric Gallery, Toronto. *Mem:* Prof Art Dealers Can (vpres, 75-78); Can Conf Arts. *Media:* Neon tubing. *Specialty:* Electric art exclusively. *Mailing Add:* Electric Gallery 226 Steelcase Rd W Markham ON L3B 1B3 Canada

MARKMAN, RONALD
PAINTER

b Bronx, NY, May 29, 31. *Study:* Yale Univ, BFA, 57 & MFA, 59. *Work:* Brooklyn Mus, New York; Art Inst of Chicago, Ill; Hirshhorn Mus & Sculpture Garden, Smithsonian Inst, Washington, DC; Metrop Mus of Art, New York; Mus of Mod Art, New York. *Exhib:* Recent Acquisitions Show, Mus of Mod Art, New York, 59 & 66; Young Am, Whitney Mus of Am Art, 60; Chicago Biennial Print & Drawing Show, Art Inst of Chicago, 64; Annual, Pennsylvania Acad of Fine Arts, Pa, 67; Am Paintings, Butler Inst, Youngstown, Ohio, 67; Print Biennial, Brooklyn Mus, 68; Humor, Satire and Irony, New Sch for Social Research, 72; Indianapolis Mus of Art, 72 & 74; Work by Students of Josef Albers, Harvard Univ, 74; Tyler Sch Art, Philadelphia, 76 & Dart Gallery, Chicago, 80. *Teaching:* Instr, Univ of Fla, 59, Art Inst of Chicago, 60-64 & Indiana Univ, 64- *Awards:* Fulbright Fel, 62-63. *Dealer:* Terry Dintenfass Inc 50 W 57 St New York NY 10019. *Mailing Add:* 719 S Jordan Bloomington IN 47401

MARKMAN, SIDNEY DAVID
ADMINISTRATOR, HISTORIAN

b New York, NY, Oct 10, 11. *Study:* Union Col, Schenectady, NY AB, 34; Columbia Univ, MA, 36, PhD, 41. *Teaching:* Prof art hist, Univ Nac de Panama, 41-45; prof art hist, Duke Univ, 47-, actg chmn dept art, 61-62 & 75-81, prof emer, 81- *Mem:* Soc Archit Historians; Soc Am Archaeol; Latin Am Studies Asn. *Res:* Colonial art and architecture of Central America and Chiapas, Mexico. *Publ:* Auth, Horse in Greek Art, Johns Hopkins Univ Press, 43; auth, San Cristobal de las Casas, Escuela de Estudios Hispano Am, Seville, Spain, 63; auth, Colonial Architecture of Antigua Guatemala, Am Philos Soc, Philadelphia, 66; auth, Colonial Central America, A Bibliography, Ariz State Univ Press, 77; auth, Architecture and Urbanization in Colonial Chiapas, Mexico, Am Philos Soc Philadelphia, 83. *Mailing Add:* 919 Urban Ave Durham NC 27701

MARKOWSKI, EUGENE DAVID
PAINTER, SCULPTOR

b St Louis, Mo, Sept 16, 31. *Study:* Wash Univ Sch Fine Art, BFA, 60; Univ Pa Sch Fine Art, MFA, 61. *Work:* Minn Mus Art, St Paul; Lauren Rogers Mus Art, Laurel, Miss; Philip Morris Corp & First & Merchants Bank, Richmond, Va; New York Bank for Savings. *Comn:* Chapel, Holy Comforter Roman Catholic Church, Charlottesville, Va, 82; stained glass windows, St Mary's Roman Catholic Church, Lovingston, Va, 83; sculpture (wood), St George's Roman Catholic Church, Scottsville, Va, 83. *Exhib:* Corcoran Gallery Art Biennial, Washington, DC, 68; Northern Ill Univ Nat Drawing Competition, 71; Nat Drawing Competition, Minn Mus Art, 71; Int Print & Drawing Competition, Alta Col Art, 72; Regional Painting Competition, Montgomery Mus Fine Arts, 75. *Pos:* Art critic, Cablevision, Charlottesville, 72- *Teaching:* Asst prof painting, Univ Pa, 61-68 & Montgomery Col, Rockville, Md, 68-70; assoc prof painting, Univ Va, Charlottesville, 70- *Awards:* Cert of Distinction, Va Mus Fine Art, 75; Univ Va Sesquicentennial Assoc Painting, 77, 84-85. *Mem:* Col Art Asn Am. *Media:* Plexiglas; Acrylic, Oil. *Publ:* Auth, The Art of Photography: Image and Illusion, Prentice-Hall Inc, 83. *Dealer:* Fontana Gallery 107 Iona Ave Narberth PA 19072. *Mailing Add:* 1007 Rugby Rd Charlottesville VA 22903

MARKS, (MR & MRS) CEDRIC H
COLLECTORS, PATRONS

Interests: Donated works to various museums and colleges in the United States and Israel. *Collection:* Far Eastern, Near Eastern, pre-Columbia medieval and classical antiquities. *Mailing Add:* 880 Fifth Ave New York NY 10021

MARKS, CLAUDE
PAINTER, WRITER

b London, Eng, Nov 13, 15; US citizen. *Study:* Trinity Col, Cambridge Univ, MA(with honors in mod lang), 36; La Grande Chaumiere, Paris; State Univ Iowa, MFA(painting), 48; also with Yves Brayer, James Lechay & Mauricio Lasansky. *Work:* Brooklyn Mus Print Collection; New York Pub Libr Prints & Drawings Collection; Mus City New York Theatre Collection; Libr & Mus Performing Arts, New York; Detroit Inst Arts Theatre Collection. *Exhib:* One-man shows, The Room (theatrical drawings), Greenwich, London, 70; Amsterdam Gallery, Libr & Mus Performing Arts, Lincoln Ctr, 71; Dimitria Gallery, Princeton, 73; Offstage & On, paintings, water colors, drawings, Margo Feiden Galleries, New York, 79; Theatre Sketchbook (auth, catalog), Langton Gallery, London, 82. *Pos:* Scenic & costume designer, Pitlochry Festival, Scotland, 54, Theatre Workshop, London, 55 & New York Shakespeare Festival, 60; guest lectr art, Metrop Mus Art, New York, 59- *Teaching:* Asst prof art hist, State Univ Iowa, 48-50; instr art hist & appreciation, Juilliard Sch Mus, New York, 57-61; instr art hist, Parsons Sch Design, New York, 64-66. *Bibliog:* Gordon Rogoff (auth), Artist's life, Theatre Arts, 11/61; Don Dunn (auth), Artist on the aisle, Playbill, 5/72; John S Patterson (auth), Marks of an actor, The Villager, New York, 12/3/79. *Mem:* United Scenic Artists' Union, New York; NY Artists Equity Asn.

Media: Oil, Watercolor. *Res:* Drawings and sketches of all periods; the Medici; art, literature of cultural background of medieval Provence. *Publ:* Auth, Calling on Gordon Craig, Theatre Arts, 9/57; auth, From the Sketchbooks of the Great Artists, Crowell, 72; auth, Pilgrims, Heretics and Lovers: A Medieval Journey, Macmillan, 75; auth, The Lute & The Sword, Camera 3, CBS-TV, 4-5/77. *Mailing Add:* 315 Central Park W New York NY 10025

MARKS, ROBERTA BARBARA
CERAMIST, PAINTER
b Savannah, Ga, Dec 2, 36. *Study:* Univ Miami, Fla, BFA, 80; Univ SFla, MFA, 81. *Work:* Smithsonian Inst, Washington, DC; Rochester Inst Technol, NY; Notre Dame Univ, South Bend, Ind; Univ Utah Mus Art, Salt Lake City; Univ South Fla, Tampa. *Comn:* Sculpture, 1800 Atlantic Condominiums, Key West, Fla, 83. *Exhib:* Craft Multiples, Renwick Gallery, Smithsonian Inst, Washington, DC, 75; 1976 Biennial Exhib, Mint Mus Art, Charlotte, NC, 76; 11th Ann Crafts, Southeastern Ctr Contemp Art, Winston-Salem, NC, 78; A Painter and a Ceramist, Galerie Du Manoir, Switzerland, 78; A Century of Ceramics in the US, Everson Mus, Syracuse, NY, 79; 50 National Women in Art, Edison Community Col Mus Fine Art, Ft Meyers, Fla, 82; The Primal Vessel, Garth Clark Gallery, Los Angeles, 83; Ceramic Echoes: Historical References in Contemporary Ceramics, Nelson-Atkins Gallery Art, Kansas City, Mo, 83; Raku-Smoke North America, Newport Col, RI, 84. *Collections Arranged:* Lake Superior Int Craft Exhib, Tweed Mus Art, Univ Minn, 72-75 & 77. *Pos:* Mem bd dirs, Grove House Gallery, 77-79. *Teaching:* Vis artist ceramics, Univ SFla, Tampa, 76; instr ceramics, Rochester Inst Technol, NY, 76; instr ceramics, Art Inst Chicago, Ill, 77; instr, NC State Univ, Raleigh, 81- *Awards:* Best in Show, Florida Craftsmen, Ceramic Monthly Publ, 73; Purchase Award, Am Crafts Coun, Am Bankers Insurance Co, 76; Merit Award, Ceramic League, Miami, Fla, 79. *Bibliog:* Garth Clark (auth), A Century of Ceramics in the US, E P Dutton, 79; Leon Nigrosh (auth), Low Fire: Other Ways to Work in Clay, 80; Susan Wechsler (auth), Low-Fire Ceramics, A New Direction in American Clay, Watson-Guptill, 81. *Mem:* Artists Equity Asn Inc; Am Crafts Coun; Nat Coun Educ Ceramic Arts; World Crafts Coun; Fla Craftsmen. *Media:* Clay; Acrylic, Collage. *Publ:* Contribr, Crafts Horizon, 71-81; contribr, Ceramics Monthly, 71-81; contribr, Archaeology in Northwest Florida, Fla Endowment Humanities, 78; contribr, The Valley of Oaxaca: The Zapotecs (exhib catalog), Univ SFla Fine Arts Prog, 81. *Dealer:* Elements Gallery 90 Hudson St New York NY 10013. *Mailing Add:* 816 Eaton St Key West FL 33040

MARKS, ROYAL S
DEALER, COLLECTOR
b Detroit, Mich, Sept 11, 27. *Study:* Wayne Univ. *Pos:* Owner & dir, Royal Marks Gallery, New York. *Specialty:* Works by contemporary artists such as Ernst, Klee, Leger, Miro, Picasso, Delaunay and Calder; also Egyptian, Oceanic and Pre-Columbian sculpture. *Mailing Add:* 29 E 64th St New York NY 10021

MARKUSEN, THOMAS ROY
CRAFTSMAN, METALSMITH
b Chicago, Ill, Jan 1, 40. *Study:* Univ Wis, Madison, BS, 65, MS, 66. *Work:* Mus of Contemp Crafts, New York; Lannan Found Art Mus, Palm Beach, Fla; Wustum Mus of Fine Arts, Racine, Wis; Hand Workshop Gallery, Richmond, Va; Vatican Mus, Rome; and others. *Comn:* Sculpture, Va Nat Bank, Norfolk, 67; acting set, Newmen Oratory, Brockport, 75-76; and others. *Exhib:* Contemp Am Silversmiths & Goldsmiths, Corcoran Gallery, Washington, DC, 73; Int Goldsmiths & Weavers, Albright-Knox Art Gallery, Buffalo, NY, 74; 275 Yrs of Am Metalsmithing, Mus of Contemp Crafts, New York & Cranbrook Acad of Arts Mus, Bloomfield Hills, Mich, 75; Fifth Marietta Col Crafts Nat, Fine Arts Ctr, Marietta Col, Ohio, 76; 41st Int Eucharistis Exhib of Liturgical Arts, Civic Ctr, Philadelphia, 76; Solid Wrought Iron, Southern Ill Univ Mus & Art Gallery, Carbondale, 76; Arts/Objects USA, Lee Nordness Gallery & Johnson Wax Found, New York, 76; and many others. *Pos:* Dir & organizer metal exhib, Fine Arts Gallery, State Univ NY Col, Brockport, 71-78; guest lectr metalsmithing, Univ Wash, Mont State Univ, Va Commonwealth Univ, Syracuse Univ, State Univ NY Col, New Paltz, US Embassy-Mexico & Seventh World Craft Conf, Mexico, 75-77. *Teaching:* Instr crafts, Univ Wis, Madison, 65-66; asst prof metalsmithing, Radford Col, Va, 66-68; assoc prof metalsmithing, State Univ NY Col, Brockport, 68-80, prof, 80- *Awards:* Fac Res Fel, State Univ NY Res Found, 71 & 79; Craftsmen Fel, Nat Endowment for the Arts, 75; Tech Res Grant, Soc NAm Goldsmiths & Nat Endowment for the Arts, 77. *Bibliog:* Leon Nigrosh (auth), Forged iron today, Craft Horizons, 2/76; Jack O'Field (filmmaker), Hands: The Arts & Crafts of America, Raymond Lowry Int Productions, 76; Dona Z Meilach (auth), Decorative and Sculpture Ironwork, Crown, 77. *Mem:* World Crafts Coun; Am Craftsmen Coun; Artist & Blacksmiths Asn of NAm; Soc NAm Goldsmiths; NY State Craftsmen. *Mailing Add:* c/o State Univ NY Col Dept Art Brockport NY 14420

MARLOR, CLARK STRANG
HISTORIAN, COLLECTOR
b Camden, NJ, Nov 18, 22. *Study:* Carnegie-Mellon Univ, BFA, 45; Univ Mich, MA, 46; NY Univ, DEduc, 61. *Collections Arranged:* John Barnard Whittaker (with catalog), Adelphi Univ, 68, Eleanor C Bannister (with catalog), 71; Benjamin Eggleston, Long Island Hist Soc, 75. *Teaching:* Prof, Adelphi Univ, 56- *Mem:* Salmagundi Club (mem, Libr Comt & Bicentennial Comt). *Res:* 19th century American artists. *Collection:* American artists of the 19th and early 20th centuries. *Publ:* Auth, A History of the Brooklyn Art Association with an Index of Exhibitions, 70; auth, John B Whittaker, Brooklyn artist, Antiques, 11/71; auth, A quest for independence: The SIA, Arts & Antiques, 81; auth, The Society of Independent Artists: Exhibition Record and History, 84. *Mailing Add:* 295 Sterling Pl Brooklyn NY 11238

MARONEY, JAMES H, JR
DEALER
b Summit, NJ, Sept 22, 43. *Study:* Columbia Univ, BA, 70. *Pos:* Dir & head Am paintings, Sotheby Parke Bernet, NY, 67-74; assoc, Hirschl & Adler, New York, 74-76. *Specialty:* American traditional paintings executed between 1812 and 1939. *Mailing Add:* 129A E 74th St New York NY 10021

MAROZZI, ELI RAPHAEL
SCULPTOR, INSTRUCTOR
b Montegallo, Italy, Aug 13, 13; US citizen. *Study:* Univ Wash, BA; Univ Hawaii, MA; also with Mark Tobey. *Work:* St Andrew's Cathedral, Honolulu; Honolulu Leeward Community Col. *Comn:* Stone Madonna and Child, St Philomena Church, Honolulu, 75; stone figure portrait, Vivekananda Vedanta Soc, Chicago; seven compositions in abstract in stone, Honolulu Stadium State Park, State Found Cult & Arts; Jefferson Elem Sch & Wainae High Sch, State Found Cult & Arts. *Exhib:* Seattle Art Mus Ann, 47 & 48; Artists of Hawaii Ann, Honolulu Acad Arts, 50-69; Assoc Artists Hawaii, Honolulu, 52-55; Hawaii Painter's & Sculptor's League, Honolulu, 55-82; two-man show, Contemp Art Ctr. *Teaching:* Art instr, Honolulu Acad Arts, 50-55; art instr, YWCA Adult Educ, Honolulu, 50-; art instr, Univ Hawaii Exten, Honolulu, 51-53. *Awards:* First Prize Sculpture, Honolulu Assoc Artists, 55. *Mem:* Hawaii Artists League; hon mem Windward Artists Guild; hon mem Honolulu Assoc Artists. *Media:* Marble, Synthetic Stone. *Publ:* Contribr, Times of India Mag, 53; contribr, Essays in Philosophy, 62; contribr, Swami Vivekananda in East and West, 68; contribr, Prabuddha Bharata Mag, 69 & 73; auth, Modern science and meditation, Vedanta Kesari Mag. *Mailing Add:* 1081 Young St Honolulu HI 96814

MARRIOTT, WILLIAM ALLEN
PAINTER, EDUCATOR
b Pontiac, Mich, July 17, 42. *Study:* Ctr Creative Studies, Col Art & Design; Wayne State Univ, BFA; Yale Univ, MFA; study with Lester Johnson, Irving Kriesberg, Nicholas Carone, Michael Goldberg, Robert Wilbert, David Mitchell, Gabor Peterdi & George Kubler. *Work:* Wayne State Univ, Detroit; The New Mus, New York. *Exhib:* Drawings USA 1975, Minn Mus Art, St Paul, 75; 5th Int Miniature Print Competition, Pratt Graphics Ctr, New York, 75; Nat Invitational Drawing Exhib, Southern Ill Univ, Carbondale, 75; 1977 Artists Biennial, New Orleans Mus Art, 77; 45th Southeastern Competition for Painting and Sculpture, Southeastern Ctr Contemp Art, 75. *Teaching:* Assoc prof painting, drawing & printmaking, Univ Ga, Athens, 67- *Awards:* Purchase Awards, Appalachian Nat Drawing Competition, Appalachian State Univ, 74 & 45th Southeastern Competition for Painting & Sculpture, Southeastern Ctr Contemp Art, 77. *Mem:* Southeastern Graphics Coun. *Media:* Oil, Charcoal. *Dealer:* Mr Dean Gillette Image South Gallery 1931 Peachtree Rd NE Atlanta GA 30309. *Mailing Add:* Dept of Art Univ of Ga Athens GA 30602

MARRON, DONALD B
COLLECTOR
b Goshen, NY, July 21, 34. *Pos:* Trustee, Calif Int Arts, Valencia, 71-, Mus Mod Art, New York, 75- & Trust Cult Resources City New York, 76- *Collection:* Nineteenth and twentieth century American artists. *Mailing Add:* 140 Broadway New York NY 10005

MARROW, JAMES HENRY
HISTORIAN, EDUCATOR
b New York, NY, Mar 27, 41. *Study:* Univ Minn, BA(magna cum laude), 63; Columbia Univ, MA, 66, PhD(with distinction), 75. *Teaching:* Assoc prof hist art, State Univ NY, Binghamton, 70-76 & Yale Univ, 76-80; prof, Univ Calif, Berkeley, 80- *Mem:* Col Art Asn Am. *Res:* Northern European art of the late Middle Ages and early Renaissance, with special interest in religious iconography, manuscript illumination and early prints. *Publ:* Coauth, The James A de Rothschild Collection at Waddesdon Manor: Illuminated Manuscripts, Office Livre, 77; coauth, Medieval and Renaissance Manuscripts at Yale: A Selection (exhib catalog), Yale Univ Press, 78; auth, Passion Iconography in Northern European Art of the Late Middle Ages and Early Renaissance, Van Ghemmert, 79; coauth, Hans Baldung Grien: Prints and Drawings (exhib catalog), Yale Univ Press, 78; auth, Simon Bening in 1521: A group of dated miniatures, Liebaers Festschrift, 84. *Mailing Add:* Hist Art Dept 405 Doe Libr Univ Calif Berkeley CA 94720

MARSH, ANNE STEELE
PAINTER, PRINTMAKER
b Nutley, NJ, Sept 7, 01. *Study:* Cooper Union Art Sch; plus others. *Work:* Brooklyn Mus; New York Pub Libr; NJ State Mus, Trenton; Metrop Mus Art; Mus Mod Art; plus others. *Exhib:* Metrop Mus Art; Nat Acad Design; Art Inst Chicago; Am Watercolor Soc; Soc Am Graphic Artists; plus others. *Teaching:* Newark Sch Fine & Indust Art, 46-48; Huntardon Art Ctr, 56-60. *Awards:* Phillips Mill, Pa, 71 & 82; Pen & Brush Awards, 72-82; Soc Am Graphic Artists, 82. *Mem:* New York Soc Women Artists; Nat Asn Women Artists; Boston, Albany & Washington Soc Printmakers; Soc Am Graphic Artists (past pres). *Mailing Add:* RD 1 Fiddlers Forge Pittstown NJ 08867

MARSH, DAVID FOSTER
EDUCATOR, PAINTER
b Salkum, Wash, Jan 24, 26. *Study:* Cent Wash Univ, BA; Univ Ore, MS. *Work:* Westminster Col, Fulton, Mo; Inst Mexicana-NAm, Guadalajara, Mexico. *Exhib:* NW Watercolor Soc Exhib, 58, 62 & 77; NW Ann, 63 & 66. *Teaching:* Prof drawing & painting, Western Wash Univ, 57-; dean, Fine and Performing Arts, 83- *Mem:* Col Art Asn; Nat Art Educ Asn. *Mailing Add:* Dept of Art Western Wash Univ Bellingham WA 98225

MARSH, (EDWIN) THOMAS
POTTER, EDUCATOR
b Winchester, Ky, Feb 11, 34. *Study:* Univ Louisville, BS(fine arts), 60; apprentice to Totaro Sakuma, Mashiko, Japan & Kei Fujiwara, Imbe, Bizen, 61-63; Ind Univ, MAT(ceramics), 70, also with Karl Martz. *Work:* Ashland Oil Collection, Louisville, Ky; Ind Univ, Bloomington; Smithsonian Inst; Columbus Gallery Fine Art; Brown Univ. *Comn:* 14 holy water fonts and other ceramic pieces (with David Day, architect), Abbey of Gethsemani, Trappist, Ky, 66; holy water font (with David Day), St Margaret of Cortona Church, Columbus, Ohio, 68; baptismal font, New Harmony, Ind, 74; sculpture, Our Lord's Woods, New Harmony, Ind, 78. *Exhib:* One-man exhibs, The Gallery, Bloomington, Ind, 71 & 74; Notre Dame Univ, 76; Greenwich House Pottery, New York, 78; Univ Louisville, 79; Concorso Int della Ceramica d'Arte, Faenza, Italy, 79; and others. *Teaching:* Prof ceramics, Univ Louisville, 70-; vis prof ceramics, Purdue Univ, summers, 70 & 72. *Awards:* Merit Award, Gen Elec Co, 72; Hands of Man, Ind Potters Guild Special Clay Award, 78; Distinguished Professor, Univ Louisville, 83. *Mem:* Nat Coun Educ Ceramic Arts; Am Asn Univ Prof; Am Craftsmen's Coun. *Media:* Ceramics. *Publ:* Auth, The folk potters of Mashiko, 10/61, Marsh pottery, 3/74 & Bardstown pottery, 9/73, Ceramics Monthly. *Mailing Add:* c/o Marsh Pottery RR 2 Box 657 Borden IN 47106

MARSHALL, BRUCE
PAINTER, ILLUSTRATOR
b Athens, Tex, Dec 23, 29. *Study:* Univ Ariz, Tucson; Southern Ariz Sch of Art (full scholar). *Work:* First Cavalry Mus, Ft Hood, Tex; Confederate Res Ctr, Hill Jr Col, Hillsboro, Tex; San Jacinto Monument, Tex; The Alamo, San Antonio. *Comn:* Portrait of Dick Dowling, Dowling Sch, Houston, 70, comn by Sons of Confederate Veterans; paintings, Inst of Texan Cult, Univ Tex, San Antonio, 70-75; Tex Citizen Soldier (mural), Tex Nat Guard for Nat Infantry Mus, Ft Benning, Ga, 76. *Exhib:* Smithsonian Inst, Washington, DC, 54; Panhandle-Plains Mus, Canyon, Tex, 77; Chamizal Nat Mem, El Paso, Tex, 77; Mus of the Big Bend, Alpine, Tex, 77; San Jacinto Monument, Houston, Tex, 78; Star of the Repub Mus Washington State Park, Tex, 78. *Pos:* Auth & illusr, The Texas Star, 72-73; assoc ed, Military Hist Tex & South West, 72- *Awards:* Knighted by King Peter II, Yugoslavia, 66; Artist of the Confederacy, United Daughters of the Confederacy, 74; Nat Artist, Confederate State of Am, Sons of Confederate Veterans, 76. *Bibliog:* Robert St Johns (auth), article in Argosy Mag, 74; Renee Klentz (auth), article in San Angelo Times, 79; Frank Woods (auth), article in Austin Mag, 80. *Mem:* South Western Watercolor Soc; Tex Fine Arts Asn; Tex Watercolor Soc. *Media:* Watercolor, Oil. *Publ:* Illusr, Military History of Texas and the Southwest, Presidial Press, 71-78; illusr, Sabers on the Rio Grande, Presidial Press, 75; illusr, The Texas Rangers: Their First 150 Years, Encino, 75; illusr, History of Hood's Texas Brigade, Hill Jr Col, 78; illusr, All-Texas telephone book cover, Southwestern Bell Tel Co, 79. *Mailing Add:* PO Box 5512 Austin TX 78763

MARSHALL, JAMES DUARD
CONSERVATOR, PAINTER
b Springfield, Mo, Sept 29, 14. *Study:* Kansas City Art Inst, Mo, dipl painting, 40, with Thomas Hart Benton; Colo Col, BA(art), 45, with Boardman Robinson, Lawrence Barrett & Ricco Lebron; Univ Denver, MA(art), with Julio de Deigo & Ruth Reeves. *Work:* Libr of Cong, Washington, DC; Tex Fine Arts Asn, Austin. *Comn:* Murals, History of Mo (7 ft x 30 ft), comn by City of Neosho, Mo, for pub libr, 39, Children's Stories (500 ft long), Officer's Wives Nursery, Ft Worth, Tex, 52 & Beginning of a New Day (two 4 ft x 6 ft mosaics), Jones Store, Prairie Village, Kans, 62. *Exhib:* San Francisco Mus of Art Ann, Calif, 38; Philadelphia Print Club Ann, Pa, 40, 45 & 52; one-man shows, Santa Fe Art Mus, NMex, 43 & Oklahoma City Art Ctr, 43; Carnegie Inst Int, Pittsburgh, 45; Denver Art Mus Ann, Colo, 45-47; Nat Acad of Design, New York, 46; Artists West of the Mississippi, Colorado Springs, Colo, 47. *Pos:* Chmn art dept, Ft Worth Children's Mus, Tex, 51-53; crafts dir, US Army, Ger, 54-60; asst to Thomas Hart Benton, Truman Libr & New York Power Authority Murals, 60. *Teaching:* Mem, Fed Teaching Prog, Fayetteville, Ark, 33-34; teacher summer and Saturday classes, Kansas City Art Inst, 36-40; asst prof drawing & painting, Univ Denver, Colo, 46-51; instr summer art sessions, Kansas City Univ, 63. *Awards:* Honorable Mention, Denver Ann, Colo, 46 & Philadelphia Print Club, 46 & Benedictine Art Awards, New York, 70-74. *Mem:* Am Inst for Conservation; Appraisers Asn of Am. *Media:* Woodcut, lithography and egg tempera painting. *Mailing Add:* 5927 Brookside Blvd Kansas City MO 64113

MARSHALL, JOHN CARL
CRAFTSMAN
b Pittsburgh, Pa, Feb 25, 36. *Study:* Cleveland Inst Art, BFA; Syracuse Univ, MFA. *Work:* Everson Mus, Syracuse, NY; Objects USA. *Comn:* Cruets & lavabo bowl, Cathedral of Immaculate Conception, Syracuse, 67; chancellors bowl, Syracuse Univ, 69; gold bowl, Hendricks Chapel, Syracuse, 69; mace, State Univ NY Col Cortland, 71; cross, standing candle holders & baptismal bowl, Our Redeemers Lutheran Church, Seattle, Wash, 72. *Exhib:* American Metalsmiths, DeCordova Mus, Lincoln, Mass, 74; North American Goldsmiths, Renwick Gallery, Washington, DC, 74; Enamel Guild Show, Univ Md, 74; Spangle, Sheffield Polytechnic Sch Art & Design Gallery, Eng, 74; Forms in Metal, Mus Contemp Crafts, New York, 75. *Teaching:* Asst prof metalworking, design & enamel, Syracuse Univ, 65-70; assoc prof, Univ Wash, 70-75, prof, 75- *Awards:* Nat Merit Award, Am Craftsmen Coun, Craftsmen USA, 66; Thomas C Thompson Prize 45th Ceramic Nat Competition, 68; Am Metalcraft Award, Nat Enamels Exhib, 70. *Mem:* Northwest Designer Craftsmen; Am Craftsmen's Coun; Soc North Am Goldsmiths. *Media:* Gold, Silver. *Mailing Add:* 23312 Robinhood Dr Edmonds WA 98020

MARSHALL, MARA
PAINTER
b Nice, France, July 21, 26; US citizen. *Study:* With Rosamond Gaydash, Washington, DC. *Exhib:* 25th Biennial Art Exhib, Nat League Am Pen Women, Salt Lake City, 70; one-man shows, First Fed Gallery, Chicago, 71, Nat League Am Pen Women, Washington, DC, 72 & Arts Club of Washington, 77; 41st Ann Exhib, Miniature Painters, Sculptors & Gravers Soc, Washington, DC, 74; Am Art League Exhib, Rehoboth Art League Galleries, Del, 75. *Awards:* State Art Exhib First Prize, 71, President's Citation, 74 & DC Br Ann Award First Prize, 75, Nat League Am Pen Women. *Bibliog:* Article in Les Editions de la Revue Moderne, 6/73. *Mem:* Nat League Am Pen Women, Inc (corresp secy, 68-70, pres, 70-72, chmn hospitality, Nat Hq, 72-74, state pres, 74-76, co-chmn, Biennial Conv, 76); Am Art League; Artists Equity Asn; Nat Soc Arts & Lett (Washington Chap pres, 78-80); Miniature Painters, Sculpture & Gravers Soc. *Media:* Oil, Acrylic. *Mailing Add:* 2929 Ellicott St NW Washington DC 20008

MARSHALL, RALPH
EDUCATOR, PHOTOGRAPHER
b Yorkshire, Eng, Nov 23, 23. *Study:* Saltley Col, Birmingham Univ, England, cert(educ), 56. *Exhib:* One-man show, Design Ctr Gt Brit, Manchester, 63; one-man retrospective, Cleveland Inst Art, Ohio, 81. *Pos:* Chief adjudicator photog, Duke of Edinburgh's Award, 64-66. *Teaching:* Brit Secondary Sch System, 56-60; teacher photog, Manchester Regional Col, Eng, 60-66, chmn dept, 62-66; teacher photog & chmn dept, Cleveland Inst Art, 66- *Mem:* Am Inst Graphic Arts; assoc Royal Photog Soc London. *Publ:* Contribr, Graphis Annual, Graphis, Zurich, 71; auth, article, Nikon World, 76. *Mailing Add:* 2340 Delaware Dr Cleveland Heights OH 44106

MARSHALL, RICHARD DONALD
CURATOR, HISTORIAN
b Los Angeles, Calif, May 5, 47. *Study:* Calif State Univ, Long Beach, BA, MA; Univ Calif, Irvine. *Collections Arranged:* Clay (auth, catalog), 74 & Continuing Abstraction in American Art (contribr, catalog), 74, Whitney Mus Am Art; Handmade Paper: Prints & Unique Works, 76, Mus Mod Art, New York; Calder's Universe (contribr, catalog), 76-77, Robert Irwin (ed & contribr, catalog), 77, Art About Art (coauth, catalog), 78, New Image Painting (auth, catalog), 78, Biennial Exhib (coauth, catalog), 79, Isamu Noguchi (ed & contribr, catalog), 80, Louise Nevelson: Atmospheres and Environments (contribr, catalog), 80, Biennial Exhib (coauth, catalog), 81, Developments in Recent Sculpture (auth, catalog), 81, Ceramic Sculpture: Six Artists (coauth, catalog), 81, Joel Shapiro (coauth, catalog), 82-83, Biennial Exhib (coauth, catalog), 83, American Art Since 1970 (auth, catalog), 84-85 & Jonathan Borofsky (coauth, catalog), 84-85, Whitney Mus Am Art. *Pos:* Consult, Art Adv Serv, Mus Mod Art, New York, 74-76; exhib coordr, Whitney Mus Am Art, New York, 74-76, asst cur exhib, 76-78, assoc cur, 78-; art ed, Paris Rev Mag, 78- *Mailing Add:* Whitney Mus of Am Art 945 Madison Ave New York NY 10021

MARSHALL, ROBERT LEROY
EDUCATOR, PAINTER
b Mesquite, Nev, Dec 15, 44. *Study:* Brigham Young Univ, BA, 66, MA, 68; studies in Europe, primarily Spain & England. *Work:* Mus of the Southwest, Midland, Tex; Brigham Young Univ, Provo, Utah; Webster Oil Co, Springfield, Mo; Springville Mus, Utah; Am Savings & Loan. *Exhib:* Watercolor West; Watercolor USA, Springfield, Mo; Utah Coun Arts, Salt Lake City; Am Watercolor Soc, New York; Butler Inst Am Art; Scottsdale Biennial, Ariz. *Teaching:* Assoc prof painting & drawing, Brigham Young Univ, 69-, chmn dept art & design, 76-81. *Awards:* Purchase Award, Watercolor USA, Webster Oil Co. *Mem:* Nat Watercolor Soc; Nat Coun Art Adminrs; Springville Mus Art (mem bd dirs, 77-). *Media:* Watercolor, Acrylic. *Mailing Add:* 35 N 1300 E Springville UT 84663

MARSICANO, NICHOLAS
PAINTER, EDUCATOR
b Shenandoah, Pa, Oct 1, 14. *Study:* Pa Acad Fine Arts & Barnes Found, 31-34. *Work:* Mus Mod Art; Art Inst Chicago; San Francisco Mus Art; Larry Aldrich Mus; Dallas Mus Fine Arts; and many others. *Exhib:* Whitney Mus Am Art, 60-62; Mus Mod Art, New York, 61, 62 & 69; Larry Aldrich Mus Contemp Art, Ridgefield, Conn, 64; Univ Tex, Austin, 64, 66 & 68; solo exhib, Munson-Williams-Proctor Inst, Utica, NY, 79; Gruenebaum Gallery, New York, 80; and many others. *Teaching:* Assoc prof art, Cooper Union, 48-76, prof, 77-; instr, Univ Mich, summer 50, Yale Univ, summers, 51-54, Brooklyn Mus Sch, 51-58, Pratt Inst, 57-60, Cornell Univ, summer 59 & Silvermine Col Fine Arts, 65-69; prof art, State Univ NY Col Purchase, 77-82. *Awards:* Cresson Fel & Barnes Found Scholar to Europe, Pa Acad Fine Arts, 33-36; Second Prize, 5th Hallmark Int Competition, 60; Guggenheim Award, 74. *Publ:* Contribr cover, Art News, 60; contribr, Man and His Image, 68. *Dealer:* Gruenebaum Gallery 38 East 57th St New York NY 10028. *Mailing Add:* 42 West 15th St New York NY 10011

MARSTELLER, WILLIAM A
COLLECTOR
b Champaign, Ill, Feb 23, 14. *Pos:* Trustee, Whitney Mus Am Art, New York, currently. *Mem:* Life mem Art Inst Chicago. *Collection:* Modern American art. *Mailing Add:* 1060 Fifth Avenue New York NY 10028

MARTELL, BARBARA BENTLEY
PAINTER
b Trenton, NJ. *Study:* Philadelphia Col Art, Pa. *Exhib:* Philadelphia Sketch Club Ann, 68-; Philadelphia Plastic Club, 71-72; Long Beach Island Found Arts & Sci; Long Beach Island Hist Mus, 79; NJ State Ann, 81; and others. *Awards:* Second Prize for Oils, Willingboro Pa Art Alliance, 72. *Media:* Mixed Media. *Mailing Add:* 333 Kentford Ave Beach Haven NJ 08008

MARTER, JOAN
HISTORIAN, CRITIC
b Philadelphia, Pa, Aug 13, 46. *Study:* Temple Univ, BA; Univ Del, MA, PhD(art hist). *Collections Arranged:* Vanguard Am Sculpture 1913-1939 (guest cur, catalog), Rutgers Univ Art Gallery, 79; Design in America: The Cranbrook Vision 1925-1950, Detroit Inst Arts & Metrop Mus Art, 83; Beyond the Plane (auth, catalog), American Constructions 1930-1965, NJ State Mus, 83. *Teaching:* Assoc prof art hist, Rutgers Univ, 77- *Awards:* Chester Dale Fel, Nat Gallery of Art, Washington, DC, 73-74. *Mem:* Col Art Asn; Women's Caucus for Art; Int Asn Art Critics (mem Am Sect). *Res:* 20th Century art. *Publ:* Auth, Jose De Rivera Construction, Wittenborn, 80; coauth, Vanguard Am Sculpture 1913-1939, Rutgers Univ Art Gallery; auth, Alexander Calder, Abbeville Press, 84. *Mailing Add:* 220 Madison Ave New York NY 10016

MARTIN, AGNES BERNICE
PAINTER
b Maklin, Sask, Can, Mar 22, 12; US citizen. *Study:* Columbia Univ; Univ NMex. *Work:* Mus Mod Art, Whitney Mus Am Art & Guggenheim Mus, New York; Tate Gallery, London, Eng; Kunstraum Munich, Ger; Stedlelijk Mus, Amsterdam, Mus Fine Arts, Canberra, Australia, Art Mus of Ontario, Can. *Exhib:* Retrospective, Inst Contemp Art, 73; Mus Mod Art, prints, 73; Kumstraum Munich, Ger; Retrospective, Heyward Gallery, London, Eng, 77; Stedlelijk Mus, Amsterdam, Holland, 77; and others. *Media:* Acrylic. *Publ:* Auth, The Perfection Underlying Life & The Untroubled Mind, 73, Univ Pa Press. *Dealer:* Pace Gallery 32 E 57th St New York NY 10022. *Mailing Add:* Lamy NM 87540

MARTIN, ALEXANDER TOEDT
EDUCATOR, PAINTER
b Kinderhook, NY, Mar 11, 31. *Study:* Albright Art Sch, cert, 52; Univ Buffalo, BFA, 57; Tulane Univ, MFA, 63. *Work:* Neuberger Mus, State Univ NY Col, Purchase; Whitney Mus Am Art, Union Carbide Corp, Salomon Brothers, New York; Schenectady Mus, NY; Continental Transport Inc, White Plains, NY; and others. *Exhib:* Albright-Knox Art Gallery, Buffalo, 59; Southeastern Exhib, Delgado Mus, New Orleans, La, 63; Wadsworth Atheneum, Hartford Conn, 66; Convocation of Arts Exhib, State Univ NY, Albany, 69; Cooperstown Ann, NY, 75; Plaza Gallery, State Univ NY Central, Albany, 82; one-man show, Barrett House, Poughkeepsie, NY, 83; and others. *Teaching:* Prof painting & drawing, State Univ NY Col, New Paltz, 63- *Awards:* First Prize Painting, Schenectady Mus, 58 & Cooperstown Ann, 75. *Bibliog:* Hilton Kramer (auth), article in New York Times, 3/25/78; article, Am Artist, 5/82. *Media:* Oil, Watercolor. *Mailing Add:* 14 Watch Hill Rd New Paltz NY 12561

MARTIN, BERNARD MURRAY
PAINTER, EDUCATOR
b Ferrum, Va, June 21, 35. *Study:* Wake Forest Col, NC; Richmond Prof Inst, Va, BFA; Hunter Col, MA. *Work:* Va Mus Fine Arts, Richmond; Walter Rawls Mus, Courtland, Va; Chrysler Mus, Norfolk, Va; Nat Collection, Washington, DC; First & Merchants Nat Bank, Richmond, Va. *Exhib:* Nostalgia and the Contemporary Artist, Am Fedn Arts Traveling Exhib, 68; American Painting 1970, Va Mus Fine Art, 70; Friends of the Corcoran, Corcoran Gallery Art, Washington, DC, 71; one-man show, Gallery K, Washington, DC, 78 & 80; 32nd Southeastern Exhib, Gallery Contemp Art, Winston-Salem, 72. *Teaching:* Assoc prof painting, Va Commonwealth Univ, 61- *Awards:* Cert distinction, Va Artists Exhib, Va Mus Fine Arts, 64, 66, 68 & 70; First Prize, Southeastern Exhib, Gallery Contemp Art, 70 & 71. *Media:* Oil. *Dealer:* Gallery K Washington DC 20013. *Mailing Add:* 3329 Hanover Ave Richmond VA 23221

MARTIN, CHARLES E
DESIGNER, PAINTER
b Chelsea, Mass, Jan 12, 10. *Study:* Self taught. *Work:* Mus City New York; Metrop Mus, NY; Princeton Mus, NJ; Archives, Syracuse Univ, NY; Libr Cong. *Exhib:* One-man shows, Brooklyn Mus Art Sch, 54, Rockland Found, 56-57, Graham Gallery, 74 & Nicholls Gallery, 75; Ruth White Gallery, 60. *Pos:* Illusr, PM newspaper, 39-42; art dir, air drop newspapers, New York, London, Naples & Paris, 42-45. *Teaching:* Instr watercolor painting, Brooklyn Mus Art Sch, 63-65. *Bibliog:* Monograph, Art Dept, Syracuse Univ. *Mem:* Mag Cartoonist Guild Am. *Media:* All Media. *Publ:* Contribr, New Yorker Mag, New York Times, Playboy, Sat Rev, Life & Time Mags, 35-; illusr childrens books, Bradbury Press, Random House, Western Publ & Greenwillow. *Mailing Add:* 39-22 47th St Sunnyside NY 11104

MARTIN, DENISE B
EDITOR
b West Springfield, Mass, Sept 15, 40. *Study:* Smith Col, with Ruth & Clarence Kennedy & Leonard Baskin, BA(magna cum laude), 61; Radcliffe Col, with Agnes Mongan, MA(art hist), 62. *Pos:* Arts ed, Soho News, New York, 78-79; assoc ed, Portfolio, New York, 79-80, exec ed, 80- *Mailing Add:* 35 Bond St New York NY 10012

MARTIN, DORIS-MARIE CONSTABLE
DESIGNER, SCULPTOR
b New York, NY, July 5, 41. *Study:* Miami-Dade Community Col, S Campus, Miami, Fla, AA, 71; Univ Miami; Univ NC, Asheville, BA, 76; Penland Sch Crafts, NC; Arrowmont Sch Crafts, MA, 81. *Work:* Miami-Dade Community Col; Durham Art Guild, M Biddle Gallery for the Blind, NC State Mus, Raleigh; Chrysler Mus, Norfolk, Va; Miami Herald, Fla; Univ NC, Asheville; and others. *Comn:* Soft sculpture, Unitarian/Universalist Church of Asheville, 78. *Exhib:* Ann Painting & Sculpture Exhib, Mint Mus, Charlotte, 73 & 76; Marietta Col Int, Grover M Hermann Fine Arts Ctr, Ohio, 76 & 77; Springs Mills Traveling Show, Ft Mill, SC, 77 & 78; one-man shows, Chrysler Mus, 73 & Beyond Craft: Fiber/Form/Fabric, Univ NC, Asheville, 75; and many others. *Teaching:* Instr soft construction sculpture, Asheville Art Mus, 76-, instr beginning printmaking, 77- *Awards:* Best Sculpture, Craft Work 76, Am Crafts Coun, 76; Best Sculpture & One-Man Show, Durham Arts Guild, Inc, Allied Arts Ctr, NC, 76; Award for Sculpture, Springs Mills Traveling Show, 75 & 77. *Bibliog:* R Clermont (auth), Poloities & Expositions Diverses, Les Editions de la Revue Moderne Des Arts, Paris, France, 73; article, Miami Herald, 76. *Mem:* Am Crafts Coun; Fla Craftsmen, Miami; Western NC Fibers/Handweavers Guild (bd dirs); Handweavers Guild Am; NC Art Soc; and others. *Media:* Fiber. *Publ:* Contribr, Shuttle, Spindle & Dyepot, Handweavers Guild Am, 76. *Mailing Add:* 65 Woodland Rd Asheville NC 28804

MARTIN, DOUG
PAINTER
b Newton, Kans, Dec 10, 47. *Study:* Kans State Univ, BFA; Univ Nebr, MFA. *Work:* Power Inst Fine Arts, Sydney, Australia; Sheldon Art Gallery, Lincoln, Nebr; Mulvane Art Gallery, Topeka; Henderson Mus, Boulder, Colo; State Univ NY Col Potsdam. *Exhib:* William Rockhill Nelson Gallery Art, Kansas City, 72; St Louis Art Mus, Mo, 72; Mulvane Art Ctr, Topeka, 74; Sheldon Art Gallery, Lincoln, Nebr, 75; Robert Hull Fleming Mus, Univ Vt, 81; solo exhibs, Oscarsson Hood Gallery, New York, 81 & Edward Thorp Gallery, New York, 82; Aldich Mus Contemp Art, Ridgefield, Conn, 81; Herbert Johnson Mus, Ithaca, NY, 81. *Pos:* Vis artist, Cornell Univ, Ithaca, NY, 81- *Awards:* Fel, Nelle Cochrine Woods, 74; Artistic Merit Award, F W Vreeland Estate, 74; Esteban Vicente Fel, Yaddo, Saratoga Springs, NY, 83. *Mem:* Artists Equity Asn. *Dealer:* Edward Thorp Gallery 419 W Broadway New York NY 10013. *Mailing Add:* 457 Broome New York NY 10013

MARTIN, FRED THOMAS
PAINTER
b San Francisco, Calif, June 13, 27. *Study:* Univ Calif, Berkeley, BA, 49, MA, 52; San Francisco Art Inst, with David Park, Clifford Still & Mark Rothko. *Work:* Whitney Mus Am Art, Mus Mod Art, New York; San Francisco Mus Art; Oakland Art Mus, Calif; Fogg Art Mus, Cambridge, Mass. *Exhib:* San Francisco Mus Art Ann, 50-60; Whitney Mus Am Art, 70 & 73; one-man shows, M H DeYoung Mus, San Francisco, 54 & 64, San Francisco Art Inst, 72 & San Francisco Mus Mod Art, 58 & 73; Hansen Fuller Gallery, San Francisco; and others. *Pos:* Dir, San Francisco Art Inst, 66-76; contrib cd, Art Week, 77- *Teaching:* Instr hist painting, San Francisco Art Inst, 79- *Awards:* Nat Found Arts Artists Grant, 70-71. *Bibliog:* Dan Tooker (auth), article, Art Int, 11/75. *Media:* Miscellaneous. *Publ:* Auth, Beulah Land, A Book of Etchings, Hansen Fuller & Crown Press, 74; auth, A Travel Book, Arion Press, San Francisco, 77; auth, From an Antique Land, Green Gates Press, Oakland, Calif, 79. *Dealer:* Quay Gallery 254 Sutter St San Francisco CA 94108. *Mailing Add:* 232 Monte Vista Oakland CA 94611

MARTIN, G W
DESIGNER, PAINTER
b Tacoma, Wash, Apr 19, 13. *Study:* Herron Art Sch, Millikan Europ travel scholar & BFA, 38; State Univ Iowa, with Philip Guston, Fletcher Martin & Emil Ganso, MFA; Boston Mus Art Sch, with Karl Zerbe. *Work:* Lithograph Libr Cong, Washington, DC; Watercolor Wadsworth Atheneum, Hartford, Conn; Conn Printers, Hartford. *Comn:* Mural, US Post Off, Danville, Ind; portrait, Chancellor Coffin, Univ Hartford; double mural comn, 75. *Exhib:* Mus Mod Art, New York, 42; Color Print Soc, Philadelphia, 42; Carnegie Inst Int, 42 & 43; Conn Acad Fine Arts, 47-57 & 62; Mus Am Art, New Brit, Conn, 68. *Teaching:* Prof art & head dept, Lindenwood Col, 41-43; assoc prof art, Hartford Art Sch, 47, Univ Hartford, 57-83, retired. *Awards:* New Eng Drawing Exhib Award, 58; mural competition, Gengras Campus Ctr, Univ Hartford, 68. *Media:* Oil. *Mailing Add:* Box 61 Ocracoke NC 27960

MARTIN, JANE
PAINTER
b Montreal, Que, Mar 31, 43. *Study:* Bishop's Univ, Lennoxville, Que, BA, 65; Carleton Univ, Ottawa, Ont, MA, 66. *Work:* Univ Alberta, Calgary; Can Coun Art Bank, Ottawa, Ont; Canadian Art Archives, Vancouver Art Gallery, British Columbia; Mem Univ Art Gallery, St John's, Nfld; Dept External Affairs, Ottawa. *Exhib:* Solo exhibs, Contact, AGO Exten Div Touring Show, 79-80 & Wallack Galleries, Ottawa; Art Bank Works, Steward Hall Gallery, Pointe Claire, Que, 82; Artfemme I, Can Adv Coun Status Women, 82; Art Bank Exhib, Harbourfront, 83; and others. *Pos:* Artist-in-residence, Ont Arts Coun Project, 77; coordr, SAW Gallery, Ottawa, 78. *Teaching:* Lectr, UAAC Conf, Concordia Univ, Montreal, 81, Univ Ottawa, 81 & Powerhouse Gallery, Montreal, 81. *Awards:* Ont Arts Coun Grant, 75, 76, 77 & 80; Visual Arts Ont Award, 76; Can Coun Short Term Grants, 78, 79 & 83. *Bibliog:* Peter Bell (auth), The Paintings of Jane Martin, St John's Telegram, 9/4/77; Cyrel Troster (auth), Jane Martin, Artmag, 1-2/78; Suzanne Joubert (auth), L'amour au Jr regard, Le Droit Ottawa, 80. *Mem:* Can Artists Representation/Le Front Artistes Can (nat coun, 77-79, chairperson, Ottawa local, 81). *Media:* Oil. *Publ:* Illusr, 77 Best Canadian Stories, Oberon, 77; auth, Who judges whom, Atlantis, 79; illusr, Stories of Quebec, Oberon, 80; auth, Woman Visual Artists on Canada Council Juries, Can Artists Representation/Le Front Artistes Can, 81; illusr, Fat Woman, General, 82. *Mailing Add:* 134 McLeod St Ottawa ON K2P 0Z7 Canada

MARTIN, KNOX
PAINTER, SCULPTOR

b Barranquilla, Colombia, Feb 12, 23; US citizen. *Study:* Art Students League, 4 yrs. *Work:* Corcoran Gallery Art, Washington, DC; Mus Mod Art, New York; Whitney Mus Am Art, New York; Mus Art, Austin, Tex; Univ Calif, Berkeley. *Comn:* 19 story wall painting, City Walls, Inc, West Side Hwy, New York, 71; wall painting, Mercor, Inc, Merritt Complex, Ft Lauderdale, Fla, 72; wall painting, Houston & McDougal Streets New York, 79; wall painting, Nieman Marcus, White Plains, NY, 80; John Wayne Mural, John Wayne Sch, Brooklyn, 82. *Exhib:* Santa Barbara Mus Art, Calif, 64; Yale Univ Art Gallery, 66; Whitney Mus Am Art, 72; River Gallery, Irvington, NY, 80; Nat Gallery, Yugoslavia, 81; Ingber Gallery, New York, 81; and many others. *Teaching:* Asst prof drawing & painting, Yale Univ, 65-70; instr, Art Students League, 74-76. *Awards:* Balloonist Award, Mat Wiedekehr, St Paul, Minn, 72; Nat Endowment Arts, 72; Creative Artists Pub Serv, 78. *Bibliog:* Knox Martin Super Creation (collage/film, color), Yale Univ Art Dept, 67; George Parrino (auth), Knox Martin, The Deadalian Work, 72. *Mem:* Visual Artists Group Asn. *Dealer:* Don Raviv 515 Madison Ave New York NY; Dubelle Fine Art 40 W 17th St New York NY 10011. *Mailing Add:* 128 Ft Washington Ave New York NY 10032

MARTIN, LARRY KENNETH
PAINTER, DEALER

b Anniston, Ala, June 7, 39. *Study:* Jacksonville State Univ, BS, 61; Tulane Univ, MS, 64, PhD, 70. *Work:* Gov's Mansion, Montgomery, Ala; and others. *Comn:* Pteranodon (sculpture, with James Hagler), 79, Archaeopteryx (painting), 80, Anniston Mus Natural Hist, Ala; In Pursuit (mural), US Dept Interior, Richard Russell Bldg, Atlanta, Ga, 80. *Exhib:* Ala Zoological Soc, Birmingham, 82-83; Fernbank Sci Ctr, Atlanta, 82-83; Southern Wildfowl Festival, Point Mallard, Ala, 82-83; Oklahoma Wildlife Art Festival, Tulsa, 83-84; Southeastern Wildlife Expos, Charleston, SC, 84; and others. *Pos:* Co-founder/co-owner, Nance's Creek Proj: Preserv Rustic Homes (pre-1860) & Hist Structures, 70-; cur, Anniston Mus Natural Hist, 76-79; owner/founder, Wren's Nest Gallery, Jacksonville, Ala, 78- *Bibliog:* Stinson (auth), Wildlife artists promotes conservation, Midweek, 12/82; Kite (auth), cover story, Ala Purchasor, 9/82 & 10/83; Myers (auth), American characters: Eccentrics offer artist challenge and rewards, Art Bus News, 10/83. *Media:* Miscellaneous. *Mailing Add:* c/o Wren's Nest Gallery 507B N Church Jacksonville AL 36265

MARTIN, LORETTA MARSH
CALLIGRAPHER, CARTOONIST

b Plymouth, Ind, Jan 22, 33. *Study:* Art Inst Chicago, BAE, 55; Univ Notre Dame, MA, 68. *Work:* Many pvt collections in US & other countries. *Exhib:* One-woman show, First Unitarian Church, South Bend, Ind, 62; Northern Ind Artists; Alumni Asn Art Inst Chicago; Artists 70 & 71, Citrus Co, Fla; El Paso Centennial Mus. *Pos:* Asst cur, El Paso Mus Art, currently. *Mem:* Guild Bookworkers; Ctr Book Arts; Escribiente; Pencrafters' Guild El Paso. *Media:* All Media. *Publ:* Graphic work included in Mangan Publ. *Mailing Add:* Martin Studio 2521 Catnip El Paso TX 79925

MARTIN, LUCILLE CAIAR
PAINTER, MURALIST

b Carlsbad, NMex, June 7, 18. *Study:* With La Vora Norman; Frederic Taubes Workshops, Cloudcroft & Ruidoso; Merlin Enabnit Art Sch, Chicago, dipl; workshop with Olaf Wieghorst, Puerto Vallarta, Mex, dipl, 75. *Work:* Carlsbad Libr & Mus, NMex; Houston Med Ctr, Tex. *Comn:* Jordan River (mural), Hillcrest Baptist Church, Carlsbad, 62; Sacred River (mural), First Baptist Church, McCrory, Ark, 63; El Capitan (mural), Security Savings & Loan, Carlsbad, 64; NMex State Bird-Roadrunner, Young Democrats for Gov Off, State Capitol, Santa Fe, 64; roadrunner painting, comn by Gov Campbell for aircraft carrier Constellation, 64. *Exhib:* Fla Int Art Exhib, Lakeland, 52; Nat Palo Duro Art Show, WTex State Univ, Canyon, 64; Nat Sun Carnival Art Exhib, El Paso Mus Art, 64; Boulder City Art Festival, Nev, 70; one-man show, NMex State Univ, Las Cruces, 65. *Awards:* Grand Sweepstakes, Tri-State Art Exhib, El Paso, 57; First Place, Carlsbad Area Art Asn Exhibs, 64, 65 & 66; First Place, Nat Parks Show, 73, 75 & 76. *Bibliog:* Articles in NMex Newspaper & El Paso Times, 64 & 65; Elena Montes (auth), Lucille Martin's art, NMex Mag, 4/65. *Mem:* Charter mem Carlsbad Area Art Asn; Tucson Art Ctr. *Publ:* Contribr, Ariz Highways Mag, 3/70 & NMex Mag, 54 & 65. *Mailing Add:* 5901 E Third St Tucson AZ 85711

MARTIN, MARGARET M
PAINTER, DESIGNER

b Buffalo, NY, Aug 15, 40. *Study:* Boston Univ, BFA; watercolor workshops with John Pike, Robert E Wood, John Pellew, Rex Brandt & Milford Zornes. *Work:* M & T Bank, Buffalo, NY; Pierce Arrow Restaurant, Williamsville, NY; Olkahoma Christian Col, Oklahoma City. *Exhib:* Rocky Mountain Nat Watermedia, Foothills Art Ctr, Golden, Colo, 75; Far Away Places, Old Bergen Art Guild Travel Tour, 75-80; Allied Artists of Am, 76; Midwest Watercolor Soc, 78-81; Riverside Art Ctr, Calif, 78; and others. *Pos:* Designer, Wagner Folding Box, Buffalo, NY, 62-64; art dir-designer, Concept Group, Inc, Buffalo, 64-77; freelance graphic designer & illusr, 77- *Teaching:* Watercolor classes & workshop sessions in many areas of US. *Awards:* Grumbacher Silver Medallion Award, Midwest Watercolor Soc, 81; Grumbacher Silver Medallion Award, Nat Arts Club, 82; Hardie Gramatky Memorial Award, Am Watercolor Soc, 83; and others. *Bibliog:* R Stevens (auth), Contemporary Art in America, La Revue Modern, France, 3/71; John Hanchette (auth), The art of watercolor, Buffalo Evening News, 10/72. *Mem:* Am Watercolor Soc; Nat League of Am Pen Women; Pen & Brush; Nat Arts Club; Salmagundi Club; and others. *Publ:* Contribr, Designers Dictionary, 74; illusr, Buffalo & Erie County Arts Resource Directory, 74. *Mailing Add:* 78 Summer St Buffalo NY 14209

MARTIN, MARIANNE WINTER
HISTORIAN, EDUCATOR

b Vienna, Austria; US citizen. *Study:* Hunter Col, New York, BA, 45; Univ Chicago, MA, 47; Bryn Mawr Col, MA, 53, PhD, 62; studied with J C Sloane, R Bernheimer & A C Soper. *Pos:* Chmn & prof of Fine Arts, Boston Col, 77- *Teaching:* Asst prof art hist, Rutgers Univ, 63-65; assoc prof art hist, Bard Col, 65-66; assoc prof art hist, NY Univ, 66-77. *Awards:* Am Asn Univ Women Fel, 56-57; Bunting Fel, Radcliffe Col, 81-82; Guggenheim Fel, 82-83; and others. *Mem:* Col Art Asn Am; Jesuit Inst Art. *Res:* Modern Italian art; relationship of modern art and dance. *Publ:* Auth, The Walter and Louise Arensberg Collection, Philadelphia Mus, 54; auth, Futurist Art and Theory, 1909-1915, Clarendon Press, 68; auth, Torello Ancillotti, Lemonnier, 72; coauth, A Modern Focus: Futurism, Guggenheim Mus, 73; coauth, Great Drawings of All Times: The 20th Century, Shorewood, New York, 78; and others. *Mailing Add:* Dept of Fine Arts Boston Col Newton Campus Newton MA 02159

MARTIN, MARY FINCH
DIRECTOR, PAINTER

b Glens Falls, NY, Sept 7, 16. *Study:* Pvt tutoring with Isabel La Freniere. *Exhib:* Rockport Art Asn, Mass, 71-; Hamilton-Wenham Art Show, S Hamilton, Mass, 74-; Newbury Art Asn, Mass, 75-; Gloucester & Cape Ann Exhib, Gloucester, Mass, 72; N Shore Art Asn, Gloucester, Mass. *Pos:* Art dir, Harbor Gallery, Rockport, Mass, 71- *Mem:* Rockport Art Asn; Newbury Port Art Asn. *Media:* Oil. *Mailing Add:* 8 Clark Ave Rockport MA 01966

MARTIN, RICHARD (HARRISON)
HISTORIAN

b Bryn Mawr, Pa, Dec 4, 46. *Study:* Swarthmore Col, BA(art hist), 67; Columbia Univ, MA(art hist), 69 & MPhil(art hist), 71. *Pos:* Assoc curator art hist & archaeol, Columbia Univ, 68-70; exec ed, Arts Mag, 73-74, ed, 74-; exec dir, Shirley Goodman Resource Ctr, Fashion Inst Technol, 80- *Teaching:* Instr art hist, William Paterson Col, 72-73; instr hist civilization & art, Fashion Inst Technol, State Univ NY, 73-76, asst prof, 76-80, assoc prof, 80-; lectr art hist, Sch Visual Arts, 75-80; adj asst prof, NY Univ, 77-80; adj fac, New Sch Social Res, 81- *Awards:* Arts & Soc Fel, Grad Ctr City Univ NY, 83. *Mem:* Col Art Asn Am (nominating comt); Costume Soc Am (bd dirs, 83-); Soc Archit Historians; Victorian Soc Am (bd dirs, 80-); Art Libr Soc NAm; and others. *Res:* Contemporary art and fashion. *Publ:* Auth, articles in Arts Mag, Art & Artists, Art Educ, Dress & Art J. *Mailing Add:* 235 E 22nd St New York NY 10010

MARTIN, ROGER
PAINTER, INSTRUCTOR

b Gloucester, Mass, Sept 3, 25. *Study:* Boston Mus Fine Arts Sch. *Work:* Pvt collections in New Eng, New York & the West Coast. *Comn:* graphic art, D C Heath & Co, Allyn & Bacon, Beacon Press, 65-68 & United Church Teaching Pictures; designed cases & executed carvings, C B Fisk Pipe Organs, Harvard Univ & Pohick Church, Lorton, Va, 65-69; House of Hope Presby Church, St Paul, Minn, 79; Stanford Univ, 83. *Exhib:* De Cordova Mus, 66-67, 69, 72 & 75-78; one-man shows, Marion Art Ctr, Mass, 75, Galleria Rosanna, Boston, 76, Stagecoach House Gallery, Gloucester, Mass, 77, Montserrat Sch Visual Art, 79 & Pingree Sch, 79; plus others. *Teaching:* Instr design & drawing & head freshman dept, New Eng Sch Art, Boston, 67-69; instr design & illus to chmn drawing & design dept, Montserrat Sch Visual Art, Beverly, Mass, 69-83, mem found fac. *Awards:* Eric Hudson Mem Award, Rockport Art Asn, 83. *Bibliog:* Article, Gloucester Daily Times, 5/83. *Mem:* Rockport Art Asn. *Publ:* Contribr, illus in New Yorker Mag, Atlantic Monthly & New York Times; contribr, articles & illus in Child Life Mag & textbks. *Mailing Add:* 16 Mt Locust Ave Rockport MA 01966

MARTIN, RON
PAINTER

b London, Ont, April 28, 1943. *Study:* H B Beal Tech Sch, with Herb Ariss, John O'Henley & M Cryderman, 60-64. *Work:* London Pub Art Gallery, Ont; Art Gallery Vancouver; Nat Gallery Can, Ottawa; Art Gallery, Ont, Toronto; Agnes Etherington Art Ctr, Kingston, Ont; and others. *Exhib:* Solo exhibs, Carmen Lamanna Gallery, Toronto, 71-80, 82 & 83, Art Gallery Ont, Toronto, 76, Ctr for Inter-Am Relations, New York, 78 & 37th Venice Biennale, Italy, 78; Boucherville, Montreal, Toronto, London 1973, Nat Gallery Can, Ottawa, Ont, 73; 10 Can Artists in the 70's, Travelling Exhib, 80; 20th Century Can Painting, Japan, 81. *Teaching:* Instr children's art, London Pub Art Gallery, Ont, 67-, York Univ, Toronto, 69-72. *Awards:* Ont Arts Coun Grant, 73-76; Can Coun Sr Arts Grant, 76, 77, 80 & 81; Can Coun-Victor Martyn Lynch-Stauton Award, 80. *Bibliog:* Walter Klepac (auth), Ron Martin-water on paper (catalog), 76; Roald Nasgaard (auth), New work by 4 Ont Artists, The Gallery, 6-7/81. *Mem:* Can Artists Representation. *Media:* Acrylic, Watercolor. *Mailing Add:* c/o Carmen Lamanna Gallery 840 Yonge St Toronto ON M4W 2H1 Canada

MARTIN, STEFAN
PRINTMAKER, COLLAGE ARTIST

b Elgin, Ill, Jan 10, 36. *Study:* Art Inst Chicago, cert(fine arts), 58. *Work:* Smithsonian Inst; Metrop Mus Art, New York; Philadelphia Mus Fine Arts; Geraldine R Dodge Found, Morristown, NJ. *Comn:* Portrait Ben Shahn, Ben Shahn Found, New York, 70; Holocaust, Coun Jewish Orgn, Windsor, NJ, 75; print landscape & bldgs, Princeton Univ, 75; prints landscape & bldg, Printmaking Coun NJ, 81 & Univ Pa Dental Col, 82. *Exhib:* Washington Printmakers, Libr Cong, 57, 59, 60 & 67; Ann Boston Printmaker Exhib, Mus Fine Ars, Boston, 59, 60 & 62; Am Acad Arts & Lett Print Exhib, New York, 59, 71 & 72; Metropolitan Young Artists, Metrop Mus Art, New York, 60;

Nat Print Exhib, NJ State Mus, Trenton, 66-83; Northwest Printmakers, Seattle Mus Fine Arts, 67; Xylon's Int, Winterthur Mus, Geneva, Switz, 69-71 & 83; Holzstiche, Hamburg Mus, Ger, 76 & 77. *Teaching:* Instr engraving, Printmaking Coun NJ, 79-, Beaver Col & Mercer Co Col. *Awards:* Tiffany Fels, 61-64; Purchase Prize, Tenth Nat Print Exhib, NJ State Mus, 66; 18th Ann Award Excellence Publ, Art Dirs Club NJ, 80. *Bibliog:* Anne Commire (auth), Something About the Author, Gale Res Co, 83. *Mem:* Visual Artists & Galleries Asn; Soc Am Graphic Artists (vpres, 72-74); Philadelphia Print Club; World Print Coun; Printmaking Coun NJ. *Publ:* Illusr, The Sparrow Bush: Rhymes, Horn Book Inc, 66; illusr, Small Pond, E P Dutton, 67; illusr, They Walk in the Night, W W Norton, 69; illusr, Panoramas of Literature, Random House, 69; illusr, Garrity US History, Harcourt, 82. *Dealer:* Kennedy Galleries 40 W 57th St New York NY 10019. *Mailing Add:* PO Box 304 Roosevelt NJ 08555

MARTIN, THOMAS
PAINTER, INSTRUCTOR
b Amsterdam, NY, Feb 24, 43. *Study:* State Univ NY Col Buffalo, BS(art educ); Syracuse Univ, MFA(painting). *Work:* State Univ NY Col Buffalo; Syracuse Univ. *Exhib:* Allegorical Portraits, Univ Maine, Portland-Gorham, 74; Unordinary Realities, Xerox Corp, Rochester, NY, 75; Art on Paper, Weatherspoon Ann Exhib, Univ NC, Greensboro, 76; Artists Draw, Artists Space, New York, 79; 9th St Survival Show, New York, 81; and many one-man shows. *Pos:* Cur exhibs, Mus of the Am Indian, New York, NY, 75-*Teaching:* Instr fine arts, Western Conn State Col, Danbury, 74-75; asst prof fine arts, New York Inst Technol, Old Westbury, 80- *Bibliog:* David Pascal (auth), Comics, An American Expressionism, Graphis, Zurich, 72; Rev of 77 New York Exhib, Arts Mag, 4/77; rev of Artists Draw, SoHo Weekly News, 1/79. *Mailing Add:* 237 Lafayette St New York NY 10013

MARTINEZ, ALFRED
PAINTER
b Ennis, Tex, Dec 24, 44. *Study:* Southern Methodist Univ, Dallas, BFA, 68; Syracuse Univ, MFA, 71. *Comn:* Mr London (drawings), comn by Joe London, Dallas, 74; Coil-Fence (prints), comn by Lanny Brooks, West Hartford, Conn, 78 & Leah Rayblatt, New York, 78; Invisible-Lips (painting), comn by Gerry Dorman, New York, 81; Electric Fans (painting), comn by William Maxwell, New York, 82. *Exhib:* Dallas Mus Fine Arts Ann, 63; Finger Lakes Exhib, Rochester Mus & Sci Ctr, 70; Artist-Initiate, Bronx Mus Arts, 78; Artists Books--Franklin Furnace, Walker Art Ctr, 81; History of Art Works Gallery Coop, Wadsworth Atheneum, 81; Summer Invitational, O K Harris Gallery, New York, 81; Prints Benefit, Ctr Inter-Am Arts, New York, 82; Appalachian Nat Drawing Competition, Appalachian Col, NC, 83. *Teaching:* Assoc prof art, Univ Conn, West Hartford, 73-, dir, Campus Art Gallery, 81- *Awards:* Traveling Artist Fel, Syracuse Univ, 69; Res Grant, Univ Conn, 74; Vis Artist Grant, Castle Gallery, Col New Rochelle, Artists Space Inc, 80. *Bibliog:* Robyn Brentano & Mark Savitt (auths), One Hundred and Twelve Workshop, 112 Green Street, NY Univ Press, 81; Roger Winter (auth), Indroduction to Drawing, Prentice-Hall, 83. *Mailing Add:* 9 Chatham Sq Third Floor New York NY 10038

MARTINEZ, ERNESTO PEDREGON
INSTRUCTOR, MURALIST
b El Paso, Tex, Feb 26, 26. *Study:* Self-taught. *Work:* New Bowie High Sch, El Paso; St Joseph Church, Houston; Mil Bldgs, Ft Bliss, Tex; also in pvt collections. *Comn:* Mural, War Mem Honoring Recipient Recipients of Cong Medal of Honor, Vet Hosp, El Paso, Tex. *Exhib:* One-man shows, N Mex State Univ, 74, Univ Tex, El Paso, 74, Chamizal Nat Mus, 74-75 & Officer's Clubs, White Sands Missile Proving Base, 75; Exhib for First Ladies of US & Mex, Chamizal Nat Mus, El Paso, 77; and others. *Teaching:* Art consult, Boy Scouts Am, 60-; prof Chicano art, El Paso Community Col, 74-; instr free classes for underprivileged & senior citizens. *Awards:* Artist of Year, Lulac Coun, 74 & 79; City Coun Recognition, El Paso, 77. *Bibliog:* Interview world television, Mexico City, 78; Art Diary, 82. *Media:* Oil, Pen & Ink. *Mailing Add:* 4753 El Campo Dr El Paso TX 79924

MARTINEZ, HECTOR ARTECHE See Arteche

MARTINO, ANTONIO P
PAINTER
b Philadelphia, Pa, Apr 13, 02. *Study:* Philadelphia Mus Col Art; La France Art Inst; also with Albert Jean Adolphe. *Work:* Nat Acad Design, New York; Pa Acad Fine Arts, Philadelphia; Butler Art Inst, Youngstown, Ohio; Springville Art Mus, Utah; IBM Collection. *Exhib:* Sesqui-Centennial, Philadelphia, 26; Nat Acad Design Ann, 26-; Golden Gate Int Expos, San Francisco, 40; Carnegie Inst Int, Pittsburgh, 40-44; Corcoran Gallery, Washington, DC, 40-47. *Awards:* Saltus Gold Medal Merit, Nat Acad Design, 64; Gold Medal, Calif State Expos, 73; First Award, 11th Traditional, San Bernardino Mus, Calif, 77. *Bibliog:* Joseph Finigan (auth), article, Am Artist Mag, 25; Henry Pitz (auth), Antonio P Martino, G Alan Chidsey, 1/53; Ernest Watson (auth), Composition, Landscape and Still Life, Watson-Guptill, 59. *Mem:* Nat Acad Design; life mem Nat Arts Club; Am Watercolor Soc. *Media:* Oil, Watercolor. *Publ:* Auth, Prize winning watercolors, Allied Fla, 63. *Mailing Add:* 1864 Rutgers Dr Thousand Oaks CA 91366

MARTINO, BABETTE
EDUCATOR, PAINTER
b Philadelphia, Pa. *Study:* L'Accademia di Belle Arti, Florence, Italy, dipl, 68; Temple Univ, Philadelphia, BA, 72; Inst Alllende, Mexico, MFA, 75. *Work:* Camden Co Cult & Heritage Comn, NJ; Municipal Ctr, Lawton, Okla; Mohawk Valley Community Col, Utica, New York. *Exhib:* Nat Acad Design, New York; Allied Artists, New York; Audubon Artists, New York; Butler Inst Am Art, Ohio; Tex Fine Arts Asn, Laguna Gloria Mus, Austin; one-woman show, Mohawk Valley Community Col, Utica, 80; and others. *Teaching:* Instr painting & drawing, Munson-Williams-Proctor Inst, Utica, 78-80; instr drawing, Mohawk Valley Community Col, Utica, 78-81. *Awards:* Purchase Award, Owensboro Nat Bank, 82; Gilberts Purchase Award, Reading Mus, Pa, 82; Best of Show, Frederick Co Art Asn, Md, 83. *Mem:* Fel Pa Acad Fine Arts; Col Arts Asn. *Mailing Add:* 1435 Manor Ln Blue Bell PA 19422

MARTINO, EDMUND
PAINTER, DESIGNER
b Philadelphia, Pa, June 21, 15. *Study:* LaFrance Art Inst, Graphic Sketch Club & Poor Richard Club, Philadelphia. *Work:* Allentown Art Mus, Pa. *Exhib:* Pa Acad Fine Arts, Philadelphia; Philadelphia Art Alliance; Corcoran Art Gallery, Washington, DC; Butler Inst Am Art, Youngstown, Ohio; Allentown Art Mus; one-man shows, Chester Co Art Ctr, West Chester, Pa, Universalist Church, Germantown, Pa & Pa Military Col, Chester; and others. *Pos:* Freelance designer, Franklin Mint, Franklin Ctr, Pa, formerly. *Awards:* Two Lloyd Van Scriver Prizes, Woodmere Art Gallery, 57, 59 & 60; First Prize, Wilmington Art Mus, 65; First Prize, Woodmere Art Gallery, 68. *Media:* Oil. *Mailing Add:* 4920 W Chester Pike Newtown Square PA 19073

MARTINO, EVA E
PAINTER, SCULPTOR
b Philadelphia, Pa. *Study:* Gwynedd Mercy Col; Montgomery Co Community Col; also with Giovanni Martino. *Exhib:* Pa Acad Fine Arts; Nat Acad Design, New York, 65; William Penn Memorial Mus, Pa; Butler Inst Am Art, Ohio; Indiana Univ, Pa. *Awards:* Second Prize, Greater Norristown Art League, 76; Charles J Romans Mem Award, Allied Artists Am, New York, 81; Third Nat Bank Award, Springfield Art League, Mass, 82. *Mem:* Nat Forum Prof Artists; Artists Equity Asn. *Media:* Oil, Wood. *Mailing Add:* 1435 Manor Lane Blue Bell PA 19422

MARTINO, GIOVANNI
PAINTER
b Philadelphia, Pa, May 1, 08. *Study:* Spring Garden Inst, Pa; La France Inst, Pa; Philadelphia Graphic Sketch Club. *Work:* Nat Acad Design, New York; Pa Acad Fine Arts, Philadelphia; Va Mus Fine Art; Springfield Art Mus, Mo; Butler Art Inst, Youngstown, Ohio. *Exhib:* Royal Acad Eng; Carnegie Inst Int, Pa; Whitney Mus Am Art, New York; San Francisco Int Expos; Nat Acad Design. *Teaching:* Instr painting, Lehigh Univ, 57-58. *Awards:* Elmer Fox Purchase Award, Springfield Art Mus, 72; Hallmark Award, 72 & Benjamin Altman Prize, 75, Nat Acad Design. *Mem:* Nat Acad Design; Am Watercolor Soc; Woodmere Art Gallery. *Media:* Oil, Watercolor. *Mailing Add:* 1435 Manor Lane Blue Bell PA 19422

MARTINO, NINA F
PAINTER
b Philadelphia, Pa. *Study:* Univ Florence, Italy, dipl, 68; Temple Univ, BA 72; Univ Guanajuato, Mexico, 75. *Comn:* Seascape (oil), Mercantil de Irapuato, Mexico, 80; landscape (oil), Mercantil de Irapuato, Mexico, 80. *Exhib:* Woodmere Gallery, Pa; Panarama, Audubon Artists, 79; Marshall & Dekalb, Butler Inst Am Art, 79; Airy Street, Mus Civic Center, Philadelphia, 80. *Teaching:* Grad asst painting & drawing, Inst Allende, Mex, 75, grad instr, 77-80. *Awards:* Second Prize, Esposicion Iaurino, 80. *Media:* Oil, Watercolor. *Mailing Add:* 1435 Manor Lane Blue Bell PA 19422

MARTINSEN, IVAR RICHARD
PAINTER, EDUCATOR
b Butte, Mont, Dec 9, 22. *Study:* Mont State Col; Univ Ore; Univ Wyo. *Exhib:* Wyo Artists Traveling Exhib, Sheridan & Laramie, Wyo; Scottsbluff, Nebr; Sheridan Inn Gallery, 75-76, 78 & 79. *Teaching:* Prof art & chmn humanities div, Sheridan Col, currently. *Awards:* Prizes, Wyo-Nebr Exhib, 58 & 59 & Wyo State Fair, 60. *Mem:* Sheridan Artist Guild; Wyo State Art Asn. *Mailing Add:* 1422 Big Horn Ave Sheridan WY 82801

MARTON, PIER
VIDEO ARTIST, EDUCATOR
b Dec 1, 50; US citizen. *Study:* Univ Calif, Los Angeles, MFA(film, video), 79; also in Paris. *Work:* Inst Contemp Arts, London, England; Otis Inst, Parsons Sch Design, Los Angeles; Long Beach Mus Art, Calif; Japan Victo Corp, Tokyo; Seattle Arts Comn, Wash. *Exhib:* Biennale de Paris, Mus Art Mod, Paris, France, 80; Ithaca Video Festival, 80 & 83; Tokyo Video Festival, Japan, 81; Worldwide Video Festival, Kujkhuis, The Hague, Netherlands, 83; Art Video Retro-Perspective, Palais des Beaux Arts, Brussels, Belg, 83; US Nat Film & Video Festival, Park City, Utah, 83. *Pos:* Dir, Found Art Resources, 81- *Teaching:* Asst prof film, video & photog, Occidental Col, 78-79 & 82-; vis lectr video, Univ Calif, Los Angeles, 80-83 & Art Inst Chicago, 84. *Awards:* Video Art Merit Award, Athens Video Festival, 79; Awards, Ithaca Video Festival, Imagine Video Inc, 80 & 83; Video Award, Just Above Midtown, New York, Gallery D Visions, 81. *Bibliog:* Jim Hoberman (auth), Videosyncracies, Village Voice, 12/79; Douglas Blau (auth), article, Arts Mag, 3/80; Jean Paul Fargier (auth), Une Chambre d'Enregistrement, Le Monde, 9/81. *Mem:* Found Art Resources (bd dirs, 81-82). *Publ:* Auth, Ephemera #3, U Carrion, Amsterdam, 79; auth, Cahiers du cinema #5, Cahiers, Paris, 81; auth, Dreamwork #4, Human Sci Press, 81; contrib, TV for Advanced TV Viewers, Dutch TV Network, Netherlands, 83. *Dealer:* Art Metropole Toronto ON Canada; The Kitchen New York NY. *Mailing Add:* 613 1/2 N Harper Los Angeles CA 90048

MARTON, TUTZI
PAINTER
b Bucharest, Rumania, Oct 13, 36; US citizen. *Study:* Acad Journalism, Budapest, grad, 71. *Work:* Nat Arch, Washington, DC; Mus Art State Fla; Tomaquag Indian Mem Mus, Dove Crest, RI; Romanian Libr, New York; Vatican, Rome. *Exhib:* Int House Christmas Show, New Orleans, 78; one-person show, Kar Gallery Fine Art, Toronto, 78 & Galleria Laurina, Haag, Neth, 81; Ann Show, Mus Art, Long Beach, NY, 79 & 81; and others. *Pos:* Art dir, Foaia Noastra Mag, Budapest, 59-71; textiles designer, Loweinstein Inc, 72-75. *Awards:* First Prize, Ann Show, Mus Art, Long Beach, 81; Ioan & Maria Constantinescu Grant, Fondatia Cult Neth, 81; Caplazz, Romagma Italy, Soc Passator, 82. *Bibliog:* Agnes Hirschi (auth), Eine Meisterinder Goldmalerei, Bermer Tagblatt Bern, 77; Charles Z Offini (auth), Pictures on Exhibit, Pictures Publ Co, 80. *Mem:* Int Asn Art; Audubon Artists; Artists Equity Asn. *Media:* Mixed Media, Oil. *Dealer:* Paul K Kovesdy 16 E 73 St New York NY 10021. *Mailing Add:* 319 W 74 St New York NY 10023

MARTONE, MICHAEL
PHOTOGRAPHER
b New York, NY, Nov 8, 41. *Study:* Self-taught. *Work:* Mus Mod Art, New York; Fogg Mus, Harvard Univ; High Mus Art, Atlanta; Wheeler Col Photography Collection, Boston, Mass. *Comn:* AIR Light Work, Syracuse Univ, NY, 78. *Exhib:* Die Welt Ausstellung der Photographie, Akad der Kunste, Berlin, 64; New Acquisitions, Mus Mod Art, New York, 70; Multiple Image Show, Mass Inst Technol, Cambridge, 72; New Acquisitions, Fogg Mus, Harvard; solo show, Hirshhorn Mus, Washington, DC, 79; Fifth Vienna Biennale Contemp Photog, Austria, 81. *Awards:* Purchase Awards, Art Festival Atlanta, 66 & 67; Photography Fel Grant, Nat Endowment Arts, 75; AIR Exhibitor & Lectr Grant for Light Work, Syracuse Univ, 78. *Bibliog:* A D Coleman (auth), Latent image, Village Voice, New York, 4/71 & article, New York Times, 3/74. *Publ:* Auth, Dark Light, Lustrum Press, 74; contribr, Creative Camera Mag, 74; contribr, The Grotesque in Photography, Summit Press, 78; contribr, Light Readings, Oxford Univ Press, 79; contribr, Altered photographs, Art News Mag, 81. *Mailing Add:* 342 E 15th St New York NY 10003

MARTONE, WILLIAM ROBERT
PAINTER, INSTRUCTOR
b Wilmington, Del, Nov 30, 45. *Study:* Pa Acad Fine Arts, Cressen Traveling Scholar, 64-68; Univ Pa, BFA, 69; also with Morris Blackburn, Walter Stuempffig & Franklin Watkins. *Work:* Many pvt collections in US & South Am; US State Dept, Gen Serv Admin. *Comn:* Portrait of Fredrick Joseph Kinsman, Third Episcopal Bishop, comn by Mr & Mrs Charles Proctor, Warren, Ohio, 72; Resurrection, St Mark's Lutheran Church, Wilmington, 73; Sen J Caleb Boggs, comn by Sen & Mrs J Caleb Boggs, Wilmington, 73; Joe Frazier (portrait), comn by Cloverlay, Philadelphia, 74; Joe Frazier & Family, 81. *Exhib:* Ann Exhib, Nat Acad Design, New York, 67 & 75; Pa Acad Fine Arts, 75 & 79; Cottage Tour, Rehoboth Art League, Del, 75; solo exhibs, Grand Opera House, Wilmington, Del, 77 & Hardcastles, Wilmington, Del, 79; Rockwood Mus, Wilmington, Del, 81; and others. *Teaching:* Instr oil painting, Bancroft Studios, Schoonover Galleries, Wilmington, 68-70; instr & chmn dept, Mt Pleasant Upper & Middle Schs, Wilmington, 69-74; instr oil & watercolor, Howard Pyle Studios-Studio One, Wilmington, 70-; instr, Pa Acad Fine Arts, 73-80; instr art & chmn upper sch dept, Wilmington Friends Sch, 74-77; instr, Mus Alumni Prog, Philadelphia Art Inst, 79-81. *Awards:* First Prize, Philadelphia Watercolor Club, 72; First Prize, 31st Ann Chestertown Arts League, Washington Col, 79; First Prize Oils, Soc NJ Artists, 79; and others. *Mem:* Del Archaeol Soc; Fel Pa Acad Fine Arts; Philadelphia Watercolor Club (mem bd mgr, 75-77); Int Soc Artists; assoc Am Inst Conserv Hist & Artistic Works. *Media:* Oil, Watercolor. *Mailing Add:* c/o Howard Pyle Studios-Studio One 1305 N Franklin St Wilmington DE 19806

MARTYL (MARTYL SCHWEIG LANGSDORF)
PAINTER, MURALIST
b St Louis, Mo, Mar 16, 18. *Study:* Washington Univ, AB; Colorado Springs Fine Arts Ctr, with Arnold Blanch & Boardman Robinson. *Work:* Whitney Mus Am Art, New York; Art Inst Chicago; Colorado Springs Fine Arts Ctr; Los Angeles Co Mus; St Louis Art Mus. *Comn:* Recorder of Deeds (mural), comn by Sect Fine Arts, Washington, DC, 43; Darkness into Light (mural), Unitarian Church, Evanston, Ill, 62; 22 projections for Pierrot Lunaire, Fine Arts Quartet, Ill, 62. *Exhib:* Painting in the USA, Carnegie Inst Int, Pittsburgh, 43-45; New Accessions, 9th Biennial Exhib Contemp Paintings, Colorado Springs Fine Arts Ctr, 62; American Drawing Biennial XXIV, Norfolk Mus Arts, 71; one-person shows, Art Inst Chicago, 76, Fairweather-Hardin Gallery, 77, 81 & 83, Ill State Mus, 78 & Lake Forest Col, 79. *Pos:* Art ed, Atomic Sci Bulletin, 45-72; mem artists comt, Art Inst Chicago, 69; exec comt, Artists Equity Asn Chicago, 58-60. *Teaching:* Instr painting, Univ Chicago, 65-70; artist in residence, Tamarind Inst, Univ NMex, 74. *Awards:* Logan Award & Medal, 50 & William Bartels Award, 57, Art Inst Chicago; Am Inst Archit Honor Award, 62. *Bibliog:* George McCue (auth), Martyl, St Louis Dispatch, 69; interview (film), WTTW Pub TV, 79; Michael Bonesteel, article, New Art Examiner, 83. *Mem:* Arts Club Chicago; Renaissance Soc (pres, 70-71); New Art Asn; Oxbow Sch Art. *Media:* Acrylic, Ink. *Publ:* Contribr, Methods and Techniques of Gouache Painting, 46; auth, Cliches, old and new, St Louis Post-Dispatch, 67; auth, Art Scene--Fred Sweet, 68. *Dealer:* Fairweather-Hardin Gallery 101 E Ontario St Chicago IL 60611. *Mailing Add:* Box 228 645 S Meacham Rd Schaumburg IL 60193

MARTZ, KARL
CERAMIST, EDUCATOR
b Columbus, Ohio, June 24, 12. *Study:* Ind Univ, AB, 33; Ohio State Univ, 33-34 & 39, grad study in ceramic art; sabbaticals in Kyoto, 62, & Mashiko, 71, Japan. *Work:* Nat Collection Art, Smithsonian Inst, Washington, DC; Mus Mod Art, Tokyo; Am Craft Coun Mus, New York; Mus Dec Arts, Lisbon, Portugal; Walker Art Ctr, Minneapolis. *Exhib:* 20th Int Ceramic Exhib, Syracuse Mus & Metrop Mus, New York, 59; Cult Exchange Exhib, Smithsonian Inst & many European museums, 60; Ninth Int Exhib Ceramic Art, Smithsonian Inst, Washington, DC, 63; Int Ceramic Exhib, Mus Mod Art, Tokyo, 64; Twenty Five Years of Art in Clay, USA, Scripps Col, Claremont, Calif, 69. *Teaching:* Prof ceramic art, Ind Univ, Bloomington, 45-77, emer prof, 77-; Bingham prof humanities, Allen R Hite Art Inst, Univ Louisville, 75. *Awards:* First Prize, Ind Biennial Ceramic Exhib, Herron Mus, Indianapolis, 53, 55 & 57; Third Prize, Miami Nat Ceramic Exhib, Fla, 56; Award of Merit, Nat Fiber-Clay-Metal Exhib, St Paul Gallery Fine Arts, Minn, 57. *Bibliog:* Karl Martz retrospective, Ceramics Monthly, 5/77; Paul S Donhauser (auth), Photographs of work, History of American Ceramics, The Studio Potter, Kendall/Hunt Publ Co, 78; Richard Zakin (auth), Electric Kiln Ceramics, Chilton, 81. *Mem:* Nat Coun Educ for Ceramic Arts (pres, 65-66); World Craft Coun; Am Craft Coun (chmn, NCent Regional Assembly, 65-66); Int House of Japan; Acad Independent Scholars. *Media:* Porcelain, Stoneware. *Dealer:* The Gallery 102 N Grant St Bloomington IN 47401. *Mailing Add:* 105 N Overhill Dr Bloomington IN 47401

MARX, EVELYN
TAPESTRY ARTIST, PAINTER
b Pine Bluff, Ark. *Study:* Wash Univ Sch Fine Arts; Brooklyn Acad; Univ Cincinnati; Cincinnati Art Acad. *Work:* Cincinnati Art Mus; Royal Mus, Copenhagen; Mod Art Mus, Haifa, Israel; Va Mus Art; Rochester Mem Art Ctr. *Comn:* Fabric collage, comn by Fred Grossman, Cleveland, 80-81, Mr & Mrs Peter Miller, Lexington, Mass, 81, Dr & Mrs Jaliare Galvin, Sarasota, 82, Mrs Joseph Roach, Sarasota, 83 & Fine Arts Soc, Sarasota, 83. *Exhib:* Cincinnati Art Mus; Dayton Art Mus; Toledo Art Mus; Boston Printmakers; Libr Cong; New York Pub Libr. *Teaching:* Instr printmaking, Manatee Art League, Bradenton, Fla, 65-68 & Colson Sch Art, Sarasota, Fla, 68; instr art, Longboar Art Ctr, Longboat Key, Fla, 69- *Bibliog:* Diana Colson (dir), Fabricollage (film), Colson & Swain, 76; Meilach (auth), Soft Sculpture, Crown Publ. *Dealer:* Joan Hodgell Gallery 46 S Palm Ave Sarasota FL 33577. *Mailing Add:* 1750 Ben Franklin Dr Apt 2-D Sarasota FL 33577

MARX, NICKI D
PAINTER, PHOTOGRAPHER
b Los Angeles, Calif, Oct 3, 43. *Study:* Univ Calif, Riverside; Univ Calif, Santa Cruz. *Work:* Palm Springs Desert Mus, Calif; Cedars-Sinai Hospital, Los Angeles, Calif; Bank Am, Calif; Calif Farm Bureau. *Comn:* Fairchild Sci Ctr, Stanford Univ, Calif, 77. *Exhib:* Calif Women in Craft, Craft & Folk Art Mus, Los Angeles, 77; one-man shows, Markham Gallery, San Jose, 81, Weston Gallery, Carmel, 81, Bruised Reed Gallery, Monterey, 81; Kirk De Gooyer, Los Angeles, 82; and other group and one-man shows. *Awards:* Calif Crafts IX, 75; MacDowell Colony Fel, NH, 75. *Bibliog:* Bea Miller (auth), Fine feathers, Los Angeles Times Home Mag, 6/14/73; M Gottschalk (auth), Fiery feathers, Calif Today, 10/74. *Mem:* Am Crafts Coun; Artists Equity Asn. *Dealer:* The Weston Gallery PO Box 655 Carmel CA 93921; Kirk De Gooyer 830 South Central Los Angeles CA 90021. *Mailing Add:* 417 Cliff St Santa Cruz CA 95060

MARX, ROBERT ERNST
PAINTER, PRINTMAKER
b Northeim, Ger, 1925. *Study:* Univ Ill, BFA, 51, MFA, 53; study & travel in Ger, Austria, Italy, Switz & France, 1 yr. *Work:* Mus Mod Art, New York; Philadelphia Mus Art; Dallas Mus Art, Tex; Seattle Art Mus; Munson-Williams-Proctor Inst, Utica, NY; and many others. *Exhib:* One-man show, Gallery 696, Rochester, NY, 77; 4th Int Exhib Graphic Art, Kunstverein zu Frechen, Ger, 76; Franz Bader Show, Baway Found, Vienna, Austria, 76; Art of Poetry, Nat Collection Fine Arts, Smithsonian Inst, 76; Premio Int Biella, l'Incisione, Italy, 76; plus many others; and other group & one-man shows. *Pos:* Artist attached to exhib in Prague & Bratislava, Czech, 65; dir, Flint Inst Art, 57; dir, Impressions Workshop, Boston, 69. *Teaching:* Instr, Univ Wis, 53; chmn dept art, Flint Jr Col, 56; instr, Sch Art, Syracuse Univ, 58; assoc prof art, State Univ NY Binghamton, 66-69, prof, 69-70; assoc prof, State Univ NY Col Brockport, 70-72, prof, 72- *Media:* Intaglio. *Dealer:* Zaner Gallery 100 Alexander St Rochester NY 14620; Bellair Gallery 25 Bellair St Toronto ON M5R 3I3. *Mailing Add:* Dept of Art State Univ NY Col Brockport NY 14420

MARZANO, ALBERT
PAINTER, DESIGNER
b Philadelphia, Pa, Aug 22, 19. *Study:* Philadelphia Graphic Sketch Club; Philadelphia Plastic Club. *Comn:* Murals, Dept Pub Health, Philadelphia, 67 & 69; portrait Riccardo Muti, Friends & Admirers Maestro Riccardo Muti, Philadelphia, 78; portrait Louis A DeSimone, Grand Lodge Pa, Order Sons Italy, Philadelphia, 81. *Exhib:* Ann Mid-Year Show, Butler Inst Am Art, Youngstown, Ohio, 60; one-man shows, St Joseph's Col, Philadelphia, 70, La Salle Col, Philadelphia, 71, Philadelphia Sketch Club, 74, Waldron Acad, 75 & Episcopal Acad, 77; plus others. *Pos:* Designer & consult, Philadelphia Asn Blind, 53-56; art dir & consult, J Cunningham Cox Agency, Bala-Cynwyd, Pa, 58; art consult & graphic designer, Philadelphia Pub Health Dept, 58-60; art dir & consult, Benn Assocs, Philadelphia, 60. *Teaching:* Instr drawing & painting, Sons Italy in Am, Philadelphia, 65-70. *Awards:* Gold Medals, Philadelphia Art Dirs Club, 54, 55 & 56; Gold Medal, Haddonfield Art Ctr, NJ, 59; Gold Medal, Nat Soc Painters in Casein, 61. *Mem:* Watercolor Club Philadelphia; Philadelphia Art Alliance. *Media:* Mixed. *Mailing Add:* 1809 Delancey Pl Philadelphia PA 19103

MARZIO, PETER CORT
HISTORIAN, MUSEUM DIRECTOR
b New York, NY, May 8, 43. *Study:* Juniata Col, BA, 65; Univ Chicago, MA, 66 & PhD, 69. *Pos:* Historian, Smithsonian Inst, 70-72, cur of prints, 73-78; dir, Corcoran Gallery & Sch Art, 78-82 & Mus Fine Arts, Houston, 82- *Awards:* Smithsonian Fel, 68-69; Woodrow Wilson Sr Fel, Italy, 73-74. *Res:* Relationship of political democracy and fine art in America. *Publ:* Auth, Men and Machines of American Journalism, Smithsonian, 73; auth, Rube Goldberg: His Life and Work, 75 & auth & contribr, A Nation of Nations, 76, Harper & Row; auth, The Art Crusade, Smithsonian, 76; auth, The Democratic Art, David Godine, 79. *Mailing Add:* Mus Fine Arts 1001 Bissonnet PO Box 6826 Houston TX 77265

MARZOLLO, CLAUDIO
SCULPTOR
b Milan, Italy, July 13, 38; US citizen. *Study:* Columbia Col, BA. *Work:* Windsor Art Gallery, Ont; Neiman-Marcus Exec Off, Dallas, Tex; Mus Sci & Indust, Chicago; Ft Wayne Mus Art, Ind. *Comn:* Kinetic piece, ARCO Hq, Philadelphia, 74. *Exhib:* Loan Exhib, Everson Mus, Syracuse, NY, 72; one-man shows, Tafts Mus, Cincinnati, Ohio, 74, traveling exhib, Nat Acad Sci, Washington, DC, 77; Illum, Whitney Mus Am Art, New York, 74; New Acquisitions, Windsor Gallery Art, Ont, 75; The Logic & Nature of Color, Akron Art Inst, Ohio, 75; Hudson River Mus, Yonkers, NY, 76; one-man show, Virginia Beach Arts Ctr, 79. *Teaching:* Instr three-dimensional design, Sch Visual Arts, New York, 74 & Univ Bridgeport, Conn, 75-77; Mather vis scholar, Case Western Reserve Univ, Cleveland, 75; vis artist, US Mil Acad, West Point, 78- *Bibliog:* Joseph Horning (dir), Metamorphoses (film), Ohio Arts Comn, 75. *Media:* Plexiglas, Aluminum. *Dealer:* Luis K Meisel Gallery 141 Prince St New York NY 10012; Gallery Nuki 800 25th St NW Washington DC 20037. *Mailing Add:* Lane Gate Rd Cold Spring NY 10516

MASER, EDWARD ANDREW
HISTORIAN, MUSEUM DIRECTOR
b Detroit, Mich, Dec 23, 23. *Study:* Univ Mich, 41-43; Univ Chicago, MA, 49, PhD, 58. *Collections Arranged:* German and Austrian Painting of the 18th Century, 78 & Drawings by Johann Michael Rottmayr, 80, Univ Chicago. *Pos:* Dir, David & Alfred Smart Gallery, Univ Chicago, 72-; mem int comt, Franz Anton Maulbertsch Exhib, Vienna, 74. *Teaching:* Assoc prof art hist, Univ Kans, 53-61; prof art hist, Univ Chicago, 61-, chmn dept art, 61-64. *Awards:* Fulbright Res Fel, 50-52 & Sr Res Scholar, 65-66; Guggenheim Res Fel, 69-70; and others. *Mem:* Col Art Asn Am; Am Asn Univ Prof. *Res:* Italian, German and Austrian art of the 17th and 18th centuries. *Publ:* Co-auth, Il Museo del Opificio delle Pietre Dure, 53; auth, Giovan Domenico Ferretti, Florence, Marchi & Bertolli, 68; ed & auth, Baroque and Rococo Pictorial Imagery, Dover Press, 71; auth, Disegni inediti di Johann Michael Rottmayr, Monumenta Bergomensia XXX Bergamo, 71. *Mailing Add:* 5318 S Hyde Park Blvd Chicago IL 60615

MASHECK, JOSEPH DANIEL
HISTORIAN, CRITIC
b New York, NY, Jan 19, 42. *Study:* Columbia Univ, AB, 63, MA, 65, PhD, 75, doctoral study with Dorothea Nyberg & Rudolf Wittkower. *Pos:* Ed, Artforum Mag, 77-80. *Teaching:* Lectr liberal studies, Col Art, Kent, Eng, 68-69, Harvard Univ, 83; preceptor art hist, Columbia Col, Columbia Univ, New York, 69-71; instr art hist, Barnard Col, 71-73, asst prof, 73-83. *Awards:* Art Critics' Fel, Nat Endowment Arts, 72-73, 75-76; Guggenheim Mem Found Fel, 77. *Mem:* Soc Fel Humanities Columbia Univ. *Res:* Abstract painting and sculpture. *Publ:* Ed, Marcel Duchamp in Perspective & essay, Chance Is zee fool's name for fait, Prentice-Hall, 75; auth, The carpet paradigm--critical prolegomena to a theory of flatness, Arts Mag, 9/76; auth, Iconicity, Artforum, 1/79; auth, Raw art: Primitive authenticity and German Expressionism, Res, autumn 82; auth, Historical Present: Essays of the Seventies, UMI Res Press (in press); and others. *Mailing Add:* 405 W 118th St New York NY 10027

MASON, ALDEN C
PAINTER, EDUCATOR
b Everett, Wash, July 14, 19. *Study:* Univ Wash, MFA. *Work:* Seattle Art Mus, Wash; San Francisco Mus Art; Denver Art Mus. *Comn:* Mural, 80 ft, Senate Chambers, State Capitol, Olympia, Wash, 81. *Exhib:* One-man shows, Portland Ctr for Visual Arts, Ore, 73, Denver Art Mus, 73 & Chas Cowles Gallery, New York, 81; Allan Stone Gallery, New York, 74 & 78; 14 Abstract Painters, Frederick Wight Art Galleries, Univ Calif, Los Angeles, 75; Univ Art Galleries, Univ NDak, Grand Forks, 78; and others. *Teaching:* Prof art, Univ Wash, 47- *Awards:* Purchase Award, 44th Northwest Ann, 63 & 54th Northwest Ann, 68, Seattle Art Mus. *Media:* Acrylic. *Dealer:* Greg Kucera Gallery 608 Second Ave Seattle WA 98104; Tortue Gallery Santa Monica CA. *Mailing Add:* 3131 Western Ave 503 Seattle WA 98121

MASON, BENJAMIN LINCOLN
MUSEUM DIRECTOR
b Boston, Mass, Jan 13, 40. *Study:* Harvard Univ, AB, 63, MEd, 75. *Pos:* Dir, Shelburne Mus, Vt, 79- *Mailing Add:* Shelburne Mus Rte 7 Shelburne VT 05482

MASON, BETTE
PAINTER, EDUCATOR
b Tex. *Study:* Trinity Univ; Syracuse Univ; Stephens Col, BA; Art Students League; Mus Mgt Sem, Mus Mod Art, New York; post grad work, Univ New Orleans. *Exhib:* 5th Int Exhib, New Orleans, 75; Jefferson Parish Bicentennial Exhib, New Orleans, 76; Univ New Orleans, 78; Womanart, Nat Art Ctr,

New York, 80 & 82; Ctr Performing Arts, New Orleans, 81. *Pos:* Dir, Assoc Artists Gallery, Syracuse, 66-68; art consult, Delgado Col, 76-78. *Teaching:* Dir art dept, Westchester Learning Ctr, Fleetwood, NY, 70-72; chmn fine arts dept & asst prof art, Delgado Col, New Orleans, 78-81. *Awards:* Beaux-Arts Award, Federated Woman's Clubs, New York, 71; Award, New Orleans Art Asn, 82-83. *Mem:* New Orleans Art Asn (vpres); Col Art Asn; Women in the Arts, New York; Women's Caucus Art; Westchester Art Soc (former pres). *Media:* Acrylic, Oil. *Mailing Add:* 527 St Philip New Orleans LA 70116

MASON, FRANCIS SCARLETT, JR
ADMINISTRATOR
b Jacksonville, Fla, Sept 9, 21. *Study:* St John's Col, Annapolis, Md, BA, 43; grad study art hist with Nikolaus Pevsner; Birkbeck Col, Univ of London, 61-64. *Pos:* Cult attache & exhibs officer, US Info Agency Foreign Serv, 54-64; chief US exhibs to USSR & E Europe, US Info Agency, 65-67; pres experiments in art & technol, New York, 68; asst dir, Pierpont Morgan Libr, New York, 75- *Mem:* New York Studio Sch Drawing & Sculpture (chmn, 71-74); Archit Asn, London; Gallery Asn New York (trustee, 77-). *Publ:* Ed, Steuben, Seventy Years of Glassmaking, Praeger, 74; co-auth, Balanchine's Complete Stories of the Great Ballets, Doubleday, 77. *Mailing Add:* 46 Morton St New York NY 10014

MASON, FRANK HERBERT
PAINTER, INSTRUCTOR
b Cleveland, Ohio, Feb 21, 21. *Study:* Nat Acad Design, New York, with George Nelson, 37-38; Art Students League, with Frank Vincent DuMond, 37-51. *Work:* Eureka Col Mus, Ill; Butler Inst Am Art, Youngstown, Ohio; Am Embassy, London; Hall of Governors, State Capitol, Albany, NY; US War Dept, Washington, DC. *Comn:* Life of St Anthony of Padua (eight large canvases), 11th Century Church of San Giovanni di Malta, Venice, Italy, 64; Resurrection, Old St Patrick's Cathedral, New York, 72; San Rocco, Church of Santa Vittoria, Italy; 3 murals, King Faisal Naval Acad, Saudi Arabia, 81. *Exhib:* Expos Intercontinentale, Palais des Congres, Monaco, 68; Nat Arts Club, New York, 73; Mood Gallery, Milan, Italy, 75; John Pence Gallery, San Francisco, 77 & 79; Metrop Mus Art, New York, 79. *Teaching:* Instr fine arts, Art Students League, New York, 50- *Awards:* Popular Prize, Assoc Artists Pittsburgh, Carnegie Inst Mus Art, 46; figure composition-St Anthony, Penn-National, Ligonier, 68; Prix d'Amerique du Nord, Expos Intercontinentale, Monaco, 68. *Bibliog:* Condon Riley (auth), Frank Mason, painter, Am Artist, 6/64; Alexander Eliot Frank Mason: Allegiance to the old masters, Am Artist, 12/73; David L Bell (auth), Frank Mason, Artists of the Rockies and the Golden West, fall 83. *Mem:* Art Students League; Nat Soc Mural Painters; Int Inst Conserv of Hist & Artistic Works; Academician Nat Acad Design. *Media:* Graphics, Watercolor. *Mailing Add:* 385 Broome St New York NY 10013

MASON, HAROLD
PRINTMAKER, PAINTER
b Springfield, Mo, Feb 1, 37. *Study:* Calif State Univ, Fresno; Art Ctr Sch Design, Pasadena, Calif, BFA. *Work:* Included in major corp collections throughout the US, including Chicago, Phoenix, Los Angeles & Seattle. *Exhib:* Gold Spike Centennial, Pac Railroad, Provost, Utah, 69; 29th Ann Soc Western Artist, de Young Mus, San Francisco, Calif, 71; Western Asn of Art Mus Traveling Exhib, 73; Watercolor Int, Dazell Hatfield Galleries, Los Angeles, 74; West Coast Watercolor Soc Exchange Exhib, Royal Watercolor Soc, London, 75. *Teaching:* Chmn art dept, Ursuline High Sch, Santa Rosa, Calif, 65-70; prof art, Santa Rosa Jr Col, 68-70. *Awards:* Best of Show, 29th Ann Soc Western Art, de Young Mus, 71; Best Watercolor, Atrium 72, Santa Rosa, 72. *Mem:* Carmel Art Asn; Fine Arts Evaluation Comt, Carmel, Calif. *Media:* Watercolor, Graphics. *Publ:* Coauth, Flight: Poems & Drawings, India House of Calif, 70; contribr, Transparent Watercolor: Ideas & Techniques, Davis Publ, 72. *Dealer:* Carmel Art Association Carmel CA 93921; Gallery Three 3819 Third St Phoenix AZ 85013. *Mailing Add:* 24650 Cabrillo Carmel CA 93921

MASON, JOHN
SCULPTOR
b Madrid, Nebr, Mar 30, 27. *Study:* Otis Art Inst, Los Angeles, 49-52; Chouinard Art Inst, Los Angeles, 53-54. *Work:* Art Inst Chicago; Los Angeles Co Mus Art; San Francisco Mus Art; Mus Contemp Crafts, New York; Nat Mus Mod Art, Kyoto, Japan; and others. *Comn:* Ceramic relief, Palm Springs Spa, Calif, 59; ceramic relief, Tishman Bldg, Los Angeles, 61; ceramic doors, Sterling Holloway, South Laguna, Calif; and others. *Exhib:* One-man shows, Pasadena Art Mus, Calif, 60 & 74; Whitney Mus Am Art, 64, 73 & 76; Retrospective, Los Angeles Co Mus Art, 66; Kompas 4, Van Addemuseum Eindhoven, Netherlands, 69; Nat Mus Mod Art, Kyoto, Japan, 71; and others. *Teaching:* Assoc prof art, Univ Calif, Irvine, 67-73; prof art & chmn dept studio art, 73-74; prof studio art, Hunter Col, New York, 74- *Awards:* Ford Found Award, 67th Am Exhib, Art Inst Chicago, 64; Univ Calif Award, Creative Arts Inst, 69-70; and others. *Bibliog:* John W Mills (auth), The Technique of Sculpture, Reinhold Corp, NY, 65; John Coplans (auth), John Mason--Sculpture, Los Angeles Co Mus Art, 66; Glenn C Nelson (auth), Ceramics, Holt, Rinehart & Winston, 71. *Media:* Ceramics. *Dealer:* Hansen-Fuller Gallery 228 Grant Ave San Francisco CA 94108. *Mailing Add:* 1521 S Central Ave Los Angeles CA 90021

MASON, LAURIS LAPIDOS
LECTURER, WRITER
b New York, NY, Apr 21, 31. *Study:* Syracuse Univ, AB, 52; State Univ NY New Paltz, MS, 55. *Pos:* Dir, Mason Fine Prints, 72- *Teaching:* Lectr, art appraisal prog, Hofstra Univ, 78- *Specialty:* American and European original

prints. *Publ:* Auth, Print Reference Sources: A Select Bibliography, 18th-20th Centuries, 75, second ed, 79; coauth (with Cecile Shapiro), Fine Prints: Collecting, Buying & Selling, co-ed, Joan Ludman's Print Collector's Quarterly: An Anthology of Essays of Eminent Printmakers of the World & auth, The Lithographs of George Bellows: A Catalogue Raisonne, KTO Press. *Mailing Add:* 16 Quaker Ridge Dr Glen Head NY 11545

MASON, NOVEM M
SCULPTOR, DESIGNER
b North Wildwood, NJ, Nov 22, 42. *Study:* NC State Univ Sch Design, BA(archit), 68; ECarolina Univ Sch Art, MFA, 74. *Work:* Relief sculpture, ECarolina Univ. *Comn:* Sculptural screen, Southern Bank, Richmond, Va, 76; relief sculptures, Richmond Fredericksburg Petersburg Railroad, Richmond, Va, 77, Southern Univ, 80 & First Fed Savings & Loan, Lake Charles, La, 81; entrance sculpture, Mid-States Wood Preserving Inc, Simsboro, La, 82. *Exhib:* Va Artist Biennial, Va Mus Fine Arts, 73; 13th Ann Painting & Sculpture Exhib, Mint Mus Art, 73; La Grange Nat Competition, La Grange Art Mus, 75; Peninsula Arts Asn Artists Exhib, Hampton Mus, Hampton Roads, Va, 76; Anderson Gallery Summer Invitational, Richmond, Va, 76; Three Artists, Wyly Tower Gallery, Ruston, La, 81; Alumni Masonic Temple Studios, Anderson Gallery, Richmond, Va, 83. *Pos:* Partner, artist & designer, Design Collaborative Richmond, Va, 74-79; designer & artist, Woodsmith, Ruston, La, 79- *Teaching:* Asst prof art, Va Commonwealth Univ, Richmond, 68-79; assoc prof, La Tech Univ, 79- *Mem:* Southern Asn Sculptors; Col Art Asn Am. *Media:* Wood; Mixed Media. *Mailing Add:* Rte 4 Box 5AA Ruston LA 71270

MASON, PHILLIP LINDSAY
PAINTER, ADMINISTRATOR
b St Louis, Mo, Sept 20, 39. *Study:* Calif Col Arts & Crafts, Oakland, Calif, BFA(painting, with high distinction), 69, MFA (painting), 70. *Work:* Art Gallery, Howard Univ, Washington, DC; Art Gallery, Vincennes Univ, Ind; Art Gallery, Ind State Univ, Terre Haute; Canterbury Sch, Walnut Creek, Calif. *Comn:* Illustrated front & back covers of jazz album, Those Who Chant, Blue Thumb Records, 72. *Exhib:* One-man exhibs, Wichita Art Mus, Kans, 70 & Tex Tech Univ, 81; Contemp Black Artists in Am, Whitney Mus Am Art, 71; A Question of Surrealism?, San Francisco Mus Art, 72; Directions in Afro-Am Art, Herbert F Johnson Mus, Cornell Univ, 74; Huntsville Mus Art, Ala, 79; Oakland Mus, 80; and others. *Teaching:* Instr painting & drawing, Calif Col Arts & Crafts, 69-71; asst prof painting & drawing, Ind State Univ, 72-73; assoc prof & chmn dept art, NC Cent Univ, 73-77; prof art, Fisk Univ, Nashville, 77- *Awards:* Purchase Awards, 68 & 70, Oakland Mus Art; Tangley Oaks grad fel, Tangley Oaks Educ Ctr, 70. *Bibliog:* Lewis & Waddy (auth), Black artists on art, Vol 1, Contemp Crafts, 69; Samella Lewis (auth), Art: African-American, Harcourt, Brace, Jovanovich, 77. *Media:* Acrylic; Prismacolor Pencil. *Publ:* Auth, Art and Black consciousness, Negro Dig Mag, 69; auth, Black Art, Tangley Oaks Educ Ctr, 71. *Mailing Add:* c/o Dept Art/Fisk Univ 1000 17th Ave N Nashville TN 37203

MASON, WILLIAM CLIFFORD
FILMMAKER, PAINTER
b Winnipeg, Man, Apr 21, 29. *Study:* Univ Man Sch Art, dipl. *Awards:* Best Film, Soc Film & TV Awards; Three Blue Ribbons, Am Film Festival; plus numerous nat and int awards. *Mem:* Royal Can Acad Arts; Asn Int Film Animation. *Media:* Oil. *Mailing Add:* Meach Lake Rd Old Chelsea PQ J0X 2N0 Can

MASSARO, KAREN THUESEN
CERAMIST, SCULPTOR
b Copenhagen, Denmark, Oct 23, 44; US citizen. *Study:* State Univ NY, Buffalo, BSEd, 66; Univ Mass, Amherst, 67-68; Univ Wis, Maidson, with Don Reitz, MFA, 72. *Exhib:* One-man shows, Kresge Art Gallery, Univ Mich, East Lansing, 79, Rochester Art Ctr, Minn, 80 & Synopsis Gallery, Winnetka, Ill, 80; Am Porcelain, Renwick Gallery, Smithsonian Inst, Washington, DC, 81; Scripps Col 40th Ann Exhib, 84; Rocklands Gallery, Monterey, Calif, 84. *Teaching:* Vis fac mem fine art & art hist, Beloit Col, Wis, 72-77; vis artist ceramic arts, Ohio State Univ, 77; vis artist, Kohler Co, Wis, fall 79 & 84; vis fac mem, Scripps Col, Claremont, Calif, 80. *Awards:* Purchase Prize, 51st Exhib Wis Crafts, Milwaukee Art Ctr, 72; Best in Ceramics & Outstanding Wis Craftsman, Beaux-Arts Designer/Craftsman 72, Columbus Mus Fine Arts, 72. *Bibliog:* Articles, Ceramic Mo, 10/79 & 2/84; article, Am Craft, 4/82. *Mem:* Nat Coun Educ in Ceramic Arts (exhib chmn, 78-80). *Media:* Porcelain Clay; Low-Fire Clay. *Mailing Add:* 617 Arroyo Secco Santa Cruz CA 95060

MASSEY, CHARLES WESLEY, JR
PRINTMAKER, EDUCATOR
b Lebanon, Tenn, Aug 21, 42. *Study:* Mid Tenn State Univ, BS, 64; Univ Ga, MFA, 72. *Work:* Philadelphia Mus Art; Art Inst Chicago; Pushkin Mus, Moscow, USSR; Bradford City Art Gallery, Eng; Libr of Cong, Washington, DC. *Exhib:* 8th Dulin Nat Print & Drawing Competition, Smithsonian Inst Traveling Exhib, 73-74; American Drawings III, IV Smithsonian Traveling Exhib, 81-85; Philadelphia Print Club Int Competition, 81 & 82; Second Int Print Exhib, Seoul, Korea, 82; Miami Int Print Biennial, 82; Boston Printmakers Nat Print Exhib, 82 & 83; Ninth Int Prints, Kanagawa, Japan, 83; and others. *Teaching:* Instr art printmaking, Univ Ga, Athens, 72-74; assoc prof printmaking, Ohio State Univ, 74-, chairperson, 82- *Awards:* Purchase Award, Philadelphia Print Club, 82; Purchase Award, Nat Drawing, 82; Purchase Award, 35th Nat Print, Boston, 83. *Bibliog:* Albert Christ-Janer (auth), Artist--Charles Massey, Jr, Printer (film), Univ Ga, 71. *Mem:* Philadelphia Print Club; Boston Printmakers; Conn Acad Fine Arts; Col Art Asn; Columbus Art League (pres, 82-). *Media:* Lithography, Drawing. *Publ:* Illusr, The Complete Screenprint & Lithography, Macmillan & Free Press, 74; illusr, Sing with Understanding, Broadman Press, 80; illusr, J Higher Educ, OSU Press, 83. *Dealer:* Assoc Am Artists 663 Fifth Ave New York NY 10022; 1614 Latimer St Philadelphia PA 19103. *Mailing Add:* 93 E Lincoln St Columbus OH 43215

MASSEY, ROBERT JOSEPH
PAINTER, EDUCATOR
b Ft Worth, Tex, May 14, 21. *Study:* Okla State Univ, with Doel Reed, BA, 47; Univ Havana, 47-48; Univ Mich, fall 48; Syracuse Univ, MFA, 52; Univ Tex, Austin, PhD, 62. *Work:* Dallas Mus Fine Art; Syracuse Univ; Soc Am Graphic Artists; El Paso Mus Art; Univ NMex; plus others. *Comn:* Enamel mosaic, State Nat Bank El Paso; applique hanging (with Sally Bishop), 69 & polyester-coated polyurethane sculpture, 69, Univ Tex, El Paso Union Bldg. *Exhib:* Nat Small Painting Exhib, Univ of the Pac, Stockton, Calif, 70; 5th Ann Gulf Coast Art Exhib, Mobile, Ala, 70; 11 State Small Painting Show, Albuquerque, NMex, 70; 12th, 13th & 14th Ann Painting Exhib, Longview, Tex, 70-72; 5 State Art Exhib, Port Arthur, Tex, 71; and others. *Teaching:* Asst, Okla State Univ, 47; instr, Inst Cult Cubano-Norte-Americano, 48; teaching fel, Univ Mich, 48-49; vis prof art, Fla State Univ, 49-50; instr, Syracuse Univ, 52-53; prof art, Univ Tex, El Paso, 53- *Awards:* Purchase Award for Painting, 6th Nat Arts Exhib, Tyler, Tex, 69; Third Award, 11 State Small Painting Show, 70. *Media:* Egg Tempera. *Publ:* Auth, Formulas for Painters, 67 & auth, Notes for American readers, In: Notes on the Technique of Painting, 69, Watson-Guptill; auth, Formulas for Artists, B T Batsford, London, 68; auth, Painting, drawing & printmaking supports, 9/70 & auth, The artist's ideal studio, 1/71, Am Artist. *Dealer:* Two-Twenty-Two Gallery 6109 Pinehurst El Paso TX 79902. *Mailing Add:* 708 McKelligon St El Paso TX 79902

MASSIE, LORNA
PRINTMAKER, GRAPHIC ARTIST
b Milwaukee, Wis, Dec 27, 38. *Study:* Layton Sch Art, Milwaukee; Smith Col; Univ Calif, Berkeley, BA, 61; Marshall Glazier, New York, 67; Woodstock Sch Art, 74-76; Albert Handell Sch, 77; Art Students League, 78. *Exhib:* Mohawk Hudson Regional, Schenectady Mus, NY, 80 & Albany Inst Hist & Art, NY, 81; Prints and Drawings, Berkshire Mus, Pittsfield, Mass, 81; Audubon Artists, Nat Arts Club, New York, 81 & 83; Works on Paper, Berkshire Mus, Pittsfield, Mass, 82; Salmagundi Club Exhib, New York, 82. *Awards:* Hudson Valley Art Asn Award, 81. *Mem:* Woodstock Artists Asn; Ulster Co Art Asn. *Media:* Serigraphs. *Mailing Add:* Rt 1 Old Mill Rd Accord NY 12404

MASSIN, EUGENE MAX
PAINTER, EDUCATOR
b Galveston, Tex, Apr 10, 20. *Study:* Art Inst Chicago; Univ Chicago, BFA, 48; Escuela Univ Bellas Artes, Mex, MFA, 49; first asst to David Alfara Sequeiros, Mex muralist. *Work:* Brandeis Univ, Boston; Lowe Mus, Univ Miami; Escuela Univ Bellas Artes, Mex; Ringling Mus, Fla; Norton Gallery, Palm Beach, Fla. *Comn:* Acrylic/canvas mural, City Nat Bank of Miami, Fla, 66; acrylic sheet mural (with Julia Busch), City Nat Bank of Miami Beach, Fla, 72; acrylic mural, Southern Gen Builders Inc, 72; painting of Fla, World Bk Encycl, 72; Sculpture in Steel, Temple Israel, Miami, Fla. *Exhib:* Metrop Mus Art, 53 & Whitney Ann, New York, 55; Art USA, 59; Am Fedn Art Traveling Exhib, 62; Southeastern Ann, Atlanta, Ga, 64. *Pos:* Pres, Artist Equity Asn, 55-58, founder, Fla Chap; adv, Arts Coun, 60-64; adv, Cafritz Found for Arts, Washington, DC, 66; juror, Nat Scholastic Art Awards, 71. *Teaching:* Instr art, Univ Wis, 49-50 & Univ SC, 52; prof art, Univ Miami, 54- *Awards:* Humanities Award, Univ Miami, 64 & 71; artist in residence, Univ WVa, 66; Res Award, Esso, 71. *Bibliog:* Julia Busch (auth), A painter's plastic sculpture, Art J, 70; Thelma Newman (auth), Plastics as design form, Chilton, 72; Julia Busch (auth), A Decade of Sculpture, Art Alliance Press, 74. *Media:* Acrylic Sheet, Metal. *Publ:* Contribr, Art Techniques, Reinhold, 65 & Lucite Spectrum, Du Pont Co Mag, 67-68. *Mailing Add:* 3891 Little Ave Coconut Grove FL 33133

MASTERFIELD, MAXINE
PAINTER
b Los Angeles, Calif, 1933. *Study:* Cleveland Inst Art, grad 55. *Work:* First Chicago Trust of Ariz & St Joseph Children's Ctr, Phoenix; Nat Watercolor Soc; Bancohio Nat; Ohio Savings & Loan. *Comn:* Trip-tyche, Off-the-Wall Racket Club, Strongsville, Ohio, 79; wall mural, Security Fed Savings & Loan, Parma, Ohio, 79. *Exhib:* Watercolor USA, Springfield Art Mus, Mo, 68; Aqueous Open, Arts & Crafts Ctr, Pittsburgh, Pa, 76-79; Butler Midyear Exhib, Butler Inst Am Art, Youngstown, Ohio, 77; Rocky Mountain Nat Watermedia, Foothills Art Ctr, Golden, Colo, 77-79; Nat Watercolor Soc, Los Angeles, 77-79; Ky Watercolor, Owensboro Mus Fine Arts, Ky, 78 & Mid-Am Art Exhib, 79. *Awards:* Purchase Award, Nat Watercolor Soc, 78; High Winds Medal, Am Watercolor Soc, 81; Grand Buckeye Leaf Award, Ohio Watercolor Soc, 82. *Mem:* Am Watercolor Soc; Nat Watercolor Soc; Ky Watercolor Soc; Ohio Watercolor Soc. *Media:* Water-Media. *Publ:* Illusr, Watercolor Bold and Free, 80; illusr, Creative Seascape Painting, 81, Watson-Guptill. *Dealer:* C G Rein Galleries 4235 N Marshall Way Scottsdale AZ 85251. *Mailing Add:* 22404 Fairlawn Circle Fairview Park OH 44126

MASTER-KARNIK, PAUL JOSEPH
MUSEUM DIRECTOR, CRITIC
b New York, NY, Nov 20, 48. *Study:* Rutgers Univ, BA, 70, MA, 71, PhD, 78; NY Univ, cert(mus studies), 79. *Pos:* Art critic, Staten Island Advan, Newhouse Publ, 76-81; dir, Summit Art Ctr, NJ, 81- *Teaching:* Adj prof cult

& art hist, Rutgers Univ, New Brunswick, NJ, 71-78; adj prof mus studies, New York Univ, 80- *Awards:* Nat Endowment Arts Internship, Neuberger Mus, State Univ NY Col Purchase, 80-81. *Mem:* Am Asn Mus; NJ Mus Coun; Col Art Asn; Nat Asn Schs Art & Design. *Res:* Methods and styles of contemporary art criticism; social history of the art museum; contemporary American art. *Publ:* Auth, Art criticism in the suburban context, Artview, Vol 3, No 1, 79; auth, Philip Pearlstein: Progress of a Painter (exhib catalog), 82, American Realism 1930's/1980's: A Comparative Perspective (exhib catalog), 83 & William Zorach: Sculpture and Drawings (exhib catalog), 83, Summit Art Ctr. *Mailing Add:* 96 Essex Ave Montclair NJ 07042

MASUROVSKY, GREGORY
DRAFTSMAN, PRINTMAKER
b Bronx, NY, Nov 26, 29. *Study:* Art Students League, New York, study with Will Barnet; Parsons Sch of Design, New York; Black Mountain Col, NC, study with Ilya Bolotowsky. *Work:* Mus Mod Art, New York; Minneapolis Inst Art, Minn; Fogg Art Mus, Cambridge, Mass; Mus Nat Art Mod, Paris; Libr Cong, Washington, DC. *Comn:* Decor, Costumes & Lighting, Ballet Theatre Contemp d'Angers, France, 75. *Exhib:* Druck Graphic, 71, Nurenberg Nat Mus, Ger, 70; Estampe Contemp, Bibliotheque Nat, Paris, 73; Third Int Biennale Nat Graphique, Kunstverein, Frechen, W Ger, 74; Minneapolis Inst Arts, Minn, 67; Mus de Pontoise, France, 82. *Pos:* Graphics monitor to Will Barnet, Art Students League, New York, 52-53. *Teaching:* Vis prof drawing, Minneapolis Col Art & Design, Minn, 66-67; prof drawing, Am Ctr, Paris, 80-83. *Awards:* Grant, William & Noma Copley Found, 63; Int Jury Prize, Etching III Biennial de Paris, 63; Fel, Tamarind Lithography Workshop, Los Angeles, 69. *Bibliog:* Georges Boudaille (auth), article, Cimaise, 5/65; Michel Conil Lacoste (auth), Masurovsky, an American in Paris, Studio Int, 3/65; Michel Buter (auth), article, Opus Int, 71. *Mem:* Centre Georges Pompidou, Paris; Artists Equity Asn, New York. *Media:* Pen & Ink; Etching. *Publ:* Illusr, Western Duo, Tamarind Litho, Los Angeles, 69; illusr, Seven Poems (Carl Sandburg), Asn Am Art, 70; auth, Obliques, Numero Special, pvt publ, 76; ed, Obliques, Nyons, France. *Dealer:* Assoc Am Artists 663 5th Ave New York NY 10022; Galerie des Editions de l'Ermitage Paris France. *Mailing Add:* 43 Rue Liancourt Paris 75014 France

MATASSA, JOHN P
PAINTER, INSTRUCTOR
b Norwich, Conn, Sept 13, 45. *Study:* Sch Mus Fine Arts, Boston, BFA, 67; Tufts Univ, with T Lux Feininger & Jan Cox, MFA, 73; Ind Study Mus Pre History, France. *Work:* Del Division of Public Libraries; Blount Collection, Ala; Logan Int Airport, Boston; Historical Soc Del; Eleutheran Mills Hagley Foundation. *Comn:* Concrete & neon wall, Eastern Airlines, Mass, 71; welded steel sculpture, Univ City Arts League, Pa, 74; sculptural relief, Del State Arts Coun, 80. *Exhib:* State Awards Wadsworth Atheneum, Conn, 63; Boston Area Show, Inst Contemp Art, Mass, 66; Traveling Scholars, Boston Mus Fine Arts, 68; one-man show, Del State Arts Coun, 80; Regional juried, Del Art Mus, 75, 78 & 81; Regional juried, Univ Del, Newark, 79 & 81; Nat Acad Design, New York, 82; Am Watercolor Soc, 82 & 83. *Pos:* Exhib dir, Club 47 Gallery, Mass, 66-68; art dir, auth & illusr, Del Steamboater Mag, Steamboat Found, 81-; chmn, Dept Visual Arts, Wilmington Friends Sch, Del, 77- *Teaching:* Grad instr painting, Sch Mus Fine Arts, Boston, 67-68; instr painting, drawing & sculpture, Wilmington Friends Sch, Del, 74- *Awards:* Grand Prize, Del Trust Co, 81; Nat Soc Painters Nauman Medal, 82; Artist of Year, Christiana Cult Arts Ctr, 84. *Bibliog:* Jean Gilmour (auth), Feature Artist, Del State Arts Council, 80; Nancy Muhr (auth), Delaware artist, Art Voices South Mag, 80. *Mem:* Philadelphia Watercolor Club; Nat Soc Painters Casein & Acrylic; assoc Am Watercolor Soc; Rehoboth Art League. *Media:* Watercolor, Acrylic. *Publ:* Photo illusr, Seventeen Mag, 76. *Dealer:* Mary Shea 3922 Kennett Greenville DE 19803. *Mailing Add:* c/o 101 Sch Rd Wilmington DE 19803

MATHEWS, NANCY MOWLL
HISTORIAN, CURATOR
b Baltimore, Md, Feb 11, 47. *Study:* Goucher Col, BA, 68; Cleveland Mus Art, fel, 70-71; Case-Western Reserve Univ, MA, 72; NY Univ Inst Fine Arts, Goldwater fel, 73-74, PhD, 80. *Collections Arranged:* The World Through 19th Century Eyes, 19th Century Am Still Life & Genre Painting, 78; The Tradition of American Folk Art (auth, catalog), Am Folk Painting & Sculpture, 79; Aspects of Photorealism (auth, catalog), Photorealist Painting, 80; Abstract Art in the 80s (auth, catalog), 81; Quilts and Collages: American Art in Pieces, 82. *Pos:* Sr cur, Maiem Mus Art, Randolph-Macon Womans Col, 77- *Awards:* Katherine Graves Davidson Award, 80; Smithsonian Postdoctoral Fel, 82; and others. *Mem:* Col Art Asn; Women's Caucus for Art; Am Asn Mus. *Res:* 19th century European and American painting; impressionism; Mary Cassatt, the 19th century Madonna. *Publ:* Auth, Mary Cassatt, In: Women Artists 1550-1950, Knopf, 76; auth, Four new books on Mary Cassatt, Woman's Art J, 81; ed, Mary Cassatt and Her Circle: Selected Letters, Abbeville Press, 84; auth, Mary Cassatt, Abrams, 85. *Mailing Add:* 400 Arlington St Lynchburg VA 24503

MATHIS, EMILE HENRY, II
DEALER, COLLECTOR
b Superior, Wis, Feb 25, 46. *Study:* Dominican Col, Univ Wis, Superior, BFA, MFA. *Collections Arranged:* J A Mon Whistler, (etchings & lithographs), 81; Rubber stamps by contemp Am artists, 81; 19th Century French Etching, 82. *Pos:* Asst dir, La Porte Gallery, Racine, 70-71; dir, New Gallery One, Racine, 71-72; gallery owner, Mathis Gallery, Racine, 72- *Teaching:* Instr art, Sheboygan Sch Syst, Wis, 68-69. *Mem:* Racine Urban Aesthetics. *Specialty:* Old and modern masters; contemporary graphics. *Collection:* American nineteenth and twentieth century contemporary drawings and paintings. *Mailing Add:* 735 Center St Racine WI 53403

MATISSE, PIERRE
DEALER
Pos: Owner & dir, Pierre Matisse Gallery Corp, currently. *Mailing Add:* 41 E 57th St New York NY 10022

MATLICK, GERALD ALLEN
PAINTER, ADMINISTRATOR
b Ft Wayne, Ind, Aug 18, 47. *Study:* Western Ky Univ, BA, 69, MA, 74; Bowling Green State Univ, MFA. *Work:* Bowling Green State Univ, Ohio; Owensboro Mus Fine Art, Ky; Brown & Williamson Tobacco Co, Louisville, Ky; Western Ky Univ. *Exhib:* Eight State Ann Graphics Painting, J B Speed Art Mus, Louisville, Ky, 77 & 78; Mid-States Art Exhib, Evansville Mus Art & Sci, Ind, 78, 81 & 83; Nat Watermedia, Ohio State Univ, Newark, 81; Alternatives, Art Inst of Boston, Mass, 81; Watercolor USA, Springfield Art Mus, Mo, 82; Aqueous 83 & one-man show, 83, Owensboro Mus Fine Art, Ky; and others. *Teaching:* Instr art, Crittenden Co Schs, Marion, Ky, 69-73; instr, co art supervisor, & head fine arts div, 76-79; vis instr, Western Ky Univ, Bowling Green, 74-76; asst prof painting, drawing & art educ & coordr art dept, Brescia Col, 81- *Awards:* Molly Morpeth Canady Award & Third Place Merit Award Watercolor, 62nd Ann Toledo May Show, Toledo Art Mus, 80; Merit Award Watercolor, Spring Show, Art Asn Lima, Ohio, 80; and others. *Mem:* Ky Asn Art Administrators; Col Art Asn Am. *Media:* Watercolor. *Dealer:* Swearingen Art Gallery 4806 Brownsboro Ctr Louisville KY 40207. *Mailing Add:* 127 West 17th St Owensboro KY 42301

MATSON, GRETA (GRETA MATSON KHOURI)
PAINTER
b Claremont, Va. *Study:* Grand Cent Sch Art, New York; also with Jerry Farnsworth, Cape Cod. *Work:* New Britain Mus Am Art, Conn; Va Mus Fine Arts, Richmond; Little Rock Mus, Ark; Tex Technol Col, Lubbock; Longwood Col, Farmville, Va. *Comn:* Portraits, Dean Grace Landrum, William & Mary Col, Williamsburg, Va, 46 & Mary Calcott, Calcott Sch, Norfolk, Va, 53. *Exhib:* Nat Drawing Ann, Albany Inst Hist & Art, NY, 40 & 45; Oil Nat, Carnegie Inst, Pittsburgh, 41, 44 & 45; Oil & Watercolor Nat, Art Inst Chicago, 42, 43 & 46; Oil Nat, Butler Art Inst, Youngstown, Ohio, 43, 45, 57 & 59; Oil Nat, Va Mus Fine Arts, Richmond, 53 & 57. *Awards:* Altman Figure Prize, Nat Acad Design, 45; Am Artist Mag Medal, Am Watercolor Soc, 55; Allied Artists Am Gold Medal, 62. *Mem:* Nat Asn Women Artists (pres, 61-65); Audubon Artists (corresp secy, 61-62); Allied Artists; Am Soc Contemp Artists (first vpres, 61); Am Watercolor Soc. *Media:* Oil, Watercolor. *Publ:* Auth, Painting in watercolor at the seashore, Am Artist Mag, 56. *Mailing Add:* 8750 Old Ocean View Rd Norfolk VA 23503

MATSUBARA, NAOKO
PRINTMAKER, ILLUSTRATOR
b Kyoto, Japan, Apr 5, 37. *Study:* Kyoto Acad Fine Arts, BFA, 60; Carnegie-Mellon Univ, MFA, 62; Royal Col Art, London, 63. *Work:* British Mus, London; Mus Fine Arts, Boston; Tokyo Nat Mus Mod Art; Cincinnati Mus Art; Libr Congress. *Comn:* Mural, Kyoto Univ Hosp, 59; mural, Carnegie-Mellon Univ, Pittsburgh, 62; woodcut print, Smithsonian Inst, Washington, DC, 67; woodcut print, Boston Winter Festival, 69; Solitude (portfolio), Aquarius Press, New York, 71. *Exhib:* Solo shows, Hart House Gallery, Univ Toronto, 74, Art Gallery Hamilton, Ont, 79, Hewlett Gallery, Carnegie-Mellon Univ, 80 & Wako Art Gallery, Tokyo, 81; Munakata & Matsubara Traveling Show, 76-77; and others. *Teaching:* Instr woodcut, Pratt Graphic Art Ctr, 65-67; instr woodcut, Univ RI, 67-68; asst prof woodcut, Univ Victoria, BC, summer 77. *Awards:* Kegon Shou, Hangain Ten, Shiko Munakata, 63; Samuel Gold Award, Soc Am Graphic Artists, 68. *Bibliog:* Fritz Eichenberg (auth), The two worlds of Naoko Matsubara, Am Artist, 66; Fritz Eichenberg (auth), Naoko Matsubara, Xylon, Switz, 70; Joan Stanley-Baker (auth), The woodcuts of Munakata and Matsubara, Art Gallery Greater Victoria, 76. *Mem:* Soc Am Graphic Artists; Royal Can Acad Arts. *Media:* Woodcut; Watercolor. *Publ:* Auth-illusr, My woodcuts and myself, Univ Tex Quart, 63; illusr, The Tale of the Shining Princess, 66 & illusr, Kyoto Woodcuts, 78, Kodansha Int; illusr, Nantucket Woodcuts, Barre Publ, 68; illusr, In Praise of Trees, Mosaic Press, 84. *Dealer:* AAA Gallery 663 5th Ave New York NY. *Mailing Add:* 324 Coral Terr Oakville ON L6J 4C4 Canada

MATTERN, PENNY GREIG
LIBRARIAN, PRINTMAKER
b Jersey City, NJ, Aug 24, 43. *Study:* Clark Univ, AB, 65; Simmons Col, SM, 69. *Pos:* Asst librn, Worcester Art Mus, 70-72; librn, 72-77; head cataloger, Worcester Pub Libr, 77-79; New Eng Libr Info Network mem serv librn, 79-81; instructional coordr, OCLC Inc, 81- *Mem:* Art Libr Soc NAm (treas, New Eng Chap, 75-76). *Mailing Add:* 1950 Mackenzie Dr Columbus OH 43220

MATTERNES, JAY HOWARD
PAINTER, ILLUSTRATOR
b Corregidor, Philippines, Apr 14, 33; US citizen. *Study:* Carnegie Mellon Univ Col Fine Arts, Mellon Found scholar & BFA, 55. *Work:* Cleveland Mus Natural Sci, Ohio; Kenya Nat Mus, Nairobi; Carnegie Mus, Pittsburgh; Bedloe Island Mus Immigration, New York. *Comn:* NAm Tertiary Murals (four), Smithsonian Natural Hist Mus, DC, 60-64, Hagerman (Idaho) Pliocene Mural, 69 & Alaska Ice Age Mural, 76; Morristown Revolutionary War Mural, Nat Park Serv, NJ, 75. *Exhib:* Art & the Animal, Royal Ont Mus, Ottawa, Can, 75; Nat Acad Western Art at Cowboy Hall of Fame, Oklahoma City, 79; Leigh Yawkey Woodson Art Mus, Wausau, Wis, 80, 81 & 83; bird art, Royal Scottish Acad, Edinburgh; Brit Mus, London, 82. *Pos:* self-employed free-lance artist, 60- *Awards:* Award Merit, 68 & Gold Medal,

82, Art Dir Club Washington; Award Merit, Soc Animal Artists, 79. *Bibliog:* Dr L B Leakey (auth), The dawn of man (film TV), 65 & Dr Clark Howell (auth), Man hunters (film TV), 68, Nat Geographic Soc; John Heminway (auth), The Three Million Year Clue (film TV), Survival Anglia Ltd, 76. *Mem:* Artists Equity Asn. *Media:* Oil and Acrylic; Charcoal and Pencil. *Publ:* Illusr, American Cowboy, 72 & Vanishing Wild Life of North America, 74, Nat Geographic Soc Bk Div; illusr, A New Look at Early Man in North America, World Yr Bk, 73; illusr, Lost Empires, Living Tribes, 82; illusr, Peoples & Places of the Past, 83. *Dealer:* Carson Gallery 730 17th St Denver CO 80202. *Mailing Add:* 4328 Ashford Lane Fairfax VA 22032

MATTESON, IRA
SCULPTOR, DRAFTSMAN
b Hamden, Conn, June 26, 17. *Study:* Art Students League, with Arthur Lee, 37-42, also with William Zorach, 46-51; Nat Acad, with John Flanagan, 46-47. *Work:* Akron Art Inst, Ohio; Cleveland Mus Art; Chrysler Mus, Provincetown, Mass; Norfolk Mus, Va; Case Western Reserve Univ, Cleveland, Ohio. *Comn:* Figure-Bend, Cascade Plaza, Akron, 77; Back, Case Western Reserve, Univ Cleveland, Ohio, 81. *Teaching:* Fac, Sch of Art, Kent State Univ, Kent, 68- *Awards:* Prix de Rome, Am Acad Rome, 53-55, Louis Comfort Tiffany, 56 & 60; Ohio Arts Coun grant, 78. *Media:* Wood, Metal. *Mailing Add:* 621 S Depeyster St Kent OH 44240

MATTHEWS, GENE (EUGENE EDWARD)
PAINTER, EDUCATOR
b Davenport, Iowa, Mar 22, 31. *Study:* Bradley Univ, 48-51; Univ Iowa, BFA, 53, MFA, 57. *Work:* Nat Mus Am Art, Washington, DC; Butler Inst Am Art, Youngstown, Ohio; Denver Art Mus, Colo; Nat Mus Poland; Chrysler Mus, Norfolk, Va. *Exhib:* Am Watercolors, Drawings & Prints, Metrop Mus Art, New York, 52; Int Drawing Biennale, Middlesbrough Art Gallery, Eng, 77; Int All on Paper, AAO Gallery, Buffalo, NY, 80; American Drawings, Smithsonian Inst, Washington, DC, 80-82; one-man show, Dubins Gallery, Los Angeles, 81; Galeria Wielka, Poznan, Poland, 82-83; Brena Gallery, Denver, Colo, 83. *Teaching:* Prof fine arts, Univ Colo, Boulder, 61- *Awards:* Univ Colo Fac Fel for Creative Res, Boulder, 66; Quartana Purchase Award, Int Watercolor Exhib, Baton Rouge, La, 73; Purchase Award, American Drawings IV, 82. *Bibliog:* Wendon Blake (auth), Acrylic Watercolor Painting, 70 & L C Goldsmith (auth), Watercolor Bold and Free, 80, Watson-Guptill. *Mem:* Fel Am Acad, Rome. *Media:* Acrylic. *Dealer:* Brena Gallery 313 Detroit Denver CO 80206. *Mailing Add:* 2865 Jay Rd Boulder CO 80301

MATTHEWS, HARRIETT
SCULPTOR
b Kansas City, Mo, June 21, 40. *Study:* Sullins Jr Col, Briston, Va, AFA; Univ Ga, BFA & MFA; with Leonard DeLonga. *Work:* Univ Ga Art Mus; Colby Col Art Mus & Libr; Cascoe Bay Bank, Portland, ME. *Comn:* Designed awards for the Maine Arts & Humanities Comn, 69. *Exhib:* Colby Col Art Mus, 71, 75, 77 & 79; one-person shows, Vanderbilt Univ, 74, Treat Gallery, Bates Col, Lewiston, Maine, 79, Univ Southern Maine, Gorham, 82, Sanford Gallery, Clarion State Univ, Pa, 83 & Montpelier Cult Arts Ctr, Laurel, Md, 83; Univ Georgia, 71, 75, 77, 79 & 82; and others. *Teaching:* Vis instr sculpture, Univ Okla, 64-65; from instr to asst prof sculpture & drawing, Colby Col, 66-75, assoc prof, 75- *Awards:* Colby Travel Grants, 71, 76, 78 & 81; Ingram Merrill grant, 80; Colby Mellon Grant, 80. *Mem:* Maine State Comn Arts & Humanities; Col Art Asn. *Media:* All. *Mailing Add:* RFD 2 Clinton ME 04927

MATTHEWS, WANDA MILLER
PRINTMAKER
b Barry, Ill, Sept 15, 30. *Study:* Bradley Univ, Peoria, Ill, BFA, 52; Univ Iowa, Iowa City, with Mauricio Lasansky, MFA, 57. *Work:* Libr of Cong; Philadelphia Mus of Art; Los Angeles Co Mus; Boston Pub Libr; Portland Art Mus, Ore. *Exhib:* Inst Grafik Biennale, Frechen, WGer, 76; 6th, 7th & 8th Int Print Biennale, Cracow, Poland, 76, 78 & 80; New Talent in Printmaking 1980, Asn Am Artists, New York & Philadelphia, 80; retrospective, Prints: 1955-1982, Jane Haslem Gallery, Washington, DC, 82; solo exhib, Am Printmaker, Am Ctr Gallery US Info Agency, Belgrade & Piran, Yugoslavia, 82; and others. *Pos:* Res assistantship printmaking, Univ Iowa, 56-57. *Awards:* Benton Spruance Prize, Print Club of Philadelphia, 71; Purchase Award, Soc Am Graphic Artists Nat Exhib, New York, 79; Stella Drabkin Award & Medallion, Am Color Print Soc Nat Exhib, Philadelphia, 81. *Mem:* Print Club of Philadelphia; Calif Soc of Printmakers. *Media:* Intaglio. *Dealer:* Jane Haslem Gallery 2121 P St NW Washington DC 20037; Assoc Am Artists 663 Fifth Ave New York NY 10022. *Mailing Add:* 2865 Jay Rd Boulder CO 80301

MATTIL, EDWARD L
EDUCATOR, WRITER
b Williamsport, Pa, Nov 25, 18. *Study:* Pa State Univ, BS, 40, MA, 46 & DEd, 53; also with Viktor Lowenfeld & Hobson Pittman. *Pos:* Ed, Everyday Art, 57- *Teaching:* From asst prof to assoc prof, Pa State Univ, 48-60, prof art educ & head dept, 60-70; prof art, NTex State Univ, 71-, chmn art dept, 71-76. *Awards:* Distinguished Serv Award, Nat Gallery Art, 65; Nat Art Educators Asn Distinguished Fel, 83. *Mem:* Nat Art Educ Asn (pres, 63-65). *Publ:* Auth, Meaning in Crafts, Prentice-Hall, 59, 65 & 71; coauth, Providing for individual differences in the elementary schools, 60 & The arts in higher education, 69; El valor educativo de las manualidades 73: The Cuna Mola, 74; coauth, Meaning in Children's Art, Prentice-Hall, 81. *Mailing Add:* Dept Art NTex State Univ Denton TX 76203

MATTINGLY, (JAMES THOMAS)
PRINTMAKER, EDUCATOR
b Southgate, Calif, Mar 14, 34. *Study:* San Jose State Univ, with Fred Spratt, Terry Frost, Ken Auvil, Jeff Bowman, Robert Collins & Robert Freemark, BA, 63, MA(art), 66. *Work:* Montreal Mus Fine Arts; Honolulu Acad Arts; State Ore Capitol Bldg, Salem; Coos Art Mus, Coos Bay, Ore; Wash State Arts Comn, Seattle. *Comn:* Box (wood sculpture), comn by Glenda Milton, Salem, Ore, 80. *Exhib:* Introduction 78, R L Kidd Assoc Gallery, Birmingham, Mich, 77; 24th Nat Print Exhib, Hunterdown Art Ctr, Clinton, NJ, 80; 4th Miami Int Print Biennale, Metrop Mus Art Ctr, Miami, 80; Northwest Prints 82, Portland Art Mus, Ore, 82; Rockford Int Print & Drawing Biennale, Rockford Col, 83; and others. *Teaching:* Asst art, San Jose State Univ, 63-66; instr, Alta Col Art, Calgary, 66-68; prof, Western Ore State Col, 68-, art dept head, 78- *Awards:* Reid Mem Award, Int Exhib Graphics, Montreal Mus Fine Arts, 71; Statewide Serv Travel Award, 74 & Visual Arts Resources Award, 77, Mus Art, Univ Ore. *Mem:* Northwest Print Coun (pres, 83-); Salem Art Asn, Ore (mem bd dirs, 77-). *Media:* Intaglio, Mixed Media. *Mailing Add:* 15440 Strong Rd Dallas OR 97338

MAU, HUI-CHI
PAINTER
b Chekiang, China, Oct 1, 22; US citizen. *Study:* Hangchow Nat Art Acad; with Hsu Pei Hung & Chi Pai Shih. *Work:* San Diego Mus; Elliott Mus. *Exhib:* Chekiang Univ, 43; Chinese Embassy, Berlin, Ger, 48; San Diego Mus, 68; Wash Sq Art Exhib, New York, 69; Cocoanut Grove Art Exhib, Miami, Fla, 73; Elliott Mus, Stuart, Fla. *Teaching:* Art dir, Mil Acad China, 42-54. *Awards:* Monterey Art Exhib Award, Calif, 68; Wash Sq Art Exhib Award, New York, 73; Church of Ascension Award, New York, 74. *Bibliog:* Diana Kan (auth), The artist and his work, Villager, New York, 74; Ann D Browne (auth), Art circle, Directions Mag, 74. *Mem:* Suffolk Co Artist League, New York; Chinese Artists & Writers Soc, Taiwan. *Media:* Watercolor, Graphics. *Mailing Add:* 90-22 193rd St Hollis NY 11423

MAUGHELLI, MARY L
PAINTER, LITHOGRAPHER
b Glen Lyon, Pa, Nov 20, 35. *Study:* Univ Calif, Berkeley, BA & MA; Pratt Graphic Ctr. *Exhib:* 85th Ann San Francisco Art Inst Exhib, San Francisco Mus Art, 66; Images & Ideas: Printmakers, Calif State Univ, Hayward, 80; Western Edge, Capricorn Asunder, San Francisco, 81; Fac Show, Calif State Univ, Fresno, 79 & 81; Drawing on Fresno, Fresno Arts Ctr, 83; Small Works Show, Painted Bride Art Ctr, Philadelphia, 83; and others. *Teaching:* Prof art, Calif State Univ, Fresno, 62-; lectr design, Univ Calif, Berkeley, summer 63. *Awards:* Fulbright Fels, Italy, 59-60 & 60-61; Helene Wurlitzer Found Fel, Taos, NMex, summer 76, 77 & 83; Humanities Res Grant, Calif State Univ, Fresno, 82; and others; and others. *Mem:* Col Art Asn; Calif Soc Printmakers; Artists Equity. *Media:* Acrylic. *Dealer:* Fig Tree Gallery 1536 Fulton St Fresno CA 93721. *Mailing Add:* 1114 W Keats Ave Fresno CA 93711

MAULDIN, BILL
CARTOONIST, WRITER
b Mountain Park, NMex, Oct 29, 21. *Study:* Chicago Acad Fine Arts; Conn Wesleyan Univ, Hon MA, 46; Albion Col, Hon LittD, 70; Lincoln Col, Hon LHD, 70. *Pos:* Cartoonist, Chicago Sun-Times, 62- *Awards:* Pulitzer Prize, 44 & 58; Sigma Delta Chi Award, 64. *Mem:* Nat Cartoonists Soc. *Publ:* Auth, What's Got Your Back Up, 61 & I've Decided I Want My Seat Back, 65, Harper-Row; auth, Up Front, 68 & Brass Ring, 71, Norton; auth & illusr, articles in Life, Sat Eve Post, Sports Illus, Atlantic Monthly, New Repub & many others. *Mailing Add:* Chicago Sun-Times 401 N Wabash Ave Chicago IL 60611

MAURER, EVAN MACLYN
DIRECTOR, HISTORIAN
b Newark, NJ, Aug 19, 44. *Study:* Amherst Col, BA, 66; Univ Minn, MA, 68; Univ Pa, PhD, 74. *Collections Arranged:* Fakes and Forgeries (auth, catalog), Minneapolis Inst Arts, 73; The Native American Heritage (auth, catalog), Art Inst Chicago, 77; Gerome Kamrowski Retrospective, 83. *Pos:* Cur & asst to dir, Minneapolis Inst Arts, 71-73; cur primitive art, Art Inst Chicago, 73-81; dir, Univ Mich Mus Art, 81- *Teaching:* Vis prof primitivism & mod art, Univ Chicago, 76; lectr primitivism, mod art & mus studies, Art Inst Chicago, 78-81, assoc prof, 81. *Mem:* Col Art Asn; Am Asn Mus. *Publ:* Auth, Metaphysical Landscape by G de Chirico, Minneapolis Inst Arts, 73; auth, North American Indian clothing, In: The Fabric of Culture, Mouton, 80. *Mailing Add:* Mus Art Univ Mich Ann Arbor MI 48109

MAURER, NEIL DOUGLAS
PHOTOGRAPHER
b New York, NY, Jan 12, 41. *Study:* Brown Univ, BA, 62; RI Sch Design, MFA, 75. *Work:* Mus Mod Art, New York; Corcoran Gallery Art; San Antonio Mus Art; Mus Art, RI Sch Design; Libr Cong. *Exhib:* Solo exhib, Corcoran Gallery Art, 73 & Madison Art Ctr, 73; Texas Photographers, Washington Proj Arts, 81; New Photographics 82, Cent Wash Univ, 82; 12th Ann Works on Paper, Southwest Tex State Univ, 83; Amarillo Competition, Amarillo Art Ctr, Tex, 83; Contemporary Works Series, San Antonio Mus Art, 83. *Teaching:* Instr, Corcoran Sch Art, 75, Dept Fine Arts, Univ Bridgeport, Conn, 77-78 & Dept Arts & Humanities, Ocean Co Community Col, 78; asst prof, Div Art & Design, Univ Tex, San Antonio, 78- *Awards:* Fulbright-Hays Grant, 75-76. *Mem:* Soc Photog Educ. *Dealer:* Marcuse Pfeifer Gallery 825 Madison Ave New York NY 10021. *Mailing Add:* 723 E Woodlawn San Antonio TX 78212

MAURICE, ALFRED PAUL
PAINTER, EDUCATOR
b Nashua, NH, Mar 11, 21. *Study:* Univ NH, 40-42; Mich State Univ, BA, 47, MA, 49. *Comn:* Murals (with Raymond Pinet), Nat Youth Admin, Jr High Sch, Hudson, NH & Community Chest Bldg, Nashua, 39-40. *Exhib:* Butler Inst Ann, 81-83; one-man shows, Univ Ill, Chicago, 82, Bradley Univ, 82, Mich State Univ, 83, Chicago Pub Libr Cult Ctr, 83 & Anderson Art Ctr, 83; and others. *Pos:* Dir art ctr, Kalamazoo Inst Arts, Mich, 59-65. *Teaching:* Instr printmaking, calligraphy & drawing, Macalester Col, 47-49; asst drawing, Mich State Univ, 49-50; from asst prof to assoc prof drawing, painting, printmaking & design, State Univ NY Col New Paltz, 50-57, actg chmn art dept, 55-56; exec dir, Md Inst Col Art, Baltimore, 57-59; chmn art dept, Univ Ill, Chicago Circle, 65-67, prof printmaking painting & drawing, 65-, assoc dean faculties, 69-72, actg dean, Col Archit & Art, 75-77. *Awards:* Dr David Soletsky Award, Nat Soc Painters Casein & Acrylic Ann, 83. *Mem:* Nat Soc Painters Casein & Acrylic. *Collection:* American prints of all periods and in all print media. *Publ:* Auth, Four Printmakers, 62; auth, Miklos Suba, 64; auth, Oliver Chaffee, 64. *Dealer:* Joy Horwich Gallery 226 E Ontario Chicago IL 60611. *Mailing Add:* 2725A S Michigan Ave Chicago IL 60616

MAURICE, E(LEANOR) INGERSOLL
PAINTER, DESIGNER
b East Orange, NJ, Sept 4, 01. *Study:* Arts Student League, with F V Du Mond & Allen Tucker, 22-30; Montclair Mus, with Estelle Armstrong & Arerg Johnson, 45-47. *Work:* Montclair Mus, NJ; Bloomfield Libr, NJ. *Exhib:* Traveling shows, Am Watercolor Soc, New York, 63; Nat Acad Design; Audubon Artist Annuals; Allied Artist Annuals; Portland Mus, Maine; Butler Inst Annuals. *Awards:* Nat Acad Ann Award, 63; Audubon Artist Ann, 65; Butler Int Ann, 67. *Bibliog:* Norman Keat (auth), 100 Watercolor Techniques, Watson-Guptill. *Mem:* Life mem Am Watercolor Soc; Art Students League; Allied Artists of Am; Audubon Artists Am; NJ Watercolor Soc. *Media:* Watercolor, Oil. *Dealer:* The Chime Art Gallery 39 Maple St Summit NJ 07901. *Mailing Add:* 215 S Mountain Ave Montclair NJ 07042

MAVIAN, SALPI MIRIAM
PAINTER
b Mar 27, 08; US citizen. *Study:* Sch Practical Arts, Boston; Art Students League; also with Robert Brackman, Joseph Hirsch & Robert Philipp. *Work:* Three mus, Armenia, USSR. *Comn:* St John the Baptist & St Gregory the Illuminator, St John Church of Detroit, 68; Archbishop Garigin, Diocese of Armenian Church NAm, New York, 63; portrait of Archbishop Tiran Nersoyan; side altar paintings of St Nersess Shnorhali & St Gregory the Enlightener, Diocese of Armenian Church of Am, New York, 73; side altar paintings, St James Armenian Church, Richmond, Va, 80. *Exhib:* Knickerbocker Artists, 59-60 & Allied Artists Am, New York, 63; one-man shows, Armenia, USSR & Panaras Gallery; Artists Equity Asn, 65; J George Mayer Gallery, Ft Lauderdale, Fla, 79; and others. *Teaching:* Private instr, currently. *Awards:* Silver Trophy, 74 & Gold Trophy, 76, Golden Age Art Exhib, New York. *Mem:* Art Students League. *Media:* Oil. *Mailing Add:* 435 E 57th St New York NY 10022

MAVIGLIANO, GEORGE JEROME
HISTORIAN, EDUCATOR
b Chicago, Ill, Oct 24, 41. *Study:* Western Ill Univ, BA, 64; Northern Ill Univ, MA, 67. *Teaching:* Assoc prof art hist, Southern Ill Univ, 70- *Awards:* Smithsonian Inst Fel, 81; Nat Endowment Humanities Summer Sem Award, 81. *Res:* New Deal art programs. *Publ:* Auth, A Matter of History: New Deal and the Arts (exhib catalog), 73; auth, On Painting, Sculpture and Architecture, Stipes, 73; auth, Governmental patronage of the arts, Southern Illinoisan, 78; auth, Fred Myers, Woodcarver, Southern Ill Univ, 80; auth, The Herrin Massacre revisited, Ill Mag, 83. *Mailing Add:* Sch Art Southern Ill Univ Carbondale IL 62901

MAVROUDIS, DEMETRIOS
SCULPTOR, EDUCATOR
b Thasos, Greece, Nov 18, 37. *Study:* Jersey City State Col, BA; Teachers Col, Columbia Univ, MA & EdD. *Comn:* Bronze sculptures, Bus Comt for Arts, Esquire, 73-76; sculpture, Lifestyles Mag, 77. *Exhib:* Albright-Knox Art Gallery, Buffalo, NY, 70 & 71; Artists-in-Residence Traveling Exhib, Del Art Mus, Wilmington, 75 & 76; Sculpture in the Fields, Storm King Art Ctr, Mountainville, NY; one-man shows, Philadelphia Art Alliance, Pa, Anchorage Hist & Fine Arts Mus, Alaska & Alaska State Mus. *Pos:* Artist-in-residence, NJ Coun Arts, 71-73. *Teaching:* Asst prof sculpture, NY Univ, New York, 69-71 & Teachers Col, Columbia Univ, 67-69 & 73-74; assoc prof sculpture & artist-in-residence, Univ Richmond, Va, 74- *Awards:* Dow Purchase Award, Columbia Univ, 69. *Mem:* Am Foundrymen's Soc; Nat Art Educ Asn; Col Art Asn. *Media:* Cast Metal, Wood. *Mailing Add:* 9712 Cherokee Rd Richmond VA 23235

MAWICKE, TRAN
PAINTER, ILLUSTRATOR
b Chicago, Ill, Sept 20, 11. *Study:* Art Inst Chicago, with Louis Ritman; Am Acad Art, Chicago; Acad Fine Art, Chicago. *Work:* USAF Collection, Washington, DC; Mus Am Illus, New York; Schenectady Mus, NY; Bronxville New York Library; Charleston Mus. *Comn:* Portraits, Gen Elec Corp Knolls Lab, 48, NY Nat Guard, Schenectady, 53, Ingersoll-Rand, 75 & Roper Hosp, 82. *Exhib:* Am Watercolor Soc, 48 & 69-74; Soc Illusrs; Am Watercolor Traveling Exhib, 70 & 74; Am Watercolor Soc Invitational, Edward Dean Mus, Cherry Valley, Calif, 78; SC Watercolor Soc, 78. *Bibliog:* S Meyer (auth), Fairfield watercolor group, Am Artist, 7/72; article in Southwest Art, 4/80. *Mem:* Am Watercolor Soc (dir, 70 & 72); life mem Soc Illusrs (pres, 60-61); Fairfield Watercolor Group; life mem Joint Ethics Comn (chmn, 55-60). *Media:* Oil, Watercolor. *Publ:* Illusr, South America Illustrated, 60 & More Answers, 61, G & D; illusr, Little Britches, Norton, 62; illusr, Andre, Putnams, 67; illusr, Captain, Garrard, 75. *Dealer:* Carolina Print & Frame Charleston SC 29401. *Mailing Add:* 452 Golf Villas Rt 1 Johns Island SC 29455

MAX, LOPE (LOPE MAX DIAZ RIVERA)
PAINTER, EDUCATOR
b Santurce, PR, Dec 13, 43. *Study:* Univ PR, BA, 66; Hunter Col, New York, MA, 71. *Work:* Inter-Am Univ PR Art Gallery, Rio Piedras; Mus Latin Am Print, PR Inst Cult, San Juan. *Comn:* Three-Dimensional Mural, Govt PR, Aguadilla, 75; painted mural, Las Am Expressway, San Juan Munic Govt, PR, 79. *Exhib:* Second Wiener Graphikbiennale, Vienna, Austria, 75; First Ann Exhib PR Painting & Sculpture, Inst PR Cult, San Juan, 77; Art in PR, Mus Fine Arts, San Juan, 78; Contemp PR Painting, Inter-Am Univ, Rio Piedras, 82; solo exhib, Mus Univ PR, Rio Piedras, 83. *Teaching:* Prof art, Inter-Am Univ PR, 74- & Univ PR, 77- *Awards:* First Prize for Watercolor, Christmas Art Festival, Ateneo, PR, 66; First Prize for Painting, IBEC Group Show, 68; Honorary Award, Second Latin Am Graphic Biennale, Int PR Cult, 73. *Bibliog:* Manuel Perez-Lizano (auth), Dos Pintores Abstractos de PR, Roberto Laureano y Lope Max, Cruz Ansata Univ, Ctr de Bayamon, 82; Myrna Rodriguez (auth), Lope Max: One of the best, San Juan Star Mag, 2/13/83; Efrain Perez-Chanis (auth), Lope Max y la magia de su Universo, El Nuevo Dia, 3/6/83. *Media:* Acrylic, Oil. *Publ:* Contribr, Kasimir Malevich: Revolucionario, Frente, 78. *Dealer:* Forma Art Gallery 305 Alcazar Ave Coral Gables FL 33134. *Mailing Add:* PO Box 1866 San Juan PR 00903

MAX, PETER
PAINTER, PRINTMAKER
b Berlin, Ger, Oct 19, 37; US citizen. *Study:* Art Students League; Pratt Inst; Sch Visual Arts. *Comn:* World's Fair US postage stamp, Spokane, Wash, 74; Border Station Welcoming Billboards, erected at points of entry along Can and Mex borders, Gen Serv Admin, 76; Kentucky Derby poster, 81; cachet, UNICEF Int Flags Stamp Program, 81; and others. *Exhib:* Munic Art Gallery, Los Angeles, The World of Peter Max, M H De Young Mem Mus, San Francisco & US Tour, 70; London Arts Gallery Peter Max Exhibs, 12 major world cities, 70; two Smithsonian Inst Peter Max Exhibs, US, 72-74; Corcoran Gallery Art, Washington, DC, 81; and many others. *Pos:* Dir, Daly-Max Design Studio; designer, Gen Foods, Elgin Nat Industs, Takashimaya Ltd Japan, Van Heusen, UN & other major orgns. *Awards:* Award, Am Inst Graphic Arts; Award, Soc Illusr; Award, Int Poster Competition Poland; plus many others. *Media:* Mixed. *Publ:* Auth, Peter Max Posterbook & Peter Max Superposterbook, Crown; auth, Peter Max Astrological Calendar, Grosset & Dunlap; auth, The Peter Max Paints America, Acropolis; Peter Max Japan Book; drawings & meditations syndicated in 176 papers in US & Can, two yrs; and many others. *Mailing Add:* Peter Max Enterprises 118 Riverside Dr New York NY 10024

MAXFIELD, ROBERTA MASUR
SILVERSMITH
b Chicago, Ill, Oct 30, 52. *Study:* Northern Ill Univ, with Eleanor Caldwell & Lee Peck, BFA, 74, MA, 75; Ind Univ, with Alma Eikerman, MFA, 77. *Work:* Ill State Mus, Springfield; Village Art Collection, Oak Park & River Forest High Sch, Ill. *Exhib:* Goldsmiths Show, Phoenix Art Mus, Ariz, 77; Ill Craftsmen, Ill State Mus, Springfield, 79; Everyday Metal Exhib, Nat Ornamental Mus, Memphis, Tenn, 80; Young Americans Metal, Am Crafts Mus, New York, 81; Calso, traveling, 81. *Awards:* Honorable Mention, Soc North Am Goldsmiths, 77; Purchase Award & Third Place, Village Art Fair, Village Art Comt, 79; Honorable Mention, Ill Crafts Exhib, Ill State Mus, 80. *Bibliog:* Craft Horizons, Am Coun Crafts, 4/77. *Mem:* Assoc mem Soc North Am Goldsmiths. *Media:* Sterling Silver. *Mailing Add:* 548 Kendall Ln De Kalb IL 60115

MAXWELL, JOHN
PAINTER
b Rochester, NY. *Study:* Rochester Inst Technol; Univ Rochester; Provincetown Workshop; privately with nationally known instructors. *Work:* Philadelphia Mus Art; Nat Acad Design; Butler Inst Am Art; Wichita State Univ; Allentown Art Mus, Pa; and others. *Exhib:* Butler Inst Am Art; Richmond Mus, Va; Norfolk Mus, Va; Smithsonian Inst; Chicago Art Inst; Lehigh Univ; San Francisco Palace Legion Honor; Corcoran Gallery; Rutgers Univ; William Penn Mus, Harrisburg, Pa; and others. *Awards:* Altman Prize, Nat Acad Design; Silver & Bronze Medals Hon, Am Watercolor Soc; Dana Medal, Pa Acad Fine Arts; and others. *Bibliog:* Articles in Arts, Art News, Am Artist & others. *Mem:* Nat Acad Design; Am Watercolor Soc; Audubon Artists; Philadelphia Watercolor Club; Allied Artists Am; and others. *Media:* Oil, Watercolor. *Publ:* Writer on art & artists, with national magazine articles on: Giorgio Morandi, Henry C Pitz, Watercolors of John Maxwell; and others. *Dealer:* Newman & Saunders Galleries Wayne PA 19087. *Mailing Add:* 415 Holly Lane Wynnewood PA 19096

MAXWELL, ROBERT EDWIN
b Mt Vernon, NY, Dec 31, 29. *Study:* Art Students League; Franklin Sch Art; Nat Acad Design, with Robert Philipp, Hallgarten travel scholarship, 51; Escuela de Bellas Artes with James Pinto, etching with Guilermo Silva Santamaria. *Work:* Galeria Moderna, Banjalvka, Yugoslavia; Inst Norteamericano de Relaciones Culturales, Mexico City; Vincent Price Col. *Exhib:* Am Watercolor Soc, New York, 49; 14th Am Drawing Ann, Norfolk Mus, Va, 56; Nat Acad Design, 57; Acapulco Pictorial Festival, Mex, 64;

Galeria Moderna, 74. *Teaching:* Instr drawing & landscape, Inst Allende, Mex, 55-56. *Awards:* Stacey Found Scholarship, 52. *Bibliog:* Image of Mexico II, Univ Tex, Austin; Crespo de la Serna (auth), Exhibit Paintings, 67 & Erasto Cortez Juarez (auth), Color and drawing, 69, Novedades, Mexico City. *Media:* Oil, Acrylic; Etching, Pastel. *Publ:* Contribr, Oil Painting-Traditional & New, 59; contribr, Painters Workshop, 69. *Dealer:* Galeria San Miguel C San Francisco San Miguel de Allende Guanajuato Mexico. *Mailing Add:* San Pedro 18 San Miguel de Allende Guanajuato Mexico

MAXWELL, WILLIAM C
PAINTER, PRINTMAKER
b Yonkers, NY, Sept 3, 41. *Study:* Wagner Col, Staten Island, NY, BFA, 70; Columbia Univ, New York, MA, 71, EdM, 72, EdD, 76; study with Paul Pollaro, Clare Romano & Deli Sacilotto. *Work:* Hudson River Mus, Yonkers, NY; Brooklyn Mus, NY; Arthur Wesley Dow Collection & Federico Castellon Mem Collection, Columbia Univ; Univ Mass, Amherst; State Dept of Educ, Trenton, NJ; and others. *Exhib:* Printmakers 1973, Metrop Mus of Art, New York, 73; 19th Nat Print Exhib Traveling Show, Brooklyn Mus, 74-75; Elizabeth Weiner Galleries, New York, 79-81; Cardet Gallery, Coral Gables, Fla, 81; Brooklyn Acad Music, 82; Univ Conn, Hartford, 83; Bernice Steinbaum Gallery, New York, 83; and others. *Pos:* Master printer, Bank St Atelier, 68-71; cur, Federico Castellon Mem Collection, Columbia Univ, New York, 75- *Teaching:* Vis assoc prof art & educ, Teachers Col, Columbia Univ, New York, 71-; assoc prof painting & printmaking, Col of New Rochelle, NY, 75- *Awards:* President's Award, Nat Arts Club, New York, 75; Shields Award, New York, 75; Purchase Award, Univ Dallas, Irving, Tex, 80. *Bibliog:* Edgar Bournagurio (auth), rev in Arts, 6/79; Peter Frank (auth), rev in Village Voice, 6/79; Helen Thomas (auth), rev in Arts, 10/80. *Mem:* Col Art Asn; Nat Art Educ Asn; Artist's Equity; Soc Layerists; and others. *Media:* Mixed Aqueous, Oil; Polymer, Oil Print. *Publ:* Contribr, Elizabeth Harris & Sue Vardin (auths), Urban Education, Open Univ, London, 74; auth, Printmaking: A Beginning Handbook, Prentice-Hall, 77. *Dealer:* Bernice Steinbaum Gallery 903 Madison Ave New York NY 10021; Robert L Kidd Assocs Inc Birmingham MI 48011. *Mailing Add:* 307-9 Canal St New York NY 10012

MAY, DANIEL STRIGER
DEALER
b Decatur, Ill, Sept 5, 42. *Study:* State Univ NY, Buffalo, BA, 64, MBA, 66 & MEd, 68. *Pos:* Dir, Jackson Hole Art Gallery, 70-72; owner & dir, May Gallery, Scottsdale, Ariz, 72- *Specialty:* Western Americana and wildlife. *Mailing Add:* 7149 Main PO Box 1058 Scottsdale AZ 85252

MAY, MORTON DAVID
COLLECTOR, PATRON
b St Louis, Mo, Mar 25, 14. *Study:* Dartmouth Col, BA, 36. *Awards:* Great Cross of Ger Govt for Interest in Ger Painting in US, 63. *Collection:* German expressionism; oceanic and pre-Columbian collections; other primitive sculpture; twentieth century painting and sculpture. *Mailing Add:* 12 Brentmoor Park St Louis MO 63105

MAY, WILLIAM L
COLLECTOR
b La Grange, Ga, Apr 4, 13. *Study:* Columbia Univ, BS; Spencer Bus Col, art hist with Robert E Day. *Pos:* Prof photog participation, New York, 45-48; bd dirs, La Interior Design Inst, 69. *Awards:* Int Patron Art, Boston Mus Fine Arts, 69. *Collection:* Graphic prints by old masters; works by contemporary artists; oils, watercolors, gouache, polymer, including works by Moore, Rockmore. *Publ:* Auth, A businessman looks at art, Register, 68; auth, brochures for artists & galleries, New Orleans, La, 68. *Mailing Add:* 5034 Whitehaven Baton Rouge LA 70808

MAYEN, PAUL
DESIGNER
b La Linea, Spain, May 31, 18. *Study:* Cooper Union Art Sch; Art Students League; Columbia Univ; New Sch Social Res. *Work:* Mus Mod Art. *Exhib:* Brooklyn Mus; Mus Mod Art; Nelson Gallery Art; Ann Adver Art. *Pos:* Design consult, var indust orgns; bk designer, leading publ, ads, booklets & others; art dir, Agfa, Inc, Orradio & NAm Philips Co; design coordr, Cadre Industs & Habitat, Inc; designer for exhibs, US Info Agency; staff designer, Intrex, Inc; furniture designer, Archit Suppl Inc; designer, Visitor Ctr, Fallingwater House. *Teaching:* Instr advert design, Cooper Union Art Sch; former instr advert design, Parsons Sch, New York. *Awards:* Art Dirs Club Award, NY; and others. *Publ:* Contribr, Indust Design, Interiors, Progressive Archit, Art News Ann, Progressive Archit & others. *Mailing Add:* 61 Cedar Rd Cresskill NJ 07626

MAYER, BENA FRANK
PAINTER
b Norfolk, Va, May 31, 1900. *Study:* Cooper Union; Hunter Col; Art Students League; portrait painting with Cecelia Beaux; also with George Luks & Kenneth Hayes Miller. *Work:* Norfolk Mus Arts & Sci, Va; Whitney Mus Am Art, New York; Butler Inst Am Art; also pvt collections of Mrs Charles Love, Rochester, NY & Mrs David Levy, New York; and others. *Comn:* Portraits, comn by Mrs Edward Rohr, Norfolk, 24, World Med Asn, New York, 59, Dr Nachtigall, New York, 59, Dr William M Hitzig, New York, 70 & Katharine Trenchard, New York, 70; and others. *Exhib:* New York Soc Women Artists Ann, 47-; Nat Asn Women Artists Ann, 50-; Am Soc Contemp Artists Ann, 50-; New York Watercolor Soc, 53; one-person show, Simon's Rock Col, Great Barrington, Mass, 73. *Pos:* Admin asst, Artists Tech Res Inst, 59- *Teaching:* Pvt lessons. *Awards:* Silver & Bronze Medals for Drawing, Cooper Union Art Sch, 1920; Marcia Brady Tucker Prize, 51 & Lena Newcastle Prize,

59, Nat Asn Women Artists. *Bibliog:* Ann Geracimos (auth), An odessey for art, New York World Telegram, 61; J Harvey Rosenthal (auth), article, Travel in Fashion, spring 59; Bena Frank Mayer--The art of life, Am Artist Mag, 5/82. *Mem:* Am Soc Contemp Artists; Nat Asn Women Artists; New York Soc Women Artists (pres, 52-53); Artists Equity Asn. *Media:* Oil, Watercolor. *Mailing Add:* 207 W 106th St New York NY 10025

MAYER, EDWARD ALBERT
EDUCATOR, SCULPTOR
b Union, NJ, Oct 30, 42. *Study:* Brown Univ, Providence, RI, BA, 64; Univ Wis, Madison, MFA, 66. *Work:* Milwaukee Art Mus, Wis; Huntington Galleries, WVa; Rose Art Mus, Waltham, Mass; Ohio State Univ. *Comn:* Ohio Bldg Authority, Columbus, 74. *Exhib:* One-man shows, Kunsthalle Darmstadt, WGer, 78, Nassau Co Mus Fine Art, Roslyn, NY, 80 & Rose Art Mus, Waltham, Mass, 81; Architectural Sculpture, Los Angeles Inst Contemp Art, Calif, 80; Five Ohio Sculptors, Contemp Art Ctr, Cincinnati, 80; Columbus Mus, 82; Akron Art Mus, 83; and others. *Teaching:* Asst prof art, Carthage Col, Kenosha, Wis, 66-70; prof sculpture, Ohio Univ, Athens, 70-83; vis sculptor, Tyler Sch Art, Rome, Italy, 73-74; prof sculpture, State Univ NY, Albany, 83- *Awards:* Regional Fel, Nat Endowment Arts, 78; Fel, Ohio Arts Coun, 78, 79 & 81; Nat Fel, Nat Endowment Arts, 79. *Bibliog:* Ronald J Onorato (auth), review, Artforum, 12/78; Deborah Perlberg (auth), review, Artforum, 1/79. *Mem:* Col Art Asn. *Dealer:* Zabriskie Gallery 724 Fifth Ave New York NY 10019. *Mailing Add:* 46 Hawthorne Ave Delmar NY 12054

MAYER, GRACE M
CURATOR, COLLECTOR
b New York, NY. *Study:* Pvt schs & tutors, US & abroad. *Collections Arranged:* Currier & Ives & the New York Scene, 39, Philip Hone's New York, 40, New York Between Two Wars, 44, Stranger in Manhattan, 50, Charles Dana Gibson's New York, 50 & Currier & Ives Printmakers to the American People, 57-58, Mus of City of New York; 70 Photographers Look at New York (with Edward Steichen), 57-58, The Sense of Abstraction, 60, Steichen, The Photographer, 61 & others, Mus Mod Art, New York. *Pos:* Cur, New York Iconography, Mus of City of New York, 31-59; spec asst to dir dept photog, Mus Mod Art, New York, 59-60, assoc cur dept photog, 61-62, cur dept photog, 62-68, cur, Edward Steichen Arch, Dept Photog, Mus Mod Art, 68-72, vol cur, 72- *Mem:* Print Coun Am (treas); resident mem Cosmopolitan Club New York. *Res:* New York subjects; history of photography. *Collection:* Posters and lithographs and autographed letter signed Toulouse-Lautrec; photographs, especially those of Edward Steichen; books on photography. *Publ:* Auth articles, Mus of City of New York Bulletin, Mus Mod Art Bulletin & var photog mags; auth, Once Upon a City, Macmillan, 58. *Mailing Add:* 35 E 76th St New York NY 10021

MAYER, ROSEMARY
SCULPTOR, GRAPHIC ARTIST
b Ridgewood, NY, Feb 27, 43. *Study:* State Univ Iowa, Iowa City, AB, 64; Brooklyn Mus Art Sch, 65-67; Sch of Visual Arts, New York, 67-69. *Work:* Sidney Lewis Collection, Richmond, Va; Herbert Johnson Mus, Cornell Univ, Ithaca, NY; Allen Mem Art Mus, Oberlin Col, Ohio; Hartwick Col Collection, Oneonta, NY. *Comn:* Spell (temp outdoor work with weather balloons), Queens Coun Arts & Greater Jamaica Develop Coun, 77; Balloon, Rose Hill Property Assoc, New York, 78; plans for Orfeo, Soho Baroque Opera Co, New York, 82. *Exhib:* One-person show, Whitney Mus Am Art Resources Ctr, New York, 75, 55 Mercer St, New York, 79, Cornell Univ, 80 & Locrian Mode, Interart Ctr, NY, 80; Times Square Show, 80; Moontent (outdoor installation), Lansing, NY, 82; and others. *Pos:* Art writer & reviewer, Arts Mag, 71-73 & Art in Am, 74-75. *Teaching:* Visiting artist painting, Art Inst Chicago, 74; vis artist painting & drawing, Hartwick Col, Oneonta, 76; Artist's Workshop Program, Nat Endowment Arts, 81- *Awards:* Creative Artists Pub Serv Grant, NY State Coun Arts, 76-77, 80-81 & 82; Nat Endowment Arts Grant, 79-80. *Bibliog:* Bruce Kurtz (auth), Rosemary Mayer, Art Am, 3-4/77; Valentin Tatransky (auth), Rosemary Mayer, Arts Mag, 4/78; Ballerini & Milazzo (eds), Pontormo's Diary/Rosemary Mayer; and others. *Media:* Fabric, Metal Screening; Watercolor, Pencil. *Publ:* Contribr, Spell, White Walls, Vol 1, No 2, 79; contribr, Those, White Walls, winter 80; auth, Pontormo's Diary, Out of London Press, 82; auth, Moontent, White Walls, winter 83; auth, Beauty and Critique, TSL Ltd, 83. *Mailing Add:* 55 Leonard St New York NY 10013

MAYER, SONDRA
PRINTMAKER, WRITER
b New York, NY, July 12, 33. *Study:* Syracuse Univ, BA, 51; Columbia Univ, MA, 55; Mus Mod Art, 57-58; Pratt Inst, 68; Art Students League, 72. *Work:* Los Angeles Co Mus Art, Los Angeles; Syracuse Univ Lowe Gallery, NY; MacDowell Colony Collection, Peterborough, NH; Portland Art Mus, Ore; Crocker Nat Bank, San Francisco, Calif. *Comn:* Greeting card design, Mus Mod Art, New York, 76 & 78; design for Star & Snowflake Jewelry, Metrop Mus Art, New York 77 & 81; greeting card design, UNICEF, 79 & 81. *Exhib:* Philadelphia Print Club, Widener Mus, Rutgers Univ, 79 & 81; Boston Printmakers Ann, DeCordova Mus, Lincoln, Mass, 79; Current Works, Everson Mus, Syracuse, NY, 80; Heckscher Mus, Huntington, NY, 79-82; Int Miniature Show, Seoul, Korea, 80; Queens Mus, 81; and others. *Teaching:* Instr printmaking, Ruth Leaf Studio, Douglaston, NY, 76- *Awards:* MacDowell Colony fel, Peterborough, NH, 78; Leila Sawyer Mem Prize in Graphics, Nat Asn Women Artists, 79; Graphics Award, Firehouse Gallery, Garden City, New York, 81. *Mem:* Artists Equity New York; Philadelphia Print Club; Pratt Graphics Fellows. *Media:* Etching, Intaglio. *Publ:* Illusr, Intaglio Printmaking Techniques, Watson-Guptill, 76; contribr, Graphis Ann, Graphis Press, 78-79; and others. *Mailing Add:* 6 Wooley Lane Great Neck NY 11023

MAYER, SUSAN MARTIN
EDUCATOR, MUSEOLOGIST
b Atlanta, Ga, Oct 25, 31. *Study:* Am Univ; Univ NC, BA(art); Univ Del; Ariz State Univ, MA(art educ); Atelier Grande Chaumier, Paris; Kans State Univ. *Teaching:* Mus educ, Univ Tex Art Mus, 70- *Awards:* Museum Educators Award, Nat Art Educ Asn, 83. *Mem:* Nat Art Educ Asn; Tex Art Educ Asn; Tex Asn Mus. *Media:* Oil. *Publ:* Auth, What about museums?, Art Educ, 74; coauth, What is a Hologram, 76 & Robert Indiana: An American Artist, 76, Univ Tex Art Mus; coauth (with B Reese), A Woman's Place, 77, American Images, 81 & Texas, 83; Art to Heart Talk (film). *Mailing Add:* 4816 Rollingwood Dr Austin TX 78746

MAYES, ELAINE
PHOTOGRAPHER, FILMMAKER
b Berkeley, Calif, Oct 1, 38. *Study:* Stanford Univ, BA, 59; San Francisco Art Inst, with Paul Hassel, John Collier & Minor White. *Work:* San Francisco Art Inst; Mus Mod Art & Metrop Mus Art, New York; Minneapolis Inst Arts, Minn; Oakland Mus, Calif; and many others. *Exhib:* Women Artists Ann, San Francisco Mus Art, 64 & 65; Collection of Portraits, doc exhib, Mass Inst Technol, 69; New Acquisitions, Mus Mod Art, New York, 70 & Photographs of Women, 71; Landscape-Cityscape, Metrop Mus Art, New York, 74; 50 Photographs, Pratt Inst, 76 & Fac Exhib, 79; Photog & Landscape, George Eastman House, Rochester, NY, 77; Baltimore Mus Art, Md, 77; Photographs from Collection of Sam Wagstaff, Corcoran Gallery Art, DC, Grey Gallery, NY Univ, St Louis Mus, Mo, Seattle Mus Art, Wash & Berkeley Mus Art, Calif, 78-79; plus many others. *Teaching:* Instr photog & filmmaking, Univ Minn, 68-70; assoc prof film & photog, Hampshire Col, 71-81; assoc prof photog & film, Bard Col, 82- *Mem:* Soc Photog Educ; Col Art Asn. *Media:* Photography; Film. *Publ:* Auth, Portfolio, Aperture, Vol 15, No 2, 70; auth, A Portfolio of Photographs, Popular Photog Ann, 75-76; auth, chap, In: Darkroom, Lustrum Press, New York, 77; contribr, Faces: A History of Photographic Portraiture, Chanticleer Press, New York, 77; contribr, A Book of Photographs, by Sam Wagstaff, New York, 78; and others. *Mailing Add:* 18 Mercer St New York NY 10013

MAYES, STEVEN LEE
ADMINISTRATOR, PRINTMAKER
b Los Angeles, Calif, Nov 7, 39. *Study:* Wichita State Univ, BFA & BAE, 62, MFA, 65. *Work:* SDak Mem Art Ctr, Brookings; Sioux City Art Ctr, Iowa; Wichita Art Mus, Kans; Tamarind Inst, Univ NMex, Albuquerque; Univ NDak, Grand Forks. *Exhib:* 13th Midwest Biennial, Joslyn Mus, Omaha, Nebr, 72; Fourth Nat Print & Drawing Exhib, Minot State Col, NDak, 74; 12th Ann Paper Works, Waterloo Munic Galleries, Iowa, 76; Amarillo Art Ctr, Tex, 79 & 81; Catskill Ctr Photography, Woodstock, New York, 81; and many others. *Collections Arranged:* Portraits and Self-Portraits, Civic Fine Arts Ctr, Sioux Falls, SD, 74; The Artist-Teacher, Sioux City Art Ctr, Iowa, 75. *Teaching:* Assoc prof printmaking & drawing, SDak State Univ, Brookings, 71-77; prof printmaking & design & head art dept, WTex State Univ, Canyon, 77- *Awards:* Purchase Awards, Fifth NDak Ann, Univ NDak, 61, 33rd & 35th Ann Fall Show, Sioux City Art Ctr, Iowa, 71 & 73. *Media:* Multimedia. *Mailing Add:* Dept of Art West Tex State Univ Canyon TX 79016

MAYHEW, EDGAR DE NOAILLES
EDUCATOR, MUSEUM DIRECTOR
b Newark, NJ, Oct 1, 13. *Study:* Amherst Col, BA, 35; Yale Univ, MA, 39; Johns Hopkins Univ, 39-41, PhD(Carnegie Fel), 41. *Collections Arranged:* Contents of Lyman Allyn Mus, check list published. *Pos:* Dir, Lyman Allyn Mus, New London, 50- *Teaching:* Instr art hist, Wellesley Col, Mass, 44-45; prof art hist, Conn Col, New London, 45- *Awards:* Am Philos Soc Grant for Res, 68. *Mem:* New London Co Hist Soc (bd mem, 60-); Conn Antiqn & Landmarks Soc (furnishings chmn, 60-); plus many hist soc & preserv groups. *Collection:* Approximately one hundred Old Masters drawings. *Publ:* Co-auth, The Book of the Courtier, 58; auth, Sketches by Thornhill in the Victoria & Albert Museum, 67; A Documentary History of the American Interior, 80. *Mailing Add:* 613 Williams St New London CT 06320

MAYHEW, ELZA
SCULPTOR
b Victoria, BC. *Study:* Univ BC, Can, BA; Univ Ore, MFA; also with Jan Zach, Victoria, BC. *Work:* Univ Victoria; Art Gallery Gtr Victoria; Nat Gallery Can, Ottawa; Simon Fraser Univ, Vancouver; Meditation Ctr, Expo, Montreal. *Comn:* Bronze column, Victoria Arch & Mus, BC, 67; Coast Spirit (bronze), Univ Victoria, 67; bronze mural, Bank Can Lobby, Vancouver, 68; Concordia (bronze column), Brock Univ, Ont, 68; Column of the Sea, Confederation Ctr, Charlottetown, 73. *Exhib:* Outdoor Sculpture, Quebec, 60; Contemporary Sculpture Show, Ottawa, 62; Canadian Pavilion, Venice Biennale, 64; Sculpture Today, Dorothy Cameron Gallery, Toronto, 65; Int Trade Fair, Tokyo, 65. *Pos:* Bd dirs, Nat Sculpture Ctr, Univ Kans, 68-79; BC Govt Comt for Art, 74. *Awards:* Sir Otto Beit Medal, Royal Soc Brit Sculptors, 62; Purchase Award, BC Centennial Sculpture Exhib, 67. *Bibliog:* Tony Emery (auth), Elza Mayhew, Arts Can, Vol XX, No 4; Robin Skelton (auth), A language for humanity, 4/71 & Karl Soreitz (auth), Making of the Column of the Sea, 72, Malahat Rev, Univ Victoria Quart. *Mem:* Sculptors Soc Can, BC; Royal Can Acad Arts. *Mailing Add:* 330 St Lawrence St Victoria BC V8V 1Y4 Canada

MAYHEW, RICHARD
PAINTER
b Amityville, NY, Apr 3, 34. *Study:* Art Students League; Brooklyn Mus Art Sch, with Edwin Dickinson & Reuben Tam, 48. *Work:* Whitney Mus Am Art; Newark Mus; Brooklyn Mus; Mus Mod Art; Nat Acad Design; and many others. *Exhib:* Butler Art Inst, Youngstown, Ohio, 61; Brooklyn Mus, 61; Whitney Mus Am Art Ann; Univ Ill, 63; retrospective, Studio Mus, New York, 78; one-man shows, San Jose Mus Art, 80, Young Gallery, San Jose, 83 & Pa State Univ Mus, 83; Midtown Galleries, New York, 82. *Teaching:* Instr art, Brooklyn Mus Art Sch, 63-68 & Art Students League, 65-71; instr, Smith Col, 69-70; asst prof, Hunter Col, 71-75; prof, Pa State Univ, 77- *Awards:* Benjamin Altman Award, Nat Acad Design, 70; Merit Award, Nat Acad Design, 77; Grumbacher Gold Medal, Nat Acad Design, 83. *Mem:* Nat Acad Design; MacDowell Colony Asn. *Dealer:* Midtown Galleries 11 E 57th St New York NY 10022; Young Gallery 140 W San Carlos San Jose CA 95113. *Mailing Add:* 102 Visual Art Bldg University Park PA 16802

MAYNARD, WILLIAM
PAINTER, EDUCATOR
b Brookline, Mass, Dec 31, 21. *Study:* Mass Col Art; Sch Mus Fine Arts, Boston, dipl, 50. *Work:* Boston Mus Fine Arts; Springfield Mus Fine Arts, Mass; Fairleigh Dickinson Univ; Fitchburg Mus Fine Arts, Mass. *Exhib:* Shore Studio Galleries, Charles Childs Gallery & Vose Gallery, Boston; De Cordova Mus, Lincoln, Mass; Busche Reisinger Mus, Cambridge, Mass. *Teaching:* Instr drawing & painting, Boston Mus Fine Arts, 60-67, instr painting, currently; chmn dept fine arts, New Eng Sch Art & Design, 74- *Mem:* Boston Watercolor Soc; Provincetown Art Asn; Copley Soc; Brookline Soc Artists. *Media:* Watercolor, Acrylic. *Mailing Add:* 223 Freeman St Brookline MA 02146

MAYO, MARGARET ELLEN
CURATOR
b Charlottesville, Va, May 18, 44. *Study:* Randolph-Macon Womans Col, AB, 66; Rutgers Univ, PhD, 73. *Collections Arranged:* Ancient Portraiture: The Sculptor's Art in Coins and Marble, 80 & The Art of South Italy: Vases From Magna Graecia (auth, catalog), 82, Va Mus; Wealth of the Ancient World: The Nelson Bunker Hunt and William Herbert Hunt Collections (coauth, catalog), 83. *Pos:* Res assoc, Iconographical Lexicon, Rutgers Univ, 73-76; dir, Summa Galleries, Beverly Hills, 76-78; cur, Ancient Art, Va Mus, 78- *Mem:* Archaeol Inst Am; Soc Promotion Hellenic Studies. *Res:* Greek art; Greek and south Italian vase-painting. *Mailing Add:* Va Mus Boulevard & Grove Ave Richmond VA 23221

MAYO, MARTI
CURATOR, HISTORIAN
b Bluefield, WVa, Oct 17, 45. *Study:* Am Univ, BA, 70, MFA, 74. *Collections Arranged:* Vernon Fisher Story Paintings & Drawings (auth, catalog), 80; The New Photography (auth, catalog), 80; Placements and Performances: Works for Washington, 80; Other Realities: Installations for Performance (auth, catalog), 81; 4 Painters: Jones, Smith, Stack, Utterback (auth, catalog), 81; Robert Morris: Selected Works 1970-1980 (auth, catalog), 81; Paintings by Pat Steir (auth, catalog), 83; Michael Tracy: Requiem Para Los Olvidados (auth, catalog), 83; Southern Fictions, 83. *Pos:* Coordr exhib, Corcoran Gallery Art, DC, 74-80; cur, Contemp Arts Mus, Houston, 80- *Mem:* Am Asn Mus; Col Art Asn. *Mailing Add:* Contemp Arts Mus 5216 Montrose Blvd Houston TX 77006

MAYO, ROBERT BOWERS
DEALER
b Phoenixville, Pa, Apr 26, 33. *Study:* Art Students League, 49; Chicago Art Inst, 51; Richmond Prof Inst (Va Commonwealth Univ), BA, 59. *Collections Arranged:* Thomas Sully & His Contemporaries (auth, catalog), 78; Mrs Susan Waters, 19th Century Itinerant Painter (auth, catalog), 81; American Paintings from Virginia Collectors (auth, catalog), 81. *Pos:* Cur, Jamestown Festival Park, Va, 59-61; exhibs designer, Hall Hist, Raleigh, NC, 61-66; dir, Valentine Mus, Richmond, 66-75; owner, Gallery Mayo Inc, Richmond, presently. *Teaching:* Guest lectr, NY Hist Soc, Cooperstown, summer 72; guest lectr, Longwood Col, Farmville, Va, 79. *Mem:* Am Asn Mus (nat coun, 73-77); SEastern Mus Conf Inc (pres, 74); Am Soc Appraisers; Va Mus Fedn (pres, 72-73); Antiquarian Soc Richmond (pres, 74-75). *Specialty:* American and European paintings, 18th, 19th and early 20th century. *Publ:* Auth, Exhibit techniques for small museums, Mus News, 73; auth, Painting collection of the Valentine Museum, Mag Antiques, 73. *Mailing Add:* 5705 Grove Ave Richmond VA 23226

MAYORGA, GABRIEL HUMBERTO
PAINTER, SCULPTOR
b Colombia, SAm, Mar 24, 11; US citizen. *Study:* Nat Acad Design, painting with Leon Kroll & Ivan Olinsky, etching with Aerobach-Levi & sculpture with Robert Aikin; Art Students League, with Brackman; Grand Cent Art Sch, New York, with Harvey Dunn. *Work:* Inst Ingenieros, Bogota, Colombia, 37; Art Gallery of Barbizon-Plaza, New York, 55; West Point Mus, NY. *Comn:* Many painting & portrait comns, 55- *Exhib:* Inst Ingenieros, Bogota, Colombia, 37; Art Gallery of Barbizon Plaza, New York, 55; Mayorga Art Gallery, 60; Int Expos, Paris, 62; Int Art Show, New York, 70. *Pos:* Art dir & illusr, Revista Estrellas, Bogota, 37-38 & Mannequins by Mayorga Inc, New York, 40-65; art dir & illusr, Revista Temas, 53-54. *Teaching:* Instr painting & fashion, Pan-Am Art Sch, New York, 60-72. *Bibliog:* Morton Cooper (auth), How to be an artist & still eat, Art & Photog, 57 & Gabriel Mayorga, New York angry artist, Figure, 60; J Rothschild (auth), Artists create with plastics, By Gum, 70. *Media:* Oil, Watercolor; Epoxy Plastic, Polyester Plastic. *Publ:* Illusr, Theory & Practice of Fencing, 37; illusr, Popular Publ, 38; illusr, Don Mag. *Mailing Add:* Mayorga Art Gallery 331 W 11th St New York NY 10014

MAYRS, DAVID BLAIR
PAINTER, EDUCATOR
b Winnipeg, Man, May 2, 35. *Study:* Vancouver Sch Art, dipl(hon), 57. *Work:* Vancouver Art Gallery; London Pub Libr & Art Mus, Ont; Etherington Art Ctr. *Exhib:* New Talent Show, Vancouver Art Gallery, 64; Young Contemporaries, London Art Mus, Ont, 65; Canadian Group of Painters, Montreal Mus Fine Art, 67; Nat Gallery Can Bi-Ann, 68; Young Vancouver Artists, Victoria Art Gallery, 68; H Marc Moyens Collection, Corcoran Gallery Art, 69; West Coast Artists, Sadie F Bronfman Ctr, Montreal, 75; BC Artists, Vancouver Art Gallery, 83. *Teaching:* Instr painting & silkscreen, Emily Carr Col Art, Vancouver, 67- *Awards:* Purchase Award, Burnaby Art Gallery Print Show, 71. *Media:* Acrylic. *Mailing Add:* c/o Bau-Xi Gallery 3045 Granville St Vancouver BC V6H 3J9 Canada

MAYS, VICTOR
PAINTER, ILLUSTRATOR
b New York, NY, July 2, 27. *Study:* Yale Univ, BA, 49. *Work:* De Grummond Collection of Children's Book Illus, Univ Southern Miss; Kerlan Collection, Univ Minn; Peabody Mus, Salem, Mass. *Comn:* Illus for children's bks, major US publ, 55- *Exhib:* Nat Oceans Week Exhib, Washington, DC, 78; Am Soc Marine Artists Ann Exhibs, 78-82; Mystic Seaport, Conn, 79-82; Peabody Mus, 81. *Awards:* Best in Show, 80, First & Second Prize Watercolor, 81 & Best in Show, 83, Mystic Int Marine Art Exhib, Mystic Seaport, Conn. *Mem:* Fel, Am Soc Marine Artists (vpres). *Media:* Watercolor, Wood; Casein. *Publ:* Auth & illusr, Fast Iron, 53, Action Starboard, 55, Dead Reckoning, 65. *Dealer:* Annapolis Marine Art Gallery Annapolis MD 21401; Ragged Sailor Block Island RI 02807. *Mailing Add:* Box 207 Clinton CT 06413

MAYTHAM, THOMAS NORTHRUP
MUSEUM DIRECTOR, LECTURER
b Buffalo, NY, July 30, 31. *Study:* William Col, BA, 54; Yale Univ, MA, 56. *Collections Arranged:* Ernst Ludwig Kirchner Retrospective (148 works), Seattle Art Mus, Pasadena Art Mus & Boston Mus, 68-69; Great American Paintings from the Boston & Metropolitan Museum (100 paintings, with catalog), Nat Gallery Art, City Art Mus St Louis & Seattle Art Mus, 70-71; and others. *Pos:* Asst, Wadsworth Atheneum, summer 55; res asst, Prof Carroll L V Meeks, Yale Univ, summer 56; asst in dept paintings, Mus Fine Arts, Boston, 56-57; head dept paintings, Boston Mus, 57-67, asst cur paintings, 67; assoc dir, Seattle Art Mus, 67-74; dir, Denver Art Mus, 74-82. *Teaching:* Lectr, mus, clubs, groups & art asns, Boston & Seattle areas. *Mem:* Am Fedn Art; Am Asn Mus; Asn Art Mus Dir; Int Exhib Found. *Publ:* Auth articles in Boston Mus Bulletin, Antiques & Can Art; ed, American Painting in the Boston Museum (catalog), Vols I & II, 68; auth, TV Prog for Nat Educ TV, produced by Boston Mus. *Mailing Add:* 2317 S Jackson Denver CO 80210

MAZUR, MICHAEL
PAINTER, PRINTMAKER
b New York, NY, Nov 2, 35. *Study:* Amherst Col, BA, 58, with Leonard Baskin; Yale Univ Sch Art & Archit, BFA, 59 & MFA, 61, with Gabor Peterdi & Bernard Chaet. *Work:* Mus Mod Art, New York; Boston Mus Fine Arts; Fogg Art Mus, Harvard Univ; Art Inst Chicago; Libr Congress, Washington DC; and others. *Comn:* Painting of Wassaw & Ossabaw Islands, Dept of Interior Bicentennial Exhib, 75-76. *Exhib:* Painters & Sculptors as Printmakers, Mus Mod Art, 64; Nine American Printmakers, US Info Serv Agency Traveling Exhib in Europe, 64; Young Americans, Whitney Mus Am Art, 65; Two Painters on Two Aspects of Illusion, Finch Col Mus, 71; American Landscape for Bicentennial, Corcoran Gallery, 76; Am Monotype, Phillips Collection, 79; The Painterly Print, Metrop Mus Art, 80. *Pos:* Bd mem, Mass Coun on Arts & Humanities. *Teaching:* Instr prints & drawing, RI Sch Design, 61-64; asst prof prints & drawing, Brandeis Univ, 65-76; vis artist, Yale Sch Art & Archit, 71 & Harvard Univ, 76-78. *Awards:* Louis Comfort Tiffany Grant, 62; Nat Inst Arts & Lett Award, 64; Guggenheim Fel, 65. *Bibliog:* J Canaday (auth), rev in New York Times, 65, 66, 68 & 77; C Belz (auth), Mazur at ICA, Art Forum, 9/70; Franklyn Robinson (auth), Michael Mazur--The Vision of a Draughtsman (catalog), Brockton Art Mus, Montreal Mus Fine Arts; Grace Glueck (auth), article, New York Times, 81. *Mem:* Boston Visual Artists Union. *Publ:* Auth, Prints by M Mazur, Artist Proof, 70; auth, The Monoprints of Naum Gabo, Print Collections Newsletter; and others. *Dealer:* Barbara Krakan Gallery Boston MA 02116; Barbara Maches Gallery 851 Madison Ave New York NY 10021. *Mailing Add:* 5 Walnut Ave Cambridge MA 02140

MAZZE, IRVING
SCULPTOR, MEDALIST
b New York, NY. *Study:* With Beth Benton, 72 & Hermann Gass & Richard Hahn, 77. *Work:* Residenz Mus Munzsammlung, Munich; Cabinet Medailles, Bibliot Nat, Paris; Proust Mus, France. *Comn:* Citrine portrait, comn by Alice Whitfield, New York, 74; moonstone portrait, comn by Louise Benton, Chicago, 75; moonstone portrait Marcel Proust, comn by Mr & Mrs Milton Stern, Long Island, 75; crystal engraving, comn by James Van Aken, New York, 83; topaz engraving, comn by John Sinkankas for Smithsonian Inst, 84. *Exhib:* Fedn Int Medaille, Palazzo Ricardi, Florence, Italy, 83; Am Medallic Sculpture Asn Traveling Exhib, Am Numismatic Soc, New York, 83 & Denver, 84 & US Mint, San Francisco, 84. *Pos:* Consult engraved gemstones, Dept Mineralogy, Am Mus Natural Hist, 79- *Bibliog:* Beverly Philip Mazze (auth), The making of a gem engraver, Lapidary J, 6/73. *Mem:* Am Medallic Sculpture Asn; Royal Soc Arts. *Media:* Gemstone. *Mailing Add:* 7 W 45 St New York NY 10036

MAZZOCCA, GUS (AUGUSTUS NICHOLAS MAZZOCCA)
PRINTMAKER, EDUCATOR
b Boston, Mass, Jan 2, 40. *Study:* Univ Conn, BA, 64, BFA, 65; RI Sch of Design MFA, 70. *Work:* Mus Mod Art, Munich; City Hartford Fine Arts Collection. *Exhib:* Parish Art Mus, Southampton, NY, 67; RI Col, Providence, 69; Mus of RI Sch of Design, Providence, 70; New Talent, New Eng, De Cordova Mus, Lincoln, Mass, 72; Conn Col, New London, 74. *Teaching:* Art teacher, Riverhead Cent Sch Dist, NY, 65-68; instr, RI Sch of Design, Providence, 70; assoc prof lithography & drawing, Univ Conn, Storrs, 70- *Awards:* Purchase Award, Hartford Fine Art Festival, Conn, 70; Conn Artists, Slater Mus, Norwich, 73. *Mem:* Graphic Arts Tech Found, Pittsburgh. *Media:* Charcoal, Pastel. *Mailing Add:* 333 Prospect St Willimantic CT 06226

MAZZONE, DOMENICO
SCULPTOR, PAINTER
b Rutigliano, Italy, May 16, 27. *Work:* Vatican Collection, Italy; John F Kennedy Ctr Performing Arts, Washington, DC; UNESCO Collection, Paris, France; Westchester Mus, NY; United Nations Bldg, New York; and others. *Comn:* Medallion for Peace (gold bas relief), US Govt, 80. *Exhib:* Nat Exhib Marble, Carrara, Italy, 62; Nat Exhib, San Remo, Italy, 63; Int Exhib Metal, Gubbio, Italy, 65; Exhib Tree State, Silvermine Conn, 66; Ital Club Exhib, UN Bldg, 67. *Awards:* Gold Medal, Accad Italia, Salsomaggiore Terme, 81; Asn Cult Artistica Vadese, 82; Gold Medal & Dipl, Accad Italia Ctr Rodino, Naples, Italy, 83; and others. *Bibliog:* Articles, Art West, 82, Communita Viva, 83 & La Folia di New York, 83; and many others. *Mailing Add:* 44 Lembeck Ave Jersey City NJ 07305

MEADER, JONATHAN GRANT See Ascian

MEAD-LOPEZ, BEATRIZ See Lopez, Bea

MEADMORE, CLEMENT L
SCULPTOR
b Melbourne, Australia, Feb 9, 29. *Study:* Royal Melbourne Inst Technol. *Work:* Art Inst Chicago; Nat Gallery Australia; J B Speed Mus, Ky; Atlantic Richfield Collection; Chase Manhattan Bank Collection; and others. *Comn:* Large outdoor sculptures, Australian Mutual Provident Soc, 68, Mexico City, 68, Columbia Univ, 68, NY State, Albany, 71 & Princeton Univ, 71. *Exhib:* Guggenheim Mus, 67; Aldrich Mus, Ridgefield, Conn, 68; Rockefeller Collection, Mus Mod Art, 69 & Whitney Mus Am Art Ann, 69, New York; J B Speed Mus, 80; Columbus Mus Art, 80; Albuquerque Mus, 81; Davenport Art Gallery, 81; Amarillo Art Ctr, 81; Princeton Univ, 83; and many others. *Pos:* Instr, Studio Sch, 77-80, State Univ NY, Purchase, 83. *Bibliog:* Hughes (auth), article in Time Mag, 4/71; Segal (auth), Clement Meadmore: circling the square, Art News, 2/72; H H Arnason (auth), History of Modern Art, Prentice-Hall, 77. *Mem:* Archit League New York. *Media:* Steel, Bronze. *Mailing Add:* Deer Hill Lane Briarcliff Manor NY 10510

MEADOWS, P B (PATRICIA B)
ADMINISTRATOR, PAINTER
b Amarillo, Tex, Nov 12, 38. *Study:* Univ Tex, BA, 60; studied with Ramon Froman, 76-80, William Henry Earle, Victor Armstrong, Julius Zsohar, Joe Dawley, Ann cushing Gantz & Dorothy Barta. *Work:* Harlingen Court House, Tex; State Bar Tex Hq, Austin; Univ Tex Health Sci Ctr, Tyler. *Collections Arranged:* Presenting Nine (auth, catalog), 84. *Pos:* Co-founder, ed newsletter & prog dir, D-Art Visual Art Ctr, Dallas, 81-, pres bd dirs, 82- *Mem:* Artists & Craftsmen Asn (vpres bd dirs, 81-82, pres bd dirs, 82-83); Tex Fine Arts Asn; Pastel Soc Southwest. *Mailing Add:* 2917 Swiss Ave Dallas TX 75204

MECKLENBURG, VIRGINIA MCCORD
CURATOR, LECTURER
b Dallas, Tex, Nov 11, 46. *Study:* Univ Tex, Austin, BA, 68, MA, 70; Univ Md, College Park, PhD, 80. *Collections Arranged:* John R Grabach, Seventy Years an Artist (auth, catalog), 80; Across the Nation: Fine Art for Federal Buildings, 72-79 (auth, catalog), 80; Roosevelt's America: New Deal Paintings from Nat Mus Am Art (auth, catalog), 82; Jose de Creeft: Sculpture and Drawings (auth, catalog), 83. *Pos:* Assoc cur 20th century painting & sculpture, Nat Mus Am Art, 79- *Teaching:* Instr Am art, Univ Md, 79. *Mem:* Col Art Asn; Am Asn Mus; Am Asn Univ Women. *Res:* American art of the 20th century; New Deal art; theory and criticism; public art. *Publ:* Auth, The Public as Patron, A History of the Treasury Department Murals, Univ Md Art Gallery, 79; contribr, Recent Trends in Collecting: 20th Century Painting, Sculpture from National Museum American Art, 82 & Franklin D Roosevelt: The Intimate Presidency (catalog), 82, Smithsonian Press. *Mailing Add:* 8217 Larry Pl Chevy Chase MD 20815

MEDEARIS, ROGER
PAINTER, LITHOGRAPHER
b Fayette, Mo, Mar 6, 20. *Study:* Kansas City Art Inst, with Thomas Hart Benton & John S DeMartelly. *Work:* DC Munic Ct, Washington, DC; Nat Mus Am Art; Butler Inst Am Art, Youngstown, Ohio; Hunt Inst, Carnegie-Mellon Univ; San Jose Mus Art, Calif. *Comn:* Painting, Nat Recreation & Park Asn, 82. *Exhib:* American Painting Today, Metrop Mus Art, New York, 50; West Coast Exhib, Frye Art Mus, Seattle, 66; Midyear Show, 69-81 & Four American Artists, 74, Butler Inst Am Art, Youngstown, Ohio; 148th Ann, Nat Acad Design, 73; Hunt Inst 5th Int, Carnegie-Mellon Univ, 83; and others. *Bibliog:* Roger Medearis, Drawings, Desind, 81; Stephen M Doherty (auth), Roger Medearis: Turning life into art, Am Artist, 10/82; Roger Medearis, J Print World, fall 82. *Media:* Tempera, Acrylic; Graphite. *Dealer:* Capricorn Galleries 4849 Rugby Ave Bethesda MD 20014. *Mailing Add:* 2270 Melville Dr San Marino CA 91108

MEDICINE FLOWER, GRACE
POTTER
b Santa Clara Pueblo, NMex, Dec 13, 38. *Exhib:* Am Indian Show, Los Angeles; Seven Families in Pueblo Pottery, Maxwell Mus of Anthrop, Univ NMex, 74; one-person shows, Gila River Arts & Crafts Ctr, Sacaton, Ariz, 73; Gov Gallery, Santa Fe, NMex, 77; Wheelwright Mus, 79; and many others. *Awards:* First Prize, Best of Show Award & Cert of Merit, Inter-Tribal Indian Ceremonials, Gallup, 71; First Prize, Scottsdale Nat Indian Arts Exhib, Ariz, 71. *Bibliog:* TV artists film series, KAET PBS, Phoenix, Ariz, 76. *Media:* Clay. *Mailing Add:* Box 1128 Espanola NM 87532

MEDINA, ADA
DRAWER
b Carrizo Springs, Tex, June 4, 48. *Study:* Layton Sch Art & Design, BFA, 72; Univ Iowa, MA, 73, MFA, 74. *Work:* Equitable Life Assurance Soc, New York; Mint Mus Art; Springfield Art Mus, Mo; Fairweather Hardin Gallery, Chicago. *Exhib:* The Downtown Dog Show, Fine Arts Mus San Francisco, 78; Small Works Nat 81, Zaner Gallery, Rochester, NY, 81; solo exhib, WARM Gallery, Minneapolis, 82 & Artemisia Gallery, Chicago, 82; Works on Paper, Art Inst Boston, 83; Awards in the Visual Arts Two, Mus Contemp Art, Chicago, 83, Mint Mus Art, 83, DeCordova & Dana Mus, Lincoln, Mass, 83 & Equitable Gallery, New York, 84. *Teaching:* Instr drawing, Northern Ill Univ, 75-77; instr, Drake Univ, 77-79, asst prof, 79-84, assoc prof, 84- *Awards:* Fine Arts Work Ctr Fel, 77; Yaddo Fel, 78; Awards in the Visual Arts Two, 83. *Bibliog:* Margarita Donnelly (ed), illus, Calyx, 79; John Hawkes (ed), illus, Fedora, 80. *Publ:* Co-ed, Native American and Chicana-Hispanic Women's Art and Literature Issue, Calyx, 84. *Mailing Add:* 1427 25th St Des Moines IA 50311

MEDOFF, EVE
PAINTER, WRITER
b Philadelphia, Pa. *Study:* Pa Acad Fine Arts; Tyler Sch Art; Pratt Graphics Ctr. *Work:* Wagner Col for Women, Staten Island, NY; Holmes Pub Sch, Mt Vernon, NY; Gestetner Corp, Yonkers; Fellowship of Reconciliation, Nyack, NY. *Exhib:* ACA Gallery, New York, 62; Riverside Mus, New York, 65; Albany Inst Art & Hist, 66; Westchester Printmakers, Fordham Univ, 67; Katonah Gallery, NY, 72. *Pos:* Ed arts page, Yonkers Rec, 66-70; ed Artslett & Interarts, Coun Arts Westchester, 68-69; contribr, Am Artist Mag, 68- *Awards:* Hudson River Mus Purchase Awards, 57 & 70; Hon Title, Mus Assoc in Art, Hudson River Mus, 64; Gestetner Corp Print Competition Award, 71. *Media:* Oil, Acrylic; Watercolor. *Publ:* Auth, John Moore, Joseph Solman, In: 20 Oil Painters and How They Work, 78. *Mailing Add:* Apt D9 7300 Cresheim Rd Philadelphia PA 19119

MEDRICH, LIBBY E
SCULPTOR
b Hartford, Conn. *Study:* NY Univ, 31; Vassar Col, 49 & 54; Silvermine Guild Sch, 51; Art Students League, 52-55; White Plains Co Ctr, 57 & 58; also with John Hovannes, Helen Beling, Domenico Facci, George Koras & Harold Castor. *Work:* Univ Chicago; First Church Christ, Wethersfield, Conn; numerous pvt collections in US & abroad. *Exhib:* Solo shows, Ward-Nasse Gallery, New York, 77, Hastings-on-Hudson, NY, 83 & others; Am Soc Contemp Artists, World Trade Ctr, New York, 81; Women & Arts, Lincoln Ctr, 82; Audubon Artists, Nat Arts Club, 82; Silvermine Art Northeast USA, 82; Texaco Hq, Purchase, NY, 83; Metrop Mus Art, New York; and others. *Awards:* Int Women's Year Award Slide Exhib, 75-76; Am Soc Contemp Artists Sculpture Award Merit, 82; Audubon Artists Donors Sculpture Award, 82. *Bibliog:* Nina Roustayi (auth), article, ArtSpeak, 9/30/82, Virginia Jones (auth), Sculptural Forms of Selected 20th Century American Women, Tex Woman's Univ, 82; Helen Harrison (auth), article, New York Times Long Island Ed, 5/15/83. *Mem:* Artists Equity Assn New York; Mamaroneck Artists Guild (pres, 68-70); Metrop Painters & Sculptors; Am Soc Contemp Artists; Women & Arts. *Media:* Bronze, Polyester Resin. *Dealer:* Ward-Nasse Gallery 178 Prince St New York NY 10003; Mag Gallery 150 Larchmont Ave Larchmont NY 10538. *Mailing Add:* 88 Carleon Ave Larchmont NY 10538

MEEHAN, WILLIAM DALE
PAINTER, EDUCATOR
b Decatur, Ill, Oct 23, 30. *Study:* Art Inst Chicago, BFA; Bradley Univ, MA; Inst de Allende, Mex, MFA. *Work:* Ohio Univ; Bradley Univ; Evansville Mus Arts & Sci; DePauw Univ; Earlham Col. *Comn:* Mural design (with Richard Peeler & students), DePauw Univ Art Ctr, 72; Mem Sculpture to Chauncey Rose, Founder of Rose-Hulman Inst Technol for 100th Year of Sch, 75. *Exhib:* Works on Paper, Indianapolis Mus Art, 71; one-man shows, Ind Cent Col, 71 & 79, Galleria Pergola, San Miguelde Allende, Mex, 78, The Gallery, Bloomington, Ind, 79 & Indianapolis Art League, 79; and others. *Pos:* Art dir, Southwestern Press, Ft Smith, Ark, 55-56; advert designer, Caterpillar Tractor Co, Peoria, 56-60; art dir, Nichols Advert, Decatur, summer 61; design consult, DePauw Univ, 64-; design consult for several industs. *Teaching:* Instr design & drawing, Syracuse Univ, 60-64; prof art & dept chmn, DePauw Univ, 64- *Awards:* Purchase Award, Ohio Valley Oil & Watercolor Show, Athens, 59; First Prize, 22nd Ann Cent Ill Exhib, Decatur, 66; First Prize Watercolor, 62nd Ind Artists Exhib, Indianapolis, 67. *Media:* Oil, Gouache. *Mailing Add:* RR 1 Greencastle IN 46135

MEEK, A J
PHOTOGRAPHER, EDUCATOR
b Beatrice, Nebr, Aug 29, 41. *Study:* Art Ctr Col Design, Los Angeles, with Todd Walker, BFA, 70; Ohio Univ, Athens, with Arnold Gassan, MFA, 72; further study with Paul Caponigro & Oliver Gagliani; Louisiana State Univ Teaching Fel, 81. *Work:* New Orleans Mus Art, La; Chrysler Mus, Norfolk, Va; Inverness Mus & Art Gallery, Scotland & Royal Comn Ancient Monuments, Edinburgh; Aberdeen City Art Gallery, Scotland; Int Mus Photo/George Eastman House. *Exhib:* Portrait of Am, Paine Art Ctr, Smithsonian Traveling Exhib, Oshkosh, Wis, 75; Photog at Chrysler Mus, Norfolk, Va, 78; The Highlands, Inverness Mus & Art Gallery, Scotland, 79; Photog in La 1800-1980, New Orleans Mus Art, 80; Four Southeastern Photographers, Contemp Arts Ctr, New Orleans, 81; The Highlands, Aberdeen City Art Gallery, 82; and others. *Collections Arranged:* Spirit of Utah 1860-1976 (ed, catalog), Utah State Univ, 76. *Teaching:* Asst prof photog, Utah State Univ, Logan, 72-77; head photog film area, La State Univ, 77- *Awards:* Nat Endowment for Arts Exhib aid, 76. *Bibliog:* Rev of Night Creatures, 7/75 & rev of British Views, 3/78, Artweek; article in Orcadian, Kirkwall, Scotland, 11/77. *Mem:* Soc Photog Educ; Friends of Photog. *Media:* Silver Prints, Alternative Processes. *Publ:* Contribr, Exposure, J Soc for Photog Educ, 74; contribr, Combinations, J of Photog, Greenfield Ctr, NY, 79; contribr, The Highlands--Limited Edition Portfolio of Fine Prints, 80; contribr, A Chronology of Photography, 80; contrib, New Orleans, Yesterday and Today, La State Univ Press, 83; and others. *Dealer:* Gallery for Fine Photography 5423 Magazine St New Orleans LA 70115. *Mailing Add:* 1278 Sharlo Ave Baton Rouge LA 70820

MEEK, J WILLIAM, III
DEALER, CONSULTANT
b Aberdeen, Md, Nov 8, 50. *Study:* Fla Southern Col, BA, 72. *Pos:* Asst dir, Harmon Gallery, Naples, Fla, 72-77; dir-owner, Harmon-Meek Gallery, 78-; pres, Fine Art Consultants Naples, Inc, 81- *Mem:* Fel Royal Soc Arts, London. *Specialty:* Paintings, drawings and sculpture by major American artists of the 20th century. *Collection:* Private collection of 20th century American art. *Mailing Add:* c/o Harmon-Meek Gallery 1258 Third St S Naples FL 33940

MEEKER, BARBARA MILLER
EDUCATOR, PAINTER
b Peru, Ind, Dec 31, 30. *Study:* DePauw Univ, BA; also with Jack Pellow, Ray Loos, Edgar A Whitney, Claude Croney, Charles Reid, Ed Fitzgerald, Frank Webb, Millard Sheets, Robert Landry, Robert A Wood, Miles Batt, Dong Kingman & Glen Bradshaw. *Work:* DePauw Univ Art Ctr Print Collection, Greencastle, Ind; Purdue Univ, Calumet & Hammond Pub Schs, Ind; Tri-State Col, Angola, Ind; Oak Park River Forest High Sch, Ill; Lake Co Pub Libr. *Exhib:* Ft Wayne Art Mus; Lafayette Art Mus; Artists Guild Chicago Watercolor Show, Chicago & Northern Ind Art Salon, Hammond; Contemp Artists Ind, Indianapolis; Ind State Mus Invitational, Indianapolis; Ind Univ Northwest Area Fac Show, Gary; and many others. *Pos:* Mem Art Comn, Ind State House, 63-65. *Teaching:* Assoc prof freehand drawing & painting, Purdue Univ, Calumet, 65- *Awards:* Purchase & Merit Award, Ind Artists Club; Award for The Gold Pitcher (collage), Northern Ind Art Salon; Hon Mention, Outstanding Teacher Awards, Purdue Univ, Calumet, 71, 75, 76 & 81. *Bibliog:* Hawkins & McClarren (auth), Indiana lives, Hist Rec Asn, 67. *Mem:* Artists Guild Chicago; Midwest Watercolor Soc (mem bd dirs, 83-85); Ind Heritage Arts; Northern Ind Art Asn; Artists Equity Asn. *Media:* Watercolor, Collage. *Publ:* Auth, Freehand Drawing, 72, 2nd ed, 75, 3rd ed, 80. *Mailing Add:* 8314 Greenwood Ave Munster IN 46321

MEEKER, DEAN JACKSON
PRINTMAKER, PAINTER
b Orchard, Colo, May 18, 20. *Study:* Art Inst Chicago, BFA & MFA; Northwestern Univ; Univ Wis. *Work:* Boston Mus Fine Arts; Libr Cong, Washington, DC; Mus Mod Art, New York; Dallas Mus Fine Arts; Denver Art Mus. *Exhib:* Seattle Art Mus, 53-55; Munic Mus, The Hague, 54; Boston Mus Fine Arts, 54-56; Mus Mod Art, New York, 55; La Gravure, 59; Los Angeles Mus Art, 59; Libr Cong; Art Inst Chicago; Metrop Mus Art, New York; plus others. *Teaching:* Assoc prof art educ, Univ Wis-Madison, 46-70, prof, 70-80. *Awards:* Medal of Honor, Milwaukee Art Inst, 52 & 56; Guggenheim Fel, 58. *Bibliog:* S W Hayter (auth), About Prints, Oxford Univ, 62. *Mailing Add:* c/o Jane Haslem Gallery 1669 Wisconsin Ave NW Washington DC 20007

MEIER, RICHARD ALAN
ARCHITECT
b Newark, NJ, Oct 12, 34. *Study:* Cornell Univ, BArch, 57. *Comn:* Olivetti Corp; Mus Mod Art, Villa Strozzi, Florence, Italy; Cornell Univ; High Mus Art, Atlanta, Ga; Hq La Regie Nat des Usines Renault, Boulogne-Billancourt, France; and others. *Exhib:* Graham Found, Chicago, 77; 200 Yrs of Am Architectural Drawing, Art Inst Chicago & others, 78; Masterworks of Bronx Architecture, Bronx Community Col, 79; Modernism Gallery, San Francisco, 80; Wadsworth Atheneum, Hartford, Conn, 80; High Mus Art, Atlanta, 80; Max Protetch Gallery, New York, 80; Harvard Univ, 80; and many others. *Pos:* Resident architect, Am Acad in Rome, 73-74; mem adv coun, Col Art, Archit & Planning, Cornell Univ, Ithaca, NY, 71- *Teaching:* William Henry Bishop Vis Prof archit, Yale Univ, New Haven, Conn, 75-77; vis prof archit, Harvard Univ, Cambridge, Mass, 77, Eliot Noyes vis critic archit, 80-81. *Awards:* Bartlett, First Honor, Am Inst Architects, 65-81; Progressive Archit Design Award, 79; Medal Hon, New York Am Inst Archit, 80. *Bibliog:* Suzanne Stephens (auth), Architecture cross-examined, Progressive Archit, 7/77; Paul Goldberger (auth), Architecture: Richard Meier, Archit Digest, 9/78; Andrew McNair (auth), Quien es Quien en New York en 1979, Arquitectura, 5/79. *Mem:* Nat Acad Design; col fel Am Inst Architects; Century Club New York. *Publ:* Coauth, Five Architects: Eisenman/Graves/Gwathmey/Hejduk/Meier, Wittenborn Co, 72; auth, Richard Meier, Architect, Oxford Univ Press, 76; and others. *Mailing Add:* 136 E 57th St New York NY 10022

MEIGS, JOHN LIGGETT
PAINTER, COLLECTOR
b Chicago, Ill, May 10, 16. *Study:* Univ Redlands; Acad Grande Chaumiere, Paris. *Work:* Roswell Mus, NMex; Univ Tex, Austin; WTex Mus, Lubbock; Mus NMex, Santa Fe; El Paso Mus Art, Tex. *Comn:* Pioneer Frescoes (with Peter Hurd), Tex Tech Univ, Lubbock, 51-54; murals, Nickson Hotel, Roswell, 51, F O Masten Farms, Tex, 60, N Jr High Sch, Abilene, Tex, 61 & Weatherford First Nat Bank, Tex, 71; and others. *Exhib:* One-man shows, Honolulu Acad Fine Arts, Calif Palace of Legion of Honor, San Francisco, Dayton Art Inst, Ohio, Mus NMex & Ball State Mus, Muncie, Ind; O S Ranch Exhib, Tex, 77. *Media:* Egg Tempera, Watercolor. *Res:* American graphics, especially 1930-1950. *Collection:* American graphics and drawings; Peter Hurd; Henriette Wyeth; American Realists; American quilts; coverlets; books. *Publ:* Ed, Peter Hurd--the Lithographs, Baker Gallery, 70; ed, Peter Hurd--Sketchbook, 71 & ed, The Cowboy in American Prints, 72, Swallow; contribr, NMex Mag, Ford Times, Southwest Art Gallery Mag & Ariz Highways. *Mailing Add:* c/o Baker Gallery 13th & Ave L Lubbock TX 79401

MEIGS, WALTER
PAINTER
b New York, NY, Sept 21, 18. *Study:* Syracuse Univ, BFA; Ecole Beaux-Arts, Fontainebleau, France, dipl; Univ Iowa, MFA. *Work:* Amherst Col, Mass; Denver Art Mus, Colo; Va Mus Fine Arts, Richmond; Smithsonian Inst, Washington, DC; Ohio Univ, Athens. *Exhib:* Boston Fine Arts Festival, 56; Carnegie Int, Pittsburgh; Whitney Mus Am Art Ann; Univ Ill, Champaign; Univ Iowa, Iowa City. *Teaching:* Asst prof art, Univ Nebr, 49-53; prof oil painting & chmn art dept, Univ Conn, 53-61. *Awards:* Purchase Prize, Birmingham Art Mus, 54; Best Exhib, Springfield Art Mus, Mass, 57; First Prize for Drawing, Boston Fine Arts Festival, 59. *Bibliog:* A J Weller (auth), Art: USA: Now, C J Bucher, 62. *Media:* Plastic Paint. *Dealer:* Harmon Gallery Naples FL. *Mailing Add:* Candelaria Tenerife Canarias Spain

MEISEL, LOUIS KOENIG
DEALER, PUBLISHER
b Brooklyn, NY, Sept 4, 42. *Study:* Tulane Univ; Columbia Univ; New Sch Social Res. *Collections Arranged:* Photo Realism 1973, Stuart M Speiser Collection (with catalog), Smithsonian Inst; Photo-Realism, Guggenheim Mus. *Pos:* Pres, Louis K Meisel Gallery, New York, currently; pres & publ, Editions Lasiter Meisel, New York. *Bibliog:* Les Levine (auth), New dealer, Arts Mag, 1/74; Judy Beardsall (auth), Louis Meisel, Art Gallery Mag, 9/73. *Res:* Photo realism. *Specialty:* Photo realism; abstract illusionism. *Publ:* Auth, Nathan Wasserberger, 67; auth, Watercolors and drawings, Am Realists, 74; auth, American Photo Realism in New Zealand and Australia, 75; auth, Photorealism, Harry N Abrams, 80; auth, 15 Years of Photorealism, Horizon Mag, 11/80. *Mailing Add:* 141 Prince St New York NY 10012

MEISELMAN, MARILYN NEWMARK See Newmark, Marilyn

MEISTER, MICHAEL WILLIAM
HISTORIAN, EDUCATOR
b West Palm Beach, Fla, Aug 20, 42. *Study:* Harvard Col, BA, 64; Harvard Univ, MA, 71, PhD, 74; Univ Pa, Hon MA, 79. *Teaching:* Asst prof art hist, Univ Tex, Austin, 74-76; asst prof, Univ Pa, 76-79, cur, South Asia Art Archive, 78-, assoc prof, 79- *Awards:* Fulbright Scholar India, 76-77; Nat Endowment Humanities Award, 79-85; Smithsonian Develop Grant, 81. *Mem:* Am Comt South Asian Art (mem bd dirs, 76-79 & 83-); Am Inst Indian Studies; Asn Asian Studies. *Res:* South Asian art, particularly Hindu temple architecture and sculpture. *Publ:* Auth, The pearl roundel in Chinese textile design, Ars Orientalis, 70; auth, An essay in Indian architecture, Roopa Lekha, 73; auth, Phamsana in western India, Artibus Asiae, 76; auth, Mandala and practise in Nagara architecture ..., J Am Oriental Soc, 79; ed, Encyclopaedia of Indian Temple Architecture, Vol 1, Univ Pa Press, 83. *Mailing Add:* Hist Art Dept G-29 Meyerson Hall Univ Pa Philadelphia PA 19104

MEITZLER, (HERBERT) NEIL
PAINTER, DESIGNER
b Pueblo, Colo, Sept 14, 30. *Study:* With Kenneth Callahan. *Work:* Seattle Art Mus, Wash; Memphis Acad Art, Tenn. *Exhib:* Art in USA, New York, 59; one-man show, Seattle Art Mus, Wash, 59; Seattle World's Fair, Wash, 62; Pac Coast Exhib, Santa Barbara Mus Art, Calif, plus five other mus, 62-63; Artists of the Northwest, Japanese World's Fair, 71. *Pos:* Designer, Seattle Art Mus, 57-78. *Awards:* Katharine Baker Award, Seattle Art Mus, 58; Nat Coun Theatres Award, US Govt, 67. *Media:* Acrylic, Tempera, Watercolor. *Dealer:* Foster-White Gallery 311 1/2 Occidental Ave S Seattle WA 98104. *Mailing Add:* PO Box 118 Wildwood GA 30757

MEIXNER, MARY LOUISE
PAINTER, EDUCATOR
b Milwaukee, Wis, Dec 7, 16. *Study:* Milwaukee-Downer Col, BA; State Univ Iowa, MA; Art Students League, with Hale; Univ Minn & Bowling Green Univ, with Max Weber; Mills Col, with Yasuo Kuniyoshi; Am Sch, Fontainebleau, France; Carpenter Ctr Visual Arts, Harvard Univ. *Work:* Nat Am Home Econ Asn, Washington, DC; Des Moines Art Ctr, Iowa; Denison Arts Asn Gallery, Iowa. *Exhib:* Des Moines Art Ctr Ann, 54, 55 & 62; Mid Am Ann, Kansas City, Mo, 55; solo show, Nat Design Ctr, New York, 69; MacNider Mus Ann, Mason City, Iowa, 70-75; solo show, Western Ill Univ, Macomb, 79; and others. *Teaching:* Prof art hist, Milwaukee-Downer Col, 45-52; prof color, environ arts & painting, Iowa State Univ, Ames, 53-75, distinguished prof, 75- *Awards:* Regional exhib awards. *Mem:* Col Art Asn Am; Intersoc Color Coun; and others. *Media:* Oil, Acrylic. *Res:* Experiments in light and color. *Publ:* Auth articles in Art J, 53-71, Lyrical Iowa Poetry Mag, 62-83, Design Mag, 67 & 68 & Leonardo, 75; Film documentary, Sky Event, 79; auth, Geometry of F L Wright at Richland Center, Wis Acad Rev, 82; La Chagallite: The style in tapestry, Iowa State Univ Res J, 82. *Mailing Add:* 1007 Lincoln Way 4 Ames IA 50010

MEIZNER, PAULA
SCULPTOR
b Belchatow, Poland; US citizen. *Study:* Westchester Workshop, White Plains, NY. *Exhib:* New Eng Exhibs, New Canaan, Conn; Critics Choice, Sculpture Ctr, New York, 72; Contemporary Reflections 1972-1973, Larry Aldrich Mus, Ridgefield, Conn; Modern Maxis, New Brit Mus Am Art, Conn, 74; Sculpture in the Fields, Storm King Art Ctr, Mountainville, NY, 74-75; and others. *Teaching:* Pvt adult art classes. *Awards:* Claudia & Maurice L Stone Mem Award, 72, New Eng Exhib, New Canaan; Charles N Whinston Mem Award, Nat Asn Women Artists, New York, 72, 78, 79 & 83; Paper on Paper, Katonah Gallery, NY, 77, 78 & 79; and others. *Bibliog:* National community arts program, HUD, 74. *Mem:* Audubon Artists; Silvermine Guild Artists; Nat Asn Women Artists. *Media:* Fieldstone, Aluminum. *Mailing Add:* 126 Seacord Rd New Rochelle NY 10804

MEJER, ROBERT LEE
PAINTER, EDUCATOR
b South Bend, Ind, Nov 8, 44. *Study:* South Bend Art Ctr; Ball State Univ, BS; Miami Univ, MFA; Kent State Univ, 73; Kalamazoo Art Inst, 75; Oxbow Summer Sch Art, 76-78 & 81; Notre Dame Univ, 79; Washington Univ, 80; Skidmore Col, 82-83. *Work:* Ball State Univ, Muncie, Ind; Quincy Art Ctr, Ill; Int Arts League Youth, New York; Anderson Art Ctr, Ind; Col Dupage, Ill. *Exhib:* New American Monotypes, Smithsonian Inst Traveling Exhib, 77-80; Retrospective 1969-1979, Quincy Art Ctr, 79; Krannert Art Mus, Ill, 80; Pensacola Nat Watermedia Exhib, Fla, 82; Shreveport Nat Art Biannual, La, 82; 15th Ann Washington & Jefferson Col Nat Painting Show, Pa, 83; Intermont Nat Works on Paper, Va, 83. *Collections Arranged:* Q C Alumni Invitational, 73, Middlewestern Cardscape, 74, Religious in the Arts, 77, Alps, 81, Keith Achepohl, 81 & Sylvia Solochek Waters, 82, Quincy Col; Director's Choice, Quincy Art Club, 77. *Pos:* Gallery asst, Ball State Art Gallery, 62-66 & Quincy Art Ctr, Ill, 70- *Teaching:* Instr painting & drawing, Ball State Univ, summers 66 & 67; instr drawing, Miami Univ, 66-68; prof art & gallery dir, Quincy Col, 68-; instr, John Wood Community Col, Pittsfield, 75 & Quincy, 76; vis res fac, Skidmore Col, 82-83. *Awards:* Quincy Col Fac Develop Grants, 75-83; Fel Va Ctr Creative Arts, 82; Best Show, 33rd Ann Quincy Art Ctr, 83; and others. *Bibliog:* Terrence Riddell (auth), Bob Mejer an artist, Riverword 1, 77; Richard Mammel (auth), Progressive variations of a theme: Space and Robert Lee Mejer, Quincy Art Club First Quart Bulletin, 79. *Mem:* Nat Art Educ Asn; Ill Art Educ Asn (exec coun, 70-72 & 75-77); Quincy Art Club (bd dirs, 76-80, 1st vpres, 76); Midwest Watercolor Soc; Ill Arts Coun. *Specialty:* Contemporary artists. *Media:* Watercolor, Monotypes. *Publ:* Illusr, Salt-Lick Mag, 68-71; illusr, Riverword Mag, Vols 1, 2, & 3, 77. *Dealer:* Nornberg Gallery Contemp Art St Louis MO; Prairie House IL. *Mailing Add:* Art Dept Quincy Col Quincy IL 62301

MEKLER, ADAM
DEALER, CURATOR
b Haifa, Israel, Feb 1, 41; US citizen. *Study:* Calif State Univ, Northridge, BA, MA; Univ Southern Calif. *Collections Arranged:* Jack Zajac, Retrospective 1955-74, Fine Arts Gallery San Diego; Jack Zajac, Retrospective 1955-77, Palm Springs Desert Mus; Jack Zajac, Retrospective 1966-74, Santa Barbara Mus Art; William Dole, Retrospective 1960-75, Munic Art Gallery Los Angeles, Colo Springs Fine Arts Ctr, Fine Arts Gallery San Diego & Santa Barbara Mus Art. *Pos:* Owner-dir, Mekler Gallery. *Specialty:* Contemporary and 20th century sculpture and paintings. *Mailing Add:* Mekler Gallery 651 N La Cienega Blvd Los Angeles CA 90069

MELAMED, ABRAHAM & HOPE
COLLECTORS, PATRONS
Dr Melamed b Chicago, Ill, Nov 19, 14. *Study:* Mrs Melamed, Univ Wis, Madison, 38-40; Goodman School, Art Inst Chicago, 40-42. *Pos:* Dr Melamed, Mem, Gov Coun Arts, Wis, 63-65; trustee, Arch Am Art, Smithsonian Inst, 66-82; trustee, John Michael Kohler Arts Center, Sheboygan, Wis, 79-82; Mrs Melamed, trustee, Milwaukee Art Museum, Wis, 74-83; council, Elvehjem Art Mus, Univ Wis, Madison. *Bibliog:* Cubist Prints in Collection of Dr and Mrs Abraham Melamed, Univ Wis, 72; Selections from Collection of Hope and Abraham Melamed, Milwaukee Art Mus, 83. *Mem:* Am Fedn Arts; Chicago Art Inst; Am Asn Mus. *Interests:* Visual arts; contributors and patrons to art organizations and institutions. *Collection:* Contemporary and modern works-graphics, paintings, sculpture. *Mailing Add:* 1107 E Lilac Lane Milwaukee WI 53217

MELBERG, JERALD LEIGH
CURATOR, COLLECTOR
b Minneapolis, Minn, Aug 17, 48. *Study:* Pillsbury Col, Owatonna, Minn; Bob Jones Univ, Greenville, SC. *Collections Arranged:* Biennial Exhibition of Piedmont Painting & Sculpture (ed, catalog), 77, 79 & 81; Biennial Exhibition of Piedmont Crafts (ed, catalog), 78, 80 & 82; Romare Bearden 1970-1980 (ed, catalog), 80; Mint Mus Art, Charlotte, NC; Seymour Lipton: Sculpture (ed, catalog), 82; Herb Jackson: Drawings (ed, catalog), 83; Ed Buonagurio: Recent Paintings (auth, catalog), 83. *Pos:* Dir, Hampton III Gallery, Ltd, Greenville, SC, 73-74; exec dir, Anderson Co Arts Coun, SC, 75-76; cur exhib, Mint Mus Art, 77- *Mem:* Int Coun Mus; Am Asn

Mus; assoc Smithsonian Inst, Washington, DC. *Res:* Herb Jackson, Jacques Lipchitz, Romare Bearden. *Collection:* Paintings, sculpture, graphics and crafts by Southeastern United States artists, and graphics by nationally known American artists. *Mailing Add:* 518 1/2 Clarice Ave Charlotte NC 28204

MELBY, DAVID A
PAINTER, PHOTOGRAPHER
Study: Kansas City Art Inst; Wichita State Univ, BFA, 67; Univ Nebr, MFA, 70. *Work:* Am Express Corp, Salt Lake City; Hallmark Corp, Mutual Benefit Life, Kansas City, Mo; McDonald Corp, Chicago; Sheldon Mem Art Gallery. *Exhib:* A Sense of Place, Joslyn Art Mus, Sheldon Mem Art Gallery, Mid-Am Arts Alliance & others, 73; Landscape, Gallery One, Bergen, Norway, 73; solo exhibs, Limassol Munic Cult Arts Ctr, Cyprus, 73 & Valdres Folk Mus, Fagernas, Norway, 77; Cyprus, Sheldon Mem Art Gallery, 77; Coos Art Mus, Coos Bay, Ore, 79; Passages, Wichita Art Mus, Kans, 79; Mid-Four, Nelson Atkins Mus, 80-83. *Collections Arranged:* Artists Behind Bars, Jewish Community Ctr, Kansas City, Mo, 76; In Respect of Space, 79, Groups: A Public Face, 79 & Gold Rush: Work of Hal Parker, 80, Swan River Mus; Points of View: Six Artists, St Mary Col, 81. *Pos:* Artist in residence, Leavenworth Fed Penitentiary, Kans, Nat Endowment Arts, 75-76; dir exhibs, Swan River Mus, Paola, Kans, 79-80. *Teaching:* Instr drawing & painting, Iowa State Univ, Ames, 70-75; instr painting, drawing & photog, St Mary Col, Kans, 80-82. *Awards:* First Prize, Kansas Two, Kans Arts Comn, 82; Award Merit, Mid-Four Exhib, Nelson Atkins Mus, 82; Jurors Award, Nat Small Works Exhib, NY Univ, 83. *Bibliog:* Knut Førsund (auth), article, Fotograft, 11/77; Victoria Melcher (auth), Kansas City: Dizzying directions, Art News, 10/80. *Mem:* Kansas City Artists Coalition; Print Soc, Nelson Atkins Mus. *Media:* Oil; Black and White 35mm Film. *Publ:* Contribr, A Sense of Place: The Artist and the American Land, Mid-Am Arts Alliance, 73; co-dir, videotape, Artist in Residence Prog, US Bur Prisons, 76; contribr, Poets on Photography, Dog Ear Press, 81. *Mailing Add:* c/o Midwestern Light PO Box 508 Leavenworth KS 66048

MELCHERT, JAMES FREDERICK
SCULPTOR, EDUCATOR
b New Bremen, Ohio, Dec 2, 30. *Study:* Princeton Univ, AB; Univ Chicago, MFA; Univ Calif, Berkeley, MA; ceramics with Peter Voulkos. *Work:* San Francisco Mus Art; Mus Mod Art, Kyoto, Japan; Victoria & Albert Mus, London; Oakland Mus Art, Calif; Stedelijk Mus, Amsterdam. *Exhib:* Abstract Expressionist Ceramics, Univ Calif, Irvine, 66; Contemporary American Sculpture, Whitney Mus Am Art, New York, 66, 68 & 70; Documenta 5, Kassel, Ger, 72. *Pos:* Dir visual arts prog, Nat Endowment Arts, 77- *Teaching:* Chmn dept ceramics, San Francisco Art Inst, 61-64; prof art, Univ Calif, Berkeley, 64-, chmn dept art, currently; vis sculptor, Univ Wis-Madison, spring 71. *Awards:* Louis Comfort Tiffany Found Grant, 63; Nealie Sullivan Award, San Francisco Art Inst, 70; Nat Found Arts Grant, 72. *Media:* Clay. *Mailing Add:* Dir Visual Arts Prog Nat Endowment for the Arts Washington DC 20506

MELIKIAN, MARY
PAINTER
b Worcester, Mass. *Study:* RI Sch Design, Providence, BFA, 55; Columbia Univ Teachers Col. *Work:* Worcester Mus Art, Mass; Mint Mus, Charlotte, NC; Yerevan Mus, Armenia; Vassar Col Art Mus; Art for US Embassies, State Dept. *Exhib:* Nat Arts Club, New York, 69 & 70; Galerie de Tours, San Francisco & Ankrum Gallery, Los Angeles, 70, Calif; retrospective, Centenary Col, Hackettstown, 75; one-man shows, Bodley Gallery, New York, 78 & 81 & Quadrangle Gallery, Dallas, 80; group show, Nicholas Gallery, Palm Beach, Fla, 79. *Pos:* Asst designer, Fuller Fabrics, NY, 56; asst dir, Grand Cent Moderns, New York, 60-61; dir pub rels, Grand Cent Art Galleries, New York, 61-67. *Teaching:* Instr art, Nutley High Sch, 57-60. *Awards:* First Prize, Kit Kat Club, 61, Armenian Student Asn, 61 & 62 & Women's Nat Repub Club, 70, 72, 73 & 75. *Bibliog:* Stan Haste (auth), Mary Melikian, RI Sch Design Mag, 9/68; Colette Roberts (auth), article, France-Am; N Stepanian (auth), Paintings of Mary Melikian, Voice of Am, 68. *Mem:* Am Watercolor Soc; Burr Artists. *Media:* Pastel, Watercolor. *Publ:* Auth, article, Ararat Mag. *Mailing Add:* 429 E 52nd St Rivercourt 27H New York NY 10022

MELL, ED (EDMUND PAUL JR)
PAINTER, PRINTMAKER
b Phoenix, Ariz, Sept 17, 42. *Study:* Phoenix Col, AA, 63; Art Ctr Col Design, Los Angeles, BFA(advert illus), 67. *Work:* Scottsdale Ctr Arts, Ariz. *Comn:* Oil painting, Mary Kay Cosmetics, Dallas, 80; oil murals, Empire Bank, Denver, 82, Farm Bank Ctr, Denver, 82 & Courson Oil, Perryton, Tex, 83. *Exhib:* Ariz Invitational, Scottsdale Ctr Arts, 82; Artists of Arizona, Ctr Mod Art, Guadalajara, Mex, 82; solo exhibs, Art Resources Gallery, Denver, 82, Dewey-Kofron Gallery, Santa Fe, 83 & Long Beach Mus Art, Calif, 83. *Pos:* Art dir, Kenyon & Eckhardt Advert, 68-70; artist & co-dir, Sagebrush Studio, New York, 70-73. *Teaching:* Instr art, Bacavi Community Sch, Hotevilla, Ariz, summers 71 & 73. *Bibliog:* Article, Art Voices S, 80; Ed Mell--Mesas man made, Southwest Art, 82; A portfolio of regional landscape painting, Am Artist, 84. *Media:* Oil on Canvas, Pastel; Lithography. *Mailing Add:* c/o Suzanne Brown Gallery 7160 Main St Scottsdale AZ 85251

MELLON, JAMES
PRINTMAKER, PAINTER
b New York, NY, Feb 14, 41. *Study:* Creative Graphic Workshop, with Chaim Koppleman, 56-59; Art Students League, 57-58. *Work:* Smithsonian Inst; Univ Pa. *Exhib:* Sch Visual Arts Gallery, NY, 62; Soc Am Graphic Artists Traveling Exhib, SAm, 62; Everson Mus Art, 68; Int Miniature Print Exhib,

Pratt Inst, 67 & 68; Cranbrook Acad Art, Bloomfield Hills, Mich; plus others. *Teaching:* Instr media, Dept Adult Educ, Brooklyn Col, 64-67; instr graphics, Sch Visual Arts, 65- *Awards:* Pennell Purchase Prize, Libr Cong, 58 & 61; Warren Mack Mem Award, 65; Purchase Prize, Everson Mus Art. *Mem:* Soc Am Graphic Artists. *Mailing Add:* 81 Irving Pl New York NY 10003

MELLON, PAUL
COLLECTOR, ADMINISTRATOR
b Pittsburgh, Pa, June 11, 07. *Study:* Choate Sch, Wallingford, Conn, 19-25; Yale Univ, BA, 29, Hon LHD, 67; Clare Col, Cambridge Univ, BA, 31, MA, 38; Oxford Univ, Hon LittD, 61; Carnegie Inst Technol, Hon LLD, 67. *Pos:* Trustee, Nat Gallery Art, 38-39 & 45-, pres, 38-39 & 63-; trustee, Va Mus Fine Arts, Richmond, Va, 38- *Awards:* Nat Inst Arts & Lett Award for Distinguished Serv to Arts, 62; Benjamin Franklin Medal, Royal Soc Arts, 65; Gertrude Vanderbilt Whitney Award, Skowhegan Sch Painting & Sculpture, 72. *Interests:* Major financial contributor to Yale Center and Paul Mellon Centre for Studies in British Art, London, England. *Collection:* (Paul Mellon) English paintings, 1700-1850; (Mr and Mrs Paul Mellon) impressionist and post-impressionist paintings. *Mailing Add:* 1729 H St NW Washington DC 20006

MELLOR, GEORGE EDWARD
EDUCATOR, SCULPTOR
b Bronxville, NY, Sept 13, 28. *Study:* Oberlin Col, AB(fine arts), 54; Atelier Zadkine, 52-53; Tyler Sch Fine Arts, MFA, 65. *Work:* Nat Collection Fine Art, Smithsonian Inst; Danvers Security Nat Bank, Lynn, Mass, Southeastern Mass Univ. *Exhib:* Regional Exhib, Pa Acad Fine Arts, Philadelphia, 64; one-man shows, Lamont Gallery, Exeter, NH, 68, Tufts Univ, Medford, Mass, 69 & Kanegis Gallery, Boston, 70; RI Sch Design, 75. *Pos:* Dir art gallery, Exeter Acad, NH, 65-68. *Teaching:* Instr art, Solebury Sch, New Hope, Pa, 57-65; prof art, Southeastern Mass Univ, 68- *Bibliog:* Fred Stein (dir), Sketches-Some American Sculpture (film), US Info Agency, 70. *Mailing Add:* R7 West Blvd Onset MA 02558

MELLOW, CYNTHIA STAN See Stan, Cynthia

MELTZER, ARTHUR
PAINTER
b Minneapolis, Minn, July 31, 1893. *Study:* Minneapolis Sch Fine Art; Pa Acad Fine Arts, Cresson traveling scholar, 21, fel prize, 25. *Work:* Art Alliance, Pa Acad Fine Arts, Philadelphia; Moore Inst; Woodmere Art Gallery, Columbus Gallery Fine Art. *Comn:* Budd Trains (murals) & Stephen Girard (murals), Girard Fed, Philadelphia. *Exhib:* Pa Acad Fine Arts; Nat Acad Design, New York; Art Inst Chicago. *Teaching:* Head fine arts dept, Moore Col, Philadelphia, 25-49. *Awards:* Gold Medal, Ligonier Art League, 61; Williamson Prize, Phillips Mill, New Hope, Pa, 63; First Prize, Jenkintown Art Festival, 73; and others. *Mem:* Fel Pa Acad Fine Arts; Artists Equity Asn. *Media:* Oil, Watercolor. *Mailing Add:* 1521 Old Welsh Rd Huntingdon Valley PA 19006

MELTZER, ROBERT HIRAM
INSTRUCTOR, PAINTER
b New Rochelle, NY, Oct 18, 21. *Study:* Jean Morgan Sch Art, 46-47; Sch Art Studies, 46-47; Art Students League, 46-47; Southern Methodist Univ, BFA, 50; Univ Hawaii, 52-56; also with Jean Charlot, Robert Beverly Hale, Ernest Fiene, Robert Benney & Charles Kinghan. *Work:* Edward-Dean Mus, Cherry Valley, Calif; San Bernardino City Hall, Calif; US Naval Archives, Washington, DC; Armed Forces Pub Info Officers Inst, Ft Slocum, NY; Southern Methodist Univ, Dallas, Tex. *Comn:* Oil portrait of Admiral John Hoskins, Mil Air Transport Serv, 52; oil on masonite Hukilau scene, Hukilau Hotel, Hilo, Hawaii, 54; oil portrait of W A S Smith, Lethbridge Col, 63. *Exhib:* Knickerbocker Artists, 81; Am Art Annual, Middletown, Ohio, 81; Watercolor Okla, 81; Tex Watercolor Soc, 81; San Diego Watercolor, 81; and others. *Pos:* Mem bd dir, Edward-Dean Mus, Cherry Valley, 72-74. *Teaching:* Coordr, Crafton Hills Col Watercolor Sem, 75-82; lectr & demonstr watercolors, Wenatchee Vallery Col, 77; instr art, Jackson State Community Col Workshop, Tenn, 80, Southwestern Watercolor Soc, 81; Jade Fon Watercolor Workshop, 81 & Banning Unified Sch Dist Watercolor Sem, 83; instr workshops, SOre State Col, 82 & Utah Watercolor Soc, 84. *Awards:* Art Newton Mem Award, 81; First Purchase Award, San Bernadino Co Mus, 82; Strathmore Award, Inland Empire XVIII, 82; and others. *Mem:* Am Watercolor Soc (vpres Far West, 76-); Salmagundi Club; Int Platform Asn; and others. *Media:* Watercolor, Oil. *Publ:* Auth & illusr, Drawing for the Fun of It, newspaper series, Banning Record, 65. *Dealer:* Oak Glen Art Gallery 39576 Lincoln Cherry Valley CA 92223. *Mailing Add:* PO Box 2132 Beaumont CA 92223

MELVILLE, GREVIS WHITAKER
PAINTER, PRINTMAKER
b Damariscotta, Maine, Dec 23, 04. *Study:* Yale Sch Art & Archit; Art Students League; also with Will Barnet & William C Palmer. *Work:* William A Farnsworth Libr & Art Mus, Rockland, Maine; Pierson Col, Yale Univ, New Haven, Conn; Damariscotta Region Info Bur. *Comn:* Designed seal, co comnr, Lincoln Co, Maine, 75. *Exhib:* Pa Acad Fine Art, Philadelphia; one-man show, Smith Col Mus, Northampton, Mass; Maine State Art Festival, Augusta; Maine Artists Shows, Portland Mus Art; Maine Art '75, Bowdoin Col Mus Art, 75; Retrospective, Maineart Gallery, 79; and others. *Teaching:* Artist in residence, Hackley Sch, Tarrytown, NY, 41-42. *Mem:* Maine Art Gallery (bd dirs, 68-72); Pemaquid Group Artists (dir, 66). *Media:* Oil, Lithography. *Publ:* Illusr, Windswept, Macmillan, 63; Illusr, Maine Memories, Greene, 68. *Dealer:* Jacques Seligmann Galleries 5 E 57th St New York NY 10022; Ogunquit Gallery US Rte 1 Ogunquit ME 03907. *Mailing Add:* 38 Main St Damariscotta ME 04543

MELVIN, RONALD MCKNIGHT
MUSEUM DIRECTOR

b Regina, Sask, Oct 25, 27. *Study:* Univ British Columbia, BComm, 49. *Collections Arranged:* Important Western Art from Chicago Collections, 80; Five American Masters of Watercolor (auth, catalog), 81; American Naive Paintings from the Nat Gallery Art (auth, catalog), 82; Solitude--Inner Visions in American Art, 82; Woman, 84. *Pos:* Dir, Terra Mus Am Art, Evanston, Ill, 80- *Mailing Add:* 2600 Central Park Evanston IL 60201

MENDELSON, HAIM
PAINTER, PRINTMAKER

b Semiatich, Builsk, Poland, Oct 15, 23; US citizen. *Study:* Am Artists Sch, 36-40; Saul Baizerman Art Sch, 40-43; Educ Alliance Art Sch, 46; pvt study with Saul Baizerman, 43-52. *Work:* Contemp Drawing Collection, Minn Mus Art, St Paul; Print Collection of New York Pub Libr; Print Collection of St Vincent Col, Latrobe, Pa; Griffiths Art Ctr of St Lawrence Univ, Canton, NY; Edwin A Ulrich Mus, Wichita State Univ, Kans. *Exhib:* The Artist as Reporter, Mus Mod Art, New York, 40-41; Drawings USA, St Paul Art Ctr, Minn, 61 & 66; Pa Acad Fine Arts, 65; Butler Inst Am Art, Youngstown, Ohio, 65 & 67; Nat Acad of Design, New York, 65, 68, 75 & 77; 10th Nat Exhib of Prints & Drawings, Okla Art Ctr, 68; Fedn of Mod Painters & Sculptors (traveling exhib), Gallery Asn New York, 76-78; Prints USA, Pratt Graphics Ctr Traveling Exhib, 82. *Pos:* Dir, Hudson Guild Art Gallery, New York, 71-72 & 73- *Awards:* First Prize, Graphics, Knickerbocker Artists Ann, New York, 64; Purchase Award, Drawings USA, St Paul Art Ctr, 66; Graphics Award, Painters & Sculptors Soc of NJ, 74. *Mem:* Fedn of Mod Painters & Sculptors (pres, 74-); Knickerbocker Artists; Painters & Sculptors Soc of NJ. *Media:* Oil, Acrylic; Intaglio. *Mailing Add:* 234 W 21st St New York NY 10011

MENDENHALL, JACK
PAINTER, INSTRUCTOR

b Ventura, Calif, Apr 7, 37. *Study:* Calif Col Arts & Crafts, BFA, 58 & MFA(painting), 70. *Work:* Univ Calif Art Mus, Berkeley; San Francisco Art Comn; Gallery Ostergren, Malmo, Sweden; Butler Inst of Am Art, Ohio; Va Mus of Fine Arts, Richmond; plus numerous pvt collections, individual & industrial, US & Europe. *Comn:* Rainbows, Waldo Tunnels, Calif Div Hwy, San Francisco, 70. *Exhib:* Amerikanske Realister, Panders Kunstmuseum, Sweden, 73; Tokyo Biennale 74, Japan, 74; New Photo Realism, Wadsworth Atheneum, Hartford, Conn, 74; one-man show, O K Harris Gallery, New York, 74, 78 & 81; Realist Painting in California, John Berggruen Gallery, San Francisco, 75; Watercolors & Drawings, American Realists, Meisel Gallery, New York, 75; plus others. *Teaching:* Assoc prof painting & drawing, Calif Col Arts & Crafts, 70- *Awards:* Purchase Award, San Francisco Art Comn, 70. *Bibliog:* William C Seitz (auth), The real and the artificial: Painting of the new environment, Art in Am, 12/72; Linda Chase (auth), Les hyperrealistes Americans, Paris, Ed Filipacchi, 73; Ellen Lubell (auth), article, Arts Mag, 2/75; and others. *Media:* Oil, Watercolor. *Dealer:* O K Harris Gallery 383 W Broadway New York NY 10012. *Mailing Add:* 5824 Florence Terr Oakland CA 94611

MENDES, BARBARA
PAINTER

b Montclair, NJ, Jan 30, 48. *Study:* Hunter Col, 67-69; Univ Calif, Riverside, BA, 80. *Work:* Beserkley Record Co, Berkeley, Calif. *Exhib:* One-person shows, Africa Woman, Inland Empire Gallery, Riverside, Calif, 80 & Phyllis Needlman Gallery, Chicago, 81 & 82; Hundred Thousand Images, Cicchinelli Gallery, New York, 82; All California Biennial, Riverside, 82; and others. *Awards:* Weisglass Mem Award, Spring Show, Staten Island Mus, 74. *Bibliog:* Susan Threlkeld (auth), rev, KSCI TV, San Bernardino, 79; Mark Lundahl (auth), Africa woman shines on canvas, San Bernardino Sun, 80; Harold Haydon (auth), Top of the weekend, Chicago Sun Times, 3/13/81 & rev, 4/16/82. *Media:* Oil. *Publ:* Coauth, It ain't me babe, Last Gaspeco, 70; coauth, All Girl Thrills, 71 & auth, Illuminations, 72, Print Mint. *Dealer:* Factory Place Gallery 1308 Factory Pl Los Angeles CA 90013. *Mailing Add:* 870 S Acacia Ave Rialto CA 92376

MENDOZA, ANTONIO G
PHOTOGRAPHER

b Havana, Cuba, July 21, 41; US citizen. *Study:* Yale Univ, BA, 63; Harvard Grad Sch Design, MA(archit), 68. *Work:* Mus Mod Art, New York; Mus Fine Arts, Boston; Fogg Art Mus; Addison Gallery Am Art. *Exhib:* Cats & Dogs, Arco Ctr Visual Art, Los Angeles, 80; Light Gallery, New York, 81; Kathleen Ewing Gallery, Washington, DC, 81; Jacksonville Art Mus, Fla, 82; New Mus, New York, 83. *Teaching:* Photog, Int Ctr Photog, 82- *Awards:* Nat Endowment Arts Photog Grant, 81; Creative Artists Pub Serv Grant, 81. *Bibliog:* Ben Lifson (auth), Young dog, old tricks, Village Voice, 3/17/80; Owen Edwards (auth), Dog bites psyche, Saturday Rev, 6/80 & Tony Mendoza's animal farm, Am Photogr, 11/83. *Dealer:* Virginia Miller Galleries 169 Madeira Coral Gables FL 33134. *Mailing Add:* 53 Park Pl Brooklyn NY 11217

MENEELEY, EDWARD
PAINTER, SCULPTOR

b Wilkes Barre, Pa, Dec 18, 27. *Study:* Murray Art Sch, Wilkes Barre, 52-56; Sch of Visual Arts, New York, 57-58; pvt study with Jack Tworkov, New York, 58-59. *Work:* Metrop Mus Art, New York; Mus Mod Art, New York; Whitney Mus, New York; Chrysler Mus, Norfolk, Va; Victoria & Albert Mus, London, Can. *Exhib:* Recent Acquisitions, Whitney Mus, New York, 69; Machine Art, Mus Mod Art, New York, 70; Victoria & Albert Mus, London, 71; Photography into Art, Camden Arts Ctr, London, Can, 72; Paper Show, Ericson Gallery, New York, 79; one-man shows, Susan Caldwell Gallery, New York, 76, Vivian Brant, New York, 79 & Ericson Gallery, New York, 80; retrospective, Frank Marino Gallery, New York, 78; and others. *Teaching:* Instr, Central Sch Art, London, 68-73; instr, Winchester Sch of Art, England, 69-; instr, Art Students League, New York, 74; lectr, Belleville Col, St Louis, Mo, 79 & Art Students League, New York, 79. *Awards:* Nat Endowment Arts Grant, Washington, DC, 71; Arts Coun Grant, London, 71. *Bibliog:* Anthony Howell (auth), Ed Meneeley, Vogue, London, 8/75; Grace Glueck (auth), Instant Art, New York Times, 11/75; Barbara Cavaliere (auth), Edward Meneeley: Liverpool Paintings, Arts Mag, 12/79. *Dealer:* Frank Marino Gallery 489 Broome St New York NY 10013. *Mailing Add:* 156 Lafayette Ave Brooklyn NY 11238

MENG, WENDY
PAINTER

b Fla, Feb 15, 44. *Study:* Seishen Daibako, Tokyo, 61-62; Kansas City Art Inst, BFA, 67; Md Inst Col Art, MFA(with honors), 69. *Work:* Chase Manhattan Bank, New York; Nat Gallery Am Art, Washington, DC; Libr of Cong, Washington, DC. *Comn:* School of Fish (lithograph), Spec Proj Group for Bicentennial, Chicago, 75. *Exhib:* One-woman shows, Gallery of July & August, Woodstock, 75, James Yu Gallery, 76 & Alpha Gallery, Boston, 77; 41st Ann Midyear Show, Butler Inst Am Art, Youngstown, Ohio, 77; Space/Color/Place, Brockton Art Mus, Mass, 77-78; Shayne Gallery, Montreal, Que, 78; and many others. *Teaching:* Art instr, Berkeley Inst, Brooklyn, 71-74. *Awards:* Print Honorarium, Spec Proj Group, 75. *Media:* Oil, Watercolor. *Dealer:* Alpha Gallery 121 Newbury St Boston MA 02116; Hodgell Hartman Gallery 48 S Palm Ave Sarasota FL. *Mailing Add:* 45 Bond St New York NY 10012

MENIHAN, JOHN CONWAY
PAINTER, PRINTMAKER

b Rochester, NY, Feb 14, 08. *Study:* Wharton Sch, Univ Pa, 30; St John Fisher Col, LLD, 83. *Work:* Libr of Cong, Washington, DC; Carnegie Inst, Pittsburgh; Mem Art Gallery, Rochester. *Comn:* Triptych, St Thomas the Apostle Roman Cath Church, Rochester, NY, 78; ceremonial mace, St John Fisher Col, Rochester, NY, 81, D'Youville Col, Buffalo, NY, 81 & Community Col Air Force, 81; Life of St Elizabeth Seton (triptych), St Thomas Apostle Church, Rochester, NY. *Exhib:* Finger Lakes Show, Mem Art Gallery, Rochester, 30 & 71; Art Inst Chicago, 39; World's Fair, New York, 39; Nat Acad Design, 48; Am Watercolor Soc, 54, New York; retrospective, Nazareth Col, Rochester, NY, 83. *Teaching:* Asst prof drawing & painting, Univ Rochester, 46-65. *Awards:* Lillian Fairchild Award, Univ Rochester, 40; Marion Stratton Gould Award, Univ Rochester Mem Art Gallery, 46. *Bibliog:* Norman Kent (auth), John C Menihan, lithographer, Am Artist, 45. *Mem:* Nat Acad Design; Am Watercolor Soc; Asn Am Inst Architects. *Publ:* Illusr, How Scientists Find Out, Little, 65; illusr, Historic St Mary's Church, Albany, NY, 73; illusr, St Ann's of Hornell, 76. *Mailing Add:* 208 Alpine Dr Rochester NY 14618

MENKES, SIGMUND
PAINTER

b Lwow, Poland, May 7, 1896; US citizen. *Study:* Inst Art Decorative, Lwow, 14; Acad Fine Art, Krakow, Poland, 19. *Work:* Metrop Mus Art & Whitney Mus Am Art, New York; Pa Acad Fine Arts, Philadelphia; Hirshhorn Mus, Washington, DC; Brooklyn Mus. *Exhib:* Carnegie Inst, Pittsburgh; Metrop Mus Art & Whitney Mus Am Art, New York; Corcoran Gallery Art, Washington, DC; Pa Acad Fine Arts, Philadelphia; and many other group & one-man shows. *Awards:* First Prize & Gold Medal, Corcoran Gallery Art, Washington, DC, 47; Nat Inst Arts & Letters Award, 55; Polish Inst Arts & Sci Prize, 68; and others. *Bibliog:* Emily Genauer (auth), Best of Art, Doubleday, 48; Arthur Zaidenberg (ed), The Art of Artists, Crown, 51; Nathaniel Pousette-Dart (ed), American Painting Today, Hastings, 56. *Mem:* Nat Acad Design. *Media:* Oil, Acrylic. *Mailing Add:* 5075 Fieldstone Rd Riverdale NY 10471

MENSES, JAN
PAINTER, PRINTMAKER

b Rotterdam, Netherlands, Apr 28, 33; Can citizen. *Study:* Rotterdamse Kunst Akademie; Univ Delle Arti, hon degree, 81. *Work:* Mus Mod Art & Guggenheim Mus, New York; Art Inst Chicago; Brooklyn Mus; Munic Mus, Amsterdam, Holland; Victoria & Albert Mus, London. *Comn:* Mural, Montreal Holocaust Mem Centre, Can. *Exhib:* Montreal Mus Fine Arts, 61, 65 & 76; 5th & 7th Biennial Can Painting, 63 & 68 & 1st & 2nd Biennial Can Watercolours, Drawings & Prints, 64 & 66, Nat Gallery Can, Ottawa; 20 New Acquisitions, Mus Mod Art, New York, 66; 9th & 11th Int Exhib Drawings & Engravings, Lugano, Switz, 66 & 72; Rotterdam Art Found, Netherlands, 74; Univ British Columbia, Vancouver, 81; Mead Art Mus, Amherst, Mass, 83; and others. *Teaching:* Vis lectr, var Can univs. *Awards:* Award, 9th Int Exhib Drawings & Engravings, City of Lugano, Switz, 66; Prize, Perspective 67, Prov of Ont, 67; Gold Medal, Accademia Italia Delle Arte, Italy, 80. *Bibliog:* Jerrold Morris (auth), The Nude in Canadian Painting, New Press, Toronto, 72; Jan Menses--Peintre et prophete, Johathan, 82; La peinture de Jan Menses: Kadish, Klikppoth, Tikkoune, Tribune Juive, Montreal, 83. *Mem:* Royal Can Acad Arts; Print & Drawing Coun of Can; Soc Artistes en Arts Visuels de Que; Accademia Italia Delle Arte, Italy; Accademia D'Europa, 83. *Media:* Tempera, Acrylic. *Dealer:* Galerie Don Stewart 1460 Sherbrooke St W Montreal PQ H3G 1K4 Can; Michel Tetreault Art Contemporain 4260 Rue Saint Denis Montreal PQ H2J 2K8. *Mailing Add:* 5571 Woodbury Ave Montreal PQ H3T 1S6 Canada

MENTHE, MELISSA
LIBRARIAN, PHOTOGRAPHER
b Hackensack, NJ, June 16, 48. *Study:* Montclair State Col, NJ, BA; Rutgers Univ, MLS. *Pos:* Reference librn, Art Dept, Newark Pub Libr, Newark, NJ, 71-76; reference librn, Rutgers Univ, New Brunswick, 76-82. *Awards:* Nat Educ Asn Arts Grant, 81. *Mem:* Art Libr Soc of NAm; Asn Col & Res Libr, Am Libr Asn; Col Art Asn; Spec Libr Asn; Indust Photographers of NJ. *Res:* Methodology in history of photography. *Interests:* History of photography, incunabula and fine printing, historic preservation. *Mailing Add:* 3210 Carbon St #75 Whitehall PA 18052

MEREDITH, DOROTHY LAVERNE
WEAVER, EDUCATOR
b Milwaukee, Wis, Nov 17, 06. *Study:* Layton Sch Art, Milwaukee; Univ Wis-Milwaukee, BAE; Cranbrook Acad Fine Art, Bloomfield Hills, Mich, MFA. *Work:* Objects USA, Johnson Found; Milwaukee Art Ctr; Cranbrook Acad Art; Fedn Handweavers Gallery, Wellington, NZ; Univ Wis-Milwaukee. *Exhib:* 22 Wis Designer Craftsmen, 46-72; Nippon Gendai Koghi Bijutsu Int, Japan, 67 & 68; Six Midwest Designer Craftsmen; Am Crafts Coun Craftsmen of Midwest; Fiber Clay Metal; and others. *Teaching:* Prof weaving, Univ Wis-Milwaukee, 53-75, emer, 75- *Awards:* Miss River Crafts Award, 62; Nippon Gendai Koghi Bijutsu Award, Japan, 66; 9 Wis Designer Craftsmen Award, Milwaukee Art Ctr, 71. *Mem:* World Crafts Coun; fel Am Crafts Coun (trustee, 58-61, state rep, 62-63, emer trustee bd, 80-); Am Crafts Coun NCent Regional; Midwest Designer Craftsmen; Wis Designer Craftsmen. *Media:* Fibers. *Mailing Add:* 2932 North 69th St Milwaukee WI 53210

MEREDITII, JOHN
PAINTER
b Fergus, Ont, 1933. *Work:* Art Gallery, Ont; Nat Gallery Can; Univ Waterloo, Ont; Mus Mod Art, New York; Montreal Mus Fine Arts; and others. *Exhib:* Canada 101, Edinburgh Festival, Scotland, 68; 10th Int Black & White Exhib, Lugano, Switz, 68; Winters Col, York Univ, Toronto, 69; Rothmans Art Gallery, Stratford, Ont, 70; Eight Artists From Canada, Tel Aviv Mus, Israel, 70; and others. *Mem:* Royal Can Acad Arts. *Mailing Add:* c/o Isaacs Gallery 832 Yonge St Toronto ON M4W 2H1 Canada

MERFELD, GERALD LYDON
PAINTER
b Des Moines, Iowa, Feb 19, 36. *Study:* Am Acad Art, with William Mosby, 54-57. *Work:* Marietta Col, Ohio; McDonough Collection Am Art; US Navy Arch; John Deere & Co. *Exhib:* Hope Show, Butler Inst Am Art, 72, 74, 76, 78 & 80; Okla Mus Art 14th Ann Artists Salon, 75; Allied Artists Am Ann, New York, 75-77; Civic Fine Arts Asn, Sioux Falls, SDak, 77; Vanishing Landmark Exhib, Springfield Art Mus, Mo, 77; Nat Acad Western Art, 79; Artists of the Rockies & Golden West Retrospective Exhib, Sangre de Cristo Arts Ctr, Pueblo, Colo, 83; and others. *Pos:* Studio asst, Dean Cornwell, New York, 57-60; combat artist, US Navy, Vietnam, 69 & Mediter, 71. *Teaching:* Pvt lessons painting, drawing & sculpture, studio. *Awards:* Louis E Seley Gold Medal, Salmagundi Club, 71; Okla Mus Art Award, 75; 1st Prize, Butler Inst Am Art, 81. *Bibliog:* Charles Movalli (auth), Gerald Merfeld's teaching tenets, Am Artist, 12/78; Betty Harvey (auth), Gerald Merfeld, Artists of the Rockies & Golden West, fall 81. *Media:* Oil, Pastel, Conte Crayon. *Dealer:* DeColores Art Gallery 2817 E Third Ave Denver CO 80206. *Mailing Add:* 228 Oak St New Lenox IL 60451

MERKEL, JAYNE (SILVERSTEIN)
HISTORIAN, CRITIC
b Cincinnati, Ohio, Sept 28, 42. *Study:* Simmons Col, with Wylie Sypher, BS, 64; Smith Col, with Henry-Russell Hitchcock, MA(art hist), 68; Univ Mich, with Leonard K Eaton, 66-68; Univ Cincinnati, 78-80. *Collections Arranged:* Early Works: Alexander Calder (auth, catalog), Taft Mus, 72; Behind the Queen's Skirt, Taft Mus, 72; Drawn by Cincinnati (auth, catalog), Collection of the Cincinnati Hist Soc, Contemp Arts Ctr, 80; 1930's Remembered, Part I, The High Style, Taft Mus, 82. *Pos:* Asst cur, Univ Mich Mus Art, Ann Arbor, 65-68; cur, Contemp Arts Ctr, Cincinnati, 68-69; dir educ, Taft Mus, Cincinnati, 68-74; archit critic, Cincinnati Enquirer, 77-; reviewer, Artforum, 80-; archit critic, WGUC (pub radio), 83- *Teaching:* Adj instr art hist, Univ Cincinnati, 70-72; instr art hist, Art Acad Cincinnati, 73-78; vis instr art hist, Miami Univ, 78-79 & 81-82. *Awards:* Award for Excellence in Archit Writing, Am Inst Archit, Cincinnati, 73. *Mem:* Col Art Asn. *Res:* Contemporary American architecture, art and criticism. *Publ:* Auth, var bk reviews, Art J, 76-77 & J Aesthetics & Art Criticism, 80; auth, articles & reviews, Am Inst Archit J, 78, Prog Archit, 80-82, Artforum, 81-82 & Inland Archit, 83. *Mailing Add:* 1908 Dexter Ave Cincinnati OH 45206

MERKIN, RICHARD MARSHALL
PAINTER, PRINTMAKER
b Brooklyn, NY, Oct, 1938. *Study:* Syracuse Univ Sch Art, BFA, 60; RI Sch Design, MFA(teaching fel), 63. *Work:* Mus Art, RI Sch Design; Mus Mod Art; Finch Col, NY; Rose Art Mus, Brandeis Univ; Mass Inst Technol. *Comn:* Seven murals, Blackstone Park Pub Sch, Boston, Mass. *Exhib:* Whitney Mus Am Art, 67, 69 & 72; one-man exhibs, Terry Dintenfass Inc, 73-74, 78 & 80-81, Chrysler Mus, Norfolk, Va, 80, Gallery Camino Real, Boca Raton, Fla, 81 & Eric Makler Gallery, Philadelphia, 81; Painting and Sculpture Today, Indianapolis Mus Art, 76; Alumni Artists Exhib, Syracuse Univ, 79; Nat Ann Midyear Show, Butler Inst Am Art, 79; and others. *Teaching:* Asst prof painting, RI Sch Design, 61-70, adj prof, 70-; vis artist in residence, Syracuse Univ, 72. *Awards:* Purchase Award, Soc Washington DC Printmakers Show, Smithsonian Inst, 62; Tiffany Found Fel Painting, 62-63; Rosenthal Found Award, Nat Inst Arts & Lett, 75. *Dealer:* Terry Dintenfass Gallery New York NY. *Mailing Add:* 500 West End Ave New York NY 10024

MERMIN, MILDRED (SHIRE)
PAINTER
b New York, NY. *Study:* Nat Acad Design; Art Students League, with Boardman Robinson & George Grosz; also with Charles W Hawthorne & Philip Evergood. *Work:* Israel Mus, Jerusalem; Chrysler Mus Art, Norfolk, Va; Springfield Mus Fine Arts, Mass. *Exhib:* Pa Acad Fine Arts, Philadelphia; Japanese-Am Exchange Exhib, Nat Mus, Tokyo, Japan, 61; Silvermine Guild Artists Nat Exhib, New Canaan, Conn, 62; Nat Acad Design, New York, 63; New Haven Festival Art, Conn, 69. *Awards:* Am Art Mag Award, 57 & Marian Haldenstein Award, 77, Nat Asn Women Artists; Grumbacher Award, Am Soc Contemp Artists, 68. *Mem:* Fel MacDowell Colony; Artists Equity Asn; Am Soc Contemp Artists; Nat Asn Women Artists; Provincetown Art Asn. *Media:* Oil, Watercolor. *Mailing Add:* 605 S US Hwy One Apt T920 Juno Beach FL 33408

MERRICK, JAMES KIRK
PAINTER, EDUCATOR
b Philadelphia, Pa, Oct 8, 05. *Study:* Philadelphia Col Art, dipl; Cape Sch Art, Provincetown, Mass, with Henry Hensche. *Work:* Philadelphia Mus Art; State Mus Art, Harrisburg, Pa; State Mus NJ, Trenton; Lehigh Univ, Bethlehem, Pa; Du Pont Collection, Wilmington, Del. *Comn:* Murals, pvt home, Bryn Mawr, Pa, 73 & outside wall, Drake Hotel, Philadelphia, Pa, 74. *Exhib:* Pa Acad Fine Arts, Philadelphia, 35-; Philadelphia Mus Art, 40-; Nat Acad Design Watercolor Shows, New York, Audubon Artists, New York; Art Inst Chicago, 40-49; plus many one-man shows. *Pos:* Exec dir, Philadelphia Art Alliance, 60-70. *Teaching:* From instr to prof art, Philadelphia Col Art, 29-60. *Awards:* Gold Medal, Philadelphia Col Art Alumni Asn, 54; Gold Medal Award of Merit, Philadelphia Watercolor Club, 55; Dawson Medal, Pa Acad Fine Arts, 64. *Mem:* Hon vpres & life mem Philadelphia Art Alliance; hon life pres Philadelphia Watercolor Club; founding mem Am Nat Theater Acad. *Media:* Watercolor, Oil. *Mailing Add:* 341 S Hicks St Philadelphia PA 19102

MERRILL, DAVID KENNETH
PAINTER, MURALIST
b Bridgeport, Conn, Oct 18, 35. *Comn:* Monroe Green, Town of Monroe, Conn, 72; ann report cover, William R Berkley Corp, New York, 73; IBM, Burlington, Vt, 74; 43 scenes of Southbury's past & present (mural), Southbury, Conn Town Hall Bldg Comt, 78; mural, Edmond Town Hall, Newtown, Conn, 83-85; and others. *Exhib:* Kent Art Asn, Conn, 69, 73 & 74; Northern Vt Artists Asn, 71-74; Mainstreams '74, Marietta, Ohio; Conn Acad Fine Art, 74; Douglas Gallery, Stamford, Conn, 74 & 75. *Teaching:* Instr art, Southbury Training Sch, Conn, 63-67. *Awards:* First Place, 72 & First & Second Place, 74, Northern Vt Artists Asn; First Prize Acrylic, Scan Art Exhib, 78 & 82. *Mem:* Kent & Washington Art Asns; Northern Vt Art Asn; New Haven Paint & Clay Club. *Media:* Acrylic. *Publ:* Auth, article in This New Eng, Yankee Mag; auth, article in Int Mag Marifacts, 10/78. *Dealer:* Douglas Gallery 1117 High Ridge Rd Stamford CT 06905; Lillian Haversat Jericho VT 05465. *Mailing Add:* PO Box 188 Southbury CT 06488

MERRILL, ROSS M
CONSERVATOR, PAINTER
b Abilene, Tex, 43. *Study:* Pa Acad Fine Arts; Oberlin Col, Ohio, MA; Intermus Conserv Asn, conserv cert. *Pos:* Admin head of conserv dept, Cleveland Mus Art, 74-81; head painting conserv, Nat Gallery Art, Washington, DC, 81- *Teaching:* Lectr mus conserv for var mus & conserv orgns. *Mem:* Am Inst Conserv; Int Inst Conserv; Nat Conserv Adv Coun (chmn energy comt). *Media:* Oil, Watercolor. *Res:* Fifteenth century northern European painting techniques. *Interests:* Early European paintings. *Publ:* Co-auth, Honeycomb Core Construction for Supporting Panels, 72 & An Information Retrieval System for Painted Works of Art, 73, Am Inst Conserv; auth, Juan deFlandes, a technical study, Cleveland Mus Bull, 76; co-auth, A History of Painting Forgery From 1500 to Present, 78 & auth, Technical Investigation of Cleveland Museum's Recent Forgery, St Catherine of Alexandria, 78, Am Inst Conserv. *Mailing Add:* 1643 Warrensville Ctr South Euclid OH 44121

MERRIN, EDWARD H
DEALER
Specialty: Classical and pre-Columbian antiquities. *Mailing Add:* Edward H Merrin Gallery 724 Fifth Ave 3rd Floor New York NY 10019

MERRITT, FRANCIS SUMNER
PAINTER, DESIGNER
b Danvers, Mass, Apr 8, 13. *Study:* Vesper George Sch Art; San Diego Acad Fine Art; Mass Sch Art; Boston Mus Sch; Yale Univ Sch Fine Arts; Colby Col, Hon DFA, 71. *Work:* Univ Southern Maine; William A Farnsworth Art Mus. *Comn:* Murals, Bd Educ, New London High Sch, NH, 43 & Knox Co Med Ctr, Rockland, Maine, 52. *Exhib:* Directions in American Art, Am Fedn Arts Traveling Unit, Carnegie Inst, 42; Int Watercolor Show, Art Inst Chicago, 42-43; Artists for Victory, Metrop Mus Art, 42; Butler Art Inst Ann, Youngstown, Ohio, 47; Greetings Exhib, Mus Mod Art, New York, 57; Maine Biennial, 79; Mus Northern Ariz, 79; Farnsworth Print Ann, 80; and others. *Pos:* Cur, John Esther Art Gallery, Andover, Mass, 37-39; dir, Flint Inst Art, Mich, 47-51; dir, Haystack Mountain Sch Crafts, Deer Isle, Maine, 51-77, emer dir, 77- *Teaching:* Instr painting & drawing, Abbot Acad, Andover, Mass, 37-39, Colby Jr Col, New London, 40-44, Kingswood, Cranbrook, Bloomfield Hills, Mich, 46-47 & Bradford Jr Col, Mass, 53-57; instr experimental printmaking & monotype, Haystack Mountain Sch Arts, 79 & 81; instr, Penland Sch Crafts, 80-81. *Bibliog:* Crafts tomorrow, standards, quality, design, Can Crafts Coun Artisan News, 9-10/79; The

Haystack Tradition, Art Craft Media, Bowdoin Col Mus Art, 80; and others. *Mem:* Artists Equity (regional bd mem, 47-48); fel Am Crafts Coun (trustee, 56-62 & 80-81); fel Royal Soc Arts; Penland Sch Crafts (trustee, 80-); World Craft Coun. *Mailing Add:* Centennial House Deer Isle ME 04627

MERTIN, ROGER
PHOTOGRAPHER
b Bridgeport, Conn, Dec 9, 42. *Study:* Rochester Inst Technol, BFA, 65; Visual Studies Workshop, MFA, 72. *Work:* Nat Gallery Can, Ottawa; Int Mus Photog & Visual Studies Workshop, Rochester, NY; Mus Mod Art, New York; Boston Mus Fine Arts. *Exhib:* Past into Present, Seattle Art Mus, Wash, 76; Great West: Real/Ideal, Univ Colo, Boulder, 77; Mus Mod Art, New York, 78 & 81; One-of-a-Kind Am Photog, Corcoran Gallery Art, Washington, DC, 79; Photog in the 70's, Art Inst Chicago, 79; Light Gallery, New York, 80; Friends of Photog, Carmel, Calif, 81. *Teaching:* Asst prof fine arts & photog, Univ Rochester, NY, 73-81, assoc prof, 81- *Awards:* Guggenheim fel photog, 74; Nat Endowment for Arts fel photog, 76. *Publ:* Auth, Records 1976-78, Chicago Ctr Contemp Photog, 78. *Mailing Add:* Fine Arts Dept Univ Rochester Wilson Blvd Rochester NY 14627

MESCHES, ARNOLD
PAINTER, EDUCATOR
b New York, NY, Aug 11, 23. *Study:* Art Ctr Sch; Chouinard's Art Inst; Jepson's Art Inst. *Work:* Philadelphia Mus Art; San Francisco Mus Art; Brooklyn Mus Art; Arco Collection, La; Palm Springs Mus, Calif. *Comn:* Murals, Hotel Newhouse, Salt Lake City, Utah, 50, Dr & Mrs August Maymudes, La, 70, Temple Isaiah, La, 73 & Bank of Am, Beverly Hills, Calif, 75. *Exhib:* Solo exhib, Palm Springs Mus, 72, Arco Ctr Visual Arts, La, 76, Mount St Mary's Col Fine Arts Gallery, Los Angeles, 78, Newport Harbor Mus Art, 81 & Municipal Art Gallery, La, 83. *Pos:* Art dir, Frontier Mag, 54-60. *Teaching:* Instr painting & drawing, Univ Southern Calif, summer 50; instr & dir, New Sch Art, Los Angeles, 54-57; instr, Otis Art Inst, Los Angeles, 63-67 & 77-78, Otis/Parsons Art Inst, 79-; instr, Univ Calif Exten, Los Angeles, 72-78. *Awards:* Purchase Award, Home Savings & Loan, Los Angeles Munic Exhib, 69 & San Francisco Mus Art, 69; Nat Endowment Arts Grant, 82. *Bibliog:* Thomas Leavitt (auth), Preface to Arnold Mesches & his paintings, Santa Barbara Mus of Art, 66; Michael Kurcfeld (auth), A flurry of codes, Arnold Mesches, Images & Issues, summer 81; Susan C Larsen (auth), Arnold Mesches at Karl Bornstein, Art News, 1/83. *Mem:* La Inst Contemp Art. *Media:* Acrylic. *Publ:* Auth, interview with James Welling, Mount St Mary's Fine Arts Gallery Catalog, 78; auth, Municipal Art Gallery Catalog, 83. *Mailing Add:* 4727 W Washington Blvd Los Angeles CA 90016

MESEROLE, VERA STROMSTED (MRS MILTON D BLOCK)
PAINTER, ADMINISTRATOR
b New York, NY, Aug 10, 27. *Study:* Wellesley Col, Mass, BA(hist art, painting), with A Abbot, B Swann & E Frisch & archit with J MacAndrew; Univ Vt, Burlington, adult educ with Francis Colburn; critique with Stan Marc Wright, Vt & father, Alf Stromsted, NY & NJ. *Work:* IBM, Montpelier, Vt. *Exhib:* Northern New Eng Artists, Univ Vt, Burlington, 54; New Eng Artists, New York World's Fair, 64; Nat League Am Pen Women, Tulsa, Okla, 66 & Salt Lake City, Utah, 70; Vt Pavilion, Expo, Montreal, 70. *Pos:* Supt art, Champlain Valley Expos, Vt, 67; juror, Cracker Barrel Exhib, Newbury, Vt, 67; chmn, Ann State, Fleming Mus, Burlington, 66-73; mgr art ctr exhib, Burlington, 72-74; auth, Newsletter Northern Vt Artists Asn, 67-73. *Awards:* First Prize, Champlain Valley Expos, 60; First Prize Portraits, Nat League Am Pen Women, Vt, 66 & 70; First Prize Watercolor & Portrait, Nat League Am Pen Women, Ga, 81 & 82. *Bibliog:* Stuart Perry (auth), TV interview, WCAX, Burlington, 71; article in Burlington Free Press, 67 & 72. *Mem:* Northern Vt Artist Asn; Nat League Am Pen Women, Atlanta Branch. *Mailing Add:* 10 Colony Ridge Pl Alpharetta GA 30201

MESIBOV, HUGH
PAINTER, INSTRUCTOR
b Philadelphia, Pa, Dec 29, 16. *Study:* Fleischer Mem Art Sch, Philadelphia, 34-35; Pa Acad Fine Arts, Philadelphia, 35-37; Albert C Barnes Found, Merion, Pa, 36-40. *Work:* Metrop Mus Art & NY Univ Collection Contemp Am Art, New York; Philadelphia Mus Art; Pa Hist Mus; Albert C Barnes Found, Merion, Pa; Whitney Mus Am Art; and others. *Comn:* Mural design, Benjamin Franklin High Sch, 37-40; mural, Work Progress Admin Art Proj, Bennet Hall, Univ Pa, 37-40; mural, Steel Indust, US Treas, US Post Off, Hubbard, Ohio, 41; color lithograph, New York Hilton Art Collection, 62; acrylic on canvas mural, Job, Temple Beth El, Spring Valley, NY, 72. *Exhib:* Pa Acad Fine Arts, 40, 58 & 67; Whitney Mus Am Art, New York, 46, 56 & 59; Hallmark Int Water Color Show, New York, 52; Corcoran Gallery Art, Washington, DC, 59; Am Acad Arts & Lett, New York, 67. *Teaching:* Art therapist, Wiltwyck Sch Boys, NY, 57-66; prof art, Rockland Community Col, Suffern, NY, 66- *Awards:* May Audubon Post Prize for Oil, Fel of Pa Acad Fine Arts, 58; First Prize Oil Painting, Tappan Zee Bank, Rockland Found Award Show, 64; Thornton Oakley Mem Prize, Philadelphia Watercolor Club, 76. *Mem:* Philadelphia Water Color Club; fel Pa Acad Fine Arts. *Media:* Acrylic, Watercolor. *Mailing Add:* 377 Saddle River Rd Monsey NY 10952

MESSER, THOMAS M
MUSEUM DIRECTOR, HISTORIAN
b Bratislava, Czech, Feb 9, 20; US citizen. *Study:* Thiele Col exchange student, Inst Int Educ, 39; Boston Univ, BA, 42; Sorbonne, Paris, France, 47; Harvard Univ, MA, 51; spec fel, Brussels, Belg, 53; Univ Mass, hon DFA, 62. *Collections Arranged:* First US mus shows, Egon Schiele & New Departures: Latin America, Inst Contemp Art. *Pos:* Dir, Roswell Mus, 49-52; asst dir, Am Fedn Arts, 52-53; dir exhibs & dir, 53-56; dir, Inst Contemp Arts, Boston, 57-61; dir, Solomon R Guggenheim Found, 61-; pres, MacDowell Colony, Peterborough, NH, 77-80. *Teaching:* Sr fel advan studies, Wesleyan Univ Ctr Advan Studies, 66; vis prof mod art, Barnard Col, 66 & 71. *Awards:* Knight First Class, Order of St Olaf, 66; Officer's Cross of Order of Merit, Fed Repub Ger, 75; Officer of the Order of Leopold II, Belgium, 78; and others. *Mem:* Asn Art Mus Dir (pres, 74-75); Am Arts Alliance; Int Coun Mus; Am Asn Mus; Arts Int. *Publ:* Auth, Edvard Munch, Abrams, 73. *Mailing Add:* Solomon R Guggenheim Mus 1071 Fifth Ave New York NY 10028

MESSERSMITH, FRED LAWRENCE
PAINTER, EDUCATOR
b Sharon, Pa, Apr 3, 24. *Study:* Ohio Wesleyan Univ, BFA, 48, MA, 49. *Work:* Addison Gallery Am Art, Andover, Mass; Cummer Gallery, Jacksonville, Fla; Butler Inst Am Art, Youngstown, Ohio; Springfield Art Mus, Mo; Huntington Galleries, WVa. *Exhib:* Am Watercolor Soc, 57-; Mid-Year Show, Butler Inst Am Art, 65; Yale Univ, 71; World Bk Encyclopedia; Daytona Beach Mus Art; one-man shows, Arno Gallery, Florence, Italy, 70, Vaccarino Gallery, Florence, Italy, 78 & Old Sculpin Gallery, Edgartown, Mass, 83. *Teaching:* Chmn dept art, WVa Wesleyan Col, 49-59; chmn dept art, Stetson Univ, 59- *Awards:* Spec Watercolor Award, Mead Packaging, Atlanta, 60; First Award, Fla State Fair, 67 & Winter Park, 75. *Bibliog:* Norman Kent (auth), Fred Messersmith paints on rice paper, Am Artist Mag, 12/60. *Mem:* Am Watercolor Soc; Fla Artist Group (pres, 64-66); Ala Watercolor Soc; Fla Watercolor Soc. *Publ:* Auth, Pottery of Gene Bunker, 62 & Francis Chapin, 65, Am Artist Mag; contribr, Artist and Advocate, Renaissance Ed Inc, 67; contribr, 100 Watercolor Techniques, 68; contribr, Acrylic Watercolor Painting, 70; contribr, Eyewitness to Space, 71. *Dealer:* Harmon Gallery 1415 Main St Sarasota FL 33577; Galleries International 401B Park Ave Winter Park FL 32789. *Mailing Add:* Dept of Art Stetson Univ De Land FL 32720

MESSICK, BEN (NEWTON)
PAINTER, INSTRUCTOR
b Strafford, Mo, Jan 9, 01. *Study:* Los Angeles Sch Art & Design, 23; Chouinard Art Inst, 25-32; anatomy with F Tolles Chamberlain. *Work:* San Francisco Mus Art; Springfield Mus Art, Mo; Los Angeles Co Mus Art; Long Beach Mus Art; Nat Mus, Washington, DC. *Comn:* Three murals, US Treas Dept, 35-40. *Exhib:* Long Beach Art Mus, 57; Springfield Art Mus, 67; Pomona Valley Art Asn, Calif, 75; one-man show, Gold West Park, Victorville, Calif, 79; Messick-Hay Studio Gallery, Apple Valley, Calif. *Pos:* Sketch artist, Disney Studios, Los Angeles, 40; sketch artist, Metro-Goldwyn-Mayer, Culver City, Calif, 42. *Teaching:* Instr life drawing, Chouinard Art Inst, Los Angeles, 43-51; instr drawing & painting, San Diego Sch Arts & Crafts, La Jolla, Calif, 48-53 & Messick-Hay Studio, Long Beach & Apple Valley, 52- *Awards:* Calif Graphics Award, Fla Southern Col, 51; Seton Hall Univ Key Award, 58. *Bibliog:* Michael M Engel (auth), Sketching the spec, Design Mag, 56; Vera Williams (auth), Art is a way of life, Southland Mag, 66; Geraldine H Wheeler (ed), Ben Messick & Velma Hay-Messick, Athelings Mag, 75. *Mem:* Fel Royal Soc Arts; Int Arts Guild, Monte Carlo. *Media:* Oil. *Mailing Add:* 20930 Lone Eagle Rd Apple Valley CA 92307

MESSICK, DALE
CARTOONIST
b South Bend, Ind, 1906. *Study:* Art Inst Chicago & Ray Vogue Sch. *Pos:* Designer greeting cards, Chicago; creator comic strip Brenda Starr, Reporter, Chicago Tribune-NY News Syndicate, Sunday & daily feature, 40- *Mailing Add:* c/o Chicago Tribune 435 N Michigan Ave Chicago IL 60605

MESSINA, JOSEPH R
PAINTER
b Newark, NJ, Sept 24, 04. *Study:* Nat Acad Design, New York, 20-23; Art Students League, with Bridgeman, 24. *Exhib:* Hudson Valley Art Asn, White Plains, New York, 71; Audubon Soc, Nat Acad, New York, 73; Bayberry Art Gallery, Southern Pines, NC, 77; Seventh Ann Nat Miniature Show, 81; Nat Western Small Show, Bosque Farms, NM, 81 & 83. *Awards:* Collectors Award, Seventh Ann Miniature Show, 81; First Prize Ivory, Nat Western Small Show, Bosque Farms, NM, 81; First Prize, Miniature Painters, Sculptors & Gravers Soc Washington, DC, 82. *Bibliog:* Spiritual qualities pervade Messina portraits of three Apollo astronauts, Montclair Times & Newark News, 8/69. *Mem:* Am Artist Prof League; Miniature Art Soc, NJ, Washington, DC, Fla & Mont. *Media:* Oil, Watercolor. *Mailing Add:* 71 Valley St South Orange NJ 07079

METCALF, CONGER A
PAINTER, INSTRUCTOR
b Cedar Rapids, Iowa, Apr 27, 14. *Study:* Stone City Art Colony, with Grant Wood, 31-33; Coe Col, with Marvin Cone, BMus, 36; Boston Mus Fine Arts Sch, with Alexandre Iacovleff & Karl Zerbe, 36-40; Coe Col, Hon DFA, 64; Gordon Col, Hon DFA, 78. *Work:* Boston Athenaeum, Mass; DeCordova Mus, Lincoln, Mass; Cedar Rapids Art Ctr & Coe Col, Cedar Rapids, Iowa; Phoenix Art Mus, Ariz. *Exhib:* Fifteen Years Museum Sch Alumni, Boston Mus Fine Arts, Mass, 40; Margaret Brown Mem Exhib, DeCordova Mus, Lincoln, Mass, 56; Retrospective, Brockton Art Mus, Mass, 69; Centennial Exhib, Boston Mus Fine Arts, Mass, 76; Boston Draftsmen, Boston Athenaeum, Mass, 78; Centennial Exhib, Boston Copley Soc, Mass, 79. *Teaching:* Asst to head painting & drawing dept, Boston Mus Sch, Mass, 40-41; assoc prof art drawing & painting, Boston Univ Sch Fine Arts, Mass, 56-72. *Awards:* Tiffany Found Prize, 38; Paige Travelling Scholarship, 40. *Media:* Oil, Graphite. *Mailing Add:* 2 Otis Pl Boston MA 02108

METCALFE, ERIC WILLIAM See Dr Brute

METSON, GRAHAM
PAINTER, WRITER

b London, Eng, June 24, 34. *Study:* Cambridge Sch Art; Chelsea Col Art; Univ London. *Work:* Mus Contemp Art, Chicago; Manchester City Art Col; Ga Mus Art; Mus of d'Art Mod, Skopje, Yugoslavia; Can Coun Art Bank. *Exhib:* 76 Essex Festival of Conceptual Artists, Univ Essex, Eng; Morbus, Dalhousie Univ Art Gallery, 73; Videoslope, Art Gallery of Ont, 74; one-man shows, Nancy Poole Studio, Toronto, Ont, 77-81, Eye Level Gallery, Halifax, NS, 78 & Art Gallery NS, 79. *Collections Arranged:* Quilts, Yesterday, Today, Possibilities, Mt St Vincent Univ Art Gallery, 74; Gleams of Remoter Worlds, 18th Century Metaphysical Art, Dalhousie Univ Art Gallery, 76; Nova Scotia Folk Art, Art Gallery of NS, Halifax, 76; Halifax 0906 Dec 6 1917 (auth, illusr, catalogue), A Photodoc on the Halifax Explosion, West House Mus, 77. *Awards:* Recreation Grant, NS Govt Dept of Recreation, 77; Can Coun Grant, 80; Gold Medal, Accademia Italia delle Arti de Lavoro, Italy, 80. *Bibliog:* Ron Shuebrooke (auth), article in Arts Atlantic J, 78; What we did in the world, Halifax Mag, 12/80; Lucy Lippard (auth), Overlays, Pantheon Books, 82. *Media:* Oil, Watercolor. *Res:* Alternative modes, essays in alternative interpretation of 20th century art and cultural ecology; war drawings of Alex Colville. *Publ:* Auth, Halifax Explosion, McGraw-Hill, fall 78; auth, East Coast Port, McGraw Hill Ryerson, 2nd ed, 80; auth, Alex Colville: Diary of a War Artist, Nimbus Publ, 81; auth, East Coast Port, McGraw Hill Ryerson, 81; auth, Alex Colville: Personal Realist, Nat Film Bd Can, 81. *Dealer:* Dresden Gallery Halifax NS Can. *Mailing Add:* c/o Sanford N Medford RR 2 Canning NS B0P 1H0 Canada

METYKO, MICHAEL JOSEPH
MUSEUM DIRECTOR, SCULPTOR

b Port Arthur, Tex, Feb 27, 45. *Study:* Houston Mus Fine Arts Sch; St Thomas Univ, Houston, with Dominique de Menil & Jermyne McAgy; Pratt Inst, Brooklyn; San Francisco Art Inst, MFA(printmaking). *Comn:* Tatto Parlor: Segment I (15 minute film) & Segment II (15 minute film with architect, Thomas Burke), David Gallery, Houston, 70; participation/doc event piece, Main St 76, Houston CofC, 76; installation piece, Houston Festival, 79. *Exhib:* The Bosch Show, Univ St Thomas, Houston, 76; Contemp Icons, Mus Mod Art, Houston, 76; Made in Houston, La Gallery, 78 & 79; group show, Art Ctr, Waco, Tex, 79; minatures, Univ Houston Lawndale Gallery, 79; Univ Houston Thomas Gallery, 79; and many others. *Collections Arranged:* Texas Week in San Francisco, Festival & Exhib of Texas Art & The Artist's Archives, Exhib of Materials Collected by Artists, San Francisco Art Inst, 72; Main St/Houston Festival art & video exhibitions, 78 & 79; Texas Crafts touring exhibition (ed, contribr & illusr, catalog & producer media presentation), S C Blaffer Gallery, 78; Embroidery: Houston Emb Guild, Craft & Folk Arts Adv Comt, 79, Lone Star Sampler: Works by Texas Craftsmen, 79, Art/Craft: 6 Houston Craft Guilds, 79, Selected Works: Texas Designer Craftsmen, 79 & Dimensions in Glass, 79. *Pos:* Asst to chmn, Dept of Art, Rice Univ, 66-67; cur, Grad Print & Photo Gallery, San Francisco Art Inst, 71-72; asst to dir/cur, S C Blaffer Gallery, Univ Houston, 73-78; dir crafts events, Houston Festival, 79- *Awards:* Tex Comn Arts exhib support grant, 78 & Cult Arts Coun Houston proj support grant, 79. *Bibliog:* Niomi Berman (auth), Interview & article in Southwestern Craftsman Mag, 76; Charlotte Moser (auth), Review of Houston Artists, Art News, 76. *Mem:* Artists Equity Asn (pres chap, Houston, 75-77); Cult Arts Coun Houston; Tex Asn Mus; Am Coun Arts; Western Asn Art Mus. *Media:* Various Media & Combinations of Media. *Publ:* Contribr & illusr, 9th Congress of European Exchange Students Journal, Int Cult Exchange Serv, 66; contribr & illusr, Conceptual Excerpts, Guano Mag, Univ Houston, 70; contribr & illusr exhib catalogues, S C Blaffer Gallery, 73-78; contribr introd, exhib catalogue for Donald Thornton, Col of the Mainland, 76; illusr, New Cultural Decision Makers in Houston, Art News, 77. *Mailing Add:* 1634 Branard St Houston TX 77006

METZ, FRANK ROBERT
PAINTER, DIRECTOR

b Philadelphia, Pa, July 3, 25. *Study:* Philadelphia Mus Sch, with Ezio Martinelli; Art Students League, with Will Barnet. *Work:* Olsen Found, Guilford, Conn; Ball State Teachers Col, Muncie, Ind; Philadelphia Mus Art; Nass Inst Technol. *Exhib:* Drawing & Small Sculpture Ann, Ball State Teachers Col, 62-63 & 64-65; Am Acad Arts & Lett, Childe Hassam Fund, 66; The American Landscape--A Living Tradition, Peridot Gallery, New York, 68; one-man shows, Alonzo Gallery, 74, 77 & 79; Monhegan Artists, Allentown Mus, Pa, 74. *Pos:* Art dir, Simon & Schuster, 50- *Awards:* Elisabeth Ball Purchase Award, Ball State Teachers Col, 64. *Bibliog:* Jules Perel (auth), Landscape drawings of Frank Metz, Am Artist, 5/62; Doreen Managan (auth), Landscape paintings of Frank Metz, Am Artists, 3/78 & Twenty Oil Painters and How They Work, Watson-Guptill, 78. *Media:* Oil, Watercolor. *Dealer:* Vered International Gallery 70 A Park Pl East Hampton NY 11937; Haber Theodore Gallery 24 W 57th St New York NY 10019. *Mailing Add:* 800 West End Ave New York NY 10025

METZ, GERRY MICHAEL
PAINTER, SCULPTOR

b Chicago, Ill, July 22, 43. *Study:* Wright Jr Col, Chicago; Sch Prof Art, Chicago. *Work:* Mt Whitney Mus Western Art, Calif; Favell Mus Western Art, Klamath Falls, Ore. *Exhib:* Death Valley Western Art Show, Calif, 73-79; Ariz Artists State Competition, Phoenix, 74; George Phippen Mem Western Art Show, Prescott, Ariz, 75-81; Western Heritage, Colo, 77-78. *Teaching:* Dir, Village Art Sch, Skokie, Ill, 68-72; instr oils & life drawing, Phoenix Art Mus, Ariz, 73-76. *Awards:* First Place Blue Ribbon Watercolor, 78 & Third Place, 79, Death Valley Western Art Show; First Place Watercolor, Western Heritage Show, 78. *Mailing Add:* 8437 E Monterey Way Scottsdale AZ 85251

METZGER, EVELYN BORCHARD
PAINTER, SCULPTOR

b New York, NY, June 8, 11. *Study:* Vassar Col, AB, 32, with C K Chatterton; Art Students League, with George Bridgman & Rafael Soyer; also George Grosz, sculpture with Sally Farnham, Guzman de Rojas in Bolivia & Demetrio Urruchua in Arg. *Work:* Fine Arts Gallery San Diego, Balboa Park, Calif; Ariz State Mus, Tucson; Lyman Allyn Mus, New London, Conn; Univ Mo-Columbia; Butler Inst Am Art, Youngstown, Ohio; and others. *Exhib:* One-man shows, Galeria Muller, Buenos Aires, 50, Gallerie Bellechasse, Paris, 63; Norfolk Mus Art, Va, 65; Mex-Am Cult Inst, Mexico City, 67; Van Diemen-Lilienfeld Gallery, New York, 66; Bartholet Gallery, New York, 73. *Bibliog:* Aymel Seghers (auth), New York news (and cover), Arts Rev, 4/63; M L D'Otrange Mastai (auth), An American flowering, 5/63 & Evelyn Metzger--recent works, 12/66, The Connoisseur. *Mem:* Artists Equity Asn; Am Fedn Art; Arch Am Art. *Media:* Oil, Acrylics; Enamel, Mixed Media. *Mailing Add:* 815 Park Ave New York NY 10021

METZGER, ROBERT PAUL
CURATOR, EDUCATOR

b Detroit, Mich. *Study:* Wayne State Univ, BA, MA; Columbia Univ, with T Reff; Univ Calif, Los Angeles, with Fred Wight, PhD; Am Film Inst, with Jean Renoir. *Pos:* Cur, Lydia Winston Malbin Collection of Art, New York, 74-76; dir art, Stamford Mus, Conn, 76- *Teaching:* Asst prof art hist survey, Univ Detroit, Mich, 65-66; assoc prof Am art hist, Univ Bridgeport, Conn, 77- *Awards:* Univ Calif Arts Coun Traveling Grant, 69; Mich State Univ Art Hist Res Grant, 74. *Mem:* Col Art Asn Am. *Res:* Biomorphism in the 20th century, American painting and sculpture 18th through 20th century, Reuben Nakian. *Publ:* Ed, Directory of American Periodicals, Oxbridge Press, 76; auth, Karl Struss, American Cinematographer, 76, Nakian's Place in History, 77 & The Case for Pop Art as Neo-Dada, 78, Stamford Mus. *Mailing Add:* 39 Scofieldtown Rd Stamford CT 06903

METZKER, RAY K
PHOTOGRAPHER, EDUCATOR

b Milwaukee, Wis, Sept 10, 31. *Study:* Beloit Col, BA, 53; Ill Inst Technol, MS, 59, with Aaron Siskind & Harry Callahan. *Work:* Mus Mod Art, New York; Art Inst Chicago; Smithsonian Inst; Bibliot Nat, Paris; Philadelphia Mus Art. *Exhib:* My Camera and I in the Loop, Art Inst Chicago, 59; Persistence of Vision, Int Mus Photog, George Eastman House, 67; one-man shows Mus Mod Art, New York, 67, Delpire Gallery, Paris, 79, Light Gallery, 79 & 81, Pa Acad Fine Arts, 80 & Marion Locks GAllery, 78 & 82; Milwaukee Art Ctr, 70; New Photog USA Traveling Exhibit, Mus Mod Art, New York, 70-72; Landscape/Cityscape, Metrop Mus Art, New York, 73; Philadelphia: Three Centuries of Am Art, Philadelphia Mus of Art, 76; The Photographer and the City, Mus Contemp Art, Chicago, 77; Venezia '79, La Fotografia, Venice, Italy, 79. *Teaching:* Prof photog, Philadelphia Col of Art, 62-81; assoc prof photog, Univ NMex, 70-72; adj photog, RI Sch Design, 77; adj photog, Columbia Col, Chicago, 80-83. *Awards:* Guggenheim Fel, 66 & 79; Nat Endowment Arts Fel, 74. *Bibliog:* Peter C Bunnell (auth), Ray Metzker, Print Collector's Newsletter, Vol IX, No 6, 79; Chuck Isaacs (auth), Ray K Metzker: An interview, Afterimage, 11/80; Andy Grundberg (auth), Ray K Metzker: form as expression, Mod Photog, 11/81; and others. *Publ:* Illusr, Razerol, Janus, 73; auth, Sand creatures, Aperture, 79. *Dealer:* Laurence G Miller Inc 38 E 57th St New York NY 10019. *Mailing Add:* 733 S Sixth St Philadelphia PA 19147

MEW, TOMMY
PAINTER, CONCEPTUAL ARTIST

b Miami, Fla, Aug 15, 42. *Study:* Fla State Univ, BS, MA; NY Univ, PhD. *Work:* Am Tel & Tel, New York; Jacksonville Art Mus, Fla; Middleburg Netherlands Mus; Mildura Art Ctr, Australia; Meridian Mus Art, Miss. *Exhib:* One-man shows, Montgomery Mus Fine Arts, Ala, 70 & Meridian Mus Art, Miss, 76; Paintings, Mus Art, Macon, Ga, 72; Kunst Informatie Centrum, Netherlands, 75; 37th Venice Biennale, 76; Nat Gallery Can, Ottawa, 77; Gallery 34, Kassel, Germany; and others. *Teaching:* Grad asst art, Fla State Univ, 64-65; asst prof art, Troy State Univ, Ala, 66-68 & Jacksonville Univ, Fla, 68-70; prof painting & chmn art dept, Berry Col, 70-; vis artist & lectr drawings, Nat Endowment for the Arts, 72. *Awards:* Grant, Cowperthwaite Corp, 72 & Ga Coun Arts, 80. *Bibliog:* Annette Kuhn (auth), Scar art, Village Voice, 75; Peter Frank (auth), Auto-art-and how, Art News, 76; Alan Storey (auth), Tommy Mew, Art Voices S, 3/78. *Mem:* Col Art Asn; Southeastern Col Art Asn; Popular Cult Asn South; Nat Art Educ Asn; Am Fedn of the Arts. *Media:* Acrylic; Fome-cor. *Publ:* Ed & contribr, Third Floor Love Poems, 66 & auth & ed, Le Voyage, 68, Troy State Press; ed & contribr, Dramatika, New York Press, 70; ed & contribr, Scartissue, Troy State Press, 76; auth, Ray Johnson, Col Art Asn J, 77; contribr, Intermedia Mag, Can, 77. *Dealer:* Marianne Lambert 3280 Farmington Dr NW Atlanta GA 30339. *Mailing Add:* Box 580-Art Mt Berry GA 30149

MEYER, CHARLES EDWARD
HISTORIAN, CERAMIST

b Detroit, Mich, Sept 7, 28. *Study:* Wayne State Univ, BFA, 50 & MA, 52; Free Univ, Berlin, Ger, 52-54; Univ Wurzburg, Ger, 58-59; Univ Mich, PhD, 67. *Work:* Mus Contemp Crafts, New York; Detroit Inst Arts; Boston Mus Fine Arts; South Bend Art Ctr, Ind; Ann Arbor Potters Guild, Mich. *Exhib:* Fiber, Glass, Clay & Metal Exhib, Wichita, 52; Midwest Crafts Exhib, Ceramics, South Bend, 53 & 54; Opening Exhib, Ceramics, Mus Contemp Crafts, New York, 57. *Pos:* Bd dirs, Kalamazoo Inst Arts, 78- *Teaching:* Assoc prof art hist, head dept & dir, Div Fine Arts, Mich State Univ, 59-66; chmn dept, Western Mich Univ, 66-77, prof art hist, 66-83; dir div art, Bradley Univ, 83- *Awards:* Purchase Award in Ceramics, Opening Exhib, Mus Contemp

Crafts, New York, 57. *Mem:* Nat Asn Schs Art (dir Div II, 72-80); Col Art Asn Am; Mid-Am Col Art Asn Am (vpres, 60-61, exec bd, 60-63, treas, 61-62); Ann Arbor Potters Guild (dir, 54-57); fel Nat Asn Schs Art & Design, 83. *Res:* European baroque architecture. *Publ:* Auth, Sebastiano Riccio, 57, A new group of ceramics, 57 & A Rodin portrait, 58, Detroit Inst Arts Bulletin; auth, Seymour Lipton and His Place in 20th Century Sculpture, 62. *Mailing Add:* 6620 N Greenmont Peoria IL 61614

MEYER, ELMER FREDERICK
PAINTER, WRITER
b Twin Falls, Idaho, May 24, 10. *Study:* Fed Schs Com Design, diploma, 29; Calif Sch Fine Arts, 30-31 & 54; studies with Eliot O'Hara, Rex Brandt, Millard Sheets, Tom Hill, Ken Potter, Morris Shubin, Barbara Nechis & Jason Williamson. *Work:* Santa Rosa City Hall, Calif; 1st Nat Bank Ariz & Tucson Realty & Trust Co, Tucson; Arts Coun, Phoenix. *Exhib:* California Art, State Fair Galleries, Sacramento, 80; 32nd Ann Soc Western Artists, Hall Flowers, San Francisco, 80; 18th Ann Statewide Exhib, Santa Rosa Art Guild, Veterans Mem, Calif, 81; Am Watercolor Soc, Nat Acad, New York, 81; Watercolor West, Riverside Art Ctr, 82. *Teaching:* Instr watercolor, on-location workshops, Forestville, Calif, 78-; instr watercolor, Arts Guild, Arts Sch Belvedere, Calif, 80-81; instr watercolor, Wine Country Workshops, Calistoga, Calif, 82. *Awards:* Gerry Pierce Mem, 4th Ann Southern Ariz Watercolor Guild, 71; Special Award, 31st Ann Soc Western Artists, House of Hatch Covers, 78; Neva Rall Mem, 32nd Ann Soc Western Artists, 80. *Mem:* Am Watercolor Soc; Soc Western Artists; Santa Rosa Art Guild (pres, 79-80); Santa Cruz Valley Art Asn (pres, 62-65); SWestern Watercolor Soc (vpres, 70-71). *Media:* Watercolor. *Publ:* Auth, Making watercolor work, private pub, 78; auth, Watercolor painting on location, private pub, 82. *Dealer:* Occidental Fine Art Gallery 200 Main St Occidental CA. *Mailing Add:* 5929 Van Keppel Rd Forestville CA 95436

MEYER, FRANK HILDBRIDGE
PRINTMAKER, DESIGNER
b Fitchburg, Mass, Jan 21, 23. *Study:* Art Students League, with Wallace Morgan, Robert Brackman, Reginald Marsh, Will Barnet & George Grosz; City Univ New York, with Julius Portnoy, BA; Cent Conn State Col, MS(art). *Exhib:* Bay Printmakers 1st Traveling Show, Oakland Munic Art Mus, Calif, 55; Soc Washington Printmakers 20th Exhib, Nat Gallery, Smithsonian Inst, 56; Fundacion Ynglada-Guillet Exposition de Obras, Palacio de la Virreina, Spain, 60; 25th Ann Nat Exhib Acad Artists Asn, Mus Fine Arts, Springfield, Mass, 74; plus many others in Conn area, 75-77; Conn Chap Artists Equity Asn Ann Show, Old State House, Hartford, 80. *Pos:* Artist, framer & restorer, Morristown Fine Arts Ctr, NJ, 54-56; state art consult, Ariz Dept Educ, Phoenix, 64; lectr-demonstr cellograph printmaking, Silvermine Guild of Artists Inc, 77 & New Eng Regional Art Educ Conf, 77. *Teaching:* Instr art, Eng & jour, Penasco Independent High Sch, NMex, 62-63; head art counr, Camp Tapawingo, Sweden, Maine, 64-68; instr art, Windsor High Sch, Conn, 67- *Awards:* Best in Show, Fall Exhib, Springfield Art League, Mass, 52; Alice Collins Dunham Award, 69 & Sage Allen Award, 72, Conn Acad Fine Arts. *Bibliog:* Ref shows, Art News, 9/54; Junior Jottings, Monday Afternoon Club Mag, 3/56; Janet Gaston (auth), Frank Hildbridge Meyer, Rev Moderne, Paris, 4/1/61. *Mem:* Conn Art Educ Asn (regional chmn, 74-76); Art Students League; Conn Acad Fine Arts; Artists Equity Asn (founder & 1st pres Conn chap, 76-); Visual Artists & Galleries Asn Inc. *Media:* Oil, Cellograph. *Publ:* Coauth, League Mag, Art Students League, 50; coauth, Comprehensive study on facilities, physical plot and philosophy of secondary and elementary art departments, NJ Art Educ Asn, 57; coauth, New Mexican Rev, 63; illusr, Our America, Ariz Dept Educ, 65; auth, Cellographic process of printmaking, Elihu Burritt Libr, 72. *Mailing Add:* 470 Wolcott Ave Windsor CT 06095

MEYER, FRED (ROBERT)
SCULPTOR, PAINTER
b Oshkosh, Wis. *Study:* Univ Wis; Harvard Grad Sch Bus Admin; Cranbrook Acad Art, BFA & MFA. *Work:* New York State Theatre, Lincoln Ctr Performing Arts; Everson Mus, Syracuse, NY; Allentown Art Mus, Pa; Little Rock Mus Art, Ark; Wichita Art Mus, Kans. *Comn:* Murals, Schrafft's Motor Inn, Binghamton, NY, 58, Exec Motel, Buffalo, NY, 59 & Holiday Inn, Niagara Falls, NY, 60; two bronze sculptural groups, Lazarus Mall, Columbus, Ohio, 67; two murals, Sarah Coventry Int Hq, Newark, NJ, 71. *Exhib:* One-man shows, Midtown Galleries, New York, 47, 48, 69, 74, 78 & 82, Philadelphia Art Alliance, 64, Everson Mus, Syracuse, NY, 65 & Allentown Art Mus, Pa, 81; Scripps Col Ceramic Invitational, 66; Ann Arbor Film Festival Tour, 68; 156th Ann, Nat Acad Design, 81. *Teaching:* Prof & special asst to dean for grad affairs, Col Fine & Appl Arts, Rochester Inst Technol, 55- *Awards:* Ford Found Fel, 55; Carborundum Award, Western NY State Exhib, 64. *Media:* Bronze, Terracotta; Gouache. *Publ:* Auth, Sculpture in Ceramic, Watson-Guptil, 71; illusr, Beck Third-Worlds It, Playboy, 8/75; illusr, The Great Gatsby, 81 & illusr, Tender is the Night, 82, Limited Editions Club. *Dealer:* Midtown Galleries 11 E 57th St New York NY 10022. *Mailing Add:* 17 Church St Scottsville NY 14546

MEYER, JERRY DON
HISTORIAN, EDUCATOR
b Carbondale, Ill, Nov 19, 39. *Study:* Southern Ill Univ, Carbondale, BS, 62, MA(art hist), 64; New York Univ, Inst Fine Arts, PhD(art hist), 73. *Teaching:* Prof art hist, Northern Ill Univ, 68- *Mem:* Col Art Asn; Mid-Am Col Art Asn; Asn Art Historians. *Res:* Late 18th & 19th century English & American Art. *Publ:* Auth, Benjamin West's Chapel of Revealed Religion, Art Bull, 75; auth, Benjamin West's St Stephen altar-piece, Burlington Mag, 76; auth, Benjamin West's window designs for St George's Chapel, Am Art J, 79; auth, Painter and the craftsman: Late 18th century stained glass, Stained Glass, 81. *Mailing Add:* Dept Art Northern Ill Univ De Kalb IL 60115

MEYER, RUTH KRUEGER
HISTORIAN, ADMINISTRATOR
b Chicago Heights, Ill, Aug 20, 40. *Study:* Univ Cincinnati, Col Design, BFA, 63; Brown Univ, MA, 68; Univ Minn, PhD, 81. *Collections Arranged:* Proposals for Sawyer Point Park, 77; Arabesque (auth, catalog), 78; Walls, 80; The Pattern Principle, 81; Inner/Urban: How the Artist Saw the City in the 70's (auth, catalog), 81; New Epiphanies: Contemporary Religious art. *Pos:* Cur, Contemp Arts Ctr, Cincinnati, 76-80; dir, Ohio Found Arts, Columbus, 80-83. *Mem:* Col Art Asn; Am Asn Mus; Int Asn Art Critics; Ohio Mus Asn. *Res:* Contemporary art, monumental and environmental sculpture. *Publ:* Auth, Pat Adam's paintings, Contemp Arts Ctr, 79; ed & contribr, The modern art society: the center's early years, Contemp Arts Ctr, 79; contribr, A meeting place of humanistic experience, Natur Skulptur, Kunstverein, Stuttgart, 81. *Mailing Add:* Taft Mus 316 Pike St Cincinnati OH 45202

MEYER, SEYMOUR W
SCULPTOR
b Brooklyn, NY. *Study:* With Louise Nevelson. *Work:* C W Post Col, Long Island Univ, Brookville, NY; Arlen Industs, New York; Mus Mod Art, Rio de Janeiro, Brazil; Tel-Aviv Mus & Bat-Yam Mus, Israel; Temple Beth-El, Great Neck, NY; and others. *Exhib:* Metrop Mus Art, New York, 76; Heath Gallery, 77-78; D Justin Lester Gallery, Los Angeles, Calif, 78-80; Royal Acad, London, Eng, 79; Galeria of Sculpture, Palm Beach, Fla, 79-80; Engel Gallery, Jerusalem, 81. *Mem:* Am Fedn Arts; Mus Mod Art New York; Sculptors League of NY; Guggenheim Mus. *Media:* Bronze. *Dealer:* Soufer Gallery 1015 Madison Ave New York NY 10021; Frances Aronson Gallery Atlanta GA. *Mailing Add:* 495 E Shore Rd Great Neck NY 11024

MEYER, SUSAN E
EDITOR, WRITER
b New York, NY, Apr 22, 40. *Study:* Univ Perugia, 60; Univ Wis, BA, 62. *Pos:* Managing ed, Watson-Guptill Publ, New York, 63-70; ed in chief, Am Artist, New York, 71-79, retired; ed dir, Am Art & Antiques, New York, 78-80; trustee, Artists' Fel, 78-; ed dir, Am Artist, Art & Antiques & Interiors & Residential Interiors, New York, 79-80; treas, Art Table, 81-; founder, Roundtable Press, Inc, 81. *Teaching:* Adj prof, Empire State Col/Union Col, 76-78. *Mem:* Artists Fellowship; Art Table. *Publ:* Auth, James Montgomery Flagg, 74; auth, Three Generations of the Wyeth Family, 75; auth, America's Great Illustrators, 78, auth, Will Barnet, 79; auth, Norman Rockwell's People, 81; auth, Treasury of the Great Children's Books Illustrators, 83. *Mailing Add:* 20 E Ninth St New York NY 10003

MEYER, THOMAS VINCENT
DEALER
b San Francisco, Calif, Dec 28, 43. *Study:* Inst Allende, San Miguel Allende, Mex, 61; Univ Denver, BSBA(marketing). *Pos:* Co-owner, Grapestake Gallery, 74-; vpres, San Francisco Art Dealers Asn, 77- *Specialty:* Contemporary painting, sculpture and 20th century American photography. *Mailing Add:* c/o Grapestake Gallery 2876 California St San Francisco CA 94115

MEYER, URSULA
SCULPTOR, PHOTOGRAPHER
b Hannover, Ger. *Study:* New Sch Social Res, BA, 60; Columbia Univ Teachers Col, MA, 62. *Work:* Brooklyn Mus; Finch Col Mus; Newark Mus; Larry Aldrich Mus; Grad Ctr, City Univ New York. *Exhib:* One-person shows, Hunter Col, 69, Lehman Col, 71 & Grad Ctr, City Univ New York, 74; Schemata 7, Finch Col Mus, 67; Listening to Pictures, Brooklyn Mus, 68; Cool Art of 1967, Larry Aldrich Mus, 68, Highlights of 1967-1968 Art Season; Cool Art, Abstractions Today, Newark Mus, 68. *Teaching:* Asst prof, Hunter Col, 66-68; assoc prof sculpture, Lehman Col, 68- *Awards:* Estelle Goodman Award for Best Sculpture, Nat Design Ctr, 66; City Univ New York Res Grant, Lehman Col, 70. *Bibliog:* Christopher Andreae (auth), Exhibition by Ursula Meyer at A M Sachs Gallery, Christian Sci Monitor, 2/26/68; Gregory Battcock (auth), Minimal Art, 68; Al Rogers (auth), Ursula Meyer, Alre-Films, 70. *Mem:* Women's Interart Ctr; Women in Arts. *Media:* Metal. *Publ:* Auth, De-objectification of the object, Arts Mag, summer 69; auth, Conceptual Art, 70 & The eruption of anti-art, In: Idea-Art, 73, Dutton; auth, How to explain pictures to a dead hare, Art News, 1/70; auth, Towards feminist art, Women & Art, summer-fall 72. *Mailing Add:* Lehman Col City Univ New York Bedford Park Blvd W New York NY 10468

MEYEROWITZ, JOEL
PHOTOGRAPHER
b New York, NY, Mar 6, 38. *Work:* Mus Mod Art, New York; Art Inst Chicago; Boston Mus Fine Arts; Philadelphia Mus; St Louis Art Mus. *Comn:* St Louis and the Arch, St Louis Art Mus, 80. *Exhib:* One-man shows, Eastman House, Rochester, NY, 66, Mus Mod Art, New York, 68, Akron Art Inst, Ohio, 79 & Stedelijk Mus, Amsterdam, 80; Cape Light, Boston Mus Fine Arts, 78; St Louis Art Mus, Mo, 80. *Teaching:* Adj prof, Cooper Union, 71-78; lectr, Princeton Univ, 78. *Awards:* Guggenheim Fel, 71 & 79; Nat Endowment Arts Fel, 78; Photogr of Yr, Friends of Photog, 81. *Publ:* Auth, Cape light, 78, auth, St Louis and the arch, 80 & auth, Wild flowers, 83, New York Graphic Soc. *Dealer:* Witkin Gallery 41 E 57th St New York NY. *Mailing Add:* 817 W End Ave New York NY 10025

MEYERS, DALE (MRS MARIO COOPER)
PAINTER, INSTRUCTOR
b Chicago, Ill, Jan 24, 22. *Study:* Corcoran Gallery Sch Art; Art Students League; watercolor with Mario Cooper; graphics with Seong Moy. *Work:* Smithsonian Inst; Nat Air & Space Mus, Washington, DC; Owensboro Mus

Fine Art, Ky; Univ Utah, Logan; Schumacher Gallery, Capital Univ, Columbus, Ohio. *Comn:* Apollo 11 Moon Flight (painting), 69 & Project Viking (landing on Mars), 75, for NASA, Nat Gallery Art, Washington, DC; ecology paintings, Environ Protection Agency, Washington, DC, 72; paintings, US Coast Guard, 83-84. *Exhib:* Smithsonian Inst, Washington, DC, 62-63; 200 Years of Watercolor Painting in America, Metrop Mus Art, New York, 66; Nat Acad Design, 68-; Butler Inst Am Art, Youngstown, Ohio, 69-70; Eyewitness to Space, Nat Gallery Art, 70. *Pos:* Ed newsletr, Am Watercolor Soc, 62-79, chmn awards, 67-79, chmn traveling exhibs & scholarships, 78-; academician, Nat Acad Design, 79. *Teaching:* Instr watercolor, Kefauver Sch Art, Washington, DC, 61-62 & Art Students League, 79-; workshops in NMex, Calif, Maine, New York, Tex, Pa & Fla, 70-77 & 79-81. *Awards:* Adolf & Clara Obrig Awards, 76 & 81; Arches Papers Award, 81; Medal of Honor, Knickerbocker Artists, 82. *Mem:* Allied Artists Am (pres, 75-78); hon mem Miami Watercolor Soc; dolphin fel, Am Watercolor Soc; hon mem Soc Mex de Acuarelistas; fel Royal Soc Arts, Gt Brit; and others. *Media:* Watercolor. *Publ:* Auth, articles, Am Artist Mag, 69 & Today's Art Mag, 70 & 74; contribr, Eyewitness to Space, Abrams, 71; contribr, Nat Sculpture Rev, 77; contribr, Watercolor Bold & Free, Watson Guptill, 80; auth, The Sketchbook, Van Nostrand Reinhold, 83. *Mailing Add:* 1 W 67th St New York NY 10023

MEYERS, FRANCIS JOSEPH
PAINTER, SCULPTOR
b Cleveland, Ohio, Feb 19, 21. *Study:* Fenn Col, 40; John Huntington Inst, 47; Cleveland Inst Art, BFA, 50. *Work:* Cleveland Mus Art; Akron Art Inst; Avis World Hq, Garden City, NJ; Speed Mus, Louisville, Ky; Westminster Col, New Castle, Pa. *Comn:* Prog cover, Cleveland Symphony Orchestra, 70; painting, Good Samaritan Hosp, Sandusky, Ohio, 74; sculpture, Visconsi & Sons, Cleveland; portrait, Cleveland Playhouse; bank mural, Third Fed Savings & Loan, Cleveland. *Exhib:* One-man shows, Toledo Mus Art, 65 & Westminster Col, 71; Juried Regional, Cleveland May Show, 61; group shows, Wooster Col, Ohio, 77 & Atlanta Col Art, Ga, 78; Juried Nat, Butler Inst Am Art, Youngstown, Ohio. *Pos:* Chmn dept drawing & med illus, Cleveland Inst Art, 78- *Teaching:* Prof drawing, Cleveland Inst Art, 51-80; assoc prof painting & sculpture, Notre Dame Col, 60-75. *Awards:* Second Prize, Ind State Fair; First Prize, Cleveland Jay Show. *Bibliog:* Katherine White (auth), Extension 18, Fine Arts Mag, 61; Paul Mooney (auth), Meyers art proves fine talent, Cleveland Press, 61; Paul B Metzler (auth), Artist showing runs the gamut, Cleveland Plain Dealer, 64. *Media:* Egg Emulsion, Acrylic; Bronze, Aluminum. *Collection:* Pre-Columbian art objects (Nyarit, Jalisco, Zapotec, Tarascan); oriental bronzes, polychrome wood, Santos and Roman glass. *Publ:* Auth, Drawing is the soul of art, Am Artist, 61; auth, Charcoal Drawing (Pitman), Grosset & Dunlap, 65. *Dealer:* Ross Widen Gallery Mayfield Lyndhurst OH 44124. *Mailing Add:* 2897 Plymouth Rd Cleveland OH 44124

MEYERS, RONALD G
EDUCATOR, CERAMIST
b Buffalo, NY, Nov 4, 34. *Study:* State Univ NY, Col Buffalo, BS, 56, MS, 60; Sch Am Craftsmen, Rochester Inst Technol, with Frans Wildenhain, MFA, 65. *Work:* High Mus Art, Atlanta; Lamar Dodd Art Ctr, LaGrange, Ga; SC Arts Comn, Columbia. *Exhib:* Guild Prize Winners, Columbia Mus Art, SC, 71; Southeastern Crafts, Greenville Mus Art, SC, 74; 25 Southeastern Artists, High Mus, Atlanta, 75; Artist-Craftsmen Invitational, Southeastern Ctr Contemp Art, Winston-Salem, NC, 76; Tribute to Hands, Springfield Art Asn, Ill, 78; Drinking Companions, J M Kohler Art Ctr, Sheboygan, Wis, 79. *Teaching:* Asst prof ceramics, Univ SC, Columbia, 67-72; assoc prof, Univ Ga, Athens, 72- *Awards:* Best of Show, Mid-South Ceramic & Crafts, 71 & SC Craftsmen, 71; Guild Purchase Award, Columbia Mus, 71. *Media:* Clay. *Mailing Add:* 230 Milledge Circle Athens GA 30606

MICALE, ALBERT
PAINTER, SCULPTOR
b Punxsutawney, Pa. *Study:* Pratt Inst Fine & Applied Art, cert(illus). *Work:* Riveredge Found, Calgary; First Fed Savings & Loan Asn, Valley Nat Bank & Ariz Bank, Phoenix; Dartmouth Col. *Exhib:* Mountain Oyster Club Western Art Show, Tucson, Ariz, 74-79; one-man show, Lincoln Thrift Asn Pres Club, Phoenix, 75; Cody Co Art League Ann Prof Show, Wyo, 75; Western States Art Show, Cody, 75; Nebraskaland Days Western & Wildlife Art, North Platte, Nebr, 75. *Awards:* Outstanding Science Bks for Children Award, Nat Sci Teachers Asn, 76. *Bibliog:* Profile: Ariz horseman, 5/77. *Publ:* Illusr, The Sign of the Open Hand, Scribners, 62; illusr, The First Book of the Spanish American West, Franklin Watts, 63; illusr, Lets Go with Lewis and Clark, Putnam, 63; contribr, Western Horseman Mag, 72-76; illusr, Something About the Author, Gale Res Co. *Mailing Add:* 7574 N Mockingbird Lane Paradise Valley AZ 85253

MICHAEL, GARY
WRITER, PAINTER
b Denver, Colo, Apr 17, 37. *Study:* Denver Univ, BA; Colo Univ, MA; Syracuse Univ, with Sydney Thomas, PhD. *Work:* Denver Pub Libr Permanent Collection, Colo; Denver Art Mus; Mus Natural Hist, Denver; Colorado Springs Fine Arts Ctr, Colo; Miron Collection, Poughkeepsie, NY. *Comn:* Mural, Perlmaco Corp, Regent Plaza, Denver, 75; bus panel design, Bill & Dorothy Harmsen Collection, Denver, 78. *Exhib:* One-man shows, First of Denver, Farraginous V, 76 & United Bank, Denver, 75 & 76; Northern Colo Invitational Art Exhib, 79; Pastel Soc Am, New York, 79; Faces and Places, Denver Nat Bank, 82; Of Lilies and Ladies, Kontny Studio, Englewood, Colo, 83. *Pos:* Demonstrating artist, Spree Arts Festival, 75-; lectr & demonstr, Grumbacher, New York, 77- *Teaching:* Prof humanities, Metrop State Col, Denver, 70-73; instr painting, Colo Univ, Denver, 75-76.

Awards: Popular Vote Award, Pastel Soc Am Ann Exhib, 79; First Place, Glenwood Art Festival, Colo, 79; Merit Award, Colo State Fair, Pueblo, 79. *Bibliog:* Joan Gould (auth), Academician turned artist, Southwest Art, 5/75; Irene Clurman (auth), Farraginous artist, 11/76 & Marjorie Barrett (auth), Traditional artist with a rebellious streak, 11/79, Rocky Mountain News. *Mem:* Pastel Soc Am. *Publ:* Auth, Dorothy Mandel: Her woodcut magic, Am Artist, 1/79; auth, Journey to the Magi, Colo Quart, 7/79; auth, The Art Institute of Chicago at 100, Denver Post, 8/26/79; auth, Markings, Southwest Art, 3/81; auth, Imagination in realist painting, Am Artist, 1/83. *Mailing Add:* 1440 Columbine Denver CO 80206

MICHAELS, GLEN
SCULPTOR, PAINTER
b Spokane, Wash, July 21, 27. *Study:* Yale Sch Music, 50-52; Eastern Wash Col Educ, BA, 57; Cranbrook Acad Art, with Zoltan Sepeshy, MFA, 58. *Work:* Detroit Inst Arts; Johnson's Wax Collection. *Comn:* Tapestry, Henry Ford Mem Libr, Dearborn, Mich, 75; mural, Renaissance Ctr, Manufacturer's Nat Bank, Detroit, 77; bronze fountain, Bicentennial Proj, Alpena, Mich, 77; mural, New Detroit General Hosp, Mich, 79; assemblage, Oakwood Hospital, Dearborn, Mich; and others. *Exhib:* Thirteenth Trienale, Milan, Italy, 64; Archit League New York Gold Medal Exhib, 65; Plastic as Plastic, Mus Contemp Crafts, 68; Objects: USA, 69-70; Smithsonian Plastic Exhib, 69-70. *Teaching:* Supvr art for children, Cranbrook Acad Art, 59-65; asst prof sculpture, Wayne State Univ, 67-69 & Univ Windsor, 70-71. *Awards:* Stuttgart Handcraft Exhib Award, 66. *Bibliog:* Slivka (auth), The crafts in the modern world, Horizon, 68; Redstone (auth), Art in Architecture, McGraw, 68; Nordness (auth), Objects: USA, Viking Press, 70. *Mailing Add:* 4800 Beach Rd Troy MI 48098

MICHAELS-PAQUE, JOAN
DESIGNER, SCULPTOR
b Menominee, Mich. *Study:* Layton Sch Art, Milwaukee, Wis, scholar, 55-57; Marquette Univ, 56-57. *Work:* Nat Mus Am Art & Nat Collection Fine Arts, Washington, DC; Univ Wis Hosp & Clinics; Objects USA, Johnson Wax Co, Racine, Wis; Dr J Wear Mem Libr, Madison, Wis; and others. *Comn:* Med Col Wis, Milwaukee, 80; President's Conference Room, Wis Tel Co, 82; ASEA, Indust Systems Inc Hq, Milwaukee, 83; CCSI-LBM Enterprises, St Cloud, Minn, 83; First Bank of Milwaukee Corp Hq, 83. *Exhib:* Michigan 72, Cranbrook Art Ctr, Bloomfield Hills, 72; Midwest Contructed Fiber Traveling Exhib, Northern Ill Univ, Univ Wis, Oshkosh & Lafayette Art Ctr, 80-81; one-man shows, Dayton Art Inst, 81, Viterbo Col, Lacrosse, Wis, 81 & Ariel Gallery, Chicago, 83; Wisconsin Now, Milwaukee Art Ctr, 81; and many others. *Teaching:* Vis artist, Miami Univ, Ohio, 81, Dayton Art Inst, 81, St Cloud State Univ, Minn, 82 & Kawashima Textile Sch, Kyoto, Japan, 83. *Awards:* Manpower Award, Wis Art Teachers, 71; Lily Mills Award, Belding-Lily Mills, Shelby, NC, 76; Bush Found Grant, 82. *Bibliog:* Rich Mathews (auth), Joan Michaels-Paque: An Appreciation, Fiberarts, 11-12/76; Judith M Kaiser (auth), New Dimensions in Wisconsin Art, Fiberarts, 11-12/76. *Mem:* Am Crafts Coun; Int Guild Journalists, Auths & Photogrs; Wis Painters & Sculptors; Handweavers Guild Am; Nat Stand Coun Am Embroiderers. *Media:* Flexible Linear Material. *Res:* Universal principles and concepts and their application in original, one-of-a-kind visual statements. *Publ:* Auth, ed & illusr, Design Principles/Fiber Techniques, 73 & A Creative/Conceptual Analysis of Textiles, 79, pvt publ. *Dealer:* Fanny Garver Gallery 230 State St Madison WI 53703. *Mailing Add:* 4455 N Frederick Ave Milwaukee WI 53211

MICHALS, DUANE
PHOTOGRAPHER
b McKeesport, Pa, Feb 18, 32. *Study:* Univ Denver, BA. *Work:* Mus Mod Art; Nat Libr, Paris; Mus Folkwang, Essen; Chicago Art Inst; George Eastman House, Rochester, NY. *Exhib:* Chicago Art Inst, 68; Mus Mod Art, 70; Am Pavilion Osaka Fair, 70; Cologne Kunstverein, 73; Frankfurt Kunstverein, 74. *Bibliog:* Carol Stevens (auth), Series photographs, more is more, Print Mag, 10/70; Arnold Gassan (auth), A conversation with Duane Michals, Image, George Eastman House, 1/71; Carter Ratcliffe (auth), Duane Michals, Print Collector's Newslett, 9/75. *Publ:* Auth, Sequences, Doubleday, 70; auth, The journey of the spirit after death, Winterhouse, 71; auth, Things are queer, Wilde, Koln, 73. *Dealer:* Sidney Janis Gallery 110 W 57th St New York NY. *Mailing Add:* 109 E 19th St New York NY 10003

MICHAUX, RONALD ROBERT
DEALER
b Holyoke, Mass, Aug 8, 44. *Pos:* Dir, Rolly-Michaux Galleries, Boston & New York. *Specialty:* 20th century masters & contemporaries, including paintings, sculpture & graphics. *Mailing Add:* c/o Rolly-Michaux Galleries 943 Madison Ave New York NY 10021

MICHELI, JULIO
PAINTER, ASSEMBLAGE ARTIST
b Ponce, PR, Aug 14, 37. *Study:* Univ Miami, BA, 62; Claremont Grad Sch, MFA, 65. *Work:* Mus Art Ponce; Mus San Juan, Ateneo Puertorriqueno, San Juan, PR; Inst Cult Puertorriquena. *Comn:* Serigraphs (three ed), Hotel San Juan, 69 & (five ed), Hotel Caribe Hilton, San Juan, 71. *Exhib:* First Nat Painting Exhib, Joe & Emily Lowe Art Gallery, Coral Gables, Fla, 63; Expos Pan-Am Art Graficas, Cali, Colombia, 70; Primera Bienal San Juan Grabado Latin Am, San Juan, 70 & Segunda Bienal, 72; XII Sao Paulo Biennial. *Teaching:* Prof art, Cath Univ PR, 65-, chmn dept, 71-78. *Awards:* First Prize in Painting, IBEC Corp, San Juan, 65; First Prize in Painting, Ateneo Puertorriqueno, San Juan, 66 & First Prize in Prints, 69. *Bibliog:* Nine Artists of Puerto Rico (film), Orgn Am States, 68; Pintores Contemporaneos Puertorriquenos. *Mem:* Col Art Asn Am. *Media:* Assemblage. *Publ:* Contribr, How to Make Your Own Greeting Cards, 68. *Mailing Add:* 14 Baldorioty St Ponce PR 00731

MICHELS, EILEEN MANNING
EDUCATOR, HISTORIAN

b Fargo, NDak, Mar 27, 26. *Study:* Univ Minn, BA, 47, MA, 53, MA, 59, PhD, 71; Inst Fine Arts, NY Univ, 50-51; Sorbonne, 56-57. *Collections Arranged:* Edwin Hugh Lundie, FAIA (auth, catalog), 72. *Pos:* Free-lance cur, Minn Mus Art, 72-73, assoc dir, 73-74; free-lance cur, Minneapolis Inst Arts, 73-74. *Teaching:* Vis asst prof art hist, Stanford Univ, 72-73; assoc prof & chair dept, Col St Thomas, 78- *Mem:* Soc Archit Historians (dir, 76-79, secy 82-); Col Art Asn; Women Historians Midwest. *Res:* Nineteenth and twentieth century architecture; American art. *Publ:* Auth, An Architectural View, Minneapolis Society of Fine Arts 1883-1974, Minneapolis Inst Arts, 74; auth, A Landmark Reclaimed, Minn Landmarks, 77. *Mailing Add:* 2183 Hendon Ave St Paul MN 55108

MICHOD, SUSAN A
PAINTER

b Toledo, Ohio, Jan 3, 45. *Study:* Smith Col; Univ Mich, BS; Pratt Inst, MFA. *Exhib:* Artemisia Gallery, Chicago, 74-; Painting & Sculpture Today, Indianapolis Mus Art, 76; Watercolor USA, Springfield Mus, Mo, 77; Pattern Painting, PS1, Flushing, NY, 77; Jan Cicero Gallery, Chicago, 77-; Andre Zarre Gallery, New York, 78-; Mus Contemp Art, Chicago, 79. *Pos:* Pres, Artemisia, Inc, 74-75; dir, Artemisia Fund, 74- *Teaching:* Instr painting, Chicago Acad Fine Arts, 69-74. *Awards:* Purchase Prize, Ill State Mus, 74; Purchase Prize, Carleton Col Exhib, 75. *Mem:* Chicago Artists Coalition; West-East Bay-Nat Network of Women's Aid Registries. *Media:* Acrylic, Watercolor. *Dealer:* Jan Cicero Gallery 433 N Clark St Chicago IL 60610; Andre Zarre Gallery 41 E 57th St New York NY 10019. *Mailing Add:* 118 S Clinton Chicago IL 60606

MIDANI, AKRAM
ADMINISTRATOR, EDUCATOR

b Damascus, Syria, Dec 7, 27; US citizen. *Study:* High Inst Dramatic Arts, Cairo, Egypt, BFA, 50; New York Univ, MA, 63. *Pos:* Dean col fine arts, Carnegie-Mellon Univ, 72- *Teaching:* Prof aesthetics, Carnegie-Melon Univ, 65- *Mem:* Pittsburgh Plan Art; Arts & Crafts Ctr (bd mem, 74-78). *Res:* Art criticism; history of Islamic art. *Publ:* Numerous art criticism essays and reviews, 60-67. *Mailing Add:* 2227 Beechwood Blvd Pittsburgh PA 15217

MIDDAUGH, ROBERT BURTON
PAINTER

b Chicago, Ill, May 12, 35. *Study:* Univ Ill, 54-55; Art Inst Chicago, BFA, 64. *Work:* Art Inst Chicago; Boston Mus Fine Art; Los Angeles Co Mus; Phoenix Art Mus; Worcester Art Mus, Mass. *Comn:* Prehistoric Project (permanent educ display, with Martyl Langsdorf & Prof Robert Braidwood), Oriental Inst, Univ Chicago, 68. *Exhib:* Chicago & Vicinity Show, Art Inst Chicago, 64, 66 & 73; Ill Biennial Exhib, Krannert Art Mus, Urbana, 65; Ill Exhib, Ill State Mus, Springfield, 66, 68, 69 & 71; Am Painting Exhib, Va Mus Fine Arts, Richmond, 66; 162nd Ann Exhib, Pa Acad Fine Arts, Philadelphia, 67; and others. *Pos:* Asst cur, Art Collection First Nat Bank Chicago, 71-78, cur, 79- *Mem:* Arts Club Chicago. *Publ:* Contribr, Buying Art on a Budget, Hawthorn, 68; contribr, Living World History, Scott Foresman. *Dealer:* Fairweather Hardin Gallery 101 Ontario Chicago IL 60657. *Mailing Add:* 1318 W Cornelia Chicago IL 60657

MIDDLEBROOK, DAVID A
SCULPTOR, EDUCATOR

b Jackson, Mich, May 1, 44. *Study:* Albion Col, BA, 66; Univ Iowa, with Jerry Rothman, Paul Soldner & Stuart Eddie, MA, 69, with Don Reitz, Byron Burford & Hans Braeder, MFA, 70. *Work:* Univ Wash Mus Art, Seattle; Koehler Mus, Sheboygan, Wis; San Jose Mus Art, Oakland Mus Art & San Francisco Mus Art, Calif; San Francisco Mus Mod Art; Fresno Mus; and others. *Exhib:* Nine Calif Artists, Everson Mus Art, Syracuse, NY, 78; A Century of Ceramics in US, Smithsonian Mus, traveling, DC, 78-80; NCCR: Sculpture Now, San Francisco Mus Mod Art, 79; Joshua Wedgwood Invitational, Philadelphia Mus Art, 80; Illusionism in Am, Los Angeles Co Mus Art, Los Angeles, 80; Reconstructions, San Jose Mus Art, 81; Klein Gallery, Chicago, 81 & 82; one-person show, Fresno Mus, 83; RAU Sculpture Court, Johannesburg, 83; Asn Gallery, Capetown, 83; and others. *Teaching:* Asst prof art, Univ Ky, Lexington, 70-74; prof art, San Jose State Univ, 74-; vis prof art, Notre Dame Univ, 72 & 76, Mills Col, Oakland, Calif, 77; artist-in-residence, Darwin Community Col, Australia, 80, Shefield Polytechnic, Eng, 81; artist-in-residence, Shefield Polytechnic, Eng, 81; vis artist, SAfrica, 82. *Awards:* Westinghouse res award, Koehler Mus, Purdue Univ, 73; Nat Endowment for Arts artist grant, 77; Lucy Stern fel, Mills Col, 78. *Bibliog:* Elsbeth Wood (auth), Handbuilding, McGraw Hill, 78; Harvey Brody (auth), Low Fire Ceramics, 80; Susan Peterson (auth), Modern ceramic concerns, 81. *Mem:* Nat Cong Educ Ceramic Art; Col Art Asn; Am Crafts Coun. *Dealer:* Klein Gallery 356 Huron Chicago IL 60610. *Mailing Add:* 18404 Montevina Rd Los Gatos CA 95030

MIDDLEMAN, RAOUL F
PAINTER, MURALIST

b Baltimore, Md, Apr 3, 35. *Study:* Johns Hopkins Univ, BA, 55; Pa Acad Fine Arts, 59-61; Brooklyn Mus Art Sch, 61. *Exhib:* Human Concern/Personal Torment, Whitney Mus Am Art, New York, 69; Painterly Landscape, Jersey City Mus, NJ, 82; one-man shows, Water Gap Art Gallery, NJ, 82 & Swain Sch Art, Mass, 83; Bodies & Souls, Artists Choice Mus, New York, 83; and many others. *Teaching:* Chmn painting dept, Md Inst Col Art, Baltimore, 61- *Bibliog:* Gerrit Henri (auth), rev in Art News, 72; Pat Mainardi (auth), rev in Art in Am, 7/74. *Media:* Oil, Watercolor. *Dealer:* Allan Stone Gallery 48 E 86th St New York NY. *Mailing Add:* Dept Art/Md Inst Col Art 1300 Mount Royal Ave Baltimore MD 21217

MIDENER, WALTER
SCULPTOR, INSTRUCTOR

b Ger, Oct 11, 12; US citizen. *Study:* Vereinigten Staats Schulen Fine & Appl Art; Berlin Acad, 32-36; Wayne State Univ, MA, 50. *Work:* Whitney Mus Am Art & House Living Judaism, New York; Detroit Inst Art & Flint Inst Art, Mich. *Comn:* Justice Butzel (portrait bust), Mich Supreme Court, 62; monument, Temple Bethel Mem Park, 62; sculpture, Bundy Corp, Detroit, 63; carved wood relief, Detroit Pub Libr, 64; hammered metal screen, Pontiac Motor Div, Gen Motors Corp, 68-69. *Exhib:* Mich Artists Shows, 46-61; Modellers, Carvers, Welders, Mus Mod Art, New York, 49-50; American Sculpture, Metrop Mus, New York, 51; Pa Acad, Philadelphia, 59; Friends of Whitney Collection, Whitney Mus Am Art, 64. *Teaching:* Instr sculpture, Henry St Settlement, 39-41; head sculpture dept, Soc Arts & Crafts Art Sch, 46-66, asst dir, 58-61, actg & assoc dir, 61-67, dean fac, 67-68, dir, Ctr Creative Studies, Col Art & Design, 68-76, pres, 76-77, pres emer & prof sculpture, 77-79. *Awards:* Mus Purchase Prize, Mich Artists Show, 50 & Founders Prize, 52, Founders Soc; Scarab Club Gold Medal, 60. *Media:* Metal, Wood. *Mailing Add:* 2568 N M-66 Box 603 East Jordan MI 49727

MIECZKOWSKI, EDWIN
PAINTER

b Pittsburgh, Pa, 1929. *Study:* Cleveland Inst Art, BFA; Carnegie Inst, MFA. *Work:* Cleveland Mus Art; Robert Hull Fleming Mus, Vt. *Exhib:* One-man shows, Robert Hull Fleming Mus, 74, New Gallery, Cleveland, 74, Tyler Sch Art, Pa, 74 & Mansfield Art Ctr, Ohio, 75; All-Ohio Show, 74; Cleveland Mus Art, 75; Park Ctr Show, Cleveland, 75. *Mem:* Founding mem Anonima Group; Nat Organization Visual Artists, Cleveland. *Media:* Acrylic. *Mailing Add:* 268 Bowery New York NY 10012

MIEZAJS, DAINIS
PAINTER, INSTRUCTOR

b Latvia, Kaucminde, Mar 11, 29. *Study:* Ont Col of Art, 56. *Work:* Nat Gallery of Can, Ottawa, Ont; Art Gallery of Ont, Toronto; Mus Fine Arts, Montreal, Que; Art Gallery of Winnipeg, Man; Vancouver Art Gallery, BC. *Comn:* Series of 18 paintings, Trans-Can Pipeline, Toronto, Ont, 71. *Exhib:* Ann Can Soc of Painters in Watercolors, 61-78; Can Painters in Watercolor & Am Watercolor Soc Exchange Show, 73; Can Painters in Watercolor & Watercolor Soc of Japan, 77. *Collections Arranged:* Across Canada in Watercolor, Art Gallery of Ont, 69-71. *Teaching:* Instr drawing & painting, Ont Col of Art, Toronto, 60-, chmn fine art, 83-; dir landscape, Madawaska Valley Sch Art, Maynooth, Ont, 65- *Awards:* Merit Award, Can Soc of Painters in Watercolor Ann; Purchase Awards, Can Soc of Painters in Watercolor. *Bibliog:* F Barwick (auth), Pictures from the Douglas Duncan Collection, Univ Toronto Press, 75. *Mem:* Can Painters in Watercolor (dir, 65-67); Latvis Soc Artists (vpres, 62-64). *Media:* Watercolor, Tempera. *Dealer:* Robert Art Gallery 641 Yonge St Toronto ON M4Y 1Z9 Can. *Mailing Add:* 380 Sackville St Toronto ON M4X 1S5 Canada

MIGNOSA, SANTO
CERAMIST, SCULPTOR

b Siracusa, Italy, Nov 14, 34; Can citizen. *Study:* Scuola d'Arte, Italy, Cert; Inst Statale d'Arte Firenze, Italy, Dipl: NY State Univ Alfred, MFA. *Work:* Univ Calgary Art Gallery, Can; Govt of Alta Art Found, Can; Govt of Tenn Ceramic Collection; Pall Mall of Can Art Collection; Art Centrum, Prague, Czech. *Exhib:* Int Ceramic Exhib, Ostend, Belg, 58, Prague, Czech, 61 & Gdansk, Poland, 73; Syracuse Nat, NY, 60, 62 & 66; Smithsonian Inst, Washington, DC; Faenza Int Concorso, Italy; Int Ceramic Exhib, Calgary, 73. *Collections Arranged:* Int Ceramic 73, Calgary, Can; Nat Ceramic 76, Calgary, Can. *Pos:* Co-chmn, Nat Ceramic Exhib, Calgary, Can, 75-76. *Teaching:* Instr ceramics & sculpture, Kootenay Sch of Art, Nelson, BC, 60-68; assoc prof ceramics, Univ Calgary, Alta, Can, 69- *Awards:* Gold Medal, Int Ceramic Exhib, Ostend, 58, Silver Medal, Prague, 61 & Second Prize Ex-Aequo, Calgary, 73, Int Acad Ceramics; Achievement Awards, Gov Alberta, 70 & 72. *Bibliog:* Al Riegger (auth), Featured Artist, Ceramic Mo, 63; article in, La Revue Mod des Arts et de la Vie, 67. *Mem:* Alta Potters' Asn (vpres, 70-71); Int Acad Ceramics, Geneva, Switz (coun mem). *Media:* Clay. *Mailing Add:* 5835 Bowness Rd NW Calgary AB T3B 0C5 Canada

MIKUS, ELEANORE
PAINTER, EDUCATOR

b Detroit, Mich, July 25, 27. *Study:* Art Students League; study in Cent Europe; Univ Denver, BFA & MA. *Work:* Mus Mod Art, Whitney Mus Am Art, New York; Victoria & Albert Mus, London; Los Angeles Co Mus Art; Indianapolis Mus Art, Ind; Nat Gallery Art, Washington, DC; and others. *Exhib:* One-woman shows, Pace Gallery, New York, 63, 64 & 65, O K Harris Gallery, New York, 70-74 & Mary Baskett Gallery, Cincinnati, 83; Mus Mod Art, New York, 74; Richmond Mus, Va, 77; Weatherspoon Art Gallery, Greensboro, NC, 77; Johnson Mus, Ithaca, 79-83; O K Harris Gallery, New York, 80-83; Mary Baskett Gallery, Cincinnati, 82-83; and others. *Teaching:* Asst prof painting, Monmouth Col, 66-70; vis lectr painting, Cooper Union, 70-72; lectr painting, Cent Sch Art & Design, London, Eng, 73-77; assoc prof, Cornell Univ, 79- *Awards:* Guggenheim Found Fel Painting, 66-67; Ford Found Tamarind Fel Lithography, 68; MacDowell Colony Fel, 69. *Dealer:* O K Harris 383 W Broadway New York NY 10012. *Mailing Add:* 645 First Ave New York NY 10016

MILANT, JEAN ROBERT
DEALER

b Milwaukee, Wis, Dec 27, 43. *Study:* Univ Wis, Milwaukee, BA & BFA, 66; Univ NMex, Albuquerque, MA, 69; Lithography Workshop, Los Angeles. *Pos:* Dir & owner, Cirrus Ed Ltd, 70-; dir & owner, Cirrus Gallery Ltd, 70-;

mem bd, Los Angeles Inst Contemp Art, 74-76; vpres, Los Angeles Visual Arts. *Awards:* Tamarind Master Printer, 69. *Specialty:* Contemporary painting, sculpture, performance, environments of Southern California artists; publisher of lithographs and screenprints of noted California artists. *Publ:* Ed, Artists/Prints 1976-1977, Contemp Art Publ Inc, 78. *Mailing Add:* 542 S Alameda St Los Angeles CA 90013

MILDER, JAY
PAINTER, SCULPTOR
b Omaha, Nebr, May 12, 34. *Study:* The Sorbonne; with Ossip Zadkine; with Andre L'Hote, Paris, France; Chicago Art Inst. *Work:* Tel Aviv Mus, Israel; Chrysler Mus, Norfolk, Va; Skidmore Col, NY. *Comn:* Sculpture, Sinai Temple, Los Angeles, Calif, 64; litho, Greenwich Light Opera, Conn, 70; etching, Rainbow Arts Found, NY, 77. *Exhib:* Mus PR; Dayton Art Inst, Ohio; Chrysler Mus, Norfolk, Va; Mint Mus Art, Charlotte, NC; Joslyn Art Mus, Omaha, Nebr; Art for the Olympics, Mus Mod Art, New York. *Collections Arranged:* Rhino Horn Exhib, New Sch for Social Res, New York; Oakley Collection, Skidmore Col; 50 American Contemporary Drawings, Ann Arbor Mus, Mich. *Teaching:* Asst prof art, City Col, New York, 77-81, assoc prof, 81- *Awards:* Gutman Award, 60; First Prizes, All Ohio Artists, 64 & Am Figurative Artists, Bayonne, NJ, 77. *Bibliog:* Dorothy Beskind (auth), Jay Milder Paints (film), 67; Rudy Stern (auth), Paintings and Life of Jay Milder (film), 70; George Preston (auth), article, Arts Mag, 11/76. *Media:* Oil; Mixed. *Dealer:* Oscarsson Hood Gallery 41 W 57th St New York NY 10019. *Mailing Add:* 108 Wooster St New York NY 10012

MILES, ELLEN GROSS
HISTORIAN, CURATOR
b New York, NY, July 28, 41. *Study:* Bryn Mawr Col, BA, 64; Winterthur Summer Inst, 67; Yale Univ Grad Sch, MPh, 70 & PhD, 76. *Pos:* Pub relations asst & registr, Corcoran Gallery Art, Washington, DC, 64-66; asst to dir, Nat Portrait Gallery, Washington, DC, 72-77, assoc cur, 77- *Mem:* Col Art Asn; Am Soc Eighteenth Century Studies. *Res:* Eighteenth and nineteenth century British and American portrait painting and drawing. *Publ:* Ed, Portrait painting in America: the 19th century, Main St/Universe, 77; auth, The Iveagh Bequest, Kenwood, Greater London Council (England): Thomas Hudson, 1701-1779, Portrait Painter and Collector, a bicentenary exhib, 79; auth, Portraits of the heroes of Louisbourg, 1745-1751, Am art J, winter 82-83; contribr, Masterpieces from Versailles: Three Centuries of French Portraiture, Nat Portrait Gallery, 83; and others. *Mailing Add:* c/o Nat Portrait Gallery Eighth & F Sts Washington DC 20560

MILES, JEANNE PATTERSON
PAINTER, SCULPTOR
b Baltimore, Md, 08. *Study:* George Washington Univ, BFA; Grande Chaumiere, Paris; also with Marcel Gromaire, Paris. *Work:* Guggenheim Mus, New York; Newark Mus; Munson Williams Proctor Mus, Utica, NY; Andrew C White Mus, Cornell Univ; Santa Barbara Mus, Calif. *Comn:* Mural designs for Kentile Co, Kansas City, 60, Los Angeles, 62 & Atlanta, Ga, 63; mural symbolic design, Chicago, 64 & room divider in geometric design, NY, 65. *Exhib:* Eight exhibs, Betty Parsons Gallery, New York, 43-82; Mysticism in Art, Rome-New York Found, Rome, 57; Geometric Art, Whitney Mus Am Art, New York, 63; The Square in Art Traveling Show, Am Fedn Art, 68-69; retrospective, Three American Purists, Mus Fine Arts, Springfield, Mass, 75. *Collections Arranged:* Purist Painting Exhib, Yale Univ, 57. *Teaching:* Docent, Mus Non Objective Art, New York, 45-50; dir art dept, Moravian Col Women, 48-51; docent, Guggenheim Mus, New York, 51-52; asst dir painting & life drawing, Oberlin Col, 52-53; instr painting, NY Inst Technol, 68-69. *Awards:* C C Ladd Study Scholar, 39-40; Am Inst Arts & Lett Emergency Grant, 69; Mark Rothko Found Grant, 71. *Bibliog:* Article in Arts Mag, 11/79; Listing as Special Event, Art Gallery Guide, 11/79; article, New York Times, 79. *Mem:* Am Abstract Artists; Fine Arts Federation, NY. *Interests:* Research into use of mandala as an art form throughout history. *Publ:* Auth, article in Arts Mag, 4/77; illus, cover, Art Gallery Guide; Auth, Three America Purists (catalog), Springfield Mass Mus, 75; auth, Past, Present & Peculiar (catalog), Ingber Gallery, 79; auth, page, American Women Painters, 82. *Dealer:* Betty Parsons Gallery 24 West 57th St New York NY 10022. *Mailing Add:* 463 West St Apt A 1103 New York NY 10014

MILES, M MARIANNE See Marianne

MILEY, LES
CERAMIST, EDUCATOR
b Petersburg, Ind, Nov 1, 34. *Study:* Purdue Univ, ceramics with Bill Farrell; Ind State Univ, BA & MA; Southern Ill Univ, with Nicholas Vergette & Brent Kington, MFA. *Work:* DePauw Univ, Greencastle, Ind; Evansville Mus Arts & Sci, Ind; Mitchell Gallery, Southern Ill Univ, Carbondale; Boris Wine Collection Contemp Am Ceramics, Peoria, Ill; Morehead State Univ, Ky. *Comn:* Archit ceramics, Robert L Blaffer Trust, New Harmony, Ind, 74. *Exhib:* Alliance Gallery, Indianapolis Mus Art, 77; Clayfest, Leah Ramborg Gallery, Indianapolis, 82; Salzbrand 83, Handwerkskammer Galerie, Koblenz, Ger, 83; Nat Functional Ceramics, Wooster Mus, 83; Hands of Man, Indianapolis Art League, 83; Ninth Clay Nat, Millersburg Univ, 83. *Pos:* Dir, Blafter Trust ceramic workshop, New Harmony, Ind, 67-; mem bd dirs, Evansville Mus Arts & Sci. *Teaching:* Prof art, Univ Evansville, 61-, chmn dept, 65-66 & 69- *Awards:* Purchase Awards, Owensboro Mus Art Exhib, Ky, 82 & Clayfest, Indianapolis, 83. *Bibliog:* Stanley Lee (auth), A sprigging variation, Ceramics Monthly Mag, 74; Thomas Schafer (auth), Pottery Decoration, 75 & Jack Troy (auth), Salt-Glazed Ceramics, 77, Watson-Guptill. *Mem:* Nat Coun Educ Ceramic Arts; Nat Coun Art Adminr. *Media:* Clay, Metal. *Mailing Add:* 447 S St James Blvd Evansville IN 47714

MILEY, MIMI CONNEEN
CURATOR
b Bryn Mawr, Pa, Aug 17, 46. *Study:* Western Col, Oxford, Ohio, BA(art hist). *Collections Arranged:* Winter Scenes by 19th Century Lithographers, 74; Pennsylvania Folk Art (auth, catalog), Allentown Art Mus, Pa, 74; Discover Texture, 75-77, Discover Color, 77-78 & Discover Design Elements, 79-80; A Salute to Walter Emerson Baum, 76; Howard Chandler Christy: Artist/Illustrator of Style (auth, catalog), 77; The Perceptive Eye: Art/Math (auth, catalog), 79. *Pos:* Cur educ, Allentown Art Mus, Pa, 70- *Mem:* Nat Arts Club; Am Asn Mus. *Mailing Add:* Box 117 Fifth & Court Sts Allentown PA 18105

MILGROM, BETTY
PAINTER
b New York, NY. *Study:* New York Univ, BA & MA; privately at Mus Mod Art & Brooklyn Mus. *Work:* Nat Energy Found & New York Public Libr, NY. *Exhib:* Jersey City Mus Art, NJ, 75; Montgomery Co Art Mus, Md, 75; Mus du Luxembourg, Paris, France, 76; Goldsboro Art Ctr, NC, 77; Percy H Whiting Art Mus, Fair Hope, Ala, 78; Metrop Mus Art, New York, 79. *Pos:* Founder & dir, Eleanor Gay Lee Gallery Found, 76- *Awards:* First Prize, Composers, Authors & Artists Am, 81. *Mem:* Burr Artists (bd dirs, 77-); Nat League Am Pen Women; Nat Arts Club; Composers, Authors & Artists Am (mem nat bd, 78-). *Media:* Watercolor, Oil. *Dealer:* Hansen Galleries 561 Broadway New York NY 10012. *Mailing Add:* 185 E 85th St New York NY 10028

MILHOAN, RANDALL BELL
ADMINISTRATOR, PAINTER
b Overton, Nebr, Feb 24, 44. *Study:* Kearney State Teachers Col, 64; Univ Nebr, Lincoln, BFA, 68; Univ Calif, Santa Barbara, Calif Regents Scholar, 70. *Work:* Sheldon Mem Gallery, Lincoln, Nebr; Joslyn Gallery, Omaha, Nebr. *Exhib:* Modern Trends Exhib, Elder Gallery, Lincoln, 67; Mulvane Mus, Topeka, Kans, 68; Tenth Midwest Biennial, Joslyn Mus, Omaha, 68; Summervail Faculty Exhib, Summervail Gallery, Vail, Colo, 75 & 82; Creatures in Print, STex Artmobile, Corpus Christi, 83. *Pos:* Founder & dir, Summervail Workshop for Art & Critical Studies, Colo Mountain Col, 71- *Teaching:* Instr advan studies & special proj painting, Colo Mountain Col, 70- *Awards:* Purchase Award, Tenth Midwest Biennial, 68. *Mem:* Eagle Valley Arts Coun (vpres, 71-76); Colo Art Educ Asn; Am Asn Community & Jr Col; Col Art Asn Am. *Media:* Oil, Pastel. *Dealer:* Summervail Workshop Gallery 1310 Westhaven Dr Vail CO 81658. *Mailing Add:* 483 E Gore Creek Dr Box 1114 Vail CO 81658

MILHOLLAND, RICHARD ALEXANDER
PAINTER
b Paterson, NJ, Apr 30, 46. *Study:* Neward Sch fine Fine & Indust Arts, NJ, 64-68; Brooklyn Mus Art Sch, with Reuben Tam; Univ of the Americas, Mexico City, BFA & MFA(teaching fel). *Work:* Honolulu Acad Arts, Hawaii; Gibbes Art Gallery, Charleston, SC; Grinnell Col; Ball State Univ Art Gallery. *Exhib:* Childe Hassam Fund Exhib, Am Acad Arts & Lett, New York, 72; Mem Gallery Exhib, Albright-Knox Art Gallery, Buffalo, NY, 72; one-man show, Babcock Galleries, New York, 72, 73 & 75; 21st Ann Drawings & Sculpture, Ball State Univ Art Gallery, 74. *Teaching:* Instr sculpture, drawing & painting, Univ of the Americas, 69-70; instr painting & drawing, Univ SFla, 72. *Awards:* Childe Hassam Fund Purchase Award, Am Acad Arts & Lett, 72. *Mailing Add:* 20 E 67th St New York NY 10021

MILLARD, CHARLES WARREN, III
CURATOR, WRITER
b Elizabeth, NJ, Dec 20, 32. *Study:* Princeton Univ, BA; Harvard Univ, MA & PhD. *Pos:* Dir, Washington Gallery Mod Art, 66-67; cur 19th century European art, Los Angeles Co Mus Art, 71-74; art ed, Hudson Rev, 72-; chief cur, Hirshhorn Mus & Sculpture Garden, 74- *Teaching:* Adj prof art hist, Johns Hopkins Univ, 82- *Res:* Nineteenth century French sculpture, particularly Degas and Preault; various topics in modern painting and sculpture. *Publ:* Auth, Sculpture of Edgar Degas, Princeton Univ, 76; and many other articles & rev in var art periodicals. *Mailing Add:* Hirshhorn Mus & Sculpture Garden Eighth St & Independence Ave SW Washington DC 20560

MILLEA, TOM (THOMAS FRANCIS)
PHOTOGRAPHER
b Bridgeport, Conn, Sept 30, 44. *Study:* Univ Western Conn, BA, 66; studied with Paul Caponigro, 68-73. *Work:* Mus Mod Art, New York; Victoria & Albert Mus; Ctr Creative Photog, Tucson; Oakland Mus; Philadelphia Mus Art. *Exhib:* Solo exhibs, Friends Photog, Carmel, Calif, 78; DeSaisset Art Mus, Santa Clara, Calif, 80, Arco Ctr Arts, Los Angeles, 80, Camden Arts Ctr, London, 81 & Ctr Creative Photog, Tucson, 82; and others. *Teaching:* Guest lectr photog, Friends Photog, Carmel, Calif, 75- & San Francisco Art Inst, 83. *Awards:* Ruttenberg Grant, 82 & Publ Workshop Grant, 83, Friends Photog. *Bibliog:* John Hafey & Tom Shillea (auths), The Platinum Print, Rochester Inst Technol, 80; interview, New Pictorialist Soc, 83; Alan Plone (auth), The Life and Work of Tom Millea, Vis Art Films Inc, 84. *Mem:* Friends Photog; Soc Photog Educ. *Media:* Platinum, Palladium. *Publ:* Auth, The Technique of Platinum and Palladium, Platinum Workshops, 76. *Dealer:* Light Gallery 724 Fifth Ave New York NY; Weston Gallery Carmel CA. *Mailing Add:* PO Box 4212 Carmel CA 93921

MILLER, BARBARA DARLENE
PAINTER, PRINTMAKER
b Jarbidge, Nev. *Study:* Univ Wash, BA; Univ Hawaii, MEd; etching with Rudy Pozzatti & Gabor Peterdi; design with Clayton Rippey; painting with

Tadashi Sato & Tseng Yu-Ho. *Work:* State Found Cult & Arts, Honolulu; Univ Hawaii Art Dept Etching Collection. *Comn:* Acrylic mural, KPOI Radio, Waikiki, Honolulu, 68; Christ with Thorns (acrylic painting), Church of Good Shepherd, Kahului, Maui, 70; Buddha (acrylic painting), Kahului Hongwanji Mission, Maui, 72; Mosaics (film), State Found & Maui Arts Coun, 72. *Exhib:* Walker Art Ctr Nat, Minneapolis, 65; Painters of Hawaii Circulating Exhib, 69; Etchings, Hawaii State Libr, 70; Regional Ethel Baldwin Mem, Wailuku, 72-81; Art Maui, Hawaii State Invitational Show, 81; plus others; Invitational Show, Honolulu Cult Plaza, 82. *Pos:* Artist, Logos Layouts, KPOI Radio, 65-67; art dir, KHVH Radio-TV, Honolulu, 67-68. *Teaching:* Art instr, Hilo High Sch, 57-60; elem art specialist, Kahului Elem Sch, 64-68; art instr & art program coordr, Maui Community Col, 68- *Awards:* Hawaii Artists Exhibs Awards & Prizes, 65-77; State Found Cult & Art Purchase Award, 72; Grand Prize, Best in Show, Hui Noeau Art Soc, 77. *Bibliog:* Eileen Webster (auth), Milady of the week--Barbara Miller, 68 & Darrell Neilson (auth), Works of Mrs Miller, 68, Maui News; Tim Mitchell (auth), Art news--Barbara Miller painter, Honolulu Mag, 69. *Mem:* Maui Arts Coun (visual arts chmn, 68-80); Hui Noeau Art Soc; Nat Art Educ Asn; Maui Mayors' Comt Cult and Art. *Media:* Acrylic, Intaglio. *Publ:* Illusr cover, Festival of Arts, 69; coauth, Grass Roots, Poetry & Art, 70; illusr cover, Our Changing Times, Univ Hawaii Div Continuing Educ, 70. *Dealer:* Village Gallery-Whalers Village Kaanapali Maui HI 96753. *Mailing Add:* Maui Community Col 310 Kaahumanu Ave Kahului HI 96732

MILLER, BRENDA
SCULPTOR, ENVIRONMENTAL
b Bronx, NY. *Study:* Univ NMex, BFA, 65; Tulane Univ, MFA, 67. *Work:* Mus Boymans-Van Beuningen, Rotterdam, Holland; Haag Gemeente Mus, Holland; Hartford Atheneum, Conn; Univ Tex, Austin; Newport Harbor Art Mus, Newport Beach, Calif. *Exhib:* Untitled IV, Mus Mod Art, New York, 72; Untitled, Mus Boymans-Van Beuningen, Rotterdam, Holland, 73; Discussions: Works, Words, Clocktower, New York, 74; solo exhib, Whitney Mus Am Art, 75; Four Sundays, PS1, Long Island City, NY, 76; Studies and Other Initial Works, Vancouver Art Gallery, 77; two-person exhib, Portland Ctr Visual Art, 78; The Minimal Tradition, Aldrich Mus Contemp Art, 79. *Awards:* Creative Artists Pub Serv Grant, 75; Fels, Guggenheim Found, 78 & Nat Endowment Arts, 79. *Bibliog:* Susan Tower (auth), The object perceived, the object apprehended, Art Forum, Vol XII, No 5, 74; Lucy Lippard (auth), Brenda Miller: Woven stamped, Art in Am, Vol 64, No 3, 76; Ted Castle (auth), About Brenda Miller & her art, Mus J, Ser 22, No 1, 77. *Media:* All. *Dealer:* Sperone Westwater 142 Greene St New York NY 10012. *Mailing Add:* 36 W 26th St New York NY 10010

MILLER, DANIEL DAWSON
PAINTER, SCULPTOR
b Pittsburgh, Pa, July 7, 28. *Study:* Lafayette Col, BA, 51; Pa State Univ, summers with Hobson Pittman; Pa Acad Fine Arts, 55-59; Univ Pa, MFA, 58. *Work:* Pa Acad Fine Arts, Philadelphia; Philadelphia Mus Art; Rutgers Mus, New Brunswick, NJ; Wilmington Soc Fine Arts, Del; Dickinson Col, Carlisle, Pa. *Exhib:* 11 Modern American Artists, Rahr Mus, Manitowoc, Wis, 63; 158th-162nd Ann Exhib, Pa Acad Fine Arts, Philadelphia, 63-67; one-man shows, Peale House, Pa Acad Fine Arts, 67, Drexel Inst, 68, Rutgers Mus, Rutgers Univ, 70 & Univ Maine, 72 & Rosenfeld Gallery, Philadelphia, Pa, 81. *Pos:* Asst dean faculty, Pa Acad Fine Arts, 83- *Teaching:* Instr life painting, Pa Acad Fine Arts, 64-; instr art & head fine arts dept, Eastern Col, St Davids, Pa, 64-; instr woodcut, Pa Acad Fine Arts, 83- *Awards:* Prize for Oil, Del Ann, Del Soc Fine Arts, 60; May Audubon Post Prize, 61, Bertha M Goldberg Mem Award, 70 & 75 & Leona Karp Brauerman Prize, 76, Fel of Pa Acad Fine Arts. *Mem:* Philadelphia Watercolor Club. *Dealer:* Rosenfeld Gallery 113 Arch St Philadelphia PA 19106. *Mailing Add:* Box 41 Christiana PA 17509

MILLER, DAVID
DEALER
b Mich, 1948. *Study:* Art Inst Chicago; Princeton Univ, BA, 70. *Collections Arranged:* Many exhibitions of works in various mediums in New York and Fla. *Pos:* Asst cur, United Nations Educ, Sci, & Cult Orgn, Paris, 74-75; asst dir, Max Hutchinson Gallery & Sculpture Now, New York, 77-78; asst dir, Irving Galleries, Palm Beach, Fla, 78-80; dir, Art Investors Int, West Palm Beach, Fla, 80- *Specialty:* Contemporary American art. *Mailing Add:* c/o Art Investors Int 324 Datura St West Palm Beach FL 33401

MILLER, DOLLY (ETHEL B)
PAINTER
b Johnstown, Pa, June 14, 27. *Study:* Brooklyn Col, NY, BA(chemistry); NY Univ, MA(Fr lit); art hist, The Sorbonne & the Louvre, Paris, France; studied painting with Andre Lhote, Paris; Art Students League, with Julian Levi; also with Leo Manso, NY Univ. *Work:* Johnson & Johnson, Surgico, Inc, Piscataway, NJ; The Friends Acad, Locust Valley, NY. *Exhib:* Butler Inst Am Art Ann, Youngstown, Ohio, 68 & 69; one-person shows, Art Exhib Consult, Princeton, NJ, 77, Northeast Kingdom Arts Ctr, St Johnsbury, Vt, 81, Wood Art Gallery, Montpelier, Vt, 82 & Copley Gallery, Morrisville, Vt, 83; Award Winners of Fence Show, Brooklyn Mus Fine Arts, 75; Candidates for Art Award, Am Acad Nat Inst Art, New York, 76. *Awards:* Hon Mention, Garden State Art Ctr, NJ, 70; Barney Paisner Mem Award, Painters & Sculptors Soc NJ, 75; Salmagundi Club Award, Nat Acad Galleries, 79. *Mem:* Audubon Artists, Inc; Art Students League New York; Art Resources Asn Vt. *Mailing Add:* RFD 1 Barton VT 05822

MILLER, DONALD
CRITIC, WRITER
b Pittsburgh, Pa, Dec 21, 34. *Study:* Univ Pittsburgh, AB, 56, MA(art hist), 75; Harvard Inst in Arts Admin, 76. Am Fedn Art Critics Workshop, with Barbara Novak, 70. *Pos:* Art critic, Pittsburgh Post-Gazette, 66- *Teaching:* 19th & 20th century art, Carnegie-Mellon Univ, 79-80. *Awards:* Golden Quill Award, Pittsburgh Press Club, 80. *Bibliog:* Amy Laurent-Vanderah (auth), Art surgeon, Pittsburgh Mag, 81. *Mem:* Hon mem 100 Friends Pittsburgh; Associated Artists Pittsburgh. *Publ:* Auth, Irene Rice Pereira, 78, Eduardo Chillida, 79 & Gary Jurysta, 79, Arts Mag; auth, A W Mellon Charitable Trust 1930-1980, Davis & Warde, 81; and many others. *Mailing Add:* Pittsburgh Post-Gazette Pittsburgh PA 15230

MILLER, DONALD RICHARD
SCULPTOR, MEDALIST
b Erie, Pa, June 30, 25. *Study:* Dayton Art Inst, 47-52; Pratt Inst, 55-57; Art Students League, 58-61; also with Ulysses A Ricci, 56-60. *Work:* Dayton Art Inst, Ohio; William Farnsworth Art Mus, Rockland, Maine; Medallic Art Co, New York; Div Numismatics, Smithsonian Inst. *Comn:* Thoreau Medal, Soc Medalists, 67; two bronze reliefs, Cincinnati Zoo, 75; nickel-bronze relief, Philadelphia Zoo, 73; four gargoyles, Washington Cathedral, 76; raccoon sculpture, Ridge Sch, NJ, 79. *Exhib:* Mus Fine Arts, Springfield, Mass, 63-70; Allied Artists Am, 63-; Nat Acad Design, 67-74; Nat Sculpture Soc, 67-; Soc Animal Artists, 68- *Teaching:* Adj asst prof sculpture, Fashion Inst Technol, 72- *Awards:* Mrs Louis Bennett Prize, Nat Sculpture Soc, 68; Lindsey Morris Memorial Prize & Dr Maurice B Hexter Prize, Nat Sculpture Soc. *Mem:* Nat Sculpture Soc; Soc Animal Artists; Nat Acad Design; Allied Artists Am; Audubon Artists. *Dealer:* Fisher Galleries 1509 Connecticut Ave NW Washington DC. *Mailing Add:* RD 2 Box 229 Warwick NY 10990

MILLER, DOROTHY CANNING
CONSULTANT
b Hopedale, Mass. *Study:* Smith Col, BA & LHD, 59. *Collections Arranged:* Many exhibs, Mus Mod Art, 36-69. *Pos:* Asst to dir, Mus Mod Art, 34, assoc cur painting & sculpture, 35-43, cur painting & sculpture, 43-47, cur mus collections, 47-67, sr cur painting & sculpture, 67-69; mem art comt, Chase Manhattan Bank, 59- & Port Authority of NY & NJ, 59-; art adv, var collectors, cols & corp, 69-; dir, Mark Rothko Found, currently. *Publ:* Ed, 12 Americans, 56; ed, The New American Painting, 58; ed, 16 Americans, 59; ed, Americans 1963; ed, 20th Century Art from the Nelson Aldrich Rockefeller Collection, 69-79; and many others. *Mailing Add:* 400 W 128th St New York NY 10027

MILLER, EARL B(EAUFORD)
GRAPHIC ARTIST, DESIGNER
b Chicago, Ill, Sept 19, 30. *Study:* Pratt Inst, with Richard Lindner, 54-56; Brooklyn Mus Art Sch, with Reuben Tam, 56; Akad Bildenden Kunst, Munich, with Jean Deyrolle & Robert Jacobsen, 62-63. *Work:* Mus Mod Art, Chase Manhattan Bank, New York; Ore State Capitol, Salem; Danish Labor Union, Copenhagen; Ctr Nat Art & Cult, Paris. *Comn:* Ann Commerative Gov Award, Ore Arts Comn, 79. *Exhib:* Solo exhib, Phoenix Gallery, New York, 61; Biennial, Stadt Wolfsburg, Ger, 63; Als Artists, Mus Mod Art, New York, 67-77; 30 Contemporary Black Artists Traveling Exhib, Minneapolis Inst Arts, 68-70; The Studio Museum in Harlem, Martha Jackson Gallery, New York, 70; Gallery Group, Genesis Gallery, 76. *Teaching:* Asst prof painting & decorative design, Munich Studio, 63-64; instr, Art Students League & Ford Found, 68-69; assoc prof, Univ Wash, Seattle, 69- *Awards:* Grand Concourse, Ann Painting Show, Art Students League, 58; Bavaria Ministry Cult Grant, 63; Original Ed, Graphics Competition, Ore Arts Comn, 78. *Media:* Oil, Acrylic; Collage, Assemblage Construction. *Mailing Add:* 5026 22nd Ave NE Seattle WA 98105

MILLER, GEORGE
CONCEPTUAL ARTIST, WRITER
b Wooster, Ohio, June 12, 44. *Study:* Ohio State Univ, BFA, 66; Rutgers Univ, MFA, 68. *Work:* Los Angeles Co Mus; Guggenheim Mus. *Exhib:* Whitney Biennial, 76; Word Works, Bergman Gallery, Chicago, 81; Trenton Mus, NJ, 82; Photo-Alchemy Show, Freidus Gallery, New York, 82; Los Angeles to New York, 83 & two-person exhib, 83, Koplin Gallery, Los Angeles; Michael Blankfort Collection, Los Angeles Co Mus, 83. *Teaching:* Asst prof painting & graphics, Univ Ore, Eugene, 68-70; instr art, Calif Inst Art, 70-72 & Citrus Community Col, 77-78. *Awards:* NJ Coun Arts Grant, 82. *Bibliog:* Robert Pincus (auth), article, Los Angeles Times, 9/83. *Media:* Charcoal, Typography. *Publ:* Auth, California White Walls, 74, Circa, 75, The Great Themes of Literature, 76, The Morocco Story, 82 & The Changeling Series, 83, pvt publ. *Dealer:* Koplin Gallery 8225 1/2 Santa Monica Blvd Los Angeles CA 90046. *Mailing Add:* 139 Park Ave Hoboken NJ 07030

MILLER, (RICHARD) GUY
SCULPTOR
b Pittsburgh, Pa. *Study:* City & Guilds of London Art Coun, Eng, with Ennis Fripps, 58; Art Students League, New York, with Will Barnet & Robert Hale; Pratt Inst, Brooklyn, NY, with Calvin Albert, MFA, 65. *Work:* State Univ NY Col New Paltz; Pratt Inst, Brooklyn; New Sch, New York; Bennington Col, Vt; Long Island Hall of Fame, Stony Brook, NY. *Comn:* Cast aluminum wall sculpture, Birchwood Park Corp, Bayside, NY, 71; free standing stainless steel sculpture, Jackson Heights, NY, 74 & environ stainless steel sculpture, Elmhurst, NY, 78; stainless steel wall sculpture, New Sch, New York, 74; free standing stainless steel dual form, Sky Island Club, Plainview, NY, 79. *Exhib:* Ann Exhib, Guild Hall, East Hampton, NY, 75 & 81; Ann Group Show, Parish Mus, Southampton, NY, 76; Caumsett Park, Long Island, NY, 78;

Long Island Exhib, Hecksher Mus, Huntington, NY, 79; Betty Parsons Gallery, New York, 79, 80 & 81; and others. *Teaching:* Instr sculpture, Pratt Inst, Brooklyn, summer 64; prof art, Monmouth Col, West Long Branch, NJ, 64-65, prof sculpture, 66-69; artist-in-residence, Friends World Col, Lloyd Harbor, NY, 77-79. *Awards:* Tiffany Found Grant, 66; MacDowell Colony Found Fel, 68; Award, Long Island Hall Fame, Sky Island Club, 79. *Bibliog:* William Allen (auth), Miller's bright metal frames, Artsmag, 4/68; Jeanne Paris (auth), Emotional sculpture, 8/79; Malcolm Preston (auth), Public building as a gallery, 8/81, Newsday; and others. *Mem:* Art Students League, New York; Huntington Twp Art League, NY (bd dirs, 78-81). *Media:* Stainless Steel; Lucite. *Dealer:* Himelfarr Gallery Southampton NY. *Mailing Add:* 25 Minetta Lane New York NY 10012

MILLER, INGE MORATH See Morath, Inge

MILLER, J(OHN) BROUGH
SCULPTOR, EDUCATOR
b Emerson Twp, Mich, Apr 4, 33. *Study:* Central Mich Univ, BS, 60; Cranbrook Acad Art, MFA, 64; Indust Welding Trade Sch, Dallas, Tex, cert, 68. *Work:* Tex Woman's Univ, Denton & Dallas; Richland Col, Richardson, Tex; Lakewood Branch, Dallas Pub Libr. *Comn:* Outdoor steel sculptures, Aztec Products Inc, Mansfield, Tex, 82 & Peyco Products Inc, Arlington, Tex, 82. *Exhib:* One-person exhibs, Central State Univ, Edmond, Okla, 74, NTex State Univ, 76, Univ Dallas, 79, Richland Col, Tex, 80 & Tyler Mus Art, Tex, 84. *Teaching:* Prof art, Texas Woman's Univ, 61-, chmn dept art, 79-82; instr, Dallas Mus Fine Arts Mus Sch, 68-69. *Awards:* Purchase Award, Outdoor Sculpture Competition, Northlake Col, 83; Connemara Conservancy Found Grant, 84. *Media:* Welded Steel. *Mailing Add:* Box 289 Route 1 Argyle TX 76226

MILLER, JAN
PAINTER, DESIGNER
US citizen. *Study:* Grand View Col, Des Moines, Iowa; Fenger Jr Col, Chicago; St Xavier Col, Chicago, BA. *Work:* Ill State Fine Arts Mus, Springfield; Mus Fine Arts, Ft Lauderdale, Fla; Springfield Civic Collections, Ill; Union League Club, Chicago; Kemper Ins Co, Long Grove, Ill. *Exhib:* Ill State Exhib, Springfield, 74; Contemporary Still Life, Renaissance Soc, Univ Chicago, 74; Mainstreams in American Art, Marietta Col, 74; 75th Chicago & Vicinity Exhib, Art Inst Chicago, 75; New Horizons in Art, Chicago, 75. *Awards:* First Place for Prof Art, Ill State Fair, 73; Best of Show, Rockford & Vicinity, Ill, 75; First Place, Lakehurst Exhib, Waukegan, Ill, 75. *Mem:* Artists, Residents of Chicago; NShore Art League. *Media:* Acrylic. *Mailing Add:* 9424 S Turner Ave Evergreen Park IL 60642

MILLER, JEAN JOHNSTON
LIBRARIAN, HISTORIAN
b New York, NY, Feb 19, 18. *Study:* Barnard Col, AB, 39. *Pos:* Art librn, Univ Hartford, West Hartford, Conn, 64- *Mem:* Art Libr Soc NAm. *Mailing Add:* c/o Art Library Univ Hartford West Hartford CT 06117

MILLER, JOAN VITA
MUSEUM DIRECTOR, ADMINISTRATOR
b New York, NY, Jan, 46. *Study:* Syracuse Univ, BA(art hist), MA(art hist); independent res in Italy. *Collections Arranged:* New York Eleven, 74; Louise Nevelson (auth, catalogue), 74; Gertrude Stein and Her Friends (auth, catalogue), 75; Wreck, 75; The Long Island Art Collector's Exhibit (auth, catalogue), 75; European Masters in Portraiture, 76; An Exploration of Photography 1839-1976 (auth, catalogue), 76; The Arts of China, 77; Marsden Hartley, 1877-1943, 77; Double Exposure: Alfredo Valente as Photographer and Collector, 78; The First 4000 Years: The Ratner Collection of Judaean Antiquities, 79; Realist Space, 79; African Sculpture: The Shape of Surprise, 80; Auguste Rodin, 80 & 81. *Pos:* Asst dir, Michael Rockefeller Arts Ctr, State Univ NY Col, Fredonia, 71-72; dir gallery & cur permanent collection, C W Post Art Gallery, C W Post Col, 73-80; dir, B G Cantor Sculpture Ctr, New York, 80- *Teaching:* Mus & gallery mgt, C W Post Col, Long Island Univ, 76- *Mem:* Am Asn Mus; Long Island Mus Asn (pres, 79); Gallery Asn NY State; Contemp Print Soc New York. *Mailing Add:* B G Cantor Sculptor Ctr One World Trade Ctr New York NY 10048

MILLER, JOHN FRANKLIN
ADMINISTRATOR
b Hagerstown, Md, June 4, 40. *Study:* St Johns Col, Annapolis, BA, 62; Yale Univ, with Edgar Munhall, 65; Univ Md, with Ruth Butler, 69-72. *Work:* Hampton Nat Historic Site, Md; Stan Hywet Hall Foundation, Ohio. *Pos:* Resident cur, Hampton Nat Historic Site, Md, 72-75, admin, 76-79; cur of educ, Stann Hywet Hall Foundation, Akron, Ohio, 79-80, exec dir, 81. *Mem:* Am Asn Mus; Nat Trust for Hist Preserv; Am Asn State and Local Hist; Intermuseum Conserv Asn (trustee, 81). *Res:* European and domestic architecture of the late 17th and early 18th centuries and its influence in America. *Mailing Add:* 714 North Portage Path Akron OH 44303

MILLER, JOHN PAUL
JEWELER, INSTRUCTOR
b Huntingdon, Pa, Apr 23, 18. *Study:* Cleveland Inst Art, cert indust design; and with Baron Eric Fleming. *Work:* Cleveland Mus Art, Ohio; Mus Contemp Crafts, New York; Huntington Gallery, WVa; Minn Mus, St Paul; Johnson Wax Collection. *Exhib:* Int Jewelry Exhib, London, 61; Objects USA Traveling Exhib, US, Europe & Japan, 69; 15 Jewelers, Schmuck-Objekte, Mus Bellevue, Zurich, 71; Metal Exhib, DeCordova Mus, Boston, 74; Goldsmiths '74, Smithsonian Inst, Washington, DC, 74; Am Craftsmen, Vatican Mus, Rome, Italy, 78. *Pos:* Gallery dir, Cleveland Inst Art, 60-81.

Teaching: Instr design & jewelry, Cleveland Inst Art, 40- *Bibliog:* Von Neumann (auth), Design and Creation of Jewelry, Chilton, 61; Graham Hughes (auth), Modern Jewelry, Crown; J Anderson Black (auth), Story of Jewelry, Morrow, 74. *Mem:* Fel Am Craftsmen Coun; Soc NAm Goldsmiths. *Mailing Add:* 9333 Highland Dr Brecksville OH 44141

MILLER, LAURENCE GLENN
PHOTOGRAPHER, DEALER
b New York, NY, Oct 8, 48. *Study:* Univ Wis, BS, 72, MA, 73; Univ NMex, 74. *Work:* Art Inst Chicago; Madison Art Ctr, Wis; Northwestern Univ Libr; Univ Wis, Madison; C W Post Col. *Exhib:* Photography West, Utah State Univ, Logan, 74; The Book--A New Direction for Photography, Quivira Gallery, Albuquerque, 74; Five Color Photographers, Jorgenson Gallery, Univ Conn, Storrs, 77; The Great American Foot, Contemp Crafts Mus, New York, 78; Attitudes: Photography in the 1970s, Santa Barbara Mus Art, 79; Industrial Sites, Whitney Mus, New York, 79. *Pos:* Assoc dir, Light Gallery, New York, 74-80; dir, Laurence Miller Gallery, New York, 84- *Teaching:* Instr hist photog, New Sch Social Res, 76-80; vis prof, Univ Tex, San Antonio, 80. *Awards:* Creative Artists Pub Serv Grant, 77-78. *Mem:* Asn Int Photog Art Dealers (bd dirs, 83-). *Specialty:* Contemporary art, especially photography. *Publ:* Auth, More galleries, but the competition is keen, New York Times, 75. *Mailing Add:* 38 E 57 St New York NY 10022

MILLER, LILLIAN DUNN
PAINTER, COLLECTOR
b Brooklyn, NY. *Study:* Pratt Inst, Art Students League, New York, scholar, 30; Univ Southern Calif, fine arts with Edgar Ewing & Francis De Erdely. *Exhib:* Painting Exhib, Los Angeles Co Mus Art, Los Angeles, 60, 61, 62 & 71; Painting, Nat Orange Show, San Bernardino, Calif, 65-66; Painting, Laguna Beach Art Asn, Calif, 67-68; Exhib I, Otis Art Inst, 68 & Exhib II, 69; Painting in Oil, Los Angeles Art Asn, 71-79; and others. *Awards:* Merit Award, Home Savings & Loan Asn, 63; Cash Award, Otis Art Inst, 68; 2nd Place, San Bernardino Art Mus, 81. *Bibliog:* Jules Langsner (auth), Scary image, Los Angeles Times, 68. *Mem:* Los Angeles Art Asn. *Media:* Oil, Watercolor. *Collection:* Primitive art, American Indian art. *Mailing Add:* 1637 Vine Los Angeles CA 90028

MILLER, MELISSA WREN
PAINTER
b Houston, Tex, Mar 3, 51. *Study:* Univ Nmex, BFA, 74. *Exhib:* Visions and Figurations, Calif State Univ, Fullerton, 80; New Orleans Triennial, New Orleans Mus Art, 80; solo exhib, Contemp Arts Mus, Houston, 81 & Art Mus STex, Corpus Christi, 81; New Works, Summer 82, Laguna Gloria Art Mus, Austin, Tex, 82; End of the World, New Mus, New York, 83; Whitney Biennial Exhib, Whitney Mus Am Art, 83; Venice Bienniale, Italy, 84. *Awards:* Nat Endowment Arts Grants, 74 & 79; Anne Giles Kimbrough Award, Dallas Mus Fine Arts, 82. *Bibliog:* Susie Kalil (auth), article, Art News, 82; Susan Freudenheim (auth), Uniting art and allegory: The energetic paintings of Melissa Miller, Tex Homes, 82. *Media:* Oil, Acrylic. *Mailing Add:* 167 N Tumbleweed Trail Austin TX 78733

MILLER, MELVIN O, JR
PAINTER
b Baltimore, Md, May 16, 37. *Study:* Md Inst Art, dipl, 59. *Comn:* Paintings, Equitable Trust Co, Baltimore, 63-64; painting, Mercantile Bank & Trust, Baltimore, 82. *Exhib:* Corcoran Gallery, Washington, DC, 58; Butler Inst Am Art, Youngstown, Ohio, 65; Am Soc Marine Artists, New York, 78-80; Greenwich Workshop Gallery, Southport, Conn, 79-83; Kirsten Gallery, Seattle, 80-83; John Pence Gallery, San Francisco, 80-83; Foxhall Gallery, 83; and others. *Awards:* Second Prize, John F & Anna Lee Stacey Scholar Fund, 65. *Bibliog:* E J J Archibald (auth), Dictionary of Sea Painters, Nat Maritime Mus, London (in prep). *Mem:* Am Soc Marine Artists; Charcoal Club Baltimore. *Media:* Oil; Pen & Ink. *Dealer:* Foxhall Gallery 3301 New Mexico Ave NW Washington DC 20016; John Pence Gallery 750 Post St San Francisco CA 94109. *Mailing Add:* 2001 Alto Vista Ave Baltimore MD 21207

MILLER, NANCY TOKAR
PAINTER
b Detroit, Mich, June 13, 41. *Study:* Chouinard Art Inst & Otis Art Inst, scholar, 56-59; Univ Calif, Los Angeles, AF, 64; Univ Ariz, MFA, 71. *Work:* Otis Elevator Co, Farmingdale, Conn; Tucson Mus Art, Ariz; Valley Nat Bank, Tucson, Ariz; Yuma Fine Arts Asn, Ariz; and others. *Comn:* Maui Intercontinental Hotel, Hawaii, 75; Int Bus Machines Corp, Tucson, Ariz, 78; Western Savings, Tucson, 81. *Exhib:* Univ Ariz Mus Art, Tucson, 77; Elaine Horwitch Gallery, Scottsdale, Ariz, 81 & 83; Amarillo Art Ctr, 82; and others. *Teaching:* Instr painting, drawing & design, Cambridge Ctr Adult Educ, Mass, 65-68; instr, Tucson Art Mus Sch, 72-78; vis artist, Ariz Western Col, 77. *Awards:* Purchase Award, Yuma Fine Arts Asn, 75; Fel, Western States Arts Found, 75-76; Juror's Cash Award, Four Corners States Biennial, Phoenix Art Mus, 77. *Bibliog:* Barbara Cortright (auth), Nancy Tokar Miller, Artspace Mag, 10/81; Dave Gallagher (prod), Five Women Artists, KUAT-TV, Univ Ariz, 79; Sarah J Moore (auth), articles, Art Week, 10/83; and others. *Media:* Acrylic. *Dealer:* Elaine Horwitch Gallery 4200 N Marshall Way Scottsdale AZ 85251. *Mailing Add:* 2710 E Mabel St Tucson AZ 85716

MILLER, RICHARD KIDWELL
PAINTER
b Fairmont, WVa, Mar 15, 30. *Study:* Pa Acad Fine Arts; Am Univ, BA; Columbia Univ, MFA. *Work:* Phillips Collection, Washington, DC; Edward

Joseph Gallagher, III Mem Collection, Univ Ariz, Tucson; Hirschhorn Mus & Sculpture Garden, Washington DC; Rochester Mus Art, NY; Albrecht Gallery, St Joseph, Mo. *Comn:* Painting, Plessey Corp, Gen Motors Bldg, New York, 71. *Exhib:* Pa Acad Fine Arts Ann, Philadelphia, 56-62; Whitney Mus Am Art Ann, New York, 60; Carnegie Inst, 62; Tokyo Int, Japan, 66; one-man shows, Baltimore Mus of Art, 52, Albrecht Gallery of Art, St Joseph, Mo, 69, Long Island Univ, 73, Westreth Gallery, 82 & Adron Berman Gallery, 83; Alternative Mus, New York, 81; and others. *Teaching:* Asst prof painting, Kansas City Art Inst, 68-69; adj prof painting & drawing, Westchester Community Col, 80-83. *Awards:* Gertrude Vanderbilt Whitney Scholar, Nat Inst Arts & Lett, 48-56; Washington Times-Herald Scholar, 47; Fulbright Fel, 53. *Media:* Oil, Acrylic. *Dealer:* Peter Rose Gallery 200 E 58th St New York NY 10022. *Mailing Add:* 222 W 83rd St Apt 8C New York NY 10024

MILLER, RICHARD MCDERMOTT
SCULPTOR
b New Philadelphia, Ohio, Apr 30, 22. *Study:* Cleveland Inst Art, 40-42, 49-51, grad, 51. *Work:* Sheldon Mem Art Gallery, Lincoln, Nebr; Univ Houston; Whitney Mus Am Art; Canton Art Inst, Ohio; Hirshhorn Mus, Washington, DC. *Exhib:* One-man shows, Feingarten Gallery, Los Angeles, 66 & Alwin Gallery, London, 68; Contemporary American Realism Since 1960, Pa Acad Fine Arts & traveling, 81-82; Contemporary Realism, One Penn Plaza, New York, 82; Narrative Sculpture, Sculpture Ctr, New York, 82; Bodies & Souls, Artists Choice Mus, New York, 83. *Teaching:* Instr sculpture, Queens Col, 67- *Awards:* Purchase Award, Butler Inst Am Art, 70; Gold Medals, Nat Acad Design, 74 & 81; Sculpture Award, Am Acad & Inst Arts & Lett, 78. *Bibliog:* Sidney Tillim (auth), Richard Miller, primary realist, Artforum, summer 67; Gabriel Laderman (auth), Unconventional realists, Artforum, 3/71; Grace Glueck (auth), A new realism in sculpture?, Art in Am, 12/71. *Mem:* Alliance of Figurative Artists; Sculptors Guild; Nat Acad Design. *Publ:* Auth, Figure Sculpture in Wax & Plaster, Watson-Guptill, 71; auth, The Vanishing Armature, Sculpture Int, summer 82. *Mailing Add:* 53 Mercer St New York NY 10013

MILLER, ROBERT PETER
DEALER
b Atlantic City, NJ, Apr 17, 39. *Study:* Rutgers Col, BS & MFA. *Pos:* Exec vpres, Andre Emmerich Gallery Inc, New York, NY, 75-77; pres, Robert Miller Gallery Inc, New York, NY, 77- *Mailing Add:* Robert Miller Gallery Inc 724 Fifth Ave New York NY 10019

MILLER, (MRS) ROBERT WATT
PATRON
b Oakland, Calif, July 20, 98. *Pos:* chmn, San Francisco Opera Guild, 50-52; chmn, Ital Festival, San Francisco, 59; chmn, De Young Mem Mus Soc, 61-63. *Awards:* Ital Cross Solidarity, San Francisco, 59. *Mem:* United Bay Area Crusade (bd trustees, currently). *Interests:* Presentation of shows in museums. *Mailing Add:* 1021 California St San Francisco CA 94108

MILLER, SAMUEL CLIFFORD
MUSEUM DIRECTOR
b Roseburg, Ore, May 6, 30. *Study:* Stanford Univ, BA; Inst Fine Arts, NY Univ, grad study; Seton Hall Univ, DFA(hon), 76; also in Japan, Europe & Mex. *Pos:* Asst to dir, Albright-Knox Art Gallery, Buffalo, NY, 64-67; asst dir, Newark Mus Asn, 67, mus dir, 68- *Mem:* Am Asn Mus; Northeast Mus Conf; Mus Coun NJ; Am Fedn Arts; Asn Art Mus Dirs; and others. *Mailing Add:* Newark Mus Asn 49 Washington St Newark NJ 07101

MILLETT, CAROLINE DUNLOP
ADMINISTRATOR
b Kansas City, Mo, Feb 14, 39. *Study:* Univ Edinburgh, 59-60; Univ Wis, BA, 61; Stanford Univ, MA, 63. *Collections Arranged:* Coordinator, US Contribution Sao Paulo Bienal, 73. *Pos:* Cultural attache, Brasilia, 69-70; film dir, US Information Agency, 73; asst adv arts, Dept State, 74-80; adv arts, US Int Communication Agency, 81-; vpres, Philadelphia Col Art, 84- *Teaching:* Assoc prof US cultural hist, Univ Sao Paulo, Brazil, 66-69. *Mailing Add:* Philadelphia Col Art Broad & Spruce Sts Philadelphia PA 19102

MILLIE, ELENA GONZALEZ
CURATOR
b Greenwich, Conn. *Study:* Univ NC, BA, 64. *Collections Arranged:* Travel Then & Now, 70, The Paper Weapon (auth, catalog), 76, On View, 79 & American & European Posters (auth, catalog), 80. *Pos:* Cur, Libr Cong, 65- *Publ:* Auth, Charlot, L'As des Comiques, 68, coauth, Tomorrow night, East Lynne!, 80 & auth, Posters: A collectible art form, 82, Libr Cong Quart J; auth, College poster art, Art J, 84. *Mailing Add:* 5152 Manning Place NW Washington DC 20016

MILLIGAN, JOAN ARNOLD
PAINTER
b New Haven, Conn, Mar 13, 25. *Study:* George Washington Univ, with Lamarr Dodd & Jerry Farnsworth; Smith Col, BA, 46; Stanford Univ, Calif, with Victor Arniftauff, MA(art), 47; Corcoran Sch Art, with Richard Lahey & Wilbur Niewald. *Work:* Dept Cult, Raleigh, NC. *Comn:* Flute Player (painting), Columbus Col Music, Ga, 71; painting, Dept Justice, Washington, DC, 73; Water Lilies, Ernst & Ernst Inc, Raleigh, NC, 78. *Exhib:* Retrospective, Cairo Mus Contemp Art, 66; solo shows, Columbia Mus, SC, 71, Corcoran Gallery Art, Washington, DC, 72, Asheville Art Mus, NC, 77, Fayetteville Mus, NC, 78, Morehead Planetarium, Chapel Hill, NC, 78 & Anderson Hopkins Gallery, Washington, DC, 79; and many other group and

solo exhibs. *Teaching:* Chmn dept art, Potomac Sch, McLean, Va, 66-67; dir painting, New Sch, Washington, DC, 67-68; instr painting, Sandhills Community Col, Southern Pines, NC, 74-80. *Awards:* Second Prize, Norfolk Mus Art Ann, 56. *Mem:* Artists Equity Asn; NC Watercolor Soc; Copley Soc, Boston. *Media:* Oil, Watercolor. *Dealer:* C C Price 15 East 48th St New York NY 10017; Prince Royal Gallery 204 South Royal St Alexandria VA 22202. *Mailing Add:* Youngs Rd Southern Pines NC 28387

MILLIKEN, ALEXANDER FABBRI
DEALER, COLLECTOR
b Boston, Mass, Feb 14, 47. *Pos:* Owner, Alexander F Milliken Inc, 76- *Mem:* Solomon Guggenheim Mus; Mus Mod Art, New York; Metrop Mus Art, New York; Whitney Mus Am Art, New York; Skowhegan Sch Painting & Sculpture (co-chmn jr comt). *Specialty:* Contemporary painting & sculpture. *Collection:* Jean DuBuffet, Keith Haring, Jean-Michel Basquiat, Anthony Caro, Herbert Ferber, Martin Disler, Ed Ruscha, Morris Graves & Sandro Chia. *Mailing Add:* 98 Prince St New York NY 10012

MILLIKEN, GIBBS
PAINTER, EDUCATOR
b Houston, Tex, Dec 15, 35. *Study:* Scheiner Inst; Univ Colo; Trinity Univ, BSc; Cranbrook Acad Art, MFA. *Work:* Cranbrook Acad Art; Montgomery Mus Fine Arts, Ala; Serv League, Longview, Tex; Butler Inst Am Art. *Exhib:* San Antonio Artists, Witte Mus, 60-68; Tex Ann Painters & Sculptors, Witte Mus, Corpus Christi, Beaumont Mus & Dallas Mus Fine Arts, 62-66; Bucknell Univ, 67; Tex Fine Arts Comn, Hemisfair, San Antonio, 68; and many others. *Pos:* Asst, Univ Colo Mus, formerly; artist, photographer, asst cur, cur & head dept exhibs, Witte Mem Mus, San Antonio, formerly. *Teaching:* Instr painting & drawing, Cranbrook Acad Art, Bloomfield Hills, Mich, 64 & 65; instr art, Univ Tex, Austin, 65-69, asst prof, 69-73, assoc prof, 74-82, prof, currently. *Awards:* Grumbacher Award, Tex Watercolor Soc, Witte Mem Mus, 64, Naylor Award, 66 & Freeman Purchase Prize, 67; and many others. *Mem:* Am Fedn Arts; Am Asn Univ Prof; Men of Art Guild; Contemp Artists Group. *Mailing Add:* Dept of Art Univ of Tex Austin TX 78712

MILLS, AGNES
SCULPTOR, PRINTMAKER
b New York, NY. *Study:* Cooper Union Art Sch, dipl; Pratt Inst, BFA; NY Univ Sch Archit; Art Students League; Design Lab; studied with Raphael Soyer, Yasuo Kuniyoshi, Ruth Leaf, Krishna Reddy & Betty Holliday. *Work:* Libr Performing Arts, Friends Tampa Ballet; Univ Maine, Amhurst; Calif Sch Arts & Crafts, Oakland; C W Post Col; Lincoln Ctr Performing Arts. *Exhib:* Butler Inst Am Art Ann, 71-72; Pa Acad Art Ann, 73; Okla Art Mus Ann Printmaking Exhib, 73 & 74; Seattle Art Mus Ann, 74; Friends Tampa Ballet, 82. *Pos:* Art dir, Mills Agency Inc. *Teaching:* Art coordr & art instr, NShore Community Art Ctr, Great Neck, NY, 57-75. *Awards:* First Prize in Printmaking, Washington Miniature Prints & Sculpture, 70; Purchase Prize, Hunterdon Co Art Mus, 72; Purchase Award, Nassau Community Col, 74. *Bibliog:* Article, Art News Mag, Oct, 81; article, New York Times, Mar, 81; article, Playbill, City Ctr Theatre, Mar, 81. *Mem:* Print Club; Nat Asn Women Artists; Artists Equity. *Media:* Color Etching, Cast Paper; Colograph, Monoprint. *Dealer:* Lincoln Ctr Art Gallery 65th St & Broadway New York NY 10023; Nvance Gallery Tampa Fla 33609. *Mailing Add:* 323 Melbourne Rd Great Neck NY 11021

MILLS, FREDERICK VAN FLEET
ADMINISTRATOR, EDUCATOR
b Bremen Fairfield, Ohio, June 5, 25. *Study:* Ohio State Univ, BS, 49; Ind Univ, MS, 51, EdD, 56. *Pos:* Pres, Ind Art Educ Asn, 56; ed, Western Arts Bull, 58-62. *Teaching:* Prof art & art educ & chmn dept art educ, Ind Univ, Bloomington, 59-66; chmn dept related arts, crafts & interior design, Univ Tenn, Knoxville, 66-68; prof art & chmn dept, Ill State Univ, 68- *Mem:* Nat Art Educ Asn (bd dirs, 63-64); Col Art Asn Am; Western Arts Asn (pres, 62-64); Ill Art Educ Asn; Nat Coun Art Admin. *Publ:* Contribr, Arts & Activities Mag, 61, 66, 68 & 69; coauth, As an Artist Sees, Ind Univ AV Ctr, 65; ed, Nat Coun Art Admin Report, 75, The Status of the Visual Arts in Higher Education, 76 & New Perspectives of Visual Arts Administration, 77, Nat Coun Art Admin. *Mailing Add:* Dept of Art Ill State Univ Normal IL 61761

MILLS, JAMES
CRITIC, COLLECTOR
b Chaseburg, Wis, Jan 17, 24. *Study:* Univ Wis, BS; Fordham Univ, MFA; Cent Sch Speech & Drama, London, Eng. *Pos:* Art ed, The Denver Post Inc, 55- *Mem:* Greater Denver Coun Arts & Humanities (treas, 73-76); Larry Tajiri Mem Found (treas, 71-78); Alliance for Contemp Art. *Collection:* Twentieth century American and European paintings, sculpture and graphics; pre-Columbian ceramics; 18th-20th century Japanese paintings, prints. *Mailing Add:* The Denver Post Inc 650 15th St Denver CO 80202

MILLS, LEV TIMOTHY
PRINTMAKER, SCULPTOR
b Wakulla Co, Fla, Dec 11, 40. *Study:* Fla A&M Univ, BA(art educ); Univ Wis, Madison, MA & MFA; Slade Sch Fine Art, Univ London, Eng; Atelier 17, Paris, France, with Stanley W Hayter. *Work:* High Mus Art, Atlanta; Victoria & Albert Mus, London; Libr of Cong, Washington, DC; Bibliot Nat, Paris; Mus Mod Art, New York. *Comn:* Three glass mosaic designs, Ashby St Subway Sta, City of Atlanta, Metrop Atlanta Rapid Transit Authority, 78. *Exhib:* Slade Centenary Exhib, Royal Col Art, London, 71; Artists in Ga, High Mus Art, Atlanta, 74; 20th Century Black Artist, San Jose Mus Art, 76; Retrospective, Studio Mus in Harlem, New York, 75; Mississippi Mus Art,

Jackson; Birmingham Mus Art, Ala; and others. *Pos:* Mem bd trustees, Art Festival of Atlanta Inc, 77- *Teaching:* Instr gen art, Everglades Jr High, Ft Lauderdale, Fla, 62-68; asst prof printmaking, Clark Col, Atlanta, 73-78; asst prof art, Spelman Col, Atlanta, 79. *Awards:* Outstanding Postgrad Fel, Univ Wis, 69; Europ Study & Travel Fel, Ford Found, 70; Bronze Jubilee Award for Cult Achievement, City of Atlanta, 78. *Bibliog:* Pat Gilmour (auth), Lev Mills, Arts Rev, London, 72; Lewis & Waddy (auth), Black artists on art, Contemp Crafts Inc, Calif, 76; Samella Lewis (auth), Graphic Processes, Art: African American, Harcourt, Brace & Jovanovich Inc, New York, 78. *Mem:* Nat Col Art Asn; Black Artists Atlanta. *Publ:* Auth, I Do, A Book of Etchings & Poems, Cut Chain Press, 71. *Dealer:* Assoc Am Artists 663 Fifth Ave New York NY 10022. *Mailing Add:* 3378 Ardley Rd SW Atlanta GA 30311

MILLS, MARGARET M
ADMINISTRATOR
Pos: Exec dir, Am Acad & Inst of Arts & Lett, currently. *Mailing Add:* c/o Am Acad & Inst of Arts & Lett 633 W 155th St New York NY 10032

MILLS, PAUL CHADBOURNE
MUSEUM DIRECTOR
b Seattle, Wash, Sept 24, 24. *Study:* Reed Col, 45-48; Univ Wash, BA, 53; Univ Calif, Berkeley, MA, 61; Calif Col Arts & Crafts, Hon PhD, 71. *Pos:* Reporter, Bellevue Am, Wash, 48-51; asst cur, Henry Gallery, Univ Wash, 52-53; cur art, Oakland Mus, Calif, 53-70; vpres, Western Mus Conf, 56 & 59; dir, Santa Barbara Mus Art, 70-; dir, New Glory Bicentennial Flag Hist & Design Proj, 74-77. *Awards:* Ford Found Fel, 60-61; grants from Spain, 77-79. *Mem:* Western Asn Art Mus (vpres, 56-57, treas, 71-72, trustee, 79); NAm Vexillological Asn; Heraldry Soc; Am Asn Mus; Am Asn Art Mus Dirs (trustee, 71-72, secy, 73). *Publ:* Auth, Early Paintings of California, 56; auth, An Introduction to the Art of William Keith, 56; auth, Contemporary Bay Area Figurative Paintings, 58; coauth, The California Missions of Edwin Deakin, 66; auth, Colonial and Revolutionary Era Flags. *Mailing Add:* 638 Las Alturas Rd S Santa Barbara CA 93103

MILLSAPS, DANIEL See Nuki

MILNES, ROBERT WINSTON
SCULPTOR, EDUCATOR
b Washington, DC, Apr 1, 48. *Study:* Claremont Men's Col, BA(philosophy, fine arts), 70; Univ Wash, MFA, 74. *Work:* Smithsonian Inst; Erie Art Mus, Pa; Seattle Arts Comn. *Comn:* Wall-mounted sculpture, comn by Dr & Mrs P Rosenberg, Morristown, NJ, 80; wall-mounted sculpture, comn by Mr & Mrs Warner Bacon, Erie, Pa, 81. *Exhib:* Solo shows, Theo Portnoy Gallery, New York, 80, Pittsburgh Ctr Arts, 81, Meredith Contemp Art, Baltimore, 83, Erie Art Mus, Pa, 83 & Clay Place, Pittsburgh, 83; American Porcelain, Smithsonian Inst, 80. *Teaching:* Instr ceramics, Penland Sch Crafts, NC, 72 & 79; assoc prof, Edinboro State Col, 74-, art dept chmn, 81- *Awards:* Ceramic Sculpture Nat Juror Award, Stockton State Col, 74; Res grant, Edinboro State Col, 82; Juror Award, Erie Art Ctr, 83. *Media:* Ceramics, Copper. *Dealer:* Meredith Contemp Art 805 N Charles St Baltimore MD 21201. *Mailing Add:* 232 Church St Cambridge Springs PA 16403

MILRAD, AARON M
COLLECTOR
b Toronto, Ont, Can, May 17, 35. *Study:* Univ Toronto, BA & LLB; Law Soc Upper Can, grad lawyer. *Pos:* Pres Art Gallery at Harbourfront, Toronto, Ont, 79; pres, Koffler Art Gallery, Koffler Ctr, Toronto, 83; Comt City Toronto Pub Art. *Teaching:* Vis prof art & the law, York Univ, Toronto, Ont, 72-; instr art & the law & art management, Banff Ctr Sch Fine Arts, Alta, Can, 73-; vis prof art & the law, Concordia Univ, Montreal, 76. *Awards:* Can Coun Grant, Exploration Prog for bk on Can Art Law. *Collection:* Modern American and Canadian, 1945 to the present, primarily in the color field area, Noland, Olitski, Motherwell and others. *Publ:* Auth, The New Cultural Property Export and Import Act of Canada, 75 & Gifts to Museums, 75, Gazette; coauth, The Art World: Law, Business and Practice in Canada, Merritt Publ, Toronto, 79. *Mailing Add:* 20 Queen St West Suite 1104 Toronto ON M5H 3R3 Can

MILTON, PETER WINSLOW
PRINTMAKER
b Lower Merion, Pa, Apr 2, 30. *Study:* Yale Univ, with Josef Albers, BFA, 54, MFA, 62. *Work:* Mus Mod Art, Metrop Mus, New York; Philadelphia Mus Art; Libr Cong, Washington, DC; Tate Gallery, London. *Exhib:* Primera Bienal Americana de Artes Graficas, Mus La Tertulia, Cali, Colombia, 71; one-man shows, Corcoran Gallery Art, Washington, DC, 72 & Drawing Toward Etching, Brooklyn Mus, 80; Extraordinary Realities, Whitney Mus Am Art, 73; Norsk Internasjonal Grafikk Biennale, Gamlegyen, Norway, 74; 4th Int Exhib Original Drawings, Mus Mod Art, Rijeka, Yugoslavia, 74; and many other one-man shows. *Teaching:* Instr drawing & basic design, Md Inst Col Art, Baltimore, 61-68; instr printmaking, Yale Univ Summer Sch Music & Art, 70. *Awards:* Louis Comfort Tiffany Found Grant in Graphics, 64; First Prize in Graphics, 9th Columbian Festival de Arte, Mus La Tertula, 69; Grand Prize, Int Biennial Exhib Prints, Seoul, Korea, 72. *Bibliog:* Harriet Shapiro (auth), All realism is visionary: A reach into the ambiguous realm of Peter Milton, Intellectual Digest, 11/72; Piri Halasz (auth), The metaphysical games of Peter Milton, Art News, 12/74; Kneeland McKnulty (auth), Peter Milton: Complete Etchings 1960-1976, Impressions Workshop Inc, Boston, 77. *Media:* Etching, Engraving. *Dealer:* Franz Bader Gallery 2124 Pennsylvania Ave NW Washington DC 20037; Impressions Workshop 27 Stanhope St Boston MA 02116. *Mailing Add:* PO Box 137 Francestown NH 03043

MIM, ADRIENNE C (ADRIENNE CLAIRE SCHWARTZ)
SCULPTOR, PAINTER
b Brooklyn, NY, Feb 4, 31. *Study:* Brooklyn Mus Art Sch & Brooklyn Col, NY, 50; Hofstra Univ, 65. *Work:* Mus Section, Guild Hall, East Hampton, NY; Sculpturesites, Amagansette, NY. *Comn:* Murals, Southampton Col, NY, 69. *Exhib:* Parrish Mus, Southampton, NY, 69; Heckscher Mus, Huntington, NY, 77; Wards Island, New York, 80; Nabisco Sites, East Hanover, NJ, 81; Brooklyn Mus, 81; Fordham Univ, Lincoln Ctr, New York, 81; and others. *Teaching:* Asst instr painting, Parrish Art Mus, 66-67; adj prof sculpture, Southampton Col, NY, 73-74. *Awards:* Fel, MacDowell Colony, 72-74; Helen B Ellis Mem Prize, Nat Asn Women Artists, 80; Silver Medal, Audubon Artists, 80. *Bibliog:* Carrie Rickey (auth), Stalking the wild sculpture, Village Voice, 7/1/80; Grace Glueck (auth), Guide to what's new in outdoor sculpture, New York Times, 9/12/80; Vivienne Wechter (interviewer), WFUV Radio, 6/81. *Mem:* Fedn Mod Painters & Sculptors; Nat Asn Women Artists; Sculptors Guild. *Media:* Fiberglass, Steel; Oil, Mixed Media. *Publ:* Auth, Helicomodmim, pvt publ, 79; illusr, Audubon Artists 38, Audubon Artists, 80; illusr, Area Sculpture: Wards Island, Artists Representing Environmental Art, 80; illusr, Sculpturesites, Roger Wilcox, 81; illusr, Appearances, Independent Publ, 12/81. *Dealer:* Roger Wilcox Sculpturesites Box 534 Amagansette NY 11930. *Mailing Add:* 69 Skimhampton Rd East Hampton NY 11937

MINA-MORA, DORISE OLSON
PAINTER
b New York, NY, June 8, 32. *Study:* Art Students League, with Hale & Louis Bosa; Salmagundi Club scholar & study with Daniel Greene. *Work:* Southampton High Sch; William Cook Shipping Co & R Chapdelaine & Co, New York; Dewey, Ballatine, Bushby, Palmer & Wood Co. *Exhib:* Brooklyn Mus Community Galleries, 68-71; Winners Circle, Brooklyn Mus, 75; Community Gallery, Metrop Mus Art (with Burr Artists), 77; one-woman & joint shows with husband, Different Drummer Gallery, Conn, Wickford Art Gallery, RI & Stony Brook Univ; William Ric Galleries, NJ; Rosequist Gallery, Tucson, Ariz. *Teaching:* Instr, Isliptown Council Arts, Brookwood Hall. *Awards:* Grumbacher Award for Watercolor, Nat Arts Club, 70; Gold Medal Knickerbocker Artists, 78; Am Artists Professional League Award, 79; Nat Soc Acrylic Painters Award, 82; Forbes Award, 82; and others. *Mem:* Nat Soc Painters Casein & Acrylic; Allied Artists Am; Catharine Lorillard Wolfe Art Club; Nat Arts Club; Knickerbocker Artists; Am Artists Prof League; Audubon Artists. *Media:* Watercolor, Acrylic. *Mailing Add:* 87 Central Blvd Oakdale NY 11769

MINA-MORA, RAUL JOSE
PAINTER, ILLUSTRATOR
b Santa Anna, El Salvador, Mar 13, 14; US citizen. *Study:* San Francisco Acad Advan Arts; Art Students League, with Howard Traffton; also with Daniel Gree, Harte, Austria. *Work:* South Hampton High Sch, NY; Freid Corp. *Exhib:* Nat Soc Casein Painters; Salmagundi Club; Parrish Art Mus, NY; Nat Acad Design; Community Gallery, Metrop Mus Art, New York, 77; Brooklyn Mus, NY; Goldsboro Mus, NC, 77; and others. *Teaching:* Archit design & visual archit, Rudolph Shapher Sch Design; instr design, San Francisco Sch Design. *Awards:* Best of Show, Am Artist Prof League Grand Nat & Washington Square Art Show, 75; Knickerbocker Award, 75, 78 & 80; Leinwand Award, First Place Watercolors, 79. *Mem:* Salmagundi Art Club; Am Artist Prof League; Nat Soc Casein & Acrylic Painters; Allied Artists Am; Audubon Artists; and others. *Media:* Watercolor, Oil. *Publ:* Illusr, Fortune Mag, Rutledge, Macmillan, Cromwell-Colliers & Holt. *Mailing Add:* 87 Central Blvd Oakdale NY 11769

MINICK, ROGER
PHOTOGRAPHER, WRITER
b Ramona, Okla, July 13, 44. *Study:* Univ Calif, Berkeley, BA(hist), 69. *Work:* Mus Mod Art, Metropolitan Mus Art, New York; San Francisco Mus Mod Art; Los Angeles Co Mus Art; Houston Mus Fine Arts. *Comn:* Photo Survey, Nat Endowment Arts, 77, 78 & 80; Paramount Theater, Lancaster-Miller, Berkeley, 82. *Exhib:* Delta and Ozark Photos, Friends Photog, Carmel, Calif, 71; Sacramento Delta Photos, Int Ctr Photog, New York, 75; American Photographers and National Parks, Corcoran Gallery, 81, Amon Carter Mus, Ft Worth, 82 & Los Angeles Co Mus Art, 83; Espejo: Photographs of the Mexican-American Community, Ctr Creative Photog, Tucson, 83; Photography in California: '45 to 80, San Francisco Mus Mod Art, 84 & Ctr Georges Pompidou, Paris, 85. *Teaching:* Dir & instr photog, Assoc Students Univ Calif Studio, Berkeley, 66-75; instr, Ansel Adams Workshop, Yosemite, 74, 75, 76 & 82 & Owens Valley Workshop, Sacramento Delta, Calif, 79 & 81. *Awards:* Am Inst Graphic Arts Award, New York, 70; Guggenheim Fel, 72; Nat Endowment Arts Grant, 80. *Bibliog:* A D Coleman (auth), Light Readings, Oxford Univ Press, 79; Hal Fischer (auth), article, Art Forum, summer 81. *Publ:* Auth, Delta West: Land and People of Sacramento-San Joaquin Delta, 69 & Hills of Home: Rural Ozarks of Arkansas, 75, Scrimshaw Press; contribr, American Photographers & the National Parks, Viking Press, 81; auth, Paramount Theater, Lancaster-Miller, 82; coauth, In the Fields, Harvest Press, 82. *Dealer:* Grapestake Gallery 2876 California St San Francisco CA 94115. *Mailing Add:* 732 Kentucky St Vallejo CA 94590

MINISCI, BRENDA (EILEEN)
SCULPTOR, CERAMIST
b Gowanda, NY, June 15, 39. *Study:* RI Sch Design, Rome, Italy, 60-61, Providence, BFA, 61; Cranbrook Acad of Art, Bloomfield Hills, Mich, MFA, 64; Provincetown Fine Arts Workshop, with Harry Hollander. *Work:* Everson Mus, Syracuse, NY; Fitchburg Art Mus, Mass; Univ Mass, Amherst; Antonio Prieto Mem Collection, Mills Col, Oakland, Calif; N Adams State Col, Mass.

Comn: Fiberglass fountain sculpture, Murray D Lincoln Campus & clear cast polyester resin sculpture, Hampden Dining Commons, Univ Mass, Amherst; ceramic relief panels, Burnside Bldg, Worcester, Mass, 62; welded steel sculpture, Mercantile Trust Co, St Louis, Mo, 65-66; and others. *Exhib:* Wit & Whimsey in Am Art, Cranbrook Art Mus, Bloomfield Hills, 63; Craftsmen of the East (traveling exhib), Mus Contemp Crafts, New York & Smithsonian Inst, Washington, DC, 64-65; Nat Ceramic Exhib, Everson Mus, Syracuse, 64 & 68; G W V Smith Mus Nat Exhib, Springfield, Mass, 70-72; Seven Sculptors, Boston City Hall Galleries, Mass, 74; and others. *Teaching:* Instr ceramics, Craft Ctr, Worcester, 61-62; instr ceramics & sculpture, Univ Mass, Amherst, 67-71; instr ceramics & sculpture, Williston-Northampton Sch, Easthampton, Mass, 71-; instr ceramics & sculpture, Summer Grad Sch, Wesleyan Univ, Conn, 75. *Awards:* First Prize for Bronze Sculpture, 52nd Nat Exhib, G W V Smith Mus & Springfield Art League, 71; Juror's Award for Sculpture, Providence RI Art Club, 71; Purchase Prize for Sculpture, 22nd Exhib Painting & Sculpture, Berkshire Mus, N Adams Col, 73. *Mem:* Am Crafts Coun, NE Assembly (treas, 73-75); Mass Asn Crafts. *Media:* Multimedia. *Dealer:* Baracca Gallery 197 Pantry Rd North Hatfield MA 01066. *Mailing Add:* Box 85 North Hatfield MA 01066

MINNICK, ESTHER TRESS
PAINTER

b Chicago, Ill. *Study:* Art Students League; also with Edgar Whitney, Wong Suiling & Barbara Vassilioff. *Work:* Va State Col; Mem Hosp, New York; also in many pvt collections. *Exhib:* Nat Women's Republican Club, New York, 67; Nat Soc Painters Casein & Travel Exhib, New York, 68; Garden State Watercolor Soc, Princeton, NJ, 70; Princeton Art Asn, 71; two one-man exhibs, 74; plus others. *Awards:* First Award, Larchmont, 60; First & Third Prizes, Nat Women's Republican Club, 67; Princeton Bank Award, 70. *Mem:* Knickerbocker Artists; Catharine Lorillard Wolfe Art Club. *Media:* Watercolor. *Mailing Add:* Mease Manor Dunedin FL 33528

MINO, YUTAKA
HISTORIAN, CURATOR

b Kanagawa City, Japan, Oct 23, 41. *Study:* Keio Univ, Tokyo, Japan, BA(art hist), 65; Harvard Univ, PhD(art hist), 77. *Pos:* Cur asst, Royal Ont Mus, Toronto, Ont, 69-71; assoc cur, Montreal Mus Fine Arts, Que, 76-77; cur Oriental art dept, Indianapolis Mus Art, Ind, 77- *Awards:* Koyama Fujio Mem Prize, 81. *Mem:* Oriental Ceramic Soc, London & Hong Kong; SE Asian Ceramic Soc, Singapore; China House Gallery. *Res:* Development of Tz'u-chou type wares, important group of northern Chinese ceramics. *Publ:* Auth, Ceramics in the Liao Dynasty, China House Gallery, New York, 73; coauth, An Index to the Chinese Ceramic Kiln Sites From the Six Dynasties to the Present, 73 & auth, Chinese Stoneware in the Royal Ontario Museum, Pre-Sung Dynasty, 74, Royal Ont Mus; auth, Kogo: Japanese Incense Boxes Rediscovered, Montreal Mus, 77; auth, Freedom of Clay and Brush through Seven Centuries in Northern China: Tz'u-chou Type Wares, 960-1600 AD, Indianapolis Art Mus, 80. *Mailing Add:* 715 E 70th Place Indianapolis IN 46220

MINSKY, RICHARD
BOOKBINDER, CONCEPTUAL ARTIST

b New York, NY, Jan 7, 47. *Study:* Brooklyn Col, BA(cum laude), 68; New Sch Social Res, 69-71; Brown Univ, MA, 70. *Work:* Victoria & Albert Mus; Hirshhorn Mus & Sculpture Garden; New York Pub Libr Rare Book Room; Los Angeles Mus Craft & Folk Art. *Comn:* Leather & ivory binding for The Unicorn Tapestries, Metrop Mus Art, New York, 76; binding on Sha'arei Tefilch, Donglomur Found, Villanova, Pa, 76; Program Book, White House, Washington, DC, 77; binding for Buckminster Fuller's Tetrascroll, Universal Limited Art Ed, West Islip, NY, 77. *Exhib:* Creative Arts Workshop, Ctr Book Arts, New Haven, Conn, 75; The Book as Art, Fendrick Gallery, Washington, DC, 75; The Object as Poet, Renwick Gallery, 77 & Mus Contemp Crafts, New York, 77; Crafts in the White House, Los Angeles Mus Craft & Folk Art, 77; The Artist and the Book, Dayton Arts Inst, Ohio, 78; The Open and Closed Book, Victoria & Albert Mus, 79; Int Leather Arts Exhib, Sawtooth Ctr Visual Design, Winston-Salem, NC, 84. *Pos:* Founder, Ctr Book Arts, 74, pres, 74-78, chmn, 74-82. *Teaching:* Instr book arts, Sch Visual Arts, New York, 77- *Awards:* Nat Endowment Arts Fels, 77-81. *Bibliog:* Rolland Smith (dir), Modern work with an ancient art, WCBS-TV Six O'Clock News, 5/17/72; Shelley Rice (auth), Minsky in London, Artforum, 1/81; Ed McCormack (auth), From neo-conceptual to bodies, Artspeak, 4/21/81. *Media:* Books; Gold, Gems. *Publ:* Contribr, The decade: Change and continuity, Craft Horizons, 6/76. *Mailing Add:* 115-25 Metropolitan Ave Kew Gardens NY 11418

MINTICH, MARY RINGELBERG
SCULPTOR, CRAFTSMAN

b Detroit, Mich. *Study:* Albion Col; Ind Univ, BA; Queens Col; Univ Tenn; Univ NC, Greensboro, MFA. *Work:* Everson Mus Art, Syracuse, NY; Mint Mus Art, Raddisson Plaza, Charlotte, NC; R J Reynolds World Hq, Winston-Salem, NC; St Johns Art Mus, Wilmington, NC; and others. *Comn:* Sculpture, NC Arts Coun, Waterworks Gallery, Salisbury, 84. *Exhib:* Arts Showcase '79, Mint Mus Art, Charlotte, NC; McKissick Mus, Columbia, SC, 81; Greenville Mus Art, SC, 81; Southeastern Ctr Contemp Art, Winston-Salem, NC; NC Mus Art, Raleigh; Clemson Univ; and others. *Teaching:* Sacred Heart Col, 67-73; Penland Sch Crafts, 72; assoc prof sculpture, design & metals, Winthrop Col, 72- *Awards:* Purchase Awards, Ceramics Nat & 8th Regional Piedmont Crafts Exhib. *Mem:* Visual Arts Coalition. *Media:* Multimedia. *Publ:* Illusr, Art Works for Urban Development, 73. *Dealer:* Gilliam & Peden Assocs 1322 New Hope Church Rd Raleigh NC 27609; Art South Inc 613 Felder Ave Montgomery AL 36106. *Mailing Add:* PO Box 913 Belmont NC 28012

MINTZ, BARON (RONALD EARL)
CONSERVATOR, PAINTER

b Rocky Mount, NC, Jan 21, 26. *Study:* Univ NC, Chapel Hill, AB, 48; MI Sch & P-Einst Group, Haus der Kunst, Munich, Ger, cert, 55; Brit Mus, London, conserv apprentice & asst to Hans Griesche, cert, 56; George Washington Univ, MS, 64; Jackson State Univ, PhD, 75. *Work:* Has treated works in var mus, galleries & pvt collections. *Exhib:* Los Angeles, 68; Chapel Hill, 80; New Orleans, 82-83; Palm Beach, Fla, 82-83; Seattle, 83. *Pos:* Conservator, US Govt Worldwide, 56-74; pvt practice, 75-81. *Teaching:* Instr, US Govt Schs Worldwide, 52-74; instr, Chapel Hill, NC, 75-80. *Awards:* Legion of Merit, US Govt, 73 & Meritorious Serv Award, 74. *Mem:* Am Inst Conserv Hist & Artistic Works; Int Inst Conserv Hist & Artistic Works; Ordre pour le Merite (chancellor, 76-83); Inst Preserv Decorative Art (bd adv, 82-83). *Res:* Analysis of artist techniques; chromoform technique. *Publ:* Auth, A Global Model for Simulation and Analysis, 66, Integration Approach: Design and Development Factors, 68, Quality Control, 69, Basic Probability Theory and Its Applications, 72 & Reliability Probability Based upon the Use of Small Sample Data, 73, US Govt. *Mailing Add:* 14510 SE 167th St Renton WA 98055

MINTZ, HARRY
PAINTER

b Sept 27, 09; US citizen. *Work:* Art Inst Chicago; New Evansville Mus, Ind; Whitney Mus Am Art, New York; Tel Aviv Mod Mus Art, Israel; Rio de Janeiro Mus Art, Brazil; and others. *Exhib:* Art Inst Chicago, 34-63; Whitney Mus Am Art, New York; Venice Biennale, Italy; Denver Art Mus, 63; Corcoran Gallery Art, Washington, DC; and many others. *Teaching:* Assoc prof, Art Inst Chicago. *Awards:* Jules F Brower Prize, 52 & 54 & Silver Prize, 62, Art Inst Chicago. *Media:* Oil. *Mailing Add:* 429 W Briar Pl Chicago IL 60657

MION, PIERRE RICCARDO
ILLUSTRATOR, PAINTER

b Bryn Mawr, Pa, Dec 10, 31. *Study:* George Washington Univ; Corcoran Gallery Sch of Art, With Elliot O'Hara; also privately with Norman Rockewell. *Comn:* Solar System Evolution (mural), Smithsonian Inst, Washington, DC; team portrait of Apollo astronauts, Nat Geographic Soc; paintings of space futures, Look Mag, 69; cover painting, Reader's Digest, Pleasantville, NY, 68; Bicentennial Flag, Nat Park Serv, Washington, DC, 76. *Exhib:* Nat Ann Watercolor Exhib, Smithsonian Inst, 51 & 63; Robots to the Moon, Hayden Planetarium, New York, 63; Artist & Space, Nat Gallery Art, Washington, DC, 69; Space Art, Smithsonian Inst Air & Space Mus, 71 & Hudson River Mus, Yonkers, NY, 72; one-man shows, Acad of the Arts, Easton, Md, 72 & Metropolis Bldg Asn, Washington, DC, 76. *Pos:* Art dir illus, Creative Arts Studio, Washington, DC, 57-60; vpres art-design, Northern Sci Indust Exhibs, 64-66. *Teaching:* Instr illus, Marine Corps Inst, Washington, DC, 53-54. *Awards:* Third Prize, Outdoor Art Fair, Times Herald, 47; Second Prize/Drawing, Corcoran Art Sch, 56. *Bibliog:* Pierre Mion presents one-man show, Baltimore Sun, 72; Ev Gardner (auth), article in Washington Daily News, 72; Mary Runde (auth), Intensity brings detail to Mion's paintings, Star-Democrat, 72. *Mem:* Soc Illustr. *Media:* Acrylic and gouache; acrylic and watercolor. *Publ:* Illusr, Night driving, Popular Sci, 67; illusr, The death of a president Part III, Look Mag, 67; illusr, The squalus is down, Reader's Digest, 68; illusr, All-girl team tests the habitat, 71 & First Colony in space, 76, Nat Geographic. *Mailing Add:* 7401 Westlake Terrace Bethesda MD 20817

MIOTKE, ANNE E
PAINTER, INSTRUCTOR

b Milwaukee, Wis, Aug 31, 43. *Study:* Mount Mary Col, Milwaukee, BA, 65; Univ Wis-Milwaukee, with John N Colt & Laurence Rathsack, MS, 70 & MFA, 73. *Work:* Univ Wis-Madison & Milwaukee; Cincinnati Art Mus; Wehr Corp & Joseph P Jansen Co, Milwaukee; Hyatt Regency Hotel & Liberty Nat Bank, Louisville, Ky; and others. *Exhib:* J B Speed Art Mus, Louisville, 74; Watercolor USA, Springfield Art Mus, 77, 80, 82 & 83; Bradley Gallery, Milwaukee, 78, 81 & 83; Contemp Art Ctr, Cincinnati, 79 & 83; Cincinnati Art Mus, 75, 77 & 81; Marietta Nat, Ohio, 82; and others. *Pos:* Bd mem, Milwaukee Area Teachers of Art, 67-70; contrib ed, Midwest Art, 75-77. *Teaching:* Instr art, Mount Mary Col, Milwaukee, 70-72; Layton Sch Art & Design, Milwaukee, 73-74; Art Acad Cincinnati, 74- *Awards:* Nat Endowment Arts Vis Specialist Grant, Milwaukee Art Mus, 75-79; Cash Award, John Michael Kohler Arts Ctr, 79; Ohio Arts Coun Fel, 80 & 81. *Mem:* Col Art Asn Am; Am Asn Univ Prof; Phi Kappa Phi. *Dealer:* Bradley Galleries 2565 N Downer Ave Milwaukee WI 53211; Toni Birckhead Gallery Cincinnati OH. *Mailing Add:* 5639 Macey Ave-N-C Cincinnati OH 45227

MIRALDA, ANTONI
SCULPTOR

b Barcelona, Spain, Oct 2, 42. *Study:* Sch Textile Engineers, Tarrasa, 56-61; Cours de Methode Comparee des Arts Plastiques; Ctr Int d'Etudes Pedagogiques, Sovres, France, 62-64. *Work:* Moderna Museet, Stockholm; Ctr Nat Art Cult, Paris; Musee Cantini, Marseilles, France; Art Gallery of New South Wales, Australia. *Exhib:* Mus Mod Art, Paris, 66, 68 & 69; Les Assises du Siege Contemp, Musee des Arts Decoratifs, Paris, 68; one-man shows, Mus Contemp Crafts, New York, 71 & 72, Metrop Mus Art, New York, 73, Ctr Cult, Villeparsis, 75, Documenta 6, Kassel, Ger, 77 & Contemp Arts Mus, Houston, 77; and many others. *Awards:* City of Barcelona Bursary, 62-63; Laureate of 5th Biennale de Paris, 67. *Bibliog:* Douglas Davis (auth), A new world of art, Newsweek, New York, 73; Bill Dyckes (auth), Contemporary Spanish art, Arts Mag, New York, 76; Pierre Restany (auth), Miralda artiste en tous genres, Artitudes Int, 77. *Publ:* Auth & ed, Album, pvt publ, Majorca, Spain, 73 & Food Coloring Cards, pvt publ, Paris, 75; coauth, Ceremonials, Galeria Vandres, Madrid & Centre Beaubourg, 75-78; auth, The Last Supper, Art Enlla, Barcelona, Spain, 76; coauth, Situation-color, Galeria Vandres, Madrid, 77. *Mailing Add:* 24 Harrison St New York NY 10013

MIRANO, VIRGIL MARCUS
PHOTOGRAPHER, EDUCATOR
b Los Angeles, Calif, Jan 3, 37. *Study:* Calif State Univ, Fullerton, BA, 74; Univ Calif, Los Angeles, MA, 76. *Work:* Univ NMex Art Mus; Fla State Univ Fine Arts Gallery, Tallahassee. *Comn:* Edition, offset and color litho prints (with Robert Fichter), Fla State Univ, 74-75. *Exhib:* Emerging Artists, Fredrick S Wight Gallery, Univ Calif, Los Angeles, 76; New Blues, Mem Union Art Gallery, Univ NMex, 76; Emerging Los Angeles Photogr, Friends of Photog, Carmel, Calif, 76; Fla State Univ Fine Arts Gallery, 76 & 77. *Teaching:* Teaching asst photog, Univ Calif, 74-76; asst prof art/photog, Fla State Univ, 76-77; vis artist, Art Inst Chicago, 78. *Bibliog:* Terry Huseby (auth), Light and Substance, Univ NMex Press, 74; Joan Murray (auth), New photographics/75, Artweek, 5/75. *Mem:* Soc Photographic Educ; Visual Studies Workshop; Int Mus Photog. *Mailing Add:* 912 Vernon Ave Venice CA 90291

MIRKO (WOLODYMYR PYLYSHENKO)
COLLECTOR, PAINTER
b Ukraine, July 28, 34; US citizen. *Study:* Rochester Inst Technol, BFA, 58 & MFA, 63; NY State Univ Col Buffalo, teaching cert, 59. *Exhib:* Finger Lakes Regional, Rochester Mem Art Gallery, 63; Western NY Show, Albright-Knox Art Gallery, Buffalo, 63; Everson Mus, Syracuse, 63; Barnard Col, Columbia Univ, 65; Philadelphia Print Club, 65. *Teaching:* Assoc prof drawing & painting, NY State Univ Brockport, 63-, chmn art dept. *Awards:* First Prize Print Award, Rochester Mem Art Gallery, 62. *Bibliog:* Jean Reeves (auth), Ukrainian artist uses the myths, Buffalo Eve News, 12/13/66; Dr D K Winebrenner (auth), Mirko show at Tomac Gallery, Buffalo Courier, 12/66. *Media:* Oil, Relief. *Collection:* Collection of prints from Ukrainian Soviet Socialist Republic and 19th century Ukrainian folk costumes. *Mailing Add:* 1162 Main Ave Brockport NY 14420

MISCH, ALLENE K
PAINTER
b Utica, NY, Jan 27, 28. *Study:* Chicago Art Inst; Ind Univ; Purdue Univ; also with Tom Hill, Robert E Wood, John C Pellew & George Cherepov. *Comn:* Oil, Mem Hospital, Michigan City, Ind, 65. *Exhib:* Las Vegas Art Mus, Nev, 72-78; State Capitol, Carson City, Nev, 76; one-man shows, Green Apple Gallery, 78 & Las Vegas Art Mus, 80. *Pos:* Gallery dir, Dunes Art Found, 66-70 & Las Vegas Art Mus, 72-73; visual arts chmn, Festival: The Arts, Allied Arts Coun, Las Vegas, 77. *Teaching:* Instr oils & acrylics, Dunes Art Found, Michigan City, 65-70 & Las Vegas Art Mus, 71- *Awards:* Oils Award, Dunes Regionals, Dune Art Found, First Merchants Bank, 63, 65 & 68; Purchase Prize, Elkhart Art Festival, CofC, Ind, 65; Oil Award, Michiana Regional, South Bend Art Ctr, 67. *Bibliog:* Festival: The Arts, Las Vegas Sun, 77. *Mem:* Las Vegas Artists' Coop; Advocate for the Arts. *Media:* Acrylic, Oil; Lithograph. *Dealer:* Fine Arts Assocs 8153 Billowvista Dr Playa del Rey, CA 90291; Lewis Galleries 29835 Redwood Drive Box 4816 Canyon Lake CA 92380. *Mailing Add:* 3806 Forestcrest Dr Las Vegas NV 89121

MISRACH, RICHARD LAURENCE
PHOTOGRAPHER
b Los Angeles, Calif, July 11, 49. *Study:* Univ Calif, Berkeley, BA, 71. *Work:* Victoria & Albert Mus, London; Chase Manhattan Bank, New York; Mus Mod Art, San Francisco; Ctr Creative Photog, Tucson, Ariz; IBM Corp, San Jose, Calif; and others. *Comn:* Photography, Am Tel & Tel, Washington, DC, 78. *Exhib:* Bent Photog, Australian Ctr for Photog, Sydney, 77; Night Landscape, Oakland Mus, Calif, 77; one-man show, Desert Photographs, Ctr Georges Pompidou, Mus Art Mod, Paris, 79; Am Images, Corcoran Gallery Art & traveling, 79; Mirrors & Windows, Mus Mod Art (traveling), New York, 79-80; Beyond Color, San Francisco Mus Mod Art, 80; Whitney Biennial, Whitney Mus Am Art, New York, 81; Los Angeles Co Mus Art, 83; Honolulu Acad Arts, 84; 10-year retrospective, Friends of Photog, Carmel, 84. *Teaching:* Instr photog, Assoc Students Studio, Univ Calif, Berkeley, 71-77; vis lectr landscape archit, Univ Calif, Berkeley, 82. *Awards:* Nat Endowment Arts Photog Fel, 73 & 77; Friends of Photog Ferguson Grant, 76; Guggenheim Found Fel, 78. *Bibliog:* David Fahey (auth), Interview with Richard Misrach, G Ray Hawkins Newsletter, 79; Carter Ratcliff (auth), Richard Misrach: Words and images, Print Collectors Newsletter, 1-2/80; Irene Borger (auth), Richard Misrach, Exposure Mag, 80. *Publ:* Auth, Richard Misrach 1979, Grapestake Gallery, 79; contribr, American Images: New Work by Twenty Contemporary Photographers, Am Tel & Tel, 79; contribr, Mirrors and Windows: American Photography Since 1960, Mus Mod Art, New York, 79; Hawaii Portfolio, 80 & Graecism Portfolio, 83, Grapestake Gallery; and others. *Dealer:* Grapestake Gallery 2876 California St San Francisco CA 94115; Light Gallery 724 5th Ave New York NY. *Mailing Add:* 3588 Appaloosa Tr Pinole CA 94564

MISS, MARY
SCULPTOR
b New York, NY, May 27, 44. *Study:* Univ Calif, Santa Barbara, BA, 66; Rinehart Sch Sculpture, Md Art Inst, Baltimore, MFA, 68. *Work:* Allen Mem Art Mus, Oberlin Col, Ohio; RI Sch Design Mus. *Exhib:* Nine Artists: Theodoran Awards, Guggenheim Mus, 72; Max Protech Gallery, New York, 80; Utopia & City, Neuer Berliner Kuntsuerein, Berline, 82; Architechtural References, Los Angeles Inst Contemp Art; and others. *Teaching:* Instr, Sch Visual Arts, New York, 72-83; Pratt Inst, 73; Hunter Col, 72-75; Sarah

Lawrence Col, 76-83, Cooper Union, 83; vis artist, Pratt Inst, Brooklyn, NY, 73. *Awards:* NY State Coun on Arts CAPS Grant, 73 & 76; Nat Endowment Awards, 74 & 75; Brandeis Univ Creative Arts Award, 82. *Bibliog:* Laurie Anderson (auth), Mary Miss, Artforum, 11/73; Lucy Lippard (auth), Mary Miss: an extremely clear situation, Art Am, 3-4/74; Ronald Onorato (auth), Illusive Spaces: The art of Mary Miss, Artforum, 12/78. *Mailing Add:* Box 304 Canal St Sta New York NY 10013

MISSAL, JOSHUA M & PEGGE
DEALERS, COLLECTORS
Mr Missal, b Hartford, Conn, Apr 12, 15; Mrs Missal, b Denver, Colo, Nov 25, 23. *Study:* Mr Missal, Univ Rochester, BM, 37, MM, 38; London Inst, Hon DM, 72; Mrs Missal, NTex State Univ, BA, 44. *Pos:* Dirs & owners, Gallery M, Farmington, Conn, 70-76 & Missal Gallery Ltd, Scottsdale, Ariz, 76- *Teaching:* Mr Missal, assoc prof interrelated arts, Wichita State Univ, 52-70. *Mem:* Am Fedn Art; Appraisers Asn Am. *Specialty:* American Barbizon and Impressionist painters; British Victorian painters; French Postimpressionist artists and important graphics by major artists. *Publ:* Mrs Missal, auth, On Collecting Art, Guest Informant, 76 & auth, An Introduction to Printmaking for the Layman, 82; Mr Missal, auth, American art--the continuing boom, Art Talk, 12/81 & auth, articles on art collecting, World Fine Art, 82-83. *Mailing Add:* Missal Gallery Ltd 7134 Main St Scottsdale AZ 85251

MISSAL, STEPHEN J
PAINTER, INSTRUCTOR
b Albuquerque, NMex, Apr 23, 48. *Study:* Wichita State Univ, BFA, 70, MFA, 72; Marymount Col, 72. *Work:* New Britain Mus Am Art, Conn; Wichita Mus Art & Ulrich Mus, Kans; Jefferson Federal Savings & Loan Gallery, Meriden, Conn. *Comn:* Mural, Jed Nolan's Music Hall, Scottsdale, Ariz, 79-80; stage art & backdrop, Phoenix Little Theater, 78; jewelry, Franklin Mint, 80; wildlife diorama, Stanley Short Corp, Rose, Ore, 81; Shakespeare Mural, Scottsdale Ctr Arts, 82. *Exhib:* Mid-West Competitive Exhib, Tulsa Art Mus, Okla, 71; Civic Ctr Exhib, Wichita Civic Ctr, Kans, 72; Tulsa Invitational Exhib, Tulsa Art Mus, Okla, 72; Midwest Biennial 14th Ann, Joslyn Mus Art, Omaha, Nebr, 76; Festival VIII, Scottsdale Ctr Arts, Ariz, 77; and many others. *Pos:* Illusr & staff artist, Scottsdale Daily Progress, Ariz, 79-; illusr & staff artist, Ariz Arts & Lifestyles, Phoenix, 80. *Teaching:* Head, Art Dept, White Mountain Sch, Littleton, NH, 72-74; instr painting & drawing, Northeast Mo State Univ, 74-77; instr painting, drawing & design, Scottsdale Community Col, Ariz, 79- *Awards:* Purchase Awards, Tulsa Invitational, 72 & 14th Ann Midwest Exhib, 76; Best Drawing, Scottsdale Ctr Arts, 77. *Mem:* Nat Col Art Asn; Midwest Col Art Asn. *Media:* Oil, Pen & Ink. *Publ:* Illusr, The Field Book of Mountaineering & Rock Climbing, Winchester, 75; illusr & contribr, Musical Six-Six Newsletter, 77-79; illusr, Alpha/Omega, 78-79; illusr, Phoenix Mag, 82; illusr, Ariz Mag, 82. *Dealer:* Missal Gallery Ltd 7373 Scottsdale Mall Scottsdale AZ 85251; Winter Gallery 3050 N Country Club Rd Tucson AZ 85716. *Mailing Add:* 3102 North 81st Pl Scottsdale AZ 85251

MITCHELL, CLIFFORD
PAINTER, ARCHITECT
b Birmingham, Ala, Sept 22, 25. *Study:* Tuskegee Inst, BS, 49; Univ Hartford Art Sch, BFA, 58. *Work:* New Brit Mus Am Art; Univ Conn Sch Pharm, Storrs; Stamford Mus & Nature Ctr; Conn Gen Life Ins Co, Bloomfield; Mattatuck Mus, Waterbury, Conn; and others. *Exhib:* Silvermine Guild Artists New Eng Exhib, New Canaan, Conn, 64; Conn Pub Television, Hartford, Conn, 76; Univ Conn, Waterbury, 77; Huntsville Mus Art, Ala, 79; De Cordova Art Mus, Lincoln, Mass, 79; John Slade Ely House Gallery, New Haven, Conn, 81; and others. *Pos:* Architect, Clifford Mitchell, Hartford, 75- *Teaching:* Instr interior design, Univ Hartford Art Sch Eve Course, 68-69. *Awards:* Larry Aldrich Award, Silvermine Guild Artists, 60; Past Pres Prize, Conn Watercolor Soc, 70 & First Prize, 74; Hartford Arts Festival Purchase Award, 72; and others. *Bibliog:* Janet Gaston (auth), Aux etats-unis/a New York salon audubon, La Rev Mod, 60; J V W B (auth), Works by Mitchell at local museum, New Brit Herald, 68; Jolene Goldenthal (auth), Look at art/an architect turns artist, Hartford Courant, 71. *Mem:* Conn Acad Fine Arts; Conn Watercolor Soc (pres, 70-72); Silvermine Guild Artists. *Media:* Oil, Watercolor; Graphics. *Dealer:* Silvermine Guild Artists Silvermine New Canaan CT 06840. *Mailing Add:* 1024 Trout Brook Dr West Hartford CT 06119

MITCHELL, DANA COVINGTON, JR
COLLECTOR
b Bluefield, WVa, Feb 22, 18. *Study:* Univ WVa, BA & MD. *Pos:* Pres bd trustees, Columbia Mus Art, 60-61. *Collection:* Contemporary American art. *Mailing Add:* 600 Spring Lake Rd Columbia SC 29206

MITCHELL, DONALD
ADMINISTRATOR, DEALER
b Mt Vernon, NY, Mar 5, 22. *Study:* Wichita State Univ, art hist; Abbe Inst, painting with George DeGroat; Monterey Peninsula Col, painting with Fay Hopkins. *Pos:* Vpres, Universal Arts, Inc, Carmel, Calif, 60-; dir, Zantman Galleries, Ltd, Carmel, 60-; co-owner, Highlands Gallery, Carmel, 60- *Specialty:* Quality works, mostly representational, in all media, style and technique. *Mailing Add:* PO Box 3731 Carmel CA 93921

MITCHELL, ELEANOR
CONSULTANT, LIBRARIAN
b Orange, NJ, Apr 4, 07. *Study:* Douglass Col, New Brunswick, NJ, BA, 28, LittD, 68; Columbia Univ Sch Libr Serv, BS, 29; Inst Art & Archaeol, Univ

Paris, Carnegie summer scholar, 32; Harvard Univ, 34; Smith Col, MA, 36; additional studies art, languages & music, Univ Florence, Carnegie Inst, Univ Pittsburgh & George Washington Univ. *Pos:* Asst cur bks & photog, Art Dept, Smith Col, 29-36; asst, Grad House, Florence, Italy, 36-37; librn, Dept Fine Arts, Univ Pittsburgh, 37-42; asst to dir, Bibliot Pub Estado Jalisco, Guadalajara, Mex, 42-43; chief art div, NY Pub Libr, 43-51; prog specialist, Cult Activities Dept, UNESCO, Paris, 48-49; dir libr serv, US Info Serv, Italy, 51-53; consult fine arts, Libr of Cong, Washington, DC, 54-55; consult, Montclair Free Pub Libr, 55; US specialist, Int Educ Exchange Serv, Dept State, Bibliot Pub Dept, Cali, Colombia, 55-56; US specialist, Univ Antioquia, Medellin, Colombia, 56-57; exec dir fine arts comt, People-to-People Prog, Corcoran Gallery, 57-61; specialist, Bks for the People Fund, Inc, Pan Am Union, Washington, DC, 61-62; bibliog asst, Rockefeller Found, Proj Int Rice Res Inst-Philippines, Washington, DC, 62-63; consult, Hisp Found, Libr of Cong, 63; libr consult, Univ Catolica, Quito, Ecuador, under St Louis Univ-Agency Int Develop Contract, 63-68; proj officer, Int Rels Off, Am Libr Asn, Washington, DC, 69-72; libr consult, United Nations Educ, Sci & Cult Orgn, Brazil, 74-75. *Mem:* Am Libr Asn; Soc Woman Geogr. *Publ:* Contribr, Gazette Beaux-Arts, Col Res Libr, NY Pub Libr Bull, Art Educ Bull & Douglass Alumnae Bull, 37-61. *Mailing Add:* 730 24th St NW Washington DC 20037

MITCHELL, FRED
PAINTER
b Meridian, Miss, Nov 24, 23. *Study:* Carnegie Inst Technol, scholar, 42-43; Cranbrook Acad Art, 46-48, BFA, 48, MFA, 56; Acad Fine Arts, Rome. *Work:* Columbus Gallery of Fine Arts, Ohio; Cranbrook Acad of Art, Bloomfield Hills, Mich; Munson-Williams-Proctor Mus Art, Utica, NY. *Comn:* Cast concrete screen, Miss State Col Women. *Exhib:* Younger Am Painters, Solomon R Guggenheim Mus, New York, 54; Dallas Mus Fine Arts, Tex, 54; Vanguard 55, Walker Art Ctr, Minneapolis, Minn, 55; Painter, Sculptor & Printmaker, New York Ink Drawings, 73; Painters in Watercolor, Hunterdon Art Ctr, Clinton, NJ, 75; one-man shows, Univ Maine, Machias, 74; State Univ NY at Binghamtom Art Gallery, 76 & Munson-Williams-Proctor Sch Art Gallery, 77; and many others. *Pos:* Co-founder, Tanager Gallery, New York, 52-62; founder and artist-teacher, Downtown Art Ctr, FDR Inst, Battery Park, New York, 61 & South St Seaport Mus, New York, formerly; artist-in-residence, Columbia Mus of Art, SC, 65; artist-in-residence, Aspen Sch Contemp Art, Colo, 65. *Teaching:* Prof drawing and painting, Cranbrook Acad Art, Bloomfield Hills, Mich, 55-59; vis critic, Cornell Univ, Ithaca, 68-69; vis prof art, Ithaca Col, New York, 69-70; adj assoc prof art, New York Univ, 61-71; assoc prof art, Queens Col, New York, 73-74; vis prof art, Univ Maine, Machias, 74; vis artist, Univ Oregon, Eugene, 75; prof art, NYU Grad Sch in Venice, Italy, 75; vis assoc prof art and dir, Univ Art Gallery, State Univ NY, Binghamton, 76-77; vis artist, Munson-Williams-Proctor Sch Art, Utica, NY, 77. *Awards:* Traveling Fel, Italy, 48-51; Ford Found Artist-in-Residence, Columbia Mus Art. *Media:* Watercolor and Oil. *Mailing Add:* 92 Hester St New York NY 10002

MITCHELL, JAMES E
ILLUSTRATOR, PAINTER
b New York, NY, Jan 1, 26. *Study:* Pratt Inst, Brooklyn, NY, cert; Acad Grande Chaumiere, Paris. *Work:* US Navy Art Collection, Washington, DC; Mariners Mus, Newport News, Va; Submarine Mus, New London, Conn; US Merchant Marine Acad, Kings Point, NY. *Comn:* Operation Sea Orbit, Mariners Mus, Newport News, Va, 65; DASO-Cape Kennedy, USN, 69; Tall Ships (paintings), Texaco, 76. *Exhib:* One-man shows, Lord & Taylor Gallery, New York, 66-69; The Gallery, Essex, Conn, 73-74; South St Seaport Mus, New York, 76; Texaco Tall Ships Paintings Traveling Exhib, London, Madrid, Lisbon, Amsterdam, Copenhagen, Oslo, Goteborg & New York, 77; Third Ann Exhib, Am Soc Marine Artists, 80. *Awards:* Cert of Award for Paintings for Shell Oil Co Series, Printing Industs Am, 68 & 69; Cert of Achievement for Paintings for Texaco Co Series, Printing Industs Metrop New York, 74-77. *Media:* Gouache, Oil. *Publ:* Auth & illusr, Hydrofoils: A sketchbook of the future, Motor Boating, 62; auth & illusr, Sketchbook: SORC '72, Rudder Mag, 72. *Dealer:* South St Seaport Mus Gallery 215 Water St New York NY 10016; Trend House Gallery 717 South Dakota Ave Tampa FL 33606. *Mailing Add:* 422 S Columbus Ave PO Box 236 Mt Vernon NY 10553

MITCHELL, JOAN
PAINTER
b Chicago, Ill, 1926. *Study:* Smith Col, 42-44; Columbia Univ; Art Inst Chicago, BFA, 47; NY Univ, MFA, 50. *Work:* Walker Art Ctr; Albright-Knox Art Gallery, Buffalo; Art Inst Chicago; Mus Mod Art, New York; Phillips Collection, Washington, DC. *Exhib:* Pa Acad Fine Arts, Philadelphia, 66; Two Decades of American Painting, Mus Mod Art, New York & traveling, 67; solo exhibs, Everson Mus, 72, Ruth S Schnaffner Gallery, Los Angeles, 78, Webb & Parsons, Bedford Village, NY, 78, Paule Anglim Gallery, San Francisco, 79 & Richard Hines Gallery, Seattle, 80; Va Mus Fine Arts, Richmond, 70; Younger Abstract Artists of the Fifties, Mus of Mod Art, New York, 71; American Drawings 1963-1973, 73 & retrospective, 74, Whitney Mus Am Art; Indianapolis Mus Art, Ind, 74; Corcoran Gallery Art, Washington, DC, 75; Albright Col, Pa, 78; Albright-Knox Mus, 78. *Bibliog:* Carter Ratcliff (auth), New York letter, Art Int, 1/78; Paul Brach (auth), Joan Mitchell at Fourcade, Art in Am, 3-4/78; Merle Schipper (auth), French painting, American style, Artweek, 4/15/78. *Mailing Add:* c/o Xavier Fourcade 35 E 75th St New York NY 10021

MITCHELL, JOAN ELIZABETH See Robertson, Joan E

MITCHELL, JOHN BLAIR
PAINTER, EDUCATOR
b Brooklyn, NY, Jan 30, 21. *Study:* Pratt Inst, cert, 39-43, Pratt Inst Sch Educ, 46-47; Columbia Univ Teachers Col, BS, 48, Univ, MA, 49; Pratt Graphic Arts Ctr, 60-61, with Edmondson, Rogalski & Ponce de Leon; NY Univ Sch Educ, PhD, 63. *Work:* Metrop Mus Art, New York; Libr of Cong, Washington, DC; Silvermine Guild Artists, Conn; Baltimore Mus Art; Notre Dame Col, Baltimore. *Comn:* Mural, Baltimore City Hosp, 72. *Exhib:* Six shows, Corcoran Gallery Art, Washington, DC, 54-63; Libr of Cong 19th Nat Exhib Prints, 63; Silvermine Guild Artists 5th Nat, 64; one-man show, Baltimore Mus Art, 64; Hochschild Kohn Md Artists Today Anniversary, 72; one-man show, Towson State Univ, 77. *Teaching:* Prof graphics drawing, painting & photog & coordr grad art prog, Columbia Univ Teachers Col, 49-80, instr art, summers 50, 53 & 54; chmn art dept, Towson State Col, 51-57 & 63-65; instr graphics, Baltimore Mus Art, 63-73. *Awards:* First Awards, Intercollegiate Art Exhib, Coppin State Col, 72 & Easton Acad Art, 75; Md State Arts Coun Works in Progress Grant, 80; and others. *Bibliog:* Lincoln Johnson (auth), articles, Baltimore Sun, 12/71 & 2/24/77. *Mem:* Artists Equity Asn; Baltimore Print Club. *Publ:* Auth, Art Education, 52; coauth, Art in Our Maryland Schools, State Manual, State Dept Educ, 53; auth, School Arts, 2/57; auth, Eastern Arts Quart, 1-2/63. *Mailing Add:* 9918 Finney Dr Baltimore MD 21234

MITCHELL, KATHERINE
PAINTER
b Memphis, Tenn, Oct 25, 44. *Study:* Atlanta Col Art, BFA, 68; Tyler Sch Art, Rome, 68; Ga State Univ, MVA, 77. *Work:* High Mus Art; Ga Coun Arts & Humanities; Richard B Russell Fed Off Bldg, Ga State Univ, Atlanta; Tyler Sch Art. *Exhib:* Ga Artists of the 20th Century, Madison-Morgan Cult Ctr, Ga, 79; Hassam Fund Purchase Exhib, Am Acad & Inst Arts & Lett, New York, 79; Avant-Garde: 12 in Atlanta, 79 & Artists in Georgia, 80, High Mus Art; solo exhib, Notes on the Working Process, Atlanta Col Art Gallery, 81 & The New York Series and Beyond, Chastain Gallery, Atlanta, 83; American Drawings IV, Portsmouth Community Arts Ctr, Va, 82 & Smithsonian Inst Nat Tour, 82. *Teaching:* Vis artist, Emory Univ, 80. *Awards:* Hassam Fund Exhib Purchase Award, Am Acad & Inst Arts & Lett, 79. *Bibliog:* John Howett (auth), Katherine Mitchell at Atlanta College of Art, Art in Am, 1/82; Tom Patterson (auth), Art of the state, Browns Guide Ga, 8/82. *Mem:* Twentieth Century Art Soc (mem bd, 83). *Media:* Pencil, Ink. *Publ:* Auth, article, Contemp Art Southeast, Vol II, No 1, 78. *Dealer:* Heath Gallery. *Mailing Add:* 1200 Foster St NW Atlanta GA 30318

MITCHELL, MARGARETTA K
PHOTOGRAPHER, WRITER
b Brooklyn, NY, May 27, 35. *Study:* Smith Col, BA(magna cum laude), 57; Boston Mus Sch, 58; Escuela de Bellas Artes, Madrid, Spain, 59. *Work:* Int Ctr Photog, New York; Performing Arts Archive, San Francisco, Calif; Bannoft Libr, Univ Calif, Berkeley; Royal Print Collection, Windsor, England. *Comn:* Mural, Anixter Corp, San Francisco, Calif, 74; mural, Amax Corp, San Francisco, Calif, 74; mural, San Francisco Art Comn, Calif, 78. *Exhib:* San Francisco Dance Film Festival, San Francisco Mus Mod Art, Calif, 78; Recollections: Ten Women of Photog, Int Ctr Photog, New York, 79. *Collections Arranged:* Recollections: Ten Women of Photog (auth, catalog), Int Ctr Photog, 79. *Teaching:* Instr photog, Univ Calif Extension, 76-78; instr writing & photog, Vista Col, 77-82; instr photog, City Col San Francisco, Calif, 80-81. *Awards:* Nat Endowment Arts Mus Grant, 78-79; Calif Coun Arts Grant, Berkeley Art Ctr, 81-82; Grant, L J & Mary C Skaggs Found, 81. *Mem:* Am Soc Mag Photog; Soc Photog Educ; San Francisco Women Artists; Inst Hist Study. *Media:* Black & White, Color. *Res:* Photographers, particularly rediscoveries. *Publ:* Auth, Gift of Place, Scrimshaw Press, 69; co-auth, To A Cabin, Grossman Publ, 73; introduction to: After Ninety, Univ Washington Press, 77. *Mailing Add:* 280 Hillcrest Rd Berkeley CA 94705

MITCHELL, MICHAEL JOHN
PHOTOGRAPHER, EDUCATOR
b Hamilton, Ont, Nov 3, 43. *Study:* Univ Toronto, Hon BA, 67, MA, 68; Ryerson Polytech Inst, Toronto, advan studies dipl(photog arts), 71. *Work:* Art Gallery Ont; Nat Film Bd Can, Ottawa; Mod Mus, Fotog Mus, Stockholm. *Comn:* Photo mural, Cadillac-Fairview Corp, Eaton Centre, Toronto, 77. *Exhib:* Exposure, 75, Zoosight, 75, Focal Point, 76 & Nightlife, 78, Art Gallery Ont; Imagees Colorees, Optica Gallery, Montreal, 78; Tusen Och en Bild, Mod Mus, Stockholm, 78; Farbwerke, Kunsthaus, Zurich, 80; Photojournalism, Nat Film Bd Gallery, Ottawa, 81; Staying Home, Harbourfront Art Gallery, Toronto, 83. *Pos:* Dir, Fine Art Photography Publ, Toronto, 83. *Teaching:* Lectr art hist, Sheridan Col, Oakville, Ont, 75-76; instr colour photog, Banff Sch Fine Art, Alta, 79; instr contemp photog, Ont Col Art, Toronto, 81- *Awards:* Ont Arts Coun Photog Grants, 71 & 83. *Bibliog:* Allan Porter (auth), article, Camera, Switz, 1/78; William Boyle & J Parkin (auths), Art in Architecture, Visual Arts Ont, 82; Gail Fisher-Taylor (auth), article, Photo Communique, fall 83. *Mem:* Can Artists Rep; Toronto Photogr Workshop. *Media:* Colour. *Publ:* Contribr, Fighting Back, Hakkert Press, 72; ed & contribr, Nightlife, Art Gallery Ont, 79; auth, Monsters of the Gilded Age: Photography of Charles Eisenmann, Gage-Macmillan, 79; ed & contribr, Singing Songs to the Spirit, Govt Can, 80. *Mailing Add:* 641 Queen St E Toronto ON M4M 1G4 Canada

MITCHELL, PETER TODD
PAINTER
b New York, NY, Nov 16, 29. *Study:* Acad Bellas Artes, Mexico City, Mex, with Lozano & Galvan; Groton; Yale Art Sch. *Work:* Metrop Mus Art, New

York. *Comn:* Murals, Von Wrangell, Malaga, Spain, 55 & Thomas Murphy, St Tropez, France, 70. *Exhib:* Am Painters in Philadelphia Collections, 62; Smithsonian Traveling Show Graphics, 71; London Bridge Show, Guildhall-London, 72. *Awards:* First Tiffany Found Award for Painting, 52. *Bibliog:* Berg (auth), L'oeuvre de P T Mitchell, Jardin Arts, 69. *Media:* Oil. *Dealer:* Eric Galleries 61 E 57th St New York NY 10022. *Mailing Add:* 116 E 57th St New York NY 10022

MITCHELL, R(OBERT ELLIS)
GOLDSMITH, LECTURER
b Decatur, Ill, Feb 5, 42. *Study:* Ill Wesleyan Univ, Bloomington, BFA, 64; Southern Ill Univ, Carbondale, MFA, 66; with Nicholas Vergette & Brent Kington. *Work:* Goldsmiths' Hall, London, Eng; Ark Art Ctr, Little Rock. *Comn:* Presidential Badge, Ark State Univ, 79; silver mace, Sigma Phi Epsilon Fraternity, Ark State Univ, 81; silver mace, Univ Southern Ark, 83. *Exhib:* Young Americans, New York, 69; Goldsmiths, Smithsonian Inst, Washington, DC & travel tour, 75; Gold Now, Boston, Pa, 79. *Teaching:* Instr jewelry & design, St Leo Col, Fla, 66-67; assoc prof jewelry & silversmithing, Ark State Univ, Jonesboro, 67-80. *Awards:* Res Grants, State of Ark, 72, 75 & 76. *Mem:* Soc NAm Goldsmiths (exec secy, currently). *Media:* Gold, Silver. *Publ:* Auth, Metal Spinning and Castable Plastics, 72; auth, Periodic Reverse Cycles for Silver Electroforming, 75. *Mailing Add:* 2849 St Ann Dr Green Bay WI 54301

MITRA, GOPAL C
PAINTER, PRINTMAKER
b Patna, Bihar, India, Nov 1, 28. *Study:* B N Col, Patna Univ, PHES & IA; Govt Sch of Arts & Crafts, Patna, Dipl FA; Univ Minn, MFA & PhD, also with Roy Chordhury, B B Mukherji in India & Edward Courbet, Lorenz Either, Cameron Booth & Malcolm Myers in US. *Work:* Youth Gallery, Bucharest, Rumania; Litchfield Art Gallery, London & Cambridge, Eng; Walker Art Ctr, Minneapolis, Minn; Minneapolis Art Inst; Univ Minn Art Gallery, Minneapolis; and others. *Comn:* Life & Enlightenment of Lord Buddha (mural), Movie Theaters in India, 49-56; murals, All India Children Art Festivals, Bengal, Bihar & UP, India, 49-53; Indian Ways of Life (murals), Govt Bihar, Patna, New Delhi & Maddhya Pradesh, 53-57; murals, All India Cult Festivals, Bengal & Bihar, 54-57; Creation, Preservation & Destruction (mural), Edinboro State Col, Pa, 78. *Exhib:* Walker Art Ctr, Minneapolis; Art Exhib, Patna, Calcutta & New Delhi; one-man shows, Litchfield Gallery, London & Cambridge, Chicago State Univ, Acad Fine Arts, Calcutta & Hamline Univ, St Paul, Minn; and many others. *Collections Arranged:* All India Art & Craft Exhib, Patna & Calcutta, 47, 48 & 53; All India Children Art Exhib, Patna, Calcutta & New Delhi, 54, 56 & 57; Indian Art & Culture Exhib, Worthington, Minn, 61; Indo-American Art & Crafts Exhib, Minneapolis, 62, 65 & 67; Himalayan Art, Edinboro State Col, 77. *Teaching:* Artist & lectr, Walker Art Ctr, Minneapolis, 64-65, instr painting, 65-66; assoc prof & lectr painting & printmaking, Chicago State Univ, 67-69; prof art, art hist of India & China, painting & drawing, Edinboro State Col, 69-; and many others. *Awards:* First Prize Awards in Contemp Landscape Painting & Still Life, All India Art Exhib, Patna, Govt School of Arts & Crafts Show, 53; and many others. *Mem:* Am Soc Aesthetics; Am Asn Asian Studies; Int Soc for Comparative Study of Civilizations. *Res:* Art and culture of India and China, Himalayan art and impirical studies in attitude development and attitude change. *Mailing Add:* 12530 Cedar Dr Edinboro PA 16412

MIX, WALTER JOSEPH
PAINTER, INSTRUCTOR
b Chicago, Ill, Oct 14, 28. *Study:* Ariz State Col, Tempe, BAEd(fine arts), 53; Claremont Grad Sch, MFA, 57; studied with Phil Dike, Millard Sheets, Roger Kuntz & Jean Goodwin Ames. *Work:* Brigham Young Univ, Provo, Utah; Scripps Col, Claremont, Calif; Long Beach Munic Mus, Calif; Mt San Antonio Col, Walnut, Calif; Bakersfield Col, Calif. *Exhib:* Pa Acad Fine Arts, 58 & 60; one-man shows, Comara Gallery, Los Angeles, 58-66, Palazzo delle Esposizione, Rome, Italy, 61 & Gallery 8, Claremont, Calif, 77; Los Angeles Co Mus, Los Angeles, Calif, 59-61; Contemp Urban Visions, New Sch for Social Res, New York, 66; Los Angeles Munic Art Gallery, 71. *Pos:* Cur, Mt San Antonio Col, Walnut, Calif, 57- *Teaching:* Instr painting & drawing, Mt San Antonio Col, Walnut, Calif, 57- *Awards:* Second Award, All Calif Invitational, Laguna Beach Art Gallery, 59; Purchase Awards, Religious Dimensions, Brigham Young Univ, 61 & Bakersfield Col, Calif, 62. *Bibliog:* Gerald Nordland (auth), One-man show rev, Arts, 62; R G Wholden (auth), rev of one-man show, Artforum, 63; Jules Langsner (auth), rev of one-man show, Art News, 67. *Media:* Oil, Enamel. *Mailing Add:* 1903 Academy Ct Claremont CA 91711

MIYAMOTO, WAYNE AKIRA
PAINTER, PRINTMAKER
b Honolulu, Hawaii, Sept 6, 47. *Study:* Rensselaer Polytech Inst, 65-68; Univ Hawaii, BA & BFA, 70, MFA, 74. *Work:* State Found Cult & Arts, Honolulu; Univ Hawaii, Honolulu; Fine Arts Mus, Univ Alaska, Fairbanks; Leeward Community Col, Pearl City, Hawaii; Univ Cent Fla, Orlando. *Exhib:* 2nd Ann Honolulu Printmakers Exhib, 77; Int-Nat Drawing Exhib, Edinboro, Pa, 77; 11th Dulin Nat Print & Drawing Exhib, Knoxville, Tenn, 77; Eye of 25, Twenty-five Painters of Fla, Boca Raton Art Ctr, 78; Robert Else Gallery, Calif State Univ, Sacramento, 80; and others. *Pos:* Visual arts consult, State Found Cult & Arts, Hawaii, 81- *Teaching:* Vis asst prof art, Univ Hawaii, Hilo, 76; asst prof, Fla Technol Univ, Orlando, 76-78; vis asst prof, Calif State Univ, Sacramento, 80-81, Univ Hawaii, Hilo, 81-; asst prof, Univ Hawaii, Hilo, dept chmn, 83- *Awards:* Purchase Awards, 4th Col Regional Exhib, 74 & 47th Ann Honolulu Printmakers Exhib, 75, State Found Cult & Arts; State Found Cult & Arts Grants, 82-84. *Mem:* Col Art Asn; Honolulu Printmakers Asn

(mem bd & treas, 71-72); Kalani Honua Cult Ctr, Pahoa, (bd dirs, 81-82). *Media:* Acrylic, Oil; Intaglio, Woodblock. *Publ:* Auth, Unique art of Akaji, Honolulu Star Bulletin Advertiser, 76; Lee Chesney, 25 Years of Printmaking, Univ Presses Fla, Gainesville, 78. *Dealer:* Texann Ivy Inc 122-H N Orange Ave Orlando FL 32802. *Mailing Add:* PO Box 1176 Hilo HI 96720

MIYASAKI, GEORGE JOJI
PRINTMAKER, PAINTER
b Kalopa, Hawaii, Mar 24, 35. *Study:* Calif Col Arts & Crafts, BFA & BAEd, 57 & MFA, 58. *Work:* San Francisco Mus Art, Calif; Brooklyn Mus Art, NY; Mus Mod Art, New York; Art Inst Chicago; Pasadena Art Mus, Calif. *Teaching:* Assoc prof painting & printmaking, Univ Calif, Berkeley, 64. *Awards:* John Simon Guggenheim Fel, 63-64; Nat Endowment Arts, 80. *Bibliog:* Rudy Turk (auth), George Miyasaki, monograph, 81. *Dealer:* Stephen Wirtz Gallery 356 Sutter St San Francisco CA. *Mailing Add:* Dept Art Univ Calif Berkeley CA 94720

MOCK, RICHARD BASIL
ILLUSTRATOR, PAINTER
b Long Beach, Calif, Aug 2, 44. *Study:* Univ Mich, BS(design), 65; New York Studio Sch, with Philip Guston, 66-67. *Work:* Mus Mod Art, New York; Ft Worth Art Mus, Tex; Brooklyn Mus. *Comn:* 120 portraits of athletes at the winter Olympics, Lake Placid, NY, 80. *Exhib:* Solo exhib, Houston Contemp Arts Mus, Tex, 71-77; Portraits, Otis Art Inst, Los Angeles, 78; Block Prints, Whitney Mus Am Art, 82; American Artist as Printmaker, Brooklyn Mus, 83. *Pos:* Illusr, New York Times, 79- *Awards:* Fel, Roswell Mus, NMex, 69-70; Painting Grant, Nat Endowment Arts, 73. *Media:* Block Prints; Oil, Watercolor. *Dealer:* Brooke Alexander 20 W 57th St New York NY 10019. *Mailing Add:* 67 Furman St Brooklyn NY 11201

MODE, CAROL A
PAINTER, PRINTMAKER
b St Louis, Mo, Mar 27, 43. *Study:* Washington Univ, BFA, 65, Summer Art Inst, 80; Vanderbilt Univ, 81-82. *Work:* Tenn State Mus, Nashville; Hosp Corp Am, Nashville; Northern Telecon, Nashville. *Exhib:* Eight State Ann Graphics, J B Speed Mus, 81; Benefit Show, Tenn Fine Arts Ctr, Nashville, 82; Early Eighties Purchase Show, Tenn State Mus, Nashville, 82; Recent Works, Cumberland Gallery, Nashville, 82; two-person exhib, Marnie Sheridan Gallery, Nashville, 83; First Regional Art Exhib, Spartanburg Art Ctr, SC, 83; 47th Ann Nat Midyear Exhib, Butler Inst Am Art, 83. *Teaching:* Instr painting, Cheekwood Fine Arts Ctr, Nashville, 81-82, instr printmaking, 83- *Dealer:* Cumberland Gallery 2213 Bandywood Dr Nashville TN 37215. *Mailing Add:* 3811 Richland Ave Nashville TN 37205

MODEL, ELISABETH D
SCULPTOR, PAINTER
b Bayreuth, Bavaria; US citizen. *Study:* Ryksacademy, Amsterdam, with Prof Jurgens; also with Prof Walter Thor & Prof Cericioli, Munich & Moissi Kogan, Paris. *Work:* Corcoran Galleries, Washington, DC; Wadsworth Atheneum, Hartford, Conn; Jewish Mus, New York; Rose Collection, Brandeis Univ; Rykspreuteu Cabinet, Amsterdam; and others. *Exhib:* Mus Fine Arts, Philadelphia; Mus Fine Arts, Boston; Brooklyn Mus; Stedelyk Mus, Amsterdam, Holland; Riverside Mus, New York; plus others. *Teaching:* Pvt lessons, Amsterdam, 30-38 & New York, 42-48. *Awards:* Gold Medal of Honor, Nat Asn Women Artists, 50; plus many awards & prizes. *Bibliog:* Meilach (auth), Contemporary Sculpture & Sculpture Casting, Crown. *Mcm:* Fedn Mod Sculptors & Painters (vpres). *Media:* Stone, Wood. *Dealer:* Bodley Gallery 1063 Madison Ave New York NY 10023. *Mailing Add:* 340 W 72nd St New York NY 10023

MOE, RICHARD D
ADMINISTRATOR
b Fargo, NDak, May 7, 28. *Study:* Concordia Col, Moorhead, Minn, BA, 51; Univ Colo, MEd, 53, EdD, 60. *Pos:* Dean, Sch Fine Arts, Pac Lutheran Univ, Tacoma, Wash, 68- *Mem:* Tacoma Art Mus (pres, 77-79); Pac Northwest Dance; Int Coun Fine Arts Deans. *Mailing Add:* 304 N Stadium Way Tacoma WA 98444

MOEHL, KARL J
PAINTER, WRITER
b Oberlin, Ohio, June 24, 25. *Study:* Univ Colo, Boulder, BFA, 50; State Univ Iowa, Iowa City, MFA, 52. *Work:* Currier Mus Art, Manchester, NH; Ill State Mus, Springfield; Lakeview Mus, Peoria, Ill; Dirksen Research Libr, Pekin, Ill. *Exhib:* 15th Ann Int, Pa Acad Fine Arts, Philadelphia, 52; one-man shows, Lakeview Mus, Peoria, Ill, 75 & Tower Park Gallery, Peoria Heights, Ill, 82; Ill Landscape Art, Lakeview Mus & traveling, 76; 31st Ill Invitational, Ill State Mus, Springfield, 79; Miss Corridor 1981, Davenport Art Gallery, Iowa, 81. *Pos:* Contrib ed, New Art Asn, 80. *Teaching:* Instr studio, Univ NH, Durham, 53-55 & Brown Univ, Providence, RI, 56-57; prof art hist, Bradley Univ, Peoria, Ill, 57- *Awards:* Purchase Award, Springfield Art Mus, Mo, 71; Merit Award, State Mus Ill, 81; First Prize Painting, Ill Art League, 81 & 82. *Bibliog:* Dee Kilgo (auth), Karl Moehl Recent Work, New Art Examiner, 75. *Mem:* Chicago Art Coalition; Peoria Art Guild (bd mem, 72-81); Am Asn Univ Prof. *Media:* Acrylic, Graphite. *Publ:* Auth, 200 Years of American Painting, 65 & auth, Edward Henry Pothast, 67, Lakeview Mus; auth, Roger Annear Mem Exhib, Peoria Art Guild, 74; auth, Metalsmith: Illini Metal, Soc NAm Goldsmiths, 83. *Dealer:* Tower Park Gallery 4709 N Prospect Rd Peoria Heights IL 61614. *Mailing Add:* 1700 W Ayres Peoria IL 61606

MOELLER, ROBERT CHARLES, III
HISTORIAN, ADMINISTRATOR

b Providence, RI, Jan 22, 38. *Study:* Washington & Lee Univ, BA(hist art), 59; Harvard Univ, with John Beckwith, Dr Hanns Swarzenski, J M Delaisse & J H Plummer, MA(art hist), 63. *Collections Arranged:* Brummer Collection, Duke Univ Art Mus. *Pos:* Res assoc dept art, Duke Univ, 67-68, dir, Duke Univ Art Mus, 68-69; asst cur dept decorative arts & sculpture, Mus Fine Arts, Boston, 70-71, cur decorative arts & sculpture, 71-82. *Teaching:* Teaching fel hist art, Harvard Univ, 64-65; instr art, Duke Univ, 68, asst prof, 68-69; instr sem medieval sculpture, Univ NC, Chapel Hill, spring 68. *Mem:* Int Coun Mus; Am Asn Mus; Am Ceramic Circle; Soc Silver Collectors; Int Ctr Medieval Art. *Res:* Study of mid-twelfth century sculpture in Burgundy concentrating on Narthex sculpture of Charlieu, seventeenth century sculpture and decorative arts. *Publ:* Contrib, The Brummer Collection at Duke University, Art J, 68; auth foreword, The Graphic Art of Edvard Munch, Duke Univ Art Mus Exhib, 12/69; auth, Sculpture from Brive & Sculpture from Savigny, RI Sch Design, 7/69; auth, L'iconographie de la facade nord du narthex de Charlieu, Actes des Journees d'etudes d'histoire et d'archeologie, Charlieu, Soc Amis Arts, 73. *Mailing Add:* 110 Francis Boston MA 02115

MOERSCHEL, CHIARA
PAINTER

b Trieste, Italy; US citizen. *Study:* Lindenwood Col, with Robert Hansen & Sandra Del Munch. *Work:* Mead Gallery, Amherst Col, Mass; First Northwest Bank, St Ann, Mo; Western Ill Univ; Adria Club, Trieste, Italy; Adams Mark, Houston. *Exhib:* Span Int Pavillion, 69; one-man shows, Springfield Col, Ill, 71, Galleria Il Velocipede, Venice, Italy, 72 & Lynn Kottler Gallerie, New York, 73; Trieste Corinta, Italy, 76, 78 & 80; and many others. *Teaching:* Instr workshops, US & abroad. *Awards:* Gustave Geotch Mem Prize, St Louis Artists Guild, 69; First Prize for Watercolor, Am Bar Asn, St Louis, 70; First Prize for Watercolor, Sesquicentennial Show, Northeast Mo State Col, 71; over 200 awards. *Mem:* Acad Prof Artists (mem bd, 70-75); St Charles Artists' Guild (pres, 69-75); St Louis Artists' Guild (vchmn art sect, 70); Am Watercolor Soc; Southern Watercolor Soc; and others. *Media:* Watercolor, Oil. *Dealer:* La Petite Galerie Ltd Clayton MO; Old Frontenac Galleries 10411 Clayton Rd Clayton MO 63131. *Mailing Add:* 121 College Dr St Charles MO 63301

MOFFITT, JOHN FRANCIS
HISTORIAN, PAINTER

b San Francisco, Calif, Feb 25, 40. *Study:* Calif Col Arts & Crafts, BFA, 63; Calif State Univ, San Francisco, MA, 64; Fac Lett & Philos, Univ Madrid, PhD, 66. *Exhib:* 13th Ann NC Artists Exhib, NC State Mus Art, Raleigh, 68; 1st Biennial 5-State Exhib, Gates Gallery, Port Arthur, Tex, 71; 12th Midwest Biennial, Joslyn Art Mus, Omaha, Nebr, 72; 21st Ann Exhib, Beaumont Art Mus, Tex, 72; 50th Regional Exhib, R S Barnwell Art Ctr, Shreveport, La, 72; plus others. *Teaching:* Asst prof art, E Carolina Univ, Greenville, NC, 66-68; asst prof art, Sonoma State Col, Cotati, Calif, 68-69; vis prof landscape painting, Mendocino Art Ctr, Calif, 69; assoc prof art, NMex State Univ, Las Cruces, 69-; vis prof art, Fla State Univ, 78; vis prof art, Univ Valencia, Spain, 81. *Mem:* Col Art Asn Am; Hispanic Art Hist Studies in US; Mid-Am Col Art Asn; Rocky Mountain Medieval & Renaissance Hist Asn. *Interests:* Field of 16th and 17th century Spanish art. *Publ:* Auth, Post-Cubistic pictorial themes: Suggestions for iconographic investigations in non-abstract twentieth century painting, J Theory & Criticism Visual Arts, Vol 1, No 2, 83; auth, The poet and the painter: J H W Tischbein's perfect portrait of Goethe in der Campagna, Art Bulletin, Vol 65, No 2, 83; auth, Velazquez in the Alcazar Palace in 1656: The meaning of the mise-en-scene of Las Meninas, Art Hist (London), 9/83; auth, Velazquez's Forge of Vulcan: The Cuckold, the poets, and the painter, Pantheon: Int Zeitschrift Kunst (Munich), Vol 41, No 4, 83; auth, Who is the old man in a golden helmet?, Art Bulletin, summer 84 (in press); plus numerous critical reviews in Art Quart, Art J, Burlington Mag, Leonardo, etc. *Mailing Add:* 1104 Luna St Las Cruces NM 88001

MOGAVERO, MICHAEL JAMES
PAINTER

Study: Buffalo State Univ, BS, 73; Hoffberger Sch Painting, Md Inst Col Art, MFA, 75. *Work:* Rochester Mem Art Gallery, NY. *Exhib:* Md Biennial, Baltimore Mus Art, 74 & 75; Maryland Artists--A New Look, Baltimore Mus Art, 79; New Directions: Contemporary American Art from the Commodities Corp Collection Traveling Exhib, 81-83; 36-18-6-1, Sarah Lawrence Col Gallery, 82; one-person exhib, Holly Solomon Gallery, 83; Back to the USA Traveling Exhib, Kunstmus, Lucerne, Rheinische Landesmus, Bonn & Kunstverein, Stuttgart, 83; Made in America: 200 Years of Drawing, Minneapolis Inst Art, Minn, 83; and others. *Bibliog:* Ken Sofer (auth), article, Art News, 5/82; Marcia Tucker (auth), An iconography of recent figurative painting: Sex, death, violence and the apocalypse, Artforum, summer 82; Jon R Friedman (auth), Mark Milloff/Michael Mogavero, Arts Mag, 6/83. *Media:* Acrylic, Oil on Canvas. *Mailing Add:* c/o Holly Solomon Gallery 724 Fifth Ave New York NY 10019

MOGENSEN, PAUL
PAINTER, PRINTMAKER

b Los Angeles, Calif, Dec 3, 41. *Work:* Mus Mod Art, New York; High Mus Art, Atlanta, Ga; Houston Mus Fine Arts, Tex. *Exhib:* One-man shows, Bykert Gallery, New York, 67-69 & 75, Weinberg Gallery, San Francisco, 77 & 80 & Janus Gallery, Los Angeles, 81; Romantic Minimalism, Inst Contemp Art, Philadelphia, 67; Modular Painting, Albright-Knox Art Gallery, Buffalo, NY, 70; A View of a Decade, Mus Contemp Art, Chicago, 77; Retrospective, Houston Mus Fine Arts, 78-79. *Collections Arranged:* Structural Art, Am Fedn of Art Traveling Exhib, 67. *Awards:* John Simon Guggenheim Mem Found Fel, 76; Nat Endowment Arts, 80. *Bibliog:* H Rosenstein (auth), Total and complex, Art News, 5/67; Phyllis Derfner (auth), Paul Mogensen at Bykert, Art Am, 7-8/75; Valentin Tatransky (auth), Paul Mogensen: rectangles spirals, Arts Mag, 5/79. *Mailing Add:* 159 Mercer St New York NY 10012

MOGLIA, LUIGI (JOHN)
PAINTER, INSTRUCTOR

b Dover, NJ. *Study:* Pratt Inst, dipl(interior design); Berkshire Summer Sch Art; also with Ernest Watson, Edgar Whitney, John Rogers & Rutledge Bate. *Exhib:* Am Watercolor Soc, Audubon Artists & Allied Artists, Nat Acad Galleries, New York; Am Artists Prof League, Lever House, New York. *Pos:* Interior designer, W & J Sloane, New York; pvt practice, 26 yrs. *Teaching:* Instr interior design, Pratt Inst, Brooklyn, 10 yrs. *Awards:* Nat Art League; Manhasset Art Asn; Port Washington Art Coun. *Mem:* Audubon Artists; Knickerbocker Artists; Am Artists Prof League; Nat Art League; Manhasset Artists Asn. *Mailing Add:* 14 Baker Hill Rd Great Neck NY 11023

MOHN, CHERI (ANN)
PAINTER, INSTRUCTOR

b Akron, Ohio, Aug 12, 36. *Study:* Akron Art Inst, Ohio; Youngstown State Univ, BA. *Work:* Phoenix Gallery, Philadelphia; Johnny Artcher's Ghost Town Gallery, Mogollon, NMex. *Exhib:* Peter Hurd Water Color Show, Artesia, NMex, 68; Butler Inst Am Art Midyear Show, Youngstowns & Guest Artist at Studio 09, Cleveland, 70; John Young Invitational, Youngstown, 72-81; one-woman show, Village Art Gallery, 76; Trumbull Art Guild Art Show, 79-81. *Pos:* Ed, Niles Times, 58; auth & illusr, articles in Pigment & Form, 67-68; asst ed, writer & illusr, Paintin' Place News Inc, 72; illusr, Village Life Inc, 72; dir, Village Art Gallery, Village Market Place, Columbiana, Ohio, 76-77. *Teaching:* Dir & instr fine arts, Cheri Mohn Sch Arts, Youngstown, 63-67; instr fine arts, Cheri Mohn Studio, 68-81. *Awards:* Mademoiselle Mag Top Twenty Women Artists in USA, 60; Gallerie des Champignons Purchase Award, 68; Butler Inst Am Art Purchase Prize, 70; and others. *Bibliog:* Rakocy (auth), Artist of the month, Pigment & Form, 67. *Mem:* Copley Soc Boston; Soc NAm Artists; Friends Am Art; and others. *Mailing Add:* 12691 South Ave North Lima OH 44452

MOHR, PAULINE CATHERINE
CONSERVATOR, RESTORER

b Sheboygan, Wis, May 7, 48. *Study:* Northwestern Univ, BA; Cooperstown Grad Prog, State Univ NY, MA(cert art conserv), with Sheldon & Caroline Keck. *Pos:* Conservator, San Francisco Mus Mod Art, Calif, 76-; conservator, Western Regional Paper Conserv Lab, Calif Palace Legion Honor, San Francisco, 76- *Mem:* Int Inst Conserv Hist & Artistic Works; Am Inst Conserv Hist & Artistic Works. *Mailing Add:* San Francisco Mus Mod Art San Francisco CA 94102

MOIR, ALFRED
HISTORIAN, ADMINISTRATOR

b Minneapolis, Minn, Apr 14, 24. *Study:* Harvard Univ, AB, 48, AM, 49, PhD, 53; Univ Rome, 50-51. *Pos:* Art historian in residence, Am Acad Rome, 69-70 & 80; dir, Univ Calif Educ Abroad Prog, Italy, 78-80. *Teaching:* From instr to assoc prof hist art, Newcomb Col, Tulane Univ, 52-62; from assoc prof to prof, Univ Calif, Santa Barbara, 62-, chmn dept art, 63-69. *Mem:* Col Art Asn Am; Soc Archit Historians; Renaissance Soc; Medieval Acad Am; Southern Calif Art Historians. *Res:* Italian baroque art, particularly Caravaggio and his followers; drawings. *Publ:* Ed, European Drawings in the Collection of the Santa Barbara Museum of Art, 76; auth, Caravaggio and His Copyists, 76; ed, Regional Styles of Drawing in Italy 1600-1700, 77; auth, Caravaggio, 82; ed, Old Master Drawings from the Feitelson Collection, 83. *Mailing Add:* Dept of Art Hist Univ of Calif Santa Barbara CA 93106

MOISE, WILLIAM SIDNEY
PAINTER

b Carlinville, Ill, Feb 22, 22. *Study:* Univ South, BA, 43; Cooper Union Art Sch, CFA, 49; Teachers Col, Columbia Univ, MA, 52. *Work:* US State Dept; Univ of South; Mas d'Aigrat, Les Baux de Provence, France; Mus Art, Columbia, SC; Univ Maine, Orono. *Exhib:* Jordan Marsh Juried Regional, Boston, Mass, 67; Kennebec Valley Art Asn, Hollowell, Maine, 74; Maine 75, Bowdoin Mus Art, Brunswick, Maine, 75. *Teaching:* Instr art, Downtown Community Sch, New York, 50-52 & Mt Desert Pub Schs, Maine, 52-54; head dept art, Grovton High Sch, Fairfax Co, Va, 55-57; head dept art, Northern Conserv Music, Bangor, Maine, 60-69. *Media:* Oil. *Publ:* The taste of color, a touch of love, 72. *Mailing Add:* Hancock ME 04640

MOLDROSKI, AL R
PAINTER, EDUCATOR

b Terre Haute, Ind, Aug 27, 28. *Study:* Ind State Univ, BSc; Mich State Univ, MA; Southern Ill Univ, grant. *Exhib:* Pa Acad Fine Arts; Detroit Mus Art; City Art Mus, St Louis; De Waters Art Ctr; Boston Festival Arts; and many others. *Teaching:* Lectr art, Southern Ill Univ, formerly; asst prof, Glenville State Col, formerly; from instr to assoc prof art, Eastern Ill Univ, 63-; exchange prof, Portsmouth Polytechnic Fine Arts, Portsmouth, Eng. *Awards:* Tiffany Found Grant; Purchase Award, Pa Acad Fine Art; Mary Richart Mem Award in Painting & Art Directors Award, Detroit Mus Art; and many others. *Mailing Add:* Dept of Art Eastern Ill Univ Charleston IL 61920

MOLELLA, PATRICIA ANN
VIDEO & PERFORMANCE ARTIST
b Akron, Ohio, Mar 6, 40. *Study:* Ohio Wesleyan Univ, BA, 62; Syracuse Univ, New York, 62-65; Corcoran Sch Art, Washington, DC, with Gene Davis, Sam Gilliam & Rockne Krebs, 4 Yr Dipl, 73. *Work:* Mus Temporary Art, Washington, DC. *Exhib:* Women are Many Faces, Everson Mus, Syracuse, NY, 74; Women Who are Artists First, Anderson Gallery, Univ Richmond, Va, 78; Bologna Art Fair, Italy, 78; Int Centrum Cultural, Antwerp, Belgium, 78; A Different Light: Ten Yrs of Washington Photog, Washington Projector Arts, Washington, DC, 80; Photographers x Photographers, Washington Proj Arts, 81; 23rd Area Exhib: Video, Corcoran Gallery Art, 82. *Pos:* Adv comt performance art, Washington Project Arts, Washington, DC, 82-; adv comt video art, Fondo del Sol Gallery and Osiris Media Ctr, 82; video arts ed, Televisions Mag, 76-78; column, Artists Spaces, Art Ink Mag, 79-81. *Teaching:* Vis artist video art, Corcoran Sch Art, 74-76, Smithsonian Inst, 75; artist in residence, Visual Studies Workshop, Rochester, 83. *Awards:* Sculpture Award, Student Exhib, Corcoran Sch Art, 72; Outstanding Student, Corcoran Sch Art, 73; Washington, DC Commission Arts & Humanities Grant, 82. *Bibliog:* J Garrett Glover (auth), There's a price for everything, Live Mag, 80; Jane Addams Allen (auth), In search of video aesthetics, Washington Times, 9/22/82; Jim Cassell (auth), Corcoran features video exhibition, New Art Examiner, 11/82; and others. *Media:* Video. *Res:* History of video & performance art. *Publ:* Auth, Joan Jonas in Philadelphia, 76, The Sao Paulo Bienal and US video art, 76 & Video artists present themselves, 76, Televisions Mag. *Dealer:* Visualizations Gallery 130 West 72nd St New York NY. *Mailing Add:* 1357 F St NE Washington DC 20002

MOLINARI, GUIDO
PAINTER, SCULPTOR
b Montreal, PQ, Oct 12, 33. *Study:* Ecole Beaux-Arts, Montreal; Sch Art & Design, Montreal Mus Fine Arts. *Work:* Kunstmuseum, Basel, Switz; Mus Mod Art, Guggenheim Mus & Chase Manhattan Bank, New York; Nat Gallery Art, Ottawa, Ont. *Comn:* Murals, comn by Dept of Pub Works, Ottawa for Vancouver Int Airport, BC, 68 & Dept Nat Defence Hq Bldg, Ottawa, 72. *Exhib:* 4th Guggenheim Int Exhib, New York, 64; The Responsive Eye, Mus Mod Art, 65; Canada: Art Aujourdui, Rome, Paris, Lausanne, Bruxelles, 68; Venice 34th Biennial, Italy, 68; Can 101, Edinburgh, Scotland, 68; Retrospective Exhib, Nat Gallery, Ottawa, Montreal, Toronto & Vancouver, 76; 15th Anniversary Paris Biennial, Mus Mod Art, Paris & Seibu Art Mus, Tokyo, Japan, 77-78; Contemp Can Painters Exhib, Dept External Affairs World Tour, 77-78. *Pos:* Founder & pres, L'Actuelle, 55-57. *Teaching:* Head painting sect, Sir George Williams Univ, 70- *Awards:* Robertson Award, Montreal Mus Fine Arts, 65; Guggenheim Mem Found fel, 66; Bright Found Award Painting, 68. *Bibliog:* Gros Plan (film), Radio-Can, Montreal, 71. *Mem:* Academician Royal Can Acad Arts; Soc Esthetique Experimentale, Paris; Soc Color Res, Nat Coun Res (dir, 72). *Publ:* Coauth, Debats sur la Peinture Quebecoise, Univ Montreal, 71. *Mailing Add:* 1611 Visitation Montreal PQ H2L 3C2 Canada

MOLLER, HANS
PAINTER
b Wuppertal, WGer, Mar 20, 05; US citizen. *Study:* Kunstgewerbeschule Wuppertal-Barmen, 19-27; Acad Fine Arts, Berlin, 27-28. *Work:* Mus Mod Art & Whitney Mus Am Art, New York; Detroit Inst Art, Mich; Joseph Hirshhorn Mus, Washington, DC; Minneapolis Mus; and many others. *Comn:* Stained glass window, Am Fedn Arts, 53; tapestry, comn by Mr & Mrs Lawrence Buttenwieser, New York, 66; seven stained glass windows, comn by Mr & Mrs Neil Carothers, III, Washington, DC, 69. *Exhib:* Contemp Am Painting, Univ Ill, Urbana, 49-59; Third Art Int, Japan, 55; solo exhibs, Allentown Art Mus, Pa & Norfolk Mus, Va, 69; Contemp Painting, Sculpture & Graphics, 69. *Teaching:* Instr painting, Cooper Union Sch Art, 44-56. *Awards:* Andrew Carnegie Prize, Nat Acad New York, 74; A Hibbard Mem Award, 75; Purchase Prizes (three), Childe Hassam Fund-Acad Arts & Lett, NY. *Bibliog:* Abram Kampf (auth), Contemporary synagogue art, Union Am Hebrew Congregation, 66; Edward Betts (auth), Creative Landscape Painting, 78. *Mem:* Nat Acad Design. *Media:* Oil, Watercolor. *Dealer:* Midtown Galleries 11 E 57th St New York NY 10022. *Mailing Add:* 2207 Allen St Allentown PA 18104

MOLLETT, MICHAEL M
ASSEMBLAGE ARTIST, WRITER
b Pasadena, Calif, Jan 28, 46. *Study:* Calif State Plytech Univ, Pomona, BS, 67; Univ NC, Chapel Hill, 69-70; Mt San Antonio Col, Walnut, Calif, 70-72; Santa Monica City Col, 83-84. *Work:* Los Angeles Co Mus Art & Los Angeles Inst Contemp Art; Mus Mod Art, New York; Cavellini Mus, Brescia, Italy. *Comn:* Paintings, Los Angeles Pub Art Dept, 76-77; sculpture, Community Gardens Proj, Los Angeles, 77; wall graffito, Northampton Mus Mod Art, Amherst, Mass, 79. *Exhib:* Word Show, Los Angeles, Calif, 80; Not Hip, Uncool & Not Stupid, The 64 VW Bus, Zero Zero Gallery, Hollywood, 81; and others. *Collections Arranged:* Test the Post Office, Int Mail Art Exhib, 79; Dadafest, Los Angeles, 80. *Pos:* Co-founder, Los Angeles Dada, 78-; Westside agent, Int Corresp Newtwork, 78-; coordr, Dadafest, Los Angeles, 80; dir, ZTZU Art Sapce, Los Angeles, 83. *Teaching:* Lectr/workshop, Univ Calif, Irvine, 81. *Awards:* Outstanding Mail Artist, Trustees, Los Angeles Community Cols, 79; Peter Ivers Award, New Wave Theatre, 81; Rogue Award, High Performance, 83. *Bibliog:* Lon Spiegelman (auth), California Dada, 80; Judith Hoffberg (auth), Artists march in the Doo Dah Parade, Umbrella, 1/80; Ray Zone (auth), The Zone show (interview & performance), 83. *Mem:* Int Iconoclasts (archivist, 77-80); Junk Club Los Angeles; Dog Men, Los Angeles. *Media:* Collage, Xerography. *Publ:* Coauth, Smokey Bear Matchbooks, Diamond Press, 74; auth, Do You Have a Question(s) to Run

Around Town for a Week? privately publ, 76; auth, Isn't it about time you did something with all those questions? Orworks, 79; coauth (with Neal Taylor), The Disappearing God, ZTZU Publs, 81; auth, Semiotics #1, Zoinoid Illustories, Ray Zone Publs, 83. *Dealer:* Artworks 170 S La Brea Los Angeles CA 90036. *Mailing Add:* 2624 W Seventh St Los Angeles CA 90057

MOMADAY, AL
PAINTER
b Mountain View, Okla, July 2, 13. *Work:* Philbrook Art Ctr, Tulsa, Okla; Dallas Fine Arts Mus, Tex; Mus NMex, Santa Fe; Heard Mus, Phoenix, Ariz; Denver Art Mus, Colo. *Comn:* St Luke's Mission, 56 & Curtiss-Wright, 60, Albuquerque, NMex; Franklin Mint, Franklin Ctr, Pa, 75. *Exhib:* Mus NMex, Santa Fe, 60; Philbrook Art Ctr, Tulsa, Okla, 63; Smithsonian Inst, Washington, DC, 65; one-man show, Heard Mus, Phoenix, Ariz, 73. *Awards:* Outstanding Indian Artist, Western NY Art Asn, 65; Grand Award, Gallup Indian Ceremonials, NMex, 67; Waite Phillips Trophy, Philbrook Art Ctr, Tulsa, 75. *Bibliog:* Joanne Snodgrass (auth), American Indian Painting, Heye Found, NY, 68; N Scott Momaday (auth), The Way to Rainy Mountain, Univ NMex Press, 69. *Mem:* Artists Equity; NMex Artists Asn. *Media:* Mixed. *Publ:* Illusr, Rainbows in the Sky, Willoye & Brown, 62; illusr, The Way to Rainy Mountain, Univ NMex Press, 62. *Mailing Add:* c/o Lovena Ohl Gallery 7373 Scottsdale Mall Scottsdale AZ 85261

MOMENT, JOAN
PAINTER, EDUCATOR
b Sellersville, Pa, Aug 22, 38. *Study:* Univ Conn, BS, 60; Univ Colo, with Roland Reiss & William Wiley, MFA, 70. *Work:* E B Crocker Art Mus, Sacramento, Calif; Blue Cross of Southern Calif, Los Angeles; NY State Develop Corp, New York; Oakland Mus, Calif; Allen Mem Art Mus, Oberlin Col, Ohio, and others. *Exhib:* Contemp Am Art Biennial, Whitney Mus Am Art, New York, 73; one-person show, Whitney Mus Am Art, 74, Crocker Art Mus, Sacramento, Calif, 81 & Quay Gallery, San Francisco, Calif, 82; Touching All Things, Walnut Creek Civic Arts Gallery, Calif, 77; Crocker Kingsley, Crocker Art Mus, 78; Drawings by Painters, Long Beach Mus Art, Calif, 82; Sacramento State: The Early Seventies, Joseph Chowning Gallery, San Francisco, Calif, 82; and many others. *Teaching:* Assoc prof art, Calif State Univ, Sacramento, 70-; guest lectr, Wash State Univ & Univ Calif, Davis, 74; vis artist, Univ Colo, Boulder, 75, Ill State Mus, Bloomington, 77, Claremont Col, Calif, 80 & Long Beach State Univ, 80; vis lectr, Univ Mont, Missoula, 77 & Diablo Valley Col, Pleasant Hill, Calif, 78. *Bibliog:* Victoria Dalkey (auth), Moment in transition, Art Week, 11/79; Beverly Terwomen (auth), Two artists and the potent hit, Art Week, 4/80; Charles Shere (auth), Four exhibits by women artists, Oakland Tribune, 4/80; and many others. *Media:* Acrylic on Watercolor Board and Canvas; Painted Clothing; Gouache on Vellum. *Dealer:* Quay Gallery 254 Sutter St San Francisco CA 94108. *Mailing Add:* 1617 26th St Sacramento CA 95816

MOMIYAMA, NANAE
PAINTER, EDUCATOR
b Tokyo, Japan. *Study:* Bunka Gakuin Col, Tokyo; Tokyo Women's Col; Art Students League. *Work:* Nat Mus Mod Arts, Tokyo; Metrop Mus Arts, Tokyo; City Mus Kyoto, Japan; Munic Mus Osaka, Japan; Newberger Mus, Purchase, NY. *Exhib:* Mod Arts Asn Japan, 51-81; Grand Prix Humanitaire de France, 75; one-man shows, Seibu Gallery Tokyo, 74, 77, 79, 82 & 84, Ligoa Duncan Gallery, New York, 75 & Galeries Raymond Duncan, Paris, 75 & 76; plus many others. *Pos:* Permanent juror, Mod Art Asn, Japan, Nat Asn Women Artists, 68-77 & Salone Int di Pittura, Rome, 72. *Teaching:* Instr painting, Westchester Art Workshop, White Plains, NY, 71-; instr, State Univ NY Col, Purchase, 73-; lectr, Philadelphia Mus, Brooklyn Mus, Pittsfield Mus, Columbia Univ, Pratt Inst & numerous other institutions in US & Japan. *Awards:* Madaille d'Argent, Grand Prix Humanitaire de France, 75; Charles Woodbury Mem Prize, Nat Asn Women Artist Ann, Nat Acad, New York, 78; Gold Medal, Accademia Italia delle Arti, 79. *Bibliog:* Takachiyo Uemura (auth), Mizue, Bijitsu Shuppan-Sha, 54 & 74; Kaoru Yamaguchi (auth), Geijitsu Shincho, Shincho-Sha. *Mem:* Mod Arts Asn Japan; Japanese Artists Asn NY (pres, 78-79); Asn Int Artists Plastiques; Japanese Artist Asn; Nat Asn Women Artists; Contemp Artist Guild. *Media:* Oil, Mixed Media. *Publ:* Auth, Sumi-e, An Introduction to Ink Painting, 67; illusr, Makura-no-Soshi of Sei Shonagon, 67; illusr, Rev Paris, 68; illusr, As I Cross Bridge of Dreams, 71. *Mailing Add:* PO Box 44 Glenville Sta Greenwich CT 06830

MONAGHAN, KATHLEEN MARY
HISTORIAN, CURATOR
b Waterville, Maine, Sept 6, 36. *Study:* Univ Calif, Santa Barbara, BA, 78, Ma(Humanities Res Grant), 81. *Collections Arranged:* Faces & Figures: European Drawings, Santa Barbara Mus Art, 81; American Modernism 1910-1945, Santa Barbara Mus Art, 81; The Gloria & Donald B Marron Colllection of Am Prints, Santa Barbara Mus Art, 81; Rufino Tamayo-The Pre-Columbian Heritage, Santa Barbara Mus Art, 82. *Pos:* Curatorial asst, Whitney Mus Am Art, 78-79; asst cur collections, Santa Barbara Mus Art, Calif, 80-81; cur exhibs, 81- *Awards:* Rubinstein Fel, Whitney Mus Am Art, 78. *Mem:* Am Asn Mus; Western Asn Art Mus; Southern Calif Art Historians Asn. *Res:* 19th-20th century American art; 18th century British art; Joseph Wright of Derby. *Publ:* Ed, A Winter's Tale: Snow Scenes in Art, 81, contribr, The Gloria & Donald B Marron Collection of American Prints, 81 & contribr, The Preston Morton Collection of American Art, 81, Santa Barbara Mus. *Mailing Add:* 1130 State St Santa Barbara CA 93101

MONAGHAN, KEITH
PAINTER, EDUCATOR
b San Rafael, Calif, May 15, 21. *Study:* Univ Calif, Berkeley, BA & MA. *Work:* Wash State Univ; and many corp & pvt collections. *Exhib:* San Francisco Mus, 46-48, 50 & 53; 29th Ann Butler Inst Am Art, Youngstown, Ohio, 64; one-man shows, Wenatchee Art Ctr, Wash, 67, Wash State Univ, 68 & Univ Idaho, 69; Gov Invitational, 79 & 81; Woodside Gallery, Seattle, Wash, 79; and others. *Teaching:* Lectr art, Univ Calif, Berkeley, 46-47; prof art, Wash State Univ, 47- *Awards:* San Francisco Art Asn Award, 48; Seattle Art Mus Award, Northwest Watercolor Soc, 51; and others. *Mailing Add:* NE 1705 Lower Dr Pullman WA 99163

MONAGHAN, WILLIAM SCOTT
PAINTER, SCULPTOR
b Philadelphia, Pa, Nov 1, 44. *Study:* Yale Univ, BA; Harvard Grad Sch Design, MA. *Work:* Addison Gallery Am Art, Andover, Mass; Brockton Fuller Mem Art Mus, Mass; Fed Reserve Bank, Boston; Hyatt Hotel, Boston; Aldrich Mus Contemp Art, Ridgefield, Conn. *Comn:* Sculpture, Boston 200 Bicentennial Art Collection, 76. *Exhib:* Sculptors' Workshop Show, Addison Gallery Am Art, 74 & Berkshire Mus, Pittsfield, Mass, 75; one-man show, Inst Contemp Art, Boston, 75; Contemp Reflections, Aldrich Mus Contemp Art, 76; Davidson Art Mus, Wesleyan Univ, Conn, 77; two-man show, Soho Ctr for Visual Artists, New York, 77. *Mem:* Boston Visual Artists' Union. *Mailing Add:* 161 Perry St New York NY 10014

MONDALE, JOAN ADAMS
CRAFTSPERSON
b Eugene, Ore, Aug 8, 30. *Study:* Macalester Col, St Paul, Minn, BA, 52; hon degrees from Barnard Col, 77, Macalester Col, 77, RI Sch Design, 78, Pomona Col, 79, Beloit Col, 81, Col New Rochelle, 81, San Francisco Inst Arts, 82, Corcoran Sch Art, 83 & Savannah Col Art & Design, 83. *Work:* Boston Mus Fine Arts; Minneapolis Inst Arts; Nat Gallery Art, Washington, DC. *Mem:* Am Coun of the Arts (bd dir, 73-75); Inst Mus Serv (bd, 77-); Fed Coun on Arts & Humanities (hon chairperson, 78-81); Kennedy Ctr (bd mem, currently); Am Crafts Coun (bd mem, currently). *Interests:* Ways the goverment can help the arts; use of contemporary American art and craft items in federal buildings and offices. *Publ:* Auth, Politics in Art, Lerner, 72. *Mailing Add:* 3421 Lowell St NW Washington DC 20016

MONES, ARTHUR
PHOTOGRAPHER
b New York, NY, Aug 26, 19. *Study:* NY Inst Photog, 39. *Work:* Metrop Mus Art, New York; Brooklyn Mus; Mus Art, Carnegie Inst, Pittsburgh; New Orleans Mus Art; Grey Gallery, NY Univ, New York. *Exhib:* Photographs, Zenith Gallery, Pittsburgh, 81; one-person shows, Artists in Photographs, Mus Art, Carnegie Inst, 81, Sicily-Legacy of a Civilization, Brooklyn Mus, 82, From NY Studios, Pace Univ, New York, 82 & Photographs, City Univ New York Grad Ctr, 82-83. *Bibliog:* Fred McDarrah (auth), Voice Choices, Village Voice, 5/7/79; Palmer Poroner (auth), Artists in photographs, Artspeak, 11/26/81; Natalie Canavor (auth), Books, Popular Photog, 3/82. *Publ:* Artists in Photographs by Arthur Mones, Horizon Press, 81. *Dealer:* Ledel Gallery 168 Mercer St New York NY 10012. *Mailing Add:* 178 Prince St New York NY 10012

MONGAN, AGNES
ADMINISTRATOR, HISTORIAN
b Somerville, Mass. *Study:* Bryn Mawr Col, AB; Smith Col, AM, Hon LHD, 41; Wheaton Col, Hon LittD, 54; Univ Mass, Hon DFA, 70; LaSalle Col, Hon DFA, 73; Colby Col, Hon DFA, 73; Univ Notre Dame, Hon DFA, 80 . *Pos:* Res asst, Fogg Art Mus, Harvard Univ, 28-37, cur drawings, 37-75, assoc dir, 64-69, dir, 69-71; vis dir, Timken Art Gallery, San Diego, Calif, 71-72; mem adv comt, I Tatti; mem, Coun of Fel of Pierpont Morgan Libr; vis dir, Metrop Mus & Art Ctr, Coral Gables, Fla, 79-80. *Teaching:* Lectr fine arts, Harvard Univ; vis prof, Univ Tex, Austin, 81; vis lectr fine arts, Mt Holyoke Col, 66-67; vis lectr fine arts, Oberlin Col, 67-; vis prof, Northwestern Univ, spring 76, Univ Louisville, Ky, fall 76, Univ Tex, Austin, spring 77 & Univ Calif, Santa Barbara, 79; Kress prof in residence, Nat Gallery Art, Washington, DC, 77-78. *Awards:* Palms d'Acad, Fr Govt, 47; Cavaliere, Order of Merit, Repub Italy, 71. *Mem:* Col Art Asn Am; Asn Art Mus Dirs; hon fel Morgan Libr; Benjamin Franklin fel Royal Soc Arts. *Res:* Relation to drawings by the Masters, especially Tiepolo, Fragonard, Watteau, Ingres, Daumier and Degas. *Publ:* Co-auth, Drawings in the Fogg Museum, 41; co-auth, Ingres Drawings, 67; co-auth, Tiepolo Drawings, 70; auth articles in Burlington Mag, Art Quart, Art News, Gazette Beaux-Arts, Master Drawings & others. *Mailing Add:* Fogg Art Mus Harvard Univ Cambridge MA 02138

MONGERSON, SUSAN C
DEALER
b Indianapolis, Ind, Jan 30, 42. *Study:* Colby Col. *Pos:* Dir, Mongerson Gallery, currently. *Mem:* Chicago Art Dealers Asn. *Specialty:* Nineteenth and 20th century American art, such as: Frederic Remington, C M Russell, Nicolai Fechin, Leon Gaspard, Taos Founders and the American impressionists; illustrators, N C Wyeth and Howard Pyle; sporting art; sculpture. *Mailing Add:* Mongerson Gallery 620 N Michigan Ave Chicago IL 60611

MONK, ROBERT EVAN, JR
DEALER, CURATOR
b New York, NY, Aug 20, 50. *Study:* Pratt Inst, Brooklyn, NY. *Collections Arranged:* Dimitry Merinoff, Paintings: 1950-1970, Clocktower, New York, 80. *Pos:* Cur, Merinoff Estate, Merinoff Studio, New York, 74-; dir graphics,

Castelli Graphics, New York, 77- *Specialty:* Exhibitions of the graphic works of Robert Rauschenberg, Jasper Johns, Andy Warhol, Roy Lichtenstein, Ellsworth Kelly, Frank Stella, Edward Ruscha and Kenneth Noland. *Mailing Add:* 70 W 95th New York NY 10021

MONNIER, JACQUELINE MATISSE
CONCEPTUAL ARTIST
b Nevilly-sur-Seive, France, July 12, 31; US citizen. *Exhib:* Kites: A Summer Celebration, Inst Contemp Art, London, Eng, 76; Festival d' Automne, Paris, France, 76; Artistes--Artisms, Mus des Arts Decratifs, Paris, France, 77; Flags, Banners & Kites, Allied Arts Found, Seattle, Wash, 77; Drachen, Rhein Landesmuseum, Bonn, Germany, 77. *Bibliog:* Newman (auth), Kite Craft, Crown Publ Inc, 74; Jean-Michel Folon, Aquiloni, Alice Editions, Switzerland, 76; Suzi Gablik (auth), Cosmic kites, Art in Am, 11/80. *Dealer:* Betty Parsons Gallery 24 West 57th St New York NY 10019. *Mailing Add:* 1 Rue R Lefebvre Villiers-sovs-Grez France

MONONGYE, PRESTON LEE
SILVERSMITH, PRINTMAKER
b Los Angeles, Calif, Sept 6, 27. *Study:* With Gene Pooyouma, 35-55; with Fred Kabotie, 40-43. *Work:* Mus of Northern Ariz, Flagstaff; Heard Mus, Phoenix, Ariz; Smithsonian Inst, Washington, DC; Walter Bimpson Collection, Valley Nat Bank, Valley Ctr, Phoenix, Ariz; Fred Harvey Collection, Chicago. *Comn:* Altar set, St Luke's Hosp, Phoenix, Ariz, 72; woodcarvings, Cottonwood Branch, Valley Nat Bank, Ariz, 74. *Exhib:* Inter-Tribal Ceremonials, Gallup, NMex, 50-81; Scottsdale Nat Indian Art Show, Ariz, 68-74; Tanners Invitational, Scottsdale, Ariz, 70-77; one-man show, Heard Mus, Phoenix, 74; Indian Art Show, Heard Mus, 75; Navajo Turquoise Gallery, Paris, France, 81. *Teaching:* Instr silversmithing, Phoenix Indian Ctr, Ariz, 75. *Awards:* Best of Show, NMex State Fair, 68-71; Inter-Tribal Ceremonials, 70-72 & Scottsdale Nat, 71; Three Awards, Santa Monica Indian Ceremonials, 78; First & Second Prize, Lithographs, Inter-Tribal Ceremonials, 81. *Bibliog:* M Bedinger (auth), Indian Silver, Univ NMex Press, 73; Carl Rosnek & Joseph Stacy (co-auth), Skystone & Silver: The Collector's Book of Southwest Indian Jewelry, Prentice Hall, 76. *Mem:* Indian Artists Am. *Media:* Silver, Gold; Acrylic, Lithographs. *Publ:* Auth, The new Indian art jewelry of the Southwest, 6/72 & After fifty-one miracles, 7/72, Ariz Hwys Mag; contribr, Southwest Indian Paintings: A Changing Art, Univ Ariz Press, 73; contribr, Carl Rosnek & Joseph Stacy, co-auth, Skystone and Silver: The Collector's Book of Southwest Indian Jewelry, Prentice Hall, 76. *Dealer:* Christopher's Enterprises Inc PO Box 25621 Albuquerque NM 87125. *Mailing Add:* c/o Christopher Cates Enterprises Inc PO Box 25621 Albuquerque NM 87125

MONROE, BETTY IVERSON
EDUCATOR
b Ames, Iowa, May 3, 22. *Study:* Iowa State Univ, BS, 44, MS, 50; Univ Mich, MA, 64, PhD, 73. *Collections Arranged:* Chinese Ceramics in Chicago Collections, 82-83. *Teaching:* Asst prof art hist, Wash Univ, St Louis, 66-67; asst prof, Northwestern Univ, 68-74, chmn dept, 74-78, assoc prof, 74- *Mem:* Col Art Asn; Midwest Art Hist Soc; Am Comt S Asian Art. *Res:* Asian art history; Japanese painting. *Publ:* Ed & translr, Japanese Painting in the Literati Style, Weatherhill, New York & Heibonsha, Tokyo, 74; auth, Chinese Ceramics in Chicago Collections, Northwestern Univ Press, 82. *Mailing Add:* Art Hist Dept Kresge Hall Northwestern Univ Evanston IL 60201

MONROE, GERALD
PAINTER, EDUCATOR
b New York, NY, Aug 17, 26. *Study:* Art Students League; Cooper Union; NY Univ, EdD. *Work:* NY Univ Collection; NJ State Mus; Newark Mus, NJ; and others. *Exhib:* William Paterson Col, 73; NJ State Mus, 75; Wagner Col, 76; Newark Mus, NJ, 78; Parish Art Mus, 81; and others. *Pos:* Assoc prof art, Glassboro State Col, 68- *Awards:* Nat Endowment for Humanities Fel, 73-74, Grant, 75; Ossabaw Island Proj, 77; Va Ctr Creative Arts, 78; and others. *Media:* Oil. *Res:* Influence of left-wing politics on art and artists during Great Depression; strategies for drawing instruction. *Publ:* Auth articles in Art J, Arch Am Art J, Studio Int & Art in Am; illusr, Am Artist. *Mailing Add:* 463 West St New York NY 10014

MONTAGUE, JAMES L
PAINTER, PRINTMAKER
b New Rochelle, NY, May 6, 06. *Study:* Dartmouth Col, AB, 28; Art Students League, with Kimon Nicolaides; also with Leger, Ozenfant & Galanis, Paris. *Work:* US Mil Acad; Southern Vt Artists Permanent Collection; Dartmouth Col. *Comn:* Private portraits. *Exhib:* Various group shows & one-man exhibitions throughout New England states and New York. *Pos:* Dir, Sharon Art Ctr, NH, 61-63; dir, Southern Vt Art Ctr, 64-75. *Awards:* Fitchburg Mus Award, 62; Print Club Albany Award, 70; Award, Norwich Univ, 71. *Mem:* Art Students League; Nat Arts Club; Salmagundi Club, New York; Print Club Albany; Northern Vt Artists. *Media:* Oil, Graphics. *Mailing Add:* PO Box 926 Manchester Center VT 05255

MONTAGUE, RUTH DUBARRY See   Criquette

MONTANO, LINDA (MARY)
CONCEPTUAL ARTIST, VIDEO ARTIST
b Saugerties, NY, Jan 18, 42. *Study:* Villa Schifanoia, Florence, MA(sculpture), 66; Univ Wis, Madison, MFA(sculpture), 69. *Exhib:* How to Become a Guru, Womens Bldg, Los Angeles, 75; Learning to Talk, Univ Calif, San Diego, 76; Talking About Sex: For My Father, Kitchen, New York, 80;

Mitchell's Death, Mus Mod Art, New York, 81; Palm Reading, Real Art Ways, Hartford, Conn, 82; Readings: Visual Collaborations, Chicago Art Inst, 83. *Teaching:* Instr performance, San Francisco State Univ, 78-79, San Francisco Art Inst, 79-80, Womens Bldg, 81 & Chicago Art Inst, 83. *Awards:* Nat Endowment Arts Grant, 77; Womens Studio Workshop Grants, 82 & 83. *Bibliog:* Moira Roth (auth), Towards a history of college performance, Arts Mag, 12/78; Marcia Tucker (auth), Not just for laughs, New Mus, 11/81; Tony Whitfield (auth), Dressing up, acting out, Live Mag, 82. *Publ:* Contribr, High Performance, 77- & auth, Art in Everyday Life, 80, Astro Artz; co-ed, Fuse Mag, Franklin Furnace, 82; auth, Before and after art-life counseling, Womens Studio Workshop, 83. *Mailing Add:* 111 Hudson St New York NY 10013

MONTGOMERY, CLAUDE
PAINTER, ETCHER
b Portland, Maine, Jan 25, 12. *Study:* Portland Sch Fine Art, Maine, with Alexander Bower; Nat Acad New York, with Leon Kroll, Arthur Covey & Gifford Beal; Pratt Inst. *Comn:* Portraits of Sen Edmund Muskie & Gov Kenneth Curtis, State Maine, Augusta; portrait of Maj Gen Fritz Borum, Hall Fame, Oklahoma City; portrait of President J F Kennedy, Harvard Club, Boston; portraits of Mr & Mrs J A Chapman for Children's Med Ctr & Chapman Found, Tulsa, Okla, 75; portrait of Charles Shipman Payson, Portland Art Mus; and others. *Exhib:* Nat Acad, New York, 37-48; Paris Expos, France, 37; New York World's Fair, 64; Am Watercolor Soc, New York, 65-75; Mex Watercolor Soc, Mexico City, 70-74. *Awards:* Suydam Silver Medal, Nat Acad, 35; Silver Medal, Repub France, 37; Grand Prize, Mus Conserv Art, Oklahoma City, 64. *Bibliog:* Carmen Lopez (auth), Montgomery, his work in Spain, Diario Majorca, Spain, 67; Jenken Lloyd Jones (auth), People and portraits, Tulsa Tribune, Okla, 70; Isabel Currier (auth), Montgomery: His art, Down East Mag, 72. *Mem:* Am Watercolor Soc; Salmagundi Club; Royal Soc Art; Mex Watercolor Group; Southwestern Art Asn. *Media:* Watercolor, Oil. *Publ:* Majorca Sketchbook, Spain, 57. *Mailing Add:* Box 225 Georgetown ME 04548

MONTGOMERY, E J (EVANGELINE JULIET)
CURATOR, MEDALIST
b New York, NY, May 2, 33. *Study:* Calif State Univ, Los Angeles, 58-62; Calif Col Arts & Crafts, BFA, 69; Univ Calif, Berkeley, 69-71. *Work:* Los Angeles Bd Educ; Oakland Mus, Calif; Mus Nat Ctr for Afro-Am Artists, Inc, Boston; Univ Southern Ill, Normal; Rainbow Sign Gallery, Berkeley, Calif. *Exhib:* Seven Black Artists, Univ Southern Ill, Normal, 72; one-man show, Bowie State Col, Md, 73; Ten Metal Craftsmen, Berkeley Art Ctr, Calif, 74; African Am Crafts, Brook Mem Gallery, Memphis, Tenn, 79; plus many others. *Collections Arranged:* Sargent Johnson Retrospective (auth, catalog), Oakland Mus, 71; Elizabeth Catlett (auth, catalog), Rainbow Sign Gallery, Berkeley, Calif, 72; Black Graphics (auth, catalog), Western Asn Art Mus, 73-75; and others. *Pos:* Ethnic art consult, Oakland Mus, Calif, 68-74; art consult, Rainbow Sign Gallery, Berkeley, Calif, 71-77. *Awards:* Merit Award, San Francisco Art Festival, San Francisco Art Comn, 68. *Bibliog:* S Lewis & R Waddy (auth), Black Artists on Art, Vol 1, Contemp Crafts, Inc, 69; Samella Lewis (auth), Art African American, Harcourt, 78. *Mem:* Nat Conf Artists; An Asn Mus; Am Crafts Coun; Metal Arts Guild Calif. *Media:* Fiber, Metal. *Dealer:* The Gallery 3271 W Pico Blvd Los Angeles CA 90019. *Mailing Add:* 259 W Radcliffe Dr Claremont CA 91711

MONTHAN, GUY
PHOTOGRAPHER, EDUCATOR
b Tucson, Ariz, Apr 17, 25. *Study:* Syracuse Univ, BFA, 50; Calif State Univ, Los Angeles, MA, 67. *Exhib:* Los Angeles Co Mus Ann, 61; San Gabriel Valley Ann, Pasadena Art Mus, 61; Tucson Festival Art Show, 62 & 65; Southwestern Photog Exhibit, Dallas Mus Fine Arts, 73; Yuma Invitational, Ariz, 73-78. *Pos:* Advert design, Los Angeles, 50-68. *Teaching:* Asst prof advert design, Northern Ariz Univ, Flagstaff, 68- *Awards:* For Art and Indian Individualists, Rounce & Coffin Book Award, 76, Border Regional Libr Asn Southwest Book Award, 76 & Bookbuilders W Award, 76. *Publ:* Designer-illusr, Art and Indian Individualists, 75; designer-illusr, Nacimientos: Nativity Scenes by Southwest Indian Artisans, Northland Press, Flagstaff, 79. *Mailing Add:* PO Box 1698 Flagstaff AZ 86002

MONTLACK, EDITH
PAINTER
b New York, NY. *Study:* Metrop Mus Art Sch, with Michael Jacobs, scholar; Nat Acad Design, with Louis Bouche; Art Students League. *Exhib:* Nat Acad; Parrish Mus; Riverside Mus; Grand Central Art Gallery; Knickerbocker Artists; and many others. *Teaching:* Instruction in own studio. *Awards:* Emil Kohn Medal; St Gaudens Medal; First Prize Watercolors, Nat Asn Women Art. *Mem:* Life fel Royal Soc Art, London; Nat Asn Women Artists. *Media:* Oil. *Mailing Add:* 90 Taymil Rd New Rochelle NY 10804

MONTMINY, (ELIZABETH) TRACY
MURALIST, PAINTER
b Boston, Mass. *Study:* Radcliffe Col, Cambridge, Mass, BA, 33; Art Students League, New York, with Rico Lebrun, 34-35. *Comn:* Mural, Post Office, Sect Fine Arts Treasury Dept, Kennebunkport, Maine, 41; murals, Salinas y Rochas y Cia, Raymond Loewy Assocs, Mexico, 45; four staircase murals, Biology Bldg, 78-80 & mural, Engineering Bldg, 81, Univ Mo, Columbia; mural, Humanities Dept, Stephens Col, Columbia, Mo, 82. *Exhib:* Third Biennial, Worcester Art Mus, Mass, 37; Corcoran Gallery, Washington, DC, 39; Twelfth Ann, Joslyn Art Mus, Omaha, Nebr, 72; Am Painters in Paris, Ctr Int Paris, 75-76; Cross Country '81: Artists Who Draw, Lorretto-Hilton Gallery, St Louis, 81; Bridges, Elder Gallery, Lincoln, Nebr, 81; and others.

Teaching: Prof art, Univ Mo, Columbia, 48-, prof emer, currently; vis prof drawing, painting & art hist, Am Univ of Beirut, Lebanon, 63-64. *Awards:* Guggenheim Mem Found Fel Painting, 40; Honorable Mention for mural design, Soc Security Bldg, DC, Sect Fine Arts, Treasury Dept, 40. *Bibliog:* Charles Movalli (auth), Tracy Montminy Myth and Form, Am Artist, 3/76; K A Marling (auth), Wall-to-wall America, Minneapolis Mag, 82. *Mem:* Nat Soc Mural Painters; Artists' Equity. *Media:* Acrylic, Oil; Conte Crayon, Pastel. *Mailing Add:* 1506 Paris Rd Columbia MO 65201

MONTOYA, GUSTAVO (GUSTAVO MONTOYA CARRANCO)
PAINTER, COLLAGE ARTIST
b Mexico City, Mex, July 9, 05. *Study:* Nat Sch Fine Arts Mexico City, MA, 22. *Work:* Mus Mod Art, Mus Fine Arts Secy Treasure, Mexico City. *Comn:* Portrait Judge J Douglas, US Supreme Court, Washington, DC, 39; 12 portraits secretaries treasure, Secy Treasure, Mexico City, 50. *Exhib:* Exhibition of Masters, Nat Acad Fine Arts, Mexico City, 59; Second Panamerican Biennial, 60 & Mexican Portrait, 61, Palace Fine Arts, Mexico City; Masters of Drawing, Nat Acad Fine Arts, Mexico City, 61; retrospective, Mus Mod Art, Mexico City, 82. *Teaching:* Prof coloring, Nat Sch Fine Arts, 36-38, prof painting, 53-69. *Awards:* Second Prize, Mexico City and Its Painters, Palace Fine Arts, 49. *Media:* Oil, Collage. *Dealer:* Leonardo Martinez Lanz Cda de Bezares #50 Lomas de Beazres Mexico City Mex 11910. *Mailing Add:* 157 Lopez St Dept 41 Mexico 1 DF 06050 Mexico

MOODY, ELIZABETH CHAMBERS
DEALER, GALLERY DIRECTOR
b Memphis, Tenn, Nov 20, 44. *Study:* Univ Ky, Lexington, BFA, 66. *Pos:* Gallery attendant, Univ Ky Art Gallery, 65-66; sales consult, DuBose Gallery, Houston, 69-72; asst mgr & vpres, 72-73; mgr & vpres, Ars Longa Gallery, Houston, 73-75; dir & owner, Moody Gallery, Houston, 75- *Teaching:* Instr, Mus Fine Arts, 76- *Mem:* Art Dealers Asn of Houston; Mus Fine Arts Sch Bd. *Specialty:* Contemporary art, paintings, prints and sculpture; Houston representative. *Mailing Add:* 2015-J West Gray Houston TX 77019

MOON, JIM (JAMES MONROE)
PAINTER, PRINTMAKER
b Graham, NC, June 7, 28. *Study:* Cooper Union, 45-48; Acad Vannucci, Italy, cert, 55; Richmond Prof Inst William & Mary, BFA, 57. *Work:* Mus Mod Art, New York; NC Mus Art, Raleigh; Peggy Guggenheim Mus, Venice, Italy; Winston-Salem Pub Libr, NC; Northwood Inst, Midland, Mich. *Teaching:* Instr fine arts, Hofstra Univ, New York, 60-61; head dept visual arts, Barber Scotia Col, NC, 65-66 & NC Sch Arts, Winston-Salem, 67-71. *Bibliog:* Jenny Sharpe (auth), Jim Moon's art, Student, 79; Norman E Pendergraft (auth), Jim Moon, Art Voices, 81. *Media:* Egg Tempera, Oil; Serigraph. *Dealer:* Calvert Collection 2301 Calvert St NW Washington DC 20008; Alber 2004 Pine St Philadelphia PA 19103. *Mailing Add:* RT 3 Box 410-A Lexington NC 27292

MOON, MARC
PAINTER, INSTRUCTOR
b Middletown, Ohio, Apr 6, 23. *Study:* Appl Art Acad. *Work:* Canton Art Inst; Masillon Mus, Ohio; Richmond Mus, Va; Springfield Mus, Mo; Taylor Mem Libr, Cuyahoga Falls, Ohio. *Comn:* Mural, Canton Hall of Fame, Canton Hist Soc, Ohio, 70; mural, Lawson Milk Co, 75; McDonalds Resteraunts, Akron, Ohio, 79. *Exhib:* Am Watercolor Soc, New York, 66-70; Nat Acad Design, 74; Watercolor USA, Springfield Mus, 74; Butler Art Inst, Youngstown, Ohio, 75; Nat Soc Painters Casein & Watercolor, New York, 81. *Teaching:* Instr watercolor, Hilton Leech Art Sch, Sarasota, Fla, 68-76; Marc Moon Gallery, Cuyahoga Falls, Ohio, 82-84, Fort Meyer Branch Art Asn, 84. *Awards:* Mario Cooper Award, Am Watercolor Soc; Best in Show, Va Beach Art Asn; Purchase Award, Watercolor USA. *Bibliog:* R Fabri (auth), Medal of Merit, Todays Art, 66. *Mem:* Am Watercolor Soc; Ohio Watercolor Soc; Nat Soc Painters Casein & Acrylic; Rockport Art Asn. *Media:* Watercolor, Acrylic. *Publ:* Auth, Watercolor page, Am Artist Mag, 74. *Mailing Add:* 198 W Portage Trail Ext Cuyahoga Falls OH 44223

MOONIE, LIANA (MARIA)
PAINTER, INSTRUCTOR
b Trieste, Italy. *Study:* Istituto Magistrale G Carducci, Univ Trieste, BA(educ), 45; Art Student League, with Robert Brachman, 69; New York Univ, cert(interior decorating), 70. *Work:* State Assembly, Albany, NY; Greenburgh Libr, NY. *Exhib:* Nat Allied Artists Am, Nat Acad Galleries, New York, 77; Nat Acad Design, Nat Acad Galleries, New York, 78; Ann New England, Silvermine Artists Guild, New Canaan, Conn, 79; Hudson River Contemp Artists, Hudson River Mus, Yonkers, NY, 79; Nat Asn Women Artists Ann, Federal Bldg, New York, 79-82; Nat Audubon Artists, Nat Arts Clubs, 80. *Teaching:* Private instruction, 79-81. *Awards:* Mary Canaday Mem, Nat Asn Women Artists, Canaday, 80; Marlow Ferris Mem, Mamaroneck Artists Guild, Ferris, 81; First Oil, First Watercolor, First Mixed Media & Best in Show, Scarsdale Art Asn, 81. *Mem:* Mamaroneck Artists Guild (pres, 76-78); Hudson River Contemp Artists (vpres, 81-83); Nat Asn Women Artists (historian, 82-84); Salmagundi Club; Silvermine Artists Guild. *Media:* Watercolor, Oil. *Publ:* Contribr, Beaux Arts Mag, Westchester Fedn Women's Clubs, 74-76; contribr, Philosophizing about art, Beaux Arts Mag, Westchester Fedn Women's Clubs, 75. *Dealer:* Somerstown Studios and Gallery Route 100 Somers NY 10589; Pelham Art Center Gallery 153 Fifth Ave Pelham NY 10803. *Mailing Add:* 40 Taunton Rd Scarsdale NY 10583

MOORE, BARBARA
HISTORIAN, WRITER

b New York, NY, Sept 30, 36. *Study:* RI Sch Design, BFA. *Collections Arranged:* Collectors of the Seventies, Part III, The Sohm Archive, 75 & Alternative Gestures: Another Look at Dance Photography, 78-79, Inst Art & Urban Resources; The Page as Alternative Space 1950-1969, Franklin Furnace, New York, 81. *Pos:* Admin dir, Archives Experimental Art, New York, 62-; ed in chief, Something Else Press, New York, 65-66; co-owner, Backworks, New York, 76-83; owner, ReFlux Editions, 83- *Mem:* Am Soc Picture Prof (secy, 75-77). *Res:* Experimental art from the early 1960's to the present, particularly performance art by artists and publications by artists. *Publ:* Auth, George Maciunas: A finger in fluxus, Artforum, 10/82; articles & reviews in SoHo Weekly News, Art & Artists, Express & other publications. *Mailing Add:* 351 W 30th St New York NY 10001

MOORE, BEVERIDGE
PAINTER

b Richmond, Va, July 25, 15. *Study:* Univ Va, BA; Art Students League, with Yasuo Kuniyoshi, Morris Kantor & William Zorach. *Work:* Va Commonwealth Univ, Richmond; Fordham Univ, New York; Rutgers Univ, New Brunswick, NJ; Evansville Mus Arts & Sci; Phoenix Art Mus, Ariz; and others. *Exhib:* Nat Acad Design, New York, 48; Va Mus Fine Arts, Richmond, 53, 55 & 57; Art Alliance, Philadelphia, Pa, 65; Butler Inst Am Art, Youngstown, Ohio, 67; Artist of the Mo Exhibs, Solebury Nat Bank, New Hope, 72, 73, 75, 76, 78 & 80; five one-man shows at Bodley Gallery, New York, 62-73; Phillips Mill Exhib, New Hope, Pa. *Media:* Oil. *Dealer:* Bodley Gallery 1063 Madison Ave New York NY 10028. *Mailing Add:* Star Rte New Hope PA 18938

MOORE, ETHEL
CURATOR, HISTORIAN

b Chicago, Ill. *Study:* Vanderbilt Univ, BA; Va Commonwealth Univ; Art Students League; State Univ Iowa. *Pos:* Ed publ, Albright-Knox Art Gallery, Buffalo, NY, 64-70, ed publ & admin officer, 70-73; cur, Ga Mus Art, Univ Ga, 74-82, ed, Bull; guest cur, Atlanta Arts Festival, 82 & 84. *Awards:* Yaddo Fel, 63; Ossabaw Found Project Mem, 82; Va Ctr Creative Arts Fel, 82. *Mem:* Am Asn Mus (mem cur comt & ed cur newslett); Southeastern Mus Conf; Ga Asn Mus & Galleries (vpres, 78, pres, 79); Lyndon House Art Ctr. *Publ:* Auth, Clyfford Still: Thirty-Three Paintings in the Albright-Knox Art Gallery, 66; ed, Contemporary Art, 1942-72: Collection of the Albright-Knox Art Gallery, Praeger, 73; ed, Wallpapers of Charles Burchfield, Burchfield Center, 73; ed, Albert Christ-Janer, Ga Mus, 76; articles in Arts Mag, Mus News, Ga Mus Art Bull & others. *Mailing Add:* 140 University Dr Univ Ga Athens GA 30605

MOORE, FAY
PAINTER, ADMINISTRATOR

b Cambridge, Mass. *Study:* Henry Hensche Sch, Provincetown; Boston Mus Sch; Phillips Gallery Sch, Washington, DC; Bennington Col, Vt, with Stephan Hirsch & Paul Feeley; Yale Grad Sch with Donald Oenslager. *Work:* NY Racing Asn & Nat Hockey League, New York; Detroit Race Course, Mich; Univ Va, Charlottesville. *Comn:* Portraits, Univ Va, Charlottesville, 67; portraits, Hockey Hall Fame, Can, 70; portraits, New York Giants, 71 & seven murals, Kelso Rm, NY Racing Asn, 78, New York; murals, Rockwell Rm, Three Rivers Stadium, Pittsburgh, 76. *Exhib:* Saratoga Mus Racing, NY, 65; solo exhibs, Pittsburgh Plan Art, Pa, 69 & Nat Arts Mus Sport, New York, 70; Mus Contemp, Madrid, Spain, 72; Housing & Urban Develop Comn Arts Prog, Washington, DC, 75; and others. *Teaching:* Instr, Univ Kansas City, Mo, 55-57; instr, Carnegie-Mellon Univ, Pittsburgh, 57-59; instr, Yale Univ Grad Sch, New Haven, Conn, 59-60. *Awards:* Gold Medal, Nat Arts Club Ann, 75; Hawthorne Award, Nat Arts Club, 77; Purchase Award, Metrop Print Publ, 79. *Bibliog:* K Hollingsworth (auth), Equine art of Fay Moore, Blood Horse Mag, 68; Humphreys (auth), Racing art of America, South Bend, 69; A Painter Goes to the Races (film), R Algis Prod, 70. *Mem:* Nat Soc Mural Painters (bd mem, currently); Nat Arts Club (gov, currently); Artists Fel (trustee, currently); Nat Art Mus Sport (vpres, currently); Fine Arts Fedn NY (deleg, currently); and others. *Media:* Oil, Acrylic. *Dealer:* The Racing Scene 29 E 61st New York NY; James Hunt Barker Galleries Worth Ave Palm Beach FL. *Mailing Add:* Nat Arts Club 15 Gramercy Park New York NY 10003

MOORE, INA MAY
INSTRUCTOR, PAINTER

b Hayden, Ariz, Feb 20, 20. *Study:* Univ Ariz, BA(educ, art & music); Ariz State Univ, MA(art educ). *Work:* First Interstate Bank, Valley Nat Bank, Ariz Bank & Thunderbird Bank, Phoenix; First Fed Savings & Loan Asn, Yuma. *Exhib:* Phoenix Art Mus; Invitational Exhib, Univ SDak, 68; Nat League Am Pen Women, Salt Lake City, Utah, 71; Nat Watercolor Exhib, Ctr Performing Arts, Scottsdale, Ariz, 77; Southwest Watercolor Fedn Exhib, San Diego, 83; Kerr Ctr, Scottsdale, Ariz, 83. *Teaching:* Part-time instr art, Elem Pub Schs, 40-50; pvt classes, 50-64; instr watercolor, Phoenix Art Mus, 65-; Phoenix Col, 78- *Awards:* Merit Award, Southwest Watercolor Biennial, 76; Purchase Award, Empire Machinery Co, 77; Purchase Award, Thunderbird Bank, 79. *Mem:* Ariz Watercolor Asn (pres, 66-68); Nat League Am Pen Women; Ariz Artist's Guild. *Media:* Watercolor. *Mailing Add:* 5718 N Tenth Ave Phoenix AZ 85013

MOORE, JOHN J
PAINTER, EDUCATOR

b St Louis, Mo, Apr 25, 41. *Study:* Washington Univ, Nat Found Arts & Humanities grant, BFA, 66; Yale Univ, Milliken foreign travel fel & MFA, 68. *Work:* Philadelphia Mus Art; Pa Acad Fine Arts, Philadelphia; Yale Univ Art Gallery, New Haven; Neuberger Mus, Purchase, NY; Metrop Mus Art, New York. *Comn:* Lincoln Ctr, New York, 80; Fabric Workshop, Philadelphia, 81. *Exhib:* Fischbach Gallery, New York, 69, 73, 75, 78 & 80; Figure in Recent American Painting, Pa Coun Arts Traveling Exhib, 74-75; Real, Really, Super Real, San Antonio Mus Art, Tex, 81; Contemporary American Realism Since 1960, Pa Acad Fine Arts, 82; Hirschland Adler Mus, New York, 83; Realism-Photorealism, Philbrook Art Ctr, Tulsa. *Teaching:* Prof painting & drawing, Tyler Sch Art, Temple Univ, 68-; artist in residence, Yale Summer Sch, 68 & 69; fac, Skowhegan Sch Painting & Sculpture, summers, 74, 80 & 84; vis prof painting, Univ Calif, Berkeley, 81-82. *Awards:* Nat Found Arts and Humanities, 66; Hassam Award, Am Acad Arts & Lett, 73; Vis Artist Fel Painting, Nat Endowment Arts, 82. *Bibliog:* John Yau (auth), Introduction to exhib catalog, Hirschland Adler Galleries, 83; Carol Zemes (auth), Still Life and City View, Buscaglia-Castellani Art Gallery, 83. *Media:* Oil, Watercolor. *Dealer:* Hirschland Adler Mus 851 Madison Ave New York NY 10021. *Mailing Add:* 111 Woodland Rd Wyncote PA 19095

MOORE, MARJORIE
PAINTER, ASSEMBLAGE ARTIST

b Akron, Ohio, Mar 17, 44. *Study:* Syracuse Univ, BFA, 66. *Work:* Portland Mus Art, Maine; Butler Inst Am Art; Joan Whitney Payson Gallery, Westbrook Col; Filenes Inc, Boston. *Comn:* Cowstructure, Artpark, Lewiston, NY, 80; Walker Art Museum Reinterpreted, Bowdoin Col, 81; Random Snapshots, One Percent For Art, Portland, Maine, 83. *Exhib:* Butler Art Inst Mid-Year Show, 68; Paper and Clay, Memphis State Univ Gallery, 80; Haystack: Art in Craft Media, Rose Art Mus, Bowdoin Col, Williams Col & RI Sch Design, 81; Selected Women Artists, Philadelphia Mus Art, 82; New Architecture, Maine Traditions, Joan Whitney Payson Gallery, Westbrook Col, 83; Sticks, Addison Gallery Am Art, 83; Elements of Landscape, Boston Univ Art Gallery, 83. *Mailing Add:* 37 School St Brunswick ME 04011

MOORE, MICHAEL SHANNON
PAINTER, PRINTMAKER

b Los Angeles, Calif, Mar 30, 42. *Study:* Stanford Univ, BA(art), 64; Yale Univ, 64-65; also with Diebenkorn, Boyle & Tworkov. *Work:* Stanford Univ Mus Art; Arco World Hq, Los Angeles, Calif. *Comn:* 1956 Ford School Bus, Anonymous Artists Am, 69; interior mural, Foto Graphix, San Francisco, 71. *Exhib:* Krannert Biennial, Univ Ill, 69; Folio '73, Calif Col Arts & Crafts World Print Competition, San Francisco Mus Art, 73; ten-year retrospective, Stanford Univ Mus Art, 74; one-man shows, Smith Andersen Gallery, Palo Alto, 73, 74, 76 & 77 & San Francisco, 76, William Sawyer Gallery, San Francisco, 75 & 79, Linda Farris Gallery, Seattle, Wash, 75 & 76. *Pos:* Publisher & asst printmaker, Cactus Patch Press, 71-77. *Awards:* Art Purchase Award, Stanford Univ, 63; Mem Bequest Excellence, Desert Art Colony, 65-66. *Bibliog:* A Frankenstein (auth), Michael Moore acrylic show, 3/30/74 & A master looks at the desert, 1/16/75, San Francisco Chronicle; Hellmon (auth), article, Artweek, 8/25/79. *Media:* Ink on Paper, Watery Acrylic on Canvas; Low Fire Clay. *Publ:* Illusr, Media of Various Herbals, Grossett & Dunlap, 72 & 78; auth & illusr, Trying talking with Art Banditz, Vol 1, No 1, Other bodies of water, Vol 2, No 1 & Five autobiographies, Vol 3, No 1, Place; plus others. *Dealer:* Smith/Andersen Gallery 200 Homer St Palo Alto CA 94305; Michael F Fagan PO Box 1154 Boulder CO 80306. *Mailing Add:* c/o Smith/Andersen Gallery 200 Homer St Palo Alto CA 94305

MOORE, OLGA
PAINTER

b Chicago, Ill. *Study:* Roosevelt Univ, BA, 64; Art Inst Chicago, MFA, 69; Univ Wis, MA, 74. *Work:* Kemper Group Insurance, Chicago; US Trust Co, New York; Am Steel Foundries, Ind; Rachael Bok Seymour Collection, Philadelphia; Sony Corp Int, NJ. *Exhib:* Philadelphia Drawings, Philadelphia Mus Art, 79; solo exhibs, Jan Cicero Gallery, Chicago, 81, Newark Mus, NJ, 82, NJ State Mus, Trenton, 82 & Douglass Col, New Brunswick, NJ, 83; Eccentric Constructivists, Jan Cicero Gallery, Chicago, 82. *Teaching:* Assoc prof painting & drawing, Rutgers Univ, 78- *Awards:* Ford Found Fel, 79; NJ State Coun Fel, 82. *Bibliog:* David Shirey (auth), article, New York Times, 7/11/82; Judy Stein (auth), article, Re-dact, 1/84. *Media:* Gouache, Watercolor. *Dealer:* Jan Cicero Gallery 437 Clark St Chicago IL 60610; Condesco-Lawler 76 Greene New York NY 10012. *Mailing Add:* 292 Lafayette St New York NY 10012

MOORE, PETER
PHOTOGRAPHER, ARCHIVIST

b London, Eng, Apr 28, 32; US citizen. *Study:* Mass Inst Technol; Haverford Col. *Work:* Int Mus Photog, George Eastman House, Rochester, NY; Archiv Sohm, Ger & Archive Jean Brown, Tyringham, Mass; Dance Collection, New York Pub Libr & Mus Perform Arts, NY; Mus Contemp Art, Chicago; and others. *Exhib:* Alternative Gestures, Another View of Dance Photography, PS 1 Galleries, New York; Tangelmann Gallery, Cincinnati; Four Dance Photographers, Bruce Mus, Stamford, Conn; The Judson Project, Bennington Col Mus; Gray Art Gallery; and many others. *Pos:* Artistic dir, Archives Experimental Art, New York, 62-; sr ed, Modern Photog Mag. *Teaching:* Instr photog, New Sch, New York, 70-74; instr photog, pvt classes, New York, 70-74. *Awards:* Cash Grant, Finch Col Mus Art, 74. *Bibliog:* Ronald Argelander (auth), Photo-Documentation, An Interview with Peter Moore, Drama Rev, NY Univ, Sch of Arts, 9/74. *Mem:* Am Soc Mag Photogs; and others. *Res:* Experimental performance art, particularly that created by artists usually associated with the visual arts. *Publ:* Contribr, Modern Photog, Photomethods & Leica Photog. *Mailing Add:* 351 W 30th St New York NY 10001

MOORE, ROBERT ERIC
PAINTER

b Manchester, NH, Oct 13, 27. *Study:* Univ NH; New Eng Sch Art, Boston. *Work:* Farnsworth Mus, Rockland, Maine; Mus Fine Arts, Springfield, Mass; Headley Mus, Lexington, Ky; Colby Col Art Mus; Butler Mus Fine Arts. *Exhib:* Am Watercolor Soc Ann, New York; Guild of Boston Artists, Mass, 77 & 79; New Eng in Winter Invitational, De Cordova Mus, Lincoln, Mass, 77; Seasons Gallery, Tehran, 78; Maine Artists, US Embassy, Ottawa, Can, 79; Exchange Prog, Brazil, 79. *Awards:* Arches Paper Award, Nat Watercolor Soc, Calif, 77; Mustard Seed Award, Rocky Mountain Nat Watermedia Exhib, Golden, Colo, 77; Kowalsky Award, Adirondacks Nat Exhib Am Watercolors, 83. *Bibliog:* Ralph Fabri (auth), History of American Watercolor Society the first 100 years, Am Watercolor Soc; Field Art Collection, Chicago, Ill, reproduced in World Bk Encycl, under Maine, 66; Ed Betts (ed), Work reproduced in Creative Landscape Painting, Watson-Guptill Publ, 78. *Mem:* Am Watercolor Soc; Nat Watercolor Soc; Guild Boston Artists; Allied Artists Am; Ky Watercolor Soc. *Media:* Watercolor, Acrylic. *Publ:* Auth, Creative Seascape Painting by Edward Betts, Watson & Guptill Press, 81. *Mailing Add:* Cider Hill York ME 03909

MOORE, ROBERT JAMES
PAINTER, PHOTOGRAPHER

b San Jose, Calif, July 24, 22. *Study:* USAAF Photo Sch, Lowry Field, Colo, grad; San Jose State Col, BA; NY Inst Fine Arts, with Salmony, Schoenberger, Panofsky & Offner; Columbia Univ Teachers Col, MFA; Art Students League, with Brackman, Miller & Will Barnet. *Exhib:* Pa Acad Fine Arts, Philadelphia, 50; James D Phelan Awards Competition, San Francisco Art Mus, 51; 11 Yr Retrospective of Prizewinners, Village Art Ctr, Whitney Mus Am Art, New York, 54; NY City Ctr Gallery, 59; Audubon Artists, Nat Acad Design, New York, 62; one-man shows, Ruth Sherman Galleries, New York, 64 & Adele Bednarz Galleries, Los Angeles, 65; Berkshire Mus, Pittsfield, Mass, 66; Art Students League & Ford Found Show, New York, 75; and others. *Teaching:* Assoc prof art, Goddard Col, 54-57; instr art & photog, Battin High Sch, Elizabeth, NJ, 59-64; instr art, Julia Richman High Sch, New York, 64-79. *Awards:* Second Prize, Village Art Ctr 7th Ann Graphic Art Show, Village Art Ctr, New York, 52; Blue Ribbon, New Talent Show, Ruth Sherman Gallery, New York, 64; Berkshire Mus Award, 66. *Mem:* Artists Equity Asn of New York; life mem Art Students League. *Media:* Oil, Graphics. *Mailing Add:* 246 E 51st St New York NY 10022

MOORE, RUSSELL JAMES
MUSEUM DIRECTOR, ADMINISTRATOR

b Stockton, Calif, Jan 13, 47. *Study:* Univ Calif, Davis, BA, 69, Los Angeles, MA, 72; Harvard Univ Inst in Arts Admin, 77. *Collections Arranged:* Winslow Homer's Work in Black & White (ed, catalog), 74-76; Ernest Haskell (1876-1925) A Retrospective Exhibition (auth, catalog), 76, Nancy Hemenway: Textures of Our Earth (coauth, catalog), 77-78 & Calvert Coggeshall: Paintings, 77, all circulated nationwide, Bowdoin Col. *Pos:* Asst cur, Utah Mus Fine Arts, Salt Lake City, 72-74; acting dir, Bowdoin Col Mus Art, Brunswick, Maine, 74-78; dir, Long Beach Mus Art, Calif, 78-; exec dir, San Jose Mus Art, currently. *Mem:* Am Asn Mus; Col Art Asn; Pejepscot Hist Soc. *Res:* American art history; early 20th century. *Mailing Add:* c/o Long Beach Mus of Art 2300 E Ocean Blvd Los Angeles CA 90803

MOORE, SCOTT MARTIN
PAINTER, INSTRUCTOR

b Los Angeles, Calif, Oct 13, 49. *Study:* Calif State Univ, Long Beach, 67, 72 & 73; USMC, Hawaii, 70-72; John Pike Watercolor Sch, Woodstock, NY, 78. *Work:* Archives, Smithsonian Inst, Washington, DC; Hunt-Wesson Corp, Fullerton, Calif; Rutan & Tucker Law Firm, Costa Mesa, Calif. *Exhib:* Am Watercolor Soc Ann, Nat Acad, New York, 78, 80, 81, 82 & 83; Midwest Watercolor Soc, Rahr-West Mus, Manitowoc, Wis, 79; Watercolor USA, Springfield Mus Art, Mo, 79; Nat Watercolor Soc, Los Angeles, 79-83; Allied Artists, Am Acad Arts & Letters, New York, 80. *Pos:* Illusr, USMC, Hawaii, 70-72; graphic designer, Scott Moore Studio, 73-78. *Teaching:* Instr transparent watercolor workshops, 76-83. *Awards:* Walser S Greathouse Medal, Am Watercolor Soc, 81; Strathmore Paper Award, Nat Watercolor Soc, 81; Walter Bronson Crandell Memorial Award, Nat Watercolor Soc, 83. *Bibliog:* Julia P Chase (auth), Scott Moore: sheer color and light, Orange Co Illustrated, 8/79; Charles Dickens Phillips (auth), Gallery: Scott Moore, Westways Mag, 7/81; Jane Summer (auth), Familiar moments, Showcase Mag. *Mem:* Nat Watercolor Soc; Watercolor West; Am Watercolor Soc. *Media:* Transparent Watercolor. *Mailing Add:* 1435 Regatta Rd Laguna Beach CA 92651

MOOS, WALTER A
DEALER

b Karlsruhe, Ger, Sept 6, 26. *Study:* Ecole Superieure Com, Geneva, Switz, BA; New Sch Social Res, with Paul Zucker & Meyer Shapiro. *Pos:* Dir, Gallery Moos Ltd; vpres, Arts Mag, 77, pres, 82-83. *Mem:* Prof Art Dealers Asn Can (pres, 71-74); Can Eskimo Arts Coun. *Specialty:* Contemporary Canadian, European and American paintings, sculpture and graphics. *Mailing Add:* Gallery Moos Ltd 136 Yorkville Ave Toronto ON M5R 1C2 Canada

MOOSE, PHILIP ANTHONY
PAINTER, ILLUSTRATOR

b Newton, NC, Jan 16, 21. *Study:* Nat Acad Design; Columbia Univ; Skowhegan Sch Painting; Taxco Sch Arts, Mex; Acad Fine Arts, Munich, Ger. *Work:* Atlanta Mus Art, Ga; Norfolk Mus, Va; NC State Mus Art, Raleigh; Colchester Mus, Eng; Mint Mus Art, Charlotte, NC. *Comn:* Mural, Montreat-Anderson Col, NC, 72. *Exhib:* Am Watercolors, Metrop Mus, New York; Corcoran Biennial, Washington, DC; Southeastern Ann, Atlanta, Ga; Fulbright Artists, WGer; Piedmont Ann, Charlotte. *Teaching:* Assoc prof art, Davidson Col, 51-53 & Queens Col, NC, 56-67; assoc prof art, Queens Col, NC, 56-67. *Awards:* Pulitzer Award, 48; Tiffany Found Award, 49; Fulbright Award, 53-63. *Media:* Oil, Acrylic. *Publ:* Illusr, History of Catawba County, 52; illusr, Exploring the Mountains, 72. *Mailing Add:* Linville Rd Blowing Rock NC 28605

MOOSE, TALMADGE BOWERS
PAINTER, ILLUSTRATOR

b Albemarle, NC, June 4, 33. *Study:* Va Commonwealth Univ, BFA. *Work:* Knight Publ Co, Charlotte, NC. *Exhib:* 34th Semi-Ann Southeastern Print & Drawing Show, 71; Ann NC Artists Exhib, 71, 73 & 74; Art on Paper 1972, Weatherspoon Gallery, Greensboro, 72; Davidson Nat Print & Drawing Competition, 73; Retrospective Exhib, Pfeiffer Col, Misenheimer, 78. *Pos:* Pres, Gallery Uwharrie Artists, Ltd, 74-76; dir, Artists/Writers Dialogue, 75. *Teaching:* Instr drawing & painting, Stanly Tech Inst, Albemarle, 72-76; instr, Montgomery Tech Inst, 80-82. *Awards:* First Prize, 34th Semi-Annual Southeastern Print & Drawing Show, 71; Honorable Mention, 9th Ann Piedmont Graphics Exhib, 72; Honorable Mentions, 36th & 37th Ann NC Artists Exhib, 73-74. *Bibliog:* Clyde Burnett (auth), Limited art exhibit, Atlanta J & Constitution, 2/15/70; Elizabeth S Smith (auth), He never left Stanly County, State Mag, 7/73; mem of the issue, NLight Mag, 2-3/78. *Media:* Watercolor, Acrylics; Pencil, Alkyds. *Publ:* Contrib, Charlotte Observer, 69; contrib, Uwharrie Rev, 74; illusr, The State Mag, 77-82; illusr, Sandlapper, 77; illusr, Tar Heel Mag, 77-80; illusr, Exploring the Piedmont of North Carolina, 80. *Mailing Add:* Rte 2 Stony Mountain Albemarle NC 28001

MOOZ, R PETER
MUSEUM DIRECTOR

b New York, NY, Mar 6, 40. *Study:* Wesleyan Univ, BA(with distinction; art hist); Boston Univ, MA; Univ Pa, PhD. *Collections Arranged:* Twentieth Century American Watercolors, 73; Art of American Furniture, 74; The Winslows: Pilgrims, Patrons and Portraits, 74; Painting in the South, 83. *Pos:* Teaching assoc, Winterthur Mus, Wilmington, Del, 67-73, mus coordr, Winterthur Prog, 71-73, dir, Winterthur Summer Inst, 72-73; dir, Am Painting Summer Inst, 73, Bowdoin Col Mus Art, 73-77 & Va Mus Fine Arts, 77-82; pres, Fine Arts Am, 82-; cur, Wilton House Mus, 83. *Teaching:* Asst prof art hist, Univ Del, 67-73; vis lectr, Univ Bath, Eng, 69; vis asst prof, Univ Vt, 71; sr lectr, Bowdoin Col, 73-; vis prof, Univ Va, 81 & Va Commonwealth Univ, 82-83. *Mem:* Am Asn Mus (conmr, 80-82); Col Art Asn; Soc Archit Historians; Soc Preserv New Eng Antiquities (mem adv coun, 75); Nat Trust Hist Preserv. *Res:* American art, especially colonial painting and American furniture; American painter Robert Feke. *Publ:* Auth, New clues to the art of Robert Feke, Antiques, 68; contrib, Country and Simple City Furniture, 69; auth, Smibert's Bermuda group--a re-evaluation, Art Quart, 70; contrib, American Painting to 1776: A Reappraisal, 71; coauth, The Genius of American Painting, 73. *Mailing Add:* Fine Arts Am 404 W Franklin St Richmond VA 23220

MOQUIN, RICHARD ATTILIO
SCULPTOR

b San Francisco, Calif, July 1, 34. *Study:* City Col San Francisco, AA; San Francisco State Col, with Seymour Locks, BA & MA. *Work:* Sacramento State Col; Sacramento State Fair; Oakland Mus; Can Ceramic Int; San Francisco Mus Art. *Exhib:* 24th Ceramic Nat, Everson Mus, Syracuse, NY, 66; 23rd Scripps Col Invitational, Claremont, Calif, 67; Col Marin Invitational, Kentfield, Calif, 69; M H De Young Mus Show, San Francisco, 70; Stanford Univ Sculpture Invitational, 71 & 72; A G Gardner Gallery, 77-78. *Pos:* Vpres, Asn San Francisco Potters, 67-68. *Teaching:* Instr sculpture, City Col San Francisco, 69- *Awards:* Purchase Awards, Sacramento State Fair, 68, San Francisco Art Fair, 69 & M H De Young Mus, 70. *Bibliog:* Albright (auth), Ceramic sculpture, San Francisco Chronicle, 68 & 70; A Meisel (auth), Ceramic sculpture, Craft Horizons, 72; Charlotte Speight (auth), article in Ceramics Text Book. *Media:* Clay, Plastic. *Dealer:* H Gardner Gallery Stinson Beach CA. *Mailing Add:* 3 Herbing Lane Kentfield CA 94904

MORALES, ARMANDO
PAINTER, PRINTMAKER

b Granada, Nicaragua, Jan 15, 27. *Study:* Sch Fine Arts, Managua, Nicaragua; Pratt Graphic Art Ctr, New York. *Work:* Mus Mod Art, Guggenheim Mus, New York; Inst Art, Detroit; Mus Art, Philadelphia; Mus Fine Arts, Houston. *Exhib:* Bienal Mod Art, Sao Paulo, Brazil, 53, 55 & 59; Carnegie Int, Pittsburgh, 58, 64 & 67; Arte Am y Espana, Madrid, Barcelona, Rome & Berlin, 61; Guggenheim Int, New York, 60; The Emergent Decade, Cornell Univ & Guggenheim Mus, 66. *Teaching:* Instr adv painting, Cooper Union, New York, 72 & 73. *Awards:* Ernest Wolf Award, V Bienal, Sao Paulo, Brazil, 59; Award, Arte Am y Espana, Madrid, 63; J L Hudson Award, Carnegie Int, 64. *Bibliog:* Dore Ashton (auth), Visual pleasure from austerity, Studio Int, London, 2/65; Heinz Ohff (auth), Anleitung zum optimismus: Begegnung mit Armando Morales in Berlin, Der Taggespiegel, Berlin, 6/19/65; Esperanza Brault (auth), Armando Morales, El Sol Mex, Mexico City, 10/4/68. *Dealer:* CDS Gallery 13 E 75th St New York NY 10021. *Mailing Add:* 23 Murray Place Princeton NJ 08540

MORATH, INGE (INGE MORATH MILLER)
PHOTOGRAPHER

b Graz, Austria, May 27, 23; US citizen. *Study:* Univ Berlin, BA; asst to Henri Cartier-Bresson. *Work:* Metrop Mus Art, New York; Boston Mus Fine Arts,

Mass; Art Inst Chicago; RI Sch Design; Bibliot Nat, Paris, France; and many others. *Exhib:* Chicago Art Inst, 64; Univ Miami, Coral Gables, Fla, 72; Neikrug Galleries, New York, 77; one-woman show, China, Grand Rapids Art Mus, 79, Mus Mod Art, Vienna, 80; plus many group showings. *Teaching:* Guest instr photog & compos, Cooper Union, New York; and others. *Awards:* Photog Excellence, Stuttgart Bkwks, Bucher Publ, Switz, 11/76. *Bibliog:* Article, Saul Steinberg & Inge Morath, Creative Camera, 2/69; Allen Porter (auth), article, Camera Mag, 11/69; Olga Carlisle (auth), Great Photographers of Our Time--Inge Morath, Bucher, Switz, 75. *Mem:* Magnum Photos; Am Soc Mag Photogr. *Publ:* Illusr, From Persia to Iran, 61 & In Russia, 69, Viking Press; illusr, Boris Pasternak: My Sister Life, Harcourt, Brace, Jovanovich, 76; illusr, In the Country, Viking Press, 77; illusr, Chinese Encounters, Arthur Miller (text), Farrar Straus & Giroux, 79; and others. *Dealer:* Marge Neikrug 224 E 68th St New York NY 10021. *Mailing Add:* Tophet Rd Roxbury CT 06783

MORCOS, MAHER N
SCULPTOR, PAINTER
b Cairo, Egypt, Feb 23, 46; US citizen. *Study:* Cairo Univ, BA(archit), 69; Leonardo de Vinci, Italy, 70. *Comn:* Bust Egyptian President Nasser, Ministry of Educ, Cairo, Egypt, 62; religious paintings, Heliopolis Cathedral, Cairo, Egypt, 64; mural, Valley Nat Bank, Scottsdale, Ariz, 84. *Exhib:* Charles Russell Show, Charles Russell Mus, Great Falls, Mont, 80 & 81; Am Inst Contemp Art, San Dimas, Calif, 80 & 81; Western Artists Am, Coliseum, Reno, Nev, 80 & 81; Western Heritage Show, Arapahoe Co, Littleton, Colo, 80 & 81; George Phippen Show, CofC, Prescott, Ariz, 80 & 81. *Awards:* Gold Medal, Death Valley Show, 80; Best of Show, Western Heritage Show, Arapahoe Co Asn, 81; Best of Show, Western Artists Am, City Reno, 81. *Bibliog:* William E Freckleton (auth), Guided by imagination, Southwest Art, 4/78; Scene, Tulsa Tribune, 78; Dick Spencer (auth), Western heritage, The Western Horseman, 80. *Media:* Bronze; Oil, Watercolor. *Mailing Add:* PO Box 22659 San Diego CA 92122

MOREHOUSE, WILLIAM PAUL
PAINTER, SCULPTOR
b San Francisco, Calif, May 27, 29. *Study:* Studied with Clyfford Still, 47-50; Calif Sch of Fine Art, cert, 50; San Francisco Art Inst, BFA, 54; San Francisco State Col, MA, 56. *Work:* San Francisco Mus Mod Art; Oakland Art Mus, Calif; Univ Art Mus, Berkeley, Calif; San Francisco Art Comn Collection; Whitney Mus. *Exhib:* Younger Am Painters, Solomon R. Guggenheim Mus, New York, 54; Biennial, Whitney Mus of Am Art, New York, 59; San Francisco Mus of Art Ann, 55-60; Ill Biennial, Urbana & Art Inst of Chicago Ann, 61; 72nd Western Painters Ann, Denver Art Mus, 66; Funk, Univ Art Mus, Berkeley & Ctr for Contemp Art, Boston, 67; Interstices, San Jose Art Mus, Calif, 75 & 77 & Cranbrook Mus, Mich, 75; Lincoln Arts Ctr, Calif, 78. *Teaching:* Instr art, San Francisco Art Inst, 58-67; prof art, Sonoma State Univ, 67-83, chmn art dept, 70-73 & 79-81, retired. *Media:* Oil; Fiberglass. *Mailing Add:* PO Box 210 Bodega CA 94922

MORENO, ORDUNA NICOLAS
MURALIST, EDUCATOR
b Mexico, Dec 28, 36. *Study:* Escuela Nac Artes Plasticas, Univ Nac Autonoma Mex, prof, 45. *Work:* Mus Antropologia Mex; Univ Nac Autonoma Mex; Secretaria Relaciones Exten Mex; Escuela Nac Artes Plasticas; Secretaria Educ Publ. *Comn:* Escuela Ezequel A Chavez (mural), Secretaria Educ Publ, 51; three murals, Inst Antropologia, Mex, 64. *Exhib:* Fifty Paisajes de la Sierra Tarahomara, Galeria Mez Kup, Mex, 75; Paisaje y Naturalezz, Palacio Mineria, Mex, 81; Naturalezz y Paisaje, Escuela Nac Artes Plasticas, Univ Mex, 82; Oleas Dibujos y Grabades Univ Mex, Escuela Nat Prep, Univ Nac Autonoma Mex, 82; Obra Sixth Fica, Galeria Teorema, Florence, Italy, 83. *Collections Arranged:* Valle de Mexico, 64; Bandera Mexicana, 65. *Teaching:* Prof art, Escuela Pintura Escultura Esmeralda, 53-64 & Escuela Nac Artes Plasticas, Univ Nac Autonoma de Mex, 72-83. *Awards:* Purchase Awards, Salon Plastica Mex, 55 & Inst Nac Bellas Artes, 66. *Bibliog:* Carlos Pellier (auth), Catalog Bellas Artes, Secretaria Educ Publ, 72; Andres Henestrosa (auth), Catalog Galleria Meridians, 74; Salvador Elizondo (auth), Paisaje y Naturaliezz, Univ Nac Autonoma Mex, 80. *Mem:* Salon Plastica Mex; Movimiento Pictorico Contemp; Soc Mex Artes Plasticas. *Media:* Acrylic, Oil. *Mailing Add:* 5 de Mayo 345 Mexico Xochimilio D F 16020 Mexico

MORGAN, ARTHUR C
SCULPTOR
b Riverton Plantation, La, Aug 3, 04. *Study:* Beaux Arts Inst Design; also with Gutzon Borglum, Mario Korbel and others. *Work:* Centenary Col, Shreve Mem Libr & Civic Theater, Shreveport, La; Civic Ctr & Hist Libr, Thibodaux, La; plus numerous pvt collections. *Comn:* Heroic figure, Chief Justice Edward Douglass White, Edward Douglass White Mem Comn, US Capitol, Washington, DC, 55; Paul Geisler Mem, Comt Friends of Paul Geisler, Stadium Gounds, High Sch, Burwick, La, 65; Henry Miller Shreve Monument, City of Shreveport & Pub Subscription, River Pkwy, Shreveport, 66; A J Hodges Commemorative Bust, Trustees of Hodges Gardens, Hodges Gardens, Many, La, 72; monumental bust, Clyde E Fant, Clyde Fant Parkway, Shreveport, La, 76; and others. *Exhib:* One-man shows, La State Univ, Baton Rouge, 27, La State Exhib Mus, Shreveport, 40 & 50; Philbrook Art Ctr, Tulsa, Okla, 52 & Centennial Mus, Corpus Christi, Tex, 57; Mem Exhib, Nat Arts Club, New York, 60-; Mem Exhib, Dartmouth House Club, London, 77. *Teaching:* Instr drawing, painting, sculpture & art hist & dir dept art, Centenary Col La, 28-34; dir sculpture & drawing, Southwestern Inst Arts, 34-74. *Bibliog:* Patsi Farmer (auth), Biographer in bronze, Shreveport Mag, 12/58; Mary Gray Morris Walker (auth), Portrait of an artist, NLa Hist Asn J, 7/65; Edwin Adams Davis (auth), Louisiana, the pelican state, La State Univ Press. *Mem:* Nat Arts Club; Dartmouth House Club. *Media:* Bronze, Marble. *Mailing Add:* 657 Jordan St Shreveport LA 71101

MORGAN, BARBARA BROOKS
PHOTOGRAPHER
b July 8, 1900. *Study:* Univ Calif, Los Angeles, 19-23; Marquette Univ, Hon DFA, 78. *Work:* Nat Gallery of Can, Ottawa; Marquette Univ; Fotografiska Museet, Stockholm; Univ Calif Los Angeles Libr; Mus Fine Arts, St Petersburg, Fla. *Exhib:* Ohio Univ, Athens, 79; Baldwin Street Gallery, Toronto, 79; George Eastman House/Int Mus Photog, 79-80, traveling US, 80-81; Recollections Exhibit, Int Ctr Photog, 79, touring US, 80-81; one-person exhibs, Vision Gallery, Boston, 80 & Photomontages et Danses, Galerie Zabriskie, Paris, 81; and others. *Teaching:* Instr art, Univ Calif, Los Angeles, 25-30. *Awards:* Fel, Philadelphia Mus Art, 70; Soc Photog Educ Plaque, 79. *Bibliog:* Cecil Beaton & Gail Buckland (auths), The Magic Image, London & Boston, 75; Ruth Spencer (auth), article, Brit J Photog, London, 6/13/75; Petr Tausk, Photography in the 20th Century, Cologne, 77 & London, 80. *Publ:* Auth, photogr & designer, Summer's Children: A Photographic Cycle of Life at Camp, 51; ed, photogr & designer, Barbara Morgan (monogr), 72; photogr, Barbara Morgan Dance Portfolio, Morgan & Morgan, 77; contribr, Recollections: Ten Women of Photography, Viking, 79; photogr, auth & designer, Barbara Morgan: Photomontage, Morgan & Morgan, 80. *Mailing Add:* 120 High Point Rd Scarsdale NY 10583

MORGAN, DARLENE
PAINTER
b Salt Lake City, Utah, Feb 1, 43. *Study:* With Merle Olson. *Work:* Pac Northwest Indian Ctr. *Exhib:* Flathead Int Art Festival & Show, 71; Pac Northwest Indian Ctr Art Auction Ann, 71-78; Charles Russell Exhib & Auction Ann, 72-74 & 77-79; Nat Parks Centennial Exhib, Glacier Park, Mont, 72; Exhib of Drawing, Hockaday, 79. *Awards:* Best in Show, Pac Northwest Indian Art Auction, 72. *Bibliog:* Dave Crowell (auth), Montana's Own, Gateway, 70. *Media:* Ink, Oil. *Mailing Add:* 429 Peaceful Dr Bigfork MT 59911

MORGAN, FRANCES MALLORY
SCULPTOR
b Memphis, Tenn. *Study:* Art Students League; Nat Acad Design; Pa Acad Fine Arts; also with John Hovannes & Alexander Archipenko. *Work:* Brooks Mem Art Gallery, Memphis; IBM Corp. *Comn:* Neely Grant (bronze), Mrs Neely Grant, Memphis, 34; Sen Gilbert Hitchcock, 45 & bronze fountain, 49, Mrs Gilbert Hitchcock, Washington, DC; bronze fountain, Vance Norfleet, Memphis, 52; many portraits of children. *Exhib:* World's Fair, New York, 39-40; Whitney Mus Am Art, New York, 40; Artists for Victory, Metrop Mus, New York, 42; Philadelphia Art Alliance, 46; Pa Acad Fine Arts, 47. *Awards:* Anna Hyatt Huntington Award for Olympia, 41; Prize for Peace Again, 44, Nat Asn Women Artists; Award for Fish, Audubon Artists, 61. *Mem:* Nat Asn Women Artists; Sculptors Guild; Audubon Artists. *Media:* Multimedia. *Mailing Add:* 50 Mendota Ave Rye NY 10580

MORGAN, HELEN BOSART (MRS EDWIN M WAGSTAFF)
SCULPTOR
b Springfield, Ohio, Oct 17, 02. *Study:* Wittenberg Univ, AB; Dayton Art Inst; Art Inst Chicago. *Work:* Snyder Park, Springfield, Ohio; Springfield Art Ctr; Springfield New City Bldg; Cincinnati Mus Art; Butler Inst Am Art. *Comn:* Wittenberg Univ, 73. *Exhib:* Nat Acad Design; Nat Asn Women Artists; Cincinnati Mus Art; Columbus Gallery Fine Art; Butler Inst Am Art, Youngstown, Ohio. *Awards:* Least Imitative in Concept & Execution Award, Columbus Gallery, 63; Sculpture Prize, Ohio Liturgical Arts Guild, 71; First Prize-Sculpture, Springfield Art Asn, 71. *Mem:* Nat Asn Women Artists; Artists Equity Asn; Columbus Art League. *Media:* Bronze, Plastic. *Mailing Add:* 845 E High St Springfield OH 45505

MORGAN, JAMES SHERROD
COLLECTOR
b Birmingham, Ala, Sept 11, 36. *Study:* Univ Ala, BA. *Collection:* Art Nouveau, Art Deco, American Indian, Mission furniture, contemporary painting, sculpture, prints, art pottery and Tiffany. *Mailing Add:* 5332 W 67th St Mission KS 66208

MORGAN, LILIANE See Decock, Liliane

MORGAN, MARITZA LESKOVAR
PAINTER, ILLUSTRATOR
b Zagreb, Yugoslavia, Nov 20, 21; US citizen. *Study:* Cornell Univ, 42; Art Students League, 43. *Work:* Wilson Mus, Dartmouth Col, Hanover, NH; All Souls Unitarian Church, Tulsa, Okla; First Presby Church, Warren, Pa; St Luke's Chapel, Chautauqua, NY; Hurlbut Mem Church, Chautauqua. *Comn:* Murals, Smith-Wilkes Mem Libr, Chautauqua Inst, 70. *Exhib:* Nat Jury Show, Chautauqua, 66; Festival Arts Northwest Pa, 72; Gallery 100, Princeton, NJ, 75; Deson-Zaks Gallery, Chicago, 75; Lighthouse Gallery, Tequesta, Fla, 75. *Pos:* Artist in residence, Chautauqua Inst, 66- *Teaching:* Supvr art, Warren Co, Pa, 51-57; instr pvt classes, Chautauqua, NY, 66- *Mem:* Chautauqua Art Asn (bd mem, currently). *Publ:* Illusr, The Chautauqua Cookbook for the Elegant Eighties; co-translr, Rudolph Tesnohlidek's The Cunning Little Vixen, Viking Press. *Mailing Add:* Box 168 Chautauqua NY 14722

MORGAN, MYRA JEAN
DEALER
b Birmingham, Ala, Jan 26, 38. *Study:* Univ Ala, BA. *Pos:* Dir, Morgan Gallery, Kansas City, Mo, 69- *Specialty:* Fine contemporary art including painting, sculpture, drawings and prints; major representation of established artists, primarily American. *Mailing Add:* Morgan Gallery 1616 Westport Rd Kansas City MO 64111

MORGAN, NORMA GLORIA
PAINTER, ENGRAVER

b New Haven, Conn. *Study:* Art Students League, with Julian Levi; Hans Hofmann Sch Fine Art, New York; Atelier 17, New York, with Stanley W Hayter. *Work:* Nat Gallery Art & Pennell Collection, Libr of Cong, Washington, DC; Mus Mod Art, New York; Victoria & Albert Mus, London; Philadelphia Mus Art; Metrop Mus Art, New York; Art Inst Chicago. *Comn:* Engraving, Woodstock Artists Asn, 83; Moorland Sanctuary (oil mural), Old White Lion Inn, Haworth, Eng, 63; Grand Canyon (acrylic mural), Mary Ellen Petlee Collection, Salisbury, Conn, 80. *Exhib:* New York World's Fair, 65; Soc Am Graphic Artists, 67; Assoc Am Artists; traveling show, Old Bergen Art Guild, Bayonne, NJ, 70-; one-man shows throughout US, 70- & ann exhibs with Audubon Artists, New York; Vixen Tor (engraving), Dartmoor Pres Asn Centenary, England, 83; Dunstanburgh Castle, England (engraving), Nat Women's Print Show, Philadelphia, 83. *Teaching:* Private lessons in drawing. *Awards:* Gold Medal for Graphics, Painters & Sculptors Soc NJ 26th Ann, 67; Blue Ribbon-First Prize for Graphics, Composers, Authors & Artists Conv, 69; Medal of Honor-Gold Medal, Audubon Artists, New York, 76. *Bibliog:* Fritz Eichenberg (auth), The Art of the Print, Abrams Publ, 76. *Mem:* Print Coun Am; Soc Am Graphic Artists (coun mem, 74-75); Audubon Artists, New York; Assoc Am Artists; Woodstock Artists Asn. *Media:* Oil, Watercolor; Copper. *Mailing Add:* 239 W 63rd St New York NY 10023

MORGAN, ROBERT COOLIDGE
PAINTER, CRITIC

b Boston, Mass, July 10, 43. *Study:* Univ Redlands, BA, 64; Northeastern Univ, EdM, 68; Univ Mass, Amherst, MFA, 75; NY Univ, PhD, 78. *Work:* Mus Mod Art, New York; Univ SC, Columbia; Clark Art Inst, Williamstown, Mass; New York Pub Libr; and many pvt collections. *Comn:* Painted Forms on Steel, Mayor's Off Cult Affairs, Boston, 72; Curved Curbs, Mass Coun on Arts, Boston, 74. *Exhib:* Interventions in Landscape, Hayden Gallery, Mass Inst Technol, Cambridge, Mass, 74; Performances: 4 Evenings, 4 Days, Whitney Mus Am Art, New York, 76; one-man show, Artists Space, New York, 77; Artists Bks USA, Independent Cur Inc, DC (traveling exhib), 78-80; Artists & Bks, Ulrich Mus Art, Wichita State Univ, 79; McKissick Mus, Univ SC, 81; Wash Place Artists Gallery, New York, 81; and others. *Teaching:* Instr mod art hist, NY Univ, 76; asst prof art hist, Rochester Inst Technol, NY, 81- *Awards:* Nat Endowment Humanities Fel, 80. *Bibliog:* Walter Robinson (auth), Homespun version of mass media, Art-Rite, No 19, 78; Tom Lawson, article, Artforum, 9/83; David Craven, article, Arts Mag, 9/83. *Mem:* Col Art Asn Am; Nat Art Educ Asn. *Media:* Conceptual Art and Criticism. *Res:* Role of documentation in conceptual art; structural interactions, literal time and progressive sequence, often manifested in swimming. *Publ:* Auth, Learning to Swim (Le Style Francais), 76, rev 77 & The Scissors Kick, 76, rev 77, New Welsh Bks; auth, Conceptual art and the continuing quest for a new social context, J Los Angeles Inst Contemp Art, 6/7/79; auth, The pleasure in photographs/ components of language, Kans Quart, fall 79; auth, Conceptual art and photo installations, Afterimage, 12/81; auth, essay, In: The Unnecessary Image, MIT Press & Tanam Press, 83. *Dealer:* Galleri Bellman 41 E 57th St 5th Fl New York NY 10022. *Mailing Add:* Col Fine & Applied Arts Rochester Inst Technol Rochester NY 14623

MORGAN, SYBIL ANDREWS See Andrews, Sybil

MORGAN, THEODORA
WRITER

b Brooklyn, NY. *Study:* Packer Collegiate Inst, Brooklyn; NY Univ. *Pos:* Bd dir, Nat Arts Club, New York, formerly; pub relations dir, Crayon, Watercolor & Craft Inst, 57-60; managing ed, Nat Sculpture Review, 56-; co-dir, Sculpture Libr Bk Club, Mt Vernon, NY, 79- *Mem:* Nat Sculpture Soc. *Res:* Representational sculpture, American and worldwide. *Mailing Add:* c/o Nat Sculpture Review 15 E 26th St New York NY 10010

MORGAN, WILLIAM
HISTORIAN, WRITER

b Princeton, NJ, June 13, 44. *Study:* Dartmouth Col, AB; Columbia Univ, MA & cert in restoration & preservation hist archit; Univ Del, PhD. *Pos:* Chmn, Ky Hist Preservation Rev Bd, 75-; archit critic, Courier-J, 75-80; bk rev ed, Landscape Archit Mag, 76-78. *Teaching:* Lectr art & archaeol, Princeton Univ, 71-74; asst prof fine arts, Allen R Hite Art Inst, Univ Louisville, 74-76, assoc prof, 76-81, prof, 81- *Awards:* Nat Collection Fine Arts Vis Res Fel, Smithsonian Inst, 71. *Mem:* Soc Archit Historians; Nat Trust Hist Preservation; Nat Trust Gr Brit & Northern Ireland; and others. *Res:* American art and architecture; Gothic revival. *Publ:* Coauth, Bucks County Photographs of early architecture, Horizon, 74; coauth, Old Louisville: The Victorian Era, Courier-J, 75; auth, Louisville--Architecture and the Urban Environment, Bauhan, 79; auth, Portals: Photographs by William Morgan, Bauhan, 81; auth, The Almighty Wall: Architecture of Henry Vaughan, Archit Hist Found, 83. *Mailing Add:* Dept of Fine Arts Univ of Louisville Louisville KY 40208

MORGANSTERN, JAMES
HISTORIAN, EDUCATOR

b Pittsburgh, Pa, Oct 16, 36. *Study:* Williams Col, BA, 58; NY Univ, MA, 64, PhD, 73. *Teaching:* Asst prof hist art, Univ Wis, Milwaukee, 70-73; asst prof, Ohio State Univ, Columbus, 73-80, assoc prof, 80- *Mem:* Col Art Asn; Soc Archit Historians; Archaeol Inst Am; Medieval Acad; Int Ctr Medieval Art. *Res:* Byzantine art, architecture and archaeology; western medieval architecture. *Publ:* Auth, The church at Dereagzi: A preliminary report, Vol 22, 68 & The church at Dereagzi: A preliminary report on the mosaics of the Diaconicon, Vols 23 & 24, 69 & 70, Dumbarton Oaks Papers; auth, The church at Dereagzi: Its date and its place in the history of Byzantine architecture, Actes, XIV Congres Int Etudes Byzantines, 76; coauth, The settlement at Dereagzi: A preliminary report on the 1974 and 1975 seasons, Turk Arkeoloji Dergisi 25, 79; auth, The Byzantine Church at Dereagzi and its Decoration, Ernst Warmuth, 83. *Mailing Add:* Dept Hist Art Ohio State Univ Columbus OH 43210

MORGENLANDER, ELLA KRAMER
PAINTER, INSTRUCTOR

b Bronx, NY, Aug 7, 31. *Study:* Brooklyn Col, 53; Brooklyn Mus Art Sch, with Reuben Tam, 60-70; New York Univ, 62; Barnes Found, Merion, Pa, 74-76; Art Students League, with Will Barnett, 78-79. *Exhib:* Ann Nat Asn Women Artists, Nat Acad Arts Gallery, New York, 71-81; Brooklyn Mus, NY, 76; one-woman show, Nicholas Roerich Mus, New York, 76; Artists Depicting the Humanities, Henry St Settlement, New York, 82. *Teaching:* Instr art, St George's Pre-Sch NY, 62-67; instr, Ethical Culture Sch, Brooklyn, NY, 63-66; instr art, Bank St Sch Childhood Educ, 68-72. *Awards:* Adelle M Schiff Award, 84th Ann Nat Asn Women Artists, 73; Ziuta & Joseph James Akston Found, 88th Ann Nat Asn Women Artists. *Mem:* Artists Equity Asn, NY; Nat Asn Women Artists; Contemp Artists New York. *Media:* Oil, Watercolor. *Dealer:* Brooklyn Mus Community Gallery File 188 Eastern Parkway Brooklyn NY. *Mailing Add:* 210 Park Pl Apt 2C Brooklyn NY 11238

MORIN, JAMES CORCORAN
CARTOONIST, EDITOR

b Washington, DC, Jan 30, 53. *Study:* Syracuse Univ Sch Art, BFA, 75. *Work:* Mus Cartoon Art, Portchester, NY; Emerson Col, Boston, Mass. *Pos:* Ed cartoonist, Beaumont Enterprise & J, 76-77, Richmond Times Dispatch, 77-78 & Miami Herald, 78- *Awards:* Overseas Press Club Award, Foreign Affairs Cartoons, 79 & Hon Mention, 81; and others. *Bibliog:* Dick Comer (auth), A baker's dozen questions for one of America's brightest young cartoonists, Cartoonist Profiles, 9/79; David Finkel (auth), Etching political, Miami Mag, 8/79. *Mem:* Assoc Am Ed Cartoonists. *Media:* Pen, Ink. *Publ:* Contribr, Best Editorial Cartoons of the Year, Pelican, 78 & 79; contribr, America's Political System, Random House, 79. *Mailing Add:* One Herald Plaza Miami FL 33101

MORIN, THOMAS EDWARD
SCULPTOR, EDUCATOR

b Malone, NY; Sept 22, 34. *Study:* Mass Col Art, BS(educ), 56; Cranbrook Acad Art, MFA, 57; Brown Univ, cert(basic metal), 66, cert(plastics technol), 67. *Work:* Richmond Mus Art, Va; Brown Univ, Providence, RI; Barn Gallery Assoc, Ogunquit, Maine; NY Univ, Oneonta. *Comn:* Cast aluminum high relief, Brown Univ, 64; bronze sculpture & bronze screen, Am Tube, 72. *Exhib:* Inst Contemp Art Invitational, Boston, 60; Whitney Mus Am Art Ann, New York, 61; 11 New Eng Sculptors, Wadsworth Atheneum, Hartford, Conn, 63; Contemp Box & Wall Sculpture Invitational, RI Sch Design Mus Art, 65; Univ Conn Mus Art, Storrs, 70. *Teaching:* Head dept sculpture, Silvermine Guild Artists Col Art, 58-60; assoc prof sculpture & head sculpture grad prog, RI Sch Design, 61- *Awards:* First Prize & Best in Show, Silvermine Guild Artists, 60; First Prize, RI Art Festival, 63; First Prize, New Haven Art Festival, 66. *Mem:* Union Independent Cols Art; Am Foundrymens Soc. *Mailing Add:* 62 Waterman St Providence RI 02906

MORISHITA, JOYCE CHIZUKO
HISTORIAN, PAINTER

b Newell, Calif, Aug 22, 44. *Study:* Northwestern Univ, Evanston, Ill, BA(painting), 64, MA(painting), 65, PhD(art hist), 79. *Work:* Michael Reese Hosp & Med Ctr, Chicago, Ill. *Comn:* Oil-vaporous nudes, Michael Reese Hosp & Med Ctr, 72. *Exhib:* One-woman show, OrdMeyer Gallery, Chicago, 69; 31st Ill State Invitational, Ill State Mus, Springfield, 79; Mid-America Biennial Nat Exhib, Owensboro Mus Fine Arts, Ky, 82; 4/4 Invitational, ARC Gallery, Chicago, 82; Chicago/Chicago Artists, Hayes Gallery, Chicago, 83; and others. *Collections Arranged:* Third World Art Exhib, Gov State Univ, 76 & 77. *Pos:* Mem adv comt, Renovation of Chicago Pub Libr, 73. *Teaching:* Prof art, painting & art hist, Gov State Univ, Park Forest South, Ill, 73- *Awards:* Artists & Lectrs Grant, 74 & Craftsman in Residence Grant, 75, Nat Endowment Arts; Acquisition Prog Grant, Ill Arts Coun, 76. *Mem:* Col Art Asn Am; Chicago Artist Coalition; Turner Soc, London. *Media:* Oil, Mixed. *Res:* Study of J M W Turner at Petworth, 1802-1837. *Mailing Add:* 1360 E 52nd St Chicago IL 60615

MORLEY, MALCOM
PAINTER

b London, Eng, 1931. *Study:* Royal Col of Art, London, 54-57. *Work:* Whitney Mus, New York; Neue Galerie, Cologne, Ger; Wadsworth-Atheneum, Hartford, Conn; Mus Mod Art, New York; Musee d'Art Moderne, Paris; Victoria & Albert Mus, London. *Exhib:* The Photographic Image, Guggenheim Mus, New York, 66; Aspects of New Realism, Milwaukee Art Ctr, Wis, 69; 22 Realists, Whitney Mus, New York, 70; Kunst des 20 Jahrhunderts, Stadtische, Kunsthalle, Dusseldorf, 70; Contemp Am Painting, Whitney Mus, New York, 72; Documenta V, Kassel, Ger, 72; Projekt 74, Cologne, Ger, 74; one-man shows, Kornblee Gallery, New York, 64, 67 & 69. *Teaching:* Instr, Royal Col Art, London, 56; instr, Ohio State Univ, Columbus, 65-66; Sch Visual Arts, New York, 67-69 & State Univ NY, Stony Brook, 72. *Bibliog:* Barry Lord (auth), The Eleven O'Clock News in Colour, Artscanada, Toronto, 6/70; Nicholas & Elena Calas (auths), Icons and Images of the Sixties, New York, 71; K Levin (auth), Malcolm Morley: Post Style Illusionism, Artsmagazine, New York, 2/73. *Mailing Add:* Two Spring St New York NY 10012

MOROZ, MYCHAJLO
PAINTER

b Ukraine, July 7, 04; US citizen. *Study:* Art Sch, Lviv, Ukraine; Conservatoire National des Arts et Metiers, Paris & Acad Julian, Paris, 28-29; additional study, var mus, Italy, 32. *Work:* State Mus, Lvov & Kiev, Ukraine; State Mus, Moscow; St Sergii et Vacci Mus, Rome; Ukrainian Inst Am, New York; White House, Washington, DC; plus many others. *Exhib:* Ukrainian Artists from all European Countries Exhib, Lviv, 34; Artists Exhib, Moscow, 40-41; Exhib, Regensburg & Munich, Ger, 47-48; Int Group Exhib, Locust Valley, NY, 58; one-man shows, Panoras Gallery, New York, 59-63 & W & W Art Gallery, Toronto, 64-65; Ukrainian Inst Am, New York, 81. *Teaching:* Asst prof drawing & painting, Ukrainian Art Sch, Lviv, 30-35; also pvt lessons, Europe & US, 50- *Awards:* Silver Cap Second Award, Dem Club, Locust Valley, NY, 58; Prix de Paris, Galeries Raymond Duncan, 61; Most Artistic Christmas Card Prize, Onondaga Bank, Syracuse, NY, 62; Gold Medal, Accademica Italia delle Arti, 80. *Bibliog:* Max M Rhoude (auth), M Moroz, Mittelbayerische Zeitung, Regensburg, Ger, 47 & 48; Prof J Leschko (auth), Mychajlo Moroz--an appreciation, Ukrainian Weekly, JC, 6/81; plus many articles in US, Ukrainian, Russian & French papers, 30- *Mem:* Orgn Ukrainian Artists Am; Accademia Italia delle Arti. *Media:* Oil, Pastel. *Mailing Add:* 76 Coursen Pl Staten Island NY 10304

MORPHESIS, JIM (JAMES GEORGE)
PAINTER

b Philadelphia, Pa, Aug 26, 48. *Study:* Tyler Sch Art, with Stephen Greene, BFA, 70; Calif Inst Arts, with Paul Brach, Miriam Schapirow & Allan Kaprow, MFA, 72. *Work:* Los Angeles Co Mus Art; San Diego Mus Art. *Comn:* The Fall of Icarus (mural), Loyola Sch Law, Los Angeles, 83-84. *Exhib:* Los Angeles Artists, 76 & Eight Artists, 76, Los Angeles Co Mus Art; Newcomers, 76 & It's All Called Painting, 80, Los Angeles Munic Art Gallery; Contemporary Triptychs, Montgomery Art Gallery, Pomona, Calif, 82; Facings, Downey Mus Art, Calif, 83; Young Talent Awards: 1963-1983, Los Angeles Co Mus Art, 83; solo exhib, Tortue Gallery, Santa Monica, Calif, 83. *Teaching:* Instr painting, Calif Inst Arts, Valencia, 72-73; Los Angeles City Col, 74-83 & Otis Art Inst, Parsons Sch Design, 77- *Awards:* Nathan Margolis Mem Award Painting, Tyler Sch Art, 70; Purchase Award, Calif Small Images Exhib, Calif State Univ, Los Angeles, 71; Los Angeles Co Mus Art Young Talent Purchase Award, 83. *Bibliog:* Suzanne Muchnic (auth), article, Arts Mag, 9/79; Peter Clothier (auth), article, Art in Am, summer 82; Neal Menzies (auth), Jim Morphesis: The triumph of spiritual expression, Artweek, 3/83. *Mem:* Col Art Asn Am. *Media:* Oil, Mixed Media. *Dealer:* Freidus-Ordover Gallery 70 Greene St New York NY 10012; Tortue Gallery 2917 Santa Monica Blvd Santa Monica CA 90404. *Mailing Add:* 118 S Hobart Blvd Los Angeles CA 90004

MORRELL, WAYNE (BEAM)
PAINTER

b Clementon, NJ, Dec 24, 23. *Study:* Philadelphia Sch Indust Art; Drexel Inst. *Work:* Sloan Kettering Cancer Res Ctr, New York; Clark Mus, Carversville, Pa. *Exhib:* Expos Intercontinentale, Monoco, France; one-man shows, Gateway Gallereis, Palm Beach, Fisher Gallery, Washington, DC, O'Brian's Emporium, Scottsdale, Ariz & Americana Gallery, Santa Fe, NMex, 79; and many others. *Pos:* Art dir, John Oldham Studios, Conn, 55-61; owner & dir, Wayne Morrell Gallery, currently. *Awards:* Jane Peterson Prize, 69 & 74 & Coun Am Art Socs Award, 71, Allied Artist Am; Gold Medal, Rockport Art Asn, 70. *Bibliog:* R Kolby (auth), A stand for nature, Am Artist, 3/72. *Mem:* Allied Artist Am; Springfield Acad Artist (coun, 60-61); Salmagundi Club; Rockport Art Asn. *Media:* Oil, Watercolor. *Publ:* Illusr, Readers Digest, 67. *Dealer:* Newman Galleries 1625 Walnut Philadelphia PA 19103; Grand Central Galleries 40 Vanderbilt Ave New York NY 10017. *Mailing Add:* 25 Main St Rockport MA 01966

MORRIN, PETER PATRICK
HISTORIAN, CURATOR

b St Louis, Mo, Oct 31, 45. *Study:* Harvard Univ, AB, 68; Princeton Univ, MFA, 72. *Pos:* Dir, Vassar Col Art Gallery, 74-78; cur 20th century art, High Mus, 78- *Teaching:* Instr art hist, Vassar Col, 74-78. *Awards:* Nat Collection Fine Arts Res Fel, Smithsonian Inst, 73-74. *Res:* Modern and American art. *Publ:* Coauth (with Dr Eric M Zafran), Drawings from Georgia Collections: 19th and 20th Centuries (catalog), 81, auth, J J Haverty: The Taste of a Southern Collector (catalog), 81, auth, 20th Century Paintings from the Collection of the Museum of Modern Art: A Viewer's Guide (catalog), 82, auth, Chase Manhattan: The First Ten Years of Collection, 1959-1969 (catalog), 82 & auth, Content in Abstraction: The Uses of Nature (catalog), 83, High Mus Art, Atlanta. *Mailing Add:* High Mus of Art 1280 Peachtree St NE Atlanta GA 30309

MORRIS, CARL
PAINTER

b Calif. *Study:* Art Inst Chicago; Kunstgewerbeschule, Vienna; Akad Bildenden Kuenste, Vienna. *Work:* Guggenheim Mus, Metrop Mus, Mus Mod Art & Whitney Mus Am Art, New York; Nat Gallery Art & Joseph Hirshhorn Collection, Washington, DC. *Comn:* Murals, US Treas Dept, Post Off Bldg, Eugene, Ore, 41; murals, Ore Centennial Comn, Hall of Relig Hist, 59. *Exhib:* Carnegie Int, Pittsburgh; Rome-New York Art Found Exhib; Pittsburgh Int; San Francisco Mus Art; Art USA Int. *Awards:* Ford Found Award, Retrospective Exhib, 60-62; Purchase Award, Ford Found, 60 & Nat Inst Arts & Lett. *Bibliog:* G L M Morley (auth), article for Ford Found, 60; David Wagoner (auth), The journey of Carl Morris, Malahat Rev, 10/74; Robin Skelton (auth), Encore Mag of Arts, 78. *Media:* Oil, Acrylic. *Publ:* Illusr covers & drawings, Poetry Northwest, summers 61 & 63; illusr cover

& drawings, Five Poets of the Pacific Northwest, Univ Wash, 64; Ore Symphony poster, 76-77. *Dealer:* Kraushaar Galleries 1055 Madison Ave New York NY 10021; Fountain Gallery 115 SW Fourth Ave Portland OR 97204. *Mailing Add:* 919 NW Skyline Blvd Portland OR 97229

MORRIS, DONALD FISCHER
DEALER

b Detroit, Mich, Apr 12, 25. *Pos:* Owner & dir, Donald Morris Gallery Inc, Birmingham, Mich, currently. *Mem:* Art Dealers Asn Am; Mich Coun Arts; Detroit Art Dealers Asn (pres, 71-). *Specialty:* Twentieth century American and European painting and sculpture; African art. *Mailing Add:* Donald Morris Gallery Inc 105 Townsend Birmingham MI 48011

MORRIS, FLORENCE MARIE
DEALER

b Detroit, Mich, Apr 30, 28. *Study:* Wayne State Univ, BS. *Pos:* Dir, Donald Morris Gallery, Detroit, 58- *Mem:* Art Dealers Asn Am; New Detroit (mem visual arts comt, 77-); Detroit Art Dealers Asn. *Specialty:* 20th century painting, sculpture and drawings; African sculpture. *Mailing Add:* 105 Townsend Birmingham MI 48011

MORRIS, HILDA
SCULPTOR

b New York, NY. *Study:* Art Students League; Cooper Union Sch Art & Archit. *Work:* Chase-Manhattan Bank; Calif Palace of Legion of Honor, San Francisco; Munson-Williams-Proctor Inst Mus; Walter P Chrysler, Jr Collection, Va Mus; San Francisco Mus Art. *Comn:* Sculpture, Seattle Opera House, 63; bronze, Standard Plaza Bldg, Portland, 67; bronze, Pac Nat Bldg, Tacoma, Wash, 71; bronze, Mem Art Gallery, Univ Rochester, 75; bronze, Reed Col, Portland, Ore, 80. *Exhib:* American Sculpture, Metrop Mus Art, 51; 3rd Pac Coast Biennial, Santa Barbara Mus Art, 60; Northwest Art Today, Seattle World's Fair, 62; Nat Print Show, Brooklyn Mus, 64; many exhibs, San Francisco Mus Art. *Awards:* Ford Found Fel, 60. *Bibliog:* Robin Skelton (auth), Sculpture as metaphor: five bronzes by Hilda Morris, Malahat Rev, 7/69; Carolyn Kizer (auth), Hilda Morris: Recent Bronzes, 73; Encore Mag Arts, 77. *Publ:* Illusr cover drawings, Poetry Northwest, spring & summer 68 & spring 69. *Dealer:* Fountain Gallery Art 117 NW 21st Portland OR 97209; Triangle Gallery 95 Minna St San Francisco CA 94105. *Mailing Add:* 919 NW Skyline Blvd Portland OR 97229

MORRIS, JACK AUSTIN, JR
MUSEUM DIRECTOR, WRITER

b Macon, Ga, Sept 29, 39. *Study:* Univ SC, AB, with Edmund Yaghjian, Augusta Wittkowski & Catherine Rembert; Univ SC; Harvard Univ Inst Arts Admin. *Collections Arranged:* Arnold H Maremont Collection (20th Century American & European Painting & Sculpture), 65; Ida Kohlmeyer (one-man exhib), 67; Jasper Johns Prints (with catalog), Harbor Town Mus, Hilton Head Island, SC, 71; Andrew Wyeth in Southern Collections, 78; Select Works by Andrew Wyeth: The Arthur and Holly Magill Collection, 79. *Pos:* Curatorial assoc, Columbia Mus Art, 62-63, asst to dir, 63-65; exec dir, Greenville Co Mus Art, 65-80; exec dir, Greenville Co Art Asn, 75-80; mem exec bd, Metrop Arts Coun, 78-80; exec dir, Period Gallery West, 80-81; owner, Morris Fine Arts, 81-83; exec dir, Connally/Altermann Art Gallery, 83- *Teaching:* Lectr, Kress Collection, Columbia Mus Art, SC, 62-65; instr drawing & painting, Richland Art Sch, Columbia, 64-65. *Mem:* Am Asn Mus; Guild SC Artists (pres, 68); founder, SC Fedn Mus (vpres, 71-72, pres, 73-74); SC Arts Comn (chmn exec comt, 72-73); SC Arts Found (pres, 75-80); and others. *Res:* Contemporary American art; art of the American West. *Publ:* Ed, Museum News, 64-65 & illusr, Two-Hundred Years of the Arts of France, 65, Columbia Mus Art; auth, Contemporary Artists of South Carolina (catalog), 70; auth, William M Halsey: Retrospective (catalog), 72. *Mailing Add:* Carriage Square No 9 2320 McCue Houston TX 77056

MORRIS, ROBERT
SCULPTOR

b Kansas City, Mo, Feb 9, 31. *Study:* Kansas City Jr Col; Kansas City Art Inst, 48-50; Univ Kansas City; San Francisco Art Inst; Reed Col, 53-55; Hunter Col, MA, 66. *Work:* Dallas Mus Fine Arts, Tex; Whitney Mus Am Art, New York; Tate Gallery, London, Eng; Wadsworth Atheneum; Detroit Art Inst. *Comn:* Earth Proj, Nat Planning Comn, Ottawa; Steam Piece, Western Wash Univ, Bellingham, 69; Grand Rapids Proj, City of Grand Rapids, Mich, 74; Observatory, Sonsbeek Unlimited, Oost-Flevoland, Holland, 77. *Exhib:* Guggenheim Int, Solomon R Guggenheim Mus, 67; The Art of the Real, Mus Mod Art, 68; one-man shows, Corcoran Gallery Art, Washington, DC, 69, Whitney Mus Am Art, New York, 70, Leo Castelli Gallery, New York, 72 & 76, Max Protetch Gallery, Washington, DC, 73 & Stedelijk Mus, Amsterdam, Holland, 77 & Florence Wilcox Art Gallery, Swarthmore Col, Pa, 78; Whitney Mus Am Art, 72, 73, 75 & 76; Art Inst Chicago, 74, 76 & 77; Some Recent American Art, Mus Mod Art, New York & traveling, 74; Galerie Ricke, Cologne, Ger, 74; Sculpture, Am Directions 1945-1975, Nat Collection Fine Arts, Smithsonian Inst, Washington, DC, 75; High Mus Art, Atlanta, Ga; NY State Mus, Albany, 77; Madison Art Ctr, Wis, 77; New Gallery Contemp Art, Cleveland, Ohio, 77; Kansas City Art Inst, Mo, 78; Mus Contemp Art, La Jolla, Calif, 78; plus many others. *Teaching:* Instr, Hunter Col, 67- *Awards:* Prize, Guggenheim Mus, 67; Guggenheim Found Fel, 69; Sculpture Award, Soc Four Arts, 75. *Bibliog:* Annette Michelson (auth), Three notes on an exhibition as a work, Artforum, 6/70; Jack Burnham (auth), Robert Morris: Retrospective in Detroit, Artforum, 3/70 & Voices from the gate, Arts Mag, Vol 46 summer 72; Jeremy Gilbert-Rolfe (auth), Robert Morris: The complication of exhaustion, Artforum, 9/74. *Publ:* Auth, The art of existence, 1/71, Some splashes in the ebb tide, 2/73 & Aligned with Nazca, 10/75, Artforum; auth, The present tense of space, Art in Am, 1-2/78. *Mailing Add:* c/o Castelli Gallery 4 E 77th St New York NY 10021

MORRIS, ROBERT CLARKE
PAINTER, EDUCATOR
b New York, Apr 2, 31. *Study:* Yale Univ, with Josef Albers, BFA; Univ Tex, MFA. *Work:* Allentown Art Mus, Pa; Okla Art Ctr, Oklahoma City; Mus Fine Arts Houston, Tex; Beaumont Art Mus, Tex. *Exhib:* One-man shows, Washburn Gallery, New York, 76 & 79, Artist's Postcards-Drawing Ctr, New York, 77 & Conn Painting, Drawing & Sculpture, 78; New Eng Ann, Silvermine Guild, 78 & 79; Award Candidates, Am Acad Inst Arts & Letters, New York, 81; and others. *Collections Arranged:* Out of the Ordinary, Contemp Arts Mus, Houston, 58, Tenth St, 58 & Architectural Graphics, 59. *Pos:* Dir, Contemp Art Mus, Houston, 58-60; vis design cur, Univ Tex Art Mus, Austin, 68-69. *Teaching:* Instr painting, Univ Houston, 57-59; instr painting & drawing, Mus Sch, Mus Fine Arts Houston, 58-59; prof art, Univ Bridgeport, 61-; vis critic, Columbia Univ, 81. *Media:* Multimedia. *Dealer:* Washburn Gallery 42 E 57th St New York NY 10022. *Mailing Add:* 285 Park Ave Univ Bridgeport Bridgeport CT 06602

MORRIS, WRIGHT
WRITER, PHOTOGRAPHER
b Central City, Nebr, Jan 6, 10. *Study:* Pomona Col, 30-33; Westminster Col, Dr Lit, 68; Univ Nebr, Lincoln, Dr Lit, 68; Pomona Col, Dr Lit, 73. *Work:* Mus Mod Art, New York; Sheldon Mem Art Gallery, Univ Nebr, Lincoln; San Francisco Mus Art; Corcoran Gallery Art. *Exhib:* Solo exhib, Sheldon Mem Art Gallery, Univ Nebr, Lincoln, 75 & Corcoran Gallery Art, 83. *Teaching:* Prof lit, San Francisco State Univ, 62-74. *Awards:* Nat Book Award, 56; Am Book Award, 80; Commonwealth Award Lit, 82. *Bibliog:* David Madden (auth), Wright Morris, Wayne Publ, 64; Leon Howard (auth), Wright Morris, Univ Minn, 68; Robert Knoll (ed), Conversations with Wright Morris, Univ Nebr Press, 77. *Publ:* Auth, The Inhabitants, 46 & The Home Place, 48, Charles Scribner; auth, Photographs and Words, Friends Photog, 82. *Mailing Add:* c/o Friends Photog PO Box 500 Carmel CA 93921

MORRISON, BEE (BERENICE G)
WEAVER
b Florence, Italy, Jan 16, 08. *Study:* Self taught, also with Porfirio Lopez & Ted Hallman. *Work:* State Collection Found Cult & Arts, Honolulu, Hawaii. *Exhib:* Volcano Art Ctr, Volcanoes Nat Park, 74-75 & 79; Queen Emma Gallery, Honolulu, 81; Hawaii Women Artists, 82; Fiber Artists Hawaii, 82; Consortium Hawaii, 82. *Teaching:* Instr floorloom & offloom weaving, free design knitting & crochet, Volcano Art Ctr, Kalani Honua, currently. *Mem:* Hawaii Craftsmen; Honolulu Weavers Hui; Kiluea Weavers Guild (pres, 74); Fibers Hui of Hawaii (pres 76-79, bd, 79-). *Dealer:* Volcano Art Ctr Volcano HI 96785. *Mailing Add:* Box 335 Volcano HI 96785

MORRISON, BOONE M
PHOTOGRAPHER, DESIGNER
b Berkeley, Calif, Jan 28, 41. *Study:* Stanford Univ, BA(hist), 62, BA(commun), 63; Yosemite Photog Workshops, with Ansel Adams, 71-73. *Work:* Honolulu Acad Art, Hawaii; Bishop Mus, Honolulu; State of Hawaii Collection; US Nat Park Serv; Nat Gallery Art, Washington, DC. *Comn:* Mural photographs, Kauau Mus, 71 & C Brewer & Co, 73; interior wall mural, State of Hawaii, Ka'u Hosp, 75. *Exhib:* Artists of Hawaii, 71-75; Mountains and the Shore, Honolulu Acad Traveling Exhib, 75; A Most Hawaiian Place Traveling Exhib, 75; Time on the Land Traveling Exhib, 76-77 & American Photographers and the National Parks, 81-83, Nat Park Serv. *Pos:* Owner-founder, The Foundry Gallery, Honolulu, 69-71; dir, Hawaii Photog Workshops, 71-; dir, Volcano Art Ctr, Hawaii, 74-81; pres & publ, Summit Press, currently. *Teaching:* Instr photog, Univ Hawaii, Manoa Campus, 69-71; instr archit, 70-72; instr photog, Hawaii Photog Workshops, 71- & State Hawaii Artists Schs, 74; lectr, Univ Hawaii Ford Found, 80 & Art Dept, Univ Hawaii, Hilo, 82. *Awards:* Purchase Awards, Hawaii State Found Cult & Arts, 70-75. *Bibliog:* Joan Murray (auth), Photography in Hawaii, Art Week, 73; Portfolio, 1979 Popular Photog Ann; The Photographers Eye (film), Hawaii, 80. *Mem:* Image Continuum Group. *Publ:* Contribr, Beautiful Hawaii, Lane, 72; illusr, Hawaiian Legends, Bishop Mus Press, 75; illusr, Dillingham Corp Tide Calendar, 75; auth, Journal of a Pioneer Builder, Hawaii Nat Hist Asn, 77; auth, Images of the Hula, Summit Press, 83. *Mailing Add:* PO Box 131 Volcano HI 96785

MORRISON, C L
WRITER, CRITIC
b Evanston, Ill, Jan 14, 46. *Study:* Roosevelt Univ, BA; Field Mus Nat Hist. *Collections Arranged:* The Life and Work of Henry J Darger, 77; Abstract Art in Chicago (auth, catalog), Mus of Contemp Art, Chicago, 76. *Pos:* Res ed, Inst for Philosophical Res, Chicago, Ill, 67-74; contrib ed, Midwest Art, Milwaukee, 74-77; Chicago corresp, Artforum; ed, Format: Art and the World, Chicago, 78- *Teaching:* Workshop post-conceptual art, Mus Contemp Art, Chicago, 76; seminar, art writing, Univ of Wis, Stevens Point, 77; hist art & medicine, Rush Univ, Chicago, 80. *Bibliog:* Margaret Key Biggs (auth), interview, Earthwise, Vol 3, No 7, 81. *Res:* The New Bauhaus; design structure and social interaction; the effect of audience relationships & patronage on art styles. *Publ:* Auth, Chicago dialectic, Artforum, 78; auth, Yes, they really do want a Richard J Daley Memorial, Art Forum, 79; auth, Defilement, Chicago, 78; auth, Discrimination against the artist who has everything, Format, 10/80; auth, Why critics are inaccessible, NOVA J, 81; and others. *Mailing Add:* Seven Oaks 405 S 7th St St Charles IL 60174

MORRISON, DORIS
PAINTER, ADMINISTRATOR
b Alameda, Calif. *Study:* Calif Sch Fine Arts; Cleveland Inst Art, BFA, 49; Col of Marin, printmaking with a protege of S W Hayter, 61-62; printmaking with Ron Robertson, Santa Barbara City Col, 80-82; enameling with Floy Meyers, 82-83. *Work:* Col Fine Arts, Ohio Univ, Athens; Cleveland Mus Art; Womens City Club of Cleveland; Ross Valley Hosp, Calif; Oak Knoll Naval Hosp, Oakland, Calif. *Exhib:* De Young Mus, San Francisco Mus Art & Butler Inst Am Art Annuals; San Francisco Art Inst Traveling & Ann Exhib; East Bay Artists Asn Traveling Exhib; Invitationals, Jack London Sq, Oakland, Calif; Arts Coun Ann Exhibs, 78, 79 & 80 & four-person show, 84, Mus Natural Hist Galleries, Santa Barbara. *Collections Arranged:* Still Life, Cabillo Arts Ctr, 84. *Pos:* Started Santa Barbara Mus Art Rental Gallery, 71; founder, Co-op Gallery 113, 73; Co-dir, Cabillo Arts Ctr, currently. *Teaching:* Instr color, design & drawing, Dominican Col, 56. *Awards:* San Francisco Women Artists Award, 68; 12 awards, Santa Barbara Art Asn, 70-79. *Mem:* Life mem Marin Soc Artists; life mem Santa Barbara Art Asn; Contemp Art Forum (dir, 78); Arts Coun, Santa Barbara Chap; Artists Equity, Santa Barbara (vpres, 83-84). *Media:* Mixed. *Mailing Add:* 333 Old Mill Rd 204 Santa Barbara CA 93110

MORRISON, FRITZI MOHRENSTECHER
PAINTER, LECTURER
b Quincy, Ill. *Study:* Art Inst Chicago; Univ Chicago; also with Charles W Hawthorne, Anthony Thieme, Karl Knaths, watercolor with Eliot O'Hara & John Pike. *Work:* St Louis Art Mus, Mo; Carpenter Gallery, Dartmouth Col, Hanover, NH; City Hall, Quincy, Mass; and others. *Exhib:* A Century of St Louis Art & Artists, St Louis Art Mus, Mo, 58; Salmagundi Club Non-Mem All-Media Exhib, New York, 79; Krannert Art Mus, Irwin Collection, Univ Ill, Champaign, 80; 42 solo exhibs including Western Ill Univ, Macomb, 80 & Elizabeth Sinnock Gallery, Quincy Art Ctr, Ill, 81; and others. *Pos:* Resident artist, Quincy Art Club, Ill. *Awards:* Sixteenth Ann Artists Salon Award, Okla Mus Art, Oklahoma City, 77. *Mem:* Am Watercolor Soc; Philadelphia Watercolor Club; Washington DC Watercolor Asn; Quincy Art Club; Watercolor Soc Ala. *Media:* Transparent Watercolor. *Mailing Add:* 1845 Jersey St Quincy IL 62301

MORRISON, GEORGE
PAINTER
b Grand Marais, Minn, Sept 30, 19. *Study:* Minneapolis Sch Art, MFA (hon), 69; Art Students League; Univ Aix-Marseille, Aix-en-Provence, France. *Work:* Whitney Mus Am Art, New York; Philadelphia Mus Art; Va Mus Fine Arts, Richmond; Heard Mus, Phoenix, Ariz; Amon Carter Mus, Ft Worth, Tex; and others. *Comn:* Cedar wood mural, Minneapolis Regional Native Am Ctr, 75; redwood mural, City Seattle, Daybreak Star Art Ctr, 77; found wood collage, Hennepin County Med Ctr, Minneapolis, 77. *Exhib:* Corcoran Biennial, Washington, DC, 50; Whitney Mus Am Art Ann, New York, 52; Joslyn Art Mus, Omaha, Nebr, 55; Los Angeles Co Mus Art, 58; Dallas Mus Fine Arts, 58; Brooklyn Mus, 61; RI Sch Design Mus Art, Providence, 68; Mus Am Indian, New York, 71. *Collections Arranged:* Morrison Drawings Traveling Exhib, Walker Art Ctr, Minneapolis, 73, Heard Mus, Phoenix, 73, Mus STex, Corpus Christie, 73 & Amon Carter Mus, Ft Worth, 74. *Teaching:* Vis prof, Cornell Univ, 62 & Pa State Univ, 63; assoc prof painting & drawing, RI Sch Design, Providence, 63-70; prof painting & drawing, Univ Minn, Minneapolis, 70- *Awards:* Fulbright Scholarship, 51. *Bibliog:* Dragos Kostich (auth), George Morrison: The Story of an American Indian, Dillon Press, 76; Encounter with Artists: George Morrison (film), KTCA-TV, Minn Educ TV, 77. *Mem:* Audubon Soc; Fedn Mod Painters & Sculptors; Native Am Coun Arts; Minneapolis Soc Fine Arts (trustee, 78). *Media:* Oil, Weathered Wood. *Mailing Add:* Box 376 Grand Portage MN 55605

MORRISON, KEITH ANTHONY
PAINTER, EDUCATOR
b Jamaica, West Indies, May 20, 42; US citizen. *Study:* Art Inst Chicago, BFA, 63, MFA, 65; Univ Ill; DePaul Univ; Loyola Univ. *Work:* Jamaica Inst Art, Kingston, West Indies; Nat Govt Collection Liberia, West Africa; Fisk Univ Gallery, Nashville; Art Inst Chicago. *Comn:* Painting for Liberian Govt, 64 & Dusable Mus Afro-Am Hist, 71; mural commissioned by Phyllis Kind Gallery for Main Bank, Chicago, 72; and others. *Exhib:* Chicago Prints, Allan Frumkin Gallery, 69; Nat Exhib Black Artists, Smith-Mason Gallery, Washington, DC, 71; Black American Artists 71, Ill Bell/Ill Arts Coun, 71; Biennial Chicago & Vicinity, Art Inst Chicago, 71; Cicero Gallery, Chicago, 79; Osuna Gallery, Washington, DC, 83; Corcoran Gallery Art, 83; and others. *Collections Arranged:* Toussaint L'ouverture (paintings of Jacob Lawrence, with catalog), DePaul Univ, Chicago, 69; Black Experiences in Art (exhib of painting & sculpture, with catalog), Bergman Gallery Univ Chicago, 71; Afro-Am Artists, Washington Proj Arts, 79; Wisconsin 80, Univ Wis, 80. *Pos:* Assoc ed, New Art Examiner, 82-; cur, Whiskey Painters Am Gallery, 83-84. *Teaching:* Instr art, Hyde Park Art Ctr, Chicago, 65-67; asst prof drawing, Fisk Univ, Nashville, Tenn, 67-68; assoc prof printmaking & chmn dept, DePaul Univ, 68-71; assoc prof, Univ Ill, Chicago Circle, 71-79; prof, Univ Md, College Park, 79- *Awards:* Prize, Jamaica Inst, 59; Bicentennial Award Painting, City Chicago, 76; Int Painting Award, Orgn African Unity, Liberia, 79. *Bibliog:* Robin Glauber (auth), Keith Morrison at Black Hawk, Skyline, 9/70; Harold Hayden (auth), article, Chicago Sun-Times, 10/79; Paul Richard (auth), article, Washington Post, 83. *Mem:* Col Art Asn; Nat Conf Artists; Int Asn Art Critics. *Media:* Oil, Watercolor. *Res:* Role of black institutions in modern art of Washington, DC, 1940-1970; contemporary black artists in America. *Publ:* Auth, art criticism: A Pan-American point of view, 79, guest ed, Afro-American Art, 81 & auth, Kitai: The sword of Don Quixote, 81, New Art Examiner; auth, 200 Years of Afro-American Women Art: A Critic's View, Ill State Univ, 80; auth, Poetic objects, New Art Examiner, 82. *Dealer:* Jan Cicero Gallery 437 North Clark St Chicago IL 60610. *Mailing Add:* 1214 Randolph St NE Washington DC 20017

MORRISON, ROBERT CLIFTON
PRINTMAKER, CALLIGRAPHER
b Billings, Mont, Aug 13, 24. *Study:* Carleton Col, BA; Univ NMex, MA. *Work:* Harvard Univ Libr Print Collection, Cambridge, Mass; Ministry Art & Cult, Ghana; Rocky Mt Col, Billings; Int Col Copenhagen, Denmark; Centre Medieval Studies, Oxford, Eng. *Comn:* Mosaic murals, Mont State Unemployment Comn, Helena, 61 & Lucerne Pub Schs Wyo; mural, Lockwood Pub Schs, Billings; Bicentennial mural, Yellowstone Co Courthouse, Billings; mural, Rocky Mountain Col, Billings. *Pos:* Ed, Rocky Mt Rev, 63-69; pres bd dirs, Yellowstone Art Ctr, Billings, 64-65. *Teaching:* Dir art educ, Billings Pub Schs, 57-67; prof art, Rocky Mt Col, 67-; artist in residence, Herning Folk Skole, Denmark, 83. *Awards:* Mont Artist-Teacher of Yr, Am Artists Prof League, 64. *Media:* Wood; Acrylic, Oil. *Publ:* Translr & illusr, Maxims of LaRochefoucauld, 67. *Dealer:* Castle Gallery Billings MT 59101. *Mailing Add:* 2815 Woody Dr Billings MT 59102

MORRISS, MARY RACHEL
PAINTER
b Memphis, Tenn. *Study:* Memphis State Univ, BS, 27; Univ Colo, Boulder, Grad Sch, 31, 34, 37 & 40; Maxine Masterfield, cert, 81. *Work:* Parkway Village Branch, First Tenn Bank, Memphis; Memphis Eastwood Hospital. *Exhib:* Mid-South, Brooks Mem Art Gallery, Memphis Tenn, 58, 59, 61 & 64; one-woman show, Parthenon Art Gallery, Nashville, Tenn, 71; Central South, Parthenon, Nashville, Tenn, 76, 78 & 79; Mid-Am, Owensboro Mus Art, Ky, 79; Tenn Watercolor Soc Traveling Exhib, 80-82; Southern Watercolor, Patrons Watercolor Gala, Oklahoma City, 83; and others. *Teaching:* Instr art, Memphis City Sch System, Bellevue, 36-66; pvt classes. *Awards:* Mid-South Fair Purchase Award, 71; Best Cotton Design, Brooks Mem Art Gallery; Cash Award, Tenn Watercolor Soc, 81; and many others. *Mem:* Tenn Watercolor Soc; Memphis Watercolor Group; Southern Watercolor Soc. *Media:* Watercolor, Acrylic. *Dealer:* Forest Hill Gallery 9076 Poplar Pike Germantown TN 38138; Art Gallery East 426 Perkins Rd Ext Memphis TN 38117. *Mailing Add:* 911 Newell St Memphis TN 38111

MORROW, ROBERT EARL
DESIGNER, MURALIST
b Milan, Ohio, Mar 21, 17. *Study:* Cleveland Inst of Art, Ohio; Ohio State Univ, Columbus. *Work:* Cleveland Mus of Art; Butler Inst of Am Art, Youngstown, Ohio; Akron Art Inst, Ohio; Canton Art Inst, Ohio; Massillon Mus, Ohio. *Comn:* Hanging banners, Kent State Univ, Ohio, 62; murals (tile mosaic), Firestone High Sch, Akron, 63; murals (sgraffito), Temple Univ, Philadelphia, Pa, 66; mural (polyester resin, polydrome), Akron Pub Libr, 69; mural (portland cement sgraffito), II Cascade Plaza, Akron, 70. *Exhib:* Cleveland Mus of Art Ann Regional; Butler Inst of Am Art, Youngstown. *Teaching:* Prof drawing & painting, Kent State Univ, 46-; vis prof mural design, Tyler Sch of Art, Temple Univ, Philadelphia, 64-66. *Awards:* Second Award/Painting, Army Art Show, Nat Gallery, Washington, DC, 44; Purchase Awards, Cleveland Mus of Art, 64; Second Award, Butler Inst of Am Art, Youngstown, 50. *Media:* Concrete; Constructions. *Publ:* Illusr, Orchestra Mice, Reilly & Lee, Chicago, 70. *Mailing Add:* 141 Crain Ave Kent OH 44240

MORROW, TERRY
DRAFTSMAN, PRINTMAKER
b Austin, Tex, Oct 1, 39. *Study:* Univ Tex, BFA; Univ Wis; Ind Univ, MS, study with Rudy Pozzatti. *Work:* Univ Tex, Austin; Tex Christian Univ, Ft Worth; Western Tex Col, Snyder; Odessa Col, Tex. *Exhib:* Appalachian Nat Drawing Competition, Boone, NC, 78 & 79; two-person exhibs, Sch Galleries, Houston Mus Fine Arts, 71 & Art Dept Teaching Gallery, Univ Tenn, Knoxville, 77; one-person exhib, Clara M Eagle Gallery, Price Doyle Fine Art Ctr, Murray State Univ, 73; and many others. *Pos:* Consult in litho printing, Tex Christian Univ, Ft Worth, 69; Western Tex Col, Snyder, 74 & San Angelo Col, Tex, 78; guest artist, ETex State Univ, Commerce, 79. *Teaching:* Instr painting & printmaking, Univ Pa, Philadelphia, 65-66; asst prof drawing & printmaking, Univ Chattanooga, Tenn, 67-68; assoc prof drawing, printmaking, Tex Tech Univ, Lubbock, 68-, prof art, currently. *Awards:* Cash awards, 16th Ann Drawing and Small Sculpture exhib, 70 & Tri-State Art Exhib, 76; 12th Ann Del Mar Drawing & Small Sculpture, 78. *Media:* Pen and Ink; Intaglio. *Dealer:* Dorothy Katz c/o Sol Del Rio Gallery 1020 Townsend San Antonio TX 78209. *Mailing Add:* 5217 15th St Lubbock TX 79416

MORSE, MARCIA ROBERTS
PRINTMAKER, WRITER
b Detroit, Mich, Mar 14, 44. *Study:* Radcliffe Col, BA(cum laude), 66; Stanford Univ, MFA, 74; with S W Hayter, Misch Kohn, Adela Akers, Leonore Tawney, Walter Nottingham & Ed Rossbach. *Work:* Honolulu Acad Arts & Contemp Arts Ctr, Honolulu, Hawaii; Smithsonian Inst, Div Graphic Arts, Washington, DC; Int Paper Co, New York; Greenville Co Mus Art, SC. *Comn:* Ann gift print, Honolulu Printmakers, Hawaii, 77; prints, Hawaii State Found Culture & Arts, Honolulu, 78. *Exhib:* Collectors' Choice, Joslyn Art Mus, Omaha, Nebr, 68; New Am Graphics, Madison Art Ctr, Wis, 75; one-woman show, Contemp Arts Ctr, Honolulu, Hawaii, 78; Textures, Contemp Artisans Gallery, San Francisco, Calif, 81; Nat Crafts, Greenville Co Mus Art, SC, 81; First Int Shoebox Sculpture, Univ Hawaii Art Gallery, Honolulu, 82. *Pos:* Freelance art writer, Artweek, 78-; art columnist, Honolulu Star Bulletin, Hawaii, 79- *Teaching:* Instr printmaking, Univ Calif, Santa Cruz, 69-74; lectr printmaking & textiles, Univ Hawaii, 79-; instr papermaking, Honolulu Acad Arts, Hawaii, 80- *Awards:* Craftsmen's Fel, Nat Endowment Arts, 81-82. *Mem:* Honolulu Printmakers (pres, 76-79, bd mem, 75-80); Hawaii Craftsmen (secy, 78); Surface Design Asn; Nat Soc Arts & Letters; Am Crafts Coun. *Media:* Handmade Paper. *Res:* Contemporary craft art; Japanese art both historical and contemporary. *Publ:* Illusr, Writing from the Inside, Addison-Wesley, 73; illusr, The Eight Rainbows of Umi, Topgallant Press, 76; auth, Nature distilled and distorted, 78 & auth, Language of materials, 81, Artweek; auth, Filaments of the imagination, Fiberarts, 81. *Dealer:* The Source Gallery Folsom St San Francisco CA; Art Loft Honolulu HI. *Mailing Add:* PO Box 61069 Honolulu HI 96822

MORSE, MITCHELL IAN
DEALER, RESTORER
b Brooklyn, NY, Mar 10, 26. *Study:* Himeji Univ, 45-46; City Col New York, BBA, 47. *Pos:* Pres, Art Gallery on Wheels, New York, 53-54; pres, Mitch Morse Gallery, Inc, 69-; pres, Mitch Morse Graphics, Inc, New York, 69-; pres, Graphic Source I, 71-; pres, China Spectrum, Inc, 81. *Awards:* Designer Official Seal, Village Lawrence, 67. *Mem:* Am Soc Interior Designers; Prof Picture Framers Asn; Calhoun's Collectors Soc Inc. *Specialty:* Artists agents, publishers of limited edition, original graphics. *Publ:* Auth, Graphics as an original art form, Designer, 8/73. *Mailing Add:* Mitch Morse Gallery Inc 305 E 63rd St New York NY 10021

MORSE, PETER
HISTORIAN, COLLECTOR
b Chicago, Ill, Oct 29, 35. *Study:* Yale Univ, BA, 57. *Pos:* Assoc cur graphic arts, Smithsonian Inst, Washington, DC, 65-67; res assoc, Honolulu Acad Arts, 67-; consult Charlot Collection, Univ Hawaii Libr, Honolulu, 81-83. *Mem:* Appraisers Asn Am; Tamarind Inst. *Res:* Prints and printmaking; Hokusai; Daumier; American, Mexican and French art of the 20th century. *Publ:* Auth, John Sloan's Prints, Yale Univ Press, 69; auth, Jean Charlot's Prints, Univ Press Hawaii, 75; auth, Popular Art, Capra Press, 78; coauth, Netherlandish Artists, Vol 2, Abaris Press, 77; auth, Daumier's early lithographs, Print Review 11, 80. *Mailing Add:* 1717 Mott-Smith No 3207 Honolulu HI 96822

MORTELLITO, DOMENICO
PAINTER, SCULPTOR
b Newark, NJ, Sept 1, 06. *Study:* Newark Sch Fine Arts, cert, 21; Pratt Inst, BA, 26; Harvard Univ Bus Sch, cert, 42. *Work:* Mus Mod Art, New York; Newark Mus, NJ; Univ Del, Newark; Freedom Bell, Berlin, Ger; DuPont Co, Wilmington, Del. *Comn:* Murals, Works Progress Admin, Port Chester, NY, 34; exterior murals, B Altman & Co, New York, 38; murals, 8 pavilions, NY World's Fair, New York, 39; white Teflon sculpture, DuPont Co, Houston, 60; Crucifix & Altar, St Joseph on the Brandywine, Wilmington, Del, 76. *Exhib:* Wilmington Savings Fund Soc, Del, 75; Plastic as Plastic, Mus Contemp Crafts, New York, 69; Bicentennial Exhib, Philadelphia Mem Hall, 76; Am Freedom Caravan, Southern Vt Art Ctr, Manchester, 76; Ann Exhib, Nat Sculpture Soc, New York, 77, 78 & 79; and other group & one-man shows. *Pos:* Master designer, Mack, Jenny & Tyler, Archit Decor, New York, 26-31; creative dir, Mortellito Studio, New York, 31-42; dir graphic presentation, US Army Air Force, DC, 42-45; mgr design sect & chmn color coun, E I du Pont de Nemours & Co, Inc, Wilmington, Del, 45-77, Mobay Chemical Corp, 45-77. *Awards:* Creative Printing Award, Graphic Arts Rev, 66. *Bibliog:* Ernest Watson (auth), New mediums, Am Artist Mag, 38, 42 & 65; Time-Life ed, New medium in art, Life/Sci Libr, 66; Howard L Slater (auth), Cromalin, new art medium, Leonardo Mag, Paris, 76. *Mem:* Nat Soc Mural Painters; Am Artists Prof League; Artists Equity Asn; Inter-Soc Color Coun; Nat Sculpture Soc. *Media:* Oil; New Synthetics, Stone. *Publ:* Auth, Symbology and the corporate image, 59 & Graphics in a three-dimensional setting, 60, Print Mag; coauth, New medium for modern art, DuPont Mag, 63; auth, Sculpture overboard, Indust Design, 68; auth, How to produce cromal in art, Graphic Arts Mo, 73. *Mailing Add:* 716 W Matson Run Pkwy Wilmington DE 19802

MORTENSEN, GORDON LOUIS
PRINTMAKER, PAINTER
b Arnegard, NDak, Apr 27, 38. *Study:* Minneapolis Col of Art & Design, BFA; Univ Minn. *Work:* Nat Mus Am Art, Washington, DC; Honolulu Acad Art; Minn Mus Art, St Paul; Philadelphia Mus Art; Walker Art Ctr, Minneapolis; and others. *Exhib:* Brooklyn Print Show, Brooklyn Mus, 76 & Eight West Coast Printmakers, 78; Plains Art Mus, Moorhead, Minn, 76 & 78; Boston Printmakers Nat Exhib, De Cordova Mus, 77 & 79; Tokyo Cent Mus Art, Japan, 78; Ten West Coast Printmakers, RI Sch Design Mus; Rockford Int, Ill, 81; and others. *Awards:* Juror's Award, Rockford Int, Ill, 81; Merit Award, 62nd Nat Exhib, Springfield Art League, Mass, 81; Purchase Award, Boston Printmakers 35th Nat Print Exhib, 83; plus others. *Bibliog:* Robert McDonald (auth), Four West Coast woodcut artists, Graphics, 8-9/79. *Mem:* Boston Printmakers; Philadelphia Print Club; World Print Coun. *Media:* Oil, Watercolor; Woodcut. *Dealer:* Assoc American Artists 663 Fifth Ave New York NY 10022; C G Rein Galleries Commerce Bldg St Paul MN 55101. *Mailing Add:* 4153 Crest Rd Pebble Beach CA 93953

MORTON, RICHARD H
PAINTER, GRAPHIC ARTIST
b Dallas Tex, Aug 8, 21. *Study:* Pratt Inst, cert, 42; Oklahoma City Univ, BA, 57; Univ Tulsa, MA, 57; Inst Allende, Mexico, MFA, 68. *Work:* Okla Art Ctr, Oklahoma City; Univ Tulsa, Okla; Northeast Mo State Univ, Kirksville. *Exhib:* Watercolor USA, Springfield Art Mus, Mo; Eight State Exhib, Okla Art Ctr; Bicentennial Art Show, Mus Great Plains, Lawton, Okla; Okla Bicentennial Competition, State Capitol, Oklahoma City; Bicentennial Competition Selections, Kennedy Ctr, Washington, DC. *Pos:* Illusr, US Army, Ft Sill, Okla, 76-79, graphic artist, 79-81; self-employed artist, Aberdeen, Md, 81- *Teaching:* Instr design, Southern Ill Univ, Carbondale,

55-59; asst dean, Columbus Col Art & Design, Ohio, 59-60; asst prof design, Cent State Univ, 61-65; assoc prof painting, Northeast Mo State Univ, Kirksville, 65-72; art workshops, Southwest US, 72-76. *Awards:* John Marin Mem Award, Watercolor USA, 74; Award of Excellence, Okla Bicentennial Competition, State Capitol, Oklahoma City, 76; and others. *Mem:* Hartford Artists Asn Md; Art Guild Md. *Media:* Watercolor. *Mailing Add:* 623 W Bel Air Ave Aberdeen MD 21001

MORTON, ROBERT ALAN
PUBLISHER, WRITER
b Jersey City, NJ, May 20, 34. *Study:* Dartmouth Col, BA, 55. *Pos:* Series ed, Time-Life Libr of Art, New York, 66-70; ed dir, New York Graphic Soc, Inc, 70-73; ed in chief, Harry N Abrams, Inc, 76-78, dir spec proj, 78- *Teaching:* Western Conn State Col, 80-81; Int Ctr Photography, 82-83. *Res:* American decorative arts. *Publ:* Auth, Southern Antiques and Folk Art, Oxmoor House, 76. *Mailing Add:* Box 16 Redding Ridge CT 00876

MOSBY, DEWEY FRANKLIN
MUSEUM DIRECTOR, HISTORIAN
b San Augustine, Tex, Jan 2, 42. *Study:* Lamar Univ, BS, 63; Univ Calif, Los Angeles, MA, 69; Harvard Univ, PhD, 74. *Collections Arranged:* Degas in the Detroit Inst of Arts, Detroit Inst Arts, 74; French Painting 1774-1830: The Age of Revolution, 75 & Master Paintings from the Hermitage and the State Russian Museum Leningrad, 75; Cinco Siglos de Obras maestras de la pintura en colecciones norteamericanas cedidas en prestamo a Costa Rica, 78; The Second Empire: Art in France under Napoleon III, 1852-1870, Detroit, 79; Gods, Saints & Heroes: Dutch Paintings in the Age of Rembrandt, Detroit, 81. *Pos:* Cur European art, Detroit Inst Arts, 74-81; dir, Picker Art Gallery, Colgate Univ, Hamilton, NY, 81- *Teaching:* Asst prof art hist, State Univ NY Buffalo, 73-74; asst prof art hist, Harvard Univ, summer 74. *Awards:* Chevalier, Ordre des Arts et des Lettres, 79; Silver Medal of Merit, Order of Costantiniano Di S Giorgio, 81. *Mem:* Col Art Asn Am; Am Asn Mus. *Res:* 18th and 19th century art with an emphasis on Alexandre-Gabriel Decamps (1803-60). *Publ:* Contribr, The Homburger Collection (catalog), Fogg Art Mus, 71; auth, Master Drawings, Vol 12, 74; auth, article in Arts Mag, 9/75; auth, Alexandre-Gabriel Decamps 1803-1860, 2 Vols, New York, 77; auth, The Figure in Nineteenth-Century French Painting, Detroit, 79; and others. *Mailing Add:* Picker Art Gallery Colgate Univ Hamilton NY 13346

MOSCA, AUGUST
PAINTER, INSTRUCTOR
b Naples, Italy, Aug 19, 07; US citizen. *Study:* Yale Sch of Fine Arts; Pratt Inst; Art Students League; Grand Cent Art Sch. *Work:* Libr of Congress, Washington, DC; Butler Inst of Am Art, Youngstown, Ohio; Brooklyn Mus; Forham Univ; New York Pub Libr. *Comn:* Portrait of Heywood Brown, Newspaper Guild of New York, 55 & Newspaper Guild of Am, Washington, DC, 57. *Exhib:* Portrait of America, Metrop Mus of Art, New York, 43; Calif Palace of the Legion of Honor, 45; Brooklyn Mus Watercolor Int Ann, 59; Butler Inst of Am Art, Youngstown, Ohio, 62; one-man shows, Harry Salpeter Gallery, New York, 57, Far Gallery, New York, 74, St Michaels Col, Winooski, Vt, 74; St Mary's Col, Md, 76; and others. *Teaching:* Instr art & drawing, Pratt Inst, Brooklyn, NY, 55; instr art & painting, Tuxedo Park Sch, NY, 68-72; instr art, drawing & painting, pvt studio. *Awards:* Calif Palace of the Legion of Honor Silver Medal, 45; Audubon Artists Presidents Award, 76; Soc Am Graphic Artists Purchase Award, 77. *Bibliog:* George A Perret (auth), August Mosca, New York Cult Ctr, 73. *Mem:* Painters & Sculptors Soc NJ (pres, 72-75); Audubon Artists. *Media:* Multimedia. *Publ:* Auth, Our artists and writers, Suffolk Times, 75; auth, Art of Post-impressism, M Grumbacher, 76; auth, Artist explains Lithography, Shelter Island Reporter, 77. *Mailing Add:* Shelter Island NY 11964

MOSCATT, PAUL N
PAINTER, INSTRUCTOR
b Brooklyn, NY, July 9, 31. *Study:* Cooper Union Art Sch; Yale Univ Sch Fine Arts, BFA & MFA. *Work:* Univ Bridgeport, Conn; Yale Univ Art Dept; Earlham Col, Richmond, Ind; Cincinnati Art Mus; Allegheny Col, Meadville, Pa. *Exhib:* One-man shows, Univ Md, Baltimore, 70, Towson State Col, Md, 70, Portrait Drawings of the American Indian, Md Inst Col Art, 73 & Interiors & Nudes, C Grimaldis Gallery, Baltimore, Md, 78; Hassam Exhib, Am Acad Arts & Lett, 79. *Teaching:* Instr painting & drawing, Univ Bridgeport, 62-64; instr painting & drawing, Art Acad Cincinnati, 64-66; instr painting & drawing, Md Inst Col Art, 67-, chmn, painting dept, 77-79. *Media:* Oil, Acrylic. *Mailing Add:* Md Inst Col of Art 1300 Mt Royal Ave Baltimore MD 21217

MOSELEY, RALPH SESSIONS
PAINTER
b Kingston, NY, June 5, 41. *Study:* Williams Col, BA; Hunter Col, MA. *Work:* Whitney Mus Am Art, New York; Aldrich Mus, Ridgefield, Conn. *Exhib:* Ann, 69 & Lyrical Abstraction, 70, Whitney Mus Am Art; Aldrich Mus, 70; one-man show, A M Sachs Gallery, New York, NY, 78. *Media:* Acrylic. *Mailing Add:* 438 Broome St New York NY 10013

MOSELEY, SPENCER ALTEMONT
PAINTER
b Bellingham, Wash, July 18, 25. *Study:* Univ Wash, BA, 48, MFA, 51; Ecole Fernand Leger, Paris, 49. *Work:* Seattle Art Mus, Wash; Henry Art Gallery, Univ Wash. *Exhib:* Kobe Exchange Show, Japan, 65; Art Across America, San Francisco Mus Art, 65; The West--80 Contemporaries, Univ Ariz Art Gallery, Tucson, 67; 73rd Western Ann, Denver Art Mus, 71; Pac Cities Loan Exhib, Auckland Art Mus, NZ, 71; and others. *Teaching:* Dir, Sch Art, Univ

Wash, 66-77. *Awards:* First Prize, Pac Northwest Arts & Crafts Fair, 65; Ford Found Purchase Award, 66; Purchase Prize, 54th Ann Northwest Painting & Sculpture, 68; and others. *Bibliog:* Carraher (auth), Optical Illusions and the Visual Arts, 66 & Proctor (auth), Principles of Pattern, 69, Reinhold; Gombrich & Gregory (auth), Illusion in Art and Nature, Duckworth & Co, 74. *Mem:* Nat Coun Art Adminr; Col Art Asn; Nat Asn Sch of Art. *Media:* Oil, Acrylic. *Publ:* Coauth, Crafts Design, Wadsworth, 52; auth, History of Painting in the Western World, Frontier Press, 64; auth, Wendell Brazeau: A Search for Form, Univ Wash, 77. *Mailing Add:* 4312 Baker NW Seattle WA 98107

MOSER, BARRY
GRAPHIC ARTIST, PRINTMAKER
b Chattanooga, Tenn, Oct 15, 40. *Study:* Auburn Univ; Univ Tenn Chattanooga, with George Cress; also studied with Leonard Baskin & Jack Coughlin. *Work:* Brit Mus, London, Eng; Boston Athenaeum, Mass; Libr Cong, Washington, DC; Harvard Univ, Cambridge, Mass; Cambridge Univ, Eng. *Exhib:* Boston Printmakers, Waltham, Mass, 72; one-man shows, Berkshire Mus, Pittsfield, Mass, 73 & Boston Athenaeum, Mass, 76; Los Angeles Nat Print Show, Calif, 74; Libr Cong Nat Print Exhib, Washington, DC, 75-76; History of Printed Books, San Francisco Pub Libr, Calif, 76; 4th Int Exhibit of Botanical Art, Hunt Inst, Carnegie-Mellon Univ, Pittsburgh, Pa, 77-78. *Collections Arranged:* New York Pub Libr; Swarthmore Col, Pa; Harvard Univ, Cambridge, Mass; Univ Iowa, Ames (collection of illus bks); Smith Col, 76. *Teaching:* Head studio art, Williston Northampton Sch, Easthampton, Mass, 67- *Awards:* Second Prize, Cape Cod Ann, 71; Award of Merit, New Hampshire Int, 74. *Mem:* Am Printing Hist Asn. *Media:* Ink; Wood. *Publ:* Illusr, Chelmaxions, David R Godine, 77; illusr, Song of Songs, Harcourt Brace Jovanovich, 77; illusr, Thistles & Thorns, Abbatior Ed, Univ Nebr, 77; illusr, Moby Dick, Arion Press, 78; illusr, The Divine Comedy of Dante, Inferno, 80, Alice's Adventures in Wonderland, 82 & Through the Looking Glass, 83, Univ Calif Press. *Mailing Add:* c/o Wenniger Graphics 174 A Newbury St Boston MA 02116

MOSER, CHARLOTTE
CRITIC, WRITER
b Texarkana, Tex, June 19, 47. *Study:* Univ Tex Austin, MA, BA(art) & BA; Sweet Briar Col; Kansas City Art Inst, Inst d'Art et Archeol, Paris. *Pos:* Art critic, Houston Post, Tex, 73-74; art critic, Houston Chronicle, Tex, 74-79; corresp, Art News, New York, 76-; ed Leader Newspapers, formerly. *Teaching:* Lectr new frontiers in southwestern art, Univ Houston, 77. *Awards:* Nat Endowment Arts Critic Fel, 77. *Mem:* Asn Int des Critiques d'Art; Visual Arts Panel, Cult Arts Coun Houston. *Res:* Contemporary and historical art trends in Texas, Southwestern United States and the deep South. *Publ:* Auth, Deep in the art of Texas, Ms Mag, 2/77; auth, Houston's cultural leadership, 2/77 & auth, New Mexico: Psychic elbow room, 12/77, Art News; auth, Richard Thompson (catalog essay), Tyler Mus, 3/78; auth, Women art patrons in Women in Texas, Univ Tex Press, 79. *Mailing Add:* 723 Monticello Pl Evanston IL 62208

MOSER, JOANN
CURATOR, HISTORIAN
b Chicago, Ill. *Study:* Smith Col, BA(art hist), 69; Univ Wis, Madison, MA(art hist), 72, PhD(art hist), 76. *Collections Arranged:* Atelier 17 (50 yr retrospective traveling exhib to five mus; auth, catalog), 77-78. *Pos:* Cur of collections, Univ Iowa Mus Art, 76-, actg dir, 80- *Awards:* Ford Fel, Dept Art Hist, Univ Wis, 71-73; Kress Fel, Nat Gallery Art, Washington, DC, 75-76. *Mem:* Iowa Mus Asn; Col Art Asn; Midwest Art Hist Soc; Am Assoc Mus. *Res:* Prints and twentieth century art. *Publ:* Auth, Eaux-fortes Theatrales pour Monsieur G....by Louis Marcoussis, Elvehjem Art Ctr Bulletin, 74; contribr, Mauricio Lasansky and Intaglio Printmaking (catalog), Univ Iowa Mus Art, 76; auth, The impact of Stanley William Hayter on Post-war American art, Archives Am Art J, Vol 18, No 1. *Mailing Add:* 3058 Hastings Ave Iowa City IA 52240

MOSER, JULON
PAINTER
b Schenectady, NY. *Study:* Binghamton Fine Arts, 25, with Frank Taylor Bowers; Chouinard Sch Art, 29-30, with Pattie Patterson; Univ Calif, Berkeley, 43-44, with Wessels; Scripps Col, 47, grad sch with Millard Sheets; pvt study with Nicolai Fechin. *Work:* More than 575 paintings in pvt & pub collections. *Exhib:* Golden Gate Int, Treasure Island, San Francisco, 39; Calif Nat Watercolor Soc Current Exhib, Nat Acad Design, 72 & Ann Exhib, Laguna Beach Gallery, 72; Invitational Exhib touring Sweden, 72-73; and others. *Awards:* Purchase Award, City Santa Paula, Calif, 76; Second Award, Oxnard Art Asn Exhib, 77; Award for Oil, San Bernadino Art Mus, 83; and others. *Mem:* Calif Nat Watercolor Soc (rec secy, 72-73); Women Painters of the West (pres, 56-58, corresp secy, 72-73, mem bd, 78); Los Angeles Art Asn. *Media:* Watercolor, Oil. *Dealer:* Goldfield Galleries Los Angeles CA; Housefield Gallery Oxnard CA 93031. *Mailing Add:* 288 Homer Ave Ventura CA 93003

MOSER, REX
ADMINISTRATOR
b Webster City, Iowa, Dec 4, 47. *Study:* Univ Santa Clara, BA(hist), 70; Univ Calif Berkeley, BA(art hist), 72, MA(art hist), 74. *Work:* Art Inst Chicago; Walker Art Ctr, Minneapolis; Los Angeles Co Mus Art, Los Angeles; Nat Gallery Art, DC; Univ Calif Art Mus, Berkeley. *Pos:* Rockefeller Fel, Walker Art Ctr, Minneapolis, 74-76; cur educ, Los Angeles Co Mus Art, Los Angeles, 76-79; exec dir mus educ, Art Inst Chicago, 79- *Awards:* Phi Beta Kappa Award, Phi Beta Kappa Soc, 72. *Mem:* Am Asn Mus; Col Art Asn. *Res:*

Iconography of Roman Imperial portraiture, especially Hadrian. *Publ:* Auth, A Re-dating of the Portraits Busts of the Emperor Hadrian, Univ Calif, 74; auth, Anti-gravity study: a video work by Nam June Paik, 76 & auth, Alluvial fan: a water and sand sculpture by Andrew Leicester, 76, Design Quart; auth, New film reviews, Art & Cinema, 79; auth, Picasso: The American connection, Nat Arts Guide, 80; auth, Pocketguide to the Art Institute of Chicago, 83. *Mailing Add:* Art Inst Chicago Michigan Ave & Adams St Chicago IL 60603

MOSES, BETTE J
PAINTER, DEALER
b Blackwell, Okla. *Study:* Northwestern State Univ, Alva, Okla, BFA, 46; Inst Allende San Miguel, Guanajuato, Mexico, with James Pinto, 74-75. *Exhib:* Smoky Hill, Ft Hays Univ, Kans, 74 & Women Aware Show, 75; Am Painters in Paris, Centre Int de Paris, France, 75-76; Kans I, Hutchinson Art Asn, Kans, 78; Kans Pub TV Juried, Wichita, 78. *Collections Arranged:* Soc Prof Painters, West, State Capitol, Topeka, Kans, 78-80 & Wichita Art Mus, Kans, 79-81. *Pos:* Founder, Art Inc, Barton Co Community & Col, 70, pres, 71-72 & bd adv, 78-81; owner, Bette Moses Art Gallery, 75- *Awards:* First & second prizes, mixed media, Art Inc, Barton Community & Col, 71-73; first prize, Prof Painters, Russell Original Art Revue, 73; and others. *Mem:* Kans Soc Prof Painters, West; Int Soc Painters; Kans Watercolor Soc. *Media:* Mixed. *Specialty:* Promote work of talented unknown state and area artists, particularly those working in an unusual manner. *Mailing Add:* 2110 Tenth Great Bend KS 67530

MOSES, ED
PAINTER
b Long Beach, Calif, 1926. *Study:* Univ Calif, Los Angeles, MA; Tamarind Lithography grant. *Work:* Art Inst Chicago; Corcoran Gallery Art, Washington, DC; Pasadena Mus, Calif; Walker Art Ctr, Minneapolis, Minn; San Francisco Mus Art. *Exhib:* Mus Mod Art, New York, 69; Corcoran Gallery Art Biennial, Washington, DC, 71; Current Am Artists, Art Inst Chicago Ann, 72, 70th Am Exhib, 73; one-man shows, Los Angeles Co Mus Art, 76, Corcoran Gallery, Los Angeles, 79-81 & Janus Gallery, 83; Brooklyn Mus, 77; Mus Mod Art, Paris, 82; and others. *Teaching:* Instr art, Univ Calif, Irvine, 68-71; Skowhegan Sch Painting & Sculpture, 83. *Awards:* Nat Endowment Arts Grant, 76; Guggenheim Fel, 80. *Bibliog:* J Loring (auth), Print as surface, Arts Mag, 9/73; P Derfner (auth), article in Art Int, 4/74; article in Artforum, 5/74. *Mailing Add:* c/o Emmerich Gallery 41 E 57th St New York NY 10022

MOSES, FORREST (LEE), JR
PAINTER
b Danville, Va, May, 1934. *Study:* Washington & Lee Univ, BA, 56; Pratt Inst, 60-62; Houston Mus Sch Fine Arts, 63-64. *Exhib:* Abilene Fine Arts Mus, Tex, 74; Tyler Mus, Tex, 74; Okla Art Ctr, Oklahoma City, 75; Monotypes, Ill State Univ, Normal, 79; NMex Mus Fine Arts, Santa Fe, 79. *Teaching:* Instr drawing, Pratt Inst, 61-62; instr drawing & watercolor, Univ Houston, 69. *Awards:* Selected Juror's Award & Museum Purchase, Mus NMex Biennial, 74. *Media:* Oil. *Dealer:* Watson/de Nagy 1106 Berthea Houston TX 77006; Tibor de Nagy 29 W 57th St New York NY 10019. *Mailing Add:* 837 El Caminito Santa Fe NM 87501

MOSKOWITZ, IRA
PAINTER, PRINTMAKER
b Turka, Poland, March 15, 12; US citizen. *Study:* Art Students League, 30-33. *Work:* Metrop Mus Art & Whitney Mus Am Art, New York; Nat Gallery Art, Washington, DC; Biblioteque Nationale, Paris. *Exhib:* One-man shows, Bernhard Crystal Galleries, New York, 67; Waddington Galleries, Montreal, Can, 69, traveling show, Paris, Scotland, Ireland, 74 & Weintraub Gallery, New York, 79; Drawings of Ira Moskowitz, Haifa Mus, Israel, 69; 45 Yrs of Graphics (retrospective), Brooks Mem Art Gallery, Memphis, 75; John Davis Hatch Collection, Nat Gallery Art, Washington, DC, 79. *Pos:* Ed Fine Arts Books, Shorewood Publ, New York, 55-62; dir publs, Am Art Collections Ltd, 83. *Awards:* Am at War, prize for Lithograph, 44; Libr Congress Award, Pennell Show, 45; fel creative art, Guggenheim, 43. *Bibliog:* John Davis Hatch (auth), The Drawings of Ira Moskowitz, Shorewood Publ, 66; Isaac Bashevis Singer (auth), Reaches of Heaven, Landmark Publ & Ferrar, Strauss & Giroux, 80; Joseph S Czestochowski (auth), 55 Years of Drawings of Ira Moskowitz, Alpine Fine Arts Collections Ltd, 84. *Media:* All Media. *Publ:* Coauth, La Mythe de Pygmalion, Mourlot, Paris, 66; ed, Great Drawings of All Time, Am, German, English, Italian, Swedish, Japanese, 62 & 75; coauth, Hasidim, Crown Publ, 73; coauth, A Little Boy in Search of God, Doubleday, 76; coauth (with Isaac Bashevis Singer), Satan In Goray, Sweetwater Eds, 82. *Dealer:* Brewster Gallery 41 W 57th St New York NY 10019. *Mailing Add:* 390 W End Ave New York NY 10024

MOSKOWITZ, ROBERT S
PAINTER
b New York, NY, June 20, 35. *Work:* Mus Mod Art & Whitney Mus Am Art, New York; Albright-Knox Art Gallery, Buffalo; Rose Art Mus, Brandeis Univ, Waltham, Mass. *Exhib:* Art of Assemblage, Mus Mod Art, New York, 61; Whitney Mus Am Art Ann, 69 & New Image Painting, 78; Painting the 80's, Grey Art Gallery, New York, 79; one-man shows, Daniel Weinberg Gallery, San Francisco, 79, Margo Levin Gallery, Los Angeles, 79 & La Jolla Mus Contemp Art, Calif, 79. *Awards:* Guggenheim Fel, 67; Award, NY State Coun Arts, 73; Award, Nat Endowment Arts, 75. *Mailing Add:* 81 Leonard St New York NY 10013

MOSKOWITZ, SHIRLEY (MRS JACOB W GRUBER)
PAINTER, COLLAGE ARTIST
b Houston, Tex, Aug 4, 20. *Study:* Mus Sch Art, Houston; Rice Univ, BA, 41; Oberlin Col, MA, 42; Philadelphia Col Art, 74-76; also with Morris Davidson, New York. *Work:* Allen Mus Art, Oberlin, Ohio; Museo Roma, Italy; Free Libr of Philadelphia; Robert I Kahn Mus, Houston, Tex; William Penn Mus, Harrisburg, Pa. *Exhib:* One-man shows, Paley Libr, Temple Univ, Philadelphia, 70 & Nocara, Italy, 77; William Penn Mem Mus, 74-75; Univ Pa, Philadelphia, 81. *Teaching:* Instr art hist, Univ Tex, Austin, spring 43; lectr art, Houston Pub Schs, 43-46; dir art, Oberlin Pub Schs, 46-47. *Awards:* IBM Painting Prize, Expressions, Earth Art III, Philadelphia Civic Ctr, 79; Mid-Atlantic Regional Collage Show Prize, Univ Del, 79; Watercolor Prize, Artists Equity Triennial, Philadelphia, 81; and others. *Mem:* Philadelphia Watercolor Club (secy, 68-70); Print Club; Philadelphia Art Alliance; Am Color Print Soc; Philadelphia Chap Artists Equity (secy, 80-82); and others. *Media:* Watercolor, Acrylic; Ink, Intaglio. *Dealer:* Assoc Am Artists' Philadelphia Print Gallery. *Mailing Add:* 2211 Delancey Pl Philadelphia PA 19103

MOSLEY, ZACK T
ILLUSTRATOR, CARTOONIST
b Hickory, Okla, Dec 12, 06. *Study:* Chicago Acad Fine Arts, 26-27; Art Inst Chicago, 27-28. *Pos:* Creator syndicated comic strip, Smilin' Jack, Chicago Tribune-New York News, 33-73. *Mem:* Nat Cartoonists Soc. *Publ:* Auth & illus, Brave Coward Zack, 76, Hot Rock Glide, 79 & De-Icers Galore, 80. *Mailing Add:* PO Box 375 Stuart FL 33495

MOSS, GARY WILLIAM
PAINTER
b Minneapolis, Minn, Dec 15, 46. *Study:* Minn Col Art Design, with Harlem Holland, 66-67, BFA, 68. *Work:* US Marine Corps, Washington, DC; current work in pvt collections. *Exhib:* Portrait of Vietnam, traveling, Smithsonian Inst & US Marine Corps, 71-72; Bird Art, Smithsonian Inst, 78-80, Leigh Yawkey Woodson Mus, Wausau, Wisc, 79-81 & traveling, Royal Scottish Acad, Edinburgh, British Mus, London & Mus Art, Carnegie Inst, 82. *Awards:* Artist of Year, US Marine Corps, 70; First Place Duckstamp, Minn State, 83. *Bibliog:* S H McGarry (auth), article, SW Art, 11/80. *Media:* Oil, Watercolor. *Dealer:* Collectors Covey Dallas TX; Wild Wings Lake City MN 55041. *Mailing Add:* Rt 2 Box 485 Cambridge MN 55008

MOSS, IRENE
PAINTER
b Eperjes, Czech; US citizen. *Study:* Brooklyn Mus Sch Art; also with Moses Soyer & Dmitri Romanofsky, New York. *Work:* Akron Art Inst, Ohio; Rose Art Mus, Brandeis Univ, Mass; New Brit Mus Am Art, Conn; Norfolk Mus, Va. *Exhib:* Ft Worth Art Ctr, Tex, 68; Rochester Mem Art Gallery, NY, 68; one-woman show, Suffolk Mus, Stony Brook, NY, 71; Stamford Mus, Conn, 72; Philadelphia Civic Ctr Mus, 74. *Pos:* Co-ed, Feminist Art J, 72-73. *Bibliog:* John Gruen (auth), Friday tour of art, World J Tribune, 66; Jacqueline Barnitz (auth), Images, 68 & Gordon Brown (auth), Irene Moss & the repetition of the natural image, 3/74, Arts Mag; and others. *Dealer:* Peter Rose Gallery 200 E 58th St New York NY 10022. *Mailing Add:* 271-15H Grand Cent Pkwy Floral Park NY 11005

MOSS, JACQUELINE
HISTORIAN, EDUCATOR
b New York, NY. *Study:* Univ Bridgeport, Conn; New York Univ; Cooper Union, New York, cert, 50, BFA, 75; Queen's Col, New York, MA(art hist), 80. *Collections Arranged:* American Women Painters (auth, catalog), Housatonic Community Col, 76. *Pos:* Cur educ, Aldrich Mus Contemp Art, Ridgefield, Conn, 66-80; art critic & spec corresp, The Advocate, Stamford, Conn, 81- & Greenwich Time, Conn, currently. *Teaching:* Chairperson, Dept Art, Daycroft Sch, Greenwich, Conn, 60-75; instr art hist, Univ Bridgeport, Conn, 69 & 80-82 & Housatonic Community Col, Bridgeport, Conn, 72-73; instr art hist, Housatonic Community Col, Bridgeport, Conn, 72-73. *Awards:* Conn Comn Arts Grant, 78. *Mem:* Col Art Asn; Women's Caucus Art. *Res:* Modernist; concentration on geometric abstraction and constructivism of the 1930s and 1940s and its connection with the contemporary period (post World War II); contemporary art outside the United States; the women's movement. *Publ:* Auth, Anatomy of a brushstroke, Christian Sci Mon, 74; contribr, Sculpture 76, Greenwich Arts Coun, 76; auth, Subjects and objects, Conn Comn Arts, 78; auth, Gertrude Greene: Constructions of 1930s and 1940s, Arts Mag, 81; contribr, Abstract Painting and Sculpture in America: 1927-1944, 83. *Mailing Add:* 131 Davenport Ridge Lane Stamford CT 06903

MOSS, JOE (FRANCIS)
SCULPTOR, PAINTER
b Kincheloe, WVa, Jan 26, 33. *Study:* WVa Univ, AB, 51, MA, 60. *Work:* Del Art, Wilmington; Johnson Mus, Ithaca, NY; Martin Fine Villa, Art in Pub Places, Miami, Fla; and others. *Comn:* Sound sculpture, Martin Fine Villa, Miami, Fla, 80; and others. *Exhib:* Members Exhib, Mus Mod Art, New York, 65; one-man shows, J B Speed Mus, Louisville, Ky, 77 & Madison Square Park, New York, 80; Leading Contemp Sculptors Exhib, Sculpture Now, New York, 79; Beginnings Exhib, Laumeier Int Sculpture Park, St Louis, Mo, 79; Soundins, Neuberger Mus, Purchase, New York; Sculpture on Shoreline Sites, Wards Island, New York, 82; and other group & one-man shows. *Pos:* Vis res fel, Ctr Advan Visual Studies, Mass Inst Technol, Cambridge, 73. *Teaching:* Assoc prof art, WVa Univ, 60-70; vis prof, Univ Md, summer 67; prof, Univ Del, 70- *Awards:* Prize for Environ Design, Three Rivers Arts Festival, Pittsburgh, 68; Sculpture Award, Appalachian Corridors Exhib, Charleston, 70. *Bibliog:* Alan Gerstle (auth), Joe Moss, Arts Mag; James Kelly (auth), The Sculptural Idea, Third Ed; Quintessence, Alternative Spaces Residency Prog, Dayton, Ohio & Wright State Univand others. *Media:* Plastic, Metal. *Dealer:* Max Hutchinson Gallery 138 Greene St New York NY 10012. *Mailing Add:* 801 Valley Rd Newark DE 19711

MOSS, JOEL C
PAINTER, EDUCATOR
US Citizen. *Study:* Ft Hays Kans State Col, BS, 38; George Peabody Col, MA, 42; Columbia Univ, EdD, 53. *Work:* Wichita Art Mus, Kans; Wichita Asn Gallery; Gallery Art, Hastings Col, Nebr; Hutchinson Art Asn, Kans; over 500 paintings in pvt collections. *Exhib:* Nelson Gallery Mid Am Exhib, Kansas City, Mo, 55; San Francisco Art Mus, 56; Joslyn Mus, Omaha, Nebr, 65; Watercolor USA, Springfield, Mo, 68; Wichita Art Mus Artist Ann, 70; and others. *Teaching:* Instr art, Parsons Jr Col, Kans, 39-42; prof art, Ft Hays Kans State Univ, 46-77, chmn dept, 50-73; retired. *Awards:* First Purchase Prize, Wichita Art Asn Statewide Watercolor, 69 & 70; Amsden Award & Cult Arts Award, Kans Watercolor Soc, 71; Gov Artist, Kans Distinquished Artist, 81-82. *Mem:* Kans Watercolor Soc (bd dirs, 68-70); Kans Cult Arts. *Media:* Watercolor. *Dealer:* Sign of the Acron Gallery Wichita KS; Geo Nix Gallery Colorado Springs CO. *Mailing Add:* 408 W Fourth Hays KS 67601

MOSS, KAREN CANNER
PAINTER, EDUCATOR
b Boston, Mass, May 2, 44. *Study:* RI Sch Design, BFA, 66; Tufts Univ, Boston Mus Sch, MFA, 74. *Work:* Boston Mus Fine Arts, Mass; Addison Gallery Am Art, Andover, Mass; Vassar Col Art Gallery, Poughkeepsie, NY; Rose Art Mus, Brandeis Univ, Waltham, Mass; Bristol Community Col, Fall River, Mass. *Comn:* Outdoor mural, Mass Bay Transportation Authority, Boston, Mass, 77; ceramic tile mural, First Nat Bank Boston, 83. *Exhib:* Edinburgh Festival, Queens Col, Scotland, 74; Works on Paper, Fogg Mus, Harvard Univ, Cambridge, Mass, 74; Primitive Presence in the '70's, Vassar Col, Poughkeepsie, NY, 75; Boston Watercolor Today, Boston Mus Fine Arts, 76; one-woman show, Addison Gallery Am Art, Andover, Mass, 76; Contemp Issues: Works on Paper by Women, traveling show to Los Angeles, Salt Lake City & Houston, 77; Prints & Drawings, Mus Mod Art, New York, 78; one-woman show, Kathryn Markel Gallery, New York, 83; and others. *Pos:* Artist, trustee & rep, Boston Visual Artists Union, Inst Contemp Art, Boston, Mass, 71-73. *Teaching:* Instr drawing, Boston Mus Fine Arts Sch, 83. *Awards:* Blanche E Coleman Award, 72; First Prize for Watercolor, Silvermine Art Guild, 73; Finalist in State, Mass Arts & Humanities Found, 76-77. *Bibliog:* Wolf Kahn (auth), The subject matter in new realism, Am Artist, 11/79; Pam Allara (auth), Boston: shedding its inferiority complex, Art News, 11/79; Sarah McFadden (auth), Report from Boston, Art Am, 5/83. *Mem:* Boston Visual Artists Union. *Media:* Painting. *Dealer:* Kathryn Markel Fine Art 50 W 57th St New York NY 10019. *Mailing Add:* 141 Pearl Boston MA 02110

MOSS, MILTON
PAINTER
b New York, NY. *Study:* Cooper Union; Ecoles Beaux Arts, Paris. *Work:* Phoenix Mus Fine Arts, Ariz; Norfolk Mus Art & Sci, Va; Miami Mus Mod Art, Fla; Univ Maine; Houston Mus. *Exhib:* Butler Inst Am Art, Youngstown, Ohio, 63; one-man shows, Gallery Die Drie Hendricken, Amsterdam, Netherlands, 65; Harry Salpeter Gallery, New York, 67; Wickersham Gallery, New York, 69 & Syosset Pub Libr, New York, 71. *Mailing Add:* c/o Harbor Gallery 43 Main St Cold Spring Harbor NY 11724

MOTHERWELL, ROBERT
PAINTER, PRINTMAKER
b Aberdeen, Wash, Jan 24, 15. *Study:* Stanford Univ, BA, 36; Harvard Univ Grad Sch Philos, 37; Columbia Univ, 40, with Meyer Schapiro. *Work:* Mus Mod Art, Metrop Mus Art & Whitney Mus Am Art, New York; San Francisco Art Mus; Tate Gallery Art, London; and others. *Comn:* Mural, J F Kennedy Fed Bldg, Boston, 66; diptych, S Edelstone, Chicago, 71; A la Pintura (suite of aquatints), Universal Art Ed, Long Island, 72; mural, Univ Iowa Art Mus, Iowa City, 73; mural, Nat Gallery, Washington, DC. *Exhib:* Retrospective, Mus Mod Art, New York, 65; Collage Exhib, Whitney Mus Am Art, 68; Recent Paintings, with Matisse Sculpture, Walker Art Ctr, Minneapolis, 72; Robert Motherwell's A la Pintura: The Making of a Book, Metrop Mus, New York, 72; Stedelijk Mus, Netherlands, 80; Mazur Mus, Monroe, La, 80; Roanoke Mus, Va, 80; Cleveland Mus, Ohio, 80; William Benton Mus, Storrs, Conn, 80; Graphics 1 & Graphics 2, Boston, 80; Mus Mod Art, New York, 80; M Knoedler & Co, New York, 81; and others. *Pos:* Conroy Fel, St Paul's Sch, NH, 70; educ adv, John Simon Guggenheim Found, formerly; art dir, Partisan Rev, 62-65; adv ed, Am Scholar, Washington, DC, 68-; ed, Documents of 20th Century Art, 68- Belgian Art Critics Prize, Brussels, 66; La Grande Medaille de Vermeil de la Villa de Paris, 77; Gold Medal, Pa Acad Fine Art, 79. *Teaching:* Instr painting, Black Mountain Col, 45 & 51; prof painting, Hunter Col, 50-58, distinguished prof, 71-72; Columbia Univ, 64-65. *Awards:* Belgian Art Critics Prize, Brussels, 66; La Grande Medaille de Vermeil de la Villa de Paris, France, 77; Gold Medal, Pa Acad Fine Art, 79. *Bibliog:* Bryan Robertson & Octavio Paz (auth), Robert Motherwell paintings & collages 1967-70, Galerie I M Erker, 71; H H Arnason (auth), Robert Motherwell, Abrams, 77; E A Carmean, Jr (auth), American Art at Mid-Century, Nat Gallery Art, 78. *Mem:* Smithsonian Inst; Nat Collection Fine Arts; fel Royal Soc Arts. *Media:* Mixed; Aquatint, Lithography. *Dealer:* M Knoedler & Co 19 E 70th St New York NY 10021; Andre Emmerich Gallery 41 E 57th St New York NY 10022. *Mailing Add:* 909 North St Greenwich CT 06830

MOUFARREGE, NICOLAS A
PAINTER, CRITIC
b Alexandria, Egypt, Mar 23, 47; Lebanese & US citizen. *Study:* Am Univ Beirut, Lebanon, MSc(Goethe Inst Scholar), 69; Harvard Univ, MA(Fulbright Grant), 70. *Work:* Mus Arts Decoratifs, Paris; Mus Chateau d'Annecy, France. *Exhib:* The New York Times Front Page, PS1, Long Island City, 82; On Pins and Needles, Gabrielle Bryers, New York, 83; solo exhib, Swart Gallery, Amsterdam, 83; Fun Gallery Spring Invitational, New York, 83; Artists-Critics, White Columns, New York, 83. *Collections Arranged:* A Flag for the 80s (auth, catalog), PS1, 83; Intoxication (auth, catalog), Monique Knowlton Gallery, New York, 83; Extra-Critical Role (auth, catalog), Gabrielle Bryers Gallery, New York, 83. *Bibliog:* Jean Marie Dunoyer (auth), D'apres nature, Le Monde, Paris, 17/12/78; Kim Levin (auth), N A Moufarrege, The New York Times Front Page, Village Voice, 11/2/82; Grace Glueck (auth), One man's biennial assembles 102 artists, New York Times, 4/15/83. *Media:* Paint and Thread. *Publ:* Auth, X equals zero, everybody wins at tic-tac-toe, Arts Mag, 2/83; auth, East Village, Flash Art, 3/83; auth, Intoxication; April 9, 1983, 4/83; Face a face: Dust, spit and thread; the pastels of Lucas Samaras, 5/83 & The mutant international (ser), 9-12/83, Arts Mag. *Mailing Add:* 37 1/2 St Marks Pl New York NY 10003

MOULTON, ROSALIND KIMBALL
PHOTOGRAPHER, COLLAGE ARTIST
b Buffalo, NY, Nov 25, 41. *Study:* Photog with Minor White, 66; Art Inst Chicago, BFA(Anna Louise Raymond Traveling Fel), 71; State Univ NY, Buffalo, MFA, 76; numerous photog workshops. *Work:* Mass Inst Technol, Cambridge; Art Inst Chicago; Int Mus Photog, George Eastman House, Rochester, NY; Univ Art Mus, Univ NMex, Albuquerque; Apeiron Workshops, Millerton, NY. *Exhib:* Camera Infinity Exhib, Lever House, New York; Western New York Exhib, Albright-Knox Art Gallery, Buffalo, 74 & 75; 18th Dixie Ann, Montgomery Mus of Fine Arts, Ala, 77; Ten Women, Traveling Exhib, Women's Caucus for Art, Columbia Chap, Mo, 78-79; 7th Nat Exhib, Second St Gallery, Charlottesville, Va, 79; one-woman show, Weber State Col, Utah, 80. *Teaching:* Vis instr photog, Purdue Univ, West Lafayette, Ind, 71; instr photog, Empire State Col, Buffalo, 75, State Univ NY, Buffalo, 76 & Stephens Col, 76-; vis artist, Univ Mo, Columbia, 81. *Awards:* Stephens Grants, 78 & 82. *Mem:* Col Art Asn; Soc Photog Educ; Ctr Creative Studies, Ariz; Friends Photog. *Publ:* Contribr, Vision and Expression, Horizon Press, 69; contribr, Octave of Prayer, Aperture, 72; contribr, Insights/Self-Portraits by Women, David R Godine, 78; contribr, Fotografie, A German Quarterly for Creative Photography, 8/79; contribr, Phoography for Collectors: The Midwest, 83. *Mailing Add:* Dept of Art Stephens Col Columbia MO 65201

MOULTON, SUSAN GENE
HISTORIAN, PAINTER
b Long Beach, Calif, June 7, 44. *Study:* Univ Calif, Davis, study with Wayne Thiebaud, BA(art), 66; Univ Padua, Italy, 64-65; Accad, Venice, Italy, with Prof Balest, 64; Stanford Univ, MA(art hist; Carnegie Found Fel), 69, PhD(art hist), 77. *Teaching:* Assoc prof Renaissance & mod art, Sonoma State Univ, 71-, chairperson dept art, 75-79 & 83- *Mem:* Col Art Asn; Women's Caucus Art; San Francisco Mus Soc. *Res:* Sixteenth century Venetian painting, specifically Titian and the evolution of donor portraiture in Venice. *Publ:* Contribr, From Frontier to Fire, Univ Calif, Davis, 64; auth, Interdisciplinary Women's Studies Courses, Women's Caucus Art, 77; auth, Titian and the Evolution of Donor Portraiture, Stanford Univ, 77; auth, Four From California, Edinburg, Scotland, 81. *Mailing Add:* 7736 Elphick Rd Sebastopol CA 95472

MOUNT, MARSHALL WARD
HISTORIAN, ADMINISTRATOR
b Jersey City, NJ, Dec 25, 27. *Study:* Columbia Col, AB, 48; Columbia Univ, with Paul S Wingert, MA, 52, PhD, 66. *Pos:* Leader art study tours to Mali, Cameroun, India, Explorer Tours, Montreal, 69-77; dir art hist prog, Finch Col, San Marino, Italy, 73-75; cataloguer, Zim Collection of African Art, Children's Mus, Brooklyn, NY, 77 & 79; dir, L Kahan Gallery African Art, New York, 81-82. *Teaching:* Prof & chmn art hist dept, Finch Col, New York, 58-75; vis prof, Univ Iowa, Iowa City, summer 70 & Parsons Sch of Design, New York, 70-72; vis assoc prof, Hunter Col, New York, 72-73; prof and chmn creative arts dept, Univ Benin, Nigeria, 77-80; prof art hist, Fashion Inst Technol, New York, 82- *Awards:* Rockefeller Found Fel, 61, 62 & 68; Fac Scholar Int Studies, Columbia, 66-67; Am Coun Learned Soc Grant, 73. *Mem:* Col Art Asn; fel African Studies Asn. *Res:* Traditional and contemporary art of sub-Saharan Africa. *Publ:* Auth, African Art: The Years Since 1920, Ind Univ Press, 73; auth, African Art from New Jersey Collections, Montclair Art Mus, 83. *Mailing Add:* 74 Sherman Pl Jersey City NJ 07307

MOUNT, WARD
PAINTER, SCULPTOR
b Batavia, NY. *Study:* Art Students League; NY Univ; also with Albert P Lucas & Joseph P Pollia. *Work:* Jersey City Mus; Roosevelt Mus, Hyde Park, NY; Delgado Mus; Mus of Mod Art; Hudson River Mus. *Comn:* Bronze medal, Painters & Sculptors Soc, Jersey City Mus; holiday card for 1971 (casein), Am Heart Asn, 71; and others. *Exhib:* Audubon Artists, New York, 40-42, Nat Acad Design, 44 & Nat Sculpture Soc, 45-48; Pa Acad Fine Arts, Philadelphia, 49; Smithsonian Inst, Washington, DC, 51; New York Hist Soc; Allied Artists Am; and others. *Pos:* Former founder & head painting & sculpture, Jersey City Med Ctr, NJ; dir, Ward Mount Art Classes, Jersey City, 39- *Teaching:* Head dept painting & sculpture, NJ State Teachers Col, 41-45. *Awards:* First Prize for Sculpture, Kearney Mus, 47; First Prize Sculpture, Art Fair, New York, 50; Gold Medal, Jersey J Woman of Achievement, 71. *Bibliog:* Peyton Boswell (auth), article in Arts Digest; articles in Cue Mag, Saturday Eve Post & Rev Mod Francaise; and others. *Mem:* Founding mem Artists Equity Asn; Painters & Sculptors Soc NJ; fel Royal Soc Art; founding mem Audubon Artists; Acad Italy. *Mailing Add:* 74 Sherman Pl Jersey City NJ 07307

MOURE, NANCY DUSTIN WALL
CURATOR, WRITER
b Dayton, Ohio, Feb 26, 43. *Study:* San Diego State Col, BA; Univ Calif, Los Angeles, MA. *Collections Arranged:* Los Angeles Painters of the Nineteen Twenties (auth, catalog), Pomona Col Art Gallery, 72; California Watercolor Society Prizewinners (auth, catalog), 73, Western Scene (auth, catalog), 75, Pertaining to the Sea (auth, catalog), 76, Los Angeles Co Mus Art; William Wendt (auth, catalog), Laguna Beach Mus Art, 77; Painting and Sculpture in Los Angeles 1900-1945 (auth, catalog), Los Angeles Co Mus Art, 80. *Pos:* Curatorial aide, Los Angeles Co Mus Art, 68-72, asst cur Am art, 72- *Res:* American art executed before 1920 with an emphasis on pre-1930 Southern California art. *Publ:* Auth, California Watercolor Society, 73 & Artists Clubs and Exhibitions in Los Angeles, 74; coauth, American Narrative Painting, Los Angeles Co Mus Art, 74; auth, Dictionary of Art and Artists in Southern California Before 1930, 75; coauth, Index to Reproductions of American Paintings, Scarecrow Press, Inc, 77; auth, Southern Calif Artists, 1890-1940, Laguna Beach Mus Art, 79. *Mailing Add:* 935 W Mountain St Glendale CA 91202

MOVALLI, CHARLES JOSEPH
WRITER, PAINTER
b Gloucester, Mass, Aug 20, 45. *Study:* Clark Univ, BA; Univ Conn, MA & PhD; spec study with Emile Gruppe, Roger Curtis, Zygmund Jankowski & Betty L Schlemm. *Pos:* Contributing ed, Am Artist Mag, 76- *Awards:* Gorton Award, N Shore Arts Asn, 75; Goldberg Award, 77, Cooley Award, 77 & Gold Medal, 82, Rockport Art Asn. *Mem:* Acad Artists; Guild of Boston Artists; Rockport Art Asn; N Shore Arts Asn; Rocky Neck Art Colony (pres, 76). *Media:* Oil. *Res:* Contemporary and older painters working in plein-air tradition. *Publ:* Ed & coauth, Gruppe on Painting, 76; auth, Brushwork, 77, Color in Outdoor Painting, 77 & Painting with Light, 78 & Art of Landscape Painting, 79, Watson-Guptill; auth, Croney on Watercolor, North Light, 82. *Mailing Add:* 237 Western Ave Gloucester MA 01930

MOXEY, KEITH PATRICIO FLEMING
HISTORIAN
b Buenos Aires, Arg, Jan 4, 43; Brit/Arg citizen. *Study:* Univ Edinburgh, MA, 65; Univ Chicago, MA, 68, PhD, 74. *Teaching:* From instr to asst prof art hist, Tufts Univ, 71-74; from asst prof to assoc prof art hist, Univ Va, 74-, chmn, Art Hist, 76-79. *Awards:* Nat Endowment Humanities Fel, 78-79; sen fel, Ctr Advan Study Visual Arts, Nat Gallery Art, 80-81. *Mem:* Col Art Asn; Renaissance Soc. *Res:* Late medieval and Renaissance art in Northern Europe. *Publ:* Auth, The humanist market scenes of Joachim Beuckelaer, Antwerp JBH, 76; auth, Reflections on unusual subjects in work of Aertsen, Berliner JBH, 76; auth, Aertsen & Beuckelaer, Secular Painting & the Reformation, Garland, 77; auth, Image criticism in the Netherlands before the Iconoclasm of 1566, Nederlands Archief voor Kerkgeschiedenis, 77; auth, Master E S and the folly of love, Simiolus XI, 81. *Mailing Add:* 500 Court Sq 904 Charlottesville VA 22901

MOY, MAY (WONG)
PAINTER, INSTRUCTOR
b New York, NY, Dec 2, 13. *Study:* Parsons Sch Fine & Appl Arts, NY; Montclair Teacher's Col; Oriental Artists Sch. *Exhib:* Chinese Women Painters in Am, St John's Univ, NY, 79; Show Castle '79, Sands Point, NY, 79; 16th Ann Exhib Sumi-e Soc Am, Am Inst Architects, DC, 79; Huntington Arts Coun, NY, 83; Sumi-e Soc Am, Meridian House Int, Washington, DC, 83. *Pos:* Lectr & demonstr Chinese brush painting, Sr Citizens Groups, Huntington Schs, 71- *Teaching:* Lectr Oriental ink, Half Hollow Hills High Sch, Dix Hills, NY, 67-74; lectr Oriental brush painting, Artisan House, Northport, NY, 72-74 & Huntington Hist Soc, NY, 74- *Awards:* Zen, 63, Bamboo, 69 & Heart of Winter, 75, Sumi-e Soc Am. *Bibliog:* Sally Miller (auth), May W Moy exhibits Chinese painting, Half Hollow Hills Community Libr, 72; Hedda Friedman (auth), May Moy Chinese Exhibition, Long Islander Newspaper, 72; Rhoda Amon (auth), Long Island Sumi-e style, Newsday, 74. *Mem:* Sumi-e Soc Am, New York. *Mailing Add:* 27 Maryland St Dix Hills NY 11746

MOY, SEONG
PAINTER, GRAPHIC ARTIST
b Canton, China, Oct 20, 21; US citizen. *Study:* St Paul Sch Art, with Cameron Booth, 36-40; Art Students League, with Vaclav Vytacil, 41-42; Hofmann Sch, with Hans Hofmann, 41-42; Atelier 17, New York, 48-50. *Work:* Mus Mod Art; Brooklyn Mus; Metrop Mus Art; Pa Acad Fine Arts; NY Pub Libr; plus others. *Comn:* Three ed, Int Graphic Arts Soc; New York Hilton Hotel. *Exhib:* Metrop Mus Art, 50; Whitney Mus Am Art, 50; Univ Ill, 51, 53 & 54; Carnegie Inst, 52 & 55; New York World's Fair, 64-65; plus many other group & one-man shows. *Pos:* Dir, Seong Moy Sch Painting & Graphic Arts, Provincetown, Mass, summers 54- *Teaching:* Instr, Univ Minn, 51, Ind Univ, 52-53, Smith Col, 54-55, Univ Ark, 55, Vassar Col, 55, Cooper Union Art Sch, 57-70, Columbia Univ, 59-70 & Art Students League, 63-; prof, City Col New York, 70- *Awards:* John Hay Whitney Found Grant, 50-51; Guggenheim Fel, 55-56. *Mem:* Art Students League; Am Fedn Arts; Artists Equity Asn; Col Art Asn Am; Fedn Mod Painters & Sculptors. *Mailing Add:* 100 La Salle St New York NY 10027

MOYER, ROY
PAINTER, ADMINISTRATOR
b Allentown, Pa, Aug 20. 21. *Study:* Columbia Col, BA, Columbia Univ, MA. *Work:* Rochester Mem Art Gallery, NY; Brandeis Univ Art Gallery, Waltham, Mass; Wichita Art Mus, Kans; Sara Roby Found, New York; Fordham Univ, Lincoln Ctr, NY. *Exhib:* Nat Acad Design, New York, 77; Sneed Gallery, 79; Carl Battaglia Gallery, 80; Fordham Univ, 81; Rolly-Michaux Gallery, Boston, 81; and others. *Collections Arranged:* Inverse Illusionism, traveling exhib; numerous others for Am Fedn Arts. *Pos:* Dir, Am Fedn Arts, 63-72; chief art & design, UNICEF, 72- *Teaching:* Lectr art hist, Univ Toronto, 53-55. *Awards:* First Prize, Butler Inst Am Art, 73 & Nat Acad Design, 77. *Mem:* Nat Coun Arts (exec comt, 65-72). *Media:* Oil. *Res:* Byzantine art and architecture; sixteenth century painting and sculpture. *Dealer:* Sneed Gallery 2024 Harlem Blvd Rockford IL 61103. *Mailing Add:* 440 Riverside Dr New York NY 10027

MOYERS, WILLIAM
PAINTER, SCULPTOR
b Atlanta, Ga, Dec 11, 16. *Study:* Adams State Col, major fine arts; Otis Art Inst. *Work:* Gilcrease Inst, Tulsa, Okla; Nat Cowboy Fame, Oklahoma City; Adams State Col; Albuquerque Mus; Sangre Cristo Arts Ctr, Pueblo, Colo. *Exhib:* Cowboy Artist of Am Shows, Cowboy Hall of Fame & Phoenix Art Mus, since 68; one-man shows, Adams State Col, Alamosa, Colo, 71 & Nat Cowboy Hall of Fame, Oklahoma City, 73; group show, Mont Hist Soc, Helena, 72 & 73. *Awards:* Gold Medals-Sculpture, Nat Cowboy Hall of Fame, 68 & 72; Gold Medal for Sculpture & Co-Winner Best of Show Award, Cowboy Artists Am Show, Phoenix Art Mus, 75; Silver Medal sculpture, Cowboy Artists Am 1979 Exhib, Phoenix Art Mus, 79 & 80. *Bibliog:* Ainsworth (auth), Cowboy in Art, World Publ, 68; Harmsen (auth), Western America, Northland, 71; Broder (auth), Bronzes of the American West, Abrams, 74. *Mem:* Cowboy Artists Am (vpres, 82-83, pres, 83-84). *Media:* Oil, Watercolor; Bronze Sculpture. *Publ:* Illusr bks for nat publ, 45-62. *Dealer:* Taos Art Gallery Inc PO Box 1007 Taos NM 87571; Trailside Galleries 7330 Scottsdale Mall Scottsdale AZ 85251. *Mailing Add:* 1407 Morningside Dr NE Albuquerque NM 87110

MOZLEY, ANITA VENTURA
CURATOR, HISTORIAN
b Washington, DC, Aug 29, 28. *Study:* Northwestern Univ, Evanston, Ill, BA; Art Students League, with Morris Kantor. *Collections Arranged:* Ansel Adams: The Portfolios, Stanford Univ Mus Art, Calif, 72; Eadweard Muybridge: The Stanford Years, 1872-1882 (ed & co-auth, catalog), 72; Mrs Cameron's Photographs from the Life (auth, catalog), 74; Monsen Collection of American Photography (auth, catalog), Seattle Art Mus, Wash, 76; Nadar: Portraits and Catacombs, 78; The Grand Tour: Mid-19th Century Photographs from the Leonard/Peil Collection, 79; Paintings by Joseph Raphael (1869-1950), 80; Ansel Adams: Ski Experience, 83. *Pos:* Reviewer, managing ed & West Coast corresp, Arts Mag, New York, 55-64; poster designer, Leo Castelli Gallery, New York, 55-62; film librn, Sextant, Inc, New York, 60-61; curatorial asst & ed, SEA Letter, San Francisco Maritime Mus, 62-67; registr, Stanford Univ Mus Art, Calif, 70-78; cur photog, 71- *Teaching:* Hist photogr, Stanford Univ, spring 81. *Mem:* Friends Photog. *Res:* Nineteenth and twentieth century photographers, particularly the works of Eadweard Muybridge, Julia Margaret Cameron, Thomas Annan, Imogen Cunningham, Joe Deal & Lorie Novak. *Publ:* Auth, Thomas Annan, Photographs of the Old Closes and Streets of Glasgow, Dover, 77; auth, Muybridge's Complete Human and Animal Locomotion, Dover, 79; auth, Harry Smith's Magic Moments, White, 81; auth, The Fault Zone, Joe Deal's Portfolio, 81. *Mailing Add:* 601 Laurel Ave Menlo Park CA 94025

MUCCIOLI, ANNA MARIA
PAINTER, SCULPTOR
b Detroit, Mich, Apr 23, 22. *Study:* Soc Art & Crafts; with Sarkis Sarkisian, Charles Culver & Hay Holland. *Exhib:* Butler Inst Am Art, Youngstown, Ohio, 69; Nat Acad Galleries, New York, 71; Nat Small Painting Exhib, traveling, 72-78; Birmingham Mus Arts, 74; one-man show, Univ Liggett Sch, Grosse Point, Mich, 74; Mich Watercolor Soc, Detroit Inst Arts, 76; Art Ctr Fibers Exhib, Mt Clemens, 77. *Awards:* Third Place, Scarab Club, 71, Hon Mention, Silver Medal Exhib, 76 & 79; Second Place, Ford Motor Co Art Exhib, 76, First Place, 77, & Second Place, 79. *Mem:* Mich Watercolor Soc; Watercolor Soc Ala; Women's Caucus of Art. *Media:* Watercolor; Bronze, Stone. *Mailing Add:* c/o Muccioli Studio Gallery 511 Beaubien Detroit MI 48266

MUCHNIC, SUZANNE
CRITIC, INSTRUCTOR
b Kearney, Nebr. *Study:* Scripps Col, BA, 62; Claremont Grad Sch, MA, 63. *Pos:* Ed, Artweek, Los Angeles, 77-78, contrib ed, 78-80; art critic & staff writer, Los Angeles Times, 78- *Teaching:* Instr art hist, Los Angeles City Col, 74-82. *Mem:* Int Asn Art Critics; Col Art Asn. *Res:* Contemporary art. *Mailing Add:* c/o Los Angeles Times Times Mirror Square Los Angeles CA 90053

MUDFORD, GRANT LEIGHTON
PHOTOGRAPHER
b Sydney, Australia, Mar 21, 44. *Study:* Univ New South Wales, Australia, 63-64. *Work:* Mus Mod Art, New York; Int Mus Photog, George Eastman House, Rochester, NY; Victoria & Albert Mus; Australian Nat Gallery, Canberra; Nat Mus Am Art, Washington, DC. *Comn:* Ten photog prints, Calif State Univ, Long Beach, 80 & CSR Ltd, Sydney, 81. *Exhib:* The Land: 20th Century Landscape Photographs, Victoria & Albert Mus, 75-76; solo exhib, Hirshhorn Mus & Sculpture Garden, 79; Long Beach: A Photographic Survey, Art Mus & Galleries, Calif State Univ, Long Beach, 80; Biennial Exhib, Whitney Mus Am Art, 81; Double Take: A Comparative Look at Photographs, Int Ctr Photography, New York, 81; Photography: A Sense of Order, Inst Contemp Art, Univ Pa, 81. *Awards:* Nat Endowment Arts Photogr Fel, 80. *Bibliog:* Photographs by Grant Mudford, Interview Mag,

6/79; Celebrating the seldom-noticed, Los Angeles Times, 3/6/83; article, Artforum, summer 83. *Dealer:* Rosamund Felsen Gallery 669 N La Cienega Blvd Los Angeles CA 90069. *Mailing Add:* 5619 W 4 St #2 Los Angeles CA 90036

MUDGE, EDMUND WEBSTER, JR
COLLECTOR
b Pittsburgh, Pa, Nov 29, 04. *Study:* Harvard Univ, AB. *Collection:* Impressionist and post-impressionist paintings; English, French and German antique porcelain and pottery; antique Chinese snuff bottles and Chinese export porcelains; porcelain birds of Dorothy Doughty and Edward Marshall Boehm. *Mailing Add:* 5926 Averill Way Dallas TX 75225

MUELLER, HENRIETTA WATERS
PAINTER, SCULPTOR
b Pittsburgh, Pa, Apr 13, 15. *Study:* Art Inst Chicago, with Helen Gardner, BFA, 38; Univ Wyo, MA, 48, MEd, 60; Art Students League, with Will Barnet; Univ Colo, Boulder, with Wendell Black; also with George McNeil & Ilya Bolotowsky. *Work:* Joslyn Mus, Omaha, Nebr; New York Pub Libr, NY; William Rockhill Nelson Gallery, Kansas City, Mo; Mills Col Collection, New York; Univ Wash, Seattle. *Comn:* Stainless steel monument, Commemorative Wyo Women's Rights 1890-1970, Albany Co Courthouse, Laramie, Wyo, 72. *Exhib:* Six shows, Print Club Philadelphia, Philadelphia Mus Art, 52-61; Western Art Ann, Denver Art Mus, 52-55; 22nd Drawing & Print Ann, San Francisco Mus Art, 58; Metrop Mus Art, New York, 60 & 61; Own Your Own Exhibs, Denver Art Mus, 67; 11th Art Ann, Pioneer Mus, Stockton, Calif, 71. *Teaching:* Asst prof art & design, Univ Wyo, 50-61; asst prof art, Univ Nebr, 56-57; asst prof art, Univ Pac, 70-71. *Awards:* Int Textile Exhib Award, Univ NC, Greensboro, 48; Wilson Daly Prize, 50 Ind Prints, John Herron Art Inst, Indianapolis, 52; Purchase Award, Univ Wyo Art Mus, 73. *Mem:* Wyo Artists' Asn; Artists Equity Asn (secy-treas, Wyo Chap, 50-65); Laramie Art Guild. *Media:* Oil, Watercolor; Steel, Aluminum. *Dealer:* Overland Art Gallery Ivinson Ave Laramie WY 82070; Three Twenty Three Gallery 232 S David Casper WY 82601. *Mailing Add:* 1309 Steele St Laramie WY 82070

MUELLER, M GERARDINE
CALLIGRAPHER, STAINED GLASS ARTIST
b Newark, NJ. *Study:* Caldwell Col, BA; Univ Notre Dame, MA & MFA, with A Lauck & K Milonadis; also with W Otto, Berlin; Inst Cult, Guadalajara, Mex. *Comn:* Sculpture, St Dominic Acad, 60; windows, Sisters Chapel, Caldwell, 62; six-panel mosaic mural, Caldwell Col, NJ, 70; Sculpture & Design Chapel, All Saints Church, Jersey City, 73; windows, Puyo Cathedral, Ecuador, 77; stained glass, Dominican Sisters, Caldwell, NJ, 82. *Exhib:* Old Bergen Art Guild Tour, 79-81; NAm Calligraphers, Dallas, Tex, 74, Nat Miniature Art Soc, Fla, 75; Art by US Relig Women, Indianapolis, 81; Contemp Relig Art, Newark, 81; and others. *Pos:* Pres, Cath Fine Arts Soc, 69-71; mem, Archdiocese Comn Div Worship (art & archit), 74-77; dir art & design, Liturgy Convention, 81; consult, Archdicese Newark, 81-83. *Teaching:* Lectr lettering & crafts, Fordham Univ, 61; prof art, Caldwell Col, 63-, chmn art dept, 63-79. *Bibliog:* Article, Todays's Art, 1/81; article, Newark Advocate, 10/81; article, Newark Star Ledger, 11/81. *Mem:* Cath Fine Arts Asn; Soc Scribes; and others. *Media:* Multimedia; Stained Glass, Mosaic. *Publ:* Auth, Yearbook production, Photolith Mag, 61; auth, Art in Latin America & Art in Indian Mission of US, Cath Youth Encycl, McGraw-Hill, 62; auth, New mosaic evolvement, Cath Fine Arts Soc, 68; contribr, Stained Glass Quarterly, summer 78. *Mailing Add:* Caldwell Col Caldwell NJ 07006

MUELLER, TRUDE
SCULPTOR
b Bielsko, Poland, Jan 2, 13; US citizen. *Study:* County Art Ctr, White Plains; Greenwich House, New York; New Sch Social Res, New York; with H Beling, Lu Duble, M Pascual & P Graussman. *Work:* Palm Springs Desert Mus, Calif; Ben-Gurion Univ, Israel. *Exhib:* NY Univ, 68; Allied Artists Am, Nat Acad Gallery, New York, 68; Artist-Craftsmen Am, Lever House, New York, 68-72 & 73; Bruce Mus, Conn, 74; Petits Formats des Maitres Contemporains, Chantilly, 75. *Pos:* Art therapist, Child Sch, New York, 73. *Awards:* Beaux Arts Award, Macy's, 64 & 65; Best Piece in Firing, Greenwich House, New York, 65; plus numerous prizes in Westchester Co, 64-74. *Bibliog:* Meditation, Beaux Arts, 65; R Stevens (auth), Aux Etats-Unis, La Revue Mod, Paris, 69; K Beals (auth), articles in Daily Times, Westchester. *Mem:* Artist-Craftsmen New York; Greenwich House Sculptors (treas, 68-69); Norton Gallery Artists Guild, West Palm Beach, Fla; Allied Artists Am; Mamaroneck Artists Guild. *Media:* Wood, Clay. *Dealer:* Hilde Gerst Gallery 681 Madison Ave New York NY 10021. *Mailing Add:* 1200 S Flagler Dr West Palm Beach FL 33401

MUENCH, JOHN
PAINTER, PRINTMAKER
b Medford, Mass, Oct 15, 14. *Study:* Art Students League; Acad Julian, Paris. *Work:* Metrop Mus Art, New York; Victoria & Albert Mus, London; Bibliot Nat, Paris; Nat Collection & Smithsonian Inst, Washington, DC; Nat Mus, Jerusalem; and others. *Exhib:* Nine shows, Libr Cong, 45-56; Soc Am Graphic Artists, 47 & 50-52; Audubon Artists, 47, 48 & 56; Pa Acad Fine Arts, 49, 50 & 53-55; Cincinnati Mus, 54 & 56; and many others. *Teaching:* Dir, Portland Sch Fine & Appl Arts, Maine, 58-65; assoc prof art, RI Sch Design, 65-77; artist-in-residence, Westbrook Col, Portland, Maine; dir, Maine Printmaking Workshop. *Awards:* John Taylor Arms Award & Medal, 65, Audubon Artists; Vis Fel, Tamarind Lithography Workshop, Los Angeles, 62; US Dept State Specialist Grant, 66; and others. *Mem:* Soc Am Graphic Artists; Audubon Artists; Am Color Print Soc; Nat Acad Design. *Media:* Multimedia. *Publ:* Auth, The painter's guide to lithography, Northlight-Writers Digest, 83. *Dealer:* Assoc Am Artists 663 Fifth Ave New York NY 10019. *Mailing Add:* Westbrook Col Portland ME 02903

MUENSTERBERGER, WERNER
COLLECTOR, WRITER
Pos: Cur asst, Stedeljk Mus, Amsterdam, Holland, 45-47. *Awards:* Wenner-Gren Found Fel, 48; Guggenheim Fel, 69; Grant Found, 74-75. *Mem:* Fel Pierpont Morgan Libr; fel Am Anthrop Asn; fel Royal Anthrop Inst Gt Brit. *Res:* Primitive art of Oceania and Africa; relationship between artist, artistic themes and personality development. *Collection:* West African and Oceanic sculpture; Old Master drawings. *Publ:* Auth, Sculpture of Primitive Man, Thames & Hudson, London-Abrams, NY, 55; auth, The creative process..., Psychoanalytic Study Soc II, 62; auth & ed, Between Reality and Fantasy, Preliminary Notes on Collecting, New York, 78; auth, Universality of Tribal Art, 79; auth, The Meaning of Masking, 84; and others. *Mailing Add:* 8 Eaton Sq London England United Kingdom

MUHLBERGER, RICHARD CHARLES
MUSEUM DIRECTOR
b Englewood, NJ, Jan 20, 38. *Study:* Calif Concordia Col, AA; Wayne State Univ, BA(art hist); Johns Hopkins Univ, Baltimore, MA(art hist). *Pos:* Cur mus educ, Worcester Art Mus, Mass, 66-72; chmn educ, Detroit Inst Arts, 72-75; dir, Mus Fine Arts & George Walter Vincent Smith Art Mus, Springfield, Mass, 76- *Awards:* Phi Beta Kappa, 65; Woodrow Wilson Nat Fel, 65-67. *Mem:* Am Asn Mus; Asn Art Mus Dirs. *Res:* Dutch seventeenth century bird painters. *Mailing Add:* c/o Mus of Fine Arts 49 Chestnut St Springfield MA 01103

MUHLERT, CHRISTOPHER LAYTON
PAINTER
b Brooklyn, NY, Mar 24, 33. *Study:* Case Western Reserve, BA, 64; Oberlin Col, MA, 66; Pratt Inst; Union Col; Cleveland Inst Art. *Work:* Cleveland Mus Art; Allen Mem Art Mus, Oberlin, Ohio; Phillip Morris Corp, Estate Joseph Hirshhorn, Washington, DC; Prudential Insurance Co, Merrillville, Ind. *Exhib:* Black and White, Smithsonian Inst, 70-72; 19th Area Exhib, Corcoran Gallery Art, 74; two-person show, Barbara Fiedler Gallery, Washington, DC, 76; one-man show, Davenport Munic Art Gallery, Iowa, 77, Barbara Fiedler Gallery, Washington, DC, 78 & Carlin Gallery, Ft Worth, 83. *Pos:* Preparator, Cleveland Mus Art, 60-64. *Teaching:* Instr design & painting, Oberlin Col, 66-68; instr found, Corcoran Sch Art, 70, asst prof drawing & design, 71-75. *Media:* Acrylic. *Dealer:* Electra Carlin Seventh St Ft Worth TX 76107. *Mailing Add:* 3825 Clarke Ft Worth TX 76107

MUHLERT, JAN KEENE
MUSEUM DIRECTOR, HISTORIAN
b Oak Park, Ill, Oct 4, 42. *Study:* Neuchatel Univ, Inst European Studies, Paris; Sorbonne, with Andre Chastel; Inst de Phonetique; Acad Grande Chaumiere, 62-63; Albion Col, BA, 64; Oberlin Col, with Ellen H Johnson & Wolfgang Stechow, MA, 67. *Collections Arranged:* H Lyman Sayen (with catalog), Nat Collection Fine Arts, 70, Romaine Brooks, Thief of Souls (with catalog), 71 & William H Johnson 1901-1970 (with catalog), 71; The Ninth Level: Funerary Art from Ancient MesoAmerica (with catalog), 78 & African Sculpture, The Stanley Collection (with catalog), 79, Mus of Art Univ Iowa. *Pos:* Asst cur collections, Allen Mem Art Mus, Oberlin Col, 66-68; asst cur contemp art, Nat Col Fine Arts, 68-73; assoc cur 20th century paintings & sculpture, 74-75; dir, Mus Art, Univ Iowa, 75-79; dir, Amon Carter Mus, Ft Worth, Tex, 80- *Awards:* Grant, Asn Art Mus Dir, 79. *Mem:* Asn Art Mus Dir; Am Asn Mus; Art Table; Am Arts Alliance. *Res:* Federal art projects, 1933-1943; Arthur G Dove, 1880-1946. *Publ:* Contribr, An Exhibition of Paintings, Bozzetti and Drawings by Baciccio (catalog), Oberlin Col, 67; coauth, Tribute to Mark Tobey (catalog), Nat Collection Fine Arts, 74; contrib, Mauricio Lasansky, A Retrospective Exhibition, Univ Iowa, 76. *Mailing Add:* Amon Carter Mus PO Box 2365 Ft Worth TX 76113

MUIR, EMILY LANSINGH
PAINTER, SCULPTOR
b Chicago, Ill. *Study:* Art Students League, with Richard Lahey & Leo Lentelli; Univ Maine, LHD, 69. *Work:* Brooklyn Mus; Univ Maine. *Comn:* Design of contemporary summer homes, year-round homes, mosaics & interior design, portraits and portrait busts for private owners. *Exhib:* Int Watercolor Soc; Maine Art Gallery; Univ Maine; Farnsworth Mus Art. *Teaching:* Lectr art, Asn Am Cols, 50-60. *Awards:* Outstanding Achievement in Commercial Venture, Contrib to Visual Arts, Maine Comt Skowhegan Sch, 72. *Bibliog:* Martin Dibner (auth), People of the Maine Coast, Doubleday; William Caldwell (auth), article in Portland Press Herald; J R Wiggins (auth), article in Bangor Daily News. *Media:* Oil, Mosaic; Clay, Wood. *Publ:* Auth, Small Potatoes, Scribner, 40. *Mailing Add:* Muir Studios Stonington ME 04681

MULCAHY, KATHLEEN
GLASS ARTIST, SCULPTOR
b Newark, NJ, June 23, 50. *Study:* Kean Col NJ, Union, BA, 72; Alfred Univ, NY, MFA, 74. *Work:* Corning Mus Glass, NY; pvt collections, Westmoreland Co Mus Art, Pa. *Exhib:* 8th Biennial Invitational, Visual Arts Gallery, Ill State Univ, Normal, 80; Masters in Glass, Craftsmens Gallery, Scarsdale, NY, 80; American Art at its Best, Am Art Inc, Atlanta, Ga, 81; Nat Glass 81, Pittsburgh Ctr Arts ; New Works, Pittsburgh Plan Art Gallery, Pa, 82; and others. *Teaching:* Dir & assoc prof art, Glass Art Prog, Carnegie-Mellon Univ, Pittsburgh, 76-; artist in residence, Haystack My Sch Crafts, summer 79 & 83, Artpark, Lewiston, NY, summer 80; lectr, Portcon Glass Conf, 82 & 83. *Awards:* Nat Endowment for Arts visual arts fel, 79-80; Pa Coun Arts Fel, 81 & 83; and others. *Mem:* Glass Art Soc; Am Crafts Coun. *Media:* Glass; Mixed Media. *Publ:* Profile, Glass Studio Mag, 11/81. *Mailing Add:* 1047 Shady Ave Pittsburgh PA 15232

MULLEN, JAMES MARTIN
EDUCATOR, PRINTMAKER
b Altoona, Pa, May 14, 35. *Study:* Pa State Univ, BA, 57, MA, 63. *Work:* NJ State Mus, Trenton; Portsmouth Va Mus; Everson Mus, Syracuse, NY; Pa State Univ, Univ Park; Pushkin Mus, USSR. *Exhib:* Am Drawings III, Portsmouth Arts Ctr, Va, 80; World Print III, San Francisco Mus Mod Art, Calif, 80; 5th Nat Print, Honolulu Acad Art, Hawaii, 80; Small Works, Wash Square Gallery, New York Univ, 80; Silvermine Guild Prints, New Canaan, Conn, 80. *Pos:* Gallery dir, State Univ Col, Oneonta, NY, 76- *Teaching:* Prof art, State Univ Col, Oneonta, NY, 63- *Awards:* Chancellor's Award for Teaching Excellence, State Univ NY, 73; Chaning Hare Award, Soc Four Arts, Palm Beach, Fla. *Mem:* Soc Am Graphic Artist; Am Color Print Soc; Cooperstown Art Asn. *Publ:* Auth, Subject matter, 66 & auth, Student work, 69, Sch Arts Mag. *Dealer:* Miriam Perlman Inc Lake Point Tower Suite 1902 505 N Lakeshore Dr Chicago IL 60611. *Mailing Add:* 2 Brigham Road Rd 4-24C Oneonta NY 13820

MULLEN, PHILIP EDWARD
ARTIST, EDUCATOR
b Akron, Ohio, Oct 10, 42. *Study:* Univ Minn, BA; Univ NDak, MA; Ohio Univ, PhD. *Exhib:* Over 200, including 1975 Biennial of Contemp Am Art, Whitney Mus Am Art, New York & Smithsonian Inst Traveling Exhib. *Teaching:* Prof, Univ SC, currently. *Awards:* 46 Awards incl Russell Award for Research in Humanities, 76. *Dealer:* David Findlay Gallery 984 Madison Ave New York NY 10021; Dubins Gallery 11948 San Vicente Blvd Los Angeles CA 90049. *Mailing Add:* 1611 Hollywood Dr Columbia SC 29205

MULLER, JEROME KENNETH
COLLECTOR, DEALER
b Amityville, NY, July 18, 34. *Study:* NY Univ; Marquette Univ, BS; Layton Sch Art; Brandt Painting Workshop. *Collections Arranged:* Cartoon Show, Original Works by 100 Outstanding American Cartoonists, Laguna Beach Mus Art, Calif, 72, Bowers Mus, Santa Ana, Calif, 76, E B Crocker Art Gallery, Sacramento, Calif, 77, Indianapolis Mus Art, Ind, 77, Tweed Mus Art, Duluth, Minn, 78, Everson Mus Art, Syracuse, NY, 78, Montgomery Mus Fine Arts, Ala, 78, South Bend Art Ctr, Ind, 79, Mem Art Gallery, Univ Rochester, 79, Neville Pub Mus, Wis, 79, Cooper-Hewitt Mus, NY, 81 & Nelson Gallery Art, Kansas City, 81; Mickey Mouse: 1928-1978 (cur), Bowers Mus, 78; The Moving Image, art used in animated films, San Jose Mus Art, Calif, 80; The Engravings of William Hogarth, Bowers Mus, 81; The American Comic Strip, Univ Tex, Arlington, 81 Univ Chicago, 83. *Pos:* Photogr, New York, 53-56; art dir, Orange Co Illustrated, 62-68, art ed, 70-79. *Teaching:* Instr photog, Lindenhurst High Sch, NY, 53-54; instr, The Cartoon & the Comic Strip in Am, Univ Calif, Irvine, 79. *Awards:* Two Silver Medals, 20th Ann Exhib of Advert & Ed Art in the West, Los Angeles Art Dir Club, 64; Award of Merit, Illustration West, Los Angeles Illusr Club, 72-74. *Biblig:* Steven Parker (auth), Comics are collectible, Acquire Mag, 7/77; and others. *Mem:* Int Animated Film Soc; Art Mus Asn. *Collection:* Cartoons, comic art and original animation art, exhibited regularly in major museums throughout America. *Publ:* Auth, It's Rex Brandt, 10/73 & The comics: worth a second look, 11/73, SW Art; contribr, Mark Rothko, 74 & The Artist as Collector, 75, Newport Harbor Art Mus, Newport Beach, Calif; contribr, Arts of Oceania, Shells of Oceania, Bowers Mus, 75. *Mailing Add:* Box 743 Costa Mesa CA 92627

MULLER, PRISCILLA ELKOW
HISTORIAN, CURATOR
b New York, NY, Feb 15, 30. *Study:* Brooklyn Col, BA, 50; New York Univ, Inst Fine Arts, MA, 59, PhD, 63. *Pos:* Asst cur, Hispanic Soc Am, 64-68, cur paintings & metalwork, 68-, cur 70-; consult, Time-Life Bks, 68-69. *Teaching:* Lectr, Brooklyn Col, 66. *Awards:* Fel, Nat Endowment Arts, 77. *Mem:* Corresp mem Real Acad de Ciencias, Bellas Letras y Nobles Artes de Cordoba; Hispanic Soc Am; corresp mem Real Acad de Bellas Artes de San Fernando, Madrid; Am Soc Hispanic Art Hist Studies (gen secy, 78-80). *Res:* Spanish and Hispanic fine arts, 15th-20th centuries. *Publ:* Auth, The Drawings of Antonio del Castillo y Saavedra, Ann Arbor, 64; contribr, Francisco Goya's Portraits in Paintings, Prints and Drawings, Richmond, 72; auth, Jewels in Spain 1500-1800, New York, 72; auth, numerous articles in art-hist periodicals. *Mailing Add:* Hispanic Soc Am Mus Broadway & 155th St New York NY 10032

MULLICAN, LEE
PAINTER, EDUCATOR
b Chickasha, Okla, Dec 2, 19. *Study:* Abilene Christian Col; Univ Okla; Kansas City Art Inst, with Fletcher Martin, dipl; San Francisco Art Inst, study with Stanley Hayter. *Work:* San Francisco Mus Art; Phillips Mem Gallery, Washington, DC; Santa Fe Art Mus, NMex; Santa Barbara Mus Art, Calif; Mus Mod Art, New York; Oklahoma Art Ctr, Oklahoma City; Univ Calif, Los Angeles. *Exhib:* Art Inst Chicago, 51; Whitney Mus Am Art, 53 & Calif Artists, 62; Pa Acad Fine Arts, Philadelphia, 68; one-man shows, Okla Art Ctr, Oklahoma City, 51 & 67, Univ Calif, Los Angeles, 69, Jodi Scully Gallery, 73, Contemp Art Gallery, Santa Fe, 73 & Paule Anglim Gallery, San Francisco, 79; The Artists Collects, Newport Harbor Mus Art, 75; Five Footnotes to Art History, Los Angeles Co Mus Art, 77; and others. *Teaching:* Prof painting & drawing, Univ Calif, Los Angeles, 62-78. *Awards:* Guggenheim Fel, 59; Award, Inst Creative Arts, Univ Calif, 63; Tamarind Fel, 64-65. *Biblig:* Wolfgang Paalen & G Onslow Ford (auth), Dynaton, San Francisco Mus Art, 51; Langsner (auth), Mullican paints a picture, Art News, 52; Fink Tuchman (auth), Three Footnotes to California Art History, Los Angeles Co Art Mus, 77. *Media:* Oil. *Dealer:* Paule Anglim Gallery 710 Montgomery San Francisco CA 94111. *Mailing Add:* 370 Mesa Rd Santa Monica CA 90402

MUNDT, ERNEST KARL
SCULPTOR, EDUCATOR
b Bleicherode, Ger, Oct 30, 05; US citizen. *Study:* Berlin Inst Technol, dipl archit, 30; Univ Calif, PhD, 61. *Work:* San Francisco Mus Art. *Exhib:* Detroit Inst Art, 44; San Francisco Mus Art, 46; Calif Palace of Legion of Honor, 49; Metrop Mus Art, 50; Whitney Mus Am Art, 51; plus others. *Teaching:* Asst prof, Univ Mich, 41-44; instr, Brooklyn Col, 45-46; instr, Calif Sch Fine Art, 47-50, dir, 50-55; from asst prof to prof art, Calif State Univ, San Francisco, 55-76, chmn dept, 58-61, emer prof, 76- *Awards:* Gold Medal Honor, Am Inst Archit, 56. *Publ:* Auth & illusr, A Primer of Visual Art, 50; auth & illusr, Art, Form, & Civilization, 52; auth & illusr, Birth of a Cook, 56; contribr, Arts & Archit, Col Art J, Art Quart & J Aesthet Mags; and others. *Mailing Add:* 574 Congo St San Francisco CA 94131

MUNIOT, BARBARA KING
DEALER, COLLECTOR
b New Orleans, La. *Study:* Sullins Col, Bristol, Va, art degree; Newcomb Col, spec study with Prof Franklin Adams. *Pos:* Asst dir, Orleans Gallery, 68-70, dir, 70-73; asst dir, Galerie Simonne Stern, 73-75, dir, 75- *Specialty:* Contemporary art. *Collection:* Paintings, drawings, prints and photographs. *Mailing Add:* c/o Galerie Simonne Stern 2727 Prytania St New Orleans LA 70130

MUNO, RICHARD CARL
SCULPTOR, DIRECTOR
b Arapaho, Okla, July 2, 39. *Study:* Okla State Univ Sch Tech Training, cert com art. *Work:* Diamond M Mus, Snyder, Tex. *Comn:* Sculpture of Cavalry Man and Horse, Winchester Firearms, Hartford, Conn, 68; Western Heritage Awards Wrangler Trophy, Nat Cowboy Hall Fame, Oklahoma City, 68; Sculpture of a Lawman, Colt Firearms, Hartford, 73; Sculpture of Cowboy Branding Calf, Oklahoma City CofC, 75; Lifesize Sculpture of Pioneer Man, Bicentennial Comn of Clinton, Okla, 75. *Exhib:* Philbrook Mus Art Exhib, Tulsa, Okla, 67; Sci & Arts Found Exhib, Oklahoma City, 68; Oklahoma City Zoological Exhib, 68; Okla Mus Art Five State Salon, Oklahoma City, 71-72; Solon Borglum Mem Sculpture Exhib, Nat Cowboy Hall of Fame, Oklahoma City, 75. *Pos:* Preparator, Gilcrease Inst Am Hist & Art, Tulsa, 60-64; cur, Nat Cowboy Hall Fame, Oklahoma City, 65-69, art dir, 70-77, dep dir, 77-78, managing dir, 78- *Biblig:* Marcia Preston(auth), Orbit Mag, Okla Publ Co, 68; Dean Krakel (auth), End of the Trail, Okla Univ Press, 73. *Media:* Sculpture. *Collection:* Nat Acad Western Art Ann Exhibs, 73-75. *Publ:* Contribr, Persimmon Hill Mag, 72-75. *Mailing Add:* Nat Cowboy Hall of Fame & Western Heritage Ctr 1700 NE 63rd St Oklahoma City OK 73111

MUNOZ, RIE (MARIE ANGELINA MUNOZ)
PAINTER, PRINTMAKER
b Los Angeles, Calif. *Study:* Washington & Lee Univ; Univ of Alaska; pvt lessons. *Work:* Alaska State Mus; Anchorage Hist & Fine Arts Mus; Gov Off, Alaska. *Comn:* Alaska Coun Churches Mural, Univ Alaska Libr, Fairbanks, 67; Reindeer Round-Up, Reindeer Serv Bur Indian Affairs, 68; Ethnic People of Alaska Mural, Alaska State Libr, Juneau, 69; Covers, Jr Scholastics, 76. *Exhib:* Anchorage Mus Fine Arts, 71 & 78; Alaska State Mus, Juneau, 71 & 76; Ketchikan Mus, Alaska, 72; Charles & Emma Frye Mus, Seattle, Wash, 73, 75 & 81; Contemp Art from Alaska, Smithsonian Inst, Washington, DC, 78. *Pos:* Political cartoonist, SE Alaska Empire, 52-67; cur exhib, Alaska State Mus, Juneau, 68-72. *Awards:* Outstanding Alaska Artist, Anchorage Fine Arts Mus Asn, 77. *Biblig:* Artist in Juneau captures Alaska, Alaska Log, 73; Yvonne Mozee (auth), An interview with Rie Munoz, Alaska J, 74; Yvonne Mozee (auth), Rie Munoz--the artist from Juneau who gets around, Alaska Woman, 77. *Media:* Water-Base Colors; Silkscreen and Stone Lithography. *Publ:* Illusr, Juneau & its development, Alaska Develop Bd, 56; illusr, Alaska Camp Cook Book, Alaska Northwest, 62; illusr, Alaska Mag, 62-67; auth & illusr, Nursing in Alaska 1867-1967, Alaska Nurses Asn, 67; illusr, Kahtatah, Alaska Northwest Publ, 76. *Mailing Add:* 622 Fourth St Juneau AK 99801

MUNRO, ELEANOR
WRITER, CRITIC
b Brooklyn, NY, Mar 28, 28. *Study:* Smith Col, BA, 49; Columbia Univ, MA, 65; Sorbonne, Paris. *Collections Arranged:* The Eye of Eleanor Munro, Washington Women's Arts Ctr, 82. *Pos:* Assoc ed, Art News, New York, 53-59; managing ed, Art News Ann, New York, 54-59. *Mem:* Am Asn Art Critics; Int Asn Art Critics; Authors Guild; Women's Caucus Art; PEN Am. *Res:* Imagination and the creative process in the visual arts; pilgrimage in myth and art. *Publ:* Auth, Encyclop Art, Western Printing, 61; auth, Through the Vermilion Gates, Pantheon, 71; auth, Originals: American Women Artists, Simon & Schuster, 79 & Touchstone Press, 82; auth, Siva, the armed vision, Art in Am, 5/82; auth, Breaking stars: A collaboration in quilts, In: The Artist and the Quilt, Alfred Knopf, 83; auth, articles & reviews, var nat mags & newspapers. *Mailing Add:* 1095 Park Ave New York NY 10028

MUNRO, JANET ANDREA
PAINTER
b North Reading, Mass, Dec 8, 49. *Study:* Self-taught artist. *Work:* The White House & Smithsonian Inst, Washington, DC; Am Mus, Bath, Eng; Jay Johnson Am Folk Heritage Gallery, New York; and others. *Exhib:* One-woman shows, Country Art Gallery, Locust Valley, NY, 80, Fowler Mills Galleries, Santa Monica, Calif, 80, Art World Gallery, Acton, Mass, 80-81 & Americas Folk Heritage Gallery, New York, 81; Easter Egg Roll, White House, Washington, DC, 81; and others. *Biblig:* Carolyn Norwood (auth), Mrs Munro paints for the White House, Islander Weekly, 81; Kevin Dean (auth), Mrs Munro, Art Voices, 11-12/81; Contemporary primitives, Colonial Homes Mag, 1-2/82. *Media:* Oil, Egg Tempera. *Mailing Add:* c/o Americas Folk Heritage Gallery 1044 Madison Ave New York NY 10021

MUNSTERBERG, HUGO
HISTORIAN, EDUCATOR
b Berlin, Ger, Sept 13, 16; US citizen. *Study:* Harvard Col, AB, 38, Harvard Univ, PhD, 41. *Pos:* Art critic, Arts Mag, 57-60. *Teaching:* Asst prof fine arts, Mich State Univ, 46-49, assoc prof, 49-52; prof art hist, Int Christian Univ, Tokyo, 52-56; prof art hist, State Univ NY Col New Paltz, 58-78, chmn dept, 68-78; vis lectr, Bard Col & Parsons Sch Design, 79- *Mem:* Oriental Ceramic Soc London; Japan Soc. *Res:* Oriental art, China and Japan. *Collection:* Oriental art, especially ceramics. *Publ:* Auth, The Sculpture of the Orient, Dover, 72; auth, A History of Women Artists, 75; auth, The Modern Art of Japan, 78; contribr, Dictionary of Chinese and Japanese Art, 81; auth, Japanese Prints, 82; and others. *Mailing Add:* 48 Elting Ave New Paltz NY 12561

MUNZNER, ARIBERT
PAINTER, EDUCATOR
b Mannheim, Ger, Jan 9, 30. *Study:* Syracuse Univ, BFA; Cranbrook Acad Art, MFA. *Exhib:* Nat & regional shows, 53-63. *Teaching:* Instr painting & design, Minneapolis Sch Art, 55-68, assoc prof painting, Div Fine Arts, 68- *Mailing Add:* 2749 Bryant Ave S Minneapolis MN 55408

MURANAKA, HIDEO
PAINTER, PRINTMAKER
b Mitaka-shi, Tokyo, Japan, Feb 4, 46. *Study:* Tokyo Nat Univ Fine Arts & Music, BFA, 70, MFA, 72, cert, 74. *Work:* Brooklyn Mus; Achenback Found, Calif Palace Legion Hon. *Exhib:* One Hundred New Acquisitions, Brooklyn Mus, 78; 150 New Acquisitions, Achenback Found, Calif Palace Legion Hon, 80; Pacific Coast States Collection From the Vice President's House, Nat Mus Am Art, 81; Third Alaskan Wildlife Art Exhib, Anchorage Hist & Fine Art Mus, 82; 17th Nov Ann, Coos Art Mus, Coos Bay, Ore, 82; Rockford Int Biennale, Rockford Col, Ill, 83; Alabama Works on Paper Traveling Exhib, Auburn, 83; IEEE Centennial Art Contest, New York, 83. *Teaching:* Instr sumie, Acad Art Col, San Francisco, 74-75 & 84; teacher sumie & calligraphy, Acad Muranaka, San Francisco, 76-79. *Awards:* Purchase Prizes, Wesleyan Int Exhib Prints & Drawings, 80, Mid-Am Biennial, Owensboro Mus Fine Art, 82 & IEEE Centennial Art Contest, 83. *Bibliog:* Tom Kent (auth), Visuals, City, 5/14/75; Thomas Albright (auth), Art, San Francisco Chronicle, 5/14/75. *Collection:* Old American prints; old Oriental paintings. *Mailing Add:* 179 Oak St #W San Francisco CA 94102

MURASHIMA, KUMIKO
EDUCATOR, DESIGNER
b Nishinomiya, Japan. *Study:* Women's Col Fine Arts, Tokyo, BFA(textiles), 63; Serizawa Dyed Paper Inst, Tokyo, 63-67; Ind Univ, Bloomington, MFA(textiles), 69. *Work:* Evansville Mus Arts & Sci, Ind; Wills Eyes Hospital, Philadelphia; Flour Corp Hq, Irvine, Calif; Hackensack Medical Ctr, NJ; North Am Re-Insurance Co, New York; and others. *Comn:* Mural (woven tapestry), Disneyland Hotel Convention Ctr, Anaheim, Calif. *Exhib:* Artists Equity Triennial Juried Exhib, Mus Philadelphia, Civic Ctr, 81; Oriental Influence in Contemp Am Crafts, The Craftman's Gallery, Scarsdale, NY, 81; Wool Bureau, New York, 81; Fairmount Inst, Philadelphia, 82; Craftsman's Gallery, Scarsdale, NY, 82; and others. *Pos:* Freelance textile desinger, Izumi Archit Design, Co, Tokyo, 65-67 & Saphier, Lerner, Schindler, Inc, Environetics, 70-71. *Teaching:* Instr textile design, Glassboro State Col, 71-75, asst prof, 75-82, assoc prof, 82- *Awards:* Purchase Award, Mid-States Crafts Show, Malcolm Koch Mus, 69; Mr & Mrs Paul Arnold Merit Award, Mid-States Crafts Show '70. *Bibliog:* Dona Meilach (auth), Art Fabric: Its Form/Design, Crown Publ, 77; Eva Balassa (auth), article, Fibre Arts, 1-2/79; Burton Wasserman (auth), article, Artcrafts Mag, 8-9/80. *Mem:* Am Crafts Coun; Col Art Asn Am; Artists Equity Asn; Women's Caucus Art; New Jersey Designer/Craftsmen, Inc. *Media:* Weaving, Dyeing. *Publ:* Contribr, Pamela Scheiman's American Crafts, Am Crafts Coun, 78; contribr, Courier Post, Gloucester Times, Philadelphia Inquirer & Philadelphia Bulletin. *Mailing Add:* PO Box 515 Williamstown NJ 08094

MURATA, HIROSHI
PAINTER, PRINTMAKER
b Tokyo, Japan, Jan 18, 41. *Study:* RI Sch Design, BFA, 64; Yale Univ Sch Art, MFA, 66. *Work:* Larry Aldrich Mus Contemp Art, Ridgefield, Conn; Tokyo Univ Col Art; Nat Mus Mod Art, Kyoto; Nat Mus Mod Art, Tokyo; Kamakura Mus Mod Art, Japan. *Exhib:* Made with Paper Exhib, Mus Contemp Crafts, NY, 67; 17th Nat Print Exhib, Brooklyn Mus, 70; Contemporary Reflections, 71-72; Aldrich Mus, 72; Japanese Artists in the Americas, Nat Mus Mod Art, Tokyo & Kyoto, 73-74; Biennial Contemp Am Art, Whitney Mus, 75. *Teaching:* Asst prof art, Western Mich Univ, 66-70; from asst prof to assoc prof art, Trenton State Col, 72- *Awards:* Creative Arts Artists Pub Serv Grant, NY State Coun Arts, 72-73; Nat Endowment Arts Grant, 75-76. *Media:* Acrylic on Canvas; Silkscreen, Lithography. *Publ:* Illusr, Asahi J, 69 & Shincho-Sha Publ, 70. *Dealer:* Donna Schneier Inc E 71st St New York NY 10021. *Mailing Add:* 423 Broome St New York NY 10013

MURCH, ANNA VALENTINA
CONCEPTUAL ARTIST, PHOTOGRAPHER
b Dunbarton, Scotland, Dec 7, 48. *Study:* Leicester Polytechnic, BA, 71; Royal Col Art, London, MA, 73; Archit Asn, London, dipl, 74. *Exhib:* Holiday Exhib, San Francisco Mus Mod Art, Calif, 78; Sculpture in Public Places, San Mateo Co Arts, Belmont, 80; Three Sculptors, Kaiser Ctr, Oakland, Calif, 81; Installation, 80 Langton St Gallery, San Francisco, 81; Floating Mirrors, Mills Col, 82; Illuminated Building, Pro Arts, Oakland, 83; and others. *Teaching:* Lectr, Cal Polly Archit Dept, San Luis Obiso, 83; vis

instr, San Franciso Art Inst, 83. *Awards:* Rotaflex Award, Royal Col Art, London, 73; Honorarium Award, 80 Langton St Gallery, 81; Nat Endowment Arts, 83. *Bibliog:* Ruth Askey (auth), Inside & outside the women's building, Art Week, 4/78; Eric Hellman (auth), Materials made alive, Art Week, 11/78; Frank Cebuiski (auth), Similarities of space & place, Art Week, 8/81. *Media:* Multimedia. *Mailing Add:* 499 Alabama St Studio 306 San Francisco CA 94110

MURCHIE, DONALD JOHN
LIBRARIAN
b Plainfield, NJ, Nov 23, 43. *Study:* Univ Colo, BA; Dalhousie Univ, MLS. *Pos:* Libr dir, NS Col Art & Design, Halifax, 72- *Mem:* Art Libr Soc/NAm (mem exec bd, 75-78, chmn, 76). *Res:* Contemporary art; Canadian art history. *Publ:* Auth, Lines, Eye Level Gallery, 79; auth, A Quiet Evening, 79; auth, Opening, Open, Closed, Eye Level Gallery, 80; auth, An Invitation; or One-Way Ticket, 83. *Mailing Add:* 5163 Duke St Halifax NS B3J 3J6 Canada

MURDOCK, ROBERT MEAD
CURATOR
b New York, NY, Dec 18, 41. *Study:* Trinity Col, BA, 63; Yale Univ, MA(hist art), 65. *Pos:* Ford Found Mus Curatorial Training Prog interne, Walker Art Ctr, Minneapolis, 65-67; cur, Albright-Knox Art Gallery, Buffalo, 67-70; cur contemp art, Dallas Mus Fine Arts, 70-78; dir, Grand Rapids Art Mus, 78-83; chief cur, Walker Art Ctr, 83- *Awards:* Nat Endowment for the Arts Fels for Mus Prof, 73. *Res:* 20th century, especially constructivism, and recent American painting and sculpture. *Publ:* Auth, Today's half-century in Buffalo, Arts Mag, 3/68; Berlin/Hanover: The 1920s, Dallas Mus Fine Arts, 77; auth, Contemporary art in Europe, Art J, summer 81; Pioneers: Early 20th Century Art from Midwestern Mus, Grand Rapids Art Mus, 81; and others. *Mailing Add:* Walker Art Ctr Vineland Pl Minneapolis MN 55403

MURPHY, CATHERINE E
PAINTER
b Cambridge, Mass, Jan 22, 46. *Study:* Pratt Inst, BFA, 67; Skowhegan Sch Painting & Sculpture, with Elmar Bichoff, summer 66. *Exhib:* Whitney Mus Am Art Ann, New York, 71; Am Fedn Arts Group Traveling Landscape Show, 71-72; Whitney Mus, New York, 73; Storm King Arts Ctr, New York, 73; Indianapolis Mus, Ind, 74; Smithsonian Inst traveling exhib, 74-76; Mus Contemp Art, Chicago, 77; Am Acad Inst Arts & Letters, New York, 79; and others. *Awards:* Purchase Award, Am Fedn Arts, 71. *Media:* Oil. *Mailing Add:* c/o Xavier Fourcade Inc 36 E 75th New York NY 10021

MURPHY, CHESTER GLENN
PAINTER
b Harper, Kans, May 28, 07. *Study:* With Clyde Keller, Portland, Ore. *Comn:* Mural, Little World's Fair, Damascus, Ore, 62; two murals, Lake Oswego Shopping Ctr, Ore, 67; Ore scene in oil, USS Sperry, 69; two Ore scenes in oil, Western Elec, Vancouver, Wash, 72; George Fox Col, Newberg, Ore, 75. *Exhib:* Four-man show, Maryhill Mus Fine Arts, Wash, 60; three-man show, Dedication, Anna Hyatt Huntington Statue, Lincoln City, Ore, 65; Coun Am Artist Soc, 66; Vis Exhib of Ore Art, NMex State Capitol Bldg, 69; Am Artists Prof League Grand Nat, 71-77. *Teaching:* Instr oil painting, Willamette View Manor, 69-78; instr oil painting, Summer Workshops, Ore; guest lectr oil painting, Ore & Wash Pub Schs. *Awards:* First Prize, Lake Oswego Ann Arts & Flowers Festival; First in Prof Div, All-Ore Art Show, State Fair; Best of Show, Oak Grove Ann, 75. *Mem:* Fel Am Artists Prof League (pres, Ore Chap, 71); Ore Soc Artists; Coun Am Artist Soc. *Media:* Oil. *Publ:* Contribr, Art is For Everybody, 60; co-auth, An Artist Paints the Northwest, 71. *Mailing Add:* 19076 Midhill Dr West Linn OR 97068

MURPHY, DUDLEY C
EDUCATOR, GRAPHIC DESIGNER
b Danville, Ky, Apr 16, 40. *Study:* Univ Tulsa, BA, 65, MA, 69; Univ Okla, MFA, 71. *Exhib:* Okla Art Ctr, Oklahoma City, 70; Contemp Int Landscape Sculpture, traveling, Mo Arts Coun, 72; Nelson Gallery Art, St Louis, Mo, 74; Joslyn Art Mus, Omaha, Nebr, 74; SDak Art Ctr, Brookings, 75; Pittsburg State Univ, Kans, 79; and others. *Pos:* Design & layout artist, Litho Art Serv, Tulsa, Okla, 66-68; design & layout artist, Pub Relations Int Ltd, 68-69. *Teaching:* Instr design, SW Mo State Univ, Springfield, 69-70; cur educ, Springfield Art Mus, Mo, 71-78; assoc prof, Drury Col, Springfield, Mo, 78- *Awards:* First Place, 80 & Merit Award, 82, Springfield Ad Club; and others. *Bibliog:* Edgar A Albin (auth), Dudley Murphy, Artcraft Mag, 80. *Mem:* Springfield Ad Club; Nat Coun Ceramic Arts. *Publ:* Auth, Straw, private publ, 71. *Mailing Add:* 1418 East Portland Springfield MO 65804

MURPHY, GLADYS WILKINS
PAINTER, CRAFTSMAN
b Providence, RI, Apr 15, 07. *Study:* RI Sch Design. *Exhib:* Hope Show, Butler Inst Am Art; Am Watercolor Soc; Nat Acad Design; Libr Cong; Philadelphia Print Club; Philadelphia Art Alliance; and others. *Pos:* Owner, Art Gallery Rockport, Mass, 46-74. *Awards:* Burnett & Moore Award, Rockport Art Asn, 78. *Mem:* Providence Watercolor Club; North Shore Arts Asn; Rockport Art Asn. *Mailing Add:* 17 King St Rockport MA 01966

MURPHY, HASS
SCULPTOR, DRAFTSMAN
b Boston, Mass, Nov 1, 50. *Study:* Pratt Inst. *Exhib:* Romantic Abstraction, Brandeis Univ, Waltham, Mass, 71; Works on Paper, Logic Transformations, Contemp Arts Gallery, New York, 74; Biennial Exhib, Whitney Mus Am Art, New York, 75; New Drawings, New York, Grapestake Gallery, San Francisco, 75; Spare, Cent Hall Gallery, New York, 75. *Bibliog:* Interview,

Seven Painters, Artrite, spring 75; Judy Rifka & Willy Lenski (dirs), Ten Studios (film), Basel Art Fair, 75. *Media:* Steel, Limestone. *Dealer:* Nancy Lurie Gallery 1632 N La Salle Chicago IL 60614; Nancy Lurie Gallery 230 E Ohio St Chicago IL 60611. *Mailing Add:* 399 Washington St New York NY 10013

MURPHY, HERBERT A
ARCHITECT, PAINTER
b Fall River, Mass, June 13, 11. *Study:* RI Sch Design, 32. *Exhib:* Rockport Art Asn; NShore Art Asn; Providence Art Club; Providence Watercolor Club; RI Sch Design; and others. *Pos:* Registered architect, pvt practice, 41-83; co-dir, Art Gallery Rockport, Mass, 44- *Mem:* Rockport Art Asn (vpres, 60-62, pres, 63-65); Providence Watercolor Club. *Mailing Add:* 17 King St Rockport MA 01966

MURPHY, SUSAN (SUSAN MURPHY COLOMBINI)
PAINTER, CONCEPTUAL ARTIST
b New London, Conn, Sept 18, 50. *Study:* Col New Rochelle, with William Maxwell, 78-79. *Work:* Kresge Found, US Gypsum, Int Harvester, Quaker Oats, Mich Bell, Chicago. *Exhib:* Catharine Lorillard Wolfe Art Club, New York, 79; Southern Watercolor Soc, La Tech Univ, 81; Allied Artists Am, Nat Arts Club, New York, 81 & 82; Am Watercolor Soc, Nat Acad Design, New York, 82; Butler Inst Am Art Midyear Show, 82 & 83. *Pos:* Mgr, Gallery-Go-Round, Laurel, Md, 80-82. *Awards:* Gold Medal, Catharine Lorillard Wolfe Art Club 87th Ann, 79; Matching Funds Award, Allied Artists Am, 82; Abstract Award, Baltimore Watercolor Soc Mid-Atlantic Exhib, 83. *Mem:* Watercolor Soc, Southern, Baltimore & Midwest; Potomac Valley Watercolorists; Laurel Art Guild (pres, 82-83). *Media:* Watercolor. *Dealer:* Capricorn Galleries 4849 Rugby Ave Bethesda MD; Miriam Perlman Inc Lake Point Tower Suite 5410 Chicago IL. *Mailing Add:* 6915 Woodstream Lane Lanham-Seabrook MD 20706

MURRAY, ALBERT (KETCHAM)
PAINTER
b Emporia, Kans, Dec 29, 06. *Study:* Cornell Univ; Syracuse Univ, BFA(cum laude), 30; Eng & France, 31; also with Wayman Adams, NY & Mex, 34-38. *Work:* Nat Gallery Art, Nat Portrait Gallery & Nat Fine Arts Collection, Washington, DC; Departments of Defense, Com, Treasury & Attorney Gen, Washington, DC. *Comn:* Portrait of Laurance Rockefeller, NY Zool Soc, New York, 60; portrait of Arthur Ochs Sulzberger, New York Times, 63; portrait of R K Mellon, Pittsburgh, 64; portrait of Arthur K Watson, 75; portrait of H O Oppenheimer, Johannesburg, SAfrica, 77. *Exhib:* Carnegie Inst Int, Pittsburgh, 37; Corcoran Gallery Biennial, Washington, DC, 37; Your Navy, Metrop Mus Art, 48; American War Paintings, Salon Marine, Paris, 48; Men Who Made Washington, Nat Gallery Art, 51. *Awards:* US Navy Meritorious Pub Serv Award, 78. *Media:* Oil, Watercolor. *Dealer:* Grand Central Art Galleries Hotel Biltmore 40 Vanderbilt Ave New York NY 10017; Portraits Inc, 41 E 57th St New York NY 10022. *Mailing Add:* 33 W 67th St New York NY 10023

MURRAY, ELIZABETH
PAINTER
b Chicago, Ill, 1940. *Study:* Art Inst Chicago, BFA, 62; Mills Col, MFA, 64. *Work:* Detroit Inst Arts; Guggenheim Mus, New York; Hirshhorn Mus, Washington, DC; McCrory Corp, New York. *Exhib:* Whitney Mus 72-74, 77, 79 & 82; Baltimore Mus Art, 76; Nine Artists, Guggenheim Mus, 77; Boston Mus Fine Arts, 82; Art in Our Time, High Mus Art, Atlanta, 82; 74th Am Exhib, Art Inst Chicago, 82; Directions 83, Hirshhorn Mus, 83; and others. *Teaching:* Instr painting, Bard Col, 73-; vis prof painting, Calif Inst Arts, Valencia, 75-76; instr, Princeton Univ, NJ, 77. *Bibliog:* Donald Kuspit (auth), Elizabeth Murray's dandyish abstraction, Artforum, 2/78; Jeff Perone (auth), rev in Artforum, 1/79; John Russell (auth), Elizabeth Murray's shaped canvases, New York Times, 6/9/81. *Media:* Oil on Canvas. *Mailing Add:* c/o Paula Cooper 155 Wooster New York NY 10012

MURRAY, FLORETTA MAY
PAINTER, EDUCATOR
b Minn. *Study:* Winona State Univ, BEd; Univ Minn, MA & PhD; Minneapolis Col Art & Design; Univ Chicago; also in France, Belg & Italy. *Work:* Watkins Retirement Home; Univ Chicago; private collections of Benjamin & Abbey Grey, Dr & Mrs Truman Porter & Charles B Sweatt. *Comn:* History of Winona County (mural), Winona Co Hist Mus; pres medallion, Winona State Col. *Exhib:* St Paul Gallery Art, 60; Northrup Gallery, Univ Minn, 62; Nat League Am Pen Women, 68; Smithsonian Inst, 69; Minn Mus Art, 71-74; one-artist show, Jewish Community Ctr, St Paul, Minn, 76; plus others. *Teaching:* Prof art & chmn dept, Winona State Col, 38-76; prof art & actg head dept, Bemidji State Col, 49-50; prof, Col St Teresa, Winona, 55-58; instr painting, Univ Minn, Minneapolis, 58; lectr, St Mary's Col (Minn), 70. *Awards:* Merit Award, Minn State Fair, 38 & Rochester Art Ctr. *Mem:* Am Asn Univ Prof (secy-treas, 69-71); Nat Art Educ Asn; Am Asn Univ Women; Col Art Asn Am; Int Platform Asn; plus others. *Media:* Watercolor, Oil. *Mailing Add:* 65 West Lake Blvd Winona MN 55987

MURRAY, IAN STEWART
SCULPTOR, CONCEPTUAL ARTIST
b Pictou, NS, Nov 4, 51. *Study:* NS Col Art & Design, BFA(fine art), 72. *Work:* Art Gallery Ont; Can Coun Art Bank, Ottawa; Nat Gallery Can; Banff Ctr Walter Phillips Gallery; Mus Soladid, Santiago, Chile. *Exhib:* Record as Art, Royal Col Art, London, 73; Audio Scene, Mod Art Galerie, Wein, Austria, 79; Books by Artists, 80-82; Biennale of Sydney, Australia, 82; Second Link, Banff Mus Art & traveling, 83. *Collections Arranged:* Attitudes

Toward Photography (auth, catalog), Ann Leonowens Gallery, 72; Video From Eastern Canada, Forest City Art Gallery, 76; Radio by Artists (auth, catalog), Fine Art Broadcast Serv, 80. *Awards:* Can Coun Awards, 73, 76, 79 & 81. *Bibliog:* Phillip Monk (auth), Television by artists, Can Forum, 81; Nancy Tousley (auth), Complex piece stirs ..., Calgary Herald, 3/2/83; Mary-Beth Laviolette (auth), Audio by artists, Vanguard Mag, 4/83. *Mem:* Nightingale Arts Coun (vchair, 80-81). *Publ:* Auth, Twenty Waves in a Row, Straw Books, 71. *Mailing Add:* 51 Macdonell Ave Toronto ON M6R 2A3 Canada

MURRAY, JOAN
CRITIC, PHOTOGRAPHER
b Annapolis, Md, Mar 6, 27. *Study:* Calif Col Arts & Crafts, San Francisco Art Inst; Ruth Bernard Insight Studio; Univ Calif Exten; also studied with Wynn Bullock. *Work:* Int Mus Photog, Eastman House, Rochester, NY; San Francisco Mus Mod Art; Oakland Mus, Calif. *Exhib:* Brother and Sister, Focus Gallery, San Francisco, 69; Portraits of California Photographers, 72 & Photography/Film Center West, 72, Friends Photog Gallery, Carmel; Male Nudes--One Man, Mind's Eye Gallery, Vancouver, BC, 73. *Pos:* Photog ed, Artweek, 69-; WCoast critic, Popular Photog, 75-77; contrib ed, Am Photogr, 78- *Teaching:* Instr photog, Univ Calif Exten, 70-; instr photog, City Col San Francisco, 75- *Awards:* Nat Endowment Arts Grant Art Criticism, 78. *Mem:* Soc Photog Educ; Soc for Encouragement of Contemp Art of San Francisco Mus of Art. *Mailing Add:* 120 Blair Ave Piedmont CA 94611

MURRAY, JOHN MICHAEL
PAINTER
b Tampa, Fla, May 28, 31. *Study:* Univ Tampa, BA, 63; Ohio Univ, MFA, 65. *Work:* Staten Island Mus, NY; Bundy Art Mus, Watefield, Vt; NS Col Art, Halifax; NJ Mus. *Exhib:* Int Print Exhib, Crakow, 75; Langsam Gallery, Melbourne, Australia, 75; 19 Nat Print Exhib, Brooklyn Mus, 75; one-man shows, Dorsky Gallery, New York, 72, Halifax, 72, Blue Parrot, New York, 74 & Am Ctr, Belgrade, 81. *Teaching:* Chmn dept fine arts, New York Inst Technol, 66- *Awards:* First Prize in Painting, Fla State Ann, 63. *Mem:* Am Asn Univ Prof; Col Art Teachers. *Publ:* Contribr, Art Work--No Commercial Value, Grossman, 72; Pratt Graphics Reprint, 74. *Dealer:* James Yu Gallery 393 W Broadway New York NY 10012. *Mailing Add:* 124 W Houston St New York NY 10012

MURRAY, JUDITH
PAINTER
b New York, NY, Feb 22, 41. *Study:* Pratt Inst, Brooklyn, NY, BFA, 62, MFA, 64; Acad Fine Arts, Madrid, Spain, 63. *Work:* Brooklyn Mus, New York; Libr Congress; Honolulu Acad Fine Arts; New York Pub Libr; Chase Manhattan Bank, New York. *Exhib:* Print Exhib, Brooklyn Mus, New York, 62; A Painting Show & Works (traveling in ten countries), PS I, Project Space One, New York, 77; solo exhib, The ClockTower, Inst Art & Urban Resources, New York, 78; New York/a Selection from the Last Ten Yrs, Otis Art Inst, Los Angeles, 79; 1979 Biennial Exhib, Whitney Mus Am Art, New York, 79. *Media:* Oil. *Dealer:* Pam Adler Gallery 50 W 57th St New York NY 10019. *Mailing Add:* 598 Broadway New York NY 10012

MURRAY, RICHARD DEIBEL
PAINTER, SCULPTOR
b Youngstown, Ohio, Dec 25, 21. *Study:* Univ Notre Dame, BS, 42; Georgetown Univ, Md, 46; Univ Pa, 53. *Work:* Am Col Surgeons, Chicago; Staatsoper, Vienna, Austria; Medart Collection, Youngstown; Archduke Otto Von Hapsburg, Starnbergsee, Ger. *Comn:* Four limestone sculptures on four seasons, Mill Creek Park, Youngstown, 62; four murals & three limestone sculptures, Youngstown Symphony Ctr, 69. *Exhib:* Several exhibs, Butler Inst Am Art, Youngstown; several exhibs, Canton Art Inst, Ohio; several exhibs, Ohio State Fair, Columbus; Int, Galerie Int, New York, 72. *Awards:* Frank Punnell Award, Youngstown, Ohio, 66; Citation, City of Youngstown, Ohio, 79. *Media:* Mixed Media. *Mailing Add:* 2125 Glenwood Ave Youngstown OH 44511

MURRAY, RICHARD NEWTON
MUSEUM DIRECTOR
b Bartlesville, Okla, Aug 7, 42. *Study:* San Jose State Univ, Calif, BA, 68; Univ Chicago, MA, 70. *Collections Arranged:* Art for Architecture: Washington DC 1895-1925 (auth, catalog), Nat Collection Fine Arts, Smithsonian Press, 75; America as Art, 76; Elihu Vedder (auth, catalog), 78; American Renaissance: 1876-1917 (auth, catalog), Brooklyn Mus, 79. *Pos:* Asst dir, Nat Collection Fine Arts, DC, 76-79; dir, Birmingham Mus Art, Ala, 79-83 & Arch Am Art, Smithsonian Inst, 83- *Publ:* Auth, The drawings of Kenyon Cox, Drawing Mag, 80; auth, Art of the American West, Birmingham Mus Art, 82. *Mailing Add:* Arch Am Art Smithsonian Inst Washington DC 20560

MURRAY, ROBERT (GRAY)
SCULPTOR, PAINTER
b Vancouver, BC, Mar 2, 36. *Study:* Univ Sask Sch Art, 55-58; Mex, 59; Emma Lake Artist's Workshops. *Work:* Whitney Mus Am Art, Metrop Mus Art, New York; Walker Art Ctr, Minn; Everson Mus, Syracuse; Hirshhorn Mus, Washington, DC; and others. *Comn:* Sculpture, Dept External Affairs, Ottawa, 72; Wayne State Univ, Detroit, 74, Univ Mass, Amherst, 75, Alaska Court Bldg, Juneau, 78, Honeywell Inc, Minn, 79 & Univ Toronto, 83. *Exhib:* Whitney Mus Ann Exhib Contemp Sculpture, 64, 66, 68 & 70; American Sculpture of the Sixties, Los Angeles Co Mus, 67; 14 Sculptors: The Industrial Edge, Walker Art Ctr, Minn, 69; Condition of Sculpture, Hayward Gallery, London, 75; Sewall Gallery, Rice Univ, Houston; Dayton Mus; Columbus Mus; Art Gallery Greater Victoria. *Teaching:* Lectr, cols throughout US.

Awards: Can Coun Bursary, 60 & Sr Grant, 69 & 83; Second Prize, X Sao Paulo Biennial, Brazil, 69; Nat Endowment Arts Grant, 69. *Bibliog:* Krainin-Sage (auth), ArtIs (film), NY State Coun Arts, 71; Neil Marshall (auth), Robert Murray sculpture, Dayton Art Inst, 79; G Bellerby (auth), Robert Murray: Sculpture & Working Models, Art Gallery Greater Victoria, 83. *Media:* Steel, Aluminum. *Mailing Add:* First Floor 66 Grand St New York NY 10013

MUSGRAVE, SHIRLEY H
EDUCATOR, PHOTOGRAPHER
b Lexington, Ky, Nov 28, 35. *Study:* Miss State Col Women, BFA, 57; Colorado Springs Fine Arts Ctr, summer 56; Univ Kans, scholar, 57-58, MS, 63; Univ Ark, 64-65; Univ Iowa, 66-67; Fla State Univ, PhD(fel), 70. *Exhib:* One-artist photog exhib, Iowa City Civic Ctr, 65, Univ Ala-Huntsville, 72, Athens Col, Ala, 73 & Lambuth Col, Tenn, 74; Professional Women Artists of Florida, Lowe Art Mus, Miami, 76; Photograph, Huntsville Art League & Mus Asn Ann, Huntsville Art Mus, 79; and others. *Teaching:* Art supvr, Linwood Pub Schs, Kans, 58-60; assoc prof art educ, Memphis State Univ, 70-72 & Fla Int Univ; prof art educ & chairperson dept, Univ Ala, 78. *Awards:* Ark Artists Ann First Prize in Graphics, Little Rock Mus Fine Arts, 56; Fla Int Univ Found Grant, 76. *Mem:* Nat Art Educ Asn; Southeastern Col Art Conf; Ala Alliance Arts Educ; Ala Art Educ Asn. *Publ:* Coauth, Experiences in the Arts, 77; coauth, Annotated sources for Afro-American arts and the ancestral African background, Art Teacher, spring 80. *Mailing Add:* 1651 Northwood Lake Northport AL 35476

MUSGROVE, STEPHEN WARD
ADMINISTRATOR, CURATOR
b Pittsfield, Mass, Mar 28, 49. *Study:* Lenoir-Rhyne Col, BA(hist), 73; State Univ NY, Oneonta, 73-74, Cooperstown Grad Progs, MA(mus studies). *Pos:* Dir, Catawba Sci Ctr, Hickory, NC, 74-75; asst dir, Mint Mus of Art, Charlotte, NC, 75- *Mem:* Am Asn Mus; Am Asn for State & Local Hist; Southeastern Mus Conf; NC Mus Coun. *Publ:* Auth & illusr, Making exhib labels: a mechanical lettering system, 76 & Electrifying exhibits: low voltage techniques, 78, Hist News; The almanac: neglected witness of the American experience, 79 & For the fun of it, 80, Southeastern Mus Conf J. *Mailing Add:* PO Box 6011 Charlotte NC 28207

MUSICK, PAT
PAINTER, EDUCATOR
b Los Angeles, Calif, Sept 14, 26. *Study:* Cornell Univ, MA(design), 73, PhD(psychol), 74; with Paul Sample, Alan D'Arc Angelo. *Work:* Dartmouth Col, Hanover, NH; Exeter Acad, NH; Univ Houston; Univ Houston, Clear Lake City, Tex. *Comn:* Mural, oil on canvas, Ya I'ma Kan, Cancun, Mex. *Exhib:* Regional Exhib, Everson Mus, Syracuse, NY, 71; Q Roo, O'Kane Gallery, Houston, 81; Pizzo Calabro Ann, Italy; solo exhib, Amalfi Antichi Arsenali, Italy; Tex Only Exhib & Traveling Exhib; Jewish Community Ctr Ann Eighteenth. *Pos:* Pres, Carr-Musick Inc, Houston, currently; regist art therapist, Univ Houston, Clear Lake City, 77- *Teaching:* Teacher fine arts, Kimball Union Acad, 63-66; instr art, Dartmouth Col Alumni Prog, 64-65; instr drawing, Cornell Univ, 67-68; assoc prof creativity, Univ Houston, Clear Lake City, 76-; vis prof painting, Univ Houston Downtown, 82-83. *Awards:* Second Prize, Jewish Community Ctr Houston Ann Nat, 83; Gold Medal, Best Foreign Entry, Pizzo Calabro, Italy, 83. *Bibliog:* Art eases pain of parting, Houston Chronicle, 10/28/79; Artist puts violence in perspective, Houston Post, 8/16/81; Juried art exhibition cohesive and exciting, Houston Chronicle, 2/22/83. *Mem:* Am Art Therapy Asn; Div Psychol & Arts, Am Psychol Asn; Tex Fine Arts Asn; Women's Caucus Arts. *Media:* Oil on Canvas, Mixed Media. *Res:* The creative potential of psychotic patients. *Collection:* Kollwitz, Modigliani, Sample, Dorceley, Nottebaum, Mestrovic, Kennedy, Bott, Zuniga, Picasso & Matisse. *Publ:* Auth-illusr, Paintings and Poetry: A Teaching/Learning Experience, 77 & Creative Emergence: A Synthesis, 80, Pergammon Press; Imagery: A Metaphor for Health, Asn Study Mental Imagery, 79; auth, Greek Gods and the Unconscious, 81; auth, Creativity: Abreaction for the Therapist, 81; auth, Huracan: Paintings & Poetry Impressions of the Maya, 83. *Dealer:* Anakena Galleries Cancun Mex. *Mailing Add:* 2138 Colquitt Houston TX 77098

MUSSELMAN, DARWIN B
PAINTER
b Selma, Calif, Feb 16, 16. *Study:* Fresno State Col, AB, 38; Art Ctr Col Design, Los Angeles, 38-39; Calif Col Arts & Crafts, MFA, 50; Univ Calif, Berkeley, MA, 52; also with Lyonel Feininger, 37 & Yasuo Kuniyoshi, 49. *Work:* Oakland Art Mus, Calif; Fresno Arts Ctr, Calif; Reedley Jr Col, Calif; Sloan-Kettering Hosp, New York; Harvey Mudd Col. *Comn:* Mural of cotton indust, Prod Cotton Oil Co, Fresno, 54. *Exhib:* 3rd Ann Legion of Honor Exhib, San Francisco, 48; Calif Watercolor Soc Exhib, Riverside Gallery, NY, 48; Calif Artists Exhib, Los Angeles Mus, 49; Denver Mus Ann, Colo, 54; Butler Inst Art Nat, Youngstown, Ohio, 56; Fresno Arts Ctr, 82; Wichita Art Asn, 82; and others. *Pos:* Artist & art dir, Thomas Advert, Fresno, 39-41 & 45-46. *Teaching:* Assoc prof painting & art educ, Calif Col Arts & Crafts, 48-53; prof painting & commercial art, Fresno State Univ, 53-78. *Awards:* First Prize Painting, San Joaquin Valley Art Contest, Rouze Gallery, Fresno, 47, Northern Calif Arts, Crocker Gallery, Sacramento, Calif, 56 & Ann Show, Fresno Arts Ctr, 61. *Bibliog:* Emil Kosa, Jr (auth), California painters, Am Artist Mag, 3/50; Barbara Cott (auth), Darwin Musselman, Fresno Arts Ctr, 62. *Mem:* Am Watercolor Soc; Calif Nat Watercolor Soc; Am Portrait Soc. *Media:* Oil, Egg Tempera, Watercolor. *Publ:* Illusr, Valley of the Yokuts, 40. *Dealer:* Portraits Inc New York NY; Ratliff Gallery Ft Worth Texas. *Mailing Add:* 5161 N Sequoia Dr Fresno CA 93711

MYER, PETER LIVINGSTON
KINETIC ARTIST, EDUCATOR
b Ozone Park, NY, Sept 19, 34. *Study:* Brigham Young Univ, BA, 56; Univ Utah, MFA, 59; summers with Harry Sternberg & Joseph Hirsch. *Work:* Colorado Springs Fine Arts Ctr & Denver Art Mus, Colo; Univ Nev, Las Vegas; Phoenix Art Mus, Ariz. *Exhib:* Light, Motion, Space, Walker Art Ctr, Minneapolis, 67; Some More Beginnings, Brooklyn Mus, 68; Art & Technology, High Mus Art, Atlanta, Ga, 69; Art of the 60's, Denver Art Mus, 70; Kinetic Light Show, Phoenix Art Mus, Ariz, 73; Utah Valley Sculptors Invitational Exhib, Springville Art Mus, 77; retrospective, Springville Art Mus, Utah, 79; Glass and Light (one-man show), Salt Lake City, 81; Eccles Art Ctr, Ogden, Utah, 83; and others. *Teaching:* Assoc prof art & chmn dept, Univ Nev, Las Vegas, 62-72; art gallery dir, Brigham Young Univ, 72-78, prof art, 72- *Awards:* Best in Show for Ars Moriendi, Spring Art Roundup, 65; Second Prize/Painting, Utah State Inst of Fine Arts Exhib, 74; Purchase Award, Utah Biennial/Salt Lake City Art Ctr, 75. *Bibliog:* Kranz (auth), Science and Technology and the Arts, Rheinhold, 74. *Mem:* Western Asn Art Mus; Am Asn Art Mus; Utah Mus Asn (mem adv comt, 77). *Media:* Kinetic Light Art/Sculpture. *Mailing Add:* Dept Art Harris Fine Arts Ctr Brigham Young Univ Provo UT 84602

MYERS, C STOWE
DESIGNER, PAINTER
b Altoona, Pa, Dec 7, 06. *Study:* Univ Pa, BFA; Grand Cent Sch Art, New York; Chouinard Sch Art, Los Angeles, Calif. *Exhib:* Int Exhib Indust Design, Mus Mod Art, Buenos Aires, Arg, 63; Int Exhib Indust Design, Salle Arts Decoratif, Louvre, Paris, 64; var design exhibs, USA & Abroad, 64-80; Art Inst Chicago, Sales & Rental Gallery, 81- *Pos:* Designer, Norman Bel Geddes, 33-35; partner, Walter Dorwin Teague, 35-49; assoc, Raymond Loewy, 49-53; owner, Stowe Myers Design, 54-72; owner, Design Planning Group/Chicago, Ill, 72-74; consult, 74-77; retired, 78; partic artist, US Air Force Art Prog, 79- *Teaching:* Lectr design, Sch Design, Ill Inst Technol. *Mem:* Indust Designers Soc Am; Munic Art League of Chicago; Artists Guild Chicago; Am Watercolor Soc; and others. *Mailing Add:* 2828 N Burling St Chicago IL 60657

MYERS, CAROLE ANN
PAINTER, INSTRUCTOR
b Shawnee, Okla, Dec 28, 34. *Study:* Instituto Allende, San Miguel de Allende, Mexico, 71; Univ Okla, Extension Div Colima, Mexico with Milford Zornes, 75-76; with Edgar Whitney, Robert E Wood & Tom Nicholas, 77-79. *Work:* Monsanto World Headquarters, St Louis, Mo; Sinclair Research, Tulsa, Okla; Ft Smith Art Ctr, Ark; Commercial Nat Bank, Muskogee, Okla; US Nat Bank, Omaha, Nebr. *Exhib:* Eight States Exhib Painting & Sculpture, Okla Art Ctr, Okla City, 66, 68 & 72; Mid-Year Show, Butler Inst Am Art, Youngstown, Ohio, 70; La Watercolor Soc Int, Int Trade Mart Bldg, Baton Rouge, 74 & 76; Nat Soc Painters Casein & Acrylic Ann, Am Acad Inst Arts & Letters, NY, 79, 82 & 83; Am Watercolor Soc 112th Ann, Nat Acad Galleries, New York, 79; Open Watercolor Exhib, Nat Arts Club, New York, 81 & 83; San Diego Watercolor Soc Int Exhib, 83. *Collections Arranged:* Christian Art by St Louisans, Bellefontaine United Methodist Church, Mo, 75. *Teaching:* Instr painting & drawing, 17 Schs Stoddard Co, Mo, 71; instr watercolor, Private Workshops, Valles, Mex, 79-80; instr watercolor & acrylic/collage, Private Workshops, Oaxaca, Mex, 81 & 83. *Awards:* Eliz Erlanger Mem, Nat Soc Painters Casein & Acrylic 26th Ann, 79; John Young-Hunter Mem, Am Watercolor Soc, 79; The Marion de Sola Mendes Award, Nat Soc Painters in Casein & Acrylic, 82. *Bibliog:* Chrystal Jackson (dir), Painting with Carole Myers (film), Chrystal Jackson, 78. *Mem:* Am Watercolor Soc; Acad Professional Artists; Southern Watercolor Soc; St Louis Artists' Guild; Nat Soc Painters in Casein & Acrylic. *Media:* Watercolor, Acrylic-Collage. *Dealer:* Puccio's Gallery W 13496 Clayton Rd St Louis Mo 63131. *Mailing Add:* 12870 Ellsinore Bridgeton MO 63044

MYERS, FORREST WARDEN
SCULPTOR
b Long Beach, Calif, Feb 14, 41. *Study:* San Francisco Art Inst. *Work:* Whitney Mus Am Art, New York; Hirshhorn Mus, Washington, DC; Storm King Art Ctr, NY; Walker Art Ctr, Milwaukee; Aldrich Mus Contemp Art, Ridgefield, Conn; and others. *Exhib:* Calif Sch Fine Arts, San Francisco, 58-59; Jewish Mus, 67; Philadelphia Mus Art, 68; Los Angeles Co Mus, 68; Whitney Mus Am Art, 68, 70 & 73; Middleheim Mus, Antwerp, Belg; and others. *Teaching:* Instr sculpture, San Francisco Art Inst, 67; instr, Sch Visual Art, NY, 68; instr sculpture, Kent State Univ, 78. *Awards:* Guggenheim Fel, 73; Creative Artists Pub Serv Prog Grant, 77; Nat Endowment Arts Grant, 78; and others. *Mailing Add:* 238 Park Ave S New York NY 10003

MYERS, FRANCES
PRINTMAKER
b Racine, Wis, Apr 16, 36. *Study:* Univ Wis, MFA; San Francisco Art Inst. *Work:* Libr Cong, Washington, DC; Victoria & Albert Mus, London; Metrop Mus Art, New York; Chicago Art Inst; Nat Collection Fine Arts, Washington, DC. *Comn:* Limited ed print, Wis Arts Coun, 71 & Madison Print Club, 79; ed of prints, Frank Lloyd Wright Portfolio, Perimeter Press, 80 & Gov Wis Arts Awards, 81. *Exhib:* Biennial of Prints, Mus d'Art Mod, Paris, 70; 20th & 22nd Print Biennale, Brooklyn Mus, 76 & 81; Fifth & 8th Brit Int Print Biennale, 76 & 84; New Acquisitions, Brooklyn Mus, 79; Haslem Gallery, Washington, DC, 81; Madison Art Ctr, Wis, 81; Am Biennial Graphic Arts, Cali, Colombia, 81; 14th Int Biennial Graphic Arts, Ljubljana, Yugoslavia, 81; and others. *Pos:* Cur, Printed by Women Exhib, Port Hist, Penn's Landing, Philadelphia, 83. *Teaching:* Lectr printmaking, St Martin's Sch Art, London, 66-67 & Col Art & Design, Birmingham, Eng, 66; vis lectr, Art Dept, Univ

Wis-Madison, 75, 76, 80 & 82-84; distinguished prof art, Mills Col, Oakland, Calif, 79; vis lectr, Art Dept, Univ Calif, Berkeley, 82. *Awards:* Nat Endowment Arts Graphics Fel, 74-75; H Lester Cooke Found Fel, 77; Wis Arts Bd Grant, 77-78. *Dealer:* Jane Haslem Gallery Washington DC. *Mailing Add:* Hollandale WI 53544

MYERS, FRED A
MUSEUM DIRECTOR
b Lancaster, Pa, Dec 21, 37. *Study:* Harvard Univ, BA, 59, MA, 62. *Pos:* Asst to dir, Mus Art, Carnegie Inst, Pittsburgh, 62-70; dir, Grand Rapids Art Mus, Mich, 70-78; dir, Thomas Gilcrease Inst of Am Hist & Art, Tulsa, 78- *Mem:* Asn Art Mus Dir. *Mailing Add:* Gilcrease Inst 1400 N 25th West Ave Tulsa OK 74127

MYERS, JACK FREDRICK
PAINTER, EDUCATOR
b Lima, Ohio, Feb 17, 27. *Study:* Cleveland Art Inst, Ohio; Kent State Univ, MFA. *Exhib:* May Show, Cleveland Mus of Art, 49-54, 76-81; Freedson Gallery, Lakewood, Ohio, 69; Mid-Year Show, Butler Inst of Am Art, Youngstown, Ohio, 76, 78, 79 & 82; Nat Print Competition, San Diego State Univ, Calif, 80; Birke Art Gallery, Marshall Univ, Huntington, WVa, 81; Colorprint USA, Mus Tex Tech Univ, Lubbock, 83. *Pos:* Art dir, Premier Industrial Corp, 56-70. *Teaching:* Instr graphics & film, Cooper Sch Art, Cleveland, 70-80; prof art & dir commercial design, Univ Dayton, 82- *Awards:* First Prize Art Category, Doc Film Competition, Bolex-Newsweek Mag, 69; First Prize (one minute animated film), ASIFA Festival, New York, 74; Purchase Prize, Mid-Year Show, Butler Inst of Am Art, 79; Special Mention, May Show, Cleveland Mus Art, 79 & 80; and others. *Media:* Oil, Tempera. *Dealer:* Miller Gallery 2722 Erie Ave Cincinnati OH 45208. *Mailing Add:* 4420 Woodner Rd Kettering OH 45440

MYERS, JOEL PHILIP
ARTIST IN GLASS, EDUCATOR
b Paterson, NJ, Jan 29, 34. *Study:* Parsons Sch Design, NY, grad with honors, 54; NY State Col Ceramics, Alfred Univ, BFA, 62, MFA, 67. *Work:* Corning Mus Glass, NY; Ill State Mus, Springfield; Mus du Verre, Liege, Belg; Mus Stadt Dusseldorf, WGer. *Exhib:* One-man shows, George Walter Vincent Smith Art Mus, Springfield, Mass, 72; Columbia Col Gallery, Chicago, 79 & Habatat Gallery, Dearborn, Mich, 79; Glas Heute, Mus Bellerive, Zurich, Switz, 72; Enmansglas, Rosska Konstlojdsmuseet, Sweden, 74. *Pos:* Dir design, Blenke Glass Co, Milton, WVa, 63-70. *Teaching:* Prof art, ceramics & glass, Ill State Univ, Normal, 70- *Awards:* Fed Glass Award, Columbus Gallery Fine Arts, 73; craftsmen's fel, Nat Endowment Arts, 76-77; Purchase Award, Evansville Mus Arts & Sci, 79. *Bibliog:* Julie Hall (auth), Tradition and Change: The New American Craftsman, Dutton, 77; Illinois Artists at Work (WTVP video tape prog), Ill Valley Pub Telecomm Corp, Peoria, 79; Compositions in black: Joel Philip Myers, Am Craft, 10-11/80. *Mem:* Glass Art Soc. *Media:* Glass. *Mailing Add:* RR 2 Bunn St Rd Bloomington IL 61701

MYERS, LEGH
SCULPTOR
b Ventnor, NJ, Nov 11, 16. *Study:* Pa State Univ, 35-36; Lehigh Univ, 36-39; also with J Wallace Kelly, 52-54. *Work:* Numerous pvt collections in Tokyo, Japan & throughout US. *Exhib:* 13 shows, Knickerbocker Artists Ann, Nat Arts Club, New York, 57-81; 17 shows, Audubon Artists Ann, Nat Acad Design, New York, 60- & Allied Artists Ann, 61 & 62; Sculptors Guild Ann Mem Show, Lever House, New York, 71-; plus four one-man shows in New York. *Awards:* Audubon Artists Medal Creative Sculpture, 28th Ann Exhib, 70 & Margaret Hirsch Levine Mem Prize Sculpture, 30th Ann Audubon Artists Exhib, 72, Nat Acad Design. *Mem:* Sculptors Guild (dir & secy, 72-); Audubon Artists; Knickerbocker Artists; Artists Equity Asn of New York. *Media:* Marble, Wood. *Mailing Add:* 9 S Mansfield Ave Margate NJ 08402

MYERS, MALCOLM HAYNIE
PRINTMAKER, PAINTER
b Lucerne, Mo, June 19, 17. *Study:* Wichita State Univ, BFA; Univ Iowa, MA & MFA. *Work:* Libr Cong, Washington, DC; St Louis Art Mus; Walker Art Ctr, Minneapolis; Seattle Art Mus; Brooklyn Art Mus; plus others. *Exhib:* Ford Found Award, USA, 57; Am Prints Today, Print Coun; New York World's Fair Art Exhib; retrospective, Mr Possum and Friends, 1940-1983, Mus Art, Univ Minn, 82; one-person exhib, Walking the Dog, Dolly Fiterman Fine Art Gallery, Minneapolis, 82; and others. *Teaching:* Instr art, Univ Iowa, 45-47; prof art, Univ Minn, Minneapolis, 48-, chmn dept art, 65-70. *Awards:* Guggenheim Fels, 50-51 & 54-55; Ford Found Award, 57; Alumni Achievement Award, Wichita State Univ, Kans, 73. *Bibliog:* Article in Artists Proof, 60; Kenneth Campbell (dir), Malcolm Myers (film), Wis State Univ-Eau Claire, 69. *Mem:* Artists Equity Asn (pres Twin City chap, 53-55). *Dealer:* Dolly Fiterman Fine Art Gallery Minneapolis MN. *Mailing Add:* Dept of Studio Arts Univ Minn Minneapolis MN 55455

MYERS, MARTIN
SCULPTOR, PAINTER
b Syracuse, NY, April 21, 51. *Study:* Va Commonwealth Univ, BFA, 73; Calif Col Arts & Crafts, MFA, 74. *Work:* Oakland Mus; San Francisco Mus Mod Art. *Exhib:* Virginia Artists--1973, Va Mus Fine Arts, 73; Cityscapes, Fine Arts Mus San Francisco, 77; 35th Biennial Contemp Painting, Corcoran Gallery Art, 77; A Sense of Scale, Oakland Mus, 77; Viewpoint/77--Options in Painting, Cranbrook Mus, 77-78; Sculpture in California, 1975-1980, San Diego Mus, 80; New Bay Area Painting & Sculpture, Calif State Univ, Northridge, 82 & San Francisco Art Inst, 83. *Bibliog:* Judith Dunham (auth), Sculpture as painting as sculpture, Artweek, 77; Morris Yarowsky (auth), article, Art in Am, 79; Richard Armstrong (auth), catalog, Modernism, 81. *Media:* Painted Sculpture. *Dealer:* Wanda Hansen 615 Main St Sausalito CA 94110. *Mailing Add:* 178 Suffolk St #5 New York NY 10002

MYERS, RICHARD LEWIS
PHOTOGRAPHER, FILMMAKER
b Massillon, Ohio, Dec 1, 37. *Study:* Mexico City Col, 57; Art Students League, New York, 57; Kent State Univ, Ohio, BFA, 59, MA, 61. *Comn:* Doc film, Massillon Mus, Ohio, 75. *Exhib:* Detroit Art Inst, Mich; Univ Calif Los Angeles; Akron Art Inst, Ohio; Chicago Film Festival, Ill; Univ Calif Berkeley; Yale Univ, New Haven, Conn; Mus Mod Art, New York; Whitney Mus Art; and others. *Teaching:* Prof art & cinematography, Kent State Univ, 64- *Awards:* Guggenheim Fel for Film-making, 69 & 71; Am Film Inst Grant, 70; Nat Endowment Arts Grant, 75, 77 & 83. *Bibliog:* Amos Vogel (auth), Film as Subversive Art, Random, 75; Kevin Thomas (auth), Panorama of Imagination, Los Angeles Times, 10/14/75; other reviews in Hollywood Reporter, Los Angeles Free Press, Take One Mag, Film Makers Newsletter, Village Voice, Film Quart Mag & Variety. *Mailing Add:* Independent Films 1224 N Mantua St Kent OH 44240

MYERS, VIRGINIA ANNE
PRINTMAKER, PAINTER
b Greencastle, Ind, May 8, 27. *Study:* Corcoran Sch Art & George Washington Univ, Washington, DC, BA, 49; Calif Col Arts & Crafts, MFA, 51; Univ Ill, Champaign; Univ Iowa, Iowa City, printmaking with Mauricio Lasansky; Atelier 17, Paris, printmaking with Stanley William Hayter. *Work:* San Francisco Art Mus; Nelson-Atkins Mus, Kansas City, Kans; Toledo Mus Art, Ohio; Lehigh Univ Art Collection, Bethlehem, Pa; US State Dept. *Exhib:* Eighty-three one-woman shows, 53-79; Engravings America 1974, Albrecht Art Gallery, St Joseph, Mo, 74; West '79/The Law Exhibition, Minn Mus Art, St Paul; Nat Invitational Exhib, Univ Hawaii, Hilo, 82; and others. *Teaching:* Instr printmaking, Univ Iowa, Iowa City, 62-68, asst prof, 68-71, assoc prof, 71-80, prof, 81- *Awards:* Fulbright Grant to Paris, 61; Develop Leave Award, Univ Iowa, 73, 78 & 84; Arts Endowment Grants, State Iowa Arts Coun & Nat Endowment Arts, 74, 77 & 82. *Bibliog:* Denis O'Brien Van (auth), Iowan seeks perfections in art, teaching, Des Moines Register, 8/29/72; Joan Liffering and John Zug (auths), Virginia Myers, printmaker, Iowan Mag, winter 81. *Media:* Copper Plates; Oil on Canvas. *Publ:* Creator, A Time of Malfeasance (21 engravings & drypoints), 77; creator, Views from Tenacre: The Seasons (66 paintings & drawings on landscape themes); contribr, Handmade ink: A primer of basic principles, Printnews, 4-5/79, reprinted in Imprint, Print Coun Australia, fall 79; and others. *Mailing Add:* Tenacre Rte 3 Solon IA 52333

MYFORD, JAMES C
SCULPTOR, EDUCATOR
b Brackenridge, Pa, Aug 9, 40. *Study:* Edinboro Univ Pa, BS(art educ), 62; Ind Univ Pa, MEd(art educ), 66, MA(sculpture), 78. *Work:* Westmoreland Co Mus Art, Greensburg, Pa; Carnegie Libr, Pittsburgh, Pa. *Comn:* Outdoor aluminum sculptures, Aluminum Co Am, Pittsburgh, Pa, 75, First Nat Bank Pa, Erie, 78, Bloomsburg Univ, 80 & Manufacturing Data Systems Inc, Ann Arbor, Mich, 81; sculpture (stone & aluminum), City Pittsburgh, Pa, 83. *Exhib:* Assoc Artists Pittsburgh, Mus Art, Carnegie Inst, 70-83; 25th Ann Ball State Exhib, 79; Aluminum Sculpture, William Penn Mem Mus, Harrisburg, Pa, 79, Westmoreland Co Mus Art, Greensburg, Pa, 79 & Butler Inst Am Art, 83; Cast Aluminum Sculpture, Mus Art, Carnegie Inst, Pittsburgh, Pa, 80; Art Gallery Ont, 83; Sculptors Who Teach, Gov Mansion, Harrisburg, Pa, 83. *Teaching:* Assoc prof art, Slippery Rock Univ, 68- *Awards:* Alcoa Award, Assoc Artist Pittsburgh, 78; Jurors Award, Pittsburgh Soc Sculptors, 80; Second Prize Sculpture, Great Lakes Art Exhib, 82. *Bibliog:* Richard Sutphen (producer), Preparation for Museum Show (videotape), 81; Marilyn Evert (auth), Discovering Pittsburgh's Sculpture, Univ Pittsburgh Press, 83. *Mem:* Int Sculpture Ctr; Pittsburgh Soc Sculptors (bd mem, 80-82); Assoc Artists Pittsburgh. *Media:* Aluminum. *Mailing Add:* 327 State St Grove City PA 16127

MYRON, ROBERT
HISTORIAN
b Brooklyn, NY, Mar 15, 28. *Study:* NY Univ, BA, 49, MA, 50; Ohio State Univ, PhD(fel), 53. *Teaching:* Prof art hist & chmn art appraisal, Hofstra Univ, Hempstead, NY, 54- *Awards:* Belgium-Am Found Awards, 53. *Mem:* Am Soc Appraisers; Appraisers Asn Am. *Res:* Tribal arts; American-Asian and Western art. *Publ:* Auth, Prehistoric Art, 59 & Italian Renaissance, 61, Pitman; auth, Mounds, Towns, Totems, 63 & Two Faces of Asia: India, China, 65, World; auth, American Art, 2 vols, Crowell-Collier, 70. *Mailing Add:* Dept Art, Hist & Humanities Hofstra Univ Hempstead NY 11550

N

NAAR, HARRY I
PAINTER, EDUCATOR
b New Brunswick, NJ, July 28, 46. *Study:* Philadelphia Col Art, BFA, 68; Ind Univ, MFA, 70. *Work:* Ind Univ, Bloomington; Morris Mus Arts & Sci, Morristown, NJ; Rutgers Univ Art Mus; NJ State Mus, Trenton; Continental Life Insurance Corp, Piscataway, NJ. *Exhib:* Nat Drawing Exhib, Indianapolis Mus Art, 70, Corcoran Gallery Art, 70, High Mus Art, 70 & Trenton State Col, 83; NJ Landscape Show, Hunterdon Art Ctr, Clinton, 74; Biennial NJ Exhib, 74, 75 & 79 & solo exhib, 77, NJ State Mus, Trenton; Artists Choice Exhib, A M Sachs Gallery, New York, 80. *Teaching:* Instr painting & drawing, Beaver Col, Pa, 75-78 & Rutgers Univ, 78-80; asst prof painting, drawing & printmaking, Rider Col, NJ, 80- *Bibliog:* Rachel Mullen

(auth), Strength from nature, Bernardsville News, 4/77; Doris Brown (auth), Focus on still life, Sunday Home News, NJ, 1/7/79. *Mem:* Col Art Asn Am; Printmaking Coun NJ (bd mem, 83). *Media:* Oil, Watercolor. *Publ:* Auth, Prich Matthews Color in Space, NJ State Mus, 82; contribr, Graphite: A Collector's Choice, An Idea About Contemporary Drawing, Montgomery Col, 83; auth, ... Enjoyable to Sense, Beautiful to See, Ericson Gallery, 83. *Dealer:* David Adamson Gallery Washington DC. *Mailing Add:* 300 B Crowells Rd Highland Park NJ 08904

NADALINI, (LOUIS ERNEST)
PAINTER
b San Francisco, Calif, Jan 21, 27. *Study:* City Col San Francisco; Art Students League, with George Grosz; also with Martin Baer, San Francisco, 58-60; San Francisco Art Inst, Hon MA, 70. *Work:* Oakland Art Mus, Univ Calif, Berkeley, San Francisco Pub Sch & Wells Fargo Bank, San Francisco, Calif; Veterans Administration Hospital, Seattle, Wash. *Exhib:* One-man shows, Village Art Ctr, New York, 53 & Am Student & Artist Ctr, Paris, 54; San Francisco Mus Art Painting Ann, 57-59 & 66; Calif Palace Legion Honor, San Francisco, 63-67; Pa Acad Fine Arts 161st Ann, 66; Oakland Art Mus Painting Ann, 66-69; La Galerie Mouffe, Paris, France; Minami Gallery, Tokyo, Japan; El Crito Gallery, Caracas, Venezuela. *Teaching:* Instr art, San Francisco Pub Sch, 69-70. *Awards:* James D Phelan Award, Calif Palace Legion Honor, 65 & 67; Salon Int Diploma, D Honneur, Paris, France, 81; Merit Award Art, London, Eng, 80; Gold Medal, Acad Italy, 80. *Bibliog:* A Fried (auth), article, San Francisco Examr, 58; A Frankenstein (auth), article, San Francisco Chronicle, 66; W Ramsey (auth), Paintings, KPIX-TV, San Francisco, 1/66. *Mem:* Artists Equity Asn (vpres Seattle chap, currently). *Media:* Oil, Acrylic. *Publ:* Auth, Catalogue of the Art Bank, San Francisco Art Inst Sch, 59-60; auth, From the West, San Francisco Art Inst, 64; auth, articles & rev in Artforum, 3/66 & 5/71 & San Francisco Arts, 6/67. *Dealer:* Gordon Woodside Galleries 803 E Union St Seattle WA 98122; La Galerie Mouffe 67 Rue Mouffetard 75005 Paris France. *Mailing Add:* 1726 15th Ave #10 Seattle WA 98122

NADLER, HARRY
PAINTER, EDUCATOR
b Los Angeles, Calif, Feb 17, 30. *Study:* Univ Calif, Los Angeles, BA, 56, MA, 58. *Work:* Univ Mass, Amherst; Guild Hall Mus, East Hampton, NY; Okla Art Ctr, Oklahoma City; Detroit Inst Arts; Los Angeles Co Mus; and others. *Exhib:* American Drawings of the Sixties, New York, 69-70; one-man shows, Bertha Schaefer Gallery, New York, 69, 72 & 74; Childe Hassam Purchase Show, Nat Inst Arts & Lett, 71 & 72; 15th Ann Eight State Invitational, Okla Art Ctr, 73; Gruenebaum Gallery, 79 & 81; Cantor-Lemberg Gallery, Birmingham, Mich, 81; and others. *Teaching:* Asst prof painting & drawing, Wesleyan Univ, 65-71; assoc prof, Univ NMex, 71-80, prof art, 81- *Awards:* Childe Hassam Purchase Award, Nat Inst Arts & Lett, 72. *Dealer:* Gruenebaum Gallery Ltd 38 E 57th St New York NY 10022. *Mailing Add:* 4820 Guadalupe Trail NW Albuquerque NM 87107

NADOLSKI, STEPHANIE LUCILLE
PAINTER, PRINTMAKER
b Sacramento, Calif, Feb 21, 45. *Study:* San Jose State Col, 62-68; Sch Art, Bellevue, Nebr, 72; with Edgar Whitney, Robert E Wood & Glen Bradshaw, 78-83. *Work:* Univ Miss Libr, Oxford; Tex Commerce Bank, Scurlock Towers, Weslayan Bank, Tenneco Inc, Houston; Power Rig Drilling Co, Lafayette, La. *Comn:* Abstract collage, comn by Carl Silvani, Sugarland, Tex, 83. *Exhib:* Art, Two Houston Ctr, 80; solo exhib, Brazosport Ctr Arts & Sci, Lake Jackson, Tex, 80 & 83 & Two Houston Ctr, 81; XV Ann Art Exhib, Baytown Civic Ctr, Tex, 81; Sixth Ann Open Exhib, Houston Pub Libr, 82. *Pos:* Dir, Archway Gallery Houston, 76- *Awards:* Cash Award, Art, 76; Merit Award, XIII Ann Art Exhib, City Baytown, Tex, 79; Grumbacher Award, XV Ann Art Exhib, Baytown, Tex, 81. *Bibliog:* Mary Jean Fowler (auth), Mixed media gallery, Craft Reports, 84 & Shuttle, Spindle & Dyepot, 84. *Mem:* Houston Art Dealers Asn (dir, 83-85); Art League Houston; Watercolor Art Soc Houston; Tex Fine Arts Asn; NE Houston Prof Artists Asn. *Media:* Watercolor, Acrylic; Monoprint, Collograph. *Dealer:* Archway Gallery 2517 University Blvd Houston TX 77005. *Mailing Add:* 8250 Magnolia Glen Humble TX 77346

NAEVE, MILO M
ADMINISTRATOR, HISTORIAN
b Ness Co, Kans, Oct 9, 31. *Study:* Univ Colo, BFA; Univ Del, Winterthur Prog Am Studies & MA. *Pos:* Mem staff, Winterthur Mus, Del & Colonial Williamsburg, Va; dir, Colorado Springs Fine Arts Ctr, Colo; Art Inst Chicago; ed bd, Am Art J. *Mem:* Brit Mus Asn; Royal Soc Arts; Am Asn Mus; Nat Trust for Hist Preservation; Victorian Soc Am; and others. *Res:* American painting, sculpture, architecture, and decorative arts from the seventeenth to the twentieth century. *Publ:* Contribr, art mags & prof jour; ed, Winterthur Portfolio, Vol I-III; auth, The Classical Presence in American Art, Art Inst Chicago, 78; auth, Identifying American furniture: A pictorial guide to styles and terms, Am Asn State & Local Hist, 81; and others. *Mailing Add:* 1240 N Lake Shore Dr Chicago IL 60610

NAFTULIN, ROSE
PAINTER
b Philadelphia, Pa. *Study:* Philadelphia Col Art, 43-45; Barnes Found, 62-64. *Work:* Woodmere Art Gallery, Philadelphia; Philadelphia Free Libr, Pa; Burlington Indust, NY; Johnson & Johnson, NJ; Fidelity Bank, Pa. *Exhib:* Philadelphia Mus Art, Pa, 58; Nat Watercolor Exhib, Pa Acad Fine Art, Philadelphia, 67; Cheltenham Art Ctr Ann Award Show, Pa, 59-81; Allied Artists Am, Nat Acad Design, New York, 76; Nat Acad Design Ann Exhib,

New York, 76 & 80; Juried Ann, Allentown Art Mus, Pa, 80; solo show, Gross McCleaf, 81 & 83. *Teaching:* Instr painting, Cheltenham Art Ctr, 64-80; instr painting, Woodmere Art Gallery, 77-81. *Awards:* David Humphreys Prize, Nat Acad Design, 76; Cert of Merit, Nat Acad Design, 80; Blumenthal Award, Cheltenham Art Ctr, Pa, 83. *Mem:* Philadelphia Watercolor Club; Philadelphia Artist Equity. *Media:* Oil, Watercolor. *Dealer:* Gross McCleaf Gallery 1713 Walnut St Philadelphia PA 19103. *Mailing Add:* 1301 Stotesbury Ave Philadelphia PA 19118

NAGANO, PAUL TATSUMI
PAINTER, DESIGNER
b Honolulu, Hawaii, May 21, 38. *Study:* Columbia Col, BA, 60; Pa Acad Fine Arts, Philadelphia, 63-67. *Work:* Hawaii State Found of Cult & the Arts, Honolulu; William Rockhill Nelson Gallery, Kansas City, Mo; New Brit Mus Am Art, Conn; Boston Public Libr. *Exhib:* Pa Acad Fine Arts 75th Ann Fel Exhib, 72; Pucker/Safrai Gallery, 74 & 76-81; Contemp Arts Ctr, Honolulu, 74; Japanese Artist in Hawaii, 78-81; Fine Art of Business, Boston, 81; Duxbury Art Complex Mus, Mass, 82; and others. *Pos:* Art dir, Pucker/Safrai Gallery, Boston, 67- *Awards:* First Prize Landscape with Figures, Popular Photog, 63; Packard Prize Drawing, 64 & Lewis S Ware Traveling Scholar, 67, Pa Acad Fine Arts. *Mem:* Fel Pa Acad Fine Arts. *Media:* Watercolor. *Mailing Add:* 57 University Rd Brookline MA 02146

NAGANO, SHOZO
PAINTER
b Kanazawa, Japan. *Study:* Kanazawa Fine Arts Univ, AB; Art Students League, with Julian Levi; Pratt Inst, New York. *Work:* Allentown Art Mus, Pa; Berkshire Mus, Pittsfield, Mass; Citicorp, New York; Hudson River Mus, Yonkers, NY; State Univ NY Albany. *Comn:* It is Finished (painting), comn by Richard Hirsch, cur James Michener Collection, 71. *Exhib:* Nat Inst Arts & Lett, 72; Brooklyn Mus, 75, 77 & 78; one-man show, Squibb Art Ctr, 76; Japan Today, 79; Sindin Gallery, 82; Newark Mus, 83; and others. *Teaching:* Instr painting, Seibu Gakuen, Tokyo, 60-65. *Bibliog:* Alvin Smith (auth), article in Art Int, 5/72; David Shirey (auth), articles in New York Times, 9/75 & 3/76. *Mem:* Japanese Artists Asn NY (pres, 75). *Media:* Acrylic. *Publ:* Illusr, Kiristo-Kyo-Hoiku, 61-72; contribr, Haha no Hikari, 69-72. *Mailing Add:* c/o Sindin Gallery 1035 Madison Ave New York NY 10021

NAGENGAST, WILLIAM JOSEPH
PAINTER, DESIGNER
b Newark, NJ, May 28, 34. *Study:* Newark Sch Fine & Indust Arts, cert, 53; studied with Hans Weingartner & H Gasser, 54-60; with James Carlin & John Grabach, 55-57. *Work:* Advert Marketing Corp, Sparta, NJ. *Comn:* Abstract painting, Spinello Construction Co, Morristown, NJ, 76; Shaw Plastic Corp, Berkeley Heights, NJ, 79; painting, Advert Marketing Corp, Sparta, NJ, 80. *Exhib:* Ocean City Mus, NJ, 73; one-man show, Kean Col, NJ, 74; Am Bicentennial Exhib, Paris, France, 75; Newark Pub Libr, 75, Montclair Art Mus & Newark Mus, NJ; and others. *Pos:* Illusr/art consult, Advert Marketing Corp, Sparta, NJ, 75-; spec effects coordr, Chicksilva, New York, 78-79; spec effects coordr, Peter Runfolo Asn NJ, 80-81. *Teaching:* Instr, Newark Sch Fine & Indust Arts, 60-72. *Awards:* Grand Prizes, Atlantic City 12th Ann Nat, NJ, 75, South Orange Nat Art Show, 80 & Irvington State Nat Art Show, NJ, 80. *Bibliog:* Ruth Ann Williams (auth), article, NJ Music & Arts, spring 73; Eileen Watkins (auth), New Jersey artist, Newark Star Ledger, 75. *Mem:* Irvington Art Assocs NJ (bd dirs, 76-78, pres, 77-79); Nat Soc Painters Casein & Acrylics (bd dirs, 75-76). *Publ:* Illusr, contribr, Out of our past, Am Graphic Inc, 74; and others. *Dealer:* Offices Unlimited Gallery Morristown NJ. *Mailing Add:* 159 Park Pl Irvington NJ 07111

NAGLER, EDITH KROGER
PAINTER
b New York, NY. *Study:* Nat Acad Design, with Douglas Volk, Francis Jones & George Deforest Brush; Art Students League, with Frank Vincent DuMond, Kenneth Hayes Miller & Robert Henri. *Work:* Mus Fine Arts, Springfield, Mass; George Walter Vincent Smith Art Mus, Springfield; Wadsworth Atheneum, Hartford, Conn; Highland Park Mus, Dallas, Tex; Fed Ct House, Boston. *Exhib:* Corcoran Gallery Art, Washington, DC, 23; Nat Acad Design, New York, 28; Art Inst Chicago, 30; Philadelphia Arts Club; Pa Acad Fine Arts; Dallas Womens Club. *Pos:* Mem bd control, Art Students League. *Awards:* Crowninshield Prize, Stockbridge, Mass; First Watercolor Purchase Prize, Springfield. *Mem:* Am Watercolor Soc; Am Artists Prof League; Audubon Artists. *Media:* Oil, Watercolor. *Dealer:* Grand Central Art Galleries 40 Vanderbilt Ave New York NY 10017. *Mailing Add:* 5742 Berkshire Lane Dallas TX 75209

NAGLER, FRED
PRINTMAKER, SCULPTOR
b West Springfield, Mass. *Study:* Art Students League; also with Henri, Dumond & Bridgman. *Work:* Cathedral of St John the Divine, New York; Southern Methodist Univ; Vanderbilt Univ; Temple Univ; Metrop Mus of Art, New York; also in many pvt collections. *Exhib:* Carnegie Inst Int, Pittsburgh; Corcoran Gallery Art, Washington, DC; Art Inst Chicago; Pa Acad Fine Arts, Philadelphia; Nat Acad Design, New York. *Awards:* Carnegie Award, Nat Acad of Design; LaMont Award & Fabri Award, Audubon Artists; Am Acad Arts & Lett grant; plus many others. *Media:* Oil. *Dealer:* Midtown Galleries 11 E 57th St New York NY 10022; Valley House Galleries 6616 Spring Valley Rd Dallas TX 75240. *Mailing Add:* 5742 Berkshire Lane Dallas TX 75209

NAIMAN, LEE
DEALER, CONSULTANT
b Baltimore, Md. *Study:* Goucher Col, BA; Sorbonne, Paris; Johns Hopkins Univ; NY Univ. *Collections Arranged:* Etchings of Gunter Grass. *Pos:* Owner, Naiman Fine Arts & Tapestry Assocs, 70- *Teaching:* Instr, workshops, New Sch Social Res, NY & Glassboro Col. *Specialty:* Represent Gunther Grass in US; fibre and fabric artists; architectural glass; corporate collections; public sculpture. *Mailing Add:* 300 Central Park W New York NY 10024

NAKACHE-LYNCH, MARGARET
PAINTER
b Hartford, Conn, Dec 17, 32. *Study:* RI Sch Design, BFA, 54; Beaux-Arts, Paris, cert, 56; Atelier Chapelain-Midy. *Work:* RI Sch Design Mus, Providence; L'Ambassade du Liban, Paris; Our Lady Victory Church, Centerville, Mass; Les Embrunts, Les Essembres, France. *Comn:* Blown Tulips, Sargi, Dakar, Senegal, 78; Paris Cityscape, Cameron, Royal Oak, Mich, 78; Roses, Dagommer Cie, Paris, 78; Madonna, Ostronic, Potomac, Md, 79; Green Dunes, McDonald, Wellesley, Mass, 83. *Exhib:* One-woman show, La Galerie du Meridien, Paris, 79 & Hunter House, Vienna, Va, 82; All New Eng 1979, 79; Coun of Arts Invitational, Colvin Mill Run, Va, 80; Long Branch Nature Ctr, 81; Cape Cod Art Asn, 83; and others. *Pos:* Artist, Universal Films, New York, 56-57 & Girl Scouts USA, Hq New York, 59-61; artist-in-residence, Art Barn, DC, 79; pres, Network For Artists, Kindred Art Collection & Host Exhib Ltd, McLean, Va, 79- *Awards:* Second Place, Cape Cod Art Asn, 56; Second Place, McLean Art Club, 79; Second Place, Dennis Art Festival, 81. *Bibliog:* L Chauvin (auth), Margaret Nakache, Galerie Jardin des Arts, 2/75; E Holgren (auth), Whisperings and sharings, Alexandrian Mag, spring 78; J de Recqueville (auth), Carnet des arts, Paris-Tel, 1/79. *Mem:* McLean Art Club; Vienna Art Soc. *Media:* Watercolor. *Publ:* Contribr, Cadette Girl Scout Handbook, Girls Scouts USA, 63; auth, Art royalties, Int Herald Tribune, 5/16/77; auth, Art game letters, Washington Post Mag, 11/5/78. *Dealer:* Network For Artists Ltd 1448 Woodacre Dr McLean VA 22101. *Mailing Add:* c/o Network Artists Ltd 1448 Woodacre Dr McLean VA 22101

NAKAMURA, KAZUO
PAINTER
b Vancouver, BC, Oct 13, 26. *Study:* Cent Tech Sch, Toronto. *Work:* Nat Gallery Can, Ottawa; Art Gallery Ont, Toronto; Mus Mod Art, New York; Winnipeg Art Gallery; R McLaughlin Art Gallery, Oshawa. *Comn:* Two sculptures, Toronto Int Airport, 63; mural panel, Queen's Park Complex, Toronto. *Exhib:* 20th Biennial Int Watercolor, Brooklyn Mus, 59; 5th Int Hallmark Art Award Exhib, New York, 61; 2nd Bienniale Mus Art Mod, Paris, 61; Recent Acquisitions, Mus Mod Art, New York, 63; Can Artists 68, Art Gallery Ont, Toronto, 68; Nakamura 1951-1974, R McLaughlin Art Gallery, Can tour, 74-75. *Awards:* Prizewinner, 4th Int Exhib Drawings & Engravings, Lugano, Switz, 56. *Bibliog:* Andrew Bell (auth), The art of Nakamura, Can Art, 8/59; J M Careless (ed), The Canadians, Macmillan Co, Can, 67. *Media:* Oil, Watercolor. *Dealer:* Moore Gallery 24 Hess St S Hamilton Ont Can. *Mailing Add:* 3 Langmuir Crescent Toronto ON M6S 2A6 Canada

NAKAZATO, HITOSHI
PAINTER, PRINTMAKER
b Tokyo, Japan, Mar 15, 36. *Study:* Tama Col Art, Tokyo, BFA(painting); Univ Wis, MS(art, printmaking); Univ Pa, MFA, painting with Piero Dorazio. *Work:* Mus Mod Art, New York; Philadelphia Mus Art; Nat Mus Mod Art, Kyoto, Japan; Pa Acad Fine Arts, Philadelphia; Brooklyn Mus, New York. *Comn:* Mural, Furukawa Pavilion, Expo 70, Osaka, Japan. *Exhib:* Artists in Americas, Nat Mus Mod Art, Kyoto, 74; Three Hundred Years of American Art, Philadelphia Mus, 76; Contemporary Japanese Painting, Japan Art Festival 10th Anniversary, Tokyo, 77; Prints in Series: Idea into Image, Brooklyn Mus, New York, 77; one-man shows, Mercer Col, 78; West Chester Col, 79 & Pa Acad Fine Arts, 79; Contemporary Drawings: Philadelphia II, Philadelphia Mus Art, 79. *Teaching:* Asst prof painting, Tama Col Art, Tokyo, 68-71; asst prof printmaking, Grad Sch of Fine Arts, Univ of Pa, Philadelphia, 73-79, assoc prof, 79- *Awards:* John D Rockefeller 3rd Grant, 66-67; Creative Artists Public Service Grant, 74-75. *Bibliog:* Joseph Love (auth), Tokyo Letter, Art Int, 3-12/71; Ruth Lehrer (auth), Three Hundred Years of American Art: Philadelphia, Philadelphia Mus, 76; Teruazu Suenage (auth), Art 78, Bijutsu Techo, 1/78. *Mem:* Am Color Print Soc. *Mailing Add:* 361 W 36th St New York NY 10018

NAKIAN, REUBEN
SCULPTOR
b College Point, NY, Aug 10, 1897. *Study:* Robert Henri Sch, with Homer Boss & A S Baylinson; Art Students League, 12; also with Paul Manship & Gaston Lachaise. *Work:* Mus Mod Art, Whitney Mus Am Art, New York; Chicago Art Inst; Los Angeles Co Mus; Hirshhorn Mus, Washington, DC; and many others. *Comn:* Sculpture, NY Univ, 60. *Exhib:* Corcoran Gallery; Albright Art Gallery; Mus Mod Art, New York; Wadsworth Atheneum; Guggenheim Mus; Los Angeles Co Mus; Nat Portrait Gallery; Art Inst Chicago; Pa Acad Fine Arts; one-man retrospective, Mus Mod Art, New York, 66; Bergen Community Mus, Paramus, NJ, 81; Rolly-Michaux, New York, 81; Laumier Found, St Louis, 82; David Settles Gallery, Houston, 82; Addison Ripley Gallery, Washington, DC, 83; and many others. *Teaching:* Newark Sch Fine & Indus Arts, 46-51 & New York Studio Sch, 72-74. *Awards:* Athena Award, RI Sch Design, 79; Skohegan Sch Sculpture Award, 81; Nat Endowment Arts Grant, 81. *Bibliog:* Sam Hunter (ed), New Art Around the World: Painting and Sculpture, Abrams, 66; Wayne Craven (auth), Sculpture in America, Crowell, 68; and others. *Mem:* Am Inst Arts & Lett. *Mailing Add:* 810 Bedford Stamford CT 06901

NAMA, GEORGE ALLEN
PRINTMAKER, SCULPTOR
b Pittsburgh, Pa, Feb 23, 39. *Study:* Carnegie Mellon Univ, BFA & MFA; Atelier 17, Paris, with Stanley William Hayter. *Work:* Philadelphia Mus Art; Smithsonian Inst, Libr Cong, Washington, DC; Brooklyn Mus; Butler Inst Am Art, Youngstown, Ohio. *Exhib:* Original Prints, Calif Palace of Legion of Honor, San Francisco, 64; Pratt Graphic Art Ctr Serigraph Exhib, 65; Northwest Printmakers Int Exhib, 65-67; Contemp Am Prints, Gt Brit, 69-71; US Info Agency Exhibs, Japan Expo, 70. *Awards:* David Berger Mem Prize, Mus Fine Arts, Boston, 67; Stuart M Egnal Prize, Philadelphia Print Club, 68; Stella Drabkin Mem Award, Am Color Print Soc, 71. *Bibliog:* Leonard Slatkes (auth), Printmakers on exhibit, Art Scene, 68; Richard Shelton (auth), Journal of return, Kayak, 69; S Hazo (auth), Poets & prints, Artist Proof Mag, 71. *Mem:* Soc Am Graphic Artists. *Media:* Intaglio, Collograph; Casting. *Publ:* Illusr, Journal of Return Kayak, 69; illusr, Twelve Poems with Twelve Prints, 70; illusr, Monuments, 71; illusr, Seascript, 71; illusr, Origin of Language, Nine Etchings, 79. *Dealer:* Assoc Am Artists 663 Fifth Ave New York NY 10022. *Mailing Add:* RFD 1 Box 72 Montauk NY 11954

NAMINGHA, DAN
PAINTER, PRINTMAKER
b Polacca, Ariz, May 1, 50. *Study:* Kans Univ, Lawrence, 67; Inst Am Indian Arts, Santa Fe, NMex, 67-69; Am Acad Art, Chicago, Ill, 69. *Work:* US Dept Interior Arts Collection, Washington, DC; Mus Am Indian Arts and Culture, Chicago, Ill; Mus Northern Ariz, Flagstaff; Heard Mus, Phoenix, Ariz. *Comn:* View from Walpi (mural), City Phoenix, Ariz, 79. *Exhib:* Mus Northern Ariz, Flagstaff, 77; one-man show, Orange Coast Col, Costa Mesa, Calif, 77; Extensions of the Nampeyo Creative Spirit, Calif; Contemp Am Indian Painting, Chile, Bolivia, Peru, Columbia, Ecuador, South Am, 79; Hopi Kachina Spirit of Life, Calif Acad Sci, San Francisco, Calif, 80-82; Carnegie Mus, Pittsburgh; Am Mus Natural Hist, New York; Smithsonian Inst, Washington, DC; Field Mus, Chicago, Ill; Am Indian Art in the 1980's, Native Am Ctr Living Arts, Niagara Falls, 80; and many others. *Bibliog:* Mary Carroll Nelson (auth), Dan Namingha--the migration of a Hopi artist, Am Artist Mag, 79; Jamake Highwater (auth), The Sweet Grass Lives On, Lippincott and Crowell, 80; Jack Peterson (dir), Am Indian Artist II (film series), Native Am Public Broadcasting Consortium, Inc, 82. *Dealer:* Glenn Green 7051 Fifth Avenue Scottsdale AZ 85251. *Mailing Add:* PO Box 845 San Juan Pueblo NM 87566

NAMUTH, HANS
PHOTOGRAPHER, FILMMAKER
b Essen, Ger, Mar 17, 15; US citizen. *Work:* Mus Mod Art, Metrop Mus Art, New York; Tulane Univ, New Orleans; Cleveland Mus Art, Ohio; Va Mus Fine Arts, Richmond. *Exhib:* Jackson Pollock, Mus Mod Art, 67; solo exhibs, Corcoran Gallery, 74, Mus Art Mod, Paris, 79, Galerie Fiolet, Amsterdam, 80, Castelli Graphics, New York, 80 & Pace Gallery, New York, 81. *Pos:* Founder & secy, Museum-at-Large, New York, 70- *Awards:* Citation in Recognition of Pub Serv, US Dept State, 58; Grand Prix de Bergamo, 58. *Collection:* Prints, drawings and lithographs by Rauschenberg, J Johns, Albers, Robert Indiana, Lee Bontecou, George Segal, Constantine Nivola, Richard Lindner, Robert Morris, Robert Motherwell and W de Kooning; paintings by de Kooning, Jackson Pollock, Josef Albers, Joseph Cornell, Mary Bauermeister, Kenzo Okada, Ludwig Sander and others. *Publ:* Auth, Fifty Two Artists (portfolio of photog), 73, coauth, Eight American Masters, 74, Early American Tools, 75, The Voice and the Myth by Brian O'Doherty: Photographed by Hans Namuth, Random; auth, Calder's Universe, 77. *Mailing Add:* 157 W 54th St New York NY 10019

NARANJO, MICHAEL ALFRED
SCULPTOR
b Santa Fe, NMex, Aug 28, 44. *Study:* Wayland Col, Plainview, Tex; Highland Univ. *Work:* Heard Mus, Phoenix, Ariz; Mus of the Horse, Patagonia, Ariz; Indian Pueblo Cult Ctr, Albuquerque, NMex. *Exhib:* NMex Fine Arts Biennial, 75; Southwest Indian Arts & Crafts Fair, 75; Governor's Gallery, Santa Fe, NMex, 78; Scottsdale, Ariz, 79; Chicago, 79; Invitational, Native Am Cult Ctr, Buffalo, NY, 81. *Pos:* Bd mem, NMex Arts Comn, 71-73. *Awards:* Gov Award for Excellence in Sculpture, NMex Arts Comn, 75; First in Sculpture, Southwest Indian Arts & Crafts Fair, 75; First Prize in Sculpture, Celebration 81 Arts Festival, Atlanta, 81; and others. *Bibliog:* Guy & Doris Monthan (auth), Art & Indian Individualists, Northland Press, 75; Jamake Highwater (auth), The Sweet Grass Lives On, Lippincott and Crowell, 80; Peggy & Harold Samuels (auths), Contemporary Western Artists, Southwest Art Publ. *Media:* Bronze. *Mailing Add:* PO Box 747 Espanola NM 87532

NARDIN, MARIO
COLLECTOR, SCULPTOR
b Venice, Italy, Mar 17, 40. *Study:* Acad Belle Arti, Venice, with Guido Manarin. *Work:* Hudson River Mus, Yonkers, NY; Fordham Univ; also in pvt collections. *Exhib:* One-man shows, Fordham Univ, 69, Lesnick Gallery, 70, Sindin Galleries, 77 & Village Gallery at Gallimafry, Croton-on-Hudson, NY, 78; State Univ NY Col Plattsburg, 71; and others. *Pos:* Asst to Jacques Lipchitz, 64-71; asst mgr, Avent-Shaw Art Foundry, 64- *Awards:* New Rochelle Art Asn Award, 67; Greenburgh Arts & Cult Comt Award, 71 & 72; Mamaroneck Artist Guild Award, 73. *Bibliog:* Noel Frankman (auth), Nardin at the Hudson River Museum, Arts Mag, 3/72; Successo a Nuova York di uno scultore Veneziano, Gazzetino Venice, 72; David L Shirey (auth), Sculptor as master builder, New York Times, 3/78. *Mem:* Am Soc Contemp Artists; Sculptors League; Yonkers Art Asn; Artists Equity Asn. *Media:* Bronze. *Dealer:* Sindin Galleries 1035 Madison Ave New York NY 10021. *Mailing Add:* 184 Warburton Ave Hastings-on-Hudson NY 10706

NARDONE, VINCENT JOSEPH
PAINTER, INSTRUCTOR
b South Orange, NJ, Oct 19, 37. *Study:* Montclair State Col, NJ, BA, 61; Univ Southern Calif, Los Angeles, MFA, 66; Paris Am Acad of Fine Arts, France, 78, with Genieve Secord, Joseph Domareki, Isa Petrozzani, Mildred Taylor, Paul Harris & Arnauld D'hauterives. *Work:* Newark Mus, NJ; Newark Pub Libr, NJ; Rome Daily Am News, Italy; Isadora & Raymond Duncan Mus, Paris. *Comn:* Western pastel mural, Bonanza Restaurant Chain, Bloomfield, NJ, 68; wall inserted stone carving, Music & Art Corp, NJ, 70; original litho mag insert, NJ Music & Arts Mag, 72; relig watercolor painting, Christ the King Parish, Ploughe, Sardenia, 72. *Exhib:* Le Salon, Grand Palais, Paris, 78 & 80; Corp Art Consults NJ Traveling Show, 81-82; Il Centro Artistico San Niccolo, Florence, 81; La Galerie Esplande, La DeFense, France, 82; Whistler's Daughter Gallery, 82 & 83; and others; Whitney Counterweight, New York, 77-78. *Pos:* Illusr & art consult, NJ Music & Art Mag, Chatham, NJ, 69-73. *Teaching:* Art specialist K-5 art educ, Tuscan Sch, South Orange/Maplewood Sch Dist, NJ, 61-; instr painting adult sch, Maplewood, NJ, 66-70; adj instr art educ, Seton Hall Univ, South Orange, NJ, 68-74. *Awards:* Raymond Duncan Medal, Prix de Paris, France, 78; Painting Award, Le Salon, Grand Palais, Paris, 78; Queen Fabiola, Prix Ruebens Medal, Belg, 78; and others. *Bibliog:* Francois Perche (auth), critique, La Revue Moderne des Arts, Paris, 78; Dorothy Hall (auth), critique, Park East, 11/78; Nardone the artist, NJ Art Form Mag, 8-9/82. *Mem:* Les Surindependants Soc, Paris; Allied Artists Am; Art Educ NJ; and others. *Media:* Multimedia, Watercolor. *Publ:* Illusr (16 issues), NJ Music & Arts Mag, 70-73; auth, Panning for federal funds, 12/71 & auth & illusr, Graven images, 4/72, NJ Music & Arts Mag; auth & illusr, Ecological Genesis (portfolio), Rubicon Graphics, 72. *Dealer:* Whistler's Daughter Gallery 88 S Finley Ave Basking Ridge NJ 07920. *Mailing Add:* 75 Essex Ave Maplewood NJ 07040

NAROTZKY, NORMAN DAVID
PAINTER, PRINTMAKER
b Brooklyn, NY, Mar 14, 28. *Study:* Brooklyn Col, BA(cum laude); Art Students League; Cooper Union, BFA; Atelier 17, Paris; Kunstakademie, Munich; New York Univ Fine Arts. *Work:* Univ Tex Art Mus, Austin; Philadelphia Mus Art; Mus Contemp Art, Madrid, Spain; Mills Col Art Gallery, Oakland, Calif; Museo Popular de Arte Contemporaneo de Villafames, Spain. *Comn:* Mural, Banco de Guipuzcoa, San Sebastian, 63; ltd ed lithograph, Collectors Guild Ltd, 69 & Fine Arts 260, 72 & 76; ltd ed etchings, Galeria Fort, Barcelona, 75 & 83; Ediciones Jesus 14, Barcelona, 78. *Exhib:* Mus Mod Art, 62; Whitney Mus Am Art Ann, New York, 62; Arte Am y Espana, traveling Europe, 63-64; San Francisco Mus Art, 68; Grosse Kunstler Ausstellung, Haus der Kunst, Munich, 71; Retrospective, Elvehjem Art Ctr, Univ Wis, 77; and 31 one-man shows. *Pos:* Staff, Collector's Guild Inc, 69-71 & Fine Arts 260, 71-80; dir art gallery, Cadaques, 73; dir painting workshop, Northern Mich Univ, summer 79. *Teaching:* Pvt studio, Cadaques, Spain, 59-69; Barcelona, 76- *Awards:* French Govt Fel, Paris, 55-56; Fulbright Fel, Ger, 57-58; Painting Grant, Dept Cult, Spain, 83. *Bibliog:* Jose M, Moreno Galvan (auth), Spanish painting, the latest avant-garde, NY Graphic Soc, 69; Meilach & Ten Hoor (auth), Collage & Assemblage, Crown Publ, 73; Knigin & Zimiles (auth), The Contemporary Lithographic Workshop Around the World, Van Nostrand Reinhold, 74. *Mem:* Art Students League; Cercle Artistic de Sant Lluc, Barcelona. *Media:* Acrylic, Oil; Etching, Lithography. *Publ:* Auth, Spain: A disenchantment with materia, 9-10/65, Conversation with Cuixart, 3/66 & The Venice Biennale: Pease porridge in the pot nine days old, 9-10/66, Arts Mag; auth, Ibiza--from art refuge to art center, Art Voices, fall 65; auth, Form & communication in my art work, Leonardo Mag, 7/69. *Dealer:* Clara Londoner 185 East 85th St New York NY 10028. *Mailing Add:* Corcega 198-6 Barcelona 36 Spain

NASGAARD, ROALD
CURATOR, HISTORIAN
b Denmark, Oct 14, 41; Can citizen. *Study:* Univ BC, BA, MA, 67; Can Coun Fels, 67-71; NY Univ Inst Fine Arts, PhD, 73. *Pos:* Cur contemp art, Art Gallery Ont, 75-78, chief cur, 78- *Teaching:* Asst prof art hist, Univ Guelph, Ont, 71-75. *Mem:* Col Art Asn; Univ Art Asn Can; Int Art Critics Asn (Canadian secy-gen, 76-78). *Res:* Late 19th century to contemporary art. *Publ:* Auth, Structures for Behaviour, New Sculptures by Robert Morris, David Rabinowitch, Richard Serra and George Trakas, 78, auth, Garry Neill Kennedy: Recent Works, 78, auth, Yves Gaucher: Fifteen Year Perspective, 79 & auth, 10 Canadian Artists in the 1970's, 80, Art Gallery Ont; auth, The Mystic North: Symbolist Landscape Painting in Northern Europe and North America, 1890-1940, Art Gallery Ont & Univ Toronto Press, 84. *Mailing Add:* 317 Dundas St W Toronto ON M5T 1G4 Canada

NASH, ALICE LOUISE
CONSULTANT
b Mattoon, Ill, June 21, 15. *Study:* James Millikin Univ, Decatur, Ill, 35-36; Heatherleys Sch Fine Art, London, Eng, 47-48; Atelier Zadkine, with Ossip Zadkine, Paris, France, 48-49; Chelsea Col Art, London Univ, with Henry Moore & Bernard Meadows, 49-51; Anglo-French Art Sch, London, 52. *Pos:* Exec secy, Edward MacDowell Assocs, 57-60; asst dir, Contemporaries Gallery, New York, 60-62; dir, Osgood Gallery, New York, 62-63; dir, Alice Nash Gallery, New York, 63-65; staff mem for exhibs & librn, Am Acad & Inst Art & Lett, New York, 65-72; assoc, Harmon Gallery, Naples, Fla, 78- *Bibliog:* Art ed, Gulf Shore Life Mag, Naples, Fla. *Mem:* Fel Royal Soc Arts, Eng; Naples Art Asn (bd mem 78-). *Specialty:* Contemporary American and European paintings and sculpture. *Publ:* Auth, Collectors Handbook, Harmon-Meek Gallery, 82. *Mailing Add:* 1950 Golf Shore Blve Apt 115 Naples FL 33940

NASH, KATHERINE E
SCULPTOR, EDUCATOR
b Minneapolis, Minn. *Study:* Univ Minn, BS; Minneapolis Sch Art; Univ NMex, computer graphics with Richard Williams; Doane Col, Hon DFA. *Work:* Walker Art Ctr, Minneapolis; US Arts & Humanities Coun, Washington, DC; Joslyn Art Mus, Omaha, Nebr; Nebr Art Asn, Univ Nebr, Lincoln; Univ Minn, Minneapolis. *Comn:* Welded steel, Wright Co Ct House Foyer, Buffalo, Minn, 60 & Student Union, Doane Col, 64; welded copper, steel & brass, Epworth Church, Council Bluffs, Iowa, 66; welded copper & brass, Edina Village Coun, Edina Libr, Minn, 69; welded copper, Fed Land Bank, St Paul, Minn, 70. *Exhib:* Walker Art Ctr, 50-72; Joslyn Art Mus, 50-65; World's Fair, Brussels, 58; US Embassy Exhibs, 66-69; Nebr Centennial, 67; plus others. *Teaching:* Asst prof sculpture, Univ Nebr, Lincoln, 47-53; vis assoc prof sculpture, San Jose State Col, 61-62; prof sculpture/computer graphics, Univ Minn, 64-79. *Awards:* Minn State Arts Coun Artists Award, 69-70; McMillan Award Travel Grant, 69 & 72; Dedication of Univ Minn Gallery to Katherine E Nash Gallery, 79. *Bibliog:* Marcel Brion (auth), Art fantastique, Albin Michel, 61; Paul Vogt (auth), Stand plastiken aus stahl, Herausgeber & Verlag, 62; Reichardt (auth), The Computer in Art, Van Nostrand Reinhold, 71. *Mem:* Hon mem Artists Equity Asn (regional dir exec bd, 57-61); Mid-Am Col Art Asn (secy, 67-68); Sculptors Guild; Int Computer Arts Soc; Am Asn Univ Prof. *Media:* Cast Metals. *Dealer:* Seligman Galleries 5 E 57th St New York NY 10022. *Mailing Add:* 21450 Excelsior Blvd Excelsior MN 55331

NASH, MARY (HARRIET)
PAINTER, LECTURER
b Washington, DC, May 8, 51. *Study:* George Washington Univ, BA, 73; Wash State Univ, Pullman, with Gaylen Hansen, Patrick Siler, Robert Helm & Francis Ho, MFA, 76. *Work:* Dimock Gallery, George Washington Univ; Cleveland State Univ; Erie Art Ctr, Pa. *Exhib:* Twentieth Century Artists, Janet Fleisher Gallery, Philadelphia, 79; New Talent, Artists Invitational Mus, Washington, DC, 80; About Faces, Southern Ohio Mus, Portsmouth, 81; Living With the Volcano: The Artists of Mt St Helens, Mus Art, Wash State Univ, Pullman, 83; Eccentrics, Southeastern Ctr Contemp Art, Winston-Salem, 83. *Pos:* Guest lectr, Mus Art, Wash State Univ, 76-, Second St Gallery, Charlottesville, Va, 78-, Univ Ala, Tuscaloosa, 81- & Southeastern Women's Studies Asn Conf, Univ Va, Charlotteville, 83. *Awards:* MacDowell Colony Fel, 77; Honorable Mention, Southeastern Ctr Contemp Art, 79; Purchase Award, Wash State Arts Comn, Olympia, 82. *Bibliog:* Mary H Nash, Fork Art Finder, 80; Lenore D Miller (auth), The symbolic narrative images of Mary H Nash, Art Voices South, 80; Janet Isaacs Ashford (auth), Mary H Nash, Whole Birth Catalog, 83. *Media:* Oil, Alkyd. *Mailing Add:* 8536 Aponi Rd Vienna VA 22180

NASH, STEVEN ALAN
HISTORIAN, CURATOR
b Wadsworth, Ohio, Apr 8, 44. *Study:* Darmouth Col, BA; Stanford Univ, PhD. *Pos:* Res cur, Albright-Knox Art Gallery, Buffalo, 73-77, chief cur, 77-80; asst dir & chief cur, Dallas Mus Fine Arts, 80- *Teaching:* Adj prof, State Univ NY Buffalo, 73-80. *Awards:* Mabel McCloud Lewis Found Fel, 71; Fr Govt Res Grant, 71. *Mem:* Col Art Asn Am; Am Asn Mus. *Publ:* Jacques-Louis David; Picasso; auth, Ben Nicholson: Fifty Years of His Art, Buffalo Acad, 78; auth, Albright-Knox Collection (catalog), 79. *Mailing Add:* Dallas Mus Fine Arts PO Box 26250 Dallas TX 75226

NASH, VERONICA F
DEALER, COLLECTOR
b Leonardtown, Md, Jan 3, 27. *Study:* Four yrs study with John Chapman Lewis, Arlington, Va. *Pos:* Owner, Prince Royal Gallery, Inc, currently. *Specialty:* Contemporary, original works of art in oil, watercolor, enamel and prints and sculpture. *Collection:* Oils, watercolors and etchings of nationally and internationally known artists. *Mailing Add:* c/o Prince Royal Gallery Inc 204 S Royal St Alexandria VA 22314

NASHER, PATSY R
COLLECTOR, CONSULTANT
b Dallas, Tex, Sept 15, 28. *Study:* Hockaday Jr Col, 46; Smith Col, BA, 49. *Collections Arranged:* Calder Tapestries; American Indian Rugs; Southeast Asian Art; Leo Castelli Show, NorthPark Nat Bank, 78; Selected prints from the Collection of Mr & Mrs Raymond D Nasher, Dallas City Hall, 78. *Bibliog:* Article, Saturday Rev, 9/80. *Mem:* Dallas Mus Fine Arts; Ft Worth Mus Art. *Collection:* Pre-Columbian and primitive art, twentieth century sculpture and paintings, Guatemalan textiles and twentieth century prints. *Publ:* Auth, Close encounters of architectural kinds, Art J, summer 80. *Mailing Add:* 4701 Miron Dr Dallas TX 75220

NASISSE, ANDY S
SCULPTOR, WRITER
b Pueble, Colo, Nov 1, 46. *Study:* Inst Allende, Mex, 69; Colo Univ, MFA, 73. *Work:* High Mus Art. *Comn:* Four Walls, City Altanta, 81. *Exhib:* Southeast Ctr Contemp Arts Exhib, Winston-Salem, NC, 79; Ga Artists, High Mus, 79, 80 & 83; More than Land or Sky, Nat Mus Am Art, 82; Southern Fervor, Anderson Gallery, Richmond, Va, 83; Birmingham Mus Biennial, 83; New Epiphanies, Colo Univ Mus, 83; New Talent, Nexus Space, Atlanta, 83; solo exhib, La Mar Dodd Ctr, La Grange, Ga, 84. *Teaching:* Assoc prof, Univ Ga, Athens, 76-, gallery dir, 82-83. *Awards:* Nat Endowment Arts Grant, 79; Creative Res Award, Univ Ga, 82; Ga Coun Grant, 84. *Media:* Ceramic. *Res:* Folk art. *Dealer:* Fay Gold Gallery 3221 Cains Hill Pl Atlanta GA 30305. *Mailing Add:* 256 Georgia Dr Athens GA 30605

NATHANS, RHODA R
PHOTOGRAPHER

b Detroit, Mich, May 29, 40. *Study:* Wayne State Univ, BS; NY Univ Sch Continuing Educ, photog under Dr Roman Vishniac. *Exhib:* Neidrug Gallery, New York UN Woman's Yr, 74; one-woman exhibs, Avanti Gallery, New York, 74 & Nikon House, Rockefeller Ctr, New York, 78; Mus City New York, 74. *Publ:* Contribr, Time, Fortune, Newsweek & Print Mag, 9/75; contribr, Camera 35, 12/75. *Dealer:* Mrs Frances Wynshaw 157 E 72nd St New York NY 10022. *Mailing Add:* 141 E 89th St New York NY 10028

NATKIN, ROBERT
PAINTER

b Chicago, Ill, Nov 7, 30. *Study:* Art Inst Chicago, BA, 52. *Work:* Guggenheim Mus, Whitney Mus Am Art & Mus Mod Art, New York; Los Angeles Mus Art; Mus Fine Art, Houston; and others. *Exhib:* Whitney Mus Am Art, 60, 66 & 68; Carnegie Inst, 63; Int Biennale, Japan, 63; Mus Fine Arts, Houston, 63; retrospective, San Francisco Mus Art, 69; and others. *Teaching:* Ford Found artist in residence, Kalamazoo Inst Arts, formerly. *Dealer:* Andre Emmerich Gallery 41 E 57th St New York NY. *Mailing Add:* 24 Mark Twain Lane West Redding CT 06896

NATZLER, OTTO
CERAMIST, SCULPTOR

b Vienna, Austria, Jan 31, 08; US citizen. *Work:* Mus Mod Art & Metrop Mus Art, New York; Art Inst Chicago; Kunstgewerbemuseum, Zurich, Switz; Victoria & Albert Mus, London; Nat Mus Am Art, Washington, DC; and others. *Exhib:* One-man exhibs, Art Inst Chicago, 63 & San Francisco Mus Art, 63; retrospective exhibs, Los Angeles Co Mus Art, 66, M H De Young Mem Mus, San Francisco 71 & Renwick Gallery, Smithsonian Inst, Washington, DC, 73 (co-auth all catalogs). *Bibliog:* Article, Natzler exhibition, Ceramics Monthly, 5/78; Sarah Booth Conroy (auth), article, Washington Post, 9/20/81; Florence Rubenfeld (auth), Otto Natzler--solo, Am Craft, 2-3/82. *Media:* Multimedia. *Dealer:* Louis Newman Galleries 322 N Beverly Dr Beverly Hills CA 90210; Franz Bader Gallery 2001 Eye St NW Washington DC 20006. *Mailing Add:* 7837 Woodrow Wilson Dr Los Angeles CA 90046

NATZMER, CHERYL LYNN
DEALER, HISTORIAN

b Detroit, Mich, May 14, 47. *Study:* Mich State Univ, BA, 69. *Collections Arranged:* Zuniga, drawings, graphics & sculpture, 78; Sebastian/Geometric Transformables, steel sculpture, 79; A Tribute to Rufino Tamayo, recent works, 79; Dibujos/Drawings, survey of Latin Am drawings, 79; The New World and the Beast, animal imagery in Latin Am art, 79; Tamayo's Mexico, 80; The Imaginary Surface, paintings by Manuel Felguerez, 81; El Zodiaco-- Sculpture by Sebastian Travelling Exhib, 82-83; and others. *Pos:* Dir & pres, Gryphon Galleries, Ltd, Denver, 71-78; dir & mem bd dirs, Rutherford Barnes Collection, Ltd, Denver, Colo, 78-; adv Mex art, Denver, 82- *Mem:* Metro-Denver Arts Alliance; Rocky Mountain Inst Pre-Columbian Study; Alliance Contemp Art. *Res:* Public art in Mexico today. *Specialty:* Twentieth century Mexican and Latin American art; works of the Masters Tamayo and Cuevas. *Publ:* Co-producer, Columbian Art in the 80's (video). *Mailing Add:* 737 S Williams St Denver CO 80209

NAUMAN, BRUCE
SCULPTOR

b Ft Wayne, Ind, Dec 6, 41. *Study:* Univ Wis, Madison, with Italo Scanga, BS, 64; Univ Calif, Davis, with William Wiley, Robert Arneson, Frank Owen & Stephen Kaltenbach, MFA, 66. *Work:* Whitney Mus, New York; Wallraf-Richartz-Mus, Cologne, Ger; Kunstverein, Aachen, Ger; St Louis Mus, Mo; Los Angeles Co Mus Art, Calif. *Exhib:* Am Sculpture of the sixties, Los Angeles Co Mus Art, Calif, 67; Corcoran Gallery of Art, Washington, DC, 69; Anti-Illusion: Procedures/Materials, Whitney Mus of Art, New York, 69; Soloman R Guggenheim Mus, New York, 69; Information, Mus Mod Art, New York, 71; Art & Image in Recent Art, Art Inst, Chicago, 74; Art/Voir, Centre Beaubourg, Paris, 74; Mus Contemp Art, Chicago, 75 & 77; Drawing Now, Mus Mod Art, New York, 75; 200 Yrs Am Sculpture, Whitney Mus, New York, 76; Los Angeles Inst Contemp Art, 80; Calif Inst Technol, Pasadena, 80; Flow Ace Gallery, Venice, Calif, 81; Carol Taylor Gallery, Dallas, Tex, 81; Tex Gallery, Houston, 81; and others. *Teaching:* Instr, San Francisco Art Inst, 66-68; instr sculpture, Univ Calif, Irvine, 70. *Awards:* Nat Endowment Grant, Washington, DC, 68; Aspen Inst for Humanistic Studies Grant, Colo, 70. *Bibliog:* Robert Pincus-Witten (auth), Bruce Nauman: Another kind of reasoning, Artforum, 2/72; Jurgen Harten (auth), T for technics, B for body, Art & Artists, London, 11/73; J Minton (auth), Bruce Nauman: Gunslinger, Artweek, 6/74. *Publ:* Auth, Pictures of Sculptures in a Room, Davis, Calif, 66; auth, Clear Sky, San Francisco, 68; auth, Burning Small Fires, San Francisco, 68; auth, LA Air, Los Angeles, 70; auth, Body Works, Interfunktionen, Cologne, Ger, 9/71. *Mailing Add:* c/o Leo Castelli Gallery 420 W Broadway New York NY 10012

NAUMER, HELMUTH
PAINTER

b Ger, Sept 1, 07; US citizen. *Study:* Frank Wiggins Art Sch; Otis Art Inst, Los Angeles. *Work:* NMex State Art Mus; Bandelier Nat Monument; Univ Wyo; Univ NMex; Mus Sci & Hist, Ft Worth, Tex; and many others worldwide. *Exhib:* Am Asn Mus & Can Mus Asn Meeting, Toronto, 67. *Bibliog:* Articles in Am Ger Rev, NMex Mag & El Palacio. *Media:* Oil, Pastel, Watercolor. *Mailing Add:* Rancho de San Sebastian Rte 3 Santa Fe NM 87501

NAVARETTA, CYNTHIA
LECTURER, EDITOR

b New York. *Study:* Univ Wis; NY Univ; Columbia Univ, BA, 46, MA, 48. *Collections Arranged:* Women Choose Women (auth, catalog), Cult Ctr, New York, 73; Artists of Long Island (contribr, catalog), Guild Hall, East Hampton, NY, 79; Int Festival Women Artists, Copenhagen, 80; A Lifetime of Art: Six Women of Distinction, Women's Caucus Art, New York, 82. *Pos:* Ed, Women Artist News, Midmarch Assocs, 75- *Awards:* Nat Orgn Women, 80. *Mem:* Coalition of Women's Art Orgns (chmn, 77-78); Nat Women's Caucus for Art (bd mem, 78-81); Found for Community of Artists; Women Artists Filmmakers. *Res:* Women artists; women's art groups; art and politics. *Publ:* Auth, Guide to Women's Art Organizations, 79; ed, Voices: Three on Three, Midmarch Assocs, 80. *Mailing Add:* 300 Riverside Dr New York NY 10025

NAVRAT, DEN (DENNIS EDWARD)
PRINTMAKER, EDUCATOR

b Marion, Kans, May 15, 42. *Study:* Kans State Univ, Manhattan, BA, 64; Wichita State Univ, Kans, MFA, 66; Univ Iowa, Iowa City, 69, with Virginia Myers; Photographer's Place, Derbyshire, Eng, 77, with Paul Hill & Ralph Gibson; Anderson Ranch Arts Ctr, Aspen, 83, with Catherine Reeve, Marilyn Sward, Bernie Vinzani, Katie McGregor and Terry Allen. *Work:* Mus of Fine Art, Houston, Tex; Atkinson Art Gallery, Metrop Bur of Sefton, Eng; Plains Art Mus, Moorhead, Minn; Univ Iowa Gallery, Iowa City; Blue Cross, Fargo, NDak. *Comn:* Sexist serigraph series, NDak Coun on the Arts, Fargo, 74; Colorado Papers, NDak Art Gallery Asn, 83-85. *Exhib:* NDak Artists Touring Exhib, 78-80; Eighth Colorprint USA, Tex Tech Univ, 78; Double Exposure Touring Exhib, 80-81; and others; Yellowstone Print Club, Yellowstone Art Ctr, Billings, Mont, 78. *Collections Arranged:* Images on Exchange travelling exhib, (illusr, catalogue), 78-80. *Teaching:* Instr, Inst of Logopedics, Wichita, Kans, 65-66; from instr to asst prof art, Dickinson State col, 66-71; assoc prof art & chmn art dept, 71-79; prof art, 79-; Fulbright-Hays Exchange prof art, Southport Col of Art, Eng, 76-77. *Awards:* Medal Award & Purchase Award, 17th Ann Exhib of Midwest Artists, Rourke Gallery, Moorhead, Minn, 76; Cash Award & Reproduction, Calendar Competition, Northwestern Bell Tel Co, Omaha, Nebr, 73. *Mem:* NDak Gallery Asn; Fulbright Alumni Asn. *Media:* Oil, Serigraphy. *Publ:* Auth, Images on Exchange, Mind's Eye Gallery, 78. *Mailing Add:* Lakeview Estates RR 1 Box 816 Dickinson ND 58601

NAVRATIL, AMY See Ciccone, Amy Navratil

NAWARA, JIM
PAINTER, PRINTMAKER

b Chicago, Ill, Jan 25, 45. *Study:* Sch Art Inst Chicago, BFA, 67; Univ Ill, Champaign, MFA, 69. *Work:* Boston Mus Fine Arts; Detroit Inst Arts; Bradford City Art Gallery, Eng; City Art Mus, Aukland, NZ; Nat Mus, Warsaw, Poland. *Comn:* Screenprints (with Curtis Rhodes), Western Mich Univ, Kalamazoo, 74; etchings, Mich Workshop Fine Prints, 75; wall drawing, Dept Recreation, 78; billboard, First Fed Savings, Detroit, 80. *Exhib:* San Francisco Mus Art, 70; Butler Inst Am Art, Youngstown, Ohio, 72, 73 & 75; Minn Mus Art, St Paul, 73 & 75; Brooklyn Mus, 76; Boston Mus Fine Arts, 79; Victoria & Albert Mus, London, 79; Detroit Inst Arts, 80 & 81; Cranbrook Acad, Bloomfield Hills, Mich, 80. *Teaching:* Assoc prof drawing, Wayne State Univ, 69- *Awards:* Purchase Awards, Butler Inst Am Art Mid-Yr, 72 & Mich Printmakers, Detroit Inst Arts, 77; Research Awards, Wayne State Univ, 78 & 81. *Media:* Oil, Watercolor; Intaglio. *Dealer:* Cantor-Lemberg Gallery 538 N Woodward Birmingham MI 48011. *Mailing Add:* 13343 Kingston Huntington Woods MI 48070

NAWARA, LUCILLE PROCTER
PAINTER, EDUCATOR

b Oklahoma City, Okla, June 26, 41. *Study:* Smith Col, with Leonard Baskin, BA, 62; Boston Univ, Sch Fine & Applied Arts, with Walter Murch & Arthur Polonsky, BFA, 67; Univ Ill, Champaign, MFA, 69. *Work:* Mich Coun Arts & Detroit Inst Arts, Detroit; Springfield Col, Mass; Grand Rapids Art Mus, Mich; Univ Mich Art Mus, Ann Arbor. *Comn:* Sea Squirts (intaglio), Oxbow Portfolio, Mich Coun Arts, Detroit, 73; Prisms (intaglio), Women's Portfolio, Nat Educ Asn & Mich Workshop Fine Prints, Detroit, 76. *Exhib:* San Francisco Mus Art, 70; Watercolor USA, Springfield Art Mus, 71; Los Angeles Printmaking Soc, Otis Art Inst, 74; Mid-Yr Ann, Butler Inst Am Art, Youngstown, Ohio, 75; Krannert Art Mus, Champaign, Ill, 76; Mich Asn Printmakers 7th Biennial, Detroit Inst Arts, 77; Spokane Nat Exhib, Cheney-Cowles Mem Mus, 77; and others. *Collections Arranged:* Moving Images (auth, catalog), 80; Int of Detroit (auth, catalog), 80; Art/Words, Words/Art (auth, catalog), 80; 8 at 1010 (auth, catalog), 80. *Pos:* Exhib coordr, Detroit Focus Gallery, 80. *Teaching:* Asst prof drawing, Wayne State Univ, Detroit, 69-76; instr drawing, Macomb Co Community Col, 77-82, Henry Ford Community Col, 82 & Ctr Creative Studies, 82-83. *Awards:* First Prizes, Scarab Club, Detroit, 75 & Art Ctr, Mt Clemens, Mich, 77; Visual Artists Grant landscape painting, Mich Coun Arts, 81 & 83. *Mem:* One Percent for Art; New Detroit Arts Comt. *Media:* Oil, Watercolor. *Mailing Add:* 13343 Kingston Huntington Woods MI 48070

NAWROCKI, THOMAS DENNIS
PRINTMAKER, EDUCATOR

b Milwaukee, Wis, June 26, 42. *Study:* Univ Wis-Milwaukee, BFA, 64, MA, 66, MFA, 66. *Work:* Univ Wis-Madison; Northern Ill Univ; Brand Libr Art Galleries, Glendale, Calif; Montgomery Mus Art, Ala; Miss Art Asn, Jackson. *Exhib:* Seattle Int Print Exhib, Seattle Art Mus, 68 & 71; Hawaii Nat Print

Exhibs, Honolulu Acad Arts, 73, 75 & 79; World Print Competition, San Francisco Mus Mod Art, 77; Int Print Bienniale, Krakow, Poland, 78 & 80; Wesleyan Int Exhib, 80; Rockford Int, Ill, 81; Bradley Univ Nat Exhib, Peoria, Ill, 81; 57th Ann Int, Print Club, Philadelphia, 81; and many others. *Teaching:* Instr printmaking, Southwest Tex State Univ, 67-70; asst prof printmaking, Miss Univ Women, 70-74, assoc prof, 74- *Awards:* Dixie Annual Print Competition Award, Montgomery Mus Art, 74; Purchase Award, Nat Print Competition, Edinboro State Col, Pa, 79; Okla Nat Print Award, Okla Art Ctr, 82; and others. *Bibliog:* Artist's Proof-A Journal of Printmaking, Pratt Graphic Art Ctr, New York, 67. *Mem:* Graphics Soc, Hollis, NH; Southern Graphics Coun; Los Angeles Printmaking Soc; Am Color Print Soc, Philadelphia; Print Club, Philadelphia. *Media:* Printmaking, Textiles. *Publ:* Contribr, 1st Nat Invitational Color Blend Exhib Catalog, Univ Miss Press, 79. *Mailing Add:* 112 Shane St Columbus MS 39701

NAY, MARY SPENCER
PAINTER, EDUCATOR
b Crestwood, Ky, May 13, 13. *Study:* Art Ctr Asn Sch, Louisville, Ky, 34-40; Cincinnati Art Acad, 41; Univ Louisville, BA, 41; Art Students League, 42; with Boris Margo, Provincetown, Mass, 50-51; Univ Louisville, MA, 60. *Work:* Speed Art Mus, Louisville; Ky Wesleyan Col, Owensboro; Univ Louisville; Ohio Univ, Athens. *Comn:* Mural for children's room, Louisville Pub Libr, Fed Art Proj, 34. *Exhib:* IBM Exhib, New York World's Fair, 40; Artists for Victory, Metrop Mus Art, 41; Contemp Color Lithography Int Biennials, 50, 52 & 54; 60th Ann Am Exhib, Art Inst Chicago, 51; Terry Nat Exhib, Miami, Fla, 52. *Pos:* Supvr, Puppet Proj, Nat Youth Admin, 37-39. *Teaching:* Instr painting & printmaking, Art Ctr Asn Sch, 40-59, dir, 44-49; prof art educ & painting, Univ Louisville, 59-71, distinguished prof art educ, 71-, Marcia S Hite prof painting, 75- *Awards:* Ashland Oil Co Purchase Awards, Art Ctr Asn Regsonal, 45, 50 & 58; Evansville Mus Purchase Awards, Tri-State Ann, 52, 56 & 58; Ky State Fair Bd Purchase Awards, 54, 56 & 58. *Mem:* Ky Arts & Crafts Guild (bd dirs, 67-70); Art Ctr Asn (librn & bd dirs, 71-72); J B Speed Art Mus; Provincetown Art Asn; Ky Art Educ Asn. *Mailing Add:* Dept Art Univ Louisville Louisville KY 40292

NAYLOR, JOHN GEOFFREY
SCULPTOR, EDUCATOR
b Morecambe, Eng, Aug 28, 28; US citizen. *Study:* Leeds Col Art, nat dipl design; Hornsey Col Art, ATD; Univ Ill, MFA. *Comn:* Smithsonian Inst & Nat Collection Art, Washington, DC; Pub Libr, Chattanooga, Tenn; Columbis Mus Art, Ohio; Lincoln Ctr, Dallas, Tex. *Exhib:* Gallery Contemp Art, Winston-Salem, NC, 74; Hirshhorn Mus & Sculpture Gardens, Washington, DC, 77; Univ Ariz, Tucson. *Pos:* Cur, Ft Wayne Art Mus, Ind, 65-66. *Teaching:* Instr drawing, Fla Southern Col, 67-69; assoc prof sculpture, Univ Fla, 69- *Awards:* Fulbright Travel Grant, 54; Nat Found Arts Award, 67; Fine Art Grant, State of Fla, 80. *Media:* Mixed. *Dealer:* Art Sources Gulf Life Bldg Jacksonville FL 32207. *Mailing Add:* 1741 NW 12th Rd Gainesville FL 32605

NAZARENKO, BONNIE COE
PAINTER
b San Jose, Calif, Oct 26, 33. *Study:* San Jose State Col; Carmel Art Inst, under John Cunningham. *Work:* Mint Mus, Charlotte, NC. *Exhib:* Gallery Contemp Art, Winston-Salem, NC, 70; Am Artists Prof League, New York, 72 & 83; Soc Animal Artists, Grand Cent Art Gallery, New York, 72, 74 & 75; Game Conservation International, San Antonio, Tex, 80. *Awards:* Beaufort Art Festival Award, SC, 66; Mint Mus Purchase Award, 68. *Mem:* Soc Animal Artists; Am Artists Prof League. *Media:* Oil. *Mailing Add:* 8314 Pocahontas St Tampa FL 33615

NEAL, ANN PARKER See Parker, Ann

NEAL, (MINOR) AVON
WRITER, PRINTMAKER
b Indiana, July 16, 22. *Study:* Long Beach Col; Escuela Bellas Artes, Mex, with Siquieros, MFA. *Work:* Metrop Mus Art, New York; Libr Cong & Smithsonian Inst, Washington, DC; Abby Aldrich Rockefeller Mus Am Folk Art, Williamsburg, Va; Winterthur Mus, Wilmington, Del. *Comn:* 500 original rubbings, 70, 250 original rubbings, 71 & ed 350 original rubbings, 74, Am Heritage; ed 100 original rubbings, 70 & ed 70 original rubbings, 74, for Arton Assocs (all with Ann Parker); ed 100 original rubbings, Mead Art Gallery, Amherst Col, 76. *Exhib:* New Eng Gravestone Rubbings, Mead Art Gallery, 76; Gravestone Art, William Benton Mus Art, Univ Conn, 76; Molas, Art of the Cuna Indians, Alternative Ctr Int Arts, New York, 76; and others. *Awards:* Ford Found Grants, 62-63 & 63-64. *Bibliog:* M J Gladstone (auth), New art from early American sculpture, Collector's Quart Report, 63 & Pedestrian art, Art in Am, 4/64; Stephen Chodorov (auth), Know Ye the Hour, Camera Three, CBS-TV, 11/68. *Interests:* Stone rubbing and folk art. *Publ:* Contribr, Fritz Eichenberg's Art of the Print, Abrams, 76; contribr, How to Know American Folk Art, Dutton, 77; coauth, Molas, Folk Art of the Cunas Indians, Barre, 77; auth, Scarecrows, Barre, 78; auth, Pigs & Eagles, Thistle Hill Press, ltd ed, 78. *Dealer:* Gallery of Graphic Arts 1603 York Ave New York NY 10028. *Mailing Add:* 126 School North Brookfield MA 01535

NEAL, FRANK WINGFIELD
PAINTER, INSTRUCTOR
b Greenwood, Miss, Nov 4, 55. *Study:* Delta State Univ, BFA, 77; Cape Sch Art, with Henry Henshe, 77 & 78; Univ Miss, MFA, 83. *Work:* Houston Plaza Club; Southern Graphics Coun, Oxford, Miss; Delta State Univ; Sch Book Supply Inc, Jackson, Miss. *Comn:* Paintings, comn by Mr & Mrs Jack Garner, Grenada, Miss, 80, Timothy L Sanders, Blue Mountain, Miss, 81 & Mr & Mrs

J R Heilman, Oxford, Miss, 83. *Exhib:* Southern Realism Traveling Exhib, 79-81; Seventh Ann Bi-State Competition, Meridian Mus Art, Miss, 80; Second Ann Miss Artists Exhib, W C Woods Gallery, Univ Southern Miss, 80; Four Painters, Ctr Study Southern Cult, University, Miss, 81; Colorist, Miss Mus Art, Jackson, 83. *Teaching:* Fac mem painting, Miss Mus Art Sch, 82-83; adj fac painting & printmaking, Jackson Pub Sch Acad & Performing Arts Complex, 82-84. *Awards:* Elizabeth Greenshields Found Study Grant, 78; Award Merit, Seventh Bi-State Competition, Meridian Mus Art, 80; First Place Painting, 13th Crosstie Arts Festival, 82. *Bibliog:* O C McDavid (auth), New exhibits, Clarion Ledger & Jackson Daily, 3/27/83. *Media:* Oil, Pastel. *Dealer:* Art South 613 Felder Ave Montgomery AL 36106. *Mailing Add:* 957 E Fortification Jackson MS 39202

NEAL, REGINALD H
PAINTER, PRINTMAKER
b Leicester, Eng, May 20, 09. *Study:* Yale Univ, 29-30; Bradley Univ, BA, 32; State Univ Iowa, summer 36; Univ Chicago, MA, 39; Colorado Springs Fine Arts Ctr, summer 41. *Work:* Libr Cong; Mus Mod Art; Newark Mus Art; NJ State Mus; Wadsworth Atheneum; Cincinnati Art Mus; plus many others. *Comn:* Two ed lithographs & two ed screen prints, AAA Gallery, New York; one ed lithographs, Bk of Mo Club; City Walls Inc, Jersey City. *Exhib:* Pa Acad Fine Arts, 36, 38 & 41; Metrop Mus Art, 45 & 52; Cincinnati Art Mus, 54, 56 & 58; Houston Mus Art, 56; Houston Mus of Fine Arts, 56; Gallery Mod Art, Ljubljana, Yugoslavia, 59 & 61; Grenchen Art Soc, Switz, 58; Responsive Eye Exhib, Mus Mod Art, New York, 65; Albright-Knox Gallery, Buffalo, 65; NJ State Mus, 65-68 & 71-72; Newark Mus, 66, 68, 69, 71 & 77; one-man shows, A M Sachs Gallery, NY, 68, Jane Haslem Gallery, Washington, DC, 73. *Teaching:* Prof, Millikin Univ, 40-48, Univ Miss, 51-57 & Southern Ill Univ, 58-59; & 67; chmn dept art & dir grad MFA prog, Douglass Col, Rutgers Univ, New Brunswick, 59-77, emer prof, 77- *Awards:* Golden Reel Award, Film Coun Am, 56; Gov Award, Trenton State Mus, 72. *Bibliog:* Oto Bihalji-Merin (auth), Adventures of Modern Art, Abrams, 66; Daniel M Mendelowitz (auth), History of American Art, Holt, Rinehart & Winston, 70; Fritz Eichemburg (auth), The Art of the Print, Abrams, 76. *Mailing Add:* Circle Dr RD 4 Box 21 Lebanon NJ 08833

NEALS, OTTO
PAINTER, SCULPTOR
b Lake City, SC, Dec 11, 30. *Study:* Basically self-taught, studied briefly at Brooklyn Mus Art Sch with Isaac Soyer; Printmaking Workshop, studied with Bob Blackburn, Robert DeLamonica & Krishna Reddy. *Work:* Ghana Nat Mus, Accra; Prime Minister Forbes Burnham, Guyana Statehouse; and others. *Exhib:* Resurrection, Studio Mus, NY, 71; Millenium, Philadelphia Mus of Art, Pa, 73; Selections 73, 74, Brooklyn Mus, 74; 14 Black Artists, Pratt Inst Gallery, Brooklyn, 76; Migrations, Museo De Arte Moderno, Cali, Colombia, S Am, 76 & Caraeas, Venezuela, 77. *Bibliog:* Peter Bailey (auth), Ten Black artists depict Christ, Ebony Mag, 4/71; Diane Weathers (auth), Black artists taking care of business, New York Times, 8/19/73; Elton Fax (auth), Black Artists of the New Generation, Dodd/Mead & Co, 77. *Mem:* Nat Conf of Artists. *Media:* Oil, Acrylic; Wood, Stone. *Publ:* Illusr, African Heritage Cookbook, MacMillian Publ, 71; illusr, The Adventures of Tony, David & Marc, Exposition Press, 76. *Dealer:* Dorsey's Gallery 553 Rogers Ave Brooklyn NY 11225. *Mailing Add:* 138 Sullivan Pl Brooklyn NY 11225

NECHIS, BARBARA
PAINTER, LECTURER
b Mt Vernon, NY, Sept 25, 37. *Study:* Univ Rochester, BA, 58; Alfred Univ, MS, 59; Parsons Sch Design. *Work:* Butler Inst Am Art; Slater Mem Mus, Conn; Banco de Crefisul, Sao Paulo, Brazil. *Comn:* Citicorp, New York; Int Bus Machines, New York; Westinghouse; New York Graphic Soc. *Exhib:* Am Watercolor Soc Exhib, Nat Acad Design, New York, 70-81; Audubon Artists Exhib; Mainstreams, Marietta Col, Ohio; Nat Acad Design Ann; Hudson River Mus; Tweed Mus, Minn; and others. *Teaching:* Fac mem, Parsons Sch Design, Long Island Univ, 82 & Univ Alaska, 83; guest lectr, Can Soc Painters Watercolor; lectr workshops, currently. *Bibliog:* Artist in residence, Am Artist, 5/83. *Mem:* Am Watercolor Soc; Artists Equity; Philadelphia Watercolor Club; Audubon Artists. *Media:* Watercolor, Mixed. *Publ:* Illusr, American Artists Group Reproduction, 73; auth, Watercolor, The Creative Experience, North Light/Van Nostrand Reinhold, 79; auth, article, North Light Mag, 6/79. *Mailing Add:* 100 Kingsbury Rd New Rochelle NY 10804

NEDDEAU, DONALD FREDERICK PRICE
PAINTER, DESIGNER
b Toronto, Ont, Jan 28, 13. *Study:* Ont Col Art; also with J W Beatty, Franklin Carmichael & Archibald Barnes. *Exhib:* 11 shows, Royal Can Acad, 36-61; 20 shows, 42-65 & traveling exhibs, 44-48 & 51-65, Ont Soc Artists; group shows, 43 & 48-65 & traveling exhibs, 49-65, Can Soc Painters in Watercolor; Can Soc Painters in Water Colour & Calif Watercolor Exhib, 50-75; Can Group Painters, 55, 56, 58 & 61; plus others. *Teaching:* Head dept art & prin art summer sch, Cent Tech Sch, Toronto, Ont, 48-78, emer, 78- *Awards:* Scholar, 36 & Rous & Mann Award, 36, Ont Col Art. *Mem:* Can Soc Painters in Water Colour (past pres); Can Guild Potters; Arts & Lett Club, Toronto; Royal Can Acad of Arts; fel Int Inst Arts & Lett; and others. *Mailing Add:* 21 Sherwood Ave Toronto ON M4P 2A6 Canada

NEEDLMAN, JOEL G
DEALER
b Chicago, Ill, Dec 6, 35. *Study:* Univ Ill, BS, 57. *Pos:* Asst dir, Phyllis Needlman Gallery, 78- *Specialty:* Contemporary American art. *Mailing Add:* 125 Whitebridge Winnetka IL 60093

NEEDLMAN, PHYLLIS L
DEALER
b Chicago, Ill, Jan 25, 38. *Study:* Vanderbilt Univ, 55; Univ Ill, BA, 59. *Pos:* Dir, Phyllis Needlman Gallery, Chicago, 76- *Specialty:* Contemporary American art. *Mailing Add:* 125 Whitebridge Winnetka IL 60093

NEEL, ALICE
PAINTER
b Merion Square, Pa, Jan 28, 1900. *Study:* Philadelphia Sch Design for Women, 21-25; Moore Col Art, hon Dr, 71. *Work:* Metrop Mus Art, Mus Mod Art & Whitney Mus Am Art, New York; Hirshhorn Mus; Am Mus, Moscow; and others. *Exhib:* Retrospectives, Moore Col Art, 71 & Whitney Mus Art, 74; Whitney Mus Am Art, 77, 80 & 82; Pa Acad Fine Arts, 80 & 81; Newport Harbor Art Mus, Newport Beach, Calif, 81-82; Hirshhorn Mus, Washington, DC, 82; Metrop Mus, New York, 82; Robert Miller Gallery, 82; Eleanor Ettinger Inc, New York, 82; Vanderwoude Tananbaum Gallery, 82. *Pos:* Easel painter, Fed Works Agency, 33-43. *Teaching:* Lectr painting sem, Univ Pa Grad Sch, 71-72; lectr, Skowhegan Sch Painting & Sculpture, summer 72. *Awards:* Longview Found Award, 62; Am Acad Arts & Lett Award, 69; Benjamin Altman Figure Prize, Nat Acad Design, 71. *Bibliog:* Ted Berrigan (auth), Double portraits, Art News, 1/66; Jack Kroll (auth), Curator of souls, Newsweek, 1/31/66; Nancy Baer (producer), Alice Neel: Collector of Souls (film), 76. *Mem:* Artists Equity Asn. *Media:* Oil. *Dealer:* Graham Gallery 1014 Madison Ave New York NY 10021. *Mailing Add:* 300 W 107th St Apt 3A New York NY 10025

NEES, LAWRENCE
EDUCATOR, HISTORIAN
b Chicago, Ill, Aug 9, 49. *Study:* Univ Chicago, BA, 70; Harvard Univ, MA, 73, PhD, 77. *Teaching:* Vis lectr, Univ Victoria, BC, 76-77; lectr, Univ Mass, Boston, 77-78; from asst to assoc prof, Univ Del, Newark, 78- *Mem:* Col Art Asn Am; Int Ctr Medieval Art; Byzantine Studies Asn; Medieval Acad Am. *Res:* Medieval manuscript illumination; art at the court of Charlemagne. *Publ:* Auth, Two illuminated Syriac manuscripts, Cahiers archeol, 81; auth, The iconographic program of decorated chancel barriers, Zeitschrift Kunstgeschichte, 83; auth, The colophon drawing in the book of Mulling, Cambridge Medieval Celtic Studies, 83; auth, From Justinian to Charlemagne, G K Hall, 84; auth, The Gundohinus Gospels at Autun, Medieval Acad Am, 84. *Mailing Add:* Dept Art Hist Univ Del Newark DE 19711

NEFF, EDITH
PAINTER, INSTRUCTOR
b Philadelphia, Pa, Aug 27, 43. *Study:* Philadelphia Col Art, BFA, 65. *Work:* Philadelphia Mus of Art; Pa Acad of Fine Arts; Minn Mus of Art, St Paul; Washington & Jefferson Col; Westminster Col, New Willmington, Pa. *Comn:* Lobby mural, Univ City Sci Ctr, Philadelphia, 74. *Exhib:* Am Family Portraits, Philadelphia Mus of Art, 76; Contemp Reflections, Aldrich Mus Contemp Art, Ridgefield, Conn, 76; one-woman show, Pa Acad Fine Arts, Philadelphia, 77; About Face, Squibb Gallery, Princeton, NJ, 78; Contemp Philadelphia Drawing, Philadelphia Mus Art, 79; Twenty-Five Women Artists, Southern Mus Alleghenies, Loretto, Pa, 79; Ten Pa Artists, Allentown Art Mus, 79; American Realism Since 1960, Pa Acad Fine Arts, Richmond Mus Art, Oakland Mus & Europe, 81-82; and many other group and one-person shows. *Pos:* Guest lectr, Pa Acad Fine Arts, 80-81. *Teaching:* Lectr painting, Philadelphia Col of Art, 71- *Awards:* Philadelphia Art Alliance Exhib Award, 79; Artists Fel, Pa Coun Arts, 82; Faculty Venture Award, Philadephia Col Art, 83; and others. *Bibliog:* Barbara Whipple (auth), Edith Neff: Nostalgic New Realist, Am Artist, 1/74; Edith Neff, a portfolio, Painted Bride Quart, Summer 77; Patricia Stewart (auth), Edith Neff: Subverted realism, Philadelphia Arts Exchange, 3-4/79; Victoria Donohoe (auth), Philadelphia Inquirer, article, 2/12/82. *Media:* Oil, Pastel. *Mailing Add:* 730 Kater St Philadelphia PA 10147

NEFF, JOHN A
PAINTER, DESIGNER
b Lebanon, Pa, May 5, 26. *Study:* Whitney Sch Art, New Haven, Conn, cert; Paier Col Art, Hamden, Conn, with Herbert Gute. *Work:* New Brit Mus Am Art, Gtr Hartford Arts Coun & Mus Art, Sci & Indust, Bridgeport, Conn; Mus Fine Arts, Springfield, Mass; First Nat Bank Boston. *Exhib:* Landscape I, De Cordova Mus, Lincoln, Mass, 70; Am Watercolor Soc, New York, 75; Watercolor USA, Springfield, Mo, 75; New England in Winter, De Cordova Mus, Lincoln, Mass, 78; Allied Artists, New York, 83; Hudson Valley Nat Exhib, White Plains, NY, 83. *Pos:* Sr graphic designer, Muirson Label Co, North Haven, Conn, 50-71; owner, Crossmark Assocs, Wallingford, Conn, 72. *Teaching:* Watercolor, privately. *Awards:* Salmagundi Club Award, New York, 77; Wm Church Osborne Award, Am Watercolor Soc, 75; Best Show, US Coast Guard Acad, 82. *Bibliog:* T F Potter (auth), A proxy visit, Meriden Rec-J, Conn, 69. *Mem:* Am Watercolor Soc; Allied Artists Am; New England Watercolor Soc; Silvermine Artists Guild; Conn Watercolor Soc (bd dirs, 71-72). *Media:* Transparent Watercolor. *Mailing Add:* 17 Parkview Rd Wallingford CT 06492

NEFF, JOHN HALLMARK
HISTORIAN, MUSEUM DIRECTOR
b Miami, Fla, Mar 28, 44. *Study:* Wesleyan Univ, Middletown, Conn, BA, 66; Harvard Univ, MA, 68, PhD, 74. *Collections Arranged:* 180 Beacon Collection (auth, catalog), Boston, Mass, 67. *Pos:* David E Finley fel, Nat Gallery Art, Washington, DC, 69-72; asst cur, Sterling & Francine Clark Art Inst, Williamstown, Mass, 72-73; cur mod art, Detroit Inst Arts, 74-78; dir, Mus Contemp Art, Chicago, 78- *Teaching:* Teaching fel 19th & 20th century

art hist, Harvard Univ, 67-69; asst prof 19th & 20th century art, Williams Col, Williamstown, Mass, 72-74, vis lectr, grad prog, 73-74. *Bibliog:* Hilton Kramer (auth), Rediscovering the genius of Henri Matisse, New York Times, 7/27/75; Robert Pincus-Witten (auth), Detroit notes, Arts Mag, 78. *Mem:* Asn Art Mus Dirs (trustee, currently); Nat Endowment Arts. *Res:* Matisse scholar, currently finishing book of Matisse studies and articles; advertising in twentieth century; occult sources for abstract and non-objective art; catalogs on nineteenth and twentieth century art. *Publ:* Auth, Matisse and decoration: The Schchukin Panels, Art Am, 75; co-auth & ed, Charles Simonds, Mus Contemp Art, Chicago, 81; auth, Elyn Zimmerman (brochure), 79; auth, Contemporary Art From the Netherlands, 82; auth, Peter Joseph (catalog), 83; and others. *Mailing Add:* Mus of Contemp Art 237 E Ontario St Chicago IL 60611

NEFFSON, ROBERT
PAINTER
b New York, NY, Dec 28, 49. *Study:* Art Students League, 64-67; Skowkegan Sch Painting, 69; Boston Univ, BFA(cum laude), 71, MFA, 73. *Work:* Roswell Mus, NMex; Boston Univ; Bristol Col, Mass; Charlestown Savings Bank, Boston. *Exhib:* Butler Inst Am Art 45th Ann Midyear Show, 81; The Realist Vision, Joanna Dean Gallery, New York, 82; Nocturnes, First St Gallery, New York, 82; solo exhib, Capricorn Gallery, Bethesda, Md, 83; New Faculty, Pa State Univ Mus Art, 83; Artists Studio 1840-1983, Allentown Mus, Pa, 83-84. *Pos:* Artist in residence, Roswell Mus, NMex, 77-78. *Teaching:* Asst prof art, Ariz State Univ, 81-82 & Pa State Univ, 82- *Awards:* Fulbright-Hays Fel, Rome, 76-77; Pa Coun Arts Visual Artists Grant, 83. *Mem:* Col Art Asn. *Media:* Oil. *Dealer:* Capricorn Galleries 4849 Rugby Ave Bethesda MD 20014. *Mailing Add:* PO Box 605 Lemont PA 16851

NEGRI, ROCCO ANTONIO
ILLUSTRATOR, PAINTER
b Reggio Calabria, Italy, June 26, 32. US citizen. *Study:* Aurel Kessler Acad, Arg, BsAs; Art Students League; Sch of Visual Arts, New York; Pratt Graphic Ctr, New York. *Work:* Univ Minn, Minneapolis; Cedar Rapids Pub Libr, Iowa; Univ Tokyo, Japan; Fed Home Loan Bank, New York; Albert Einstein Sch, Bronx, NY. *Exhib:* Painter's Mill Gallery, Rochester, NY, 74; one-man shows, Ratafia Gallery, Ft Lauderdale, Fla, 75 & Mainstream Gallery, Westhampton, NY, 75; Studio Gallery, Greenport, NY, 76; Reece Galleries Inc, New York, 76. *Awards:* Sixth Place, WSOAE, Kiwanis Club, 72; Excellence Award, Long Beach Art Asn, NY, 74; Merit Award, Coconut Grove Merchants Asn, Miami, Fla, 76. *Bibliog:* June Dixon (auth), Fantasy of a better place, Chattanooga Times, 6/69; A critic's choice of the year's best, New York Times, 12/70; Picture books, Hornbook, 2/71. *Publ:* Illusr, Journey Outside, 69 & Fee, Fi, Fo, Fum, 69, Viking; illusr, The One Bad Thing About Father, Harper & Row, 70; illusr, The Magic Pumpkin, Four Winds, 71; illusr, The Son of the Leopard, Crown, 74. *Dealer:* Reece Galleries Inc 39 W 32nd St New York NY 10001. *Mailing Add:* 1668 Norman St Ridgewood NY 11385

NEHER, FRED
CARTOONIST
b Nappanee, Ind, Sept 29, 03. *Study:* Chicago Acad Fine Arts. *Work:* Syracuse Univ; Butler Inst Am Art; Albright Col, Reading, Pa. *Exhib:* Humor Festival, World Cartoon Exhib, Knokke, Heist, Belg, 70 & 71. *Pos:* Cartoonist, Life's Like That, 34- *Teaching:* Instr cartooning, Univ Colo, Boulder, 64- *Mem:* Nat Cartoonist Soc; Soc Illusr. *Mailing Add:* One Neher Lane Boulder CO 80302

NEIDHARDT, CARL RICHARD
ADMINISTRATOR, PAINTER
b Chattanooga, Tenn, May 4, 21. *Study:* Ga Sch Tech, 39-41; Univ Tenn, Chattanooga, BA, 49; Univ Fla, MFA, 52; Rijksacademie, Amsterdam, Netherlands, 53-54; Ohio State Univ, PhD, 61. *Exhib:* Fifty Florida Artists, Ringling Mus, Sarasota, 60; Artist Teachers in Southeastern Univs, Jacksonville Mus, 60; Ark Art Ctr Mus, Little Rock, 61-63 & 69; Dallas Mus of Fine Arts, Tex, 63; Okla Art Ctr Mus, Oklahoma City, 64-69; Hunter Mus Art, Chattanooga, Tenn, 80; Mus Art, Sci & Industry, Bridgeport, Conn, 81. *Pos:* Chmn dept art, Hardin-Simmons Univ, Abilene, Tex, 60-65; dir dept art, Angelo State Univ, San Angelo, Tex, 65-66; chmn dept art, Austin Col, Sherman, Tex, 66- *Awards:* Fulbright Award to Netherlands, 53-54; Danforth Grant Res Painting, 58-59. *Mem:* Col Art Asn Am; Tex Asn Schs Art. *Media:* Acrylic on Canvas. *Mailing Add:* 321 N Grand Ave Sherman TX 75090

NEIKRUG, MARJORIE
DEALER, APPRAISER
b New Rochelle, NY. *Study:* Sarah Lawrence Col. *Pos:* Owner & dir, Neikrug Photographica Ltd. *Teaching:* Teacher, The Photographer's Eye (class), NY Univ, four yrs. *Mem:* Am Soc Appraisers (pres & sr mem, 80-81, dep state dir, 82); Am Arbitration Soc; Am Soc Mag Photogr; Am Soc Picture Professionals; Photog Adminr Inc. *Specialty:* Contemporary photography; photographica; rare books; portfolios; daguerreotypes; important historical photographs. *Mailing Add:* 224 East 68th St New York NY 10021

NEILL, BEN E
PAINTER
b Quincy, Mass, Dec 11, 14. *Study:* Sch Practical Art, Boston, Mass, 33; Mass Col Art, Boston, 34. *Exhib:* Am Soc Marine Artists, Grand Cent Art Galleries, Inc, New York, 80 & 82; Int Maritime, Gallery/Mystic Seaport; Contemp Marine Art, Peabody Mus, Salem, Mass, 81; Of Ships & the Sea, Greenwich Workshop Gallery, Southport, Conn, 81-83; Annapolis Marine Art Gallery Ltd, 82-84; and others. *Pos:* Editorial artist, Boston Herald

Traveler, Mass, 46-73. *Bibliog:* John S Carter (auth), Contemporary Marine, Nimrod Press, 81. *Mem:* Am Soc Marine Artists; Int Soc Marine Painters. *Media:* Acrylic. *Mailing Add:* c/o Misty Marsh Studio 88 Wood Ave Rd 1 Sandwich MA 02563

NEILL, JOE
SCULPTOR

b New Eagle, Pa, Aug 29, 44. *Study:* Westminster Col, BA, 66; Bowling Green State Univ, MFA, 68. *Work:* Mem Art Gallery, Rochester, NY; Tyler Mus, Tex; Everson Mus; Phillip Morris, McCrory Corp, New York. *Exhib:* Solo exhibs, Robert Freidus Gallery, New York, 77, 79 & 80, Vanderwoude Tananbaum Gallery, New York, 82 & Butler Inst Am Art, 84; Current New York, Lowe Gallery, Syracuse Univ, 80; Works on Paper, Weatherspoon Art Gallery, Greensboro, NC, 82-83; Suspended Object, Berkshire Mus, Pittsfield, Mass, 83. *Bibliog:* Jean Feinberg (auth), article, 79 & Margaret Sheffield (auth), Joe Neill--the kinetic and the indeterminate, 82, Arts Mag. *Media:* Wood, Plastics. *Dealer:* Vanderwoude Tananbaum Gallery 24 E 81 New York NY 10028. *Mailing Add:* 392 Broadway New York NY 10013

NEIMAN, LEROY
PAINTER, PRINTMAKER

b St Paul, Minn, June 8, 27. *Study:* Art Inst Chicago; Univ Chicago; Univ Ill; Franklin Pierce Col, Rindge, NH, LHD, 76; St Johns Univ, NY, Hon DFA. *Work:* Ill State Mus; Joslyn Art Mus; Wodham Col, Oxford, Eng; Mus Sport in Art, New York; Hermitage, Leningrad, USSR; and others. *Comn:* Murals, Continental Hotel, Chicago, 63; Mercantile Nat Bank, Hammond, Ind, 65; Swedish Lloyd Ship-Patricia, Stockholm, Sweden, 66; Sportsman's Park, Cicero, Ill, 76; and others. *Exhib:* American Exhibition of Oil Painting, Corcoran Gallery Am Art, Washington, DC, 57; Chicago American Exhibit of Painting & Sculpture, Art Inst Chicago, 60; Meredith Long Galleries, Houston, 78; Hammer Gallery, 79; retrospective, Oklahoma City Mus Art, 81; Neiman-Warhol, Los Angeles Inst Contemp Art, 81; and other group & one-man shows. *Pos:* Resident artist, New York Jets Prof Football Team, 68-; artist reporter, ABC-TV Wide World of Sports, 69-; official artist, Major League Baseball Promotions, 71-; ABC-TV official artist, XX Olympiad, Munich, Ger, 72 & XXI Olympiad, Montreal, 76; computer artist, Superbowl 78, CBS Sports Spectacular, 79; official artist, US Olympic Games, Calif, 84. *Teaching:* Instr figure drawing, Art Inst Chicago, 50-60; instr painting, Winston-Salem Art Ctr, 64 & Atlanta Poverty Art Prog, 67-68. *Awards:* Gold Medal, Salon d'Art Mod, Paris, 61; Award of Merit as Nation's Outstanding Sports Artist, Amateur Athletic Union; and others. *Bibliog:* LeRoy Neiman Art & Life Style, Felicie Press, 74; Prints of LeRoy Neiman, Knoedler Publ, 80. *Media:* Oil, Enamel; Serigraph, Etching. *Publ:* Auth, Horses, 79 & Winners, 84, Harry N Abrams Inc. *Dealer:* Hammer Galleries 33 W 57th St New York NY 10022; Knoedler Publ Co 19 E 70th St New York NY 10021. *Mailing Add:* 1 W 67th St New York NY 10023

NELLIS, DAVID L
COLLECTOR

b Tacoma, Wash, Sept 29, 34. *Collection:* Contemporary drawings, mainly American and British. *Dealer:* Tortue Gallery 2917 Santa Monica Blvd Santa Monica CA 90401. *Mailing Add:* 1540 7th St Santa Monica CA 90401

NELLIS, JENNIFRED GENE
SCULPTURE

b Lincoln, Nebr. *Study:* Univ Nebr, Lincoln, BFA, 70; Univ Iowa, Iowa City, MA, 76, MFA, 77. *Work:* Masur Mus, Monroe, La; Fine Arts Gallery, Univ Minn, Morris; Sprague Art Gallery, Joliet Jr Col. *Exhib:* Marietta Nat, Marietta Col, Ohio, 79; Minn Energy, Tweed Mus, Duluth, 80; one-woman show, Women's Art Registry, Minneapolis, Minn, 81; Urban Landscape, Peter M David Gallery, Minneapolis, 82; Not Your Typical Landscape Show, Womens Art Registry Minn, 83. *Teaching:* Asst prof sculpture, drawing, basic studio & ceramics, Univ Minn, Morris, 78- *Awards:* Sculpture Award, 29th Ann Iowa Artists, 77; Purchase Award, Monroe Nat, 79. *Mem:* Women's Art Registry Minn; Col Art Asn. *Media:* Mixed Media. *Mailing Add:* 533 1/2 Atlantic Morris MN 56267

NELSON, CAREY BOONE
SCULPTOR

b Lexington, Mo. *Study:* Wellesley Col, BA; Univ Mo; Wagner Col, MSEd; Art Students League, with John Hovannes, Arturo Lorenzani & John Terken; Nat Acad Design. *Work:* Wagner Col, Staten Island, NY; R F Shelare Libr, St Joseph Hill Acad, Staten Island; Sheldon Swope Mus, Terre Haute, Ind; Durban Art Mus, SAfrica; Victoria Libr, Melbourne, Australia. *Comn:* Zinc Miner, Franklin Mineral Mus, NJ, 80; Reading is Fundamental, Trails Regional Libr, 80; Dr Harris Levine, Israel Friendship House, New York, 81; Chuck Yeager, USAF, Pentagon, 82; Gen Hubert Harmon, USAF Acad, Colorado Springs, 83; and others. *Exhib:* Allied Artists Am, Nat Acad Design Galleries, 57-72; Int Art Exchange, Monte Carlo, Monaco, Paris & Cannes, 66-68; Salmagundi Club, New York, 75-83; Am Artists Prof League Grand Nat, 68-83; Burr Artists, New York, 70-83; over 150 other group shows & twelve one-man shows, New York. *Teaching:* Instr sculpture seminars, Snug Harbor Cult Ctr, 82 & 83. *Awards:* Wagner Col Achievement Award, 76; and others. *Bibliog:* Articles, Key, spring 69 & fall 71 & 74; article, Art News, 11/70; Nat Collection Fine Arts, Smithsonian Inst, Washington, DC. *Mem:* Catherine Lorillard Wolfe Art Club (bd dirs, 69-83); Nat League Am Pen Women; life fel Am Artists Prof League; Composers, Authors & Artists Am; Soc Illusr; fel Royal Soc Arts. *Media:* Bronze, Marble. *Mailing Add:* 282 Douglas Rd Staten Island NY 10304

NELSON, DONA RAE
PAINTER

b Grand Island, Nebr, Aug 2, 47. *Study:* Ohio State Univ, BFA, 68; Independent Study Program, Whitney Mus Am Art, 68. *Exhib:* Twenty-Six Contemporary Woman Artists, Larry Aldrich Mus Contemp Art, Conn, 70; 10 Young Artists: Theodoran Artists, Solomon R Guggenheim Mus, New York, 71; Personal Visions: Places and Spaces, Bronx Mus Art, NY, 78; Body Language: Recent Figuration, Mass Inst Technol, Cambridge, 81. *Awards:* Theodoran Purchase Award, Guggenheim Mus, 71; Creative Artists Pub Serv Prog Grant, 78-79; Nat Endowment Arts Grant, 79-80. *Mem:* Found Community Artists. *Media:* Oil. *Publ:* Contribr, Body Language: Recent Figuration, MIT Press, 81; contribr, Contemporary Painting/Figuration, Univ Calif, 81. *Dealer:* Oscarsson/Hood Gallery 57th St New York NY 10019. *Mailing Add:* 349 Greenwich St New York NY 10013

NELSON, HARRY WILLIAM
PAINTER, PRINTMAKER

b New York, NY, June 9, 08. *Study:* Yale Univ, BA, 33; New London Art Students League, with Harve Stein, 49-59; with Katherine Howe, 53; with Clarence Brodeur, 63-70; Lyman Allyn Mus, New London, Conn, with Beatrice Cuming, 64-67; Stonington Workshop, with Robert A Cale, 74 & 77. *Work:* Lyman Allyn Mus; also in many pvt collections. *Exhib:* Mystic Art Asn, Conn, 50-81; Boston Mus of Fine Arts, 53; one-man show, Lyman Allyn Mus, 68; Lyme Art Asn, Old Lyme, Conn, 68-78; Essex Art Asn, Conn, 64-79; retrospectives, Karash Mem, Lawrence Mem Hosp, New London, Conn, 73 & 80 & Groton Libr, 80; Bicentennial 1700-1950, Bicentennial Comn, Mystic Art Gallery, Conn, 76; Retrospective, Liberty Bank, Old Mystic, Conn, 77; Invitational Print Exhib, Mystic Art Asn, 79; plus others. *Pos:* Pres, New London Art Students League, 65-68. *Teaching:* Spec demonstrations monotypes, Mystic Art Asn, 68 & 70. *Awards:* Am Cancer Soc Show Silver Trophy, Mitchell Col, 68, Am Cancer Soc Show Spec Prize Design & Graphics, 71; Wimpfheimer Prize, Regional Exhib, Mystic Art Asn, 79; Maxwelton Award, 81. *Bibliog:* Tom Ingle (auth), One man show is delight, New London Day, 3/15/68; Leslie Pfeil (auth), Groton's award-winning multi-media man, Groton News, 7/27/71; John Kelley (auth), An Artist in Retrospect: Nelson Struggles with...Conquers Communication Medium, Norwich Bull, 3/23/80. *Mem:* Mystic Art Asn; Essex Art Asn; Lyman Allyn Mus; Lyme Art Asn. *Media:* Oil, Aquamedia. *Publ:* Illusr, The Moon is Near, 44, Blame the Skulk of Night, 74 & Encounter at the Aquarium, 78. *Mailing Add:* 213 Pleasant Valley Rd Groton CT 06340

NELSON, JACK D
SCULPTOR, GRAPHIC ARTIST

b Chicago, Ill, Jan 26, 29. *Study:* Art Inst Chicago, dipl, 54; Goodman Theatre. *Work:* Mus Mod Art, Stockholm, Sweden; Everson Mus, Syracuse; also in pvt collections of Joseph H Hirshhorn, Malcolm S Forbes & Yves Tanquey, Kay Sage Estate. *Comn:* Sculptural wall, Philips Electronics Corp, Lidingo, Sweden, 63; kinetic clock sculpture, Halprin Assoc for City of Minneapolis, 66. *Exhib:* International Movement in Art Show, Stockholm, Paris & Amsterdam, 61; Nat Aspect '61 Show, Stockholm, 61; Retrospective Show, Everson Mus, 72; Circuit Existential Videotape Exhib, Cologne, Ger, Boston & Los Angeles, 74-75. *Pos:* Asst art dir, Visualscope, Inc, New York, 56-59; dir & designer children's TV show, G K Films Studio, Swedish TV-Radio, Stockholm, 60-63. *Teaching:* Assoc prof sculpture & film video, Col Visual & Performing Arts, Syracuse Univ, 66-78, emer prof, 78- *Bibliog:* Gunnar Berefelts (auth), Ord och bild, Sartrvck, Stockholm, 62; article, Time Mag, 65; Lawrence Halprin (auth), The RSVP Cycles, Braziller, 69. *Media:* Vacuum Formed Plastic, Stretched Muslin Membrane; Videotape, Film. *Dealer:* Krasner Gallery 1043 Madison Ave New York NY 13210. *Mailing Add:* 819 Comstock Ave Syracuse NY 13210

NELSON, JANE GRAY
LIBRARIAN

b Kankakee, Ill, Oct 10, 28. *Study:* Univ Calif, Berkeley, MLS, 63, MA(classical archeol), 71. *Pos:* Librn, Fine Arts Mus, San Francisco, 71-, asst cur in charge, Dept Ancient Art, 74-76, cur in charge, Images for Eternity: the Art of Ancient Egypt, 75. *Mem:* Am Inst Archaeol; Soc Promotion Hellenic Studies; Art Libr Soc NAm. *Res:* Gnathia ware; English vernacular furniture. *Publ:* Contribr, Three Centuries of French Art, 73, Claude Monet, 73, Africa, Ancient Mexican Art: The Loran Collection, 74 & Two Early Hittite Theriomorphic Vessels of the Karum-Period, 82. *Mailing Add:* Fine Arts Mus San Francisco Golden Gate Park San Francisco CA 94118

NELSON, JON ALLEN
CURATOR, HISTORIAN

b Omaha, Nebr, July 9, 36. *Study:* Univ Nebr, Lincoln, BFA, 59; museology, Univ Minn. *Collections Arranged:* Etchings of J Alden Weir (auth, catalog), 67, Thomas Coleman, Printmaker (auth, catalog), 72 & Sigmund Abeles: The First Twenty Years (auth, catalog), 79, Sheldon Mem Art Gallery, Univ Nebr, Lincoln. *Pos:* Pres, Nebr Mus Conf, 73; cur, Ctr Great Plains Studies Art Collection, Univ Nebr, currently. *Publ:* Auth, Art of Printmaking, Univ Nebr, Lincoln, 66. *Mailing Add:* c/o Ctr Great Plains Studies Art Collection Univ Nebr Lincoln NE 68588

NELSON, LEONARD
PAINTER

b Camden, NJ, Mar 5, 12. *Study:* Pa Acad Fine Arts, 36-40; Barnes Found, 36-41; Philadelphia Col Art, BFA, 52. *Work:* Mus Mod Art; Philadelphia Mus Art; Dallas Mus Mod Art; Walker Mus Art; Portland Mus; plus many others. *Exhib:* Fifty one-man shows, New York & Philadelphia; many exhibs, Pa Acad Fine Art; Mus Mod Art; Art Inst Chicago; Maj Retrospective Exhib,

Moore Col of Art, Philadelphia, 78. *Teaching:* Prof printmaking, Moore Col Art, 52-83, head dept, 69-80, prof emer, 83- *Awards:* European Fel, Bd Fine Art, 39; Nat Wood Block Award, 42. *Mem:* Print Club (mem bd trustees, 52-57). *Media:* Oil, Metal. *Dealer:* Moore Gallery Philadelphia PA. *Mailing Add:* 825 N 27th St Philadelphia PA 19130

NELSON, MARY CARROLL
WRITER, PAINTER
b Bryan, Tex, Apr 24, 29. *Study:* Barnard Col, BA(fine arts), 50, art hist with Julius Held & painting with Peppino Mangravite & Dong Kingman; Univ NMex, MA(art educ), 63, painting with Kenneth M Adams; art educ with Alexander Masley; grad studies art hist with John Tatschl, 69-70. *Exhib:* Nat Small Painting Exhib, 62, 70 & 73-75; Heidelberg Kunstverein, Ger, 65; NMex State Fair, 70 & 73; Nat League of Am Pen Women, 70; Southwestern Watercolor Soc, Dallas, 73. *Pos:* Pres, Livermore Art Asn, Calif, 63. *Awards:* First Place, NMex State Fiar Show, 73; First in Mixed Media, NMex Biennial Nat League of Am Women, 81. *Bibliog:* Charlotte Black (auth), She writes, paints & teaches children, Albuquerque Tribune, 75. *Mem:* Nat League of Am Pen Women; NMex Watercolor Soc; Soc Layerists Multi-Media (pres, 82-). *Media:* Mixed Media. *Res:* Artists of New Mexico and the surrounding area; the relationship of artists' philosophy and their technique. *Publ:* Coauth (with Robert E Wood), Watercolor Workshop, 74, coauth (with R Kelley), Ramon Kelley Paints Portraits, Figures, 77, Legendary Artists of Taos, 80 & auth, Masters of Western Art, 82, Watson-Guptill; auth, Connecting, the art of Beth Ames Swartz, Northland Press, 84; and others. *Mailing Add:* 1408 Georgia NE Albuquerque NM 87110

NELSON, ROBERT ALLEN
PRINTMAKER, PAINTER
b Milwaukee, Wis, Aug 1, 25. *Study:* Art Inst Chicago, BAE, 50 & MAE, 51, lithography with Max Kahn; John Herron Sch Art, Indianapolis, Ind, 64, lithography with Garo Antresian, NY Univ, EdD, 71. *Work:* Walker Art Inst, Minneapolis, Minn; Joslyn Mus, Omaha, Nebr; Sheldon Mus, Lincoln, Nebr; Butler Inst Am Art, Youngstown, Ohio; Mint Mus, Charlotte, NC; and others. *Comn:* Murals, outdoor mosaics, Viking Sch, Grand Forks, NDak, 58 & Bridston Savings & Loan, Grand Forks, 59, Univ NDak, Chester Fritz Libr, Grand Forks, 60 & State of NDak Hwy Dept Bldg, Bismarck, 68. *Exhib:* Butler Inst Ann, Youngtown, Ohio, 63-75; Boston Printmakers, Boston Mus, Mass, 65-80; New Vein, Smithsonian Inst, Washington, DC, 68; Watercolors USA, Springfield, Mo, 72-78; Cleveland Mus, 74-75. *Teaching:* Instr drawing, Art Inst Chicago, 52-53; asst prof lithography & painting, Univ Man Sch Art, 53-56; prof painting & drawing, Univ NDak, 56-72; prof printmaking, Cleveland State Univ, 72-75; assoc prof art, Univ NC, Chapel Hill, 75-79 & Millersville State Col, Pa, 79-; assoc prof art, Millersville State Col, Pa, 79- *Awards:* First Prizes for painting & R J Reynolds Purchase Prize, Secca Gallery, NC, 77; First Prize for drawing at Spring Mills, SC, 77; and others. *Bibliog:* Garo Antreasian & Clinton Adams (auth), The Tamarind Book of Lithography: Art and Techniques, Abrams, 72. *Mem:* Boston Printmakers; Soc Am Graphic Artists; Philadelphia Print Club. *Media:* Stone; Typesetting. *Publ:* Illusr cover, Rec, 71 & Supertooth, 72. *Dealer:* Franz Bader Galleries 2124 Pennsylvania Ave NW Washington DC 20037; Impressions Gallery 275 Dartmouth St Boston MA 02116. *Mailing Add:* RD1 Letort Rd Washington Boro PA 17582

NELSON, SIGNE (SIGNE NELSON STUART)
PAINTER
b New London, Conn, Dec 3, 37. *Study:* Univ Conn, BA, 59; Yale-Norfolk Summer Art Sch, 59; Univ NMex, MA, 60; Univ Ore, sem with Ad Reinhardt, 63. *Work:* Tacoma Art Mus, Wash; Roswell Mus & Art Ctr, NMex; 3-M Co, St Paul; First Fed Reserve Bank Minneapolis; Sheldon Mem Art Gallery; and others. *Comn:* Mural, Five Seasons Community Ctr, Cedar Rapids, Iowa, 77 & 78-79. *Exhib:* 50th Ann Exhib Northwest Art, Seattle Art Mus, 64; solo exhib, Montgomery Mus Art, 77; two-person exhib, Joslyn Art Mus, 80 & 84; The American Land, Pillsbury Invitational, 81; Jan Cicero Gallery, Chicago, 81 & 83; Northwest Women Artists, Univ Mont, 82; Vessels and Paper, Minneapolis Art Inst, 82 & others. *Teaching:* Asst prof, Visual Arts Dept, SDak State Univ, 80- *Awards:* Nat Endowment Arts Fel, 76-77; Purchase Prizes, SDak Mem Art Ctr Biennial, 77 & Pillsbury Invitational, 81. *Bibliog:* Jan Vander Marck (auth), The chromatic waves of Signe Nelson, Artscanada, 71; Mosaic: Interview with Signe Stuart (TV film), KESP-TV, 77. *Media:* Acrylic on Canvas Constructions. *Mailing Add:* 719 Eighth St Brookings SD 57006

NEMEC, NANCY
PRINTMAKER
b Pinehurst, NC, Nov 30, 23. *Study:* Colby-Sawyer Col, New London, NH; Vesper George Sch Art, Boston, grad 44; Columbia Univ Sch Gen Studies, 48. *Work:* Libr Cong; New York Pub Libr; Philadelphia Free Libr; Greenville Mus, SC; Ga Mus Art; plus others. *Comn:* Print ed, Collectors Am Art, Silvermine Guild Artists, Hudson River Mus, Print Club Albany & New York Graphic Soc. *Exhib:* One-man shows, Hudson River Mus, 59, 62 & 65; Albany Inst Hist & Art, 62 & 63; Silvermine Guild Artists; Westfield Atheneum, Jasper Rand Mus & Fremont Found; plus many others. *Teaching:* Instr, Westchester Art Workshop, White Plains, NY, Hudson River Mus & Manhattanville Col, formerly. *Awards:* Acad Artists Asn Award, 65-67 & 73-78; NJ Painters & Sculptors Soc, 67 & 74; Miniature Art Soc NJ, 71 & 72; plus others. *Mem:* Am Color Print Soc; Copley Soc Boston; Nat Asn Women Artists; Miniature Painters & Gravers Soc; NH Art Asn; plus others. *Mailing Add:* Kearsarge Mountain Rd Warner NH 03278

NEMEC, VERNITA ELLEN
PERFORMANCE ARTIST, PRINTMAKER
Painesville, Ohio, Nov 30, 42. *Study:* Ohio Univ, BFA, 64; New York Univ, MA, 66. *Exhib:* Trends, Cayman Gallery, New York, 78; Post Card Sized Art, PS 1, New York, 78; Miniaturtextil Biennale, Savaria Mus, Szombathely, Hungary, 80; Renderings of Modern Woman, Univ Hartford, Conn, 80; solo exhib, Fiatal Muveszek Klubja, Budapest, 80; Copycat Show, Franklin Furnace, 82 & The Autumn of Her Descent (performance), AIR Gallery, 83, New York. *Pos:* Exhib coordr, Mus, A Project for Living Artists, New York, 69-70; contrib ed, Womanart, New York, 76-77; co-dir, Whitney Counterweight, New York, 77-81. *Teaching:* Prof art, City Univ New York, 73-79. *Awards:* Exhib Grant, Artists Space, 79 & 83; Artist in Residence, Millay Colony Arts, 81. *Bibliog:* Grace Glueck (auth), Art people, New York Times, 2/13/81; Jerry Tallmer (auth), On the town: Thumb your nose but think small, New York Post, 2/28/81; High Performance, spring-summer, 82. *Mem:* Found Community Artists; Women's Caucus Art; Orgn Independent Artists. *Media:* Collage; Xerography, Monoprint. *Publ:* Auth, Unmaled, private pub, 78; contribr, Re-View: Artists on art, Vered Lieb, 78; contribr, Tenth assembling, Richard Kostelanetz, 80. *Mailing Add:* 361 Canal St New York NY 10013

NEMSER, CINDY
CRITIC, WRITER
b Brooklyn, NY, Mar 26, 37. *Study:* Brooklyn Col, BA, 58, MA, 64; Inst Fine Arts, NY Univ, with Walter Friedlander, Charles Sterling & Donald Posner, MA(art hist). *Pos:* Curatorial intern, NY State Coun Arts, Mus Mod Art, 67; contrib ed, Arts Mag, 71-; ed, Feminist Art J, 72- *Teaching:* Guest lectr, Pratt Inst, Md Inst, RI Univ, NY Univ & others. *Awards:* Am Fedn Arts Tuition Grant, Art Critics Workshop, 68. *Mem:* Founding mem Women Arts; Col Art Asn Am; Women's Caucus Art. *Res:* Position of women in the art world. *Publ:* Auth, Stereotypes and women artists, Feminist Art J, 4/72; auth, Art criticism and gender prejudice, Arts Mag, 3/72; auth, The Washington Women's Conference, Art in Am, 1/73; auth, Art Talk Conversations with 12 Women Artists, Scribners, 75; auth, Eve's Delight, Pinnacle Books, 82; and others. *Mailing Add:* Feminist Art Jour 41 Montgomery Pl Brooklyn NY 11215

NEPOTE, ALEXANDER
PAINTER
b Valley Home, Calif, Nov 6, 13. *Study:* Calif Col Arts & Crafts, BA, 39; Univ Calif, Mills Col Grad Div, MA, 42. *Work:* San Francisco Mus Art; Metrop Mus Art, New York; Denver Mus Art; Univ Mich. *Exhib:* Metrop Mus Art, 52; Art USA, 58; Am Art of Our Time, 60; Int Watercolor Invitational, 72; Royal Soc Watercolor Painters, 75; Calif White Paper Painters, 76. *Teaching:* Prof art & dean fac, Calif Col Arts & Crafts, 45-50; prof art, San Francisco State Univ, 50-77, emer prof, 77- *Awards:* San Francisco Mus Art, 52; Denver Art Mus, 60; Nat Watercolor Soc, 78 & 79. *Mem:* Nat Watercolor Soc; W Coast Watercolor Soc. *Mailing Add:* 410 Taylor Blvd Millbrae CA 94030

NERI, MANUEL
SCULPTOR
b Sanger, Calif, Apr 12, 30. *Study:* San Francisco City Col, 49-50; Calif Col Arts & Crafts, 52-57; Calif Sch Fine Arts, 57-59. *Work:* Oakland Mus, Calif; Mus of Art, San Francisco; Crocker Art Mus, Sacramento, Calif; Seattle Art Mus. *Comn:* Marble sculpture, State Calif Gen Serv Admin, Bateson Bldg, Sacramento, 81-82. *Exhib:* Solo exhibs, Oakland Mus, Calif, 76, Seattle Art Mus, 81 & Western Asn Art Mus Travelling Exhib, 81-83; One-man shows, Davis Art Ctr, Calif, 72 & San Jose State Univ, Calif, 74; Bay Area Art of the 60s & 70s, the Gift of Dr Sam West, Univ NMex Art Mus, Albuquerque, 78; Gallery Paule Anglim, San Francisco, 78 & 79; Related Figurative Drawings, Hansen Fuller Gallery, 79; Ann Drawing Invitational, Cent Wash State Col, Ellensburg, 79; and others. *Teaching:* Instr, Calif Sch Fine Arts, 59-64; prof art, Univ Calif, Davis, 64- *Awards:* Guggenheim Fel, 79; Nat Endowment Arts Fel, 80; Am Acad & Inst Arts & Lett Award, 82. *Bibliog:* Thomas Albright (auth), Manuel Neri's survivors: Sculpture for the age of anxiety, Art News, 1/81. *Dealer:* John Berggruen Gallery 228 Grant Ave San Francisco CA 94108; Charles Cowles Gallery 420 W Broadway New York NY 10012. *Mailing Add:* c/o Anne Kohs & Assocs Inc 251 Post St Suite 300 San Francisco CA 94108

NESBITT, ALEXANDER JOHN
EDUCATOR, CALLIGRAPHER
b Paterson, NJ, Nov 14, 01. *Study:* Art Students League; Cooper Union; also with Harry Wickey; Southeastern Mass Univ, hon DFA, 79. *Work:* Cooper Union Mus; Houghton Libr, Boston; Providence Pub Libr; Klingspor Mus, Offenbach am Main, Ger; Deutche Bucherei, Leipzig. *Comn:* Mem tablet, comn by Col Truman Smith, St John's Church, Stamford, Conn, 52; mem tablet, comn by John D Skilton, Trinity Chapel, Southport, Conn, 56; mem doc, Pilgrim John Howland Soc, presented to Lady Churchill, 66; designs for four gravestones, comn by John D Skilton, Monroeville, Ohio, 66. *Exhib:* Working Calligrapher & Lettering Artist, Brown Univ, 61; Calligraphy & Handwriting, Peabody Inst, 63, 2000 Years Calligraphy; Alexander Nesbitt--Lettering, Calligraphy, Typographic Design, Crapo Gallery, New Bedford, 66; Int Buchkunst-Ausstellung. Leipzig, 71; Work of the Third & Elm Press, Redwood Libr, Newport, RI, 77 & Alexander Nexbitt--Writing & Lettering, 79. *Collections Arranged:* Working Calligrapher & Lettering Artist, Brown Univ, 61. *Pos:* Tech art dir, Jordanoff Aviation Co, 42-44; art dir, Technographic Publ, 44-45; owner, Third & Elm Press, 65- *Teaching:* Instr typography & lettering, Cooper Union, 50-57; assoc prof graphic design & chmn dept, RI Sch Design, 57-65; prof design, Southeastern Mass Univ, 65-74, emer prof, 74- *Awards:* Travel & Study Grant, 59; Bronze Medal, Int

Buchkunst-Ausstellung, 71. *Bibliog:* Leo Joachim (auth), Nesbitt reviews recent European graphics safari, Printing News, 3/5/60; Leona G Rubin (auth), Nesbitt calligraphy exhibit praised, New Bedford Standard-Times, 2/20/66; Walter Plata (auth), Alexander Nesbitt, Polygraph, 72; William Flanagan (auth), The Third & Elm Press, Yankee Mag, 1/77. *Mem:* Soc Printers, Boston; Type Dirs Club New York; Am Printing Hist Asn; Newport Art Asn; Goethe Soc New Eng. *Publ:* Auth, Lettering--the History and Technique of Lettering as Design, 50; ed, Decorative Alphabets and Initials, 59; ed, 200 Decorative Title-Pages, 64; ed, Color Order and Harmony, 64; co-auth, Weathercocks and Weathercreatures, 70. *Mailing Add:* 29 Elm St Newport RI 02840

NESBITT, LOWELL (BLAIR)
PAINTER, SCULPTOR
b Baltimore, Md, Oct 4, 33. *Study:* Tyler Sch Fine Arts, Temple Univ, BFA; Royal Col Art, London, Eng. *Work:* Nat Collection Fine Arts, Smithsonian Inst, Washington, DC; Mus Mod Art, New York; NASA, Washington, DC; Nat Gallery Art, Washington, DC; Philadelphia Mus; and others. *Comn:* Posters, List Found, New York City Ctr, 68, Lincoln Ctr, 78 & Jewish Mus, 79; Apollo 9 & 13 (oils), NASA, 69 & 70; poster of Renwick Mus, Smithsonian Inst, 71; Clearing Sky 72 (oil), Environ Protection Agency, Washington, DC, 72. *Exhib:* Whitney Mus Am Art Ann, New York, 67; one-man shows, Corcoran Gallery Art, Washington, DC, 73, Mus de Bellas Artes, San Juan, PR, 74, Univ Rochester, 75, New York Cult Ctr, 75 & Rochester Mus, NY, 75; Traveling Bicentennial Exhib, 76; Ulrich Mus Art, Wichita, Kans, 77; Kent State Univ, 78; McNay Art Inst, San Antonio, Tex, 80; plus many others. *Pos:* Asst set designer, Ogunquit Playhouse, Maine, 53 & 54; art dir TV, Walter Reed Med Ctr, 56-60. *Teaching:* Instr printmaking, Towson State Col, 66-67; instr printmaking, Baltimore Mus Art, 67-68; honorarium lectr, Univ Miami, Univ Richmond & Baltimore Mus Art, 68, 69 & 71; instr painting, Sch Visual Arts, 70-71. *Awards:* Purchase Awards for Oils & Prints, Baltimore Mus Art, 56; Award for Ben Berns Studio (oil), Nat Collection Fine Arts, 69, Baker Brush Co (drawing), 71. *Bibliog:* Coverage of Studio series, Time Mag, 69; The Ruins (film), John Huzar Prod, 71. *Media:* Oil on Canvas. *Mailing Add:* c/o Andrew Crispo Gallery 41 E 57th St New York NY 10022

NESLAGE, OLIVER JOHN, JR
ART DEALER
b Joplin, Mo, Mar 8, 25. *Study:* Univ Pittsburgh, AB, 50, Grad Sch, 51-52, Sch Law, 52-53; Oxford Univ, 51. *Pos:* Pres & managing dir, Venable Neslage Galleries, Washington, DC, 63-; pres, Neslage Assocs, Washington, DC, 68-. *Mem:* Prof Picture Frames Asn. *Specialty:* Contemporary European and American artists in oil, graphics and drawings. *Mailing Add:* 1714 19th St NW Washington DC 20009

NESS, EVALINE (MRS ARNOLD A BAYARD)
ILLUSTRATOR, WRITER
b Union City, Ohio, Apr 24, 11. *Study:* Muncie State Teachers Col, Ind, 31; Art Inst Chicago, 33; Corcoran Art Sch, 45; Art Students League, 47; Acad Belle Arti, Rome, Italy, 50. *Pos:* Fashion illusr, Saks Fifth Ave, New York, 46-49; mag & adv illusr, 46-49; free lance illusr, 59- *Teaching:* Teacher children's art classes, Corcoran Sch Art, Washington, DC, 45-46; teacher art classes, Parsons Sch Design, New York, 59-60. *Awards:* First Prize Painting, Corcoran Sch Art, 45; Caldecott Medal Children's Books, 67. *Publ:* Designer-illusr, Paper Palace, 76, Four Rooms from the Metropolitan Museum, 77, Victorian Paper House, 78 & Shaker Paper House, 79; auth & illusr, Marcella's Guardian Angel, 79; Fierce: The Lion, 80; and others. *Mailing Add:* 303 Coconut Row Palm Beach FL 33480

NESS, (ALBERT) KENNETH
PAINTER, DESIGNER
b Saint Ignace, Mich, June 21, 03. *Study:* Univ Detroit, 23-24; Detroit Sch Appl Art, 24-26; Wicker Sch Fine Art, 26-28; Art Inst Chicago, with Boris Anisfeldt, dipl, 32. *Work:* NC State Art Mus, Raleigh; R J Reynolds Collection, Winston-Salem, NC; Ackland Art Ctr, Chapel Hill, NC; Duke Univ Mus Art. *Exhib:* Int Watercolor Exhibs, Art Inst Chicago, 34-39, Am Painting Ann, 35 & 37; Golden Gate Int Expos, San Francisco, 39; Am Painting Ann, Butler Inst Am Art, Youngstown, Ohio, 51; Pa Acad Fine Arts Ann, 53 & 54. *Pos:* Dir, War Art Ctr, Univ NC, Chapel Hill, 42-44, actg head dept art & actg dir, Person Hall Art Gallery, 44, 45, 55, 57 & 58. *Teaching:* Resident artist, Univ NC, Chapel Hill, 41-73, assoc prof, 43-49, prof art, 49-73, emer prof art, 73- *Awards:* Purchase Award, NC State Mus Ann, 54; NC Award, 73; Purchase Award, R J Reynolds Competition, 77; and others. *Mem:* Hon assoc NC Chap Am Inst Architects; life fel Int Inst Arts & Lett. *Media:* Oil, Tempera. *Publ:* Ed, Student Art at the University of North Carolina, Chapel Hill, 64; producer, Mona Lisa Rides Again (film), 69; producer, Art is Where You Mind It (film), 71-72. *Mailing Add:* PO Box 14 Chapel Hill NC 27514

NESTOR, LULA B
PAINTER, ADMINISTRATOR
b Weirton, WVa. *Study:* WVa Univ, 55-56; West Liberty State Col, WVa, BAE; Eastern Mich Univ, MA(art), 73. *Work:* Pittsburgh Plate & Glass Co; Mt Lebenon Greek Orthadox Church, Pittsburgh; WVa Univ; Mich Educ Asn, State Collection Art; Ins Com & Galleries, Michalskis Gallery, Washington, DC. *Exhib:* Butler Inst Art, Butler Mus, Youngstown, Ohio, 73 & 75; Nat Soc Painter in Casien, Nat Gallery of Acad, NY, 76; Audubon Artist 35th Ann Exhib, Nat Acad Gallery, New York, 76; Nat Watercolor Soc 57th Ann, Calif State Univ, 77; one-woman exhibs, Univ Mich, 75, Univ WVa, Morgantown, 75 & Constantine Grimaldis Gallery, 80 & 81. *Pos:* Dir, Hartland Regional Fine Arts Festival, 68-77; past pres & trustee mem,

Hartland Art Show, Mich. *Teaching:* Instr, Richie Jr High Sch, Wheeling, WVa, 57-58, Elida High Sch, Elida, Ohio, 58-59 & South Lima Jr High Sch, Lima, Ohio, 60-62; art instr & dir art dept, Hartland High Sch, Mich, 68-81; instr adult educ classes, Hartland Consolidated Schs. *Awards:* First Place, Nat Pittsburgh Watercolor Aqueous Open Competition, 74 & 76; International Artist in Watercolor Competition, London, 82; Award, Nat Watercolor Soc Ann, 82. *Mem:* Mich Watercolor Soc (mem bd); Midwest Watercolor Asn, Minn; Nat Watercolor Soc. *Media:* Watercolor; Casien. *Mailing Add:* 9865 Edwards Dr Brighton MI 48116

NETO, GILDA REIS (GILDA REIS NETOPULETTI)
PAINTER
b Rio de Janeiro, Brazil. *Study:* Ceramic Tecnic Sch, Rio de Janeiro; Mod Art Mus, Rio de Janeiro, with Ivan Serpa; Andre Lhote, Atelier 17 & Gerard Passett, Paris; Acad de la Grande Chaumiere, Paris. *Work:* Cult Div of Brazilia; Pedro Ernesto Hosp, Rio de Janeiro; Embassy of Senegal; Bank of Brazil in San Francisco, Calif. *Comn:* Mural, Reception Salon of the Ministry of Educ & Cult, Brasilia, 60; Yacht Club (mural), with architect, Sergio Rodrigues, Yacht Club, Brasilia, 60; mural, Theatre of Parque Sch, Brasilia, 61. *Exhib:* Univ San Francisco, 73; Arline Lind Gallery, San Francisco, 72; Puletti Gallery, San Francisco, 75; one-woman show, Mus Fine Arts, Rio de Janeiro, 80, Witcomb Galeria, Buenos Aires, Argentina, 81; and many others. *Awards:* Bronze Medal, Salon de SAPS, Brazilian Govt, 55 & Silver Medal, Salon Oficial de Parana, 58. *Mem:* San Francisco Women Artists. *Media:* Oil and India ink. *Publ:* Roberto Pontual (auth), Dicionario das artes plasticas no Brasil, Civilizacao, 69. *Mailing Add:* 73 Santa Paula Ave San Francisco CA 94127

NEUBERGER, ROY R
COLLECTOR, PATRON
b Bridgeport, Conn, July 21, 03. *Study:* NY Univ; Univ Sorbonne; State Univ NY, Purchase, DFA, 82. *Pos:* Bd dir, City Ctr Music & Drama, Inc, 57-74, finance chmn, 71-74, trustee, 74-; pres, Am Fedn Arts, 58-67, hon pres, 68-; mem, Friends of Whitney Mus Am Art, 60-62, chmn acquisitions comt; chmn adv coun arts, New York City Housing Authority, 60-68; mem exec comt, Coun of Friends of the Inst Fine Arts, NY Univ, 61-; trustee, Whitney Mus Am Art, 61-68, emer trustee, 69-; fine arts gifts comt, Nat Cult Ctr, 62-68; art ctr comt, New Sch Social Res, 62-69, 70-, trustee, 67-; adv comt art, Mt Holyoke Col, 63-78; fine arts adv comt, Amherst Col, 63-70; hon trustee, Metrop Mus Art, 68-; pres coun, Mus City New York, 71-; mem bd dirs, Bard Col Ctr, 79. *Teaching:* Lectr art, Wadsworth Atheneum, Vassar Col, Brooklyn Mus, Detroit Inst Art, Mass Inst Technol Alumni Assocs, State Univ NY, Purchase. *Awards:* Art in America Award, 59; NShore Community Arts Ctr Award, 61; Artists Equity Asn Award, 72. *Mem:* Benjamin Franklin Fel Royal Soc Arts; life fel Nat Acad Design; fel RI Sch Design, 81; Century Asn. *Collection:* Primarily American art, substantial part being given to the Roy R Neuberger Museum of the State University of New York College at Purchase; parts of private collection have been exhibited in museums, universities and galleries in the United States and abroad. *Publ:* Contribr, Art in Am & var other art catalogs. *Mailing Add:* 522 Fifth Ave New York NY 10036

NEUBERT, GEORGE WALTER
SCULPTOR, CURATOR
b Minneapolis, Minn, Oct 24, 42. *Study:* Hardin-Simmons Univ, BS, 65; San Francisco Art Inst, 67; Mills Col, MFA(Trefethen Found Fel), 69. *Work:* Oakland Mus, Calif; Richmond Art Ctr, Calif. *Exhib:* Contemporary Sculpture, San Francisco Art Inst, 67; Invisible Painting & Sculpture, Richmond Art Ctr, 69, one-man show, 70; 11 Bay Area Sculptors Under 35, Michael Walls Gallery, San Francisco, 69; Univ Calif, Davis, 73; Univ Calif, San Francisco, 74. *Collections Arranged:* Pierres de Fantaisie (with catalog), 70, Color and Scale (with catalog), 71, Off the Stretcher, 72, 4 Real, 72, Larry Bell, 73, Oakland Mus; Tropical, Oakland Mus & Santa Barbara Mus, 72. *Pos:* Cur art, Oakland Mus, 70-81; mem adv bd, Archives Am Art, Smithsonian Inst, 72-; assoc dir art, San Francisco Mus Mod Art, Calif, 81-83; dir, Sheldon Mem Art Gallery, Univ Nebr, Lincoln, 83- *Bibliog:* C McCann (auth), Six, six, six, 6/71 & J Dunham (auth), article, 4/73, Artweek; article, Washington Post, 3/13/75; plus others. *Mem:* Am Asn Mus; Western Asn Art Mus; Asn Art Mus Dir. *Publ:* Ed, Tropical, 71; ed, Xavier Martinez, 74; ed, Public Sculpture/Urban Environment, 74. *Mailing Add:* Sheldon Mem Art Gallery Univ Nebr Lincoln NE 68588

NEUGEBAUER, MARGOT
DESIGNER, CRAFTSMAN
b Gottingen, Ger, Nov 14, 29; US citizen. *Study:* RI Sch Design, BFA, 52, cert, 65; Syracuse Univ, MFA, 54; Haystack Mountain Sch Crafts, 57-70; Werkkunstschule, Ger, 71. *Exhib:* New England Invitational, DeCordova Mus, Lincoln, Mass, 62; Brockton & Fall River Ann, 63-67; RI Craftsmen, Providence, 65-66 & 69; Haystack Invitational, Flint, Mich, 69; Northeast Regional, ACC Gallery, New York, 72. *Teaching:* Art supvr, Cortland Pub Schs, 53-55; instr art, New Bedford Inst Technol, 55-58; asst prof art, Southeastern Mass Technol Inst, 58-72; asst prof art, Southeastern Mass Univ, 58-72, assoc prof, 72-77, prof, 77-, chmn dept design, 73- *Mem:* Am Craftsmen Coun; Boston Weavers Guild; Soc Arts & Crafts, Boston. *Mailing Add:* 133 State St New Bedford MA 02740

NEUMAN, ROBERT S
PAINTER
b Kellogg, Idaho, Sept 9, 26. *Study:* Calif Col Arts & Crafts; Calif Sch Fine Arts; Univ Idaho; Mills Col; also in Stuttgart, Ger. *Work:* San Francisco Mus Art; Boston Mus Fine Arts; Worcester Mus Art, Mass; Mus Mod Art, New York; Addison Gallery Am Art, Andover, Mass; plus others. *Exhib:* De

Cordova & Dana Mus, 60-65; New England Art Today, 63 & 65; Mus Mod Art, 64; Art Across America, Boston, 65; Allan Stone Gallery, New York; plus others. *Teaching:* Instr, Calif Cols Arts & Crafts, 51-53, Brown Univ, 61-63 & Carpenter Ctr Visual Arts, Harvard Univ, 64-65; prof art & chmn dept, Keene State Col, NH, 72-77. *Awards:* Fulbright Grant, 53-54; Prize, San Francisco Mus Art; Guggenheim Fel, 56-57; and others. *Mailing Add:* 4 Gordon St Waltham MA 02154

NEUMANN, HANS
COLLECTOR

b Venezuela, Feb 9, 21. *Mem:* Mus Mod Art (coun mem); Guggenheim Mus (assoc mem); World Future Soc. *Collection:* Modern paintings; antique sculpture and modern sculpture; antique jewelry and watches. *Mailing Add:* Apartado 5475 Caracas Venezuela

NEUMANN, WILLIAM A
EDUCATOR, GOLDSMITH

b Cleveland, Ohio, Oct 12, 24. *Study:* Cleveland Inst Art, study with John Paul Miller, BFA; Syracuse Univ, study with John Marshall, MFA. *Work:* Cleveland Mus Art; Dallas Mus Fine Arts; Massillon Mus Art, Ohio. *Comn:* Wedding bracelets (18K gold and enamel), Mr & Mrs Patrick Dougherty, Akron, Ohio, 77; diamond necklace (gold and silver enamel), Dr & Mrs Moshe Amitay, Kent, Ohio, 77. *Exhib:* One-man shows, Illums, Copenhagen, Denmark, 52 & Lowe Art Ctr, Syracuse Univ, 68; Goldsmith 74 Nat Exhib, Renwick Gallery, Smithsonian Inst, Washington, DC, 74; Blossom-Kent Univ Art Exhib, Kent, Ohio, 75-77; Nat Jewelry Competition, Tex Univ, Lubbock; and others. *Collections Arranged:* Collabr, Design & Aesthetics in Wood, 67 & Harry Wickey Drawing & Prints, 69, Lowe Art Ctr, Syracuse Univ. *Pos:* Pres & design dir, Dimensional Design, Inc, Cleveland, 57-64; resident design dir, Aid to Int Develop, Bogota, Colombia, 66-67. *Teaching:* Prof design, Syracuse Univ, 67-70; prof metalsmithing, Univ Akron, 70. *Awards:* Second Prize, All Ohio Show, Canton Art Inst, Ohio, 71; Special Award, 53rd Ann May Exhib, Cleveland Mus of Art, 72. *Bibliog:* Joseph Ordos (auth), Three American Goldsmiths (film), Univ Minn, 75. *Mem:* World Craft Coun; Am Craft Coun; Soc NAm Goldsmiths; Nat Asn Handcraftsmen. *Mailing Add:* Dept of Art Univ Akron Akron OH 44325

NEUSTEIN, JOSHUA
PAINTER, PRINTMAKER

b Danzig, Poland, Oct 16, 40; US citizen. *Study:* City Col New York, 57-61, BA, 61; Art Students League, 59-61; Pratt Inst, Brooklyn, NY, 60-63. *Work:* Mus Mod Art, Whitney Mus Am Art, New York; Jerusalem Mus of Israel; Tel Aviv Mus of Art, Israel; Louisiana Mus, Copenhagen, Denmark. *Exhib:* Travel Art, Mus of Mod Art, Oxford, Eng, 71; Documenta V, Kassel, Ger, 72; Photog into Art, Camden Art Centre, London, 72; Photog Triennale, Israel Mus, Jerusalem, 76; one-man shows, Mus Art, Worcester, Mass, 75 & Neustein-Ten Years, Tel Aviv Mus, Israel; and others. *Awards:* Willem Sandberg Prize, Jerusalem, 74. *Bibliog:* Pincus Witten (auth), Sons of light, 9/75, Six propositions, 12/75 & Neustein papers, 10/77, Arts Mag. *Res:* Art criticism. *Dealer:* Mary Boone 420 W Broadway New York NY 10012; B Urdang 23 E 74th St New York NY 10021. *Mailing Add:* 300 W 108th St New York NY 10025

NEVELSON, LOUISE
SCULPTOR, PRINTMAKER

b Kiev, Russia, 1900; US citizen. *Study:* Art Students League, 29-30; Hans Hofmann Sch, Munich, 31; Smith Col, MA, Hon DFA, 71, Hon DFA, 73; Hamline Univ, Hon DHL. *Work:* Mus Mod Art, Whitney Mus Am Art, New York; Princeton Univ; Tate Gallery Art, London; Art Inst Chicago; and many others. *Comn:* Aluminum sculpture, South Mall Proj, Albany, NY, 68; Corten steel sculptures, Binghamton, NY, 72 & Scottsdale, Ariz, 72; monumental wood sculpture, World Trade Ctr, New York, 72; Bicentennial Dawn (white painted wood), Fed Courthouse, Philadelphia, Pa; St Peter's Church, New York. *Exhib:* Pa Acad Fine Arts, 44; six Whitney Mus Am Art Ann, 47-69; Mus Mod Art, New York, 59; one-person exhibs, Pace Gallery, Boston, 60, 64 & Columbus, 78, Whitney Mus Am Art, 70, Wildenstein & Co, New York, 80, Scottsdale Ctr Arts, 80, Phoenix Art Mus, 80, Seattle Art Mus, 80, Winnipeg Art Gallery, 80, Univ Iowa, 80, Dayton Art Inst, 80 & others; Contemp Painters & Sculptors as Printmakers, Mus Mod Art, 64; Dallas Mus Fine Arts, 65; retrospectives, Whitney Mus Am Art, 66 & 80 & Walker Art Ctr, 73; Whitney Mus Am Art, 66, 69 & 73; Chicago Art Inst, 66 & 67; Am Sculpture of the Sixties, Los Angeles Co Mus Art, 67; Guggenheim Mus, 67; Tamarind Homage to Lithography, Mus Mod Art, New York, 69; American Art--Third Quarter Century, Seattle Art Mus, 73; The 20th Century: 35 Artists, Whitney Mus Am Art, 74; and many others. *Teaching:* Instr, Educ Alliance, New York, Adult Educ Prog, Great Neck, NY & New York Sch Deaf, formerly. *Awards:* Tamarind Fel, 63; MacDowell Colony Medal, 69; Creative Arts Award, Brandeis Univ, 71. *Bibliog:* Glimcher (auth), Louise Nevelson, Praeger, 72; Mackown (auth), Dawns & Dusks, Louise Nevelson, Scribner's, 76. *Mem:* Artists Equity Asn; Am Acad Inst Arts & Lett; Fedn Mod Painters & Sculptors; Am Abstract Artists; Sculptors Guild. *Dealer:* Pace Gallery 32 E 57th St New York NY 10022. *Mailing Add:* 29 Spring St New York NY 10012

NEVELSON, MIKE
SCULPTOR

b New York, NY, Feb 23, 22. *Work:* Colby Col; Wadsworth Atheneum; Whitney Mus Am Art; Strater Mus; Stratford Col. *Exhib:* Staempfli Gallery; Whitney Mus; Grand Cent Moderns; Amel Gallery; Expo 68, Montreal; plus others. *Media:* All. *Mailing Add:* PO Box 8952 New Fairfield CT 06810

NEVIA (JOSEPH SHEPPERD ROGERS)
PAINTER

b Washington, DC. *Study:* Longfellow Sch with Theodora Kane and Berthold Schmutzart, 63; Greensboro Col, with Irene Cullus and Callie Braswell, BA, 67; Univ NC, Greensboro, with Will Insley, Peter Agostini, Walter Barker, Andrew Martin, Gilbert Carpenter & Stephen Antonagis, MFA, 69. *Comn:* Mural, Bishop O'Connell Sch, Arlington, Va, 79; also pvt comns. *Exhib:* Nevia Art, Studios Gallery, 82 & Rotunda Gallery, Pan Am Health Orgn, 83, Washington, DC; Collage Invitational, Montgomery Col Gallery, Rockville, Md, 83; Spectrum Gallery, Washington, DC, 83; Arts Club Wash, Washington, DC, 83; and others; and others. *Pos:* Dir, Garfinckle's Art Gallery, Washington, DC, 72-74; dir, Porcelaine Galleries, A H Fetting Co, Baltimore, Md, 74-75. *Teaching:* Teacher art, Prince George Co Bd Educ, Upper Marlboro, Md, 69-70; teacher art, Corcoran Sch Art, Washington, DC & Col Inst Art, Columbia, Md, 70-71. *Awards:* First Mixed Media, Fall Show, Woman's Democratic Club, Washington, DC, 82; Best Oil, Miniature Show, Art League, Alexandria, Va, 82. *Bibliog:* Mrs Frank Christmas (auth), Art in a barn, Evening Star, Washington, DC, 69; Mrs Marie Bailey (auth), County show, Evening Capitol, Annapolis, Md, 70. *Mem:* Arts Club Washington, DC; NVa Fine Arts Asn; Am Asn Mus; Soc Archit Hist; Am Art League (vpres, 83-84); and others. *Media:* Oil, Acrylic. *Dealer:* Spectrum Gallery 1132 29th St NW Washingtonton DC 20007; Zebra One Gallery Perrins Court Hampstead NW3 London England. *Mailing Add:* Beall's Pleasure PO Box 1268 Landover MD 20785

NEVITT, RICHARD BARRINGTON
EDUCATOR, ILLUSTRATOR

b Montreal, Que, Aug, 36. *Study:* Ont Col of Art, study with Eric Freifeld & John Alfsen; Univ of Toronto, studied Art as Applied to Medicine with Nancy Joy, Dr W Brown & Dr C Ower; York Univ, BA, studied with Dr R Jarrell, Dr H Leith. *Work:* Nat Gallery in Ottawa, Can; Ont Col of Art Gallery; Sch of Archit, Univ of Toronto; Belville Pub Art Gallery, Ontario. *Comn:* Drawings, Military, Can govt, Cyprus, 68 & Halifax, NS, 69; Scientific Illus of the Brain, Educ TV, 72; promotional drawing, Seagram's Mus, Can, 83. *Exhib:* Military Artist Prog, Nat Gallery of Can, Ottawa, 77; Art as Applied to Medicine, Anatomical Illus, 77-78. *Pos:* Hon appt, Art Applied Medicine Dept, 76- *Teaching:* Instr anatomy & drawing, Ont Col Art, Toronto, 65-; prof drawing, Ministry Educ, Toronto, 65- *Awards:* Can Coun, Can govt, 69. *Mem:* Arts & Lett Club. *Mailing Add:* RR 2 Alton ON L0N 1A0 Canada

NEW, LLOYD H (LLOYD KIVA)
ADMINISTRATOR, DESIGNER

b Fairland, Okla, Feb 18, 16. *Study:* Okla State Univ; Univ NMex; Art Inst Chicago; Univ Chicago, BAE, 38; Harvard Univ; textile printing & dyeing with D D & Leslie Tillett. *Work:* Indian Arts & Crafts Bd Collection, Washington, DC; Heard Mus, Phoenix, Ariz. *Exhib:* 1st & 2nd Int Fashion Shows, Philadelphia Mus, 51 & 52; Textile Exhib, Mus Mod Art, New York; Edinborough Festival, 66; Cult Olympics, Mexico City, 68; The Real People, Casa de Las Americas, Havana, Cuba, 79; plus others. *Pos:* Chmn, Indian Arts & Crafts Bd, US Dept Interior; owner-operator, Lloyd Kiva Inc, Scottsdale, Ariz, 46-62; pres, Inst Am Indian Arts, 67-; mem, Indian Adv Coun, Buffalo Bill Hist Ctr, Cody, Wyo; mem adv coun, Mus Am Indian, Heye Found, New York. *Teaching:* Dir arts & instr arts & crafts, Inst Am Indian Arts, Santa Fe, NMex, 62-67. *Awards:* Cult Serv Medal, Univ Ariz, 59; Merit Award, Mus Mod Art, New York, 62. *Bibliog:* Articles in Life Mag & London Herald. *Mem:* Heard Mus, Phoenix (bd trustees, currently); fel Am Crafts Coun; World Crafts Coun. *Res:* Indian arts research; history of art, crafts and performing arts; contemporary expression of the Indian artist. *Interests:* Lecturing and painting. *Publ:* Auth, The crafts of the Indian, House Beautiful, 6/71; auth, Performing arts and the American Indian, Am Way, 7/72; auth, Arts and minorities, Arts in Soc, 8/72. *Mailing Add:* PO Box 5217 Santa Fe NM 87501

NEWBILL, AL
PAINTER

b Springfield, Mo, Jan 13, 21. *Study:* Society of Arts and Crafts, Detroit, study with John Caroll; Brooklyn Mus Sch, study with John Ferren; Hofmann Sch, study with Hans Hofmann. *Work:* Detroit Inst of Art; Univ of Kans; Mus of Mod Art, New York; Marist Col, Poughkeepsie, NY; Southern Ill Univ. *Exhib:* Detroit Inst of Art; Cleveland Mus of Art, Ohio; Mus of NMex Art Gallery, Santa Fe; one-man show, Univ of Kans, 68. *Pos:* Dir, art prog, Rodman Job Corps, 66-67. *Teaching:* Instr, Queens Col, 47, Southern Ill Univ, Univ of Calif, Berkeley, Univ of Kans, 67-68, Ohio State Univ, 68 & privately. *Mailing Add:* c/o Benson Gallery Bridgehampton NY 11932

NEWER, THESIS
PAINTER

b New York, NY. *Study:* Acad Delle Belle Arte, Florence, Italy, 4 yrs; Pratt Inst Interior Design, grad. *Exhib:* Allied Artists Am; Knickerbocker Artists; Jersey City Mus; Hudson Valley Art Asn. *Awards:* Best in Show, Catharine Lorillard Wolfe Art Club, 68; Top Award for Polymer, Am Artists Prof League, 68; Nat Art League Gold Medal, Nat Arts Club, 69 & First Prizes, 72 & 75. *Bibliog:* Articles, La Rev Mod, Paris, 70-71. *Mem:* Am Artists Prof League; Catharine Lorillard Wolfe Art Club; Nat Art League; Allied Artists Am. *Media:* Oil. *Dealer:* Thomson Gallery 19 E 75th St New York NY 10021. *Mailing Add:* 876 Adams Ave Franklin Square NY 11010

NEWHALL, BEAUMONT
PHOTOGRAPHER, EDUCATOR

b Lynn, Mass, June 22, 08. *Study:* Harvard Col, AB(cum laude fine arts), 30; Grad Sch Arts & Sci, Harvard Univ, MA, 31, Hon DA, 78; Inst Art &

Archeol, Univ Paris, 33; Courtauld Inst Art, Univ London, 34. *Work:* Victoria & Albert Mus, London; Oesterrische Landesbank, Vienna; Univ Ariz; Int Ctr photog, New York; Mus Mod Art, New York. *Exhib:* G Ray Hawkins Gallery, Los Angeles, 79; Addison Gallery, Andover, Mass, 80; Univ NMex Art Mus, 81; one-man shows, Santa Fe Gallery Photog, NMex, 81 & Univ Art Mus, Univ NMex, Albuquerque, 81. *Collections Arranged:* Permanent collections of photog in Mus Mod Art, 37-45 & George Eastman House, 48-71; also collection of Exchange Nat Bank, Chicago (with Nancy Newhall). *Pos:* Asst in dept decorative arts, Metrop Mus Art, 33-34; librn, Mus Mod Art, 35-42, cur photog, 40-45; cur, Int Mus Photog, George Eastman House, 48-58, dir, 58-71. *Teaching:* Lectr, Philadelphia Mus Art, 32-33; lectr photog hist, Univ Rochester, 54-56; lectr photog hist, Rochester Inst Technol, 56-68; vis prof, State Univ NY Buffalo, 68-71; prof art, Univ NMex, 71-79, vis prof, 79- *Awards:* Guggenheim Mem Found Fel, 46 & 75; Kulturpreis, Deutsche Gesellschaft fur Photographie, 70; Progress Medal, Royal Photog Soc, 75. *Bibliog:* Bibliography (of over 600 titles), Trustees of George Eastman House, 71; auth, The History of Photography, 5th ed, 82; auth, Latent Image, reprint ed, 83; auth, In Plain Sight: Photographs by Beaumont Newhall, 83; and others. *Mem:* Hon fel Royal Photog Soc; hon master photog, Prof Photogr Am; corresp mem Deutsche Gesellschaft Photographie; fel Photog Soc Am; fel Am Acad Arts & Sci. *Res:* History of photography. *Publ:* Coauth (with Diana C Edkins), William H Jackson, 74; ed & photogr, Essays & Images, 80. *Mailing Add:* Rte 7 Box 126C Santa Fe NM 87501

NEWHOUSE, CLYDE MORTIMER
DEALER, HISTORIAN
b St Louis, Mo, Jan 25, 20. *Study:* Yale Univ, BA(cum laude). *Pos:* Owner, Newhouse Galleries. *Mem:* Art Dealers Asn of Am, Inc (pres, 76); Nat Antique & Art Dealers Asn of Am, Inc (exec officer). *Specialty:* Old Masters from the 14th century through the 18th century; American paintings of the 18th and 19th centuries. *Mailing Add:* 19 E 66th St New York NY 10021

NEWMAN, ARNOLD
PHOTOGRAPHER
b New York, NY, Mar 3, 18. *Study:* Univ Miami, hon DFA. *Work:* Metrop Mus Art, New York; Mus Mod Art, New York; Art Inst Chicago; Nat Portrait Gallery, London; Israel Mus, Jerusalem; Moderna Museet, Stockholm. *Exhib:* one-man shows, Art Inst Chicago, 53, George Eastman House, Rochester, 72 & Galerie Fiolet, Amsterdam, 77; Faces in American Art, Metrop Mus Art, 57; Arnold Newman Portraits, 4th Int Biennale Fotografia, Venice, Italy, 63; Camera & Human Facade, Smithsonian Inst, 70; Arnold Newman Portrait Photog, Israel Mus, Jerusalem & Tel Aviv, 78; The Great Great Brit, Nat Portrait Gallery, London, 79; Photo Gallery Int, Tokyo, 81. *Pos:* Actg cur & adv photog dept, Israel Mus, Jerusalem, 67- *Teaching:* Vis prof, Cooper Union, 69- *Awards:* Newhouse Citation, Syracuse Univ, 61; Gold Medal, 4th Biennale Int Fotografia, 63; Life Achievement in Photography Award, Am Soc Mag Photogr, 75; plus others. *Bibliog:* H M Kinzer (auth), Arnold Newman biography, In: The Encyclopedia of Photography, Hawthorn, 64; Peter Pollack (auth), Arnold Newman, In: The Picture History of Photography, Abrams, 69; David R Godine (publ), One Mind's Eye--The Portraits and Other Photographs of Arnold Newman, 74; plus others. *Mem:* Am Soc Mag Photogr. *Media:* Multi-Media. *Publ:* Auth, Bravo Stravinsky, World, 67; auth, Faces USA, Amphoto, 78; auth, The Great British, Weidenfeld & Nicholson, London & NY Graphic Soc, Boston, 79; Artists: Portraits from Four Decades, New York Graphic Soc, Boston, 80. *Dealer:* Light Gallery 724 Fifth Ave New York NY 10019. *Mailing Add:* 33 W 67th St New York NY 10023

NEWMAN, ELIAS
PAINTER
b Stashow, Poland, Feb 12, 03; US citizen. *Study:* Nat Acad Design, 18-20; Educ Alliance Art Sch, 20-25; Acad Grande Chaumiere, Paris, France, 29. *Work:* Nat Mus Am Art, Smithsonian Inst; Brooklyn Mus Art; Boston Mus Fine Arts; Addison Gallery Am Art, Andover, Mass; Joslyn Mus, Omaha, Nebr; and others. *Exhib:* One-man shows, Tel Aviv Mus, 34, 38, 49 & 62, Babcock Galleries, New York, 47, 49, 51, 53 & 60, Doll & Richards Gallery, Boston, Mass, 47, 50 & 60; Am Acad Arts & Lett, New York, 59; Butler Inst Am Art, Youngstown, Ohio, 60; New Accessions USA, Colorado Springs Fine Arts Ctr, 62. *Pos:* Art dir, Palestine Pavilion, New York World's Fair, 38-40; art consult, Palestine Sect, Int Expos, Cleveland, 41; ed, Improvisations, 50-52; art consult, Am Fund for Israel Inst, 54-55. *Teaching:* Instr painting, Educ Alliance Art Sch, 46-48; instr painting, YMHA 92nd St Art Sch, New York, 49-51; instr painting, Elias Newman Sch Art, Rockport, Mass, 51-64; extensive lecturing on art of Israel & trends in American art. *Awards:* Stanley Grumbacher Mem Medal & Prize, Audubon Artists, 77; Morilla Co Award Casein, Am Soc Contemp Artists, 81; Award Merit, Artists Welfare Fund & New York Artists Equity, 83. *Bibliog:* Stephen S Kayser (auth), Elias Newman Exhibition, Jewish Mus, 49; Henry A La Farge (auth), Elias Newman exhibition, Art News, 2/49; Ralph Fabri (auth), Medal winner in casein ann, Today's Art, 7/71. *Mem:* Artists Equity Asn New York (pres, 70-75, pres emer, 75-); Conf Am Artists (chmn, 71-); Audubon Artists (dir, 71-74 & 78, treas, 77, vpres, 79-); Nat Soc Painters Casein & Acrylics (pres, 66-70, hon pres, 71-); Am Soc Contemp Artists (dir, 71). *Media:* All Media. *Res:* Art of Israel; economic and cultural problems of American artists. *Publ:* Auth, Art in Palestine, 39; auth, Art in Israel, Reconstructionist Mag, 6/29/56; ed, Directory of Open Exhibitions, 57. *Mailing Add:* 215 Park Row New York NY 10038

NEWMAN, JOHN BEATTY
PAINTER, INSTRUCTOR
b Toronto, Ont, Apr 6, 33. *Study:* Ontario Col Art; Art Acad Cincinnati, scholarship. *Work:* Art Gallery Hamilton, Ont; Rodman Hall Art Ctr, St Catharines, Ont; Montreal Mus Fine Art; Art Bank, Can Coun; and others. *Exhib:* Soc Int Beaux Arts, Grand Palais, Paris, 77; Palazzo Strozzi, Florence, 77; Prince Arthur Galleries, Toronto, 79 & 81; Hett Gallery, Edmonton, 81; Madison Gallery, Toronto, 83. *Pos:* Exhib designer, Royal Ont Mus, Toronto, 58-63; mem gov coun, Ont Col Art, 73-76 & 79-81, chmn fine arts dept, 79-83. *Teaching:* Instr figure painting, Ont Col Art, 63- *Awards:* Int Painting Competition First Prize, Can Soc Graphic Art, 56; John Alfsen Award for Drawing, 73; Honour Award, Can Soc Painters Watercolour, 74; and others. *Bibliog:* Kay Kritzwiser (auth), A tender look at little girls, Globe & Mail, Toronto, 73; Peter Bell (auth), The transition to maturity, Evening Telegram, St John's, Nfld, 74; Henry Lehman (auth), To write a painting, Montreal Star, 75. *Mem:* Royal Can Acad; Can Soc Graphic Art (secy); Can Soc Painters Watercolour. *Media:* Oil, Watercolor. *Dealer:* Madison Gallery 334 Dundas St W Toronto Can M5T 1G5; Masters Gallery 815C 17th Ave SW Calgary AB T2T O1A. *Mailing Add:* 170 Hammersmith Ave Toronto ON M4E 2W8 Canada

NEWMAN, LIBBY
PAINTER, PRINTMAKER
b Rockland, Del. *Study:* Tyler Sch Fine Arts, Philadelphia, 54; Philadelphia Col Art, 62; also with Julius Block, Sam Feinstein & Victor Lauschin. *Work:* Nat Mus Belgrade, Yugoslavia; Philadelphia Mus Art; Mus Philadelphia Civic Ctr; Mus Mod Art, Buenos Aires, Argentina; Glassboro State Col. *Exhib:* Nat Watercolor & Drawing Exhib, Pa Acad Fine Arts, 64; Eastern Cent Drawing Exhib, Philadelphia Mus Art, 65; Benjamin Mangel Gallery, Bala Cynwyd, Pa, 70-75; Pa State Mus, Harrisburg, 71; Twenty-Five Pa Women Artists, Southern Alleghenies Mus Art, Loretto, Pa, 79; Am Colorprint Soc Exhib, 79; Gov Thorburgh's Inaugural Art Comt--Cur of Contemp Sculpture Exhib, 79; and others. *Awards:* Best Picture of Year Award, Philadelphia Art Alliance, 65; National Print Award, Cheltenham Art Ctr, Pa, 70; Carl Zigrosser Award, Am Color Print Soc, 81. *Bibliog:* Burton Wasserman (auth), Fine print exhibition, Courier-Post, 71; Victoria Donohoe (auth), Gallery's finest hour, Philadelphia Inquirer, 72; Dorothy Grafly (auth), Impressions of Israel, Art in Focus, 72. *Mem:* Artists Equity Asn (pres, Philadelphia Chap, 68-70, nat vpres, 71-75); Philadelphi Art Alliance; Am Color Print Soc; Philadelphia Watercolour Soc; and others. *Media:* Acrylic; Woodcut. *Publ:* Auth, Obtaining art grants, Artists Equity Nat Newslett, 74. *Dealer:* Benjamin Mangel Gallery 1604 Locust St Philadelphia PA 19103. *Mailing Add:* 327 Meeting House Lane Merion Station PA 19066

NEWMAN, LOUIS
DEALER, GALLERY DIRECTOR
US citizen. *Study:* Ariz State Univ, BA, 70; Univ Southern Calif, Los Angeles, MA, 74. *Pos:* Art dealer, Beverly Hills. *Mem:* Artist Equity; Southern Calif Art Dealers Asn. *Specialty:* Contemporary paintings, prints, drawings and sculpture. *Dealer:* Louis Newman Galleries 322 Beverly Dr Beverly Hills CA 90210. *Mailing Add:* Louis Newman Galleries 322 N Beverly Drive Beverly Hills CA 90210

NEWMAN, RALPH ALBERT
CARTOONIST, WRITER
b Newberry, Mich, June 27, 14. *Study:* Albion Col, BA. *Pos:* Illusr, Old Timer (weekly cartoon panel), Indust Press Serv, 54-; comic bk writer, Harvey, 56-; freelance advertising, editorial cartoons. *Media:* Ink. *Mailing Add:* 189 Old Kings Hwy South Darien CT 06820

NEWMAN, SOPHIE
PAINTER, SCULPTOR
b Brooklyn, NY, Mar 4, 25. *Study:* Kreloff Art Sch, Brooklyn, 66-69; Brooklyn Mus Art Sch, NY, 69-71; Brooklyn Mus, NY, 71-72 & 79; Women's Interart Ctr, New York, 73; Creative Women's Collective, New York, 74. *Exhib:* Contemp Reflections, Aldrich Mus Contemp Art, Ridgefield, Conn, 74; Brooklyn Mus, 77; Paperworks, Hudson River Mus, Yonkers, NY, 80; Cichinelli Gallery, New York, 80; Am State Arts Gallery, New York, 80; Hudson River Mus, Yonkers, 81; Belt Buckle Gallery, Los Angeles, Calif, 81; Survival Show, Am State Arts Gallery, New York, 81; 12 Women Artists, Downtown Cultural Ctr, Brooklyn, NY, 82; one-woman show, Brooklyn Col, 82; and others. *Teaching:* Instr painting & crafts, Jewish Asn Services Aged, 75- *Awards:* Curator's Choice, Brooklyn Mus Art Sch, 72; First Prize Oils, Int Pen Women's Club, 74. *Mem:* Women's Caucus Art; Creative Women's Collective (bd mem, 73-); Women in the Arts (bd mem, 74); Artists League Brooklyn (vpres, 73). *Mailing Add:* 2680 E 29th Brooklyn NY 11235

NEWMAN-RICE, NANCY
PAINTER, CRITIC
b New York, NY, Mar 28, 50. *Study:* Cornell Univ; Washington Univ, BFA, 72, MFA, 74. *Exhib:* Drawing & Sculpture, Ball State Univ, Ind, 76; St Louis Artists, Cervantes Convention Ctr, St Louis, 78; Painting Invitational, Salisbury State Univ, Md, 79; solo exhib, Currents 2, St Louis Art Mus, 79; Mississippi Corridor, Davenport Art Gallery, Iowa, 80; Works On/Of Paper, Bixby Gallery, Washington Univ, 80. *Pos:* Ed in chief, St Louis Seen, Newspaper for Visual Arts, 75-77; St Louis ed & critic, New Art Examiner, 78- *Teaching:* asst painting, Washington Univ, 72-74; assoc prof, Maryville Col, 74- *Bibliog:* Sidra Stitch (auth), Nancy Rice & Yvette Woods, New Art Examiner, 79; Mary King (auth), Rice's floating lattice spheres, St Louis Post Dispatch, 80. *Mem:* Col Art Asn; Midwest Col Art Asn; Women's Caucus for Art (bd mem, 76-77); St Louis Arts Coord Coun (bd mem, 76-77). *Media:* Acrylic, Oil. *Dealer:* Van Straaten 361 W Superior St Chicago IL; Carol Shapiro 329 N Euclid St Louis MO. *Mailing Add:* 6322 Pershing St Louis MO 63130

NEWMARK, MARILYN (MARILYN NEWMARK MEISELMAN)
SCULPTOR
b New York, NY, July 20, 28. *Study:* Adelphi Col; Alfred Univ; also with Paul Brown, Garden City, NY. *Comn:* Majestic Light, comn by Ogden Phipps, 76; Man o' War, comn by Franklin Mint, 77; Will Shriver, comn by Broomley farm, 79; Affirmed, comn by Thoroughbred Racing Asn, 79; Ruffian & Genuine Risk, Int Mus Horse, 83; and others. *Exhib:* Allied Artists Am, New York, 70-83; Nat Sculpture Soc, New York, 70-73 & 75-83; James Ford Bell Mus Natural Hist, Minneapolis, Minn, 71; Nat Acad Design, New York, 71, 72 & 74-82; Foothills Art Ctr, Denver, Colo, 80-81. *Awards:* Coun Am Artists Soc Award, 72, 73, 79 & 80; Am Artists Prof League Gold Medal, 74 & 77; Gold Medal Award, Allied Artists Am, 81; plus others. *Bibliog:* The Horse in bronze, Horsemans J, 76; Horsewoman & artist extrardinare, Horse of Course, 77; The horse in bronze, Saddle & Bridle, 79. *Mem:* Fel Nat Sculpture Soc (mem coun, 73-75 & 81-83, rec secy, 76, secy, 77-79); Am Artists Prof League; Soc Animal Artists; Allied Artists Am; Pen & Brush. *Media:* Bronze. *Publ:* Contribr, Equine Sculpture, A Mixed Medium, Morning Telegraph, 8/9/71; contribr, Equine Sculpture, Chronicle of the Horse, 9/10/71; contribr, Horse in sculpture, Am Horseman, 12/72. *Dealer:* Arthur Ackermann & Son Inc 50 E 57th St New York NY 10022. *Mailing Add:* Woodhollow Rd East Hill NY 11577

NEWPORT, ESTHER
PAINTER
b Clinton, Ind, May 17, 01. *Study:* Art Inst Chicago, BA; St Mary of the Woods Col, AB; Syracuse Univ, MFA; St Mary's Col, Ind, LLD, 56. *Comn:* Mosaic, Dun Blane Sch, Washington, DC, 76. *Exhib:* Five shows, Hoosier Salon, 33-42; John Herron Art Inst, 38; Metrop Mus Art, 44; Contemp Relig Art, Tulsa, Okla, 49; Int Expos Sacred Art, Rome, Italy, 50. *Pos:* Founder, Cath Art Asn, 36, dir, 36-40, bd adv, 40-58; founder & ed, Cath Art Quart, 37-40; chmn US comn, Holy Yr Exhib, 49-51. *Teaching:* Head dept art, St Mary of the Woods Col, 32-64; mem staff, Cath Univ Am, 52-57; retired. *Awards:* Prizes, Hoosier Salon, 37, 39 & 42; First Place, Am & Int Needlepoint Exhib, Chicago, 74. *Publ:* ed, Reevaluating Art in Education, 60; auth, Art Teaching Plans (3 bks), 60; auth, Art Appreciation and Creative Work, 61; plus many others. *Mailing Add:* St Mary of the Woods Col St Mary of the Woods IN 47876

NEWSOM, BARBARA YLVISAKER
ADMINISTRATOR, WRITER
b Madison, Wis, July 14, 26. *Study:* Bethany Lutheran Col, Mankato, Minn, AA; Univ Minn, BA; Hunter Col, MA. *Pos:* Pub affairs consult to 100th Anniversary Comt, Metrop Mus Art, New York, 67-70; consult to vdir for educ, 70-71; study dir, Coun Mus Educ, 71-73; proj dir, Coun Mus & Educ in Visual Arts, New York & Cleveland, Ohio, 73-78; staff assoc, Rockefeller Brothers Fund, 73-80, consult, 80- *Mem:* Am Asn Mus (coun mem, 75-78). *Res:* Art museum education; art museum and urban aesthetics. *Publ:* Auth, The museum as the city's aesthetic conscience, Metrop Mus Bull, 68; auth, The Metropolitan Museum as an Educational Institution, 70; ed, The Art Museum as Educator, 78. *Mailing Add:* Box 536 Ashland NH 03217

NEWTON, DOUGLAS
ADMINISTRATOR, MUSEUM DIRECTOR
b Malacca, Malaysia, Sept 22, 20. *Collections Arranged:* Art Styles of the Papuan Gulf, (with catalog), 61; Art of the Massim Area, New Guinea, 64; Art of Africa, Oceania and the Americas, Metrop Mus Art, 69. *Pos:* Dir & trustee, Mus Primitive Art, currently; chmn dept primitive art, Metrop Mus Art, New York, currently. *Res:* Relationships of art and oral traditions in New Guinea. *Publ:* Auth, New Guinea Art in the Museum of Primitive Art, 67; auth, Crocodile and Cassowary, 72; auth, Art of the Massim Area, 72. *Mailing Add:* Metrop Mus Art Fifth Ave at 82nd St New York NY 10028

NEWTON, EARLE WILLIAMS
ADMINISTRATOR, EDUCATOR
b Cortland, NY, Apr 10, 17. *Study:* Amherst Col, AB; Columbia Univ, MA. *Collections Arranged:* British Painting 17th-18th Centuries, 57, 62, 69 & 70; Jacob Eicholtz: Pennsylvania Painter, 58; Hogarth & His School, 59. *Pos:* Ed, Vermont Life, 46-50; ed, Am Heritage, 49-54; dir, Inst Archival Admin (Harvard & Radcliffe), 54-56; Pa State Mus, 56-59, Mus Art Sci & Indust, Conn, 59-62 & St Augustine & Pensacola Hist Preserv Bd, 62-72; pres, Col Am, 72- *Teaching:* Vis prof, Univ London, 55-56; lectr, Univ Upsala, Sweden, 56; adj prof, Norwich Univ, 79- *Awards:* Award of Merit, Am Inst Graphic Arts, 50-52; comdr, Order of Isabel la Catolica, Spain, 65 & Order of Merit, Spain, 68. *Mem:* Soc Archit Historians; Am Asn State & Local Hist (secy-treas, 47-53); Soc Am Historians (secy, 48-50); New Eng Mus Asn (chmn, 53-54); NE Mus Asn (vpres, 58-59). *Res:* Anglo-American art. *Collection:* Anglo-American art of the 17th and 18th centuries; pre-Columbian art; Latin American folk art; American maps; Americana. *Publ:* Auth, Before Pearl Harbor, 42; auth, The Vermont Story, 1749-1949, rev ed 83; ed, Gulf Coast Conf Proc, 70-72. *Mailing Add:* Rt 14 Brookfield VT 05036

NEWTON, JOHN NEIL
PHOTOGRAPHER, PRINTMAKER
b Montreal, Que, Oct 30, 33. *Study:* St Martins Sch Art, London, England, 53-55; Open Studio, 72-73; Visual Studies Workshop, Rochester, NY, with Nathan Lyons, 73. *Work:* Nat Gallery Can; Nat Film Bd Can, Can Coun Art Bank, Pub Arch Can, Ottawa; Mod Mus Stockholm. *Exhib:* Solo exhib, Shaw Rimmington Gallery, Toronto, 74; Exposure--Canadian Contemporary Photography, Art Gallery Ont, 75; Photographs From the Permanent Collection, Nat Gallery Can, 75; 1001 Photographs, Mod Mus Stockholm, 78; retrospective, Can House Exhib Ctr, London, England, 80; Academic Images, Can Ctr Photog, Toronto, 82; Art Forms, Kitchener-Waterloo Art Gallery, Ont, 83. *Pos:* Founding dir, Photog Gallery, Bowmanville, Ont, 71-78 & Newcastle Visual Arts Ctr, Bowmanville, Ont, 74-76. *Teaching:* Lectr photog, York Univ, Toronto, 70-72 & Ryerson Polytech Inst, Toronto, 77-78. *Bibliog:* Annette Snowdon (auth), Holdouts, Can Mag, 7/22/78. *Mem:* Royal Can Acad Arts (coun mem, 83-85); Visual Arts Ont; Can Artists Rep. *Media:* Silver and Non-Silver Printmaking. *Dealer:* Margo Samuel 10 St Edmunds Dr Toronto ON. *Mailing Add:* 246 Oshawa Blvd S Oshawa ON L1H 5R8 Canada

NIBLETT, GARY LAWRENCE
PAINTER
b Carlsbad, NMex, Jan 9, 43. *Study:* Art Instruction Inc, Minneapolis, Minn; Eastern NMex Univ, Portales; Art Ctr Col of Design, Los Angeles, Calif. *Exhib:* Mungerson Gallery Invitational, Chicago, Ill, 78; The Enduring West, Mus of Albuquerque, 78; one-man show, Texas Art Gallery, Dallas, 75 & 76; Western Heritage Show, Houston, 78-81; Biltmore Gallery Show, Los Angeles, Calif, 79-81; and others. *Awards:* Silver Medals, Cowboy Artists Am Show, Phoenix Art Mus, 77, 82 & 83. *Bibliog:* Charles Poling (auth), article, NMex Business J, 7/81; Mary Carroll Nelson (auth), article, Am Artist, 10/81; Pam Hait (auth), article, Art W, 11-12/83. *Mem:* Cowboy Artist of Am. *Media:* Oil. *Mailing Add:* 308 Vistoso Pl Santa Fe NM 87501

NIBLOCK, PHILL
FILMMAKER, COMPOSER
b Anderson, Ind, Oct 2, 33. *Study:* Ind Univ, BA(econ). *Exhib:* Everson Mus, Syracuse; Kirkland Art Ctr, Clinton, NY; Wadsworth Atheneum, Hartford, Conn; Multimedia Performances: Hundred Mile Radius, Kirkland Art Ctr & Whitney Mus Am Art, 71; Ten Hundred Inch Radii, Everson Mus, 72; Cineprobe, films and music, Mus Mod Art, New York, 73; Sur, Wadsworth Atheneum, Hartford, Conn; Trabajando, Herbert F Johnson Mus, Cornell Univ, 76. *Teaching:* Assoc prof film, Staten Island Community Col. *Awards:* NY State Coun Arts Grant, Kirkland Art Ctr, 70, Exp Intermedia Found, 72-74; Nat Endowment Arts Pub Media Prog, 75-76. *Bibliog:* Tom Johnson (auth), Music reviews, Village Voice, 72, 73 & 74; John Rockwell (auth), What's new, High Fidelity/Musical Am, 5/74; Abigail Nelson (auth), Who's Who in Film, Sight Lines, winter 74. *Mem:* Exp Intermedia Found. *Mailing Add:* 224 Centre St New York NY 10013

NICE, DON
PAINTER
b Visalia, Calif, June 26, 32. *Study:* Univ Southern Calif, BFA, 54; Yale Univ, MFA, 64. *Work:* Del Art Mus, Wilmington; Minneapolis Inst Art; Mus Mod Art, New York; Walker Art Ctr; Whitney Mus Am Art. *Comn:* Wall murals, Nat Fine Arts Comn, Lake Placid, NY; Art in Archit Prog, Veterans Admin, White River Junction, NY. *Exhib:* Solo exhibs, Peacable Kingdom, Beasts and Demons, Newport Harbor Art Mus, Newport Beach, Calif, 80, Hood Mus Art, Dartmouth Col, 82 & Palm Springs Desert Mus, Calif, 83; Views Over America, Mus Mod Art, New York, 81; McNay Art Inst, San Antonio, Tex, 81; Real, Really Real and Super Real, San Antonio Mus Asn, Tex, 81-82; Contemporary American Realism Since 1960, Pa Acad Fine Arts, 81-83. *Teaching:* Instr, Minneapolis Sch Art, 60-62; instr, Sch Visual Arts, New York, 63-, dean, 64-66. *Awards:* Ford Found Purchase Award, 63. *Bibliog:* Todd Strasser (auth), interview, Ocular, fall 79; Suzanne Muchnic (auth), Really big show in Newport, Los Angeles Times, 80; Donald B Kuspit (auth), What's real in realism, Art in Am, 81. *Mailing Add:* c/o Nancy Hoffman Gallery 429 W Broadway New York NY 10012

NICHOLAS, DONNA LEE
CERAMIST, SCULPTOR
b South Pasadena, Calif, Mar 30, 38. *Study:* Pomona Col, BA(cum laude), 59; apprentice with Hiroaki Morino, Kyoto, Japan, 60-64; Claremont Grad Sch & Univ Ctr, with Paul Soldner & MFA, 66. *Work:* Flint Inst Arts, Mich; Edinboro State Col, Pa; Lowe Gallery, Miami; Calif Polytechnic Univ; Plains Art Mus, Moorhead, Minn. *Exhib:* Salt Glaze Ceramics, Mus Contemp Crafts, New York, 72; Brand V Ceramic Conjunction, Brand Art Ctr, Glendale, Calif, 75; Object as Poet, Renwick Gallery, Smithsonian Inst, Washington, DC & Mus Contemp Crafts, New York, 76; Clay, Fiber, Metal, Women Artists, Bronx Mus, NY, 78; A Century of Ceramics in the US 1879-1979, Everson Mus, Syracuse, NY, 79; and other group & one-man shows. *Teaching:* Instr ceramics, Mott Community Col, Flint, 66-69; prof ceramics, Edinboro State Col, 69-; vis artist/instr, Penland Sch Crafts, NC, summer 71; vis artist/instr, Scripps Col, 74; vis artist/instr, Moore Col Art, Philadelphia, 75. *Awards:* Award, Outstanding Educators Am, 75; Distinguished Teaching Chair, Comn Pa Teachers, 81. *Bibliog:* Susan Wechsler (auth), Low Fire Ceramics, Watson-Guptill, 81; Elsbeth Woody (auth), Handbuilding Ceramic Forms, Farrar Strauss & Giroux, 78. *Mem:* Am Craftsmen's Coun (Pa rep to NE Assembly, 75-78); Northwest Pa Artists Asn; Assoc Artists of Pittsburgh; Nat Coun Educ Ceramic Arts; Am Crafts Coun. *Media:* Clay. *Publ:* Auth, 27th Syracuse Nat, Craft Horizons, 12/72. *Mailing Add:* 119 Valley View Dr Edinboro PA 16412

NICHOLAS, THOMAS ANDREW
PAINTER
b Middletown, Conn, Sept 26, 34. *Study:* Studied with Ernest Lohrmann, Mariden, Conn, 50-53; Sch Visual Arts, NY, scholar, 53-55. *Work:* Butler Inst Am Art, Youngstown, Ohio; Ga Mus, Athens; Farnesworth Mus, Rockland, Maine; Adelphi Univ; Greenshields Mus, Montreal; and others. *Comn:* Four ten-colored lithographs, Franklin Mint, 77. *Exhib:* Major exhibs, New York, New Eng & Washington, DC, 59- *Teaching:* Instr, Famous Artists Schs, Westport, Conn, 58-61; Jade Fon Watercolor Workshop, Carmel, Calif, 78-

Awards: Elizabeth T Greenshields Mem Found Grants, 61 & 62; Gold Medal Honor, Allied Artists Am, 68; Gold Medal Honor, Am Watercolor Soc, 69; and many others. *Bibliog:* Articles in Am Artist, 3/60 & 8/72; article in North Light Mag, fall 70; John L Cooley (auth), article in The Old Watercolor Soc, Eng, 71; plus others. *Mem:* Nat Acad Design; Am Watercolor Soc; Allied Artists Am; Salmagundi Club; Knickerbocker Artists; and others. *Media:* Oil, Watercolor. *Publ:* Auth, article, SW Art, 12/82. *Dealer:* Tom Nicholas Gallery 8 B Main St Rockport MA 01966; A Huney Gallery 3746 6th Ave San Diego CA 92103. *Mailing Add:* 7 Wildon Heights Rockport MA 01966

NICHOLS, DONALD EDWARD
DESIGNER, EDUCATOR

b Buffalo, NY, Nov 20, 22. *Study:* Albright Art Sch, dipl(graphic design), 47; Univ Buffalo, BFA, 49; Summer Design Prog, Mass Inst Technol, 67. *Comn:* Graphics for ann catalog, NY State Coun Arts, Albany, 62; cover design, J Creative Behavior, Creative Educ Found, 69; commun graphics, Am Acad Arts & Sci, Cambridge, Mass, 69; corp graphic prog, Amarillo Art Ctr Asn, Tex, 70-72. *Exhib:* Four Western NY Exhibs, Albright-Knox Gallery, Buffalo, 54-67; Convocation on the Arts, State Univ NY Albany, 69; Int IONALES Design Zentrum, Berlin, Ger, 70; Ciba-Geigy Corp Int Display, San Francisco, Calif, 77; Int Design Conf, Aspen, Colo, 77. *Teaching:* Instr art, Albright Art Sch, 49-54; prof art & head commun design option, State Univ NY, Buffalo, 54- *Awards:* Western NY Exhib Lyman Prize & Kittinger Award, Albright-Knox Gallery, 54; Osborn Award Creative Excellence, 81; Chancellor's Award Excellence in Teaching, 82. *Mem:* Art Dir/ Communicators of Buffalo; Am Asn Univ Prof. *Publ:* Illusr, CA J Commun Arts, 59; illusr, Sch Arts Mag, 59 & 67; illusr, J Creative Behavior, 69; illusr, Humanist Mag, 69; illusr, Trademarks/G, Ann Trademark Design, 78. *Mailing Add:* 530 Mt Vernon Rd Buffalo NY 14226

NICHOLS, EDWARD EDSON
PAINTER

b Chicago, Ill, Nov 6, 29. *Study:* Univ Kans, BFA, 57, MFA, 59. *Work:* Miss Art Asn, Jackson; Tex Instruments Collection, Dallas; McAllen Int Mus, Tex. *Exhib:* Tenth Washington Area Show, Corcoran Gallery Am Art, 56; 22nd Ann, Butler Inst Am Art, 57; 154th Ann, Pa Acad Fine Arts, 59; Third Ann Delta Exhib, Ark Arts Ctr, Little Rock, 60; 23rd Am Drawing Biennial, Norfolk Mus Art, Va, 65; Art Mus STex Ann, Corpus Christi, 70; Tex Painting & Sculpture, Dallas Mus Fine Art, 71; Tex Watercolor Soc Travel Award Exhib, San Antonio, 80. *Teaching:* Assoc prof art, Pan Am Univ, Edinberg, Tex, 65- *Awards:* Aquarelle Award, Nat Watercolor Show, Miss Art Asn, 63; First Purchase Award, 59th Ann, Tex Fine Arts Asn, 70; Winsor Newton Award, Tex Watercolor Soc Exhib, 80. *Mem:* Tex Watercolor Soc; Southern Watercolor Soc. *Media:* Watercolor. *Mailing Add:* 2018 Shary Rd Mission TX 78572

NICHOLS, ELEANOR CARY
DESIGNER, SILVERSMITH

b Madison, Wis, Feb 27, 03. *Study:* Univ Wis, BS(appl art); Goldsmith Co, Stockholm, Sweden; Brookfield Craft Ctr, Conn. *Work:* Del Art Mus, Wilmington; Winterthur Mus, Wilmington. *Comn:* Twenty bronze medallions for door, St Mark's Lutheran Church, Wilmington, 54; commemorative plaque, Del Swedish Colonial Soc, 63; 30 chalices, 17 patens, 2 processional crosses & 8 torches, Lutheran Church Am, 74; ambry door plaque, St Peters Church, Smyrna, Del, 77; mem plaque, St Mark's Church, Wilmington, Del, 77; cross, missal stand & altar vases, Ascension Lutheran Church, Baltimore, Md, 79. *Exhib:* Five State & Nat Shows, 66-74 & Cult Show in Mex, 67, Nat League Am Pen Women; World Crafts Coun, Peru, SAm, 68. *Teaching:* Instr woodshop, Mt Pleasant Jr High Sch, 43-44; instr silversmithing, Del Art Mus, Wilmington, 43-; instr woodshop, Conrad Sr High Sch, 44-46. *Awards:* Second Metals, 66, Second Jewelry, 70 & First & Second Jewelry, 70, Nat League Am Pen Women. *Bibliog:* Delta Zeta & her unusual talent bring beauty to her community, Delta Zeta Lamp, spring 56; Isabel Church (auth), Profile of the week, Town Talk, 9/71; Eileen Spracker (auth), Lutheran Convention gets Delaware touch, Eve J, 6/74. *Mem:* Am Crafts Coun; Nat League Am Pen Women (br treas, 67-72, br pres, 72-74, state pres, 74-76). *Media:* Silver, Gold. *Mailing Add:* 1505 River Rd Bellevue Manor Wilmington DE 19809

NICHOLS, FRANCIS N, II
PRINTMAKER, EDUCATOR

b July 2, 35. *Study:* Wichita State Univ, MFA; also with David Bernard & Robert Kiskadden. *Exhib:* Watercolor USA, Springfield, Mo, 69; Nat Print & Drawing Exhib, Gallery 8, Erie, Pa, 70; one-man shows, Limited Ed Gallery, Durham, NC, 75 & Duke Univ, 75; Kans 5th Ann Small Painting, Drawing & Print Exhib, 80; and others. *Teaching:* Fel, Wichita State Univ, 65-67; prof printmaking, Ft Hays State Univ, 67- *Media:* Intaglio, Lithography. *Mailing Add:* 1100 Amherst Hays KS 67601

NICHOLS, JAMES WILLIAM
PAINTER

b Pasadena, Calif, Nov 22, 28. *Study:* Univ Calif, Los Angeles, BA, 50; Univ Calif, Berkeley, with Worth Ryder & Estaben Vicente, MA, 54. *Work:* Mus Mod Art, New York; Long Beach Mus Art, Calif; Aldrich Mus Contemp Art, Ridgefield, Conn; Westmoreland Co Mus Art, Greensburg, Pa; Wichita Art Mus. *Comn:* Eight collage paintings, Henkel Factory, Dusseldorf, Ger, 66-67; two collage constructions, Singer Co, New York, 67; metal mural painting, Lombard Wall, New York, 71; four panel screen & new logo, Long Beach Mus Art, 73; metal mural painting, Gotham Audio, New York, 75. *Exhib:* Jim Nichols' Metal Collage Constructions, New York Cult Ctr, 74, Long Beach Mus Art, 75, Wichita Art Mus, 75, Scottsdale Ctr Arts & Civic Ctr Gallery,

75 & Everson Mus Art, Syracuse, NY, 75. *Publ:* Illusr, About the House, London, 3/65; illusr, Art & artists, London, Vol 2, No 7 & Vol 3, No 8; illusr, Works, New York, Vol 1, No 3; illusr & contribr, Mag 4, New York, 69. *Mailing Add:* 215 Bowery New York NY 10002

NICHOLS, JEANNETTIE DOORNHEIN
PAINTER

b Holland, Mich, July 27, 06. *Study:* Art Inst Chicago, BA; Ill Inst Technol; Univ Chicago; lithography with Francis Chapin; painting with Carl Hoeckner; mural painting with Peppino Mangravite. *Work:* Smithsonian Inst Libr-Contemp Am Artists, DC; Washington Pub High Sch, Chicago; Prince William Co Pub Sch, Manassas, Va; Portage Pub Schs, Ind; Albrecht Art Mus, St Joseph, Mo. *Exhib:* Pa Acad Fine Arts, Philadelphia, 37; one-man show, Kreig Art Gallery, Lombard, Ill, 71-73; Ann Ceramic Show, South Bend, Ind, 66; Am Painters in Paris Exhib, France, 76; Artist Equity, Dallas, 77; Prof Artists of Dallas, Allen St Gallery, 77. *Pos:* Mem, Woodbridge Art Guild Workshop, 75; demonstr acrylic & mono-printmaking, Prince William Co Pub Sch & Woodbridge Art Guild, 77. *Teaching:* Art supvr, Belvedere Pub Sch Syst, Ill, 29-33; chmn art, Hyde Park High Sch, Chicago, 40-57; chmn art, Washington High Sch, Chicago, 57-72; instr art, Gary Art League, Ind & Va Community Col, 75- *Awards:* Award for Washington School Playground of 1959 (oil), Tri-Kappa, 67; First Award Acrylics, Ellis Co Art Asn, Tex, 78 & Third Award, 79. *Bibliog:* Charles A Wagner (auth), World of art, New York Mirror, 9/20/59; Helen Ruth Huber (auth), Outstanding area artists, Gary Post Tribune, 61; Will & Jean Heidorn (auth), Art renaissance in progress, Potomac News, Va, 76. *Mem:* Assoc Artists & Craftsmen of Porter Co; Art Inst Chicago Alumni Asn; Artists Equity Asn; life fel Int Inst Arts & Lett; Ellis Co Art Asn. *Publ:* Auth, Arts and activities, In: Mural Painting in High School, 56. *Mailing Add:* Rt 1 Buttonwood Village Waxahachie TX 75165

NICHOLS, MAXINE MCCLENDON See McClendon, Maxine

NICHOLS, WARD H
PAINTER

b Welch, WVa, July 5, 30. *Study:* WVa Univ. *Work:* Integon Corp & R J Reynolds Co, Winston-Salem, NC; Gutenberg Mus, Mainz, WGer; Huntington Gallery Art, WVa; Springfield Mus Art, Mass. *Exhib:* Allied Artist Exhib, Nat Acad Galleries, New York; El Paso Mus Art, Tex; Russell Centenary Exhib, Nottingham, England; NC Mus Art, Raleigh; Mainstreams, Fine Arts Ctr, Marietta Col, Ohio; and others. *Teaching:* Guest lectr, many cols in eastern US. *Awards:* Grumbacher Award Merit, El Paso Mus Art, 70; Jurors Merit Award, Miss Mus Art, 71; PICA Award, Printing Indust Carolinas, 82. *Bibliog:* Article, Pace Mag, Piedmont Airlines, 78; article, Todays Art, 80; Invitation to a Country Walk (film), Assoc Images, 80. *Mem:* Wilkes Art Guild; Assoc Artists. *Media:* Oil. *Dealer:* Wilkes Art Gallery Elizabeth St North Wilkesboro NC 28659. *Mailing Add:* 318 Elm St Beaumont Wilkesboro NC 28659

NICHOLS, WILLIAM ALLYN
PAINTER, EDUCATOR

b Chicago, Ill, Apr 1, 42. *Study:* Art Inst Chicago, BFA(painting & drawing), 66; Univ Ill, Urbana, MFA(painting), 68; Slade Sch Art, Univ Col, London, Fulbright Grant, 68-69. *Comn:* Earth (acrylic landscape painting), Third Nat Bank & Trust Co, Dayton, Ohio, 79. *Exhib:* One man exhibs, O K Harris Gallery, 79, 81 & 83; Watercolors 1980, Frumkin-Struve Gallery, Chicago, 80; Contemporary American Landscape, Taft Mus, Cincinnati, Ohio, 81; Contemporary American Realism Since 1960, Pa Acad Fine Arts, Philadelphia & traveling in US & Europe, 81-82; Painterly Realism, Rahr-West Mus, Manitowoc, Wis, 82; Watercolor USA, Springfield Art Mus, Mo, 83. *Teaching:* Assoc prof art, Univ Wis-Milwaukee, 70- *Bibliog:* Carter Radcliff (auth), article, Art Int Mag, 5/6/77; Catherine LaMagna (auth), article, Arts Mag, 79; Frank H Goodyear, Jr (auth), Contemporary American Realism Since 1960, NY Graphic Soc, 81. *Media:* Acrylic, Watercolor. *Dealer:* O K Harris Works of Art 383 W Broadway New York NY 10012. *Mailing Add:* 4210 N Maryland Ave Milwaukee WI 53211

NICHOLSON, NATASHA
ASSEMBLAGE ARTIST, SCULPTOR

b St Louis, Mo, May 29, 45. *Study:* Ringling Sch Art, 64-65. *Work:* Oakland Mus Art, Calif; Addison Gallery Am Art, Phillips Acad, Andover, Mass. *Exhib:* Solo exhibs, Addison Gallery Am Art, 74, Asher-Faure Gallery, Los Angeles, 81 & 83 & Perimeter Gallery, Chicago, 83; Collage and Assemblage in Southern California, Los Angeles Inst Contemp Art, 75; Eggsibition, Calif Place Legion Hon, 75; A Sense of Space, Oakland Mus Art, 77; Global Space Invasions, San Francisco Mus Mod Art, 78; Our Own Artists: Art in Orange County, Newport Harbor Art Mus, 79; Tableau, Middendorf-Lane Gallery, Washington, DC, 80; Forgotten Dimension: A Survey of Small Sculpture in California Now, Fresno Art Ctr, traveling, 82; and others. *Collections Arranged:* The Other Things That Artists Make, San Francisco Mus Mod Art, 76; Useable Art, Decorative Arts, Quay Gallery, San Francisco, 77; Decorative Arts of Dane County, Madison Art Ctr, Wis, 82. *Awards:* Individual Artist Grant, Nat Endowment Arts, 77; Artists Fel, 83 & Proj Grant, 83, Wis Arts Bd. *Bibliog:* Alfred Frankenstein (auth), For the magical love of oddities, San Francisco Chronicle, 77; Melinda Wortz (auth), Los Angeles, Art News Mag, 12/79; Hunter Drohojowski (auth), Pick of the week, Los Angeles Weekly, 81. *Media:* Mixed. *Dealer:* Asher-Faure Gallery 612 N Almont Dr Los Angeles CA. *Mailing Add:* 205 Princeton Ave Madison WI 53705

NICHOLSON, ROY WILLIAM
PAINTER, PRINTMAKER
b Cambridge, Eng, Mar 21, 43. *Study:* Hornsey Col Art, London, Eng, with John Hoyland, NDD, 65; Brooklyn Mus Sch Art, Max Beckman Mem Scholar, 66. *Work:* Guild Hall Mus & State University Stony Brook, NY; Royal Col Heralds & Abbot Hall Art Gallery Mus, Eng. *Exhib:* One-person shows, Kingsborough Community Col, Brooklyn, NY, 78-79, Abbot Hall Art Gallery, Kendal, Eng, 79; Four/II: A Shifting Focus, Heckscher Mus, Huntington, NY, 81; 28th Ann, Parrish Art Mus, Southampton, NY, 81-82; Winterscape, Guild Hall Mus, East Hampton, NY, 81-82; and others. *Collections Arranged:* The Art of Claude Lorrain, Newcastle & London, 69; The Art of Paul Nash, Newcastle, 71; Alan Davie/David Hockney: Watercolors & Drawings, touring, 71; The Craftsman's Art, Victoria & Albert Mus, London, 73; Watercolor & Pencil Drawings by Paul Cezanne, Hayward Gallery, London & Newcastle, 73. *Pos:* asst dir, Brook Street Gallery, London, 66-68; visual arts officer, Northern Arts, Newcastle, Eng, 68-74; bd gov, Lancaster Col Art, Eng, 72-74. *Teaching:* Vis artist, State Univ New York, Stony Brook, 78-79; adj assoc prof art, Southampton Col, NY, 81-, Victor C'Amico Art Inst, Easthampton, NY, 83- *Bibliog:* David L Shirey (auth), article, New York Times, 7/80; Jeanne Paris (auth), article, Newsday, 1/81; Kenny Mann (auth), article, Sunstorm. *Media:* Oil, Alkyd; Lithography, Etching. *Dealer:* Condeso/Lawler Gallery 76 Greene St. *Mailing Add:* Box 447A RD 1 Sag Harbor NY 11963

NICK, GEORGE
PAINTER, EDUCATOR
b Rochester, NY, Mar 28, 27. *Study:* Cleveland Inst Art, with Frank Wilcox; Brooklyn Mus Art Sch; Art Students League, with Edwin Dickinson; Yale Univ, BFA & MFA. *Work:* Hirshhorn Mus, Washington, DC; Boston Mus Fine Arts; Joslyn Art Mus, Omaha, Nebr; Rose Art Gallery, Brandeis Univ, Waltham, Mass; Galleria Sant' Onofrio, Rome, Italy. *Exhib:* Md Artists Ann Exhib, Baltimore, 66; Pa Artists Ann, Philadelphia Acad Fine Arts, 67. *Teaching:* Assoc prof drawing, Carnegie-Mellon Inst, 64-65; assoc prof painting, Univ Pa, 66-69; assoc prof painting, Mass Col Art, Boston, formerly, prof two-dimensional art, currently. *Awards:* Mass Coun Arts Grant, 74; Nat Endowment Arts Award, 76; Am Acad Arts & Lett Award, 76. *Media:* Oil. *Mailing Add:* c/o Richard Gray Gallery 620 N Michigan Ave Chicago IL 60611

NICKERSON, RUTH (RUTH NICKERSON GREACEN)
SCULPTOR, INSTRUCTOR
b Appleton, Wis, Nov 23, 05. *Study:* Simcoe Col Inst, Ont; Nat Acad Design; also with Ahron Ben-Smuel, New York. *Work:* Arlington Br, Brooklyn Pub Libr; Cedar Rapids Art Asn, Iowa; Montclair Art Mus, NJ; Interchurch Ctr, New York. *Comn:* Many portrait comns for pvt collectors, 32-; Learning (stone group), Fed Art Proj, Brooklyn, 34; Tympanum, Fed Govt, New Brunswick Post Off, NJ, 36; American Oriental Rug Weaving (ceramic mural), Fed Art Proj, Leaksville Post Off, NC; mem plaque, New Rochelle Art Comt for City Hall, 60. *Exhib:* Nat Acad Design Ann, New York, 32-; Whitney Mus Am Art, New York, 34; Mus Mod Art, New York, 39; Artists for Victory, Metrop Mus Art, New York, 42; Pa Acad Fine Arts, Philadelphia, 48; Audubon Artists, 81. *Pos:* Charter mem & secy pro tem, White Plains Civic Art Comn, 48-60. *Teaching:* Instr sculpture, Roerich Mus, New York, 34-35; instr sculpture, Westchester Art Workshop, 45-47 & 48-69; instr modeling & sculpture, Nat Acad Design Sch, New York, 80 & 81. *Awards:* Guggenheim Fel, 46-47; Vincent Glinsky Award, 81; Therese Richard Prize, Allied Artists, 82. *Bibliog:* Jacques Schneir (auth), Art in Modern America. *Mem:* Nat Sculpture Soc; Nat Acad Design; Audubon Artists; Hudson Valley Art Asn. *Mailing Add:* 106 Woodcrest Ave White Plains NY 10604

NICKFORD, JUAN
SCULPTOR, EDUCATOR
b Havana, Cuba, Aug 8, 25. *Study:* Acad Art, Havana, MFA, 46; Sch Archit, Univ Havana. *Work:* Smith Col Mus Art; Spaeth Found, New York; also in collections of Roy Neuberger, New York & Phil Berg, Los Angeles. *Comn:* Welded metal sculptures, Socony Oil Bldg, New York, 56; metal mural, Trade Show Bldg, New York, 56; free standing group, Philco Corp Trade Mart, Chicago, Ill, 57; screens, Grace Line, SS Santa Rosa, 60; outdoor sculpture, Tappan Town Soc, NY, 72. *Exhib:* Whitney Mus Am Art Ann, 50-57; Junior Council, Mus Mod Art, New York, 61; Man Came This Way, Los Angeles Co Mus Art, 71; one-man exhibs, Manhattanville Col, Purchase, NY, 75, Emanuel Col, Boston, 77, The Sculpture Gallery, Palo Alto, Calif, 81, James Gallery, Summit, NJ, 81 & Sculptor's Guild, New York, 81; and others. *Pos:* Trustee, Sculpture Ctr New York, 70-; mem exec comt, City Col New York, 75- *Teaching:* Vis artist, Univ Hartford, 65-66; vis artist, Smith Col, 66-69; asst prof sculpture, City Col New York, 70-75, assoc prof art, 75-80, prof, 80- *Awards:* Honorable Mention, Pa Acad Fine Arts, 58; Bronze Medal, NY State Expos, 64; Inst Int Educ Grant for Creative Sculpture, Cintas Found, 71. *Bibliog:* Meilach & Seiden (auth), Direct Metal Sculpture, George Allen & Unwin, Ltd, London, 66; Nathan Cabot Hale (auth), Welded Sculpture, Watson-Guptill, 68; Wayne Andersen (auth), American Sculpture in Process: 1930/1970, NY Graphic Soc, 75. *Mem:* Sculptor's Guild; Rockland Found Art. *Media:* Metal, Mixed Media. *Dealer:* Sculpture Center Inc 167 E 69th St New York NY 10021. *Mailing Add:* 161 Old Tappan Rd Tappan NY 10983

NICODEMUS, CHESTER ROLAND
SCULPTOR, DESIGNER
b Barberton, Ohio, Aug 17, 01. *Study:* Cleveland Sch Art, grad, 25; Univ Dayton; Ohio State Univ. *Work:* Dayton Art Inst; Columbus Gallery Fine Arts, Ohio; Capital Univ. *Comn:* Wright Bros Tablet, Wilbur Wright High Sch, Dayton, 28; Francis C Sessions Tablet, Columbus Gallery Fine Arts, 32; Columbus Art League Medal, 47; Edward Orton Tablet, Unitarian Church, Columbus, 63; Butler Inst Am Art Medal, Youngstown, Ohio, 72. *Exhib:* Ceramic Nat, Syracuse, NY, 54; Ceramic Int, 58; Columbus Art League, 63; Butler Inst Am Art, 65. *Pos:* Designer & producer, Ferro-Stone Ceramics, 43- *Teaching:* Instr sculpture, Dayton Art Inst, 25-30; instr sculpture, Columbus Art Sch, 30-43, dean, 31-32. *Mem:* Nat Sculpture Soc; Columbus Art League (pres, 33-36). *Media:* Ceramics, Bronze. *Mailing Add:* 447 Clinton Heights Ave Columbus OH 43202

NIELSEN, NINA I M
DEALER
b Riverdale, NY, Nov 5, 40. *Study:* Bucknell Univ, BA, 62; Univ Vienna. *Pos:* Owner, Nielsen Gallery, Boston, currently; vis comt mem, Boston Mus Sch, 79-80. *Specialty:* Contemporary abstract art; German expressionist and 19th and 20th century prints and drawings. *Mailing Add:* Nielsen Gallery 179 Newbury St Boston MA 02116

NIEMANN, EDMUND E
PAINTER, SCULPTOR
b New York, NY. *Study:* Nat Acad Design; Art Students League. *Work:* Slater Mus, Norwich, Conn; Butler Inst Am Art, Youngstown, Ohio; Storm King Art Mus, Mountainville, NY; Syracuse Univ Art Mus; Swarthmore Col. *Exhib:* Directions of American Painting, Carnegie Inst, Pa, 41; Nat Acad Design Ann, 62-68; Pa Acad Fine Arts Watercolor & Drawing Ann, 64; Butler Inst Am Art Painting Nat, 68, 74, 77 & 80; Watercolor USA, 72. *Awards:* New Eng Ann Lyon Award, 77; Audubon Artist Ann Hirsch Mem Award, 78; Young-Hunter Mem Award, Allied Artists, 80; and others. *Mem:* Audubon Artists; Am Watercolor Soc; Allied Artists Am; Nat Soc Painters Acrylic & Casein. *Publ:* Contribr, Todays Art, 7/68 & 8/73; auth, Drawing with unusual tool, Am Artists, 1/70. *Mailing Add:* 38-15 208th St Bayside NY 11361

NIEMEYER, ARNOLD MATTHEW
COLLECTOR, PATRON
b St Paul, Minn, Mar 7, 13. *Pos:* Trustee, Minn Mus Art. *Collection:* All media, especially fine graphics. *Mailing Add:* 1186 St Clair Ave St Paul MN 55105

NIERMAN, LEONARDO M
PAINTER, SCULPTOR
b Mexico City, Mex, Nov 1, 32. *Study:* Nat Univ Mex, BA. *Work:* Ft Worth Art Mus, Tex; Mus Arte Mod, Mexico City; The Wave, Detroit Inst of Arts; Bird in Flight, Acad Fine Arts, Honolulu; Genesis, Israel Mus, Jerusalem; and others. *Comn:* Murals Sch Com, Univ City, Mex, 56 & Golden West Savings, San Francisco, Calif, 65; stained glass windows, two temples, Mexico City, 66-67; Cosmic Meditation (mural), Physics Bldg, Princeton Univ, NJ, 68; Eagle (bronze sculpture), Toronto, Can, 72. *Exhib:* Paris Biennale, Mus Mod Art, France, 61; Marlborough-Gerson Gallery, New York, 64; Pittsburgh Int, Carnegie Inst, Pa, 64 & 67; El Paso Mus Art, Tex, 64 & 71; Mus Arte Mod, 72; and many one-man shows. *Awards:* First Prize, Art Inst Mex, 64; Palm D'Or Beaux Arts, Monaco, 69; Gold Medal, Tomasso Campanella Found, Italy, 72. *Bibliog:* Enrique Gual (auth), Leonardo Nierman, Ed Monterrey, 64; Jose Gomez Sicre (auth), Nierman, Artes Mex, 71; Julio Cortazar & Max Pol Fouchet (auth), Leonardo Nierman, A Capell & A Elmayan Ed, Paris, 75. *Mem:* Royal Soc Arts, London; Int Biog Asn: UK; Int Arts Guild, Monte Carlo; Salon Plastica, Mex. *Media:* Acrylic; Onyx, Bronze. *Dealer:* Nahan Galleries 540 Royal St New Orleans LA 70115. *Mailing Add:* Amsterdam 43 PH Mexico 11 DF Mexico

NIESE, HENRY ERNST
PAINTER
b Jersey City, NJ, Oct 11, 24. *Study:* Cooper Union, cert, with Robert Gwathmey & Morris Kantor; Acad Grande Chaumiere, cert, with Othon Friesz; Columbia Univ, BFA, with Leo Manso, John Heliker & Meyer Schapiro. *Work:* Whitney Mus Am Art, New York; Corcoran Gallery, DC; Albright-Knox Mus; Nat Mus Am Art, Washington, DC; Filmkundliches Arkiv, Cologne, WGer; and others. *Exhib:* Young Am, Whitney Mus Am Art, 62 & 40 Artists Under 40, 64; 4th Int Exp Film Festival, Brussels, Belg, 69; New York Avant Garde Festivals, 69-78; Six Nations Mus, NY & Corcoran Gallery, 76; Foundry Gallery, DC, 80. *Pos:* Dir, Eagle Voice Ctr, Glenelg, Md, currently. *Teaching:* Spec lectr grad humanities, NY Univ, 65-69; asst prof studio art, Ohio State Univ, 66-69; assoc prof studio art, Univ Md, 69-; guest fel, Yale Univ, 79; vis artist, Univ Calif, Santa Barbara, 81. *Awards:* Pulitzer Found Traveling Fel, 55; Int Cinema Prize, Mus Arte Mod, Vitoria, Brasil, 69; Creative & Performing Arts Grant, Univ Md, 71 & 73. *Media:* Multimedia. *Dealer:* Foundry Gallery 2121 P St Washington DC 20037. *Mailing Add:* Rte 2 Box 12924 Glenelg MD 21737

NIETO, JOHN W
PAINTER, SCULPTOR
b Denver, Colo, Aug 6, 36. *Study:* Pan Am Univ, 55-56; Southern Methodist Univ, 57-59; Dallas Mus Fine Arts, 60. *Work:* Heard Mus, Phoenix, Ariz; Smithsonian Inst, Washington, DC; NMex Mus Fine Arts, Santa Fe; Wagner Corp Collection, Austin, Tex. *Comn:* Murals, Lakewood State Bank, Dallas, 61; Bronze Bust of Chairman of the Board, Tex Power & Light, Dallas, 80; Portrait of Barry Goldwater, Goldwaters, Phoenix, Ariz, 83. *Exhib:* Annual Contempory Art, Dallas Mus Fine Arts, Tex, 63; 20th Century American Indian Artist, Kimball Art Mus, Park City, Utah, 81; American Indian Contempory Art, Smithsonian Inst, Washington, DC, 82; Night of the First American, John F Kennedy Ctr, Washington, DC, 82; Salon d'Automne,

Grand Palais, Paris, 82; one-man show, US Embassy, Barbados, 82; Images of Ranchos de Taos Church, NMex Fine Arts Mus, Santa Fe, 83. *Teaching:* Art, NTex State Univ, Denton, 64-65 & Southern Methodist Univ, Dallas, 74-75. *Awards:* Blue Ribbon Award, Arts & Crafts Show, Heard Mus, Phoenix, 81; Artist of Year, Santa Fean Mag, 82. *Bibliog:* Erica Benis (auth), John Nieto Artist, Voice Am, US Int Commun Agency, 81; Ms Goldman (auth), Artist in Santa Fe, Nat Pub Radio Washington, DC, 82; William Carpenter (auth), Profile of John Nieto, Carpenter & Assoc, 83. *Media:* Oil, Watercolor; Clay. *Dealer:* Enthios Gallery 1111 Paseo de Peralta Santa Fe NM 87501; Gallery Yves Arman 817 Madison Ave New York NY. *Mailing Add:* Rt 9 Box 86N Santa Fe NM 87501

NIGROSH, LEON ISAAC
CERAMIST, INSTRUCTOR
b Cambridge, Mass, Aug 7, 40. *Study:* Carnegie Inst Technol, 58-59; RI Sch Design, BFA, 63; Rochester Inst Technol, MFA, 65. *Comn:* ceramic, metal & glass panels, comn by Mr & Mrs Benjamin Cooperstein, Belmont, Mass, 64; ceramic & acrylite sculpture, comn by Mr & Mrs George Klomberg, Long Island, NY, 70; five ceramic fountains, Group One Inc, New Seabury, Mass, 73; ceramic sculpture, Temple Shalom Emeth, Burlington, Mass, 83; porcelain wall panel, comn by Mr & Mrs Joseph Epstein, Carlsbad, Calif, 83. *Exhib:* Branch Gallery, Washington, DC, 80; Greenwood Gallery, Washington, DC, 80; Artworks, Worcester, Mass, 81; Peters Valley Gallery, Layton, NJ, 82; Mirage Collectables, Miami, Fla, 82. *Teaching:* Instr ceramics, Auburn Community Col, 64-65; instr ceramics & studio mgr, Greenwich House Pottery Sch, New York, 65-66; instr ceramics & head dept, Craft Ctr, Worcester, 67-78; vis prof, RI Col, 78-79; lectr art, Clark Univ, Worcester, Mass, 81- *Awards:* Mass Arts Lottery Coun Grant, 82. *Mem:* Int Guild Craftjournalists, Authors & Photogr; Am Crafts Coun; Mass Asn Crafts; Worcester Cult Assembly (bd dirs, 81-). *Media:* Ceramic. *Publ:* Contribr, Craft Horizons, 71-78; auth, Claywork, 75 & Low Fire, 80, Davis; auth, five articles in Sch Arts, 76-77. *Mailing Add:* 11 Chatanika Ave Worcester MA 01602

NIIZUMA, MINORU
SCULPTOR
b Tokyo, Japan, Sept 29, 30. *Study:* Tokyo Univ Arts, BFA. *Work:* Mus Mod Art, New York; Nat Mus Mod Art, Tokyo; Albright-Knox Gallery, Buffalo; Guggenheim Mus, New York; Hirshhorn Mus & Sculpture Garden, Washington, DC; and others. *Comn:* Stone monuments, Metrop Tokyo, 56, Asia House, Tokyo, 58; Int Sculpture Symp, Vt, 68, St Margarethen, Austria, 69 & New York, 71. *Exhib:* Mus Mod Art, 65 & 66 & Whitney Mus Am Art Sculpture Ann, 66 & 68, New York; one-man shows, Howard Wise Gallery & Gimpel & Weitzenhoffer Gallery, New York, 66, 68 & 72-78 & Rockefeller Univ, 71; Carnegie Inst Int, 67; Seibu Mus Art, Tokyo, 76; Mekler Gallery, Los Angeles, 83; and others. *Teaching:* Instr sculpture, Brooklyn Mus Art Sch, 64-69; adj prof, Columbia Univ, 72- *Awards:* Mod Art Asn Award, Japan, 55 & 56. *Mem:* Mod Art Assoc Japan (permanent juror, 57-); Sculptors Guild. *Media:* Marble, Granite. *Dealer:* Gimpel & Weitzenhoffer Gallery 1040 Madison Ave at 79th New York NY 10021. *Mailing Add:* 463 West St New York NY 10014

NILSSON, GLADYS
PAINTER
b Chicago, Ill, May 6, 40. *Study:* Art Inst Chicago, dipl, 62. *Work:* Mus Mod Art, New York; Whitney Mus Am Art; Mus Contemp Art, Chicago; Art Inst Chicago; Mus Mod Kunst, Vienna. *Exhib:* The Hairy Who, Dupont Ctr, Corcoran Gallery Art, 69; Poetic Fantasy, San Francisco Mus Art, 71; Chicago Imagist Art, Mus Contemp Art, Chicago, 72; one-person exhib, Whitney Mus Am Art, 73; The Koffler Foundation Chicago Currents, Smithsonian Inst, 79. *Media:* Watercolor. *Mailing Add:* 1035 Greenwood Ave Wilmette IL 60091

NIND, JEAN
PAINTER, PRINTMAKER
b Miri, Sarawak, Borneo, June 17, 30; Can citizen. *Study:* Chelsea Art Sch, London, Eng; Univ Sask, Can, studied with Otto Rogers & Eli Bornstein. *Work:* Sask Power Corp, Regina; Court House, Edmonton, Alta, Can; Trent Univ, Peterborough, Ont; Volvo Corp, Halifax, NS; Sir Sandford Fleming Col, Peterborough, Ont. *Comn:* Symphony (oil), comn by mem bd, Saskatoon Symphony, Sask, 64; five serigraphs (for presentation to guest speakers), Trent Univ, Peterborough, Ont, 69. *Exhib:* Art Gallery, Halifax, NS, 72; one-person shows, Art Space, Ont, 75, Sisler Gallery, Toronto, Ont, 76, Art Gallery of Peterborough, 77 & 78 & Bau-Xi Gallery, Toronto, Ont, 78-79; and others. *Teaching:* Instr child art classes, Mendel Art Gallery, Saskatoon, Sask, 65-66; instr early childhood art, Sir Sandford Fleming Col, Peterborough, Ont, 69-71; instr painting, 73-77; instr painting, Trent Univ, Peterborough, Ont, 73-77. *Awards:* Prize Winner, Sask Exhib, Sask Arts Coun, 65; Purchase Award, Sir Sandford Fleming Col, Peterborough, Ont, 75; Merit Award, Ont Arts Coun, 75. *Mem:* Art Gallery Peterborough (mem bd, 72-78); Artspace, Peterborough, Ont (mem steering comt, 75); Visual Arts Ont. *Media:* Oil on Canvas; Serigraphy. *Publ:* Contribr, Artipaction, Ont Arts Coun, 74; contribr, Parachute Mag, 74; contribr, Rags to Riches, Ont Arts Coun, 77; contribr, Art Mag, Heritage Press, 77; Early Childhood Education Conference, Ont Public Sch Teachers' Fedn, 77. *Dealer:* Sisler Gallery 35 Baldwin St Toronto ON M5T 1L1 Can; Bau-xi Gallery 340 Dundas St W Toronto ON M5T 1G5 Can. *Mailing Add:* 29 Merino Rd Peterborough ON K9J 6M8 Canada

NISHIZAWA FLORES, LUIS
PAINTER
b San Mateo, Mex, Feb 2, 18. *Study:* Nat Autonomous Univ Mex, dipl(fine arts), 46; Japanese Artists Ctr, 64. *Work:* Mus Mod Art, Carrillo Gil Mus, Mus Nat Inst Fine Arts, Mexico City; Mus Mod Art, Kyoto, Japan; Fine Arts Mus, Toluca, Mex. *Comn:* Mural (acrylic), 58 & mural (ceramic), 69, Mex Inst Soc Security, Guanajuato; mural (acrylic), Cent Dept, Mexico City, 76; mural (ceramic), Japanese Cult & Traffic, Tokyo, 81. *Exhib:* Expo 67, Montreal; Lean Cows and Broken Dreams, Mus Mod Art, Mexico City, 72; Mexican Contemporary Art, Mus Mod Art, Tokyo & Kyoto, Japan, 74; First Engraving Triennial, Buenos Aires, 79; Contemporary Latin American Art and Japan, Mus Mod Art, Osaka, 81. *Teaching:* Instr materials & tech, Nat Autonomous Univ Mex, 55- *Awards:* Spec Award, Second Inter-Am Biennial, Inst Fine Art, Mexico City, 60; First Prize, Slon Guerra, 63 & Solar Exhib, Cult Olympics, 68. *Mem:* Salon Plastica Mexicana. *Media:* Tempera. *Mailing Add:* Cuadrante de San Francisco #27 Mexico DF 04320 Mexico

NIVOLA, CONSTANTINO
SCULPTOR
b Orani, Sardinia, July 5, 11. *Study:* Inst Superiore Arte, Monaz, Italy, with Marino Marini & Marcello Nizzoli, MA, 36. *Work:* Hirshhorn Mus, Washington, DC; Philadelphia Mus Art; Mus Mod Art, New York; Whitney Mus Am Art. *Comn:* Murals, Motorola Bldg, Chicago, 60; 35 sculptures, Saarinen Dormitories, Yale Univ, 62; designed a mem plaza, Nuoro, Italy, 66; sculpture, Pub Sch 320, Brooklyn, 67; sculpture, 19th Olympiad Nac, Mexico City, Mex, 68. *Exhib:* Whitney Mus Am Art, 57; Carnegie Inst, 58; Mus Contemp Crafts, 62; Nat Gold Medal Exhib Bldg Arts, New York, 62; American Drawing Traveling Exhib, Am Fedn Arts, 64; solo exhib, Marlborough Galleria d'Arte, Rome, 73, Willard Gallery, 73, Cagliari Univ, Italy, 73, Inst Contemp Art, Boston, 74 & Gallery Paule Anglim, San Francisco, 78. *Pos:* Dir design workshop, Harvard Univ Grad Sch, 53-57. *Teaching:* Instr, Columbia Univ, 61-63, Harvard Univ, 70-73, Dartmouth Col, 78 & Univ Calif, Berkeley, 78-79. *Awards:* Gold Medal, Regional Exhib Figurative Art, Cagliari, Italy; Cert Commendation, Park Asn New York, 65; Fine Arts Medal, Am Inst Architects, 68. *Bibliog:* Michel Seuphor (auth), The Sculpture of This Century, Dictionary of Modern Sculpture, A Zwemmer Ltd, London, 59; Fred Licht (auth), Sculpture, 19th and 20th Centuries, NY Graphic Soc, 67; Eduard Trier (auth), Form and Space: Sculpture in the 20th Century, Praeger, 68. *Mem:* Nat Inst Arts & Lett; Archit League New York. *Mailing Add:* 410 Stone Rd Springs East Hampton NY 11937

NIX, PATRICIA (LEA)
SCULPTOR, PAINTER
US citizen. *Study:* NY Univ, BA; New Sch Social Research, with Anthony Toney; Art Students League. *Work:* Nat Mus Am Art, Smithsonian Inst, Washington, DC; Santa Fe Mus Art, NMex; Lamesa Nat Bank, Tex; San Antonio Mus Art, Tex; Heckscher Mus, Huntington, NY. *Exhib:* Mystery Containment & The Box, Univ Conn, Storrs, 79; One-woman show, New York Univ Contemp Arts Gallery, 80; Joseph Cornell & Kindred Spirits, Heckscher Mus, Huntington, NY, 81; Bodies & Souls, Artists Choice Mus, 83; New Acquisitions, Smithsonian Inst, 83; New Eng Ctr Contemp Art, 83; and others. *Awards:* Salzman Prize, Nat Arts Club Ann, 78; Exhib Comt Award, Nat Arts Club Ann, 79; Tex Fine Arts Citations, 66, 69, 73 & 74. *Bibliog:* Elizabeth S Sasser (auth), Patricia Nix, Art Voices, 9/80; Box Assemblage, the work of Patricia Nix (film), Tower Gallery, 81; Carla Sternbaum (auth), Patricia Nix's art of boxing, Ultra, 1/83. *Mem:* Nat Arts Club; New York Artists Equity; assoc mem Audubon Artists. *Media:* Wood, Found Objects; Mixed. *Dealer:* Sutton Gallery 29 West 57th St New York NY 10019; Baumgartner Gallery. *Mailing Add:* 1308 N Bryan Lamesa TX 79331

NOA, FLORENCE
PRINTMAKER, EDUCATOR
b New York, NY, June 19, 41. *Study:* High Sch Music & Art, 59; City Col New York, BA(fine arts), 63; Pratt Inst, MFA(printmaking), 78. *Work:* Newark Mus & Newark Public Libr, NJ; NJ State Mus, Trenton; New York Public Libr; Wharton Sch, Univ Pa, Philadelphia. *Comn:* Print Edition, Merlin Communications, Inc, New York, 81. *Exhib:* 59th Ann Exhib Soc Am Graphic Artists, New York, 82; Rockford Int Biennial, Rockford Col, 83; one person exhibs, Baron Art Ctr, Woodbridge, NJ, 83, St Peter's Church, New York, 83 & Nicholas Roerich Mus, New York, 84; and others. *Pos:* Exhib coordr, Art Ctr Northern NJ, 76. *Teaching:* Instr printmaking, Montclair Art Mus, NJ, 78-80; adj asst prof printmaking, Co Col Morris, 79; adj instr art hist, Bergen Community Col, Paramus, NJ, 80- *Awards:* Fel Award, Pratt Inst, 76; Fel Grant, NJ State Coun Arts, 79; Residency, Jay Hanbidge Art Found, 82. *Mem:* Am Colorprint Soc; Women's Caucus Art, NJ; Printmaking Coun NJ. *Media:* Collagraph, Etching. *Dealer:* Marden Fine Arts 41 Union Square New York NY; Opper-Nacht Assocs Englewood NJ. *Mailing Add:* 189 Larch Ave Teaneck NJ 07666

NOBILI, LOUISE
EDUCATOR, PAINTER
b Detroit, Mich. *Study:* Wayne State Univ, BFA(painting), 39 & MA(painting), 41; Univ Wis, summers 39-41; Chicago Sch Design, with Moholy Nagy, 43-44; Chicago Inst Art, 43-44. *Work:* Scott Hall, Wayne State Univ Med Bldg, Inst Art, Detroit; Scott Hall, Wayne State Univ Med Bldg, Detroit, Mich; The Ford Times Collection of American Art, Dearborn, Mich; Steelcase Collection Contemp Art, Grand Rapids, Mich; Butler Art Inst Am Art, Youngstown, Ohio; Univ Mich Mus Art, Ann Arbor. *Exhib:* Fifty-ninth Nat Ann Am Exhib Watercolor, Art Inst Chicago, 48; Seventeenth Int Watercolor Exhib, Brooklyn Mus, NY, 53; First Columbia Painting Biennial,

Columbia Mus Art, SC, 57; The One Hundred & Fifty-third Ann Exhib of Am Painting & Sculpture, Pa Acad Fine Art, Philadelphia, 58 & Detroit Inst Art, Mich, 58; Okla Nat Exhib of Contemp Am Art, Okla Art Ctr, 60; Watercolor Panorama, An Int Survey of Watercolor, Flint Inst Arts, Mich, 62; Ravinia Festival Exhib, Ravinia Gallery, Ill, 62. *Teaching:* Asst prof art, Northwestern Univ, Evanston, Ill, 43-44; prof painting, Wayne State Univ, Detroit, Mich, 44-82, prof art, currently. *Awards:* John L Newberry Award, Mich Artist Ann Exhib, 45; Founders Soc Prize, Mich Artist Ann Exhib, Detroit Inst Art, 56; Top Merit Award, Fifth Nat Exhib Contemp Art, Okla Art Ctr, 63. *Mem:* Mich Watercolor Soc; Washington Watercolor Soc; Mich Acad of Sci, Arts & Letters; Grosse Pointe Art Asn; Am Asn of Univ Prof. *Media:* Watercolor, Oil. *Mailing Add:* 17140 E Jefferson Ave Grosse Pointe MI 48230

NOBLE, HELEN (HARPER)
PRINTMAKER, PAINTER
b Northville, Mich, Mar 27, 22. *Study:* Wayne State Univ, 39-41; Western Reserve Univ, 42-43; Santa Barbara Art Inst, 70-72. *Exhib:* Nat Competition Watercolor Soc Ala, Birmingham Mus, 77, 79 & 81; Small Works National 81, Rochester, NY; Second Nat Print Exhib, Springfield, Ill, 82; 24th Ann Exhib Prints & Drawings, Oklahoma City, 82; Third Women in Art Exhib, Springfield, Ill, 83. *Awards:* Eight Awards, Santa Barbara Art Asn, 71-79; Third Place, 41st Ann Miniature Art Soc, Washington, DC, 74. *Mem:* Pratt Graphics Ctr; Ala Watercolor Soc; Contemp Arts Forum Santa Barbara. *Media:* Watercolor; Wood. *Dealer:* Meredith Niles Gallery 1114 State St Number 24 Santa Barbara CA 93101; Byck Gallery 609 W Main St Louisville KY 40202. *Mailing Add:* 1702 Cliff Dr Santa Barbara CA 93109

NOBLE, JOSEPH VEACH
MUSEUM DIRECTOR, MUSEOLOGIST
b Philadelphia, Pa, Apr 3, 20. *Study:* Univ Pa. *Collections Arranged:* Drug Scene, 71; Cityrama, 72; Revolution, 75; The Big Apple, 79. *Pos:* Vdir, Metrop Mus Art, 56-70; trustee, Corning Mus Glass, 69-; dir, Mus City of New York, 70- *Teaching:* Instr filmmaking, City Col New York, 46-49. *Awards:* Medals, Nat Acad Design, 76 & Nat Sculpture Soc, 78; Am Watercolor Soc Award, 82. *Mem:* Am Asn Mus (pres, 75-78); NY State Hist Trust (chmn, 72-75); NY State Asn Mus (pres, 70-72); Archaeol Inst Am (treas, 63-70); Brookgreen Gardens (pres, 76-). *Publ:* Auth, The Historical Murals of Maplewood, 61; coauth, An Inquiry into the Forgery of the Etruscan Terra-cotta Warriors, 61; auth, The Techniques of Painted Attic Pottery, 65. *Mailing Add:* Mus of City of New York Fifth Ave at 103rd St New York NY 10029

NOCHLIN, LINDA (POMMER)
HISTORIAN, EDUCATOR
b New York, NY, Jan 30, 31. *Study:* Vassar Col, BA; Inst Fine Arts, NY Univ, PhD. *Teaching:* Mary Conover Mellon prof art, Vassar Col, 63-80; distinguished prof art hist, City Univ New York Grad Ctr, 80- *Awards:* Kingsley Porter Prize Best Article in Art Bulletin, 67; E Harris Harbison Award Gifted Teaching, 72; Am Coun Learned Soc Fel, 72-73. *Res:* Painting and sculpture of 19th and 20th century. *Publ:* Auth, Mathis at Colmar, Red Dust, 63; auth, Realism and Tradition in Art, 1848-1900, 66 & Impressionism and Post-Impressionism, 1874-1904, 66, Prentice-Hall; auth, Realism, Penguin, 72; auth, Gustave Courbet: A Study of Style & Society, 76; contribr, Art Bull, Art News, Art News Ann & Artforum. *Mailing Add:* 875 West End Ave New York NY 10001

NODINE, JANE ALLEN
PAINTER, DESIGNER
b Spartanburg, SC, Mar 14, 54. *Study:* Western Carolina Univ, Cullowhee, 72-73; Univ SC, Columbia, BFA, 76, MFA, 79; Kent State Univ, 78. *Work:* Equitable Life Corporate Collection, New York; SC Arts Commission State Collection, Columbia; Bankers Trust of SC & Spartanburg Art Coun, Spartanburg, SC; Palmetto Bank & Trust, Simpsonville, SC. *Exhib:* Ninth Ann Prints & Drawings, Second Street Gallery, Charlottesville, Va, 81; Awards Visual Arts, Southeastern Ctr Contemp Art & Whitney Mus Art, 82-83; Drawing Southeast, Arts Festival Atlanta, 83; Two-D Nat, Angels Gate Cult Ctr, San Pedro, Calif, 83; Fourth Biennial Exhib Paper & Clay, Memphis State Univ, 83; and others. *Teaching:* Instr, Greenville Mus, SC, 79-80; Presby Col, Clinton, SC, 80-; Wofford Col, Spartanburg, SC, 81 & 83 & Sacred Heart Col, Belmont, NC, 82- *Awards:* Juror's Top Seven, Appalachian State Univ, 80; SC Arts Comm Individual Artist Fel, 81-82; Best in Show, Spoleto Competition, Charleston, SC, 83. *Media:* Acrylic; Metal. *Dealer:* Heath Gallery 416 E Paces Ferry Rd Atlanta GA 30305. *Mailing Add:* 113 Rockwood Dr Spartanburg SC 29301

NOE, JERRY LEE
SCULPTOR, EDUCATOR
b Harlan Co, Ky, Sept 27, 40. *Study:* Univ Ky, BA; Art Inst Chicago, Ford Found Scholar, MFA. *Exhib:* Sculpture 70, Art Inst Chicago, 70; Forty Years of American Landscape, Gimpel-Wietzenhoffer Gallery, New York, 73; Nat Sculpture Traveling Exhib, 73-75; Contemporary Reflections, 1973-74, Aldrich Mus Art, Ridgefield, Conn, 74; Southeast 7, Southeastern Ctr Contemp Art, Winston-Salem, NC, 77; one-man shows, Henri Gallery, 77 & Mercer Gallery, 77. *Teaching:* Sculptor, Young Artists Studio, Art Inst Chicago, 69-71; vis lectr sculpture, Wis State Univ, Whitewater, 70-71; assoc

prof art, Univ NC, Chapel Hill, 71- *Awards:* John Quincy Adams Traveling Fel, 71; First Place, 73 & Third Place, 75, Southern Asn Sculptors; Nat Endowment Arts Grant, 77; and others. *Bibliog:* B J Ott (auth), Artist builds bridge, Buffalo Courier Newspaper, 75; Fun & games at art park, New York Times Sunday Ed, 75; and others. *Mem:* Southern Asn Sculptors (mem bd dirs, 74-75, conf chmn, 75, exhib chmn, 75); Col Art Asn; Southeastern Col Art Conf; Southeastern Ctr Contemp Art. *Media:* Neon, Mixed. *Publ:* Coauth, Neon--The Artist (film), Res Coun, Univ NC, 75. *Dealer:* Henri Gallery 1500 21st St NW Washington DC 20036. *Mailing Add:* c/o Dept Art Univ NC Chapel Hill NC 27514

NOEL, GEORGES
PAINTER, SCULPTOR
b Beziers, France, Dec 25, 24; US citizen. *Study:* France. *Work:* Albright-Knox Art Gallery, Buffalo, NY; Chase Manhattan Bank, New York; Aldrich Mus of Contemp Art, Ridgefield, Conn; Centre Nat d'Art,, Contemporain, Paris; Mus Mod Art, New York. *Comn:* Wall relief, high sch, LeLuc, France, 68; mosaic mural, High Sch, Mulhouse, France, 69. *Exhib:* Retrospectives, Ludwigshafen Mus, 65 & Mannheim, Ger, 80; Sao Paulo Bienal, 65; Montreal World's Fair, 67; Krannert Art Mus, Univ Ill, Champaign, 74. *Bibliog:* Barbara Rose (auth), Article, New York Mag, 3/12/73; Lugano (auth), article, Art Int, 2/74; Hilton Kramer (auth), article, New York Times, 12/75. *Media:* Multimedia. *Dealer:* Pace Gallery 32 E 57th St New York NY 10022. *Mailing Add:* 16 Greene St New York NY 10013

NOERDLINGER, JANAU NAU
PAINTER, PHOTOGRAPHER
b St Louis, Mo, Mar 24, 42. *Study:* George Peabody Col, 61-63; Sch Art, Inst Chicago, BFA, 67; Univ Colo, MFA, 79. *Work:* Mich Montessori Int & United Ministries Higher Educ, Lansing, Mich; Univ Colo, Boulder; Impression Five Mus, Lansing; Sante Fe Mus Fine Arts. *Comn:* Mural, Impression Five Mus, Lansing, Mich, 75; diptych, comn by Cyrus & Jane Hoffman, 84. *Exhib:* Multiple Elements, Castilleya Sch Mus, Palo Alto, Calif, 81; Myth Dominates Memory, Artemesia Place, Chicago, 81 & 83; Memorywork, A Retrospective, Univ Colo, Boulder, 84; Personal Visions, Gilman Gallery, Chicago, 84; Recent Paintings, Macey Gallery, Sante Fe, 84; and others. *Pos:* Dir exhibs, Impression Five Mus, Lansing, Mich, 72-76. *Teaching:* Lectr art, Lansing Community Col, 78-80; vis artist, Blackhawk Mountain Sch Art, 81; vis prof drawing, Univ Colo, Boulder, 81-82; instr painting, Univ NMex, 84. *Awards:* First Merit Award for painting, Boulder Art Asn 17th Ann, 78; Third Place, Menlo Civic Ctr, Menlo Arts Comn, 80; First Place, Pajarito Painting & Drawing Exhib, Fuller Ctr Arts, Sante Fe, 83. *Mem:* Col Art Asn Am; Front Range Women Visual Arts; Womens Caucus Art; Fuller Art Ctr. *Media:* Multimedia. *Publ:* Illusr, Guide to the five senses, Impression Five, 75. *Dealer:* Sebastian-Moore Gallery 1411 Market St. Denver CO 80202; Gilman Galleries 277 E Ontario St Chicago IL 60611. *Mailing Add:* 195 El Rayo Los Alamos NM 87544

NOGGLE, ANNE
PHOTOGRAPHER, EDUCATOR
b Evanston, Ill, June 12, 22. *Study:* Univ NMex, BFA(art hist), MA(art), with Van Deren Coke. *Work:* San Francisco Mus Mod Art; Univ Mich; Minneapolis Inst Arts; Bibliot Nat, France; Denver Art Mus; plus others. *Exhib:* One-person show, San Francisco Mus Mod Art, 80; Gallery Photog Hist, Smithsonian Inst, Washington, DC, 73; two-person show, Focus Gallery, San Francisco, 74; The Great West, Real/Ideal, Univ Colo, 77; Light 2, Humboldt State Univ, Calif, 77; Contemp Panoramic Views, Northwestern Univ, 78; Perception: a Field of View, Los Angeles Ctr Photog Studies, 79. *Collections Arranged:* Laura Gilpin Retrospective (with catalog), 74; Women of Photography: A Historical Survey (catalog, with Margery Mann). *Pos:* Cur photog, Fine Arts Mus, Santa Fe, NMex, 70-76. *Awards:* Nat Endowment Art fels photog, 75 & 78; Guggenheim Fel Grant, 82. *Bibliog:* J Z Grover (auth), Anne Noggle's insightful images, Artweek, 10/76; Self-Portrayal: the Photographers Image, Friends of Photog, Carmel, Calif, 78; Van Deren Coke (auth), History of Photography in New Mexico, Univ NMex Press, 79; plus others. *Mem:* Soc Photog Educ. *Res:* Three years travel and research for Women of Photography: A Historical Survey. *Publ:* Auth, Prestidigitation, eyesight & hindsight, Album Mag, 70; auth, The long skinny photography of Captain Anne Noggle, Camera 35, 73; photographs, Silver Lining, Univ NMex Press, 84. *Mailing Add:* 1204 Espanola NE Albuquerque NM 87110

NOGUCHI, ISAMU
SCULPTOR
b Los Angeles, Calif, Nov 17, 04. *Study:* Columbia Univ, 23-25; Leonardo da Vinci Art Sch, New York, East Side Art Sch, New York; apprentice to Brancusi, Paris, 27-29. *Work:* Guggenheim Mus, Metrop Mus Art, Mus Mod Art, Whitney Mus Am Art, New York; Brooklyn Mus; and many others. *Comn:* Billy Rose Garden, Jerusalem; Detroit Civic Ctr Mem Fountain, 74; Pepsico, Purchase, NY, 74; Horace E Dodge & Son Mem Fountain, Philip A Hart Plaza, Detroit, 73-79; stepped garden for Sogetsu Sch Flower Arrangement, Tokyo, 77-78; and many others. *Exhib:* Cordier & Ekstrom, NY, 63 & 68; Claude Bernard Gallery, Paris, 64; Gulbenkian Exhib, Tate Gallery, London, 64; retrospectives, Whitney Mus Am Art, 66 & 68; Los Angeles Co Mus Art, Los Angeles, 67; Whitney Mus Am Art, 70; Venice Biennial, Italy, 72; one-man shows, Minami Gallery, 73, Pace Gallery, New York, 75 & 80, Mus Mod Art, New York, 77, Walker Art Ctr, 78-79 & Andre Emmerich Gallery, 80; Masters of Mod Sculpture, Guggenheim Mus, 74; 200 Years of Am Sculpture, Whitney Mus Am Art, 76. *Awards:* Guggenheim Fel;

Bollingen Fel, 50-51; Soc Four Arts Sculpture Award, 75; and others. *Bibliog:* Shuzo Takiguchi (auth), Noguchi (monogr), Bijutsu Shippan-Sha, Tokyo, 53; Eduard Trier (auth), Form and Space: Sculpture in the 20th Century, Praeger, 68; and many others. *Mem:* Archit League; Nat Sculpture Soc. *Publ:* Auth, A Sculptor's World, Harper & Row, 68. *Mailing Add:* 32-37 Tenth Long Island City NY 11106

NOLAN, MARGARET PATTERSON
LIBRARIAN
b New York, NY. *Study:* Col Mt St Vincent, BA(magna cum laude); Columbia Univ, MA. *Pos:* Asst librn photog & slides, Metrop Mus Art, New York, 58-61, chief photog & slide libr, 61-68, chief librn photog & slide libr, 68- *Teaching:* Vis lectr, Queens Col City Univ New York, 74-75. *Mem:* Asn Am Mus; Col Art Asn; Art Libr Soc North Am. *Res:* Color film: its properties and conservation; organization of collections of visual resources for art history. *Interests:* Western decorative arts, particularly 19th and 20th century American. *Mailing Add:* Slide Libr Metrop Mus Art Fifth Ave at 82nd St New York NY 10021

NOLAND, KENNETH
PAINTER
b Asheville, NC, 24. *Study:* Black Mountain Col, 46-48; also with Ossip Zadkine, Paris, 48-49. *Work:* Mus Mod Art & Metrop Mus, New York; Mus Fine Arts, Boston; Art Inst Chicago; Los Angeles Co Mus Art; and others. *Exhib:* Three American Painters: Noland, Olitski & Stella, Fogg Art Mus, Cambridge & Pasadena Art Mus, 65; Morris Louis, Anthony Caro & Kenneth Noland, 68 & New York Painting & Sculpture: 1940-1970, 70, Metrop Mus Art, New York; Selections from the Guggenheim Museum Collection 1900-1970, New York, 70; retrospective, Visual Arts Gallery, New York, 75; Kenneth Noland: A Retrospective Traveling Exhib, 77. *Bibliog:* Michael Fried (auth), Recent work by Kenneth Noland, Artforum, summer 69; Kenworth Moffett (auth), Noland vertical, Art News, 10/71; Ken Worth Moffett (auth), Kenneth Noland, Harry N Abrams, 77. *Dealer:* Andre Emmerich Gallery 41 E 57th St New York NY 10022. *Mailing Add:* South Salem NY 10590

NOLAND, WILLIAM
SCULPTOR
b Washington, DC, May 13, 54. *Study:* Hampshire Col, with Gary Hudson & Leonard Delonga, 72-74; Sarah Lawrence Col, with Lou Sgroi & Mary Miss, BA, 77. *Exhib:* Solo exhib, Va Polytechnic Inst Art Gallery, 81; New Works in Clay III, Everson Mus Art, 81; Sculpture Invitational, Tibor de Nagy Gallery, New York, 81; Contemporary Art in Detroit Collections, Detroit Inst Arts, 82; Five American Artists, Galeria Joan Prats, New York, 83. *Bibliog:* Gene Baro (auth), article, Art Int, 8-9/81; Jo Ann Lewis (auth), article, Washington Post, 11/5/81; Valentin Tatransky (auth), article, Arts, 1/84. *Media:* Metal. *Dealer:* Salander-O'Reilly Galleries 22 E 80th St New York NY 10021. *Mailing Add:* 262 Bowery New York NY 10012

NONG
PAINTER, SCULPTOR
b Seoul, Korea, Oct 10, 30; US citizen. *Study:* Self-taught. *Work:* Nat Mus Hist, Taipei, Taiwan; Musee Nat Beaux-Arts, Monte Carlo, Monaco; Nat Gallery Mod Art, New Delhi, India; Asian Art Mus San Francisco; Nat Mus Mod Art, Seoul, Korea; and others. *Exhib:* Nat Collection Fine Arts, Smithsonian Inst, 61; Denver Art Mus, 65; Oakland Art Mus, 71; one-man exhibs, Nat Mus Hist, Taipei, Taiwan, 71, Nat Mus Mod Art, Seoul, Korea, 75 & Consulate Gen Repub Korea, New York, 83; San Francisco Mus Art, 72; Consulate Gen Repub Korea, Los Angeles, 82; and many others including Salons in Paris. *Awards:* Lett Appreciation Achievement Art, Minister Cult & Info, Repub Korea, 71; Cert Distinguished Achievement, State Calif, 82; Proclamation, City & Co San Francisco, 82. *Media:* Multimedia. *Publ:* Auth, Nong Questions, 82. *Mailing Add:* 999 Green St No 2701 San Francisco CA 94133

NOORDHOEK, HARRY CECIL
SCULPTOR, PAINTER
b Moers, Ger, Feb 10, 09; Can citizen. *Study:* Gemaelde Galerie, Kassel, Ger, 27-28. *Work:* Quebec Prov Mus, Quebec City; City of Alma, Que; Museo Giorgi, Florence, Italy; Elmwood Corp, Montreal; Mus Arte Mod, Milan, Italy; and others. *Comn:* Serenite Deux (sculpture), City of Alma, Que, 65; Cult Affairs Coun, Liberty Hill, Tex; Kreis Ostholstein, Eutin, WGer. *Exhib:* One-man show, Mus Contemp Art, Montreal, 66; 6th Int Open Air Sculpture Exhib, Milan, 70; Galerie Buerdeke, Zurich, Switz, 70; 1st Int Sculpture Show, Carrara, Italy, 72; Can Cult Centre, Paris, France, 77; Int Bildhauer Symp, Eutin, WGer, 77 & Norderstedt, WGer, 80; and others. *Awards:* President of Republic of Italy Gold Medal, Ital Nat Prize, 72; Gold Medal, Accademia Italia Delle Arti, 80; Statue of Victory, World Prize Arts, Letters & Sci, 84. *Bibliog:* M Ballantyne (auth), A sculptor of cool serenity, Montreal Star, 2/27/65; T Krieber (auth), Violence at serenite s'opposent, Progres-Dimanche, Chicoutimi, PQ, 8/8/65; R Montbizon (auth), Harry C Noordhoek, sculptor, The Gazette, Montreal, 5/21/66; A zum Winkel & Harry Noordhoek (co-auths), Kunst ohne Kompromiz, Ostholsteiner Anzeiger, Eutin, WGer, 7/7/77. *Mem:* Royal Can Acad Arts; Accademia Italia Delle Arti e del Lavoro. *Media:* Stone, Oil; Bronze, Aluminum. *Publ:* Ed, Enciclopedia Universale Seda Dell' Arte Moderna, Milan, 72; auth, Eine

Dokumentation, Internationales Bildhauer Symposium, Eutin, WGer, 77. *Mailing Add:* PO Box 263 Carrara Italy

NORDHAUSEN, A HENRY
PAINTER
b Hoboken, NJ, Jan 25, 01. *Study:* NY Sch Fine & Appl Art; Royal Acad Fine Art, Munich, Ger; Kunst Geverve Schule, Munich; Mass Inst Technol; New Sch Social Res. *Work:* Cleveland Mus Fine Art; Columbus Art Mus, Ga; New Brit Mus, Conn; Syracuse Univ; Pentagon, Washington, DC; and others. *Comn:* Several portraits, Syracuse Univ, Pentagon, Royal Crown Cola Co, Columbus, Ga, Ga Inst Technol, Atlanta & Ga Power Co, plus many others. *Exhib:* Metrop Mus Art; Nat Acad Design, New York; Glass Palace, Munich; Art Inst Chicago; Corcoran Gallery, Washington, DC; and others. *Pos:* Lectr, Metrop Mus Art & Brooklyn Mus Art. *Teaching:* Instr portraits, Roerich Mus; instr art, New York High Schs; instr art, Musemont, Columbus. *Awards:* MacDowell Colony Fel; Trask Found Fel; Tiffany Found Fel; and others. *Mem:* Am Watercolor Soc; Salmagundi Club; Artist Fel (vpres); Dutch Treat Club; Explorers Club; plus others. *Media:* Oil, Watercolor. *Dealer:* Grand Cent Art Gallery Biltmore Hotel Madison Ave E & 43rd New York NY 10017; Capricorn Gallery 8003 Woodmont Ave Bethesda MD 20014. *Mailing Add:* 1108 16th Ave Columbus GA 31906

NORDIN, PHYLLIS E
SCULPTOR, DESIGNER
b Chicago, Ill. *Study:* Wayne State Univ, 54-56; Univ Toledo, BS, 62, BA(magna cum laude), 74; Toledo Mus Art, dipl, 74. *Work:* Sylvania Chamber Commerce, Ohio; Stranahan Arboretum, Toledo, Ohio; Univ Toledo; Beloit Col, Wis; First Methodist Church, LaGrange, Ill. *Comn:* Storytime (bronze), Ronald McDonald House, Toledo; Exalted (bronze), First England Evangelical Lutheran Church, Grosse Pointe Woods, Mich; Tree of Life (bronze), Toledo Hosp; East & West (steel), First Fed Savings & Loan, Toledo; Beloved Son (bronze), Christ Presby Church, Toledo. *Exhib:* Ann Sculpture & Ceramic Show, Butler Inst Am Art, 68-78; Salmagundi Club Ann, Nat Club Galleries, New York, 81; Catharine Lorillard Wolfe Art Club, Nat Arts Club, New York, 81 & 83; Liturgical Arts Nat, McFall Gallery, Bowling Green State Univ, 81 & 83; Liturgical Art Guild Ohio Ann, Schumacher Galery, Capital Univ, 81 & 83; Shreveport Art Biennial Nat, Meadows Mus Art, La, 82; and others. *Awards:* First Prize, 43rd Ann Nat Art Exhib, Cooperstown Art Asn, NY, 78; Alpha Award, Best of Show, Energy Art Nat Exhib, Foothills Art Ctr, Golden, Colo, 83. *Bibliog:* Louise Bruner (auth), Toledo, city of sculptures, Blade, 80; M Biedron (ed), On the cover, Radio Listener, WGTE Pub Radio, 80; J Hayes (auth), Contemporary sculpture alive, Columbus Dispatch, 82. *Mem:* Nat Asn Women Artists; Ohio Designer Craftsmen; Interfaith Forum Religion, Art & Archit; Liturgical Art Guild Ohio; Toledo Arts Comn. *Media:* Bronze, Welded Steel. *Publ:* Auth, Downtown churches house treasures, Accent Arts, 80; contribr, Centennial Mall's crowning jewel, Alumnus, Univ Toledo, 80; contribr, Auxiliary presents sculpture, Toledo Hosp News, 81. *Mailing Add:* 4035 Tantara Rd Toledo OH 43623

NORDLAND, GERALD JOHN
GALLERY DIRECTOR, CRITIC
b Los Angeles, Calif, July 10, 27. *Study:* Univ Southern Calif, AB & JD. *Collections Arranged:* Gaston Lachaise (with catalog), Los Angeles Co Mus Art & Whitney Mus Am Art, 63-64; Richard Diebenkorn Retrospective (with catalog), 64, Josef Albers (with catalog), 65, Washington Color Painters, 65, Washington Gallery Mod Art, Washington, DC; John Altoon (with catalog), Julius Bissier (with Guggenheim Mus), Robert Natkin, Al Held, Fritz Glarner, Paul Jenkins (with catalog), Peter Voulkos Bronzes (with catalog), and others, San Francisco Mus Art; Gaston Lachaise Retrospective (with Cornell Univ; catalog), 74, Alberto Burri (with Guggenheim Mus; catalog), 77, and others, Frederick S Wight Art Gallery, Univ Calif, Los Angeles; Richard DeVore 1972-1982 (with catalog), 83, Controversial Public Art (with catalog), 83, and others, Milwaukee Art Mus. *Pos:* Dean, Chouinard Art Sch, Calif Inst Arts, 60-64; dir, Washington Gallery Mod Art, 64-66, San Francisco Mus Art, 66-72, Frederick S Wight Galleries, Univ Calif, Los Angeles, 73-77 & Milwaukee Art Ctr, 77- *Awards:* Lachaise Found Grant, 73. *Mem:* Nat Endowment Arts; Asn Art Mus Dirs. *Res:* More than forty museum publications on twentieth century artists and movements, emphasizing American painting, sculpture and photography. *Publ:* Auth, Gaston Lachaise: The Man and His Work, Braziller, 74. *Mailing Add:* c/o Milwaukee Art Mus 750 N Lincoln Mem Dr Milwaukee WI 53202

NORDSTRAND, NATHALIE JOHNSON
PAINTER
b Woburn, Mass. *Study:* Bradford Jr Col; Barnard Col; Columbia Univ; also with Jay Connaway, Roger Curtis, Paul Strisik & Don Stone. *Work:* First Nat Bank Boston; Commercial Union Assurance Co, Boston; Am Tel & Tel Co, New York; Int Business Machines, New York; Peabody Mus, Salem, Mass; and others. *Exhib:* Acad Artists Am, 67-83; Am Watercolor Soc Ann, 69-82; Allied Artists Am, 69-83; Mainstreams 71, Ohio, 71; New England Art in Hong Kong, Am Chamber Com, 74 & 76; De Cordova Mus, Lincoln, Mass; Butler Inst of Am Art, Youngstown, Ohio; and others. *Awards:* Bronze Medal, Catharine Lorillard Wolfe Art Club, 70; Gold Medal, Am Artists Prof League, 71 & 75; Award, Salmagundi Club, 83; and over 125 other awards. *Bibliog:* Robert Kolbe (auth), Nathalie J Nordstrand poetry of the sea, Am Artist Mag, 9/72. *Mem:* Am Watercolor Soc; Allied Artists Am; Am Artists Prof League; Salmagundi Club; Guild Boston Artists (sec, 82-83); and others. *Media:* Watercolor, Oil. *Publ:* Contribr, La Rev Mod, Paris, 72; auth, The salt wind and I, Palette Talk, winter 73 & 74. *Mailing Add:* 384 Franklin St Reading MA 01867

NORELLI, MARTINA ROUDABUSH
CURATOR
b Washington, DC, Oct 2, 42. *Study:* Mary Washington Col, Fredericksburg, Va, 60-62; George Washington Univ, DC, BA(art hist), 69, MA(museology), 72. *Collections Arranged:* Artist-Naturalists: Observations in the Americas (auth, catalog), 72, Selections from the Natural Museum of American Art Graphic Arts Collection, 78, 80 & 83, Birds: Works from the 1979 Annual Exhibitions of Art Depicting Birds (auth, catalog), 80 & An American Perspective: Selections from the Bequest of Frank McClure (auth, catalog), 81, Nat Mus Am Art, Washington, DC. *Pos:* Curatorial asst, Dimock Gallery, George Washington Univ, DC, 68-69; secy, Dept Graphic Arts, Nat Mus Am Art, Smithsonian Inst, DC, 70-71; mus technician, 71-74; asst cur, 74-78, assoc cur, 78- *Mem:* Print Coun Am. *Res:* Wildlife art; American prints and drawings; Estonian graphic art. *Publ:* Auth, American Wildlife Painting, Watson-Guptill, 75, Galahad Bks, 83; contribr, Europe 1980-Europe 1983, sect on Moscow and Leningrad, Houghton Mifflin, 79-82. *Mailing Add:* Nat Mus Am Art Smithsonian Inst Washington DC 20560

NORFLEET, BARBARA PUGH
CURATOR, EDUCATOR
b Lakewood, NJ. *Study:* Swarthmore, BA, 47; Harvard-Radcliffe, MA, 50 & PhD, 51. *Work:* Mus of Mod Art, New York City; Harvard Univ, Cambridge, Mass; Mus Fine Arts, Boston; Corcoran Gallery Art. *Exhib:* DeCordova Mus, 72; Carl Siembab Gallery, Boston, 81; Marjorie Neikrug Gallery, New York, 82; Marcus Pfeiffer Gallery, New York, 83; Boston Mus Fine Arts Ach, 83; Inst Contemp Art, Boston, 83. *Collections Arranged:* The Photography Archive on the Photographic Social History of the US; The Social Question: Social Reform at the Turn of the Century, Harvard & Mus Mod Art, 73. *Pos:* Cur, Harvard Univ, 72-; consult on art, numerous organizations, 73-; auth, photo-essays, St Louis Post Dispatch, 73- *Teaching:* Senior lectr photog, Harvard Univ, Cambridge, 70-78. *Awards:* Nat Endowment Arts, 75, 79, 81 & 83; Artists Found Mass. *Media:* Photog. *Res:* Have compiled an archive of over 30,000 negatives and prints on the social history of the US from 1900-1970. *Publ:* Auth, Wedding, Simon & Schuster, 76 & 77; auth, The Head and the Heart, Harvard Press, 78; auth, The Champion Pig; auth, Killing Time, Godine, 83. *Dealer:* Marjorie Neikrug Gallery New York NY; Carl Siembab Gallery Boston MA. *Mailing Add:* Carpenter Ctr for the Visual Arts Harvard Univ Cambridge MA 02138

NORMAN, DOROTHY (S)
WRITER, PHOTOGRAPHER
b Philadelphia, Pa, Mar 28, 05. *Study:* Smith Col; Univ Pa. *Work:* Philadelphia Mus Art; Mus Mod Art, New York. *Exhib:* Captions, Family of Man, Mus Mod Art & Tour, 55 & Forms of Israel, Am Fedn Arts & Tour, 58-60; 60 Photographs & New Workers, Mus Mod Art; Selections from Dorothy Norman Collection, Philadelphia Mus Art, 68. *Pos:* Ed & publ, Twice a Yr, 37-48. *Bibliog:* William Wasserstrom (auth), Introd in Civil Liberties and the Arts, Syracuse Univ Press, 64. *Collection:* Contemporary and ancient symbolical art. *Publ:* Co-ed, America and Alfred Stieglitz, 34, rev ed, 79; ed, Selected Writings of John Marin, 49; auth, Alfred Stieglitz--introduction to an American Seer, 60; auth, The Hero: Myth/Image/Symbol, 69; auth, Alfred Stieglitz an American Seer, winter 73. *Mailing Add:* 124 E 70th St New York NY 10021

NORMAN, EMILE
PAINTER, SCULPTOR
b El Monte, Calif, Apr 22, 18. *Work:* Oakland Mus. *Comn:* Mosaic window & marble relief, Calif Masonic Mem Temple, San Francisco, 56-58; Horse (wood sculpture), Crown Zellerbach Bldg, San Francisco, 59; St Francis (bronze sculpture), 67 & wood inlay mural, 68, Bank Calif Bldg, San Francisco. *Exhib:* Archit Art Exhib, Pasadena Art Inst, 49; Relig Art Show, De Young Mus, San Francisco, 53; 20th Ann Soc Contemp Art, Art Inst Chicago, 60; Contemp Am Painting & Sculpture, Krannert Art Mus, Univ Ill, 61; Design & Esthetics in Wood, Lowe Art Ctr, Syracuse Univ, 67. *Pos:* Owner-dir, Emile Norman Gallery, Carmel, Calif, currently. *Bibliog:* Eliz Gordon (auth), The flowering of our times, House Beautiful, 10/58; Janice Lovoos (auth), The art of Emile Norman, Am Artist Mag, 11/61. *Mem:* Carmel Art Asn; Nat Soc Mural Painters. *Media:* Oil, Acrylic; Wood, Precious Metals. *Mailing Add:* Mission & Sixth Ave Carmel CA 93921

NORQUIST, RYL
ART DEALER
b Los Angeles, Calif, Feb 25, 51. *Pos:* Dir, Droll/Kolbert Gallery, 77- *Specialty:* Contemporary American art. *Mailing Add:* PO Box 543 Bridgehampton NY 11932

NORRIS, ANDREA SPAULDING
HISTORIAN, CURATOR
b Madison, Wis, Apr 2, 45. *Study:* Wellesley Col, BA, 67; NY Univ, MA, 69, cert(mus training), 70, PhD, 77; Mus Mgt Inst, Univ Calif, Berkeley, 80. *Pos:* Asst to dir, Yale Univ Art Gallery, 77-80; chief cur, Archer M Huntington Art Gallery, Univ Tex, Austin, 80- *Teaching:* Lectr art hist, Queens Col, City Univ New York, 73-74; adj instr art hist, NY Univ, 76-77; lectr art hist, Yale Univ, 78-79. *Awards:* Ford Foundation Mus Training Grant, 69-72. *Mem:* Col Art Asn Am; Renaissance Soc Am. *Res:* Italian Renaissance painting and sculpture; medals; Gian Cristoforo Romano; Lombard Renaissance sculpture; art patronage in America. *Publ:* Coauth, Medals and Plaquettes from the Molinari Collection at Bowdoin Col, 76; contribr, Dizionario Biografico degli Italiani, Treccani, 77-81; auth, New-found works and Pollock's career, In: Jackson Pollock: New-Found Works, Yale Univ Art Gallery, 78. *Mailing Add:* c/o Huntington Art Gallery Univ Tex Austin TX 78712

NORRIS, (ROBERT) BEN
PAINTER
b Redlands, Calif, Sept 6, 10. *Study:* Pomona Col; Harvard Univ; Inst Art & Archeol, Sorbonne, Paris; also with Stanton MacDonald Wright, Jean Charlot, Max Ernst & Josef Albers. *Work:* Nat Collection Fine Arts, Washington, DC; Am Fedn Arts Mus Collection; Weatherspoon Mus, Greensboro, NC; Hawaii State Comn Cult & Arts; McNay Art Inst, San Antonio, Tex. *Comn:* Murals, First Hawaiian Bank, Honolulu, Royal Hawaiian Hotel, Honolulu & Royal Lahaina Hotel, Maui. *Exhib:* Six one-man shows, Honolulu Acad Arts, 36-58; Chicago Int Watercolor Exhib, 38-42; Metrop Mus Mid-Century Exhib, 51; Whitney Mus, 61; Pacific Heritage, West Coast Mus & Berlin, Ger, 65; A M Sachs Gallery, New York, 79, 80 & 83. *Teaching:* From instr to prof art, Univ Hawaii, 37-76. *Awards:* Mary S Litt Medal, Am Watercolor Soc, 82. *Media:* Oil, Watercolor. *Dealer:* A M Sachs Gallery 29 W 57th St New York NY 10019. *Mailing Add:* 231 Bedford Ave Brooklyn NY 11211

NORRIS, LEONARD MATHESON
CARTOONIST, ILLUSTRATOR
b London, Eng, Dec 1, 13; Can citizen. *Study:* Ont Col Art; Univ Windsor, Hon LLD, 74. *Work:* Nat Libr Can; Univ Mo; Pavilion of Humor, Montreal, Que; Winnipeg Art Gallery, Man. *Pos:* Art dir, Maclean Hunter, Toronto, Ont, 45-50; ed cartoonist, Vancouver Sun, 50- *Awards:* Nat Newspaper Award, Can Newspapers, Toronto, 62; Can News Hall of Fame, 79. *Bibliog:* Nat Film Bd, The Hecklers, Cartoon History of Can, 75; articles, Time Mag & Punch. *Mem:* Asn Am Ed Cartoonists; Royal Can Acad Art. *Publ:* Illusr, Johan's Gift to Christmas, Scrivner US MacIntyre Douglas Can, 75. *Mailing Add:* 4227 Almondel Pl West Vancouver BC V7V 3L8 Canada

NORRIS, WILLIAM A
COLLECTOR
b Turtle Creek, Pa, Aug 30, 27. *Study:* Princeton Univ, BA, 51; Stanford Univ, JD, 54. *Pos:* Founding pres & mem, bd trustees, Mus Contemp Art, Los Angeles, 79-; trustee, Craft & Folk Art Mus, Los Angeles, 79- *Collection:* Contemporary California paintings and sculpture. *Mailing Add:* 1653 US Courthouse 312 N Spring St Los Angeles CA 90012

NORTH, JUDY (JUDITH K RAFFAEL)
PAINTER, PRINTMAKER
b Los Angeles, Calif, June 24, 37. *Study:* Los Angeles Art Inst; San Francisco Art Inst. *Work:* Los Angeles Co Mus, Security Pacific Bank, Los Angeles; Mus Contemp Art, Chicago; Oakland Mus, Calif. *Comn:* Stained Glass, Northbrae Community Church, 59; stained glass, Holy Name Jesus Christ, 63; stained glass, Salvation Army, 72; Portrait of Dean of Law Sch, Stanford Univ, 77. *Exhib:* Middle, East, West, South, Corcoran Gallery of Art, Washington, DC, Ft Worth Art Mus, Tex & La Jolla Mus of Contemp Art, Calif, 75; Other Work, San Francisco Mus Art, 76; one-woman shows, Quay Gallery, San Francisco, 76 & Purdue Univ, 79; Recent Acquisitions, Oakland Mus, 77; and others. *Pos:* Staff designer, Actors Workshop, 60-64 & Cummings Stained Glass Studio, 63-65; designer, Bennington Col, 66-69. *Teaching:* Instr theatre design & stained glass, Bennington Col, 66-69; instr theatre design, Actors Workshop, San Francisco, 60-64. *Awards:* L C Tiffany, Stained Glass, 66. *Bibliog:* Otto Regan (auth), New Glass, San Francisco Book Co, 77; Giacopetti (auth), Native Funk and Flash, Scrimshaw Press, 74 & Craze for quilts, Life Mag, 5/5/72. *Media:* Watercolor. *Dealer:* Roy Boyd Gallery 233 E Ontario St Chicago IL 60611. *Mailing Add:* PO Box 210 San Geronimo CA 94963

NORTON, MARY JOYCE
PAINTER
b Tampa, Fla. *Study:* Akron Univ; Ariz State Univ; color theory with Dorothy Fratt. *Work:* First Nat Bank, Phoenix; Houston Oil & Mineral Corp, Tex; IBM, Endicott, NY; Drexel, Burnham, Lambert, Scottsdale, Ariz. *Exhib:* Watercolor Biennial, Phoenix Art Mus, 70-72, Four-Corners Biennial, 71-73; 8 West Biennial, Colo Ctr Arts, 72-74; Southwestern Fine Arts Biennial, Mus NMex, 72-74; Joslyn Mus, Omaha, Nebr, 74; and others. *Awards:* Southwestern Purchase Prize, Yuma Fine Arts Ctr, 67 & 73; 19th Nat Sun Carnival Exhib, El Paso Mus Art, 77; Ariz Painting Nat Competition, Scottsdale Ctr Arts, Ariz, 77. *Bibliog:* Barbara Cortright (auth), Meet the circle, Phoenix Mag, 2/75 & The look of nature, the flow of paint, Artweek, 5/75; Rosemary Holusha (auth), Mary Joyce Norton, Art Voices S, 5-6/79. *Mem:* Nat Women's Caucus Art. *Media:* Acrylic. *Dealer:* C G Rein Gallery Scottsdale AZ; Choice Inc 101 Kansas St San Francisco CA 94103. *Mailing Add:* 10648 N 100th St Scottsdale AZ 85260

NORTON, PAUL FOOTE
HISTORIAN, EDUCATOR
b Newton, Mass, Jan 23, 17. *Study:* Oberlin Col, BA, 38; Princeton Univ, MFA, 47, PhD, 52. *Pos:* Mass State Hist Comn, 80-83. *Teaching:* From asst prof to assoc prof hist art, Pa State Univ, University Park, 47-58; from assoc prof to prof hist art, Univ Mass, Amherst, 58-, chmn dept, 58-71. *Awards:* Fel, Am Coun Learned Socs, 51-52; Fulbright Sr Res Fel, 53-54; Nat Endowment Humanities Sr Fel, 71-72; and others. *Mem:* Soc Archit Historians (dir & ed jour, 59-64); Soc Archit Historians Gr Brit; Soc Francaise Archeol; Archeol Inst Am; fel Royal Soc Arts; and others. *Res:* History of architecture; England and America in the 18th and 19th centuries; stained glass windows in America. *Publ:* Co-auth, Arts in America: the Nineteenth Century, 69; auth, Amherst: A Guide to its Architecture, 75; auth, Latrobe, Jefferson and the National Capitol, 77; ed, The Papers of Samuel McIntire, Architect, Salem, Mass, 78; auth, articles in J Soc Archit Historians, Art Bull, Britannica Encycl Am Art & Encycl World Biog; and others. *Mailing Add:* Dept of Art Univ of Mass Amherst MA 01003

NORVELL, PATSY
SCULPTOR, ENVIRONMENTAL ARTIST
b Greenville, SC, July 13, 42. *Study:* Bennington Col, Vt, BA; study with David Smith; San Francisco Art Inst; Hunter Col, MA. *Comn:* Lobby, Nicholas Music Hall, Douglas Col, NJ, 81-82; outdoor sculpture, Fed Courthouse, Bridgeport, Conn, Gen Serv Admin, 83-84. *Exhib:* Wood, Nassau Co Mus, Roslyn, NY, 77; retrospective, Vassar Col Art Mus, 79; Hair, 80 & Gardens of Delight, 81, Cooper-Hewitt Mus, NY; two-person exhib, Norton Gallery Art, West Palm Beach, 83; Content in Abstraction, High Mus Art, 83; The Folding Image, Nat Gallery Art, 84. *Teaching:* Instr sculpture & drawing, Rutgers Univ, Newark, NJ, 69-70; instr materials & printmaking, Montclair State Col, Upper Montclair, NJ, 70-74; panelist, lectr & instr workshops, Nassau Co Mus, Aldrich Mus, Sarah Lawrence Col, City Univ New York, Skidmore Col, Mt Holyoke Col, Grad Sch Sculpture, Yale Univ & Wooster Col, Ohio, 71-79; assoc in sculpture, Columbia Univ, New York, 77; adj instr sculpture, Queens Col, NY, 77-78; adj & vis asst prof sculpture & drawing, Hunter Col, NY, 78-; vis artist, Experimental Galss Workshop, New York, 80, 83 & 84. *Awards:* Nat Endowment for the Arts Grant, 76-77. *Bibliog:* Jane Heit (auth), Patsy Norvell, Arts Mag, 81; Grace Glueck (auth), The screen comes into its own, 9/19/82 & Patsy Norvell & Robert Zakanitch, 2/83, New York Times. *Media:* Plexiglas, Glass. *Publ:* Contribr, Six Years ... Lucy Lippart, Praeger, 69. *Dealer:* AIR Gallery 63 Crosby St New York NY 10012. *Mailing Add:* 78 Greene St New York NY 10012

NORWOOD, MALCOLM MARK
PAINTER, EDUCATOR
b Drew, Miss, Jan 21, 28. *Study:* Miss Col, BA & MEd; Univ Ala, MA; Univ Colo, painting with Mark Rothko. *Work:* Miss Mus Art, Jackson; Miss Collection, First Nat Bank, Jackson; Miss Col; Belhaven Col; Jackson Country Club. *Comn:* Landscapes & watercolors, First Nat Bank, Cleveland, Miss, 64 & 66; Rosalie (painting), comn by Daughters Am Revolution for USS Miss, 78; 5 Mile Run, comn by Governor's Coun on Physical Fitness, 81; and others. *Exhib:* SMU Invitational, Ft Worth, Tex, 62; Washington Watercolor Asn, Smithsonian Inst, 63; Contemp Southern Art Exhib, Weatherspoon Art Gallery, Univ NC, 66; Artists Registry Exhib, Brooks Art Gallery, Memphis, Tenn, 69; La State Art Comn, Baton Rouge, 69. *Pos:* Bd dirs, Miss Mus Art, Jackson; dir festival, Grosstie Arts Council, 70-75; pres 79-80; mem bd dir, Miss Arts Comn, 80- *Teaching:* Prof & chmn dept art, Delta State Univ, 62- *Awards:* First Prize, Nat Oil Festival, 63; Painting Award, Holiday Inns Am Arts Festival, 69; First Prize in Drawing, Edgewater Merchants Asn Ann, 71. *Mem:* Miss Art Asn; Cross-Tie Arts Couns. *Media:* Watercolor, Oil. *Publ:* Auth, article in Jackson Daily News/Clarion Ledger, 64; illusr, 64 & cover, 68, Delta Rev; coauth, The Art of Marie Hull, 75; auth, Guide to the Roberts Library Art Collection, 77. *Mailing Add:* 600 Canal Ave Cleveland MS 38732

NOSOFF, FRANK
PAINTER
b Brooklyn, NY, Apr 10, 19. *Study:* Nat Acad Design, 38-40; Art Students League, 43-45; Art Career Sch, 53-56. *Exhib:* Painters & Sculptors Soc, NJ, Jersey City Mus, 67; Am Watercolor Soc Exhib & Traveling Show, New York, 68; L'Exposition Intercontinentale Traveling Show, 68; Nat Soc Painters Casein, New York, 71-74; Am Veterans Soc Artists, New York, 74. *Awards:* Mildred & Tommy Atkin Cash Award, 72; Simmons Award, Am Vet Soc Artists, 74; Grumbacher Cash Award, 77. *Media:* Oil, Casein. *Mailing Add:* 50 Riverside Dr New York NY 10024

NOTARBARTOLO, ALBERT
PAINTER, ENVIRONMENTAL ARTIST
b New York, NY. *Study:* Nat Acad Fine Arts, scholar, 50; apprenticeship to mural painter Ignacio La Russa, 51-53. *Work:* Fort Bragg, NC; Aldrich Mus Contemp Art, Ridgefield, Conn; Nat Gallery Art, Washington, DC. *Comn:* Series of paintings, comn by Larry Aldrich, New York, 67; painting, Radio Corp Am, New York, 71; drawing, Newsweek, 72; tapestry, Aubusson, France. *Exhib:* Corcoran Gallery Art, Washington, DC, 68; Mus Mod Art, New York, 68-70; 21 Am Artists, Del Art Mus, 70; Aldrich Mus Contemp Art, 72; Aubusson Tapestry Exhib, Norton Gallery Mus, Fla; Nat Gallery of Art, Washington, DC, 76; plus others. *Awards:* First Prize, New York Intercult Soc, 53; Dept Housing & Urban Develop Nat Community Art Competition Award, Washington, DC, 73; Nat Award, New Glory Bicentennial Flag Design Competition (for flag for first lunar colony), Santa Barbara Mus of Art, 76. *Mem:* Nat Soc Lit & Arts. *Media:* Acrylic, Mixed Media. *Publ:* Contribr, Art Workers News, 4/74; contribr, Leonardo Mag, spring 75; contribr, Art World newspaper, 1-2/78. *Mailing Add:* 215 W 98th St New York NY 10025

NOTARO, ANTHONY
SCULPTOR
b Italy, Jan 10, 15; US citizen. *Study:* Rinehart Sch Sculpture, Md Inst, Baltimore, scholar, 35-39, with William Mark Simpson & Herbert Adams, grad, 39; also with Melvina Hoffman, 40. *Work:* Hall of Fame for Great Americans; Seton Hall Univ Student Ctr; Nat Commemorative Soc; State Univ Iowa; and others. *Comn:* Wrestling Group, Coun Am Artists Soc, 67; Winter (figure), Nat Sculpture Soc, 76 & portrait of President Jimmy Carter, 78; Football Players, Allied Artists Am, 77; Hockey Players (sport sculpture), Kalos Kagathos Found; and others. *Exhib:* Greenwich Soc Artists; Ital Cult Ctr, Chicago; one-man shows, Seton Hall Univ Student Ctr, NJ, Morris Co Libr & Orange Free Pub Libr; plus many others. *Awards:* John Spring Art Founder Award, Bicentennial Art Nat Sculpture Soc, 76, Cert of Merit, 78; Gold Medal of Honor, Hudson Valley Art Asn, 81; and others. *Mem:* Fel Nat Sculpture Soc; Am Artists Prof League; Allied Artists Am. *Media:* Multimedia. *Mailing Add:* 14 Brookfield Way Mendham NJ 07945

NOTESTINE, TOM W
PAINTER, INSTRUCTOR
b Oxford, Kans, Dec 1, 19. *Study:* Southwestern Col, Winfield, Kans, 38-40; Univ Houston, 48-50; John Pike Watercolor Sch, summer 75 & 76; also with Millard Sheets, Robert E Wood, Edgar Whitney & others. *Comn:* Mural, San Antonio Bd Realtors, Tex, 76. *Exhib:* Coppini Acad Fine Arts, San Antonio, Tex, 75-81; Int Art Show, Brownsville Art Mus, Tex, 77; World Wide Air Force Show, San Francisco, Calif, 77; one-man shows, Dahl Fine Arts Mus, Rapid City, SDak, 78, Int Art Mus, McAllen, Tex, 79; and others. *Pos:* Ed, San Antonio Water Color Slurp, 75-76; dir to pres, Coppini Acad Fine Arts, San Antonio, 77- *Teaching:* Instr watercolor, numerous art workshops, 76-81; instr, Carrizo Lodge Art Sch, Ruidoso, NMex, 83- & Cedarvale Art Sch, Davis, Okla, 84- *Awards:* Best of Show & 1st Place Watercolor, Int Art Show, Brownsville Art League & Mus, 77; 1st Place, World Wide Air Force Show, 77. *Bibliog:* Pamela Bell (auth), Artists take step into history, Alamo Artist, 76; Judy Veach (auth), Famous artist workshop, Sand Dollar Watch, 77; The pro's nest, Palette Talk #40, 79. *Mem:* San Antonio Watercolor Group (chmn, 75-76); Coppini Acad Fine Arts, San Antonio. *Media:* Watercolor, Oil. *Mailing Add:* 358 Ave Maria San Antonio TX 78216

NOTKIN, RICHARD T
SCULPTOR, CERAMIST
b Chicago, Ill, Oct 26, 48. *Study:* Kansas City Art Inst, with Dale Eldred & Ken Ferguson, BFA, 70; Univ Calif, Davis, with Robert Arneson, MFA, 73. *Work:* Stedelijk Mus, Amsterdam, Holland; Nat Collection Fine Arts, Smithsonian Inst, Washington DC; Kohler Arts Ctr, Sheboygan, Wis; City Seattle. *Exhib:* Clay, Whitney Mus Am Art, New York, 74; one-man shows, Frumkin Gallery, New York, 75, Quay Gallery, San Francisco, 81 & Mus Art, Univ Ore, Eugene, 81; The Object as Poet, Renwick Gallery, Smithsonian Inst, DC, 77; Another side to Art: a Hist of Northwest Ceramics, Seattle Art Mus, 79; West Coast Ceramics, Stedelijk Mus, Amsterdam, Holland, 79; American Porcelain, Renwick Gallery, Smithsonian Inst, Washington DC, 80; Echoes ... Historical References in Contemporary Ceramics, Atkins Mus Art, Kansas City, Mo, 83; and others. *Pos:* Artist in residence, Kohler Co, Wis, 76 & 78; artist in residence, Archie Bray Found, Helena, Mont, 81. *Teaching:* Vis asst prof sculpture & ceramics, Univ Utah, Salt Lake City, 75; acting chmn & vis lectr ceramics, Md Inst Col Art, Baltimore, 77; adj asst prof, Montana State Univ, Bozeman, 81; vis artist/lectr, Ohio State Univ, 82. *Awards:* Western States Art Found fel, 76; Nat Endowment for Arts fel, 79 & 81. *Bibliog:* Lynn Eder (auth), Ceramics Monthly, 11/82. *Mem:* Nat Coun Educ of Ceramic Arts; Am Crafts Coun. *Media:* Ceramics, Porcelain; Mixed Media, Terra Cotta. *Dealer:* Alan Frumkin Gallery 50 W 57th St New York NY 10019; Garth Clark Gallery 5820 Wilshire Blvd Los Angeles CA 90036. *Mailing Add:* Bridge Rte Box 145-C Myrtle Point OR 97458

NOVACK, FRANK T
PAINTER, ADMINISTRATOR
Norwich, Conn, June 21, 40. *Study:* Tufts Univ, BS, 71, MFA, 75; Sch Mus Fine Arts, dipl, 67, cert, 68. *Work:* Slater Mus, Norwich, Conn. *Exhib:* Ann Conn Artists Exhib, Converse Gallery, 72-81; Conn Painters & Sculptors Ann Exhib, Stamford Mus, Conn; 81st Ann New Haven Paint & Clay Exhib, Conn; Regional Exhib, Mystic Art Asn, Conn, 77-83; one-man exhib, Paul Mellon Arts Ctr, Choate-Rosemary Hall, Wallingford, Conn, 82. *Pos:* Dir, Norwich Art Sch, 77- *Teaching:* Instr oil painting, Norwich Art Sch, 70- *Awards:* Directors Prize, Slater Mem Mus, 74; Dorothy Schweyer Award, Best of Show, 9th Ann Arts & Crafts Show, Conn, 75; First Place, 26th Ann Regional Exhib, Mystic Art Asn, 82. *Mem:* Conn Comn Arts; Conn Art Educ; Friends of Slater Mem Mus; Mystic Art Asn (bd dirs, 81-85). *Media:* Oil. *Mailing Add:* Norwich Art Sch Norwich CT 06360

NOVAK, BARBARA (MRS BRIAN O'DOHERTY)
HISTORIAN, EDUCATOR
b New York, NY. *Study:* Barnard Col, Columbia Univ, BA, 51; Radcliff Col, MA, 53, PhD, 57. *Teaching:* Prof art hist & chmn dept, Barnard Col, Columbia Univ, 58-; vis Mellon prof, Univ Pittsburgh, fall 78. *Awards:* Belg-Am Educ Found Fel, 53; Fulbright Award to Belg, 53-54; Guggenheim Award, 74. *Mem:* Col Art Asn Am. *Res:* Nineteenth century American painting. *Publ:* Auth, American Painting of the Nineteenth Century, Praeger, 69; contribr, Metropolitan Museum Symposium on 19th Century American Art, 72; auth, Nature and Culture: American Landscape and Painting 1825-75, Oxford Univ Press, 80; contribr to numerous art hist periodicals. *Mailing Add:* Dept Art Hist Barnard Col New York NY 10027

NOVINSKI, LYLE FRANK
PAINTER, EDUCATOR
b Montfort, Wis, June 23, 32. *Study:* Wis State Univ, BA; Univ Wis, MS & MFA; Marquette Univ. *Comn:* Thomas Aquinas Chapel, 69 & Albert the Great Priory, 72, Univ Dallas; Major Leather Wall Construct, Amarillo & Dallas, Tex, 77; chapel, Holy Trinity Sem, 79; and others. *Exhib:* Tex Gen, 64 & 72; Okla Eight State Exhib, 68; Okla Invitational, 70; Fort Worth Art Ctr, 71; Nat Interfaith Conf on Relig & Archit, 75; and others. *Teaching:* Prof art & dir dept art, Univ Dallas, 60- *Awards:* Purchase Award, Okla Eight State, 68; Top Award, Tex Gen, 72. *Bibliog:* Articles, Christian Arts, 68, Liturgical Arts, 70 & Art Gallery, 71-72. *Mem:* Western Arts Asn; Col Art Asn Am; Guild Relig Archit. *Media:* Leather, Acrylic. *Dealer:* Valley House Gallery 6616 Spring Valley Rd Dallas TX 75240. *Mailing Add:* 1101 Owenwood Irving TX 75061

NOVOTNY, ELMER LADISLAW
PAINTER, EDUCATOR
b Cleveland, Ohio, July 27, 09. *Study:* Cleveland Sch Art, dipl; Case Western Reserve Univ, BA; Kent State Univ, MA; Slade Sch, Univ London; Acad Zagreb, Yugoslavia; Yale Univ. *Work:* Cleveland Mus Art; Butler Inst Am Art, Youngstown, Ohio; Akron Art Inst; Canton Art Inst; Cleveland Munic Collection. *Comn:* Mural for game room, comn by John Sherwin, Jr, Waite Hill Village, Ohio, 37; History of Kent (mural), Portage Nat Bank, Ohio, 49; portrait of Gov Martin L Davey, comn by family, Kent, 50; portrait of Robert Carr, Oberlin Col, 70; portrait of James A Michener for Michener Libr, Univ Northern Colo, 71. *Exhib:* Cleveland Mus Ann May Show, 29-71; Butler Inst Am Art Ann Nat, 35-71; Canton Art Inst Ann Show, 37-65; Akron Art Inst Ann May Show, 37-71; Directions in American Painting, Carnegie Mus, Pittsburgh, 42. *Teaching:* Instr portraiture, Cleveland Inst Art, 33-43; prof painting & drawing, Kent State Univ, 36-46, dir sch art, 46-74, emer prof & emer dir, 74- *Awards:* First Prize for Nancy (portraiture), Cleveland Mus Art, 37; Purchase Award for Wingaersheer Beach, Butler Inst Am Art, 60; Jurors Award for Chateaux, Akron Art Inst, 69. *Mem:* Hon life mem Akron Soc Artists; life fel Int Inst Arts & Lett; Cleveland Soc Artists. *Media:* Oil, Polymer. *Publ:* Auth, Byways of Southern Europe, Kent State Univ, 69. *Mailing Add:* 7317 Westview Rd Kent OH 44240

NOVROS, DAVID
PAINTER
b Los Angeles, Calif, 41. *Exhib:* Systemic Painting, Solomon R Guggenheim Mus, New York, 66; Sound, Light & Silence, William Rockhill Nelson Gallery of Art, Kansas City, Mo, 66; A Romantic Minimalism, Inst Contemp Arts, Univ Pa, 67; Rejective Art, Am Fedn Art, 67; Whitney Mus Am Art, 67, 69 & 73; Modular Painting, Albright-Knox Art Gallery, Buffalo, NY, 70; The Structure of Color, Whitney Mus Am Art, 71; Corcoran Biennial, Washington, DC, 71; White on White, Mus Contemp Art, Chicago, Ill, 71-72; Art Inst of Chicago, 72; Five Artists: A Logic of Vision, Mus Contemp Art, 74; one-man exhibs, Sperone Westwater Fischer Inc, New York, 76 & 78. *Mailing Add:* 433 Broome New York NY 10013

NOWACK, WAYNE KENYON
PAINTER, ASSEMBLAGE ARTIST
b Des Moines, Iowa, May 7, 23. *Study:* Drake Univ, 43-45; State Univ Iowa, BA(summa cum laude), 47, MA, 48, MFA, 50. *Work:* Joseph H Hirshhorn Found, Greenwich, Conn; Yale Univ Art Gallery, New Haven, Conn; Des Moines Art Ctr, Iowa; Williams Col, Williamstown, Mass; Ft Worth Art Mus, Tex. *Exhib:* Gallery Mod Art, Washington, DC, 63; Albright-Knox Art Gallery, Buffalo, NY, 63 & 71; Recent Am Drawings, Rose Art Mus, Brandeis Univ, 64; one-man shows, Allan Stone Gallery, New York, 67, 70 & 74; Human Concern, Whitney Mus Am Art, New York, 69; Unordinary Realities, Xerox Sq Exhib Ctr, Rochester, NY, 75; Am Drawings: 1927-1977, Minn Mus Art, St Paul, 77; Thirty Years of Box Construction, Sunne Savage Gallery, Boston, 79. *Teaching:* Assoc prof art hist & painting, Union Col, Schenectady, NY, 57-65. *Awards:* Danforth Found Grant, 63-64; Nat Endowment Arts Painting Grant, 73-74. *Dealer:* Allan Stone Gallery 48 E 86th St New York NY 10028. *Mailing Add:* RD 1 346 Spencer NY 14883

NOWAK, LEO
ILLUSTRATOR, CARTOONIST
b Elizabeth, NJ, Dec 24, 07. *Study:* Cleveland Sch Art, Ohio; John Huntington Sch Art, Cleveland. *Comn:* Mural (105 ft long), Brotherhood of Locomotive Engineers' Bldg, Cleveland, 34; many portraits comn by pvt parties & collectors. *Exhib:* May Show, Cleveland Mus Art, Cleveland, 30-36; Traveling Show, US, 36; Traveling Show, US Navy, Australia, NZ & US, 44-45; Art Festival, Laguna Beach Art Asn, Calif, 50-53; Los Angeles Co Mus Art, Los Angeles, 51-52. *Pos:* Illusr, children's bks, Nat Illustrating Studios, World Syndicate, 29-34; illusr, Superman Cartoon, Action Comics, 41-43; chief illusr, Stamps-Conhaim Newspaper Serv, Los Angeles, 47-73; illusr/cartoonist, Ridgecrest Daily Independent, Calif, 76- *Awards:* Second Award-Figure, Laguna Beach Art Asn, 52; Presidential Award, Calif Art Club, 68; and many others. *Bibliog:* Western paintings, 5/76 & cover painting, 1/77, Desert Mag. *Mem:* Calif Art Club (vpres, 63-65); Valley Artists' Guild (vpres, 62-66); Desert Art League. *Media:* Oil, Watercolor; Pen. *Mailing Add:* Star Route Box 137 Inyokern CA 93527

NOWYTSKI, (SLAVKO) SVIATOSLAV
FILMMAKER, PHOTOGRAPHER
b Oct 19, 34; Can citizen. *Study:* Pasadena Playhouse Col Theatre Arts, BA(theatre), 58; Columbia Univ, MFA(motion pictures), 64. *Work:* Educ Film Libr Asn, New York; Libr Cong; Dept Tourism, Recreation & Cult Affairs, Govt Man; Fedn Assoc Arts, Man; Ont Ministry Educ, Toronto. *Comn:* Reflections of the Past (film), Ukrainian Cult & Educ Ctr, Winnipeg, 74; Last of the Jacks (film), Minn Hist Soc, 76; Immortal Image (film), Filmart Prod, 78; Grass on the Roof (film), Underground Space Ctr, Univ Minn, 79; The Helm of Destiny (film), UNA, NJ, 81. *Exhib:* Sheep in Wood (film), Am Film Festival, New York, 71; Reflections of the Past (film), Can Film Awards, Niagara on the Lake, Ont, 75 & 11th Int Chicago Film Festival, Ill, 75; Pysanka: The Ukrainian Easter Egg (film), Chicago Int Film Festival, 76. *Pos:* Ed, Ukrainian, Polish & Russian Sect, Cinema & TV Digest, 63-; pres, Filmart Prod, St Paul, Minn, 71-82. *Awards:* Blue Ribbon Award for Sheep in Wood, Am Film Festival, 71; Gold Hugo for Pysanka: The Ukrainian Easter Egg, Chicago Int Film Festival, 76 & Silver Venus Medal, Virgin Islands Int Film Festival, 77; Bronze Medal for Immortal Image, Int Film & TV Festival, NY, 78. *Mem:* Minn Soc Fine Arts; Twin Cities Metrop Arts Alliance. *Mailing Add:* 200 S Winthop 199 E Annapolis St St Paul MN 55119

NOYES, DIANA H See Holmes, Wendy

NOYES, SANDY
PHOTOGRAPHER
b New York, NY, Dec 18, 41. *Study:* Yale Univ, with Bud Leak, BA, 63; with Paul Caponigro, 73 & Minor White, 74; New Sch Soc Research, with George Tice, 74. *Work:* Metrop Mus Art, New York; Bibliot Nat, Paris; Addison Gallery Am Art; High Mus Art; NJ State Mus, Trenton. *Exhib:* Two-person exhibs, Addison Gallery Am Art, 78 & Santa Fe Gallery Photog, 78; Seven Photographers, NJ State Mus, Trenton, 79; Contemporary Platinotype, Rochester Inst Technol, NY, 79; Intervals, 22 Wooster St Gallery, New York, 82; 1983 Creative Artists Pub Serv Proj Award Photogr, Nikon House, New York, 84. *Teaching:* Instr, Int Ctr Photog, New York, 76-81. *Awards:* Proj Grant for Seven Photographers Exhib, Nat Endowment Arts, 77; Ossabaw Island Proj Fel, Ga, 79; Creative Artists Pub Serv Proj Grant, 83. *Mailing Add:* RD 1 Box 183 Chatham NY 12037

NUGENT, BOB L
PAINTER, SCULPTOR
b Santa Monica, Calif, Aug 15, 47. *Study:* Col Creative Studies, Univ Calif, BFA, 69; Univ Calif, Santa Barbara, MFA(Regents Grant), 71. *Work:* Bank Am Headquarters, San Francisco, Calif; Washington State Art in Public Places, Spokane; Indianapolis Mus Art, Ind; Ariz State Univ, Tempe; Brooklyn Mus, NY. *Exhib:* One-man shows, Antiscope, Brussels, Belgium, 79; Kathryn Markel Fine Arts, New York, 80; Los Angeles Municipal Art Gallery, Calif, 80 & Tucson Mus Art, Ariz, 81; Paper Art, Smithsonian Inst, Washington DC, 80; Painting & Sculpture Today, Indianapolis Mus Art, Ind, 80. *Collections Arranged:* California Collage (auth, catalog), 81; California Clay (auth, catalog), 81; Sculpture 82 (auth, catalog); Chicago Abstract Painting (auth, catalog). *Pos:* Dir art gallery, Sonoma State Univ, Calif, 81- *Teaching:* Prof art painting, Pepperdine Univ, Calif, 73; prof art painting, Col Siskiyavs, Calif, 73-81. *Awards:* Louis Comfort Tiffany Found Fel, 77; Individual Artists Fel, Nat Endowment Arts, 79. *Media:* Mixed Media. *Publ:* Contribr, Paper Art, E B Crocker Art Mus, 80. *Mailing Add:* c/o Grapestake Gallery 2876 California Street San Francisco CA 94115

NUGENT, JOHN CULLEN
SCULPTOR, EDUCATOR
b Montreal, Que, Jan 5, 21. *Study:* St Thomas Col, St Paul, Minn, 40-41; Cost House, Calgary, Alta, 46; St John's Univ, Collegeville, Minn, 47-48. *Work:* Norman McKenzie Gallery, Regina, Sask; Can Coun Art Bank, Ottawa, Ont; Univ Sask, Saskatoon. *Comn:* Hist site sculpture, comn by Can Govt, Ft Esperance, Rocanville, Sask, 62; relief in steel, Police Bldg, Prince Albert, Sask, 65; fountain, Mid Town Centre, Regina, 67; steel sculpture, Can Govt Dept Works, Grain Comn Bldg, Winnipeg, Man, 76. *Exhib:* Christian Art Today, Toronto, Ont, 66; Waddington Gallery, Montreal, Que, 69; Outdoor Sculpture, 72, Emma Lake Exhib, 73; one-man show, 74, Norman McKenzie Gallery, Regina; Sculpture on the Prairies, Winnipeg Gallery, 77. *Teaching:* Prof sculpture, Univ Regina, Sask, 70- *Awards:* Sr Arts fel, Can Coun, 61. *Bibliog:* Troff-Swiston (film), Another Language, 73. *Mem:* Can Artists Rep; Royal Can Acad Art. *Media:* Welded Steel. *Mailing Add:* Box 24 Regina SK S0G 3C0 Canada

NUKI (DANIEL MILLSAPS)
PAINTER, WRITER
b Darlington, SC, June 30, 19. *Study:* Univ SC, AB; Art Students League, with Kuniyoshi, Sternberg, Martin Lewis & Nahum Tchbasov. *Work:* Va Mus Fine Arts, Richmond; US State Dept & Libr Cong, Washington, DC; Columbia Mus Art, SC; Berkshire Mus, Pittsfield, Mass. *Exhib:* Va Mus Fine Arts, 47; Delgado Mus, New Orleans, La, 48; Am Inst Graphic Arts, New York, 48; Univ Colo, Denver, 58; 10 yr retrospective, Columbia Mus Art, 56. *Pos:* Ed & publ, Washington Int Arts Lett, 62- *Awards:* Anthony Hampton Award, 40; Best Woodcut & Purchase Prize, Va Mus Fine Arts, 48; Am Inst Graphic Arts Award for 50 best, 48. *Media:* Mixed Media. *Res:* Patronage of the arts; government and arts relationships. *Publ:* Auth, National Directory of Grants and Aid to Individuals in the Arts, 4th ed, 80, 5th ed, 83; auth, National Directory of Arts Support by Private Foundations, Vol 4, 80, Vol 5, 83; auth, National Directory of Arts and Education Support by Business Corporations, 2nd ed, 81, 3rd ed, 84. *Mailing Add:* PO Box 9005 Washington DC 20003

NULF, FRANK ALLEN
PAINTER, EDUCATOR
b Lima, Ohio, Sept 23, 31. *Study:* Ariz State Univ, BS, 59; Mich State Univ, MA, 60; Fulbright Grant, Madrid, Spain, 62-63; Ohio Univ, PhD, 69. *Exhib:* Soc Washington Printmakers 24th Int, 62; Boston Printmakers Ann, Boston Mus Fine Arts, 65; Int Miniature Print Exhib, Assoc Am Artists Gallery, 71; Can Printmakers Showcase, Ottawa, Ont, 72; Third Int Drawing Biennale, Cleveland, United Kingdom, 77. *Teaching:* Assoc prof art, State Univ NY Col Potsdam, 60-69; prof art & dean fine arts, Univ Regina, 69- *Awards:* Can Coun Travel Grant, 77. *Mem:* Fel Royal Soc Arts; Col Art Asn Am; Univ Art Asn Can. *Res:* Film history and film criticism. *Publ:* Auth, Report on the Bergamo film festival, Vol 5, No 3, ed, Network television and the personal documentary, Vol 6, No 1 & ed, The intensification of reality, Vol 6, No 1, Film Comment; auth, Luigi Pirandello and the cinema, Film Quart, winter 70-71. *Mailing Add:* Dept of Fine Arts Univ of Regina Regina SK S4S 0A2 Canada

NUSE, OLIVER WILLIAM
PAINTER, PHOTOGRAPHER
b Oberlin, Ohio, Jan 20, 14. *Study:* Pa Acad Fine Art, BFA, 38 & MFA, 41; Univ Pa. *Work:* Philadelphia Watercolor Club in Philadelphia Mus Art, Samuel Fleischer Art Mem, Delaware Co Mus & Wm Penn Charter Sch, Philadelphia, Pa. *Comn:* Ten Sculptors, Pa Acac Fine Arts, Philadelphia, 70;

Chinese Calligraphy, Philadelphia Mus Art, Pa, 71; Moving Sculpture, comn by sculptor Hortense Baer, Philadelphia, Pa, 72. *Exhib:* Ann Butler Art Inst, Youngstown, Ohio, 59; Oil, Drawing, Watercolor, Philadelphia Art Alliance, Pa, 59 & 64; Allied Artists, Nat Acad Design, New York, 61; Ann Pa Acad Oil & Sculpture, Pa Acad Fine Arts, Philadelphia, 61; Am Watercolor Soc, Nat Acad Design, New York, 62; Bi-Annuals Print & Watercolor, Pa Acad Fine Arts, Philadelphia, 62-67; Artists Equity Regional, Philadelphia Mus Art, Pa, 66; Painters of Maine, Carnegie Gallery, Univ Maine, Orono, 76. *Teaching:* Chmn art dept studio & art hist, Wm Penn Charter Sch, 41-74; instr painting, Samuel Fleischer Art Mem, 58-65; instr filmmaking, Philadelphia Mus Art, 70-71. *Awards:* Hon Mention Watercolor, Audubon Artists, New York, 57; Philadelphia Watercolor Prize, Philadelphia Watercolor Club, 64; Harrison S Morrison Prize, H S Morrison, 66. *Mem:* Artist Equity Asn (pres, 63-64); Philadelphia Watercolor Club (pres, 64-67); Bangor Art Soc. *Media:* Acrylic, Pastel. *Mailing Add:* Box 283 A Stockton Springs ME 04981

NUSHAWG, MICHAEL ALLAN
PRINTMAKER, EDUCATOR

b Dayton, Ohio, Oct 31, 44. *Study:* Miami Univ, Ohio, BFA, 66; Ohio Univ; Univ Iowa, MFA, 70. *Work:* Honolulu Acad Arts; Joslyn Art Mus, Nebr; Dulin Gallery Art, Tenn; Midwest Mus Am Art, Ind; Des Moines Art Ctr, Iowa. *Exhib:* 21st Nat Print Exhib, Brooklyn Mus, NY, 78; 31st Nat Exhib, Boston Printmakers, Mass, 79, 82 & 83; Mus Mod Art, Parana, Brazil; World Print III, World Print Council, Calif, 80; Smithsonian Inst Traveling Exhib, 80; 15th Nat Print Exhib, Univ NY, Potsdam, 80; one-person exhib, Miriam Perlman Gallery, Chicago. *Teaching:* Assoc prof printmaking, Univ Nebr, Lincoln, 72-. *Awards:* Sunday Times Award, 79; Purchase Awards, 6th Hawaii Nat, Honolulu & Rockford Int, Ill. *Bibliog:* Janice McCullagh (auth), Six prints by Michael Nushawg, Kans Quart, Vol 14, 82. *Mem:* Col Art Asn; Philadelphia Print Club; Chicago Artists Coalition. *Media:* Etching, Miscellaneous Media. *Dealer:* Jane Haslem 2121 P St NW Washington DC 20037; Miriam Perlman 505 N Lake Shore Dr Chicago IL 60611. *Mailing Add:* 332 S Cuyler Oak Park IL 60302

NUTT, JIM (JAMES TUREMAN)
PAINTER, DRAFTSMAN

b Pittsfield, Mass, Nov 28, 38. *Study:* Wash Univ, St Louis, 58-59; Art Inst Chicgo, with Whitney Halstead & Dominic DiMeo, dipl, 65. *Work:* Whitney Mus Am Art; Mus Contemp Art, Chicago; Mus Mod Kunst, Vienna; Mus Mod Art, New York; Philadelphia Mus Art. *Exhib:* Pictures to be Read, Poetry to be Seen, Mus Contemp Art, Chicago, 67; Venice Biennale, Am Pavillion, Italy, 72; Am Exhib, Art Inst Chicago, 72 & 76; XII Bienal de Sao Paolo, Am Pavillion, Brazil, 73; Who Chicago?, Sunderland Arts Ctr, England, 80; solo exhib, Rotterdamse Kunststichting, Holland, 80; American Painting 1930-1980, Haus Kunst, Munich, Ger, 81; and others. *Teaching:* Assoc prof painting & drawing, Calif State Univ, Sacramento, 68-75. *Dealer:* Phyllis Kind Gallery 313 W Superior Chicago IL 60610. *Mailing Add:* 1035 Greenwood Ave Wilmette IL 60091

NUTZLE, FUTZIE (BRUCE JOHN KLEINSMITH)
ARTIST, CARTOONIST

b Lakewood, Ohio, Feb 21, 42. *Study:* Self-taught. *Work:* Mus Mod Art, New York; San Francisco Mus Mod Art; Oakland Mus, Calif; Santa Cruz City Mus, Calif; Whitney Mus Am Art, New York. *Exhib:* Corresp Sch Art, Whitney Mus, New York, 70; Empty Canoes, Lithographs, San Francisco Mus Mod Art, 72; Opening, Santa Cruz Artists' Mus Proj, 73; Twin Rocker Paper Exhib, Indianapolis Mus Art, Ind, 75; Caffe Pergolesi, Santa Cruz, 75-76 & 79-80; Laica, Los Angeles, 78; one-man shows, Santa Barbara Mus Art & Univ Calif, special collection, 80. *Teaching:* Artist in residence, Victor Valley Col, 83. *Bibliog:* S Subtle & B Lee (auths), My art belongs to Dada, Esquire Mag, 8/74; feature article in Quest, 6/79; Spaceco (auth), Video, 80-81. *Media:* Pen and Ink, Wash on Paper; Acrylic on Canvas. *Publ:* Contribr, Balloon Newspaper, 68-72; Rolling Stone, 75-80, San Francisco Bay Guardian, 81-83 and numerous others; contribr, Quarry West, Number 8, 77; auth, Modern Loafer (cartoons & drawings) Thames & Hudson, Inc, 81; auth & illusr, Futzie Nutzle, Jazz Press, 83. *Mailing Add:* PO Box 325 Aromas CA 95004

NYGREN, JOHN FERGUS
GLASS ARTIST

b Big Springs, Nebr, Oct 8, 40. *Study:* Univ Nebr, BFA, 65; Cranbrook Acad Art, Bloomfield Hills, Mich, MFA(ceramics), 67; Penland Sch of Crafts, spec study in glass, 68. *Work:* Corning Mus of Glass, NY; Sheldon Art Gallery, Lincoln, Nebr; Chrysler Mus, Norfolk, Va; Mint Mus Art, Charlotte, NC; Smithsonian Inst. *Exhib:* One-man show, Sheldon Art Gallery, 71; NC Glass 78, Western Carolina Univ, Cullowhee, NC, 76; Contemp Art Glass 78, Lever House, New York, 76; New Am Glass, Focus WVa, Huntington Galleries, 76; Contemp Glass: John Nygren/Flora Mace, Chrysler Mus at Norfolk, 77; and others. *Awards:* Vreeland Award, Univ Nebr, 64; Nat Merit Award, Craftsmen USA 66, Am Crafts Coun, 66; Purchase Award, NC Glass 76, NC Nat Bank, 76. *Bibliog:* Sidney Rosenblatt (auth), The Art Glass of Tomorrow-Today, Hobbies-Mag for Collectors, 3/75; John Mebane (auth), The Glass of John Nygren, Antiques J, 6/76. *Mem:* Am Crafts Coun; Glass Art Soc; Piedmont Crafts, Inc. *Dealer:* Heller Gallery 965 Madison Ave New York NY 10021. *Mailing Add:* The New Branch Walnut Cove NC 27052

O

OAKES, JOHN WARREN
PAINTER, ADMINISTRATOR

b Bowling Green, Ky, Feb 26, 41. *Study:* Art Instr Sch Minneapolis; Art Students League, New York, Albert Dorne Scholar; Western Area Voc Sch; Western Ky Univ, AB, 64; Univ Iowa, MA, 66, MFA, 73. *Work:* Numerous works in pub & pvt collections. *Exhib:* Twenty one-man shows. *Pos:* Gallery dir, Western Ky Univ Gallery, 66-, staff asst, off dean, Potter Col Arts & Humanities, 73-75; asst dean admin, 75- *Teaching:* Instr art, Western Ky Univ, 66-71; asst prof art, 71-76; assoc prof art, 76- *Mem:* Kappa Pi; Ky Alliance Arts Educ; Ky Arts Admin (pres, 82-83); Ky Art Educ Asn; Ky Citizens for Arts; and others. *Media:* Acrylic. *Dealer:* J B Speed Mus Louisville KY 40208. *Mailing Add:* c/o Ivan Wilson Ctr Fine Arts Western Ky Univ Bowling Green KY 42101

OAKES, WILLIAM LARRY
ILLUSTRATOR, EDUCATOR

b Richmond, Va, Apr 16, 44. *Study:* Univ Md, 69-70; Cornish Sch Allied Art, 64-65; Burnly Sch Art, 65-67. *Work:* US Navy Fine Art Collection, US Info Agency, Washington, DC; Libr Cong; Franklin Mint, New York; US Naval Acad, Annapolis, Md. *Comn:* Portrait, Secy of Navy, US Naval Mus, Washington, DC, 69; Court Art, Watergate Hearings, Washington Post, ABC News, Nat Geographic & Christian Sci Monitor, Washington, DC & Boston, 74. *Exhib:* Imaginations, Corcoran Gallery Art, DC, 71; Naval Hist, Navy Mus, DC, 71; Illusr 13, traveled, New York, 72 & Art Dirs' Show 50, 72; Combat Art, Salmagundi Gallery, New York, 72; Painter as Illusr, Old Town Hall Gallery, Salem, Mass, 79-80. *Teaching:* Instr art, Comt for Community Improvement, Washington, DC, 68-71; instr drawing & painting, pvt classes, Washington, DC & Boston, 71-76; dean freshman found & illus, New Eng Sch Art & Design, 76-80; instr, Art Inst Boston, 80- *Awards:* Scholar Award, Salmagundi Club, New York, 70; Award of Merit, Soc Illusr, New York, 71; Award of Excellence, Art Dirs Club, New York, 71. *Bibliog:* Peggy Thompson (auth), Pick a dot, Am Mag, 72; David Windor (auth), Morocco: a visual documentary by Bill Oakes, Christian Sci Monitor, 78; David Wiegand, (auth), Bill Oakes, Illustrator Extraordinaire, Divisions, 79. *Publ:* Auth, The Lesson Sketcher, 78, auth, Imagination 2, Cowleybinder, 80 & auth, Art by Design, 81, Acorn Press; illusr, Sound and the Fury, by Faulkner, 77 & illusr, The Plays of Shakespeare, 78-79, Franklin Libr. *Dealer:* Upstairs Gallery East St Middleton MA 01949. *Mailing Add:* 136 Main St Kingston NH 03848

O'BANION, NANCE
ASSEMBLAGE ARTIST

b June 7, 49; US citizen. *Study:* Univ Calif, Berkeley, BA, 71, MA, 73. *Work:* Seattle Art Mus; Mus Arts Decoratifs Ville Lausanne, Switz; City Palo Alto, Calif. *Comn:* Billboard (handmade paper & bamboo), City & Co San Francisco, 83. *Exhib:* Fiber Structures & Fabric Surfaces, Herron Art Gallery, Univ Ind, 79; The Art Fabric: Mainstream, San Francisco Mus Mod Art & traveling, 81; Making Paper, Am Craft Mus, New York, 82; Papier, Mus Arts Decoratifs Ville Lausanne, Switz, 83; On and Off the Wall: Shaped and Colored, Oakland Mus, 83; Papier: Un Nouveau Langage Artistique, Mus Bellerive, Zurich, 83. *Pos:* Founding staff mem, Fiberworks Ctr Textile Arts, Berkeley, 74-79. *Teaching:* Instr, Univ Calif, Davis, 72-79; assoc prof, Calif Col Arts & Crafts, 74- *Awards:* Designer Craftsman Award, Richmond Art Ctr, Calif, 73 & 75; Nat Endowment Arts Fels, 79 & 82-83. *Bibliog:* Mary Stofflet (auth), Illusions and ambiguities, Am Craft Mag, 82; Melinda Levine (auth), article, Oakland Mus Asn J, 83. *Media:* Handmade Paper and Bamboo. *Publ:* Coauth, Fiberfinder: A Guide to Bay Area Sources, Fiberworks, 77. *Mailing Add:* c/o Allrich Gallery 251 Post St San Francisco CA 94610

O'BEIL, HEDY
PAINTER, CRITIC

b New York, NY. *Study:* Art Students League, 53; Brooklyn Mus Art Sch, 58 & 59; Empire State Col, State Univ NY, BS, 77; Goddard Col, MFA, 79. *Work:* Guild Hall, Easthampton, NY; also private collections of Eva Gatling, Ruth Solomon & Therese Parkinson. *Exhib:* Long Island Painters, Guild Hall, Easthampton, NY, 69; one-person exhib, Guild Hall, Easthampton, NY, 70 & Heckscher Mus, Huntington, NY, 72; Artists of Suffolk County, Heckscher Mus, Huntington, NY, 71; Realism, Marymount Manhattan Col, 82; Contemporary Art, Philadelphia Mus Art, 82 & 83; and others. *Collections Arranged:* Contemporary Art Exhibs, Ethical Humanist Soc, 63; The Symbolic View, Soho 20 Gallery, 82. *Pos:* Critic, Arts Mag, 76- *Teaching:* Instr art, Nassau Community Col, 74; lectr, Art Ctr Northern NJ, 76-; lectr art hist, 92nd St Y, New York, 81-82. *Awards:* First Award, Long Island Artists, Hofstra Univ, 65 & Long Island Painters, Guild Hall, Easthampton, NY, 69. *Bibliog:* Silvia Tennenbaum (auth), article, Arts Mag, 76; William Zimmel (auth), article, Soho News, 79; Elaine Wechsler (auth), article, Arts Mag, 83. *Mem:* Womens Caucus Art. *Media:* Acrylic, Charcoal. *Res:* Classical and modern art history with emphasis on surrealism. *Publ:* Contribr, Beaux Arts, 70-75, Arts, 76-, Artspeak, 82 & Art Express, 83. *Dealer:* Ingber Gallery 460 W Broadway New York NY. *Mailing Add:* 45 W 86 St New York NY 11746

OBERHUBER, KONRAD J
HISTORIAN, CURATOR

b Linz, Austria, Mar 31, 35. *Study:* Univ Vienna, DrPhil, Dozent; Univ Cologne. *Pos:* Cur, Albertina, Vienna, 61-71; cur, Nat Gallery Art, Washington, DC, 71-75; cur, Fogg Art Mus, Cambridge, Mass, 75-82. *Teaching:* Instr art hist, Smith Col, 64-65, Cambridge Univ, Eng, winter 68 & Univ Vienna, fall 70 & spring 72; prof, Fogg Art Mus, Harvard Univ, spring

74 & fall 75- *Awards:* Kress Fel, I Tatti, Florence, Italy, 65-66; fel, Inst Advanced Study, Princeton Univ, 74-75; Nat Endowment Humanities Res Fel, 79-80. *Res:* Prints, drawings and paintings of the sixteenth century in Italy and the Netherlands and seventeenth century France. *Publ:* Auth, Parmigianino und Sein Kreis (catalog), 63, auth, Die Kunst der Graphik III, Renaissance in Italien, 66 & auth, Die Kunst der Graphik IV, Zwischen Renaissance und Barock, 68, Albertina; coauth, The Famous Italian Drawings of the Albertina, New York-Milan, 72; auth, Raphaels Zeichnungen, Berlin, 72; and others. *Mailing Add:* 40 Bellis Cir Cambridge MA 02140

OBLER, GERI
PRINTMAKER, GRAPHIC ARTIST
b New York, NY May 1, 42. *Study:* Pratt Inst, with Richard Lindner & Fritz Bultman, BFA, 63; Hunter Col, with Ron Gorchov, MA, 66; Columbia Univ, with Peter Golfinopolis, EdD(fine arts & fine arts educ), 74. *Work:* Berkshire Mus, Pittsfield, Mass; Univ Wyo Art Mus, Laramie; US Embassy, Nairobi, Kenya; Conf Bd, Scottish Develop Agency, New York. *Exhib:* Nat Asn Women Artists, New York Dept Cult Affairs, 81; 67th Hudson River Mus Ann, Yonkers, NY, 82; Traveling Graphics Exhib, Jesse Besser Mus, Alpena, Mich, 83; Pratt Graphics Ctr Ann, New York, 83; Hunterdon 27th Nat Print Exhib, Wallingford Art Ctr, Pa, 83. *Bibliog:* Malcolm Preston (auth), Three printmakers on display, Newsday, 6/18/79; Helen Harrison (auth), Many shades of white, New York Times, 1/11/81; Jeanne Paris (auth), A showing of Long Island's best graphics, Newsday, 10/6/81. *Mem:* Nat Asn Women Artists; Philadelphia Print Club; Graphic Eye Artists (pres, 78-80, bd dirs, 81). *Dealer:* Ars Graphica 138 Bayview Ave Port Washington NY 11050. *Mailing Add:* 26 Brokaw Lane Great Neck NY 11023

OCAMPO, MIGUEL
PAINTER
b Buenos Aires, Arg, Nov 29, 22. *Study:* Architecture. *Work:* Albright-Knox Collection, Buffalo; Mus Mod Art, New York; State Collection, France; Mus Fine Arts, Montevideo, Uruguay; Mus Fine Arts, Buenos Aires. *Exhib:* Stedelijk Mus, Amsterdam, 53; one-man shows, Mus Mod Art, Rio de Janeiro, 59, Galeria Aele, Madrid, 74 & Jacques Kaplan Gallery, NY, 75; Mus d'Art Mod, Paris, 73. *Media:* Acrylic, Oil. *Dealer:* Jacques Kaplan 19 E 71st St New York NY 10021. *Mailing Add:* 135 Hudson St New York NY 10013

OCEPEK, LOU (LOUIS DAVID)
PRINTMAKER, PAINTER
b Detroit, Mich, Aug 27, 42. *Study:* Wayne State Univ, BFA, 64; Univ Iowa, Iowa City, with Lasansky, MA, 67. *Work:* Portland Art Mus, Ore; Portland State Univ, Ore; San Diego State Univ; State Univ NY, Oswego; Western Mich Univ, Kalamazoo. *Comn:* Paintings, Metrop Arts Comn, Portland, Ore, 78 & Art Advocates Inc, Portland, Ore, 78; prints, Clairmont Hotel Collection, Berkeley, 78, Seattle Arts Comn, 80 & Wash Arts Comn, Olympia, 81. *Exhib:* Northwest Printmakers Int, Seattle Art Mus, 70; Testimony to a Process, 74 & Constructions, Drawings and Prints, 76, Portland Art Mus; 12 Northwest Artists, 77 & A Directors Choice, 81, Portland Ctr Visual Arts, 81. *Teaching:* Prof design & printmaking, Portland State Univ, 71-83; prof design & illus, Mont State Univ, Bozeman, 83- *Awards:* Purchase Awards, The Artist Teacher Today, State Univ NY, 68, San Diego State Print Exhib, 69 & Multiples USA, Western Mich Univ, 70. *Bibliog:* David Stewart (producer), Lou Ocepek, artist, teacher, eckist, ECK World News, 78. *Mem:* Northwest Print Coun (bd dirs, 83). *Media:* Silkscreen; Gouache, Acrylic. *Dealer:* Lawrence Gallery 913 SW Broadway Portland OR 97205. *Mailing Add:* 74515 Gallatin Rd Gallatin Gateway MT 59730

OCHS, ROBERT DAVID
COLLECTOR, PATRON
b Bloomington, Ill, Mar 27, 15. *Study:* Ill Wesleyan Univ, AB, 36; Univ Ill, MA, 37, PhD, 39. *Pos:* Trustee, Columbia Mus of Art, 66-69 & 74-77; chmn mus comt, Univ SC, Columbia, 74-76. *Interests:* Contemporary art. *Collection:* Contemporary paintings, prints and sculpture, including Johns, Rauschenberg and Twombly. *Publ:* Co-ed, The Columbia Art Association 1915-1975, The Columbia Museum of Art 1950-1975, A History, Columbia Mus Art, 75. *Mailing Add:* 15D Cornell Arms Columbia SC 29201

OCKENGA, STARR
PHOTOGRAPHER, EDUCATOR
b Boston, Mass, June 14, 38. *Study:* Wheaton Col, Ill, BA, 60; RI Sch Design, with Harry Callahan & Aaron Siskind, MFA, 74. *Work:* Sheldon Art Gallery, Univ Nebr; Bibliot Nat, Paris. *Exhib:* Photography as a Fine Art, William Hayes Fogg Art Mus, Harvard, 75; Addison Gallery Am Art, Mass, 76; Group Invitational, Bowling Green State Univ, Ohio, 81; one-person shows, Robert Samuel Gallery, New York, 81 & Photoworks Gallery, Boston, 81; Second Sight, Carpenter Ctr, Harvard, 81; Catskill Ctr Photog, 81; article, Mass Review, vol XXIV, no 1. *Mem:* Soc Photog Educ. *Media:* Cibachrome Prints, Polaroid Prints. *Publ:* Auth, Mirror After Mirror, Amphoto, 75; auth, Dressup, Addison House, 78. *Mailing Add:* 94 St Botolph Street Boston MA 02116

OCKERSE, THOMAS
DESIGNER, EDUCATOR
b Holland, Apr 12, 40; US citizen. *Study:* Ohio State Univ, BFA; Yale Univ, MFA; with Norman Ives, Herbert Matter, Walker Evans, Paul Rand & Alvin

Eisenman. *Work:* Mus Mod Art, New York; Stedelijk Mus, Amsterdam; Jean Brown Arch; Richard Demarco Gallery, Edinburg, Scotland; Indianapolis Mus Art. *Exhib:* Language & Structure, Kensington Arts Asn, Toronto; Int Omaha Flow Systems, Joslyn Art Mus, Omaha; Expo Int de Novisma Poesia, Inst Ditella, Buenos Aires, 69; Kronkrete Poezie, Stedelijk Mus, Amsterdam, 70; Edinburgh Festival, Richard Demarco Gallery, Scotland, 72, 74 & 75. *Teaching:* Asst prof graphic design, Ind Univ, Bloomington, 67-71; assoc prof graphic design, RI Sch Design, Providence, 71-, head graphic design dept, 73- *Awards:* 50 Best Bks, Am Inst Graphic Arts; Scottish Trust Educ Grant. *Bibliog:* J Bowles (auth), This Book is a Movie, Dell, 71; Kostelanetz (auth), Breakthrough Fictioneers, Something Else Press, 72; Camera Three (NY TV prog), 74. *Mem:* Semiotic Soc Am; Am Inst Graphic Arts; Indust Designers Soc Am; Soc Typographic Arts. *Publ:* Auth, The A-Z Book, 69, TOP, 70, TV Documentracing, 73, Time, 73 & 26 Poems, 75, pvt publ; and many others. *Mailing Add:* 37 Woodbury St Providence RI 02906

O'CONNELL, ANN BROWN
PAINTER, COLLECTOR
b Worcester, Mass, June 3, 31. *Study:* Bradford Col, AA; Boston Univ Exten; Sumi-e with Evalyn Aaron, Port Washington, NY; Chinese brush painting with Audrey Nossal, Potomac, Md; also with Roddy McLean, Annandale, Va. *Exhib:* Sumi-e Soc Am Inc Ann Exhibs; Sixth Ann Exhib, Bank of Tokyo Trust Co, New York, 69; 7th Ann Exhib, Nippon Club, New York, 70; Am Inst Architects, 79 & 80. *Awards:* President's Prize, Sumi-e Soc Am, Inc, 69. *Mem:* Sumi-e Soc Am, Inc (mem secy, 71-73, founder, Wash Chap, 72, nat vpres, 72-73, nat pres, 74-78). *Collection:* Print collection specializing in early 20th century American printmakers; 19th and early 20th American and European paintings. *Mailing Add:* 1341 Woodside Dr McLean VA 22101

O'CONNELL, EDWARD E
PHOTOGRAPHER, PRINTMAKER
b New York, NY. *Study:* Hofstra Univ, BS; Pratt Inst, MFA. *Work:* Metrop Mus Art, New York; Brooklyn Mus, NY; Philadelphia Free Libr, Pa; Univ Mass, Amherst; Univ Tenn, Knoxville; plus others. *Exhib:* Photography into Sculpture, Mus Mod Art, New York, 70; 17th Nat Print, Brooklyn Mus, 70; US Pavilion, World's Fair, Osaka, Japan, 70; New Talent in Printmaking, Am Artists, New York, 70; Oversize Prints, Whitney Mus, New York, 71. *Teaching:* Asst prof photog & graphics, Montcla Sch Visual Arts, New York, 69-71; asst prof photog & printmaking, Fordham Univ, 70- *Awards:* Found Grant in Printmaking, Louis Comfort Tiffany Found, 66; Purchase Award, Brooklyn Mus, 70. *Bibliog:* James R Mellow (auth), Contemporary prints, the medium is not the message, New York Times, 6/28/70. *Mem:* Col Art Asn Am. *Media:* Silkscreen; Acrylic. *Dealer:* Assoc Am Artists Gallery 663 Fifth Ave New York NY 10022. *Mailing Add:* 119 Spring St New York NY 10021

O'CONNELL, GEORGE D
PRINTMAKER, EDUCATOR
b Madison, Wis, Oct 16, 26. *Study:* Univ Wis, BS, 50, MS, 51; Ohio State Univ; Rijksakademie Van Beeldende Kunsten, Amsterdam, Netherlands, Fulbright fel, 59-60. *Work:* Baltimore Mus Art; Smithsonian Inst, Washington, DC; Libr Cong, Washington, DC; Gemeentemuseum Van Schone Kunsten, The Hague, Netherlands; Brit Mus, London, Eng; and others. *Comn:* Volunteer artist prog, Dept Hist Army, 71; presentation print ed, Rochester Print Club, 83. *Exhib:* Am Embassy, Dublin, Ireland; Baltimore Mus; John & Mabel Ringling Mus Art; Contemporary American Graphic Art, Corcoran Gallery Art, Washington, DC; US Info Agency Traveling Exhib Contemp Prints. *Teaching:* Assoc prof printmaking, Univ Md, 61-68; prof printmaking, State Univ NY Col Oswego, 69-, chmn dept art, 71-, grad prog dir, 73-; vis artist, Tamarind Inst, Univ NMex, 79. *Awards:* Creative Arts & Crafts Award, Univ Md, 68; Rembrandt Graphic Arts Purchase Award, Nat Print Exhib, 80. *Mem:* Boston Printmakers; Print Club, Philadelphia. *Media:* Releif, Lithography. *Mailing Add:* 39 Baylis St Oswego NY 13126

O'CONNOR, FRANCIS VALENTINE
HISTORIAN, LECTURER
b Brooklyn, NY, Feb 14, 37. *Study:* Manhattan Col, New York, BA, 59; Johns Hopkins Univ, MA, 60, PhD(art hist), 65. *Pos:* Sr vis res assoc, Nat Collection of Fine Arts, Smithsonian Inst, Washington, DC, 70-72; ed & publ, Federal Art Patronage Notes, 74-; dir, Raphael Res Enterprises, 79- *Teaching:* Jr instr art hist, Johns Hopkins Univ, 59-62, 66-67 & 70-71; lectr art hist, Univ Md, 64-66, asst prof, 66-70; instr art, Am Univ, Washington, DC, 71; adj prof, Union Grad Sch, Antioch Col, 74-78. *Mem:* Founding mem Asn Independent Hist Art (pres, 83-); Am Soc of Aesthetics; Am Studies Asn; Soc for the Arts, Relig & Contemp Cult (mem bd, 74-); Acad Independent Scholars. *Res:* Twentieth century American art; New Deal Art Projects; abstract expressionism; projected history of American mural; art of old age. *Publ:* Auth, Jackson Pollock, Mus of Mod Art, New York, 67; auth, Federal Support for the Visual Arts: The New Deal and Now, NY Graphic Soc, 69; ed, The New Deal Art Projects: An Anthology of Memoirs, Smithsonian Press, 72; ed, Art for the Millions, NY Graphic Soc, 73; coauth & co-ed (with Eugene V Thaw), Jackson Pollock: A catalogue raisonne of paintings, drawings and other works, Yale Univ, 78. *Mailing Add:* 250 E 73rd St 11C New York NY 10021

O'CONNOR, JOHN ARTHUR
PAINTER, ADMINISTRATOR
b Twin Falls, Idaho, Jan 23, 40. *Study:* Univ Calif, Davis, AB(with honors) & scholarship, 61, with Wayne Thiebaud & William T Wiley, MA, 63; San Francisco Art Inst, scholarship, with James Weeks, 61. *Work:* Ringling Mus Art, Sarasota, Fla; State Calif Collection, Sacramento; Bates Gallery, Edinboro State Col, Pa; Archives of Calif Art, Oakland Art Mus; Kemper

Gallery, Kansas City Art Inst, Mo. *Comn:* Carr Van Anda Award for New York Times, Ohio Univ, 68; triptych, comn by Mr & Mrs George Varian, Palo Alto, Calif, 71. *Exhib:* 20th Ann Nat Exhib of Prints & Drawings, Oklahoma Art Ctr, Oklahoma City, 78; 46th Southeastern Competition: Drawing, Photog & Printmaking, Southeastern Ctr Contemp Art, Winston-Salem, NC, 78; Southern Realism, Miss Mus Art, Jackson, 79; Personal Statements: Drawing, Southeastern Ctr Contemp Art, 79; Reality of Illusion, Denver Art Mus, touring; State Univ Syst Painting Fac, Visual Arts Gallery, Fla Int Univ, Miami, 80; and many other group & one-man shows. *Pos:* Dir, Art Gallery, Univ Calif, Davis, 62-63; dir, Art Gallery, Ohio Univ, 67-68; sr investr, Ctr Creative & Optimal Design, Univ Fla, 72-; dir art dept gallery, 79-80; artist in residence, Col Creative Studies, Univ Calif, Santa Barbara, 74; dir, Appalachian Ctr Crafts, Smithville, Tenn, 81-; fac prog consult, Bd Regents, State Univ System Fla, 83- *Teaching:* Instr painting & drawing, Univ Calif, Santa Barbara, 63-64; instr painting & drawing, Ohio Univ, 65-69; assoc prof painting & contemp art hist, Univ Fla, 69- *Awards:* Modular Systems Theory & Design Analysis Award, Air Force Off Sci Res, 74. *Bibliog:* Hariette von Breton (auth), O'Connor show, artforum Mag, 64. *Media:* Acrylic, Watercolor. *Publ:* Ed, Graphics 1968-Ultimate Concerns, 68; ed, David Hosteler, Yousuf Karsh, Dana Loomis, 68; coauth, Unbottle Your Creative Ideas-A Cooperative Venture of Engineering and Art, 72; contribr, A Pictorial History of the World, 75. *Dealer:* Dana Reich Gallery 278 Post St Suite 506 San Francisco CA 94108; Capricorn Galleries 4849 Rugby Ave Bethesda MD 20814. *Mailing Add:* 3144 Tipperary Dr Tallashassee FL 32308

O'CONNOR, STANLEY JAMES
HISTORIAN, EDUCATOR
Study: Cornell Univ, BA, 51, PhD, 64; Univ Va, MA, 54. *Pos:* Dir, Southeast Asia Program, Cornell Univ, 79- *Teaching:* Prof art hist, Cornell Univ, 64- *Mem:* Col Art Asn; Asn Asian Studies (SE Asia Coun, 78-81); Borneo Res Soc; Malaysian Br, Royal Asiatic Soc. *Res:* Early trade of Southeast Asia; Buddhist and Hindu art. *Publ:* Auth, Hindu Gods of Peninsular Siam, Artibus Asiae, 72; contribr, Buddhist Votive Tablest & Caves in Peninsular Siam, Nat Mus Bangkok, 74; contribr, Iron working as spiritual inquiry in Indonesia, Hist of Relig, 75; contribr, Tambralinga and the Khmer Empire, Siam Soc J, 75. *Mailing Add:* Dept of Art Hist Cornell Univ Ithaca NY 14850

O'CONNOR, THOM
PRINTMAKER
b Detroit, Mich, June 26, 37. *Study:* Fla State Univ, BA; Cranbrook Acad Art, MFA; Tamarind Printery Fel, 64; State Univ NY Res Found Fel, 65 & 72. *Work:* Mus Mod Art, New York; Whitney Mus Am Art, New York; Brooklyn Mus; Philadelphia Mus Art; Puskin Mus, Moscow. *Comn:* Witches of Salem (suite), State Coun Arts, NY, 72. *Exhib:* Brooklyn Print Ann, 68; San Diego Print Invitational, 72. *Teaching:* Prof lithography, State Univ NY Albany, 62-; vis artist, Swedish Acad Fine Arts, 78 & Cranbrook Acad Art, 81. *Awards:* Rissanen Prize, Kuopio, Finland, 83. *Dealer:* Associated American Artists 663 Fifth Ave New York NY 10002. *Mailing Add:* Moss Rd Voorheesville NY 12186

OCVIRK, OTTO G
SCULPTOR, PRINTMAKER
b Detroit, Mich, Nov 13, 22. *Study:* State Univ Iowa, BFA & MFA. *Work:* Dayton Art Inst, Ohio; Detroit Inst Art, Mich; Dayton Co, Minneapolis, Minn. *Exhib:* Walker Art Ctr, Minneapolis, Minn, 47-49; Brooklyn Nat Print, NY, 49; Northwest Printmakers, Seattle, Wash, 49; San Francisco Ann Print & Drawing, Calif, 49-50; Libr Cong Nat Print Show, Washington, DC, 50. *Teaching:* Prof art, Bowling Green State Univ, 50- *Awards:* Sculpture Exhib, Walker Art Ctr, Minneapolis, Minn, 47; Mich Artist Exhib, Hal H Smith, Detroit, 50; Broadcast Media Award, WBGU-TV, 19th Ann Broadcasters, San Francisco. *Media:* Stone; Intaglio. *Publ:* Coauth, Art Fundamentals, Theory and Practice, Brown, 60, 68, 75 & 81. *Mailing Add:* 231 Haskins St Bowling Green OH 43402

ODATE, TOSHIO
CONCEPTUAL ARTIST, INSTRUCTOR
b Tokyo, Japan, July 9, 30. *Study:* Art Sch, Tokyo, 50-54; Nat Chiba Univ, 57-58. *Work:* Rochester Mem Art Gallery, NY; Bundy Art Gallery, Waitsfield, Vt; Great Southwest Atlanta Corp, Atlanta, Ga; Brooklyn Mus, NY. *Exhib:* Waning Moos and Rising Sun--Japanese Artists, Houston Mus Art, Tex, 59; Joseph H Hirshhorn Collection, Solomon R Guggenheim Mus, New York, 63; The Artists Reality, New Sch Social Res, New York, 64; Whitney Mus Am Art Sculpture Ann, 65-66; Attitudes, Brooklyn Mus, 70. *Teaching:* Instr sculpture, Brooklyn Mus Art Sch, 61-; instr sculpture, Pratt Inst, 68-82, adj asst prof, currently; guest lectr, Denver Mus Art, 67, Univ Wis, Wausau, 68 & Univ Ky, 69. *Publ:* Contribr, Modern sculpture from the Joseph H Hirshhorn Collection, 62; contribr, Modern American sculpture, 67. *Mailing Add:* c/o Stephen Radich Gallery 56 E 11th St New York NY 10021

O'DELL, ERIN (ANNE)
PAINTER, DESIGNER
b Phoenix, Ariz, Dec 7, 38. *Study:* Moore Col Art, BFA(textile design); Ariz State Univ; also with John Pike in Mexico, Jamaica, Ireland, Italy & Guatemala. *Work:* Ariz Bank, Phoenix; Colo Nat Bank, Colorado Springs; First Nat Bank, Mesa, Ariz; Valley Nat Bank, Scottsdale & Mesa, Ariz. *Exhib:* Two Flags Festival Arts, Douglas, Ariz, 73-79; Dagres Gallery Watercolor Show, Phoenix, 75; Phippen-O'Brien Gallery Watercolor Show, Scottsdale, 75; Laramie Nat Miniature Show, 78 & 79; Ariz State Fair, 81; and others. *Pos:* Designer, Henry Cantor, Inc, Philadelphia, Pa, 61-64; free lance designer, C A Reed Co, Williamsport, Pa & Beach Prod, Kalamazoo, Mich, 64-75; artist, Modern Color Printing, Mesa, 69-74. *Teaching:* Instr hist

textiles, Moore Col Art, 63-65. *Awards:* Mesa Artist of the Year, Mesa Art League, 73 & 79; Watercolor Award, Douglas Art Asn, 73; Artist of the Year, Ariz Saguaro Artists League, 77. *Mem:* Southwestern Watercolor Soc; Scottsdale Artists League; Midwest Watercolor Soc; Mesa Art League; Ariz Artists Guild. *Media:* Watercolor. *Mailing Add:* 938-D North Orange St Mesa AZ 85201

O DONOHUE, TEIGE ROS
PAINTER, PRINTMAKER
b New York, NY, Apr 15, 42; US & Irish citizen. *Study:* City Univ New York, with Arun Bose, BFA(cum laude), MFA(summa cum laude). *Work:* Art Inst Chicago; Brooklyn Mus; Hugh Lane Municipal Gallery, Dublin, Ireland; Nat Collection Fine Arts, Washington, DC; Tate Gallery, London. *Exhib:* Nat Arts Club, New York, 76; Hudson River Mus, Yonkers, NY, 77; Magic Realism, Utah Mus Fine Art, traveling, 79-81; Gallery Mod Art, Ljubljana, Yugoslavia, 79 & 81; Art Inst Chicago, 80-81. *Bibliog:* William Zimmer (auth), article, Arts Mag, 2/76. *Media:* Oil, Mixed Media; Etching, Aquatint. *Dealer:* Vorpal Gallery 465 W Broadway New York NY 10013. *Mailing Add:* 228 Twin Lane E Wantagh NY 11793

OECHSLI, KELLY
ILLUSTRATOR
b Butte, Mont, Feb 23, 18. *Study:* Cornish Sch of Art, Seattle, Washington, cert. *Awards:* Ann Children's Picture Storybook Award, Univ Ga, 83. *Media:* Multimedia. *Publ:* Illusr, Old Mother Hubbard, Random House, 80; illusr, Too Many Monkeys, Western Publ, 80; illusr, Herbie's Troubles, Dutton, 80; illusr, Red and the Pumpkins, Muppet Press, 83; auth & illusr, Home Sweet Home, Carnival Press, 83; and others. *Mailing Add:* 115 Sherman Ave Hawthorne NY 10532

OEHLSCHLAEGER, FRANK J
DEALER
b Paducah, Ky, Sept 8, 10. *Study:* Cornell Univ, grad, 33. *Pos:* Dir, Chicago Galleries of Assoc Am Artists, 45-47; dir, Marshall Fields & Co Art Gallery, Chicago, 47-49; dir & owner, Oehlschlaeger Gallery, Chicago, 49-, Sarasota, Fla, 62- *Specialty:* Contemporary American and European art. *Mailing Add:* PO Box 6108 Sarasota FL 33578

OENSLAGER, DONALD MITCHELL
STAGE DESIGNER
b Harrisburg, Pa, Mar 7, 02. *Study:* Harvard Univ, AB, 23; Sachs Fine Arts Traveling Fel; also with George Pierce Baker, Denman Ross & Maurice Sterne; Colo Col, Hon DFA, 53. *Work:* Metrop Mus Art & Mus Mod Art, New York; Boston Mus Fine Arts; Detroit Inst Arts; Mus of City of New York. *Comn:* Designed over 250 theatrical productions in New York, 26-75; consult on 15 new theatres incl Lincoln Ctr, Kennedy Ctr & Albany South Mall. *Exhib:* One-man exhibs, Marie Sterner Galleries, 36, Feragil Galleries, 49, Yale Gallery Fine Arts, 49, Detroit Inst Arts, 56 & Am Fedn Arts Traveling Exhib, 57. *Pos:* Trustee, Brooklyn Mus & Pratt Inst; pres, Art Comn City New York, 65-75; trustee, Mus of City of New York, 64-75. *Teaching:* Prof stage design, Sch Drama, Yale Univ, 25-70, emer prof, 70-; lectr theatre, Salzburg Sem Am Studies, 68 & 71; prof theatre, Grad Ctr, City Univ New York, 71-72. *Awards:* Pa Ambassador Award, State of Pa, 50; Antonette Perry Award, Am Theatre Wing, 58-59. *Mem:* Am Fedn Arts; Brooklyn Inst Arts & Sci; Benjamin Franklin fel Royal Soc Arts; Int Exhibs Found. *Collection:* Books, drawings and manuscripts of the 16th to 20th century American theatre. *Publ:* Auth, Scenery, then and now, 36; ed, Notes on scene painting, 52. *Mailing Add:* 825 Fifth Ave New York NY 10021

OESTERLE, LEONHARD FRIEDRICH
SCULPTOR, INSTRUCTOR
b Bietigheim, Ger, Mar 3, 15; Can citizen. *Study:* With Fritz Wotruba, Otto Muller & Hans Aeschbacher, Kunst Gewerbeschule, Zurich, Switz. *Work:* Württembergischer Kunstverein, Staats Gallery, Stuttgart, Ger; Nat Gallery, Ottawa, Can; London Art Gallery, Ont; Kitchener Waterloo Art Gallery, Can. *Comn:* Four figure group in bronze, Col McLaughlin Collegiate, Oshawa, 63; bronze statuary, St Augustin Chapel, Scarborough, Can, 64; wall sculpture & mural, Cent Labs, Toronto, 67; sculpture in lobby, Can Trust Bldg, London, Ont, 69; large sculpture for park, Sarnia, Ont, 79. *Exhib:* Young Sculptor's Exhib, Helmhaus, Zurich, 49; Schwebische Maler und Bildhauer, Zurich, 51. *Teaching:* Instr sculpture, Ont Col Art. *Awards:* Ont Soc Artists Spec Award, 68. *Bibliog:* John Sommer (auth), Leonhard Oesterle, Peter Shore, 11/71. *Mem:* Sculptor's Soc Can (vpres, 58 & 70-72); Ont Soc Artists; Royal Can Acad Arts. *Media:* Stone, Diverse Metals. *Dealer:* Sussex Gallery 515 Sussex Dr Ottawa ON Can; Del Bello Gallery 307 Queen St W Toronto ON Canada M5V 2A4. *Mailing Add:* 27 Alcina Ave Toronto ON M6G 2E7 Canada

OFFIN, CHARLES Z
COLLECTOR, CRITIC
b New York, NY, Feb 5, 1899. *Study:* City Col New York; Nat Acad Design; Art Students League; Ecole des Beaux-Arts, Fontainebleau, France. *Work:* Metrop Mus Art, Mus Mod Art, New York; Princeton Univ Art Mus; Univ Notre Dame Art Gallery; Univ Calif, Berkeley, Art Gallery. *Exhib:* One-man shows, Paris, Barcelona, Spain & New York. *Pos:* Art critic, Brooklyn Eagle, 33-36; ed & publ, Pictures on Exhibit, 37-; pres & treas, Charles Z Offin Art Fund. *Teaching:* Instr, City Col New York, 32-35. *Collection:* Twentieth century European art. *Mailing Add:* 30 E 60th St New York NY 10022

OFFNER, ELLIOT
SCULPTOR, PRINTMAKER
b Brooklyn, NY, July 12, 31. *Study:* Cooper Union; Yale Univ, with Josef Albers & Rico Lebrun, BFA & MFA. *Work:* Brooklyn Mus; De Cordova Mus, Lincoln, Mass; Lowe Art Mus, Syracuse Univ; Metrop Mus Art, New York; Joseph Hirshhorn Mus. *Comn:* Eight hammered bronze sculpture, Kehilleth Israel, Brookline, Mass, 59; Ten Commandments (bronze facade sculpture), B'Nai Israel, Northampton, Mass, 63; ten bronze plaques, Veda, Inc, Arlington, Va; pub sculptures: Holocaust Mem Figure (bronze), Cathedral St John The Divine, New York, 78; Cockerell (bronze), Springfield, Mass, 81. *Exhib:* One-man shows, Forum Gallery, New York, 64, 67, 72 & 79, Int Fine Arts Galleries, Washington, DC, 68, 73 & 79, Slater Mem Mus, Norwich, Conn, 76, Boston Atheneum, 79, Jorgensen Gallery, Univ Conn, 80 & Springfield Mus Fine Arts, 84; and other one-man and group shows. *Pos:* Dir, Rosemary Press, 67- *Teaching:* Instr art, Univ Mass, 59-60; prof art, Smith Col, 60-74, Andrew W Mellon prof humanities, 74- *Awards:* Tiffany Found Grants, 64 & 65; Nat Coun Arts & Humanities Grant, 67; Ingram Merril Found grant, 71; plus others. *Bibliog:* Cathedral's death camp sculpture, One World, 9/78; Other's dimensions, Valley Advocate, 5/23/79; The sculpture of Elliot Offner, Hampshire Life, 5/26/79. *Mem:* Printing Hist Soc; William Morris Soc; Am Printing Hist Asn; Bibliog Soc. *Media:* Wood, Bronze; Mixed. *Publ:* Auth & illusr, The Granjon Arabesque, Rosemary Press, 69. *Dealer:* Forum Gallery 1018 Madison Ave New York NY 10021. *Mailing Add:* 74 Washington Ave Northampton MA 01060

OGILVIE, WILL (WILLIAM ABERNETHY)
PAINTER
b Cape Province, SAfrica, Mar 30, 01; Can citizen. *Study:* With Erich Mayer, Johannesburg, SAfrica; Art Students League, with Nicolaides. *Work:* Nat Gallery Can, Ottawa; Art Gallery of Ontario, Toronto; Art Gallery, London; Art Gallery, Hamilton; Winnipeg Art Gallery. *Comn:* Mural, Chapel of Hart House, Univ Toronto, 36, stained glass windows in Massey Mem, 69. *Exhib:* Nat Gallery Can, Ottawa; Art Gallery Ont, Toronto; Tate Gallery, London, 38; War Art, Nat Gallery, London, 44; UNESCO, 46. *Pos:* Official Can war artist, 42-46. *Teaching:* Dir drawing & painting, Montreal Mus Fine Arts, 37-41; instr painting & murals, Ont Col Art, Toronto, 47-55; spec lectr hist techniques painting, Univ Toronto, 59-68. *Awards:* Mem Order Brit Empire; Can Coun Fel, Italy, 57-58; Order of Can. *Mem:* Royal Can Acad; Can Group Painters; Can Soc Painters in Watercolour. *Mailing Add:* 70 Heath St W Apt 212 Toronto ON M4V 1T4 Canada

OGINZ, RICHARD
SCULPTOR, INSTRUCTOR
b Philadelphia, Pa, Feb 7, 44. *Study:* Tyler Sch Art, Temple Univ, BFA, 66; Univ Wis-Madison, MA, MFA, 68. *Work:* Los Angeles Co Mus Art, Calif; Arts Coun Gt Brit, London; Bradford Mus, Yorkshire; London Borough of Camden, Eng. *Exhib:* Ellie Blankfort Gallery, Los Angeles, 77; Newcomers, Munic Art Gallery, Barnsdal Park, Los Angeles, 78; Molly Barnes Gallery, Los Angeles, 80; Arco Ctr Visual Art, Los Angeles, 83; Edge Gallery, Fullerton, Calif, 83. *Pos:* Bd dirs, Los Angeles Contemp Exhibs. *Teaching:* Principal lectr sculpture, Middlesex Polytech, London, 74-76; instr sculpture, Otis Art Inst Parsons Sch Design, Los Angeles, 76- *Awards:* Gregory fel, Leeds Univ, Yorkshire, Eng, 70-73; Ann Purchase Award, Los Angeles Co Mus Art, 79; Ford Found Grant, 79. *Media:* Mixed Media. *Mailing Add:* 4721 Washington Blvd Los Angeles CA 90016

O'GORMAN, JAMES FRANCIS
HISTORIAN
b St Louis, Mo, Sept 19, 33. *Study:* Washington Univ, Mo, BArch; Univ Ill, Urbana, MArch; Harvard Univ, PhD. *Teaching:* Grace Slack McNeil Prof of Am Art, Wellesley Col, 75- *Mem:* Soc of Archit Historians (pres, 70-72); Col Art Asn; Victorian Soc in Am. *Res:* American art and architecture. *Publ:* Auth, The Architecture of the Monastic Library in Italy, NY Univ Press, 72; coauth, The Architecture of Frank Furness, Philadelphia Mus of Art, 73; auth, H H Richardson and His Office: Selected Drawings, Harvard Col, 74; auth, This Other Gloucester, pvt publ, 76. *Mailing Add:* Dept of Art Wellesley Col Wellesley MA 02181

O'HANLON, RICHARD E
SCULPTOR, PAINTER
b Long Beach, Calif, 1906. *Study:* Santa Barbara Art Sch, Calif; Calif Col Arts & Crafts; Calif Sch Fine Arts; pvt study in Europe, Near East, India, Japan & Mex. *Work:* Worcester Mus Art, Mass; Walker Art Ctr, Minneapolis; Smith Col Collection; Chicago Art Inst; Oakland Mus Art, Calif; plus others. *Comn:* Black granite sculpture, Mill Valley Pub Libr, 66; Clark Kerr Award Gold Medallion, Univ Calif, Berkeley, 67; granite sculpture, San Rafael, Calif, 73; granite sculpture, Oakland Mus Art, 74; granite sculpture, Lawrence Hall Sci, Univ Calif, Berkeley, 77; plus others. *Exhib:* Whitney Mus Am Art Ann, New York, 48; Critics Choice Exhib, New York, 50; San Francisco Art Asn Ann, 50-71; Sao Paulo Biennial, Brazil, 55; Retrospective, San Francisco Mus Art, 61; one-man shows, Carnegie Inst, Pittsburgh, 67 & Santa Barbara Mus Art, 69. *Teaching:* Prof sculpture, Univ Calif, Berkeley, 48-74, emer prof, 74- *Awards:* First Prize for Sculpture, San Francisco Art Asn, 58. *Bibliog:* A Frankenstein (auth), Sculpture of Richard O'Hanlon, Mag Art, 48. *Mem:* San Francisco Art Inst (bd dirs, 50-62). *Media:* Stone, Bronze. *Dealer:* Brook House Gallery Orinda Calif 94563. *Mailing Add:* 616 Throckmorton Ave Mill Valley CA 94941

O'HARA, SHEILA MARY
WEAVER, DESIGNER
b Kobe, Japan, Dec 29, 53; US citizen. *Study:* Philadelphia Col Art, Pa, fall 74; Calif Col Arts & Crafts, Oakland, with Trudi Guermonprez & Kay Sekimachi, BFA(with distinction), 76. *Work:* AT&T, Richmond, Va; Bank Am, San Francisco; Crocker Bank, San Francisco, Los Angeles & Sacramento; Cyclotron Corp, Berkeley, Calif; Dean Witter, San Francisco. *Comn:* Treesweet Orange Juice, Miami, Fla, 79; Crocker Bank, Walnut Creek, Calif, 80; InterWest Partners, San Francisco, 81; Mesa Engineering, Petaluma, Calif, 81; Reid & Reige, Hartford, Conn. *Exhib:* Three Weavers, Fogelson Art Ctr, Col Santa Fe, 80; Statement II, Following Sea Gallery, Honolulu, 81; 28th Ann Designer Craftsmen, Richmond Art Ctr, Calif, 81; solo exhib, Mod Master Tapestries, New York, 82; two-person show, Mattingly-Baker Gallery, Dallas, 83; and others. *Teaching:* Lectr, Pac Basin Sch Textile Arts & Calif Col Arts & Crafts; instr, Fiberworks, Ctr Textile Arts. *Awards:* Fourth Place, 78 & First Place, 80, Calif State Expos. *Bibliog:* Teliha Draheim (auth), Sheila O'Hara: Triangles, squares and other landmarks, Interweave Loveland Co, winter 80; Kathleen Rowley (auth), Sheila O'Hara: Geometrics, Shuttle Spindle & Dyepot, fall 81; Betty Park (auth), Sheila O'Hara: Wry humor & virtuoso weaving, Fiberarts, 1/2/83. *Media:* Wool, Rayon. *Dealer:* Suzy Locke & Assocs 201 Estates Piedmont CA 94610; Mod Mastern Tapestries Inc 11 E 57th St New York NY 10022. *Mailing Add:* 2562 26th Ave San Francisco CA 94116

O'HARE, BERTA MARGOULIES See Margoulies, Berta

OHASHI, YUTAKA
PAINTER
b Kure City, Japan, Aug 19, 23. *Study:* Tokyo Acad Fine Art, Japan, BFA, 46; Sch Mus Fine Arts, Boston, 50-55. *Work:* Mus Fine Arts, Boston; Solomon R Guggenheim Mus, New York; Nat Mus Mod Art, Tokyo; Addison Gallery Am Art, Andover, Mass; Art Gallery, Yale Univ. *Exhib:* Carnegie Inst Int, Pittsburgh, 59; Summer Selection, 1962, Solomon R Guggenheim Mus, 62; Japanese Artists Abroad, Nat Mus Mod Art, Tokyo, 65; A Painter-A Potter, Montclair Art Mus, NJ, 70; Ohashis, Boston Athenaeum Gallery, 75; Art in Transition, Mus Fine Arts, Boston, 77; Half Century of Japanese Artist in New York, Azuma Gallery, 77; Salon de Tokyo, Japan, 81; and others. *Teaching:* Vis lectr critics, painting & design, Col Archit, Cornell Univ, 61, vis lectr, Col Human Ecol, 67 & 69. *Awards:* William Page Traveling Scholar, Mus Fine Arts, Boston, 56-57; Guggenheim Fel, 59-60. *Media:* Collage, Acrylic. *Mailing Add:* 5 Great Jones St New York NY 10012

OHE, KATIE (MINNA)
SCULPTOR, INSTRUCTOR
b Peers, Alta, Can, Feb 18, 37. *Study:* Alta Col Art, dipl(fine arts); Montreal Sch Art & Design, with Dr Lismer; Sculpture Ctr, New York, with Sahl Swarz & Dorothy Denslow. *Work:* Can Coun Art Banks, Ottawa, Ont Alta Art Found, Edmonton; Visual Arts, Cult Activities, Edmonton; Shell Can Art Collection, Calgary; Alta Col of Art. *Comn:* Michael the Archangel (cast stone sculpture relief), Church, Calgary, Alta, 64; cast stone sculpture fountain, City of Calgary, 66; chromed steel sculpture, Univ Calgary, 67 & 75; cast stone sculpture relief, Fed Western Regional Bldg, Calgary, 67; bronze sculpture, Sch Bd, City of Calgary, 75. *Exhib:* Sculpture Ctr, New York, 62-70; Brit Int Print Show, London, Eng, 71; Venice Biennial, Italy, 72; Alta Art Found Traveling Exhib, Can House Gallery, London, Brussels, Paris & New York, 75-76; Changes: 11 Artists Working on the Prairies Traveling Exhib, 75-76; and many other group & one-man shows. *Teaching:* Instr sculpture, Mt Royal Col, Calgary, 70-, Alta Col Art, Calgary, 70- & Univ Calgary, 79. *Awards:* Nat Gallery Study Grant, 58; Can Coun Grants, New York, 63, Europe, 68 & Verona, 74. *Bibliog:* Clement Greenburg (auth), View of art on the prairies, Can Art, 63; Anita Aarons (auth), Allied Art Catalogue, Vol 2, Arts and Architecture, Royal Archit Inst Can, 68; Barb Kwasney (auth), Canadian Golden West, Western Artist, Spring 76. *Mem:* Royal Can Acad Arts; Alta Soc Artists. *Media:* Multimedia. *Mailing Add:* c/o KO Arts Ltd Box 10/Site 27/RR12 Calgary AB T3E 6W3 Canada

OHLSON, DOUGLAS DEAN
PAINTER, EDUCATOR
b Cherokee, Iowa, Nov 18, 36. *Study:* Univ Minn, BA, 61. *Work:* Corcoran Gallery Art, Washington, DC; Mus Purchase Fund Collection, Am Fedn Arts; Minneapolis Inst Art; Dallas Mus Fine Art; Metrop Mus Art, New York; and others. *Exhib:* Art of the Real: USA 1948-1968, Mus Mod Art, New York, 68-69; Structure of Color, Whitney Mus Am Art, New York, 71; American Art Since 1960, Art Mus, Princeton Univ, 70; The Way of Color, 33rd Biennial Exhib, Corcoran Gallery Art, Washington, DC, 73; 14 Abstract Painters, Wight Gallery, Univ Calif, Los Angeles, 75; and others. *Teaching:* Prof art, Hunter Col, 64- *Awards:* Guggenheim Fel, 68; Nat Endowment Arts, 76. *Bibliog:* G Battcock (ed), Minimal Art (critical anthology), Dutton, 68; Britannica Encyl Am Art, Simon & Schuster, 73; Carter Ratcliff (auth), Doug Ohlson's color condensations, Art in Am, 5-6/78; and others. *Media:* Oil. *Dealer:* Susan Caldwell Gallery 383 W Broadway New York NY 10012. *Mailing Add:* 35 Bond St New York NY 10012

OHNO, MITSUGI
GLASSBLOWER
b Tochigi, Japan, June 28, 26; US citizen. *Work:* Smithsonian Inst, Washington, DC; Independence Hall, White House, 72; US Capitol, 75; Anderson Hall, Kans State Univ, 77; Dwight D Eisenhower Libr. *Comn:* Ohno Klein Bottle, Smithsonian Inst, Washington DC, 75, given to Emperor

of Japan, 79. *Pos:* Full-time technician, Kans State Univ. *Awards:* Yoshikawa-Eiji Prize for Cult Merit, Tokyo, Japan, 79; Walter E Morrison Award, Kans State Univ, 79. *Mailing Add:* 2808 Nevada St Manhattan KS 66502

OHRBACH, JEROME K
COLLECTOR
b New York, NY, Dec 17, 07. *Study:* Cornell Univ, AB, 29. *Collection:* Impressionist and post-impressionist art and sculpture. *Mailing Add:* 5 W 34th St New York NY 10001

OI, MOTOI
PAINTER, INSTRUCTOR
b Osaka, Japan, Nov 4, 10; US citizen. *Study:* Pac Fine Art Col, Tokyo, dipl, 28. *Work:* Metrop Mus Art, New York; Nat Gallery Art, Washington, DC; Philadelphia Mus Art; Cincinnati Art Mus; Nagaoka Mus Mod Art, Japan. *Comn:* Indust map mural, Foreign Dept of Govt, Tokyo, 50; indust map mural, Yokohama Expo, Japan, 51. *Exhib:* Nippon Bijutsuten, Japanese Govt, 36-38 & 50; Int Exhib, Educ Dept of Govt, Japan, 38; Ann exhib, Lincoln Ctr Plaza, New York, 82 & 83. *Pos:* Founder & chmn, Oi's Sch Japan-Am Sumi-e Club Inc. *Teaching:* Instr painting, Queens Col, City Univ New York, 60-72; instr painting, Brooklyn Inst Art & Sci, 67-78. *Awards:* Rising Sun, Emperor Japan, 81. *Bibliog:* Fusetsu Nakamura (auth), Upset hat, Educ Art, Japan, 38. *Media:* Sumi-e Ink. *Publ:* Auth, Sumi-e Painting & Life, 58; auth, Step by Step in Sumi-e Painting (7 vols), 58-62; auth, Brush Strokes in Sumi-e Painting, 63-; auth, Work by Motoi Oi, 65; auth, Suiboku Landscape, 68, and others. *Mailing Add:* 24-50 95th St East Elmhurst NY 11369

OKAMURA, ARTHUR
PAINTER
b Long Beach, Calif, Feb 24, 32. *Study:* Art Inst Chicago, scholar, 50-54; Univ Chicago, 51 & 53; Yale Univ Summer Art Sem, 54; Edward L Ryerson Travel Fel, 54; Univ Chicago, 57. *Work:* Corcoran Gallery Art, Washington, DC; Nat Collection Fine Arts, Smithsonian Inst; Nat Inst Arts & Lett; Hirshhorn Mus, Washington, DC; San Francisco Mus Art, Calif; and others. *Exhib:* Painters Behind Painters, Calif Palace Legion Honor, San Francisco, 67; one-man shows, San Francisco Mus Art, 68, Calif Col Arts & Crafts, 72, Southern Idaho Col, 72, Kent State Univ, Ohio, 73 & Honolulu Acad Arts, 73; Takashima 1970 Expos, Osaka, Tokyo, Japan, 70; Asian Artists, Oakland Mus, 71; and others. *Pos:* Dir, San Francisco Studio Art, 58. *Teaching:* Instr, Cent YMCA Col, Chicago, 56 & 57; instr, Evanston Art Ctr, Ill, 56 & 57; instr, Art Inst Chicago, 57; instr, NShore Art League, Winnetka, Ill, 57; instr, Acad Art, San Francisco, 57; instr, Calif Sch Fine Arts, San Francisco, 58; prof, Calif Col Arts & Crafts, 58, 59 & 66-83; instr, Saugatuck Summer Art Sch, Mich, 59 & 62; guest lectr, Univ Utah, 64 & 75. *Awards:* Schwabacher-Frey Award, 79th Ann, San Francisco Mus, 60; Neysa McMein Purchase Award, Whitney Mus Am Art, 60; Purchase Award, Nat Soc Arts & Lett; plus many others. *Bibliog:* Lee Nordness (ed), Art: USA: Now, C J Bucher, 62. *Mem:* Am Fedn Arts. *Dealer:* Ruth Braunstein Gallery 254 Sutter St San Francisco CA 94108. *Mailing Add:* 210 Kale St Bolinas CA 94924

O'KEEFFE, GEORGIA
PAINTER
b Sun Prairie, Wis, Nov 15, 1887. *Study:* Art Inst Chicago, with John Vanderpoel, 05-06; Art Students League, with William M Chase, 07-08; Univ Va, with Alon Bement, summer 12; Columbia Univ, with Arthur Dow & Alon Bement, 14-16; Mills Col, 52; Randolph-Macon Women's Col, 66; hon DFA, William & Mary Col, 38, Univ NMex, 64, Brown Univ, 71 & Minneapolis Col Art & Design, 72; hon LittD, Univ Wis, 42 & Mt Holyoke Col, 71; hon LHD, Columbia Univ, 71. *Work:* Metrop Mus Art; Mus Mod Art; Whitney Mus Am Art; Brooklyn Mus; Art Inst Chicago; and others. *Exhib:* One-man retrospectives, Art Inst Chicago, 43, Mus Mod Art, 46, Worcester Mus Art, 60, Amon Carter Mus, Ft Worth, Tex, 66, Mus Fine Arts Houston, 66 & Whitney Mus Am Art, 70; Guggenheim Mus, New York; plus many others. *Teaching:* Supvr art, Amarillo Pub Schs, Tex, 13-16; instr art, Univ Va, summers 13-16; head dept art, WTex Normal Col, Canyon, 16-18. *Awards:* Gold Medal for Painting, Nat Inst Arts & Lett, 70; M Carey Thomas Award, Bryn Mawr Col, 71, Edward MacDowell Medal, 72; and others. *Bibliog:* Barbara Rose (auth), Georgia O'Keeffe's late paintings, Artforum, 11/70; and others. *Mem:* Nat Inst Arts & Lett; Am Acad Arts & Lett; Am Acad Arts & Sci. *Publ:* Auth, The Work of Georgia O'Keeffe (portfolio of 12 paintings), 37; auth, Georgia O'Keeffe Drawings (ltd ed of 10 drawing reproductions signed & numbered by artist), 68; auth, Georgia O'Keeffe, Viking Press, 76; Georgia O'Keeffe--A Portrait by Alfred Stieglitz, Metropolitan Museum Art, New York, catalogue, Viking Press, 79. *Mailing Add:* Abiquiu NM 87510

OKOSHI, EUGENIA SUMIYE
PAINTER, PRINTMAKER
b Seattle, Wash. *Study:* St Margaret & Futaba Col, Tokyo; Seattle Univ, with Fay Chang & Nicholas Damascus; Henry Frye Mus Sch & New Sch Workshop. *Work:* Miami Mus Mod Art; Lowe Gallery, Univ Miami; Nat Women Educ Ctr, Japan. *Exhib:* Japanese Artists Exhibs, Japan & USA, 76-81; Hudson River Mus, Yonkers, NY, 77; Metrop Mus Art, New York, 77; Tokyo-To Nat Mus, Japan, 79; Newark Mus, NJ, 83; Bergen Mus Art & Sci, NJ, 83. *Media:* Oil, Acrylic; Woodcut, Etching. *Mailing Add:* Westbeth Studio G226 463 West St New York NY 10014

OKULICK, JOHN A
SCULPTOR
b New York, NY, Mar, 1947. *Study:* Univ Calif, Santa Barbara, BA; Univ Calif, Irvine, MFA. *Exhib:* Options, Cincinnati, Ohio, 73; Nancy Hoffman

Gallery, New York, 73-75, 77-79 & 83; Phyllis Kind Gallery, Chicago, 76; Asher/Faure Gallery, 80 & 83; John Berggruen Gallery, 83. *Bibliog:* B Smith (auth), Illusion & substance, ArtWeek, 73; J Russell (auth), John Okulick/ Carlos Villa, NY Times, 75. *Dealer:* Nancy Hoffman 429 W Broadway New York NY 10012; Asher/Faure Gallery 612 N Almont Dr Los Angeles CA 90069. *Mailing Add:* 706 Marine Santa Monica CA 90405

OKUMURA, LYDIA
PAINTER
b Sao Paulo, Brazil. *Study:* Fac Plastic Arts, Armando Alvares Penteado Found, Sao Paulo, Brazil, BFA, 73; Pratt Graphics Ctr, New York, 74-77. *Work:* Metrop Mus Art, New York; Hara Mus Contemp Art, Tokyo; Pinacotheca of State, Sao Paulo, Brazil; Mus Mod Art, Bogota, Colombia. *Exhib:* Solo exhibs in Sao Paulo, Tokyo, Osaka & New York, 68-83; Sao Paulo Biennial, Brazil, 73, 77, 79 & 83; Graphic Biennials, Europe, 76-82; Recent Acquisitions, Metrop Mus Art, New York, 79; Cranbrook Acad Art Mus, Bloomfield Hills, Mich, 79; Atlantic Capital Corp, NY, 81; Biennial Art, Medellin, Colombia, 81; Nat Mus Osaka, Japan, 81; and others. *Awards:* Creative Artists Pub Serv Prog Graphic grant, 78; Japan Found fel, 79; Norway Graphic Biennial, 80. *Bibliog:* Barbara Rose (auth), Environmental art, Vogue, 4/79; L G Redstone (auth), Public Art, New Directions, McGraw-Hill, 80; Deborah Phillips (auth), article, Art News, 82. *Publ:* Coauth, Dialogue with the contemporary, Mizue Mag, No 904, Tokyo, 80. *Dealer:* Condeso & Lawler Gallery 119 West 25th St New York NY 10001. *Mailing Add:* 114 Franklin St New York NY 10013

OLDENBURG, CLAES THURE
SCULPTOR
b Stockholm, Sweden, Jan 28, 29. *Study:* Yale Univ, BA, 51; Art Inst Chicago, 52-54. *Work:* Albright-Knox Art Gallery, Buffalo; Mus Mod Art, New York; Art Gallery Ont, Toronto; Art Inst Chicago; Whitney Mus Am Art, New York; plus many others. *Comn:* Sculptures, Oberlin Col, Ohio, 70, City St Louis, Mo, 71, Morse Col, Yalc Univ, 74, Walker Art Ctr, Minneapolis, 74 & Hirshhorn Mus, Washington, DC, 75; plus others. *Exhib:* Metrop Mus Art, New York, 69; Retrospective, Mus Mod Art, New York, 69, Pasadena Art Mus, Calif, 71, Walker Art Ctr, 75 & Kunsthalle, Tubingen, WGer, 75; Los Angeles Co Mus Art, Los Angeles, 71; Expo 70, Osaka, Japan; Documenta, Kassel, WGer, 72; Seattle Art Mus, Wash, 73; Am Pop Art, Whitney Mus Am Art, 74; Newport Art Mus, RI, 74; plus many other group & one-man shows. *Bibliog:* Barbara Rose (auth), Claes Oldenburg, Mus Mod Art, 70; Ellen Johnson (auth), Claes Oldenburg, Penguin, 71; articles in Art in Am, 5/74 & 9/74. *Publ:* Auth, Store Days, Something Else Press, 68; auth, Notes in Hand, Dutton & Petersburg, 71; auth, Object into monument, Pasadena Art Mus, 71. *Mailing Add:* 556 Broome St New York NY 10013

OLDENBURG, RICHARD ERIK
MUSEUM DIRECTOR
b Stockholm, Sweden, Sept 21, 33; US citizen. *Study:* Harvard Col, AB, 54. *Pos:* Dir publ, Mus Mod Art, New York, 69-72, dir mus, 72- *Mailing Add:* 11 W 53rd St New York NY 10019

OLDHAM, BERTON JEPSEN
PRINTMAKER, INSTRUCTOR
b Ross, Calif, Oct 23, 25. *Study:* San Francisco City Col, AA; Univ Calif, Berkeley, BA & MA. *Comn:* Hist bas-relief for freeway overpass, Cal-Trans, Redding, Calif, 73. *Exhib:* California Printmakers, Calif Palace Legion Honor, San Francisco, 71; San Francisco Bay Area Print Exhib, Cincinnati, Ohio, 72; 5th & 6th Ann Printmaking West, Utah State Univ, 74 & 75; Graphics Gallery, San Francisco, 74. *Teaching:* Instr art, Shasta Col, 55- *Mem:* Valley Art Ctr, Walnut Creek, Calif; Northern Calif Art Ctr, Redding. *Media:* Watercolor, Serigraphy. *Mailing Add:* c/o Shasta Col 1065 N Old Oregon Trail Redding CA 96001

OLDS, ELIZABETH
PAINTER, PRINTMAKER
b Minneapolis, Minn, Dec 10, 1896. *Study:* Univ Minn, 2 yrs; Minneapolis Sch Art, 3 yrs; Art Students League, 2 yrs; also with George Luks, Paris, France, 2 yrs. *Work:* Metrop Mus Art, New York; Brooklyn Mus; Baltimore Mus Art; Philadelphia Mus Art; San Francisco Mus Art; and others. *Comn:* Drawings on World War II years & Pa Coal Country, New Repub, 40-49; war material paintings, Fortune Mag, 52-53, series of paintings on Lykes Indust, 54. *Exhib:* Artists for Victory, Metrop Mus Art, 42; Mus of Mod Art, 40s; Whitney Mus Am Art Watercolors & Drawings, 45-47 & 56; Prints & Books for Children, Mus Mod Art, New York; Brooklyn Mus Int Watercolor Exhibs, 49, 53, 55 & 57; Seven American Women: The Depression Decade, Vassar Col, 76; Arch Am Art, Smithsonian Inst, Washington, DC, 77; one-woman show, Staten Island Mus, 69; also many other one-woman shows, New York. *Awards:* Guggenheim Fel for Painting in Europe, 26-27; First Prize for Lithograph, Philadelphia Print Club, 37 & Art Aliance, 38; Third Prize for Mexican Village (watercolor), Baltimore Mus Art, 44. *Publ:* Auth & illusr, The Big Fire, 45, Riding the Rails, 48, Feather Mountain, 51 & Deep Treasure, 58, Houghton Mifflin; auth & illusr, Plop Plop Ploppie, 62 & Little Una, Scribner. *Mailing Add:* 2221 Alvarado Ln Sarasota FL 33581

OLENICK, DAVID CHARLES
DEALER, ADMINISTRATOR
b Rockville Centre, NY, Apr 21, 47. *Study:* NY Univ; Hofstra Univ; New Sch Social Res; State Univ NY. *Pos:* Co-dir, Mansight Educ, Full Circle Assocs, 68-69; owner/dir, Park Gallery, Brooklyn, 69-71; ed consult & field prog coordr, Projects Am Develop, US AID State Dept, 69-70; asst dir, Brooklyn Mus Art Sch, 74-77, admin head, 77-81, adminr educ & prog develop, 78-; gallery dir, Adam L Gimbel Gallery, New York, 81-83; cur contemp art, Saks Fifth Ave, New York, 81-83; pvt dealer, 83- *Specialty:* Contemporary paintings and sculpture. *Mailing Add:* 120 Park Pl Brooklyn NY 11217

OLIN, FERRIS
LIBRARIAN, HISTORIAN
US citizen. *Study:* Douglass Col, BA, 70; Rutgers Univ, MLS, 72, MA, 75. *Work:* Hopewell Mus, NJ. *Collections Arranged:* Architecture of New Brunswick and its Environs, 79; Women in the Community, series exhibs, 82; Artists Books: From the Traditional to the Avant-Garde, 82; Women's Spheres (co-ed, catalog), 83. *Pos:* Researcher/consult, New York Feminist Art Inst, 77-78; bk reviewer, Leonardo, 77-82; lectr on women artists, Dept Educ, State of NJ, 78-; ed prof lit column, Art Libr Soc NAm Newslett, 80- *Teaching:* Assoc prof & art librn, Rutgers Univ, New Brunswick, 76- *Mem:* Art Libr Soc North Am (chmn, NJ chap, 79-80); Soc Archit Historians (treas, NJ chap, 78-79, pres, 79-80); Womens Caucus for Art; Col Art Asn; Nat Women's Studies Asn. *Res:* Contributions of women artists to art history; issues facing art librarians; regional history and material culture. *Interests:* Architectural history and preservation; women's art history. *Publ:* Auth, Fair Play I: A Bibliography of Nonstereotyped Resources, Training Inst for Sex Desegregation, 76 & Educ Resources Info Ctr, 79; contribr, A History of East Amwell, 1700-1800, East Amwell Bicentennial Comt, 76; auth, Coping with the Chicken Little Syndrome: AACRZ and catalogs, Art Libr Soc NAm Occasional Paper #1, 81; guest ed, Drexel Libr Quart, vol 19, no 3, 83. *Mailing Add:* Art Libr Voorhees Hall Rutgers Univ New Brunswick NJ 08901

OLIPHANT, PATRICK
POLITICAL CARTOONIST
b Adelaide, Australia, July 24, 35; US citizen. *Study:* Dartmouth Col, DHL. *Pos:* Copyboy, press artist, Adelaide Advertiser, 53-55, ed cartoonist, 53-64; ed cartoonist, Denver Post, 64-75, Washington Star, 75-81; syndicated cartoonist, Los Angeles Times Syndicate, 65-79; syndicated cartoonist, Universal Press Syndicate, 79- *Awards:* Pulitzer Prize for Editorial Cartooning, 67; Nat Headliner Asn Award, 79; Reuben Award, Nat Cartoonists Soc, 68 & 72; and others. *Mem:* Int Salon Cartoons (jury chmn). *Publ:* Auth, Oliphant An Informal Gathering, 78; auth, Oliphant, 80, The Jelly Bean Society, 81, Ban This Book & But Seriously Folks, 83, Andrews & McMeel. *Mailing Add:* c/o Universal Press Syndicate 4400 Johnson Dr Kansas City KS 66215

OLITSKI, JULES
PAINTER, SCULPTOR
b Snovsk, Russia, Mar 27, 22. *Study:* Beaux Arts Inst, New York, 40-42; Acad Grande Chaumiere, Paris, France, 49-50; Nat Acad Design, New York, 50-51; NY Univ, BS & MA. *Work:* Art Inst Chicago; Corcoran Gallery Art, Washington, DC; Whitney Mus Am Art, New York; Mus Mod Art, New York; Chrysler Mus at Norfolk, Va. *Exhib:* Whitney Mus Am Art Ann, 62, 64, 67, 69 & 72; Post Painterly Abstraction, Los Angeles Co Mus Art, Walker Art Ctr, Minneapolis & Art Gallery Toronto, Can, 64; Olitski, Paintings 1963-67, Corcoran Gallery Art & Pasadena Mus, 67; Boston Mus of Fine Arts, 77 & Hirshhorn Mus, 77; Whitney Mus Am Art Ann, 69; Sculpture of Jules Olitski, Metrop Mus Art, New York, 69; Art Inst Chicago, 70; Inst Contemp Art, Philadelphia, 70; Albright-Knox Art Gallery, Buffalo, NY, 70; Abstract Painting in the 70's, Boston Mus Fine Arts, 72; Mus Fine Arts, Houston, 74; Indianapolis Mus Art, Ind, 74. *Teaching:* Assoc prof, State Univ NY Col New Paltz, 54-55; prof & chmn dept fine arts, C W Post Col, Long Island Univ, 56-63; instr art, Bennington Col, 63-67. *Awards:* Second Prize for Painting, Pittsburgh Int Painting & Sculpture, 61; 33rd Int Biennial Exhib Art, US Pavilion, Venice, Italy, 66; First Prize for Painting, Corcoran Gallery Art, 67. *Bibliog:* Gregory Batcock (auth), Minimal Art—A Critical Anthology, 68 & Henry Geldzahler (auth), New York Painting & Sculptures 1940-1970, 69, Dutton; Kenworth Moffett (auth), Jules Olitski's sculpture, Artforum, 4/69. *Dealer:* Knoedler Contemporary Art 19 E 70th St New York NY 10021; Andre Emmerich Gallery 41 E 57th St New York NY. *Mailing Add:* RFD 1 Bear Island Lovejoy Sands Rd Meredith NH 03253

OLIVEIRA, NATHAN
PAINTER
b Oakland, Calif, Dec 19, 28. *Study:* Mills Col, Calif Col of Arts & Crafts, MFA, 52. *Work:* Hirshhorn Mus & Sculpture Garden, Smithsonian Inst, Washington, DC; Mus of Mod Art, New York; San Francisco Mus Mod Art; Solomon R Guggenheim Mus, New York. *Exhib:* Art Inst Chicago, Ill; Annual, Corcoran Gallery Art, Washington, DC; Annuals, Whitney Mus Am Art, New York, 58-61 & 67-68; I Paris Biennial, 59; New Images of Man, 59 & Recent Painting USA: The Figure, 62-63, Mus Mod Art; Solomon R Guggenheim Mus, 61; one-man shows, Univ Ill, 61, Walker Art Ctr, Minneapolis, Minn, 61, Stanford Univ, 68, San Francisco Mus Mod Art, 69, Galerie Veith Turske, Cologne, Ger, 78, Basel, Switz & FIAC, Grand Palaise, Paris, 79; retrospectives: Univ Calif Los Angeles, 63 & Oakland Art Mus, 73; and others. *Teaching:* Prof art, San Francisco Art Inst, Calif Col Arts & Crafts, 55-56, Univ Ill, 61-62, Univ Calif Los Angeles, 63-64, Cornell Univ, 64, Stanford Univ, 64-84, Univ Colo, 65, Univ Hawaii, 71, Cranbrook Acad Art, Bloomfield Hills, Mich, 72, Baltimore Art Inst, 72, John Herron Art Inst, Indianapolis, Ind 72 & Kent State Univ, 73. *Awards:* Guggenheim Found Fel, 58; Norman Wait Harris Bronze Medal, Art Inst of Chicago, 60; Tamarind Fel, 64. *Mailing Add:* 785 Santa Maria Ave Stanford CA 94305

OLIVER, RICHARD BRUCE
ARCHITECT
b San Diego, Calif, Sept 14, 42. *Study:* Univ Calif, Berkeley, BA(archit); Cambridge Univ, England; Univ Pa, with Louis Kahn, MA(archit). *Exhib:* Drawing Toward a More Mod Archit, Drawing Ctr, New York, 77 & Otis Art Inst, Los Angeles, 78; The Presence of the Past, Venice Biennial, 80; and others. *Pos:* Cur contemp archit & design, Cooper-Hewitt Mus, Nat Mus Design, Smithsonian Inst, 77-80. *Teaching:* Asst prof archit, Univ Tex,

Austin, 67-70; vis studio critic, Univ Calif, Los Angeles, 70-71; vis critic archit, 74-75; vis studio critic, Rice Univ, 79 & Univ Nebr, 81; adj asst prof archit, Columbia Univ, 82- *Awards:* Fulbright Scholar, US Govt, 65-66; Arnold W Brunner Scholar, NY Chap, Am Inst Archit, 77. *Mem:* Archit League New York; Soc Archit Historians; Am Inst Archit. *Publ:* Coauth, Architectural Drawings: The Art and the Process, Whiting Libr Design, 81; ed, The Making of an Architect, Rizzoli, 81; auth, Bertram Grosvenor Goodhue, Archit Hist Found, 83. *Mailing Add:* 23 East 26th St New York NY 10010

OLKINETZKY, SAM
PAINTER, MUSEUM DIRECTOR
b New York, NY, Nov 22, 19. *Study:* Brooklyn Col; Inst Fine Arts, NY Univ. *Work:* Philbrook Art Ctr, Tulsa, Okla; Okla Art Ctr, Oklahoma City; Mus Art, Univ Okla, Norman; Sch Bus, Okla State Univ, Stillwater; Lawton Munic Collection, Okla. *Exhib:* Philbrook Art Ctr Ann, 50-70; Int Painting & Sculpture Exhib, Mus Non-Objective Art, New York, 51-52; Recent Drawings, USA, Mus Mod Art, New York, 55; Momentum Midcontinental, Chicago Inst Design, 55; Southwestern Painting and Sculpture Ann, Okla Art Ctr, 60-70; Artsplace II, Oklahoma City, 79. *Pos:* Art consult, Kerr-McGee Indust, 64-; dir, Mus Art, Univ Okla, 59-; art consult, Okla Art Ctr, 72- *Teaching:* Asst prof art, Okla State Univ, 47-57; prof art, Univ Okla, 57-; vis prof art & humanities, Univ Ark, 62-67; lectr humanities, Langston Univ, 69-70. *Awards:* St Gaudens Medal for Draughtsmanship, 37; Purchase Award for Painting, Philbrook Art Ctr, 51; Purchase Award for Drawing, Okla Art Ctr, 65. *Mem:* Am Asn Mus; Okla Mus Asn; Art Mus Asn. *Media:* Collage. *Publ:* Auth, Oklahoma Designer Craftsman Exhibition, Craft Horizons, 71; contribr, The Art of Doublas Warner (catalog essay), 80. *Mailing Add:* Rte 1 Box 151 A Norman OK 73069

OLLMAN, ARTHUR L
PHOTOGRAPHER, HISTORIAN
b Milwaukee, Wis, Mar 6, 47. *Study:* Univ Wis-Madison, BA, 69; Visual Studies Workshop, Rochester, 72; San Francisco Art Inst, 74; Lone Mountain Col, MFA, 77. *Work:* Mus Mod Art, New York; Bibliot Nat, Centre Georges Pompidou, Mus Nat d'Art, Paris, France; Mus Mod Art, San Francisco; Mus Fine Arts, Houston. *Exhib:* Contemp Am & Can Photog, Monas Heiroglyphicas, Milan, Italy, 78; Mirrors & Windows, Mus Mod Art, New York, 78; Grapestake Gallery, San Francisco, 79; Beyond Color, San Francisco Mus Mod Art, 80; Whitney Mus, New York, 81; one-man shows, Contemp Art Ctr, New Orleans, 80, Photography Gallery, New York, 81. *Awards:* Special Proj Award, Calif Arts Coun, 77; Nat Endowment Arts Fel, 79. *Bibliog:* Charles Whitin (auth), Arthur Ollman, Am Photog|Image Nation, 11/78; Arnaud Claass (auth), Arthur Ollman, Zoom/Publicness, 6/79; Arthur Ollman, Time-Life Photog Yr, 79. *Mem:* Soc for Photog Educ; Friends of Photog. *Media:* Photography; Video Tape. *Dealer:* Grapestake Gallery 2876 California St San Francisco CA 94115; Photograph Gallery 724 5th Ave New York NY. *Mailing Add:* 6509 Raymond St Oakland CA 94609

OLMSTED, SUZANNE M
PHOTOGRAPHER, PRINTMAKER
b Palo Alto, Calif, April 15, 56. *Study:* Univ Calif, Santa Cruz, BA, 79; Southern Ill Univ, MFA, 82. *Exhib:* Photo Regional, Speed Art Mus, 82; Nat Print Exhib, Fredrick Wright Gallery, Los Angeles, 82; Invitational Auction, Yellowstone Art Ctr, 83; Recent Works, Castle Gallery, Billings, Mont, 83; Recent Brownprints, Montalvo Ctr Arts, Saratoga, Calif, 83; Experimental Photo, Pacific Grove Art Ctr, Calif, 84; and others. *Teaching:* Instr photog, Eastern Mont Col, 82- *Mem:* Col Art Asn. *Publ:* Contribr, Photogr Forum, 81. *Mailing Add:* 512 Clark St Billings MT 59101

OLOFFSON, WERNER OLAF
PAINTER, PHOTOGRAPHER
b Port-au-Prince, Haiti, June 21, 05; US citizen. *Study:* With H J Staude, Florence, Italy. *Exhib:* Hamburg, Ger, 58; Monte Carlo, 59; New York, 60, 62 & 74; Nat Acad Design; Philadelphia Acad Fine Arts; Audubon Artists Soc; Allied Artists of Am; Knickerbocker Artists Soc; Nat Arts Club. *Awards:* First Prize, NJ Painters & Sculptors, 52; Winsor & Newton Award, Nat Arts Club, 64; Second Prize, Am Art Prof League, 68. *Mem:* Am Watercolor Soc; Salmagundi Club; Am Artists Prof League; NJ Painters & Sculptors Soc; Jackson Heights Art Club. *Media:* Watercolor; Black and White Pen and Brush. *Mailing Add:* 35-33 83rd St Jackson Heights NY 11372

OLPIN, ROBERT SPENCER
HISTORIAN, CURATOR
b Palo Alto, Calif, Aug 30, 40. *Study:* Univ Utah, BS, 63; Boston Univ, AM, 65, PhD, 71. *Work:* Utah Mus Fine Arts, Univ Utah. *Collections Arranged:* Alexander Helwig Wyant, 1836-1892 (with catalog), 68, Mainstreams of American Architecture-Reflections on Salt Lake City (with catalog), 73 & Am Painting Around 1850, 76, Utah Mus Fine Arts; Contemporary Utah Artists Exhibition, Billboard Art, Tracy Collins Bank (with catalog), 74 & The Art Life of Utah, 1776-1976 (with catalog), 76, Salt Lake Art Ctr; A Retrospective of Utah Art (with catalog), Utah Arts Coun, Utah Mus Fine Arts, 81; Waldo Midgley Retrospective (with catalog), Utah State Univ, Univ Utah & Springville Mus Art, 83. *Pos:* Consult cur Am art, Utah Mus Fine Arts, Univ Utah, 73- *Teaching:* Lectr art hist, Boston Univ, 65-67; from asst prof to assoc prof art hist, Univ Utah, 67-77, prof, 77-, chmn art hist prog, 68-, actg chmn dept art, 71-72 & 75-76, chmn art dept, 76-82. *Mem:* Col Art Asn; Utah Acad Sci, Arts & Lett. *Res:* Nineteenth and 20th century American art, with special emphasis on 19th century American landscape painting. *Collection:* Eighteenth and 19th century European and American prints. *Publ:* Auth, Painting an environment, Southwest Art, 9/75; auth, Dictionary of Utah Art, Salt Lake Art Ctr, 80; coauth, Portrait of a portraitist, Univ Utah, Col Fine Arts, 81. *Mailing Add:* Art & Archit Ctr 161 Univ of Utah Salt Lake City UT 84112

OLSEN, ERNEST MORAN
DESIGNER, PAINTER
b Pittsfield, Mass, May 5, 10. *Study:* Pratt Inst, pictorial illus; portraiture with Ivan Moschowitz; Boothbay Harbor Summer Sch Art, landscape study with Frank Allen. *Work:* Berkshire Mus, Pittsfield, Mass; Fine Arts Mus, Asbury Park, NJ. *Exhib:* Int Print Exhib, Chicago World's Fair, 30; Pittsfield Art League, Berkshire Mus, 31-36; Stockbridge Art Exhib, Berkshire Playhouse, Mass, 35-38; Williams Col, Williamstown, Mass, 37; Yonkers Mus Exhib, NY, 55. *Collections Arranged:* Fine Arts Mus, Asbury Park, NJ, 77. *Pos:* Art dir, Leica (house organ), Pallard Corp, 45-50, Copper & Brass Res Asn, 45-65, Bolex (house organ), E Leitz Corp, 50-55, Maxwell House Messenger, Gen Foods, 60-76 & Sculpture Mag Nat Sculpture Review, Nat Sculpture Soc, 62-; designer, Union Carbide Corp, New York, 52- *Awards:* Cert of Merit, Folmer Graflex Corp, 40 & Printing Indust of Metrop New York, 65-74. *Mem:* Art Dir Club of New York; fel Am Artists Prof League. *Media:* Oil, Wash. *Mailing Add:* 465 Westchester Ave Mt Vernon NY 10552

OLSEN, FREDERICK L
POTTER, SCULPTOR
b Seattle, Wash, Feb 25, 38. *Study:* Univ Redlands, BA; Univ Southern Calif, MFA; Kyoto City Col Fine Art, Japan; also apprenticeship with Tomimoto Kenkichi & Kondo Yuzo, Kyoto, 3 yrs. *Work:* Gallery New South Wales, Sydney, Australia; Contemp Craft Mus, Denmark; Sturt Collection, Mittigong, Australia; Palm Springs Desert Mus, Calif; Bowan Collection, San Marcos, Calif. *Exhib:* Kyo-Ten, Kyoto Mus Mod Art, 62; also one-man exhibs, Sydney, 63, 64 & 69; Melbourne, 63 & 69, Adelaide, 69, Copenhagen, 65, Seattle, 71 & 73, Portland, Ore, 71, Los Angeles, 71, 73 & 74 & Palm Springs Art Mus, 77 & 80; Mt Jacinto Col Gallery, Jacinto, Calif, 81. *Pos:* Owner, Pinyon Crest Pottery & Olsen Kiln Kit Co, 67- *Teaching:* Lectr kiln bldg, Univ Southern Calif, 66-68; asst prof, Univ Puget Sound, summer 71 & 73; prof, Mt San Jacinto Col, Calif, 82-83. *Bibliog:* American Potter in Japan, Asahi TV Corp, 63. *Media:* Ceramics. *Publ:* Auth, The Kiln Book, Chilton Books, 81. *Dealer:* Serisawa Gallery 8320 Melrose Ave Los Angeles CA 90069; Cal Vanderwould Gallery Palm Springs CA. *Mailing Add:* Pinyon Crest Box 205 Mountain Center CA 92361

OLSEN, SHARON A
DEALER, GALLERY DIRECTOR
b Oklahoma City, Okla, June 29, 40. *Study:* Scripps Col, 58-61; Sorbonne, Paris, 61-62; Univ Calif, Los Angeles, 62-63. *Collections Arranged:* Roger Kuntz Retrospective (auth, catalog), Laguna Beach Mus Art, Calif, 77. *Pos:* Asst, Phyllis Morris Originals, Los Angeles, 64-66; mgr, Challis Galleries, Laguna Beach, Calif, 75-82, dir, 82- *Mem:* Nat Asn Cert Appraisers; Laguna Beach Festival Arts. *Specialty:* Twentieth century paintings and sculpture. *Mailing Add:* PO Box 1356 Laguna Beach CA 92652

OLSHAN, BERNARD
PAINTER, PRINTMAKER
b New York, NY, Jan 31, 21. *Study:* Am Artists Sch, New York, 37-40; Ozenfant Sch Fine Arts, New York, 47; Academie de la Grande Chaumiere, Paris, 48-51. *Work:* Emily Lowe Mus, Coral Gables, Fla; New York City Community Col & Health & Hosp Corp, Lincoln Hosp, New York. *Comn:* Mural, Theodore Roosevelt High Sch & WPA, New York, 39-40. *Exhib:* Camp Maxey Art Exhib, Dallas Mus Fine Arts, 43; Whitney Mus Am Art, New York, 48; Art USA, Madison Sq Garden, New York, 58; 144th Ann Exhib, Nat Acad Design, New York, 69; Hudson River Mus, New York, 71; Seven Bronx Artists, Herbert H Lehman Col, New York, 74; and others. *Pos:* chmn visual arts comt, Amalgamated Houses, New York, 80- *Teaching:* Instr, Crafts Students League, New York, 53; instr, New York City Community Col, 65-69; teacher & dir, Cult Arts Dept, Mosholu-Montefiore Community Ctr, New York, 66-79. *Awards:* Inter-city Mural Award, Theodore Roosevelt High Sch & Work Progress Admin, 39-40; Emily Lowe Award 1st Prize, 2nd Ann, 50. *Bibliog:* Dr Lawrence J Hatterer (auth), The Artist in Society, Grove Press, New York, 65; Barry Schwartz (auth), The New Humanism in Time of Change, Prager Publ, 74; articles in New York Times, Art News, Herald Tribune, Art Digest & others. *Mem:* New York Artists Equity Asn; Am Soc Contemp Artists; Bronx Soc Sci & Lett. *Mailing Add:* 80 Van Cortlandt Park S Bronx NY 10463

OLSON, BETTYE JOHNSON
PAINTER, INSTRUCTOR
b Minneapolis, Minn, Jan 16, 23. *Study:* Univ Minn, BS(art educ), 45, MEd, 49; Univ NMex, Taos, 47; Cranbrook Acad Art, Mich, 48. *Work:* Minn Mining & Mfg; Lutheran Brotherhood Insurance Collection; Vaxjo, Sweden; Pillsbury World Hq, Minneapolis; Augsburg Col. *Exhib:* Art Biennial, 47 & Minneapolis Soc Fine Arts Biennial, 47, Walker Art Ctr; Metamorphose One, Minn Mus Art, St Paul, 76; Mid Year Show Ann, Butler Inst Am Art, Youngstown, Ohio, 77; Watercolor USA, Springfield Art Ctr, Mo, 77; Women Invite Women, Minneapolis, 77; Am Artists Selected for Kuopio, Finland, Univ Minn Gallery, 81; Centennial Exhib, Boston Univ Mus, 81; Smaland Mus, Vaxjo, Sweden, 82. *Teaching:* Instr, Summit Sch Girls, 45-47; instr, Univ Minn, 47-49; artist in res, Holden Village, Chelan, Wash, 67-79; instr, Concordia Col, St Paul, 75-78. *Awards:* Merit Award, Twin City Show, Minn Mus Art, 61; 3rd Prize, Merit Award, Minn State Fair, 76 & 77; Grand Prize, Purchase Award, Northern Lights Show, White Bear Arts Coun, Lakewood Col, 77. *Mem:* Delta Phi Delta (pres, 46); Artists Equity Asn (secy, 74). *Media:* Watercolor, Acrylic. *Dealer:* Art Acquisitions Inc 867 Fairmont St Paul MN 55105. *Mailing Add:* 1855 Hunter Ave St Paul MN 55118

OLSON, DOUGLAS JOHN
PAINTER, EDUCATOR
b Wausau, Wis, Aug 26, 34. *Study:* Layton Sch Art, BFA; Univ Cincinnati, MFA. *Work:* Montgomery Mus of Fine Arts, Ala; Pope & Quint Corp; Gallery S; First Nat Bank of Ala; South Central Bell, Birmingham, Ala. *Exhib:* Chiaha Sixth Ann Show, Nat City Bank, Rome, Ga, 78; Honored Artists Exhib, South Central Bell Bldg, Birmingham, Ala, 79; 19th Ann Mus Show, Montgomery Mus Fine Artrs, Ala, 80; one-man shows, Univ Wis Ctr, Sheboygan, 81 & Ctr Music, Drama and Art, Lake Placid, NY, 83; LaGrange National Show VII, Chattahoochee Valley Art Gallery, Ga, 82; and many others. *Teaching:* Instr drawing, Univ Cincinnati, 67-68; prof drawing & design, Auburn Univ, 68- *Awards:* Mary Houghton Memorial Award, Montgomery Mus Fine Arts, 78; First Prize, Birmingham Mus Fine Arts, 78 & Montgomery Mus Fine Arts, 80; Purchase Award, 13th Ann Mus Exhib, Gallery S, 74; and others. *Bibliog:* Guild art exhibit opens, Montgomery Advertiser, 3/80; One-man show, Auburn Univ Report, 5/81. *Mem:* Montgomery Art Guild, Ala Art League; Birmingham Art Asn. *Media:* Enamel, Masonite. *Mailing Add:* 302 E Thach Ave Auburn AL 36830

OLSON, JOSEPH OLAF
DESIGNER, PAINTER
Study: Tadama Art Sch, Seattle, Wash; Nat Acad, New York; Art Students League. *Work:* Brooklyn Mus; also in pvt collections of Whitney, Pratt, Morgan, Harriman, Frick & Dupont families. *Exhib:* One-man shows, Corcoran Gallery, Washington, DC; Carnegie Inst, Pittsburgh; Chicago Art Inst. *Pos:* Stained glass designer, Rambusch Decorating Co, New York, 45-69. *Awards:* Isidor Prize, Salmagundi Club. *Media:* Oil, Watercolor. *Mailing Add:* RFD 1 Mystic CT 06355

OLSON, RICHARD W
PRINTMAKER, EDUCATOR
b Rockford, Ill, Aug 14, 38. *Study:* Univ Wis-Madison, BS & study with R Knipschild, Leo Steppat & Italo Scanga, 60, MS(studio art/painting & graphics) & study with Warrington Colescott, 61 & MFA(studio art/painting & graphics) & study with Warrington Colescott, 62; Dieudonne, New York, with Paul Wong, 80; Letterpress Ctr Book Arts, with Dikko Faust, 81. *Work:* Mus Contemp Art, Chicago; Nat Gallery; Albright-Knox Gallery; Walker Art Ctr; Mus Mod Art, New York; and others. *Exhib:* Soc Etchers Ann, Calif Palace of the Legion of Honor, San Francisco, 64; 25th Print Nat, intaglio, Nat Collection Fine Arts Div, Smithsonian Inst, Washington, DC, 64; Drawing & Small Group Sculpture Show, Ball State Univ, 69; Postage Sized Art, Art Fiera, Italy, 78; Book as Object, Visual Studies Workshop, 79; Books as Art, Eaton Shoen Gallery, San Francisco, 81; and others. *Teaching:* From asst prof to assoc prof, Beloit Col, Wis, 63-77, chmn art dept, 69-77, prof art drawing, printmaking, painting & sem, 77-, cur prints & drawings, 80-, chmn dept art, 80-82, dir, Artery Gallery Wright Art Mus, currently. *Awards:* Gimbels Award, Wis Painters & Sculptors, Gimbels-Milwaukee, 62; Gimbels-Schusters Award, Wis Salon Art, Gimbels-Schusters, 68; Purchase Award, Nat Juried, Waterloo Art Ctr, 65. *Bibliog:* Books in an expanded context, Artweek, 7/81. *Media:* Collage, Offset. *Publ:* Illusr covers, Beloit Poetry J, 64 & 69; Artifacts at the End Decade, Ed Watson & Heubner, 81. *Mailing Add:* Dept of Art Beloit Col Beloit WI 53511

OLUGEBEFOLA, ADEMOLA
PAINTER, DESIGNER
b Charlotte Amalie, St Thomas, VI; US citizen. *Study:* Fashion Inst of Technol, New York, AA, 61; Weusi Acad of Arts & Studies, New York, PhD, 69; Printmaking Workshop, New York, study with Krishna Reddy & Bob Blackburn. *Work:* VI Coun Arts; Schomberg Ctr, New York; Port Authority NY & NJ; Harlem State Off Bldg, New York; Mus Guyana, South Am. *Comn:* Murals, New York Dept of Cultural Affairs, Marcus Garvey Cultural Ctr, 69, Teleprompter Cable TV Corp, Pub Access Ctr, 72 & Nat Arts Consortium (lobby entrance), 78. *Exhib:* Sun Festival, Corcoran Gallery, Washington, DC, 69; 14 Artists, Pratt Inst, Main Gallery, Brooklyn, NY, 76; one-man shows, 20-20 Vision, Benin Gallery, 81-82, 20th Anniversary Exhib, Reichold Ctr Arts, St Thomas, VI, 81 & 4th Int Caribbean Festival Arts, Barbados, WI; Retrospective 12 Yrs, New York State Harlem Gallery, 81; Impressions/ Expressions, Smithsonian Inst Traveling Exhib, 80-82; and many others. *Pos:* Art dir, New Lafayette Publ, New York, 69-74. *Teaching:* Instr contemp black art, Wesleyan Univ, Middleton, Conn, 73-75 & NY Found for the Arts, 78-80. *Awards:* Fredrick Douglas Award, First Ann Harlem, 20th Century Creators, 64; Lois Noel Award, New Directions, Carnegie Inst, 72; First Prize Printmaking, Lakeview Art Soc, 75. *Bibliog:* Barbara Rose (auth), Black Art in Am, Art in Am, 9/71; Dick Young (filmmaker), Festac 77, US Info Agency, 2/78; Rosalind Jeffries (auth), The Art of Ademola, Black Art--An Int Quart, 12/78. *Mem:* Nat Arts Consortium (bd of dirs, 78-80); Nat Conference of Artists (nat vpres, 73-77); Weusi Acad of Arts & Studies (co-dir, 78-). *Publ:* Illusr, The Art Gallery Magazine, Hollycroft Press, 70; illusr, The Duplex/A Love Fable, William Morrow, 71; illusr, The Reluctant Rapist, Harper & Row, 73; illusr, Natural History, Am Mus of Natural Hist, 2/74; illusr, Art: African American, Harcourt-Brace & Jovanovich, 78. *Dealer:* Kathy Gibson Fine Arts 1561 Metropolitan Ave Bronx NY. *Mailing Add:* 800 Riverside Dr Studio 5E East New York NY 10032

OMAR, MARGIT
PAINTER, EDUCATOR
b Berlin, Ger, May 17, 41; US citizen. *Study:* Art Inst Chicago, Ill; Univ NDak, Grand Forks, BA, 66; Univ Colo, Boulder, MFA, 71. *Work:* Los Angeles Co Mus Art, Lloyds Bank London & Polygram Pictures, Los Angeles; Atlantic Richfield Co, Denver; Turtle Creek Mansion, Dallas; and others. *Exhib:* Spectrum, Los Angeles Co Mus Art, 75; New Abstract Painting

in Los Angeles, Los Angeles Co Mus Art, 76; one-man shows, Janus Gallery, Venice, Calif, 77, 78, 80 & 82; Fresh Paint, San Francisco Mus Mod Art, 82; Drawings by Painters, Oakland Mus Art, 83; Young Talent Awards 1963-1983, Los Angeles Co Mus Art, 83; and others. *Teaching:* Assoc prof graduate studies & painting, Univ Southern Calif, Los Angeles, 73- *Awards:* Young New Talent Award, Los Angeles Co Mus Art, Contemp Art Coun, 77. *Bibliog:* Susan C Larsen (auth), Margit Omar's California Suite, Arts Mag, 9/78; Water Gabrielson (auth), Pasadena pluralism: The painting Seventies, Art Am, 5/81; Ruth Weisberg (auth), Margit Omar at Janus, Images & Issues, 10/82. *Mem:* Los Angeles Inst of Contemp Art. *Media:* Acrylic. *Dealer:* Janus Gallery 8000 Melrose Ave Los Angeles CA 90046. *Mailing Add:* c/o Art Dept Univ Southern Calif Los Angeles CA 90007

O'MEALLIE, KITTY (KATE CHAMNESS JOHNSON)
PAINTER, PRINTMAKER
b Bennettsville, SC, Oct 24, 16. *Study:* Newcomb Art Sch, with Xavier Gonzales and Will Stevens, BFA(design), 37, advan painting with Pat Trivigno, George Rickey, John Taylor & Edward Corbett, 54-59. *Work:* New Orleans Mus Art & Tulane Univ, New Orleans; Meridian Mus Art, Miss; Masur Mus Art, Monroe, La; Wake Forest Univ, Winston-Salem, NC. *Comn:* Oil painting, Sellers & Sanders Clinic, New Orleans, 60; oil painting, Eustis Engineering Co, New Orleans, 67; acrylic painting, New Orleans Pub Libr, 77; mixed media painting, Houston Athletic Ctr, 81; and other pvt comns. *Exhib:* Southeastern Ctr Contemp Art, Winston-Salem, NC, 71; New Orleans Mus Art, 73; Contemp Arts Ctr, New Orleans, 77; solo exhibs, Masur Mus Art, Monroe, La, 79 & Meridian Mus Art, Miss, 81; and many others. *Awards:* Hon Mention, 5th Monroe Ann, Masur Mus Art, 68; Award Merit, 51st Regional, R S Barnwell Ctr, 73; Ann Art Auction Award, WYES Pub Television, New Orleans, 79. *Bibliog:* Keith Marshall (auth), A fresh look at art in the city that care forgot, Art Voices South Mag, 3/78; George Jordan (auth), A portrait of three artists, Merci Mag, 9/80; New Orleans Art: Three Attitudes (film), WYES Pub Television, 80. *Mem:* Artists Equity Asn; Nat Women's Caucus Art; New Orleans Women's Caucus Art. *Media:* Acrylic, Mixed Media; Silkscreen. *Publ:* Illusr, A time to die, a time to mourn, St Charles Ave Presby Church, 78. *Dealer:* Beall/Lambremont Gallery 3434 Magazine St New Orleans LA 70115; ArtSouth Inc 613 Felder Ave Montgomery AL 36106! *Mailing Add:* 211 Fairway Dr New Orleans LA 70124

OMWAKE, LEON, JR
PAINTER, SCULPTOR
b New Rochelle, NY, June 14, 46. *Study:* Pa Acad Fine Arts, 64-68. *Work:* Whitney Mus Am Art, New York; Philadelphia Mus Art, Pa Acad Fine Arts, Philadelphia. *Exhib:* Philadelphia Mus Art, 70; Whitney Ann Am Painting, New York, 72; Cheltenham Ann Painting Exhib, 72; one-man show, Marian Locks Gallery, 72; Marcel Duchamp Retrospective, Philadelphia Mus Art, 74; Tehran, Iran, 76; Dusseldorf, Ger, 76; Austin, Tex, 77; plus others. *Teaching:* Instr painting, Pa Acad Fine Art, Cheltenham Art Ctr, Pa & Chaddsford Art Sch, formerly. *Media:* Mixed. *Mailing Add:* c/o Marian Locks Gallery 1524 Walnut St Philadelphia PA 19100

O'NEAL, ROLAND LENARD
ILLUSTRATOR, GRAPHIC ARTIST
b Meridian, Miss, Feb 1, 48. *Study:* Meridian Mus Art, Miss, 68; Jackson State Univ, BS(art educ), 72. *Work:* Afro-Am Studies Dept, Harvard Univ; Prof Football Hall Fame, Canton, Ohio; Wyo Univ Art Mus, Laramie; Idaho Univ Art Mus, Moscow; Sch Archit, Univ Southern Calif. *Exhib:* Ball State Univ Drawing & Sculpture Exhib, 74; Colo Print & Drawing Exhib, Sch Art, Univ Colo, Boulder, 75; Wind River Nat, Wind River Artist Guild, Ladner, Wyo, 76; Meridian Pub Libr, 77; Afro-Am Art Show, Ala A&M Univ, 78. *Teaching:* Volunteer arts & crafts, Miss Action Progress, Meridian, 72-79; substitute teacher art educ, Meridian pub schs, Miss, 72-80. *Mem:* Wind River Valley Artist Guild; Athenian Art Club, Jackson State Univ. *Media:* Pencil, Charcoal; Watercolor, Mixed Media. *Mailing Add:* Apt E #4 Highway Village Meridian MS 39301

O'NEIL, BRUCE WILLIAM
PAINTER, INSTRUCTOR
b Winnipeg, Man, Can, July 14, 42. *Study:* Alta Col of Art, dipl(fine art painting), 59-64; Instituto Allende, San Miguel De Allende, Mex, 65. *Work:* Can Coun Art Bank, Ottawa, Ont, Can; Edmonton Art Gallery, Alta, Can; Shell Oil Resources Ltd, Calgary, Alta; Alta Culture (Alta govt); Mem Univ, St Johns Nfld; and others. *Exhib:* Abstraction West, Emma Lake & After, Nat Gallery of Can, 76; 14 Can, A Critics Choice: Hirschhorn Mus and Sculpture Garden, Washington, DC, 77; New Abstract Art, Edmonton Art Gallery, 77; one-man shows, Layola Col, Montreal, 68; Bruce O'Neil, 1973-76, traveling, Univ of Saskatchewan, Southern Alta Art Gallery, Lethbridge, Edmonton Art Gallery, 75, Mira Godard Gallery, Toronto, 77 & 80, Montreal, 78 & Calgary, 80 & Can Art Galleries, Calgary, 77-78. *Pos:* Chmn, Alberta Soc of Artists, Calgary, Alta, 72-73. *Teaching:* Instr painting, Alta Col Art, 68-80; guest instr, painting, Mount Allison Univ, Sackville, New Brunswick, 76; guest instr painting, Emma Lake Artists Workshop, Emma Lake, Saskatchewan, 76. *Awards:* Instituto Allende, Post Grad Exhib, Instituto Allende, Mex, 64; Can Coun Arts Grant, 75, 78 & 80. *Bibliog:* Dale McConathy (auth), The Can Cultural Revolution, Art Can Art Mag, 75; Karen Wilkin (auth), Bruce O'Neil, Art Mag, 77; Mike Hepburn (producer), Alberta Character-Bruce O'Neil-Artist, Can Broadcasting Corp, 78. *Mem:* Alta Soc Artists (Calgary chmn, 72-73); Can Artists Representatives. *Media:* Acrylic on Canvas. *Dealer:* Mira Godard Gallery 22 Hazelton Ave Toronto ON M5R 2E2 Can; Virginia Christopher Galleries Ltd 640 12 Ave SW T2R 0H5. *Mailing Add:* 2006 30th Ave SW Calgary AB T2T 1R2 Canada

O'NEIL, JOHN
PAINTER, EDUCATOR
b Kansas City, Mo, June 16, 15. *Study:* Univ Okla, BFA & MFA; Colorado Springs Arts Ctr, with Boardman Robinson, Paul Burlin & Henry Varnum Poor; Taos Sch Art, with Emil Bisttram; Studio Hinna, Rome, Italy. *Work:* Denver Art Mus; Dallas Mus Fine Arts; Libr Cong, Washington, DC; Univ Mich Mus Art; Seattle Art Mus. *Exhib:* Directions in American Painting, Carnegie Inst, Pittsburgh; Abstract & Surrealist Art, Art Inst Chicago; Contemporary American Painting, Univ Ill; Mid-Am Ann, Nelson-Atkins Gallery, Kansas City, Mo; Watercolor USA, Springfield Art Mus, Mo; SW Am Art, Kyoto Mus, Japan; Main St II Exhib, Contemp Arts Mus, Houston, Tex; Troisieme Salon Int des Realites Nouvelles, Paris, France; M-59 Exhib, Copenhagen, Denmark. *Pos:* Dir, Sewall Art Gallery, Houston, 71-77. *Teaching:* Prof painting, Univ Okla, 39-65 & Rice Univ, 65-83. *Awards:* 23 awards in regional & nat exhib. *Mem:* Col Art Asn Am. *Media:* Acrylic, Watercolor. *Publ:* Contribr, Oklahoma: a guide to the Sooner State, Art & Archit, 57; contribr, Thoughts on Light, Kunst, 63; contribr, On color, Cimarron Rev, 72. *Dealer:* Kauffman Galleries Houston TX 77013. *Mailing Add:* 2224 Wroxton Rd Houston TX 77005

O'NEIL, JOHN JOSEPH
ADMINISTRATOR, DESIGNER
b Brooklyn, NY, Apr 20, 32. *Study:* State Univ NY, Brooklyn, BA; State Univ NY, Buffalo, BS; Columbia Univ, MA, prof dipl & EdD. *Work:* Florence Mus, SC; Furman Mus, Greenville, SC; Beaufort Mus, SC; SC Arts Comn. *Exhib:* Piedmont Ann Crafts, 68 & Ann Graphics Exhib, 69-71, Mint Mus Art, Charlotte, NC; 24th Ann Southeastern Exhib, High Mus Art, Atlanta, Ga; 37th Southeastern, Gallery Contemp Art, 72. *Pos:* Mem, Panel Fed Graphics Progs, Nat Endowment Arts, currently; bd trustees, Columbia Mus Art & Sci, currently. *Teaching:* Prof graphic design, Univ SC, 63-, assoc head dept art, 65-75, head dept art, 75- *Mem:* SC Craftsman; Southeastern Art Conf; Columbia Artists Guild (vpres, 67, treas, 73-74); Guild SC Artist; Southeastern Print Coun. *Mailing Add:* 4225 Sequoia Rd Columbia SC 29206

O'NEILL, JOHN PATTON
PAINTER, CURATOR
b Houston, Tex, Apr 12, 42. *Study:* Univ Okla, Norman, BS; La State Univ, Baton Rouge, MS & PhD. *Exhib:* Denver Mus Nat Hist; Houston Mus Nat Sci; Leigh Yawkey Woodson Art Mus, 81. *Pos:* Curatorial asst, La State Univ Mus Zoology, Baton Rouge, 74-76, cur higher vertabrates, 76-78 & dir & cur, 78-82, coordinator field studies, 82- *Teaching:* Grad asst gen zoology, La State Univ, 64-73; asst prof ornithology, 78. *Bibliog:* Jonathan Fisher (auth), John O'Neill doesn't just paint birds, Int Wildlife, 77; Painting of John O'Neill, Cornell Lab Ornithology, 77; Frank Graham (auth), Outpacing Extinction, Audubon Mag. *Media:* Watercolor, Gouache. *Publ:* Illusr, Finding the Birds in Western Mexico, Univ Ariz Press, 69; illusr, Grouse and Quails of North America, Univ Nebr Press, 73; various illus for Encycl Britannica, 76; illusr, A Guide to the Birds of Trinidad and Tobago, Harrowood Bks, 77; illusr, National Geographic Field Guide to the Birds of North America. *Dealer:* Mill Pond Press Inc 204 S Nassau St Venice FL 33595. *Mailing Add:* 569 Maxine Dr Baton Rouge LA 70808

O'NEILL, PAT
FILMMAKER, PHOTOGRAPHER
b Los Angeles, Calif, June 28, 39. *Study:* Univ Calif, Los Angeles, with Robert Heinecken, BA, 62, MA, 64. *Work:* Art Coun Great Britain, London; Centre Georges Pompidou, Paris, France; Australian Nat Libr, Syndey; New York Pub Libr; Chicago Art Inst. *Exhib:* One-man film screenings, Carnegie Inst, Pittsburgh, 72, San Francisco Mus Art, 76 & Walker Art Ctr, Minneapolis, 77; one-man shows, Cineprobe, Mus Mod Art, New York, 73 & 79 & Univ Calif, Santa Barbara, 79; Filmworks, Eyemusic, San Francisco, 77; Poetic Eye, Los Angeles Co Mus, 77. *Pos:* Co-founder & partner, Lookout Mountain Films, Los Angeles, 77- *Teaching:* Asst prof photog, Univ Calif, Los Angeles, 67-68; asst dean & instr film, Calif Inst Arts, Valencia, 70-76. *Awards:* First Prize, Ann Arbor Film Festival, 69, 72 & 77; Am Film Inst Filmmakers Grant, 75; Nat Endowment Arts Grant, 78. *Bibliog:* Scott Hammen (auth), Pat O'Neill's Saugus Series, Afterimage, 10/75; J Hoberman (auth), Flash in the panorama, Village Voice, 6/19/78; Weinbren & Brinker (auth), The O'Neill landscape, Millenium Film J, No 4 & 5, fall 79. *Publ:* Producer films, including Saugus Series (color sound), Canyon Cinema Co-op, Filmmakers' Co-op, Serious Business Co, Cooperative des Cieastes Independants & Picture Start, 74, Sidewinder's Delta (color sound), Canyon Cinema Co-op, Filmmakers' Co-op & Serious Business Co, 76, Two Sweeps (color silent), 77, Foregrounds (color sound), 78 & Sleeping Dogs (Never Lie) (black & white & color, silent & sound), 78, Canyon Co-op, Filmmakers' Co-op & Picture Start. *Mailing Add:* 8331 Lookout Mountain Ave Los Angeles CA 90046

O'NEILL-CONTINI, ANITA See Contini, Anita

ONLEY, TONI
PAINTER
b Douglas, Isle of Man, England, Nov 20, 28. *Study:* Douglas Sch Art; Inst Allende, Mex. *Work:* Tate Gallery, London; Nat Gallery Can; Victoria & Albert Mus, London; Mus Mod Art, New York; Seattle Mus, Wash. *Comn:* Oil mural, Queen Elizabeth Playhouse, Vancouver, BC, 62. *Exhib:* Seattle World's Fair, 62; Contemporary Canadian Art, Nat Gallery Can & Africa, 62-63; Fifteen Canadian Artists, Mus Mod Art & traveling in US, 63-64; Two Canadians, Commonwealth Inst, London, 64; 36th Venice Biennale, Italy, 72. *Teaching:* Asst prof fine arts, Univ BC, 67-76. *Awards:* Jessie Dow Award, Montreal Spring Exhib, 60; Sam & Ayala Zacks Award, 83rd Ann, Royal Can Acad, 63; Sr Can Coun Fel, 63. *Mem:* Royal Can Acad Arts. *Dealer:* Kenneth G Heffel Fine Arts Inc 2247 Granville St Vancouver BC Canada. *Mailing Add:* 4279 Yuculta Crescent Beach BC V6N 4A9 Canada

ONO, YOKO
CONCEPTUAL ARTIST
b Tokyo, Japan, Feb 18, 33; US citizen. *Study:* Peers' Sch, Gakushuin Univ, Tokyo; Sarah Lawrence Col, New York; Harvard Univ, Cambridge, Mass. *Exhib:* Fluxshoe, Sch Art, Falmouth, Cornwall, Eng, 72; one-person shows, Alchemical Wedding, Albert Hall, London, 67, Evening with Yoko Ono, Birmingham 68, Event, Univ Wales, 69 & Everson Mus, Syracuse, NY, 71; and many others. *Bibliog:* P Devlin (auth), Yoko Ono, Vogue, New York, 12/71; Michael Benedikt (auth), Yoko Notes, Art & Artists, London, 1/72; E Wasserman (auth), This is not here: Yoko Ono at Syracuse, Artforum, New York, 1/72. *Publ:* Auth, Six Film Scripts, Tokyo, 64, Thirteen Film Score Scores, London, 67, John & Yoko Calendar, New York, 70, Grapefruit, London, 70 & A Hole to See the Sky Through, New York, 71. *Mailing Add:* Dakota 1 West 72nd St New York NY 10023

ONORATO, RONALD JOSEPH
HISTORIAN, CRITIC
b Jersey City, NJ, Jan 26, 49. *Study:* Rutgers Col, AB, 70; Brown Univ, MA, 73, PhD(Kress Found Grant), 77. *Collections Arranged:* Labyrinths, 75; Watson Gallery, Wheaton Col, 75-77; Mary Miss Interior Works, 82. *Pos:* Asst cur, New York Cult Ctr, 73-74; chmn & dir exhib, Univ RI, 77- *Teaching:* Vis lectr art hist, Wheaton Col, 75-77; assoc prof art hist, Univ RI, 77-; adj prof criticism & art hist, RI Sch Design, 81- *Awards:* Wyeth Found Grant, 77; Visiting Specialist Grant, Nat Endowment Arts, 78; Nat Endowment Humanities Grant, 83. *Res:* Nineteenth century American art, especially Thomas Eakins and Philadelphia; contemporary art criticism; public sculpture. *Publ:* Auth, The modern maze, Art Int, 75; auth, Photography and teaching: Eakins at the Academy, Am Art Rev, 76; auth, Illusive spaces: The art of Mary Miss, Arforum, 78; auth, Eakins assistantship to Schuessele, Arts Mag, 79; auth, A dictionary of assumptions: Drawings by contemporary sculptors, Drawing, 83. *Mailing Add:* Dept of Art Univ RI Kingston RI 02881

ONSLOW FORD, GORDON M
PAINTER
b Wendover, Eng, Dec 26, 12; US citizen. *Study:* Surrealist Group, 38-43. *Work:* Tate Gallery, London; Solomon R Guggenheim Mus, New York; Whitney Mus of Am Art, New York; San Francisco Mus of Mod Art; Fogg Art Mus, Cambridge; and others. *Exhib:* Karl Nierendorf Gallery, New York, 46; Retrospective, 48, Drawings and Watercolors, 64 & Large Paintings, 71, San Francisco Mus of Mod Art; Rabow Gallery, 56-73; Paintings 1950-1962, M H de Young Mem Mus, San Francisco, 62; Gallery of Art, Victoria, BC, 71; Pyramid Galleries Ltd, Washington, DC, 75; Retrospective of 100 paintings, Oakland Mus, 77. *Teaching:* Lectr surrealist painting, New Sch Social Res, NY, 40; lectr mod art, Blaisdell Inst Conf, 79. *Bibliog:* Madeline Tourtelot (contribr), Island Time (20 minute film), Oakland Mus, 66. *Publ:* Contribr, London Gallery Bull, 40; auth, Towards a New Subject in Painting, San Francisco Mus of Art, 48; auth, Painting in the Instant, Thames & Hudson, London & Harry Abrams, New York, 64; co-auth, The Dynaton 25 Years Later (catalogue), Los Angeles Co Mus, 77; auth, Creation, Schreiner Galerie, Basel, Switz, 78. *Mailing Add:* PO Box 128 Inverness CA 94937

OPIE, JOHN MART
PAINTER
b Sandusky, Ohio, Dec 10, 36. *Study:* Kent State Univ, BFA, MA. *Work:* Allentown Art Mus, Pa; Akron Art Inst, Ohio; Fordham Univ, NY; New Orleans Art Mus, La; St Lawrence Univ, NY. *Exhib:* Pa Acad Fine Arts, 65; Butler Mus Mid-Year Ann, 76; In Praise of Space, Westminster Col, Corcoran Gallery, 76; Personal Visions, Places, Spaces, Bronx Mus, 78; one-man shows, New Orleans Art Mus, 68, Galerie Simonne Stern, New Orleans, 69, 70, 72, 75, 80 & 83 & Bowery Gallery, New York, 73, 76 & 79; Charles More Gallery, Philadelphia, 82. *Teaching:* Instr painting, Pasadena City Col, Calif, 63-65; assoc prof painting, La State Univ, Baton Rouge, 65-70. *Awards:* Nat Endowment Arts Award, 67. *Bibliog:* Leonard Edmondson (auth), Etching, Van Nostrand Reinhold, 73. *Media:* Acrylic on Paper, Oil on Canvas. *Dealer:* Charles More Gallery 1630 Walnut Philadelphia PA 19103; Galerie Simonne Stern The Rink 2727 Prytania New Orleans LA 70130. *Mailing Add:* Pleasant Valley St Rt Quakertown PA 18951

OPPENHEIM, DENNIS A
SCULPTOR
b Mason City, Wash, Sept 6, 38. *Study:* Calif Col Arts & Crafts, BA; Univ Hawaii; Stanford Univ, MFA. *Work:* Mus Mod Art, New York; Boymans Mus, Rotterdam, Holland; Centre Georges Pompideau, Paris; Kunsthaus, Zurich, Switz; Detroit Art Inst, Mich. *Comn:* Sculpture, Cranbrook Acad Art, Bloomfield Hills, Mich, 81; sculpture, Rijksmuseum Kroller-Muller, Oterio, Holland, 82; sculpture, Pattoria di Celle, Pistoia, Italy, 83. *Exhib:* When Attitude Becomes Form, Kunsthalle, Bern, Switz, 69; A Report--Two Ocean Projects, Mus Mod Art, New York, 69, Information, 70; Am Drawings 1963-73, Whitney Mus Am Art, 73; Mass Inst Technol, 74; Retrospective, Palais des Beaux-Arts, Brussels, Belg, 75; Mus Boymans-van Beuningen, Rotterdam, Holland, 75, Art Gallery Ont, Toronto, Can, Kunsthalle Basel, Switz, 79; Louisiana Mus, Stockholm, Sweden, 78; Mus Art Contemp, Montreal, Que; Israel Mus, Jerusalem; Ace Gallery, Los Angeles, 81; Rijksmus, Holland, 81; Musee d'art etd'histoire, Geneva, Switz, 80; and others. *Teaching:* Guest artist sculpture, Yale Univ, 69; guest artist, Pratt Inst Art, Brooklyn, 69; guest artist, Calif Col Arts & Crafts, 70; guest artist, RI Col Design, 70; guest artist, Univ Wis-Whitewater, 70; guest artist sculpture, Art Inst Chicago, 71-72; guest artist sculpture, NS Col Art, 71-72. *Awards:* Newhouse Found Grant, Stanford Univ, 65; John Simon Guggenheim Found Fel, 71-72; Nat Endowment for the Arts, Grant, 74 & 81. *Dealer:* Sonnabend Gallery New York NY. *Mailing Add:* 54 Franklin St New York NY 10013

OPPENHEIM, SAMUEL EDMUND
PAINTER
Study: Nat Acad Design; Art Students League. *Work:* Chrysler Mus Art, Va; White House; West Point Mil Acad, NY; Nat Acad Design, New York; Pentagon, Washington, DC; plus many others. *Exhib:* Nat Acad Design; Audubon Artists; Allied Artists Am; Hudson Valley Art Asn; Grand Cent Art Galleries; and many others. *Teaching:* Instr art, Art Students League, 67-72. *Awards:* Prizes, Allied Artists Am, Hudson Valley Art Asn & Grand Cent Art Prof League; and others. *Mem:* Salmagundi Club; Allied Artists Am; Grand Cent Art Gallery; Artists Fel; Hudson Valley Art Asn. *Media:* Oil. *Mailing Add:* 580 E Lake Dr Naples FL 33940

OPPENHEIMER, SELMA L
PAINTER
b Baltimore, Md, Jan 13, 98. *Study:* Goucher Col, AB; Md Inst Col Art. *Work:* Baltimore Pub Schs; Loyola Col, Md; Univ Md. *Exhib:* Retrospective, Jewish Community Ctr, Baltimore, Md, 67; Mus Art Ann & Invitational, 68; one-person show, Has Sinai Synagogue, 77, McDonough Sch, 78, Cleveland Mem Gallery; Corcoran Gallery Art Biennials, Washington, DC; Western Md Col; Art Inst Chicago; Va Mus Art, Richmond; Mus Mod Art, New York. *Awards:* Lillian Cotton & Susan Kahn Awards, Nat Asn Women Artists, 52, 60 & 65; Purchase Award, Loyola Col, 67. *Mem:* Artists Equity Asn (past pres, Baltimore Chap); Nat Asn Women Artists; Baltimore Watercolor Club; Am Fedn Art. *Media:* Oil. *Mailing Add:* 7121 Park Heights Ave Baltimore MD 21215

OPPER, JOHN
PAINTER
b Chicago, Ill, Oct 29, 08. *Study:* Cleveland Sch Art; Case Western Reserve Univ, BS; Columbia Univ, MA & EdD; also with Hans Hofmann. *Work:* Mus Mod Art, New York; James Michener Found Mus, Austin, Tex; Milwaukee Art Ctr, Wis; NY Univ Collection; Montclair Mus Art, NJ. *Exhib:* Int Watercolor Exhib, Art Inst Chicago, 60; Int Watercolor Exhib, Brooklyn Mus; Int Exhib Paintings, Carnegie Inst, Pittsburgh, 61; American Drawings, Moore Inst, 68; Recent Acquisitions, Mus Mod Art, New York; Corcoran Gallery Art, 78; and others. *Teaching:* Assoc prof art, Univ NC, 52-57; prof art, NY Univ, 57-74, emer prof, 74- *Awards:* First Prize for Oil Painting, High Mus Art, 55; John Simon Guggenheim Fel, 69; Nat Endowments Arts Grant Painting, 74. *Media:* Oil, Watercolor, Acrylic. *Dealer:* Borgenicht Gallery 724 Fifth Ave New York NY 10019. *Mailing Add:* Box 347 Amagansett NY 11930

ORDER, TRUDY
PAINTER
b Munich, Ger, Nov 22, 44; US citizen. *Study:* Akad Malkunst, Munich; Scoula di Pictura, Ancona, Italy; Nat Acad Design, New York, with Maxwell Starr & Umberto Romano. *Work:* Columbia Mus Art, SC; Mt St Vincent Col; Ft Tyron Jewish Ctr, New York; Holy Rood Episcopal Church, New York. *Comn:* The Gift (oil), comn by Mme Trau, Antwerp, Belg, 70; Bar Mitzwa (oil), comn by Signora Cagli, Ancona, 72; Bar Mitzwa (graphic), comn by Mme Tilli le Brewster, Paris, 73; In the Park (oil), comn by Ernest Raaschou, St Thomas, VI, 73. *Exhib:* Audubon Artists, New York, 61; Allied Artists, New York, 62; Knickerbocker Artists, New York, 64; one-man shows, Mt St Vincent Col, 66-74 & Pietrantonio Gallery, New York, 68; Metrop Mus Art, New York, 79. *Awards:* First Prize for Oil, Twilight Park Artists, 63, Second Prize for Pastel, 63 & First Prize for Watercolor, 63. *Bibliog:* Peggy London (auth), Trudy Order, Nat Soc Arts & Lett, 64. *Mem:* Nat Soc Arts & Lett; Kappa Pi; fel Royal Soc Arts. *Media:* Oil, Watercolor. *Dealer:* Town Gallery 1036 Lexington Ave New York NY 10021. *Mailing Add:* 250 Cabrini Blvd New York NY 10033

ORENSANZ, ANGEL L
SCULPTOR, CERAMIST
b Larues, Spain, Feb 11, 41. *Study:* San Jorge Royal Fine Arts Sch, Barcelona, MA(fine arts), 64; Ecole Nat Beaux Arts, Paris, dipl(advan studies), 67; Royal Sch Fine Arts, London, dipl(advan studies), 68. *Work:* Calif Mus Sci & Indust, Los Angeles; Mus Art Mod Ville Paris; Mus Arte Contemp, Madrid, Spain; Univ Madrid, Spain; Mus Resistencia Salvador Allende, Paris. *Comn:* Refractory Facade, Dean & Mgt, Barcelona, Spain, 78; Metal Environment, Mgt Defense, Paris, 80; American Landscapes, IBM Corp, Boca Raton, Fla, 81; Purple Environment, comn by Martin Gelber, Los Angeles, 82; Kenji Growth, Steel Three, Los Angeles City Coun, 83. *Exhib:* Landscape Retrieval, Bienal Sao Paulo, Brazil, 77; Environmens, Ankrum Gallery, Los Angeles, 81; Indoor Outdoor Links, Boston City Hall Art Gallery, 81; solo exhib, Flying Sculpture, Calif Mus Sci & Indust, Los Angeles, 81; Sculpture Today, Mus Luxemburg, Paris, 83. *Awards:* Prix Everitube, Int Exhib, City Everitube, 75; Gold Medal, City Saragossa Bienale, 76; Arts, Sci, Lett, City Paris, 77. *Bibliog:* Charles Spencer (auth), Art as a public work, 80, James Sweeney (auth), Orensanz's sculpture, 81 & Pierre Restany (auth), The great interplay, 81, Sculpture & Environment. *Mem:* Royal Acad St Louis, Saragossa; Asn Artists & Ecrivains, Paris; Artists Social Responsibility. *Mailing Add:* 193 Tenth Ave New York NY 10011

ORENSTEIN, GLORIA FEMAN
EDUCATOR, HISTORIAN
b New York, NY, Mar 8, 38. *Study:* Brandeis Univ, BA(romance lang & lit), 59; Radcliffe Col, MA(Slavic lang & lit), 61; NY Univ(Danforth Grad Fel for Women), 66-71, PhD(comp lit), 71. *Pos:* Contrib ed, Womanart & Chrysalis Mag; co-founder, The Woman's Salon. *Teaching:* Lectr women of surrealism, Cornell Univ, 73, Pa State Univ, 74, Inst 20th Century Studies, Univ Wis, 75, Sheridan Col, 75 & Artists Space, New York, 75; asst prof women in contemp

arts, Douglass Col, 74-, asst prof Eng, 75-, chairperson women's studies prog, 76-78; dir Rutgers Jr Yr in France, 78-79; assoc prof compos, lit & prog for study of women & men in soc, Univ Southern Calif, Los Angeles, 81-82. *Bibliog:* Article in Female Artists: Past & Present, Women's Hist Res Ctr, 74; coordr panel, Women Artists: Preparing for Changing our Future, Centre Cult Am, Paris, 79. *Mem:* Mod Lang Asn; Soc Rel Higher Educ; Nat Women's Studies Asn; Am Soc French Prof; Int Comparative Lit Asn; Int Asn Study Dada & Surrealism. *Res:* Surrealism; women's art history; women in the arts; art and psychic phenomena. *Publ:* Auth, A renaissance of goddess-culture art, Fireweed: A Women's Lit & Cult J, No 1, 78; coauth (with Miriam Brumer), Americans in Paris revisited, Women Artists News, 79; auth, The goddess in art by contemporary women, Women's Resource & Res Ctr, London, England, 79; auth, Reclaiming the great mother: A feminist journey to madness and back in search of a goddess heritage, Symposium, spring 82; auth, Towards a bifocal vision in surrealist aesthetics, Trivia, fall 83; and others. *Mailing Add:* 435 S Maple Dr Beverly Hills CA 90212

ORENTLICHER, JOHN
VIDEO ARTIST, SCULPTOR
b Roanoke, Va, June 7, 43. *Study:* Goddard Col, BA, 68; Art Inst Chicago, MFA, 70. *Work:* Art Metropole, Toronto, Ont, Can; Everson Mus, Syracuse, NY; US Info Agency, DC; Sch Art Inst Chicago; Video Collection, Long Beach Mus, Calif. *Exhib:* Outrageous Film, Whitney Mus Am Art, New York, 74; Everson Video Revue, Everson Mus & traveling, Syracuse, NY, 79-80; one person exhibs, Art Metropole, Toronto, 82, Ctr Art Tapes, Halifax, NS & Hallwalls (video), Buffalo, NY, 82; Basil Art Fair, Basil, Switz; Athens Int Film & Video Festival, Ohio, 82. *Pos:* Peace Corps, Chile, 64-66; bd trustees, Synapse Video, Syracuse, NY, 78- *Teaching:* Prof video, Col Visual & Performing Arts, Syracuse Univ, 76-81, chmn dept experimental studies, 81-83. *Awards:* Purchase Award, Royal Film Arch Belg, 75; Nat Endowment for Arts video fel, 76; New York Coun Arts Proj Grant, 82-83. *Bibliog:* Dale Hoyt (auth), Getting close to a distant feeling, Syracuse New Times, 78; Sarah McFadden (auth), Detroit, Art in Am, 79; Victor Anconia (auth), Ithaca video, Videography, 79. *Mem:* Media Alliance, New York. *Media:* Video. *Mailing Add:* 2109 S Geddes St Syracuse NY 13207

ORKIN, RUTH (MRS MORRIS ENGEL)
PHOTOGRAPHER, FILMMAKER
b Boston, Mass, Sept 3, 21. *Work:* Mus Mod Art, New York; Metrop Mus Art, New York. *Exhib:* Lovers & Lollipops, Venice Film Festival, 55; one-woman shows, 175 Photos, Nikon House, New York, 74, Witkin Gallery, Rizzoli Bookstore Galleries, New York; Photo League, 78; and many others. *Awards:* Silver Lion of San Marco for Co-Direction of Little Fugitive, Venice Film Festival, 53; Academy Nomination for Co-Writing Little Fugitive, 53; Top Ten Women Photographers in US, Prof Photogr Am, 59. *Bibliog:* Cecil Starr (auth), The invisible women, Sight & Sound, 80; article, Harpers Bazaar, 9/82; Candor and candids, Darkroom Mag, 9/82; and others. *Mem:* Acad Motion Picture Arts & Sci; Am Soc Photogr in Commun; Am Soc Mag Photogr. *Publ:* Photogr, A World Through My Window, Harper & Row, 78; photogr, A Photo Journal, Viking Studio Bks, 81; photogr, More Pictures From My Window, Rizzoli Pub, 83; and others. *Mailing Add:* 65 Central Park W New York NY 10023

ORLAND, TED N
PHOTOGRAPHER
b San Francisco, Calif. *Study:* Univ Southern Calif, BS(industrial design), 63; San Francisco State Univ, Calif, MA(interdisciplinary arts), 74. *Work:* Corcoran Gallery Art, Washington, DC; San Francisco Mus Mod Art, Calif; Stanford Mus Art, Calif; Santa Barbara Mus Art, Calif; Univ Ariz Ctr Creative Photog, Tucson. *Exhib:* Polaroid Images, Franklin Inst, Philadelphia, Pa, 78; The Mechanical Eye, Oakland Mus, Calif, 80; The Out of State Portfolio, Crocker Art Mus, Sacramento, Calif, 81; New Acquisitions, Corcoran Gallery Art, Washington, DC, 81; Am Photog & Nat Parks, national tour, 81-83; Univ Ore Art Mus, Eugene, 82. *Pos:* Apprentice, Saul Marks, Los Angeles, Calif, 62-63; asst, Charles Eames, Venice, Calif, 68-71; asst, Ansel Adams, Carmel, Calif, 72-75; ed, Image Continuum Press, 74- *Teaching:* Photog workshops on varied subjects, Univ Calif Extension, 73-; asst prof & dir undergrad and grad prog, Univ Ore, 81- *Awards:* Artist-in-Residency, Volcanoes Nat Park, Volcano Arts Ctr, Hawaii, 76; Grant to pursue creative work, The Polaroid Corp, 77-78 & Walnut Creek Civic Arts Gallery, 78-79. *Bibliog:* Joel Pickford (auth), Ansel Adams & Ted Orland: A critical comparison, Image Continuum J, 79; David Robertson (auth), The Art & Literature of Yosemite, Yosemite Nat Hist Asn, 82. *Media:* Silver-Base Prints. *Publ:* Illusr, Yosemite Reflections, Flying Spur Press, 77; contribr, Combinations Magazine, Combinations Press, 77 & 80; contribr, Other Realities, Jerry Uelsmann, 81; auth, T Orland's Compendium of Photographic Truths, Image Continuum Press, 81. *Dealer:* Weston Gallery PO Box 655 Carmel CA 93921. *Mailing Add:* Univ Ore Eugene OR 97403

ORLING, ANNE
CONSULTANT, PAINTER
b New York, NY. *Study:* Art Students League; Empire State Univ, Old Westbury, NY, BA(art admin). *Work:* UN, New York; C W Post Col. *Exhib:* Osgood Gallery, New York, 70; Fordham Univ, Bronx, NY, 74; C W Post Art Gallery, Hillwood Commons, Greenvale, NY, 77; Silvermine Guild, New Canaan, Conn; Univ Ariz, Tucson; Baldwin Wallace Col, Berea, Ohio. *Teaching:* Instr art & art hist, North Shore Community Arts Ctr, Great Neck, NY, 63-69. *Mem:* Prof Artists Guild (vpres, 70, pres, 76-78). *Media:* Oil, Acrylic. *Interests:* Service as art consultant to help collectors acquire 19th & 20th century paintings, sculpture and graphics; work with museums, dealers and artists plus corporate consultations. *Mailing Add:* 69 Shelter Lane Roslyn Heights NY 11577

ORR, ARTHUR (LESLIE)
PAINTER, GRAPHIC ARTIST
b Rockport, Mass, Nov 12, 38. *Study:* Mass Col Art, BFA, 63; Univ Ill, Urbana, MFA, 65. *Work:* Tenn Fine Arts Collection, Opryland Hotel, Nashville; High Mus; Taubman Corp, Detroit; Colonial Corp Am, New York. *Comn:* Paintings, Bass & Assoc, Nashville, 76 & Commerce Union Bank, Nashville, 76. *Exhib:* Southeastern Ann, High Mus, 68; Whitney Mus Art Ann, 70; Southeastern Ctr Contemp Art Invitational, Winston-Salem, NC, 79; Tenn Valley Invitational, Washington, DC, 79; solo exhibs, Parallel Realities, Tenn Botanical Ctr, Nashville, 79, Recent Works, Fisk Univ, 81 & Systems & Cutouts, Tenn Fine Arts Ctr, Nashville, 83. *Teaching:* Instr fine arts, Mass Col Art, 65-66; asst prof, Moore Col Art, 66-67 & Peabody Col, 67-72. *Awards:* Jury Awards, Hunter Mus Ann, 69 & Mazur Mus Ann, Monroe, La, 69; Purchase Award, Century III Fine Art Exhib, Nashville, 80. *Media:* Acrylic. *Mailing Add:* 1804 Ashwood Ave Nashville TN 37212

ORR, ELLIOT
PAINTER
b Flushing, New York, June 26, 04. *Study:* Grand Cent Art Sch, with George Luks & Charles W Hawthorne. *Work:* Brooklyn Mus; Whitney Mus Am Art, New York; Addison Gallery, Andover, Mass; Ill State Mus, Springfield; Chrysler Mus, Norfolk, Va. *Exhib:* Romantic Painting in America, Mus Mod Art, New York, 43; Painting in the United States, Carnegie Inst, Pittsburgh, 48; American Painting Today, 50 & American Watercolors, Drawings & Prints, 52, Metrop Mus Art, New York; Golden Anniversary, Provincetown Art Asn, 64; By the People, For the People: New England, DeCordova Mus, Lincoln, Mass, 77; retrospective, 1929-1983, Harmon-Meek Gallery, Naples, Fla, 83; American Art of the 1930's & 1940's, Mitchell Mus, Mt Vernon, Ill, 83. *Awards:* Joseph Lewis Weyrich Mem Prize, Baltimore Mus, 30; Crossett First Prize, Cape Cod Art Asn, 48. *Bibliog:* F F Sherman (auth), Notes on Elliot Orr, Art in Am, 40; Rosamund Frost (auth), Contemporary Art, Crown, 42; John I H Baur (auth), Revolution and Tradition in Modern American Art, Harvard Univ, 51. *Mem:* Life mem Provincetown Art Asn. *Media:* All Media. *Dealer:* Harmon-Meek Gallery 1258 Third St S Naples FL 33940. *Mailing Add:* 442 Broad Ave S Naples FL 33940

ORR, JOSEPH CHARLES
PAINTER
b Tokyo, Japan, Oct 31, 49; US citizen. *Study:* With Anthony Allison, 71; Univ Mo, Columbia, with Frank Stack, 77-78. *Work:* State Mo Hist Soc, Columbia; Mus West Plains, Mo; Amedco Inc, Springfield, Mo. *Comn:* Paintings, Community Fed Savings, Mexico, Mo, 80 & Mercantile Bank, Eldon, Mo, 81; centennial painting, City Eldon, Mo, 82. *Exhib:* Rocky Mountain Nat Watermedia Competition, Foothills Art Ctr, Golden, Colo, 80; 30th Ann Knickerbocker Artists Exhib, 80 & Nat Soc Painters Casein & Acrylic, 80 & 82, Nat Arts Club, New York; Fifth Ann Midwest Watercolor Exhib, Burpee Mus, Rockford, Ill, 81; Nature Interpreted, Mus Hist, Cincinnati, 82. *Awards:* Best of Show, Fine Arts Exhib, Bolingbrook, Ill, 83 & Beverly Art Ctr, First in Painting, Chicago, 83; Canterbury Arts Exhib, Edmond, Okla, 83. *Bibliog:* Rita Mathews-Orr (auth), My husband the artist, Mo Life, 75; Nancy Smeltzer (auth), Missouri landscapes, Columbia Missourian, 7/30/80; Tracey Garrison (auth), The gallery, Okla Arts Gallery, 10/83. *Media:* Acrylic on Masonite. *Dealer:* Flusche Gllery Fine Art 5401 S Harvard Tulsa OK 74135. *Mailing Add:* 25 N Oak St Eldon MO 65026

ORR-CAHALL, ANONA CHRISTINA
CURATOR, HISTORIAN
b June 12, 47. *Study:* Mt Holyoke Col, BA; Oxford Univ; Ecole du Louvre; Yale Univ, MA, MPhil, PhD. *Collections Arranged:* Am Drawing 1970-1973, Yale Univ Art Gallery, 73; Addison Mizner Architect of Dreams and Realities and Contemp Views of the Am Family, Norton Gallery Art, 77. *Pos:* Chief cur art, Oakland Mus, 81- *Teaching:* Asst prof art hist & mus studies, Calif Polytechnic State Univ, San Luis Obispo, 78-81. *Res:* California art 1925-present. *Mailing Add:* c/o Oakland Mus 1000 Oak St Oakland CA 94607

ORSINI (GWENDOLYN ORSINGER ANDERSON)
ENAMELIST, INSTRUCTOR
b Chicago, Ill, May 31, 12. *Study:* Univ Calif, Los Angeles, 34-35; Univ Ill, BS, 37; Univ Va, 55. *Work:* Va Mus Fine Arts, Richmond; Baltimore Mus; Corcoran Gallery Art, Washington, DC; Thomas C Thompson Collection Contemp Am Enamelists, Chicago. *Exhib:* Nat League Am Pen Women 22nd Biennial Art Exhib, 64, Smithsonian Inst, Washington, DC; 7th Creative Craft Biennial, Norfolk Mus, Va, 66; 14th Ann Rochester Festival Relig Arts, 72; 1st Va Craftsmen Biennial, Richmond Mus of Fine Arts, 77; Int Shippo (enamel) Exhib, Tokyo, Japan, 78; and others. *Teaching:* Instr enameling, 1000 Island Mus Craft Sch, Clayton, NY, 66-67; instr enameling, Am Art Assocs, Washington, DC, 67-73; instr enameling, Lake Worth Art League, Fla, winters 73-; instr, Nat Park Serv, Glen Echo, Washington, DC, 79- & Smithsonian Inst Assoc Prog, 80- *Awards:* First Prize in Enamels, Nat League Am Pen Women, 69 & 71; Award, 1st Va Craftsmen Biennial, Richmond Mus of Fine Arts, 77; Second Prize, 30th Creative Crafts Coun, Washington, DC, 76; and many others. *Mem:* Kiln Club, Washington, DC (vpres, 68-69); Nat League Am Pen Women (vpres, 56-58, pres, 58-60); Va Craftsmens Coun; Goldsmiths Guild Washington, DC; World Craft Coun. *Media:* Multimedia. *Dealer:* Enamelists' Gallery Torpedo Art Ctr Alexandria VA; Va Mus Fine Arts Coun Shop Richmond VA. *Mailing Add:* 5906 Wood Sorrel Ct Burke VA 22015

ORTIZ, RAFAEL MONTANEZ
SCULPTOR, EDUCATOR
b New York, NY, Jan 30, 34. *Study:* Brooklyn Mus Art Sch; Art Students League; Pratt Inst, BS & MFA; Columbia Univ, EdD. *Work:* Whitney Mus Am Art, Finch Mus, Mus Mod Art, New York; Syracuse Mus Contemp Art, NY. *Exhib:* Traveling Assemblage Exhib, Mus Mod Art, New York, 63; Young America Exhibition, Whitney Mus Am Art, New York, 65; The Destruction in Art Symposium, London, Eng, 66; Everson Mus, Syracuse, NY, 79; San Antonio Mus, Tex, 79; Chicago Mus Contemp Art, 79; Palacia de Mineria, Mexico City, 80; and others. *Pos:* Dir & cur, El Museo del Barrio, New York, 69-70; comt mem, Ghetto Arts Panel, NY State Coun Arts, 70-71; vchmn, Planning Corp Arts, New York, 71; chmn bd, Fondo Del Sol, DC, 79-81. *Teaching:* Assoc prof art, Mason Gross Sch Arts, Rutgers Univ, 72- *Awards:* John Hay Whitney Fel Grant, 65. *Media:* Mixed Media. *Publ:* Auth, Disassemblage, Art & Artists, 66; ed & auth, Ritual theatre, Aspen Mag, 69; auth, Culture and the people, Art in Am, 71. *Mailing Add:* Mason Gross Sch Arts Rutgers Univ New Brunswick NJ 08903

ORTLIEB, ROBERT EUGENE
SCULPTOR, GRAPHIC ARTIST
b San Diego, Calif, July 4, 25. *Study:* Univ Southern Calif, with Merrell Gage, Francis de Erdely & Glen Lucens, BFA & MFA; independent study, Europe, Mex & SAm; San Francisco State Col. *Work:* Calif Palace Legion Honor Mus, San Francisco; Laguna Beach Art Mus; Univ Calif, Riverside; Riverside Community Col; Loma Linda Univ. *Comn:* First Presbyterian Church, Culver City, Calif, 52; Los Angeles High Sch, 53; Community Church, Palos Verde, Calif, 68; Apothecaries (bronze), Dr MacFarlane, Univ Southern Calif, 75; and others. *Exhib:* Int Graphic Exhib, Cincinnati, Ohio, 53; Los Angeles Co Mus Calif; Denver Art Mus; one-man shows, Ill State Mus, Springfield, 64 & Dean Mus, Cherry Valley, Calif, 75; Dallas Mus Fine Arts; Oakland Art Mus, Calif; Palm Springs Desert Mus, Calif, 81; and others. *Teaching:* Instr sculpture, Riverside Art Ctr, Univ Calif, 62-75 & Univ Southern Calif, Idyllwild, 64-75; inst prof de Stato per l'Industria de l'Artigianato del Marmo in, Carrara, Italy, 72; Village Ctr for the Creative Arts, Palm Springs, Calif, 68- *Awards:* First Awards, Calif State Fair & Expos, 48 & 57, Long Beach Art Mus, 57 & 77 & 50th Nat Orange Show, San Bernardino, 65. *Bibliog:* Robert Ortlieb, La Rev Mod, Paris, France, 62; Janice Lovoos & Felice Paramore (co-auth), Wood carving and wood mosaic, In: Modern Mosaic Techniques, Watson-Guptill, 65; Betje Howell (auth), Twelve California artists, Am Artist, R Riedinger, 68; and others. *Mem:* Hon life mem Inglewood Art Asn, Calif. *Media:* Stone, Wood Carving; Bronze, Plexiglas. *Dealer:* Adagio Galleries 193 South Palm Canyon Drive Palm Springs CA 92262. *Mailing Add:* 11111 Jerry Lane Garden Grove CA 92640

ORTLIP, PAUL DANIEL
PAINTER
b Englewood, NJ, May 21, 26. *Study:* Houghton Acad; Art Students League; with Louis Bouche, 47, Reginald Marsh, 48, Robert Brackman & Edwin Dickinson, 49; Acad Grande Chaumiere, 50. *Work:* US Navy Art Collection, Pentagon, Washington, DC; Bergen Community Mus, Paramus, NJ; Air & Space Mus, Smithsonian Inst, Washington, DC; Am Col Clin Pharmacology, NY Acad of Med, New York; Fairleigh Dickinson Univ; and others. *Comn:* Mem portrait of JFK, Fairleigh Dickinson Univ Libr, 64; Gemini 5 Astronauts, Off Info, USN, 65, Vietnam (painting), 67, Apollo 12 Astronauts, 69 & Apollo 17 Astronauts, 72; and others. *Exhib:* Salon L'Art Libre Ann, Paris, France, 50; Allied Artists Am Ann, 60-71; Collection of Fine Arts, Smithsonian Inst, Washington, DC; Galerie Vallombreuse, Biarritz, France, 74; La Galerie Mouffe, Paris, 75; James Hunt Barker Galleries, New York, Palm Beach & Nantucket, 83. *Pos:* Off US Navy artist, Off Info, Washington, DC, 63-; art cur, Fairleigh Dickinson Univ, 67-70. *Teaching:* Instr painting, Montclair Acad, NJ, 57-58; artist in residence, Fairleigh Dickinson Univ, 57-67; instr painting, Montclair Mus, 58-59 & 76-80. *Awards:* Franklin Williams Award, Salmagundi Club, 67; Oil Painting Award Outstanding Achievement, US Navy, 68; Artist of the Year Award, Hudson Artists, Jersey City Mus, 70; and others. *Bibliog:* Marg Dulac (auth), Odyssey of an artist, NJ Mus & Arts, 5/71; Int Naval Rev, 76; M Stephen Doherty (auth), Paul Ortlip, His Heritage and His Art, Phoenix Pub, 83. *Mem:* Life mem Art Students League; Allied Artists Am; Salmagundi Club; US Navy Liaison Comt (off artist); Nat Soc Mural Painters; and others. *Media:* Mixed Media. *Dealer:* James Hunt Galleries Five E 57th St New York NY 10022. *Mailing Add:* 95 Main St Ft Lee NJ 07024

ORTMAN, GEORGE EARL
PAINTER, SCULPTOR
b Oakland, Calif, Oct 17, 26. *Study:* Ariz State Univ; Calif Col Arts & Crafts; Atelier 17, New York; Acad Andre Lhote, Paris; Hans Hofmann Sch, New York. *Work:* Guggenheim Mus, Mus Mod Art, New York; Walker Art Ctr, Minneapolis, Minn; Albright-Knox Art Gallery, Buffalo; Milwaukee Art Ctr; Nat Gallery Art; and others. *Comn:* Mural, comn by Bd Educ, PS 192, New York, 67; Reredo, Unitarian Church, Princeton, NJ, 68; banners, Ind Univ Opera House, 71; Oracle (three panels), Mfrs Hanover Trust, 71; Albert Kahn & Assoc Inc, 81; and others. *Exhib:* Carnegie Inst Int, Pittsburgh, 60, 64 & 70; Toward a New Abstraction, Jewish Mus, New York, 63; Tokyo Biennial, Japan, 64; 100 Years of Amerian Art, Whitney Mus Am Art, 64 & Two Decades of Geometric Abstraction, 65. *Teaching:* Sr fel painting, Princeton Univ, 66-69; head painting dept, Cranbrook Acad Art, 70- *Awards:* Guggenheim Fel, 65; First Prize Religion Art, Birmingham Mus Art, 66; First Prize, NJ State Mus Second Ann, 67. *Bibliog:* J Borgzinger (auth), Analytical art, Time Mag, 4/64; Martin Friedman (auth), Symbols, Art News, 10/65. *Dealer:* Gimpel-Weitzenhoffer Galleries 1040 Madison Ave New York NY 10021. *Mailing Add:* Box 192 Castine ME 04421

ORTMAYER, CONSTANCE
SCULPTOR, EDUCATOR
b New York, NY, July 19, 02. *Study:* Royal Acad Fine Arts & Royal Acad Master Sch, Vienna, Austria, MFA. *Work:* Am Numismatic Soc, New York; Brookgreen Gardens, SC. *Comn:* Bronze group, State of SC, Brookgreen Gardens, 34; US Half Dollar, Stephen Foster Commemorative, 36; bas reliefs, US Post Off, Arcadia, Fla, 39 & Scottsboro, Ala, 41; Award Medals, Fla Acad Sci & Rollins Col, 52-62. *Exhib:* Vienna Secession, 32; Nat Asn Women Painters & Sculptors, New York, 35; Allied Arts, Brooklyn Mus, 36; Nat Sculpture Soc, Whitney Mus Am Art, New York, 40; Pa Acad Fine Arts, Philadelphia, 41. *Teaching:* Prof sculpture, Rollins Col, 37-68, head dept art, 60-68, emer prof, 68- *Awards:* Anna Hyatt Huntington Prize, Nat Asn Women Painters & Sculptors, 35; Henry O Avery Archit Prize, Nat Sculpture Soc, 40; Award of Merit, Fla Fedn Art, 48. *Mem:* Morristown Art Asn; emer mem Nat Sculpture Soc; Fla Fedn Art; hon mem Orlando Ceramic Soc. *Media:* Wood, Ceramic. *Mailing Add:* 617 W Second N St Morristown TN 37814

ORZE, JOSEPH JOHN
ADMINISTRATOR, SCULPTOR
b Exeter, Pa, Dec 11, 32. *Study:* Syracuse Univ, BFA(magna cum laude), 55, MS, 56; George Peabody Col, EdD, 70. *Work:* Munson, Williams, Proctor Inst, Utica, NY; Sch Benedictine Fathers, Rome, Italy; Mass Maritime Acad, Buzzards Bay. *Exhib:* One-man & two-man shows, J B Speed Art Mus, Louisville, Ky, 65, Dana Arts Ctr, Colgate Univ, Hamilton, NY, 69; Brooks Mem Gallery, Memphis; Hunter Gallery, Univ Chattanooga; Syracuse Univ, NY; Conn Acad Fine Arts, Wadsworth Atheneum, Hartford; Everson Mus Fine Art, Syracuse; and others. *Pos:* Vpres & dir, Southern Asn Sculptors, 64-66; chmn, Conn Col Coun Arts, 67-69; vpres & dir, Marion Art Ctr, Mass, 73-75; dir & treas, Pub Art Proj, Inc, New Bedford, Mass, 74- *Teaching:* Instr art & educ, Syracuse Univ, 56-59; assoc prof sculpture & art educ, State Univ NY Col New Paltz, 59-61; assoc prof art & head dept, Middle Tenn State Univ, 61-66; prof art & chmn dept, Southern Conn State Col, 66-69; dean, Col Fine & Applied Arts, Southeastern Mass Univ, 69-75; pres, Worcester State Col, 75- *Awards:* Purchase Award for Sculpture, Munson, Williams, Proctor Inst, 58; R A Rathbone Best in Show Award, New Haven Print & Clay Club, 66; First Prize in Sculpture, New Eng Arts Festival, Waterbury, Conn, 67 & 68. *Mem:* Col Art Asn; Nat Art Educ Asn. *Publ:* Auth, Understanding children's art, Instr Mag, 5/64; auth, Enigma of modern art, Peabody Reflector, 5/66; auth, Role of the Fine Arts in the University, Middle Tenn State Univ, 69; auth, Visual arts in higher education, Mass Art Educ Asn, 70; co-auth, Art From Scrap, Davis, 2nd ed, 73. *Mailing Add:* Worcester State Col 486 Chandler St Worcester MA 01602

OSBORN, ELODIE C
ADMINISTRATOR, FILM CONSULT
b Brooklyn, NY, Dec 6, 11. *Study:* Packer Col Inst; Wellesley Col, BA; Sch Fine Arts, NY Univ; Sorbonne, cert. *Collections Arranged:* Many exhibs at Mus Mod Art, New York, and touring to other mus, cols & schs; Klee Mem Exhib, Mus Mod Art, New York, 41. *Pos:* Dir traveling exhibs, Mus Mod Art, New York, 33-48; dir, Salisbury Film Soc, 51-81. *Mem:* Am Fedn Arts; Mus Mod Art; Int Film Seminars (bd trustees, 68-); MacDowell Colony (mem bd dirs, 70-, secy bd, 72-, vpres, 73-75, pres, 75-77); Am Fedn Film Socs (vpres, 57-58). *Publ:* Auth, Modern Sculpture (portfolio), 51; auth, Manual of Traveling Exhibitions, UNESCO, 53; contribr, Art in Am, 66; contribr, Film Quart, 68; contribr, Film Libr Quart, 72; auth, program notes for Modern Arts and Artists Traveling Exhib, Mus Mod Art, 79. *Mailing Add:* RFD 1 Box 140 Salisbury CT 06068

OSBORN, KEVIN RUSSELL
BOOK ARTIST, PRINTMAKER
b Boston, Mass, July 3, 51. *Study:* Ecole Nat Arts Decoratifs, Nice, France, 71-72; Univ Vt, Burlington, BA(cum laude), 73; Visual Studies Workshop, State Uiv NY, Buffalo, MFA, 77. *Work:* Mus Mod Art, New York; Mus Nat Art Mod, Paris; Whitney Mus; Art Inst Chicago; DeYoung Mus, San Francisco. *Comn:* Parallel (artist book), Ga State Arts Coun, Atlanta, 80. *Exhib:* Words and Images, Philadelphia Art Alliance, 80; solo exhib, Washington Proj Arts, 80; Ex Libris, Traction Gallery, Los Angeles, 81; Re/pages, New England Found Arts Touring Exhib, 81-82; Cent Livres d'Ailleurs, Ed Jean-Michel Pl, Paris, 82; 12th Biennale Paris, Mus Mod Art, Paris, 82. *Pos:* Dir, Bookworks Prog, Writer's Ctr, Bethesda, Md, 77- *Teaching:* Instr workshops, Calif Col Arts & Crafts, 80, Va Commonwealth Univ, 83 & State Univ NY, Purchase, 83. *Awards:* Grant Vector Rev (artist book), Found Todays Art, 83; Va Mus Fel, 83; Nat Endowment Arts Fel, 84. *Bibliog:* Clive Phillpot (auth), Real lives, Artforum, 5/82; Paul Zelevansky (auth), Visual literature, Am Book Rev, spring 83; Nancy Solomon (auth), The layered look, Afterimage, summer 83. *Media:* Artists Books; Experimental Offset. *Mailing Add:* PO Box 11147 Arlington VA 22210

OSBORN, ROBERT
ILLUSTRATOR, PAINTER
b Oshkosh, Wis, Oct 26, 04. *Study:* Yale Univ; Brit Acad, Rome; Acad Scandinav, Paris; also with Friesz, Varoquier & Despiau; Md Inst Art, Hon DFA, 63. *Work:* Mus Mod Art, New York; Addison Gallery Art, Andover, Mass; Paine Art Mus, Oshkosh, Wis; Corcoran Gallery Art, Washington, DC; Wadsworth Atheneum, Hartford, Conn. *Comn:* Mural, Quinta da Bacalhoa Azeitao, Port, 38-39; mural, Am Mus Natural Hist, New York, 55; mural, comn by Stonoroff for Planning Comn Philadelphia, 56; two murals for Puerto Rico Planning Comn, 70 & three murals for Smithsonian Exhib on Productivity, 72, comn by Ivan Chermayeff. *Exhib:* Wartime

Posters, Art Inst Chicago, 46; Va Mus Fine Arts, Richmond, 52; Wadsworth Atheneum, 58; Whitney Mus Am Art, New York, 60; Brooklyn Mus, 61; Live From Conn, Whitney Mus, Stamford, Conn; Nuclear Conflict, Carpenter Ctr, Harvard Univ, 84. *Pos:* Presented first show of Edward Weston in the East, Hotchkiss Sch, 31. *Teaching:* Founder & head dept art, Hotchkiss Sch, Lakeville, Conn, 29-35; chmn Yale Coun, Sch Art & Archit, Yale Univ, 60-65, alumni exec coun, 70- *Awards:* Gov Medal, Wis; Distinguished Pub Serv Award, Legion of Merit. *Bibliog:* Leo Lionni (auth), Osborn, Print, Vol 5; Russell Lynes (auth), Osborn's Americans, Horizon, 9/60; Fritz Eichenberg (auth), Osborn, Am Graphic Artist, 65; Drawings Robert Osborn, Houghton Mifflin (in prep); plus others. *Mem:* Elizabethan Club; Scroll & Keys; Century Asn. *Media:* Pen, Crayon, Watercolor. *Collection:* Despiau, Miros, Klees, Calders, Marinni, MacIver, Hartley, Picasso, Dubuffets, Friedmans, Shahns and others. *Publ:* Auth, Osborn on Osborn, Ticknor & Fields, Houghton Mifflin, 82; and others. *Mailing Add:* Salisbury CT 06068

OSBORNE, CYNTHIA A
PRINTMAKER, EDUCATOR
b New Milford, Conn, Dec 13, 47. *Study:* Conn Col, New London, BA, 69; Univ Wis-Madison, MFA, 73. *Work:* Bradley Univ, Peoria, Ill; Davidson Col, NC; Security Pac Nat Banks, Calif; State Univ NY Buffalo; US Info Agency, Selected US Embassies. *Exhib:* Miami Graphics Biennial, Metrop Mus, Fla, 76 & 80; Current Directions in Southern Calif Art, Los Angeles Inst Contemp Art, 77 & 78; Nat Print Exhib, Soc Am Graphic Artists, New York, 77 & 79; Drawings & Prints, Space, Los Angeles, 79; Paper in Particular, Columbia Col, Mo, 80; and many others. *Pos:* Vis artist, Nat Print Symp, Cranbrook Acad Art, Detroit, spring 80. *Teaching:* Assoc prof printmaking, Calif State Univ, Long Beach, 75-82, assoc prof art, currently; lectr printmaking, Otis Art Inst, Los Angeles, 77. *Awards:* Purchase Awards, Griffin Press Co, Oakland, Calif, 75 & Los Angeles Printmakers Int Exhib, Graphic Chemical, Chicago, 77. *Mem:* Los Angeles Printmaking Soc (bd mem, 77); Soc Am Graphic Artists; World Print Coun, San Francisco. *Media:* Printmaking; Lithography. *Mailing Add:* 2577 Delta Ave Long Beach CA 90810

OSBORNE, ELIZABETH
PAINTER, INSTRUCTOR
b Philadelphia, Pa, June 5, 36. *Study:* Pa Acad Fine Arts, cert(Schiedt Traveling Scholarship), 58; Univ Pa, BFA(with hons), 59. *Work:* Chase Manhattan Bank, New York; Philadelphia Mus Art, Pa; Pa Acad Fine Arts, Philadelphia; Delaware Art Mus, Wilmington. *Comn:* Etching Edition 100 Prints, Philadelphia Print Club, Pa, 81; Lithograph Ed 125 Prints, Friends of the Philadelphia Mus Art, Pa, 79. *Exhib:* Philadelphia: Three Centuries of Am Art, Philadelphia Mus Art, Pa, 76; Painting and Sculpture Today, 1978, Indianapolis Mus Art, 78; Contemporary Drawings: Philadelphia II, Philadelphia Mus Art & Pa Acad Fine Arts, 79; The New American Still Life, Westmoreland Co Mus, Pa, 79; A Feast for the Eyes, Heckscher Mus, NY, 81; Contemporary American Realism Since 1960, Pa Acad Fine Arts, 81; Collectors Gallery, McNary Art Inst, San Antonio, Tex, 82; Realist Watercolors Fla, Univ Miami, 83. *Teaching:* Critic painting, Pa Acad Fine Art, Philadelphia, 61- *Awards:* Fulbright Scholarship Paris, 63; Rosenthal Foundation Award, Nat Inst Arts & Letters, 71; MacDowell Fel, 83. *Bibliog:* Gordon Brown (auth), Painting with light Elizabeth Osborne, Arts Mag, 77; Eve Medoff (auth), article, Am Artist, 77; Christine Hopf (dir), In Praise of Women Artists (film), Bo-Tree Productions, 79. *Mem:* Philadelphia Print Club. *Media:* Watercolor, Oil. *Dealer:* Fischbach Gallery 29 West 57th St New York NY; Marian Locks Gallery 1524 Walnut St Philadelphia PA 19103. *Mailing Add:* 2125 Cypress Street Philadelphia PA 19103

OSBORNE, ROBERT LEE
PAINTER, EDUCATOR
b Chandler, Ind, June 24, 28. *Study:* Ind Univ, with Pickens, Marx, Engel, Ballinger & Hope, MA; Univ Iowa, with Lechay, Hecksher, Longman, Ludens & Tomasini, MA. *Exhib:* Fac Shows, Ringling Sch Art, Sarasota, Fla; Venice Art League, Fla; one-man shows, Beaux Arts Gallery, St Petersberg, Hilton Leech Gallery, Sarasota, South Fla Col, Lakeland & Manatee Art League, Bradenton, Fla. *Pos:* Designer, Olszewski Art Glass Co, St Louis, formerly; dir, Manatee Art League, Bradenton, 71-72; dean fac, Ringling Sch Art, currently. *Teaching:* Lectr, Evansville Mus; asst prof art & head dept, Evansville Col; instr, Evansville Mus; instr, Ringling Sch Art, currently. *Awards:* Gold Key Award, Evansville, Ind, 46; Prize, Ind Univ, 52. *Mem:* Tri-State Art Guild (pres, 58-66); Fla Artists Group. *Media:* Oil, Acrylic. *Publ:* Illusr, Organization Aquatic Clubs, 55; var illus in Image Mag. *Mailing Add:* Ringling Sch Art 1191 27th St Sarasota FL 33580

OSBY, LARISSA GEISS
PAINTER
b Artemowsk, Russia, June 7, 28; US citizen. *Study:* Lyceum & Univ Goettingen, Ger; Univ Munich; Acad Fine Arts, Munich, Ger. *Work:* Carnegie Inst, Pittsburgh; Alcoa Collection; US Steel Collection; Westinghouse Elec Co Collection; plus others. *Comn:* Am for Democratic Action, 69; Koppers Co & First Fed Savings & Loan Asn, Pittsburgh, 72; United Steelworkers of Am, 73; Nat Steel Corp, 77. *Exhib:* One-man shows, Carnegie Inst Mus of Art, 72 & Pa State Unit, New Kensington, 73; Walker Art Ctr Biennial, Minneapolis, 66; Assoc Artists Ann, 55-78; Mid-Yr Nat, Butler Inst Am Art, Youngstown, Ohio, 58, 59 & 79; Guest of Hon Exhib, Birmingham Arts Festival, Mich, 61; Drawings USA, St Paul Art Ctr, Minn, 63; Chautauqua Art Ctr Ann, NY, 64; Am Artists in France, Palais des Congres, Paris, 75-76; solo exhib, Pittsburgh Ctr Arts, 83. *Awards:* Jury Award of Distinction, Mainstreams Int, 68 & Assoc Artists Pittsburgh Ann, 69; Pittsburgh Artist of the Year, 83; and others. *Mem:* Assoc Artists Pittsburgh. *Mailing Add:* 4218 Maple Ln Allison Park PA 15101

OSCARSSON, VICTORIA CONSTANCE GUNHILD
DEALER, CONSULTANT
b Stamford, Conn, Dec 18, 51. *Study:* The Sorbonne; Trinity Col, Hartford, Conn, BA(art hist & languages), 73; Sotheby's Works of Art Course, London, 74. *Pos:* Researcher, Guggenheim Mus, New York, 73; personal asst to Richard Nathanson, dealer, London, 74-76; manager, Noonday Graphics, London, 76-77; dir, Landmark Gallery, New York, 77-80; art consult, Boston Mutual Life Insurance Co, 78-79; dir, Oscarsson-Hood Gallery, New York, 80- *Mem:* Art Table. *Specialty:* Contemporary art, all media. *Mailing Add:* Oscarsson Hood Gallery 41 West 57th St New York NY 10019

O'SHEA, TERRENCE PATRICK
PAINTER, SCULPTOR
b Los Angeles, Calif, Sept 8, 41. *Study:* Holy Cross Col; Boston Mus Sch; Chouinard Art Inst. *Work:* Los Angeles Co Mus Art; Patrick Lannan Mus, Palm Beach, Fla; Am Tel & Tel Collections, Chicago; Metromedia Collection, Los Angeles; Atlantic Richfield Corp, Los Angeles, Calif. *Exhib:* A Plastic Presence, Jewish Mus, New York, 69-70; Permutation, Light & Color, Mus Contemp Art, Chicago, 70; Pierres de Fantaisie, Oakland Mus, 70; Temple Street, Long Beach Mus, 71; First Int Biennial Small Sculpture Show, Budapest, Hungary, 71. *Teaching:* Instr, Otis Art Inst, Los Angeles, 76, Art Ctr Col Design, Pasadena, 80-81. *Awards:* Contemp Art Coun Purchase Award, Los Angeles Co Mus Art, 65. *Bibliog:* Jerry Rosen (auth), Terry O'Shea (video taped interview), 74. *Media:* Polyester Resin; Methane Base Liquid Pigment on Paper. *Dealer:* AAA Gallery 1001 E First St Los Angeles CA. *Mailing Add:* 555 Rose Ave Venice CA 90291

O'SICKEY, JOSEPH BENJAMIN
PAINTER, EDUCATOR
b Detroit, Mich, Nov 9, 18. *Study:* Cleveland Sch Art, with Paul Travis, Henry G Keller, Carl Gaertner, Frank N Wilcox & Hoyt L Sherman, cert. *Work:* Cleveland Mus Art; Pepsi Cola, New York; Cleveland Arts Asn; Canton Art Inst, Ohio; Westmoreland Art Mus. *Exhib:* Two-person show, Butler Inst Am Art; Pa Acad Fine Art, Philadelphia; one-man shows, Akron Art Inst, Canton Art Inst, Butler Inst Am Art, Youngstown, Ohio, seven shows, Jacques Seligman Galleries, New York, 64-78, Cleveland Inst Art, 82; and others. *Pos:* Art dir & graphic designer, pvt co, 49-64. *Teaching:* Instr art, Ohio State Univ, 46-47 & Akron Art Inst, 49-52; lectr art, Case Western Reserve Univ, 56-64; prof art, Kent State Univ, 64-, coordr painting & sculpture, 68-73. *Awards:* Cleveland Arts Cash Prize for Outstanding Achievement in the Arts, 74; Medal, Cash Award & Purchase Award, Butler Inst Am Art, Ohio, 74; First Prize Cash Wards, All-Ohio Exhibs, 74 & 77 & Best in Show Cash Prize, 74. *Media:* Oil, Watercolor. *Mailing Add:* Dept Art Kent State Univ Kent OH 44240

OSSORIO, ALFONSO A
PAINTER, SCULPTOR
b Manila, Philippines, Aug 2, 16; US citizen. *Study:* Harvard Col, AB, 38; RI Sch Design, 38-39. *Work:* Philadelphia Mus Art; NY Univ Art Collection; Guggenheim Mus, Mus Mod Art, Whitney Mus Am Art, New York. *Comn:* Murals, Church St Joseph, Victorias, Negros, Philippines, 50-51 & Washington Square Village, New York, 54; large circular assemblage, New York Hilton Hotel, 64. *Exhib:* Whitney Mus Am Art Painting & Sculpture Ann, 53-; Osaka Art Festival, Japan, 58 & 60; Structure & Style, Turin, Italy & Bochum, WGer, 62; Documenta, Kassel, WGer, 64; The New American Painting & Sculpture, Mus Mod Art, 69. *Pos:* Dir exhibs, Exec House, New York, 56-57; co-founder & dir, Signa Gallery, East Hampton, NY, 57-60. *Bibliog:* Jean Dubuffet (auth), Peintures Initiatiques d'Ossorio (monogr), La Pierre Volante, Paris, 52; Michel Tapie (auth), Ossorio (monogr), Ed Arte Fratelli Turin, 61; B H Friedman (auth), Ossorio (monogr), Abrams, 72. *Collection:* Contemporary painting and sculpture; art brut, primitive and Oriental. *Mailing Add:* PO Box 70 Wainscott NY 11975

OSTENDORF, (ARTHUR) LLOYD, JR
PAINTER, INSTRUCTOR
b Dayton, Ohio, June 23, 21. *Study:* Dayton Art Inst; Lincoln Mem Univ, Lincoln Dipl Hon, 66, hon ArtD, 74; Lincoln Col (Ill), LittD, 68. *Work:* Gov William Lee De Ewing (oil portrait) & Speaker W Robert Blair (oil portrait), Ill State Capitol, Springfield; Msgr Harry Ansbury (oil portrait), Parish Recreation House, Corpus Christi; Msgr Joseph D McFarland (oil portrait), Holy Angels Sch, Dayton, Ohio; Dr Herbert Y Livesay (oil portrait), Lincoln Mem Univ; Gen George Rogers Clark (oil), Restored Gov Mansion, Springfield. *Comn:* The Jesuit Martyrs (oil), Jesuit Retreat Chapel, Milford, Ohio, 49; six religious oil paintings, Hoyne Funeral Chapel, Dayton, 55. *Exhib:* Dayton Art Inst, 41. *Pos:* Art ed, Lincoln Herald, 57- *Teaching:* Instr com art & painting & dir, Ostendorf Art Acad, 69- *Awards:* Winner in Design for Chicago Lincoln (statue), Lincoln Sq C of C, 58. *Mem:* Montgomery Co Hist Soc (vpres, 56); Civil War Round Table of Dayton (pres, 55-56 & 58-59). *Media:* Watercolor, Ink, Oil. *Publ:* Auth, Mr Lincoln Came to Dayton, 59; auth & illusr, A Picture Story of Abraham Lincoln, 62; coauth, Lincoln in Photographs, An Album of Every Known Pose, 63; auth, The Photographs of Mary Todd Lincoln, 69. *Mailing Add:* 225 Lookout Dr Dayton OH 45419

OSTER, GERALD
PAINTER, KINETIC ARTIST
b Providence, RI, Mar 24, 18. *Study:* Brown Univ, ScB, 40; Cornell Univ, PhD, 43. *Work:* Milwaukee Art Ctr; San Francisco Mus Art; Tel Aviv Mus. *Exhib:* Mus Mod Art, 64; Walker Art Ctr, Minneapolis, 67; Milwaukee Art Ctr, 68; Inst Contemp Art, Chicago, 68; Tel Aviv Mus, 71; and others. *Pos:* Res assoc, Mass Inst Technol, 43-44, Princeton Univ, 44-45, Rockefeller Inst, 45-49; assoc, Birkbeck Col, London, 49-50; Rockefeller Fel, Royal Inst,

London, 50-51; vis scientist, Sorbonne, Paris, 51. *Teaching:* Prof, Poly Inst Brooklyn, 51-69; prof biophysics, Mt Sinai Sch Medicine, New York, 69-*Publ:* Auth, Physical Techniques in Biological Research, 56; auth, The Science of Moire Patterns, 64 & 69; contribr, Art Int & Sci Am. *Mailing Add:* 241 W 11th St New York NY 10014

OSTIGUY, JEAN-RENE
PAINTER, CURATOR
b Marieville, PQ, Aug 14, 25. *Study:* Univ Montreal, BA; Ecole des Beaux-Arts, Montreal; Sch Art & Design, Montreal, dipl. *Work:* Carleton Univ, Ottawa; Ottawa Univ. *Exhib:* Montreal Spring Exhib, 51 & 52. *Collections Arranged:* Leon Bellefleur, 68, Adrien Hebert, 71 & Ozias Leduc, 74, Nat Gallery Can. *Pos:* Cur Can art, Nat Gallery Can, 64- *Teaching:* Prof, Ecole des Beaux-Arts, Montreal, 53-55; prof Can art, Ottawa Univ, 66-71; vis prof Can art, Laval Univ, 71-72. *Awards:* Chriss Award, 62. *Mem:* Can Mus Asn (councillor, 63-65); Int Comt Mus. *Res:* Nineteenth and early twentieth century Canadian art. *Mailing Add:* Nat Gallery Can Ottawa ON H1N 9G9 Canada

OSTROW, STEPHEN EDWARD
HISTORIAN, MUSEUM DIRECTOR
b New York, NY, May 7, 32. *Study:* Oberlin Col, BA, 54; NY Univ Inst Fine Arts, MA, 59, PhD, 66. *Collections Arranged:* Baroque Painting: Italy and Her Influence (with catalog), 68; Visions and Revisions (with catalog), 68; Raid the Icebox I, with Andy Warhol, (with catalog), 69-70; Days Gone By, 71. *Pos:* Cur collections, Herron Mus Art, 66-67; chief cur, Mus Art, RI Sch Design, 67-71, dir, 71-78; dean Sch Fine Arts, Univ Southern Calif, 78-, dir mus studies prog, 79-82; exec dir, Portland Art Asn, 82- *Teaching:* Lectr art hist, Rutgers Univ, New Brunswick, 58-62; asst prof art hist, Univ Mo-Columbia, 62-66; vis lectr art hist, Brown Univ, 70, 71, 74, 76 & 77; prof art hist, Univ Southern Calif, 78-82. *Mem:* Asn Art Mus Dirs; Alliance Arts Educ, RI (exec comt, 74-76); RI Hist Preserv Comn, 75; Nat Coun Art Adminrs (bd dirs, 79-). *Publ:* Auth, Annibale Carracci and the Jason frescoes: Toward an internal chronology, Art Bulletin, 64; auth, Diana or Bacchus in the Palazzo Riario, Marsyas, 65; auth, A drawing by Annibale Carracci for the Jason frescoes and the S Gregorio baptism, Master Drawings, 70; auth, prefaces and introductions, In: The Selection Series & Classical Collection (10 catalogs), Mus Art RI Sch Design, 72-77. *Mailing Add:* Portland Art Asn 1219 SW Park Ave Portland OR 97225

OSTUNI, PETER W
PAINTER
b New York, NY, Oct 9, 08. *Study:* Cooper Union Sch Art & Archit, cert. *Comn:* Vitreous enamel mural, SS United States, US Steamship Lines, 51; enamel murals, Children's Mus, Ft Worth, 52; laminated stained glass, Prudential Life Ins Main Off, Newark, NJ, 59; seven cast stone bas-reliefs, for Grace Lines SS Santa Maria, 65; six windows in laminated plastics, Phipps Plaza, Atlanta, Ga, 70. *Exhib:* New Work in Stained Glass, Am Fedn Arts, 53; Craftsmen USA, 63 & Enamels USA, 65, Mus Contemp Crafts, New York; New York State Artists, Munson-Williams-Proctor Inst, 70; retrospective, List Arts Ctr, Kirkland Col, 70. *Teaching:* Instr painting, Cooper Union Sch Art & Archit, 37-38; instr painting & sculpture, Simon's Rock Col, 66-68; prof painting & sculpture, Kirkland Col, 68-73, emer prof, 73- *Bibliog:* Eugene Clute (auth), Murals in vitreous enamels, 12/52 & Priscilla Ginsberg (auth), Peter Ostuni, 1/61, Craft Horizons. *Media:* Oil, Vitreous Enamel. *Publ:* Contribr, Dimensions of design, 58 & The craftsmans world, 59. *Mailing Add:* 40 Harrison St Apt 22K New York NY 10013

O'SULLIVAN, DANIEL JOSEPH
PAINTER
b Brooklyn, NY, Aug 18, 40. *Study:* Fordham Col; Brooklyn Mus Art Sch; Pratt Graphics Ctr. *Work:* Commerce Trust Co, Kansas City, Mo; Wichita Art Mus; Mus of Albuquerque, NMex; also in pvt collections of Hirshhorn & Neuberger. *Comn:* Portraits, Brooklyn Bar Asn & Pace Univ. *Exhib:* Brooklyn Mus, 64; New Talent Exhib, Kraushaar Galleries, New York, 73; Kalamazoo Inst Art, Mich, 74; US Dept State Art in Embassies Prog, Korea, 75; Am Acad Arts & Lett, New York, 75 & 76; one-man show, Kraushaar Galleries, New York, 75 & 79. *Teaching:* Instr, Brooklyn Mus Art Sch, formerly; instr, New York City Cath High Schs, presently. *Awards:* Purchase Award, Am Acad Arts & Lett, New York, 76. *Media:* Oil, Acrylic. *Dealer:* Kraushaar Galleries 724 Fifth Ave New York NY 10019. *Mailing Add:* 17 Camanche La Comac Setauket NY 11733

OSVER, ARTHUR
PAINTER
b Chicago, Ill, July 26, 12. *Study:* Northwestern Univ, 30-31; Art Inst Chicago, with Boris Anisfeld, 31-36. *Work:* Mus Mod Art; Whitney Mus Am Art; Davenport Munic Art Gallery; Peabody Mus, Salem, Mass; plus many others. *Comn:* Cover, Fortune Mag, 60. *Exhib:* Whitney Mus Am Art, 44, 45 & 63; one-man shows, Univ Fla, 52; Art: USA: Now, 64-65 & Coe Col, Cedar Rapids, Iowa, 66; retrospective, Iowa State Col, Ames, 68; plus many other group & one-man shows. *Teaching:* Instr painting, Brooklyn Mus Art Sch, 49-51; instr, Columbia Univ, 52 & Univ Fla, 54-55; instr painting, Cooper Union Art Sch, 55 & 58; vis critic painting, Yale Univ, 56-57; painter in residence, Am Acad Rome, 57-58; instr, Washington Univ, 60- *Awards:* Medal, Art Dirs Club, Chicago, 61; J Henry Schiedt Mem Prize, Pa Acad Fine Arts, 66; Sabbatical Grant, Nat Endowment Arts, Washington, DC, 66; plus many others. *Bibliog:* Ray Bethers (auth), How Paintings Happen, Norton, 51; Lee Nordness (ed), Art: USA: Now, C J Bucher, 62. *Mailing Add:* 465 Foote Ave St Louis MO 63119

OSYCZKA, BOHDAN DANNY
PAINTER, ILLUSTRATOR
b Herkimer, NY. *Study:* Vesper George Sch Art; Col Fine Arts, Syracuse Univ, BFA; Art Students League. *Work:* Syracuse Univ, NY; Prudential Insurance Co Am, Mass; Hoffman-La Roche, Nutley, NJ; Am Tel & Tel Co, New York; Int Bus Machines, New York. *Comn:* Religious murals, St Peter & Paul Ukranian Orthodox Church, Utica, 48; Painting (watercolor), Pepsico World Hq, NY, 71. *Exhib:* Am Watercolor Soc, 68 & 70; one-man shows, Katonah Gallery, NY, 71, 76 & 82 & Silvermine Guild Artists, New Canaan, Conn, 71; Huson River Mus, Yonkers, NY, 74 & 76; New England Ann, Silvermine Guild, Conn, 71, 73, 76 & 80; and others. *Pos:* Juror, Westchester Art Soc, Tarrytown, NY, 71; Lectr-demonstr, The Katonah Gallery, 71-74, Kirkland Col, Clinton, NY, 74 & Hudson River Mus, Yonkers, NY, 74; instr, Parsons Sch of Design, New York, 75- *Teaching:* Instr, Parsons Sch Design, NY, 75-; lectr, Katonah Gallery, 71-83, Kirkland Col, 74-, Hudson River Mus, 74. *Awards:* Agusta Hazard Fel, Syracuse Univ, NY, 43; Watercolor Award, Westchester Art Soc, 67-70; Sindin Harris Gallery Award, 71 & Mus Purchase Award, 76, Hudson River Mus. *Bibliog:* Joan Hanauer (auth), Osyczka watercolors are a Maine event, NY J Am, 3/6/65; Noel Frackman (auth), Process: earthy and oozing, Patent Trader, 4/1/71; Bella O'Hara (auth), World of arts, Stamford Advocate, 9/23/71. *Mem:* Silvermine Guild Artists; Artist Equity Asn, New York; Hudson River Contemp Artists; Soc Illustr. *Publ:* Contribr, Am Artist, 9/65. *Dealer:* Gallery Nine 9 E 19th St New York NY 10003. *Mailing Add:* Summit Ave Peekskill NY 10566

OSZE, ANDREW E
SCULPTOR
b Nagykanizsa, Hungary, Jan 14, 09; US citizen. *Study:* Acad Art, Budapest; Acad D'Ungheria, Rome, fel, 47-49. *Work:* Denver Art Mus; Hanley Collection, Pa; Mus Budapest; and numerous others. *Comn:* St John of Cross, Church, Budapest, 42; Arpad Toth, comn by Nyugat, 43; Veronica (gravestone), Budapest, 43; fountain, Rome, 48; T S Eliot Relief, St Louis, 80. *Exhib:* Montclair Art Mus, 61; Far Gallery, New York, 64 & 70; De Young Mus, San Francisco, 73; Denver Art Mus, 75. *Teaching:* Prof sculpture, Fra Angelico Art Sch, 59-60; prof sculpture & dir, Acad Mus Arte, Lima, 63-64; prof sculpture, Cath Univ, Peru, 63-64. *Awards:* Grant, Peru, 62-64; Grant, France & Greece, 67. *Bibliog:* William Yuhasz (auth), A Osze, Hungarian Quart, 62; George Szabo (auth), A Osze, New Horizons, 70; I Soter (auth), Osze, Jelenuor, 80. *Mem:* Col Art Asn Am. *Media:* Stone, Bronze, Wood. *Publ:* Auth, Universal Thought and the Arts in Modern Time, Philos Question Series 10, Learned Publ, Inc, New York. *Mailing Add:* 855 Dahlia Ln Apt 7 Vero Beach FL 32963

O'TOOLE, JAMES ST LAURENCE
DEALER, HISTORIAN
b Baltimore, Md, Nov 5, 1895. *Study:* Md Art Inst; Loyola Col, Baltimore; Trinity Col, Dublin, Ireland, Celtic archaeol. *Pos:* Jacques Seligmann et Fils, Paris, France, 21-25; De Hauke et Cie, New York & Paris, 25-35; co-dir, James St L O'Toole Art Gallery, New York, 35- *Mem:* Sr mem Am Soc Appraisers; fel Royal Soc Antiq of Ireland, Dublin. *Specialty:* American, European and Asian pre-17th to 20th century paintings, prints, drawings, sculpture and photographs. *Mailing Add:* 200 East 57th New York NY 10022

OTT, JERRY
PAINTER
b Albert Lea, Minn, July 31, 47. *Study:* Mankato State Col, 65-70; Univ Minn, 71. *Work:* Walker Art Ctr, Minneapolis; Smithsonian Inst; Mus Contemp Art, Tokyo, Japan; Univ Kans Mus; Metrop Mus, New York; and others. *Exhib:* One-man shows, Louis K Meisel Gallery, New York, 73, 75 & 79, Morgan Gallery, Kansas City, Mo, 77 & 79 & Smith Fine Art Gallery, Monte Carlo, Monaco, 74; Tokyo Biennale '74, 74; Three Centuries of American Nudes, New York Cult Ctr, 75. *Teaching:* Artist in residence, St Cloud State Univ, 79. *Media:* Airbrush, Acrylic. *Dealer:* Styria Studio 419 Broome St New York NY; Morgan Gallery 5006 State Line Rd Shawnee Mission KS 66205. *Mailing Add:* 1251 Barclay St Paul MN 55106

OTT, ROBERT WILLIAM
EDUCATOR, WRITER
b Sharon, Pa, Mar 14, 34. *Study:* Pa State Univ, BS, 56, MEd, 63, DEd, 73; Univ London, Eng, 75. *Pos:* Ed, The Museologist: Official Museum Journal, Am Asn Mus, Northeast Conf, 78- *Teaching:* Instr art educ, Pa State Univ, 68-73, asst prof, 73-77, assoc prof art & mus educ, 77- *Mem:* Am Asn Mus; Northeast Mus Conf; Nat Art Educ Asn; fel Royal Soc Arts, London, 76; Int Asn Advan Educ, Belgium, 78. *Publ:* Auth, Museum Education and Society: Relevance Today, Concordia Univ, 81; auth, Interdisciplines in the Art Museum, Int Coun Mus, Sweden, 82; auth, Museums: The Encyclopedia of Education Research, Am Soc Educ Res, 82; ed, Art in Education: An International Perspective, Pa State Press, 84. *Mailing Add:* 273 Chambers Bldg University Park PA 16802

OTT, WENDELL LORENZ
MUSEUM DIRECTOR, PAINTER
b McCloud, Calif, Sept 17, 42. *Study:* San Francisco Art Inst, 60-61; Trinity Univ, San Antonio, Tex, BA, 68; Univ Ariz, Tucson, MFA, 70. *Work:* Witte Mem Mus, San Antonio, Tex. *Exhib:* Tex Painting & Sculpture, Dallas Mus Fine Arts, 66; 11th Ariz Ann, Phoenix Art Mus, 69; Yuma Fine Arts Asn, Ariz, 69; Juarez Mus Art, Mex, 73; one-man shows, George Walter Vincent Smith Art Mus, Springfield, Mass, 73 & Eastern NMex Univ, Portales, 74. *Pos:* Dir, Roswell Mus & Art Ctr, NMex, 70- *Teaching:* Instr painting, NMex Mil Inst, Roswell, 74-80. *Awards:* Onerdonk Award, Witte Mem Mus Ann, 68; Purchase Award, 11th Ariz Ann, Phoenix Art Mus, 69; Nat Mus Act Travel Grant, 73. *Mem:* Am Asn Mus; NMex Asn Mus (chmn, 73-75). *Media:* Oil. *Mailing Add:* PO Box 907 Roswell NM 88201

OTTIANO, JOHN WILLIAM
JEWELER, SCULPTOR
b Medford, Mass, July 23, 26. *Study:* Mass Col Art, BS, 54; Boston Univ, MFA, 60; Pa State Univ, DEd, 63. *Work:* Viktor Lowenfeld Mem, Pa State Univ; Univ Western Ill; Gloucester Co Col; Glassboro State Col. *Comn:* Mimosa & The Age of Miracles (murals) & two other large exterior murals, Glassboro State Col, 67, sculpture, 74; Art Educator Award, Sculpture, NJ Art Educ Asn, 69. *Exhib:* Pa Acad Fine Arts, Philadelphia, 64; Nat Acad Galleries, New York, 65; Art From NJ, NJ State Mus, 66-70; Sculpture in the Park, Van Suan Park, Paramus, NJ, 71; Artists Equity, Philadelphia Civic Ctr, 72. *Teaching:* Instr three-dimensional design & jewelry, Boston Univ, 54-60; asst prof, Mass Col Art, 61-62; prof, Pa State Univ, University Park, 62-63; prof, Glassboro State Col, 63- *Awards:* First for Sculpture, NJ Tercentenary, 64; Award for Sculpture, Somerset Art Asn, 73. *Bibliog:* Artist/Educator, Sch Arts, 2/66; article in La Rev Mod, 3/1/66. *Mem:* Am Asn Univ Prof; NJ Art Educ Asn (pres, 70-); NJ Designer-Craftsmen Asn (Pres, 70-72, NJ state pres, 75-); Artists Equity Asn; Nat Art Educ Asn (NJ state rep, 63-). *Media:* Bronze, Gold, Silver. *Res:* The relationship between surface texture preference, personality characteristics and three-dimensional art performance. *Mailing Add:* 1115 Glen Lake Blvd Pitman NJ 08071

OTTO, CATHERINE K(LEMANN)
SCULPTOR
b April 27, 47; US citizen. *Study:* Fla Atlantic Univ, BA, 69; Univ Miami, MA, 72. *Work:* Delray Beach Pub Libr, Fla. *Comn:* Black African Stone Fish, John H Surovek Fine Arts, Palm Beach, Fla, 82-83; Reef Series #1, comn by Mrs Harry Kline, Abaco, Bahamas, 82-83; Alabaster Self-Portrait, comn by Artine Artinian, Palm Beach, Fla, 83; Mythical Fish, comn by Mr & Mrs Gunter Schulz-Franke, Osnäbruck, WGer, 83; archit sculpture & wall reliefs, comn by Sally Gingras, West Palm Beach, Fla, 83 & 84. *Exhib:* Boca Raton Mus Arts Ann Exhib, 82 & 83; Allied Artists Am, 83 & Catharine Lorillard Wolfe Art Club, 83, Nat Arts Club; Generic Art, Broward Art Guild, Ft Lauderdale, Fla, 83; State Show, Nat League Am Pen Women, Sarasota, Fla, 83. *Awards:* First Prize Sculpture, Delray Art League, 82 & 83. *Bibliog:* Nancy Miller (auth), Hands, heart and head all work to create beauty, Delray Beach News-J, 4/15/82; Gary Schwan (auth), New exhibits worth taking in, Palm Beach Post, 2/6/83. *Mem:* Catharine Lorillard Wolfe Art Club; Nat League Am Pen Women; Prof Artists Guild; Norton Artists Guild. *Media:* Stone, Metals. *Dealer:* John H Surovek Fine Arts Palm Beach FL. *Mailing Add:* 111 Periwinkle Lane Delray Beach FL 33444

OUBRE, HAYWARD LOUIS
SCULPTOR, EDUCATOR
b New Orleans, La. *Study:* Dillard Univ, BA; Univ Iowa, MFA; also with Hale Woodruff, Nancy E Prophet, James Lechay, Mauricio Lasansky & Humbert Albrizio. *Work:* Univ Iowa Gallery, Iowa City; Atlanta Univ Gallery, Ga. *Comn:* Ram (wire sculpture), Winston-Salem State Univ Libr, 65. *Exhib:* Six States Exhib, Joslyn Mem Mus, Omaha, Nebr, 47; Northwest Printmakers, Seattle Art Mus, Wash, 48; John & Mable Ringling Mus, Sarasota, Fla, 48; Ball State Ann Exhib, Muncie, Ind, 60-62; Madison Gallery Exhib, New York, 62; and many others. *Pos:* Arranger & cur, Selma Burke Gallery, Winston-Salem State Univ, NC, 83- *Teaching:* Chmn painting & sculpture, Fla A&M Univ, Tallahassee, 48-49; chmn drawing & painting, Ala State Univ, Montgomery, 49-65; chmn drawing & painting, Winston-Salem State Univ, 65- *Awards:* First Prize for Trailerview (oil), Iowa State Fair, 47; First Prize for Crown of Thorns (wire), 58 & Second Prize for Equivocal Fox (painting), 68, Atlanta Univ; and many others. *Bibliog:* Art of wire sculpture, Design Mag, 62, 68 & 71. *Mem:* Southeastern Art Asn; Nat Conf Artists. *Res:* Designed & copyrighted Colorwheel with Four Intensity Bands, 62 & Colorchart with Three Intensity Bands, 66; corrected color triangle devised by Johann Wolfgang Von Goethe, 76; designed Four Intensity Bank Color Wheel, 77. *Publ:* Auth, Directions of modern art, Art Rev Mag, 66. *Mailing Add:* 2422 Pickford Ct Winston-Salem NC 27101

OUTTERBRIDGE, JOHN WILFRED
ADMINISTRATOR, PAINTER
b Greenville, NC, Mar 12, 33. *Study:* Agr & Tech Univ, Greensboro, NC; Am Art Acad, Chicago, with Vernon Stakey. *Work:* Oakland Mus, Mills Col, Oakland, Calif; Calif State Col, San Jose; Compton Community Col, Calif; Med Facility, Watts, Univ Southern Calif, Los Angeles. *Comn:* Mural collages (mixed-media), Communicative Arts Acad, Compton, 70; Ethnic Heritage Doll Ser (five units), Studio Watts Endowment Fund, 77. *Exhib:* Oakland Mus, 67; 6th & 9th Southern Calif Ann, Long Beach Mus Art, 68 & 70; Los Angeles Co Mus Art, Los Angeles, 69; Dimensions in Black Art, La Jolla Mus Contemp Art, Calif, 70; St Art by Black Am, Merabash Mus, Willingboro, NJ, 75; W Coast Artists, Studio Mus of Harlem, New York, 77. *Pos:* Painter/designer, Art Craft, Div Traid Corp, Burbank, 64-68; artistic dir, Communicative Arts Acad, Compton, 69-75, mem bd dir, presently; dir, Watts Towers Arts Ctr, Munic Arts Dept, City of Los Angeles, 75- *Teaching:* Instr assemblage & sculpture, Pasadena Art Mus, 67-70; lectr art hist, Calif State Col, Dominguez Hills, 67-71. *Awards:* First Place/Sculpture, Westwood Art Asn, 67; Our Auth Study Club Award, Los Angeles Area Artists, 67; Nat Conf Artists Award, 75. *Bibliog:* Samella Lewis (auth), John Outterbridge/ Black Artist (film), Contemp Crafts Inc, 68; article, Wilson Libr Bulletin, 4/69; Elton C Fax (auth), Black Artists of the New Generation, Dodd, Mead & Co, 77. *Mem:* Calif Confedn of Arts, Los Angeles; Advocates for the Arts; Mus African Am Art; Nat Conf Artists, Va Commonwealth Univ. *Media:* Mixed. *Mailing Add:* PO Box 1445 South Pasadena CA 91030

OVERLAND, CARLTON EDWARD
CURATOR, HISTORIAN
b Stoughton, Wis, Feb 28, 42. *Study:* St Olaf Col, BA; Univ Wis-Madison, MA. *Collections Arranged:* 20th Century Graphics: The Hollaender Collection, 74. *Pos:* Cur prints & drawings, Elvehjem Art Ctr, Madison, Wis, 72-77, cur collections, 77- *Teaching:* Instr art hist, Univ Northern Iowa, Cedar Falls, 68-70. *Mem:* Am Asn Mus. *Mailing Add:* 5113 Sherwood Rd Madison WI 53711

OWEN, BILL
PAINTER, SCULPTOR
b Gila Bend, Ariz, Jan 23, 42. *Work:* Whitney Mus, Buffalo Bill Hist Ctr, Cody, Wyo; Phoenix Art Mus; Leanin' Tree Mus, Boulder, Colo. *Exhib:* Cowboy Artists Am, Phoenix, Ariz, 74-77; Tex Art Gallery, Dallas, 74 & 75; Marlboro Bicentennial Traveling Show, Louisville, Ky, 75; Whitney Mus, Buffalo Bill Hist Ctr, 75; Trailside Gallery, Scottsdale, Ariz, 75-77; Tex Art Gallery, Dallas, 76. *Awards:* Franklin Mint Gold Medal for Western Art, Pa, 74; Gold Medal, drawing, 78 & 79; Silver Medal, Cowboy Artists Am Exhib, 78; and others. *Bibliog:* Bill Owen, Franklin Mint, 74; Cowboy Artists of America 1974, 75-77 & Ten Years with the Cowboy Artists of America, 76, Northland Press. *Mem:* Cowboy Artists Am (secy-treas, 74-75, bd dir, 76-77, pres, 77-78). *Media:* Oil; Wax, Clay. *Mailing Add:* PO Box 95 Flagstaff AZ 86001

OWEN, FRANK (FRANKLIN CHARLES)
PAINTER
b Kalispell, Mont, May 13, 39. *Study:* Antioch Col; Calif State Univ Sacramento; Univ Calif, Davis, BA & MA. *Work:* Corcoran Gallery of Art, Washington, DC; Albright-Knox Art Gallery, Buffalo, NY; St Louis Art Mus, Mo; Des Moines Art Ctr, Iowa; Madison Art Ctr, Wis; plus others. *Exhib:* 32nd Corcoran Biennial, Washington, DC, 71; Madison Art Ctr Exhib, 73; 15th Nat Exhib of Contemp Am Painting & Sculpture, Univ Ill, 74; 71st Ann Exhib, Art Inst Chicago, 74; Soho in Berlin, Berlin Kunstmuseum, WGer, 76; one-man shows, Leo Castelli Gallery, 72, 75 & Sable-Castelli Gallery, Toronto, 77. *Teaching:* Instr painting, Calif State Univ, Sacramento, 67-68; instr fine arts, Sch Visual Arts, New York, 70- *Bibliog:* Peter Schedjahl (auth), Six painters of the 70s, Ackland Art Ctr, NC, 73; Douglas Davis (auth), Painter's painters, Newsweek, 5/13/74. *Mailing Add:* c/o Leo Castelli Gallery 420 W Broadway New York NY 10012

OWENS, GWENDOLYN JANE
CURATOR, WRITER
b Baltimore, Md, July 8, 54. *Study:* Tufts Univ, BA, 76; Williams Col, MA, 79. *Collections Arranged:* Watercolors by Maurice Prendergast from New England Collections (auth, catalog), 78 & Master Drawings from the Collection of Ingrid and Julius Held (co-auth, catalog), 79, The Dr and Mrs Milton Lurie Kramer Collection (auth, catalog), 81, Clark Art Inst; Golden Day, Silver Night, Perceptions of Nature in American Art, 1850-1910 (with catalog). *Pos:* Ed asst, Am Asn Mus, Washington, DC, 76-77; registr, Williams Col Mus Art, Mass, 78-79; asst cur, Herbert F Johnson Mus, Cornell Univ, Ithaca, NY, 79-81, assoc cur, 81- *Mem:* Col Art Asn; Asn Historians Am Art. *Res:* 19th and 20th century American art and architecture. *Publ:* Contirbr, Harvard Honors Lafayette, Fogg Art Mus, 75; auth, bk revs in Baltimore Sun, Art & Antiques & Mus News, 77-; auth, Pioneers in American Museums: Bryson Burroughs, Mus News, 79; auth, H Siddons Mowbray, Easel Painter, Art & Antiques, 80; auth, Alive, Well and Prospering, Cooperative Conservation Centers Come of Age, Mus New, 82. *Mailing Add:* Herbert F Johnson Mus Cornell Univ Ithaca NY 14853

OWENS, MARY (MARY LOUISE SCHNORE)
PAINTER
b Des Moines, Iowa, Dec 4, 35. *Study:* State Univ NY, Buffalo, BS, 57; Albright-Knox Art Sch, with Sam Amato, Buffalo, 53-54. *Work:* Los Angeles Water & Power Credit Union Corp Hq, Los Angeles; Citybank Int, San Francisco; Fluor Corp Hq, Irvine, Calif; State Univ NY, Buffalo. *Exhib:* Watercolor Calif Ann Exhib of Artists, Los Angeles Co Mus Art, Los Angeles, 61; one-person shows, Pac Basin Ser, Janus Gallery, Los Angeles, Calif, 76 & Watercolor Exhib, Brand Libr Art Galleries, Glendale, Calif, 77; Am Watercolor Soc 112th Ann Exhib, Nat Acad Galleries, New York, 79; Watercolor Ann, Brand Art Galleries, Glendale, Calif, 80-82; Nat Watercolor Soc Travel Show, 81; Mt San Jacinto Open, 83; and others. *Awards:* Golden CofC Award, Rocky Mt Watermedia Exhib, 77; Cash Award, Mt San Jacinto Open, 83. *Mem:* Nat Watercolor Soc. *Media:* Watercolor, Oil. *Mailing Add:* 2443 Yosemite Dr Los Angeles CA 90041

OWENS, TENNYS BOWERS
DEALER
b Washington, DC, June 25, 40. *Study:* St Mary's Jr Col, Raleigh, NC; Eastern Carolina Univ, Greenville, NC. *Pos:* Owner, Artique Ltd, 71- *Specialty:* General art merchandise, prints, paintings, sculpture and pottery. *Mailing Add:* c/o Artique Ltd 314 G St Anchorage AK 99501

OWENS, WALLACE, JR
ADMINISTRATOR, PAINTER
b Muskogee, Okla. *Study:* Langston Univ, BA(art educ), 59; Cent State Univ, Edmond, Okla, Masters(teaching), 65; Inst Allende, San Miguel de Allende, Mex, MFA(painting), 66. *Work:* Okla State Permanent Collection, Oklahoma City; Gainesville Col, Ga. *Exhib:* Cent State Univ, Edmond, 65; Univ Okla, Norman, 69. *Teaching:* Dept chmn visual arts, Langston Univ, Okla, 66- *Awards:* Fulbright Scholar Italy, Univ Rome, 70; Study Tour Award, African Am Inst, New York, 74. *Mem:* Okla Art Ed Asn; Nat Conf Artist (charter mem, 60). *Media:* Acrylic. *Collection:* Contemporary paintings in acrylic and oil; fine prints in lithography woodcut and etching; some metal sculpture. *Mailing Add:* 4304 Sycamore Ln Edmond OK 73034

OWSLEY, DAVID THOMAS
CONSULTANT

b Dallas, Tex, Aug 20, 29. *Study:* Harvard Col, AB, 51; Inst Fine Arts, NY Univ, MFA, 62. *Collections Arranged:* Decorative Arts Collection & Ailsa Mellon Bruce Collection, Carnegie Inst Mus Art. *Pos:* Fel, Am Wing, Metrop Mus Art; asst cur decorative arts & sculpture, Mus Fine Arts, Boston; visitor, Victoria & Albert Mus, London, Eng; cur antiquities, Oriental & decorative arts, Carnegie Inst Mus Art. *Teaching:* Decorative arts, Univ Pittsburgh Ext. *Awards:* Cert Appreciation, Am Soc Appraisers, 83. *Mem:* Sr mem Am Soc Appraisers; Knickerbocker Club. *Publ:* Auth, article, Antiques, 12/72 & 4/73 & Apollo, 8/73. *Mailing Add:* 116 E 68th St New York NY 10021

OXMAN, MARK
SCULPTOR, EDUCATOR

b New York, NY, Mar 9, 40. *Study:* Adelphi Univ, Long Island, NY, 58-61; Pa Acad Fine Arts, Philadelphia, 61-65; Showhegan Sch, summer 65; City & Guilds London, 65; Art Sch, London, 67. *Comn:* Large sculpture relief, Bellmore Mem Libr, Long Island, NY, 73; large sculpture relief, Queens Plaza Complex, New York, 76. *Exhib:* Outdoor Sculpture Series, Portland Sch Art, 74; one-man show, Port Washington Libr, Long Island, NY, 74; New Faces, Franz Bader Gallery, Washington, DC, 78; 21st Area Show Sculpture, Corcoran Mus, Washington, DC, 78; Int Monetary Fund, Washington, DC, 78. *Teaching:* Lectr art, Haverford Col, Pa, 67-70; asst prof art, Amherst Col, Mass, 70-76; assoc prof sculpture, American Univ, Washington, DC, 76- *Media:* Bronze. *Mailing Add:* 620 Gist Ave Silver Spring MD 20910

OZONOFF, IDA
PAINTER, COLLAGE ARTIST

b La Crosse, Wis, July 27, 04. *Study:* State Teachers Col, Milwaukee, grad, 24; Milwaukee Downer Col, 58 & 59; Univ Wis-Milwaukee, 60-64 & 69-70. *Work:* Print Div, Smithsonian Inst, Washington, DC; Milwaukee Pub Schs; Univ Wis, Fond du Lac Campus; Abilene Fine Arts Mus, Tex; Carleton Col, Northfield, Minn. *Exhib:* Walker Art Ctr Exhib, Minn, 64; Butler Inst Am Art, Ohio, 65, 67 & 68; Audubon Artists Exhib, New York, 66, 68 & 69; Nat Acad Design Exhib, New York, 68 & 69; Allied Artists Am Exhib, New York, 70; West Bend Gallery Fine Arts, Wis, 76 & 77; Univ Wis Alumni Exhib, 78. *Awards:* Purchase Award, Western Publ, 66; Benjamin Altman First Prize, Nat Acad Design, 68; Carleton Col Purchase Award, Charles E Merrill Trust Fund, 75. *Bibliog:* Gerald F Brommer (auth), The Art of Collage, 78; and others; Wis Acad Rev (spec ed), Wis Painters & Printmakers, 3/83. *Mem:* Wis Arts Coun; Collectors Gallery, Milwaukee Art Ctr. *Dealer:* Bradley Galleries 2565 N Donner Milwaukee WI 53211. *Mailing Add:* 500 W Bradley Rd C216 Milwaukee WI 53217

P

PABLO (PAUL BURGESS EDWARDS)
PAINTER, EDUCATOR

b Moulton, Iowa, Feb 18, 34. *Study:* Iowa Wesleyan Col, with S Carl Fracassini, BA, 55; Wichita State Univ, with Robert Kiskadden, MA, 59. *Work:* Iowa Wesleyan Col Art Dept; Wichita State Univ Art Dept; Wichita Art Mus; Miami Beach Pub Libr; Citizens Libr, Washington, Pa. *Comn:* Mosaic mural, Halstead Hosp Lobby, 59; mural, Tosco Mining Co, Washington, Pa, 78. *Exhib:* Ann Nat Graphics Art Show, Wichita Art Asn, 60; Ann Juror's Award Show, Huntington Gallery, WVa, 65; Ann Nat Decorative Arts Show, Wichita Art Asn, 66; Max 24, Nat Small Painting Show, Purdue Univ, 66; 2nd Nat Polymer Exhib, Eastern Mich Univ, 68. *Collections Arranged:* Washington & Jefferson Col Nat Painting Show, 67-82. *Pos:* Co-dir, Bottega Art Gallery, Wichita, 60-62; pres, Wichita Artists Guild, 61-62; dir, Gallery 319, Wichita, 62-63. *Teaching:* Instr ceramics, Wichita State Univ, summer 62; asst prof sculpture & ceramics, West Liberty State Col, 63-66; chmn art dept, Washington & Jefferson Col, 66- *Awards:* E D Caldwell Award First Prize, Bethany Col Ann, 64; First Prize, Oglebay Inst Summer Show, 64; Juror's Best of Show Award, Huntington Gallery, 65. *Mem:* Arts Coun Washington Co (pres & founding mem, 69-73); Am Asn Univ Prof; Am Council Art Administrators. *Media:* Acrylic, Oil. *Publ:* Illusr, Nonverbal Communication, Vol 5, In: Communication Science & Technology Series, Marcel Dekker Inc, 74. *Mailing Add:* 268 E Wheeling Washington PA 15301

PACE, MARGARET BOSSHARDT See Willson, Margaret (Bosshardt) Pace

PACE, STEPHEN S
PAINTER, PRINTMAKER

b Charleston, Mo, Dec 12, 18. *Study:* Inst Arte, San Miguel Allende, Mex; Acad Grande Chaumiere, Paris; Inst Arte Statale, Florence, Italy; Art Students League, with Cameron Booth & Morris Cantor; Hans Hofmann Sch. *Work:* Metrop Mus Art & Whitney Mus Am Art, New York; Univ Calif, Berkeley; James Michener Found, Univ Tex, Austin; Walker Art Ctr, Minneapolis, and others. *Exhib:* Int Watercolor Exhib, Brooklyn Mus, 53 & 55; Whitney Ann, 53, 54, 57, 58 & 61; Int Biennial, Japan, selected by Mus of Mod Art, New York, 57; Walker Art Ctr, 62; Abstract Watercolors by 14 Americans, Mus of Mod Art, tour of Europe, Asia & Australia, 64-66; 10-Yr Retrospective, Des Moines Art Ctr, 70; Univ Tex Art Mus, 70; Recent Acquisitions, Boston Mus of Fine Arts, 77; one-man shows, Howard Wise Gallery, New York, 60, 61, 63 & 64 & A M Sachs Gallery, New York, 74,

76, 78, 79 & 81; and others. *Teaching:* Artist in residence, Washington Univ, spring-summer 59; instr art, Pratt Inst, 61-68; instr art sem, Univ Calif, Berkeley, spring 68; prof art, Am Univ, 75- *Awards:* Dolia Lorian Award to promising painters, 54; Hallmark Co Purchase Award, 61; Guggenheim fel, 80-81; and others. *Bibliog:* Hubert Crehan (auth), A change of pace, Art News, 4/64; Russell Arnold (auth), Paintings by Stephen Pace, Crucible, fall 65; Denver Lindley (auth), In a landscape (film), 69-71. *Media:* Oil, Watercolor; Monotype, Prints. *Mailing Add:* 164 11th Ave New York NY 10011

PACHNER, WILLIAM
PAINTER

b Brtnice, Czech, Apr 7, 15; US citizen. *Study:* Acad Arts & Crafts, Vienna, Austria; Univ Tampa, DFA AC, 81. *Work:* Whitney Mus Am Art, New York; Butler Inst Am Art, Youngstown, Ohio; Fort Worth Art Ctr, Tex; Iowa State Teacher's Col. *Exhib:* Carnegie Inst Int, Pittsburgh; Whitney Mus Am Art Ann; Corcoran Gallery Art Biennial, Washington, DC; Pa Acad Fine Arts, Philadelphia; US Fine Arts Pavilion, New York World's Fair, 65; Univ Tampa, 81; one-man show, Pachner Landscapes, Mus Fine Arts, St Petersburg, Fla, 83. *Teaching:* Instr painting & drawing, Art Students League, 69-70. *Awards:* Am Acad Arts & Lett Award, 49; Ford Found Awards, 59-64; Guggenheim Fel, 60. *Bibliog:* Kenneth Donahue (auth), William Pachner, Am Fedn Arts, 59. *Media:* Oil, Watercolor. *Mailing Add:* 962 Ohayo Mountain Rd Woodstock NY 12498

PACIFIC, GERTRUDE
PAINTER, DESIGNER

b Victoria, BC, July 21, 42. *Study:* Univ Wash, BA(painting), 64, MFA(painting), 65; with Alden Mason. *Work:* Nat Capitol Comn, Govt Can, Ottawa; Whatcom Mus Hist & Art, Bellingham, Wash; Seattle City Light, City Seattle, Wash; Wash State Dept Hwys, Olympia. *Comn:* Paintings, Schoenfeld Industries, Corp Collection, William & Sue Justen, Seattle & Anne Clark, Bainbridge Island. *Exhib:* Art of the Pacific Northwest, Smithsonian Inst, Washington, DC, 74; Skagit Valley Artists, Seattle Art Mus, Wash, 74; Am Landscape, Trenton Art Mus, NJ, 76; Gertrude Pacific, Art Gallery of Greater Victoria, BC, 77. *Pos:* Cur design, Thomas Burke Mem, Wash State Mus, 69- *Bibliog:* Charles Cee Brown (auth), Gertrude Pacific Oyster Light, Art Gallery of Greater Victoria, BC, 77; Jessica Maxwell (auth), Memoirs from the Pacific Northwest, Playgirl, 82 & Oyster light, United Mag, 83. *Media:* Acrylic. *Mailing Add:* 2538 31st St Seattle WA 98144

PADOVANO, ANTHONY JOHN
SCULPTOR, DRAFTSMAN

b Brooklyn, NY, July 19, 33. *Study:* Carnegie Inst Technol; Pratt Inst; Columbia Univ, with Oronzio Maldarelli; Hunter Col, MA, 80. *Work:* Whitney Mus Am Art; Nat Collection Fine Arts, Washington, DC; Univ Ill; John Herron Art Inst; Storm King Art Ctr, NY. *Comn:* Sculpture In The Park, Parks Dept, New York, 68; design, NY State Art Awards, NY State Coun Arts, 69; sculpture, World Trade Ctr, Port Authority NY & NJ, 70; three arcs, donated by Trammel & Crow Co for City of Dallas, 72; sculpture, Nebr Bicentennial Sculpture Corp, 76. *Exhib:* 3rd Mostra Arte Figurative Int, Rome, Italy, 61; Young Am, Whitney Mus Am Art, 65; Am Sculpture, Mus Mod Art, 66; Am Express Pavilion, New York World's Fair, 66; Inauguration of Nat Collection Fine Arts, Washington, DC, 67. *Pos:* Adv mem, NJ State Coun Arts, 65-67. *Teaching:* Asst prof sculpture, Columbia Univ, Univ Conn, 72 & Kingsborough Community Col, 83; adj asst prof sculpture, Queens Col, City Univ New York, 72. *Awards:* Guggenheim Found Fel, 64; Ford Found Purchase Award, 66; Inst Arts & Lett Award, 76. *Bibliog:* Young talent, Art Am, 65; James Mellow (auth), article in New York Times Sun Rev, 4/70. *Mem:* Sculptors Guild (vpres, 68-69); Silvermine Guild Artists. *Media:* Metal, Stone. *Publ:* Auth, Process of Sculpture, Doubleday Co, 81. *Dealer:* James Graham Gallery 1014 Madison Ave New York NY 10021. *Mailing Add:* RD 1 Box 64 Putnam Valley NY 10579

PADULA, FRED DAVID
FILMMAKER, PHOTOGRAPHER

b Santa Barbara, Calif, Oct 25, 37. *Study:* Univ Calif, Santa Barbara; Calif State Univ, San Francisco, BA(music), with Jack Welpott, Don Worth & Wynn Bullock, MA(art). *Work:* George Eastman House, Rochester, NY; San Francisco Mus Art; Oakland Mus Art; Kalamazoo Art Ctr, Mich; Crocker Mus Art, Sacramento, Calif; and many pvt collections. *Comn:* Children's Letters to God (film), Lee Mendelson, San Francisco, 68; Navaho (film), Pub Broadcast Lab, KQED-TV, San Francisco, 68; S F Mix (film), Ford Found, 70; film, Am Film Inst. *Exhib:* 30 Photographers Nat Exhib, Buffalo, NY, 64; one-man shows, San Francisco Mus, 64, George Eastman House, 68 & DeYoung Mus, San Francisco, 69; Mus Mod Art, New York, 67; completion & premiere showing of El Capitan (film), San Francisco Mus of Mod Art, 78; and others. *Pos:* Mem selection comt, US Art in the Embassies, 65; mem bd dirs, Canyon Cinema Coop, 71- *Teaching:* Lectr photo & film making, San Francisco State Univ, 63- & Univ Calif, San Francisco, 66-71; resident artist, Univ Minn, Minneapolis, 70. *Awards:* Awards for film El Capitan: Grand Prize, Banff Festival Mountain Films, Can, 79, Gold Medal, Festival Int Film Alpin, Les Diablerets, Switz, 79 & Silver Medal, Int Bergfilm Munchen, Munich, Ger, 79; and others. *Bibliog:* Callenbach (auth), Ephesus, Film Quart, Univ Calif, winter 66-67; Winston (auth), American film maker, Melbourne Art Rev, fall 68; Hoffmann (auth), Ephesus, Weg Zum Nachbarn, Oberhausen, Ger, 68. *Dealer:* Canyon Cinema Coop Rm 220 Indust Ctr Bldg Sausalito CA 94941. *Mailing Add:* 47 Shell Rd Mill Valley CA 94941

PAGE, ADDISON FRANKLIN
MUSEUM DIRECTOR

b Princeton, Ky, Oct 9, 11. *Study:* Wayne State Univ, BFA & MA. *Collections Arranged:* 19 Canadian Painters, 62; Reg Butler: A Retrospective Exhibition, 63; Treasures of Chinese Art, 65; The Figure in Sculpture 1865-1965, 65; Treasures of Persian Art, 66; Indian Buddhist Sculpture, 68; The Sirak Collection, 68; Ciechanowiecki Collection of Gilt and Gold Medals and Plaquettes, 69; 19th Century French Sculpture: Monuments for the Middle Class, 71. *Pos:* Jr cur educ, Detroit Inst Arts, 47-58, cur contemp art, 58-62; dir, J B Speed Art Mus, 62- *Teaching:* Instr sculpture, Wayne State Univ, 47-55, instr hist sculpture, 55-58; instr hist mod art, Cranbrook Acad Art, 58-62. *Mem:* Mich Sculpture Soc (chmn, 50); Mich Watercolor Soc (bd mem, 60); Asn Art Mus Dirs. *Publ:* Auth, Modern Sculpture: A Handbook, 50 & Diego Rivera's Detroit Frescoes: a Handbook, 55, Detroit Inst Arts. *Mailing Add:* J B Speed Art Mus 2035 S Third St Louisville KY 40208

PAGE, JEAN JEPSON
COLLECTOR

b Minneapolis, Minn, Aug 22, 24. *Study:* With Walter S Baum; Minneapolis Inst Arts; San Francisco Inst; Smith Col, BA, 46. *Pos:* Comnr, Dist Columbia Comn Arts & Humanities, 76-80. *Res:* American painting, particularly 19th century artists; political aspects of art patronage during ante-bellum years; Frank Mayer. *Collection:* American paintings, prints and drawings, primarily representational; books illustrated by painters. *Publ:* Auth, Francis Blackwell Mayer, Antiques, 2/76; auth, Frank Blackwell Mayer: Painter of the Minnesota Indian, Minn Hist, 78; auth, Notes on the contributions of Francis Blackwell Mayer and his family to the cultural history of Maryland, Md Hist Mag, 81. *Mailing Add:* 3219 Chesapeake St NW Washington DC 20008

PAGE, JOHN HENRY, JR
PRINTMAKER, EDUCATOR

b Ann Arbor, Mich, Jan 18, 23. *Study:* Minneapolis Sch Art; Art Students League; Univ Mich, BDesign; Univ Iowa, MFA. *Work:* Libr Cong, Washington, DC; Walker Art Ctr, Minneapolis; Des Moines Art Ctr, Iowa; Joslyn Art Mus, Omaha, Nebr; Carnegie Inst, Pittsburgh. *Comn:* Memberships Print, Des Moines Art Ctr, 69. *Exhib:* Young American Printmakers, Mus Mod Art, New York, 53; 10th Nat Print Show, Brooklyn Mus, 56; Nine Iowa Artists, Gov Exhib, 71-72; Midwest Printmaker Invitational, Walker Art Ctr, Minneapolis, 73; one-person exhib, Muskegon Mus Art, Mich, 83; and others. *Teaching:* Prof printmaking, Univ Northern Iowa, 54-; chmn dept art, Univ Omaha, 60-61. *Awards:* Younker Prize for Prints, Des Moines Art Ctr, 71; Nat Endowment Arts, Individual Artist Fel, 74; Purchase Prize & Cash Award, Fourth Ann Midwestern Printmaking & Drawing Competition, Tulsa, Okla, 77; plus others. *Mem:* Col Art Asn Am. *Dealer:* Percival Galleries Inc 210 Shops Bldg Des Moines IA 50309. *Mailing Add:* 1615 Tremont Cedar Falls IA 50613

PAIK, NAM JUNE
VIDEO ARTIST

b Seoul, Korea, 1932. *Study:* Univ Tokyo, grad, 56. *Exhib:* Fluxus Festival, Mus Wiesbaden, WGer, 62; Cybernetic Serendipity, Inst Contemp Arts, London, Eng, 68; The Machine as Seen at the End of the Mechanical Age, Mus of Mod Art, New York, 68; Vision & Television, Rose Art Mus, Brandeis Univ, Waltham, Mass, 69; St Jude Video Int, de Saisset Art Gallery & Mus, Univ Santa Clara, Calif, 71; solo exhibs, Mus Mod Art, New York, 72 & Kitchen, New York, 73; Circuit: a Video Invitational, Everson Mus of Art, Syracuse, NY, 73; Open Circuits: The Future of Television, Mus of Mod Art, New York, 74. *Teaching:* Artist-in-residence, WGBH-TV, Boston, 69 & GNET-TV, New York, 71. *Bibliog:* Patricia Sloane Discusses the Work of Nam June Paik, Art & Artists, London, 3/72. *Mailing Add:* c/o Galerie Bonino Ltd 48 Great Jones St New York NY 10012

PAJAUD, WILLIAM ETIENNE
PAINTER

b New Orleans, La, Aug 3, 25. *Study:* Xavier Univ, New Orleans, BFA; Chouinard Inst, Los Angeles, grad; also with Tyrus Wong & Charles White. *Work:* Norton Simon Collections, Los Angeles; Pushkin Mus, Moscow; Atlanta Univ, Ga; Westside Jewish Community Ctr, Los Angeles; Golden State Mutual Afro-Am Art Collection. *Exhib:* National Watercolor Soc; Watercolor USA; Carnegie Inst; Los Angeles Co Art Mus; Butler Art Inst. *Awards:* Westside Jewish Community Ctr; Atlanta Univ Ann; Calif Watercolor Soc. *Mem:* Nat Watercolor Soc (pres, 74-75); Los Angeles City Art Asn; Tutor Art, Los Angeles (pres). *Media:* Oil. *Dealer:* Heritage Gallery 718 La Cienega Los Angeles CA 90048. *Mailing Add:* 3767 Grayburn Ave Los Angeles CA 90018

PAL, PRATAPADITYA
CURATOR, HISTORIAN

b Sylhet, Bangladesh, Sept 1, 35. *Study:* Delhi Univ, BA(hons), 56; Calcutta Univ, MA, 58, DPhil, 62; Cambridge Univ, PhD, 65. *Collections Arranged:* The Sensuous Line (with catalog), 76; The Sensuous Immortals (with catalog), 77; The Divine Presence (with catalog), 78; The Classical Tradition in Rajput Painting (with catalog), 78; The Ideal Image (with catalog), 78; Elephants and Ivories (catalog), 81. *Pos:* Sr res assoc, Am Acad Benares, 66-67; keeper of Indian collections, Mus Fine Arts, Boston, 67-69; curator Indian & Islamic art, Los Angeles Co Mus Art, 70- *Teaching:* Lectr Indian art, Harvard Univ, 68-69; lectr Nepali art, Univ Calif, Los Angeles, 70; adj prof SE Asian art, Univ Southern Calif, 70- *Awards:* Most Distinguished Indian (fine arts award), Fed Indian Asn NAm, 80. *Mem:* Asiatic Soc; Nat Soc Arts & Lett. *Res:* Arts, architecture and cultural history of India, Islamic countries, Nepal, Tibet & Southeast Asia. *Publ:* Auth, Bronzes of Kashmir, 75; auth, The Ideal Image, 78; auth, The Classical Tradition in Rajput Painting, 78; auth, A Buddhist Paradise: The Murals of Alchi, 82; auth, Court Painting in India, 83. *Mailing Add:* Los Angeles Co Mus Art 5905 Wilshire Blvd Los Angeles CA 90036

PALADIN, DAVID CHETHLAHE See Chethlahe

PALAIA, FRANC (DOMINIC)
PAINTER, PHOTOGRAPHER

b New Rochelle, NY, Sept 18, 49. *Study:* Newark State Col, Union, NJ, BA(fine arts), 71; Univ Cincinnati, Ohio, MFA(scholar, teaching asst), 73. *Work:* Newark Mus, NJ; Univ Cincinnati, Ohio; NY Univ; Newark Libr, NJ; Mus Mod Art Libr; and others. *Comn:* Mural, Boyle Realty Co, Elizabeth, NJ, 80; mural (5ft x 80ft), Grand Bldg Supply, Elizabeth, NJ, 82. *Exhib:* NJ Photog, Princeton Art Mus, 74; Jersey City Mus, Jersey City, NJ, 77; 1st & 3rd NJ Biennial, Newark Mus, NJ, 77 & 81; Morris Mus, Morristown, NJ, 79; Young Emerging Italian-Am Artists, Museo Italo-Americano, San Francisco, 81; Salon Show, Alternative Mus, New York, 81; and many others. *Teaching:* Instr art hist, Essex Co Col, Newark, NJ, 76-77; instr sculpture, Upsala Col, East Orange, NJ, 76; instr painting, Kean Col, NJ, 78-82. *Awards:* Jurors Award, Rutgers Univ, 74; NJ State Coun Arts Fel, 82. *Bibliog:* Ann Sargent Wooster (auth), Village Voice, 80; Robert Yoskowitz (auth), Franc Palaia, Arts Mag, 80; John Caldwell (auth), review, New York Sunday Times, 81. *Publ:* Contribr, Trylon & Perisphere, Gregory Battcock, 78; contribr, Art Am, Appearances Mag, Umbrella Mag & NJ Monthy Mag, 83. *Dealer:* Royal Palm Gallery 125 Worth Ave Palm Beach FL; City Without Walls Gallery 140 Halsey St Newark NJ 07102. *Mailing Add:* 330 Morris Ave Elizabeth NJ 07208

PALAU, MARTA
TAPESTRY ARTIST, SCULPTOR

b Albesa, Lerida, Spain, July 17, 34. *Study:* La Esmeralda, Inst Nat Bellas Artes, Mex; San Diego State Col; Barcelona Escuela Artes Oficios. *Work:* Secretaria Relaciones Exteriores, Mexico City; Mus Mod Art, Mexico City; Casa Americas, La Habana, Cuba; Tamayo Mus, Mexico City; Museo Arte Contemporaneo, Morelia, Michoacan, Mex. *Comn:* Mural, Ctr Mod Art, Guadalajara, 71; tapestry mural, Hotel El Cid, Mazatlan, Sin Mex, 80; mural tapestry, Hotel Sheraton, Cancun, Mex, 80; metal sculpture, Chapultepec Park, Mexico City, 81; metal sculpture, Univ Metropolitana, Xochimilco, DF Mex, 81; ambiental tapestry, First & Second Int Festival Poetry, Morelia, Michoacan, Mex, 83. *Exhib:* Biennale Int de la Gravure, Krakow, Poland, 74; Mod Art Mus, Tokyo & Mod Art Mus, Kyoto, Japan, 77; Eighth Biennial Int de la Tapiserie, Lausanne, Switz, 78; one-woman show, Mod Art Mus, Mexico City, Mex, 78; Trienal De Lodz, Poland, 81; and others. *Pos:* Collabr spec events, Inst Michoacano Cultura, Mex. *Teaching:* Artist in Residence, Casa Americas, La Habana, Cuba, 82. *Awards:* Exhibit Purchase Award, Inter-Am Mus Graphic Art, San Juan, PR, 73. *Bibliog:* Raquel Tibol (auth), Marta Palau renueva el arte del tapiz, Excelsior Sunday Mag, Mexico City, 1/74 & Los tejidos multi-multidimensionales de Marta Palau, Del Tapiz a la Escultura, Inbal, Mexico City, 74; Juan Acha (auth), Fiber Works, Americas-Japan, Mus Mod Art, Kyoto, Japan, 78. *Mem:* Ford De Arte Contemporaneo, Mexico City. *Media:* Oil, Etching. *Publ:* Auth, Lo Mas Antiguo Y Lo Mas Moderno En El Arte De Marta Palau, Antonio Rodriguez, 73; auth, Eighth Biennale de la Tapisserie, Int Musee Cantonal Beux Arts, Switz, 77. *Dealer:* Independent Galileo 16-6 Mex DF 11560. *Mailing Add:* Galileo 16-6 Mexico DF 11560 Mexico

PALEY, ALBERT RAYMOND
GOLDSMITH, DESIGNER

b Philadelphia, Pa, Mar 28, 44. *Study:* Tyler Sch Art, Temple Univ, BFA, 66, with Stanley Lechtzin, goldsmithing, MFA, 69. *Work:* Minn Mus Art, St Paul; Wilmington Soc Fine Arts, Del; Temple Univ; Univ Ill; Mem Art Gallery, Univ Rochester. *Comn:* Wrought iron portal gates, Renwick Gallery, Smithsonian Inst, Washington, DC, 74; wrought iron fence, Hunter Art Mus, Chattanooga, Tenn, 75. *Exhib:* Tendencies, Schmuchmuseum un Reuchlinhaus, Pforzheim, Ger, 70; Jewelry 71, Art Gallery Ont, Toronto, 71; Goldsmiths' 74, Smithsonian Inst, 74; one-man shows, Cornell Univ, 74 & Goldsmiths' Hall, London, Eng, 76. *Teaching:* Asst prof goldsmithing, Sch Am Craftsmen, Rochester Inst Technol, 69-72; assoc prof goldsmithing, State Univ NY Col Brockport, 72- *Awards:* Purchase Award, Goldsmiths' 74, Minn Mus Art, 74; Nat Endowment Arts Master Apprentice Grant, 75; Am Iron & Steel Inst Design in Steel Award, 75. *Bibliog:* A Peterson (auth), Metalwork of Albert Paley, Craft Horizons, 73; H Hollander (auth), Plastics for jewelry, 74; Craftsman in Am, Nat Geog Soc, 75. *Mem:* Soc NAm Goldsmiths; Am Crafts Coun. *Media:* Ferrous & Nonferrous Metals. *Publ:* Contribr, Goldschmiede Zeitung, 1/69 & 10/70, Body Jewelry, 73 & Jewelry Making, 75. *Mailing Add:* 1237 E Main Rochester NY 14609

PALEY, (MR & MRS) WILLIAM S
COLLECTORS

Mr Paley, b Chicago, Ill, Sept 28, 01. *Study:* Mr Paley, Univ Chicago, 18-19; Univ Pa, BS, 22; Hon LLD, Adelphi Univ, 57, Bates Col, 63, Univ Pa, 68, Columbia Univ, 75, Brown Univ, 75, Pratt Inst, 77, Dartmouth Col, 79; Ithaca Col, LHD, 78. *Pos:* Mr Paley, trustee, Mus Mod Art, New York, pres, 68-72, chmn, 72- *Mem:* Fel Royal Soc Arts. *Collection:* Contemporary paintings. *Mailing Add:* 51 W 52nd St New York NY 10019

PALLEY, REESE
DEALER

b Atlantic City, NJ, Jan 26, 22. *Study:* New Sch Social Res, BA, 48; London Sch Econ, 49-52. *Pos:* Owner, Reese Palley Gallery, San Francisco, Atlantic City & Palm Beach, Fla, currently. *Specialty:* Avant-garde American art and porcelain objet d'art. *Publ:* Auth, The Porcelain Art of Edward Marshall Boehm, Abrams. *Mailing Add:* Reese Palley Inc Park Place & The Boardwalk Atlantic City NJ 08401

PALMER, FRED LOREN
COLLECTOR, PATRON

b Richmond Hill, NY, Sept 12, 01. *Study:* Hamilton Col, AB. *Pos:* Trustee, Am Fedn Arts, 55-63, mem exec comn, 57-63; chmn bd adv, Edward W Root Art Ctr, Hamilton Col, 58-; mem adv coun, State Mus NJ, 60-63; trustee, Summit Art Ctr, NJ, 70-, chmn, 75- *Collection:* Watercolors by Robert Parker, Kingman, Fredenthal and others; drawings by Baskin, Kuniyoshi, Tam, Shahn, Hirsch, Liberman, Thomas George and others; oils by William Palmer, Rattner, Kerkam, Venard, Meigs and others; prints and etchings by Isabel Bishop, Matisse, Picasso and Beckmann; sculpture by Maldarelli and Hardy. *Mailing Add:* 105 New England Ave Summit NJ 07901

PALMER, HERBERT BEARL
DEALER, COLLECTOR

b New York, NY, June 23, 15. *Study:* NY Univ Inst Fine Arts, with A P McMahon, BA(Carnegie Scholar), MA(Michael Friedsam Scholar, Charles Hayden Scholar); Univ Southern Calif; Univ Calif, Los Angeles. *Collections Arranged:* The Film and Modern Art (auth, catalog), Los Angeles Munic Art Gallery, 69; Tantric Art, Twentieth Century Masters & many solo exhibs incl Bridget Riley, Allen Jones & George Grosz, Herbert Palmer Gallery. *Pos:* Western ed, Minicam Photogr, Cincinnati, 46-50; mgr, Feigen Palmer Gallery, Los Angeles, 63-68; owner & pvt art dealer, Herbert B Palmer & Co, Los Angeles, 68-75 & 81- & Beverly Hills, 75-81. *Teaching:* Lectr collecting & investing in art, Univ Calif, Los Angeles Exten. *Mem:* Am Asn Mus; Col Art Asn; Ethnic Arts Coun Los Angeles (bd dirs, 69-71); Int Coun Mus; Art & Antique Dealers League Am. *Specialty:* Modern and contemporary painting, sculpture and drawings. *Collection:* Twentieth century abstract American painting. *Publ:* Auth, Art museums face crisis of identity, Los Angeles Times; auth, Anti-educational influence of pictorial communication, J Sec Educ; auth, Perspective and optical illusions, Design; auth, The mollusk in art, Nature Mag; and others. *Mailing Add:* 802 N La Cienega Blvd Los Angeles CA 90069

PALMER, LUCIE MACKAY
PAINTER, LECTURER

b St Louis, Mo, May 23, 13. *Study:* Boston Mus Fine Arts Sch; St Louis Sch Fine Arts, Washington Univ; Art Students League, with Rapheal Soyer, J N Newell & Robert Brackman. *Exhib:* One-man show, Akari Gallery, Cuernavaca, 76; McAllen Int Mus, Tex, 79; spec group show for Pres of Mex Portillo, Plastica de Morelos Gallery, Cuernavaca, 78; Borda Gallery, Cuernavaca, 81; Univ Morelos, 81; and other group & one-man shows. *Awards:* Prize, Nat Asn Women Artists, 44; Governor's Award for Best Landscape, Morelos State Art Exhib, 77. *Mem:* Nat Asn Women Artists; St Louis Art Guild; Orlando Art Asn; Art League Orange Co. *Media:* Oil. *Res:* Underwater painting. *Mailing Add:* Apartado 1205 Cuernavaca, Morelos 62000 63112 Mexico

PALMER, MABEL (EVELYN)
PAINTER

b Denver, Colo, Oct 19, 03. *Study:* With Richard Yip, Warren Brandon, Vernon Nye & Michael Green. *Work:* Revue Studios Hollywood; Nat Cowgirl Hall of Fame, Hereford, Tex; City Santa Rosa; Bank Am Regional Off, Santa Rosa; Security Bank Antioch, Calif; and others. *Comn:* First Telegraph Line, Union Pac Gold Spike Centennial, Calif & Nev, 69. *Exhib:* M H De Young Mem Mus, San Francisco, 65-66, 68-69 & 71; Watercolor USA, Springfield, Mo, 69; 141st Ann Exhib, Nat Acad Design, New York, 66; Charles & Emma Frye Mus, 71; Los Angeles Mus of Sci & Indust, 76; Nat Cowgirl Hall of Fame, Tex, 77; and others. *Pos:* Dir, Occidental Art Gallery, Calif, 68-; mem adv coun, Artists Round Table, Santa Rosa, 72-; mem art comt, Sonoma Co Fair, Santa Rosa, 75; dir & prog chmn, Santa Rosa Art Guild, 75- *Awards:* Villa Palette Award, de Young Mus, 66; Best of Show & First Award, All Western Art Show, Ellensburg, Wash, 72; Best in Show, Las Vegas Art Mus, 79; and many others. *Mem:* Soc Western Artists; Am Watercolor Soc; Women Artists Am West (historian). *Media:* Acrylic, Transparent Watercolor. *Publ:* Illusr, La Revue Mod, 66, Southwest Art, 79, 82 & 83 & Artwest, 81. *Dealer:* Occidental Fine Arts Gallery 200 Main St Occedental CA 95465. *Mailing Add:* 10395 Barnett Valley Rd Sebastopol CA 95472

PALMER, MICHAEL ANDREW
PAINTER, DEALER

b Mt Sterling, Ky, Dec 8, 42. *Study:* Univ Ky; Univ Hawaii; Univ NH, BA, 70. *Work:* Ogunquit Mus Art, Maine; DeCordova Mus Art, Lincoln, Mass; Colby Col Mus, Waterville, Maine; Elliott Mus Art, Stuart, Fla; Univ Maine, Orono. *Comn:* Auburn (portrait of city), Scammon & Gould, Inc, Maine, 78. *Exhib:* Nat Drawing & Small Sculpture, Ball State Col, Muncie, Ind, 72; Artists of Our Time, Ogunquit Mus Art, Maine, 75, 76 & 78; Am Artists Paris, State Dept, France, 76; one-man shows, Bates Col, Lewiston, Maine, 78 & Elliott Mus, Stuart, Fla, 80. *Pos:* Dir, Bray-Hampton Gallery, Atlanta, Ga, 65-67; co-owner, dir, PS Galleries, Ogunquit, Maine, 78- & Dallas, Tex, 81- *Awards:* Dr Morton M Shur Mem Award, Nat Soc Painters Casein & Acrylic, 75; Purchase Award, DeCordova Mus, 76; First Prize, Bankers Int Collection,

Orlando, Fla, 78. *Bibliog:* A young artist in Georgia, Southern Living, 68; Kathleen Hawk (auth), Michael A Palmer in Dallas, Art Voices, 81. *Mem:* Nat Soc Painters Casein & Acrylic; Ogunquit Art Asn (pres, 74-77). *Media:* Ink, Acrylic. *Specialty:* Primarily representational contemporary artists as well as late 19th, early 20th century American artists. *Dealer:* PS Galleries 2525 Fairmount Dallas TX. *Mailing Add:* PO Box 2381 Ogunquit ME 03907

PALMER, WILLIAM C
PAINTER, LECTURER

b Des Moines, Iowa, Jan 20, 06. *Study:* Art Students League; Ecole Beaux-Arts, Fontainebleau, France; Hamilton Col, Hon DFA, 75. *Work:* Whitney Mus Am Art, New York; Metrop Mus Art, New York; Des Moines Art Ctr; Munson-Williams-Proctor Inst, Utica, NY; plus others. *Comn:* Murals, Post Off Bldg, Washington, DC, First Nat City Bank New York, Queens Gen Hosp, Jamaica, NY & Homestead Savings & Loan Asn, Utica, NY. *Exhib:* Corcoran Gallery Art, Washington, DC; Va Mus Fine Arts, Richmond; Carnegie Inst, Pittsburgh; one-man shows, Midtown Galleries, New York, 63-69, 74 & 77, Two Decades of Painting, Munson-Williams-Proctor Inst, 71, Cummer Art Gallery, Jacksonville, Fla, 71 & Root Art Ctr, Hamilton Col, 75; recent paintings, Midtown Galleries, New York, 81-82; plus others. *Teaching:* Dir, Munson-Williams-Proctor Inst Sch Art, 41-73, emer dir, 73- *Awards:* Prize, Nat Acad Design, 46 & 80; Medal, Audubon Artists, 47; Am Acad Arts & Lett Grant, 53; plus others. *Mem:* Nat Acad Design; Audubon Artists. *Publ:* Contribr, Am Artist Mag. *Mailing Add:* Box 263 Clinton NY 13323

PALMGREN, DONALD GENE
PAINTER, PHOTOGRAPHER

b Moline, Ill, Nov 22, 38. *Study:* Augustana Col, BA; Lutheran Sch Theol, Chicago, MDiv; Detroit Soc Arts & Crafts; Cranbrook Acad Art, with George Ortman, MFA. *Work:* St John's Univ; Anoka-Ramsey Col; Gustavus Adolphus Col. *Exhib:* Davidson Nat Print & Drawing Competition, 72; Drawings USA, 73; Magic Silver Show, Murray State Univ, Ky, 77; Appalachian Nat Drawing Competition, Appalachian State Univ, Boone, NC, 77; one-man show, St John's Univ, 74; Rutgers Nat Drawing, 79; plus many others. *Teaching:* Vis asst prof drawing & design, Murray State Univ, 72; assoc prof drawing & photog, Gustavus Adolphus Col, 72- *Awards:* Res grants, Gustavus Adolphus Col, 73, 75 & 76. *Media:* Charcoal, Oil; Black & White Film. *Mailing Add:* Dept of Art Gustavus Adolphus Col St Peter MN 56082

PANTELL, RICHARD KEITH
PAINTER, PRINTMAKER

b Bronx, NY, May 2, 51. *Study:* Univ Bridgeport, Conn, 69-71; Art Students League, with David Leffel, Frank Mason & Earl Mayan, 74-75. *Work:* Woodstock Hist Soc, NY. *Exhib:* Audubon Artists Ann, Nat Acad & Nat Arts Club, New York, 80 & 81; Ann Mid-Year Show, Butler Inst Am Art, 81-83; 157th Ann Exhib, Nat Acad Design, New York, 82; 69th Ann, Allied Artists Exhib, Nat Arts Club, New York, 83; solo exhib, Gallery Rondout, Kingston, NY, 83; Bernard & S Dean Levy Gallery, New York, 83. *Teaching:* Instr painting & drawing, Continuing Educ, Univ Uppsala, Sweden, 76-77 & Woodstock Sch Art, NY, 79- *Awards:* Julius Hallgarten First Prize, 157th Ann Exhib, Nat Acad Design, 82; Woodstock Artist Asn Award, 82. *Bibliog:* Palmer Paroner (auth), The art of Richard Pantell, 7/23/81 & A transplanted New Yorker, 7/7/83, Artspeak; Tram Combs (auth), Pantell's luminous urbanities, Woodstock Times, 7/21/83. *Mem:* Allied Artists Am; Audubon Artists; Woodstock Artists Asn (mem bd dirs, 79-80 & 82-83). *Media:* Oil; Etching. *Dealer:* Bernard & S Dean Levy 981 Madison Ave New York NY 10021. *Mailing Add:* 37 Cooper Lake Rd Bearsville NY 12409

PAONE, PETER
PRINTMAKER, PAINTER

b Philadelphia, Pa, Oct 2, 36. *Study:* Philadelphia Col Art, BFA, 58. *Work:* Libr Cong; Philadelphia Mus Art; Mus Mod Art; Atlantic Richfield Visual Arts Ctr; Victoria & Albert Mus, London, Eng; and others. *Exhib:* Brooklyn Mus, 62 & 64; Butler Inst Am Art, 65; New York World's Fair, 65; Otis Art Inst, Los Angeles, 64 & 66; one-man shows, Contemp Art Mus, Houston, 76, Roswell Mus, NMex, 77 & Hooks-Epstein Galleries, Houston, 78; Pa Acad Fine Arts, 83; and many others. *Teaching:* Instr, Philadelphia Col Art, 59 & Pratt Inst, 59-66; instr art hist, Positano Art Sch, Italy, 61; instr drawing & chmn graphics dept, Pa Acad Fine Arts, 78- *Awards:* Purchase Prize, Syracuse Univ, 64; Guggenheim Fel, 65-66; Print Club Award of Merit, Philadelphia, 83; and others. *Bibliog:* Selden Rodman (auth), The Insiders, La State Univ, 60. *Mem:* Soc Am Graphic Artists; assoc mem Nat Acad Design, New York. *Publ:* Auth & illusr, Paone's Zoo, 61, Five Insane Dolls, 66 & My Father, 69; auth, Kachina--Paone, 76; and others. *Dealer:* Hooks-Epstein Gallery 1200 Bissonnet Houston TX 77005. *Mailing Add:* 1027 Westview St Philadelphia PA 19119

PAPAGEORGE, TOD
PHOTOGRAPHER

b Portsmouth, NH, Aug 1, 40. *Study:* Univ NH, BA; Yale Univ, Hon MA. *Work:* Mus Mod Art; Art Inst Chicago; Bibliot Nat, Paris; Boston Mus Fine Arts; Seagrams Inc, New York. *Comn:* The American Courthouse Bicentennial Doc, Seagrams, Inc, 75; American Images, AT&T, 78. *Exhib:* Recent Acquisitions, Mus Mod Art, 71, 73 & 79 & Pub Landscapes, 74; 14 Am Photogr, Baltimore Mus of Art, 75; Ten Am Photogr, Galerie Zabriskie, Paris, France, 77; Mirrors & Windows, Mus Mod Art, 78; one-man exhibs, Light Gallery, New York, 73 & 79, Art Inst Chicago, 78, Galerie Zabriskie, Paris, 80, Daniel Wolf Gallery, New York, 81 & Akron Art Mus, 81. *Pos:* Cur, Mus Mod Art, 77; Akron Art Mus, 81. *Teaching:* Prof photog, Yale Univ, 79. *Awards:* Guggenheim Found Fel Photog, 70 & 77; Nat Endowment Arts Fel Photog, 73 & 75. *Publ:* Contribr, articles, Aperture, Vol 19, No 1 & No 85,

81; auth & ed, Public Relations, The Photographs of Garry Winogrand, Mus Mod Art, 77; auth, Walker Evans and Robert Frank: An Essay on Influence (catalog), Yale Art Gallery, 80; and others. *Mailing Add:* 100 York St #4-K New Haven CT 06511

PAPO, ISO
PAINTER
b Sarajevo, Yugoslavia, May 2, 25; US citizen. *Study:* Polytech Milan; Brera Acad Fine Arts, Milan, Italy, grad, 51; Boston Mus Sch; also with Carlo Carra. *Comn:* Paintings for films & posters, United Church of Christ, 64-65. *Exhib:* Inst Contemp Art, Boston, 68; Brockton Art Ctr, 70; Tanglewood, 71; one-man shows, Boston Athenaeum, 73 & Boston Psychoanal Soc & Inst, 75. *Teaching:* Instr art, Kirkland House & Quincy House, Harvard Univ, 64-69; assoc prof painting, Boston Univ, 67-75; instr painting & drawing, Pine Manor Col, 68- *Awards:* Nat Scholastic Competition First Prize, Govt of Italy, 50. *Mem:* Boston Visual Artists Union. *Media:* Watercolor, Oil. *Mailing Add:* 212 Aspinwall Ave Brookline MA 02146

PAPPAS, GEORGE
ADMINISTRATOR, PAINTER
b Boston, Mass, Jan 25, 29. *Study:* Mass Col of Art, BS, 52; Harvard Univ, MA, 53; Mass Inst of Technol, with Gyorgy Kepes, 52-53; Pa State Univ, PhEduc, 57. *Work:* De Cordova Mus, Lincoln, Mass; St Paul Gallery of Art, Minn; Tampa Bay Art Ctr, Fla; Pa State Univ, University Park. *Exhib:* Corcoran Biennial, Washington, DC; De Cordova Mus Art, Lincoln, Mass; Ringling Mus Art, Sarasota, Fla; Detroit Inst of Art, Mich; Boston Mus Fine Arts, Mass; Kanegis Gallery, Boston; Nordness Gallery, New York. *Teaching:* Asst prof painting & art educ, Pa State Univ, 55-56; prof painting & chmn dept art, Univ South Fla, 66- *Awards:* Purchase Awards, Drawing USA, St Paul Gallery of Art, Chautaqua Nat, Chautaqua Art Asn & Tampa Bay Art Ctr, Fla. *Mem:* Col Art Asn; Nat Conf of Art Adminr; Nat Art Educ Asn. *Media:* Oil. *Publ:* Co-auth, Design, It's Form and Function, Pa State Univ, 65; auth, Concepts in Art & Education, McMillian, 70. *Mailing Add:* Dept of Art Univ S Fla Tampa FL 33620

PAPPAS, MARILYN
COLLAGE ARTIST, EDUCATOR
b Brockton, Mass, Jan 1, 31. *Study:* Mass Col Art, BSEd; Pa State Univ, MEd. *Work:* Objects USA, Am Craft Mus, New York, NY; Viktor Lowenfeld Mem Collection, Pa State Univ; Krannert Art Mus, Univ Ill; Dayton Traveling Mus, Ohio. *Comn:* Wall covering, comn by Lee Nordness, New York, 67; theater curtain, Temple Israel, Miami, 68; fabric collage, Pan Am Int, 70; wall relief, Musa Isle Residence for the Elderly, Miami, Fla, 76. *Exhib:* Craftsmen of the Eastern States, 63, Fabric Collage, 65 & Craftsmen USA, 66, Mus Contemp Crafts; History of Collage, Kunstgewerbemus, Zurich, Switz, 68; Objects USA, Smithsonian Inst, 69; solo exhibs, Helen Shlien Gallery, Boston, 80 & 82. *Teaching:* Asst prof art educ, Pa State Univ, 59-64; assoc prof art, Miami-Dade Jr Col, 65-74; assoc prof art & chmn three-dimensional fine arts dept, Mass Col Art, 74- *Awards:* Nat Endowment Arts Craftsman Grant, 73; Fel, Bunting Inst, Radcliffe Col, 78-80; Artists Found Grant, Mass, 81; and others. *Bibliog:* Bartlett Hayes (auth), Drawings of the Masters: American Drawings, Shorewood Publ, 65; Nik Krevitsky (auth), Stitchery: art and craft, Art Horizons, 66; Lee Nordness (auth), Objects USA, Viking Press, 70. *Mem:* Am Crafts Coun. *Publ:* Contribr, Sch Arts Mag, 62-67; auth, The Temples of William Wyman, Am Craft Mag, 2-3/82. *Dealer:* Helen Shlien Gallery Newbury St Boston MA. *Mailing Add:* 67 Walker St Cambridge MA 02138

PARADISE, PHIL (HERSCHEL)
PAINTER, SCULPTOR
b Ontario, Ore, Aug 26, 05. *Study:* Chouinard Art Inst, grad; also with F Tolles Chamberlain, Rico Lebrun & Leon Kroll. *Work:* Libr Cong, Washington, DC; Philadelphia Watercolor Club; San Diego Fine Arts Soc. *Exhib:* Los Angeles Co Mus Art, 40; San Francisco Art Asn, 41; Art Inst Chicago, 43; Carnegie Inst Int, Pittsburgh, 43-44; Whitney Mus Am Art, New York, 45. *Pos:* Art dir & prod designer, Sol Lesser Prod, Paramount Studios, 41-48; dir, Greystone Galleries, 62-75. *Teaching:* Prof painting, Chouinard Art Inst, 31-40, dir fine arts, 36-40; lectr painting & drawing, Univ Tex, El Paso, 52; lectr painting & drawing, Scripps Col, 56-57. *Awards:* Purchase Award for Goleta, Philadelphia Watercolor Club, 39; Purchase Award for Landscape, San Francisco Int Exhib, 41; Dana Medal for Suburban Supper, Philadelphia Watercolor Club, 43. *Bibliog:* Janice Lovos (auth), Guatemala journey, Am Artist Mag, 50; Beverly Johnson (auth), Phil Paradise and his works, Los Angeles Times Home Mag, 67; Janice Lovos (auth), Phil Paradise serigraphs, Am Artist Mag, 69. *Mem:* Assoc Nat Acad Design. *Media:* Graphics. *Publ:* Illusr, Fortune Mag, Westways Mag, True Mag & others, 40-60. *Mailing Add:* PO Box 11105 Bakersfield CA 93389

PARDEE, WILLIAM HEARNE
PAINTER, EDUCATOR
b Pittsburgh, Pa, Aug 25, 46. *Study:* Yale Univ, with Sewell Sillman, BA, 69; New York Studio Sch, with Philip Guston, George McNeil & Leland Bell, 69-73; Columbia Univ, with Meyer Schapiro, MFA, 75. *Exhib:* Ann Exhib, Maine Coast Artists Gallery, Rockport, 81; Hudson River Contemp Art, Hudson River Mus, 81; Paintings, Bowery Gallery, New York, 81 & 82; Paintings, Univ Maine, Farmington, 82; Recent Paintings, Colby Col Mus Art, 83. *Collections Arranged:* Linens, Wall-Clothing and Straw Sculpture, sculptures by Maureen Connor, 82; Aspects of Abstraction, sculpture by Deborah de Moulpied, Gerald DiGiusto & Lawrence Fane, 83. *Pos:* Consult contemp art, Colby Col Mus Art, Maine, 82- *Teaching:* Lectr painting, Univ Southern Maine, Portland, 81-82; asst prof painting & design, Colby Col, Maine, 82-; vis asst prof, Col William & Mary, 83. *Bibliog:* Gerard

Haggerty (auth), Hearne Pardee: Paintings and cut-ups, Art New England, 4/82; Edgar Allen Beem (auth), Approaching landscape from two directions, Maine Times, 2/18/83; Mark Erickson (auth), Landscape show gives new look to reality, Va Gazette, 9/14/83. *Mem:* Col Art Asn Am. *Media:* Oil. *Publ:* Auth, Proust's visual imagery, Yale French Studies, 65; auth, On color, 83, A reading of Marsden Hartley, 83 & Six painters at the Hudson River Museum, 83, Arts Mag. *Dealer:* Bowery Gallery 121 Wooster St New York NY 10012; Barridoff Galleries 242 Middle St Portland ME 04101. *Mailing Add:* 549 W 123rd St #15A New York NY 10027

PARDINGTON, RALPH ARTHUR
CERAMIST, SCULPTOR
b Highland Park, Mich, June 14, 38. *Study:* Albion Col, BFA, 60; Alfred Col Ceramics, summers 61 & 65; Cranbrook Acad Art, MFA, 62; with Hal Reiger & Palo Soleri, 64 & Dominic Labino, 67. *Work:* Inst Contemp Arts, Washington, DC; Mus Int Folk Art, Santa Fe; Mus Fine Arts, Div Mus NMex, Santa Fe; Mus Albuquerque; Mus Fine Art, Univ Okla. *Comn:* Bas-relief wall sculpture of patron saint, 69, holy water fountain, 69, Christ Desert Monastery, Albuquerque; sculpture, comn by Fritz Scholder, Galisteo, NMex, 70; outdoor planters, comn by A J O'Brien, Harbor Springs, Mich, 73; two large punch bowls, Int Folk Art Mus, Santa Fe, 73. *Exhib:* 25th Ceramic National, Syracuse, NY, 68; Object Makers, Univ Utah, 71; Int Am Indian Arts Fac Exhib, Smithsonian Inst, Washington, DC, 73; Christmas Exhib, ACC Gallery, New York, 74; NMex Exhib, Univ Albuquerque, 74. *Teaching:* Instr applied arts, Inst Am Indian Arts, 62-; instr ceramics, Penland Sch Crafts, summers 67 & 69. *Awards:* First Prize, Int Folk Art, 68; Outstanding Work Award, Mus Albuquerque, 70; Commission Prize, Mus NMex, 71. *Bibliog:* Article in NMex Mag, winter 71. *Mem:* NMex Potters Asn; Am Crafts Coun; NMex Designer Craftsmen (pres, Santa Fe Chap, 64-65, state pres & vpres, 65-66). *Media:* Clay, Wood. *Publ:* Auth, 30-minute demonstration prog, KNME TV, 66. *Mailing Add:* c/o Inst Am Indian Arts Mus Cerrillos Rd Santa Fe NM 87501

PARDON, EARL B
CRAFTSMAN, EDUCATOR
b Memphis, Tenn, Sept 6, 26. *Study:* Memphis Acad Art, BFA; Syracuse Univ, MFA. *Work:* Mus Contemp Crafts; St Paul Mus & Sch Art; Lower Art Ctr, Syracuse; Memphis Acad Art; Skidmore Col. *Comn:* Mus Contemp Crafts & Prudential Life Ins Co, Newark, NJ. *Exhib:* Mus Contemp Crafts; Wichita Craft Biennial; Syracuse Ceramics Nat; Skidmore Col; Schenectady Mus Art; plus others. *Teaching:* Lectr painting, jewelry & design, art schs, craftsmens orgns & col alumni groups; prof art, Skidmore Col, currently. *Mailing Add:* Dept Art Skidmore Col Saratoga Springs NY 12866

PARELLA, ALBERT LUCIAN
PAINTER, INSTRUCTOR
b Youngstown, Ohio, Mar 21, 09. *Study:* Cleveland Sch Art, dipl art; Am Acad, Chicago. *Work:* Butler Inst Am Art; Hoyt Inst; Westminster Col; Youngstown Pub Libr. *Comn:* Set designs, Youngstown Playhouse, 33; emblem design, Youngstown YMCA, 60; emblem design, Youngstown Symphony Soc, 70; plague design, Choffin Voc Sch, 73; medal design, Butler Inst Am Art, 73. *Exhib:* Am Vet Art Soc, 74; Nat Acad, 74; Am Watercolor Soc, 74; Audubon Artists, 75; Soc Painters Casein, 75; Retrospective Show Winners of Prizes, Nat Arts Gallery, 78. *Pos:* Cartoonist, Youngstown Telegram, 32-34; art dir, Wearstler Advertising, Youngstown, 34-45; advertising dir, Century Foods, Youngstown, 45-50; art dir, WKBN TV, Youngstown, 50- *Teaching:* Instr art, Butler Inst Am Art, 46-48; instr art, Youngstown State Univ, 65-67. *Awards:* Gold Medal, Butler Inst Am Art, 73; President's Award, Audubon Artists, 74; Strathmore Watercolor Award, 77. *Mem:* Am Watercolor Soc; Audubon Artists; Artists in Casein & Acrylic; Knickerbocker Artists; Ohio Watercolor Soc. *Media:* Casein, Watercolor. *Publ:* Auth, Art in television, Today's Art, 73. *Mailing Add:* 208 Evergreen Dr Poland OH 44514

PARFENOFF, MICHAEL S
EDUCATOR, LITHOGRAPHER
b Gary, Ind, Aug 8, 26. *Study:* Art Inst Chicago, with Boris Anisfeld & Max Kahn, BFA & MFA. *Exhib:* Print Exhib, Libr Cong, Washington, DC; Momentum, Art Inst Chicago; Philadelphia Print Club. *Pos:* Dir, Blackhawk Mountain Sch Art, 63- *Teaching:* Instr lithography, Art Inst Chicago, 58-65; prof art, Chicago City Col, 58- *Mem:* Am Asn Univ Prof; Ill Art Educators. *Media:* Stone. *Mailing Add:* 453 W Roslyn Chicago IL 60614

PARIS, JEANNE C
CRITIC, CONSULTANT
b Newark, NJ. *Study:* Newark Sch Fine Arts; Tyler Sch Art, Temple Univ; Columbia Univ; NY Univ. *Collections Arranged:* Organized & directed The Artist of the Month, providing lecturers & demonstrators in all the arts for organizations & schools; organized exhibs of American art for Latin America, Italy & USA. *Pos:* Assoc dir, Valente Gallery, New York, currently; art critic, Long Island Press, 63-; art critic, Newsday, 77- *Teaching:* Lectr art, univs, cols, art leagues, women's clubs, mus asns, radio & NBC-TV series, You're a Part of Art. *Mem:* Glen Cove Pub Libr; Coun Arts North Shore; New York Reporters Asn; Newspaper Women's Club; Sea Cliff Chamber Soc; and others. *Collection:* Twentieth century painting & sculpture. *Publ:* Auth articles for Weekly Newspaper Chain, Record Pilot & Newsday; auth, article, Cue Mag, 7/72. *Mailing Add:* 21 Whitney Circle Glen Cove NY 11548

PARIS, KAY
MUSEUM EXECUTIVE DIRECTOR, CONSULTANT
b Kans City, Mo, Feb 6, 30. *Study:* Stephens Col, AA, 48; Carnegie-Mellon Univ, BA, 49 & MA, 50. *Collections Arranged:* Gloria dell'Arte: A Renaissance Perspective (auth, catalog), 79; The Frederick W Schumacher Collection (ed, catalog), 76; Conserving Our Cultural Heritage, 76; Common Clay to Ceramic, 75; Environment for Living, 73. *Pos:* Administrator of tour programs & docent, Nelson Gallery, Kans City, Mo, 61-69; cur & registrar, Columbus Gallery Fine Arts, Ohio, 70-78; bd dirs, Ohio Mus Asn, 76-78; guest cur, Philbrook Art Ctr, Tulsa, Okla, 78-79; dir, Beaumont Art Mus, Tex, 80- *Mem:* Am Asn Mus; Tex Mus Asn; Mt Plains Mus Asn; Int Coun Mus. *Publ:* Auth, Transfer Printed Ware, 70, Common Clay to Ceramic: A Brief History of English Pottery, 75, & ed, Catalog of the Collection, 78, Columbus Mus Art. *Mailing Add:* 1111 Ninth Street Beaumont TX 77702

PARIS, LUCILLE M
PAINTER, PRINTMAKER
b Cleveland, Ohio, Apr 8, 28. *Study:* Univ Calif, Berkeley, BA(Taussig Traveling Fel), 51, MA(McEnerney Grad Fel), 52; Atelier 17, Paris. *Work:* Butterfield Collection; NJ State Mus Contemp Art; Newark Mus Collection Contemp Art. *Exhib:* San Francisco Mus of Art, 50, 51, 53, 54, 55, 61 & 62; SFW Annuals, San Francisco Mus Art, 52, 53, 56, 57 & 58; one-person shows, Aegis Gallery, New York, 65, NJ State Mus, Trenton, 73 & Bronx Mus Art, New York, 76; Rutgers Univ, 81; NJ Soc Archit Hq, WCalif group, 81; ETS Corp, Princeton, 84; and others. *Teaching:* Prof painting & graphics, Ball State Univ, 55-57; prof art, William Paterson Col, 59- *Mailing Add:* Dept Art William Paterson Col Wayne NJ 07470

PARISH, BETTY WALDO
PAINTER, WRITER
b Dec 6, 10; US citizen. *Study:* Art Students League, with Kenneth Hays Miller & John Sloan; Acad Julian, Paris; Grand Cent Sch, New York; Chicago Acad Fine Arts. *Work:* Metrop Mus Art, New York; Libr Cong, Washington, DC; Brit Mus, London; Mus d'Art, Brussels, Belg; Pa Acad Fine Arts, Philadelphia; and others. *Exhib:* Pa Acad Fine Arts Ann, 39-41; US Asn Women Artists, 39-45; Libr Cong; Nat Acad Design, New York; Nat Arts Club, 68-72; and others. *Awards:* Second Prize, Am Artists Prof League, 64; Nat Arts Graphic Prize, 70; David Humprys Mem Prize, Allied Artists Am, 72; and others. *Mem:* Audubon Artists (bd dirs, 60-); Allied Artists Am; Nat Asn Women Artists; Art Students League; Pen & Brush; and others. *Publ:* Auth, Rome, 58, England Again, 59 & Paris, 60. *Mailing Add:* 69 Fifth Ave New York NY 10003

PARIZEK, JARO
DEALER, COLLECTOR
b Prague, Czech, Mar 16, 34; US citizen. *Study:* Art & Tech Col Vienna, 56; Art Students League, with Brackman, 66-69. *Pos:* Art dealer-mgr, Wally Findlay Galleries Inc, New York, 70-75; art dealer-owner, Jaro Art Galleries, New York, 75- *Mem:* Am Artists Asn. *Res:* History of the Yugoslav Naive School of Art. *Specialty:* Yugoslav naive art and American contemporary primitives. *Collection:* Yugoslav naive art, to be eventually shown in different museums throughout the country. *Mailing Add:* Jaro Art Galleries 955 Madison Ave New York NY 10021

PARKE, WALTER SIMPSON
PAINTER, PRINTMAKER
b Little Rock, Ark, Dec 30, 09. *Study:* Art Inst Chicago; Am Acad Art; also with Wellington Reynolds. *Work:* Univ Ill Col Dentistry; Union League Civic & Arts Found; plus others in pvt collections. *Exhib:* Union League Club Art Show, Chicago; Allied Artists Am 52nd Ann, New York; Munic Art League, Chicago; Am Artists Prof League, New York; Denver Art Mus; plus many others. *Teaching:* Instr portrait painting, Palette & Chisel Acad. *Awards:* Six Purchase Awards, Union League Club Exhib, 55-78; Gold Medal, Munic Art League, 71; Gold Medal, Diamond Medal & Silver Medal, Palette & Chisel Acad, 76-79. *Mem:* Brown Co Art Guild; Palette & Chisel Acad; Munic Art League; Oak Park Art League; Union League Civic & Arts Found. *Media:* Oil, Watercolor; Etching. *Mailing Add:* 30 W 225 Argyll Ln Naperville IL 60540

PARKER, ALFRED
ILLUSTRATOR
b Saint Louis, Mo, Oct 16, 06. *Study:* St Louis Sch Fine Arts, Washington Univ, 23-28; Acad Art San Francisco, Hon MFA, 78; RI Sch Design, Hon PhD, 78; Calif Sch Arts & Crafts, Hon PhD, 78. *Comn:* Creator mother & daughter covers, Ladies Home J, 38-51. *Exhib:* Exhibs in major cities of US & Can. *Pos:* Founder & mem, Famous Artists Schs, Westport, Conn, 47- *Teaching:* Lectr, major cities US & Can; mem grad fac, Illus Dept, Acad Art Col, San Francisco, 78- *Awards:* Named to Hall of Fame, Soc Illusr, 65; Life Achievement Award, Soc Illusrs, Los Angeles, 80; and others. *Bibliog:* Article, Commun Arts Mag, 6/77; Walt Reed (auth), Great American Illustrators, 79; Sister Cor Immaculatum Heffernan (auth), A Comparative Study of American Illustrators, 81; and others. *Mem:* Fel Int Inst Arts & Lett; hon mem Soc Illusr; St Louis Art Dirs Club; Art Dirs & Artists Club San Francisco; Westport Artists Group (founder & past pres). *Publ:* Contribr, mag and advert art, 29-; plus others. *Mailing Add:* 56 Rancho Rd Carmel Valley CA 93924

PARKER, ANN (ANN PARKER NEAL)
PHOTOGRAPHER, GRAPHIC ARTIST
b London, Eng, Mar 6, 34; US citizen. *Study:* RI Sch of Design; Yale Univ, BFA. *Work:* Metrop Mus Art, New York; Libr of Cong, Washington, DC; Smithsonian Inst, Washington, DC; Mus Mod Art, New York; Mus Int Folk

Art, Santa Fe, NMex. *Comn:* Arton Assoc, 70 & 74; Mead Art Gallery, Amherst, Mass, 76. *Exhib:* Ephemeral Image, Mus Am Folk Art, New York, 70; Worlds Beyond the Echo, Friends of Photog, Carmel, Calif, 71; Portuguese Portfolios, 73 & Guatemalan Portfolio, 76, Siembab Gallery; Flowering of Am Folk Art, Whitney Mus Am Art, New York, 74; plus many others. *Awards:* Fifty Best Books Award, Am Inst Graphic Artists, 57 & 79; Ford Found Grant in Arts & Humanities, 62-64; First Prize in Photog, Americana Bicentennial Photog Contest, 76 & Mass Open, 77. *Bibliog:* M J Gladstone (auth), New art from early American sculpture, Collector's Quart Report, 63 & Pedestrian art, Art in Am, 4/64; Stephen Chodorov (producer), Know ye the Hour, Camera Three, CBS-TV, 11/68. *Mem:* Friends of Photog. *Dealer:* Gallery of Graphic Arts 1603 York Ave New York NY 10028. *Mailing Add:* Thistle Hill North Brookfield MA 01535

PARKER, CAROLYN JOHNSON
PAINTER, GRAPHIC ARTIST
b Cleveland, Ohio, Nov 22, 42. *Study:* Skidmore Col, BA(art hist), 65. *Work:* Berkshire Mus, Pittsfield, Mass; Needham, Harper, Steers Advert, Chicago; Am J Psychiatry, Washington, DC; Sybil & Stephen Stone Collection, Brocton Mus, Mass. *Exhib:* Ann Exhib, Springfield Mus, Mass, 78; Hood Col, Frederick, Md, 82; Professional & Amateur Maryland Artists, Md Art Place, Baltimore, 82; Ann Exhib, Allied Artists, New York, 82; Mem Ann Exhib, Albright-Knox Gallery, 83; one-artist show, Peel Gallery, Danby, Vt, 83. *Awards:* Collection Award, Berkshire Mus, Pittsfield, Mass, 77. *Media:* Acrylic. *Dealer:* Elain Starkman 465 W Broadway New York NY 10012; Harris & Peggy Peel Rt 7 Danby VT 05739. *Mailing Add:* 239 Dill Ave Frederick MD 21701

PARKER, HARRY S, III
MUSEUM DIRECTOR
b St Petersburg, Fla, Dec 23, 39. *Study:* Harvard Univ, BA; Inst Fine Arts, NY Univ, MA. *Pos:* Asst to dir, Metrop Mus Art, New York, 63-67, vdir educ, 68-73; dir, Dallas Mus Fine Arts, 74- *Teaching:* Lectr mus educ. *Mem:* Am Asn Mus; Am Fedn Arts; Int Coun Mus. *Publ:* Contribr, Metrop Mus Art Bul. *Mailing Add:* 9612 Rockbrook Dr Dallas TX 75220

PARKER, JAMES
PAINTER
b Butte, Mont, Oct 20, 33. *Study:* Columbia Col, BA, 55; independent study, Spain, 60-62. *Work:* Whitney Mus Am Art, New York; Aldrich Mus, Ridgefield, Conn; Carnegie Inst; Chase Manhattan Bank Collection, New York; Santa Barbara Mus. *Exhib:* Whitney Mus Am Art, 72 & 74; Soho Ctr Visual Artists, 74; Schaffner Gallery, 74; Univ Calif, Santa Barbara, 74; Parsons Sch Design Fac Exhibs, 77 & 79; and others. *Teaching:* Instr art, Metrop State Col, 65-67; instr color theory, Parsons Sch Design, New York, 74- *Media:* Acrylic, Pastel. *Publ:* Auth, Pop's ancestors, Denver Quart, 67. *Mailing Add:* 466 Washington St New York NY 10013

PARKER, JAMES VARNER
ADMINISTRATOR, DESIGNER
b Senath, Mo, June 27, 25. *Study:* Phoenix Community Col, AA; Ariz State Univ, BFA & MA. *Work:* Southeast State Teachers Col; City of Phoenix Civic Art Collection; Alhambra High Sch Art Collection, Ariz; Heard Mus, Phoenix; Scottsdale Art Collection. *Comn:* Carl Hayden High Sch Student Body, Phoenix, 60; Greater Ariz Savings Bank, Tucson; Heard Mus. *Exhib:* Tucson Art Ctr, 66; Phoenix Art Mus, 66; Stanford Res Inst, Palo Alto, Calif, 66; Yuma Art Asn, Ariz, 70; Into White, Scottsdale, Ariz; plus others. *Collections Arranged:* Indian Art Collection, 68 & 72; African Art, Heard Mus, 6/72 & 9/72; Indian Art of the Americas. *Pos:* Curator educ, Heard Mus, 58-68, illusr, 58 & 71, curator art, 68-75; consult adminr, Phoenix Mus Hist, 75-77; mus dir, Southeast Mo State Univ Mus, 77- *Teaching:* Instr art, Phoenix Col, 68-70; instr art, Glendale Community Col, 71-72; instr, Southeast Mo State Univ, 76- *Awards:* Nat Vet Award, Santa Monica Recreation Dept, 53; O'Brien Art Award, Ariz State Fair, 60; UNICEF Award, 68. *Bibliog:* Design-Crafts-Education (film), KAET TV, Ariz State Univ, 60. *Mem:* Ariz Art Asn (secy, 60); Nat Art Educ Asn; Ariz Watercolor Asn (founder & pres, 59); Ariz Art Asn (pres, 60). *Publ:* Illusr, The Story of Navaho Weaving, 61; illusr, Pima Basketry, 65; illusr, Women in 1970, 70. *Mailing Add:* 445 Marie Cape Girardeau MO 63701

PARKER, NANCY WINSLOW
ILLUSTRATOR, WRITER
b Maplewood, NJ, Oct 18, 30. *Study:* Mills Col, Calif, BA, 52; Art Students League & Sch Visual Arts, New York. *Exhib:* 3rd Ann Art Exhib, Mills Col, 69; Audubon Artists 29th Ann Exhib, New York, 71; Webb & Parsons, Bedford Village, NY, 76; Master-Eagle Gallery, NY, 80 & 83; Webb & Parsons, New Canaan, Conn, 83. *Pos:* Art dir, Appleton, Century, Crofts, New York, 68-70; graphic designer, Holt Rinehart & Winston, New York, 70-72. *Awards:* Am Libr Asn Notable Book Award, 80; My Mom Travels A Lot, New York Times Ten Best Illustrated Books, 81; Chistopher Award, 81; and others. *Mem:* Soc Illusr; Authors Guild. *Media:* Watercolor, Wood. *Publ:* Auth & illusr, The Spotted Dog, 80, Cooper, The McNallys' Big Black Dog, 81, Love from Aunt Betty, 83 & The Christmas Carol, 83, Dodd Mead; auth & illusr, The President's Car, Crowell, 81; and others. *Mailing Add:* 51 E 74th St New York NY 10021

PARKER, OLIVIA
PHOTOGRAPHER
b Boston, Mass, June 10, 41. *Study:* Wellesley Col, BA, 63. *Work:* Victoria & Albert Mus, London; Boston Mus Fine Arts; Mus Mod Art, New York; Art Inst Chicago; Int Mus Photog, Eastman House, Rochester; and others. *Comn:*

Photographic Resource Ctr, Boston, 81. *Exhib:* 14 New Eng Photogr, Boston Mus Fine Arts, 78; Loans to the Collection, Art Inst Chicago, 78; One of a Kind Traveling Exhib, Mus Fine Arts, Houston; 20 x 24, Light Gallery, New York, 79; one-person shows, Friends Photog, Carmel, Calif, 79 & 81, Eastman House, Rochester, 81, Mus Art, Univ Ore, 82, Catskill Ctr Photog, Woodstock, 82 & Art Inst Chicago, 82; and others. *Awards:* Artists Found fel, 78; Cert of Excellence, Am Inst of Graphic Arts Bk Show, 79; Ferguson Grant, 81. *Bibliog:* Owen Edwards (auth), The clear Yankee eye, Saturday Rev, 79; Vicki Goldberg (auth), Signs of (still)life, Am Photogr, 79; David Featherstone (auth), Olivia Parker, Mod Photog, 80. *Mem:* Soc for Photog Educ; Friends Photog. *Media:* Photography. *Publ:* Auth, Signs of Life, 78 & contribr, One of a Kind, 79, David Godine; contribr, Darkroom Dynamics, Curtin & London, 79; auth, Under the Looking Glass, New York Graphic Soc, 83. *Mailing Add:* c/o Vision Gallery 216 Newbury St Boston MA 02116

PARKER, RAY(MOND)
PAINTER
b Beresford, SDak, Aug 22, 22. *Study:* Univ Iowa, BA, 46, MFA, 48. *Work:* Solomon R Guggenheim Mus, Mus Mod Art, Whitney Mus Am Art, & Metrop Mus Art, New York; Tate Gallery, London, Eng; and 33 others. *Exhib:* One-man exhibs, Walker Art Ctr, Minneapolis, Minn, 50, Kootz Gallery, New York, 60-66 & Solomon R Guggenheim Mus, 61; Retrospective, Dayton Art Inst, Ohio, 65, San Francisco Mus Art, Calif, 67 & Sch Visual Arts, New York, 71; Mus Mod Art, New York, 68 & 71; Univ Tex, 72; and others. *Teaching:* Prof art, Hunter Col, 55- *Awards:* Ford Found Purchase Award, Corcoran Biennial, 63; Nat Coun on Arts Award, 67; Guggenheim Fel, 67 & 81. *Bibliog:* L Campbell (auth), Parker paints a picture, Art News, 11/62; G Nordland (auth), exhib catalog, San Francisco Mus Art, 67. *Media:* Oils. *Publ:* Contribr, Student, teacher, artist, Col Art J, 53; contribr, Direct painting, spring 58 & Intent painting, fall 58. *Mailing Add:* 101 Prince St New York NY 10012

PARKER, ROBERT ANDREW
PAINTER
b Norfolk, Va, May 14, 27. *Study:* Art Inst Chicago, BAE, 52; Skowhegan Sch Painting & Sculpture; Atelier 17, New York, 52-53. *Work:* Los Angeles Co Mus; Metrop Mus Art; Morgan Libr, New York; Mus Mod Art; Whitney Mus Am Art; plus others. *Comn:* Designer sets, William Shuman Opera, Mus Mod Art, 61. *Exhib:* Brooklyn Mus, 55; Mus Mod Art, 57; Laon Mus, Aisne, France, 56; New Sch Social Res, 65; Sch Visual Arts, NY, 65; and many others. *Awards:* Rosenthal Found Grant, Nat Inst Arts & Lett, 62; Tamarind Lithography Workshop Fel, 67; Guggenheim Fel, 69-70; plus others. *Publ:* Illusr, hand colored ltd ed poems, Mus Mod Art, 62; illusr poetry, The days of Wilfred Owen (film), 66. *Dealer:* Terry Dintenfass Inc 50 W 57th St New York NY 10021. *Mailing Add:* Box 114 West Cornwall CT 06796

PARKER, SAMUEL MURRAY
PAINTER
b Madison, Wis, Aug 6, 36. *Study:* Wis State Univ, Eau Claire, BA(art), 63; Univ Wis, MS(painting & drawing), 64, MFA(painting), 65. *Work:* Springfield Mus; Playboy Club; Laura Musser Mus, Muscatine, Iowa; Container Corp Am. *Comn:* Serigraphy, Ill Print Comn, Ill Arts Coun, 73. *Exhib:* Univ Pac Nat Small Painting Show, 71; 3rd Nat Drawing Show, Oshkosh, Wis, 71; New Talent: Midwest USA, Gallery 1640, Montreal, Que, 72; Dong a Ibo Korean Int Print Show, Seoul, 72; Nat Print Invitational, Artists Contemp Gallery, Sacramento, Calif, 73. *Teaching:* Assoc prof painting & drawing, Western Ill Univ, 65-78, prof, 78- *Awards:* First Prize for Painting, Ill State Fair Show, 72, 25th Ill Invitational, Ill State Mus, 72 & Laura Musser Mus, 73. *Media:* Acrylic Polymer. *Mailing Add:* 216 E Jefferson Macomb IL 61455

PARKER, WILL (WILLIAM CRAWFORD)
DRAFTSMAN, EDUCATOR
b Augusta, Ga, Sept 24, 44. *Study:* Clemson Univ, drawing with Robert Hunter, 61-63; Univ SC, Columbia, painting with Edmund Yaghjian, AB, 65; Sch Boston Mus Fine Arts, printmaking with Ture Bengtz, advan study, 65-67; Imageworks Sch Photog, Cambridge, Mass, with Ron MacNeil, 73. *Work:* SC Chap Am Inst Architects, Columbia, SC. *Exhib:* New Eng Artists, DeCordova Mus, Lincoln, Mass, 69; 9th, 10th & 11th Ann Piedmont Graphics Shows, Mint Mus Art, Charlotte, NC, 72, 73 & 74; NH Art Asn Ann, Currier Gallery Art, Manchester, 78 & 80-83; one-man show, Recent & Other Works on Paper, Nashua Arts & Sci Ctr, NH, 79; 30th Ann Exhib, Guild SC Artists, Gibbs Art Gallery, Charleston, SC, 80; 2nd NH Arts Biennial, Manchester Inst Arts & Sci, 81; Plymouth State Col Art Gallery, NH, 84; and others. *Pos:* Actg head dept art, Nathaniel Hawthorne Col, 75-78. *Teaching:* Instr drawing & printmaking, Nathaniel Hawthorne Col, Antrim, NH, 75-78; instr drawing & design, Sharon Arts Ctr, Peterborough, NH, 76-81 & Arts & Sci Ctr, Nashua, NH, 76-83. *Awards:* Selection for Traveling Show, Springs Mill, Inc, Lancaster, SC, 72; First Prize for Drawing, 34th Ann Exhib NH Art Asn, Currier Gallery Art, Manchester, NH, 81; First Prize for Drawing, Sharon Arts Ctr, 83. *Bibliog:* Barbara Center (auth), Amherst artist explores painting, drawing, printmaking, Milford Cabinet, 5/8/80; Artist etches 3-way career, Nashua Telegraph, 12/13/83; Chris Chinlund (auth), Artists plotting strategy for change, Boston Globe, 10/9/83. *Mem:* NH Art Asn. *Media:* Pastel, Pencil. *Mailing Add:* 203 Cannongate Rd Nashua NH 03063

PARKER, WILMA JOAN
PAINTER
b Springfield, Mass, May 15, 41. *Study:* RI Sch Design, with John Lafarge, BFA, 63; Art Inst Chicago, with Prof Whitney Halsted, MFA, 66. *Work:* Springfield Mus Fine Art, Mass; Ariz State Univ, Tempe; 3-M Corp, St Paul,

Minn; and others. *Comn:* Autumn Dance (painting), Dionex Corp, Hayward, Calif, 76; Soweto (painting), Int Plasma Corp, Hayward, Calif, 79; Desert Gold (painting), Durrum Instruments, Sunnyvale, Calif, 80; painting, IBM Corp, Tucson, Ariz, 81. *Exhib:* Realist Painting, Walnut Creek Civic Arts Gallery, Calif, 80; New West 80, Suzanne Brown Gallery, Scottsdale, Ariz, 80; Bay Area Artists Invitational, Oakland Mus, Calif, 80; Poster Biennale, Warsaw, Poland, 81; Springfield Mus Art, Mass, 81; and others. *Bibliog:* Thomas Albright (auth), Realism, San Francisco Chronicle, 80; Frank Cebulski (auth), Rendering the real, Artweek, 80; and others. *Mem:* Artists Equity Asn. *Media:* Oil, Lithography. *Publ:* Auth, Wilma Parker, an interchange in life, Southwest Art Mag, 81. *Mailing Add:* c/o Suzanne Brown Gallery 7156 Main St Scottsdale AZ 85251

PARKHURST, CHARLES
ADMINISTRATOR, CURATOR
b Columbus, Ohio, Jan 23, 13. *Study:* Williams Col, BA, 35; Oberlin Col, MA, 38; Princeton Univ, MFA, 41. *Pos:* Asst to dir, Albright Art Gallery, Buffalo, 45-47; dir, Allen Mem Art Mus, Oberlin Col, 49-62; dir, Baltimore Mus Art, 62-70; asst dir & chief curator, Nat Gallery Art, 71-83; co-dir, Williams Col Mus Art *Teaching:* Asst prof art & archaeol, Princeton Univ, 47-49; prof hist & art appreciation & head dept art, Oberlin Col, 49-62; vis lectr, Univ Minn, Univ Calif, Los Angeles & Johns Hopkins Univ; lectr. *Awards:* Chevalier, Legion of Honor, Fr Govt, 47; Ford Found Fel, 52-53; Fulbright Res Fel, Univ Utrecht, 56-57; plus others. *Bibliog:* H Matile (auth), Die Farbenlehre P O Runges, Munich, 79. *Mem:* Col Art Asn Am (past pres); Intermus Conserv Asn (co-founder & past pres); Asn Art Mus Dirs (vpres); Am Asn Mus (pres). *Res:* History of scientific color theories and their relationship to visual arts. *Publ:* Coauth (with Robert L Feller), Who invented the color wheel?, Color Res & Application, 82; coauth, Alberti's color scheme and some possible roots, Temple Univ, in press. *Mailing Add:* Williams Col Mus Art Williamstown MA 01267

PARKINSON, ELIZABETH BLISS (MRS HENRY IVES COBB)
PATRON, COLLECTOR
b New York, NY, Sept 25, 07. *Pos:* Trustee, Mus Mod Art, New York, 39-, pres int coun, 57-65, pres mus, 65-68, vchmn, 69-; mem art comt, Addison Gallery, Phillips Acad, Andover, Mass, 55-72, trustee, Archives Am Art, 69-80. *Collection:* Twentieth century American paintings and drawings. *Mailing Add:* 215 E 72nd St New York NY 10021

PARKS, CHARLES CROPPER
SCULPTOR
b Va, June 27, 22. *Study:* Pa Acad Fine Arts. *Comn:* Boy and dogs, H B du Pont, Wilmington, Del, 69; James F Byrnes, Byrnes Found, Columbia, SC, 70; Boy with Hawk, Brandywine River Mus, 73; Boy with Gulls, Mystic Seaport Mus, 75; Sunflowers, Equitable Bldg, New York, 76. *Exhib:* Nat Sculpture Soc Ann, 62-77; Nat Acad Design, 65-77; six-city tour, Equitable Life Assurance Soc, 76-77. *Pos:* Mem adv comt, John F Kennedy Ctr, 68- *Awards:* Wemys Found Travel Grant, Greece, 65; Am Artists Prof League Gold Medal, 70; Nat Sculpture Soc Gold Medal, 71. *Bibliog:* Nancy Mohr (auth), The Parks family, Del Today Mag, 72. *Mem:* Fel Nat Sculpture Soc (pres, 76-78); Allied Artists Am; Nat Acad Design; Del State Arts Coun. *Publ:* Contribr, Sights and sounds of Easter, TV film produced by Wilmington Coun Churches, 64. *Mailing Add:* 44-A Bancroft Mills Wilmington DE 19850

PARKS, JAMES DALLAS
HISTORIAN, PAINTER
b St Louis, Mo, Aug 25, 07. *Study:* Bradley Univ, BS; State Col Iowa, MA; Chicago Art Inst; also with Jean Charlot, Philip Guston & Thomas Hart Benton. *Work:* Howard Univ; Tex Southern Univ; Springfield Art Mus, Mo; Dunbar Sch, Kansas City. *Comn:* Early presidents mural, Lincoln Univ (Mo). *Exhib:* Mid-America; Atlanta Ann; Joslyn Six State Show; Ill State Fair; Mo State Fair. *Pos:* Art ed, Sphinx Mag, 26-50. *Teaching:* Head dept art, Lincoln Univ, Mo, 27-77, emer prof, 77- *Awards:* First Prize for Lithographs, Springfield Mus, Mo, 45; Second Prize for Oils, Mo State Fair, 45; First Prize for Watercolors, Nat Conf Artists, 63. *Bibliog:* Cedric Dover, American Negro art, Graphic Arts, 65; Wadder & Lewis (auth), Black Artists on Art, 70. *Mem:* Nat Art Educ Asn; Col Art Asn Am; Mo Col Art Asn (pres, 55-56); Nat Conf Artists (pres, 55-56); Mid-West Col Art Asn. *Media:* Oil, Watercolor. *Publ:* Coauth, Comprehensive Examination for Undergraduate Majors in Art, Educ Testing Serv, Princeton, NJ. *Mailing Add:* 923 E Dunklin St Jefferson City MO 65101

PARNALL, PETER
DESIGNER, ILLUSTRATOR
b Syracuse, NY, May 23, 36. *Study:* Cornell Univ; Pratt Inst. *Exhib:* Contemp Illusr, Rutgers Mus, Newark, NJ, 75; Int Illusr Show, Bratislava, Czech, 76; Alphabets, Mus Fine Arts, Houston, Tex, 78. *Pos:* Art dir, ed & advert consult, 58-67. *Teaching:* Instr design, Lafayette Col, Easton, Pa, 66-76. *Awards:* Caldecott Honor Bk, Am Libr Asn, 76, 77 & 79; Horn Bk Award, Boston Globe, 76. *Media:* Pen & Ink; Watercolor Wash. *Publ:* Auth & illusr, The Mountain, 71 & The Great Fish, 73, Doubleday; illusr, The Nightwatchers, Four Winds, 71; auth & illusr, Alfalfa Hill, Doubleday, 75; auth & illusr, The Dogs Book of Birds, Scribners, 77; and 54 others. *Dealer:* Greenwich Workshop 30 Lindeman Dr Trumbull CT 06611. *Mailing Add:* RD 3 Waldoboro ME 04572

PARRA, CARMEN
PAINTER, PRINTMAKER
b Mexico City, Mex, Nov 12, 44. *Study:* Escuela Nac Antropologia e Hist, Mexico City, BA, 64; Acad Belles Artes, Rome, BFA, 67; Esmeralda, 67.

Work: Mus Hombre, Paris; Casa Lago, Univ Nac Autonoma Mex; Mus Arte Mod, Mexico City. *Exhib:* Decima Bienalde Paris, Mus D'Art Mod, France, 77; Las Ventanas, Mus Art Mod, Mexico City, 79; Mexico de Manana, Mus Bibliot Pape, Monetove, Coahuila, 79; La Creacion Femenina, Kunstller Haus Behanien, Berlin, 80; Musica y Angeles, Metrop Cathedral Mex, Mexico City, 83; and others. *Awards:* Primavera Otono, Fiesta Primavera Otono, City Mexico, 81. *Bibliog:* China Mendoza (auth), Maquinita de hacer ruido, Arvil, 70; Gonzalo Celorio (auth), Tiempo Cautivo, La Cathedral Mex, 82; Images (videotape), Carton Papel Mex, 82. *Publ:* Illusr, La Grafostatica u Oda a Eiffel, Talleres Graficos Nacion, 78; illusr, Tiempo Cautivo, La Cathedral de Mexico, Ed Arvil, 80; illusr, De la Pluma al Angel, Ed Nayaqui, 83; illusr, Templo Mayor, Ed Multiarte, 83; illusr, La Eternidad to lo Efimero, Miquel Angel Porrua, 83. *Dealer:* Lurdes Chumacero Estocolmo 34 Mexico DF Mex 06600. *Mailing Add:* Primera Cerrada de Galeana 13 San Angel Mexico DF 01000 Mexico

PARRINO, GEORGE
PAINTER, ADMINISTRATOR
b New York, NY, Sept 25, 42. *Study:* Cooper Union Art Sch, BFA, 64; Yale Univ Art Sch, MFA, 70; Acad Fine Art, India, Fulbright Res Fel Painting, 71-72. *Work:* Metrop Mus Art & Guggenheim Mus, New York; Brooklyn Mus, NY; Marion Koogler McNay Art Mus, San Antonio, Tex. *Exhib:* Solo exhibs, Ingber Gallery, New York, 74 & 76 & Univ Tex, San Antonio, 79; Fac Exhib, Brooklyn Mus, NY, 73; Fulbright Artists, Inst Int Educ, New York, 77; Cubist Syntax in the 70's, Ingber Gallery, 78; Artists' Kites, Danforth Mus, Conn, 78; and others. *Teaching:* Instr painting, Brooklyn Mus Art Sch, NY, 73; asst prof humanities, St John's Univ, New York, 74-75; lectr painting, N Tex State Univ, Denton, 77-78; lectr painting, Univ Tex, San Antonio, 78-79; dean, San Antonio Art Inst, 78- *Awards:* Residence fels, Yaddo, 75 & 76. *Bibliog:* Phyllis Derfner (auth), New York letter, Art Int, 1/75; Modris Ramans (auth), George Parrino, Arts Mag, 11/76; Lawrence Alloway (auth), Cubist syntax in the 70's, Nation, 78. *Mem:* Col Arts Asn; Nat Coun Art Adminr; Nat Asn Sch Art & Design; bd mem Tex Arts Alliance. *Media:* Acrylic. *Dealer:* Ingber Gallery 3 E 78th St New York NY 10021. *Mailing Add:* 355 E Terra Alta San Antonio TX 78209

PARRIS, NINA GUMPERT
CURATOR, EDUCATOR
b Berlin, Ger, Sept 11, 27; US citizen. *Study:* Bryn Mawr Col, BA(art hist); Woodrow Wilson Fel), 68; Univ Pa, MA(art hist), 69, PhD(art hist), 79. *Collections Arranged:* Prints & Paintings in Permanent Collection (auth, catalog), Robert Hull Fleming Mus, 71. *Pos:* Cur, Robert Hall Fleming Mus, Univ Vt, 71-79; chief cur, Columbia Mus Art, 79- *Teaching:* Lectr art hist, Philadelphia Col Art, 70-71; lectr mus studies, Univ SC, Columbia, 72- *Mem:* Am Asn Mus; Southeastern Regional Mus Conf; Int Coun Mus; SC Crafts Guild (bd mem, 81-82). *Res:* Late 19th and 20th century art including contemporary art. *Publ:* Auth, Van de Velde, Obrist, Hölzel: The Basic Course at the Bauhaus, McMaster Colloquium, 81. *Mailing Add:* 1723 Devine St Columbia SC 24201

PARRISH, DAVID BUCHANAN
PAINTER
b Birmingham, Ala, June 19, 39. *Study:* Univ Ala, with Melville Price & Richard Brough, BFA. *Work:* Brooks Mem Art Gallery, Memphis; Wadsworth Atheneum, Hartford, Conn; Partheon, Nashville; Monsanto Chem Co, Decatur, Ala. *Exhib:* One-man shows, Galerie Francois Petit, Paris, 73 & Sidney Janis Gallery, 75; Sharp Focus Realism, Sidney Janis Gallery, New York, 72 & 75; Painting & Sculpture Today, Indianapolis Mus Art, 72; Phases of New Realism, Lowe Mus, Coral Gables, 72; Realists Revival, Am Fedn Arts Traveling Show, 72-73; New/Photo Realism, Wadsworth Atheneum, Hartford, Conn, 74; Super Realism, Baltimore Mus Art, 75. *Awards:* Award of Merit, 23rd Southeastern Ann Exhib, High Mus, Atlanta, 68; Top Award, 61st Ann Exhib, Birmingham Mus Art, 69; Top Award, Mid-South Ann, Brooks Mem Art Gallery, 70. *Media:* Oil. *Dealer:* Nancy Hoffman Gallery New York NY 10012. *Mailing Add:* 700 Cleermont Dr SE Huntsville AL 35801

PARRISH, JEAN
PAINTER
b Plainfield, NH, June 26, 11. *Study:* with father, Maxfield Parrish, 25-35. *Work:* Mus NMex, Santa Fe; WTex Mus, Lubbock; NMex State Fair Permanent Collection Art Gallery, Albuquerque. *Exhib:* NMex State Fair Art Exhib, Art Gallery, Albuquerque, 55, 57, 58 & 64; Cracker Barrel Bazaar, Newbury, Vt, 59; Paintings & Sculpture, Okla City Junior League, Okla, 66; Margaret Jamison Presents, Sweeney Auditorium, Sante Fe, NMex, 80 & 81; Sante Fe Festival of the Arts, Sweeney Auditorium, Sante Fe, NMex, 82. *Awards:* Grand Award, NMex State Fair, 55; First Prize, NMex State Fair, 55; Purchase Prize, NMex State Fair, 55. *Bibliog:* Margaret I Meaders (auth), The art of Jean Parrish, Empire Mag & Denver Post, 69; Susan E Meyer (ed), 20 Landscape Painters & How they Work, Watson-Guptill Publ, 80; Mary Carroll Nelson, Masters of Western Painting (in prep). *Media:* Oils. *Dealer:* Woodrow Wilson Fine Arts 319 Read St Sante Fe NM 87501. *Mailing Add:* 4815 Guadalupe Tr NW Albuquerque NM 87107

PARRY, ELLWOOD COMLY, III
HISTORIAN
b Abington, Pa, Aug 9, 41. *Study:* Harvard Univ, AB, 64; Univ Calif, Los Angeles, MA, 66; Yale Univ, PhD, 70. *Collections Arranged:* American Paintings: A Gathering from Three Centuries, Hist Soc of Princeton, NJ, 75. *Teaching:* Asst prof, Dept Art Hist & Archaeol, Columbia Univ, 69-75; assoc prof, Sch Art & Art Hist, Univ Iowa, 76-81; prof, Dept Art, Univ Ariz,

Tucson, 81- *Awards:* Nat Endowment Humanities Fel, 75-76. *Mem:* Col Art Asn; Mid-Am Col Art Asn; Mid-West Art Hist Soc; Asn Historians Am Art. *Res:* Iconography of American art and the interface between 19th-century painting and the popular arts, such as panoramas and photography. *Publ:* Auth, The Image of the Indian and the Black Man in American Art, 1590-1900, George Braziller, 74; coauth, Reflections of 1776: The Colonies Revisited, Viking Studio, 74; auth, The Thomas Eakins portrait of Sue and Harry: Or, when did the artist change his mind?, Arts Mag, 5/79; auth, Thomas Cole's imagination at work in The Architect's Dream, Am Art J, 80. *Mailing Add:* Dept Art Univ Ariz Tucson AZ 85721

PARRY, MARIAN (MARIAN PARRY FELD)
ILLUSTRATOR, PRINTMAKER
b San Francisco, Calif, Jan 28, 24. *Study:* Univ Calif, BA, 46; Contemporaries Gallery, etching & lithography with Michael Ponce de Leon, stone engraving with Ben Shahn. *Work:* Houghton Libr, Harvard Univ, Cambridge, Mass; Metrop Mus Art Print Collection, New York; Smith Col Rare Bk Collection; Wellesley Col Rare Bk Collection; Univ Mass Rare Bk Collection, Northampton. *Exhib:* Boston Visual Artists Union, 74; Cambridge Art Asn; one-man show, Smith Col Rare Bk Rm, 77; Los Angeles Inst of Contemp Art, 78. *Teaching:* Lectr illus & writing, Radcliffe Sem Prog, 74-, lectr hist of the bk, 77-; lectr writing, Emmanuel Col, 74- *Awards:* Scholar, Radcliffe Inst, 65-67; Best Illus Bk Award for Birds of Basel, New York Times Bk Panel, 69; One of 50 Bks of the Yr (Birds of Basel), Am Inst of Graphic Arts, 69. *Mem:* Soc Children's Bk Writers; New England Authors & Illusrs Children's Bks. *Media:* Pen and Ink; Watercolor; Printmaking with Linoleum; Xerox Watercolor. *Publ:* auth & illusr, Birds of Basel, Pharos Verlag, 67 & Knopf, 69; auth & illusr, Roger & the Devil, Knopf, 72; auth & illusr, King of the Fish, MacMillan, 77; auth & illusr, I Am a Big Help, Greenwillow, 80; illusr, The Education of a Mouse, Countryman Press, 83; and others. *Mailing Add:* 60 Martin St Cambridge MA 02138

PARRY, PAMELA JEFFCOTT
LIBRARIAN, ADMINISTRATOR
b New York, NY, Mar 6, 48. *Study:* Univ Ariz, BA, 69; Columbia Univ, MA(art hist & archaeol), 71, MLS, 73. *Pos:* Asst fine arts librn, Columbia Univ, New York, 72-76; ed, The Art Reference Collection, 78-, Art Libr Soc NAm Newsletter, 78-81 & Art Documentation, 82; librn, Dada Arch & Res Ctr (vice-pres), 79-81. *Mem:* Art Libr Soc NAm (exec secy, 80-83, exec dir, 83-); Col Art Asn; Women's Caucus for Art; Am Soc Assoc Execs; and others. *Publ:* Contribr, From Realism to Symbolism: Whistler and His World, Columbia Univ/Philadelphia Mus Art, 71; auth, Contemporary Art and Artists, 78 & Photography Index, 79, Greenwood Press. *Mailing Add:* 3775 Bear Creek Circle Tucson AZ 85749

PARSONS, DAVID GOODE
SCULPTOR, EDUCATOR
b Gary, Ind, Mar 2, 11. *Study:* Chicago Art Inst, 30; Univ Wis, Experimental Col, BS, 34 & MS(art & art hist), 37. *Comn:* Christus Rex, St Michael & All Angels Church, Lake Charles, La, 57-58; Birdforms, Moody Nat Bank, Galveston, Tex, 62-63; Patterned Brick for Space Sci, Space Sci Bldg, Rice Univ, 65-66; Large Cellist, Rice Univ, 74-75; Quartet, Rice Univ, 83. *Exhib:* Chicago & Vicinity Exhib, Art Inst Chicago, 37-39, 40 & 44; Am Sculpture, Carnegie Inst Int, 39; Am Exhib, Art Inst Chicago, 38-40; Six State Sculpture Exhib, Walker Art Ctr, Minneapolis, 45; Pa Acad Fine Arts Ann Exhib, 45; The Artist & His World, Denver Art Mus, Colo, 49; Houston Mus Fine Arts Ann, 53, 54 & 58; 11th Ann Midwest Exhib, Joslyn Art Mus, Omaha, Nebr, 67; one-man shows, Beaumont Mus, Tex, 53-67 & Witte Mus, 56; 50 Yr Retrospective Show, Bellaire City Hall, Tex, 82. *Pos:* Sculptor, Pub Works Art, 33-34, Fed Art Proj, Milwaukee, Wis, 38-42; sculptor & visual educ aid designer, US Army, Camp Lee, Va, 24-44; surgical artist asst in plastic surgery, Civil Serv US Army Valley Forge Gen Hospital, 44-47. *Teaching:* Dir mus sch, Denver Mus Art, Colo, 47-49; asst prof sculpture, drawing & ceramics, Bradley Univ, Peoria, Ill, 49-52; assoc prof sculpture, drawing & art educ, McNeese State Univ, Lake Charles, La, 52-53; prof sculpture & drawing, Rice Univ, Houston, 53-81, emer prof, 81- *Awards:* First in Sculpture, Va Biennial, Va Mus Art, Richmond, 42; Sculptor Award, Houston Mus Art Ann, 54; Mus Dir Award, Beaumont Regional, Beaumont Mus Art, Tex, 70. *Mem:* Col Art Asn Am; Tex Soc Sculptors (pres, Gulf Coast Sect, 75-76); Artists Fedn of Wis (pres, 40-42); Houston Munic Art Comn. *Media:* All Media. *Mailing Add:* 645 Mulberry Ln Bellaire TX 77401

PARSONS, MERRIBELL MADDUX
CURATOR, ADMINISTRATOR
b San Antonio, Tex. *Study:* Newcomb Col, BFA; Ecole du Louvre, cert; Inst Fine Arts, NY Univ, MA; Metrop Mus & Inst Fine Arts, dipl (mus training). *Pos:* Contribr, Minn Inst Arts Bulletin, 69-74; Bell Mem cur decorative arts, Minn Inst of Arts, 69-74, chief cur & cur sculpture & decorative arts, 74-79; chmn & curatorial liaison for educ, Metrop Mus Art, 79- *Awards:* Longhi Fel; Ford Found Fel; Nat Endowment Arts Fel. *Mem:* Col Art Asn; Decorative Arts Chap, Soc Archit Hist; Am Asn Mus; Int Asn Study of Textiles. *Res:* European sculpture, 1600-1900. *Publ:* Auth, Sculpture in the David Daniels Collection, Minn Inst Arts Bulletin. *Mailing Add:* c/o Metrop Mus of Art Fifth Ave at 82nd St New York NY 10028

PARTCH, VIRGIL FRANKLIN, II
CARTOONIST, ILLUSTRATOR
b St Paul Island, Alaska, Oct 17, 16. *Study:* Chouinard Art Inst, Los Angeles. *Pos:* Illusr, syndicated comic strip & daily panel Big George, currently. *Awards:* First Prize, Brussels Cartoon Exhib, 64. *Publ:* Auth & illusr, VIP tosses a party, S&S, 59; auth & illusr, New faces on the bar room floor, 61; contribr, VIP's Quips, 75; contribr, cartoons in Look & True Mags; and others. *Mailing Add:* Box 725 Corona Del Mar CA 92625

PARTIN, ROBERT (E)
PAINTER, EDUCATOR
b Los Angeles, Calif, June 22, 27. *Study:* Univ Calif, Los Angeles, with Clinton Adams, Gordon Nunes & S Macdonald-Wright, BA, 50; Yale-Norfolk Art Sch, fel & study with Conrad Marca-Relli, 55; Columbia Univ, with Andre Racz, John Heliker, Meyer Shapiro, Paul Tillich, MFA, 56; Tamarind Lithography Workshop, Herron Art Sch, fel & study with Garo Antreasion, 63. *Work:* Solomon R Guggenheim Mus Art, New York; Jonson Gallery, Univ NMex; Weatherspoon Art Gallery, Univ NC. *Exhib:* Whitney Mus Am Art Ann, New York, 63; San Francisco Art Asn Centennial Exhib, De Young Mus, 71; Visual Poetics/Abstract Space, Calif State Univ, Los Angeles, 79; Stage One Gallery, Orange, Calif, 80; one-man show, Sherman Oaks, Calif, 81; Perceptions on Paper/A Visual Dialogue, Long Beach Gallery, Calif, 81; and others. *Teaching:* Assoc prof art, Univ NC, Greensboro, 57-66; vis assoc prof art, Univ NMex, 63-64; prof art, Calif State Univ, Fullerton, 66- *Awards:* Ford Found Purchase Prize, Whitney Mus Am Art Ann, 63; Purchase Prize, NC Mus Art Ann, 64 & 65; Purchase Award, Viewpoints Five, Colgate Univ, 71. *Bibliog:* Van Deren Coke (auth), Robert Partin, The Painter and The Photograph, 65; Robert Ewing (auth), Reticence clarified, Artweek, 4/80; Suzanne Muchnic (auth), The valley, Los Angeles Times, 1/81; and others. *Media:* Mixed. *Dealer:* Stage One Gallery 420 W Chapman Ave Orange CA 92666; Orlando Gallery 14553 Ventura Blvd Sherman Oaks CA 91403. *Mailing Add:* Dept Art Calif State Univ 800 N State College Blvd Fullerton CA 92634

PARTON, NIKE
PAINTER
b New York, NY, June 23, 22. *Study:* Ringling Sch Art, fine art cert; also sculpture with Lesley Posey & painting with Jay Connaway. *Work:* Univ Fla; Stetson Univ; S Fla Mus, Buadenton. *Exhib:* One-man shows, Sarasota Art Asn, 69 & Longboat Art Ctr, 72; Art League of Manatee Co, 73; Beaux Arts Gallery, Pinellas Park, Fla, 80; Selby Pub Libr, Sarasota, Fla, 83; and others. *Teaching:* Instr painting, Art League Manatee Co, 54-74; instr pvt studio, 63- *Awards:* First Prize in Watercolor, Festival of States, St Petersburg, Fla, 79; 1st Place Oil, Beaux Arts Gallery, 80; Grand Prize, Beaux Arts Gallery, 82. *Mem:* Fla Artist Group; Sarasota Art Asn; Art League of Manatee Co; Fla Watercolor Soc; Fla Suncoast Watercolor Soc. *Media:* Watercolor, Oil. *Dealer:* Ralph Wells 1322 Fourth Ave W Bradenton FL 33505; Art Uptown Inc 1369 Main St Sarasota FL. *Mailing Add:* 840 Edgemere Lane Sarasota FL 33581

PARTON, RALF
SCULPTOR, EDUCATOR
b New York, NY, July 2, 32. *Study:* Albright Art Sch, Buffalo, dipl, 53; NY Univ Col Buffalo, BS(art educ), 54; Columbia Univ, MA(art), 55. *Work:* Civic Ctr, Turlock, Calif; City Hall, Turlock, Calif; Northwestern Mich Col Gallery, Traverse City, Mich. *Comn:* Tree of Life (steel sculpture), Beth Shalom Synagogue, Modesto, Calif, 79; and many pvt commissions. *Exhib:* Sisti Gallery Ann, Buffalo, NY, 57; Calif State Fair Art Exhib, Sacramento, Calif, 64; San Francisco Mus Art, San Francisco, Calif, 72; Art Fac Exhib, Calif State Col Stanislaus, Turlock, Calif, 73; Calif State Col Stanislaus Art Fac Exhib, Univ of the Pac, Calif, 76. *Teaching:* Chmn dept painting & sculpture, Northwestern Mich Col, 58-62; prof sculpture, Calif State Col, Stanislaus, 63-, chmn dept art, 63-70. *Awards:* Horohoe Prize Originality Sculpture, Sisti Gallery, Buffalo, NY, 57; Reynolds Prize Sculpture, Stockton Art Show, Calif, 66. *Bibliog:* David Otth (auth), Monoliths to miniatures, Toy Train Operating Soc Bulletin, Vol 2, No 2. *Media:* Bronze, Steel. *Mailing Add:* 1900 Clemson Ct Turlock CA 95380

PARTRIDGE, DAVID GERRY
PAINTER, SCULPTOR
b Akron, Ohio, Oct 5, 19; Can citizen. *Study:* Univ Toronto, BA; Queen's Univ, Kingston, Ont; Art Students League; Slade Sch, London; Atelier 17, Paris, with W S Hayter. *Work:* Tate Gallery, London; Nat Gallery Can, Ottawa; Libr Cong, Washington, DC; Art Gallery Ont, Toronto; Gallery NSW, Sydney, Australia. *Comn:* Nail murals, York Univ, Toronto, 70, Westminster Cathedral, London, 71 & foyer, Toronto City Hall, 77, Bell Trinity, Toronto, 83 & Can Capital Cong Ctr, Ottawa, 83; and others. *Exhib:* Montreal Mus Spring Show, 62; Int Print Exhib, Cincinnati, 62; Art of the Americas & Spain, Madrid & Barcelona, 63; Carnegie Int, Pittsburgh, 65; Sculpture '67, Toronto; Art Gallery Windsor, 79. *Teaching:* Art master, Ridley Col, St Catharines, Ont, 44-56; instr art, Queens Univ, Ont, summers 56-60 & Ont Col Art, 74-75; instr art, Ont Col Art, 74-75. *Awards:* Brit Coun Scholar to Slade Sch, 50-51; Sculpture Prize & Purchase Award, Montreal Mus Fine Arts, 62. *Bibliog:* Alan Jarvis (auth), Configurations, Can Art, autumn 60; Charles S Spencer (auth), David Partridge's Nail Mosaics, Studio Int, 7/65; Kenneth Coutts-Smith (auth), David Partridge, Quadrum, 65. *Mem:* Fel Royal Soc Arts; Royal Can Acad. *Media:* Miscellaneous; Wood, Nails. *Dealer:* Gallery Quan 112 Scollard St Toronto ON Can. *Mailing Add:* 77 Seaton St Toronto ON M5A 2T2 Canada

PARTRIDGE, ROI
PRINTMAKER
b Centralia, Territory Wash, Oct 14, 1888. *Study:* Nat Acad Design, NY. *Work:* Libr Cong, Washington, DC; Smithsonian Inst, Washington, DC; Honolulu Acad of Art; Calif Legion of Honor Mus, San Francisco; Mills Col Art Gallery, Oakland, Calif. *Teaching:* Instr art, Mills Col, 20-23, prof art, 23-46. *Awards:* Los Angeles Gold Medal, Los Angeles Print Makers Soc, 28; Joseph Pennell Purchase Prize, Libr Cong, 43; Henry B Shope Prize, Soc Am Etchers, New York, 48. *Bibliog:* D W Prall (auth), Aesthetic Judgement, Crowell, 29; Aline Kistler (auth), Roi Partridge, Etcher, Prints, New York, 34;

Frederic Whitaker (auth), The etchings of Roi Partridge, Am Artist Mag, 11/73. *Mem:* Nat Acad Design, New York. *Media:* Etchings; Drawings, Pen & Ink. *Publ:* Contribr, articles in Sierra Club Bull & Am Mag of Art. *Mailing Add:* 1601 Skycrest Dr No 2 Walnut Creek CA 94595

PARTZ, FELIZ (RON GABE)
PAINTER
b Winnipeg, Man, 45. *Study:* Univ Man Sch Fine Arts, 63-67. *Work:* Can Coun Art Bank, Nat Gallery Can, Ottawa; Ctr d'Art Contemporain, Geneva, Switz; Lucio Amelio Gallery, Naples, Italy; Mod Art Gallery, Vienna, Austria. *Comn:* Ursa Major and Taurus: Pavillion Fragments from the Starry Vault, Toronto Stock Exchange, 83. *Exhib:* Solo exhibs, Carmen Lamanna Gallery, Toronto, 72-84; Canadian Trajectoires, Mus d'Art Mod de la Ville, Paris, 73; Projects Video VIII, Mus Mod Art, London, England, 78; Glamour, Inst Contemp Art, London, England, 78; Reconstructing Futures, Carmen Lamanna Gallery, Toronto, 78; Artistic Collaboration on the 20th Century, Hirshhorn Mus, Washington, DC, 84; P is for Poodle, Nat Gallery Can, Ottawa, 84; and others. *Awards:* Can Coun Grants, 68-83. *Bibliog:* German Celant (auth), General idea in Canada: Un Gruppo Canadese, Domus, 11/74; Elke Town (auth), Fiction, Art Gallery Ont, 82; John Bentley Mays (coauth), Visions: Contemporary Art in Canada, Douglas & McIntyre, 83. *Mailing Add:* c/o Carmen Lamanna Gallery 840 Yonge St Toronto ON M4W 2H1 Canada

PASCAL, DAVID
PAINTER, CARTOONIST
b New York, NY. *Study:* Am Artists Sch. *Exhib:* One-man shows, Mus Art, Sao Paulo, Brazil, Mus Mod Art, Rio de Janeiro, Brazil, Graham Gallery, New York, 73, Man and His World, Montreal, 74 & Mus Art, Angouleme, France, 83. *Pos:* Int rep, Newspaper Comics Coun, New York, 69-; US rep of Phenix Mag, France, Comics, Italy & RanTanPlan, Belg, 70- *Teaching:* Instr graphic journalism, Sch Visual Arts, 55-58. *Awards:* Dattero D'Oro, Salone Int dell Umorismo, Italy, 63; Award for Illus Excellence, Nat Cartoonists Soc, 69 & 77, Silver T-Square, 72. *Bibliog:* Sergio Trinchero (auth), Visit to funland, Sgt Kirk Mag, 68; Rinaldo Traini (auth), Incontro con David Pascal (slide prog), Immagine, 3/15/69; Claude Moliterni (auth), David Pascal, Phenix Mag, 70. *Mem:* Nat Cartoonists Soc; Cartoonists Asn; Int Comics Orgn. *Media:* Ink, Acrylic, Oil. *Publ:* Illusr, Fifteen Fables of Krylov, 65; auth & illusr, The Silly Knight, 67; auth, Comics: An American Expressionism, Mus Arts, Brazil, 70; ed, Graphis Mag, 72; auth, Goofus, Paris, 75; and others. *Dealer:* Graham Gallery 1014 Madison Ave New York NY 10024. *Mailing Add:* PO Box 31 Village Sta New York NY 10014

PASCHALL, JO ANNE
PRINTMAKER, LIBRARIAN
b Murray, Ky, Mar 9, 49. *Study:* Memphis State Univ, BFA, 71; Univ GA, MFA, 74; Art Studies Abroad-Cortona, Italy, Dodd-Carnegie scholar, 73-74; Univ Ala, 76-77; Atlanta Univ, MLS, 81. *Work:* Huntsville Mus Art, Ala; Memphis State Univ Collection; Univ Ga Collection. *Comn:* 3 ed of 3 color intaglio etchings & 15 watercolor paintings, St Joseph's Infirmary, Atlanta, Ga. *Exhib:* Invitational Exhib, Atlanta Artworkers Coalition Gallery, Ga; Invitational Print Exhib, Huntsville Mus Art, Ala; one-person exhib, Memorabilia, Univ Ala Gallery, Huntsville; group exhib, Inst Prof Femminile di Stato Gino Severini, da Cortona, Italy; Eleven Printmakers, Southeastern Ctr for Contemp Art, Winston-Salem, NC. *Pos:* Grad asst printmaking, Univ Ga Art Dept, 73-74; intern, Art for Exceptional Children, Ga Retardation Ctr, 77; cur, Visual Collections, Atlanta Col Art Libr, 78-79, head librn, 79-; orgn consult, High Mus Art, 83- *Teaching:* Assoc instr printmaking, Art Studies Abroad, Cortona, Italy, 74; div head printmaking dept, Univ Ala, 75-77. *Awards:* Third Place, painting, Tenn All-Artists Exhib, Nashville, 71; Special Purchase Award, Inst Prof Femminile di Stato Gino Severini da Cortona, Italy, 74. *Mem:* Art Libr Soc NAm; Am Libr Asn; Anarchist Librns Group Am. *Media:* Lithography, Intaglio. *Interests:* 20th century; contemporary issues; artists books and publications, bookworks. *Publ:* Contribr, Macmillan Encyclopedia Archits, Macmillan Pub Co, 82. *Dealer:* Heath Gallery 416 E Paces Ferry Atlanta GA 30305. *Mailing Add:* Atlanta Col Art Libr 1280 Peachtree St NE Atlanta GA 30309

PASCHKE, EDWARD F (ED)
PAINTER, ILLUSTRATOR
b Chicago, Ill, June 22, 39. *Study:* Art Inst Chicago, BFA(Raymond Fel), 61 & MFA(Ponte del Arte Fel), 70. *Work:* Art Inst Chicago; Mus Contemp Art, Chicago; Mus Boymans, Rotterdam; Musee d'Art Moderne Nationale, Paris; Baltimore Art Mus, Md. *Exhib:* Soc for Contemp Art, Art Inst Chicago, 70-72; Whitney Annuals, Whitney Mus Am Art, New York, 72-74 & Biennial Contemp Am Art, 73; Made in Chicago, Mus Contemp Art, Chicago, Mexico City & Washington, DC, 74 & 75 & View of a Decade, 77; Am Show, Art Inst Chicago, 74; Nat Collection of Fine Arts, Washington, DC, 75; Ed Paschke Retrospective, Contemp Art Ctr, Cincinnati, Ohio, 75. *Teaching:* Instr painting, Art Inst Chicago, 74-76; instr painting, Columbia Col, Chicago, Ill, 76-78; prof drawing, Northwestern Univ, Evanston, Ill, 77-78. *Awards:* Cassandra Grant, Cassandra Found, 72; Logan Medal, Art Inst Chicago, 73. *Bibliog:* Barry Schwartz (auth), Humanism in 20th Century American Art, Praeger, 72; Sheldon Williams (auth), Made in Chicago, Art & Artists, 75; Peter Schjeldahl (auth), Letter from Chicago, Art in Am, 76; and others. *Media:* Oil; Pencil. *Dealer:* Phyllis Kind Gallery 226 E Ontario Chicago IL 60611. *Mailing Add:* 1927 E Estes Chicago IL 60626

PASCUAL, MANOLO
SCULPTOR, INSTRUCTOR
b Bilbao, Spain, Apr 15, 02; US citizen. *Study:* Acad Fine Arts, San Fernando, Madrid, Spain, MA. *Work:* Mus Fine Arts, Santo Domingo, Dominican Repub; Emily Lowe Gallery, Coral Gables, Miami Univ, Fla; Hofstra Univ, New York; Mus, World Univ, Tucson, Ariz; and others. *Comn:* Miguel de Cervantes (sculpture), Govt of Santo Domingo, 40; Thri Relieves (sculpture), Dominican Party Bldg, 45; Trinidad Sanchez (sculpture), Santo Domingo, 46; Duarte (sculpture), Cathedral of Santo Domingo, 48; The Goddess of Pete, Harlan Collection, Mich, 58. *Exhib:* Int Art, Paris, 25; Royal Acad Fine Arts, Madrid, 36; Int Biennal of Venice, 37; Nat Acad Fine Arts, Santo Domingo, 44; Retrospective, 50 Years of Sculpture, Hofstra Univ, NY, 68; and many others. *Teaching:* Dir & teacher sculpture, Nat Acad Fine Arts, Santo Domingo, 40-50; instr, New Sch Social Res, New York, 51-82. *Awards:* Gold Medal, Acad San Fernando, Madrid, Spain, 18; Grand Prix de Rume, Spanish Govt, 31; First Prize & Gold Medal, Biennial Santo Domingo, Dominican Repub, 45. *Media:* Iron, Stone. *Publ:* Coauth, Album of the Victory, 45. *Dealer:* New Bertha Schaefer Gallery 41 E 57th St New York NY 10022. *Mailing Add:* 84-26 Homelawn St Jamaica NY 11432

PASINSKI, IRENE
PAINTER, SCULPTOR
b Pittsburgh, Pa, Oct 14, 23. *Study:* Carnegie-Mellon Univ, BFA, 45; Ecole du Louvre & Inst d'Art Applique a l'Industrie, cert, 51. *Work:* Chase Manhattan Bank, New York; WVa Univ Collection, Morgantown; Pittsburgh Bd Educ; Univ Pittsburgh; Nat Steel Co, Pittsburgh. *Comn:* Poster, Int Poetry Forum, Pittsburgh, 74; outdoor wall mural, Community Savings Asn, Pittsburgh, 75; scene design & costume, Steel City Symphony, Pittsburgh Ballet Co, 76; poster, Poetry on the Buses, Pa Coun on Arts, 76; plexiglas wall mural, Westinghouse Credit Corp, Pittsburgh, 79. *Exhib:* Carnegie Inst, 44-79; Albright-Knox Gallery, 57; Inst Contemp Crafts, New York, 57; Butler Inst Am Art, 62 & 77; Silvermine Guild Ann, New Canaan, Conn, 63; Westmoreland Co Mus Art, 64-78; New Glass, Corning Mus, NY, 79. *Teaching:* Instr fundamentals of design, Carnegie-Mellon Inst, Pittsburgh, 68-73. *Awards:* Outstanding Work, Assoc Artists of Pittsburgh, 47-50, 70 & 72; Purchase Award, Erie Art Ctr Ann, 69; Best of Show, Pa Sculpture Exhib, Southern Alleghenies Mus Art, Loretto, Pa, 77. *Mem:* Assoc Artists Pittsburgh; Western Pa Soc Sculptors; Indust Designers Soc Am; Pittsburgh Art Comn. *Media:* Mixed, Acrylics; Mirrored Plexiglas, Diffraction Gratings. *Dealer:* Gallery G 408 Blvd of Allies Pittsburgh PA 17219. *Mailing Add:* 4951 Centre Ave Pittsburgh PA 15213

PASSANTINO, GEORGE CHRISTOPHER
PAINTER, INSTRUCTOR
b New York, NY. *Study:* Art Students League, 48-53. *Work:* Adelphi Univ, Garden City, NY. *Exhib:* Conn Acad Fine Arts, Wadsworth Antheneum, Hartford, 75-76; Audubon Artists, Nat Acad, New York, 76; 49th Ann Exhib, Hudson Valley Art Asn, White Plains, NY, 77. *Teaching:* Instr drawing, painting & compos, Famous Artists Sch, Westport, Conn, 57-63, supervisor, 63-74; instr, Univ Bridgeport, Conn, 74-75; instr drawing & painting, Art Students League, 78- *Awards:* Charles Noel Flagg Mem Prize, Conn Acad Fine Arts, 76. *Mem:* Life mem, Art Students League. *Media:* Oil, Watercolor. *Publ:* Coauth, Six artists paint a portrait, Northlight, 74; coauth, The Portrait and Figure Painting Book, Watson-Guptill, 79. *Dealer:* Portraits Inc 985 Park Ave New York NY 10022. *Mailing Add:* 30 Rising Ridge Rd Ridgefield CT 06877

PASSUNTINO, PETER ZACCARIA
PAINTER, PRINTMAKER
b Chicago, Ill, Feb 18, 36. *Study:* Art Inst Chicago, scholar, 54-58; Oxbow Sch Painting, summer 58; Inst Art Archeol, Paris, 63. *Work:* Walter P Chrysler Mus; Hirshhorn Mus, Washington, DC; Norfolk Mus, Va; Titan Steel Corp. *Exhib:* Corcoran Mus, Washington, DC; Knowlton Gallery, New York, 76; Gallery K, Washington, DC, 76; Joseph Gallery, New York; Gallery 187, Englewood, NJ; Art Latitude, New York, 79; and many others. *Pos:* Chmn, Momentum, Chicago, 57-58. *Awards:* Fulbright Fel, 63-64; Guggenheim Award, 71; Nat Endowment Arts Grant, 84. *Bibliog:* Article, Arts Mag, 1/72, Humanism, 72 & Urban Explorations 1975, Curant, 3/76; article in Urban Explorations 1975, Currant, 3/76. *Dealer:* Gallery Marc Alexandria VA 22313; Gallery Bienville New Orleans LA 70130. *Mailing Add:* 530 La Guardia Pl New York NY 10012

PATCH, PEGGIE (MARGARET THOMPSON WILLIAMSON)
PAINTER, DEALER
b St Paul, Minn. *Study:* Univ Minn, 36-39; Johns Hopkins Univ, Art as Applied to Med Cert; also with Paul Penczner, Marilyn Lehman, Ray Ridaback, Jason Williamson & Max Broedel. *Exhib:* Tenn Watercolor Soc, 71-75; 12th Tenn All State Exhib, 72. *Pos:* Chmn-docent, Brooks Mem Art Gallery, Memphis, Tenn, 65-66; free lance med illusr, 66-; vpres, Brooks Mem Art League, 72-73; owner-dir, Golden Fleece Art Gallery, Memphis, 72-75, Carefree, 76- *Awards:* First Prize in Watercolor, Tenn All State Exhib, 72; Fowler Purchase Prize, Tenn Watercolor Soc, 73. *Mem:* League Am Pen Women & Artists; Ariz Watercolor Assoc. *Media:* Watercolor, Oil; Pen & Ink. *Specialty:* Prints, watercolor, oils and acrylics. *Publ:* Illusr (Margaret T Guthrie, pseudonym), Memphis Med J, 67-69; illusr, (Peggy Williamson, pseudonym), Sourcebook of Medical Communication, FACS, 81. *Mailing Add:* c/o Golden Fleece Art Gallery 42 Easy St Carefree AZ 85377

PATEMAN, KIM See Levin, Kim

PATERNOSTO, CESAR PEDRO
PAINTER
b La Plata, Buenos Aires, Arg, Nov 29, 31. *Study:* Nat Univ La Plata, Sch Fine Arts, 57-59, Inst Philos, 61. *Work:* Mus Mod Art, New York; Nat Fine Arts Mus, Buenos Aires; Plastic Arts Mus, La Plata; Albright-Knox Gallery, Buffalo; Hirshhorn Mus, Washington, DC; and others. *Exhib:* Latin American Art Since Independence, Yale Univ, Conn, 65; 3rd Biennial Am Art, Cordoba, Arg, 66; The 1960's, Mus Mod Art, New York, 67; 2nd Biennial Coltejer, Medellin, Colombia, 70; one-man shows, Dusseldorf, WGer, 72, New York, 73 & Paris, 74; and others. *Awards:* First Prize, 3rd Biennial Am Art, Cordoba, 66; Acquisition Award, 15th Exhib, Mar Del Plata, Arg, 66. *Bibliog:* Sam Hunter (auth), The Cordoba biennial, Art Am, 4/67; J R Mellow (auth), New York letter, Art Int, 11/68; K Kline (auth), Reviews, Art News, 1/70. *Media:* Acrylic on Canvas. *Dealer:* Galerie Denise Rene 6 W 57th St New York NY 10019 & Hans Mayer Dusseldorf West Germany. *Mailing Add:* 135 Hudson St New York NY 10013

PATERSON, ANTHONY R
SCULPTOR, EDUCATOR
b Albany, NY, Dec 17, 34. *Study:* Sch of Mus Fine Arts, Boston, dipl & grad dipl; study with Harold Tovish, Ernest Morenon, Peter Abate; La Grande Chaumier Sch Drawing, Paris; Mass Inst Technol, welding; Univ Guadalajara, Mex. *Work:* Sch Mus Fine Arts, Boston; Kalamazoo Inst Arts, Mich. *Comn:* Portrait of Seymour H Knox (bronze torso), comn by Buffalo Found, 78-79. *Exhib:* Dark Mirror, Am Fedn Arts Travel Exhib, 64; Young Talent Show, Mass Coun Arts, Boston, 67; Mainstreams, Marietta Col, Ohio, 69; Small Sculpture & Drawing, Ball State Univ, 71; Nat Drawing, Pottsdam, NY, 73; 150 Years of Portraiture in Western NY, Burchfield Ctr, Buffalo, NY, 81. *Teaching:* Instr sculpture, Sch Mus Fine Arts, Boston, 62-65; instr sculpture, Mt Ida Jr Col, Newton Ctr, Mass, 64-68; asst prof sculpture, State Univ NY Buffalo, 68-71, assoc prof, 71- *Awards:* Alumni Travel Fcl, Boston Mus Fine Arts, 69; MacDowell Colony Fel, NH, 71; Fac Res Fel, State Univ NY, 70-73. *Mem:* Artists Comt, Buffalo. *Media:* Bronze. *Mailing Add:* 530 Norwood Ave Buffalo NY 14222

PATNODE, J SCOTT
PRINTMAKER, EDUCATOR
b Seattle, Wash, Oct 19, 45. *Study:* Gonzaga Univ, AB, 68; Pratt Inst, fel, 68, MFA, 70; also with George McNeil, Walter Rogalski & Clare Romano. *Work:* Cheney Cowles Mem Mus, Spokane; Kalamazoo Inst Arts, Mich; Evergreen State Col, Olympia, Wash; Pac Nat Bank of Wash, Seattle. *Exhib:* Hawaii Nat Print Exhib, Honolulu Acad Art, 71 & 73; CCAC World Print Competition, San Francisco Art Mus, 73; New Generation Drawings Exhib, circulated by Western Asn Art Mus, 73-75; 59th Ann Exhib Northwest Artists, Seattle Art Mus, 74; Gov Invitational, 78. *Pos:* Dir, Ad Art Gallery, Gonzaga Univ, 71- *Teaching:* Assoc prof art, Gonzaga Univ, 70-, chmn dept art, 79- *Awards:* Print Purchase Award, Honolulu Acad Art, 71; Fremont Lane South Award for Painting, Spokane Art Mus, 72. *Mem:* Western Asn Art Mus; Spokane Allied Arts; Art Mus Asn. *Media:* Mixed. *Mailing Add:* 901 E Nora Spokane WA 99207

PATRICK, ALAN K
CERAMIST, PAINTER
b Richmond, Ind, June 16, 42. *Study:* Ball State Univ, with Byron Temple, BS, 64, MA, 66. *Work:* Ball State Univ Art Gallery; Earlham Col, Richmond, Ind; Richmond Art Asn Gallery. *Exhib:* Ind Univ Bicentennial Craft Exhib, Bloomington, 76; Ball State Univ Art Gallery, 76; Beaux Arts Designer Craftsman Exhib, Columbus, Ohio, 75 & 77; Functional Pottery, Wooster Col, Ohio, 78; The Gallery, Bloomington, Ind, 83. *Bibliog:* Ruth Chin (auth), Bethel Pike Potters, Ceramics Mo, 74; Kathleen R Postle (auth), Bethel Pike Pottery, Spinning Wheel, 6/79. *Mem:* Ind Artist-Craftsmen; Ind Potters Guild. *Media:* Stoneware, Porcelain; Oil. *Mailing Add:* Rt 1 Box 80-B Albany IN 47320

PATRICK, CHARLES WILLIAM
CONCEPTUAL ARTIST, WRITER
b Indianapolis, Ind, Feb 20, 37. *Study:* Purdue Univ, BA; Art Students League, New York; John Herron Art Inst, Indianapolis; Sch Visual Arts, New York, 53-59; Harvard Univ, MBA, 57; Univ Geneva, Switz, PhD, 66. *Work:* Carnegie Endowment Int Peace, New York; Rutgers Univ, New Brunswick; New York Univ; Univ PR, San Juan; George Washington Univ, DC. *Comn:* Performance with Color Poems (film), Nat Endowment Arts, Washington, DC, 79; Art in America (film), Nat Film Inst, Washington, DC, 83. *Exhib:* Group shows, Walker St Gallery, Craftmans Gallery & Azuma Gallery, New York, 74; Aames Gallery, New York, 75 & 76; Letter Poem, New York Univ, New York, 76; Words & Images, Smithsonian Inst, DC, 76-77; Learning to Read Through the Arts, Guggenheim Mus, New York, 77. *Pos:* Consult, Nat Endowment Arts, 77-79; fel, Ctr for Advan Visual Studies, Smithsonian Inst/Mass Inst Technol Centerbeam Proj, 78; consult, Am Inst Architects Found, 78 & Washington DC Slide Registry for the Visual Arts, 78-79. *Teaching:* Lectr art in Am, Harvard Univ Club, New York, Am Univ & others, 77-83; lectr visual arts & poetry, Va Poetry Soc, Univ Va, Rutgers Univ, Harvard Club & others, 77-83. *Awards:* Nat Endowment Arts Special Proj Grant, Performances with Color Poems, 79. *Bibliog:* Leslie Jacobson (auth, text) & Pat Mollela (auth, film), Color Poems in the Dramatic Arts, Nat Endowment Arts, 80. *Mem:* Artists Equity Asn; Cult Alliance Washington DC. *Media:* Acrylic, Collage. *Publ:* Auth, Art in America--The Great Happening, pvt publ, 78; auth, New Forms of Poetry in the Visual Arts, George Washington Univ, 79; auth, Public Poem About America, Libr Cong, 80. *Mailing Add:* 1214 Lyndale Dr Alexandria VA 22308

PATRICK, DARRYL L
HISTORIAN, ADMINISTRATOR
b Havre, Mont, Oct 5, 36. *Study:* Northern Mont Col, BS, 62; Univ Wash, MA, 70; N Tex State Univ, PhD, 78. *Teaching:* Instr art hist, Factory of Visual Arts, Seattle, Wash, 69-71; asst instr, Sam Houston State Univ, Huntsville, Tex, 71-, dir dept art, 78- *Mem:* Col Art Asn; Nat Coun Art Adminr. *Res:* Investigation in areas of 19th and 20th century American paintings, Italian Baroque architecture and Venitian architecture. *Publ:* Auth, Venitian Palaces (2-part filmstrip), Educ Filmstrips, 73; auth, The Texas Hill Country, Tex A&M Press, 81. *Mailing Add:* Dept of Art Sam Houston State Univ Huntsville TX 77340

PATRICK, GENIE HUDSON
PAINTER, INSTRUCTOR
b Fayetteville, Ark, Nov 25, 38. *Study:* Miss State Col Women, 56-58; Univ Ga, BFA, 60; Univ Ill, Urbana-Champaign, 60-61; Univ Colo, MA, 62. *Exhib:* Walker Ann, Minneapolis, 66; Mid-Miss Invitational, Davenport Munic Art Gallery, 79; two-man exhib, Drawing & Painting, Coe Col Galleries, Cedar Rapids, Iowa, 71, Laura Musser Mus, Muscatine, Iowa, 72 & 77, Fine Art Ctr, Univ Mo-Columbia, 75 & Myers Fine Art Gallery, State Univ NY, Plattsburgh, 76; and others. *Pos:* Fel in Residence, Huntington Hartford Found, Pacific Palisades, Calif, summer 64. *Teaching:* Instr art, Northeast Miss Jr Col, Booneville, 62-64; instr art, Radford Col, Va, 64-65; instr children's art classes, Cedar Rapids Art Ctr, Iowa, 65-70; instr drawing & painting, Univ Iowa Exten, 74-, instr drawing, Sch Art & Art Hist, Univ Iowa, Iowa City, 74 & 80. *Media:* Oil, Drawing. *Mailing Add:* 1190 E Court St Iowa City IA 52240

PATRICK, JOSEPH ALEXANDER
PAINTER, EDUCATOR
b Chester, SC, Feb 10, 38. *Study:* Univ Ga, BFA, 60; Univ Colo, Boulder, MFA, 62. *Work:* Keokuk Art Asn, Iowa; Luther Col, Iowa; SDak Mem Art Ctr, Brookings; Laura Musser Mus, Muscatine, Iowa; Univ Mo Alumni Collection, Columbia. *Exhib:* One-man shows, Augustana Col, SDak, 72, Univ Iowa Mus Art, 73, Iowa State Univ Design Ctr, Ames, 74, Kans State Univ, Manhattan, 75, Northwest Mo State Univ, Maryville, 77 & Friends Gallery, Minneapolis Inst Arts, Minn, 77; and others. *Pos:* Mus asst, Univ Ga Mus Art, Athens, 58-60. *Teaching:* Asst art, Univ Colo, Boulder, 60-62, instr drawing & painting, 61-62; instr & head dept, Northeast Miss Jr Col, Booneville, 62-64; instr, Radford Col, 64-65; instr, Univ Iowa, 65-68, asst prof drawing & painting, 68-71, assoc prof drawing, 71, head dept drawing, 79- *Awards:* Residence Fel, Huntington Hartford Found, 64; Summer Fac Fel, 69 & Fac Grants, 73, 77 & 78-79, Univ Iowa Found. *Mem:* Mid-Am Art Asn; Col Art Asn Am. *Media:* Oil, Watercolor. *Mailing Add:* 1190 E Court St Iowa City IA 52240

PATTEE, ROWENA
SERIGRAPHER, FILMMAKER
b Ft Wayne, Ind, Oct 29, 35. *Study:* Lewis & Clark Col; Edinburgh Col Art, Scotland; Univ Ore, BA & MFA; Univ Calif, Berkeley. *Work:* Nat Gallery Israel, Jerusalem. *Comn:* Marcus Whitman Mural, Presbyterian Church, Portland, Ore; six mosaic murals, Cave-of-Dawning, Montecito, Calif. *Exhib:* American Artists in Britain, New Vision Ctr Gallery, London, 58; one-woman show, Marylhurst Col, 59; two-man shows, Seligmann Gallery, Seattle, 66 & Coos Art Mus, 68; Portland & Seattle Art Mus, 67-70. *Teaching:* Instr vis commun, Univ Portland, 70-71; instr drawing & painting, Clackamas Community Col, 70-72; lectr myths & symbols, Univ Calif & Juno Inst, 73-74, John F Kennedy Univ, 81-83, Calif Inst Integral Studies, 82-83. *Awards:* Art Award, Lewis & Clark Col, 53-54; Art Award, Coos Art Mus, Ore, 68. *Res:* Archetypal themes in cross-cultural manner. *Publ:* Auth & illusr, Song to Thee: Divine Androgyne, Celestial Arts, 73; auth & illusr, Our living earth, Maitraya, Shambhalla, 74; films include Song to Thee: Divine Androgyne, Interspace, Metamorphosis I & The Tree of Life. *Mailing Add:* PO Box 784 Point Reyes Station CA 94956

PATTEN, DAVID JOHN
EDITOR, LIBRARIAN
b Bancroft, Iowa, May 14, 38. *Study:* Univ Nebr, Omaha, BFA; Univ Iowa, with Chu-Tsing Li, MA; Univ Mich, with Oleg Graber & Walter Spink, AMLS. *Pos:* Design, art & archit librn, Univ Cincinnati, 66-68; art & archit librn, Washington Univ, St Louis, 68-70; ed, Art Index, H W Wilson Co, Bronx, NY, 70-80; art librn, Oberlin Col, Ohio, 80-82 & Clark Art Inst, Mass, 82- *Mem:* Col Art Asn Am; Art Libr Soc NAm (secy, 73-74, chmn NY chap, 73-74). *Res:* Iranian architecture; art reference works; indexing in the visual arts. *Interests:* Islamic art; India art; Old Master prints; Japanese prints. *Publ:* Ed, Art Libraries Society of North America Directory of Members, 1973-74, Art Libr Soc NAm, 73-74; ed, Library Classification Systems and the Visual Arts, Art Libr Soc NAm, 76; ed, ARLIS/New York News, 78-79. *Mailing Add:* 1560 Massachusetts Ave North Adams MA 01247

PATTERSON, CURTIS RAY
SCULPTOR, INSTRUCTOR
b Shreveport, La, Nov 11, 44. *Study:* Grambling State Univ, BS, 67; Ga State Univ, MVA, 75. *Comn:* Coretin steel, Bur Cult & Int Affairs, 77; mild steel, Atlanta Rapid Transit Authority, 78. *Exhib:* Thirty-five Artists in the SE (contribr, catalog), High Mus Art, Atlanta, Ga, 76; 35 Artists in the SE Traveling Show, 77-78; Festival of Arts & Cult, Lagos, Nigeria, 77; Fourteen Sculptors, High Mus Art, Atlanta, 77. *Pos:* Vpres, Thirteen Minus One, 76-77. *Teaching:* Teacher sculpture & pottery, Therrell High Sch, Atlanta, 70-76; instr sculpture, Atlanta Col of Art, 76- *Awards:* Bronze Jubilee Award Visual Arts, WETV, Channel 30, Atlanta, Ga, 79. *Mem:* Black Artist of Atlanta; Thirteen Minus One. *Media:* Metal, Clay. *Mailing Add:* 1091 Flamingo Dr SW Atlanta GA 30311

PATTERSON, PATRICIA
FILM CRITIC, PAINTER
b Jersey City, NJ, Mar 17, 41. *Study:* Parson's Sch of Design, grad cert. *Exhib:* Houston Mus Contemp Art, Tex, 77; La Jolla Mus Contemp Arts, Calif, 78; Inst for Art & Urban Resources, PS 1, New York, 78; Cleveland Mus Art, Ohio, 78; Fine Arts Gallery, Univ Calif, Irvine, 78; and others. *Pos:* Contrib writer, Film Comment Mag, New York, 75- *Teaching:* Asst prof painting, drawing & art criticism, Univ Calif, San Diego, 76- *Media:* Casein, Enamel; Watercolor. *Publ:* Coauth, Werner Herzog, The cinema of Fata Morgana, 75 & The new breed of filmmakers: A multiplication of myths, 75, City Mag; auth, Fassbinder, 75 & coauth, Gun crazy--Part II, 76 & Beyond the new wave: I (Kitchen without Kitsch), 77, Film Comment; auth, Aran kitchen, aran sweaters, Heresies, 78. *Dealer:* Ellie Blankfort Gallery 2341 Ronda Vista Dr Los Angeles CA 90027. *Mailing Add:* Art Dept Univ Calif San Diego La Jolla CA 92093

PATTERSON, SHIRLEY
PAINTER, INSTRUCTOR
b Buffalo, NY, Dec 13, 23. *Study:* Albright Sch Fine Art, Buffalo, NY, dipl, 44; New York State Univ, Buffalo, BS(art educ), 45. *Work:* E I Dupont deNemours & Co, Del Trust Co & Blue Cross-Blue Shield, Wilmington, Del; Widener Col Mus, Chester, Pa; State Del Div Libr, Dover. *Exhib:* Regional Art Exhib, Del Art Mus, Wilmington, 75, 78, 79 & 81; Regional Art Exhib, Univ Del, Newark, 75, 76, 77, 79 & 81; Pa Soc Watercolor Painters, Harrisburg, 79; Am Watercolor Soc, Nat Acad Galleries, New York, 79; Ky Watercolor Soc, Louisville Water Tower Mus, 80-81. *Collections Arranged:* Mid-Atlantic Regional Exhib Collage, Univ Del, 79. *Teaching:* Instr art, Griffith Inst Cent Sch, Springville, NY, 45-46; critic instr art, Kenmore Pub Sch, NY, 46-49; instr art, privately, 58-70. *Awards:* Artist of the Year, Hotel DuPont, Wilmington Christmas Comt, 76; First Prize, Del State Biennial, Nat League Am Pen Women, 77, 79, 81 & 83. *Bibliog:* Mary Sam Ward (ed), Delaware Women Remembered, Modern Press, 77; Lise Monty (auth), article, Sunday News J, 4/8/79; article, Artists register, Del Artline, 7/79; Delaware Artists Series (slides), Univ Del, 83. *Mem:* Nat League Am Pen Women, Diamond State Branch (pres, 78-80); Studio Group Inc, Wilmington, Del (pres, 78-80); Pa Soc Watercolor Painters; Ky Watercolor Soc. *Media:* Watercolor, Mixed Media. *Dealer:* Grace McFarren 3 Winterbury Circle Wilmington DE 19808. *Mailing Add:* 3405 S Rockfield Dr Wilmington DE 19810

PATTERSON, WILLIAM JOSEPH
PAINTER, PRINTMAKER
b Albany, NY, Mar 16, 41. *Study:* Hartford Art Sch, BFA, 65; Am Acad Rome, Abbey Found Fel, 65-67; Syracuse Univ, MFA, 69. *Work:* Libr Cong; Honolulu Acad Art; New Britain Mus; State Univ NY Col Potsdam; Northern Ill Univ. *Comn:* Five drawings, Third Nat Bank, Springfield, 75; ed of prints, Mass Bar Asn. *Exhib:* One-man shows, Nat Acad Design, New York, 68 & New Britain Mus, 81; Assoc Am Artists, New York, 70 & 72; NY State Univ, 72; 23rd Nat Exhib Prints, Libr of Cong & Nat Col Fine Arts, 73. *Teaching:* Instr printmaking, Hartford Art Sch, Univ Hartford, 69-71; assoc prof printmaking & drawing, Univ Mass, Amherst, 71- *Awards:* Mass Coun Arts Fel, 75; Purdue Univ Award, 80; New Britain Mus, Conn, 81. *Bibliog:* Florence Berlman (auth), Prints of Patterson, Hartford Courant, 7/71; Tom Hart (auth), Bank commissions painting, Springfield Daily News, 75. *Mem:* Boston Printmakers. *Media:* Intaglio; Watercolor, Tempera. *Publ:* Young Man, 71, Four Artists, 72, After Rembrandt, 73 & Daumier, 75, Assoc Am Artists; Self Portrait Near a Window, 74. *Dealer:* Assoc Am Artists 663 Fifth Ave New York NY 10021. *Mailing Add:* c/o Dept Art Univ Mass Amherst MA 01002

PATTI, TOM
SCULPTOR
Study: Pratt Inst Sch Art & Design, BID, 67, Grad Sch Art & Design, MID, 69; New Sch Social Res, with Roudolph Arheim, 69. *Work:* Metrop Mus Art & Mus Mod Art, New York; Toledo Mus Art, Ohio; Kunstmuseum Dusseldorf, WGer; Victoria & Albert Mus, London. *Exhib:* Art & Relig, Vatican Mus, Rome; Mex-NAm Cult Inst, Mexico City, 82; Recent Aquisitions: Archit & Design, Mus Mod Art, New York, 79; New Glass: A Worldwide Survey, Corning Mus Glass, 79. *Awards:* Nat Endowment Arts, 79; 1st Prize, Glaskunst 81, Kassel, WGer. *Publ:* Auth, articles, Neues Glas, 3/81 & Art News, summer 81. *Mailing Add:* Maple St Plainfield MA 01070

PATTISON, ABBOTT
SCULPTOR, PAINTER
b Chicago, Ill, May 15, 16. *Study:* Yale Col, BA, 37, Yale Sch Fine Arts, BFA, 39. *Work:* Whitney Mus Am Art; Israel State Mus, Jerusalem; San Francisco Mus; Buckingham Palace, London; Art Inst Chicago; and others. *Comn:* Sculpture, Cent Nat Bank, Cleveland; Ill State Capitol, Springfield; Lincoln Libr, Springfield; Chicago State Univ; US State Dept; and others. *Exhib:* Art Inst Chicago, 40-69; Metrop Mus Art, 51 & 52; four shows, Whitney Mus Am Art, 53-59; one-man shows, Holbrook Mus, Univ Ga, 54 & Sculpture Ctr, NY, 56; Pa Acad Fine Arts, Philadelphia; Calif Palace Legion of Honor, San Francisco; and many others. *Teaching:* Instr, Art Inst Chicago, 46-52; sculptor-in-residence, Univ Ga, 54; instr, Skowhegan Sch Art, 55-56. *Awards:* First Logan Prize, Art Inst Chicago, 42; Prize, Metrop Mus Art, New York, 50; Prize, Bundy Mus, Vt, 67. *Mem:* Chicago Art Club. *Mailing Add:* c/o Fairweather-Hardin Gallery 101 E Ontario St Chicago IL 60611

PATTON, SHARON FRANCES
HISTORIAN, LECTURER
b Chicago, Ill. *Study:* Roosevelt Univ, BA(studio art), 66; Univ Ill, Urbana, MA, 69; Northwestern Univ, with Frank Willett & Ivor Wilks, PhD(art hist), 80. *Collections Arranged:* Contemporary Afro-American Artists, Lake Forest Col, 72; Traditional Forms & Modern Africa: West African Art at the Univ Md, College Park (auth, catalog), 83. *Teaching:* Asst prof art hist, Va Commonwealth Univ, Richmond, 72-73; instr African-Am & African art, Univ Houston, 76-79; asst prof African art hist, Univ Md, College Park, 79- *Bibliog:* Dana Grabiner (auth), New look at traditional African art, Precis, Vol 14, No 8, 83. *Mem:* African Studies Asn; Arts Coun African Studies Asn; Nat Conf Artists; charter mem African & African-Am Hist Soc. *Res:* Sub-Saharan west Africa, especially Asante; African art as political emblem; antebellum Louisiana African-American art. *Publ:* Auth, The Asante stool, African Arts, 79; auth, Development of culture by black artisans, Negro Hist Bulletin, 83; auth, African heritage: Afro-American art and architecture in the US, Colorlines, 83; auth, Traditional Forms and Modern Africa, Univ Md, 83; auth, Asante chiefly regalia: The umbrella, African Arts, 84. *Mailing Add:* 1832 Metzerott Adelphi MD 20783

PAUL, ARTHUR
DESIGNER, PAINTER
b Chicago, Ill, Jan 18, 25. *Study:* Art Inst Chicago, 41-43; Inst Design, Chicago, 46-50. *Exhib:* Kunstverein Munchen, Munich, WGer, 72, Btsee des Art Decoratifs, Lausanne, Switz, 72, Lowe Mus Art, Coral Gables, Fla, 73, Munic Art Gallery, Los Angeles, 74 & New York Cult Ctr, 74. *Pos:* Self-employed freelance designer, 50-53; art dir, Playboy Mag, 53-, vpres corp art & graphics dir, Playboy Enterprises, Inc, 78- *Teaching:* Guest lectr mag design & illus, Art Inst Chicago, 78, Syracuse Univ, NY, 79 & hon teacher, Tokyo Design Sch, Japan, 81. *Awards:* Top Award, Soc Typographic Arts, 64; Gold Medal, City Milan, Italy, 72; Polycube Award, Art Dirs Club Philadelphia, 75; and others. *Bibliog:* Jerome Snyder (auth), Playboy, Graphis, Switz, 10/72; Akiko Hyuga (auth), Art Paul linear drawings, Idea Mag, Japan, 7/73; Don Holden (auth), Interview with Art Paul, Am Artist (cover story), 5/75. *Mem:* Alliance Graphique Int; Mus Contemp Art (bd trustees, exhib & educ comt); Alumni Asn ITT-Inst Design (bd mem-liaison); hon mem Artists Guild Chicago; Chicago 27 Designers. *Media:* Acrylic, Watercolor. *Publ:* Auth, Problems of art direction, Comment 200, 60; auth, The high art of low art, Print Mag, 72; auth, The world of work: An artists-design view, In: National Art Education Association Carrer Education Handbook, Purdue Univ. *Mailing Add:* 175 E Delaware Pl Chicago IL 60611

PAUL, GREG (GREGORY WILMER)
DIRECTOR, ILLUSTRATOR
b Cleveland, Ohio, Nov 7, 50. *Study:* Kent State Univ, BFA, 72. *Exhib:* Type Dirs Club 26, New York, 80; Communication Arts, Palo Alto, Calif, 79-81; Photographis, Zurich, Switz, 80 & 81; Graphis, Zurich, Switz, 81 & 82; 24th Ann Exhib, Soc Illusrs, New York, 82; and others. *Pos:* Illusr, Cleveland Mag, 73-76 & Indust Week, 76-77; graphic designer, Plain Dealer Mag, Cleveland, 76-77, design dir, 79- & illusr, 80-; art dir, Ohio Mag, Columbus, 77-79, illusr, 78-79; illusr, Scottsdale Mag, 80- *Teaching:* Instr type design, Cooper Sch Art, Cleveland, 76-77; instr illus, Kent State Univ, Ohio, 79-81. *Awards:* Bronze Medal, Indust Graphics Int '78; three Gold Medals & one Silver Medal, Cleveland Soc Communicating Artists, 80; Gold Medal, 24th Ann Exhib, Soc Illusrs, New York, 82; and others. *Bibliog:* Daniel Kagan (auth), Variations in simplicity, 3/79 & Karen Jacobsen (auth), Going into depth, 8/79, Art Direction Mag; Barbara Love (auth), Graphic Solutions, Folio Mag, 2/80; Jean Coyne (auth), article, Communication Arts Mag, 5/81. *Media:* Mixed. *Mailing Add:* 852 Englewood Rd Cleveland Heights OH 44121

PAUL, KEN (HUGH)
PRINTMAKER, PAINTER
b Ogden, Utah, Apr 24, 38. *Study:* Univ Utah, 58-59; Univ Wyo, BA(with honors), 61, MA, 65. *Work:* Art Gallery SAustralia, Adelaide; Art Gallery Tasmania, Hobart, Australia; Univ Ore Mus of Art, Eugene; Portland Art Mus, Ore. *Comn:* Translucent painting, Adelaide Arts Festival, 67; ceiling panel restoration, Sacred Heart Chapel, Geelong, Australia. *Exhib:* First Springfield Col Nat Print Exhib, Mass, 65; Denver Art Mus Nat Show, 65; Calif Soc Printmakers Ann, Richmond, 71; Seattle Print Int, 71; Ore Artists Ann, Portland, 72-73 & 75; one-man show, Cheney Cowles Mus, Spokane, 79. *Teaching:* Lectr art, Gordon Inst Technol, Geelong, 66-67; lectr printmaking, SAustralian Sch Art, Adelaide, 67-69; assoc prof printmaking, Univ Ore, 70-; vis instr, M I Kerns Art Ctr, Eugene, Ore, summer 71; vis instr, Pac Northwest Graphics Workshop, Cheshire, Ore, 74. *Awards:* Printmakers Ore Exhib First Prize, M I Kerns Art Ctr, 72; Prize for Painting, Ore Col Educ, Monmouth, 72; Graduate School Summer Res Grant, Univ Ore, 73. *Mem:* Contemp Art Soc SAustralia (vpres, 68-69). *Media:* Lithography, Silkscreen; Oil, Acrylic. *Mailing Add:* 2585 Taylor St Eugene OR 97405

PAUL, SUZANNE
PHOTOGRAPHER
b Houston, Tex, Feb 13, 45. *Study:* Univ Houston, BFA, 68; post-grad studies: Univ Calif, Berkeley & San Francisco Art Inst. *Work:* Mus Fine Arts & First City Nat Bank, Houston, Tex; Chase Manhattan Bank, New York. *Exhib:* One-woman show, Contemp Arts Mus, Houston, Tex, 76 & Ft Worth Art Mus, 83; Tex Fine Arts Asn, Laguna Gloria Art Mus, Austin, Tex, 80; A Texas Photo Sampler, Washington Project Arts, Washington, DC, 81; The Ties that Bind: Photog Portray the Family, Doughtery Cultural Arts Ctr, Austin, Tex, 81; In Our Time, Contemporary Arts Mus, Houston, 82; Thirteen Artists: A Look at Houston, Ga State Univ, Atlanta, 82. *Awards:* Purchase Award, Tex Fine Arts Asn Exhib, Laguna Gloria Art Mus, Austin,

Tex, 80; Photog Survey Grant, The Ties that Bind: Family Relationships, Nat Endowment Arts, 81-82. *Bibliog:* Women See Woman, Thomas Y Crowell Co, New York, 76; Marcia Tucker (auth), Woman in Sight: New Art in Texas, Women & Their Work, Inc, 79; Marcia Tucker (auth), 1980 New Orleans Triennial, New Orleans Mus Art, 80. *Media:* Black & White Silver Prints, Cibachrome. *Publ:* Photogr, Juarez Series: Terry Allen, 75, photogr, Norman Bluhm, 76, photogr, Donald Schule, 76 & photogr, American Narrative/Story Art: 1967-1977, 78, Contemp Arts Mus, Houston; photogr, Frank Gillette: Aransas/Axis of Observation, Points of View, Houston, 78. *Dealer:* Texas Gallery 2012 Peden Houston TX 77019. *Mailing Add:* 1508 Indiana Houston TX 77006

PAUL, WILLIAM D, JR
PAINTER, PHOTOGRAPHER
b Wadley, Ga, Sept 26, 34. *Study:* Atlanta Col of Art, BFA; Univ Ga, AB & MFA; Emory Univ; Ga State Col; Univ Rome, Italy. *Work:* General Mills, Inc, Minneapolis; Hallmark Cards, Kansas City, Mo; Little Rock Art Ctr, Ark; Univ Ga, Ga Mus Art, Athens; and others. *Exhib:* Southeastern Ann, Atlanta; Va Intermont Col, Bristol; Birmingham Ann, Ala; Corcoran Gallery Art, Washington, DC; Art of Two Cities, Nat Traveling Exhib, Am Fedn Arts; and many others. *Collections Arranged:* Sixty small original exhibs, Charlotte Crosby Kemper Gallery, Kansas City Art Inst, 61-65; Art of Two Cities, Am Fedn Arts Traveling Exhib, 67; The Visual Assault, 67, Drawings by Richard Diebenkorn, Selections: The Downtown Gallery, Drawing and Watercolors by Raphael Soyer, Recent Collages by Samuel Adler, 20th Anniversary Exhibition & Art of Ancient Peru, The Paul Clifford Collection, Ga Mus Art; American Painting: the 1940's, 68; American Painting, the 1950's, 68; American Painting: the 1960's, 69; Philip Pearlstein, Retrospective Exhibition (auth, catalog), 70; Alice Neel, Retrospective Exhib (auth, catalog), 75; and many others. *Pos:* Dir exhibs & cur study collections, Kansas City Art Inst, 61-65; cur, Ga Mus Art, 67-69; dir, Ga Mus Art, 69-70. *Teaching:* Instr art & art hist, Kansas City Art Inst, Park Col & Univ Ga. *Awards:* Macy's Ann, Kansas City, 59, 61, 63 & 64; Atlanta Paper Co Ann, 61; Hallmark Award, Mid-Am Ann, 62; and others. *Mem:* Am Fedn Arts (trustee, 69-80); Col Art Asn; Southeastern Mus Conf; Am Asn Mus; Arts Festival Atlanta (vpres, 82-). *Publ:* Auth foreward, Alice Neel, Harry N Abrams, 83. *Mailing Add:* 150 Bar H Ct RR 3 Athens GA 30605

PAULIN, RICHARD CALKINS
MUSEUM DIRECTOR, CRAFTSMAN
b Chicago, Ill, Oct 25, 28. *Study:* DePauw Univ, BA; Univ Denver, MA; Inst Fine Arts, NY Univ; also in Guadalajara, Mex. *Exhib:* Univ Ill, 60; Rockford Art Asn, 61; Beloit Col, 61-63 & 65; two-man show, Nat Col Educ, Evanston, Ill, 64. *Collections Arranged:* Teachers Who Paint, 59; Chicago Painters, 60; Six Chicago Painters, 61; Picasso Preview, 62; George Rouault-His Aqua Tints and Wood Engravings, 63; Collectors Showcase, 64; 30 Contemporary Living American Painters, 64; First National Invitational Painting Exhibition: Fifty States of Art, 65; Swedish Handcraft, 61. *Pos:* Dir, Harry & Della Burpee Art Gallery, Rockford, Ill, formerly; dir mus art & asst prof art hist, Univ Ore, currently. *Teaching:* Instr arts & crafts, Roosevelt Jr High Sch, Rockford, Ill; former instr basic & intermediate art courses, Rockford Art Asn. *Awards:* Canfield Award, Rockford Art Asn, 61. *Mem:* Nat Educ Asn; Nat Coun Art Educ; Mus Dirs Asn NAm; Western Art Asn; Mid-Western Mus Dirs Asn; plus others. *Mailing Add:* Mus of Art Univ Ore Eugene OR 97403

PAULSEN, BRIAN OLIVER
PAINTER, PRINTMAKER
b Seattle, Wash, Mar 29, 41. *Study:* Univ Wash, BA, 63; Wash State Univ, MFA, 66. *Work:* El Paso Art Mus; Amoco Oil Co, Denver; Rothmans Art Gallery, Stratford, Ont; Western Ill Univ; Pioneer Mus & Haggin Galleries, Stockton; and others. *Exhib:* San Francisco Art Int Centennial Exhib, San Francisco Mus Art, 70; Extraordinary Realities, Whitney Mus Am Art, New York, 73; touring exhib, 5 Atlantic Provincial Can Mus, 74; Artrain Traveling Art Exhib, Cent US, 75; Smithsonian Traveling Drawing Exhib, 79-80; solo exhib, Rochester Art Ctr, Minn, 80; New American Graphics 82-83, Butler Inst Am Art, 82. *Teaching:* Asst prof printmaking & drawing, Calif State Univ, Chico, 66-71; asst prof painting & drawing, Univ Calgary, 71-73; assoc prof, Univ NDak, 73- *Awards:* Purchase Awards, Lagrange, Ga, 78, Owensboro Mus, Ky, 79 & Masur Mus, La, 79; Watercolor USA, 77, 80 & 81; Nat Endowment Arts Fel, 81-82. *Bibliog:* Article, Art Express Mag, 1-2/82. *Media:* Acrylic, Watercolor; Engraving. *Mailing Add:* 320 N 16th St Grand Forks ND 58201

PAYNE, JOHN D
SCULPTOR, EDUCATOR
b Pontotoc, Miss, Sept 17, 34. *Study:* Beloit Col, BA, studied with Franklin Boggs, O V Shaffer & A D Popinsky; Univ Wis-Madison, MS, studied with Dean Meeker, W Colescott, A Sessler & others, MFA, Danforth Study Grant; Univ Kans, Lawrence, studied with Elden Teft. *Work:* Univ Wis Union Collection, Madison; Beloit State Bank, Adams Collection, Wis; Atlanta Univ, Ga; Loyola Univ, New Orleans; La State Univ, Union Collection, Baton Rouge. *Comn:* Steel sculpture, comn by John Pyros, Tarpon Springs, Fla, 67; wood sculpture, Baton Rouge, La, 68; The Sculptor, The Campus & The Prairie (three steel works), Govs State Univ, Park Forest South, Ill, 70-76. *Exhib:* Burpee Mus, Rockford, Ill, 80; Tampa Mus, 81; Beloit Col, Wis, 81; Lakeview Mus, Peoria, Ill, 81; Univ Ind, Gary, 81; and many others. *Teaching:* Chmn dept art, Langston Univ, Okla, 61-63; assoc prof sculpture & 3-D design, Southern Univ & La Inst Interior Design, 63-71; prof art, Southern Univ, New Orleans, La, 63-65 & Southern Univ, Baton Rouge, 66-71; sculptor in residence, chmn dept art & coordr art, music & theatre, Gov State Univ, 71-82, prof sculpture & ceramics, currently. *Awards:* Top Award,

State Fair, Milwaukee, Wis, 61; All Wis Exhib, 61; Second Award, Atlanta Univ Ann, Ga, 64, 65 & 66. *Bibliog:* American Printmaker, Graphic Group, Calif, 74; Afro-American Artist 1800 to Present, Boston Univ Libr, Mass, 75; Art: African American, Harcourt Brace Jovanovich, Inc, 78. *Mem:* Col Art Asn; Nat Coun Art Adminr. *Media:* Mixed. *Mailing Add:* 25645 Western Ave Park Forest IL 60466

PEABODY, AMELIA
SCULPTOR
b Marblehead, Mass, July 3, 90. *Study:* Boston Mus Fine Arts Sch, with Charles Grafly; Northeastern Univ, Hon DFA. *Work:* Mus Fine Arts, Boston; Children's Med Ctr, Boston; Audubon Soc Laughing Brook Reservation. *Comn:* Victory Medal, Joslin Clin, Boston; baptismal font, church in Oxford, Mass; portrait plaque of Dr Hsein Wu, Harvard Med Sch, Cambridge; Woodchucks and Pheasants, cast stone for entrance gate of Groton Mem Park, Mass; granite setter in animal graveyard for Mrs Frank C Paine, Wayland, Mass. *Exhib:* New York World's Fair, two yrs; Whitney Mus Am Art, New York, 40; Carnegie Inst Int, 41; Nat Asn Women Artists, 53. *Teaching:* Chmn arts & skills, Am Red Cross, Boston. *Awards:* Mrs Oakleigh Thorne Medal, Garden Club Am. *Mem:* Guild Boston Artists; Nat Asn Women Artists; Nat Sculpture Soc; New Eng Sculptors' Asn; Copley Soc. *Media:* Stone, Bronze. *Mailing Add:* 120 Commonwealth Ave Boston MA 02116

PEACE, BERNIE (KINZEL)
PAINTER, PRINTMAKER
b Williamsburg, Ky, Oct 20, 33. *Study:* Berea Col, AB(art), 54; Ind Univ, MFA(painting), 57. *Work:* Fed Reserve Bank, Richmond, Va; Ind Univ; WVa Univ; State WVa, Charleston; Washington & Jefferson Col; and others. *Comn:* Painting, WVa Arts & Humanities Coun, Charleston, 72. *Exhib:* 11th Ann Piedmont Painting & Sculpture Exhib, Mint Mus, Charlotte, NC, 71; 45th Southeastern Competition-Painting & Sculpture, Southeastern Ctr for Contemp Art, Winston-Salem, NC, 77; retrospective exhib, Delf Norona Mus, WVa, 80; 42nd Ann Exhib Comtemp Am Paintings, Palm Beach, Fla, 80; 12th Nat Painting Show, Washington & Jefferson Col, Pa, 80; 14th Ann Nat, Marietta Col, Ohio, 81; and many others. *Teaching:* Prof drawing & painting, West Liberty State Col, 60- *Awards:* Purchase Awards, WVa Arts & Humanities Coun, 72, 73 & 75; Judge's Choice Award, Bethany Col Fall Ann & Hon Mention, Bethany Col Bicentennial Exhib, Bethany, WVa, 76; Merit Awards, 43rd Ann Upper Ohio Valley Art Show, Wheeling, WVa, 81 & Bethany Col Fall Ann, 81. *Mem:* Col Art Asn WVa; Allied Artists WVa. *Media:* Acrylic; Silkscreen. *Dealer:* Gallery G 408 Blvd Allies Pittsburgh PA. *Mailing Add:* Washington Farms Wheeling WV 26003

PEAK, ELIZABETH JAYNE
PRINTMAKER, EDUCATOR
b Ft Belvoir, Va, May 19, 52. *Study:* Univ Calif, Santa Barbara, BA, 74; Brandeis Univ, Waltham, Mass, with Michael Mazur, 75; Yale Univ, New Haven, Conn, with Gabor Peterdi, MFA, 77. *Work:* Yale Univ Mus Art, New Haven, Conn; Kent State Univ Gallery, Ohio; Smithsonian Inst and Libr Cong, Washington, DC; Brigham Young Univ, Logan, Utah; Bowdoin Col; and others. *Comn:* Catalog frontispiece, Bowdoin Col Mus, Brunswick, Maine, 81; monotype, Michael Cleary, Washington, DC, 81. *Exhib:* 25th Nat Print Show, Smithsonian Inst, Washington, DC, 77; 10th Ann Works on Paper, SW Texas State Univ, San Marcos, 80; Va Mus, Richmond, 81; 8th Int Miniature Print Exhib, Pratt Graphics, New York, 81; one-person shows, Jane Haslem Gallery, Washington, DC, 81 & Bowdoin Col Mus Art, Brunswick, Maine, 82. *Teaching:* Asst prof drawing, Kent State Univ, Ohio, 79-80; asst prof, Bowdoin Col, Brunswick, Maine, 80-82, Col Holy Cross, 83- *Awards:* Helen G Wintnermitz Award, Yale Univ, 77. *Mem:* Intaglio Relief Soc; Col Art Asn; Los Angeles Printmaking Soc. *Media:* Intaglio; Oil Monotype. *Dealer:* Jane Haslem Gallery 2121 P St NW Washington DC 20037. *Mailing Add:* Dept Art Holy Cross Col Worcester MA 01610

PEAKE, CHANNING
PAINTER, MURALIST
b Marshall, Colo, Oct 24, 10. *Study:* Calif Col Arts & Crafts, 28; Santa Barbara Sch Art, 29-31; Art Students League, with Rico Lebrun, 35-36. *Work:* Santa Barbara Mus Art; Everson Mus Art, Syracuse, NY; Los Angeles Co Mus Art; Portland Art Mus, Ore. *Comn:* Murals (with Louis Rubenstein), Germanic Mus, Harvard Univ, 36, (with Rico Lebrun), Pa Sta, New York, 36-38 & (with Howard Warshaw), Santa Barbara Pub Libr, 58; Santa Barbara Biltmore Hotel, 77-79. *Exhib:* Pa Acad Fine Arts; Los Angeles Co Mus Art; Santa Barbara Mus Art, 74; solo exhib, Santa Barbara Mus Art, 75, Chelsea Galleries, Venice, Calif, 76, Bradley Gallery, Saanta Barbara, 78 & Everson Mus, 78. *Pos:* Founder, Santa Barbara Mus Art. *Mailing Add:* Box 662 Santa Ynez CA 93460

PEARL, MARILYN
DEALER
b Akron, Ohio. *Study:* Hunter Col, BA; Columbia Univ, MA. *Pos:* Dir & pres, Marilyn Pearl Gallery, 76- *Teaching:* Asst prof hist, New York Inst Technol, New York & Old Westbury, NY, 68-74. *Mem:* Art Dealers Asn. *Specialty:* Contemporary American painting, sculpture, drawing. *Mailing Add:* 38 E 57th St New York NY 10022

PEARLMAN, ETTA S
PAINTER
b New York, NY, Mar 30. *Study:* Brooklyn Col, BA, 60; Brooklyn Mus Art Sch. *Work:* Power Gallery Contemp Art, Univ Sydney, Australia; Brooklyn Mus; Temple Univ, Pa. *Exhib:* One-woman shows, Brooklyn Mus Little Gallery Series, 73 & 74 & Pleiades Gallery, 75-76, 78-80 & 82; Gallery 91, Brooklyn, 75; Brooklyn Mus Art Sales & Rental Gallery, 75. *Media:* Multimedia. *Publ:* The Art of Collaging, G F Brommer, Davis Publ, 78. *Dealer:* Pleiades Gallery 164 Mercer St New York NY 10012. *Mailing Add:* 2934 Clubhouse Rd Merrick NY 11566

PEARLSTEIN, PHILIP
PAINTER, EDUCATOR
b Pittsburgh, Pa, May 24, 24. *Study:* Carnegie Inst, with Sam Rosenberg, Robert Lepper & Balcomb Greene, BFA, 49; Inst Fine Arts, NY Univ, MA, 55. *Work:* Whitney Mus Am Art; Mus Mod Art, New York; Corcoran Gallery Art, Washington, DC; Hirshhorn Collection, James Michener Found; Art Inst Chicago; also in pvt collections. *Exhib:* One-man exhibs, Carnegie Mellon Univ, 79, Reed Col Art Mus, Portland, Ore, 79 & others; The Opposite Sex: A Realistic Viewpoint travelling exhib, Univ Mo-Kansas City, 79; The Figure of Five, Western Asn Art Mus, travel through western US, 79-80; Biennial Exhib, Whitney Mus Am Art, New York, 79; Figurative/Realist Art, Artists' Choice Mus, 79; and many others. *Teaching:* Instr, Pratt Inst, 59-63; from asst prof to prof art, Brooklyn Col, 63-82, distinguished prof art, currently. *Awards:* Fulbright Fel to Italy, 58-59; Nat Endowment Arts Grant, 69; Guggenheim Fel, 71 & 72. *Bibliog:* Robert Duffy (auth), Philip Pearlstein: Is he an enemy of realism?, St Louis Post-Dispatch, 2/27/77; John Perreault (auth), Philip Pearlstein: Naked nudes, a profile, Soho Weekly News, 4/20/78; Franz Schulze (auth), An artist who likes the body, Sunday Sun-Times, 6/17/79; and others. *Dealer:* Allan Frumkin Gallery 41 E 57th St New York NY 10022. *Mailing Add:* 163 W 88th St New York NY 10024

PEARLSTEIN, SEYMOUR
PAINTER, EDUCATOR
b Brooklyn, NY, Oct 14, 23. *Study:* Pratt Inst; Art Students League; also pvt study with Jack Potter, New York. *Work:* Mus of NMex, Santa Fe; Mint Mus Art, Charlotte, NC; Nat Acad of Design, New York; Fine Arts Gallery of San Diego, Calif; Adelphi Univ, Garden City, NY. *Exhib:* Butler Inst Am Art, Youngstown, Ohio, 75; Art in Embassies Prog, Nicaragua, 76-78; Am Watercolor Soc, New York, 77; Nat Arts Club, Nat Acad of Design & Queens Mus, New York, 78; New York Historical Society, 81; Colo Heritage Ctr Mus, Denver, 81; and many one-man shows. *Teaching:* Prof art, City Univ New York, New York City Community Col, Brooklyn, 70- *Awards:* Childe Hassam Purchase Award, 69 & 77 & Grant, 75, Am Acad of Arts & Lett; Henry Ward Ranger Purchase Award, Nat Acad of Design, 71 & 82. *Bibliog:* Malcolm Preston (auth), Seumour Pearlstein rev, Newsday, 5/4/79; David L Shirey (auth), Seymour Pearlstein, New York Times, 5/13/79. *Mem:* Nat Acad of Design (bd dirs, 82-84); Allied Artists of Am (dir, 76-78); Alliance of Figurative Artists (chmn, 76-77); Am Watercolor Soc (dir, 78-80); Audubon Artists (dir, 82-84). *Publ:* Auth, Acrylics, Am Artist Mag, 2/79. *Mailing Add:* 52 Dartmouth St Forest Hills NY 11375

PEARMAN, SARA JANE
HISTORIAN, LIBRARIAN
b Dallas, Tex, Sept 6, 40. *Study:* Univ Wichita, BAE; Univ Kans, MA(art hist); Case-Western Reserve Univ, PhD(art hist). *Collections Arranged:* Glass Collection of the University of Kansas (auth, catalog). *Pos:* Slide librn, Cleveland Mus of Art. *Teaching:* Instr art hist, Kearney State Col, 64-66; lectr, Akron State Univ, 68-, Cleveland State Univ, 77- & Kent State Univ, currently. *Mem:* Col Art Asn; Midwest Art Hist Asn; Cleveland Medieval Soc; Art Libr Soc NAm; Mid-Am Col Art Asn. *Res:* Iconography of all periods; Late Medieval and northern Renaissance art history; slide classification systems and visual resources; history of graphic design. *Publ:* Auth, Mirror of Art, Ralph, Vol 4, 77; auth, Otto Dix, A Self Portrait (exhib catalog), Univ Kans. *Mailing Add:* 2120 Hampstead Rd Cleveland Heights OH 44118

PEARSON, CLIFTON
SCULPTOR, INSTRUCTOR
b Birmingham, Ala, June 24, 48. *Study:* Ala A&M Univ, BS, 70; Ill State Univ, MS, 71, EdD, 74; also with Joel Myers, Timothy Mather, Ruddy Audio, Thomas Malone, Max Rennels, M M Chambers. *Work:* Peoria Art Guild, Ill. *Comn:* Salt glaze sculptures, comn by Dr & Mus E W Womack, Huntsville, Ala & Wayman AME Church, Bloomington, Ill; Celebrated Lady (mural), comn by Mrs Jane Rhinehart, Huntsville; Slavery Chains (ceramic bust), Ala A&M Univ, Normal. *Exhib:* Black Artists/South, Huntsville Mus Art, 79; Ala Craftsmen Invitational, Birmingham Mus Art, 79; Black Artists of the South: Dimensions & Directions, Miss Mus Art, 79; and many others. *Collections Arranged:* Twenty-one exhibs, Ala A&M Univ Gallery Art. *Teaching:* Asst ceramics & art educ, Ill State Univ, 71-73; asst prof ceramics, drawing & art educ, Ala A&M Univ, 73-74, assoc prof, 74-76. *Awards:* Purchase Award, Ill State Mus, Springfield, 73; Southern Fel Grant, 74; House of Bamboo Award in Sculpture, Tenn Art League, 75. *Bibliog:* C Pearson (auth), 60 programs on ceramics, Educ TV/Ala A&M Univ TV Commun, 8/75. *Mem:* Nat Conf Artists; Am Crafts Coun; Nat Educ Asn; Ala Craftsmen Coun (trustee, 75). *Media:* Clay Stoneware, Salt Glaze. *Mailing Add:* 6503 Greenmeadow Rd Huntsville AL 35810

PEARSON, HENRY C
PAINTER, INSTRUCTOR
b Kinston, NC, Oct 8, 14. *Study:* Univ NC, BA, 35; Yale Univ, MFA, 38; Art Students League, 53-56. *Work:* Mus Mod Art, Metrop Mus Art & Whitney Mus Am Art, New York; Albright-Knox Art Gallery, Buffalo; NC Mus Art, Raleigh. *Comn:* World University Service (poster), List Art Posters, 65; 6th New York Film Festival--Lincoln Center (poster), List Art Posters, 68;. *Exhib:* The Responsive Eye, Mus Mod Art, New York, 65; 29th Biennial

Exhib, Corcoran Gallery Art, Washington, DC, 65; Drawings USA, Minn Mus Art, St Paul, 71-73; Betty Parsons Gallery, New York, 71-76; Color Painting, Amherst Col, Mass, 72; Art Students League Centennial Exhib, 75; Truman Gallery, New York, 76-79; Marilyn Pearl Gallery, New York, 79-; and others. *Teaching:* Instr painting, New Sch Social Res; gen critic, Pa Acad Fine Arts. *Awards:* Tamarind Lithography Workshop, Ford Found, 64; Kreeger Purchase Prize, Corcoran Gallery Art, 65; J Henry Scheidt Award, Pa Acad Fine Arts, 69. *Bibliog:* Lippard (auth), Henry Pearson, Art Int, 65. *Mem:* Am Abstract Artists; Century Asn. *Media:* Oil, Watercolor. *Dealer:* Marilyn Pearl Gallery 38 E 57th St New York NY 10022. *Mailing Add:* 1601 Cambridge Dr Kinston NC 28501

PEARSON, JAMES EUGENE
INSTRUCTOR, SCULPTOR
b Woodstock, Ill, Dec 12, 39. *Study:* Northern Ill Univ, BS(educ), 61, MS(educ), MFA, 64; Tyler Sch Art, Temple Univ; Ithaca Col. *Work:* Northern Ill Univ, DeKalb; Palais des Beaux Arts, Charleroi, Belg; Taft Field Campus, Northern Ill Univ, Oregon; Dixon State Sch, Ill; Sch Dist 15, McHenry, Ill. *Comn:* Lorado Taft, Taft Field Campus, Northern Ill Univ, 67; Vicki Unis, Sarasota, Fla, 69; Mae Stinespring, Harry Stinespring, McHenry, Ill, 69; portraits in oils of Mr & Mrs Francis Hightower, comn by Mrs Nancy Langdon, Woodstock, Ill, 71. *Exhib:* 21st Am Drawing Biennial, Norfolk Mus Arts & Sci, Va, 65; 54th Ann Exhib, Art Asn Newport, RI, 65; 2 eme Salon Int de Charleroi, Palais des Beaux Arts, Belg, 69; 5th Int Grand Prix Painting & Etching, Palais de la Scala, Monte Carlo, Monaco, 69; one-man show sculpture, Mitchell Art Mus, Mt Vernon, Ill, 75. *Teaching:* Instr art, Woodstock High Sch, Ill, 61-; instr art, McHenry Co Col, Crystal Lake, Ill, 70- *Awards:* Best of Show Award, William Boyd Andrews, 61; Purchase Prize, Mr & Mrs Allen Leibsohn, 63; Mary E Just Art Award, Waukegan News-Sun, 69. *Bibliog:* F Tramier (auth), James E Pearson, La Rev Mod, 65; Sally Wagner (auth), Volume tells McHenry history, Chicago Tribune, 69. *Mem:* Col Art Asn Am; Ill Art Educ Asn; Ill Craftsmen's Coun; Am Fedn Arts; Centro Studi E Scambi Internazionali, Rome. *Publ:* Illusr, McHenry County 1832-1968, 68; auth, A dream never realized, 69 & Eagle's nest colony, 70, Outdoor Ill; auth, Perspective: outdoor education from an artists point of view, J Outdoor Educ, 71; illusr, The rectangle, 72. *Mailing Add:* 5117 Barnard Mill Rd Ringwood IL 60072

PEARSON, JOHN
PAINTER, INSTRUCTOR
b Boroughbridge, Yorkshire, England, Jan 31, 40. *Study:* Harrogate Col Art, Yorkshire, nat dipl design, 60; Royal Acad Schs, London, cert, 63; Northern Ill Univ, MFA, 66. *Work:* Mus Mod Art, New York; Bochumer Mus, Stuttgart, WGer; Pasadena Mus Fine Art, Calif; Kleye Collection, Doertmund, WGer; Kunstverien, Hannover, WGer. *Exhib:* American Drawing 1963-73, Whitney Mus Am Art, New York; one-man shows, Gray Gallery, Chicago, 67, 68 & 82, Paley & Lowe Gallery, 71; Fischbach Gallery, 74 & 76, New York & Akron Art Mus, 83. *Teaching:* Instr painting, Univ NMex, 66-68; assoc prof painting & head dept, NS Col Art & Design, Halifax, 68-70; int artist in residence, Cleveland Inst Art, Ohio, 70-72; prof art & chmn dept art, Oberlin Col, 72- *Awards:* Can Coun Grant, 70; Cleveland Arts Prize, 75; Nat Endowment Arts, 76. *Bibliog:* Jock Wittet (auth), Editorial, Studio Int, 3/68; Harry Borden (auth), John Pearson, Artforum, 2/72; James R Mellon (auth), article, New York Times, 2/3/75; Edward Henning (auth), The art of John Pearson: an analogy of works of art & general systems, Art Int, 4-5/77. *Publ:* Contribr, Art: The measure of man, Directions 66/67; contribr, article in Mus Educ J, 66. *Dealer:* DBR Gallery 13225 Shaker Square Cleveland OH 44120; Richard Gray Gallery 620 N Michigan Ave Chicago IL 60611. *Mailing Add:* Dept Art Oberlin Col Oberlin OH 44074

PEART, JERRY LINN
SCULPTOR
b Winslow, Ariz, Feb 26, 48. *Study:* Ariz State Univ, BFA(sculpture); Southern Ill Univ, Carbondale, MFA(sculpture). *Comn:* Three large-scale pub sculptures, comn by Dayton Hudson Properties of Minneapolis, Minn for Novi, Mich, Grand Forks, NDak & Las Vegas, Nev; large-scale pub sculpture, comn by Nat Endowment Arts for City of Park Forest South, Ill. *Exhib:* The Chicago Connection, E B Crocker Art Gallery, Sacramento, Calif, 76; The Sculptor, the Campus, and the Prairie, Governors State Univ, Park Forest South, Ill, 76; Masterpieces of Recent Chicago Art, Chicago Pub Libr Cult Ctr, 77; one-man shows, Con Struct Gallery, Chicago, 79 & Riverview Park Comn, City of Chicago, 79. *Awards:* Jeannette Sacks Art Achievement Medal, Ariz State Univ, 70; First Chicago Art Awards for Best Body of Work Over the Yr, Chicago Art Asn, 76-77. *Dealer:* Con Struct 233 E Ontario St Chicago IL 60611. *Mailing Add:* 1544 N Sedgwick St Chicago IL 60610

PEASE, DAVID G
ADMINISTRATOR, PAINTER
b Bloomington, Ill, June 2, 32. *Study:* Univ Wis-Madison, BS, 54, MS, 55, MFA, 58. *Work:* Whitney Mus Am Art, New York; Philadelphia Mus Art; Pa Acad Fine Arts, Philadelphia; Power Gallery, Univ Sydney, Australia; Des Moines Art Ctr, Iowa. *Exhib:* Carnegie Int Exhib Painting & Sculpture, Carnegie Inst, Pittsburgh, 61; Corcoran Biennial Painting, Corcoran Gallery Art, Washington, DC, 61 & 63; Whitney Ann Exhib Painting, Whitney Mus Am Art, New York, 63; Nat Drawing Exhib, San Francisco Mus Art, Calif, 69; Drawings USA, Minn Mus Art, St Paul, 71, 73 & 75. *Pos:* Dean, Tyler Sch Art of Temple Univ, 77-83; dean, Sch Art, Yale Univ, 83- *Teaching:* Prof painting dept painting & sculpture, Tyler Sch Art, Temple Univ, 60-83; prof painting, Yale Univ, 83- *Awards:* William A Clark Award, Corcoran Gallery Art, 63; Guggenheim Fel, 65-66; Childe Hassam Fund Purchase Award, Am Acad Arts & Lett, 70. *Mem:* Col Art Asn Am; Nat Coun Arts Adminr. *Media:* Acrylic, Gouache. *Mailing Add:* 1497 Huntingdon Rd Abington PA 19001

PEASE, ROLAND FOLSOM
CRITIC, COLLECTOR
b Boston, Mass, Dec 11, 21. *Study:* Dartmouth Col; Columbia Univ, BS. *Pos:* Reporter, United Press Int, 52-55; exec ed, Art Voices, 62, assoc ed, 62-63, contrib ed, 63; managing ed, Harry N Abrams, Inc, 63-64; mem, Denhard & Stewart, Inc, New York, currently. *Collection:* Works by Diego Rivera, Grace Hartigan, Larry Rivers, Robert Goodnough, Fairfield Porter, Jane Wilson, Sherman Drexler, Red Grooms, Ron Gorchov, Jane Freilicher, George L K Morris, Nancy Wisseman-Widrig, Ray Ciarrochi, Robert Rauschenberg, Helen Frankenthaler, Elaine de Kooning, Maurice Golubov, Betty Parsons, Stanley Boxer, George Nick, Richard Chiriani, Ann Purcell & Church Magistro. *Publ:* Contribr, art criticisms in Art Int, Metro, Pictures on Exhib & Auth Guild Bulletin. *Mailing Add:* 45 E 72nd St New York NY 10021

PECCHENINO, J RONALD
PAINTER, EDUCATOR
b Murphy, Calif, April 3, 32. *Study:* Col Pac, BA, 56; Calif Col Arts & Crafts, MFA, 69. *Work:* Univ Calif, Chico; Univ Pac. *Comn:* Acrylic lacquer paintings, Hilton Hotel, Stockton, Calif, 81 & Sheraton Hotel, Boston, 83. *Exhib:* Third Ann Art Invitational, Pleasant Hill, Calif, 69; Northern Calif Arts Exhib, Crocker Mus Art, Sacramento, 72; solo exhib, Lyon Art Gallery, San Francisco, 79 & 81. *Pos:* Mem, Art Adv Panel, Calif State Comn, 71-80. *Teaching:* Instr art, Manteca Unified Sch District, Calif, 56-70; prof painting, Univ Pac, 70-, chair art, 83- *Awards:* Purchase Awards, Lodi Ann Exhib, M Neufield & Sons, 68, Third Ann Art Invitational, City Pleasant Hill, 69 & Northern Calif Arts Exhib, Crocker Art Gallery, 72. *Media:* Acrylic Lacquer, Air Brush. *Dealer:* Arteam 3126 A St Loft 4 Boston MA 02210. *Mailing Add:* 5310 Wood Duck Ct Stockton CA 95207

PECHE, DALE C
PAINTER
b Long Beach, Calif, Nov 28, 28. *Study:* Long Beach City Col, BPA; Art Ctr Col Design, Los Angeles; also with Reckless, Tyler, Legakes, Feitelson, Polifka, Williamaoski & Kramer. *Comn:* California City, 73 & Off Highway One, 75, Glendale Fed Savings & Loan Permanent Collection; Wild Blackberries & Hay Barn, McCleary-Cummings, Artists Am Collection, 74. *Exhib:* One-man shows, Challis Galleries, Laguna Beach, Calif, 72, 73 & 74; 149th Nat Acad Design, New York, 74; 206th & 207th Summer Exhib, Royal Acad Arts, London, 74 & 75; 61st Ann Exhib, Allied Artists Am, New York, 74. *Awards:* Two awards, Los Angeles Art Dirs Show, 63 & 70; Pageant of the Oaks Award, 74; Brea Art Asn Award, 75. *Mem:* Nat Watercolor Soc; Allied Artists Am; Royal Soc Arts. *Media:* Gouache. *Mailing Add:* 4330 La Portalada Dr 1390 S Coast Hwy Carlsbad CA 92008

PECK, JAMES EDWARD
PAINTER, DESIGNER
b Pittsburgh, Pa, Nov 7, 07. *Study:* Cleveland Inst Art, cert. *Work:* Cleveland Mus Art, Ohio; US Govt, Carville, La; Dayton Art Inst, Ohio; Am Acad Arts & Lett, New York; Seattle Art Mus, Wash. *Exhib:* Am Watercolor Soc, New York; Seattle Art Mus Northwest Ann; Pepsi-Cola Drawing & Watercolor Exhib, Metrop Mus Art, New York; Dayton Art Inst. *Pos:* Illusr, Fawn Art Studios, Cleveland, 36-46; art dir, Miller, McKay, Hoeck & Hartung, Seattle, 54-60; graphic designer, 60-66; graphic designer, Boeing Co, 66-70. *Teaching:* Head dept art, Cornish Sch, Seattle, 47-52; instr painting & graphic design, Burnley Sch Art, Seattle, 66-76. *Awards:* Awards for watercolors, Dayton Art Inst, 42-45; award for painting, Guggenheim Found, 42 & 46; Seattle Art Mus Awards, var shows & yrs. *Mem:* Puget Sound Group Northwest Painters (past pres). *Media:* Watercolor, Enamel; Wood. *Publ:* Illusr, Ford Times Mag. *Mailing Add:* 19155 130th Ave NE Bothell WA 98011

PECK, JUDITH
SCULPTOR, EDUCATOR
b New York, NY, Dec 31, 30. *Study:* Adelphi Col, BA; Art Students League; Sculpture Ctr, New York; Columbia Univ, MA & EdM; New York Univ, EdD. *Work:* Yale Univ; Ghetto Fighters Mus, Acco, Israel. *Comn:* Monuments, Temple Beth El, Spring Valley, NY, 71; James Richard Elster Mem Courtyard, Tenafly High Sch, NJ, 72 & Temple Oheb Sholom, Baltimore, Md, 75. *Exhib:* 23rd Ann Md Exhib, Baltimore Mus Art, 55; Art USA 58, Madison Sq Garden, 58; 2nd Biennial of Am Painting & Sculpture, Detroit Inst Arts, 60; 155th Ann Exhib Am Painting & Sculpture, Pa Acad Fine Arts, 60; NJ 33rd Ann State Exhib, Montclair Art Mus, 64; 53rd Ann Nat Exhib, Allied Artists of Am, Nat Acad Galleries, NJ, 66; Audubon Artists 21st Ann Nat Exhib, Nat Acad Galleries, New York, 66; solo sculpture shows, Barzansky Galleries, New York, 65, Unicorn Gallery, New York, 75 & 76 & NJ State Mus, Trenton, 78; Reyn Gallery, New York, 78, 81 & 82. *Pos:* Designer/dir, Art on Outside, Ramapo Col NJ, 75-80. *Teaching:* Asst prof art, Rampo Col NJ, 71-, Rockland Community Col, Suffern, NY, 83. *Awards:* First Prize Sculpture, 33rd Ann NJ State Exhib, 64; First Prize Sculpture, Art in the Park, Paterson, NJ, 69; Grants, Art on the Outside, 75, 76, 77. *Bibliog:* Margaret Harold (auth), Prize Winning Sculpture, Book II, Allied Publ, 65; New York Art Yearbook, 76; Mildred Jailer (auth), Ramapo Project Helps Institutionalized, New York Times, 12/75. *Mem:* Author's Guild; Mod Artists Guild; Am Asn Artists/Therapists; Am Art Therapy Asn. *Media:* Wax, Bronze. *Publ:* Auth, Leap to the Sun: Learning through Dynamic Play, Prentice-Hall, 79; Sculpture as Experience, Van Nostrand Reinhold (in publ). *Mailing Add:* 60 Armour Rd Mahwah NJ 07430

PECK, LEE BARNES
JEWELER, EDUCATOR
b Battle Creek, Mich, Sept 21, 42. *Study:* Kellogg Community Col, AA, 63; Western Mich Univ, BS(art educ), 65; Univ Wis, MFA(art metal), 69. *Work:* Johnson Wax Co. *Exhib:* The Goldsmith, Renwick Gallery, Smithsonian Inst, Washington, DC, 74; Am Goldsmiths Now, Washington Univ, St Louis, 78; Sangree De Cristo Art Ctr, Pueblo, Colo, 78; Northeast Mo State Univ, Kirksville, 78; Visual Arts Ctr Alaska, Anchorage, 78; one-man show, Mich Tech Univ, Houghton, 78; Objects 79, Western Colo Arts, 79; and many others. *Teaching:* Assoc prof jewelry & metalwork, Northern Ill Univ, 70-82, prof art, currently; lectr in jewelry, Rosary Col, 72- *Awards:* Lakefront Festival Art Prize, Milwaukee Art Ctr, 75; The Metalsmith Award, Phoenix Art Mus, Ariz, 77; First Prize in Metal, Cooperstown Art Asn, NY, 77. *Mem:* Am Crafts Coun (Ill rep, 72-74); Wis Designer Craftsman; Soc NAm Goldsmiths. *Media:* Precious Metals. *Publ:* Auth & illusr, Jewelry Making, Vol 3, In: Illustrated Libr of Arts & Crafts, 74. *Mailing Add:* 121 Mason Ct Sycamore IL 60178

PECK, STEPHEN ROGERS
INSTRUCTOR, PAINTER
b Cortland, NY, Dec 18, 12. *Study:* Syracuse Univ, BFA(painting), 34; Acad Julian, Paris, fresco painting with Unterstellar, 38. *Comn:* Many portraits. *Teaching:* Instr drawing, Col Fine Arts, Syracuse Univ, 37-42, asst prof drawing & painting, 46-47; instr anat & life drawing, Parsons Sch Design, New York, 47-55; instr anat, Pratt Inst, 52-60; instr drawing, painting & anat, Westchester Art Workshop, White Plains, NY, 62-81; retired. *Mem:* Artists Equity Asn. *Media:* Oil, Pastel. *Publ:* Auth, Atlas of Human Anatomy for the Artist, Oxford Univ Press, 51, Japanese transl, Iwasaki Bijutsu-sha, Tokyo, 80 & Galaxy ed, 82. *Mailing Add:* 55 Sarles Lane Pleasantville NY 10570

PECK, WILLIAM HENRY
CURATOR, HISTORIAN
b Savannah, Ga, Oct 2, 32. *Study:* Ohio State Univ, 50-53; Wayne State Univ, BFA, 60, MA, 61. *Collections Arranged:* Mummy Portraits from Roman Egypt (with catalog), 67, Detroit Collects: Antiquities, 73 & Akhenaten and Nefertiti, 73-74, Detroit Inst Arts; plus many others. *Pos:* Jr cur educ, Detroit Inst Arts, 60-62, asst cur educ, 62-64, assoc cur, 64-68, cur ancient art, 68-; mem, Brooklyn Mus Theban Exped, 78-, assoc field dir, 80- *Teaching:* Lectr art hist, Cranbrook Acad Art, 63-65; adj prof art hist, Wayne State Univ, 66-; vis lectr classics, Univ Mich, 70. *Awards:* Travel Grant, Ford Motor Co, Eng, 62; Am Res Ctr Egypt Fel, 71; Travel Grant, Smithsonian Inst, 75. *Mem:* Am Asn Mus; fel Am Res Ctr Egypt; Cranbrook Acad Art (mem bd gov, 74-); Archaeol Inst Am; Int Asn Egyptologists. *Res:* Ancient Near East and classical world with a particular specialty in Egyptian art and archaeology. *Publ:* Auth, The present state of Egyptian art in Detroit, 12/70 & The arts of the Ancient Near East in Detroit, 7/73, Connoisseur; auth, A seated statue of Amun, J Egyptian Archaeol, 71; auth, The problem of restoration in teaching ancient art, Art J, summer 73; auth, Drawings From Ancient Egypt, Thames & Hudson, 78, German transl, 79, French transl, 80; and others. *Mailing Add:* Detroit Inst of Arts 5200 Woodward Ave Detroit MI 48202

PECKHAM, NICHOLAS
ARCHITECT, EDUCATOR
b Teaneck, NJ, Apr 11, 40. *Study:* US Merchant Marine Acad, BS, 62; Univ Calif, Berkeley, 63; Univ Pa, BArch, 67, MArch, 73, with Louis Kahn, PhD cand with R Buckminster Fuller. *Pos:* Pres, Peckham & Wright Architects, Columbia. *Teaching:* Prof design, Stephens Col, Columbia, 75- *Awards:* Cycle-4 Solar Award & Passive Cycle Award, Dept Housing & Urban Develop; Com Solar Award, Dept Energy. *Mem:* Construct Specifications Inst; Am Inst Architects; Int Solar Energy Soc. *Res:* Optimization in architecture. *Publ:* Auth, Evolution in architecture, Pass-Age, summer 75. *Mailing Add:* 1104 E Broadway Columbia MO 65201

PEEPLES, MAIJA GEGERIS ZACK See Woof, Maija

PEERS, GORDON FRANKLIN
PAINTER, EDUCATOR
b Easton, Pa, Mar 17, 09. *Study:* RI Sch Design, BFA, 33; Art Students League; Beaux-Arts Inst Design; also with John R Frazier; Portland Sch Art, Hon DL, 82. *Work:* RI Sch Design. *Exhib:* Univ Ill; Boston Art Festival, 58; Carnegie Inst, Pittsburgh, Pa; Pa Acad; New York World's Fair; Va Biennial. *Pos:* Chief critic, RI Sch Design Europ Hons Prog, Rome, 61-62. *Teaching:* Head dept painting, RI Sch Design, 34-36 & 38-69, prof painting & chmn div fine arts, 69-73, artist in residence, 74- *Awards:* Prizes, Boston Art Festival, 55 & Newport Art Asn, 56 & 58. *Media:* Oil. *Mailing Add:* 65 Halsey St Providence RI 02906

PEI, I M (IEOH MING)
ARCHITECT, DESIGNER
b Canton, China, Apr 26, 17; US citizen. *Study:* Mass Inst Technol, BArch, 40; Harvard Univ, MArch, 46; Hon DFA degrees from NY Univ, Univ Pa, Rensselaer Polytechnic Inst, Brown Univ & Univ Rochester; DHL degrees from Columbia Univ & Univ Colo; Chinese Univ, Hong Kong, DL. *Comn:* JFK Library, Boston, 79; NY Expos & Conv Ctr, New York, 79-; West Wing, Mus Fine Arts, Boston, 81; Dallas Symphony Hall, 81; Fragrant Hill Hotel, Beijing, China, 82; and others. *Pos:* Head Archit division, Webb & Knapp Inc, New York, 48-55; archit, New York, 55-; mem, Nat Coun Humanities, 66-70; mem, Urban Design Coun, 67-72. *Teaching:* Instr, Harvard Grad Sch Design, 45-48. *Awards:* Gold Medal for Archit, Am Acad Arts & Lett, 79; La Grande Medaille D'Or, Acad Archit, France, 81; Pritzker Archit Prize, 83; and others. *Mem:* Fel Am Inst Architects; Am Acad Arts & Lett (chancellor, 78-80); hon fel Am Soc Interior Designers; Am Acad Arts & Sci; Nat Coun Arts; and others. *Mailing Add:* c/o I M Pei & Partners 600 Madison Ave New York NY 10022

PEII, AHMAD OSNI
SCULPTOR, DESIGNER
b Palembang, Indonesia, Sept 7, 30; US citizen. *Study:* Craft Students League; New Sch Social Res, scholar, 66; Educ Alliance; Haystack Mountain Sch Arts & Crafts; Fairfield Univ. *Work:* Freidus Gallery, New York; New Eng Ctr Contemp Arts, Brooklyn, Conn; Univ Conn Libr, Storrs; Peter Scotese pvt collection, New York; Int Rotary Club, Toronto. *Comn:* Eleven piece sculpture, Johnson & Wales Col, Providence, RI, 79; and others. *Exhib:* Int Art Exhib, Minneapolis/St Paul, 72; American Craft Coun Gallery, New York, 73; Brooklyn Mus, 73; Yonkers Mus, NY, 74; Silvermine Guild, Conn, 74; Wadsworth Antheneum, Hartford, Conn, 78; Slater Mem Mus, Conn; and others. *Pos:* Display consult, Johnson & Wales Col, 79- *Teaching:* Instr sculpture, Craft Students League, New York, 76-77, Johnson & Wales Col, Providence, 79- & New Sch Soc Res, 80. *Awards:* Best Sculpture Award, Artist-Craftsmen of New York Ann Show, 72 & 74; grant, Conn Comn on Arts, 78; Groton Arts Comt Award, Conn, 79; and others. *Bibliog:* Steven Slosberg (auth), Penumbra, New London Day, Conn, 79; Julie Rogers (auth), Hampton sculptor, Willimantic Chronicle, 79; Ruth Lamp Ross (auth), Profile, Norwalk News, Conn, 82. *Mem:* Am Craft Coun; Artists Equity Asn; Sculptors Guild (exhib chmn, 76-). *Media:* Cast & Welded Metals. *Publ:* Auth, Should the public get the art it likes?, Norwich Bulletin, 6/17/79; auth, Art as an elevation of life, Norwalk News, 3/11/82. *Dealer:* Renata Shapiro 60 Sutton Place S New York NY 10022. *Mailing Add:* PO Box 174 Norwalk CT 06856

PEIPERL, ADAM
KINETIC ARTIST, VIDEO ARTIST
b Sosnowiec, Poland, June 4, 35; US citizen. *Study:* George Washington Univ, BS, 57; Pa State Univ, 57-59. *Work:* Nat Mus Am Hist, Nat Mus Am Art & John F Kennedy Ctr Performing Arts, Washington DC; Pa Acad Fine Arts, Philadelphia; Boymans-Van Beuningen Mus, Rotterdam, Holland. *Exhib:* Corcoran Gallery Art, 68; one-man shows, Baltimore Mus Art, 69, Pa Acad Fine Arts, 69, Nat Mus Am Hist, 72-73, Philadelphia Art Alliance, 78, Nat Mus Am Art, 81; Mem Art Gallery, Univ Rochester, 78; Inst Contemp Art, Boston, 73. *Awards:* Popular Award & Special Prize, 82, Silver Medal, 83, Int Platform Asn Art Show. *Bibliog:* Frank Getlein (auth), He defied tradition and made it work, Sun Star, 7/21/68; Diane Chichura & Thelma Stevens (auths), Super Sculpture, Van Nostrand-Reinhold, 74; Victoria Donohoe (auth), Kinetic art lives on, Philadelphia Inquirer, 10/27/78. *Media:* Miscellaneous. *Dealer:* Richard Mann Gallery Los Angeles CA. *Mailing Add:* 1135 Loxford Terr Silver Spring MD 20901

PEKAR, RONALD WALTER
PAINTER, SCULPTOR
b Cleveland, Ohio, Oct 9, 42. *Study:* Cleveland Inst Art; Wash Univ, BFA, fel, 66-67, MFA. *Work:* Ark State Univ; Miss Art Asn, Jackson; Carroll Reece Mus, ETenn State Univ; State Tenn Arts Comn Collection, Nashville; Brooks Mem Art Gallery, Memphis. *Comn:* Tommy stage design, Memphis State Univ, 70; illuminated painting, Gen Pub Utilities, Pa, 72; two 3-story illuminated sculptures, Lemoyne-Owen Col, 73; mural, St Jude Children's Res Hosp, 74; two urban wall graphics, CofC, Memphis, 74-75. *Exhib:* Young Light Artists 68, Gallery Loretto-Hilton Ctr, Webster Col, St Louis, 68; one-man shows, Miss Art Asn, 69 & Brooks Mem Art Gallery, Memphis, 73; EAT/ATL 69 & 70, Exp in Art & Technol, High Art Mus, Atlanta, Ga, 69-70; Artrain-Southeastern Tour, Nat Endowment Arts Southern Growth Policies Bd, Research Triangle Park, NC, 74; Memphis Pink Palace Mus Commemorative Painting, 77; Spirit of the River (audio/visual environment), Brooks Mem Art Gallery, 77-78. *Pos:* Floor dir, KMOX-TV CBS, St Louis, 64-67; visual arts lectr, WKNO-TV, Memphis, 73- *Teaching:* Studio asst to Prof Arthur Osver, Wash Univ, 65-67, teaching asst, 66; dir workshop oil painting, Tenn Arts Comn, Jackson, 70, dir workshop watercolor, Arts & Crafts Guild, Helena, Ark, 74; prof painting, Memphis Acad Arts, 67- *Media:* Photography; Audio/Visual. *Publ:* Illusr, Air poster, Memphis Acad Arts, 69; illusr rec label, Ardent Rec, 72; ed & illusr, Homage to the Land and Sky, 73; illusr rec label, Privilege Rec, 74. *Mailing Add:* Memphis Acad Arts Memphis TN 38112

PEKARSKY, MEL (MELVIN HIRSCH)
PAINTER, EDUCATOR
b Chicago, Ill, Sept 18, 34. *Study:* Art Inst of Chicago; Northwestern Univ, BA, MA. *Work:* Corcoran Gallery of Art, Washington, DC; Indianapolis Mus of Art; Columbus Gallery of Fine Arts, Ohio; Weatherspoon Mus, Univ NC; Yale Univ Mus Fine Arts. *Comn:* Exterior murals, Kaplan Fund, 70 & US Dept Housing & Urban Develop, 74. *Exhib:* Oversize Prints, Whitney Mus of Am Art, New York, 71; Am Prints, Brooklyn Mus, NY, 74-75; Am Prints, San Diego Fine Arts Gallery, Calif, 75; New Editions 74-75, New York Cult Ctr, 75; Drawings by Seven Am Artists, Cleveland Mus, 78; one-man shows, G W Einstein, New York, 75, 77, 78, 80 & 81 & Gallery 112 Green St, New York, 80; The Am Landscape, Recent Developments, Whitney Mus Am Art, New York, 81; and others. *Pos:* Founding mem & mem bd, City Walls, Inc, 69-75, vpres, 70-75. *Teaching:* From asst to assoc dean art, Sch of Visual Arts, New York, 67-69; prof art, State Univ, NY, Stony Brook, 75-, chmn, 76-78, dir studio programs, 75-78. *Bibliog:* Ann Lockhart (auth), Mel Pekarsky, Arts Mag, 3/78; Ronny Cohen (auth), Mel Pekarsky, Arts, 10/82; and others. *Mem:* Col Art Asn. *Media:* Oil and mixed media drawings. Interest: Painting, public art. *Publ:* Illusr, The Curious Cow, 60, Little Quack, 61, The Three Goats, 63, & The Little Red Hen, 63, Follett; illusr, Handbook of Gestures, Mouton, The Hague, 72. *Dealer:* G W Einstein Co Inc Fine Art 243 E 82nd St New York NY 10028. *Mailing Add:* Ashley Lane Shoreham NY 11786

PELADEAU, MARIUS BEAUDOIN
WRITER, MUSEUM DIRECTOR
b Boston, Mass, Jan 27, 35. *Study:* St Michael's Col, Winooski Park, Vt, BA(cum laude), 56; Boston Univ, Mass, MS, 57; Georgetown Univ, Washington, DC, MA(fel), 61. *Pos:* Dir, Maine League of Hist Soc & Mus, 72-76; dir, William A Farnsworth Libr & Art Mus, 76- *Mem:* Am Asn Mus; New Eng Mus Asn; New Eng Doc Conserv Ctr. *Res:* American art and the decorative arts. *Publ:* Ed, The Verse of Royall Tyler, Univ Va Press, 68; ed, The Prose of Royall Tyler, Vt Hist Soc, 72; auth, Chansonetta: The Photographs of Chansonetta Stanley Emmons, 1858-1937, Morgan & Morgan, 77; auth, Stephen R Deane: Early Maine Folk Calligrapher, Kennebec River Press, 84. *Mailing Add:* Box 466 Rockland ME 04841

PELLAN (ALFRED)
PAINTER
b Quebec City, Can, May 16, 26. *Study:* Ecole des Beaux Arts, Quebec City, grad, 20. *Work:* Mus Nat d' Art Mod, Paris; Mus Grenoble, France; Que Mus, Quebec City; Nat Gallery Can, Ottawa; Montreal Mus Fine Arts, PQ. *Comn:* Painting, Winnipeg Airport, Man, 63; stained glass, La Place des Arts, Montreal, 63; stained glass, Church Saint Theophile, Laval-Quest, PQ, 64; two paintings, Nat Libr & Archives, Ottawa, 67; polychromy of bldgs, Vt Constructions Inc, Laval City, 68. *Exhib:* Retrospectives, Mus Nat d'Art Mod, Paris, 55; Hall of Hon, Montreal, PQ, 56 & Nat Gallery Can, Art Gallery Toronto & Montreal Mus Fine Arts, 60-61; one-man shows, Musee Que, Laval Univ & Galerie de Montreal, 72; and many others. *Teaching:* Instr painting, Ecole Beaux Arts, Montreal, 43-52; instr painting, Art Centre Sainte Adele, PQ, summer 57. *Awards:* Centenary Medal, Can Confederation, 68; Prix Philippe Hebert, Soc Jean Baptiste, 72; Molson Prize, 73. *Bibliog:* A letter from Gilles Toupin, Artscanada, 11-12/72; Germain Lefebrere (auth), Pellan, Toronto, 73; The tale of the comet, Vie des Arts, autumn 75. *Mem:* Soc Artistes Prof Que; Royal Can Acad Arts. *Media:* Oil. *Publ:* Contribr, Les iles de la nuit, Parizeau Ed, 44; contribr, Le voyage d'Arlequin, Cahiers File Indienne, 46. *Dealer:* La Guilde Graphique 4677 St-Denis Montreal PQ Can; Galerie l'Art Francais 370 Ouest Laurier Montreal PQ Can. *Mailing Add:* 649 Des Mille-Iles Blvd Auteuil Laval PQ H7L 1K5 Canada

PELLETTIERI, MICHAEL JOSEPH
PRINTMAKER, PAINTER
b New York, NY, Nov 25, 43. *Study:* Art Students League New York, with Robert B Hale, Edwin Dickinson, Harry Sternberg & Joseph Hirsch, 63-66; City Col New York, BA, 65; City Univ New York, MA, 69. *Work:* De Cordova Mus, Lincoln, Mass; Taz Gallery & Co, Boston; Newark Art Libr, NJ; Ben Goldstein Collection, New York; and others. *Exhib:* Boston Printmakers 32nd Nat, De Cordova Mus, Lincoln, Mass, 79; Hunterdon Art Ctr 23rd & 25th, Newark Art Libr, NJ, 79 & 81; Nat Acad & Inst Arts & Letters, 80; Charlotte Printmakers, NC, 81; and others. *Teaching:* Instr lithography, Art Students League New York, 77-79, instr graphics, 79-, instr intaglio, Summit Art Ctr, 82- *Awards:* John Taylor Arms Award, Audubon Artists 37th, Joseph R Fazzano, 79; Strathmore Paper Co Award, Boston Printmakers 32nd, 79; Grumbacher Silver Medallion, Audubon Artists, 82. *Bibliog:* Garry Simpson (auth), Currier & Ives (film for television), Univ Vt, 76. *Mem:* Audubon Artists; Artist Equity New York; Art Students League New York (bd control, 65, treas, 66-67); Philadelphia Print Club. *Media:* Intaglio, Lithography; Oil. *Publ:* Contribr, Print Review Ten, Pratt Graphic Art Ctr, 79. *Dealer:* Anna Comolli 4 Gibbon Ave Milford MA 01757; Miriam Pearlman Inc Suite 5410 505 N Lake Shore Dr Chicago IL 60611. *Mailing Add:* 325 W 77th St New York NY 10024

PELLEW, JOHN CLIFFORD
PAINTER
b Heamoor, Eng, Apr 9, 03; US citizen. *Study:* Penzance Sch Art, Eng. *Work:* Metrop Mus Art, New York; Butler Inst Am Art, Youngstown, Ohio; Ga Mus Fine Arts, Athens; Adelphi Col, NY; New Brit Mus Am Art, Conn; and others. *Exhib:* Nat Acad Design, New York, 48-72; Butler Inst Am Art, Youngstown, Ohio, 64; 200 Years of Watercolor Painting in America, Metrop Mus Art, New York, 67; Landscape 1, De Cordova & Dana Mus, Lincoln, Mass, 70; Am Watercolor Soc Exchange Exhib, Can, 72. *Awards:* Adolph & Clara Obrig Prize, Nat Acad Design, 61; First Award Watercolor, Butler Inst Am Art, 64; Silver Medal, Am Watercolor Soc, 70. *Bibliog:* Norman Kent (auth), Watercolor Methods, Watson-Guptill, 55; Wendon Blake (auth), Complete Guide to Acrylic Painting, Watson-Guptill, 71. *Mem:* Nat Acad Design; Am Watercolor Soc; Allied Artists Am; Southwestern Watercolor Soc. *Media:* Watercolor, Oil. *Publ:* Auth, Acrylic Landscape Painting, 68; Painting in Watercolor, 69; Oil Painting Outdoors, 71; Painting Maritime Landscapes, 73. *Dealer:* Grand Central Art Galleries 40 Vanderbilt Ave New York NY 10017. *Mailing Add:* 123 Murray St Norwalk CT 06851

PELLI, CESAR
ARCHITECT
b Tucuman, Arg, Oct 12, 26; US citizen. *Study:* Univ Tucuman, Dipl in Archit(cum laude), 49; Univ Ill, MS(archit), 54. *Comn:* Indiana Tower, White River Park, Indianapolis, 80; Battery Park, New York, 81; World Financial Ctr, New York, 81; Herring Hall, Rice Univ, Houston, Tex, 82; Norwest Ctr, Minneapolis, 83. *Exhib:* Houses for Sale, Castelli Galleries, New York, 80; Late Entries, Chicago Tribune Competition, Ill, 80; Art & Archit Exhib, New York, 80; Lingotto-Fiat Proposal, Turin, Italy, 83. *Pos:* Designer, Eero Saarinen & Assoc, 54-64; dir & vpres design, Daniel Mann, Johnson & Mendenhall, 64-68; partner in charge of design, Gruen Assoc, Los Angeles & New York, 68-77; partner, Cesar Pelli & Assoc, New Haven, 77- *Teaching:* Dean, Sch Archit, Yale Univ, 77- *Awards:* First Prize, Int Archit Competition, United Nations City, Repub of Austria, City of Vienna, 69;

Honor Award, Pac Design Ctr, 76. *Bibliog:* Moholy-Nagy, Sybil (auth), Cesar Pelli: Public Architect, Spec Publ; Walter Wagner (ed), Architectural Record, US Embassy, Tokyo, 4/77; John Pasher (auth), Cesar Tilli, Whitney Libr Design, 82. *Mem:* fel Am Inst Archit; Am Acad & Inst Arts & Lett. *Publ:* auth, Open line city, Progressive Archit, 6/70; auth, Eero Saarinen, 1/79, Philip Johnson, 6/79 & Joseph Paxton's Crystal Palace, 2/80, Architecture & Urbanism; auth, Skyscrapers, Perspecta #19, 81. *Mailing Add:* 1056 Chapel St New Haven CT 06510

PELLICONE, MARIE
GALLERY DIRECTOR
b New York, NY. *Study:* Fordham Univ, BA(Eng). *Pos:* Dir, Marie Pellicone Gallery, New York, 76- *Specialty:* Paintings, sculptor drawings and contemporary prints. *Mailing Add:* 47 Bond St Gallery New York NY 10012

PELLICONE, WILLIAM
PAINTER, MURALIST
b Philadelphia, Pa, Apr 12, 15. *Study:* Pa Acad Fine Arts, Philadelphia; Barnes Found, Merion, Pa. *Work:* Boston Mus, Mass; Smithsonian Inst, Washington, DC; Am Broadcasting Co, NY. *Comn:* Murals, Abraham & Strauss, Brooklyn, NY, 69 & 70. *Exhib:* Pa Acad Fine Arts, 39; Nat Acad Design, New York, 39; Woodmere Art Gallery & Art Alliance, Philadelphia; Baltimore Mus, 71. *Media:* Oil. *Publ:* Auth, reviews & critiques for ArtSpeak Publ, New York & Dan's Papers, Bridgehampton, NY. *Dealer:* Capricorn Gallery 8003 Woodmont Ave Bethesda MD 20014; Allan Stone Gallery 48 E 86th St New York NY 10028. *Mailing Add:* 47 Bond St New York NY 10012

PELS, ALBERT
PAINTER, ADMINISTRATOR
b Cincinnati, Ohio, May 7, 10. *Study:* Art Acad Cincinnati; Univ Cincinnati; Beaux Arts Sch; Art Students League, six scholarships; also with Thomas Hart Benton, Kenneth Hayes Miller & Bridgeman. *Work:* Butler Inst Am Art; NY State Mus Art; Smithsonian Inst, Washington, DC; West Moreland Mus Art, Greensburg, Pa. *Comn:* The Landing of the Swedes, Courthouse, Wilmington, Del, 42; Early History of Normal, Ill, in post off; Africa scene for ship, North African Line, 50; History of Norfolk, Va, for naval base; gen hist of Anniston, Ala area, YMCA. *Exhib:* Whitney Mus Am Art Ann, 40-50; Carnegie Int Exhib, 42-48; Nat Acad Design, 45-52; Butler Inst Am Art Ann, 45-55; Chicago Ann, 49; Cincinnati Mus world tour; and many other group & one-man shows. *Pos:* Dir & owner, Albert Pels Sch Art Inc, 72-; demonstr oil painting on educ TV. *Teaching:* Instr art, Jones Mem Sch & Hessian Hills Sch; instr fine art, Albert Pels Sch Art, Inc, 46- *Awards:* First Prize for Sea Disaster, Butler Inst Am Art, 46; Schackenberg Scholar, 49. *Media:* Mixed. *Publ:* Contribr, Art News, 46; illusr, Easy puppets, 52 & Water pets, 56. *Dealer:* Gorwit Galleries Roslyn NY 11576; Rainone Art Galleries 1212 Park Row Arlington TX 76013. *Mailing Add:* 2109 Broadway New York NY 10023

PEN, RUDOLPH
PAINTER
b Chicago, Ill, Jan 1, 18. *Study:* Art Inst Chicago; BFA; also Europe, SAm, Mex & NAfrica. *Work:* Davenport Mus, Iowa; Libr of Cong, Washington, DC; Philadelphia Mus, Pa; Vincent Price Collection; Art Inst Chicago. *Exhib:* Carnegie Inst, Pittsburgh, 46; Contemp Artists Exhib, Art Inst Chicago, 61-; Watercolor Print Exhib, Pa Acad Fine Arts, Philadelphia; Am Watercolor Soc, Nat Acad Design, New York; Corcoran Gallery Art, Washington, DC. *Pos:* Pres, Alumni Asn, Art Inst Chicago, 60-62; dir, Summer Sch Painting, 64-65. *Teaching:* Asst prof painting, Art Inst Chicago, 48-63; dir pvt sch, 63- *Awards:* Huntington Hartford Found Grant, 58; Ryerson Traveling Fel, 63; plus many others. *Bibliog:* Marilyn Hoffman (auth), Art, Christian Sci Monitor, 1/3/51; Kay Loring (auth), Pen named director of art school, 7/24/64 & Edith Weigle (auth), Art critic, 11/28/65, Chicago Tribune. *Mem:* Am Watercolor Soc; Arts Club Chicago; hon mem Union League Civic & Arts Found. *Media:* Oil, Watercolor. *Publ:* Auth, Whipping boy or cultural spokesman, 54 & The tongue is quicker than the mind, 66, Art League; auth, Artist-teacher blasts tycoons and pretenders, Chicago Sun Times, 71. *Dealer:* Art Inst Sales & Rental Gallery S Michigan & E Adams Chicago IL 60603. *Mailing Add:* 55 W Schiller St Chicago IL 60610

PENA, AMADO MAURILIO, JR
PAINTER, ILLUSTRATOR
b Laredo, Tex, Oct 1, 43. *Study:* Tex A&I Univ, BA(art), 65, MA, 71. *Work:* Tex A&I Univ; Dept Foreign Lang, Univ Ky; Univ Tex, Austin; Juarez-Lincoln Univ, Austin; Los Pinos, Pres Palace, Mexico. *Comn:* Mural, Laredo Independent Sch Dist, Serv Ctr, 70; mural, City Hall, Crystal City, 72; painting, City Coun Crystal City, 72; centennial poster, Univ Tex, Austin, 83; Amarille Art Ctr, Tex, 83; and others. *Exhib:* Chicago Art Exhib, Nat Lulac Conf, Washington, DC, 73 & Univ Tex Student Ctr, 74; Chicano Artists of the Southwest, Inst Mex Cult, San Antonio, 75; one-man retrospectives, Mus Nuevo Santander, Laredo, Tex, 83 & Laguna Gloria Art Mus, Austin, Tex, 83; and others. *Teaching:* Teacher art, Laredo Independent Sch Dist, 65-71; Crystal City Independent Sch Dist, 71-73 & L C Anderson High Sch, Austin, 73- *Awards:* Citation Award, Laguna Gloria Art Mus, 68; Corpus Christi Art Found Award, 69; Rio Grande Art Festival Award, Laredo Art Asn, 71, 72 & 74. *Bibliog:* Kelly Fearing (auth), Art & the Creative Teacher, Univ Tex, 69; Jacinto Quirarte (auth), The Art of Mexican Americans, The Humble Way, Exxon Oil Co, 69 & Mexican American Artists, Univ Tex, 73. *Mem:* Laredo Art Asn (pres, 68-69); Austin Art Teachers Asn (treas, 74-75). *Media:* Serigraphy; Watercolor. *Publ:* Contribr & auth, Chicano Art of the Southwest, Chicano Slide Collection, 73; contribr, Tejidos, Magazin & Calendario Chicano; illusr, Cuenots, 75. *Dealer:* El Taller Gallery 723 E Sixth St Austin TX 78701; Gallery Mack Seattle WA. *Mailing Add:* 11511 Catalonia Austin TX 78759

PENCE, JOHN GERALD
DEALER, PATRON
b Ft Wayne, Ind, Feb 8, 36. *Study:* Wabash Col, BA(econ), 58; Am Univ, MA(int relations), 63. *Collections Arranged:* Douglas Fenn Wilson, Worcester Mus, Dartmouth Col, Janus Gallery, Santa Fe, San Francisco Mus, Hibernia Bank, San Francisco & Deloitee, Haskins, Sells, New York; Michael Bergt, Pence Gallery, San Francisco & San Francisco Mus; Frank Mason, Clorox Co & Pence Gallery, San Francisco; Robert Maione, Pence Gallery, San Francisco, Clorox Co, Standard Oil of Calif, Hering & Assoc, Portland & Allen-Pacific Co, San Francisco; Gillian Wiles, Pence Gallery, San Francisco & URS Corp, Dallas; Donald Davis, Cellocon Inc, San Francisco, Deloitee, Haskins, Sells, New York & James Malott Architects; Will Wilson, Buckeye Petroleum, NJ & Butler Inst Am Art. *Interests:* American contemporary realists--advance support prior to initial presentations. *Publ:* Auth, Will Wilson, Am Artist Mag, 5/83. *Mailing Add:* Pence Gallery 550 Suttor St San Francisco CA 94102

PENCZNER, PAUL JOSEPH
PAINTER
b Hungary, Sept 17, 16; US citizen. *Study:* In Hungary & Austria. *Work:* Vatican, Rome; Capitol Bldg, Jefferson City; Univ Tenn, Memphis; Univ Mo, Cape Girardeau; Fla State Univ, Talahassee. *Exhib:* Pa Acad Fine Arts, Philadelphia; Brooks Mem Art Gallery, Memphis; Jersey City Mus; Smithsonian Inst, Washington, DC; El Delgado Mus, New Orleans; Tenn Botanical Gardens & Fine Art Ctr, Nashville. *Teaching:* Owner & dir, Penczner's Fine Art Sch, Memphis. *Mem:* Nat Soc Painters Casein; Tenn Watercolor Soc; Am Artist Prof League; Southern Watercolor Soc. *Media:* Multimedia. *Dealer:* Round Corner Gallery 1684 Poplar Ave Memphis TN 38104; Forest Hill Gallery 9076 Old Poplar Pike Germantown TN 38138. *Mailing Add:* 2383 Strathmore Circle Memphis TN 38112

PENDERGRAFT, NORMAN ELVEIS
MUSEUM DIRECTOR, HISTORIAN
b Durham, NC, Mar 4, 34. *Study:* Univ NC, Chapel Hill; Conservatorio di Musica G Rossini, Pesaro, Italy, with Maestra Raggi-Valentini; Mus Mgt Inst, Univ Calif, Berkeley. *Pos:* Art reviewer, Durham Sun, 75-; dir art mus, NC Cent Univ, Durham, 76- *Teaching:* Assoc prof art hist, NC Cent Univ, Durham, 66- *Mem:* Am Asn Mus; Southeastern Mus Coun; Col Art Asn; NC Mus Coun. *Res:* Italian Renaissance, Afro-American and American art. *Publ:* Auth, Heralds of Life: Artis, Bearden & Burke, NC Cent Univ Mus Art, 77; auth, Tracing the rise of Afro-American art in North Carolina, & other articles in Art Voices/South; auth, On tour in Winston-Salem North Carolina, Am Artist, 10/81. *Mailing Add:* 208 Watts St Durham NC 27701

PENDLETON, MARY CAROLINE
HANDWEAVER, WRITER
. b Rochester, Ind. *Study:* Dayton Art Inst, Ohio; Cranbrook Acad Art; also with Lili Blumenau & Mary Meigs Atwater. *Comn:* Over the years, many pieces for pvt homes, bus & churches such as drapery fabrics, upholstery, dividers & paraments. *Exhib:* Int Textile Exhib, Woman Col, Univ NC, 52 & 54; Ann Women's Int Expos, New York, 59 & 60; Crafts Western US, Southern Calif Expos, Del Mar, 61; one-man show, Charles W Bowers Mem Mus, Santa Ana, 65; two-man show, Stanford Med & Res Inst, 63; Six Craftsmen Exhib, Heard Mus, Phoenix, Ariz, 63. *Pos:* Mem bd dirs, Handweavers Guild Am, 70; auth & ed, The Looming Arts, Nat Handweavers. *Teaching:* Teacher handweaving, Pendleton Fabric Craft Sch, 58-; weaving instr, Northern Ariz Univ, Flagstaff, 76-81; teach workshops all over the country. *Awards:* Int Textile Exhib, Women's Col, Univ NC, 52; Contemporary Craftsmen Far West, Mus Contemp Crafts, 62; Ariz State Fair, 62. *Bibliog:* Isabel Stroud (auth), Couple finds weaving and full-time career, Christian Sci Monitor, 1/6/75. *Mem:* Nat League Am Pen Women; Ariz Designer Craftsmen; Am Crafts Coun. *Publ:* Auth, Navajo & Hopi Weaving Techniques, Macmillan, 74; auth, Double Weave Series, 74 & Overshot Weave Series, 77. *Mailing Add:* PO Box 233 Sedona AZ 86336

PENKOFF, RONALD PETER
EDUCATOR, PAINTER
b Toledo, Ohio, May 18, 32. *Study:* Bowling Green State Univ, BFA, 54; Ohio State Univ, MA, 56; Stanley William Hayter's Atelier 17, Paris, 65-66. *Work:* Libr Cong, Washington, DC; Columbus Gallery Art, Ohio; Munson-Williams-Proctor Inst, Utica, NY; Montclair Mus, NJ; Ball State Art Gallery, Muncie, Ind. *Exhib:* Pennell Int English Prints, Libr Cong, Washington, DC, 55-57; Notre Dame Mus, 70; Skylight Gallery, 73; Madison Art Ctr, 75; Alvejihem Mus, 77 & 83; Milwaukee Art Mus, 78. *Teaching:* Asst prof art, State Univ NY Col, Oneonta, 56-59; asst prof, Ball State Univ, 59-67; vis prof, Bath Acad Art, Corsham, England, summer 66; prof, Univ Wis, Waukesha, 67-, chmn, Ctr Syst Art Dept, 70- *Awards:* Munson-Williams-Proctor Inst Award, Cent NY Artists, 58-59; First Award Painting, Eastern Ind Artists, 64; Nat Endowment Humanities Grant, 78. *Bibliog:* W Fabricki (auth), Prints and drawings of Ronald Penkoff, Quartet, 63; M E Young (auth), Profile, Wis Acad Rev, 69; Donald Key (auth), Color printing is an elusive endeavor, Milwaukee J, 71. *Media:* Intaglio. *Publ:* Auth, The eye and the object, Forum, 62; auth, Roots of the Ukiyo-E, 65; auth, Sign, Signal, Symbol, 70. *Mailing Add:* 1500 University Dr Waukesha WI 53186

PENN, IRVING
PHOTOGRAPHER
b NJ, 17. *Work:* Mus Mod Art & Metrop Mus Art, New York; Art Inst Chicago; Victoria & Albert Mus, London. *Exhib:* One-man shows, Mus Mod Art, New York, 75, Galleria Civica D'Arte Moderna, Torino, 75 & Metrop Mus Art, New York, 77. *Publ:* Auth, Moments Preserved, 60; auth, Worlds in a Small Room, 74; auth, Inventive Paris clothes, 1909-1939, 77; auth, Flowers, 80. *Mailing Add:* c/o Irving Penn Studios PO Box 934 FDR Station New York NY 10150

PENNEY, BRUCE BARTON
PAINTER
b Laconia, NH, Aug 9, 29. *Study:* Worcester Mus Sch; Cleveland Woodward, illusr; with Eldon Rowland, Well Fleet, Mass; New York-Phoenix Sch Design. *Work:* Worcester Polytech Inst, Mass; Stockholm Mus, Sweden; Dartmouth Col, Hanover, NH. *Exhib:* Hanover Gallery, NH; Southern Vt Art Asn, Manchester, 67; one-man shows, Wiener Gallery, New York, 68, Center St Gallery, Winter Park, Fla, 69 & Gallery 2, Woodstock, Vt, 69-71. *Awards:* Creative Communication's Award, Art Inst of Boston, 76. *Media:* Oil. *Dealer:* Hobe Sound North Galleries One Milk St Portland MA 04101; Center St Gallery 136 Park Ave S Winter Park FL 32789. *Mailing Add:* 27 West St Portland ME 04102

PENNEY, CHARLES RAND
COLLECTOR, PATRON
b Buffalo, NY, July 26, 23. *Study:* Yale Univ, BA; Univ Va, LLB & JD. *Collections Arranged:* Prints from the Charles Rand Penney Found, traveling NY & Tex, 64-75; Selections from the Charles R Penney Collection, Lakeview Gallery, NY, 70; Prints From the Charles Rand Penney Foundation, Niagara Co Community Col Mus, 71 & 77; Staffordshire Pottery Portrait Figures, Niagara Co Hist Soc, 72; 44 Charles Burchfield Drawings & two paintings, Charles Burchfield Ctr, Buffalo, 73; Decade, Graphics in the Sixties, 74; NY State Photographers, 74; Victorian Staffordshire Figurines, Carborundum Mus of Ceramics, Niagara Falls, 74 & Columbus Gallery of Fine Arts, Ohio, 76; Charles Burchfield: The Charles Rand Penney Collection, traveling throughout US, 78-81; The Graphic Art of Emil Ganso, Univ Iowa Mus Art, 79; The Charles Rand Penney Collection: Twentieth Century Art, traveling throughout US. *Awards:* Distinguished Service to Culture Award, State Univ NY Col Potsdam, 83. *Mem:* Smithsonian Inst, Washington, DC; Am Ceramic Circle; hon life mem Rochester Art Club; Gallery Asn NY; hon trustee Buffalo Soc Artists; and many others. *Collection:* International contemporary art; works of Charles E Burchfield and Emil Ganso; Western New York artists; Spanish-American Santos and Retablos; Victorian Staffordshire pottery portrait figures; American antique historic glass and textiles; American antique pressed glass; international primitive art. *Mailing Add:* 538 Bewley Bldg Lockport NY 14094

PENNEY, JACQUELINE
PAINTER, INSTRUCTOR
b Roslyn, NY, Mar 26, 30. *Study:* Phoenix Sch Design, New York, 48; Black Mountain Col, 49; Inst Design, Chicago, 50. *Work:* Port Authority, World Trade Ctr, New York; Stony Brook Sch, NY; Eastern Long Island Hosp, Greenport, NY; Unitarian Universalist Church Oak Park, Ill. *Exhib:* Me (self portraits), Heckscher Mus, Huntington, NY, 81; Still Life on a Checkered Tablecloth, Parrish Art Mus, Southampton, NY, 81; Blue, Nat Soc Painters in Casein & Acrylic, New York, 82; Printer's Devil, Salmagundi Club, New York, 82; Still Life After Death, Heckscher Mus, Huntington, NY, 81. *Teaching:* Art classes all media, 77- *Awards:* Award Excellence, Locust Valley Art Show, 76; First Prize, East End Arts Open Competition, 80, 81 & 82 & Gallery 21, WLIW-TV, 82. *Bibliog:* Kathleen Sullivan (auth), Scream painting, Sun Newspaper, 1/28/82; Paul Demery (auth), An artist dreams in Cutchogue, Long Island Traveler-Watchman, 3/17/83. *Mem:* Artist Equity New York. *Media:* Acrylic, Watercolor. *Publ:* Auth, A painting in progress-- from far to near, Palette Talk Mag, 81. *Dealer:* Gallery East 257 Pantigo Rd East Hampton NY 11937. *Mailing Add:* 270 North St PO Box 10 Cutchogue NY 11935

PENNINGTON, MARY ANNE
MUSEUM DIRECTOR, EDUCATOR
b Franklin, Va, Apr 12, 43. *Study:* Va Commonwealth Univ, BFA, MFA, 66. *Collections Arranged:* Work Prog Admin Graphics Collection, 82; For the Sake of a Single Verse, 84. *Pos:* Exec dir, Greenville Mus Art, NC, 80-; columnist, Pitt-Greenville Times, 81- *Teaching:* Instr art, Presby Col, 66-70; asst prof sculpture & art hist, Pembroke State Univ, 76-80. *Mem:* Am Asn Mus; Southeastern Mus Conf; NC Mus Coun. *Publ:* Auth, Sand casting in sculpture, Foundry, 7/67; auth, Art in eastern NC, Carolina Arts, summer 81. *Mailing Add:* PO Box 8022 Greenville NC 27835

PENNUTO, JAMES WILLIAM
CONCEPTUAL ARTIST, CONSERVATOR
b Joliet, Ill, June 15, 36. *Study:* Art Students League. *Work:* Oakland Mus, Calif; San Francisco Mus Mod Art. *Exhib:* Butler Inst Am Art, Youngstown, Ohio, 66-67; Oakland Mus, 69-70; Mus Mod Art, New York, 70; St John's Univ, New York, 70; Joslyn Art Mus, Omaha, Nebr, 70; San Francisco Mus Mod Art, 71. *Bibliog:* Palmer French (auth), San Francisco, Artforum, 2/70; New dimensions, Time, 4/13/70; Carter Ratcliff (auth), Report from San Francisco, Art in Am, 5-6/77. *Media:* Miscellaneous. *Mailing Add:* 500A Cole San Francisco CA 94117

PENNY, AUBREY JOHN ROBERT
PAINTER, GALLERY DIRECTOR
b London, Eng, July 30, 17; US citizen. *Study:* Univ Calif, Los Angeles, BA(art & art hist), 53, MA(art), 55. *Work:* Contemp Art Soc, London; Edward Dean Mus, Cherry Valley, Calif; Mt San Jacinto Col Gallery Art. *Exhib:* Corcoran Gallery Art, Washington, DC, 57; Am Watercolor Soc, New York, 57-58; two-man shows, Madison Gallery, New York, 63 & Int De Deauville, France, 72; one-man shows, Mt San Jacinto Col, Calif, 72 & 82; Los Angeles Inst Contemp Art, 81. *Pos:* Owner, Aubrey Penny Fine Art, Los Angeles, 55-; mem art coun, Univ Calif, Los Angeles, 55- *Awards:* Award of merit, Nat Watercolor Soc, 55; Gold Seal Award, Los Angeles Inst Contemp Art, 81. *Mem:* Contemp Art Soc, London; Victoria Inst, London; Am Soc

Aesthetics & Art Criticism; Los Angeles Inst Contemp Art. *Media:* Acrylic. *Publ:* Auth, The Mind-Line Approach of Aubrey Penny, 76; auth, Sculpture-Halcyon Series, 79 & Geneva Series, 80. *Mailing Add:* c/o Penny Fine Art 16134 Sherman Way Van Nuys CA 91406

PENNY, DONALD CHARLES
CRAFTSMAN, EDUCATOR
b Atlanta, Ga, Oct 5, 35. *Study:* Ga Inst Technol, 57-58; Ga State Univ, with Joe Perrin & Joe Almyda, BBA, 61; Fla State Univ, with Karl Zerbe & Ralph Hurst, MS, 63. *Work:* Middle Tenn State Univ, Murfreesboro; Metrop Mus Art, Miami; Ahmadu Bello Univ, Zaria, Nigeria. *Comn:* Ga Coun Arts & Humanities, Valdosta, 81-82; Emory Univ, Atlanta, Ga, 81-82. *Exhib:* High Mus Art, Atlanta, Ga, 60, 68, 71 & 72; Mint Mus Art, Charlotte, NC, 67, 69 & 70; Smithsonian Inst, Washington, DC, 70; solo exhib, Metrop Mus & Art Ctr, Miami, Fla, 70; Greenville Co Mus, SC, 74; Furman Univ/R J Reynolds, Winston-Salem, NC, 77; Mus Arts & Sci, Macon, Ga, 82; and others. *Teaching:* Instr, Palm Beach Jr Col, West Palm Beach, Fla, 61-63; prof art, Valdosta State Col, Ga, 63-; sr lectr, Ahmadu Bello Univ, Zaria, Nigeria, 72-73. *Awards:* Best Show, Columbus Mus Arts & Crafts, Ga, 69; First Prize, St Augustine Festival, Fla, 70; Purchase Award, High Mus Art, Atlanta, Ga, 71. *Bibliog:* Barclay F Gordon (auth), Record houses: 1978, Archit Record Mag, 5/78; The connection, Atlanta Impressions Mag, summer, 81; Alexandra Mettler (auth), Emory's Cannon Chapel: Master touches, Atlanta Mag, 12/81. *Mem:* Am Crafts Coun (trustee, 80-82); Ga Designer Craftsman (vpres, 68); founding mem Ga Crafts Prof; Nat Coun Educ Ceramic Arts; World Crafts Coun. *Media:* Miscellaneous. *Dealer:* Signature Shop Roswell Rd Atlanta GA. *Mailing Add:* 2005 Bay Tree Rd Valdosta GA 31601

PENNYPACKER, JAMES S
DESIGNER, PUBLISHER
b Sellersville, Pa, Oct 11, 51. *Study:* Va Polytechnic Inst & State Univ, 69-72; Temple Univ, with Joseph Margolis, BA(magna cum laude), 78, fel, 78-80; Ariz State Univ, with Beth Luey, 83-84. *Comn:* Mural, Shelly's Hardware Inc, Perkasie, Pa, 71; logos, Emil's Diner, Sellersville, Pa, 72 & Interlude, Philadelphia, 77; posters, Nat Endowment Humanities Summer Inst, Phoenix, 83. *Pos:* Dir, Ctr Study Normative Futures, Philadelphia, 80-82, ed & designer, Crotonan Times, 82; publ designer, Pecksnipp's Ed Serv, Tempe, Ariz, 82-84; newspaper designer, Gentle Strength Food Coop, Tempe, Ariz, 82-84; publ & designer, Wizard Press, Philadelphia, 84- *Teaching:* Asst, Temple Univ, 79-80; lectr, Univ Colo, Boulder, 82. *Mem:* Writers Guild; World Future Soc Philadelphia (bd dirs, 80-82). *Media:* Pen and Ink, Colored Pencils. *Res:* The future of culture. *Publ:* Designer, Rudyard Kipling's Plain Tales From the Hills, 84, Stephen Crane's Last Words, 84 & Winston Churchill's The River War, 84, Renaissant Books; lead ed, Who's Who in American Art, R R Bowker, 84; designer, Deborah Weiss's Monsters and Ogres, Wizard Press (in prep). *Dealer:* Dr William Weiss 3912 Netherfield Rd Philadelphia PA 19129. *Mailing Add:* 2609 W Southern #242 Tempe AZ 85282

PENTAK, STEPHEN
PAINTER, EDUCATOR
b Denver, Colo, Aug 24, 51. *Study:* Union Col, NY, BA, 73; Tyler Sch Art, with Stephen Greene, MFA, 78. *Work:* Schenectady Mus, NY; Free Libr Philadelphia. *Exhib:* New Drawing in America, Drawing Ctr, New York, 82; Selected Works, Sutton Place, London, 82 & Gallerie D'Arte Mod Ca'Pesaro, Venice, 83; solo exhib, Jan Cicero Gallery, Chicago, 83 & Noel Butcher Gallery, Philadelphia, 83. *Teaching:* Vis asst prof, Art Inst Chicago, 81-82; asst prof, Ohio State Univ, Columbus, 83- *Bibliog:* Edward Sozanski (auth), article, Philadelphia Inquirer, 6/8/83. *Media:* Oil on Canvas and Paper. *Publ:* Auth, Gregory Amenoff's new pictures, 81 & Daryl Hughto, 81, Arts Mag. *Dealer:* Noel Butcher Gallery 17th St Philadelphia PA 19103. *Mailing Add:* 1835 F Northwest Ct Columbus OH 43212

PENTELOVITCH, ROBERT ALAN
PAINTER
b Minneapolis, Minn, Oct 13, 55. *Study:* Minneapolis Col Art & Design, BFA, 78; San Francisco Art Inst, MFA, 80. *Work:* Walker Art Ctr & Regis Corp, Minneapolis, Minn; l'art et l'automobile, New York; Chicago Inst Arts; Martin Marietta Corp, New York; Maslon, Kaplan, Borman & Brand, Minneapolis. *Exhib:* ACA Galleries, New York, 80; Music & Art Found, Woodmere, NY, 81; Dyansen Gallery, New York, 81; Ivan Karp, Soghor, Leonard & Assocs, New York, 82-83; Mari Galleries, Westchester, NY, 83. *Awards:* First Place, Minneapolis Col Art & Design, 77. *Mem:* Artists Equity Asn; Ulster Co Coun Arts. *Media:* Acrylic. *Publ:* Contribr, Edsel Owners News, 79 & 80, & Automotive Showcase, 1/82. *Mailing Add:* 340 W 55th St, No 2D New York NY 10019

PENTZ, DONALD ROBERT
PAINTER, PRINTMAKER
b Bridgewater, NS, Sept 18, 40. *Study:* Mt Allison Univ, Sackville, NB, BFA, 66; Univ Regina, Sask, MFA, 79; Banff Sch Fine Art, Alta, 77. *Work:* Art Gallery NS, NS Art Bank, Halifax; Can Coun Art Bank, Ottawa; Confederation Ctr Art Gallery, Charlottetown, PEI; Imperial Oil, Calgary, Alta. *Comn:* Selected Birds, Parks Can, Newfoundland, 82. *Exhib:* Young Artists of the Prairies, Walter Phillips Gallery, Banff, Alta, 79; Force Field Series, Art Gallery NS, Halifax, 79; RCA Centennial Exhib, CNE Bldg, Toronto, 80; Emerging Canadian Artists, Muttart Gallery, Calgary, Alta, 81; Atlantic Artists, Shell Can, Calgary, Alta, 81. *Teaching:* Instr art, privately, 70-72, Univ Regina, Sask, 77-79 & Mt St Vincent Univ, Halifax, NS, 80. *Awards:* Prof Artists Award, 75 & NS Talent Trust, 78, NS Govt; Can Coun Grant, 80. *Bibliog:* Janet Smith (producer), D Pentz--Wildlife Artist, CBC-TV, 83. *Mem:* Visual Arts NS; Royal Can Acad. *Media:* Acrylic, Pen and Ink. *Dealer:* Gallery 1667 1869 Upper Water St Halifax NS B3J 1S9. *Mailing Add:* RR1 Pleasantville Lunenburg County NS B0R 1G0 Canada

PEPE, MARIE SOPHIE HUPER
ADMINISTRATOR, HISTORIAN
b Wichita Falls, Tex, Sept 16, 22. *Study:* Univ Iowa, BFA, 47, MA, 48, PhD, 56. *Teaching:* Instr art hist & studio, Univ Tenn, Knoxville, vis lectr, Ont Dept Educ, Toronto, Can, summers 50-62; from asst prof to prof art, Agnes Scott Col, Decatur, Ga, 51-; chmn art dept, 70- *Awards:* Named Charles A Dana prof art, Agnes Scott Col, spring 74. *Mem:* Col Art Asn Am; Soc Archit Historians; Southeastern Col Art Conf (pres, 72). *Res:* Architectural monuments of the Hypnerotomachia Poliphili. *Mailing Add:* Dept of Art Agnes Scott Col Decatur GA 30030

PEPPER, BEVERLY
SCULPTOR, PAINTER
b Brooklyn, NY, Dec 20, 24. *Study:* Pratt Inst; Art Students League; also with Fernand Leger & Andre L'hote, Paris; Pratt Inst, Hon PhD, 82; Md Inst, Hon PhD, 83. *Work:* Albright-Knox Art Gallery, Buffalo, NY; Mass Inst Technol, Boston; Fogg Art Mus, Cambridge, Mass; Walker Art Ctr, Minneapolis; Metrop Mus Art, New York; and others. *Comn:* Excalibur (painted steel), San Diego Fed Courthouse, Calif, 74; Amphisculpture 75 (site sculpture), Bedminster, NJ, 75; Thel (site sculpture), Dartmouth Col, 77; Nat Endowment Arts, Toledo City Hall, 79; Spirit of Place, John Deere Co, Moline, Ill, 81; and others. *Exhib:* Plus by Minus, Today's Half Century, Albright-Knox Art Gallery, 68; San Francisco Mus Art, Calif, 76; Seattle Mus Contemp Art, 77; Princeton Art Mus, 78; Andre Emmerich Gallery, 79; Sala delle Pietra & Todi Piazza, 79; Earthworks as Land Reclamation, Seattle Mus, 79; Int Sculpture Conf, Washington, DC, 80; Nat Collection Arts, Smithsonian Inst, Washington, DC, 80; and many others. *Awards:* Best Art in Steel, Iron & Steel Inst, 70; Nat Endowment for the Arts Grant, 75 & 79; Gen Serv Admin Grant, 75. *Bibliog:* Wayne Andersen (auth), Sculpture Today, Mass Inst Technol Press, 70; Vittorio Armentano (auth), B P Making Sculpture (film), G Ungaretti, narrator, 70; Amphisculpture (film), Barbara Rose & Beverly Pepper, narrators, 77; Eleanor Munro (auth), Originals: American Women Artists, Simon & Schuster, 79; and others. *Media:* Cast Iron, Cast Steel. *Dealer:* Andre Emmerich Gallery 41 E 57th St New York NY 10022. *Mailing Add:* Torre Gentile Di Todi (PG) Italy

PEPPER, KATHLEEN DALY See Daly, Kathleen

PERA, ISABELLA
SCULPTOR
b Trivero, Italy, Sept 24, 45. *Study:* State Univ NY Cortland, BA, 73; Univ Ill Urbana-Champaign, MFA, 77. *Work:* Sheldon Swope Art Mus, Terre Haute, Ind; Del Mar Col, John Seaman Collection, Corpus Christi, Tex; Kirkland Fine Arts Ctr, Millikin Univ, Decatur, Ill; Almidones Mejicanos Bldg, Guadalajara, Mex; Italian Cultural Ctr, Chicago. *Exhib:* One-woman shows, Gilman Galleries, Chicago, 77, Freeport Art Mus, Ill, 79, Sheldon Swope Art Mus, Terre Haute, 80, Italian Cult Ctr, Chicago, 80 & Burpee Art Mus, Rockford, Ill, 81; 30th & 31st Ann Mid-States Art Exhib, Evansville Mus Art & Sci, Ind, 77-78; and others. *Collections Arranged:* 7th Ann Mid-States Traveling Art Show, Evansville Mus Art & Sci, 77-78. *Awards:* Best Casting of Colo Award, Foothills Art Ctr, 79; First Prize Sculpture, La Junta Fine Arts League, 79; First Prize Sculpture, Italian Cultural Ctr, Chicago, 81; and others. *Bibliog:* Janelle Hirchert (auth), Artistry in bronze wins recognition, News Gazette, 76; Harold Haydon (auth), Art, Sun Times, Chicago, 77; Nina Rubel (auth), Relief in bronze, Heartland Beat, Kerning Arts Press, 81. *Mem:* Int Sculpture Ctr. *Media:* Bronze; Epoxy. *Dealer:* Gilman Galleries 277 E Ontario St Chicago Ill 60611. *Mailing Add:* 1303 Belmeade Dr Champaign IL 61821

PERCY, ANN BUCHANAN
CURATOR, HISTORIAN
b Lynchburg, Va, Nov 13, 40. *Study:* Sweet Briar Col, BA, 62; Pa State Univ, MA, 65; Courtauld Inst Art, Univ London, with Anthony Blunt, PhD, 74. *Collections Arranged:* Giovanni Benedetto Castiglione: Master Draughtsman of the Italian Baroque (auth, catalog), Philadelphia Mus Art, 71; Contemporary Drawings: Philadelphia (coauth, catalog), Philadelphia Mus Art & Pa Acad Fine Arts, 78-79; A Scholar Collects: Selections from the Anothy Morris Clark Bequest (coauth, catalog), Philadelphia Mus Art, 80; and many others. *Pos:* Art hist ed, Pa State Univ Press, 69-72; asst cur drawings, Philadelphia Mus Art, 72-74, assoc cur drawings, 74-81, acting cur drawings, 81- *Mem:* Print Coun Am; Col Art Asn Am. *Res:* Seventeenth and eighteenth century Italian drawings and paintings; American illustration. *Publ:* Auth, Castiglione's chronology: Some documentary notes, Burlington Mag, 67; auth, Magic and melancholy: Castiglione's Sorceress in Hartford, Wadsworth Atheneum Bulletin, Vol 6, No 3, 70; coauth, Philadelphia: Three Centuries of American Art, Philadelphia Mus Art, 76. *Mailing Add:* Philadelphia Mus Art PO Box 7646 Philadelphia PA 19101

PEREHUDOFF, WILLIAM W
PAINTER
b Saskatoon, Sask, Apr 21, 19. *Study:* Colorado Springs Fine Arts Ctr; Ozenfant Sch Art, New York; Univ Sask, Emma Lake, workshops with Cherry, Noland & Greenberg. *Work:* Norman MacKenzie Art Gallery, Regina; Mendel Art Gallery, Saskatoon; Edmonton Art Gallery; London Art Gallery, Ont; Univ Calgary, Alta. *Comn:* Mural, Toronto Dominion Bank, Regina, 75. *Exhib:* Mendel Art Gallery, 65; Edmonton Art Gallery, 72; Waddington Art Gallery, Montreal, 73; Noah Goldowsky Inc, New York, 74. *Bibliog:* Clement Greenberg (auth), Painting and Sculpture in Canada, Can Art, 63; Karen Wilkin (auth), W Perehudoff recent paintings, Arts Can, 72. *Mem:* Royal Can Acad Art. *Media:* Acrylic on Canvas. *Dealer:* Noah Goldowsky Inc New York NY; Waddington Art Gallery Montreal Can. *Mailing Add:* 1131 Second St E Saskatoon SK S7H 1R4 Canada

PEREZ, VINCENT
PAINTER, INSTRUCTOR
b Jersey City, NJ, July 17, 38. *Study:* Pratt Inst, BFA; Univ Am, Mex; Calif Col Arts & Crafts, MFA. *Work:* Mus Art, Calif Palace Legion Hon, San Francisco; Oakland Art Mus, Calif; Playboy Enterprises, Chicago; Time Inc, New York; and many others. *Comn:* Mural, Arleigh Gallery, San Francisco, 69; portrait of State Supreme Court Judge Peters, comn by Clerks of Supreme Court for Univ Calif, Berkeley Law Sch, 74; woodcuts, Civic Arts Asn, Walnut Creek, Calif, 74. *Exhib:* One-man shows, Calif Col Arts & Crafts, 77 & Hoover Gallery, 80; 12 Artists, Calif Col Arts & Crafts, 78; Human Form, Walnut Creek Col, 78; Palo Alto Cult Ctr, 80; and many others. *Teaching:* Assoc prof drawing & printmaking & chmn dept drawing, Calif Col Arts & Crafts, 66-; instr anat, Univ Calif, Berkeley, 73-82. *Awards:* Union Independent Col Art Res Grant, 70; Best of Show, Tech Writers Convention, Los Angeles, 72; Gold Medal, Acad Italy, 80; and others. *Bibliog:* Fred Martin (auth), San Francisco letter, Art Int, 66; Cecille McCann (auth), Vincent Perez, FMb Fine Arts, 69; Palmer French (auth), San Francisco artists, Artforum, 69. *Mem:* Artists Equity; Union Independent Col Art. *Media:* Mixed. *Publ:* Illusr cover, Time Mag, 69; illusr, Art & Tools, 72; illusr, Archives of Institutional Change Humanizing Technology, 73; illusr, Psychol Today, 73; illusr, Playboy, 74. *Mailing Add:* 1279 Weber St Alameda CA 94501

PEREZNIETO, CASTRO FERNANDO
PRINTMAKER, PAINTER
b Aug 12, 38; Mexican citizen. *Study:* Nat Univ Mexico, archit, 62, arts, 76; Villa Schifandia, Florence, Italy, 77. *Work:* Museo de La Ciudad de Mexico, Mexico City; Dixon Art Ctr & Int Student Ctr, Univ Calif, Los Angeles; Banobras, Mex; Orion Bank, London, Eng. *Exhib:* Mexico--Tenochtitlan, Museo de La Ciudad de Mex, Mexico City, 75; Architects in Art, Nat Palace Fine Arts, Mexico City, 78; one-man show, Univ Calif, Los Angeles, 80 & Teorema Gallery, Florence, Italy, 83; Images of the Conciousness, Musee Goya, Castres, France, 81. *Teaching:* Master space geometry, Nat Univ Mex, 59-63. *Awards:* Luis Bunuel, Luis Bunuel Film Co, 68; Editorial Art, Camara Nat Ind Editorial, 80; First Place Etching, Pelago, Italy, 83. *Bibliog:* Ecu D'Arte Moderna No 44, 83; Segnalati, Il Candelaio, Florence, Italy, 83 & 84. *Media:* Watercolor, Etching. *Publ:* Auth, Apuntes de La Ciudad de Mexico, 72 & auth, Coyoacan, 73, Mortiz Publ; auth, Florence, History of a Surrender, UNAM, 79 & Il Candelaio, Florence, Italy, 83; auth, Images of the Conciousness, UNAM, 80; auth, Capital sins, Lacourriere et Frelaut, 80. *Dealer:* Galleria D'Arte Teorema Via Del Corso 21-R Florence Italy; Galeria Misrachi Genova 20 Mexico DF 06600 Mex. *Mailing Add:* PO Box 41-897 Mealo DF 10 Mexico

PERHAM, ROY GATES
PAINTER
b Paterson, NJ, Apr 18, 16. *Study:* Grand Cent Art Sch; also with Frank V Dumond & Frank J Reilly. *Work:* Americana Mus, Univ SC; Plimoth Plantation, Plymouth, Mass; Salisbury Pub Libr, Md; Maywood Pub Libr, NJ. *Comn:* Portrait of Dr O Howard, comn by friends at Diocesan Col, McGill Univ, 56; Jordan River (mural), Rutherford Baptist Church, NJ, 57; portrait of Dr Arthur Armitage, S Jersey Col, Rutgers Univ, 61; portrait of Dr Milton Hoffman, Cent Col, Iowa, 66; portrait of H Bruce Palmer, Conf Bd, New York, 71. *Exhib:* Allied Artists Am, New York, 66; Fairleigh Dickinson Univ, NJ, 67; Fair Lawn Art Asn, NJ, 68; Bergen Mall Exhib, Paramus, NJ, 70. *Awards:* Purchase Prize, Bergen Mall, 64. *Mem:* Hackensack Art Club. *Media:* Oil. *Mailing Add:* 268 Raymond St Hasbrouck Heights NJ 07604

PERINE, ROBERT HEATH
PAINTER, WRITER
b Los Angeles, Calif, Nov 30, 22. *Study:* Univ Southern Calif; Chouinard Art Inst, cert; watercolor with Rex Brandt & Phil Dike. *Work:* Butler Inst Am Art, Youngstown, Ohio; Univ Mass, Amherst; Brigham Young Univ; Utah State Univ; San Diego Mus Art. *Exhib:* Nat Watercolor Soc Ann, 49-53 & 71-77; San Diego Art Inst Ann, 71-; Butler Inst Ann, 72; Nat Orange Show Ann, 73-; Brand Libr Art Ctr, Glendale, Calif, 75 & 80; Cal State, Fullerton, 76; Pierce Col, Los Angeles, 77; Laguna Beach Mus, 77; San Diego Mus, 80. *Awards:* First Place & Purchase Award, 58th Ann Nat Orange Show, San Bernardino, 73; First Place in Watercolors & Purchase Award, 21st Ann San Diego Art Inst Show, 74; Purchase Award, 13th Ann Riverside Art Ctr Show, 75. *Bibliog:* Donovan Maley (auth), The delicate balance, San Diego Mag, 2/73 & A one-man renaissance for watercolor, Southwest Art Mag, summer 73; Fran Preisman (auth), Robert Perine's Geoglyphica Revisited, Artweek, 4/75. *Mem:* Nat Watercolor Soc; Watercolor West; West Coast Watercolor Soc; San Diego Art Inst; San Diego Art Guild. *Media:* Watercolor. *Mailing Add:* 628 San Dieguito Dr Encinitas CA 92024

PERKINS, A ALAN
CERAMIST, ENAMELIST
b Toronto, Ont, Nov 30, 15. *Study:* Danforth Tech Sch, Toronto, dipl; Ont Col Art, Toronto, scholar; Brookfield Craft Ctr, Conn, with Margaret Seeler & Francis Felton. *Work:* Ont Inst of Studies, Toronto; Ont Craft Coun Permanent Collection, Toronto, Confedn Centre Gallery & Mus, Charlottetown, PEI, Can; Jean A Chalmers Can Collection, Toronto. *Comn:* Mural, Cochran Murray Co, Toronto, 69; modular assemblage, Cadillac Develop Corp, Toronto, 72, Crown Life Insurance Head Off, Toronto, 73 & Whitney Public Sch, Toronto, Ont, Can, 81; and others. *Exhib:* First World Craft Exhib, Ont Sci Centre, Don Mills, 74; Design Can Award, Can Gov, Ottawa, 74; Visage du Can, Guilde Can des Metiers d'art Que, 76; Ont Craft Coun Traveling Exhib, 77-78; Artisan 78 Nat Travelling Show, 79; and other group and one-man shows. *Pos:* Tread bd dirs, Ont Craft Found, Toronto,

68-69. *Teaching:* Instr enameling & jewelry arts, George Brown Col, Toronto, 68-; instr glazes on metal, Toronto Bd Educ, 68-78. *Awards:* Adelaide Merriot Award of Excellence, Can Nat Exhib, 70; Award of Excellence, MAKE Exhib, Ont Can Guild of Crafts, 71; Best in Show, Graphics, Aviva Art Show, 81; and others. *Bibliog:* Una Abrahamson (auth), Crafts Canada, The Useful Arts, Clarke Irwin & Co Ltd, Toronto, 74; David Piper (ed), Canadian Interiors, Maclean Hunter Publ, 74; J Hartley Newman (auth), Wire Art, Crown Publ, New York, 75. *Mem:* Soc Can Artists (chmn exhib comt, 76-77); Ont Soc Artists; Ont Crafts Coun (secy-treas bd dirs, 68-70); Can Craftsmen's Coun; assoc mem, Soc NAm Goldsmiths. *Media:* Multimedia. *Dealer:* Nerton Gallery Toronto ON Can; Gallery House Sol Georgetown ON Can. *Mailing Add:* 29 Glen Davis Toronto ON M4E 1X6 Canada

PERKINS, ANN
HISTORIAN, EDUCATOR
b Chicago, Ill, Apr 18, 15. *Study:* Univ Chicago, AB, 35, AM, 36, PhD, 40. *Teaching:* Res assoc ancient art, Yale Univ, 55-65; assoc prof ancient art, Univ Ill, Urbana, 65-69, prof ancient art, 69-78, emer prof, 78- *Awards:* Guggenheim Fel, 54-55. *Mem:* Archaeol Inst Am; Col Art Asn Am. *Res:* Greek and Roman art. *Publ:* Auth, The Art of Dura-Europos, 73. *Mailing Add:* 1009 W Clark St Champaign IL 61821

PERKINS, CLARENCE JAMES
PAINTER, INSTRUCTOR
b Baton Rouge, La, June 16, 35. *Study:* Cooper Sch Art, Cleveland, with Fred Leach. *Work:* Pa State Bd Educ; Massillon Art Mus, Ohio; Springfield Art Mus, Mo; Canton Inst Art, Ohio. *Comn:* Monthly mag cover, Ohio Bell Telephone Co, Cleveland, 69; Int Bus Machines Corp, Cleveland, 81. *Exhib:* Several exhib, Butler Mid-Years, Butler Inst Am Art, Youngstown, Ohio; Watercolor USA, Springfield Art Mus, Mo, 68; Am Watercolor Soc, Nat ACA Galleries, New York, 68, 69, 72 & 75 & Nat ACA Art, 72; Massillon Mus Ann, Massillon Art Mus, Ohio, 70; Nat Watercolor Soc, Los Angeles, 73. *Teaching:* Instr watercolor, Cooper Sch Art, Cleveland, 70-73 & Valley Art Ctr, Chagrin Falls, Ohio, 73- *Awards:* Roy Wilhelm Mem Award, Ohio Watercolor Soc, Akron Soc Artists, 79; First Award Mixed Media, Boston Mills Arts Festival, 83; Bronze Medallion, Ohio Watercolor Soc, 83. *Mem:* Am Watercolor Soc; Ohio Watercolor Soc. *Media:* Watercolor, Gouache. *Dealer:* Garden Gallery 4556 Warrensville Ctr, Warrensville Heights OH 44122. *Mailing Add:* 13413 Maplerow Dr Garfield Heights OH 44105

PERKINS, CONSTANCE M
EDUCATOR, CRITIC
b Denver, Colo, Dec 20, 13. *Study:* Univ Denver, BA, 35; Mills Col, MA, 37. *Collections Arranged:* Pacific Profile, Pasadena Art Mus, Calif & Western Asn Art Mus, 61; Jose Louis Cuevas, 64 & The Edge of Pop, 65, Western Asn Art Mus; The New Vein: The Figure 1963- 1968 (traveling Latin Am), 68-70, The New Vein: The Figure 1964-1968 (traveling Europe), 69-70 & Variaciones Fotograficas, 75, Smithsonian Inst, Washington, DC. *Teaching:* Inst art, Univ Denver, 37-42; prof art hist, Occidental Col, Los Angeles, 47-83, prof emer, 83- *Publ:* Contribr articles in Los Angeles Times, 63-65 & Artforum 62-64; auth, Fact or fiction? the legacy of Oriental art, 65 & Los Angeles: the way you look at it, 66, Art in Am; contribr reviews, Artweek, 77-80. *Mailing Add:* 1540 Poppy Peak Dr Pasadena CA 91105

PERKINS, G HOLMES
ARCHITECT, EDUCATOR
b Cambridge, Mass, Oct 10, 04. *Study:* Harvard Univ, AB, 26, MArch, 29, LLD, 72. *Pos:* Ed, J Am Inst Planners, 50-52; chancellor col fels, Am Inst Architects, 64-66. *Teaching:* Chmn dept archit & dean grad sch fine arts, Univ Pa, 51-71, chmn grad prog archit & prof archit & urbanism, 71- *Mem:* Fel Am Inst Architects; hon corresp mem Royal Inst Architects Can. *Mailing Add:* Dept of Archit Univ Pa Philadelphia PA 19104

PERKINS, ROBERT EUGENE
ADMINISTRATOR
b Pittsfield, Mass, Oct 20, 31. *Study:* Sioux Falls Col, BA, 56; Columbia Univ, MA, 57; Univ SDak; Sioux Falls Col, LHD, 74. *Pos:* Asst prin, Canton High Sch, SDak, 59-61; dir admis, Sioux Falls Col, 61-63, dean students, 63-70; pres, Ringling Sch Art, Sarasota, Fla, 71-81; exec dir, William G Selby Found, currently. *Publ:* Coauth, Profile of the South Dakota High School Graduate of 1968, 69; auth, The Maestro, 70; auth, 50 Year History, Ringling School of Art and Design, 81. *Mailing Add:* 3424 S Lockwood Ridge Rd Sarasota FL 33579

PERLESS, ROBERT
SCULPTOR
b New York, NY, Apr 23, 38. *Study:* Univ Miami, Coral Gables, Fla. *Work:* Whitney Mus Am Art, New York; Aldrich Mus Contemp Art, Ridgefield, Conn; Chrysler Mus at Norfolk, Va; Everson Mus, Syracuse, NY; Okla Art Ctr, Oklahoma City. *Comn:* Am Tel & Tel, Atlanta, Ga; Tauberman Co, Lake Forest Shopping Mall; Guggenheim Int, New York; Avon Corp, New York; Nat Chemsearch, Irving, Tex; and others. *Exhib:* Bodley Gallery, New York, 68 & 74; New Acquisitions Exhib, Whitney Mus Am Art, New York, 70; Houston Gallery, Tex, 75; Forum Gallery & Galleria Bonino, New York, 75; Aldrich Mus Contemp Art, 78; Taft Mus, 80. *Media:* Miscellaneous. *Mailing Add:* 37 Langhorne Lane Greenwich CT 06830

PERLIN, BERNARD
PAINTER, ILLUSTRATOR
b Richmond, Va, Nov 21, 18. *Study:* Nat Acad Design, with Leon Kroll, 36-37; Art Students League, with Isabel Bishop, William Palmer & Harry

Sternberg, 36-37; also in Poland. *Work:* Tate Gallery, London; Nat Collection Fine Art, Smithsonian Inst; Mus Mod Art & Whitney Mus Am Art, New York; Va Mus Fine Arts; and others. *Comn:* US Post Off Dept, 40; US Treas Dept. *Comn:* Cincinnati Mus Asn, 58. *Exhib:* Brussels World's Fair, 58; Detroit Inst Art, 60; Pa Acad Fine Arts, 60; retrospective, Univ Bridgeport, 69; and many other group & one-man shows. *Teaching:* Instr, Wooster Community Art Ctr, Danbury, Conn, 67-69. *Awards:* Fulbright Fel, 50; Guggenheim Fels, 54-55 & 59; Nat Inst Arts & Lett Award, 64; and others. *Bibliog:* Lloyd Goodrich & John I H Baur (auths), American Art of Our Century, Whitney Mus Am Art, 61; Daniel M Mendelowitz (auth), A History of American Art, Holt, 61; Selden Rodman (auth), Conversations with Artists, Capricorn Press, 61; and others. *Publ:* Illusr, Life & Fortune Mags. *Mailing Add:* 56 Shadow Lake Rd Ridgefield CT 06877

PERLIN, RAE
PAINTER
b St John's, Nfld. *Study:* With Samuel Brecher, 41, 42 & 46 & Hans Hofmann, 47 & 48, New York; Acad Grande Chaumiere, Paris. *Work:* Mem Univ Nfld Permanent Collection, Can. *Exhib:* Mem Univ Northfield Art Gallery, 71; solo retrospective, Mem Univ Northfield, 82; and others. *Pos:* Art critic, St John's Daily News, 60-71; art critic, St John's Eve Telegram, 64-67. *Awards:* Arts & Lett, Nfld Govt, 56 & 62-67; Can Coun Grant, 70. *Media:* Oil, Acrylic. *Collection:* Contemporary works of Canadian artists; prints, drawings, constructions and paintings. *Publ:* Illusr, Spindrift and morning light, 68. *Mailing Add:* 11A Monkstown Rd St John's NF A1C 3T1 Canada

PERLIN, RUTH RUDOLPH
CURATOR, HISTORIAN
b Washington, DC. *Study:* Wellesley Col, BA, 57; Metrop Mus Art, Inst Fine Arts, 61-62; New York Univ Inst Fine Arts, MA, 64. *Pos:* Chief, mus educ, Baltimore Mus Art, 69-72; cur dept exten progs, Nat Gallery Art, Washington, DC, 74-80, chair ed bd, 76-82, head dept exten progs, 80-; officer bd, Mus Educ Roundtable, 78-81; contrib ed, Sch Arts Mag, 78-82. *Teaching:* Head docent training art hist, Baltimore Mus Art, 65-69; instr art hist, Towson State Col, Md, 67-69. *Mem:* Am Asn Mus; Nat Art Educ Asn; Col Art Asn. *Res:* Collections, exhibitions of National Gallery; 15th & 16th century Italian painting; late 19th & 20th century painting. *Publ:* Auth, The Far North, 76, auth, Index of American Design: Pottery, Textiles and Furniture, 77, auth & ed, Thomas Jefferson: Art and Reason, 78, co-auth & ed, Venetian Painting, 80, Nat Gallery Art, Washington, DC. *Mailing Add:* c/o Nat Gallery Art EB 503 Washington DC 20565

PERLMAN, BENNARD BLOCH
PAINTER, INSTRUCTOR
b Baltimore, Md, June 19, 28. *Study:* Carnegie-Mellon Univ, BFA, 49; Univ Pittsburgh, MA, 50. *Work:* Libr Cong, Washington, DC; Peale Mus & Baltimore Mus Art, Baltimore, Md; Univ Ariz, Tucson; Univ Md, College Park. *Comn:* Mural, 66 & History of Gardenville (oil), 80, City Baltimore. *Exhib:* Baltimore Mus Art; Corcoran Gallery Art, Washington, DC; Carnegie Mus, Pittsburgh; Pa Acad Fine Arts, Philadelphia. *Teaching:* Prof & chmn dept art, Community Col Baltimore, 54-; vis lectr, Oxford Univ, Eng, 75 & Dartmouth Col, 81. *Awards:* Freeland Art Award, Md Artists Exhib, Baltimore Mus Art; First Prize & Mus Purchase, Peale Mus Ann. *Mem:* Artists Equity Asn (nat vpres, 69-71 & 77-79); Baltimore Mus Art Artists Comt (chmn, 59-61 & 69-70); Greater Baltimore Arts Coun (pres, 64-66). *Media:* Oils, Ink. *Res:* American art; Robert Henri and the Eight. *Publ:* Auth, One Percent Art in Civic Architecture, Nat Endowment Arts, 72; auth, The Golden Age of American Illustration, 78 & The Immortal Eight: American Painting from Eakins to the Armory Show, rev ed 79, North Light; auth, The Eight and Its Influence (cxhib catalog), Art Students League New York, 83; auth, 75th Anniversary of The Eight (exhib catalog), Whitney Mus Am Art, 83. *Mailing Add:* 6603 Baythorne Rd Baltimore MD 21209

PERLMAN, JOEL LEONARD
SCULPTOR, INSTRUCTOR
b New York, NY, June 12, 43. *Study:* Cornell Univ, BFA, 65; Cent Sch of Art & Design, London; Univ Calif, Berkeley, MA, 68. *Work:* Larry Aldrich Mus Contemp Art, Ridgefield, Conn; Storm King Art Ctr, Mountainville, NY; Johnson Mus, Cornell Univ; Hirshorn Mus & Sculpture Garden. *Comn:* Outdoor sculpture, RTKL Inc, Baltimore, 71; Night Traveler (outdoor sculpture), Storm King Art Ctr, 77; High Peaks, 80 Winter Olympics, Lake Placid. *Exhib:* Axiom Gallery, London, 69; Bennington Col, Vt, 70; Whitney Mus Am Art Biennial, 73; Contemp Reflections, Aldrich Mus Contemp Art, 73; Andre Emmerich Gallery, New York, 73, 76, 78, 80 & 82 & Zurich, 77; Storm King Art Ctr, 74 & 75; Roy Boyd Gallery, Chicago & Los Angeles, 78, 80, 81 & 83; Gloria Luria Gallery, Fla, 83. *Teaching:* Instr sculpture, Sch Visual Arts, 73- *Awards:* Guggenheim Found Fel Sculpture, 74; Nat Endowment Arts Grant, 79. *Bibliog:* Barbara Zucker (auth), article, Artnews, summer 76; Jon Cayman (auth), article, summer 76 & Gene Kaplan (auth), Joel Perlman's new sculpture, 10/82, Arts Mag; and others. *Media:* Welded Steel, Cast Bronze. *Mailing Add:* c/o Emmerich Gallery 41 E 57th St New York NY 10022

PERLMAN, RAYMOND
EDUCATOR, ILLUSTRATOR
b Sheboygan, Wis, May 17, 23. *Study:* Univ Ill, Champaign, BFA, 48 & MFA, 53; Art Ctr Col Design, Pasadena, Calif, MPA, 52. *Work:* Watercolors, Univ Ill, Champaign; serigraphs, Standard Oil Cos of Ind; Tulsa City-Co Libr Syst; Kankakee Community Col, Ill; IBM Corp. *Exhib:* Creativity on Paper, Mead Paper Co, New York, 65; Chicago 3, Ill, 70; Art Dir Club New York 49th Ann, 70; Printing Job of the Year, 3M Co, 70; TDC 17, Type Dir Club New

York, 71; numerous group and solo exhibs in painting, photography and printmaking, 75- *Pos:* Illusr, World Book & Childcraft, Field Enterprises, 58-73. *Teaching:* Prof art, Univ Ill, Champaign, 49-, head graphic design, 60-83. *Awards:* UN Int Poster Competition, 49; Purchase Award, Print & Drawing Exhib, Artists Guild Chicago, 77; Center for Advan Study Fel, Univ Ill, 75. *Mem:* Soc Typographic Arts, Chicago. *Media:* Watercolor, Serigraphy. *Publ:* Illusr, Rocks and Minerals, 57, Fossils, 62, Light and Color, 71, Geology, 72 & Ecology, 73, Golden Guides, Western Publishing, NY; and others. *Mailing Add:* RR 3 Park Hills Mahomet IL 61853

PERLMUTTER, JACK
PAINTER, PRINTMAKER
b New York, NY, Jan 23, 20. *Work:* Nat Gallery Art, Phillips Collection & Corcoran Gallery Art, Washington, DC; Metrop Mus Art, New York; Nat Mus Mod Art, Tokyo. *Comn:* First Saturn Moon Rocket Launching (painting), 67 & Saturn V, Apollo 6 (painting), 68, NASA, Kennedy Space Ctr, Fla; Woodcuts for Apollo 16, Mission Control Ctr, Houston, Tex, 72; Columbia Space Shuttle (painting), NASA, 81; Voyager II (painting), NASA, 81. *Exhib:* Four Corcoran Gallery Art Am Biennials, 49-61; American Prints Today, Print Coun Am, exhibited in ten cities, 59-60; 3rd & 4th Expos Gravure, Ljubljana, Yugoslavia, 59 & 61; 3rd Nat Exhib Printmaking, Univ Wis, 71; 2nd Nat Print Show, Fine Arts Gallery, San Diego, 71. *Pos:* Dir, Dickey Gallery Art, DC Teachers Col, 56-68; contrib ed, Art Voices. *Teaching:* Chmn dept graphics, Corcoran Sch Art, 60-82; vis prof, Univ Costa Rica, 83. *Awards:* Fulbright Grant in art & printmaking to Tokyo, 59-60; Print Prize, 1st Int Exhib Fine Arts Saigon, 62; also numerous purchase awards. *Bibliog:* Reproduction, Art Today, Holt, Rinehart & Winston, 4th ed; Eyewitness to Space, Abrams, 72; The Art of the Print, Abrams, 76. *Mem:* Soc Am Graphic Artists; Cosmos Club (art comt, 63-). *Publ:* Contribr, Transactions of 5th International Conference of Orientalists (Toho Gakkai), Japanese Prints Today, 7/60; auth, Western art influences in Japan, Today's Japan Orient/West, 8/60; auth, Painting in a land of transition (with reproductions), Inst Int Educ Mag, 1/61. *Mailing Add:* 2511 Cliffbourne Pl NW Washington DC 20009

PERLMUTTER, MERLE
PRINTMAKER, INSTRUCTOR
b London, England, Apr 16, 36; US citizen. *Study:* Art Students League, with Ethel Katz; Pratt Inst, Brooklyn, NY; Ruth Leaf Graphic Workshop, Douglaston, NY. *Work:* Museo de Arte Moderno Chapultepec, Mexico City; DeCordova Mus, Mass; Univ Dallas, Irving; Nassau Community Col, NY; New York City Pub Libr, 42nd St Branch Print Collection. *Exhib:* Boston Printmakers Nat Competition, Mass, 74, 76 & 80; Pratt Int Miniature Graphics Exhib, 75, 77 & 81; Premio Internazionale Biella Por L'Incisione, Italy, 76 & 80; Miami Int Biennial, Metrop Mus & Art Ctr, Fla, 77 & 80; Martha Jackson Gallery, New York, 79; NY State Mus, Albany, 81; and others. *Teaching:* Instr etching & printmaking, Ruth Leaf Graphic workshop, Douglaston, NY, 76-; guest printmaker prints & techniques, Grey Art Gallery & Study Ctr, NY Univ, New York, 76. *Awards:* Two Gold Medals & Silver Medal, Audubon Artist Nat Competition, New York, 75, 77 & 80; Creative Artist Pub Serv Prog Fel, 76; Soc Am Graphic Artists Award, 78 & 80; and many others. *Bibliog:* Robert Taylor (auth), article, Boston Globe, 76; Ruth Leaf (auth), Intaglio Printmaking Techniques, Watson-Guptill, 77; Jacquline Brody (auth), Prints Published, Print Collectors News Lett, 9-10/78. *Mem:* Boston Printmakers, Mass; The Print Club, Philadelphia, Pa; Audubon Artists; Soc Am Graphic Artists. *Media:* Intaglio, etching. *Mailing Add:* 20 Cherry Ave New Rochelle NY 10801

PERLS, KLAUS G
DEALER
b Berlin, Ger, Jan 15, 12; US citizen. *Study:* Univ Basel, Switz, PhD, 33. *Pos:* Partner, Perls Galleries, 37- *Mem:* Art Dealers Asn Am. *Specialty:* Modern masters. *Publ:* Auth, Complete works of Jean Fouquet, 40; auth, Maurice de Vlaminck, 41. *Mailing Add:* 1016 Madison Ave New York NY 10021

PERNOTTO, JAMES ANGELO
PAINTER, ENVIRONMENTAL ARTIST
b Youngstown, Ohio, Oct 20, 50. *Study:* Ohio State Univ, BFA(cum laude), 73; Univ Wis, MFA, 75. *Work:* Art Inst Chicago; Univ Dallas; Indianapolis Mus Art. *Exhib:* Paper as Medium, Smithsonian Inst Traveling Exhib, 78; Int Papermakers, Boston Univ, 80; solo exhib, Love Hurts, Butler Inst Am Art, 81 & Walking the Line Between Heaven and Hell, Fendrick Gallery, Washington, DC, 81; New Directions, Ft Lauderdale Mus & traveling, 82; Int Art Exposition, Navy Pier, Chicago, 82; Dynamix, Cincinnati Contemp Mus, 82. *Awards:* First Award, Wis Bienalle, Madison Art Ctr, 78, Midyear Show, Butler Inst Am At, 81 & Nat Show, Hoyt Inst, 82. *Bibliog:* Jules Heller (auth), Papermaking, Watson-Guptill, 78; Jo Ann Lewis (auth), Steelyard stories, Washington Post, 10/8/81; David Tannous (auth), James Pernotto at Fendrick, Art in Am, 2/82. *Media:* Multi. *Dealer:* Barbara Fendrick Gallery 3059 M St NW Washington DC 20007. *Mailing Add:* 27 1/2 Federal Plaza W Youngstown OH 44503

PERREAULT, JOHN
CRITIC, CURATOR
b New York, NY, Aug 26, 37. *Pos:* Art critic, Village Voice, New York, 66-74; sr art critic, Soho News, New York, 75-82; cur contemp art, Everson Mus, 83- *Teaching:* Vis prof, Univ Calif, San Diego, 76; prof art criticism, Univ Ariz, Tucson, 79 & State Univ NY, Binghamton, 81. *Awards:* Art Criticism Fels, Nat Endowment Arts, 73 & 79. *Bibliog:* Alex Gildzen (ed), John Perreault issue, Serif, Kent State Univ Libr, Ohio, Vol XI, fall 74. *Mem:* Am Sect Int Asn Art Critics (pres, 78-81). *Res:* Contemporary art. *Publ:* Auth, articles in Artforum, Art Am, Arts, Artscanada & Art Int & many others. *Mailing Add:* 318 E 7th Suite 222 New York NY 10003

PERRET, GEORGE ALBERT
WRITER, APPRAISER

b New York, NY. *Study:* Munson-Williams-Proctor Inst, Utica, NY; Utica Col, Syracuse Univ; Art Students League; Nat Acad Design Sch Art, New York. *Collections Arranged:* Artists of the South Fork, 65; The Wyeth Family, 66 & Mary Cassat, 67, Parrish Mus, Southampton, NY. *Pos:* Dir, Parrish Art Mus, 63-68; cur, Am Contemp Artists Gallery, 68-72; dir publ, Assoc Am Artists, 72-; cur, Andrew Crispo Gallery, New York, 73-; dir, Metrop Art Appraisers Am, New York, 73- *Teaching:* Instr art hist, Southampton Col, Long Island Univ, 63-68. *Res:* American painting, 1860-1950. *Publ:* Contribr, Art news and reviews (weekly column), Suffolk Sun, 65-68; auth, Levon West, 66; auth, George Elmer Browne, 66; co-auth, Tully Filmus Drawings, 71; auth, Moses Soyer Drawings, 71. *Mailing Add:* Metrop Art Appraisers America Inc 595 Madison Ave New York NY 10022

PERRET, NELL FOSTER
PAINTER, PRINTMAKER

b Brooklyn, NY, Dec 22, 16. *Study:* Pratt Inst; Art Students League; Design Lab. *Work:* Southampton Col, Long Island Univ; East Hampton Guild Hall; St Mary's Univ; Wichita State Univ; Pace Univ. *Exhib:* Westbeth Graphics Workshop, Palacio Bellas Artes, Mex, 71-72; East Hampton Guild Hall Ann; Chung Hsing Galleries, Taiwan, 73; Roko Gallery, New York, 76; solo show, Westbury Gallery, 79; and others. *Teaching:* Instr graphics, Parrish Art Mus, Southampton, 60-68; adj grad graphics, Southampton Col, 68-70. *Awards:* Two awards, East Hampton Guild Hall, 61 & 62; three awards for graphics, Parrish Art Mus, 63, 64 & 67; Graphics Award, Painters & Sculptors Soc, 78. *Bibliog:* Jean Paris (auth), Review of my work, Newsday, 63; Gordon Brown (auth), Review, Arts Mag, summer 71 & 76. *Mem:* Westbeth Graphic Artists Workshop; Painters & Sculptors Soc; Audubon Artists; Artists Equity Asn New York. *Media:* Egg Tempera, Oil; Etching, Aquatint. *Mailing Add:* 463 West St 628A Westbeth New York NY 10014

PERRIN, C ROBERT
PAINTER, ILLUSTRATOR

b Medford, Mass, July 13, 15. *Study:* Sch Practical Art, scholar, also with John Wharf & Lester Stevens, four yrs. *Work:* Ford Motor Co Collection Am Watercolors; Lyman Allyn Mus, New London, Conn. *Exhib:* Mus Fine Arts, Boston, 52; Am Watercolor Soc, 58-; US Info Agency World Tour, 59; Boston Watercolor Soc, 60-; Nat Acad Design. *Pos:* Freelance illusr, Boston, 39-42 & 46-68. *Teaching:* Artist, lectr & demonstr, Boston & Nantucket Island, Mass, 50. *Awards:* Richard Mitton Mem Award, 32nd Ann Exhib Painting by Contemp New Eng Artists, 61; First Award, Copley Soc, 65; six First Prizes, Artist Asn Nantucket, 73-82. *Bibliog:* James S Geggis (auth), Art studio on wheels, United Press, 47; Patricia Boyd Wilson (auth), The home forum, Christian Sci Monitor, 66; Norman Kent (auth), 100 Watercolor Techniques, Watson-Guptill, 68. *Mem:* Am Watercolor Soc; New Eng Watercolor Soc; Artist Asn Nantucket; Guild Boston Artists. *Publ:* Coauth, Watercolor page, 59 & Making a rug mural, 66, Am Artist Mag; contribr, The Folk Arts and Crafts of New England, 65 & Creating Art From Anything, 68. *Mailing Add:* 91 Washington St PO Box 1335 Nantucket MA 02554

PERROT, PAUL N
ADMINISTRATOR, LECTURER

b Paris, France, July 28, 26; US citizen. *Study:* Inst Fine Arts, NY Univ, 46-52. *Collections Arranged:* Three Great Centuries of Venetian Glass, 58; most exhibs shown at The Corning Mus Glass, 60-72. *Pos:* Asst, The Cloisters, Metrop Mus Art, 48-52; asst to dir, Corning Mus Glass, 52-55, asst dir, 55-60, dir, 60-72; ed, J Glass Studies, 59-72; asst secy mus progs, Smithsonian Inst, 72-84; dir, Va Mus Fine Arts, 84- *Teaching:* Instr glass hist, Corning Community Col & Alfred Univ. *Awards:* Chevalier Ordre des Arts et Lettres, France. *Mem:* Am Asn Mus; US Int Coun Mus; Am Archaeol Inst; Int Ctr Study Preserv & Restoration Cult Property; and others. *Publ:* Auth, Three great centuries of Venetian glass, 58; auth, articles, Antiques, Apollo, Arts Va, col Art J and others. *Mailing Add:* Smithsonian Inst Washington DC 20560

PERRY, CHARLES O
SCULPTOR

b Helena, Mont, Oct 18, 29. *Study:* Yale Univ, BA(archit). *Work:* Art Inst Chicago; Oakland Mus, Calif; San Francisco Mus Art, Calif; Mus Mod Art, New York; de Young Mus, San Francisco. *Comn:* Univ SC, 73; Gen Elec Hq, Conn, 74; Ministry of Defense, Riyadh, Saudi Arabia, 75; Nat Air & Space Mus, Washington, DC, 76; City of Miami Beach, Fla, 78. *Exhib:* Milwaukee Art Ctr, Wis, 69; Chicago Mus Contemp Art, 69; Whitney Mus Am Art, New York, 64 & 66; Venice Bienale, 70; Quadriennale di Roma, Italy, 77; one-man shows, Alpha Gallery, 70, Hopkins Art Ctr, Dartmouth, 72, Arts Club of Chicago, 72; and others. *Pos:* Sculptor in residence, Am Acad Rome, 68 & Hopkins Art Ctr, Dartmouth, 72. *Awards:* Prix de Rome in Archit, 64-66; Am Inst Steel Design Award, 68 & 70. *Media:* Metal. *Mailing Add:* Shorehaven Rd Norwalk CT 06855

PERRY, DONALD DEAN
PRINTMAKER, EDUCATOR

b Hutchinson, Kans, Sept 29, 39. *Study:* Pittsburg State Univ, BFA, 62; Kans State Univ, MS, 67; Univ Wis-Madison, MFA, 67. *Comn:* Wildlife Panorama, Marshfield Libr, Wis, 70. *Exhib:* Nat Print Exhib, State Univ NY, Potsdam, 67; Miami Graphics Biennial Int, Metrop Mus, Fla, 74; Nat Print & Drawing Exhib, Univ NDak, Minot, 76; New Photographics '76, Cent Wash State Univ, Ellensburg, Wash, 76; Ann Printmaking West, Logan Utah, 78; and others. *Pos:* Mem bd dirs, Community Arts Inc, Emporia, 73-74; dir, Univ Art Galleries, Emporia State Univ, 79- *Teaching:* Instr drawing & printmaking,

Univ Wis, Marshfield, 67-72; assoc prof, Emporia State Univ, Kans, 72, chmn art dept, 77- *Awards:* Purchase Award, Miami Graphics Biennial, 74. *Mem:* Emporia Arts Coun, Kans. *Media:* Screenprint; Acrylic. *Mailing Add:* 1908 Coronado Ave Emporia KS 66801

PERRY, EDWARD (TED) SAMUEL
ADMINISTRATOR

b New Orleans, La, June 4, 37. *Study:* Baylor Univ, BA, 61; Univ Iowa, MA, 66, PhD, 68. *Pos:* Dir film dept, Mus Mod Arts, New York, 75-78. *Teaching:* Prof cinema & chmn dept, Univ Iowa, Univ Tex & NY Univ, 69-75; Luce vis prof cinema, Harvard Univ, spring 75; Middlebury Col, 78- *Mem:* Soc Cinema Studies; Speech Commun Asn (mem res bd, 74-). *Publ:* Ed, Performing Arts Resources, 75; coauth, New Film Index, Dutton, 75; auth, Filmguide to 8-1/2, Ind Univ, 75; auth, The passenger, Film Comment, Vol 2, No 4; auth, Formal strategies as an index to the evolution of film history, Cinema J, 75. *Mailing Add:* 49 South St Middlebury VT 05753

PERRY, FRANK
SCULPTOR

b Vancouver, BC, Jan 15, 23. *Study:* Univ BC, BA, 49; Cent Sch Arts & Crafts, London, Eng; Regent Poly, Chelsea Sch Art, London. *Work:* Nat Gallery, Ottawa; Vancouver Art Gallery; Univ BC Sch Archit; Art Gallery Greater Victoria, BC; Univ Victoria. *Comn:* Granite carving, Burnaby Art Gallery, BC, 58; bronze fountain, Crescent Apts, West Vancouver, 61; cor-ten welded, Fed Govt Bldg, Victoria, 66; bronze cast, Playhouse Theatre, Vancouver, 67 & BC Govt for Prov Bldgs, 73. *Exhib:* Montreal Mus Fine Arts, 58; Winnipeg Show, 58; BC Centennial Outdoor Show, 58; BC Centennial Outdoor Sculpture Show, 67. *Pos:* Pres, Northwest Inst Sculpture, 59-60. *Awards:* First Prizes, Montreal Mus Fine Arts, Winnipeg Show & BC Centennial Outdoor Show, 68; Grand Prize, BC Centennial Outdoor Sculpture Show, 67; Rothman Award, 67. *Mem:* Sculptor's Soc Can; Sculptor's Soc BC; Royal Can Acad Art. *Media:* Bronze, Welded Steel. *Mailing Add:* 3526 Everglade Pl North Vancouver BC V7P 3T9 Canada

PERRY, JUDITH ELAINE
PAINTER

b North Tonawanda, NY, Feb 19, 47. *Study:* Self-taught painter; Ohio State Univ, Columbus, BA, 69. *Exhib:* Fabian Gallery, New York, 79; solo exhib, Naive Art Gallery, San Francisco, 80; Occidental Ctr Gallery, Los Angeles, 80-81; Trans Am Tower, San Francisco, 80-81 & 81-82; Cochise Fine Arts, Bisbee, Ariz, 82. *Bibliog:* Frances Ring (auth), Gallery: Judy Perry, Westways Mag, 7/79; Betje Howell (auth), Judy Perry, Art Voices Mag, 11/81. *Media:* Acrylic. *Dealer:* Johnson Gallery 69 Main St Bisbee AZ 85603. *Mailing Add:* PO Box 1722 Bisbee AZ 85603

PERRY, KATHRYN POWERS
GRAPHIC ARTIST, PAINTER

b Chico, Calif, Mar 13, 48. *Study:* Concordia Col, seminar in Italy with Barbara Glasrud, 69, with Cy Running, BA(art, Eng), 70; Stanford Univ, 68; Art Students League, with Will Barnet, Earl Mayan, Knox Martin & Gregory d'Alessio, 71-74, Emily Ferrier-Spear scholarship, 73-74; Sch of Visual Arts, 78-79. *Exhib:* Solo exhib, Aames Gallery, New York, 76; Berg Art Ctr, Moorhead, Minn, 77; Orgn Independent Artists, Arte Fiera, Bologna, Italy, 78; Marietta Nat, Ohio, 79; Ligoa Duncan Gallery, New York, 79; and others. *Pos:* Asst art dir, Metrop Opera Guild, 81-83, art dir, 83- *Bibliog:* Review of four Concordia College artists, Fargo Forum, 5/70; Rob Edelman (auth), Three Brooklyn artists probe their role in society, Courier-Life, 7/74. *Mem:* Art Students League; New York Artists Equity Asn; assoc mem Audubon Artists. *Media:* Acrylic, Watercolor; Charcoal, Pencil. *Mailing Add:* 145 Lincoln Pl Brooklyn NY 11217

PERRY, REGENIA ALFREDA
HISTORIAN

b Virgilina, Va, Mar 30, 41. *Study:* Va State Col, BS, 61; Case Western Reserve Univ, MA(Va Mus Fine Arts Out of State Fel), 62; Univ Pa, 63-64, PhD(art hist), 66; Yale Univ, 70-71. *Pos:* Spec res asst, Cleveland Mus Art, 64-65; vis scholar, Piedmont Univ Ctr, Winston-Salem, 71-72. *Teaching:* Asst prof art hist, Howard Univ, 65-66; asst prof art hist, Ind State Univ, Terre Haute, 66-67; prof art hist, Va Commonwealth Univ, 67- *Awards:* Danforth Found Post-Doctoral Fel, 70-71. *Mem:* Col Art Asn Am; Am Asn Mus; Soc Archit Historians; Am Asn Univ Prof. *Publ:* auth, James Van Derzee-- Photographer, 73; Auth, A History of Afro-American Art 1619-1976, 78. *Mailing Add:* c/o Art Dept Va Commonwealth Univ 910 W Franklin St Richmond VA 23284

PERRY, RICHARD C
DEALER, COLLECTOR

b Atlanta, Ga, June 15, 40. *Pos:* Dir, Merrill Chase Galleries, Oak Brook, Ill, 70-81, vpres, 81- *Specialty:* Fifteenth through twentieth century graphic art works. *Collection:* Chagall, Dali, Delacroix, Durer, Legrand, Manet, Picasso, Rembrandt, Renoir, Toulouse-Lautrec, Villon & Whistler, and many others. *Mailing Add:* c/o Merrill Chase Gallery 89 Oak Brook Ctr Oak Brook IL 60521

PERSHAN, MARION
PAINTER

b New York, NY. *Study:* Hunter Col, with William Starkweather, BA, 38; Nat Acad Fine Arts, with Louis Bouche, 53; Art Students League, with Edwin Dickinson & Frank Mason, 54. *Work:* Dow Chemical Corp, Midland, Mich; Cardiology Assoc, Westport, Conn. *Exhib:* Brooklyn Artist Biennial, Brooklyn Mus, NY, 53; Catharine Lorillard Wolfe Arts Club, Nat Arts Club,

New York, 76-83; Brooklyn Watercolor Soc, Metrop Mus Art, New York, 76 & 77; Allied Arts Am, Nat Acad Design, New York, 78; Hudson Valley Art Asn, Westchester Co Ctr, NY, 78-80; Knickerbocker Artists, Salmagundi Club, New York, 81; 157th Ann, Nat Acad Design, New York, 82. *Pos:* Art dir, Camp Roselake, Honesdale, pa, 54-55. *Teaching:* Instr & coordr art, New York City Public Sch System, 60-77. *Awards:* Gold Medal of Honor, 79 & Silver Medallion, 82, Catharine Lorillard Wolfe Club Inc, 79; First Award, Nat Arts Club, 82; Second Prize Watercolor, Knickerbocker Artists, 82. *Bibliog:* Walter Cruickshank (auth), Art Review, Flatbush Life, 5/8/71; Claude Leseur (auth), article, Artspeak, 83. *Mem:* Malverne Artists Inc; Catharine Lorillard Wolfe Art Club Inc; Knickerbocker Artists; Hudson Valley Art Asn; assoc Am Watercolor Soc. *Media:* Watercolor. *Publ:* Auth, Language Arts in the Art Curriculum, Fac News Asn, 4/72; illusr, Career Opportunities Exposition, Am Educ Asn, 10/73. *Dealer:* Grand Central Art Galleries New York NY. *Mailing Add:* 209-25 18th Ave Bayside New York NY 11360

PERSHING, LOUISE
PAINTER, SCULPTOR
b Pittsburgh, Pa. *Study:* Pa Acad Fine Arts; Carnegie-Mellon Univ; Univ Pittsburgh; Hans Hoffman. *Work:* Gulf Oil Corp, Alcoa Aluminum Corp, Jones & Laughlin Steel Corp & Westinghouse Corp, Pittsburgh; Univ WVa. *Comn:* Large outdoor sculpture, City Pittsburgh Corten Steel. *Exhib:* Carnegie Int, 37 & 50; Painting in the US, Carnegie Inst Int, 43-49; one-man shows, Westinghouse Corp, 65 & Gulf Oil Corp, 66, Pittsburgh; Mus Art, Carnegie Inst Int, Pittsburgh, 74. *Awards:* Twelve awards, Assoc Artists Pittsburgh, 30-72; Nat Soc Arts & Lett Award of Merit, 69; Distinguished Daughter Pa for Work in Arts, 83. *Media:* Mixed. *Mailing Add:* 916 College Ave Pittsburgh PA 15232

PERSKY, ROBERT S
WRITER, DEALER
b Jersey City, NY, Jan 5, 30. *Study:* NY Univ, 49; Harvard Law Sch, JD, 52. *Pos:* Dir, Images...A Gallery of Contemp Photog Art, 76-; ed, Photograph Collectors Newsletter, 80-; publ, Photograph Collectors Resource Directory, currently. *Mailing Add:* c/o The Photograph Collector 127 E 59th St New York NY 10022

PESNER, CAROLE MANISHIN
DEALER
b Boston, Mass, Aug 5, 37. *Study:* Ecole du Louvre, Inst d'Art et d'Archit, Paris, 58; Smith Col, Northampton, Mass, BA, 59. *Pos:* Mgr, Kraushaar Galleries, New York, 59- *Specialty:* 20th century American art. *Publ:* Auth & coauth, Kraushaar Gallery Publ & Catalogs. *Mailing Add:* Kraushaar Galleries 724 Fifth Ave New York NY 10019

PETER, FRIEDRICH GUNTHER
CALLIGRAPHER, EDUCATOR
b Dresden, Ger, Feb 23, 33. *Study:* Hochschule fuer Bildende Kuenste, W Berlin, Ger, 50-56; Meisterschueler Dipl in lettering & graphic design, 56-57. *Comn:* Postage stamp designs, Can Post Off, 70, 79-80 & 82; mural, World Coun Churches Sixth Assembly, Vancouver, BC, 83. *Exhib:* Royal Can Acad Arts Exhib, Spectrum Can, 76, Olympics, Montreal, 76; Royal Can Acad Exhib, Toronto, 81. *Collections Arranged:* 26 Letters (traveling exhib), Fine Arts Gallery, Univ BC, Vancouver. *Pos:* Chmn graphic design, Vancouver Sch of Art, BC, 76; chmn dept graphic design, Emily Carr Col Art, 76- *Teaching:* Instr graphic design, Vancouver Sch Art, BC, 59-78, chmn graphic design, 76; chmn graphic design, Emily Carr Col Art, Vancouver, BC, 76-, instr, 78- *Awards:* Second Prize for Magnificat Typeface, Int Typeface Design Competition, Letraset Corp, 72; Regina Silver Dollar, 81; 100 Dollar Gold Coin, 82. *Mem:* Royal Can Acad; Graphic Designers Can; Can Postage Stamp Adv Comt. *Publ:* Auth & ed, Idea Mag, No 110, Yoshinobu Kawasaki, 72; auth & ed, Novum education Vancouver School of Art, Novum/Gebrauchsgraphik Mag, 3/75; contribr (calligraphy), Im Aufwind, Oncken, Ger, 77; contribr (calligraphy), Searching for You, Harper & Row, 78; illusr, Der Turm, Ulrich Schaffer (auth), Oncken, Ger, 79; and others. *Mailing Add:* 193 E St James Rd North Vancouver BC V7N 1L1 Canada

PETER, GEORGE
PAINTER, INSTRUCTOR
b New York, NY. *Study:* Brooklyn Mus Art Sch, with Reuben Tam, Abraham Rattner & Gabor Peterdi. *Work:* Butler Inst Am Art, Ohio; Ga Mus Art; Norfolk Mus Art & Sci, Va; Telfair Acad Arts & Sci, Ga; Univ Mass. *Comn:* Paintings, Sea Fare of the Aegan Restaurant, 63-75, Broadway Maintenance, 68, Winslow Construct Corp, 75 & HBSA Indust, Inc, 65-75, New York. *Exhib:* Am Embassy, Athens, Greece; 6th & 7th Ann Print, Brooklyn Mus, NY; Berkshire Mus, Mass; New York World's Fair, 65; Artists Equity Asn, Union Carbide Corp Bldg, 74. *Pos:* Founder, George Peter Sch Art. *Teaching:* Teacher contemp painting, Westchester Art Workshop, White Plains, NY, 69-; lectr & demonstr contemp painting, many cols & schs. *Mem:* Artists Equity Asn, New York. *Media:* Oil, Acrylic. *Mailing Add:* Westchester Art Workshop County Ctr B1/Tarrytown Rd White Plains NY 10606

PETERDI, GABOR F
PAINTER, PRINTMAKER
b Pestujhely, Hungary, Sept 17, 15; US citizen. *Study:* Hungarian Acad, Budapest; Acad Julien, Paris; Atelier 17, Paris, with Hayter. *Work:* Whitney Mus Am Art, Mus Mod Art & Metrop Mus Art, New York; Art Inst Chicago; Boston Mus Fine Arts; and others. *Exhib:* Retrospectives, Brooklyn Mus, 59, Cleveland Mus, 62, Corcoran Gallery Art & Yale Univ Art Gallery, 64 & Honolulu Acad Arts, 68; Suzanne Brown Gallery, Scottsdale, Ariz, 81;

Jacques Baruch Gallery, Chicago, 81; Conn Fine Arts, Westport, 81; over 100 solo exhibits and 22 retrospectives. *Teaching:* Instr, Brooklyn Mus Art Sch, 48-52; assoc prof, Hunter Col, 52-59; prof art, Yale Univ, 60- *Awards:* Prix du Guggenheim Fel, 64-65 *Bibliog:* V Johnson (auth), Graphic Work 1934-69, Touchstone, 69. *Mem:* Silvermine Guild Artists; Florentine Acad Design; Nat Drawing Soc. *Media:* Oil, Intaglio. *Publ:* Auth, Printmaking, 59 & Great Prints of the World, 69, Macmillan; auth, Printmaking, Encycl Britannica. *Dealer:* Grace Borgenicht Gallery 1018 Madison Ave New York NY 10021. *Mailing Add:* 108 Highland Ave Rowayton CT 06853

PETERS, DIANE (PECK)
PAINTER, DESIGNER
b Corpus Christi, Tex, May 14, 40. *Study:* Univ Okla Art Workshop, with Milford Zornes, 75; Master Class in Watercolor, with Edward Betts, 78; La Tech Univ, with Douglas Walton, 78. *Work:* Corpus Christi Mus, Tes. *Comn:* Stained glass window series, Olszewski Stained Glass Studio, Corpus Christi, 71, mural, 73; and others. *Exhib:* 39th Watercolor Soc of Ala Ann nat Competition, Birmingham Mus Art, Ala; Southern Watercolor Soc 2nd Ann Exhib, Columbus Mus Arts & Sci, Ga; Allied Artists Am 65th Ann Exhib, Nat Acad Galleries, New York; Salmagundi Club 2nd & 3rd Ann Non-member Exhib, Salmagundi Galleries, New York; Southwestern Watercolor Soc 18th Ann Membership Exhib, Dallas; Watercolor Southwest Three, Houston Pub Libr, Tex; and others. *Pos:* Reporter, Southwestern Watercolor Soc, Tex Chap, 76-78. *Awards:* John Herweck Award, John Herweck Co, 77; Merchants Award, Green Printing Co, 77; Third Prize, West Tex Watercolor Asn, 79. *Bibliog:* Jay Rosser (auth), Woman's art is more than a pastime, Corpus Christi Caller Times, 2/79; Lee Dodds (auth), Tonkaland a winner, Corpus Christi Times, 6/79; Spotlight Ed (auth), Local artist has show in New York, Corpus Christi Times, 12/79. *Mem:* Assoc Allied Artists Am; assoc Am Watercolor Soc; Southwestern Watercolor Soc; Southern Watercolor Soc; Audubon Artists. *Media:* Watercolor, Acrylic; Stained Glass. *Publ:* Illusr, cover, Star to Star, 1/72. *Dealer:* Sundial II Gallery 508 S Austin St Rockport TX 78382. *Mailing Add:* 531 Chamberlain St Corpus Christi TX 78404

PETERS, LARRY DEAN
CURATOR, ADMINISTRATOR
b Manhattan, Kans, July 15, 38. *Study:* Washburn Univ, BFA, 62; Southern Ill Univ, with Nicholas Vergette, MFA, 65. *Work:* Afghanistan Embassy, Kabul; Singapore Embassy. *Exhib:* 16th Mid-Am Exhib, William Rockhill Nelson Gallery, Kansas City, Mo, 66. *Collections Arranged:* Artists of the American West, 74, Topeka Crafts Exhib 1-8, 77-84, Recent Acquisitions, 78, Ukiyo-E, Pictures of the Floating World (The Japanese Woodblock Print), 78, Precolumbian Figurative Clay, Carpets of the Caucasus, Robert Motherwell's a la pintura & The Age of Art Nouveau, Gallery Fine Arts, Topeka Pub Libr. *Pos:* Readers adv, Dept Fine Arts, Topeka Pub Libr, 65-73, gallery dir, Gallery Fine Arts, 73- *Teaching:* Instr pottery, Washburn Univ Topeka, Kans, 69-70. *Mem:* Am Asn Mus; Mountain Plain Mus Asn; Kans Mus Asn (bd mem, 79-); Kans Art Comn; Kans Artist Craftsmen Asn (sec, 69-71, pres, 71-73). *Mailing Add:* Topeka Pub Libr 1515 W Tenth St Topeka KS 66604

PETERSEN, ROLAND CONRAD
PAINTER, PRINTMAKER
b Endelave, Denmark, Mar 31, 26; US citizen. *Study:* Univ Calif, Berkeley, AB, 49 & MA, 50; San Francisco Art Inst, 51; Calif Col Arts & Crafts, summer 54; Atelier 17, Paris, with Stanley W Hayter, 50, 63 & 70; Islington Studio, London, 77; The Print Workshop, London, 80. *Work:* Mus Mod Art & Whitney Mus Am Art, New York; Philadelphia Mus Art, Pa; Nat Collection Fine Arts, Washington, DC; Univ Reading, Eng; San Francisco Mus Mod Art. *Comn:* Dams of the West (portfolio of 25 color prints), US Dept Interior, Bur Reclamation, Washington, DC, 70. *Exhib:* Carnegie Inst Int, Pittsburgh, 64; 25th Ann Exhib Contemp Art, Art Inst Chicago, 65; one-man shows, Phoenix Art Mus, Ariz, 72, Santa Barbara Mus, Calif, 73 & Rorick Gallery, San Francisco, 81-83. *Pos:* Mem educ process, Col Lett & Sci, Univ Calif, Davis, 65, mem exec comt, 65-66. *Teaching:* Instr painting, Wash State Univ, 52-56; prof painting & printmaking, Univ Calif, Davis, 56-; instr printmaking, Univ Calif, Berkeley, summer 65. *Awards:* Guggenheim Fel, 63; appointee, Inst Creative Arts, Univ Calif, 67 & 70; Fulbright Travel Award, 70. *Bibliog:* James Mellow (auth), article, Art Int, 67; William Wilson (auth), article, Los Angeles Times, 76; Andree Marchal-Workman (auth), article, Artweek, 81; and others. *Mem:* Intercontinental Biog Asn; Calif Soc Etchers. *Dealer:* Staempfli Gallery 47 E 77th St New York NY 10021; Brubaker Gallery 300 John Ringling Blvd Sarasota FL 33577. *Mailing Add:* Art Dept Univ Calif Davis CA 95616

PETERSEN, WILL
PRINTMAKER, PAINTER
b Chicago, Ill, Dec 9, 28. *Study:* Mich State Univ, BA, 51, MA, 52; Calif Col Arts & Crafts, MFA, 56; Kawamura Noh Theatre, Kyoto, Japan, 57-65. *Work:* Oakland Mus, Calif; Victoria & Albert Mus, London, Eng; Portland Art Mus, Ore; Baltimore Mus of Art; Bibliot Nat, Paris. *Comn:* Two hundred forty paintings, Burroughs Corp, Detroit, Mich; Dark Dancer Watcher Suite (etchings), comn by Jan Murdock, Flint, Mich, 83; and others. *Exhib:* Ten Yrs of Am Prints, Brooklyn Mus Art, NY, 56; 15th, 16th & 17th Kyoto Art Exhib, Japan, 63-65; Int Soc Plastic & AV Art Int, Seoul, Korea, 67; Brit Int Print Biennial, Bradford Art Mus, Yorkshire, Eng, 70; 30 American Printmakers, Ohio State Univ, 82; The Figure: Continuing Tradition, Fairweather-Hardin Gallery, 83; and others. *Pos:* Founder & pres, Bay Printmakers Soc, Oakland, Calif, 55-57; publ, Plucked Chicken Press, Chicago, Ill, currently. *Teaching:* Instr, Ohio State Univ, 65-69 & WVa Univ, 70-77. *Awards:* Best-of-the-Yr, Kyoto, Japan, Mainichi Newspaper, 63; Suda Prize Painting, Kyoto Fine Arts

Mus, 65; and others; and others. *Bibliog:* Nancy Wilson Ross (ed), The World of Zen, Random House, 60; Jack Kerouac (auth), Heaven & Other Poems, Grey Fox Press, 77; Ron Jones (auth), article, Art Voices/South, 3/78; and others. *Publ:* Auth, Stone Garden, Evergreen Rev, Grove Press, rev 57; translr, Akutagawa's A Fool's Life, Mushinsha, 70; translr, Zeami's Noh: Yashima, Mushinsha, 77; auth, The Mask, The Return, Day of the Hundred Dances, Kazuraki. *Dealer:* Fairweather Hardin Gallery 101 E Ontario Chicago IL 60611. *Mailing Add:* Plucked Chicken Press PO Box 5941 Chicago IL 60680

PETERSON, A E S
PAINTER, PRINTMAKER
b Northampton, Mass, June 30, 08. *Study:* Herman Itchkawich, Providence, RI & C Gordon Harris, Lincoln, RI. *Work:* Attleboro Mus, Md; Grant Capitol Mgt Corp, Providence; RI Hosp Trust Co, Providence & Pawtucket; Tillinghast-Stiles Co, East Providence; RI Group Health Asn, Providence. *Exhib:* Butler Inst Am Art, Youngstown, Ohio, 70; Rocky Mountain Nat Watermedia Exhib, Foothills Art Ctr, Golden, Colo, 74; Nat Acad Design, New York; Springfield Mus, Mass; Jersey City Mus, NJ; Riverside Mus, NY; and others. *Awards:* Gold Medal for Cabanas, Catharine Lorillard Wolf Art Club, 71; Kathleen Grumbacher Medal for Urban Renewal, 73; Medal of Honor for Urban Renewal, Painters & Sculptors Soc NJ, 73. *Bibliog:* R Stevens (auth), Nobody home, La Rev Mod, 11/1/65; Ralph Fabri (auth), Old barn, Syndicate Mag, 6/69 & Cabanas, Today's Art Mag, 5/72. *Mem:* Am Watercolor Soc; Nat Soc Painters Casein & Acrylic (dir, 70-77); Allied Artists Am; Nat Asn Women Artists; Salmagundi Club, New York. *Media:* Watercolor, Casein. *Mailing Add:* 27 Holbrook Ave Rumford East Providence RI 02916

PETERSON, DAVID WINFIELD
PAINTER
b Chicago, Ill, Feb 7, 13. *Study:* Northwestern Univ & Univ Wis, BS, 35; with David R Peterson, Carroll Berry, Edmond J Fitzgerald, Emile A Gruppe & S E Oppenheim. *Work:* Brevard Art Mus, Melbourne, Fla; Gold Room, Easton, Md; Salmagundi Club, New York; City Hall, Naples, Fla. *Exhib:* Salmagundi Club Ann, New York, 77-83; Int Soc Marine Painters, Brevard Mus, Mass & Fla, 79-83; Am Soc Marine Artists Nat Anns, NY, 80-83; Grand Central Art Galleries, New York; Am Art Prof League. *Teaching:* Pvt classes. *Awards:* Award, Ft Myers Beach Art Asn, Elizabeth Niven, 78. *Mem:* Int Soc Marine Painters; Salmagundi Club; Naples Art Asn (bd dirs, 76-81); Artists Fel; Am Artists Prof League. *Media:* Oil. *Publ:* Illusr, Hunting is for the Birds, Naples Printing Co, 81. *Dealer:* Mc Nichols Art Gallery 1170 Third St S Naples FL 33940; Arnold Art 210 Thomas St Newport RI 02840. *Mailing Add:* 2750 Gulf Shore Blvd N Naples FL 33940

PETERSON, HAROLD PATRICK
LIBRARIAN, EDITOR
b Chicago, Ill, Aug 27, 35. *Study:* Harvard Col, AB; Univ Wis, MA. *Pos:* Art librn & ed-in-chief, Minneapolis Inst Arts, 72- *Mem:* Art Libr Soc NAm; Col Art Asn; Midwest Art Hist Asn. *Interests:* Decorative arts, history of printing, illustration of books. *Publ:* Ed, Victorian High Renaissance, 78, New Treasures at the Institute, 78, Millet's Gleaners, 78 & Treasures of the Hermitage Museum of Leningrad, 79, Minneapolis Inst Arts; ed, Chinese Jades: Archaic & Modern, Tuttle, 77; and many others. *Mailing Add:* Minneapolis Inst of Arts Minneapolis MN 55404

PETERSON, JOHN DOUGLAS
ADMINISTRATOR, MUSEUM DIRECTOR
b Peshtigo, Wis, July 9, 39. *Study:* Univ Wis, 58; Layton Sch Art, cert indust design, BFA, 62; Cranbrook Acad Art, 62-64, MFA, 66; Oakland Univ, 64-65. *Exhib:* Made of Plastic, Bloomfield Art Asn, 70; Detroit Artists, Mkt, 71; James Yaw Gallery, 71; Bloomfield Art Asn, 71. *Collections Arranged:* Dr & Mrs Hilbert De Lawter-African Collection, 67; Miaja Grottel Retrospective-Ceramics, 71; Wallace Mitchell Retrospective-Painting, Memorial--Painting 77; Concept and Manufacture of Decorative Arts, 78; Survey of Illinois Fiber, 78; Survey of Illinois Photography, 78. *Pos:* Pres, Romaine Gallery, 64-65; asst dir, Cranbrook Acad Art/Mus, 68-70, assoc dir, 70-71, dean students, Acad, 72-74, dir mus, 71-77; pres, VCI Inc, 77-; dir, Lakeview Mus Arts & Sci, 77- *Teaching:* Instr exhib design, Cranbrook Acad Art, 70-72. *Mem:* Ill Arts Coun; Mich Coun Arts; Advocates for the Arts; Am Asn Mus; Midwest Mus Conf; and others. *Mailing Add:* Lakeview Mus Arts & Sci 1125 W Lake Ave Peoria IL 61614

PETERSON, LARRY D
PAINTER, EDUCATOR
b Holdrege, Nebr, Jan 1, 35. *Study:* Kearney State Col, BA, 58; Northern Colo Univ, MA, 62; Univ Kans, EdD, 75. *Work:* Univ Minn; US Nat Bank, Omaha; Kearney State Col; 425 works in pvt collections. *Comn:* Acrylic & oil paintings, First Methodist Church, Kearney, 72; watercolor paintings, Kearney State Bank, 80. *Exhib:* 13th Midwest Biennial, 74 & Nebraska '75 Exhib, Joslyn Art Mus, 75, Omaha; Ann Am Nat Miniature Exhib, Laramie, Wyo, 77 & 80-81; Elder Gallery, Nebr Wesleyan Univ, Lincoln, 80; Augustana Col, Sioux Falls, SDak, 80; Col St Mary, Omaha, 80; Tenth Ann Nat Fall Art Fete, Scottsbluff, Nebr, 80-81; and others. *Teaching:* Instr art, North Platte Pub Schs, 58-65; instr art, North Platte Col, 66-67; prof art, Kearney State Col, 67-; grad asst, Univ Kans, Lawrence, 70-71. *Awards:* Gov Art Award, State Nebr, 81; Nebr Art Educator Year, 83. *Bibliog:* Nancy Kalis (auth), article, Art Rev, 68; Reva Remy (auth), one-man rev in Rev Mod Art, Paris, 68 & 72; Tom Norwood (auth), Contemporary Nebraska Art and Artists, Univ Nebr, 78. *Mem:* Nat Art Educ Asn (nat comt, 83-84); Nebr Art Teachers Asn (past pres); Asn Nebr Art Clubs (past pres); Kappa Pi (past pres,

Beta Beta Chap); Nat Educ Asn. *Media:* Watercolor, Acrylic. *Publ:* Coauth, Nebraska Art Guide K-6, Elem Art Curric, State Nebr, 66; coauth, Nebraska Art Collection, Rural Artreach Catalog, 81-83. *Dealer:* Studio 44 4 Seminole Lane Kearney NE 68847; Art Ctr 4844 St Paul St Lincoln NE 68504. *Mailing Add:* 4 Seminole Lane Kearney NE 68847

PETERSON, ROGER TORY
ILLUSTRATOR, WRITER
b Jamestown, NY, Aug 28, 08. *Study:* Art Students League; Nat Acad Design; DSc Degrees from Franklin & Marshall Col, 52, Ohio State Univ, 62, Fairfield Univ, 67, Allegheny Col, 67, Wesleyan Univ, 70, Colby Col, 74 & Gustavus Adolphus Col, 78; Hamilton Col, Hon PhD(Humanities), 76; LHD Degrees, Amherst Col, 77 & Skidmore Col, 81; Univ Hartford, Hon DFA, 81. *Work:* New Britain Mus Am Art, Conn; Am Mus Natural Hist, New York; Calif Acad Arts & Sci, San Francisco; Carnegie Mus Natural Hist, Pittsburgh, Pa; Metrop Mus Art, New York; and many others. *Exhib:* Leigh Yawkey Woodson Art Mus, Wausau, Wis, 76, 78 & 81; Smithsonian Inst, 79; Mass Audubon Soc, 81; Univ Conn, Storrs, 81; Univ Hartford, Conn, 81; Calif Acad Sci, San Francisco, 81-82; and many others. *Pos:* Art ed, Audubon Mag, 34-43; art dir, Nat Wildlife Fedn, 46-75; ed, Houghton Mifflin Co, Am Naturalist Series, 65-; spec consult, Nat Audubon Soc, 70-; roving reporter, Int Wildlife Mag, 70; mem, Galapagos Int Sci Proj, 64. *Teaching:* Instr art & sci, Rivers Sch, Brookline, Mass, 31-34; educ dir, Nat Audubon Soc, 34-43; lectr, Audubon Screen Tour, Nat Audubon Soc, 46-72; fel, Davenport Col, Yale Univ, 66- *Awards:* Presidential Medal of Freedom, 80; Ludlow Griscom Award, 80; Bradford Washburn Award, Boston Mus Sci, 81. *Bibliog:* Jerry Bowles (auth), Artist profile: Roger Tory Peterson, Acquire, 76; Sevlin/Naismith (auth), The world of Roger Tory Peterson, Times Bks, 77; John Diffily (auth), A field guide to Roger Tory Peterson, Am Artist, 77. *Mem:* Soc Animal Artists; Soc Wildlife Artists, Eng (vpres, currently); Nat Audubon Soc (bd dirs, 58-60, 65-67 & 68-70); patron Am Ornithologists Union (1st vpres, 62-63); Int Comt Bird Protection (chmn, 65-70); and others. *Publ:* Auth, ed & illusr, A Field Guide to the Birds, 34, 39, 47 & 80; ed, A Field Guide to Western Birds' Nests, 79; coauth & illusr, Audubon's Birds of America, Abbeville Press, 81; ed, A Field Guide to the Atmosphere, 81 & A Field Guide to Coral Reefs of the Caribbean and Florida, 82; and many other field guides and ornithology books. *Dealer:* Mill Pond Press Inc 204 S Nassau St Venice FL 33595. *Mailing Add:* Neck Rd Old Lyme CT 06371

PETERSON, SUSAN HARNLY
EDUCATOR, CERAMIC ARTIST
b McPherson, Kans, July 21, 25. *Study:* Monticello Col, Alton, Ill, AA, 44; Mills Col, Oakland, Calif, AB, 46; New York State Col Ceramics, Alfred Univ, NY, MFA, 50. *Work:* Mus Art, Oakland, Calif; Mus Art, Long Beach, Calif; Mus Art, Lausanne, Switzerland; Smithsonian Inst, Washington, DC; Mengei-kan Mus, Tokyo, Japan. *Exhib:* Nat Decorative Arts & Ceramic, Wichita Art Asn Mus, 47-62; Ceramic Art of the 60's, Los Angeles Co Mus Art; Smithsonian Exhib Ceramics; Am Ceramic Soc; Int Ceramic, Brussels Worlds' Fair; World Craft Coun, Lima, Peru; Mus Contemp Craft, New York. *Collections Arranged:* Indian Artists: Five Matriarchs (auth, catalog), ACA Gallery, New York, 80; Maria Martinez: Five Generations of Potters (auth, catalog), Smithsonian Inst, Renwick Gallery, Washington, DC. *Teaching:* Instr ceramics, Wichita Art Asn Sch, Kans, 47-49; instr & chmn ceramics, Chouinard Art Inst, Los Angeles, 52-55; assoc prof ceramics, Univ Southern Calif, Los Angeles, 55-72; prof studio art, Hunter Col, New York, 72- *Awards:* Wrangler Award for Best Western Art Book, Nat Cowboy Hall Fame, 79; Nat Endowment Arts Critics Fel, 80; Fel Award, Hunter Col, City Univ New York, 80-81. *Bibliog:* F Carlton Ball (auth), Terra-sigilatta of Susan Peterson, Ceramics Monthly, 56. *Mem:* Nat Coun Ceramic Educ; World Craft Coun; Am Craft Coun; Southern Calif Design Div Am Ceramic Soc (pres, 66). *Media:* Ceramics. *Res:* Glaze technology and indigenous folk art. *Publ:* Auth, Wheels, Kilns, and Clay, Univ Southern Calif, Press, 69; auth, Shoji Hamada: A Potter's Way and Work, 74 & auth, The Living Legend of Maria Martinez, 77, Kodansha Int; contribr, Studio Potter, Am Craft & Ceramics Monthly. *Mailing Add:* c/o Hunter Col Box 1251 New York NY 10021

PETHEO, BELA FRANCIS
PAINTER, PRINTMAKER
b Budapest, Hungary, May 14, 34; US citizen. *Study:* Univ Budapest, MA, 56; Acad Fine Arts, Vienna, with A P Guetersloh, 57-59; Univ Vienna, 58-69; Univ Chicago, MFA, 63. *Work:* Hungarian State Mus Fine Arts, Budapest; Kunstmus, Bern, Switz; Univ Minn Art Mus, Minneapolis; Tweed Mus, Duluth, Minn; Rhodes Nat Gallery, Salisbury, Zibabwe; and others. *Comn:* Kindliche Untugenden (mural), Asn Austrian Boyscouts, Vienna, 58; The History of Handwriting (exhib panel), comn by Noble & Noble Publ for Hall of Educ, New York World's Fair, 64; plus others. *Exhib:* Hamline Univ, 66; Coffman Gallery, Univ Minn, 66; Moorhead State Col, 69; Biennale Wis Printmakers, 71; Duluth: A Painterly Essay, Tweed Mus Art, Minn, 75; B P Themes: 1953-1983, CSB Gallery, St Joseph, Minn, 83; and others. *Teaching:* Instr art, Univ Northern Iowa, 64-66; assoc prof art & artist in residence, St John's Univ, 66- *Awards:* Belobende Anerkennung, Acad Fine Arts, Vienna, 58; graphic prize, Univ Chicago, 62; Purchase Award, Pillsbury Invitational, 81; and others. *Bibliog:* Arturo Carlo Quintavalle (auth), Bela Petheo, Univ Parma & St John's Univ Res Coun Publ, 67; plus others. *Mem:* Col Art Asn Am; Los Angeles Printmaking Soc. *Media:* Lithography; Oil, Acrylics. *Publ:* Auth, Rembrandt's pupils in the Museum of Fine Arts in Budapest, Szabad Muveszet, 6/56; auth, Polymer-coated lithographic transfer paper, In: Five artists--their printmaking methods, Artists Proof, 68; auth, The college art gallery, Art J, summer 71; auth, Manuscript illuminations and the modern stained glass painter, Stained Glass, winter 75; auth, Lithography: an Introduction, traveling exhib, 78, In: The Tamarind Papers, Vol 2, No 2, Spring, 79. *Dealer:* Groveland Gallery 25 Groveland Terrace Minneapolis MN 55403. *Mailing Add:* 400 NE Riverside Dr St Cloud MN 56301

PETLIN, IRVING
PAINTER
b Chicago, Ill, Dec 17, 34. *Study:* Art Inst of Chicago, BFA, 52-56; Yale Univ, MFA, with Josef Albers, 59. *Work:* Art Inst Chicago; Jewish Mus, New York; Mus Mod Art, New York; Mus d'Art Mod, Paris, France; Metrop Mus, New York. *Exhib:* Art Inst of Chicago, 53, 56 & 72; Mus d'Art Mod, Paris, 61-66; Chicago Imagist Art, Mus Contemp Art, Chicago, 72; Whitney Mus Am Art, New York, 73; Retrospective, Palais des Beaux-Arts, Brussels, Belg, 65; Neuberger Mus, State Univ NY Col, Purchase, 78; Arts Club Chicago, 78. *Teaching:* Instr, Univ Calif, Los Angeles, 63-66; vis prof, Cooper Union, New York, 78-83; artist in residence, Dartmouth Col, fall 83. *Awards:* Ryerson Fel, 56; Copley Found Grant, 61; Guggenheim Found Fel, 71. *Media:* Oil on Canvas; Pastel on Paper. *Dealer:* Marlborough Gallery 40 W 57th St New York NY 10019. *Mailing Add:* 267 W 11th St New York NY 10014

PETRIE, FERDINAND RALPH
PAINTER, ILLUSTRATOR
b Hackensack, NJ, Sept 17, 25. *Study:* Parsons Sch Design, New York, cert advert, 49; Art Students League, with Frank Reilly; Famous Artists Course Illus, cert, 59. *Work:* Nat Collection Fine Art, Smithsonian Inst, Washington, DC; Indianapolis Mus Art; J F Kennedy Libr, Boston; US Navy Combat Art Gallery, Washington, DC. *Exhib:* Allied Artists Am, Nat Acad Design Gallery, New York, 71-77; Am Artists Prof League Grand Nat, New York, 71-79; Am Watercolor Soc Travel Exhib, 73, 75-78; White House Loan Exhib from Smithsonian Inst, Washington, DC, 73-75. *Pos:* Illusr, J Gans Assoc Studio, New York, 50-69. *Teaching:* Pvt instr watercolor, 72-78; instr, DuCret Sch Art, 75-77. *Awards:* Salmagundi Club Awards, 70-83; US Navy Gold Medal for Watercolor, 74; Gold Medal, Hudson Valley Art Asn, 76. *Mem:* NJ Watercolor Soc; Artists Fel; Salmagundi Club; Rockport Art Asn; Am Watercolor Soc. *Media:* Watercolor, Oil. *Publ:* Illusr, Salvation Army, 75-83; illusr, Reader's Digest covers, 77 & 79; auth, Drawing Landscapes in Pencil, 79, The Color Book, 81 & The Alkyd Book, 82, Watson-Guptill. *Dealer:* Petrie Gallery 57 Main St Rockport MA 01966; Grand Central Galleries New York NY 10017. *Mailing Add:* 51 Vreeland Ave Rutherford NJ 07070

PETRIE, SYLVIA SPENCER
PRINTMAKER, PAINTER
b Wooster, Ohio, June 15, 31. *Study:* Col Wooster, BA; State Univ Iowa, with Mauricio Lasansky & Eugene Ludens; Univ RI. *Work:* Graphics Soc, Hollis, NH; Art Ctr Mus, Wooster Col; Gilbert Stuart Birthplace, Saundertown, RI; Providence Public Libr. *Exhib:* 4th Midwest Biennial, Joslyn Art Mus, Omaha, Nebr, 56; Mo Valley Exhib Oil Painting, Mulvane Art Mus, Topeka, Kans, 56; 9th Nat Print Exhib, Silvermine Guild, New Canaan, Conn, 72; Images on Paper, Springfield Art Asn, Ill, 73; 64th & 66th Am Annuals, Art Asn Newport, RI, 75 & 77; 16th Bradley Nat Print & Drawing Exhib, Peoria, Ill, 77; and others. *Pos:* Vis artist, Title III Prog, Coventry Elem Schs, RI, 75-77. *Awards:* Netta Strain Scott Prize Art, Wooster Col, 53; First Prize & Purchase Award, Fantle's, 56; First Prize Graphics, Westerly Art Festival, 75; and many others. *Bibliog:* Elizabeth Findley (auth), Petrie prints and pastels depend on point of view, Eve Bulletin, Providence, 10/15/77; Edward Sozanski (auth), Print forms offer intriguing tones, Providence Sunday J, 10/15/78; Arline Aissis (auth), Peace Dale artist to open show Saturday, Narragansett Times, 9/3/81. *Mem:* Cambridge Art Asn; Graphics Soc; Artists Guild & Gallery; Art Asn Newport; South County Art Asn. *Media:* Intaglio, Collagraph; Oil, Pastel. *Publ:* Illusr, From under the Hill of Night, Vanderbilt Univ, 69; illusr, The Idol, Biscuit City Press, 73; illusr, Time Songs, Biscuit City Press, 79. *Dealer:* Artists Guild & Gallery Rte 1 Charlestown RI 02908. *Mailing Add:* 66 Dendron Rd Peace Dale RI 02879

PETRO, JOSEPH (VICTOR), JR
PAINTER, ILLUSTRATOR
b Lexington, Ky, Nov 4, 32. *Study:* Transylvania Col, with Victor Hammer; grad art, Cincinnati Med Sch, art as appl to med. *Work:* Hermitage Mus, Leningrad, USSR. *Comn:* Panorama of American Medicine (mural), Hardin Hosp, 83; Brown & Bigelow calendars; 32 paintings, Keeneland Collection, Keeneland Racing Asn, Lexington, Ky; 28 portraits of pres of Transylvania Col, 1794-1980, Transylvania Col; series of paintings of all Triple Crown winners for Oaklawn Park, 73-77; mural, Hardin Mem Hospital, 82; and others. *Pos:* Publ, series ltd number collector prints, 54-79; consult, Spindletop Res, Inc, Lexington, 65-68; head, Dept Appl Art, Loyola Univ of Chicago, Rome Ctr, Italy, 69-77; vis prof art, John Cabot Int Col, Rome, Italy, 75-76; cult adv, US Info Serv, Am Embassy, Rome, Italy, 73-77; designer, Franklin Mint, Franklin Ctr, Pa, 80- *Teaching:* Prof art, Transylvania Univ, Lexington, Ky, 78-; artist in residence, Transylvania Univ, 82- *Awards:* Morrison Medallion, Transylvania Univ, 83. *Mem:* Soc Illusr; Southeastern Ctr Contemp Art; Artists Equity, Washington, DC. *Publ:* Illusr, var publ including Thoroughbred Rec, Nat Geog, Holiday, Better Homes & Gardens & others. *Mailing Add:* 357 Henry Clay Blvd Lexington KY 40502

PETTET, WILLIAM
PAINTER
b Whittier, Calif, Oct 10, 42. *Study:* Chouinard Art Inst, Los Angeles. *Work:* Whitney Mus Am Art, New York; Mus Mod Art, New York. *Exhib:* Nicholas Wilder Gallery, Los Angeles, 66; Whitney Mus Am Art, New York, 67 & 73; Corcoran Mus Art Biennial, 69; Aldrich Mus Art, 69; Recent Acquisitions, Mus Mod Art, New York, 70 & 74; Spray, Santa Barbara Mus Art, Calif, 71; Art of the 70s, Seattle Art Mus, Wash, 72; one-man shows, Willard Gallery, New York, 75 & S & G Mathews Gallery, San Antonio, Tex, 78 & 79; New in the 70s, Austin Art Mus, Tex, 77; and others. *Teaching:* Instr painting, Skowhegan Sch Paintings & Sculpture, summer 72; fac mem mentor prog, Empire State Col, 77. *Awards:* Tamarind Fel, 70. *Media:* Liquitex. *Mailing Add:* 14 Beach 213th St Rockaway Point NY 11697

PETTIBONE, JOHN WOLCOTT
CURATOR, GRAPHIC ARTIST
b Springfield, Ohio, Jan 30, 42. *Study:* Wittenberg Univ, 62-63; Cleveland Inst Art, 63-65, Ford grant, 64. *Work:* Am Red Cross, Washington, DC; Town of Rockport, Mass. *Exhib:* Rockport Art Asn, 71-; Am Fortnight Exhibition, Hong Kong, 73. *Pos:* Dir marketing, Hammond Castle Mus, Gloucester, Mass, 83- *Teaching:* Instr drawing, Lakewood Pub Schs, Ohio, 59; instr drawing, Springfield Art Asn, Ohio, 61-63; instr drawing, Rockport Pub Schs, 73-78. *Mem:* Rockport Art Asn; Arms & Armour Soc, London; Co Mil Historians, Washington, DC. *Media:* Conte Crayon, Silverpoint. *Dealer:* Rockport Art Asn 12 Main St Rockport MA 01966. *Mailing Add:* 196-A Main St Rochester MA 01966

PETTIBONE, RICHARD H
PAINTER
b Los Angeles, Calif, Jan 5, 38. *Study:* Pasadena City Col, AA, 59; Otis Art Inst, MFA, 62. *Work:* Israel Mus, Jerusalem; Lowe Art Ctr, Syracuse, NY; De Mennil Found, Houston; Rose Art Mus, Brandeis Univ. *Exhib:* One-man show, O K Harris, New York, 70-78; Small Images, Art Inst Chicago, 75; Max Protetch Gallery, Washington, DC, 76; Small Objects, Whitney Mus Downtown, New York, 77; Art About Art, Whitney Mus Am Art, New York, 78; Elhrich Gallery, New York, 79-80; Tortue Gallery, Los Angeles, Calif, 80-82; 20 Yr Survey, Los Angeles Valley Col; and others. *Media:* Oil on Canvas; Silkscreen on Canvas. *Dealer:* Tortue Gallery 2917 Santa Monica Blvd Santa Monica CA 90404. *Mailing Add:* Star Route Charlotteville NY 12036

PETTUS, JANE MESSICK
PAINTER
b St Louis, Mo, Oct 9, 08. *Study:* With Wallace H Smith & William Quinn. *Work:* Butler Inst Am Art, Youngstown, Ohio; Clopton Auditorium, Wash Univ, Mary Inst Ctr Arts & Jr League Club Rooms, St Louis, Mo; Sheldon Swope Mus, Terre Haute, Ind. *Comn:* Portrait (oil) Dr Walter Ballinger, Barnes Hospital, St Louis, Mo, 79, portrait Dr William Newton, 81. *Exhib:* One-woman shows, St Louis Artists Guild, Mo, 61 & 80, Chase Gallery, New York, 62 & 68, Sheldon Swope Mus, Terre Haute, Ind, 69, Camptell House Found, St Louis, Mo, 71 & Busch Mem Ctr, St Louis Univ, Mo, 81. *Awards:* Award for Semi Realistic Painting, St Louis Artists Guild, Jean T Knowles, 65; Portrait Exhib, St Louis Artist Guild, Clay Eugene Jordan, 68. *Bibliog:* Alexis Wallace Carton (auth), St Louis: middle of the road, Art in Am, 60; C N W (auth), article, Art News, 68; TV Newsbeat, NBC, 81. *Mem:* St Louis Artists Guild; Nat Soc Arts & Letters. *Media:* Oil, Ink. *Mailing Add:* 3 York Hills St Louis MO 63144

PEZZATI, PIETRO
PAINTER
b Boston, Mass, Sept 18, 02. *Study:* Child-Walker Sch Art; also with Charles Hopkinson; in Europe. *Work:* Med Sch & Bus Sch, Harvard Univ; Sch Med & Sch Educ, Univ Pa; Children's Hosp Medical Ctr, Boston; Yale Sch Med; Mass Hist Soc; and others. *Exhib:* Exhibited regionally and nat in group and one-man shows. *Teaching:* Instr, schs and pvt classes & demonstr techniques. *Mailing Add:* c/o Fenway Studios 30 Ipswich St Boston MA 02215

PFAHL, CHARLES ALTON, III
PAINTER
b Akron, Ohio, May 15, 46. *Study:* With Robert Brackman, Madison, Conn, John Koch, New York & Jack Richard, Cuyahoga Falls, Ohio. *Exhib:* Audubon Artist Ann, 70-72; Butler Inst Am Art Ann, Youngstown, Ohio, 72-74; FAR Gallery, New York, 73 & 78; Three Centuries of American Nude Traveling Exhib, 75; Westmorland Co Mus, 79; Retrospective, Grand Central Galleries, 80; and others. *Teaching:* Instr painting, Art Students League, New York, 81- *Awards:* Halgarten Awards, Nat Acad Design, 76 & 81; Andrew Carnegie Prize, Nat Acad Design, 78; Isaac N Maynard Prize, Nat Acad Design, 80; plus others. *Bibliog:* Article, Am Artist Mag, 3/73; J Singer (auth), Charles Pfahl: Artist at Work, Watson-Gutpill, 77; article, After Dark, 3/81. *Mem:* Allied Artists Am; Audubon Artists; Salmagundi Club. *Media:* Pastel, Oil. *Dealer:* Grant Central Art Galleries 24 W 57th St New York NY. *Mailing Add:* 525 West 45th St New York NY 10036

PFEIFER, MARCUSE
DEALER, GALLERY DIRECTOR
b Little Rock, Ark, Nov 4, 36. *Study:* Sarah Lawrence Col, AB, 58. *Collections Arranged:* Gravure, 74; American Indian Photographs from the 19th & Early 20th Century, 74; Cyanotype, 75; The Male Nude (auth, catalog), Marcuse Pfeifer Gallery, 78. *Pos:* Asst to dir, New Sch Art Ctr, New York, 66-70; dir photog art, Robert Schoelkopf Gallery, New York, 70-76; gallery owner, Marcuse Pfeifer Gallery, 76- *Mem:* Asn Int Photography Art Dealers (pres, 80-82). *Specialty:* Photography. *Publ:* Auth, Thank Heaven for Little Girls/Lewis Carroll, Bk Forum, 79. *Mailing Add:* 825 Madison Ave New York NY 10021

PFISTER, HAROLD FRANCIS
ADMINISTRATOR
Evanston, Ill, Dec, 25, 47. *Study:* Harvard Col, BA, 69; Univ Del, MA, 74. *Collections Arranged:* Facing the Light: Historic American Portrait Daguerrotypes, 78; American Portrait Drawings (with Marvin S Sadik), 80. *Pos:* Asst dir, Nat Portrait Gallery, Washington, DC, 80-83, actg dir, 82-83; asst dir, Cooper-Hewitt Mus, New York, 83- *Mem:* Col Art Asn; Soc Archit Historians. *Res:* American architectural history; portraiture. *Publ:* Auth, Burlingtonian architectural theory in England & America, Winterthur Portfolio II, 76; auth, Facing the Light: Historic American Portrait Daguerrotypes, 78 & coauth, American Portrait Drawings, 80, Smithsonian Press. *Mailing Add:* 65 Nassau St Apt 4C New York NY 10038

PFRIEM, BERNARD
PAINTER, DIRECTOR
b Cleveland, Ohio, Sept 7, 16. *Study:* John Huntington Polytech Inst, 34-36; Cleveland Inst Art, 36-40; Europ study, 50-52. *Work:* Mus Mod Art, Chase Manhattan Bank, Metrop Mus Art, New York; Brooklyn Mus; Columbia Banking, Savings & Loan Asn, Rochester, NY. *Comn:* Murals, Guerrero & Mexico City, Mex. *Exhib:* Six shows, Iolas Gallery, NY, 49-63; Whitney Mus Am Art, 52 & 65; retrospective, Cleveland Inst Art, 63; Richard Feigen Gallery, Chicago, 67; Am Drawing Soc, 70; Cleveland Inst Art, 73; Pa State Univ, 74; plus others. *Pos:* Dir, studio arts sessions in Southern France, Cleveland Inst Art. *Teaching:* Instr drawing & painting, Peoples Art Ctr, Mus Mod Art, 46-51; instr drawing, Cooper Union Sch Art & Archit, 63-71; instr, Sarah Lawrence Col, 69-76. *Awards:* Mary Ranney Traveling Scholar, Western Reserve Univ; Copley Award Painting, 59; Prize Drawing, Norfolk Mus Arts & Sci. *Bibliog:* Patrick Waldberg (auth), Bernard Pfriem (monogr), William & Noma Copley Found, 61 & Main et marvielles, Mercure, France, 61; Patricia Allen Dreyfus (auth), The inward journey (monogr), Am Artist, 9/72. *Mailing Add:* 115 Spring St New York NY 10012

PHELAN, ANDREW L
EDUCATOR, PAINTER
b May 8, 43. *Study:* Pratt Inst, Brooklyn, NY, BA(art educ), 65, MFA, 69; New York Univ, post-grad, 77- *Exhib:* Finger Lakes, Mem Art Gallery, Rochester, NY, 65 & 66; New York State Exposition, Syracuse, NY, 66 & 67; two-man show, Houghton Col, NY, 68; Landscape, Still Life & Figurative Photog, Pratt Manhattan Ctr Gallery, New York, 78; one-man show, Snug Harbor Cultural Ctr, Staten Island, NY, 80. *Pos:* Dir, Saturday Art Sch, 72-77. *Teaching:* Acting chair, Art Educ Dept, Pratt Inst, Brooklyn, NY, 73-74, chmn, Art Educ Dept, 74-79, from asst dean to assoc dean, Sch Art & Design, 77-82, actg dean, 82- *Mem:* Col Art Asn; Nat Asn Sch Art; Nat Art Educ Asn; NY State Art Teachers Asn. *Media:* Oil, Ink Wash. *Res:* Historical development and current state of studio art education on the university or college level. *Publ:* Auth, The Bauhaus and studio art education, 81 & Post modern art and its influence on studio art education, 84, Art Educ. *Mailing Add:* Sch Art & Design Pratt Inst 200 Willoughby Ave Brooklyn NY 11205

PHELAN, ELLEN DENISE
PAINTER
b Detroit, Mich, Nov 3, 43. *Study:* Wayne State Univ, BFA, 69, MFA, 71. *Work:* Detroit Inst Arts; Mus Mod Art, Chase Manhattan Bank, New York; Mass Inst Technol. *Exhib:* Soho, Acad Kunste, West Berlin, 76; Pittura Ambiente, Palazzo Reale, Milan, 79; Matrix #48, Wadsworth Atheneum, 79; 3 Dimensional Painting, Mus Contemp Art, Chicago, 80; solo exhib, Clocktower, New York, 80; Kick Out the Jams: Detroit's Cass Corridor 1963-1977, Detroit Inst Arts, 80 & Mus Contemp Art, Chicago, 81; New Drawing in America, Drawing Ctr, New York, Sutton Place, London & Galerie d'Arte Mod Ca Pesaro, Venice, 82. *Teaching:* Instr painting, Calif Inst Arts, 78-79 & 83; instr painting & drawing, Sch Visual Arts, 81-83. *Awards:* Nat Endowment Arts Grant, 78-79. *Bibliog:* Barry Kahn (auth), John Egner & Ellen Phelan: Reconstructing the jams, New Art Examiner, 81; Richard Armstrong (auth), Un tour d'horizon: Mary Heilman & Ellen Phelan, Bomb Mag, 82. *Media:* Oil, Gouache. *Dealer:* Barbara Toll Fine Arts 146 Greene St New York NY 10012. *Mailing Add:* 284 Lafayette St New York NY 10012

PHELAN, LINN LOVEJOY
DESIGNER
b Rochester, NY, Aug 25, 06. *Study:* Rochester Inst Technol, dipl, 28; Ohio State Univ, BFA(ceramic art), 32; Alfred Univ, MS, 55. *Exhib:* Rochester Mem Art Gallery, 28-58; Everson Mus, Syracuse, 32-50; Albright-Knox Mus, Buffalo, 51; New York State Craftsman, Ithaca Col, 54-75; NY State Fair, Syracuse, 60-75; Hornell Area Arts Coun Summer Festival, NY, 82; 55 Years of Potting Exhib, 82 & I Love New York Ceramics Show, 82, State Univ NY Alfred. *Pos:* Owner & operator, Linnwood Pottery, 50-; mgr fair, York State Craftsmen, Inc, 57-59. *Teaching:* Instr pottery, Sch Am Craftsman, 44-50; instr art, Alfred-Almond Cent Sch, 50-67; lectr art, State Univ NY Col Ceramics, Alfred Univ, 67-72. *Awards:* NY State Fair Awards, 75. *Bibliog:* Mel Bernstein (auth), Phelan's first pottery retrospective in 55 years a delight, Alfred Sun, 10/14/82. *Mem:* NY State Art Teachers (pres, 60-61); Almond Hist Soc (mus chmn, 65-, pres, 78-80). *Media:* Ceramics. *Mailing Add:* 114 S Main St Almond NY 14804

PHELPS, NAN DEE
PAINTER
b London, Ky. *Study:* Self-taught; scholar to Cincinnati Art Mus, Ohio. *Work:* The Henry Ford Collection, Dearborn, Mich; CofC, Pulaski, Va; also in pvt collections. *Comn:* The Shepherd and Sheep, Orphanage, Trinidad Island, 65; 20 murals, comn by churches, Hamilton, Ohio, Middletown, Ohio, New Miami, Ohio & Toledo, Ohio; Tenn; numerous paintings in Peru, SAm. *Exhib:* All-American Fine Art Show, Cincinnati, Ohio; Cincinnati Art Mus, 42-56; Lynn Kottler Galleries, New York, 75. *Awards:* First Place, Ford Motor Co, 60; First Place mag cover, Kiwanis Club, Cincinnati, 60; Greater Hamilton Art Club Award. *Media:* Oil. *Publ:* Auth, Self-taught artist, Ford Times News, 58. *Mailing Add:* 1721 Green Wood Ave Hamilton OH 45011

PHELPS, ROSEMARIE BECK See Beck, Rosemarie

PHILBRICK, MARGARET ELDER
PRINTMAKER
b Northampton, Mass, July 4, 14. *Study:* Mass Col Art, grad; De Cordova Mus Workshop, with Donald Stoltenberg. *Work:* Libr of Cong, Washington, DC; Wiggin Collection, Boston Pub Libr; Nat Bezalel Mus, Jerusalem; First Nat Bank, Boston; New Brit Mus, Conn. *Exhib:* US Info Agency Serv Exhib to Far East, 58-59; 2nd Int Miniature Print Exhib, Pratt Graphic Art Ctr, New York, 66; Soc Am Graphic Artists 51st Nat, Kennedy Galleries, New York, 71; retrospective, Ainsworth Gallery, Boston, 72; Boston Printmakers 32nd Nat Exhib, De Cordova Mus, Lincoln, Mass, 79; 40 Yr Retrospective Exhib of Graphics, Westenhook Gallery, Sheffield, Mass. *Pos:* Artist & designer, Wedgwood Commemorative Plates, 44-55. *Awards:* John Taylor Arms Mem Prize, Nat Acad Design, 72; Ralph Fabri Award, Nat Acad Design, 77; Best in show, Southern Berkshire Arts Council Exhib, 81; and many others. *Mem:* Boston Printmakers (exec bd, 50-79); New England Watercolor Soc (exec bd, 75-77); Soc Am Graphic Artists; Nat Acad Design; Am Color Print Soc. *Media:* Intaglio, Watercolor. *Publ:* Illusr, On Gardening, 64 & In Praise of Vegetables, 66, Scribners; illusr, Natural Flower Arrangements, Doubleday, 72; illusr, Sheffield: Frontier Town, 76; illusr, Robert Frost's Spring Pools, Lime Rock Press, 83. *Dealer:* Ainsworth Gallery 42 Bromfield St Boston MA 02170; Westenhook Gallery Sheffield MA 01257. *Mailing Add:* Sheffield MA 01257

PHILIP, LOTTE BRAND
HISTORIAN
b Hamburg, Ger, May 27, 10; US citizen. *Study:* Univ Munich, Ger; Univ Heidelberg, Ger; Univ Freiburg, Ger; Univ Hamburg, Ger, PhD, 37. *Teaching:* Prof art hist, Queens Col, City Univ New York, 61- *Awards:* Fulbright fel; Bollingen fel; Nat Endowment for Humanities fel; plus others. *Mem:* Col Art Asn Am; Verband Deutscher Kunsthistoriker. *Res:* Medieval and Renaissance art in Northern Europe. *Publ:* The Prado Epiphany by Jerome Bosch, Art Bull, 53; Hieronymus Bosch, Abrams, New York, 55; The Peddler by Hieronymus Bosch, a Study in Detection, Netherlands Kunsth Jaarbook, 58; The Ghent Altarpiece and the Art of Jan Van Eyck, Princeton Univ Press, 71; The Portrait Diptych of Dürer's Parents, Simiolus, 79. *Mailing Add:* 58 W 68th St New York NY 10023

PHILLIPS, ALICE JANE
PAINTER
b New York, NY, Aug 30, 47. *Study:* NY Univ, with Chuck Close & John Opper, BS, 70, MA, 72. *Work:* Aldrich Mus Contemp Art; Mus City New York; Brooklyn Mus; Chase Manhattan Bank, Lehman Brothers Kuhn Loeb, New York. *Exhib:* Works on Paper--Women Artists, Brooklyn Mus, 75; Contemporary Reflections, 77 & 15 New Talents, 79, Aldrich Mus; solo shows, David Findlay Galleries, New York, 82, Van Straaten Gallery, Chicago, 83 & Dubins Gallery, Los Angeles, 83 & 84; Printed by Women, Port Hist Mus, Philadelphia, 83; Contemporary Views 84, Queens Mus, NY, 84. *Bibliog:* William Zimmer (auth), article, Soho Weekly News, 9/20/79; Carol Donnel-Kotrozo (auth), Women and art, 3/81 & Mary Vaughn (auth), article, 1/82, Arts Mag. *Mem:* Women in Arts Found (exec coordr, 78-80), secy, 80-82); Womens Caucus Art. *Media:* Acrylic, Mixed Media. *Dealer:* Dubins Gallery 11948 San Vicente Blvd Los Angeles CA 90049; van Straaten Gallery 361 W Superior Chicago IL 60610. *Mailing Add:* 32 Greene St New York NY 10013

PHILLIPS, BERTRAND D
PAINTER, PHOTOGRAPHER
b Chicago, Ill, Nov 19, 38. *Study:* Art Inst Chicago, with Paul Wieghardt & Leroy Neiman, BFA; Northwestern Univ, MFA. *Work:* Governors State Univ, Park Forest South, Ill; David & Alfred Smart Gallery, Univ Chicago, Ill; Du Sable Mus African Am Hist, Chicago; Art Inst Chicago; Erie Art Ctr, Pa; and others. *Exhib:* Art Inst Chicago, 78-80; Ill State Mus, 78 & 80; Nat Mus Haitian Art, 79-80; Cult Ctr Guyana, 79-80; NAME Gallery, Chicago, 81; Mid-America Biennial Nat Exhib, Owensboro Mus Fine Arts, Ky, 82; and many others. *Teaching:* Instr drawing & painting, Elmhurst Col, 70-72; asst prof drawing & painting, Northwestern Univ, 72-79; vis artist, Sch Art Inst Chicago, 81- *Awards:* George D Brown Foreign Traveling Fel, Art Inst Chicago, 61; Governor's Purchase Award, State Ill. *Bibliog:* Elton Fax (auth), Black Artists of the New Generation, Dodd Mead & Co, 77; and others. *Media:* Oils, Acrylic. *Mailing Add:* 6617 S Perry Chicago IL 60621

PHILLIPS, BONNIE
DEALER, PAINTER
b Salt Lake City, Utah, July 8, 42. *Study:* Univ Utah, BA. *Work:* Salt Lake Art Ctr, Utah; Utah Mus Fine Arts, Salt Lake City; Braithwaite Gallery, Southern Utah State Col, Cedar City. *Exhib:* Intermountain Biennial, Salt Lake Art Ctr, 66-77. *Pos:* Co-owner, Phillips Gallery, Salt Lake City. *Awards:* Purchase Prize, Utah 81. *Mem:* Utah Watercolor Soc. *Media:* Watercolor, Gouache. *Mailing Add:* Phillips Gallery 444 E Second South Salt Lake City UT 84111

PHILLIPS, DICK (RICHARD CORTEZ)
PAINTER, INSTRUCTOR
b Ft Worth, Tex, May 6, 33. *Study:* Texas A & M Univ, BBA, 55; with Milford Zornes, 73; also with Robert E Wood, 74, 77 & 78. *Comn:* Drawings, Arapaho Petroleum Co, Denver, Colo, 75; paintings, Valley Nat Bank, Phoenix, Ariz, 76. *Exhib:* Watercolor Exhib, US State Dept, toured Taiwan, 75; Rocky Mountain Nat, Golden, Colo, 78; Am Watercolor Soc Ann, Nat Acad Design, New York, 78; Watercolor Biennial, Ctr Arts, Scottsdale, Ariz, 78 & 80; and others. *Teaching:* Private lessons, Phoenix, Ariz, 72-; instr, Sch Int Training, Univ Okla, 77 & 78. *Awards:* Merit Awards, Western Fedn Watercolor Anns, 75, 79, 80 & 83; Best of Show, Southwest Watercolor Soc, 77; First Place, Watercolor West, 82. *Bibliog:* Paul Perry (auth), One artist's metamorphosis, Southwest Art, 78; Barbara Pearlman (auth), Making changes, Ariz Arts & Lifestyle, 81. *Mem:* Scottsdale Artists League; Ariz Artists Guild; Ariz

Watercolor Soc (bd dirs, 73-77); Southwest Watercolor Soc; San Diego Watercolor Soc. *Media:* Watercolor, Acrylic. *Publ:* Illusr, Si! Si! Mrs Crusoe, Franklin Publ, 70. *Dealer:* Austin Gallery 7103 Main St Scottsdale AZ 85251. *Mailing Add:* 7829 E Hubbell Scottsdale AZ 85257

PHILLIPS, DUTCH (JAMES O, JR)
GALLERY DIRECTOR, DEALER
b Ft Worth, Tex, Mar 29, 44. *Study:* Univ Tex, Austin, BA, 67. *Pos:* Dir, Ft Worth Gallery, currently. *Specialty:* Contemporary painting and sculpture; Pre-Columbian and African art. *Mailing Add:* Ft Worth Gallery 901 Boland Ft Worth TX 76107

PHILLIPS, GIFFORD
COLLECTOR, WRITER
b Washington, DC, June 30, 18. *Study:* Stanford Univ, 36-38; Yale Univ, BA, 42. *Mem:* Trustee Mus Mod Art, New York; trustee Phillips Collection, Washington, DC; trustee Rothko Found, New York; trustee Pasadena Art Mus (pres, 73-74, secy-treas, 75-76); Mus Mod Art Int Coun (bd dirs); Los Angeles Co Mus Art Contemp Art Coun. *Collection:* Contemporary American painting and sculpture. *Publ:* Auth, Arts in a Democratic Society, 66; auth, articles, Art News, Artforum & Art Am. *Mailing Add:* 2501 La Mesa Santa Monica CA 90402

PHILLIPS, HELEN (ELIZABETH)
SCULPTOR, GRAPHIC ARTIST
b Fresno, Calif, Mar 3, 13. *Study:* Calif Sch Fine Arts, San Francisco, with Ralph Stackpole, 32-36. *Work:* Mus Mod Art, Bank Am World Hq, San Francisco; De Young Mus; Victoria & Albert Mus; Dallas Mus Contemp Art. *Exhib:* San Francisco Art Asn Ann, San Francisco Mus Mod Art, 36, 48 & 60; Salon de Mai, Mus Art Mod, Paris, 70-74; II Int Bianalle Sculpture, Middleheim, Belg, 53; Womens Int Art Club, New Burlington Gallery, London, 55; Int Biannalle Sculpture, Mus Rodin, Paris, 56, 61 & 65; Formes Francaises, Mus Art Mod, Zurich, 57; 14 Americaines En France, Smithsonian Traveling Exhib, 60-62; Salon de Mai en Holland, Stedleck Mus, Amsterdam, 61. *Awards:* Phelan Traveling Award Sculpture, San Francisco Art Asn, 36; Copley Found Int Sculpture Prize, 58. *Publ:* Contribr, Ides of March, Tigers Eye Mag, 49. *Mailing Add:* 737 Washington St New York NY 10014

PHILLIPS, IRVING W
CARTOONIST, ILLUSTRATOR
b Wilton, Wis, Nov 29, 05. *Study:* Chicago Acad Fine Arts. *Work:* Smithsonian Inst. *Comn:* Stage play adaptations, One Foot in Heaven, Gown of Glory, Mother was a Bachelor & Rumple, Alvin Theatre, New York, 55; and others. *Exhib:* Nat Cartoonist Soc; New York World's Fair; one-man shows, Comedy in Art, Ariz State Univ & El Prado Gallery, Sedona, Ariz. *Pos:* Cartoon humor ed, Esquire Mag, 37-39; cartoon staff, Chicago Sun-Times Syndicate, 40-52; motion picture assignments with Warner Bros, RKO, Charles Rodgers Prod & United Artists, formerly; auth & illusr, syndicated strip appearing int in 180 papers in 22 countries, The strange world of Mr Mum, formerly; auth & illusr, Syndicated Allied Feature Syndicate, Barnaby Bungle, 79. *Teaching:* Instr cartooning & humor writing, Maricopa Tech, Phoenix, currently. *Awards:* Int First Prize & Cup, Salone dell'Umorismo of Bordighera, Italy, 69. *Mem:* Writers Guild Am; Dramatists Guild; Nat Cartoonists Soc; Mag Cartoonists Guild; Newspaper Cartoon Coun; and others. *Publ:* Auth & illusr, The Strange World of Mr Mum, 65; auth, The Twin Witches of Fingle Fu, 69; auth, No Comment by Mr Mum, Popular Libr, 71; auth & co-auth, 260 TV scripts; contribr, scripts & animation to ABC-TV children's prog, Curiosity Shop; and many others. *Mailing Add:* 2807 E Sylvia St Phoenix AZ 85032

PHILLIPS, JAMES
HISTORIAN, PAINTER
b Black River Falls, Wis, Aug 11, 29. *Study:* Layton Sch Art, Milwaukee, Wis; Univ Wis-Madison, BS; Art Students League; Acad de Grande Chaumiere; Ecole dy Louvre, Paris; Univ Tex, Austin, MA, MFA & PhD. *Work:* Art Inst Chicago. *Exhib:* Forty Artists Under Forty, Fulbright Painters (nationwide showings) & Young America, Whitney Mus Am Art, New York; one-man show, G Gallery, New York, 62. *Teaching:* Instr art hist, Kearney State Univ, Nebr, 66-68; instr, Univ Tex, Austin, 68-79; asst prof art hist, Va Commonwealth Univ, Richmond, currently. *Awards:* Fulbright Prize Award, US State Dept, 56-57; Louis Comfort Tiffany Award, Tiffany Found, 57-58; Neysa McMein Purchase Award, Whitney Mus Am Art, 60. *Mem:* Col Art Asn; Am Archaeol Soc; Soc Archit Historians. *Media:* Egg Tempera; Oil. *Res:* Roman and late antique art, emphasis on architecture. *Publ:* Contribr, Temoin de France, Appleton, 66. *Mailing Add:* 2024 W Main Richmond VA 23220

PHILLIPS, JAMES M
MUSEUM DIRECTOR, COLLECTOR
b Philadelphia, Pa, July 18, 46. *Study:* Glassboro State Col, BA, 75. *Work:* Antietam Nat Mus, Sharpsburg, Md; and others. *Pos:* Dir, Antietam Nat Mus, 68- *Teaching:* Lectr, Univ Wyo, 83. *Mem:* Co of Military Historians; Am Bladesmiths' Soc. *Collection:* Artifacts of soldiers who fought in the Civil War through the Viet Nam Wars; uniforms, weapons, photographs, paintings, documents and writings of participants. *Publ:* Auth, The Nunchaku II, 74 & ed, Bail Out Over North Africa, 80, Phillips Publ; contribr, Art Cop-Robert Volpe-Art Crime Detective, Dodd, 75; ed, Moran: Fire and Steel, 82; publ, The Airborne Album, Vol I, 82. *Mailing Add:* PO Box 168 Williamstown NJ 08094

PHILLIPS, LAUGHLIN
MUSEUM DIRECTOR
b Washington, DC, Oct 20, 24. *Study:* Yale Univ, 42-43; Univ Chicago, MA(philos), 49. *Pos:* Pres & trustee, Phillips Collection, Washington, DC, 67-, dir, 72- *Mem:* Am Asn Mus Dirs. *Mailing Add:* 1600 21st St Washington DC 20009

PHILLIPS, MARJORIE
PAINTER
b Bourbon, Ind, Oct 25, 1894. *Study:* Art Students League; additional study with Kenneth Hayes Miller & Boardman Robinson; Smith Col, hon DFA, 72. *Work:* Whitney Mus Am Art, New York; Corcoran Gallery Art, Washington, DC; Santa Barbara Mus, Calif; Phillips Collection, Washington, DC; Mus Fine Arts, Boston. *Exhib:* American Painting, Tate Gallery, London, 46; Carnegie Inst Int, Pittsburgh; one-woman shows, Calif Palace of Legion of Honor, San Francisco, 59; Edward Root Art Ctr, Munson-Williams-Proctor Inst, Utica, NY, 65 & retrospective, Marlborough Galleries, London, 73; Franz Bader Gallery, Washington, DC, 77; Phillips Collection Exhib, 78; Cosmos Club, 78. *Collections Arranged:* Seymour Lipton's Sculpture, 64; Giacomotti Sculpture and Painting, 65; Alexander Calder Sculpture, 67; Contemporary Sculpture, 68; Cezanne Exhib (with Art Inst Chicago & Boston Mus Fine Arts), to celebrate 50th Anniversary of Phillips Collection opening, 71; Forty Paintings by Washington, DC, Artists, 71-72; plus others. *Pos:* Assoc dir, Phillips Collection, 25-66, dir, 66-72, dir emer & trustee, 72- *Awards:* Award of Merit, Pa Mus Sch Art, 59. *Mem:* Am Fedn Arts. *Media:* Oil. *Publ:* Auth, Duncan Phillips and his Collection, Atlantic, Little, Brown, 72. *Mailing Add:* 2101 Foxhall Rd NW Washington DC 20007

PHILLIPS, MATT
PAINTER, EDUCATOR
b New York, NY. *Study:* Univ Chicago, MA; Stanford Univ; Barnes Found. *Work:* Nat Collection Fine Art in Pub Libr, Whitney Mus Am Art, Metrop Mus Art, New York; Nat Gallery Art; Philadelphia Mus Art. *Exhib:* Retrospective, Baltimore Mus Art, 61-75; Princeton Gallery Fine Art, 71; Smithsonian Inst Traveling Exhib, 72; William Zierler Gallery, New York, 72-73; Retrospective, Phillips Collection, Washington, DC, 76-77; Middendorf/Lane, Washington, DC, 78; Donald Morris Gallery, Birmingham, Mich; and others. *Teaching:* Prof & head dept art, Bard Col, 64- *Publ:* Auth, Maurice Prendergast: The Monotypes (catalog), 67 & Milton Avery: Works on Paper (catalog), 71, Bard Col; auth, The monotype today, Artist's Proof, 69; auth, The Monotype: An Edition of One, Smithsonian Inst Traveling Exhib, 72. *Dealer:* Marilyn Pearl 29 W 57th St New York NY 10019. *Mailing Add:* Bard Col Annandale-on-Hudson NY 12504

PHILLIPS, ROBERT J
FILMMAKER, EDUCATOR
b Montclair, NJ, Feb 28, 46. *Study:* Jersey City State Col, BA(art educ), 68; New York Univ Grad Sch Arts, MFA(photog, film & TV), 72; Found for Mind Res, Pomona NY, creative actualization with Dr Jean Houston & Dr Robert Masters, Res & Teaching Assoc, 75- *Pos:* Designer of high sch film educ prog, identified as exemplary model curriculum site by Am Film Inst, DC, 68-70; coordr, Film Festival, 19th Congress Int Soc for Educ Through Art, 69; asst proj dir, NJ State Coun on Arts, Inner City Arts Proj, Hoboken, NJ, 70; proj dir, Summer Arts Workshop for Mentally Handicapped, Title VI grant, East Orange, NJ, 71; chmn, Comt for Creative Actualization, New Ways of Being Inst Conf, Minneapolis, Dallas, Los Angeles & NJ, 78-79. *Teaching:* Instr art, Photog & film, Woodbridge Sr High Sch, NJ; educator-at-large, master classes & teacher-in-service training in creative actualization, camera arts & fine arts, schs, communities & cols throughout the east, 72-; adj instr, creative actualization & camera arts, Caldwell Col, NJ, 72-; adj instr, camera arts & still life, New York Univ Sch Educ, 75- *Awards:* Bronze Phoenix Award for outstanding creative achievement in filmmaking, Atlanta Int Film Festival, Ga, 74; Award for Outstanding Achievement in film direction, in graphic design, Int Creativity Ann, Art Direction Mag, 74; Cert Excellence, filmmaking, NJ Art Dir's Club, 75; plus others. *Media:* Video Tape, Multi Media. *Publ:* Filmmaker & photog, Qualify (film), Net Channel 13, New York, 71; Choice Not Chance (film), 74 & Daydreams and Indecision, 79, NJ State Dept Educ; Asbury Park--A Renaissance, Asbury Park Dept Community Affairs, 79; Art and Multi-Sensory Learning (filmstrip), Educ Frontiers Assocs, 80. *Mailing Add:* Dept Art Caldwell Col Caldwell NJ 07006

PHILLIS, MARILYN HUGHEY
PAINTER, INSTRUCTOR
b Kent, Ohio, Feb 1, 27. *Study:* Ohio State Univ, BS, 49; Toledo Mus Art Sch Design, 61; studied with Fred Leach, Jeanne Dobie, Edward Betts, Glenn Bradshaw, Robert Laessig & Nita Engle. *Work:* Springfield Art Ctr, Kissell Co, Springfield, Ohio; E F McDonald Co, Gem Plaza Bldg, Dayton; Rolls Royce Ltd, Palmyra, NY. *Exhib:* Allied Artists Am, Nat Acad & Nat Arts Galleries, New York, 74-77, 80 & 81; Am Watercolor Soc, Nat Acad Gallery, New York & traveling, 74, 76, 78, 79 & 82; Nat Watercolor Soc, Laguna Beach Mus & Palm Springs Mus, Calif, 74, 80 & 83; solo exhib, Columbus Mus Art, Ohio, 81; Watermedia Exhib, Springfield Art Ctr, Ohio, 81 & 83; Ga Watercolor Soc, High Mus Mem Arts Ctr, 83; and others. *Pos:* Illusr, Western Reserve Mag, 74-78. *Teaching:* Instr art, Edison State Community Col, 76; instr watercolor, Springfield Art Ctr, Ohio, 76- & Boston Mills Workshops, Peninsula, Ohio, 81- *Awards:* William Church Osborne Award, Am Watercolor Soc, 74; Nat Watercolor Soc Award, Watercolor West Exhib, 82; Papercraft Corp Award, Pittsburgh Aqueous, 83. *Bibliog:* Fred Kalister (auth), Directions in watercolor dialogue, Ohio Arts J, 1-2/81; Jacqueline Hall (auth), Phillis art works offer poetic look at nature, Columbus Dispatch,

5/2/82; Maxine Masterfield (auth), Painting the Spirit of Nature, Watson-Guptill, 84. *Mem:* Watercolor Soc, Am & Nat; Allied Artists Am; Watercolor West; Ohio Watercolor Soc (rec secy, 78-82, vpres, 82-84). *Media:* Watermedia. *Publ:* Illusr, Historic Piqua: An Architectural Survey, Piqua Br, Am Asn Univ Women, 76; auth, article on Glenn Bradshaw, Ohio Watercolor Soc, 83. *Dealer:* Windon Gallery 1644 W Fifth Ave Columbus OH 43212. *Mailing Add:* 9744 N Country Club Rd Piqua OH 45356

PHILLPOT, CLIVE JAMES
LIBRARIAN, WRITER
b Thornton Heath, Eng, June 26, 38. *Study:* Polytech of N London, ALA, 67; Univ London, Dipl HA(with distinction), 74. *Collections Arranged:* Artists' Bookworks, touring exhib in Ger (auth, catalog), 75; Ways of Making, touring exhib in Wales (auth, catalog), 75; Artists' Books (auth, catalog), Inst Contemp Arts, London, 76; The Art Press (auth, catalog), Victoria & Albert Mus, London, 76 & Art Gallery of Ontario, Toronto, 79; The Page as Alternative Space, Franklin Furnace, New York, 80; Collaborations (auth, catalog), Ctr Bk Arts, new York, 82 & State Univ NY, Purchase, 82. *Pos:* Librn, Chelsea Sch Art, London, 70-77; dir libr, Mus Mod Art, New York, 77-; mem bd dirs, Printed Matter, Inc; mem adv comt Arch Am Art. *Bibliog:* The New York Times, 10/10/80; article, Mus Mod Art, No 26, spring 83. *Mem:* Art Librs Soc, United Kingdom; Art Libr Soc North Am (secy, 79-81); Col Art Asn; Asn Art Critics. *Res:* Visual language, visual communication. *Interests:* Contemporary art. *Publ:* Contribr, Art Library Manual, Resources and Practice, Bowker, 77; contribr, Visual Literature Criticism, Southern Ill Univ Press, 79; guest ed, Art J, summer 82; plus many articles and reviews in various art magazines and library journals. *Mailing Add:* Mus Mod Art 11 W 53rd St New York NY 10019

PIATEK, FRANCIS JOHN
PAINTER, INSTRUCTOR
b Chicago, Ill, Dec 9, 44. *Study:* Sch Art Inst Chicago, BFA & MFA. *Work:* Art Inst Chicago. *Comn:* Mural, Main State Bank Chicago, 72. *Exhib:* Whitney Mus Am Art Ann Exhib Contemp Am Painting, 68; one-man shows, Hyde Park Art Ctr, 69, Phyllis Kind Gallery, 72, Merrimac Col, 74 & NAME Gallery, Chicago, 75. *Teaching:* Instr painting, Art Inst Chicago, 70-71 & 75-; instr painting, Washington Univ, St Louis, 73-74. *Awards:* Art Inst Traveling Fel, Francis Ryerson, 67; Pauline Potter Palmer Award, 68 & John G Curtis Prize, 69, Chicago & Vicinity Shows. *Media:* Oil, Acrylic. *Mailing Add:* 3925 N Troy St Chicago IL 60618

PICCILLO, JOSEPH
PAINTER
b Buffalo, NY, 1941. *Study:* State Univ NY Col Buffalo, MFA, 64, fel, 68, 69 & 72. *Work:* Mus Mod Art, New York; Brooklyn Mus; Art Inst Chicago; Butler Inst Am Art, Youngstown, Ohio; Minn Mus Art, Minneapolis. *Exhib:* One-man show, Albright-Knox Art Gallery, Buffalo, 69; Smithsonian Inst Traveling Drawing Exhib, 71; Monique Knowlton Gallery, 80, 81 & 83; Betsy Rosenfield Gallery, 80 & 83. *Pos:* Consult, NY State Coun Arts, 75-77. *Teaching:* Prof art, State Univ NY Col Buffalo, currently. *Awards:* Childe Hassam Purchase Award, Am Acad Arts & Lett, 68; Nat Endowment for Arts fel, 79. *Publ:* Diane Cochrane (auth), J Piccillo's game structures, Am Artist, 12/73. *Publ:* Illusr, covers, Poverty in America, 5/17/68 & Black vs Jew-A tragic confrontation, 1/31/69, Time Mag. *Dealer:* Monique Knowlton Gallery 153 Mercer St New York NY 10012. *Mailing Add:* 257 Franklin St Buffalo NY 14202

PICCOLO, THOMAS FRANK
SCULPTOR, JEWELER
b Bridgeport, Conn, June 3, 45. *Study:* NTex Univ; Tex Tech Univ; El Centro Col; Univ Tex, Dallas, BA(summa cum laude), 77; E Tex State Univ. *Comn:* Bronze-wood combinations, Fryburger Collection, San Antonio, Tex, 75; Brookhaven Country Club, Dallas, 76; Jewish Community Ctr, San Antonio, Tex, 79. *Exhib:* One-man shows, Expos Gallery, 80, Contemp Gallery, Dallas, 80 & El Centro Col, 80; and others. *Teaching:* Prof sculpture, El Centro Col, 73-; prof, Community Serv Prog, Dallas, 74-; jeweler workshops at var univs. *Awards:* Richardson Bank First Sculpture Award, NTex Regional, 74. *Bibliog:* Article in Tex Mo, 12/76; Janet Kutner (auth), articles in Art News, 4/77 & 11/80; Two galleries spotlight innovative sculpture, Dallas Morning News, 10/80. *Media:* Wood, Stone; Silver, Gold. *Publ:* Auth, Wood and metal flow in modern sculpture, San Angelo Standard Times, 75. *Mailing Add:* 6410 Dykes Way Dallas TX 75230

PICHER, CLAUDE
PAINTER, CURATOR
b Quebec City, Que, May 30, 27. *Study:* Que Fine Arts Sch, 45-46; New Sch Social Res, New York, with Julian Levi, 48; Ecole du Louvre, Paris, with Jean Cassou, 48-49; Ecole Nat Superieure des Beaux-Arts de Paris, with Demeter Galanis. *Work:* Nat Gallery Can, Ottawa; Art Gallery Ont, Toronto; Lord Beaverbrook Art Gallery, Fredericton, NB; Agnes Etherington Art Gallery, Kingston, Ont. *Comn:* Mural of Old Que, Hall of the Claridge, Quebec City, 67. *Exhib:* Montreal Mus Fine Arts, 58 & 64; 2nd Int Biennial, Mus Mod Art, Paris, France, 61; Lord Beaverbrook Art Gallery, 62; Que Mus, Quebec City, 67. *Pos:* Eastern rep, Nat Gallery Can, 58-61; assoc dir, Que Mus, 63-64. *Awards:* Jessie Dow Found Award, 73rd Spring Exhib, Montreal Mus Fine Arts, 56; Acquisition Prize, Nat Gallery Can, Govt of Can, 57 & Lord Beaverbrook Art Gallery, Can Art Coun, 62. *Bibliog:* Robert Fulford (auth), Twenty-four young Canadian artists, Can Art Mag, 61; Guy Viau (auth), La peinture au Canada-Francais, Ministere des Affaires Culturelles, 64; Guy Robert (auth), La peinture au Quebec depuis 1940, Ed La Presse, 73. *Mem:* Royal Can Acad Arts. *Media:* Oil. *Interests:* Pre-1920 art work. *Dealer:* Walter Klinkhoff Gallery 1200 Sherbrooke St W Montreal PQ Can. *Mailing Add:* St-Leandre RR 8 Matane PQ G0J 2V0 Canada

PICKENS, ALTON
PAINTER, INSTRUCTOR
b Seattle, Wash, Jan 19, 17. *Study:* Reed Col. *Work:* Mus Mod Art. *Teaching:* Prof art, Vassar Col, 56-83; retired. *Mailing Add:* 35 Smith St Poughkeepsie NY 12601

PICKFORD, ROLLIN, JR
PAINTER
b Fresno, Calif. *Study:* Calif State Univ; Stanford Univ, BA; also with Alexander Nepote, Ralph DuCasse, James Weeks & Joseph Mugnaini. *Work:* Springfield Art Mus, Mo; State of Calif Collection, Sacramento; Ford Motor Co, Dearborn, Mich; City of Santa Paula, Calif; Monterey Peninsula Mus Art; and others. *Exhib:* Watercolor USA, Springfield, Mo, 62, 65 & 66; Mainstreams Marietta, Ohio, 68; Austrian-Am Exchange Exhib, Linz, Salzburg & Vienna, Austria, 72; Taiwan-Am Exchange Exhib, 73; Royal Watercolor Soc, London-WCoast Watercolor Soc Exchange Exhib, 75-76; and others. *Teaching:* Instr art, Fresno State Col, 48-62. *Awards:* Best of Show, All-California Exhib, 60; First Prize & Purchase Award, Watercolor USA, 62; First Prize & Purchase Award, Calif State Fair, 63; and others. *Mem:* West Coast Watercolor Soc; Carmel Art Asn. *Media:* Multimedia. *Publ:* Illusr, stories by William Saroyan, Lincoln-Mercury Times & Ford Times, 50's; auth, A philosophical approach to watercolor, Am Artist, 69. *Mailing Add:* 930 E Sierra Madre Fresno CA 93704

PICKHARDT, CARL
PAINTER, PRINTMAKER
b Westwood, Mass, May 28, 08. *Study:* Harvard Univ, AB, 31; study with Harold Zimmerman, 30-35. *Work:* Mus Mod Art, New York; Mus Fine Arts, Boston; Newark Art Mus, NJ; Libr Cong, Washington, DC; Brooklyn Art Mus, NY. *Exhib:* Int Biennial of Color Lithography, 51; Carnegie Inst Int, 52; Int Exhib, Japan, 52; Am Drawing Biennial, Norfolk, Va, 66; Pa Acad Fine Arts, Philadelphia, 67; Radcliffe Col, 83. *Teaching:* Instr printmaking, Worcester Mus Art Sch, 49-50; instr printmaking, Art Students League, 51; instr painting, Fitchburg Art Mus, 51-62. *Awards:* Shope Prize, Nat Acad Design, 42. *Bibliog:* Parker Tyler (auth), Carl Pickhardt, Horizon, 72; and others. *Mailing Add:* 66 Forest St Sherborn MA 01770

PIEHL, WALTER JASON, JR
PAINTER, EDUCATOR
b Marion, NDak, Aug 1, 42. *Study:* Concordia Col, BA, 64; Univ NDak, MA, 66; Univ Minn, 69. *Work:* Pillsbury Co, St Paul, Minn; Fed Reserve Bank Minneapolis; NDak Governor's Collection, Bismarck; Plains Art Mus, Moorhead, NDak. *Comn:* Mosaic mural, Devils Lake Sioux Tribe, NDak, 71; Univ NDak Mobile Art Gallery Graphic, Art Gallery Asn, NDak statewide tour, 79. *Exhib:* 19th Ann Drawing, Ball State Mus, Muncie, Ind, 73; Ann Images, Anoka Ramsey Col Gallery, Minn, 73; Midwestern Graphics, Tulsa City Libr Mus, Okla, 74; 15th Ann Nat Graphics, Okla Art Ctr, Oklahoma City, 74; one-man shows, Dynamics of Rodeo & Landscape, Univ Art Galleries, Grand Forks, NDak, 75 & 81 & Rodeo Imagery, Plains Art Mus, Moorhead, Minn, 66, 69, 70 & 76. *Collections Arranged:* Great Plains Traveling Exhib, 70-71; Northwest Biennial Invitation (auth, catalog), 71; Artrain (traveled), 75; Dakota Made, Mobile Gallery, 79; Nat Watercolor Invitation (auth, catalog), 79-80. *Teaching:* Instr art, Valley City State Col, NDak, 67-68; from asst prof to assoc prof art, Minot State Col, NDak, 69-. *Awards:* Purchase Awards, Nat Graphics, Univ NDak, 72 & Northwestern Bak Corp, 74 & Drawing USA, Minn Mus Art, 73. *Bibliog:* Nancy Edmonds Hanson (auth), Contemporary artists of the west, NDak Horizons, 75; article, Art Voices South, 81. *Mem:* NDak Art Gallery Asn (vpres, 79-80); NDak Coun on Arts. *Media:* Mixed. *Dealer:* Wildine Gallery 903 Rio Grande Blvd NW Albuquerque NMex 87104. *Mailing Add:* RR 4 Box 108 Minot ND 58701

PIENE, OTTO
SCULPTOR, PAINTER
b Laasphe, Westphalia, Ger, Apr 18, 28. *Study:* Blocherer Art Sch & Acad of Fine Arts, Munich, 48-50; Dusseldorf Art Acad, WGer, 50-53; Univ Cologne, WGer, 53-57. *Work:* Albright-Knox Art Gallery, Buffalo, NY; Mus Mod Art, New York; Carnegie Inst Int Mus Art, Pittsburgh, Pa; Nat Gallery of Can, Ottawa, Ont; Stedelijk Mus, Amsterdam, Holland; and others. *Comn:* Olympic Rainbow, Munich, 72. *Exhib:* Sixteen German Artists, Corcoran Gallery of Art, Washington, DC, 62; Mus am Ostwall, Dortmund, WGer retrospective, 67; Earth, Air, Fire, Water: Elements of Art, Mus Fine Arts, Boston, Mass, 71; Westphalian Art, Westfalisches Landsmuseum, Munster, Ger, 73; Documenta 6, Ctr Advan Visual Studies, Mass Inst Technol, 77, Kassel, Ger; one-man shows, Trumbull Col, Yale Univ, New Haven, Conn, 69, Centro de Arte y Communicacion, Buenos Aires, Art, 72 & Kolnischer Kunstverein, Cologne, 73; Hayden Gallery, Mass Inst Technol, Cambridge, Mass, 75; Fitchburg Art Mus, Mass, 77; and many others. *Pos:* Dir, Ctr Adv Visual Studies, Mass Inst Technol, Cambridge, currently. *Teaching:* Prof environmental art, Sch Archit & Planning, Mass Inst Technol, 72. *Awards:* Konrad von Soest Prize, Munster, 68; Tamarind Fel, Los Angeles, Calif, 69; Prize, Tokyo Graphics Biennale, Mus Mod Art, Tokyo, Japan, 72. *Bibliog:* Dietrich Mahlow, et al (auth), Otto Piene--Werkverzeichnis der Druckgrafik 1960-76, Karlsruhe, WGer, 77; Lawrence Alloway (auth), Otto Piene, St Gallen, Switz, 79; Heiner Stachelhaus & Jurgen Claus (auth), Otto Piene, Essen, Ger, 83. *Publ:* Auth, Rainbows, 71, More Sky, 73 & co-auth, Zero, 73, Cambridge, Mass; coauth & co-ed, Sky Art (conference catalogs), Cambridge, Mass, 81, 82 & 83; and others. *Mailing Add:* c/o Mass Inst Technol 40 Massachusetts Ave Cambridge MA 02139

PIEPENBURG, ROBERT
SCULPTOR
b Detroit, Mich, Oct 28, 41. *Study:* Eastern Mich Univ, BS, 64, MA, 65, MFA, 73. *Work:* Detroit Inst Arts; Smithsonian Inst. *Comn:* Sculpture, Cadillac City Co Bldg, Mich, 79; mural, Liberty State Bank, Clinton, Mich, 81; sculpture, Fed Mogul World Hq, Southfield, Mich, 82; fountain, Sheraton Hotel, Novi, Mich, 82. *Exhib:* Solo exhib, Robert Kidd Gallery, Birmingham, Mich, 80; Wichita Art Mus, Kans, 81; Duluth Art Inst, Minn, 81; Eastern Ill Univ, 82; Univ Mich, Ann Arbor, 83. *Teaching:* Instr ceramics, Oakland Community Col, Ill, 69-, Vancouver Sch Art, 76 & Tyler Sch Art, 77. *Awards:* Nat Endowment Arts Fel, 80; Mich Coun Arts Creative Artist Grant, 81. *Bibliog:* Nino Caruso (auth), Ceramic Raku, Hoepli, 82. *Mem:* Nat Coun Educ Ceramic Arts. *Media:* Ceramics, Welded Steel. *Publ:* Auth, Raku Pottery, Macmillan, 72. *Mailing Add:* 1313 N Main Ann Arbor MI 48104

PIERCE, ANN TRUCKSESS
PAINTER, EDUCATOR
b Boulder, Colo, Aug 28, 31. *Study:* Univ Colo, Boulder, BFA, 53, MFA, 55; Yale Univ summer sch, fel, 53; study with Bernard Chaet, Gabor Peterdi, Jimmy Ernst, N Marsicano; workshops with Harold Gretzner, Robert E Wood, Morris Shubin, Jade Fon, George Post, Millard Sheets, Tom Hill, Tom Nicholas & Millard Sheets. *Work:* Tri-Counties Bank, Mangrove; Pillsbury Branches, Chico, Calif; Yale Univ, New Haven, Conn; Forum Gallery, New York; Calif State Univ, Chico; and others. *Exhib:* Rocky Mt Nat Watermedia Exhib, Foothills Art Ctr, Golden, Colo, 74, 77-81; San Diego Watercolor Soc Nat, Cent Fed Tower Plaza Gallery, 76, 77, 78, 80 & 81; Scottsdale Watercolor Biennial, Scottsdale Ctr for Arts, Ariz, 78 & 80; Ann Exhib Watercolor Soc Ala, Birmingham Mus Art, 78 & 79; Watercolor West, Riverside Art Ctr, Calif, 79 & 81; Nat Watercolor Soc, Desert Mus, Palm Springs, Calif, 79-81 & traveling exhib, 79 & 80. *Teaching:* Grad asst drawing & watercolor, Univ Colo, Boulder, 53-54, instr, summers, 59 & 62; prof drawing & watercolor, Calif State Univ, Chico, 64- *Awards:* First & Second Prize, Calif State Fair, 82; Award of Excellence & Purchase Award, Lodi Ann, 83; Silver Recognition, San Diego Watercolor Soc, 83. *Bibliog:* Paintings reproduced, Visual Dialog Mag, fall, 75 & Int Soc Artists Communicator, fall, 79; Practical Guide for Beginning Painters, Prentice-Hall, 81. *Mem:* Nat Watercolor Soc; Watercolor Soc Ala; Watercolor West; Rocky Mountain Nat Watermedia Soc; Nat Asn Wonmen Artists. *Mailing Add:* 545 W Shasta Ave Chico CA 95926

PIERCE, DANNY P
SCULPTOR, PAINTER
Study: Chouinard Inst Art, Los Angeles; Am Art Sch, New York; Brooklyn Mus Art Sch; Univ Alaska. *Work:* Mus Mod Art, New York; Nat Libr, Paris; Nat Mus Sweden, Stockholm; Huntington Libr, San Marino, Calif. *Comn:* Eskimo scene panels, 62, abstract design in concrete for cafeteria bldg, 63, Univ Alaska. *Exhib:* Traveling Exhib Prints, Europe, Eurasia, 59-62; Northwest Printmakers Int, Seattle Art Mus, 68; Washington Art, Worlds Fair, Osaka, Japan, 70; Edge of the Sea, Bradley Gallery, Milwaukee, 73, 75, 77, 79 & 81; one-man show, Small Bronzes, 74 & Oost Duinkerke, Belgium, 80. *Pos:* Artist in residence, Univ Alaska, 59-63. *Teaching:* Assoc prof art, Univ Wis-Milwaukee, 65- *Awards:* Green Memorial Award for Best Oil, Conn Acad Art, 49; Purchase Award, Libr Cong, 52, 53 & 58; Northwest Printmakers International Award, Seattle Art Mus, 68. *Publ:* Auth & illusr, Cattle Drive, 76, 77, Shepherdess of Monument Valley, 79, Man, Horse, Sea, 80, Sea Wreck, 81 & Birds, 81, pvt publ. *Dealer:* Bradley Galleries Downer Ave Milwaukee WI; Assoc Am Artists New York NY. *Mailing Add:* 3547 N Murray Ave Milwaukee WI 53211

PIERCE, DELILAH W
PAINTER, EDUCATOR
b Washington, DC, Mar 3, 04. *Study:* DC Teachers Col, dipl; Howard Univ, BS; Columbia Univ, MA; also Lois Jones, Celine Tabary, Ralph Pearson, James Lesene Wells & Jack Perlmutter. *Work:* Howard Univ Gallery Art, Washington, DC; Barnett-Aden Gallery Collection; Anacostia Mus, Smithsonian Affil; Smith-Mason Gallery Collection. *Comn:* Portrait of Dr Eugene A Clark, comn by family for Eugene A Clarke Pub Sch, Washington, DC, 69. *Exhib:* Area Show, 57-59 & Travel Exhib, 60-61; Corcoran Gallery Art; Howard Univ Gallery, 76; Afro-Am Hist & Cult Mus, Philadelphia, Pa, 76; Frick Fine Arts Mus, Univ of Pittsburgh, 77; Nat Mus Am Art, Washington, DC, 81; Univ Md Art Gallery, Ill State Univ Traveling Exhib, 81-82; and many others. *Teaching:* Instr art, sec pub schs, Washington, DC, 25-52; instr art & art educ, DC Teachers Col, 52-56, prof art & art educ, 56-69, vis prof art educ, 70-71; vis prof art educ, Howard Univ Sch Educ, 64-67. *Awards:* Achievement Award, Phi Delta Kappa, 63; Achievement Award, Phi Delta Kappa, 63; Award, Nat Conf Artists, 81; and others. *Bibliog:* Cedric Dover (auth), American Negro art, NY Graphic Soc, 60; J E Atkinson (auth), Black dimensions in contemporary American art, Carnation Co, 71; Profile of Delilah W Pierce, Artist/Educator (videotape), Howard Univ Pub TV. *Mem:* Soc Washington Artists (treas, 69-); Artists Equity Asn; Washington Watercolor Asn; Nat Conf Artists (nat treas, 73-81); DC Art Asn. *Media:* Oil, Acrylic. *Publ:* Auth, Can art serve as a balance wheel in education?, Educ Arts Asn J, 49; auth, The significance of art experiences in the education of the Negro, J Negro Life & Hist. *Dealer:* Smith-Mason Gallery 1207 Rhode Island Ave NW Washington DC 20005; Evans-Tibbs Gallery 1910 Vermont Ave NM Washington DC 20001. *Mailing Add:* 1753 Verbena St NW Washington DC 20012

PIERCE, DIANE
ILLUSTRATOR, SCULPTOR
b Lakewood, Ohio, Mar 6, 39. *Study:* Cleveland Inst Art, Ohio, dipl, 61; Western Reserve Univ, BA, 62. *Work:* Ward Found Mus, Salisbury, Md; Heard Mus, McKinney, Tex; Ind State Mus, Indianapolis; Prime Minister Indira Ghandi, New Delhi, India; Clairson Int, Ocala, Fla. *Comn:* Christmas card, Nat Audubon Soc, New York, 77 & Nat Wild Turkey Fedn, 77; warbler calendar, Nat Wildlife Fedn, 79-81; postal stamp design, Govt India. *Exhib:* One-person show, Cornell Lab of Ornithology, 73; Int Exhib Wildbird Artists, Woodson Art Mus, Wausau, Wis, 76-82; Wildfowl Art Exhib, Ward Found, 76, 77 & 79; Soc Animal Artists Mem Show, New York, 76-82; Midwest Wildlife Art Show, Kansas City, Mo, 76-78; Waterfowl Festival, Easton, Md, 77-79 & 83; Game Coin Int, San Antonio, Tex, 79; NAm Wild Animal Art Exhib, Cowboy Hall of Fame, Oklahoma City, Okla, 79. *Awards:* First Place, Ind Duck Stamp Contest, 79; First Place, Long Island Duck Stamp Contest, 80. *Bibliog:* Stalking birds with pen & brush, Explorer Mag, Cleveland Mus Natural Hist, 78. *Mem:* Soc Animal Artists; Nature Conservancy; Outdoor Writers Asn Am. *Media:* Watercolor, Oil; Scratchboard. *Publ:* Contribr, The Living Bird, Cornell Univ Lab Ornithology, 72-83; illusr, An Introduction to Ornithology, Macmillan, 75; contribr (illus), Children's Sci Mag, 77; illusr, Endangered Birds/Temple, Wis Press, 78; illusr, Nat Geographic Field Guide to the Birds of North America, 83; and others. *Mailing Add:* c/o Edge of the Wild Spring Creek Dr Bonita Springs FL 33923

PIERCE, DONALD (BENJAMIN)
PAINTER, INSTRUCTOR
b Toms River, NJ, Jan 23, 16. *Study:* Pratt Inst, cert, 37; Grand Cent Sch Art, 38-40; with Edgar Whitney & Frederic Taubes, 47-48. *Work:* San Diego Mus Art; Rutgers Univ; Slater Mem Mus, Norwich, Conn; Celanese Corp Am, New York; Butler Inst Am Art. *Comn:* Mural (oil on canvas), Cavanaughs Restaurant, New York, 49. *Exhib:* Audubon Artists Ann, Nat Acad Design, New York, 70-82; Pratt Faculty Show, Pratt Inst Gallery, New York, 79; solo exhib, Westbeth Galleries, New York, 81; Small Works, NY Univ, 82; Am Soc Contemp Artists, Jacob Javits Bldg, New York, 83. *Teaching:* Instr painting, Donald Pierce Sch Painting, Provincetown, Mass, 55-78 & Plateau Cirque, Bronxville, NY, 58-; instr life drawing, Pratt Inst, New York, 74-79. *Awards:* Allied Artists Am Award, 67; Ranger Fund Purchase Award, Audubon Artists Ann, 68. *Bibliog:* Norman Kent (auth), Seascapes and Landscapes in Watercolor, 56 & Ernest W Watson (auth), Composition in Landscape Still Life, 59, Watson-Guptill; Frederic Taubes (auth), A Guide to Traditional and Modern Painting Methods, Viking Press, 63. *Mem:* Artists Equity Asn; Audubon Artists Am; NJ Soc Painters & Sculptors; Am Soc Contemp Artists. *Media:* Oil, Watercolor. *Publ:* Auth, Watercolor Ser, Am Artist, 54. *Mailing Add:* 463 West St D-806 New York NY 10014

PIERCE, ELIZABETH R
PAINTER
b Brooklyn, NY. *Study:* Art Students League, with John Groth, John Stewart Curry & Anne Goldthwaite; Art League Long Island, NY, with Edgar A Whitney; Columbia Univ Exten. *Work:* Children's room, Jamaica Pub Libr, NY. *Exhib:* Nat Asn Women Artists Ann, Nat Acad Design Galleries; NS Soc Artists, Halifax; Nat Mus, Washington, DC; Yarmouth Art Soc, NS; Royal Bank Can, Th'Yarc, Yarmouth, NS. *Teaching:* Instr adult educ oil painting, NS Dept Educ, Yarmouth, 59-67. *Mem:* Nat Asn Women Artists; life mem Art Students League; Yarmouth Art Soc; Visual Arts NS, Halifax. *Media:* Oil. *Mailing Add:* RR 1 Yarmouth NS B5A 4A5 Canada

PIERCE, JAMES SMITH
HISTORIAN, SCULPTOR
b Brooklyn, NY, Apr 26, 30. *Study:* Oberlin Col, AB, 52; Harvard Univ, PhD, 62. *Comn:* Earthwork, Arts Festival Atlanta Asn, 83. *Exhib:* Univ Ky Art Galleries, 74-83; Ohio State Univ, Columbus, 76; Hirshhorn Mus, Smithsonian Inst, Washington, DC, 77-78; La Jolla Mus Contemp Art, Calif, 78; Seattle Art Mus, Wash, 78; Art Ctr Asn, Louisville, Ky, 83; Contemp Arts Ctr, Cincinnati, 83; Maine Coast Artists Gallery, Rockport, 83. *Collections Arranged:* Jim Campbell (with catalog), 70, Deborah Frederick (with catalog), 71, David Middlebrook (with catalog), 71, Recent Early American, 73, Sacred Symmetry: Ancient Earthworks of the Ohio Valley (with catalog), 73, Evan Decker: Kentucky Folk Carver, 82, Ctr Contemp Art, Univ Ky. *Pos:* Dir, Ctr Contemp Art, Univ Ky, 70-71, Crossroads Mus Art, Lexington, Ky, 78-79. *Teaching:* From asst prof to assoc prof art hist, Case Western Reserve Univ, 59-69; prof art hist, Univ Ky, 69-, chmn dept art, 69-73. *Awards:* America the Beautiful Fund Grant, 72; Best Images and Fantasy Award, Nat Film Soc, 73; Nat Endowment for the Humanities independent study fel, 76. *Bibliog:* John Beardsley (auth), Probing the Earth: Contemporary Land Projects, Hirshhorn Mus, Smithsonian Inst, Washington, DC, 77; John Beardsley (auth), James Pierce and the picturesque landscape, Art Int, XXIII, 12/79; John Beardsley (auth), Traditional aspects of new land art, Art J, fall 82. *Media:* Earth, Rock. *Res:* Relation of past to the present; American Native and folk art. *Publ:* Auth, Visual and auditory space in baroque Rome, J Aesthetics & Art Criticism, 59; auth, Architectural drawings and the intent of the architect, Art J, 67; auth, Contemplating parallax, Art Int, Vol 12, No 7; auth, From Abacus to Zeus: A Handbook of Art History, Prentice-Hall, 68; auth, Paul Klee and Primitive Art, Garland, 75. *Mailing Add:* Dept of Art Univ of Ky Lexington KY 40506

PIERCE, PATRICIA JOBE
DEALER, HISTORIAN
b Seattle, Wash, May 18, 43. *Study:* Univ Conn, 64; Boston Univ Sch Fine & Appl Arts, BFA, 65. *Pos:* Pres, Pierce Galleries, Inc, Hingham, Mass, 66-80; owner, Pierce Galleries Publ Co, 80- *Awards:* Citation for Excellence, El Paso

Mus Art, Tex. *Mem:* Adv Coun of Archives Am Art; Appraisers Asn Am; Frick Art Ref Libr; Victorian Soc; patron Brockton Art Ctr. *Res:* Edmund Charles Tarbell and the Boston School of painting; John Joseph Enneking; Rockport painters; surrealism and the current work of Samuel Rose. *Specialty:* Eighteenth to twentieth century American painting, specializing in American impressionism; supports and promotes Boston living painters and their work; agent for Samuel Rose, J W S Cox, Roy Thompsen and Arnold Carl Savrann. *Collection:* Nineteenth century American impressionists, William S Barrett, W Metcalf, E C Tarbell, William Paxton, J J Enneking and Twachtman; wildlife by A C Savrann; surreal paintings by Samuel Rose; sculpture by Kahlil Gibran. *Publ:* Auth, The Ten American Painters, 76; auth, Edmund C Tarbell and the Boston School, 81; auth, The Phophetic Odessey of Richard Thompson, Am Impressionist, 82; auth, The Watercolored World of J W S Cox, 81; auth, Edward Henry Potthast: American Impressionist, 84. *Mailing Add:* c/o Pierce Galleries Inc 721 Main St Rte 228 Hingham MA 02043

PIEROTTI, JOHN
CARTOONIST
b New York, NY. *Study:* Art Students League; Cooper Union; Mechanics Inst. *Work:* Collection of All Works, Syracuse Univ; Wayne State Univ; Univ Wis. *Exhib:* Man and this World, Montreal, Can; Yugoslavia; Metrop Mus Art, New York. *Pos:* Illusr, sports & ed cartoonist, New York Post, retired. *Awards:* Six Silurian Awards for Best Ed Cartoon, 65-72; Page One Awards for Best Ed Cartoon, 67-76; Best Ed Cartoonist Award, Nat Cartoonists Soc, 75. *Mem:* Nat Cartoonists Soc (pres, 57-59); Artists & Writers. *Mailing Add:* 2004 Ocean Ave Brigantine NJ 08203

PIEROTTI, RAY (RAYMOND CHARLES)
PAINTER, ADMINISTRATOR
b Bountiful, Utah, Aug 5, 32. *Study:* La Sorbonne, Paris, France, Sci Lett, 60; Univ Utah, BS, 62, MA, 63. *Work:* Kemper Gallery, Kansas City Art Inst, Mo, 74; Dade Co Col, Miami, Fla, 77; Mich Educ Asn Hq, East Lansing, Mich, 80; St Clair Co Community Col, Port Huron, Mich, 81. *Exhib:* Solo exhibs, SC Mus Art, Columbia, 69; Hunter Art Mus, Chattanooga, Tenn, 70; Univ South, Swanee, Tenn, 78; Fairfax Art Acad, Mobile, Ala, 79 & Dulin Gallery Art, Knoxville, Tenn, 83; Three Artists, Southeastern Ctr Contemp Art, Winston-Salem, NC, 82; and others. *Collections Arranged:* The Door, 68, Feel It, 68, Sound, 69, Contemplation Environments, 70 & Photo Media, 70, Am Craft Mus. *Pos:* Asst dir, Am Craft Mus, New York, 66-70 & Mus Contemp Crafts, New York, 68-71; dir regional prog, Am Craft Coun, New York, 70-77; dir, Arrowmont Sch Arts & Crafts, Tenn, 77-79; exec dir, Sawtooth Ctr Visual Design, Winston-Salem, NC, 81- *Teaching:* Instr visual arts, Sch Visual Arts, New York, 66-69; assoc prof, Univ Tenn, Knoxville, 77-79; chmn art dept, St Clair Co Community Col, Mich, 79-81. *Awards:* Nat Endowment Humanities, 82. *Media:* Ink. *Publ:* Auth, articles on nat children's competition, Leadership Mag, annually, 74-; auth, Figure as image, J Am Goldsmiths, 80; auth, Visual arts in the educational development of the child, 81 & National competition in ceramics for the child, 82, Leadership Mag; auth, Director's corner, Arts J, 10/82. *Dealer:* Mid-town Gallery 209 Third St W Winston-Salem NC 27102. *Mailing Add:* PO Box 1359 Winston-Salem NC 27102

PIERRE-NOEL, VERGNIAUD
DESIGNER, GRAPHIC ARTIST
b Port-au-Prince, Haiti, Aug 2, 10; US citizen. *Study:* Cent Sch Damien, Univ Haiti, dipl; Columbia Univ, cert; Casa de Moneda, Buenos Aires, cert. *Work:* Nat Mus Haiti, Port-au-Prince; Am Mus Nat Hist, New York; UN, New York; Pan Am Health Orgn, Washington, DC; Wingspread Collection, Racine, Wis. *Comn:* Insects of Haiti, Serv Tech Damien, 33; Caribbean Cong commemorative stamp designs, Govt Haiti, 40; bicentennial commemorative stamp designs 1749-1949, Haiti Postal Admin, 49; World Health Orgn commemorative poster design, Washington, DC, 68. *Exhib:* Am Mus Natural Hist Staff Artists Exhib, New York, 36; Mil Club Haiti, Port-au-Prince, 40; Women Club Arg, Buenos Aires, 48; Nat Asn Indust Artists, Washington, DC, 65; Washington Tech Inst, DC, 68. *Pos:* Graphic designer, Dept Educ, Haiti, 30-34, Am Mus Natural Hist, 35-40, Haiti Postal Admin, 40-54 & Pan Am Health Orgn, 56-75. *Awards:* Gold Medal Award for Bicentennial of City of Port-au-Prince, 49; First Award for UN Postage Stamp Design, 65; First Award, Nat Asn Indust Artists, 65. *Bibliog:* Albert F Kunze (auth), V Pierre-Noel, creator of stamp designs for Haiti, Linn's Weekly Stamp News, 10/52; Belmont Faries (auth), Philatelic news, Washington Star, 2/62. *Mem:* Indust Graphics Int; Washington Tech Inst Advert Design. *Media:* Pen & Ink. *Publ:* Contribr illus, Am Mus Natural Hist, New York, 31, Entom Soc Am, 31, Haiti Postal Admin, 40, UN Postal Admin, 65 & Pan Am Health Orgn, 75. *Mailing Add:* 4706 17th St NW Washington DC 20011

PIET, JOHN FRANCES
SCULPTOR, INSTRUCTOR
b Detroit, Mich, Feb 23, 46. *Study:* Detroit Soc Arts & Crafts, BFA, 73; Wayne State Univ, MFA, 75. *Comn:* Detroit Bank & Trust, Mich, 72; Pingree City Park, Detroit, Mich, 73; Grand Circus Park, Mich Coun Arts, 75; sculpture, KMart Courtyard, KMart Int, Troy, Mich, 79; Oakland Univ, Rochester, Mich, 81. *Exhib:* Tradition & Invention, Kresge Art Gallery, Mich State Univ, East Lansing, Mich, 77; Kick Out the Jams, Detroit Inst Arts, 80 & Mus Contemp Art, Chicago, 81; Detroit Artists, Cranbrook Acad Art, West Bloomfield, Mich, 80; Meadowbrook Invitational, Oakland Univ, Rochester, Mich, 81; and others. *Awards:* Nat Endowment Arts Grant, Oakland Univ Festival, 81. *Bibliog:* Robert Pincus-Witten (auth), Islands in the blight, Arts Mag, 1/78; Mary S Smyka (auth), Dreams in steel, Detroit Monthly Mag, 80; Dennis A Nawrocki (auth), Art in Detroit public places, Wayne State Press, 80. *Media:* Steel. *Dealer:* Cantor-Lemberg Gallery 538 N Woodward Ave Birmingham MI 48010. *Mailing Add:* 1440 Gratiot Detroit MI 48226

PIGOTT, MARJORIE
PAINTER
b Yokohama, Japan; Can citizen. *Study:* Master Artists of Nanga Sch Art, Japan, 12 yrs, teachers dipl. *Work:* London Art Gallery & Mus, Ont; Univ Western Ont; Atlantic Inst Educ, Halifax, NS; Confedn Art Gallery, Charlottetown, PEI; Nat Gallery Can, Ottawa; and others. *Exhib:* Eleven Can Soc Painters Watercolour Ann, 61-74; 4th Biennial Exhib, Nat Gallery Can, 61; 10 Ont Soc Artists Ann, 63-74; Art Galleries, Hamilton, London & Montreal, 67-74; Royal Can Acad, 70; and others. *Awards:* Sumi-ye Soc Am Award for Northern Woods, 67; Hamilton Spectator Award for Liquid Rhythm 4, Can Soc Painters Watercolour. *Mem:* Can Soc Painters Watercolour; Ont Soc Artists; Royal Can Acad Arts. *Media:* Watercolor. *Dealer:* Roberts Gallery 641 Yonge St Toronto ON Can. *Mailing Add:* Apt 1503 77 St Clair Ave E Toronto ON M4T 1M5 Canada

PIJANOWSKI, EUGENE M
EDUCATOR, CRAFTSMAN
b Detroit, Mich, Oct 5, 38. *Study:* Wayne State Univ, BFA, 65, MA, 67; Cranbrook Acad Art, Bloomfield Hills, Mich, MFA, 69; Tokyo Univ Art, 69-71. *Work:* Kalamazoo Inst of Art, Mich; Ga State Univ Art Gallery, Atlanta; Worshipful Co of Goldsmiths Hall, London; Tex Tech Univ Art Gallery, Lubbock; Vienna Mus Applied Arts. *Exhib:* 75 in US & 20 in Japan, England, Germany & other countries, 69-83; Work by Eight Am Metalsmiths & Jewelers, traveling exhib, 74; Six Am Jewelers, Electrum Gallery, London, Eng, 76; Modern Jewelry, Mikimoto Pearl Co, Tokyo, Japan, 78; The 4th Int Jewelry Art Exhib, Tokyo, Japan, 79; Int Jewelry 1900-1980, Kunstlerhaus, Vienna, Austria, 80; Good as Gold, Smithsonian Inst, Washington DC, 81. *Teaching:* Instr metalwork, jewelry & crafts design, San Diego State Univ, Calif, 72-73; lectr Japanese metalworking, over 60 workshops throughout the US, Japan & Vienna, 73-83; assoc prof metalwork, jewelry & three-dimensional design, Purdue Univ, West Lafayette, 73-81; adj assoc prof, Sch Art, Univ Mich, Ann Arbor, 81- *Awards:* Award, Profiles in Jewelry, USA, Tex Tech Univ, 73 & 77; Ind Artist-Craftsman Award, Objects & Crafts 1975, Indianapolis Mus Art, 75; Beaux Arts Designer-Craftsmen Award, Columbus Mus Art, Ohio, 79. *Bibliog:* Mokume-Gane (film), Oberon Films, 81. *Media:* Non-ferrous metals. *Publ:* Contribr to 12 books on metalwork, 73-83; coauth, Lamination of nonferrous metals by diffusion: Adaptations of the traditional Japanese technique of Mokume-Gane, Goldsmiths J, 77; coauth, Mofume-Gane, Craft Horizons, 78, update, Goldsmiths J, 79 & Goldschmiede Zeitung, 81; coauth, Refractory metals, Jewel, Japan, 82; Update II: Mokume-Gane, Metalsmith, 83. *Mailing Add:* 1829 Sheffield Dr Ypsilanti MI 48197

PILAVIN, SELMA F
COLLECTOR, PATRON
b Providence, RI, Sept 20, 08. *Pos:* Bd dirs, Mus Art, RI Sch of Design, 68-; trustee, RI Sch of Design, 74- *Awards:* Providence Art Club Medal, Providence Art Club, 71; Hon PhD (fine arts), 79. *Bibliog:* The Albert Pilavin. *Mem:* Providence Art Club. *Interests:* 20th century American. *Collection:* Twentieth Century, Am Art, Vol I, 69, Vol II, 73; article in The Connoisseur, 2/70. *Mailing Add:* 601 Elmgrove Ave Providence RI 02906

PILGRIM, DIANNE H
CURATOR, HISTORIAN
b Cleveland, Ohio, July 8, 41. *Study:* Pa State Univ, University Park, BA(art hist), 63; New York Univ, Inst Fine Arts, MA, 65; City Univ New York Grad Ctr, 71. *Exhib:* Am Renaissance 1876-1917 (auth, catalog), traveling, Brooklyn Mus, Nat Collection Fine Arts, DC, Fine Arts Mus San Francisco, Denver Art Mus, 79-80. *Collections Arranged:* American Impressionist and Realist Paintings and Drawings from the Collection of Mr & Mrs Raymond J Horowitz (auth, catalog), Metrop Mus Art, New York, 73. *Pos:* Asst to dir, Pyramid Galleries, Ltd, DC, 69-71; researcher, Metrop Mus Art, New York, spring, 71 & res consult, 72-73; asst to dir, Finch Col Mus Art, New York, summer, 71; cur, Decorative Arts, Brooklyn Mus, 73- *Teaching:* Adj asst prof Museological problems: the period rooms, Columbia Univ Sch Archit & Planning, 76-78. *Awards:* Chester Dale Fel, Metrop Mus Art, 66-68. *Mem:* Decorative Arts Soc; Decorative Arts Trust; Friends of Clermont; Victorian Soc in Am, New York Chap. *Res:* American 19th and 20th century decorative arts and paintings. *Publ:* Auth, Alexander Roux, his plain and artistic furniture, Antiques, 2/68; auth, Inherited from the past: the American period room, 5/78 & The revival of pastels in nineteenth century America: the Society of Painters in Pastel, 10/78, Am Art J; auth, Eighteenth century American interiors, Apollo, 4/82. *Mailing Add:* Brooklyn Mus 188 Eastern Pkwy Brooklyn NY 11238

PILGRIM, JAMES F
CURATOR, HISTORIAN
b Richmond, Ind, Feb 19, 41. *Collections Arranged:* American Impressionist Paintings, Corcoran Gallery, 68; John Storrs Retrospective, 69; Robert Morris (coauth, catalog), 69; Alexander Liberman (coauth, catalog), 70; The Vincent Melzac Collection, 70; Paintings from the Metrop, 71; Treasured Masterpieces from the Metrop Mus, Loan to Japan, summer 72. *Pos:* Cur Am art, Corcoran Gallery Art, 68-70, chief cur, 70-71; assoc cur Am painting, Metrop Mus Art, 71, asst cur in chief, 71-74, deputy vdir curatorial affairs, 74-79, deputy dir, 79- *Teaching:* Asst prof mus studies, George Washington Univ, 70-71. *Awards:* Ford Found Fel Mus Training, NY Univ, 64-66; Clawson Mills Fel, Metrop Mus Art, 67-68. *Mem:* Am Inst Conserv; Col Art Asn; Am Asn Mus; Int Coun Mus. *Res:* Late 19th & 20th century art. *Publ:* Contribr, J William Middendorf Collection (catalog), 67; auth, Recent Paintings of Leon Berkowitz, 68; auth, H Marc Moyens Collection (catalog), 70. *Mailing Add:* c/o Metrop Mus Art Fifth Ave & 82nd St New York NY 10028

PILLET, MICHEL LOUIS
ARCHITECT, EDUCATOR

b Toulon, France, Oct 31, 26; US citizen. *Study:* Ecole Nat Superieure des Beaux Arts, Paris, DPLG, 58; Univ Calif, Berkeley, MArchit, 59; Univ NMex. *Work:* Indiens d'Amerique du Nord-les Anasazi, Mus de l'Homme, Paris. *Teaching:* Assoc prof hist archit & design, Univ NMex, 69-77; prof design & archit & prof & dir Sch Art & Archit, Univ SW La, Lafayette, 77-83; vis prof archit, Univ NMex, Albuquerque, 83. *Awards:* Lercaro Prize, Religious Archit Am, Pittsburgh, 60; Second Prize, Painting, NMex Art League, 75. *Mem:* Soc des Americanister, Paris. *Media:* Mixed. *Res:* Pre-Columbian art and architecture; Pueblo art and architecture. *Publ:* Auth, Pueblo Housing, Response to Design on Arid Land, Archit Press, 80. *Mailing Add:* 330 St Joseph Lafayette LA 70506

PILLIN, POLIA
PAINTER, CERAMIST

b Czenstochowa, Poland, Sept 1, 09; US citizen. *Study:* Jewish People's Inst, Chicago; Studio of Todros Geller, Chicago. *Work:* Long Beach Mus, Calif; Syracuse Mus Art, NY; Otis Art Inst, Los Angeles, Calif; Dallas Art Mus, Tex; Univ Maine. *Exhib:* Art Inst of Chicago; San Francisco Art Mus; Pa Acad Fine Arts; Butler Inst Am Art, Youngstown, Ohio; Los Angeles Art Mus; Seattle Art Mus, Wash; De Young Art Mus, San Francisco; Syracuse Art Mus, NY; Adele Bednarz Galleries, Los Angeles; Wichita Art Asn, Kans; Portland Art Mus, Ore; Cincinnati Art Mus, Ohio. *Awards:* Award, Los Angeles Co Art Inst, 48; Awards, Syracuse Mus, 51 & 53; Awards, Calif State Fair, 55, 57 & 60. *Bibliog:* Dennis Burns (auth), Like a Jewel (film), 72; Dale Wilson Smith (auth), The American Artist, Paintings on Clay, 55; articles in Los Angeles Times Home Sect. *Mem:* Nat Watercolor Soc. *Media:* Oil. *Dealer:* Richard Challis c/o Challis Galleries 1390 S Coast Hwy Laguna Beach CA 92652. *Mailing Add:* 4913 Melrose Ave Los Angeles CA 90029

PILSK, ADELE INEZ
CERAMIST, ADMINISTRATOR

b Nashville, Tenn, Jan 21, 37. *Study:* Peabody Col, MA; Richmond Art Ctr, Calif; Univ Mo; also with leading ceramists in country. *Pos:* Crafts res & educ coordr, Tenn Arts Coun, 77-78; interium dir visual arts prog, Tenn Arts Comm, 83. *Teaching:* Instr ceramics, pvt studies, Sarratt Crafts Ctr, Vanderbilt Univ, 77; instr clay, Metrop Pub Sch, Davidson Co, 77. *Mem:* Am Crafts Coun; Tenn Artists-Craftsmen's Asn (student vpres, 76, regional vpres, 77, secy, 82); Tenn Crafts Marketplace (pres, 79); Cumberland Valley Artist-Craftsmen's Asn (pres, 78); Int Guild Craft Journalists, Authors & Photogr. *Publ:* Auth, Kai Walters: Eccelesiastical fibers, 77, A tribute: Mary Frances Davidson, 78 & Jimmie Benedict, 78, Fiberarts; auth, Jan Havens: A profile, Olen Bryant, Ceramics Mo. *Mailing Add:* 2211 Bandywood Dr Nashville TN 37315

PIMENTEL, DAVID DELBERT
GOLDSMITH, EDUCATOR

b Plymouth, Mass, June 29, 43. *Study:* Mass Col Art, BS(art educ), 65; Sch Am Craftsmen, Rochester Inst Technol, MFA, 72. *Comn:* Three holloware pieces, Hawaii State Found Cult & Arts, Honolulu, 72; Mace (pres chain off), Ariz State Univ, 81. *Exhib:* The Goldsmiths '74, Renwick Gallery, Smithsonian Inst, DC, 74; Contemp Crafts Americas, Colo State Univ, Ft Collins, 75; The Metalsmith, Phoenix Art Mus, 77; Soc NAm Goldsmiths, Minn Mus Art, St Paul, 79-80; Europ Exhib, Schmuck Mus, Pforzheim, Ger & others; Viewpoint '80 Art in Craft Media, Mus Tex Tech Univ, Lubbock, 80. *Teaching:* Asst prof jewelry metalworking, Ariz State Univ, 73- *Awards:* Cash Award, Scottsdale Ctr Arts, 76; Pat Mutterer Award, Tucson Mus Art, 77. *Mem:* Soc NAm Goldsmiths; Am Crafts Coun; World Crafts Coun. *Media:* Jewelry, Metal. *Mailing Add:* Sch Art Ariz State Univ Tempe AZ 85287

PINARDI, ENRICO VITTORIO
SCULPTOR, PAINTER

b Cambridge, Mass, Feb 11, 34. *Study:* Apprentice with Pelligrini & Cascieri, five yrs; Boston Archit Ctr; Sch Mus Fine Arts, Boston; Mass Col Art, BS(educ); RI Sch Design, MFA. *Work:* Worcester Art Mus, De Cordova Mus, Lincoln & Boston Inst Contemp Art, Mass; Chase Manhattan Bank, New York. *Exhib:* New England Art Part IV Sculpture, 64 & Surrealism, 70, De Cordova Mus; 21 Sculptors & Painters, Boston Univ, 64; New England Art Today, Northeastern Univ, 65; 10 Sculptors, Nashua, NH, 68. *Teaching:* Instr sculpture, Worcester Art Mus Sch, 63-67; prof RI Col, 78. *Media:* Wood. *Dealer:* Pucker Safrai Gallery 171 Newbury Boston MA 02116; Vorpal Gallery 465 W Broadway New York NY 10012. *Mailing Add:* 87 Child Hyde Park MA 02136

PINCHBECK, PETER G
PAINTER

b London, England, Dec 9, 40; US citizen. *Study:* Twickenham Col Art, Eng, 57-58; Polytechnic Art Sch, London, Eng, 58-59. *Work:* Corcoran Mus, Washington, DC; Mutual Benefit Insurance Co, Newark, NJ. *Exhib:* Primary Structures, Jewish Mus, New York, 66; American Painting: The Eighties, Grey Art Gallery, New York, Contemp Arts Mus, Houston, Am Cult Ctr, Paris & touring Europe & Japan, 80-; Painting Up Front, Johnson Mus, Cornell Univ, Ithaca, NY, 81; Newcastle Salutes New York, Newcastle Polytechnic Gallery, Newcastle-on-Tyne, Eng, 83. *Awards:* Nat Endowment Arts Fel, 81; Albee Found, 80-82. *Bibliog:* Anita Feldman (auth), Space and subjectivity, Art Forum Mag, 79. *Mem:* Artists Equity Asn. *Media:* Oil. *Publ:* Auth, Structures of reality in word and image, Arts Mag, 72; auth, Believing is seeing, ARTextreme, summer, 82. *Mailing Add:* 69 Greene St New York NY 10012

PINCKNEY, STANLEY
PAINTER, TAPESTRY ARTIST

b Boston, Mass, Sept 30, 40. *Study:* Famous Artist Sch, Westport, Conn, 57-61; Mus Sch Fine Arts, Boston, Mass, 67. *Work:* Nat Ctr African-Am Art, Roxbury, Mass; Mus Dynamique, Dakar, Senegal, W Africa; Palace de l'Pres, Dakar. *Comn:* Wood sculpture, Boston Mus Fine Arts, 74; tapestry, Mus Sch Fine Arts, Boston, 75. *Exhib:* A Century of the Mus Sch, Boston Mus Fine Arts, 77; African-Am Master Artists-in-Residency Prog Exhib, Dodge Libr Gallery, Northwestern Univ, 78 & Univ Lowell, 79; Recent Tapestries, Mus Sch Fine Arts Gallery & Boston Mus Fine Arts, 78; Resist-Dyed Tapestries, Stanley McCormick Gallery, Boston Archit Ctr, 79; Traveling Scholarship Exhib, Mus Fine Arts, Boston, 81; and many others. *Collections Arranged:* Twelve Black Artists, Rose Art Mus, Brandeis Univ, 69; Osubamba (auth, catalog), Boston Ctr for the Arts, 76 & Cyclorama Gallery, Boston, 76; A Century of the Museum School (auth, catalog), Boston Mus Fine Arts, 77. *Teaching:* Instr African & traditional arts, Mus Sch Fine Art, Boston, 72- *Awards:* 19th Albert H Whitin Fel, Boston Mus Fine Arts, 69; Ford Found Fac Enrichment-Artist Grant, Mus Sch Fine Art, 78; Blance E Colman Fel, 78; and others. *Bibliog:* and others. *Media:* Watercolor. *Mailing Add:* c/o Mus Fine Arts Sch 230 Fenway Boston MA 02115

PINCUS, DAVID N
COLLECTOR

b Philadelphia, Pa. *Pos:* Trustee, Philadelphia Mus Art, 74-, Fairmount Park Art Asn, 76- & Pa Acad Fine Arts, 79- *Collection:* Contemporary sculpture; New York school of abstract expressionists; recent realist painters. *Mailing Add:* 1319 Remington Rd Wynnewood PA 19096

PINCUS, ROBERT L(AWRENCE)
CRITIC, EDUCATOR

b Bridgeport, Conn, June 5, 53. *Study:* Univ Calif, Irvine, BA, 76; Univ Southern Calif, MA, 80 & currently. *Collections Arranged:* Cultural Excavations: Recent and Distant (auth, catalog), 83. *Pos:* Contrib reviewer, Artweek, 79; art critic, Los Angeles Times, 81-; contrib critic, Art in Am, 82- *Teaching:* Instr art & lit hist, Univ Southern Calif, 79- *Mem:* Mod Language Asn. *Res:* Twentieth century American art history. *Publ:* Auth, Edward Kienholz's assemblages and tableaux, Images & Issues, 81. *Mailing Add:* Calendar Sect Los Angeles Times Times Mirror Sq Los Angeles CA 90053

PINCUS-WITTEN, ROBERT A
EDUCATOR, WRITER

b New York, NY, Apr 5, 35. *Study:* Cooper Union, Emil Schweinburg Grant, 56; Univ Chicago, MA(dept fel), 60, PhD(dept fel), 63; Univ Paris, Sorbonne, exchange fel, 63-64. *Pos:* Ed, Artforum Mag, 66-76; assoc ed, Arts Mag, currently. *Teaching:* Prof art hist, Queens Col & Grad Ctr, City Univ New York, currently. *Res:* Symbolism; the history of contemporary art and photography. *Publ:* Auth, Occult Symbolism in France, Josephin Peladan and the Salons de la Rose-Croix, Garland Press, 76; auth, Post-Minimalism, Art of the Decade, 77 & auth, Entries (Maximalism), Art at the Turn of the Decade, 83, Out of London Press; auth, Eye Contact, Twenty Years of Art Criticism, Univ Mich Press, 84; and others. *Mailing Add:* Dept of Art Queens Col Flushing NY 11367

PINDELL, HOWARDENA DOREEN
PAINTER, EDUCATOR

b Philadelphia, Pa, Apr 14, 43. *Study:* Boston Univ Sch Fine & Applied Arts, BFA, 65; Cumminton Sch Arts, 63; Sch Art & Archit, Yale Univ, MFA, 67. *Work:* Mus Modern Art, New York; Fogg Art Mus, Harvard Univ; Whitney Mus Am Art & Metrop Mus of Art, New York; Philadelphia Mus of Art; Chase Manhattan Bank, New York & Tokyo. *Exhib:* New Am Graphic Art, Fogg Art Mus, Cambridge, Mass, 73; Painting & Sculpture Today, Indianapolis Mus, Ind & Taft Mus, Cincinnati, 74; Five Americans in Paris, Gerald Piltzer Gallery, Paris, 75; 9th Paris Biennale, Mus Mod Art, Paris, 75; H Pindell: Video Drawings, Sonja Heine Onstad Found, Oslo, Norway, 76; Vassar Col Art Gallery, 77. *Collections Arranged:* Pop Art Prints, Drawings and Multiples, 70, California Prints, 72 & tour, 73, Projects: Chuck Close and Liliana Porter, 73, Published in Germany (co-dir), 74, Printed, Cut, Folded and Torn, 74, Felix Vallotton (co-dir), 74, Points of View, 75, Projects: John Walker, 75, Projects: Mary Miss and Charles Simonds, 76, Narrative Prints, 76 & Abstraction-Creation, 77, Mus Mod Art, New York. *Pos:* Exhib asst, Mus Mod Art, New York, 67-69, cur asst, 69-71 & asst cur, prints & illus books, 71-77, assoc cur, 77-79. *Teaching:* Assoc prof, State Univ NY, Stony Brook, 79- *Awards:* Painting Award, Nat Endowment for Arts, 72-73. *Bibliog:* Marina Urbach (auth), Paris Biennale, 9th catalog, Paris, 9/75; Francoise Eliet, Five Americans in Paris, Art Press, Paris, 4/75; Carter Radcliff (auth), The paint thickens, Artforum, summer 76. *Media:* Acrylic on Canvas. *Res:* Twentieth century prints. *Publ:* Auth, Mary Quinn Sullivan, Notable American Women, Harvard Univ, 72; auth, California Prints, Arts Mag, New York, 5/72; auth, Ed Ruscha: Words, Print Collectors Newsletter, 1/73; auth, Robert Rauschenberg: Link, Mus Mod Art, 10/75; auth, Alan Shields: Tales of Brave Ulysses, 1/75 & Artists' Periodicals: Alternative Space, 9/77, Print Collector's Newsletter. *Mailing Add:* 322 Seventh Ave New York NY 10001

PINEDA, MARIANNA
SCULPTOR

b Evanston, Ill, May 10, 25. *Study:* Cranbrook Acad with Carl Milles, Mich, 42; Univ Calif, Berkeley with Raymond Puccinelli, 43-45; Columbia Univ, New York with Oronzio Maldarelli, 45-46; Ossip Zadkine Sch Sculpture, Paris, Frnace, 49-50. *Work:* Mus Fine Arts, Boston, Mass; Walker Art Ctr, Minneapolis, Minn; Munson, Williams Proctor Inst, Ithaca, NY; Wadsworth Atheneum, Hartford, Conn; Fogg Art Mus, Harvard Univ, Cambridge, Mass.

Comn: Bronze medallian, Jan Veen Dance Libr, Boston Conservatory Music, 65; bronze relief, Newton Col class of 74, Mass, 75; Twirling (bronze figures), Boston Redevelopment Authority, 76; Queen Lili'uokalani (bronze), State Hawaii, Honolulu, 82. *Exhib:* American Sculpture, Metrop Mus Art, New York, 51; one-man shows, Walker Art Ctr, Honolulu Acad Art, 52 & 70 & Contemp Arts Ctr, Honolulu; Sculpture Biennials, Whitney Mus Am Art, New York, 53, 55, 57 & 59; Pittsburgh Int, Carnegie Inst, Pa, 58; Recent Sculpture, Mus Mod Art, New York, 59-60; 64th Exhib, Art Inst Chicago, 61; Works by Women, Los Angeles Co Mus, Calif, 76; Boston Portraits, Boston Univ Art Gallery, 82. *Pos:* Bd mem, Ft Point Arts Community, Boston, Mass, 80- *Teaching:* Instr sculpture, Newton Col Sacred Heart, 72-75; adj prof, Boston Univ, Mass, 75-83; instr, Boston Col, Mass, 76-77. *Awards:* First Prize, San Francisco Art Asn, 55; Mather Prize Sculpture, Art Inst Chicago, 57; Fel Independent Study, Bunting Inst, Radcliffe Col, 62-64. *Bibliog:* Duane Preeble (auth), We Create Art Creates Us, Canfield Press, 76; Nathan Goldstein (auth), The Art of Responsive Drawing, Prentice-Hall, 78; CharlotD. *Mem:* Artists Equity (secy, NE chapter, 62-64); Sculptors Guild New York; Boston Visual Artists Union; Artists Equity; Nat Acad Design. *Media:* All. *Mailing Add:* 380 Marlborough Street Boston MA 02115

PINES, NED L
COLLECTOR
b Malden, Mass, Dec 10, 05. *Collection:* Modern art. *Mailing Add:* 355 Lexington Ave New York NY 10017

PINK, MARILYN OVERMAN
DEALER, EDITOR
b Rumania; US citizen. *Study:* NY Univ, BS, 50. *Collections Arranged:* Louis Lozowick: American Precisionist, 77 & Paul Kelpe, 80, Long Beach Mus Art; Images of Women, 78; The Color Print-Eighteenth to Twentieth Century, 79; Innovative Pr Printmaking, 80. *Pos:* Ed Newslett, Los Angeles Co Mus Art, 65-81; vpres, Southern Calif Art Dealers Asn, 73-82. *Teaching:* Guest lectr grad sem, Univ Southern Calif, 82. *Mem:* Graphic Arts Coun, Los Angeles Co Mus Art; Am Art Coun, Los Angeles Co Mus Art; Col Art Asn; Southern Calif Art Dealers Asn; Inst Paper Conserv, London. *Specialty:* Prints and drawings, watercolors, monotypes and unique works of art on paper from the 15th to the early 20th century. *Publ:* Auth, How to Catalogue Works of Art: A Guide for the Private Collector, Mus Systems, 72. *Mailing Add:* 817 N La Cienega Blvd Los Angeles CA 90069

PINKEL, SHEILA MAE
PHOTOGRAPHER, SCULPTOR
b Newport News, Va, Aug 21, 41. *Study:* Univ Calif, Berkeley, BA, 63; Univ Calif, Los Angeles, with Robert Heinecken, Bart Parker, Bea Nettles, Gary Lloyd & Carl Chiarenze, MFA, 77. *Work:* Walker Art Ctr, Minn; Los Angeles Co Mus, Calif; Ctr Creative Photog, Tucson; Mus Mod Art & Int Mus Photog, George Eastman House, New York. *Comn:* Cyanotype mural, Park La Brea Towers, Los Angeles, Calif, 76. *Exhib:* The Artist and the Computer, Long Beach Mus, Calif, 83; two-women show, Santa Barbara Mus Art, Calif, 83; Lensless Photography, Franklin Inst, Philadelphia, 83; Contemporary Collage: Extensions, Claremont Col, Calif, 83; Restoring the Balance on Earth, Univ Southern Calif Gallery, 83; Thermonuclear Garden Installation, Long Gallery, Claremont Col, Calif, 83; Form as Content, Visual Studies Workshop, Rochester, NY, 81; Photofusions, Pratt Inst, Brooklyn, NY, 81. *Collections Arranged:* Multicultural Focus (auth, catalog), Cross Cultural Photog Exhib. *Teaching:* Instr photog, Univ Calif Exten, Los Angeles, 76-; instr photog, Otis Parsons Art Inst, 81- *Awards:* Nat Endowment Arts Emerging Artist Grant, 79 & 82. *Bibliog:* Thelma Newman (auth), Innovative Printmaking, Crown Publ, 78; 1980 Ann, 80 & The Print Revised, 81, Time-Life Publ. *Mem:* Los Angeles Ctr Photog Studies (vpres, 78-81); Soc Photog Educ. *Media:* Black & White, Xeroradiography. *Publ:* Contribr, Centerfold, Arton's Publ, 3/79; contribr, Los Angeles Inst Contemp Art J, 10/79; auth, Multicultural Focus, 81 & contribr, Obscura, 82, Los Angeles Ctr Photog; contribr, Afterimage, Visual Studies Workshop, 5/81. *Dealer:* G Ray Hawkins 7224 Melrose Los Angeles CA 90046. *Mailing Add:* 126 Hart St Santa Monica CA 90405

PINKERTON, CLAYTON (DAVID)
PAINTER
b San Francisco, Calif, Mar 6, 31. *Study:* Calif Col Arts & Crafts, BAEd & MFA; Harwood Found, Univ NMex. *Work:* De Young Mus & Calif Palace Legion of Honor, San Francisco; Ill Bell Tel, Chicago; also some pvt collections. *Exhib:* Recent Paintings USA: The Figure, Mus Mod Art, New York, 63; one-man shows, San Francisco Mus Art, Calif, 67, Esther Robles Gallery, Los Angeles, 68, Arleigh Gallery, San Francisco, 70 & Whitney Mus Am Art, 71; Contemp Am Painting & Sculpture, Univ Ill, 67 & 69; Three Centuries of American Painting, Calif Palace Legion of Honor, 71; First Soap Box Derby, San Francisco Mus Art, 75; Central Calif Biennial, Pacific Grove Arts Ctr, 83; and others. *Pos:* Free-lance cur, currently. *Teaching:* Prof fine arts, Calif Col Arts & Crafts, 60-; cur, Richmond Art Ctr, formerly. *Awards:* Fulbright Scholar, 57-58; James Phelan Award, 57 & 61. *Bibliog:* Joan Mondale (auth), Politics in art, Lerner, 77. *Mailing Add:* PO Box 133 Carmel CA 93921

PINKNEY, HELEN LOUISE
CURATOR, LIBRARIAN
b Decatur, Ill. *Study:* Dayton Art Inst Sch, grad. *Collections Arranged:* The Camera, the Paper and I, Collection of Photographs by Jane Reece, 52; The Wonderful World of Photography, Jane Reece Mem Exhib, 63; Oriental & Europ Textiles Exhib, 72; Am Indian Textiles & Baskets, 73; Hidden Treasures: Textiles from the Dayton Art Institute Collection, 83. *Pos:* Registr

of collections, Dayton Art Inst, 36-45, cur, 45-59, librn, 45-, assoc cur textiles, 59- *Mem:* Art Libr Soc/NAm; Am Asn Mus; Spec Libr Asn, Mus Div. *Res:* Jane Reece Photographic Collection; textiles; bibliographies. *Publ:* Auth, articles and catalogues on Jane Reece Collection in Dayton Art Inst Bulletin, 52 & 63. *Mailing Add:* 37 Stoddard Ave Dayton OH 45405

PINTO, ANGELO RAPHAEL
PAINTER, PRINTMAKER
b Casal Velino, Italy, Sept 27, 08; US citizen. *Study:* Pa Mus & Sch Indust Arts, Philadelphia; Barnes Found, Merion, Pa, Europ Study Scholar, 31-33. *Work:* Pa Acad Fine Arts, Philadelphia; Metrop Mus Art, New York; Libr Cong, Washington, DC; Boston Pub Libr; Chrysler Mus, Norfolk, Va; and others. *Comn:* Ballets & costumes, Philadelphia Ballet Co, 37. *Exhib:* One-man shows, Bignou Gallery, Paris, France, 33, Valentine Gallery, New York, 34, Mellon Galleries, Philadelphia, 35, Makler Gallery, Philadelphia, 60, Medici II Gallery, Miami, Fla, 70 & 74 & Marion Locks Gallery, Philadelphia, 83; and others. *Teaching:* Fac mem, Barnes Found, 35- *Awards:* First Prize American Painters, Four Arts Club, Miami Beach, 38; Silver Medal, Da Vinci Alliance, Philadelphia, 40. *Bibliog:* Helen McCloy (auth), Art of Pinto Brothers, Parnassus, 35; Mildred Lee-Ward (auth), Reverse Paintings on Glass, Spencer Mus Art. *Mem:* Art Alliance, Philadelphia; United Scenic Artists, New York. *Dealer:* Marion Locks Gallery Philadelphia PA; Mary Ryan Gallery New York NY. *Mailing Add:* 28 W 69th St New York NY 10023

PINTO, BIAGIO
PAINTER
b Philadelphia, Pa, Oct 6, 11. *Study:* Graphic Sketch Club, Philadelphia; Sch Indust Arts, Philadelphia; Barnes Found, Merion, Pa; also study in Italy & France. *Work:* Barnes Found; Dallas Contemp Mus Art, Tex; Pa Acad Fine Arts, Philadelphia; Mus Art, Eugene, Ore; Philadelphia Mus Art. *Comn:* Posters, USAF, Washington, DC, 43 & Pa Opera Co, Philadelphia, 73. *Exhib:* Whitney Mus Art, New York; Chicago Art Inst; Del Art Mus, Wilmington; Mus Mod Art, Miami, Fla; Metrop Mus Art, New York; Tweed Mus Art, Duluth, Minn; William Penn Mem Mus, Harrisburg, Pa; Lakeview Ctr for the Arts & Sci, Peoria, Ill; Pa Acad Fine Arts; Corcoran Gallery Art, Washington, DC; also one-man shows in Philadelphia, New York & Paris. *Teaching:* Instr painting, Philadelphia Col Art, 62-72 & Main Line Ctr Art, Haverford, Pa, 64-72. *Awards:* European Fels, Albert C Barnes Found, 31 & 32; John A Lee Cult Award, City of Philadelphia, 62; Philadelphia Sketch Club Medal. *Bibliog:* Albert C Barnes (auth), The Art in Painting, Harcourt Brace, 37; Valerie Seward (auth), Art as I see it, Lancaster Mag, 57; Irine Patai (auth), Encounters, Life of Jacques Lipchitz, Funk & Wagnalls, 61. *Mem:* Artists Equity Asn (dir, Philadelphia Chap, 65-66); Friends of Barnes Found; Philadelphia Art Alliance (juror, 66-72); Fla Artists Group; Philadelphia Print Club. *Media:* Oil. *Publ:* Illusr & auth, articles, Town & Country, Harper's Bazaar & Art News. *Dealer:* Benjamin Mangel Gallery 202 Bala Ave Bala-Cynwyd PA 19004. *Mailing Add:* 229 Lisbon St Venice FL 33595

PINTO, JAMES
PAINTER, SCULPTOR
b Bijelina, Yugoslavia, Apr 24, 07; US citizen. *Study:* Chouinard Art Inst, Los Angeles; mural painting with David Alfaro Siqueiros. *Work:* Witte Mem Mus, San Antonio, Tex; Musej Savremene Umjetnosti, Belgrad, Yugoslavia; Berg Art Ctr, Concordia Col, Moorehead, Minn; Umjetnicka Galerija Bosne; Hercegovine, Sarajevo, Yugoslavia; and others. *Comn:* Two outdoor murals, Inst Allende, San Miguel, 58; indoor mural, Hotel Inst Allende, 70. *Exhib:* American Painting Today, Metrop Mus Art, New York, 52; 15th Ann Contemp Art, Art Inst Chicago, 55; Nat Acad of Sci, Washington, DC, 76; Univ Miss, Oxford, 79; Galeria Jugoslovenskog Portreta, Tuzla, Yugoslavia, 79; McAllen Int Mus, Tex, 80; Evanston Art Ctr, Ill, 81; and others. *Teaching:* Emer prof art & dean fac, Inst Allende, 50- *Awards:* First Prize, 1st Nat Vet Exhib, Santa Monica, Calif, 47; First Prize, Nat Univ Mex & US Embassy, Mexico City, 49; Purchase Prize, Life-Day Exhib Contemp Art, Fargo, NDak, 57. *Bibliog:* Brooks (auth), Painting and Understanding of Abstract Art, 64 & Baldwin (auth), Contemporary Sculpture Techniques, 67 & Reinhold: Archives of American Art, Smithsonian Inst J, 76. *Media:* Acrylic, Bronze. *Mailing Add:* Apdo Postal 12 San Miguel de Allende Guanajuato Mexico

PINTO, JODY
SCULPTOR
b New York, NY, Apr 8, 42. *Study:* Pa Acad Fine Arts, Cresson fel, 67, 68; Philadelphia Col Art, BFA, 73. *Work:* Philadelphia Mus Art & Pa Acad Fine Arts, Philadelphia; Newberger Mus, Purchase, NY; Whitney Mus Am Art, New York; Des Moines Art Ctr, Des Moines, Iowa. *Comn:* Temp Outdoor Sculptures, Insert Chamber for H C, Art Inst Chicago, 78; Serpentine Corridor, Wooster Col, Ohio; Widow's Perch, Art on the Beach, New York; Split-Tongue Pier, Swarthmore Col, Pa; Colorado Corridor, Univ Colo; and others. *Exhib:* 1979 Biennial Exhib, Whitney Mus Am Art, New York, 79; Venice Biennial 1980, Italy, 80; NY on Paper, Douglass Drake Gallery, Kans City, 81; Large Format Drawings, Barbara Toll Gallery, New York, 81; Ritual and Landscape, Touchstone Gallery, New York, 81; Whitney Mus Am Art, 81. *Teaching:* Instr drawing & sculpture, Univ Guelph, Can, 77; vis artist critic, Pa Acad Fine Arts, 80- & RI Sch Design, 80- *Awards:* Nat Endowment for Arts Fel, 79-80; Pa Coun Arts Grant, 80-81; NJ Coun Arts Grant, 82-83. *Bibliog:* Grace Glueck (auth), New York Times, 12/24/81; Lucy Lippard (auth), Overlay, Pantheon Bks, 83; Janet Karvon (auth), Connections, ICA, 83; and others. *Media:* Industrial Materials (Building). *Publ:* Coauth, Excavations and Constructions: Notes for the Body/Land, Marian Locks Gallery, 79. *Dealer:* Marian Locks Gallery 1524 Walnut St Philadelphia PA 19102; Hal Bromn Gallery 90 W Broadway New York NY 10007. *Mailing Add:* 101 W 15th St 6M NO New York NY 10011

PINZARRONE, PAUL
PAINTER, FILMMAKER
b Grand Rapids, Mich, Nov 19, 51. *Study:* Univ Ill, BFA(painting), 73. *Work:* Butler Inst Am Art, Youngstown, Ohio; Ill State Mus, Springfield; Kemper Ins Co, Chicago; St Xavier Col, Chicago, Ill; Union League, Chicago. *Exhib:* New Horizons in Art, Chicago, 75, 76 & 80; 28th Ill Exhib, Springfield, 75; 39th & 40th Midyear Exhibs, Butler Inst, 75 & 76; Mainstreams 75-, Marietta Int, Ohio, 75; one-man show, Joy Horwich Gallery, Chicago, Ill, 76, 77 & 80. *Teaching:* Instr art, Rock Valley Col, Rockford, Ill, 75-76 & 78, Rockford Col, 76; guest lectr, Univ Miami, 77, Gloria Curia Gallery, Miami, 77, Regent Art Asn, 78, St Xavier Col, Chicago, 80 & Highland Col, 81. *Awards:* First Prize, Ill State Fair Prof, 75, New Orleans Int, 75 & Rockford Juried, Ill, 82; First Prize, New Orleans Int, 75; First Prize, Ill State Fair Prof, 75. *Bibliog:* Article, New Art Examiner, Chicago, 12/80; Carrie Rebora & Laura Cottingham (auths), The Chicago Art Review, 81. *Dealer:* Art Independent Gallery Lake Geneva WI; Joy Horwich Gallery Chicago IL. *Mailing Add:* 103 Paris Ave Rockford IL 61107

PIPER, JANE
PAINTER, LECTURER
b Philadelphia, Pa, Aug 21, 16. *Study:* Pa Acad Fine Arts, 35-36; Studio Arthur B Carles, Philadelphia, 39-42; Hans Hofmann Sch, Provincetown, 41. *Work:* Mus Art, Carnegie Inst, Pa; Corcoran Gallery, Washington, DC; Philadelphia Mus Art, Pa; Pa Acad Fine Arts, Philadelphia; Allentown Art Mus, Pa. *Exhib:* Recent Acquisitions, Pa Acad, Peale House, 75; Recent Acquisitions, Philadelphia Mus Art, Pa, 77; one-woman shows, Jane Piper, Gross McCleaf Gallery, Pa, 77-78 & 81-83 & Bodley Gallery, New York, 81; 5 1/2 Artists, Landmark Gallery, New York, 79; Long Point Gallery, Mass, 81; Recent Acquisitions, Mus Art, Carnegie Inst, 83; and others. *Teaching:* Instr painting, Philadelphia Mus Art, Pa, 54-56; instr painting & drawing, Philadelphia Col Art, Pa, 56- *Awards:* Saltus Gold Medal, Nat Acad Design, New York, 82. *Bibliog:* W P Scott (auth), Conversations with Jane Piper, Am Artist, 11/78; Larry Day (auth), Jane Piper, Gross McCleaf Gallery, 81; Michael Florescu (auth), Jane Piper, Arts, 5/81. *Media:* Oil, Oil Pastel. *Mailing Add:* c/o Gross McCleaf Gallery 1713 Walnut St Philadelphia PA 19103

PIRKL, JAMES JOSEPH
DESIGNER, EDUCATOR
b Nyack, NY, Dec 27, 30. *Study:* Pratt Inst, cert adv design, 51 & BID, 58; Wayne State Univ; Syracuse Univ; Univ Monterrey, Hon diploma, Mexico, 81. *Pos:* Jr designer, General Motors Design staff, 58-59, designer, 59-60, sr designer, 61-64 & asst chief designer, 64-65; principal, James J Pirkl/Design, Cazenovia, NY, 65- *Teaching:* Instr, Ctr for Creative Studies, Detroit, Mich, 63-65; asst prof indust design, dept of design, Syracuse Univ, 65-68, assoc prof, 69-73, prof, 74-, prof in charge, Indust Design Prog, 79- *Mem:* Indust Designers Soc Am (mem bd dirs, 77-, vchmn, Cent NY Chap, 75-76 & chmn, 77-78); Human Factors Soc; Am Asn Univ Prof. *Publ:* Co-ed, State of the Art and Science of Design, 71; auth, Design is seen entering a new humane stage, Instrial Design, 7-8/78; auth, A focus on form, Indust Designers Am Papers, 7/81. *Mailing Add:* Meadow Hill Rd Cazenovia NY 13035

PISANI, JOSEPH
MURALIST, PAINTER
b New Rochelle, NY, Oct 1, 38. *Study:* San Francisco Art Inst; Calif Col Arts & Crafts, with George Post, Richard Diebenkorn, Nathan Oliveira & Ralph Borge, BFA. *Work:* Dept of Defense, The Pentagon, Arlington, Va; The White House, Washington, DC, 81; Hq Dept of the Army, Pentagon. *Comn:* Mondavi Tomb, Caesar Mondavi Family, St Helina, Calif, 62; General Marshall Mem Corridor, comn by Secy of the Army, Pentagon, 75; Army Bicentennial Murals, comn by Secy of Defense, 75-76; Gen Pershing mural, comn by Gen Yerks, Ft Myer, Va, 77-78; Gen MacArthur Mem, 81, Anzus Mem Corridor, 82 & Military Womens Corridor, 83, comn by Sec of Defense Weinberger, Pentagon. *Exhib:* Army Wide Art Exhib, Pentagon, 63, 65; Corcoran Washington Area Show, 69; Artist Equity Group Shows, Washington, DC, 72 & 73; Va Beach Art Shows, 73 & 75. *Pos:* Chief graphic arts, Chief of Staff (Personnel), Pentagon, 67-73; graphic designer, Dept of Defense, 73-75; art dir, US Army Hq, 75- *Awards:* Outstanding Achievement in Art, Bank of Am, 61; Scholar to Study Fine Arts, Scholastic Mag, 62; First Prize for Painting, Art League Va, 70; and many other awards. *Bibliog:* Article, Art Voices/South, 5-6/78. *Mem:* Art League of Va; League of Reston Artist; Art Guild of Woodbridge, Va. *Media:* Mixed. *Publ:* Illusr, Yorktown 1781/1981 Poster, 81; illusr, 1980 & 1981 Army Weapon Systems Covers; and others. *Dealer:* Second Story Gallery 10629 Main St Fairfax VA 22030. *Mailing Add:* 2658 Quincy Adams Dr Herndon VA 22071

PISANO, RONALD GEORGE
HISTORIAN, CONSULTANT
b New York, NY, Dec 19, 48. *Study:* Adelphi Univ, Garden City, NY, BA; Univ Del. *Collections Arranged:* An American Place (auth, catalog), 81, The Long Island Landscape, 1865-1914: The Halcyon Years (auth, catalog), 81 & The Long Island Landscape, 1914-1946: The Transitional Years (auth, catalog), 82, Parrish Art Mus, Southampton, NY; American Paintings from the Parrish Museum, (auth, catalog), Coe-Kerr Gallery, New York, 82; A Leading Spirit in American Art: William Merritt Chase, 1849-1916, Henry Art Gallery & Metrop Mus Art, 83-84. *Pos:* Dir exhib, Baruch Col, New York, 74-76; consult cur of Am art, Heckscher Mus, Huntington, NY, 75-77; guest cur, Mus of Stony Brook, NY, 77 & 78; assoc cur, Parrish Art Mus, Southampton, NY, 77-79, dir, 79-81, pvt art consult, 81- *Awards:* A Conger Goodyear Award, Adelphi Univ, 71; Stebbins Family Res Grant, Heckscher Mus, 72-73; Distinguished Art Historian Award, Grand Cent Art Gallery, 79.

Mem: Col Art Asn. *Res:* Late 19th and early 20th century American art; William Merritt Chase; artists of Long Island. *Publ:* Auth, Catalog of the Heckscher Museum, Part I: American Art, Heckscher Mus, 78; auth, William Merritt Chase, Watson Guptill, 79; auth, Prince of Pastels, Portfolio, 83; auth, A Leading Spirit in American Art: William Merritt Chase, 1849-1916, Henry Art Gallery, 83. *Mailing Add:* 353 Riverside Dr 4-A New York NY 10025

PISKOTI, JAMES
PRINTMAKER, PAINTER
b Logan, WVa, July 5, 44. *Study:* Univ Mich, Ann Arbor, BS(design), 67; Yale Univ, MFA, 69. *Exhib:* Color Print USA, Tex Tech Univ Gallery, Lubbock, Tex, 78; Stockton Nat 1978, Haggin Mus, Calif, 78-79; Southwest Print & Drawing Competition, NMex State Univ Gallery, Las Cruces, 79; 13th Dulin Prints & Drawings Competition, Dulin Gallery Art, Knoxville, Tenn, 79; Boston Printmakers 32nd Nat Exhib, DeCordova Mus, Lincoln, Mass, 80; and many others. *Teaching:* Lab asst Intaglio Printmaking Studio, Univ Mich, 65-67; teaching asst printmaking, Yale Univ, 68-69; vis lectr printmaking, Southern Conn State Col, spring 69; prof fine art, Calif State Col Stanislaus, Turlock, 69- *Awards:* Bennard F Walker Prize, Mich Asn Printmakers, 66; Purchase Award, Bradley Univ, 75; First Prize Cash Award, NMex State Univ, 79. *Bibliog:* Peter Fierz (auth), Young American Painter, Der Kunst, 69; Gabor Peterdi (auth), Four prints, Eye-Mag of Yale Arts Asn, 69. *Mem:* Los Angeles Printmaking Soc. *Media:* Oils; Color Intaglio. *Mailing Add:* Dept of Art Calif State Stanislaus 800 Monte Vista Ave Turlock CA 95380

PITCHER, JOHN CHARLES
PAINTER, ILLUSTRATOR
b Kalamazoo, Mich, Aug 6, 49. *Work:* Anchorage Hist & Fine Arts Mus, Alaska; Nat Wildlife Fedn, Washington, DC; Univ Alaska Mus; Leigh Yawkey Woodson Art Mus, Wausau, Wis. *Exhib:* Leigh Yawkey Woodson Art Mus, 81; Royal Scottish Acad, Edinburgh, Scotland, 82; British Mus Nat Hist, London, 82; Carnegie Mus Nat Hist, 82; Alaska's Artists in Washington, DC, Capitol Rotunda Rm, 83; Denver Mus Hat Hist, 84; and many others. *Awards:* Award Merit, Soc Animal Artists, 79; 1st Place, Wildlife Art Show, Seattle Audubon Soc, 81; First Place, Wildlife Art Show, Audubon Soc, 82. *Bibliog:* Elaine Rhode (auth), John Pitcher: In perspective with nature, Alaska J, autumn 79; Peggy & Harold Samuels (auth), Contemporary Western Artist, Southwest Art Pub, 82; Eric Wallace (dir), Exploring the Arts with John Pitcher Kakm (film), Alaska Public TV, 11/83. *Mem:* Soc Animal Artists Inc. *Media:* Watercolor, Gouache; Oil, Acrylic. *Collection:* Limited edition lithographic reproduction wildlife prints. *Publ:* Illusr, A Guide to the Birds of Alaska, Alaska NW Publ Co, 80; Contribr-illusr, bird sect rev, World Bk Encycl, 81; illusr, Field Guide Birds of NAm, Nat Geographic Soc, 83. *Dealer:* Mill Pond Press 204 S Nassau St Venice FL 33595; Artique Ltd 314 G St Anchorage AK 99501. *Mailing Add:* 2839 Telequana Apt 1 Anchorage AK 99503

PITT, SUZAN (LEE)
PAINTER, FILMMAKER
b Kansas City, Mo. *Study:* Cranbrook Acad Art, BFA, 65. *Work:* Mus Mod Art, New York; Walker Art Ctr; Whitney Mus Am Art. *Exhib:* Solo exhib, Holly Solomon Gallery, New York, 79, Whitney Mus Am Art, 79, Galerie Denise-Rene Hansmayer, Düsseldorf, 81 & Delahunty Gallery, New York, 82. *Teaching:* Prof art, Psychopolis Vrije Akad Haag Holland, 74-75; guest lectr film animation, Harvrd Univ, 75-76. *Awards:* Best Animated Film 1979, Asparagus, Int Asn Film Animation, 79; First Prize, Oberhausen Festival Short Films, WGer, 79. *Mailing Add:* c/o Delahunty Gallery 291 Church St New York NY 10013

PITTORE, CARLO
PAINTER, MURALIST
b New York, NY, May 14, 43. *Study:* Tufts Col, BA, 66. *Work:* Mus Mod Art Libr, New York; Jen Brown Arch; Dr Sackner Arch; Sohm Arch; New York Pub Libr. *Exhib:* Works in Progress, Brooklyn Mus, 77; Postcard Size Art, PS1, New York, 78; Artists Publication, Tweed Mus Art, 80; Int Mail Art Exhib, Art Inst Chicago Libr, 82; Oxfordshire Int Mail Art Exhib, Gallery, England, 82; and others. *Collections Arranged:* Bern Porter Retrospective, Franklin Furnace & travelling, 79. *Pos:* Ed, Me Mag, 80- *Awards:* Max Beckman Scholar, 77; Portland Sch Art Award, 83. *Bibliog:* Articles, Art News, 12/81, Rubber Stamp Madness, 7/82 & Nat Stampographic, 7/83. *Mem:* Artists Equity; Union Maine Visual Artists; Found Community Artists. *Publ:* Ed, Colleagues, 80 & illusr, The Adventures of Carlo Pittore, 80, Pittore Euforico; illusr, Boxers, 82 & The Man With an Egg, 83, Bern Porter. *Mailing Add:* PO Box 1132 Peter Stuyvesant Sta New York NY 10009

PITTS, RICHARD G
PAINTER, PRINTMAKER
b Ft Monmouth, NJ, Oct 15, 40. *Study:* Newark Sch Fine Arts, 61; Pratt Inst, BFA, 68; New York Studio Sch, Paris, 72. *Exhib:* Jacque Kaplan Collects, Finch Col Mus, 70; Then and Now, Guild Hall, Easthampton, NY, 74; Charleston Ann, Weatherspoon Gallery, Univ NC, Greensboro, 77; Area Artists, Nelson Mus, 81; Painted Light, Queens Mus, 83; Painters of Content, Artists Choice Mus, 80 & 83; solo exhib, David Findlay Jr, 83. *Teaching:* Asst prof painting, Kansas City Art Inst, 70-73 & Fashion Inst Technol, 73- *Bibliog:* Ruth Bass (auth), Richard Pitts, Arts Mag, 9/79; John Russell (auth), Richard Pitts, New York Times, 2/25/83; Sarah King (auth), Richard Pitts, Art World, 2/83. *Media:* Oil on Canvas. *Dealer:* David Findlay Jr Inc 41 E 57 St New York NY 10022. *Mailing Add:* 233 W 18 St New York NY 10011

PIZITZ, SILVIA
COLLECTOR, PATRON
b Birmingham, Ala. *Study:* Painting with George Elmer Browne, Europe; Cornell Univ; Columbia Univ; Nat Acad Sch Fine Arts; Grand Cent Art Sch; Univ Munich & Art Sch. *Collections Arranged:* New York Painter (auth, catalog), Marlborough Gallery, 67. *Pos:* Assoc chmn, Cornell Friends Mus. *Interests:* Started collections at New York University and University of Alabama in Birmingham; made donations to Guggenheim Museum and Museum of Modern Art, New York, New York University, Cornell University, New York and Birmingham Museum of Art, Alabama. *Collection:* Neoplastic, constructivist, minimal. *Mailing Add:* 45 E 72nd St New York NY 10021

PIZZAT, JOSEPH
EDUCATOR, CRAFTSMAN
b Creekside, Pa, Nov 4, 26. *Study:* Kalamazoo Col, Mich, BA, 49, MA, 50; Columbia Univ Teachers Col, New York, EdD, 55; Pratt Inst, New York, 61. *Exhib:* One-man show, Gannon Col, Erie, Pa, 75, Americana, 76 & T is for Taping, Grafika Gallery, Erie, Pa, 81; one-man show, Tapings 1975, Ivy Sch Prof Art, Pittsburgh, 76; Liturgical Arts, Neuman Ctr, Bowling Green State Univ, Ohio, 79; Indiana Univ Pa Exhib, 83; and others. *Teaching:* Prof art & chmn art prog, Southwest Minn State Col, Marshall, 67-71; prof art, Mercyhurst Col, Erie, Pa, 71-78, chmn creative arts div, 71-78, coordr creative arts therapy prog, 79. *Awards:* Outstanding Art Educator Award, Pa Art Educ Asn, 81. *Mem:* Artists' Equity Asn; Am Art Therapy Asn; Pa Art Educ Asn; Nat Art Educ Asn; SDak Art Educ Asn (pres, 55-57). *Media:* Tape, Contact Sheet. *Res:* Implications of the duality of the human brain as it relates to art, arts, creativity and athletics. *Publ:* Auth, Teacher as artist, Arts & Activities, 9/80; auth, Ten commandments of child art, Arts and Activities, 9/81; auth, I'm a right brained person, Why me God? Nat Art Educ Asn Art Educ J; auth, Tennis as therapy, ADDvantage Mag, 11/12/79; auth, Artmaking with tape, Sch Arts Mag, 83-84. *Mailing Add:* 2046 Charleston Ave Erie PA 16509

PLACE, BRADLEY EUGENE
EDUCATOR
b Rule, Tex, Nov 4, 20. *Study:* Tex A&M Univ, 38-40; NTex Univ, with Carlos Merida & Ivan Johnson, BS, 42. *Pos:* Mem visual arts adv panel, Okla Arts & Humanities Coun, 72-; mem selection comt, Art for Pub Places, Tulsa, 75- *Teaching:* From asst prof to prof lettering & typography, Univ Tulsa, 47-, chmn dept art, 64- *Awards:* Brad Trust Scholar, 73. *Bibliog:* Jenk Jones, Jr (auth), Honor roll for May, Tulsa Tribune, 71; Connie Cronley (auth), Profile of a teacher of artists, Tulsa, 6/14/73; Myrna Smart (auth), Dilemma of penal reform, Arts & Humanities Coun Tulsa & KTEW-TV, 5/74. *Mem:* Tulsa Advert Fedn; Tulsa Art Dir Club (exec bd, 70-75, 77 & 81-, pres, 74-75); Tulsa Arts & Humanities (mem bd, Chmn Mayor's Arts Comn, 77). *Mailing Add:* 2156 S Fulton Pl Tulsa OK 74114

PLACZEK, ADOLF KURT
LIBRARIAN, HISTORIAN
b Vienna, Austria, Mar 9, 13; US citizen. *Study:* Univ Vienna, 31-38; Inst Art History, 34-38; Sch Libr Serv, Columbia Univ, 41-42. *Pos:* Asst librn, Avery Archit & Fine Arts Libr, Columbia Univ, 48-60, librn, 60-80, librn emer, 80- *Teaching:* Adj prof archit hist, Columbia Univ, 65-80, prof emer, 80- *Awards:* Award Merit, Am Inst Archit, New York Chap, 79; Munic Art Soc, 81. *Mem:* Soc Archit Hist (pres, 78-80). *Res:* Eighteenth century European and nineteenth century American architecture. *Publ:* Ed, Avery Index to Architectural Periodicals, 63 & Catalog of the Avery Architectural Library, 68, G K Hall Press; contribr, Palladio, The Four Books of Architecture, Dover Press, 65; coauth, Piranesi, Drawings & Etchings, Sackler Found, 75; contribr, Hitchcock, American Architectural Books, DaCapo Press, 76; contribr, Macmillan Encyclopedia of Architects, 82. *Mailing Add:* 176 W 87th St New York NY 10024

PLAGENS, PETER
PAINTER, EDUCATOR
b Dayton, Ohio, Mar 1, 41. *Study:* Univ Southern Calif, BFA, 62; Syracuse Univ, MFA, 64. *Work:* Baltimore Mus Art; Albright-Knox Mus; Continental Grain Corp, New York; Dechert, Price & Rhodes, Philadelphia; Newark Mus. *Exhib:* Solo exhib, John Berggruen Gallery, San Francisco, 74 & 77, Nancy Hoffman Gallery, New York, 75, Hirshhorn Mus, 76, Baum-Silverman Gallery, Los Angeles, 77, Marianne Deson Gallery, Chicago, 78 & Inst Contemp Art, Los Angeles, 79; Butler Mus, 76; San Francisco Mus Art, 77; Inst Contemp Art, Los Angeles, 77. *Pos:* Cur, Long Beach Mus, Calif, 65-66; contrib ed, Artforum, 66-76. *Teaching:* Assoc prof art, Calif State Univ, Northridge, 69-79. *Awards:* Nat Endowment Arts Grant, 77. *Publ:* Auth, Ecology of evil, 12/72, Peter and the pressure cooker, 6/74 & None dare call it BoHo, 9/75, Artforum; auth, Soft touch of hard edge, LAICA J, 4/75; auth, Sunshine Muse: Contemporary Art on the West Coast, Praeger Publ, 75. *Mailing Add:* c/o Nancy Hoffman Gallery 429 W Broadway New York NY 10012

PLAMONDON, PETER M
PAINTER
Study: San Francisco Art Inst, BFA, 67; Boston Univ, MFA, 75. *Work:* Mus Fine Arts, Boston; DeCordova Mus, Lincoln, Mass; Worcester Art Mus, Mass; Rose Art Mus, Brandeis Univ. *Exhib:* Solo exhibs, Alpha Gallery, Boston, 76, 78 & 81 & Touchstone Gallery, New York, 83; Collectors Exhib, Inst Contemp Art, Boston, 77; Still-Life, Lamont Gallery, Phillips Exeter Acad, NH, 79; Directions in Realism, Danforth Mus, Framingham, Mass, 80; Triennial Boston Artists, Brockton Art Mus, Mass, 83. *Awards:* Grants,

Blanche E Colman, 75 & Mass Coun Arts & Humanities, 77 & 80. *Bibliog:* Wolf Kahn (auth), Subject matter in new realism, Am Artist, 11/79. *Media:* Oil on Canvas. *Dealer:* Touchstone Gallery 29 W 57th St New York NY 10019; Alpha Gallery 121 Newbury St Boston MA. *Mailing Add:* c/o Alpha Gallery 121 Newbury St Boston MA 02116

PLASTER, ALICE MARIE
PAINTER, INSTRUCTOR
b Hickory, NC. *Study:* Md Inst, Col Art, BFA, 77. *Work:* George Washington House Mus, Bladensburg, Md. *Comn:* Mural, Md Nat Capital Park & Planning Comn, Riverdale, 79. *Exhib:* Nat Soc Arts & Letters, Washington DC, 73-76; Md Inst Printmaking Exhib, Baltimore, 77; Frostburg State Col, Md, 79. *Pos:* Graphic artist, Prince George's Co Mem Libr System, Hyattsville, Md, 80- *Teaching:* Instr drawing & painting, Md Nat Capital Park, 77-79. *Awards:* Cash Award, Nat Soc Arts & Letters, 73; and others. *Bibliog:* Richard Carter (auth), Spectrum, The Post, 9/15/78; Joanne Hoover (auth), The arts, Washington Post, 3/22/79; William N Swetcharnik (auth), The view from my easel, The Post, 11/19/80. *Mem:* Arlington Arts Ctr; Artists Equity Asn. *Media:* Oil, Pencil. *Mailing Add:* 3925 Winchester Ln Bowie MD 20715

PLATH, IONA
WRITER, WEAVER
b Dodge Center, Minn, May 24, 07. *Study:* Westmoreland Col; Art Students League; Art Inst Chicago. *Teaching:* Instr art & design, 30-; instr handweaving, 65- *Mem:* Handweavers Guild Am; STex Fiver Arts Guild; Byliners. *Publ:* Auth & illusr, Decorative Arts of Sweden, Scribner's, 48 & Dover, 65; auth & illusr, Hand Weaving, 64 & The Craft of Handweaving, 72, Scribner's; auth, The Handweaver's Pattern Book, Dover, 81. *Mailing Add:* 2949 Lawnview Corpus Christi TX 78404

PLATUS, LIBBY
FIBRE & PAPER SCULPTOR
b Los Angeles, Calif. *Study:* Univ Calif, Los Angeles, BA. *Comn:* Fibre sculpture wall, Irvine Co's Big Canyon Country Club, Newport Beach, Calif; fibre sculpture ceiling environment, Holiday Inn Airport Lakes, Miami; fibre sculpture wall hangings, McCulloch Properties, Silver Lakes Resort Hotel, Victorville, Calif, Sheraton Nat Hotel, Arlington, Va, Security Pac Bank, South Pasadena, Calif, Blue Cross of Southern Calif, Woodland Hills, Discovery Bay, Hawaii & Corp Hq, Faberge, NY; plus others. *Exhib:* Laguna Beach Mus Art, 73; Riverside Art Ctr, Calif, 74; Calif State Univ, Fullerton, 74; Calif Design 76, Los Angeles, 76; Fiberworks Int Exhib, Cleveland Mus of Art; plus others. *Pos:* Los Angeles Olympics '84 Cult & Fine Arts Comn; Los Angeles Artists Equity Adv Bd. *Teaching:* Guest lectr, numerous insts in US & abroad, 76- *Awards:* Winner, Tex Christian Univ Nat Invitational Competition for Fiberwork Comn. *Bibliog:* Article, Craft Horizons, 12/74; Sandra Winston (auth), The Entrepreneurial Woman, Newsweek Bks, 79; The Fiberarts Design Book, Fiberarts Mag, 80; and others. *Mem:* Am Crafts Coun; Artists Equity; Women's Caucus Art. *Media:* Cast Paper. *Publ:* Contribr, Shuttle, Spindle & Dyepot, fall 75 & spring 77. *Mailing Add:* 1359 Holmby Ave Los Angeles CA 90024

PLAUT, JAMES S
ART ADMINISTRATOR, WRITER
b Cincinnati, Ohio, Feb 1, 12. *Study:* Harvard Univ, AB, 33, AM, 35; Wheaton Col, hon DFA, 74. *Collections Arranged:* In charge of all exhib planning, US Pavilion, Brussels World's Fair, 58, New York World's Fair, 64, Montreal, 67 & Osaka, 70; First World Crafts Exhib, Ont Sci Ctr, Toronto, 74. *Pos:* Asst cur paintings, Mus Fine Arts, Boston, 35-39; dir, Inst Contemp Art, Boston, 39-56; vpres, Old Sturbridge Village, Mass, 59-62; secy gen, World Crafts Coun, 67-76; adv, NJ State Mus & Pac Northwest Arts Ctr; pres, Aid to Artisans Inc, 76-; planning consult, New York Pub Libr, 76-; mem vis comt, Prog in Artisanry, Boston Univ, 75- *Teaching:* Lectr hist art, Harvard Univ, 34-35, 37-38; lectr hist art, New Eng Conserv Music, 38-39. *Awards:* Off, Royal Order St Olav, Norway, 50; Comdr, Royal Order of Leopold, Belg Govt, 58. *Mem:* Art Vis Comt of Wheaton Col (chmn); MacDowell Colony; Coun Arts, Mass Inst Technol. *Publ:* Auth, Oskar Kokoschka, 48; auth, Steuben glass, 48, 51 & 72; auth, Assignment in Israel, 60; In Praise of Hands (with Octavio Paz), 74. *Mailing Add:* 64 Fairgreen Pl Chestnut Hill MA 02167

PLEAR, SCOTT EDWARD
PAINTER, PRINTMAKER
b Vancouver, BC, Mar 26, 52. *Study:* Univ BC, BFA, 76; Univ Sask, with Emma Lake, 77 & 80; Triangle Artists Workshop, Pine Plains, NY, 82. *Work:* Edmonton Art Gallery, Alta. *Exhib:* Ninth Burnaby Biennial Print Show, Burnaby Art Gallery, BC, 77; Malaspina Printmakers Fifth Ann, Presentation House, NVancouver, BC, 79; The West Face, Charles H Scott Gallery, Emily Carr Col Art, Vancouver, BC, 81; BC Currents, Sarnia Art Gallery, Ont, 81; Royal Can Acad Invitational, Kenneth G Heffel Gallery, Vancouver, BC, 81; The Current Generation, Edmonton Art Gallery, 83. *Teaching:* Instr, Univ BC, 78-79; asst prof, Univ Alta, 83. *Media:* Acrylic. *Dealer:* Martin Gerard Gallery 10416 80th Ave Edmonton AB T6E 5T7. *Mailing Add:* 1947 Adanac St Vancouver BC V5L 2E5 Canada

PLETCHER, GERRY
PAINTER, PRINTMAKER
b State College, Pa. *Study:* Edinboro State Univ, BS; Pa State Univ, MA(fine arts); also with Montenegro, Carol Summers, Harold Altman, Nelson Sandgren & Shobaken; George Peabody Col, Nashville, PhD. *Work:* Evansville Mus Arts & Sci, Ind; Fisk Univ, Tenn; Jacksonville State Univ,

Ala; Tenn Arts Comn; Tenn Botanical Gardens; and others. *Exhib:* Cent South Art Exhib, Nashville, 69-71 & 83; Nat Acad Design 145th Ann, New York, 70; Wonderworks Four, Nat Print Show, Nashville, 79; Women in Art, Springfield Nat Exhib, Ill, 79; Summer Lights Art Exhib, Nashville, 83; and others. *Teaching:* Assoc prof, Tenn State Univ, currently. *Awards:* Graphics Purchase Award, 22nd Ann Mid-States Art Exhib, Evansville Mus Arts & Sci, 69; seven Purchase Prizes, Tenn Arts Comn, 72; Purchase Award, 13th Ann Tenn All-State, 73; and others. *Bibliog:* Sweimal drei, Aufbau, 3/19/71; Artists USA, 1972-73; Am Printmakers, 74. *Media:* Etchings, Woodcuts, Acrylic, Oil. *Mailing Add:* 605 Brook Hollow Rd Nashville TN 37205

PLETKA, PAUL
PAINTER, PRINTMAKER
b San Diego, Calif, 1946. *Study:* Ariz State Univ, Tempe; Colo State Univ, Ft Collins. *Work:* San Antonio Mus Art, Tex; Milwaukee Fine Arts Ctr, Wis; St Louis Art Mus, Mo; Minneapolis Inst Art, Minn; Phoenix Art Mus, Ariz; and others. *Comn:* Ghost Dancer (lithograph), Phoenix Art Mus, Ariz, 77; Those Living at the Sunrise (lithograph), Heard Mus, Phoenix, Ariz, 79; Papageno (poster), St Louis Opera Theater, Mo, 80. *Exhib:* Four Corners Biennial, Phoenix Art Mus, Ariz, 77; one-man show, El Paso Mus Art, Tex, 78; A Sense of Space, Univ NMex Art Mus, 79; Eiteljorg Collection, Indianapolis Mus Art, 79; Here and Now, Albuquerque Art Mus, NMex, 80. *Awards:* Certificate of Excellence, Chicago, 76; Nat Watercolor Soc Award, Watercolor USA, 77. *Bibliog:* Edna Gundersen (auth), Pletka bares Indian souls on canvas, El Paso Times, 5/13/78; Ed Montini (auth), Unmasking a dedicated artist, The Ariz Republic, 3/22/81; Edna Gundersori (auth), Pletka, Northland Press, 83. *Media:* Acrylic, Watercolor. *Mailing Add:* c/o ACA Galleries 21 E 67th St New York NY 10021

PLETSCHER, JOSEPHINE MARIE
LIBRARIAN, SERIGRAPHER
b Muscatine, Iowa. *Study:* Immaculate Heart Col, BA, 62, MA, 64; Univ Calif, Los Angeles. *Comn:* Feel Free (poster), Wilson Libr Bulletin, Bronx, NY, 69. *Exhib:* Iowa Artists 4th Ann Exhib, Des Moines Art Ctr, 52 & 11th Ann Iowa Artists Exhib, 59; Calif State Fair, Sacramento, 62. *Collections Arranged:* Mexican Festival--Arts and Crafts, Pasadena Pub Libr, 72. *Pos:* Fine arts coordr, Pasadena Pub Libr, 64-82; reference librn, Rio Hondo Col Libr, Whittier, Calif, 83- *Awards:* Watercolor Hon Award, Des Moines Art Ctr, 59 & State Calif, 62; Recognition Award, Pasadena Pub Libr, 68. *Bibliog:* Larry Palmer (auth), Local art and artists, Pasadena Star News, 7/13/69; Jack Birkinshaw (auth), Joy of children painting is captured on librarian's film, Los Angeles Times, 9/4/69; Arthur Plotnik (auth), This is a library feel free, Wilson Libr Bulletin, 11/69. *Mem:* Art Libr Soc NAm; Hollywood Art Coun; and others. *Media:* Serigraph, Oil. *Interests:* Architecture, graphics, printmaking and rare art objects. *Publ:* Illusr, Immaculate Heart College--Announcement of Courses, Immaculate Heart Col, 63-64; illusr & contribr, Painting from the heart, Business: Pasadena C of C, 5/69. *Mailing Add:* 1917 Rodney Dr Los Angeles CA 90027

PLOCHMANN, CAROLYN GASSAN
PAINTER, GRAPHIC ARTIST
b Toledo, Ohio, May 4, 26. *Study:* Toledo Mus Art Sch Design, 43-47; Univ Toledo, BA, 47; State Univ Iowa, MFA, 49; with Alfeo Faggi, 50; Southern Ill Univ, 51-52. *Work:* Evansville Mus Arts & Sci, Ind; Fleishmann Found Collection, Cincinnati, Ohio; Butler Inst Am Art, Youngstown, Ohio; pvt collection of Mr & Mrs Arthur Magill, Greenville, SC; and others. *Comn:* Mural, North Side Old Nat Bank, Evansville, 53. *Exhib:* One-man shows, Witte Mus, San Antonio, Tex, 68 & Toledo Mus Art, 68 & Kennedy Galleries, New York, 83; 164th Prints & Drawings Ann, Pa Acad Fine Arts, Philadelphia, 69; 52nd Ann Mem Exhib, Philadelphia Watercolor Club, 69. *Teaching:* Supvr art, Allyn Training Sch, Southern Ill Univ, Carbondale, 49-50. *Awards:* George W Stevens Fel, Toledo Mus Art, 47-49; Tupperware Art Fund First Award, 53; Emily Lowe Found Competition Award, 58. *Bibliog:* Louise Bruner (auth), Art notes, Toledo Blade, 10/10/65; Thomas Hoving (auth), article, Connoisseur, 83; Ilene Susan Fort, article, Arts Mag, 83. *Mem:* Woodstock Art Asn; Philadelphia Watercolor Club; Toledo Fedn Art Socs. *Media:* Oil, Acrylic; Graphics. *Publ:* Auth, University Portrait: Nine Paintings by Carolyn Gassan Plochmann, Southern Ill Univ Press, 59; auth, cover article, Prize-Winning Graphics, 66. *Dealer:* Kennedy Galleries 40 W 57th St New York NY 10019. *Mailing Add:* Rte 9 Box 104 Carbondale IL 62901

PLOSSU, BERNARD
PHOTOGRAPHER
Dalat, S Vietnam, Feb 26, 45. *Work:* Bibliotheque Nat, Paris; Amon Carter Mus, Ft Worth, Tex; George Eastman House, Rochester, NY; Ctr Creative Photography, Tucson, Ariz; Niepce Mus, Chalon, France. *Exhib:* Plossu by Atelier Fresson, Eaton-Shoen Gallery, San Francisco, 82; solo exhib, Etherton Gallery, Tucson, Ariz, 82; The Spirit of Travelling, Arles Photo Fest, Arles, France, 82; In Place, Albuquerque Mus, NMex, 82; two-person show, Hoshour Gallery, Albuquerque, NMex, 83. *Teaching:* Photography workshops, Okla Summer Arts Inst, 83. *Bibliog:* Gilles Mora (auth), La rupture creatrice du Voyage Mexicain, Cahiers Photo, 81; L Sherman & S Parks (auths), I photograph the weather, Artlines, 81; M Foley (auth), Bernard Plossu, Artspace, 81. *Publ:* Photogr, Surbanalism, Chene, France, 72; Go West, Chene, France, 72; Le Voyage Mexicain, Contrejour, France, 79; Egypte, Photoeil, France, 79; New Mexico Revisited, Univ NMex Press, 83. *Mailing Add:* c/o Eaton-Shoen Gallery 500 Paul Ave San Francisco CA 94124

PLOUS, PHYLLIS
CURATOR
b Green Bay, Wis. *Study:* Univ Wis, with Oskar Hagen & James Watrous, BA, 47; Univ London; Univ Calif, Santa Barbara. *Collections Arranged:* Ralph A Blakelock retrospective & tour (coauth, catalog); Charles Demuth retrospective & tour (coauth, catalog); 19 Sculptors of the 40's; 5 American Painters; Sculptors in the 50's, tour; Jack Tworkov Recent Paintings; Guy Williams Recent Paintings; Sculptural Perspectives in the 70's; Richard Diebenkorn, Intaglio Prints 1961-1978; Dark/Light: Extensions of Photography, tour; and many others. *Pos:* Asst to dir, Santa Barbara Mus Art, 54-56; asst to dir, Univ Art Mus, Univ Calif, Santa Barbara, 63-72; cur exhibs & contemp art, 72- *Awards:* Nat Endowment Arts Fel, Mus Professionals, 80. *Mem:* Santa Barbara Contemp Arts Forum; Col Art Asn Am; Southern Calif Art Writers Asn. *Mailing Add:* 375 Toro Canyon Rd Carpinteria CA 93013

PLUMB, JAMES DOUGLAS
PAINTER, CURATOR
b New Haven, Conn, Dec 20, 41. *Study:* Univ Va; Philadelphia Col Art, BFA. *Work:* Acad Arts, Easton, Md. *Exhib:* Ann Md Show, Acad Arts, Easton, Md, 74, 78, 79 & 81; Art Asn Newport Ann Show, RI, 75; Conn Acad Arts Ann Show, Wadsworth Atheneum, 75; Five From the Eastern Shore, 76 & Md Biennial, 78, Baltimore Mus Art. *Collections Arranged:* Collection of the Academy of the Arts, 175 Works (auth, catalog), 79; College Show (auth, catalog), Contemporary Maryland Photographers (auth, catalog), 79; Eight Artists' Invitational Shows (auth, catalog), 79; Contemporary Works on Paper, 80. *Pos:* Cur, Acad Arts, Easton, Md, 78- *Teaching:* Instr painting & drawing, Acad Arts, Easton, MD, 71-76; lectr art hist, State Extension Home Economics & Improvement, Univ Md, 73-76. *Awards:* Acad Arts Ann Show Awards, 74, 78 & 80; Best in Show, Easton Lions' Club Show, 75. *Media:* Oil on Canvas, Pencil on Paper. *Mailing Add:* PO Box 1088 Easton MD 21601

PODUSKA, T F
LECTURER, PAINTER
b Cedar Falls, Iowa, Dec 6, 25. *Study:* Univ Northern Iowa, BA(art educ). *Work:* Denver Art Mus, Contemp Collection; Atlantic Richfield Corp; Amoco; Int Bus Machines; Exeter; and others. *Exhib:* Colo Womens Col, 79; Aspen Inst, 79; Univ Wyo, 80; Watercolor USA, Springfield, Mo, 80; Carson-Sapiro Gallery, Denver, 82; and others. *Pos:* Lectr, consult & proj asst, Colo Coun Arts & Humanities, 73. *Teaching:* Bus skills workshops, 75. *Awards:* Colo Governor's Award for Arts & Humanities, 77; Merit Award, Nat Acad of Design, 77. *Mem:* Alliance Contemp Art; Asian Art Asn. *Media:* Water Media, Paper. *Publ:* Coauth, Insuring the artist's work, Am Artist Bus Lett, suppl, 74; coauth, Business Practices for Artists, Artists Equity Asn, 75. *Mailing Add:* c/o Art/Beasley Gallery 2802 Juan St Ste 16 San Diego CA 92110

POEHLMANN, JOANNA
PAINTER, PRINTMAKER
b Milwaukee, Wis, Sept 5, 32. *Study:* Layton Sch Art, four-year dipl, 54; Kansas City Art Inst, 55; Marquette Univ, 58; Univ Wis, Milwaukee, 65. *Work:* Milwaukee Art Mus; Charles A Wustum Mus Fine Arts, Racine, Wis; Metrop Mus & Art Ctr, Coral Gables, Fla; Univ Hosp Gallery, Madison, Wis; Int Print Biennial, Embragel, Cabo Frio, Brazil. *Comn:* Kiosk posters, Performing Arts Ctr, Milwaukee, 68; animal postal cards, Milwaukee Co Zoological Soc, 72; greeting cards, H George Caspari Inc, New York, 72-83 & Riveredge Nature Ctr, Milwaukee, 72 & 75; animal note cards, Recycled Paper Co, Chicago, 81-83. *Exhib:* Retrospective, Drawings, Collages, Mindscapes, Milwaukee Art Mus, 66; Wisconsin Directions I & II, Milwaukee Art Mus, 75 & 78; Works on Paper, Art Inst Chicago, 78; one-man exhib, John Michael Kohler Art Ctr, Sheboygan, Wis, 79; Prints, Multiples, Art Inst Chicago, 81 & Nat Mus Am Art, 82; Fifth Miami Int Print Biennial, Metrop Mus & Art Ctr, Coral Gables, Fla, 82; Wis Biennial, Madison Art Ctr, 82. *Awards:* Award Excellence, Wis Painters & Sculptors, 81; Second Award, Watercolor Wis, Wustum Mus Fine Arts, Racine, Wis, 83. *Bibliog:* Tom Lueders (producer), JoAnna Poehlmnn Retrospective (film), Channel 4, 12/66; Verna Curtis (auth), New dimensions in Wisconsin art: JoAnna Poehlmann, Exclusively Yours Mag, 1/2/80; James Auer (auth), Independent artists of Wisconsin, Wis Acad Rev, 3/83. *Mem:* Print Club Philadelphia; Printforum Milwaukee Art Mus; Illustrators & Designers Milwaukee (secy, 62-63); Wis Painters & Sculptors. *Media:* Watercolor, Collage; Stone Lithograhy. *Publ:* Illusr, The Happy Book, 65 & Just Alike Princes, 66, Western Publ Co; illusr, The chimp who went fishing, Int Wildlife Mag, 78; auth & illusr, The Day Before Christmas, Western Publ Co, 79; illusr, A Nutrition Monograph for Taking Off Pounds Sensibly, Tops Club, 80. *Dealer:* Bradley Galleries 2565 N Downer Ave Milwaukee WI 53211; van Straaten Gallery 361 W Superior St Chicago IL. *Mailing Add:* 1231 N Prospect Ave Milwaukee WI 53211

POGZEBA, WOLFGANG H
PAINTER, SCULPTOR
b Planegg, Ger, July 7, 36; US citizen. *Study:* Colo Sch Mines; Univ Mex; Sorbonne, Paris; Kunstakademie, Munich, Ger; Univ Colo, BA(hist), 61, MA(educ), 63. *Work:* Denver Art Mus; Univ Wyo Art Mus, Laramie; Indianapolis Mus Fine Art; Russell Mus Gallery, Great Falls, Mont. *Exhib:* Art in the Embassy, US Govt-Mus Mod Art, 66; Amon Carter Mus, Ft Worth, 68; Russell Gallery Mus, Great Falls, Mont, 71; sculpture-painting, Loretto Heights Col-Ctr Performing Arts, Denver, 75; Photog of Am W, State Mus Wyo, 77-78; and others including one-man shows. *Pos:* Owner-mgr, Pogzeba Art Studios, 61-81. *Awards:* Patron's Award, Mus of NMex, Santa Fe, 64; Purchase Award, Salt Lake Art Ctr, 65; Nat Cert of Merit, Ann Bookbinders Western Bk Show, 77. *Media:* Watercolor, Oil; Etching.

Specialty: Western Americana; American impressionism; modern. *Publ:* Auth & ed, Painting-Drawings-Sculpture, Leonard Hutton Galleries, NY, 62 & Amon Carter Mus, 63; auth, New Vision: Photographs of the American West, Northland Press, 77; auth, Rancho De Taos, Lowell Press, 81. *Mailing Add:* PO Box 3022 Taos NM 87571

POINDEXTER, ELINOR FULLER
DEALER
b Montreal, Can; US citizen. *Pos:* Dir, Poindexter Gallery, currently. *Mem:* Art Dealers Asn Am. *Specialty:* Contemporary painting and sculpture, especially American. *Mailing Add:* 1160 Fifth Ave New York NY 10029

POINIER, ARTHUR BEST
CARTOONIST
b Oak Park, Ill, Feb 9, 11. *Study:* Drake Univ, 34; Ohio Wesleyan Univ, AB, LHD, 55. *Pos:* Sports cartoonist, Columbus Dispatch, Ohio, 29-32; cartoonist, Des Moines Register & Tribune, Iowa, 34-36; cartoonist comic strip, Jitter, 36-43; political cartoonist, Detroit Free Press, 40-51 & Detroit News, 51-76; mem, Bell-McClure Syndicate & United Features Syndicate, 50- *Mem:* Asn Am Ed Cartoonists. *Mailing Add:* 5470 Miller Rd Ann Arbor MI 48103

POLAN, LINCOLN M
COLLECTOR
b Wheeling, WVa, Feb 12, 09. *Study:* NY Univ; Univ Va; Ohio State Univ. *Pos:* Mem bd dirs, Huntington Galleries, WVa. *Mem:* Mus of Mod Art; Metrop Mus Art. *Collection:* Line and wash drawings by Rodin; drawings by French impressionists; American paintings, predominantly of the Ash Can School; Renaissance portraits of men; Renaissance prints and engravings. Collections exhibited at Huntington Galleries Art Museum, Charleston Art Gallery, University of West Virginia Art Museum, Museum of Fine Arts, Houston, Texas and Phoenix Art Museum, Arizona. *Mailing Add:* 2 Prospect Dr Huntington WV 25701

POLAN, NANCY MOORE
PAINTER
b Newark, Ohio. *Study:* Marshall Univ, AB; Huntington Galleries, with Fletcher Martin, Hilton Leech, Paul Puzinas & Robert Friemark; Al Schmidt, Fla. *Work:* Huntington Galleries; OVAR Mus, Portugal; Cabell Huntington Hospital. *Exhib:* Nat Arts Club, New York, 62-81; Joan Miro Graphics, Barcelona, 70 & Travel Exhib, 70-71; 21st Contemp Art, La Scala, Florence, Italy, 71 & 77; one-woman show, New York World's Fair, 65; and many other group & one-woman shows. *Pos:* Mem, Art Comn Int Platform Asn, 68-83; hon vpres, Centro Studi e Scambi Internazionali, Rome, Italy, 78-81; fel, Intercontinental Biog Asn, 75-83. *Awards:* Int Platform Asn Award, 77; Grumbacher Watercolor Award, Pen & Brush, Inc, 78; Gold Medal, Acad Italy, 79 & 83. *Mem:* Nat Arts Club; assoc Allied Artists Am; Pen & Brush, Inc; assoc Am Watercolor Soc; Acad Internazionali Leonardo da Vinci. *Media:* Watercolor, Oil. *Publ:* Contribr, cover, La Rev Mod, 61 & 66; Talent Mag Int Platform Asn, 77; spec issue, WVa Hillbilly, 73. *Mailing Add:* 2 Prospect Dr Huntington WV 25701

POLCARI, STEPHEN
HISTORIAN
b Boston, Mass, Jan 22, 45. *Study:* Columbia Col, BA, 67; Columbia Univ, MA, 71; Univ Calif, Santa Barbara, PhD, 80. *Pos:* Cur, DeCordova Mus, Lincoln, Mass, 76. *Teaching:* Asst prof mod art, Univ Ill, Urbana, 79-83; State Univ NY, Stony Brook, 83- *Awards:* Rubinstein Mus Fel, Whitney Mus Art, 77; Nat Endowment Humanities, 82; Inst Advan Study, Princeton, 82. *Mem:* Col Art Asn. *Res:* Relationship between intellectual history and the development of modern art, especially abstract expressionism. *Publ:* A newly-found drawing by Saraceni, Burlington Mag, 79; Intellectual roots of abstract expressionism: Mark Rothko, 79, Jackson Pollock and Thomas Hart Benton, 79 & Mark Rothko, 79, Arts Mag; Intellectual roots of abstract expressionism: Clyfford Still, Art Int, 82. *Mailing Add:* Dept Art State Univ NY Stony Brook NY 11777

POLESKIE, STEPHEN FRANCIS
ENVIRONMENTAL ARTIST, PRINTMAKER
b Pringle, Pa, June 3, 38. *Study:* Wilkes Col, BA(econ), 59; New Sch Social Res, 61. *Work:* Whitney Mus Art, Metrop Mus Art & Mus Mod Art, New York; Victoria & Albert Mus; Tate Gallery, London. *Exhib:* Word & Image-Posters and Typography (1879-1967), Mus Mod Art, New York, 68; Recent Acquisitions: Prints and Drawings, Metrop Mus Art, 69; Oversize Prints, Whitney Mus Am Art, 71; Louis K Meisel Gallery, New York, 78 & 80; Int Commun Agency tour of USSR, 79; one-man exhib, Palace of Cult & Sci, Warsaw, Poland & Gallery of Mod Art, Gdansk, 79; Sky Art Conference, Mass Inst Technol, 81; Int Biennial Graphic Art, Ljubljana, Yugoslavia, 81 & 83; Anderson Gallery, Col William & Mary, 83; and others. *Teaching:* Instr, Sch Visual Arts, New York, 66-68; assoc prof silk-screen & contemp art issues, Cornell Univ, 68-81, prof, 81-; vis prof, Univ Calif, Berkeley, 76. *Awards:* Am Fedn Arts, 72; Creative Artists Public Service, 78. *Bibliog:* Pierre Restany (auth), Christo and Poleskie, D'Ars, Milano, 83. *Dealer:* Marian Goodman Gallery 24 W 57th St New York NY 10019; New Acquisitions Gallery 120 E Washington St Syracuse NY 13202. *Mailing Add:* 306 Stone Quarry Rd Ithaca NY 14850

POLING, CLARK V
MUSEUM DIRECTOR, HISTORIAN
US citizen. *Study:* Yale Univ, BA, 62; Columbia Univ, MA, 66, PhD, 73. *Collections Arranged:* Bauhaus Color, 76, Contemporary Art in Atlanta Collections, 76 & Contemporary Art in Southern California, 80, High Mus Art; Kandinsky: Russian and Bauhaus Years, 1915-1933, Guggenheim Mus, 83. *Teaching:* Vis lectr art hist, Cooper Union, 70-73; asst prof mod art, Emory Univ, 73-79, assoc prof, 79-, dir, Mus Art & Archaeol, 82- *Awards:* Kress Found Fel, 64-65; Deutscher Akad Austauschdienst Grant, 77 & 81; Nat Endowment Humanities Stipend, 78. *Mem:* Am Asn Mus; Col Art Asn. *Res:* Early 20th century European art and theory, especially at the Bauhaus; contemporary American art and architecture. *Publ:* Auth, Geometric abstraction: A new generation, Inst Contemp Art, Boston, 81; auth, Kandinsky--Unterricht am Bauhaus, Kunstverlag Weingarten, 82. *Mailing Add:* Mus Art & Archaeol Emory Univ Atlanta GA 30322

POLISZCZUK, OREST STEPHAN
EDUCATOR, SCULPTOR
b Lviv, Ukraine, Jan 7, 42; US citizen. *Study:* Univ Md, BA, 66, MA, 68. *Work:* Montgomery Col, Rockville; Garden Patriots, Cape Coral, Fla. *Comn:* Sculpture (steel), St Stephan's Lutheran Church, White Oak, Md, 75; two sculptures, Bank Va, Richmond, 77. *Exhib:* Md Artist's Ann, Baltimore Mus Art, 64 & 65; Young Sculptors Invitational, Sculptors Guild, New York, 69; Artists Equity Asn Invitational, Peale Mus, Baltimore, 71; one-man shows, Wash Co Mus Fine Arts, Hagerstown, Md, 73 & Ukrainian-Canadian Art Found, Toronto, 78; Sculpture Invitational, Textile Mus, Washington DC, 74. *Pos:* Artist consult, Johnson, McCordic & Thompson, PA, Engineers, Planners, Surveyors, 80. *Teaching:* Assoc prof sculpture, Montgomery Col, Rockville, Md, 69- *Awards:* Nat Col Sculpture Competition, Garden Patriots, Fla, 66; David Smith Mem Award, Young Sculptors Competition, Sculptors Guild, NY, 69; Best in Show, Loyola Col Ann Invitational, Loyola Col, Md, 70. *Mem:* Am Asn Univ Profs; Southern Sculptors Asn; Artists Equity Asn Md (vpres, 74-75). *Media:* Chrome Plated Welded Steel; Gouache, Oils. *Mailing Add:* 5531 High Tor Hill Columbia MD 21045

POLK, FRANK FREDRICK
SCULPTOR
b Louisville, Ky, Sept 1, 08. *Study:* With Hughlette Wheeler, George Phippen & J R Williams. *Work:* Colorado Springs Fine Arts Ctr; John Ascuaga's Nuggett, Sparks, Nev & pvt collection Ezra Brooks. *Exhib:* Cowboy Artists Am Ann Show, Cowboy Hall Fame, Oklahoma City, 68-72 & Phoenix Art Mus, Ariz, 73-75; Matthews Traveling Exhib to eastern mus & galleries, including the Kennedy Gallery, New York, 71. *Awards:* Golden Spur Award, Bronze, Nat Rodeo Cowboy's Asn, 68; Silver Medal, George Phippen Mem Ann Art Show, Prescott, Ariz, 76. *Bibliog:* Anne Grose (auth), Cowpoke sculptor, Quarter Horse J, 1/68; Patricia Broder (auth), Bronzes of the American West, Abrams, 74; Ten Years with the Cowboy Artists of America, Northland Press, 76. *Mem:* Cowboy Artists Am. *Publ:* Auth, F-F-F-Frank Polk: An Uncommonly Frank Autobiography, Northland Press, 78. *Dealer:* Texas Trails Gallery 255 Losoya San Antonio TX 78205. *Mailing Add:* Box 126 Mayer AZ 86333

POLLACK, REGINALD MURRAY
PAINTER, SCULPTOR
b Middle Village, NY, July 29, 24. *Study:* Apprentice to Moses Soyer, 41; study with Wallace Harrison, 46-47; Acad Grande Chaumiere, Paris, 48-52. *Work:* Whitney Mus Am Art & Mus Mod Art, New York; Tel Aviv Mus, Jerusalem Mus & Haifa Mus, Israel; plus many other pub & pvt collections. *Comn:* Peace (greeting card), Jewish Mus, New York, 61; painting for Great Thoughts of Western Man series, Container Corp Am, 64; cover for State of NY Dir, Bell Tel Co, 68-69; Chinese animal destiny calendar, Colgate-Palmolive Co, 72; Jacob's Dream (103 ft painting), Washington Cathedral, 74. *Exhib:* 46 one-man shows, 12 at Peridot Gallery, New York, 49-69, Felix Landau Gallery, Los Angeles, Washington Project for Arts: Retrospective, 77 & Jack Rasmussen Gallery, Washington, DC, 78-82; Summit Gallery, New York, 83; and many other group shows. *Pos:* Mem bd trustees, Washington Proj for the Arts, DC, 75-80. *Teaching:* Vis critic art, Yale Univ, 62-63; instr art, Cooper Union, 63-64; staff mem, Human Rels Training Ctr, Univ Calif, Los Angeles, at Lake Arrowhead, 66; pvt art classes, 67-69; instr, Quaker Half-Way House, Los Angeles, 68; vis artist, Mat Res Lab, Pa State Univ, 77 & 78. *Awards:* Prix Othon Friesz-V, Paris, 56; Prix des Peintres Etrangers - Laureate, Paris, 58; Ingram-Merrill Found Grants in painting, 64 & 70-71. *Media:* Oil; Laser Light, Multimedia. *Publ:* Auth & illusr, The Magician and the Child, Atheneum, 71; illusr, Ctr for Dem Insts Mag, 3/72; auth, To artists with love & Brancusi's sculpture versus his home, Art News; illusr, Sounds Freedomring, Martin, Holt-Rinehart & Winston; illusr, Ted Knight (auth), Oedipus, 73. *Mailing Add:* 205 River Bend Rd Great Falls VA 22066

POLLAK, THERESA
PAINTER, DRAFTSMAN
b Richmond, Va, Aug 13, 1899. *Study:* Westhampton Col, Univ Richmond, BS; Art Students League; Fogg Mus, Harvard Univ, Carnegie Fel; with Hans Hofmann, Provincetown, Mass; Univ Richmond, Hon DFA, 73; Va Commonwealth Univ, Hon DH, 78. *Work:* Va Commonwealth Univ, Richmond; Va Mus Fine Arts, Richmond; Chrysler Mus Norfolk, Va; Univ Va, Charlottesville; Washington & Lee Univ, Lexington, Va. *Exhib:* 12th Biennial Exhib Contemp Am Painting, Corcoran Gallery Art, Washington, DC, 30; 1st Biennial Contemp Am Painting, Whitney Mus Am Art, New York, 32; New Eng Soc Contemp Art, Boston Mus Fine Arts, 33; Oakland Art Gallery, Calif, 41, 42 & 43; Butler Inst Am Art, Youngstown, Ohio, 47; 20th Century Gallery, Williamsburg, Va, 64; 19th Irene Leache Mem Regional Painting Exhib, Chrysler Mus Norfolk, 68; Virginia Artists 1971, Va Mus Fine Arts, Richmond, 71; one-person show, Scott-McKennis Fine Art, Richmond, Va, 77 & Reynolds/Minor Gallery, Richmond, 83. *Teaching:* Instr drawing & painting, Va Commonwealth Univ, 28-35, prof drawing & painting, 35-69, fac chmn, 42-50, emer prof, 69-; instr drawing & painting,

Westhampton Col, Univ Richmond, 30-35. *Awards:* Cert Distinction, Va Mus Fine Arts, 71; Theresa Pollak Bldg of Fine Arts, Va Commonwealth Univ, 71; First Laureate Award, Peer Eminent in art, Va Cult Laureate Ctr, 77. *Bibliog:* Portrait of a very special woman, Commonwealth, Mag Va, 2/80. *Mem:* honorary mem Richmond Artists Asn; life mem Art Students League. *Media:* Oil; Miscellaneous Media. *Publ:* Contribr, art criticisms in Richmond Newsleader & Richmond Times Dispatch, 31-49; auth, An Art School--Some Reminiscences, Va Commonwealth Univ, 69. *Mailing Add:* 3912 Stuart Ave Richmond VA 23221

POLLAND, DONALD JACK
SCULPTOR
b Los Angeles, Calif, May 24, 32. *Work:* C M Russell Mus, Great Falls, Mont; Favell Mus Western Art & Artifacts, Klamath Falls, Ore; Mont Hist Soc Mus, Helena. *Comn:* 18 sculptures, Lance Corp, Boston, 74; four western sculptures, Am Express Corp, 75. *Exhib:* Three-man show, Troy's Cowboy Art Gallery, Scottsdale, Ariz, 72; retrospective, R W Norton Mus, Shreveport, La, 74; C M Russell Mus, Great Falls, Mont, 71; Rancho Calif Art Show, Temecula, 72; George Phippen Mem Art Exhib, Prescott, Ariz, 75. *Pos:* Art dir, Control Dynamics, North Hollywood, Calif, 62-63; free lance illusr, Space Age Indust, 64-68. *Awards:* Best of Show & Second Place in Sculpture, Rancho Calif Art Comt, 72; Gold Medal for First Place in Sculpture, George Phippen Mem Art Show, 75; Western Heritage Award, Favell Mus Western Art & Artifacts, 80. *Bibliog:* R W Norton (auth), The Old West in Miniature, R W Norton Art Found, 74; Patricia J Broder (auth), Bronzes of the American West, Harry N Abrams, Inc, 75; Fielding L Greaves (auth), Old West in miniature, SW Art Mag, 75. *Mem:* George Phippen Mem Art Found (pres, 79-80); Wildlife Artists Int (vpres, 79). *Media:* Metal. *Mailing Add:* PO Box 609 Prescott AZ 86302

POLLARD, DONALD PENCE
DESIGNER, PAINTER
b Bronxville, NY, Sept 13, 24. *Study:* Pvt study with Harriet Lumis; RI Sch Design, BFA; Brown Univ. *Work:* Eisenhower Mus; Kennedy Collection; Govt of Can, Ottawa, Ont; also in pvt collections in the US, Europe, Asia & the Far East. *Comn:* Design of the Great Ring of Canada (with Alexander Seidel); other comns as assigned by Steuben Glass. *Exhib:* Conn Nat Acad, 42; all major Steuben Exhibs, 53-; Phillips Mall Ann, 72. *Pos:* Sr designer, Steuben Glass, 50- *Media:* Crystal, Oil. *Mailing Add:* c/o Steuben Glass 5th Ave & 56th St New York NY 10022

POLLARO, PAUL
PAINTER
b Brooklyn, NY. *Study:* Flatiron Sch Art, New York; Art Students League. *Work:* Corcoran Mus, Phillips Collection, Wasington, DC; Newark Mus; Mus Mod Art, New York; MacDowell Colony Collection, Peterborough, NH. *Exhib:* Ann, Pa Acad Fine Arts, Philadelphia, 64; Am Acad Arts & Lett, 66 & 72; Nat Inst Arts & Lett, 69 & 72; Artists of the 20th Century, Gallery Mod Art, New York, 70; Artists at Work, Finch Col Mus, 71. *Teaching:* Instr painting, New Sch Social Res, 64-69; asst prof painting, Wagner Col, 69-76; vis artist, Notre Dame Univ, summers 65 & 67. *Awards:* Second Prize, Jersey City Mus, 62; MacDowell Colony Fels, 66, 68 & 71; Tiffany Found Grant, 67. *Mailing Add:* c/o Babcock Galleries 20 East 67th St New York NY 10021

POLLITT, JEROME JORDAN
HISTORIAN, EDUCATOR
b Fair Lawn, NJ, Nov 26, 34. *Study:* Yale Univ, New Haven, Conn, BA, 57; Columbia Univ, New York, PhD, 63. *Pos:* Ed-in-chief, Am J Archaeol, 74-78. *Teaching:* Prof classic art & archaeol, Yale Univ, 64- *Publ:* Auth, The Art of Greece: Sources and Documents, 64 & auth, The Art of Rome: Sources and Documents, 65, Prentice-Hall; auth, Art and Experience in Classical Greece, Cambridge Univ Press, 72; auth, The Ancient View of Greek Art, Yale Univ Press, 75; auth, The Impact of Greek Art on Rome, Tapa, 79. *Mailing Add:* Dept of Classics 1967 Yale Station New Haven CT 06520

POLLOCK, BRUCE WALTER
SCULPTOR, DESIGNER
b Painesville, Ohio, July 7, 51. *Study:* Carnegie-Mellon Univ, 70; Cleveland Inst Art, BFA, 76; Tyler Sch Art, with Italo Scanga, MFA, 78. *Work:* Philadelphia Mus Art. *Exhib:* Morris Gallery, Pa Acad Fine Art, 79; May Show, Cleveland Mus Art, 81; Karen Lennox Gallery, Chicago, 82; solo exhib, Alan Stone Gallery, New York, 82, Jeffery Fuller Fine Art, Philadelphia, 82 & Swarthmore Col, 83; Pertaining to Philadelphia, Philadelphia Mus Art, 83. *Teaching:* Instr, Philadelphia Col Art, 79-81, exhib designer, 81-83. *Awards:* Best of Show, Small Works Ann, NY Univ, 80; Artist Fel, Pa Coun Arts, 83. *Bibliog:* Articles, Artforum, 10/79 & Art in Am, 10/82. *Media:* Wood, Polychrome. *Dealer:* Jeffery Fuller Fine Art 2108 Spruce St Philadelphia PA 19103; Alan Stone Gallery 48 E 86 New York NY 10028. *Mailing Add:* 35 S 3rd Philadelphia PA 19106

POLLOCK, MERLIN F
PAINTER, EDUCATOR
b Manitowoc, Wis, Jan 3, 05. *Study:* Art Inst Chicago, BFA & MFA; Ecole Beaux Arts, Paris; Sch Fine Arts, Fontainebleau, France. *Work:* Syracuse Univ; Munson-Williams-Proctor Inst, Utica; Everson Mus, Syracuse; State Univ NY Col Environ Sci & Forestry, Syracuse; Archives Am Art, Smithsonian Inst. *Comn:* Steel (fresco), Tildon Tech High Sch, Chicago; mural, O'Fallon Ill Post Off, comn by US Treas Dept. *Exhib:* 125 Years of New York State Painting & Sculpture, NY State Fair, 66; one-man shows, Mich State Univ, East Lansing, 59, Everson Mus, Syracuse, 66, Lubin House, New York, NY, 70 & Lowe Art Ctr, Syracuse Univ, 71; and others. *Pos:* Supvr

mural painting, Ill Art Proj, Works Proj Admin, 40-43; chmn grad prog, Sch Art, Syracuse Univ, 47-71, actg dean, Sch Art, 60-61, 67-68 & 69-70. *Teaching:* Instr mural painting, fresco & drawing, Art Inst Chicago, 35-43; prof painting, Syracuse Univ, 46-71. *Awards:* James Nelson Raymond Fel, Art Inst Chicago, 30; Syracuse Ann, Everson Mus, 50, 60, 64 & 66; Finger Lakes Ann, Rochester Mem Mus, 56-58 & 60. *Media:* Mixed. *Mailing Add:* 120 Wellwood Dr Fayetteville NY 13066

POLONSKY, ARTHUR
PAINTER, EDUCATOR
b Lynn, Mass, June 6, 25. *Study:* Boston Mus Sch, with Karl Zerbe, dipl (with highest honors), 48; Europ Traveling Fel, 48-50. *Work:* Fogg Mus, Harvard Univ, Cambridge; Mus Fine Arts, Boston; Addison Gallery Am Art, Andover; Walker Art Ctr; Stedelijk Mus, Amsterdam, Holland. *Comn:* Portrait of Dr William Dameshek, Tufts-New Eng Med Ctr, Boston, 66; Stone with the Angel (portfolio of ten original lithographs), Impressions Workshop, Inc, Boston, 69; portrait of Dr Sidney Farber, Harvard Med Sch for Boston Children's Hosp, 71. *Exhib:* Salon des Jeunes Peintres, Paris, 49; Art Today-50, Metrop Mus Art, New York, 50; Exhib Am Art, Stedelijk Mus, Amsterdam, Holland, 50; Carnegie Inst Int Expos, Pittsburgh, 51; nineteen one-man exhibs in Boston, New York & Washington, 51-81; Chateau Rohans, Strasbourg, 58. *Pos:* Founding mem & dir, Artists' Equity Asn, 48-67; mem, Boston Visual Artists' Union, 73-79. *Teaching:* Instr painting, Boston Mus Sch, 50-60; asst prof painting, drawing & design, Brandeis Univ, 54-65; assoc prof painting, drawing & design, Boston Univ, Sch for the Arts, 65- *Awards:* Tiffany Found Grant for Painting, 51-52; First Prize, Boston Arts Festival, 54; Purchase Award, Drawings '74, Wheaton Nat Exhib, Wheaton Col, 74. *Bibliog:* Article, Life Mag, 12/48; reviews of exhibs in Art News, Arts Mag, New York Times, Time Mag, New Yorker Mag & others, 48-81; Archives Am Art, Smithsonian Inst, 72. *Publ:* Illusr, Lincoln, A Big Man, Hastings House Publ, 58; illusr, The Sling and the Swallow, United Church Press, 63; illusr, More Time to Grow, Beacon Press, 77; illusr, Sexual Decisions, Little, Brown & Co, 80. *Dealer:* Francesca Anderson Gallery 32 Newbury St Boston MA 02116. *Mailing Add:* 364 Cabot St Newtonville MA 02160

POLSKY, CYNTHIA
ADMINISTRATOR, COLLECTOR
b New York, NY, Feb 16, 39. *Study:* Art Students League; New Sch Social Res; Marymount Manhattan Col, BA; Fordham Univ, MBA. *Work:* Corcoran Gallery Am Art, Washington, DC; Israel Mus, Jerusalem; Ulrich Mus of Art, Wichita, Kans; Fogg Art Mus, Cambridge, Mass; American Embassy, London, Eng; and others. *Exhib:* One-woman shows, Benson Gallery, Bridgehampton, Long Island, NY, 68, Comara Gallery, Los Angeles, 69, Artisan Gallery, Houston, Tex, 70, Palm Springs Desert Mus, 72-73 & Crispo Gallery, New York, 73 & 74; Ulrich Mus of Art, Wichita, Kans, 77. *Pos:* Trustee, Storm King Art Ctr, Mountainville, NY, currently. *Bibliog:* Judith Denham (auth), article, Art Week, 73; Alfred Frankenstein (auth), article, San Francisco Chronicle, 73. *Media:* Acrylic, Watercolor. *Dealer:* Andrew Crispo Gallery 41 E 57th St New York NY 10022. *Mailing Add:* 50 E 79th St New York NY 10021

POLSTER, JOANNE F
LIBRARIAN, WRITER
b New York, NY, Feb 3, 30. *Study:* Hunter Col, New York, BA, 52; Pratt Inst, Brooklyn, NY, MLS, 72. *Pos:* Head librn, Am Craft Coun Libr, 73- *Awards:* Field librn, Nat Endowment Arts. *Mem:* Art Libr Soc NAm (chairperson New York Chap, 79); Am Asn Mus. *Res:* Post World War Two American crafts and craftspeople. *Interests:* Preservation and documentation of exhibition publications of New York galleries and museums through work with the New York Chapter of the Librarians Society of North America. *Publ:* Contribr, Contemporary Crafts Market Place 1975-76, 75 & Contemporary Crafts Market Place 1977-1978, 77, R R Bowker; coauth, Master's Theses: Crafts, 76, auth, Crafts Business Bookshelf, 77 & auth, Grant References for the Craftman, 78, Am Craft Coun; and others. *Mailing Add:* Am Craft Coun Libr 44 W 53rs St New York NY 10019

POLZER, JOSEPH
HISTORIAN
b Vienna, Austria, May 7, 29. *US* citizen. *Study:* Univ Iowa, BA(art), 50, MA(art hist), 52; Inst Fine Arts, NY Univ, PhD(art hist), 63. *Teaching:* Instr, Univ Kans, 57-58; lectr, Univ Buffalo, 58-62; from asst prof to prof, Univ Louisville, 62-73; prof art, Queen's Univ, Kingston, 73- *Res:* Late Rome, Renaissance. *Publ:* Auth, articles in Late Antique & Renaissance Art. *Mailing Add:* Dept of Art Univ Calgary Calgary AB T2N 1N4 Canada

POMERANTZ, LOUIS
CONSERVATOR
b Brooklyn, NY, Sept 26, 19. *Study:* Art Students League; Acad Julian; Rijksmuseum, Amsterdam, Holland, with H H Mertens; Worcester Art Mus, with G Stout; Brooklyn Mus, with C & S Keck; Cent Lab of Belg Mus. *Collections Arranged:* Know What You See, Univ Chicago, Ill Arts Coun, 70-72 & Found of the Am Inst for Conserv, Smithsonian Inst, 76-80; Learning to See, Univ Iowa Mus Art, 77. *Pos:* Conservator, Dept of Paintings & Sculpture, Art Inst of Chicago, 56-61; consult, UN Develop Prog in Israel, Israel Mus, Jerusalem, UNESCO, 68, Mus Contemp Art, Chicago, 76, Minn Hist Soc, 76 & SITES, Smithonian Inst, Washington, DC, 77; founder pres, Pomerantz Inst Advanc Fine Arts Conserv, 82. *Mem:* Fel Int Inst for Conserv of Hist & Artistic Works; fel Am Inst for Conserv (bd dirs, 79-82); Int Inst for Conserv-Am Group (founding mem, secy-treas, 59-61, treas, 62-63, vchmn, 64-65, chmn, 66-68); Int Inst Conserv; and others. *Publ:* Auth, Is Your Contemporary Painting More Temporary Than You Think?, Int Bk Co, 62;

auth, Know What You See--The Examination of Paintings by Photo-Optical Techniques, Univ Chicago & Ill Arts Coun, 70; auth, Preventive Care of Paintings: What to Do About It, Midwest Mus Conf, 71; co-auth, Conservators advise artists, Col Art Asn J, 77; contribr, Mus News, Bulletin of Am Group & Am Inst for Conser Bulletin. *Mailing Add:* 6300 Johnsburg Rd Spring Grove IL 60081

POMEROY, JAMES CALWELL, JR
PERFORMANCE ARTIST, PHOTOGRAPHER
b Reading, Pa, Mar 21, 45. *Study:* Univ Mont; Univ Tex, Austin, BFA, 68; Ariz State Univ; Univ Calif, Berkeley, MFA, 72. *Work:* Longview Mus & Art Ctr, Tex; Mus Conceptual Art, San Francisco; Univ Calif Art Mus, Berkeley; Mildura Art Ctr, Australia; Exploratorium, San Francisco. *Comn:* Edition of Unique Binders, Soc Encouragement Comtemp Art, San Francisco Mus Mod Art, 73; Lightweight Phantoms (stereoscopic installation), The Exploratorium, San Francisco, 76. *Exhib:* DFW/SFO Exchange, San Francisco Mus Mod Art, 75-76; Biennial of Sydney, Gallery of New South Wales, Australia, 76; Bay Area--New Strengths, Univ Calif Santa Barbara, 79; San Jose Mus Art, 80; 80 Langton St Performance Festival, San Francisco, 81; Albright-Knox Art Mus, Buffalo, 81; The Kitchen Gallery, New York, 81; and many others. *Collections Arranged:* Rushmore--Another Look (auth catalog), San Francisco Art Inst, 76; 77-78 San Francisco Art Inst Ann, (auth, catalog), 77. *Teaching:* Lectr, Calif State Univ, San Jose, 74-76. *Awards:* Eisner Prize, Univ Calif, Berkeley, 71; Nat Endowment for Arts Visual Arts Fel, 75 & 79. *Bibliog:* Jill Silverman (auth), Jim Pomeroy at Artists Space, Art in am, 3-4/79; and others. *Mem:* New Music Alliance. *Mailing Add:* PO Box 6145 San Francisco CA 94101

POMMER, RICHARD
EDUCATOR, HISTORIAN
b New York, NY, Nov 4, 30. *Study:* Columbia Univ, BS, 53; New York Univ Inst Fine Arts, MA, 57, PhD, 61. *Teaching:* Instr, Williams Col, 60-62; asst prof, NY Univ Inst Fine Arts, 62-66; prof, Vassar Col, 66- *Awards:* Alice Davis Hitchcock Award, Soc Archit Historians, 67. *Mem:* Soc Archit Historians (dir, 81-). *Res:* 20th century architecture. *Publ:* Auth, Eighteenth Century Architecture in Piedmont, New York Univ, 67; auth, The architecture of housing in the United States in the early 1930's, J Soc Archit Historians, 78. *Mailing Add:* 875 W End Ave New York NY 10025

PONCE DE LEON, MICHAEL
PRINTMAKER, PAINTER
b Miami, Fla, July 4, 22. *Study:* Univ Mex, BA; Art Students League; Nat Acad Design; Brooklyn Mus Art Sch; also in Europe. *Work:* Mus Mod Art & Metrop Mus Art, New York; Nat Gallery Art & Smithsonian Inst, Washington, DC; Brooklyn Mus; and others. *Comn:* Many print editions, 60-; ten prints, US State Dept, 66; glass sculpture, Steuben Glass, 71; 100 prints, Pioneer Moss, Inc, annually, 68-83. *Exhib:* Mus Arte Mod, Paris; Victoria & Albert Mus, London; Venice Bienale, 70; Mus Mod Art & Metrop Mus, New York; Smithsonian Inst, Washington, DC; and others. *Pos:* Int Cult Exchange, US State Dept, teaching, lect & travel, Yugoslavia, 65, India & Pakistan, 67-68, Spain, 71 & SAmerica. *Teaching:* Instr printmaking, Hunter Col, 59-66; prof, New York Univ, 77 & Pratt Inst, 78; instr printmaking, Art Students League, 78-, Berkeley Univ, Calif, Univ Calif, Los Angeles, and others. *Awards:* More than 65 medals & awards, incl Tiffany Found Grants, 54 & 55; Fulbright Grants, 56 & 57; Guggenheim Found Grant, 67. *Bibliog:* G Peterdi (auth), Printmaking, Macmillan, 72; F Eichenberg (auth), The Art of the Print, Abrams, 77; D Saff, Printmaking History and Process, Holt, Rinehart & Winston, 78. *Mem:* Soc Am Graphic Artists (treas, 68); Asn Am Univ Prof. *Publ:* Contribr, Experiments in three dimensions, Art Am, 68; auth, The collage intaglio, 72; The collage-intaglios of Michael Ponce de Leon, Am Artist, 8/74; History of an Art, Skira (in 4 languages), 81; History of International Art, Academia Italia (in 4 languages), 81. *Dealer:* Jane Haslem Gallery 2121 P St NW Washington DC 20036; AAA Gallery 663 Fifth Ave New York NY. *Mailing Add:* 463 West St New York NY 10014

POND, CLAYTON
PAINTER, PRINTMAKER
b Long Island, NY, June 10, 41. *Study:* Carnegie Inst Technol, BFA, 64; Pratt Inst, MFA, 66. *Work:* Nat Collection Fine Arts, Washington, DC; Mus Mod Art, New York; Boston Mus Fine Arts; Philadelphia Mus Art; Art Inst Chicago; and many others. *Exhib:* Whitney Mus Am Art Ann, New York, 67; Int Exhib Colored Graphics, Mus Mod Art, Paris, 70; New Am Prints Traveling Exhib, US Info Agency, Vienna, 71; 23rd Libr Cong Exhib, Nat Collection Fine Arts, Smithsonian Inst, 73; Linden Gallery, New York, 81; one-man shows, Gallery North, Setauket, Long Island, 81 & Haan Gallery, Chestnut Hill, Philadelphia, Pa, 81; and many other group & one-man shows. *Teaching:* Instr photog & printmaking, C W Post Col, Long Island Univ, 66-68; adj instr serigraphy, Sch Visual Arts, New York, 68-70; guest lectr, Univ Wis-Madison, spring 72. *Awards:* State Dept Grant, Smithsonian Inst Int Art Prog & Abby Gray Found, 67; Boston Mus Purchase Award, Boston Printmakers 20th Ann, 68; Color Print USA Purchase Award, WTex Mus, 69. *Bibliog:* Richard S Field (auth), Silkscreen, the media medium, Art News Mag, 1/72; Jules Heller (auth), Printmaking Today, Holt, Rinehart & Winston, 72; Marshall B Davidson (auth), Artists' America, Am Heritage, 73. *Mem:* Am Color Print Soc; Print Coun Am; Boston Printmakers; Philadelphia Print Club. *Dealer:* Martha Jackson Gallery 521 W 57th St New York NY 10019. *Mailing Add:* 130 Greene St New York NY 10012

PONSOT, CLAUDE F
EDUCATOR, PAINTER
b Rabat, Morocco, May 29, 27; US citizen. *Study:* Atelier Perrier/Jaudon, 47-50; Atelier Andre L'hote, 48-50; Atelier Fernand Leger, 49-50. *Work:* Associated Metals & Minerals Corp, New York; also pvt collections. *Comn:* Graphics, LaGuardia Community Col, NY, 79-80 & St John's Univ, 81; South Oaks Hospital, Amityville, 81; and others. *Exhib:* One-man show, Galerie Maitre Albert, Paris, 76; Cabinet des Estampes, Biblioteque Nat, Paris, 78; Brand X, Glendale, Calif, 80; In the Best Tradition, Heckscher Mus, Huntington, 81; Firehouse Gallery, Nassau Community Col, NY, 82 & 83; and others. *Teaching:* Prof art, St John's Univ, New York, 60- *Awards:* Pat Lambert Award, Shreveport Art Guild; Purchase Award, Images/Shapes 76, Plattsburgh; Patron Purchase Award, Watercolor USA, Springfield Mus, 77. *Bibliog:* Jean Parris (auth), articles, Newsday, 79-81. *Mem:* Nat Drawing Asn. *Media:* Oil, Watercolor. *Dealer:* Ruth Solomon Art Connections Unlimited. *Mailing Add:* 41 Clifford Ct Huntington NY 11743

POOLE, LESLIE DONALD
PAINTER, PRINTMAKER
b Halifax, NS, May 3, 42. *Study:* Prince of Wales Col, Charlottetown, PEI, 60; Univ Alta, Edmonton, BFA, 67; Yale Univ, MFA, 70. *Work:* Can Coun Art Bank, Ottawa; Beaverbrook Art Gallery, Fredericton, NB; Confederation Ctr Art Gallery, Charlottetown, PEI; BC Art Access, Victoria; Ring House Gallery, Univ Alta, Edmonton. *Comn:* Portrait lieutenant gov, Prov Alta, 73. *Exhib:* Solo exhib, Confederation Ctr Art Gallery, Charlottetown, PEI, 73 & Edmonton Art Gallery, 74; Alberta Artists, Can House, Paris, Brussels, London, New York & Montreal, 76; Whats New, 76 & Collectors Choice, 78, Edmonton Art Gallery; Confessions, Vancouver Art Gallery, 79; Insights, Simon Fraser Univ Art Gallery, Vancouver, 81; Vancouver: Art and Artists, Vancouver Art Gallery, 83. *Teaching:* Lectr design, Univ Alta, Edmonton, 71-72; instr painting, Banff Sch Fine Arts, 73; lectr drawing, Vancouver Comunity Col, 75- *Bibliog:* Glenn Howarth (auth), An ecumenical intent, Vanguard Mag, Vancouver, 78; Lawrence McCarthy (auth), article, Arts West, Alta, 81; David Watmough (auth), Not exactly limpid Pooles, Interface, Alta, 81. *Media:* Acrylic; Lithography. *Dealer:* Kenneth G Heffel Fine Arts 2247 Granville St Vancouver BC V5T 2E9; Gilman Galleries 277 E Ontario St Chicago IL 60611. *Mailing Add:* 922 E 11 Ave Vancouver BC V5T 2E9 Canada

POOLE, RICHARD ELLIOTT
PAINTER, INSTRUCTOR
b Pasadena, Calif, Feb 26, 31. *Study:* Otis Art Inst, Calif State Univ, Los Angeles, BA, MA(painting), 58. *Exhib:* Nat Watercolor Soc Ann, Los Angeles Art Mus, San Francisco De Young Mus & Calif Palace Legion Honor, 64-73; US Embassy Sweden Invitational, 72; 5th Ann Watercolor West, 73; one-man shows, Heritage Gallery, Los Angeles, 70, 71 & 73 & Mittwoch Gallery, Bonn, Ger, 74, and others. *Teaching:* Instr painting & drawing, Pasadena City Schs, 60- *Awards:* Uecker Award, Ann Pasadena Art Mus, 63; Katharine Steale Dan Award, Pasadena Art Mus, 64. *Mem:* Los Angeles Art Asn; Nat Watercolor Soc. *Media:* Mixed. *Mailing Add:* 4504 W Washington Dr Los Angeles CA 90016

POONS, LARRY
PAINTER
b Tokyo, Japan, Oct 1, 37. *Study:* Boston Mus Fine Arts Sch, 58. *Work:* Mus Mod Art; Albright-Knox Art Gallery; Stedelijk Mus, Holland; Woodward Found, Washington, DC. *Exhib:* Art Inst Chicago, 66; Corcoran Gallery Art, 67; Carnegie Inst, 67; Documenta IV, Kassel, Ger, 68; Whitney Mus Am Art Ann, 68 & 72 & Whitney Biennial, 73; Albright-Knox Art Gallery, Buffalo, NY, 68 & 70; Pasadena Art Mus, Calif, 69; and many others. *Teaching:* Vis fac, NY Studio Sch, 67. *Bibliog:* Lawrence Alloway (auth), Systemic Painting, Guggenheim Mus, 66; Gregory Battcock (ed), Minimal Art: A Critical Anthology, Dutton, 68; E C Goosen (auth), The Art of the Real USA 1948-1968, Mus Mod Art, 68; and others. *Publ:* Auth, The Structure of Color, 71. *Dealer:* Andre Emmerich Gallery Inc 41 E 57th St New York NY 10022. *Mailing Add:* 831 Broadway New York NY 10003

POOR, ANNE
PAINTER
b New York, NY, Jan 2, 18. *Study:* Bennington Col; Art Students League, with Alexander Brook, William Zorach & Yasuo Kuniyoshi; Acad Julian, Paris, painting with Jean Lurcat & Abraham Rattner. *Work:* Whitney Mus Am Art; Brooklyn Mus; Art Inst Chicago; Wichita Mus; Des Moines Art Ctr. *Comn:* Murals, Pub Works Admin, 37; murals, Skowhegan Sch Painting & Sculpture, 54, South Solon Free Meeting House, Maine, 57. *Exhib:* Artists for Victory, Metrop Mus Art, 42; Am Brit Art Ctr, New York, 44, 45 & 48; Maynard Walker Gallery, New York, 50; seven shows, Graham Gallery, New York, 57-79; plus others. *Teaching:* Mem fac painting & dir, Skowhegan Sch Painting & Sculpture, 47-61, gov & trustee, 63- *Awards:* Edwin Austin Abbey Mem Fel for Mural Painting, 48 & First Prize for Landscape Painting, 70, Nat Acad Design; Nat Inst Arts & Lett Grant in Art, 57. *Bibliog:* Alan Gussow (auth), A sense of place, Friends of Earth, Sat Rev Press, 72. *Mem:* Artists Equity Asn. *Media:* Oil, Watercolor. *Publ:* Illusr, Greece, Viking Press, 64. *Dealer:* Graham Gallery 1014 Madison Ave New York NY 10021. *Mailing Add:* 92 S Mountain Rd New York NY 10956

POOR, ROBERT JOHN
HISTORIAN
b Rockport, Ill, July 10, 31. *Study:* Boston Univ, BA, 53 & MA, 57; Univ Chicago, with Ludwig Bachhofer, PhD(art hist), 61. *Collections Arranged:* Art of India (exhib catalog), 69 & Far Eastern Art in Minnesota Collections

(exhib catalog), 70, Univ Minn Gallery; Hanga, The Modern Japanese Print (exhib catalog), Minn Mus Art, St Paul, 72. *Pos:* Consult Asian art, Minneapolis Inst Art, formerly; cur Asian art, Minn Mus Art, St Paul, formerly. *Teaching:* Asst prof Asian art, Dartmouth Col, 61-65; from assoc prof Asian art to prof art hist, Univ Minn, formerly, 65- *Res:* Chinese bronzes. *Publ:* Auth, Notes on the Sung archaeological catalogs, 65 & auth, Some remarkable examples of I-Hsing ware, 66-67, Arch of Chinese Art Soc Am; auth, Ancient Chinese Bronzes, Inter-Cult Arts Press, 68; auth, Evolution of a secular vesseltype, 68 & On the Mo-tzu-Yu, 70, Oriental Art. *Mailing Add:* Dept Art Hist Univ Minn Minneapolis MN 55455

POPE, ANNEMARIE HENLE
ADMINISTRATOR
b Dortmund, Ger; US citizen. *Study:* Heidelberg Univ, PhD, 32; Radcliffe Col, Harvard Univ, exchange fel, 33-34. *Pos:* Asst dir, Portland Art Mus, Ore, 41-42; dir in charge exhibs, Am Fedn Arts, 47-51; chief traveling exhibs, Smithsonian Inst, 51-64; pres, Int Exhibs Found, 65- *Awards:* Royal Swedish Order of Polar Star, 57; Order of Merit, First Class, Ger, 64; Officer, Order Brit Empire, 79; and others. *Mem:* Am Asn Mus; Washington Friends of Am Mus Bath, Eng (chmn); Am Fedn Arts; Master Drawings Asn; Drawing Soc; and many others. *Publ:* Auth, acknowledgments for catalogues publ by Int Exhibs Found in connection with traveling exhibs. *Mailing Add:* Int Exhibs Found 1729 H St NW Washington DC 20006

POPE, MARY ANN IRWIN
PAINTER, PRINTMAKER
b Louisville, Ky, Mar 8, 32. *Study:* Art Ctr, Louisville; Univ Louisville; Cooper Union. *Work:* Nat Collection Fine Art, Washington, DC; Mint Mus, Charlotte, NC; Huntsville Mus of Art; Fine Arts Mus S, Mobile, Ala. *Exhib:* Mid-South, Brooks Art Gallery, Memphis, Tenn, 71-74; Piedmont Painting & Sculpture Exhib, Mint Mus, Charlotte, NC, 72 & 73; Artrain, Southeast Tour, 74; Calif Nat Watercolor Show, Laguna Beach Mus, 74 & Palos Altos Mus, Calif, 75; Watercolor USA 1982, 83; Birmingham Biennial, 83; and others. *Teaching:* Instr painting, Art Ctr, 59; instr painting, Huntsville Art League, Ala, 66-, dir adult classes, 67-; part-time instr, Univ Ala in Huntsville. *Awards:* Shaw Warehouse Award, 32nd Nat Watercolor Exhib, 72; Mint Mus Purchase Award, Piedmont Painting & Sculpture Exhib, 72; Mus Award, Watercolor USA 1982, 83. *Mem:* Kentucky Watercolor Soc; Ala Watercolor Soc; Calif Nat Watercolor Soc; Ala Art League. *Media:* Acrylic, Watercolor. *Mailing Add:* 1705 Greenwyche Rd SE Huntsville AL 35801

POPESCU, CARA
SCULPTOR, PRINTMAKER
b Munich, Bavaria, Ger; Can citizen. *Study:* Fine Arts Acad, Acad di Belle Arti, Florence, Italy; Fine Art Acad, Berlin, Ger; Fine Art Acad, Stuttgart, Ger, with painter, Willi Baumeister & sculpture masterclass with Otto Baum; L'Ecole des Beaux-Arts, Montreal, Que, with printmaker, A Dumouchel. *Work:* Cult Ctr Montreal-Verdun, Que; Gallery Hellhof, Frankfurt, WGer; Bell Tel Co of Can, Toronto; Bank of Commerce, Montreal; plus pvt collections in US, Brazil, WGer & Can. *Comn:* Fifteen Stations of the Cross, St Rock Church, Montreal, 68; bronze sculpture, Bell Can, Trinity Sq, Toronto, 83. *Exhib:* Three Sculptors Exhib in Goethe Inst, Toronto, 78, Montreal, 78 & Ottawa, 78; Sculpture Canada 78, London, Paris & Brussels; plus others. *Teaching:* Prof perception & three-dimensions for painters, L'Univ du Que, Montreal, 69-71; vis guest artist & lectr, Confederation Centre, Charlottetown, PEI & Sch Visual Arts, Holland Col, PEI, 79; lectr sculpture, YHA, Toronto, 80-82. *Awards:* Best Sculpture Exhib, Multi-Cultural Exhib, O'Keefe Centre, Toronto, 79. *Bibliog:* Working Sculpture (film), Charlottetown, PEI, 79; Jean-Luc E'Pivent (auth), Cara Popescu--Une Harmonie Interieur, Vie Des Arts, 81; On Techniques of Sculpture (film), Cable Oakville, 83. *Mem:* Ont Soc Artists (exec mem, 78-80 & 82-84); Visual Arts Ont; Sculptor's Soc Can (exec mem, 78-80); Sculptor's Soc WGer; Soc des Sculpteurs du Que (exec mem, 65-70). *Media:* Stone, Bronze. *Publ:* Coauth, Sculptures in Expo: Seen by sculptor, Cara Popescu, Karusell-Montreal CFMB Radio, Que, 67. *Dealer:* Dominion Gallery of Can Montreal PQ Can; Galerie Kastel Westmount Que Can. *Mailing Add:* One Woodland Heights Toronto ON M6S 2W3 Canada

POPINSKY, ARNOLD DAVE
SCULPTOR, CERAMIST
b Bronx, NY, Aug 21, 30. *Study:* Albright Art Sch, State Univ NY, Buffalo, BS; Univ Wis-Madison, MS; Alfred Univ. *Comn:* Metal sculpture, Wright Art Ctr, Beloit, Wis, 64; 3 cast iron plaques, 64 & aluminum sculpture, 68, Beloit Col, Wis. *Exhib:* Colt & Popinsky, Wright Art Ctr, Beloit, Wis, 67; one-man shows, Lang Art Ctr, Claremont, Calif, 69, Univ WFla, Pensacola, 73 & Fishey Whale Gallery, Milwaukee, Wis, 75; Wis Designer-Craftsman, Milwaukee Art Ctr, 73. *Pos:* Artist-in-residence, Inst Artes Plasticas, Univ Guadalajara, Mex, 64-65; vis sculptor, Scripps Col & Claremont Grad Sch, Calif, 68-69; artist-in-residence, Univ WFla, Pensacola, 72-73; owner, Clarksville Pottery, Austin, Tex. *Teaching:* Prof sculpture & ceramics, Beloit Col, Wis, 57-76. *Mem:* Col Art Asn; Am Craft Coun; Austin Contemp Visual Arts Asn (mem bd dirs, 78); Rock Prairie Arts Coun. *Media:* Clay; Metal. *Mailing Add:* 1004 Eason Austin TX 78703

PORADA, EDITH
HISTORIAN
b Vienna, Austria, Aug 22, 12; US citizen. *Study:* Univ Vienna, PhD, 35; Smith Col, DLitt, 67. *Work:* Pierpont Morgan Libr, New York. *Pos:* Hon cur seals & tablets, Pierpont Morgan Libr, 55- *Teaching:* Instr art hist, Queens Col, NY, 49-55; asst prof, 50-58; asst prof art hist & archaeol, Columbia Univ, 58-62, assoc prof, 62-64, prof, 64-73, Arthur Lehman prof, 73-84, Arthur

Lehman prof emer, 84-; chmn, Columbia Univ Sem Archaeol Eastern Mediterranean, Eastern Europ & Near E, 66- *Awards:* Guggenheim Found Fel, 50 & 83-84; Award Distinguished Archaeol Achievement, Archaeol Inst Am, 77. *Mem:* Fel Am Acad Arts & Lett; Am Philos Soc. *Publ:* Auth, Seal Impressions of Nuzi, Am Schs Orient Res; auth, Corpus of Ancient Near Eastern Seals in North American Collections, Bollingen, 48; auth, Alt-Iran, Holle, 62; auth, Art of Ancient Iran, Crown, 65; auth, Tchoga Zanbil IV: La Glyptique, Mem Deleg Arch Iran, 70. *Mailing Add:* Dept Art Hist & Archaeol Columbia Univ New York NY 10027

PORTER, ALBERT WRIGHT
EDUCATOR, PAINTER
b Brooklyn, NY, Nov 25, 23. *Study:* Ecole Des Beaux-Arts, Paris; Chouinard Art Inst; Univ of Calif, Los Angeles, BA; Calif State Univ, Los Angeles, MA; Otis Art Inst. *Work:* Los Angeles City Col; Utah State Univ. *Exhib:* Nat Watercolor Soc, Laguna Beach, Calif, 69; Southern Calif Expo, Del Mar, 72; Watercolor West, Riverside Art Mus, Calif, 74; Nat Watercolor Soc, Northridge, Calif, 77; Nat Watercolor Soc, Palm Springs, 83. *Pos:* Art supervisor, Los Angeles City Schs, 58-71. *Teaching:* Prof art, Calif State Univ, Fullerton, 71- *Awards:* Cash Award, Nat Watercolor Soc, Del Mar Col, 72. *Mem:* Nat Watercolor Soc (1st vpres, 77); Watercolor West; Calif Art Educ Asn; Orange Co Art Asn. *Media:* Watercolor, Pen & Ink. *Publ:* Auth, Shape and Form: Design Elements, 74, auth, Pattern: A Design Principle, 75, auth, The Art of Sketching, 77, team auth, Exploring Visual Design, 78 & auth, Expressive Watercolor Techniques, 82, Davis Publ. *Mailing Add:* 8554 Day St Sunland CA 91040

PORTER, (EDWIN) DAVID
PAINTER, SCULPTOR
b Chicago, Ill, May 18, 12. *Work:* Whitney Mus Am Art; Miami Mus Mod Art; Chrysler Art Mus; Norfolk Mus Arts & Sci; Parish Art Mus, Southampton. *Exhib:* Solo exhib, Am Inst Archit, NY Chap, 69 & Guild Hall, East Hampton, 70; Outdoor Sculpture, Artists of the Region, Guild Hall, NY, 70; Artists at Dartmouth Retrospective, City Hall, Boston, 71; Artists of Suffolk County, Part V, New Directions, Heckscher Mus, Huntington, NY, 71. *Teaching:* Artist in residence, Dartmouth Col, 64-65 & Cooper Union, 67-68; lectr art, Corcoran Gallery Art, Washington, DC, 68 & 69; instr painting, Guild Hall, East Hampton, 75-78; lectr painting techniques, Wainscoth, NY, 76. *Awards:* Gold Medal of Pres Gronchi of Italy, Sassoferrato, Italy, 61; Beaux Arts Award in Painting, Beaux Arts Club, 69; Nat Inst Arts & Lett Grant, 70. *Bibliog:* Today's living, New York Herald Tribune, 56; The Making of a Construction (TV film interview), Voice Am, 57; maj articles on work publ in newspapers in Norway & Sweden, 60. *Publ:* Auth, Why I ran away, Am Weckly, 7/10/60. *Mailing Add:* Wainscott NY 11975

PORTER, ELIOT FURNESS
PHOTOGRAPHER, WRITER
b Winnetka, Ill, Dec 6, 01. *Study:* Harvard Univ, BS, 24; Harvard Med Sch, MD, 29; Colby Col, Hon DFA, 69. *Work:* Metrop Mus Art & Mus Mod Art, New York; George Eastman House, Rochester, NY; Worcester Mus Art, Mass; New Orleans Mus Art; plus many pvt collections. *Comn:* In Wildness is the Preservation of the World (book), Sierra Club, 62; Forever Wild-The Adirondacks (book), Harper & Row, 66; Appalachian Wilderness (book), 69 & Birds of North America (book), 72, E P Dutton; photo-murals, Independent Life Ins Bldg, Jacksonville, 75. *Exhib:* An American Place, New York, 39; The Seasons, George Eastman House, 60; The Photographer & the American Landscape, Mus Mod Art, New York, 63; M H De Young Mem Mus, San Francisco, 65; Traveling Retrospective, Univ Art Mus, Albuquerque, NMex, 73. *Awards:* Silver Plaque, Wild Life Photography, Country Life Int Exhib, 50; Am Acad Arts & Sci Fel, 71; Acad Natural Sci Gold Medal Distinction Natural Hist Art, 83. *Mem:* Advocates for the Arts; Friends of Photog. *Media:* Color Photography; Nature Writing. *Publ:* Coauth, The Tree Where Man was Born, a Personal Experience, 72, auth, Birds of North America, 72 & auth, Antarctica, 78, Dutton; auth, Intimate Landscapes, Metrop Mus Art & Dutton, 79; coauth (with Jonathan Porter), All Under Heaven--The Chinese World, Pantheon, 83. *Mailing Add:* Rte 4 Box 33 Santa Fe NM 87501

PORTER, ELMER JOHNSON
PAINTER, EDUCATOR
b Richmond, Ind, May 5, 07. *Study:* Art Inst Chicago, BAE; Ohio State Univ, MA; Earlham Col; Univ Cincinnati; Univ Colo; Butler Univ; San Carlos Univ, Guatemala. *Exhib:* Hoosier Salon, Chicago; Art League, Columbus, Ohio; Art Asn Richmond, Ind; also in Cincinnati & New York. *Teaching:* Instr art, McKinley High Sch, Cedar Rapids, Iowa, 30-37; instr art, Hughes High Sch, Cincinnati, 38-46; prof art, Ind State Univ, Terre Haute, 46-73, emer prof, 73- *Awards:* Appl Arts Prize, Indianapolis Art Asn, 29; Watercolor Award, Art League, Columbus, 38; Bonsib Purchase Prize, Hoosier Salon, 39. *Mem:* Art Educ Asn Ind (pres, 52-53, secy-treas, 54-67); Kappa Pi (int secy, 70-); Nat Art Educ Asn; Am Soc Bookplate Collectors & Designers; Pen & Brush Club. *Media:* Watercolor. *Publ:* Auth, Bookplates of Ernest Haskel, Bookplate Ann, 51. *Mailing Add:* 3115 Margaret Ave Terre Haute IN 47802

PORTER, J ERWIN
PAINTER
b Medina, NY, Jan 13, 03. *Study:* Rochester Inst Technol. *Work:* Marine Midland Bank; Monroe Co Savings Bank; Rochester Savings Bank; New Paltz Savings Bank; Charles Rand Penny Found; plus others. *Comn:* Paintings depicting Bicentennial events surrounding restoration of Ft Stanwix, comn by Oneida Co Savings Bank of Rome, NY, 77. *Exhib:* Four shows, Am Watercolor Soc, 61-68; Nat Acad Design, 63 & 65; six shows, Allied Artists

Am, 63-77; one-man show, Smithsonian Inst, 67; Nat Arts Club Ann, 67-70; plus others. *Awards:* Rochester Art Club Awards, 64, 65, 68 & 69; Widmer Wine Co Award, Mem Art Gallery Finger Lakes Exhib, 68. *Bibliog:* Article in Am Artist, 6/66. *Mem:* Fel Rochester Mus & Sci Ctr; Am Watercolor Soc; Allied Artists Am; Pastel Soc of Am. *Mailing Add:* 116 El Pinon Green Valley AZ 85614

PORTER, JEANNE CHENAULT
EDUCATOR, HISTORIAN
b New York, NY, Mar 18, 44. *Study:* Barnard Col, Columbia Univ, BA, 65; Univ Mich, Ann Arbor, MA, 66 & PhD(Ford Found Graduate Fel), 71; Univ Florence, Rome & Ghent. *Collections Arranged:* Bradley Tomlin: A Retrospective View, traveling exhib (auth, catalog), Hofstra Univ, 75-76. *Teaching:* Assoc prof, Finch Col, New York, 72-74 & Pa State Univ, 74- *Awards:* Fulbright Grant to Rome, 68-69; Belgian Govt Grant, 68. *Mem:* Col Art Asn Am. *Res:* Abstract Expressionism (American), and Spanish, French and Italian Baroque Painting. *Publ:* Auth, Bradley Walker Tomlin: Early paintings & intimations, Archives Am Art J, 74; auth, Bradley Walker Tomlin: A painter's painter, Arts Mag, 75; auth, Jusepe de Ribera and the Order of Christ, Burlington Mag, 76; Painting and Sculpture in the Samuel Gallu Collection (catalog), 80 & Works on Paper: Henry Varnum Poor (catalog), 83, Pa State Press. *Mailing Add:* 239 E Irvin Ave State College PA 16801

PORTER, LILIANA
PAINTER, PRINTMAKER
b Buenos Aires, Arg, Oct 6, 41; US citizen. *Study:* Sch of Fine Arts, Buenos Aires; printmaking, Iberoamerican Univ & La Ciudadela, Mexico City & Pratt Graphic Art Ctr, New York. *Work:* Mus of Mod Art, New York; Mus of Fine Arts, Philadelphia; Museo de Bellas Artes, Caracas, Venezuela & Santiago, Chile; La Bibliot Nat, Paris. *Exhib:* Museo de Bellas Artes, Caracas, 69; Museo de Bellas Artes, Santiago, 69; Info, Mus of Mod Art, New York, 70; Bks Made by Artist (traveling show), US, 72; Proj Ser, Mus of Mod Art, New York, 73; Museo de Arte Moderno, Bogota, Colombia, 74; Biennial of Paris, 75; and others. *Pos:* Co-dir, Studio Porter-Wiener, 79- *Teaching:* Instr etching, New York Graphic Workshop, 65-68; instr art tutorials, State Univ NY, Old Westbury, 75-76; instr graphics, Lucca, Italy, summers, 75-77. *Awards:* Park Sq Gallery Award, Fourth Brit Int Print Bienniale, 74; First Prize, Argentinian Art 78, Mus Fine Arts, Buenos Aires, 78; Guggenheim Fel, 80; and others. *Bibliog:* James Collins (auth), articles in Artforum, 73 & Arts Mag, 5/77. *Publ:* Contribr, Wrinkle, 68, Nail, 73 & String, 73, New York Graphic Workshop. *Dealer:* Barbara Toll New York NY. *Mailing Add:* 178 Franklin St 5th Fl New York NY 10013

PORTER, RICHARD JAMES
ADMINISTRATOR, HISTORIAN
b Bellefonte, Pa, Jan 2, 50. *Study:* Pa State Univ, BA, 71, MA, 73, PhD, 83. *Collections Arranged:* Sidney Goodman: Paintings, Drawings & Graphics 1959-1979 (coauth, catalog), Mus Art, Pa State Univ, Queens Mus, Columbus Mus Art & Del Art Mus, 80-81; Henry Varnum Poor (coauth, catalog), Mus Art, Pa State Univ, Burchfield Ctr, Everson Mus & Nat Acad Design, 83-84. *Pos:* Deputy dir, Project Soho, New York, 71-72. *Teaching:* Instr art hist, Middle Tenn State Univ, 73-76. *Mem:* Am Asn Mus; Northeast Mus Conf; Asn Col Univ Mus Galleries; Col Art Asn. *Res:* American and European art, 17th century to present, particularly American 18th-20th centuries. *Publ:* Auth, A newly discovered painting by Ammi Phillips, Conn Hist Soc Bulletin, 79; auth, Introduction selected works from the collection of Samuel Gallu, Pa State Univ, 80; auth, Jerome Witkin, A Decade of Work (exhib catalog), 82. *Mailing Add:* 239 E Irvin Ave State College PA 16801

PORTER, SHIRLEY
PAINTER
b Tallahassee, Fla. *Study:* Fla State Univ, BS(educ), 62; Univ SFla, MA(educ), 69. *Work:* Tweed Mus, Duluth, Minn; Montgomery Co Dept Parks, Rockville, Md; Utah State Univ. *Exhib:* Am Watercolor Soc, Nat Acad Gallery, New York, 75-77 & 79; Allied Artists, Nat Acad Gallery, 75-77; Nat Acad Design, Nat Acad Gallery, 77-81; Rocky Mountain Nat Watermedia, Foothills Art Ctr, Golden, Colo, 78, 80 & 81; Watercolor USA, Springfield Art Mus, Mo, 79. *Awards:* David Soloway Mem Award, 77 & Gold Medal, 78, Allied Artists; Silver Medal, 80 & Gold Medal, 81, Baltimore Watercolor Soc. *Mem:* Am Watercolor Soc; Allied Artists Am; Audubon Artists; Nat Watercolor Soc; Midwest Watercolor Soc; and others. *Media:* Watercolor. *Dealer:* Prince Royal Gallery Alexandria VA 22313. *Mailing Add:* 14315 Woodcrest Dr Rockville MD 20853

PORTNOY, THEODORA PREISS
DEALER
b New York, NY. *Study:* Manhattanville Col; Sarah Lawrence Col, BA. *Pos:* Dir, Theo Portnoy Gallery, currently. *Specialty:* Sculpture with emphasis on work that has evolved from craft media, clay, glass, wood and forged steel. *Mailing Add:* Theo Portnoy Gallery 162 W 56th St New York NY 10019

POSEN, STEPHEN
PAINTER
b St Louis, Mo, Sept 27, 39. *Study:* Washington Univ, BFA(Milliken Traveling Scholar; Fulbright Grant Italy), 66; Yale Univ, MFA. *Work:* Va Mus Fine Arts; Chase Manhattan Collection; Pa Acad Fine Arts. *Exhib:* Highlight of the 1971 Season, Aldrich Mus Contemp Art, Ridgefield, Conn, 71; The New Realsits, Chicago Mus Contemp Art, 71; Whitney Mus Am Art Ann, New York, 72; Chicago Art Inst, 74; Taft Mus, 75; Canberra Nat, 77-78; Pa Acad Fine Arts, 77; solo exhib, Robert Miller Gallery, New York, 78. *Teaching:* Instr drawing, Cooper Union. *Bibliog:* Ivan Karp (auth), Rent is the

only reality, Arts Mag, 1/72; Dore Ashton (auth), Stephen Posen and the mixed metaphor, Arts Mag, 10/78; A Mackie (auth), Dialectic in modernism: The paintings of Stephen Posen, Art Int, 1/80. *Mailing Add:* c/o Robert Miller Gallery 724 Fifth Ave New York NY 10019

POSES, (MR & MRS) JACK I
COLLECTORS
Mr Poses, b Russia, Dec 28, 1899; US citizen; Mrs Poses, b New York, NY, June 5, 08. *Study:* Mr Poses, NY Univ, BCS, 23 & MBA, 24; Brandeis Univ, LLD, 68; Mrs Poses, Hunter Col, BA, 27; Bryn Mawr Col, (Susan B Anthony Fel), 28; Sch Law, NY Univ, LLB, 30. *Pos:* Mr Poses, vchmn, New York Bd Higher Educ, 63-; mem bd trustees, mem educ & budget comts, founder Poses Inst Fine Arts & chmn coun fine arts, Brandeis Univ; founder, Einstein Med Sch; Mrs Poses, mem & secy, New York City Charter Rev Comn, 61; mem bd visitors, Grad Ctr, City Univ New York, 77-78; practicing attorney, New York, currently. *Awards:* Mr Poses, Chevalier, Legion of Honor, 58; Citation Distinguished & Exceptional Serv to City New York, Mayor Lindsay, 67; and others. *Interests:* Established numerous scholarships at many leading universities, as well as devoting active support to major art museums. *Collection:* French and American. *Mailing Add:* 1107 Fifth Ave New York NY 10028

POSEY, ERNEST NOEL
PAINTER
b New Orleans, La, 1937. *Study:* Tulane Univ, Art Ctr Col; La State Univ, BFA. *Work:* San Francisco Mus Art; Santa Barbara Mus Art; New Orleans Mus of Art; Brooklyn Mus; Oakland Mus; plus numerous pvt collections. *Exhib:* Looking West, Joslyn Art Mus, 70; New Accessions, San Francisco Mus Art, 73; Achenbach Found, Calif Palace of the Legion of Hon, 77; Aesthetics of Graffiti, San Francisco Mus Mod Art, 78; solo exhibs, Palace of the Legion of Honor, 71, Bank of Am Concourse, San Francisco, 77, Nuage Gallery, Los Angeles, 78, Walnut Creek Civic Arts Gallery, 78 & Los Robles Gallery, Palo Alto, Calif, 78; plus others. *Teaching:* Instr painting & design, San Francisco Acad Art, 72- *Mailing Add:* 1253 Pacific Ave San Francisco CA 94109

POSEY, LESLIE THOMAS
SCULPTOR, INSTRUCTOR
b Harshaw, Wis, Jan 20, 1900. *Study:* Wis Sch Fine & Appl Arts, with Ferd Koenig, 19-23; Pa Acad Fine Art, with Albert Laessle, 23; Art Inst Chicago, 24, with Albin Polasek, 29-30. *Work:* Manatee Art League, Bradenton, Fla; Contemp Arts Gallery, Pinellas Park, Fla; Longboat Key Art Ctr, Fla. *Comn:* Beethoven (limestone), Dr O Seivert, Wildwood Park, Wis, 33; decorative cast stone, Church of the Redeemer, Sarasota, Fla, 52; garden figure in cast stone, Nat Coun Garden Clubs, Athens, Ga, 54; Kellogg portrait (stone), Dept Fire Control, Oneco, Fla, 58; Terry portrait (bronze), Longboat Key Art Ctr, 70. *Exhib:* Wis Sculptors & Painters, 23 & Lincoln Int, 30, Milwaukee Art Inst; Am Artists Exhib, Art Inst Chicago, 30; Hoosier Salon, Marshall Fields Gallery, Chicago, 30; Fla Int, Lake Land, 50. *Pos:* Sculptor, Am Terra-Cotta Co, Chicago, 25-26; head sculpture & design, Indianapolis Terra-Cotta Co, Ind, 26-29. *Teaching:* Dir sculpture, Posey Sch Sculpture, 37-; instr sculpture, Manatee Art League, Bradenton, Fla, 52-61 & Longboat Key Art Ctr, 61-71. *Awards:* Medal & Award, Milwaukee Art Inst, 23; First Prize, Hoosier Salon, Katherine Barker Hickox, 30; First Prize, Sarasota Art Asn, Fla Fedn Art, 40. *Mem:* Sarasota Art Asn (dir, 71-73). *Media:* Stone, Bronze. *Mailing Add:* 401 N Tuttle Ave Sarasota FL 33577

POSNER, DONALD
HISTORIAN
b New York, NY, Aug 30, 31. *Study:* Queens Col, AB, 56; Harvard Univ, AM, 57; NY Univ, PhD, 62. *Pos:* Art historian in residence, Am Acad Rome, 68-69; ed-in-chief, Art Bull, 68-71; deputy dir, NY Univ Inst Fine Arts, 83- *Teaching:* Instr art hist, Queens Col, 57; asst prof art hist, Columbia Univ, 61-62; Ailsa Mellon Bruce prof art hist, NY Univ Inst Fine Arts, 62-; Robert Sterling Clark vis prof, Williams Col, 73; William R Kenan Jr vis prof, Univ Va, 76-77. *Awards:* Phi Beta Kappa Award, 56; Rome Prize Fel, Am Acad Rome, 59-61; C R Morey Bk Award, 72. *Mem:* Col Art Asn Am (dir, 70-74);. *Res:* Italian painting of 16th through 18th century; French painting of 18th century. *Publ:* Auth, Annibale Carracci, 71; coauth, 17th & 18th Century Art, 72; auth, Watteau's Lady at her Toilet, 73; auth, Jacques Callot and the dances called Sfessania, Art Bull, 77; auth, Antoine Watteau, 84. *Mailing Add:* NY Univ Inst Fine Arts 1 E 78th St New York NY 10021

POSNER, JUDITH L
DEALER, PUBLISHER
b Milwaukee, Wis, Sept 22, 41. *Study:* Univ Wis, BA(fine arts). *Pos:* Dir & pres, Judith L Posner & Assocs, Inc, currently. *Teaching:* Instr, Comprehensive Employment & Training Act, Milwaukee, currently. *Bibliog:* Curtis Casewitt (auth), Making a Living in the Fine Arts, Macmillan. *Mem:* Industrial Found Am Soc Interior Designers; Prof Picture Framers Asn; Int Soc Appraisers. *Specialty:* Nineteenth and twentieth century American and European painting, sculpture and graphics. *Publ:* Publisher of posters and prints. *Mailing Add:* 152 W Wisconsin Ave Milwaukee WI 53203

POST, ANNE B
SCULPTOR, GRAPHIC ARTIST
b St Louis, Mo. *Study:* Bennington Col, BA(fine arts); study with Simon Moselsio, Stephen Hirsch & Edwin Park; study in Europe. *Work:* Israel Mus, Jerusalem; Art Dept Mus, Wellesley Col; Dept Fine Arts Mus, Univ Chicago; Maison Francaise; Cooper Union Mus Gallery. *Exhib:* St Louis Mus Art; Univ NJ Mus; benefit exhib, Acad Medicine, New York; Bennington Mus Art;

Bennington Col Visual Arts Mus; AIR Gallery, New York. *Teaching:* Drawing & sculpture, Army Hosps, WVa, Tex, Mo & Settlement House, St Louis, 42-46. *Bibliog:* Gunter Klotz (auth), Zeichnunsen und skulpturen der Anne Post, Klotz-Makowckie, 65. *Mem:* Artists Equity. *Media:* Wood, Stone. *Mailing Add:* 29 Washington Sq W New York NY 10011

POST, GEORGE (BOOTH)
PAINTER
b Oakland, Calif, Sept 29, 06. *Study:* Calif Sch Fine Arts. *Work:* San Francisco Mus Art; Seattle Art Mus; Calif Palace of Legion of Honor; San Diego Fine Arts Soc; Metrop Mus Art; and many others. *Exhib:* Metrop Mus Art; San Francisco Mus Art; DeYoung Mem Mus; Seattle Art Mus; San Diego Fine Arts Gallery; and others. *Teaching:* Instr, Stanford Univ, 40; prof fine arts, Calif Col Arts & Crafts, 47-73; instr, San Jose Col, 51-52; class workshops conducted in Spain, 74, Oaxaca & Taxco, Mex, 75, Albuquerque, NMex, 75, 76 & 77, Salt Lake City, Utah, 76, Aspen, Colo, 76, Sorrento, 76, Little Rock, Ark, 77 & San Miguel, Mex, 78. *Awards:* Purchase Awards, Watercolor USA, Springfield Mus Art, Mo, 66 & Jack London Square Art Festival, 68; First Award, Zellerbach Show, 75; and others. *Mem:* Am Watercolor Soc; San Francisco Art Asn; Calif Nat Watercolor Soc; Int Inst Arts & Lett; Southwest Watercolor Soc. *Publ:* Contribr illus in Fortune, Calif Arts & Archit, Art Digest, Am Artist & Ford Times Mags. *Mailing Add:* 327 Cumberland St San Francisco CA 94114

POST, MARION (MARION POST WOLCOTT)
PHOTOGRAPHER
b Montclair, NJ, June 7, 10. *Study:* NY Univ; Univ Vienna, BA, 34; with Ralph Steiner, 35-36. *Work:* Metrop Mus Art, Mus Mod Art, Int Ctr Photog, New York; Nat Gallery Can; San Francisco Mus Contemp Art. *Exhib:* FSA Anniversary Show, Brooklyn Mus, 55; The Bitter Years, Mus Mod Art, New York, 62; Women Look at Women, Libr Cong Traveling Exhib, 77; Everson Mus Art, 78; solo exhib, Univ Calif Mus Art, Berkeley, 78; Image de l'Amerique en Crise: Photos de la FSA, Ctr George Pompidou, Paris, 79; American Photography and Social Conscience, Victoria, Australia, 80. *Bibliog:* Hal Fischer (auth), MPW's spectrum of the depression, Artweek, 5/27/78; Martha Chahroudi (auth), From the FSA to today, Afterimage, 11/78; Joan Murray (auth), FSA veteran gets back to work, Am Photogr, 3/80. *Mem:* Friends Photog; Friends Imogen Cunningham. *Publ:* Contribr, Hometown on the Face of American, Alliance Book Corp, 40; contribr, 12 Million Black Voices, Viking Press, 41; contribr, Portrait of a Decade, La State Univ Press, 72; contribr, In This Proud Land, New York Graphic Soc, 73; contribr, A Vision Shared, St Martins Press, 76. *Dealer:* Lee Witkin Gallery 41 E 57th New York NY 10022. *Mailing Add:* 1755 Filbert 3B San Francisco CA 94123

POSTIGLIONE, COREY M
PAINTER, EDUCATOR
b Chicago, Ill, July 35, 43. *Study:* Univ Ill, Circle Campus, BFA; also with Martin Hurtig & Roland Ginzel. *Exhib:* One-man shows, Evanston Art Ctr, Ill, 72 & Jan Cicero Gallery, Chicago, 76, 78 & 83; Cool Abstraction, Richard Gray Gallery, Chicago, 76; Works on Paper, Chicago & Vicinity Show, Art Inst Chicago, 78; Ill State Mus, Springfield, 83; and many others. *Pos:* Contribr ed, New Art Examiner, New Art Asn, 75-76 & illusr the little artist cartoon, 75-76; asst dir, Jan Cicero Gallery, Chicago, 77- *Teaching:* Instr painting, Evanston Art Ctr, Ill, 71-79, Ill Inst Technol, 75-83, Columbia Col, Chicago, 79-, Art Inst Chicago, 81-83 & Univ Ill, Chicago, summer 83; Art Inst Chicago, 81- *Awards:* 3rd Prize, Italian American Exhib. *Bibliog:* Franz Schultz (auth), Jan Cicero Group Show, Chicago Daily News, 77; C L Morrison (auth), One person show Jan Cicero Gallery, Artforum, 79; Alan G Artner (auth), article, Chicago Tribune, 83. *Media:* Multimedia. *Publ:* Auth, Interview with five abstract painters, New Art Examiner, 76. *Dealer:* Jan Cicero 437 N Clark St Chicago IL 60610. *Mailing Add:* 1943 N Damen Chicago IL 60647

POTTER, (GEORGE) KENNETH
PAINTER, DESIGNER
b Bakersfield, Calif, Feb 26, 26. *Study:* Acad Art, San Francisco, 47 & 48; Acad Frochot, Paris, with Metzinger, 50-52; Inst Statale Belli Arte, Florence, Italy, summer 51; study in Sicily, 53; San Francisco State Univ, BA, 74. *Work:* Univ San Francisco Collection; hist mural (ink & acrylic on canvas), Corte Madera Town Hall; Fed Housing & Urban Development, Regional Off, San Francisco. *Exhib:* Phelan Awards Competition, San Francisco Mus Art, 49; Am Watercolor Soc Ann, New York, 61 & 74, 76 & 79; A City Buys Art, Calif Palace Legion Hon, San Francisco, 63; Watercolor USA, Springfield Art Mus, Mo, 73 & 74. *Pos:* Art dir, McCann-Erikson Inc Advert, Rio de Janeiro, 54-55; art dir, Johnson & Lewis Advert, San Francisco, 57; art dir, Michelson Advert, Palo Alto, Calif, 59-60; artist demonstr, Grumbacher Inc, New York, 78-79. *Teaching:* Instr watercolor, Civic Art Ctr, Walnut Creek, Calif, 68-70, Acad Art, San Francisco, 70, San Francisco State Univ, 74 & 75 & Richmond Art Ctr, Calif, 78-79; pvt watercolor coach, currently. *Awards:* Non-Purchase Award for Watercolor, Calif State Fair & Expos, 58 & 72; First Award for Watercolor, Delta Ann, Antioch, Calif, 69; First Award Watercolor, Alameda Co Fair Statewide Competition, 74 & 79. *Bibliog:* Harold Rogers (auth), Color out of the West, Christian Sci Monitor, 2/26/49; Mabel Greene (auth), I began to draw, then to talk, San Francisco News-Editorial, 11/13/52; Milton Goldring (auth), O pintor Americano Kenneth Potter, Correio da Manha, Rio de Janeiro, 6/2/55. *Mem:* West Coast Watercolor Soc (pres, 68-70). *Media:* Watercolor, Oil, Acrylic. *Publ:* Contribr, Golden Gate Bridge, 5/27/62, A walk in Chinatown, 6/10/62 & A walk in the art world, 9/29/63, Bonanza, San Francisco Chronicle; contribr, Mission San Antonio, Calif Automobile Asn, 9/67; contribr, Marin portfolio, Image Mag, 10/67. *Mailing Add:* 105 Sonora Way Corte Madera CA 94925

POTTER, TED
PAINTER, ADMINISTRATOR
b Springhill, Kans, Dec 6, 33. *Study:* Chicago Art Inst; Northwestern Univ; Univ Kans; Baker Univ, BFA; Univ Calif, Berkeley; Calif Col Arts & Crafts, MFA. *Work:* Calif Col Arts & Crafts, Oakland; Univ Kans Art Gallery, Lawrence; Rockefeller Found, New York; Wake Forest Univ, Winston-Salem; Vanderbilt Univ, Nashville; and many pvt collections. *Exhib:* Solo exhibs, State Univ, Salem Col, Winston-Salem, Barbara Fiedler Gallery, Washington, DC & Morehead Galleries, Greensboro, NC; New Orleans Acad Fine Art, 84. *Pos:* Dir art, Glide Found, 65-67; dir, Southeastern Ctr Contemp Art, Winston-Salem, 68-; dir, Awards Visual Arts, Nat Artist Fel Prog, currently. *Mem:* NC State Arts Soc (adv coun, 69-72); NC State Arts Coun. *Dealer:* Judith Selkowitz Fine Arts Inc New York NY; Barbara Fiedler Galleries Washington DC. *Mailing Add:* Southeastern Ctr Contemp Art 750 Marguerite Dr Winston-Salem NC 27106

POTTS, DON
SCULPTOR
b San Francisco, Calif, Oct 5, 36. *Study:* San Jose State Col, BA, 36, MA, 65; Univ Iowa, 63. *Work:* Joslyn Art Mus, Omaha; La Jolla Mus Art, Calif; Pasadena Art Mus, Calif; Oakland Mus, Calif; San Francisco Mus Art; and others. *Exhib:* Mus Mod Art, New York, 69; Univ Art Mus, Univ Calif, Berkeley, 70; San Francisco Mus Mod Art, Calif, 71 & 76; one-man shows, Denver Art Mus, 72, Walker Art Ctr, Minneapolis, 72, Whitney Mus Am Art, New York, 72 & Garden of the Literarizchez Colloquium & Gallery Andre, West Berlin, Ger, 76; Inst of Contemp Art, Boston, Mass, 74; Stadtische Kunsthalle Dusseldorf, Ger, 76; Documenta, Kasel, Ger, 77; Stedelijk Mus, Amsterdam, 78; and many others. *Awards:* Nat Endowment Arts Fel Grant, 70; Lewis Comfort Tiffany Found Grant, 73-74; Berliner Kunstler Prog, Deutscher Acad Austauschdienst, Buro Berlin, Ger, 75-76. *Bibliog:* Robert Hughes (auth), My first car, Time Mag, 7/3/72; Peter Plagens (auth), Sunshine Muse: Contemporary Art on the West Coast, Praeger, 74; Wayne Anderson (auth), American Sculpture in Process 1930/1970, Little Brown & Co, 75. *Mailing Add:* c/o Fuller Goldeen Gallery 228 Grant Ave San Francisco CA 94108

POUCHER, ELIZABETH MORRIS
SCULPTOR
b Yonker, NY. *Study:* Vassar Col, AB; NY Univ; Columbia Univ; Art Students League; with Alexander Archipenko; Acad Grande Chaumiere, Paris, France; Ecole Animalier, Paris; also with Andre L'Hote. *Work:* Smithsonian Inst, Washington, DC; Taylor Art Gallery, Vassar Col, Poughkeepsie, NY; Mus City New York; and others. *Exhib:* Bronxville Ann, NY, 68-78; Hudson Valley Art Asn, White Plains, NY, 68, 76-79; Pen & Brush, New York, 68, 75-79; Allied Artists Am, New York, 68, 75-79; Nat Sculpture Soc Exhibs, 68, 75-78; one-man show, Bronxville Pub Libr, NY, 80. *Awards:* First Prize for Sculpture, Bronxville Ann, NY, 71 & 73; Mrs John Newington Award for Sculpture, 75. *Mem:* Fel Nat Sculpture Soc; Allied Artists Am; Pen & Brush; Hudson Valley Art Asn. *Mailing Add:* 9 Brooklands Bronxville NY 10708

POULOS, BASILIOS NICHOLAS
PAINTER, EDUCATOR
b Columbia, SC, Dec 15, 41. *Study:* Atlanta Sch Art, BFA; Tulane Univ, MFA; Univ SC. *Work:* Houston Mus Fine Arts; Chase Manhattan Bank, New York; Voorus Mus, Athens; Tulane Univ, New Orleans, La; New Orleans Mus Art; and others. *Exhib:* One-man exhibs, High Mus Art, Atlanta, Ga, 65; Columbia Mus Art, SC, 67, Simonne Stern Gallery, New Orleans, La, 73, 74, 76 & 79, Greenville Co Mus Art, SC, 79; Watson de Nagy & Co, Houston, Tex, 75, 76 & 79; Tibor De Nagy Gallery, New York, 80; 35th Biennial, Corcoran Gallery Art, Washington, DC, 77. *Teaching:* Assoc prof painting, Rice Univ, 75- *Awards:* Fine Arts Found Grant, Atlanta, Ga, 65; French Govt Grant, 65-66; Guggenheim Found Fel, 73-74. *Bibliog:* Mimi Crossley (auth), Poulos at Watson De Nagy, Art in Am, 77. *Media:* Acrylic on Canvas. *Dealer:* Heath Gallery 416 E Paces Perry Rd Atlanta GA 30305; Grapestake Gallery 2876 California St San Francisco 94115. *Mailing Add:* 1430 W 23rd Houston TX 77008

POUNIAN, ALBERT KACHOUNI
PAINTER, CURATOR
b Chicago, Ill, Mar 7, 24. *Study:* Art Inst Chicago, BFA, 48 & MFA, 49. *Work:* Borg-Warner Corp, Chicago; Ill Bell Tel, Chicago; Harper Col, Palatine, Ill; Barat Col, Lake Forest, Ill. *Exhib:* Chicago & Vicinity, Art Inst Chicago; Ringling Mus, Sarasota, Fla; Northwest Territory, Springfield, Ill; Violence in Contemp Am Art, Mus Contemp Art, Chicago, 68. *Pos:* Consult & contribr, Am Educ Encycl; coordr, Nat Upward Bound Exhib, Off Econ Opportunity, 66 & consult, 67-68; corp art cur, Continental Ill Nat Bank & Trust Co, Chicago, 79-; founding chmn, asn Corp Art Curators, Chicago, 80. *Teaching:* Instr, painting & drawing, Art Inst Chicago, 48-56; lectr art hist, Lake Forest Col, 50-65; prof painting & drawing, Barat Col Lake Forest, 49-79 & chmn art dept, 70-74; Fulbright-Hays Exchange Prof, Sch Fine Arts, Ulster Col, Northern Ireland Polytechnic, Belfast, Northern Ireland. *Mem:* Am Asn Univ Prof. *Publ:* Auth, articles, Am Educ Encycl. *Mailing Add:* 46 N Washington Circle Lake Forest IL 60045

POUSETTE-DART, RICHARD
PAINTER
b St Paul, Minn, June 8, 16. *Study:* Bard Col, 36, Hon DHL, 65. *Work:* Mus Mod Art, Whitney Mus Am Art, New York; Addison Gallery Am Art, Andover, Mass; Albright-Knox Art Gallery; Nat Collection Fine Arts, Washington, DC; and many others. *Exhib:* Abstract Painting & Sculpture in

America, 44 & Traveling Exhibs, 69 & 71, Mus Mod Art, New York; The New Decade, 55 & Retrospective Exhib, 63 & 74, Whitney Mus Am Art, New York; New York School Exhibition, Los Angeles Mus Fine Arts; Documenta 2, Kassel, WGer, 59; Walker Art Ctr, Minneapolis, 60; Mus Mod Art, 61 & 69; Corcoran Gallery Art, Washington, DC, 64; American Abstract Expressionists & Imagists, Solomon Guggenheim Mus, 61; Wadsworth Atheneum, Hartford, Conn, 62; Nat Gallery, Washington, DC, 73; The Magic Circle, Bronx Mus, 77; and others; Perceptions of the Spirit in 20th Century Am Art, Indianapolis, 77; Abstract Expressionists: Formative Years, Cornell Univ, 78. *Teaching*: Lectr, Boston Mus Sch Fine Arts, 59; instr painting, New Sch Social Res, 59-61; instr advan paintings, Sch Visual Arts, New York, 65; lectr, Minneapolis Inst Fine Arts, 65; guest critic, Columbia Univ, 68; instr painting, Sarah Lawrence Col, 70-74. *Awards*: Comstock Prize, Art Inst Chicago, 65; Nat Arts Coun Award, 66; Nat Endowment Arts Grant, 67; and others. *Bibliog*: Richard Pousette-Dart: Transcendental expressionist, 61, Lawrence Campbell (auth), Pousette-Dart: Circles and cycles, 63 & Charlotte Willard (auth), Yankee Vedanta, 67, Art News; and many others. *Dealer*: Marisa del Re Gallery 41 East 57th St New York NY 10022. *Mailing Add*: 286 Haverstraw Rd Suffern NY 10901

POWELL, DAN T
PHOTOGRAPHER

b Richland, Wash, July 12, 50. *Study*: Cent Wash Univ, with Jim Sahlstrand, BA, 73, MA(art), 77; Univ Ill, with Art Sinsabaugh & Luther Smith, MFA(art), 80. *Work*: Hallmark Collection, Kansas City, Mo; Calif Inst Arts; Rainier Collection 20th Century Am Photog, Seattle; Midwest Mus Am Art, Elkhart, Ind; Ill State Univ, Normal. *Exhib*: Iowa Artists Ann, Des Moines Art Ctr, 82; Summer Light, Light Gallery, New York, 82; Fifth Vienna Int Biennial, Austria, 82; four-person exhib, San Francisco Camerawork, 83; Susan Spiritus Gallery, Los Angeles, 83. *Teaching*: Asst photog, Cent Wash Univ, 76-77 & Univ Ill, 79-80; asst prof, Univ Northern Iowa, 80- *Awards*: Second Award, Contemp Photoworks, Univ NMex, 80; Best of Show, Midwest Photo 80, Midwest Mus Am Art, 80; Best of Prints & Drawings, Iowa Artists, Des Moines Art Ctr, 82. *Bibliog*: Joan Murray (auth), rev of New Photographics, 79 & Diane Neumaier (auth), Visual & Verbal Language, 80, Artweek. *Mem*: Soc Photog Educ. *Dealer*: Ledel Gallery 168 Mercer St New York NY. *Mailing Add*: 114 1/2 Main St Cedar Falls IA 50613

POWELL, EARL ALEXANDER, III
CURATOR, HISTORIAN

b Spartanburg, SC, Oct 24, 43. *Study*: Williams Col, BA, 66; Harvard Univ, MA, 70, PhD, 74. *Pos*: Cur Michener Collection, Univ Tex, Austin, 74-76; mus cur & asst to asst dir, Nat Gallery of Art, Washington, DC, 76-, exec cur, 79-80; dir, Los Angeles Co Mus Art, 80- *Teaching*: Asst prof Am art, Univ Tex, Austin, 74-76. *Mem*: Col Art Asn; Am Asn Mus; Am Asn Mus Dirs. *Res*: English influences in the art of Thomas Cole. *Publ*: Coauth, American Art at Harvard (catalog), 72; auth, Catalogue Raisonne of the Michener Collection, 78; auth, articles, catalogue essays on Am art. *Mailing Add*: Los Angeles Co Mus Arts 5905 Wilshire Blvd Los Angeles CA 90036

POWELSON, ROSEMARY A
INSTRUCTOR, PAINTER

b La Junta, Colo. *Study*: Univ Nebr, Lincoln, BFA, 71; Mich State Univ, East Lansing, MFA, 74. *Work*: Art Inst Chicago; Cranbrook Acad Art, Bloomfield Hills, Mich; Hackley Art Mus, Muskegon, Mich; Kalamazoo Inst Art, Mich; Sioux City Art Ctr, Iowa. *Comn*: Mich bicentennial portfolio prints in collotype, Nat Endowment Arts, Alma, Mich, 76; Prints 83 (portfolio), Lower Columbia Col Found, Longview, Wash, 83. *Exhib*: Saginaw Ann Area Art Exhib, Saginaw Art Mus, Mich, 77; Paintings & Drawings, Lee Hall Gallery, Northern Mich Univ, Marquette, 77; one-woman show, Alma Col, Mich, 78; Kans 5th Nat Small Paintings & Drawings, Art Gallery, Ft Hayes State Univ, 81; Wash Women Art, Art Gallery, Eastern Wash Univ, Cheney, 81; Print Exhib, Fort Steilacoom Community Col, Tacoma, Wash, 83. *Pos*: Humanities consult, Wash Humanities Project, Olympia, 81- *Teaching*: Instr painting & drawing, Alma Col, Mich, 75-78; instr design & drawing, Ft Steilacoom Community Col, Tacoma, Wash, 78-79; instr art hist & design, Lower Columbia Col, Longview, Wash, 79- *Awards*: Purchase Award, 33rd Ann Fall Show, 71; Merit Award, Saginaw Ann Area Art Exhib, 77. *Media*: Acrylic, Video Tape. *Publ*: Producer, Women in Art (film), Wash State Humanities Project, Olympia, 81. *Mailing Add*: Art Dept Lower Columbia Col Longview WA 98632

POWER, MARK
PHOTOGRAPHER, EDUCATOR

b Washington, DC, Mar 6, 37. *Study*: Bowdoin Col; Art Ctr Col. *Work*: Bibliotheque Nat, Paris; Libr Cong, Washington, DC; Corcoran Gallery of Art, Washington, DC; Smithsonian Inst, Washington, DC; New Orleans Mus Art, La. *Exhib*: One-man shows; Corcoran Gallery, Washington, DC, 70 & 74; Rita Hayworth series, Diane Brown Gallery, Washington, DC, 77, Friends & Family, Ewing Gallery, Washington, DC, 79; Mexican Photographs, Jefferson Place Gallery, Washington, DC, 74; Color Work, Galerie Chambre Clair, Paris, 83; Palladium Work, Contrasts Gallery, London, 80; and others. *Collections Arranged*: Marcel Bardon Photographs, 74 & Wright Morris: Words and Pictures (contribr, catalog), 82, Corcoran Gallery. *Pos*: Photog critic, Washington Post, 74-75; Washington Correspondent, After Image, 76; assoc ed, Washington Review. *Teaching*: Assoc prof photog, Corcoran Sch Art, Washington, DC, 70-; vis prof art, Univ Tex, San Antonio, 82. *Awards*: Grant in Aid Fel, Washington Gallery Mod Art Fund, 70-72; Materials Grant, Polaroid Corp, 72-75. *Bibliog*: David Tannous (auth), Art America, 12/77-1/78; Paul Richard (auth), Beasts of Beauty, Washington Post, 10/6/79; John Brumfield (auth), Washington's strongest, Artweek, 7/83.

Publ: Photographs, Camera Mag, Switz, 67, 69, 74, 78 & 79; photogr, Glooskap's Children, 71; photographs, Creative Camera, Great Britain, 5/70; auth, introd, George Krause-1, 72; auth, introd, Nancy Rexroth, Iowa, 77. *Dealer*: Kathleen Ewing Gallery 3243 P St NW Washington DC 20007. *Mailing Add*: c/o Corcoran Sch Art 17th & NY Ave NW Washington DC 20006

POWER, S BRENDA JOAN
SCULPTOR, PAINTER

b New York, NY, May 12, 41. *Study*: St Johns Univ, BS, 62; Pratt Inst, with Calvin Albert, George McNeil & Walter Rogalski, MFA(sculpture), 77. *Exhib*: Brooklyn 77, Brooklyn Mus, 77; Audubon Artists Ann Exhib, Nat Acad Galleries, New York, 77; Brighton Beach Maquettes & Ethnifest, Downtown Cult Ctr, Brooklyn, 81; Salmagundi Gallery, 81 & 82; Images and Symbols, Cork Gallery, New York, 82; and others. *Pos*: Dir art gallery, Harriman Col, 77-80. *Teaching*: Asst prof art hist, St Johns Univ, Jamaica, NY, 83- & Mercy Col, Dobbs Ferry, NY, 83- *Awards*: Ford Found Award Sculpture, 76; Long Beach Mus Art Creativity Award, 76. *Bibliog*: Alternative spaces--some highlights, 1/21/82, Claude Lesuer (auth), Brenda Power: Drawing in space & beyond, 1/6/83 & Will Grant (auth), Belanthi, growing & maturing, 10/16/83, Art Speak. *Mem*: Am Soc Contemp Artists; Metrop Painters & Sculptors (pres, currently); New York Artists Equity; Found Community Artists; Col Art Asn. *Media*: Polychromed Sculpture. *Dealer*: Belanthi Gallery 143 Court St Brooklyn NY 11201. *Mailing Add*: PO Box 251 Brooklyn NY 11215

POZZATTI, RUDY O
PRINTMAKER, PAINTER

b Telluride, Colo, Jan 14, 25. *Study*: Univ Colo, BFA & MFA; Hon LHD, Univ Colo, 73; also with Wendell H Black, Max Beckman & Ben Shahn. *Work*: Mus Mod Art, New York; Libr Cong, Washington, DC; Art Inst Chicago, Ill; Sheldon Mem Art Gallery, Lincoln, Nebr; Cleveland Mus Art, Ohio. *Comn*: Spec Print Eds, Cleveland Print Club, Cleveland Mus Art, 54; Int Graphic Arts Soc, New York, 58-61 & 63; Conrad Hilton Hotel, New York, 61; Clairol, Inc, comn for New York World's Fair, 63; Ferdinand Roten Galleries, Baltimore, Md, 67 & 68. *Exhib*: Work of Rudy Pozzatti, Cleveland Mus Art, 55; Young Americans, Whitney Mus Am Arts, New York, 61; Stampe di Due Mondi: Prints of Two Worlds, Tyler Sch Art, Rome, Italy, 67; 20 Year Retrospective, Sheldon Mem Art Gallery, Univ Nebr, 69; Artists Abroad, Inst Int Educ, Am Fedn Arts, New York, 69. *Pos*: US State Dept Cult Exchange Proj, USSR, 61, Yugoslavia, 65 & Brazil, 74; artist-in-residence, Roswell Mus & Art Ctr, 79. *Teaching*: Asst prof printmaking & painting, Univ Nebr, 50-56; prof printmaking, Ind Univ, 56-72, distinguished prof, 72- *Awards*: Guggenheim Fel, 63-64; George Norlin Silver Medal, Assoc Alumni of Univ Colo, 72. *Bibliog*: Norman Geske (auth), Rudy Pozzatti; American Printmaker, Univ Kans, 71; Richard Taylor (auth), Pozzatti (film), Artists in America, NETV, 71; Nancy Carroll (auth), A visit with Rudy Pozzatti, North Shore Art League, 72. *Mem*: Soc Am Graphic Artists; Am Color Print Soc; Col Art Asn, New York (bd dirs). *Media*: All Media. *Dealer*: Jane Haslem Gallery 2121 P St NW Washington DC 20007; David Heath Gallery 416 E Paces Ferry Rd Atlanta GA 30305. *Mailing Add*: 117 S Meadowbrook Ave Bloomington IN 47401

POZZI, LUCIO
PAINTER

b Milano, Italy, Nov 29, 35; US citizen. *Study*: Sculpture with Michael Noble. *Teaching*: Asst prof art & art hist, Cooper Union, 69-75; vis prof art, Princeton Univ, 75; instr art, Sch Visual Arts, 78- *Awards*: Nat Endowment Arts Fel, 83. *Bibliog*: David Shapiro (auth), An interview with Lucio Pozzi, NY Art J, 11/79. *Res*: Modern movement. *Publ*: Auth, five stories, 75 & 78. *Dealer*: John Weber Gallery 420 W Broadway New York NY 10012. *Mailing Add*: 142 Greene St New York NY 10012

PRACZUKOWSKI, EDWARD LEON
PAINTER, EDUCATOR

b Norwich, Conn, May 25, 30. *Study*: Norwich Art Sch, fine arts dipl, 50; Sch Mus Boston, cert with hons in painting, 56, Clarrisa Bartlett travel fel & grad cert, 59; Tufts Univ, BS(art educ), 58; Cranbrook Acad, MFA, 65. *Work*: Slater Mem Mus, Norwich, Conn, 81; City of Seattle, Wash. *Exhib*: Drawing USA, St Paul Art Ctr, Minn, 66 & 69; Nat Polymer Exhib, EMich Univ, 67 & 68; 11th Ann Nat Drawing Exhib, Oklahoma Art Ctr, 69; one man shows, Greenwood Gallery, Seattle, Wash, 81 & 83; Living With the Volcano, The Artists of Mt St Helens, Mus Art, Wash State Univ, 83. *Teaching*: Assoc prof drawing & painting, Univ Wash, 65- *Awards*: First Prize Painting, Int Arts Festival, Detroit, 65; MacDowell Colony Grants, 66 & 69; Wash Water Power Award, Spokane Ann, 81. *Mem*: Edward MacDowell Colony, New York; Allied Artists, Seattle, Wash. *Media*: Oil, Acrylic. *Mailing Add*: 5707 26th Ave N Seattle WA 98105

PRAEGER, FREDERICK A
COLLECTOR, PUBLISHER

b Vienna, Austria, Sept 16, 15; US citizen. *Study*: Univ Vienna; Univ Denver, LHD. *Pos*: Pres, Frederick A Praeger Publ, New York, 50-68; chmn, Phaidon Publ, Ltd, London, 67-68; gen mgr, Ed Praeger, Munich, 69-74; pres, Westview Press, Boulder, 75- *Teaching*: Adj prof, Grad Sch Librarianship, Univ Denver, Colo. *Mem*: Cosmos Club. *Collection*: Contemporary art; Gothic and Baroque sculpture. *Mailing Add*: Westview Press 5500 Central Ave Boulder CO 80301

PRAGER, DAVID A
COLLECTOR
b Long Branch, NJ, July 25, 13. *Study:* Columbia Univ, BA & LLD; also with Jack Tworkov. *Pos:* Asst secy, Friends of Whitney Mus Am Art, New York, 59-63, secy, 63-67; mem acquisitions comt, Whitney Mus Am Art, 60-61, 67-68 & 70-71; bd trustees, Am Fedn Arts, 67-82, treas, 69-79; treas, Munic Art Soc, 67-69, bd dirs, 69-, pres, 72-74, vpres, 74-; bd dirs, Mark Rothko Found, 77- *Mem:* Century Asn. *Collection:* Contemporary American painting. *Mailing Add:* 14 E 90th St New York NY 10028

PRAKAPAS, EUGENE JOSEPH
DEALER, EDITOR
b Lowell, Mass, July 29, 32. *Study:* Yale Univ, BA, 53; Oxford Univ, Eng, with Balliol, MA, 59. *Pos:* Dir, Prakapas Gallery, New York, currently. *Specialty:* Twentieth century modernism, with special emphasis on photography. *Mailing Add:* 19 E 71st St New York NY 10021

PRAMUK, EDWARD RICHARD
PAINTER
b Akron, Ohio, Feb 14, 36. *Study:* Kent State Univ, BFA, MA; Queens Col, grad study; Akron Art Inst; also with John Ferren, James Brooks & Louis Finkelstein. *Work:* Kent State Univ; Pan Am Life Corp. *Comn:* Paintings, James Talcott Inc, New York, 74. *Exhib:* New Orleans Mus Art Biennial, 73; Westbeth Gallery, New York, 75; Pelham-Von Stoffler Gallery, Houston, Tex, 78; Edinboro State Univ, Edinboro, NY, 78; one-man shows, Contemp Art Ctr, New Orleans, 80 & First St Gallery, New York, 83; and others. *Teaching:* Prof art, La State Univ, 64- *Awards:* Award, La Prof Artists, Baton Rouge, 71; Purchase Award, 7th Nat Drawing & Sculpture Show, 73; Purchase Award, New Orleans Mus Art, 74. *Media:* Acrylic. *Mailing Add:* 1152 Aberdeen Ave Baton Rouge LA 70808

PRANGE, SALLY BOWEN
CERAMIC ARTIST
b Valparaiso, Ind, Aug 11, 27. *Study:* Univ Mich, Ann Arbor, BA; workshops with Paul Soldner, Karen Karnes, Warren McKenzie, Don Reitz & Michael Cardew. *Work:* Victoria & Albert Mus, London, Eng; William Hayes Ackland Mem Art Ctr, Univ NC, Chapel Hill, NC Mus Art, Raleigh; Smithsonian Inst, Washington, DC; Mus Art, Pa State Univ, University Park. *Exhib:* Ann Ceramic & Sculpture Show, Butler Inst Am Art, Youngstown, Ohio, 67-68 & 71; Am Porcelain Show, Renwick Gallery, Smithsonian Inst, Washington, DC, 78; one-woman shows, Sumter Gallery Art, SC, 82 & Greenwich House Pottery, New York, 83; New Directions: Clay & Fiber 1982, ECarolina Univ Mus Art, 82; and others. *Teaching:* Instr ceramic pottery, Univ NC, Chapel Hill, 57-66; instr, Arrowmont, Gatlinburg, Tenn, 79 & 80, Penland Sch Crafts, NC, 81; NC State Univ Crafts Ctr, Raleigh, 82, Univ Calif, San Diego Craft Ctr, 82 & Greenwich House Pottery, New York, 83; instr, Penland Sch Crafts, NC, 81; guest lectr, Brit Craftsmen Potters Asn, London, 80, Int Mus Ceramics, Faenza, Italy, 80 & Porcelain Symposium, Herron Sch Art, Indianapolis, 82. *Bibliog:* Peter Lane (auth), Studio Potter, 83; Elaine Levin (auth), History of American Ceramics, 83; Katherine Pearson (auth), American Crafts, 83. *Mem:* Piedmont Crafts Inc; Am Crafts Coun; World Crafts Coun; Carolina Designer Craftsmen; Nat Coun Educ Ceramic Art. *Mailing Add:* 1804 Rolling Rd Chapel Hill NC 27514

PRASCH, RICHARD JOHN
PAINTER, EDUCATOR
b Seattle, Wash, Sept 11, 18. *Study:* Univ Wash, Seattle, BFA, 49; Univ Okla, with Emilio Amero, 50; Univ Ore, Eugene, MFA, 51. *Work:* Seattle Mus Art; Portland Art Mus, Ore; Marylhurst Col, Ore; First Nat Bank of Ore, Portland; Portland State Univ. *Exhib:* One-man show, Univ Okla Art Gallery, 50; Northwest Ann, Seattle Art Mus, 53 & 55; Drawings USA, Walker Art Ctr, Minneapolis, 64; San Francisco Drawing Ann; Denver Art Mus; and others. *Teaching:* Prof art, Portland State Univ, Ore, 55-82, currently. *Awards:* Katherine Baker Mem Award, Seattle Art Mus, 53. *Bibliog:* David Smeltzer (auth), Portland Rev Publ Bd, Vol 23, Portland State Univ, 77-78. *Mem:* Ore State Employees Asn; Am Asn Univ Profs. *Media:* Mixed. *Dealer:* Rental Sales Gallery, Portland Art Mus Portland Art Asn 1219 SW Park Ave Portland OR 97205. *Mailing Add:* 1817 NW Aspen Portland OR 97210

PRATT, DALLAS
PATRON, COLLECTOR
b New York, NY, Aug 21, 14. *Study:* Yale Univ, BA; Columbia Univ, MD. *Pos:* Ed, Columbia Libr Columns, 51-80; co-founder & trustee, Am Mus Britain, 59-; ed, Am in Britain, 63-64; founder, John Judkyn Mem, Bath, Eng, 64- *Collection:* Renaissance maps and manuscripts. *Publ:* Auth, Discovery of a world-early maps of America, Antiques Mag, 12/69 & 1/70; auth, Angel-motors, Columbia Libr Columns, 5/72; auth, The Best Books, Col Libr Columns, 5/74; auth, This stone and these flowers, Am Brit, XVII, 1/79. *Mailing Add:* 228 E 49th St New York NY 10017

PRATT, FRANCES (FRANCES ELIZABETH USUI)
PAINTER, ILLUSTRATOR
b Glen Ridge, NJ, May 25, 13. *Study:* New York Sch Appl Design for Women; Art Students League, with Richard Lahey; Hans Hofmann Sch Art. *Work:* Brooklyn Mus, NY; Va Mus Fine Arts, Richmond. *Exhib:* Denver Art Mus Ann, 42; Addison Gallery, 45; Cleveland Mus Art, 47; Brooklyn Mus Watercolor Int, 47, 49 & 51; Corcoran Gallery Art Biennial, 49. *Collections Arranged:* Ancient Mexico in Miniature, Am Fedn Arts, 64-66; Guerrero, Stone Sculpture from the State of Guerrero, Mex, Finch Col Mus Art, 65. *Pos:* Owner-dir, Frances Pratt, Inc, Gallery. *Teaching:* Instr painting, Ballard Sch New York, 42-59; instr painting, Parsons Sch Design, 48-51. *Awards:* Anne

Payne Robertson Prize, 46 & Prize for Oil, 50, Nat Asn Women Artists Ann; Audubon Prize for Crayon Mixed Media, Audubon Artists Ann, 52. *Res:* Pre-classic cultures of Mexico (1600 BC-300 AD). *Specialty:* Decorative arts, sculpture and painting of the 20th century. *Publ:* Illusr, Mezcala Stone Sculpture: the Human Figure, Mus Primitive Art, 67; illusr, Chalcacingo, 71 & 260 illus for Ceramic Figures of Ancient Mexico, 80, Akad Druck--U Verlagsanstalt, Graz, Austria; illusr, Paleolithic & Megalithic Traits in the Olmec Tradition of Mexico, Inst Canarium, Hallein, Austria, 72; illusr, Olmec hieroglyphic writing, Archaeology, 73; illusr, The Aztec treasure house, Harper's, 77. *Mailing Add:* 33 W 12th St New York NY 10011

PRATT, MARY FRANCES
PAINTER, PRINTMAKER
b Fredericton, NB, Can, Mar 15, 35. *Study:* Mount Allison Univ, Sackville, NB, studied with Alex Colville & Lawren Harris, Jr. *Work:* Nat Gallery Can, Ottawa, Ont; NB Mus, St John & Univ NB, Fredericton; Mem Univ, St John's, NF; Confederation Centre, Charlottetown, PEI; and others. *Exhib:* The Acute Image in Can Art, Owens Art Gallery, Mt Allison Univ, Sackville, NB, 74; Towards a New Reality, Art Gallery Ont, Toronto, 75; Some Can Women Artists, Nat Gallery Can, Ottawa, Ont, 75; Rothman's Realist Show, int traveling show, 76-77; one-person shows, Aggregation Gallery, Toronto, 81 & traveling through Canada, 82; and others. *Pos:* Dir art prog, Fredericton Recreation Comn, 55-57; instr exten dept, Mem Univ, NF, 61-63; mem staff, Art in the Sch, CBC TV Series, St John's, NF, 68-70; lectr & vis artist, Nat Gallery Can, Dalhousie Univ & Mt Allison Univ, 74-77. *Bibliog:* Bob Smith (producer), Take 30 (film), 70 & The Pratts of Newfoundland (film), 73, CBC-TV; Harry Bruce (auth), The fine art of familiarity, Can Mag, 11/75. *Mem:* Royal Can Acad Art. *Media:* Silkscreen, Lithography. *Dealer:* Aggregation Gallery 83 Front St East Toronto On Can M5E 1B8; Gallery Mira Godard Calgary AB Can. *Mailing Add:* PO Box 87 Mt Carmel NF A0B 2M0 Canada

PRATT, VERNON GAITHER
PAINTER, EDUCATOR
b Durham, NC, Dec 9, 40. *Study:* Phillips Acad, Andover, Mass; Duke Univ; Univ NC; San Francisco Art Inst with James Weeks & Richard Diebenkorn, hon BFA, 62, MFA, 64. *Work:* Duke Univ Mus of Art; San Francisco Art Asn; R J Reynolds World Hq, Winston-Salem, NC; NC Mus Art. *Comn:* Paintings, Brainstorm, MGM production, 81. *Exhib:* Piedmont Painting Anns, Mint Mus of Art, Charlotte, NC; DeGestlo Gallery, Hamburg, Ger, 73; Basel Int Art Fair, Switz, 73; Award Winners, NC Mus of Art, Raleigh, 74; New Orleans Mus, La, 77; John Weber Gallery, 80; and others. *Collections Arranged:* Real Cool-Cool Real, Duke Univ Mus of Art, 73. *Pos:* Dir, Duke Univ-New York Arts Program, currently. *Teaching:* Asst prof art, Duke Univ, 64- *Awards:* Nealie Sullivan Award for Drawing, San Francisco Art Inst, 62; First Purchase Award, NC Mus of Art, NC Art Soc, 72; Duke Univ Outstanding Professor, 73. *Bibliog:* John Russell (auth), article, New York Times, 7/80. *Media:* Acrylic, Oil. *Collection:* Works by William Bailey, Walker Evans, Friedlander, Gillespie, Groover, Hambourg, Lewitt, Wade, Warhol, Zakanitch. *Dealer:* Somerhill Gallery Durham NC; John Weber Gallery New York NY. *Mailing Add:* 416 W Markham Ave Durham NC 27701

PREBLE, MICHAEL ANDREW
CURATOR, ADMINISTRATOR
b Tampa, Fla, July 27, 47. *Study:* Cornell Univ, BA(art hist); Calif State Univ, Dominguez Hills, MA(art hist & mus studies). *Collections Arranged:* William Baziotes Retrospective (auth, catalog introd), Newport Harbor Art Mus, Newport Beach, Calif, 78; Elizabeth Duveneck, 79 & Sculpture, 79, Muckenthaler Cult Ctr, Fullerton, Calif; Theodore Wores Retrospective, Huntsville Mus Art, 80; James Brooks, Paintings and Works on Paper, 1946-1982, 83. *Pos:* Dir, Art Gallery, Mt San Antonio Col, Walnut, Calif, 74-78; exhib supvr, Muckenthaler Cult Ctr, 79; cur exhibs & collections, Huntsville Mus Art, 79-81; cur collections, Portland Mus Art, Maine, 81- *Teaching:* Instr, Portland Sch Art, 82. *Res:* Museum studies; American art, 1940 to present. *Mailing Add:* Portland Mus Art Seven Congress Square Portland ME 04101

PRECHTEL, DON (DONALD CONRAD)
PAINTER
b Los Angeles, Calif, Dec 16, 36. *Study:* Famous Artists Sch, 64. *Work:* Univ Pac, Hist Studies Dept, Stockton, Calif; Pac NW Indian Ctr, Spokane, Wash; Golden Gate Univ, San Francisco; Mt Hood Community Col, Ore. *Exhib:* NW Rendezvous Group, Mont Hist Soc, Helena, 74-81; American Indian/Cowboy Artist, Civic Ctr, San Dimas, Calif, 80; Cowboy and Western Art, State Mus, Munich, Ger, 81; Western Heritage Art Classic, Western Heritage Ctr, Billings, Mont, 82. *Awards:* Judges Comt Award, Mus Native Am Cult/Pac NW Indian Ctr, 78; Purchase Award, Western Art Exhib, Western Art Asn, 79. *Bibliog:* Fred Crafts (auth), article, Eugene Register Guard, 77 & Transitional art, Art West Mag, 80. *Mem:* NW Rendezvous Group, Helena, Mont. *Media:* Oil. *Mailing Add:* 83647 N Pacific Highway Creswell OR 97426

PREIS, ALFRED
ARCHITECT, ADMINISTRATOR
b Vienna, Austria, Feb 2, 11; US citizen. *Study:* Vienna Inst Technol, Archit. *Work:* USS Ariz Mem, Pearl Harbor, Hawaii; Honolulu Zoo Entrance Bldg; First United Methodist Church, Honolulu; Laupahoehoe High & Elementary Sch, Hawaii; Wahiawa Intermediate Sch, Oahu. *Pos:* Designer, Dahl & Conrad, 39-41; designer, Hart Wood, 42-43; principal archit, Alfred Preis, 43-63; state planning coordr, Dept Planning & Econ Develop, 63-67; exec dir, State Found Cult & the Arts, 67-80. *Awards:* Am Church Archit Award, 56; Honor Awards, Am Inst Archit, Hawaii, 52-63. *Mem:* Fel Am Inst Archit (pres, Hawaii Br), 51). *Mailing Add:* 3233 Melemele Pl Honolulu HI 96022

PREKOP, MARTIN DENNIS
SCULPTOR, EDUCATOR
b Toledo, Ohio, July 2, 40. *Study:* Cleveland Inst Art; Cranbrook Acad Art, MFA; RI Sch Design, MFA; Slade Sch Art, London, Eng. *Exhib:* Roof Works, Mus Contemp Art, 72; Art Inst Chicago, 74 & 75; one-man shows, Photographs, Yale Univ, 75, Name Gallery, Chicago, 75; Jan Cicero Gallery, Chicago, 79; LYC Gallery, Cumbria, Eng, 81. *Teaching:* Prof & grad prog chmn painting, sculpture & photog, Art Inst Chicago, 66-, chmn Freshman Found, 70-73 & chmn grad div, 73-77, chmn painting dept, 78-, chmn undergrad div, 82- *Awards:* Fulbright Fel, US State Dept, 65. *Bibliog:* Jan Vendermark (auth), Roof Works Rev, Artforum, 72. *Mailing Add:* c/o Art Inst Chicago S Michigan Ave & E Adams Chicago IL 60603

PREMINGER, MARY G(ARDNER)
SCULPTOR, PAINTER
b Grand Rapids, Mich. *Study:* Kans City Art Mus (scholar); Academie des Beaux Arts, Paris; Univ Calif, Los Angeles with Fritz Faiss. *Work:* Collectors Gallery, Mus Mod Art, New York. *Comn:* Monumental steel sculpture, Sears/Homart Co, Westminister Mall, Calif, 76; functional sculptures, Golden Gate Park, San Francisco, 78; wall sculpture (steel), Great Western Savings, San Francisco, 77; monumental bronze, Taubman Co, Briarwood Mall, Ann Arbor, Mich, 74; bronze sculpture, foote Cone & Belding Corp, Chicago, 73. *Exhib:* West Coast Mus Tour, Fresno Mus Fine Art, 58; Los Angeles Co Mus, Calif, 63; M H De Young Mem Mus, San Francisco, 65; Mus Fine Arts, Denver, 67; Mus Mod Art, New York, 68; Architectural art, Corcoran Gallery, Washington, DC, 73. *Awards:* Honor Award, Golden Gate Park, San Francisco Am Soc Landscape Architects, 78. *Bibliog:* Skira Semeta Watson (auth), Mary Preminger, Art Voices, 5-6/81; and others. *Media:* Oil, Acrylic; Bronze, Steel. *Mailing Add:* 20444 Roca Chica Drive Malibu CA 90265

PRENT, MARK
ENVIRONMENTAL ARTIST, SCULPTOR
b Montreal, PQ, Can, Dec 23, 47. *Study:* Sir George Williams Univ, Montreal, 66-70, BFA, 70, study with John Ivor Smith. *Work:* Art Gallery of Ont, Toronto; Art Bank of Can; Sir George Williams Art Galleries; Musee D'Art Contemporain, Montreal, Que. *Exhib:* Eighth Biennale de Paris, Nat Mus Mod Art, France, 73; one-man show, Musee d'Art Contemporain, Montreal, 79; Birmingham Festival Arts, Ala, 79; 11th Int Sculpture Conf, Dupont Ctr, Cochran Gallery, Washington, DC, 80; Maison Cult Rennes, France, 80-81; Issacs Gallery, Toronto, 81; Art Against Represssion Traveling Exhib, 82-83; and others. *Awards:* Guggenheim Mem Found Fel, 77; Can Coun Sr Arts Award, 78-79, 80-81 & 81-82; Victor M Lynch-Staunton Award, 78. *Bibliog:* Joyce Zeemans (auth), Freedom and the artist, Can Forum, 8/74; Werner Rhode (auth), Mark Prents macabre manipulation, Mag Kunst, No 3, 75; Hartmut Kraft (auth), Antiasthetica 1978, Helmut Braun Kg, Koln, WGer, 78; and others. *Mem:* Can Artists Representatives. *Media:* Polyester Resin, Fiberglass. *Dealer:* Isaacs Gallery 832 Yonge St Toronto ON M4W 2H1 Can. *Mailing Add:* 1610 Sherbrooke St W Apt 54 Montreal PQ H3H 1E1 Canada

PRENTICE, DAVID RAMAGE
PAINTER, PRINTMAKER
b Hartford, Conn, Dec 22, 43. *Study:* Hartford Art Sch. *Work:* Wadsworth Atheneum, Hartford; Yale Univ, New Haven, Conn; Mus Mod Art, New York; Corcoran Gallery Art, Nat Gallery, Washington, DC; Aldrich Mus, Ridgefield, Conn. *Exhib:* One-man shows, Livingstone-Learmonth Gallery, 75, New York & Genesis Gallery, New York, 78; Other Ideas, Detroit Inst Fine Arts, Mich, 69; Prospect, Dusseldorf, Ger, 69; Whitney Mus Am Art Ann, New York, 70; From Los Angeles & other places, Silverman Gallery, Los Angeles, 78. *Teaching:* Guest instr painting, Hartford Art Sch, Univ Hartford, fall 70. *Media:* Acrylic. *Mailing Add:* 654 Broadway New York NY 10012

PRESCOTT, KENNETH WADE
EDUCATOR, WRITER
b Jackson, Mich, Aug 9, 20. *Study:* Western Mich Univ, BS; Univ Del, EdM; Univ Mich, MA & PhD. *Collections Arranged:* Ben Shahn Retrospective Exhib, Nat Mus Mod Art, Tokyo & other Japanese mus (with catalog), 70; Jack Levine Retrospective Exhib, Jewish Mus, New York, 79-80; Burgoyne Diller Exhibs, Meredith Long & Andre Emmerich Gal, 79-81. *Pos:* Dir, Kansas City Mus, Mo, 54-58; managing dir, Acad Nat Sci, Philadelphia, 58-63; dir, NJ State Mus, Trenton, 63-71; prog officer, Div Arts & Humanities, Ford Found, New York, 71-74. *Teaching:* Adj prof changing perspectives in the humanities, Temple Univ, 60-70; prof art & chmn dept, Univ Tex, Austin, 74-84. *Mem:* Tex Asn Schs Art; Am Color Print Soc (hon vpres, 68-71); Col Art Asn Am; Nat Coun Art Adminr (chmn, 79-80); Am Fedn Arts. *Res:* Preparation of catalog resumes on contemporary American artists (Shahn, Levine, Diller & Hunt). *Collection:* Works of contemporary American artists. *Publ:* Auth, Ben Shahn: A Retrospective (catalog), 76-77; auth, Jack Levine: A Retrospective (catalog), 78; auth, Burgoyne Diller 1938-1962, Paintings, Drawings and Collages (catalog), 79; auth, The Prints and Poster of Ben Shahn, 82; auth, The Prints and Posters of Jack Levine, 83. *Mailing Add:* Dept of Art Univ of Tex Austin TX 78712

PRESSLY, NANCY LEE
CURATOR, ADMINISTRATOR
b Suffern, NY, Feb 11, 41. *Study:* Goucher Col, BA, 62; Columbia Univ, with T Reff, L Hawes & O Brendel, MA, 69; Inst Fine Arts, with W Rubin, R Rosenblum & G Schiff, 69-71. *Collections Arranged:* The Pursuit of Happiness: A View of Life in Georgian England (auth, catalog), 77 & The Fuseli: Circle in Rome: Early Romantic Art of 1770s (auth, catalog), 79, Yale Ctr Brit Art; A Birthday Celebration: Recent Gifts and Acquisitions, 1981 (auth, catalog), 82, Salome: La belle dame sans merci (auth, catalog), 83 & Revealed Religion: Benjamin West's Commissions for Windsor Castle and Fonthill Abbey (auth, catalog), 83, San Antonio Mus Art. *Pos:* Cataloguer Am art, Metrop Mus Art, New York, 69-71; assoc res & asst cur, Yale Ctr Brit Art, 71-79; chief cur, San Antonio Mus Art, 81- *Bibliog:* Hilton Kraemer (auth), Henry Fuseli: A leader in Romanticism, Sunday New York Times, 9/16/79; John Ashbery (auth), Dark satanic mills, New York Mag, 10/6/79; Gert Schiff (auth), article, Arts Mag, 12/79. *Mem:* Col Art Asn; Am Asn Mus; Soc 18th Century Studies. *Publ:* Auth, Whistler in America: An album of early drawings, Metrop Mus J, 72; auth, James Jefferys and the Masks of the Giants, Burlington Mag, 4/77; auth, Guy Head and his Echo Flying from Narcissus: A British artist in Rome in the 1790s, Bulletin Detroit Inst Arts, 82. *Mailing Add:* 332 Prinz Dr San Antonio TX 78213

PRESSLY, WILLIAM LAURENS, JR
HISTORIAN, EDUCATOR
b Chattanooga, Tenn, Apr 1, 44. *Study:* Princeton Univ, BA, 66; Inst Fine Arts, New York Univ, PhD, 73. *Teaching:* Assoc prof 18th-20th century European art, Yale Univ, 73-82, sr lectr, Univ Tex, Austin, spring 82 & 83. *Awards:* Morse Fel, Yale Univ, 75-76; Guggenheim Memorial Fel, 83-84. *Mem:* Fel Royal Soc Arts, London; The Am Soc for Eighteenth Century Studies; Col Art Asn. *Publ:* Auth, Samuel Palmer and the Pastoral Convention, Record of the Art Mus, Princeton Univ, Vol 28, 69; auth, The praying mantis in surrealist art, Art Bull, 12/73; auth, A portrait of Joseph Nollekens reattributed to John Francis Rigaud, Connoisseur, 2/78; auth, The Life and Art of James Barry, Yale Univ Press; auth, James Barry: The Artist as Hero, Tate Gallery, London, 83. *Mailing Add:* 332 Prinz Drive San Antonio TX 78213

PRESTINI, JAMES LIBERO
SCULPTOR, DESIGNER
b Waterford, Conn, Jan 13, 08. *Study:* Yale Univ, BS, 30, Sch Educ, 32; Univ Stockholm, with Carl Malmsten, 38; Inst Design, Chicago, with L Moholy-Nagy, 39; also study in Italy, 53-56. *Work:* Nat Collection Fine Arts, Smithsonian Inst, Washington, DC; San Francisco Mus Art; Brooklyn Mus, New York; and others. *Comn:* Aluminum sculpture, R S Reynolds Mem Sculpture Award, Richmond, Va, 72. *Exhib:* James Prestini, Sculpture from Structural Steel Elements, San Francisco Mus Art, 69; James Prestini, Art Inst Chicago, 69; Excellence: Art from the University, Univ Calif, Berkeley, 70; International Collection of 20th Century Design, Mus Mod Art, New York, 72; Twentieth Century Accessions 1967-1974, Metrop Mus Art, New York, 74; Philadelphia Mus Art, 79; Mus Fine Arts, Boston, 80; Brooklyn Mus, 81. *Teaching:* Instr design, Lake Forest Acad, 33-42 & Inst Design, Chicago, 39-46 & 52-53; assoc res & asst cur, NTex State Univ, 42-43; prof design, Univ Calif, Berkeley, 56-, res prof, Creative Arts Inst, 67-68 & Bauhaus-Archiv, WBerlin, 77. *Awards:* Guggenheim Fel for Sculpture, 72-73; Award for Excellence in Fine Art in Steel, Am Iron & Steel Inst, New York, 71; Univ Calif Berkeley Award, 75. *Bibliog:* Edgar Kaufmann (auth), Prestini's Art in Wood, Pantheon, 50; Gerald Nordland (auth), James Prestini, Sculpture from Structural Steel Elements, San Francisco Mus Art, 69; George Staempfli (auth), James Prestini, Recent Sculpture, Staempfli Gallery, 71 & 74. *Mem:* Life fel Metrop Mus Art. *Media:* Steel, Aluminum, Wood. *Publ:* Co-auth, The Place of Scientific Research in Design, 48; co-auth, Research in Low-cost Seating for Homes, 48; co-auth, Survey on Construction Materials Demonstration & Training Center, 51; auth, Survey of Italian Furniture Industry (Milan), 54; auth, Proposed policy statement on architectural research for the College of Architecture of the University of California, Berkeley, 58. *Mailing Add:* 2324 Blake St Berkeley CA 94704

PRESTON, GEORGE NELSON
HISTORIAN, EDUCATOR
b Dec 14, 38; US citizen. *Study:* City Col New York, BA, 62; Columbia Univ, MA, 68, PhD, 73. *Collections Arranged:* African Art: Rare and Familiar Forms (auth, catalog), State Univ New York Art Gallery, Potsdam, 76; The Innovative African Artist (auth, catalog), Ithaca Col Mus Art; Permanent Installation, African Hall, Brooklyn Mus, 66-78; Ancient Terracottas of Ghana and Mali (with catalog), 81-82. *Pos:* Spec consult, Brooklyn Mus, 68. *Teaching:* Asst prof art, Rutgers Univ, Livingston Col, 70-72; asst prof art, City Col, City Univ New York, 72-80, assoc prof, 81- *Awards:* Fels, Ford Found, 68-70 & 72 & Kress Found, 69; Res Award, Res Found City Univ New York, 81-82. *Mem:* Columbia Univ Seminar Primitive & Pre-Columbian Art; Washington Hq Asn, New York (bd dirs, 79-); Int Asn Art Critics. *Res:* Conceptual and culture historical aspects of African art; contemporary American artists whose styles are outside the definition of the most popular isms. *Publ:* Auth, Dynamic/Static, African Art as Philosophy, Interbook, New York, 74; auth, Jay Milder: Painter of discovery, resolution and rediscovery, 11/76 & auth, Against the grain: The paintings of Ann Tabachnik, 2/79, Arts Mag; auth, Reading the art of Benin, Images of Power: Royal Court Art of Benin, New York Univ, 81. *Mailing Add:* c/o Art Dept City Col City Univ New York New York NY 10031

PRESTON, MALCOLM H
CRITIC, PAINTER
b West New York, NJ, May 25, 19. *Study:* Univ Wis, BA; Columbia Univ, MA & PhD. *Work:* Hofstra Univ Collection; Dayton Art Inst; Hofstra Univ; Portland Mus; Living Arts Found, New York. *Exhib:* Kendall Gallery; Tower Gallery; Linden Gallery; Kendall Gallery; Himelfarb Gallery; Benson Gallery; and others. *Pos:* Dir, Inst Arts, Hofstra Univ, 60-64; art critic, Newsday, 68-; art critic, Boston Herald Traveler, 70-72. *Teaching:* Asst instr fine arts, New Sch Social Res, 40-41; instr fine arts, Adelphi Univ, 47-48; prof

fine arts, Hofstra Univ, 49-74. *Awards:* Joe & Emily Lowe Found Educ Res Grant, 50; Ford Found Grant, 56 & 57; Shell Oil Res Grant, 64. *Media:* Oil. *Publ:* Contribr, Christian Sci Monitor, Boston Globe & other mag & newspapers; writer, producer & principal performer, Arts Around Us & American Art Today (Ford Found-sponsored nat educ television series), 55-56. *Dealer:* Linden Gallery 11 E 57th St New York NY ; Customs House Gallery Wellfleet MA. *Mailing Add:* Box 182 Truro MA 02666

PRESTOPINO, GREGORIO
PAINTER
b New York, NY, June 29, 07. *Study:* Nat Acad Design. *Work:* Whitney Mus Am Art, New York; Walker Art Ctr, Minneapolis, Minn; Joseph H Hirshhorn Collection, Washington, DC; Art Inst Chicago; NJ State Mus, Trenton. *Comn:* Mosaic, comn by Dr Rebecca Notterman, Prof Bldg, Princeton. *Exhib:* Whitney Mus Am Art, Am Painting Ann, 45; Mus Mod Art, New York; Pa Acad Fine Arts, Philadelphia; Corcoran Gallery Art, Washington, DC; Phillips Acad, Andover, Mass. *Teaching:* Instr painting, Brooklyn Mus Sch, 46-51; artist in residence, Mich State Univ, 60. *Awards:* B Altman Figure Painting Award, 72 & William A Paton Prize, 77, Nat Acad Design; Emily Goldsmith Award, Am Watercolor Soc, 77; and others. *Bibliog:* J Hubley (auth), Harlem Wednesday (film), Storyboard, Inc, 56; J G Smith (auth), Watercolors of Gregorio Prestopino, Am Artist, 10/57. *Mem:* MacDowell Colony (dir, 71); academician Nat Acad Design. *Media:* Oil, Watercolor. *Dealer:* Midtown Galleries Inc 11 E 57th St New York NY 10003. *Mailing Add:* Roosevelt NJ 08555

PRETSCH, JOHN EDWARD
CARTOONIST, ILLUSTRATOR
b Philadelphia, Pa, Apr 14, 25. *Pos:* Sun supplement, news & promotional layout artist, Philadelphia Bulletin, 47-63, news, ed & advert artist, 66-80; advert layout artist, Sears Roebuck & Co, 63-66; dir, Pretsch Art Serv, 80- *Publ:* Illusr, Five Years, Five Countries, Five Campaigns with the 141st Infantry Regiment, 45; illusr cartoons, Colliers, Sat Eve Post & Philadelphia Bulletin. *Mailing Add:* 4337 H St Philadelphia PA 19124

PREUSS, ROGER
PAINTER, WRITER
b Waterville, Minn, Jan 29, 22. *Study:* Minneapolis Col Art & Design, BFA. *Work:* Nat Wildlife Gallery, Washington, DC; Mont Hist Soc Mus, Helena; Smithsonian Hall Philately, Washington, DC; Mont State Univ, Missoula; US Fed Bldg & Minn State Capitol, St Paul; and others. *Comn:* 1949-50 Fed Duck Stamp Design, US Dept Interior, Washington, DC, 48; 16 painting wildlife series, Shedd-Brown Collection, Minneapolis, 50; 150 paintings of wildlife, Thos D Murphy Co, Red Oak, Iowa, 54; 72 paintings, The Haas Corp, Sleepy Eye, Minn, 73; Commemorative Centennial Pheasant Stamp Design, 81; and others. *Exhib:* Minneapolis Inst of Arts, 49; Mont Hist Soc Mus, Helena, 64; Inst Contemp Arts, London, 68; Harris Fine Arts Ctr, Brigham Young Univ, Provo, 69; Animal Artists, Grand Cent Art Galleries, New York, NY, 72; one-man shows, US Bicentennial Exhib, Le Sueur Co Hist Soc Mus, Elysian, Minn, 76; and many others. *Teaching:* Sem lectr wildlife painting, Minneapolis Col Art. *Awards:* Fed Duck Stamp Design Award, US Fish & Wildlife Serv, 49; named US Bicentennial Wildlife Artist, Am Heritage Asn, 76; Knight of Mark Twain, Mark Twain Soc, 78. *Bibliog:* Vivian A Paladin (auth), Roger Preuss: Delineator and defender of the wild, Art W, 11/80 & 12/82; Bob Bushnell (auth), Roger Preuss: King of the wildlife artists, Sports & Recreation, 9/81; and others. *Mem:* Soc Animal Artists; fel Int Inst Arts; Minn Artists Asn (dir & vpres, 53-56); Deep Portage Conserv Found (bd dirs, 77-); found charter mem Wildlife Artists World. *Media:* Oil, Watercolor. *Publ:* Auth & illusr, The official wildlife of America calendar, 53-; auth & illusr, Outdoor Horizons, 57; auth & illusr, American game birds, 64; illusr, Twilight over the wilderness, 71; contribr/illusr, Nat Wildlife, Country Gentleman, The Farmer, Western Can Outdoors, Colliers, Sports Afield, Today's Art & many other nat periodicals & ltd ed prints by Wildlife Am. *Dealer:* Wildlife of America Box 556-WA Minneapolis MN 55440. *Mailing Add:* 2224 Grand Ave Minneapolis MN 55405

PREUSSER, ROBERT ORMEROD
PAINTER, EDUCATOR
b Houston, Tex, Nov 13, 19. *Study:* Pvt study with McNeill Davidson, Houston, 30-39; Inst Design, Chicago, 39-40 & 41-42; Newcomb Sch Art, Tulane Univ, 40-41; Art Ctr Sch, Los Angeles, 46-47. *Work:* Mus Fine Arts, Houston; Contemp Arts Mus, Houston, Witte Mem Mus, San Antonio, Tex; Tex Christian Univ, Ft Worth; Addison Gallery Am Art, Andover, Mass. *Exhib:* Directions in American Painting, Carnegie Inst, Pittsburgh, 41; Int Watercolor Exhib, Art Inst of Chicago, 42, Abstract & Surrealist American Exhib, 47 & Am Artists Ann, 51; Fifth Biennial Contemp American Exhib, 46; Contemp American Artists Ann, 46 & 47; Gulf-Caribbean Exhib, Houston Mus of Fine Arts Circulating Exhib, 56-57; Survey of American Painting, Am Fedn Arts Circulating Exhib, 57-58; Texas Painting & Sculpture--the 20th Century, Owens Arts Ctr Circulating Exhib, Dallas, 71-72. *Pos:* Art ed, Tex Cancer Bull, 48-50; co-dir, Contemp Arts Mus, Houston, 49-51; stage set designer, Tex Stage, Houston, 50-51; assoc cur educ, Mus Fine Arts, Houston, 52-54; dir educ, Ctr Advan Visual Studies, Mass Inst Technol, 74-; co-ed, Leonardo, 74- *Teaching:* Instr painting, Houston Mus Fine Arts Sch, 47-54; instr painting, Univ Houston, 51-54; prof visual design, Mass Inst Technol, 54-; instr drawing, Harvard Univ Grad Sch Design, 55-56. *Awards:* Purchase Prize, 16th Ann Houston Artists Exhib, Mus Fine Arts, Houston, 40; Contemp Arts Mus Purchase Prize, 27th Ann Houston Artists Exhib, 52. *Bibliog:* Ralph M Pearson (auth), Chap 3, In: The Modern Renaissance in American Art, Harper & Row, 54; Vision in engineering (interview), Int Sci & Technol, 10/65. *Media:* Mixed Media. *Publ:* Auth, Visual education for

science & engineering students, In: Education of Vision, Braziller, 65, Fr & Ger ed, 67; auth, Art & the engineer, Mech Eng, 12/67; auth, Relation of art to science and technology: an educational experiment at MIT, Leonardo, Vol 6, No 3, 73; auth, Revitalizing art & humanizing technology: an educational challenge, Impact, Vol 24, No 1, 74; auth, Coloured illumination and the environment, in: Colour for Architecture, Studio Vista, 76. *Mailing Add:* 2 Willard St Ct Cambridge MA 02138

PREZIOSI, DONALD A
HISTORIAN, CRITIC
b New York, NY, Jan 12, 41. *Study:* Fairfield Col, BA, 62; Harvard Univ, MA, 63, PhD, 68. *Teaching:* Asst prof art hist, Yale Univ, 67-73 & Mass Inst Technol, 73-77; assoc prof, State Univ NY, Binghamton, 78- *Awards:* Fels, Nat Endowment Humanities, 73-74, Ctr Advan Study Visual Arts, Nat Gallery, 81-82 & Ctr Advan Study, Stanford Univ, 83-84. *Mem:* Col Art Asn Am; Archaeol Inst Am; Semiotic Soc Am (vpres, 83-84, pres, 84-85). *Res:* Ancient art and architecture; contemporary theory and criticism. *Publ:* Auth, The Semiotics of the Built Environment, Ind Univ Press, 79; auth, Architecture, Language and Meaning, 79 & Minoan Architectural Design, 83, Mouton; auth, Constru(ct)ing the origins of art, Art J, 83. *Mailing Add:* Dept Art & Art Hist State Univ NY Binghamton NY 13901

PRIBBLE, EASTON
PAINTER, INSTRUCTOR
b Falmouth, Ky, July 31, 17. *Study:* Univ Cincinnati. *Work:* Whitney Mus Am Art, New York; Munson-Williams-Proctor Inst, Utica; Hirshhorn Mus, Washington, DC; Parrish Mus, Southampton, NY; State Univ NY. *Comn:* Painted wood relief mural, Munson-Williams-Proctor Inst Sch Art, 61; painted wood relief mural, Oneida Co Off Bldg, NY, 69. *Exhib:* Whitney Ann Am Painting, Whitney Mus Am Art, 50, 54 & 55; Univ Nebr Ann, Lincoln, 56; Everson Mus, Syracuse, 63; Retrospective Exhib, Munson-Williams-Proctor Inst Mus Art, 76; one-man exhib, Munson Williams Proctor Inst Mus, 82. *Teaching:* Instr painting, Munson-Williams-Proctor Inst Sch Art, 57-; instr hist art, Utica Col, 60-73. *Awards:* Painting Award, Everson Mus, 60 & 64; Painting Award, Munson-Williams-Proctor Inst, 63. *Media:* Oil, Acrylic, Pastel. *Publ:* Contribr, Contemporary American culture, Chicago Rev, 54; contribr, New talent in America, Art Am, 56. *Mailing Add:* Munson-Williams-Proctor Inst 310 Genesee St Utica NY 13502

PRICE, ANNE KIRKENDALL
CRITIC
b Birch Tree, Mo, June 14, 22. *Study:* Univ Mo, Columbia, BJ; Univ Ga, Athens, art seminars; Southern Regional Educ Bd workshop for art critics. *Pos:* Art critic, Morning Advocate, Baton Rouge, La, 60- *Awards:* Award for Arts Coverage, La Coun Music & Performing Art, 74; Communicator of the Yr Award, Pub Relations Soc La, 78. *Mem:* Capitol Corresp (pres, 68); Baton Rouge Arts Coun. *Mailing Add:* c/o Morning Advocate 525 Lafayette Baton Rouge LA 70802

PRICE, BARBARA GILLETTE
ADMINISTRATOR, PAINTER
b Philadelphia, Pa, June 26, 38. *Study:* Univ Ala, BFA, 66, MA, 68. *Work:* Univ Ala, Tuscaloosa; Dept Health, Educ & Welfare N Portal Bldg, DC; Ferris State Col, MI. *Exhib:* One-person shows, Univ Ala Gallery Art, Tuscaloosa, 68, Works on Paper, Cranbrook Acad Art Mus, Bloomfield Hills, Mich, 80 & Ferris State Art Gallery, Big Rapids, Mich, 81; Washington Painting, Rutgers Univ Mus Art Gallery, NJ, 75; The Genius of Corcoran, Corcoran Gallery Art, DC, 76; Col Notre Dame, 83; and others. *Pos:* Dean, Cranbrook Acad Art, 78-82; vpres, Acad Affairs, Maryland Inst, Col Art, 82- *Teaching:* Asst prof art, Corcoran Sch Art, DC, 70-78, dir summer prog, 75-78. *Mem:* Nat Coun Art Adminr; Col Art Asn; NASAD. *Media:* Oil, Acrylics, Mixed-Media. *Publ:* Ed, Sculpture at Cranbrook (catalog), Cranbrook Acad Art Mus, 79; ed, Spiritscapes (catalog), Ferris State Col, 81. *Mailing Add:* Md Inst Col Art 1300 Mt Royal Ave Baltimore MD 21217

PRICE, GEORGE
CARTOONIST
b Coytesville, NJ, June 9, 01. *Pos:* Cartoonist & bk illusr. *Publ:* Auth of 10 books & illusr of 24 books; illusr, Life, Vogue, New York Times, Forbes and others. *Mailing Add:* 81 Westervelt Ave Tenafly NJ 07670

PRICE, JOAN WEBSTER
ENVIRONMENTAL ARTIST, SCULPTOR
b Camden, NJ, Jan 8, 31. *Study:* Tyler Sch Art, Temple Univ, BFA, 54; Columbia Univ, MA, 58, EdD, 71. *Exhib:* Abstraction in Action, Am Abstract Artists, City Gallery, 82; On and Off the Wall, Women's Caucus Art NJ, Newark Mus, 82; Am Abstract Artists Exhib, Weatherspoon Gallery, Greensboro, NC, 83; Am Abstract Artists Exhib, Art Gallery, Univ Ala, 83; Modern Mythology, Fordham Univ, 83-85. *Collections Arranged:* University Artists/Teachers (auth, catalog), Bronx Mus Art, 76; Women Artists 78, City Univ New York Grad Ctr, 78; Works on Paper Am Abstract Artists, Betty Parsons Gallery, 79. *Pos:* Vpres & bd gov, Inst Study Art in Educ, 76-78. *Teaching:* Asst prof painting & design, Suffolk Community Col, NY, 65-67; lectr art educ, Queens Col, NY, 67-68; prof environmental art, City Col New York, 68- *Bibliog:* Stephen P Breslow (auth), Art/price show has its own energy, Staten Island Advance, 9/24/81; Palmer Paromer (auth), article, Artspeak, 1/12/82; Irene Rousseau (auth), Abstraction in action, American abstract artists, Arts Mag, 5/82. *Mem:* Am Abstract Artists; Women's Caucus Art; Col Art Asn; Univ Coun Art Educ; New York City Art Teachers Asn. *Media:* All. *Publ:* Auth, A Response for an Environmental Response Center, NY State Arts & Humanities, 71; auth, VTR/The Observed and the Observer, NY State Publ, 75; auth, Light Boxes, NY State Art Teachers, 75; coauth, Sun altar, Landscape Archit, 11/80. *Mailing Add:* 35 Ridgewood Terrace Maplewood NJ 07040

PRICE, JOE (ALLEN)
SERIGRAPHER, INSTRUCTOR
b Ferriday, La, Feb 6, 35. *Study:* Northwestern Univ, Evanston, Ill, BS, 57; Art Ctr Col Design, Los Angeles, with Glenn Vilppu, 67-68; Stanford Univ, Calif, MA, 70. *Work:* Philadelphia Mus Art, Pa; New Orleans Mus Art, La; Oakland Mus Art, Calif; Huntsville Mus Art, Ala; San Francisco Mus Mod Art; and others. *Exhib:* Int Triennal Colored Graphics, Haldenschuhaus, Grenchen, Switzerland, 79; Int Print Biennale, Nat Mus Cracovie, Poland, 78 & 80; Miami Int Print Biennale, Metrop Mus, Fla, 80; Great Gifts, Oakland Mus Art, Calif, 80; The Familiar Eye, Huntsville Mus Art, Ala, 81. *Teaching:* Prof studio drawing, Col San Mateo, Calif, 70- *Awards:* Louis Lozowick Mem Award, Audubon Artists 36th Ann, 78; Lessing J Rosenwald Prize, Philadelphia Print Club Int, 79; Kempshall Clark Purchase Award, 17th Bradley Nat Print Exhib, Peoria Art Guild, 81. *Bibliog:* Duane Wakeham (auth), Joe Price: serigraphs in light and tone, Am Artist, 10/77; Tom Cervenak (auth), Bay area printmakers, Visual Dialog, spring 78. *Mem:* Calif Soc Printmakers; Los Angeles Printmaking Soc; Boston Printmakers; Am Color Print Soc; Assoc mem Audubon Artists. *Media:* Serigraphy. *Dealer:* Editions Limited West Gallery 1 Market Plaza San Francisco CA 94105. *Mailing Add:* 2031 Belle Monti Belmont CA 94002

PRICE, KENNETH
PRINTMAKER, SCULPTOR
b Los Angeles, Calif, 1935. *Study:* Univ Calif; Otis Art Inst; Chouinard Art Inst; Univ Southern Calif, BFA, 56; State Univ NY Albany, MFA, 58. *Work:* Los Angeles Co Mus Art. *Exhib:* Two-man shows, 66 & American Sculpture of the Sixties, 67, Los Angeles Co Mus Art; Ten from Los Angeles, Seattle Art Mus, 66; Whitney Mus Am Art, New York, 72; Mus Mod Art, New York, 71; Philadelphia Mus Art, 72; Ronald Greenberg Gallery, St Louis, 76; James Corcoran Gallery, Los Angeles, Calif, 76; Los Angeles Co Mus Art, 78; Gallery Contemp Art, Taos, NMex, 78; Tex Gallery, Houston, 79; Stedelijk Mus, Netherlands, 80; Whitney Mus Am Art, 80; and many others. *Awards:* Tamarind Fel, 68-69. *Bibliog:* Thomas Hess (auth), Art, New York Mag, 12/74; Judith Tannenbaum (auth), Kenneth Price--Willard, Arts Mag, 2/75; Kenneth Price at Willard, Art in Am, 5-6/75. *Dealer:* Willard Gallery 29 E 72nd St New York NY 10021. *Mailing Add:* Box 1356 Taos NM 87571

PRICE, LESLIE KENNETH
PAINTER, EDUCATOR
b New York, NY. *Study:* Sch Visual Arts, NY, 63-64; Pratt Inst, with James Gahagan, Ernest Briggs, G Laderman, BFA, 69; Mills Col, Oakland, Calif, MFA, 71. *Work:* Oakland Mus, Calif; Johnson Publ Co, Chicago. *Exhib:* Blacks USA, New York Cult Ctr, 73; New Directions in Afro-Am Art, Cornell Univ, Ithaca, NY, 74; Berkeley Art Ctr, Calif, 76; San Jose Mus, Calif, 76; Studio Mus in Harlem, NY, 77. *Teaching:* From assoc prof painting to prof art, Humboldt State Univ, Arcata, Calif, 72- *Awards:* Painting Award, Pratt Inst, 68; Award of Merit, Calif Palace Legion Honor, 73; Honorarium, Cornell Univ, 74. *Bibliog:* Alfred Frankenstein (auth), article, San Francisco Chronicle, 11/77. *Mem:* Nat Conf of Artists. *Media:* Acrylic, Graphite. *Publ:* Contribr, Black Artists on Art, Vol II, Contemporary Crafts, 72; contribr, Existance Black, Southern Ill Univ, 72; contribr, Directions in Afro-American Art, Cornell Univ, 74. *Mailing Add:* 3414 Fernway Arcata CA 95521

PRICE, MICHAEL BENJAMIN
SCULPTOR, EDUCATOR
b Chicago, Ill, Oct 21, 40. *Study:* Univ Ill, Urbana-Champaign, with Frank Gallo, AB, 63, MA, 64; Tulane Univ, MFA(sculpture). *Work:* Art Gallery Mus, Mobile, Ala; Hamline Univ Gallery; Gov Mansion, St Paul. *Comn:* St Johns of the Cross Church, Western Springs, Ill; Plymouth Congregational Church, Minneapolis, Minn; Morris Arboretum, Philadelphia; Ursinus Col, Collegeville, Pa; and many pvt comn. *Exhib:* One-man shows, Vincent Price Gallery, Chicago, 69 & Krasner Gallery, New York, 73-74, 76-77 & 80; Encounter V, Minn Mus Art, St Paul, 71; Living American Artists and the Figure, Mus Art, Pa State Univ, University Park, 74; Esculturas, Maison Bernard, Caracas, Venezuela, 75; Copper & Graphite, Friends Gallery, Minneapolis Inst Art, 78; C G Rein Gallery, Scottsdale, Ariz, 79. *Teaching:* Instr sculpture, Univ Ala, Huntsville, 66; assoc prof sculpture, drawing & art hist, Hamline Univ, 70-, chmn art dept, 80- *Awards:* Purchase Prize, Gulf Coast Art Exhib, 68. *Media:* Cast Bronze. *Dealer:* Krasner Gallery 1043 Madison Ave New York NY 10021; C G Rein Galleries Scottsdale AZ & Minneapolis MN. *Mailing Add:* 1954 Laurel Ave St Paul MN 55104

PRICE, ROSALIE PETTUS
PAINTER
b Birmingham, Ala. *Study:* Birmingham-Southern Col, AB; Univ Ala, MA. *Work:* Birmingham Mus Art, South Trust Bank, Bell South, Spain Ctr Collection, Univ Ala, Birmingham; Springfield Art Mus, Mo. *Exhib:* Nat Watercolor Soc Ann, 45-48 & 70; Am Watercolor Soc, Nat Acad Design, New York, 47; Watercolor & Print Exhib, Pa Acad Fine Arts, Philadelphia, 48; solo shows, Birmingham Mus Art, Ala, 66, 73 & 82-83; 35th Ann Midyear Show, Butler Inst Am Art, Youngstown, Ohio, 70; Ann Drawing & Small Sculpture Show, Ball State Univ, Muncie, Ind, 72, 74 & 78-82; Rocky Mountain Nat, Golden, Colo, 74 & 80; Audubon Artists Ann, New York, 81; and others. *Awards:* W Alden Brown Mem Prize, Nat Soc Painters in Casein, 70; Purchase Award, Watercolor USA, 72; Joseph A Cain Mem Prize, Nat Soc Painters Casein & Acrylic, 83. *Mem:* Nat Watercolor Soc; Watercolor Soc Ala (secy, 48-49); La Watercolor Soc; Birmingham Art Asn (pres, 47-49); Nat Soc Painters Casein & Acrylic. *Media:* Acrylic, Oil. *Mailing Add:* 300 Windsor Dr Birmingham AL 35209

PRICE, VINCENT
COLLECTOR, DEALER
b St Louis, Mo, May 27, 11. *Study:* Yale Univ, BA, 33; Univ London, Courtauld Inst, 34-35; Ohio Wesleyan, Hon LLD; Calif Col Arts & Crafts, Hon DFA; Columbia Col, Hon DFA. *Pos:* Founder, Mod Inst Art, 45; former pres, Univ Calif, Los Angeles Art Coun; dir, Vincent Price Art Gallery; former mem bd, Archives Am Art; mem, Whitney Mus Friends Am Art; mem, US Indian Arts & Crafts Bd; former mem fine arts comt, White House; bd dir, Ctr Arts of Indian Affairs; adv comt, Friends of Art, Univ Southern Calif; art consult, Sears Roebuck & Co. *Mem:* Royal Soc Art; Indian Arts & Crafts Bd, Dept Interior (chmn, 68-72). *Publ:* Auth, Vincent Price on art, syndicated column, Chicago Tribune, 3 yrs; auth, many articles on art in nat mags & newspapers; auth, I Like What I Know, The Book of Joe & Treasury of American Art; co-ed (with Ferdinand V Delacroix), Drawings of Delacroix; plus others. *Mailing Add:* 315 S Beverly Dr Beverly Hills CA 90212

PRIEST, HARTWELL WYSE
PAINTER, PRINTMAKER
b Brantford, Ont, Jan 1, 01; US citizen. *Study:* Smith Col, 24; Paris-Atelier, with Andre L'Hote; also with Hans Hofmann, New York. *Work:* Libr Congress; Neward Pub Libr; Smith Col Art Mus Pvt Collection; Univ Maine; Hunt Botanical Libr, Richmond Mus Fine Art; and others. *Comn:* Murals, Children's Ward, Univ Va Hosp, Charlottesville, 55; flowers & woodland scene for ann report, Hunt Botanical Libr, Pittsburgh, 71. *Exhib:* Nat Asn Women Artists Ann, 44-; Soc Am Graphic Artists Ann, 56-; Nat Asn Women Artists Foreign Exhib, Palazzo Vechio, Florence, Italy, 72; solo shows, Pen & Brush, 73 & McGaffey Art Ctr, Charlottesville, Va, 84; and others. *Teaching:* Instr, Va Art Inst, 69-75. *Awards:* Edna Stauffer Mem Prize for Etching, 77; First Painting Award, 79 & First Graphics Award, 82, Blue Ridge Sch An Exhib; and others. *Mem:* Nat Asn Women Artists; Soc Am Graphic Artists; Washington Printmakers; Pen & Brush. *Mailing Add:* 41 Old Farm Rd Charlottesville VA 22901

PRIEST, T (THERESA KHOURY STRUCKUS)
PAINTER, PRINTMAKER
b Worcester, Mass, Jan 20, 28. *Study:* Worcester Art Mus Sch, Mass, 47-48; Quinsigamond Community Col, Worcester, 72 & 73; Univ Mass, Amherst, BFA(painting), 75, MFA(painting), 77. *Work:* Worcester Art Mus, Mass; Aldrich Mus Contemp Art, Ridgefield, Conn; DeCordova Mus, Lincoln, Mass; Bundy Art Ctr, Waitsfield, Vt; Brockton Art Mus; and others. *Comn:* Three color serigraph, Worcester Art Mus, 77; ltd ed print, Holy Cross Col, Worcester, 81; and others. *Exhib:* New Eng Women, DeCrodova Mus, Lincoln, 75; Painting Invitational, Brockton Art Ctr, Mass, 75; one-person shows, Drawings, Worcester Art Mus, Mass, 76 & Washington World Gallery, Washington, DC, 81; Paperworks, Hudson River Mus, New York, 80; and others. *Pos:* Color integrated sem, Hampshire Col, Amherst, Mass, 75. *Teaching:* Asst prof intermediate painting, visual design & color, Col Holy Cross, Worcester. *Awards:* Kinnicutt Travel Award, Worcester Art Mus, 74; Charles & Roseanna Batchelor Summer Fel, Holy Cross Col, Worcester, 81; Res & Publ Award, Holy Cross Col, 82. *Bibliog:* Nina Kaiden & Bartlett Hayes (auth), Artist and Advocate, Renaissance, 67. *Mem:* Boston Visual Artists Union; Col Art Asn. *Media:* Acrylic, Oil; Silkscreen. *Dealer:* Gallery at Oui Boston MA 02109; Thronja Art Gallery Springfield MA. *Mailing Add:* 5 Pratt St Worcester MA 01609

PRINCE, ARNOLD
SCULPTOR, EDUCATOR
b Basseterre, West Indies, Apr 17, 25. *Study:* Brit Coun with John Harrison, Jose DeGreeft, William Zorach, John Hovvannes; Art Students League. *Work:* First Vest Pocket Park, New York; Art Students League. *Comn:* Concrete sculpture, City North Adams, Mass, 68; gate post sculpture, Spruces Residential Park, 72; concrete sculpture, comn by Robert Potrin, Stamford, Vt, 73. *Exhib:* St Marks on the Bowery, 64; Sculptors Guild Exhib, 69-; Slide Show Collection of Afro-Am Artists, Univ Ala, 71; Boston Pub Libr, 73; one-man show, RI Sch Design, 75. *Teaching:* Dir sculpture educ, Fed Govt Poverty Proj Harlem, HARYOU, 64-67; adj prof sculpture, North Adams State Col, 70-72; asst prof fine arts & sculpture, RI Sch Design, 72-82. *Bibliog:* Article in Village Voice, 12/65; article in NAdams Transcript, 66-71. *Mem:* Sculptors Guild NY. *Media:* Wood, Stone. *Dealer:* Sculptors Guild Inc 75 Rockefeller Plaza New York NY 10020. *Mailing Add:* 207 Wickenden St Providence RI 02903

PRINCE, RICHARD EDMUND
SCULPTOR, EDUCATOR
b Comox, BC, Apr 6, 49. *Study:* Univ BC, BA(art hist), 71 & study, 72-73; Emma Lake Artists Workshop, Sask, with Ron Kitaj, 70. *Work:* Nat Gallery Can, Ottawa; Vancouver Art Gallery, BC; Govt of BC, Victoria Art Collection; Can Coun Art Bank, Ottawa; Vancouver Art Collection, Can; and others. *Exhib:* One-man shows, Issacs Gallery, Toronto, 78 & 82 & Figure Structures, Burnaby Art Gallery, BC, 79; A New Decade: Vancouver, Alta Col Art Gallery, Calgary, 79; Agnes Etherington Arts Centre, Kingston, Ont, 81; Vancouver Heritage, Vancouver Art Mus, 81-83; and others. *Teaching:* Instr sculpture, Vancouver Community Col, BC, 74-75; instr fine arts & sculpture, Univ BC, 75-; vis lectr sculpture, Univ of BC, 77-78; asst prof sculpture, 78-83, assoc prof, 83- *Awards:* Art Vancouver for 74 Award, City of Vancouver, 74; Can Coun Arts Grant, Govt Can, 75; Can Coun Arts Grant, 77-78. *Bibliog:* Joan Lowndes (auth), Richard Prince: bringing the outdoors in, Artscanada, Toronto, 10-11/78; Arthur Perry (auth), Richard Prince: figure structures, Vanguard Vancouver, BC, 11/79; and others. *Mem:* Life mem Royal Can Acad; Univ Art Asn Can. *Media:* Multimedia. *Dealer:* Equinox Galleries Penthouse 1525 W Eighth Ave Vancouver BC Can. *Mailing Add:* 285 W 18th Ave Vancouver BC V5Y 2A8 Canada

PRINTZ, BONNIE ALLEN
PHOTOGRAPHER, PAINTER
b Luray, Va. *Study:* Va Commonwealth Univ, Richmond, BFA, 68; Hunter Col, New York, MA, 70. *Work:* Baltimore Mus Art; Corcoran Gallery Art, Washington, DC. *Exhib:* Open Space Gallery, Victoria, BC, 78; Baltimore Mus Art, 78-80 & 83; Blue Sky Gallery, Portland, Ore, 79; Corcoran Gallery Art, Washington, DC, 79 & 82; William Penn Mem Mus, Harrisburg, Pa, 79-80 & 82; Va Mus Fine Arts, Richmond, 80; D H Dalsheimer Gallery Ltd, Baltimore, 83. *Pos:* Tech asst spec collections, Mus Mod Art, New York, 68-70. *Teaching:* Instr fine arts, Md Inst, Col Art, Baltimore, 72-73, 76 & 79. *Awards:* Departmental Award, Va Commonwealth Univ, 68; Fel, Va Mus Fine Arts, 79-80; First Place, Women Arts, Pa, 82. *Bibliog:* Allan Ripp (auth), Polaroid photos allow artists to develop their talents, News Am, Baltimore, 12/31/78. *Media:* Oils. *Publ:* Illusr, Frank Young's Visual Studies: A Foundation Course for the Visual Arts, Minneapolis Col Art & Design, 81/82. *Mailing Add:* 2208 Maryland Ave Baltimore MD 21218

PRITZLAFF, (MR & MRS) JOHN, JR
COLLECTORS
Mr Pritzlaff, b Milwaukee, Wis, May 10, 25; Mrs Pritzlaff, b St Louis, Mo. *Study:* Mr Pritzlaff, Princeton Univ, BA, 49; Mrs Pritzlaff, Briarcliff Col. *Pos:* Mr Pritzlaff, US Ambassador to Malta, 69-72; Ariz State Sen, formerly; mem bd dirs, Heard Mus, Phoenix, Ariz, 76-77; Mrs Pritzlaff, pres, bd dirs, Phoenix Art Mus, formerly. *Mailing Add:* 4954 E Rockridge Rd Phoenix AZ 85018

PROCHOWNIK, WALTER A
EDUCATOR, PAINTER
b Buffalo, NY, Dec 12, 23. *Study:* Art Inst of Buffalo; Art Students League. *Work:* Albright-Knox Art Gallery, Buffalo, NY; Norfolk Mus Arts & Sci, Va; Minn Mus Arts, St Paul; Burchfield Ctr, State Univ NY, Buffalo; Ball State Univ Art Gallery, Muncie, Ind. *Comn:* You the People (mural), Co of Erie, Rath Off Bldg, Buffalo, 74. *Exhib:* One-man shows, Member's Gallery, Albright-Knox Art Gallery, Buffalo, 64; Col of Wooster, Ohio, 66; Chautauqua Art Asn Gallery, NY, 68 & Burchfield Ctr, Buffalo, 75; Smithsonian travel tour, 68-69. *Teaching:* Lcctr art, State Univ NY, Buffalo, 63-81, adj prof, 81- *Awards:* First Oil Award, Chautauqua Art Asn, 58; Purchase Prize, Drawings USA, 63 & 66; Perkin-Elmer Corp Award, Silvermine Guild, 69. *Mem:* Patteran Artists. *Media:* Oil, Multimedia. *Dealer:* More-Rubin Gallery 36 Norwood Ave Buffalo NY 14222. *Mailing Add:* 1885 Hertel Ave Buffalo NY 14214

PROHASKA, ELENA ANASTASIA
DEALER, CONSULTANT
b Southampton, NY, Sept 3, 46. *Study:* NY Univ, Washington Sq Col, BA, 70; Univ Va, Charlottesville, with William Seitz, MA, 72; New Sch; NY Univ. *Collections Arranged:* Monthly exhibs, Upstairs Gallery (auth, catalogs), East Hampton. NY, 72-74 & Twelve Americans: Masters of Collage, Andrew Crispo Gallery, New York, 77. *Pos:* Owner, Elena Prohaska Fine Arts. *Teaching:* Docent & art lectr, Guggenheim Mus, New York, 74-76; instr art, The Town Sch, New York, 74-77. *Mem:* Appraisers Asn Am, New York. *Specialty:* Contemporary paintins, sculptures and photographs; also specialize in advising private and corporate clients on art acquisitions. *Mailing Add:* 41 Central Park W New York NY 10023

PROKOPOFF, STEPHEN STEPHEN
MUSEUM DIRECTOR, HISTORIAN
b Chicago, Ill, Dec 24, 29. *Study:* Univ Calif, Berkeley, BA & MA; NY Univ, PhD. *Collections Arranged:* Romantic Minimalism, 67; Spirit of the Comics, 68; Highway, 69; Two Generations of Color Painting, 70; Against Order, 71; White on White, 72; Post-Mondrian Abstraction in America, 73; Logic of Vision, 74; Made in Chicago, 75; and others. *Pos:* Dir, Hathorn Gallery, Skidmore Col, 66-67, Inst Contemp Art, Univ Pa, 67-71, Mus Contemp Art, Chicago, 71-77, Inst Contemp Art, Boston, 78-82 & Krannert Art Mus, Univ Ill, 82- *Teaching:* Robert B Mayor prof art hist, Univ Chicago, 75, Boston Univ & Univ Ill. *Mem:* Am Asn Mus Dirs; Am Asn Mus; Col Art Asn Am. *Publ:* Coauth, 19th Century Architecture of Saratoga Springs, NY, 72. *Mailing Add:* Krannert Art Museum Univ Ill Urbana-Champaign Champaign IL 61820

PROMUTICO, JEAN
PAINTER
b Baltimore, Md, Nov 23, 36. *Study:* Md Inst Art, with Lila Katzen & Jon Schueler, BFA(painting & drawing), 66; Univ NMex, Albuquerque, with John Kacere, MA(painting & drawing), 68. *Work:* Fine Arts Mus NMex, Santa Fe; Art Gallery, Univ NMex, Albuquerque; Mus Albuquerque; Roswell Mus & Art Ctr, NMex; Lynn Mahew Gallery, Ohio Wesleyan Univ. *Exhib:* Md Ann Exhib, Baltimore Mus Art, 71; New Work-New Mexico, Arco Ctr Visual Arts, Los Angeles, 76; solo exhib, L Mahew Gallery, Ohio Wesleyan Univ, 76 & Roswell Mus & Art Ctr, NMex, 79; First Western States Biennial, Denver Art Mus, San Francisco Mus Mod Art & others, 79-80; Santa Fe-Taos Traveling Exhib, Sheldon Gallery, Univ Nebr, Lincoln, 82-83. *Pos:* Artist in residence painting, Roswell Mus & Art Ctr, 78. *Awards:* Purchase Award, Fine Arts Mus NMex, 72; Nat Endowment Arts Grant, 74. *Bibliog:* William Peterson (auth), article, Artspace, spring 79; Gerit Henry (auth), article, Art News, 9/81; William Peterson (auth), article, Artspace, fall 83. *Media:* Linen, Acrylic. *Dealer:* Kornblee Gallery 20 W 57th St New York NY; Linda Durham Gallery 400 Canyon Rd Santa Fc NM. *Mailing Add:* 104 W 17th St 3S New York NY 10011

PROPERSI, AUGUST J
ADMINISTRATOR, PAINTER
b Bronx, NY, Apr 3, 26. *Study:* Sch Art Studies, with Isaac Soyer & Sol Wilson, 46-47; Sch Visual Arts, with Jack Sheridan, Ben Dale & Francis Criss, grad, 50; Conference Conservation of Paintings, Brooklyn, Mus, 62. *Work:* Veterans Administration Hospital, Montrose, NY. *Exhib:* Artists USA, Bohman Gallery, Stockholm, Sweden, 68; 50 State Competition, Duncan Galleries, Paris, France, 68; Am Artists, Propersi Gallery D'Arte, Scarsdale, NY, 68 & 80; Propersi Galleries, Greenwich, Conn, 77-84. *Pos:* Founder & dir, The Little Studio and Art Gallery Art Sch, 59-68; founder and dir, Propersi Galleria D'Art, Scarsdale, NY, 68-70; founder & pres, Propersi Galleries & Sch Art Inc, 70-84. *Teaching:* Dir & instr life drawing, The Little Studio, Pelham, NY, 59-68; dir & instr fine arts, Propersi Gallerie D'Arte, 68-70; chmn fine and commercial art, Propersi Sch Art, Inc, 70-84. *Awards:* Prix d'Paris, 50 States Competition, Raymond Duncan Galleries, 68. *Bibliog:* Kathie Beals (auth), Dealer bullish on American art, Gannett Westchester Newspaper, 6/13/75; Dorothy Friedman (auth), Personal attention key to success, Greenwich Time Newspaper, 10/13/75; John Branca & Steve Acunto, Profiles, WVOX-WFAS Radio Westchester, 76-77. *Mem:* Artist Guild (bd dirs, 53); Am Veterans Soc Artists (bd dirs, 68). *Media:* Pastels, Oils. *Specialty:* Listed American painters and European painters--19th & 20th centuries. *Mailing Add:* 225 Magnolia Ave Mt Vernon NY 10552

PROSS, LESTER FRED
EDUCATOR, PAINTER
b Bristol, Conn, Aug 14, 24. *Study:* Oberlin Col, BA, 45, MA, 46; Ohio Univ, with Ben Shahn, summer 52; Skowhegan Sch Painting & Sculpture, summer 53; with Simon, Zorach, Levine, Hebald & Bocour; Univ Colo Kyoto Sem, Japan, 75-76; study painting with Kono Shuson. *Exhib:* Midstates Ann, Evansville, 64; Face of Kentucky I & II Traveling Exhib, 68-70; Appalachian Corridors II Traveling Exhib, 70-71; Morehead State Univ, 73; Ky Bicentennial, 74; More than Land or Sky: Art from Appalachia, Nat Mus Am Art, Smithsonian Inst, Washington DC, 81-82, Traveling Exhib, 82-84. *Pos:* Chmn adv bd, Appalachian Mus, Berca Col, 69-; bd dirs, Doris Ulmann Found, currently. *Teaching:* Prof art, Berea Col, 46-, chmn dept, 50-; Fulbright lectr painting & art hist, Univ Panjab, Pakistan, 57-58; vis assoc prof art educ & hist, Union Col, summer 61; vis prof art, Am Univ Cairo, 67-68. *Awards:* Haskell Traveling Fel, Oberlin Col, 57-58. *Mem:* Col Art Asn Am; Am Comt SAsian Art; Ky Guild Artists & Craftsmen (pres, 61-63); Asn Asian Studies; Asia Soc. *Media:* Oil, Watercolor. *Mailing Add:* 1287 CPO Berea KY 40404

PROVDER, CARL
PAINTER, INSTRUCTOR
b Brooklyn, NY, Feb 7, 33. *Study:* Pratt Inst, BFA; Columbia Univ, MA, prof dipl; Inst Allende, MFA; Educ Alliance Art Sch; Art Students League; NY Univ; Acad Belli Arti, Perugia; also with Samuel Adler. *Exhib:* Contemp Artists Brooklyn, Brooklyn Mus, 72; Painters & Sculptors Soc, Jersey City Mus, NJ, 72; La Jolla Mus, 74 & 75; San Diego Mus, 75 & 79; Laguna Beach Mus, Calif, 77; and others. *Teaching:* Instr fine arts, Bd Educ, New York, 64-73; instr fine arts, San Diego Community Col, 74-; instr, Mira Costa Col, 76-77; instr, Mendocino Art Ctr, 80-81. *Awards:* First Prize/Mixed Media, Southern Calif Expo, Del Mar, 77 & Third Prize Mixed Media, 79; Purchase Award, Small Image Art Show, San Diego, 78, 79 & 80; First Prize painting, San Diego Art Inst Ann, 80 & Honorable Mention, 81. *Bibliog:* Denise Draper (auth), An exhibit that passes the test, Coast Dispatch, 1/21/78; Richard Reilly (auth), Artist's work is from within, 1/22/78, Joan Lcvine (auth), Art on a cul-de-sac, 10/19/78, San Diego Union. *Mem:* Artists Equity Asn (vpres, 76-79); San Diego Art Guild; Art Inst San Diego; San Diego Watercolor Soc; San Diego Mus of Art. *Mailing Add:* 1416 Elva Terr Encinitas CA 92024

PROWN, JULES DAVID
HISTORIAN
b Freehold, NJ, Mar 14, 30. *Study:* Lafayette Col, AB, 51, 79; Harvard Univ, AM(fine arts), 53; Univ Del, AM(early Am cult), 56; Harvard Univ, PhD(fine arts), 61; Lafayette Col, Hon DFA, 79. *Collections Arranged:* John Singleton Copley Traveling Exhib (auth, catalog), 65-66 & American Art from Alumni Collections, 68, Yale Univ Art Gallery; travelling exhib), 65-66 & American Art from Alumni Collections, 68, Yale Univ Art Gallery. *Pos:* Asst to dir, William Hayes Fogg Art Mus, Harvard Univ, 59-61; cur, Garvan & Related Collections of Am Art, Yale Univ, New Haven, 63-68; dir, Yale Brit Art Ctr, New Haven, 68-76; assoc dir, Nat Humanities Inst, New Haven, 77. *Teaching:* Fel art hist, Harvard Univ, Cambridge, Mass, 56-57; from instr art hist to prof art hist, Yale Univ, 61-71, Yale Univ. *Awards:* Blanche Elizabeth MacLeish Billings Award, Yale Univ, 66; Robert C Smith Award, Soc Arch Historians, 83. *Mem:* Am Asn Mus; Am Soc 18th Century Studies (exec bd mem, 73-76); Col Art Asn (bd dir, 75-79); Benjamin Franklin fel Royal Soc Arts; Am Antiquarian Soc (mem coun, 77-). *Res:* American and English art; John Singleton Copley; Benjamin West. *Publ:* Auth, John Singleton Copley, two vols, Harvard Univ Press, 66; auth, American Painting from Its Beginnings to the Armory Show, Skira, 69; auth, The architecture of the Yale Center for British Art, Yale Ctr for Brit Art, 77; auth, Style as evidence, 80 & Mind in matter, 82, Portfolio. *Mailing Add:* Dept of Art Hist Box 2009 New Haven CT 06520

PRUITT, LYNN
SCULPTOR, ASSEMBLAGE ARTIST
b Washington, DC, May 24, 37. *Work:* Marlboro Hall, Prince George Com Col, Largo, Md, 76. *Comn:* Sculptured canvas wall relief, Naval Acad, Annapolis, Md, 76. *Exhib:* Corcoran Gallery Art, Washington, DC, 65 & 72; one-person shows, Md Artists Today, East Coast Univ Tour, Baltimore Mus, 75 & 76, Nat

Audubon Soc, Chevy Chase, Md, 77 & Nourse Gallery, Washington, DC, 80; Am Chairs, Form, Function & Fantasy, John Michael Kohler Arts Ctr, Sheboygan, Wis, 78; Washington Proj for the Arts, DC, 80; and others. *Pos:* Juror, Prince George's Community Col, 72-75, Nat Inst Health, 73-75, Md Col Art, 76 & Scholastic Art Awards, Washington, DC, Md & Va, 77-78; Dir & consult, Holden Gallery, Inc, Kensington, Md, 76- *Teaching:* Instr basic art, Jewish Community Ctr, Rockville, Md, 74- *Awards:* First in Painting, 68, 69 & 70, Best in Show, 68, 69 & 70 & First in Sculpture, 70, 71, 73 & 74, Nat Inst Health, Bethesda, Md. *Mem:* Washington Womens Arts Ctr; Am Crafts Coun. *Media:* Sculpture, plaster. *Dealer:* Nourse Gallery Washington DC 20013. *Mailing Add:* 303 Nimitz Ave Rockville MD 20851

PUCCINELLI, RAIMONDO
SCULPTOR, GRAPHIC ARTIST
b San Francisco, Calif, May 5, 04. *Study:* Calif Sch Fine Arts, San Francisco; Rudolph Schaeffer Sch Design, San Francisco; apprentice to woodcarvers, stone cutters & masters of plaster; Univ Calif, Berkeley. *Work:* Bocholt Mus, Ger; Jugenberg Mus, Gemen, Ger; Stedelijk Mus, Zutphen, Neth; Hirshhorn Mus, Smithsonian Inst, Washington, DC; Israel Mus, Jerusalem Music Ctr; and others. *Comn:* Salinas Col, Calif, 40; Mills Col, Oakland, Calif, 41; Univ Calif, Berkeley, 44; House of Theology, Franciscan Monastery, Centerville, Ohio; St Andrew's Church, Mayo, Md, 60. *Exhib:* Contemporary American Sculpture, Whitney Mus Am Art, New York, 48 & 49; Biennale Int del Bronzetto, Padova, Italy, 67; Modern Sculpture, Corcoran Gallery Art, Washington, DC, 62; one-man exhibs, Duke Univ Mus Art, Durham, NC, Salon D'Automne, Paris, 78-81 & Chiostro di San Marco, Florence, Italy, 79; and others. *Teaching:* Instr sculpture & drawing, Mills Col, 38-47; prof sculpture & drawing, Univ Calif, Berkeley, 42-47; asst prof sculpture & drawing, Univ NC, Chapel Hill, 47-48; instr design & art hist, Queens Col, New York, 48-51; dean sculpture & drawing, Rinehart Sch Sculpture, Peabody Inst & Md Inst Col Art, 58-60; prof sculpture, Int Univ Arts, Florence, formerly. *Awards:* Sculpture Prize, San Francisco Mus Art, 37 & 38; Sculpture Award, Los Angeles Co Mus Art, 39; Medaglio d'Oro for Il Fiorino, Palazzo Strozzi, Florence, Italy, 66; and many others. *Bibliog:* William S Heckscher (auth), Puccinelli, Duke Univ, 74; Selhorst & Modlmayr (coauth), Raimondo Puccinelli, Kulturamt, Ger, 76; Edwin Birnmayer (auth), Graphische Kunst: Puccinelli, Ed Curt Visel, Ger, 78; and others. *Mem:* Hon mem Florentine Acad; Soc Salon D'Automne, Paris, France; Chelsea Arts Club, London. *Publ:* Auth, Bronze sculpture, Arts & Archit, 39; auth, Sculpture, a visual language, Architects' Report, winter 61; auth, We Think with Entire Being, Duke Univ. *Mailing Add:* Piazza Donatello 18 Florence Italy

PUCKER, BERNARD H
ART DEALER
b Kansas City, Mo, Oct 19, 37. *Study:* Columbia Univ, BA, 59; Hebrew Univ, Jerusalem, 60; Brandeis Univ, MA, 66. *Pos:* Dir, Pucker Safrai Gallery, Boston, currently. *Specialty:* Contemporary artists; Chagall graphics; Israeli artists; New England artists; fantastic realist painters; African artists; bronzes by David Aronson, Kieff & David Chamberlain. *Mailing Add:* 171 Newbury St Boston MA 02116

PUFAHL, JOHN K
EDUCATOR, PRINTMAKER
b Urbana, Ill, Nov 6, 42. *Study:* Wesleyan Univ, Ill, BFA(hon), 65; Northern Ill Univ, MA & MFA, studied with David F Driesbach, 67. *Work:* Univ Wis, Platteville; Art Gallery of Windsor, Ont; Bd Educ, Windsor, Ont. *Exhib:* Chicago & Vicinity Exhib, Art Inst Chicago, 66; 162nd Ann Exhib, Philadelphia Acad Fine Arts, 67; Can Print Exhib, Windsor, Ont, 74; Calgary Int Drawing Exhib, Alta, 74; Imprint 76 (in conjunction with Olympic Games), Montreal, Que, 76; Fourth Biennale Int de l'Image, Epinal & Paris, France, 77 & 78. *Collections Arranged:* Can Printmakers, Art Gallery Toronto, Ont, 70; Imprint 76, Art Gallery Ont, 76-77. *Pos:* Pres, Pufahl & Krassov Ltd, Press Manufacturers, 74-; actg dir, Sch Fine Arts, Univ Windsor, Ont, 76-77; artist-in-residence, Sch of Art, Yeovil Col, Somerset, Eng, 78. *Teaching:* Asst instr intaglio, Ill Wesleyan Univ, Bloomington, 64-65; assoc prof intaglio & drawing, Univ Windsor, Ont, 67- *Awards:* Can Coun Grant, Adaptation of Stainless Steel to Intaglio Printmaking, 77. *Mem:* Can Univ Art Asn; Print & Drawing Coun Can; Royal Soc Arts, London, Eng. *Media:* Intaglio, Wood Engraving. *Publ:* Contribr, Canadian print workshops, Art Mag, 77. *Mailing Add:* 1111 Garden Ct Dr Windsor ON N8S 2S1 Canada

PUGH, GRACE HUNTLEY
PAINTER, GRAPHIC ARTIST
b Schenectady, NY, Sept 25, 12. *Study:* Wellesley Col, 30-32; Barnard Col, BA(fine arts), 34; Nat Acad Design, with Leon Kroll, Charles Hinton & Ivan Olinsky, 34-36; with Samantha Littlefield Huntley, 34-38; Parsons Sch Design, summer 37; Art Students League, with Reginald Marsh, summer 38. *Work:* Barnard Col; 100 Friends of Pittsburgh & Montefiore Hop, Pittsburgh; Mamaroneck Free Libr, NY; Westchester Co Art in Pub Places, White Plains, NY. *Comn:* Harbor mural, St Thomas Episcopal Church, Mamaroneck, NY, 63-66; paintings, Mamaroneck Harbor, Union Savings Bank, Mamaroneck, 75, Mill Stream, Harrison, NY, 76 & Scarsdale Summer, Scarsdale, NY, 77. *Exhib:* Artist Equity Exhib, Whitney Mus Am Art, New York, 51 & Riverside Mus, New York, 53; Ann, Nat Acad Design, New York, 57 & Am Watercolor Soc Ann, 57, 59 & 61; NY State Painters, NY State Bldg-World's Fair, Flushing, 65; one-woman shows, Sails, Wildcliff Mus, New Rochelle, NY, 75 & Rockport Art Asn, Mass, 76 & 80; and others. *Pos:* Chmn art, Mamaroneck Free Libr, 50-; artist-in-residence & adv fine arts, Village of Mamaroneck, 77- *Teaching:* Artist-in-residence & head dept art, Briarcliff Jr Col, Briarcliff Manor, NY, 36-40; art instr, Westchester Co Workshop, White Plains, 61-63.

Awards: Ernest Longfellow Award, Rockport Art Asn Ann, 44; First Prize, New Rochelle Art Asn, 51; First Prize, Beaux Art, Westchester Co Womens Clubs, 54, 57 & 64. *Bibliog:* Jim Kinter (auth), Show mirrors artists strong moods, Intel J Newspaper, 74; Herb Rosoff (auth), The pro's nest meet with Grace Huntley Pugh, Palette Talk Mag, 77. *Mem:* Am Watercolor Soc; Rockport Art Asn; Mamaroneck Artists Guild (pres, 53-55, 61-63, dir, 53-80); Artists Equity. *Media:* Oil, Watercolor. *Publ:* Illusr, Know the UN members: China, Facts Int, 50; illusr, More Power for Your Church, Farrar, Straus & Young, 52; contribr, Portfolio '78, Howard Publ Co, 77; illusr, Archaeology Inst Am-Westchester Soc Newslett, 77-80; and others. *Mailing Add:* 823 Stuart Ave Mamaroneck NY 10543

PUJOL, ELLIOTT
EDUCATOR, MEDALIST
b Memphis, Tenn, June 4, 43. *Study:* Southern Ill Univ, BS(theatre), 68, with Brent Kington, MFA(art), 71; Penland Sch, with Arline Fisch, 70. *Work:* Minn Mus Art, St Paul; Sheldon Mem Art Gallery, Lincoln, Nebr; Topeka Public Libr; Wichita Art Mus; Louisiana Sch Visually Impaired. *Comn:* Pendulum (sculpture), Kansas State Univ Col Eng, 83. *Exhib:* Drinking Companions, John Michael Kohler Art Ctr, Sheboygan, Wis, 77; 1st Nat Spoon & Ash Tray Show, Sangre de Cristo Art Ctr, Pueblo, Colo, 78; 3rd Ann Jewelry and Small Sculpture Invitational, Ogden, Utah, 79; Visual Arts Ctr Alaska, Anchorage, 80; Brookfield Craft Ctr, Conn, 80; and many others. *Collections Arranged:* First Blacksmith Conference, Carbondale, Ill, 70; Third National Student Metal International (auth, catalog), Tyler Sch Art, 72; Summer Vail Metal Symposium, Colo, 74; American Metal Work (auth, catalog), Sheldon Mem Art Gallery, 76; First National Ring Show, Athens, Ga & Manhattan, Kans, 77. *Pos:* Guest artist, Penland Sch, NC, 71, 73 & 76, Arrowmont Sch, Gatlinburg, Tenn, 73 & 79, Brookfield Craft Sch, Conn, 73, 76 & 79, Summer Vail, Colo, 74-82. *Teaching:* Instr jewelry & silversmithing, Tyler Sch Art, Philadelphia, 71-73; prof metalsmithing, Kans State Univ, Manhattan, 73- *Awards:* First Place, Mus Contemp Crafts, Copper Develop Asn, 71; 50 Outstanding Craftsmen, Penland Sch, Nat Endowment for Arts, 71; Purchase Award, Renwick Gallery, DC, 74. *Bibliog:* Philip Morton (auth), Contemporary Jewelry, Holt, Rinehart, Winston, 70; Modern silver, Craft Horizons, 71; plus var newspaper articles. *Mem:* Am Crafts Coun; Artist Blacksmith Asn NAm; Kans Artist Craftsmen Asn (pres, 76-78); Soc NAm Goldsmiths. *Media:* All Media. *Dealer:* Silversmiths of Vail Vail CO 81657. *Mailing Add:* 1609 Leavenworth Manhattan KS 66502

PULOS, ARTHUR JON
INDUSTRIAL DESIGNER, DESIGN EDUCATOR
b Vandergrift, Pa, Feb 3, 17. *Study:* Carnegie Inst Technol, BFA, 39; Univ Ore, MFA, 43. *Work:* Walker Art Ctr, Minn; Newark Mus Fine Arts, NJ; Detroit Inst Art, Mich; Mus Mod Art, New York; Utrecht Mus Decorative Arts, Holland. *Exhib:* Brussels World Fair, 60; Metrop Mus, 66; Smithsonian Inst, 66; Louvre, Paris, 66; US Info Agency Exhib, 66. *Pos:* Pres, Pulos Design Assoc, Inc, 58- *Teaching:* Prof indust design, Univ Ill, 46-55; prof indust design & chmn dept, Syracuse Univ, 55-82, prof emer, 82- *Awards:* Award Ceramics, Pittsburgh Art Asn, 39; Award Flatware, Wichita Art Asn, 48; Award Hollow Ware, Chicago Art Inst, 52. *Mem:* Fel Indust Designers Soc Am (pres, 73-75, chmn bd, 75-77); Int Coun Soc Indust Design (pres, 80-81, past pres, 81-). *Publ:* Auth, Opportunities in Industrial Design, 70 & 78; auth, Contact--Selling Design Services, 75; auth, Ethics of aesthetics, Indust Design, 3-4/79; auth, Post materialism, Japan Int Trand & Indust, 81; auth, American Design Ethic, MIT Press, 83; auth articles on design in American and foreign design publications; auth, articles on design in Am & foreign design publ. *Mailing Add:* 1939 E Genesee St Syracuse NY 13210

PUNIA, CONSTANCE EDITH
PAINTER
b Brooklyn, NY. *Study:* Brooklyn Mus Art Sch; oil with Edwin Dickinson & Yonia Fain; oil and sumi-e with Murray Hantman. *Exhib:* Les Surindependants, Paris, 75; Grand Prix Humanitaire de France, Paris, 75; Des Artistes Francais, Grand Palais, Paris, France, 76 & 77; Sun Yat Sen Ctr of Asian Studies at St John's Univ, Jamaica, NY, 76; Nat A Arts Club, New York, NY, 77; and others. *Awards:* Silver Medal & Laureate of Honor, Grand Prix Humanitaire de France, 75; Bronze Medal, Akad Raymond Duncan, 75; Order of Merit Medal, Acad of Sci & Human Rels, Dominican Repub; and others. *Mem:* Nat League Am Pen Women; Sumi-E Soc Am; Asn Belgo-Hispanique; Les Surindependants; Guild Creative Art, Shrewsbury, NJ; and others. *Media:* Oil, Sumi-e. *Dealer:* Galeries Raymond Duncan 31 Rue de Seine Paris France. *Mailing Add:* 215 Adams St Brooklyn NY 11201

PURA, WILLIAM PAUL
PRINTMAKER, PAINTER
b Winnepeg, Man, Dec 19, 48. *Study:* Sch Art, Univ Man, BFA, 70; Ind Univ, Bloomington, MFA, 73. *Work:* Art Bank, Can Coun, Ottawa, Ont; Miller Brewing Co, Milwaukee, Wis; Prudential Life Insurance Co, Minneapolis; Gallery III, Univ Man, Winnipeg; Wilfred Laurier Univ, Kitchener, Ont. *Exhib:* Winnipeg Art Gallery, Man, 75; solo exhibs, Alternative Space Gallery, Winnipeg, 78 & Gallery III, Univ Man, Winnipeg, 80; Virginia Beach Art Ctr, Va, 79; Charlotte Printmakers, NC, 79; Edmonton Art Gallery, Alta, 80; and others. *Teaching:* Assoc prof, Sch Art, Univ Man, 73- *Awards:* Print & Drawing Coun Can, Opus Frames Ltd, Vancouver, 80. *Dealer:* Miriam Perlman Inc Lake Point Tower Suite 5410 505 North Lake Shore Dr Chicago IL 60611. *Mailing Add:* 1182 Markham Rd Winnipeg MB R3T 3Z8 Canada

PURCELL, ANN
PAINTER
b Arlington, Va, Nov 18, 41. *Study:* Corcoran Sch Art, DC; George Washington Univ, BA(fine arts), 73. *Work:* Corcoran Gallery Art, DC; Phillips Collection, DC; Albright-Knox Mus, Buffalo, NY; AT&T; Milwaukee Art Mus; and others. *Exhib:* 19th Area Exhib, Corcoran Gallery Art, DC, 74, one-woman show, 5 Washington Artists, 76 & Corcoran Fac Exhib, 76; Group Show, Selected, Southern Alleghenies Mus Art, Loretto, Pa, 78; 5 Artists, Mus Fine Arts, St Petersburg, Fla, 78; Selected Works from Tibor de Nagy, Mint Mus, Charlotte, NC, 79; plus many others. *Teaching:* Instr painting & drawing, Smithsonian Inst, DC, 74-78, Corcoran Sch Art, 74-79, Parsons Sch Art & Design, 83- *Bibliog:* Jane Livingston (auth), Five Washington Artists, Garamond Press, 76; article, Arts, 11/83. *Mem:* New York Artists Equity Asn. *Media:* Acrylic. *Dealer:* Tibor de Nagy Gallery 29 W 57th St New York NY 10019; Osuna Gallery 2121 P St NW Washington DC 20037. *Mailing Add:* 655 Sixth Ave Number 407 New York NY 10010

PURDY, DONALD R
PAINTER
b Conn, Apr 10, 24. *Study:* Univ Conn, BA; Boston Univ, MA. *Work:* New Britain Mus; Colby Col; Chase Manhattan Bank Collection; Univ Kans; Chrysler Mus. *Exhib:* USA Int Show; Silvermine Guild Artists; Audubon Artists; Allied Artists Am. *Awards:* Gold Medal, Allied Artists Am; First Prize, Silvermine Guild Artists; Jane Peterson Award, Audubon Artists. *Bibliog:* F Whitaker (auth), article, Am Artist. *Mem:* Am Fedn Arts; Allied Artists Am; Silvermine Guild Artists. *Media:* Oil. *Collection:* American and Barbizon. *Dealer:* Hammer Gallery E 57th St New York NY 10022; Flemington Art Gallery Main St Flemington NJ 08822. *Mailing Add:* 163 Westport Rd Wilton CT 06897

PURDY, HENRY CARL
PAINTER, EDUCATOR
b Wolfville, NS, Nov 6, 37. *Study:* NS Col Art, Halifax, assoc, 58. *Work:* Confederation Ctr Arts, Island Art Collection, Charlottetown, PEI; Dofasco Steel, Hamilton, Ont; NB Mus, St John; Art Ctr Gallery, Univ NB, Fredericton. *Comn:* Steel sculpture, Fathers of Confederation Trust, Charlottetown, NB, 73; steel fountain sculpture, Parkdale, PEI, 73; acrylic painted mural, Univ PEI, Charlottetown, 79; stained glass windows, St Dunstan's Basilica, Charlottetown, 81; carved wooden mural, Can Coast Guard Col, Sydney, NS, 81. *Exhib:* Ars Sacra Int, St Mary's Art Gallery, Halifax, 77; Maritime Art Asn, Eptek Exhib Ctr, Summerside, PEI, 79; Royal Can Acad Arts Ann, Toronto Exhib Ctr, 80; Between Two Islands, Visby Art Gallery, Sweden, 81; solo exhib, St John City Hall Gallery, NB, 83; and others. *Collections Arranged:* Arts East '79 (maritime art work), PEI, 79; Arts East '80 (work from Atlantic provs), Memracook, NB, 80; Island Visual Artists, 82 & 83. *Teaching:* Instr commercial design, Holland Col, 69-77, dir art & crafts, Sch Visual Arts, 77- *Awards:* Centennial Awards, Gold Medal Sculpture, 63 & Gold Arts Medal, 73, Prov PEI; Silver Medal for Contrib to Art in Atlantic Can, Royal Soc Arts, 81. *Bibliog:* Robert Percival (auth), Purdy in the Maritimes, Art Mag, 74; Pat Murphy (auth), Look out! Here comes Henry Purdy, Axiom Mag, 3/76; Rich Smith (dir), Henry Purdy--Artist (video), Confederation Ctr Arts, 78. *Mem:* Royal Can Acad Art (vpres Atlantic region, 78-); Can Soc Educ Through Art; Can Artists Rep; Royal Soc Arts; PEI Coun Arts (chmn bd, 78-83). *Media:* Acrylic, Welded Steel. *Publ:* Auth, Me Too!, Holland Press, 74; illusr, Icons of Poverty & Riches, 81 & Francis, 83, A Arsenault; contribr, Sand Patterns--A Commemorative Issue, Sand Patterns Group, 83. *Mailing Add:* 6 St Peters Rd Parkdale PE C1A 5N2 Canada

PURSER, STUART ROBERT
PAINTER, EDUCATOR
b Stamps, Ark, Feb 8, 07. *Study:* La Col, BA, 28; Art Inst Chicago, BFA, 32, MFA, 33; Ohio State Univ, 44; also with Boris Anisfeld, 30-33. *Work:* Nat Gallery, Melbourne, Australia; High Mus Art, Atlanta, Ga; Hunter Gallery Art, Chattanooga, Tenn; Univ Miss. *Comn:* Mural, Gretna, La Post Off, 38, Forty-Eight State Mural, Leeland, Miss Post Off, 39, Bankhead Memorial Mural, Carrolton, Ala Post Off, 40 & mural, Ferriday, La Post Off, 41, US Treas Dept. *Exhib:* Nat Oil Exhib, 38 & Nat Watercolor Ann Exhib, 41, Art Inst Chicago; Pa Acad Ann, Philadelphia, 38-40; 1st Ann Oil Exhib, Metrop Mus, New York, 50; Am Drawing Ann, Norfolk Mus, Va, 61-63. *Teaching:* Instr art, Wash State Univ, 34-35; prof art & chmn dept, La Col, 35-45; prof art, Art Inst Chicago, summers 36-37; prof art & chmn dept, Univ Chattanooga, 45-49; prof art & chmn dept, Univ Miss, 49-51; prof art, Univ Fla, 51-, chmn dept art, 51-56; vis prof art, Univ Calif, Northridge, 58 & 61; prof art, Cent Wash State Col, summer 61; head, Idyllwild Found, Univ Southern Calif, summer 62; prof art, Eastern Wash State Col, summers 65-67. *Awards:* First Award, Delgado Mus, New Orleans, 42-44; Southeastern Annual First Award, High Mus Art, 60; First Award, Ocala Arts Festival, 68. *Mem:* Southeastern Col Arts Asn (pres, 45); Southeastern Arts Asn (pres, 53); Nat Art Educ Asn (mem coun, 53-55). *Media:* Oil. *Publ:* Auth, Applehead, 74; auth & illusr, Jesse J Aaron-Sculptor, 75; auth, Drawing Handbook, 75; auth, Applehead Number Two, 76. *Mailing Add:* 2210 NW Second Ave Gainesville FL 32603

PURTLE, CAROL JEAN
HISTORIAN, EDUCATOR
b St Louis, Mo, Feb 20, 39. *Study:* Maryville Col, St Louis, BA(magna cum laude), 60; Manhattanville Col, MA, 66; Washington Univ, St Louis, PhD, 76. *Teaching:* Instr art hist, Washington Univ, St Louis, 70-76; assoc prof art & coordr art hist, Memphis State Univ, 77- *Awards:* Advan Res Fel, Belgian-Am Educ Found, 74-75; Nat Endowment Humanities Summer Fel, Columbia Univ, 82; Fac Res Grant, Memphis State Univ, 83. *Mem:* Historians Netherlandish Art (nat pres, 83-85); Col Art Asn Am; Southeastern Col Art Conf; Midwest Art Hist Soc; Renaissance Soc Am. *Res:* Painting of Jan van Eyck; 15th century devotional images; Bernini; funerary chapels; relationship between word and image in church-related art. *Publ:* Auth, The Marian Paintings of Jan van Eyck, Princeton Univ Press, 82; ed & contribr, 600 Years of Netherlandish Art: Selected Symposium Lectures, Memphis State Univ, 82; auth, Monumentality and twentieth century art: A case of apples and oranges, Interpretations, 82. *Mailing Add:* 767 Mt Moriah #32 Memphis TN 38117

PUSEY, MAVIS
PAINTER, PRINTMAKER
b Jamaica, WI. *Study:* Art Students League, with Will Barnet, Harry Sternberg, 61-65; Printmaking Workshop, with Robert Blackburn, 69-72; Birgit Schold Printmaking Workshop, London, 67-68; New Sch Social Res, New York, 74 & 76. *Work:* Citibank, Pub Libr, Mus Mod Art, New York; First Nat Bank of Chicago; Cleveland State Univ. *Exhib:* Whitney Mus, New York, 71; Fla Int Univ North Miami Campus Traveling Exhib, 77; Tamiami Campus Fine Arts Gallery Traveling Exhib, 77; one-woman exhibs, Grimaldis Gallery, Baltimore, Md, 77, Rainbow Art Found, New York, 77 & Franklin & Marshall Col, Pa, 79; and many others. *Teaching:* Guest artist, Pa Acad Fine Arts, 72-75; instr painting, New Sch Social Res, 73-, asst prof fine arts, currently; asst prof painting, State Univ NY Stony Brook, 74-77; instr, Rutgers State Univ, NJ, formerly. *Awards:* Louis Comfort Tiffany Found Grant, 72 & Purchase Award, 74; Award, Staten Island Mus, 75; Award, Int Woman's Yr, 76; plus others. *Bibliog:* Studio Int J Mod Art, London, 67; Linda Blandford (auth), Four 1970s successes, Quee Mag, London, 68; article, New York Times, 74; and others. *Mem:* Fedn Mod Painters & Sculptors, Inc. *Media:* Oil. *Mailing Add:* 116 W 21st St New York NY 10011

PUTNAM, (MRS) JOHN B
COLLECTOR
b Cleveland, Ohio, June 19, 03. *Mem:* Art Collectors Club. *Collection:* Paintings and modern art. *Mailing Add:* 12817 Lake Shore Blvd Cleveland OH 44108

PUTNAM, MARION WALTON See Walton, Marion

PUTTERMAN, FLORENCE GRACE
PAINTER, PRINTMAKER
b Brooklyn, NY, Apr 14, 27. *Study:* NY Univ, BS; Bucknell Univ; Pa State Univ. *Work:* Metrop Mus Art, New York; Art Inst Chicago; Washington Co Mus Fine Arts, Hagarstown, Md; Everson Mus, New York; Brooklyn Mus. *Exhib:* Everson Mus, Syracuse, NY, 76; Libr Cong Biennial Print Exhib, Nat Collection Fine Arts, Washington, DC, 77; Chatauqua Nat, NY, 80; Boston Printmakers, 81; Potsdam Drawing Exhib, 81; Audubon Artists Ann, Nat Acad Design, New York, 83; New Acquisitions, Jacksonville Mus, Fla, 83; and others. *Pos:* Founder & pres, Arts Unlimited, Selinsgrove, Pa, 65-78; cur, Milton Shoe Co Print Collection, Pa, 70-; bd dirs, Fetherston Mus, Lewisburg, Pa, 75- *Teaching:* Artist in residence, Fed Title III Prog, 67-68 & 69-70; instr, Lycoming Col, Williamsport, Pa, 73-75. *Awards:* Gold Medal of Honor, Audubon Artists, 79; Nat Endowment Arts, 79-80; Va Ctr Creative Arts Fel. *Bibliog:* New American Monotypes, 79-80; articles, Am Artist, 7/79 & 2/81; The Nation, Art News, 1/83. *Mem:* Los Angeles Printmaking Soc; Print Coun NJ; Soc Am Graphic Artists; Nat Colorprint Soc; Audubon Artists. *Media:* Oil, Acrylic; Etching, Lithography. *Mailing Add:* 3 Fairway Dr Selinsgrove PA 17870

PYLYSHENKO, WOLODYMYR See Mirko

Q

QUANDT, ELIZABETH (ELIZABETH QUANDT BARR)
PRINTMAKER
b Oxfordshire, England, July 13, 22; US citizen. *Study:* San Francisco Art Inst, BFA, MFA. *Work:* Bibliot Nat, Paris; Stanford Univ Art Mus; Libr Cong; Achenbach Found & Transamerica Corp, San Francisco; Atlantic Richfield Corp, Los Angeles. *Comn:* Edition of 20 Prints, City of San Francisco, 74. *Exhib:* One-woman exhib, Monoprint Drawings, Achenbach Found, Calif Palace Legion Honor, 75; Silvermine Guild of Artists Nat Exhib, Conn, 78; West Coast Artists, New Gallery of Contemp Art, Cleveland, 78; Footprint 1978, NW Int Small Format Print Competition; 1st Invitational Print Exhib, Univ Calif, Hayward, 79; Boston Printmakers Ann, 79; Paul Anglim Gallery, San Francisco, 83; and others. *Teaching:* Instr printmaking, Santa Rosa Jr Col, Calif, 70- *Mem:* Calif Soc Printmakers. *Publ:* Illusr, Ten Poems of Frances Ponge, Greenwood Press, 83. *Dealer:* Smith Andersen Gallery 200 Homer St Palo Alto CA 94301; Annex Gallery 604 College Ave Santa Rosa CA 95404. *Mailing Add:* 920 McDonald Ave Santa Rosa CA 95404

QUAT, HELEN S
PRINTMAKER, PAINTER
b Brooklyn, NY, Oct 2, 18. *Study:* Skidmore Col; Columbia Univ; Art Students League; also with Raphael Soyer, Joseph Solman, Leo Manso, Ruth Leaf & Krishna Reddy; Empire State Col, State Univ NY, grad. *Work:* Univ

Mass, Amherst; NJ State Mus, Trenton; Nassau Community Col; Butler Inst Am Art, Youngstown, Ohio; Slater Mus, Norwich, Conn. *Exhib:* Pratt Graphics Ctr Third Int Miniature Print Exhib, 68; 164th Ann, Pa Acad Fine Arts, 69; Int Exhib Women Artists, Ont & France, 69; State Univ NY Potsdam 10th Print Ann, 69-70; Nat Exhib Prints & Drawings, Okla Art Ctr, 69-72; Brooklyn Mus. *Awards:* Vadley Art Co Award for Graphics, Catharine Lorillard Wolfe Art Club, 67; Purchase Prize, Hunterdon Art Ctr, NJ, 70; Mr & Mrs Benjamin Ganeles Prize, Nat Asn Women Artists, 71. *Mem:* Nat Asn Women Artists; Soc of Am Graphic Artists; fel MacDowell Colony. *Media:* Mixed. *Mailing Add:* 16 Elliot Rd Great Neck NY 11021

QUAYTMAN, HARVEY
PAINTER
b Far Rockaway, NY, Apr 20, 37. *Study:* Syracuse Univ; Tufts Univ; Boston Mus Fine Arts Sch, BFA. *Work:* Tate Gallery, London; Whitney Mus Am Art & Mus Mod Art, New York; Israel Mus, Jerusalem; Carnegie Inst of Technol, Pittsburgh, Pa; and others. *Exhib:* Whitney Mus Am Art Ann, 69 & 72 & Structure of Color, Whitney Mus Am Art, 70; Young Am Artists, Gent of Te Radhus, Charlottenborg, Denmark, 73; Painting Endures, Inst Contemp Art, Boston, 75; 14 Abstract Painters, Univ Calif, Los Angeles, 75; New Painting in New York, Univ of Tex, Austin, 77; one-man shows, David McKee Gallery, New York, 75, 77, 78 & 80 & Nordenlake Galerie, Malmo, Sweden, 81; and others. *Teaching:* Former instr, Boston Mus Fine Arts Sch, Middlebury Col, Essex Col Art, Colchester, Eng & Sch Visual Arts, New York; instr, Cooper Union, Parsons Sch Design, New York; vis lectr, Harvard Univ, 82 & 83; adj asst prof, Hunter Col, 83. *Awards:* Creative Artists Pub Serv Prog Award, 72 & 75; Guggenheim Fel, 79; Nat Endowment Arts, 83. *Mailing Add:* c/o David McKee Inc 41 E 57th St New York NY 10021

QUEST, CHARLES FRANCIS
PAINTER, EDUCATOR
b Troy, NY, June 6, 04. *Study:* Washington Univ Sch Fine Arts, St Louis, Mo, 24-29; advan study in Paris, 29; summer study, Spain, France & England, 60. *Work:* Brit Mus, London; Victoria & Albert Mus, London; Nat Mus, Stockholm; Bibliot Nat, Paris; Mus Mod Art & Metrop Mus Art, New York; plus 41 mus & many pvt collections throughout world. *Comn:* Altar painting, St Mary's Church, Helena, Ark, 34; baptistry murals, St Michael & St George Episcopal Church, St Louis, Mo, 34; altar painting, Trinity Episcopal Church, St Louis, 35; altar painting, Old Cathedral, St Louis, 59-60. *Exhib:* Soc Am Graphic Artists Ann, New York, 46-; Les Peintres Graveurs Actuels Aux Etats-Uni, Bibliot Nat, Paris, 51; Am Watercolor, Drawings & Prints Exhib, Metrop Mus Art, New York, 52; Art in the Embassies Prog, Dept of State, Washington, DC, 67; one-man show, Mint Mus, NC, 79; plus many group & one-man exhibs in mus & galleries throughout world. *Teaching:* Instr art, St Louis Pub Schs, Mo, 29-44; prof art, Washington Univ Sch Fine Arts, 44-71, emer prof, 71- *Awards:* Purchase Prizes, 3rd Ann Nat Print Exhib, Brooklyn Mus, 49, Nat Print Exhib, Libr Cong, 52 & 51st Ann Print Exhib, Soc Am Graphic Artists, 71; and others. *Bibliog:* Article, St Louis Post Dispatch, 60; Art in St Louis, KMOX-TV, St Louis, 68; article, Greenville News, SC, 72. *Mem:* St Louis Artists Guild; Soc Am Graphic Artists, New York; Philadelphia Color Print Soc; Print Club Philadelphia. *Media:* Oil. *Dealer:* Hampton III Gallery Taylors SC 29678; Bethesda Art Gallery 7950 Norfolk Ave Bethesda MD 20814. *Mailing Add:* 200 Hillswick Rd Tryon NC 28782

QUEST, DOROTHY (JOHNSON)
PAINTER, EDUCATOR
b St Louis, Mo, Feb 28, 09. *Study:* Washington Univ Sch Fine Arts, St Louis, Mo, 28-33; study in Europe, 29; Columbia Univ, summer 37. *Work:* Erskine Col, Due West, SC; St Luke's Hospital, Columbus, NC; Washington & Lee Univ, Va; Bob Jones Univ, Greenville, SC; Univ Eastern Ill, Charleston. *Comn:* Portrait of Dr John S Bradshaw & Dr Wm R Bosien, comn by St Luke's Hosp, Columbus, NC, 79; portrait, J Fred Buzhardt, Pres Nixon's atty, 79; portrait, Dr Iranaeus McCane, Erskine Col, 80; portrait, Ralph H Cuthbertson, pres Stevens Beechcraft, Greenville Airport, 80; plus over 650 other portraits, 31- *Exhib:* St Louis City Art Mus Ann; St Louis Artists Guild Ann; one-man shows, St Louis Club, Pierre Laclede Ctr, Mo, 64, Tryon Fine Arts Ctr, NC, 72 & Fine Arts Ctr, Anderson, SC, 75. *Pos:* Lectr painting, St Louis City Art Mus, radio sta KMOX & KSD. *Teaching:* Instr art, Community Sch, St Louis, 36-38; head art dept, Acad Sacred Heart, St Louis, 39-41 & Maryville Col, St Louis, 44-45; instr art, Tryon Fine Arts Ctr, 71-78. *Bibliog:* Walter Orthwein (auth), article, 67 & Lynn Hawkins (auth), articles, 69 & 82, St Louis Globe Democrat; feature article in Spartanburg Herald, 10/4/79. *Mem:* Tryon Painters & Sculptors, Inc. *Media:* Oil. *Dealer:* Hampton III Gallery Taylors SC 29678. *Mailing Add:* 200 Hillswick Rd Tryon NC 28782

QUICK, BIRNEY MACNABB
PAINTER, INSTRUCTOR
b Proctor, Minn, Nov 9, 12. *Study:* Vesper L George Sch, Boston; Minneapolis Col Art Design; Louis Comfort Tiffany fel & Chaloner fel, 38. *Work:* Minneapolis Inst Art; Univ Minn Art Gallery; Gen Mills Collection; Int Multifood Corp Collection; Northwestern Nat Life Collection. *Comn:* Oil on canvas, Med Arts Bldg, Duluth, Minn, 46, Minn Mutual Life Ins Co, St Paul, 58, Minn Fed Savings Loan, St Paul, 60, Grand Marais St Bank, Minn, 68 & St John's Catholic Church, Grand Marais, 72. *Exhib:* Am Painters & Sculptors Show, Art Inst Chicago; Minn Biennial, Minneapolis Art Inst; Independent Artist's Show, Boston; one-man shows, Walker Art Ctr & Minneapolis Art Inst; Tweed Gallery, Univ Minn, Duluth. *Pos:* Dir studies abroad, Am Cols Art, 70-71. *Teaching:* Prof painting, Minneapolis Sch Art, 46-77, emer prof, 77- *Awards:* Biennial Award in Drawing, Minneapolis Art Inst, 60. *Media:* Oil, Watercolor. *Mailing Add:* 4537 Dupont Ave S Minneapolis MN 55409

QUIGLEY, MICHAEL ALLEN
ADMINISTRATOR
b Buffalo, NY, Oct 28, 50. *Study:* Univ Pa, BA(art hist), 71. *Collections Arranged:* Joan Jonas/Stage Sets, 76, Material Pleasures/The Fabric Workshop, 79 & Art Materialized, 81, Independent Curators Inc, Inst Contemp Art, Univ Pa. *Pos:* Mus asst, Nat Collection of Fine Arts, Smithsonian Inst, Washington, DC, summer 1971; curatorial asst, Inst of Contemp Art, Univ Pa, 71-75, asst dir, 75-79; assoc dir, The Fabric Workshop, Philadelphia, 79-80, dir, 80- *Mailing Add:* 2238 Bainbridge St Philadelphia PA 19146

QUILLER, STEPHEN FREDERICK
PAINTER, PRINTMAKER
b Osmond, Nebr, Aug 15, 46. *Study:* Colo State Univ, BA, 68. *Work:* City Medford Art Collection, Ore; Petro-Lewis Corp Gallery, Colo Coun Arts, United Bank Denver Pub Collection & Cent Bank Denver, Colo. *Comn:* Gov's Export Award (painting), Colo Coun Arts, Denver, 79. *Exhib:* One-man show, Foothills Art Ctr, Golden, Colo, 73; Am Watercolor Soc, 73 & 76 & Nat Soc Painters Casein & Acrylic, 74 & 76-78, Nat Acad Design, New York; Rocky Mountain Nat, Foothills Art Ctr, Golden, Colo, 74-75, 77-79 & 81; Watercolor USA, Springfield Art Mus, Mo, 77; American & Italian Printmakers, Sangre de Cristo Art Ctr, Pueblo, Colo, 80; and others. *Teaching:* Instr art, SW Watercolor Soc, Dallas, spring 76; instr art, NMex Watercolor Soc, Albuquerque, spring 79; guest artist-in-res intaglio, Adams State Col, Alamosa, Colo, fall 81. *Awards:* John Wegner Mem Award, Nat Soc Painters Casein & Acrylic, 76; Alta Woodcarvers Award, Rocky Mountain Nat Watermedia, 78; Gov's Award, Colo Coun Arts, 79. *Bibliog:* Web Allison (auth), Steve Quiller: Creede's artist in residence, Colo Country Life, San Luis Valley, 11/72; G A Minshew (auth), Spotlight on the artist, Scene, SW Watercolor Soc, 4/75; Susan Meyer (auth), 40 Watercolorists And How They Work, Watson-Guptill, 78. *Mem:* Rocky Mountain Nat Watermedia; Nat Soc Painters Casein & Acrylic; Watercolor West; Artists Equity Asn; Watercolor Asn Ala. *Media:* Watercolor, Casein; Intaglio. *Publ:* Auth, Watercolor Page, Am Artist Mag, 5/75; coauth, Watermedia, Watson-Guptill, 5/83. *Mailing Add:* c/o Pen & Quill Gallery PO Box 307 Creede CO 81130

QUINN, AYSHA
VIDEO ARTIST
b New London, Conn, Jan 5, 45. *Work:* Utah Media Ctr, Salt Lake City. *Comn:* Satellite Transmission Interactive Performance, Univ Iowa, Iowa City, 82; performance, Long Beach Mus Art, 83; video-performance, Los Angeles Co Mus Art, 83. *Exhib:* Solo exhib, Utah Media Ctr, Salt Lake City, 81; Second Intermedia Arts Festival, Univ Iowa, Iowa City, 82; Ninth Ann Ithaca Video Festival Traveling Exhib, 83; Haunted Womanhouse, 83 & At Home, 83, Long Beach Mus Art. *Teaching:* Instr video, Utah Media Ctr, Salt Lake City, 82-83; vis artist & lectr video & performance, Univ Iowa, Iowa City, 82-83; vis artist performance, Art Inst Chicago, 83. *Awards:* Western States Media Arts Fel Video, Nat Endowment Arts & Am Film Inst, 83; Winner, Utah Short Film & Video Festival, Utah Arts Coun, 83. *Bibliog:* Jackie Apple (auth), Art and techno-consciousness, Artweek, 10/1/83; Michael Nash (auth), Present tense rites of passage, Art Com, fall 83; Kathy Huffman (auth), The artist and television, Los Angeles Inst Contemp Art J, winter 83. *Mem:* Screen Actors Guild; Am Fedn TV & Radio Artists. *Media:* Video, Performance. *Mailing Add:* 1903 Burdett Ave Troy NY 12180

QUINN, BRIAN GRANT
SCULPTOR, PAINTER
b Wahoo, Nebr, Oct 21, 50. *Study:* Nebr Wesleyan Univ, with Maynard Whitney, BAE; Ariz State Univ, with Ben Goo, MFA. *Work:* Weber State Col, Odgen, Utah; Ariz State Univ, Tempe; Tucson Art Mus, Ariz; Univ NMex. *Comn:* Sculpture, Blue Ribbon Food, Phoenix, Ariz, 81 & Median Inst, Pittsburgh, Pa, 83. *Exhib:* Jewelry/Small Sculpture Invitational Exhib, Weber State Col, Ogden, Utah, 77 & 81; Fac Exhib, Ariz State Univ, 80; 14th & 16th Southwest Invitational, Yuma Arts Ctr, 80 & 82; Ariz Biennial, Tucson Art Mus, 80; 1st & 2nd Northern Ariz Univ Sculpture Invitational, 80 & 81; 13th Midwestern Invitational, O'Rourke Gallery, Moorhead, Minn, 81; and many others. *Pos:* Preparator, Phoenix Art Mus, 75; asst to Fritz Scholder, 75-82. *Teaching:* Vis instr sculpture, Glendale Community Col, 76-82; lectr sculpture, Ariz State Univ, Tempe, 80 & 81. *Awards:* Artist-in-Residence, Nat Endowment Art, 75-76; Fred Wells Purchase Award, Small Sculpture and Drawing Exhib, Nebr Wesleyan Univ, 76; Jurors Award, First & Third Ariz Wood-in-Art Exhib, 77-79. *Bibliog:* James Mills (auth), Quinn works express beauty, lyricism yet remain lighthearted, Roundup, Denver Post, 10/9/77; Barbara Cortright (auth), article, Artspace, winter 82-83; Kelly Walton (auth), Sculptor, painter? Always an artist, City Life, Phoenix Gazette, 12/21/83. *Mem:* Southern Asn of Sculptors. *Dealer:* Gallery of Contemp Art 2 Ledout St Taos NM 87571; Leslie Levy Gallery 7141 Main St Scottsdale AZ 85251. *Mailing Add:* 2925 E St Johns Rd Phoenix AZ 85032

QUINN, HENRIETTA REIST
COLLECTOR, PATRON
b Lancaster, Pa, Dec 11, 18. *Study:* Edgewood Park Jr Col. *Collection:* American primitive paintings; eighteenth century porcelain; eighteenth century miniature memoribilia; eighteenth century American and English furniture. *Mailing Add:* Rollings Meadows Cornwall PA 17016

QUINN, NOEL JOSEPH
PAINTER, INSTRUCTOR
b Pawtucket, RI, Dec 25, 15. *Study:* RI Sch Design, grad, 36, fel, Paris; Parsons Sch Fine & Appl Arts, Paris & Italy, cert dipl; Ecole Beaux Arts; also

with Andre L'hote & Andre Cassandre; Nat Gallery & Kaiser Frederick Mus, Berlin, Ger. *Work:* Butler Art Inst, Youngstown, Ohio; Air Force Acad, Denver; Pentagon, Libr of Cong & House of Rep, Washington, DC; and others. *Comn:* Thoroughbred Racing (portfolio of paintings), Los Angeles Turf Club, 60. *Exhib:* American Paintings & Prints, Metrop Mus Art, New York, 52; Hallmark Int Show, Wildenstein Galleries, New York, 53; Southwest Watercolor Soc Show, Southern Methodist Univ, Dallas, 69; one-man show, Yoseido Gallery, Tokyo, 55; plus many others. *Teaching:* Instr watercolor, Otis Art Inst, 53-75; guest instr, Palo Verdes Art Ctr, 76-77. *Awards:* Cert of Esteem for work in Korea & Japan, Secy Defense Charles E Wilson, 55; Watercolor USA Award, Springfield Art Mus, 64; Alumni of the Year Award, RI Sch Design, 81; and others. *Bibliog:* Norman Kent (auth), 100 American Watercolorists, Watson-Guptill, 69; feature article, Today's Art Mag, 2/80; California Watercolorists 1930-1960, Hillcrest, 84. *Mem:* Nat Watercolor Soc; Soc Motion Picture illusr (pres, 65-68); fel Int Inst Arts & Lett. *Media:* Watercolor. *Interests:* Creator of new language of symbols for color and value in bas-relief. *Publ:* Auth, article, Am Artist Mag, 5/63; auth, Scene, Southwestern Watercolor Soc Mag. *Mailing Add:* 3946 San Rafael Ave Los Angeles CA 90065

QUINN, WILLIAM
PAINTER, PRINTMAKER
b St Louis, Mo, Sept 5, 29. *Study:* Washington Univ, BFA, study with Paul Burlin & Carl Holty; Univ Ill, MFA, 57. *Work:* Butler Inst of Am Art, Youngstown, Ohio; Brooks Mem Art Gallery, Memphis, Tenn; Nelson-Atkins Gallery, Kansas City, Mo; St Louis Art Mus; Weatherspoon Art Gallery, Univ NC; and others. *Comn:* High Mus, Atlanta, Ga; Mulvane Art Ctr, Topeka, Kans; Univ Mo, Columbia; Mus Art, Ft Lauderdale, Fla; Mexican-Am Cult Inst, Mexico City; and many others. *Exhib:* Nineteen one-man shows. *Teaching:* Prof painting & drawing, Washington Univ, 58- *Awards:* Thirty-six awards in regional museums and galleries. *Media:* Oil and acrylic. *Mailing Add:* Sch of Fine Arts Washington Univ St Louis MO 63130

QUINSAC, ANNIE-PAULE
HISTORIAN, WRITER
b Bouches du Rhone, France, Aug 2, 45. *Study:* Univ Montpellier, 59-61; Paris, DES, 63; Sorbonne, Paris, PhD, 68. *Collections Arranged:* Ottocento Painting in Am Collections (auth, catalog), NY Cult Ctr, Columbia Mus Arts & Mass Inst Technol, 72-73; Exhib Segantini: Japan 1978, Japan, 78; Millet Corot and the Sch of Barbizon (auth, catalog), Japan, 82; An Anthology of Occidental Landscape (auth, catalog), Japan, 83-84. *Pos:* Mitarbeiter, Inst Kunstwissenshaft, Zurich, 74-75. *Teaching:* Prof art history, Univ SC, 70- *Awards:* Mellon Fel, Univ Pittsburgh, 78-79. *Mem:* Nat Soc Lit & Arts; Col Art Asn Am; Arte Lombarda Milan; Soc Amis de Segantini. *Res:* 19th century Italian studies; currently working on Rosa Boneur and Giuseppe Pellizza da Volpedo. *Publ:* Auth, Peinture Divisionniste Italienne: Origines et premiers developpements, Klincksieck, 72; auth, Catalogue raisonne di Giovanni Segantini, Electa Editcice, Milan, 82; auth, Vent'anni di vita artistica europea nei cartegi inediti de Giovanni Segantini e suoi mecenati a cura di Annie-Paule Quinsa, Milan (in press). *Mailing Add:* 2210 Lincoln Columbia SC 29201

QUIRARTE, JACINTO
HISTORIAN, ADMINISTRATOR
b Jerome, Ariz, Aug 17, 31. *Study:* San Francisco State Col, BA, 54, MA, 58; Nat Univ Mex, PhD, 64. *Pos:* Dir cult affairs, Ctr Venezolano Am, Caracas, 64-66; bd mem & vpres, San Antonio Arts Coun, 73-77; mem visual arts & humanities panel, Tex Comn on the Arts & Humanities, 76-80. *Teaching:* Art instr, Colegio Americano, Mexico City, 59-61; asst to Alberto Ruz Lhuillier, Seminario de Cultura Maya, Nat Univ Mex, 61-62; dir cult affairs, Centro Venezolano Americano, Caracas, 64-66; vis prof hist contemp art Latin Am & pre-Columbian art, Yale Univ, New Haven, Conn, 67; prof hist pre-Columbian, Colonial & contemp art of Mex & Guatemala, Univ Tex, Austin, 67-72; vis prof hist pre-Colombia art of Mesoamerica & Colonial art of Latin Am, Univ NMex, 71; dean, Col of Fine & Applied Arts, Univ of Tex, San Antonio, 72-78; dir & prof art hist, Research Ctr Arts & Humanities, 77- *Mem:* Mid-Am Col Art Asn; Soc for Am Archaeol; Int Cong of Americanists; Int Cong of the Hist of Art; Int Cong of Ethnology & Anthrop. *Publ:* Auth, El estilo artistico de Izapa, Cuadernos de Historia del Arte, No 3, Instituto de Investigaciones Esteticas, Univ Nac Autonoma de Mexico, 73; auth, Izapan style art--a study of its form and meaning, Studies in Pre-Columbian Art & Archaeology, No 10, Dumbarton Oaks, Washington, DC, 73; auth, Mexican American Artists, 73 & Maya Vase, (in prep), Univ Tex Press, Austin. *Mailing Add:* Research Ctr Arts & Humanities Univ of Tex San Antonio TX 78285

QUIRK, THOMAS CHARLES, JR
PAINTER, EDUCATOR
b Pittsburgh, Pa, Dec 31, 22. *Study:* Edinboro State Col, BS, 48; Univ Pittsburgh, MEd, 64. *Work:* Butler Inst Am Art, Youngstown, Ohio; Chatham Col, Pittsburgh; Pittsburgh Pub Schs; Millersville State Col, Pa; Rutgers Univ, Camden, NJ. *Exhib:* Pa Acad Fine Arts Ann, Philadelphia, 69; Drawing & Small Sculpture Ann, Ball State Univ, 71; Nat Acad Design Ann, New York, 74; Philadelphia Watercolor Club Ann, 74 & 79; Philadelphia Watercolor Club, 76; Ann Nat Soc of Painters in Casein & Acrylic, New York, 76 & 79; and others. *Pos:* Artist in residence, Everhart Mus, Scranton, Pa, 72- *Teaching:* Asst prof painting & drawing, Kutztown State Col, 66- *Awards:* Prizes, Drawing Ann, Ball State Univ, 71 & Millersville State Col Watercolor Show, 76; Dawson Mem Prize, Philadelphia Watercolor Club, 74. *Mem:* Soc Painters in Casein & Acrylic; Philadelphia Watercolor Club. *Media:* Multimedia. *Mailing Add:* 310 E Main St Kutztown PA 19530

QUISGARD, LIZ WHITNEY
PAINTER, SCULPTOR
b Philadelphia, Pa, Oct 23, 29. *Study:* Md Inst Col Art, dipl, 49, BFA(summa cum laude), 66; studied with Morris Louis, 57-60; Rinehart Sch Sculpture, MFA, 66. *Work:* Univ Ariz Ghallager Mem Collection; Lever House, New York; Univ Baltimore; Johns Hopkins Univ; Hampton Sch, Towson, Md. *Comn:* Mural painting, William Fell Sch, Baltimore, 78. *Exhib:* Corcoran Biennial Am Painting, 63; Univ Colo Show, 63; Am Painting & Sculpture Ann, Pa Acad Fine Arts, 64; Art Inst Chicago Ann, 65; solo exhibs, South Houston Gallery, New York, 74; Arts & Sci Ctr, Nashua, NH, 75; Gannon Col, Pa, 78 & Mechanic Gallery, Baltimore, 78; Baltimore Mus Traveling Show, 78. *Pos:* Theatre designer, Goucher Col, Theatre Hopkins & Ctr Stage, Baltimore, 66-; art critic, Baltimore Sun, 69 & 70; area reviewer, Craft Horizons Mag, 69- *Teaching:* Instr painting & design, Baltimore Hebrew Congregation, 62-; instr painting & color theory, Md Inst, Baltimore, 65-; lectr design, Goucher Col, 66-69; lectr art hist, Univ Md, Catonsville, 69-70; instr painting, Baltimore Jewish Community Ctr, 74. *Awards:* Artists Prize, Baltimore Mus Regional Exhib, 58; Rinehart Fel, Md Inst, 64-66; Best in Show, Loyola Col, 66. *Bibliog:* B Rose (auth), article, Art Int, 11/62; articles, Arts Mag, 11/62 & Art News, 11/62. *Publ:* Auth, Baltimore's top twelve, Baltimore Mag, 5/69; auth & illusr, An artist's travel log, Baltimore News Am, 71. *Mailing Add:* 321 Rossiter Ave Baltimore MD 21212

R

RABB, (MR & MRS) IRVING W
COLLECTORS
Study: Mr Rabb, Harvard Univ, AB, Harvard Bus Sch; Mrs Rabb, Smith Col, AB; Radcliffe Col, AM. *Collection:* Twentieth century sculpture, including Henry Moore, Giacometti, Maillot, Arp, Lipshitz, Calder, Dubuffet, Nevelson and Laurens; twentieth century drawings and collages, with emphasis on Cubism and sculpture drawings. *Mailing Add:* 1010 Memorial Dr Cambridge MA 02138

RABBIT, WILLIAM E
PAINTER, SCULPTOR
b Casper, Wyo, Dec 3, 46. *Study:* Self taught. *Work:* Tsa-La-Gi Cherokee Nat Mus, Tahlequah, Okla; St Gregory's Mus, Shawnee, Okla; Red Cloud Indian Sch, Pine Ridge, SDak. *Exhib:* Trail of Tears Show, Cherokee Nat Mus, Tahlequah, Okla, 79-83; The Turtle, Native Am Ctr Living Arts, Niagara Falls, NY, 81; Red Cloud Ann, Pine Ridge, SDak, 81-83; Night of the First Americans, Kennedy Ctr, 82 & Smithsonian Inst, 82, Washington, DC; 61st Ann Gallup Ceremonial, NMex, 82-83. *Awards:* First Place for Cherokee Div, Five Tribes Mus, Ft Howard Paper Co, 81; Al Momaday Award, 61st Gallup Ceremonial, 82; Jerome Tiger Award, Trail of Tears Exhib, Getty Oil Co, 83. *Bibliog:* Pat Wall (auth), Oklahoma Art Gallery, 80 & Art Gallery, 82; Beverly Hutton (auth), Art Voices, 81. *Mem:* Indian Arts & Crafts Asn; Southwestern Asn Indian Affairs. *Media:* Acrylic. *Dealer:* Okla Indian Art Gallery 2335 SW 44th Oklahoma City OK 73119. *Mailing Add:* PO Box 34 Pryor OK 74362

RABINOVICH, RAQUEL
PAINTER, SCULPTOR
b Buenos Aires, Arg, Mar 30, 29. *Study:* Univ Cordoba, Arg; Univ Edinburgh; Atelier Andre LHote, Paris. *Work:* Mus Mod Art, Buenos Aires; Genaro Perez Mus, Cordoba; Best Products Co; Container Corp Am; and others. *Comn:* Homage to R C Murphy (glass outdoor monumental sculpture); glass indoor monumental sculpture, Banco Provincia Buenos Aires, New York. *Exhib:* New Directions (Artists of Suffolk Co), Hecksher Mus, Huntington, NY, 71; Benson Gallery, Bridgehampton, NY, 73; Hecksher Mus, Huntington, NY, 74; Susan Caldwell Gallery, New York, 75; City Univ New York Grad Ctr, 78; Jewish Mus, 79; PS 1, 79; Galeria Garces Velasquez, Bogota; Columbia Ctr Int-Am Relations, NY; plus others. *Awards:* Fondo Nac Art Fel, 64; McDowell Colony Fel, 80. *Bibliog:* John Gruen (auth), article, Soho Weekly News, 75; Grace Glueck (auth), article, New York Times, 79; Joh Stringer (auth), article, Arte Informa, 83; George Collins (auth), article, Arts, 83. *Mem:* Abstract Am Artists. *Mailing Add:* 52 Warren St New York NY 10007

RABINOVICH, RHEA SANDERS See Sanders, Rhea

RABINOVITCH, WILLIAM AVRUM
PAINTER, SCULPTOR
b New London, Conn, Sept 16, 36. *Study:* Worcester Polytech Inst, BSME; Boston Mus Sch Fine Arts; San Francisco Art Inst, MFA; Whitney Mus, independent study prog, 73. *Work:* Monterey Peninsula Col, Calif; Monterey Conf Ctr, Calif; Fairmont Hotel, San Francisco & New Orleans; Best & Co; New York Roadrunners Club. *Comn:* Mural, Fairmont Hotel, 74. *Exhib:* One-man shows, Monterey Peninsula Mus Art, 65, Whitney Mus, 73, Rabinovitch & Guerra Gallery, New York, 75 & 76 & Worcester Polytechnic Inst, 83; Whitney Counterweight, Soho Gallery, New York, 77, 79, 81 & 83; Running Show, New York, 81-83; Terminal New York, New York, 83; and others. *Pos:* Dir, Rabinovitch Gallery, New York, Whitney Counterweight, 77, 79 & 81. *Teaching:* Instr, Gallatin Prog, New York Univ, 82. *Awards:* First Prize, Monterey Peninsula Mus Art, 65; Nat Endowment Arts Grant, 77; Grant, Artists Space, New York, 83. *Bibliog:* Rabinovitch Gallery, Anderson

& Archer's SoHo, 79; Charles Dexter (dir), Body and Soul (film), 82; Valentin Tatransky (auth), Group show, Novo arts, New York, Arts Mag, 2/83; and others. *Mem:* Artists Equity Asn; and others. *Media:* Multimedia. *Publ:* Cover artist, Jacob Boehme & Gregory of Nyssa: The Life of Moses, Paulist Press, 78. *Mailing Add:* PO Box 403 New York NY 10013

RABINOWITCH, DAVID
SCULPTOR
b Toronto, Ont, Mar 6, 43. *Study:* Univ Western Ont, BA, 66; self-taught. *Work:* St Louis Mus Art, Mo; Nat Gallery, Berlin, Ger; Mus Mod Art, Vienna; Ruhr Univ, Bochum, Ger; Stucke Mus, Lodz, Poland; and many other pvt & pub collections. *Comn:* Plaster installations, Clocktower, New York & PS 1, New York, 76; elliptical sculpture, Bruckner Festival, Austria, 77; sculpture, Documenta VI, Kassel, WGer, 77; sculpture, City of Dusseldorf, WGer, 81; and others. *Exhib:* Bienniale de Paris, Mus Mod Art, Paris, 77; Recent Acquisitions, Mus Mod Art, New York, 77; Structures for Behavior, Art Gallery Ont, Toronto, 78; Int Sculpture of the 20th Century, Basel, Switzerland, 80; Ten Canadian Artists, Art Gallery Ont, 80; Construction in Process, Lodz, Poland, 81; and many other group & one-man shows. *Collections Arranged:* Dorothy & Herbert Vogel Traveling Exhib; Henry Levison, York Univ, Toronto; and many others. *Teaching:* Instr sculpture, Yale Univ, 74-75. *Awards:* Guggenheim Fel, 75; Can Coun Lynch Staunton Award, 77; and others. *Bibliog:* Article, Vie des Arts, 77; Thomas Lawson (auth), article, Arts Mag, 77; Philip Monk (auth), articles, Parachute, 77 & 78; and others. *Dealer:* Oil & Steel Gallery 157 Chambers St New York NY. *Mailing Add:* 49 E First St New York NY 10003

RABINOWITCH, ROYDEN LESLIE
SCULPTOR
b Toronto, Ont, Mar 6, 43. *Study:* Self taught. *Work:* Mus Ludwig, Cologne, Ger; Mus Contemp Art, Gent, Belgium; Mönchengladbach Mus, Ger; Ulster Mus, Belfast, NIreland; Scottish Nat Gallery Mod Art, Edinburgh. *Exhib:* 10th Paris Biennial, Mus d'Art Mod, France, 77; Brooklyn Mus, 80; Mus Ludwig, Mus Contemp Art, Gent, Belgium, 83 & 84; Lodz Mus, Poland, 84; Mus Ludwig, Cologne, 84; Mönchengladbach Mus, Ger, 84; and others. *Teaching:* Vis assoc, Clare Col, Cambridge Univ, currently. *Awards:* Can Coun Arts Bursary, 67-69 & 71-72 & Sr Arts Grant, 74, 76-77 & 79-80. *Bibliog:* David Bellman (auth), The Barrel Constructions of Royden Rabinowitch: Their Meaning and Effect, Orchard Press, Londonderry, N Ireland, 83. *Media:* Mixed. *Publ:* Auth, Development of the Early Sculpture Leading to the Most Recent Sculpture, Orchard Press, 83; auth, Notes on the handed - limited - numbered, developed manifold, In: Sculptors' Drawings, The Seagram Collection, 83. *Dealer:* John Weber 420 W Broadway New York NY 10013. *Mailing Add:* PO Box 210 New York NY 10013

RABKIN, LEO
COLLECTOR, PAINTER
b Cincinnati, Ohio, July 21, 19. *Study:* Univ Cincinnati; NY Univ. *Work:* Mus Mod Art, Whitney Mus Am Art & Guggenheim Mus, New York; Smithsonian Inst; LaJolla Mus Contemp Art, Calif; plus others. *Exhib:* Seven Painting & Sculpture Biennials, 59-69 & Drawings & Watercolor, 74 & 75, Whitney Mus Am Art; A Plastic Presence, San Francisco Mus Art, Milwaukee Art Ctr & Jewish Mus, 70; one-man shows, La Jolla Mus Contemp Art, 81 & Marilyn Pearl Gallery, New York, 83; American Folk Art Int, 82-85; Art Concrete, Nuremberg, WGer, 83; and others. *Awards:* Ford Found Award for Watercolor, 61; First Prize for Watercolor, Silvermine Guild Artists, 61; Award Sculpture, First Ann Westchester, 67. *Mem:* Am Abstr Artists (pres, 64-78); US Comn Int Asn Art (secy, 68-70); Fine Arts Fedn New York (mem bd dirs, 70-). *Media:* Box Constructions; Watercolor. *Collection:* Whirligigs; Shaker furniture; American primitive sculpture; paintings of Black artists. *Publ:* Ed, American Abstract Artists, 1936-1966. *Mailing Add:* Marilyn Pearl Gallery 38 E 57th St New York NY 10022

RACITI, CHERIE
PAINTER, SCULPTOR
b Chicago, Ill, June 17, 42. *Study:* Univ Ill, Urbana, 60-61; Memphis Acad Arts, Tenn, 63-65; San Francisco State Univ, BA, 68; Mills Col, Oakland, MFA, 79. *Work:* San Francisco Mus of Mod Art, Calif; Mills Col, Oakland. *Exhib:* One-woman shows, Adaline Kent Award Exhib, San Francisco Art Inst, 77, Hansen Fuller Goldeen Gallery, San Francisco, 79 & Marianne Deson Gallery, Chicago, 79; Whitney Mus Am Art Biennial, New York, 75; Los Angeles Inst Contemp Art, Calif, 76 & 78; Univ Calif Art Mus, Berkeley, 77; Long Beach Mus, Calif, 82; and others. *Teaching:* Lectr, Calif State Univ, Hayward, 74; instr, San Francisco Art Inst, Calif, 78; lectr, San Francisco State Univ, Calif, 77-80, asst prof art, 80- *Awards:* Adaline Kent Award, 76; Tregethen Fel, Mills Col, 79. *Bibliog:* Lynn Hershman (auth), Resin painters, Artweek, 9/23/72; Claudia King (auth), 5 Women Artists in Las Vegas, Univ Nev, 3/75; Phillip Linhares (auth), interview, Currant, 4-5/75. *Mem:* San Francisco Art Inst Artist Comt. *Media:* Mixed. *Mailing Add:* 1045 17th St San Francisco CA 94107

RACKUS, GEORGE (KEISTUS)
PAINTER, MURALIST
b Lithuania, May 29, 27; Can citizen. *Study:* Wayne Univ, 48-50; Ont Col Art, 50-52; with Andre L'Hote, 52-55. *Work:* Victoria & Albert Mus, London; New York Cent Libr; Nat Gallery Can; NB Mus, St John; Contemp Mus, Sao Paulo, Brazil. *Comn:* Murals (anodized aluminum), Howoco, Brussels, 69, Alcan Aluminum Ltd, Toronto, 70, Shell Can, Oakville, Ont, 70, Univ Western Ont, London, 71 & Dental Arts Bldg, Dunnville, Ont, 75. *Exhib:* Fifth Ann Exhib Can Art, Montreal Mus, 62; Can Nat Art Gallery Tour, Nat

Art Gallery Victoria, Australia, 67, Nat Gallery SAustralia, Adelaide, 67 & Art Gallery New South Wales, Sydney, 68; Anodized Aluminum Works, Commonwealth Inst Art Gallery, London, 70; Anodized Aluminum Works & Prints, NB Mus, St John, 73; Graphics, Vilnius Contemp Mus, Lithuania, 79; solo exhib, Brand Libr Art Gallery, Glendale, Calif, 81. *Teaching:* Instr art, Dundas Valley Art Sch, Ont, 65-66, McMaster Univ, Hamilton, Ont, 68-69 & Brock Univ, St Catharines, Ont, 77-78. *Awards:* Print of Year, Soc Can Painter-Etchers & Engravers, 71; Graphic Award, Baltic Roots, Baltic Studies Asn, 78; First Prize Anodized Aluminum Work, Colour & Form Exhib, 81. *Bibliog:* Robert Ayre (auth), article, Montreal Star, 62. *Mem:* Ont Soc Artists; Colour & Form Soc (pres, 74-76 & 79-84). *Media:* Anodized Aluminum, Lithography. *Publ:* Auth, British sculpture at Montreal Museum, Weekly, 61; auth, Works of E Gaputyte, Painter & Sculptor, 61; auth, A painter speaks up, Globe & Mail, 62; auth, Toronto painters & sculptors, Review, 62; auth, Anodized aluminum as an art media, Arts Mag, 71. *Dealer:* Merton Gallery 68 Merton Toronto ON. *Mailing Add:* 1998 Lakeshore Rd W Mississauga ON L5J 1J8 Canada

RACZ, ANDRE
PAINTER, PRINTMAKER
b Cluj, Romania, Nov 21, 16; US citizen. *Study:* Univ Bucharest, BA, 35. *Work:* Mus Mod Art, Whitney Mus Am Art & New York Pub Libr, New York; Libr Cong, Washington, DC; Bibliot Nat, Paris. *Exhib:* 50 Yrs Am Art, Mus Mod Art, Paris, London, Belgrade & Barcelona, 55; Int Watercolor Biennial, Brooklyn Mus, 61; Nat Inst Arts & Lett, New York, 68; 50 Yrs American Printmaking, Mus Mod Art, 74; Surrealism & American Art 1931-1947, Rutgers Univ, 77; 50th Anniversary Retrospective, Atelier 17, Univ Wis, 77; Columbia Univ, 83; and others. *Teaching:* Prof painting, Columbia Univ, 51-83, chmn div painting & sculpture, 64-73 & 75-77, prof emer, 83-. *Awards:* Fulbright Res Scholar, Chile, 57; Ford Found Award, 62; Bankroft Award for Distinguished Teacher, Columbia Univ, 83. *Bibliog:* Carmen Valle (auth), Poets on painters & sculptors, Tiger's Eye, 49; Rosamel del Valle (auth), Una tarde con el pintor Andre Racz, Nacion, 49; Antonio Romera (auth), Andre Racz pintor y grabador, Ed Pacifico, 50. *Mem:* Am Asn Univ Prof. *Publ:* Auth, The Reign of Claws, 45, XII Prophets of Aleijadinho, 47, Via Crucis, 48, Mother & Child, 49 & Canciones Negras, 53. *Mailing Add:* PO Box 43 Demarest NJ 07627

RADECKI, MARTIN JOHN
CONSERVATOR
b South Bend, Ind, Jan 4, 48. *Study:* Ind Univ, AB, 70; Intermuseum Conserv Lab (spec study), 74-75. *Collections Arranged:* Conservation of Indiana Governors Portraits, Indianapolis Mus Art, 78. *Pos:* Apprentice conservator, Indianapolis Mus Art, 71-73, asst conservator, 73-74 & chief conservator, 75-; conserv intern, Intermuseums Conserv Lab, 74-75. *Mem:* Am Inst Conserv Historic & Artistic Works; Int Inst Conserv Historic & Artistic Works. *Res:* Treatment of blanched paintings. *Mailing Add:* 1217 Pickwick Pl Indianapolis IN 46208

RADES, WILLIAM L
PAINTER, SCULPTOR
b Milwaukee, Wis, Aug 13, 43. *Study:* Univ Wis, Milwaukee, BFA, 65, MFA, 68; San Francisco Art Inst, with Ron Nagle & Jack Jefferson, 66. *Work:* Santa Barbara Mus Art, Calif; Am Telephone & Telegraph, New York; Minneapolis Inst Art, Minn; Georgia Pacific Corp, Portland, Ore; Eastern Wash Univ, Cheney. *Comn:* Drawing on paper, Wash State Arts Comn & Evergreen State Col, Olympia, 79; Painting on paper, Wash State Arts Comn, Olympia, 80; Painted wood relief, Wash State Arts Comn, Spokane, 82. *Exhib:* Oregon Artists Under 35, Portland Art Mus, 74 & 77; Drawing USA, Minn Mus Art, 77; Washington Painting, Tacoma Art Mus, 77, 79 & 81; 21st Nat Chautauqua Exhib Am Art, New York, 78; Illusionism: Handmade, Henry Art Gallery, Univ Wash, Seattle, 81; Northwest Perspectives, traveling exhib in US, 82-84. *Teaching:* Instr drawing, Univ Wis, Milwaukee, 65-68; asst instr ceramics, San Francisco Art Inst, 66; vis asst prof drawing, Ore State Univ, 72-74. *Awards:* Purchase Awards, Pensacola Nat Drawing Competition, Visual Arts Gallery, 76, Drawing USA, Minn Mus Art, 77 & Fourth LaGrange Nat Competition, CVAA Gallery, 78. *Bibliog:* Bill Rades paintings, Artweek, 74; Mus interview, KTRS Pub TV, 82; Harvey West (auth), The Washington Year, Univ Wash Press, 82. *Mem:* Col Art Asn. *Mailing Add:* 12709 Lake City Blvd SW Tacoma WA 98498

RADICE, ANNE-IMELDA MARINO
HISTORIAN, CURATOR
b Buffalo, NY, Feb 29, 48. *Study:* Wheaton Col, Norton, Mass, AB, 69; Villa Schifanoia, Florence, Italy, MA, 71; Univ NC, Chapel Hill, PhD, 76. *Collections Arranged:* Two on Two at the Octagon (auth, catalog), Drawings from the Collection of the Architect of the Capitol, US Capitol, 80. *Pos:* Asst cur & staff lectr, Nat Gallery Art, 72-76; archit historian for the architect, US Capitol, 76-80, cur, 80- *Res:* Italian renaissance architecture, architecture of Thomas Jefferson and US Capitol. *Publ:* Auth, Il Cronaca: Fifteenth Century Florentyne Architect, Univ Microfilms, 76; ed, ann reports of architect of Capitol, 76- & contribr, The Capitol, Govt Printing Off, 80; auth, US Capitol, Art J, fall 80, The Original Libr Congress, 81. *Mailing Add:* 234 G St SW Washington DC 20024

RADIN, DAN
PAINTER, INSTRUCTOR
b New York, NY, May 12, 29. *Study:* Queens Col; Cranbrook Acad Art, BFA & MFA. *Work:* Cranbrook Mus, Bloomfield Hills, Mich; Detroit Inst Arts, Mich; Butler Inst Am Art, Youngstown, Ohio. *Exhib:* Butler Inst Am Art 26th Ann, 61; Painting Part II, 63 & Landscape II, 71, De Cordova Mus; Am Acad

Ann, Rome, 64; Contemp Surv, J B Speed Mus, Louisville, Ky, 66; The Figure Today, Slater Mus, Norwich, Conn, 77; Invitational, Slater Mus, Norwich, Conn, 80; 25th Ann Regional Exhib, Mystic Art Asn, Conn, 81. *Teaching:* Instr painting, Swain Sch Design, New Bedford, Mass, 64-71; instr painting & drawing, Univ Conn, 72; instr drawing, RI Sch Design, 72. *Awards:* Louis Comfort Tiffany Found Awards in Painting, 62 & 64; Second Purchase Award, Lowe Gallery, 63. *Media:* Oil, Acrylic. *Mailing Add:* Rte 6 Norwich CT 06360

RADOCZY, ALBERT
PAINTER
b Stamford, Conn, Oct 24, 14. *Study:* Parsons Sch Design; Cooper Union, grad. *Work:* Brooklyn Mus, NY; Ball State Teachers Col, Ind; Lyman Allyn Mus, Conn; Sloan-Kettering Mem. *Comn:* Tapestry murals, Allegheny Col, Meadville, Pa, 66. *Exhib:* NJ State Mus Ann, Trenton, 61; Whitney Mus Am Art Ann, New York, 62; Brooklyn Mus Nat Print Exhib, NY, 62; Mus Mod Art Lending Collection, 65; Bergen Community Mus, 73; The Figure in Drawing, Univ of Bridgeport, 77. *Teaching:* Lectr drawing, Cooper Union, 50-55; prof design, City Col New York, 55- *Awards:* Purchase Award, Ball State Teachers Col, 59. *Media:* Oil. *Dealer:* Barbara Walter Gallery 1015 Madison Ave New York NY 10021. *Mailing Add:* 61 Cedar St Cresskill NJ 07626

RADOVICH, DONALD
EDUCATOR, PAINTER
b Nazareth, Pa, Jan 3, 32. *Study:* Univ NMex, BFA, 56, with Randall Davey & Kenneth Adams, MA, 60; also in San Miquel Allende, Mex, 70. *Work:* Univ NMex Mus, Albuquerque; State Capitol, Santa Fe, NMex; Cedar City Art Collection, Utah. *Exhib:* Int Art Exhib, San Antonio, Tex, 69; Midwest Wildlife Art, Kansas City, Mo, 72; Nat Audubon Art Exhibs, Estes Park, Colo, 78 & Denver, 80; Am Ornithologist Union, Ft Collins, Colo, 81; Wave Hill Mus, Bronx, NY, 82; and others. *Teaching:* Assoc prof painting, Western State Col, Gunnison, Colo, 64-; instr, Nat Wildlife Fedn, Washington, DC & Estes Park, Colo, 78- *Awards:* Gold Medal, Nat Exhib, Tubac, Ariz, 65; Purchase Award, Nat Exhib, Cedar City, Utah, 68. *Bibliog:* David Jackson (auth), Radovich paints a cover, NMex Wildlife Mag, 63; J W Campbell (auth), Donald Radovich: Artist, naturalist, teacher, Southwestern Art, Vol IV, No 4, 74. *Mem:* Kappa Pi (sponsor, 65-). *Media:* Oil, Watercolor. *Publ:* Illusr, Birds of New Mexico: Where To Find Them, Univ NMex Press, 63; illusr, Birds of Colorado's Gunnison Country, Western State Found Press, 80. *Mailing Add:* 720 North Spruce St Gunnison CO 81230

RADULOVIC, SAVO
PAINTER, TAPESTRY ARTIST
b Montenegro, Yugoslavia, Jan 27, 11; US citizen. *Study:* St Louis Sch Fine Arts, Wash Univ, 30-32; Fogg Mus Art, Harvard Univ, Carnegie Fel, 37; Acad Belle Arte, Rome, Italy, Fulbright Fel, 49-50. *Work:* City Art Mus St Louis; Univ Ariz; Hist Sect, War Dept, Pentagon, Washington, DC; Col William & Mary, Williamsburg, Va; Mus Mod Art, Miami Beach, Fla; also in pvt collections US & abroad. *Exhib:* Nat Acad Design; Pa Acad Fine Arts; Whitney Mus Am Art; City Art Mus St Louis; Philadelphia Mus Art; and others. *Pos:* Owner & dir, Artists Little Gallery, New York, 46-75. *Awards:* Purchase Prize, City Art Mus St Louis, 41. *Mem:* Nat Soc Lit & Arts; Artists Equity Asn. *Mailing Add:* 140 E 56th New York NY 10022

RADY, ELSA
CERAMIST, SCULPTOR
b New York, NY, July 29, 43. *Study:* Chouinard Art Sch, 62-66. *Work:* Boston Mus Fine Arts; Bank Am, San Francisco; Prudential Insurance, Newark, NJ; Joan Mannheimer Collection, Des Moines. *Comn:* Sculptures, Jules Stein Eye Inst, Univ Calif, Los Angeles, 66 & Disneyland, 67. *Exhib:* Craftsmen USA, Los Angeles Co Mus Art, 66; Design, Pasadena Art Mus, 68-71; Contemporary Porcelain, Philadelphia Art Alliance, 73; Ceramics, Oakland Mus, 74; For the Table Top, Am Crafts Mus, New York, 80; American Porcelain, Renwick Gallery, 80; Ceramic Echoes, Nelson Gallery, Atkins Mus, 83; A Personal View: Selections From the Joan Mannheimer Collection, Univ Mo, Kansas City, 83. *Awards:* Nat Endowment Fel, 81; Calif State Arts Comn Grant, 83. *Mem:* Inst Ceramic Hist. *Media:* Ceramics; Porcelain. *Publ:* Contribr, Ornaments and Surfaces on Ceramics, Kunst & Handwerk, 77; contribr, Studio Porcelain, Chilton Book Co, 80; contribr, Porcelain: Traditions and New Visions, Watson-Guptill, 81; contribr, Ceramics of the 20th Century, Rizzoli, 82; contribr, American Crafts: A Source Book for the Home, Stewart, Tabori, Chang, 83. *Mailing Add:* 1500 Andalusia Ave Venice CA 90291

RADYCKI, J(OSEPHINE) DIANE
HISTORIAN, LECTURER
b Chicago, Ill, Dec 4, 46. *Study:* Univ Ill, Chicago Circle, BA, 69; Hunter Col, City Univ NY, MA, 76; Harvard Univ, MA, 83- *Collections Arranged:* The Legacy of Raphael, Fogg Art Mus, 83. *Pos:* Staff aid, New York City Dept Cult Affairs, 80; res assoc, Metrop Mus Art, 80-81. *Mem:* Col Art Asn; Women's Caucus Art. *Res:* Nineteenth and twentieth century European and American art. *Publ:* Coauth, Voices of women: Three critics, three poets, three heroines, Midmarch Assoc, 80; ed, The Letters and Journals of Paula Modersohn-Becker, Scarecrow Press, 80; auth, The life of lady art students: changing art education at the turn of the century, Art J, 82; auth, Jahrhundertwende, In: Deutsche Kunst des 20 Jahrhunderts aus dem Busch-Reisinger Museum, Harvard University, USA, Städtische Galerie im Städelschen Kunstinstitut Frankfurt am Main, 82. *Mailing Add:* One Langdon St Apt 3 2 Washington Square Village Cambridge MA 02138

RAFFAEL, JOSEPH
PAINTER, PRINTMAKER
b Brooklyn, NY, Feb 22, 33. *Study:* Cooper Union Art Sch, cert; Yale Univ, BFA. *Work:* Metrop Mus Art, New York; San Francisco Mus of Mod Art; Libr of Cong, Hirshhorn Mus & Smithsonian Inst, Washington, DC. *Exhib:* Human Concern, Personal Torment, Whitney Mus Am Art, New York, 70; Tokyo Biennial Figure Art, 74 & Bicentennial Exhib, Dept Interior, originating at Corcoran Gallery Art, 76-77 & 78; one-man exhibs, Calif Yrs 1969-78 (catalog), San Francisco Mus Mod Art, 78, Des Moines Art Ctr, Iowa, 78, Joslyn Art Mus, Nebr, 78, Newport Harbor Art Mus, Newport Beach, Calif, 78, Denver Art Mus, Colo, 78. *Teaching:* Instr art, Sch Visual Arts, 66-69; assoc prof art, Univ Calif, Berkeley, 69; prof art, Sacramento State Univ, 69-73. *Awards:* Fulbright Award, 58-60; L C Tiffany Found Fel, 60; First Prize, Tokyo Biennial Figure Art, 74; First Prize & Purchase Award, Oakland Mus, Calif, 75. *Bibliog:* Gloria Smith (auth), The Eyes Have It: Joseph Raffael (film), NBC-TV, 72; Wm S Wilson (auth), The paintings of Jos Raffael, Studio Int, 5/74; Jerome Tarshis (auth), Nature upclose, Horizon, 9/78. *Media:* Oil, Watercolor; Pastel, Lithography. *Dealer:* Nancy Hoffman Gallery 429 W Broadway New York NY 10012. *Mailing Add:* PO Box 210 San Geronimo CA 94963

RAFFAEL, JUDITH K See North, Judy

RAFFEL, ALVIN ROBERT
PAINTER, INSTRUCTOR
b Dayton, Ohio, Dec 25, 05. *Study:* Chicago Acad Fine Arts; Art Inst Chicago, with F DeForest Schook. *Work:* Dayton Art Inst; Canton Art Mus, Ohio. *Comn:* Seascape (oil), George E Morris, Chicago, 33; portrait of A H Allen, comn by Mrs A H Allen, Chicago, 34; portrait of Karl Koeker, Dayton, Ohio, 35; portrait of S H McCoy, Springfield High Sch, Ohio, 56; landscape (oil), Widow's Home, Dayton, 58. *Exhib:* Cincinnati Ann, Cincinnati Art Mus, 45; Portrait of America, New York, 46; Carnegie Ann, Pittsburgh, 46-48; Provincetown Arts Festival, Mass, 58; Images Age, Ohio, 81. *Teaching:* Prof painting & life drawing, Sch of Dayton Art Inst, 46- *Awards:* First Purchase Prize for Fellaheen, Dayton Art Inst, 45; Award for Holiday on the Ice, Mrs G S Weng, 48; Award for The Lesser Light to Rule the Night, Jefferson Patterson, 51. *Mem:* Am Asn Univ Prof; Dayton Soc Painters & Sculptors. *Media:* Oil, Watercolor. *Publ:* Auth, Art, Exponent, 61. *Mailing Add:* 6720 Mad River Rd Dayton OH 45459

RAFFO, STEVE
PAINTER, DRAFTSMAN
b Hoboken, NJ, Aug 21, 12. *Study:* Cooper Union Sch Art, New York, 2 certs, 33 & 37. *Work:* Delgado Mus, New Orleans, La; Fla Gulf Coast Art Ctr, Clearwater; Pa Acad Fine Arts, Philadelphia; Legal Aid Offices, New York; Citibank, New York; and others. *Exhib:* Whitney Mus Am Art, New York, 47, 48, 49 & 51; Corcoran Gallery, Washington, DC, 47 & 51; Pa Acad, Philadelphia, 48, 49, 53, 61, 62 & 69; Carnegie Inst, Pa, 49; Am Acad Inst Arts, 51, 58 & 60; Art Inst Chicago, Ill, 52 & 61; 4 Young Americans Exhib, RI Mus Art, 55; Nat Acad Design, New York, 60, 67, 69, 75 & 76. *Teaching:* Instr painting, Cooper Union, New York, 39-43 & 47-50; instr painting, Parsons Sch Design, New York, 56-63. *Awards:* Scheidt Mem Prize, Pa Acad, 48; Guggenheim Fel, 50 & 51; Prix de Rome, 52-54. *Bibliog:* Emily Genauer (auth), Art Review, NY World Telegram, 4/25/49; David Friend (auth), Case History--Raffo--Composition, 75; John Corry (auth), East Harlem Artist, New York Times, 9/8/80. *Media:* Oil; Pen & Ink. *Publ:* Contribr, How Paintings Happen, Norton, 51; contribr, Composition--A Painters Guide, Watson Guptill, 75. *Mailing Add:* 503 E 116th St New York NY 10029

RAFSKY, JESSICA C
COLLECTOR
b New York NY, Sept 18, 24. *Study:* George Washington Univ; NY Univ. *Mem:* Whitney Mus; sustaining mem Mus Mod Art; assoc Metrop Mus Art; assoc Am Fedn Arts. *Interests:* Benefactor of Foundation Maeght and friend of Tate Gallery, British Mus, & Victoria & Albert Mus, London. *Collection:* Contemporary art. *Mailing Add:* 200 E 62nd St New York NY 10021

RAGAN, CONNIE SEABOURN
PAINTER, PRINTMAKER
b Purcell, Okla, Sept 20, 51. *Study:* Univ Okla, BFA, 81. *Work:* Gilcrease Mus, Tulsa; Talley Indust, Phoenix; Southwestern Bell Tel Co, Washington, DC; Heritage Ctr, Red Cloud Indian Sch, Pine Ridge, SDak; Tyson Foods Corp, Fayetteville, Ark. *Exhib:* Ann Artists Salon, Okla Mus Art, 79; Nat Printmaking & Drawing Show, Okla Art Ctr, 81; Night of the First Americans, John F Kennedy Ctr, Washington, DC, 82; Selected Works from Night of the First Americans, Smithsonian Mus, 82; Traditions & Transformations, Somerstown Gallery, Somers, NY, 83; Native American Art--Three Artists, Twenty Six Horses, New York, 83; two-person exhib, New Trends Gallery, Santa Fe, 83. *Awards:* Powers Award, Red Cloud Art Show, 83. *Bibliog:* Jimmie Marshall (auth), The emerging of an artist, Art Gallery Mag, winter 80; Jimmie Marshall (auth), The best of both worlds: Connie Seabourn Ragan, Okla 81, 11/81; Dick Frontain (auth), The rising star of Connie Seabourn Ragan, Indian Trader, 10/82. *Media:* Watercolor, Serigraphy. *Mailing Add:* 2605 Southwest 99th St Oklahoma City OK 73159

RAGGIO, OLGA
HISTORIAN, CURATOR
b Feb 5, 26. *Study:* Liceo E O Visconti, Rome, BA(with hon), 44; Lycee Chateaubriand, Rome, Baccalaureat I, 45; Vatican Libr, dipl, 47; Sch Art Hist & Archaeol & Sch Mod Lang, Univ Rome, PhD(cum laude), 49; Inst Fine

Arts, NY State Univ, 51-52. *Collections Arranged:* Renaissance Sculpture from Northern Italy, 72, Patterns of Collecting: Selected Acquisitions 1965-1975 (coauth & ed, catalog), 75, Bernini: A Bacchanal Group, 77, Highlights from the Untermeyer Collection, 77-78, The Splendor of Dresden, 78-79, Treasures from the Kremlin, 79 & European Terracottas from the Arthur M Sackler Collections, 81, Metrop Mus Art, New York. *Pos:* Jr res fel, Metrop Mus Art, New York, 50-52, curatorial asst, Dept of European Sculpture & Decorative Arts, 52-54, asst cur, 54-63, assoc res cur, 63-68, cur, 68-71, chmn, Dept of European Sculpture & Decorative Arts, 71- *Teaching:* Adj asst prof fine arts, Inst Fine Arts, NY Univ, 64-67, adj assoc prof fine arts, 67-68, adj prof fine arts, 68- *Publ:* Coauth (with T Hoving and others), The Chase, The Capture: Collecting at Metropolitan, New York, 76; ed, Notable Acquisitions, 1965-1975, Metrop Mus Art, New York, 76; auth, Sculptuer in the grand manner: Two groups by Anguier & Monnot, 11/77 & A new Bacchic group by Bernini, 12/78, Apollo. *Mailing Add:* Dept of Europ Sculpture Inst Fine Arts Fifth Ave at 82nd St New York NY 10028

RAGINSKY, NINA
PAINTER, PHOTOGRAPHER
b Montreal, Que. *Study:* Rutgers Univ, BA, 62. *Work:* Nat Film Bd Can; Edmonton Art Gallery; George Eastman House; Nat Gallery Can. *Exhib:* International Photo Show, Nat Gallery Can, 68; Vision and Expression, George Eastman House, Rochester, NY, 69; solo exhibs, San Francisco Mus Art, 75 & Art Gallery Ont, 79; Between Friends, Field Mus, Chicago, 76. *Teaching:* Instr photog, Emily Carr Col Art, Vancouver, 72-81; workshops, Univ Ottawa, Univ Victoria & Banff Sch Fine Arts. *Awards:* Can Coun Grant, 76. *Bibliog:* Geoffrey James (auth), An inquiry into the aesthetics of photography, Arts Can, 12/74. *Mem:* Royal Can Acad Art. *Media:* Oils. *Dealer:* Nancy Hoffman W Broadway New York NY. *Mailing Add:* 102 S Turner St Victoria BC V8V 2J8 Canada

RAGLAND, BOB
PAINTER, LECTURER
b Cleveland, Ohio, Dec 11, 38. *Study:* Rocky Mountain Sch Art, Denver, Colo; study with Phil Steele. *Work:* Denver Pub Libr; Karamu House, Cleveland; Irving St Ctr, Cult Arts Prog, Denver. *Comn:* Logo, Metro State Col Black Student Union, 74; art print, Big Sisters of Colo, 75. *Exhib:* 16th Ann Drawing Exhib, Dallas Mus Fine Art Traveling Exhib, 67; one-man show, Cleveland State Univ, 68, Denver Nat Bank, Colo, 80-81, Century Bank Cherry Creek, Denver, 80-81; Juried Jewish Community Ctr Collector's Mart, 80; Group Exhib, Boston, Mass Tubman Gallery, 81. *Pos:* Chmn, Arts & Humanities Comt, 68-69; founding fac mem, Auraria Campus, Community Col, Denver, 70-72; lectr Afro-American art of the 60's & 70's; visual arts coordr, City Spirit Proj, 72. *Teaching:* Instr painting & drawing, Denver Pub Libr, 69-71 & Eastside Action Ctr, Denver, 69-71; artist-in-residence, Model Cities Cult Arts Ctr Workshop, 71-73; artist/teacher, KRMA-TV; instr, Gove Community Sch, 79-81; instr, Metrop State Col, Denver, Colo; instr, Arapahoe Community Col, Littleton, Colo. *Bibliog:* Arlynn Nellhaus (auth), Ragland turns out survival tips for artists, Denver Post, 1/81; Diane Wengler (auth), Bob Ragland--He's learned to survive by using his wits and considerable talent, Gazette-Telegraph, Colo Springs, 4/81; Alexandra King (auth), article, Street Talk Mag, Denver, 10/81. *Mem:* Colo Black Umbrella. *Collection:* Traditional renderings of the figure and landscape in all mediums. *Publ:* Auth, The Artists Survival Handbook or What to do till you're rich and famous, 80; publ, Colorado Gallery Guide, 78-; contr, Black Umbrella/Black Artists Denver. *Mailing Add:* 1723 E 25th Ave Denver CO 80205

RAGLAND, JACK WHITNEY
PAINTER, PRINTMAKER
b El Monte, Calif, Feb 25, 38. *Study:* Ariz State Univ, BA & MA, with Dr Harry Wood, Arthur Jacobson & Ben Goo; Univ Calif, Los Angeles, with Dr Lester Longman, Sam Amato & William Brice; Akad Angewandte Kunst; Akad Bildenden Kunste; Graphische Bundes-Lehrund Versuchsanstalt, Vienna. *Work:* Albertina Mus, Vienna, Austria; Phoenix Art Mus, Ariz; Bibliotheque Nat, Paris; Kunsthaus, Basel, Switz; Los Angeles Co Mus, Calif. *Comn:* Portrait, Henry Nollen, Equitable Life Insurance, 73; stained glass windows, Methodist Church, Derry, Iowa, 74. *Exhib:* Ariz Ann Exhib, Phoenix, 61; Exhib Nat Recognized Artists, Seattle, 63 & Ft Lauderdale, Fla, 64 & 65; Iowa Ann Exhib, Des Moines, 70 & 72; Artists Fedn Traveling Exhib, Eight Midwest States, 75; Southern Calif Exhib, Del Mar, Calif, 81 & 83; and many one-man shows. *Teaching:* Grad asst drawing & painting, Univ Calif, Los Angeles, 61-64; instr drawing & painting, Ariz State Univ, summer 63; assoc prof art hist, drawing, printmaking & painting, Simpson Col, 64-76. *Awards:* Grand Purchase Prize, Ariz Ann, Phoenix Art Mus, 61; Painting Selected as One of Top Representational Paintings in USA, Allied Publ, 62; First Prize, Prints & Graphics, Iowa State Fair, 74. *Bibliog:* Applause, NY Mag of Arts, 11/3/71; New woman, Fla Mag, 11-12/74. *Media:* Acrylic, Oils; Serigraphy. *Mailing Add:* 5490 Rainbow Heights Rd Fallbrook CA 92028

RAGUSA, ISA
HISTORIAN
b Rome, Italy, Dec 30, 26; US citizen. *Study:* NY Univ, BA(magna cum laude), 47, Inst Fine Arts, MA, 51, PhD, 66. *Pos:* Reader & acting dir, Index Christian Art, formerly; res art hist, Princeton Univ, formerly. *Teaching:* Vis scholar, Inst Fine Arts, NY Univ, 83-84. *Mem:* Medieval Acad Am; Col Art Asn; Renaissance Soc; Int Ctr Medieval Art. *Publ:* Coauth (with R B Green), Meditations on the Life of Christ, Princeton Univ Press, 61 & 77; auth, An illustrated psalter from Lyre Abbey, Speculum 64, 71; auth, The Egg reopened, Art Bulletin 53, 71; auth, Terror demonum and terror inimicorum: The two lions of the throne of Solomon and the open door of Paradise, Zeitschrift Kunstgeschichte 40, 77; auth, Art, Americana Ann, 77-84. *Mailing Add:* 30 W 12 St New York NY 10011

RAHILL, MARGARET FISH
CURATOR, CRITIC
b Milwaukee, Wis, Feb 21, 19. *Study:* Univ Wis, Milwaukee. *Collections Arranged:* Karl Priebe Retrospective (with catalog), 68, Marc Chagall Painting and Prints from Milwaukee Collections (with catalog), 70, Eskimo Sculptures and Stone Prints from Baffin Island, Canada (with catalog), 70, Wisconsin Art of the 1920's and 1930's (with catalog), 75 & American Plains Indians, Paintings and Drawings (with catalog), 76, Charles Allis Mus. *Pos:* Art ed & critic, Milwaukee Sentinal, contribr reviewer, Milwaukee Art J & art critic, Wis Archit, 46-61; pub relations, Milwaukee Art Ctr, 62; pub relations & exhibs, Layton Sch of Art, 62-68; cur, Charles Allis Mus, 68-; vpres, City Milwaukee Art Comn, 81-83, councilor at large, 82-86; vpres, City Milwaukee Art Comn, 81-82. *Awards:* Four Milwaukee Press Club Ann Awards for articles on art, museums, art education, 55-60; Milwaukee Art Comn Award for Excellence, 76; Commendation Award, Milwaukee Co Hist Soc, 82. *Mem:* Hon mem Wis Painters & Sculptors Inc; hon mem Wis Designer-Craftsman Inc; Wis Women in Art; Wis Acad Sci, Arts & Lett. *Res:* American 19th century landscapists; Wisconsin art and artists. *Publ:* Auth, Richard Lorenz, Milwaukee Art Ctr, 65. *Mailing Add:* 1630 E Royall Pl Milwaukee WI 53202

RAHJA, VIRGINIA HELGA
PAINTER, ADMINISTRATOR
b Aurora, Minn, Apr 21, 21. *Study:* Hamline Univ, BA, 44; Sch Assoc Arts, DFA, 66. *Exhib:* Many exhibs & ann, Walker Art Ctr, Minn Art Inst, Minn State Fair & Hamline Galleries. *Pos:* Asst supt fine arts, Minn State Fair, 44-48. *Teaching:* Assoc prof painting, Hamline Univ, 43-48 & dir, Hamline Galleries, 45-48; prof painting, Sch Assoc Arts, St Paul, 48-65, dean, 48-73, dir, 73-, pres, 75- *Mem:* Col Art Asn Am; Am Asn Univ Women; Midwest Col Art Conf; Am Fedn Arts. *Media:* Oil. *Mailing Add:* Art Dept Sch Assoc Arts 344 Summit Ave St Paul MN 55102

RAIMONDI, JOHN RICHARD
SCULPTOR
b Boston, Mass, May 29, 48. *Study:* Mass Col Art, BFA, 73. *Work:* Nat Mus Am Art, Washington, DC; Milwaukee Art Mus, Wis; Mus Fine Arts, Boston; Newark Mus, NJ; Okla Mus Art, Oklahoma City. *Comn:* Michael, Canal Nat Bank, Portland, Maine, 75; Erma's Desire, Bicentennial Sculpture Proj, Grand Island, Nebr, 76; Peter John, Blue Cross/Blue Shield, Milwaukee, 78; Evelyn, Spaulding & Sly Corp for IBM, Burlington, Mass, 78; Ran, Levi Strauss & Nat Educ Asn, San Angelo, Tex, 79. *Exhib:* Heritage Art, Brockton Mus Art, Mass, 73; Works in Progress, Boston City Hall Plaza, 74; one-man show, Sunne Savage Gallery, Boston, 78, Dolly Fiterman Gallery, Minneapolis, 83 & Virgina Miller Artspace, Coral Gables, Fla, 83; Art for Architectural Spaces, Art Gallery, Baltimore, 80; New Accessions, Smithsonian Inst, Washington, DC, 81. *Bibliog:* John Raimondi: Artist-in-Residence, Guggenheim Productions, Washington, DC, 75; 500 Mile Sculpture Garden (film), Nebr Educ Television, 76; Harry Rand (auth), cover story, Arts Mag, 4/83. *Mem:* Mass Coun Arts & Humanities. *Media:* Mixed Media. *Mailing Add:* Seal Harbor Winthrop MA 02152

RAKOCY, WILLIAM (JOSEPH)
PAINTER, MURALIST
b Youngstown, Ohio, Apr 14, 24. *Study:* Butler Inst Am Art, with Clyde Singer, 39-41; Am Acad Art, 44; Kansas City Art Inst, with Ross Braught, Ed Lanning & Bruce Mitchell, MFA, 51. *Work:* US Naval Training Sta, Great Lakes, Ill; YMCA, Youngstown; Butler Inst Am Art; El Paso Mus Art, Tex. *Comn:* Mural, Woodrow Wilson High Sch, Youngstown, 46; four murals (with Robert Sonoga & Chet Kwiecinski), McSorleys Colonial Rest, Pittsburgh, Pa, 55; three murals, YMCA, Youngstown; three murals, Mesa Inn, El Paso, Tex, 75; six dioramas, Cavalry Mus & Wilderness Park Mus, El Paso, Tex, 78. *Exhib:* Butler Inst Am Art Ann, 55; one-man show, Juarez, Mexico, 79. *Pos:* Installation cur, Wilderness Park Mus, 77; founder, Bill Rakocy Sch Art. *Teaching:* Instr painting & drawing, Mohn Sch Art, 54-56; asst prof painting & drawing, Col Artesia, 66-67, assoc prof, 67-71. *Awards:* Art Travel Grant to Study in Italy, Ital Businessmen, Kansas City, Mo, 53; Area Award in Watercolor, Butler Inst Am Art, 56. *Mem:* Kansas City Area Artists Asn; El Paso Art Asn; founder Rio Bravo Watercolorists; Western Asn Art Schs & Univ Mus; El Paso Hist Soc. *Media:* Oil, Watercolor. *Interests:* Promote art auctions to assist artists via sales and scholarships. *Publ:* Auth, A Western Portfolio, 65; auth, Art Reporter, 72; auth, Sketches & Observations, 72. *Mailing Add:* 4210 Emory Way El Paso TX 79925

RAKOVAN, LAWRENCE FRANCIS
PRINTMAKER, PAINTER
b Eleria, Ohio, Oct 26, 39. *Study:* Detroit Soc Arts & Crafts; Wayne State Univ, BS; RI Sch Design, MA. *Work:* Brooklyn Mus, NY; Colby Col; Calif Col Arts & Crafts, Oakland; Univ Southern Maine; Univ Maine, Orono. *Comn:* 14 Stations of the Cross & exterior monumental cross with stoneware reliefs of The Four Evangelists, St Charles Borromeo Church, Brunswick, Maine, 75. *Exhib:* Two-man show, St Peter's Ctr, New York, 73; Maine 75, Bowdoin Col, 75; Sculpture in Wood, Maine Festival of Arts, Bowdoin Col, 77; two-man exhib, Benbow Gallery, Newport, RI, 77; one-man show, Treat Gallery, Bates Col, 76; and others. *Teaching:* Assoc prof painting & printmaking, Univ Southern Maine, 67-; vis prof art, Univ Maine, Augusta, 79-80. *Awards:* State of Maine Res Grant, 73. *Mem:* Col Art Asn Am; Skowhegan Sch Painting & Sculpture. *Media:* Oil, Stone Lithography. *Dealer:* Benbow Gallery Newport RI 02840; Barridoff Gallery Portland ME. *Mailing Add:* Upper Maine St Brunswick ME 04011

RALEIGH, HENRY PATRICK
PAINTER, WRITER
b New York, NY, Feb 5, 31. *Study:* Pratt Inst, BS, 56 & MS, 59; New York Univ, PhD, 63. *Exhib:* Ten Artists Under Thirty, Riverside Mus, New York, 64; Artists of the Mid-Hudson Valley, Albany Inst of Art, NY, 70-75 & 82; First Street Gallery, New York, 83-84. *Teaching:* Chmn art dept, Pratt Inst Art Sch, 61-68; prof film hist, art criticism & aesthet, State Univ NY, New Paltz, 68-, co-dean fac fine & performing art, 71-73 & chmn studio art & art hist, 68-74. *Awards:* Travel Grant, 7th Int Am Coun Learned Soc, Cong, Rumania, 72. *Mem:* Am Soc Aesthet. *Media:* Oils. *Res:* Application of value study to examinations of contemporary art and art criticism. *Publ:* Auth, Exhaustion thresholds of painting, Bucknell Rev, 72; auth, Revival of aesthetic symbolism, 74 & Aesthethic of chance, 75, J Aesthet & Art Criticism; auth, Art and the public, 79 & The Ambiguous Art (film), 82, J Aesthetic Educ. *Mailing Add:* State Univ NY New Paltz NY 12561

RALEY, ROBERT L
COLLECTORS
b Baltimore, Md, Aug 22, 24. *Study:* Univ Pa, MArch, with Louis Kahn; Univ Del, MA. *Pos:* Mem bd dir, Del Art Mus; mem Am art comt, Philadelphia Mus Art; state adv, Nat Trust for Hist Preserv; bd trustees, Hist Soc Del; mem, State Rev Bd Hist Preserv, Del. *Mem:* Am Inst Architects; Am Asn Mus (mem trustees comt). *Collection:* Twentieth century European and American paintings and drawings and contemporary sculpture. *Mailing Add:* 800 Center Mill Rd Greenville DE 19807

RALSTON, JAMES KENNETH
PAINTER, ILLUSTRATOR
b Choteau, Mont, Mar 31, 1896. *Study:* Art Inst Chicago; Rocky Mountain Col, Hon DFA, 71. *Work:* Jefferson Nat Expansion Mem, St Louis, Mo; Custer Battlefield Nat Monument, Mont; Mont Hist Soc Mus & Galleries, Helena; Buffalo Bill Hist Ctr, Whitney Gallery Western Art, Cody, Wyo; Western Heritage Mus Treasures of West Collection, Billings, Mont. *Comn:* Murals, The Crossing, Jordan Hotel, Glendive, Mont, 52 & Billings Munic Airport, Logan Field, 58; paintings, After the Battle, Treasures of West Collection, 55, Into the Unknown, Jefferson Nat Expansion Monument, 64 & The Return, First Westside Nat Bank, Great Falls, Mont, 71. *Exhib:* Gainsborough Gallery, Calgary, Alta, 59; Charles M Russell Gallery, Great Falls, 62 & 71; Mont Hist Soc, 64; Galeries Lafayette, Paris, 66; Yellowstone Art Ctr, Billings, 67 & 71. *Awards:* Inducted into Nat Cowboy Hall of Fame of Great Westerners, 78; William F Cody Award, Old West Trail Found, 78. *Bibliog:* Ed Ainsworth (auth), The Cowboy in Art, Bk World Publ, 68; James Graff (producer), The Old West of J K Ralston (doc film), Rendezvous 75, Mont Hist Soc, 76; Bob Eide (auth), Cowboy artist, Northern Natural Gas Publ, 79. *Mem:* Mont Inst Arts; Billings Arts Asn; Yellowstone Art Ctr. *Media:* Oil, Ink, Watercolor. *Publ:* Auth & illusr, Rhymes of a Cowboy, Rimrock Publ, 69. *Mailing Add:* 2103 Alderson Ave Billings MT 59102

RAMANAUSKAS, DALIA IRENA
PAINTER, DRAFTSMAN
b Kaunas, Lithuania, Jan 10, 36; US citizen. *Study:* Southern Conn Col, BS(art educ). *Work:* Am Tel & Tel; Prudential Insurance Co; Smithsonian Inst, Washington, DC; Va Mus, Richmond; New Britain Mus Am Art, Conn. *Comn:* Sepia drawing, Rebekah Harkness Kean Dance Theater, New York, 64. *Exhib:* Realism, Ulrich Mus Art, Wichita, 75; Drawings by Four Artists, DM Gallery, London, 75; Art 77, Root Art Ctr, Hamilton Col, Clinton, NY; Am Drawing 1927-1977, Minn Mus of Art, St Paul; solo shows, O K Harris Gallery, New York, 77-79 & Capricorn Gallery, Washington, DC, 77-82; Stockholm Int Art Expo, 81; and others. *Awards:* Am Drawing 20th Ann Purchase Award, Norfolk Mus Arts & Sci, 63. *Bibliog:* Rev in Artforum, 4/74; M L D'Otrange Mastai (auth), Illusionism in Art, Abaris, 76. *Media:* Color Inks, Watercolor. *Dealer:* O K Harris 383 W Broadway New York NY 10012; Payson Weisberg 822 Madison Ave New York NY 10021. *Mailing Add:* PO Box 264 Main St Ivoryton CT 06442

RAMBERG, CHRISTINA
PAINTER
b Camp Campbell, Ky, Aug 21, 46. *Study:* Art Inst Chicago, BFA, 68, MFA, 72. *Work:* Art Inst Chicago; Whitney Mus Am Art, New York; Nat Collection Fine Art, DC; 20th Century Mus, Vienna, Austria; Mus Contemp Art, Chicago. *Exhib:* Spirit of the Comic in the 50's & 60's, Univ Pa, Philadelphia, 69; False Image II, Hyde Park Art Ctr, Chicago, 69; Whitney Ann, Whitney Mus Am Art, New York, 72, 73 & 79; Made in Chicago, Sao Paulo Biennial, Brazil, 73; one-person shows, Phyllis Kind Galleries, 75 & 77; Who Chicago, 80-81, traveling to London, Sunderland, Glasgow, Edinburgh, Belfast & Boston; and others. *Teaching:* Vis artist-instr painting, Univ Colo, Boulder, 72; vis artist drawing, Sch Art Inst Chicago, 75-; vis artist drawing & painting, Northwestern Univ, Evanston, 79-80. *Awards:* Nat Endowment for Humanities, 78 & 83. *Media:* Acrylic, Masonite. *Dealer:* Phyllis Kind Gallery 313 W Superior St Chicago IL 60611. *Mailing Add:* 3454 N Damen Chicago IL 60618

RAMES, STANLEY DODSON
PAINTER, EDUCATOR
b Woodson, Ark, Aug 11, 23. *Study:* Chicago Art Inst, cert, 45-49; also with Edgar Whitney, Robert E Wood, Henri Casselli, Bud Shackelford, Tom Hill. *Comn:* Mural, 375th Fighter Squadron, England, 44. *Exhib:* New Orleans Art Asn, Delgado Mus, La, 55; Southern Watercolor, Tenn Fine Arts Ctr Cheekwood, Nashville, 77; Southern Watercolor, Columbus Mus Art, Ga, 78; Southern Watercolor, Columbia Mus Art, SC, 80. *Pos:* Set designer, NBC-TV, Chicago, 49-54; art dir, WDSU-TV, New Orleans, La, 54-72. *Teaching:* Instr

art, Tulane Univ Col, New Orleans, La, 72-79. *Awards:* Watercolor Award, Southern Watercolor Ann, La Watercolor Soc; Best of Show, Southern Artists, Hot Springs Art Ctr, 81. *Bibliog:* Article, Wayne King sets, Popular Mechanics, 53. *Mem:* La Watercolor Soc (pres, 71); Cooperstown Art Asn; Southern Watercolor Soc; Southern Artists Asn; Ky Watercolor Soc. *Media:* Watercolor, Oil. *Dealer:* Collectors Showroom Inc 325 N Wells Chicago IL 60610. *Mailing Add:* PO Box 2005 Albert Pike Station Hot Springs AR 71913

RAMIREZ, JOEL TITO
CALLIGRAPHER, ILLUSTRATOR
b Albuquerque, NMex, June 3, 23. *Study:* Univ NMex, with Randall Davey, Kenneth M Adams & Ralph Douglass; also with Enrique Montenegro & Raymond Jonson. *Work:* Mus NMex, Santa Fe; Univ Albuquerque; NMex State Univ. *Comn:* La Hacienda, Ford Motor Co, Dearborn, Mich, 73; Keep New Mexico Beautiful, Kennecott Copper Corp, 74; Tex Int Airlines; Paramont Pictures. *Exhib:* War with Japan, 47; Fiesta Show, Mus NMex, 62; Art Intimates, Galerie de Paris, New York, 65; and others. *Pos:* First vpres, NMex Art League, 58-59; assoc ed & art dir, El Clarin. *Teaching:* Teacher oil painting, Ramirez Art Studio, 65-73. *Awards:* Devocion, Rodeo de Sante Fe, Paul F Rutledge, 59; Anitiqua, Fine Arts Mus, Santa Fe, James T Forrest, 62; Los Trampas, Fiesta Show, Bernique Longley, 63. *Bibliog:* Jacinto Quirate (auth), Southwest Artists, Exxon Oil Co, 73 & Mexican-American Artists, Univ Tex, Austin, 74; Frank Duane (auth), Pilgrims to the West, KLRN-TV, San Antonio, Tex, 73. *Mem:* Int Soc Artists. *Publ:* Contribr, After Cortez, 73; illusr, Juan Diego and the Virgin of Guadalupe, 75; illusr, St Bernadette of Lourdes, 75. *Mailing Add:* 10305 Santa Paula NE Albuquerque NM 87111

RAMOS, MELVIN JOHN
PAINTER, EDUCATOR
b Sacramento, Calif, July 24, 35. *Study:* Sacramento Jr Col, with Wayne Thiebaud, 54; San Jose State Col, 55; Sacramento State Col, MA, 58. *Work:* Mus Mod Art, New York; Neue Galerie, Aachen, Ger; Oakland Art Mus & San Francisco Art Mus, Calif; Univ Mus, Potsdam, NY. *Comn:* Paintings, Time Inc, New York, 68 & Syracuse Univ, NY, 70. *Exhib:* Pop Art USA, Oakland Mus & Six More, Los Angeles Co Mus, Calif, 63; Human Concern, Personal Torment, Whitney Mus Am Art, New York, 69; Pop Art Revisited, Hayward Gallery, London, 69; Looking West, Joslyn Art Mus, Omaha, Nebr, 70; Am Pop Art, Whitney Mus Am Art, 74; Krannert Mus, Univ Ill, Champaign, 74; Cornell Univ, Ithaca, NY, 74; Retrospective, Kaiser Wilhelm Mus, Krefeld, WGer, 75; and others. *Teaching:* Assoc prof painting, Calif State Univ, Hayward, 66-80, prof art, 80- *Bibliog:* John Perreault (auth), Classic pop revisited, Art in Am, 3-4/74; Liz Claridge (auth), Mel Ramos, Mathews Miller Dunbar, London, 75; Mel Ramos--Watercolors, Lancaster-Miller, 79. *Media:* Oil, Watercolor. *Publ:* Contribr, History of Modern Art, 69, Erotic Art 2, 70, Art Now/New Age, 71, The High Art of Cooking, 72 & Art as Image & Idea, 72. *Dealer:* Calle Moragrega 38 Horta de San Juan Spain; Louis K Meisel Gallery 141 Prince St New York NY 10012. *Mailing Add:* 5941 Ocean View Dr Oakland CA 94618

RAMSAUER, JOSEPH FRANCIS
PAINTER, EDUCATOR
b Chicago, Ill, Aug 12, 43. *Study:* Southern Ill Univ, Carbondale, BA, 67, MFA, 69; also with David Slivka. *Work:* Univ Galleries, Southern Ill Univ; Louisville Arts Club; Standard Oil Co Ind; McDonald Corp Indianapolis. *Comn:* Jr Theatre Show Wagon, Davenport Park Bd, Iowa, 71; Saukenuk Indian Mem, Ill State Bicentennial Comn, Black Hawk Col, Ill, 76. *Exhib:* Mid-Am Two, City Art Mus of St Louis, 69; Mid-Miss Valley Ann, Davenport Munic Art Gallery, Iowa, 70, 74-77, 80 & 81; 19th Mid-South Biennial, Brooks Mem Art Gallery, Memphis, 75; Washington & Jefferson Nat, Washington & Jefferson Col, Washington, Pa, 76; Am Painters in Paris, Paris Convention Ctr, France, 76; Ann Seven State Competition, Univ Wis, Platteville, 77; 41st Nat Ann Midyear Show, Butler Inst of Am Art, Youngstown, Ohio, 77; 69th Ann Jury Exhib, Birmingham Mus of Art, Ala, 77; Tex Fine Arts Asn Traveling Exhib, 78. *Collections Arranged:* Spectrum Invitational, Davenport Munic Gallery, Iowa, 72; Black Hawk Col & Ill Cent Col Art Fac Exhib, 74; 31st Ill Invitational, Ill State Mus, 79; Two Midwest Artists, Sangamon State Univ, Springfield, Ill, 81. *Teaching:* Prof art, Black Hawk Col, 69-, chmn art dept, 71-83. *Awards:* Second Place, 14th Mid-Miss Ann, Quad-Cities Times, 76; Best of Show, Ann Seven State Competition, 77; First Place in Acrylic Division & The Judges Award, Pilot Club of Golden Sands Int Fine Arts Exhib, 77. *Mem:* Col Art Asn; Chicago Artists Coalition. *Media:* Acrylic on Canvas. *Mailing Add:* 5701 38th Ave Moline IL 61265

RANALLI, DANIEL
PHOTOGRAPHER, CONSULTANT
b New Haven, Conn, Oct 17, 46. *Study:* Clark Univ, Worcester, Mass, BA, 68; Boston Univ, Mass, MA, 71. *Work:* Polaroid Europa Collection, Amsterdam; Boston Mus Fine Arts; San Francisco Mus Mod Art; Worcester Art Mus, Mass; Mus Mod Art, New York; and others. *Comn:* Stage set projections, James Cunningham & Acme Dance Co, New York, 78; New Works, Mass Council Arts, Photographic Resource Ctr, 81. *Exhib:* One-man shows, Mass Inst of Technol Photog Gallery, 77, Foto Gallery, New York, 78, Carl Siembab Gallery, Boston, 78, 79 & 82 & Vision Gallery, Boston; Inst Contemp Art, Boston, 81; Boston Mus Fine Arts, 81; San Francisco Mus Mod Art; Baltimore Mus Fine Arts; and others. *Pos:* Program dir, The Artists Found, 75-79; executive dir, Truro Ctr Arts, 79-81; actg dir, Boston Univ Art Gallery, 82-83. *Awards:* Nat Endowment Arts, Visual Arts in the Performing Arts, 78; Individual Photog Fel, 80. *Bibliog:* Jessica Alonso (auth), Expressions of Finesse, The Boston Globe, 4/26/77; Candida Finkel (auth), Light Lines, Afterimage, Rochester, NY, 6/77; article, Camera Arts, 5/83. *Mem:* Boston Visual Artists Union (vpres, 77); Photog Resource Ctr, Boston;

Mass Alliance Art Educ (bd trustees, 76-79). *Publ:* Auth, Trail Pouch, Right Hemisphere, 77; contribr, Panopticon, Panopticon Gallery, 77; coauth, Darkroom Dynamics, Curtin & London, 78; contribr, Patron's Choice, Mus Calender, De Cordova Mus, 77. *Dealer:* G H Dalsheimer Gallery 519 N Charles Baltimore MD; Vision Gallery 216 Newbury St Boston MA. *Mailing Add:* 76 Sumner St Newton MA 02159

RAND, ARCHIE
PAINTER, MURALIST
b New York, NY, 49. *Study:* City Col New York, 65-66; Brooklyn Col, 67; Art Students League NY, 67-68; Pratt Inst, Brooklyn, BFA, 70. *Work:* Brooklyn Mus & Pratt Inst, NY; Israel Mus, Jerusalem; Mint Mus Art, Charlotte, NC; Carnegie Inst; Art Inst Chicago. *Comn:* Mural wall panels, Yeshivah of Flatbush, New York, 73-77; murals in stone, Congregation B'nai Yosef, New York, 75-77 & fresco & mosaic interior, 78-79; 12 stained glass windows, Anshe Emet Synagogue, Chicago, 80; three stained glass windows, Temple Sholom, Chicago, 83; exterior murals, Michlalah Col, Jerusalem, 83. *Exhib:* One-man shows, Tibor de Nagy Gallery, New York, 72, 74, 78, 79, 80, 82 & 84 & Dart Gallery, Chicago, 80; Selected Works from Tibor de Nagy Gallery, Mint Mus Art, Charlotte, NC, 78; New York Collection, Mem Gallery, Albright-Knox Art Gallery, Buffalo, NY, 78-79 & 79-80; Young Am Painters, Salon des Independents, Paris, 80; Artists Choice Mus, New York, 79 & 83; Urban Works, Phyllis Kind Gallery, New York, 84. *Pos:* Designer, Rambusch Stained Glass Studios, formerly, Edward Fields Tapestries Inc 83-84. *Teaching:* Instr, Westchester Community Col, 82- *Awards:* Creative Artists Pub Serv Prog, NY State Coun Arts, 75; Clayworks Residency, Nat Endowments Arts, 83. *Bibliog:* Ross Feld (auth), On the hook: The work of Archie Rand, Arts, 12/77; John Ashbery (auth), A joyful noise, New York Mag, 6/79; John R Lane (auth), Archie Rand, the consistency of choice, Arts, 11/79. *Media:* Acrylic on Canvas; Stained Glass, Fresco. *Mailing Add:* Tibor de Nagy Gallery 29 W 57th St New York NY 10019

RAND, HARRY
HISTORIAN, EDUCATOR
b New York, NY, Jan 10, 47. *Study:* City Col New York, BA, 69; Harvard Univ, AM, 71, PhD, 74. *Pos:* Contrib ed, Arts Mag, New York, 75-; cur 20th century painting & sculpture, Nat Mus Am Art, DC, 79- *Teaching:* Asst prof mod art & methodology, State Univ NY Buffalo, 74-78. *Awards:* Andrew W Mellon Postdoctoral fel in Humanities, 76-77. *Bibliog:* Hilton Kramer (auth), The pictures in the paintings, 6/21/81 & A true museum of record, 2/14/82, New York Times. *Mem:* Explorers Club, New York. *Res:* History of modern art; problems of methodology and implications. *Publ:* Coauth, The Genius of American Painting, Morrow & Co, New York, 73; auth, Seymour Lipton; Aspects of Sculpture, Smithsonian Inst, 79; auth, Arshile Gorky: The Implications of Symbols, A Schram & Co, 81; auth, The Beginning of Things, Dryad Press, 83. *Mailing Add:* Nat Mus Am Art Eighth & G St NW Washington DC 20560

RAND, PAUL
PAINTER, DESIGNER
b New York, NY, Aug 15, 14. *Study:* Pratt Inst; Art Students League, with George Grosz; Parsons Sch Design; Philadelphia Col Art, Hon DFA, 79. *Work:* Mus Mod Art; Libr Cong, Washington, DC. *Exhib:* One-man shows, Composing Room, 47, Am Inst Graphic Arts Gallery, 58 & IBM Gallery, 71; Pratt Inst, 72; many shows, Art Dirs Club New York. *Pos:* Art dir, Esquire Apparel Arts, 37-41; art dir, Weintraub Advert Agency, 41-54; design consult, IBM Corp, 56, Westinghouse Elec Corp, 60-81 & Cummins Engine Co, 63- *Teaching:* Instr design, Cooper Union, 42; instr graphic design, Pratt Inst, 46-47; prof graphic design, Yale Univ, 56-69 & 74- *Awards:* Gold Medal, Am Inst Graphic Arts, 66; Art Dirs Hall of Fame, 72. *Bibliog:* Georgine Oeri (auth), article, Graphis Mag, 47; Y Kamekura (auth), The work of Paul Rand, Zokeisha, Tokyo & Knopf, NY, 59; article in Am Artist, 70. *Mem:* Art Dirs Club New York; Am Inst Graphic Arts; Alliance Graphique Int, Paris; Benjamin Franklin fel, Royal Soc Arts & Sci, London. *Publ:* Auth, Thoughts on design, Wittenborn, 47 & Van Nostrand Reinhold, 70; auth, Black in the Visual Arts, Harvard Univ, 49; illusr, I Know a Lot of Things, 56, Sparkle & Spin, 57, Little 1, 62 & Listen, Listen, 70, Harcourt. *Mailing Add:* 87 Goodhill Rd Weston CT 06883

RAND, STEVEN JAY
SCULPTOR
b Yonkers, NY. *Study:* State Univ NY, Buffalo, BFA, 75; Univ Ariz, MFA, 77. *Work:* Phoenix Art Mus; Tucson Mus Art; Colorado Springs Fine Arts Ctr; Plains Art Mus, Moorhead, Minn; City Palo Alto, Calif. *Comn:* Sculptures, City Scottsdale, 79, City Phoenix, 81 & City Casa Grande, 82. *Exhib:* Six Artists Invitational, Tucson Mus Art, 79; Okla Arts Ctr Ann Competition, 81; solo exhibs, Scottsdale Ctr Arts, Ariz, 82 & Plains Art Mus, Moorhead, Minn, 83; Sept Competition, Alexandria Mus, La, 83; Coos Mus Ann, Coos Bay, Ore, 83. *Mem:* Artists Equity Asn. *Media:* Painted Welded Metal. *Dealer:* John Berggruen Gallery 228 Grant Ave San Francisco CA 94108. *Mailing Add:* 2639 N 28 Pl Phoenix AZ 85008

RANDALL, LILIAN M C
CURATOR
b Berlin Germany, Feb 1, 31. *Study:* Mt Holyoke Col, BA(cum laude), 50; Radcliffe Col, MA, 51, PhD, 55. *Work:* Walters Art Gallery, Baltimore, Md. *Collections Arranged:* Armenian Manuscripts, Walter Art Gallery, Baltimore, Md, 74; Printed Books before 1500, Walters Art Gallery, 77; Splendor in Books, Grolier Club, New York, 77-78; An American Art Agent in Paris, George A Lucas (1857-1909), Walters Art Gallery, 78-79. *Pos:* Asst dir, Md Arts Coun, 72-73; cur manuscripts & rare books, Walters Art Gallery, 74.

Teaching: Vis lectr medieval illumination, Johns Hopkins Univ, 64-68. *Mem:* Medieval Acad Am; Col Art Asn; Int Ctr Medieval Art (bd dirs, 78-82); Baltimore Bibliophiles (pres, 81-83). *Res:* Medieval European illumination. *Publ:* Auth, Exempla and their influence on Gothic marginal art, Art Bull, 57; auth, Images in the margins of Gothic manuscripts, Univ Calif, 66; co-ed & contribr, Gatherings in honor of Dorothy Miner, Walters Art Gallery, 74; auth, The Diary of George A Lucas: An American Art Agent in Paris, (2 vols), Princeton Univ Press, 79; auth, A Nineteenth-Century Medieval Prayerbook Woven in Lyon, In: Art the Ape of Nature: Studies in Honor of H W Janson, Harry N Abrams, 81. *Mailing Add:* c/o Walters Art Gallery 600 N Charles St Baltimore MD 21201

RANDALL, (LILLIAN) PAULA
SCULPTOR, DESIGNER
b Plato, Minn, Dec 21, 1895. *Study:* Minneapolis Inst Arts; Univ Southern Calif; Otis Art Inst, Los Angeles. *Work:* Western Div, Nat Audubon Soc, Sacramento, Calif; Off Tournament Roses, Pasadena, Calif. *Exhib:* Form & the Inner Eye Tactile Show, Calif State Univ, Los Angeles & Pierce Col, San Fernando, Calif, 72; 22-Nation Bicentennial Show, Galerie Int, New York, NY, 76; one-person shows, Galerie Vallombreuse, Biarritz, France, 75 & Pacificulture Asian Art Mus, Pasadena, Calif, 77; and others. *Teaching:* Pvt sculpture classes, 69-; instr sculpture, Pasadena Sch Fine Arts, 70. *Awards:* Laguna Beach Art Mus Award, All Calif Show, 64; Spec Achievement Award, All Calif Exhib, Indio, 66; Pasadena Soc Artists Spec Award, 71. *Bibliog:* Louise Bouett (auth), An approach to understanding art: Paula Randall, Daily News; Carla Tomaso (auth), Ageless art: The inner circuits of Paula Randall, Pasadena Guardian, 75; Meet this lady sculptor, Senior World, San Diego, 7/75. *Mem:* Pasadena Soc Artists (secy-treas publicity, 62-72); Laguna Beach Art Mus; Los Angeles Co Art Gallery. *Media:* Mixed; Welded Metals. *Mailing Add:* 441 Ramona Ave Sierra Madre CA 91024

RANDALL, RICHARD HARDING, JR
CURATOR, HISTORIAN
b Baltimore, Md, Jan 31, 26. *Study:* Princeton Univ, AB(archit); Harvard Univ, MA(fine arts). *Collections Arranged:* American Furniture in the MFA (with catalog), Mus Fine Arts, Boston, 64; reinstallation of the entire collection of the Walters Art Gallery, 74. *Pos:* Assoc cur, Cloisters, Metrop Mus Art, New York, 53-59; asst cur, Mus Fine Arts, Boston, Mass, 59-64; asst dir, Walters Art Gallery, Baltimore, 64-65, dir, 65-81, cur, medieval art, 81- *Res:* American furniture, medieval art, arms and armour. *Publ:* Auth, Bestiary of the Cloisters, 59. *Mailing Add:* 301 Kendall Rd Baltimore MD 21210

RANDALL, RUTH HUNIE
DESIGNER
b Dayton, Ohio, Sept 30, 1896. *Study:* Cleveland Art Inst, design & art educ; Syracuse Univ, BFA & MFA; State Univ NY Col Ceramics, Alfred Univ; Kunstgewerbe Schule, Vienna; also with Ruth Reeves & Ivan Mestrovic. *Work:* Syracuse Univ, Everson Mus, Syracuse, NY; Walker Art Mus, Youngstown, Ohio; San Antonio Mus, Tex. *Comn:* Ceramic sculpture relief, Exterior Br Libr, Syracuse Bd Educ Bldg Comt, 60. *Exhib:* World's Fairs, San Francisco & New York; Paris Decorative Arts; Nat Ceramic Exhibs, 30-62; Everson Mus, 81. *Teaching:* Prof design & crafts, Syracuse Univ Sch Art, 30-62; adult educ instr crafts & design, Charlotte Co, 64-78. *Awards:* Second Prize Awards, Nat Ceramic Show, 30, 36 & 56; First Prize for Ceramic Sculpture, Rochester Mus, NY, 62. *Bibliog:* Article on personal ceramic collection, Syracuse Mus Bulletin, 60; A Century of Ceramics in the USA, Dutton, 78. *Mem:* Southwest Fla Craft Guild; NY State Craftsmen (bd dirs, 58-60); Syracuse Ceramic Guild (pres, 56). *Media:* Ceramics. *Collection:* Japanese Mingei ceramics and Peruvian ceramics for Syracuse University Art School Collection. *Publ:* Illusr ceramics page, Craft Horizons, 39 & 73; auth, Ceramic Sculpture, Watson Guptill, 46. *Mailing Add:* 146 Sunset Dr Glastonbury CT 06033

RANDALL, THEODORE A
SCULPTOR, EDUCATOR
b Indianapolis, Ind, Oct 18, 14. *Study:* Yale Univ, BFA, 38; State Univ NY Col Ceramics, Alfred Univ, MFA, 49, Hon DFA, 83. *Comn:* Pottery, Syracuse Mus Fine Arts & St Stephens Church, Albany, NY. *Exhib:* Solo exhibs, Elements Gallery, New York, Rodell Retreat Gallery, Los Angeles, Gumps Gallery, San Francisco, DBR Gallery, Cleveland and others. *Pos:* Sculptor/potter, Cooper-French Gallery, Newport, RI, presently. *Teaching:* Lectr motives & meaning in art & ceramics today; instr, State Univ NY Col Ceramics, Alfred Univ, 52-53, asst prof, 53-56, head div art, 56-73, prof ceramics, 60- *Awards:* Prizes, Smithsonian Inst & Everson Mus; Ceramic Symp Award, 82; and others. *Mem:* Fel Am Ceramic Soc; fel Acad Int Ceramics; fel Nat Coun Educ Ceramic Arts; fel Nat Asn Schs Art. *Publ:* Auth, Notions about the usefulness of pottery, Pottery Quart, 61; auth articles in Am Ceramic Soc J & Bulletin, Ceramic Age, Ceramic Indust & Ceramics Monthly. *Mailing Add:* Box 774 Alfred NY 14802

RANDLETT, MARY WILLIS
PHOTOGRAPHER
b Seattle, Wash, May 5, 24. *Study:* Whitman Col, BA, 47; photog with Hans Jorgensen, Seattle, 48. *Work:* Dept Photog & Prints, Metrop Mus Art, New York; Arch Am Art, Nat Collection Fine Arts, Nat Portrait Gallery, Washington, DC; Manuscripts Div, Univ Wash Collections, Seattle. *Comn:* Wash State Writers (photographs), Wash State Libr, Olympia, 68; doc ser photographs Noguchi Skyviewing sculpture, Western Wash Univ, Bellingham, 70; nature photos, comn by Fred Bassetti, 71. *Exhib:* One-woman shows, Action/Better City, Am Inst Architects, Seattle Art Mus, 68, Artists of Pac Northwest, Seattle Art Mus Pavilion, 71 & Seattle Sci Ctr, 71; Art in

Pub Places, Henry Gallery, Univ Wash, Seattle, 71 & Imogene Cunningham Exhib, 74; Wood, Paper & Metal, Contemp Works from Northwest Coast, Heard Mus, Phoenix, Ariz, 79; Royal Photog Soc Mem Exhib, London, Eng, 79 & Int Exhib Photog, 79. *Pos:* Free-lance photogr, 48- *Awards:* Gov Award, Wash, 83. *Mem:* Am Soc Mag Photogr. *Publ:* Illusr, Selected Letters of Theodore Roethke, Univ Wash, 66; illusr, Beautiful Northwest, Lane Publ, 70; illusr, My Life And Times, Playboy Press, 72; illusr, Isamu Noguchi: The Life of a Sculptor, Crowell Publ, 75; illusr, Northwest Traditions, Seattle Art Mus, 78. *Mailing Add:* Box 10536 Bainbridge Island WA 98110

RANDOLPH, LYNN MOORE
PAINTER
b New York, NY, Dec 19, 38. *Study:* Univ Tex, Austin, BFA, 81. *Exhib:* Okla Eight State Exhib, Ohla Art Ctr, 71 & 74; Mid-Year Exhib, Butler Inst Am Art, 72; Chautauqua Art Asn Exhib, NY, 74; Houston Area Ann Exhib, Univ Houston, 74 & 75; solo exhib, Contemp Arts Mus, Houston, 78; Texas Artists, Contemp Arts Ctr, New Orleans, 80; Ten Houston Artists in Dallas, 500 Exposition Gallery, 80; Thirteen Artists: A Look at Houston, Ga State Univ Gallery, Atlanta, 82. *Awards:* Purchase Prize, 71 & First Prize, 74, Okla Eight State Exhib. *Bibliog:* Charlotte Moser (auth), Four Houston women artists, MS Mag, 2/77; Lucy Lippard (auth), Texas red hits, Art in Am, 7-8/79 & Overlay: Contemporary Art and the Art of Prehistory, Pantheon, 83. *Mem:* Nat Womens Caucus Art (regional vpres, 82-83); Houston Womens Caucus Art (pres, 79-80). *Media:* Oil. *Publ:* Auth, Beyond political and economic equality, Women Artists News, 83. *Dealer:* Bill Graham 2411 Bartlett Houston TX 77098. *Mailing Add:* 1803 Banks Houston TX 77098

RANES, CHRIS
PAINTER
b Warsaw, Poland; US citizen. *Study:* Pratt Inst, New York, Art Cert; Univ Santa Clara, BA & MA. *Work:* Arco Ctr Visual Arts, Los Angeles; Bank Am & Crown Zellerbach, San Francisco; Triton Mus Art, Santa Clara, Calif; de Saisset Mus, Santa Clara Univ, Calif; and others. *Exhib:* Solo shows, de Saisset Mus, Calif, 78, La Galerie Bleue, Grenoble, France, 80, Ivory/ Kiurpton Gallery, San Francisco, 80, La Galerie d'Art UNA, Geneva, Switz, 80 & Fine Arts Mus, Alexandria, Egypt, 83; and others. *Pos:* Textile designer & stylist, Riverdale Fabrics, Blanc Studios, New York, 51-55. *Teaching:* Lectr painting & graphic printmaking, Univ Santa Clara, Calif, 68-73, lectr French, 72-73. *Awards:* Second Prize, Calif State Competition, 66 & Nat Award of Merit, Nat Biennial, 66, Nat League Am Pen Women. *Bibliog:* Ada Garfinkel (auth), Oils are distinctive, Independent J of Marin, Calif, 78; Premiere Exposition Europeenne de Chris Ranes, Le Dauphine Libere, Grenoble, France; F Cebulski (auth), The adequate symbol, Artweek, 7/82; and others. *Mem:* San Francisco Women Artists (exec bd, 79-81). *Media:* Oil. *Mailing Add:* 3973 Bibbits Dr Palo Alto CA 94303

RANKAITIS, SUSAN ANNE
PHOTOGRAPHER, PAINTER
b Cambridge, Mass, Sept 10, 49. *Study:* Univ Ill, Champaign, BFA(painting), 71; Univ Southern Calif, Los Angeles, MFA(painting & photography), 77. *Work:* Ctr Creative Photog, Tucson, Ariz; San Francisco Mus Mod Art, Calif; Los Angeles Co Mus Art, Calif; Santa Barbara Mus Art, Calif; Int Mus Photog George Eastman House; and others. *Exhib:* Mask Show, Craft and Folk Art Museum, Los Angeles, Calif, 77; Attitudes: Photography in the 1970's, Santa Barbara Mus Art, Calif, 79; The US Eye, Winter Olympics & traveling, 80-82; Nat Endowment Arts Purchase Award Artists, Ctr Creative Photog, Tucson, Ariz, 80; SECA Photog Invitational, San Francisco Mus Mod Art, Calif, 80; one-woman show, Fire River Series, Light Gallery, Los Angeles, Calif, 81; Lately in LA, Washington Project for the Arts, Washington, DC, 82; one-woman shows, Los Angeles Co Mus Art & Int Mus Photog George Eastman House. *Teaching:* Assoc prof art, Chapman Col, currently. *Awards:* Nat Endowment Arts Grant, 80. *Bibliog:* Dr Susan Larsen (auth), Where technology meets earth and sky, artists the critics are watching, Art News, 5/81; Mark Johnstone (auth), Susan Rankaitis's materiality and Jan Groovers structuralism, Artweek, 2/81. *Mem:* Soc Photographic Educ; Los Angeles Ctr Photographic Studies; Graphic Arts Council, Los Angeles Co Mus Art. *Mailing Add:* 707 E Hyde Park Blvd Inglewood CA 90302

RANKIN, DON
PAINTER, PRINTMAKER
b Dec 9, 42. *Study:* Famous Artists' Sch; also with Bill Yeager; Samford Univ, BA(fine art & psychol). *Comn:* Birmingham Centennial Commemorative Coins, Arlington Shrine, 70, Univ Ala Med Complex, 71 & Birmingham-Jefferson Civic Ctr, 71; prints, First Nat Bank, Tuskaloosa, 74-76; painting, Country Club Birmingham, 79; and others. *Exhib:* One-man show, Birmingham Mus Art, 74 & 79; First Ann Juried Exhib, Southern Watercolor Soc, Cheekwood, Tenn, 77; Second Ann Juried Exhib, Southern Watercolor Soc, Columbus Mus Arts & Sci, 78; The Am Barn & It's Translation in Watercolor, Chautauqua Art Asn Exhib Am Art, NY, 79; 3rd Ann Exhib Southern Watercolor Soc, N Tex State Univ Galleries, Denton, 79; Ga Watercolor Soc Ann, 83; and others. *Teaching:* Instr techniques of watercolor & drawing, Univ Ala, Birmingham Col Special Studies. *Bibliog:* Featured artist, watercolor page, Am Artist, 3/80. *Mem:* Ala Watercolor Soc; charter mem La Watercolor Soc; Southern Watercolor Soc. *Media:* Watercolor, Egg Tempera. *Mailing Add:* 3412 Wellford Circle Birmingham AL 35226

RANKINE, V V
SCULPTOR, PAINTER
b Boston, Mass. *Study:* Amedee Ozenfant Sch, New York; Black Mt Col, with Albers & De Kooning. *Work:* Nat Mus Am Art, Washington, DC; Corcoran Gallery Art, Washington, DC; Oklahoma City Mus; Indianapolis Mus Art,

Woodward Found, Washington, DC; Guild Hall Mus, East Hampton, NY. *Comn:* Altar painting, Robert Owen Shrine, New Harmony, Ind, 65. *Exhib:* Betty Parsons Gallery, New York, 66-81; 30th Corcoran Biennial, Washington, DC, 67-68; Four Americans, Axiom Gallery, London, Eng, 68; Painting & Sculpture Today, Indianapolis Mus, 65; one-person show, Fraser's Stable Gallery, Washington, DC, 78; 21st Area Exhib, Corcoran Gallery Art, DC, 78; Outdoor Sculpture, Northern Va Community Col, 78; Women Artists of Eastern Long Island, Mus sect, Guild Hall, East Hampton, NY, 79. *Teaching:* Dir art dept, Madeira Sch, Greenway, Va, 67-70; artist in residence, Inst Man & Sci, Rensselaer, NY, summer 68; instr humanities art, Hunter Col High Sch, New York, 70-71; instr painting & drawing, Univ Md, College Park, 79-81. *Awards:* Sculpture Prize, Corcoran Gallery Ann Exhib, 55; Maurice Tuchman Juror Award, Corcoran Gallery Art, 78. *Bibliog:* Leslie Judd Ahlander (auth), article, 11/64 & Legrace Benson (auth), article, 12/69, Art Int; Lawrence Campbell (auth), article, Art News, 3/69. *Media:* Plexiglas; Acrylic on Wood. *Dealer:* Betty Parsons Gallery 24 W 57th St New York NY 10019. *Mailing Add:* 3524 Williamsburg Ln Washington DC 20008

RANSOM, HENRY CLEVELAND, JR
PAINTER
b Chattanooga, Tenn, Aug 19, 42. *Study:* Univ Ga, BFA, 64, MFA, 72. *Work:* Montgomery Mus Fine Art, Ala; Mint Mus Art, Charlotte, NC; Hunter Mus Art, Chattanooga, Tenn; Columbus Mus Art, Ohio. *Exhib:* Artists in Ga III, High Mus Art, Atlanta, Ga, 74; 1975 Art Acquisition Nat, Univ Tex, Arlington; 40th Ann Exhib, Soc Four Arts, Palm Beach, Fla, 78; New Am Still Life, Westmoreland Co Mus Art, Greenburg, Pa, 79; Southern Realism, Miss Mus Art, Jackson, 79; one-man shows, Mint Mus Art, 76, Hunter Mus Art, Chattanooga, 76, Montgomery Mus Fine Art, 76 & Far Gallery, New York, 78. *Awards:* Purchase Award, Mint Mus Art Ann, NC Nat Bank, 73; Atwater Kent Award, 39th Ann Exhib, Soc Four Arts, Palm Beach Fla, 77; Purchase Award, Mint Mus Art Biennial, 77. *Media:* Oil. *Publ:* Contribr, Ga Rev, Univ Ga Press, 76. *Dealer:* Far Gallery 22 E 80th St New York NY 10028. *Mailing Add:* PO Box 25 Good Hope GA 30641

RANSON, NANCY SUSSMAN
PAINTER, SERIGRAPHER
b New York, NY, Sept 13, 05. *Study:* Pratt Inst Sch Art & Design, BFA; Art Students League; Brooklyn Mus Art Sch; also with Alexander Brook; Robert Laurent & Jean Charlot. *Work:* Fogg Mus Art, Harvard Univ, Cambridge, Mass; Butler Inst Am Art, Youngstown, Ohio; Smithsonian Inst; New York Mus; Nat Art Gallery, Sydney, Australia; Nat Mus Mod Art, New Delhi, India; and others. *Exhib:* Brooklyn Mus, 50, 54 & 56; Whitney Mus Am Art, New York, 51; Pa Acad Fine Arts, 57; Color Prints of Americas, NJ State Mus, 70; Nat Soc Painters in Casein & Acrylics, Am Inst & Acad Arts & Lett, 79; solo shows, George Binet Gallery, New York, 48-50, Brooklyn Pub Libr Main Br, 51 & Univ of Maine, Orono, 64-78; traveling exhibs in Israel & Egypt, 81; and many others. *Awards:* Medal of Honor in Graphics, Nat Asn Women Artists, 56; MacDowell Found Fel, 64; First Prize in Graphics, Am Soc Contemp Artists, 70; Best Silk Screen, Audubon Artists, 82. *Mem:* Am Soc Contemp Artists (pres, 69-71, mem permanent bd, 71-); Nat Asn Women Artists (chmn foreign exhibs, 63-67, chmn admis, 69-71, chmn nominations, 75-77, mem adv bd, 77-80 & chmn graphics, 80-82); Audubon Artists (dir graphics, 70-73 & 75-78); Int Asn Art (deleg, US comt, 64-78, rec secy, 78-80); Audubon Artists (dir grphics, 70-73, 75-78). *Media:* Oil, Acrylic; Serigraphy. *Mailing Add:* 400 Rugby Rd Brooklyn NY 11226

RAPOPORT, SONYA
PAINTER, CONCEPTUAL ARTIST
b Boston, Mass. *Study:* Mass Col Art; New York Univ, BA; Univ Calif, Berkeley, MA. *Work:* Stedelijk Mus, Amsterdam, Holland; Grey Art Gallery, New York Univ; Indianapolis Mus Art, Ind; Oakland Art Mus, Calif; Crocker Art Mus, Sacramento, Calif. *Comn:* Abstract painting (acrylic/canvas), Hall of Justice, Hayward, Calif, 76. *Exhib:* One-person shows, Calif Palace Legion Honor & Crocker Art Mus, 64 & 74 & Peabody Mus, Harvard Univ, Cambridge, Mass, 76; Art Scene, San Francisco Mus Mod Art & Baltimore Mus Art, 65 & 73; Recent Acquisitions & Loans & Calif Landscape, Oakland Art Mus, Calif, 74; USA Women Artists, Mus Art Contemporanea, Sao Paulo, Brasil, 80; Painting and Sculpture Now, Indianapolis Mus Art, Ind, 80; Survey of Contemp Artists Books, Art Alliance Mus Pa, 81. *Awards:* Vera Adams Davis Mem Award, 63 & Rhea Keller Mem Prizes, 65, San Francisco Mus Art; Individual Juror's Award, Richmond Art Ctr Ann, Calif, 66. *Bibliog:* Stephen Moore (auth), Sonya Rapoport--An Aesthetic Response, Union Gallery, San Jose State Univ, 78; Kirsten Murray (auth), Behind Those Computer Etchings, Sonya Rapoport, Ctr Visual Arts, 79; Edgar Buonagurio (auth), Interaction art & science, Truman Gallery review, Arts Mag, 4/79. *Mem:* Womens Caucus Art. *Media:* Computer, Pen & Ink. *Publ:* Auth, About Me, 79, Surface, 80, Chelate, 80 & The Remainder, 80, pvt publ. *Mailing Add:* 6 Hillcrest Court Berkeley CA 94705

RAPP, LOIS
PAINTER
Study: Philadelphia Col Art, dipl(teacher's training) & cert(illus), 29; also with Earl Horter. *Work:* Woodmere Art Gallery, Philadelphia; Valley Forge Mem Chapel, Pa; Gwynedd-Mercy Col, Gwynedd Valley, Pa; Norristown Pub Libr, Pa; Montgomery Hosp, Norristown; and others. *Exhib:* Am Drawing Ann XV, Norfolk, Va, 57; Am Watercolor Soc 91st Ann, New York, 58; Regional Exhib, Philadelphia Mus Art, 59; Philadelphia Watercolor Club, 71; Woodmere Art Gallery, 72. *Teaching:* Instr art, Mater Misericordiae Acad, Merion, Pa, 33-45; Collegeville-Trappe Pub Schs, Pa, 35-48, Conshocken Art League, Pa, 35-37 & Greater Norristown Art League, 73-81. *Awards:* Gold Medal for Along the Schuylkill River, Lansdale Art League,

52; Awards for Meeting House Interior, 60 & Falls of the Potomac, 63, Woodmere Art Gallery. *Mem:* Am Watercolor Soc; Philadelphia Watercolor Club (bd dirs, 68-70). *Media:* Watercolor, Oil. *Mailing Add:* 116 Haws Ave Norristown PA 19401

RAPPIN, ADRIAN
PAINTER

b New York, NY, Jan 20, 34. *Study:* Acad Fine Arts, Rome; Brandeis Univ, BA; Art Acad Cincinnati; Art Students League. *Work:* Staten Island Mus, New York; Gibbes Gallery, Charleston Mus, SC; Lincoln Univ, Oxford, Pa; Randolph Macon Col, Lynchburg, Va; Mus City New York; and others. *Exhib:* Allied Artists Am, Nat Acad Design Galleries, 61-79; Audubon Artists, 74-77; one-man exhibs, Barzansky Gallery, 64, 66 & 69; 50 Am Artists, New York, 65-69; UNICEF Int, Monaco, 65-67; Kalamazoo, Mich, 70; Capricorn Gallery, 75; and others. *Mem:* Allied Artists Am; Salmagundi Club; 50 Am Artists; Intercontinental Artists; Am Artists Prof League. *Media:* Oil on Canvas & Masonite. *Publ:* Reproductions painting, Christmas Fund, New York Times, 67-70, Songs of Our Times, Hansen, 73 & The Bookshelf for Boys & Girls, Univ Soc Press, 73-74; The Gershwin Song Book, 76; and others. *Mailing Add:* 14 W 68th St New York NY 10023

RASCOE, STEPHEN THOMAS
PAINTER, EDUCATOR

b Uvalde, Tex, May 8, 24. *Study:* Univ Tex, Austin; Art Inst Chicago, BFA & MFA. *Work:* Dallas Mus Fine Arts; Southern Methodist Univ, Dallas; Ford Motor Co, Dearborn, Mich; Ling-Temco-Vought Res Ctr, Grand Prairie, Tex. *Comn:* Rancho Seco Land & Cattle Co, Corpus Christi, Tex, 67; Tex Instruments Corp, Dallas, 67; Arlington Bank & Trust Co, Tex, 69; First Nat Bank, 69 & Lakewood Bank, 71, Dallas. *Exhib:* Longview Ann, Tex, 57-72; Artists West of the Mississippi, Denver, 67; San Antonio Hemisphere, Tex, 68. *Teaching:* Assoc prof art, Univ Tex, Arlington, 64- *Awards:* Houston Mus Fine Arts Purchase Award, Tex Show, 56; First Prize, Tex Painting & Sculpture Show, Dallas Mus, 57; D D Feldman Award, 58. *Mem:* Dallas Art Asn; Ft Worth Art Asn; STex Art League (pres, 60-61); Arlington Art Asn (pres, 67-68). *Media:* Oil. *Dealer:* Mary Nye Contemporary Art 5906 Norway Rd Dallas TX 75230. *Mailing Add:* 2002 Westview Terr Arlington TX 76013

RASH, NANCY
HISTORIAN, WRITER

b Louisville, Ky, Nov 19, 40. *Study:* Radcliffe Col, BA(magna cum laude), 62; Bryn Mawr Col, MA, 65, with Charles Mitchell, PhD, 71. *Teaching:* Prof art hist, Conn Col, 72-, chmn dept, 79- *Mem:* Col Art Asn; Renaissance Soc Am. *Res:* Apulian Romanesque art; Florentine Renaissance art. *Publ:* Auth, A Note on the Stanza della Segnatura, Gazette des Beaux Arts, 79; auth, The months at Lentini, J Warburg & Courtauld Inst, 79; coauth, Orcagna's tabernacle in Orsanmichele in context, Art Bulletin, 81. *Mailing Add:* 123 York St 10A New Haven CT 06511

RASKIN, ELLEN
ILLUSTRATOR, GRAPHIC ARTIST

b Milwaukee, Wis. *Study:* Univ of Wis, Madison. *Work:* Milwaukee Public Libr; Univ Minn, Kerlan Collection. *Exhib:* Fifty Years of Graphic Arts in America, Am Inst Graphic Arts, 66; Biennale of Illus, Bratislava, Czech, 69; Biennale of Applied Graphic Arts, Brno, Czech, 72; Contemp Am Illurs of Children's Bks (shown in five US cities), Rutgers Univ, 74-75. *Teaching:* Instr graphic arts, Pratt Univ, 65 & illus, Syracuse Univ, 76-77. *Awards:* Best Picture Bk, World-J-Tribune, 66; Citations of Merit, Soc of Illusr, 66, 70 & 71; Brooklyn Mus of Art Citation-Children's Bk, 73-74. *Bibliog:* Kingman (auth), Illustrators of Children's Books, The Horn Bk, 57-66 & 67-76; Hopkins (auth), Books Are By People, Citation Press, 69. *Mem:* Graphic Artists Guild. *Media:* Woodcut; Pen & Ink. *Publ:* Auth & illusr, Nothing Ever Happens on My Block, 66 & Spectacles, 68, Atheneum; auth & illusr, The Mysterious Disappearance of Leon (I Mean Noel), E P Dutton, 71; auth & illusr, Who, Said Sue, Said Whoo?, 73 & Twenty-two, Twenty-three, 76, Atheneum. *Mailing Add:* 12 Gay St New York NY 10014

RASKIND, PHILIS
SCULPTOR, INSTRUCTOR

b New York, NY. *Study:* Art Students League; Nat Acad Sch Fine Arts, cert, 73. *Work:* Elizabeth T Greenshields Mem Found, Montreal, Can. *Comn:* Peace Medal US & N Vietnam, pvt comn, New York, 73; theatre masks for New York City Opera, Conn Opera Co, 73-75; bust: Pompidou, Waxworks, Can, 74; miniature series, Quantum Arts, New York, 78-79. *Exhib:* Catharine Lorillard Wolfe Art Club, Nat Arts Club, New York, 72-79; Nat Sculpture Soc, New York, 72-80; Pen & Brush Club, New York, 75, 76, 78 & 79; Nat Acad Fine Arts Bldg, Nat Acad Fine Arts, 76-78; Salmagundi Club, New York, 79. *Pos:* Ed newsletter, Catharine Lorillard Wolfe Art Club, 75-78. *Teaching:* Instr sculpture, Manhattan Community for Psychotherapy, 73-75; instr sculpture, Am Telegraph & Telephone Adult Educ Prog, New York, 73-74. *Awards:* Gold Medal, Pen & Brush Club, 78; Bronze Medal, Catharine Lorillard Wolfe Art Club, 77; Kalos Kagathos Found Award, Nat Sculpture Soc, 82; and others. *Mem:* Catharine Lorillard Wolfe Art Club (sculpture chmn, 75-78); Nat Art League; Vis Artists & Galeri Galleries Asn; Int Soc of Artists; Artists Equity Asn. *Media:* Clay; Wood. *Mailing Add:* 37 East 28th St New York NY 10016

RASMUSSEN, ANTON JESSE
PAINTER, ADMINISTRATOR

b Salt Lake City, Utah, Nov 12, 42. *Study:* Univ Utah, BFA, 67, MFA, 74. *Work:* Utah Mus Fine Arts, Eccles Health Sci Libr, Univ Utah, Salt Lake City; Davis Co Libr, Farmington, Utah. *Comn:* Oil paintig, Bountiful, 76 & three

panels, Clearfield, 77, Davis Co Libr, Utah; oil painting, four panels (4ft x 5ft), Salt Lake Int Airport, Utah. *Exhib:* Utah Painting 75, Utah Mus Fine Arts, Salt Lake City, 75; one-man exhibs, Davis Co Libr, S Davis Br, Bountiful, Utah, 76, N Davis Br, Clearfield, Utah, 76 & Eccles Health Sci Libr, Univ Utah, Salt Lake City, 76; Two Utah Artists, Boise State Univ, Idaho, 77. *Pos:* Dir, Bountiful Art Ctr, Univ Utah Exten, Bountiful, 74-; asst dir, Prog for Higher Educ, Davis Co/Univ Utah, Bountiful, 75- *Teaching:* Adj asst prof art, Univ Utah, Salt Lake City, 74- *Bibliog:* Claudia Sisemore (producer, color film), Anton J Rasmussen--painter of abstractions from nature, pvt publ, 77. *Media:* Oil. *Mailing Add:* c/o Bountiful Art Ctr 2175 S Main Bountiful UT 84010

RASMUSSEN, KEITH ERIC
PRINTMAKER, EDUCATOR

b Madelia, Minn, July 29, 42. *Study:* Minneapolis Col Art & Design, BFA, 66; Pa State Univ, MFA, 70. *Work:* Minneapolis Inst Arts, Minn; High Mus Art; Brooklyn Mus; Inst Man & Sci, Rennsaelerville, NY; Atlanta Br, Int Bus Machines Corp. *Exhib:* Davidson Nat Print & Drawing Exhib, NC, 75; 20th Printmakers Exhib, Brooklyn Mus, 76; Boston Printmakers Exhib, Delgado Mus, Boston, 77; Visiting Artists, Col Art, Md Inst, 81-82; Mo State Univ Nat Print Invitational, Cape Girardean; Southeastern Graphics Invitational, Mint Mus, 81; Silvermine Printmaking Competition, 81 & 82. *Pos:* Cur, Art Ctr Gallery, Univ Wis, Stout, 70-72; mem, Atlanta Arts Festival Bd, 77-80. *Teaching:* Fac mem printmaking & drawing, Atlanta Col Art, 72- *Media:* Lithography, Watercolor. *Mailing Add:* 1015 Rosedale Rd NE Atlanta GA 30306

RASMUSSEN, ROBERT NORMAN See Redd Ekks

RASTO (RASTISLAV HLAVINA)
SCULPTOR, CONSERVATOR

b Topolcany, Czech, June 5, 43; Can citizen. *Study:* Art Col, Bratislava, with A Drexler & L Korkos, dipl(sculpture), 62; Nat Conservation & Restoration Inst, Pelhrimov, with Vaclav Vanek, dipl(conservation), 66. *Comn:* Restorations: Altarpiece Dobra Voda, 64-65, Loreta, Royal Summer Palace, Prague, 65 & Monastery Libr Cistercian Abbey, Vyssi Brod, 65-66, Nat Heritage Inst, Prague. *Exhib:* Look, Pub Art Gallery Sarnia, Ont, 82; Synthesis: Idea and Form, Multicult Mus & Gallery, Toronto, 82; New Artists, New York, 82; Artists of Czechoslovak Origin, Univ Pittsburgh, 82; CKOC Arts Hamilton, Art Gallery Hamilton, 82-83. *Pos:* Conservator & restorer fine arts, Nat Conservation & Restoration Inst Fine Arts, Pelhrimov, Czech, 64-66; art dir, MIER Nat Enterprise, Topolcany, Czech, 67-68. *Awards:* Merit Distinction, Expo Brno, 67. *Bibliog:* Jenny Bergin (auth), Sculptor ... takes your all, Ottawa Citizen, 10/28/72; Nancy Baele (auth), Perseverance pays off, Citizen, 11/26/81; Margarat Virany (auth), Aylmer sculptor starts art movement, Aylmer Bulletin, 12/17/81. *Mem:* Sculptors Soc Can; Czech Soc Arts & Sci. *Media:* All. *Publ:* Auth, Legacy of Vinland: The Multiple Sculpture, pvt publ, 81. *Mailing Add:* 67 Terrasse Eardley Aylmer PQ J9H 6B5 Canada

RATCLIFF, CARTER
CRITIC, WRITER

b Seattle, Wash, Aug 20, 41. *Study:* Univ Chicago, BA, 63. *Pos:* Ed assoc, Art News, 69-72; adv ed, Art Int, 70-75; contrib ed, Art in Am, 77- *Teaching:* Workshop dir, Poetry Proj, St Mark's Church, New York, 69-70; instr art hist & art criticism, Sch Visual Arts, 71- *Awards:* Poets Found Grant, 69; Nat Endowment Arts Fels, 72 & 78; Guggenheim Mem Found Fel, 76. *Res:* History of American art criticism. *Publ:* Auth, Art Criticism: Other Minds, Other Eyes (6 parts), 74-75; auth, Willem de Kooning, 75; auth, Alexander Liberman, 78; auth, Robert Smithson, 79; auth, Rafael Ferrer, 80; and others. *Mailing Add:* 77 Blecker New York NY 10003

RATH, HILDEGARD
PAINTER, LECTURER

b Freudenstadt, Württemberg, Ger; US citizen. *Study:* Atelier House, Stuttgart, Ger, with Adolf Senglaub; Kunstgewerbe Sch, Stuttgart; Akad Bildenden Kunste, Berlin, Ger; also with Otto Manigk, Berlin; Cambridge, England, IBC dipl, 76. *Work:* Württembergisches Kultministerium, Stuttgart; Metrop Mus Art, Pub Libr, New York; Brooklyn Mus, NY; Libr Cong, Washington, DC; over 800 works in mus & pvt collections. *Comn:* Oil paintings, portraits & landscapes, comn by Willi Eiselen, Ulm, Donau, Ger, 32; portraits, landscapes & still lifes, comn by Walter Freudenberg, Baden, Ger, 46; Triplets, comn by Mrs Sig Buchmeyer, Paris, 48; Mrs Siegtraut Gauss-Glock, Wurttemberg, Ger, 54; Madonna, comn by Klaus Heuck, Frankfurt, Ger, 59. *Exhib:* Allied Artists Am, Nat Acad Design, New York, 51; Artists Equity Bldg Fund Exhib, Whitney Mus Am Art, 51; 15th Nat Print Exhib, Libr Cong, 57; murals, traveling exhibs, throughout US, 57-84; Salon des Nations, Paris, 83; 260 nat & int one-man shows in Stuttgart, Paris, New York, Washington, DC, and others. *Teaching:* Dir painting, Europ Sch Fine Art, NY, 49-54; lectr hist art, Great Neck Pub Schs, formerly; lectr serigraphy, NShore Art Ctr, formerly. *Awards:* Prix de Paris, 63; Cert Merit for Distinguished Serv to the Community, Cambridge, Eng, 76; Gold Medal, Accad Italia, 80; and others. *Bibliog:* Hennemann-Bayer (auth), Zur Ausstellung, Schwarzwalder Bote Stuttgart, 59; Dannecker (auth), Von werker, Stuttgarter Nachrichten, 59; P H Buhner (auth), Hildegard Rath im Kunsthaus Schaller, Stuttgarter Zeitung, 59. *Mem:* Wurttembergischer Kunstverein, Stuttgart; Landesverband Würtemburg Kunstler, Tübingen, Ger; Nat Asn of Adult Educators; Nat Soc of Mural Painters; and others. *Media:* Mixed. *Publ:* Auth articles in Art Digest, 52, Schwarzwald Zeitung, 59 & Am Artist, 63; contribr, Enciclopedia Int Degli Artisti, 70-71; contribr, Artisti Contemporaney, Accad Italia, 80. *Dealer:* Weintraub Gallery 992 Madison Ave New York NY 10021. *Mailing Add:* PO Box 298 Manchester Center VT 05255

RATHBONE, PERRY TOWNSEND
MUSEUM DIRECTOR
b Germantown, Pa, July 3, 11. *Study:* Harvard Col, AB, 33, Harvard Univ, 33-34; Wash Univ, Hon DFA, 58; Northeastern Univ, Hon DHL, 60; Bates Col, Hon DFA, 64; Suffolk Univ, Hon DHL, 69; Williams Col, Hon DHL, 70; Boston Col, Hon DFA, 70; RI Sch Design, Hon DFA, 72. *Pos:* Cur, Detroit Inst Art, 36-40; secy & dir masterpieces of art, New York World's Fair, 39; dir, City Art Mus St Louis, 40-55; dir, Boston Mus Fine Arts, 54-72; dir, Christie's USA, 73-, sr vpres, 77- *Awards:* Chevalier, Legion of Honor. *Mem:* Am Asn Mus (vpres, 60-); Asn Art Mus Dirs (pres, 59-60 & 69-70); Benjamin Franklin fel Royal Soc Arts, London; Fogg Art Mus. *Publ:* Auth, Max Beckmann, 48, Mississippi Panorama, 49, Westward the Way, 54, Lee Gatch, 60 & Handbook for the Forsyth Wickes Collection, 68; contribr art mags & mus bulletins. *Mailing Add:* 151 Coolidge Hill Cambridge MA 02138

RATHBUN, WILLIAM JAY
CURATOR
b Sioux City, Iowa, June 19, 31. *Study:* Univ Wash, BA, 54, MA(art hist), 66. *Collections Arranged:* Song of the Brush: Japanese Paintings from Sanso Collection (auth, catalog), 79, Treasures of Asian Art from the Idemitsu Collection (auth, catalog), 81, Yo no Bi: The Beauty of Japanese Folk Art (auth, catalog), 83 & 50 Years: A Legacy of Asian Art, 83, Seattle Art Mus. *Pos:* Asst cur, Seattle Art Mus, 73-76, assoc cur Asian painting, 76-78, cur Japanese art, 78- *Teaching:* Asst art hist, Univ Wash, Seattle, 66-67; asst prof, Portland State Univ, 70-71. *Mem:* Oriental Ceramic Soc, London; Japan Soc. *Publ:* Coauth, Asiatic Art in the Seattle Art Museum, Seattle Art Mus, 73; contribr, A Myriad of Autumn Leaves, New Orleans Mus Art, 83. *Mailing Add:* Seattle Art Mus Volunteer Park Seattle WA 98112

RATHLE, HENRI (AMIN)
PAINTER
b Cairo, Egypt, Nov 4, 11; US citizen. *Study:* Self-taught; Royal Palace, with El Hawawini, 29-30; with Henri Matisse, Nice, France, 33; with Henry Gasser, 70. *Work:* Phoenix Fire Mus, Mobile, Ala. *Comn:* President Nixon, Washington, DC, 69; Oakley and Southern Belle, Emperor Clocks, West Germany, 73; President Charles deGaulle, comn by J F Bezou, New Orleans, La. *Exhib:* One-man shows, Percy Whiting Art Ctr, Fairhope, Ala, 68, Biloxi Municipal Art Gallery, Miss, 68, Jackson Co Col, Gautier, Miss, 68 & Fine Arts Mus South, Mobile, Ala, 72. *Awards:* Purchase Award, Bellingrath Gardens, Mobile, Ala, 70; Purchase Award, Fine Arts Mus South, Mobile, Ala. *Bibliog:* John Fay (auth), Masculinity found in art, Mobile Register, 3/67; J F Bezou (auth), Exposition a Biloxi, France-Amerique, 2/68; German & Swedish Monographs, 78. *Mem:* Mobile Art Asn; Eastern Shore Art Asn. *Media:* Oil, Acrylic. *Mailing Add:* 756 Sullivan Ave Mobile AL 36606

RATKAI, GEORGE
PAINTER, SCULPTOR
b Budapest, Hungary, Dec 24, 07. *Work:* Tel-Aviv Mus, Israel; Abbott Labs Collection; Univ Ill; Butler Inst Am Art; Univ Nebr; and others. *Exhib:* Pa Acad, Philadelphia, 48-53 & 61; Carnegie Inst, Pittsburgh, Pa, 49; Whitney Mus Ann, New York, 49, 50 & 56; Mint Mus, Charlotte, NC; Metrop Mus Ann, New York, 50; Univ Ill, Urbana, 51, 53, 55 & 57; Dayton Art Inst, Ohio, 56; Recent Drawing Show, Mus Mod Art, Spoleto, Italy, 61; Butler Inst Art, Youngstown, Ohio, 62; Provincetown Art Asn Golden Anniv, 64; and many others. *Awards:* Gold Medals, 53 & 65 & Mem Medal, 56, Audubon Artists; Childe Hassam Award, 59. *Mem:* Artists Equity Asn; Audubon Artists; fel Int Inst Arts & Lett; Am Fedn Arts; Nat Soc Painters in Casein; and others. *Mailing Add:* 350 W 57th St New York NY 10019

RATNER, DAVID M
PAINTER, EDUCATOR
b Minneapolis, Minn, June 14, 22. *Study:* Minneapolis Sch Art; Skowhegan Sch of Painting & Sculpture; Acad de la Grande Chaumiere. *Comn:* Illus for Mathematics Presentation Project, Nat Sci Found, 61-63; Diorama, Am Mus Immigration, New York, 71. *Exhib:* Painting Biennial, Walker Art Ctr, Minneapolis, 56 & 58; solo exhibs, Minneapolis Inst Art, 61 & Carl Siembab Gallery, Boston, 68; Boston Arts Festival, Boston, 63 & 64; The Skowhegan Sch, Inst Contemp Art, Boston, 76; Cont Still-Life, Newport Art Asn, Newport, RI, 78; Helen Bumbus Gallery, Duxbury, Mass, 82. *Teaching:* Instr painting & drawing, Minneapolis Sch Art, 53-62; prof art, Boston Univ, 62- *Awards:* Minn State Fair, 55-57; Purchase Award, Walker Art Ctr, 58; Esther Conant Memorial Prize, Helen Bumbus Gallery, 82. *Media:* Oil, Gouche. *Mailing Add:* 22 Richard Rd Natick MA 01760

RAUCHER, HAVA
PAINTER, PRINTMAKER
b Bulgaria, June 5, 44; Israeli citizen. *Study:* Tel Aviv Univ, Israel, BA, 71; Avni Inst Fine Arts, Tel Aviv, 72-76; Washington Univ, MFA, 81. *Work:* Evansville Mus Arts & Sci, Ind. *Exhib:* Solo exhibs, Gallerie Ninety-Nine, Bay Harbor, Fla, 80, NAME Gallery, Chicago, 81 & Timothy Burns Gallery, St Louis, Mo, 83; Self Portrait, Timothy Burns Gallery, St Louis, Mo, 81; Mid-States Art Exhib, Evansville Mus Arts, Ind, 81; Mid-States Art, Mitchel Mus, Mt Vernon, IL, 82. *Awards:* Bronstein Award, Mid-State Art Exhib, Evansville Mus Arts, 81. *Bibliog:* Nancy N Rice (auth), Self portrait, New Art Examiner, 81; Robert W Duffy (auth), The punk phenomenon, St Louis Post Dispatch, 81; Johan MacFarland (auth), article, New Art Examiner, 83. *Mailing Add:* 1042 Willowbrook Dr St Louis MO 63141

RAUSCHENBERG, ROBERT
PAINTER, PHOTOGRAPHER
b Port Arthur, Tex, Oct 22, 25. *Study:* Kansas City Art Inst & Sch Design, 46-47; Acad Julian, Paris, 47; Black Mt Col, with Josef Albers, 48-49; Art Students League, with Vaclav Vytlacil & Morris Kantor, 49-50. *Work:* Albright-Knox Art Gallery; Whitney Mus Am Art; Wadsworth Atheneum; Tate Gallery, London; Mus Mod Art, New York. *Exhib:* Retrospective, Nat Collection Fine Art, 76; Mus Mod Art, New York, 76 & 78; Whitney Mus Am Art, 76-78; Minn Mus Art, 77; Nat Collection Fine Art, 78; Albright-Knox Gallery, 78; Corcoran Biennial, 79; solo exhib, Tucson Mus Art, 79, Palm Springs Desert Mus, 79, Galerie Mathilde, Amsterdam, 79, Ohio State Univ, 80 & West Coast Gallery, Newport Beach, 80; Hirshhorn Mus, 80; Baltimre Mus, 80. *Awards:* Grand Prix D'Honneur, 13th Int Exhib Graphic Art, Ljubljana, Yugoslavia; Gold Medal, Oslo, Norway; Officier, Ordre des Arts et Lettres, Ministry Culture & Commun, France; and others. *Bibliog:* Gregory Battcock (ed), Minimal Art: a Critical Anthology, Dutton, 68; Hal Foster (auth), Review, Artforum, 9/79; Calvin Tomkins (auth), Off the Wall, 80; plus many others. *Mailing Add:* c/o Leo Castelli Gallery 420 W Broadway New York NY 10012

RAUTBORD, DOROTHY H
COLLECTOR, PATRON
b Winamac, Ind, Aug 13, 06. *Study:* Univ Ill; self-taught. *Mem:* Arts Club, Chicago. *Collection:* Post impressionism. *Mailing Add:* 44 Cocoanut Row Palm Beach FL 33480

RAVE, GEORGIA
PAINTER, TAPESTRY ARTIST
b Mt Vernon, NY, June 3, 36. *Study:* Hunter Col, BFA, 57 & MA, 66. *Pos:* Dir grad art educ, Hunter Col, 67-70; coordr MAT in art, Manhattanville Col, Purchase, NY, 75-80. *Teaching:* Instr drawing & art educ, Hunter Col, New York, 66-70; lectr drawing & art educ, Newark State Col, Union, NJ, 72-73; lectr drawing, painting & art educ, Manhattanville Col, Purchase, NY, 73-80. *Awards:* City Univ Fac Summer Grant, City Univ New York, 68; Shuster Grant, Hunter Col, 69; Manhattanville Col res grants, Spain, 76 & London, 79. *Bibliog:* Kosia Orloff (auth), Reforming Fabric, Women Artists News, fall 82. *Mem:* Col Art Asn; Graphic Arts Coun. *Media:* Acrylic, Watercolor; Silk. *Mailing Add:* c/o Westbeth Gallery 463 West St New York NY 10014

RAVEN, ARLENE
WRITER, HISTORIAN
b Baltimore, Md, July 12, 44. *Study:* Hood Col, BA, 65, HHD, 79; Univ Madrid; Md Inst Col Art; George Washington Univ, MFA, 67; Johns Hopkins Univ, NDEA, Kress & Gilman fels, 69-73, MA, 71; Int Col, PhD, 75. *Pos:* Co-founder, Ctr Feminist Art Hist Studies, 73-; vpres, Women's Community Inc, Los Angeles, 73-; co-founder & dir, Woman's Bldg, Los Angeles, 73-; ed, Chrysalis Mag, cur innovative exhibs, Los Angeles, 80 & Artemisia Gallery, Chicago, 80. *Teaching:* Tutor, Calif Inst Arts, 72-74, Otis Art Inst Parsons Sch Design, 81-83, New Sch Soc Res, 83- *Awards:* Nat Endowment Arts Critic Fel, 79; Vesta Award, Woman's Bldg, 83; Calif Coun Humanities Grant, 83-84; and others. *Bibliog:* Shirley Koploy (auth), Art: the woman's building, MS Mag, 10/74; Focus, KNBC-TV, 74; Female imagery, MS Mag, 5/75. *Mem:* Col Art Asn Am; Women's Caucus Art (bd dirs, 74-78). *Res:* Washington color school; theoretical perspective on women's art; abstract expressionist men's and women's art; Georgia O'Keeffe and Romaine Brooks. *Publ:* Auth, The circle: Ritual and the occult in women's performance art, New Art Examiner, 11/80; auth, Dark horse: New paintings by Tom Knechtel, Arts, 4/81; auth, The eye of the be*hold*her, Sinister Wisdom, spring 81; auth, Soldier of fortune--Rachel Rosenthal, Artweek, 8/29/81; auth, Passion/passage, High Performance, Vol 6, No 21, 83; and others. *Mailing Add:* 105 Eldridge St New York NY 10002

RAWLINSON, JONLANE FREDERICK
PAINTER, INSTRUCTOR
b Memphis, Tenn, Feb 12, 40. *Study:* Memphis State Univ, 58-59; Memphis Acad Arts, BFA, 63; Syracuse Univ, MFA, 75. *Work:* Parthenon, Nashville, Tenn; Watkins Collection of Tenn Art; Fall Creek Falls Collection of Tenn Art; Memphis Acad Art Collection. *Comn:* Mississippi River Bridge (painting), comn by Young Republican Party, US House of Rep, 73; paintings of farm, Pin Oak Farms, Versailles, Ky, 75. *Exhib:* Mid-South Exhib, Memphis, 71; Tenn All-State Competition, 71-73; Cent South Exhib, Nashville, 72-73; Tenn Watercolor Soc, 72-75; Watercolor USA, Springfield, Mo, 75. *Teaching:* Graphic art instr, Univ Tenn, 65-75; instr art, Memphis Acad Arts, 72- *Awards:* Second Purchase Prize for Mixed Media, Tenn All-State Competition, 71; Art Dirs Club Memphis First Prize, Art South, 72; First Award & Gold Medal of Merit, Tenn Watercolor Soc, 75. *Mem:* Tenn Watercolor Soc (vpres, 75). *Media:* Watercolor. *Mailing Add:* 1918 Peabody Memphis TN 38104

RAY, CHRISTOPHER T
SCULPTOR, CRAFTSMAN
b Albany, NY, May 7, 37. *Study:* Pa Acad Fine Arts, 60; studied with Howard Keyser, master blacksmith, 64-66. *Work:* Mus Am Jewish Hist & Port of Hist Mus, Philadelphia. *Comn:* Sculptured gates, Penn's Landing Sq, Philadelphia, 73; pub sculpture, Scheie Eye Inst, Philadelphia, 75, First Pa Bank, Philadelphia, 76 & Great Valley Corp Ctr, Malvern, Pa, 79; sculptured gate/bas-relief, Chestnut St Park, Philadelphia, 79. *Exhib:* Figure & Fantasy, Smithsonian Inst, DC, 75; Am Craft Show, Philadelphia Mus Art, 77; Sculpture Outdoors, Temple Univ, Ambler, Pa, 79; Animal Art, Smithsonian Inst, 81; Mod Wrought Ironwork & Sculpture Int Exhib, Lindau, Ger, 81;

Ornamentalism, Hudson River Mus, Yonkers, NY, 83; and others. *Pos:* Pres/founder, GENUS Collab, Philadelphia, 77- *Bibliog:* Donna Z Meilach (auth), Decorative & Sculptural Ironwork, Crown Publ; R Jensen & P Conway (auth), Ornamentalism, Potter Inc; and others. *Mem:* Artists' Equity Asn (vpres, 76-78); fel Pa Acad Fine Arts; Artists-Blacksmiths Asn NAm; Am Crafts Coun. *Mailing Add:* 315 E Wister Philadelphia PA 19114

RAY, DEBORAH See Kogan, Deborah

RAY, JIM
MUSEUM DIRECTOR
b Hayti, Mo, Sept 16, 24. *Study:* Univ Mo, Columbia, BS. *Collections Arranged:* Drawing America--1973 (with catalog); Architecture of St Joseph (with catalog); Engraving America 1974 (with catalog). *Pos:* Dir, Albrecht Art Mus, St Joseph, Mo, 73- *Mem:* Am Asn Mus; Mo Mus Assocs. *Publ:* Auth, The Stained Glass Windows of St Joseph, 76; auth, Drawing Missouri, 76. *Mailing Add:* 2706 Union St St Joseph MO 64506

RAY, ROBERT (DONALD)
PAINTER, SCULPTOR
b Denver, Colo, Oct 2, 24. *Study:* Univ Southern Calif, BFA(cum laude); Centro Estudios Universitarios, Mexico City, MA(magna cum laude). *Work:* Baltimore Mus Art, Md; Brooklyn Mus Art, NY; Denver Art Mus, Colo; Mus NMex, Santa Fe; Columbia Mus Art, SC. *Exhib:* Denver Art Mus, 53-; 13th Nat Exhib Prints, Libr Cong, Washington, DC, 55; Taos Now, San Diego Mus Fine Arts, Calif, 60; Art & The Atom, Calif Palace of Legion of Honor, 65; The West--80 Contemporaries, Univ Ariz Art Gallery, Tucson, 67; one-man show, Mus NMex, Santa Fe, 59 & 67 & Colorado Springs Fine Arts Ctr, Colo, 68; Three Cultures--Three Dimensions, 69 & Southwestern Artists Biennial, 70, Mus NMex; 73rd Ann Exhib Western Art, Denver Art Mus, 71; and many others. *Awards:* Purchase Award, Ball State Teachers Col, 59; First Prize for Sculpture, Mus NMex, 69; Graphics Award, Taos Art Asn, NMex, 72. *Bibliog:* Fels (auth), Compression & expansion in the works of Blackburn & Ray, 72; Harmsen (auth), Harmsen's Western Americana, Northland, 72. *Mem:* Taos Art Asn. *Dealer:* Mission Gallery Taos NM 87571. *Mailing Add:* 115 Los Cordovas Rte Taos NM 87571

RAYBURN, (BOYD) DALE
PAINTER, PRINTMAKER
b Carriere, Miss, May 12, 42. *Study:* Univ Southern Miss, BS, 64; Univ Miss, MFA, 70. *Work:* DeCordova Mus, Lincoln, Mass; High Mus, Atlanta; Mint Mus, Charlotte, NC; Southeastern Ctr Contemp Art, Winston-Salem, NC; Miss Mus Art, Jackson. *Exhib:* 20th Southeastern Exhib, High Mus, Atlanta, 65; Piedmont Painting & Sculpture, Mint Mus, Charlotte, NC, 71; Audubon Artist Ann, Nat Acad Gallery, New York, 73; two-person show, Mint Mus, Charlotte, NC, 74 & Miss Mus Art, Jackson, 77; Hunterdon Print Exhib, Hunterdon Art Ctr, Clinton, NJ, 78. *Teaching:* Instr art, Univ Miss, 69-70; instr printmaking, Ga Southwestern Col, 72-73; asst prof, La State Univ, Shreveport, 80-82. *Awards:* Honorable Mention, Westchester Art Soc, 70; Purchase Award, DeCordova Mus, 77 & Southeastern Ctr Contemp Art, 78. *Mem:* Boston Printmakers; Southeastern Printmakers Asn. *Media:* Oil; Etching. *Dealer:* Lagerquist Gallery 3235 Paces Ferry Place NW Atlanta GA 30305. *Mailing Add:* 3901 Lynhurst Marietta GA 30062

RAYDON, ALEXANDER R
DEALER, COLLECTOR
Study: Tech Univ Munich, grad. *Pos:* Dir, Raydon Gallery. *Mem:* Am Asn Mus; Int Coun Mus. *Res:* American art of the nineteenth and early twentieth centuries. *Specialty:* Paintings, sculpture, prints and drawings from the Renaissance to the present, with emphasis on the nineteenth and early twentieth centuries. *Publ:* Ed, America the Beautiful, 71; ed, Americans Abroad, 72; ed, Charles Burchfield--Master Doodler, 72; ed, American Scene--American Artists Abroad, 75-77; ed, Masters in European Portraiture, 76. *Mailing Add:* 1091 Madison Ave New York NY 10028

RAYEN, JAMES WILSON
PAINTER, EDUCATOR
b Youngstown, Ohio, Apr 9, 35. *Study:* Yale Univ, BA, BFA & MFA; with Josef Albers, Seawell Sillman & Rico Lebrun. *Work:* Addison Gallery Am Art, Andover, Mass; Yale Univ, New Haven, Conn; Wellesley Col, Mass; First Nat Bank, Boston. *Exhib:* One-man shows, Durlacher Brothers Gallery, New York, 66 & Eleanor Rigelhaupt Gallery, Boston, 68; Landscape II, De Cordova Mus, Lincoln, Mass, 71; 10 Year Retrospective, Brockton Art Ctr, Mass, 73; Recent & Revised, Wellesley Col Mus, 78; Chapel Gallery, Boston, 84; and others. *Teaching:* Prof, Wellesley Col, 61-, Elizabeth Christy Kopp chair in studio art, 83. *Awards:* Ital Govt Grant in Painting, 59-60; Ford Found Grant in the Humanities, 69-70; Wellesley Col Fac Grant, summer 75, spring 84 & 85. *Mem:* Boston Visual Artists Union. *Media:* Acrylic, Watercolor. *Dealer:* Ginzburg-Hallowell Boston. *Mailing Add:* 108 Fox Hill St Westwood MA 02090

RAYMOND, LILO
PHOTOGRAPHER
b Frankfurt, Ger, June 23, 22; US citizen. *Study:* Photog Sem, with David Vestal, 61-63. *Work:* Sheldon Mus Art Gallery, Mus Mod Art & Metrop Mus, New York; High Mus, Atlanta; New Orleans Mus Art. *Exhib:* Still Life in Photog, Helios Gallery, New York, 76; Contrasts Gallery, London, Eng, 80; Woodman Gallery, Morristown, NJ, 81; Photo West, Carmel, 82; Baker Gallery, Kans, 82; and many one-woman shows. *Teaching:* Mem sem photog, Sch Visual Arts, New York, 78-, Maine Photog Workshop, Rockport, summer 79 & Int Ctr Photog, New York, winter 79. *Awards:* Creative Artists Pub Serv

Prog Grant, 78. *Bibliog:* Sir Cecil Beaton (auth), The Magic Image, Little Brown & Co, 75; Alicia Wille (auth), Lilo Raymond, gravure portfolio, Popular Photog, 77; Richard Blodgett (auth), A Collectors Guide, Ballatine Bks, 79. *Publ:* Photogr, Classic County Inns of America, Knapp Press & Holt, Rinehart & Winston, 78. *Dealer:* Marcuse Pfeifer 825 Madison Ave New York NY 10021. *Mailing Add:* 212 E 14th St New York NY 10003

RAYNER, ADA (ADA RAYNER HENSCHE)
PAINTER
b London, England, Feb 9, 01; US citizen. *Study:* Grand Cent Art Sch, New York, with Wayman Adams, 27-29; Art Students League, with Ivan Olinsky, 30; Cape Sch Art, with Henry Hensche, 32-36. *Work:* Grand Cent Art Gallery, New York; Walter Chrysler Mus, Norfolk, Va; Ft Wayne Mus; Paper Mill Playhouse, NJ; and pvt collections. *Exhib:* New York Watercolor Exhib; Provincetown Art Asn, 35-; Okla Asn Conservative Artists; Copely Soc Boston, 67-68; Miniature Painters Washington, 71-72. *Awards:* Founders Second Place for Best Painting, Miniature Painters, 73. *Media:* Oil, Watercolor. *Mailing Add:* Conwell St Provincetown MA 02657

RAYNER, GORDON
PAINTER
b Toronto, Ont, 1935. *Work:* Philadelphia Mus Art; Mus Mod Art, New York; Can Coun, Ottawa, Ont; Hirshhorn Collection, Nat Gallery Can, Ottawa. *Comn:* Wall Mural, Bank of Montreal, Toronto, 70; building facade & canopy, Ontario Hydro/Ont Place, Toronto, 71; outdoor wall mural, Benson & Hedges Tobacco Co, Toronto, 71; Tempo (ceramic tile mural), Toronto Transit Comn, 77. *Exhib:* Sixth Biennale of Can Painting, Nat Gallery Can, Ottawa, 65; Mus Mod Art, New York, 67; Coughtry/Rayner/Markle, Nat Gallery Can (traveling), Ottawa, 68; Toronto Painting 1953-1965, Nat Gallery Can, 72; Artists Jazz Band, Mus d'Art Contemporian, Montreal, 74-75; Survey Can Painting, Art Gallery Ont, Toronto, 75; Artists Jazz Band, Beaubourg Centre, Can, Paris, France, 78; Paradise, The Isaacs Gallery, 79. *Teaching:* Painting, Three Schs Art, Toronto, 68-77; teacher painting & founder, For Art's Sake Inc, Toronto, 77-80. *Awards:* First Prize, Graphics 12th Winnipeg Art Show, 70; Can Coun Sr Arts grant, 73 & 75. *Bibliog:* Barrie Hale (auth), Gordon Rayner: The first decade, 2/70 & Theodore Heinrich (auth), Edging up to paradise, 5/6/79, Artscanada. *Media:* Acrylic, Collage. *Mailing Add:* The Isaacs Gallery 832 Yonge St Toronto ON M4H 2H1 Canada

READ, DAVE (DAVID DOLLOFF)
PHOTOGRAPHER, EDUCATOR
b Belfast, Maine, July 14, 38. *Study:* Ohio Univ, BFA, 63, MFA, 65. *Work:* Mus Mod Art, New York; Libr Cong, Washington, DC; Mus Fine Arts, St Petersburg, Fla; Univ Mich, East Lansing; Univ Louisville, Ky. *Exhib:* Photog Fine Arts, Metrop Mus Art, New York, 67; Photog Art Form, Ringling Mus, Sarasota, 77; Dave Read Photog, Mich State Univ, 77 & Light Factory, Charlotte, NC, 78; Dave Read: 1st Mid-west Photogs, Sheldon Art Gallery, Lincoln, Nebr, 80; Photographs by Dave Read, Friends Photog, Carmel, Calif, 83. *Collections Arranged:* Flash (photog by Mertin, Hume, Cohen & Bishop, auth, catalog), Miami Dade Community Col, 76. *Teaching:* Instr photog, Univ NMex, Albuquerque, 65-66; assoc prof photog, Miami-Dade Community Col, Fla, 69-77; assoc prof photog, Univ Nebr, Lincoln, 78- *Awards:* Artist's Fel, Mid-Am Arts Alliance & Nat Endowment Arts, 83. *Mem:* Soc Photog Educ; Friends of Photog; Visual Studies Workshop; Print Club, Philadelphia. *Media:* Silver Prints. *Publ:* Contribr, Afterimage, Visual Studies Workshop, 81; contribr, Electronic Flash Photography, Van Nostrand Reinhold, 80; contribr, Exposure, 79. *Mailing Add:* 5550 S 32nd Circle Lincoln NE 68516

REALE, NICHOLAS ALBERT
PAINTER, INSTRUCTOR
b Irvington, NJ, Mar 20, 22. *Study:* Pratt Inst; Art Students League; New Sch Social Res, New York; Workshop Sch Design, New York. *Work:* Nat Acad Design, New York; Newark Mus, NJ; Univ of Ariz; Jersey City Mus; Morgan Guarrantee & Trust Co, New York. *Exhib:* Metrop Mus Art, New York; New York Worlds Fair, 65; Everhart Mus, Scranton, Pa, 67; Pa Acad Fine Arts, Philadelphia, 68; Montclair Mus, NJ, 69; Butler Inst Am Art, Youngstown, Ohio, 72; Frye Mus, Seattle, Wash, 75; NJ State Mus, 75; Nat Acad Design, New York, 78. *Teaching:* Instr graphic design, Newark Sch Fine & Indust Art, 67; instr painting, Summit Art Ctr, NJ, 69- *Awards:* High Winds Award, Am Watercolor Soc Nat, 76; Assoc Mems Award, Allied Artist Nat, New York, 77; Sadie & Max Tessler Award, Audubon Artist Nat, New York, 78. *Mem:* Am Watercolor Soc; Allied Artist Am; Audubon Artists; Assoc Artist NJ; Nat Casein Soc. *Media:* Oil, Acrylic. *Dealer:* c/o George Dembo Gallery Nine 9 Passaic Ave Chatham NJ 07928. *Mailing Add:* 81 Wilder St Hillside NJ 07205

REARDON, MARY A
PAINTER, MURALIST
b Quincy, Mass. *Study:* Radcliffe Col, AB; Yale Univ Sch Fine Arts, BFA; also with Eugene Savage, Jean Charlot & David Siqueiros; New Eng Sch Law, LHD, 74. *Work:* Mural drawings, De Cordova Mus, Lincoln, Mass; Radcliffe Col, Cambridge, Mass. *Comn:* Creation & Last Judgement (mosaic ceilings), Nat Shrine Immaculate Conception, Washington, DC, 73; Chapel of the Patrons, St Mary's Cathedral, San Francisco, Calif; portraits, Judge Edmund Dewing, 78 & Cardinal Humberto Medeiros, 80; stained glass window, First Church, Weymouth, Mass, 81, and others. *Exhib:* Int Exhibs Relig Art, Trieste, Italy, 61 & 66; 7th Centennial Exhib, Basilica St Anthony, Padua, Italy, 63; one-man exhib, Trieste, 71; additional exhibs in Boston, New York & Richmond, Va. *Pos:* Design consult, San Francisco Cathedral, 74- *Teaching:* Instr adult educ, Boston Mus Fine Arts; assoc prof studio courses,

Emmanuel Col, Boston, 51-70. *Awards:* President's Medal, 2nd Int Exhib Relig Art, 66. *Bibliog:* Frank De Frederico (auth), The Mosaics of the National Shrine of Immaculate Conception, Decatur House Press, 81. *Mem:* Nat Soc Mural Painters; Cambridge Art Asn; Harvard Club of Boston; NShore Arts Asn; Copley Soc. *Media:* Oil, Watercolor; Mosaic. *Dealer:* South Shore Art Centre Cohasset MA. *Mailing Add:* 12 Martin's Lane Hingham MA 02043

REBBECK, LESTER JAMES, JR
PAINTER, SCULPTOR
b Chicago, Ill, June 25, 29. *Study:* Art Inst Chicago & Univ Chicago, hist with K Blackshear, BAEd, MAEd, 59; also painting with Wieghardt, drawing with Isoble McKinnon. *Comn:* Paintings & prints, comn by William Fischer, 69. *Exhib:* Boston Soc Independent Artists, 56; Sculptors Gallery, St Louis, 67; Ball State Teachers Col, 75; Mus Sci & Industry, Chicago, 83; Ill State Mus, Springfield, 83; Peace Mus, Chicago, 83; and others. *Pos:* Gallery dir, Countryside Art Gallery, Arlington Heights, Ill, 63-68; gallery dir, Chicago Soc of Artists Gallery, 67-68. *Teaching:* Asst prof art appreciation & painting, Harper Col, 67-71. *Awards:* GI Show Medal Award, Art Inst Chicago, 53; First Place Oils, McHenry Art Fair, 60, Best of Show, 62. *Bibliog:* Dona Z Meilach (auth), Creating Art from Anything, Reilly & Lee, 68; Louise D Yochim (auth), Role and impact, Chicago Soc Artists. *Mem:* Col Art Asn Am. *Media:* Oil on Canvas; Wood Sculpture. *Mailing Add:* 2041 Vermont St Rolling Meadows IL 60008

REBER, MICK
SCULPTOR, PAINTER
b St George, Utah, June 6, 42. *Study:* Brigham Young Univ, BFA & MFA; independent studies in San Francisco, Chicago, Montreal & New York. *Work:* NMex Jr Col Art Mus, Hobbs; Nev State Bank, Las Vegas. *Comn:* Brigham Young Univ, Provo, Utah, 68; paintings, 20th Century Fox, 73; sculptural park, City of Las Vegas, Nev, 78; sculptural playground, Clark Co Sch Dist, Las Vegas, 78. *Exhib:* Mainstreams Exhib, Marietta Col, Ohio, 74; Western State Art Found Traveling Exhib, San Francisco Mus of Mod Art, Denver Art Mus & Seattle Art Mus, 78; one-man shows, Brigham Young Univ, 68 & 72, Tameron-Durango, Ft Lewis Col, Colo, 76, Recent Paintings & Sculptures, NMex Civic Ctr, 77 & Main Gallery World Hq of Bank of Am, San Francisco, 78; and others. *Teaching:* Prof advan painting & sculpture, Ft Lewis Col, Durango, Colo, 68-76. *Awards:* Painting Award, Springville Nat, Springville Mus of Art, Utah, 70; First Cash Award, Four Corners Biennial, Phoenix Art Mus, 73. *Bibliog:* H Lester Cooke (auth), A Biennial of Painting & Sculpture (catalog), 73; Cassy Cohen (auth), Mick Reber, Nevadan, 7/11/76; Paul Abe (auth), ...And Then There's Mick Reber, NMex Daily Times, 77. *Media:* Acrylic, Wood, Steel. *Mailing Add:* 8725 W El Campo Grande Las Vegas NV 89108

RECANATI, DINA
SCULPTOR
b Cairo, Egypt. *Study:* Art Students League, with Jose de Creft, 59-62. *Work:* Israel Mus, Jerusalem; Tel Aviv Mus; President's Garden Collection, Jerusalem; Ben Gurion Airport, Tel Aviv. *Comn:* Gate (bronze), Ministry of Transportation, Israel, 74 & Gates (spec bronze ed), Am-Israel Cult Found, New York, 76; Israel Chancellery, Washington, DC, 80. *Exhib:* Padua Biennale, Italy, 77; Gray Gallery, NY Univ, 78; Gurewitsch Gallery, 78; American Israel Cult Found, New York, 81; July M Gallery, Tel-Aviv, 81; and many others. *Bibliog:* Paul Waldo Schwartz (auth), Scrooge in style in Paris, New York Times, 65; Zvi Sas (auth), Sculptor of powerful temperament, L'Info, 70; Emanuel Bar Kadma (auth), Yediot Ahronot, The source of inspiration, ancient Eqypt, 77. *Media:* Bronze, Wood. *Publ:* Contribr, The Artist's Notebook, Gordon Galleries, Israel, 75. *Dealer:* E P Gurewitsch Works of Art 55 E 74th St New York, NY 10021. *Mailing Add:* 944 Fifth Ave New York NY 10021

REDD, RICHARD JAMES
PAINTER, EDUCATOR
b Toledo, Ohio, Oct 22, 31. *Study:* Toledo Mus Sch; Univ Toledo, BEd, 53; Univ Iowa, MFA, 58, study with Eugene Ludins & Mauricio Lasansky. *Work:* Allentown Art Mus, Pa; Lehigh Univ, Bethlehem, Pa; Philip & Muriel Berman Collection, Allentown; Kutztown State Col, Pa. *Exhib:* One-man shows, Allentown Art Mus, 61, Kutztown State Col, 68, Moravian Col, Bethlehem, Pa, 71 & Kemerer Mus, Bethlehem, 80; 20 Yr Retrospective, Lehigh Univ, 78; Mushroom Magic, Reading Mus, 82; Breaking with Tradition, Int Quit Exhib, 83; and others. *Teaching:* Prof art, Lehigh Univ, 58-; chmn dept fine art, 70-77. *Awards:* Garth Howland Award, Lehigh Art Alliance, 63 & 75; First Award, Lehigh Art Alliance, 64; First Award, Mid-Atlantic Regional Col, Univ Del, 79. *Mem:* Lehigh Art Alliance (bd dir, 72-75, pres, 76-78); Col Art Asn; Artists Equity Asn; Kemerer Mus, Bethlehem (bd dirs, 78-). *Mailing Add:* RD 3 Stonesthrow Rd Bethlehem PA 18015

REDD EKKS (ROBERT NORMAN RASMUSSEN)
SCULPTOR, CERAMIST
b Oslo, Norway, Feb 11, 37. *Study:* San Francisco Art Inst, BFA, 59; Calif Col Arts & Crafts, MFA, 70. *Exhib:* Mix, San Francisco Mus Art, 73; Ceramic Sculpture, San Francisco Art Inst, 74; Newport Harbor Art Mus, Newport Beach, Calif, 81; New Mus, New York, 81; Artists Space, New York, 82; Joseph Chowning Gallery, San Francisco, 83; and others. *Teaching:* Instr ceramics, San Francisco Art Inst, 71-; instr ceramics, Univ Wis-Madison, summer, 75. *Awards:* Nat Endowment Arts, 81. *Mailing Add:* c/o San Francisco Art Inst 800 Chestnut St San Francisco CA 94133

REDDINGTON, CHARLES LEONARD
PAINTER, EDUCATOR
b Chicago, Ill, Mar 22, 29. *Study:* Art Inst Chicago, with Paul Wieghardt, dipl, 54, BFA, 58; Southern Ill Univ, MFA, 70. *Work:* Commonwealth Govt Collection, Canberra, Australia; Art Gallery NSW, Sydney; Nat Gallery Victoria, Melbourne; Western Australian Art Gallery, Perth; Southern Ill Univ, Carbondale. *Comn:* Harold Mertz Pub Collection, New York, 63; Four Color Lithographs, Nat Gallery Victoria, Melbourne, 64. *Exhib:* Australian Painting Today, 64; Young Contemporaries of Australia, Japan, 65; Travel Exhib of Art, Ind, 71; one-man show, Swope Art Gallery, Terre Haute, Ind, 73; Nat Drawing, USA, 75. *Pos:* Dir Education Abroad, Ind State Univ, Terre Haute, 75- *Teaching:* Lectr drawing & painting, NSW Univ, Sydney, 63-66; prof painting, Ind State Univ, Terre Haute, 70- *Awards:* Willis Painting Award, H O Willis Corp, Inc, Sydney, 65; Louis Comfort Tiffany Grant, 70; Works on Paper Prize, Indianapolis Mus, 72. *Bibliog:* Daniel Thomas (auth), Australian Prints, Art Gallery, NSW, 65; Robert Hughes (auth), Art in Australia, Pelican Books, 70; James Gleeson (auth), Modern Painters, Landsdowne Press, 71. *Mem:* Col Art Conf; Art Inst Chicago Alumnae; Int Inst Conserv Historic & Artistic Works; Ind Arts Comn. *Media:* Acrylic; Oil. *Dealer:* Gallery A 21 Gipps St Paddington NSW Sydney Australia; Ronald Hunnings 139 Spring St New York NY. *Mailing Add:* 504 Hulman St Terre Haute IN 47802

REDDIX, ROSCOE CHESTER
PAINTER, EDUCATOR
b New Orleans, La, Nov 15, 33. *Study:* Southern Univ, BA; Univ New Orleans; Ind Univ, Bloomington, MS(art educ); Univ Southern Miss; also with Dr Eddie Jordan & Dr Arthur Britt. *Comn:* Plastic painting, Southern Univ New Orleans. *Exhib:* Expo 72, La Artist Exhib, Ill State Univ; NJ State Mus; Black Artist, Ind Univ; one-man shows, Ala State Univ & Southern Univ New Orleans. *Teaching:* Instr art, Shreveport, La & New Orleans, La; from asst prof to assoc prof art, Southern Univ New Orleans, 74- *Bibliog:* Samella S Lewis & Ruth Waddy (auth), Black Artist on Art, Contemp Crafts. *Mem:* Nat Conf Artist (state dir, 73); Col Art Asn; Creative Artists Alliance New Orleans. *Media:* Oil. *Publ:* Contribr, Black Artist on Art, Vol 2, 71. *Mailing Add:* 1330 Cambronne St New Orleans LA 70118

REDDY, KRISHNA N
PRINTMAKER, SCULPTOR
b Chittoor, Andhra State, India, July 15, 25. *Study:* Int Univ Santiniketan, India, dipl(fine arts), 47; Univ London Slade Sch Fine Arts, cert(fine arts), 52; Acad Grande Chaumiere, Paris, with Zadkine, cert(fine arts), 55; Atelier 17, Int Ctr Gravure, Paris, 55; Academie DiBelle Arti DiBrera, Milan, with Marino Marini, cert(fine arts), 57. *Work:* Mus Mod Art, New York & Paris; Libr Cong, Nat Galleries, Smithsonian Inst, Washington, DC; and others. *Comn:* Monumental sculpture in marble, Int Sculpture Symposium, St Margarethan, Austria, 62 & Montreal, 64. *Exhib:* Brooklyn Mus of Art, 78; one-man shows, Madison Art Ctr, 73, Assoc Am Artists, New York, 74, Univ Calif Gallery, Santa Cruz, 75 & Galerie Vivant, Tokyo, 78; retrospective, Bronx Mus Arts, New York, 81; and others. *Pos:* Dir art dept, Col Fine Arts, Kalakshetra, Madras, 47-49. *Teaching:* Prof & co-dir printmaking, Atelier 17, Int Ctr Graphics, Paris, 57-76; coordr & assoc prof printmaking, Dept Art & Art Educ, NY Univ, 77-81, artist in residence, prof art & dir graphics & printmaking, 81- *Awards:* Padma Shree, Pres India, 72. *Bibliog:* S W Hayter (auth), About Prints, 64 & New Ways of Gravure, 66, Oxford Univ Press, London; Gabor Peterdi (auth), Printmaking, Macmillan Co, New York, 71. *Media:* Engraving, Etching; Stone. *Dealer:* Assoc Am Artists 663 Fifth Ave New York NY 10022; Weintraub Gallery 992 Madison Ave New York NY 10021. *Mailing Add:* 80 Wooster St New York NY 10012

REDEIN, ALEX S
PAINTER, INSTRUCTOR
b Bridgeport, Conn, Jan 21, 12. *Study:* Yale Univ Sch Art, 32-35; Arts Students League, 36. *Work:* Butler Art Inst, Ohio; Smithsonian Inst, Washington, DC; Albany Inst, NY; Cornell Univ; Ainharod Mus, Israel. *Exhib:* Am Watercolor Soc, Nat Acad, 50; Recent Oils & Gouaches, Philadelphia Art Alliance, 51 & 65; 21st Int Watercolor Biennial, Brooklyn Mus, 61; Pa Acad Ann, 68; Drawings and Paintings 1970-1982, St Marys Col, Md. *Media:* Oil, Acrylic. *Mailing Add:* Paintings & Drawings Ltd 343 E 30 St New York NY 10016

REDGRAVE, FELICITY
PAINTER, CRITIC
b UK, 1920. Can citizen. *Study:* Sheridan Col, Oakville, Ont, dipl(hon; graphic design), 70; Univ Guelph, Ont, BA(hon; fine arts), 73; Univ Toronto, BEd(art), 75. *Work:* Can Art Bank, Ottawa; Esso Resources Ltd, Calgary, Alta; Lavalin Inc, Montreal; Art Gallery NS, Halifax; Confederation Ctr Art Gallery & Mus, Charlottetown, PEI. *Exhib:* Solo exhib, Woodimensions, Mt St Vincent Univ Art Gallery, Halifax, NS, 76 & Images of Nova Scotia & Newfoundland, Harbourfront Art Gallery, Toronto, 77, Art Gallery NS, Halifax, 78, Confederation Ctr Art Gallery, Charlottetown, 78 & Mem Univ Art Gallery, St Johns, Newfoundland, 78; Land & Sea: Viewpoints of Prince Edward Island, Confederation Ctr, Univ Waterloo, Charlottetown, PEI, 80; Art Gallery Waterloo, Ont, 81; Mt St Vincent Univ Art Gallery, Halifax, NS, 81. *Pos:* Contrib ed, Artmagazine, 78-; mem bd dirs, Art Gallery NS, 81-82. *Teaching:* Vis artist, NS Col Art & Design, 78, Univ Waterloo, Ont, 79 & 81 & Confederation Ctr Art Gallery, Charlottetown, 78 & 81; chairperson, Visual Arts NS, 80-81. *Awards:* Purchase Award, Atlantic Graphics, Mt St Vincent Univ, 76; Can Coun B Grant, 83-84. *Bibliog:* Patrick Laurette (auth), article, Artmagazine, 78; Peter Bell (auth), article, Evening Standrd St Johns, 79. *Mem:* Visual Arts NS; Can Artists Representation; Prof Artists NS. *Publ:*

Auth, Tom Forrestal, Arts Atlantic, 79; contribr, Visual Arts News, Visual Arts NS, 79; auth, Survival Atlantic Style, Artmagazine, 80; contribr, Halifax-Dartmouth Artists Supplement, Visual Arts NS, 83; auth, Paraskeva Clark, Artmagazine, 83. *Dealer:* Martin Gerard Gallery 10416-80 Ave Edmonton AB Can T6E 5T7. *Mailing Add:* 1688 Henry St Halifax NS B3H 3T8 Canada

REDINGER, WALTER FRED
SCULPTOR, MURALIST
b Wallacetown, Ont, Jan 6, 42. *Study:* Beal-Spec Art, London, Ont; Meinsinger Sch Art, Detroit; Ont Col Art, Toronto. *Work:* Nat Art Gallery, Ottawa; Art Gallery Ont, Toronto; Can Coun, Ottawa; Univ Western Ont; Univ Sask. *Comn:* Caucasian totems (set of 5), Rothman's, Stratford, 72; caucasian totems (set of 4), Samuel Bronfman, Can Jewish Cong, 73; Xabis (monument, 6 units), Ct House, London, Ont, 74; Montagne (monument), Pinetree Develop, Toronto, 75; Umbria (monuments, 3 units), Univ Guelph, 75. *Exhib:* Survey, Montreal Mus Fine Arts, 68; Plastic Presence, Jewish Mus, New York, Milwaukee Art Ctr, 70; Venice Biennale, 72; Owens Art Gallery, Mt Allison, NB, 75; Birmingham Festival Arts, Ala, 79; Harbourfront Art Gallery-Toronto, 82. *Pos:* Resident artist, Univ Western Ont. *Awards:* Sculpture Prize, Montreal Mus, 69; Can Coun Jr Awards, 68-71, Sr Awards, 73-74; Victor Lynch-Stauton Award, 77. *Bibliog:* Robert Arn (auth), Rebirth of humanism, Arts Can, 74; Document Venice Biennale (film), film, Educ TV Toronto, 74; film, Can Broadcasting Co, 74. *Mem:* Royal Can Acad Arts. *Media:* Fiberglass, Steel. *Dealer:* Isaacs Gallery 832 Yonge St Toronto ON Can. *Mailing Add:* Rte 3 West Lorne ON N0L 2P0 Canada

RED STAR, KEVIN See Running Rabbit

REDSTONE, LOUIS GORDON
ARCHITECT, WRITER
b Grodno, Poland, Mar 16, 03; US citizen. *Study:* Univ Mich, BS(archit), 29; Cranbrook Acad Art, MArch & Urban Design, 48. *Comn:* Brick mural, Jewish Community Ctr, West Bloomfield, Mich, 75 & First Federal Savings & Loan of Detroit, Operations Ctr, Troy, Mich, 76; Tapestries (woven in Mex by Mr Delgado), Manufacturers Bank & 333 W Fort Off Bldg, Detroit, Mich, 78. *Exhib:* Ann Mich Artists Water Color Exhib, Detroit, 28 & 42; The Levant Fair, Israeli Inst Exhib, Tel Aviv, Israel, 34; Watercolor USA, 69; Mich Watercolor Soc, 72; and others. *Awards:* Robert F Hastings Award for Outstanding Achievement, Mich Soc Archit. *Bibliog:* William Tall (auth), L G R: Minor Miracles in Watercolors, 11/22/69 & Marsha Miro (auth), Art in Architecture, 2/22/77, Detroit Free Press; Joy Hakanson (auth), Louis G Redstone: Fighting His Own War on Ugliness, Detroit News, 72. *Mem:* Patron Mich Foundation Arts, 77 (bd mem, 78); Mich Gov Spec Comn on Art in State Bldg; hon fel Royal Acad Fine Art, The Hague; corresponding acad Royal Acad Fine Arts, San Fernando, Spain; Mich Soc Archit. *Media:* Watercolor. *Interests:* Support of Michigan Society of Ceramic Artists. *Collection:* Pre-Columbian Art, Aztec, Inca. *Publ:* Auth, New Dimensions in Shopping Centers and Stores, 73; The New Downtowns, 76 & 80 & Public Art-New Directions, 81, McGraw-Hill; contribr, Art in Public Places in the US, Bowling Green Univ, 75; contrib, Masonry in Architecture, 84; and others. *Mailing Add:* 19303 Appoline Detroit MI 48235

REECE, MAYNARD
PAINTER, ILLUSTRATOR
b Arnolds Park, Iowa, Apr 26, 20. *Work:* Cent Nat Bank, Des Moines, Iowa; Iowa Des Moines Nat Bank. *Comn:* Designs for postage stamps, Govt of Bermuda, 65; First Iowa Duck Stamp, State Conserv Comn, 72; Marshlander Mallards, Ducks Unlimited Inc, 73; Canada Geese & Mallards, Winnebego Indust; Canada Geese, Remington Arms, Bridgeport, Conn, 76. *Exhib:* Various mus throughout the US & Can. *Awards:* Five Time Winner, Fed Duck Stamp Competition; Ark Duck Stamp Award, 82; Tex Duck Stamp Award, 83. *Bibliog:* George Harrison (auth), Iowa artist Maynard Reece: Bringing art out of the blind, Acquire, 77; Diane Milobar (auth), Maynard Reese: Wildlife artist, The Iowan, 77; John Diffely (auth), Maynard Reece: Wildlife artist, Am Artist, 78. *Mem:* Grand Cent Art Galleries New York; hon trustee Ducks Unlimited Inc; Soc Animal Artists; Nat Audubon Soc; Outdoor Writers Asn Am (past bd mem). *Media:* Oil, Watercolor; Stone Lithography. *Publ:* Illusr, Life, Outdoor Life, Sports Afield & others; auth & illusr, Fish & Fishing, Meredith, 63; illusr, Waterfowl in Iowa & Iowa Fish & Fishing, Iowa Conserv Comn. *Dealer:* Mill Pond Press Inc 201 S Nassau St Venice FL 33595. *Mailing Add:* 5315 Robertson Dr Des Moines IA 50312

REED, DAVID FREDRICK
PAINTER
b San Diego, Calif, Jan 20, 46. *Study:* Reed Col, BA; New York Studio Sch; Skowhegan Sch Painting & Sculpture. *Work:* Roswell Mus & Art Ctr, NMex; La Jolla Mus Contemp Art, Calif; Musee Nat d'Art Moderne, Centre George Pompidou, Paris. *Exhib:* Whitney Mus Biennial Contemp Am Art, New York, 75; one-man show, Susan Caldwell Inc, New York, 75 & Clock Tower, New York, 80; Max Protetch Gallery, New York, 77, 79 & 83; Investigations: Probe, Structure, Analysis, New Mus, 80 & Bertha Urdang Gallery, 81, New York; Gael Granson Gallery, Chicago, 82; and others. *Awards:* Rockefeller Found Grant, 66; Roswell Mus & Art Ctr Grant, 69. *Bibliog:* Peter Schjeldahl (auth), David Reed at Susan Caldwell, Art in Am, 7-8/75; James Sherry (auth), David Reed's paintings, ArtForum, 1/80; William Zimmer (auth), Artbreakers, New York's emerging artist, Soho Weekly News, 9/79; and others. *Media:* Oil with Wax, Acrylic on Canvas. *Publ:* Auth, On jumping, spring 75 & auth, On intermediate cases, spring 75, Art-Rite. *Dealer:* Max Protetch Gallery 37 W 57th St New York NY 10019. *Mailing Add:* 315 Broadway New York NY 10007

REED, DOEL
PAINTER, PRINTMAKER
b Logansport, Ind, May 21, 94. *Study:* Art Acad Cincinnati, with L H Meaken, James R Hopkins & H H Wessel. *Work:* Bibliot Nat, Paris; Victoria & Albert Mus, London; Metrop Mus Art, New York; Rosenwald Collection, Philadelphia; Pa Acad Fine Arts, Philadelphia. *Comn:* Six murals, Okla State Off Bldg, Oklahoma City, 41. *Exhib:* Many ann, Nat Acad Design, Audubon Artists, Allied Artists Am, Soc Am Graphic Artists & Nat Soc Painters Casein. *Teaching:* Prof art & chmn dept, Okla State Univ, 24-59, emer prof, 59- *Awards:* Gold Medal of Honor, 51 & John Taylor Arms Mem Medal, 54, Audubon Artists; Samuel Morse Medal, Nat Acad Design, 65. *Bibliog:* Doel Reed makes an aquatint, Mus NMex Press, 65. *Mem:* Nat Acad Design; Allied Artists Am; Audubon Artists; Soc Am Graphic Artists; Nat Soc Painters Casein. *Media:* Graphics. *Dealer:* Mission Gallery Taos NM 87571; Cremer Gallery 8575 E 31st Pl Tulsa OK 74145. *Mailing Add:* Box 1244 Taos NM 87571

REED, HAL
PAINTER, SCULPTOR
b Frederick, Okla, Feb 22, 21. *Study:* Trade Tech Col Los Angeles; Art Ctr Col Design; Art League San Francisco; also with Nicolai Fechin & Burt Proctor. *Work:* State of Calif Gov Off, Sacramento; Los Angeles City Hall Permanent Collection; and other pub & pvt collections. *Comn:* Brea in Progress (bronze), Brea, Calif, 79; Jonas Salk Commemorative Medal & Levi Strauss Commemorative Medal, Magnes Mus, Berkeley, Calif, 79; Albert Einstein Bust, Permanent Collection, Los Angeles Co Mus Sci & Indust, 79; Bicentennial bronze medals, US Navy & US Marine Corps, US Mint; bronze plaque of Jesse Owens, Los Angeles Coliseum; two portrait bronzes, St Mary's Hospital, Long Beach, Calif; and many others. *Exhib:* Nat Open, Miniature Painters, Sculptors & Gravers Soc, Washington, DC, 72; Nat Open, Miniature Art Soc NJ, 72; Am Artists Prof League, New York, 72; plus many others. *Teaching:* Founder & instr color, compos, anat, perspective & advan painting, Art League Los Angeles, 65-; instr art, 35 TV programs, 83. *Awards:* Best in Sculpture & Col King Award, Miniature Painters & Sculptors Soc Washington, DC, 72; selected NACAL artist, US Navy, 74; Award of Highest Merit, Miniature Art Soc of NJ, 74; and many others. *Mem:* Coun Traditional Artists Soc (pres, 71-72); fel Am Artists Prof League; fel Am Inst Fine Arts. *Media:* Oil, Acrylic; Bronze. *Publ:* Auth, How to Compose Pictures & Achieve Color Harmony, Walter Foster Publ, 69; auth, art instruction videotapes, Art Video Productions. *Mailing Add:* 20914 Pilar Rd Woodland Hills CA 91364

REED, HAROLD
DEALER
b Newark, NJ, Jan 11, 37. *Study:* Stanford Univ, BA; Art Students League. *Pos:* Dir, Harold Reed Gallery, New York, currently. *Mailing Add:* 120 East 78th St New York NY 10021

REED, JESSE FLOYD
PAINTER, PRINTMAKER
b Belington, WVa, July 25, 20. *Study:* Grand Cent Sch Art, 39-42; Art Students League, 45-47; Davis & Elkins Col, BA; WVa Univ, MA. *Work:* Huntington Galleries, WVa; Rosenberg Libr, Galveston, Tex. *Exhib:* Print Show, Brooklyn Mus, 49; Libr Cong, 55; Print Club Albany Ann; Soc Washington Printmakers Ann; Boston Printmakers Ann. *Teaching:* Prof art & hist, Davis & Elkins Col, 49- *Awards:* Purchase Award, Print Club Albany, 74; Merit Award & Purchase Award, Charleston Art Gallery, WVa, 75; Merit Award, Cult Ctr, WVa, 79. *Mem:* Salmagundi Club; Boston Printmakers; Print Club Albany. *Media:* Watercolor; Aquatint Etching. *Mailing Add:* PO Box 650 Elkins WV 26241

REED, MICHAEL ARTHUR
WRITER, EDITOR
b South Bend, Ind, May 5, 47. *Study:* Kalamazoo Col, BA. *Pos:* Contribr, Southwestern Art, Austin, Tex, 76-; co-ed & designer, Artspace Mag, Albuquerque, 76- *Res:* The history of modern ceramics in mainstream am; interviews with major contemporary ceramists. *Publ:* Auth, History of fine art printmaking in the Southwest (3 parts), Southwestern Art, 76; auth, Tamarind Institute (2 part series), Artspace, 76; auth, Roger Sweet, Artspace, 78. *Mailing Add:* Box 4547 10516 Trevino Loop NE Albuquerque NM 87106

REED, PAUL ALLEN
PAINTER, INSTRUCTOR
b Washington, DC, Mar 28, 19. *Study:* San Diego State Col; Corcoran Sch Art. *Work:* In 40 pub collections, including: San Francisco Mus of Art; Everson Mus of Art, Syracuse, NY; Corcoran Gallery Art & Nat Mus Am Art, Washington, DC; Detroit Inst Art; Walker Art Ctr, Minneapolis; Albright-Knox Art Gallery, Buffalo, NY. *Exhib:* 25th Ann Soc Am Art, Art Inst Chicago, 65; Washington Color Painters, Washington, DC, Tex, Calif, Mass & Minn, 65-66; 250 Yrs American Art, Corcoran Gallery Art, 66; Jackson Pollock to the Present, Steinberg Gallery, Wash Univ, St Louis, 69; Inaugural Exhib, Wadsworth Atheneum, Hartford, Conn, 69; Washington 20 Yrs, Baltimore Mus Art, 70; one-man exhib, Phoenix Art Mus, 77. *Teaching:* Instr painting, Art League Northern Va, 71-74; asst prof & coordr first yr prog, Corcoran Sch Art, 71-80. *Bibliog:* Barbara Rose (auth), The primacy of color 5/64 & Legrace Benson (auth), The Washington scene, 69, Art Int; Walter Hopps (auth), The Vincent Melzac Collection, Corcoran Gallery Art, 71. *Media:* Acrylic, Unprimed Canvas. *Mailing Add:* 3541 N Utah St Arlington VA 22207

REED, WALT ARNOLD
HISTORIAN, DEALER

b Big Spring, Tex, July 21, 17. *Study:* Pratt Inst; Phoenix Art Inst; also with Franklin Booth. *Comn:* Designer US postage stamp series, 50 state flags, US Postal Serv, 76. *Pos:* Art dir, CARE, New York, 52-55; ed, North Light Publ, Westport, 72-78; proprietor, Illus House, 75- *Teaching:* Art instr, Famous Artists Sch, Westport, Conn, 57-66, asst to dir, 66-72. *Awards:* Wrangler Award for Best Western Art Book, Cowboy Hall Fame & Western Heritage Ctr, 72. *Mem:* Westport Artists; New York Soc Illusr; Westport-Weston Arts Coun; Sanford Low Mem Collection Am Illus, New Brit Mus Am Art. *Res:* American illustrations, 1880 to the present. *Publ:* Auth, The Illustrator in America 1900-1960's, Reinhold, 65; auth, Harold Von Schmidt Draws and Paints the Old West, Northland, 72; auth, John Clymer, Northland, 76; auth, The magic pen of Joseph Clement Coll, North Light, 78; Fifty Great American Illustrators, Artabras, 79. *Mailing Add:* 7 Belaire Dr Westport CT 06880

REEP, EDWARD ARNOLD
PAINTER, EDUCATOR

b Brooklyn, NY, May 10, 18. *Study:* Art Ctr Col Design, cert, 41; also with E J Bisttram, Stanley Reckless & Willard Nash. *Work:* Los Angeles Co Mus, Calif; 66 works, US War Dept, Pentagon; Grunwald Graphic Arts Collection, Univ Calif, Los Angeles; Lytton Collection, Los Angeles; State of Calif Collection, Sacramento. *Comn:* Three panels of early conquests in Calif, SAm & US (with Gordon Mellor), USA Private's Club, Ft Ord, Calif, 41; Painter's Impression of International Airports (10 pages in full color), Life Mag, 6/56; Impressions of the Berlin Wall, Ger, US Govt, 71. *Exhib:* Whitney Mus Am Art Ann, New York, 46-48; Los Angeles Co Mus Ann, 46-60; Corcoran Gallery Art Biennial, Washington, DC, 49; Nat Acad Design, New York; Nat Gallery Art, Washington, DC. *Pos:* Coord art chmn, Los Angeles City Art Festival Exhibs, 51. *Teaching:* Instr painting & drawing, Art Ctr Col Design, Los Angeles, 46-50; instr painting & drawing & chmn, Dept Painting, Chouinard Art Inst, Los Angeles, 50-69; prof painting, artist in residence, E Carolina Univ, 70- *Awards:* First Purchase Prize for Watercolor, Los Angeles Co Mus, 51; First Prize in Oil Painting, Los Angeles All City Ann, 63; Nat Endowment Arts Grant, 75. *Bibliog:* Schaad (auth), Realm of Contemporary Still-life, 62 & Mugnaini (auth), Drawing, a Search for Form, 65, Van Nostrand Reinhold; James Jones (auth), Grosset & Dunlap, 75. *Mem:* Nat Watercolor Soc (pres, 51-52). *Media:* Oil, Watercolor. *Publ:* Auth, The Content of Watercolor, Van Nostrand Reinhold, 83. *Mailing Add:* 201 Poplar Dr Greenville NC 27834

REESE, PEARL HARDAWAY See Hardaway, Pearl

REESE, THOMAS FORD
HISTORIAN, EDUCATOR

b New Orleans, La, Oct 9, 43. *Study:* Fac Filosofia y Letras, Univ de Madrid, 63-64; Tulane Univ, BA, 65; Yale Univ, MA, 69, PhD, 73. *Teaching:* Asst prof art hist, Univ Tex, Austin, 70-76, assoc prof art hist, 76- *Awards:* John Simon Guggenheim fel, 76-77; Acad corresp, Real Acad Bellas Artes San Fernando, Madrid, 77. *Mem:* Am Soc Spanish & Portuguese Art Hist Studies (exec secy, 75-76). *Res:* History of the arts of Spain and Portugal; Latin American Colonial Art; European architecture since 1400. *Publ:* Co-ed, Newsletter of the Am Soc Hispanic Art Hist Studies, 74-76; auth, The Architecture of Ventura Rodriguez, New York, 76. *Mailing Add:* 1408 Northwood Rd Austin TX 78703

REESE, WILLIAM FOSTER
PAINTER

b Pierre, SDak, July 10, 38. *Study:* Wash State Univ; Orange Coast Col; Los Angeles Trade Tech Sch; Art Ctr Sch Design, Los Angeles. *Work:* Frye Art Mus, Seattle, Wash. *Comn:* Painting, Walter Lommell Hosp, Woodburn, Ore, 72; paintings, St Francis Hotel, San Francisco, 72. *Exhib:* Rocky Mountain Nat, Golden, Colo, 75, 76 & 77; Am Watercolor Soc Show, 76; Pastel Soc Show, 76-77; NAWA Show, Cowboy Hall of Fame, Oklahoma City, 77; one-man show, Frye Art Mus, 77; and others. *Awards:* Leon Augustine Hermitte Award, Puget Sound Exhib, Frye Mus, 75 & 77; House of Heydenryk Award, Nat Arts Club, 77; Best Show, Mus Great Plains, 78. *Bibliog:* Mary N Balcomb (auth), William F Reese: Form follows function, Am Artist Mag, 12/78; Laurel Andrews (auth), The visual poetry of William F Reese, Art West Mag, fall 79; Mary N Balcomb (auth), The art of painting, Southwest Art Mag, 10/82. *Mem:* Puget Sound Group Northwest Painters (secy, 70-71, treas, 71-72); Nat Acad Western Art; Whiskey Painters Am; Pastel Soc Am; Soc Animal Artists. *Media:* Oil, Watercolor. *Mailing Add:* 15511 SE 44th Ct Bellevue WA 98006

REESER, ROBERT D
EDUCATOR

b Orangeville, Ill, Mar 4, 31. *Study:* Northern Ill Univ, BS, 53; Univ Denver, MA(art), 59; Ohio State Univ, PhD(art educ), 74. *Work:* Burpee Art Gallery, Rockford, Ill. *Teaching:* Prof art, Calif State Univ, Los Angeles, 71- *Mem:* Calif Art Educ Asn (pres, 76-78); Nat Art Educ Asn; Artists Equity Asn; Int Soc Educ Art. *Res:* Teaching of secondary school art; aesthetics, art criticism and art history. *Mailing Add:* 1435 Edgecliff Ave Pasadena CA 91107

REEVE, JAMES KEY
HISTORIAN, CONSULTANT

b Lewistown, Mont. *Study:* Univ Tulsa, Okla, BA, 50; NY Univ Inst Fine Arts, MA, 54; Univ London Courtauld Inst, postgrad, 61-63. *Collections Arranged:* Masters of the Landscape: 1650-1900 (auth, catalog), 77, 100

Years of Native American Painting, 78, Oklahoma Sculpture Today (auth, catalog), 78 & Masters of the Portrait (auth, catalog), 79, Okla Mus Art. *Pos:* Cur, Univ Notre Dame Art Gallery, 58-61; cur/dir, Anglo-Am Art Mus, La State Univ, Baton Rouge, 63-67; cur Am art, Toledo Mus Art, Ohio, 67-72; cur art, Philbrook Art Ctr, Tulsa, Okla, 72-74; dir, Okla Mus Art, Oklahoma City, 75-81; art consult, Oklahoma City, 81-83; independent art & mus consult, Tulsa, 83- *Teaching:* Asst prof art hist, Univ Notre Dame, Ind, 58-61; asst prof art hist & museology, La State Univ, Baton Rouge, 63-67; adj prof art hist, Univ Tulsa, Okla, 72-74; adj prof, Oklahoma City Univ, 77-80; vis assoc prof, Univ Okla, 81-82. *Mem:* Am Asn Mus; Okla Mus Asn (coun mem, 79-81); Int Coun Mus; Soc Archit Historians. *Res:* American and English art and architecture, eighteenth century to present; museology. *Publ:* Coauth, Nineteenth century religious architecture in Toledo, Ohio, Northwest Ohio Hist Soc Quart, 71. *Mailing Add:* 4913 E 27th St Tulsa OK 74114

REEVES, JAMES FRANKLIN
HISTORIAN, COLLECTOR

b Huntsville, Ala, July 4, 46. *Study:* Univ Ala, Huntsville, BA(art hist), 72; Vanderbilt Univ, Nashville, Tenn, MA(art hist), 75. *Collections Arranged:* Gilbert Gaul, (with catalog), Tenn Fine Arts Ctr, Nashville & Huntsville Mus Art, 75. *Pos:* Asst, P L Hay House Mus, Macon, Ga, 66-67; asst to dir, 73-75, cur Huntsville Mus Art, 75-77. *Mem:* Col Art Asn Am; Southeastern Col Art Conf; Kappa Pi (pres local chapter, 71-72). *Res:* Gilbert Gaul, 1855-1919; Huntsville architecture, 1820-1975. *Collection:* 19th and 20th century American paintings; 18th and 19th century American decorative arts; 19th century European paintings; Oriental porcelains and sculpture. *Mailing Add:* 2005 Kildare St Huntsville AL 35811

REEVES, JOHN ALEXANDER
PHOTOGRAPHER

b Burlington, Ont, Can, Apr 24, 38. *Study:* Sir George Williams Art Sch, Montreal, 56-57; Ont Col Art, Toronto, 57-61, AOCA. *Work:* Nat Film Bd Can, Ottawa; Archives Canada; Dept Indian & Northern Affairs, Ottawa. *Exhib:* One-man shows, Deja Vue Gallery, Toronto, 77, Magic Word, Archives Canada, 81, Inuit Art World, Can Ctr Photog, Toronto, 82 & Corning Gallery, Toronto, 83; and others. *Teaching:* Instr photog, Ontario Col Art. *Awards:* Am Inst Graphic Arts Award, 63 & 68; Award of Merit, Art Dir Club, Toronto, 72; Can Nat Mag Award for Photo-journalism, Can Fiction Mag. *Bibliog:* Charles Oberdorf (auth), article, Camera Can Mag, 11/72 & 6/77; Gary Michael Dault (auth), Toronto Star, 6/77; Gary Michael Dault (auth), Inuit Art World Catalogue, 82. *Mem:* Royal Can Acad Art. *Publ:* Auth, John Fillion--Thoughts About My Sculpture, Martlet Press, 68. *Dealer:* Jane Corkin Gallery 144 Front St W Toronto ON Can. *Mailing Add:* 11 Yorkville Ave Toronto ON M4W 1L1 Canada

REFF, THEODORE
HISTORIAN

b New York, NY, Aug 18, 30. *Study:* Columbia Col, BA, 52; Harvard Univ, MA, 53, PhD, 58. *Collections Arranged:* Cezanne Watercolors (ed, catalog), M Knoedler & Co, New York, 63; Degas in the Metropolitan, Metrop Mus, New York, 77; Cezanne: the Late Work, Mus Mod Art, New York, 77; Manet and Modern Paris, Nat Gallery, Washington, DC, 82-83. *Teaching:* Prof art hist & mod art, Columbia Univ, 57-; vis Vis prof, Univ Mich, Princeton Univ, NY Univ, Hebrew Univ, Jerusalem, plus others. *Mem:* Col Art Asn Am (dir, 77-81); Int Found Art Res (dir, 80-). *Res:* 19th and 20th century art; relations between art and literature. *Publ:* Ed, Unpublished Correspondence of Toulouse-Lautrec, Phaidon Press, 69; auth, The Notebooks of Edgar Degas, Clarendon Press, 76; auth, Degas: the Artist's Mind, Harper & Row, 76; auth, Manet: Olympia, Penguin, 76; auth, Manet and Modern Paris, Univ Chicago Press, 83. *Mailing Add:* Dept of Art Hist Columbia Univ New York NY 10027

REGAT, JEAN-JACQUES ALBERT
SCULPTOR, MURALIST

b Paris, France, Sept 11, 45. *Study:* Univ Alaska, BA; Soc Beaux Arts, France. *Work:* Sheik Zayed Ben Sultan Al-Nahyan, Pres of United Arab Emirates, Abu Dabi; Fairbanks North Star Borough Pub Libr, Alaska; Soroptimist Int of Anchorage; RCA Alascom, Anchorage; Kobuk Valley Jade Co, Alyeska. *Comn:* The Man Who Became Caribou (bas relief wood), Noatak Artic Sch Dist, 81; Miners of the Yukon (tryptic bas relief wood), Yukon Off Supplies Co, 82; Delta Pastoral (bas relief wood), Delta Greely Sch Dist, 82; The Rsolution (bronze & bas relief wood), Carr-Gottstein Ltd; St Joseph & St Francis, St Anthony Cath Church Anchorage, 83. *Exhib:* One-man show, Artique Ltd, Anchorage, 72-77; Heritage Northwest Gallery, Juneau, 73-74; House of Wood, Fairbanks, 74-80; Erdon Gallery, Houston, Tex; Rendezvous Gallery, Anchorage. *Bibliog:* Judy Shuler (auth), Jacques & Mary Regat, Alaska J autumn 77; Nancy Cain Schmitt (auth), Ancient legend of Sedna is captured in bronze, Anchorage Times, 5/20/79; Mary Sawyer-Albert (auth), Stories carved in wood and stone, Jacques and Mary Regat, Southwest Art, 8/79; plus others. *Media:* Stone, Wood. *Dealer:* House of Wood 529 Fourth Fairbanks AK 99701. *Mailing Add:* c/o Regat Studio 518 Pearl Dr Anchorage AK 99502

REGAT, MARY E
SCULPTOR, MURALIST

b Duluth, Minn, Nov 12, 43. *Study:* Univ Alaska. *Work:* Anchorage Fine Arts Mus, Alaska; Soroptimist Int of Anchorage; Kobuk Valley Jade Co, Alyeska, Alaska; Fairbanks North Star Borough Pub Libr; RCA-Alascom, Anchorage. *Comn:* Trail of 98 (bas relief wood), Pioneers Asn Alaska, 79; Creek Woman (bas relief wood & bronze), Kokanok, Peninsula Sch Dist, 80; Huskies (bronze), Kotzebue Artic Sch Dist, 82; Dance of the Oomialik (sculpture),

Gottstein Inc, 82; High, Wild and Free (sculpture), Greyling, Iditarod Sch Dist, 83. *Exhib:* One-woman show, Artique Ltd, Anchorage, 72-77; Heritage Northwest Gallery Juneau, 73-74; House of Wood, Fairbanks, 74-80; Erdon Gallery, Houston, Tex; Rendezvous Gallery, Anchorage; plus others. *Awards:* Sculpture Award, Design I, 71; Purchase Award, Anchorage Fine Arts Mus, 71. *Bibliog:* Judy Schuler (auth), Jacques and Mary Regat, Alaska J, autumn, 77; Nancy Cain Schmitt (auth), Ancient legend of Sedna is captured in bronze, Anchorage Times, 5/20/79; Mary Sawyer-Albert (auth), Stories carved in wood and stone, Jacques and Mary Regat, Southwest Art, 8/79; plus others. *Mem:* Artist Guild; Anchorage Fine Arts Mus Asn. *Media:* Stone, Wood. *Dealer:* Rendezvous Gallery 600 W 6th Ave Anchorage AK 99501; House of Wood 529 Fourth Fairbanks AK 99701. *Mailing Add:* Regat Studio 518 Pearl Dr Anchorage AK 99502

REGENSTEINER, ELSE (FRIEDSAM)
DESIGNER, WEAVER
b Munich, Ger, Apr 21, 06; US citizen. *Study:* Univ Munich; Inst Design, Chicago; Black Mountain Col, with Moholy-Nagy, Marli Ehrman & Anni & Josef Albers. *Work:* Cooper-Hewitt Mus, New York; Art Inst Chicago; Ill State Univ; Univ Houston. *Exhib:* Designer-Craftsmen USA, Smithsonian Inst, 53; Designer-Craftsmen Ill, Ill State Mus, Springfield, 66; Decorative Arts Nat, Wichita, Kans, 70; Textiles for Collectors, Art Inst Chicago, 71; Fabrications, Cranbrook Acad Art, 72; Am Crafts, Philadelphia Mus of Art, 77; Midwest Constructed Fiber, 80. *Pos:* Ed bd, The Working Craftsman, Northbrook, Ill, 75-78. *Teaching:* Instr weaving, Hull House, Chicago, 41-45; instr weaving, Inst Design, Chicago, 42-46; prof weaving, Art Inst Chicago, 45-71; workshops & lect throughout US, Can & Greece, 71-; consult, Am Farm Sch, Thessaloniki, Greece, 72-78. *Awards:* Five Citations of Merit, Am Inst Interior Design, 47, 48 & 51; Hon Mention, State Mus Art, Springfield, 66; Regensteiner Award, Midwest Weavers Asn, 80. *Bibliog:* Naomi Whiting Towner (auth), Interview: Else Regensteiner, Shuttle, Spindle & Dyepot, spring 79. *Mem:* Am Crafts Coun; Handweavers Guild Am. *Publ:* Contribr, Weaving in Illinois, Directions 1970, Ill Art Educ Asn, 70; auth articles in Handweaver & Craftsman, 65 & 69; auth, articles, Shuttle, Spindle & Dyepot, 71-80; auth, Weaving Sourcebook, Ideas and Techniques, Weaver's Study Course, 83; Geometric Design in Weaving, Van Nostrand Reinhold, 84. *Mailing Add:* 1416 E 55th St Chicago IL 60615

REGER, LAWRENCE L
ADMINISTRATOR
b Lincoln Nebr, June 23, 39. *Study:* Univ Nebr; Vanderbilt Univ, JD, 64. *Pos:* Dir prog development & coordination, Nat Endowment Arts, DC, 71-78; dir, Am Asn Mus, DC, 78- *Mailing Add:* 1055 Thomas Jefferson St NW Washington DC 20007

REGINATO, PETER
SCULPTOR
b Dallas, Tex, Aug 19, 45. *Study:* San Francisco Art Inst, 63-66. *Work:* Metrop Mus Art; Houston Mus of Fine Arts; Mint Mus Art; Chase Manhattan Bank, New York, NY; Brown Univ, RI; and others. *Comn:* High Plains Drifter (large sculpture), Allen Ctr, Houston, Tex, 73; Outdoor Sculpture Exhib (sculpture), Rutgers State Univ, Camden, NJ, 78. *Exhib:* Park Place Invitational, New York, 67; Whitney Mus of Am Art Biennial, 70; Highlights of the Season, Aldrich Mus, Ridgefield, Conn, 71; Univ of RI, Providence, 73; Sculpture in the Park, North Jersey Cult Coun, 74; Modern Sculpture in Houston Collections, 74 & Geometry: A Summer Exhibition, Mus Fine Arts, Houston; Sculpture Now, Gallery Ariadne, New York, 75; The Condition of Sculpture, Hayward Gallery, London, Eng, 75; plus others. *Teaching:* Adj lectr sculpture, Hunter Col, 71-73. *Awards:* John Simon Guggenheim Mem Found fel, 76; Purchase Award, Hirshhorn Mus, DC, 79; Clayworks Residency, Nat Endowment Arts, 83. *Bibliog:* Tony Tovle (auth), article, Art Am, 9/79; Vivien Raynor (auth), article, New York Times, 7/19/80; John Russell, article, New York Times, 7/81; plus others. *Media:* Painted Welded Steel, Clay. *Dealer:* Salander-O'Reilly Galleries Inc 22 E 80 St New York NY 10012; Diane Brown 100 Greene St 10012 New York NY 10012. *Mailing Add:* 60 Greene St New York NY 10012

REHBERGER, GUSTAV
PAINTER, DRAFTSMAN
b Riedlingsdorf, Austria, Oct 20, 10; US citizen. *Study:* Art Inst Chicago, scholar; Art Instr Schs, Minneapolis, scholar. *Work:* Lyman Allyn Mus, New London, Conn; St Johns Univ, NY; Sports Hall, Peking, China; numerous pvt collections in US, Can, Mex, Europe, Saudi Arabia & China. *Exhib:* One-man shows, Soc of Illusrs, New York, 57 & 65; Wickersham Gallery, New York, 71 & Jacques Seligman Gallery, New York, 77. *Teaching:* Instr & lectr, Art Students League, 72- *Awards:* Awards, Art Directors Club of New York, 54 & 55; Award, Allied Artists of Am, 74; Awards, Pastel Soc of Am, 76, 79 & 81; and others. *Mailing Add:* Studio 1206 Carnegie Hall New York NY 10019

REIBACK, EARL M
SCULPTOR, KINETIC ARTIST
b New York, NY, May 30, 43. *Study:* Lehigh Univ, BA & BS; Mass Inst Technol, MS. *Work:* Whitney Mus Am Art, New York; Philadelphia Mus Art; Milwaukee Art Ctr; New Orleans Mus Art; Wichita Art Mus, Kans. *Exhib:* Milwaukee Art Ctr, Wis, 67; Experiments in Light & Technology, Brooklyn Mus, NY, 68; Metrop Mus Art, New York; Philadelphia Mus Art; Albright-Knox Art Gallery, Buffalo, NY; New Orleans Mus Art, La; Long Beach Mus Contemp Art, Calif; Aldrich Mus Contemp Art, Ridgefield, Conn; Mus d'Art Contemporain, Montreal, Que; Am Cult Ctr, Beirut, Lebanon; US Cult Ctr, Tel Aviv, Israel; Fine Arts Gallery, Ankara, Turkey; and others. *Publ:* Auth, articles, House & Garden, 1/69 & Electronics Age, spring 70. *Mailing Add:* 20 E Ninth St New York NY 10003

REIBEL, BERTRAM
SCULPTOR, GRAPHIC ARTIST
b New York, NY, June 14, 01. *Study:* Art Inst Chicago; also with Alexander Archipenko. *Exhib:* Metrop Mus Art & Nat Acad Design, New York; Pa Acad Fine Arts, Philadelphia; Northwest Printmakers; Libr Cong, Washington, DC; plus many others, incl one-man shows at Univ d'El Salvador, San Salvador, Korean Design Ctr, Seoul, Merrick Art Gallery, New Brighton, Pa & La Casa Cultura, Puebla, Mex. *Mem:* Artists Equity Asn; Asn Int Arts Plastiques. *Media:* Wood, Bronze. *Mailing Add:* 1127 Hardscrabble Rd Chappaqua NY 10514

REICH, DON
PAINTER
b Martinez, Calif, 1931. *Work:* Legion of Honor; Oakland Mus, Calif; Dallas Mus Fine Arts; San Francisco Mus Mod Art; E B Crocker Art Gallery. *Exhib:* One-man shows, Calif Palace Legion of Honor, San Francisco & others; group shows, Crocker-Kingsley 50-Yr Retrospective, Sacramento, Bay Area Artists on Paper, San Francisco Art Inst, Carnegie Inst Ann, Poindexter Gallery, New York & Nat Invitational Drawing Show, Univ Ill, plus others. *Bibliog:* Various articles in Art in Am, Artforum & Artweek. *Mailing Add:* c/o Graphics Gallery 2140 Bush St Suite 6 San Francisco CA 94115

REICH, NATHANIEL E
PAINTER, COLLAGE ARTIST
b Brooklyn, NY. *Study:* Art Students League; Pratt Inst; Brooklyn Inst Arts & Sci. *Work:* Huntington Hartford Collection, Gallery Mod Art, New York; Joe & Emily Lowe Mus, Univ Miami; Washington Co Mus Fine Arts, Hagerstown, Md; Evansville Mus Arts & Sci, Ind; New York Heart Asn; and others. *Exhib:* Eighth Serv Command Competition USA, 44; 4th Har Zion Temple Art Show, Philadelphia, 66; Prospect Park Centennial, 66; Mus Mod Art, Paris, 70; Boston Inst Fine Arts, 71; two retrospectives, NY Univ; and others. *Awards:* St Gaudens Medal, 23; First Prize, Eighth Serv Command Competition, USA, 44. *Mem:* Artists Equity Asn. *Media:* Oil. *Mailing Add:* 1620 Ave I Brooklyn NY 11230

REICH, SHELDON
HISTORIAN, LECTURER
b Brooklyn, NY, Sept 5, 31. *Study:* Univ of Miami, BA, 54; New York Univ, MA, 57; Univ of Iowa, PhD, 66. *Pos:* Prof of art hist, Univ of Ariz, Tucson, 60-68; dept head of art hist, Univ of Cincinnati, 68-72; prof of art hist, Univ Ariz, 72- *Awards:* Arch Am Art Res Grant, 63; Sr Res Fel, Nat Mus Art, Smithsonian Inst, 71-72. *Mem:* Col Art Assoc; Am Asn of Univ Prof; Mid-Am Col Art Asn. *Res:* Specialize in early 20th century American painting. *Publ:* Auth, John Marin: A Stylistic Analysis and a Catalogue Raisonne, Univ Ariz, 70; auth, A H Maurer, Smithsonian, 73; auth, Isabel Bishop, Univ Ariz, 74; auth, Graphic Styles of the American Eight, Univ Utah, 76; auth, Francisco Zuniga, Sculptor, Univ Ariz, 80. *Mailing Add:* 710 N Alamo Ave Tucson AZ 85711

REICHARD, STEPHEN BRANTLEY
ADMINISTRATOR
b Salisbury, Md, Mar 6, 49. *Study:* Sch Foreign Serv, Georgetown Univ, BSFS, 71; Diplomatic Acad, Vienna, Austria, dipl, 73; Grad Sch Bus, Columbia Univ, MBA, 74. *Pos:* Pres, Stephen Reichard Inc, New York, 74-79; vpres & admin dir, Inst Art & Urban Resources Inc, 75-79; co-founder & dir, Livet Reichard Co Inc, New York, currently. *Mem:* Artists Cable TV (bd mem, 77-78); Deutscher Akademischer Austauschdienst, Berlin; Am Coun on Ger. *Interests:* Provide administration services for artists & art organizations. *Publ:* New Yorks New Realism, Art Gallery, 75; Alternative art spaces: One to one politics/or the avant-garde, Soho Downtown Manhattan, 76; Art Spaces by and for the Artist, Berlin Festival Cent Nat SE, 77; Works and Projects of the Seventies, The New York Avant-Garde, Inst Art & Urban Resources Inc, 78. *Mailing Add:* 87 Franklin St New York NY 10013

REICHEK, ELAINE
CONCEPTUAL ARTIST
b Brooklyn, NY, Apr 30, 43. *Study:* Brooklyn Col, BA, 63; Yale Univ Sch Art & Archit, BFA, 64. *Work:* Norton Gallery Art, West Palm Beach, Fla; Portland Art Mus, Ore; Best Products Co Inc, Ashland, Va. *Exhib:* Out of the House, Whitney Mus, New York, 78; Small is Beautiful, Freedman Gallery, Reading, Pa, 79; USA Women Artists 1980, Mus De Arte Contemp, Sao Paulo, Brasil, 80; Home Work, Women's Hall Fame, Schenectady, NY, 81; Day In/Day Out, Freedman Gallery, Reading, Pa, 83; Walls of the Seventies, Queensborough Community Col, NY, 83. *Awards:* Creative Artists Pub Serv Grant, NY State Coun Arts, 83. *Bibliog:* Corinne Robins (auth), Verbal image/written object, Arts Mag, 2/81; Kim Levin (auth), article, Flash Art, 1/83; Ann-Sargent Wooster (auth), article, Art in Am, 3/83. *Mem:* Women's Caucus Art. *Dealer:* AIR Gallery 63 Crosby St New York NY 10013. *Mailing Add:* 140 Riverside Dr New York NY 10024

REICHEK, JESSE
PAINTER, EDUCATOR
b Brooklyn, NY, Aug 16, 16. *Study:* Inst Design, Chicago, 41-42; Acad Julian, Paris, 47-51. *Work:* Amon Carter Mus Western Art, Ft Worth, Tex; Art Inst Chicago; Bibliot Nat, Paris; Los Angeles Co Mus Art, Los Angeles; Mus Mod Art, New York; and others. *Exhib:* Mus Mod Art, 62, 65 & 69; one-man shows, Am Cult Ctr, Florence, Italy, 64 & Univ NMex Mus, 66; retrospective, Univ Southern Calif Art Mus, 67; San Francisco Mus Art, 69; and others. *Teaching:* Assoc prof design, Univ Calif, Berkeley, 58-60, prof, 60-; artist in residence, Tamarind Lithography Workshop, Los Angeles, 66; res prof,

Creative Arts Inst, Univ Calif, 66-67. *Awards:* Co-partic, Graham Found Grant, 62; Res Travel Grant, Creative Arts Inst, Univ Calif, summer 63; Tamarind Fel, 66. *Publ:* Auth, Jesse Reichek-Dessins, Ed Cahiers Art, Paris, 60; auth, La Montee de la Nuit, 61 & Fontis, 61, P A Benoit, Alex; auth, Etcetera, New Directions, 65; auth, The Architect & the City, Mass Inst Technol, 66; plus many others. *Dealer:* Betty Parsons Gallery 24 W 57th St New York NY 10019. *Mailing Add:* 5925 Red Hill Rd Petaluma CA 94953

REICHERT, DONALD KARL
PAINTER, EDUCATOR
b Libau, Man, Jan 11, 32. *Study:* Univ Man Sch Art, with Robert A Nelson & George Swinton, BFA, 56; Inst Allende, Mex, with James Pinto; Emma Lake Artist's Workshops, with Jules Olitzki, Stepan Wolpe, Lawrence Alloway, John Cage & Frank Stella. *Work:* Nat Gallery Can; Art Gallery Ont; Winnipeg Art Gallery; Mt Allison Univ; Montreal Mus Fine Arts. *Exhib:* Winnipeg Show Nat Biennial; Montreal Spring Show Nat; Nat Gallery Biennial; Visua '67, Nat Exhib; Midwest Painters. *Teaching:* Artist in residence, Univ NB, 61-62; prof painting, Univ Man Sch Art, 64- *Awards:* Can Coun Bursary, 62 & Sr Nat Awards, 67 & 74. *Mem:* Royal Can Acad Arts. *Media:* Acrylic, Oil. *Mailing Add:* 228 Glenwood Crescent Winnipeg MB R2L 1J9 Canada

REICHMAN, FRED
PAINTER
b Bellingham, Wash, Jan 28, 25. *Study:* Univ Calif, Berkeley, BA(cum laude) & MA; San Francisco Art Inst. *Work:* San Francisco Mus Art; Oakland Mus Art, Calif; Santa Barbara Mus Art, Calif; Edwin A Ulrich Mus Art, Wichita, Kans; Milwaukee Art Mus, Wis; and others. *Comn:* Murals, Stanford Univ Med Sch, Palo Alto, Calif, 61 & San Francisco Art Festival, Civic Ctr, 68. *Exhib:* One-man shows, San Francisco Mus Art, 56 & 69 & Santa Barbara Mus Art, 74; 50 Calif Artists, Whitney Mus Am Art, New York, 62; Gallery Paule Anglim, San Francisco, 78 & 80; Chikyudo Gallery, Tokyo, 80; The New Gallery, Taos, NMex, 82. *Teaching:* Instr art, Univ Calif Exten, San Francisco, 66- *Awards:* Artist's Coun Prize, San Francisco Art Asn Ann, 54; Purchase Award, San Francisco Art Festival, 64; Award of Merit, Art Festival City & Co San Francisco, 68. *Bibliog:* Judy Stone (auth), interview, San Francisco Chronicle, 10/15/63; Mimi Jacobs (auth), interview, Pac Sun, 1/16/75. *Media:* Oil, Acrylic. *Dealer:* Charles Campbell Gallery 647 Chestnut San Francisco CA 94133; The New Gallery Box 1408 Taos NMex. *Mailing Add:* 1235 Stanyan St San Francisco CA 94117

REID, CHARLES
WRITER, PAINTER
b Cambridge, NY, Aug 12, 37. *Study:* S Kent Sch; Univ of Vt; Art Students League, study with Frank Reiley. *Work:* Yellowstone Art Ctr, Billings, Mont; Brigham Young Univ, Salt Lake City, Utah; Smith Col Mus, South Hampton, Mass. *Comn:* US Postage Stamp to Commemorate Family Planning, US Postal Dept. *Exhib:* Nat Acad of Design, Am Watercolor Soc & Am Inst of Arts & Letters, New York. *Awards:* First Altman Figure Award, 72 & Second Altman Figure Award, 74; Nat Acad of Design, New York; Childe Hassam Purchase Awards, Am Acad of Arts & Letters, 76 & 77. *Mem:* Assoc Nat Acad of Design. *Media:* Watercolor; Oil. *Publ:* Auth & illusr, Figure Painting in Watercolor, 72, Portrait Painting in Watercolor, 73, Flower Painting in Oil, 76 & Flower Painting in Watercolor, 79, Watson-Guptill. *Dealer:* Far Gallery 2 E 80th St New York NY. *Mailing Add:* Box 113 Greens Farms CT 06436

REID, LESLIE MARY MARGARET
PAINTER, PRINTMAKER
b Ottawa, Ont, Feb 8, 47. *Study:* Queen's Univ, Kingston, Ont, BA(art hist), 67; Byam Shaw Sch Art, London, Eng, LCAD, 70; Chelsea Sch Art, London, Eng, grad dipl, 71; Slade Sch Art, London, Eng, 77. *Work:* Nat Gallery Can, Ottawa; Can Coun Art Bank, Ottawa; Winnipeg Art Gallery; Dept External Affairs, Ottawa; Montreal Mus Fine Arts; and others. *Exhib:* Nat Gallery Can, Ottawa, 75 & 78; 7th Int Print Biennale, Cracow, Poland, 78; one-man shows, Can Cult Ctr, 80, Can House Gallery, London, 80, Mira Godard Gallery, Toronto, 78 & 81 & Galerie Jolliet, Montreal, 82. *Teaching:* Assoc prof painting & printmaking, Univ Ottawa, Ont, 72- *Awards:* Can Coun Proj Grant, 74, 75, 76 & 80; Ed Award, First Can Biennial Prints & Drawings, Ont Arts Coun, 78; Ont Arts Coun Prog Grant, 83. *Bibliog:* Anna Babinska (auth), Light distilled, Arts Mag, 78; Richard Simmins (auth), Leslie Reid, 80 & Jean-Louis Paudrat (auth), Quelques Felures..., 80, Can Cult Centre, Paris. *Mem:* Royal Can Acad; Can Artist Representation (Ottawa exec, 77); Univ Art Asn Can. *Media:* Acrylic; Lithography. *Dealer:* Mira Godard Gallery 22 Hazelton Ave Toronto ON M5R 2E2 Can. *Mailing Add:* Dept of Visual Arts Univ Ottawa Ottawa ON K1N 6N5 Canada

REID, ROBERT DENNIS
PAINTER, INSTRUCTOR
b Atlanta, Ga, 1924. *Study:* Clark Col, 41-43; Art Inst Chicago, 43-46; Parson Sch Design, New York, 48-50. *Work:* Myers Col, Birmingham, Ala; Studio Mus Harlem; Cornell Univ, Ithaca, NY; Montclair Art Mus, NJ; Mus et Galerie des Beaux-Arts, Bordeaux, France; and others. *Exhib:* US Info Serv Tour, Paris, Brest, Vannes & Tours, 71; Black Artists: Two Generations, 71 & Recent Acquisitions, 71, Newark Mus; Black Artists Am, Whitney Mus Am Art, 71; Artists Postcards, Drawing Ctr, New York & Smithsonian Inst-sponsored tour, 78-79; one-man shows, Alonzo Gallery, 72, Leslie Rankow Gallery, New York, 74-75 & Lenore Gray Gallery, Providence, RI, 77; and many other group & one-man shows. *Teaching:* Asst prof drawing, RI Sch Design, 70-; instr painting, State Univ NY Col Purchase, summer 75; vis instr, Parsons Sch of Design, New York, 77 & Drew Univ, Madison, NJ, 78. *Awards:* Childe Hassam Purchase Award, Am Acad Arts & Lett, 69. *Media:* Oil, Watercolor. *Dealer:* Elaine Benson Gallery Bridgehampton Long Island NY. *Mailing Add:* 233 Lafayette St New York NY 10012

REIF, (F) DAVID
SCULPTOR, EDUCATOR
b Cincinatti, Ohio, Dec 14, 41. *Study:* Univ Cincinatti, 60-63; Sch Art Inst Chicago, BFA, 68; Yale Univ, with James Rosati, Robert Morris & Al Held, MFA, 70. *Work:* Weatherspoon Art Gallery, Univ NC, Greensboro; Univ Wyo Art Mus, Laramie. *Exhib:* Joslyn Art Mus, Omaha, Nebr, 78 & 79; Springville Art Mus, Utah, 79; one-man shows, Slusser Gallery, Univ Mich, Ann Arbor, 80 & Dorsky Gallery, New York, 80; Miss Mus Art Traveling Show, 81-; Flatworks, Washington Project Arts, Washington, DC, 83-84; and others. *Teaching:* Assoc prof, Univ Wyo, Laramie, 70-80, prof, 81-; assoc prof, Univ Mich, Ann Arbor, 80-81. *Awards:* Third Prize, Southern Asn Sculptors, 78; Best Sculpture Award, Joslyn Art Mus, Omaha, 78; Emerging Artist Grant, Nat Endowment Arts, 79-80. *Bibliog:* George P Tomko (auth), Regionalism, Seven Views, Joslyn Art Mus, 7-8/79; Martha Keller (auth), Art, a catalyst to thought and dialog, Ann Arbor News, Mich, 8/16/81. *Mem:* Col Art Asn; Southern Asn Sculptors; Int Sculpture Ctr, Washington, DC. *Media:* Mixed Media. *Publ:* Auth, Contemporary art on the Wyoming frontier: 1978, Wyo News Mag, 8/78. *Dealer:* Henri Gallery 1500 21st NW Washington DC 20036. *Mailing Add:* 1117 Curtis St Laramie WY 82070

REIF, RUBIN
PAINTER, EDUCATOR
b Warsaw, Poland, Aug 16, 1910. *Study:* Cooper Union Art Sch; Art Students League; Hans Hofmann Sch Fine Arts; Acad Fine Arts, Florence, Italy. *Work:* Ohio Univ; Art Students League; Cooper Union Collection; Ark Indust Develop Comn; also in many pvt collections. *Exhib:* Am Fedn Arts Traveling Exhib, 48-49 & 67-69; Cincinnati Mus Asn; Ark Art Ctr, Little Rock, 60, 61 & 67-69; Springfield Art Mus, Mo, 67-69; Okla Art Ctr, 67-69; and many other group & one-man shows. *Teaching:* Assoc prof art, Univ Ark, Fayetteville, formerly, emer prof, currently. *Awards:* Prizes, Ohio State Fair, 52, Ark Festival Arts, 62 & 63 & Okla Ann, 64; and many others. *Mailing Add:* 416 Gunter St Fayetteville AR 72701

REILAND, LOWELL KEITH
SCULPTOR
b Wahpeton, NDak, May 11, 48. *Study:* NDak State Univ, Fargo, 66-68; Moorhead State Univ, with Lyle Laske, BA, BS, 71; Cornell Univ, with Jack Squire & Jason Seley, dipl, 74. *Work:* Claire M Eagle Mus, Murray, Ky. *Comn:* Sculptures, Moorhead State Univ, 78 & City Fargo, NDak, 78. *Exhib:* Plains Art Mus, Moorhead, Minn, 79-83; Mus Monterrey, Mex, 83; Alexandria Mus, La, 83; Univ Ore Mus, Eugene, 83; Univ Okla Mus, Norman, 83. *Bibliog:* Glen Tornell (auth), Sculptor ... drops off a vision, Moorhead State Univ, 78; Fargo sculptor ... stepping stone, Fargo Sunday Forum, 79; Tony Towle (auth), article, Condeso-Lawler Newslett, 83. *Dealer:* Condeso-Lawler Gallery 76 Green St New York NY 10013. *Mailing Add:* 83 Grand St New York NY 10013

REILING, SUSAN WALLACE
CURATOR, HISTORIAN
b Denver, Colo, Aug 2, 40. *Study:* Moore Inst of Art, Philadelphia, BFA(interior design), 62; Univ Miami, MA(art hist & mus studies), 72, DA(Europ hist), 78. *Collections Arranged:* Religious Masks from Indonesia, Antique Europ Fans, 71, Two Centuries of Oriental Art in the Deering Collection, 72, 17th & 18th Century South American Colonial Religious Sculpture, 72 & Antique Costumes, 73, Vizcaya Mus & Gardens, Miami, Fla. *Pos:* Cur decorative arts, Vizcaya Mus & Gardens, 71-76, cur of the collections, 76- *Teaching:* Guest lectr interior design & decorative arts, Miami-Dade Community Col, 74-, coordr mus intern prog, Museology, 75- *Mem:* Am Asn Mus; Int Inst for Conserv of Hist & Artistic Works; Am Inst for Conserv of Hist & Artist Works; Am Soc of Interior Designers; Comite Int de Photogrammetrie Architecturale. *Res:* Conservation methods; European decorative arts, architecture and landscape architecture, archaeology; cultural anthropology. *Publ:* Auth, The Restoration of a 17th century mantelpiece, Proj Quart, 75; auth, Vizcaya, Compass Mag, 75; auth, Vizcaya Mus & Gardens (official mus bk), Fla Natural Color, 76. *Mailing Add:* 11 Edgewater Dr Apt 418 Coral Gables FL 33133

REILLY, BERNARD FRANCIS
HISTORIAN, CURATOR
b Philadelphia, Pa, June 7, 50. *Study:* Villanova Univ, BA, 72; Bryn Mawr Col, with Arthur Marks, MA(hist art), 74. *Exhib:* Caricature Since 1870, Libr Cong, DC, 79. *Collections Arranged:* American Political Prints (cataloged), Libr Cong, 78; Applied Graphic Art, Libr Cong; Photographs from 1845 to 1876 (cataloged), Libr Co Philadelphia. *Pos:* Cur prints & drawing, Libr Co Philadelphia, 74-77; cur popular & applied graphic art, Prints & Photographs Div, Libr Cong, 78- *Teaching:* Am political art, Humanities Program, Georgetown Univ, 81. *Mem:* Print Coun Am; Am Print Conf; Asn Historians of Am Art. *Res:* History of 19th century painting, graphic art and photography, particularly landscape; history of political art from Renaissance to current times with emphasis on theory of expression. *Publ:* Contribr, Philadelphia: Three Centuries of American Art, Philadelphia Mus Art, 76; auth, Drawings of Nature and Circumstance; Caricature Since 1870, auth, Popular and Applied Graphic Art in the Library of Congress & contribr, Posada's Mexico, Libr Cong, 79. *Mailing Add:* Prints & Photographs Div Libr of Cong Washington DC 20540

REILLY, JACK
PAINTER
b Pittsburgh, Pa, Nov 4, 50. *Study:* Fla State Univ, BFA, 76, MFA, 77. *Work:* Oakland Mus Art, Calif; Matthews Ctr Mus, Ariz State Univ, Tempe; Arco Ctr Visual Arts, Los Angeles; Triton Mus Art, Santa Clara, Calif; Fresno

Metrop Mus, Calif. *Exhib:* Reality of Illusion, Denver Art Mus, Colo, Oakland Mus Art, Calif & Toledo Art Mus, Ohio; Am Painters in Paris, Ctr Int, Paris, France, 75; New Floridians, Jacksonville Art Mus, 77; Eyes and Ears, Calif Mus Sci, Los Angeles, 78; one-man show, Matthews Ctr Mus, Ariz State Univ, Tempe, 80; Laguna Beach Mus Art, Calif; Downtown LA, Palm Springs Mus, Calif. *Teaching:* Adj instr painting, Fla State Univ, 78; vis prof painting, Ariz Western Col, Yuma, 80-81. *Awards:* Painting Award, Marietta Nat, Marietta Col, Ohio, 78; Best of Show, Belleair, Fla Nat, 78; Exhib Travel Grant, Nat Endowment Arts & Ariz Commission Arts, 81. *Bibliog:* Linda Jacobson (auth), article, 12/81 & Betty Brown (auth), article, 11/83, Arts Mag; Stephen Grossman (auth), article, Artweek, 11/83. *Mem:* Col Art Asn Am; Los Angeles Contemp Exhibs. *Media:* Acrylic, Shaped Canvas. *Dealer:* Aaron Berman Gallery 50 West 57th St New York NY 10019; Stella Polaris Gallery 303 Boyd St Los Angeles CA 90013. *Mailing Add:* 443 S San Pedro St 5th Floor Los Angeles CA 90013

REILLY, RICHARD
CRITIC, CURATOR
b New York, NY, Mar 13, 26. *Pos:* Art critic, San Diego Union; cur, James S Copley Libr & Art Collection, La Jolla. *Publ:* Auth, A Promise Kept, 83. *Mailing Add:* PO Box 1530 La Jolla CA 92037

REIMANN, WILLIAM P
SCULPTOR, EDUCATOR
b Minneapolis, Minn, Nov 29, 35. *Study:* Yale Univ, BA, 57, BFA, 59, MFA, 61; with Josef Albers, Rico Lebrun, Robert M Engman, James Rosati, Gilbert Franklin, Seymour Lipton, Gabor Peterdi, Neil Welliver & Bernard Chaet. *Work:* Mus Mod Art, Whitney Mus Am Art & Rockefeller Univ, New York; Boston Mus Fine Arts. *Comn:* Suspended sculpture, Rockefeller Univ, 70-71; courtyard sculpture, Harvard Col Observ, Cambridge, Mass, 72; relief-mural, First Church of Christ, Boston, Mass, 81; suspended sculpture, Shell Oil Corp, Houston, Tex, 81; and others. *Exhib:* Structured Sculpture, Galerie Chalette, New York, 61-68; Sculpture Ann, 64-65 & Young Americans, 65, Whitney Mus Am Art; Int Exhib Contemp Painting & Sculpture, Carnegie Inst, Pittsburgh, 67-68; one-man show, Sculpture & Drawings, State Univ NY, 75. *Pos:* Vis critic, Univ Pa, Philadelphia. *Teaching:* Asst prof art, Old Dom Col, 61-64; lectr visual & environ studies, Harvard Univ, 64-, actg coordr studies, Carpenter Ctr Visual Arts, spring 71, sr preceptor visual & environ studies, 75- *Media:* Plexiglas, Stainless Steel. *Dealer:* Galerie Chalette 9 E 88th St New York NY 10028; Estelle Dodge Associates 301 East 47th St New York NY 10017. *Mailing Add:* One Gerry's Landing Cambridge MA 02138

REINDORF, SAMUEL
PAINTER
b Warsaw, Poland, Sept 1, 14; US citizen. *Study:* Cent Tech Sch, Toronto; Am Artists Sch, New York, with Saul Wilson Nahum Tschacbasov & Saul Baizerman, scholar. *Work:* Fairfield Mus, Conn; Toronto Art Gallery, Ont; Riverside Mus & Hall Art, New York; Tygeson Gallery, Toronto. *Exhib:* Toronto Art Gallery, 34-38; Riverside Mus, 39-40; New York World's Fair, 63-65; Butler Inst Am Art, 63-65; 26th Ann Exhib Contemp Am Painting, Palm Beach, 64; Palace Fine Art, Guadalajara, Mex; Retrospective, Palace Fine Arts, Mexico City, 81; and 28 one-man shows in US, Can & Mex. *Awards:* First Prize, 26th Exhib Contemp Am Painting, 64. *Bibliog:* Article, El Ocidental, Guadalajara, 2/76, Times-Picayune, New Orleans, 11/76 & Excelsior, Mexico City, 76-79. *Mem:* Artists Equity Asn. *Media:* Multimedia. *Publ:* Auth, article, Art News, 64, Toronto Star, 65, Toronto Globe & Mail, 66, Excelsior, Mexico City, 67 & Dallas Morning News, 67; and others. *Dealer:* Galeria de Arte Siles Las Hadas Manzanillo Couma Mex; Veerhoff Gallery Washington DC. *Mailing Add:* Apartado 285 San Miguel de Allende Guanajuato Mexico

REINER, GLADYS & JULES
COLLECTORS, PATRONS
Mr Reiner, b New York, NY, Mar 3, 18. *Study:* Mr Reiner, St Johns Univ, LLB; Mrs Reiner, NY Univ, BA. *Mem:* Friends Whitney Mus Am Art; assoc Guggenheim Mus; Mus Mod Art; Metrop Mus Art; Friends Hofstra Univ Mus. *Collection:* Late nineteenth century art; twentieth century art. *Mailing Add:* 295 Madison Ave New York NY 10017

REINHARDT, SIEGFRIED GERHARD
PAINTER, DESIGNER
b Eydkuhnen, Ger, July 31, 25; US citizen. *Study:* Wash Univ, AB. *Work:* Am Acad Arts & Lett; City Art Mus St Louis; Concordia Teachers Col; Southern Ill Univ; Whitney Mus Am Art; plus many others. *Comn:* Murals, Rand McNally, Skokie, Ill, Edison Bros Shoe Co, St Louis, Teamsters Local 88 Med Bldg & Nooter Corp, St Louis; Man's Conquest of Space Aviation--An American Triumph (mural), Lampert Int Airport, St Louis, 83. *Exhib:* 14 shows, City Art Mus St Louis, 43-61; Whitney Mus Am Art, 51-55 & 60; Cincinnati Art Ctr, 55, 58 & 61; Pa Acad Fine Arts, 60-61; plus many other group & one-man shows. *Pos:* Designer & executor stained glass windows, Emil Frei, Inc, 48-; painting Man of Sorrows, weekly TV show, 55, 57 & 58. *Teaching:* Lectr, pvt groups, TV & radio; instr painting & drawing, Wash Univ, 55-70. *Awards:* Six Awards, St Louis Art Guild, 51-58; Awards, Cincinnati Contemp Art Ctr, 58 & Int Exhib Sacred Art, Trieste, Italy, 61; plus many others. *Bibliog:* Nathaniel Pousette-Dart (ed), American Painting Today, Hastings, 56; Lee Nordness (ed), Art: USA: Now, C J Bucher, 62. *Mem:* St Louis Art Guild. *Dealer:* Midtown Galleries 11 E 57th St New York NY 10022; Albrecht Gallery of Art 2818 Frederick Blvd St Joseph MO 64506. *Mailing Add:* 635 Craig Woods Dr Kirkwood MO 63122

REINHART, MARGARET EMILY
PAINTER
b De Pere, Wis, May 19, 08. *Study:* Fontbonne Col, AB; Univ of Mo, MA; studied with Jean Charlot, Walter Quirt, Boris Margo, Ben Cunningham & Gaell Lindstrom. *Work:* Green Bay Wis Pub Sch Collection; Avila Col Collection; K C Plaza Public Libr; Cardinal Ritter Inst, St Louis. *Comn:* Calligraphic design for Pope Pius XII, comn by Bishop Edwin O'Hara, 49; calligraphic design for Bishop Marling, comn by Kansas City Diocesan Confraternity, 50; fresco mural, O'Shaughnessy Hall, work with Jean Charlot, comn by Notre Dame, 55; Stations of the Cross in metal, comn by S Dallavis, Foyle Chapel, Kansas City, 64. *Exhib:* One-woman shows, Neville Art Mus, Green Bay, 47 & Blue Springs City Hall, Mo, 75; Jr League Voters, Kansas City, Mo, 68 & 69; Am Assoc Univ Women, Kansas City, 74. *Collections Arranged:* Women Religious of the Congregation of St Joseph at Avila Col, 70; Faculty of Cols, Kansas City Regional Coun for Higher Educ, 75. *Pos:* Art supervisor, St Louis & St Joseph parochial schs, 38-39. *Teaching:* Instr painting & design, St Teresa Acad, Kansas City, 45-50; asst prof painting, art hist & humanities, Avila Col, 50-65, chmn dept fine arts, 63-64, prof painting & art educ, 65-67, coordr art, 69-76, artist in residence, 76-; art inst, Vita Int Col Tour, Europe, 68 & 69. *Awards:* Medal of Honor, Pres Dallavis, Avila Col, 63; Grant for Study in New York, Kansas City Regional Coun for Higher Educ, 70; Service Award, Dean Richard Scott, Avila Col, 75. *Mem:* Nat Art Educ Assoc; Fed Religious Artists. *Media:* Oil, Watercolor. *Mailing Add:* Avila Col 11901 Wornall Rd Kansas City MO 64145

REININGHAUS, RUTH (RUTH REININGHAUS SMITH)
PAINTER
b New York, NY, Oct 4, 22. *Study:* Nat Acad Design, with Morton Roberts, 62; Frank Reilly Sch Art, with Frank Reilly, 63; Art Student's League, with Robert Philip & Robert Beverly Hale, 68; New York Univ, 68. *Exhib:* Am Artists Professional League Ann, Lever House & Customs House, New York, 69-75; Hudson Valley Art Asn Ann, Westchester Co Ctr, New York, 69-72; Allied Artists Am Ann, Nat Acad Design, New York, 72; Salmagundi Club Ann, New York, 74-; Catharine Lorillard Wolfe Art Club Ann, New York, 78-. *Teaching:* Instr oil painting, Bankers Trust, New York, 71-77 & Kittredge Club for Women, 72-77. *Awards:* Claude Parson's Mem Award, Am Artist's Professional League Ann, 75; Phil Isenberg Award, Salmagundi Club Ann, 77; Best in Show, Catharine Lorillard Wolfe Art Orgn Ann, 78. *Bibliog:* Lucien Mandose (auth), 58th Ann Allied Artists Am Exhib, La Rev Mod, Paris, 72; Dorothy Varrone (auth), Former chemist becomes noted as an artist, Adelphian, Alpha Delta Pi, 75; Robin Lengman (auth), People, places & events, Am Artist Mag, 10/83. *Mem:* Salmagundi Club (dir at large, 74-77, pres, 83-); Washington Sq Outdoor Art Orgn, New York (bd dirs, 83-); fel Am Artist's Professional League; hon mem Nat Arts Club. *Media:* Oils. *Mailing Add:* 222 East 93rd St Apt 26A New York NY 10128

REISMAN, PHILIP
PAINTER
b Warsaw, Poland, July 18, 04; US citizen. *Study:* Art Students League, illus & compos with Wallace Morgan, life drawing with George Bridgeman; also etching & compos with Harry Wickey. *Work:* Metrop Mus Art Print Collection, New York; Wadsworth Atheneum, Hartford, Conn; Hirshhorn Mus, Washington, DC; Butler Inst Am Art, Youngstown, Ohio; City New York Mus. *Comn:* Mural, Bellevue Psychiat Hosp, New York, 38. *Exhib:* Mural Show, Mus Mod Art, New York, 32; Whitney Mus Am Art, New York; Nat Acad Design, 56 & 79; Pa Acad Fine Arts, Philadelphia; one-man retrospective, City New York Mus, 79-80; S Vt Art Ctr, Manchester, 75; Mid-Hudson Mus Sci, Poughkeepsie, NY, 80; Munic Art Gallery, Berlin, WGer, 83. *Pos:* Academician, Nat Acad Design, 82. *Teaching:* Instr art, Workshop Sch, New York, 54-56, Five Towns Arts Found, 68-70 & Educ Alliance, New York, 71-79. *Awards:* Joseph Isidor Gold Medal, Nat Acad Design, 56; Childe Hassam Purchase Prize, 68; Philip Reisman Day, New York, 11/13/79. *Bibliog:* Illus reproduced by Life, 41; Diane Klemin (auth), The Illustrated Book, Its Art and Craft; article, Am Artist Mag, 10/79. *Mem:* Audubon Artists New York; Artists Equity Asn New York; Am Soc Contemp Artists. *Media:* Watercolor, Oil. *Publ:* Illusr, Anna Karenina, Vols I & II, 40 & Crime and Punishment, 44, Random. *Dealer:* Mary Ryan Gallery 452 Columbus Ave New York NY 10024. *Mailing Add:* 4 W 18th St New York NY 10011

REISS, LIONEL S
PAINTER, WRITER
b Jarowslaw, Austrian Regime, Jan 29, 94; US citizen. *Work:* Harvard Univ Libr, Mass; Jewish Mus, New York; New York Historical Mus, NY; Brandeis Univ, Mass; Nat Portrait Gallery, Washington, DC; and others. *Exhib:* Carnegie Int, Carnegie Mus; Art Inst Chicago; Brooklyn Mus; Pa Acad Fine Arts; Nat Acad Design; Baltimore Mus; Whitney Mus; Mus Mod Art, New York. *Awards:* First Prize, Artist as Reporter Nat Competition, 40; First Prize, War Paintings Nat Competition, Mus Mod Art, 42. *Mem:* Am Watercolor Soc; Audubon Artists; Poetry Soc Am. *Media:* Oil, Watercolor. *Publ:* Auth, My Models Were Jews, Gordon Press, 38; auth, New Lights Old Shadows, Reconstructionist Found, 54; auth, A World at Twilight, MacMillan Co, 71. *Mailing Add:* 370 Central Park West New York NY 10025

REITZENSTEIN, REINHARD
ENVIRONMENTAL ARTIST
b Uelzen, Ger, May 27, 49; Can citizen. *Study:* Ont Col Art. *Work:* Art Gallery of Ont; Can Coun Art Bank; Nat Gallery Can. *Exhib:* Nat Gallery Can, 74 & 77; Landscape Canada Traveling Exhib, Art Gallery Ont & Edmonton, 76; 17 Can Artists: A Protean View, Vancouver Art Gallery, 76; Carmen Lamanna Gallery, Bologne Art Fair, Italy, 77; one-man shows,

Carmen Lamanna Gallery, Toronto, Can, 75-81 & London Art Gallery, Ont; Nat Film Bd Can, Ottawa, 81; and others. *Teaching:* Instr, Univ Guelph, 80-82, Univ Waterloo, 83- *Awards:* Can Coun Proj Cost Grants, 74 & 76-77 & Art Grants, 78-80. *Bibliog:* John Bentley Mays (auth), Reinhard Reitzenstein, Globe & Mail, Toronto, 11/80; Jeanne Randolphe (auth), Reinhard Reitzenstein, Artforum, 9/82; Jerry McGrath (auth), Reinhard Reitzenstein, Vanguard, 5/83. *Media:* Mixed Media. *Publ:* Natural Areas Divisions Charter, 75; According (record album), 80. *Dealer:* Carmen Lamanna Gallery 840 Yonge St Toronto ON Can. *Mailing Add:* 146 Ridge Rd W RR 1 Grimsby ON L3M 4E7 Canada

REMBERT, VIRGINIA PITTS
EDUCATOR, HISTORIAN
b Birmingham, Ala, Nov 15, 21. *Study:* Univ Montevallo, BA, 42; Columbia Univ, MA, 44, univ traveling fel, 67, Am Asn Univ Women fel, 67, PhD, 70; Univ Wis, MA, 59. *Work:* NC State Mus, Raleigh. *Exhib:* Ala State Exhib, Birmingham, 43; NC State Exhib, Raleigh, 48 & 49; Ala Watercolor Soc, Birmingham, 62. *Pos:* Pres, Ala Watercolor Soc, 62-63; pres, Birmingham Art Asn, 70-71. *Teaching:* Instr art, Beloit Col, 53-55; asst prof art hist, Mass Col Art, 56-60; from asst prof to prof art & chmn dept, Birmingham Southern Col, 60-73; prof art & chmn dept, Univ Ala, Birmingham, 74-75, Univ Ala, Tuscaloosa, 81-; Donaghey Distinguished prof art & art hist, Univ Ark, Little Rock, 75-81; lectr, Fine Arts Club, Vanderbilt Univ, 79, Birmingham Mus Art, 82-83, Montgomery Mus Art, 83. *Awards:* Silver Bowl Award, Birmingham Area Chamber of Com, 70; Pres Award, Univ Montevallo, 81; and others. *Mem:* Col Art Asn; Southeastern Col Art Asn (bd dirs, 74-76, pres, 77-78). *Res:* Mondrian's life, work and influence in America; Bolotowsky, Von Wiegand, Baber & Gillespie; post-modernism in art and architecture. *Publ:* Column, Birmingham News, 66-73; contribr, Mass Col Art Alumni Bulletin, 58 & Southeastern Col Art Asn Rev, 68-78; contribr, Arts Mag, 80; and others. *Mailing Add:* Dept Art Univ Ala University AL 35486

REMBSKI, STANISLAV
PAINTER, WRITER
b Sochaczew, Poland. *Study:* Technol Inst, Warsaw, Poland; Ecole Beaux Arts, Paris; Royal Acad Fine Arts, Berlin, Ger. *Work:* Woodrow Wilson House, Washington, DC; Franklin D Roosevelt Mem Libr, Hyde Park, NY; Archbishop's House, Baltimore; Hist Soc, Madison, Wis; Nat Acad Design, New York. *Comn:* Conversion of William Duke of Acquitaine, Trustees of St Barnard's Sch, Gladstone, NJ, 31; I Am the Life, Mem Episcopal Church, 62; Jefferson and the Four Maryland Signers of the Declaration of Independence (large hist painting), 76-77; Brigham Young, Mormon Church, Salt Lake City, Utah. *Exhib:* One-man shows, Dudensing Galleries, New York, 27, Carnegie Hall Gallery, New York, 34, Arthur U Newton Galleries, New York, 35, Baltimore Mus Art, 47; Baltimore Inst Art, Md, 50; Engineering Ctr, Baltimore, Md, 81. *Pos:* Vis critic, Md Inst Art, 52-55. *Mem:* Salmagundi Club; Allied Artists Am; Nat Soc Mural Painters; Am Artists Prof League. *Media:* Oil, Crayon. *Publ:* Auth, Mysticism in Art, Leonardo da Vinci Forum, 36; auth, Freedom, New Age, 72. *Mailing Add:* 1404 Park Ave Baltimore MD 21217

REMENICK, SEYMOUR
PAINTER, INSTRUCTOR
b Detroit, Mich, Apr 3, 23. *Study:* Tyler Sch Fine Arts, 40-42; Hans Hofmann Sch, 46-48. *Work:* Philadelphia Mus; Pa Acad Fine Arts; RI Sch Design; Phoenix Art Mus; Dallas Mus Contemp Art. *Exhib:* Am Painting, Rome, Italy, 55; Four Young Americans, RI Sch Design, 56; 11 Contemp Am Painters, Paris, France, 56; Art Inst Chicago Ann, 61; Drawing Show, Philadelphia Mus, 65. *Teaching:* Instr painting & drawing, Pa Acad Fine Arts, 77- *Awards:* Louis Comfort Tiffany Found Grant, 55; Benjamin Altman Landscape Prize, Nat Acad Design, 60; Hallmark Purchase Award, 60. *Mem:* Nat Acad Design, New York. *Media:* Oil, Watercolor. *Dealer:* Pearl Fox Gallery 103 Windsor Ave Melrose Park PA 19126. *Mailing Add:* 1836 Pine St Philadelphia PA 19103

REMINGTON, DEBORAH WILLIAMS
PAINTER
b Haddonfield, NJ, June 25, 35. *Study:* San Francisco Art Inst, BFA, 57; studies in Asia, 57-59. *Work:* Whitney Mus Am Art, New York; Mus Boymans von Beuningen, Rotterdam, Holland; Centre d'Art et de Cult George Pompidou, Paris; Nat Mus Am Art; Art Inst Chicago. *Exhib:* One-person shows, Bykert Gallery, New York, 67, 69, 72 & 74, Galerie Darthea Speyer, Paris, 68, 71 & 73, Hamilton Gallery, New York, 77 & Portland Ctr for the Visual Arts, Ore, 77; Whitney Mus Ann Exhib, 72; 71st Am Exhib, Art Inst Chicago, 74; Painting Endures, Inst Contemp Art, Boston, 75; 20 Year Retrospective, Newport Harbor Art Mus, Calif, 83; 20 Year Retrospective, Oakland Mus Art, Calif, 84; and others. *Awards:* Fel, Tamarind Inst, Albuquerque, 73; Nat Endowment Fel, 79-80. *Bibliog:* R C Kenedy (auth), Deborah Remington, Art Int, summer 74; Corinne Robins (auth), Deborah Remington, Paintings without answers, Arts Mag, 4/77; Donald J Kuspit (auth), Deborah Remington: Autonomy and absences in the visual koan, Art Int, summer, 79. *Media:* Oil; Lithography. *Mailing Add:* 309 W Broadway New York NY 10013

REMSEN, JOHN EVERETT, II
CONSULTANT, PAINTER
b Glen Cove, NY, Apr 21, 39. *Study:* Pratt Inst, BFA; NY Univ, MA(art educ). *Exhib:* Parish Art Mus, Southampton, NY, 68, 69 & 71; one-man exhibs, Suffolk Community Col, Selden, NY, 66, State Univ at Stony Brook, NY, 77-78 & Burlington Bookshop, New York, 81. *Specialty:* Nineteenth-twentieth century American painting and graphic arts. *Mailing Add:* 77 Main St Box 803 Setauket NY 11733

REMSING, (JOSEPH) GARY
PAINTER, SCULPTOR
b Spokane, Wash, Sept 18, 46. *Study:* San Jose State Univ, BA & MA. *Work:* De Saisset Mus, Univ Santa Clara; Oakland Mus. *Comn:* Maj sculptural comn, State of Calif, 78. *Exhib:* One-man exhibs, Atherton Gallery, Menlo Park, Calif, 70 & 72 & William Sawyer Gallery, San Francisco, 71, 73 & 74; Project Proposals: Art in Public Buildings, Sacramento Community Arts Gallery, Calif, 78; Int Sculpture Competition, State of NJ, traveling, 79-80; Calif Invitational, House of Rep, Washington, DC, 82; and others. *Teaching:* Instr, Modesto Jr Col, 71- *Awards:* Award, Maryville Col, Tenn, 70; Award, Calif Arts Comn, 70. *Bibliog:* Articles in San Francisco Chronicle, 9/8/69 & 5/7/71, Artforum, 11/69 & Art Wk, 5/71, 4/72 & 6/74; and others. *Mailing Add:* 1418 Oakwood Dr Modesto CA 95350

RENICK, CHARLES COOLEY
SCULPTOR, EDUCATOR
b Williamsburg, Va, Apr 29, 25. *Study:* Va Commonwealth Univ, BFA & MFA. *Teaching:* Prof sculpture, Va Commonwealth Univ, 53- *Mailing Add:* PO Box 74 Bumpass VA 23024

RENK, MERRY
GOLDSMITH, SCULPTOR
b Trenton, NJ, July 8, 21. *Study:* Sch Indust Arts, Trenton, NJ; Inst Design, Chicago. *Work:* San Francisco State Col Libr; San Francisco Art Comn; Univ Wis; Oakland Mus Art, Calif, Calif Craft Mus, Palo Alto. *Comn:* Wedding crown, Am Craft Mus, New York. *Exhib:* One-woman show, De Young Mem Mus, San Francisco, 71 & Mus Hist & Technol, Smithsonian Inst, 71-72; Objects USA Traveling Exhib, US & Europe, 70-72; retrospective, Calif Craft Mus, Palo Alto, 81. *Awards:* San Francisco Art Comn Awards, 54 & 59; San Francisco Women Artists Award, 65; Craftsman Grant, Nat Endowment Arts. *Bibliog:* C McCann (auth), Three fine craftsmen, Artweek, 2/71; A Fried (auth), article in San Francisco Examr, 3/71; Joan Watkins (auth), article, Am Crafts Mag, 4/81; and others. *Mem:* Metal Arts Guild (pres, 53); distinguished mem Soc NAm Goldsmiths. *Mailing Add:* 17 Saturn St San Francisco CA 94114

RENNER, ERIC
PAINTER, PHOTOGRAPHER
b Philadelphia, Pa, Nov 6, 41. *Study:* Univ Cincinnati, BS, 64; Cranbrook Acad Art, MFA, 68. *Work:* Mus Mod Art, New York; Nat Gallery Can, Ottawa; Mus Mod Art, Mexico City; Mus Art Sao Paulo, Brazil; Inst Contemp Art, Chicago. *Comn:* Photographs, State Ohio, State Off Tower, 74. *Exhib:* Nat Gallery Can, 71, 73 & 75; solo exhib, Mus Mod Art, Mexico City, 71 & Mus Sao Paulo, Brazil, 78; The Great West, Univ Colo, Denver, 79; The Extended Frame, Visual Studies Workshop, Rochester, NY, 80; Handmade Cameras, Tyler Sch Art, Temple Univ, 82; The Panoramic Image, Univ Southampton, England, 82; The Pinhole Image, Va Mus, Richmond, 83. *Teaching:* Asst prof design, State Univ NY, Alfred, 68-71; adj prof photog, Visual Studies Workshop, 75. *Awards:* Nat Endowment Arts Fel, 76 & 79-80. *Publ:* Auth, From the Stars, the Sun, and the Air for Laurie, 75 & auth, The Horsefetter, 77, Visual Studies Workshop. *Dealer:* Jeffrey Fuller Fine Art 2108 Spruce St Philadelphia PA. *Mailing Add:* Star Rte 15 Box 1655 San Lorenzo NM 88057

RENNICK, DAN
ASSEMBLAGE ARTIST, SCULPTOR
b July 3, 05; US citizen. *Study:* NY Univ, BA; New Sch Social Res, with Henry Pearson & Licio Isolani. *Work:* Yad Labinim Mus, Israel; Univ Med Ctr, Boston; St Vincent's Hosp, Toledo; Indianapolis Mus Art; Munson-Williams-Proctor Inst, Utica; and others. *Pos:* Mag design consult; formerly vpres & ed, Hearst Mag, New York, retired. *Teaching:* Lectr constructions as an art form, col groups & womens clubs. *Mem:* Artists Equity Asn of NY (dir, 79-81); Audubon Artists; Nat Soc Painters Casein & Acrylic; Allied Artists Am; Am Soc Contemp Artists (treas, 81-82); and others. *Media:* Mixed Media, Acrylic. *Mailing Add:* 1415 Glenwood Rd Brooklyn NY 11230

RENNIE, HELEN (SEWELL)
PAINTER, DESIGNER
b Cambridge, Md. *Study:* Corcoran Sch Art, hon student; Nat Acad Design; also with Charles W Hawthorne, Provincetown. *Work:* Phillips Gallery Collections, Washington, DC; C Law Watkins Collection, Am Univ; US Dept Com, Washington, DC; US Dept State, Washington, DC; Clarendon Trust Co, Arlington, Va. *Comn:* Mural design, Roosevelt High Sch, Washington, DC, Pub Works Art Proj, 33-34. *Exhib:* Mus Mod Art, New York, 46, Recent Drawings USA, 56; Corcoran Gallery Art Biennial, Washington, DC, 59; Baltimore Mus Regional, 64; Washington Artists, Phillips Gallery, 71-72; six one-person shows, Baltimore Mus of Art, Phillips Gallery, Washington, DC, Univ PR, San Juan & Franz Bader Gallery, Washington, DC. *Pos:* Artist-designer, War Food Admin, Washington, DC, 40-45; art dir, US Navy Dept, Washington, DC, 48-51; visual info officer, US Off Price Stabilization, Washington, DC, 51-53. *Teaching:* Instr drawing & painting, Phillips Gallery Sch; instr drawing & painting, Art League Washington. *Awards:* Five awards from various donors, Soc Washington Artists, 48-71; Baltimore Mus Regional, 59 & 60; First Prize for Oil Painting, Bicentennial Exhib, Jewish Community Ctr, DC, 76. *Mem:* Soc Washington Artists (vpres); Women in the Visual Arts; Deer Isle Art Asn, Maine. *Media:* Oil, Acrylic; Watercolor. *Mailing Add:* 1306 30th St NW Washington DC 20007

RENNINGER, KATHARINE STEELE
PAINTER

b Philadelphia, Pa, Feb 26, 25. *Study:* Moore Col Art, Philadelphia, BFA, 46; Univ Pa, with Paul Domville, 48. *Work:* William Penn Mem Mus, Harrisburg, Pa; Rutgers Univ Mus, New Brunswick, NJ; SmithKline Beckman Corp, Philadelphia, Pa; Devecchi Collection, Bucks Co Educ Serv, Doylestown, Pa; Woodmere Gallery, Chestnut Hill, Pa. *Exhib:* Butler Inst Am Art, Youngstown, Ohio, 63, 68 & 74; traveling exhib, Nat Drawing Soc, New York, 65; Childe Hassam Purchase Mem, Am Acad Arts & Lett, New York, 69, 75 & 78; Nat Acad Design, New York, 69, 74-75 & 80; Allied Artists Am, New York, 70-83; Allentown Mus, Pa, 79-80; and others. *Awards:* Grumbacher/Kreidler, Ann Exhib, Nat Soc Painters Casein & Acrylic, 73, 74 & 82; Hassam Mem Purchase Award, Am Acad Arts & Lett, 79; Salmagundi Award, Allied Artists Am, 82. *Mem:* Artists Equity Asn Philadelphia (bd dir, 74 & 79); Allied Artists Am; Nat Soc Painters Casein & Acrylic; Philadelphia Watercolor Club; Bucks Co Coun Arts (chmn, 74-75 & 78). *Media:* Casein. *Publ:* Auth, Watercolor page, Am Artist, 77. *Dealer:* Mickelson Gallery 707 G St Washington DC 20001; Noel Butcher Gallery 132 S 17th St Philadelphia PA 19103. *Mailing Add:* 148 N State St Newtown PA 18940

RENOUF, EDDA
PAINTER, PRINTMAKER

b Mexico City, Mex, June 17, 43; US citizen. *Study:* Acad Julian, Paris, 63-64; Sorbonne, Paris, 63-64; Inst D'Art & D'Archeol, Paris, 63-64; Sarah Lawrence Col, BA, 65; Art Students League, 67-68; Sch Arts, Columbia Univ, MFA, 71; Gurgundfund Fel Paris. *Work:* Mus Mod Art, Metrop Mus Art, Whitney Mus Am Art, New York; Art Inst of Chicago; Musee De Grenoble, Grenoble, France; and others. *Exhib:* Recent Acquisitions, Mus of Mod Art, New York, 73; Eighth Paris Biennial, Musee D'Art Moderne, Paris, 73; Fundamental Painting, Stedelijk Mus, Amsterdam, Holland, 75; Extraordinary Women, Mus of Mod Art, New York, 77; Matrix 36, Wadsworth Atheneum, Hartford, Conn, 78; Contemp Drawing/New York, Univ Calif Santa Barbara, 78; Biennial Exhib, Whitney Mus of Am Art, 79; New Works of Contemp Art & Music, Fruit Market Gallery, Edinburgh, Scotland; and others. *Bibliog:* Henry Martin (auth), In Milan Spring, Art Int, 5/75; Margaret Betz (auth), New Editions, Art News, 9/77; Anne Dagbert (auth), Edda Renouf, Art Press, 2/81. *Media:* Acrylic, Pastel Chalk. *Publ:* Auth, Lines, Flash Art Edition, 74; auth, Lines and Non-Lines, Lapp Princess Press Ltd, New York, 77; auth, Echoes, Graeme Murray Gallery, Scotland, 79. *Dealer:* Blum-Helman Gallery 20 W 57th St New York NY 10019; Yvon Lambert Gallery 5 Rue Grenier-St-Lazare 75003 Paris France. *Mailing Add:* 20 W 30th St New York NY 10001

RENOUF, EDWARD
PAINTER, SCULPTOR

b Hsiku, China, Nov 23, 06; US citizen. *Study:* Phillips Andover Acad, 24; Harvard Univ, 28; Columbia Univ, 36-40; also drawing & painting with Carlos Merida, Mex, 41. *Comn:* Steel sculpture, 65 & mural painting, 67, Horace Mann Sch, Riverdale, NY. *Exhib:* Whitney Mus Am Art Sculpture Ann, 60 & 64; Conn Acad Show, Wadsworth Atheneum, Hartford, 61; Pa Acad Fine Arts 161st Ann, Philadelphia, 66; one-man shows, Allan Stone Gallery, New York, 73, 78, 80 & 82; Sculptors Guild Ann; Fedn Mod Painters & Sculptors Ann; and others. *Teaching:* Vis artist painting, Akad Bildenden Kunste, Munich, Ger, 70. *Awards:* Second Prize Sculpture, Sharon Creative Arts Found, 64. *Bibliog:* Gordon Brown (auth), article, 5/78, John Deckert (auth), article, 5/78 & Mathew Licht (auth), article, 11/82, Arts; plus others. *Mem:* Sculptors Guild; Fedn Mod Painters & Sculptors. *Media:* Multimedia. *Publ:* Contribr, Dyn, Mex, 42. *Dealer:* Allan Stone Gallery 48 E 86th St New York NY 10028. *Mailing Add:* East St Washington Green CT 06793

RENSCH, ROSLYN (ROSLYN MARIA ERBES)
HISTORIAN, WRITER

b Detroit, Mich. *Study:* Northwestern Univ, BM & MM; Univ Ill, MA(art hist); Univ Wis-Madison, PhD(art hist), 64. *Pos:* Bd dirs, Sheldon Swope Art Gallery, Terre Haute, Ind, 77-82. *Teaching:* Lectr art hist & humanities & chmn div humanities, Nat Col Educ, 62-65; prof art hist & humanities, Ind State Univ, 65- *Mem:* Col Art Asn Am; Midwest Art Hist Soc; Int Ctr Medieval Art. *Res:* Pre-Romanesque stone carving in the British Isles; representations of the harp in art monuments; American landscape painting. *Publ:* Auth, Harp, its History, Technique & Repertoire, Duckworth, 69; auth, Development of the medieval harp: A re-examination of the evidence of the Utrecht Psalter and its progeny, Gesta, Vol 11, No 2; auth, Harp carvings on the Irish crosses, Am Harp J, winter 74; auth, Landscape painting in America to c 1900, Ind State Univ, 75. *Mailing Add:* 701 Delaware Ave Terre Haute IN 47804

RENTSCHLER, SARAH YORKE
DEALER, COLLECTOR

b Minneapolis, Minn, Mar 23, 50. *Study:* Sarah Lawrence Col, Bronxville, NY. *Pos:* Owner/dir, Sarah Y Rentschler Gallery, New York, 78-; co-owner/dir, Sarah Y Rentschler Gallery, Bridgehampton, NY, currently. *Specialty:* Contemporary artists, specializing in paintings and sculpture. *Mailing Add:* S Y Rentschler Gallery Penthouse 450 W 24th St New York NY 10011

REOPEL, JOYCE
DRAFTSMAN

b Worcester, Mass, Jan 21, 38. *Study:* Ruskin Sch Drawing & Fine Arts, Oxford Univ; Yale-Norfolk Art Sch, fel; Worcester Mus Art Sch, grad; Radcliffe Inst, scholar. *Work:* Ohio State Univ; Fogg Art Mus, Cambridge, Mass; Pa Acad Fine Arts, Philadelphia; Addison Gallery Am Art, Andover, Mass; Univ Mass, Amherst; and others. *Exhib:* Boston Arts Festival; Nat Inst

Arts & Lett; Worcester Mus Art; De Cordova & Dana Mus, Lincoln, Mass; Victoria & Albert Mus, London, Eng; plus others. *Awards:* Nat Inst Arts & Lett; Wheaton Col Award for Res; Ford Found Grant. *Mailing Add:* c/o Forum Gallery 1018 Madison Ave New York NY 10021

REPLINGER, DOT (DOROTHY THIELE)
WEAVER, DESIGNER

b Chicago, Ill, Jan 30, 24. *Study:* Sch Art Inst Chicago, BA(educ), study with Carolyn Howlett & Else Regensteiner. *Work:* Amerinvesco, Chicago; Caterpillar Int, Peoria, Ill; Haskins & Sells, Stand Oil Bldg, Chicago; Allstate Insurance Co, Northbrock, Ill. *Comn:* Ark curtain, Sinai Temple, Champaign, Ill, 76; wall piece, Friends of Champaign Pub Libr, Ill, 78; Citizens Bank, Ind. *Exhib:* Craft Multiples, Renwick Gallery, Smithsonian, Washington, DC, 75; Marietta Crafts Nat, Ohio, 75 & 77; Miss River Crafts Show, Brooks Mem Art Gallery, Memphis, Tenn, 76; Mid-States Craft Exhib, Evansville Mus Arts, Ind, 77; Clay & Fiber--15 Viewpoints, Wustum Mus Fine Arts, Racine, Wis, 78. *Awards:* Craftsmen's Fel, Nat Endowment Arts, 76-77; Creativity Award, Miss River Craft Show, 76; Purchase Award, Mid-States Craft Exhib, Evansville, Ind, 77. *Mem:* Am Crafts Coun (state rep, 70-76); Handweavers Guild Am; Midwest Weavers Cong. *Media:* Fiber. *Mailing Add:* 4 Burnett Circle Urbana IL 61801

RESEK, KATE FRANCES
PAINTER

b Cleveland, Ohio. *Study:* Univ Wis, Madison, BS(fine arts); Columbia Univ, MFA, 69. *Work:* Aldrich Mus of Contemp Art, Ridgefield, Conn; Neuberger Mus, Purchase, NY; Housatonic Mus, Bridgeport, Conn; Columbia Univ. *Exhib:* One-man shows, Soho 20, New York, 74 & 76, Noyes, Van Cline & Davenport, New York, 77 & Bertha Urdang Gallery, New York, 77; Contemporary Reflections 1974-1975, Aldrich Mus of Contemp Art, 75; 40th Ann Show, Butler Inst of Am Art, Youngstown, Ohio, 76; New Acquisitions, Neuberger Mus, 76; New Acquisitions, Aldrich Mus of Contemp Art, 78; Penthouse Show, Mus Mod Art, 80-81; Adam Gimbel Gallery, New York, 81; and others. *Teaching:* Instr drawing/painting, State Univ NY, Purchase, 75-76, Fairleigh Dickinson Univ, Teaneck, NJ, 78-82; Brooklyn Mus, 83. *Awards:* Silver Hill Award/Painting, & Inez Leon Greenberg Award/Drawing, Silvermine 22nd New Eng Exhib; Yaddo Fel, 78 & 82; NJ State Coun Arts Grant, 83. *Bibliog:* Ellen Lubell (auth), Kate Resek, Arts Mag, 12/76; Holland Cotter (auth), article in NY Arts J, 9/77; Carrie Rickey (auth), Village Voice, 10/82. *Mem:* Women's Caucus of Art; Women in the Arts; Col Art Asn. *Media:* Pastel on Canvas. *Dealer:* Adam Gimbel Gallery 17 E 49th St New York NY. *Mailing Add:* 354 Bowery New York NY 10012

RESIKA, PAUL
PAINTER

b New York, NY, Aug 15, 28. *Study:* With S Wilson, 40-44 & Hans Hofmann, 45-47, New York; also in Venice & Rome, 50-54. *Work:* Indianapolis Mus Art; Metrop Mus Art, New York; Chase Manhattan Bank; Sheldon Mem Gallery, Univ Nebr-Lincoln; Joseph H Hirshhorn Collection, Washington, DC. *Exhib:* Am Landscape, Smithsonian Inst, Washington, DC, 68; Hassam Exhib, Am Acad Arts & Lett, 69-71, 73 & 78, Award Exhib, 75; Calton Gallery, New York, 75; Art of Pastel, Graham Gallery, New York, 77; Next to Nature, Nat Acad Design, New York, 80; and others. *Pos:* Artist in residence, Dartmouth Col, 72; chmn masters prog, Parsons Sch Design, NY, 78- *Teaching:* Adj prof painting & drawing, Cooper Union, 66-78; instr painting, Art Students League, 68-69; instr, Skowhegan Sch Painting, 73 & 76; instr Grad Sch, Univ Pa, 74 & 79. *Awards:* Ingram Merrill Prize, 69; Hassam Purchase Prize, Am Acad Arts & Lett, 71 & Award, 77; Benjamin Altman Landscape Prize, Nat Acad Design, 82; and others. *Bibliog:* Articles, Art in Am, Am Artist, Art News & others. *Mem:* Nat Acad Design; Century Asn, NY; Longpoint. *Dealer:* Graham Gallery 1014 Madison Ave New York NY 10021. *Mailing Add:* 114 E 84th St New York NY 10028

RESNICK, MARCIA AYLENE
PHOTOGRAPHER, CONCEPTUAL ARTIST

b New York, NY, Nov 21, 50. *Study:* NY Univ, 67-69; Cooper Union, BFA, 72; Calif Inst Arts, MFA, 73. *Work:* Metrop Mus Art & Mus Mod Art, New York; George Eastman House, Int Mus Photog; Contemp Arts Mus, Houston; San Francisco Mus. *Exhib:* Photography Unlimited, Harvard Fogg Mus, 74; Women of Photography, San Francisco Mus & Traveling Show, 75; two-person show, Chicago Ctr Contemp Photog, 78; Punk Art, Washington Proj Arts, 78; Book Art, Art Inst Chicago, 78; Kunst als Photographie 1879-1979, Tiroler Landesmuseum Ferdinandeum, Innsbruck, Austria, 79; Galerie Wilde, Cologne, 81; and others. *Teaching:* Instr photog, Queens Col, New York, Cooper Union, New York & Int Ctr of Photog. *Awards:* Nat Endowment Arts Photography Grants, 75 & 78; Creative Artists Pub Serv Prog Grant, 77. *Bibliog:* Pop up people, Time-Life Yearbk, 74; Layered eye, Camera 35 Mag, 7/74; Peter Frank (auth), Picture books, Soho Weekly News, 7/17/75. *Publ:* Auth, Landscape, 75; auth, See, 75; auth, Tahitian Eve, 75; auth, Re-visions, 78; auth, Landscape-Loftscape, 78. *Dealer:* Light Gallery 724 Fifth Ave New York NY 10019. *Mailing Add:* 530 Canal St New York NY 10013

RESNICK, MILTON
PAINTER

b Bratslav, Russia, Jan 8, 17; US citizen. *Study:* Paris & New York. *Work:* Calif Mus Fine Arts, Berkeley; Mus Mod Art, Whitney Mus Am Art, New York; Wadsworth Atheneum; Wake Forest Col, Winston-Salem, NC; also many others including pvt collections. *Exhib:* One-man show, M H DeYoung Mem Mus, San Francisco, 55; four shows, Whitney Mus Am Art, 57-67 & Whitney Biennial, 73; San Francisco Mus Art, 63; Univ Tex Art Mus, 64 & 68; Jewish Mus, NY, 67; Mus Mod Art, New York, 69; Univ Calif, Santa

Barbara, 74; plus many other group & one-man shows. *Teaching:* Instr, Pratt Inst, Brooklyn; vis lectr & critic, var schs, RI, Yale Summer Sch, Wagner Col & Silvermine; vis prof, Univ Calif, Berkeley, 55-56; instr, NY Univ, 64-; vis lectr & critic, NY Studio Sch, 65-; vis prof, Univ Wis-Madison, 66-67. *Dealer:* Max Hutchinson Gallery 138 Greene St New York NY 10012. *Mailing Add:* 80 Forsyth St New York NY 10002

RETZER, HOWARD EARL
PAINTER
b Rochester, Pa, Jan 31, 25. *Study:* Geneva Col, Pa; Univ Colo, BA; Temple Univ Sch of Med, MD; study for five years with Pawel A Kontny. *Exhib:* Fur Rendevous, Anchorage, Alaska, 75; Zang Mus, Denver, Colo, 77-78. *Bibliog:* John Jellico (auth), Howard Retzer, Southwestern Art, 77. *Media:* Multimedia. *Collection:* Many works of Kontny, as well as Fechin, Frank Hoffman, Timmermans, Frank Tenny Johnson & others. *Dealer:* O'Briens Art Emporium 7122 Stetson Dr Scottsdale AZ 85251. *Mailing Add:* c/o Elk Mountain Ranch PO Box 340 Parshall CO 80468

REUTER, LAUREL J
GALLERY DIRECTOR
b Devils Lake, NDak, Oct 17, 43. *Study:* Univ NDak, MA, 74. *Collections Arranged:* American Women Artists (with catalog), 73; Kenneth Patchen (with catalog), 74; Indian Images, 76; John Ihle Retrospective (with catalog), 76; Jiri Anderle (with catalog), 77; Allan Graham: Fifteen Paintings (with catalog), 79; and numerous others. *Pos:* Founder & dir, Univ NDak Gallery, Univ NDak, 70-, dir & head, NDak Mus Art, currently; founder & exec dir, NDak Art Gallery Asn, 77- *Awards:* Mus Internship Fel, Minneapolis Inst Arts, 72; Nat Endowment Arts Mus Prof Fel, 73. *Mem:* Am Asn Mus. *Mailing Add:* Univ NDak Art Gallery Box 8136 Univ Station Grand Forks ND 58202

REVINGTON-BURDICK, BETTY, III
COLLECTOR
Collection: Modern American painting and sculpture exhibited at major museums throughout the United States. *Mailing Add:* 3000 WoodKirk Dr Columbia MO 65201

REVOR, REMY
DESIGNER, EDUCATOR
b Chippewa Falls, Wis, Sept 17, 14. *Study:* Mt Mary Col, BA; Sch Art Inst Chicago, BFA & MFA. *Work:* Milwaukee Art Ctr; St Paul Art Ctr, Minn; Mus Tex Tech Univ; Sheldon Art Gallery. *Exhib:* Wis Designer Craftsmen Ann, 53-72; Mus Contemp Crafts, New York, 62, 63 & 66-68; Wichita Art Asn, 64; Chicago Pub Libr, 64 & 74. *Teaching:* Prof textile design, Mt Mary Col, 52-70, prof, 70-; instr textile design, Arrowmont Sch Arts & Crafts, Gatlinburg, Tenn, summers 69-81; vis lectr, Univ Tenn, Knoxville, 73-74; instr, Sch Am Craftsmen, Rochester Inst Technol, NY, summer 79; Notre Dame Women's Col, Kyoto, Japan, 80. *Awards:* Louis Comfort Tiffany Found Award for Textiles, 62; Am Inst Architects Gold Medal Award for Craftsmanship, 67; Fulbright Award for Res Textile Design, Finland, 69-70. *Mem:* Wis Designer Craftsmen (publ chmn, 66-68); Col Art Asn Am; Am Craft Coun. *Mailing Add:* Mt Mary Col Milwaukee WI 53222

REWALD, JOHN
HISTORIAN, EDUCATOR
b Berlin, Ger, May 12, 12; US citizen. *Study:* Univ Hamburg, 31; Univ Frankfurt am Main, 31-32; Sorbonne, 36; DFA Univ Mich, 82. *Pos:* Cur pvt collection, the late John Hay Whitney; assoc, Mus Mod Art, 43-, hon trustee, 83. *Teaching:* Lectr on visits with artists in Europe & forgeries of modern art; vis prof, Princeton Univ, 61; prof art hist, Univ Chicago, 64-71; dist prof art hist, Grad Ctr, City Univ New York, 71- *Awards:* Prix Charles Blanc, Acad Francaise, 41; Knight, Legion of Honor, 54; Comdr, French Order of Arts & Lett, 79. *Publ:* Auth, The History of Impressionism, 46, 55, 61, & 73 & Post-Impressionism--from Van Gogh to Gauguin, 56, 62 & 78, Mus Mod Art; auth bks on Cezanne, Bonnard, Pissarro, Seurat, Manzu, Degas & Maillol; ed, Cezanne, Gauguin, Pissarro Letters; auth, Watercolors of Paul Cezanne, 83; and many others. *Mailing Add:* 1075 Park Ave New York NY 10028

REXROTH, NANCY LOUISE
PHOTOGRAPHER
b Washington, DC, June 27, 46. *Study:* Marietta Col, Ohio, 64-65; Am Univ, BFA, 65-69; Ohio Univ, MFA(photog), 69-71. *Work:* Mus Mod Art, New York; Smithsonian Inst & Libr Cong, DC; Biblioteque Nat, Paris, France; Ctr Creative Photog, Tucson, Ariz. *Exhib:* One-person shows, Corcoran Gallery Art, Washington, DC, 73, Light Gallery, 75, 77 & 80, Grapestake Gallery, San Francisco, 78 & Ctr Creative Photog, Tucson, 82; group show, Baltimore Mus Art, Md, 73; Smithsonian Inst, Washington, DC, 73; Kennedy Art Ctr, Washington, DC, 74; Halstead 381 Gallery, Birmingham, Mich, 77; Int Ctr Photog, New York, 78. *Teaching:* Mem staff beginning-advan photog, Antioch Col, Yellow Springs, Ohio, 77-79; mem staff beginning-advan photog, Wright State Univ, 79-82. *Mem:* Soc Photog Educ; Am Asn Univ Women. *Media:* Photography. *Publ:* Auth, IOWA, 76 & The Platintotype 1977, 76, Violet Press; contribr, The Diana and the Nikon, Godine, 79; contribr, The Platinum Print, Graphic Arts Res Ctr-RIT, 80; and others. *Dealer:* Light Gallery 724 Fifth Ave New York NY 10019; Grapestake Gallery 2876 California St San Francisco CA 94115. *Mailing Add:* 1228 South 24th St Arlington VA 22202

REYNAL, JEANNE
MOSAIC ARTIST
b White Plains, NY, Apr 1, 03. *Study:* Atelier, Paris, France, apprentice with Boris Anrep, 30-38. *Work:* Ford Found, White Plains; Mus Mod Art, New York; Walker Art Ctr, Minneapolis; Whitney Mus Am Art; Rockefeller Univ; plus many others. *Comn:* Ford Found Prog Adult Educ, White Plains, 59; Our Lady of Florida, Palm Beach, 62; Cliff House, Avon, Conn, 62; Nebr State Capitol, Lincoln, 65 & 66; SS Joachim & Ann Church, Queens Village, NY, 67; plus many others. *Exhib:* San Francisco Mus Art Traveling Exhib, Lincoln, Nebr, Amarillo, Tex, Boston & Montreal, 64; Betty Parsons Gallery, 71; Newport Art Asn, RI, 71; Craft Horizons, 71 & 76; Bodley Gallery, New York, 76; plus many others. *Awards:* Emmanuel Walter Fund Purchase Prize for Yuba (mosaic), San Francisco Art Asn, 45. *Bibliog:* Hans Unger (auth), Practical Mosaic, 65; Barbara Poses Kafka (auth), Art & architecture, Craft Horizons, 1-2/68; Paul Falkenberg (producer & ed), Mosaics: The Work of Jeanne Reynal (film), 68. *Mailing Add:* 240 W 11th St New York NY 10014

REYNARD, CAROLYN COLE
PAINTER, INSTRUCTOR
b Wichita, Kans, Aug 6, 34. *Study:* Wichita State Univ, BFA; Ohio Univ, MFA. *Work:* Wichita State Univ; State Univ NY Col Oswego. *Exhib:* Air Capitol Annual, Wichita Art Mus, Kans, 56; Exhibition 80, Huntington Galleries, WVa, 57-59; Santa Barbara Art Mus, Calif, 60; Artists of Santa Barbara, Faulkner Gallery, Santa Barbara, 60-62; Artists of Central New York, Munson-Williams-Proctor Inst Mus Art, Utica, NY, 64-65 & 67. *Teaching:* Instr art, Ohio Univ, 58-59; asst prof art, State Univ NY Col Oswego, 63-69; instr art, Wappingers Cent Sch Dist, NY, 69-, adminr/coordr fine arts dept, 78-79. *Mem:* NY State Art Teachers Asn; Dutchess Co Art Asn. *Media:* Acrylic. *Publ:* Auth, I can't draw, 71 & auth, Getting it all together, 74, Sch Arts. *Mailing Add:* 110 College Ave Poughkeepsie NY 12603

REYNOLDS, JAMES ELWOOD
PAINTER
b Taft, Calif, Nov 9, 26. *Study:* Kann Inst Art, Beverly Hills, Calif; Sch Allied Arts, Glendale, Calif. *Work:* Phoenix Art Mus, Ariz; Cowboy Hall Fame, Oklahoma City; Mus Southwest, Midland, Tex. *Comn:* Design gold & silver medals for Cowboy Artists Am 8th Ann Exhib & future competition, Cowboy Artists Am & Franklin Mint, 73; painting used by Marlboro for spec Christmas advert, Philip Morris Co, 74. *Exhib:* Cowboy Hall Fame, Oklahoma City, 69-73; Ann Cowboy Artists Am Show, Phoenix Art Mus, 73-75. *Awards:* Gold Medal First Prize, Cowboy Hall Fame, 71 & 78; Most Outstanding Western Painter, 74-75; Artist of the Yr, Tucson Festival of Arts, Ariz, 77; plus others. *Mem:* Cowboy Artists Am (secy, 72-73, vpres, 74-75, pres, 75-76); Western Art Asn, Phoenix; Ariz Artists in Action. *Media:* Oil. *Publ:* Contribr, Cowboy in Art, 68; contribr, West & Walter Bimson, Univ Ariz, 71; contribr, American cowboy in life & legend, Nat Geographic, 72; contribr, Renaissance of Western Art, Franklin Mint, 74; contribr, Western Painting Today, Watson-Guptill, 75. *Mailing Add:* RR3 Jacks Canyon Rd Sedona AZ 86336

REYNOLDS, NANCY DUPONT
SCULPTOR
b Greenville, Del, Dec 28, 1919. *Study:* Goldey-Beacom Col, grad, 38. *Work:* Lutcrine Towers Bldg, Wilmington, Del. *Comn:* Fifteen panels carved lucite, Stephenson Sci Ctr, Nashville, Tenn; lucite carved panel, Goldsborough Bldg, Wilmington, Del; Bronze fountain head, Longwood Gardens, Kennett Square, Pa; watercolor painting, E I duPont de Nemours & Co, Wilmington, Del; bronze statue of child, Childrens Bur, Wilmington, Del. *Exhib:* Corcoran Gallery, Washington, DC, 43; Nat Sculpture Soc, New York, 64; Metrop Mus Art, New York, 77; Lever House, New York, 79; one-man show, Del Mus Art, Wilmington, 80. *Mem:* Burr Artists, New York; Pen Women Am, Del Chapt. *Media:* Bronze, Lucite. *Mailing Add:* PO Box 3919 Greenville DE 19807

REYNOLDS, PATRICIA ELLEN
PAINTER
b Portchester, NY, April 6, 34. *Study:* State Univ NY; studied with Mario Cooper, 79, Barbara Necchia, 81 & Jeanne Dobie, 82. *Work:* Temple Univ; State Univ, Montpelier; IBM Corp, Burlington, Vt; Gen Electric Corp, Schenectady, NY; Int Trade & Commerce, Montreal, Que & Waitsfield, Vt. *Comn:* Acrylic collage mural, Pizzagalli Construction Corp, Burlington, Vt, 79; Lake Champlain (watercolor), comn by Richard Spire, Washington, DC, 83. *Exhib:* Audubon Artists Exhib, Nat Arts Club, New York, 80; solo exhib, US Nat Tour Univs, 80-82; Am Watercolor Soc, Nat Acad, New York, 82; Salmagundi Club Invitational, New York, 83; Mid-West Watercolor Soc, Davenport Art Gallery, Iowa, 83; and others. *Pos:* Treas, Adirondack Art Asn, 62-65, dir gallery, 66-77. *Awards:* Best of Show, Fleming Mus, 70 & 71 & Wood Mus, 76, 78 & 79; Traveling Exhib Award, Am Watercolor Soc, 82. *Bibliog:* Peg Byrne (auth), Patricia Reynolds experiments, Adirondack Life Mag, 71; JoAnn Taylor (producer), Patricia Reynolds Work, Educ TV, 79-81; Mal Boright (interviewer), Good Morning Am, 81. *Mem:* Copley Soc Boston; Watercolor Soc, Cent NY, Am & Nat; assoc Allied Artists Am. *Dealer:* Hohe Sound Galleries Hohe Sound FL & Portland ME; River Oaks Gallery Houston TX. *Mailing Add:* East Side Studio Point Rd Willsboro NY 12996

REYNOLDS, RALPH WILLIAM
PAINTER
b Albany, Wis, Nov 10, 05. *Study:* Art Inst Chicago, 25-27 & 31; Beloit Col, BA, 38; State Univ Iowa, MA, 39; also with Grant Wood, Jean Charlot, Eliot O'Hara, Charles Burchfield, William Thon, Clarence Carter & Millard Sheets.

Work: Indiana Univ Pa; Westminster Col (Pa); One Hundred Friends Pittsburgh Art; Univ Club, Pittsburgh; Univ Pittsburgh, Johnstown; also pub schs, banks & indust concerns in western Pa & numerous pvt collections. *Exhib:* Assoc Artists Pittsburgh, Carnegie Mus, 42-67; Pittsburgh Watercolor Soc, Pittsburgh Ctr Arts, 51-72; Am Watercolor Soc, Nat Acad Design Galleries, 59; Am Artists Prof League's Grand Nat, Lever House, New York, 72 & 73; 20 one-man shows and many other group exhibs; and many other group and one-man exhibs. *Pos:* Com artist, var studios, Chicago & Cleveland, 27-33. *Teaching:* Student instr art, Beloit Col, 33-38; head dept art, SDak State Univ, 40-41; prof art, Indiana Univ Pa, 41-71, emer prof, 72- *Awards:* Awards, Ann Allied Artists Johnstown, Pa, 51-72; 5 Ida Smith Mem Awards & First Prize, Pittsburgh Watercolor Soc, 51-63; Purchase Awards, Penelec & US Bank Shows, 60-76; and others. *Mem:* Indiana Art Asn, Pa (pres, 42); Allied Artists Johnstown, Pa; Pittsburgh Watercolor Soc (vpres, 52); Assoc Artists Pittsburgh; fel Am Artists Prof League (vpres, Pa Chap, 74 & 75, pres, 76 & 77). *Media:* Miscellaneous Media, Watercolor. *Dealer:* Pittsburgh Ctr Arts Fifth & Shady Ave Pittsburgh PA 15232. *Mailing Add:* 363 S Third St Indiana PA 15701

REYNOLDS, RICHARD (HENRY)
SCULPTOR, PAINTER
b New York, NY, May 16, 13. *Study:* San Bernardino Valley Col, AA, 33; Univ Calif, Berkeley, BA, 36, cert, 39; Univ Calif, Los Angeles, 39; Mills Col, with Moholy-Nagy, 40; Univ Pac, Calif, MA, 42; Rudolph Schaefer Sch; Ore State Univ, Shell grant; Morningside Col, Sioux City, Iowa, Hon DFA, 76. *Comn:* Steel Viking symbol, Edison High Sch, Stockton, Calif, 64; metal Bengal tiger, Class of 1950, Univ of the Pac, 65; cast stone buffalo, Manteca Union High Sch, Calif, 65; bronze relief, New Wing Stockton Rec Bldg, 66. *Exhib:* Northern Calif Arts Painting Open, Sacramento, 70, 80 & 81; Stockton Art League Ann Exhib, Haggin Mus, 74-80. *Teaching:* Instr art & asst chmn div arts & lett, Stockton Col, 39-48; prof art, Univ Pac, Calif, 48-81, chmn dept art, 48-73, sr prof, 73-80; guest prof art educ, Univ Idaho, summer 54; guest lectr, Alaska Methodist Univ, 62; retired. *Awards:* Sculpture Prizes, Crocker-Kingsley Exhib, Sacramento, 80 & 82; Purchase Awards, Lodi Acampo Shows, 80-82; Second Prize Painting, Unitarian Ann Art Fest, 82 & San Joaquin Co Fair, 83. *Mem:* Life fel Int Inst Arts & Lett; Pac Arts Asn (ed, Journalette & pres, Northern Calif Sect, 51-52); Nat Art Educ Asn (chmn nat mem comt, 52-53); hon mem Stockton Art League (pres, 52-53 & 80-82); Nat Soc Lit & Arts. *Media:* Mixed. *Publ:* Contribr, Arts & Archit, 1/48; auth, A plea for wider distribution of art values, Col Art J, winter 51-52; auth, A buffalo sculpture for a California high school, Am Artist, 1/66; auth, Auto paint art, Design, spring 73; contribr poster design, fall 74 & cover design, 83, Pythian Mag; and others. *Dealer:* Stockton Fine Arts Gallery 2310 Pacific Ave Stockton CA 95207. *Mailing Add:* 1656 W Longview Ave Stockton CA 95207

REYNOLDS, ROBERT
PAINTER, EDUCATOR
b San Luis Obispo, Calif, Mar 7, 36. *Study:* Art Ctr Col of Design, Los Angeles, Calif, BPA; Calif Polytech State Univ, San Luis Obispo, MA; also with Lorser Fettelson, Harry Carmean, Robert Clark, Arne Nybak & Joe Henninger. *Work:* City of Stockton, Calif; Spec Collections, Chancellor's Off, Calif State Univ & Col System. *Comn:* Bicentennial coin, 71 & bicentennial off seal, 71, City of San Luis Obispo, Calif; off co seal, Co of San Luis Obispo, 74; painting & limited print, Calif Polytech State Univ, 76; large mural, Mus Natural Hist, Morro Bay, Calif, 82; ltd ed print, Natural Hist Asn Central Coast, Calif, 82. *Exhib:* Int Wildlife Art Show, Safari Club Int, Las Vegas, Nev, 75-78; one-man retrospective art exhib, Art Ctr, San Luis Obispo, Calif, 75; traveling exhib, Ford Motor Co, Dearborn, Mich, 77-78; Cunningham Art Mus Watercolor Exhib, Bakersfield, Calif, 78; one-man show, Allan Hancock Col, Santa Maria, Calif, 80; and many other group & one-man shows. *Pos:* Pres, Art Asn, San Luis Obispo, Calif, 68-69; mem design & review bd, City of San Luis Obispo, 68-73; mem bd of trustees, San Luis Obispo Art Ctr, 69-78; founding mem, Cent Coast Watercolor Soc, Calif, 77-, pres, 80-81. *Teaching:* Prof art, drawing & painting, Dept Art, Calif Polytech State Univ, 64-, actg dept head, 82-83; art instr drawing & painting, Evening Div, Cuesta Community Col, 72-76; instr watercolor, artist-in-residence, Stockton City, Calif, 76- *Awards:* Best of Show Award, Art Festival, City of Pismo Beach, Calif, 70; Purchase Award, Art Exhib, Fair Bd Asn, Paso Robles, 72; Award Winner, Calif Survey Drawing & Watercolor, Humboldt Cult Ctr, Eureka, Calif, 83. *Bibliog:* James Hayes (auth), A retrospective, Telegram-Tribune, 74; Morning Show, KEY-T, Santa Barbara, Calif, 82; Artist's artist, Santa Maria Times, 8/83. *Mem:* Allied Art, Cambria, Calif; Artist's Equity. *Media:* Multimedia. *Publ:* Illusr, VEP Productions, Calif Polytech State Univ, 64-74; illusr, Vocational Report, Vocational Div State of Calif, 67; contribr, WestCoast Graphics, WestArt, 70; illusr, Disappearing windmill, 74 & California Mendocino Coast, 77, Ford Times, Ford Motor Co. *Dealer:* Olive Tree Gallery 705 G E Main Santa Maria CA 93454. *Mailing Add:* Dept Art Calif Poly Univ San Luis Obispo CA 93407

REYNOLDS, VALRAE
CURATOR
b San Francisco, Calif, Dec 18, 44. *Study:* Univ Calif, Davis, BA, 66; NY Univ, MA, 68, cert mus training, 69. *Collections Arranged:* Silk, Tea and Porcelain, Trade Goods from the Orient, 75-76 & Two Worlds of Japanese Art, 78, Newark Mus; Tibet, A Lost World (auth, catalog), US Tour, Am Fedn Arts, 78-80; Chinese Art from the Newark Museum, China Inst, 80. *Pos:* Ford Fel arms & armor dept, Metrop Mus Art, New York, fall 68; Ford Fel Islamic ceramics, Asian Art Mus, San Francisco, spring 69; asst cur Oriental collection, Newark Mus, 69-70, cur Oriental collection, 70- *Awards:* Nat Endowment Humanities Grant Film Production, 72-74; Nat Endowment

Arts Grant Publ, 82-83. *Mem:* Comt SAsian Art; Asia Soc; Japan Soc; China Inst Am; Tibet Soc. *Res:* Arts of Tibet, India and Himalayas. *Publ:* Auth, Journey to Tibet: Dr Albert L Shelton, Newark Mus, spring-summer 72; auth, Tibet, A Lost World, Ind Univ Press, 79; auth, Chinese Art from the Newark Museum, China Inst, 80; auth, The Newark Museum Tibetan Collection, Vol I, 83; auth, Japan, the enduring heritage, Newark Mus Quart, 83. *Mailing Add:* Newark Mus 43 Washington St Newark NJ 07101

REYNOLDS, WADE
PAINTER
b New York, NY. *Study:* Self-taught. *Work:* Santa Barbara Mus Art, Calif; Cleveland Mus Art, Ohio; Miami Inst Fine Art, Fla; Times-Mirror Corp, Los Angeles. *Exhib:* Realism, Calif Palace Legion Honor, 75; California Visions, Santa Barbara Mus, Calif, 77; Prints, Miami Inst Art, 79; Retrospective, Pioneer Mus, Stockton, Calif, 82. *Awards:* Best Show, Madonna Festival, San Luis Obispo, Calif, 77 & Miami Print Biennial, 79. *Bibliog:* Frankenstein (auth), New realists, San Francisco Chronicle, 77; Stowens (auth), Intense realism, Am Artist, 1/81; Pincus (auth), Los Angeles Times, 6/25/82. *Media:* Oil, Acrylic. *Mailing Add:* c/o Louis Newman Galleries 322 N Beverly Dr Beverly Hills CA 90210

RHODEN, JOHN W
SCULPTOR
b Birmingham, Ala, 1918. *Study:* With Richmond Barthe, 38; Columbia Univ Sch Painting & Sculpture, with Oronzio Maldarelli, Hugo Robus & William Zorach. *Work:* Stockholm Mus; Carl Milles Collection; Heinz Collection, Pittsburgh; Steinberg Colletion, St Louis, Mo; Del Mus; and many others. *Comn:* Curved bronze & glass wall, Sheraton Hotel, Philadelphia, 57; bronze monument, comn by City of New York, 66; Clifton Sr High Sch, Baltimore, Md, 71; CliftonD; monumental bronze, Bellevue Hosp, New York, 75; monumental sculpture, Afro-Am Mus, Philadelphia, Pa, 76; and others. *Exhib:* Metrop Mus Art; Audubon Ann; Pa Acad Fine Arts; Nat Acad Design; Am Acad Arts; and many others. *Pos:* Specialist, US Dept State Tour Iceland, Europe & NAfrica, 55-56; mem artist deleg, US Dept State Tour USSR, Poland & Yugoslavia, 59 & Asia, 60; consult, Seni-Rupa Inst Teknol, Bandung, Indonesia, 62. *Awards:* Rockefeller Grant, 59; Medal Pro Sculptura Egregia, Howard Univ, 61; Guggenheim Fel, 61; and others. *Mem:* Life mem Munic Art Soc; Am Soc Contemp Artists. *Media:* Mixed. *Mailing Add:* 23 Cranberry St Brooklyn NY 11201

RHODES, CURTIS A
PAINTER, PRINTMAKER
b Butler, Mo, Nov 5, 39. *Study:* Univ Kans, BFA, 62; Ohio Univ, MFA, 66. *Work:* Univ Kans Art Mus, Lawrence; Flint Inst Art, Mich; Grand Rapids Art Mus, Mich; Kalamazoo Art Ctr, Mich. *Comn:* Multi-color lithograph, Oxbox Sch Art, Sagituck, Mich, 73; multi-color photo-etching, Detroit Print Workshop, Mich, 76. *Exhib:* Butler Ann, Butler Inst Art, Youngstown, Ohio, 60; And Another, Western Mich Univ, Kalamazoo, 66; Nat Painting & Sculpture Invitational, Flint Inst Art, Mich, 66-67 & 70; Paper as Medium, Smithsonian Invitational & Traveling Exhib, Washington, DC, 79-81. *Collections Arranged:* 3rd Nat Drawing-Prints (auth, catalog), Juried Drawing-Prints, 68; Multiples USA (auth, catalog), Nat Juried Invitational Exhib of Prints, 70; Markings, Major Int Exhib of Prints, 75. *Pos:* Visual arts advisor, Mich Council for Arts, 75-78. *Teaching:* Prof, Western Mich Univ, Kalamazoo, 66- *Awards:* Purchase Award, Flint Inst Art, 67; Nat Endowment Arts Fel, 74-75; Ford Found Awards, 77-82. *Bibliog:* Kathy Clark (auth), Twinrocker: Collaboration in Custom Papermaking, Fine Print, 77 & Pigments and Dyes in Hand Papermaking, Tamarind Tech Papers, 78. *Media:* Color Lithography. *Publ:* Mayan Legends/Replys, Limited Ed, Twinrocker Paper Mill, 81. *Mailing Add:* 10526 Cranberry Rd Marcellus MI 49067

RHODES, JAMES MELVIN
GLASS BLOWER, SCULPTOR
b Gorman, Tex, Dec 1, 38. *Study:* Univ Wis, Mechanical eng; Univ Hawaii, BA. *Work:* State Found on Cult & the Arts, Hawaii. *Comn:* Glass mural, Steven B Dixon, 83. *Exhib:* Honolulu Acad Arts, Hawaii, 72; two-man shows, The Foundry, Honolulu, Hawaii, 72 & 74, Metes & Bounds, Sausalito, Calif, 74, Hand & Eye, Honolulu, 74, Downtown Gallery, Honolulu, Hawaii, 77 & Sculptore, HI, 80. *Pos:* Chmn, Easter Art Festival, Hawaii, 76; vpres, Big Island Artists Guild, Hawaii, 76. *Teaching:* Instr arts & crafts, Schofield Arts & Crafts, Wahiawa, Hawaii, 70-74; instr off hand glass blowing, The Foundry, Honolulu, Hawaii, 70-74. *Awards:* Am Fac Award, Hawaii Craftsmen Show, 73; Campus Ctr Bd Award, Univ Hawaii Show, Univ Hawaii, 74. *Mem:* Hawaii Concert Soc; E Hawaii Cult Coun. *Media:* Blown glass. *Mailing Add:* Box 1131 Keaau HI 96749

RHODES, REILLY PATRICK
MUSEUM DIRECTOR
b Bloomington, Ill, Mar 28, 41. *Study:* Kansas City Art Inst, BFA, 66; Wichita State Univ, MFA, 68; Sterling Inst, Boston, art gallery mgt, 69; Syracuse Univ, mus mgt, 70; Univ Mo-Columbia, 70. *Pos:* Dir, Albrecht Gallery, St Joseph, Mo, 68-71; dir, Canton Art Inst, Ohio, 71-73 & Charles W Bowers Mem Mus, Santa Ana, Calif, 73-82. *Mem:* Int Coun Mus; Am Asn Mus; Western Asn Art Mus; Am Fedn Arts; Art Mus Develop Dirs Asn. *Publ:* Auth, Public Relations Catalogue, Albrecht Gallery; auth introd to var catalogs, including L E Shafer Bronzes, An Exhibition of Sculpture & Drawings by O V Shaffer, Moses Soyer: A Selection of Paintings 1960-1970, The Art of Irving Ramsey Wiles (1861-1948) & All Ohio (Canton Art Inst Ann); and others. *Mailing Add:* Charles W Bowers Mem Mus 2002 N Main St Santa Ana CA 92706

RHYNE, CHARLES SYLVANUS
HISTORIAN
b Philadelphia, Pa, Mar 29, 32. *Study:* Wittenberg Col, AB, 54; Univ Chicago, MA, 56, advan study, 56-60; Fulbright fels, Courtauld Inst, Univ London, 62-64. *Work:* Mr & Mrs Paul Mellon; Yale Ctr British Art. *Collections Arranged:* Andrew Leicester: Earth Drawings, 9/76, Lee Kelly: Outdoor Public Sculpture in the Northwest, 10/76, Miriam Schapiro: Anatomy of a Kimono, 4/78 & Francoise Grossen: Fiber as Sculpture, 8/78, Reed Col Art Gallery. *Pos:* Chief reader, Advan Placement Prog, Art Hist of Art Educ Testing Serv, Princeton, NJ, 70-75; bd dirs, Portland Ctr for the Visual Arts, 73-80; dir art gallery, Reed Col, 74-80; mem long-range planning comt, Portland Art Mus, 75-77. *Teaching:* Instr art hist & humanities, Reed Col, 60-62, from asst prof to assoc prof art hist, 62-68, prof, 68-; vis teacher art hist, Mus Art Sch, Portland, 74-75. *Awards:* Younger Humanities Fel, Nat Endowment Humanities, 72-73; Resident fel, Yale Ctr for Brit Art, 78; and others. *Mem:* Col Art Asn; sr fel Ctr Adv Study Visual Arts; Soc Archi Historians; Soc of Indust Archaeol; res fel Yale Ctr British Art. *Res:* Landscape painting, especially John Constable (preparing catalogue raisonne); architecture of bridges. *Publ:* Auth, Fresh light on John Constable, Apollo, 68; co-auth, Advanced Placement Art, Col Entrance Exam Bd, 70; Lionel Constable's East Berlin Sketchbook, Art News, 78; and others. *Mailing Add:* Reed Col Portland OR 97202

RICCI, JERRI
PAINTER
b Perth Amboy, NJ. *Study.* New York Sch Appl Design for Women, 35; Art Students League, with Scott Williams, George Bridgman, Mahonri Young & others, 35-38. *Work:* Fairleigh Dickinson Col; Parrish Mus, Southampton, NY; Am Acad Arts & Lett; Butler Art Inst, Clark Univ; Addison Gallery Am Art, Andover, Mass; and others. *Exhib:* Toledo Mus Art; Pa Acad Fine Arts; Art Inst Chicago; Dayton Art Inst; Addison Gallery Am Art; and others. *Awards:* Silver Medal, Catharine Lorillard Wolfe Art Club, 54; Clara Obrig Award, Nat Acad Design; Gold Medal, Audubon Artists, 55; and others. *Mem:* Am Watercolor Soc; Allied Artists Am; assoc Nat Acad Design; Philadelphia Watercolor Club; Audubon Artists; and others. *Mailing Add:* 1 Atlantic Ave Rockport MA 01966

RICE, ANTHONY HOPKINS
SCULPTOR, PAINTER
b Angeles Pampanga, Philippine Islands, July 21, 48. *Study:* Va Commonwealth Univ, Richmond, BFA, 70; Univ NC, Chapel Hill, MFA, 72. *Work:* High Mus Art, Atlanta, Ga; Nat Mus Am Art, Smithsonian Inst, Washington, DC. *Comn:* Outdoor environmental sculpture, Wright State Univ, Dayton, Ohio, 74. *Exhib:* New Sculpture, Washington, Baltimore, Richmond, Corcoran Gallery, Washington, DC, 70; Translucent and Transparent Art, St Petersburg Mus Art, Fla, 71; one-man show, Cochise Col, Douglas, Ariz, 73; Ga Artists Show, High Mus Art, 74; Nat Sculpture '75 Traveling Exhib, Huntsville Mus Art, Ala, 75; Renwick Gallery, Smithsonian Inst, Washington, DC, 81; Morgan Gallery, Kansas City. *Teaching:* Asst prof art, Wesleyan Col, Macon, Ga, 72-81, assoc prof art, 81-, chmn dept art, currently. *Awards:* Purchase Award, Charlotte Printmakers Soc, NC. *Bibliog:* Greg Thielew (auth), article, Art Voices, 3/81. *Mem:* Col Art Asn; Am Asn Univ Prof; Southeastern Col Art Asn; Southern Asn Sculptors; Popular Cult Asn South. *Media:* Steel, Wood. *Dealer:* Morgan Gallery Kansas City MO. *Mailing Add:* c/o Wesleyan Col 4760 Forsyth Rd Macon GA 31201

RICE, HAROLD RANDOLPH
EDUCATOR, WRITER
b Salineville, Ohio, May 22, 12. *Study:* Univ Cincinnati, BSAA & BS(art educ), 34, MEd, 42; Columbia Univ, EdD(Arthur Wesley Dow Scholar), 44; Moore Col Art, Hon LHD, 63. *Pos:* Contrib art ed, Jr Arts & Activities, 37-46; chmn comt on art, Ohio Elem Educ Policies Comt, 40-42; chmn arts & skills corps, Am Red Cross, Ala, 44-46; dir, Philadelphia Art Alliance, 47-63; nat scholar juror, Scholastic Arts Awards, nine yrs, 49-75, nat jury chmn, ann, 74-; adv art ed, Bk Knowledge, 50-63; mem bd dirs, Contemp Arts Ctr, 64-69, mem adv bd, 69-72. *Teaching:* Art supvr, Wyoming Pub Schs, Ohio, 34-42; adj instr, Univ Cincinnati, 40-42; teaching fel, Columbia Univ, 42-44; head dept art, Univ Ala, 44-46; dean, Moore Inst Art, 46-62, first pres, 51-62; pres & dean, Moore Col Art, 62-63; dean, Col Design, Archit & Art, Univ Cincinnati, 63-72, prof design, art & educ, 72-78, dean & emer prof, 78- *Mem:* Fel & life mem Nat Asn Schs Art (secy, 50-55, pres, 55-57); life mem Eastern Arts Asn (vpres, 56-58, pres, 58-60); Nat Art Educ Asn (coun mem, 60-63); hon mem Cincinnati Art Club; Int Coun Fine Arts Deans; and others. *Publ:* Auth, numerous articles for prof mag & jour, 29- *Mailing Add:* 640 Evening Star Lane Cincinnati OH 45220

RICE, M ROBERT & BARBARA MENEN
DEALERS, COLLECTORS
b New York, NY. *Pos:* Owners, Robert Rice Gallery, Houston. *Specialty:* Nineteenth and twentieth century American/French traditional. *Collection:* Hassem, Potthast, Carlson, Martha Walter, W M Chase, A Bierstadt, Boldini, Jean Bernaud, F Freiseke, F Church, T Cole, M Luce and K Von Dongen. *Publ:* Ed, C K Chatterton, 77 & ed, Emil Carlson, NA, 78; Graphics Houston; ed, William S Horton, Fox Press, 79; ed, Gallery Collection, 82; ed, Thomas Cole and Frederick Church, 83; and others. *Mailing Add:* 2627 Kipling Suite 201 Houston TX 77098

RICE, NANCY NEWMAN See Newman-Rice, Nancy

RICE, NORMAN LEWIS
PAINTER, EDUCATOR
b Aurora, Ill, July 22, 05. *Study:* Univ Ill, BA, 26; Art Inst Chicago, 26-30; Otis Art Inst, DFA, 67. *Pos:* From asst dean to dean, Art Inst Chicago, 30-43; dir, Sch Art, Syracuse Univ, 46-54; dean, Col Fine Arts, Carnegie-Mellon Univ, 54-72, emer dean, 72- *Teaching:* Instr drawing & design, Art Inst Chicago, 28-43; prof painting, Syracuse Univ, 46-54; prof painting & hist art, Carnegie-Mellon Univ, 54-73. *Mem:* Fel Nat Asn Schs Art; fel Am Coun Arts in Educ; plus others. *Mailing Add:* 5850 Meridian Rd Apt 107C Gibsonia PA 15044

RICE, SHELLEY ENID
CRITIC, HISTORIAN
b Bronx, NY, Aug 20, 50. *Study:* Smith Col, 68-69; State Univ NY, Stony Brook, BA(summa cum laude), 72; Inst Fine Arts, NY Univ, MA, 75; Princeton Univ. *Pos:* Photog critic, Village Voice, 76-77; columnist, SoHo Weekly News, 78-79; staff writer, Artforum, 80-82; free lance cur, 78- *Teaching:* Instr art hist, Brooklyn Col, NY, 72-77; mem fac photog hist & criticism, Sch of Visual Arts, New York, 75-78 & 81-; instr art hist & criticism, Tyler Sch Art, Temple Univ, 78-80; adj asst prof photog, NY Univ, 82- *Awards:* Nat Endowment Arts Art Critics Fel, 80; Nat Endowment Arts, Service Field Grant, 81; NY State Coun Arts Video Writing Grants, 82 & 83. *Mem:* Womens Caucus Art; Col Art Asn; Am Sect Int Asn Art Critics. *Res:* Historical and contemporary photography; contemporary multi-media art. *Publ:* Auth, Essential differences: A comparison of the portraits of Lisette Model and Diane Arbus, Artforum, 5/80; auth, Deconstruction-Reconstruction (catalog), New Mus, New York, 7/80; auth, Schemes: A Decade of Installation Drawings (catalog), Elise Meyer Gallery, New York, 6/81; auth, Mythic space: Video installations of Rita Myers, Afterimage, 1/82; auth, New York: A pictorial history, Picture Mag, Issue 19, 82. *Mailing Add:* 255 W 12th St New York NY 10014

RICH, FRANCES L
SCULPTOR, DRAFTSMAN
b Spokane, Wash, Jan 8, 10. *Study:* Smith Col, BA, 31; sculpture with Malvina Hoffman, drawing & frescoes with Angel Zarraga, Paris, France, 33-35; Beaux Art Acad; Boston Mus Sch, with Alexander Iacovleff, 35-36; Cranbrook Acad Art, sculpture with Carl Milles, 37-40; Claremont Col, with Millard Sheets, 46; Columbia Univ, 47. *Work:* Palm Springs Desert Mus, Calif; Santa Catalina Sch, Monterey, Calif; bronze portrait head, Virgil Thomson, Thomson Rm, NY Univ; also pvt collection of Father Edward Boyle, Holy Trinity Church, Bremerton, Wash; Bronze Portrait Head, Virgil Thomson, Thomson Rm, NY Univ. *Comn:* Christ of the Sacred Heart, St Sebastian's Church, West Los Angeles, 74; bronze plaque honoring Dr Mario Gonzalez Ulloa, 77; 15 bronze flying birds, Aviary Wall, Living Desert Reserve, Palm Desert, Calif, 78; nine bronzes, Cranbrook Acad Art Mus, 81; and others. *Exhib:* One-man shows, Santa Barbara Mus Art, 52, Calif Palace Legion Hon, 55, Palm Springs Desert Mus, 69 & 77; Calif Relig Artists, De Young Mem, 52; Lenten Exhib Liturgical Arts, Denver Art Mus, 55; Smith Col Mus Art, 81. *Bibliog:* Articles in Liturgical Arts Quart; Sculpture of Frances Rich, Manzanita Press, 74; and others. *Mem:* Archit League New York; Alumna Cranbrook Acad Art. *Media:* Bronze, Stone. *Mailing Add:* PO Box 213 Palm Desert CA 92261

RICH, GARRY LORENCE
PAINTER
b Newton Co, Mo, Nov 11, 43. *Study:* Kansas City Art Inst, BFA; NY Univ, MA. *Work:* Whitney Mus Am Art, New York, NY; Aldrich Mus Contemp Art, Ridgefield, Conn; Phoenix Art Mus, Ariz; Nelson Gallery Art, Kansas City, Mo; Miami Art Ctr, Fla. *Exhib:* Whitney Mus Am Art Ann, 71; Highlights of the Season, Aldrich Mus Contemp Art, Ridgefield, 71; one-man shows, Max Hutchinson Gallery, New York, 71-72 & 74, Henri Gallery, Washington, DC, 72 & Gallery A, Sydney, Australia, 72. *Teaching:* Asst prof painting, NY Univ, 65-71; asst prof painting, Hofstra Univ, 71-72; asst prof painting, Bard Col, 72- *Awards:* Max Beckman fel, Brooklyn Mus, 66; Nat Coun Arts Nat Endowment, 67 & 74; Anderson fel, NY Univ, 68. *Bibliog:* Domingo (auth), Color abstractionism, 12/70 & Bowling (auth), Color & recent painting, 72, Arts Mag; Ratcliff (auth), Young New York painters, Art News, 70. *Dealer:* Max Hutchinson Gallery 127 Green St New York NY 10013. *Mailing Add:* 167 Crosby St New York NY 10012

RICHARD, JACK
PAINTER, GALLERY DIRECTOR
b Akron, Ohio, Mar 7, 22. *Study:* Chicago Prof Sch Art, scholar; Univ Ohio, Athens; Kent Univ; Akron Univ; also with R Brackman, A Bohrod, Y Kunioshi, B Shahn, J Carroll & many others. *Work:* Canton Art Inst, Ohio; Umbaugh Pole Bldg Collection, Ravenna, Ohio; Woodrum Ins Collection, Stow, Ohio. *Comn:* President & Mrs Eisenhower, Tupperware Int, Orlando, Fla; mural, Central Christian Church Kettering, Dayton; mural, Valley Savings & Loan, Cuyahoga Falls; mural, First United Church of Christ, Akron; portraits, comn by Bing & Katherine Crosby, Byron Nelson, Juan Rodrigues; and others. *Exhib:* Retrospective, Ambassador Col, Pasadena, 70; City Ctr Gallery, New York; Fifty Am Artists, Gallerie Int & Salmagundi Club, New York; Butler Inst Am Art Nat, Youngstown, Ohio. *Pos:* Illusr, Stevens-Gross Studios, Chicago. *Teaching:* Instr painting & design & dir, Cuyahoga Valley Art Ctr, Cuyahoga Falls, 53-63; instr, Woman's City Club, Akron, Ohio, 60-; instr painting & design & dir, Almond Tea Galleries, Cuyahoga Falls, 63-; instr, Madison Sch Art, Conn, 81. *Awards:* Purchase Award & Second Award Painting, Canton Art Inst; Best in Show Award, Akron Art Inst, 48; Huntington Hartford Fel, 58. *Bibliog:* Six Rotos, Beacon J, Knight Newspapers; M M (auth), Jack Richard Al Lavoro, Il Pungold Verde, Italy, 74. *Mem:* Artists, Ohio; Ohio Arts & Crafts Guild; Tri-County

Art Soc, Ohio; Akron Soc Artists. *Media:* Multimedia. *Interests:* Assisting in training of young artists and rehabilitation use of arts. *Collection:* R Brackman, L Grell, R Skemp, G Eluegren, D Cornwell, Ball, Japanese Prints, A Loomis & 60 others. *Publ:* Illusr, Staley J, Ind, 43-45; illusr, The Helm Mag; illusr, Ohio Edison Ann Report, 60; illusr, Ohio Story, TV prog, Ohio Bell Tel. *Mailing Add:* c/o Almond Tea Galleries 2250 Front St Cuyahoga Falls OH 44221

RICHARD, PAUL
CRITIC
b Chicago, Ill, Nov, 22, 39. *Study:* Harvard Col, BA, 61; Univ Pa Grad Sch Fine Arts. *Pos:* Art critic, Washington Post, DC, 67- *Mailing Add:* 1673 Columbia Rd NW Washington DC 20009

RICHARDS, BILL
PAINTER
b Grantsville, WVa, July 15, 36. *Study:* Ohio Univ, with Dwight Mutchler, BFA; Ind Univ, with Leon Golub & James McGarrell, MFA; Skowhegan Sch Painting & Sculpture. *Work:* Philadelphia Mus Art; Brooklyn Mus; NJ State Mus Art, Trenton; Westinghouse Corp, Pittsburgh; Solomon R Guggenheim Mus, New York; and others. *Exhib:* Friends Collect 20th Century, Philadelphia Mus Art, 67; Pa Acad Fine Arts Ann, 68; Whitney Mus Am Art Biennial, 75; one-man shows, Marian Locks Gallery, Philadelphia, 75, Olympia Galleries Ltd, Philadelphia, 76 & Ohio Univ, Athens, 79; 19 Artists--Emergent Americans, Exxon Nat Exhib, Guggenheim Mus, 81; Westinghouse Collection, Loch Haven Art Ctr, Orlando, Fla, 83; New York Painting Today, Three Rivers Arts Festival, Pittsburgh, 83; and others. *Teaching:* Assoc prof, Moore Col Art, 67-81, prof 81-82. *Bibliog:* Victoria Donohoe (auth), rev in Philadelphia Inquirer, 5/75; Ann Jarmusch (auth), article, Art News 1/77; Peter Frank (auth), article, Art Am, 3/77. *Media:* Acrylic. *Mailing Add:* 40 W 24th St New York NY 10010

RICHARDS, BILL (WILLIAM A)
DRAFTSMAN
b Brooklyn, NY, Sept 19, 44. *Study:* Pratt Inst, BFA, 66; Univ Iowa, MA, 68; Univ NMex, MFA, 70. *Work:* Chase Manhattan Bank, New York; Ill Bell Tel, Chicago. *Exhib:* Drawings, Del Art Mus, Wilmington, 77; On Paper, Va Mus Fine Arts, 80; American Drawing in Black and White: 1970-1980, Brooklyn Mus, 80; The American Landscape: Recent Developments, Whitney Mus Am Art Fairfield Co Br, Stamford, Conn, 81; Contemporary American Realism Since 1960, Pa Acad Fine Arts, Va Mus Fine Arts, Oakland Mus Art & mus in Europe, 81-83; Nature Transformed, Anderson Gallery, Va Commonwealth Univ, 82; solo exhib, Hite Art Inst, Univ Louisville, 83; Perspectives on Contemporary Realism ..., Pa Acad Fine Arts & Art Inst Chicago, 83. *Teaching:* Asst adj prof drawing, State Univ NY, Purchase, 77-78; instr, Sch Visual Arts, 77-79. *Awards:* Creative Artists Pub Serv Grant, 75-76; Nat Endowment Arts Fel, 77-78. *Bibliog:* Ruth Bass (auth), The illusion of reality, Art News, 12/81; Vivian Raynor (auth), Art: A tranquil show of American landscape, New York Times, 5/15/82. *Dealer:* Nancy Hoffman Gallery 429 W Broadway New York NY 10012. *Mailing Add:* 77 Seventh Ave Apt 8P New York NY 10011

RICHARDS, EUGENE
PHOTOGRAPHER, LECTURER
b Dorchester, Mass, Apr 25, 44. *Study:* Northeastern Univ, Boston, BA(Eng), 67; Mass Inst Technol, grad level study with Minor White. *Work:* Mus Mod Art, New York; Mus Fine Arts, Boston; Addison Gallery Am Art, Andover, Mass; J B Speed Art Mus, Louisville, Ky; Everson Mus, Syracuse, NY. *Comn:* Art in Public Places, Mass Artists Found, Boston, 78. *Exhib:* We the People, Smithsonian Inst, DC, 75; Photogs, J B Speed Art Mus, Louisville, Ky, 76; Recent Acquisitions, Mus Fine Arts, Boston, 76 & Fourteen New Eng Photogrs, 78; Recent Acquisition Show, Addison Gallery Am Art, Andover, Mass, 77; one-man show, Photogs, Folkwang Mus, Essen, WGer, 79; Mass Art Found Winners, Worcester Art Mus, Mass, 80. *Pos:* Artist-in-residence, Maine Photo Workshop, Rockport, 77-78 & Int Ctr Photog, New York, 78-79; nominee mem, Magnum Photos, New York, 78- *Teaching:* Instr photog, Art Inst Boston, 74-76 & Union Col, Schenectady, NY, 77. *Awards:* Nat Endowment for Arts grant, photog, 74; Mass Artists Found, 78 & fel, 79; Guggenheim fel, photog, 80. *Bibliog:* Lou Stettner (auth), A look at forgotten books, Camera 35, 3/78; Vickie Goldberg (auth), Half dirty realities, Am Photogr, 78; Julia Scully (auth), Dorchester days, Mod Photog, 6/79. *Mem:* Photog Resource Ctr. *Publ:* Auth, Few Comforts or Surprises: The Arkansas Delta, Mass Inst Technol, 73; contribr, Photographer's Choice, Addison House, 76; contribr, Family of Children, 77 & contribr, Family of Women, 78, Ridge Press; auth, Dorchester Days, Many Voices Press, Wollaston, Mass, 78. *Mailing Add:* 20 Chase St Dorchester MA 02125

RICHARDS, GLENORA
PAINTER
b New London, Ohio, Feb 18, 09. *Study:* Cleveland Sch Art, with Rolf Stohl. *Work:* Philadelphia Mus Art; Waterbury Mus Collection, Mattatuck Hist Soc, Conn; Nat Collection Fine Arts, Smithsonian Inst; US Post Off. *Exhib:* Philadelphia Watercolor Soc Show, 47; Nat Asn Women Artists, Nat Acad, New York, 53-74; Royal Soc Miniature Painters Exhib, London, 58; Smithsonian Mus Traveling Show, 66. *Awards:* Leuantia White Boardman Mem Medal, Am Soc Miniature Painters, 47; Philadelphia Watercolor Soc Prize, 47; Medal Hon Watercolor, Nat Asn Women Artists Ann Show, 74. *Bibliog:* Frederick Whitaker (auth), The art of painting portraits in miniature, Am Artist Mag, 58. *Mem:* Miniature Painters, Sculptors & Gravers Washington, DC; Whiskey Painters Am; Soc Miniature Painters, NJ & Fla. *Media:* Watercolor on Ivory. *Publ:* Auth, Good things come in small packages, North Light, 72; auth, The magic of miniatures, Dynamic Maturity, 76; auth, North Light Collection II, 79. *Mailing Add:* 87 Oak St New Canaan CT 06840

RICHARDS, JEANNE HERRON
ETCHER, PAINTER
b Aurora, Ill. *Study:* Univ Iowa, with Mauricio Lasansky, BFA, 52, MFA, 54; Atelier 17, Fulbright grant, 54-55, with Stanley William Hayter. *Work:* Lessing J Rosenwald Collection, Nat Gallery Art; Prints & Photographs, Libr Cong, Washington, DC; Nat Mus Am Art, Washington, DC; Sheldon Mem Art Galleries, Univ Nebr-Lincoln; British Mus, London, Eng. *Exhib:* L C Pennell Exhib, 47, 54, 57, 58 & 61; Contemporary Prints, Drawings & Watercolors, Metrop Mus Art, New York, 52; NW Printmakers, Seattle Art Mus, 53 & 61; Bay Printmakers, Oakland Mus Art, Calif, 56-59; Boston Printmakers, Boston Mus Fine Arts, 56-57, 59 & 61; Prints From Brooklyn Mus Nat, Am Fedn Arts US Tour, 56; Intaglio Prints USA, US Info Agency Tour SAm, 59; Nat Print & Drawing, Dulin Gallery of Art, Knoxville, Tenn, 68; one-man show, Univ Ill, Champaign, 69; Sheldon Mem Art Galleries, Univ Nebr, Lincoln, 70; 19th Area Exhib, Corcoran Gallery Art, Washington, DC, 74; plus others. *Teaching:* Asst instr drawing, Univ Iowa, 55-56; asst prof prints & drawing, Univ Nebr-Lincoln, 57-63. *Awards:* Purchase Award, Corcoran Gallery Art, 57; Purchase Award, Print Club Albany 13th Nat, 69; SW Printmakers Purchase Prize to Philadelphia Mus of Art in hon of Carl Zigrosser, 76. *Bibliog:* Archives of American Art, Smithsonian, 83. *Mailing Add:* 9526 Liptonshire Dallas TX 75238

RICHARDS, JOSEPH EDWARD
PAINTER
b Des Moines, Iowa, Oct 10, 21. *Study:* Am Acad Art, Chicago, 46-49; Chicago Art Inst, 49-50; Pa Acad Fine Arts, Philadelphia, 50-52. *Work:* American Republic Insurance Co, Des Moines, Iowa; Mobil Oil Co; United Airlines; Am Oil Co; and pvt collections. *Exhib:* Audubon Artists Ann, Nat Acad Design, New York, 75, 77 & 78; Ann Midyear Exhib, Butler Inst Am Art, Youngstown, Ohio, 76, 77, 78 & 81; Tex Fine Arts Asn 66th Ann, Laguna Gloria Mus, Austin, 77; Fel Exhib, Pa Acad Fine Arts, Philadelphia, 78; Nat Acad Design Ann, New York, 78; New Eng Exhib, Silvermine Guild Artists, New Canaan, Conn, 78 & 79; Va Artists 27th Biennial, Va Mus Fine Art, Richmond, 79; two-person show, OK Harris West, Scottsdale, Ariz, 81 & 82; Spring Invitational, OK Harris, New York, 82. *Awards:* Distinguished Artist, Va Mus Fine Arts, Richmond, 79. *Mem:* Fel Pa Acad Fine Arts. *Media:* Oil. *Dealer:* OK Harris West 4200 N Marshall Way Scottsdale AZ 85251. *Mailing Add:* PO Box 374 Hillsdale NY 12529

RICHARDS, KARL FREDERICK
DRAFTSMAN, PAINTER
b Youngstown, Ohio, June 14, 20. *Study:* Cleveland Inst Art, dipl, 44; Western Reserve Univ, BSEd, 44; State Univ Iowa, MA, 47; Ohio State Univ, PhD, 56. *Teaching:* Asst prof art, Bowling Green State Univ, 47-56; prof art & chmn dept, Tex Christian Univ, 56-71; prof art & chmn dept, Ark State Univ, 71- *Mailing Add:* PO Box 640 State University AR 72467

RICHARDS, TALLY
DEALER, WRITER
b Clarkston, Ga. *Pos:* Instr, Tally Richards Gallery, Taos, 69-, Tally Richards Gallery, Palm Desert, 83- *Specialty:* Contemporary art by Southwest artists. *Publ:* Auth, Scholder, Dartmouth: Renewed commitments, Southwest Art Mag, 74; auth, Larry Bell, 75; auth, Indian in Paris, Am Indian Art Mag, 77; auth, Tally 13, collected stories, 80; auth, Three AM, Puerto Del Sol, 82. *Mailing Add:* PO Box 1734 2 Ledoux St Taos NM 87571

RICHARDS, WALTER DUBOIS
PAINTER, PRINTMAKER
b Penfield, Ohio, Sept 18, 07. *Study:* Cleveland Sch Art, grad, 30. *Work:* Cleveland Mus Art; Whitney Mus Am Art, New York; New Britain Mus Am Art, Conn; Nat Mus Sports, Bridgeport, Conn; Johnson Mus. *Comn:* Am Trees (four stamps), 78, 100th Anniversary Nat Park Serv stamp design, Cape Hatteras, 72 & American Architecture (16 stamps), 79-82, US Postal Serv; James Hoban Stamp, White House painting, 81; and others. *Exhib:* Int Watercolor Exhib, Art Inst Chicago, 38; 12th Biennial, Brooklyn Mus Art, 43; Royal Soc Painters in Watercolor, London, 62; Am Prints Around the World, various nations, 63; 200 Years of Watercolor Painting, Metrop Mus Art, New York, 66; Mystic Int, Mystic Maritime Gallery, Conn, 83. *Pos:* Illusr, Tranquillini Studios, Cleveland, 31-36 & Charles E Cooper Studios, New York, 36-50. *Teaching:* Instr pvt classes drawing & watercolor, 68- *Awards:* Lily Saportas Award, Am Watercolor Soc, 62; First Graphics, Hudson Valley Art Asn, 75; Environ Improvement Award, Conn Soc Archit, 83. *Bibliog:* Howard Munce (auth), One artist: one subject: endless variations, N Light Mag, 11/12/72; Susan E Meyer (auth), On location with the Fairfield Watercolor Group, Am Artist, 7/72; 200 Years of American Illustration, NY Hist Soc Mus, 77. *Mem:* Am Watercolor Soc (recording secy, 60-61, vpres, 62-70); assoc Nat Acad Design; Conn Watercolor Soc; Soc Illusr; Fairfield Watercolor Group (pres, 48-). *Media:* Watercolor; Lithography. *Publ:* Illusr, Divided South searches its soul, 56 & The age of psychology in the US, 57, Life Mag; illusr, Readers Digest, Colliers, Am Legion & Fortune Mag; auth, 200 Years of American Illustration, NY Hist Soc Mus, 77. *Mailing Add:* 87 Oak St 87 Oak St New Canaan CT 06840

RICHARDSON, BRENDA
MUSEUM CURATOR
b Howell, Mich, July 15, 42. *Study:* Univ Mich, Ann Arbor, BA, 64; Univ Calif, Berkeley, MA, 66. *Collections Arranged:* Eighties, 70, William T Wiley (with catalog), 71, Eight New York Painters, 72, Terry Fox (with catalog), 73, Joan Brown (with catalog), 74 & Stephen A Davis, Howard Fried, Steven J Kaltenbach, 74, Univ Art Mus, Berkeley; Fourteen Artists, 75 & Andy Warhol, 75, Baltimore Mus Art; Mel Bochner (with catalog), 76; Frank Stella

Black Paintings (with catalog), 76; Barnett Newman Complete Drawings (with catalog), 79; Mondrian Drawings, 81; Bruce Nauman Neons (with catalog), 82; Gilbert & George (with catalog), 84; and many others. *Pos:* Cur exhib, Univ Art Mus, Berkeley, 66-72, asst curatorial dir, 72-74; cur painting & sculpture, Baltimore Mus Art, Md, 75-77, asst dir art, 77- *Awards:* Distinguished Alumni Lectureship, Univ Calif, Berkeley, 73. *Publ:* Auth, Howard Fried: Paradox of approach-avoidance, summer 71 & Nancy Graves: a new way of seeing, 4/72, Arts Mag; plus many others. *Mailing Add:* 4300 N Charles Baltimore MD 21218

RICHARDSON, CONSTANCE (COLEMAN)
PAINTER

b Indianapolis, Ind, Jan 18, 05. *Study:* Pa Acad Fine Arts. *Work:* Detroit Inst Arts; Santa Barbara Mus Art; John D Rockefeller III Collection; Columbus Gallery Fine Arts; Pa Acad Fine Arts, Philadelphia. *Comn:* This Land is Ours (painting), Omaha Nat Bank, 66. *Exhib:* Am Painting Today, Metrop Mus Art, New York, 50; Am Landscape, A Changing Frontier, Nat Collection Fine Arts, Washington, DC, 66; Fifty Artists from Fifty States Circulating Exhib, Am Fedn Arts, 67-68; Am Paintings of Ports & Harbors, 1774-1968, Jacksonville-Norfolk, 69; Remnants of Things Past, Jacksonville-St Petersburg, 71. *Bibliog:* Louise Bruner (auth), Constance Richardson, Am Artist, 1/61; Alan Gussow (auth), A sense of place: the artist & the American land, Sat Rev, 71. *Media:* Oil. *Mailing Add:* c/o Kennedy Galleries 40 West 57th St New York NY 10019

RICHARDSON, EDGAR PRESTON
HISTORIAN

b Glens Falls, NY, Dec 2, 02. *Study:* Univ Pa; Williams Col; Pa Acad Fine Arts; six hon doctorates. *Pos:* Ed, Art Quart, 38-64; dir, Detroit Inst Arts, 45-62; dir, H F du Pont Winterthur Mus, 62-66; chmn, Smithsonian Art Comn, 63-66; pres, Pa Acad Fine Arts, 68-70. *Awards:* Distinguished Servic Medal, Am Asn Mus; Smithson Medal, Smithsonian Inst; Chevalier Legion of Honor, France. *Mem:* Arch Am Art (dir); Am Philos Soc; Hist Soc Pa (vpres); Nat Portrait Gallery Comn; Am Antiquarian Soc. *Publ:* Auth, The Way of Western Art, 39 & 67; auth, American Romantic Painting, 44; auth, Washington Allston, 48 & 67; auth, Painting in America--the Story of 450 Years, 56 & 65; auth, A Short History of Painting in America, 63. *Mailing Add:* 285 Locust St Philadelphia PA 19106

RICHARDSON, FRANK, JR
MURALIST

b Baltimore, Md, Jan 14, 50. *Study:* Community Col Baltimore, AA; Md Inst Col Art, BFA; Towson State Col; Riverside Art Ctr with Jacob Laurence, Romare Bearden. *Work:* ILE-IFE Mus Afro-American Cult, Philadelphia; ThirdWorld Mus, 111 & Assoc, Baltimore; Merabash Mus, Inc, Willingboro, NJ; Old Slave Mart Mus, Charleston, SC; Nat Ctr Afro-American Artists, Inc, Dorchester, Mass. *Comn:* Mural for film Amazing Grace, 74; mural, Enoch Pratt Free Libr, Baltimore, 74; Black Art (murals), FAN: Baltimore Arts Tower, 74; Amen America, (murals with Berkeley S Thompson), Asn Black Arts/East, Nat Endowment Arts, 75. *Exhib:* First and Second Wide-Regional, Black Art Show, Baltimore; Black Mural Painter, Inst Art Ctr, Lima, Peru, 75; Mural Painter, Univ Pretoria, Repub South Africa, 75. *Collections Arranged:* An Evening With the Links, 74; Awards Extravaganza 74. *Teaching:* Dir graphics, Sinai Druid Camp, Baltimore, 71-72; dir, Mus Prep Sch, 72-; instr printing, Career Opportunities Inc, Baltimore, 71- *Awards:* Best Black Art Work in Show, Black Cult Endowment, 69; Children's Hour Prog, Md Art Coun, 74; Third World Prep Sch, Nat Endowment Arts, 75. *Bibliog:* Averil Jordan-Kadis (auth), Colorful mural, Baltimore Sun, 67; Priscilla Coger (auth), Mr Richardson's beautiful wall, Baltimore Afro-American, 72; James Kelmartin (auth), Museum unit to expand, News American, 75. *Mem:* Asn Black Arts/East. *Media:* Paint. *Mailing Add:* 3024 Westwood Ave Baltimore MD 21216

RICHARDSON, GRETCHEN (MRS RONALD FREELANDER)
SCULPTOR

b Detroit, Mich. *Study:* Wellesley Col, BA; Acad Julian, Paris, France; Art Students League, with William Zorach & Jose de Creeft. *Exhib:* Int Arts Club, London, Eng; Pa Acad Fine Arts, Audubon Artists & Knickerbocker Artists, Lever House, New York; and several one-man shows. *Awards:* Amelia Peabody Prize, 55, Nat Asn Women Artists, & Mary Kellner Mem Prize, 59 & 72; Award, Knickerbocker Artists, 70. *Mem:* Audubon Artists; Nat Asn Women Artists (exec comt, 52-55); Artists Equity Asn New York. *Media:* Stone, Marble. *Mailing Add:* 530 Park Ave New York NY 10021

RICHARDSON, JOHN ADKINS
HISTORIAN, EDUCATOR

b Gillette, Wyo, Oct 24, 29. *Study:* Eastern Wash State Univ, BA, 51; Columbia Univ, New York, MA, 52, EdD, 58. *Teaching:* Asst prof art hist, State Univ NY, 57-58; asst prof art hist, Fresno State Col, Calif, 58-59; prof art hist, Southern Ill Univ, Edwardsville, 59- *Mem:* Col Art Asn; Am Soc Aesthetics. *Res:* Art as intellectual-cultural history in late nineteenth and earlier twentieth centuries. *Publ:* Auth, Modern Art and Scientific Thought, Univ Ill Press, 71; auth, Art: The Way It Is, Abrams/Prentice-Hall, 74, rev ed, 80; contribr, Technology as Institutionally Related to Human Values, Acropolis Books, 74; auth, The Complete Book of Cartooning, Prentice-Hall, 76; auth, Design: Systems, Elements, Applications, Prentice-Hall, 83. *Mailing Add:* 802 W High St Edwardsville IL 62025

RICHARDSON, SAM
SCULPTOR, EDUCATOR

b Oakland, Calif, July 19, 34. *Study:* Calif Col Arts & Crafts, BA, 56 & MFA, 60. *Work:* Dallas Mus Fine Art, Tex; Denver Art Mus; M H De Young Mem Mus, San Francisco; Milwaukee Art Ctr; Nat Mus Am Art, Smithsonian Inst, Washington, DC. *Exhib:* Plastic as Plastic, 63 & Creative Casting, 73, Mus Contemp Crafts, New York; New Media, New Methods, Mus Mod Art, New York, 69; Whitney Mus Am Art, 68-69; Stanford Univ, Calif, 72; Vassar Col, 72; Rutgers Univ, 75; Vpres US Home, Artists Pac Coast States, 80; and others. *Teaching:* Instr art, Oakland City Col, 60-61; art dir, Mus Contemp Crafts, New York, 61-63; asst prof art, San Jose State Univ, 63-66, assoc prof art, 67-72, prof art, 72- *Dealer:* Martha Jackson Gallery 521 W 57th St New York NY 10019; Hansen Fuller Goldeen Gallery 228 Grant Ave San Francisco CA 94108. *Mailing Add:* 4121 Sequoyah Rd Oakland CA 94605

RICHENBURG, ROBERT BARTLETT
PAINTER, SCULPTOR

b Boston, Mass, July 14, 17. *Study:* George Washington Univ; Boston Univ; Corcoran Sch Art; Art Students League; Ozenfant Sch Art; Hans Hofmann Sch Fine Art. *Work:* Chrysler Mus Art; Aldrich Mus Contemp Art, Ridgefield, Conn; Berkeley Mus Art, Univ Calif; Whitney Mus Am Art; Mus Mod Art, New York; and many others. *Exhib:* Dayton Art Inst, 62 & Cornell Univ, Ithaca, New York, 64; Am Fedn Arts Traveling Exhibs, 60-61, 64-65 & 68-69; Mus Mod Art, New York, 61 & 63-64; Whitney Mus Am Art Painting Ann, 61, 64 & 68, Sculpture Ann, 68; Retrospective, Dana Arts Ctr, Colgate Univ, 70 & Ithaca Col Mus Art, 71; plus many other one-man & group shows. *Teaching:* Instr art, Pratt Inst, Cooper Union & NY Univ, formerly; assoc prof art, Cornell Univ, 64-67; assoc prof art & grad adv art dept, Hunter Col, 67-70; prof art, Ithaca Col, 70- *Mem:* Am Asn Univ Prof; Col Art Asn Am; life mem Art Students League. *Mailing Add:* 121 E Remington Rd Ithaca NY 14850

RICHMAN, ROBERT M
ADMINISTRATOR, WRITER

b Connersville, Ind, Dec 22, 14. *Study:* Western Mich Univ, AB(Eng) & AB(hist); Univ Mich, AM. *Collections Arranged:* Arranged over 100 exhibits of recent work by contemporary artists from Europe, Asia and the Americas. *Pos:* Founder & pres, Inst Contemp Arts, Washington, DC, 47, trustee, mem exec comt & bd trustees, 47-; lit & art ed, New Repub Mag, 51-54; mem, President's Arts & Letters Comt, 56-60, chmn, 60-67; mem, Washington Festival, 57-, dir, 58; mem, Am Nat Theatre & Acad, 58-; exec comt, J F Kennedy Ctr, 59-; trustee, Opera Soc Washington, 59-; trustee, Meridian House Found, 60-; trustee, Arena Stage, Washington Drama Soc, 60-; consult arts, Dept State, 61; trustee, Ctr Arts Indian Am, 65- *Teaching:* Instr, Univ Mich, 38-45; prof, Adelphi Col, 45-47; lectr philos art, Nat Gallery Art, Phillips Gallery & Libr Cong. *Awards:* Hopwood Awards, 42-44; Cosmos Club Award, 55; Comdr Brit Empire, 59. *Mem:* Am Asn Mus Dirs; Am Asn Mus; fel Inst Arts & Lett; Col Art Asn Am; Artists Equity Asn; plus others. *Publ:* Publ, The Potter's Portfolio, 50; ed, The Arts at Mid-Century, 54; auth, The Endangered Phoenix, 76; contribr, New Repub & Kenyon Rev; and others. *Mailing Add:* 3102 R St NW Washington DC 20007

RICHMOND, REBEKAH
PRINTMAKER

b Ashland, Ky. *Study:* Ringling Sch Art, 60-61; Univ Ky, Lexington, 61-62; Art Inst Pittsburgh, 62-64. *Work:* Coos Art Mus, Coos Bay, Ore; Albany Inst Hist & Art. *Comn:* Presentation Print, Print Club Albany, 76-77. *Exhib:* Ann Artists Salon, Okla Mus Fine Art, 75 & 77; Montgomery Mus Fine Art Ann, 76; Int Print Competition, Pratt Graphics Ctr, New York, 77; solo exhib, Albany Inst Hist & Art, 77; April Salon, Springville Mus Art, Utah, 77, 78, 80 & 82; Knickerbocker Artists Ann, Nat Arts Club, New York, 78-81; Colorprint USA, Tex Tech Univ, 80; Audubon Artists Ann, Nat Arts Club, New York, 81. *Awards:* Gold Medal Hon, Acad Artists Asn, Mass, 78 & 79; Anna Hyatt Huntington Bronze Medal, Catharine Lorillard Wolfe Art Club, 79; Mrs John Newington Award, Hudson Valley Art Asn Ann, 82. *Mem:* Salmagundi Club; Hudson Valley Art Asn; Catharine Lorillard Wolfe Art Club; Print Club Albany; Acad Artists Asn. *Media:* Etching. *Dealer:* Driscol Gallery 555 17th St Denver CO 80202. *Mailing Add:* Box 878 Estes Park CO 80517

RICH-PERLOW, KATHARINA
DEALER, GALLERY DIRECTOR

b Vienna, Austria, Mar 31, 37; US citizen. *Study:* Hunter Col (art hist), 75-77. *Pos:* Dir, Jack Gallery, New York, formerly; secy in corp, A M Sachs Art Gallery, currently. *Specialty:* Contemporary art, 20th century. *Mailing Add:* A M Sachs Gallery 29 W 57th St New York NY 10019

RICHTER, HANK
PAINTER, SCULPTOR

b Cleveland, Ohio, Oct 10, 28. *Study:* Philadelphia Mus Sch of Art. *Work:* Heard Mus, Phoenix, Ariz; DeGrazia-Gonzales Cult Ctr & Mus, Casa Grande, Ariz; Valley Nat Bank Collection, Phoenix; First Nat Bank Collection, Tucson, Ariz; Read Mullan's Gallery of Western Art, Ariz State Univ. *Comn:* Green Pastures Rayetta (bronze sculpture of Champion Brown Swiss Cow), St John's Dairy, Glendale, Ariz, 77; Ted DeGrazia portrait (ltd edition pewter bas-relief plate) & Tracks Across America (series of six ltd edition pewter bas-relief sculptures), comn by Richard Smith, Century Reproductions, Inc, Wilmington, Mass, 77; three 50 year commemorative belt buckle sculptures, Western Savings & Loan, Phoenix; portrait of George Fullerton--Cowboy Biblical Roots of Man, Don Fullerton, Covina, Calif; gift of an elephant, John F Goodson, Phoenix, Ariz. *Exhib:* Mountain Oyster

Invitational Show, Tucson, 74-79; Charles M Russell Invitational Art Auction, Great Falls, Mont, 76-79; Ann San Dimas Am Indian & Cowboy Artists Soc Show, Calif, 77, 78, 79, 80 & 81; First Fed Savings & Loan Traveling Exhib; Western Gallery, 1st Interstate Bank, Tucson, Az. *Teaching:* Student instr anat, Philadelphia Mus Sch Art, 49-50; instr creative design, Kachina Sch Art, Phoenix, 54-56; sculpture inst, Principia Col, Elsah, Ill; instr pvt classes, currently. *Awards:* Gold Medal, Atlanta Film Festival, 69; Golden Eagle, CINE/USA, 69. *Bibliog:* The West & Walter Bimson, Univ Ariz Press, 72; Pat Broder (auth), Bronzes of the American West, Abrams, 75; Lil Rhodes (auth), A man and his art, Southwest Art, 78. *Mem:* Am Indian & Cowboy Artists Soc; Art Group 12, Payson, Ariz. *Media:* Bronze, Pewter; Oil, Acrylic. *Dealer:* Linda Robinson Silver-Son West Inc PO Box 647 Sedona AZ 86336; Lynn Lesvki House of Bronze Art Gallery 107 S Cortez Prescott AZ. *Mailing Add:* 219 W Montebello Phoenix AZ 85013

RICKEY, GEORGE W
SCULPTOR
b South Bend, Ind, June 6, 07. *Study:* Trinity Col, Scotland; Balliol Col, Oxford Univ, BA, 29, MA, 41; Ruskin Sch Drawing, Oxford Univ; Acad Andre L'Hote & Acad Mod, Paris; Inst Fine Arts, NY Univ; State Univ Iowa, 47; Inst Design, Chicago, 48-49; Six honorary degrees. *Work:* Albright-Knox Art Gallery, Buffalo, NY; Joseph H Hirshhorn Mus & Sculpture Garden, Washington, DC; Mus Boymans-van Beuningen, Rotterdam, Neth; Mus Mod Art, New York; Neue Nationalgalerie, Berlin, Ger. *Comn:* Kinetic sculpture, Rijksmuseum Kroller-Muller, Otterlo, Neth, 65, Nordpark, Dusseldorf, Ger, 65 & Nat Collection Fine Arts, Washington, DC, 67; Ft Worth City Hall, Tex, 74; Prince Jonah Kalanianaole Bldg, Honolulu, Hawaii, 75; and others. *Exhib:* Guggenheim Mus, 67 & 79; Albright-Knox Art Gallery, 68; St del Mus, Frankfurt, Ger, 77; Amerika Haus, Berlin, 79; Musee d'Art Contemp, Montreal, 81; Scottish Sculpture Trust, Glasgos, 82; Yorkshire Sculpture Park, Eng, 82; Tulane Univ, 83; and others. *Awards:* Nat Fine Arts Honor Award, Am Inst Architects, 72; Brandeis Univ Creative Arts Award, 79. *Bibliog:* Engineer of movement, Time Mag, 11/4/66; Peter Riedl (auth), George Rickey: kinetische objekte, Philipp Reclam J, Stuttgart, 70; Nan Rosenthal (auth), George Rickey, Abrams, New York, 77. *Mem:* Century Asn; Nat Inst Arts & Lett. *Media:* Stainless Steel. *Publ:* Auth, Constructivism: Origins & Evolution, Braziller, 67. *Mailing Add:* Rd 2 Box 235 East Chatham NY 12060

RIDDLE, JOHN THOMAS, JR
PRINTMAKER, SCULPTOR
b Los Angeles, Calif, Mar 18, 33. *Study:* Los Angeles City Col, AA, 60; Los Angeles State Col, BA, 66; Calif State Univ, MA, 73. *Work:* High Mus Art, Atlanta, Ga; Golden State Mutual Life Inst Co, Calif State Univ, Los Angeles; Oakland Mus, Calif; Albany Mus Art, Ga. *Comn:* Murals, Bank of Am (2 br), Los Angeles, 70; The Operation (welded steel), Los Angeles Co Mental Health Clinic, 72; relig murals, Shrine of Black Madonna, Atlanta, 74; Expelled Because of Their Color (bronze), State of Ga, Atlanta, 77; Spirit Bench 1, City of Atlanta, 78. *Exhib:* Black Artists, Oakland Mus, Calif, 73; Calif Artists, Calif State Univ, Sacramento, 74; Artists in Ga, High Mus Art, Atlanta, 75-80; Calif Artists, the Black Experience, State Capitol, Sacramento, Calif, 76; Black Artists S, Huntsville Mus Art, Ala, 78; 8th Ann Art Festival, Martinique, WI, Port de France, 79. *Pos:* Dir, Neighborhood Arts Ctr, Inc, Atlanta, 75-81. *Teaching:* Instr ceramics & sculpture, Pub Schs, Los Angeles & Beverly Hills, Calif, 66-73; asst prof painting, Spelman Col, Atlanta, 79-80. *Awards:* Emmy Award, TV Acad Arts & Sci, 71; Ga Gov Award Visual Art, 81. *Bibliog:* Lewis Productions, Three artists, Lewis, Riddle, Pajaud, 68; Larry Stuart (auth), Renaissance in black, KNBC, 10/71; Lewis & Waddy (coauth), Black Artists on Art, 2 vols, Contemp Crafts, 72. *Mem:* Black Artists Atlanta; Ga Coun for Arts; Gov Artist-in-Schs. *Publ:* Contribr, Prints by American Negro Artists, Cult Exchange Ctr, 67; contribr, Black Artists on Art, 2 vols, Contemp Crafts, 71; contribr, Art: African American, Harcourt-Brace, 78. *Dealer:* Art International PO Box 511 Atlanta GA 30361. *Mailing Add:* c/o Neighborhood Art Ctr 252 Georgia Ave SW Atlanta GA 30337

RIDGWAY, PEGGI
WRITER
b Hampton, Va, Feb 5, 42. *Study:* Philbrook Art Ctr, Tulsa; Tulsa Jr Col; Moody Inst, dipl, 64. *Res:* Fine artists and exhibitions. *Publ:* Auth, The legacy of Asa L Powell, Southwest Art, 79; auth, Philbrook--in the national spotlight once again, Tulsa Mag, 81; auth, Archie Blackowl, Art Voices, 81; auth, Ray Vinella--a milieu of love, life and art, Art Gallery, 83; auth, Bill Harrison--sensual freedom, Southwest Art, 83; over forty articles in national and regional publications. *Mailing Add:* PO Box 2911 Tulsa OK 74101

RIDLEY, GREGORY D, JR
PAINTER, SCULPTOR
b Smyrna, Tenn, July 18, 25. *Study:* Fisk Univ, with Aaron Douglas, 45-49; Tenn State Univ, with Frances Thompson, BS, 51; Univ Louisville, Ky, with Ulfret Wilke, Justus Bier, Creighton Gilbert & Walter Creese, 54-55. *Work:* Fisk Univ; Univ Louisville; Grambling Col; Mt Zion Baptist Church, Smyrna, Tenn; African-Am Mus, Nashville; and others. *Comn:* Directed mural, Harlem Hosp Ctr, 70; St Jaquims, Queens, NY, 71; McDonald's Restaurant, Harlem, 73-74; Carver Savings Bank, New York, 74. *Exhib:* Fisk Univ Traveling Shows, throughout US, 51-; South Cent Show, Nashville, Tenn, 67-71; Two Centuries Black American Art Traveling Exhib, Brooklyn Mus, 71-75; Amstad II, 75. *Pos:* Cult coordr, Harlem Backstreet Youth Inc, 67; consult, African-Am Mus, Nashville, 83. *Teaching:* Asst prof art, Ala State Col, 51-58; Grambling Col, 58-62; Elizabeth City State, 62-64 & Tenn State Univ, 66-71 & 75-78; adj prof, Brooklyn Col, summers 66-75, Lehman Col,

summers 71-74 & Medgar Evers Col, summers 71-75; asst prof, Fisk Univ, 66-71, assoc prof, 81- *Awards:* Six Prizes, Atlanta Univ Ann, 51-65; Battle of Gettysburg First Prize Gold Medal, Am Soc Vet, 65; Teacher of Year, Tenn State Univ, 78. *Bibliog:* Cedric Dover (auth), American Negro Art, 61; Ralph Hudson (auth), Black Artist South, 79. *Mem:* Nat Conf Artist (vchmn, 62); Am Asn Univ Prof; Nat Educ Asn. *Media:* Stone, Metal. *Res:* Great battles of the Civil War. *Collection:* African masks, textiles & prints. *Publ:* Contribr, Great Negroes Past and Present, 65 & Decision for Destiny, 74; auth, Two Centuries of Black American Art, Driskell, 77. *Mailing Add:* 1106 28th Ave N Nashville TN 37208

RIDLON, JAMES A
SCULPTOR, FILMMAKER
b Nyack, NY, July 11, 34. *Study:* Syracuse Univ, BA, 57, MFA, 65; San Francisco State Col, 58-59. *Work:* Munson-Williams-Proctor Inst, Utica, NY; Julliard Sch, New York; Rochester Mem Gallery, NY; Everson Mus, Syracuse, NY; New York Univ; and others. *Comn:* Sculptured mural, C & U Broadcasting, 58; Bert Bell Mem Trophy, Long Island Athletic Club, 68. *Exhib:* New Paintings, Everson Mus Art, 74; one-man retrospective, Logan Alexander Ctr Creative Arts, Concord Col, 75; Lubin House Gallery, New York, 77; Herbert F Johnson Mus, Cornell Univ, Ithaca, NY, 77; Two Rivers Gallery, Binghamton, NY, 77; Alan Brown Gallery, Hartsdale, NY, 81; and others. *Pos:* Dir, NY State Summer Sch Arts Sch of Visual Arts. *Teaching:* Assoc prof sculpture & studio arts, 68-74, Syracuse Univ, prof sculpture & synaesthetic educ, 74-81, prof CORE dept, 82- *Awards:* Purchase Prize, 32nd Ann Exhib, Munson-Williams-Proctor Inst, 68; First Prize in Sculpture, 10th Ann Westchester Art Soc Exhib, 70; First Prize Sculpture, NY State Fair, 80; and others. *Publ:* Contribr, Synaesthetic Education, Syracuse Univ, 71; auth, Synaesthetic education as a basis for symbolic expression, Humanities J, 5/73; co-producer & dir, Icons and Eclecticism (film), Syracuse Univ, 81; producer & dir, Artist-Athlete (film), Syracuse Univ, 82; co-producer & dir, The Wonder of Friction (film), Syracuse Univ, 83. *Dealer:* Oxford Gallery 267 Oxford Rochester NY 14607; Alan Brown Gallery 60 E Hartsdale Ave Hartsdale NY 10530. *Mailing Add:* Fire House 20 401 Elliott St Syracuse NY 13204

RIEGEL, MICHAEL BYRON
METALSMITH
b Hannibal, Mo, Nov 21, 46. *Study:* Eastern Ill Univ, Charleston, BSEd, 68, MA, 72; Southern Ill Univ, Carbondale, with Brent Kington, MFA, 74. *Work:* Ark Art Ctr, Little Rock; Ill State Mus, Springfield. *Exhib:* Biennial Lake Superior Nat Craft Exhib, Tweed Mus Art, Univ Minn, Duluth, 72; 7th Biennial Beaux Arts Designer Craftsmen Exhib, Columbus Gallery Fine Arts, Ohio, 73; Miss River Craft Exhib, Brooks Mem Art Gallery, Memphis, Tenn, 73 & 75; Baroque 74, Forms in Metal, 75 & Homage to the Bag, 75, Mus Contemp Crafts, New York; Craft Multiples, Renwick Gallery, Smithsonian Inst, Washington, DC, 75; Goldsmiths, Phoenix Art Mus, Ariz, 77. *Teaching:* Instr design & 2-D design, Southeast Mo State Univ, Cape Girardeau, 75 & instr metalsmithing, 76; instr art metals & drawing, Calif State Univ, Sacramento, 76-81, asst prof art, 81-82, assoc prof, currently. *Awards:* Exhib Award, Goldsmiths, Renwick Gallery, 74; Design in Steel Award Prog, 74-75; Steel Indust, 75 & Miss River Craft Show, Brooks Mem Art Gallery, 76. *Mem:* Artists Blacksmiths Asn of NAm; Calif Blacksmiths Asn. *Media:* Steel. *Mailing Add:* 1066 Alamos Ave Sacramento CA 95815

RIES, MARTIN
PAINTER, CRITIC
b Washington, DC, Dec 26, 26. *Study:* Corcoran Gallery Art, 40-44; Am Univ, with Jack Tworkov & Leo Steppat, BA, 50; Hunter Col, MA, 68, with Leo Steinberg, William Rubin, Ad Reinhardt & E C Goossen. *Work:* Pace Univ Mus; Riverside Mus Collection, Rose Art Mus, Brandeis Univ; Inst Cult Hisp, Madrid, Spain. *Exhib:* Corcoran Gallery Art, 52; Inst Cult Hisp, Univ Madrid, 55; Mus Mod Art, 56; Paul Gallery, Tokyo, Japan, 68; Verfeil, France, 73; and others. *Pos:* Asst prof pub rels, Nat Cong Comt, 51; asst dir, Hudson River Mus, Yonkers, NY, 57-67; adv, Westchester Cult Ctr, 65-67; contrib ed, Arts Mag; art ed, Greenwich Village News. *Teaching:* Instr medieval art hist, Marymount Col, 59; instr mod art hist, Hunter Col, 63-67; prof hist art, drawing & painting, Long Island Univ, 68. *Awards:* Honorable Mention, 52nd Nat Soc Arts & Lett Award, Corcoran Gallery Art; Critics Choice, Whyte Gallery, 57. *Mem:* Asn Int des Antiques d'Art, Am Sect. *Res:* Minotaur in Western art, from ancient Greek myth to contemporary art. *Publ:* Auth, Elusive Goya, New Repub, 57; auth, monthly articles, Hudson River Mus Bull, 57-67; auth, Endowments for great society, Art Voices Mag, 65 & New Art: Anthology, 66; Picasso and the myth of the Minotaur, Art J, winter 72-73, portion reprinted in: Picasso in Perspective, Prentice Hall, 75. *Dealer:* Aaron Berman Gallery 50 W 57th New York NY 10019. *Mailing Add:* 36 Livingston Rd Scarsdale NY 10583

RIESS, LORE
PAINTER, PRINTMAKER
b Berlin, Ger; US citizen. *Study:* Art Acad, Contempora (Bauhaus Sch), Berlin; Sumi Drawing & Calligraphy, Tokyo; Art Students League. *Work:* Corcoran Gallery Art, Washington, DC; Tel Aviv Mus & Israel Mus, Jerusalem; US Embassy, Japan & Korea; pvt collections in US, Japan, Belg, Eng & Israel; and others. *Comn:* Ed of etchings, Mickelson Gallery, Washington, DC, 71. *Exhib:* One-man shows, Old Jaffa Gallery, Israel, 70, 73, 75 & 79, Nora Art Gallery, Jerusalem, 71, 74 & 82, Jeanne Frank Gallery, New York, 78 & Park Village West, London, 79 & 80; Linden Galleries, New York, 81; and others. *Awards:* William McNulty Merit Award, Art Students League, 64; M J Kaplan Prize, Nat Asn Women Artists, 69; Gallery of Graphic Art Award, Int Miniature Print Exhib, 71. *Bibliog:* T Ichinose (auth), Colorful abstract oils by Lore Riess, Mainichi Daily News, 65; articles in Jerusalem Post, 7/70 & 3/71. *Media:* Oil. *Dealer:* Alonzo Gallery 30 W 57th St New York NY 10019. *Mailing Add:* 1200 Broadway New York NY 10001

RIFKIND, ROBERT GORE
COLLECTOR
b Beverly Hills, Calif, July 12, 28. *Study:* Univ Calif, Los Angeles, AB, 50; Harvard Univ, LLB, 54. *Collection:* Largest private collection of German Expressionist graphic arts in US; more than 6,000 graphics and 3,500 volumes. *Publ:* Contribr, German Expressionist Woodcuts, de Saisset Art Gallery & Mus, Santa Clara, 80; contribr, The Human Image in German Expressionist Graphic Art, Berkeley Univ Art Mus, 81; contribr, An Alle Künstler: War-Revolution-Weimar, San Diego State Univ Art Gallery, 83. *Mailing Add:* Robert Gore Rifkind Found Suite 704 9454 Wilshire Blvd Beverly Hills CA 90212

RIGBY, IDA KATHERINE
CRITIC, HISTORIAN
b Los Angeles, Calif, May 10, 44. *Study:* Stanford Univ, BA, MA; Ecole des Beaux Arts, Tours, France; Univ Calif, Berkeley, MA, PhD(art hist), 74. *Teaching:* Asst prof mod art hist, Univ Montana, Missoula, spring 1972; instr, Newcomb Col, Tulane Univ, New Orleans, 72-74; asst prof, Univ Victoria, BC, 74-76; assoc prof mod & contemp art, San Diego State Univ, 76- *Awards:* Kress Found Grant; Grant, Deutscher Akademischer Austauschdienst, Bonn. *Mem:* Col Art Asn; Art Historians of Southern Calif. *Res:* German Expressionism; German Expressionist artists and politics; politics of opposition and official collaboration in Germany during the 1930's; art criticism. *Publ:* Auth, Karl Hofer, Garland Publ, 76; auth, The Expressionist Artist and Revolution, 1918-1922 & Entartete Kunst, 1933-1938, In: German Expressionist Art: The Robert Gore Rifkind Collection, Univ Calif, Los Angeles Press, 77; auth, Franz Marc's wartime letters from the front, In: Franz Marc: 1880-1916, Univ Calif Berkeley, 79; auth, Wichner Collection, Long Beach Mus Art, 81; auth, An Alle Kunstler! War Revolution Weimar: German Expressionist Prints, Drawings, Posters and Periodicals from The Robert Gore Rifkind Found, San Diego State Univ Press, 83. *Mailing Add:* Dept of Art San Diego State Univ San Diego CA 92182

RIGG, MARGARET RUTH
ASSEMBLAGE ARTIST, CALLIGRAPHER
b Pittsburgh, Pa, Dec 14, 29. *Study:* Carnegie-Mellon Univ, 45-50; Fla State Univ, BA, 51; Scarrett Col; Presby Sch, MA, 55; George Peabody Col; Chicago Art Inst, 63; painting with Edmund Lewandowski & Florence Kawa; design & theory with Mathias Goeritz; Chinese calligraphy with Tsutomu Yoshida, Kim Kee-Sung, Kim Hahn & Tennyson Chang; Am calligraphy with Corita Kent & Jan Steward. *Work:* Tenn Collection, Smithsonian Inst; Yamada Gallery, Kyoto, Japan; Turku Univ Mus, Finland; NH Mus, Manchester; Korea Fulbright House, Seoul. *Comn:* Stained glass windows, Mexico City Nat Cathedral, 61; stained glass window, communion table, lectern & celtic cross, Univ NC, Chapel Hill, 62; calligraphy mural, Experiment House, Vere, Jamaica; calligraphy letterhead & gates to campus, Eckerd Col, 72. *Exhib:* Man's Disorder, God's Design, Univ Ill, 52 & Krannert Art Mus, Univ Nebr-Lincoln, 61; Am Artists, Am Cult Ctr, Seoul, 73; Bicentennial Art, Mus Fine Arts, St Petersburg, Fla, 75-76; Ringling Mus Art Arch, Sarasota, Fla; Womanspirit Ann Exhib, 79-; over 70 solo shows. *Pos:* Art dir, Bd Publ, Fla State Univ, 51-53; owner & publ, Possum Press. *Teaching:* Artist in residence, Fla Presby Col, 65-67; assoc prof visual art, Eckerd Col, 67-; dir, Elliot Teaching Gallery, Eckerd Col, 81-83. *Awards:* Fulbright-Hays Sr Res Grant in Chinese Calligraphy, Korea, 72. *Bibliog:* Meinke (auth), Very Seldom Animals, 69 & 77, Barbara Chaulk (auth), Poems & Why, 75 & Amos Wilder (auth), Imagining the Real, 78, Possum Press. *Mem:* Int Soc Women Calligraphers; Soc Italic Handwriting; Nashville Artist Guild (pres, 63-64); Fla Artist Group, Inc; St Petersburg Soc Scribes (pres, 78-81). *Media:* Quill & Ink, Brush & Chinese Ink. *Dealer:* Carol Ridge St Petersburg FL 33712. *Mailing Add:* 2960 58th Ave S St Petersburg FL 33712

RIGGS, MARY KATHRYN
DEALER, COLLECTOR
b Bakersfield, Calif, Dec 22, 35. *Study:* Calif State Univ, Fresno; New Sch, New York, 77; pvt study in Paris, 72 & 82, London, 83 & Rome, 83. *Collections Arranged:* Mayo Clinic, Rochester, Minn; Santa Fe Savings & Loan; Bank Am Southern Region; Sheraton Hotels; Hope Consult Group, San Diego; Girard Capital Group; Sun Savings & Loan Asn. *Pos:* Dir, Riggs Galleries, Des Moines, Iowa, 74-78, San Diego, 78- & Los Angeles, 83- *Teaching:* Lectr art collecting, La Jolla Newcomers Asn, Soroptimists Int, San Diego Women in Business, Artists Equity & San Diego Mus Art. *Awards:* Combined Arts Coun Award, San Diego, 80 & 81; San Diego CofC Two Percent, 83. *Bibliog:* Articles, Calif Bus J, 83, San Diego Home & Garden Mag, 83 & Calif Arts Rev, 83. *Mem:* Art Dealers Asn Southern Calif. *Specialty:* Contemporary painters, photographers, printmakers, sculptors; traditional and modern. *Collection:* Fin-de-siecle French and American painting; contemporary American, French and Italian painting. *Mailing Add:* 2550 Fifth Ave Suite 167 San Diego CA 92103

RIGSBY, JOHN DAVID
PAINTER
b Tallassee, Ala, Oct 10, 34. *Study:* Univ Ala, BFA & MS; Southern Conn State Col; Columbia Univ, with Leon Goldin. *Work:* Telfair Acad Arts & Sci, Savannah, Ga; Univ Ala Gallery Collection; Beaufort Mus, SC; US Embassy, Tunis, Tunisia; Brit Coun, Tunis. *Comn:* Sculpture, Mobil Art Ctr, Ala, 63. *Exhib:* Am Artists Tunisia, US Info Serv, 66; Guild SC Artists Ann, 71; Springs Mills, 73; two-man show, Sch Art & Archit, Yale Univ, 73 & Alabama Bag, Washington, DC, 75; plus others. *Teaching:* Nat Endowment Arts artist in residence, Beaufort Pub Sch Syst, SC, 70-73. *Awards:* Merit Award, Artists of Southeast & Tex, Delgado Mus, 63; Merit Award, Guild SC Artists Exhib, 71; Springs Mills Traveling Exhib Award, 72. *Bibliog:* Al Wardi (auth), Dans

le tournoi de l'art avec John David Rigsby, L'Action, 2/29/67; Gaynor Pearson (auth), The one room school now has wheels, Conn Educ, 2/68; Oliver & Sisk (auth), Artist in residence--a fist for South Carolina, SC Educ J, winter 71. *Mem:* Guild SC Artists; Nat Art Educ Asn; Col Art Asn Am; Nat Soc Lit & Arts. *Media:* Oil, Acrylic. *Mailing Add:* c/o 641 Gallery 641 Indiana Ave Washington DC 20004

RILEY, ART (ARTHUR IRWIN)
PAINTER, CARTOONIST
b Boston, Mass, Sept 14, 11. *Study:* Art Ctr Sch Los Angeles. *Exhib:* Am Watercolor Soc, New York; Calif Watercolor Soc, Los Angeles Co Mus Art; Springfield Art Mus, Mo; Youngstown Art Mus, Ohio; one-man show, Pacific Grove Art Mus, Calif. *Pos:* Artist, MGM Studios, 5 yrs; artist, Walt Disney Studios, 37-65. *Awards:* Am Watercolor Soc Award; Laguna Beach Art Asn Award; Butler Inst Am Art Award; plus others. *Mem:* Acad Motion Picture Arts & Sci; Am Watercolor Soc. *Publ:* Auth & illusr, article in Am Artist Mag; contribr, Sat Eve Post, Ariz Hwys, Ford Times, Life Mag & others. *Dealer:* Pebble Beach California Gallery Pebble Beach CA 93953; The Palette Carmel CA 93921. *Mailing Add:* 608 N First St Burbank CA 91502

RILEY, BARBRA BAYNE
PHOTOGRAPHER, EDUCATOR
b Brooklyn, NY, Dec 20, 49. *Study:* Sch Visual Arts, New York, cert(fine arts), 70; Calif State Univ, Sacramento, BA, 72, MA, 74. *Work:* Erie Art Ctr, Pa; Corpus Christi State Univ, Tex; Laguna Beach Mus Art; Chase Manhattan Bank, New York. *Comn:* Photographers Portray the Family, Women & Their Work, Nat Endowment Arts, Austin, Tex, 81; 24 photographs, Corpus Christi Nat Bank, 81. *Exhib:* Artworks & Bookworks, Los Angeles Inst Contemp Art, Calif, 78; one-woman shows, Art Mus STex, Corpus Christi, 79 & Amarillo Art Ctr, Tex, 81; Friends of the Gallery, Daniel Wolf Gallery, New York, 80; Sacramento State Early 1970's, Laguna Beach Mus Art, Calif, 82. *Collections Arranged:* Return to Beyond the Valley of Photography, Weil Gallery, Corpus Christi State Univ, 81. *Teaching:* Asst prof photog & design, Corpus Christi State Univ, Tex, 82- *Bibliog:* Michael Spies (auth), Color it different..., Corpus Christi Caller Times, 11/6/81; Ellen Wallenstein (auth), Ties that bind, Artweek, 12/81; Suzanne Winkler (auth), Where's the family, Tex Monthly, 1/82. *Mem:* Visual Studies Workshop; Col Art Asn. *Media:* Silver Prints & Non-Silver Processes. *Dealer:* Susan Spiritus Gallery 3336 Via Lido Newport Beach CA; Holly Solomon Editions 724 Fifth Ave New York NY. *Mailing Add:* 4222 Cott St Corpus Christi TX 78411

RILEY, BERNARD JOSEPH
PAINTER
b Bridgeport, Conn, Mar 27, 15. *Study:* Self-taught; study with Nelson Gordy & James Dougherty. *Work:* Metrop Mus Art, New York; Mus Art, Sci & Industry, Bridgeport, Conn; Corcoran Gallery Art; Municipal Court Bldg, Washington, DC; Sacred Heart Univ, Bridgeport, Conn. *Comn:* Life of St Aloysius Gonzaga, Fairfield Univ, 59; processional (gold leaf), comn by Dr Harold Wesley, Stamford, Conn, 70; History of Bridgeport, Conn Comn Arts, Bridgeport Pub Libr, 76; Medici, St Vincents Med Ctr, 77. *Exhib:* Pa Acad Fine Arts, 46, 52 & 58; New England Regional Silvermine Artists, New Cannan, 51-56; Silvermine Guild Artists, 55-75; Nat Acad Design Ann, New York, 56, 67 & 68; Detroit Inst Fine Art, 58; Fairfield Library, 68; New York Hilton Gallery, 68; NC Mus Art, 68; Am Acad Arts & Lett, New York, 75; Housatonic Community Col, 76. *Awards:* Americana, Silvermine Regional, 53; Three Carl J Blenner Awards, New Haven Paint & Clay, Blenner Foundation; Artist of the Year, Chamber Commerce, Fairfield, Conn, 80. *Bibliog:* Story of the History of the Bridgeport Mural, Burroughs Libr, 76. *Mem:* Silvermine Guild Artists (bd of trustees, 58-); Conn Acad of Fine Art; Paint & Clay Club; Third Stream Art Asn. *Media:* Oil, Acrylic. *Dealer:* Silvermine Guild of Artist 1037 Silvermine Rd New Cannan CT 06840. *Mailing Add:* 295 Figlar Ave Fairfield CT 06430

RILEY-LAND, SARAH (SARAH AGNES RILEY LAND)
PAINTER, EDUCATOR
b Richmond, Va, July 1, 47. *Study:* Tyler Sch Art, Rome, 67; Va Commonwealth Univ, BFA, 69; Univ Mo, Columbia, MA, 77, MFA, 82. *Exhib:* Albrecht Art Mus, 79; Fifth Nat Watercolor Exhib, Springfield Art Asn, Ill, 81; Va Prints & Drawings, Va Mus Fine Arts, 81; Terrance Gallery Nat Show, Palenville, NY, 82; Va Mus Fine Arts Next Show, 83; Watercolor USA, Springfield Art Mus, Mo, 83; 11th Nat Exhib, Second St Gallery, Charlottesville, Va, 83; one-woman show, Northwest Mo State Univ, 84. *Teaching:* Instr drawing & painting, Stephens Col, 82- *Mem:* Col Art Asn; Mid-Am Col Art Asn. *Media:* Pencil, Paint. *Dealer:* Reynolds-Minor Gallery Richmond VA. *Mailing Add:* 101 N Glenwood Columbia MO 65201

RINEHART, MICHAEL
LIBRARIAN, EDITOR
b Miami, Fla, Dec 27, 34. *Study:* Harvard Univ, BA, 56; Courtauld Inst, Univ London, 57-59. *Pos:* Librn, Clark Art Inst, Williamstown; ed-in-chief, RILA Int Repertory Lit art. *Teaching:* Lectr Italian Renaissance art, Williams Col, Williamstown, Mass, 67- *Mem:* Col Art Asn; ARLIS/NA. *Publ:* Ed, B Berenson, Italian Pictures of the Renaissance, Florentine School, London, 63; auth, A Drawing by Vasari for the Studiolo of Francesco I, Burlington Mag, 64; auth, Practical Support on an International Basis for the Bibliography of Art History, CNRS, Paris, 69; auth, A Document for the Studiolo of Francesco I in Art the Ape of Nature, Abrams, 81; auth, Art databases and art bibliographies: A survey, Art Librs J, 82; and others. *Mailing Add:* c/o Clark Art Inst Williamstown MA 01267

RING, EDWARD A
PUBLISHER, COLLECTOR
b New York, NY. *Collections Arranged:* Focus on Light, NJ State Mus, Trenton, 67. *Pos:* Owner, Carter Gallery, formerly; mem, NJ State Coun Arts, 67-78, chmn, 71-76; partner, Artnews, currently. *Mem:* Metrop Mus Art. *Mailing Add:* 45 Hodge Rd Princeton NJ 08540

RINGGOLD, FAITH
PAINTER, SCULPTOR
b New York, NY, Oct 8, 34. *Study:* City Col New York, BS, 55, MA, 59; with Robert Gwathney. *Work:* Chase Manhattan Bank, New York; Childrens Mus, Brooklyn; Philip Morris Collection, New York. *Comn:* For the Womens House (mural), Women House Detention, Rikers Island, NY, 71. *Exhib:* Memorial for Martin Luther King, Mus Mod Art, New York, 68; Women Choose Women, New York Cult Ctr, 73; retrospectives, Rutgers Univ Art Gallery, 73 & Studio Mus Harlem, New York, 84; Jubilee, Boston Mus, 75; Second World Black & African Festival Arts & Cult, Lagos, Nigeria, 77; one-person show, Douglass Col, Rutgers Univ, 78; and others. *Teaching:* Univ Calif, San Diego, 84. *Awards:* Creative Artists Pub Serv Prog Grant, 71; Am Asn Univ Women Artists Fel, 76; Nat Endowment Arts Grant, 78-79. *Bibliog:* Lucy Lippard (auth), From the Center, 76; Eleanore Munro (auth), The Originals: American Women Artists, Simon & Schuster, 79. *Media:* Mixed. *Publ:* Contribr, Confirmation: An Anthology of African American Women Writers, William Morrow, 83. *Mailing Add:* 345 W 145th St New York NY 10031

RINGNESS, CHARLES OBERT
EDUCATOR, PRINTMAKER
b May 2, 46; US citizen. *Study:* St Cloud State Univ, BS, 68; Univ NMex, 70; Tamarind Lithography Workshop, Los Angeles, Master Printer(Ford Fel Grant), 70; Univ Cincinnati, MFA, 83. *Work:* Mus Mod Art, New York; Los Angeles Co Mus Art, Calif; Amon Carter Mus Western Art, Ft Worth, Tex; Canada Coun Art Bank, Ottawa; Pasadena Art Mus, Calif. *Exhib:* One-man shows, Gallery Moos, Toronto, 81 & 83, Phyllis Needlman Gallery, Chicago, 83, Univ Cincinnati Art Gallery, 73; Canadian Biennial, Winnipeg Art Gallery, Man, 81; Condesso/Lawler Gallery, New York, 83. *Teaching:* Asst prof, Univ SFla, 70-76, graphics studio mgr, 71-76; assoc prof, Univ Sask, 76- *Awards:* Prizes for prints & drawing, Art Gallery Brant Inc, Brantford, Ont, 80 & 81; Kathleen Fenwick Award, Edmonton Art Gallery, 80. *Bibliog:* Marshall Webb (auth), article, Arts West, 11-12/79; Carol Phillips (auth), article, Artscanada, 4/80; Charlie Crane (auth), Anti-multiple printmaker, Artmagazine, 5-6/80. *Mem:* Col Arts Asn, New York; Print & Drawing Coun Canada. *Media:* Mixed. *Dealer:* Gallery Moos 136 Yorkville Ave Toronto ON Canada M5R 1C2; Van Straaten Gallery 361 W Superior St Chicago IL 60611. *Mailing Add:* 126 Meglund Pl Saskatoon SK S7H 4Z7

RIPPEL, M (MORRIS CONRAD)
PAINTER
b Albuquerque, NMex, Jan 23, 30. *Study:* Univ NMex, BS(Archit Eng), 58. *Work:* NMex Dept Development, Santa Fe; West Texas Mus, Lubbock; Denver Art Mus, Colo; Valley National Bank, Phoenix. *Exhib:* Retrospective, Haley Libr, Tex, 79; Nat Acad Western Art, Nat Cowboy Hall Fame, Okla, 75-81; Artists of Am Exhib, Colo Heritage Ctr, Denver, 81; Western Heritage, Houston, Tex, 81. *Pos:* Design architect, Chambers & Campbell Architects, 64-67. *Awards:* Prix de West, Nat Cowboy Hall Fame, 79; Gold Medal Watercolor, Nat Cowboy Hall Fame, 78 & 79. *Bibliog:* Susan E Meyer (auth), The watercolor page, Am Artist, 72; Mary Carroll Nelson (auth), A serious realist, Southwest Art, 80; Jean Jordan (auth), From blueprints to egg tempera, NMex Mag, 81. *Mem:* Nat Acad Western Art. *Media:* Egg Tempera; Drybrush Watercolor. *Dealer:* Settler's West Galleries 6420 North Campbell Ave Tucson AZ 85718. *Mailing Add:* 1317 Florida St NE Albuquerque NM 87110

RIPPEY, CLAYTON
PAINTER, MURALIST
b La Grande, Ore, Apr 24, 23. *Study:* Northwestern Univ; Stanford Univ, with Daniel Mendelowitz, Ray Faulkner & Aaron Refrigier, BA & MA; San Jose State Col, with George Post; Inst Allende, Mex, with James Pinto & Fred Samuelson. *Work:* Cunningham Mus, Bakersfield, Calif; Dance Mag Hq, New York; Wakayama Castle, Japan; Missions of Calif, Mexicali, Bakersfield, Calif; World of Legends, Los Altos, Calif. *Comn:* Pylon design & mural, Bakersfield Col, Calif, 58; two murals, Valley Plaza Mall, Bakersfield, 67; three-dimensional mural, Tenneco Corp Hq, Bakersfield, 69; mural, Bakersfield Californian Publ Hq, 75; mural, Nat Martinize Corp, 77; and others. *Exhib:* Lucian Labaudt Gallery, San Francisco, 55; Cunningham Mem Mus, Bakersfield, 58, 61 & 66; Circulo de Belles Artes, Palma, Spain, 60; Pioneer & Haggen Mus, Stockton, Calif, 64; Port Townsend Art Ctr, Wash, 65; and over 70 one-man shows. *Bibliog:* Clayton Rippey, Ora Press, Athens, Greece. *Media:* Acrylics; Ceramics. *Dealer:* Cezanne Gallery Int PO Box 2354 Bakersfield CA 93303. *Mailing Add:* Buckhorn Studio PO Box 581 Eastsound WA 98245

RIPPON, RUTH MARGARET
CERAMIST, EDUCATOR
b Sacramento, Calif, Jan 12, 27. *Study:* Calif Col Arts & Crafts, with Antonio Prieto, BA, 47, MFA, 51; San Francisco Sch Fine Arts, with Joan J Pearson, scholar. *Work:* Crocker Art Mus, Sacramento; Vice President's House, Washington, DC; Bemidji State Univ; Calif Expos & Fair, Sacramento; Memorial Gallery Rochester; and many pvt collections. *Comn:* Relief tile garden wall, comn by Ralph Jones, landscape archit, Piedmont, Calif, 57; relief tile garden wall, comn by Grant Duggins for Calif Expos, 58; Nativity Creche, Crocker Art Mus, Sacramento, 72; carved discs, comn by Mr & Mrs Robert Powell, 80; large clay sculpture, comn by Dr & Mrs Malcolm McHenry, 83. *Exhib:* one-person shows, Artists Contemp Gallery, Sacramento, 67, 69, 72, 74, 77 & 79, Univ Pac, Stockton, Calif, 76 & Univ Rochester, NY, 76; 20-Yr Retrospective, Crocker Art Mus, Sacramento, 71; Oakland Mus, 74; Crocker Kingsley Retrospective, Sacramento, 75; Drawing Show, Sacramento City Col, 78; Col Holy Names, 82. *Teaching:* Crafts dir, Presidio of San Francisco, 54-56; prof ceramics, Calif State Univ, Sacramento, 56- *Awards:* Many Purchase Awards, Calif State Fair & Expos, Sacramento, 48-66; Presidents Wives Series, San Francisco Potters Asn, DeYoung Mus, 69-70. *Bibliog:* Oppi Untracht (auth), Ruth Rippon, Sgraffito Through Glaze, 57 & Fred Ball (auth), Ruth Rippon Retrospective, 71, Ceramics Monthly Mag; Ruth Holland (auth), Rippon Retrospective, Creative Arts League 71 Catalog, 71. *Mem:* Creative Arts League Sacramento; Asn San Francisco Potters; Am Crafts Coun; Crocker Art Gallery Asn. *Media:* Stoneware, Porcelain Clay; Watercolor, Pencil. *Mailing Add:* 57 Sandburg Dr Sacramento CA 95819

RIPPS, RODNEY
PAINTER
b New York, NY. *Study:* York Col, BA; Hunter Col, MA. *Exhib:* Critics Choice, Munson-Williams-Proctor Inst, Utica, NY, 77; one-man shows, Nancy Lurie Gallery, Chicago, 77, Brooke Alexander Gallery, New York, 77 & 78 & Galerie Daniel Templon, Paris, 78; Holly Solomon Gallery, New York, 80-81; and many others. *Pos:* Vis artist, Art Inst Chicago, 77 & Ill State Univ, Bloomington, 78. *Teaching:* Instr painting, Brooklyn Mus Art Sch, 74-76. *Bibliog:* David Rush (auth), Paintings with a sculptural character, Artweek, 10/76; Ken Wahl (auth), The paintings of Rodney Ripps, Flash Art, 4/78; Ingeborg Schlesweig-Holstein (auth), The painter sculpts, Interview, 4/80. *Mailing Add:* 94 Mercer New York NY 10012

RISBECK, PHILIP EDWARD
GRAPHIC ARTIST, EDUCATOR
b Kansas City, Mo, July 25, 39. *Study:* Univ Kans, BFA, 62, MFA, 65. *Work:* Sheldon Gallery Art, Lincoln, Nebr; Union Soviet Artists Collections, Moscow; Libr Cong; Wilanov Poster Mus, Warsaw; Moravian Mus, Brno, Czechoslovakia. *Exhib:* Int Poster Biennale, Zacheta Mus, Warsaw, 66, 68, 70 & 72; Graphic Design Biennale, Moravian Mus, Brno, Czechoslovakia, 66, 70, 74, 78 & 82; Posters USA, Mead Libr Ideas, New York, 75; American Poster, 45-75, Smithsonian Inst, 76; Jurors Exhib, Cordegarda Gallery, Warsaw, 80; one-man exhib, Gallery Union Soviet Artists, Moscow, 83 & traveling exhib, 83-84; and many others. *Pos:* Co-dir, Colo Int Poster Exhib, 79- *Teaching:* Prof art, Colo State Univ, 65- *Awards:* Silver Medal, Int Biennale Graphic Design, Brno, Czechoslovakia, 82; Durrell Award Res, Colo State Univ, 82; Outstanding Prof, Col Arts, Humanities & Soc Sci, Colo State Univ, 83. *Bibliog:* Lanny Sommese (auth), John Sorbie and Phil Risbeck, Colo State Univ & Novum Gebrachsgraphik, Ger, 76; Richard Coyne (auth), Colorado State University Poster Exhibition, Calif Mag, 79; Lanny Sommese (auth), Colorado State University Art Program in Graphics, Graphis, Zurich, 82. *Mem:* Art Dirs Club Denver (pres, 81-82, mem bd, 81-); Univ & Col Designers Asn; Int Typography Alliance; Int Cong Graphic Design. *Publ:* Auth, Eighth International Poster Biennale in Warsaw, Graphis Press, Zurich, 80. *Mailing Add:* 3521 Canadian Pkwy Ft Collins CO 80524

RISE, JOHN ERNEST
PAINTER
b Albuquerque, NMex, Nov 30, 54. *Study:* Tamarind Litho Workshops, with Garo Antresian, 74-75; Ariz State Univ, with Jim Pile, BFA, 76; Univ NMex, with John Wenger, MA(grad asst), 77. *Work:* Mus Albuquerque; Roswell Mus & Arts Ctr, NMex; Prudential Life Insurance Co, Los Angeles; Ariz State Univ, Tempe; Am Oil Co, Denver; and others. *Exhib:* One-man shows, William Sawyer Gallery, San Francisco, 79 & traveling show in Mex, 81-82; Here and Now, Mus Albuquerque, 80; Joslyn Art Mus, Omaha, 80; New Mexico Artists, Sarah Blaffer Mus, Univ Houston, 81; and others. *Pos:* Pres & gen mgr, Best Moulding Frames, 80- *Awards:* Alumni Asn Award, Ariz State Univ, 76; Jurors Award, 8 West Biennial, Grand Junction, Colo, 80. *Bibliog:* Thomas Albright (auth), Decadence, motion, San Francisco Chronicle, 80; William Peterson (auth), New Mexico art, Portfolio Mag, 81; William Peterson (auth), New Mexico art, Art Am, 81. *Mem:* Nat Art Materials Trade Asn. *Media:* Oil, Chalk Pastel. *Dealer:* William Sawyer Gallery 3045 Clay St San Francisco CA. *Mailing Add:* 1929 Leon Ct Albuquerque NM 87107

RISELING, ROBERT LOWELL
EDUCATOR, PAINTER
b Sioux City, Iowa, June 5, 41. *Study:* Univ Northern Iowa, BA, 63, MA, 66; State Univ Iowa, 64; Univ Wis-Madison, MFA, 72. *Work:* Memphis Acad of Art, Tenn; State Tenn, Nashville; Augustana Col, Rock Island, Ill; Rochester Art Ctr, Minn; Univ Northern Iowa, Cedar Falls. *Exhib:* Images '71, Anoka-Ramsey State Jr Col, 71; State Col Fac Exhib, Minn Mus Art, St Paul, 74; Rochester Open, Rochester Art Ctr, 74; 17th Ann Delta, 74 & 11th Ann Prints & Drawings, 78, Ark Arts Ctr, Little Rock; Memphis Art Faculty, Brooks Mem Art Gallery, Tenn, 78; Tenn Artists, Western Ky State, Bowling Green, 79; Art in the Eighties, Tenn State Mus, Nashville. *Teaching:* Instr art, Monticello, Iowa, 63-65; grad asst, Dept Art, Univ Northern Iowa, 65-66; asst dir & resident artist, 66-67, dir art, Rochester Art Ctr, 67; instr, 67-71, teaching asst, Dept Art, Univ Wis, 71-72; asst prof, Dept Art, St Cloud State Univ, 72-74; asst prof, Memphis Acad Arts, Tenn, 74-78, assoc prof, 78- *Awards:* First Award Painting, 8th Ann, Waterloo, 71; Second Award Painting 40th Ann Arrowhead, Tweed Gallery, Duluth, Minn, 73; Purchase Award, Tenn Bicentennial, 76. *Media:* Oil, Dye. *Mailing Add:* 1273 N Parkway Memphis TN 38104

RISHEL, JOSEPH JOHN, JR
CURATOR
b Clifton Springs, NY, May 15, 40. *Study:* Hobart Col, BA, 62; Univ Chicago, MA, 65. *Pos:* Cur, European painting before 1900 & John G Johnson Collection, Philadelphia Mus Art, 71- *Mailing Add:* Philadelphia Mus Art Franklin Pkwy at 26th St Philadelphia PA 19101

RISING, DOROTHY MILNE
PAINTER, ILLUSTRATOR
b Tacoma, Wash, Sept 13, 1895. *Study:* Pratt Inst, dipl, 16; Cleveland Sch Art, with Henry Keller, 20; Univ Wash, BA, 32, MFA, 33. *Work:* Seattle Art Mus; Frye Art Mus, Seattle; Pac Nat Bank Washington, Tacoma; Three Grumbacher Collections; Lakeside Sch. *Exhib:* Northwest Ann, Art Mus Pavilion, 69, Northwest Watercolor Soc, 69 & 77; West Coast Oil Exhib, Frye Art Mus, 69; Puget Sound Area Exhib, 71; Pac Northwest Art Ann, 71; Erb Mem Art Gallery, Eugene, Ore, 72; plus others. *Teaching:* Instr art, Univ Puget Sound, 16-17; instr & supvr art, Western Wash Col, 17-19; instr art, Seattle High Schs, 33-66. *Awards:* Nat League Am Pen Women Best Watercolor in Show, Smithsonian Inst, 55; Women Painters Awards, 60, 75 & 76; Isabel Hansen Mem Award Watercolor, Women Painters Washington, 81. *Bibliog:* Around the world through an artist's eyes, Pen Woman, 67; Edna Daw (auth), A word about Dorothy Rising, Age of Achievement, 71. *Mem:* Fel Royal Soc Art, London; Nat League Am Pen Women (pres, Seattle Br, 70-72); Women Painters Wash (pres, 49); Northwest Watercolor Soc; President's Forum. *Media:* Oil, Watercolor. *Publ:* Auth & illusr, Contemporary versus academic art, Town Crier, 34; auth, The silver Bible, Christian Sci Monitor, 64; auth & illusr, December events in many lands, 12/74, Seeing Sweden past and present, 3/75 & Journey behind the Iron Curtain, 5/75, Age of Achievement; plus many others. *Mailing Add:* 5033 17th Ave NE Seattle WA 98105

RISLEY, JOHN HOLLISTER
SCULPTOR
b Brookline, Mass, Sept 20, 19. *Study:* Amherst Col, BA(cum laude); R I Sch Design, BFA; Cranbrook Acad Art, MFA. *Work:* Wesleyan Univ; Fred Olsen Found, Conn; Hartford Jewish Community Ctr, Conn; Rose Art Gallery, Brandeis Univ. *Comn:* Wood & metal relief, IBM Hq, New York, 65; wrought iron relief, Cleveland Garden Ctr, Ohio, 66; copper relief, Nat Bank, Quarryville, Pa, 71; wood & metal sculptures, Brookside Elementary Sch, Waterville, Maine, 70; bronze sculpture, Univ Maine, Portland, 70. *Teaching:* Prof sculpture, Wesleyan Univ, 54-, chmn dept of art, 68- *Awards:* Drakenfield Prize, 18th Ceramic Ann, 54; New Haven Arts Festival Sculpture Prize, 66; First Prize, Int Festival Humor and Satire, Bulgaria. *Mailing Add:* 30 Maple Shade Rd Middletown CT 06457

RISS, MURRAY
PHOTOGRAPHER, EDUCATOR
b Poland, Feb 6, 40; US citizen. *Study:* City Univ New York, BA; Cooper Union Sch Art; RI Sch Design, with Harry Callahan, MFA. *Work:* Mus Mod Art, New York; Bibliot Nat, Paris; Art Inst Chicago; Nat Gallery Art, Can; New Orleans Mus Fine Arts. *Comn:* Photograph Reelfoot Lake, State of Tenn, 72. *Exhib:* Mus Mod Art, New York, 70-71; one-man shows, Minneapolis Mus Fine Art, 71, Visual Studies Workshop (traveling show), New York, 76-78, Projects Inc, Cambridge, 79 & Southern Artist (worldwide traveling exhib), US Info Agency, 76; Fantastic Photography USA, six maj mus in Europe, 78. *Pos:* Vis sr lectr, Univ Haifa, Israel, 75-76. *Teaching:* Assoc prof photog, Memphis Acad Art, 68-78, prof, 78-, head dept photog, 68- *Awards:* Nat Endowment Arts Grant, 79. *Bibliog:* William Parker (auth), Introduction to my portfolio, Ctr Photog Studies, 75. *Publ:* Illusr, Sleep Book, Harper & Row, 74; illusr, Good Abode: Architectural History of Shelley County, Towery Press, 83. *Mailing Add:* 1306 Harbert Ave Memphis TN 38104

RISSER, JAMES K
DEALER, PAINTER
b Ft Collins, Colo, Nov 8, 47. *Study:* Univ Calif, Santa Barbara, MFA, 72. *Work:* Mus Mod Art, New York; Oakland Mus; Richmond Art Ctr, Calif; NJ State Mus, Clinton; Grunwald Ctr Graphic Arts, Los Angeles. *Exhib:* Photography in Printmaking, Cornell Univ Art Gallery, 77; Aesthetics of Graffiti, San Francisco Mus Mod Art, 78; Santa Barbara Artists Invitational, Santa Barbara Mus Art, 79; Drawing Show Biennale, Newcastle Upon the Tyne, Cleveland, England, 80; solo show, List Gallery, Brown Univ, 80; Love Hate Fear Suicide, Vrije Univ Gallery, Brussels, Belgium, 81; Prints: Acquisitions 1977-1981, Mus Mod Art, New York, 82. *Collections Arranged:* Work of Five Artists, Santa Barbara Mus Art, 79. *Pos:* Owner, Risser Gallery, Pasadena, currently. *Teaching:* Instr drawing & printmaking, Univ Calif, Berkeley, 74-76, Col Creative Studies, Univ Calif, Santa Barbara, 79-82 & Brown Univ, 80-81. *Awards:* Tiffany Found Grant, 77. *Dealer:* Ruth S Schaffner Gallery 128 W Ortega Santa Barbara CA 93101; Kathryn Markel Gallery 50 W 57th New York NY 10019. *Mailing Add:* 48 S Raymond Pasadena CA 91105

RITCHIE, (CELIA) ANN
PAINTER
b Providence, RI, Feb 17, 34. *Study:* Univ Wis, Madison, BA, 57; Columbia Univ, MA, 70; Art Students League, New York, with Mario Cooper & Dale Meyers; also with Leo Rabkin, Fay Spahn & Dorothy Gillespie. *Exhib:* Am Watercolor Soc, Nat Acad Galleries, New York, 74-82; Works on Paper, Brooklyn Mus, 75; Nat Arts Club Open, New York, 75-83; Paper, An Invitational Exhib, Michael C Rockefeller Arts Ctr Gallery, State Univ NY Col, Fredonia, 76-77; Nat Arts Club, 82; Salmagundi Club, 83. *Awards:* Award of Merit, Ga Watercolor Soc, 79; Merchandise Award,

Inveresk 1979 Artists in Watercolor Competition, 79; House of Heydenryk Award, Nat Arts Club, 83. *Mem:* Am Watercolor Soc (treas, 83-); Allied Artists; Nat Soc Painters in Casein and Acrylic; Audubon Artists; Nat Arts Club. *Media:* Watercolor, Acrylic. *Mailing Add:* 195 W Tenth St New York NY 10014

RITCHIE, WILLIAM (BILL)
PRINTMAKER, VIDEO ARTIST
b Yakima, Wash, Dec 24, 41. *Study:* Cent Wash State Col, BA, 64; San Jose State Col, MA, 66; studied with Rolf Nesch, Norway, 69; intern Nat Ctr for Experiments in Television, 74. *Work:* Philadelphia Mus Art, Pa; US Info Agency, Japan; New York Pub Libr; Univ Calgary, Can; Seattle Pub Libr, Wash; and others. *Comn:* Videotape, King Co Arts Commission, 80; print, Henry Gallery Asn, Seattle, Wash, 70; sculpture, City of Seattle, Wash, 77. *Exhib:* Int Print Exhib, Seattle Art Mus, Wash, 70; Nat Art Exhib, Calif Palace Legion of Honor, 71; Nat Print Exhib, Libr of Cong, Washington, DC, 71; British Int Print Biennale, Bradford Galleries, Eng, 72; NWest Film & Video Festival, Portland Art Mus, Ore, 73 & 74; Am Printmaking, Brooklyn Mus Art, NY, 76; Boston Printmakers 29th Nat, De Cordova Mus, Lincoln, Mass, 77; Portopia, Kobe, Japan, 81. *Teaching:* Prof printmaking & media arts, Univ Wash, Seattle, 66- *Awards:* Research Grants, Printmaking, Video & Computer Art, 70-76; First Prize, First NWest Film & Video Festival, Portland Art Mus, Ore, 73; Nat Endowment for the Arts Fel, 74. *Bibliog:* Korot & Schneider (coauths), Video Art, Harcourt, Brace, Jovanovitch, 76; F Eichenberg (auth), The Art of the Print, Harry N Abrams, 76; V Ancona (auth), Bill Ritchie: Video in the Northwest, Videography Mag, Vol 12, Number 6. *Mem:* World Print Coun. *Media:* All print media; video and computer graphics. *Publ:* Auth, Behind Time in the Electronic Age, Magee Sweed, 82. *Dealer:* Harrison Magee 360 Halladay Seattle WA 98109. *Mailing Add:* 360 Halladay Seattle WA 98109

RITZ, LORNA
PAINTER, EDUCATOR
Study: Worcester Art Mus, Mass, 63-65; Boston Mus Fine Arts, 65; Art Students League, New York, 66; Skowhegan Sch Painting & Sculpture, Maine, 68; Pratt Inst, Brooklyn, 69; Cranbrook Acad Art, Mich, 71. *Exhib:* Solo exhibs, Roswell Mus Art Ctr, NMex, 75, Blue Mountain Gallery, New York, 82 & Milhouse Bundy Performing & Fine Arts Ctr, Waitsfield, Vt, 82; Mus Fine Arts, Santa Fe, NMex, 78; Allan Stone Gallery, New York, 81; Regional Selections, Hood Mus Hopkins Ctr, Dartmouth Col, 82; Mills Gallery, Boston Ctr Arts, 82. *Teaching:* Adj instr sculpture, Art Inst Boston, 71; instr two-dimensional design, Rochester Inst Technol, NY, 72-73; instr painting, RI Sch Design, 73-75; vis staff mem, Fine Arts Work Ctr, Provincetown, Mass, 75, RI Sch Design, 76, Brown Univ, 78 & Dartmouth Col, 78-79; asst prof painting, Univ Minn, 76-77; instr, Univ Vt, 84. *Awards:* Blanche E Colman Grant, Boston, 81-82; Artist in Residence Grant, Vt Coun Arts, 81-82; USA Grant to exhibit & lecture in Honduras. *Media:* Oil. *Mailing Add:* Box 10 Elm & Hopson Rds Norwich VT 05055

RIVARD, J B(ERNARD)
PRINTMAKER, PAINTER
b South Bend, Ind, May 5, 30. *Study:* Chicago Acad Fine Arts; Univ Fla, BS. *Work:* El Paso Mus Art, Tex; Hammond Pub Libr, Ind. *Exhib:* Rockford Int Biennale, 83; Small Impressions Print Exhib, NJ, 83; Nat On-Paper Show, NY, 83; NJ Printmaking Coun Traveling Exhib, 83-84; and others. *Awards:* Print Award, Salmagundi Club Open, 82; and others. *Mem:* Salmagundi Club, New York. *Media:* Color Etchings, Aquatints. *Mailing Add:* c/o High Plateau Gallery 6717 Lomas Blvd NE Albuquerque NM 87110

RIVERA, FRANK
PAINTER
b Cleveland, Ohio, Aug 28, 39. *Study:* Yale Univ Grad Sch Fine Arts, with Alex Katz & Jack Tworkov, BFA, 62; Univ Pa, with Pi Dorazio, Savelli, Helen Frankenthaler & Ludwig Sander, MFA, 67. *Exhib:* Ann Am Painting & Sculpture, Pa Acad Fine Arts, 68; NJ State Mus Painting & Sculpture Ann, 72; Univ Rochester Gallery Art, 72; Susan Caldwell Gallery, New York, 74; 1975 Biennial Exhib Am Art, Whitney Mus Am Art, 75. *Teaching:* Assoc prof painting & design, Mercer Col, Trenton, NJ, 67- *Awards:* Nat Endowment Humanities Grant for Study & Travel in France, 72-73. *Bibliog:* Elizabeth Stevens (auth), Review Whitney Biennial, This Week Mag, Trenton Times, 3/23/75. *Media:* Mixed. *Mailing Add:* 110 Broad St Hightstown NJ 08520

RIVERA-VELAZQUEZ, MARIANO
PAINTER, WRITER
b Mexico City, Mex, July 4, 45. *Study:* Iberoamericana Univ, Mex, dipl(archit), 67; Atelier Friedländer, Paris, dipl(graphic arts; scholar), 67-68. *Work:* Mus Mod Art, Mus Arte Carrillo Gil, Mexico City. *Comn:* Monumental Letter, Augusto Elias Advert Agency Bldg, Mexico City, 83. *Exhib:* Codex, Tenth Biennale Paris, Mus Art Mod, France, 77; Fourth Triennial India, Mus Mod Art, New Delhi, 78; La Travesia de la Escritura, Mus Carrillo Gil, Mexico City, 80; Stockholm Int Art Expo, Sollentuna, Sweden, 81; Parafrasis, Mus Carrillo Gil, Mexico City, 83; Arte Contemporaneo de Mexico, Mus Mod Art, Mexico City, 83. *Pos:* Co-founder & adv, Arquitecto Mag, 75- *Teaching:* Prof art hist, Inst Cult Superior, Mexico City, 73-77. *Awards:* World Cult Prize, New Directions in Visual Art, Centro Studi Ricer Che-Delle Nazioni, Italy, 83. *Bibliog:* Graciela Kartofel (auth), article, Vogue Mag VIII, 82. *Mem:* Accad Ital. *Media:* All. *Publ:* Auth, The human dimension, Vol V, 77 & Sketch of the image, Vol XI, 78, Arquitecto Mag; auth, Architecture and language, Artes Visuales Mag, Mus Mod Art, Mex, 2/79; auth, On the Campidoglio, Arquitecto Mag, Vol XVII, 80. *Dealer:* Galeria Juan Martin Amberes 17 Mexico City DF Mex. *Mailing Add:* Lazcano 23 Mexico DF 01000 Mexico

RIVERON, ENRIQUE
PAINTER, SCULPTOR
b Cienfuegos, Las Villas, Cuba, Jan 31, 02; US citizen. *Study:* Acad Villate, Havana, Cuba; Acad San Fernando, Madrid, Spain; La Colarouse & Grand Chaumiere, Paris, France; travel scholar from Cuba, Spain, France, Italy & Belgium. *Work:* Fine Arts Mus, Havana, Cuba; Wichita Art Mus, Kans; Lowe Art Mus, Coral Gables, Fla; Miami Mus Mod Art, Fla. *Exhib:* Retrospective exhibs, Lowe Art Mus, Coral Gables, Fla, 80 & De Armas Gallery, Virginia Gardens, Fla, 80; one-man exhibs, Forma Gallery, Coral Gables, 82-83 & Gallery at Grove Isle, Miami, Fla, 83; Hommage a Joan Miro, Editar Cult Ctr, Geneva, Switz, 83; and others; and other one-man shows. *Pos:* Founder & dir, Index Gallery, Wichita, Kans, 58-60, Arger Gallery, Coral Gables, Fla, 60-61 & Gala (group Latin-American artists), 69- *Teaching:* Instr cartooning, Wichita Art Asn, Kans, 49-53; instr painting, Wichita Univ, Kans, 58-59. *Awards:* Sculpture Award, Sculptors of Fla, Miami, 70; Sculpture Award, Ft Lauderdale Mus Arts, Fla, 70; Painting Award, Third Ann Pan-Am, Miami, 72. *Bibliog:* Dore Ashton (auth), Art criticism, NY Times, 4/13/57; Carroll E Hogan (auth), Catalog Preface, Dir Wichita Art Mus, Kans, 5/58; J Gomez-Sicre (auth), Catalog Preface, Dir Visual Arts, Orgn Am States, Washington, DC, 74. *Media:* Steel, Iron; Collage. *Publ:* Illus & cartoons, New Yorker, NY Times, Modern Screen & Cine Mundial, New York, 27-50; contribr, Creating art from anything, 68. *Mailing Add:* 1726 Espanola Dr Miami FL 33133

RIVERS, LARRY
PAINTER
b New York, NY, 1923. *Study:* Hans Hofmann Sch Fine Arts, 47-48; NY Univ. *Work:* Brooklyn Mus; Corcoran Gallery Art; Kansas City Art Inst; Metrop Mus Art; Minneapolis Inst Art; and many others including pvt collections. *Comn:* Outdoor billboard, First New York Film Festival, 63. *Exhib:* Nine shows, Whitney Mus Am Art, 54-64; Pa Acad Fine Arts, 63; retrospective, Art Inst Chicago, 70; Two Decades Am Painting (traveling exhib to Japan, India & Australia), Mus Mod Art, New York, 66; Va Mus Fine Art, Richmond, 70; Saidye Bronfman Ctr, Montreal, 80; Hirshhorn Mus, Washington, DC, 80; Sierra Nevada Mus Art, Reno, 80; Indianapolis Mus Art, 80; Tate Gallery Art, London, England, 80; Parrish Art Mus, Southampton, NY, 80; Baum Editions, San Francisco, 80; La Jolla Mus Art, 80. *Teaching:* Artist in residence, Slade Sch Fine Arts, London, 64; Md Inst Col Art. *Awards:* Third Prize, Corcoran Gallery Art, 54. *Bibliog:* William Gaunt (auth), The Observer's Book of Modern Art From Impressionism to the Present Day, Frederick Warne & Co Ltd, London, 64; Lucy R Lippard (auth), Pop Art, Praeger, 66; Sam Hunter (auth), Larry Rivers (monogr), Abrams, 70; and many others. *Dealer:* Marlborough Gallery Inc 41 E 57th St New York NY 10022. *Mailing Add:* 92 Little Plains Rd Southampton NY 11968

RIVERS, VICTORIA Z
SCULPTOR
b Louisville, Ky, Sept 7, 48. *Study:* Murray State Univ, BFA, MACT, SCT, 70 & 74. *Work:* Evansville Mus Arts & Sci; Liberty Gallery, Louisville Gallery, Louisville, Ky; Crocker Mus Art, Sacramento; Bradley Univ Drawing Collection. *Comn:* Several private comns in Ky & Tenn, 77-79; Transcendental Landscape (textile) & Recollections (textile), Opryland Hotel, Nashville, 78. *Exhib:* Solo show, Am Gallery, Bern, Switz, 82, Mus Neon Art, Los Angeles, 83 & Crocker Art Mus, Sacramento, 84; Young Americans, Mus Contemp Crafts, New York, 82; The Magic of Neon, Smithsonian Inst Sites Show, 83-85; Art Makes Sense, Laguna Beach Art Mus, 84. *Teaching:* Asst prof art, Volunteer State Col, 74-80; assoc prof design, Univ Calif, Davis, 80-; instr workshops, Summervail, Colo, Fiberworks, Berkeley & Art Inst Chicago. *Awards:* Young Am Award, Am Crafts Coun, 77; Tenn Arts Comn Fel, 78-79. *Bibliog:* Christine Rex (auth), rev of Taming Neon, Artweek, 6/12/82; Virginia Kaild (auth), At home with art, Sacramento Mag, 4/83; Lynn Woods (auth), article, Art Week, 11/26/83. *Mem:* Surface Design Asn; Am Crafts Coun. *Media:* Painted Neon, Printed Dyed Fabric. *Mailing Add:* 2131 51st St Sacramento CA 95817

RIVOLI, MARIO
ASSEMBLAGE ARTIST
b New York, NY, Jan 31, 43. *Study:* Sch Industrial Art; Art Students League; Sch Visual Arts. *Work:* Mus of Contemp Crafts, New York; Smithsonian Inst, Washington, DC; Philadelphia Mus of Art, Pa; Denver Nat Bank; Denver Art Mus. *Comn:* Art Deco Mural, Stromberg's Penthouse Restaurant, 76; Decoration of House Organ, Carnegie Hall Cinema, Denver, Colo, 77; Mural, St Moritz Hotel, Cafe De La Paix, 80; mural, Helmsley Corp, Harley Hotel, Orlando, Fla, 80. *Exhib:* Denim Show, Smithsonian Inst, 77; Show of Wearable Art, Philadelphia Mus of Art, 77-78; Homage to the Bag, Mus of Contemp Crafts, 77; two-man show, Dolls, Julie Artisans Gallery, New York, 80; Sebastian-Moore Gallery, 81-82; Another Great Love Affair, Alliance Contemp Art Show, Denver Art Mus, 82. *Pos:* Theatre designer, Harry M Koutoukas; graphic & set designs, Sch for Gargoyles, New York, 76-77 & 77-78. *Awards:* Illus of 69, Soc of Illusrs, 69; Special merit, Washington Square Outdoor Art Exhib, 76; Most Creative Mask, Denver Art Mus. *Bibliog:* Patti Thorn (auth), Making faces (make-up), Rocky Mountain News, 82; Jeanne Jakle (auth), Behind Denver's masks, Denver Post, 82; film, From the Thrift Stores of Denver to Madison Avenue, PM Magazine, 11/82. *Media:* Mixed. *Publ:* Illusr, Song for Clowns, Atheneum, 65 & Do Tigers Bite Kings, 68, Antheneum; illusr, Best Foot Forward, E P Dutton, 70; auth, Incomplete Book of Sleaze, Slime and Supersition, pvt publ, 76. *Dealer:* Julie Artisan Gallery 687 Madison Ave New York NY 10021. *Mailing Add:* 1220 Marion St Denver CO 80218

RIZZIE, DAN (DURANT CHARLES)
COLLAGE ARTIST, PAINTER
b Poughkeepsie, NY, May 23, 51. *Study:* Hendrix Col, Conway, Ark, BA, 73; Southern Methodist Univ, Dallas, Tex, MFA, 75. *Work:* Dallas Mus Fine Arts & Univ Gallery, Southern Methodist Univ, Tex; Witte Mus, San Antonio, Tex, 79. *Exhib:* Tex Painting & Sculpture, Dallas Mus Fine Arts, 76; one-man shows, Works on Paper, Dallas Mus Fine Arts, 78 & Meadows Mus, Shreveport, La, 79; Focus, Ft Worth Art Mus, 80; On the Right Bank of the Red River, Root Art Ctr, New York, 79; Response, Tyler Mus, Tex, 80; Collage, Brooklyn Mus, 81. *Teaching:* Instr lithography & drawing, Southern Methodist Univ, Dallas, 74-75; instr drawing, Richland Col, Dallas, 75-76; instr painting & drawing, Eastfield Col, Dallas, 76-80. *Awards:* Best of Shows, Tex Painting & Sculpture, 76, Shreveport Ann, 77 & Tarrant Co Ann, 78. *Bibliog:* Janet Kutner (auth), Capricious places, Art News, 12/77; Ned Rifkin (auth), Southwest 1978, Art Week, Vol IX, No 18, 78; M J Smith (auth), Dan Rizzie, Art in Am, 2/80. *Media:* Drawing, Collage. *Mailing Add:* 2008 Laws Dallas TX 75202

ROBB, CHARLES (CHARLES ROBERT BUSH)
PAINTER
b Toronto, Ont, Can, June 28, 38. *Study:* Ont Col Art, AOCA, 59, with Jock MacDonald, John Alfson & Carl Schaefer. *Work:* Can Coun Art Bank, Ottawa; Citicorp Ltd, Toronto; Kitchener/Waterloo Art Gallery, Ont; Esso, Calgary, Alta; Art Gallery London, Ont, Can; and others. *Exhib:* One-man shows, Pollock Gallery, Toronto, 77-82; three-man show, Agnes Etherington Art Centre, Queens Univ, Kingston, Ont, 77; Art for Bus Sake, Art Gallery Ont, Toronto, 75; Lefebvre Galleries, Edmonton, Alta, 81; Kitchener/Waterloo Art Gallery, Ont, 81; and others. *Bibliog:* D Adlow (auth), Stripes by Robb, Christian Sci Monitor, 64; Kay Woods (auth), Charles Robb, Arts Canada, 77 & 81; Seeing it Our Way, Portrait of Charles Robb (film), Canadian Broadcasting Corp. *Media:* Acrylic, Paper. *Dealer:* Gallery One 121 Scollard St Toronto ON M5R 1G4 Can. *Mailing Add:* 121 Nymark Ave 104 Willowdale ON M2J 2H3 Canada

ROBB, DAVID METHENY, JR
MUSEUM DIRECTOR, HISTORIAN
b Minneapolis, Minn, Apr 12, 37. *Study:* Princeton Univ, BA, 59; Yale Univ, MA, 67; Attingham Summer Sch, 78; Mus Mgt Inst, Univ Calif, Berkeley, 83. *Collections Arranged:* The book of Hours of Charlotte of Savoy, 73; Star Spangled History..., 75-77; Louis I Kahn: Sketches for the Kimbell Art Museum (auth, catalog), 78; Elisabeth Louise Vigee Le Brun, 82. *Pos:* Res asst, Nat Gallery Art, DC, 63; cur, Collection of Mr & Mrs Paul Mellon, 63-65; curatorial fel, Walker Art Ctr, Minneapolis, 67-69; cur, Kimbell Art Mus, Ft Worth, Tex, 69-74, chief cur, 74-83 & acting dir, 79-80; dir, Telfair Acad Arts & Sci, Savannah, 84- *Awards:* Ford Found Cur Training Fel, 68-69. *Mem:* Col Art Asn; Am Asn of Mus; Soc Archit Historians. *Res:* European and American portrait painting; architectural presentation. *Publ:* Ed, Kimbell Art Mus Handbook, 81. *Mailing Add:* Telfair Acad Arts & Sci PO Box 10081 Savannah GA 31412

ROBB, PEGGY HIGHT
PAINTER
b Gallup, NMex, Sept 14, 24. *Study:* Univ NMex, BFA & MA, with Raymond Jonson & Kenneth Adams; Art Students League. *Work:* Univ NMex, Albuquerque. *Comn:* Stained glass window & portraits, Christian Ctr, Albuquerque, 75; McDonnell-Douglass Aircraft, St Louis, Mo, 79. *Exhib:* NMex State Fair, Albuquerque, 59 & 63; Southwestern Fiesta, Santa Fe, 66; Sun Carnival Art Exhib, El Paso, Tex, 71; Women in Art Invitational, 78; Nat Small Painting Show, Albuquerque, 79; and others. *Teaching:* Pvt classes, currently. *Awards:* First Prize, NMex State Fair, 59 & 63; Exhib Awards, St John's Episcopal Cathedral, Albuquerque, 78 & 79. *Mem:* Fel of Christian Artists in Media & Entertainment; Albuquerque Asn United Artists. *Media:* Miscellaneous. *Mailing Add:* 7200 Rio Grande Blvd NW Albuquerque NM 87107

ROBBIN, ANTHONY STUART
PAINTER
b Washington, DC, Nov 24, 43. *Study:* Columbia Col, BA; Yale Univ Sch Art, BFA & MFA. *Work:* Addison Gallery Am Art, Andover, Mass; Whitney Mus Am Art. *Exhib:* Bykert Gallery, New York, 71; Paley & Lowe Inc, New York, 72; Ann, Whitney Mus Am Art, 72, one-man show, 75. *Media:* Acrylic. *Publ:* Auth, Smithson sites & non sites, Art News, 69; auth, Two ocean projects, 69 & auth, A protein sensibility, 71, Arts Mag; auth, Hutchison ecological art, Art Int, 70; auth, Visual paradox & 4-D geometry, Tracts Mag, 75. *Mailing Add:* 423 Broome St New York NY 10013

ROBBINS, DANIEL J
HISTORIAN, MUSEUM DIRECTOR
b New York, NY, Jan 15, 33. *Study:* Univ Chicago, BA; Yale Univ, MA; NY Univ Inst Fine Arts, PhD; Univ Paris. *Collections Arranged:* Cezanne & Structure, 63, Albert Gleizes Retrospective, 64-65, Guggenheim Mus Art; Contemporary Wall Sculpture, 63-64, Decade of New Talent, 64-65, Am Fedn Arts. *Pos:* Cur, Nat Gallery Art, Washington, DC, 59-60; cur, Guggenheim Mus Art, 61-64; dir, Mus Art, RI Sch Design, 64-71; dir, Fogg Art Mus, Harvard Univ, 71-82. *Teaching:* Instr, Ind Univ, 55; prof, Brown Univ, 65-71; lectr, Harvard Univ, 71-75; vis prof, Dartmouth Col, 75-80 & Yale Univ, 77; Clark prof, Williams Col, 78-82. *Awards:* French Govt Fel, Paris, 58; Nat Endowment Humanities Sr Fel, 76; Guggenheim Fel, 78-79. *Mem:* Am Fedn Arts. *Publ:* Auth, Jacques Villon, Fogg Mus, 76; auth, Folk Sculpture Without Folk, Brooklyn Mus, 76; From Statues to Sculpture, 76; Cubist Drawings, 79; co-auth, Henri de Toulouse-Lautrec, 80. *Mailing Add:* Farcevol Farm Randolph VT 05060

ROBBINS, EUGENIA S
WRITER, EDITOR
b New York, NY, Apr 22, 35. *Study:* Smith Col, BA. *Pos:* Art ed, George Braziller Inc, 60-64; bk ed, Art in Am, 64-67; news ed, Art J, Col Art Asn of Am, 67 & Col Art Asn Newsletter, 76-80; ed, Art & Auction, 80; news ed, Art Express, 81-; secy, Iriquois Co, currently. *Res:* Persian art and architecture; modern art and architecture; art books. *Publ:* Auth & coauth, articles in Studio Int, Art in Am, Art and Auction & NY Post; auth, Art, Collier's Yr Bk; auth, regular column in Art J & rev in Art in Am & Art J; and others. *Mailing Add:* RR 2 Peth Rd Randolph VT 05060

ROBBINS, HULDA D
PAINTER, PRINTMAKER
b Atlanta, Ga, Oct 19, 10. *Study:* Pa Mus Sch Indust Art, Philadelphia; Prussian Acad, Berlin, with Ludwig Bartning; Barnes Found, Merion, Pa. *Work:* Metrop Mus Art, New York; Victoria & Albert Mus, London, Eng; Bibliot Nat, Paris; Art Mus Ont; Smithsonian Inst, Washington, DC. *Exhib:* Portrait of America, New York & Tour, 45-46; Current Am Prints, Carnegie Inst, Pittsburgh, 48; Nat Print Ann, Brooklyn Mus & Tour, 48-49; Nat Exhib Prints, Libr Cong, Washington, DC, 56; US Info Agency Print Exhib Europ Tour, 72- *Teaching:* Instr basic & advan serigraphy, Nat Serigraph Soc Sch, 54-60; instr creative painting, Atlantic Co Jewish Community Ctr, Margate, NJ, 60-67. *Awards:* Purchase Award, Prints For Children, Mus Mod Art, 41; Paintings by Printmakers Award, 47 & Babette S Kornblith Purchase Prize, 49, Nat Serigraph Soc. *Mem:* Print Club; Am Color Print Soc. *Media:* Oil. *Mailing Add:* 16 S Buffalo Ave Atlantic City NJ 08406

ROBBINS, LEROY (SOUTHWARD)
PHOTOGRAPHER, FILMMAKER
b St Louis, Mo, June 14, 04. *Study:* Apprenticed under artist Oscar Thalinger while working as photographer for St Louis Art Mus, 22-27; Washington Univ Sch Archit, 24-27. *Work:* Mus Mod Art, New York; San Francisco Mus Mod Art; Oakland Mus; Univ Minn Gallery, Minneapolis; Santa Barbara Mus Art; and others. *Exhib:* A Pageant of Photog, Golden Gate Int Expos, San Francisco, 40; Image of Freedom, Mus Mod Art, New York, 41; one-man shows, Mexico, San Francisco Mus Mod Art, Calif, 67, Friends of Photog, Carmel, Calif, 72 & Phoenix Art Mus, Ariz, 76; Quartet, Munic Art Gallery, Los Angeles, 73; New Deal Art: Calif, de Saisset Art Gallery & Mus, Univ Santa Clara, 76; retrospective, Sr Cye Gallery, Long Beach, Calif, 80. *Mem:* Artists Equity Asn. *Media:* Black and White Photography. *Publ:* Contribr, A Pageant of Photography, Crocker-Union, San Francisco, 40; auth, Ancient Peru Today (limited ed of photog), privately publ, 75; contribr, New Deal Art, Calif deSaisset Art Gallery, Univ Santa Clara, 76. *Dealer:* Herbert B Palmer 802 N La Cienega Blvd, Los Angeles, CA, 90069. *Mailing Add:* 10210 Legend Rock Rd Escondido CA 92026

ROBBINS, TRINA
CARTOONIST, ILLUSTRATOR
b Brooklyn, NY, Aug 17, 38. *Exhib:* Corcoran Gallery, Washington, DC, 69; Global Space Invasions, San Francisco Mus Mod Art, 78; Pork Roasts, Univ BC Fine Arts Gallery, Vancouver, 81. *Awards:* Inkpot Award, San Diego Comic Art, 77. *Bibliog:* Ronald Levitt Lanyi (auth), Trina, Queen of underground comics, Univ Calif, Davis, 78; Sharon R Gunton (ed), Contemporary Literary Criticism, Vol 21, Gale Res, 82. *Publ:* Ed & contribr, It ain't me, Babe, 70 & contribr, Wimmen's Comix No 1-6, 72-76, Last Gasp; ed, contribr, Wet Satin No 1 & 2, Krupp/Last Gasp, 76 & 78; auth & illusr, Flashback Fashions, Price, Stern, Sloan, 83; coauth, Women and the Comics, Eclipse Enterprises (in prep); and others. *Mailing Add:* 1982 15th St San Francisco CA 94114

ROBBINS, WARREN M
MUSEUM DIRECTOR
b Worcester, Mass, Sept 4, 23. *Study:* Univ NH, BA, 45; Univ Mich, MA, 49. *Hon Degrees:* Lebanon Valley Col, Pa, 75, Int Col, Los Angeles, 79 & Univ NH, 79. *Collections Arranged:* African Art--The De Havenon Collection, 71; African Art in Washington Collections, 72; Tribute to Africa--the Photography and the Collection of Elliot Elisofon, 74; African Textiles & Traditional Dress, 75; The Art of Zaire, 76; The Art of Sierra Leone, 76; Religious & Secular Art of Ethiopia, 76-77; The Sculptor's Eye, Chaim Gross Collection, 76; The Traditional Art of the Nigerian Peoples, 77; Art of Zaire: The Bronson Collection, 78; Traditional Sculpture from Upper Volta, 79; The Useful Arts of Kenya, 79; African Puppetry, 80; Permanent Collections, 80-81; Traditional Costumery and Jewelry in Africa, 81; Traditional Costumes and Jewelry of Egypt, 81. *Pos:* Sr scholar & founding dir, Mus African Art, 64- *Teaching:* Lectr African art, Mus African Art, Washington, DC, 64-; lectr influence of African sculpture on mod western art, mus & univs in US, 68- *Awards:* Rothko Chapel Int Human Rights Award, 81. *Bibliog:* John Coppola (auth), Teaching museum, Topic Mag, 12/76; Barbaralee Diamondstein (auth), Light from the Dark Continent (film), CBS TV, 3/77; The Museum of African Art, Sat Rev, 5/77. *Mem:* Asn Art Mus Dirs; DC Comn Arts & Humanities; Am Asn Mus; Libr Cong; Duke Ellington Sch Arts. *Res:* Influence of African sculpture on modern western art. *Publ:* Contribr, Art in Society, Vol 5, No 3; How to Approach Traditional African Sculpture, Smithsonian, 72; auth, Traditional American Values in a World of Hostilities, Adult Educ, 75; auth, African Art in America, Vista, 75. *Mailing Add:* 530 Sixth St SE Washington DC 20003

ROBERSON, SAMUEL ARNDT
ARCHITECTURAL HISTORIAN, EDUCATOR
b Honolulu, Hawaii, May 5 39. *Study:* Williams Col, BA, 61, MA, 63; Salzburg-Klessheim Sch, cert, 65; Yale Univ, PhD, 74. *Collections Arranged:*

American Paintings from a Private Long Meadow Collection, Amherst Col, 71; Five College Modern Architecture, Amherst Col, 72; Early Chicago Architecture, Herron Sch Art, 80. *Pos:* Consult, Eye of Thomas Jefferson Bicentennial Exhib, Nat Gallery Art, Washington, DC, 74-76; acad coordr, Nat Endowment Humanities Learning Mus Prog, Indianapolis Mus Art, 76-80; dir, Historic Indianapolis Inc, 80- *Teaching:* Instr art hist, Williams Col, 61-63, Yale Univ, 64-66, Princeton Univ, 66-68 & Amherst Col, 69-72; asst prof, Herron Sch Art, 72-76, chmn art hist, 72-80, assoc prof, 76-; vis assoc prof, Ind Univ, Bloomington, 76. *Mem:* Soc Archit Historians; Col Art Asn; and others. *Res:* Eighteenth and nineteenth century American architecture and landscape gardening. *Publ:* Auth, The Technical Creation of the Greek Slave, 65 & coauth, The Greek Slave, 65, Newark Mus; contribr, Praeger Encyclopedia of Art, Praeger Publ, 71; auth, Indiana Historic Sites and Structures Reports, 80-; auth, Historic American Buildings Survey in Indiana Catalog, 83. *Mailing Add:* Herron Sch of Art 1701 N Pennsylvania Indianapolis IN 46202

ROBERSON, WILLIAM
TAPESTRY ARTIST
b Ripley, Miss, Feb 15, 39. *Study:* Memphis State Univ; Memphis Acad Arts, BFA; Ind Univ. *Work:* Ark Art Ctr, Little Rock; Tenn Craft Collection, Craft Mus, Nashville; 1st Nat Bank, Orlando, Fla; Memphis Acad Arts; Falls Creek State Park, Tenn; and others. *Comn:* Tapestries, comn by Lausanne Sch, Memphis, 70, Jewish Community Ctr, Memphis, 71, Holiday Inns of Am, Aberdeen, Tex, 73, Opreyland Hotel, Nashville & First Tenn Bank, Memphis. *Exhib:* Young Americans, Mus Contemp Crafts, New York, 69; Piedmont Craft Exhib, Sneed Mus, Charlotte, NC; Miss Arts Festival, Jackson; Southeastern Craftmen Show, San Antonio, Tex. *Teaching:* Assoc prof fiber design, Memphis Acad Arts, 69- *Mailing Add:* 694 N Trezevant St Memphis TN 38112

ROBERT, HENRY FLOOD, JR
MUSEUM DIRECTOR
b El Dorado, Ark, Feb 26, 43. *Study:* Palomar Col, AA, 66; Ariz State Univ, BFA, 70, MFA, 73; Harvard Univ, dipl (arts admin), 77. *Collections Arranged:* Zelda Sayre Fitzgerald Retrospective, 74, Marathon Art by Three Artists, 75, Corporate Collections in Montgomery, 76, George Verdak: Eras the Dance, 76-77 & Art Inc: American Paintings from Corporate Collections, 79, Montgomery Mus Fine Arts, Ala. *Pos:* Dir, Mem Union Gallery, Ariz State Univ, Tempe, 69-70, asst dir, Univ Art Mus, 70-72; asst dir, Loch Haven Art Ctr, Orlando, Fla, 73-74; dir, Montgomery Mus of Fine Arts, 74-79; dir, Joslyn Art Mus, Omaha, 79- *Mem:* Am Asn of Mus; Asn of Art Mus Dirs; Int Conf of Mus. *Publ:* Auth, Paolo Soleri: Arcology and the Future of Man, 75, contribr, Venetian Drawings from the Collection of Janos Scholz, 76, The Throne of the Third Heaven of the Nations Millenium General Assembly, 77 & Anne Goldthwaite: 1869-1944, 77 & auth, Walter Gauknek Retrospective, 78, Montgomery Mus Fine Arts. *Mailing Add:* c/o Joslyn Art Mus 2200 Dodge St Omaha NE 68102

ROBERTS, BRUCE ELLIOTT
PAINTER
US citizen. *Study:* Art Students League, 37-39; Corcoran Sch Art, 44-45; also design with Paul Rand, New York, 49-51. *Work:* Rosenberg Libr, Galveston; Elliott Mus, Stuart, Fla; La Maritime Mus, New Orleans. *Comn:* Downwind Victory (painting), US Capitol, Washington, DC, 73; History of Florida (painting), Fla Supreme Court, Tallahassee. *Exhib:* Walker Mus Art, Brunswick, Maine, 75; one-man shows, Elliott Mus, Stuart, Fla, 71 & 76, Mus Arts & Sci, Daytona Beach, Fla, 77; 2nd Ann, Am Soc Marine Art, New York, 79. *Bibliog:* John Alexander (auth), Maritime paintings, USN All Hands Mag, 9/76; Charlotte Moser (auth), Sailing ships, Houston Chronicle, 1/77; Gary R Libby (auth), Bruce E Roberts, SW Art Mag, 1/79. *Mem:* Am Soc Marine Artists; Soc Marine Painters. *Media:* Oil. *Publ:* A Salute to Josh Slocum, Cruising World Publ, 1/77. *Dealer:* Townhouse Galleries 319 Royal St New Orleans LA 70130. *Mailing Add:* 611 Ash St Port St Lucie FL 33452

ROBERTS, CLYDE HARRY
PAINTER, EDUCATOR
b Sandusky, Ohio, June 12, 23. *Study:* Cleveland Inst Art, dipl, 46; Columbia Univ, MA, 49; also with John Pike, Robert Brackman, Edgar Whitney & William Schultz. *Work:* Washington Co Mus Fine Arts, Hagerstown, Md; Ford Times Gallery, Dearborn, Mich; State House, Annapolis, Md. *Exhib:* Many exhibs, Baltimore Watercolor Open, Cumberland Valley Exhib, Miss Art Asn Open & Cleveland Mus May Show; one-man show, Pa State Univ, 79. *Teaching:* Instr painting, Hagerstown Jr Col, 57-; supvr art, Washington Co Bd Educ, 68-81; retired; instr watercolor, Mont Alto Campus, Pa State Univ; instr art teacher educ, Shepherd Col, WVa. *Awards:* Popular Prize, Cumberland Valley Artists, 71; Artists Members Award, Baltimore Watercolor Club, 71 & 74; First Award, Pa Watercolor Soc, 81. *Bibliog:* G Horn (auth), article, Art Today, 68; feature article, Painting--Materials and Techniques, Timmon, 79; article, US News & World Report, 82. *Mem:* Baltimore Watercolor Club; Md Art Asn (secy, 62-64); Nat Art Educ Asn; fel Royal Soc Art; Pa Watercolor Soc. *Media:* Watercolor. *Publ:* Illusr, Ford Times Mag, 58; contribr, Sch Arts, 68; contribr, Artists News Unlimited, 71; contribr, Nat Geog Sch Ed, 73; auth, article, Palette Talk, 80. *Dealer:* Hill Top House Harpers Ferry WV 25425; Benjamen's Art Gallery Hagerstown MD 21740. *Mailing Add:* 219 N Colonial Dr Hagerstown MD 21740

ROBERTS, DONALD
EDUCATOR, PRINTMAKER
b Wolfeboro, NH, Nov 24, 23. *Study:* Vesper George Sch of Art, Boston, cert; RI Sch of Design, Providence, BFA; Ohio Univ, Athens, MFA. *Work:*

Cleveland Mus of Art; Tate Gallery, London; Rosenwald Collection, Los Angeles; Seattle Mus, Wash; Libr of Cong, Washington, DC. *Exhib:* Dayton Art Inst, Ohio, 60, 65 & 74; 1st-3rd Lithography Ann, Tallahassee, Fla, 64-67; The Print Club, Philadelphia, 68; Contemp Am Prints, Krannert Mus, Champaign-Urbana, Ill, 70; Huntington Galleries, WVa, 71; and others. *Teaching:* Prof printmaking, drawing & painting, Ohio Univ, Athens, 53- *Awards:* Tamarind Lithography Grant, 62; Purchase Award, 9th Ann Paint of the Yr, Mead Corp, 63; Pennypacker Award, 4th Ann Soc Am Graphic Artists, 65. *Bibliog:* William Sargent (auth), American Printmakers, Ashland Oil Corp, 76. *Mailing Add:* Dept Art Ohio Univ Athens OH 45701

ROBERTS, GILROY
SCULPTOR

b Mar 11, 05; US citizen. *Study:* Frankford High Sch Eve Art Class, Philadelphia; Corcoran Gallery Art Sch; also with John R Sinnock & Heinz Warneke. *Work:* US Mint, Philadelphia; Smithsonian Inst, Washington, DC; Franklin Mint, Franklin Center, Pa. *Comn:* Portrait of Anthony Drexel, Drexel Univ, 38; Kennedy half dollar, US Mint, 63; portrait of Albert Einstein, Inst Advan Study, Princeton; portrait of David Sarnoff, RCA Corp; portrait of Ernie Pyle, Scripps Howard News Alliance. *Exhib:* Pa Acad Fine Arts, Philadelphia, 36-37; Corcoran Gallery Art, Washington, DC, 42; Nat Sculpture Soc, New York; Madrid, Spain, 51; Rome, Italy, 61. *Pos:* Picture engraver, Bur Engraving & Painting, Washington, DC, 38-44; chief sculptor & engraver, US Mint, Philadelphia, 48-64; chmn & chief sculptor, Franklin Mint, 64- *Awards:* Honorable Mention, Nat Sculptors Soc, 51; Gold Medal & Citation, Int Exhib Coins & Medals, Madrid, Spain, 51; Gold Medal, Numismatic Asn, 51. *Bibliog:* Willard Garvin (auth), The suburb that has its own mint, Sunday Bull Mag, 1/51; Thomas Baker (auth), The creation of the Kennedy half dollar, Coin Asn Mag, 6/72. *Mem:* Fel Nat Sculpture Soc; Franklin Inst; Philadelphia Sketch Club. *Publ:* Auth, Birth of a dime design, 10/67 & Creating designs in circles, 5/68, Coins Mag. *Mailing Add:* 67 Llangollen Lane Newtown Square PA 19073

ROBERTS, HELENE EMYLOU
LIBRARIAN

b Seattle, Wash, Mar 23, 31. *Study:* Univ Wash, BA, 53, MA, 57, ML, 61. *Pos:* Art librn, Dartmouth Col, Hanover, NH, 63-66 & slide librn, 68-70; cur visual collections, Harvard Univ, 70-; adv ed, Victorian Periodical Newslett, 75-78. *Awards:* Librn Res Fel, Harvard Univ Libr, 80-81. *Mem:* Art Libr Soc NAm; Spec Libr; Res Soc for Victorian Periodicals (treas, 70-75); Am Soc Picture Professionals. *Res:* Dante Gabriel Rossetti; Victorian Art; Eighteenth and nineteenth century art periodicals; images of women in art; nineteenth century art criticism. *Publ:* Auth, The exquisite slave, Signs, spring 77; auth, The image library, Art Libr J, 3/78; auth, Victorian medievalism: Revival or masquerade, Browning Inst Studies, 8/80; auth, The sentiment of reality, Thackeray's art criticism, In: Studies in The Novel, Vol 13, 81; auth, Exhibition and review: The periodical press and the Victorian art exhibition system, In: Victorian Periodical Press, Leicester Univ Press, 82. *Mailing Add:* c/o Fogg Art Mus Harvard Univ Cambridge MA 02138

ROBERTS, LUCILLE D (MALKIA)
PAINTER, EDUCATOR

b Washington, DC. *Study:* Howard Univ; Univ Mich, AM; NY Univ; Acad Grande Chaumiere, Paris; Univ Ghana; also with Jose Gutierriez, Mexico City, Mex. *Work:* Atlanta Univ; WVa State Col; Jefferson Community Col, Water Town, NY. *Exhib:* One-man shows, Porter Gallery, Howard Univ, 71 & Col Mus, Hampton Inst, 72; Nat Exhib Black Artists, Smith-Mason Gallery, Washington, DC, 71; Black Artists Exhib, Afro-Am Cult Ctr, Cleveland State Univ, 72. *Teaching:* Asst prof art, DC Teachers Col, Washington, DC, 65-78; assoc prof African & Afro-Am art, State Univ NY Col Oswego, 70-71. *Awards:* First Prize, Mem Show, 65 & Evening Star Award, 66, Soc Washington Artists; James A Porter Award, Cleveland State Univ, 72. *Bibliog:* Lewis & Wadday (auths), Black Artists on Art, 69; J Edwin Atkinson (auth), Black Dimensions in Contemporary Art, Carnation Co, 70. *Mem:* Nat Conf Artists; Black Acad Arts & Lett; Soc Washington Artists; DC Art Asn. *Media:* Oil, Acrylic. *Mailing Add:* 2445 Lyttonsville Rd 1116 Silver Spring MD 20910

ROBERTS, PERCIVAL R
EDUCATOR, PAINTER

b Wilmington, Del, Nov 2, 35. *Study:* Univ Del, BA, 57, MA, 62; Haystack Mt Sch Art, Maine, summer 57; Ill State Univ, EdD, 68; L'Libre Univ Asie, LittD. *Work:* Univ Del; Ill State Univ; Clarion State Col; Delaware Poetry Ctr; Bloomsburg Univ. *Exhib:* US Fine Arts Registry, New York, 67; Haas Gallery Art, Bloomsburg State Col, Pa, 69; Hazel Sanford Gallery, Clarion State Col, 74; Am Painters in Paris, 76; Harrisburg Area Community Col, 80. *Pos:* Chmn, Art Comn, State Del, 62-65; dir, Broadway Gallery Art, Ill, 67-68; mem, Visual Arts Adv Panel, Pa Coun Arts, 75- *Teaching:* Instr drawing & painting, Del Art Mus & Univ Del, 60-64; lectr art, Ill State Univ, 65-68; prof art educ, art hist & visual aesthetics, Bloomsburg Univ, 68-; prof psychology art, Univ Scranton, 72-80. *Awards:* Distinguished Teaching Award, Commonwealth Pa, 75 & 76; Maya Schock Award, Doshi Ctr Contemp Art, 81. *Bibliog:* Glenn Canouse (auth), He Makes Poetry...Art...Time, Press-Enterprise, 6/74; Valery O'Connell (auth), A true artist resorts to expression in two modes, Art News, summer 68. *Mem:* Mid-State Artists Asn (bd dirs, 68-); Pa Art Educ Asn (exec coun, currently); life mem Nat Art Educ Asn. *Res:* Aesthetics and synesthesia as a component of the aesthetic experience. *Publ:* Auth, Centaurian Flight, 69 & auth, Red Sky in the Morning, 74, Mitre Press, London; auth, Birth of Venus, Lawton Press, 78; auth, Bark: A Folio of Poems and Eye Poems, Palette Press, 80; auth, Incantations, In: The Clouds Threw This Light, Am Indian Inst Arts Press, 83. *Mailing Add:* Dept of Art Bloomsburg Univ Bloomsburg PA 17815

ROBERTS, PRISCILLA WARREN
PAINTER

b Glen Ridge, NJ, June 13, 16. *Study:* Art Students League; Nat Acad Design. *Work:* Metrop Mus Art, New York; Dallas Mus Fine Arts; Walker Art Ctr, Minneapolis; Butler Inst Am Art, Youngstown, Ohio; IBM Collection, New York. *Exhib:* Carnegie Inst Int, Pittsburgh, 50; Nat Acad Design, New York, 69; Corcoran Gallery Art, Washington, DC; Univ Ill, Urbana; Allied Artists, New York. *Awards:* Hallgarten Prizes & Proctor Portrait Prize, Nat Acad Design, 47; Third Prize, Carnegie Inst Int, 50. *Mem:* Nat Acad Design; hon mem Catharine Lorillard Wolfe Asn. *Media:* Oil. *Dealer:* Grand Central Galleries 50 E 50th St New York NY 10022. *Mailing Add:* Box 281 Wilton CT 06897

ROBERTS, RICHARD
PAINTER

b Philadelphia, Pa, June 26, 25. *Work:* Nat Acad Design, New York; Butler Inst Am Art, Youngstown, Ohio. *Exhib:* 51st Ann, Pa Acad, Philadelphia, 53; March Exhib, Mus Fine Art, Springfield, Mass, 53; 19th Ann Mid Year, Butler Inst, Youngstown, Ohio, 54; Manhattan Artists, Whitney Mus, New York, 54; 54th Ann Spring Exhib, Delgado Mus, New Orleans, La, 55; The Seaport, Baltimore Mus, Md, 55; 5th Ann Exhib, Pittsfield Mus, Mass, 56; 153rd Exhib, Nat Acad Design, New York, 78. *Awards:* Louis Comfort Tiffany Found Fel, 54; Purchase Prize, Butler Inst Am Art, 54; Ward Ranger Purchase Award, Nat Acad Art, 78. *Media:* Oil, Acrylic. *Mailing Add:* 175 W 12th St New York NY 10011

ROBERTS, TOM (THOMAS KEITH)
PAINTER

b Toronto, Ont, Dec 22, 08. *Study:* Cent Tech Sch, Toronto; Ont Col Art, Toronto. *Work:* Ford Motor Co; Rio-Algom; Seagrams; plus collections of many other Can co & insts. *Exhib:* Many ann, Royal Acad Arts, Montreal & Toronto, Montreal Mus Fine Arts & Ont Soc Artists, Toronto, 29-; and one-man shows in Montreal, Toronto, Ottawa, Halifax & Vancouver, Can. *Awards:* Ralph Clarke Stone Award, 49. *Mem:* Royal Can Acad; Ont Soc Artists. *Media:* Oil, Watercolor, Acrylic. *Dealer:* Wallack Gallery 203 Bank Ottawa ON Can; Continental Gallery Montreal PQ. *Mailing Add:* 1312 Stavebank Rd Mississauga ON L5G 2V2 Canada

ROBERTS, WILLIAM EDWARD
PAINTER, EDUCATOR

b Cleveland, Ohio, July 1, 41. *Study:* Kent State Univ, BFA, 68, MA, 71; Cornell Univ, lithography with Arnold Singer, 73. *Work:* Everson Mus Art, Syracuse, NY; Kent State Univ, Ohio; IBM Corp, Albany, NY; NY Racing Asn, Elmont. *Exhib:* Midyear Show, Butler Inst Am Art, Youngstown, Ohio, 73; one-man show, Everson Mus Art, 74; 55 Mercer, New York, 81; Saratoga Performing Art Ctr, NY, 82; Hartell Gallery, Cornell Univ, 82; Dayspring Gallery, Saratoga Springs, NY, 82 & 83; Handwerker Gallery, Ithaca Col, 83; and others. *Teaching:* Assoc prof painting, Wells Col, Aurora, NY, 71-; instr painting, Auburn Prison, NY, 75-77. *Awards:* Purchase Award, State Univ NY Col Potsdam, State of Ny, 73; Purchase Award, Erie, Pa Ann, Marine Midland Bank, 73. *Bibliog:* Millie Wolff (auth), Artist's racing series has Kings' excitement, Palm Beach Daily News, 3/14/79. *Mem:* Col Art Asn; Am Asn Univ Prof. *Media:* Oil, Wash. *Mailing Add:* Wells Col Aurora NY 13026

ROBERTSON, CHARLES J
ADMINISTRATOR

b Houston, Tex, Sept 12, 34. *Study:* Univ Va, BA, 56; Harvard Univ, MA, 58; Courtauld Inst, Univ London, 60; George Washington Univ, JD, 64. *Pos:* Assoc dir, NC Mus Art, 75-77; assoc dir mus resources, Nat Mus Am Art, 77- *Mem:* Am Asn Mus (treas, 81-); Col Art Asn Am; Soc Archit Historians. *Mailing Add:* Nat Mus Am Art Smithsonian Inst Washington DC 20560

ROBERTSON, JOAN E (JOAN ELIZABETH MITCHELL)
CURATOR, GRAPHIC ARTIST

b Washington, DC, June 11, 42. *Study:* Bucknell Univ, Lewisburg, Pa, BA(art), 64; Univ Iowa, MA(printmaking), 67, studied with Mauricio Lasansky. *Work:* Kemper Group, Long Grove, Ill; Schif Hardin & Waite, Chicago; First Nat Bank, Chicago; Household Int, Ill; Ill State Mus, Springfield. *Exhib:* Works on Paper by Artists of Chicago and Vicinity, Art Inst Chicago, 78; one-person shows, Donnelly Libr Gallery, Lake Forest Col, Ill, 79 & Loyola Univ, Chicago, 81; Nat Prints & Drawing Competition, DeKalb, Ill, 81; Wustum Mus, Racine, Wis, 82. *Collections Arranged:* Kemper Group art collection, brochure preparation & monthly exhibs, 73- *Pos:* Art cur, Kemper Group, Long Grove, Ill, 73-; gallery coordr, Lake Forest Col, Ill, 81. *Awards:* 2nd Prize, Libertyville, Ill, 81; YWCA Leadership Award in the Arts, 83. *Bibliog:* Lydia Murman (auth), Joan E Robertson, New Art Examiner, 6/81; Sandy Riemer (auth), Color puts life into her pencil drawings, Sunday Herald, 4/81; article, Art (instead of soda) for insurance company, Am Artist Mag, 81; Diane Norman (auth), Palatine curator guides growing Kemper art collection, Suburban Sun-Times, 80; and others. *Media:* Colored Pencil; Intaglio. *Mailing Add:* c/o Kemper Group Long Grove IL 60049

ROBERTSON, NANCY ELIZABETH See Dillow, Nancy E

ROBINS, CORINNE
CRITIC, WRITER

b New York, NY, July 31, 34. *Study:* Walden Sch; NY Univ; New Sch Social Res. *Pos:* Asst managing ed, Mademoiselle Mag, 57-59; cur exhib, Soho Ctr

Visual Artists, 76; contrib ed, Arts Mag, 76-82, assoc ed, 82- *Teaching:* Lectr Am art, US Info Serv, Brazil, 72; lectr Drawing Now, Jamaica Art Ctr, 76; lectr art hist, criticism & social change, Pratt Inst, 77, lectr painting seminar, 79-; lectr art hist, Sch Visual Arts, 78- *Awards:* Critics Fel Award, Nat Endowment Art, 78. *Bibliog:* Grace Glueck (auth), Art people, New York Times, 5/28/76. *Mem:* Artist Talk Art (bd mem, currently); Orgn Independent Artists; Art Critics Asn. *Publ:* Auth, Late decorative: Art, artifact and the Ersatz, 4/80 & Ten months of rush hour figuration, 9/82, Arts Mag; auth, Germans and Jews, Sub-Stance, Vol 35, fall 82; auth, Walls of the '70s, In: Queensborough Community Col Catalog, 83; auth, Pluralism: American Art 1968-1981, Harper & Row, 84; and others. *Mailing Add:* 83 Wooster St New York NY 10012

ROBINSON, C DAVID
ARCHITECT, COLLECTOR
b New York, NY, June 12, 36. *Study:* Princeton Univ, NJ, BA(art, magna cum laude), 57; Sch Archit, Univ Calif, Berkeley, with hon, 61-62; Grad Sch Fine Arts, Univ Pa, MArch, 65. *Pos:* Co-owner, Robinson, Mills & Williams, Architecture & Planning, currently. *Teaching:* Fac, Mus Management Inst, Univ Calif, Berkeley, 79; mem bd overseers, Grad Sch Fine Arts, Univ Pa. *Mem:* Int Coun Mus Mod Art; Western Asn Art Mus (vis spec, 73-78, bd trustees, 79); San Francisco Art Inst (trustee, 73-, chmn bd, 76-79); San Francisco Mus Art. *Collection:* Contemporary, New York School 1960's & 1970's and West Coast. *Mailing Add:* 153 Kearny St San Francisco CA 94108

ROBINSON, CHARLOTTE
PAINTER, PRINTMAKER
b San Antonio, Tex, Nov, 24. *Study:* Art Students League, New York, 48; New York Univ, 49; Corcoran Art Sch, 51. *Work:* Mus Espanol de Arts Contemporaneo, Madrid; The New Sch for Social Res, New York; Am Telephone & Telegraph, New York & Chicago; Philip Morris Inc, New York; Inland Steel, Washington, DC. *Exhib:* The Bronx Mus, New York, 76; The Mint Mus, Charlotte, NC, 77; Collectors Choice, Sheldon Swope Gallery, Terre Haute, Ind, 77; San Jose State Univ, Calif, 77; Douglass Col of Rutgers Univ, New Brunswick, NJ, 79 & 80; Arlington Art Center, Va, 81. *Collections Arranged:* One to One, Eight Artists & Eight Cur, Washington Women's Ctr, Washington, DC, 76; Artists Co, Nine From Washington, DC, Nat Endowment for the Arts & Humanities mus traveling show, 77. *Pos:* Trustee, Bronx Mus, New York, 76-77. *Teaching:* Instr drawing, Smithsonian Assoc Prog, Washington, DC, 76-; instr art world sem, Washington Women's Art Ctr, Washington, DC, 76-80. *Awards:* Scholar, Student Exhib, Corcoran Art Sch, Washington, DC, 51; grants, Nat Endowment Arts, 77, 78 & 81. *Bibliog:* Cynthia Nadelman (auth), Not so crazy quilts, Artnews, 3/82; Dorthy Seiberling (auth), A new kind of quilt, New York Times Mag, 9/82; Jo Ann Lewis (auth), X marks the spot, Washington Post, 10/83; Paul Richard (auth), Family album, Washington Post, 5/30/81. *Mem:* Nat Women's Caucus Art (bd dirs, currently). *Media:* Silkscreen, Lithograph. *Publ:* Ed, The Artist & The Quilt, Knopf, 10/83. *Dealer:* Fendrick Gallery 3059 M St Washington DC 20007. *Mailing Add:* 6324 Crosswoods Dr Falls Church VA 22044

ROBINSON, CHRIS (CHRISTOPHER THOMAS)
CONCEPTUAL ARTIST, EDUCATOR
b Huntington, NY, Mar 18, 51. *Study:* Fla State Univ, BFA, 72; Univ Mass, MFA, 75. *Work:* Arch Am Art, Washington, DC; Univ South; SC State Art Collection, Columbia. *Comn:* Installations, Ninth Nat-Int Sculpture Conf, New Orleans, 76, Nat Sculpture Conf, Jonesboro, Ark, 77, Arcosanti Festival Art in the Environment, Cordes Junction, Ariz, 78, Col Art Asn, New Orleans, 80 & Eastern Ill Univ, 81. *Exhib:* Artists Biennial, New Orleans Mus Art, 77; solo exhib, Atlanta Art Workers Coalition Gallery, 80; Installation, Southeastern Ctr Contemp Art, Winston-Salem, NC, 81; Appalachian Nat Drawing Competition, Appalachian State Univ, 81; Netherlands-Am Contemp Exchange Exhib, 82; Printmakers in the South, Southern Arts Traveling Exhib, 83. *Collections Arranged:* Nat Sculpture Exhib, 76, 78 & 79. *Teaching:* Assoc visual arts, Univ Mass, Amherst, 73-75; from instr to asst prof, Univ SC, Cola, 75-; guest artist, Univ Ala, Huntsville, 77, Univ South, Greensboro Col & Brevard Col. *Bibliog:* Elizabeth George (auth), Laser artist beams brush towards space shuttle, Greenville Piedmont, 3/10/78; Ron Jones (auth), Techno-aesthetics in South Carolina, Art Papers, 3-4/81. *Mem:* Col Art Asn; Southern Asn Sculptors (bd mem, 75-80); Southeastern Col Art Conf. *Publ:* Auth, Astronautics as an impetus to visual art, In: Proceedings of the 33rd International Astronautical Federation Congress, 82. *Mailing Add:* 198 Sweetwood Circle Columbia SC 29210

ROBINSON, FRANKLIN W
MUSEUM DIRECTOR, HISTORIAN
b Providence, RI, May 21, 39. *Study:* Harvard Univ, BA, 61, MA, 63, PhD, 70. *Pos:* Dir, Williams Col Mus Art, 75-79 & Mus Art, RI Sch Design, 79- *Teaching:* Asst prof art hist, Dartmouth Col, 69-75; assoc prof & dir grad prog art hist, Williams Col, 75-79. *Mem:* Col Art Asn; Am Asn Mus; Am Asn Mus Dir. *Res:* Baroque art; prints and drawings. *Publ:* Auth, 100 Master Drawings from New England Private Collections, 72; auth, Gabriel Metsu, 75; auth, Dutch Life in the Golden Century, 75; auth, Seventeenth Century Dutch Drawings from American Collections, 77; auth, Dutch and Flemish Paintings, from the Ringling Museum, 80. *Mailing Add:* Museum of Art RI Sch of Design Providence RI 02903

ROBINSON, GROVE
PAINTER, EDUCATOR
b Asheville, NC, May 17, 35. *Study:* Mars Hill Col, 53-55; Univ NC, Chapel Hill, 55-56; with Kenneth Ness & Robert Howard; Yale Summer Sch Music & Art, Norfolk, Conn, 57; with Bernard Chaet, Rudy Pozzatti & Gabor

Peterdi; Columbia Univ, BFA, 58, MFA, 60, with Seong May, Edwin Dickinson, Hans Mueller, Meyer Schapiro & Ruddy Wittkower; Fulbright Fel to France, in Painting, 58-59; with Marcel Brion. *Work:* NC Mus Art, Raleigh; Carroll Reece Mus, E Tenn State Univ; Tenn State Mus, Nashville; Tenn All-State Collection, First Am Nat Bank, Nashville. *Exhib:* 8th Ann Piedmont Craft Exhib, Mint Mus, Charlotte, NC, 71; 18th Biennial Mid-South Exhib, Brooks Art Gallery, Memphis, Tenn, 73; Four Tenn Artists, Univ of Ga, Athens, 74; Painters in Tenn Univs, Middle Tenn State Univ, Murphreesboro, 77; one-man show, East Tenn State Univ, 64; Memphis State Univ Fac Show, 79; Wesleyan Int Print Exhib, 80; Early 80's, Tenn State Mus, 81; and others. *Pos:* Vpres for visual arts, Jackson Art Coun, Tenn, 72-74; crafts adv panel, Tenn Arts Comn, 72-76. *Teaching:* Instr, Meredith Col, Raleigh, 65-71; chmn & assoc prof dept of art, Union Univ, Jackson, Tenn, 71-; lectr grad art hist, Memphis State Univ, 79. *Awards:* Purchase Awards, 19th NC Artists Ann, NC Mus of Art, 56 & Tenn State Mus & Cultural Ctr, 81. *Bibliog:* M Beth (auth), 28th NC Artists Ann Art Review, Veritas Corp Inc, 66; Acquisitions from NC Anns 1946-1966 (catalog), N Mus of Art, 67; W C Burton (auth), Mixed Bag, Greensboro Daily News, 69. *Mem:* Southern Graphics Coun; Tenn Watercolor Soc. *Media:* Acrylic, Watercolor. *Publ:* Illusr, Union Univ Forum, Union Univ, 77-82. *Dealer:* Oates Gallery 91 N Tillman Memphis TN; Marson Graphics Shawan Rd Baltimore MD. *Mailing Add:* 17 Laurel Lane Jackson TN 38301

ROBINSON, JAY (THURSTON)
PAINTER
b Detroit, Mich, Aug 1, 15. *Study:* Yale Col, BA; Cranbrook Acad Art, MFA. *Work:* Cranbrook Mus, Bloomfield Hills, Mich; Detroit Inst Art; Houston Mus Fine Arts; J B Speed Mus, Louisville, Ky; Philbrook Art Ctr, Tulsa. *Exhib:* Audubon Artists, New York; Carnegie Inst Int, Pittsburgh; Corcoran Gallery Art Biennial, Washington, DC; Nat Acad Design, New York; Pa Acad Fine Arts, Philadelphia. *Awards:* Louis Comfort Tiffany Found Fel, 49; seven Childe Hassam Fund Purchase Awards, Am Acad Arts & Lett. *Mem:* Artists Equity Asn, New York. *Mailing Add:* 60 Church St Pleasantville NY 10570

ROBINSON, LILIEN FILIPOVITCH
HISTORIAN, EDUCATOR
b Ljubljana, Yugoslavia, Feb 7, 40; US citizen. *Study:* George Washington Univ, BA, 62, MA, 65; Johns Hopkins Univ, PhD, 78. *Pos:* Chmn dept art, George Washington Univ, 76- *Teaching:* Lectr art introd & surveys of Western art, George Washington Univ, 64-65, asst prof 19th century art & surveys of Western art, 65-76, assoc prof 19th century Europ art, 76-79 & prof 19th century Europ art, 80. *Bibliog:* Boris Weintraub (auth), The professor's enthusiasm is contagious, Washington Star, 10/27/79. *Mem:* Col Art Asn. *Res:* 19th-century French painting and academic painting. *Publ:* Auth, Revival of etching in the 19th century, In: Max Klinger: Art and Imagination, Dimock Gallery, 81; auth, Frank Wright (catalog), 83 & Jerry Lake (catalog), 83, Dimock Gallery; auth, La Vie MOderne: Art and Life in Nineteenth Century France (catalog), Corcoran Gallery, 83; auth, Collecting as tradition and art, In: The Intimate Scale: Paintings from the Phillips Collection, Diamock Gallery, 83. *Mailing Add:* Dept Art George Washington Univ Washington DC 20052

ROBINSON, MARGOT (MARGOT STEIGMAN)
PAINTER, SCULPTOR
b New York, NY. *Study:* Art Students League, with Harry Sternberg, 47; Robert Blackburn's Creative Workshop, 49-55; painting with John Von Wicht, 53-55; Gerard Koch Studio, Paris, 68; Donald Mavros Studio, New York, 71-72. *Work:* Am Express Co, New York; Data Processing Co, Boston & Chicago; Continental Grain Co, Columbus, Ohio. *Exhib:* Brooklyn Mus Nat Print Ann, New York; Pa Acad of Fine Arts, Philadelphia; Cincinnati Mus Color Lithography Biennial, Ohio; Riverside Mus, New York; Whitney Mus of Am Art, New York; Brooklyn Mus Community Exhib, New York; Herbert Benevy Gallery, New York, 73; Sarah Inst, New York, 80; Marymount Manhattan Col, 83. *Pos:* Dir, Creative Graphic Workshop, New York, 52-54; registr, Nat Acad Sch of Fine Arts, New York, 55-57; vpres, Noho Gallery, New York, 76-77, secy, 77-78. *Bibliog:* Valerie Natsios (auth), article, Arts J, 2/81; James T McCartin (auth), article, Arts Mag, 10/82; William Pellicone (auth), article, Artspeak, 10/82. *Mem:* New York Artists Equity; Women in the Arts. *Media:* Mixed Media. *Dealer:* Noho Gallery 168 Mercer St New York NY 10012. *Mailing Add:* 141 Joralemon St Brooklyn NY 11201

ROBINSON, MARIE RACHELLE
DEALER, PAINTER
b De Ridder, La, Oct 14, 19. *Study:* Warner Sch Art, New Orleans, La, 27; Sophie Newcomb Univ, New Orleans, 36-37; Univ Paris, France, 64. *Comn:* Road to San Jacinto, Rice Hotel, Houston, Tex, 73; Galveston Fishing Camp, Vincent Genna Enterprises, Tex, 73; Big Thicket (mural), Tex Preservation, Houston, 75. *Pos:* Owner, Bayou Art Sch, Dickinson, Tex, 70-; owner, Marie Robinson Art Gallery, Houston, Tex, 70- *Bibliog:* Mable McClure (auth), Coastal artist, Galveston News, 8/22/67; Jack Loftis (auth), Texas landscape art, Tex Mag, 12/10/68; Don Buchanan (auth), Artist comes home, New Orleans Item, 2/23/72. *Mem:* Am Soc Contemp Artists; Tex Soc Water Fowl Artists; Int Asn Appraisers; New England Appraisers Asn; Appraisers Asn Am. *Media:* Oil, Watercolor. *Specialty:* Original art, contemporary and master. *Publ:* Auth, A Walk With the Old Masters, 67, Painting Scapes--Land & Sea, 68 & The Importance of Perspective, 68, Wilson Press. *Mailing Add:* 305 West 6th St PO Box 64 Rusk TX 75785

ROBINSON, MARY ANN
ADMINISTRATOR, EDUCATOR

b McPherson, Kans, Sept 24, 23. *Study:* Kans State Univ, BS, 45; McCormick Theological Sem, MA, 55; Wichita State Univ, MA, 72; studied under Maude Ellsworth, Jan Lundgren, Robert Kisskaden, Robert Wood & James Pike. *Exhib:* Kans Biennial Art Exhib, Birger Sandzen Mem Gallery, Lindsborg, Kans, 72; Kans Ann Watercolor Exhib, Wichita Art Asn, 73; Am Contemp Arts & Crafts, Fla, 73; Kans Watercolor Soc Mem Show, Art Ctr Gallery, Hays, Kans, 77; Birger Sandzen Mem Gallery, 77 & 83. *Pos:* Supvr art pub sch, McPherson, Kans, 47-49; dir, Friendship Hall Gallery, McPherson Col, Kans, 63- *Teaching:* Assoc prof art educ & art hist & chmn dept art, McPherson Col, Kans, 63- *Mem:* Kans Watercolor Soc (bd mem, 77-79); Kans Art Educ Asn; Nat Art Educ Asn; McPherson Arts Coun. *Media:* Watercolor, Acrylic. *Mailing Add:* 601 S Walnut McPherson KS 67460

ROBINSON, SALLY W
PAINTER, PRINTMAKER

b Detroit, Mich, Nov 2, 24. *Study:* Bennington Col, BA; Wayne State Univ, MA & MFA; Cranbrook Acad Art; also with Hans Hofmann, Paul Feeley, Karl Knaths & Leon Kroll. *Work:* Chase Manhattan Bank, New York; Detroit Inst Arts; K-Mart Hq; and pvt collections. *Exhib:* Toledo Mus, Winston Traveling Show; Zella 9 Gallery, London, Eng; Troy Art Gallery, 78; Detroit Inst Arts, 78; Cliche-Verre, nat exhib, Detroit Inst Arts & Houston; and others. *Pos:* Mem, Gov Comn for Art in State Bldgs, Mich, 78-79; bd mem, Mus Art, Univ Mich, 79- *Teaching:* Instr silk screen, Wayne State Univ, 73-74. *Awards:* Second Prize, Bloomfield Art Asn, 72; Second Prize, Soc Women Painters, 74 & First Prize, 75. *Mem:* Friends Mod Art; Founders Soc; Detroit Artists Market; Soc Women Painters; Bloomfield Art Asn. *Publ:* Contribr, Mich Art J, 76; auth, Cliche-Verre: Hand Drawn, Light Printed, 80. *Dealer:* Klein-Vogel Gallery 4520 N Woodward Royal Oak MI 48053; Rina Gallery E 74th St & Madison New York NY 10021. *Mailing Add:* 708 Pine Run Dr Osprey FL 33559

ROBINSON, THOMAS V
DEALER, COLLECTOR

b Ft Worth, Tex, Feb 9, 38. *Study:* Tex Christian Univ, 56-57; Carlsbad-Oceanside Col, 57-58; Tex Wesleyan Col, 59-61. *Collections Arranged:* Ben Shahn 1930-1969, 70; Authery G Dove 1920-1940, 71; Am Landscape, 73; Westeryn Am Art 1860-1940 (auth, catalog), 74; PV Series 100 (auth, catalog), 80-82. *Pos:* Dir, Robinson Galleries, 69-77, pres & dir, 77-; dir, Ben Shahn Foundation, New York, 71-75. *Bibliog:* Thomas V Robinson, SW Art Mag, 71; Donna Tennant (auth), Gallery-Inst Exchange, Houston Chronicle, 81; Internation exchange, Artscene, Houston, 83. *Mem:* Cultural Arts Comt Houston Chamber Com; Tex Arts Alliance; Cultural Arts Coun Houston; Houston Art Dealers Asn (treas, bd-83, dir, 83-84). *Specialty:* Nineteenth and twentieth century American art; International contemporary conceptual, performance, video and all media objects. *Collection:* Nineteenth and twentieth century, American art, Mexican and regional art. *Publ:* Coauth, Kachinas-Paone, Encino Press, 76. *Mailing Add:* Robinson Galleries Inc 1200 Bissonnet Houston TX 77005

ROBISON, ANDREW
MUSEUM CURATOR, WRITER

b Memphis, Tenn, May 23, 40. *Study:* Princeton Univ, AB & PhD; Oxford Univ, MA; Fulbright Res Scholar, India. *Collections Arranged:* Giovanni Battista Piranesi & Picasso Prints, 70, Princeton Univ; diverse print & drawing exhib, Nat Gallery of Art, 74-; 18th century Venetian Illus Bks, Grolier Club, 81; Prints From an Alumni Collection, Princeton Univ Art Mus, 82. *Pos:* Cur & head dept prints & drawings, Nat Gallery Art, 74-83, sr cur, 83-; mem ed adv bd, Master Drawings, 81- *Teaching:* Instr, Univ Ill, 70-74. *Mem:* Grolier Club, NY; Col Art Asn; Print Coun Am (pres, 75-81); Washington Print Club. *Res:* Eighteenth century Italian graphic art; origins of etching. *Collection:* Prints and 18th century Italian illustrated books. *Publ:* Auth, Giovanni Battista Piranesi: The Early Architectural Fantasies, 78; auth, article, Master Drawings, 78; auth, Early German Drawings and Prints, 79; auth, Contemporary American Prints and Drawings, 81; auth, Picasso: The Bull, 82. *Mailing Add:* Dept of Graphic Arts Nat Gallery of Art Washington DC 20565

ROBLES, JULIAN
PAINTER, SCULPTOR

b Bronx, NY, June 24, 33. *Study:* Nat Acad Art & Design, with Robert Phillip; Art Students League, with Sidney Dickinson. *Work:* NMex State Permanent Collection, Albuquerque; Diamond M Mus, Snyder, Tex; 3M Collection, Houston, Tex. *Comn:* Portraits, Adm Edward O McDonnell, Lincoln Family, Oyster Bay, Long Island, 68, Ernestine Evans, Secy State NMex, 69, Margaret Jamison, Santa Fe, NMex, 70, Jean & Merle Rosenbaum, Santa Fe, 71, Bill Acheff, 81; and others. *Exhib:* NMex State Fair Art Exhib, Albuquerque, 71; Gov Galley Show, Santa Fe, 78; one man shows, Diamond M Mus, Snyder, Tex, 73, Pelham, Santa Fe, NMex, 81; Cowboy Hall Fame, 75; and others. *Awards:* Rosenthan Award, Pastel Soc Am, 83; Silver Medal for Oils & Third Place for Pastels, Nat Western Artist Show, 83; 24 national and regional awards; and others. *Bibliog:* Article, SW Art, 8/75; article, Artists of the Rockies, spring 82. *Mem:* Artists Equity; Pastel Soc Am; SW Pastel Soc. *Media:* Mixed; Wood. *Res:* Researching and recording authentic western Indian life and ceremonials. *Dealer:* Grand Central Galleries New York NY; Trailside Galleries Scottsdale AZ. *Mailing Add:* PO Box 1845 Taos NM 87571

ROCH, ERNST
DESIGNER, LECTURER

b Osijek, Yugoslavia, Dec 8, 28; Can citizen. *Study:* State Sch Appl Arts, Graz, Austria, MFA, 53; also with Hans Wagula, Graz, Austria. *Work:* Nat Poster Mus, Warsaw; Nat Gallery, Ottawa; Mus Mod Art, New York; Libr Congress, Washington, DC; and others. *Exhib:* Nat Libr, Ottawa, Ont, 77; St Mary's Univ, Halifax, 78; NB Mus, St John, 78; Alta Col of Art Gallery, Calgary, 78; York Univ, 79; and numerous other group exhibitions. *Collections Arranged:* The Visual Image of the Munich Games 1972, Montreal Mus Fine Arts, Art Gallery Ont, Toronto, 72; Alliance Graphique Int Posters, Place Ville Marie, Montreal, 82. *Pos:* Founding mem & principal, Design Collaborative, Montreal & Toronto, 65-77; principal, Roch Design, Montreal, 77- *Teaching:* Vis lectr graphic design, Ohio State Univ, Columbus. *Awards:* Fifty Books of the Year, Am Inst Graphic Arts, 72 & 75; Most Beautiful Books of the World, Leipzig, 75; Poster Biennale, Warsaw, 76, 78 & 80; and numerous other awards. *Bibliog:* John Gibson (auth), Ernst Roch, Printing Rev, 6/61; Hans Kuh (auth), Design Collaborative, Gebrauchsgraphik, Munich, 6/70; Allan Harrison & Hans Neuburg (auth), Graphic Designs by Rolf Harder & Ernst Roch, Montreal, 77. *Mem:* Royal Can Acad Arts; Alliance Graphique Int; Am Inst Graphic Arts; Int Inst Typographic Arts; Soc Graphic Designers Can. *Publ:* Ed, Arts of the Eskimo: Prints, 74; ed, Paper Zoo, 74. *Mailing Add:* PO Box 1056 Sta B Montreal PQ H3B 3K5 Canada

ROCHE, ROBERT (RICHARD)
PAINTER

b New Rochelle, NY, Dec 5, 21. *Study:* Apprenticeship, studio of Sebastian Cruset, 31-32; Nat Acad Design, New York, 33-36; Art Students League, New York, 36-40. *Work:* NY Racing Asn, Aqueduct, Long Island & Belmont, Elmwood; Nat Mus Racing, Saratoga, NY; Wilmington Race Track, Del; US Air Force, Offutt, Nebr. *Comn:* Saratoga Race Track Series, NY Racing Asn, Long Island, 60, painting of Man O War, 61 & Belmont Race Track Series, 63; plus others. *Exhib:* One-man shows, Frank K M Rehn Galleries, New York, 49 & 52; Am Watercolor Soc, New York; Silvermine Guild Artists, Norwalk, Conn, 51-54; Salmagundi Club, New York, 54 & 55. *Pos:* Cur, Mus Fine Arts, Richmond, Va, 47-48; radio art prog, WWNH, Rochester, NH, 68-70; writer, Nat Antiques Rev, Portland, Maine, 69-71. *Teaching:* Instr painting & drawing, pvt art sch, 42-64. *Bibliog:* G Leonard Gold (auth), Saratoga Prints, NY Racing Asn, 62. *Mem:* Am Watercolor Soc; Royal Soc Arts. *Media:* All Media. *Publ:* Illusr, Birds and Beasts of Mark Twain, by Robert M Rodney, Univ Okla Press, 66. *Mailing Add:* Windswept Farm York ME 03909

ROCKBURNE, DOROTHEA
PAINTER

b Verdun, PQ. *Study:* Black Mountain Col. *Exhib:* Seventeenth Am Exhib, Art Inst Chicago, 72 & Fogg Mus Art, 73; American Drawing, Whitney Mus Am Art, 73; 34th Biennial of Contemporary American Painting, Corcoran Gallery Art, DC, 75; Three Decades of American Art, Seibu Mus Art, Tokyo, 76; New York-The State of Art, NY State Mus, Albany, 77; Paper, Dayton Art Inst, Ohio, 78; Contemporary Drawing/New York, Univ Calif, Santa Barbara, 78; New York Now, Phoenix Art Mus, Ariz, 79; Prospectus: The Seventies, Aldrich Mus Art, 79; and many others. *Awards:* Guggenheim Fel, 72-73; Painting Award, Art Inst Chicago, 72; Nat Endowment Arts fel, 74-75. *Bibliog:* David Bourdon (auth), Three women manipulate geometry, earth and old masters, The Village Voice, 11/76; John Russell (auth), Gallery View, New York Times, 11/19/78; Jeff Perrone (auth), Working through, fold by fold, Artforum, 1/79. *Mailing Add:* 140 Grand St New York NY 10013

ROCKEFELLER, (MR & MRS) DAVID
COLLECTORS

Mr Rockefeller, b New York, NY, June 12, 15. *Study:* Mr Rockefeller, Harvard Univ, BS, 36; Univ Chicago, PhD, 40; LLD, Columbia Univ, 54, Bowdoin Col, 58, Jewish Theol Sem, 58, Williams Col, 66, Wagner Col, 67, Harvard Univ, 69, Pace Col, 70, St John's Univ, 71, Univ Liberia, 79. *Pos:* Trustee & chmn bd trustees, Mus Mod Art, New York. *Collection:* Paintings, modern art. *Mailing Add:* 30 Rockefeller Plaza New York NY 10112

ROCKEFELLER, (MRS) LAURANCE S
COLLECTOR

Study: Vassar Col, 27-29; Art Students League, 29-34. *Mem:* Trustee, Whitney Mus Am Art; Metrop Mus Art, New York; Mus Mod Art, New York. *Collection:* Paintings & modern art. *Mailing Add:* c/o Laurance S Rockefeller 30 Rockefeller Plaza New York NY 10112

ROCKLIN, RAYMOND
SCULPTOR, EDUCATOR

b Moodus, Conn, Aug 18, 22. *Study:* Educ Alliance, New York, with Abbo Ostrovsky; Cooper Union Art Sch, with Milton Hebald & John Havannes, BFA(Skowhegan Scholar). *Work:* Whitney Mus Am Art, New York; Provincetown Mus Art, Mass; Temple Israel, St Louis; Skowhegan Sch Painting & Sculpture. *Comn:* Wall brass, comn by Mrs Beskind, New York, 62; wall brass, comn by Mrs Nina Waller, Baltimore, 63; four religious sculptures, White Plains Hosp, NY, 79. *Exhib:* Young Americans, Whitney Mus Am Art, 56; Oakland Art Mus, 59; Gallerina Tiberina, Rome, 59; Univ Calif, Berkeley, 60; Claude Bernard Gallery, Paris, 60. *Teaching:* Guest artist, Am Univ, 56; asst prof art, Univ Calif, Berkeley, 59-60; guest artist, Ball State Teachers Col, summer 64; prof art, Borough Manhattan Community Col, City Univ New York, currently. *Awards:* Fulbright Grant, Italy, 52-53; Yaddo Found Fel, 56. *Bibliog:* M Seuphor (auth), Raymond Rocklin, The Sculpture of this Century, 61; F Hazan (auth), article, Dictionary Mod Sculpture; and others. *Mem:* Sculptors Guild; Am Abstract Artists; Fedn Mod Painters & Sculptors. *Media:* Mixed. *Dealer:* Sculptors Guild 10 E 53rd St New York NY 10022. *Mailing Add:* 232B Watch Hill Rd Peekskill NY 10566

ROD, BRUCE JOHN
SCULPTOR, PAINTER

b Fargo, NDak, Oct 18, 47. *Study:* Moorhead State Univ, Minn, BA, 69; Univ Wis-Madison, MFA, 72. *Work:* Springfield Art Mus, Mo; Walnut Creek Civic Art Ctr, Calif; Ball State Univ Art Mus, Muncie, Ind; Univ Wis-Madison Mem Gallery; Roswell Mus & Art Ctr, NMex. *Exhib:* Current Directions, Tucson Mus Art, 77; solo exhib, San Jose Mus Art, 78; Colored Directions, Walnut Creek Civic Art Ctr, Calif, 78; Watercolor USA, Springfield Art Mus, Mo, 79; solo exhib, Scottsdale Ctr Arts, Scottsdale, Ariz, 79; and others. *Pos:* Dir, Harry Wood Art Gallery, Ariz State Univ, Tempe, 78-81. *Teaching:* Instr ceramics, Milton Col, Wis, 72-73; assoc prof sculpture painting, Ariz State Univ, Tempe, 73-81; assoc prof, NMex State Univ, Las Cruces, 81-82. *Awards:* Am Heritage Fund Award, Matthews Ctr Gallery, Ariz State Univ, 78; Jurors Award, Phoenix Art Mus, 78; Purchase Award, Springfield Art Mus, Mo, 79. *Media:* Wood, Bronze; Oil, Acrylic. *Mailing Add:* 202 N Main Studio 220 Los Angeles CA 90031

RODA (RHODA LILLIAN SABLOW)
PAINTER, TAPESTRY ARTIST

b Port Chester, NY, Nov 26, 26. *Study:* Univ Wis; Rochester Inst Technol; Art Students League; also with Frank Vincent DuMont & Frank Reilly. *Comn:* Cranbrook 50th Anniversary (needlepoint rug), Cranbrook Acad, Bloomfield Hills, Mich, 73; needlepoint designs of main altar area & furniture, Christ Episcopal Church, Detroit, Mich, 75; needlepoint design main altar rug, Christ Episcopal Church, Detroit, 82; needlepoint designs altar seats & kneelers, St James Church, Birmingham, Mich, 83. *Exhib:* Allied Artists Am, Nat Acad, New York, 69; Ahda Artzt Gallery, New York, 70; Needle Arts Gallery, Birmingham, Mich, 71, 74 & 76; Lever House, New York, 77. *Bibliog:* Lesley Umans (auth), Encaustic painting, Reporter Dispatch, AP, 7/70 & Creative stitchery, Women's Wear Daily, 8/71; Lillian Braun (auth), 3-D needlepoint, int, Detroit Free Press, 10/74. *Media:* Oil, Acrylic. *Mailing Add:* Rural Dr Scarsdale NY 10583

RODAN, DON
PHOTOGRAPHER, PAINTER

b Cincinnati, Ohio, June 30, 50. *Study:* Cooper Union Art Sch, BFA, 74. *Work:* Int Mus Photog, George Eastman House, NY; Australian Nat Gallery, Canberra; Williams Col Art Mus, Mass; The Polaroid Collection, Cambridge, Mass; San Francisco Mus Mod Art, Calif. *Exhib:* One-man shows, The Greek Myths, Int Mus Photog, George Eastman House, 77 & Castelli Gallery, NY, 79; One of a Kind Color, Houston Mus Fine Arts & Corcoran Gallery, 79-80; Exploration of a Medium, Rheinisches Landes Mus & Frakfurter Kunst Verein, Germany, 80 & 81; Fabricated to be Photographed, San Francisco Mus Mod Art & Albright-Knox Gallery, 80; New Voices 2, Allen Mem Art Mus, Ohio, 81. *Bibliog:* Richard Whelan (auth), New York Reviews: Don Rodan, Art News, 5/79; Sally Eauclaire (auth), The New Color, Abbeville Press, 81; Carter Ratcliff (auth), Tableau photography from Mayall to Rodan, Picture Mag #18, fall 81. *Media:* Cibachrome Color. *Mailing Add:* Castelli Gallery 4 East 77th St New York NY 10021

RODBARD, BETTY
PAINTER

b Boston, Mass. *Study:* Univ Toronto, Can; Univ Buffalo, NY, with Seymour Drumlevich, Walter Prochownik & Sheldon Berlyn. *Work:* Springfield Art Mus, Mo; Univ Utah Art Gallery, Logan; Roswell Park Mem Inst, Buffalo; KFAC Radio Sta, Los Angeles; Cedars-Sinai Med Ctr, Los Angeles, & City of Hope Med Ctr. *Exhib:* Albright-Knox Art Mus, 63; Nat Juried Ann, Butler Inst Am Art, 68, 70 & 73; Languna Beach Mus Art, Calif, 80 & 82; Pasadena Mus Art; Calif Inst Technol, 80; Tuscon Mus Art, 82; Brand XIII, 83; and others. *Collections Arranged:* Under the Arches, Nat Watercolor Soc, 73; Science and Art, City of Hope Med Ctr, 76. *Teaching:* Pvt instruction in painting. *Awards:* Southwest Mo Mus Award, Mus Assocs, 68; Henry C Pitz Mem Award, Am Watercolor Soc, 77; Nat Watercolor Soc Award, 79. *Mem:* Nat Watercolor Soc (secy, 69-72, treas, 79-80); Pasadena Soc Artists (secy treas, 69-71, historian, 76-79); Women Painters of the West; Los Angeles Art Asn. *Media:* Watercolor, Oil. *Dealer:* Los Angeles Art Associal 825 N La Cienega Los Angeles CA 90069. *Mailing Add:* 1810 Wilson Ave Arcadia CA 91006

RODE, MEREDITH EAGON
PRINTMAKER, EDUCATOR

b Delaware, Ohio, Mar 27, 38. *Study:* Corcoran Sch of Art, 55-58; George Washington Univ, BA, 58; Art Students League of New York (scholar), study with George Grosz & Harry Sternberg, 59; Univ of Md, MFA, 74. *Work:* Southern Graphics Print Collection, Univ Miss, Oxford; Univ Md Col Permanent Collection; Dundalk College. *Exhib:* Baltimore Mus of Art, Md, 77; Utah Mus of Fine Arts, Salt Lake City, 77; Works on Paper, Blaffer Gallery, Univ Houston, Tex, 77; Printmakers Guild of Annapolis Exhib, Hopkins Univ, Baltimore, Md, 77; US Dept State Art in the Embassies Prog, Nassau, Bahamas, Kinshasa, Zaire; and others. *Pos:* Chmn(actg), Federal City Col, Washington, DC, 71-72; vpres (Nat), Women's Caucus for Art, 75-76. *Teaching:* Instr studio art, Corcoran Sch Art, 62-68; assoc prof studio art, Univ District Columbia, 68-78, prof, 78- *Mem:* Women's Caucus for Art (vpres, 75-76); Southern Graphics Coun; Southeastern Col Art Asn; and others. *Media:* Multimedia. *Publ:* Auth, Articles in Art J, Col Art Asn, 75. *Dealer:* Foundry Gallery 641 Indiana Ave Washington DC. *Mailing Add:* 7319 Baltimore Ave Takoma Park MD 20012

RODGERS, JACK A
ADMINISTRATOR

b Littlefield, Tex, Oct 5, 38. *Study:* Tex Tech Univ, BA(advert & design); Univ Tex Southwestern Med Sch, Dallas, MMA. *Pos:* Supvr med illus, Univ Tex Med Br, Galveston, Tex, 64-66; exec dir, San Antonio Art Inst, Tex, 76-80, bd chmn, 81-; spec adv, San Antonio Arts Coun; educ adv, Tex Comn on Arts; bd mem, Tex Arts Alliance. *Teaching:* Asst prof & deputy chmn dept med commun, Univ Tex Med Sch, San Antonio, 67-75. *Awards:* Nat Eaton Award, Nat Student Am Med Asn; First Place, Dept Neurol Exhib, Univ Tex Med Br, Galveston, Tex & Dept Surgery Exhib, Tex Med Asn. *Mailing Add:* San Antonio Art Inst PO Box 6092 San Antonio TX 78209

RODMAN, RUTH M
PRINTMAKER, TAPESTRY ARTIST

b Boston, Mass, Apr 13, 28. *Study:* Mass Sch of Art; Boston Mus Sch, with Karl Zerbe; De Cordova Mus, Lincoln, Mass, with Stoltenberg. *Work:* New York Pub Libr; Boston Pub Libr, Mass; Brockton Art Ctr, Mass; Minneapolis Inst of Art, Minn. *Comn:* Annual Appeal Print, DeCordova Mus, 78. *Exhib:* De Cordova Mus, Lincoln, Mass, 73-77; 1st Nat Bank Boston Printmaker Exhib; Silvermine Guild of Artists Nat Print Exhib, Conn, 74; Worcester Mus, Mass, 74-75; Brockton Art Ctr, Mass, 75; Boston Visual Artist Union; Boston Ctr for the Arts. *Awards:* Purchase Prizes, Boston Printmakers, Rose Art Mus, Brandeis Univ & De Cordova Mus; Nat Print Show, Silvermine Nat Print Exhib. *Bibliog:* J Silverman (auth), feature article, Boston Sunday Globe & Wayland-Weston Town Crier, 75; Carol LeBrun Danikian (auth), review in Christian Sci Monitor, 11/76; Corporations--the new medicis, Newsweek Mag, 11/76. *Mem:* Boston Printmakers; Boston Visual Artists Union; Nat Asn Am Penwomen. *Publ:* Illusr, Collagraph Printmaking, Watson-Guptill, 75; illusr, A Time for Living, Dutton, 75. *Dealer:* John Stoke 340 East 57th St New York NY 10033. *Mailing Add:* c/o AAA Gallery 663 Fifth Ave New York NY 10022

RODMAN, SELDEN
WRITER, COLLECTOR

b New York, NY, Feb 19, 09. *Study:* Yale Univ, 31. *Collection:* Contemporary figurative painting and sculpture, primitive and folk art; collection has been widely shown in the United States and Mexico, and has been catalogued by Vanderbilt University and by San Carlos Academy, Mexico. *Publ:* Auth, The Miracle of Haitian Art, 74; auth, Tongues of Fallen Angels, 74; auth, The Brazil Traveler, 75; auth, Genius in the Backlands, 77; auth, Artists in Tune with Their World, Simon & Schuster, 82; and others. *Mailing Add:* 659 Ramapo Valley Rd Oakland NJ 07436

RODRIGUEZ, GENO (EUGENE)
PHOTOGRAPHER, GALLERY DIRECTOR

b New York, NY, June 2, 40. *Study:* Hammersmith Col Art, London, NDD, 66; Int Peoples Col, Elsinore, Denmark. *Work:* Metrop Mus Art; Everson Mus Art; Int Ctr for Photog, New York; Am Mus Natural Hist, New York; Mus Contemp Art, Caracas, Venezuela. *Exhib:* Images of Puerto Rico, Wadsworth Atheneum, Hartford, Conn, 74; Feathered Gladiators, Il Diaframma Gallery, Milano, Italy, 79; Manipulated Photog, La Flaviana Gallery, Locarno, Switz, 80; Cayman Gallery, New York, 80; Miss Mus Art, Jackson, 81; Chrysler Mus Art, Norfolk, Va, 81; and others. *Collections Arranged:* Ashes to Ashes, Visions of Death, 82, Dreams, Demons Madness, 83, Showdown: Southwest Perspective, 83 & Artists of the West Coast, 84, Alternative Mus. *Pos:* Pres, founder, Inst Contemp Hispanic Art, 72-74, Enfoco: Latin Am Photog Collaborative, 73-74, Alternative Mus, 75- *Teaching:* Instr photog, Rutgers Univ, 77-78; instr photo critique, Sch Visual Arts, New York, 77- *Awards:* Distinguished Am Vis to Africa, Phelps Stokes Fund, 77; Artist Nat Endowment Arts fel, 79; Ludwig Vogelstein Found Fel, 81. *Media:* Photo-assemblage. *Publ:* The Islands: Worlds of the Puerto Ricans, Harper & Row, 74; auth, Mira Mira Mira Puerto Rican New Yorkers, Forum Press, 75. *Mailing Add:* 32 W 82nd St New York NY 10024

RODRIGUEZ, OSCAR
PAINTER, SCULPTOR

b Mexico, DF, Mex, May 14, 43. *Study:* La Esmeralda, Nat Sch Painting & Sculpture, Inst Fine Arts, Mexico, DF, 65-67; Benito Juarez Univ, Engraving Workshop, Oaxaca, Mex, 72; Pratt Graphic Ctr, New York, 72. *Work:* Eliot Felt Ballet Found, New York; Simon Fraser Univ, Vancouver, Can; Mus Casa de Los Once Patios, Patzcuaro, Michoacan, Mex; La Casa del Lago Cult Difusion Ctr, Nat Univ Mex, Mexico, DF; Benito Juarez Univ. *Exhib:* One-man shows, EDAF Salas de Arte, Madrid, Spain, 79 & Gallery Jose M Velasco, Inst Fine Arts, Mexico City, 79; Salon Nac de Artes Plasticas, Seccion Beinal de Grafico, Inst Fine Arts, Mexico City, 77 & 79; Arte Actual de IberoAmerica, Inst Cult Hispanica, Madrid, Spain, 77; Presencia de la Plastica Mexicana, Fine Arts Inst, Mexico City, 78; Primera Bienal ItaloAmericana de Tecnicas Graficas, Rome, Italy, 79; Trienal LatinoAmericana de Grabado, Buenos Aires, Arg, 79. *Bibliog:* Margarita Nelken (auth), Oscar Rodriguez, 2/2/67 & Enrique Gual (auth), Propositos y Rilicarios, 2/12/67, Newspaper Excelsior, Mexico, DF; Alfonso de Neuvillate y Oritz (auth), Oscar Rodriguez: Las Fueras y Comercio, 10/76. *Mem:* Salon de la Plastica Mex. *Dealer:* Galeria de Arte Misrachi Genova 20 Mexico 6 DF Mexico. *Mailing Add:* Edificio Condesa Calle Matehuala Entrada H Dept 2 Mexico 11 DF Mexico

RODRIGUEZ, PEDRO A
PAINTER, ADMINISTRATOR

b San Antonio, Tex, July 25, 36. *Study:* N Tex State Univ, Denton, BA, 64; Univ Dallas, Irving, MA, 68, MFA, 70. *Comn:* Acrylic murals, NMex Highlands Univ, Las Vegas, 71-72 & 72-73; acrylic mural, Wash State Arts

Comn, Granger, 76; acrylic mural, Rapid Advancement Sch, Nacogdoches, Tex, 78; painting & photog essay, Southern Fel Found, 78-79. *Exhib:* 24th Tex Ann, Dallas Mus Fine Arts, 64; one-person shows, Univ Dallas, Irving, 68-70 & Texas A&I Univ, Kingsville, 70; 6 Artists of the Southwest, Galleria de la Raza, San Francisco, 75-80; Latin Am Artists, Casa de las Americas, Havana, Cuba, 78 & 83; Caras y Cuerpos, Cheney Cowles Mem Mus, Spokane, 79; and others. *Pos:* Mgr cult arts progs, City Austin, 81- *Teaching:* Asst prof, Tex A&I Univ, Kingsville, 68-70; asst prof, NMex Highlands Univ, Las Vegas, 71-73; assoc prof, Wash State Univ, Pullman, 73-83, Dougherty Art Ctr, Austin, Tex, 83-84. *Awards:* 2nd Place, STex Mus Ann, 70. *Bibliog:* Gonzales (auth), Mural para los ninos, El Visitante Cath J, 1/28/79; White (auth), Chicano/Latino Artists of the Northwest, Metamorfosis, 83. *Media:* Acrylic, Graphite. *Publ:* Illusr, Mexican-American History and Culture, Arlington Sch Dist, Wash, 80; illusr, Revista Chicano/Riguena, Univ Houston, 80; auth, Arte para la gente, Metamorfosis, Univ Wash, Seattle, 80. *Mailing Add:* 3104 S 5th Austin TX 78704

RODRIGUEZ-LEON, ANA M See Leon, Ana

ROEBLING, MARY G
COLLECTOR, PATRON
b Collingswood, NJ, July 29, 05. *Mem:* Am Art Asn; Arch Am Art; Philadelphia Print Club; NJ Cult Ctr Adv Coun (first chmn); Metrop Mus Art. *Collection:* Paintings, sculpture, fine porcelain and glass. *Mailing Add:* Lafayette House 777 W State St Trenton NJ 08618

ROESCH, KURT (FERDINAND)
PAINTER
b Berlin, Ger, Sept 12, 05; US citizen. *Study:* Acad Art, Berlin. *Work:* Mus Mod Art, New York; Albright-Knox Art Gallery, Buffalo; Metrop Mus Art, New York; Currier Gallery, Manchester, NH; Univ Nebr. *Exhib:* Carnegie Inst, 41-58; Documenta, Kassel, Ger, 55; one-man shows, Curt Valentin Gallery, 49-53; Currier Gallery, 55. *Pos:* Mem fac, Sarah Lawrence Col, 34-72, emer, 72. *Mem:* NH Art Asn. *Mailing Add:* Richards Lane New Canaan CT 06840

ROESLER, NORBERT LEONHARD HUGO
COLLECTOR
b Plankenberg, Austria, Aug 8, 01; US citizen. *Mem:* Drawing Soc; fel Pierpont Morgan Libr. *Collection:* Drawings by Dutch, French, Italian, English and others. *Mailing Add:* 785 Park Ave New York NY 10021

ROEVER, JOAN MARILYN
ILLUSTRATOR, DIORAMIST
b Philadelphia, Pa, Dec 13, 35. *Study:* Philadelphia Mus Col Art. *Work:* State Mus, Jackson, Miss; Cameron Co Libr, La. *Mem:* Soc Animal Artists, New York. *Media:* (Painting) Acrylic; (Dioramas) Oil. *Publ:* Auth-illusr, The North American Eagles, 73, The Brown Pelican, 74, Wolves, 75 & Whales in Danger, 76, Steck-Vaughn; Snake Secrets, Walker, 79. *Mailing Add:* 5315 S US Hwy One Rockledge FL 32955

ROGALSKI, WALTER
PRINTMAKER, LECTURER
b Glen Cove, NY, Apr 10, 23. *Study:* Brooklyn Mus Sch, with Xavier Gonzalez, Arthur Osver, C Seide & Gabor Peterdi, 47-51. *Work:* Mus Mod Art; Brooklyn Mus; Cleveland Mus Art; Fogg Mus Art; Seattle Art Mus; plus many others. *Exhib:* Six shows, Brooklyn Mus, 51-68; Soc Am Graphic Artists, 66 & 69; Cincinnati Mus Asn, 68; Am Fedn Arts Traveling Exhib, 69; Nat Print Exhib, Potsdam, NY, 69; plus many others. *Teaching:* Prof graphic art, Grad Sch Art & Design, Pratt Inst, currently. *Awards:* Prizes, De Cordova & Dana Mus, 61 & Yale Gallery Fine Arts, 61; Purchase Prize, Assoc Am Artists, 66; plus others. *Mem:* Soc Am Graphic Artists. *Mailing Add:* Dept of Printmaking Pratt Inst Brooklyn NY 11205

ROGERS, BARBARA JOAN
PAINTER, EDUCATOR
b Newcomerstown, Ohio, Apr 28, 37. *Study:* Ohio State Univ, BSc; Univ Calif, Berkeley, MA. *Work:* San Francisco Mus Mod Art; Oakland Mus Art, Calif. *Exhib:* New Realist Painters, Univ Calif, Davis, 69; West Coast 70, Biennial, Crocker Art Gallery, Sacramento, Calif, 70; Twelve Painters and the Human Figure, Santa Barbara Mus of Art, Calif, 73; one-woman exhib, San Francisco Mus Mod Art, 73; Contemp Am Painting & Sculpture, Krannert Art Mus, Univ Ill, Champaign, 74; 71st Am Exhib, Art Inst of Chicago, 74; Six Painters, Six Attitudes, Oakland Mus, 75; and others. *Teaching:* Vis lectr drawing & painting, Univ Calif, Berkeley, 72-73; vis artist painting & grad sem, Univ Wash, Seattle, 75; vis artist painting & drawing, San Francisco Art Inst, 75-76; instr painting & drawing, San Jose State Univ, 78-82. *Awards:* Eisner Prize, Univ Calif, Berkeley, 63. *Bibliog:* P D French (auth), articles, Artforum, summer 68 & 1/70; Jerome Tarshis (auth), article, Art News, 11/73. *Media:* Acrylic. *Dealer:* Hansen Fuller Gallery 228 Grant Ave San Francisco CA 94108. *Mailing Add:* 6389 Colby St Oakland CA 94618

ROGERS, CHARLES B
PAINTER, MUSEUM DIRECTOR
b Great Bend, Kans, Jan 27, 11. *Study:* Nat Acad Design; Tiffany Found; Bethany Col, BFA; Calif Col Arts & Crafts, MFA; with Dong Kingman; Jay Connaway Sch Art. *Work:* Libr Cong Pennell Collection, Washington, DC; Metrop Mus Art Arms Collection, New York; Inst Mex Norteamericanos, Mexico City; Philadelphia Mus Art; Boston Pub Libr. *Comn:* Mural, US Govt Post Off, Council Grove, Kans, 40; Smoky Valley Landscape, Citizens Bank Mem, Ellsworth, Kans, 69; Splitter Farm, comn by Dr Stan Splitter, Oakland,

Calif, 71; Autumn in Kansas, C L Clark Law Off, Salina, Kans, 72. *Exhib:* One-man exhibs, US Nat Mus, Smithsonian Inst, Washington, DC; Inst Mex Norteamericanos, Mexico City, Munic Tower Galleries, Los Angeles, Galleries de Arte, Monterrey, Mex & Inst Technol, Rochester, NY; plus many other group & one-man shows. *Collections Arranged:* The Great West-Paintings & Prints by Charles B Rogers; Paintings of the Southwest by Peter Hurd, Bethany College. *Pos:* Mgr & asst dir, Huntington Hartford Found, 54-66; dir, Rogers House Mus-Gallery, 67- *Teaching:* Head sch art, Bethany Col, 47-53; head sch art, Kans Wesleyan Univ, 66-67. *Awards:* Over 138 art awards including Am Inst Fine Arts & Mikami Award. *Bibliog:* Ed Smith (auth), Charles B Rogers--Artist, Kans State Publ, 68; Art Professor Charles B Rogers, Kans State Univ, 69. *Mem:* Soc Am Graphic Artists; Carmel Art Asn, Calif; Prairie Watercolor Painters; Kans Fedn Art (bd mem, 71-). *Media:* Oil, Oriental Sumi. *Specialty:* Paintings and prints of the Great West. *Publ:* Auth, Painting the American West, Artists Mag, London; auth, Charles B Rogers pleads for the spirit in art, Am Artist Mag, 8/63; auth, Heart of art, Art & Artists, 65; auth, Art Observations, pvt publ, 80; and others. *Mailing Add:* Rogers House Mus-Gallery Snake Row Ellsworth KS 67439

ROGERS, JOHN
PAINTER
b Brooklyn, NY, Dec 9, 06. *Study:* Art Students League. *Exhib:* Am Watercolor Soc, 41-72; Brooklyn Mus Int, 46; Watercolor USA, Springfield, Mo, 62; Watercolor Soc, London, 65; Nat Acad Design, 70. *Pos:* Artist, New York Times, 28-30; artist & illusr, New York Post, 50-55. *Teaching:* Instr watercolors, Garden City Adult Sch, 55-70; instr watercolor, Elmont Adult Prog, 57-70. *Awards:* Am Watercolor Soc Silver Medal, 42; First Prize in Watercolor, Salmagundi Club, 70; Gold Medal, Am Artists Prof League. *Bibliog:* Norman Kent (auth), John Rogers watercolorist, Am Artist, 48, 52 & 64. *Mem:* Am Watercolor Soc (exhib chmn, 68-75); Am Artists Prof League; life mem Salmagundi Club; Art League Nassau Co (pres, 66-68); Art Students League. *Media:* Watercolor. *Publ:* Auth, articles in Am Artist, 48, Design Mag, 51 & Artist's Mag, London, 52; auth, Watercolor Simplified, 65. *Dealer:* Grand Central Gallery Biltmore Hotel New York NY 10017; Garden City Gallery 923 Franklin Ave Garden City NY 11530. *Mailing Add:* 59 Terry Ave Amityville NY 11701

ROGERS, JOHN H
SCULPTOR, EDUCATOR
b Walton, Ky, Dec 20, 21. *Study:* Eastern Ky Univ; Tyler Sch Art, Temple Univ, BFA & MFA. *Work:* Ala Archives, Montgomery; Marine Corps Combat Art Collection, Marine Corps Mus, Washington, DC; Auburn Univ, Ala; Dept Defense, Pentagon, Washington, DC; NDak Mill, Grand Forks, 81. *Comn:* Bust of Gen H M Smith USMC, Ala Archives, Montgomery, 69; mem plaque of Lt Gen J A Chaisson, USMC, 75; baptistry, St Paul's Episcopal Church, Grand Forks, NDak, 83. *Exhib:* Armed Forces of US as Seen by the Contemporary Artist, Smithsonian Inst, Washington, 68; Artists in Vietnam, Smithsonian Traveling Exhib Serv, 68-70; Atlanta Col Art Fac Exhib, High Mus Art, Ga, 72; Inaugural Exhib, USMC Hist Ctr, Washington, DC, 77; solo show, Art Gallery, Univ NDak, 81; and others. *Pos:* Acad dean, Minneapolis Col Art & Design, 64-68; asst head, Marine Corps Combat Art Prog, Washington, 68-69, head, 69-70; dean, Atlanta Col Art, Ga, 70-73; dean col fine arts, Univ NDak, 73-80; sculptor in residence, Syracuse Univ, 80-81. *Teaching:* Sr sem humanities, Atlanta Col Art, 70-71; prof fine arts & sr symp, Univ NDak, 73-80, prof visual arts, 81-; adj prof basic design, Syracuse Univ, 80-81. *Mem:* Nat Asn Schs Art & Design; Am Crafts Coun; Int Sculpture Ctr. *Media:* Cast Metals, Wood. *Publ:* Ed, Directory of Arts Resources in the State of North Dakota, 77; coauth, Aging & creativity, In: Lifelong Learning and the Visual Arts, Nat Art Educ Asn, 80. *Mailing Add:* Box 7202 Univ Sta Grand Forks ND 58202

ROGERS, JOSEPH SHEPPERD See Nevia

ROGERS, LEO M
COLLECTOR, PATRON
b Boston, Mass, Dec 24, 02. *Study:* Columbia Col, BA, 23; Columbia Univ, ChE, 25. *Collection:* Cezanne, Manet, Degas, Soutine, Modigliani, Sisley, Signac, Roualt, Vuillard, Picasso, Pascin, Lautrec, Cassat, Renoir, Pisarro, Van Gogh, Morisot, Daumier, Brach, Homer & Ryder. *Mailing Add:* 814 36th Ave E Bradenton FL 33508

ROGERS, MILLARD BUXTON
HISTORIAN, EDUCATOR
b Danville, Ill, Sept 1, 12. *Study:* Art Inst Chicago, BFA, 37, MFA, 40; Univ Chicago, AM, 40, PhD, 65. *Teaching:* Chmn art dept, Univ Southern Calif, 46-47; asst prof art hist, Stanford Univ, 47-50; prof, Univ Wash, Seattle, 52- *Mem:* Col Art Asn; Oriental Ceramic Soc, London; Am Comt South Asian Art. *Res:* China, Japan, India and Europe in the Middle Ages. *Publ:* Contribr, articles, Artibus Asia, 52-58; auth, Korean ceramics, Far Eastern Ceramic Bulletin, 57; auth, An archaeological pilgrimage to Santiago de Compostella, Sci Mag, 60; auth, Northwest Art Today, 62 & coauth, The Search for Form, 77, Univ Wash Press. *Mailing Add:* Univ Wash Seattle WA 98195

ROGERS, MILLARD FOSTER, JR
MUSEUM DIRECTOR, HISTORIAN
b Texarkana, Tex, Aug 27, 32. *Study:* Mich State Univ, BA(hon), 54; Univ Mich, MA, 58; Victoria & Albert Mus, London, 59, with John Pope-Hennessy. *Collections Arranged:* New Eng Glass Co, 1818-1880, Toledo Mus Art, 63; Indian Miniature Painting, 71, Canadian Landscapes, 73, Treasures From the Tower of London, 82-83, Univ Wis. *Pos:* Asst to dir, Toledo Mus Art, Ohio, 59-63; cur Am art, 64-67; dir, Elvehjem Art Ctr, Univ

Wis-Madison, 67-74; dir, Cincinnati Art Mus, 74- *Teaching:* Prof art hist dept, Univ Wis-Madison, 67-74. *Awards:* Gosline Fel, Toledo Mus Art, 58-59; Samuel B Sachs Prize, 83. *Mem:* Asn Art Mus Dirs; Am Asn Mus. *Res:* Junius Brutus Stearns, 1815-1885; 19th century American Bozzetti. *Publ:* Auth, Benjamin West and the caliph: Two paintings for Fonthill Abbey, Apollo, 6/66; auth, Nydia, popular Victorian image, Antiques, 3/70; auth, Randolph Rogers, American Sculptor in Rome, Univ Mass, 71; auth, Spanish Paintings in the Cincinnati Art Museum, 78; auth, Favorite Paintings from the Cincinnati Art Museum, Abbeville Press, 80. *Mailing Add:* Cincinnati Art Mus Eden Park Cincinnati OH 45202

ROGERS, OTTO DONALD
PAINTER, EDUCATOR
b Kerrobert, Sask, Nov 19, 35. *Study:* Sask Teacher's Col, cert, 53; Univ Wis, BSc(art educ), 58, MA(fine art), 59. *Work:* Nat Gallery Can, Ottawa; Montreal Mus Fine Arts; Nat Mus Iceland, Reykjavik; Fredericton Art Gallery, NB; Windsor Art Gallery, Ont. *Comn:* Sculpture in steel (with George Kerr, architect), Prince Albert Regional Libr, 65. *Exhib:* Biennial, Nat Gallery Can, 66; Royal Can Acad Art Exhib, 70; Directors Choice Exhib, sponsored by Can Coun, Confedn Art Gallery & Mus, Charlottetown, PEI, 68; Art in Saskatchewan, Waddington Fine Arts Gallery, Montreal, 69; Art Bank Can Exhib, Mendel Gallery, Saskatoon, 72. *Teaching:* Prof painting, Univ Sask, 59-, head dept art, 73- *Awards:* Sr Award for Study in Europe, 67-68. *Bibliog:* R Harper (auth), History of Canadian Painting, 66; W Townshend (auth), Canadian art today, Studio Int, 70; C McConnell (auth), Otto Rogers, Arts Can, 71. *Mem:* Royal Can Acad Art. *Media:* Acrylic. *Mailing Add:* 827 University Dr Saskatoon SK S7N 0J5 Canada

ROGERS, P J
PRINTMAKER, PAINTER
b Rochester, NY. *Study:* Wells Col, BA; Univ Buffalo; Acad Fine Arts, Vienna; Art Students League; also with Victor Hammer, Lazlo Szabo & Robert Brackman. *Work:* Frank J Lausche State Office Bldg, Cleveland, Ohio; Rockford Col; TRW Corporate Headquarters, Ohio; Cleveland Mus Art; Cleveland Art Asn, Ohio. *Comn:* Murals for Hall of Man, Buffalo Mus Sci, 53-55; portrait of founder, Novatny Elec Co, Akron, 67; poster for opening of new theater, Akron Weathervane Theater, 70; portrait of Dr D J Guzzetta, pres of Univ Akron, 75; spec ed aquatints, Bayvillage, Ohio, 79. *Exhib:* May Show, Cleveland Mus Art, 73-83; Rockford Int Print & Drawing III, 81 & 83; 58th Ann Philadelphia Print Club Int, 82; 60th Soc Am Graphic Artists Nat, New York, 83; Boston Printmakers Nat, 83; and others. *Pos:* Art preparator, Buffalo Mus Sci, 52-55. *Teaching:* Instr painting, Buffalo Mus Sci, 55; instr arts & crafts, Univ Akron Spec Progs, 58. *Awards:* Top Graphic Cash Award, Cleveland Mus Art, 76; Ohio Arts Coun Fel, 79; Purchase Award, Rockford Int, 83. *Bibliog:* Stevens (auth), Aux Etats-Unis, expositions diverses, P J Rogers, La Rev Mod. *Mem:* New Orgn Visual Arts, Cleveland; World Print Coun; Philadelphia Print Club; Boston Printmakers; Pratt Graphics, NY. *Dealer:* vanStraaten Gallery 646 North Michigan Ave Chicago IL 60611; Jane Haslem Gallery 2121 P St NW Washington DC 20037. *Mailing Add:* 954 Hereford Dr Akron OH 44303

ROGERS, PETER WILFRID
PAINTER
b London, Eng, Aug 24, 33. *Study:* St Martins Sch Art, London, Eng. *Work:* Bristol Art Gallery, Eng; Roswell Mus, NMex; Macnider Mus, Mason City, Iowa; Mus Southwest, Midland, Tex. *Comn:* Mural, Tex State Archives & Libr, Austin, 64; 48 paintings & drawings of Alaska, Atlantic Richfield Co, Los Angeles, 70-71; mural, Tex Tech Mus, 74; mural, Anaconda Co, Denver; mural, Arcomex, Mexico City. *Exhib:* One-man shows, Fairmount Gallery, Dallas, 69, Artium Orbis, Santa Fe, 71 & 72, Grace Cathedral, San Francisco, 73 & Janus Gallery, Santa Fe, 75; Heard Mus, Phoenix, Ariz, 75; plus others. *Publ:* Auth & illusr, The Quest. *Dealer:* Robischon Gallery 1122 E 17th Ave Denver CO 80218. *Mailing Add:* PO Box 214 San Patricio NM 88348

ROGOVIN, MARK
MURALIST, MUSEUM DIRECTOR
b Buffalo, NY, July 31, 46. *Study:* Spec study in Mexico, with Elizabeth Catlett Mora & David Alfaro Siqueiros, 64-68; RI Sch Design, Providence, BFA, 68; Art Inst Chicago, MFA, 70. *Comn:* Outdoor mural (18ft x 89ft), side of Am Nat Bank, comn by Rockford Evening Cosmopolitan Club, Ill, 75; indoor mural (8ft x 24ft), Col of DuPage, Glen Ellyn, Ill, 75; outdoor mural (10ft x 100ft), comn by several neighborhood orgn on Chicago's West Side, 76. *Exhib:* Murals for the People, Mus of Contemp Art, Chicago, 71; Street Art--Pub Murals in the USA (Bicentennial traveling exhib), Amerika-Haus, W Berlin, 76; Mural Art USA (traveling exhib), Maison de la Cult Andre Malraux, Reims, 77. *Pos:* Dir & co-founder, Pub Art Workshop, 72--81, Peace Mus, 81. *Teaching:* Sch prog artist, Urban Gateways, Chicago, 73-81; artist-in-residence murals, Col DuPage, Glen Ellyn, Ill, spring 75, Univ Nebr, Omaha, 77 & 78 & Univ Ill, Champaign, 78. *Bibliog:* Hermann Kopp (auth), Kunstler der demokratischen Offentlichkeit, Tendenzen, Fed Repub of Ger, 7/74; Macarlo Matus (auth), Mark Rogovin, muralista Norteamericano, El Dia, Mexico City, 2/76. *Mem:* United Scenic Artists Local; Chicago Artists Coalition. *Media:* Acrylics. *Mailing Add:* 5623 W Madison St Chicago IL 60644

ROGOVIN, MILTON
PHOTOGRAPHER
b New York, NY, Dec 30, 09. *Study:* Columbia Univ, BS, 31; State Univ NY, Buffalo, MA, 72. *Work:* Metrop Mus Art & Mus Mod Art, New York; Libr Cong, Washington, DC; Bibliot Nat, Paris; Albright-Knox Art Gallery, Buffalo, NY. *Comn:* Eight porcelain enamel panel portraits, Niagara Frontier Transit Authority, Buffalo, NY, 83. *Exhib:* Lower West Side, Albright-Knox Art Gallery, 75 & Photog Mus Finland, Helsinki, 77; Working People, Ctr Fotografia, Barcelona, Spain, 81, Currier Gallery Art, Manchester, NH, 82, Canon Foto Galerie Amsterdam, Netherlands, 82 & Preus Fotomus, Horten, Norway, 82. *Awards:* W Eugene Smith Mem Fund Award, 83. *Bibliog:* James N Wood (auth), Lower West Side, Albright-Knox Gallery Art, 75; Ann Rogovin (auth), Learning by Doing, Westinghouse Learning Corp, 79 & Let Me Do It, Harper & Row, 79. *Mailing Add:* 90 Chatham Ave Buffalo NY 14216

ROHLFING, CHRISTIAN
ADMINISTRATOR, CURATOR
b Philadelphia, Pa, Nov 14, 16. *Study:* Univ Chicago. *Pos:* Bd dirs & adv bd, Four Winds Mus Theatre; asst dir for collections, Cooper-Hewitt Mus Design, New York, currently. *Mailing Add:* 343 E 30th St New York NY 10016

ROHM, ROBERT
SCULPTOR
b Cincinnati, Ohio, Feb 6, 34. *Study:* Pratt Inst, BID, 56; Cranbrook Acad Art, Bloomfield Hills, Mich, MFA, 60. *Work:* Mus Mod Art, New York; Kunsthalle, Zurich, Switz; Finch Col Mus, New York; Columbus Gallery Fine Art; Whitney Mus Am Art, New York. *Exhib:* Sculpture Ann, Whitney Mus Am Art, 62, 64, 70 & 73; Works Mostly on Paper, Va Mus Art, Richmond, 70; one-man exhib, Works of Art, O K Harris, New York, 70, 72, 73, 75, 77, 80 & 82; Recent Abstract Art, Fogg Mus, Cambridge, Mass, 71; two-man show, Boston Mus Fine Art, 74; Bicentennial Collection, Inst Contemp Art, Boston, 75; New Dimensions in Drawing, Aldrich Mus Contemp Art, Ridgefield, Conn, 81; and others; The Sculptor As Draftsman, Whitney Mus Am Art, 83. *Teaching:* Instr sculpture, Columbus Col Art & Design, 56-59; instr sculpture, Pratt Inst, 60-65; prof sculpture, Univ RI, 65- *Awards:* Guggenheim Found Fel, 64; Nat Endowment Arts Award, 74; Artpark, Lewiston, NY, 77; plus others. *Bibliog:* Ralph Pomeroy (auth), An interview with Robert Rohm, Artforum, 4/70, Robert Rohm, Arts Can, 4/70 & Moving things, Art & Artists, 11/74; and others. *Dealer:* OK Harris Works of Art 383 W Broadway New York NY 10012. *Mailing Add:* 26 Lake St Wakefield RI 02879

ROHRER, WARREN
PAINTER, INSTRUCTOR
b Lancaster, Pa, Dec 4, 27. *Study:* Eastern Mennonite Col, BA; Madison Col, BS; Pa State Univ; Pa Acad Fine Arts. *Work:* Philadelphia Mus Art; Pa Acad Fine Arts; Metrop Mus Art, New York; Portland Art Mus, Ore; Allentown Art Mus, Pa; Smith Col Mus Art, Northampton, Mass. *Comn:* Commemorative Woodcut, Eastern Mennonite Col, Harrisonburg, Va, 61. *Exhib:* Pittsburgh Int, Carnegie Inst Finc Arts, 55; 154th & 163rd Ann, Pa Acad Fine Arts, Philadelphia, 59 & 68; one-man shows, Makler Gallery, Philadelphia, 63, 65, 67, 69 & 71, Marian Locks Gallery, Philadelphia, 74, 76, 78 & 80, Lamagna Gallery, New York, 76, Morris Gallery, Pa Acad Fine Arts, 82 CDS Gallery, New York, 83; A Sense of Place: The American Artist & the Land, Joslyn Art Mus, Omaha, 73; Philadelphia: Three Centuries of Am Art, Philadelphia Mus Art, 76; Philadelphia Houston Exchange, Inst Contemp Art, Philadelphia, 76; Susan Caldwell Gallery, New York, 77; Philadelphia: Contemporary Drawings, Pa Acad Fine Arts, 78. *Pos:* Mem, Pa Coun Arts, 76-79. *Teaching:* Assoc prof painting, Philadelphi Col Art, 67- *Awards:* Hon Mention, Pa Acad Fine Arts, 59; Artist Fel Grant, 81; Artist Fel Grant, Nat Endowment Arts, 81-82; and others. *Media:* Oil. *Dealer:* CDS Gallery 13 E 75th St New York NY 10021. *Mailing Add:* Box 25 Christiana PA 17509

ROJO, VICENTE
PAINTER
b Barcelona, Spain, Mar 15, 32. *Work:* Mus Mod Art, Mex; Banco Cedulas Hipotecarias SA, Mex; Casa de las Americas, Havanna, Cuba; Biblioteca Luis Arango, Bogota, Colombia; Banco Nac de Mex. *Comn:* Portfolio of five lithographs, Lublin Inc, New York, 69. *Exhib:* Second Biennial De Jovenes, Paris, 61; Mexico: The New Generation Traveling Exhib, US, 66; Expo '67, Montreal, PQ, 67; 1st Triennial India, New Delhi, 68; Contemporary Mexican Painting, Mus Mod Art, Tokyo, 74; and others. *Bibliog:* J J Gurrola (producer), Rojo (film), 66 & J Garcia Ponce (auth), Vicente Rojo, 71, Nat Univ Mex; Octavio Paz (auth), Discos visuales, Ediciones Era, 68. *Media:* Acrylic, Oil. *Dealer:* Galeria Juan Martin Amberes 17 Mexico DF Mexico. *Mailing Add:* Gallery Juan Martin Amberes 17 Mexico DF Mexico

ROLLER, MARION BENDER
SCULPTOR, PAINTER
b Boston, Mass. *Study:* Vesper George Sch Art, dipl; Art Students League, with John Hovannes; Greenwich House, with Lu Duble; Queens Col, BA; also watercolors with Edgar Whitney. *Comn:* Head of child, Nassau Ctr Emotionally Disturbed Children, Woodbury, NY, 68; Relief portrait of Ethel Traphagen & commemorative medal, Traphagen Sch, 82-83; portrait of Margaret Sussman, Pen & Brush, 83-84; sculpture of woman & youth, St Mary of Angels Home, Syopsett, NY, 84; and many private commissions of portraits, figures & animals. *Exhib:* Catharine Lorillard Wolfe, 79-81; Sculpture Ctr Gallery, 79-81; solo exhib, Hudson Valley Art Asn, 80-81; Nat Sculpture Soc, 80-81; Allied Artists, 80-81; and many others. *Teaching:* Instr art, Fashion Inst Technol, 67-72; instr, Traphagen Sch, 73-, Sculpture Ctr, 77- *Awards:* Silver Medal Hon, Allied Artists Am, 81; C Percival Dietsch Sculpture Award, Nat Sculpture Soc, 82; Tallix Foundry Award, Pen & Brush, 83; and others. *Bibliog:* Gustav Kramer (auth), Profile, Hudson Register Star, 65 & 10/3/75. *Mem:* Fel Nat Sculpture Soc (rec secy, 82-); Allied Artists Am (asst corresp secy, 66 & 83, corresp secy, 82); Pen & Brush (co-chmn, 67, chmn, 82-); assoc mem Audubon Artists; Fine Arts Fedn (bd dir, 81-, secy, 83-); and others. *Media:* Mixed. *Publ:* Auth, The challenge of space, Nat Sculpture Soc Rev, spring, 82; auth, several art book reviews, Nat Sculp Rev, summer 81-82. *Mailing Add:* 1 W 67th St New York NY 10023

ROLLER, RUSSELL KENNETH
EDUCATOR, PRINTMAKER
b Chicago, Ill, Oct 6, 38. *Study:* Ill Wesleyan Univ, BFA, 63; Southern Ill Univ, MFA, 65. *Work:* Univ Wisconsin, Eau Claire; Emporia State Col, Kans; Northern State Col, Aberdeen, SDak. *Exhib:* Int Miniature Print Exhib, Pratt Graphics, New York, 79. *Teaching:* Asst prof printmaking, Emporia State Col, Kans, 65-70; assoc prof printmaking, Northeastern Ill Univ, 70-76, prof & chmn art dept, 76- *Media:* Intaglio, Acrylic. *Mailing Add:* 2317 Brown Ave Evanston IL 60202

ROLLINS, JO LUTZ
DEALER, PAINTER
b Sherburn, Minn, July 21, 96. *Study:* Cornell Col; Univ Minn, BA & MA; Minneapolis Sch Art; Corcoran Art Sch; and with Cameron Booth, BJO Nordfeldt, Edmund Kinsinger & Hans Hofmann, Munich. *Work:* Minneapolis Art Inst. *Pos:* Founder, West Lake Gallery, Minneapolis. *Teaching:* From instr to prof studio art, Univ Minn, 28-65. *Awards:* Rockefeller Found Grant, Univ Grad Sch, 50; Grad Sch Grants, Univ Minn, 50-65. *Mem:* Artists Equity; Minn Artists Asn (pres, 63-66). *Specialty:* Women's cooperative, painting, sculpture, prints. *Dealer:* West Lake Gallery 1612 W Lake St Minneapolis MN 55408. *Mailing Add:* 7500 York Ave Apt 845 Edina MN 55435

ROLLMAN-SHAY, ED & CHARLOTTE
PAINTERS, PRINTMAKERS
Ed, b Boston, Mass, Nov 12, 47; Charlotte, b Harrisburg, Ill, Oct 15, 47. *Study:* Both, Murray State Univ, Ky, BFA, 69; Univ Ill, Champaign, MFA, 71. *Work:* Minn Mus Art, St Paul; Univ NDak, Grand Forks; Dulin Gallery Art, Knoxville, Tenn; Bradley Univ, Peoria, Ill; Calif Col Arts & Crafts, San Francisco. *Comn:* Oil Planetarium, Ponderosa Collection, Dayton, Ohio, 74; wall graphic, Skate Away, Muncie, Ind, 77; billboard, Indianapolis Art League, Ind, 78. *Exhib:* 74th Chicago Artists & Vicinity Show, Chicago Art Inst, 73; World Print Competition, Calif Col Arts & Crafts, San Francisco, 73; Works On Twinrocker Handmade Paper, Ind Mus Art, Indianapolis, 75; Crimes of Passion, Univ Ky, Lexington, 77; Rutgers Nat Drawing 77, Camden Col of Arts & Sci, NJ, 77. *Collections Arranged:* Rollman-Shay, Not In New York Gallery, Cincinnati, Ohio, 74 & 76; Krannert Gallery, Univ Evansville, Ind, 74; Nancy Lurie Gallery, Chicago, Ill, 76; Ball State Univ Art Gallery, Muncie, Ind, 76. *Awards:* Purchase Awards, 55th Soc Am Graphic Artists Nat Print Exhib, New York, 77 & Drawings & Prints 77, Miami Univ, Oxford, Ohio, 77; Bronstein Purchase Award, Mid-States Exhib, Evansville Mus Art, Ind, 77. *Bibliog:* Ellen Brown (auth), Ed & Charlotte Rollman-Shay, Art in Am, 3-4/76; Lynn Karn (auth), Ed & Charlotte Rollman-Shay, New Art Examiner, 1/77; Franz Schulze (auth), Illinois Artists, Chicago Daily News, 1/23/77. *Media:* Oil, Watercolor. *Mailing Add:* c/o Nancy Lurie Gallery 1632 N LaSalle Chicago IL 60614

ROLLY, RONALD JOSEPH
DEALER
b Waterbury, Conn, Dec 31, 37. *Pos:* Dir, Rolly-Michaux Galleries, Boston & New York. *Specialty:* 20th century masters and contemporaries; paintings, sculpture and graphics. *Mailing Add:* c/o Rolly-Michaux Galleries 290 Dartmouth St Boston MA 02116

ROLOFF, JOHN SCOTT
SCULPTOR, ENVIRONMENTAL ARTIST
b Portland, Ore, Sept 20, 47. *Study:* Univ Calif, Davis, BA; Calif State Univ, Humboldt, MA. *Work:* Oakland Mus; Univ Art Mus, Berkeley; Lannon Found, Palm Springs; Mus Mod Art, San Francisco; Herbert F Johnson Mus, Cornell Univ, Ithaca, NY; and others. *Exhib:* Clay Images, Calif State Univ, Los Angeles, 74; Clay USA, Fendrick Gallery, Washington, DC, 75; Whitney Mus Am Art, Biennial, New York, 75; Northern California Clay Routes-Sculpture Now, San Francisco Mus Mod Art, 79; solo shows, Fuller-Goldeen Gallery, 79-81, San Francisco, Theo Portnoy Gallery, New York, 81 & San Francisco Art Inst, 82; Six East Bay Artists, Oakland Mus, 82. *Teaching:* Instr ceramics, San Francisco Art Inst, 73-74 & 78-; asst prof ceramics, Univ Ky, 74-78; asst prof, Mills Col, 80- *Awards:* Craftsmens Fel, Nat Endowment Arts, 77; Visual Arts Grant, Nat Endowment Arts, 80; Guggenheim Found Fel, 83. *Bibliog:* Jan Axel & Karen McCready (coauths), Porcelain: Tradtions and New Visions, Watson-Guptill, 81; Susan Weschler (auth), Low Fire Ceramics, Watson-Guptill, 81; Joanne Burstein (auth), John Roloff Allegory/Alchemy, Am Ceramics Mag, fall 83. *Publ:* Auth, Kiln projects, Artery Mag, 2-3/83. *Dealer:* Fuller-Goldeen Gallery 228 Grant St San Francisco CA 94108. *Mailing Add:* c/o Lester Gallery PO Box 485 Inverness CA 94837

ROMAN, SHIRLEY
PRINTMAKER
b New York, NY. *Study:* Am Artists Sch; Brooklyn Mus Sch; Queens Col; also with Gregorio Prestopino, Raphael Soyer, Ruth Leaf & Agnes Mills. *Work:* De Cordova Mus, Lincoln, Mass; Readers Digest, Pleasantville, NY; Slater Mus, Norwalk, Conn; Butler Mus Am Art; Libr Cong, Washington, DC. *Exhib:* Philadelphia Print Club, 69-74; Soc Am Graphic Artists; Silvermine Guild, 73; Pratt Graphics Miniature Show; Boston Printmakers Asn, 73; Audubon Artists, 80. *Awards:* Purchase Prize, Boston Printmakers 25th Ann, 73; Medals of Hon, Nat Asn Women Artists, 76, 79 & 82; Audubon Artists, 80; and others. *Mem:* Philadelphia Print Club; Nat Asn Women Artists; Audubon Artists; Soc Am Graphic Artists; Boston Printmakers. *Dealer:* Am Artists Asn 663 5th Ave New York NY 10022. *Mailing Add:* 60-41 251 St Little Neck NY 11362

ROMANO, CLARE CAMILLE
PRINTMAKER, PAINTER
b Palisade, NJ. *Study:* Cooper Union Sch Art, 39-43; Ecole Beaux-Arts, Fontainebleau, France, 49; Inst Statale Arte, Florence, Italy, Fulbright Grant, 58-59. *Work:* Mus Mod Art, Whitney Mus Am Art & Metrop Mus Art, New York; Libr of Cong & Nat Collection Fine Arts, Washington, DC. *Comn:* Tapestry, Mfrs Hanover Bank, New York, 69. *Exhib:* 2nd Triennial Int Exhib Woodcuts, Ugo Carpi Mus, Italy, 72; American Prints, US Info Agency, Australian Nat Mus, Canberra, 72; Hane Haslem Gallery, Washington, DC, 81; Queensland Col Art, Brisbane, Australia, 82; AAA Gallery, New York, 82; and others. *Teaching:* Instr printmaking, New Sch Social Res, 60-73; adj assoc prof printmaking, Pratt Graphic Arts Ctr, 63-; assoc prof printmaking, Pratt Inst, 64- *Awards:* Citation for Prof Achievement, Cooper Union Sch Art, 66; Distinguished Teacher Award, Pratt Inst, 79; NJ State Counc Arts Grant, 80; and others. *Bibliog:* Pat Gilmour (auth), Modern prints, Studio Vista, London, 70; Jules Heller (auth), Printmaking Today, Holt, Rinehart & Winston, 72; Fritz Eichenberg (auth), The Art of the Print, Abrams, 77. *Mem:* Soc Am Graphic Artists (pres, 70-72); Print Club Philadelphia; Nat Acad Design. *Publ:* Co-illusr, Leaves of Grass, 64; auth, Artist's Proof, 64 & 66; auth, American Encyclopedia, 71; coauth, The Complete Printmaker, 72 & The Complete Collagraph, 80, Free Press. *Dealer:* Assoc Am Artists 663 Fifth Ave New York NY 10022; Jane Haslem Gallery 406 Seventh St NW Washington DC 20004. *Mailing Add:* 110 Davidson Pl Englewood NJ 07631

ROMANO, EMANUEL GLICEN
PAINTER, ILLUSTRATOR
b Rome, Italy, Sept 23, 97. *Study:* In Switz; also with Enrico Glicenstein. *Work:* Univ Art Mus, Univ Tex, Austin; Fogg Mus Art; Metrop Mus Art, New York; Detroit Inst Art; Mus Ville Paris; and others. *Comn:* Mural, Klondike Bldg, Welfare Island, NY; portraits in many pvt collections. *Exhib:* Whitney Mus Am Art; City Col New York; Ft Worth Art Asn; one-man shows, Greenville Mus Art, SC, 62 & Haifa Mus & Tel-Aviv Mus, Israel; and many others. *Teaching:* Lectr mural painting in ancient and modern times. *Mem:* Artists League Am. *Publ:* Contribr drawings, in The Waste Land, The Hollow Men, Waiting for Godot, Beckett, Rhinoceros & Ionesco; and many others. *Mailing Add:* 163 E 74th St New York NY 10021

ROMANO, JAIME (LUIS)
PAINTER
b San Juan, PR, Mar 10, 42. *Study:* Univ PR, BBA & BA(humanities), 66; Am Univ, MA, 69; New York Univ, 77-78. *Work:* Mus Bellas Artes, Ponce, PR; Pratt Graphic Ctr, New York; Inst Cult Puertorriquena, San Juan; Mus Antropologia y Arte, Univ PR, Rio Piedras; C Law Watkins Collection, Am Univ, Washington, DC. *Exhib:* One-man shows, Inst Puerto Rican Culture, San Juan, 74; Washington Project Arts, Washington, DC, 77; Humphrey Building, Washington, DC, 81 & Art Students League, New York, 83; Art 81, Jack Rasmussen Gallery, Washington, DC, 81; and others. *Pos:* Vpres, Fondo Becas Artes Plasticas, Inc, San Juan, 72-75. *Teaching:* Instr advan drawing & painting, Univ PR, Rio Piedras, 69-71, acad adv, 70-71, Art Students League, San Juan, 73-75; lectr, Am Univ, Washington, DC, 83. *Awards:* First Prize in Painting, Puerto Rican Atheneum, 68; First Prize in Watercolor, Puerto Rican Atheneum, 73; Acquisition Prize, Inst Puerto Rican Culture, 77; and others. *Bibliog:* Myrna Rodriquez (auth), Still the same style, San Juan Star, 4/17/83; Teresa Tio (auth), Jorge Romano Y el jardin hechizado, El Mundo, 4/21/83; Samuel Cherson (auth), Un aromatico jardin de flores invisibles, El Nuevo Dia, 4/22/83; and others. *Media:* Acrylic, Watercolor. *Publ:* Auth, Ernesto Alvarez, 66; auth, Art in Puerto Rico-Boom or Bust?, 71; auth, On Criticism, Critics & Criteria, 72. *Mailing Add:* 5415 Connecticut Ave NW Apt 542 Washington DC 20015

ROMANO, SALVATORE MICHAEL
SCULPTOR, KINETIC ARTIST
b Cliffside Park, NJ, Sept 12, 25. *Study:* Art Students League, with Jon Corbino; Acad Grande Chaumiere, Paris, with Edouard Georges & Earl Kerkam. *Work:* Chase Manhattan Bank, New York. *Exhib:* Highlights of the Season, 68-69, Aldrich Mus Contemp Art, Ridgefield, Conn, 69; Monumenta, A Biennial Exhib Outdoor Sculpture, Newport, RI, 74; Wave Hill Sculpture Garden Exhib, New York, 77; Shared Spaces, Bronx Mus Art, 83; Anchorage Brooklyn Bridge Ctr, 83; NJ State Mus, 83; and others. *Teaching:* Adj instr sculpture, Cooper Union Sch Arts & Archit, 68-70; lectr painting & sculpture, Lehman Col, 69-71, asst prof, 72-; lectr kinetic sculpture, US Info Serv, Brazil, 72, Rutgers Univ, 79, Col New Rochelle, 83. *Awards:* Nat Endowment Arts, 79-80; Fac Res Award, City Univ New York, Lehman Col, 80-81; McDowell Coloy Fel, 80 & 81. *Bibliog:* Lawrence Alloway (auth), Salvatore Romano's sculpture, Arts Mag, 10/77; Donald B Kuspit (auth), article, Art Am, 1-2/78; and others. *Media:* Plastics, Wood; Metal, Water. *Publ:* Auth, article, Lehman Col Art News Lett, 71. *Mailing Add:* 83 Wooster St New York NY 10017

ROMANO, UMBERTO ROBERTO
PAINTER, SCULPTOR
b Naples, Italy, Feb 26, 06; US citizen. *Study:* Nat Acad Design, New York, 21-26; Tiffany Found, summer 25; Am Acad Rome, 26-27. *Work:* Nat Collection Fine Arts & Corcoran Gallery, Washington, DC; Whitney Mus Am Art; Roosevelt Libr, Hyde Park, NY; Smith Mus, Springfield, Mass. *Comn:* Mural, Three Centuries of New England History, Springfield Post Off, 38; portrait of Sara Delano Roosevelt, March of Dimes, Hyde Park Libr, 42; mosaic mural, After Chaos Came Order, Munic Ct House, New York, 61; Pupil Learns from Past & Looks Toward the Future, PS 234, Brooklyn, 64; Mother and Child (stained glass window), Allen Stevenson Sch, New York, 67. *Exhib:* Carnegie Inst Int, Pittsburgh, 33-49; one-man shows, Worcester Art Mus, Mass, 35 & Galerie Andre Weil, Paris, 49; Oriental Fragment, US

Govt Traveling Show, Orient, 50-52; Fragment--Man Weeps, US Govt Traveling Relig Show, Italy, Fr, Spain & Ger, 58-61. *Pos:* Dir, Abbey Found, 66- *Teaching:* Instr painting & sculpture & dir, Worcester Art Mus Sch, 33-40; pvt instr, Gloucester, Mass, 33-60, New York & Chatham, Mass, 50- *Awards:* Pulitzer Prize, Columbia Univ, 26; Carnegie Award, Nat Acad Design, 54; Gold Medal of Honor, Century Asn, 69. *Bibliog:* Edward Alden Jewell (auth), Romano portrays horrors of war, New York Times, 44; Harry Salpeter (auth), Renaissance of Umberto Romano, Esquire, 45; Richard Merrifield (auth), Umberto Romano, Yankee Mag, 52. *Mem:* Century Asn; Int Asn Plastic Arts; Nat Mural Soc (dir, 62-); Provincetown Art Asn; Audubon Artists; and others. *Media:* Oil, Acrylic; Bronze, Marble. *Publ:* Illusr, Dante's The Divine Comedy, 46 & contribr, Best of Art, 48, Doubleday; contribr, Contemporary American Painting, Univ Ill, 49; contribr, Expressionism in Art, Liveright, 58; auth, Great Men, 40 Paintings, Dial Press, 79. *Dealer:* Wellfleet Art Gallery Cape Cod MA 02650; ACA Gallery 21 E 67th St New York NY 10021. *Mailing Add:* 162 E 83rd St New York NY 10028

ROMANS, VAN ANTHONY
SCULPTOR, DESIGNER
b Baltimore, Md, Jan 13, 44. *Study:* Univ Calif, Fullerton, BA(art design), studied with Dextra Frankel; Univ Southern Calif, studied 3-D arts & mus design with Lee Chesney, MFA. *Work:* Claremont Grad Sch Gallery, Calif; Univ Southern Calif, Los Angeles; Calif State Univ, Fullerton; Orange Coast Col, Costa Mesa, Calif. *Comn:* Westcliff Shopping Ctr (designed), comn by Richard Marowitz, 76; Courtyard Shopping Ctr (designed), comn by Jerry Stout, 77. *Exhib:* One-man shows, Oakland Mus Art, Calif, 71 & Univ Southern Calif, Los Angeles, 72; Six Promising Young Sculptors, Claremont Cols, Calif, 73; Environments/Spaces, Orange Coast Col, 75; Spaces, Pac Design Ctr, Calif, 76; and others. *Collections Arranged:* Thonet & Thereafter, show of chair hist incl Bauhaus (auth, catalog), Japanese Sword Show, collection from collectors & from Los Angeles Co Art Mus, Western Indian Show--Dan Namingha & Persian Rug Show (designed exhib), 57 rugs from cols & collections, Orange Coast Col Art Gallery. *Pos:* Dir display prog, Orange Coast Col, Costa Mesa, Calif, 73-, dir galleries & dir interior design, 75-; mem, Orange Co Art Alliance, Calif, 77; lectr, Newport Harbor Art Mus, Newport Beach, Calif. *Teaching:* Prof design & exhib design/visual promotion, Orange Coast Col, Costa Mesa, Calif, 73- & prof design & visual promotion, currently; asst prof design, Univ Southern Calif, Los Angeles, 73-82. *Awards:* Most Outstanding Educator, Orange Coast Col, 75. *Bibliog:* Wilson (auth), Sculpture, 74. *Mem:* Am Soc Interior Designers. *Media:* Metal. *Mailing Add:* 514 W Memory Lane Santa Ana CA 92706

ROMBOUT, LUKE
MUSEUM DIRECTOR
b Amsterdam, Neth, May 4, 33; Can citizen. *Study:* Mt Alison Univ, Sackville, NB, BFA, 67. *Pos:* Asst cur, Beaverbrook Art Gallery, Fredericton, NB, 60; chmn art comt, Comn Continuing Educ, St John, NB, 60; secy, Atlantic Prov Art Circuit, 64-67; actg cur, Owens Art Gallery, Mt Allison Univ, 65-67, cur, 67-68, dir, 68-71; organizer fine arts crafts exhib, Atlantic Pavilion, Expo '67, Montreal; mem arts supervisory comt, NB Mus, St John, 67-68; mem arts adv panel, Can Coun, Ottawa, Ont, 69-70, dir art bank, 72-74, head visual arts film sect, 74-75; mem adv comt art, Can Dept Pub Works, 73; mem design adv comt, Can Post, 73; mem fine arts comt, Can Dept External Affairs, 73-75; dir, Vancouver Art Gallery, BC, 75- *Teaching:* Lectr Can art hist, Mt Alison Univ, 68-71; lectr art hist, NS Col Art Design, 70-72; asst prof visual arts & chmn prog, Fac Fine Arts, York Univ, Toronto, Ont, 72-74; lectr Can art hist, Univ Ottawa, Ont, 74-75. *Mem:* Can Mus Asn (vpres, 70-71); Can Art Mus Dirs Orgn; Asn Art Mus Dirs; Asn Am Mus Dirs; Can Asn Mus Dirs; and others. *Mailing Add:* 750 Hornby St Vancouver BC V6Z 2H7 Canada

ROMELING, W B
PAINTER
b Schenectady, NY, Feb 26, 09. *Study:* Pratt Inst, Brooklyn; Syracuse Univ; Sch Fine Arts; also with Ogden Pleissner. *Work:* Schenectady Mus; Cooperstown Art Asn; Canajoharie Libr. *Exhib:* Central New York, Munson-Williams-Proctor Inst, Utica, NY, 62; one-man shows, Pioneer Gallery, Cooperstown, 83 & Elhoff Gallery, Syracuse, NY, 83; Cooperstown Ann, NY, 70-71; Retrospective, Muggleton Mus, 77. *Teaching:* Instr art, Owen D Young Sch, Van Hornesville, NY, 43-69. *Awards:* Purchase Prize, Schenectady Mus, 63; First Prize for Still Life, Cooperstown Art Asn, 66, Godley Watercolor Award, 70. *Mem:* Cooperstown Art Asn (pres, 70-72); Southern Vt Artists; Central NY Watercolor Soc. *Publ:* Contribr (watercolor), Am Artist Mag, 12/77. *Mailing Add:* Box 53 Van Hornesville NY 13475

ROMEU, JOOST A
CONCEPTUAL ARTIST, DESIGNER
b Bremerhaven, Ger, Jan 16, 48; US citizen. *Study:* Drexel Univ, BS. *Work:* Kansas City Art Inst; MTL Gallery, Belg. *Exhib:* Deurle, Belg, 73; Projekt '74, Koln, Ger; Diskussies Omtrent Joost A Romeu, Univ Antwerp, Belg, 75; Idea Warehouse, New York, 75. *Bibliog:* Foote (auth), The apotheosis of the crummy space, Artforum; J L Mackie (auth), The Directon of Causation; Merleau Ponty (auth), Primacy of Perception. *Publ:* Art after philosophy, 73; auth & illusr, ONCE1, ONCE2,...., ONCE24. *Mailing Add:* 38 White St New York NY 10013

ROMNEY, HERVIN A R
ARCHITECT
b Havana, Cuba, 1941; US citizen. *Study:* Cooper Union, 62-65; L'Ecole Speciale d'Architecture, Paris, 70; Catholic Univ, Washington, DC, BArchit, 73; Yale Univ Sch Archit, Master's, 75. *Comn:* Il Gattopardo, Ambassador

J A Correa, Quito, Equador, 76; Babylon (condominium), Pac Developers, Miami, 77; Atlantis (condominium), Stonecrest Development, Miami, 79; Palace (condominium), Helmsley-Spear, Miami, 79, Helmsley Ctr, 81. *Exhib:* Inst Archit & Urban Studies, Rome, 79; Cooper Hewitt, New York, 79; Yale Art Gallery, New Haven, Conn, 80; Inst Fine Arts, Chicago, 80; Mus Contemp Arts, La Jolla, 81; Contemp Arts Mus, Houston, 82. *Pos:* Designer, Harrison & Abramovitz, New York, 61-65; proj designer, Andrault-Parat, architects, Paris, 69-70; architect & environmental designer, South Am, 75-76; principal & founder, Arquitectonica Int Corp, Miami, 76- *Awards:* Cintas Fel, UN Inst Int Educ, 74-75; Design Citations, Progressive Archit, 78 & 80; Fla Am Inst Archit, 82. *Bibliog:* Article, Color/architecture, Life Mag, 4/81; articles, Newsweek 11/8/82 & House & Garden, 6/83. *Mem:* Am Inst Architects. *Publ:* Ed, Perspecta 15, Yale Archit Papers, 75. *Mailing Add:* 5758 Southwest 31st St Miami FL 33155

ROMOSER, RUTH AMELIA
PAINTER, CONCEPTUAL ARTIST
b Baltimore, Md, Apt 26, 16. *Study:* Baltimore Art Inst, grad; sculpture with Xavier Corbera, Barcelona, Spain; Robert Motherwell Workshop; graphics with Joseph Ruffo. *Work:* Miami Mus Mod Art, Fla; Lowe Mus, Univ Miami; Nat Cardiac Hosp, Miami; Int Gallery, Baltimore, Md; Marj Stoneman Douglas Purchase, Tallahassee, 81. *Comn:* Two paintings for 12 productions, Actors Studio M, Coral Gables, Fla, 63-64. *Exhib:* Nat Drawing Exhib, Cheltenham, Pa, 64; Hortt Mem Regional, Ft Lauderdale Mus Arts, 66; one-man show, Palm Beach Jr Col; Jacksonville Mus, Fla; Norton Gallery, Palm Beach, Fla. *Awards:* Dade Co Coun Arts & Sci Award, 79; Fla House of Rep Purchase Award, 79; Individual Artist Fel, Div Cult Affairs, Fla, 80-81; and others. *Bibliog:* Bernard Davis (auth), Romoser Foreward (catalog), Miami Mus Mod Art, 68; Doris Reno (auth), Lively arts, Miami Herald, 69. *Mem:* Blue Dome Art Fel; Women's Caucus of Art; Fla Artists Group; Lowe Mus; Miami Art Ctr. *Media:* Oil, Acrylic. *Publ:* Auth, All Florida artist, House Mag, 63; auth, article, Art News Mag, 67; auth, Art Voices South, 79 & Fla Visual Artists, 81. *Mailing Add:* 8025 SW 64th St Miami FL 33143

ROMPPANEN, EINO ANTTI See Eino

RONALD, WILLIAM
PAINTER
b Stratford, Ont, Aug 13, 26; US citizen. *Study:* Ont Col Art, hon grad, 51. *Work:* Mus Mod Art, Guggenheim Mus & Whitney Mus Am Art, New York; Nat Gallery Can, Ottawa, Ont; Carnegie Inst, Pittsburgh, Pa; among others. *Comn:* Acrylic mural, Nat Art Ctr, Ottawa, 70. *Exhib:* Carnegie Int, 58; Brussels World's Fair & traveling exhib, 58; Sao Paulo Biennale, Mus Arte Mod, 59; Whitney Mus Am Art Ann, 59; Can Biennial, Nat Gallery Can, 68; and many one-man shows. *Pos:* Host of TV show on arts, Can Broadcasting Corp, Toronto, Ont, 66-67. *Awards:* Watercolor Award, Hallmark Corp Art, 52; Nat Award, Can Sect, Int Guggenheim Awards, 56; Award, Second Biennial Exhib Can Painting, Nat Gallery Can, 57. *Bibliog:* David Ralston & Hugo McPherson (auth), Ronald Chapel in Toronto Harbour, Can Art, 4/66; William Cameron (auth), Portrait of the artist as a violently honest man, Macleans Mag, 2/71; From crisis to crisis with William Ronald, Sat Night, 7-8/75. *Mailing Add:* 392 Brunswick Ave Toronto ON M5R 2Z4 Canada

RONEY, HAROLD ARTHUR
PAINTER, LECTURER
b Sullivan, Ill, Nov 7, 1899. *Study:* Chicago Acad Art; Art Inst Chicago; also with Harry Leith-Ross, John Folinsbee & George A Aldrich. *Work:* Sullivan Pub Libr, Ill; Witte Mem Mus; Austin Pub Libr, Tex; South Bend Pub Sch, Ind; Southwest Tex State Univ; and others. *Exhib:* River Square Gallery, San Antonio, 71; Coppini Acad Fine Arts, San Antonio, 71; and others. *Teaching:* Instr oil landscape, Froman Sch Art, Cloudcroft, NMex, 58- *Media:* Oil. *Mailing Add:* 20025 1H 10 W San Antonio TX 78215

ROOTS, GARRISON
ENVIRONMENTAL ARTIST, EDUCATOR
b Abilene, Tex, June 25, 52. *Study:* Mass Col Art, with George Greenmayer, Harris Barron & Jana Longacre, BFA(with hon), 79; Washington Univ, with Howard Jones & James Sterritt, MFA, 81. *Work:* Washington Univ Fine Arts, St Louis. *Comn:* Model for outdoor installation, comn by Dr Beej Nirengarten-Smith, St Louis, Mo, 81. *Exhib:* Boston Area Sculptors: Out of the Woods, Rose Art Mus, Waltham, Mass, 82; solo exhibs, So Then What Have We Learned, Crapo Gallery, Swain Sch Design, 82, So Then Who is Responsible, Ctr Idea Art, Denver, 83, So You Think You're An Individual, Los Angeles Mus Contemp Art, 83, I Have So Much More to Learn, Ft Worth Mus, Tex, 83 & In Hopes of Not Being Seen, Contemp Art Ctr, New Orleans, 84; New Faculty Exhib, Univ Colo, Boulder, 83. *Pos:* Med artist/photogr, Mass Eye & Ear Infirmary, 76-79; asst to dir, Laumeier Int Sculpture Park, St Louis, 80-81. *Teaching:* Teaching/tech asst, Washington Univ, St Louis, 79-81; instr, Swain Sch Design, New Bedford, Mass, 81-82; asst prof, Univ Colo, Boulder, 82- *Awards:* Rosenthal Found Award for Sculpture, Silvermine Guild for Artists, 79; Fel Award for Sculpture, Nat Endowment Arts, 81; Grant in Aid for Res & Creative Work, Univ Colo, Boulder, 83. *Bibliog:* Jim Walsh (auth), Sculptor Carnes niche at Swain, New Bedford Standard Times, 82; Irene Clurman (auth), Eye on art, Denver Rocky Mountain News, 83; Robert L Pincus (auth), Installation art: Life as theater, Los Angeles Times, 83. *Mem:* Mid-Am Col Art Asn. *Mailing Add:* 931 Vetch Circle Lafayette CO 80026

ROREX, ROBERT ALBRIGHT
EDUCATOR, HISTORIAN
b Alexandria, La, Sept 9, 35. *Study:* Hendrix Col, BA, 57; Univ Ark, MFA, 60; Princeton Univ, MA, 69, PhD, 75. *Teaching:* Asst prof, Hendrix Col, 60-61; actg asst prof, Univ Kans, Lawrence, 68-70; instr, Univ Iowa, Iowa City, 70-75, asst prof art hist, 75-79, assoc prof, 79- *Mem:* Col Art Asn; Mid-Am Col Art Asn; Midwest Art Hist Soc. *Res:* Chinese art & archeology; Japanese art & archeology; Sung, Ming & Liao painting. *Publ:* Coauth, Eighteen Songs of a Nomad Flute: The Story of Lady Wen-Chi, Metrop Mus Art, 74; auth, Setting out at dawn on an autumn river: A painting by Wang Hui, Artibus Asiae, 79; auth, Eighteen songs of a nomad flute, 8/81 & Chunghi Choo: Works in metal and silk, 10/82, Orientations; auth, Some observations on Harold Osborne's The Aesthetics of Chinese Pictorial Art, J Theory & Criticism Visual Arts, 82. *Mailing Add:* 846 Kirkwood Ave Iowa City IA 52240

ROSAND, DAVID
HISTORIAN, CRITIC
b Brooklyn, NY, Sept 6, 38. *Study:* Columbia Col, AB, 59; Columbia Univ, MA, 62, PhD, 65. *Collections Arranged:* Titian and the Venetian Woodcut (auth, catalog), Nat Gallery Art, DC, 76. *Teaching:* Prof art hist, Columbia Univ, New York, 64- *Awards:* Fulbright Fel; Nat Endowment Humanities Fel; Guggenheim Fel. *Mem:* Col Art Asn Am; Renaissance Soc Am. *Res:* Venetian painting; Renaissance tradition; graphic arts; criticism of drawing. *Publ:* Auth, Art history and criticism: The past as present, New Literary Hist, Vol 5, 74; co-auth, Titian and the Venetian Woodcut, Int Exhib Found, DC, 76; auth, Titian, Abrams, 78; auth, Painting in Cinquecento Venice: Titian, Veronese, Tintoretto, Yale Univ Press, 82; auth, The Portrait, the Courtier, and Death in Castiglione, Yale Univ Press, 83; auth, Paint, paste, and plane, New York Literary Forum, Vol 10-11, 83. *Mailing Add:* Dept of Art Hist & Archaeol Columbia Univ New York NY 10027

ROSAS, MEL
PAINTER
b Des Moines, Iowa, June 1, 50. *Study:* Drake Univ, with Jules Kirschembalm, BFA, 71; Tyler Sch Art, with John Moore & Steven Greene, MFA, 74. *Work:* Mus Am Art, Washington, DC; Cleveland Co Coun, Middlesbrough, Eng; Carnegie-Mellon Inst, Pittsburgh; Alberta Art Found, Edmonton; Detroit Inst Art. *Comn:* Drawings, W D Gale Inc, Detroit, 78 & 79; The Road Show (billboard proj art), 1st Fed Savings & Loan, Detroit, 80. *Exhib:* Cranbrook Acad Art Mus, Bloomfield Hills, Mich, 79; The Road Show, City Detroit, 80; American Drawings in Black and White, Brooklyn Mus, 81; Mich Artists 80-81, Detroit Inst Art, 82; City Walls (solo exhib), Fendrick Gallery, Washington, DC, 82; and others. *Teaching:* Instr, Univ Calgary, Alberta, 75-76; asst prof, Wayne State Univ, Detroit, 76- *Awards:* Purchase Award, Third Int Drawing Biennale, Cleveland Co Coun, England, 77; Creative Artists Grant, Mich Coun Arts, 81. *Media:* Oil, Watercolor. *Dealer:* Cantor-Lemberg Gallery 538 N Woodward Ave Birmingham MI 48011; Fendrick Gallery 3059 M St Washington DC 20007. *Mailing Add:* 743 Beaubien Detroit MI 48226

ROSATI, JAMES
SCULPTOR, EDUCATOR
b Washington, Pa, June 9, 12. *Work:* Yale Gallery Fine Arts; NY Univ; Whitney Mus Am Art; Albright-Knox Art Gallery, Buffalo, NY; Hirshhorn Mus, Washington, DC; also in many pvt collections. *Comn:* World Trade Ctr, New York. *Exhib:* Six shows, Whitney Mus Am Art Ann, 52-66; Int Coun Mus Mod Art Exhib, France, Ger & Scandinavia, 65-66; Flint Inst, 66; Colby Col, 67; Mus Contemp Crafts Traveling Exhib, 67-68; and many others. *Teaching:* Adj assoc prof sculpture, Yale Univ, 60-73; vis critic sculpture, Hopkins Art Ctr, Dartmouth Col, spring 63. *Awards:* Logan Medal & Prize, Art Inst Chicago, 62; Carborundum Major Abrasive Mkt Award, 63; Guggenheim Fel, 64; and others. *Bibliog:* Michel Seuphor (auth), The Sculpture of This Century, Dictionary of Modern Sculpture, A Zwemmer Ltd, London, 59; Jean Selz (auth), Modern Sculpture, Braziller, 63; Herbert Read (auth), A Concise History of Modern Sculpture, Praeger, 64. *Dealer:* Marlborough Gallery 41 E 57th St New York NY 10028. *Mailing Add:* 56 Seventh Ave New York NY 10011

ROSE, DAVID
PAINTER, ILLUSTRATOR
b Malden, Mass, Mar 10, 10. *Study:* Mass Col Art, Boston, with Ernest Majors, Richard Andrews, Otis Philbrick, dipl drawing-painting, 31, BSc(art educ), 34; Mus Fine Arts, Boston, with Jocovleff, 32; etching with Herman Struck, Haifa, 33; Chouinard Art Inst, Los Angeles, 38-40; Art Ctr Col, 40-42. *Work:* Israel Mus, Jerusalem; Mus Mod Art, Haifa; Bialik Mus, Tel Aviv; Skirball Mus, Los Angeles. *Comn:* Courtroom sketches of famous trials: Pentagon Papers, Patty Hearst, Nat Broadcasting Co, New York, 74-77 & Am Broadcasting Co, New York, 77-80; film titles, Humanities & The Arts, Coast Community Col Dist, Calif, 78; and others. *Exhib:* Artists of Los Angeles & Vicinity, Los Angeles Co Mus Art, 52; Soc Illusr, Calif State Mus, Los Angeles, 70; Skirball Mus, Los Angeles, 78; one-man shows, Artist in the Courtroom, Univ Calif, Los Angeles, 79 & Univ Ariz, Tucson, 79; Artists in the Courtroom, Mandeville Gallery, Univ Calif, San Diego, 80; plus others. *Teaching:* Instr artist as reporter, Otis-Parsons Sch Design, Los Angeles, 79-81. *Awards:* US War Dept Commendation, Army Pictorial Serv, Info & Educ, 45; Two Medal Awards, Art Dirs Club Los Angeles, 59; Emmy Nomination for Pentagon Papers trial sketches, TV Acad Arts & Sci, 74; and many others. *Bibliog:* Paul Buscemi (auth), Artists in the Courtroom (videotape), Mandeville Gallery, Univ Calif, San Diego, 80; John Gorham (auth), Courtroom art: David Rose draws it as he sees it, Los Angeles Weekly,

3/14-20/80. *Mem:* Art Dirs Club Los Angeles; Nat Soc Art Dirs; Soc Illusr Los Angeles; Artists Equity. *Media:* Pen, Felt Markers; Oil, Watercolor. *Publ:* Auth, Western art, (Graphis) Int J Graphic Art, 57; auth-illusr, Yiddish poet in Denmark, Jewish Observer-Mid E Rev, 70; auth-illusr, Fairfax Avenue, Nat Jewish Mo, 71; illusr, People's Almanac No 1, Doubleday, 78 & People's Almanac No 2, William Morrow & Co, 79. *Dealer:* Tobey C Moss Fine Arts 7321 Beverly Blvd Los Angeles CA 90036. *Mailing Add:* 1623 N Curson Ave Los Angeles CA 90046

ROSE, HERMAN
PAINTER, PRINTMAKER
b Brooklyn, NY, Nov 6, 09. *Study:* Nat Acad Design, 27-29. *Work:* Whitney Mus Am Art, Mus Mod Art, New York; Univ Tex; Univ Nebr; Smithsonian Inst Print Collection; and others. *Exhib:* Mus Mod Art, 48 & 52; 15 Americans, Whitney Mus Am Art, 48-58 & 72; Pa Acad Fine Arts, 52; one-man shows, ACA Gallery, 52 & 55-56, Forum Gallery, NY, 62 & Zabriskie Gallery, 67, 69, 72 & 74. *Teaching:* Instr, New Sch Social Res, 54-55 & 63-; instr, Hofstra Col, 59-60; artist in residence, Univ Va, 66; vis prof, Univ NMex, 70-71. *Awards:* Childe Hassam Purchase Award, 71; Benjamin Altman Award, Nat Acad Design, 76; Nat Endowment Arts, 76. *Mailing Add:* 463 West Apt H821 New York NY 10014

ROSE, LEATRICE
PAINTER, INSTRUCTOR
b New York, NY. *Study:* Cooper Union, 45; Art Students League, 46; Hans Hofmann Sch, 47. *Exhib:* Artists Ann, Whitney Mus Am Art, 50; one-woman shows, Zabriskie Gallery, 65, Landmark Gallery, 74 & Tibor de Nagy Gallery, 75, 78 & 81; Pa Acad Fine Arts Ann, 66; Women Choose Women, New York Cult Ctr, 73; Nat Acad Design Ann, 74-76; Whitney Mus Am Art, Downtown, 78; Hans Hofmann as Teacher: Drawings by his Students, Metrop Mus Art, 79; Contemp Naturalism, Nassau Co Mus Fine Arts, 80. *Teaching:* Instr painting, State Univ NY, Stony Brook, 74-75 & Sch Visual Art, New York 77. *Awards:* Creative Artists Pub Serv Grant, 74; Am Asn Univ Women Grant, 75-76; Nat Endowment Arts Grant, 77. *Bibliog:* John Ashbery (auth), Dash, Dodd & Rose, Art in Am, 3/74; April Kingsley (auth), The Lugano review, Art Int, 3/20/74; Lawrence Alloway (auth), Art, Nation, 10/25/75. *Dealer:* Tibor de Nagy Gallery 29 W 57th St New York NY 10019. *Mailing Add:* 463 West St New York NY 10014

ROSE, MARY ANNE
PAINTER
b San Francisco, Calif, Aug 10, 49. *Study:* Univ Calif, Santa Cruz, AB, 70; Univ Calif, Berkeley, MA, 72, MFA, 73. *Work:* Mills Col, Oakland, Calif; Malmo Mus, Malmohus Lans Landstinget & Skandinaviska Enskilda Banken, Sweden; Art Mus Santa Cruz Co. *Exhib:* Pasadena Mus Mod Art, 73; San Francisco Mus Mod Art, 73 & 77; Los Angeles Inst Contemp Art, 76; Univ Art Mus, Berkeley, 73 & 77; two-person show, San Francisco Art Inst, 78; Art Mus Santa Cruz Co, 83; solo show, San Jose Mus Art, 83; and others. *Pos:* Gallery attendant supervisor, Univ Art Mus, Berkeley, 73-78. *Awards:* Eisner Award in the Creative Arts, Univ Calif, Berkeley, 72; Studio, Cite Int des Arts, Paris, 78-80; Nat Artist Fel, Sweden, 82; and others. *Media:* Acrylic, Watercolor. *Dealer:* Bernice Steinbaum Gallery New York NY. *Mailing Add:* 222 W 23rd St New York NY 10011

ROSE, PETER HENRY
DEALER
b New York, NY, Feb 25, 35. *Study:* Hamilton Col, BA; Univ Pa, MA; Columbia Univ; Ecole Superieure, Univ Paris. *Pos:* Co-owner, Peter Rose Gallery, currently. *Mem:* Arts & Bus Coun New York. *Specialty:* Nineteenth and twentieth century contemporary American art; major French impressionist paintings. *Mailing Add:* c/o Peter Rose Gallery 200 E 58th St New York NY 10022

ROSE, ROSLYN
PRINTMAKER, INSTRUCTOR
b Irvington, NJ, May 28, 29. *Study:* Rutgers Univ; Pratt Graphic Ctr; Skidmore Col, BS. *Work:* NJ State Mus, Trenton; McAllen Int Mus, Tex; Am Tel & Tel; Newark Mus, NJ; Citibank of New York, Moscow, Russia. *Comn:* Etchings, New York Graphic Soc, Ltd, Greenwich, Conn, 70-; Etchings, John Szoke Gallery, New York, 81-; UNICEF Card, 79-80. *Exhib:* Wadsworth Atheneum, Hartford, Conn, 65 & 75; Birmingham Mus of the Arts, Ala, 67; Seattle Art Mus, Wash, 68; Women in the Arts, Florence, Italy, 72; Newark Mus, NJ, 74; The Print Club, Philadelphia, 75; George Fredercik Gallery, Rochester, 81; Arnot Art Mus, Elmira, NY, 82; and others. *Collections Arranged:* Liberated Printmakers (traveling exhib), NJ Coun on the Arts, 72; Black/White & Color, Printmaking Coun NJ, 82. *Teaching:* Instr printmaking, Newark Mus, 72- *Awards:* Best-in-Show, Tri-State Exhib, Summit Art Ctr, NJ, 69, 71 & 75; Graphic Award, Rochester Int Religious, Coun of Churches & Synagogues, 70; Memorial Graphic Prize, Nat Asn Women Artists, Georgi & Mock, 77. *Bibliog:* J H Newman & L S Newman (auths), Plastics for the Craftsman, Crown, 72; Thelma R Newman (auth), Innovative Printmaking, Crown, 77. *Mem:* Artists Equity of NJ (mem exec bd, 71-75); Nat Asn of Women Artists; Assoc Artists of NJ; Printmaking Coun of NJ (bd dirs, 80-85). *Media:* Etching, Relief Printing. *Publ:* Auth, Outline of Printmaking, NJ Coun Arts, 72. *Dealer:* Assoc Artists of America 663 Fifth Ave New York NY 10022. *Mailing Add:* 457 Baldwin Rd Maplewood NJ 07040

ROSE, SAMUEL
PAINTER, MURALIST

b Cleveland, Ohio, Sept 17, 41. *Study:* Cape Cod Sch Art, Provincetown, with Henry Henche; Cooper Sch & Kent State Univ; Boston Atelier, with R H Ives Gammell; also with Basil Kalashnifoff, Cleveland. *Work:* Maryhill Mus Art & St Ignatius Church, Washington, DC. *Comn:* Many incl Maharaj Ji, Mrs F Lee Bailey, Patricia Barlow & Patricia Pierce. *Exhib:* Nat Arts Club, New York, 69; Copley Art Soc & Concord Art Asn, 71; Jordan Marsh, Boston, 72-73; one-man shows, Concord Art Asn, 75 & Pierce Galleries, Inc, 79; and others. *Teaching:* Pvt art classes. *Awards:* First Prize, Concord Art Asn, 63, 67 & 69; Greenshields Grant, Montreal, 63-70; and others. *Bibliog:* The Surreal World of S Rose, Am Antiques, 79. *Mem:* Copley Soc; Salmagundi Club; Guild Boston Artists; Concord Art Asn; Am Artists Prof League. *Media:* Oil. *Dealer:* Pierce Galleries Inc Hingham MA. *Mailing Add:* c/o Pierce Galleries Inc 721 Main St Hingham MA 02043

ROSE, STEPHANIE
PAINTER, EDUCATOR

b US, April 23, 43. *Study:* Skidmore Col, BS(fine art), 64; also with David Smith. *Work:* Continental Bank, Chicago; Chase Manhattan Bank, New York; Sydney Lewis Co, Richmond, Va; Prudential Insurance Co Am, Coopers & Lybrand, Boston. *Exhib:* Albright-Knox Art Gallery, 74-77; Arte Fiera, Bologna, Italy, 78; PS1, Long Island City, 79; Alternative Mus, New York, 81; Heresies, Grey Art Gallery, NY Univ, 81; Chicago Int Art Exposition, Navy Pier, 83. *Teaching:* Vis instr drawing & painting, Pratt Inst Grad Sch Fine Art, 79-80; instr, Parsons Sch Design, 80-; guest critic, Empire State Col, State Univ NY, 82- *Awards:* Ludwig Vogelstein Found Grants, 76 & 79. *Bibliog:* Ellen Schwartz (auth), article, Vol 79, No 5, 80 & Deborah Phillips (auth), article, Vol 82, No 3, 83, Art News; Mary Lee Thompson (auth), article, Arts, Vol 57, No 6, 83. *Mem:* New York Artists Equity Asn. *Media:* Oil on Canvas. *Dealer:* Getler-Pall 50 W 57th St New York NY; Mattingly-Baker Dallas TX. *Mailing Add:* 100 Grand St New York NY 10013

ROSE, THOMAS ALBERT
SCULPTOR

b Washington, DC, Oct 15, 42. *Study:* Univ Wis-Madison, 60-62; Univ Ill, Urbana, BFA, 65; Univ Calif, Berkeley, MA, 67, study grant to Univ Lund, 67-68. *Work:* Univ NMex Mus, Albuquerque; Libr Cong, Washington, DC; Minneapolis Inst Art; Walker Art Ctr, Minneapolis; Brooklyn Mus, NY; plus others. *Comn:* Park St Loft One, Springfield, Mass; chapel, St Lukes Espicopal Church, Minneapolis. *Exhib:* Walker Art Ctr, Minneapolis, 74; Small Objects, Downtown Whitney, New York; Scale & Environment, Walker Art Ctr; one-man shows, The Clocktower, Truman Gallery, New York & Directions, Hirshhorn Mus, Washington, DC, 81; outdoor sculpture exhib, Wave Hill, New York, 81; and others. *Teaching:* Instr sculpture, Univ Calif, Berkeley, 68-69; instr sculpture & graphics, NMex State Univ, 69-72; instr sculpture, Univ Minn, Minneapolis, 72-81, assoc prof, 81-83, prof, 83- *Awards:* Grants, Nat Endowment Arts, 75, 81 & 82; Bush Found Fel, 79-80; McKnight Fel, 82. *Bibliog:* John Ligon (prod), Encounters with Minnesota Artists (film). *Media:* Multimedia. *Dealer:* Rosa Esman Gallery 121 String St New York NY. *Mailing Add:* 5124 Harriet Ave Minneapolis MN 55419

ROSEBERG, CARL ANDERSSON
SCULPTOR, HISTORIAN

b Vinton, Iowa, Sept 26, 16. *Study:* Univ Iowa, BFA, 39, MFA, 47; Cranbrook Acad Arts, summers 47 & 48; Univ Va, summer 64; Univ Mysore, summer 65; Tyler Sch Art, summer 67. *Work:* Springfield Art Mus, Mo; Chrysler Mus, Norfolk, Va; Va Mus Fine Arts, Richmond; Thalhimers, Richmond; Univ Iowa. *Comn:* Bronze hwy markers, Rockingham Co Citizens Comt, Va, 55; William & Mary Medallion, Marshall-Wythe Sch Law, 67, Medallion, 68, Donald W Davis Commemorative Plaque, Life Sci Bldg, 70 & William G Guy Commemorative Plaque, Rogers Hall, 75, Col William & Mary. *Exhib:* One-man show, Norfolk Mus Arts & Sci, 63; Am Art Today, New York World's Fair, 64; Va Sculptors Traveling Exhib, 70-72; Tidewater Col Fac Exhib, Chrysler Mus, 72; 1st Int Sculpture Competition & Traveling Show, Mercer Col, 79-80. *Teaching:* Instr, Col William & Mary, 47-52, asst prof fine arts, 52-57, assoc prof, 57-66, prof & Heritage fel, 66-82, emer prof fine arts, 82- *Awards:* Fulbright Fel, India; Award of Honor, Va Chap Am Inst Architects, 68; Thomas Jefferson Award, Robert McConnell Found, 71; and others. *Mem:* Asian Soc; Audubon Artists; Twentieth Century Gallery; Tidewater Artists. *Res:* Art of India. *Publ:* Illusr, Little Red Riding Hood & Big Bad Wolf, 53; illusr roll titles for The Colonial Naturalist (film), 64. *Mailing Add:* 110 Hickory Signpost Rd Williamsburg VA 23185

ROSEMAN, STANLEY
PAINTER, DRAFTSMAN

b Brookline, Mass, Sept 4, 45. *Study:* Cooper Union Col Art & Architecture, BFA, 67; Pratt Inst, MFA, 72. *Work:* Nat Gallery Art, Washington, DC; Bibliotheque Nationale, Paris; Victoria & Albert Mus, London; Musse Beaux Arts, Bordeaux; Albertina, Vienna. *Exhib:* One-man shows, Mus Performing Arts, Lincoln Ctr, New York, 77, Peabody Mus, Yale Univ, 77, Thomas Mann Archiv, Zurich, 81 & Albertina, Vienna, 83; Bibliotheque Royale, Brussels, 80. *Awards:* Artistic Achievement Among the Saami People of Lappland, The Explorers Club, New York, 77. *Bibliog:* David Shirey (auth), Paintings by Stanley Roseman glow with a shiny dignity, New York Times, 8/21/77; Stanley Roseman, Drawing the Monastic Life (film), Thames TV, Eng, 79; John Groser (auth), How an artist captured the pure face of sanctity, The Times-London, 4/8/80. *Media:* Oil; Chalk, Pencil. *Publ:* Illusr, Stanley Roseman-Drawings: Faces Behind the Monastery Wall--The Monastic Life in Europe, Deventer, 84. *Dealer:* Ronald Davis Postfach 1348 CH 6002 Lucerne Switzerland. *Mailing Add:* c/o Ronald Davis Postfach 1348 CH 6002 Lucerne 10023 Switzerland

ROSEMAN, SUSAN CAROL
PAINTER, PRINTMAKER

b Philadelphia, Pa, June 20, 50. *Study:* Art Inst Pittsburgh, 67; Pa Acad Fine Arts, 5 yr cert, 73. *Work:* Allentown Art Mus, Pa. *Exhib:* Women's Nat Exhib, Galerie Triangle, Washington, DC, 80; Celebration: Women in the Arts, William Penn Mem Mus, Harrisburg, 81; 15th Int Grand Prix Contemp Art, Cong Ctr, Monte Carlo, Monaco, 81; Japan Int Artists Soc, Prefectural Mus, Nara, Chiba, 81-82; NJ State Mus Biennial, 83. *Pos:* Secy & bd dirs, Open Space, Allentown, Pa, 80- *Teaching:* Lectr, William Allen High Sch, Allentown, Pa, 76. *Awards:* Hendrik Vanderly Award, Doylestown Art League 17th Ann, 76; Warga Award, Princeton Art Asn 10th Ann, 79; Critic's Choice Award, Lehigh Art Alliance Ann, 83. *Mem:* Artists Equity Asn; Women's Caucus Art; Philadelphia Art Alliance. *Media:* All Media. *Dealer:* 20th Century Gallery 259 S 20th St Philadelphia PA 19103. *Mailing Add:* PO Box 925 Buckingham PA 18912

ROSEN, BEVERLY DORIS
PAINTER

b Boston, Mass. *Study:* Simmons Col, BS; Univ Colo; Univ Denver, MA. *Work:* Knight Pub Sch, Denver; Colorado Springs Fine Arts Ctr, Colo; Univ Colo, Denver; Johns Manville Collection; State Mutual Am, Worcester, Mass; and others. *Comn:* Painting, New Eng Life, Salt Lake City, 70; two outside murals, 73, two inside paintings, 73, Colo Agency, State Mutual Am, Denver; outside mural, Colo Agency, Denver, 81. *Exhib:* Southwest Biennial, Mus Fine Arts, Santa Fe, NMex, 74; Ten Take Ten, Colorado Springs Fine Arts Ctr, 77; Ariz Nat, Scottsdale Ctr for Arts, 78; Okla Art Ctr, Oklahoma City, 80; 16th Joslyn Biennial, Joslyn Art Mus, Omaha, Nebr, 80; and others. *Pos:* Dir, St Charles Contemp Art Gallery, Denver, Colo, 75-80. *Teaching:* Assoc prof painting, Univ Denver, 64- *Awards:* Purchase Prize, Gallery Fine Arts Ctr, 70; Monied Prize, Gilpin Co Art Asn, Central City, Colo, 70; Nat Educ Asn Grant & Colo Coun Grant for Gallery Exhib, Univ Denver Gallery, 75. *Bibliog:* Article, Artspace, fall 79; articles, Craft Range, 5-6/80 & 1-2/81. *Mem:* Colo Art Educ Asn; Colo Artists Asn Exhib. *Media:* Acrylic, Clay. *Mailing Add:* Dept Art Univ Denver Denver CO 80210

ROSEN, HY (HYMAN JOSEPH)
CARTOONIST, SCULPTOR

b Albany, NY, Feb 10, 23. *Study:* Art Inst Chicago; Art Students League; State Univ NY Albany; Stanford Univ, fel. *Pos:* Ed cartoonist, Albany Times-Union, 45; ed cartoonist, Hearst Newspapers. *Teaching:* Instr cartooning, State Univ NY Albany, currently. *Awards:* Top Award, Freedom Found, Valley Forge, Pa, 50, 55 & 60; Top Award, Nat Conf Christians & Jews, 62; Am Legion Fourth Estate Awards, 62nd Nat Conv, 80. *Mem:* Asn Am Ed Cartoonists (pres, 72). *Media:* Ink. *Publ:* Auth, As Hy Rosen Saw It, 70; auth, Do They Tell You What to Draw?, 80. *Mailing Add:* Times-Union Albany-Shaker Rd Albany NY 12201

ROSEN, ISRAEL
COLLECTOR

b Baltimore, Md, Dec 28, 11. *Study:* Johns Hopkins Univ, AB, 31; Univ Md Sch Med, MD, 35. *Pos:* Bd trustees, Baltimore Mus Art, 72- *Collection:* Modern art, with special emphasis on abstract expressionism, including works by Pollock, de Kooning, Still, Kline, Rothko, Baziotes, Tobey, Rauschenberg, as well as works by twentieth century European artist artists such as Picasso, Miro, Schwitters, Klee, Leger & Gris. *Publ:* Auth, Toward a definition of abstract expressionism, Baltimore Mus News, 59; auth, Edward Joseph Gallagher, III memorial collection, Baltimore Mus Art, 64 & Metrop Mus Art, 65; The pleasures and agonies of collecting art, World Fedn Friends Mus, 5/79. *Mailing Add:* 1 E University Pkwy Baltimore MD 21218

ROSEN, JAMES MAHLON
PAINTER, HISTORIAN

b Detroit, Mich, Dec 3, 33. *Study:* Cooper Union, with Franz Klein, Ludwig Sander, Leo Manso & Paul Zucker; Wayne State Univ, with Ernst Scheyer, BA; Cranbrook Acad Art, with Zoltan Sepeshy, MFA. *Work:* Mus Mod Art, New York; Whitney Mus Am Art; Newark Art Mus, NJ; Victoria & Albert Mus, London; San Francisco Mus Mod Art; and others. *Exhib:* Color Field 1890-1970, Albright-Knox Art Gallery, Buffalo, NY, 71; one-man show, Mus Mod Art Penthouse Show, 73 & Betty Parsons Gallery, New York, 74; Drawings USA, Minn Mus Art, 73; A Sense of Place, Joslyn Mus, 73; New Milwaukee Art Ctr; Dana Reich Gallery, San Francisco, 81; Thomas Babeor Gallery, La Jolla, 81; Bluxome Gallery, San Francisco. *Teaching:* Instr studio, Wayne State Univ, 61-63; asst prof studio & art hist, Univ Hawaii, 65-67; instr art hist, Santa Rosa Jr Col, 67- *Awards:* Huntington Hartford Found Fel Painting, 63; Yaddo Found Fel Painting, 68 & 72; Nat Endowment Fel, 72-73. *Bibliog:* Alfred Frankenstein (auth), Perception traps, San Francisco Chronicle, 70; John Canaday (auth), art criticism column, New York Times, 74; Thomas Albright (auth), On the edge of nirvana, San Francisco Chronicle, 81. *Media:* Oil, Watercolor. *Res:* Perception and structuring in 15th and 16th century Italian art and architecture. *Publ:* Auth, Notes From a Painter's Journal, 60; auth, Qualities of Camouflaging, 70; auth, The Sheer Nonsense of Liking Anything. *Dealer:* Betty Parsons Gallery 24 W 57th St New York NY 10019; Annex Gallery 604 College Ave Santa Rosa CA 95404. *Mailing Add:* Dept of Art Santa Rosa Jr Col Santa Rosa CA 95401

ROSEN, JOAN FISCHMAN
PAINTER

b St Louis, Mo. *Study:* Univ Iowa, with Philip Guston & Maurice Lasansky, 43-46; Wash Univ, with Arthur Osver & Fred Becker, BFA, 61, MFA, 65. *Work:* Consolidated Aluminum Corp, St Louis, Mo; Univ Iowa, Iowa City; Taft Hoffman Corp, Fla; Springfield Art Mus, Mo. *Comn:* Poster, St Louis Ice

Cream Festival, 79; portrait of Dr Irwin Levy for Barnes Hospital, comn by Maurice Handelsman, St Louis, 80. *Exhib:* William Rockhill Nelson Gallery Art, Kansas City, Mo; Joslyn Mus, Omaha; Watercolor USA (traveled); Va Traveling Exhib; Ten Mo Painters Traveling Exhib, Mo State Coun Arts. *Collections Arranged:* St Louis Artists' Exhib, Bixby Gallery, Washington Univ, 80. *Pos:* Coordr, Visual Catalog, Women's Caucus for Art, 79-80. *Teaching:* Artist-in-residence, Midwest Coun for Aging, 78. *Awards:* Purchase Award, Watercolor USA, Southwestern Mus Asn; Lena Newcastle Watercolor Award, Nat Asn Women Artists. *Bibliog:* Kenneth Shuck (auth), Joan Rosen, Ten Mo Painters, Mo State Arts Coun; R Stevens (auth), article, La Revue Mod, 2/63; Mary King (auth), article, St Louis Post Dispatch, 11/78. *Mem:* Area Coord Coun for Arts; Nat Asn Women Artists; Women's Caucus for Art. *Media:* Watercolor, Oil. *Dealer:* Schweig Galleries 4658 Maryland St Louis MO 63108. *Mailing Add:* 6320 Forsythe St Louis MO 63108

ROSENBAUM, ALLEN
MUSEUM DIRECTOR
b New York, NY. *Study:* Queens Col City New York, BA, 58; Inst Fine Arts, New York Univ, MA, 62. *Pos:* Lectr, Educ Dept, Metrop Mus Art, 64-69, sr lectr, 71-72; asst dir, Shickman Gallery, New York, 72-73; asst dir, The Art Mus, Princeton Univ, 74-, dir, 80- *Teaching:* Instr, Sch Gen Studies, Queens Col, City Univ New York, 61; instr, Sch Fine Arts, Univ Calif, Irvine, 72. *Awards:* Fulbright Fel Hist Art, Rome, 62-63. *Mem:* Asn Art Mus Dirs. *Publ:* Auth, Titian and Giotto in Padua, Marsyas, Studies Hist Art, Vol 8, 66-67; auth, Old Master Paintings from the Collection of Baron Thyssen Bornemisza, Int Exhibs Found, Washington, DC, 79. *Mailing Add:* The Art Mus Princeton Univ Princeton NJ 08544

ROSENBAUM, EVELYN ELLER See Eller, Evelyn

ROSENBERG, ALEX JACOB
PUBLISHER, DEALER
b New York, NY, May 25 19. *Study:* Philadelphia Mus Art; Albright Col. *Collections Arranged:* An American Portrait 1776-1976 Traveling Exhib (original print & multiple sculpture portfolio; ed, catalog), 76-77; Maric Tobey Retrospective, 77 & 81; James Coignard Traveling Exhib, 82-83. *Pos:* Publ & ed-in-chief, Transworld Art Corp, New York, 73-; dir & bd mem, Artists' Rights Today Inc, 76-; bd mem, Int Meeting Fine Art Dealers, 76-; dir, Alex Rosenberg Gallery, New York, 77-; assoc dir, Snug Harbor Cult Ctr, 83- *Teaching:* Lectr, New Sch Social Res, Parsons Div, 79- *Awards:* Spec Prize Publ, 7th Int Triennial Colored Graphic Prints, Kunstgesellschaft, Grenchen, Switz, 76; and others. *Mem:* Asn Artist Run Galleries (bd dirs, 79-); Visual Artists & Galleries Asn (trustee, 78-); Fine Arts Found Asn (vpres & dir, currently). *Publ:* Ed, The 12 Tribes of Isreal--Dali, 73, The Prophets--R Rubin, 73, Homage to Tobey, 74, Our Unfinished Revolution--Calder, 76 & An American Portrait 1776-1976, 76, Transworld Art; and others. *Mailing Add:* 20 W 57th St New York NY 10019

ROSENBERG, BERNARD
PUBLISHER, BOOK DEALER
b New York, NY, Aug 2, 38. *Study:* City Col of New York, cert advert. *Pos:* Owner, Olana Gallery. *Res:* American art. *Specialty:* Issues ten catalogues per year of books and exhibition catalogues on American art from Colonial period to the present. *Publ:* Auth, Olana's Guide to American Artists, A Contribution Toward a Bibliography, Olana Gallery, 2/78, supplement, vol 2, 80. *Mailing Add:* Drawer 9 Brewster NY 10509

ROSENBERG, CAROLE HALSBAND
EDITOR, DIRECTOR
b New York, NY, Nov 16, 36. *Study:* Hunter Col, Brooklyn Col, BA; Yeshiva Univ; NY Univ. *Collections Arranged:* Am American Portrait 1176-1976; Mark Tobey Retrospective (ed, catalogue), 77 & Yaacov Agam (ed, catalogue), 77. *Pos:* Art ed & exec dir, Transworld Art Corp; exec dir, Alex Rosenberg Gallery, currently. *Awards:* Spec Prize for Publ, Seventh Int Triennial of Colored Graphic Prints, Grenchen, Switz, 76. *Mem:* Visual Artists & Galleries Asn (bd mem). *Specialty:* Contemporary painting, sculpture, graphics and multiples. *Collection:* Contemporary painting, sculpture, prints and multiples. *Mailing Add:* 20 W 57th St New York NY 10019

ROSENBLATT, ADOLPH
PAINTER, SCULPTOR
b New Haven, Conn, Feb 23, 33. *Study:* Sch Design, Yale Univ, BFA, 56, with Albers, Brooks & Marca-Relli. *Work:* New York Times; Libr Cong, Washington, DC; Ft Wayne Mus Art, Ind; Carlisle Mus Art, Pa; Williamstown Mus, Mass. *Exhib:* Razor Gallery, New York, 78 & 79; one-man shows, Toledo Mus Art, Ohio, 78, Minneapolis Inst Art, 82 & Tibor de Nagy Gallery, New York, 82; Cooperstown Hall of Fame, NY, 83; and others. *Teaching:* Assoc prof, Univ Wis, Milwaukee, 66- *Awards:* Great Lakes Film Festival Award, 76. *Bibliog:* Robert Berlind (auth), Adolph Rosenblatt, Art in Am, 9-10/78. *Media:* Polychrome, Clay. *Publ:* Auth, Book of Lithographs, Peter Deitsch Gallery, New York, 71; producer, dir & ed, Underpass (film), 74; producer, dir & ed, Daydream Diner (film), 75. *Mailing Add:* 4211 N Maryland Milwaukee WI 53211

ROSENBLATT, SUZANNE MARIS
PAINTER
b Hackensack, NJ, July 2, 37. *Study:* Cent Sch Arts & Crafts, London, 57-58; Oberlin Col, Ohio, BA, 59; Cooper Union, 60; Art Students League, 61-63.

Work: City Ctr, New York; Libr Performing Arts, Dance Film Col, Lincoln Center, NY; Guggenheim Mus Artists Books Collection. *Comn:* Courtroom drawings, WISN-TV, Milwaukee, 73-77 & Milwaukee's Pub TV, 74. *Exhib:* One-woman shows, Oshkosh Pub Mus, Wis, 72, New York City Ctr Gallery, 76 & others; Ft Wayne Mus Art, Ind, 76; Performing Arts Ctr, Milwaukee, 76-82; Long Island Univ, Brooklyn, New York, 80. *Awards:* Hon Mention, Media Am, Seattle, Wash, 75. *Bibliog:* Dean Jensen (auth), Personal vision of circus magic, Milwaukee Sentinel, 71; Donald Key (auth), Show of painted people shadowed by circus, Milwaukee J, 71. *Mem:* Nat Art Workers Community; and others. *Media:* Acrylic, Ink. *Publ:* Illusr, Jumping rope, 70 & Quiet ethnics, 71, Insight, Milwaukee J; producer, dir & ed, Animated film paintings & drawings of dancers, Dance Film Festival, New York, 75 & Philadelphia Art Alliance, 76; auth, Memorandance, Marcel Dekker, 78; auth, Changes in the Lake, 82; and others. *Mailing Add:* 4211 N Maryland Milwaukee WI 53211

ROSENBLUM, JAY
PAINTER, PRINTMAKER
b New York, NY, Oct 12, 33. *Study:* Pratt Inst, with Richard Lindner; Bard Col, with Louis Schanker, BA, 55; Cranbrook Acad Art, with Fred Mitchell, MFA, 56. *Work:* Larry Aldrich Mus Contemp Art, Ridgefield, Conn; Whitney Mus Am Art, New York; Albright-Knox Mus Lending Serv, Buffalo; 180 Beacon St Collection, Cambridge, Mass. *Comn:* Painting, comn by Larry Aldrich, Phoenix, Ariz, 71. *Exhib:* Festival of Two Worlds, Spoleto, Italy, 56; Detroit Inst Art, 56; Highlights of 1970 Season, Aldrich Mus, 70; one-man shows, A M Sachs Gallery, 70 & Blue Parrot Gallery, New York, 72; Recent Prints USA, New York Cult Ctr, 72. *Teaching:* Instr painting, 92nd St YMHA, New York, 65-; adj lectr painting, Queensboro Community Col, 69-; adj lectr painting, Lehman Col, 71-, Sch Visual Arts, 78- *Awards:* Carlos Lopez Mem Prize in Painting, Detroit Inst Art, 56; Painter of Year, 1970, Larry Aldrich; City Walls Inc Grant, 72. *Bibliog:* Cindy Nemser (auth), rev in Arts Mag, 10/70; Carter Ratcliff (auth), rev in Art Int, 2/71; Ward Jackson (auth), Art now: New York, 71. *Media:* Acrylic. *Dealer:* Allan Stone Gallery 48 E 86th St New York NY 10028. *Mailing Add:* 502 E 11th St New York NY 10009

ROSENBLUM, RICHARD STEPHEN
SCULPTOR
b New Orleans, La, Dec 31, 40. *Study:* Calif Sch Art; Cleveland Inst Art; Cranbrook Acad Art. *Work:* Columbus Mus Art; Addison Gallery Am Art. *Exhib:* Three Figurative Sculptors, Pauly Art Ctr, Univ NH, 76; Profile of a Gallery, Addison Gallery Am Art, Andover, Mass, 80; Nat Acad Design Ann, New York, 80; one-man show, Columbus Mus Art, Ohio, 81 & Edwin Ulrich Mus Art, Wichita, Kans, 82; Narrative Sculpture, Artists Choice Mus, New York, 82. *Pos:* Guest cur, Artists Choice Mus, New York, 82. *Media:* Bronze. *Dealer:* Coe Kerr Gallery 49 East 82nd St New York NY. *Mailing Add:* 44 Ballard St Newton MA 02159

ROSENBLUM, ROBERT
HISTORIAN
b New York, NY, July 24, 27. *Study:* Queens Col, BA; Yale Univ, MA; NY Univ, PhD; Oxford Univ, Hon MA, 73. *Teaching:* Instr hist art, Univ Mich, 55-56; assoc prof hist art, Princeton Univ, 56-66; prof hist art, NY Univ, 67- *Awards:* Frank Jewett Mather Award Art Criticism, Col Art Asn Am, 81. *Res:* Modern art, 1760 to the present. *Publ:* Auth, Transformations in Late Eighteenth Century Art, 67, Ingres, 67, Frank Stella, 70 & Modern Painting and the Northern Romantic Tradition: Friedrich to Rothko, 75; coauth, 19th Century Art, 84. *Mailing Add:* 1 E 78th St New York NY 10021

ROSENBLUM, SADIE SKOLETSKY
PAINTER, PRINTMAKER
b Odessa, Russia, Feb 12, 1899; US citizen. *Study:* Art Students League; New Sch Social Res; also with Raphael Soyer, Kunioshr, Ben-Zion & Samuel Adler. *Work:* Philadelphia Mus Art; Ohio Univ; El Paso Mus Art; Brandeis Univ Mus; Lowe Art Mus, Univ Miami; and many others. *Exhib:* Mus Mod Art, New York; Corcoran Gallery Art, Washington, DC; one-man shows, Mus Arts, Ft Lauderdale, Fla, 62 & 65, Lowe Art Mus, Univ Miami, 64 & Columbia Mus, SC, 72; and many others. *Media:* Oil. *Mailing Add:* 5255 Collins Ave Apt L-1 Miami Beach FL 33140

ROSENBORG, RALPH M
PAINTER
b Brooklyn, NY, June 9, 13. *Study:* Sch Art League, NY; Am Mus Natural Hist. *Work:* Mus Mod Art; Guggenheim Mus; Yale Univ Art Gallery; Metrop Mus Art; Hirshhorn Mus & Sculpture Garden, DC; plus many others. *Exhib:* Retrospective, Mus of Art, Univ Notre Dame, 67; Butler Inst Am Art, 79; Whitney Mus Am Art; Guggenheim Mus Art, Hirshhorn Mus, Newark Art Mus. *Teaching:* Instr art, Brooklyn Mus, 36-38; instr, Ox-Bow Summer Sch, Saugatuck, Mich, 49. *Awards:* Purchase Award, Am Acad Arts & Lett, 60; Nat Coun Arts & Humanities Award, 66; Nat Endowment Arts. *Bibliog:* Sidney Janis (auth), Abstract and surrealist, Art in Am, 42; Belle Krasne (auth), article, Arts & Archit Mag, 1/55; Martica Sawin (auth), The achievement of Ralph Rosenborg, Arts Mag, 11/60. *Mem:* Am Abstract Artists; Fedn Mod Painters & Sculptors; Artists Equity. *Mailing Add:* 115 E 34th St New York NY 10016

ROSENFELD, RICHARD JOEL
DEALER
b Philadelphia, Pa, May 31, 40. *Study:* Pratt Inst, New York, MFA, 64; Univ Pa, Philadelphia & Pa Acad Fine Art (coordinated prog), BFA, 62. *Pos:* Mgr, Artists Galleries, Cheltenham, Pa, 67-72; co-dir, Longman Gallery, Pa, 72-75;

dir-owner, Rosenfeld Gallery, Philadelphia, Pa, 76- *Teaching:* Instr painting & art hist, Perkiomen Sch, Pennsburg, Pa, 63-65. *Bibliog:* Susan Perloff (auth), article, Pa Gazette, 6/77. *Mem:* Fel Pa Acad Fine Arts. *Specialty:* Contemporary art, all media including crafts. *Mailing Add:* Rosenfeld Gallery 113 Arch St Philadelphia PA 19006

ROSENFELD, SAMUEL L
DEALER, COLLECTOR
b New York, NY, July 27, 31. *Study:* Univ Pa, BS, 51; Harvard Univ, MBA, 53. *Pos:* Dir, Artists Unlimited Gallery & Rosenfelds Fine Arts, New York, currently; assoc, Dept Prints, Mus Mod Art. *Mem:* Appraisers Asn Am. *Specialty:* American art in the realistic tradition in all media, mainly from 1880 to World War II. *Collection:* Modern American realists; Trench art; Rogers groups; Doulton Lambeth stoneware pottery. *Mailing Add:* Artists Unlimited Gallery 44 E 82nd St New York NY 10028

ROSENFIELD, JOHN M
EDUCATOR, CURATOR
b Dallas, Tex, Oct 9, 24. *Study:* Univ Calif, Berkeley, BA, 45; Univ Iowa, Iowa City, MFA, 49; Harvard Univ, PhD, 59. *Collections Arranged:* Japanese Art of Heian Period (auth, catalog), Asia House, NY, 67; Traditions of Japanese Art (auth, catalog), Fogg Mus, Harvard, 70; Courtly Tradition in Japanese Art & Literature (coauth, catalog), Fogg Mus, Harvard, 73; Journey of the Three Jewels (coauth, catalog), Asia House, NY, 79. *Pos:* Cur oriental art, Fogg Art Mus, Cambridge, Mass, 76-; actg dir, Harvard Univ Art Mus, 82 *Teaching:* Asst prof oriental art, Univ Calif, Los Angeles, 57-60; prof japanese art, Harvard Univ, Cambridge, Mass, 65- *Publ:* Auth, Dynastic Arts of the Kushans, Univ Calif, 67; ed, Song of the Brush: Japanese Paintings from the Sanso Collecion, Seattle Art Mus, 79; coauth, The Japanese Courtier: Painting, Calligraphy and Poetry from the Fogg Art Mus, The Philip Hofer Colection, Santa Barbara Mus Art, 80. *Mailing Add:* Fogg Art Mus Harvard Univ Cambridge MA 02138

ROSENHOUSE, IRWIN
PRINTMAKER, PAINTER
b Chicago, Ill, Mar 1, 24. *Study:* Cooper Union, cert, 50, BFA, 78. *Work:* Metrop Mus Art; Cooper Union Mus; New York Pub Libr Graphics Collection; Everhart Mus, Pa; Brooklyn Col. *Exhib:* Am Fedn Arts; Libr Cong; Mus Mod Art, New York; Pa Acad Fine Arts; Boston Printmakers. *Pos:* Resident artist, Huntington Hartford Found, 59 & 61; owner & operator, Rosenhouse Gallery, New York, 63-71; free lance designer & illusr, currently. *Teaching:* Instr drawing, painting & graphics, Mus Mod Art Educ Ctr, 68-70; instr graphics, Brooklyn Col, 72; adj prof art, Nassau Community Col, 73-, New York Tech Col, 82-83. *Awards:* Award for Graphics, Louis Comfort Tiffany Found; Billboard Ann Award, Huntington Hartford Fedn. *Media:* Graphics. *Publ:* Illusr, What Kind of Feet Does a Bear Have, Bobbs, 63; illusr, Have You Seen Trees, Young-Scott, 67; illusr, Alternate Celebrations Catalogue, Pilgrims Press, 82; illusr, Teenagers Themselves, ADAMA, 83-84. *Mailing Add:* 256 Mott St New York NY 10012

ROSENQUIST, JAMES
PAINTER
b Grand Forks, NDak, Nov 29, 33. *Study:* Univ Minn, Minneapolis, scholar, 48, study with Cameron Booth; Art Students League, 54-55; Aspen Inst of Humanist Studies, Colo, Eastern philo & hist, 65. *Work:* Art Gallery Ont, Toronto; Stedelijk Mus, Amsterdam; Metrop Mus, New York; Mus Mod Art, New York; Musee Nat d'art Moderne, Paris; and others. *Exhib:* Six Painters & the Object, Solomon R Guggenheim Mus, New York, 63; Mixed-Media, 63 & Kid Stuff, 71, Albright-Knox Art Gallery, Buffalo, NY; Americans 1963, Around the Automobile, 65, The 1960s, 67 & Works from Change, 74, Mus Mod Art, New York; Sound, Light, Silence, William Rockhill Nelson Gallery of Art, Kansas City, Mo, 66; Ann, 67 & Am Pop Art, 74, Whitney Mus of Am Art, New Yrok; Documenta IV, Kassel, WGer, 68; New York: The Second Breakthrough, 1959-1964, Univ Calif, Irvine, 69; Prints by Four New York Painters, 69 & New York Painting & Sculpture: 1940-1970, 69-70, Metrop Mus of Art, New York; Am Painting, Va Mus Fine Art, Richmond, 70; Art & Technol, Los Angeles Co Mus of Art, Los Angeles, 71; Am Drawing: 1970-1973, Yale Univ, 73; Am Art--Third Quarter Century, Seattle Art Mus, Wash, 73; one-man shows, Nat Gallery Can, Ottawa, 68; Metrop Mus Art, New York, 68, Whitney Mus Am Art, New York, 72, Mus Contemp Art, Chicago, 72 & Portland Art Ctr, Ore, 73; Contemp Arts Mus, Houston, 82; Whitney Mus Am Art, 82; Mus Fine Arts, Houston, 83; and many others. *Pos:* Commercial display artist, Gen Outdoor Advert Co, 52-54 & Bonwit Teller & Tiffany & Co, New York, 59; coun mem, Nat Endowment Arts, 78- *Teaching:* Vis lectr, Yale Univ, New Haven, Conn, 64. *Awards:* Torcuato di Tella Int Prize, Buenos Aires, 65. *Bibliog:* J Siegel (auth), An Interview with James Rosenquist, Artforum, New York, 6/72; J Loring (auth), Prints: James Rosenquist's Horse Blinders, Artmagazine, New York, 2/73; P Tuchman (auth), Pop: Interview with James Rosenquist, Art News, New York, 5/74. *Media:* Oil. *Dealer:* Leo Castelli 142 Greene St New York NY 10012. *Mailing Add:* Box 4 420 W Broadway Aripeka FL 33502

ROSENQUIT, BERNARD
PAINTER, PRINTMAKER
b Hotin, Roumania, Dec 26, 23; US citizen. *Study:* Inst Art & Archeol, Paris; Fontainebleau Sch Fine Arts, France; Brooklyn Mus Sch Fine Art; Atelier 17, New York; Art Students League. *Work:* Metrop Mus Art, New York; Brooklyn Mus Fine Art; Victoria & Albert Mus, London, Eng; Smithsonian Inst, Washington, DC; New York Pub Libr Print Collection; and others.

Exhib: Honolulu Acad Fine Arts; Boston Mus Fine Arts; Mus Mod Art, New York; Newark Mus Art, NJ; seven one-man shows, Roko Gallery, New York, 51-71; and others. *Awards:* Fulbright Grant Painting, Paris, 58; Louis Comfort Tiffany Found Grant Printmaking, 59. *Mem:* Artists Equity Asn New York; life mem Art Students League. *Media:* Oil, Gouache; Wood, Etching. *Mailing Add:* Apartment 4D 1482 York Avenue New York NY 10021

ROSENTHAL, DEBORAH MALY
CRITIC, PAINTER
b New York, NY, Jan 16, 50. *Study:* Smith Col, with Leonard Baskin, 66-68; Barnard Col, BA, 71; Pratt Inst, with George MacNeil, MFA, 74; Queens Col, with Ilya Bolotowsky, 74. *Exhib:* Purdue Univ, Ind, 73; Metaphor in Painting, Fed Hall Nat Mem, New York, 78; Artists by the Sea, Snug Harbor Cult Ctr, New York, 79 & 80. *Pos:* Critic, Arts, Artforum & New York Arts J, 75-; artist & cur, Cult Coun Fedn, 78-80. *Teaching:* Guest lectr, Queens Col, Univ NH & Parsons Col, 77-; lectr, Sch Visual Arts, New York, 80-82; fac mem, New Sch Social Res, 81- *Awards:* Critic's Award, Nat Endowment Arts, 79-80. *Mem:* Col Art Asn; Int Asn Art Critics. *Media:* Oil. *Publ:* Auth, Metaphor in Painting, 78, auth, The lesson of the master: Paul Klee, 78, an Interview with Andre Masson, 80 & coauth, Zone painting, 81, Arts Mag; auth, Ilya Bolotowsky, Harry N Abrams, 82. *Dealer:* Nicholas Rizzo Fine Arts 18 Strong Pl Brooklyn NY. *Mailing Add:* 250 West 85th St New York NY 10024

ROSENTHAL, EARL EDGAR
EDUCATOR, HISTORIAN
b Milwaukee, Wis, Aug 26, 21. *Study:* Univ Wis, Milwaukee, BA, 43; NY Univ, PhD, 53. *Pos:* Asst dir, Milwaukee Art Inst & Layton Art Gallery, 52-53. *Teaching:* Prof hist art, Univ Chicago, 54- *Mem:* Col Art Asn Am; Soc Archit Historians (dir, 57-58 & 59-60); Am Soc Hispanic Art Hist Studies; corresp mem Hispanic Soc Am; corresp mem Acad San Fernando, Madrid. *Res:* Renaissance architecture and sculpture in Italy and Spain. *Publ:* Auth, The Cathedral of Granada, Princeton Univ Press, 61; auth, Michelangelo's Moses, Art Bulletin, XLVI, 64; auth, Lombard sculptor Niccolo da Corte, Art Quart, XXIX, 66; auth, Die Reichskrone, In: Jahrbuch der Kunsthistorischen Sammlungen in Wien, 71; auth, Invention of columnar device of Charles V, J Warburg Inst, 73. *Mailing Add:* Cochrane-Woods Art Ctr 5540 S Greenwood Ave Chicago IL 60637

ROSENTHAL, GERTRUDE
HISTORIAN, ADMINISTRATOR
b Mayen, Ger, May 19, 03; US citizen. *Study:* Univ Paris, 25-26; Univ Cologne & Univ Bonn, with A E Brinckmann, PhD(magna cum laude), 32; Goucher Col, hon LHD, 68; Md Inst Baltimore Col Art, hon DFA, 68. *Collections Arranged:* Bacchiacca & His Fiends, Baltimore Mus Art, 60, Four Paris Painters--Manet, Degas, Morisot & Mary Cassatt (with catalog), 62; Nineteen Hundred Fourteen (with catalog), 64; From El Greco To Pollock, Early & Late Works by American & European Artists (with catalog), 68; Cone Collection, Mary Frick Jacobs Collection, Daingerfield Collection & Wurtzburger Primitive Art Collection. *Pos:* Res asst, Courtauld Inst, Univ London, 39-40; art librn, Goucher Col, 40-45; from cur to chief cur, Baltimore Mus Art, 45-69, emer chief cur, 69-, res specialist, 75-; ed, Baltimore Mus News, 59-63; consult, Western Col Honolulu Acad Arts, 72- *Teaching:* Vis prof, Johns Hopkins Univ, 48-50, vis lectr, 52-53. *Awards:* Nat Found Arts Res Grant Am & Ger Romantic Nineteenth Century Painting, 68; Nat Endowment for the Arts Grant, 76-78; and others. *Mem:* Am Asn Mus; Col Art Asn Am. *Res:* French paintings before 1800. *Publ:* Auth, article on German Expressionism, 57, Baltimore Mus News; ed, Biennale Venezia 1960, Stati Uniti d'America, 60; ed, Annual II, Studios on Thomas Cole, Baltimore Mus Art, 68; cd, J Honolulu Acad Arts, Vol 1, No 1, 74 & Vol 3 No 3; ed & contribr, Italian Paintings XIV-XVIII, Baltimore Mus Art, 81; and many others. *Mailing Add:* 3925 Beech Ave Baltimore MD 21211

ROSENTHAL, GLORIA M
COLLAGE ARTIST, PAINTER
b Brooklyn, NY, May 24, 28. *Study:* Com Art Training, Archit Design, Univ Cincinnati; Post Col; Artist in Am Sch; Queen's Col; Provincetown Workshop; Nassau Community Col; Pratt Graphic Ctr; pvt & independent study. *Work:* Bankers Trust, New York; Sperry Gyroscope, Lake Success, NY; Weaver Schs, Milwaukee, Wis; Community Hosp, Glen Cove, NY; Transverse Nat Bank, Pa. *Exhib:* Audubon Artists; Nat Asn Women Artists; Nat Acad Design, 70-75; Silvermine Regional, Silvermine, Conn, 72; one-woman shows, Saratoga Performing Art Ctr, NY, 71 & State Univ NY Farmingdale, 79; Palazzo Vecchio, Florence, Italy, 72; Winners of the Past Ten Years, Brooklyn Mus, 75. *Pos:* Artist in residence, Gloria Rosenthal Gallery, Rocky Neck Art Colony, Mass, 71-; artist-in-residence, Col St Benedict, St Joseph, Minn. *Awards:* Medal of Honor, Nat Asn Women Artists, 75 & Grumbacher Award, 79; Am Artist Mag Nat Award, 78. *Mem:* Nat Asn Women Artists; Rocky Neck Art Colony, (vpres, 73); Syosset Players (vpres, 66, pres, 67). *Media:* Oil, Collage. *Mailing Add:* PO Box 1322 Gloucester MA 01930

ROSENTHAL, JOHN W
PHOTOGRAPHER, PUBLISHER
b Munich, Ger, Mar 25, 28; US citizen. *Study:* Univ of Chicago, BA(liberal arts). *Pos:* Commercial photogr, Koopman-Neumer, Chicago, Ill, 55-65; owner-dir, Rosenthal Art Slides, Chicago, 60- *Teaching:* Helped photograph the collections & taught photogrs at the Art Inst of Chicago & Mus of Contemp Art, 70-77. *Bibliog:* N De Laurier (auth), Slide Buyer's Guide, Col Art Asn, 80. *Media:* Slide Maker; Photographer. *Specialty:* Extensive collections of high quality slides pertaining to art and art history. *Publ:* Auth, Rosenthal Art Slides, Vol I, 74 & rev 80, Vol II, 78 & Supplements, 81 & 83, pvt publ. *Mailing Add:* 5456 S Ridgewood Court Chicago IL 60615

ROSENTHAL, JUDITH-ANN SAKS See Saks, Judith-Ann

ROSENTHAL, MARK L
CURATOR, WRITER
b Philadelphia, Pa, Aug 9, 45. *Study:* Temple Univ, AB, 63; Univ Iowa, MA, 71, PhD, 79. *Collections Arranged:* Andre, Buren, Irwin, Nordman: Space as Support (auth, catalog), 79; Franz Marc (auth, catalog), 79; Neil Jenney (auth, catalog), 81; Juan Gris (auth, catalog), 83-84; Jonathan Borofsky (auth, catalog), 84-85. *Pos:* Assoc cur, Wadsworth Atheneum, Hartford, Conn, 74-76; cur collections, Univ Art Mus, Berkeley, Calif, 76-83; cur 20th century art, Philadelphia Mus Art, Pa, 83- *Mem:* Col Art Asn. *Res:* Various topics in twentieth century art. *Publ:* Auth, Paul Klee, Phillips Collection, 81; auth, The prototypical triangle of Paul Klee, Art Bulletin, 82; auth, Picasso's night fishing at Antibes, Art Bulletin, 83. *Mailing Add:* 7033 McCallum St Philadelphia PA 19119

ROSENTHAL, RACHEL
PERFORMANCE ARTIST, SCULPTOR
b Paris, France, Nov 9, 26; US citizen. *Study:* New Sch Soc Res, New York; Sorbonne, Paris; also with Hans Hofmann, Karl Knaths, William S Hayter & John Mason. *Exhib:* Rental Gallery, Los Angeles Co Mus, 72; Five-Person Show Performance Art, Contemp Art Ctr, New Orleans, 80; Soldier of Fortune (performance), Art Inst Chicago & others, 81; Traps (performance), throughout US, 82; An Artist's Living Space, LAVA, Japanese-Am Cult Ctr, Los Angeles, 82; At Home Exhibition, Long Beach Mus, 83; Gaia, Mon Amour, throughout US, 83 & 84. *Pos:* Founding mem bd dir, Womanspace, Los Angeles, 72-74, co-chmn, 73-74; dir, Instant Theatre, Los Angeles, 56-66 & 74-76; founding mem, Double X, Los Angeles, 74-76; dir, Espace dbd, Los Angeles, 80-82. *Teaching:* Performance, Claremont Grad Sch, Calif, 79, Otis/ Parsons Inst Design, Los Angeles, 80-81, Espace dbd, Los Angeles, 81-82 & Univ Calif, Irvine, 82; vis artist, Univ Colo, Boulder, 83 & Calif State Univ, Long Beach, 83. *Awards:* Gold Medal Art, High Sch Mus & Art, New York, 45; Nat Endowment Arts Artist's Fel Grant, 83; Vesta Award, Woman's Building, Los Angeles, 83. *Bibliog:* Linda Burnham (auth), Performance art in the San Francisco International Theatre Festival, High Performance #19, 82; Irene Borger (auth), Rachel Rosenthal: Performance artist, DanceFLASH, 3-4/83 & 5-6/83; Moira Roth (auth), The amazing decade-- women and performance art in America 1970-1980, Astro Artz, 8/83. *Mem:* Artists Equity Asn; Woman's Building; Int Asn Art Critics. *Media:* Performance. *Publ:* Auth, Coiled sculpture, Ceramics Monthly, 74; Petit- Beurre, 78; auth, article in Los Angeles Inst Contemp Art J, 75; Lee that's just not cool, No Mag, Los Angeles, 81; Soldier of Fortune, self publ, 81. *Mailing Add:* 2847 S Robertson Blvd Los Angeles CA 90034

ROSENTHAL, SEYMOUR
PAINTER, LITHOGRAPHER
b New York, NY, Aug 14, 21. *Work:* Metrop Mus Art, City New York Mus, New York; Technion Bldg, Haifa, Israel; Santa Barbara Mus Art, Calif; Harry S Truman Libr, Independence, Mo. *Comn:* Drawings of children, New York Bd Educ, 57; painting of Moses, borough pres off, Queens, NY, 62; Pfizer Pharmaceutical. *Exhib:* Civil Rights Art Show, Brooklyn Mus, 62; one-man shows, Suffolk Mus, 68 & ACA Gallery, New York, 69; Major Drawings of 19th & 20th Century Exhib, Gallery Mod Art, New York, 64-65; Art Dealers Choice Exhib, 67; Indianapolis Mus Art, 72. *Awards:* Saint Gaudens Medal. *Bibliog:* Edwin Newman (commentator), Today Show, NBC TV, 70; Alfred Werner (auth, film), Directions, ABC TV, 71; Life and Works of Seymour Rosenthal, ABC TV, 10/82. *Mem:* Artists Equity Asn; Comt Arts & Lit in Jewish Life; Jewish Fedn Philanthropies & United Jewish Appeal. *Media:* Watercolor, Oil. *Publ:* Illusr, Parke Davis Med J, 56; illusr, Scope, 56; contribr, Commonweal, Vol 90, No 15. *Dealer:* Art Graphics 249-10 63rd Ave Little Neck NY 11362; Concord Art Gallery Kiamesh Lake NY 12751. *Mailing Add:* 161-08 Jewel Ave Flushing NY 11365

ROSENTHAL, STEPHEN
PAINTER
b Richmond, Va, May 28, 35. *Study:* Art Students League, with Edwin Dickinson; Tyler Sch Fine Arts, Philadelphia, with Boris Blai & BFA, 60. *Work:* Arts Club Chicago; Yale Univ Art Gallery, New Haven, Conn; Art Fund, New York. *Exhib:* Am Acad Arts & Lett, New York, 63; Amon Carter Mus, Ft Worth, Tex, 64; Int Watercolor Biennial, Brooklyn Mus, NY, 65; Herron Inst, Indianapolis, Ind, 67; Pa Acad Fine Arts Biennial Exhib, Philadelphia, 67. *Pos:* Bk reviewer, Arts Mag, New York, 71-72. *Teaching:* Instr design, Cooper Union, New York, 66-67; lectr painting, Univ NC, Greensboro, 71-72. *Awards:* Mason Lord Prize, Baltimore Mus Art, 67. *Bibliog:* Raymond Charmet (auth), Un jeune Americain, Arts Mag, 66; Leach Levy (auth), The drawn line in painting, Parker St 470, 71. *Media:* Tempera. *Dealer:* John Weber Gallery 142 Greene St New York NY 10012. *Mailing Add:* 39 Bond St New York NY 10012

ROSENTHAL, TONY (BERNARD)
SCULPTOR
b Highland Park, Ill, Aug 9, 14. *Study:* Univ Mich, BFA, 36; Cranbrook Acad Art. *Work:* Guggenheim Mus, Mus Mod Art, Whitney Mus Am Art, New York; Israel Mus, Jerusalem; Albright-Knox Art Gallery, Buffalo. *Comn:* Cube, Alamo, New York, 66; Large Cube, Univ Mich, Ann Arbor, 68; Bronze Disk, Rondo, New York Pub Libr, 69; Sun Disk, Financial Ctr Pac, Honolulu, Hawaii, 71; Police Plaza Sculpture, New York, 74. *Exhib:* Nine Whitney Mus Am Art Ann, 53-72; Recent Sculpture USA, Mus Mod Art, 59; Am Painting & Sculpture 1948-1969, Krannert Art Mus, Univ Ill, Champaign, 71; Aldrich Mus Contemp Arts, Ridgefield, Conn, 73; Stanford Mus, Calif, 76; Guild Hall,

East Hampton, NY, 76. *Awards:* Ford Found Purchase Prize, Krannert Art Mus, 63; Outstanding Achievement Award, Univ Mich, 67; First Prize, Iron & Steel Inst, 75. *Bibliog:* Gibson Danes (auth), Bernard Rosenthal, Art Int, 68; Sam Hunter (auth), Rosenthal: Sculptures, 68; Edward Albee (auth), Reacting to Rosenthal, Decade, 79. *Mailing Add:* 173 E 73rd St New York NY 10021

ROSENWALD, BARBARA K
COLLECTOR
b Norfolk, Va, July 30. *Study:* Boston Mus Sch Fine Arts; Fogg Mus, Harvard Univ; Stella Elkins Tyler Sch Fine Arts; also in Paris, France & Florence, Italy. *Collection:* Modern Italian art, including works by Afro, Campigli, Moscha; French modern art, including works by Pignon and others. *Mailing Add:* Box 496 Rushland Rushland PA 18956

ROSENWALD, CAROL
DEALER
b New Haven, Conn, Sept 4, 33. *Pos:* Pres, Art for Offices, Ltd, New York. *Specialty:* American, European and Asian 20th century paintings, prints, drawings, sculpture and photographs; framing, installations and corporate exhibitions. *Mailing Add:* Art for Offices Ltd 135 E 83rd St New York NY 10028

ROSENZWEIG, DAPHNE LANGE
HISTORIAN, MUSEUM CONSULTANT
b Evanston, Ill, July 7, 41. *Study:* Mt Holyoke Col, AB; Columbia Univ, MA & PhD; Univ Wis; Corcoran Sch Art; Nat Taiwan Univ, spec scholar. *Collections Arranged:* Art of the Orient: Eighth Century to the Present, Univ NMex, 72. *Teaching:* Lectr Oriental art, Univ NMex, Albuquerque, 69-73; asst prof Oriental art, Oberlin Col, 73-77; asst prof, Univ SFla, 78- *Awards:* Fulbright Fel, Repub China, 67-69; Columbia Univ Grant, 69; Mary E Wooley Fel, 70. *Mem:* Japan House; Int House of Japan; Asn Asian Studies; Asia House; China Inst. *Res:* Painting the Ch'ing Dynasty of China, with emphasis on court painting and modern Chinese jades. *Collection:* Chinese paintings, Oriental ceramics; modern Japanese prints. *Publ:* Auth, Landscape Painting by Hsiao Yun-ts'ung, Allen Art Mus Bulletin, 2/74; auth, Court painting and the K'ang-hsi Emperor, Ch'ing Shih Wen t'i, 12/75; auth, Court painting of the K'ang-hsi era: The socioeconomic aspects, Monumenta Serica, 75; auth, Stalking the Persian Dragon: Chinese prototypes for the miniature representations, Kunst des Orients, 80. *Mailing Add:* Dept of Art Col of Fine Arts Univ of South Fla Tampa FL 33620

ROSENZWEIG, PHYLLIS D
ASSOCIATE CURATOR
b Brooklyn, NY, Dec 27, 43. *Study:* Hunter Col, City Univ New York, BA, 64; Inst Fine Arts, New York, 65-69. *Collections Arranged:* The Thomas Eakins Collection (auth, catalog), Hirshhorn Mus & Sculpture Garden, Smithsonian Inst, Washington, DC, 77, Arshile Gorky: The Hirshhorn Museum & Sculpture Garden Collection, 79; The Fifties: Aspects of Painting in New York, 80; Larry Rivers, The Hirshhorn Mus and Sculpture Garden Collection, 81; Directions 1983, 83. *Pos:* Curatorial asst, Hirshhorn Mus & Sculpture Garden, 71-78, assoc cur, 78- *Res:* Specialty is 20th century American art. *Publ:* Contribr, Get Out Stay Away Come Back: an Exhibition by Richard Nonas, Univ Gallery, Univ Mass, Amherst, 82; auth, Big Science by Laurie Anderson, Washington Review Arts, fall 82. *Mailing Add:* Hirshhorn Mus & Sculpture Garden Smithsonian Inst Washington DC 20560

ROSER, CE (CECILIA)
PAINTER, VIDEO ARTIST
b Philadelphia, Pa. *Study:* Berlin Fine Arts Acad, 52-53. *Work:* Guggenheim Mus, New York; Prudential Insurance Co, Newark, NJ; Chase Manhattan Bank, New York; Ciba-Geigy Co, Ardsley, NY; and others. *Exhib:* Int Watercolor Biennial, Brooklyn Mus, 63; High Mus Art, Atlanta, Ga, 66; Women Choose Women, New York Cult Ctr, 73; Works on Paper--Women Artists, Brooklyn Mus, 75; Joy, Stamford Mus, Conn, 75; Art & Poetry, Tweed Mus Art, Duluth, Minn, 77; Christmas Show & Gallery, Philadelphia Mus Art, 77, 78 & 79; Kites, Danforth Mus, Farmingham, Mass, 78; Guggenheim Mus, 82; plus many others. *Pos:* Producer & pres, Artists Video Arch, New York, 77- *Bibliog:* Rosemary Daniell (auth), Elegant explosions East and West mingle in Roser act, Atlanta Constitution, Ga, 7/5/67; Lane Dunlop (auth), article, 9/77 & Joan Marter (auth), article, 2/80, Arts Mag; plus others. *Mem:* Founder Women in the Arts (first exec-coordr, 74-76, bd mem at large, 76-78); Women's Caucus for Art. *Media:* Oil, Watercolor; Collage. *Dealer:* Ingber Gallery 460 West Broadway New York NY 10013. *Mailing Add:* 355 Riverside Dr New York NY 10025

ROSKILL, MARK WENTWORTH
HISTORIAN, CRITIC
b London, Eng, Nov 10, 33. *Study:* Trinity Col, Cambridge (Eng), BA, 56, MA, 61; Harvard Univ, MA, 57; Courtauld Inst, Univ London, 57; Princeton Univ, MFA & PhD, 61. *Teaching:* Instr & asst, Princeton Univ, 59-61; from instr to asst prof, Harvard Univ, 61-68; assoc prof, Univ Mass, Amherst, 68- 72, prof, 72- *Awards:* Am Coun Learned Socs Fel, 65-66 & 74-75. *Mem:* Col Art Asn Am. *Res:* Nineteenth & twentieth century art; criticism; history of photography; methodology of art history. *Publ:* Ed, The Letters of Vincent Van Gogh, 63 & 83; auth, Dolce's Aretino and Venetian Art Theory of the Cinquecento, 68 & Van Gogh, Gauguin and the Impressionist Circle, 70; contribr, Atlantic Brief Lives, 71; auth, What is Art History, 76; and others. *Mailing Add:* Dept of Art Univ of Mass Amherst MA 01002

ROSLER, MARTHA ROSE
VIDEO ARTIST, CRITIC
b Brooklyn, NY, July 29, 43. *Study:* Brooklyn Mus Art Sch; Brooklyn Col, BA; Univ Calif, San Diego, MFA. *Work:* NS Col Art & Design, Halifax; Contemp Arts Mus, Houston, Tex; New England Found Arts; Long Beach Mus Art, Calif; Mus Mod Art, New York. *Exhib:* One-person shows, Long Beach Mus Art, Calif, 77, Whitney Mus Am Art, New York, 77, A-Space, Toronto, 79 & Interaction Arts, New York, 80; Whitney Mus Am Art Biennial, 79 & 83; Public Disclosure: Secrets From the Street, San Francisco Mus Mod Art, 80; Issue, Inst Contemp Arts London, 80; 74th Am Exhib, Art Inst Chicago, 82; Documenta 7, Kassel, WGer, 82; Video of the Seventies--The Greatest Hits, Inst Contemp Art, Boston & traveling, 83; Festival Andere Avant Garde, Brucknerhaus, Linz, Austria, 83. *Teaching:* Instr, San Diego State Univ, 75-76 & Univ Calif San Diego, 75-78; instr photog, Orange Coast Col, Costa Mesa, 77-79; instr film, photog & media, Univ Calif, Irvine, 78-79; vis prof art, Simon Fraser Univ, Vancouver, 80; NY Univ & Cooper Union; asst prof, Rutgers Univ, 80-; studio instr, Whitney Independent Study Prog. *Awards:* Nat Endowment Arts Fel, 75-77, 80 & 83. *Bibliog:* Jane Weinstock (auth), interview, October, No 17, summer 81; Bruce Barber & Serge Guilbaut (coauth), interview, Parachute, fall 81; Martha Gever (auth), interview, Afterimage, 10/81. *Media:* Images & Texts. *Res:* Relationships between representations and power in daily life and in the public sphere. *Publ:* Auth, Lee Friedlander's Guarded Strategies, 75 & Private and the public: Feminist art in California, Artforum, 77; auth, Service: A trilogy on colonization, New-Found Career, 78; auth, Lookers, buyers, dealers, and makers: Thoughts on audience, Exposure, 79; auth, Martha Rosler: Three Works, NS Col Art & Design Press, 81. *Mailing Add:* 53 Pearl St Brooklyn NY 11201

ROSS, ALEXANDER
PAINTER
b Dunfermline, Scotland, Oct 28, 08; US citizen. *Study:* Carnegie Inst Technol, with Prof Robert Lepper; Boston Col, Hon MFA, 54. *Work:* New Britain Mus, Conn; Waterbury Mus, Conn; US Air Force Collection, Denver, Colo; Nat Acad Design, New York; Mormon Church, Salt Lake City, Utah. *Comn:* Portrait of Pres John F Kennedy, comn by Romaine Pearson Publ Inc, New York, 71; paintings, Phoenix Arthritis Ctr, Ariz, 74; stained-glass doors, St Peter's Church, Danbury, Conn, 77; and others. *Exhib:* Two Hundred Yrs Watercolor, Metrop Mus Art, New York, 67; 18th Ann New Eng Exhib, Silvermine Guild, Conn, 68; Landscape One, De Cordova Mus, Lincoln, Mass, 70; 17 one-man shows, galleries in New York, Phoenix, Nashville, Palm Beach, Fla, Hilton Head, Bridgeport, Conn, Naples, Fla & others, 72-80; 200 Yrs Am Illus, NY Hist Soc, New York, 77; Royal Soc Painters, London, Eng; Smithsonian Inst, Washington, DC; Wadsworth Atheneum, Hartford, Conn; Tenn Ctr Arts, Nashville; plus others. *Pos:* Illusr covers, Good Housekeeping, 42-54, Sat Evening Post, 43-50, Cosmopolitan, 44-60, Ladies Home J, 45-60 & McCalls, 45-60. *Teaching:* Lectr creative painting, Cath Univ Am, summer 54. *Awards:* Adolph & Clara Obrig Award, Nat Acad Design Ann Exhib, 72 & 80; Columbus Award, Georgia Watercolor Soc, 81; Am Watercolor Soc, 82; and many others. *Bibliog:* Robert Ulrich Godsoe (auth), Alex Ross: reluctant prophet, Esquire, 48; Charles Daugherty (auth), Six Artists Paint A Landscape, N Light Publ, 75. *Mem:* Nat Acad Design; Conn Acad Fine Arts; Am Watercolor Soc (dir, 75-77); Silvermine Guild Artists; Conn Watercolor Soc. *Media:* Oil, Watercolor. *Publ:* auth, How I use watercolor, Am Artist, 62; auth, New Directions in Watercolor (film), Electrographic Corp, 71. *Dealer:* Thompson Gallery 815 N Central Ave Phoenix AZ 85004. *Mailing Add:* 8 Hawthorn Trail Ridgefield CT 06877

ROSS, B(EATRICE) BROOK
PAINTER, COLLAGE ARTIST
b New York, NY. *Study:* Brooklyn Mus Art Sch, with Ruben Tam; Sch Chinese Brushwork, scholar, study with Wang Chi Yuan; also with Leo Manso. *Work:* Textured Prod, New York; pvt collections of W Thornton, New York, Laura Ford, Ontario, Can, Hideo Hikawa, Tokyo, Japan, Isabelle Gardner Tate, Boston, and others. *Comn:* Two paintings, Muller, Jordan & Herricks Advert Agency, New York, 71. *Exhib:* Brooklyn Mus, 64; Libr Cong, 65; Silvermine Guild Artists, 68 & 70; St John's Univ, 76; Port Washington Libr, New York, 77; Lincoln Ctr, 78; Gallery 84, 81; solo show, Adelphi Univ, 82; and many others. *Awards:* Benjamin Altman Landscape Prize, Nat Acad Design, 68; Second Prize Oil, Heckscher Mus, 70; MacDowell Colony Fel, 75 & 80; and others. *Bibliog:* Malcolm Preston (auth), article, Newsday, 72; Addison Parks (auth), article, Arts Mag, 2/80; article, Artspeak, 81. *Mem:* Prof Artists Guild (vpres admis, 73-75, exec vpres, 75-77); Artists Equity; Women in the Arts. *Media:* Oil. *Dealer:* Gallery 84 30 W 57th St New York NY 10019; Gillary Gallery 62 Maiden Ln Jericho NY 11753. *Mailing Add:* 19 Briar Ln Jericho NY 11753

ROSS, CHARLES
ENVIRONMENTAL ARTIST, SCULPTOR
b Philadelphia, Pa, Dec 17, 37. *Study:* Univ Calif, AB, 60, MA, 62. *Work:* Whitney Mus Am Art; Univ Art Gallery, Berkeley, Calif; Univ Pa, Philadelphia; Indianapolis Mus Art; Nelson Art Gallery, Kansas City, Mo. *Comn:* Prism skylight, Dietrich Found, Philadelphia & Spectrum Bldg, Denver; and others. *Exhib:* Cartes et Figures de la Terre, Centre Georges Pompidou, Paris, 77; one-man show, Mass Inst Technol, 78; Numerals: Castelli Gallery, New York, Dartmouth Col & Yale Univ, 78; Supershow, Hudson River Mus, 79-80; and others. *Teaching:* Instr, Univ Calif, 65, Sch Visual Arts, New York, 67, 70 & 71 & Herbert Lehman Col, 68; vis prof archit, Univ Utah, 72 & 73; artist in residence, 74; artist in residence, Mass Inst Technol, 77. *Awards:* Am Inst Graphic Arts Award, 76; and others. *Bibliog:* Donald Kuspit (auth), Light's measure, Art in Am, 3-4/78; Kay Larson (auth), New landscapes in art, New York Times, 5/13/79; Katharine

Chafee & Steve Katz (auths), article, Artspace, fall 81. *Publ:* Auth, Sunlight Convergence/Solar Burn, Univ Utah Press, 76. *Dealer:* John Weber Gallery 420 W Broadway New York NY 10012. *Mailing Add:* 383 W Broadway New York NY 10012

ROSS, CLIFFORD
PAINTER, SCULPTOR
b New York, NY, Oct 15, 52. *Study:* Skowhegan Sch, 73; Yale Univ, BA(A Conger Goodyear Fine Arts Award), 74; Nat Acad Design, 81. *Work:* Metrop Mus Art, New York; Yale Univ Art Gallery; Corcoran Gallery Art, Washington, DC; Albright-Knox Mus, Buffalo, NY; J P Speed Art Mus, Louisville, Ky. *Exhib:* Award Winners, Am Acad & Inst Art & Lett, New York, 78; Figuratively Sculpting, Inst Art & Urban Resources, New York, 81. *Awards:* Rosenthal Award for Young Am Painter of Distinction, Am Acad & Inst Arts & Lett, 78. *Bibliog:* Connie Rogers (auth), article, Arts Mag, 1/79; Paul Goldberger (auth), article, Art in Am, 7/79. *Media:* Oil on Canvas; Bronze. *Dealer:* Salander/O'Reilly Galleries 22 E 80th St New York NY 10021. *Mailing Add:* 832 Broadway New York NY 10003

ROSS, CONRAD H
PRINTMAKER, EDUCATOR
b Chicago, Ill, Apr 26, 31. *Study:* Univ Ill, BFA, 53; Univ Chicago, 54; Univ Iowa, MFA, 59. *Work:* Libr Cong, Washington, DC; Springfield Art Mus, Mo; Norfolk Mus Arts & Sci, Va; Dallas Mus Fine Arts, Tex; Macon Mus Arts & Sci, Ga. *Exhib:* Monotypes Survey Exhibit, Pratt Graphics Ctr Gallery, New York, 72; 1973 Artists Biennial, New Orleans Mus Art, La; one-man show, Augusta Col, Ga, 79; Southeastern Graphics Invitational, 81; Prints, Mint Mus, Charlotte, NC; Washington & Lee Univ, Va, 81. *Pos:* Bd dirs, Southeastern Col Art Conf, 79-82. *Teaching:* Instr drawing, design, lettering & art appreciation, La Polytech Inst, 61-63; asst prof drawing & printmaking, Auburn Univ, 63-81, assoc prof, 81-; vis lectr drawing & printmaking, Kans Univ, 68. *Awards:* Louis Comfort Tiffany Found Grant printmaking, 60; Auburn Univ Res Grant-in-Aid, 65-68, 70 & 73; Purchase Award, LaGrange Nat II, Prints and Drawings, Ga, 75. *Mem:* Ala Art League (pres, 78-80); Artist Equity Asn; Col Art Asn Am; Nat Art Workers Community; Southeastern Graphics Coun (vpres, 78-80). *Publ:* Contribr, Artists' proof the annual of prints and printmaking, 70; The monoprint and the monotype: a case of semantics, Art Voices/South, 7-8/79; Approaches to Drawing: Activity in the Southeast, SECAC Rev, 81. *Mailing Add:* 447 Wrights Mill Rd Auburn AL 36830

ROSS, DAVID ANTHONY
CURATOR, LECTURER
b New York, NY, Apr 26, 49. *Study:* Syracuse Univ, BS, 71. *Collections Arranged:* Traveling exhib, Circuit: A Video Invitational (survey of video art, 68-72), 72-74; Southland Video Anthology (survey of video art in Southern Calif, 68-75, with catalog), Long Beach Mus Art, 75. *Pos:* Asst dir, Everson Mus Art, Syracuse, 71-72, cur video arts, 71-74; deputy dir TV & film, Long Beach Mus Art, 74-77; chief cur, Univ Art Mus, Univ Calif, Berkeley, 77-; dir, Sam Rayburn House, Bonham, Tex, currently; dir, Boston Inst Contemp Art, currently. *Teaching:* Lectr video performance, San Francisco Art Inst, formerly; lectr video art, Grad Sch, Univ Calif, San Diego, 74-82. *Awards:* John D Rockefeller III Found Res Study Grant, 74. *Mem:* Am Asn Mus; Advocates for Arts. *Res:* Relationship between development of new art and context that supports art in American society and development of new support structures. *Publ:* Coauth, Douglas Davis: Videotapes, Manifestos, Drawings and Objects, 72; coauth, Frank Gillette: Video Process & Metaprocess, 73; coauth, Nam June Paik: Videa & Videology, 74; coauth, Peter Campus: Video Works, 74; auth, Southland Video Anthology, 75 & 76-77. *Mailing Add:* Univ Art Mus Berkeley 2626 Bancroft Way Berkeley CA 94704

ROSS, DOUGLAS ALLAN
SCULPTOR, INSTRUCTOR
b Los Angeles, Calif, Jan 23, 37. *Study:* Carleton Col, BA, 59; Minneapolis Col Art & Design, 59-61; Univ Minn, MFA, 65. *Work:* Northrup Gallery, Univ Minn, Minneapolis; Ill State Univ, Normal; Sheldon Art Gallery, Lincoln, Nebr. *Exhib:* Mid-Am I, William Rockhill Nelson Gallery Art, Kansas City, Mo & St Louis Art Mus, Mo, 68; 19th Ann Exhib of Prints & Drawings, Okla Art Ctr, Oklahoma City, 77; 15th Joslyn Biennial, Omaha, 78; 67th Am Ann, Art Asn Newport, RI, 78; 60th Nat Exhib, Springfield Art League, Mass, 79; two-person shows, Univ Reading, Eng & Treat Gallery, Bates Col, Lewiston, Maine. *Collections Arranged:* First Great Plains sculpture Exhib, Sheldon Mem Art Gallery, Lincoln, Nebr, 75; Drawings by Sculptors, SW Mo State Univ, 75 & Syracuse Univ, NY, 76; Second Ann Great Plains Sculpture Exhib, Sheldon Mem Art Gallery, 76; Nebr Alumni, Nebr Mus Fine Arts, 76. *Teaching:* From asst prof to assoc prof sculpture/drawing, Univ Nebr, Lincoln, 66-79, prof, 79-; lectr grade II sculpture, Manchester Polytech, Eng, 69-70. *Awards:* Second Prize, 3rd Minn Artist's Biennial, Minneapolis, 63; Measuregraph Award, Mid-Am I, William Rockhill Nelson Gallery of Art, Addressograph/Multigraph, 68; Purchase Award, One-man Show, Muhlenberg Col, 76. *Mem:* Mid-Am Col Art Asn (prog dir & exhib dir, 75-76). *Media:* Mixed. *Mailing Add:* 1933 B St Lincoln NE 68502

ROSS, FRED (JOSEPH)
PAINTER, INSTRUCTOR
b St John, NB, May 12, 27. *Study:* St John Voc Sch; Pa Acad Fine Arts, with Ben Kamihira; also with Pablo O'Higgins, Mex. *Work:* Can Coun Art Bank, Ottawa, Ont; Winnipeg Art Gallery, Man; NB Mus, St John. *Comn:* Mural, NB Tourist Bur, St John, 58; mural, Prince of Wales Col, Charlottetown, PEI,

61; mural, NB Govt Centennial Bldg, 67. *Exhib:* One-man shows, Walter Klinkhoff Gallery, Montreal, 69, 71 & 75, Galerie Dresdnere, Toronto, 73, 76 & 77; Nat Gallery Ann Exhib, 53, 58 & 66; Royal Can Acad Ann Exhib, 58, 59, 61 & 70; 8th Ann, Montreal Mus, 65 & Survey Exhib, 68. *Pos:* Mem bd dir, Sunbury Shores Arts & Nature Ctr, 75- *Teaching:* Instr drawing, Exten Dept, Univ NB, Fredericton, 70-77; instr painting, summer workshop, Sunbury Shores, St Andrews, NB, 70-77; instr painting, summer workshop, Mt Allison Univ, Sackville, NB, 73-77. *Awards:* O'Keefe Art Award, 50; Price Fine Arts Award, Price Kraft & Paperboard Corp, 70; Short Term Grant, Can Coun, 73 & 76. *Bibliog:* Painting a Province, Nat Film Bd, 62; Paul Duval (auth), Four Decades, 74 & High Realism, 75, Clark Irwin Co. *Mailing Add:* c/o Galerie Dresdnere 130 Bloor St West Toronto ON M5S 1N5 Canada

ROSS, GLORIA F(RANKENTHALER)
TAPESTRY ARTIST
b New York, NY, Sept 5, 23. *Study:* Mt Holyoke Col, Mass, BA, 43; Art Students League, New York, 57-60. *Work:* Denver Art Mus; Int Bank for Reconstruction & Development, DC; Int Business Machines Corp Hq, Armonk, NY; Kennedy Int Airport, New York; Storm King Art Ctr, Mountainville, NY. *Comn:* Tapestry in collaboration with Jack Youngerman, Skidmore Owings Merrill, Upper Ave Nat Bank, Chicago, 70; tapestry in collaboration with Robert Motherwell, Westinghouse Broadcasting Co, Philadelphia, 71; tapestry in collaboration with Helen Frankenthaler, Westinghouse Broadcasting Co, Philadelphia, 71 & Winters Bank, Dayton, Ohio, 71; tapestry in collaboration with Jack Youngerman, comn by Gen Services Admin, Fed Court House, Portland, 76. *Exhib:* Tapestries & Rugs by Contemp Painters & Sculptors, Mus Mod Art, New York, 65; Art Market, Kolner Kunstmarkt, Cologne, Ger, 71; Fiber Structures, Denver Art Mus, 72; Beyond the Artists' Hand, Calif State Univ, Long Beach, 76; Tapestries, Jacksonville Art Mus, Fla, 77; solo exhib, Ringling Mus Art, Sarasota, 78 & Mt Holyoke Col Art Mus, Mass, 79. *Collections Arranged:* Gloria F Ross Tapestries, Feigen Galleries, New York & Chicago, 68-69 & 71, Pace Gallery, New York, 73, 75 & 78; Gloria F Ross/Nevelson Tapestries, Pace Gallery, New York, 78. *Bibliog:* Gene Baro (auth), Tapestry as design, Washington Post, DC, 2/2/72; Rochelle Reed (auth), Art: contemporary tapestries, Archit Dig, 5/78. *Mem:* Am Fed Arts; Textile Mus; Mt Holyoke Col Art Mus Coun; Am Crafts Coun. *Media:* Flat Weave (high & low warp), Tufted Weave (hooked & handknotted). *Mailing Add:* 21 E 87th St New York NY 10028

ROSS, JAMES MATTHEW
EDUCATOR, PAINTER
b Ann Arbor, Mich, Sept 8, 31. *Study:* Univ Mich, AB; Cranbrook Acad Art, MFA; Rockham Sch Grad Studies, Ann Arbor; Accad Belle Arti, Rome. *Work:* Butler Inst Am Art; Cranbrook Mus Art; Wustum Mus, Racine, Wis; Madison Art Ctr, Wis; Detroit Inst Art. *Exhib:* Michigan Artists, 51-60 & 63; Detroit Inst Art & Pa Acad Fine Arts, 59-60; Walker Art Ctr, 59-60; Wis Painters & Sculptors Ann, Milwaukee Art Ctr, 63-65; Univ Wis-Whitewater, 65; and others. *Teaching:* Asst prof art, Univ Wis-Platteville, 62-80, assoc prof Fine Arts, 80- *Awards:* Fulbright Grant Painting to Italy, 60 & 61; Prizes, Wis Painters & Sculptors, 63 & Mich Fine Arts Exhib, 64; and others. *Mem:* Col Art Asn Am; Wis Painters & Sculptors Soc; Am Asn Univ Prof. *Mailing Add:* Dept of Art Univ of Wis-Platteville Platteville WI 53818

ROSS, JANICE KOENIG
PAINTER
b Harrisburg, Pa. *Study:* Pa State Univ, BA; Univ Ill, MFA. *Exhib:* Piedmont Ann Crafts Exhib, Mint Mus, Charlotte, NC, 73; Cent S Exhib, The Parthenon, Nashville, Tenn, 76; Piedmont Graphic Exhib, Greenville Co Mus, SC, 76; Nat Drawing & Sculpture Show, Kutztown State Col, Pa, 77; Images, Univ Montevallo, 80; solo exhibs, Ga Inst Technol Student Ctr Gallery, 80 & Chattahoochee Valley Art Asn Gallery, 83; and others. *Teaching:* Prof art, Tuskegee Inst, Ala, 68- *Awards:* Nat Endowment Humanities Fel, 81-82. *Mem:* Col Art Asn; Women's Caucus Art; Nat Art Worker's Community; founder Studio 218; Southeastern Women's Caucus Art (mem secy-treas, 78-80); and others. *Media:* Oil, Graphic Media. *Publ:* Auth, MFA Survey, Col Art Asn, fall 78; auth, Eight from Auburn, Art Voices South, 1-2/80; auth, Agnes Bradley Taugner profile, Artcraft, 2-3/80. *Mailing Add:* 447 Wrights's Mill Rd Auburn AL 36830

ROSS, JOHN T
PRINTMAKER, EDUCATOR
b New York, NY, Sept 25, 21. *Study:* Cooper Union Art Sch, with Morris Kantor & Will Barnet, BFA; New Sch Social Res, with Antonio Frasconi & Louis Schanker; Columbia Univ, 53. *Work:* Libr Cong, Hirshhorn Mus & Nat Collection Fine Arts, Washington, DC; Metrop Mus Art, New York; Cincinnati Art Mus. *Comn:* Ed prints, Hilton Hotel, 63, Assoc Am Artists, 64, 66 & 72, Philadelphia Print Club, 67, NY State Coun Arts, 67 & Int Poetry Forum, 68. *Exhib:* Second Int Color Print Exhib, Grenchen, Switz, 61; Int Biennale Gravure, Cracow, Poland, 68; Prize-winning Am Prints, Pratt Graphic Art Ctr, New York, 68; Nat Acad Fine Arts, Amsterdam, Neth, 68; Biennial Print Exhib, Calif State Col, Long Beach, 69; and others. *Pos:* Dir, Art Ctr Northern NJ, 66-67; pres, US Comt-Int Asn Art, 67-69. *Teaching:* Instr printmaking, New Sch Social Res, 57-; instr printmaking, Pratt Graphic Ctr, 63-; prof art, Manhattanville Col, 64-; demonstr & lectr, US Info Agency Exhib, Romania & Yugoslavia, 64-66. *Awards:* Louis Comfort Tiffany Found Grant Printmaking, 54; Purchase Prize for 100 Prints of the Year, AAA Gallery, 63; citation for prof achievement, Cooper Union Art Sch, 66. *Bibliog:* Articles, Am Artist, 52-81; Artists Proof, 64 & Art in Am, 65. *Mem:* Soc Am Graphic Artists (pres, 61-65, exec coun, 65-); assoc Nat Acad Design; Boston Printmakers; Philadelphia Print Club; Am Color Print Soc. *Publ:* Illusr, many bks; coauth, The Complete Printmaker, 72 & The Complete Collagraph, 80, Macmillan. *Dealer:* Assoc Am Artists 663 Fifth Ave New York NY 10022. *Mailing Add:* 110 Davison Pl Englewood NJ 07631

ROSS, KENNETH
ADMINISTRATOR
b El Paso, Tex, Aug 1, 10. *Study:* Pasadena Jr Col; Chouinard Art Inst; Art Ctr Sch Los Angeles; Nat Acad, Florence, Italy; Acad Grande Chaumiere, Paris; Euston Rd Sch Drawing & Painting, London. *Pos:* Dir, Pasadena Art Inst, Calif, formerly; dir, Mod Inst Art, Beverly Hills, Calif, formerly; art critic, Pasadena Star News & Los Angeles Daily News, Calif, formerly; dir, Los Angeles Munic Arts Dept, (Art Gallery, Watts Tower Art Ctr, Jr Arts Ctr, Bur Music & Cult Heritage Bd), 50-82. *Teaching:* Lectr hist art & art appreciation, Univ Southern Calif. *Mem:* Jr Arts Ctr Los Angeles; Munic Art Assoc, Los Angeles; Alliance Calif State Arts Coun; Craft & Folk Art Mus. *Mailing Add:* 4804 Hollywood Blvd Los Angeles CA 90027

ROSSE, MARYVONNE
SCULPTOR, MEDALIST
b Palo Alto, Calif, Mar 4, 17. *Study:* Acad Fine Arts, The Hague, Neth, dipl. *Work:* Mus Holland, Mich. *Comn:* Plaques, J Bos, Neth, 38; medals, Koninklyk Begeer, Neth, 38; portraits, D Tutein Noltenius, Neth, 42; garden ornaments, Nederlandshe Olie Fabriek, Delft, Neth, 46; commercial prototypes, D G Williams Inc, Brooklyn, 48-66. *Exhib:* Pulchri Studios, The Hague, 36-47; New York World's Fair, 39; Pen & Brush Club, 67-80; Catharine Lorillard Wolfe Art Club, 67-80; Nat Sculpture Soc, 67-80. *Pos:* Sculpture, D G Williams, Brooklyn, NY, 48-66; ed news lett, Catharine Lorillard Wolfe Art Club, 68-72. *Teaching:* Instr sculpture, Rockland Found, Nyack, NY, 47; instr art, King Coit Theatre Sch Children, New York, 47-48. *Awards:* Pen & Brush Solo Exhib Award, 71; Gold Medal, Catharine Lorillard Wolfe Art Club Ann, 72; Tallix Award, Nat Sculpture Soc, 78. *Mem:* Nat Sculpture Soc; Pen & Brush Club (sculpture chmn, 69-72); Burr Artists (historian, 68-70); Catharine Lorillard Wolfe Art Club (bd mem, 69-73, sculpture chmn, 69-72); Am Medallic Sculpture Asn (secy, 82-84). *Media:* Clay, Plaster; Wood, Bronze. *Mailing Add:* 431 Buena Vista Rd New City NY 10956

ROSSEN, SUSAN F
HISTORIAN, EDITOR
Study: Smith Col, AB(art hist), 63; Univ of Mich, Wayne State Univ, MA(art hist), 71. *Pos:* Asst cur of educ, Detroit Inst of Arts, 64-68, assoc cur European art, 71-72, sr ed & coordr of publ, Detroit Inst of Arts, 72-81; coordr & ed publications, Art Inst Chicago, 81- *Teaching:* Lectr 19th century art, Univ of Detroit, 71. *Awards:* Am Art Mus Asn; Art Mus Asn, Chicago Book Clinic. *Mem:* Am Asn of Mus; Mus Publ of Am; Women's Caucus for Art, Col Art Asn. *Res:* Nineteenth and twentieth century art and women artists. *Publ:* Ed, Treasures from Ancient Nigeria, 80 & Cliche-Verre: A Survey of the Medium from 1839 to the Present, 80; ed, Henri Matisse Paper Cut-Outs, 77; ed, The Golden Age of Naples: Art and Civilization Under the Bourbons 1734-1805, 81; ed, Chicago Architects Design, 82; and others. *Mailing Add:* Art Inst Chicago Michigan Ave & Adams St Chicago IL 60603

ROSSI, BARBARA
PAINTER, PRINTMAKER
b Chicago, Ill. *Study:* Art Inst Chicago, MFA. *Work:* Fogg Mus; Baltimore Mus Art, Md; Nat Collection of Fine Arts, Washington, DC; Mus des 20, Jahrhunderts, Vienna; Art Inst Chicago. *Exhib:* What They're Up To In Chicago, Nat Gallery Can, Ottawa, 72; Directions, Hirshhorn Mus & Sculpture Garden, Washington, DC, 79; one-woman shows, Phyllis Kind Gallery, Chicago, 75, 76 & 80, New York, 78 & Inst Contemp Art, Boston, 80-82; and others. *Teaching:* Vis artist, Art Inst Chicago, 71- *Awards:* Nat Endowment Arts Artist's Fel, 73; Mr & Mrs Frank Armstrong Prize, 74th Artists of Chicago & Vicinity Exhib, Art Inst Chicago, 73; Vielher Award, 78th Artists of Chicago & Vicinity Exhib, Art Inst Chicago, 80. *Mailing Add:* c/o Phyllis Kind Gallery 313 W Superior Chicago IL 60610

ROSSI, JOSEPH O
PAINTER, INSTRUCTOR
b Paterson, NJ. *Study:* Newark Sch Fine & Indust Art; Grand Cent Art Sch; Columbia Univ; private study with John R Grabach, Harvey Dunn & Edgar A Whitney. *Work:* Salmagundi Club Collection; Norfolk Mus, Va; Bergen Mall Collection & Bergen Community Mus, Paramus, NJ; Newark Hospital Collection. *Exhib:* Am Watercolor Soc Ann, Nat Acad Design, New York, 79, Allied Artists Ann, 79 & Audubon Artist Ann, 79; Selected Am Watercolor Soc, Royal Acad, London; Rockport Art Asn, Mass, 79. *Teaching:* Instr watercolor, oil & life drawing, Newark Sch Fine & Indust Art; instr watercolor, Art Students League, New York. *Awards:* Malcolm Tuttle Award, Salmagundi Watercolor Exhib, 74; NJ Watercolor Award, 78; Lena Newcastle Award, Am Watercolor Soc, 79. *Mem:* Am Watercolor Soc; NJ Watercolor Soc; Allied Artists Am; Audubon Artists; Salmagundi Club. *Media:* Watercolor, Oil. *Publ:* Auth, Watercolor Page, Am Artist Mag, 8/72. *Dealer:* Grand Cent Galleries New York NY 10017. *Mailing Add:* 45 Lockwood Dr Clifton NJ 07013

ROSSMAN, RUTH SCHARFF
PAINTER, INSTRUCTOR
b Brooklyn, NY. *Study:* Cleveland Inst Art; Case-Western Reserve Univ, BS; Kahn Inst Art; Univ Calif, Los Angeles; also with Sueo Serisawa & Rico Lebrun. *Work:* Pa Acad Fine Arts; Univ Redlands; Nat Watercolor Soc; Brandeis Inst; Ahmanson Collection, Calif; plus others. *Exhib:* Recent Paintings USA: Figure, Mus Mod Art, New York, 61; one-woman shows, Heritage Gallery, Los Angeles, 63 & 66, Univ Judaism, Los Angeles, 79; Los Angeles Mus Sci & Indust, 78; Crescent Gallery, New Orleans, 77, 78; Rocky Mountain Nat, Colo, 77 & 81; Denver Art Mus; and others. *Teaching:* Teacher art, Pub Sch Syst, Canton; teacher art, Canton Art Inst; instr, Arts

& Crafts Ctr, Los Angeles. *Awards:* Purchase Award, Pa Acad Fine Arts, 65; All-City Ann Purchase Awards, Los Angeles, 65 & 69; Rocky Mountain Nat, 77; plus others. *Bibliog:* William Wilson & Henry Seldis (auths), articles, Los Angeles Times, 63 & 6/66; States Item, Times-Picayune World Art, New Orleans, 12/77. *Mem:* Nat Watercolor Soc (secy, 73-74, 1st vpres, 74-75, pres, 75-76). *Media:* Acrylic, Oil. *Mailing Add:* 401 Cascada Way Los Angeles CA 90049

ROSTER, FRED HOWARD
SCULPTOR, EDUCATOR
b Palo Alto, Calif, June 27, 44. *Study:* Gavilan Col, AA; San Jose State Col, BA & MA; Univ Hawaii, MFA & with Herbert H Sanders. *Work:* Honolulu Acad Art, Hawaii; State Found Cult & Arts, Honolulu; Contemp Arts Ctr Hawaii; Hawaii Loa Col, Kailua; St Francis Hosp, Honolulu. *Comn:* Sand cast mural, Ft Derussy, 75; bronze bust of former Gov John Burns, State Found Cult & The Arts; Kekuanaoa bronze portrait, 79; bronze & stainless steel mural, Physical Educ Facility, Univ Hawaii, Manoa, 82; bronze, stone & stainless steel sculpture, Honolulu Int Airport, 83. *Exhib:* Artists of Hawaii Ann, Honolulu Acad Art, 75-76, 79 & 81; Hawaii Craftsmen's Ann, Honolulu, 69-72 & 75-80; one-man shows, Contemp Arts Ctr Hawaii, 72; Gima's Art Gallery, Honolulu, 75 & 78 & Corpus Christi Univ, Tex, 80. *Teaching:* Instr ceramics, San Jose State Col, 68-69; asst prof sculpture, Univ Hawaii, 69-78, assoc prof, 78- *Awards:* Elizabeth Moses Award, San Francisco Potter's Asn, 68; Sculptural Grant Award, Windward Artists Guild, 71; Hawaii Craftsman Award, 74. *Mem:* Honolulu Acad Art. *Media:* Mixed. *Mailing Add:* 1841 Halekoa Dr Honolulu HI 96821

ROSTER, LAILA BERGS
MUSEUM DIRECTOR
b Dresden, Ger, Dec 12, 44; US citizen. *Study:* San Mateo Col, AA, 64; San Jose State Univ, BA, 67; Honolulu Acad Art, with Rudy Pozzatti; Mus Mgt Inst, Univ Calif, Berkeley, 79. *Work:* State Found Cult & Arts, Honolulu; Castle and Cooke; Honolulu Advertiser. *Exhib:* Honolulu Printmakers, Honolulu Acad Arts, 79-81; Contemp Arts Ctr Exhib, 79; Honolulu Printmakers Miniature, 79; Hawaii Artists League Ann, 80-81. *Pos:* Dir, Lytton Ctr Visual Arts, Palo Alto, Calif, 67-69; art critic, Honolulu Star Bull, 74-79, mus dlr, Contemporary Arts Ctr Hawaii, 75- *Teaching:* Adult educ instr paintings & drawing, Honolulu Acad Arts, 73-; instr, Continuing Col Educ, Univ Hawaii, 79. *Awards:* Honolulu Printmakers Annual, 75; Windward Artists Guild Annual, 76; Outstanding Achievement, Leader in the Arts, 79. *Bibliog:* Article, Honolulu Star Bulletin, 1/81; Cult Climate, Arts Coun of Hawaii, 9/81. *Mem:* Hawaii Craftsmen (secy, 71, 72, vpres, 73-75); Hawaii Painters & Sculptors League (pres, 77-79); Honolulu Printmakers (mem bd, 77-80); Honolulu Acad Arts; Hawaii Artists League (pres 76-80). *Media:* Acrylic, Drawing. *Specialty:* Regional contemporary art. *Publ:* Contribr, Currant Mag, 75- *Mailing Add:* 3715 Diamond Head Circle Honolulu HI 96815

ROTAN, WALTER
SCULPTOR
b Baltimore, Md, Mar 29, 12. *Study:* Md Inst; Pa Acad Fine Arts; also with Albert Laessie. *Work:* Pa Acad Fine Arts; Brookgreen Gardens, SC. *Exhib:* Nat Acad Design; Pa Acad Fine Arts; Art Inst Chicago; Philadelphia Mus Art; Carnegie Inst; and others. *Teaching:* Head art dept, Taft Sch, Watertown, Conn, 38-53. *Awards:* Cresson Traveling Scholar, 33 & Prize, 46, Pa Acad Fine Arts; four Prizes, Nat Acad Design, 36-45; Prize, Allied Artists Am, 56; and others. *Mem:* Fel Nat Sculpture Soc; Audubon Artists; fel Pa Acad Fine Arts. *Mailing Add:* 45 Christopher St New York NY 10014

ROTH, DAVID
PAINTER
b New York, NY, June 7, 42. *Study:* Ill Inst Technol, study with Harry Callahan & Aaron Siskind. *Work:* Albright-Knox Gallery, Buffalo; Ball State Univ, Ind; Mus Contemp Art, Tehran, Iran; Philadelphia Mus Art; Rockefeller Inst, New York. *Exhib:* Thirty-Second Ann for Soc Contemp Art, Art Inst Chicago, 72; Painting or Sculpture?, Newark Mus, 72; 8th Nat Print Exhib, Brooklyn Mus, 72; Small Works-Selections from Richard Brown Baker Collection, Mus Art RI Sch Design, 73; Contemp Am Artist, Cleveland Mus Art, 74; Painting & Sculpture Today, Indianapolis Mus Art, 74 & 76. *Bibliog:* Marcia Hafif (auth), A fusion of real & pictorial space, Arts Mag, 3/72; Tom Hinson (auth), Contemporary American Artists, Cleveland Mus Art, 73; Carter Ratcliff (auth), NY Leter, Art Int, summer 73. *Media:* Liquitex. *Dealer:* Robert Elkon Gallery 1063 Madison Ave New York NY 10028. *Mailing Add:* RD 4 Mt Kisco NY 10549

ROTH, FRANK
PAINTER
b Boston, Mass, Feb 22, 36. *Study:* Cooper Union, 54; Hofmann Sch, 55. *Work:* Albright-Knox Art Gallery, Buffalo, NY; Whitney Mus Am Art; Santa Barbara Mus Art, Calif; Baltimore Mus Art; Walker Art Ctr, Minneapolis; and others. *Exhib:* Va Mus Fine Arts, Richmond, 70; Indianapolis Mus Art, Ind, 70; Amherst Col, 72; Contemp Am Painting, Lehigh Univ, 72; Finch Col Mus Art, New York, 73; Louise Himmelfarb Gallery, Bridgehampton, NY, 77 & 78; plus many other group & one-man shows. *Teaching:* Instr painting, State Univ Iowa, summer 64; instr painting & drawing, Sch Visual Arts, NY, 63-; Ford Found artist in residence, Univ RI, 66; instr, Univ Calif, Berkeley, 68; instr, Univ Calif, Irvine, 71. *Awards:* Guggenheim Fel, 64; Minister Foreign Affairs Award, Int Exhib Young Artists, Tokyo, Japan, 67; Nat Endowment for Arts, 77; and others. *Bibliog:* William H Gerdts, Jr (auth), Painting & Sculpture in New Jersey, Van Nostrand-Reinhold, 64. *Dealer:* Louis K Meisel Gallery 141 Prince St New York NY 10014. *Mailing Add:* 120 Accabonac Rd East Hampton NY 11973

ROTH, JACK (RODNEY)
PAINTER
b Brockway, Pa, Mar 13, 27. *Study:* Calif Sch Fine Arts, with Mark Rothko & Clifford Still, 49-50; State Univ Iowa, with James Lechay, MFA, 51-53; Duke Univ, PhD, 62. *Work:* Mus Mod Art, New York. *Exhib:* Younger American Painters, Guggenheim Mus, New York, 54; one-man shows, Clocktower, New York, 81, Montclair Art Mus, 82 & NJ State Mus, 83. *Teaching:* Prof math, Ramapo Col, NJ, 71- *Awards:* Guggenheim Fel, 79-80. *Mem:* Artists Equity. *Media:* Acrylic, Watercolor. *Dealer:* M Knoedler 19 East 70th St New York NY 10021. *Mailing Add:* 32 Clinton Ave Montclair NJ 07042

ROTH, LELAND M(ARTIN)
HISTORIAN, WRITER
b Harbor Beach, Mich, Mar 22, 43. *Study:* Univ Ill, Urbana, BA(archit), 66; Yale, MA, 70, PhD, 73. *Teaching:* Instr, Univ Ill, Urbana, 66-67 & Ohio State Univ, Columbus, 71-73; asst prof, Northwestern Univ, 73-78; assoc prof, Univ Ore, Eugene, 78- *Awards:* Founders Award, Soc Archit Historians, 79. *Mem:* Col Art Asn; Soc Archit Historians (dir, 77-80). *Res:* American architecture, 1850-1950; history of urban America; history of American art, 1850-1930. *Publ:* Ed, Monograph of the Work of McKim, Mead & White, B Blom, 73; auth, The Architecture of McKim, Mead & White, 1870-1920: A Building List, Garland Publ, 78; auth, A Concise History of American Architecture, 79, ed, America Builds: Source Documents in American Architecture, 83 & auth, McKim, Mead & White, Architects, 83, Harper & Row. *Mailing Add:* Art Hist Dept Univ Ore Eugene OR 97403

ROTH, MOIRA
EDUCATOR, HISTORIAN
b London, Eng, July 24, 33. *Study:* New York Univ, BA, 59; Univ Calif, Berkeley, MA, 66, PhD, 74. *Teaching:* Acting asst prof art hist, Univ Calif, Irvine, 70-72; lectr art hist, Univ Calif, Santa Cruz, 73-74; from asst to assoc prof, Univ Calif, San Diego, 74-, chmn, Visual Arts Dept, 82-83. *Res:* Performance art, Marcel Duchamp & women's contemporary art. *Publ:* Auth, Marcel Duchamp in America: A self-readymade, 5/77 & auth, Toward a history of California performance, 6/78, Arts; auth, The aesthetic of indifference, 11/77 & auth, Visions and re-visions, 11/80, Artforum; ed & contribr, The Amazing Decade: Women and Performance Art in America, 1970-1980, 83. *Mailing Add:* Visual Arts Dept Univ Calif San Diego CA 92093

ROTH, RICHARD
PAINTER, EDUCATOR
b Brooklyn, NY, June 22, 46. *Study:* Cooper Union, BFA, 69; Tyler Sch Art, Temple Univ, MFA, 77. *Work:* Akron Art Inst, Ohio; Chase Manhattan Bank Collection, New York; New York Univ Art Collection; First Nat City Bank Collection, New York; Indianapolis Mus Art. *Exhib:* 1969 Ann Exhib of Contemp Am Painting, Whitney Mus Am Art, New York, 69-70; one-man shows, O K Harris Gallery, New York, 70 & 72 & Kans State Univ, Manhattan, 79; Inst Contemp Art, Boston, 71; three-person show, Jan Cicero Gallery, Chicago, 79; Ann Group Show, Columbus Mus Art, Ohio, 82; two-person show, Gallery Ohio Found Art, Columbus, 82. *Teaching:* Asst prof & dir, Prog Fundamentals & Spec Classes, Art Inst Chicago, 77-81; asst prof & dir, Found Prog, Dept Art, Ohio State Univ, 81- *Mailing Add:* 141 Walhalla Rd Columbus OH 43202

ROTH, RUBI
PAINTER
b New York, NY, Dec 1, 05. *Study:* NY Univ; Cooper Union; Columbia Univ; Brooklyn Mus; Sculptors Guild, New York. *Work:* Norfolk Mus, Va; Seton Hall, NJ; Forbes Mus, New York; Long Beach Libr. *Comn:* Mural, West End Temple, New York, 71. *Exhib:* Lever House, New York; Nat Art League, Douglaston, NY; Nat Acad Design, New York; Am Artists Prof League; Am Watercolor Soc. *Teaching:* Instr art, Nat Art League, 57, lectr, 72. *Awards:* First Prize, Am Artists League, 67; First Prize, Forbes Mus, New York. *Mem:* Am Watercolor Soc; Nat Asn Women Artists; Am Artists Prof League; Artists Equity Asn; Nat Art League. *Media:* Watercolor, Oil. *Mailing Add:* 211 Beach 134 St Belle Harbor Far Rockaway NY 11694

ROTHBEIN, RENEE
PAINTER, PRINTMAKER
b London, Eng, Aug 11, 24; US citizen. *Study:* Univ Chicago; Sch Art Inst Chicago, BFA, MFA; studied with Louis Ritman & Max Kahn. *Work:* Art Inst Chicago; Fogg Mus Art, Cambridge, Mass; Atlanta Univ Art Mus, Ga. *Exhib:* Nat Print Exhib, Libr Cong, Washington, DC, 55-57; Nat Painting Exhib, Pa Acad, Philadelphia, 57; Boston Printmakers, Mus Fine Arts, Boston, 57-58; DeCordova Mus, Lincoln, Mass, 63, 74 & 75; Nat Drawing Exhib, Smith Col Mus Art, 65. *Media:* Oil; Pen & Ink, Woodcut. *Mailing Add:* 350 Quinobequin Rd Waban MA 02168

ROTHENBERG, BARBARA
PAINTER, COLLAGE ARTIST
b New York, NY, June 21, 33. *Study:* Univ Mich, 52-54; Bennington Col, with Paul Feeley, BA(cum laude), 56; Columbia Univ Teachers Col, MA, 56; NY Univ, with Esteben Vicente & Samuel Adler, 56-58. *Work:* Housatonic Mus Art, Bridgeport, Conn; Westport Town Hall, Conn; Gen Electric Corp, Fairfield, Conn; Marketing Corp Am, Westport, Conn; Bennington Col. *Exhib:* Gruenebaum Gallery Invitational, New York, 78; Women Artists, City Univ New York, 78; Postcard-Size Art, Loyola Univ, 80; Landscape Drawing, Hurlbutt Gallery, Greenwich, Conn, 80; New Dimensions in Drawing, Aldrich Mus, 81; Northeast USA, 83 & Out of Landscape, 83, Silvermine

Guild; Stone Stream Series, Katonah Gallery, NY, 83. *Teaching:* Instr art, City Col New York, 58-60 & Silvermine Sch Arts, 80-83; adj assoc prof art, Housatonic Community Col, 70-82, Sch Visual Arts, New York, 80-82 & Sacred Heart Univ, 80- *Awards:* Top Award: Works Under Glass, New England Ann, 80 & Northeast USA, 83; Sacred Heart Univ Grant, 83. *Bibliog:* Jacqueline Moss (auth), On Landscape: A new view, Stanford Advocate, 7/3/83. *Mem:* Col Art Asn; Womens Caucus Arts; Westport-Weston Arts Coun; Silvermine Guild Ctr Arts (mem bd, 78-80). *Media:* Pastel, Oil; Collage. *Publ:* Auth, On painterly painting, Women Artists News, 81; auth, Connecticut women artists, Conn Mag, 81. *Dealer:* Brancheville-Soho Gallery Georgetown CT; Katonah Gallery Katonah NY. *Mailing Add:* 303 Bayberry Lane Westport CT 06880

ROTHENBERG, SUSAN
PAINTER, PRINTMAKER
b Buffalo, NY, Jan 20, 45. *Study:* Cornell Univ, BFA, 66; George Washington Univ, 67; Corcoran Mus Sch. *Work:* Mus Mod Art, New York; Albright-Knox Art Gallery, Buffalo; Whitney Mus Am Art, New York; Walker Art Ctr, Minneapolis; Museum Fine Arts, Houston. *Exhib:* Extraordinary Women, 77 & New Acquisitions, 77, Mus Mod Art, New York; Susan Rothenberg: Recent Work, Walker Art Ctr, Minneapolis, 78; New Image Painting, 78-79 & Whitney Biennial, 79, Whitney Mus Am art; Paintings & Sculpture Today, Indianapolis Mus Art, 80; A New Bestiary: Animal Imagery in Contemp Art, Va Mus Fine Arts, 81; Animals in Am Art, Nassau Co Mus Fine Art, 81-82; solo exhibs, Akron Art Mus, Ohio, 82, Stedelijk Mus, Amsterdam, 82, Willard Gallery, New York, 83, Los Angeles Co Mus Art, 83, San Francisco Mus Art, 83 & Carnegie Inst, Mus Mod Art, Pittsburgh, 84. *Collections Arranged:* A Guide to the Collection of the Museum Fine Arts, Houston, Tex; The Image in American Photography & Sculpture 1950-1980 (auth, catalog), Akron Art Mus. *Awards:* Creative Artists Pub Serv Prog Grant, NY State Coun Arts, 76-77; Guggenheim Fel Painting, 80; Award Painting, Am Acad Arts & Lett, 83. *Bibliog:* Peter Schjeldahl (auth), article, Artforum, summer 79; Hilton Kramer (auth), article, New York Times, 79. *Media:* Acrylic and Flashe on Canvas or Paper, Aquatint; Lithography. *Publ:* Contribr, New Image Painting, Whitney Mus, 78; contribr, American Paintings: The Eighties, Barbara Rose/ Vista Press, 79. *Mailing Add:* Willard Gallery 29 E 72nd St New York NY 10021

ROTHFARB, ED (EDWIN I)
SCULPTOR, EDUCATOR
b Brooklyn, NY, Sept 12, 50. *Study:* Boston Mus Sch, BFA, 72. *Comn:* Istra (outdoor sculpture), State Mass, Brandeis Univ, 82. *Exhib:* Whitney Mus Am Art Biennial Exhib, 75; Current Concerns, Univ Iowa Mus Art, Iowa City, 77; Two Views, Two Sculptors, Hayden Gallery, 79; Six Sculptors, Inst Contemp Art, Boston, 79; Architectural Sculpture, Los Angeles Inst Contemp Art, 80; Monumenta Merziana, Danforth Mus, Framingham, Mass, 82. *Teaching:* Instr sculpture, RI Sch Design, 79-83, asst prof, 83- *Awards:* St Gaudens Mem Fel, 78; Mass Artist Found Fel Sculpture, 78; Graham Found Award, 81. *Bibliog:* Ronald Onorato (auth), article, Art Forum, 10/79; Sarah McFadden (auth), Report from Boston, Art in Am, 5/83. *Dealer:* Stux Gallery Newbury St Boston MA 02116. *Mailing Add:* 133 Chrystie St Third Floor New York NY 10002

ROTHMAN, SIDNEY
GALLERY DIRECTOR, CRITIC
b US, May 7, 18. *Study:* Brooklyn Col; Columbia Univ, BA(lang & art hist); New York Sch Archit Design. *Collections Arranged:* New Jersey Artists Show, 68; South American Collection, 69; Yugoslavian Printmakers, 72; Collection of European Prints, Fordham Univ, 72. *Pos:* Art dealer, Philadelphia area, 46-66; gallery dir, Barnegat Light, 58-; assessor of paintings, Long Beach Found Arts & Sci, 71-72. *Teaching:* Lectr art, Women's Club Island, Beach Haven, NJ, 67-68, Deborah Hosp, Browns Mills, NJ, 69 & Long Beach Found, Loveladies, NJ, 71. *Bibliog:* Miriam Bush (auth), articles, Asbury Park Press, 6/8/75 & 9/8/81; article, Philadelphia Inquirer, 8/3/75 & 6/12/81; article, Summer Times, 6/2/82. *Mem:* Long Beach Found Arts & Sci; Ocean Co Cult & Heritage Comn, NJ; Artists Equity Asn. *Res:* Spanish art of time of Velasquez thru Ribera; ukiyo-e Japanese prints and identification. *Specialty:* Showing only living artists of all mediums, sponsoring foreign contemporary artists. *Publ:* Auth, Articles in Beach Haven Times, 67-71; contribr, Arts of Asia, Hong Kong, 71; auth, articles, New York Times, 9/9/79, Beachcomber, 6/2/82 & Summer Times, 6/3/82 & 6/2/83. *Mailing Add:* 21st on Central Ave Barnegat Light NJ 08006

ROTHOLZ, RINA
PRINTMAKER
b Israel; US citizen. *Study:* Pratt Graphic Arts Ctr, New York; Brooklyn Mus Art Sch, NY. *Work:* Boston Mus Fine Arts; Rose Art Mus, Brandeis Univ; Mus Mod Art, New York; Israel Mus, Jerusalem; Albright-Knox Art Gallery, Buffalo, NY; and others. *Comn:* Ed of 50 prints, 69 & ed of 200 prints, Commentary Libr Collection of Art Treasure; Blue Disc (greeting card design), UNICEF, 72; 36 ingots (reprod by Franklin Mint), Judaic Heritage Soc, 73-78. *Exhib:* One-man shows, Pucker/Safrai Gallery, Boston, 72, 74, 77 & 81 & Port Washington Libr, New York, 75; Boston Printmakers Ann & Traveling Shows, 67-79; Queens Mus, NY, 74; Potsdam Print Exhib, State Univ NY Col, Purchase, 76; and others. *Teaching:* Lectr & demonstr, Bd Coop Educ Serv, Scholars in Residence Prog, Nassau Co, NY. *Awards:* First Prize for Graphics, Port Washington Ann, 70; Purchase Prize, Nassau Community Graphic Exhib, 72 & 73; Prize in Graphics, Nat Asn Women Artists, 72 & 74. *Mem:* Boston Printmakers; Graphic Arts Coun NY; Nat Asn Women Artists; Prof Artists Guild. *Res:* Discovered process of Tuilegraphy, which is the carving of vinyl asbestos tiles while they are still warm, then printing the tiles as intaglio plates to achieve a variety of textures, shapes, and high reliefs. *Publ:* Auth, Tuilegraphy, Artist's Proof, Vol 7. *Mailing Add:* 42 Shepherd Lane Roslyn Heights NY 11577

ROTHROCK, ILSE SKIPSNA
LIBRARIAN
b Riga, Latvia, Feb 17, 28; US citizen. *Study:* Univ Tex, Austin, MLS, 53; Hunter Col, New York, MA, 67. *Pos:* Librn, Kimbell Art Mus, Ft Worth, 67- *Bibliog:* Ojars Kratins (auth), Society and the self in novels by Ilse Skipsna and Alberts Bels, Bks Abroad, Vol 47, No 4, 73. *Mem:* Art Libr Soc NAm; Spec Libr Asn; Tex Inst Letts. *Publ:* Auth, Veja Stabules (Latvian short stories), Tilts, Minneapolis, 61; auth, Aiz Septita Tilta (Latvian novel), 65 & Neapsolitas Zemes (Latvian novel), 70, Gramatu Draugs, New York; auth, Videja Isteniba (Latvian short stories), 74. *Mailing Add:* Kimbell Art Mus Libr PO Box 9440 Ft Worth TX 76107

ROTHSCHILD, AMALIE (ROSENFELD)
SCULPTOR, PAINTER
b Baltimore, Md, Jan 1, 16. *Study:* Md Inst Col Art, dipl; New York Sch Fine & Appl Art; and with Herman Maril. *Work:* Corcoran Gallery Art & Phillips Collection, Washington, DC; Martenet Collection, Baltimore Mus Art; Peale Mus, Baltimore; Honolulu Acad of Arts. *Comn:* Design for needlepoint ark curtain, Baltimore Hebrew Congregation, 51; design for Plexiglas & aluminum window, Forest Park High Sch, Baltimore, 81; design for needlepoint wall hanging, Sun Life Ins Co Am, Baltimore, 66; design for aggregate archit panels, Martin Luther King, Jr Elementary Sch, Baltimore, 69; design for needlepoint wall hanging, Walters Art Gallery, Baltimore, 74. *Exhib:* Synagogue Art Today, Jewish Mus, New York, 52; Living Today, 58 & Three Artists from Washington & Baltimore, 59, Corcoran Gallery Art; solo exhibs, Baltimore Mus Art, 71, Celebration for the Artists, Nat Acad Sci, 75, Kornblatt Gallery, Baltimore, 78 & 80 & Meredith Contemp Art, Baltimore, 82; Sculpture/300, Philadelphia Art Alliance, 82. *Teaching:* Instr painting, Metrop Sch Art, Baltimore, 56-59; lectr fine arts, Goucher Col, 60-68. *Awards:* Prize Painting, 50 & Prize Work in Any Medium, 54, Baltimore Mus Art; Award for Painting, Corcoran Gallery Art, 57. *Bibliog:* Peter Blake (auth), An American Synagogue for Today & Tomorrow, Union Am Hebrew Congregations, 54; Theodore L Low (auth), Man the maker, WMAR-TV & Walters Art Gallery, Baltimore, 60; Lincoln F Johnson, Jr (auth), Amalie Rothschild: Drawings, Goucher Col, 68. *Mem:* Artists Equity Asn. *Media:* Particle Board, Metal Leaf; Acrylic, Cast Handmade Paper. *Dealer:* Meredith Contemporary Art 805 N Charles St Baltimore MD 21201. *Mailing Add:* 2909 Woodvalley Dr Baltimore MD 21208

ROTHSCHILD, CAROLYN ANITA
DEALER
b Baldwin, NY, April 3, 39. *Study:* State Univ NY, Potsdam, BS, 61; Southern Ill Univ, MS(fel), 63; NY Univ, 63-65; Univ Int, Santander, Spain, 65. *Collections Arranged:* Nancy Grossman Exhib, Univ Nev, Reno, 78. *Pos:* Owner, Rothschild Fine Arts, currently. *Specialty:* European and American paintings, drawings and sculptures by the masters, from French Impressionists up through the present. *Mailing Add:* Rothschild Fine Arts Inc 205 West End Ave New York NY 10023

ROTHSCHILD, JOHN D
DEALER
b Chicago, Ill, June 22, 40. *Study:* Mass Inst Technol, BS, 62; Columbia Univ, MBA, 64. *Pos:* Owner, Rothschild Fine Arts Inc, currently. *Specialty:* European and American paintings, drawings and sculptures by the masters, from French impressionists up through the present. *Publ:* Contribr, I Love New York Guide, Macmillan. *Mailing Add:* Rothschild Fine Arts Inc 205 West End Ave New York NY 10023

ROTHSCHILD, JUDITH
PAINTER, COLLAGE ARTIST
b New York, NY. *Study:* Fieldston Sch, with Victor D'Amico & Alex Brook; Art Students League, with Reginald Marsh; Cranbrook Acad Art; Wellesley Col, BA(art hist); study with Hans Hofmann; Atelier 17, with Hayter. *Work:* Metrop Mus Art, Whitney Mus Am Art, New York; Fogg Art Mus, Harvard Univ, Cambridge, Mass; City Art Gallery, Auckland, New Zealand; First Nat Bank Chicago, Chicago & New York; and others. *Exhib:* The Non-Objective World, Annely Juda Gallery, London, Galleria Milan, Milan & Liatowich Gallery, Basle, 73-74; Gallery Gmurzynska, Cologne, 79-81; Thorne Art Gallery, NH, 82; and many other group & one-man shows. *Pos:* Staff consult, Fine Arts Work Ctr of Provincetown, 71-; corresp ed, Leonardo Mag, Europe, 71- *Teaching:* Artist in residence in painting, Univ Syracuse, 70-71; guest artist painting, Pratt Univ, summer 74 & RI Sch Design, summers 75, 76 & 77. *Awards:* Wellesley Achievement Award, 81. *Mem:* Am Fedn Arts; MacDowell Colony (mem bd). *Media:* Oil, Collage. *Mailing Add:* 345 E 93rd New York NY 10154

ROTHSTEIN, ARTHUR
PHOTOGRAPHER
b New York, NY, July 17, 15. *Study:* Columbia Col, New York, BA, 35. *Work:* Mus Mod Art, New York; George Eastman House, Rochester; Libr Cong & Smithsonian Inst, DC; Royal Photog Soc, London, Eng. *Exhib:* 1st Int Photog Expos, New York, 38; 1st Int Exhib Mod Art, Paris, 40; George Eastman House, Rochester, 56; Biblioteca Communal, Mican, 60; Smithsonian Inst, DC, 63; Western Heritage Mus, Omaha, Nebr, 79. *Collections Arranged:* Rothstein Collection, Libr Cong, 72; My Land, My People, George Eastman House, 76; The West, Forty Years Ago, Western Heritage Mus, 79; Ctr Creative Photography, Tucson, Ariz, 83. *Teaching:* Fac, Parsons Sch Design; prof Syracuse Univ & Mercy Col, 83. *Awards:* Exhib Excellence Award, 1st Int Photog Expos, New York, 38; Distinctive Merit, New York Art Dirs, 63; Int Understanding Award, Photo Soc Am, 68. *Bibliog:* Jack Hurley (auth), Portrait of a Decade, La State Press, 69; Archives

of American Art, J of Smithsonian Inst, Vol 17, No 1, 77; Hank O'Neal (auth), A Vision Shared, St Martins Press, 78. *Mem:* Fel Royal Photog Soc Gt Brit; fel Photog Hist Soc NY; Am Soc Mag Photogr (vpres, 47); Photog Adminr, New York (pres, 61-63). *Publ:* auth, Creative Color Photography, Chilton, 63; co-auth, Look at Us, Cowles, 70; auth, The Depression Years, Dover, 78; auth, Words and Pictures, Amphoto, 79; auth, The American west in the thirties, 81; and others. *Dealer:* Lee Witkin 41 E 57th St New York NY 10022. *Mailing Add:* 122 Sutton Manor New Rochelle NY 10805

ROTTERDAM, PAUL Z
PAINTER
b Austria, Feb 12, 39; US citizen. *Study:* Acad & Univ Vienna. *Work:* Graphische Sammlung Albertina, Vienna, Austria; Metrop Mus, New York; Musee Nat d'Art Moderne, Paris; Mus Mod Art, Guggenheim Mus, New York; and others. *Exhib:* 4th Biennial, Paris, 65; 8th Biennial, Tokyo, 65; Whitney Biennial Am Art, 75; Acquisitions, Guggenheim Mus, 75; Susan Caldwell Gallery, New York, 75; Mus de l'Abbaye St Croix, Les Sables d'Olonne, France, 76; Mus de Nice, France, 77; Birmingham Mus Art, Ala, 77; and others. *Teaching:* Lectr painting, Harvard Univ, 68- & Cooper Union Sch Art, 74-75. *Dealer:* Galerie Maeght Nine W 57th St New York NY; Galerie Maeght 13 Rue de Teheran Paris France. *Mailing Add:* 115 W Broadway New York NY 10013

ROUKES, NICHOLAS M
KINETIC ARTIST, WRITER
b San Jose, Calif, Nov 22, 25. *Study:* San Jose State Col, Calif; Fresno State Col, BA, 49; Stanford Univ, MA, 51. *Work:* Can Coun Art Bank, Ottawa. *Comn:* Kinetic Light, Provincial Judges Court; column, Calgary, Alta, 74. *Teaching:* Prof art educ & sculpture, Univ Calgary, Alta, 66-, prof art, currently. *Media:* Plastics. *Res:* New media for art, plastics, new art technology. *Publ:* Auth, Painting with Acrylics, 65; auth, Sculpture in Plastics, 68; auth, Crafts in Plastics, 70; auth, Plastics for Kinetic Art, 74; auth, Masters of Wood Sculpture, 80. *Mailing Add:* Dept of Art Univ of Calgary Calgary AB T2N 1N4 Canada

ROUSE, JOHN R
APPRAISER, CONSULTANT
b Cunningham, Kans. *Study:* Bethel Col, BA. *Pos:* Dir-cur, Wichita Art Asn, 72-; retired; fine arts appraiser & consult, currently. *Mem:* Am Asn Mus; Am Crafts Coun; Kans Mus Asn; Mountain Plains Mus Asn; Nat Asn Certified Antique & Art Appraisers. *Collection:* Old Staffordshire figures. *Mailing Add:* 115 S Rutan Wichita KS 67218

ROUSSEAU, IRENE VICTORIA
SCULPTOR, WRITER
Study: Hunter Col, with Tony Smith, AB; Claremont Grad Sch, MFA; NY Univ, PhD. *Work:* Scripps Col, Claremont, Calif; Univ Brazil, Campinas; and numerous pvt collections. *Exhib:* Drawing Exhib, Pa Mus Art, Philadelphia, 70; Univ Artists, Teachers 76, Bronx Mus Art, New York, 76; one-person exhib, Drew Univ, Madison, NJ, 76; New Jersey Currents, NJ State Coun Arts & Nat Endowment Arts, traveling, 79; Sculptors Exhib, Morris Mus Arts & Sci, Morristown, NJ, 79; On and Off the Wall, Newark Mus, NJ, 82. *Collections Arranged:* Language of Abstraction, 79 & Works on Paper, 79, Am Abstract Artists, Betty Parsons Gallery; American Abstract Artists: The Early Years, mus traveling show, 80 & 81; Transitions, Am Abstract Artists, Summit Art Ctr, 81; Abstraction in Action, City Gallery, New York, 82. *Teaching:* Asst prof, William Paterson Col, Wayne, NJ, 70-74 & 76. *Awards:* Squibb Sculpture Award; six First Prizes in NJ State juried exhibs in painting, sculpture, drawing, graphics and mixed media. *Bibliog:* Ruthann Williams (auth), Previews and reviews, NJ Music & Arts Mag, 4/71 & 10/72; Eileen Watkins (auth), A light touch, Sunday Star Ledger, NJ, 79; Richard Shepard (auth), Other views, In: Going Out Guide, New York Times, 1/11/82. *Mem:* Am Abstract Artists (pres, 79-82); Col Art Asn; Women's Caucus Art. *Res:* Space in light sculpture. *Publ:* Auth, American abstract artists, 9/81, Perle Fine, 6/82, De Stijl 1917-1931, 9/82, Hiroshi Murata, 1/83 & Nassos Daphnis: An artist in the art world, 5/83, Arts Mag. *Mailing Add:* 41 Sunset Dr Summit NJ 07901

ROUSSEAU-VERMETTE, MARIETTE
TAPESTRY ARTIST
b Trois Pistoles, PQ, Aug 29, 26. *Study:* Ecole Beaux Arts, Quebec, 48; Liebes Studio; Oakland Col Arts & Crafts, Calif. *Work:* Galerie Nat Can, Ottawa; Mus Quebec; Mus of Mod Art, Kyoto, Japan; Univ Vancouver Art Fac Hall; Vancouver Art Gallery. *Comn:* Theater stage curtains, J F Kennedy Ctr, Washington, DC, 71; tapestries, Macmillan Bloedel Hall, Vancouver, 68, Hall of Justice Perce, 68 & Hall of the Toronto Star, 71-72; Main Hall, Royal Bank, Toronto. *Exhib:* Biennales, Lausanne, Switz, 62, 65, 69, 71 & 76; Quebec & Ont Contemp Painters Centennial Exhib, 65; 300 Yrs Art, Nat Gallery Can, 67; Mus Mod Art, New York, 69; Mus Beaux Arts, Montreal, 61; Que Art Gallery, 72; Winnipeg Art Gallery, 76. *Pos:* Dir, Can Conf of Arts, 58-75; dir, Can Craft Coun, 74-75; dir, Royal Can Acad, 74-75. *Teaching:* Prof tapestry, ctr Art Ste-Adele, Que, 52-56; head fiber, Banff Sch art, 80- *Awards:* First Prize, PQ Art Contest, 57; Can Art Coun Traveling Bursary, 67; Cult Inst Rome, Italy Bursary, 72-73. *Bibliog:* Andre Kuenzi (auth), La Nouvelle Tapisserie, Bonvent, 73; Constantine Larsen (auth), Beyond Craft, The Art Fabric, 73; Madeleine Jarry (auth), La Tapisserie, Off du Livre, 74. *Mem:* Assoc Can Royal Acad (dir, 74-75); Asn Artistes Prof; World Craft Coun; Montreal Mus Fine Art. *Collection:* Canadian paintings, sculptures and tapestries; graphic art; Polish tapestries, icons and paintings. *Dealer:* Mira Goddard Gallery 22 Hazelton Toronto ON Can; Alice Pauli 7 ave de Rumine Lausanne 1005 Switz. *Mailing Add:* 373 Rue Morin Ste-Adele PQ J0R 1L0 Canada

ROUSSEL, CLAUDE PATRICE
SCULPTOR, INSTRUCTOR
b Edmundston, NB, July 6, 30. *Study:* Ecole Beaux-Arts, Montreal, PQ, 50-56; Can Coun Sr Traveling Fel, Europe, 61. *Work:* Smithsonian Inst, Washington, DC; NB Mus, St John; Confedn Art Gallery, Charlottetown, PEI; Portland Mus, Maine; Mt Allison Univ, Sackville, NB. *Comn:* Mural, Frederickton Airport, NB, 64; mural, NB Centennial Bldg, 66; monument, fishermen, Escuminac, NB, 69; exterior sculpture & interior mural, Univ Moncton Nursing Pavillion, 71; and 20 other archit projs. *Exhib:* Survey 69, Montreal Mus Fine Arts, 69; Confedn Art Gallery, 70; Air & Space Mus, Smithsonian Inst, 71; Man and His World, Montreal, 71; Owens Art Gallery, 75 & 79; Ctr d'Art, Drummond, 81; Ctr d'Art du Montreal, Royal, 82; and others. *Pos:* Asst cur, Beaverbrook Art Gallery, Fredericton, 59-61. *Teaching:* Instr art, Edmundston Pub Schs, 56-59 & Univ Moncton, 63- *Awards:* Allied Arts Medal, Royal Archit Soc Can, 64; St John City Hall Sculpture Competition, City of St John, 72; Winner of Sailing Olympics Sculpture Competition, Kingston, Ont, 76. *Bibliog:* Painting a province, Nat Film Bd, 60; articles, Arts Atlantic, fall 77 & spring, 83; and others. *Mem:* Can Artist Representation (Moncton rep, 72). *Media:* Wood, Stone. *Publ:* Coauth, Les Acadiens des Maritimes, In: Les Arts Visuels, 80. *Mailing Add:* 905 Amirault Dieppe Moncton NB E1A 1E1 Canada

ROVETTI, PAUL F
MUSEUM DIRECTOR, ADMINISTRATOR
b New Haven, Conn, Jan 29, 39. *Study:* Columbia Univ, BA, 61; Cooperstown Grad Prog, MA, 66. *Pos:* Dir, Mattatuck Mus, Waterbury, Conn, 66-69; dir, William Benton Mus of Art, Univ Conn, Storrs, 69- *Awards:* Scriven Found Fel, 65-66; Nat Endowment Arts Mus Prof Fel, 73. *Mem:* Am Asn Mus (mem coun, 78-81); New Eng Mus Asn (exec comt, 66-81, Conn rep, 69-78); Int Coun Mus. *Res:* Nineteenth century American painting; nineteenth century American folk art. *Publ:* Auth, Dwight W Tryon: A Retrospective Exhibition (catalog), Univ Conn Mus Art, 71; coauth, The American Earls (catalog), 72 & auth, Nineteenth Century Folk Painting: Our Spirited National Heritage, 73, William Benton Mus Art. *Mailing Add:* William Benton Mus of Art U-140 Univ of Conn Storrs CT 06268

ROWAN, DENNIS MICHAEL
PRINTMAKER, EDUCATOR
b Milwaukee, Wis, Jan 6, 38. *Study:* Univ Wis, BS, 62; Univ Ill, MFA, 64. *Work:* Art Inst Chicago; Boston Mus Fine Arts; Seattle Art Mus, Wash; Okla Art Ctr, Oklahoma City; Honolulu Acad Arts, Hawaii. *Exhib:* Boston Mus Fine Arts, 61, 64-65, 68-69 & 70; Walker Art Ctr, Minneapolis, 62; Chicago Art Inst, 62 & 66; Pa Acad Fine Arts, 63; Seattle Art Mus, Wash, 63-65, 67, 70 & 71; Okla Art Ctr, 68, 70 & 72; Miami Art Ctr, 73; Brooklyn Mus, NY, 73; Calif Palace Legion Honor, San Francisco, 73; Vienna Graphics Biennale, Austria, 73; US Nat Mus, Washington, DC, 74; Kansas City Art Inst, 75; 3rd Biennale Int de l'Image, Epinal, France, 75; and many others. *Teaching:* Prof art, Univ Ill, Urbana-Champaign, 64-, assoc ctr advan study, 71-, prof sch art & design, currently. *Awards:* Purchase Award, 2nd Biennale Int Gravure, Cracow, Poland, 68; Yorkshire Arts Asn Purchase Prize, Brit Int Print Biennale, 70; Juror's Prize, Graphikbiennale Wien, Europahaus, Vienna, Austria, 72. *Media:* Intaglio. *Publ:* Contribr, Prize-winning graphics, Vol 3, 65 & Vol 4, 66; contribr, John Ross & Clare Romano's Complete Printmaker, Free Press, New York & Collier-Macmillan Ltd, Toronto, 72; contribr, Walter Chamberlin's Etching & Engraving, Thames & Hudson, London, 72 & Viking Press, New York, 73. *Mailing Add:* 143 Fine Arts Bldg Univ Ill Champaign IL 61820

ROWAN, FRANCES PHYSIOC
PAINTER, PRINTMAKER
b Ossining, NY. *Study:* Randolph-Macon Woman's Col, 29-30; Cooper Union, cert, 36; also graphics with Harry Sternberg & woodcuts with Carol Summers. *Work:* Randolph-Macon Woman's Col, Lynchburg, Va; Freeport High Sch, NY; Cotton Inc. *Exhib:* Brooklyn Mus 11th Nat Print Show, 58; Audubon Artists, 58 & 59; Am Fedn Arts Traveling Show, 58-59; Knickerbocker Artists, 61; Silvermine Guild Artists 6th & 14th Nat Print Show, 66 & 80; one-man show, Sarasota Art Asn, 81. *Teaching:* Instr drawing & painting, Country Art Gallery, Westbury, NY, 55-66; instr drawing & painting, Five Towns Music & Art Found, 70-72; instr drawing, still life & figure, Longboat Key Art Ctr, 77- *Awards:* First Prizes, Hofstra Univ, 57 & Sarasota Art Asn, 79 & 82; Flax Award, Knickerbocker Artists, 61; and others. *Mem:* Prof Artists Guild; Silvermine Guild Artists. *Media:* Graphics. *Mailing Add:* 601 Broadway Box 453 Longboat Key FL 33548

ROWAN, HERMAN
PAINTER, EDUCATOR
b New York, NY, July 20, 23. *Study:* Cooper Union; San Francisco State Col; Kans State Col, BS; State Univ Iowa, MA & MFA. *Work:* Walker Art Ctr, Minneapolis; Brooklyn Mus, NY; Univ Notre Dame, South Bend, Ind; Columbus Mus, Ohio; San Diego Gallery Fine Arts, Calif. *Exhib:* Art USA, New York, 60; San Francisco Mus Nat Ann, 63; Southwest Ann, Houston Mus, 63; Walker Art Ctr Exhib, 65; Box-Top Art, Tour NZ Galleries, 71-72; Mitzi Landau Gallery, Los Angeles, 82. *Teaching:* Prof painting, Univ Minn, Minneapolis, 63- *Awards:* Lyman Award, Albright Gallery, 59; Purchase Prize, San Diego Gallery Fine Arts, 63. *Media:* Oil. *Mailing Add:* Dept Studio Arts Univ Minn Minneapolis MN 55455

ROWAN, (C) PATRICK
SCULPTOR, EDUCATOR
b Milwaukee, Wis, Jan 7, 37. *Study:* Univ Wis-Madison, BSArch, 62; Univ Wis-Milwaukee, BFA(painting), 69, MS(painting), 70; Univ Fla, Gainesville,

MFA(sculpture), 71. *Work:* Kearney State Col, Nebr; Univ Wis-Milwaukee; Joslyn Art Mus, Omaha, Nebr; Sheldon Art Gallery; Springfield Art Mus, Mo; and others. *Comn:* Doc sculpture, Niobrara Community Ctr, Nebr, 75; doc artwork, Weeping Water Hist Mus, Nebr, 77; outdoor sculpture, Sheldon Mem Art Gallery, Lincoln, Nebr, 79. *Exhib:* One-man sculpture exhibs, Gallery '72 & Joslyn Art Mus, Omaha, Nebr, 81; E Carolina Univ Nat Drawing Competition, Greenville, NC, 81; one-man exhibs, Concordia Col, 82, Ripon Col, 83, Univ S Colo, 83 & Adams State Col, 83; and others. *Teaching:* Instr, Univ Wis-Milwaukee, 69-70; prof sculpture, Univ Nebr-Lincoln, 71- *Awards:* Nebr Arts Coun Summer Grant, All-State Prog, 77; Woods Travel Grant, Univ Nebr-Lincoln, 79-83; and others. *Bibliog:* Art Editor (auth), Artist vs environment, Milwaukee J, 75, Weeping Water documentary, Lincoln Sun Newspapers, 76 & Patrick Rowan, Lincoln J & Star, 79. *Mem:* Nat Col Art Asn; Mid-Am Col Art Asn; Int Sculpture Ctr; Am Studies Col Asn; Archaeol Inst Am. *Media:* Wood, Pastels. *Publ:* Auth, Cybernetics and the Visual Arts, Univ Fla Press, 71; co-auth, The process of art, Weekender Mag, 76. *Mailing Add:* 5110 Lenox Lincoln NE 68510

ROWE, CHARLES ALFRED
PAINTER, DESIGNER
b Great Falls, Mont, Feb 7, 34. *Study:* Mont State Univ, 52-53; Southern Methodist Univ, 56-57; Univ Chicago, 57-58; Art Inst Chicago, BFA, 60; Tyler Sch Art, Philadelphia, MFA, 68; also with John Rogers Cox, Boris Margo & Max Brill. *Work:* Univ Del; Great Falls Pub Schs. *Comn:* Designed a coord arts coun symbol & related printed materials for Mont Arts Coun, Missoula, 73; designed numerous fabrics for major accounts for Galleon Fabrics, Inc, New York, 74- *Exhib:* One-man shows, C M Russell Mus, Great Falls, Mont, 73 & Pleiades Gallery, New York, 77; Butler Inst Art Mid-Year Show, Youngstown, Ohio, 73; Ball State Univ Nat Drawing & Small Sculpture Show, 74; Am Painters in Paris, France, 76-77; World Trade Ctr Exhib, New York, 79; and others. *Pos:* Graphic package designer, Am Can Co, Bellwood, Ill, 60-62; graphic designer, Abrams-Bannister Engraving, Inc, Greenville, SC, 62-64; artist in residence, Nat Endowment Arts & Humanities, 72-73. *Teaching:* Prof drawing & painting, Univ Del, 64-; vis artist, Univ Ariz, 83-84. *Awards:* Drawing of Distinction, Mead Painting of the Year Exhib, Atlanta, Ga, 64; Delaware Duck Stamp Winner, 81; Grant, Ctr Advanced Study, Univ Del, 81; and others. *Bibliog:* Artist in residence, Mont Arts, Vol 25, No 1; Artist employs original method and style, Great Falls Tribune, 10/72; Mary Hemple (auth), Charles Rowe, the creator of a new art form, Del Today Mag, 1/73. *Mailing Add:* 133 Aronimink Dr Chapel Hill Newark DE 19711

ROWE, REGINALD M
PAINTER, SCULPTOR
b New York, NY, Dec 8, 20. *Study:* Princeton Univ, BA, 44; Art Students League, with Louis Bosa, 46-47; Inst Allende, Univ Guanajuato, 58-59, MFA, 59. *Work:* McNay Mus, San Antonio; Arts Coun San Antonio; Univ Tex Health & Sci Ctr; San Antonio Mus Art. *Comn:* Mural & outdoor sculpture, Hemisfair 1968, San Antonio, Tex, 68. *Exhib:* One-man shows, Marion Koogler McNay Mus, San Antonio, Tex, 77, Tex Christian Univ, Ft Worth, Tex, 78; San Antonio Art Inst, 80; Robinson Gallery, Houston, 82; San Antonio Art Mus, 82. *Pos:* Chmn exhibs, Witte Mus, 65-67. *Teaching:* Instr painting & design, San Antonio Art Inst, 64-; vis artist, Univ NFla, 75. *Awards:* San Miguel Allende, 60. *Bibliog:* Ernest Hemingway (auth), catalog statement for first New York show, 52; reviews in Arts, Art News, Artweek, Pictures on Exhib, Times, Tribune & Art Int, 52-70. *Dealer:* Robinson Gallery 1200 Bissonnet Houston TX 77005. *Mailing Add:* 219 W Gramercy San Antonio TX 78212

ROWELL, MARGIT
HISTORIAN, CURATOR
b New Haven, Conn. *Study:* Inst Art Archeologie, MA; Univ Paris, PhD. *Collections Arranged:* Mondrian Retrospective, 71; Miro, Magnetic Fields (with catalog), 72; Jean Dubuffet, Retrospective (with catalog), 73; Frantisek Kupka, Retrospective (with catalog), 75; The Planar Dimension (with catalog), 79; Art of the Avant-garde in Russia: The George Costakis Collection (with catalog), 81; Julio Gonzalez, Retrospective (with catalog), 83. *Pos:* Cur, Solomon R Guggenheim Mus, 73-83 & Musee Nat Art Mod, Paris, 83- *Teaching:* Instr art hist, Sch Visual Arts, 69-72; instr contemp art, New Sch Social Res, 74. *Awards:* Frank Jewett Mather Award, Col Art Asn Am, 72; Guggenheim Found Grant, 76; Nat Endowment Arts Grant Mus Prof, 76. *Mem:* Int Asn Art Critics; Am Asn Mus; Int Coun Mus. *Res:* Twentieth century European art and aesthetics. *Publ:* Auth, Joan Miro, Abrams, 71; auth, La Peinture le geste, l'action, Klincksieck, Paris, 72. *Mailing Add:* Musee Nat Art Mod Place Beaubourg-Rue St Merri Paris 75191 10013 France

ROWLAND, MARY ADELE
PHOTOGRAPHER, EDUCATOR
b New Bedford, Mass, Dec 4, 15. *Study:* Carnegie-Mellon Univ; Univ Hawaii; Univ Southern Calif, BS, 38, MS, 42; Univ Calif, Berkeley, PhD, 49; study with Ansel Adams, Wynn Bullock, Imogen Cunningham, Jerry Uelsmann & Judy Dater. *Work:* Bibliot Nat, Paris, France; Libr Cong, Washington, DC; Oakland Art Mus, Calif; San Francisco Gen Hosp Med Ctr, Calif; Metrop Mus Mod Art, Manila, Philippines; and others. *Comn:* Wall murals, Harrah's of Tahoe, Nev, 76; color photomontages, Occidental Life, Los Angeles, Calif, 77; wall mural, Kapalua Bay Hotel, Maui, Hawaii, 79. *Exhib:* Friends of Photog Show, Carmel, Calif, 75; Haiku Imagery, Otago Art Mus, Dunedin, NZ, 79; plus others. *Teaching:* Assoc prof humanities & photog, Dom Col San Rafael, Calif, 51-74, artist in residence, 74- *Awards:* Photog Awards, Oakland Art Mus, 78, Sonoma State Univ, 78 & San Francisco Women Artists, 79. *Bibliog:* Derek Paterson (auth), Compressed images, Photo & Audio, NZ,

8/79; Jeff Greer (auth), Nun follows ancient artistic tradition, Independent-J, San Rafael, Calif, 1/80; and others. *Mem:* San Francisco Women Artists (bd dirs, 75-78); Soc Photog Educ; Friends of Photog, Carmel, Calif. *Media:* Color Photomontage. *Dealer:* Ellen Terry Lemer 1100 Park Ave New York NY 10028. *Mailing Add:* Dept of Photog Dominican Col San Rafael CA 94901

ROYSHER, HUDSON (BRISBINE)
DESIGNER, ADMINISTRATOR
b Cleveland, Ohio, Nov 21, 11. *Study:* Cleveland Art Inst, grad dipl, 34; Western Reserve Univ, MS, 34; Univ Southern Calif, MFA, 48. *Work:* Univ Buffalo, NY; Univ Southern Calif, Los Angeles; Syracuse Univ, NY; Calif State Univ, Los Angeles; Bethune-Cookman Col, Daytona Beach, Fla. *Exhib:* US State Dept Traveling Exhib, 50-52; Eleven Southern Californians, De Young Mem Mus, San Francisco, Calif, 52; Smithsonian Inst Traveling Exhib, 53-55; Designer Craftsmen of the West Traveling Exhib, 57; Masters of Contemporary American Crafts Exhib, Brooklyn Mus, 61. *Teaching:* Asst prof indust design, Univ Southern Calif, 39-42; head div indust design, Chouinard Art Inst, 45-50; prof art, Calif State Univ, Los Angeles, 50-70, chmn dept art, 70-75, prof emer, 75- *Awards:* Spec Award for Continued Excellence, Cleveland Mus Art, 40 & 46; Outstanding Professor Award, 66 & Outstanding Educator Award, 72, Trustees Calif State Univ & Col. *Bibliog:* A welded steel education, Design Mag, 1/51; H E Winter (auth), Three American silversmiths, Amerika, 5/53; Churches and temples, Progressive Archit, 10/56. *Mem:* Indust Designers Soc Am; Am Asn Univ Prof; Southern Calif Designer Craftsmen; Am Craftsman's Coun; Asn Calif State Univ Prof (chap pres, 63-65 & 71-72). *Mailing Add:* 1784 S Santa Anita Ave Arcadia CA 91006

ROZMAN, JOSEPH JOHN
PAINTER, PRINTMAKER
b Milwaukee, Wis, Dec 26, 44. *Study:* Univ Wis, Milwaukee, BFA(with honors), 67, MFA, 69. *Work:* Milwaukee Art Mus, Wis; Southwest Tex State Col; Univ Wis, Milwaukee; Charles Wustum Mus Fine Arts, Racine, Wis; and others. *Comn:* Complete ed of etchings for membership drive, Milwaukee Art Ctr, 69; Award Emblem Design, Lakefront Festival of Arts, Milwaukee Art Ctr, 73 & 77; PBS Great TV Auction (poster), WMVS TV, 78. *Exhib:* 19th, 20th & 21st Boston Printmakers Nat, Boston Mus Fine Arts, 67-69; Nat Print & Drawing Exhib, Okla Art Ctr, Oklahoma City, 67-68 & 72; Int NW Printmakers Exhib, Seattle Art Mus & Portland Art Ctr, 68 & 69; Printmaking: Wisconsin Editions, Milwaukee Art Mus, 72; one-man show, Milwaukee Art Mus, 73 & Joy Horwich Gallery, Chicago, 80 & 83; The Collagraph--A Survey, Pratt Graphics Ctr, New York, 75; Artists/Toys Exhib, Milwaukee Art Mus, 77 & 79; Works on Paper, Art Inst Chicago, 78; Wisconsin Directions Two: Here & Now, Milwaukee Art Mus, 78; Glass/ Backwards: Reverse Painting on a Transparent Support, 500-1979 AD, John Michael Kohler Arts Ctr, Sheboygan, Wis; Watercolor USA, Springfield Art Mus, 81; Prints & Multiples, Art Inst Chicago, 81; and others. *Teaching:* Instr printmaking, Milwaukee Art Mus, 68-76; instr printmaking & painting, Carthage Col, 69-72; vis lectr art, Univ Wis-Parkside, 70-71; instr printmaking & design, Layton Sch Art & Design, 73-74; assoc prof printmaking, painting, photography & film, Mt Mary Col, Wis, 75-; artist in residence, Univ Wis-Platteville, 83. *Awards:* Purchase Award, 23rd Nat Boston Printmakers Exhib, De Cordova Mus, 71; Main Award in Painting, Lakefront Festival of Arts, 77, 79 & 81-82; John G Curtis Award, Art Inst Chicago, 81. *Bibliog:* James Auer (auth), They call him the Wizard of Roz, Milwaukee J, 3/11/73; Genene Grimm (auth), Joe Rozman: The busiest boy on the block, Art Scene Mag, 2/69; Tracy Lawrence (auth), Joseph Rozman, New Art Examiner, 10/80. *Mem:* Boston Printmakers; Am Film Inst, Art Inst Chicago; Racine Art Asn. *Mailing Add:* 4419 Lindermann Ave Racine WI 53405

ROZZI (JAMES A)
PAINTER, SCULPTOR
b Pittsburgh, Pa, Jan 22, 21. *Work:* State Capitol, Carson City, Nev; Favell Mus, Klamath Falls, Ore; Elks Lodge, Las Vegas; State Bicentennial Comt, Nev. *Comn:* Mural, Valley of Fire State Park Visitors Ctr, Nev, 68. *Exhib:* US Army Nat Art Exhib, Dallas, Tex, 45; Heldorado Western Art Show, Las Vegas, 69-75; Death Valley Western Art Show, Calif, 70-75; Nev Bicentennial Calendar Competition, 75; George Phippen Mem Art Show, Prescott, Ariz, 75. *Pos:* Pres, Arts & Crafts Guild, Las Vegas, 63-65. *Teaching:* Teacher adult educ, San Bernardino Valley Col, Calif, 49-60; teacher drawing, Las Vegas Art League, 67-69. *Awards:* First Place Purchase Awards, Elks Lodge, Las Vegas, 69, 73 & 74; First Place Trophy for Oils, Death Valley 49'ers, 71; Third Place Medal, George Phippen Mem Comt, 75. *Bibliog:* Ray Chesson (auth), article, Rev J, 71; Florine Lawlor (auth), article, Las Vegas Sun Newspaper, 71. *Mem:* Nat Cowboy Hall Fame; Nat Soc Lit & Arts. *Media:* Oil, Watercolor; Bronze. *Publ:* Illusr, Loma Linda Med Col Handbook, 51; illusr, San Bernardino Valley Col Handbook, 58; auth, Screen Process Mag, 58; illusr, Las Vegas Jazz Festival Mag, 63; illusr, True West Mag, 71. *Mailing Add:* 1041 Franklin Ave Las Vegas NV 89104

RUBELLO, DAVID JEROME
PAINTER, PHOTOGRAPHER
b Detroit, Mich, Sept 3, 35. *Study:* La Accademia Di Belle Arti, Rome, with Franco Gentilini, BFA, 61; Det Kongelige Akademi, Copenhagen, with Richard Mortensen, 63-66; Univ Mich, Ann Arbor, with Guy Palazzola, MFA, 72. *Work:* Mus Erotic Art, San Francisco, Calif; Accademia Di Belle Arti, Rome, Italy; Mus Pa State Univ, University Park; New Detroit Murals, Inc, Mich; Univ Mich, Ann Arbor; and others. *Comn:* Mural-painting, New Detroit, Inc, Mich, 72; mural-painting, Residential Col, Ann Arbor, Mich, 73. *Exhib:* One-man show, Slusser Art Gallery, Univ Mich, 78; Int Juried Exhib, Coos Bay Mus Art, Ore, 79; Works on Paper, Md State Arts Coun, Annapolis,

81; Novo Gallery, New York, 82 & 83; GMB Gallery, Detroit, 82 & 83. *Teaching:* Lectr, Univ Mich, Ann Arbor, 73-74; asst prof art, Pa State Univ, University Park, 74-80; assoc prof art, Towson State Univ, Md, 80-81. *Awards:* Ford Found Grants, Pa State Univ, 79 & 80; Fel, Va Ctr Creative Arts, 81. *Bibliog:* Diane Kirkpatrick (auth), David Rubello, John Dietrich, 73; Murals in Detroit, Detroit Free Press, 8/14/74; article, Art Diary, 83. *Mem:* Col Art Asn. *Media:* Acrylic, Wood. *Dealer:* Barbara Fiedler 1621 21st St NW Washington DC 20009; Novo Gallery New York NY. *Mailing Add:* 1322 E Branch Rd State College PA 16801

RUBEN, ALBERT
PAINTER

b New Orleans, La, Dec 4, 18. *Study:* Univ Calif, Los Angeles, BA(hon; art), 41; Art Students League, with Robert Brackman & F V Dumond, 44-46. *Work:* Elizabeth Greenshields Found, Montreal. *Exhib:* Solo exhib, Regina Gallery, New York, 55, Studio Gallery Workshop, New York, 59 & Doll & Richards, Boston, 61; Butler Mus Am Art, 60; Nat Acad Ann Exhib, New York, 72; Allied Artists Am Ann Exhib, New York, 75-78. *Teaching:* Instr painting, Pels Sch Art, New York, 65-66 & Montserrat Sch Art, Mass, 73-74. *Awards:* Gold Medals, Am Veterans Art Soc, 57 & Rockport Art Asn, 68 & 80. *Mem:* Allied Artists Am; Rockport Art Asn; North Shore Art Asn. *Media:* Oils. *Mailing Add:* Bearskin Neck Rockport MA 01966

RUBEN, LEONARD
DESIGNER, EDUCATOR

b St Paul, Minn, June 3, 21. *Study:* Pratt Inst, cert, 48, BFA, 50; Columbia Univ, MA, 61; NY Univ, PhD, 70. *Work:* Designers Register, Nat Endowment Arts, Washington, DC; Mus Art Sci & Indust, Bridgeport, Conn; Young & Rubicam, NY. *Exhib:* Clio Awards, New York, 69-74; Am Inst Graphic Arts, 73; Int Broadcasters Award, Hollywood, 73; Int Film & TV Festival, New York, 73-75; Designers Register, Nat Endowment Arts, Washington, DC, 74-75. *Pos:* Art dir, Young & Rubicam, New York, 51-60; creative dir, Lake, Spiro, Shurman, Memphis, Tenn, 68-69; pres, Ruben & Ruben, Austin, Tex, 72-78. *Teaching:* Prof advert, Univ Tex, Austin, 78; F J Heyne Centennial Prof Commun, 83. *Awards:* Silver Medal, Int Film & TV Festival, 73-75; Spec Award, Houston Art Dirs Club, 79; Teaching Award, Col Commun, Univ Tex, Austin, 83. *Mem:* Dallas-Ft Worth Soc Visual Commun. *Media:* Film Video Tape. *Publ:* Designer, Augustus Vincent Tack, 72; designer, Color Forum, 72; designer, The Twenties, 73. *Mailing Add:* 16821 S Ridge Lane Austin TX 78734

RUBEN, RICHARDS
PAINTER, EDUCATOR

b Los Angeles, Calif, Nov 29, 25. *Study:* Chouinard Art Inst. *Work:* Wooster Mus, Mass; Brooklyn Mus, NY; Los Angeles Co Mus Art; Corcoran Gallery Art, Washington, DC; Pasadena Art Mus, Calif. *Exhib:* First Paris Biennial, France, 59; Whitney Mus Am Art, 62-63 & 64; Arte de America y Espana, Madrid, Spain, 63; San Francisco Mus Art, Calif, 71; one-man exhib, Johnson Mus, Cornell Univ; Harm Bouckaert Gallery, New York, 81. *Teaching:* Asst prof drawing & painting, Pomona Col, 58-62; asst prof drawing & painting, NY Univ, 63-82; instr drawing & painting, Pratt Inst, 67-71; New York Studio Sch, summer 81. *Awards:* Tiffany Grant, 54; Tamarind Fel, 61; Nat Endowment Arts Fel, 80-81. *Mailing Add:* 85 Mercer St New York NY 10012

RUBENSTEIN, LEWIS W
PAINTER, PRINTMAKER

b Buffalo, NY, Dec 15, 08. *Study:* Harvard Univ, AB, 30; Bacon Traveling Fel, 31-33; painting with Leger & Ozenfant, Paris, fresco with Rico Lebrun, Rome, lithography with Emil Ganso, New York & sumi with Keigetsu, Tokyo. *Work:* Ford Found, New York; Am Univ, Washington, DC; Vassar Col Art Gallery, Poughkeepsie, NY; and others. *Comn:* Frescoes, Fogg Art Mus, 33 & 35 & Busch-Reisinger Mus, Cambridge, Mass, 37; murals, Post Off, US Sect Fine Arts, Wareham, Mass, 40 & Jewish Ctr, Buffalo, 50; Marine Midland Nat Bank, 65; and others. *Exhib:* Whitney Mus Am Art, 38; Nat Acad Design, 46, 52, 56 & 63; Libr Cong, Washington, DC, 52-60; Soc Am Graphic Artists, New York, 52-81; Am Watercolor Soc, New York, 55 & 64; retrospective, Schenectady Mus, NY, 75 & Barrett House, Poughkeepsie, NY, 79 & 83; and others. *Pos:* Illusr, Foreign Serv J, 58-66. *Teaching:* Instr fresco painting, Boston Mus Sch Art, 37-38; prof painting, Vassar Col, 39-74. *Awards:* Am Artists Group & Knobloch Prizes, Soc Am Graphic Artists, 52 & 54; Fulbright Grant, Japan, 57-58; Fairfield Award, Silvermine Guild Artists, 59. *Bibliog:* Erica Beckh Rubenstein (auth), Lewis Rubenstein's time painting, Vassar Alumnae Mag, 5/57; Masao Ishizaka (auth), Rubenstein and his sumi painting, Hoshun, Japan, 2/25/59; Beatrice Schuller Cohen (auth), Lewis Rubenstein and his time paintings, Am Artist, 11/78. *Mem:* Soc Am Graphic Artists; Dutchess Co Art Asn. *Publ:* Auth, Fresco painting today, Am Scholar, 35; auth, Time Painting (films), 56-57 & Ceremony for a New Planet (film), 72, Vassar Col; coauth, Psalm 104 (film), Weston Woods Studios, 70. *Mailing Add:* 153 College Ave Poughkeepsie NY 12603

RUBENSTEIN, MERIDEL
PHOTOGRAPHER

b Detroit, Mich, Mar 26, 48. *Study:* Sarah Lawrence Col, BA, 70; Mass Inst Technol, with Minor White, 72-73; Univ NMex, with Beaumont Newhall, Van Deren Coke & Tom Barrow, MA, 74, MFA, 77. *Work:* Bibliotheque Nat, Paris; Ctr Creative Photog, Univ Ariz; Denver Art Mus; Mus Kunst & Gewerbe, Hamburg, Ger; NMex Mus Fine Arts, Santa Fe. *Exhib:* Solo exhibs, La Gente de la Luz, NMex Mus Fine Arts, Santa Fe, 77 & Mus Kunst & Gewerbe, Hamburg, Ger, 79, The Lowriders, NMex Mus Fine Arts, Santa Fe, 80 & Artists Space, New York, 81 & Lifelines, Ctr Creative Photog, Tucson,

83; The Portrait Extended, Mus Contemp Art, Chicago, 80; Eleven Photographers from Santa Fe, Int Festival Photog, Arles, France, 81; Unraveling Sound--A Ranch, Paris Biennale, Musee l'Art Mod, Paris, 82. *Teaching:* Instr photog, Univ NMex, Albuquerque, 76-78 & Col Santa Fe, 76-80; vis lectr photog & art hist, Univ Colo, Boulder, 80-83. *Awards:* Guggenheim Fel Photog, 81-82; Photog Survey Grant, 82 & Visual Arts Fel, 83, Nat Endowment Arts. *Bibliog:* Van Deren Coke (auth), Photography in New Mexico, Univ NMex Press, 79; Dana Asbury (auth), article, Popular Photog, 2/83. *Mem:* Soc Photog Educ; Friends Photog; Santa Fe Ctr Photog. *Publ:* Auth, La Gente de la Luz, NMex Mus Fine Arts, 77; auth, Photography in New Mexico, 1/77 & Alternative images, 9/79, Afterimage; auth, article, Newslett Friends Photog, 78. *Mailing Add:* Rte 2 Box 305A Santa Fe NM 87501

RUBEY, TONY (GEORGE ANTON)
PRINTMAKER, EDUCATOR

b Cincinnati, Ohio, May 12, 52. *Study:* Miami Univ, Ohio, BFA, 74; Univ Wis, Madison, MA, 78, MFA, 79. *Work:* Okla Arts Ctr; Alaska State Mus, Juneau; Atlantic-Richfield Co, Anchorge, Alaska; Dulin Gallery Art. *Comn:* Photo-lithographs, Alaska State One Per Cent for Arts Proj, Anchorage, 82. *Exhib:* Collage and Assemblage, Miss Mus Art, Jackson, 81; Lithographs and Constructions, Okla Arts Ctr, 81; Dulin Nat Print Exhib, 82; Colorprint Nat, Tex Tech Univ, 83; solo exhib, Alaska State Mus, Juneau, 83. *Pos:* Studio dir printmaking, Visual Arts Ctr Alaska, Anchorage, 80- *Teaching:* Vis instr printmaking & drawing, Univ Okla, Norman, 79-80; instr printmaking, Univ Alaska, Anchorage, 82- *Awards:* Alaska State Coun Arts Fel, 83. *Mem:* Col Art Asn; Northwest Printmakers Orgn. *Media:* Etching, Lithography. *Dealer:* Miriam Perlman 505 N Lakeshore Dr Suite 5410 Chicago IL 60611; Toni Birckhead Gallery 342 W Fourth St Cincinnati OH 45211. *Mailing Add:* SRA Box 2053 G Anchorage AK 99507

RUBIDOUX (RUBIDOUX EARLY JOHNSON)
PAINTER, DESIGNER

b Riverside, Calif. *Study:* Art Inst Chicago; Inst Design, Ill; Inst Technol, Chicago; with Moholy-Nagy & Archipenko, 45-46; Univ Ga, BFA, 51; also with James Johnson Sweeney. *Work:* Ga Mus Art, Univ Ga, Athens; Heublein, Farmington, Conn. *Comn:* Murals, paintings, designs in various media for two cargo ships, comn by John Conrad for Farrell Lines, New York, 80. *Exhib:* Chicago & Vicinity Shows, Art Inst Chicago, 30-41; Southeastern Ann, High Mus, Atlanta, 48-49; New Eng Ann, Silvermine Guild, Conn, 59-61; Seventh Ann New Haven Festival, Mus Art, Sci & Indust, Bridgeport, Conn, 60-61; Stamford Ann, Stamford Mus, Conn, 64-65; Eastern States Art Exhib, Springfield Mus Fine Arts, Mass, 65-67. *Pos:* Art ed & art dir magazines, Henry Holt & Co, Chicago, 51-58. *Teaching:* Instr design & crafts, Dept Art, Univ Ga, 50-51; instr & founder art prog, Bateman Pvt Sch, 60-61. *Awards:* Three Shorter Awards, Art Fac Exhib, Univ Ga, 51; Barnum Festival Award, Mus Art, Sci & Indust, Bridgeport, Conn, 66; Nat Christmas Seal Award, Am Lung Asn, 74. *Mem:* Washington Art Asn, Conn; Silvermine Guild Ctr Arts, Conn; Audubon Artists, New York. *Mailing Add:* 755A Heritage Village Southbury CT 06488

RUBIN, ARNOLD GARY
HISTORIAN

b Richmond, Va, July 24, 37. *Study:* Rensselaer Polytech Inst, 55-60, BArch; Ind Univ, Bloomington, MA(art hist), 64, PhD(art hist), 69. *Collections Arranged:* Sculpture of Black Africa: Paul Tishman Collection (with catalog), Los Angeles Co Mus Art, 68; Yoruba Sculpture in Los Angeles Collections (with catalog), Pomona Col, Claremont, Calif, 69; Sculptor's Eye: The African Art Collection of Mr & Mrs Chiam Gross, Mus African Art, Washington, DC. *Teaching:* Assoc prof art of Africa, Oceania & Native Am, Univ Calif, Los Angeles, 67- *Awards:* Foreign Area Fel Prog Dissertation Res Grant, Am Coun Learned Socs/Social Sci Res Coun, Ford Found, 64-66; Fulbright-Hays African Area Studies Ctr Fac Res Grant, Dept Health, Educ & Welfare, 69-70. *Mem:* Col Art Asn Am. *Res:* Art of Africa, Oceania, Native America, especially the Benue River Valley of Northern Nigeria. *Publ:* Auth, Bronzes of the Middle Benue, WAfrican J Archaeol, 73 & Accumulation: Power & display in African sculpture, 75, Art Forum. *Mailing Add:* Dept of Art Dickson Art Ctr Univ of Calif Los Angeles CA 90024

RUBIN, DAVID S
CURATOR, CRITIC

b Los Angeles, Calif, June 18, 49. *Study:* Univ Calif Los Angeles, AB(philos), 72; Harvard Univ, MA(art hist), 74. *Collections Arranged:* Paper Art (auth, catalog), 77, Black and White are Colors (auth, catalog), 79, Recent Los Angeles Painting, 79 & Contemporary Triptychs (auth, catalog), 82, Galleries of the Claremont Cols; Imaginative Sculpture (auth, catalog), Security Pac Nat Bank, 82; Gary Lloyd, A Survey, Santa Monica Col, 83. *Pos:* Asst dir, Galleries of the Claremont Cols; contrib ed, Arts Mag, New York, 79-81; cur, Los Angeles Visual Arts, 82; dir, Santa Monic Col Art Gallery, 82-83; dir exhibs, San Francisco Art Inst, 83-; adj cur, San Francisco Mus Mod Art, 83- *Teaching:* Lectr art hist, Sch Visual Arts, New York, 76-77; asst prof art hist, Scripps Col, Claremont, Calif, 77-82. *Awards:* Nat Endowment for Arts Mus fel, Fogg Art Mus, 75-76; summer fel, Solomon R Guggenheim Mus, 76. *Mem:* Col Art Asn; Int Asn Art Critics; Am Asn Mus; Art Mus Asn. *Res:* Contemporary art, twentieth century art, automatism, abstract expressionism, Southern Calif art. *Publ:* Contribr, Jacques Villon, Fogg Art Mus, 76; auth, critical reviews of exhibitions, 77 & auth, A case for content: Jackson Pollock's subject was the automatic gesture, 79, Arts Mag; and others. *Mailing Add:* 212 Divisadero St San Francisco CA 94117

RUBIN, DONALD VINCENT
SCULPTOR
b New York, NY, July 10, 37. *Exhib:* Soc Animal Artists Exhib/Conv, NY, 79; one-man shows, Brass Door Galleries, Houston, 77, Hunter Gallery, San Francisco, 77, Indian Paint Brush, Vail, Colo, 77-81 & Huntsville Mus Art, Ala, 78; Nat Sculpture Soc 47th Ann Exhib, New York, 80; and many others. *Pos:* Dr Dirs, Huntsville Mus Art, currently. *Awards:* Richman Award for Sculptures, Salmagundi Club, 75, 76, 77 & 80, DeBellis Award, 79; Elliot Liskin Sculpture Award, 81; and others. *Bibliog:* Ralph Perrill (auth), Capturing the freedom and toughness of the Old West, SW Art Mag, 9/77; Ralph Perrill (auth), Donald Rubin (Huntsville Alabama), Art Voices South Mag, 9-10/78; cover photog, SW Art Mag, 12/78. *Mem:* Am Artists Prof League; Soc Animal Artists; Artists Fellowship; Salmagundi Club. *Media:* Bronze. *Dealer:* J N Bartfield Art Galleries 45 W 57th St New York NY 10019; Indian Paint Brush 183 Gore Creek Dr Vail CO 81657. *Mailing Add:* 305 Meadowbrook Dr Huntsville AL 35803

RUBIN, IDA ELY
CONSULTANT, WRITER
b New York, NY. *Study:* Wells Col, Aurora, NY, BA(with high honors), 44; NY Univ Inst Fine Arts, 44-49; Belg-Am Educ fel, Brussels, 51. *Collections Arranged:* The Guennol Collection (ed, catalog), Metrop Mus Art, New York, 69; Collection of Mr and Mrs John D Rockefeller, III, NY; Collection of Mr and Mrs David Rockefeller, NY; and others. *Pos:* Exec Dir, 20th Int Cong Art Hist, Columbia Univ & NY Univ, 59-61; dir develop, Inst Fine Arts, NY Univ, 62-64; spec consult, Art Gallery, Ctr Inter-Am Rels, New York, 66-69. *Teaching:* Lectr art of Latin Am, Manhattanville Col, Purchase, NY, 70-71. *Mem:* Univ Andes Found; Am Found; Coun Arts Mass Inst Technol; and others. *Res:* Cross-cultural influences of American and European art. *Publ:* Ed, Acts of the 20th International Congress of Art History, 4 vols, Princeton Univ, 63; ed, The Drawings of Morris Graves, New York Graphic Soc, 75; auth, Text on Eduardo Ramirez Villamizar, In: Panorama Artistico Colombiano, Lithografia Arco, Bogota, 77; and others. *Mailing Add:* Indian Head Rd Riverside CT 06878

RUBIN, IRWIN
PAINTER, DESIGNER
b Brooklyn, NY, July 26, 30. *Study:* Brooklyn Mus Sch Art; Cooper Union Art Sch; Yale Univ, BFA & MFA. *Exhib:* Fla State Univ, 60; Baltimore Mus Art, 60; Bertha Schaefer Gallery, NY, 60-63; Stable Gallery, NY, 64; Byron Gallery, 65; and others. *Pos:* Art dir, McGraw-Hill Bk Co, New York, 58-63; art dir, Harcourt Brace Jovanovich, Inc, New York, 71- *Teaching:* Instr drawing & color design, Univ Tex, 55; asst prof, Fla State Univ, 56-58; instr, Pratt Inst, Brooklyn, 64-; assoc prof art Cooper Union Art Sch, 67- *Publ:* Auth, Permanency in collage, Arts Mag, 57. *Mailing Add:* Croton Lake Rd Mt Kisco NY 10549

RUBIN, LAWRENCE
DEALER, COLLECTOR
b New York, NY, Feb 22, 33. *Study:* Brown Univ, BA, 55; Univ Paris. *Pos:* Dir, M Knoedler & Co Inc, New York, currently. *Specialty:* Nineteenth and twentieth century painting and sculpture; painters Stella, Motherwell, Diebenkorn, Graves, Ferber, Bannard, Olitski, Roth, Dzubas; estates of Alexander Calder & David Smith; Adolph and Ester Gottlieb Found. *Collection:* Contemporary painting and sculpture. *Mailing Add:* 19 E 70th St New York NY 10021

RUBIN, MARJORIE J(OAN)
TEXTILE ARTIST, WEAVER
b Chicago, Ill, Jan 9, 55. *Study:* Calif Col Arts & Crafts, BFA(textile arts), 78, cert(gallery management), 78. *Comn:* Fluctuation (fiber construction), Crocker Nat Bank, San Francisco, Calif, 79; Stratosphere (fiber construction), Crocker Nat Bank, Sacramento, Calif, 80; Undercurrent (fiber construction), Home Savings & Loan, Tiberon, Calif, 80. *Exhib:* First All Colo Show, Denver Art Mus, 74; Award Exchange Exhib, Corcoran Mus, Washington, DC, 78; Designer Craftsman, Richmond Art Ctr, Calif, 77 & 78; Objects 79 Nat Exhib, Western Colo Ctr Arts, Grand Junction, 79; Tradition & Change Nat Crafts Exhib, Houston Designer Craftsman, Tex, 80; Eight Contemp Weavers, Vorpal Gallery, San Francisco, Calif, 81; Fiberous Directions Invitational Exhib, Salem Art Asn Gallery, Ore, 81. *Teaching:* Instr weaving & textiles, Walnut Creek Civic Arts Ctr, Calif, 81-; substitute instr color Xerox & textiles, Pacific Basin Sch Textile Arts, Berkeley, Calif, 81- *Awards:* Third Place Award, Calif State Exposition, 77; First Place Award, Calif State Exposition, 78. *Mem:* Am Crafts Council; Artists Equity; Handweavers Guild Am; Fiberworks Ctr Textile Arts. *Media:* Natural Fiber, Color Xerox Transfers. *Publ:* Contribr, Fiberarts design book, Fiberarts Mag, 80. *Mailing Add:* 358 50th St Oakland CA 94607

RUBIN, SANDRA
PRINTMAKER, LITHOGRAPHER
b Denver, Colo. *Study:* Stanford Univ; Tex Christian Univ, BFA, 67, MFA, 70. *Work:* Ft Worth Art Mus, Tex; Mus NMex, Santa Fe; Univ Ark Gallery, Fayetteville; Univ Colo Gallery, Colorado Springs; Artlink Artspace, Ft Wayne, Ind. *Exhib:* Handmade Paper Objects, Santa Barbara Mus Art, Calif, 76, Oakland Mus, Calif, 77, Inst Contemp Art, Boston, 77, Johnson Mus, Cornell Univ, Ithaca, NY, 77 & Jacksonville Mus Art, Fla, 77; Southwestern Prints & Drawings, Dallas Mus Fine Arts, 78; Fire & Water, Paper as Art, Rockland Ctr for Arts, West Nyack, NY, 80; and others. *Teaching:* Assoc prof printmaking & papermaking, Univ Tex, Arlington, 70-, assoc prof art, currently. *Awards:* Univ Tex, Arlington Organized Res Grant, study handmade paper in Spain, 76 & study handmade paper in Japan, 79; Nat

Endowment Arts Ctr for Book Arts Grant, Papermaking Symposium, 77. *Mem:* Col Art Asn Am. *Media:* Intaglio, Embossment. *Dealer:* Adele M Fine Arts Gallery Dallas TX. *Mailing Add:* 4312 Bellaire Dr S Apt 222 Ft Worth TX 76109

RUBIN, WILLIAM
CURATOR, HISTORIAN
b New York, NY, Aug 11, 27. *Study:* Columbia Univ, AB, MA & PhD; Univ Paris. *Collections Arranged:* Dada, Surrealism & Their Heritage (auth, catalog), 68; New Am Painting & Sculpture (auth, catalog), 69; Stella (auth, catalog), 72, Picasso (auth, catalog), 72 & Miro (auth, catalog), 73, Mus Mod Art; Gerald Murphy (auth, catalog), 74, Anthony Caro (auth, catalog), 75, Andre Masson (auth, catalog), 76 & Cezanne: The Late Work (auth, catalog), 77; Picasso: A Retrospective (auth, catalog), 80; Giorgio DeChirico (auth, catalog), 82. *Pos:* Am art ed, Art Int Mag, 59-64; chief cur painting & sculpture, Mus Mod Art, New York, 68-73; dir painting & sculpture, 73-; trustee, Sarah Lawrence College, 80- *Teaching:* Prof art hist, Sarah Lawrence Col, 52-67; prof art hist, City Univ New York Grad Div, 60-68; adj prof art hist, NY Univ Inst Fine Arts, 68- *Awards:* Chevalier French Legion of Honor, Officier dans l'ordre des Arts et Lettres, 79. *Publ:* Auth, Modern sacred art and the Church of Assy, 61, Dada and surrealist art, 69; plus others. *Mailing Add:* Museum of Modern Art 11 W 53rd St New York NY 10019

RUBINFIEN, LEO H
PHOTOGRAPHER
b Chicago, Ill, Aug 16, 53. *Study:* Reed Col; Calif Inst Arts, BFA, 74; Yale Univ Sch Art, MFA, 76. *Work:* Bibliot Nat, Paris; San Francisco Mus Mod Art, Calif; Univ Mass Art Mus, Amherst; Mus Mod Art, New York; Corcoran Gallery Art. *Exhib:* Solo exhibs, Castelli Gallery, New York, 81 & Fraenkel Gallery, San Francisco, 82; The New Color, Int Ctr Photog, New York, 81; New Am Color Photog, Inst Contemp Arts, London, 81; Color & Colored, San Francisco Mus Mod Art, Calif, 81; Color Photog, George Eastman House, Rochester, NY, 81; Color in the Street, Calif Mus Photog, 83. *Teaching:* Instr photog, Swarthmore Col, 77; instr photog, Sch Visual Arts, 78-; asst prof art, Fordham Univ, 81-; vis lectr, Cooper Union, 82. *Awards:* Guggenheim Found Fel, 82-83. *Bibliog:* Ben Lifson (auth), Cons of collections, Village Voice, 7/22/81; Pete Karmel (auth), The Anxious Moment, Soho News, 11/4/81; Prudence Carlson (auth), article, Art in Am, 3/82. *Publ:* Auth, Love-Hate Relations, Artforum, 78; auth, The Man in the Crowd, In: Photography in Print, Touchstone Press, 81. *Dealer:* Light Gallery 724 5th Ave New York NY; Fraenkel Gallery 55 Grant Ave San Francisco CA. *Mailing Add:* 230 Riverside Dr #5L New York NY 10025

RUBINS, DAVID KRESZ
SCULPTOR
b Minneapolis, Minn, Sept 5, 02. *Study:* Beaux Arts Inst Design, New York; Ecole Beaux Arts & Acad Julian, Paris, asst to James E Fraser. *Work:* Minneapolis Inst Art, Minn; Ind Univ, Bloomington; Indianapolis Mus Art, Ind. *Comn:* Figure on Steps, Arch Bldg, Washington, DC, 33; work in Riley Hosp, Indianapolis, 36-72; Lilly Monument, Crown Hill Cemetery, Indianapolis, 61; Lincoln Monument, State Off Bldg Plaza, Indianapolis, 64. *Exhib:* Archit League, New York, 33; Nat Acad Design, New York, 33; Ind Artists Ann, Indianapolis, 36-70; Am Sculpture Today, Metrop Mus Art, 51. *Teaching:* From instr to prof emer sculpture & anat, Herron Sch Art, Indianapolis, 35-73; retired. *Awards:* Fel Am Acad Rome, 28; Nat Inst Arts & Lett Grant Sculpture, 54. *Publ:* Auth, The Human Figure--An Anatomy for Artists, Viking Press, 53. *Mailing Add:* 4440 Marcy Lane Apt 136 Indianapolis IN 46205

RUBINSTEIN, CHARLOTTE STREIFER
HISTORIAN, EDUCATOR
b New York, NY, Dec 14, 21. *Study:* Brooklyn Col, BA, 41; Teachers Col, Columbia Univ, MA, 46; Otis Art Inst, Los Angeles, MFA, 69. *Collections Arranged:* Women USA Nat Exhib (with catalog), Nat Endowment Arts, 73. *Teaching:* Instr art appreciation & design, West Los Angeles Col, 69-70; instr art hist, appreciation & design, Fullerton Col, 71-74; instr art appreciation, women in art, Saddleback Col, 74- *Awards:* Best Humanities Bk of 1982, Asn Am Publ, 82. *Mem:* Col Art Asn; Women's Caucus Art; Calif Art Educ Asn; Art Lib Soc NAm. *Res:* All aspects of history of American women artists. *Publ:* Auth, Florence Arnold and Lawrence Jones, Artweek, Vol 8 No 5, 77; auth, The first American women artists, Women's Art J, spring/summer 82; auth, American Women Artists: From Early Indian Times to the Present, G K Hall/Avon Bks, 82. *Mailing Add:* 2680 Victoria Dr Laguna Beach CA 92651

RUBINSTEIN, SUSAN R
PHOTOGRAPHER
b New York, NY, May 17, 46. *Study:* Brooklyn Mus Art Sch; Am Univ, BA(fine arts & graphic design); Art Ctr Col Design, Los Angeles, with Todd Walker. *Work:* Denver Mus Art; Yale Univ Art Gallery; Exchange Nat Bank Chicago; Mus Art & Hist, Fribourg, Switz; Het Sterckhof Mus, Antwerp, Belg; and others. *Exhib:* Fac Exhib, Int Ctr Photography, 80; Independent Am Photography, Warsaw, Poland, 80; Galerie Nouvelles Image, The Hague, Holland, 81; Canon Photo Gallery, Geneva, Switz, 81; Bertha Urdang Gallery, New York, 81; and many others. *Teaching:* Instr, Hunter Col & Marymount Manhattan Col, New York, 78 & 79 & Int Ctr Photog, NY, 79; artist in residence, Apeiron Workshops, Millerton, NY, 79. *Bibliog:* John Hunter (auth), Ironic reality, Art Week, 1/75; Jacques J Halber (auth), Brief vit Belge, Foto, 3/77; Arthur Secunda (auth), article, Visual Dialogue, winter 77-78. *Mem:* Soc Photog Educators. *Media:* Light. *Dealer:* Zabriskie Gallery 29 W 57th St New York NY 10019. *Mailing Add:* 155 Bank St D816 New York NY 10014

RUBLE, RONALD L
PRINTMAKER, PAINTER
b St Louis, Mo, Aug 15, 35. *Work:* Minneapolis Inst Art, Minn; Flint Inst Arts, Mich; Honolulu Acad Arts, Hawaii; Mint Mus, Charlotte, NC; Utah Mus Fine Art, Salt Lake City; and others. *Exhib:* 21st Biennial Am Prints, Brooklyn Mus, NY; Nat Print Exhib, Univ Tex, Austin; 5th Hawaii Nat Print Exhib, Honolulu Acad Arts, Hawaii; 154th Ann Exhib, Nat Acad Design, New York; Philadelphia Print Club Ann, Pa. *Awards:* James R Marsh Mem Award, Audubon Artists, 79; Gladys Mock Mem Award, Soc Am Graphic Artists, 79; Special Purchase Award, Okla Art Ctr, 80. *Mem:* Soc Am Graphic Artists; Los Angeles Printmaking Soc; Audubon Artists, NY; Academic Artist Asn, Springfield, Mass. *Media:* Etching, Lithography; Acrylic, Watercolor. *Publ:* Contribr, Print Review 13, 25th Anniv Issue, Pratt Graphics Ctr, 81. *Mailing Add:* 1029 N Jackson St Apt 810 A Milwaukee WI 53202

RUBY, LAURA
SCULPTOR, PRINTMAKER
b Los Angeles, Calif, Dec 7, 45. *Study:* Univ Southern Calif, BA, 67; San Francisco State Col, MA, 69; Univ Hawaii, MFA(art), 78. *Work:* Contemp Arts Ctr, Musicians Asn Hawaii, Castle & Cooke Inc, Hawaii State Fedn Cult & Arts, Honolulu. *Comn:* Cromlech (exterior sculpture), Hawaii State Fedn Cult & Arts, Hilo, 80. *Exhib:* Westwood Clay Nat, Downey Mus Art, Calif, 81; Small Works Nat, Zaner Gallery, Rochester, NY, 81; First Int Shoebox Sculpture Exhib, Univ Hawaii Art Gallery & traveling, 82; Shreveport Biennial Nat Exhib, Meadows Mus Art, La, 82; 17th Ann Nat Drawing & Small Sculpture Show, Cain Mem Gallery, Corpus Christi, Tex, 83; and others. *Teaching:* Instr, Univ Hawaii, Honolulu, 77-; instr, Chaminade Univ, Honolulu, 80-81. *Awards:* Best of Show, First Ann Exhib Poets & Artists, Ga, 81; 1st Place, Easter Art Festival, Hawaii, 76; Purchase Award, Erie Clay Nat, Pa, 83. *Bibliog:* Tony Quagliano (auth), Resisting distinctions, Hawaii Observer, 8/19/75; Pat Matsueda (auth), Painted/read in retrospect, Hawaii Literary Arts Coun Newsletter, 11/79; Kathy Rethlake (auth), Out of stone rises a monument to man's mastery of materials, Evening Outlook, Santa Monica, Calif, 9/22/80. *Media:* Mixed Media; Serigraph. *Mailing Add:* 509 University Ave 902 Honolulu HI 96826

RUBYLEE (CHARLES ARMSTRONG LITTLER)
b Montrose, Colo, Jan 31, 28. *Study:* Univ NMex, BA, 49; Hans Hofmann Sch, New York, 52-54; Alfred Univ, MFA. *Work:* Phoenix Art Mus; Univ NMex Art Mus; Roswell Art Mus, NMex; Univ Ariz Art Mus; Yuma Art Mus, Ariz. *Exhib:* One-man shows, Univ Ariz Art Mus, 60 & 78 & Inst Cult, Mex, 64; Ariz Comn Arts, 78; Tucson Art Mus; Phoenix Art Mus, 81. *Pos:* Founder, pres & trustee, Rancho Linda Vista Arts Community. *Teaching:* Prof art, Univ Ariz 58-83; vis artist, Alfred Univ, 60 & Brown Univ, 62. *Awards:* First Purchase Awards, Phoenix Art Mus, 59, Roswell Mus, 61 & Yuma Art Mus. *Bibliog:* Articles in Art in Am & Artspace, fall 81; Ariz Illus, KUAT-TV, 81. *Media:* Charcoal; Mixed Media. *Mailing Add:* Rancho Linda Vista Oracle AZ 85623

RUDA, EDWIN
PAINTER
b New York, NY, May 15, 22. *Study:* Columbia Univ, MA, 49; Sch Painting & Sculpture, Mexico City, 49-51; Univ Ill, MFA, 56. *Work:* State of NY Collection, Albany Mall; Indianapolis Mus Art, Ind; Dallas Mus Fine Art, Tex; Nat Gallery of Australia, Canberra; Mass Inst Technol, Cambridge. *Exhib:* Smithsonian Traveling Exhib, Latin Am, 66; Systemic Painting, Guggenheim Mus, 66 & Whitney Mus Am Art Painting Ann, 69, New York; Paintings on Paper, Aldrich Mus Contemp Art, Ridgefield, Conn; 73 Biennial, Whitney Mus Am Art, New York; Contemp Am Painting & Sculpture, Krannert Art Mus, Univ Ill, Urbana, 74, 10th Anniversary Exhib 1964-1974, Aldrich Mus Contemp Art, 74; Baltimore Mus, 75, Drawing Show, 76; Benefit Exhib for Udine, Italy, NY Univ, 76; one-man shows, Tyler Sch Art, Philadelphia, 74 & 79, Max Hutchinson Galleries, 77 & 79 & Ohio State Univ, Columbus, 79; and others. *Pos:* Co-founder, Park Pl Gallery Art Res. *Teaching:* Instr painting, Univ Tex, Austin, 56-59, Sch Visual Arts, New York, 67-71, Pratt Inst, Univ Tex, Syracuse Univ, 78, Ohio State Univ, 78 & Tyler Sch Art, Philadelphia, 79; instr painting, Sch Visual Arts, New York, 67-71. *Awards:* Creative Artists Pub Serv Fel, 78-79. *Bibliog:* Carter Ratcliff (auth), Striped for action, Artnews, 2/72; Dore Ashton (auth), New York commentary, Studio Int, 2/70; Peter Schjeldahl (auth), In and out of step in Soho, New York Times, 10/73. *Publ:* Auth, Park Place 1963-67: some informal notes in retrospect, Art Mag, 67. *Mailing Add:* 44 Walker New York NY 10013

RUDDLEY, JOHN
ADMINISTRATOR, PAINTER
b New York, NY, Oct 29, 12. *Study:* Cooper Union Sch Art & Archit, with Tully Filmus, Ernest Fiene & Paul Feeley; DaVinci Sch Art; Columbia Univ, BS(hist art); Columbia Univ, MA(art educ). *Work:* Corcoran Sch Art, Washington, DC; Arts Club Washington. *Exhib:* Corcoran Gallery Art, Washington, DC, 63; Arts Club Washington, 63; Corcoran Sch Art, 63-64; Avant Gallery, Alexandria, Va, 64; Columbia Univ Gallery, New York, 65. *Pos:* Dean & head, Corcoran Sch Art, 62-65; supvr art, Westchester Co, White Plains, NY, 65-; dir, Westchester Art Workshop, 65-; trustee, Hammond Mus, North Salem, NY, 69-; bd gov, Cooper Union, New York, 69; bd dirs, Nippon Mus, New York. *Teaching:* Prof design & painting, Corcoran Sch Art, 62-64; prof hist art, Lab Inst Design, New York, 64-69; prof painting, Pace Col, Pleasantville, NY, 70-71. *Mem:* Am Soc Aesthetics; Arts Club Washington; Inst Study Art; Int Soc Educ Art; Nat Art Educ Asn. *Media:* Acrylic, Oil, Watercolor. *Publ:* Auth, Series of book reviews, Nat Art Educ Asn J, 64-72. *Mailing Add:* 97-40 62nd Drive New York NY 11374

RUDMAN, JOAN (COMBS)
PAINTER, INSTRUCTOR
Study: Mich State Univ, BA(art educ), MA(art); Art Student's League, Woodstock, NY, with Arnold Blanch & Walter Plate; also with Edgar A Whitney, Hans Axel Walleen, Walter DuBois Richards, Diana Kan & Charles Reid. *Exhib:* Wadsworth Atheneum; Acad Fine Arts & Watercolor Soc, New Brit Mus Am Art; Nat Arts Club Open Watercolor Show, 69 & 78; Am Watercolor Soc, 74 & 77; Mus Fine Arts, Springfield, Mass, 77; Salmagundi Club, 78; and others. *Teaching:* Instr, King Sch, Stamford, Conn, Round Hill Community House, Greenwich, Conn & Continuing Educ Classes, Stamford, currently; artist in residence, Southern Vermont Art Ctr, Manchester, currently. *Awards:* Whiskey Painters Am, 76; Pen & Brush, 77 & 78; 50th Grand Nat Exhib, Am Artists Prof League, 78. *Mem:* Southern Vt Artists; Am Artists Prof League; Hudson Valley Art Asn; Conn Watercolor Soc; Whiskey Painters Am; and others. *Media:* Watercolor. *Mailing Add:* 274 Quarry Rd Stamford CT 06903

RUDQUIST, JERRY JACOB
PAINTER, EDUCATOR
b Fargo, NDak, June 13, 34. *Study:* Minneapolis Col Art & Design, BFA, 56; Cranbrook Acad Art, MFA, 58. *Work:* Univ Minn Gallery, Minneapolis; St Cloud State Col, Minn; Anoka Ramsey State Jr Col, Minn. *Exhib:* Walker Art Ctr, Minneapolis, 58, 60, 62, 65 & 77; Minn Portfolio (traveling exhib, Middle East & Europe), St Paul Gallery, 60; Denver Art Mus, Colo, 63; Joslyn Mus Art, Omaha, Nebr, 64, 68 & 70; Birmingham Mus Art, Ala, 66; Art in the Embassies Prog, US State Dept, 68-71; Drei Amerikaner aus dem Mittleren Western, Mannheimer Symposion der Kunste, WGer, 72; one-man exhibs, Walker Art Ctr, Minneapolis, 63 & Minneapolis Inst Arts, 64, 71 & 75; Colo 1st Nat Print & Drawing Competition, 74. *Teaching:* Prof art, Macalester Col, 58-; vis lectr & critic art, Boston Univ, summer 69. *Awards:* Spec Donor & Purchase Award, Walker Art Ctr, 62; Purchase Award, Minneapolis Inst Arts, 65; Purchase Award, World Print Competition, San Francisco, 73. *Bibliog:* Dan Paris (auth), Rudquist (film), produced by Minneapolis Inst Arts, Macalester Col & Minn State Arts Coun, 71; Samuel Sachs II (auth), Jerry Rudquist: Recent works, Minneapolis Inst Arts, 71. *Media:* Oil. *Dealer:* Suzanne Kohn Gallery 1690 Grand Ave St Paul MN 55105. *Mailing Add:* 2322 Seabury Ave S Minneapolis MN 55406

RUDY, CHARLES
SCULPTOR
b York, Pa, Nov 14, 04. *Study:* Pa Acad Fine Arts, Philadelphia; York Col, DHL, 82. *Work:* Pa Mus Fine Arts; Brookgreen Gardens, Georgetown, SC; Philadelphia Mus, Pa; Metrop Mus Art, New York; Carnegie Inst, Pittsburgh, Pa. *Comn:* US Post Off, Bronx, NY, 39; US Govt Bldg, 39; five stone figures (with Roy Larson), Va Polytech Inst, Blacksburg, 54; sculpture (with Willard Hahn), Lehigh Co Ct House, 64; bronze gates (with Edward Green), William Penn Hist Mus, Harrisburg, Pa, 64. *Exhib:* Pa Acad Fine Arts, Philadelphia, 28-68; Whitney Mus Am Art, 36-53, Metrop Mus Art, 50 & Nat Acad Design, 50-71, New York; Art Inst Chicago, 39-52; 300 Years of American Art, Philadelphia, 76; one-man show, Bucks Co Arts Coun, Pa, 80. *Pos:* Mem Art Comn Pa, 49-72. *Teaching:* Head dept sculpture, Cooper Union, 31-41; instr sculpture, Pa Acad Fine Arts, 50-52, Philadelphia Mus Col Art, 60-62. *Awards:* Guggenheim Found Fel, 42; Gold Medal, Nat Sculpture Soc, 73; Citation, Legislature Pa, 80; and others. *Bibliog:* Scrap sculpture welding, Life, 12/20/43. *Mem:* Nat Acad Design; Nat Sculpture Soc. *Media:* Multimedia. *Publ:* Auth, Challenge of form, Mag Art, 40. *Mailing Add:* PO Box 92 Ottsville PA 18942

RUELLAN, ANDREE
PAINTER
b New York, NY, Apr 6, 05. *Study:* Art Students League, scholar, 20-22; Maurice Sterne Sch, Rome, scholar, 22-23; Acad Suedoise, Paris, with Per Krogh & Charles Dufresne. *Work:* Fogg Mus, Harvard Univ; Metrop Mus Art, New York; Phillips Mem Gallery, Washington, DC & Columbia Mus Art, SC; Whitney Mus Am Art; Springfield Mus Art, Utah. *Comn:* Murals, Post Off, Emporia, Va, 40 & Lawrenceville, Ga, 41. *Exhib:* 10 ann, Whitney Mus Am Art; Am Painting Today, Metrop Mus Art, 50; Storm King Art Ctr Retrospective, 66; Artists for Victory, Metrop Mus Art, New York; Pa Acad Fine Arts Ann; Mus City New York; Art Inst Chicago; Corcoran Gallery, Washington, DC; Springfield Mus Art, Mass; Libr Cong, Washington, DC; Va Mus Fine Arts, Richmond; Heckscher Mus, New York; Retrospective, Lehigh Univ; one-person show, Woodstock Artists Asn, 77; and others. *Teaching:* Vis artist, Pa State Univ, summer 57. *Awards:* Pennell Mem Medal, Philadelphia Watercolor Club, 45; Dawson Medal, 50; Guggenheim Found Fel, 50-51; and others. *Bibliog:* Harry Salpeter (auth), About Andree Ruellan, Coronet, 12/38; Ernest Watson (auth), Andree Ruellan, Am Artist, 10/43; Arthur Zaidenburg (auth), The Art of the Artist, Crown, 51. *Mem:* Woodstock Artists Asn; Art Students League. *Media:* Multimedia. *Dealer:* Kraushaar Galleries 724 Fifth Ave New York NY 10019. *Mailing Add:* Shady NY 12479

RUFFING, ANNE ELIZABETH
PAINTER
b Brooklyn, NY. *Study:* Cornell Univ, BS; Drexel Inst Technol; also studied with John Pike. *Work:* Metrop Mus Art, New York; Brooklyn Mus, NY; Nat Gallery Art, Washington, DC; Whitney Mus Am Art, New York; Libr of Nat Collection of Fine Arts, Smithsonian Inst, Washington, DC; and many others. *Comn:* Four Wildlife Drawings, Johnston Hist Mus, North Brunswick, NJ, 76; four hist landmark lithographs, NY State Senate, comn by City of Kingston, NY, 76; porcelain series, Danbury Mint, Norwalk, Conn, 81-82. *Exhib:* Rocky Mountain Nat Watermedia Exhib, Golden, Colo, 76; 25th Ann

Exhib Painting & Sculpture, Berkshire Mus, 76; one-woman shows, Art in Industry, Int Bus Machines Corp, New York, 66 & A E Ruffing Exhib, Hall of Fame, Goshen, NY, 71; 4th Ann Exhib, Midwest Watercolor Soc, Manitowoc, Wisc, 80; and others. *Awards:* Int Women's Year Award, Int Women's Arts Festival, D Gillespie, 76; Special Merit Award, Midwest Watercolor Soc, 80. *Bibliog:* Bruce Henry Davis (auth), Introducing the art of A E R, 1/77, Memories of Childhood, 2/77 & Glimpses of yesterday, 7/77, Collector's News, Am Masters Found. *Media:* Watercolor, Ink. *Publ:* Illusr, Ideals Old Fashioned Issue (title page plus two others), Ideals, 75. *Mailing Add:* Box 125 Bloomington NY 12411

RUFFNER, GINNY MARTIN NAIL
GLASSBLOWER

b Atlanta, Ga, June 21, 52. *Study:* Univ Ga, BFA(drawing, painting, cum laude), 74, with James Herbert, Edmund Feldman, Lamar Dodd, MFA, 75; Penland Sch Crafts, glassblowing with Fritz Dreisbach, 79. *Work:* Penland Sch Crafts, NC; Corning Mus Glass, NY; Kuntsmus of Dusseldorf, WGer. *Comn:* Stained glass wall, Velco Builders, 77; stained glass pieces, McDonalds, Inc, Hilton Head, SC, 78 & Winder, Ga, 78; stained glass pieces, Murdick's Fudge, Inc, Naples, Fla, 78. *Exhib:* Westlake Gallery, White Plains, NY, 80 & 81; Touch of Glass, Decatur, Ga, 81; Leigh Yawkey Woodsen Mus, Wausau, Wis, 81; Del Mano Gallery, Los Angeles, 81; Callanwolde Gallery, Atlanta, Ga, 81; and others. *Pos:* Glassblower & engraver, Lillie Glassblowers, Smyrna, Ga, 76-79; designer-craftsman, Nail Stained Glass, Marietta, 76-; glassblower & engraver, Frabel Glassblowers, Atlanta, 79- *Teaching:* Adj instr watercolor & art appreciation, DeKalb Col, Clarkston, Ga, 77; vis scholar glassblowing, Penland Sch Crafts, NC, 79. *Mem:* Glass Art Soc; Atlanta Glass Art Guild; Am Sci Glassblowers Soc. *Publ:* Contribr, Artists/USA, 77-78; auth, New Glass Review II, Corning Mus, 81; auth, Georgia Crafts/Coastal Plains, 81; and others. *Dealer:* Touch of Glass 524 Church St Decatur GA 30033. *Mailing Add:* 967 Drewry St Atlanta GA 30306

RUFFO, JOSEPH MARTIN
PRINTMAKER, ADMINISTRATOR

b Norwich, Conn, Dec 6, 41. *Study:* Pratt Inst; Cranbrook Acad Art. *Work:* Brooks Mem Art Gallery, Memphis, Tenn; Ark Art Ctr, Little Rock; Mus Mod Art, Salvador, Brazil; Memphis Acad Arts, Tenn; Miss Art Asn, Jackson. *Exhib:* Third Biennial Rutgers Nat Drawing Exhib, State Univ NJ, Camden Col Arts & Sci, 79; Images Aluminum, Tamarind Prints Traveling Exhib, Macalester Col, 79-80; Potsdam Prints, 16th Nat, 82; 11th Nat Prints & Drawing Exhib, Minot State Col, 82; La Grange Nat, 82; 23rd Nat Print Exhib, Hunterdon Art Ctr, Clinton, NJ, 79; Images Aluminum, Tamarind Prints Traveling Exhib, Macalester Col, 79-80. *Pos:* Head dept art, Univ Northern Iowa, Cedar Falls. *Teaching:* Instr art, Memphis Acad Arts, 64-68; instr art, Fla Mem Col, 69-77; asst prof art & chmn dept, Barry Col, 69-74, chmn div fine arts, 74-77. *Awards:* Fulbright Grant, Brazil, 63; Best in Show, 12th Ann Mid South Exhib, 67; Purchase Prize, 10th Dixie Ann Prints & Drawings, 68. *Mem:* Nat Coun Art Adminrs; Nat Asn Schs Art & Design; Col Art Asn; Am Arbitration Asn. *Dealer:* Miriam Pearlman Inc 505 N Lake Shore Dr Chicago IL 60611. *Mailing Add:* 2216 Clay St Cedar Falls IA 50613

RUGGLES, JOANNE BEAULE
PRINTMAKER, EDUCATOR

b New York, NY, May 19, 46. *Study:* Akron State Univ; Ohio State Univ, with Sidney Chafetz, BFA(painting) & MFA(painting, printmaking & photography); Univ of Calif, Santa Barbara; Calif Polytechnic State Univ. *Work:* Ohio State Univ, Columbus; Calif Polytech State Univ, San Luis Obispo; Calif State Library, Sacramento; Wesleyan Col, Macon, Ga. *Exhib:* Eighth Premio Biella Per L'Incisione, Italy, 80; Ibiza Graphic 80, Mus Art Contemporaneo Ibiza, Spain, 80; Second International Exhibition of Prints and Drawings, Mus Arts & Sci, Wesleyan Col, 83-84; Cabo Fio International Print Biennal, Brazil, 83; Intergraphic '84, Exhib Ctr, Berlin, 84; Printmakers, Ideas & Images, Cal State, Hayward, 80. *Teaching:* Lectr drawing & painting, Ohio State Univ, 70-71, Allan Hancock Col, 71-76 & Cuesta Col, 77-79; lectr drawing & printmaking, Calif Polytech State Univ, 73-80. *Awards:* First prize graphics, Arts Club of Washington, 81; University Purchase Award, Wesleyan Col, 83; Jurors Award, Cabo Frio Int, Brazil, 83. *Mem:* Los Angeles Printmaking Soc; Calif Soc of Printmakers; Boston Printmakers; World Print Council; Philadelphia Print Club. *Media:* Pencil. *Publ:* Co-auth, Darkroom Graphics: Creative Photographic Techniques for Photographers and Artists, Amphoto, 75; contribr, Encyclopedia of Photography, Amphoto/Eastman Kodak, 78. *Mailing Add:* Box 46 San Luis Obispo CA 93406

RUGOLO, LAWRENCE
SCREENPRINTER, EDUCATOR

b Milwaukee, Wis, Oct 2, 31. *Study:* Univ Wis, Milwaukee, BA(art & art educ), 54; Univ Iowa, MFA, 59. *Work:* Albrecht Art Mus; Springfield Art Mus, Mo; State Univ NY Col, Potsdam; Ark Arts Ctr, Little Rock; Mus Art, Univ Mo, Columbia; plus others. *Exhib:* Nat Print Exhibs, Silvermine Guild of Artists, New Canaan, Conn, 64, 72 & 80; Colorprint: USA, Nat Print Exhib, Tex Tech Univ, Lubbock, 71 & 74; Boston Printmakers 31st Nat Exhib, 79; one-man shows, Albrecht Art Mus, 75 & Visa Int Print Soc, Fresno, Calif, 80; plus many others. *Teaching:* Assoc prof screenprinting & design, Univ Mo, Columbia, 68-73, prof, 73-, chmn art dept, 73-76. *Awards:* Two Purchase Awards, 5th Ann Art Exhib, Tulsa Arts Coun, 72; Purchase Award, Potsdam Prints, State Univ NY, 72 & 74 & 44th Ann Exhib, Springfield Art Mus, 74. *Mem:* Columbia Art Legue (mem bd dir, 83-). *Mailing Add:* 415 Parkade Blvd Columbia MO 65202

RUHE, BARNABY SIEGER
PAINTER, CRITIC

b New York, NY, Aug 10, 46. *Study:* US Naval Acad, BS, 68; Md Inst, Col Art, with Ed Dugmore, Sal Scarpitta & Babe Shapiro, MFA(painting), 75; NY Univ. *Work:* Lincoln & Great Neck Schs; Muhlenberg Col, Lincoln & Great Neck. *Comn:* Marathons, City Allentown, 80. *Exhib:* Pleiades, New York, 76, 77 & 79; Terminal, New York, 83; Carnegie Mellon Mus, 84. *Collections Arranged:* St Johns Col, Annapolis, 76; WC4 Box 83 10,000, New York Mail Concept Exhib. *Pos:* Dir, cur & producer, Whitney Counterweight, New York, 77, 79, 81 & 83; Soho critic, Art World, 80-84. *Teaching:* Art hist, US Naval Acad, 72-75; instr Shamanistic painting workshops, Muhlenberg Col & Great Neck Schs, 81- *Awards:* Nat Endowment Arts Dirs Grant, 77; Prize, Allentown Art Mus, 79; Comn Visual Arts Grant, New York, 83. *Bibliog:* Vic Miles (interviewer), Ruhe marathon painting, CBS TV, New York, 1/79 & NBC TV, 2/80; Myra Goldfarb (auth), Zen in Ruhe painting, Call Chronicle, 5/79. *Mem:* Founding mem Valley Arts Coun. *Media:* Oil, House Paint. *Dealer:* Helen Turner 185 E 85th New York NY 10028. *Mailing Add:* RD 2 Box 67 Emmaus PA 18049

RUIZ DE LA MATA, ERNESTO J
CRITIC, HISTORIAN

b San Juan, PR, Aug 4, 35. *Study:* Univ PR, BA, 56; Univ Cent Madrid, Fac Filosofia y Letras, Spain, 60-61; Harvard Univ, AM, 62. *Collections Arranged:* Affiches Portoricaines 1950-1972, France & NJ State Coun Arts, 72, Trois Generations Clef dans le Developpement des Arts Graphiqies a Porto Rico: Homar, Alicea et Martorell, Biennale Int d'Art de Mentor, 76 & Quatr Latin-Americains de New York-Abularach, Belkin, Gongora et Rayo, 76; Panorama of Contemporary Latin American Artists, NJ State Mus, Trenton & other NJ Mus, 75-76. *Pos:* Contribr ed art, San Juan Rev, 65 & 66; art critic, Sunday San Juan Star Mag, 67-72 & 79-80; contribr, Rev Inst Cult Puertorriquena, 71-; art critic, El Reportero, 80-81; art critic & ed, Caribbean Business Mag, 81. *Teaching:* Asst prof art hist, Univ PR, 56-65 & 77-81; asst prof art hist & chmn dept fine arts, Inter-Am Univ PR, 65-70. *Mem:* Asn Int Critiques d'Art, US sect; Nat Trust hist Preserv; PEN. *Res:* Contemporary art in Latin America and a dictionary of contemporary Latin American painters. *Publ:* Manuel Hernandez Acevedo-Obra Grafica Completa, Inst Cult Puertorriquena, 81. *Mailing Add:* Marlin Towers I Apt 3-D Isla Verde PR 00913

RUMFORD, BEATRIX TYSON
ADMINISTRATOR

b Baltimore, Md, June 16, 39. *Study:* Wellesley Col, 58-62; State Univ NY Oneonta & NY State Hist Asn Cooperstown, 64-65; Bath Summer Sch, Courtauld Inst, Univ London travel course, 69; Nat Trust Summer Sch, Attingham Park, Shropshire, Eng & study tour, Oslo, Norway, 70. *Collections Arranged:* The Beardsley Limner, 72-73; Folk Art in America: A Living Tradition, 74-76; and organized five major exhibs on American Folk Art Ann. *Pos:* Art res ed, D C Heath & Co, Boston, 62-64; res assoc, Chicago Hist Soc, Ill, 66-67; from asst cur to assoc cur, Colonial Williamsburg, Va, 67-71, vpres & dir mus, 77-; from assoc dir to dir, Abby Aldrich Rockefeller Folk Art Collection, 71-, vpres mus, 79- *Mem:* NY State Hist Asn; Furnishings Comt, Exec Mansion, Richmond, Va; Bermuda Nat Trust; Antique Collectors Guild, Richmond, Va (exec coun, 74). *Res:* Role of death as reflected in the art and folkways of the Northeast in the eighteenth and nineteenth centuries. *Publ:* Auth, The household accessories at Colonial Williamsburg, 69 & Nonacademic English painting, 74, Antiques; auth, What is American Folk Art?, 74; auth, Folk art, In: World Bk Encycl, 75; ed, American Folk Portraits, 81. *Mailing Add:* Tayloe House 110 E Nicholson St Williamsburg VA 23185

RUMSEY, DAVID MACIVER
ENVIRONMENTAL ARTIST, PATRON

b New York, NY, Apr 29, 44. *Study:* Yale Univ, BA, 66, BFA & MFA, 69. *Exhib:* Spaces, Mus Mod Art, New York, 70; Work for New Spaces, Walker Art Mus, Minneapolis, 71; Pulsa & Television Sensoriums, Automation House, 71; Pulsa, Philadelphia Mus Fine Arts, 71; Calif Inst Arts, 72. *Teaching:* Lectr art, Yale Univ, 68-72; vis artist, Calif Inst Arts, 70-73. *Mem:* Pulsa Group; Am Soc for Eastern Arts & Ctr for World Music (assoc dir, 73-75). *Interests:* Life-involved large scale speculative sculpture; patron of Radical Lava Plateau Art Company. *Mailing Add:* 24 Beulah San Francisco CA 94117

RUNNING RABBIT (KEVIN RED STAR)
PAINTER, PRINTMAKER

b Lodge Grass, Mont, Oct 9, 43. *Study:* Inst Am Indian Art, Santa Fe, NMex, 62-65; San Francisco Art Inst, 65-67; Mont State Univ, 68-69; Eastern Mont Col, Billings, BA, 72. *Work:* Heard Mus, Phoenix, Ariz; Northern Plains Mus, Browning, Mont; Inst Am Indian Art Mus, Santa Fe, NMex; Denver Art Mus, Colo; Shenyang Nat Art Mus, Liaoning, China. *Comn:* Mural, Crow Tribal Office, Crow Agency, Mont. *Exhib:* NMex Mus Fine Art Indian Art Show, Santa Fe, 65; Wheelwright Contemp Indian Artist Show, Wheelwright Ceremonial Art Mus, Santa Fe, 78; 100 years of Native American Painting, Okla Mus Art, 78; Indian Images '80, Natural History Mus, Denver; Peking Exhibit of American Western Art, China, 81; and many others. *Collections Arranged:* 77 West Coast Experience (auth, catalog), Tokyo, Japan; American Indian Art Exhibition, Espace Pierre Cardin, Paris, 79; The Real People, Havana, Cuba, 79; Santa Fe Festival of the Arts, 78-81; American Indian Art in the 80's, Native Am Ctr Living Arts Mus (auth, catalog), Niagara Falls, NY, 81. *Teaching:* Instr art, Lodge Grass, Mont, 73-74; instr art, Inst Am Indian Art, Santa Fe, 75-76. *Awards:* Governor's Trophy, Scottsdale Nat Indian Art Exhib, 65; First Place, Cent Wash State Col Art Exhib, Ellensburg, Wash, 74. *Bibliog:* Scott E Dial (auth), Visual portrayals of Kevin Red Star,

Southwest Art, 2/76; Penny Cox (auth), Red Star: Modern mystic and on the move, Santa Fe Profile Mag, 12/79; Jamake Highwater, The Sweet Grass Lives On, Harper & Row, 79-80. *Media:* Acrylic, Oil; Lithography, Etchings. *Dealer:* Good Company Gallery 339 Columbus Ave New York NY; Louis Newman Galleries 322 N Beverly Dr Beverly Hills, CA 90210. *Mailing Add:* 2705 Camino Chueco Santa Fe NM 87501

RUSCHA, EDWARD JOSEPH
PAINTER, FILMMAKER
b Omaha, Nebr, Dec 16, 37. *Study:* Chouinard Art Inst. *Work:* Mus Mod Art & Whitney Mus Am Art, New York; Los Angeles Co Mus Art; Joseph Hirshhorn Collection, Washington, DC; San Francisco Mus Moad Art. *Exhib:* Drawings USA, Minn Mus Art, St Paul, 71; Albright-Knox Art Gallery, Buffalo, NY, 76; Stedelijk Mus, Amsterdam, Holland, 76; Ft Worth Art Mus, Tex, 77; Works of Edward Ruscha Exhib Tour, San Francisco Mus Mod Art, 82-83; Whitney Mus; Los Angeles Co Mus Art; and others. *Teaching:* Lectr painting, Univ Calif, Los Angeles, 69-70. *Bibliog:* Geoffrey Haydon (dir), Edward Ruscha (film), British Broadcasting Corp, 79; Dave Hickey (auth), Available Light, Hudson Hills Press, 82; Peter Plagens (auth), Ed Ruscha, Seriously, Hudson Hills Press, 82; plus many others. *Publ:* Auth, Twenty six Gasoline Stations, 63, Various Small Fires, 64, Real Estate Opportunities, 70, A Few Palm Trees, 71, Heavy Industry Publs; auth, Guacamole Airlines, Abrams, 80; and others. *Dealer:* Leo Castelli 420 W Broadway New York NY 10012. *Mailing Add:* 1024 3/4 N Western Ave Hollywood CA 90029

RUSH, ANDREW
PRINTMAKER
b Mich, Sept 24, 31. *Study:* Univ Ill, BFA(hons), 53; Univ Iowa, MFA, 58; Fulbright fel, Florence, Italy, 58-59. *Work:* Uffizi Mus, Florence, Italy; Libr Cong, Washington, DC; Dallas Mus, Tex; Seattle Mus, Wash. *Comn:* Law Prints (portfolio of three offset lithographs), Lawyers Publ Co, 68 & 74; ed etchings, Tucson Art Ctr, 71. *Exhib:* US Info Serv Traveling Exhib to Europe & Latin Am, 60-65; Graphic Art USA, Am prints to Soviet Union, 63; Brooklyn Mus Biennial, 64; 50 American Printmakers, Am Pavilion, New York Worlds Fair, 64-65; Intag 71, 30 Printmakers, San Fernando State Univ, 71. *Pos:* Founding mem, Rancho Linda Vista Community of the Arts, 69. *Teaching:* Assoc prof art, Univ Ariz, 59-69; vis artist in residence, Ohio State Univ, 70. *Awards:* Seattle Mus Int Printmakers Award, 63; Purchase Award, Brooklyn Mus Biennial, 64. *Bibliog:* Article, Southwest Art Gallery Mag, 3/72. *Dealer:* Assoc Am Artists 663 Fifth Ave New York NY 10022; Carlin Galleries 710 Montgomery St Ft Worth TX 76107. *Mailing Add:* Rancho Linda Vista 2360 Oracle AZ 85623

RUSH, JEAN C
EDUCATOR, PAINTER
b Bloomington, Ill, Nov 21, 33. *Study:* Ill Wesleyan Univ, BFA, 55; Univ Iowa, MFA, 58; Univ Ariz, PhD, 74. *Exhib:* 13th Nat Exhib Prints, Libr Congress, Washington, DC, 55; 11th Exhib Southwest Prints & Drawings, Dallas Mus Fine Arts, Tex, 61; Ariz Women's Caucus for Art Statewide Show, 79. *Pos:* Coordr art educ program, Univ Ariz, 78-80 & 81-; co-ed, Studies in art education, Nat Art Educ Asn, 81-83, sr ed, 83- *Teaching:* Lectr art educ, Univ Ariz, 71-75, asst prof art educ, 75-80, assoc prof, 80- *Awards:* Purchase Prize, Tucson Mus Art, 60; First Prize, Ariz State Fair, 60; Purchase Prize, Dallas Mus Fine Arts, 61. *Mem:* Nat Art Educ Asn; Am Asn Univ Prof; Am Educ Research Asn; Col Art Asn; Women's Caucus Art. *Res:* Visual perception, art learning. *Publ:* Auth, Can the arts teach thinking? A look at artistic conceptual behavior, Art Educ, 79; auth, On the Appeal of M C Escher's Pictures, Leonardo, 79; coauth, A comparison of instructional methods for teaching contour drawing to children, 80 & The perception of artistic style, 81, Studies Art Educ; coauth, Research for the classroom: An ecological impact statement, Art Educ, 82. *Mailing Add:* Dept Art Univ Ariz Tucson AZ 85721

RUSH, JON N
SCULPTOR, EDUCATOR
b Atlanta, Ga, Sept 24, 35. *Study:* Art Inst Chicago, 53-55; Cranbrook Acad Art, with Tex Schiwetz, BFA & MFA. *Work:* Columbus Mus Art, Ohio; Univ Mich, Ann Arbor. *Comn:* Sculpture, Summerset Mall, Troy, Mich, 70, Briarwood, Ann Arbor, 80 & Southwestern Mich Col, Dowagiac, 84. *Exhib:* Hong Kong Int Competition, China, 62; one-man show, Columbus Gallery Fine Art, 62; Bundy Art Gallery, Waitsfield, Vt, 63; Mich Artists, Detroit Inst Fine Art, 66; Mich Sculptors, Eastern Mich Univ, Ypsilanti, 71; All Mich Artists, Flint Art Inst, 74; Sculpture Inside & Out, Univ Mich, Ann Arbor, 75; Fifteen Mich Sculptors, City of Lansing, 76; Meadowbrook Outdoor Sculpture, Rochester, Mich, 81. *Teaching:* Prof sculpture, Univ Mich, 62- *Awards:* Detroit Foundry Prize, Mich Artists Show, Detroit Sculpture Foundry, 66; Sculpture Award, All Mich Artists, Flint Inst Art, 72; Tiffany Found Grant Sculpture, 70. *Media:* Stainless Steel, Cor-Ten Steel. *Mailing Add:* 7930 Hirth St Dexter MI 48130

RUSH, KENT THOMAS
PAINTER, PRINTMAKER
b Hayward, Calif, Jan 16, 48. *Study:* Calif Col Arts & Crafts, BFA, 70; Univ NMex, Albuquerque, MA, 75; Univ Tex, Austin, MFA, 79. *Work:* Oakland Mus, Calif; McNay Mus, San Antonio; USIA, Washington, DC; City Dallas, Tex; New Orleans Pub Libr. *Comn:* Lithographs, Tex Arts Alliance, Austin, 78; cross design, Eden United Church Christ, Haward, Calif, 81. *Exhib:* Contemporary Prints, traveling, 73; Madison Art Ctr, Wis, 77; Paperworks: An Exhibit of Texas Artists, traveling, 79-80; Cliche-Verre, Detroit Inst Arts, 80; Aspects of Realism, World Print Coun, Oakland, Calif, 81; Seventh British Int Print Biennale, Bradford Galleries, Eng; and others. *Teaching:* Instr, San

Antonio Art Inst, 76-79; lectr, Calif Col Arts & Crafts, Oakland, 80-81, San Francisco Art Inst, 82; asst prof, Univ Tex, San Antonio, 82- *Awards:* Purchase Awards, Los Angeles Printing Soc 5th Ann, 78, 1st SEastern Graphics Ann, New Orleans, 78 & Santa Barbara City Col, 80. *Bibliog:* Pamela Hammond (auth), Kent Rush at Art Space, Images and Issues, spring 82; Peter Boswell (auth), Urban Imagery, Artweek, 7/31/82. *Media:* Mixed Media; Lithography, Collotype. *Dealer:* Art Space 10550 Santa Monica Blvd Los Angeles CA 90025. *Mailing Add:* 407 Meredith Dr San Antonio TX 78228

RUSKIN, LYNNE See Caimite

RUSSELL, (GEORGE) GORDON
PAINTER
b Altoona, Pa, July 15, 32. *Study:* Pa State Univ, with Hobson Pittman; Pa Acad Fine Arts, with Walter Stuempfig; Barnes Found. *Work:* Pa Acad Fine Arts, Philadelphia; Fogg Art Mus, Harvard Univ; Mus Fine Arts, Bowdoin Col, Maine; Krannert Art Mus, Univ Ill, Urbana; New York Hosp Collection, NY. *Exhib:* Pa Acad Fine Arts Ann & Fel Ann; Contemporary Paintings, Yale Univ Art Gallery, 62; one-man shows, Durlacher Bros, New York, 57-67, Ft Worth Art Ctr, Tex, 62 & Larcada Gallery, New York, 69 & 71. *Awards:* Lewis S Ware Mem, 53, J Henry Schiedt Mem, 54 & Toppan Prize, 54, Pa Acad Fine Arts. *Mem:* Fel Pa Acad Fine Arts. *Media:* Oils, Gouache. *Dealer:* Marshall Lewis 293 Central Park W New York NY 10024. *Mailing Add:* c/o Murie de Givenchy 626 W Hortter St Philadelphia PA 19119

RUSSELL, HELEN DIANE
HISTORIAN
b Kansas City, Mo, Apr 8, 36. *Study:* Vassar Col, AB; Radcliffe Grad Sch; Johns Hopkins Univ, PhD. *Collections Arranged:* Protest and Social Comment in Prints, 70; Kathe Kollwitz, 71; Rare Etchings by Giovanni Battista & Giovanni Domenico Tiepolo, 72; Jacques Callot, Prints and Related Drawings, 75; Europ Countryside: 16th & 17th century prints; Self-Portraits in Prints, 79; Claude Lorrain 1600-1682, Washington, 82 & Paris, 83. *Pos:* Asst to chief, Smithsonian Inst Traveling Exhib Serv, Washington, 60-61; mus cur, Nat Gallery Art, Washington, DC, 64-70, asst cur graphic arts, 70-76, cur French Prints, 76-, asst head, Dept Graphic Arts, 81-; mem, Inst Adv Study, 80-81. *Teaching:* Prof 15th-17th century Europ painting & graphic arts, Am Univ, Washington, DC, 66-72 & 78, adj prof, 83. *Awards:* Woodrow Wilson Nat Fel, 58-59; Samuel H Kress Fel, 73; Mus Professional Fellowship, Nat Endowment Arts, 80-81. *Mem:* Col Art Asn Am; Women's Caucus for Art (adv bd, 77-79); Print Coun Am. *Res:* Prints and drawings of the 16th through 18th centuries. *Publ:* Auth, A museum worker speaks, Washington Print Club Newslett, 72; auth, Francoise Viatte, Dessins de Stefano della Bella, Art Bulletin, 77; auth, Claude's Psyche Pendants: London and Cologne, Studies Hist Art (in prep). *Mailing Add:* Nat Gallery Art Washington DC 20565

RUSSELL, JOHN LAUREL
DEALER, COLLECTOR
b Cochrane, Ont, Aug 14, 16. *Study:* Russell Sch Art, Toronto, 37-38. *Pos:* Owner, Beaver Hall, Gananoque, Ont, currently. *Mem:* Fel Royal Soc Arts; fel Royal Geog Soc; Can Guild Crafts; Order of Can; life gov Montreal Numis & Hist Soc. *Specialty:* General antiques. *Collection:* Early Canadian painting of the eighteenth and nineteenth centuries. *Mailing Add:* Beaver Hall Gananoque ON K7G 2W7 Canada

RUSSELL, PHILIP C
PAINTER, INSTRUCTOR
b Tulsa, Okla, July 9, 33. *Study:* Colo Springs Fine Arts Ctr, study with V Vytlacil; Univ Iowa, study with M Lasansky; Univ Calif, Berkeley, study with R Motherwell, W Kahn, MA. *Work:* Philbrook Art Ctr, Tulsa; Wichita Mus Art; Dallas Mus Fine Arts; Palace of the Legion of Honor, San Francisco; Butler Inst Am Art, Youngstown, Ohio. *Exhib:* US Info Serv (travelling exhib), SAm, 57-59; Drawings, Dallas Mus Fine Arts, 58-59; Mid Am Ann Exhib, Nelson Gallery, Kansas City, Mo, 58; Philadelphia Mus Art, 58; Calif Soc of Etchers, 44th Am Nat Exhib, 59; Area Gallery, New York, 61 & 63; New York World's Fair, 63-64. *Collections Arranged:* 10th Street Days-- Coops of the 50s, Noho Gallery & Landmark, 77. *Teaching:* Instr drawing, Univ Okla, 57-58; instr composition, Philadelphia Col Art, 62-63; instr art art hist, Edgemont Sch, Scarsdale, NY, 69-71, chmn arts, 71-79. *Awards:* Purchase Awards, Drawing and Prints, Dallas Mus, 58 & 59, Calif Soc of Etchers, Legion of Honor, San Francisco, 59 & Am Graphic Arts, Wichita Art Assoc, 59. *Bibliog:* John Canaday (auth), Art: Street of strugglers, 12/14/61 & Goodbye forever, a sad farewell to 10th street, 5/9/63, New York Times; Joellen Bard (auth), 10th Street Days, Educ Art & Serv Inc, 12/77. *Media:* Oil, Intaglio. *Mailing Add:* 145 W 79th St 16A New York NY 10024

RUSSELL, RAYMOND See Fink, Ray

RUSSELL, ROBERT PRICE
PAINTER, EDUCATOR
b Rochelle, Ill, June 23, 39. *Study:* Kansas City Art Inst, Mo, BFA, 61; Southern Ill Univ, Carbondale, MFA, 63. *Work:* Mobil Oil, NY; Roswell Mus & Art Ctr, NMex; Springfield Art Mus, Mo. *Exhib:* One-man shows, Roswell Mus and Art Ctr, NMex, 75, Humboldt State Univ, Arcata, Calif, 75 & Idaho State Univ, Pocatello, 79; Watercolor USA-1979, Springfield Art Mus, Mo; Works on Paper, Douglas Drake Gallery, Kansas City, Mo, 79; and other group & one-man shows. *Pos:* Artist-in-residence, Area arts prog, Wis, 66-67, Hanover Col, Ind, 73, Roswell Mus and Art Ctr, NMex, 74-75 & Idaho State Univ, Pocatello, 79. *Teaching:* Instr art, Univ Wis-Stevens Point, 63-66; assoc

prof art, Pittsburg State Univ, Kans, 67- *Awards:* Purchase Awards, 15th Ann Nat Sun Carnival Art Exhib, El Paso Mus Art, Tex, 70, 46th Ann Exhib, Springfield Art Mus, 76 & Chautauqua Exhib of Am Art, NY, 79. *Media:* Acrylic, Polymer. *Dealer:* Douglas Drake Gallery 4500 State Line Kansas City KS 66103. *Mailing Add:* 2610 Omaha Pittsburg KS 66762

RUSSIN, ROBERT I
SCULPTOR, EDUCATOR
b New York, NY, Aug 26, 14. *Study:* City Univ New York, BA & MA; Beaux Arts Inst Design. *Work:* Menorah Med Ctr, Kansas City; Fed Bldgs, Denver & Cheyenne; Lincoln Monument, Wyo; Evanston Post Off, Ill; Duarte Monument, Santo Domingo. *Comn:* Spirit of Life, City Hope Nat Med Ctr, Duarte, Calif; Fountainhead (steel), City Hall, Casper, Wyo; marble carving, Univ Wyo; Prometheus (bronze), Casper Pub Libr, Wyo; Herios Dallas (bronze & marble), Lincoln Ctr, Dallas. *Exhib:* Pa Acad Fine Arts Sculpture Biennial, Philadelphia, 66; one-man shows, Colorado Springs Fine Arts Ctr, 67, Palm Springs Desert Mus, 70, Magnes Mus, Berkeley, Calif, 70, Galleria d'Arte Mod, Santo Domingo, 76-77 & Fine Arts Mus, Univ Wyo, 77. *Teaching:* Instr sculpture, Cooper Union Art Inst, 44-47; prof sculpture, Univ Wyo, 47-; univ artist, 79- *Awards:* Lincoln Sesquicentennial Medal, US Cong, 59; Charles G B Steele Sculpture Award, Pa Acad Fine Arts, 66; Order of Duarte, Sanchez & Mella, by Pres Joachim Balaguer, Dominican Repub, 77. *Bibliog:* O A Sealy (auth), Russin's metal magic, Empire Mag, 2/56; Tom Francis (auth), Robert Russin, Wyoming sculptor, Am Artist, 1/60; F K Frame (auth), Russin's Lincoln, Empire Mag, 2/26. *Mem:* Nat Sculpture Soc; Sculptors Guild. *Publ:* Contribr, A new sculptural medium, Col Art J, 56; contribr, The Lincoln monument on the Lincoln highway, Lincoln Herald, 61; contribr, A university bronze foundry, Am Artist, 63. *Dealer:* Maxwell Galleries 551 Sutter Ave San Francisco CA. *Mailing Add:* 716 Ivinson Ave Laramie WY 82070

RUSSO, ALEXANDER PETER
PAINTER, EDUCATOR
b Atlantic City, NJ, June 11, 22. *Study:* Pratt Inst, 40-42; Swarthmore Col, 47; Bard Col, summer 47; Columbia Univ, BFA(Breevort-Eickenmeyer Fel), 52; Acad Fine Arts, Rome, Fulbright Grant, 52-54; Univ Buffalo, 55. *Work:* Albright-Knox Gallery, Buffalo, NY; Corcoran Gallery Art, Washington, DC; Nat Collection Fine Arts, Washington, DC; Fed Ins Deposit Corp, Washington; Acad Arts & Lett, New York. *Comn:* Encaustic mural, Telesio Interlandi, Capo San Andrea, Sicily, 53; var design comns, Doubleday Publ Co, Dutton Publ, Birge Co & Cohn Hall Marx, 56-60; acrylic painting series, US Navy Dept, 64; acrylic mural, Dr Martin Cherkasky, NY, 70; Vet Mem sculpture, Frederick, Md, 75. *Exhib:* Carnegie Nat, Pittsburgh, 46; Int Exhib, Bordighera, Italy, 53 & 54; Four Am Artists Exhib, Biblioteca, Rome, 54; Albright-Knox Gallery Regional, Buffalo, NY, 56; Corcoran Biennials, Washington, DC; and many one-man shows. *Pos:* Combat artist, US Navy Dept, Washington, 42-46; actg art dir, Sewell, Thompson, Caire Advert, New Orleans, 48-49; free-lance artist & designer, var agencies & orgns, New York, 58-60; guest lectr art, Roanoke & Hollins Cols, Univ Southern Ill, Miss Art Asn, and others; art consult, Univ Publications of Am, Frederick, Md, 80- *Teaching:* Assoc prof painting & drawing, Corcoran Sch Art, 61-70, chmn fac & painting dept, 66-69; prof art & chmn dept, Hood Col, 71- *Awards:* Purchase Award, Albright-Knox Art Gallery, Buffalo, NY, 56; David Lloyd Kreeger Award, Corcoran Gallery Art, Washington, DC, 63; Hudson Beneficiary Teaching Fel, Hood Col, 83. *Bibliog:* Carl Fortes (auth), Tape on aesthetics and teaching methods of Alexander Russo, Boston Univ, 68; Anne M Jonas (auth), Focus on Alexander Russo, The Art Scene, 70/71. *Mem:* Col Art Asn; Arts Club Washington (chmn exhibs, 70-71); Artists Equity; Soc Washington Artists; Edward McDowell Colony; Md State Arts Coun. *Media:* Acrylic, Oil. *Publ:* Illusr, To All Hands, an Amphibious Adventure, 44 & illusr, Many a Watchful Night, 45, McGraw; auth, The Italian experience, Inst Int Educ, 53; auth, Profiles on Women Artists, Univ Publ Am, 83. *Dealer:* Phoenix II 1875 Eye St NW Washington DC 20006. *Mailing Add:* 519 Culler Ave Frederick MD 21701

RUSSO, MICHELE
PAINTER
b Waterbury, Conn, Apr 30, 09. *Study:* Yale Univ, BFA, 34; Colorado Springs Fine Arts Ctr, studies with Boardman Robinson & George Biddle, fel, 37. *Work:* Portland Art Mus & Collection of Reed Col, Portland; Dayton Art Inst, Ohio; Seattle Art Mus; Univ Ore Art Mus, Eugene. *Exhib:* Santa Barbara Mus, 63; retrospective, Portland Art Mus, 66; Art of the Pacific Northwest, Smithsonian Inst, Washington, DC, 74; Portland Ctr Visual Arts, 77; one-man show, Portland Ctr Visual Arts, 78; 38th Corcoran Biennial Exhib Am Painting & Second Western States Traveling Exhib, 82-84, Corcoran Gallery, Washington, DC. *Awards:* State Ore Arts Comn Award, 81; City Portland Arts Comn Award, 83. *Bibliog:* Ron Glowen (auth), article, Artweek, 78; Jane Van Cleve (auth), World of Russo, Bigoni Books, 81; 50 Northwest Artists, Chronicle Bks, 83. *Mem:* Metrop Arts Comn, Portland (comnr, 79-81); founder Portland Ctr Visual Arts (pres bd, 71-); founder Artist Equity, Portland; Comt Art Pub Places (chmn, 75). *Media:* Acrylic, Ink. *Dealer:* Fountain Gallery 117 NW 21st Portland OR. *Mailing Add:* 3227 NW Thurman Portland OR 97210

RUST, DAVID E
CURATOR, COLLECTOR
b Bloomington, Ill. *Study:* Harvard Col, BA; NY Univ Inst Fine Arts, MA, 63. *Collections Arranged:* English Drawings & Watercolors, 62; Old Master Drawings from Chatsworth, 69; Nathan Cummings Collection, 70; Francois Boucher....100 Drawings (asst author, catalogue), 73; French Paintings from the Ailsa Mellon Bruce Collection (auth, catalogue), 78. *Pos:* Cur Fr, Brit &

Spanish Paintings, Nat Gallery Art, Washington, DC, 61-83. *Collection:* Paintings and drawings, mostly European sixteenth-nineteenth century; American nineteenth century and some contemporary. *Publ:* Auth, Twentieth Century Paintings & Sculpture of the French School in the Chester Dale Collection, 65; auth, Eighteenth & Nineteenth Century Paintings & Sculpture of the French School in the Chester Dale Collection, 65; auth, The drawings of Vincenzo Tamagni da San Gimignano, Report & Studies Hist Art, 68; auth, Small French Paintings from the Bequest of Ailsa Mellon Bruce, 78. *Mailing Add:* 2812 P St NW Washington DC 20007

RUST, EDWIN C
SCULPTOR, ADMINISTRATOR
b Hammonton, Calif, Dec 5, 10. *Study:* Cornell Univ; Yale Univ, BFA; also with Archipenko & Milles; Southwestern at Memphis, Hon DFA. *Work:* US Ct House, Washington, DC; Univ Tenn Ctr Health Serv; Univ Miss, Oxford; Univ Tenn, Knoxville; Memphis Acad Arts, Tenn. *Exhib:* Whitney Mus Am Art, New York, 40; Carnegie Inst Int, Pittsburgh, 40; Philadelphia Mus Art, 40 & 49; Mus Mod Art, New York, 42; Brooks Mem Mus, 50 & 52. *Pos:* Dir, Memphis Acad Arts, 49-75, emer dir, 75- *Teaching:* Assoc prof sculpture, Col William & Mary, 36-43, head, Dept Fine Arts, 39-43. *Mailing Add:* 3725 Waynoka Ave Memphis TN 38111

RUSTVOLD, KATHERINE JO
DEALER
b Grand Forks, NDak, Jan 24, 50. *Collections Arranged:* Equestrian Exhib, 10/77; American Impressionists, 5/78; The Impressionist Years, 10/78; Ann Biltmore Celebrity Show, 2/81; Henry Casselli, one-man show, 11/81; and others. *Pos:* Mgr, Biltmore Galleries, Los Angeles, Calif, 79- *Specialty:* Nineteenth and twentieth century American art; French Impressionists, with emphasis on American Western and Hudson River School. *Mailing Add:* c/o Biltmore Galleries 515 S Olive St Los Angeles CA 90013

RUTA, PETER PAUL
PAINTER
b Dresden, Ger, Feb 7, 18; US citizen. *Study:* Art Students League, with Morris Kantor & Jean Charlot, 38-42 & 45-46; Acad Fine Arts Venice, 47-49, degree; Acad Venice, with Guido Cadorin, 48. *Work:* Uffizi Gallery, Florence, Italy; Univ Southern Ill. *Exhib:* One-man shows, Larcada Gallery, New York, 76, Santo Domingo Convent, Mex, 78, Sunne Savage Gallery, Boston, 80, Sch House Gallery, Truro, Mass, 83 & Acad Gallery, New Orleans, 83. *Awards:* First Prize, Westchester Art Soc, 65. *Media:* Oil. *Publ:* Ed, Arts Mag, 68-71; ed, Int Art Exhibs, 69. *Dealer:* Modern Art Consultant 390 W End Ave New York NY. *Mailing Add:* 463 West St New York NY 10014

RUTHERFORD, ERICA
PAINTER, PRINTMAKER
b Edinburgh, Scotland, Feb 1, 23. *Study:* Royal Acad Dramatic Art; Slade Sch Fine Art, theatre design with I V Pulunin; Academia, Florence, theatre design with Vangetti. *Work:* Corcoran Gallery, Washington, DC; Burnaby Art Gallery, BC; Mus Contemp Art, Madrid, Spain; Arts Coun Gt Brit; Confederation Art Ctr Mus, PEI; and numerous other corp collections. *Comn:* Puppets, Telegoons, BBC Film Ser; theatre designs, Eng. *Exhib:* Landscape Abbreviations, Victoria Art Gallery, 74; Ten Years at Open Studio, Ont Gallery Art, 81; Gallery Pascal, Toronto, Ont, 77-82; First Choices, Harbour Front Gallery, Toronto, Ont, 81; Burnaby Nat, BC; and other group and one-man shows. *Pos:* Critic, Art Mag & Arts Atlantic. *Teaching:* Vis assoc prof painting & drawing, Univ WVa, 69-71; assoc prof painting, Univ Mo-Columbia, 71-83, retired; vis artist, Fanshawe Col, London, Ont; teacher art, Sheridan Col, Oakville, Ont, Guelph Univ, Ont, 76-77. *Awards:* Best of Show Award, J B Speed Mus Regional Biannual, 69; Colorprint USA Purchase Awards, Tex Tech Univ, 74 & Univ NB; Helen Wurlitzer Found Fel, 82; and others. *Bibliog:* Laura Brandon (auth), Erica Rutherford: Alchemy in art, Arts Atlantic, No 14, summer 82. *Media:* Acrylic; Screenprint. *Mailing Add:* 33 MacPherson 122 Scollard St Toronto ON M5R 1W7 Canada

RUTHLING, FORD
PAINTER, PRINTMAKER
b Santa Fe, NMex, Apr 23, 33. *Study:* With Randall Davey; largely self taught. *Work:* Mus NMex; Wichita Falls Fine Art Mus; Univ Utah Collection. *Comn:* US Pueblo Pottery Postage Stamp (4 thirteen cent stamps), 77; and others. *Exhib:* Nelson Atkins Mus, Kansas City Mus Fine Art; Dallas Mus Fine Art; Wichita Falls Mus Fine Art; Roswell Art Mus, 79; and others. *Media:* Oil, Graphics. *Mailing Add:* 313 E Berger St Santa Fe NM 87501

RUTHVEN, JOHN ALDRICH
PAINTER, LECTURER
b Cincinnati, Ohio, Nov 12, 24. *Study:* Cincinnati Art Acad; Cent Acad Com Art; Miami Univ, Ohio, DHL; St Francis Col, Loretto, Pa, DHL. *Work:* Hermitage Mus, Leningrad, Russia; Armstrong Space Mus, Wapakoneta, Ohio; Ruthven Conf Ctr, Middletown, Ohio; Smithsonian Inst, Washington, DC; Cincinnati Natural Hist Mus. *Comn:* Cardinals for Gov Conf, State Ohio, Columbus, 68, Eagle to the Moon, 69; Colonial Williamsburg Ser, Va, 70-75; Cardinal, USSR, 70; Miami Indian, Miami Univ, 74. *Exhib:* Ducks Unlimited, Hilton Head, SC, 72; Ohio State Fair, Columbus, 74; White House Reception, 76; Leigh-Yawkey-Woodson Mus, Wausau, Wis, 76 & 77; Wildlife Festival, Easton, Md, 77. *Pos:* Mem bd dir, Cincinnati Nature Ctr, 69-; trustee, Cincinnati Natural Hist Mus, 71-; trustee, Ducks Unlimited, 75- *Awards:* Sachs Fine Art Award, Cincinnati Art Acad, 69; Printing Industry Am Award, 70-77; Ohioana Career Medal, Martha Kinne Cooper Ohioana Libr,

75. *Bibliog:* Jerry Bowles (auth), John Ruthven, Acquire Mag, 73; Cincinnati Art, Town & Country, 75; Dan Johnston (auth), John Ruthven, Artist, pvt publ, 75. *Mem:* Soc Animal Artists New York. *Media:* Opaque Watercolor. *Publ:* Coauth, Topflight, 69; auth, Carolina Paraquet, Audubon Mag, 72; auth, Regal Series Prints, 68-75, North American Series Prints, 69-75 & Aquatint Series Prints, 71-81, Wildlife Int Publ. *Mailing Add:* 6290 Old State Rte 68 Georgetown OH 45121

RUTSCH, ALEXANDER
PAINTER, SCULPTOR
b Austria. *Study:* Acad Fine Art, Belgrade, Yugoslavia; studied in Vienna & Austria; govt study grant, Paris. *Work:* Albertina Graphic Art Collection, Austria; Austrian Gallery, Belvedere, Vienna; Munic Mus, Vienna; Mus Mod Art, Paris; Mus Liege, Belg. *Exhib:* Int Sculptors, Mus Rodin, Paris, 62-63; one-man show, Galerie Vendome, Brussels, Belg, 65; Int Exhib, Grand Palais de Champs Elyses, Paris, 66; Avanti Galleries, 74 & Harkness House Gallery, 75, New York. *Teaching:* Pelham Art Ctr, NY, 82 & Blumka II, New York, 82. *Awards:* Silver Medal Arts, Sci & Lett & Bronze Medal Art, City Paris, 58; First Prize, Salon Artistique Int Sceaux, 54; Int Beaux Arts Artist Year, 76 & 82. *Bibliog:* Jean Desville (producer), The world of Rutsch (film), 64; Carlton Lake (auth), In Quest of Dali, Putnams, 69; Roger Seiler (auth), Inner Eye of Alexander Rutsch (film), IBM, 72. *Mem:* Burr Artists New York; Accad Ital. *Mailing Add:* 222 Highbrook Ave Pelham NY 10803

RUTTINGER, JACQUELYN
PAINTER, EDUCATOR
b Great Falls, Mont, July 21, 40. *Study:* Univ Wash, Seattle, 58-60; Art Inst Chicago, with McKinnon, Fabian, Kauffman & Yoshida, BFA(hon), 63; Northern Ill Univ, with Mahmoud, Beard & Syrek, MA, 76, MFA, 77; Governor's State Univ, 81-83. *Work:* Ill State Mus, Springfield; State Ill Percent Art, Northern Ill Univ, DeKalb & Eastern Ill Univ, Charleston; Freeport Art Mus, Ill; Univ Wis, Waukesha. *Exhib:* Works on Paper, Art Inst Chicago, 78; 17th Nat Print & Drawing Exhib, Bradley Univ, Peoria Art Guild, Lakeview Mus, 79; 31st Ill Invitational, Ill State Mus, Springfield, 79; Prints & Multiples, Art Inst Chicago, 81; Three at the Mitchell Mus, Mt Vernon, Ill, 81; traveling exhib, Nat Acad Design, New York, Nat Mus Am Art, Smithsonian Inst, Ill State Mus, Southern Ill Univ Mus & Western Ill Univ Gallery, 82-83; Stockton Nat Print & Drawing Exhib, Haggin Mus, Calif, 83. *Teaching:* Instr art, Prairie State Col, 77-81; community prof, Governor's State Univ, 82; chmn art dept, St Mary-of-the-Woods Col, 83- *Awards:* Exhib Honorarium, Ill Painters III Traveling Exhib, Ill Arts Coun, 80-81; Merit Award for Paintings, 12th Biennial Michiana Regional, Art Ctr Inc, South Bend, Ind, 82; Proj Completion Grant for Printmaking, Ill Arts Coun, 81-82. *Bibliog:* Judith Kanin (auth), article, New Art Examiner, 1/79; Adelaide Cooley (auth), Ruttinger & O'Brien, New Art Examiner, 12/81; Nancy Rice (auth), Forecki, Ruttinger & Teczar, New Art Examiner, 12/82. *Mem:* Col Art Asn Am; Arts Illiana; Chicago Artists' Coalition; Mid-Am Col Art Asn; Women's Caucus Art. *Media:* Acrylic. *Dealer:* Contemp Art Workshop 542 W Grant Place Chicago IL 60614. *Mailing Add:* Art Dept St Mary of Woods Col St Mary of the Woods IN 47876

RUTZKY, IVY SKY
SCULPTOR
b New York, NY, Nov 19, 48. *Study:* Penland Sch, NC, 69; Univ NMex, BFA, 73. *Work:* Glacial, Macomb Community Col, Warren, Mich. *Comn:* Silver Phoenix, Detroit, Mich, 79; Hybrid, Ann Arbor, Mich, 80. *Exhib:* One-person shows, Threshold, Kiva, New York, 80; Cranbrook Acad Art, 80 & Berry Col, Ga, 83; Gilbert & Lila Silverman Collection, Cranbrook Acad Art, Bloomfield Hills, Mich, 81; Artists Invite Artists, Limnol, New Mus, New York, 81; and others. *Bibliog:* Dennis Nawrocki & Tom Holleman (auth), Art in Detroit Public Places, Wayne State Univ Press, 80; Ruth & Louis Redstone (auth), Public Art/New Directions, McGraw-Hill, 81; Keith Johnson, Threshold, Art Express, 5-6/81. *Mailing Add:* PO Box 215 New York NY 10013

RUVOLO, FELIX EMMANUELE
PAINTER, EDUCATOR
b New York, NY, Apr 28, 12. *Study:* In Catania, Sicily. *Work:* Krannert Art Mus, Univ Ill, Urbana; Art Inst Chicago; Walker Art Ctr, Minneapolis; Oakland Mus, Calif; Univ Calif Mus Fine Arts, Berkeley. *Comn:* Colored lithograph, Collectors Press, 67. *Exhib:* Abstract & Surrealist Art in America, Mus Mod Art, New York, 51; 60 Americans--1960, Walker Art Ctr, 60; American Drawing, Moore Col Art Gallery, Philadelphia, 68; Drawings 1969, Ithaca Col Art Gallery, NY, 69; American Drawing & Sculpture, 1948-1969, Krannert Art Mus, 71; Gruerrebaum Gallery, 82. *Teaching:* Prof art, Art Inst Chicago, 44-48; prof art, Univ Calif, Berkeley, 50-; prof art, Univ Southern Calif, summer 63. *Awards:* San Francisco Mus Art Award, 64; Hall of Justice Competition Award, San Francisco Art Comn, 67; Grants, Univ Calif Inst Creative Arts, 64 & 71. *Bibliog:* K Kult (auth), Felix Ruvolo, Mag Art, 47 & Painters who teach, Pictorial Living, 59; N Pousette Dart (auth), American Painting Today, Hastings, 57. *Mailing Add:* 78 Strathmoor Dr Berkeley CA 94705

RYAN, DAVID MICHAEL
MUSEUM DIRECTOR
b Lincoln, Nebr, July 10, 39. *Study:* Univ Nebr, BFA & BA, 62; Univ Nebr Law Sch, 62-63; Univ Denver, MA, 65. *Collections Arranged:* Sixth Minn Biennial, 68; Documents at, 69; Barry Le Va: Piece One and Two, 69, Richard Avedon, 70, Art Deco, 71 & American Indian Art: Form and Tradition, 72, Minneapolis Inst Art; Aycock, Holste, Singer, 80, Josef Hoffman, 82, Twentieth Century Drawings, 83, Focus Series: Cork

Marcheschi, 79, Jim Woodson, 80, Arthur France, 81, Maureen Connor, 82, Suzanne Paul, 83, Otis Jones, 83 & Garrison Roots, 83, Ft Worth Art Mus. *Pos:* Mus intern, Denver Art Mus, 64-65; cur asst, Walker Art Ctr, 65-68; cur exhibs, Minneapolis Inst Arts, 68-72; asst dir, Am Fedn Arts, New York, 73-74; asst dir mus prog, Nat Endowment Arts, 74-79; dir, Ft Worth Art Mus, 79- *Mem:* Asn Art Mus Dirs. *Publ:* Auth, Guide to the Painting and Sculpture Collection, Ft Worth Art Mus, 83. *Mailing Add:* 1309 Montgomery St Ft Worth TX 76107

RYAN, ELIZABETH THERESA
PAINTER
b New York, NY. *Study:* With Ed Whitney, Ivan Olinsky & Bruce Stevenson. *Work:* Va State Col, Richmond; Frye Mus, Seattle. *Exhib:* Am Watercolor Soc Travelling Exhib, 82-83; Nat Acad Design; Salmagundi Club; and others. *Awards:* Dorothy Laphman Ferriss Award, Pen & Brush Inc Watercolor Exhib, 83. *Mem:* Am Watercolor Soc (treas, 70-73); Allied Artists Am; Audubon Artists (mem bd dirs, 82-84); Salmagundi Club. *Media:* Watercolor. *Mailing Add:* 14 Sutton Pl S New York NY 10022

RYDEN, KENNETH GLENN
SCULPTOR
b Chicago, Ill, May 16, 45. *Study:* Univ Wis, Superior, BFA; Univ Kans, Lawrence, MFA; study with Bernard Frazer, Eldon Tefft & Victor Timmerman. *Work:* Grover Hermann Fine Arts Ctr, Marietta, Ohio; Swope Art Gallery, Terre Haute, Ind; Southern Ill Univ Art Collection, Edwardsville; Wabash Col Art Collection, Crawfordsville, Ind; Kans State Univ; and others. *Comn:* Delyte Morris Mem, Southern Ill Univ at Edwardsville, 76 & John Rendleman Mem, 76; Greenville City Sq, 80; 10 Yr Mem, Southern Ill Univ, Sch Med, Springfield. *Exhib:* Mainstreams 73, Grover M Hermann Fine Arts Ctr, Marietta, Ohio, 73; one-man exhibs, Univ Wis-Superior, Ark State Univ, Jonesboro, Univ Notre Dame, Kans State Univ, Manhattan & Roberts Wesleyan Col, Rochester; Houghton Col, New York, 80; and many others. *Teaching:* Instr sculpture, Univ Mo, Columbia, 70-73; asst prof sculpture, Southern Ill Univ, Edwardsville, 73-78; assoc prof & chmn art dept, Greenville Col, Ill, 78-; assoc prof, Anderson Col, Ind, 83- *Awards:* Purchase Award, Mainstreams 73, Grover M Hermann Fine Arts Ctr, 73; Top Purchase Award, 33rd Ann Wabash Valley Sheldon Swope Art Gallery, 77; First in Sculpture, Int Platform Asn Artists Exhib, 82. *Mem:* Nat Col Art Asn; Southern Sculptors Asn; Nat Sculpture Ctr; Int Platform Asn; Washington Arts Club, Washington, DC. *Media:* Multimedia, Metals. *Dealer:* Prairie House Gallery 213 S Sixth St Springfield IL 62701; Neville-Sargent Gallery 509 Main St Evanston IL 60202. *Mailing Add:* 310 W Eighth St Anderson IN 46016

RYDER, MAHLER BESSINGER
COLLAGE ARTIST, ILLUSTRATOR
b Columbus, Ohio, July 7, 37. *Study:* Columbus Col Art & Design, 55-58; Art Students League, 66-68; Provincetown Workshop, Mass, 64; Sch Visual Art, 67-68; RI Sch Design, 77. *Work:* E J Arnold Collection, Wis Univ, Superior; Col Art & Design, Columbus, Ohio; RI Hosp Trust, Providence; Nat Ctr Afro-Am Artists, Boston, Mass; RI Hosp, 82. *Comn:* Mural, US Army Baumholder, Ger, 62-63; RI State Coun Arts, 75 & 81; RI State Coun Arts, 83; Kwan um Zen Sch (logo design), 83. *Exhib:* One-man exhib, Whitney Mus Am Art, 73; two-man show, Two Afro-Am Artists, Nat Ctr Afro-Am Art, 77 & Ohio State Univ, 79; Am Acad & Inst Arts & Lett, New York, 79; Franklin Furnace, New York, 80; Wheeler Gallery, Providence, RI, 81; and others. *Teaching:* Instr children's sculpture, Sompsec, Bd Educ, New York, 66-67; asst prof illus & drawing, RI Sch Design, 69- *Awards:* Painting & Sculpture Award, Art Students League, Ford Found, 64-66; RI State Coun Arts Proj Award, 72, 75 & 78; Nat Endowment Arts Award, 73. *Bibliog:* Robert Doty (auth), Contemporary Black Artists in America, Dodd Mead, 71; Neal & Di Gregorio (auths), Practically speaking, Nat Libr J, 72; Barry Schwartz (auth), The New Humanism: Art in Time of Change, Praeger, 74. *Mem:* Arts RI (trustee, 71-72); RI Arts Educ; New Eng Found Arts; RI State Coun Arts; RI Vol Lawyers Arts. *Media:* Collage, Mixed Media. *Publ:* Auth, Eight by Eight (catalog), Riverside Mus, 67; illusr, Arts in Society, Univ Wis, 72-74; contribr & illusr, RI State Libr Booklet, 72; contribr, The New Humanism: Art in Time of Change, Praeger, 74; illusr & contribr, Any Art J, RI State Coun Arts, 77. *Dealer:* Suzette Schochet Gallery Brick Market Place Newport RI 02840; Gallery Seven Fisher Bldg Studio 315 Detroit MI. *Mailing Add:* c/o RI Sch of Design 2 College St Providence RI 02906

RYERSON, MARGERY A
PAINTER, PRINTMAKER
b Morristown, NJ, Sept 15, 1886. *Study:* Vassar Col, AB; Art Students League, with Robert Henri; also with Charles Hawthorne, Provincetown, Mass. *Work:* Vassar Col Gallery, Poughkeepsie; Fr Mus, Seattle, Wash; etchings, Metrop Mus Art, New York; Philbrook Art Ctr, Tulsa, Okla; Bibliot Nat, Paris. *Exhib:* Allied Artists Am, New York, 71 & 77; NJ Watercolor Soc, Morristown, 71; Am Watercolor Soc, 72 & 76; Nat Acad Design & Audubon Artists, 72 & 74, New York. *Awards:* Maynard Prize, Nat Acad Design, 59; Hook Prize, Am Watercolor Soc, 62; Silver Medal, Nat Arts Club, 71. *Bibliog:* E Hobson (auth), An artist and a child, Foster's Daily Democrat, Dover, NH, 8/15/70; Charles Morralli (auth), article, Am Artist, 1/10/76. *Mem:* Nat Acad Design; life mem Am Watercolor Soc; life mem Allied Artists Am; NJ Watercolor Soc; Nat Arts Club. *Media:* Watercolor, Oil. *Publ:* Ed, Robert Henri's The Art Spirit, 23 & Hawthorne on Painting, 36; illusr, Winkie Boo, 48; contribr, Am Artist. *Dealer:* Grand Central Art Galleries 43rd St & Madison Ave New York NY 10017; Chapellier Galleries 815 Park Ave New York NY 10021. *Mailing Add:* 15 Gramercy Park S New York NY 10003

RYMAN, ROBERT
PAINTER
b Nashville, Tenn, May 30, 30. *Study:* Tenn Polytech Inst, 48-49; George Peabody Col, 49-50. *Work:* Mus Mod Art, New York; Milwaukee Art Ctr, Wis; Wadsworth Atheneum, Hartford, Conn; Ctr Pompidou, Paris; Whitney Mus Am Art; and others. *Exhib:* One-man shows, Guggenheim Mus, New York, 72, Stedelijk Mus, 74, Palais Des Beaux-Arts, Brussels, 74 & Kunsthalle, Basel, Switz, 75; Whitechapel Art Gallery, London, 77; Centre Pompidou, Paris, 80; Kunsthalle, Ger, 81; and others. *Pos:* Mem, Art Comn New York, 82-85. *Bibliog:* Barbara M Reise (auth), Robert Ryman, Studio Int, 2/74, 3/74 & Data, Vol 4, No 11; Phyllis Tuchman (auth), An interview with Robert Ryman, Artforum, 5/71. *Mailing Add:* 17 W 16th St New York NY 10011

S

SAALBURG, ALLEN RUSSEL
PAINTER, PRINTMAKER
b Rochelle, Ill, June 25, 1899. *Study:* Art Students League. *Work:* Paintings, US Air Force Hist Art Collection, Washington, DC & Whitney Mus, Juliana Force Collection, New York; prints, Philadelphia Mus Art & Bucks Co Hist Soc, Doylestown, Pa. *Comn:* Murals, Arsenal & five park dept bldgs, New York, 36, Pa RR, Steamship Line & USS Constitution, 38 & New York World's Fair Sci Bldg, 39; movie sets, Green Pastures & Two Bouquets, Marc Connolly, Hollywood, Calif, 38; fullscale mural of Clairol Bldg, New York World's Fair, 64. *Exhib:* Decorative Panels Exhib, Bernheim Jeune Gallery, Paris, 27-30; Kraushaar Gallery, several 37-75, Whitney Mus, 38, Bodley Gallery, New York, 73-74, 79 & 81. *Bibliog:* Robert V Godsoe (auth), article, Esquire Mag; Robert Blattner (auth), article, Am Artist Mag, 58. *Media:* Oil, Gouache. *Dealer:* Bodley Gallery 1063 Madison Ave New York NY 10028. *Mailing Add:* AA Star Route Box 5 Upper Black Eddy PA 18972

SAAR, BETYE
ASSEMBLAGE ARTIST, COLLAGE ARTIST
b Los Angeles, Calif, July 30, 26. *Study:* Univ Calif, Los Angeles, BA; Univ Southern Calif; Long Beach State Col; San Fernando Valley State Col. *Work:* Univ Mass, Amherst; Wellington Evest Collection, Boston; Golden State Mutual Life Ins Collection, Los Angeles; Los Angeles Co Mus Art; Univ Calif Mus, Berkeley. *Comn:* Poster design, Los Angeles Bicentennial Ser, 79. *Exhib:* Sculpture Ann, 70 & Contemporary Black Artists in America, 71; Whitney Mus Am Art, New York; Black Artist Exhib, Los Angeles Co Mus Art, 72; one-woman exhibs, Whitney Mus Am Art, 75, Jan Baum/Iris Silverman Gallery, Los Angeles, 77 & 79, Univ Art Gallery, Univ NDak, 79 & Mandeville Art Gallery, Univ Calif, San Diego, 79; Painting/Sculpture in Calif: Mod Era, San Francisco Mus Mod Art, 76 & Smithsonian Inst, Washington, DC, 77; San Francisco Mus Mod Art, 77; Studio Mus, Harlem, New York, 80. *Pos:* Costume designer, Inner City Cult Ctr, Los Angeles, 68-71. *Teaching:* Vis artist, Calif State Univ, Hayward, fall 71; prof art, Calif State Univ, Northridge, 73-75 & Otis Art Inst, 76-; Univ Alaska, summer 79. *Awards:* Purchase Award, Calif State Col, Los Angeles, 72; Purchase Award, Downy Mus Art, 72; Nat Endowment Arts Award, 74. *Bibliog:* Spirit Catcher: The Art of Betye Saar, The Originals: Women in Art series, WNET-PBS, New York; Houston Conwill (auth), Interview with Betye Saar, Black Art, 79; Eleanor Munro (auth), Originals: American Women Artists, Simon & Schuster, 79; Lynn Miller & Sally Swenson (auths), Lives & Works: Talks with Women Artists, Scarecrow Press, NJ, 81. *Media:* Multimedia. *Publ:* Auth, Handbook, 67. *Dealer:* Monique Knowlton New York NY. *Mailing Add:* 8074 Willow Glen Rd Los Angeles CA 90046

SAARI, PETER H
PAINTER, SCULPTOR
b New York, NY, Feb 15, 51. *Study:* Sch Visual Arts, 69-70; C W Post Col, BFA, 74; Tyler Sch Art, Rome, Italy, study with Stephen Greene, 72-73; Yale Sch Art, study with William Bailey & Al Held, MFA(fel), 76. *Work:* Hirshhorn Mus, Washington, DC. *Exhib:* One-man shows, Lamagna Gallery, New York, 75 & 76 & O K Harris Gallery, New York, 77, 78 & 80; Rothmans Int Realist Traveling Exhib, Ont, Can, 76-78; This is Today: An Exhib of Works by Living Artists, Root Art Ctr, Hamilton Col, Clinton, NY, 77; Artists Look at Art, Helen Foresman Spencer Mus, Univ Kans, Lawrence, 78; Directions, Hirshhorn Mus, 79; one-man shows, Lamagna Gallery, New York, 75 & 76, O K Harris Gallery, New York, 77, 78 & 80. *Teaching:* Asst instr advan painting, Yale Sch Art, New Haven, Conn, 75-76; guest lectr, St Lawrence Univ, 78. *Bibliog:* John R Clark (auth), Peter Saari's new paintings, Arts Mag, Vol 50, No 6, 76; Gregory Battcock (auth), Why Art, E P Dutton, 77; Andrew Batey (auth), Peter Saari, Archetype, spring 79. *Mailing Add:* c/o Ivan Karp 383 W Broadway New York NY 10007

SAARINEN, LILIAN
SCULPTOR
b New York, NY, Apr 17, 12. *Study:* Art Students League, with Alexander Archipenko, 28; study with Hans Warneke, 34-36; with Albert Stewart; Cranbrook Acad Art, with Carl Milles, 36-40. *Work:* IBM Collection; Addison Mus Gallery, Andover, Mass; Fogg Art Mus, Harvard Univ. *Comn:* Sculpture for Toffennetti Restaurant, Skidmore, Owings & Merrill, Chicago, 48; eagle for Detroit Fed Reserve Bank, Leineweber Yamasaki & Hellmuth, Detroit, 52; and others. *Exhib:* World's Fair, 39; Los Angeles Co Art Fair, 44; Boston Arts Festival, 54-60; Beverly Farms Regional Art Exhib, Mass, 63; St

Gaudens Hist Park, Cornish, NH, 75. *Teaching:* Instr lang of clay, Pratt Inst, Brooklyn, 59-60, Mus Fine Arts, Boston, 63-64 & Mass Inst Technol, 63-67. *Awards:* Jefferson Nat Expansion Mem Competition Award for Sculpture Gateway to the West, 48; Walter B Ford Prize for Eagle, 54; Beverly Farms Regional Art Exhib Award for Portrait Edwin O'Connor, 61. *Bibliog:* Clay sculpture, Arts & Archit, 9/42; Emily Genauer (auth), Super sculpture, This Week Mag, Detroit News, 9/54; Mabel Colgate (auth), Visit with L Saarinen, Boston Globe, 5/7/70. *Mem:* Cambridge Art Asn; St Gaudens Nat Hist Park (trustee, 73-75); Fine Arts Work Ctr Provincetown. *Media:* Terra Cotta, Metal. *Publ:* Auth & illusr, Who Am I?, Reynal & Hitchcock, 46; design for eagle used on book jackets, Americans, 63 & Short Chronology of American History, 63. *Mailing Add:* 224 Brattle St Cambridge MA 02138

SABATELLA, JOSEPH JOHN
ADMINISTRATOR, PAINTER
b Chicago, Ill, May 5, 31. *Study:* Univ Ill, BFA(painting & graphics), 54, MFA(painting & graphics), 58. *Comn:* Acrylic painting on masonite, Campus Cafeteria, Univ Fla, Gainesville, 64. *Exhib:* Hunterdon Print Society, Nat Print Show, 57; Libr Cong, Washington, DC, 57; Society Four Arts, West Palm Beach Fla, 63; Atlantic Artist Show, Clemson Col, SC, 64; one-man shows, Atelier Chapman Kelley, Dallas, Tex, 64 & Visual Arts Comt Jacksonville Coun Arts, Fla, 69; and others. *Pos:* Mgr, Elenhank Designers Inc, Riverside, Ill, 58-59. *Teaching:* Prof drawing & design, Univ Fla, Gainesville, 59-, asst dean, Col Archit & Fine Arts, 66-75, dean, 75- *Awards:* First Award, Arts Festival Six, City of Jacksonville, Fla, 63. *Mem:* Int Coun Fine Arts Deans. *Media:* Oil. *Mailing Add:* 2510 N W 30th Terrace Gainesville FL 32605

SABATINI, RAPHAEL
PAINTER, SCULPTOR
b Philadelphia, Pa, Nov 26, 1898. *Study:* Pa Acad Fine Arts, Cresson traveling scholarships; also with Arthur B Carles, Fernand Leger, Antoine Bourdelle & Constantin Brancusi. *Work:* Philadelphia Mus Art; Pa Acad Fine Arts, Philadelphia; Sturgis R Ingersoll Collection, Pennlyn, Pa. *Comn:* Frieze for Fine Art Bldg, Sesquicentennial, Philadelphia, 26; Mother Mary Drexel Chapel, Langhorn, Pa, 29; NW Ayer Bldg, Philadelphia, 28. *Exhib:* Sesquecentennial, Philadelphia, 26; Golden Gate Expos, San Francisco; Pa Acad Fine Art Ann. *Pos:* Comnr, Philadelphia Art Comn, 65-68; consult, Fine Art Comn, Redevelop Auth, Philadelphia, 71- *Teaching:* Prof painting & sculpture, Tyler Sch Art, Temple Univ, 36-66, prof emer, 66- *Awards:* Limback Found Award for distinguished teaching, 62; Percy Owens Mem Award for distinguished Pa artist, 63; 400th Anniversary of Michelangelo Award, Am Inst Ital Cult, 64. *Mem:* Artists Equity Asn; Philadelphia Art Alliance; Philadelphia Art Mus; fel Pa Acad Fine Arts. *Publ:* Auth, Sculpture processes, Prothman Baldwin, 57. *Mailing Add:* 7318 Oak Lane Rd Melrose Park PA 19126

SABELIS, HUIBERT
PRINTMAKER, PAINTER
b Wageningen-Gelderland, Neth, Feb 28, 42; Can citizen. *Study:* Tech Sch Art, Neth, with Bloothoofd, 57-60; Art Instr Schs Inc, Minneapolis, 64; lino printmaking with Senggih, 73. *Work:* Royal Ont Mus, Toronto; Philippine Nat Mus, Manila; UNESCO of Japan, Tokyo; Nat Libr, Paris, France; HRH Prince Bernard of the Neth. *Exhib:* One-man shows, Woodstock Public Art Gallery, Can, 80, Laurier Gallery, Totonto, Can, 81 & Galerij 3, The Netherlands, 81; Saxe Gallery, Toronto, Can, 81; and many other one-man & group exhibs. *Media:* Acrylic, Watercolor, Serigraphy. *Dealer:* Holysingel 80 313 G L C Vlaardingen The Netherlands; Calle 119 No 7-47 Int 4 Bogota DE 10 Columbia. *Mailing Add:* 309 Kristin Grove Mississauga ON L5A 3E7 Canada

SABLOW, RHODA LILLIAN See Roda

SABO, BETTY JEAN
PAINTER, DEALER
b Kansas City, Mo, Sept 15, 28. *Study:* Univ NMex; also with Randall Davey, Carl von Hassler, Charles Reynolds & Al Merrill. *Comn:* Baldequino (mural), St Bernadette's Catholic Church, Albuquerque, 61; painted windows, Ascension Church, Pojoaque, NMex, 63; 15 paintings for children murals, pediatrics ward, St Joseph's Hosp, 66; Leanin' Tree Cards, Artists of the Am West, 77; Christmas Greeting, Phelps-Dodge Collection, 81. *Exhib:* Albuquerque I, Albuquerque Mus, 68; Ariz-NMex Regional Exhib, Phoenix, Ariz, 70-71; Catharine Lorillard Wolfe Exhib, Nat Acad, NY, 71 & Nat Arts Club, NY, 72-73; Allied Artists, 78-80; and others. *Pos:* Co-owner, Galeria del Sol, currently. *Awards:* Grand Award, 68 & First Prize Oils, 70, NMex State Fair; Purchase Award, Regional Art Exhib, Phoenix, 70. *Bibliog:* James Newton (auth), Chili, not chicken soup, Phoenix Gazette, 73; Flo Wilks (auth), The colorful way of the land, SW Art, 12/77; Women Artists, Southwestern Art, 4/81. *Mem:* Catharine Lorillard Wolfe Art Club; Artists Equity Asn, Albuquerque; NMex Art League; Am Artists Prof League. *Media:* Oil. *Specialty:* Regional arts and crafts; cooperative gallery. *Dealer:* Galeria del Sol 206 1/2 San Felipe NW Albuquerque NM 87102. *Mailing Add:* 705 Parkland Circle SE Albuquerque NM 87108

SABO, IRVING
SCULPTOR, DESIGNER
b New York, NY, Mar 27, 20. *Study:* Cooper Union Art Sch, cert, 40. *Work:* Elmira Col Permanent Collection. *Exhib:* New Design, Walker Art Ctr, Minneapolis, 51; Columbus Park Competition, Hudson River Mus, Yonkers, NY, 74; New Eng Ann, Silvermine Guild Artists, New Canaan, Conn, 74, 76-79; Contemporary Reflections, Aldrich Mus, Ridgefield, Conn, 78; New

Brit Mus Am Art, Conn, 78; Bridgeport Mus Art Sci & Indust, Conn, 79; solo show, Carlson Art Gallery, Univ Bridgeport, Conn, 82. *Teaching:* Instr, Cooper Union Art Sch, 47-50; instr, Brooklyn Mus Art Sch, 50-54. *Awards:* 2nd Prizes, 25th New Eng Ann, Cleworth Publ Co, 74 & 29th New Eng Ann, Olivetti Found, 78; 1st Prize, 27th New Eng Ann, Silvermine Guild, 76. *Bibliog:* Dona Z Meilach (auth), Woodworking--The New Wave Crown, 81. *Mem:* Silvermine Guild Artists (vpres, 77-80); Sculptors Guild; Orgn Independent Artists. *Media:* Wood. *Dealer:* Bell Gallery Stamford CT. *Mailing Add:* 10 Old Hill Rd Westport CT 06880

SACHS, A M
DEALER, COLLECTOR
b New York, NY. *Study:* Univ Mich, Ann Arbor, BA. *Pos:* Dir, A M Sachs Gallery. *Mem:* Art Dealers Asn Am; Confederation Inst des Negociants en Oeuvres d'Art. *Specialty:* Contemporary painters and sculptors. *Collection:* Power Boothe, Alice Dalton Brown, Dorthy Dehner, Terry Lee Dill, Alan Falk, John Ferren, John Gundelfinger, Douglas Maguire, Roger Laux Nelson, Stephen Pace, Jon Schueler, Sally Vagliano, Simon Harling & Ben Norris. *Mailing Add:* 29 W 57th St New York NY 10019

SACHS, SAMUEL, II
HISTORIAN, MUSEUM DIRECTOR
b New York, NY, Nov 30, 35. *Study:* Harvard Univ, AB(cum laude); NY Univ Inst Fine Arts, AM. *Collections Arranged:* The Past Rediscovered, XIX Century French Painting 1800-1900, 69; Fakes and Forgeries (with catalog), 73; Grant Wood, 83. *Pos:* Asst prints & drawings, Minneapolis Inst Arts, 58-60, chief cur, 64-73, dir, 73-; asst dir, Univ Mich Mus Art, 62-64. *Teaching:* Lectr art hist, Univ Mich, Ann Arbor, 62-63; lectr art hist, Minneapolis Inst Arts, 64- *Mem:* Am Asn Mus; Am Fedn Arts; Col Art Asn Am; Asn Art Mus Dir; Int Coun of Mus. *Res:* Fakes and forgeries; American 19th and 20th century painting. *Publ:* Auth, Reconstructing the whirlwind of 26th St, Art News, 2/63; auth, Drawings and watercolors of Thomas Moran, In: Thomas Moran (catalog), Univ Calif, Riverside, 63; auth, American paintings at the Minneapolis Institute of Arts, 71; auth, Art forges ahead, Auction Mag, 1/72; auth, Favorite Paintings from the Minneapolis Institute of Arts, Abbcyville Press, 81. *Mailing Add:* 2400 Third Ave S Minneapolis MN 55404

SACHSE, JANICE R
PAINTER, PRINTMAKER
b New Orleans, La, May 6, 08. *Study:* La State Univ, with Conrad Albrizio. *Work:* New Orleans Mus Art; Anglo Am Mus, La State Univ; Lauren Rogers Mus, Laurel, Miss; Pan American Life Insurance Bldg, New Orleans. *Exhib:* New York World's Fair, 65; Volkfest Exhib from New Orleans Galleries, Berlin, Ger, 68; 11th Midwest Biennial, Joslyn Art Mus, Omaha, Nebr, 70; Sally Jackson Gallery, Hong Kong, 70; 50 Year Retrospective, La State Univ, 82; Southern Works on Paper 1900-1950, Southern Arts Fed, Atlanta; Am Soc Contemp Artists Exhib, New York, 83. *Awards:* Ten juried purchase prizes; Bicentennial Exhib Purchase Prize, 76; First Prize, 65th Anniversary Celebration Exhib, Am Soc Contemp Artists, 83. *Bibliog:* Keith Cooper Marshall (auth), article, Am Artist Mag, 9/80. *Mem:* Am Soc Contemp Artists. *Publ:* Auth, article & centerfold, New Orleans Mus Art, Arts Quarterly, 81. *Dealer:* Griffith-Menard Gallery 7643 Jefferson Baton Rouge LA 70809. *Mailing Add:* 3737 Essen Lane #60 Baton Rouge LA 70809

SACKLARIAN, STEPHEN
PAINTER
b Varna, Bulgaria, Nov 25, 1899; US citizen. *Study:* Fleisher Mem Art Sch; Philadelphia Col of Art; Pa Acad of Fine Arts; Wharton Sch, Univ Pa; also studied sculpture with Paul Manship. *Work:* Smithsonian Inst, Washington, DC; Philadelphia Mus Art, Pa; Museo Arte Moderno, Mex; Everson Mus Art, Syracuse, NY; Royal Mus Fine Arts, Belg; and more than 50 other museums. *Comn:* Wood sculpture, Furman Family Trust, Washington, DC, 68; painting, Int Sci Meeting on Aging, Bulgarian Govt, Sophia, 77. *Exhib:* Notre Dame Art Gallery, Ind, 75; Greenville Mus Art, SC, 76; Everson Mus Art, Syracuse, 76-77; one-man shows, Fla Gulf Coast Art Ctr, Clearwater, 76, Moravian Col, Bethlehem, Pa, 76 & Chicago, 79. *Teaching:* Artist-in-residence painting, Univ Notre Dame, Ind, 75; guest lectr art, Moravian Col, Bethlehem, Pa, 75-76. *Awards:* Achievement in Art, Bulgarian Govt, 76. *Media:* Acrylic on Canvas. *Mailing Add:* c/o Dr A F Furman 12308 Loch Carron Cir Washington DC 20022

SACKS, BEVERLY & RAY
CONSULTANTS, COLLECTORS
b US. *Study:* Beverly: Brooklyn Col, BA; Ray: Pratt Inst. *Pos:* Beverly: Consult, Phillips & Son & Neale, Am Illusr; owners, Sacks Fine Art. *Bibliog:* Antique & Arts Weekly, 10/17/80; Maine Antique Digest, 11/80; Buying American painting, Boston Sunday Globe, 11/23/80. *Mem:* Appraisers Asn Am; Prof Antique Dealers Asn; Long Island Antique Dealers Asn; Soc Illusr; Nat Arts Club. *Specialty:* American paintings; 19th and early 20th century American illustrations and paintings. *Collection:* American symbolist, muralist and illustrator paintings. *Publ:* Auth, Rube Goldberg, Early Works, 81. *Mailing Add:* Box 141 Cedarhurst NY 11516

SADEK, GEORGE
EDUCATOR, DESIGNER
b Czech, Oct 12, 28; US citizen. *Study:* Hunter Col; City Univ New York, BA; Ind Univ, MFA. *Work:* Mus Mod Art, New York; Libr Cong; Morgan Libr. *Exhib:* Type Dir Club New York, 69; Am Inst Graphic Arts, 70; Typomondus, Frankfurt, Ger, 71. *Teaching:* From instr to asst prof graphic design, Ind Univ, 60-66; prof graphic design, Cooper Union, 66-, chmn dept art, 66-68, dean, Sch Art, 68- *Bibliog:* Articles, Am Inst Graphic Arts J, 68 & Print, 70. *Mem:* Am Inst Graphic Arts (bd mem, 69-72); Col Art Asn (vpres, 74-76, pres, 76-78). *Mailing Add:* Cooper Union Sch Art 41 Cooper Sq New York NY 10003

SADIK, MARVIN SHERWOOD
DEALER
b Springfield, Mass, June 27, 32. *Study:* Harvard Univ, AB, 54, AM, 61. *Collections Arranged:* Painting in British India, 63; The Portrayal of the Negro in American Painting, 64; Salton Collection of Renaissance & Baroque Medals & Plaquettes, 65; As Maine Goes, 66; Winslow Homer at Prout's Neck, 66; The Drawings of Hyman Bloom (with catalog), 68; Edith Halpert & the Downtown Gallery (with catalog), 68; Portrait Reliefs of Augustus St Gaudens, 69; Life Portraits of John Quincy Adams (with catalog), 70; Black Presence in the Era of the American Revolution, 73; Christian Gullager: Portrait Painter to Federal America (with catalog), 76; American Portrait Drawings (with catalog), 80; Portraits by George Bellows (with catalog), 81. *Pos:* Curatorial asst, Worcester Art Mus, Mass, 55-57; cur & dir, Bowdoin Col Mus Art, 61-67; dir, Univ Conn Mus Art, 67-69; dir, Nat Portrait Gallery, Smithsonian Inst, 69-81. *Teaching:* Instr fine arts, Harvard Col, 58-60. *Awards:* Knight of Dannebrog, Denmark. *Mem:* Colonial Soc Mass; Am Antiquarian Soc; fel Morgan Libr; Century Asn; Grolier Club. *Publ:* Auth, Colonial & federal portraits at Bowdoin Col, 66. *Mailing Add:* PO Box 6039 Falmouth Portland ME 04105

SAFER, JOHN
SCULPTOR
b Washington, DC, Sept 6, 22. *Work:* Baltimore Mus Art, Md; Corcoran Gallery Art, Washington, DC; New York Cult Ctr; Philadelphia Mus Art, Pa; San Francisco Mus Art; and others. *Exhib:* One-man shows, Westmoreland Co Mus, Greensburg, Pa, 71, Valley House Gallery, 71, US Embassy, London, 72, Findlay Galleries, 74 & 78, High Mus, Atlanta, 78, Milwaukee Art Ctr. *Bibliog:* Gerald Nordland (auth), John Safer and the light fantastic, Art Gallery Mag, 2/72; C Doug Lewis (auth), article, Arts Mag, 78; Frank Getlein (auth), John Safer. *Mailing Add:* 10401 Grosvenor Lane Rockville MD 20852

SAFF, DONALD JAY
PRINTMAKER, ADMINISTRATOR
b New York, NY, Dec 12, 37. *Study:* Queens Col, City Univ NY, BA, 59; Columbia Univ, MA, 60; Pratt Inst, MFA, 62; Teachers Col, Columbia Univ, EdD, 64; Pratt Graphic Art Workshop, 59-62. *Work:* Metrop Mus Art, Mus Mod Art, New York; William Hayes Fogg Art Mus, Harvard Univ, Cambridge, Mass; Nat Gallery Art, Washington, DC; Philadelphia Mus Art. *Comn:* Two hundred prints, 67, 200 prints, 68 & 125 prints, 71, Int Graphic Arts Soc. *Exhib:* Smithsonian Inst, 61; 15th Ann Print Show, Brooklyn Mus, 66; Ringling Mus of Art, Sarasota, Fla, 66; Boston Printmakers, Mus Fine Arts, Boston, 66; Brooklyn Mus, 69 & 76; one-man shows, Martin Gordon Gallery, New York, 65, 66 & 70, Byron Gallery, 70 & Getler/Pall Gallery, 79 & 82; Tom Luttrell Gallery, San Francisco, 80; Edison Community Col, Ft Myers, Fla, 80. *Pos:* Consult ed, Art Jour, co-dir, Pyramid Arts Ltd, Tampa, Fla, formerly. *Teaching:* Instr printmaking & design, Teachers Col, Columbia Univ, summers 65 & 66; assoc prof printmaking & design, Univ S Fla, Tampa, 65-67, chmn visual arts dept, 67-71, dir graphic studio, 68-76, dean col fine arts, 71-82, distinguished serv prof visual arts, currently. *Awards:* Fulbright Grant, Italy, 64-65; Patrick Gavin Mem Prize, Boston Printmaking Asn, 66; Grant Proj, Dir, Univ S Fla, Nat Endowment Arts, 73-77. *Bibliog:* Article, New York Herald Tribune, 12/65; John Canaday (auth), article, New York Times, 10/68; article, Print Collector's Newsletter, 7-8/72. *Mem:* Nat Coun of Art Adminrs (mem bd dirs, 73-75); Int Coun Fine Arts Deans; Col Art Asn. *Media:* Prints and drawing. *Publ:* Coauth, Images of Destruction: Monsu Desiderio and Jacques Callot, Queens Col, 64; auth, Modern Masters of Intaglio, Queens Col, 64; coauth, Printmaking History and Technique, Holt, Rinehart & Winston, Fall 1977. *Mailing Add:* 514 Riverhills Dr Temple Terrace FL 33617

SAFFORD, RUTH PERKINS
PAINTER
b Boston, Mass. *Study:* Mass Col Art, BS; also with Henry B Snell. *Work:* Nat Gallery Art, Washington, DC; Va Mus Fine Arts, Richmond; Mint Mus, Charlotte, NC; Navy Hist Mus, Washington, DC; Ball Mus, Muncie, Ind. *Comn:* Portraits of interiors, Nat Cathedral, Mt Vernon, Lee Mansion, Hyde Park & Gunstor Hall; plus many others. *Exhib:* Critics Choice, Cincinnati; New England Contemporary Art; Am Watercolor Soc; Corcoran Gallery Art; Mellon Found Traveling Exhib, three yrs. *Teaching:* Instr art, Harvard Sch Educ. *Mem:* Am & Washington Watercolor Socs; N Art Asn; Northern Art Asn; assoc Smithsonian Inst. *Media:* Watercolor. *Publ:* Auth article in Am Artist. *Mailing Add:* c/o Guild Boston Artists 162 Newbury Boston MA 02116

SAGE, BILL B
CERAMIST, EDUCATOR
b Rapid City, SDak. *Study:* Black Hills State Col, Spearfish, SDak, BS, 51; Mont State Univ, Bozeman, MAA, 59; Mills Col, Oakland, Calif, MFA(ceramics & sculpture), 65. *Work:* Crocker Art Gallery, Sacramento, Calif; Mills Col, Oakland, Calif; Archie Bray Found, Helena, Mont; Univ Utah, Salt Lake City; Mont Inst Art, State Capitol, Helena. *Comn:* Ceramic wall sculpture, Reinhardt House, Mills Col, 65; Stoneware Jar, President Dongguk Univ, Seoul, Republic Korea, 80. *Exhib:* NW Am Crafts Coun Award Winner's Exhib, Mus of Am Crafts, New York, 73; Northwest Designer Craftsmen Exhib, 70-80; The Container, Cheney Cowles Mem Mus, Wash, 78; The 1980 Governor's Invitational Art Exhib, State Capitol, Olympia, Wash, 80; Nat Ceramics Invitational, Archie Bray Foundation, State Capitol Mus, Helena, Mont, 81. *Teaching:* Instr art, pub sch, Billings, Mont, 56-62; asst prof, Eastern Washington Univ, Cheney, 65-70, assoc prof, 70-78, prof, 78-; assoc prof, Eastern Wash Univ, Cheney, 70-78, head

ceramics dept, 70-, prof art, 78- *Awards:* Nat Merit Award, NW Craftsmen USA 66, Am Crafts Coun, New York, 66; Jury Award, Ceramics/NW, Russell Gallery, Great Falls, 70; First Place Award, Verbal/Visual Exhib, Mont Inst of the Arts, 76. *Bibliog:* LaDonna Fehlberg (auth), article, Mont Inst Arts J, fall 76. *Mem:* Am Crafts Coun, New York; NW Designer Craftsmen; Archie Bray Found, Helena, Mont. *Media:* Bronze. *Publ:* Auth, Pottery, photography, poetry, Mont Inst Arts Quart, 67; auth, A potter's graffiti, Mont Arts, 67. *Mailing Add:* Rt 2 Box 142 Cheney WA 99004

SAHLSTRAND, JAMES MICHAEL
PHOTOGRAPHER
b Minneapolis, Minn, May 4, 36. *Study:* Univ Minn, BA, MFA. *Comn:* Photographs SE Wash, Walla Walla Community Col, 76-77 & photographs E Wash, Eastern Wash Univ & Turnbull Game Reserve Res Sta, 77, Wash State Arts Comn. *Exhib:* Young Photographers Traveling Exhib, 68-70; Being without Clothes, Mass Inst Technol, 70; Photo-Media, Mus Contemp Crafts, New York, 71; San Francisco Mus Art, 72; Synthetic Color, Univ Southern Ill, 74. *Pos:* Pres, Roslyn Arts, 72- *Teaching:* Assoc prof photog, Cent Wash Univ, Ellensburg, 65- *Mem:* Soc Photog Educ. *Media:* Color, Multiple Image. *Mailing Add:* Rte 4 Box 279 Ellensburg WA 98926

SAHLSTRAND, MARGARET AHRENS
PRINTMAKER, CRAFTSMAN
b Saint Louis, Mo, Oct 1, 39. *Study:* Lindenwood, Col, Saint Charles, Mo, 61; Univ of Iowa, Iowa City, printmaking with Mauricio Lasansky, MFA, 64; also in Japan, 81-83. *Work:* Kobe Mus of Fine Arts, Hygo Prefecture Mus Collection, Japan; Okla Art Ctr, Oklahoma City; Wash State Printmakers Collection, Evergreen State Col, Olympia; Nat Collection Art, Washington, DC. *Comn:* Cast paper murals, W Valley Sr High Sch, Yakima, Wash, 80 & Western Paper Co, Kent, Wash, 81. *Exhib:* 1st Editions Graphics Competition, Oregon Arts Comn, Salem, 76; World Print Competition, San Francisco Mus of Art, 77; one-man show, Cast Paperworks, Slocumb Gallery, E Tenn State Univ, Johnson City, 77; Paper as Medium, SITES, Smithsonian Inst, Washington, DC, 78-; Cast Paper, Pratt Graphics Ctr, New York, 78; Paper, Dayton Art Inst, Ohio, 78. *Pos:* Proprietor, Icosa Studio & Papermill, Ellensburg, currently. *Teaching:* Assoc prof printmaking & papermaking, Cent Wash Univ, Ellensburg, 65- *Awards:* Cannon Prize, Printmaking, Nat Acad of Design, New York, 66; Purchase Award, Statewide Services, Univ of Oregon, Eugene, 75; Fac Res Grant, Cent Wash Univ, 78. *Mem:* Am Crafts Coun, New York; Northwest Designer Craftsmen. *Dealer:* Source Gallery 1099 Folsom San Francisco CA 94103; Diane Gilson Gallery 209 Occidental S Seattle WA 98104. *Mailing Add:* Rte 4 Box 279 Ellensburg WA 98926

SAHRBECK, EVERETT WILLIAM
PAINTER, DESIGNER
b East Orange, NJ, Nov 4, 10. *Study:* NY Univ. *Work:* De Cordova Mus, Lincoln, Mass; Montclair Art Mus; Newark Art Mus; Overlook Hosp, Summit, NJ; First Nat Bank Boston. *Exhib:* Am Watercolor Soc Ann, 54-72; Montclair Art Mus Statewide Ann, 55-67; Royal Soc Painters Watercolors, London, 63; Landscape I, De Cordova Mus, 70 & 77; Boston 350th Jubilee, 80. *Pos:* Art dir, Reach, McClinton & Co, 34-68. *Teaching:* Watercolor workshops, Cape Cod Art Asn. *Awards:* Am Watercolor Soc Ann Prize, 61; Silver Medal of Honor, NJ Watercolor Soc, 70; Cape Cod Art Asn Watercolor Prizes, 71-80. *Mem:* Am Watercolor Soc; NJ Watercolor Soc; Cape Cod Art Asn (pres, 71-72). *Media:* Mixed. *Dealer:* Port Gallery Harwichport MA. *Mailing Add:* Box 401 South Harwich MA 02661

SAIDENBERG, DANIEL
DEALER
b Winnipeg, Man, Oct 12, 06. *Study:* Julliard Sch Music. *Pos:* Pres, Saidenberg Gallery. *Specialty:* Twentieth century European and American masters. *Mailing Add:* 1018 Madison Ave New York NY 10021

SAIDENBERG, ELEANORE B
DEALER, COLLECTOR
b Chicago, Ill, Apr 7, 11. *Pos:* Owner & dir, Saidenberg Gallery Inc, New York, currently. *Mem:* Art Dealers Asn Am (bd mem, 65-70). *Specialty:* Picasso, Leger, Klee, Masson, Gris, Braque & others. *Collection:* Picasso and School of Paris; Klee, Kandinsky, Feininger. *Publ:* Auth, Pablo Picasso Paintings, 57, Picasso Exhibition, 67-68, Fernand Leger-Gouaches, Watercolors, Drawings, 68, Paul Klee--A Retrospective Exhibition, 69 & Picasso--Recent Works on Paper-1967-1970, 70, (all catalogs). *Mailing Add:* Saidenberg Gallery Inc 1018 Madison Ave New York NY 10021

ST AMAND, JOSEPH
PAINTER
b New York, NY, Nov 10, 25. *Study:* Univ Calif, Berkeley; Calif Sch Fine Art, San Francisco. *Work:* Cathedral Sch, Kristiansand, Norway. *Exhib:* San Francisco Mus Art 75th Ann, 57; Palace Legion Honor Winter Exhib, Calif, 60-64; Carnegie Inst Int, Pittsburgh, 64; Univ Calif, Santa Cruz, 69; one-man retrospective, Arbes Gallery, San Francisco, 79. *Media:* Oil. *Mailing Add:* 953 Kansas St San Francisco CA 94107

ST CLAIR, MICHAEL
DEALER
b Bradford, Pa, May 28, 12. *Study:* Kansas City Art Inst, with Thomas Hart Benton, Vanderslice Scholar; Art Students League, with George Grosz; Colorado Springs Fine Arts Ctr, with Boardman Robinson, scholar. *Exhib:* One-man exhib, Okla Art Ctr, Oklahoma City. *Pos:* Dir, Babcock Galleries, New York, 59- *Teaching:* Instr drawing & painting, Okla Art Ctr Sch. *Mem:* Art Dealers Asn Am. *Specialty:* Nineteenth and twentieth century American paintings. *Mailing Add:* 20 E 67th St New York NY 10021

ST DENIS, PAUL ANDRE
PAINTER, INSTRUCTOR
b Chicago, Ill, Nov 16, 38. *Study:* Cleveland Inst of Art, BFA; Kent State Univ, MA; additional study with Julian Stanczak. *Work:* Tweed Mus, Duluth, Minn; Massillon Mus, Ohio; Utah State Univ, Logan; Columbia Mus Art, SC. *Exhib:* Butler Inst of Am Art, Youngstown, Ohio, 68 & 70; Am Watercolor Soc, Nat Acad Galleries, New York, 71-73, 75 & 77-79; Canton Art Inst, Ohio, 73; Aqueous Open, Pittsburgh Watercolor Soc, 74 & 75; Watercolor West, Utah State Univ, 76-79; Nat Watercolor Soc, Laguna Beach Mus of Art, Calif, 76; and others. *Pos:* Chmn art dept, Interlochen Ctr Arts, Mich, summers, 69-81. *Teaching:* Instr painting, Kent State Univ, Ohio, 68-70, Cooper Sch of Art, Cleveland, 70-80 & Cleveland Inst of Art, 73- *Awards:* Awards, Am Watercolor Soc, Nat Acad Galleries, New York, 72 & 78; Purchase Prize, Nat Watercolor Soc, Laguna Beach Mus of Art, Calif, 76; First Prize & Purchase Prize, Aqueous Open, Pittsburgh Watercolor Soc, 74. *Mem:* Am Watercolor Soc; Nat Watercolor Soc. *Media:* Acrylic, Watercolor. *Mailing Add:* 30601 Ashton Ave Cleveland OH 44140

ST FLORIAN, FRIEDRICH GARTLER
EDUCATOR, DESIGNER
b Graz, Austria, Dec 21, 32; US citizen. *Study:* Tech Univ Graz, dipl(archit), 58; Ecole Nat Superiure d'Archit, Brussels, Belg, 55-56; Atelier, with Victor Bourgeois; Columbia Univ, MArch, 62. *Work:* Mus Mod Art, New York; Mass Inst Technol, Cambridge; Mus Art, Providence. *Exhib:* One-man shows, Mod Museet, Stockholm, 69, Hayden Gallery, Mass Inst Technol, 73, Mus Art, Univ Tex, 76, Drawing Ctr, New York, 79 & Walker Art Ctr, Minneapolis, 80; Inst Contemp Art, London, Eng, 73; Archit Studies & Proj, Mus Mod Art, New York, 75; RI Sch Design Mus Art, 77. *Teaching:* From asst to assoc prof design, RI Sch Design, 63-77, chmn archit div, 77-78, dean archit, 78-82. *Awards:* Fulbright Fel, 61-62; Ctr for Advan Visual Studies Fel, Mass Inst Technol, 71-77; Nat Endowment Arts Awards, 73-74 & 76-77. *Mem:* Am Inst Architects. *Publ:* Auth, On my imaginary architecture, Leonardo, 77. *Mailing Add:* 305 S Main Providence RI 02917

ST JOHN, BRUCE
ADMINISTRATOR, HISTORIAN
b Brooklyn, NY, Jan 10, 16. *Study:* Middlebury Col, AB, 38; Columbia Univ, 40; NY Univ, 46; Neth Inst Art Hist Sem, 64. *Collections Arranged:* The Independents of 1910, 60; The Life and Times of John Sloan, 61; The Calder Family, 61; Jerome Myers, 66. *Pos:* Dir, Mint Mus Art, 50-55; cur, Delaware Art Mus, 55-57, dir, 57-73; assoc dean, New York Studio Sch, 73-74; art consult, St John & Co, 74-78 & St John Art Int, Inc, 78- *Res:* John Sloan. *Publ:* Ed, John Sloan's New York Scene 1906-1913, Harper & Row, 65; auth, John Sloan, Praeger, 71; auth, John Sloan in Philadelphia 1888-1904, Am Art J, 71. *Mailing Add:* Rushmore Rd Stormville NY 12582

ST JOHN, JOHN MILTON
PAINTER, MURALIST
b Oak Park, Ill, Apr 30, 11. *Study:* Univ Ky, AB; Syracuse Univ, MS; with Eliot O'Hara, Dong Kingman & Jerry Farnsworth; also with Jose Gutierrez, Mex. *Work:* Mus Art, Tel Aviv, Israel; Mus Art, Ponce, PR; Palacio de Bellas Artes, Lima, Peru; Palacio Nacional, Cartagena, Colombia; Syracuse Univ, NY; plus others. *Comn:* Epochs of Florida History (first exterior monumental mural on a pub bldg in US), City of Coral Gables, 55; Science of Highways (four murals), Ky State Off Bldg, Frankfort, 59; We, the People (two murals), Ky State Off Bldg, Louisville, 60; Landmarks of the Twenties, City Hall, Coral Gables; Man's Quest (exterior mural), Christiansen Family, Coral Gables. *Exhib:* Southeastern Regional, High Mus Art, Atlanta, 53; Mid-Am, Evansville Mus, Ind, 62; SCoast Ann, Ringling Mus, Sarasota, Fla, 63; one-man show, Dominico-Am Inst Cult, Santo Domingo, Republico Dominicano, 68; and others. *Pos:* Dir, John St John Gallery. *Bibliog:* Piero Sanavio (auth), John St John, La Casa del Arte, San Juan, PR, 62. *Media:* Oil for easel paintings, vinyl for exterior murals. *Publ:* Auth, John St John, Visions of Reality, Solvang, Calif, 81. *Mailing Add:* c/o John St John Gallery 1683 Copenhagen Dr Solvang CA 93463

ST JOHN, TERRY N
PAINTER, CURATOR
b Sacramento, Calif, Dec 24, 34. *Study:* Univ Calif, Berkeley, AB; San Francisco Art Inst, spec study with James Weeks; Calif Col Arts & Crafts, Oakland, MFA. *Exhib:* James D Phelan Award Show, Calif Palace Legion Honor, 65; one-man show, Crown Col, Univ Calif, Santa Cruz, 75; Univ Miss, 78; 20 Bay Area Painters, Western Asn Art Mus (traveling), 76-79; Berkeley Art Ctr, 78; Brookhouse, Orinda, 81; and others. *Collections Arranged:* Harry Bowden: Artist out of the Mainstream (co-cur, auth, catalog), 79. *Pos:* Asst cur, Oakland Mus, 69- *Teaching:* Outdoor Painters Proj, Univ Calif, Santa Cruz, 79-81. *Bibliog:* Thomas Albright (auth), article, San Francisco Chronicle, 2/12/75. *Media:* Oil. *Publ:* Auth, Society of Six (catalog), Oakland Mus, 72; auth, Louis Siegriest: A painter's topography, Currant Mag, 75; auth, Impressionism: The California view, Oakland Mus, 81. *Mailing Add:* 2736 Shasta Rd Berkeley CA 93308

ST MAUR, KIRK (KIRK SEYMOUR MCREYNOLDS)
SCULPTOR, PAINTER
b Quincy, Ill, July 7, 49. *Study:* Quincy Col; Univ Minn; Carleton Col, BA, 72; Academia di Belle Arti, Florence, Italy, 72-75, studied anat with Harkevitch; asst to R Puccinelli, Univ Int de Belle Arte, 73 & 74; Villa Schifanoia, Florence, MA, studied with E Manfrini; Simi Studio, Florence, 74-77. *Work:* Hinkhouse Collection, Stephens College; H M Seymour Libr, Indianola, Miss; St Michael's Citadel, Buriano, Italy; Oregon State Univ. *Comn:* oil mural of old bridge, The Abbey, Quincy, Ill, 76; heroic bronze of

St Michael, Church of Buriano, Quarrata, Italy, 76; oil mural, comn by Dr William McReynolds, Quincy, Ill, 76. *Exhib:* Anthology of the Art of Kirk McReynolds, Quincy Art Ctr, Ill, 74; The Great Collective, Centro di Arte, Florence, Italy, 75; Foreign Artists in Tuscany, Torre di Bellosguardo, Italy, 76; one-man show, Drawings, & Paintings & Sculpture of St Maur, Perseo Gallery, Florence, Italy, 77; Paintings & Sculpture of St Maur, The Abbey, Quincy, Ill, 77. *Awards:* First Prize for Relig Art, Allied Artists Am, 78. *Bibliog:* Mario Bucci (auth), Kirk McReynolds, Sansoni Editrice, Florence, Italy, 77; articles in Rome Daily American, & San Francisco Examiner, 79. *Media:* Terra Cotta, Bronze. *Dealer:* Guildhall Gallery Chicago IL; John Pence San Francisco CA. *Mailing Add:* PO Box 158 Payson IL 62360

ST TAMARA (TAMARA KOLBA)
PAINTER, PRINTMAKER
b Navahradak, Byelorussia; US citizen. *Study:* Western Col, Oxford, Ohio, BA; Columbia Univ, MFA, studied with John Heliker; Art Students League, Studied with Seong Moy. *Work:* UNICEF, United Nations, New York; New York Pub Libr, New York; Woodbridge Free Pub Libr, NJ; Columbia Univ, New York; Fine Arts Mus, Asbury Park, NJ. *Comn:* Four Icons, Byelorussian Church, Cleveland, Ohio; woodcut portrait of Dr Francisak Skaryna, Dr V Kipel, New York Pub Libr, 68. *Exhib:* Davidson Nat Print & Drawing Competition, NC, 73; First New Hampshire Graphics Ann, Nashua, 73; 2nd Miami Graphics Biennial Int Exhib, Fla, 75; 3rd Hawaii Nat Print Exhib, Honolulu, 75; 15th Ann Artists Salon, Okla Mus Art, Oklahoma City, 76; 28th Nat Exhib of Contemporary Realism in Art, Mus Fine Arts, Springfield, Mass, 77; and others. *Awards:* Gold Medal, 75th Open Exhib, Nat Acad Design, Catharine Lorillard Wolfe Art Club, Inc, 71; Ada V Wester Award, La Luz, NMex, 78; Ida Becker Fund for Graphic Award, Catharine Lorillard Wolfe Art Club, 78. *Bibliog:* Pat Hipp (auth), Woods Enhance Her Art, Asbury Park Press, 3/13/77; Zina Stankievic, Let's Get Acquainted with an Artist, Byelarus, 77. *Mem:* Printmaking Coun NJ; Catherine Lorillard Wolfe Art Club, Inc; Print Club, Albany; and others. *Media:* Oil, Etching. *Publ:* Illusr, Biography of a Polar Bear, G P Putnam's Sons, 72, Come Visit A Prairie Dog Town, Harcourt Brace Jovanovich, 76 & Animal Games, Holiday House, 76; illusr, Save That Racoon, 78 & auth & illusr, Chickaree, A Red Squirrel, 80, Harcourt Brace Jovanovich. *Mailing Add:* 235 Hockhockson Rd PO Box 97B Tinton Falls NJ 07724

SAITO, SEIJI
SCULPTOR
b Utsunomiya, Japan, 1933. *Study:* Tokyo Univ Art, BFA(sculpture) & MFA(stone carving); Brooklyn Mus Art Sch, scholar, 8 yrs; stone carving with Kametaro Akashi & granite carving with Odillio Beggi. *Work:* Pepsico Co, Purchase, NY; Methodist Hospital, Brooklyn, NY; Isaac Delgado Mus Art, New Orleans; Non-Ferros Int Corp, New York; The Toyo Trust & Banking Co, Ltd, New York. *Exhib:* Ann Exhib, Nat Sculpture Soc, NY, 70-81; Japanese Artists of Brooklyn, Brooklyn Mus, NY; Azuma Gallery, New York, 75; one-man shows, New Sch, New York, 78, Warner Commun Bldg, 79 & Yokyo Gallery, Tokyo, Japan, 79; Fedn Int Medaille, Florence, 83; and others. *Teaching:* Instr sculpture, Brooklyn Mus Art, summer 74. *Awards:* Outstanding Prize, Ann Art Festival Exhib, Tochigikaikan Gallery, Japan, 58; Cert of Merit, Ann Exhib of Nat Acad Design, New York, 73; Merit Prize, Hakone Open-Air Mus, Japan, 80. *Mem:* Nat Sculpture Soc. *Media:* Stone, Bronze, Wood. *Mailing Add:* 925 Union St Apt 1G Brooklyn NY 11215

SAKS, JUDITH-ANN (JUDITH-ANN SAKS ROSENTHAL)
PAINTER, PRINTMAKER
b Anniston, Ala, Dec 20, 43. *Study:* Tex Acad Art, Houston, 57-58, Houston Mus Fine Arts, 62; Rice Univ, 62; Sophie Newcomb Col, Tulane Univ, BFA(Arthur Q Davis Prize), 66; Univ Houston, 67. *Work:* Marine Transportation Collection, Smithsonian Inst; Royal Libr, Windsor Castle, England; Univ Houston; Harris Co Heritage Soc Mus, Houston; Johnson Manned Space Mus, Clear Lake, Tex. *Comn:* Christmas card design (oil painting), Houston CofC, 70; Drawing of the Straithard, Roberts Steamship Agency, New Orleans, 75; Am Revolution Bicentennial Proj (six oil paintings), Port of Houston Authority, 75-76; four hist paintings, Pin Oak Charity Horse Show Asn, 77. *Exhib:* 59th Ann Exhib, Birmingham Mus Art, Ala, 67; 1st Nat Space Art Show, Brown Palace Hotel, Denver, 69; Images on Paper, Miss Arts Festival & Munic Art Gallery, Jackson, 70; 7th Ann Art Exhib, Mobile Art Gallery, Ala, 72; and others. *Pos:* Cur student art collection, Univ Houston, 68-72. *Awards:* Selected Print, Miss Art Asn, 70-71. *Bibliog:* Ann Absher (auth), Painter on the roof, The Milepost, Columbia Gulf Transmission Co, 6/69; Susanna Friedman (auth), Southern artist, Bulletin Asn Jewish Libr, 9/79; Judith-Ann Saks, Arch Am Art, Smithsonian Inst, 79. *Mem:* Art League, Houston. *Media:* Oil on Linen; Pen and Ink Etchings. *Publ:* Illusr, Southwestern Art Inc, 11/67; illusr, seven covers, Port Houston Mag, 71, 75 & 76; illusr, The Catline, Desk & Derrick Club, 72; illusr, Maersk Post, A P Moller, Denmark, 8/77. *Dealer:* Galerie Barbizon 561 Town & Country Village Houston TX 77024. *Mailing Add:* c/o Mrs S B Weiner 434 Hunterwood Houston TX 77024

SAKUYAMA, SHUNJI
PRINTMAKER, PAINTER
b Harbin, Manchuria, July 29, 40, Japan citizen. *Study:* Tokyo Gakugei Univ, BA, 65; Brooklyn Col, MFA, 72; Pratt Graphics Ctr. *Work:* Brooklyn Mus; Berkshire Mus, Pittsfield, Mass; City Mus, New York; New Sch Art Ctr, New York. *Exhib:* One-man shows, Paintings, 72 & Prints, 79, Berkshire Mus; 21st Nat Print Exhib, 78 & New York Album, 79, Brooklyn Mus; New York Album, Brooklyn Mus, 79; New York Collects, City Mus, New York, 81; Gene Baro Collects, Brooklyn Mus, 83. *Teaching:* Instr Japanese brush work,

Long Island Univ, Brooklyn Ctr, 77-78. *Awards:* Painting Awards, New England Art Exhib, New Canaan, Conn, 72 & Berkshire Art Asn Exhib, 75. *Mem:* Japanese Artists Asn, NY; Contemp Artist Guild, NY. *Media:* Lithography; Acrylic, Oil. *Mailing Add:* 915 President St Brooklyn NY 11215

SAL, JACK
PHOTOGRAPHER, PAINTER
b Waterbury, Conn, Mar 28, 54. *Study:* Philadelphia Col Art, BFA, 76; Art Inst Chicago, MFA, 78. *Work:* Detroit Inst Arts, Mich; Ctr for Creative Photog, Tucson, Ariz; Mus Mod Art, New York; Int Mus Photog, Rochester, NY; Yale Univ Art Gallery, New Haven, Conn; and others. *Comn:* Earth Work, Off Cult Affairs, New Haven, Conn, 79; Grant, Conn Comn for Arts, 80. *Exhib:* One-man shows, Northlight Gallery, Tempe, Ariz, 80 & Recent Camera Works, Photographics Workshop, New Canaan, Conn, 80; Prints in the Cliche-Verre, Houston Mus Fine Art, 80; Light Gallery, New York, 81; Int Ctr Photog, New York, 81; Ferns Gallery, Hull, Eng, 82; and others. *Teaching:* Instr, Int Ctr Photog/New York Univ, Rutgers Univ, currently. *Awards:* Mellon Fel, 82. *Bibliog:* S D Peters (auth), Interview/Jack Sal, Int Mus Photog, 79; Roger Baldwin (auth), Jack Sal/camera images, Views, 80; Glassman/Symmes, Prints in the Cliche-Verre, Detroit Inst Arts, 80. *Mem:* Soc Photog Educ; Ctr Independent Study. *Media:* Pigment, Light-Sensitive Paper. *Publ:* Auth, Cliche-verre: cameraless images, Portfolio Mag, 79; contribr, Prints in the Cliche-Verre, Detroit Inst Arts, 80; contribr, Connecticut Photographers, Art Resources of Conn, 80; contribr, Photographers Hand, Int Mus Photog/George Eastman House, 80; auth, Mark/Making, Combinations Press, 81. *Mailing Add:* 362 Oliver Rd New Haven CT 06515

SALA, JORGE See Zontal, Jorge

SALAMONE, GLADYS L
PAINTER
b New York, NY. *Work:* US Army War Col, Carlisle, Pa; Lobo Arts Theater, Albuquerque; Kirtland AFB Officers Club, NMex; First Interstate Bank NMex. *Exhib:* Ouray Co Art Asn, Colo, 68-74; Denver Art Mus, 69; Lawton, Okla Art Coun Int Art Show, 70-73; Nat Art Show, Pikes Peak Art Asn, Colo, 70-74; Okla Mus Art, 75. *Awards:* Best of Show, NMex Art League, 70; First Prize Watercolor, Montrose Art League, 72; First Prize Graphics, NMex Art League, 74; plus others. *Mem:* Am Artists Prof League; NMex Art League; Nor Este Art Asn. *Media:* Oil, Watercolor. *Mailing Add:* 8301 Pickard Ave NE Albuquerque NM 87110

SALAZAR, JUAN
PAINTER, DESIGNER
b Mexico City, Mex, Apr 11, 34. *Study:* Inst Politecnico Nac; Escuela Pintura y Escultura Inst Nac Bellas Artes, with Carlos Orozco Romero. *Comn:* Design settings, Mus Ciudad Mexico, 83; engravings, Carton y Papel, S A, Mexico City, 71. *Exhib:* Mus Nac Arte Mod, Mexico City, 72; 10th Anniversary Friends of Mex Art Show, Phoenix Art Mus; Mus Albuquerque, NMex, 73-75; Bienal Ibero Americana de Pintura, Museo de Arte Alvar Carrillo Gil, Mexico City, 78; Actualidad Grafica Panorama Artistico, Museo Nacional de Arte Moderno, Mexico City, 79; and others. *Awards:* Prize, Nat Contest Furniture Design, Knoll Int, 71. *Bibliog:* Toby Joysmith (auth), The gallery goer: Table top art, News, Mexico City, 79; Alfonso de Neuvillate (auth), El Estadio Emotivo, Novedades, Mexico City, 79. *Media:* Oil. *Dealer:* Galeria de Arte Mexicano Milan 18 Mexico City Mex. *Mailing Add:* Aurora 26 Coyoacan 04000 Mexico DF Mexico

SALEMME, ANTONIO
PAINTER, SCULPTOR
b Gaeta, Italy, Nov 2, 92; US citizen. *Study:* Artists Equity. *Work:* Metrop Mus Art, Columbia Univ; Newark Mus, NJ; Syracuse Mus, NY; Man Centennial Ctr, Winnipeg; Swedish Int Trade Fair Ctr. *Comn:* Gen Dwight D Eisenhower, Columbia Univ Alumni, 65; Dr Josiah Trent, comn by Dr & Mrs James Semans, Duke Univ Med Ctr, 75; bronze portrait of Pres John F Kennedy, Kennedy Mem Library, 77. *Exhib:* Gen Int Exhib, Salon des Tuileries, Paris, France, 32, 34, 35; Gen Int Exhib, Salon d'Automne, Paris, France, 33-34; Gen Nat, Pa Acad Fine Arts, 30-50; Art in Am, Metrop Mus Art, 50; Blossom-Kent 3rd Ann Sculpture Exhib, Kent State Univ, 70; one-man shows, Edward-Dean Mus Decorative Arts, Cherry Valley, Calif, 79; Paintings and sculpture, Yellow Box Gallery, New York, 80. *Pos:* Dir, Manhattan Art Proj of WPA for Mural Painting, New York, 34-35. *Teaching:* Instr sculpture, Nat Inst Archit Educ, 20-23; instr sculpture, Roerich Mus Sch Art, New York, 20-23; Spence Sch, New York, 37-38. *Awards:* Hon Mention Sculpture, Pa Acad Fine Arts, 30 & Art Inst Chicago, 31; Guggenheim Fel, 32 & 35. *Bibliog:* Records (on sculpture & painting), Folkway Records, 78; interview, Twin Co Cable TV, Allentown, Pa, 77; interview, PM Mag, Harrisburg, Pa, 80. *Mem:* Hon life mem Nat Inst Archit. *Media:* Oil, Watercolor; Terra Cotta, Bronze. *Mailing Add:* RD 4 Box 473 Easton PA 18042

SALEMME, LUCIA (AUTORINO)
PAINTER, WRITER
b New York, NY, Sept 23, 19. *Study:* Art Students League, 38. *Work:* Whitney Mus Am Art; Nat Gallery Art, Washington, DC; Ital Embassy; New York Pub Libr Print Collection. *Comn:* Mosaic mural, Mayer & Whittlesey, New York, 58; many portraits, 59-72; art restoration, Art Students League Painting Collection, New York, 72 & Manhattan House murals, 77. *Exhib:* One-woman exhibs, Dorsky Gallery, 65, William Zierler Gallery, New York, 72 & 74, Fair Lawn Pub Libr, NJ, 76, Cape Split Place Gallery, Maine, 77 & Summit Gallery, New York, 79 & 80; and many other group exhibs. *Teaching:*

Instr, People's Art Ctr, Mus Mod Art, 57-61; adj prof painting & drawing, NY Univ, 59-70; instr painting & drawing, Art Students League, 70- *Awards:* Solomon R Guggenheim Found Scholar, 42; MacDowell Colony Fel, 62. *Media:* Oil, Watercolor. *Publ:* Auth, Color Exercises for the Painter, 70 & Compositional Exercises for the Painter, 73, Watson-Guptill; auth, The Complete Book of Painting Techniques, Macmillan, 82. *Dealer:* Summit Gallery 101 W 57th St New York NY 10019. *Mailing Add:* 112 W 21st St New York NY 10011

SALEMME, MARTHA
PAINTER
b Geneva, Ill, Aug 30, 12. *Study:* With Antonio Salemme. *Work:* New York Hosp; Svenska Massan, Swedish Int Trade Fair Ctr, Gothenburg, Sweden. *Exhib:* One-woman exhibs, New York, Paris & Sweden, 48, 63, 74-76 & 80; Hudson River Mus, Yonkers, NY, 58; Jersey City Mus, 59 & 61; Int Platform Asn Exhib, Washington, DC, 69-71, 73, 75, 77 & 81; two-person show, Community Art League and Grollmans Dept Store, Easton, Pa, 80; and other group exhibs. *Bibliog:* Hugo Johansson (auth), articles, Hyssna, Sweden, 76, 78 & 83; Sonny Mattison (auth), Vastgota-Demokraten, Kinna, Sweden, 83; interview, Twin Co Cable TV, 83. *Mem:* Artists Equity; Int Platform Asn. *Mailing Add:* RD 4 Easton PA 18042

SALERNO, CHARLES
SCULPTOR, EDUCATOR
b Brooklyn, NY, Aug 21, 16. *Study:* Art Students League; Acad Grande Chaumiere, Paris; Escuela Pintura Y Escultura, Mexico City; State Univ NY, teaching cert. *Work:* Mus Art RI Sch Design; Ariz State Univ Collection Am Art; Atlanta Art Asn, Ga; Wadsworth Atheneum, Hartford, Conn; Grand Rapids Art Mus, Mich. *Exhib:* Carvers, Modelers, Welders, Mus Mod Art, New York, 50; Am Pavilion, Brussels Fair, Belg, 58; New York World's Fair, 64; one-man shows, Weyhe Gallery, New York; retrospective, Sculpture Ctr, NY, 75. *Teaching:* Asst prof sculpture, City Col New York, 64-74 & Nat Acad Design, 78-80. *Awards:* Louis Comfort Tiffany Found Fel sculpture, 48; Purchase Prize, Staten Island Mus, 59; Margaret Hirsch-Levine Prize in sculpture, Audubon Artists Ann, 71. *Bibliog:* Frances Christoph (auth), Salerno sculpture, Weyhe Gallery, 65. *Mem:* Audubon Artists; Nat Acad Design; Sculptors Guild; Nat Sculpture Soc. *Media:* Stone. *Dealer:* Weyhe Gallery 794 Lexington Ave New York NY 10021. *Mailing Add:* 5828 Lindsay Rd Sebastian FL 32958

SALINAS, BARUJ
PAINTER, PRINTMAKER
b Havana, Cuba, July 6, 35; US citizen. *Study:* Kent State Univ, BArch. *Work:* Inst Nac Bellas Artes, Mexico City; Beit Uri Mus, Kineret, Israel; San Antonio Mus Art; Museo Arte Siglo XX, Alicante, Spain; McNay Art Inst, San Antonio; and others. *Comn:* Murals, Sephardi Sch, Mex DF; paintings, Edificio la Victoria, Mex DF, 79; paintings, European Am Bank, Miami, Fla, 82. *Exhib:* One-man shows, Harmon Gallery, Fla, 75 & 83, EditArt, Geneva, Switz, 75, 77, 79 & 83, Mus Carrillo Gil, Mex, 81, Galeria Joan Prats, New York, 82 & Barbara Gillman Gallery, Miami, 82. *Awards:* Best Watercolor, 10th Hortt Mem Ann, 68; Cintas Found Competition Grant, 70 & 71; First Prize, VI Bienal Grabado Latino Am, San Juan, PR, 83. *Bibliog:* Wifredo Fernandez (auth), Baruj Salinas su mundo pictorico, Ed Punto Cardinal, 71; Merle De Kuper (auth), Twenty-eight artists in Mexico, Ed Montauriol, 72; Gloria Moure, Carlos Franqui, Wifredo Fernandez & Jose A Valente (authors), Baruj Salinas, Ediciones Poligrafa, Espana, 79. *Media:* Acrylic, Miscellaneous Media. *Publ:* Illusr, Calendario del hombre Descalzo, 70; illusr, Resumen A I P, 71; illusr, Narradores Cubanos de Hoy, 75; illusr, Revista Escandalar, NY, 81. *Dealer:* Harmon Gallery 1415 Main St Sarasota FL 33577; Galeria Joan Prats Rbla Cataluna 54 Barcelona 7 Spain. *Mailing Add:* 2740 SW 92nd Ave Miami FL 33165

SALLA, SALVATORE
PAINTER, EDUCATOR
b Khosrovabad, Iran, Aug 3, 03; US citizen. *Study:* Fribourg Col, Switz; Royal Univ Galata, Constantinople, BA(archit); also with Chevalier Leonardo de Mango. *Work:* Springfield Mus, Ill; Grant's Mem Auditorium, Northlake, Ill; Acad Magical Arts, Hollywood, Calif; Niavaran Imp Palace, Tehran, Iran. *Comn:* Multum in Parvo (mural), Encycl Britannica, Chicago, 36; GI Heroes of Bataan, Vet Park Admin, Maywood, Ill, 49 & Last Mission (mural), Northlake, Ill, 60. *Exhib:* 33rd & 37th Ann Exhib, Artists of Chicago & Vicinity, Art Inst Chicago, 29 & 33; NShore Art Asn, Gloucester, Mass, 47-48; Combined Ins Art Gallery, Chicago, 66-68; La Jolla Art Asn, Calif, 73. *Pos:* Official portrait painter, Chicago Civic Opera Co, 29-32. *Teaching:* Life class educator constructive anat, drawing & painting, Am Acad Fine Arts, Chicago, 48-67. *Bibliog:* Jan Jennings (auth), Magical Masterpiece of the Great Masters by Salvatore Salla, 79; Dale Salwak (auth), Salla's Magical Masterpiece, Tops, 12/79; Sir Alan Snowden (auth), Salla's true magical masterpiece, Magic Circular, London, 3/81; and others. *Mem:* Fine Arts Soc of San Diego; La Jolla Art Asn. *Media:* Oil, Watercolor. *Publ:* Contribr, Look at the Art Institute, 58. *Mailing Add:* Lime Grove Apts #5 1060 Chinquapin Ave Carlsbad CA 92008

SALLE, DAVID
PAINTER
b Norman, Okla, Sept 28, 52. *Study:* Calif Inst Arts, Valencia, BFA, 73 & MFA, 75. *Work:* Boymans Mus, Rotterdam, Holland; Basel Kunst Mus, Switzerland; New York Public Libr; Whitney Mus. *Exhib:* L'Amerique aux Independants, Grand Palais, Paris, 80; Galerie Bischofberger, Zurich, Switzerland, 80; Young Americans, Allen Mem Art Mus, Oberlin, Ohio, 81; West Kunst, Koln, WGermany, 81; Figures Forms and Expressions, Albright-Knox Mus, Buffalo, NY, 81; Figurative Aspects of Recent Art, Hayden Gallery, Mass Inst Technol, 81; Mary Boone Gallery, New York, 81; Larry Gagosian Gallery, Los Angeles, 81; The Anxious Edge, Walker Art Ctr, 82; 74th Am Exhib, Chicago Art Inst, 82; Homo Sapiens, Aldrich Mus, 82; The Americans: Collage 1950-1982, Contemp Art Mus, Houston, 82; and many others. *Awards:* Creative Artists Public Service Program Grant, 79. *Bibliog:* Grace Glueck (auth), Artists who scavenge from the media, New York Times, 1/9/83; Roberta Smith (auth), Appropriation uber allies, Village Voice, 1/11/83; Michael Brenson (auth), New York vs Paris: Views of an art reporter, New York Times, 1/16/83. *Mailing Add:* c/o Mary Boone Gallery 420 West Broadway New York NY 10012

SALLICK, LUCY ELLEN
PAINTER, INSTRUCTOR
b Boston, Mass, Sep 21, 37. *Study:* Univ Mich, 55-58; New York Univ, BA, 59, painting, 60-62; Art Students League, 64-65; Corcoran Sch Art, 66-68. *Work:* County Fed Savings & Town of Westport, Conn; Brunswick Savings Inst, Maine; Housatonic Mus Art, Bridgeport, Conn; Univ Mich Art Mus, Ann Arbor. *Comn:* Painting, Brunswick Savings Inst, Maine, 75. *Exhib:* Contemporary Reflections, Aldrich Mus, Ridgefield, Conn, 75; solo exhibs, Rutgers Univ, New Brunswick, NJ, 77 & Canton Art Inst, Ohio, 80; Childe Hassam Purchase Exhib, Am Acad & Inst Arts & Lett, 76-83; Contemporary Naturalism, Nassau Co Mus Fine Arts, NY, 80; Conn Painters, Wadsworth Atheneum, 83; Contemp Landscape Painting, Wesleyan Univ, Conn, 83; and others. *Teaching:* Instr painting, Silvermine Guild Sch Arts, 77- *Awards:* Eloise Egan Mem Award, New Eng Ann Silvermine Guild, 75 & Guild Award, 79. *Bibliog:* Lawrence Alloway (auth), Lucy Sallick, Fairleigh Dickinson Univ, 75; John Russell (auth), article, New York Times, 9/23/77; Gerrit Henry (auth), article, Art in Am, 2/83. *Mem:* Women's Caucus Art; Silvermine Guild (artist mem bd trustees, 79-). *Media:* Oil, Watercolor. *Dealer:* G W Einstein Co Inc 243 E 82nd St New York NY 10028. *Mailing Add:* 77 Long Lots Rd Westport CT 06880

SALMON, LARRY
CURATOR
b Winfield, Kans, May 5, 45. *Study:* Univ Kans, BA, 67; Harvard Univ, AM, 68. *Pos:* Curatorial asst, City Art Mus, St Louis, Mo, summer 68; asst cur textiles, Mus Fine Arts, Boston, 68-69, actg cur textiles, 69-71, cur textiles, 71-82. *Mem:* Am Asn Mus; Ctr Int Etude Textiles Anciens; Costume Soc Am; Int Coun Mus. *Mailing Add:* 139 W Newton Boston MA 02146

SALMON, RAYMOND MERLE
CARTOONIST, EDUCATOR
b Akron, Colo, Sept 6, 31. *Study:* Mesa Col; Univ of Denver; Chicago Acad of Fine Arts; Univ of Colo; Calif Col of Arts and Crafts; San Francisco State Univ; Colorado Springs Fine Arts Ctr; Univ of Northern Colo, BA & MA(fine arts). *Work:* Libr Commun & Graphic Arts, Ohio State Univ. *Exhib:* Univ of Denver Art Mus, 55; Colorado Springs Fine Arts Ctr, 61; Tacoma Art Mus, Wash, 64; State Univ Mo, 65; Master Cartoonists Exhib, Parke-Bernet, New York, 71. *Pos:* Free lance graphic artist, Salmon Studios, Calif, 60-; cartoonist, assoc with Morrie Turner Wee Pals Comic Strip, 74-; creator cartoon panel, The Little Man. *Teaching:* Art educ, John F Kennedy Univ, 66-74; art educ/commercial dept, Solano Community Col, 71- *Mem:* Nat Cartoonists Soc, New York; Northern Calif Cartoon and Humor Asn; Soc Prof Journalists. *Media:* Pen and Ink; Color Wash. *Publ:* Cartoons in Saturday Review, FM and the Fine Arts Mag & Writer's Digest. *Mailing Add:* PO Box 712 Vallejo CA 94590

SALOMON, LAWRENCE
SCULPTOR, EDUCATOR
b Chicago, Ill, July 18, 40. *Study:* Art Inst Chicago; Univ Ill, BFA; Univ Chicago. *Exhib:* Chicago Bienniel, 68 & Critic Choice, 69, Art Inst Chicago; Lyman Wright Art Ctr, Beloit, Wis, 70; The Five: Public Works, Univ Chicago, 71; Art for Public Places, Dept Housing & Urban Develop Nat Competition, 73; Cool Abstraction, Richard Gray Gallery, Chicago, 76; Romantic Structures: Abstract Art in Chicago Traveling Exhib, Univs Mo & Kans, 78; and others. *Teaching:* Assoc prof fine art, Univ Ill, Chicago Circle, 65- *Awards:* Art in Public Places Award, Nat Competition, Dept Housing & Urban Develop, 73. *Bibliog:* Amy Goldin (auth), Greasy kid stuff, Art Gallery Mag, 73; articles, Art in Am, 77; C L Morrison (auth), Chicago dialectics, Art News, 2/78. *Mem:* The Five; Participating Artists Chicago (secy, 68-70); Art Pub Places (bd dir, 78-). *Media:* Metal. *Dealer:* Jan Cicero Gallery 433 N Clark Chicago IL. *Mailing Add:* 2116 N Bissell Chicago IL 60614

SALT, JOHN
PAINTER
b Birmingham, Eng, 1937. *Study:* Birmingham Col Art, Eng; Slade Sch Fine Arts, London. *Exhib:* Die Metamorphose des Dinges, Palais des Beaux-Arts, Brussels, 71; Relativerend Realisme, Stedelijk van Abbemuseum, Eindhoven, Netherlands, 72; Sharp-Forcus Realism, Sidney Janis Gallery, New York, 72; Verkehrskultur, Westfalische Kunstverein, Munster, W Ger, 72; one-man show, Univ Birmingham, Eng, 66. *Teaching:* Instr, various cols of art, Eng, 60-67 & Maryland Col Art, Baltimore, 67-68. *Bibliog:* Grace Glueck (auth), New York gallery notes, Art in Am, New York, 11-12/70; J Patrick Marandel (auth), New York Letter, Art Int, Lugano, 1/71; Juergen Weichardt (auth), Neue Landschaft, Mag Kunst, Mainz, 1, 72. *Media:* Oil. *Mailing Add:* c/o O K Harris Gallery 383 W Broadway New York NY 10013

SALTER, RICHARD MACKINTIRE
PAINTER

b Iowa City, Iowa, May 7, 40. *Study:* Northern Ariz Univ, BA, 64; Univ Guanajuato, Inst Allende, Mex, MFA, 68. *Work:* Arthur Adams Western Collection, Beloit, Wis; US Dept Interior, Washington, DC; Miller Brewing Co, Milwaukee, Wis; Univ Wis, Green Bay; Northern Ariz Univ. *Comn:* Com Design, US Borax Co, Boron, Calif, 65-66; Photography, Orput & Orput, Architects, Rockford, Ill, 71. *Exhib:* Mitchell Mus, Mt Vernon, Ill, 81; Smithsonian Inst, 82; Kennedy Ctr, 82; one-person show, Alverno Col, Milwaukee, 82; Appleton Gallery Fine Arts, Wis, 83; and many other group and one-man exhibs. *Teaching:* Instr painting, Stanislaus State Col, 68; instr creative photog, Univ Wis-Green Bay, 73. *Awards:* First Prizes, Red Cloud Indian Art Show, Pine Ridge, SDak & Heard Indian Art Show, Phoenix. *Bibliog:* Platt Cline (auth), NAU Show, Ariz Daily Sun, 73; Barbara Manger (auth), Salter Exhib, Mid-West Art Mag, 74 & 77. *Mem:* Rockford Art Asn; Wis Painters & Sculptors Asn; Col Art Asn Am. *Media:* Acrylic, Mixed. *Dealer:* Segal Gallery New York NY; Cudahy Gallery Milwaukee Art Ctr Milwaukee WI. *Mailing Add:* Rte 1 Box 902 Lake Geneva WI 53147

SALTMARCHE, KENNETH CHARLES
PAINTER, ADMINISTRATOR

b Cardiff, Wales, Sept 29, 20; Can citizen. *Study:* Ont Col Art, Toronto, assoc, 46; Art Students League, with Julian Levi; Univ Windsor, LLD, 77. *Work:* Art Gallery Hamilton, Ont; London Art Mus, Ont; Govt Ont, Toronto. *Pos:* Dir, Art Gallery Windsor, 46-; art critic, Windsor Star, 47-74. *Mem:* Ont Asn Art Galleries (pres, 68-69); Can Art Mus Dirs Orgn (pres, 75-76); Can Mus Asn. *Mailing Add:* 995 Chilver Rd Windsor ON N8Y 2K6 Canada

SALTONSTALL, ELIZABETH
PAINTER

b Chestnut Hill, Mass, July 26, 1900. *Study:* Sch Mus Fine Arts, Boston, dipl; also painting with Andre L'Hote, Paris & lithography with Stow Wengenroth. *Work:* Libr Cong; Boston Mus Fine Arts; Yale Univ Art Gallery; Bixler Mus, Colby Col, Maine; Boston Athenaeum. *Exhib:* Libr Cong, Washington, DC, 42, 44, 45 & 49; Carnegie Inst Graphics, 46, 47 & 50; Boston Printmakers, 58, 67 & 69; Audubon Artists Ann, 60, 67 & 69; Print Club Albany, 71. *Teaching:* Instr painting, Winsor Sch, Boston, 23-28 & Milton Acad, Mass, 28-65. *Mem:* Artists Equity Asn; Audubon Artists; Nat Asn Women Artists; Pen & Brush Club; Boston Printmakers. *Media:* Oil, Acrylic. *Mailing Add:* 231 Chestnut Hill Rd Chestnut Hill MA 02167

SALTZMAN, MARVIN
PAINTER, EDUCATOR

b Chicago, Ill, June 16, 31. *Study:* Art Inst Chicago, 54-56; Univ Southern Calif, BFA, 57, MFA, 59. *Work:* Nat Collection, Washington, DC; Univ Calif, Berkeley Art Mus; Ackland Art Mus, Chapel Hill, NC; Univ Southern Calif, Los Angeles; Portland Mus Art, Ore. *Exhib:* Los Angeles Artists & Vicinity Ann, Los Angeles Co Mus, 57-59; Pasadena Mus Nat Print Festival, Calif, 58; Ball State Ann, 59, 61, 66 & 67; Artists of Ore Painting & Sculpture Ann, 64-65; Northwest Printmakers, Seattle, Wash, 66-67; and many others. *Teaching:* Vis lectr printmaking, Univ Southern Calif, 66-67; prof painting & studio chmn, Univ NC, Chapel Hill, 67-74, chmn fine arts div, 76-79; Pogue Fel, 78-79. *Media:* Oil. *Dealer:* Belanthi 142 Court St Brooklyn NY 11201. *Mailing Add:* 717 Emory Dr Chapel Hill NC 27514

SALTZMAN, WILLIAM
PAINTER, SCULPTOR

b Minneapolis, Minn, July 9, 16. *Study:* Univ Minn, BS, 40. *Work:* Mayo Clin, Rochester, Minn; Minneapolis Inst Art; Walker Art Ctr, Minneapolis; Joslyn Mus, Omaha, Nebr; plus others. *Comn:* Ten Commandments, Eternal Light (welded sculpture & candelabra), B'nai Abraham Synagogue, Minneapolis, 65; stained glass windows, Univ Minn Hosps, Minneapolis, 65; copper relief sculptures, Univ Nebr Law Sch Bldg, Lincoln & First Nat Bank, Sioux Falls, SDak, 75; set designs, Minn Opera Co, St Paul, 79; copper relief sculptures, Adath Jeshurun Synagogue, Minneapolis, 79; plus others. *Exhib:* Abstract and Surrealist American Art, 58th Ann Exhib Am Paintings & Sculpture, Art Inst Chicago, 48; 13th Ann Watercolor Exhib, San Francisco Mus Art, San Francisco Mus Art, 49; Ann Exhib Contemp Am Painting, Whitney Mus Am Art, New York, 52; 1952 Pittsburgh Int Exhib Contemp Painting, Carnegie Inst Int, 52; 5th Midwest Biennial Exhib, Joslyn Art Mus, 58; one-man show, Philbrook Mus, Tulsa, Okla, 72; Watercolor USA, Springfield Mus, Mo, 77; Sculpture, Coast to Coast Stores Hq, Edina, Minn, 78; and many others. *Pos:* Supvr art, Fairmont Pub Schs, Minn; camouflage adv, USA Engrs, 42-46; mem gov comt, Minn State Art Soc, 46-50; resident artist & dir, Rochester Art Ctr, 48-64; juror, many exhibs, Iowa, Wis & Minn, 48- *Teaching:* Instr painting & drawing, Exten Div, Univ Minn, asst & actg dir, Univ Minn Gallery, Minneapolis, 46-48; guest instr, St Olaf Col, 51-54; vis prof, Univ Nebr, Lincoln, spring 64; assoc prof art, Macalester Col, 66-74, prof art, 74- *Awards:* Best in Painting Award, 48th Ann Minn State Fair, St Paul, 59; Guild for Relig Arch Award, 73; AIA Assoc Art Award, 73; plus others. *Mem:* Nat Soc Mural Painters & Sculptors. *Mailing Add:* 5140 Lyndale Ave S Minneapolis MN 55419

SAMARAS, LUCAS
SCULPTOR

b Kastoria, Greece, Sept 14, 36; US citizen. *Study:* Rutgers Univ, with Alan Kaprow, BA, 59; Columbia Univ, with Meyer Schapiro, 59-62. *Work:* Metrop Mus Art, Whitney Mus Am Art, Mus Mod Art, New York; Albright-Knox Art Gallery, Buffalo, NY; Los Angeles Co Mus Art. *Exhib:* Art Inst Chicago, 67 & 74; Mus Mod Art, New York, 68 & 78; retrospective, Mus Contemp Arts, Chicago, 71 & Whitney Mus Am Art Ann, 72; Whitney Mus Am Art,

74; Art Inst Chicago, 74; Mus Contemp Art, Chicago, 75; solo exhib, Pace Gallery, 75-, Inst Contemp Art, Boston, 76, Seattle Art Mus, 76, Walker Art Ctr, 77 & Lowe Art Mus, Univ Miami, 82; Corcoran Gallery, 79; Indianapolis Mus Art, 80; Mus Mod Art, Paris, 80; Denver Art Mus, 81. *Bibliog:* Barbara Rose (auth), Lucas Samaras: The self as icon and cultural development, 3/78 & Carter Ratcliff (auth), Modernism turned inside out: Lucas Samaras' reconstructions, 11/79, Arts Mag; Allen Robertson (auth), Singular developments: Polaroid's Paean to color, TWA Ambassador, 12/79. *Mailing Add:* c/o Pace Gallery 32 E 57th St New York NY 10023

SAMBURG, GRACE (BLANCHE)
PAINTER, LITHOGRAPHER

b New York, NY. *Study:* Art Students League, painting with Morris Kantor & Raphael Soyer; New Sch for Social Res, stage design & lighting; Contemp Art Gallery Graphic Workshop, with Michael Ponce de Leon; also with Philip Guston. *Work:* Slide Collection, Mus Fine Arts, Boston. *Exhib:* Silvermine Guild of Artists Ann, New Canaan, Conn, 59; Works on Paper, Brooklyn Mus, New York, 75; Fairleigh Dickinson Univ, NJ, 75; Artists Choice (traveling exhib), State Univ NY, Binghamton, 76; Chatham Col, Pittsburgh, Pa, 76; Randolph-Macon Women's Col, Lynchburg, Va, 77; one-artist exhib, Kornbluth Gallery, Fairlawn, NJ, 83, and others. *Bibliog:* Lawrence Campbell (auth), article, Art News, 9/73; Gordon Brown (auth), article, Arts Mag, 11/73; Lucy Lippard (auth), From the Center, Feminist Essays on Women's Art, Dutton, 76. *Mem:* Women in the Arts. *Media:* Oil on Canvas. *Publ:* Contribr, Arts Mag, 67 & Art News, 67. *Dealer:* Kornbluth Gallery Fairlawn NJ. *Mailing Add:* 63 Highwood Terrace Weehawken NJ 07087

SAMERJAN, GEORGE E
DESIGNER, PAINTER

b Boston, Mass, May 12, 15. *Study:* Art Ctr Col, grad, 38; Chouinard Art Inst, 33; Otis Art Inst, 40-41; also with Alexander Brook & Willard Nash. *Work:* San Diego Fine Arts Soc; Fla Southern Col; Abbott Labs; Ford Motor Co Collection; Cole of Calif, Los Angeles; plus others. *Comn:* Designed Arctic Commemorative Stamp, 59, Adlai Stevenson Mem Stamp, 65 & Erie Canal Sesquicentennial Stamp, 67, US Post Off Dept; SC Tricentennial, 70. *Exhib:* Nat Acad Design; Pa Acad Fine Arts, Philadelphia; Denver Art Mus; Corcoran Gallery Art, Washington, DC; Liege Belg & Paris, France; plus others. *Pos:* Chmn, Soc Illusrs Sem, 62-63. *Teaching:* Lectr, NY Univ & Pratt Inst, formerly. *Awards:* Art Dirs Clubs New York, Philadelphia, Advert Club Westchester, NY & Calif Watercolor Soc Awards; Am Watercolor Soc Award, Audubon Artists, Oakland Art Gallery; plus others. *Mem:* Am Watercolor Soc; Dirs Club; Advert Club, Westchester, NY; Audubon Artists. *Mailing Add:* Cantitoe St Katonah NY 10536

SAMPSON, FRANK
PAINTER, PRINTMAKER

b Edmore, NDak, Mar 24, 28. *Study:* Concordia Col, BA, 50; Univ Iowa, MFA, 52, printmaking with Mauricio Lasansky, 56-59. *Work:* Libr Cong, DC; Walker Art Ctr, Minneapolis; Nelson-Atkins Mus, Kansas City; Sheldon Mem Art Ctr, Lincoln, Nebr; Joslyn Art Mus, Omaha, Nebr. *Exhib:* One-man shows, Walker Art Ctr, Minneapolis, 54, Sheldon Mem Art Ctr, Lincoln, Nebr, 64 & Denver Art Mus, 75; Mid-Am, Nelson-Atkins Mus, Kansas City, 65; 13th Am Drawing Biennial, Norfolk Mus Arts, Va, 69; 21st Nat Exhib Prints, Libr Cong, DC, 69; Drawings from Nine States, Mus Fine Arts, Houston, Tex, 70; Regionalism: Seven Views, Joslyn Art Mus, Omaha, Nebr, 79. *Teaching:* Prof painting, drawing & printmaking, Univ Colo, Boulder, 61- *Awards:* Best in show, Mid-Am Purchase Fund, 62; Ford Purchase, Walker Biennial, 64; Purchase Prize, Somers Mem, 70. *Bibliog:* Michele de Ghelderode (auth), D'ou ViensTu, Beau Nuage?, Le Cahier des Arts, Bruxelles, Belgique, 4/61; Walter Simon (auth), The collector, Univ Colo, summer 77; Merrill Mahaffey (auth), Contemporary western painting, the new western art, Southwestern Art, fall 77. *Media:* Oil, Acrylic. *Dealer:* Brena Gallery 313 Detroit St Denver CO 80206. *Mailing Add:* 1912 Columbine Ave Boulder CO 80302

SAMSTAG, GORDON
PAINTER, SCULPTOR

b New York, NY, June 21, 06. *Study:* Nat Acad Design Sch; Art Students League; also schs in Paris. *Work:* Toledo Mus, Ohio; Santa Barbara Mus; Aldridge Collection, Australia. *Comn:* Paintings, Reidsville, NC Post Off & Scarsdale, NY Post Off; 23D Collage, Diamond Christensen, Adelaide. *Exhib:* Pa Acad Fine Arts; Corcoran Gallery Art, 58; Carnegie Int, 59; Contemp Art Soc Interstate, Hobart Tas, Melbourne & Sydney, 67-70. *Teaching:* Dir, Am Art Sch, New York, 51-61; sr lectr fine art, painting & sculpture, South Australian Sch Art, 61-71. *Awards:* Clarke Prize, Nat Acad Design, 49; Lippincott Prize, Pa Acad Fine Arts, 50; Woodville Critics Prize, 68. *Mem:* Nat Acad Design; Contemp Art Soc (pres, 68); Royal South Australian Soc Art; Burnside Painting Group (pres, 64); Naples Art Asn, Fla. *Publ:* Ed, Bull Australian Soc Educ Through Art, 68, Contemp Art Soc Quart, 69 & Collection, Elliot Aldridge, 70. *Mailing Add:* 2058 Snook Dr Naples FL 33962

SAMUELS, EDWARD GEORGE
PAINTER, SCULPTOR

b New York, NY, Nov 8, 41. *Study:* State Univ NY, New Paltz, painting with Ilya Bolotowsky, 60-63; with Ben Johnson, Woodstock Studio, 64-65; Boston Mus Sch, 65-66. *Work:* Whitney Mus Am Art & Finch Col Mus, New York; State Univ NY, New Paltz; Int Mus Erotic Art, San Francisco. *Comn:* Drawings, comn by Andy Williams, Los Angeles, Calif, 75; silver & gold sculpture, comn by Erica Jong, 75; silver minatures, comn by Arman Fernandez, New York, 76; silver minatures, comn by Richard Pryor, Los

Angeles, 76-77; gold minatures, comn by Jasper Johns, New York, 79. *Exhib:* Options, Milwaukee Art Ctr & Chicago Art Inst, 69; Light Group, Buffalo Mus Art, 70; Bicentennial Art of America, Tokyo Mus Mod Art, Japan & Nat Gallery, London, Eng, 76; Instituto Cult Americano-Dominicano, Santo Domingo, 82; and others. *Collections Arranged:* Paintings/Sculpture/Drawings, Allan Stone Gallery, New York, 72 & Paintings/Marble/Minatures, 73; Marble Sculpture/Drawings, Tharrington Gallery, New York, 77; Minatures/Paintings/Drawings, Au Fond de la Cour, Paris, 78 & Minatures, 79; and others. *Pos:* Master sculptor, D C Williams Display, Brooklyn, NY, 67-69; head dept sculpture, Lombardo Display, Brooklyn, NY, 68-71; owner, Cloud Screen silkscreen printing, Brooklyn, 70-72; owner, Samuels Fine Art Studios, Manhattan, 72- *Teaching:* Pvt lessons, 72-; instr metal working, New York Univ, presently; instr, Parsons Sch Design, 81. *Awards:* Best in Show, Soc Illusrs, 76. *Bibliog:* Hilton Kramer (auth), Arts & Leisure, New York Times, Sunday ed, 71. *Media:* Oil, Acrylic; Precious Metals, Marble. *Publ:* Contribr, Erotic Art by Drs Phyllis Eberhard & Ron Hausen, Nat Sex Forum, 73; contribr, Hardcore Crafts by Nancy Levine, Ballatine-Tree, 76. *Dealer:* Allan Stone Gallery E 86th St New York NY 10028. *Mailing Add:* c/o R K Parker 157 Spring St New York NY 10012

SAMUELS, GERALD
PAINTER, SCULPTOR
b Brooklyn, NY, Nov 14, 27. *Study:* Long Island Univ; City Col New York; NY Univ; Pratt Inst; also with Moses Soyer, Phillip Evergood, Hans Hofmann. *Work:* Mass Inst Technol; San Francisco Mus. *Exhib:* One-man shows, Drawing & Sculpture, Molesworth Gallery, New York, 69, Painting, River Run Gallery, Martha's Vineyard, 74 & Painting, Landmark Gallery, New York, 7577 & 81; Paintings, Maine Coast Artist, 74. *Teaching:* Instr advan painting, Arts Students League, New York, currently. *Mailing Add:* 799 Greenwich St New York NY 10014

SAMUELS, HAROLD & PEGGY
HISTORIANS, DEALERS
Harold, b Brooklyn, NY, July 9, 17; Peggy, b Brooklyn, NY, Nov 27, 22. *Study:* Harold, Ohio Univ, BA(art hist), MA; Harvard Univ, LLB; Art Students League; also with Stuart Davis & Wayne Davis; Peggy, NY Univ, BS, 44. *Pos:* Both currently writers, art dealers, antiquarian book dealers as Harold & Peggy Samuels; Peggy, ed, Woman's Day, 45-48; both have lectured on how to buy a painting, restoring paintings, how to buy western painting, buying paintings for investment and other subjects pertaining to art. *Res:* Maintain data on 200 artists of American West before 1950. *Specialty:* Paintings of the American and Canadian West before 1950, including illustrations. *Publ:* Coauth, Illustrated Biographical Encyclopedia of Artists of the American West, Doubleday, 76; Harold, auth, The Life of Frederic Remington & Catalog Raisonne of the Paintings of Frederic Remington; coauth, The Collected Writings of Frederic Remington, Doubleday, 78. *Mailing Add:* 95 Trellis Lane Wantagh NY 11793

SAMUELS, JOHN STOCKWELL, 3RD
COLLECTOR, PATRON
b Galveston, Tex, Sept 15, 33. *Study:* Tex A&M Univ, BA, 54 & MS, 54; Harvard Univ, BL, 60. *Collection:* American, French, Italian & Pre-Columbian paintings and decorative arts. *Mailing Add:* 10 E 40th St, 42nd Floor New York NY 10016

SAMUELSON, FRED BINDER
PAINTER, EDUCATOR
b Harvey, Ill, Nov 29, 25. *Study:* Sch Art Inst Chicago, BFA, 51 & MFA, 53; Univ Chicago, 46-53. *Work:* Denver Art Mus, Colo; Witte Mus, San Antonio, Tex; Ohio Univ, Athens; Tex Fine Arts Asn, Laguna Gloria Mus, Austin. *Comn:* Acrylic mural, Hemisfair 68, San Antonio. *Exhib:* 60th Ann Exhib Western Art, Denver Art Mus, 54; 20th Ann Tex Painting & Sculpture Exhib, Dallas Mus Fine Art, 58; Southwest Am Art Ann, Okla Art Ctr, 60; Segundo Festival Pictorico Acapulco, 64; 53rd Tex Fine Arts Asn Ann, 64. *Teaching:* Prof painting & drawing, Inst Allende, San Miguel de Allende, Mex, 55-63, head grad studies & painting, 65-; chmn fac, San Antonio Art Inst, 63-64. *Bibliog:* Leonard Brooks (auth), Oil Painting Traditional and New, 59 & Wash Drawings, 61, Van Nostrand Reinhold; interview, Time-Life, 65. *Media:* Acrylic. *Dealer:* Hartley Gallery Winter Park FL 32789; Odyssey Gallery San Antonio TX 78209. *Mailing Add:* 1465 S Atlantic Apt 7 Cocoa Beach FL 32931

SANABRIA, ROBERT
SCULPTOR
b El Paso, Tex, Aug 20, 31. *Study:* Univ Md, BA, 65, MFA, 79. *Work:* Snite Mus Art, Univ Notre Dame, Ind; Wichita Art Mus, Kans; SDak Mem Art Ctr, Brookings; Tweed Mus Art, Duluth, Minn; Miss Mus Art, Jackson. *Comn:* Abstract steel tree, B F Saul Co, Lexington, Ky, 75; 2 abstract concrete sculptures, City Philadelphia, 80; cast paper relief, Lane & Edson, Washington, DC, 81; concrete sculpture, Md Nat Capitol Park & Plan Comt, Prince Georges Co, 81-82; abstr concrete sculpture, M/G Archit Inc, Milford, Va, 83. *Exhib:* Works with Paper, Grace Gallery, Reston, Va, 78; Washington Art, Heidenberg Gallery, Washington, DC, 79; New Acquisitions, SDak Mem Arts Ctr, Brookings, 79; Regul Gallery, Chicago, 79; Allied Artists Am 68th Ann, Nat Arts Club, New York, 81; and others. *Teaching:* Instr sculpture, Art League Workshops, Alexandria, Va, 75-78. *Bibliog:* Jean Lawrence (auth), Outdoor sculpture, Washingtonian, 7/77; S Heldrig (auth), 900 Seconds, Storer Cable TV, 82; I Winitsky (auth), Private Dream, Public Art, Media Arts Inc, 83. *Mem:* Artists Equity Asn (pres, Washington, DC chap, 83-85). *Publ:* Auth, Fees for commissions, Sculptors' Int, Vol 1, No 6, 83. *Mailing Add:* 8100 River Bend Ct Ft Washington MD 20744

SANBORN, HERBERT J
LITHOGRAPHER, PAINTER
b Worcester, Mass, Oct 28, 07. *Study:* Nat Acad Design, Pulitzer Traveling Fel, 29; Teachers Col, Columbia Univ; Univ Chicago. *Work:* Libr Cong; Nat Mus Am Art, Smithsonian Inst; Hunterdon Co Art Ctr. *Exhib:* 10th Biennial Nat Print Exhib, Print Club Albany, 63; Jacksonville Coun Arts Festival, 64; Print Club Philadelphia Mem Exhib, 64; Va Artists, Va Mus Art, 65; Corcoran Gallery Art Area Ann, 65; West the Law, Minn Mus Art & Traveling Exhib, 79-80. *Pos:* Dir, Davenport Munic Art Gallery, 33-35; dir mus, Oglebay Inst, Wheeling, WVa, 36-42; exhibs officer, Libr Cong, Washington, DC, 46-76. *Awards:* Third Prize, 3rd Ann Va Printmakers, Univ Va, 62; Purchase Prize, Hunterdon Co Art Ctr, 64; First Prize, Washington Watercolor Soc, 80. *Mem:* Print Club Philadelphia; Artists Equity Asn. *Publ:* Auth, Hill towns of Spain (lithographs), 30; auth, Modern Art Influences on Printing Design, 56. *Mailing Add:* 3541 Forest Dr Alexandria VA 22302

SANCHEZ, BEATRICE RIVAS
ADMINISTRATOR, PRINTMAKER
b San Antonio, Tex, June 17, 41. *Study:* Del Art Ctr, 65-69; Montgomery Col, 70-71; Univ Mass, MFA, 75. *Work:* McNay Mus, Trinity Univ, Tex; Univ Tex Health Sci Ctr; Fla State House Rep; St Johns Col, Fla. *Comn:* Two Hundred Years of Graphics (poster), STex Print Soc, San Antonio, 76. *Exhib:* Nat Works on Paper, Springfield Col, Mass, 75; Color Print USA, Tex Tech Univ, 75; Women Artists of San Antonio, Univ Tex, 76; Womens Nat Exhib, Galarie Triangle, Washington, DC, 80. *Teaching:* Artist in residence printmaking & drawing, Trinity Univ, Tex, 76; coordr fine arts prog, Fla Sch Art, Palatka, 76-78; acad & assoc dean, Md Col Art & Design, 78-82; dean, Cranbrook Acad Art, 82- *Awards:* Second Prize, Eighth Ann Parkville Art Exhib, Md, 68; Third Place, Dept Commerce Exhib, Washington, DC, 69; First Prize, Creative Painting, Md Sch Art, 69. *Mem:* Nat Coun Art Admin (mem bd dirs, currently); Mich Asn Community Art Agencies (bd mem, currently); Nat Asn Schs Art & Design; Col Art Asn; Womens Caucus Arts. *Publ:* Contribr, Spectrum Fine Arts, 74 & 75 & Chomo-Uri Mag, summer 75. *Mailing Add:* PO Box 801 Bloomfield Hills MI 48013

SANCHEZ, MARY LOWE (ELIZA)
DEALER, COLLECTOR
b Taos, NMex, July 21, 14. *Pos:* Secy & assoc dir, Gallery A (Allied Artists NMex Inc), Taos, 61-70, dir, secy & treas, 70-76, pres & dir, 76- *Specialty:* Original paintings, etchings and sculpture. *Collection:* Watercolors and etchings by Gene Kloss, aquatints by Doel Reed, pastels and oils by Howard Cook and etchings, watercolors and oils by Barbara Latham and others. *Mailing Add:* De Tevis Lane PO Box 314 Taos NM 87571

SANCHEZ, THORVALD
PAINTER
b Havana, Cuba, June 11, 33; US citizen. *Work:* Milwaukee Art Ctr, Wis. *Exhib:* Pintura Cubana, Caracas, Venezuela, 72; 15th Ann Hortt Competition, Ft Lauderdale, Fla, 73; 35th Ann Exhib, Soc Four Arts, Palm Beach, Fla, 73; East Coast Painters, Longboat Key Art Ctr, Sarasota, Fla, 74; Fla Artists, Norton Mus, West Palm Beach, 75. *Awards:* Best of Show Award, Fla Gulf Coast 9th Show, High Mus Art, Atlanta, Ga, 74. *Bibliog:* Georgia Dupuis (auth), Transition theme of Sanchez work, Palm Beach Post, 74. *Mem:* Fla Artist Group. *Media:* Acrylic, Collage. *Dealer:* Center Gallery 327 Acacia Rd West Palm Beach FL 33401. *Mailing Add:* 146 Seminole Ave Palm Beach FL 33480

SANDBACK, FREDERICK LANE
SCULPTOR
b Bronxville, NY, Aug 29, 43. *Study:* Yale Univ, BA, 62-66, Sch Art & Archit, 66-69, BFA & MFA. *Work:* Mus Mod Art & Whitney Mus Am Art, New York; Nat Gallery Can, Ottawa, Ont; Kunsthalle Basel, Switz; Kaiser Wilhelm Mus, Krefeld, Ger. *Exhib:* One-man shows, Kunsthalle, Berne, Switz, 73; Folkwang Mus, Essen, WGer, 74 & Hessisches Landesmuseum, Darmstadt, 75; Sculpture Ann, Whitney Mus Am Art, 68; Mus Mod Art, 69; Inst Contemp Art, Univ Pa, 69; Actualite d'un Bilan, Galerie Yuon Lambert, Paris, 72. *Bibliog:* Peter Hutchinson (auth), Perception of illusion: object & environment, Arts Mag, 4/68; Paul Wember (auth), Frederick Lane Sandback, Mus Hauslange, Krefeld, 69; Hermann Kern (auth), Fred Sandback, Kunstaum München, 75. *Media:* Yard, Cord. *Publ:* Auth, 16 Variationen von 2 Diagonalen Linien, 72; auth, 16 Variationen von 2 Horizontalen Linien, 73. *Mailing Add:* c/o John Weber Gallery 420 W Broadway New York NY 10012

SANDBERG, HANNAH
PAINTER, LECTURER
b Safed, Upper Galilee, Israel, Aug 12, 04; US citizen. *Comn:* Ktubah (ceremonial marriage contract), Temple Emmanuel, Toronto, Ont, 74. *Exhib:* One-woman shows, East Side Gallery, New York, 64 & 67; Jewish Mus, Theological Seminary Am, New York, 67, Zacks Gallery, Strong Col, York Univ, 71, 74, 78 & 80, Hart House Art Gallery, Univ Toronto, 76 & Beit Emit/Beit Yehude Synagogue, Toronto, 78; and others. *Teaching:* Lectr 20th century painting, Yeshiva Univ, New York, 58-61; assoc fel painting, Strong Col, York Univ, Toronto, 70-82. *Awards:* Int Women's Year Grant, Genesis, Ont Arts Coun, 75. *Media:* Acrylic-Liquitex, Gouache. *Mailing Add:* 11 Catford Rd Apt 723 Downsview ON M3J 1P9 Canada

SANDE, RHODA
ART DEALER
b New York, NY. *Study:* Pratt Inst & Parsons Sch of Design. *Pos:* Owner & dir, Rhoda Sande Gallery, New York. *Specialty:* Twentieth Century American and Mexican paintings, drawings, and sculpture. *Collection:* Picasso, Valtat, antique Persian calligraphy. *Mailing Add:* 220 E 60th St New York NY 10022

SANDEN, JOHN HOWARD
PAINTER, INSTRUCTOR

b Austin, Tex, Aug 6, 35. *Study:* Minneapolis Sch Art, BFA, 56; Art Students League New York. *Work:* US Capitol & NASA Hq, Washington, DC; Fifth Ave Presby Church & New York Univ, New York; Royal Palace, Oyo, Nigeria. *Pos:* Pres & found, Portrait Inst, Washington, Conn, 74-; chmn & found, Nat Portrait Sem, 79- *Teaching:* Instr, Art Students League New York, 71- *Bibliog:* Doreen Mangan (auth), Portrait of a portraitist, Am Artist Mag, 3/75; Joe Singer (auth), Painting Men's Portraits, Watson-Guptill, 76 & 77; Eunice Agar (auth), John Howard Sanden, Am Artist Mag, 11/83. *Media:* Oil. *Publ:* Auth, Painting The Head in Oil, 76 & auth, Successful Portrait Painting, 81, Watson-Guptill. *Dealer:* Portraits Inc 41 East 57th St New York NY 10022. *Mailing Add:* c/o Portraits Inc 985 Park Ave New York NY 10028

SANDERS, ANDREW DOMINICK
PAINTER, INSTRUCTOR

b Erie, Pa, Dec 22, 18. *Study:* Philadelphia Mus Sch Art, dipl, 42. *Exhib:* Butler Inst Am Art Anns, Youngstown, Ohio, 53-55, 64, 72 & 74; Nat Acad Design 146th, 147th & 149th Anns, New York, 71, 72 & 74; Audubon Artists 30th-33rd Anns, Nat Acad Design Galleries, 72-75; Mainstreams 72 & 73, 5th & 6th Ann, Marietta Col, Ohio. *Teaching:* Instr drawing, painting & art hist, Ringling Sch Art, Sarasota, Fla, 49-59; instr drawing & painting, Columbus Col Art & Design, 60-63. *Awards:* Edward C Roberts Award, Conn Acad Fine Arts, 73; Cert Merit, Nat Acad Design & Painters & Sculptors Soc NJ, 74. *Bibliog:* Joan Tomcho (auth), article in Am Artist, 9/75; Susan E Meyer (ed), 20 Figure Painters and How They Work, Watson/Guptill, 79. *Mem:* Audubon Artists. *Media:* Oil. *Publ:* Auth, Murray Stern: social surrealist, Am Artist, 2/77. *Mailing Add:* 18 N Park Row Erie PA 16501

SANDERS, HERBERT HARVEY
CERAMIST, WRITER

b New Waterford, Ohio, Apr 29, 09. *Study:* Ohio State Univ, BS(educ), 32, MA, 33, PhD(ceramic art), 51, with Arthur E Baggs, Edgar Littlefield & Carlton Atherton. *Work:* Everson Art Mus, Syracuse, NY; Metrop Mus Art, New York; Oakland Art Mus, Calif; Mus Int delle Ceramiche, Faenza, Italy; Nat Gallery Art, Smithsonian Inst, DC. *Exhib:* One-man show, Ceramics, Calif Palace of the Legion of Honor, San Francisco, 43; Contemp Crafts Exhib, Little Rock Mus, Ark, 66; Calif Craftsmen, Calif Arts Comn Exhib, San Francisco, 66 & Oakland, 68; A Quarter Century of Ceramic Art in US, Scripps Col Art Galleries, Pasadena, 69; Ceramics '70 Plus Woven Forms, Everson Art Mus, Syracuse, NY, 70; Objects USA, Johnson Wax Collection, toured Europ & Am mus, 70-74. *Teaching:* Teacher indust arts, Groveport High Sch, 34-35; teacher crafts, Norwood High Sch, Ohio, 35-38; from asst prof to prof ceramics, San Jose State Univ, 38-74; emer prof ceramics, 74-; instr, Sch Am Craftsmen, Alfred Univ, NY, 46-47, dir sch, 47-48; Fulbright res scholar ceramic art & educ, Japan, 58-59. *Awards:* Best Design for Production, Gumps San Francisco, 46; Prize, Can Guild Potters, 62; Purchase Prize, Int Minerals, 66. *Bibliog:* Janice Lovoos (auth), California ceramics, Am Artist, 5/68; Fred Ball (auth), Herbert Sanders, 11/71 & Elaine Levin (auth), Pioneers of contemporary American ceramics, Maija Grotell, Herbert Sanders, 11/76, Ceramics Mo. *Mem:* Fel Am Ceramics Soc; hon mem San Francisco Potters Asn; hon mem Bay Area Arts & Crafts Guild. *Media:* Stoneware, Porcelain. *Publ:* Auth, Glazes from plant ash, Craft Horizons Mag, 5/48; auth, 29 articles on pottery form & decoration, Ceramic Age Mag, 52-55; auth, The World of Japanese Ceramics, Kodansha Int, Tokyo, Japan, 67; auth, How to Make Pottery, 74 & Glazes for Special Effects, 74, Watson-Guptill. *Dealer:* Collectors Gallery Oakland Mus 1000 Oak St Oakland CA 94607. *Mailing Add:* 4525 Dundee Wichita KS 67220

SANDERS, JOOP A
PAINTER

b Amsterdam, Holland, Oct 6, 22; US citizen. *Study:* Art Students League, with George Grosz; also with De Kooning. *Work:* Stedelijke Mus, Amsterdam; Munic Mus, The Hague; Belzalel Mus, Jerusalem; Dillard Univ. *Exhib:* Ninth St Show, 51; Stable Shows, 52-55; one-man retrospective, Stedelijke Mus, 60; Carnegie Inst, 60; Options, Mus Contemp Art, Chicago, 68. *Teaching:* Vis lectr, Carnegie Inst Technol, spring 65; prof painting, State Univ NY Col, New Paltz, 66-; vis lectr, Univ Calif, Berkeley, spring 68. *Awards:* Longview Found Fel, 60-61; Carnegie Inst Technol Res Found Awards, 71-72. *Media:* Oil, Acrylic. *Mailing Add:* White Lands Rd 118A Stone Ridge NY 12484

SANDERS, RHEA (RHEA SANDERS RABINOVICH)
PAINTER

b Charleston, SC, Nov 6, 23. *Study:* With Maurice Sterne, 40-44. *Work:* Governor's Mansion, Columbia, SC; Univ SC, Columbia; Univ South, Sewanee, Tenn; British Mus Libr, London; Rare Bks Collection, New York Pub Libr. *Exhib:* Paintings in Egg Tempera, Gibbes Art Mus, Charleston, SC, 79; The New Am Still Life, Westmoreland Co Mus Art, Greensburg, Pa, 79; Audubon Artists Ann, New York, 80; Realist Painting People and Objects in Women's Lives, Marymount Col, New York, 82; Works on Paper: The Still Life, Fordham Univ, 83; and others. *Bibliog:* Jerry Tallmer (auth), Public place, private faces, New York Post, 12/13/80. *Mem:* Orgn Independent Artists New York; Women's Caucus Art New York; Found Community Artists, New York. *Media:* Egg Tempera, Watercolor. *Publ:* Auth & illusr, The Fire Gardens of Maylandia, Tradd St Press, 80. *Mailing Add:* 617 West End Ave New York NY 10024

SANDERSON, CHARLES HOWARD
PAINTER, INSTRUCTOR

b Hamilton, Kans, Mar 6, 25. *Study:* Kans State Univ; Emporia State Univ, Kans; Wichita State Univ, BS(art educ); Ft Hays State Univ, Kans, MS(art educ). *Work:* Okla Art Ctr, Oklahoma City; Wichita Art Mus, Kans; Springfield Art Mus, Mo; Hockaday Ctr for the Arts, Kalispell, Mont; Birger Sandzen Mem Gallery, Lindsborg, Kans; and others. *Exhib:* One-man show, Wichita Art Mus, Kans, 65-80; Sanderson-Booty Exhib, Galerie Monti-Carlo, Charleroi, Belg, 72; Am Painters in Paris, France, 76; Charles M Russell Art Mus Art Auction, Great Falls, Mont, 77; Kalispell Art Show, Mont, 79 & 80; and others. *Collections Arranged:* Group Two--Invitational Kans Exhib, Century II Concert Hall Foyer, Wichita, 72-75. *Teaching:* Instr art, Kans Pub Schs, 51-; instr painting, Wichita Art Asn, 58-71; instr teaching methods, Friends Univ, Wichita, 68-74; lectr & instr, Kans Art Educators Workshop, Wichita, 72-75; instr watercolor, Wichita State Univ Continuing Educ, 75-81. *Awards:* Purchase awards, Air Capitol Ann, Wichita Art Mus, 56-58; Kans Watercolor Soc Tri-State Exhib Award, 70-73, 75-76 & 80-81. *Bibliog:* Larry Hatteberg (auth), Channel Ten Mag Feature, Channel Ten Television, 76; Watercolor, Acrylic, Sculpture & Demonstration (four educ videotapes), Wichita Bd of Educ, 77; Eileen O'Hara (auth), The painter and the business manager, Wichitan Mag, 5/81. *Mem:* Founder Kans Watercolor Soc (pres, 71-72 & 79); Wichita Artists Guild; Whiskey Painters Am; Kans Art Educ Asn. *Media:* Watercolor, Acrylic. *Mailing Add:* 902 Waddington Wichita KS 67212

SANDERSON, WARREN
DEALER, HISTORIAN

b Boston, Mass, Feb 9, 31. *Study:* Boston Univ, MA, 51; Univ Saarland, Saarbrucken, WGer, cert(Fulbright Scholar), 60; Inst Fine Arts, NY Univ, PhD, 65. *Pos:* Co-owner, Warren Sanderson Beaux Arts/Fine Arts, Montreal, 81- *Teaching:* Prof hist art & archit, Univ Ill, Chicago, 66-70; prof art hist & criticism, Concordia Univ, Montreal, 76-; vis prof art hist, Univ Trier, WGer, 77-78 & 83. *Awards:* Fulbright Fel, 66 & 82; Deutsche Forschungsgemeinschaft, 77, 78 & 83; Can Coun Award, 80. *Bibliog:* Jeffrey Horrell (auth), article, Art Documentation, 10/82; Diane Kay (auth), article, Art Int, 1/3/83; Elaine Cohen (auth), Sharing the joy & discovery of fine works of art, Suburban, 9/28/83. *Mem:* Int Asn Critics Art; Col Art Asn Am; Soc Archit Historians; Int Comt Hist Art; Univ Arts Asn Can. *Res:* Early medieval art and architecture; Carolingian ivories; art and architecture since 1950. *Specialty:* Twentieth centure art; old masters; impressionists. *Publ:* Auth, Die Frühmittelalterlichen Krypten von St Maximin in Trier, Trierer Zeitschrift, 68; auth, Monastic reform in Lorraine ... the outer crypt 950-1100, Transactions Am Philosophical Soc, 71; auth, Archbishop Ratbodus ... Regino of Prüm ... Art & Music circa 900, Jahrbuch Berliner Mus, 82; ed & contrib, International Handbook of Contemporary Developments, Greenwood Press, 83; auth, Japanese Avant-Garde Architecture and the West, Avant Garde & Semiotics (in prep). *Mailing Add:* PO Box 509 Champlain NY 12919

SANDESON, WILLIAM SEYMOUR
CARTOONIST

b Mound City, Ill, Dec 16, 13. *Study:* Chicago Acad Fine Arts, 31-32. *Pos:* Free-lance cartoonist for nat mags, 32-37; ed cartoonist, New Orleans Item-Tribune, 37-41; cartoonist, picture ed & art dir, St Louis Star-Times, 41-51, daily cartoon feature, Sketching Up with the News, Star-Times; ed cartoonist, Ft Wayne News-Sentinel, Ind, 51-82; retired. *Awards:* Honor Medal, 52, 53 & 56 & Distinguished Serv Award, 71-73, Freedoms Found; George Washington Honor Medal, 54, 55 & 57-60; Ind Sch Bell Award, 67; Pulitzer Prize, 83; and others. *Mem:* Nat Cartoonists Soc; Am Asn Ed Cartoonists; Cong Club; Ft Wayne Press (pres, 65). *Mailing Add:* 119 W Sherwood Terr Ft Wayne IN 46802

SANDGREN, ERNEST NELSON
PAINTER, PRINTMAKER

b Dauphin, Man, Dec 17, 17. *Study:* Univ Ore, BA & MFA; Univ Michoacan, Mex; Chicago Inst Design. *Work:* Portland Art Mus, Ore; Am Embassy Collection; Victoria & Albert Mus, London. *Comn:* Murals, Ore State Univ Libr, Corvallis & Portland. *Exhib:* Denver Art Mus; Santa Barbara Mus Art; Brooklyn Mus; Am Cult Ctr, Paris, Turin & Bordighera, Italy & Johannesburg, SAfrica; 46 USA Printmakers, New Forms Gallery, Athens, Greece, 64. *Pos:* Artist, Am Quintana Roo Mex Exped, 65 & 66 & CEDAM Exped to Durango, Mex, 70. *Teaching:* Instr art, Univ Ore, 47; prof art, Ore State Univ, 48-; guest instr printmaking, Pa State Univ, 66 & Cent Ore Col, 70-72. *Awards:* M H De Young Mem Mus, 58; Yaddo Fel, 61; K Fisher Award, NW Watercolor Soc, 79; plus others. *Mem:* Ore Artists Alliance; West Coast Watercolor Soc. *Mailing Add:* Art Dept Ore State Univ Corvallis OR 97331

SANDGROUND, MARK BERNARD, SR
COLLECTOR, PATRON

b Boston, Mass, June 6, 32. *Study:* Univ Mich, BA, 52; Univ Va, LLB, 55 & JD, 71. *Teaching:* Prof humanities & cooking, Free Col Belgravia, Lower Sch, 65-66. *Awards:* La Chaine des Les Robsier Chevalier, 71; Klip & Klop Gold Medal, 72. *Bibliog:* D Kane (auth), Killer Kane and the White Princess, McGraw, 72; The Gypsie princess (film), Anon, 72. *Mem:* Friends of Corcoran Gallery Art (bd dir, 67-, pres, 68-70); Osuna Gallery. *Res:* Graphic works of Jose Louis Cuevas. *Collection:* Cuevas, Rico Lebrun & Anne Truitt. *Publ:* Auth, Collected letters from unknown artists, 1846-1871, privately publ, 52; auth, Erotica from the Falls Church Collection, 72. *Mailing Add:* 1025 Connecticut Ave NW Suite 405 Washington DC 20036

SANDLER, BARBARA
PAINTER

b New York, NY, Sept 14, 43. *Study:* Art Students League, George Bridgeman scholar, 63, also with Edwin Dickenson & Robert Beverly Hale. *Work:* Mus Mod Art, New York; Chicago Art Inst; Joseph Hirshhorn Mus, Washington, DC; Chase Manhattan Bank; Manufacturers Hanover Trust. *Comn:* Poster & lithograph for Bicentennial, Spec Proj Group, Chicago, 75; posters, Circle in the Square Theatre, New York, 77-78; covers for Harpers & Sat Rev Mag; var record covers for Columbia & Verve Records. *Exhib:* One-person shows, Newman Southern Gallery, Conn, 78 & Segal Gallery, New York, 81, 83 & 84; Alex Rosenberg Gallery, New York, 79; Micro '83 Int Exhib, Stockholm, Sweden, 83. *Awards:* Elizabeth T Greenshields Mem Found Grant, 74. *Bibliog:* Articles, Archit Digest, 2/76; Print Mag, 79 & Arts Mag, 5/83. *Media:* Oil, Graphite. *Publ:* Illusr, The Long View, Knopf, 74; illusr, Indian Oratorio, Ballantine Bks, 75; contribr, Super Realism, Dutton, 75. *Mailing Add:* 221 W 20th St New York NY 10012

SANDLER, IRVING HARRY
CRITIC, HISTORIAN

b New York, NY, July 22, 25. *Study:* Temple Univ, BA, 48; Univ Pa, MA, 50; NY Univ, PhD, 76. *Pos:* Art critic, Art News, 56-62 & New York Post, 60-65; vis critic, State Univ NY, 69-70; contrib ed, Art Am, 72. *Teaching:* Instr art hist, NY Univ, 60-71; prof, State Univ NY Col Purchase, 71- *Awards:* Tona Shepherd Fund Grant Travel in Ger & Austria; Guggenheim Found Fel, 65; Nat Endowment Humanities Fel, 80. *Bibliog:* Jay Jacobs (auth), Of myths and men, Art Am, 3-4/70; Rosalind Constable (auth), The myth of the myth-makers, Washington Post Bk World, 11/29/70; Gesture-makers and colourfieldsmen, Times Lit Suppl, 6/8/71. *Mem:* Int Asn Art Critics (pres, 70-75); Col Art Asn Am; Inst Study Art Educ. *Res:* American art since 1930. *Publ:* Auth, The triumph of American painting, a history of abstract expressism, 70; ed, Art Criticism and Art Education, 72; contribr, Contemporary Art: 1942-1972: Collection of the Albright-Knox Gallery, 73; auth, The New York School: Painters and Sculptors of the Fifties, Harper-Row, 78; auth, Alex Katz, Abrams, 79; and others. *Mailing Add:* 100 Bleecker St New York NY 10012

SANDMAN, JO
PAINTER, SCULPTOR

b Boston, Mass, Mar 22, 31. *Study:* Brandeis Univ, AB, 52; with Hans Hofmann, 52-53; Hunter Col, with Robert Motherwell, 53; Univ Calif, Berkeley, MA(art), 54; Radcliffe Col, MAT, 56. *Work:* Aldrich Mus Contemp Art; Addison Gallery Am Art; Dallas Mus Fine Arts; NY Univ; Mass Inst Technol. *Comn:* Video piece for TV, Nat Endowment Arts, Rockefeller Found & Mass Coun Arts, Boston, 75; Removal Drawing, Bicentennial Painting Comn, Boston 200, 75. *Exhib:* Flush with the Walls, Mus Fine Arts, Boston, 71; Unstretched Paintings, Brockton Art Mus, Mass, 73-74; Drawings from Two New York Galleries, Va Mus Fine Arts, 73-75; solo exhib, O K Harris Works Art, New York, 73, 75 & 82, Addison Gallery Am Art, 74, Brockton Art Mus, Mass, 76 & Stux Gallery, Boston, 81 & 83; Prospectus: Art in the Seventies, Aldrich Mus Contemp Art, 79; Boston Now: Abstract Painting, Inst Contemp Art, Boston, 81. *Teaching:* Vis artist, lectr & critic painting, various art sch & col, 56- *Bibliog:* Kay Larson (auth), Jo Sandman, Christopher Wilmarth, 5/78 & Pamela Allara (auth), The scope of Boston art is broader than it would appear, 11/81, Art News. *Mem:* Boston Visual Artists Union; Ft Point Arts Community. *Dealer:* O K Harris Works Art 383 W Broadway New York NY 10012. *Mailing Add:* 326 A St Boston MA 02210

SANDOL, MAYNARD
PAINTER

b Newark, NJ, 1930. *Study:* Newark State Col, 52; also with Robert Motherwell. *Work:* Newark Mus Art; Wadsworth Atheneum, Hartford, Conn; Princeton Univ, NJ; Finch Col Mus, New York; Joseph Hirshhorn Collection, Washington, DC; also pvt collections. *Exhib:* Corcoran Gallery of Art, Washington, DC; Mus Mod Art, New York; NJ Pavilion, New York World's Fair; NJ State Mus, Trenton; NJ Masters, 1980; and others. *Bibliog:* William H Gerdts, Jr (auth), Paintings and Sculpture in New Jersey, Van Nostrand, 64. *Media:* Oil, Acrylic, Watercolor. *Mailing Add:* Bunn St Box 364 RR 2 Califon NJ 07830

SANDOR, JOSEPHINE (BEARDSLEY)
SCULPTOR

b New York, NY, May 21, 14. *Study:* Grand Cent Sch Art, 30-33; Art Students League, with William Zorach & John Hovannes, 49-52; Columbia Univ Sch Painting & Sculpture, with Oronzio Maldarelli, 53-58. *Exhib:* Nat Acad Design, New York, 66, 67, 72 & 80; Salmagundi Club, New York, 78; Catharine Lorillard Wolfe Art Club Ann, New York, 78; Nat Sculpture Soc, New York, 79; Am Artists Prof League, 79; and others. *Teaching:* Marlboro Hosp, NJ, three yrs. *Awards:* Gold Medal, Catharine Lorillard Wolfe Art Club Ann Exhib, 78; First Prizes, Allied Artists Am, 78 & Salmagundi Club Exhib, 78. *Mem:* Salmagundi Club; Allied Artists Am; Knickerbocker Artists; Pen & Brush Club (sculpture chmn, 70-72, bd dirs, 72-75); Catharine Lorillard Wolfe Art Club (sculpture chmn, 77-80, bd dirs, 76-79). *Media:* Stone, Clay. *Mailing Add:* Ramapo Park Oakland NJ 07436

SANDWEISS, MARTHA ANN
CURATOR

b St Louis, Mo, Mar 29, 54. *Study:* Harvard Univ, BA, 75; Nat Endowment for Humanities Fel, Nat Portrait Gallery, Washington, DC, 75-76; Yale Univ, MA, 77; Yale Univ, MPhil, 81. *Collections Arranged:* A Knot of Dreamers: The Brook Farm Community, Nat Portrait Gallery, 76; Pictures from an Expedition: Early Views of the American West (auth, catalog), Yale Univ Art Gallery, 78; Carlotta Corpron: Designer with Light (auth, catalog), 80; Masterworks of American Photography (auth, bk), 82 & Carleton E Watkins: Photographer of the American West, 83, Amon Carter Mus. *Pos:* Fel, Ctr Am Art & Mat Cult, Yale Univ, 77-79; cur photographs, Amon Carter Mus, Ft Worth, Tex, 79- *Collection:* American photography, strong in photos of the American West; includes photographic estate of Laura Gilpin (1891- 1979). *Mailing Add:* Amon Carter Mus PO Box 2365 Ft Worth TX 76101

SANGIAMO, ALBERT
EDUCATOR, PAINTER

b Brooklyn, NY. *Study:* Brooklyn Col, AB; Yale Univ, BFA & MFA. *Work:* Baltimore Mus, Md. *Exhib:* Smithsonian Traveling Exhib Am Drawing, 65; one-man shows, Baltimore Mus, 69, Towson State Col, 71, Decker Art Gallery, Md, 75 & Md Arts Coun Traveling Show, 75. *Teaching:* Instr painting & drawing, Md Inst Col Art, 61-, chmn found dept, 61-73, chmn dept fine arts, 73- *Awards:* Grand Prize, Baltimore Mus, 59; Purchase Prizes, St Paul Arts Ctr, 64. *Media:* Synthetic Charcoal, Acrylic. *Mailing Add:* 1715 Bolton St Baltimore MD 21217

SANGUINETTI, EUGENE F
ADMINISTRATOR, LECTURER

b Yuma, Ariz, May 12, 17. *Study:* Univ Santa Clara, BA, 39; Univ Ariz, 60-62. *Collections Arranged:* Selected Drawings from the Collection of Edward Jacobson, 70; Drawings by Living Americans, Objects from Buddhist Cultures & Etching Renaissance in France: 1850-1880, 71 (with catalog); Drawings by New York Artists (with catalog), Prehistoric Utah Petroglyphs & Pictographs & Ron Resch and the Computer, 72; Abraham Walkowitz Retrospective (with catalog), 74; plus other retrospectives & one-man exhibs. *Pos:* Dir, Tucson Mus & Art Ctr, Ariz, 64-67; dir, Utah Mus Fine Arts, Univ Utah, Salt Lake City, 67-; judge art shows, Colo, Utah & Idaho, 68-72, Bellevue & Seattle, Wash, 75. *Teaching:* Lectr art hist, Univ Ariz, 62-64; adj prof art, Univ Utah, 67- *Mem:* Asn Am Mus; Western Asn Art Mus; Col Art Asn Am; Asn Archit Historians; Am Fedn Arts. *Res:* American art of the first half of the 20th century. *Specialty:* Paintings, tapestries and furniture from American and European periods, Oriental material, Egyptian and Cyprist antiquities; French and English objects and decoration. *Publ:* Contribr, Alexander H Wyant Retrospective, 68; contribr, John Marin Drawings Retrospective, 69; contribr, Alex Katz Retrospective, 71; contribr, Social Concern and the Worker: French Prints from 1830-1910, 73. *Mailing Add:* 101 Arts & Archit Ctr Univ of Utah Salt Lake City UT 84112

SANKOWSKY, ITZHAK
PAINTER, SCULPTOR

b Kishinew, Romania, Mar 9, 08; US citizen. *Study:* Acad Fine Arts & Univ Florence, Italy; Univ Pa, MA; and with Arthur B Carles, Jr. *Work:* Philadelphia Mus Art; Jewish Mus Art, New York; Mus Tel Aviv; Harrisburg Mus Art; also in pvt collection of Milton Shapp. *Comn:* Stained glass windows & mem plaques, Har-Zion Temple, Philadelphia, 60-66; candelabra, Philadelphia Psychiat Hosp, 62; stained glass windows, Levine Mem Chapel, Philadelphia, 63-64; sculpture bas-relief, Home for Jewish Aged, Philadelphia, 64-65; illus for book, Jewish Publ Soc, Philadelphia, 67. *Exhib:* Int Watercolor Show, Chicago, 40-69; one-man shows, Arts & Crafts, Pittsburgh, 52, Philadelphia Art Alliance, 56-68, Agra Gallery, Washington, DC, 65 & Franklin & Marshall Col, 67; and others. *Teaching:* Instr painting & sculpture, Philadelphia Mus Art, 48-, Allens Lane Art Ctr, Philadelphia, 48-51 & Main Line Ctr Art, Philadelphia, 50-53. *Awards:* Within the Ghetto Walls, YM-YWHA, Philadelphia, 51; Purchase Prize for Print, Burr Gallery Nat Exhib, 58-59. *Mem:* Philadelphia Print Club; Artists Equity Asn; Am Color Print Soc; Philadelphia Art Alliance. *Publ:* Auth, Art in Israel, Jewish Frontier, New York, 35; auth, Art in Israel, Bull Har-Zion Temple, Philadelphia, 65; auth, Always time for art, suppl to the Jewish Exponent, Philadelphia, 73. *Mailing Add:* 217 Upland Rd Merion Station PA 19066

SAN SOUCIE, PATRICIA MOLM
PAINTER, INSTRUCTOR

b Minneapolis, Minn, Nov 4, 31. *Study:* Univ Wisc, graphics with Warrington Colescott & Alfred Sessler, painting with Dean Meeker, BS(applied art), 53; Drew Univ, NJ, with Lee Hall, 72-73; Summit Art Ctr, NJ, painting with V Fangor, R Reid, William McCartin & Wolf Kahn, 72-81. *Work:* Springfield Art Mus, Mo. *Comn:* Neuberger & Berman Off, New York; Casio Int Off, New York. *Exhib:* Watercolor USA, Springfield Mus, Mo, 65-81; Nat Asn Women Artists, Nat Acad Galleries, New York, 70-83; NJ Watercolor Soc Ann, 72-83; Am Watercolor Soc, 72-76; Solo exhib, Acad Arts, Easton, Md, 83; and others. *Pos:* Jury selection chmn, St Louis Artists Guild, 68-71; gallery exhib comt, Summit Art Ctr, NJ, 73-79. *Teaching:* Instr, Watercolor Art Asn, NJ, 75-76 & Art Ctr South Orange, NJ, 76-78; fac mem, Summit Art Ctr, NJ, 83. *Awards:* Prize & Medal Hon, Nat Asn Women Artists, 72; Purchase Award, Watercolor USA, Springfield Art Mus, 74; Strathmore Award, Watercolor West, Riverside Mus, Calif, 83. *Bibliog:* Edward Betts (auth), Master Class in Watercolor, Watson-Guptill Publ, 75. *Mem:* Nat Waterolor Soc; Nat Asn Women Artists; NJ Watercolor Soc; Am Watercolor Soc. *Media:* Watercolor. *Dealer:* Gallery 9 Chatham NJ; Norton's Fine Arts St Louis MO. *Mailing Add:* 35 Cayuga Way Short Hills NJ 07078

SANTLOFER, JONATHAN
PAINTER

b New York, NY, Apr 26, 46. *Study:* Boston Univ, BFA; Pratt Inst, MFA, studied painting with George McNeil. *Work:* Norton Simon Inc; Inst of Contemp Art, Tokyo, Japan; Prudential Corp, Grand Rapids, Mich; Indianapolis Mus Art, Ind; Chase Manhattan Bank, New York; and others. *Exhib:* Contemp Reflections, The Aldrich Mus of Contemp Art, Conn, 76;

one-man exhibs, Drawings, Inst of Contemp Art, Tokyo, 77, Drawings, The Jersey City Mus, NJ, 77, Paintings, Franklin & Marshall Col, Pa, 78 & Pam Adler Gallery, New York, 79 & 81; Betsy Rosenfield Gallery, Chicago, 81; and others. *Teaching:* Instr art hist/studio, Jersey City State Col, NJ, 74-; instr contemp art, The New Sch, New York, 76- *Awards:* Skowhegan Scholar, Summer Painting Grant, Skowhegan Sch of Painting & Sculpture, Maine, 66; Visual Artists Fel, Nat Endowment Arts, 83. *Bibliog:* Grace Glueuk (auth), article, New York Times, 10/29/82; Ronny H Cohen (auth), article, Artforum, 1/83; Steven H Madoff (auth), article, Art Am, 2/83; Deborah Perlberg (auth), The new paintings of Jonathan Santlofer, Arts, 2/81. *Media:* Multimedia. *Dealer:* Pam Adler Gallery 50 W 57th St New York NY 10019. *Mailing Add:* 151 W 28th St New York NY 10001

SAPHIRE, LAWRENCE M
WRITER, DEALER
b Brooklyn, NY, Jan 12, 31. *Study:* Yale Univ, BA, 52, writing with Robert Penn Warren; Yale Sch Fine Arts, 51-53; Univ Paris I at Sorbonne, two dipl. *Pos:* Dir, Blue Moon Gallery, New York; ed, Blue Moon Press, Yorktown Heights, NY. *Res:* Modern prints, particularly Leger, Andre Masson. *Specialty:* Modern European painting, sculpture, graphics, original print publications in books and albums. *Publ:* Auth & ed, Sea Bird Saga (including Wallace Putnam lithographs), Blue Moon Gallery, 66; auth, Poems (including Andre Masson etchings), Ed de la Lune Bleue, 74;; auth (catalogues), Andre Masson/Second Surrealist Period, 75 & the Genius of Andre Masson, 76 & auth, Fernand Leger/Complete Graphic Work, 78, Blue Moon Press. *Mailing Add:* 808 Broadway New York NY 10003

SAPIEN, DARRYL RUDOLPH
PERFORMANCE ARTIST, GRAPHIC ARTIST
b Los Angeles, Calif, Mar 12, 50. *Study:* Fullerton Col, AA, 71; San Francisco Art Inst, BA, 72, MA, 76. *Work:* Univ Art Mus, Univ Calif, Berkeley; Oakland Mus, Calif; San Francisco Mus Mod Art; Solomon R Guggenheim Mus, New York. *Comn:* This is Not A Test (participation performance), Soc Encouragement Contemp Art, San Francisco, 76. *Exhib:* Within the Nucleus (performance), San Francisco Mus Mod Art, 76; Painting & Sculpture in Calif: The Mod Era, San Francisco Mus Mod Art, 76; Gallery of the Nat Collection of Fine Arts, Washington, DC, 77; The Principle of the Arch (performance), PS 1, New York 77; A Bridge Can Also Be a Work of Art (performance), Arte Fiera di Bologna, Italy, 77; Crime in the Streets (performance), Adler Alley, San Francisco, 78; Space, Time, Sound, a Decade in the Bay Area, San Francisco Mus Mod Art, 79; Hero (performance), Newport Harbor Art Mus, Calif, 80 & Victoria Theater, San Francisco, Calif, 81; 19 Artists--Emergent Americans, Solomon R Guggenheim Mus, New York, 81; Am Roulette, Solomon R Guggenheim Mus, NY, 81. *Awards:* Nat Endowment Arts Awards, 73 & 79; Louise Riskin Award, Video Pavillion, San Francisco Art Festivel, 75. *Bibliog:* Jack Burnham (auth), Contemporary ritual, Arts Mag, 73; Robert McDonald (auth), The total art of Darryl Sapien, Artweek, 75; William Kleb (auth), Art performance San Francisco, Performing Arts J, 77. *Media:* Live Performance, Closed Circuit Video & Sound Systems. *Publ:* Auth, Splitting the axis & Video art and the ultimate cliche, La Mamelle, 76; contribr, Other Sources (catalog), San Francisco Art Inst, 76; contribr, Oggi in California, Data, 77; auth, Crime in the streets, High Performance, summer 79; auth, What is performance art?, Intersection Newsletter, 81. *Dealer:* Galerie Paule Anglim 710 Montgomery St San Francisco CA 94111. *Mailing Add:* 4333 Balboa St San Francisco CA 94121

SARDELIC, ANTE
SCULPTOR, PAINTER
b Blato, Korcula, Yugoslavia, Feb 3, 47; Can citizen. *Study:* Acad Fine Arts, Univ, Zagreb, Yugoslavia, with Krista Hegedosic & V Micheli, 71. *Work:* Osijek Art Mus, Yugoslavia; Split Art Mus, Yugoslavia. *Comn:* Mosaic murals, Hotel Lipa, Blato, Yugoslavia, 69 & Restaurant Blato, Zagreb, Yugoslavia, 70; wall relief, Hotel Alfir, Brna, Yugoslavia, 72; mosaic mural, comn by Mr M Sajeta, Blato, Yugoslavia, 77. *Exhib:* Int Friendship Exhib, Gallery Mitsubishi, Tokyo, Japan, 78-81; Int Biennial Miniature Prints, Space Art Gallery, Seoul, Korea, 80 & 82; solo exhibs, Galeria Meindl, Bogota, Colombia, 81 & Gallery Gilman, Chicago, 83; Gallery Melki, Paris, 82. *Awards:* First Prize for Sculpture, Fifth Ann Multi-cultural Art Exhib, O'Keefe Ctr, Toronto, 77; Bronze Medal for Painting, First Int Art Biennial, Acad Mondiale d'Info & Doc Artistiques, Lyon, France, 79. *Bibliog:* Toby Joysmith (auth), Gallery goer, The News, Mexico City, 78; Gerry Moses (auth), The art of Ante Sardelic (catalog), 80; F Gil Tovar (auth), Los Artistas de la Transicion, El Timepo, Bogota, Colombia, 81. *Mem:* Sculptor's Soc Can, Toronto; Print Club, Philadelphia; Print Coun Australia. *Media:* Stone, Wood, Acrylic, Oil. *Dealer:* Gallery Gilman 277 E Ontario St Chicago IL 60611. *Mailing Add:* 397 St Clements Ave Toronto ON M5N 1M2 Canada

SARET, ALAN DANIEL
SCULPTOR
b New York, NY, Dec 25, 44. *Study:* Cornell Univ, BArch, with Peter Kahn & Alan Atwell; Hunter Col, with Robert Morris. *Work:* Mus of Mod Art, Whitney Mus Am Art, New York; Detroit Inst of the Art; Art Gallery of Ont. *Exhib:* When Attitudes Become Form, Bern Kunsthalle, 69; Whitney Ann, 69 & Whitney Biannual, 77, Whitney Mus of Am Art, New York; Recent Acquisitions, Mus of Mod Art, New York, 75-76; Recent Developments in Sculpture, Whitney Mus Am Art, 81; Charles Cowles Gallery, New York, 81. *Pos:* Founder & dir, ALAEL, 74- *Teaching:* Vis artist sculpture, Univ Calif, Irvine, 78. *Awards:* Guggenheim Fel, 69. *Bibliog:* Emily Wasserman (auth), Alan Saret's studio exhib, 3/70 & Alan Saret: A synthesis, 5/70, Artforum; Jonathan Crary (auth), Alan Saret, Arts, 9/77. *Media:* Multimedia. *Publ:* Auth, The Ghosthouse, ALAEL, 76. *Dealer:* Charles Cowles Gallery 420 W Broadway New York NY 10013. *Mailing Add:* 54 Leonard St New York NY 10013

SARFF, WALTER
PAINTER, DESIGNER
b Pekin, Ill, Oct 29, 05. *Study:* Sch Mod Photog, New York, grad, 49; Sch Portrait & Commercial Photog, New York; also with Alexey Brodovitch & Adolph Fassbender; Nat Acad Art, Chicago, grad(traveling scholar); Grand Cent Sch Art, New York; Art Students League; Woodstock Sch Painting, NY; also with Hubert Ropp, Chicago & Yasuo Kuniyoshi, New York. *Work:* Collections of George Hillenbrand, M Owen Page & Anna Carolan. *Exhib:* Springfield Art Mus, Mass; Worcester Art Mus, Mass; Denver Art Mus, Colo; San Francisco Art Mus; Seattle Art Mus; and many others. *Pos:* Dir, Sawkill Gallery, Woodstock; chmn exec bd, Woodstock Artists Asn, 39; exec secy, Ulster Co Artists Union; pres, Sarff-Zumpano, Inc & Quilts by the Squares, Inc, currently. *Teaching:* Instr & asst registr, Nat Acad Art, Chicago, 29-31; pvt instr, 31-42. *Mem:* Am Soc Mag Photogr; Artists Equity Asn; Art Students League; hon mem Hypo Club; and others. *Publ:* Contribr, Am Ann Photog, cover, Am Photog, Art Photog, Cath Digest & Charm; and others. *Mailing Add:* 78 Morningside Ave Yonkers NY 10703

SARGENT, J MCNEIL See Braley, Jean

SARGENT, MARGARET HOLLAND
PAINTER
b Hollywood, Calif, 27. *Study:* Univ Calif, Los Angeles, 45-47; Tokyo, Japan, 56; with, Herbert Abrams, NY, 59-61 & Marcos Blahove, Fairfax, Va, 69; Art Students League, with John Sanden, 74. *Comn:* Portrait, President Gerald Ford, Time, Inc; portrait, Secretary of State Alexander M Haig; portrait, playwright Tennessee Williams; portrait, Jules S Stein; portrait, Prince Turki Saud; and others. *Exhib:* One-man shows, Turkish Am Asn, Ankara, 63, Frye Art Mus, 71, Woodside Gallery, Seattle, 72 & Excelsior Club, NY, 74-75; plus many others. *Pos:* Owner-dir, Portraits Int, Los Angeles, currently. *Awards:* Painter & Painting of Year, Most Popular Painting, Painters Club, NY; II M Salmagundi Award; Nacal Award Outstanding Achievement in Oil Painting, 77; First Prize Prof Oils, AFL-CIO's 10th Ann, Los Angeles, 79; and others. *Bibliog:* About Women, Los Angeles Times, 12/14/80; Three from Hollywood, SW Art, 9/82; Margaret Holland Sargent, Am Artist, 4/83. *Mem:* Salmagundi Club; Am Portrait Soc. *Mailing Add:* 2750 Glendower Ave Los Angeles CA 90027

SARGENT, RICHARD
PAINTER, PHOTOGRAPHER
b St Louis, Mo, 1932. *Study:* Univ Southern Calif, BFA & MFA. *Comn:* Mural, Audio Workshop, New York, 58; painting on environmental electricity, Int Sci & Technol Mag, 63. *Exhib:* One-man shows, Nonagon Gallery, New York, 61 & Heads, Berkeley Art Ctr, 68; Drawing & Small Sculpture, Ball State Teachers Col, 57, 58 & 62; West Coast Graphic Design, Am Inst Graphic Arts, 74; Santa Rosa Jr Col, 80. *Collections Arranged:* David Anderson Sculpture, 72; Karen Breschi, Larry Fuente Sculpture, 73; Berkeley City Limits, 73; Water Works, 75; John Battenberg, Sculpture: Flesh Sex Death Hate Skin Love, 75; Fiber Space, 75; Joseph Rees, Neon-Argon, 75; Barbara Spring, Wood Sculpture. *Pos:* Cur, Long Beach Mus Art, 64-65; cur, Berkeley Art Ctr, 69-78. *Media:* Acrylic, Indian Ink. *Publ:* Illusr, New York Times, 59, Western J Surgery, Obstet & Gyn, 59, Africa Today, 61 & 62; illusr, Poems Read in the Spirit of Peace & Gladness, 66; illusr, San Francisco Earthquake, 68. *Mailing Add:* 2316 McGee Ave Berkeley CA 94703

SARKISIAN, PAUL
PAINTER
b Chicago, Ill, Aug 18, 28. *Study:* Art Inst Chicago; Otis Art Inst, Los Angeles; Mexico City Col. *Work:* Metrop Mus Art, New York; Philadelphia Mus Arte; Santa Barbara Mus, Calif; Chicago Art Inst; Hirshhorn Mus, Washington, DC. *Exhib:* One-man exhib, Corcoran Gallery Art, 69, Santa Barbara Mus, 70 & Mus Contemp Art, Chicago, 72; Documenta, Ger, 72; San Francisco Mus, Calif, 76; Kunsthaus Zurich, 77; Nat Mus Fine Arts, Washington, DC, 79. *Teaching:* Vis prof painting, Univ Calif, Los Angeles, 70, Univ Ore, Eugene, 71 & Univ S Fla, Tampa, 72. *Media:* Air Brush. *Mailing Add:* c/o Nancy Hoffman Gallery 429 W Broadway New York NY 10012

SARNOFF, ARTHUR SARON
PAINTER
b Brooklyn, NY, Dec 30, 12. *Study:* Indust Sch Art; Grand Cent Sch Art; also with Harvey Dunne. *Work:* Bass Mus; Springfield Mus; Parrish Mus; Hartford Mus; Nat Art Mus Sport, New York. *Comn:* Fine art prints, Arthur Kaplan Co, Donald Art Co & Cataldi Fine Prints; portraits Pres Kennedy, Bob Hope and others. *Exhib:* Int Art Galleries; Continental Art Galleries; Sports in Action, Grand Cent Art Galleries; Nat Acad Art; Allied Art Show; plus others. *Teaching:* Instr Boca Raton Mus Art, currently. *Awards:* Outdoor advert award, Art Dirs Club; Art League Nassau Award. *Mem:* Soc Illusrs; Allied Artists Am. *Media:* Oil, Acrylic. *Mailing Add:* 6462 Woodbury Rd Boca Raton FL 33433

SARNOFF, LOLO
SCULPTOR, COLLECTOR
b Frankfurt am Main, Ger, Jan 9, 16; US citizen. *Study:* Reimann Art Sch, Berlin, Ger, grad, 36. *Work:* Nat Acad Sci, Washington, DC; Nat Air & Space Mus, Washington, DC; Kennedy Ctr, Washington, DC; Corning Glass Ctr, Corning, NY; Federal Nat Mortgage Asn, Washington, DC. *Comn:* Flame, Kennedy Ctr, 71; spiral galaxy, Nat Air & Space Mus, DC, 78. *Exhib:* One-person shows, Agra Gallery, Washington, DC, 68, Corning Mus Glass, NY, 76 & Franz Bader Gallery, Washington, DC, 76; Franz Bader Gallery, 76; Gallery von Bartha, Basel, 78 & 82; Salisbury State Col, Md, 79; Gallery K, Washington, DC, 82; and others. *Awards:* Gold Medal, Accademia Italia

Arti Lavoro. *Mem:* Nat League Am Pen Women; Artists Equity Asn; Women's Art Ctr, Washington, DC. *Media:* Acrylic, Fiberoptics. *Collection:* Nineteenth and twentieth century drawings, paintings and sculptures; 18th century Fayence; Chinese porcelain and snuff bottles. *Dealer:* Gallery K 2032 P St NW Washington DC 20036; Gallery von Bartha Schertlingasse 16 CH-4051 Basel Switzerland. *Mailing Add:* 7507 Hampden Lane Bethesda MD 20814

SARSONY, ROBERT
PAINTER, PRINTMAKER
b Easton, Pa, Jan 1, 38. *Work:* Butler Inst Am Art, Youngstown, Ohio; NJ State Mus, Trenton; Joslyn Art Mus, Omaha, Nebr; Sara Roby Found, New York; Univ Kans Mus Art, Lawrence; and others. *Exhib:* Allied Artist Show, New York, 63-65; one-man shows, Capricorn Galleries, Bethesda, Md, 67-78; Christopher Gallery, New York, 78-80; Meinhard Galleries, Houston, Tex, 82-83; and others. *Bibliog:* John S Le Maire (auth), Robert Sarsony, NJ Bus Mag, 69; Philip Desind (auth), article, Southwest Art, 4/80. *Media:* Oil, Watercolor; Serigraph, Lithography. *Dealer:* Meinhard Galleries 1502 Augusta Houston TX. *Mailing Add:* 60 Gristmill Rd Randolph NJ 07869

SARVIS, ALVA TAYLOR
PRINTMAKER
b Nanking, China, Nov 27, 24; US citizen. *Study:* Univ Calif, Berkeley; Calif Col Arts & Crafts, BFA; Univ NMex, MA. *Work:* US Info Agency, Beirut, New Delhi; Wachovia Bank Collection, Asheville, NC; Lewis Col, Lockport, Ill; US Steel/Ryan Homes, Pittsburgh; Huntsville Mus Art, Ala. *Exhib:* 156th Pa Acad Ann Exhib, 61; 5th Okla Printmakers Nat, 63; 5th Ann Mercyhurst Nat, 65; 162nd Pa Acad Ann, 67; 1st NH Int Graphics Ann, 74. *Teaching:* Instr gen studio, Univ NDak, 60-63; asst prof gen studio, San Diego State Col, 63-65; prof printmaking, Va Polytech Inst, 70- *Awards:* Huntington Hartford Found Fel in Residence, Los Angeles, 65; Alice McFadden Eyre Medal, 162nd Pa Acad Ann Exhib, 67; Third Prize, 4th Gtr New Orleans Nat, 74. *Mem:* SE Col Art Conf. *Media:* Etching, Intaglio. *Publ:* Coauth, Gesso Block for printmaking, Sch Arts, 12/69; coauth, Computer modulated drawing, SE Col Art Conf, 74; Prints of William Blake, SE Graphics Coun, 75; auth, Lithography on your etching press, Sch Arts, 75. *Mailing Add:* 110 Orchard View Lane Blacksburg VA 24060

SASAKI, TOMIYO
PAINTER, VIDEO ARTIST
b Vernon, BC, Can, Dec 21, 43. *Study:* Alta Col of Art, Calgary; San Francisco Art Inst, BFA, 67; Calif Col of Arts & Crafts, Oakland, MA, 69. *Work:* Nat Gallery of Art, Ottawa, Can; Can Coun, Ottawa; New York City Hospital; Synapse, Syracuse, NY; Donnell Libr Video Libr, New York. *Exhib:* Montreal Mus of Art, Can, 70; Ont Gallery of Art, Toronto, Can, 70; Nat Gallery of Art, Ottawa, Can, 72; Aldrich Mus of Art, Ridgefield, Conn, 74; Contemp Mus of Art, Chicago, 74; Painting Exhib, Mus of Mod Art, New York, 77; two-person show, Bard Col of Art Gallery, Hudson on Avon, NY, 76; one-man shows, 55 Mercer Gallery, New York, 74 & Rutgers Univ Art Gallery, NJ, 76. *Teaching:* Artist-in-residence video, Media Studies, Buffalo, NY, 76. *Awards:* Sr Arts Grant (sculpture & filmmaking), Can Coun, 74; Video Grants Creative Artists Pub Serv, New York, 76 & Can Coun, 76. *Bibliog:* Barry Lord (auth), Realism, Arts Can, 70; Ann Wooster Sargent (auth), Video, Soho News & Ithaca News, 77. *Mem:* Artists Equity. *Media:* Painting; Video. *Mailing Add:* 118 Forsyth St New York NY 10002

SASSONE, MARCO
PAINTER, PRINTMAKER
b Florence, Italy, July 27, 42. *Study:* Ist Galileo Galilei, Florence; Acad Fine Arts, with Silvio Loffredo, Florence. *Work:* Los Angeles Co Mus Art; Nat Art Gallery, Wellington, NZ; Galleria d'Arte Int, Florence; Hunt-Wesson (subsid Norton Simon, Inc); Newport Harbor Art Mus, Calif. *Comn:* California (poster/exhib), Galleria d'Arte Int, 73; Air California (mag cover), Urbanus Commun Corp, South Laguna, Calif, 74; Orange Co Illustrated (mag cover), Orange Co Illus, Newport Beach, Calif, 73-74; Only in Laguna (bk cover), Hardy House Publ, Newport Beach, 75; auction poster, KCET-TV, Los Angeles, 77 & 78. *Exhib:* Grand Nat Competition, Am Artist Prof League, New York, 73-75; Maxwell Galleries, Ltd, San Francisco, 74; one-man shows, Wally Findlay Galleries, Beverly Hills & New York, 77-79 & Laguna Beach Mus Art, 79; Nat Acad Design, New York, 77. *Pos:* Lectr-guest artist, Bowers Mus, Santa Ana, Calif, 70, Lakewood Artist Guild, Calif, 71, San Fernando Valley Art Club, Calif, 73, San Bernardino Mus Art, 78 & Laguna Beach Mus Art, 79. *Awards:* Spec Recognition in Commemorative Exhib of Great Flood of Florence, Lo Sprone Gallery, 67; First Prize, LaMirada Ann, Calif, 74; Gold Medal, Ital Acad Arts, Lit & Sci, 78. *Bibliog:* Phyllis Barton (auth), article, 10/73 & Donelson F Hoopes (auth), article, 79, Arti Grafiche Il Torchio, Florence, Italy; John Wilson (producer), I Am an Artist Sassone (film), Fine Arts Films Inc, 76. *Mem:* Am Artists Prof League, New York. *Media:* Oil, Serigraphs. *Publ:* Auth, William Wilson, Los Angeles Times, 11/14/75; auth, Sassone's Personal Renaissance, Southwest Art, Houston, Tex, 11/75; auth, article, New York Times, 7/2/78; auth, article, American Artist Mag, 5/79. *Dealer:* Wally Findlay Galleries New York Chicago Palm Beach Beverly Hills & Paris. *Mailing Add:* 1414 Mar Vista Way Laguna Beach CA 92651

SATO, MASAAKI
PAINTER
b Kofu, Japan, Feb 28, 41. *Study:* Kofu Saito Fine Arts Inst, Japan; Heatherley Sch Fine Arts, London, Eng; Brooklyn Mus Art Sch, NY; Pratt Inst. *Work:* Aldrich Mus Contemp Art, Ridgefield, Conn; Mus Honolulu Acad Art; Minn Mus Art, Minneapolis; ETenn State Univ; Mus Mod Art, La Tertulia, Cali,

Columbia; and others. *Exhib:* One-man shows, Brooklyn Mus Little Gallery, 73; Soho Ctr Visual Artists, New York, 76 & Edward Williams Col, NJ, 77; Yamanashi Prefectural Mus, Japan, 79; OK Harris West Gallery, Scottsdale, Ariz, 82; and many others. *Bibliog:* Richard Walker (auth), Gallery reviews, Art Rev, 8/31/68; Arthur Bloomfield (auth), An artist of many styles, San Francisco Examiner, 9/24/73; Malcolm Preston (auth), Westbeth connection, Newsday, 7/31/75. *Mem:* Contemp Artists Orgn; Am Soc Contemp Artists. *Media:* Acrylic, Oil. *Dealer:* Wenger Galleries 5721 La Jolla Blvd La Jolla CA 92037; OK Harris 383 W Broadway New York NY 10012. *Mailing Add:* Studio A-931 463 West St New York NY 10014

SATO, NORIE
VIDEO ARTIST
b Sendai, Japan, July 19, 49. *Study:* Univ Mich, BFA, 71; Univ Wash, MFA, 74. *Work:* Brooklyn Mus; Philadelphia Mus Art; Seattle Art Mus; Oxford Galleries, Oxford, Eng; Guggenheim Mus. *Exhib:* Thirty Yrs Am Printmaking, 76 & Eight West Coast Printmakers, Brooklyn Mus, 78; 5th Int Brit Print Biennale, Bradford, Eng, 76; Northwest '77, Seattle Art Mus, 77; Seattle Video, Pub Sch No 1, Queens & Media/Study, Buffalo, NY, 78; Proj Video XXIV, Mus Mod Art, New York, 79; Lande, Ritchie & Sato, Vancouver Art Gallery, BC, 79; Videoviewpoints, Mus Mod Art, New York, 80; Reflections & Shadows, AAA Gallery, Philadelphia, 80; 19 Artists-Emergent Americans, Guggenheim Mus, 81; solo show, Linda Farris Gallery, 81. *Awards:* Nat Endowment Arts Fel, 78 & 81. *Media:* Electronic, Mixed media. *Dealer:* Linda Farris Gallery 322 Second Ave S Seattle WA 98104. *Mailing Add:* 83 Columbia 4th Floor Seattle WA 98104

SATO, TADASHI
PAINTER, SCULPTOR
b Maui, Hawaii, Feb 6, 23. *Study:* Honolulu Sch Art; Brooklyn Mus Art Sch; New Sch Social Res, New York; also with Ralston Crawford, Stuart Davis, John Ferren & Wilson Stamper. *Work:* Albright-Knox Art Gallery, Buffalo, NY; Guggenheim Mus & Whitney Mus Am Art, New York; Honolulu Acad Arts, Hawaii; Univ Art Gallery, Tucson, Ariz. *Comn:* concrete relief wall & oil mural, State Libr, Kahului, Maui, 63; mosaic floor design, Hawaii State Capitol Bldg, Honolulu, 69; mosaic mural, West Maui Mem Gym, Maui, 72; ceramic floor mural, Tsunami Mem, Hilo; oil mural, Kapalua Bay Club, Maui, 80; and others. *Exhib:* 52 Young Painters of America, Guggenheim Mus, 54; Pacific Heritage Exhibit, Los Angeles, Calif, 63; Four Contemporary Painters, McRoberts & Tunnard Ltd, London, 64; White House Festival of Arts, White House, Washington, DC, 65; American Paintings in Berlin Art Festival, Ger, 67; one-man shows, Seattle, Wash, New York & Honolulu. *Awards:* John Hay Whitney Found Opportunity Fel, 53; McInerny Found Honolulu Community Fel, 55; Best Painting in Show, Honolulu Acad Arts, 57. *Mem:* Hawaii Painters & Sculptors League. *Media:* Oil. *Mailing Add:* PO Box 476 Lahaina HI 96761

SATORSKY, CYRIL
PRINTMAKER, ILLUSTRATOR
b London, Eng. *Study:* Leeds Col Art, nat dipl design; Royal Col Art, Royal scholar, traveling scholar, res scholar, ARCA & first class hon degree. *Work:* Cincinnati Art Mus; Wooster Col; Essex Community Col. *Exhib:* Philadelphia Print Club Ann; Rental Gallery, Baltimore Mus, 70; Sixth Dulin Nat Print Show, Knoxville, Tenn, 70; one-man show, Gallery Four, Alexandria, Va, 74 & Grimaldo Gallery, Baltimore, 78. *Pos:* Adv to univ publ, Univ Tex, Austin, 62-65. *Teaching:* Prof illus & printmaking, Md Inst Col Art, 65- *Publ:* Auth & illusr, A pride of Rabbis, Aquarius, 70; illusr, Frenchman & the Seven Deadly Sins, Scribners, 71; illusr, Sir Gawain & the Green Knight, Limited Ed Club, 72; illusr, Country J. *Dealer:* Gallery K 2032 P St NW Washington DC 20036. *Mailing Add:* 5707 Berkeley Ave Baltimore MD 21215

SATTERFIELD, JOHN EDWARD
GOLDSMITH, EDUCATOR
b Clearwater, Fla, Sept 14, 31. *Study:* Univ Fla, BDesign; Univ Kans, MFA; study with Hekki Seppa, Earl Krentzin, Fred Feuster & Eleanor Moty. *Work:* Renwick Gallery; Mint Mus, Charlotte, NC; Gilchrist Mills, NC; East Carolina Univ, NC; and others. *Exhib:* Southeastern Crafts Invitational, Greenville Co Art Mus, SC, 75; Goldsmith 1974, Renwick Gallery, Washington, DC, 74; Nine NC Jewelers, Western Carolina Univ, 77; Southeastern Ctr for Contemp Art, 78, 79 & 81; Southern Fedn Art traveling exhib, 79-82; and many others. *Pos:* Art dir, Advertising Design Studio, Clearwater, Fla, 57-63; Peace Corps Vol arts & crafts develop, Peru, SAm, 63-65. *Teaching:* Prof design & metal, ECarolina Univ, 67-, assoc prof art, Univ Abroad Prog, Univ Nac Heredia, Costa Rica, CentAm, 75- *Awards:* Mus Purchase, Mint Mus Art, 78; Kans Designer Craftsmen Exhib Award, Wichita, 83; NC Mus Hist Award, 83. *Bibliog:* American Craftsmen, John Satterfield (film), Cinemasonics Inc, 74; article, Goldsmith J, Vol 3, 12/77. *Mem:* Am Crafts Coun; Soc NAm Goldsmiths; Piedmont Craftsmen; Southeastern Ctr Contemp Art; and others. *Media:* Precious Metal. *Mailing Add:* Rte 1 Box 34 Greenville NC 27834

SATURNESKY, RUTH See Colorado, Charlotte

SATZ, JANET MAAS
PAINTER, ADMINISTRATOR
b Chicago, Ill, Apr 20, 33. *Study:* Pratt Inst, BFA, 74; New York Univ, MA, 77, PhD(art ed), 77. *Work:* Smithsonian Inst; Gen Electric Corp & Fairfield Univ, Fairfield, Conn; Housatonic Col Mus Art, Bridgeport, Conn; Town of Westport, Conn. *Comn:* Wall mural, comn by Town of Norwalk, Conn, 78. *Exhib:* Hudson Mus Ann, Yonkers, NY, 72; Drawings & Prints, Marion Koogler McHay Mus, Dallas, Tex, 76; New York Univ Presents, Int Delle

Arti Palazzo Grassi, Venice, Italy, 76; Genesis Gallery, New York, 77; Contemporary Reflections, Aldrich Mus, Ridgefield, Conn, 77; Women's Art 78, Graduate Ctr, City Univ New York, 78; Connecticut Today, Stamford Mus, Conn, 79; solo exhib, Silvermine Guild Ctr Arts, Conn, 80. *Pos:* Asst mgr, Fairfield Co Branch, Whitney Mus Am Art, 81- *Teaching:* Instr art, Parent-Child Workshop, Metrop Mus Art, New York, 76-77. *Awards:* Purchase Award, New Horizons, Chicago, Ill, 59; Winsor-Newton, Hudson River Ann, Yonkers, NY, 72. *Bibliog:* William Caxton, Jr (auth), The art of Janet Maas Satz, Am Artist, 5/64; J Burnham (auth), monograph, Arts Mag, 2/73; Jacqueline Moss (auth), Stamford Museum celebrates, The Advocate, 4/13/82. *Mem:* Westport/Weston Arts Coun, Conn; Silvermine Ctr Arts; Col Art Asn, New York; Artist Equity, New York. *Media:* Mixed. *Mailing Add:* 24 Broadview Rd Westport CT 06880

SAUL, PETER
PAINTER
b San Francisco, Calif, Aug 16, 34. *Study:* Stanford Univ; Calif Sch Fine Arts, 50-52; Wash Univ, with Fred Conway, BFA, 56. *Work:* Art Inst Chicago; Whitney Mus Am Art, New York; Mus Mod Art, New York; Univ Mass. *Exhib:* Mus Mod Art, New York, 68; Univ Ill, 69; Whitney Mus Am Art, 69 & 78; Corcoran Gallery Art, Washington, DC, 71; Art Inst Chicago, 72; Lerner-Heller Gallery, New York, 73; Krannert Art Mus, Univ Ill, Urbana, 74; Painting & Sculpture Today, Indianapolis Mus Art, Ind & Taft Mus, Ohio, 74. *Awards:* New Talent Award, Art in Am Mag, 62; William & Norma Copley Found Grant, 62; Nat Endowment Arts Grant, 80. *Dealer:* Allan Frumkin Gallery 620 N Michigan Ave Chicago IL 60611. *Mailing Add:* 383 Lovell St Mill Valley CA 94941

SAULS, FREDERICK INABINETTE
SCULPTOR, PAINTER
b Seattle, Wash, Mar 22, 34. *Study:* Stanford Univ, BA; Calif Col Arts & Crafts, MFA Prog; Univ Calif, MA. *Work:* Mus Mod Art, Skopje, Yugoslavia; Ithaca Mus Art, Cornell Univ, NY; Univ Calif Mus; Picker Art Gallery, Colgate Univ, Hamilton, NY; Univ Minn Mus Art. *Exhib:* San Francisco Mus Mod Art Ann, Calif, 60-63; Paris Biennale, Paris Mus Mod Art, 64; Sauls Sculpture, Univ Ky Mus, 66; Sauls Graphics, Univ Minn Mus, 67; UNESCO Int traveling exhib mod art, 68. *Teaching:* Assoc sculpture, Univ Calif, Berkeley, 63-64; vis artist sculpture, Univ Ky, 65-67; asst prof sculpture, Univ Minn, 68. *Awards:* Grand Prize, Am Sculptors, Paris Mus Mod Art, France, 63; Harry Lord Ford Grad Prize, Univ Calif, 65. *Media:* Bronze, Aluminum. *Mailing Add:* 1110 N Hudson Ave Hollywood CA 90038

SAUNDERS, AULUS WARD
PAINTER, EDUCATOR
b Perry, Mo, Sept 22, 04. *Study:* Westminster Col, Mo, BA; St Louis Sch Fine Arts; Washington Univ, MA; Univ Iowa, PhD; also with Charles Cagle. *Work:* State Univ NY Col Oswego; Mo Hist Soc; plus pvt collections. *Exhib:* Midwestern Ann Art Exhib, Kansas City Art Inst, 35; 30th & 31st Ann Exhib Paintings Am Artists, St Louis City Art Mus, 36 & 37; 18th Ann Exhib Artists Cent NY, Munson-Williams-Proctor Inst, Utica, NY, 55; one-man shows, Denison Univ, 51 & State Univ NY A&T Col, Morrisville, 67; Oswego Art Competition, 79 & 80. *Teaching:* Prof art, State Univ NY Col Oswego, 37-70, chmn dept, 37-68, prof emer, 74-; vis prof, Southern Ill Univ, Carbondale, summer 49; vis prof, Pa State Univ, University Park, summers 50-52. *Media:* Watercolor, Acrylic/Oil. *Res:* Psychology of art, especially genesis and stability of art talent in children. *Publ:* Auth, The stability of artistic aptitude, Psychol Monogr, 36; auth, Feeling and form, Sch Arts, 10/70. *Mailing Add:* 165 E Third St Oswego NY 13126

SAUNDERS, EDITH DARIEL CHASE
PAINTER, INSTRUCTOR
b Waterville, Maine, Mar 19, 22. *Study:* Univ NC, Greensboro, with Robert Partin, Boris Margo, Gilbert Carpenter & Madam Sun To-Ze Hsu; John Brady Sch Art, Blowing Rock, NC; studied with Maria D'Annuzio & Leroy Neiman. *Work:* Wachovia Bank; Reynolds Tobacco; Southport Libr, NC; Hunt Mfg Co Collection; Westminster Presbyterian Church, Knoxville, Tenn. *Comn:* Portraits, 55-78. *Exhib:* Island Gallery, Manteo, NC; Contemp Graphic Artists (traveling exhib); Weatherspoon Art Gallery, Greensboro; Regional Gallery, Boone, NC; Assoc Artists of NC; Mint Mus Art, Charlotte, NC; and others. *Collections Arranged:* Arts Coun Gallery, Winston-Salem, 57, 62, 64, 65, 77 & 81; Southeastern Art Festival, Winston-Salem; Arts & Sci Mus, Statesville, NC; Herman Art Gallery, Statesville, NC; Contemporary Graphic Artists (nat traveling exhib); Regional Gallery, Boone, NC; Hickory Mus of Art, NC; Greenville Art Gallery, NC; Caldwell Arts Coun, Lenoir, NC. *Pos:* Art chmn-coordr, Winston-Salem Women's Club, 60-61; columnist, Edy and Art (weekly), The Suburbanite, 74-76 & 77-78; owner, operator & instr, Art Loft, Winston-Salem, currently. *Teaching:* Instr oriental painting, Guilford Tech Inst, Jamestown, NC, 73. *Awards:* Purchase Prizes, Northwest Art Exhib, Lowe's Collection, Lowe's Co, 62 & Southport Art Festival, City of Southport, NC, 63; Hunt Mfg Purchase Award, Watercolor Soc of NC, 75. *Mem:* Assoc Artists Winston-Salem; Watercolor Soc NC. *Media:* Acrylic, Watercolor. *Dealer:* Erl Originals Winston-Salem NC; Art Leasing Int 3300 Northern Blvd Long Island City NY. *Mailing Add:* 2250 Hilltop Dr Winston-Salem NC 27106

SAUNDERS, J BOYD
PRINTMAKER, EDUCATOR
b Memphis, Tenn, June 12, 37. *Study:* Memphis State Univ, BS; Univ Miss, MFA; Bottega Arte Grafica, Florence, Italy. *Work:* Denison Univ; SC State Collection, Mus Art, Columbia; Bottega Arte Grafica; Univ Ariz. *Comn:* Mixed media altar panel, Guess Chapel, Univ Church, Oxford, Miss, 62; mem portrait comn, Tipoff Club, Columbia, SC, 69; oil mural, Univ House, Univ SC, 72. *Exhib:* Soc Washington Printmakers 24th Nat, Smithsonian Inst, 62; First Int Printmaker's Exhib, Gallerie Bottega & Arte Grafica, Florence, 67; 34th Graphic Arts & Drawing Nat, Wichita, Kans, 69; Fifth Dulin Print & Drawing Competition Nat, Knoxville, Tenn, 70; 15th NDak Print & Drawing Ann, Grand Forks, 72. *Pos:* Staff artist, Dan Kilgo & Assocs, Tuscaloosa, Ala, 59-60; designer & illusr, Chaparral Press, Kyle, Tex, 63-65. *Teaching:* Instr art, Univ Miss, 61-62; instr art, Southwest Tex State Col, 62-65; assoc prof art, Univ SC, 65- *Awards:* Third Prize, Sixth Ann Mid-South Exhib Paintings, Prints & Drawings, Memphis, Tenn, 61; Grand Prize, Guild Columbia Artists, 71; Purchase Prize, 15th NDak Ann Print & Drawing Competition, 72. *Bibliog:* Jack Morris (auth), Boyd Saunders, printmaker, Contemp Artists SC, 69; Harriet Door (auth), Two forceful exhibitions, Charlotte Observer, NC, 72; Adger Brown (auth), Boyd Saunders--vital forces, State-Rec, Columbia, 72. *Mem:* Print Coun Am; Guild SC Artists; Columbia Art Asn; Southeastern Graphics Soc; Am Asn Univ Prof. *Publ:* Illusr, Bosque Territory: A History of an Agrarian Community, 64; illusr, Lyndon Baines Johnson: The Formative Years, 65; auth, A summer's printmaking in Florence, Art Educ J, 68. *Dealer:* Hubris Press Columbia SC 29210. *Mailing Add:* Dept of Art Univ of SC Columbia SC 29208

SAUNDERS, RAYMOND JENNINGS
PAINTER
b Pittsburgh, Pa, Oct 28, 34. *Study:* Pa Acad Fine Arts, nat scholastic scholar, 53-57; Univ Pa, nat scholastic scholar, 54-57; Carnegie Inst Technol, BFA, 60; Calif Col Arts & Crafts, MFA, 61. *Work:* Mus Mod Art, New York; Whitney Mus Am Art, Andover Collection Am Art; Pa Acad Fine Arts; Nat Inst Arts & Lett. *Exhib:* One-man show, San Francisco Mus Mod Art, 71; Mus Mod Art, New York, 74; Stedelijk Mus, Amsterdam, 77; Oakland Mus, 79; Mandeville Art Gallery, Univ Calif, La Jolla, 79; Univ Calif, San Diego, 79; Seattle Art Mus, 81; Calif Inst Technol, Pasadena, 82; Ariz State Univ, 82; Stephen Wirtz Gallery, San Francisco, 82; and others. *Pos:* Nat consult urban affairs, Vol Teaching Serv, New York, 68; art consult, Dept Black Studies, Univ Calif, Berkeley, 69. *Teaching:* Prof painting, Calif State Univ, Hayward, 68-; vis critic, RI Sch Design, 68, vis artist, Yale Univ, 72. *Awards:* Nat Inst Arts & Lett Award, 63; Guggenheim Award, 76; Nat Endowment Arts Award, 77. *Bibliog:* Bearden & McNolty (auth), The Painter's Mind, Crown, 69. *Mem:* Fel Am Acad Rome. *Publ:* Auth, Black is a color, pvt publ, 68. *Dealer:* Terry Dintenfass Inc 50 W 57th St New York NY 10019; Stephen Wirtz Gallery 228 Grant Ave San Francisco CA 94108. *Mailing Add:* 6007 Rock Ridge Blvd Oakland CA 94618

SAUNDERS, WADE
SCULPTOR, CRITIC
b Berkeley, Calif, Sept 13, 49. *Study:* Wesleyan Univ, Conn, BA, 71; Univ Calif, San Diego, MFA, 74. *Work:* Philadelphia Mus Art; Baltimore Mus Art; Milwaukee Mus Art; Newport Harbor Art Mus, Newport Beach, Calif; Addison Gallery Am Art. *Exhib:* One-person shows, Newspace Gallery, Los Angeles, 77, 79, 81 & 83; Diane Brown Gallery, Washington, DC, 80 & 82, Charles Cowles Gallery, New York, 81 & 82 & Lawrence Oliver Gallery, Philadelphia, 84; Dwellings, Inst Contemp Art, Philadelphia, 78; Sculpture in California 1975-80, San Diego Mus Art, 80; Connections, Inst Contemp Art, Philadelphia, 83. *Teaching:* Asst prof sculpture, Tyler Sch Art, 78-82 & Pa State Univ, University Park, 82- *Awards:* Artist's Fel, Pa Coun Arts, 83. *Bibliog:* Carrie Rickey (auth), article, Arts Mag, 11/77; David Tannous (auth), article, Art in Am, 10/80; Reagan Upshaw (auth), article, Art in Am, 6/82. *Publ:* Auth, Art inc, 79, Hot metal, 80, Touch and eye: '50's sculpture, 82, Tom Butter, 83 & Risk & balance: Mark di Suvero, 83, Art in Am. *Dealer:* Diane Brown Gallery 100 Greene St New York NY 10012. *Mailing Add:* 930 Stratford Ave Melrose Park PA 19126

SAVAGE, NAOMI
PHOTOGRAPHER
b NJ, June 25, 27. *Study:* Bennington Col; and with Man Ray. *Work:* Mus Mod Art, New York; Fogg Mus, Boston; NJ State Mus; Univs of Kans, Ill & Princeton. *Comn:* 8 x 50 ft wall of photo engravings, LBJ Presidential Libr, Austin, Tex, 72; 60 tennis photographs, Youth Tennis Found, Princeton, NJ, 73-74. *Exhib:* Always the Young Stranger, Mus Mod Art, New York, 53; Photography as Printmaking, Mus Mod Art, 68; Two Generations of Photographs-Man Ray & Naomi Savage, NJ State Mus, 68; Light & Lens-Methods of Photography, Hudson River Mus, Yonkers, NY, 73; Women of Photography, San Francisco Mus Art, 75. *Awards:* Photography, Cassandra Found, 70; Nat Endowment Arts Grant, 71. *Bibliog:* Peggy Lewis (auth), Two Generations of Photographs-Man Ray & Naomi Savage, NJ State Mus, 68; Julia Scully (auth), Everchanging faces of Naomi Savage, Mod Photography, 1/70. *Dealer:* Witkin Gallery 41 E 57th St New York NY 10022. *Mailing Add:* 41 Drakes Corner Rd Princeton NJ 08540

SAVAGE, ROGER
PAINTER, PRINTMAKER
b Windsor, Ont, Sept 25, 41. *Study:* Mt Allison Univ, Sackville, NB, Can, BFA, 63; study with Alex Colville, Lawren Harris, Jr & E B Pulford. *Work:* Confederation Ctr Art Gallery & Mus, PEI; City of Wolfsburg Collection, WGer; Can Coun Art Bank, Ottawa, Ont; Glenbow Mus, Calgary; Gotlands Kommun, Visby, Sweden; and others. *Comn:* Can $100 Gold Commemerative Coins, Royal Can Mint, Ottawa, 78 & 81; watercolors, Bowater Mersey Paper Co, 81. *Exhib:* 3rd Int Grafik Biennale, Frechen, WGer, 74; Int of Drawings, Christchurch, NZ, 78; Art Gallery of NS, Halifax, 79; FGK Galleri, Visby, Sweden, 81; Aschaffenburg, WGer, 81; and others. *Pos:* Can Coun vis artist, Art Gallery, Corner Brook, NF, 77, Summerside, PEI, 78 & Univ Moncton, 79. *Teaching:* Instr, Holland Col Summer Art Prog,

PEI, 81 & other workshops. *Awards:* Can Coun Grants, 70 & 80; Scholarship, Brucebo Found, 80; Award, Province NS, 80. *Bibliog:* Don Curley (auth), Silk & Color (film), Univ Air, TV Series, 75; Elizabeth Jones (auth), Roger Savage: An intractable essence, Artsatlantic, 3/81; and others. *Mem:* Can Artists Representation; Visual Arts NS. *Media:* Watercolor; Serigraphy. *Dealer:* Swordstreet Gallery 10 Swordstreet Toronto ON M5A 3N2 Can. *Mailing Add:* RR 1 Liverpool NS B0T 1K0 Canada

SAVAS, JO-ANN
PAINTER, INSTRUCTOR
b Opelika, Ala, Jan 30, 34. *Study:* Auburn Univ, BS(art educ; Alpha Delta Pi Scholar). *Exhib:* New York World's Fair; Chateau de la Napole, Cannes, France; Southern Contemporaries Collection of Sears-Roebuck; Int Women's Show; Nat Women's Watercolor Exhib; and others. *Pos:* Tech illusr, Army Ballistic Missile Agency, Redstone Arsenal, Ala, 57-58; brochure designer, Huntsville Symphony Orchestra, 72-; dir art dept, Madison Acad, Huntsville, Ala, 74-77; chmn dept art, Stone Middle Sch. *Teaching:* Pvt art instr, Huntsville. *Mem:* Huntsville Art League & Mus Asn; Huntsville Art Educ Asn; Nat Asn Women Artists. *Media:* Multimedia. *Mailing Add:* 3506 Mae Dr SE Huntsville AL 35801

SAVELLI, ANGELO
PAINTER, SCULPTOR
b Pizzo Calabria, Italy, Oct 30, 11. *Study:* Liceo Artistico, Rome, Italy; Acad di Belle Arti, Rome. *Work:* Mus Mod Art, New York; High Mus Art; Philadelphia Mus Art; Nat Collection Fine Arts, Smithsonian Inst, Washington, DC; Corcoran Gallery Art. *Comn:* Fresco painting Boimond Chapel, comn by Mr Boimond, Sora, Italy, 35; outdoor work, comn by Mayor Alexander, Lincoln Sq, Syracuse, NY, 72. *Exhib:* Corcoran Art Gallery, Washington, DC, 59; Everson Mus, Syracuse, NY, 72; Tweed Mus Art, Duluth, Minn, 73; Hutchinson Gallery, New York, 78; Parsons-Dreyfuss Gallery, New York, 78; Lorenzelli Arte, Milan, Italy, 81; Gimpel-Hanover & Andre Emmerich Gallery, Zurich, Switzerland, 81; and others. *Teaching:* Asst prof drawing, Liceo Artistico, Rome, Italy, 40-43 & 48-54; asst prof painting, Univ Pa, 60-69; vis artist painting, Cornell Univ, 74; vis prof, Univ Tex, Arlington, 81-82. *Awards:* Fel Paris France, Minister Naz Educ, 48; Grand Prize per L'Incisione, XXXII Venice Biennale, 64; Guggenheim Fel, 79-80. *Mailing Add:* 22 Cornelia St New York NY 10014

SAVILLE, KEN
SCULPTOR, CRAFTSMAN
b Hanging Rock, WVa, Jan 9, 49. *Study:* Austin Peay State Univ, BS, 71. *Work:* Albuquerque Mus; Mus NMex, Santa Fe; Libr Cong. *Exhib:* Drawings USA, Minn Mus Art, 77; Artwords and Bookworks, Los Angeles Inst Contemp Art, 78; New Epiphanies, Gallery Contemp Art, Univ Colo, 82; Arteder, Muestra Int Arte Grafico, Bilboa, Spain, 82. *Awards:* Jurors Award, Southwest Fine Arts Biennial, 76; Award Merit, Craftworks V, 83. *Bibliog:* Susan Zwinger (auth), Walking the edge of precipitous sacrilege: Ken Saville, Craftrange, summer 83; Michael Reed (auth), article, Artspace, summer 83. *Dealer:* Gallery K 2032 P St NW Washington DC 20036. *Mailing Add:* Box 4662 Albuquerque NM 87196

SAVITT, SAM
PAINTER, ILLUSTRATOR
b Wilkes-Barre, Pa. *Study:* Pratt Inst; Art Students League; drawing with Paul Brown, painting with Howard Trafton & John Vickery & sculpture with Seymour Lipton. *Work:* St Lawrence Univ, Canton, NY; and pvt collections including William Randolph Hearst, Jr, Raymond Firestone, August Busch & Dr Jere Lord, Jr. *Comn:* Posters, Nat Horse Show, New York, 80 & Lipizzaner Stallions, 82. *Exhib:* Int Sports Core, Oak Brook, Ill, 75; West Returns, Grand Cent Gallery, New York, 78; one-man shows, Piccolo Mondo, Palm Beach, Fla, 74 & Gallery at Noroton, Darien, Conn, 81; Am Acad Equine Artists, Morven Park, Leesburg, Va, 81; Soc Animal Artists, Acad Natural Sci, Philadelphia, 81; and others. *Pos:* Official artist, US Equestrian Team, 60- *Teaching:* Guest lectr horses in art, 55- *Awards:* Jr Bk Award, Boys Clubs Am, 58. *Bibliog:* Anthony Amaral (auth), About cowboys and broncos, Ariz Hwy, 5/70; Nancy Boyce (auth), Sam Savitt speaks, Horse Play, 4/78; Annette Cummings (auth), Profile, Lead Line, 3/78. *Mem:* Soc Animal Artists; Soc Illusr; Graphic Artists Guild; Authors Guild; Am Acad Equine Art. *Media:* Mixed. *Publ:* Auth & illusr, Vicki and the Brown Mare, 76; Dingle Ridge Fox and Other Stories, 78 & One Horse, One Hundred Miles, One Day, 81, Dodd Mead Co; auth & illusr, Draw Horses with Sam Savitt, Viking Press, 81; auth, A Horse to Remember, Viking Press, 84. *Dealer:* Arthur Ackermann & Son Inc 50 E 57th St New York NY 10022. *Mailing Add:* PQ Box 302 North Salem NY 10560

SAVITZ, FRIEDA (FRIEDA SAVITZ LADEN)
PAINTER, INSTRUCTOR
b New York, NY, Dec 3, 31. *Study:* NY Univ, BS, MA; Cooper Union; Hans Hofmann Sch Scholar, New York & Provincetown, Mass; Accad Italia, hon dipl, 83. *Work:* Chrysler Mus; San Francisco Mus Mod Art; Sophia Smith Collection, Smith Col, Mass; Am Tel & Tel Co; World Print Coun, San Francisco. *Exhib:* Smithsonian Inst, Washington, DC, 56; Nat Gallery Art, Washington, DC, 56; Chrysler Mus, Provincetown, Mass, 58; Art USA, New York, 59-60; Brooklyn Mus, NY, 75 & 76; Ford Found Int Traveling Exhib, 75-76; Hudson River Mus, Yonkers, NY, 76; Int Women's Exhib, Copenhagen, Denmark, 76; World Print Exhib, San Francisco Mus Mod Art, 77; Multiples 80, New Orleans, La; one-person shows, Hudson River Mus, 73 & Ariz State Univ, Tempe, 78. *Teaching:* Art instr compos, painting & drawing, New York, 54-60, NJ, 73-81; instr, Newark Mus, NJ, 54-58; instr, Summit Ctr, 74-77. *Awards:* Ford Found Int Women's Award, 75; Nat

Endowment for Arts Grant, 79; Gold Medal, Accademia Italia Delle Arti-E-Del-Lauuno, Parma, Italia, 80. *Mem:* Artists Equity; World Print Coun; Int Artists Asn; Accademia Italia Delle Arti: VAGA I. *Media:* Oil, Pastel. *Dealer:* Carol Goldberg 1050 Fifth Ave New York NY 10028; Joan Nothen Meyer, Inc 5720 S Third St Arlington VA 22204. *Mailing Add:* 109 W Clarkstown Rd New City NY 10956

SAVOY, CHYRL LENORE
SCULPTOR, EDUCATOR
b New Orleans, La, May 23, 44. *Study:* La State Univ, BA(art); Acad Fine Arts, Florence, with Gallo & Berti; diploma di Profitto, Universita degli Studi di Firenze, Florence; Wayne State Univ, MFA(sculpture). *Work:* Our Lady Bayous Convent, Abbeville, La; Couvent St Dominique de la Gloire de Dieu, Maison Mere des Dominicaines, Flavigny, France; Our Lady Star of the Sea, Cameron, La; Cath Church, SAfrica; Herrod Jr High Sch Libr, Abbeville. *Comn:* St John the Baptist (sculpture design), Our Lady Star of the Sea, Cameron, La, 73; monumental sculpture, Rural Dominican Missionaries, Abbeville, La, 74. *Exhib:* 58th Exhib Mich Artists, Detroit Inst Arts Mus, 71; Biennial Exhib of Artists of Southwest & Tex, New Orleans Mus Art, 71; one-man show, New Orleans Mus Art, La, 72; 7th Ann Nat Drawing & Small Sculpture Show, Del Mar Col, Corpus Christi, Tex, 73; Am Painters in Paris, Palais des Congres, Paris, 75-76; Appalachian Nat Drawing Competition, Appalachian State Univ, Boone, NC, 76; Beaumont Art League Sculpture Show, Brown Scurlock Gallery, Tex, 78. *Teaching:* Asst prof fine arts, La State Univ, Shreveport, 73-77. *Awards:* Purchase Award, New Orleans Mus Art, 71; hon mentions, 13th Ann Piedmont Painting & Sculpture Exhib, 73; Samuel Wiener Sculpture Award, 51st Regional Exhib, 73. *Media:* Wood, Metal. *Mailing Add:* 1009 Poinciana Ave Mamou LA 70554

SAWADA, IKUNE
PAINTER
b Japan, Aug 30, 36. *Study:* Kyoto Art Univ, BFA. *Work:* Seattle Art Mus; Art Gallery Gtr Victoria, BC; Brooklyn Col; Art Univ Kyoto. *Comn:* Mural, Puget Sound Mutual Savings Bank, Seattle, 75; King Co Bldg, Seattle, Wash, 76; Safeco Insurance Co, Seattle, 80. *Exhib:* Ann Exhib Northwest Artists, Seattle Art Mus, 71-75; Wash State Artmobile Exhib, 72; Ann Puget Sound Area Exhib, Charles & Emma Frye Art Mus, Seattle, 72 & 75; Nat Art Competition, Springfield Art Mus, Utah, 75; Asian Artist Exhib, Western Wash State Col Mus, 75. *Teaching:* Teacher art & art hist, Pub High Sch, Japan, 60-65. *Awards:* Lulu Fairbanks Award, Found Int Understanding Through Students, 70; Second Place Award, Fed Way Arts Festival, Washington, 72; Honorable Mention Award, Ann Exhib Northwest Artists, Seattle Art Mus, 74. *Bibliog:* Natsuhiko Tsutsumi (auth), People in Seattle, Katei-Zenka, 75. *Media:* Oil, Watercolor. *Dealer:* Francine Seders Gallery 6701 Greenwood Ave N Seattle WA 98103. *Mailing Add:* 2129 47th Ave SW Seattle WA 98116

SAWAI, NOBORU
PRINTMAKER, EDUCATOR
b Takamatsu, Japan, Feb 18, 31; US citizen. *Study:* Augsburg Col, Minneapolis, BA, 66; Univ Minn, MFA, 69; Yoshida Hanga Acad, Tokyo, woodcut printmaking with Toshi Yoshida, 70. *Work:* Nat Gallery Can, Ottawa; Glenbow Mus, Calgary, Alta; Edmonton Art Gallery, Alta; Winnipeg Art Gallery, Man. *Comn:* Sculpture, Trinity Lutheran Congregation, Minneapolis, 67. *Exhib:* 38th Ann Exhib, Japan Printmakers Asn, Tokyo, 70; Can Nat Exhib, Toronto, 73; 1st Ann Nat Print Exhib, Los Angeles, 73; 2nd NH Int Graphics Ann, 74; 11th Int Biennial Graphic Art, Ljubljana, Yugoslavia, 75. *Teaching:* Instr printmaking, drawing & art hist, Berea Col, Ky, 70-71; asst prof printmaking, Univ Calgary, 71- *Awards:* Manisphere Award, Manisphere 10th Ann Show, 73; Purchase Award, London Mus, Ont, 74; Edition Award, Art Gallery Brant, Brantford, Ont, 75. *Bibliog:* Dennis Elliot (auth), 12th Annual Calgary Graphic Show, Arts Can Mag, 72; Ruth Weisberg (auth), Prints of wit and humor, W Coast Art Works, 5/4/74; Rino Boccaccini (auth), Noboru Sawai, Voce di Ferrara, 9/21/74. *Media:* Woodcuts, Etching. *Dealer:* Thomas Gallery 460 River Ave Winnipeg Man Can. *Mailing Add:* Dept of Art Univ Calgary Calgary AB T2N 1N4 Canada

SAWYER, ALAN R
CONSULTANT
b Wakefield, Mass, June 18, 19. *Study:* Bates Col, BS, 41; Boston Mus Fine Arts Sch; Boston Univ, 47-48; Harvard Univ, MA(art hist), 49; Bates Col, Hon DFA, 69. *Collections Arranged:* Designer-Craftsmen USA, 54, Design in Scandinavia, 56, coordr of Midwest Designer-Craftsmen Exhib, 57 & installation of all primtive art exhibs, 52-59, Art Inst Chicago; installation of rug & textile exhibs, Textile Mus, 59-71. *Pos:* Cur primitive art, Tex Woman's Univ, 49-52; asst to cur decorative arts, Art Inst Chicago, 52-54, asst cur decorative arts in charge Early Americana & pre-Columbian art, 54-56, assoc cur in charge primitive art, 56-58, cur primitive art, 58-59; dir, Textile Mus, 59-71. *Teaching:* Instr art dept, Tex Women's Univ, 49-52; group discussion leader, Looking at Modern Art, Ford Found, Art Inst Chicago, 55-57; lectr, Pub Lect Prog, Univ Chicago-Art Inst Chicago, 59; adj prof art & archaeol, Columbia Univ, 68-69; lectr, Smithsonian Assocs, 71-73; prof art, Univ BC, 75- *Mem:* Archaeol Inst Am; Soc Am Archaeol; Inst Andean Studies. *Publ:* Auth, Handbook of the Nathan Cummings Collection of Ancient Peruvian Art, 54 & Animal Sculpture in Pre-Columbian Art, 57, Art Inst Chicago; auth, A group of early Nasca sculptures in the Whyte Collection, Archaeol Mag, 62; auth, Ancient Peruvian Ceramics, Metrop Mus Art, 66; auth, Ancient Peruvian Art, 68; plus numerous other articles & catalogs on Peruvian art. *Mailing Add:* Dept Fine Arts Univ Brit Columbia Vancouver BC V6T 1W5 Canada

SAWYER, CHARLES HENRY
MUSEUM DIRECTOR

b Andover, Mass, Oct 20, 06. *Study:* Yale Univ, AB; Harvard Law Sch & Harvard Grad Sch; Amherst Col, LHD; Univ NH, DFA; Clark Univ, LHD. *Pos:* Dir, Addison Gallery Am Art, Andover, Mass, 30-40, mem art comt, 40-55; dir, Worcester Mus Art, Mass, 40-47; mem Mass Art Comn, 43-45; trustee, Corning Mus Glass, 50-76; mem, Smithsonian Art Comn, 54-80; dir, Univ Mich Mus Art, 57-72; mem art gallery coun, Univ Notre Dame, 72-. *Teaching:* Prof hist art, Sch Archit & Design, Yale Univ, 47-56; prof mus practice & hist art, Univ Mich, Ann Arbor, 57-75, prof emer, 76. *Mem:* Am Asn Mus; Asn Art Mus Dirs; Col Art Asn Am; Am Antiquarian Soc; Am Acad Arts & Sci. *Publ:* Auth, Art Education in English Public Schools, 37; auth, Report of Committee on Visual Arts at Harvard, 54-55; auth, Integration in the arts, 57 & The college art department and the work of art, 65, Col Art J; contribr, var art mags. *Mailing Add:* 2 Highland Lane Ann Arbor MI 48104

SAWYER, HELEN (HELEN SAWYER FARNSWORTH)
PAINTER, WRITER

b Washington, DC. *Study:* Masters Sch, Dobbs Ferry; Nat Acad Design Sch, with Charles Hawthorne. *Work:* Whitney Mus Am Art; Pa Acad Fine Arts; Toledo Mus; Atlanta Mus; Indianapolis Mus. *Comn:* Paintings, Blue Ridge Spring, Chesapeake & Ohio RR, New York, First Nat City Bank & Circus Parade, G Lister Carlyle. *Exhib:* Carnegie Nat & Int, Pittsburgh; Am Painting Today, Metrop Mus Art; Century of Progress, Chicago; San Francisco World's Fair; New York World's Fair; and many others. *Teaching:* Instr, Art Students League, New York, Farnsworth Sch Art, Cape Cod & Fla. *Awards:* Award for The Bareback Rider, Ringling Mus; First Hon Mention for Trees by the Turn, Art Inst Chicago, First Prize for landscape & still life, Atlanta Mus. *Bibliog:* Ernest Watson (auth), Helen Sawyer, Am Artist. *Mem:* Nat Acad Design; Fla Artists Group; Audubon Artists; Nat Asn Women Painters & Sculptors. *Media:* Oil, Watercolor. *Res:* Material on life and work in Syracuse University Archives and Archives of American Art. *Publ:* Auth, Paintings in oils on paper, Am Artists; auth, Living Among the Modern Primitives, Scribner. *Dealer:* Frank Oehlschlaeger Gallery 28 Blvd of the Presidents St Armands Key Sarasota FL 33578. *Mailing Add:* 3482 Flamingo Ave Sarasota FL 33581

SAWYER, MARIA ARTEMIS PAPAGEORGE See Artemis, Maria

SAWYER, WILLIAM
DEALER, COLLECTOR

b Lindsay, Okla, Feb 16, 20. *Pos:* Dir, William Sawyer Gallery, San Francisco, Calif. *Specialty:* Contemporary American painting, sculpture and graphics. *Collection:* Contemporary American and Mexican paintings, sculpture and graphics. *Mailing Add:* 3045 Clay St San Francisco CA 94109

SAXE, HENRY
SCULPTOR

b Montreal, Que, Sept 24, 37. *Study:* Ecole Des Beaux Arts, Montreal. *Work:* Nat Gallery Can; Montreal Mus Fine Arts; Musee Art Contemporain, Montreal; Art Gallery Ont; Musee de Quebec. *Exhib:* The Bienale De Jeune Peinture de Paris, Musee Art Moderne, 68; Can Art d'Aujourdhul, Paris, Rome, Bruxelles, Lausanne, 68; two-man show, Baxter & Saxe, Eastern Circuit, Nat Gallery Can, 68; Third Int Pioneers Exhib, Lausanne, Paris, 71; Boucherville, Montreal, Toronto, London, Nat Gallery, Can, 73; Owens Art Gallery, Sackville, NB, 76; Agnes Etherington Art Ctr, Queens Univ, 74 & 83; solo exhibs, Dunlap Libr, Univ Man, 76 & Gilles Gheerbrant, 76 & 80-82; Ron Martin & Henry Saxe, Venice Bienale & Ctr for Inter Am Activities, 78. *Awards:* Grants, 67-69 & Sr Awards, 73, 77 & 81, Can Coun Arts. *Dealer:* Gallery Gilles Gheerbrant. *Mailing Add:* PO Box 143 Tamworth ON K0K 3G0 Canada

SAXON, CHARLES DAVID
CARTOONIST, ILLUSTRATOR

b New York, NY, Nov 13, 20. *Study:* Columbia Univ, BA; Hamilton Col, LHD; William Penn Col, LHD; Wadsworth Atheneum, Hartford, Conn. *Work:* Brooklyn Mus, NY; Libr of Cong; Columbia Univ; Wadsworth Atheneum; Syracuse Univ. *Awards:* Best Advert Artist Award, Nat Cartoonists Soc, 78; Best Mag Cartoonist Award; Cartoonist of the Year, 80. *Bibliog:* Jack Dillon (auth), article, Graphis, 71; Robert Jones (auth), article in Commun Arts, 78. *Media:* Pencil, Watercolor. *Publ:* Auth & illusr, Oh, Happy, Happy, Happy, 59-60; contribr, New Yorker Anthologies; contribr, Great Cartoons of the World, 69-71; auth & illusr, One Man's Fancy, 77; auth & illusr, Honesty Is One of the Better Policies, 83. *Mailing Add:* 228 Weed St New Canaan CT 06840

SAYRE, ELEANOR AXSON
CURATOR

b Philadelphia, Pa, Mar 26, 16. *Study:* Bryn Mawr Col, AB, 38; Harvard Univ, 38-40. *Collections Arranged:* Rembrandt: Experimental Etcher, in collaboration with Morgan Library; Albrecht Duerer: Master Printmaker; Goya. *Pos:* Asst in exhibs, Yale Univ Art Gallery, 40-41; gallery asst, Lyman Allyn Mus, New London, Conn, 42; asst dept educ, RI Sch Design Mus, 42-45; asst cur prints & drawings, Mus Fine Arts, Boston, 45-67, cur, 67-. *Teaching:* Lectr, Harvard Univ & Radcliffe Col. *Awards:* Lazo de Dama of the Order of Isabel la Catolica, 75. *Mem:* Keepers Pub Collections Graphic Art; Real Academia de Bellas Artes de San Fernando; Print Coun of Am; Hispanic Soc Am. *Publ:* Auth, A Christmas Book, 66; coauth, Rembrandt: Experimental Etcher, 69; auth, Late Caprichos of Goya, 71; coauth, Goya: Master Printmaker, 71; auth, Goyas Spanian, Tiden och Historien, Nationalmuseet, Stockholm, Sweden, 80. *Mailing Add:* Dept of Prints & Drawings Museum Fine Arts Boston MA 02115

SAZEGAR, MORTEZA
PAINTER

b Teheran, Iran, Nov 11, 33; US citizen. *Study:* Univ Tex, El Paso, BA, 55, BS, 56; Baylor Univ Col Med, 56-57; Cornell Univ, 58-59. *Work:* Whitney Mus Am Art, New York; San Francisco Mus Art; Corcoran Gallery Art, Washington, DC; Prudential Ins Co, Newark, NJ; Tehran Mus Contemp Art. *Exhib:* One-man shows, Poindexter Gallery, New York, 64-77; Art Inst Chicago, 65; Whitney Mus Am Art Ann, 69-70; Cleveland Mus Art, 72; Corcoran Gallery Art, 73. *Bibliog:* Donald B Goodall (auth), Color Forum, Univ Tex Art Mus, 72; Gene Baro (auth), The Way of Color, Corcoran Gallery Art, 73; Lucy R Lippard (auth), Intricate Structural Repeated Image, Tyler Sch Art, Temple Univ, Philadelphia, Pa, 79. *Media:* Acrylic. *Dealer:* Poindexter Gallery 1160 5th Avenue New York NY 10029. *Mailing Add:* RR 1 Cochranville PA 19330

SCALA, JOSEPH (A)
SCULPTOR, MUSEUM DIRECTOR

b Queens, NY, Feb 20, 40. *Study:* C W Post Col, BS, 62; Cornell Univ, MFA(sculpture), 71. *Work:* Metrop Mus Art, New York; Herbert Johnson Mus, Ithaca, NY; Battelle Mem Inst, Acad Contemp Problems, Columbus, Ohio. *Comn:* Laser sculpture, Andrew Dickson White Mus, Ithaca, NY, 70; Sound/Light Sculpture, Rochester Jr League, 70; Cybernetic Fountain, Cornell Univ Physics Dept, 72. *Exhib:* Some More Beginnings, Brooklyn Mus, 68; Mirrors, Motors, Motion, Albright-Knox Gallery, Buffalo, NY, 70; one-person one-piece show, Everson Mus, Syracuse, NY, 72; Can Comput Show Art Exhib, Toronto, Ont, 75; one-person show, Westbroadway Gallery, New York, 78. *Collections Arranged:* Current-New York (auth, catalog), Syracuse Univ Lowe Art Gallery, 80; Tibor de Nagy Collection, Syracuse Univ Lubin House Gallery, 80. *Pos:* Pres & founder, Collaborations in Art, Sci & Technol Inc, 69-; dir, Lowe Art Gallery, Syracuse Univ, 78-, dir Lubin House Gallery, 79. *Teaching:* Instr multi-media, Cornell Univ, 70 & 71; assoc prof art & technol, Syracuse Univ, 71-, chairperson museology prog, 78-. *Awards:* Winner Young Sculptors Competition, Sculptors Guild, New York, 69; New York State Coun Arts Grants, 70-75. *Bibliog:* Milford Kime (auth), Laser art, Laser Focus, 73. *Mailing Add:* 266 W Seneca Turnpike Syracuse NY 13207

SCALISE, NICHOLAS PETER
PAINTER, SCULPTOR

b Meriden, Conn, June 4, 32. *Study:* Horace C Wilcox Tech Sch, Meriden; Paier Sch Art, New Haven, Conn. *Work:* Meriden World War II Mem Hosp, Meriden. *Exhib:* Nat Art League, New York, 69; Butler Inst Am Art, Youngstown, Ohio, 69; Nat Soc Painters in Casein, New York, 70; Wadsworth Atheneum, Hartford, Conn, 72; Silvermine Guild, Conn, 77 & 81; New Eng in Winter Watercolor Exhib, De Cordova Mus, Lincoln, Mass, 77 & 78; Addison Gallery Am Art, Phillips Acad, Andover, Mass, 81. *Teaching:* Instr drawing & painting, Famous Artists Sch, Westport, Conn, 59-69. *Awards:* First Prize, Conn Watercolor Soc, 41st Ann Exhib, 80; 1st Prize Best in Show, Meriden Arts Crafts, 57th Ann Exhib, 81; 1st Prize, Greene Art Gallery, 82. *Mem:* Springfield Acad Artist; Meriden Arts & Crafts, Conn; Conn Acad Fine Arts, Hartford; Conn Watercolor Soc, Hartford. *Media:* Oil, Watercolor. *Publ:* Auth, article, North Light, 7-8/77; auth, article, Am Artist, 7/78; auth & illusr cover, Palette Talk, 80; illusr, Executive Diary, Am Artist, 80. *Dealer:* Capricorn Gallery 4849 Rugby Ave Bethesda MD; Munson Gallery 653 Canyon Rd Santa Fe NM & Main St Chatham MA. *Mailing Add:* 59 Susan Lane Meriden CT 06450

SCANGA, ITALO
SCULPTOR, EDUCATOR

b Lago, Italy, June 6, 32; US citizen. *Study:* Mich State Univ, BA & MA. *Work:* Metrop Mus Art, New York; Fogg Mus, Cambridge, Mass; Philadelphia Mus Art; Mus Art, RI Sch Design, Providence; Mus Mod Art, New York. *Exhib:* Sculpture Ann, 70 & Biennial Exhib, 83, Whitney Mus Am Art; Mus Mod Art, New York, 71; Corcoran Gallery Art, Washington, DC, 71; one-man shows, Whitney Mus Am Art, New York, 72, Archimedes Troubles, La Jolla Mus Contemp Art, Calif, 83, Heads, Los Angeles Co Mus Art, 83 & Delahunty Gallery, New York, 83; The Anxious Edge, Walker Art Ctr, 81; Beyond Modernism, Crysler Mus, Norfolk, Va, 82; The 6th Day: A Survey of Recent Developments in Figurative Sculpture, Univ Chicago, 83; and others. *Teaching:* Asst prof sculpture, RI Sch Design, 64-66; assoc prof sculpture, Tyler Sch Art, Philadelphia, 68-78; vis assoc prof visual arts, Univ Calif, San Diego, 76-77, prof, 78-. *Awards:* Howard Found Grant, Brown Univ, 70; Cassandra Found Grant, 72; Nat Endowment Arts, 80. *Bibliog:* Eric Cammeron (auth), article, Artforum, 77; Ron Onorato (auth), article, Art in Am, 78; Christopher Knight (auth), Scanga's object cipher, Art Express Mag, 82; and others. *Media:* Mixed Media. *Dealer:* Delahunty Gallery 291 Church St New York NY 10013; Delahunty Gallery 2701 Canton St Dallas TX 75226. *Mailing Add:* 6717 Vista Del Mar La Jolla CA 92037

SCARBROUGH, CLEVE KNOX, JR
MUSEUM DIRECTOR, HISTORIAN

b Florence, Ala, July 17, 39. *Study:* Univ NAla, BS, 62; Univ Iowa, MA, 67. *Collections Arranged:* Pre-Columbian Art of the Americas, 70, Graphics by Four Modern Swiss Sculptors, circulated by Smithsonian Traveling Serv, 72- & Completed Charlotte Museum of History, 76, Mint Mus Art, Charlotte, NC. *Pos:* Dir, Mint Mus Art, 69-76; dir, Hunter Mus Art, 76-; mem visual arts adv panel, Tenn Arts Comn, 76, chmn comt, 77-81, rev comt, Art in Pub Places, 78. *Teaching:* Grad asst, Univ Iowa, 64-67; asst prof art hist, Univ Tenn, Knoxville, 67-69. *Mem:* Southeastern Mus Conf (bd mem, 76-79); Col Art Asn; Am Asn Mus; NC Mus Coun (bd mem, 70-75, pres, 76); Friends Festival Bd; and others. *Publ:* Ed, North Carolinians Collect, 71; ed, Graphics by Four Modern Swiss Sculptors, 72; ed, British Painting from NC Museum of Art, 73; ed, Mountain Landscapes by Swiss Artists, 75. *Mailing Add:* Hunter Mus Art 10 Bluff View Chattanooga TN 37403

SCARPITTA, SALVATORE
SCULPTOR
b New York, NY, 1919. *Study:* Study in Italy, 36-59. *Work:* Stedelijk Mus, Amsterdam, Holland; Albright-Knox Art Gallery, Buffalo, NY; Los Angeles Co Mus Art; Mus Mod Art, New York; Tel-Aviv Mus, Israel. *Exhib:* Corcoran Gallery Art, Washington, DC, 63; Art Inst Chicago, 64; Contemp Primitivism, Vassar Col, 76; retrospective, Houston Contemp, 77; one-man exhibs, Robinson Galleries, Houston, 78 & Portland Ctr Visual Arts, 78; Private Myths, Queens Mus, 78; Sustained Vision, The New Mus, New York, 79. *Teaching:* Vis critic, Md Inst, Col Art, 66- *Bibliog:* Harriet Janis & Rudi Blesh (auth), Collage, Personalities-Concepts-Techniques, Chilton, 62; Allen S Weller (auth), The Joys & Sorrows of Recent American Art, Univ Ill, 68; B H Friedman (auth), The ivory tower, Art News, 4/69. *Mailing Add:* c/o Leo Castelli Gallery Md Inst Col Art New York NY 10021

SCHAB, MARGO POLLINS
ART DEALER
b Cincinnati, Ohio, Aug 4, 45. *Pos:* Pres, Margo Pollins Schab, New York. *Specialty:* Important prints, drawings and paintings of the 19th and 20th century. *Mailing Add:* 1000 Park Ave New York NY 10028

SCHABACKER, BETTY BARCHET
PAINTER, LECTURER
b Baltimore, Md, Aug 14, 25. *Study:* Conn Col Women; Marian Carey Art Asn, Newport, RI; Coronado Sch Art, Calif, with Monty Lewis; also with Gerd & Irene Koch, Ojai, Calif. *Work:* B K Smith Gallery, Lake Erie Col, Painesville, Ohio; First Nat Bank Pa, Erie; Western Union, New York; McGraw Edison, Columbia, Mo; Erie Zoo, Pa; and others. *Exhib:* Mus Mod Art, Paris, 61-63; Butler Inst Am Art Ann, 64-77; Chautauqua Exhib Am Art, 66-74; Audubon Artists, 67-79; Nat Watercolor Soc Ann, 79; 14 solo shows, Nat Acad Design; Acad Natural Sci, Philadelphia, 81-82; and others. *Pos:* Artist in residence, Lake Erie Col, 71. *Awards:* Nancy Hubbard Lance Award, Lake Erie Col, 71; First Toastmaster, Ann Fine Art Series, 73; Second Award, Nature Interpreted, Cincinnati Mus Natural Hist, 80; and others. *Mem:* Nat Watercolor Soc; Northwestern Pa Artists Asn; Audubon Artists; Artists Equity Asn; Soc Animal Artists. *Media:* Watercolor, Cloth Collage. *Dealer:* The Inn Gallery Clymer NY 14724; I Michael Brown Co Erie PA 16501. *Mailing Add:* 540 Wilkins Rd Erie PA 16505

SCHACHTER, JUSTINE RANSON
GRAPHIC ARTIST, ILLUSTRATOR
b Brooklyn, NY, Dec 18, 27. *Study:* Tyler Sch Fine Arts, Temple Univ, scholar; Brooklyn Mus Art Sch, with John Bindrum, Milton Hebald & John Ferren; Art Students League, with Will Barnett. *Work:* Bellmore Pub Libr, NY; Island Trees Pub Sch, Levittown, NY; Wantagh High Sch, NY. *Comn:* Poster, NY State Parent-Teacher Asn, 70-73. *Exhib:* One-woman show, Ruth White Gallery, 61; Nat Asn Women Artists Traveling Graphics Show, US & Europe, 69-70; Am Soc Contemp Artists, New York, 69-83; and others. *Pos:* Dir graphic arts, Audio-Visual Educ TV, Mineola Pub Sch, 64-65; exec dir, Art Forms Creative Ctr, 71-73; owner, The Artist's Studio Gallery, 74- *Teaching:* Artist in residence, Community Arts Prog, Wantagh High Sch, 72 & Syosset High Sch, 74. *Awards:* Award for graphics, Brooklyn Soc Artists Ann, 49; awards for mixed media, Nassau Co Off Cult Develop, 70 & Am Soc Contemp Artists, 71 & 75. *Bibliog:* Elyse Sommer (auth), Rock and Stone Craft, Crown, 72. *Mem:* Am Soc Contemp Artists (chmn admis, 68-71); Nat Asn Women Artists; Artists Equity Asn; Int Asn Arts. *Media:* Pen, Ink; Paper, Stone. *Publ:* Illusr, Long Island Free Press, 70-71; illusr, Make a Glad Sound, Consort Music, Inc, 74; illusr, You Can Play a Recorder, Music Minus One, illusr, Treasury of Stories, Waldman, 78. *Mailing Add:* 14 Trumpet Lane Levittown NY 11756

SCHACTMAN, BARRY ROBERT
PAINTER, EDUCATOR
b Newark, NJ, May 10, 30. *Study:* Univ of Miami; Art Students League; Rutgers Univ; Tyler Sch of Art of Temple Univ; Yale Univ Sch of Art, BFA, 58, MFA, 60, study with Josef Albers & Rico Lebrun. *Work:* Yale Univ Art Mus, New Haven, Conn; St Louis Univ, Mo; Mus of Israel, Jerusalem; Minn Mus of Art, St Paul; Weatherspoon Art Gallery, Univ of NC, Greensboro. *Exhib:* Drawing Soc Nat Traveling Exhib, Am Fedn of Arts, 70-72; Drawing USA (nat traveling exhib), Minn Mus of Art, St Paul, 71-73; Nat Invitational Drawing Exhib, Mitchell Gallery, Southern Ill Univ, Carbondale, 75; Drawing Mo 1976, Bicentennial Invitational Exhib (traveling exhib), Albrecht Art Mus, St Joseph, Mo, 76; 30th Ann Hassam Purchase Fund Exhib, Am Acad & Inst of Arts & Lett, New York, 78. *Pos:* Assoc dean, Sch Fine Arts, Washington Univ, St Louis, Mo, 77-79. *Teaching:* Instr drawing & design, Univ of Tex, Austin, 59-61; prof drawing & painting, Washington Univ, St Louis, Mo, 61- *Awards:* Purchase Prize, Drawing USA, Minn Mus of Art, St Paul, 71; plus others. *Bibliog:* Gerald M Monroe (auth), Teaching drawing: The personal approach of Barry Schactman, drawing, Drawing Soc, 81 & Am Artist, 82; Bernard Chaet (auth), The Art of Drawing, Holt, Rinehart and Winston Inc, 83. *Media:* Pen and Ink, Charcoal; Oil. *Dealer:* Capricorn Galleries Bethesda Maryland. *Mailing Add:* 437 E Glendale Rd St Louis MO 63119

SCHAEFER, CARL FELLMAN
PAINTER
b Hanover, Ont, Apr 30, 03. *Study:* Ont Col Art, Toronto, with J E H MacDonald & Arthur Lismer; Cent Sch Arts & Crafts, London; Ont Col Art, Fel, 76; Univ Waterloo, Ont, Hon DLett, 76. *Work:* Nat Gallery Can; Art Gallery Ont; Art Gallery Hamilton; Art Gallery London; Va Mus Fine Arts, Richmond. *Comn:* Ser of paintings on prod, Can Packers, Ltd, Toronto, 42.

Exhib: Century of Can Art, Tate Gallery, London, 38; 18th Int Art Inst Chicago, 39; 11th Int, Brooklyn Mus, 41; 1st Biennial, Sao Paulo Mus Arte Mod, 51; Retrospective 1926-1969, Sir George Williams Univ, Montreal, 69-70; Aviation Paintings, Can War Mus, Ottawa, 72; Can Paintings to People's Repub of China, 75; Can Paintings in the Thirties, Nat Gallery Can, 75; Ont Community Collects, Art Gallery Ont, Toronto, 75; Retrospective 1932-1967, Robert McLauglin Gallery, Oshawa, 76; Can Paintings in Univ Toronto, Art Gallery Ont, 77-78; Hanover Edmonton Art Gallery, 80; and others. *Pos:* Off war artist, Europ Theatre Opers & Iceland, 43-46. *Teaching:* Instr painting, Cent Tech Sch, Toronto, 30-40; dir art, Hart House, Univ Toronto, 34-40; instr & dir painting, Ont Col Art, 48-55, emer chmn dept drawing & painting, 68- *Awards:* Queen's Coronation Medal, Elizabeth II, 53 & Can Silver Jubilee Medal, 52-77 & 78; Mem, Order of Can, 78. *Bibliog:* Donald W Buchanan (auth), The Growth of Canadian Painting, Collins, 50; J Russell Harper (auth), Painting in Canada, a History, Univ Toronto Press, 66; Can Artists Series, Carl Schaefer, Gage Publ, 77. *Mem:* Can Soc Graphic Art; Can Soc Painters Watercolour; fel Royal Soc Arts; Royal Can Acad Arts; life fel Int Inst Arts & Lett. *Media:* Watercolor, Egg Tempera. *Publ:* Auth, Iceland, Atlantis on the Arctic Circle, Can Art Mag, 46. *Dealer:* Roberts Gallery 641 Yonge St Toronto ON Can; Downstairs Gallery Edmonton Can. *Mailing Add:* 157 St Clements Ave Toronto ON M4R 1H1 Canada

SCHAEFER, GAIL
SCULPTOR
b NJ, June 11, 38. *Study:* Art Students League, with Kaz-Simon, 77-80; Ramapo Col, NJ, BA, 79; Nat Acad Design, Lucchesi scholar, 80-83. *Exhib:* Catherine Lorrilard Wolfe Nat Arts Club, New York, 78, 82 & 83; Allied Artists Am, Nat Acad Galleries, New York, 78, Am Acad & Inst Arts & Lett, 80 & Nat Arts Club, 81 & 83; Salmagundi Club, New York, 80; Nat Acad Design 157th Ann, New York, 82. *Teaching:* Instr studio classes, 77-; instr sculpture, Ctr Advanced Enrichment, Englewood, NJ, 81- *Awards:* William Averbach-Levy Award, Nat Acad Design, 81; Medal Hon, Printers & Sculptors Soc NJ, 82; Anna Hyatt Huntington Award, Catherine Lorrilard Wolfe Art Club, 83. *Bibliog:* David Spengler (auth), Women of the arts, Record, 10/28/76; Diana Drew (auth), Sculptress has a way with children, Town News, 6/21/78; Terry Meyer (auth), Gail Schaefer's talent, Sunday Post, 7/16/78. *Mem:* Allied Artists Am; Painters & Sculptors Soc NJ; Portrait Soc NJ. *Media:* Clay. *Dealer:* Whychoff Galery Whychoff NJ; Du Roche Studio Englewood NJ. *Mailing Add:* 103 Commander Black Oradell NJ 07649

SCHAEFER, RONALD H
PRINTMAKER, EDUCATOR
b Milwaukee, Wis, June 2, 39. *Study:* Univ Wis-Milwaukee, BS(art), 62; Univ Wis-Madison, MS(art), 63, MFA, 64. *Work:* Joslyn Mus, Omaha, Nebr; Tampa Pub Libr; First Nat Bank Minneapolis; and others. *Exhib:* Five Okla Printmakers Ann, 64-72; three Boston Printmakers Ann, 65-67; 12th & 19th Ball State Univ Drawing & Small Sculpture Ann, 66 & 73; Miami Biennial Print, 73; NH Int Ann, 73; and others. *Teaching:* Prof printmaking & chmn dept, Univ NDak, 65- *Awards:* Twenty-five Printmakers Nat Invitational Purchase Award, Minot State Col, 71; Graphic Chem & Ink Co Award, First NH Print Int, 73; Purchase Award, Los Angeles, Print Exhib, 73. *Mem:* Print Club. *Media:* Etching, Intaglio. *Mailing Add:* 119 Conklin Ave Grand Forks ND 58201

SCHAEFER, SCOTT JAY
CURATOR, HISTORIAN
b Chicago, Ill, Mar 30, 48. *Study:* Univ Ariz, BA, 70; Bryn Mawr Col, MA, PhD, 75. *Pos:* Asst cur paintings, Philadelphia Mus Art, 74; asst cur prints, Fogg Art Mus, Cambridge, Mass, 76-78; asst cur paintings, Mus Fine Arts, Boston, 78-80; cur paintings, Los Angeles Co Mus Art, 80- *Teaching:* Lectr, Philadelphia Col Art, 71-72; lectr, Harvard Univ, Cambridge, Mass, 76-79. *Mem:* Southern Calif Art Hist; Am Mus Asn. *Res:* Late 16th & 17th century Italian painting. *Publ:* Auth, Los Angeles, Russian avant-garde at the County Museum, Burlington Mag, 12/80; auth, A painting of the origins of gunpowder, J Warbur & Courtland Inst, XLIV, 81; auth, Drawings for the Studiolo of Francesco; a catalogue, Master Drawings, XX, 83; auth, Drawings by Martin Freminet, Gazette Des Beaux-Arts, 1371, 83; auth, Europe and beyond; some paintings for the studiolo, Coun Europe, 3/84. *Mailing Add:* 5905 Wilshire Blvd Los Angeles CA 90036

SCHAEFFER, KATE
DEALER, COLLECTOR
b Berlin, Ger; US citizen. *Collections Arranged:* Carl Hofer (auth, catalog), 35. *Pos:* Owner, Schaeffer Galleries, New York, currently. *Specialty:* Fine Old Master paintings and drawings early 19th century. *Mailing Add:* Schaeffer Galleries Inc 983 Park Ave New York NY 10028

SCHAEFFER, MARTHA JANE
DEALER
b Springfield, Mass, Jan 14, 48. *Study:* St Bonaventure Univ; Herbert Lehman Col, BA, 74. *Collections Arranged:* Jean Solombre, New Paintings, 77; Beck & Jung, Space Game Paintings, 77; Louttre, Recent Paintings, 78; Pat Hammerman, Mixed Medial Works on Handmade Paper, 81; Joan Miro, Works on Paper, 82. *Pos:* Owner, Schaffer Editions, currently. *Bibliog:* Sandra Salmas (auth), Personal finance, 1/25/81 & Good buys in fine arts, 1/25/81, New York Times. *Mem:* Art Pipeline; Women's Business Owners of NY. *Specialty:* Nineteenth and twentieth century paintings, drawings, prints & sculpture. *Mailing Add:* 500 East 77th St Suite 512 New York NY 10162

SCHAFFER, ROSE
PAINTER, LECTURER
b Newark, NJ. *Study:* Art Students League, 35-40, with George Bridgeman
& Ivan Oninsky; also with Bernard Karfiol, Sol Wilson, Seong Moy & Antonio
Frasconi. *Work:* Smithsonian Inst, Washington, DC; Chrysler Mus Arts & Sci,
Norfolk, Va; Springfield Mus Art, Mass; State NJ Cult Ctr; J F Kennedy Libr;
Montclair Mus; and others. *Exhib:* Nat Acad Design, New York; Boston Mus
Art, Mass; Delgado Mus, New Orleans; Brooklyn Mus, NY; Philadelphia
Print Club, Pa; and others. *Teaching:* Lectr mod art, adult schs & other orgn.
Awards: Terry Nat Award, Miami Beach, Fla, 55; Seton Hall Univ Award,
56; Two Purchase Prizes, Art for Overlook, 55-60; plus others. *Mem:* Nat Asn
Women Artists; Am Fed Arts; Nat Artists Equity Asn. *Media:* Acrylic, Oil.
Mailing Add: 119A Old Nassau Rd Jamesburg NJ 08831

SCHAFFNER, J LURAY See Luray, J

SCHAFFNER, RUTH S
DEALER, CONSULTANT
b Mannheim, Ger; US citizen. *Study:* Itten Art Sch, Berlin; Sorbonne, Paris;
New Sch of Soc Research, New York; Clarence White Sch of Photog, New
York. *Pos:* Owner, Ruth S Schaffner Gallery, Santa Barbara, 73-, Los Angeles,
74-80. *Specialty:* Avante-garde and contemporary paintings and sculpture.
Mailing Add: 128 W Ortega St Santa Barbara CA 93101

SCHAPIRO, MEYER
EDUCATOR, HISTORIAN
b Shavly, Russia, Sept 23, 04; US citizen. *Study:* Columbia Univ, AB, MA &
PhD. *Teaching:* Prof hist art, Columbia Univ, 28-75, prof emer, 75- *Awards:*
Comdr l'Order Artes & Lett, France. *Mem:* Fel Am Acad Arts & Scis; Am
Philos Soc; Nat Inst Arts & Lett; Medieval Acad Am. *Res:* Early Christian,
medieval and modern art. *Publ:* Auth, Words and Pictures: On the Literal and
the Symbolic in the Illustrations of a Text, Mouton, 73; auth, Romanesque
Art, 77, Late Antique, Early Christian & Medieval Art: Selected Papers, 79
& Modern Art, 82, Braziller; and others. *Mailing Add:* c/o George Braziller
Inc One Park Ave New York NY 10016

SCHAPIRO, MIRIAM
PAINTER, COLLAGE ARTIST
b Toronto, Ont, Nov 15, 23; US citizen. *Study:* Univ Iowa, BA, 45, MA, 46,
MFA, 49; Col Wooster Ohio, Hon DFA, 83. *Work:* Whitney Mus Am Art,
Mus Mod Art, New York; Stanford Univ, Palo Alto, Calif; Allen Mem Art
Mus; Oberlin Hirshhorn Mus. *Exhib:* Carnegie Int, 58; Mus Mod Art, New
York, 67; The Shrine, The Computer and The Dollhouse, retrospective, Univ
Calif, San Diego, 75; Palais des Beaux Arts, Brussels, Belg, 79; Mus Contemp
Art, Chicago, 79; Barbara Gladstone Gallery, New York, 81; Galerie Rudolf
Zwirner, Cologne, Ger, 81; Art Inst Chicago, 81; and others. *Pos:*
Co-originator feminist art prog, Calif Inst Arts, 72-75; co-found, Feminist Art
Inst, New York, 79. *Awards:* Ford Found Tamarind Fel, 64; Nat Endowment
Arts Grant, 76; Skowhegan Award, 81. *Bibliog:* Skira Annual--Actual Art, 80;
Jensen & Conway (auths), Ornamentalism, Clarkson N Potter, 82; Paula
Bradley, Miriam Schapiro (dissertation), Univ NC, 83. *Mem:* Women's
Caucus Art (nat adv bd, currently). *Publ:* Auth, The education of women as
artists project, Womanhouse, Col Art J, summer 72; coauth, Womanhouse
(catalog), 72; ed, Anonymous Was a Woman, 74 & Art: A Woman's
Sensibility, 75, Feminist Art Prog, Cal Inst Arts; auth, Women and the
Creative Process, Univ Man, 74. *Dealer:* Barbara Gladstone Gallery 152
Wooster St New York NY 10012. *Mailing Add:* 393 W Broadway New York
NY 10012

SCHAR, STUART
EDUCATOR, PRINTMAKER
b Chicago, Ill, Aug 27, 41. *Study:* Univ Chicago, BFA, 63, MFA, 64, PhD(arts
admin), 67. *Comn:* Painting for Frank Lloyd Wright house, Brookfield, Ill, 73;
lithograph for Lyons Twp High Sch, City of LaGrange, Ill, 74; painting for
Aurora Pub Libr, City of Aurora, Ill, 75. *Exhib:* Art Inst Chicago, 60-64, 70
& 74; Lexington Studios, Chicago, 64-65, 75-76; Printmaking 1969, Northern
Ariz Univ, Flagstaff, 69; John Hancock Ctr, Chicago, 73; Columbus Gallery
Fine Arts, Ohio, 76; Oberlin Col, Ohio, 77; Western Art League Asn, 77; and
others. *Pos:* Res assoc higher educ, NCent Asn Cols & Sec Schs, 65, asst to
exec secy, 66; admin asst to chmn art dept, Univ Ill, Chicago Circle, 66-69,
actg chmn art dept, 69; artist-in-residence, Joliet Art League, Ill, 70-72; dir
sch of art, Kent State Univ, 75-83; co-dir, Blossom Kent Art, Music & Theatre
summer progs, 75-83; dir, James A Michener Mus, Univ Galleries, Eells
Outdoor Gallery & Jack Lord Purchase Collections, 75-83. *Teaching:* Asst
prof rendering & drafting, Chicago Tech Col, 64, asst prof design & graphics,
65; asst prof art, Univ Ill, Chicago Circle, 66-70, assoc prof urban sci, 70-75;
prof art, Kent State Univ, 75-83; Distinguished Prof, La State Univ, 83.
Awards: Best of Show, Midway Studios, 72, Gen Motors Purchase Award,
Art Inst of Chicago, 74; Best of Show, Western Art League Asn, 77. *Mem:*
Col Art Asn; Am Asn Univ Prof; Am Inst Planners. *Publ:* Coauth, Guide for
the Evaluation of Institutions of Higher Education, NCent Asn Cols & Sec
Schs, 66; auth, The education of an art student, Tallyrand, Vol 3 (1970);
coauth, A Self Study Report: The University of Illinois at Chicago Circle,
Univ Ill, 71. *Mailing Add:* Col Design La State Univ Baton Rouge LA 70803

SCHARF, WILLIAM
PAINTER
b Media, Pa, Feb 22, 27. *Study:* Samuel Fleisher Mem Art Sch, Philadelphia,
Pa; Pa Acad of the Fine Arts, Philadelphia; The Barnes Foundation, Merion,
Pa. *Work:* High Mus, Atlanta, Ga; Neuberger Mus, Purchase, NY; Boston
Inst of Contemp Art, Ma; Solomon R Guggenheim Mus, New York; Brooklyn

Mus, New York; and others. *Exhib:* Pa Acad Anns, Philadelphia, 47-; Inst
Contemp Art, Boston, 51; Aldrich Mus, Ridgefield, Conn, 63; Brandeis Univ,
Waltham, Mass, 63; San Francisco Art Inst, 70; The Neuberger Mus,
Purchase, NY, 76; High Mus, Atlanta, Ga, 78. *Mailing Add:* 75 Central Park
W New York NY 10023

SCHARFF, CONSTANCE KRAMER
PRINTMAKER, PAINTER
b New York, NY. *Study:* Brooklyn Mus Art Sch, grad; also with Adja
Jounkers & Abraham Rattner. *Work:* Brooklyn Mus Art; Philadelphia Mus
Art; Columbia Univ; Smithsonian Inst Archives; Butler Inst Am Art,
Youngstown, Ohio. *Comn:* Ed prints, Contemp Arts Asn, NY, 56 & 60 & Am
Asn Contemp Arts, 68. *Exhib:* Potsdam Nat Print Show, 66; Soc Am Graphic
Artists, 72-81; Award Winners Show, Community Church, NY, 74; Am Acad
& Inst of Arts & Lett, New York; Traveling Juried Show, Israel & Egypt, 81
& 82. *Awards:* Medal of Honor, Nat Asn Women Artists, 68; Grumbacher
Award, Nat Asn Women Artists, 73; Edna Stauffer Award, Audubon Artists,
73. *Mem:* Soc Am Graphic Artists; Nat Soc Painters Casein & Acrylic (rec
secy, 67-); Audubon Artists; Nat Asn Women Artists; Am Soc Contemp
Artists (rec secy 75-81, exec bd, 82-). *Mailing Add:* 115 Jaffrey St Brooklyn
NY 11235

SCHARY, EMANUEL
PAINTER, PRINTMAKER
b Feb 27, 24; US citizen. *Study:* Carnegie Inst Technol Sch Fine Arts; Art
Students League; Pratt Graphics Ctr; and with Edwin Dickenson, Howard
Trafton, Frank Reilly, Ivan Olinsky, Robert Hale & Jurgen Fischer. *Work:*
Nat Fine Art Collection, Smithsonian Inst, Washington, DC; Metrop Mus
Fine Art, New York; Israel Mus, Jerusalem; Vatican Mus, Rome, Italy;
Brooklyn Mus, New York; and others. *Comn:* New York World's Fair
Pavilion, Weizmann Inst Sci, 64-65; large painting, West Hempstead
Community Ctr, NY; numerous litho ed for var group collectors. *Exhib:*
One-man shows, Tel-Aviv, Israel, 68 & Kean Col, NJ, 73; Brooklyn Mus, 70;
New York, Assoc Am Artists, 74; Kansas City Country Club Plaza, 74; Guild
Gallery, New York, 78, 79 & 81. *Bibliog:* Michael Patterson (auth), Elmont
artist ... master, New York Sunday News, 4/5/70; Ann Shapiro (auth), New
York artist comes to Kansas City, Kansas City Chronicle, 9/74; Rusty
Hoffland (auth), Art show '75, NSide News, Atlanta, Ga, 2/6/75. *Mem:* Life
mem Art Students League; Univ Mich Artists & Craftsmens Guild; Artists
Equity Asn, Inc. *Media:* Acrylic, Graphics. *Dealer:* Jem Publishers PO Box
194 Elmont New York NY 11003. *Mailing Add:* 536 Kirkby Rd Elmont NY
11003

SCHAUMBURG, DONALD ROLAND
EDUCATOR, CERAMIST
b Oakland, Calif, Aug 23, 19. *Study:* Calif Col Arts & Crafts, Oakland, BA(art
educ), 41; Claremont Col, MFA, 51; graduate studies with Marguerite
Wildenhain, 57-59. *Work:* Folk Art Mus, Santa Fe, NMex; Univ Art
Collections, Ariz State Univ, Tempe; Int Minerals Corporation Collection,
Skokie, Ill. *Comn:* Ceramic wall panel, Valley National Bank, Tempe, Ariz,
81. *Exhib:* One-man shows, Phoenix Art Mus, 62 & 68, Univ Art Collections,
Tempe, Ariz, 74 & Hand and the Spirit Gallery, Scottsdale, Ariz, 75 & 82;
Southwestern Craftsmen, Mus Int Folk Art, NMex, 65; 9th Ann Ceramic
West Nat Invitational, Utah State Univ, Logan, 80. *Pos:* Chmn, Palomar Col,
46-49. *Teaching:* Instr ceramics, San Diego State Univ, 53; prof ceramics,
Ariz State Univ, 53- *Awards:* Awards of Merit, Tucson Mus, 60-62; First
Prize, Heard Mus, 75; Mary Soule Mem, Ariz Designer Craftsman, 76.
Bibliog: Krevanic (auth), Keramos, Kendall-Hunt, 70; Glenn Nelson (auth),
Ceramics Handbook, Holt Reinhart Winston, 78; John H Conrad (auth),
Contemporary Ceramic Techniques, Prentic-Hall, 79. *Mem:* Nat Council
Educ of Ceramic Arts. *Media:* Porcelain Clay, Raku Clay. *Dealer:* The Hand
and the Spirit Crafts Gallery Scottsdale AZ. *Mailing Add:* 5410 E Vernon
Phoenix AZ 85008

SCHEER, SHERIE (HOOD)
PHOTOGRAPHER, EDUCATOR
b Estherville, Iowa, Feb 15, 40. *Study:* Univ Iowa, 58-60; Univ Calif, Los
Angeles, BA, 69, MA, 71. *Work:* Metrop Mus Art, New York; Fogg Art Mus,
Harvard Univ; Israel Mus, Jerusalem; Minneapolis Inst Art, Minn; Oakland
Mus, Calif. *Exhib:* Contemporary Hand-Colored Photography, DeSaisset
Mus, Santa Clara, Calif, 81; Summer Show V, Los Angeles Co Mus Art, 81;
Five Photographers, Los Angeles Inst Contemp Art, 82; Artists' Tribute to
Bertha Urdang, Israel Mus, Jerusalem, 82; Invitational: Bertha Urdang,
London Regional Gallery, Ont, 83. *Teaching:* Instr photog, Univ Calif, Los
Angeles Exten, 82- *Bibliog:* Barbara Noah (auth), J Golden & S Scheer at the
Womens Building, Art in Am, 3-4/78; Colin Westerbeck (auth), Reviews:
New York, Artforum, 3/81; Helen Harrison (auth), Transforming the
familiar, New York Times, 3/29/81. *Mem:* Artists Econ Opportunity; Soc
Photog Educ. *Media:* Hand-Colored Photographs. *Dealer:* Bertha Urdang
Gallery 23 E 74th St New York NY 10021. *Mailing Add:* 31 Park Ave Venice
CA 90291

SCHEIN, EUGENIE
PAINTER, PRINTMAKER
US citizen. *Study:* Hunter Col, BA; Columbia Univ, MA; Martha Graham Sch
Dance; Nat Univ Mex. *Work:* Carvell Mus, La; Ga Mus Art, Athens; Lowe
Art Mus, Coral Gables, Fla; Miami Mus Mod Art, Fla. *Exhib:* Int
Watercolors, Brooklyn Mus; Cincinnati Mus; Riverside Mus, New York; Soc
Four Arts, Palm Beach; Lowe Mus, Univ Miami, Coral Gables, Fla;
Hollywood Art & Cult Ctr, Fla; and others. *Teaching:* Instr, Hunter Col,
26-55; instr, Univ Miami, 56-60. *Mem:* Artists Equity Asn (vpres, 72-); Fla
Artists Group. *Media:* Oil, Acrylic; Graphics. *Mailing Add:* 1070 Stillwater
Dr Miami Beach FL 33141

SCHELLIN, ROBERT WILLIAM
PAINTER, CRAFTSMAN
b Akron, Ohio, July 28, 10. *Study:* Univ Wis-Milwaukee, BA, 33; with Hans Hofmann, New York, 39-40; Univ Wis-Madison, MA, 48. *Work:* Milwaukee Art Ctr; Madison Art Asn; Univ Wis-Milwaukee; Kenosha Pub Mus, Wis; Wustum Mus, Racine, Wis. *Exhib:* US Info Agency Am Crafts Exhib, Europe, 61-62; Wis Craftsmen, Smithsonian Inst, Washington, DC, 62; Four Ceramists, Tweed Gallery, Duluth, Minn, 63; Wisconsin Art, 1850 to Today, Milwaukee Art Ctr, 63, Commemorative Exhib Wis Art, 64; one-man retrospective, Univ Wis-Milwaukee, 75. *Pos:* Mem, Milwaukee Art Comn, 62-70, chmn, 68-70. *Teaching:* Instr painting & drawing, Whittier Sch Syst, Calif, 45-51; prof ceramics, Univ Wis-Milwaukee, 51-75, emer prof, 75- *Awards:* Silver Medal, Milwaukee Art Inst, 33; Design Excellence Award, Milwaukee Art Ctr, 57, First Award for Ceramics, 62. *Mem:* Wis Painters & Sculptors; Wis Designer Craftsmen; Am Craftsmen Coun. *Media:* Acrylic, Clay. *Mailing Add:* 3335 N Bartlett Ave Milwaukee WI 53211

SCHELLSTEDE, RICHARD LEE
ART DEALER
b Tulsa, Okla, Apr 3, 48. *Study:* Northeastern Okla State Univ, BA(bus mgt, tourism promotion). *Collections Arranged:* Five State Area Artists Fine Art Shows, Northeastern Okla State Univ, 75; Five State Artists, Green Country Art Assoc, Afton, Okla, 72-74; American Artists, Green Country Art Assoc, Tulsa, Okla, 67-77; Invitational to America's Outstanding Artists, Int Petroleum Exhib, 76; one-man & small group shows, Green Country Art Ctr, Tulsa, Okla, 74-78. *Pos:* Dir & exec vpres, Green Country Art Ctr, Tulsa, Okla, 75-; co-owner, Schellstede Gallery Fine Arts. *Mem:* Green Country Art Assoc (vpres). *Specialty:* Original paintings, oils, watercolors, acrylics and graphics by outstanding artists through the world; Select antiques; Special Exhibs; Fine Art Auctions. *Mailing Add:* c/o Green Country Art Ctr 1825 E 15th Tulsa OK 74104

SCHENCK, WILLIAM CLINTON
PAINTER, PRINTMAKER
b Aug 19, 47. *Study:* Columbus Col Art & Design, 65-67; Kansas City Art Inst, BFA, 69. *Work:* Va Art Mus, Richmond; Rose Art Mus, Boston; Security Pac Bank, Brussels, Belg; Nat Bank Switz, Geneva; Scottsdale Ctr Arts, Ariz. *Comn:* Paintings, Sky Harbor Int Airport, Phoenix, 79; paintings, IBM Corp, Tucson, Ariz, 81. *Exhib:* Wadsworth Atheneum, Hartford, Conn, 74; Rose Art Mus, Boston, 75; Grand Hornu Gallery, Belg, 76; Edwin Ulrich Mus, Wichita, Kans, 76; West Coast Gallery, Newport Beach, Calif, 79; Navy Pier, Chicago, 81; and others. *Bibliog:* Gregory Battcock (auth), Super-Realism: A Critical Anthology, E F Dutton, New York, 75; John Perrault (auth), Impressions of Arizona, Art Am, 81; Barbara Perlman (auth), Schenck's brand, Ariz Arts & Lifestyle, 81. *Media:* Oil; Serigraph. *Dealer:* Main Trail Gallery 90 North Center Jackson WY 83001; Elaine Horwitch Gallery 4211 North Marshall Way Scottsdale AZ 85251. *Mailing Add:* 144 South 85th St Mesa AZ 85208

SCHEPIS, ANTHONY JOSEPH
INSTRUCTOR, PAINTER
b Cleveland, Ohio, Mar 6, 27. *Study:* Cooper Sch Art, dipl; Cleveland Inst Art, cert; Kent State Univ, MA. *Work:* Akron Art Inst, Ohio; Lakeland Community Col; Massillon Mus Art, Ohio; Butler Inst Am Art, Youngstown, Ohio. *Exhib:* Nat Mid-Year Show, Butler Inst Am Art, 55-74; Avanti Gallery, New York, 71; May Show, Cleveland Mus Art, 73-82; 47th All-Ohio Exhib, Akron Art Inst, 70; Nova Invitational, 76; Cleveland/Toronto 78 Exhib, Harbourfront Gallery, Toronto, 78; one-person shows, B K Smith Gallery, 80 & Univ Columbia Fine Arts Gallery, 80, Mo; Ind Univ, 83; and others. *Teaching:* Prof drawing & painting, Cleveland Inst Art, Ohio, 79- *Awards:* Edwin C Shaw Purchase Award, 47th All-Ohio Exhib, Akron Art Inst, 70; Purchase Award, Nat Mid-Year Show, Butler Inst Am Art, 74; Individual Artists fel, Ohio Arts Coun; and others. *Bibliog:* Article, Ft Wayne J, 3/26/80; article, Cleveland Mag, 6/78. *Mem:* New Orgn Visual Arts, Cleveland. *Media:* Oil, Silkscreen. *Dealer:* Robert L Kidd Asn Inc Bermingham MI. *Mailing Add:* 34720 Sherwood Dr Solon OH 44139

SCHERER, HERBERT GROVER
LIBRARIAN, HISTORIAN
b Brooklyn, NY, May 16, 30. *Study:* Western Reserve Univ, BA(art), 53, MA(art hist), 60, MLS, 63. *Collections Arranged:* Marquee on Main Street: Jack Liebenberg's Movie Theaters, 1928-1941 (auth, catalog), Univ Minn Art Gallery, 82. *Pos:* Art librn, Syracuse Univ, 63-66 & Univ Minn, Minneapolis, 66- *Teaching:* Instr art hist & methodology, Univ Minn, Minneapolis, 66- *Awards:* Res Grant, Am Philos Soc, 67, Univ Minn, 67 & Nat Endowment Humanities, 79. *Mem:* Charter mem Art Libr NAm; Col Art Asn Am. *Publ:* Auth, Program of the thirty-nine ceiling paintings of the Jesuit Church of St Ignatius in Antwerp, painted by P P Rubens in 1620, Am Philos Soc Yearbk, 68; auth, Minneapolis art deco extravaganza, Arts Mag, summer 71; dir, Streamlined Dreams (TV doc), KTCA, 80. *Mailing Add:* 208 Walter Libr Univ of Minn Minneapolis MN 55455

SCHERPEREEL, RICHARD CHARLES
EDUCATOR, PAINTER
b Mishawaka, Ind, Dec 1, 31. *Study:* Univ Notre Dame, BFA & MFA; McMurry Col, MEd; George Peabody Col for Teachers, EdD. *Comn:* STex totems, Tex A&I Univ, Kingsville, 75. *Exhib:* Mid States Artist Exhib, 66-68; Found Exhib, Art Mus S Tex, 70-78; Del Mar Nat Drawing & Small Sculpture Exhib, 71; Tex Fine Arts Asn, 72-74. *Teaching:* Instr art, Irving Pub Schs, Tex, 59-60 & Elkhart, Ind, 60-63; prof & chmn dept art, Bloomsburg State Col, Pa, 64-68 & Tex A&I Univ, 68- *Mem:* Nat Coun Art Adminr (bd dirs, 72-78, secy-treas, 72-78); Art Mus STex (bd mem, 74-); Tex Fine Arts Asn (bd dirs, 71-74); S Tex Art League (pres, 72-73); Coastal Bend Art Educ Asn (pres, 73-74). *Mailing Add:* Dept of Art Tex A&I Univ Kingsville TX 78363

SCHEU, LEONARD
PAINTER, LECTURER
b San Francisco, Calif, Feb 19, 04. *Study:* Calif Sch Fine Arts, San Francisco; Art Students League, drawing with George Bridgeman. *Work:* Ford Motor Co Collection, Dearborn Mus, Mich. *Exhib:* Butler Inst Am Art, Youngstown, Ohio, 68; Holyoke Mus, Mass, 69; Erie Pub Mus, Pa, 70; Anchorage Fine Arts Mus, 71; Nat Drawing Exhib, Del Mar Col, Corpus Christi, Tex; Drawing & Small Sculpture Exhib, Purdue Univ, Ind. *Pos:* Juror, local & nat exhibs, 53- *Teaching:* Instr painting & drawing, Whittier Sch Syst, Calif, 61-70; prof art, Banff Sch Fine Arts, Univ Alta, 62-65; instr painting, drawing & art hist, Orange Coast Col, 62-67. *Awards:* Honorable Mention, Laguna Beach Art Asn. *Bibliog:* M Jackson (auth), article in Laguna Beach Post, 55; Margaret Paige (auth), article in SCoast News, 64; article in St Vincent, Latrobe, Pa, 66. *Mem:* Laguna Beach Art Asn (mem bd, 56-, pres, 56-57, exhib chmn, 56-58); Calif Nat Watercolor Soc; Nat Soc Painters Casein (bd mem, 56-59). *Media:* Watercolor, Oil. *Publ:* Illusr, Good ghost towns never die, Lincoln Mercury Times, 54; illusr, Saga of Cinnabar, New Almaden, 54 & Gold rush town that took its time, 61, Ford Times. *Dealer:* William D Gorman 43 W 33rd St Bayonne NJ 07002. *Mailing Add:* 309 Agate St Laguna Beach CA 92651

SCHEYER, ERNST
HISTORIAN, LECTURER
b Breslau, Ger, July 3, 1900; US citizen. *Study:* Univ Freiburg, Ger, Dr rer pol, 22; Univ Cologne, Ger, PhD(hist art), 26. *Collections Arranged:* Art at Time of Goethe, Detroit Inst Arts, 50. *Pos:* Cur asst, Mus Appl Arts, Cologne, 26-29; cur, Mus Appl Arts, Breslau, 29; hon res fel, Detroit Inst Arts, 36- *Teaching:* Prof art hist, Wayne State Univ, Detroit, 38-71. *Awards:* Bronze Plaque, Mich Acad Sci, Arts & Lett, 66; Georg Dehio Prize for Art Hist, Künstlergilde, Esslingen, Ger, 70; Great Order of Merit, Ger Fed Rep, 81. *Mem:* Life mem Thomas Mann Arch; Gerhart Hauptmann Gesellschaft; Eichendorff Gesellschaft. *Res:* Interrelation of art and literature; Northern European art of the 17th and 20th centuries. *Publ:* Auth, Lyonel Feininger, Wayne State Univ, 64 & Circle of Henry Adams, 70; auth, Mary Wigman-O Schlemmer/Dance Perspectives, New York, 70. *Mailing Add:* 201 Kirby Ave Detroit MI 48202

SCHIEBOLD, HANS
PAINTER, INSTRUCTOR
b Freiberg, Germany, Feb 12, 38; US citizen. *Study:* Brigham Young Univ, Utah, BA, 68; Hartford Art Sch of Univ Hartford, Conn, MFA, 70. *Work:* Aldrich Mus Contemp Art, Conn; New Britain Mus Am Art, Conn; Brownville Art Mus, Tex; Wichita Art Mus, Kans; Southern Conn State Col, New Haven. *Comn:* Mural, Sedgewick County Courthouse/County Commissioners, Kans, 81; 12 public murals, Kans Arts Commission & Wichita Arts Board, Kans, 80; 3 outdoor murals, Wesleyan Univ, Conn, 76. *Exhib:* Invitation Acad Exhib, Wadsworth Atheneum, Conn, 71-73; Contemporary Reflections, Aldrich Mus, Conn, 74; one-man shows, Ctr Arts, Wesleyan Univ, Conn, 74, Razor Gallery, New York, 77, Mus Art, Okla, 80 & Wichita Art Mus, Kans, 81. *Teaching:* Asst prof painting & drawing, Wesleyan Univ, Conn, 70-78; asst prof painting & drawing, Wichita State Univ, Kans, 78-82. *Awards:* Best in Show, Greater Hartford Arts Festival, 72; First Prize, Conn Acad, 74; First Prize, Springfield Art League, Mass, 75. *Media:* Acrylic, Graphite. *Dealer:* Lawrence Gallery Portland OR; Paige Gallery Dallas TX. *Mailing Add:* 13705 SW 118th Court Tigard OR 97223

SCHIEFERDECKER, IVAN E
PRINTMAKER, PAINTER
b Keokuk, Iowa, Apr 14, 35. *Study:* Univ Ill, BFA; Univ Iowa, MFA. *Work:* Colorado Springs Art Ctr; Ohio Univ; Dulin Art Gallery, Knoxville, Tenn; Springfield Art Mus, Mo; Montgomery Art Mus, Ala. *Exhib:* Pa Acad Fine Arts Am Prints & Drawings, 65; Nat Print Show, Cent Wash State Col, 75; J B Speed Art Mus, Louisville, Ky, 77; Nat Print & Drawing Competition, Minot, NDak, 79; Prints, Drawings, Watercolor Show, Eastern Ky Univ, 79; 1st Nat-Am Exhib, Owensboro Art Mus, Ky, 79; and others. *Teaching:* Assoc prof printmaking, Western Ky Univ, 64-81. *Mem:* Col Art Asn. *Mailing Add:* c/o Western Kentucky Univ Bowling Green KY 42010

SCHIETINGER, JAMES FREDERICK
SCULPTOR, EDUCATOR
b Baltimore, Md, Sept 27, 46. *Study:* Fla Presby Col, 64-66; Fla Atlantic Univ, 67; Univ SFla, BA, 68, MFA, 71. *Work:* Univ SFla; Norton Gallery Art, West Palm Beach. *Exhib:* Twenty-fifth Ceramic Nat, Everson Mus, Syracuse, 69; New Photographics, Cent Wash State Col, 71; Photo-Media Show, Mus Contemp Crafts, New York, 71; Light and Lens: Methods of Photography, Hudson River Mus, NY, 73; Images-Dimensional, Moveable, Transferable, Akron Art Inst, 73. *Teaching:* Instr art hist, Fla Atlantic Univ, 71; instr ceramics, Univ SFla, 71-72; instr art, Miami-Dade Community Col, Miami, 72-73; asst prof art, Univ Vt, Burlington, 77-78 & Millikin Univ, 78- *Awards:* Winter Park Art Show First Prize in Sculpture, 70; Technol & Artist-Craftsman Symposium Award, Octagon Art Ctr, 73; Las Olas Art Festival Best in Show, Ft Lauderdale, 75. *Mem:* Am Crafts Coun. *Media:* Clay. *Mailing Add:* Art Dept-Millikin Univ 1184 W Main St Decatur IL 62522

SCHIFF, GERT K A
HISTORIAN
b Oldenburg, Ger, Dec 24, 26. *Study:* Albertus Magnus Univ, Cologne, PhD, 57. *Teaching:* Prof mod art hist, Inst Fine Arts, NY Univ, 65- *Res:* Western art from 1750 to the present. *Publ:* Auth, Johann Heinrich Fuessli, Berichthaus-Prestel, 73; auth, Picasso in Perspective, Prentice-Hall, 76; auth, Images of Horror and Fantasy, Abrams, 79; auth, An Epoch of Longing, In: German Masters of the Metropolitan Museum, Metrop Mus, 81; auth, Picasso--the Last Years 1963-1973, Braziller, 83. *Mailing Add:* 575 West End Ave New York NY 10024

SCHIFF, JEAN
DRAFTSMAN

b Keokuk, Iowa, Oct 20, 29. *Study:* Chicago Art Inst, 49-52; Washburn Univ, 57-60; Univ Kans, 61-63; Col San Mateo, 63-64; Univ Denver, BFA, 66; Univ Colo, Boulder, MFA, 70. *Work:* St Paul Fine Art Ctr, Minn; Wichita Art Asn; Bucknell Univ; Francis McCray Gallery, Western NMex Univ; Mulvane Art Ctr, Washburn Univ. *Comn:* Illustration, Scott Printing Co, Denver, 75; illustration, Rocky Mountain Mag, 80 & 81. *Exhib:* Del Mar Col, Corpus Christi, Tex, 79; Ft Hays State Univ, Kans, 79; Minot State Col, NDak, 79; Memphis State Univ, Tenn, 81; Colo Women's Col, Technology Exhib, 81; and many others. *Teaching:* Instr drawing, Univ Colo, Denver, summer 70; instr drawing, Metrop State Col, 70-71, assoc prof, 71-; instr drawing, Temple Buell Col, 70-71 & Denver Community Col, 71; instr video workshops, Univ Colo, Colorado Springs, 75, Colo State Univ, Ft Collins, 77 & Red Deer Col, Alta, Can, 77. *Awards:* Grad Fel, Univ Colo, Boulder, 70; Purchase Award, Stanislaus State Col, 72; Video Workshop fel, Chicago Art Inst, 82; and others. *Mem:* Alliance Contemp Art. *Media:* 2-D Mixed; Electronics. *Dealer:* Sebastian-Moore Gallery 1411 Market St Denver CO 80202. *Mailing Add:* 1276 Corona N Apt B-3 Denver CO 80218

SCHIFF, JEFFREY ALLEN
SCULPTOR, ENVIRONMENTAL ARTIST

b Rolla, NDak, Aug 23, 52. *Study:* Brown Univ, with R Fleischner, BA, 74; Univ Mass, Amherst, MFA, 76. *Work:* Univ Mass, Amherst. *Comn:* Second Mesa (performance), Inst Contemp Art, Boston, 83. *Exhib:* Inst Contemp Art, Boston, 79; solo exhibs, Univ RI, Kingston, 80, Univ Mass Gallery, Amherst, 81, Stux Gallery, Boston, 82 & Danforth Mus, Framingham, Mass, 83; Boston Mus Fine Arts, 82; Brown Univ, 83; Hayden Gallery, Mass Inst Technol, 83. *Teaching:* Instr, Boston Col, 80-81; lectr, Clark Univ, Worcester, Mass, 81- *Awards:* Artist Fels, Mass Artist Found, 75 & 80, Nat Endowment Arts, 76; Rome Prize, Am Acad Rome, 76-77. *Dealer:* Stux Gallery 36 Newbury St Boston MA 02116. *Mailing Add:* 35 Harris St Cambridge MA 02140

SCHIFF, LONNY
COLLAGE ARTIST, CONSERVATOR

b Columbus, Ohio. *Study:* Univ Ill, BA(hons), 53; Worcester Art Mus Sch, fine arts cert, 64; Impressions Workshop, etching study, 65; papermaking study, Carriage House Papers, 79. *Work:* Fogg Art Mus; Rose Art Mus; Am Express Co, Boston; Publishers Clearing House, Long Island; Prudential Insurance Co, Boston; and others. *Comn:* Complete restoration of oils by Enneking, A C Goodwin, Largelliere, and others, 67; restoration painting, Longfellow's Wayside Inn, 68; wall graphics designer, Framingham Union Hosp, 76-; plus others. *Exhib:* Key Gallery, New York, 81; AAO Gallery, Buffalo, NY, 82; Memorial Art Mus, Rochester, NY, 83; Second St Gallery, Charlottesville, Va, 83; Mass Col Art, Brookline, Mass, 83; and others. *Teaching:* Instr oil painting, Adult Classes, Worcester Art Mus, 63-67; instr art appreciation & techniques, Sudbury Art Asn, 68-69; instr printmaking workshop, Charles River Art Ctr, 68, lectr & demonstrator, 69- *Awards:* Founder's Medal, Cape Cod Art Asn, 78 & 79; First Prize, Works on Paper, Fall River Mass, 82; Top Prize, Berkshire Mus, Pitts Field, Mass, 82; plus others. *Mem:* Int Inst Conservators Art, London, Eng. *Res:* Lost old masters; conservation. *Dealer:* Tanglewood Gallery 148 E 89th St New York, NY 10028. *Mailing Add:* Box 2156 Framingham Center MA 01701

SCHILLER, BEATRICE
PAINTER, GRAPHIC ARTIST

b Chicago, Ill. *Study:* Inst Design; Ill Inst Technol; Art Inst Chicago; also with Richard Florsheim, Jack Kearney, Herbert Davidson, Kwak Wai Lau & Stanley Mitruk. *Work:* Standard Oil Bldg, Chicago; Excel Packing Co, Wichita, Kans; Michael Reese Hospital, Chicago. *Exhib:* Nat Exhib Small Paintings, Purdue Univ, West Lafayette, 64; 17th Ann Nat Exhib Realistic Art, Mus Fine Arts, Springfield, Mass, 66; Butler Inst Am Art, Youngstown, Ohio, 67; New Horizons in Sculpture & Painting, Chicago, 70; Draw 82, Boulder, Colo, 82; and others. *Awards:* Reinhard Jahn Purchase Award, Union League Club Exhib; and others. *Mem:* Chicago Soc Artists; Ill Inst Technol (alumni); Arts Club Chicago; N Shore Art League; plus others. *Media:* Watercolor, Graphic. *Dealer:* Art Rental & Sales Gallery Art Inst of Chicago Michigan Ave & Adams St Chicago IL 60603. *Mailing Add:* 3150 N Lake Shore Dr Chicago IL 60657

SCHIMANSKY, DONYA DOBRILA
LIBRARIAN, HISTORIAN

b Yugoslavia; US citizen. *Study:* Univ Belgrade, Yugoslavia, BA & MA(art hist); Univ Cologna, WGer, study with Prof Hans Kaufmann; Univ Hamburg, medieval art with Prof Wolfgang Schone; City Univ New York, MLS. *Pos:* Asst to chmn, The Cloisters, New York, 69-73; asst chief librn, Metrop Mus Art Libr, 73-76, mus librn, 76- *Mem:* Int Ctr Medieval Art (secy, 69-74); Spec Libr Asn, New York (secy/treas, 78); Yugoslav Am Art Asn (bd dir, 79-); Art Libr Soc NAm. *Res:* Wall painting in Byzantine art; classification of art books. *Publ:* Auth, The study of medieval ecclesiastical costume, 71 & On stained glass, 72, Metrop Mus Art Bulletin; auth, The Metropolitan Museum of Art Library Classification System: How it works, Art Libr Soc Newsletter, 76; auth, Museum art libraries collection development policy in the United States, Art Librs J, 81. *Mailing Add:* c/o Metrop Mus of Art Fifth Ave & 82nd St New York NY 10028

SCHIPPER, MERLE SOLWAY
HISTORIAN, CRITIC

b Toronto, Ont; US citizen. *Study:* Univ Toronto, BA, 43; Univ Calif, Los Angeles, MA(art), 71, PhD(art hist), 74. *Collections Arranged:* Americans in Paris: The 50s (auth, catalog), Art Gallery, Calif State Univ, Northridge, 79;

1931 America: The Artists View (auth, catalog), Sierra Nev Mus Art, Reno, 82. *Pos:* Interviewer Los Angeles art community, Oral Hist Prog, Univ Calif, Los Angeles, 76-77; contrib ed, Images & Issues, Los Angeles, 82- *Teaching:* Lectr 20th century art, Calif State Univ, Northridge, 76-78 & Univ Calif, Los Angeles, 77-79; adj instr contemp art, Orange Coast Col, 83- *Mem:* Col Art Asn Am; Int Asn Art Critics; Art Historians Southern Calif; Southern Calif Art Writers (pres, 80-81). *Res:* Twentieth century European and American art. *Publ:* Auth, Jean Helion: The abstract decade, Art in Am, 76; contrib, California: Five Footnotes to Modern Art History, Los Angeles Co Mus Art, 77; auth, Los Angeles Art Community: Felix Landau, Univ Calif, Los Angeles Oral Hist Prog, 78; auth, Katarzyna Kobro: Sculptural innovation in Poland of the 30s, Womans Art J, 80; contrib, Abstract Art in American 1927-1943, Abrams, 83. *Mailing Add:* 768 Westholme Ave Los Angeles CA 90024

SCHIRA, CYNTHIA
WEAVER, TAPESTRY ARTIST

b Pittsfield, Mass, June 1, 34. *Study:* Rhode Island Sch of Design, BFA, 56; L'ecole D'Art Decoratif, Aubusson, France, 56-57; Univ of Kans, MFA, 67. *Work:* Mus Bellerive, Zurich, Switz; Chicago Art Inst, Ill; Columbia Mus of Art, SC; Wichita Art Mus, Kans; Metrop Mus Art, New York. *Comn:* Wall hangings, Commercial Bank of Japan, Los Angeles, 75, Galleria Bank, Houston, Tex, 77, Am Cyanamid, Wayne, NJ, 78, 3D-1 Architectural Firm, Houston, Tex, 80 & Bank Southwest, Houston. *Exhib:* 3rd Triennale Textiles, Lodz, Poland, 78; one-man shows, Mus Bellerive, Zurich, 79, Contemp Crafts Assoc Gallery, Portland, Ore, 82; Textiles 81, Linz, Austria; The Art Fabric: Mainstream, San Francisco Mus Mod Art, 81; Sixth & Eighth Int Biennale Tapestry, Lausanne, Switz; and many others. *Teaching:* Assoc prof textile design, Univ Kans, 76- *Awards:* Textron Fel, 56-57; Louis Comfort Tiffany Award, 66-67; Nat Endowment Arts Craftsman's Fel, 74-75 & 83. *Mem:* Am Crafts Coun. *Mailing Add:* 1700 New Hampshire St Lawrence KS 66044

SCHIRM, DAVID H
PAINTER, EDUCATOR

b Pittsburgh, Pa, Mar 31, 45. *Study:* Carnegie Inst Technol, BFA(painting; scholar), 67; Ind Univ, with James McGarrell & Robert Barnes, MFA, 72. *Work:* Carnegie Mus, Pittsburgh, Pa; Chase Manhattan Bank, New York; Atlantic Richfield Corp, Los Angeles; Fed Home Loan Mortgage Co, Washington, DC; Northwestern Nat Bank, St Paul, Minn. *Exhib:* Ariz Nat Painting Exhib, 77; Nat Drawing Exhib, 78; Directions 1979, Hirshhorn Mus, 79; Painting and Sculpture Today, Indianapolis Mus Art, 80; Between the Freeways, Nickle Arts Mus, Calgary, 81 & Palm Springs Desert Mus, Calif, 82; Carnegie Int, Carnegie Mus Art, Pittsburgh, 82. *Pos:* Dir, Hewitt Gallery, Carnegie-Mellon Univ, 74-75; exec dir, Monongahela Living Arts Ctr, Pittsburgh, 75. *Teaching:* Vis artist painting, Univ Calif, Los Angeles, 77-80 & Otis Art Inst, 80-81; asst prof, Univ Southern Calif, 81- *Awards:* Award for Painting, Kaufman Co, 63. *Bibliog:* Howard Fox (auth), article, Directions, 79; Garrit Henry (auth), article, Art News, 82; Susan Larsen (auth), article, Artforum, 82. *Media:* Mixed. *Mailing Add:* 810 E Third St Los Angeles CA 90013

SCHLAGETER, ROBERT WILLIAM
ADMINISTRATOR

b Streator, Ill, May 10, 25. *Study:* Univ Ill, BA & MFA; Univ Heidelberg, cert; Univ Chicago; Harvard Univ. *Collections Arranged:* Fifty Years of American Art (1900-1950), 68; Martin Johnson Heade: St Augustine Years (with catalog), 81; Robert Henri & George Bellows (with catalog), 81. *Pos:* Dir, Mint Mus Art, Charlotte, NC, 58-66; assoc dir, Downtown Gallery, New York, 67; assoc dir, Ackland Art Ctr, Univ NC, Chapel Hill, 67-; dir, Cummer Gallery Art, Jacksonville, Fla, 76- *Teaching:* Asst prof art hist, Univ Tenn, Knoxville, 52-58. *Mailing Add:* 829 Riverside Ave Jacksonville FL 32204

SCHLAM, MURRAY J
SCULPTOR

b Tyczyn, Austria, May 7, 11; US citizen. *Study:* Langfuhr Univ, Free City Danzig; Arthipenko Art Sch; New York Univ, with Prof Ross; Art Students League, with Robert Brackman; Nat Acad. *Work:* Fordham Univ, Lincoln Ctr, New York; Einstein Med Col, Bronx, NY; Mus Bat-Yam, Israel; Univ Miami, Fla; St Francis Hosp, Miami. *Comn:* Dr Bela Schick, Einstein Med Col, 59; Herman Muehlstein, Muehlstein Plastic Co, New York, 60; Dr Leo Michel, Grossinger Country Club, NY, 62; Rocky Marciano, pvt collection, 64; Leo Lowenstein, Fordham Univ, Lincoln Ctr, 68. *Exhib:* Gillary Gallery, Jericho, NY, 75; Centro Lincoln, Buenos Aires, Arg, 79; Mus Fine Arts, Arg, 79; one-man show, Nat Mus Fine Arts, Santiago, Chile, 77; Metrop Mus, New York, 79; and others. *Pos:* Art dir, Grossinger Hotel, 53-67; art dir, Second Masonic Dist, 62-64. *Teaching:* Asst dir sculpture, Art Life Sch, New York, 53-57; instr drawing, City Col New York, 61-63; instr sculpture, Albert Pels Art Sch, New York, 64-66. *Awards:* Gold Medal, Second Masonic Dist, New York, 62. *Mem:* Fel Royal Soc Art, London; Vet Art Asn, New York. *Media:* Bronze. *Mailing Add:* 25 Chateau Dr Melville NY 11747

SCHLANGER, JEFF
SCULPTOR

b New York, NY, 37. *Study:* Swarthmore Col, BA; Cranbrook Acad Art, with Maija Grotell. *Work:* Sheldon Mem Art Gallery, Univ Nebr, Lincoln; Mus Contemp Crafts, New York. *Exhib:* Total Cup, Kanazawa City, Tokyo, Kyoto, Japan, 73; Contemp Crafts of the Americas: 75, Ft Collins, Colo, 75; The Object as Poet, Renwick Gallery, Smithsonian Inst, Washington, DC & Mus of Contemp Crafts, New York, 77; one-man shows, State Col of Ceramics, Alfred, NY, 78 & City Univ New York Grad Ctr Mall Gallery, 80; and others. *Teaching:* Instr ceramics, Hunter Col, 75 & Pratt Inst Grad Sch, 77; instr sculpture, State Univ NY, Purchase, 82. *Awards:* Tiffany Found

Scholar, 67; Craftsmen's Fel, Nat Endowment for the Arts, 73; Fel, NY State Creative Artists Pub Serv, 81. *Media:* Clay, Wood. *Publ:* Auth, Maija Grotell, Craft Horizons, 11/69. *Mailing Add:* 556 Stratton Rd New Rochelle NY 10804

SCHLEEH, HANS MARTIN
SCULPTOR
b Königsfeld Schwarzwald, Ger, Oct 9, 28; Can citizen. *Work:* Montreal Mus Fine Arts; Tel Aviv Mus, Israel; Art Gallery Winnipeg; Vancouver Art Gallery; Univ Sherbrooke, Can. *Comn:* Limestone sculpture, Ciba Ltd, Montreal, 56; Swan (carrara marble), Pl Arts, Montreal, 65; copper sculptures, Arthur Maron Enterprises, Montreal, 67 & Cote Neiges Shopping Ctr, Montreal, 70; limestone sculpture, Freiman Stores, Ottawa, 73. *Exhib:* Solo exhibs, Dominion Gallery, Montreal, 60-70, Que Sculptors Asn, Montreal, 65-70; Salon Jeune Sculpture, Paris, 66-67 & Expo 67, Montreal, 67; Exposition Int, Rodin Mus, Paris, 71; and others. *Bibliog:* Guy Robert (auth), L'Art au Quebec Depuis 1940, 40 & Ecole de Montreal, 64, La Presse. *Mem:* Royal Can Acad Arts. *Media:* Stone, Metal. *Dealer:* Dominion Gallery 1438 Sherbrooke W Montreal Can. *Mailing Add:* 5 Shady Golfway #316 Don Mills ON M3C 3A5 Canada

SCHLEMM, BETTY LOU
PAINTER
b Jersey City, NJ, Jan 13, 34. *Study:* Phoenix Sch Design, New York, scholar; Nat Acad Design, New York, scholar. *Work:* United States Navy; 1st Nat Bank Boston; Andrew Mellon Collection; American Telephone & Telegraph; also in many other pvt & public collections. *Exhib:* Am Watercolor Soc; Butler Inst Am Art; Nat Acad Design; Allied Artists Am; Audubon Artists. *Awards:* Gold Medal, Rockport Art Asn, 81; Frederick B Robinson Award, Academic Artists, 81; Dolfin Fel, Am Watercolor Soc, 81; and others. *Bibliog:* Article in Christian Sci Monitor, 67; 100 Watercolor Techniques, Watson-Guptill, 69; and others. *Mem:* Am Watercolor Soc; Allied Artists Am (secy, 64-65); Rockport Art Asn (mem bd, 70-); Boston Watercolor Soc (vpres, 76-); and others. *Media:* Transparent Watercolor, Oil. *Publ:* Auth, Watercolor page, Am Artist, 64 & 76; auth, Painting With Light, Watson-Guptill, 78, 2nd ed, 79. *Dealer:* Guild of Boston Artists 162 Newbury St Boston MA 02116; Grand Central Art Galleries 57th St New York NY. *Mailing Add:* Caleb's Lane Rockport MA 01966

SCHLEMOWITZ, ABRAM
SCULPTOR
b New York, NY, July 19, 11. *Study:* Beaux-Arts Inst Design, 28-33; Art Students League, 34; Nat Acad Design, 35-39. *Work:* Chrysler Mus, Provincetown, Mass; Univ Calif, Berkeley; City Univ New York, Kingsborough Col; Univ NC, Greensboro. *Exhib:* One-man show, Howard Wise Gallery, 61 & 62; Collaboration: Artist & Architect, Mus Contemp Crafts, 62; 12 New York Sculptors, Riverside Mus, 62; Humanists of the 60's, New Sch Social Res, 63; Art in Embassies Traveling Exhib, Mus Mod Art, circulated internationally, 63-64; Retrospective 1960-1977, Kingsborough Col, City Univ New York, 77; and others. *Pos:* Organizing chmn, New Sculpture Group, 57-58. *Teaching:* Instr, Pratt Inst, 62-63; lectr, Univ Calif, Berkeley, 63-64; lectr, Univ Ky, 65; prof, Univ Wis, 65-67; Distinguished lectr, Kingsborough Col, City Univ New York, 70-76; lectr, NY Univ, 78-79, Sculpture Ctr, 80, New Sch Soc Res, 83. *Awards:* Guggenheim Fel, 63; Longview Found, 60. *Media:* Bronze, Steel. *Mailing Add:* 139 W 22nd St New York NY 10011

SCHLEY, EVANDER DUER (VAN)
CONCEPTUAL ARTIST, PHOTOGRAPHER
b Montreal, PQ, Apr 21, 41; US citizen. *Exhib:* Software, Jewish Mus, New York, 70; Information, Mus Mod Art, New York, 70; one-man show, Everson Mus, Syracuse, 73; Project 74, Kunstverein, Cologne, Ger, 74; Video Show, Arts Coun Gt Brit, London Serpentine Gallery, 75; plus others. *Teaching:* Lectr art & archit, Univ Calif, Santa Barbara, 72. *Awards:* Avalanche Mag Art Award, 72. *Bibliog:* Billy Adler (auth), In the Midnight Hour (videotape), GBF, Inc, 69; article, Ramparts Mag, 73; Willoughby Sharp Videoviews Van Schley, Elecric Arts Intermix, New York, 74. *Media:* Videotape, Film. *Publ:* Auth, Signs, 72; contribr, Avalanche Mag, 73; auth, World Run, Flash Art, 74; contribr, Art Press, 74; contribr, Los Angeles Inst Contemp Art J, 75. *Mailing Add:* Box 309 Topanga CA 90290

SCHLICHER, KARL THEODORE
PAINTER, HISTORIAN
b Terre Haute, Ind, May 14, 05. *Study:* Univ Wis, BS & MS; Colt Sch Art; Art Inst Chicago; Univ Chicago; Ohio State Univ, PhD; also with Reynolds, Giesbert, Coats, Hopkins, Grimes & others. *Exhib:* Lufkin Art League; Nacogdoches Fair; Fac Exhibs, Stephen F Austin State Univ & one-man retrospective, 75; one-man exhib of recent paintings, 78; Exhib Three, 81. *Pos:* Ed & publ, Trends in Art Educ, 51-56. *Teaching:* Prof art, Stephen F Austin State Univ, 48-82, head dept art, 48-65, prof emer, 82. *Mem:* Col Art Asn Am; Tex Fine Arts Asn; Tex Art Educ Asn (pres, 56-58); Royal Soc Arts; Nat Art Educ Asn; plus others. *Media:* Oil, Pastel. *Publ:* Contribr, Texas outlook & Texas trends in art education, Western Arts Asn Res Bulletin. *Mailing Add:* Dept of Art Stephen F Austin State Univ Nacogdoches TX 75961

SCHLIEFER, STAFFORD LERRIG
PAINTER, MURALIST
b Kingston, Jamaica, WI, Jan 29, 39; Jamaican & US citizen. *Study:* Self-taught. *Work:* Nat Mus of Jamaica, Kingston; Papal Collection of the Vatican, Italy; Nat Trust Comn of Jamaica; Olympia Int Gallery, Kingston; Bank of Jamaica, Kingston. *Comn:* Portrait, comn by Adolph R Bernstein,

Chicago, 70; mural, comn by Sinclair T Brody, Jamaica, 72. *Exhib:* Ann Nat Exhib of Painting (Jamaican), Kingston, 71; First Biennial de Sao Paulo, Brazil, 71; World Black & African Festival of Arts & Cult, 75; Artists of the Black Community of Arizona, Phoenix, 81; Atlanta Life Second Ann Nat Art Competition, Ga, 82. *Teaching:* Guest lectr Caribbean art in humanities, Mohave Community Col, Kingman, Ariz, 74-75, instr art, 75- *Awards:* Purchase Award, US Postal Service, Bicentennial Art Contest, Phoenix, Ariz, 76; Second Place Painting, Black Canyon Art Show, Boulder City, Nev, 83. *Bibliog:* Mason Carrol (auth), Desert scenery inspires artist Stafford Schliefer, Mohave Co Miner, Ariz, 74 & 75. *Mem:* Contemp Jamaican Artists Asn; Nat Conf Artists USA. *Mailing Add:* 1055 Gardencrest Dr Kingman AZ 86401

SCHLOSBERG, CARL MARTIN
DEALER
b Los Angeles, Calif, Feb 5, 36. *Study:* Univ Calif, Los Angeles, BS, 58. *Pos:* Dir, Carl Schlosberg Fine Arts, 72- *Mem:* Graphic Arts coun, Los Angeles Co Mus; Univ Calif, Los Angeles Art Coun; Los Angeles Inst Contemp Art; Nat Soc Lit & Arts; Artists Equity Asn. *Specialty:* Contemporary paintings, graphics, tapestry, sculpture; publisher of Lee Waisler editions; twentieth century master prints; twentieth century American sculpture: Aldo Casanova, George Rickey, Oliver Andrews. *Mailing Add:* 15447 Valley Vista Blvd Sherman Oaks CA 91403

SCHLOSS, ARLEEN P (ARLEEN P KELLY)
PAINTER
b Brooklyn, NY, Dec 12, 43. *Study:* Parsons Sch Design, cert; New York Univ, BA; Art Students League. *Work:* Aldrich Mus Contemp Art, Ridgefield, Conn; Am Tel & Tel Longlines, NJ. *Exhib:* Tenth Anniv Exhib, Aldrich Mus, Conn, 74; Contemporary Reflections, 1971-74 Traveling Show, Am Fedn Arts, 75-77; Artists Books USA, Allen Mem Art Mus, Oberlin Col, 79; one-woman show, Diagrams, Rush Rhees Gallery, Rochester Univ, 75. *Collections Arranged:* 10 New York Women Artists (with catalog), State Univ NY, Albany, 72; Abstraction-Alive and Well (with catalog), Brainerd Hall, State Univ NY, Potsdam, 75; Contemporary Reflections 1971-74 (with catalog), Am Fedn Arts, 75-77. *Teaching:* Artist-in-residence art & music, New York Pub Schs, 67-75; guest lectr art, Rochester Univ, 75. *Bibliog:* Robert Palmer (auth), Music: Kitchen sink, New York Times, 10/13/77; Jill Dunbar (auth), Avant-Garde--The other end, The Villager, 12/8/77. *Media:* Audio & Visual Materials. *Publ:* Contribr, Weaving: A Handbook of The Fibre Arts, Holt, Rinehart & Winston, 78. *Mailing Add:* 330 Broome St New York NY 10002

SCHLOSS, EDITH
PAINTER, WRITER
US citizen. *Study:* Art Students League. *Exhib:* Assemblage, Mus Mod Art, New York, 61; Women in Art, Stamford Mus, Conn, 72; one-woman shows, Il Segno, Rome, 68 & 74; Green Mountain Gallery, 70, 72 & 74, Am Acad Rome, 71 & Ingber Gallery, 74, 75, 77 & 79; and others. *Pos:* Ed assoc, Art News, 55-61; art critic for Italy, Int Herald Tribune, Paris, France. *Teaching:* Lectr, RI Sch Design, Rome, Temple Univ, Univ Minn, NYU, Am Acad Rome, Galleria Nazionale D'Arte, Rome and others. *Bibliog:* Allen Ellenzweig (auth), article in Arts Mag, 3/77; Charles North (auth), article in Art in Am, 6/77; Lawrence Campbell (auth), article, Art Am, 10/83; and others. *Mem:* Circolo Pace, Rome. *Media:* Oil, Watercolor, Assemblage. *Publ:* Auth & illusr, Seven Dogs Walk in Rome or More, Prove Dieci, Rome, 74; auth & illusr, The Ziggorat, 78; auth & illusr, Songs of La Serra, Vetrina, Rome, 82; Contribr, The Nation, MS, Village Voice and others. *Dealer:* Ingber Gallery 460 West Broadway New York NY 10012; Galleria Il Segno Via Capolesace 400186 Rome Italy. *Mailing Add:* Via Della Vetrina 18 Rome 00186 Italy

SCHLUMP, JOHN OTTO
EDUCATOR, PRINTMAKER
b Monroe, Mich, Oct 5, 33. *Study:* Wittenberg Univ, study with Ralston Thompson, BS & BFA; Mich State Univ, study with James McConnell, MA; Univ Toledo; Univ Calgary, study with Toshida Yoshida & Sadao Watanabe. *Work:* British Mus, London, Eng; Libr of Congress, Washington, DC; Cleveland Mus of Art, Ohio. *Comn:* Two silkscreen ed, 72-75 & four silkscreen ed, 78, Lakeside Studio, Mich; large silkscreen, Continental Cablevision Corp, Springfield, Ohio, 76; wall mural, Ohio Arts Coun, Mus Walls, Springfield; Cliff Form (print/painting), Springfield City Bldg, Ohio; Commemorative/Dedication Poster (silkscreen), Community Hosp, Springfield, Ohio. *Exhib:* Lutheran Brotherhood Exhib, Minneapolis, Minn, 72; Lakeside Traveling Exhib (50 states), 70-78; Lakeside Exhib, Univ of Mo, 77; Cincinnati Art Mus Exhib, Ohio; Columbus Art League Exhib, Ohio; and others. *Pos:* Art supervision, Delta Pub Schs, Ohio, 56-59; instr & chmn dept, Frostburg State Col, 59-61; chmn art dept, Wittenberg Univ, Springfield, 61- *Teaching:* Art instr printmaking, Frostburg State Col, Md, 59-61; prof printmaking & mod art, Wittenberg Univ, Springfield, Ohio, 61- *Awards:* Int Dimensions Grant, Wittenberg Univ, 75-76; Res & Creativity Grant, Lutheran Church in Am; Fac Develop Res Grant, 79-80. *Mem:* Nat Art Asn; Springfield Art Asn (bd dir, 71-77); Nat Art Educ Asn; Ohio Art Educ Asn (pres, 64-65); Mid-Ohio Col Art Asn. *Media:* Silkscreen, Drawing. *Res:* Hanga, Japanese relief printmaking, public school, arts & crafts techniques. *Publ:* Auth, Arts & Crafts Techniques, 78. *Dealer:* The Lakeside Studio 150 S Lakeside Rd Lakeside MI 19116. *Mailing Add:* 1240 N Limestone St Springfield OH 45503

SCHMALTZ, ROY EDGAR
PAINTER, EDUCATOR
b Belfield, NDak, Feb 23, 37. *Study:* Otis Art Inst, Los Angeles, 59-60; Univ Wash, Seattle, 60-61; Akademie Der Bildenden Kunste, Munich, Ger, 65-66; San Francisco Art Inst, BFA, 63, MFA, 65. *Work:* Frye Art Mus, Seattle; San Francisco Art Inst & M H De Young Mem Art Mus, San Francisco; Mills Col, Oakland; Amerika-Haus, Munich, Ger; Univ Hawaii, Hilo; and others. *Exhib:* M H De Young Mem Art Mus, San Francisco, 69; San Francisco Mus Mod Art, 71; Oakland Art Mus, 79; Springfield Art Mus, Mo, 81; Butler Inst Am Art, Youngstown, Ohio, 81; Crocker Art Mus, Sacramento, 82; Appalachian State Univ, NC, 82; Univ Hawaii, Manoa, 83; and others. *Teaching:* Lectr, Col Notre Dame, Belmont, Calif, 68-70; lectr, M H De Young Art Mus, San Francisco, 69-70; assoc prof, St Mary's Col, Moraga, Calif, 69- *Awards:* Fel, Fulbright, Munich, Ger, 65; Watercolor Award, Chautauqua Inst, NY, 80; KQED Calendar, Bay Area Artists, San Francisco. *Bibliog:* Robert Brawley (auth), Peaceable kingdom series, Lone Mountain Col, 75; Paul Allman (auth), Richmond visit by Art Who, Richmond Independent, 76; Carol Fowler (auth), View Northwest via painting, Contra Costa Times, 77. *Media:* Oil, Watercolor. *Dealer:* Collectors Gallery Oakland Art Mus 1000 Oak St Oakland CA 94607; Scott Gallery Orinda CA. *Mailing Add:* 1020 Whistler Dr Suisun City CA 94585

SCHMALZ, CARL (NELSON), JR
PAINTER, EDUCATOR
b Ann Arbor, Mich, Dec 26, 26. *Study:* Eliot O'Hara Watercolor Sch, summers 43 & 44; Harvard Univ, AB, 48, MA, 49, PhD, 58; Amherst Col, MA, 69. *Work:* Walker Art Mus, Brunswick, Maine; Jones & Laughlin Steel Corp, Cleveland, Ohio; Diners Club Am; Blue Cross-Blue Shield; Hampshire Col; plus others. *Exhib:* Am Watercolor Soc, 66, 68 & 70; Watercolor USA, Springfield, Mo, 70; Wichita Centennial Nat Art Exhib, Kans, 70; Wall of Fame Bicentennial Exhib, Baltimore Watercolor Soc, 76; Boston Atheneum, 79; plus others. *Pos:* Vpres & mem bd dirs, Portland Mus Art, 57-62; art consult, O'Hara Picture Trust, 69- *Teaching:* Asst prof art hist & assoc dir, Bowdoin Col, 53-62; prof art hist, Amherst Col, 62-; dir pvt watercolor workshops, Kennebunkport, Maine, 71- *Awards:* First Prize for Watercolor, Cambridge Art Asn Ann, 47; First Prize for Traditional Watercolor, Virginia Beach Boardwalk Show, 65; Southern Mo Trust Purchase Award, Watercolor USA, 70. *Mem:* Col Art Asn. *Media:* Watercolor, Serigraph. *Publ:* Contribr, A staining and transparent palette, In: Watercolor Portraiture, Putnam, 49; auth, Watercolor Lessons from Eliot O'Hara, Watson-Guptill, 74; auth, Watercolor Your Way, Watson-Guptill, 78; plus others. *Dealer:* Harmon-Meek Gallery 1258 Third St S Naples FL 33940; Mast Cove Gallery K'port ME. *Mailing Add:* 40 Arnold Rd Amherst MA 01002

SCHMANDT-BESSERAT, DENISE
HISTORIAN, ARCHAEOLOGIST
b Ay-Champagne, France, Aug 10, 33. *Study:* Ecole du Louvre, Paris, dipl(Ancienne Eleve), 65. *Collections Arranged:* Permanent exhib, Near Eastern Collections (with catalog), Peabody Mus, Harvard Univ, 68; The Legacy of Sumer, the First Civilization (with catalog & children's catalog), 75 & Ancient Persia--The Art of an Empire, 78, Univ Tex Art Mus. *Teaching:* Assoc prof Paleolithic art & ancient Near East, Univ Tex, Austin, 72- *Awards:* Radcliffe Fel, Radcliffe Inst, Cambridge, Mass, 69-71; Nat Endowment Arts Grant, 74-75 & 77-78; Nat Endowment Humanities, 79-80. *Mem:* Archaeol Inst Am (pres, Cent Tex Chap, 74-76); fel Radcliffe Inst; Am Oriental Studies; fel Am Anthropological Asn. *Publ:* Auth, The earliest uses of clay in Anatolia, Anatolian Studies, Vol 27, 78; auth, Reckoning before writing, Archaeol, Vol 32, 79; ed, Early Technologies, Undena Publ, 79; auth, Decipherment of the Earliest Tablets, Science, Vol 211, 81; auth, The Envelopes that Bear the First Writing, Technology and Culture, Vol 21, No 3, 80. *Mailing Add:* 11 Hull Circle Austin TX 78746

SCHMECKEBIER, LAURENCE E
HISTORIAN, SCULPTOR
b Chicago Heights, Ill, Mar 1, 06. *Study:* Univ Wis, BA, 27; Univ Marburg, 27-28; Sorbonne, 28; Univ Munich, PhD, 30. *Work:* Syracuse Univ Collection. *Exhib:* Cleveland Mus Ann May Show, 49-54; Rochester Mem Mus Finger Lakes Exhib, 55-57; Regional Artists Exhib, Everson Mus, Syracuse, 56, 57, 59 & 60; Cent NY Artists, 56, 58 & 59; Corning Glass Ctr Ann May Show, Munson-Williams Proctor Inst, Utica, NY, 70. *Teaching:* Asst prof art hist, Univ Wis-Madison, 31-38; prof fine arts & chmn dept, Univ Minn, Minneapolis, 38-46; prof art hist & dir, Cleveland Inst Art, 46-54; prof fine arts & dean, Syracuse Univ, 54-71, emer prof, 71- *Awards:* Cert of Merit, May Show, Cleveland Mus Art, 49-51; George L Herdle Award, Rochester Mem Mus, 55; First Prize for Sculpture, Chautauqua Art Asn Exhib, 56. *Mem:* Col Art Asn Am; Appraisers Asn Am. *Res:* Italian Renaissance painting; modern Mexican art; contemporary American art. *Publ:* Auth, Art in Red Wing, 46; auth, Ivan Mestrovic, Sculptor and Patriot, 59; auth, The Art of A Henry Nordhausen, Phoenix Publ, 80; ed & auth preface & epilogue to Alexandra K Schmeckebier's Princess in Paradise, Phoenix Publ, 81; auth, A New Handbook of Italian Renaissance Painting, Hacker, 81; and others. *Mailing Add:* RD 1 Lyme NH 03768

SCHMID, RICHARD ALAN
PAINTER
b Chicago, Ill, Oct 5, 34. *Study:* Am Acad Art, Chicago, 52-55, with William Mosby. *Exhib:* Invitational Drawing Exhib, Otis Art Inst, Los Angeles, 66; 33rd Ann, Butler Inst Am Art, Youngstown, Ohio, 68; 23rd Ann Drawing Biennial, Norfolk Mus Arts & Sci, 69; 164th Ann, Pa Acad Fine Arts, Philadelphia, 69; Am Watercolor Soc Ann, Nat Acad Design Galleries, New York, 70-71; and many one-man shows throughout US, 58-72. *Awards:* Jane

Peterson Prize, Allied Artists Am, 67; Gold Medal of Honor, Am Watercolor Soc, 71, Gold Medal of Honor for Marianne, Am Artist, 72; and others. *Media:* Oil, Watercolor. *Publ:* Auth, Richard Schmid Paints the Figure, 73 & auth, Richard Schmid Paints Landscapes, 75, Watson-Guptill. *Dealer:* Talisman Gallery 115 SE 12th Bartlesville OK 74003. *Mailing Add:* Voltaires Gallery Rte 7 New Milford CT 06776

SCHMIDT, ARNOLD ALFRED
PAINTER, SCULPTOR
b Plainfield, NJ, Jan 9, 30. *Study:* Art Students League, 49-50; Cooper Union, cert, 56; Hunter Col, BA & MA, 65; also with Hannes Beckmann, Neil Welliver & Tony Smith. *Work:* Mus Mod Art; Rose Art Inst, Brandeis Univ; Newark Mus; Fairleigh Dickinson Univ; Stedelijk Mus, Schiedam, Netherlands. *Exhib:* The Responsive Eye, 65, Optical Art, 66 & Recent Acquisitions, 66, Mus Mod Art, New York; Op Art and Others, Newark Mus, 67; Form and Color, Stedelijk Mus, 67; American Paintings of the Nineteen Sixties, Currier Mus Art, 72; plus others. *Bibliog:* Alfred Barr (auth), What is Modern Art, 67 & Painting and Sculpture in the Museum of Modern Art 1929-1967, Mus Mod Art; Ray Faulkner & Edwin Ilegfeld (auth), Art Today, Holt, Reinhart & Winston, 69. *Media:* Acrylic. *Mailing Add:* 505 La Guardia Pl New York NY 10012

SCHMIDT, CHARLES
PAINTER
b Pittsburgh, Pa, Mar 4, 39. *Study:* Carnegie-Mellon Univ, Pittsburgh, BFA(painting), 60; Cranbrook Acad Art, Bloomfield Hills, Mich, MFA(painting), 67. *Work:* Nat Air & Space Mus, Nat Gallery Art Rosenwald Collection, DC; San Francisco Mus Art; Salt Lake Art Ctr, Utah; Butler Mus, Youngstown, Ohio. *Comn:* Painting, Nat Aeronautics & Space Admin, 81, 82 & 83. *Exhib:* 164th Ann Exhib, Pa Acad Fine Arts, Philadelphia, 69; Nat Drawing Exhib, San Francisco Mus Art, 70; one-man shows, Lowe Art Mus, Syracuse Univ, NY, 73 & Salt Lake Art Ctr, Utah, 74; Mich Artrain, Midwest Touring Exhib, Upper Midwest, 74; Small Works, Newcastle upon Tyne Polytech Mus Art, Eng, 79; and many other group and one-man shows. *Pos:* Calligrapher, White House Social Staff, DC, 61-62. *Teaching:* Instr, Atlanta Col Art, Ga, 63-65; assoc prof, Tyler Sch Art, Temple Univ, Philadelphia, 67-81, prof, 81-; asst prof, Temple Abroad Tyler Sch Art Rome, Italy, 70-72. *Awards:* Dana Watercolor Medal, Pa Acad Fine Arts, 69; Purchase Awards, Rutgers Univ, Camden, NJ, 75 & Southern Ill Univ, Carbondale, 75. *Bibliog:* Art for armor, Life Mag, 9/21/53; Life on the new frontier, Look Mag, 1/2/62; The watercolor page, Am Artist Mag, 10/77. *Media:* Multimedia. *Publ:* Illusr, Bioscience, by Platt & Reid, Reinhold Publ, 67. *Dealer:* Rosenfeld Gallery 113 Arch St Philadelphia PA 19106; Capricorn Gallery Bethesda MD. *Mailing Add:* 347 Harrison Ave Elkins Park PA 19117

SCHMIDT, EDWARD WILLIAM
PAINTER, MURALIST
b Ann Arbor, Mich, April 19, 46. *Study:* Art Students League, with R Beverly Hale, 66-69; Pratt Inst, BFA, 71; Ecole Beaux Arts, Paris, with R Chaplain-midi, 67-68; Brooklyn Col, with P Pearlstein, MFA, 74. *Work:* Bayly Mus Art, Univ Va, Charlottesville; Am Acad Rome; Elizabeth Greenshields Found, Montreal. *Comn:* Posters, Pratt Inst, 75 & 76; interior murals, Allegra Indust, New York, 77; poster, New York Acad Art, 82. *Exhib:* Salon Nat Beaux Arts, Grand Palais, Paris, 68; Huit Voyages a Ners, Mus Grande Combe, Ales, France, 79; solo exhib, Bayly Mus Art, Univ Va, Charlottesville, 80; Nat Exhib, Nat Acd Design, New York, 82; Figurative Artists, Grand Cent Gallery, New York, 83. *Teaching:* Instr drawing, New York Acad Art, 84. *Awards:* Elizabeth Greenshields Found Grant, 72; Rome Prize Fel, Am Acad Rome, 82-83. *Bibliog:* Jed Perl (auth), Life of the object, 12/77 & George M Tapley (auth), Arcadian ethos, 2/83, Arts Mag; Lawrence Campbell (auth), article, Art in Am, 2/83. *Mem:* Soc Artists & Anatomists. *Media:* Oil. *Mailing Add:* c/o Robert Schoelkopf Gallery 825 Madison Ave New York NY 10021

SCHMIDT, FREDERICK LEE
PAINTER, EDUCATOR
b Hays, Kans, Dec 11, 37. *Study:* Univ Northern Colo, BA; Univ Iowa, with Eugene Ludins & Stuart Edie, MFA; also with Joe Patrick & Howard Rogovin. *Work:* Joint Educ Consortium, Arkadelphia, Ark; Worthen Bank, Little Rock, Ark; Univ Iowa; Southeast Ark Arts Ctr, Pine Bluff; Ark Arts Ctr, Little Rock; and others. *Comn:* Stuck, Frier, Lane, Scott Archit, 82. *Exhib:* Little Rock Arts & Design Fair, 77; 12th Ann Ark Artists Exhib, 78 & 79; 23rd & 24th Ann Delta Exhibs, Little Rock, Ark, 80 & 81; Arkansas Art on Exhibit, Arkadelphia, 82; Fourth Ann Nat Art Exhib, Oklahoma City; and others. *Teaching:* Asst prof art, Northwestern Col, 68-70, Western Carolina Univ, 70-72 & Va Polytech Inst & State Univ, 72-76; instr, Ark State Univ & Ark Arts Ctr, 76-77, Univ Ark, Pine Bluff, 77-78 & Ark Arts Ctr, 78- *Awards:* Purchase Awards, 12th Ann Ark Artists Exhib, 79 & 24th Ann Delta Exhib, 81; Governor's Award, Little Rock Arts & Design Fair, 80. *Mem:* Nat Col Art Asn. *Media:* Acrylic, Oil. *Dealer:* Virginia Miller Galleries Miami FL; Cromwell Interior Design & Architects Inc. *Mailing Add:* 217 W 20th Apt C Little Rock AR 72206

SCHMIDT, FREDERICK LOUIS
PAINTER, ILLUSTRATOR
b New York, NY, Mar 21, 22. *Study:* Am Sch Design, scholar, 39-41; Phoenix Sch Art, New York, 45-46. *Work:* Federal Home Loan Bank, Executive Offices, Brooklyn Union Gas Co, Hofstra Univ & Calvary Hospital, NY; Nat Bank NC. *Exhib:* Painters & Sculptors Soc NJ, Jersey City Mus, 70; Bergen Co Artists Guild, Bergen Co Mus, NJ, 75; one-man show, Hofstra Univ Club, Long Island, NY, 78; Knickerbocker Artists, Nat Arts Club, New York, 79-80; Am Artists Prof League, Equitable Life US Gallery, New York, 81.

Pos: Asst art dir, Fairchild Publ Co, New York, 65-77; art dir, Marshall/Altman Adv, New York, 77-82, Newmark, Posner & Mitchell Adv, 82- *Awards:* Second Prize, Salmagundi Spring Auction, 80; Gold Medal, Nat Art League, 80; Lee Loeb Mem Award, Knickerbocker Artists, 81. *Mem:* Nat Art League; Knickerbocker Artists; Artists Fel; Am Artists Prof League; Salmagundi Club. *Media:* Acrylic, Oil. *Mailing Add:* 82-16 34th Ave Apt 6E Jackson Heights NY 11372

SCHMIDT, JULIUS
SCULPTOR
b Stamford, Conn, June 2, 23. *Study:* Okla Agr & Mech Col; Cranbrook Acad Art, BFA & MFA; with Ossip Zadkine, Paris, France, 53; Acad Belle Arti, Florence, Italy, 54. *Work:* Mus Mod Art, New York; Art Inst Chicago; Albright-Knox Art Gallery, Buffalo; Hirshhorn Mus; Whitney Mus Am Art, New York. *Exhib:* Sixteen Americans, Mus Mod Art, New York, 59; The Hirshhorn Collection, Guggenheim Mus, New York, 62; Seventh Biennial, Sao Paulo, Brazil, 63; Sculpture in the Open Air, Battersea Park, London, Eng, 63; Biennial, Middleheim, Belg, 71. *Teaching:* Chmn dept sculpture, Kansas City Art Inst, 54-59; vis artist sculpture, RI Sch Design, 59-60 & Univ Calif, Berkeley, 61-62; chmn dept sculpture, Cranbrook Acad Art, 62-70; head dept sculpture, Univ Iowa, 70- *Awards:* Guggenheim Fel, 64. *Bibliog:* H Read (auth), Concise History of Modern Sculpture, Praeger, 64; Redstone (auth), Art in Architecture, McGraw, 68; Feldman (auth), Varieties of Visual Experience, Prentiss-Hall. *Media:* Cast Bronze & Iron. *Mailing Add:* Sch of Art Univ of Iowa Iowa City IA 52242

SCHMIDT, MARY MORRIS
LIBRARIAN
b Minneapolis, Minn, June 23, 26. *Study:* Univ Minn, BA, 47, MS(libr sci), 54 & MA(art hist), 55; Univ Paris, Fulbright fel, 56-57. *Pos:* Art librn, Univ Minn, Minneapolis, 53-55; cataloger-reference librn, Metrop Mus Art, New York, 57-58; indexer, Art Index, H W Wilson Co, Bronx, 58-65, ed, 65-69; fine arts librn, Columbia Univ, New York, 69-77; librn, Marquand Libr, Princeton Univ, NJ, 77- *Mem:* Art Libr Soc NAm; Col Art Asn Am. *Interests:* Romantic book illustration. *Mailing Add:* Marquand Libr Princeton Univ Princeton NJ 08544

SCHMIDT, RANDALL BERNARD
SCULPTOR, EDUCATOR
b Ft Dodge, Iowa, Oct 2, 42. *Study:* Hamline Univ, BA; Univ NMex, MA. *Work:* Univ NMex Art Mus, Albuquerque; Univ Art Collections, Ariz State Univ, Tempe; Col Art Collection, Ariz Western Col; Univ Art Collections, Pac Lutheran Univ, Tacoma, Wash; Yuma Fine Arts Asn. *Exhib:* Nat Crafts Exhib, Univ NMex Art Mus, 68; 25th Ceramics Nat, Everson Mus Art, Syracuse, NY, 68-70; Media 68 & Media 72, Civic Arts Gallery, Walnut Creek, Calif, 68-72; Southwest Crafts '70, Am Crafts Coun, Los Angeles, 70; Crafts 72, Richmond Art Ctr, Calif, 72. *Teaching:* Asst prof ceramics, Ariz State Univ, 68-75, assoc prof, 75-; guest artist, Pac Lutheran Univ, summer 71. *Awards:* Best of Show, 1st Ann Art Exhib, Phoenix Jewish Community Ctr, 68; Award, Media 68, Civic Arts Gallery, 68; Award, Four Corner Painting & Sculpture Biennial, Phoenix Art Mus, Ariz, 71; and others. *Mem:* Ariz Designer-Craftsmen; Nat Coun Educ Ceramic Arts. *Media:* Ceramics, Vinyl. *Res:* Exploration of expanded vinyl as a sculptural material. *Publ:* Contribr, Teaching Secondary School Art, W Brown Co, 71. *Mailing Add:* 834 W 12th St Tempe AZ 85281

SCHMIDT, STEPHEN
MUSEUM DIRECTOR
b New York, NY, Dec 11, 25. *Study:* Mohawk Col; Univ NMex, BA. *Pos:* Dir, Fire Mus of Tex; regional mus coordr & develop officer, Nat Mus Kenya, 2 yrs. *Mem:* Am Asn Mus; Mountain-Plains Mus Conf; Am Asn State & Local Hist; Nat Trust Hist Preserv; Co Mil Historians; plus others. *Mailing Add:* c/o Fire Mus of Tex 702 Safari Pkwy Grand Prairie TX 75050

SCHMITT, MARILYN LOW
HISTORIAN, EDUCATOR
b Chicago, Ill, May 24, 39. *Study:* Lawrence Univ, Wis, BA, 60; Univ Calif, Berkeley, MA, 62; Seminar, Bibliotheque Royale, Brussels, 62; Yale Univ, PhD, 72. *Pos:* Dir, Int Ctr Medieval Art. *Teaching:* Vis lectureships, Univ of Nebr, 63, Univ of Colo, 75 & Southern Methodist Univ, 77; instr, Dickinson Col, Carlisle, Pa, 64-66; actg instr, Yale Univ, 69-70; asst prof art hist, Southern Conn State Col, New Haven, 70-75; asst prof, Univ Miami, 75-78, assoc prof, 79- *Awards:* Woodrow Wilson Fel, 60-61; Am Asn Univ Women Fel, 68-69; Individual Res Fel, Nat Endowment Humanities, 81-82; and others. *Mem:* Col Art Asn Am; Women's Caucus Art; Soc Archit Hist; Mediaeval Acad of Am. *Res:* Romanesque sculpture in France. *Publ:* Auth, The carved gable of Beaulieu-les-Loches, Gesta, 75; auth, Alice Neel, Arts Mag, 78; auth, Random reliefs and primitive friezes: Re-used sources of Romanesque sculpture?, Viator, 80; auth, Traveling carvers in the Romanesque: The case history of St Benoit-sur-Loire, Selles-sur-Cher, Meobecq, Art Bulletin, 81; and others. *Mailing Add:* Art Dept Univ of Miami Coral Gables FL 33124

SCHMUCKAL, JANET BELL (CYNTHIA SIGNATURE)
MUSEUM DIRECTOR, CONCEPTUAL ARTIST
b Downers Grove, Ill, July 28, 48. *Study:* Univ Ill, Champaign-Urbana, BA, 69; Univ Mass, Amherst, MFA, 71. *Collections Arranged:* Exhibition Howard Hughes, A Legend's Artifacts, 76; Larry Longenecker's Matchcover Expos, 77; Dirt, Mus Temporary Art, DC, 78; Mus Temporary Art Mail: 1976-1978 (auth, catalog), 78 & 36 Hours, 78; Correspondence Art Archives, 76- *Pos:* Dir, Mus Temporary Art, DC, 75-, ed MOTA Mag, 75-79; publisher & ed,

Art Ink Newspaper, Washington, DC, 79-82. *Awards:* Cert of Appreciation for Outstanding Administration, Mayor Marion Barry, Washington, DC, 81. *Bibliog:* Jean Kirshenbaum (auth), Art today, gone tomorrow, Washington Times, 11/23/76; Neal Leavitt (auth), Exhibits come up on short end of things, Los Angeles Times, 7/16/78; Harry Jaffe (auth), Thirty-six hours of access, Unicorn Times, 1/79. *Mem:* Artists Developing a Partnership Today (pres, 80). *Media:* Mixed. *Publ:* Auth, The Book of Suicide, MOTA Press, 81. *Mailing Add:* PO Box 28385 Washington DC 20005

SCHMUTZHART, BERTHOLD JOSEF
SCULPTOR, EDUCATOR
b Salzburg, Austria, Aug 17, 28; US citizen. *Study:* Acad Appl Art, Vienna, Austria; masterclass for ceramics & sculpture. *Work:* Mr & Mrs Hirshhorn Collection; Fredericksburg Gallery Mod Art, Va. *Comn:* Christ (wood), St James Church, Washington, DC, 62, Christ (bronze), 64; bacchus fountain, Fredericksburg Gallery, 67; Christ (steel), St Clements Church, Inkster, Mich, 68; processional cross (bronze), 71; cross (guilded wood), Church of Reformation, Washington, DC, 74. *Exhib:* Washington Artists, Massilon Mus, Ohio, 69; Twenty Washington Artists, Nat Collection Fine Arts, Washington, DC, 70; Art Barn, US Dept Interior, Washington, DC, 71; Int Monetary Fund Exhib, Washington, DC, 75; Franz Bader Gallery, Washington DC, 78-81; and others. *Teaching:* Assoc prof sculpture & chmn sculpture dept, Corcoran Sch Art, Washington, DC, 63-81, prof, 81- *Awards:* First Prize, Washington Religious Arts Soc, 60; First Prize, Southern Sculpture, 66; First Prize Silver Medal, Audubon Soc, 71. *Bibliog:* Off Econ Opportunity (auth), A Face for the Future (film), Booker Assocs, Reston, Va, 65; Tools for Learning (film), Kingsbury Ctr, Washington, DC, 71. *Mem:* Am Asn Univ Prof; Guild Religious Archit; Artist's Equity Asn (pres, Washington, DC Chap, 73). *Media:* Multimedia. *Publ:* Auth, The Handmade Furniture Book, Prentice-Hall, 81. *Dealer:* Franz Bader Gallery 2001 Eye St NW Washington DC 20037. *Mailing Add:* 18 Ninth St NE Washington DC 20002

SCHMUTZHART, SLAITHONG CHENGTRAKUL
INSTRUCTOR, SCULPTOR
b Bangkok, Thailand, Jan 1, 34; US citizen. *Study:* Corcoran Sch Art, Washington, DC, dipl sculpture, 68, dipl ceramics, 70; Univ DC, BA(fine arts), 77; George Washington Univ, MFA(sculpture), 83. *Comn:* Polychromed wood altar relief, Sr Citizens Home, Inkster, Mich; polychromed wood relief, comn by Dr Morton Ehudin for dental off, Oxon Hill, Md, 77; Corten steel standing figure, comn by Mr & Mrs Leon Baer, Alexandria, Va, 77; polychromed wood relief, comn by James Ellison, Capitol Hill, Washington, DC, 77. *Exhib:* Nat Collection of Fine Arts, Washington, DC, 68; Textile Mus, Washington DC, 73-74; Columbus Mus, Ga; Corcoran Gallery, Washington, DC, 75; Phillips Gallery, Washington, DC, 76; one-man shows, Univ DC, 77, Mt Vernon Col, 78 & 79 & Antioch Univ, Md, 79. *Teaching:* Asst instr sculpture, Off Economic Opportunity, Job Corps, 65-66; instr art, Lab Sch, Kingsbury Ctr, Washington, DC, 68-71 & Northern Va Community Col, 78-; lectr studio art, Mt Vernon Col, 78- & Am Univ, Washington DC, 79-; instr art, sculpture, Corcoran Sch Art, Washington DC, 80. *Awards:* Ford Found Scholar in Sculpture, 66. *Bibliog:* Sarah B Conroy (auth), Living in style, Washington Post, 2/71; Benjamin Forgey (auth), Washingtons Artists, Sunday Star, 12/71; Anne Ogden (auth), New Ways with Stained glass, House Beautiful, 8/73. *Mem:* Artists Equity Asn. *Media:* Welded Steel, Woodcarving. *Dealer:* Franz Badger Gallery Washington DC. *Mailing Add:* 1011 E Capitol St Washington DC 20003

SCHNACKENBERG, ROY
PAINTER, SCULPTOR
b Chicago, Ill, Jan 14, 34. *Work:* Whitney Mus Am Art, New York; Art Inst Chicago. *Exhib:* Whitney Recent Acquisitions Show, 67 & Whitney Ann, 67-69; New American Realists, Goteberg, Sweden, 70; Beyond Illustration, The Art of Playboy World Tour, 71-; Recent Acquisitions Show, Art Inst Chicago, 71; Dept Interior Bicentennial Exhib, Corcoran Gallery, Washington, DC; and numerous one-man & group shows. *Awards:* Copley Found Award, 67. *Mailing Add:* 1919 N Orchard Chicago IL 60614

SCHNEEBAUM, TOBIAS
PAINTER
b New York, NY, Apr 25, 21. *Study:* Work Prog Admin, 35-36; City Col New York, BA, 42; Brooklyn Mus Art Sch, with R Tamayo, 46 & A Osver, 47. *Work:* Mus Estado, Guadalajara, Mex; Mus Nat, Cuzco, Peru. *Exhib:* Smithsonian Inst, Washington, DC, 55; Peridot Gallery, 55-70; Univ Nebr, 63; Art Inst Chicago, 64; Univ Colo, 65. *Teaching:* Instr painting, Ajijic Sch Art, Mex, 47-49. *Awards:* Fulbright Fel, 55 & 56; Firefly Fund Award, 75. *Media:* Oil. *Publ:* Illusr, The Girl in the Abstract Bed, 54; auth, Keep the River on Your Right, Grove Press, 69; illusr, Wild Man, Viking Press, 79. *Mailing Add:* 463 West St New York NY 10014

SCHNEEMANN, CAROLEE
PAINTER, FILMMAKER
b Fox Chase, Pa, Oct 12, 39. *Study:* Univ Ill, Urbana, MFA; Bard Col, MA; Columbia Univ Sch Painting & Sculpture, New York; New Sch Social Res, New York; Univ de Puebla, Mexico. *Work:* Mus Contemp Art, Chicago; Erotica Archives Mus, Yugoslavia; also in pvt collections of Billy Kulver, NJ, Arman, Paris & Claes Oldenburg, New York. *Exhib:* Fluxfestival, Forum Theatre, Berlin, 71; Up To and Including Her Limits, Univ Art Mus, Berkeley, Calif & Anthology Film Archives, New York, 74, Palazzo Reale, Milan, 81, Max Hutchinson Gallery, New York, 82-83; and others. *Pos:* Founder-dir, Kinetic Theatre, New York, 63-68; artist-in-residence, Art Inst Chicago, Rutgers Univ, Univ Colo & Univ Ohio, formerly. *Awards:* Nat Endowment

Arts Grants, 74 & 77; Creative Artists Pub Serv Grant, NY, 78; Visual Artist Fel, Nat Endowment Arts, 83. *Publ:* Auth, Kenneth Anger's Scorpio Rising, Film Culture No 32, New York, 64; auth, Love Paint Ritual, Technicians of the Sacred, New York, 69; auth, Banana Hands, Plays for Children to Direct, London, 70; auth, More Than Meat Joy (complete performance works & selected writings), 78 & auth, Carolee Schneemann: Early & Recent Work (monography of painting--constructions 1963-1983), 83, Documentext. *Mailing Add:* 114 W 29th St New York NY 10001

SCHNEIDER, IRA
VIDEO ARTIST, LECTURER
b New York, NY, Mar 2, 39. *Study:* Brown Univ, AB, 60; Univ Wis, MA, 64. *Work:* Mus Mod Art Film Arch, New York; Donnell Film Libr, New York; Anthology Film Arch, New York; Long Beach Mus Art, Calif. *Comn:* Wipe Cycle (video installation, with Frank Gillette), Howard Wise Gallery, New York, 69; Manhattan is an Island (video installation), 74 & Video 75 (video installation), 75, The Kitchen, New York. *Exhib:* Videotape (circuit), Los Angeles Co Mus, Los Angeles, 73; Video Art, Inst Contemp Art, Philadelphia, 75; Videotape, 13th Biennial, Sao Paulo, Brazil, 76; Manhattan is an Island (video installation), Whitney Mus Am Art, New York, 77; Proj XIII (videotape), Mus Mod Art, New York, 77; Time Zones (video presentation), 1980 Winter Olympics, Lake Placid; Time Zones, Everson Mus Art, Syracuse, 80; Whitney Mus Am Art, New York, 81. *Pos:* Ed, Radical Software, Raindance Mag, 70-74; pres, Raindance Found, New York, 72-*Teaching:* Vis lectr video art, Univ Calif, San Diego, 76-77, 78-79 & Cooper Union, New York, 79-81. *Awards:* Film Contest Award, Philharmonic Hall, Lincoln Ctr, New York, Nat Student Asn, 67; Nat Endowment Arts Individual Artist Fels, 76 & 79; Guggenheim Found Fel, 77. *Bibliog:* David Antin (auth), Aspects of the video medium?, Artforum, 76; Russell Conor (auth), Panorama--video gallery, WNET Pub Broadcasting System, 77; Grace Glueck (auth), Critics choice, New York Times, 5/3/81. *Media:* Video. *Publ:* Contribr, Guerillo Television, Holt Rinehart & Winston, 71; co-ed (with Beryl Korot), Video Art, Harcourt Brace Jovanovich, 76; and others. *Dealer:* Electronic Art Intermix 84 Fifth Ave New York NY 10011. *Mailing Add:* 51 Fifth Ave New York NY 10003

SCHNEIDER, JANET M
MUSEUM DIRECTOR, PAINTER
b New York, NY, June 6, 50. *Study:* Queens Col, City Univ New York, BA(fine arts, summa cum laude), 72; Boston Univ Tanglewood Inst, special study, fine arts, 71. *Collections Arranged:* Sons and others: Women Artists See Men (auth, catalog), 75; Urban Aesthetics (auth, catalog), 76; Masters of the Brush: Chinese Painting and Calligraphy from the Sixteenth to the Nineteenth Century (auth, catalog), 77; Symcho Moszkowicz: Portrait of the Artist in Postwar Europe (auth, catalog), 78; Shipwrecked 1622: The Lost Treasure of Philip IV (auth, catalog), 81; Michelangelo: A Sculptor's World (auth, catalog), 83. *Pos:* Curk Queens Mus, 73-75, prog dir, 75-77 & exec dir, 77- *Mem:* Gallery Asn NY State (bd dirs, 79-81); Artists Choice Inc (bd trustees, 79-82). *Media:* Oil. *Dealer:* Prince St Gallery 121 Wooster New York NY 10012. *Mailing Add:* 35-39 159th St Flushing NY 11358

SCHNEIDER, JO ANNE
PAINTER
b Lima, Ohio, Dec 4, 19. *Study:* Sch Fine Arts, Syracuse Univ. *Work:* Butler Inst Am Art, Youngstown, Ohio; Syracuse Univ; Allentown Mus, Pa; St Lawrence Univ; Metrop Mus Art, New York; and others. *Exhib:* Corcoran Gallery Art; Whitney Mus Am Art Ann; 50 Years of American Art, Am Fedn Art, 64; Childe Hassam Fund Exhib, Am Acad Arts & Lett, 71; plus one-man exhibs, 54-78. *Awards:* First Prize, Guild Hall, 67; Marion K Haldenstein Mem Prize, Nat Asn Women Artists, 70; Stanley Grumbacher Mem Award, Audubon Artists, 72. *Media:* Oil. *Mailing Add:* 35 E 75th St New York NY 10021

SCHNEIDER, JULIE (SAECKER)
PAINTER, DRAFTSMAN
b Seattle, Wash, Mar 7, 44. *Study:* Univ Wis, Madison, BS(art;honors); Univ Wis, MFA(painting, two-dimensional), 76. *Work:* Minn Mus Art, St Paul; Algur Meadcws Mus, Shreveport, La; Rutgers Univ, Camden, NJ; State Univ NY Col, Potsdam; Indianapolis Mus Art; and others. *Exhib:* Drawings USA/ 75 Nat Exhib (traveling show), 75 & Drawings USA/77 Nat Exhib (traveling show), 77, Minn Mus of Art, St Paul; American Drawings 1976 & 1978, Tidewater Art Coun & Portsmouth Community Art Ctr, Va, 76 & 78; Smithsonian Travel Exhibs, 76 & 78; Davidson Nat Print & Drawing Competition, NC, 76; Appalachian Nat Drawing Competition, Boone, NC, 76; Bradley Print & Drawing Competition, Bradley Univ, Peoria, Ill, 77 & 79; New England Drawing Competition & Tour, DeCordova Mus; and others. *Teaching:* Adj prof, Williams Col, 82- *Awards:* Purchase Awards, Rutgers Nat Drawing 77, Drawings USA/77, Minn Mus of Art, St Paul, 77 & Bradley Print & Drawing, 79. *Bibliog:* Sandra Conn (auth), Julie Schneider/Jerry Torn at the Fairweather-Hardin Gallery, Reader, 4/2/82; Susan Blake (auth), Julie Schneider/Jerry Torn, Fairweather-Hardin, New Art Examiner, 5/82. *Media:* Graphite, Silverpoint. *Dealer:* Fairweather-Hardin Galleries 101 E Ontario Chicago IL 60611; Quadrum Gallery Chestnut Hill MA 02167. *Mailing Add:* 2312 N Wakefield St Arlington VA 22207

SCHNEIDER, LISA DAWN
DEALER, CRITIC
b Brookline, Mass, Nov 16, 54. *Study:* Boston Mus of Fine Arts Sch, Mass; DeCordova Mus; Syracuse Univ, Visual & Performing Arts Sch; Finch Col; Arts Sch League; Marymount Col, BA(fine arts). *Pos:* Asst dir, Galerie Denise/Rene, 76-77; art critic & art ed, Women's Week, 77-79; dir, Robert

Freidus Gallery, New York, 78; assoc dir, Bertha Urdang Gallery, New York, 79-; exec dir, Cur Consul & Galleries, NY & Boston, 80- *Awards:* Third Annual Interiors Award, Ramco Co Art Collection. *Specialty:* Modern masters and contemporary painting, prints, photography & sculpture. *Mailing Add:* 135 E 54th St New York NY 10022

SCHNEIDER, NOEL
SCULPTOR
b New York, NY, July 31, 20. *Study:* Art Students League, with William Zorach; City Univ New York. *Comn:* Willner Memorial Bas Relief, Bergen Co YMHA, 64. *Exhib:* Two-man show, Meet Sculptor Ser, Sculpture Ctr, New York, 69; 28th Ann Nat Exhib Painters & Sculptors, Jersey City Mus, 69; Salmagundi Club, 70; Nat Arts Club, 74; Brooklyn Mus, NY, 76, 77 & 79; US Customhouse Mus, 79 & 81. *Awards:* Gold Medal Sculpture, Salmagundi Club, 70; First Prize Sculpture, Nat Arts Club, 74; First Prize Sculpture, US Customhouse Mus, 82. *Bibliog:* Feature in New York Sunday News, 4/22/56; interview in New York World Telegram & Sun, 2/21/62; article in New Writers, 9/74. *Mem:* Am Vet Soc Artists; Artists Equity Asn. *Media:* Welded Metal, Wood. *Mailing Add:* 124 Oxford St Manhattan Beach Brooklyn NY 11235

SCHNEIDER, RICHARD DURBIN
CERAMIST, CRAFTSMAN
b Toledo, Ohio, April 5, 37. *Study:* Univ Toledo, BA, 63; Bowling Green State Univ, MA, 68. *Work·* Utah Mus Fine Arts, Salt Lake City, Cleveland Mus Art; Ohio Wesleyan Univ; Libbey-Owens, Ford Collection, Toledo. *Exhib:* Eighteenth Nat Las Vegas Art Exhib, Las Vegas Art Mus, 75; Materials & Techniques of 20th Century Artists, Cleveland Mus Art, 76; Lake Superior 4th Biennial Int Exhib, Tweed Mus Art, Duluth, Minn, 77; Beaux Art Designer, Columbus Mus Art, Ohio, 79; Eighth State Ann Craft Exhibition, JB Speed Art Mus, Louisville, Ky, 80; 28th Annual National Drawing & Sculpture, Ball State Univ, Muncie, Ind, 82; First Annual American Ceramic National, Downey Mus Art, Calif, 83. *Teaching:* Asst prof ceramics, Monroe Co Community Col, Mich, 69-71; assoc prof, Cleveland State Univ, Ohio, 71- *Awards:* Special Award Sculpture, Cleveland Mus Art, 72; Purchase Award Ceramics, Butler Mus Am Art, Butler Mus, 73; Juror's Award for Drawing, Kansas 6th National Exhib, Ft Hays State Univ, 81. *Bibliog:* Lynette Rhodes (auth), Nine artisans, Craft Horizons, 74; Elizabeth McClelland (auth), Ceramic sculpture, Nat Orgn Visual Artists News, 80; Roger Welchans (auth), Dialogue, Ohio Arts J, 83. *Publ:* Auth, Large thrown forms, 76 & auth, Surface decoration on ceramic functional ware, 82, Ceramics Monthly. *Dealer:* Sylvia Ullman Gallery of American Crafts Larchmere Woodland Shaker Heights OH 44121. *Mailing Add:* 2610 Exeter Rd Cleveland Heights OH 44118

SCHNEIDERMAN, DOROTHY
DEALER
b New York, NY, Apr 11, 19. *Pos:* Dir, Harbor Gallery, 65- *Specialty:* Nineteenth & twentieth century fine prints. *Mailing Add:* 24 W 57th St New York NY 10019

SCHNEIDERMAN, RICHARD S
CURATOR, HISTORIAN
b NJ, June 27, 48. *Study:* Hartwick Col, BA, 70; Univ Cincinnati, MA, 73; State Univ NY Binghamton, PhD, 76. *Collections Arranged:* West Meets East, Impressionism in Nincteenth Century Prints, 78-80; J M W Turner Watercolors from the British Museum (auth introd, catalog), 80. *Pos:* Cur prints & drawings, Ga Mus Art, Univ Ga, Athens, 76-, dir, 81- *Teaching:* Adj prof hist art, Tompkins-Cortland Community Col, Cortland, NY, winter 76; lectr mod art, State Univ NY Binghamton, summer 76. *Mem:* Am Asn Mus; Am Soc Aesthet; Col Art Asn; Asn Art Mus Dirs; Print Coun Am. *Res:* History of prints, primarily English and northern European. *Publ:* Contribr, Strictly Academic: Academic Drawings in the Nineteenth Century, State Univ NY Binghamton Art Gallery, 73; contribr, Open to New Art: A Collection of New Art for Jimmy Carter, Ga Mus Art, 77. *Mailing Add:* Ga Mus of Art North Jackson St Athens GA 30602

SCHNEIER, DONNA FRANCES
DEALER
b St Louis, Mo, Mar 30, 38. *Study:* Brandeis Univ, BA; NY Univ, MFA. *Pos:* Pres, Gallery 6M, New York, 66-73; pres, Donna Schneier Inc, New York, 73- *Mem:* New York Hist Soc; Visual Studies Workshop, New York; Soc for Photog Educ. *Specialty:* Photography. *Mailing Add:* 251 E 71st St New York NY 10021

SCHNIER, JACQUES
SCULPTOR
b Dec 25, 1898; US citizen. *Study:* Stanford Univ, AB(civil eng); Univ Calif, MA; Calif Sch Fine Arts, San Francisco. *Work:* Oakland Art Mus, Calif; Legion of Honor Mus, San Francisco; Santa Barbara Mus Art; Honolulu Acad Art; San Francisco Mus Mod Art. *Comn:* US Half Dollar, commemorating San Francisco-Oakland Bay Bridge, 36; archit relief, Berkeley High Sch, Calif, 39; sculpture, Calif Col Arts & Crafts Founders, 72; sculpture, San Francisco Med Ctr, 75; Elizebeth S Fine Mem, Temple Emanu-El, San Francisco, 75; plus others. *Exhib:* 3rd Sculpture Int, Philadelphia Mus, 49; one-man shows, Ryder Gallery, Univ Calif, Berkeley, 65; Judah Magnes Mus, Berkeley, 71 & Willis Gallery, San Francisco, 75 & 77; Vanguard American Sculpture (traveling exhib), Rutgers Univ Mus, 79; Walnut Creek Civic Art Gallery, 83; and others. *Pos:* Chmn adv bd, Nat Sculpture Ctr, Univ Kans, 61-77; mem adv bd, Int Sculpture Symp, Eugene, Ore, 71-74. *Teaching:* Instr sculpture, Calif Col Arts & Crafts, Oakland, 35-36; from lectr to prof sculpture, Univ Calif,

Berkeley, 36-66. *Awards:* First Sculpture Prize & Gold Medal, Oakland Art Mus, 48; Berkeley Citation, Univ Calif, 70; Artist of the Year, San Francisco Art Comn, 79. *Bibliog:* Yvonne Greer Thiel (auth), Artists and People, Philos Libr, 59; Irving Stone (ed), There was Light, Doubleday, 70; Thelma Newman (auth), Plastics as Sculpture, Chilton, 74; plus others. *Media:* Acrylic, Bronze. *Publ:* Auth, The Tibetan Lamaist ritual: Chod, Int J Psychoanal, Vol 37, No 6; auth, Reinforced polyester plastic and acrylic color for sculpture, 68 & Reflection and transparency in carved acrylic sculpture, 70, Proc Nat Sculpture Conf; auth, The cubic element in my sculpture, 69 & Transparency and reflection as form entities in sculpture of carved acrylic resin, 72, Leonardo. *Mailing Add:* 4081 Happy Valley Rd Lafayette CA 94549

SCHNITZER, ARLENE
DEALER, PATRON
b Salem, Ore, Jan 10, 29. *Study:* Univ Wash, Seattle, 47-48; Portland Art Mus Sch, 59-61; studied with Michele Russo. *Pos:* Dir, Fountain Gallery of Art, Portland, Ore, currently; pres, ArtQuake, City of Portland, formerly, trustee, currently; trustee, Reed Col, currently. *Awards:* Portland Art Asn Award, 79; Aubrey Watzek Award, Lewis & Clark Col, 81. *Mem:* Portland Ctr Visual Arts; Portland State Univ Found Bd; Ore Symphony Asn (bd dirs, currently). *Specialty:* Featuring the most noted artists of the Northwest; also sculpture, paintings, prints & pottery. *Collection:* Primarily most noted artists of the Northwest; largest collection outside a museum of works by C S Price, including carvings. *Mailing Add:* 117 NW 21st Ave Portland OR 97209

SCHNITZER, KLAUS A
PHOTOGRAPHER
Study: State Univ NY, Albany, BA, 67; Ohio Univ, Athens, MFA, 71. *Work:* Mus Mod Art, New York; Witkin Gallery, New York; Brookdale Community Col, Lincroft, NJ. *Exhib:* Invitational, Bertha Urdang Gallery, New York, 77; one-man shows, Newark Mus, NJ, 77, Mem Fine Arts Ctr, Univ Colo, Boulder, 81 & Art Inst Chicago, Ill, 81; Hunterdon Art Ctr, Linton, NJ, 78; NY Univ East Galleries, 78; and many others. *Awards:* Nat Endowment Arts Photog Fel, 80; Montclair State Col Alumni Asn Grants, 78 & 80; Montclair State Col Research Grant & Release Time, 81-82. *Publ:* Ed & contribr, Sans Silver, Camera 25 Mag, 10-12/74; illusr, Ancient Glass at the Newark Mus, Newark Mus, 77; auth, New Jersey: Unexpected pleasures, United Jersey Banks & NJ Monthly, 80; auth, Capitol Story, New York State Publ, 82. *Mailing Add:* 187 Montclair Ave Montclair NJ 07042

SCHNORRENBERG, JOHN MARTIN
HISTORIAN, ADMINISTRATOR
b New York, NY, Dec 1, 31. *Study:* Univ NC, Chapel Hill, AB(Phi Beta Kappa), MA, 53; Princeton Univ, MFA, 57, PhD, 64. *Teaching:* Instr art hist, Columbia Univ, 58-59; from asst prof to prof art hist, Univ NC, Chapel Hill, 59-76; chmn & prof art, Univ Ala, Birmingham, 76- *Awards:* Tanner Award for Excellence in Teaching, Univ NC, Chapel Hill, 66; Nat Endowment for Humanities, Jr Fel, 67-68. *Mem:* Col Art Asn; Mediaeval Acad Am; Soc Archit Historians; Archeol Inst Am; Southeastern Col Art Conf (ed, Review, 66-70, pres, 75-76 & 79-80). *Res:* Late gothic architecture, gothic survival, modern architecture. *Publ:* Ed & contribr, A Medieval Treasury From Southeastern Collections, Ackland Art Ctr, 71; ed, Catalogue of Collection ... of Ackland art Center, Chapel Hill, 71; ed & contribr, Comedy in Western Art, Visual Arts Gallery, 78. *Mailing Add:* Dept Art Univ Col Univ Ala Birmingham AL 35294

SCHOELKOPF, ROBERT J, JR
DEALER
b New York, NY, Nov 9, 27. *Study:* Yale Col, BA. *Pos:* Dir & owner, Robert Schoelkopf Gallery, currently. *Mem:* Art Dealers Asn Am. *Specialty:* Nineteenth and twentieth century American painting, sculpture and photography. *Mailing Add:* 825 Madison Ave New York NY 10021

SCHOEN, (MR & MRS) ARTHUR BOYER
COLLECTORS
Mr Schoen, b Pittsburgh, Pa, Apr 17, 23; Mrs Schoen, b New York, NY, Sept 27, 15. *Study:* Mr Schoen, Princeton Univ, BA; Mrs Schoen, Columbia Univ; Grand Cent Sch Art, New York. *Pos:* Mr Schoen, bd adv, Ocean Learning Inst, West Palm Beach, Fla; dir & secr, Aqua Sol Inc; dir, Solar Micro Inc. *Mem:* Parrish Art Mus (Mrs Schoen, pres, 70-76, trustee); Meadow Club, Southampton. *Collection:* Paintings: 18th century English and American furniture; archaeological artifacts; Chinese porcelains; 10th & 12th century Persian pottery. *Mailing Add:* 17 E 89th St New York NY 10028

SCHOENBACH, BERTHA KARP
PAINTER, PRINTMAKER
b Philadelphia, Pa, Dec 1, 07. *Study:* Moscow Technicum, USSR, 34-36; Taller De Grafica Popular, 40; Pratt Inst, New York, 52. *Work:* Israeli Mus, Jerusalem; Rosenwald Col, Libr Congress, Washington, DC; Donglomur Found, Pa; Dropsie Univ, Philadelphia, Pa; Fedn Jewish Agencies, Pa. *Exhib:* Sculpture & Oil Show, Hartford Mus Art, Conn, 54; Ann Award Show, Del Soc Fine Arts, Wilmington, 60; Regional Art Festival, Philadelphia Mus Art, Pa, 63-67; Am Watercolor Soc, Nat Acad Galleries, New York, 66; Nat Watercolor Ann, Pa Acad Fine Arts, Philadelphia, 67-70; Nat Soc Painters in Casein & Acrylic, New York, 69-81; one-woman show, Stanford Univ, Calif, 78; Am Color Print Soc, Trenton Mus Art, NJ, 78. *Pos:* Supervisor of art teaching programs, Pa, 37-39; artist-in-residence, Southern NJ Schools, 70; Temple Asn Retired Professional, 79-80. *Awards:* First Prize, Wilmington Soc Fine arts, Del, 56; Silver Medal, Plastic Club, Philadelphia, 61; Marcell H Stieglitz Award, Nat Soc Casein Acrylic Painters, 69. *Mem:* Artists Equity Asn, Philadelphia Chapter (treas 61-63); Philadelphia Watercolor Club (dir 65-66); Philadelphia Print Club; Nat Color Print Soc; Nat Soc Painters Casein Acrylic. *Media:* Oil, Acrylic; Woodcut, Serigraph. *Mailing Add:* 1810 Rittenhouse Sq #501 Philadelphia PA 19103

SCHOENER, ALLON
DESIGNER, CONSULTANT
b Cleveland, Ohio, Jan 1, 26. *Study:* Yale Univ, BA, 46, MA, 49; Courtauld Inst Art, Univ London, 47-48. *Collections Arranged:* Lower East Side: Portal to American Life, Jewish Mus; Erie Canal: 1817-1967, NY State Coun Arts, 67; Harlem on My Mind, Metrop Mus Art, 69; Word From Jerusalem, Jewish Mus, 72; Life Aboard the Tall Ships for South Street, Seaport Mus, 76; The Family of Nations for the United Nations, Vienna, Austria, 79; Jewish Life in American, New York Pub Libr, 83. *Pos:* Asst dir, Jewish Mus, 66-67; visual arts prog dir, NY State Coun Arts, 67-72; consult traveling exhib, Smithsonian Inst, Washington, DC & Jewish Mus, New York; consult multiple exhib prog, Libr of Cong, Washington, DC. *Awards:* Nat Endowment Arts Proj Fel, 82. *Publ:* Ed, Portal to America, Holt, Rinehart & Winston, 67; ed, Harlem on My Mind, Random House, 69 & Dell, 79; ed, The American Jewish Album, Rizzoli Int Publ 83. *Mailing Add:* Grafton VT 05146

SCHOENER, JASON
PAINTER, EDUCATOR
b Cleveland, Ohio, May 17, 19. *Study:* Cleveland Inst Art, dipl; Western Reserve Univ, BS; Art Students League; Columbia Univ, MA. *Work:* Cleveland Mus Art; Whitney Mus Am Art, New York; Calif Palace Legion of Honor, San Francisco; Columbus Gallery Fine Art; Rochester Mem Art Gallery, De Cordova Mus, Lincoln, Nebr; and others. *Exhib:* San Francisco Mus Art Painting Ann, 53-65; Brooklyn Mus Int Watercolor Exhibs, 59 & 61; Pa Acad Fine Arts Watercolor Ann, 59-69; Calif Palace Legion of Honor Winter Invitationals, 68 & 70; Landscape I & II, DeCordova Mus, 70 & 71; Wichita Art Asn, Kans, 75; Kalamazoo Art Inst, Mich, 75; Expressions From Maine, Hobe Sound Galleries, Fla, 76; 76 Maine Artists, Maine State Mus, 76; 41st & 43rd Ann Butler Art Inst Am Art, Youngstown, Ohio; and other group & one-man shows. *Teaching:* Instr, Munson-Williams-Proctor Inst, 49-53; assoc prof, Calif Col Arts & Crafts, Oakland, 53-61, dir pub rels & spec serv, 53-55, chmn dept fine arts, 55-70, dir, Eve Col, 55-69, prof, 61-, dir, Div Fine Arts, 70-78, dean advanced studies, 78-; vis lectr, Mills Col, 62-63; vis prof, Athens Technol Inst, Greece, 64-65. *Awards:* Award, Calif State Fair, 58; Award, Maine Art Gallery, 61; Childe Hassam Award, Am Acad Arts & Lett, 78. *Mem:* Art Students League; Am Asn Univ Prof. *Media:* Multimedia. *Publ:* Contribr, Art patronage in Greece, Art J, winter 66-67. *Dealer:* Midtown Galleries 11 E 57th St New York NY 10022; Gumps Gallery 250 Post St San Francisco CA 94118. *Mailing Add:* 74 Ross Circle Oakland CA 94618

SCHOENHERR, JOHN CARL
PAINTER, ILLUSTRATOR
b New York, NY, July 5, 35. *Study:* Art Students League; Pratt Inst, BFA, study with Will Barnet & William A Smith. *Work:* Nat Park Serv, DC; US Air Force, DC. *Exhib:* One-man show, New York Zoological Soc, 68; Brandywine Mus, Chadds Ford, Pa, 73; Soc Illusr, New York, 64-68, 71 & 75; Contemp Am Illusr of Childrens Bks, Rutgers Univ, NY, 74; Royal Ont Mus, Toronto, Can, 75. *Bibliog:* Kingman, Foster & Lontoft (auths), Illustrators of Childrens Books 1957-1966, Horn Bk Inc, 68; Diana Klemin (auth), The Illustrated Book, Clarkson N Potter Publ, 70; Contemporary American Illustrators of Childrens Books, Rutgers Univ, 74. *Mem:* Soc Illusr; Illusr Guild; Soc Animal Artists; Rutgers Adv Coun Childrens Lit. *Media:* Polymer Tempera, Oil. *Publ:* Illusr, Rascal, E P Dutton, 63; auth & illusr, The Barn, Atlantic Mo Press, 68; illusr, Julie of the Wolves, Harper & Row, 72; illusr, Dune, Berkeley, 78. *Mailing Add:* RD 2 Box 260 Stockton NJ 08559

SCHOLDER, FRITZ
PAINTER, PRINTMAKER
b Breckenridge, Minn, Oct 6, 37. *Study:* Univ Kans; Wis State Univ; Sacramento City Col, with Wayne Thiebaud; Sacramento State Univ, BA; Univ Ariz, MFA. *Work:* Tucson Mus Art; Boston Mus Fine Arts; Plains Art Mus, Moorhead, Minn; Milwaukee Art Ctr, Wis; Philadelphia Mus Art. *Exhib:* Winter Invitational, Calif Palace Legion Hon, San Francisco, 61; Two Am Painters, Nat Collection Fine Art, Smithsonian Inst, 72; Two American Painters, Madrid, Berlin, Bucharest, Belgrade, Ankara, Athens & London, Dept Interior Bicentennial Exhib, Corcoran Gallery, Washington, DC, San Francisco Mus Art, plus others, 76-77; one-man shows, Oakland Mus, Calif, 77, Scottsdale Ctr Arts, 81, Fresno Art Ctr, Calif, 81, El Paso Mus Art, 82 & Tempe Fine Arts Ctr, Ariz, 83; and others. *Pos:* Artist in residence, Dartmouth Col, 73. *Teaching:* Guest artist, Okla Summer Arts Inst, Quartz Mt. *Awards:* Gov's Awards, NDak, 81, NMex, 83; Distinguished Achievement Award in the Arts, Ariz State Univ, Tempe, 83; and others. *Bibliog:* C AdamsD (auth), Fritz Scholder (film), Pub Broadcasting Serv, 76; Fritz Scholder, Rizzoli Int, 82; Fritz Scholder/An American Portrait (film), Pub Broadcasting Serv, 83; and others. *Dealer:* Marilyn Butler Fine Art 7157 Main St Scottsdale AZ 85251; ACA Galleries 21 East 67th St New York NY 10021. *Mailing Add:* 118 Cattle Track Rd Scottsdale AZ 85253

SCHOLDER, LAURENCE
PRINTMAKER, EDUCATOR
b Brooklyn, NY, Nov 23, 42. *Study:* Carnegie Inst Technol, BFA; Univ Iowa, MA. *Work:* Ft Worth Art Ctr, Tex; Houston Mus Fine Arts; Brooklyn Mus, NY; Dallas Mus Fine Arts, Tex. *Exhib:* American Graphic Workshops '68, Cincinnati Art Mus, 68; Multiples USA, Western Mich Univ, Kalamazoo, 70; Midwest Biennial, Joslyn Art Mus, Omaha, Nebr, 70 & 72; Seattle Print Int, Seattle Art Mus, 71; Libr of Cong 22nd Print Nat, Washington, DC, 71. *Teaching:* Asst prof printmaking, Southern Methodist Univ, 68-73, assoc prof, 73-81, prof, 81- *Awards:* Purchase Awards, Young Printmakers, Herron Art Inst, 67 & Print & Drawing Nat, Okla Art Ctr, 68; Merit Award, Southwest Graphics, San Antonio, 72; Nat Endowment Arts Printmaker's Fel, 75. *Media:* Intaglio. *Dealer:* Delahunty Gallery 2611 Cedar Springs Dallas TX 75201. *Mailing Add:* 3109 Drexel Dr Dallas TX 75205

SCHON, NANCY QUINT
SCULPTOR, INSTRUCTOR
b Boston, Mass, Sept 24, 28. *Work:* Easter Seal Collection, NJ; Ford Alliance Competition, New York; pvt collection of Sen Harrison Williams, Washington, DC. *Comn:* Bronze, Am Speech and Hearing Assoc, Washington, DC, 66; bronze, Easter Seal Collection, NJ, 73. *Exhib:* Univ of NH, 75; Fine Boston Area Artist, Concourse Art Gallery, Boston, 78; one-woman shows, Bristol Mus, RI, 78 & Jerusalem Theatre Gallery, Israel, 79; Richard's Galleries, Hyannis, Mass, 80 & 81; Riji Gallery, New York, 81; and many others. *Pos:* Gov's task force, Accessibility of the Arts (gov's comm), Boston Mass, 72-74; Gov's Coun on Arts & Humanities, Boston, Mass, 72-75; Newton Cultural Affairs Comn, 73-76. *Teaching:* Founder sculpture & arts classes, Jewish Community Ctr, Kansas City, Mo, 57-59; pvt sculpture classes for adults & children, 59- *Awards:* Carroll Ctr for the Blind Mem Award, Mass, 71; Good Samaritan Award, Easter Seal/Sculpture Competition, 73; First Place, Sculpture Competition, Ford Alliance, NY, 74. *Bibliog:* David Freudberg (auth), Nancy Schon Sculptures, WGBH Radio, Boston, 3/23/77; Katharine Childes Jones, Nancy Schon Sculptures, Tech Talk, 5/15/77; Edward Cooper (auth), Interview with Nancy Schon, WBUR Radio, Boston, 6/26/77. *Mem:* New Eng Sculpture Asn (pres & secy, 51); Galerie Refusee, Kansas City, Mo (pres, 55); Cambridge Art Asn; Boston Visual Arts Coun; Springfield Art League. *Media:* Bronze. *Dealer:* Schoenhaus 291 Otis St W Newton MA 02165. *Mailing Add:* 291 Otis St West Newton MA 02165

SCHONBERGER, FRED
PAINTER, SCULPTOR
b Arnhem, Holland, Dec 16, 30; Can citizen. *Study:* Kunst Nyverheid, Arnhem, with Jacob Van Arnhem & Hoff; Uffizi, Florence, Italy, with Kroller Muller. *Work:* Queens Univ, Ont; Reyerson Inst, Toronto, Ont; plus others. *Comn:* Mural, Holy Name Parish, Kirkland Lake, Ont, 59; cement fondu sculpture, County Court House, Kingston, 68. *Exhib:* Lady Dunn Int Exhib, Beaver Brook Gallery, Fredericton, 61; Kingston Art Asn Ann Spring Exhib, 63-68; Expos Provinciale Quebec, 64; Nine Kingston Artists, Can Art Coun, 67-68; two-man show, Agnes Etherington Art Ctr, Queens Univ, Ont, 68 & 75. *Pos:* Dir, Gallery Schonberger, currently. *Teaching:* Instr drawing, painting & sculpture, Ont Dept Educ, Community Prog Br, Ont, 62-71; instr drawing, painting & sculpture, Queens Univ, Ont, 63-70. *Awards:* Grand Prix for Mars-1964 & Fourth Prize for Love, Concours Nat Art Quebec, 64. *Mem:* Soc Can Artists; Can Artists Representatives. *Media:* Oil, Tempera; Fibreglass. *Dealer:* Gilhooly Galleries Billings Bridge Ottawa ON Can K1V 8R7. *Mailing Add:* Gallery Schonberger 326 King St E Kingston ON K7L 3B4 Canada

SCHONWALTER, JEAN FRANCES
PAINTER, SCULPTOR
b Philadelphia, Pa. *Study:* Moore Col Art, scholar, BFA; Pa Acad Fine Arts, grad fel. *Work:* Philadelphia Mus Art; Brooklyn Mus, NY; Slater Mus, Norwich, Conn; New York Pub Libr. *Comn:* Two paintings of Temple B'nai Jeshurun, NJ, 59. *Exhib:* Libr Cong, Washington, DC; NJ State Mus Exhibs; Boston Mus Exhibs; Butler Inst Am Art, Youngstown, Ohio; Nat Acad Design, New York. *Teaching:* Instr life painting, Newark Sch Fine & Indust Art, NJ, 69- *Awards:* Pennypacker Prize for Graphics, Soc Am Graphic Artists, 66; Purchase Prize, NJ State Mus, 67; First Prize & Medal of Honor for Graphics, Nat Asn Women Artists, 71. *Bibliog:* Dona Meilach (auth), Direct Metal Sculpture, Crown, 58; E F Singer (auth), Meet the artist--Jean Schonwalter, Suburban Life, 70. *Mem:* Artists Equity Asn NJ; Soc Am Graphic Artists; Assoc Artists NJ; Nat Asn Women Artists. *Media:* Oil; Bronze. *Dealer:* Randall Galleries 823 Madison Ave New York NY 10021. *Mailing Add:* Nob Hill Apt 1F Locust St Roseland NJ 07068

SCHONZEIT, BENJAMIN
PAINTER
b Brooklyn, NY, May 9, 42. *Study:* Cooper Union, BFA, 64. *Work:* Brooklyn Mus Art; Del Art Mus, Wilmington; Denver Art Mus; Mus Contemp Art, Chicago; Worcester Art Mus, Mass. *Exhib:* Lowe Art Mus, Univ Miami, Fla, 72; Storm King Art Ctr, Mountainville, NY, 73; Art Inst Chicago, 74; Wadsworth Atheneum, Hartford, Conn, 74; Albright-Knox Art Gallery, Buffalo, NY, 75; Whitney Mus Downtown, New York, 75; Baltimore Mus Art, 75-76; Butler Inst Am Art, Youngstown, Ohio, 76; solo exhibs, Michael Berger Gallery, Pittsburgh, 79; Tomasulo Gallery, Union Col, Crawford, NJ, 79; Gibbes Art Gallery, Charleston, SC, 80; Nancy Hoffman Gallery, New York, 81 & DeGestlo Gallery, Cologne, WGer, 81; Brooklyn Mus, 80; and many others. *Dealer:* Nancy Hoffman Gallery 429 West Broadway New York NY 10012. *Mailing Add:* 109 Mercer St New York NY 10012

SCHOOLER, LEE
COLLECTOR
b Chicago, Ill, June 15, 23. *Study:* Roosevelt Univ, BA, 46; Mundelein Col, hon LHD, 72. *Mem:* Am Fedn Arts; Mus Mod Art, New York; Art Inst Chicago; Mus Contemp Art, Chicago (trustee). *Collection:* Contemporary painting and sculpture; pre-Columbian sculpture; antique Oriental rugs. *Mailing Add:* 43 E Elm St Chicago IL 60611

SCHOOLEY, ELMER WAYNE
PAINTER, EDUCATOR
b Lawrence, Kans, Feb 20, 16. *Study:* Univ Colo, BFA, 38; State Univ Iowa, MA, 41. *Work:* Mus Mod Art, New York; Hallmark Collection, Kansas City; Mus NMex, Santa Fe; Roswell Mus Art, NMex; Metrop Mus Art, New York. *Comn:* Fresco (with Gussie Du Jardin), Las Vegas, NMex Hosp, 50. *Exhib:* Houston Southwestern Exhib, 62; Kansas City Mid-Am Exhib, 64; Tucson Festival Art Exhib, 64; Eight State Exhib, Oklahoma City, 68; Biennial Southwestern Exhib, Santa Fe, 72. *Teaching:* Asst prof, NMex Western Univ, 46-47; prof arts & crafts, NMex Highlands Univ, 47-77; artist-in-residence, Roswell Mus, NMex, 77-78. *Awards:* Purchase Prize, Ford Found, 62; Prizes, Southwest Biennial, Santa Fe, 70, 72 & 74; Honorable Mention, Kansas City Hallmark Purchase, 64. *Media:* Oil. *Mailing Add:* Rt 1 Box 245 Roswell NM 88201

SCHORR, JUSTIN
PAINTER, EDUCATOR
b New York, NY, June 10, 28. *Study:* City Col New York, BSS, 50; Columbia Univ Teachers Col, EdD, 62. *Work:* Butler Inst Am Art, Youngstown, Ohio; Waldemar Res Found; Lock Haven State Col; Columbia Univ; NY Hosp. *Exhib:* Brooklyn Mus, 58; Nat Acad Design, New York, 59; Pa Acad Fine Arts, Philadelphia, 63; Butler Inst Am Art, 64; Union Theological Seminary, 83. *Teaching:* Prof painting, Columbia Univ Teachers Col, 62- *Media:* Oil. *Publ:* Auth, Aspects of Art, Barnes, 67; auth, Toward the Transformation of Art, Fairleigh Dickinson Univ, 74. *Mailing Add:* 106 Morningside Dr New York NY 10027

SCHORRE, CHARLES
PAINTER, PHOTOGRAPHER
b Cuero, Tex, Mar 9, 25. *Study:* Univ Tex, BFA, 48. *Work:* Mus Fine Arts, Houston, Tex. *Comn:* Transworld Airways, Kansas City, Mo, 70; Borlenghi Towers, Houston; Westlake Hilton, Houston; Hyatt Regency, Houston; Transco Tower, Houston. *Exhib:* One-man show, Laguna Gloria Art Mus, Austin, Tex, 74; 20th Exhib Prints & Drawings, 75 & Works on Paper/Southwest, 78, Dallas Mus Fine Arts, Tex; New Orleans Triennial, New Orleans Mus Art, La, 80; Houston Area Exhib, Blaffer Gallery/Univ House, Houston, 80; Pages from Books Unpublished, Contemp Arts Mus, Houston, 81; Invitational 81, Longview Mus Arts Ctr, Tex; and others. *Teaching:* Instr drawing & painting, Mus Fine Arts, Tex, 50-55 & Rice Univ, Houston, 56-70. *Awards:* Award, Pages for Books Unpublished, Nat Endowment Arts, 79; Artist-in-residence/Saudi Arabia, Mobil Oil Corp, 80. *Bibliog:* Peter Schjeldahl & C Moser (auths), Art & money in the city of Future-Think, Houston City Mag, 2/81; Susie Kalil (auth), article, Art Am, 12/81. *Dealer:* DuBose Gallery 2950 Kirby Dr Houston TX 77098; Texas Gallery 2012 Peden Houston TX. *Mailing Add:* 2406 Tangley Rd Houston TX 77005

SCHOTTLAND, M
ILLUSTRATOR, PAINTER
b Brooklyn, NY, Nov 18, 35. *Study:* Pratt Inst, BFA, 57; New Sch, printmaking with Antonio Frasconi, painting with Gregorio Prestodino, 58-60. *Work:* Soc of Illustrators Permanent Collection, New York; US Army Military Hist, US Air Force Art Prog, Pentagon & Nat Parks Serv, DC. *Comn:* postage stamp, US Postal Serv, DC, 76; painting, US Air Force, DC, 77; paintings for nat advert, Ingersoll Rand Corp, NJ, 78; painting for bk illus, Franklin Libr, New York/Philadelphia, 79; NASA, 83; and others. *Exhib:* Indust Arts Methods Ann Show, New York, 76; 200 Yrs Am Illus, New York Hist Soc, 77; Soc Publ Designers Ann Show, New York, 78-79; Soc Illustrators Ann Show, New York, 78 & 79 & 50 Yrs of Award Winners, 79; Art in Sci, Cincinnati Mus Art, 79; Smithsonian Inst, 83. *Pos:* Chmn Air Force Art Prog, US Air Force/Soc Illustrators, 76-79. *Teaching:* Guest lectr illus, Soc Illustrators, New York, 77, Sch Visual Arts, New York, 78, Fashion Inst Technol, New York, 79 & Philadelphia Col Art, 79. *Awards:* Hamilton King Award, Soc Illustrators Ann Show, 71; Best of Show, Indust Arts Methods Ann Show, 76; Awards of Distinctive Merit, Soc Publ Designers Ann Show, 77 & 79. *Mem:* Soc Illusrs; Comt to Save New York Libr Picture Collection (vpres, 78-80); Graphic Artists Guild, New York. *Media:* Tempera. *Mailing Add:* 42 W 76th St New York NY 10023

SCHRAG, KARL
PAINTER, PRINTMAKER
b Karslruhe, Ger, Dec 7, 12; US citizen. *Study:* Ecole Beaux Arts, Geneva & Paris; Acad Ranson, Paris; Art Students League, with Lucien Simon, Roger Bissiere, Harry Sternberg & S W Hayter. *Work:* Nat Gallery Art; Metrop Mus Art; Mus Mod Art; Whitney Mus Am Art; Guggenheim Mus; and others. *Exhib:* Several one-man shows, Kraushaar Galleries, New York, 47-; Mod Art in US, Tate Gallery, London & other Europ mus, 56; Am Fedn Arts one-man exhib, Brooklyn Mus & Tour, 62; Whitney Mus Am Art Painting Ann, 65; Assoc Am Artists, 71 & 80; Retrospective Exhib Prints, Nat Collection Fine Arts, Washington, DC, 72. *Teaching:* Dir etching, Atelier 17, New York, 50-51; instr printmaking, Brooklyn Col, 53-54; instr drawing & printmaking, Cooper Union, 54-68. *Awards:* Purchase Awards, Brooklyn Mus Print Ann, 47 & 50; Cert of Merit for Best Exhib US, Fourth Int Exhib Contemp Art, New Delhi, India, 62; Am Acad Arts & Lett Grant, 66. *Bibliog:* US Info Agency staff (auth), Printmakers USA (film), Sidney Stiber Prod, 61. *Mem:* Soc Am Graphic Artists; Artists Equity Asn; Art Students League. *Media:* Oil, Gouache; Graphic. *Publ:* Auth, Some Thoughts on Art, Cable, 58; auth, Happiness and torment of printmaking, Artist's Proof, 66; auth, The artist alone versus the artist in the workshop, New Univ Thought, autumn 67; auth, Light & darkness in contemporary printmaking, Print Rev, 7/77. *Dealer:* Kraushaar Galleries 724 5th Ave New York NY 10019; Associated American Artists 663 Fifth Ave New York NY 10022. *Mailing Add:* 127 E 95th St New York NY 10028

SCHRAMM, JAMES SIEGMUND
COLLECTOR, PATRON
b Burlington, Iowa, Feb 4, 04. *Study:* Coe Col, hon LLD, 54; Amherst Col, hon LHD, 61; Grinnell Col, hon DFA, 72. *Pos:* Pres & trustee, Des Moines Art Ctr, 42-; trustee, Chicago Mus Contemp Art, 69-70; hon chmn, Amherst Col Asn Art, 71- *Awards:* Distinguished Serv Award, Univ Iowa, 71. *Mem:*

Am Fedn Arts (exec comt, 42-, pres, 56-58); Whitney Mus Am Art Friends; Guggenheim Mus Friends. *Interests:* Supporting art departments in colleges and universities; encouraging American contemporary artists. *Collection:* American painting and sculpture from the thirties; some European, Japanese and American prints; African sculpture. *Mailing Add:* 2700 S Main St Burlington IA 52601

SCHRECK, MICHAEL H
PAINTER, SCULPTOR

b Austria; US citizen. *Work:* Ft Lauderdale Mus of Art; Heckscher Mus, New York; Metrop Mus, Miami; Mus Fine Arts, Lausanne, Switz; Tel Aviv Mus & Mus Mod Art, Haifa, Israel; Jacksonville Art Mus; and others. *Comn:* Masada Monument, Hollywood, Fla. *Exhib:* Mus Fine Arts, Montreal, 53-56; Jersey City Mus, 59; Selected Artist Gallery, New York, 61; Mus Mod Art, Paris, 64; Gallery LaCloche, Paris, 64; Gloria Luria Gallery, Miami, Fla; Palm Beach Gallery, Fla; Rauchbach Gallery, Bay Harbor, Fla, 82. *Awards:* Grand Prix Int, Deauville, France; City of Hollywood Appreciation Award, Fla, 75; Academic Gold Medal, Accademia, Italia, 80; Diploma-Maiestro Di Pittura, 82. *Bibliog:* Alfred Werner (auth), Michael Schreck Sculpture, Univ Miami, 75; Richard A Madigan (auth), Michael Schreck Sculpture, Mus Palm Beaches, 79. *Mem:* Life fel Royal Soc Arts, London; Am Fedn Arts; Artists Equity Asn; Accademia Italia, Italy. *Mailing Add:* Artist Studio 3111 N Ocean Dr Hollywood FL 33019

SCHRECKENGOST, VIKTOR
DESIGNER, SCULPTOR

b Sebring, Ohio, June 26, 06. *Study:* Cleveland Sch Art, 25-29; Univ Vienna, Austria, 29-30. *Work:* Cleveland Mus Am Art; Metrop Mus Art; Whitney Mus Am Art; Memphis Mus Art; also in pvt collections. *Comn:* Designer K K Culver Air Trophy, Oberlin Mem Tablet; sculpture for bird bldg, Cleveland Zoo, Pachyderm Bldg, 50; Cleveland Hopkins Airport, 56. *Exhib:* Major mus in US; also Century Progress, Chicago, San Francisco & New York World's Fair, Paris Expos. *Pos:* Head designer, Murray Ohio Mfg Co, Nashville; consult designer, Harris-Intertype Corp & divs; designer, Am Artists Group, Inc, New York; mem fine arts adv comt, Cleveland Planning Comn, 61- *Teaching:* Instr, Cleveland Sch Art, 30-, head dept indust design, 36- *Awards:* Spec & First Award, Cleveland Mus Art, 55; Gold Medal Fine Arts, Am Inst Architect, 58; Visual Arts Award, Women's City Club Cleveland, 73. *Mem:* Fel Int Inst Arts & Lett; Cleveland Soc Artists; NY Archit League; Indust Designers Soc Am (past nat vpres & dir); Am Watercolor Soc; plus others. *Mailing Add:* 2265 Stillman Rd Cleveland Heights OH 44118

SCHREIBER, EILEEN SHER
PAINTER, PRINTMAKER

b Denver, Colo. *Study:* Univ Utah, 42-45; NY Univ Exten, 66-68; Montclair State Col, 75-79. *Work:* Am Tel & Tel Co; Johnson & Johnson; Georgia Pacific; Champion Int Paper; Public Serv NJ. *Comn:* NJ Beach Area, Broad Nat Bank, Newark, 70; Mitzubushi, Barclay Bank of England. *Exhib:* NJ Mus in Trenton, 69 & 73; Am Watercolor Soc Nat, Nat Acad Galleries, New York; Audubon Artists, New York; Pallazzo Vecchio, Florence, Italy; Va State Mus, 75; and others. *Awards:* Best in Show Cash Award, Short Hills State Show, 76; Purchase Award, Tri-State Exhib, Somerset Co Col, 77; Best in Show, Tri State Exhib, Somerset Col, 80; and others. *Bibliog:* M Lenson (auth), article, Newark Eve News, 4/70; article, Newark Star Ledger, 6/74; Addison Parks (auth), article, Arts Mag, 12/79. *Mem:* Nat Asn Women Artists (chmn, 73-75); Artists Equity Asn; Nat Painters & Sculptors Soc; Hunterdon Art Asn; Summit Art Asn. *Media:* Acrylic, Watercolor; Collage. *Dealer:* Reece Gallery 39 W 32nd St New York NY 10011; Laffiche Gallery 145 Spring St New York NY 10012. *Mailing Add:* 22 Powell Dr West Orange NJ 07052

SCHREIBER, MARTIN
SCULPTOR, PAINTER

b Berlin, Ger, Nov 8, 23; US citizen. *Study:* Art Students League; Brooklyn Mus Art Sch; also with Ruben Tam. *Work:* Nassau Community Col; Contemp Arts Ctr, Cincinnati, Ohio; Mary Washington Col, Univ Va; Corcoran Mus, Washington, DC. *Exhib:* Silvermine Ann; Gallery MacKay, Montreal, 68; Razor Gallery, New York, 78; Documenta Gallery, Sao Paulo, Brazil, 79; one-man show, Spectrum Gallery, New York, 71; and others. *Awards:* First Prize in Acrylic, Silvermine, Conn, 65. *Mem:* Hempstead Harbor Artists Asn. *Media:* Chrome Plated Steel; Acrylic. *Dealer:* Pleiades Gallery 164 Mercer St New York NY 10029. *Mailing Add:* 1578 Pea Pond Rd North Bellmore NY 11710

SCHRERO, RUTH LIEBERMAN
SCULPTOR, PAINTER

b New York, NY. *Study:* Columbia Univ, with Oronzio Maldarelli; Art Students League, with George Grosz; Tyler Sch Art of Temple Univ. *Work:* New York Univ Sch Law; Maywood Pub Libr, NJ; Harsen & Johns, Architects, Tenafly, NJ; Nabisco Brands Corp. *Comn:* Bronze portrait Hon Edward Weinfeld, comn by New York Univ Sch Law, 77. *Exhib:* Nat Acad Design Galleries, New York, 74, 76 & 80; Nat Arts Club, New York, 75; solo show, Bergen Mus Art & Sci, 75; Sculptors Asn NJ, Newark, 79; and others. *Awards:* Estelle Goodman Prize, Nat Painters & Sculptors Soc, 75; Hon Mention, Audubon Artists Ann, 75; Harriet J Frishmuth Mem, Catharine Lorillard Wolfe Art Club Ann, 81. *Mem:* Artists Equity Asn New York; New York Soc Women Artists; Sculptors Asn NJ; Catharine Lorillard Wolfe Art Club; life mem Art Students League. *Media:* Acrylic, Watercolor. *Mailing Add:* 377 Rutland Ave Teaneck NJ 07666

SCHREYER, GRETA L
PAINTER, PRINTMAKER

b Vienna, Austria, July 28, 23; US citizen. *Study:* Columbia Univ, with Seong Moy; Art Students League; Pratt Inst; also with Moses Soyer & Fred Taubes. *Work:* Oesterreichische Gallerie Belvedere, Vienna, Austria; Museen der Stadt Wien, Vienna, Austria; Jewish Mus, New York; Univ Windsor, Can; Loyola Marymount Univ, Los Angeles; and others. *Exhib:* Four shows, New Sch Art Ctr, New York, 60-68; Knickerbocker Artists, New York; one-man shows, St Olaf Col, 66 & Fairleigh Dickinson, Univ NJ, 79; Roko Gallery, New York, 72-78; and others. *Teaching:* Guest lectr, Mus Mod Art, Metrop Mus Art, Whitney Mus Am Art & Guggenheim Mus, New York, 69- *Awards:* Grumbacher Awards, 56 & 69. *Mem:* Arch Am Art; Artists Equity Asn New York; Art Students League. *Media:* Oil, Watercolor; Lithography. *Mailing Add:* 54 W 74th St New York NY 10023

SCHRUT, SHERRY
PAINTER, PRINTMAKER

b Detroit, Mich, Apr 27, 28. *Study:* Wayne State Univ, Detroit, BA(art), 50; Long Beach State Col, Calif & Univ Calif, Los Angeles. *Work:* Security Pac Nat Bank, Palm Desert, Calif; Cedars-Sinai Med Ctr, Thalians Bldg, Los Angeles; Int Cult Ctr for Youth, Jerusalem, Israel; Hebrew Union Col Skirball Mus, Los Angeles; Atlantic Richfield Co, Los Angeles. *Comn:* Southern Calif Psychoanalytic Inst, Beverly Hills, 71 & 74; and others. *Exhib:* Los Angeles Inst Contemp Art, Century City, 75; Laguna Beach Mus Art, 76; Works on Paper, Newport Harbor Art Mus, Calif, 77; one-woman shows, Brand Libr & Art Ctr, Glendale, 72 & 79 & Galeria Del Sol, Santa Barbara, 76. *Teaching:* Instr, Craft & Folk Art Mus, Los Angeles, 73-74. *Awards:* Second Prizes, Wayne State Univ, Detroit, 51 & Long Beach Mus Art, 53; First Prize, Westwood Ctr Arts, Calif, 68. *Bibliog:* Barbara Probstein (auth), The fiery art, Home Mag, Los Angeles Times, 73 & Cloisonne enameling, Sch Arts Mag, Davis Publ, 1/75; W F Alexander, auth, Cloisonne extraordinaire, California contemporary artists, In: Cloisonne & Related Arts, Wallace-Homestead Bk Co, 77. *Mem:* Southern Calif Designer-Crafts, Inc (treas, 75-78); Enamel Guild/West (mem bd, 77); Am Crafts Coun; World Crafts Coun; Calif Design. *Publ:* Contribr, Creative Stitchery, Crown Publ, 70; contribr, Porcelain Enamel, Historical, Contemporary, Industrial and Artistic, San Diego Univ Press, 76; contribr, Enameling for Secondary Schools, Lawrence Univ Press, RI, 76; contribr, Crafts, 1976, Southern Calif Designer-Crafts, Inc, 76; contribr, The Center Mag, Ctr for Democratic Insts, Santa Barbara, Calif, 78 & 79. *Dealer:* Lonny Gans Gallery 8225 1/2 Santa Monica Blvd Los Angeles CA 90046. *Mailing Add:* 911 Honeywood Rd Los Angeles CA 90049

SCHUCKER, CHARLES
PAINTER

b Gap, Pa, Jan 19, 08. *Study:* Md Inst Fine & Mech Arts, grad, 33; traveling scholar, Europe, 34. *Work:* Whitney Mus Am Art; Brooklyn Mus; Brooklyn Heights Libr; New Brit Mus Am Art; Archit Digest; plus others. *Comn:* Painting, Woodhull Hosp, 76. *Exhib:* Solo exhibs, Whitney Mus Am Art, 71; Camino Real, Boca Raton, Fla, 80, 81 & 84, Brooklyn Borough Hall Rotunda, 81 & Great East River Bridge Show, Brooklyn Mus, 83; Nat Watercolor Ann, Baltimore Mus Art, 49; Am Painting Today, Metrop Mus Art, New York, 50; Am Painting, Walker Art Ctr, Minneapolis, 50; Whitney Mus Am Art, 52-57, 59, 63 & 73; Art in 20th Century, San Francisco Mus Art, Calif, 55; Brooklyn Mus Biannual, NY, 56; Pratt Inst Gallery, 82; Princeton Gallery Fine Art, 83; plus many others. *Pos:* Mem Fed Art Proj, Works Prog Admin, 38-42. *Teaching:* Prof art, Pratt Inst, 56-75, emer prof, 75- *Awards:* Brooklyn Mus Prize, 48 & 60; Childe Hassam Prize, Nat Inst Arts & Lett, 52; Guggenheim Found Fel, 53. *Bibliog:* Robert Goldwater (auth), article, Mag Art, 53; Carter Ratcliff (auth), article, Art Int, 78; Anne Sharp (auth), article, Arts Mag, 78. *Media:* Oil. *Mailing Add:* Studio 33 Middagh St Brooklyn Heights NY 11201

SCHUELER, JON R
PAINTER

b Milwaukee, Wis, Sept 12, 16. *Study:* Univ Wis, BA, 38, MA, 40; Calif Sch Fine Arts, with Clyfford Still, 48-51. *Work:* Ford Found; Cleveland Mus Art; Glasgow Art Gallery, Scotland; Whitney Mus Am Art, New York. *Exhib:* Richard Demarco Gallery, Edinburgh, Scotland, 71; Whitney Mus Am Art, 75; Cleveland Mus, 75; House Gallery, London, England, 78; Talbot Rice Art Ctr, Univ Edinburgh, Scotland, 81; A M Sachs Gallery, New York, 83; and others. *Teaching:* Vis artist & lectr, Yale Sch Art, Md Inst & Univ Ill. *Awards:* Nat Endowment Arts, 80. *Bibliog:* John I H Baur (auth), Nature in Abstraction, Macmillan, 58; B H Friedman (ed), School of New York, Grove Press, 59; Lloyd Goodrich & John I H Baur (auth), American Art of Our Century, Whitney Mus Am Art, 61. *Mem:* Artists Equity. *Media:* Oil, Watercolor. *Publ:* Contribr, Letter on the Sky, It Is Mag, 60; contribr, New England Review, 79. *Dealer:* A M Sachs 29 W 57th St New York NY 10019; John Stoller 400 Marquette Ave Minneapolis MN 55402. *Mailing Add:* 40 W 22nd St New York NY 10010

SCHULE, DONALD KENNETH
SCULPTOR, INSTRUCTOR

b Madison, Minn, June 17, 38. *Study:* Univ Minn, sculpture with Richard Randall, Robert Mallory & James Wines, BFA, 64, MFA, 67. *Work:* Walker Art Ctr, Minneapolis; Sheldon Art Mus, Lincoln, Nebr; Univ Notre Dame, South Bend, Ind; Wichita Art Mus, Kans; Minn Mus Art, St Paul. *Exhib:* Walker Art Ctr, Minneapolis, 62 & 64; solo shows, Minneapolis Inst Arts, 70, Contemp Arts Mus, Houston, 75, Sheldon Art Mus, Lincoln, Nebr, 78 & Phyllis Kind Gallery, Chicago, 78; Allan Stone Gallery, New York, 73 & 77; Whitney Mus Am Art, New York, 77; Indianapolis Mus Art, 78; Nelson Mus, Kansas City, 83; Karen Lennox Gallery, Chicago, 83; Janet Fleisher Gallery, Philadelphia, 83; and others. *Teaching:* Assoc prof, Wichita State Univ, 67-78;

lectr, Southwest Tex State Univ, San Marcos, 81- *Awards:* Purchase Prizes, Ford Found, 64 & Nat Endowment Arts, 70; 1st Prize, Wichita Art Asn, 72. *Bibliog:* Dona Z Meilach (auth), Woodworking: The New Wave, Crown Publ Inc, 81. *Media:* Wood, Stone. *Dealer:* Karen Lennox Gallery 620 N Michigan Ave Chicago IL 60611. *Mailing Add:* Star Rte 1A Box 77M Dripping Springs TX 78620

SCHULER, MELVIN ALBERT
SCULPTOR, PAINTER
b San Francisco, Calif, Apr 29, 24. *Study:* Calif Col Arts & Crafts, BA, 46, MFA, 47; Danish Royal Acad Fine Arts, Copenhagen, 55-56. *Work:* Hirshhorn Mus & Sculpture Garden, Nat Collection Fine Arts, Smithsonian Inst, Washington, DC; Storm King Art Ctr, Mountainville, NY; Portland Mus Art, Ore; La Jolla Mus Contemp Art, Calif. *Comn:* Sculpture (copper over redwood), Tri-Met Mall, Portland, 77; sculpture (copper over redwood), Deschutes Co Justice Bldg, Bend, Ore, 79; sculpture (copper over redwood), Greenwood Park Mall, Indianapolis, 79; sculpture (copper over redwood), Alderwood Ctr, Lynwood, Wash, 79. *Exhib:* Portland Mus Art, Ore, 73 & 76; Henry Gallery, Univ Wash, Seattle, 75; Wash State Univ, Pullman, 75; Univ Ore Mus Art, Eugene, 76; Palm Springs Desert Mus, Calif, 78; and others. *Teaching:* Prof art, Humboldt State Univ, Arcata, 47-77. *Media:* Watercolor; Wood. *Dealer:* Fountain Gallery Art 117 NW 21st OR 97209 Portand Ave; Gumps Gallery 250 Post St San Francisco CA 94108. *Mailing Add:* c/o Ankrum Gallery 657 North La Cienaga Blvd Los Angeles CA 90069

SCHULLER, GRETE
SCULPTOR
b Vienna, Austria; US citizen. *Study:* Vienna Lyzeum; Vienna Kunstakademie; Art Students League, sculpture with W Zorach; Sculpture Ctr, New York. *Work:* Norfolk Mus Arts & Sci, Va; Mus Natural Hist, New York; Mus Sci, Boston. *Exhib:* Acad Arts & Lett, 55; Univ Notre Dame, 59; Detroit Inst Arts, 59-60; Pa Acad Fine Arts, Philadelphia, 59-60; 150 Years American Art, New Westbury Garden, NY, 60; plus many others. *Awards:* Bronze Medal, Nat Sculpture Soc, Lever House, 75; Goldie Paley Prize, Nat Asn Women Artists, 75; Top Award, Audubon Artists, 80; and others. *Mem:* Fel Nat Sculpture Soc; Allied Artists Am; Audubon Artists; Sculptors League; Nat Asn Women Artists. *Media:* Stone, Wood. *Publ:* Auth, The form is in the fieldstone, Nat Sculpture Rev, fall 71. *Mailing Add:* 8 Barstow Rd Apt 7G Great Neck NY 11021

SCHULLER, NANCY SHELBY
LIBRARIAN, HISTORIAN
b Austin, Tex, Aug 20, 42. *Study:* Univ Tex, Austin, BFA, 63, MA, 69. *Pos:* Prof librn dept art, Univ Tex, Austin, 67-77, cur visual arts, 77- *Teaching:* Lectr, Univ Tex, Austin, 78- *Mem:* Art Libr Soc NAm (pres Tex chap, 80-); Col Art Asn; Mid-Am Col Art Asn (chair, visual resources group, 77-79); Spec Libr Asn; Visual Resources Asn (vpres, 82, treas, 83-). *Res:* Automated process for slide and photograph collections in the visual arts; subject indexing of slides and photographs of works of art; the image bank in visual arts. *Publ:* Auth, Slide collections, Tex Libr J, Vol 47, No 4; auth, Strake College Book of Hours, Gothic & Renaissance Illuminated Manuscripts, Univ Tex, 71; ed, Guide to Equipment for Maintenance and Viewing of Slides, 78, ed & coauth, Guide for Management of Visual Resource Collections, 79 & auth, Conservation, 79, Mid-Am Col Art Asn. *Mailing Add:* 2709 Trail Madrones Austin TX 78746

SCHULMAN, JACOB
COLLECTOR
b New York, NY, July 2, 15. *Study:* Sch Educ, NY Univ, BS. *Collection:* Contemporary painters and sculptors, including works by Baskin, Bloom, Levine, Rattner, Shahn, Weber and Zorach. *Mailing Add:* 117 First Ave Gloversville NY 12078

SCHULSON, SUSAN
PAINTER
b Racine, Wis, Nov 21, 41. *Study:* Lawrence Univ, BA, 63; Univ Ill, MFA(teaching asst), 78. *Work:* Mus Contemp Art, Chicago. *Exhib:* With Paper, About Paper, Albright-Knox Art Gallery, Buffalo, NY, 80; Basel, Switz, 80 & 81; Navy Pier, Chicago, 81; Heresies, Grey Art Gallery, New York, NY, 81; Swen Parson Gallery, 83; Ornaments as Sculpture, Sculpture Ctr, New York, 83; and others. *Pos:* Ed, Le Corbusier Sketchbooks vols II-IV, Archit History Found, New York, 81-82. *Teaching:* Instr printmaking, Evanston Art Ctr, Ill, 75-76, Univ Ill, 76-78, Searing Sch, New York, 80-81; lectr, Univ Chicago, 75-76. *Bibliog:* Joanna Frueh (auth), Susan Schulson at Zolla/Lieberman, Art Am, 79. *Mem:* Col Art Asn; Artist Equity. *Media:* Oil, Acrylic. *Dealer:* Galerie Farideh Cadot 77 rue des Archives, Paris, France. *Mailing Add:* 121 Wooster New York NY 10012

SCHULTE, (MR & MRS) ARTHUR D
COLLECTORS
Mr Schulte, b New York, NY, 1906. *Study:* Mr Schulte, Yale Univ; Mrs Schulte, Hunter Col, Columbia Univ, NY Univ. *Collection:* French, American, Italian and Greek paintings and sculpture. *Mailing Add:* 810 Fifth Ave New York NY 10021

SCHULTZ, CAROLINE REEL
PAINTER, LECTURER
b Evansville, Ind. *Study:* Art Ctr Col Design, Los Angeles, 58; Univ Ill-Urbana, 60-62; Wellfleet Sch, with W Kennedy, 60; Art Mart Sch, Martha's Vineyard; European Sch, Mallorca, Spain, 61; also with Nichola Ziroli & Billy M Jackson. *Work:* Mt Kenya Safari Club, EAfrica; Pavillon, Scottsdale, Ariz;

New Masters, Carmel, Calif; Bruners Fine Art, Santa Rosa, Calif. *Comn:* Wildlife (screen), comn by John Batten, III, Twin Disc Corp, Racine, Wis, 75. *Exhib:* Game Coin, San Antonio, 75; Shikar Safari Club 75, San Diego Zoo, 75; Safari Int, Las Vegas, 76; Abercrombie & Fitch, San Francisco, 76; and other group and one-woman shows. *Pos:* US art dir, EAfrican Wild Life Soc, 75. *Teaching:* Lectr animal anat & Africa through the eyes of an artist, currently. *Awards:* Purchase Award, Comedians Classic, 72; three awards, Palm Springs Festival Arts & Music, 71 & 72; Lenten Art Festival, San Diego, 72; and many others. *Mem:* San Diego Art Inst; La Jolla Art Asn; Desert Art Ctr, Palm Springs, Calif. *Mailing Add:* 10405 Viacha Dr San Diego CA 92124

SCHULTZ, DOUGLAS GEORGE
CURATOR
b Oakland, Calif, Oct 3, 47. *Study:* Univ Calif, Berkeley, BA(art hist), 69, MA(art hist), 72; Inst Arts Admin, Harvard Univ, 71. *Collections Arranged:* Antoni Tapies: Thirty-Three Years of His Work, 77, In Western New York (coauth, catalog), 77, Piero Dorazio: A Retrospective, 79, Kenneth Snelson, 81, Chryssa: Urban Icons, 82 & Robert Motherwell, 83, Albright-Knox Art Gallery. *Pos:* Curatorial intern, Albright-Knox Art Gallery, 72-73, asst cur, 73-75, assoc cur, 75-76, cur, 77-79, chief cur, 80-83, acting dir, 83-; mem professional adv comt, Arts Develop Servs, Buffalo, NY. *Teaching:* Adj prof art hist, State Univ NY, Buffalo, 75-79. *Mem:* NY State Coun Arts; Arts Develop Serv. *Mailing Add:* 1285 Elmwood Ave Buffalo NY 14222

SCHULTZ, HAROLD A
PAINTER, EDUCATOR
b Grafton, Wis, Jan 6, 07. *Study:* Layton Sch Art; Northwestern Univ, BS & MA. *Exhib:* Art Inst Chicago; Chicago Soc Artists; Brooklyn Mus; Ferargil Gallery. *Teaching:* Lectr, American Art Today; head dept art, Francis W Parker Sch, Chicago, 32-40; prof art & design, Univ Ill, Urbana-Champaign, 40-75, emer prof, 75- *Publ:* Coauth, Art in the Elementary School, 48. *Mailing Add:* 2017 Burlison Dr Urbana IL 61801

SCHULTZ, SAUNDERS
SCULPTOR
b July 16, 27. *Study:* Wash Univ, St Louis, Mo, BFA, 50; Univ Ill, Urbana, MFA, 52; special study with Max Beckman, Paul Burlin & Fred Conway. *Work:* Morris Arboretum/Sculptural Park, Philadelphia; Broward Co—Art in Public Places Collection, Pompano Beach, Fla; Univ Ark Art Collection, Little Rock; Sculptured Fountains, Kansas City; Brandeis Univ Art Gallery, Waltham, Mass; and others. *Comn:* Connectors, Blue Cross, Chapel Hill, NC, 72; Solaris, Tampa Electric Co, 80; Cosmos, Juffali Headquarters, Jedda Saudi Arabia, 83; Gray Mist, Orchard Park Hotel, Singapore, 83; and others. *Exhib:* Sculpture Architectural Context, Fordham Univ, New York, 79; Centennial Alumni Exhib, Bixby Hall Gallery, Wash Univ, St Louis, Mo, 79; Sculpture Outdoors, Temple Univ, Philadelphia, Pa, 80; Int Sculpture Competition, Mercer Col, Trenton, NJ, 80; and others. *Teaching:* Guest lectr, Univ Minn Sch Archit, Minneapolis, 77, 79 & 80, Ball State Univ Col, 80 & 82, Univ Miami, 81, Clemson Univ, 82, Univ Okla, Stillwater, 83. *Awards:* First Prize, Univ Wis, Green Bay, 75; First Prize, Broward Co Housing Authority, 80; First Prize, Washington, DC Hebrew Cong, 83. *Bibliog:* Theodore F Wolff (auth), Something for all to share, The Christian Sci Monitor, 4/1/80; William McDougal (auth), Sculpture carves out audience in US, US News & World Report, 9/1/80; Louis G Redstone (auth), Public Art, New Directions, McGraw-Hill, 81. *Mem:* Int Sculpture Ctr, Washington, DC; Full Circle Foun Arts, St Louis, Mo (founder & pres). *Media:* Stainless Steel, Marble/Brick Carving. *Publ:* Contribr, Catfish and Crystal, Doubleday, 60; contribr, Nat Community Arts Program, US Dept Housing Urban Development, 73; auth, Washington Univ Mag, Washington Univ, St Louis, Mo, 79; auth, Religion and Theatre, Bethel Col, St Paul, Minn, 8/80; contribr, A Christian Response to the Holocaust, Stonehenge Books, 81. *Mailing Add:* c/o Scopia 18350 Chesterfield Airport Rd Chesterfield MO 63017

SCHULTZ, STEPHEN WARREN
PAINTER, EDUCATOR
b Chicago, Ill, Aug 28, 46. *Study:* RI Sch Design, 65-67; San Francisco Art Inst, BFA, 71; Stanford Univ, MFA(teaching fel), 74. *Work:* Equitable Life Assurance Corp, New York; Univ Iowa Mus, Iowa City; Stanford Univ; Regis Corp, Minneapolis; Syntex Corp, Saratoga, Calif. *Exhib:* Elvehjem Mus Art, Madison, Wis, 77; Walker Art Ctr, 77; Awards in Visual Arts, Nat Mus Am Art, Washington, DC, 82; Denver Art Mus, 83 & Des Moines Art Ctr, 83; Iowa Artists, Des Moines Art Ctr, 82; Sid Deutsch Gallery, New York, 83. *Pos:* Rockefeller Found artist in residence, Bellagio Ctr, Lake Como, Italy, 84; artist in residence, George Rickey Workshop, East Chatham, NY. *Teaching:* Assoc prof, Univ Iowa, 75-; vis artist, Univ Tex, Arlington, 80. *Awards:* Tiffany Found Fel, 79; Awards in Visual Arts, Southeastern Ctr Contemp Arts, 81. *Bibliog:* Southeastern Ctr Contemp Art, Awards in Visual Arts (film), PBS TV, 83; R S Coburn (auth), Raising veil of emerging artist, Smithsonian Mag, 5/82; All art considered (interview), Nat Pub Radio, 5/19/82. *Dealer:* Sid Deutsch Gallery 20 W 57th St New York NY . *Mailing Add:* 618 Bowery St Iowa City IA 52240

SCHULZ, ANN MARKHAM
HISTORIAN, EDUCATOR
b New York, NY, Mar 3, 38. *Study:* Radcliffe Col, BA, 59; New York Univ, Inst Fine Arts, MA, 62, PhD, 68. *Teaching:* Asst prof Renaissance art, Univ Ill, Chicago Circle, 67-68; vis lectr to vis asst prof & res assoc, Brown Univ, 68- *Awards:* Basic Res Grant, Nat Endowment Humanities, 82-85; Independent Study Grant, Nat Endowment Humanities, 80. *Mem:* Col Art Asn; Soc Archit Historians; Renaissance Soc; assoc mem I Tatti, Italy. *Res:* Venetian Renaissance sculpture; early Renaissance art. *Publ:* Auth, The

Columbia altarpiece & Roger van der Weyden's stylistic development, Münchner Jahrbuch, 71; auth, The Sculpture of Bernardo Rossellino and his workshop, 77 & Antonio Rizzo, Sculptor & Architect, 83, Princeton Univ Press; auth, The sculpture of Giovanni & Bartolemeo Bon, Transactions Am Philos Soc, 78; auth, Niccolo di Giovanni Fiorentino and Venetian Sculpture of the Early Renaissance, CAA Monographs, 78. *Mailing Add:* Art Dept Brown Univ Providence RI 02912

SCHULZ, CHARLES MONROE
CARTOONIST
b Minneapolis, Minn, Nov 25, 22. *Study:* Anderson Col, Hon LHD, 63. *Pos:* Cartoonist, St Paul Pioneer Press & Sat Eve Post, 48-49; created syndicated comic strip Peanuts, 50- *Awards:* Outstanding Cartoonists of the Year, Nat Cartoonists Soc, 55; Outstanding Humorist of the Year, Yale Univ, 57; Emmy Award for CBS Cartoon Spec, 66; and others. *Publ:* Auth & illusr, Boy Named Charlie Brown, 81 & Look Out Behind You Snoopy, 82, Fawcett; auth & illusr, Classroom Peanuts, 82 & You're Weird, Sir, 82, Holt, Rinehardt & Winston; auth & illusr, Some Day You'll Find Her, Charlie Brown, Random House, 82; and more than 200 others. *Mailing Add:* c/o Fawcett World 1515 Broadway New York NY 10036

SCHULZ, JUERGEN
EDUCATOR, HISTORIAN
b Kiel, Ger, Aug 18, 27; US citizen. *Study:* Univ Calif, Berkeley, BA, 50; Courtauld Inst Art, Univ London, PhD, 58. *Collections Arranged:* Master Drawings from California Collections (coauth, catalog), 68; Caricature and Its Role in Graphic Satire (coauth, catalog), 70; The Origins of the Italian Vedanta (coauth, catalog), 78. *Teaching:* From instr to prof hist art, Univ Calif, Berkeley, 58-68, assoc cur Renaissance art, Art Mus, 64-68; prof, Brown Univ, 68- *Awards:* Grande Ufficiale, Stella Solidarieta Repub Italiana, 68. *Mem:* Col Art Asn Am; Renaissance Soc Am (mem exec bd, 72-74); Soc Archit Historians. *Res:* History of Italian medieval architecture and urbanism; history of Italian 16th century art and architecture. *Publ:* Auth, Venetian Painted Ceilings of the Renaissance, Univ Calif Press, 68; auth, Printed Plans and Panoramic Views of Venice, Fondajione G Cini, 72; auth, Michelangelo's unfinished works, 74 & Jacopo de Barbari's View of Venice, 78, Art Bulletin; auth, The houses of Titian, Aretino and Sansovino, Titian, 82. *Mailing Add:* Dept Art Brown Univ Providence RI 02906

SCHULZ, KEN
PAINTER, LECTURER
b Racine, Wis, Jan 19, 20. *Study:* Layton Sch Art, Milwaukee; also with Gerhard C F Miller. *Comn:* Many pvt corp comns. *Exhib:* Ann Am Watercolor Soc, NY; Ann Allied Artists Am, NY; Ann Knickerbocker Artists, NY; Ann Audubon Artists, Inc, NY; Ann Nat Acad Design, NY; Academic Artists, Springfield, Mass. *Pos:* Artist-owner, Ken Schulz Gallery, Gatlinburg, Tenn, 66- *Teaching:* Pvt art classes & watercolor workshops, Arrowmont Sch, Gatlinburg, 66- *Awards:* Best of Show, Circa 1964, Wustom Mus Fine Arts, Wis; Kathrine M Howe Mem Prize, Knickerbocker Artists, 72; Tenn Waterfowl Stamp Print, 82-83; *Bibliog:* Karen Tansel (auth), article, Racine J Times, 72; Flo Gullockson (auth), Knoxville News-Sentinel, 75; Deborah Walther (auth), article, Decor Mag, 12/77. *Mem:* Am Watercolor Soc; Salmagundi Club; Allied Artists Am; Audubon Artists; Knickerbocker Artists. *Media:* All. *Mailing Add:* PO Box 396 Gatlinburg TN 37738

SCHULZ, WILLIAM GALLAGHER
SCULPTOR, PAINTER
b St Charles, Mo, Mar 25, 20. *Study:* St Louis Sch Fine Arts; Washington Univ, with Max Beckman, Fred Conway, Philip Guston, BFA, 48; Escuela de Pintura, Univ Michoacan, Mex, 49-53; Md Inst, Baltimore, MFA, 62. *Work:* Schutzverband Bildender Kunstler, Frankfurt, Ger; De Barndesteed, Vriji Acad, Amsterdam, Holland; Kunstverein, Erlangen, Ger. *Exhib:* Good Design Show, Mus Mod Art, New York, 50; Junge Amerikanische Kunstler, Ger, 58; St Paul Ceramic, Minn, 64; Northwest Ceramics, Seattle, Wash, 65; Sen Mike Mansfield Mont Artists Exhib, Washington, DC, 67. *Pos:* Arts & crafts dir, USAREUR, Ger & Austria, 53-59; handicrafts adv, Amman & Jerusalem, Jordan, 59-60; handicrafts expert, UNDP, Gilbert, Ellice, Solomon, New Hebrides, Fiji, Samoa & New Guinea Islands, 67-74; consult, UN Develop Adv Team, Suva, Fiji Islands, 73; manufacturer porcelain giftwares, 77- *Teaching:* Instr drawing & watercolor, Washington Univ, 48-49; instr weaving, Escuela de Pintura, Univ Michoacan, 50-53; asst prof ceramics, Eastern Mont Col, Billings, 62-67. *Awards:* Rinehart Fel, Md Inst, Baltimore, 62. *Mem:* Artists Equity Asn, Inc. *Media:* Bronze, Ceramics. *Publ:* Auth, various UN reports. *Mailing Add:* 3829 SE Washington Portland OR 97222

SCHULZE, FRANZ
EDUCATOR, CRITIC
b Uniontown, Pa, Jan 30, 27. *Study:* Northwestern Univ, 43; Univ Chicago, PhB, 45; Art Inst Chicago, BFA, 49, MFA, 50; Acad Fine Arts, Munich. *Pos:* Art critic, Chicago Daily News, 62-78; corresp ed, Art in Am, 65-; contrib ed, Art News, 75- & Inland Architect, 75-; art critic, Chicago Sun-Times, 78- *Teaching:* Instr, Purdue Univ, 50-52; prof, Lake Forest Col, 52-74, Hollender prof art, 74- *Awards:* Ford Found Critics Fel, 64; Harbison Award, Danford Found, 71; Graham Found Advan Fine Arts Fel, 71 & 80; and others. *Mem:* Col Art Asn Am (bd dirs, 81-82); Arch Am Art; Am Asn Univ Prof; Ragdale Found; Koffler Found. *Res:* Art and architecture in the Midwest, especially Chicago. *Publ:* Auth, Art, Architecture and Civilization, 68; auth, Fantastic Images: Chicago Art Since 1945, 72; auth, 100 Years of Architecture in Chicago, 76. *Mailing Add:* c/o Chicago Sun-Times 401 N Wabash Ave Chicago IL 60601

SCHULZE, JOHN H
PHOTOGRAPHER, EDUCATOR
b Scottsbluff, Nebr, June 7, 15. *Study:* Kans State Teachers Col, BS; Univ Iowa, MFA. *Work:* Nihon Univ, Tokyo; Hayden Gallery, Mass Inst Technol; Univ Ala; Oakland Mus; Libr Cong. *Comn:* Photog mural, Sci Bldg, Univ Northern Iowa, 71. *Exhib:* American Photography: The Sixties, Sheldon Mem Art Gallery, Nebr, 66; Photography in Fine Arts V, Metrop Mus Art, 67; Photography USA, DeCordova Mus, 68; Focus Gallery, San Francisco, 68; Exposure Gallery, New York, 73; and others. *Teaching:* Prof photog, Sch Art, Univ Iowa, 48-, res prof, 68-69; artist in residence, Washburn Univ, 72 & Northwest Mo State Col, 72; instr, Sun Valley Ctr Arts, 77. *Bibliog:* Elusive Shadow (film), Univ Iowa Camera, 65. *Mem:* Soc Photog Educ (chmn, 70); Col Art Asn Am; Mid Am Col Art Asn. *Publ:* Contribr, Camera Int, 65, Contemp Photographer, 67, Aperture, 69, Photog Ann, 69 & Fotografie, Int Fotokunst, 79. *Mailing Add:* 5 Forest Glen Iowa City IA 52240

SCHULZE, PAUL
DESIGNER
b New York, NY, Feb 7, 34. *Study:* Parsons Sch Design, cert; NY Univ, BS(indust design), 60. *Comn:* Crystal cross, Steuben Glass, St Clement's Episcopal Church, New York. *Exhib:* Studies in Crystal 1966, Steuben Glass, NY, 65, Islands in Crystal, 66; New Glass, Corning Mus Glass, 79. *Pos:* Off interior design, Bus Equip Sales Co, New York, 60-61; designer, Steuben Glass, 61-69, asst dir design, 69-70, dir design, 70- *Teaching:* Instr eng drawing & three dimensional design, Parsons Sch Design, 62-70. *Awards:* Student Competition Award, Am Soc Indust Designers, 59. *Mem:* Guild for Organic Environment; Nat Alumni Coun Parsons Sch Design; NY State Craftsmen. *Media:* Glass, Mixed Media. *Publ:* Illusr, Organics, Steendrukkerij & Co, Holland, 61. *Mailing Add:* 52 E Third St Corning NY 14830

SCHUPBACH, TERRY ANN
PRINTMAKER
b Verdun, France, July 27, 52; US citizen. *Study:* Ind Univ, BFA, 74, MFA, 79; Univ Ga, 76-77. *Exhib:* Dulin Print Show, Knoxville Tenn, 79; Potsdam Print Show, New York, 80; Wesleyan Int Print Show, Macon, Ga, 80; Kans 6th Nat Print Show, Hays, 81. *Teaching:* Asst prof printmaking, Kenyon Col, 79- *Awards:* Purchase Award, Potsdam Print Show, 80; Purchase Award, Wesleyan Int Print Show, 80; Jurors Prize, Kans 6th Nat Print Show, 81. *Mem:* Col Art Asn. *Media:* Multimedia. *Mailing Add:* PO Box 15 Gambier OH 43022

SCHUSELKA, ELFI
PRINTMAKER, SCULPTOR
b Vienna, Austria, Feb 13, 40. *Study:* Art hist & theatre, Univ Vienna; Acad Arts, Vienna; photog, Graphic & Experimental Inst, Vienna; studied with Oskar Kokoschka, Sch of Vision, Salzburg, Austria; Art Students League, New York; Pratt Graphics Ctr, New York. *Work:* Albertina, Vienna, Austria; Amon Carter Mus Western Art, Ft Worth, Tex; Bibliot Nat, Paris, France; Nat Mus Hist, Taipei, Taiwan; Mus Mod Art, New York. *Exhib:* Int Print Biennale, Cracow, Poland, 70, 76, 78 & 80; Brooklyn Mus Print Exhib, NY, 70 & 76; Int Exhib Graphic Art, Ljubljana, Yugoslavia, 75, 79 & 81; Int Print Biennale, Fredrikstad, Norway, 76, 78 & 80; one-man shows, 55 Mercer, New York, 77, 79 & 82; one-person show, Condeso/Lawler Gallery, New York, 80 & 83; plus others. *Teaching:* Instr printmaking, Sch Visual Arts, New York, 70-73; instr art, Pratt/Phoenix Sch of Design, New York, 74 & Pratt Graphics Ctr, 78 & 79. *Awards:* Int Exhib Graphic Art Medal, Ger, 78; Award, Ibizagrafic 82, Spain. *Bibliog:* Tiffany Bell (auth), article, Arts Mag, 1/78; Vivien Raynor (auth), New York Times, 8/6/78 & 12/26/82; Nancy Unger (auth), Gannett Newspaper, 1/21/83. *Mem:* Artist Equity of NY; Soc Am Graphic Artists (mem coun, 76 & 77). *Dealer:* Condeso/Lawler Gallery 76 Greene St New York NY 10012. *Mailing Add:* 133 Eldridge St New York NY 10002

SCHUSTER, CITA FLETCHER (SARAH E)
PAINTER, CONSULTANT
b El Paso, Tex, Sept 12, 29. *Study:* Vassar Col, AB, 50; Univ Tex, El Paso, with David Deming & Sally Bishop; Univ Calif, Los Angeles, Am Soc Appraisers sem fine arts; conservation & restoration with Nikoli Poloskov, 81. *Exhib:* One-man exhib, Univ Tex, El Paso, 75 & 78; Int Woman's Art Slide Festival, 76; 19th Ann Sun Carnival Nat, El Paso Mus Art, Tex, 76-77; El Paso Designer Craftsmen Invitational, Univ Tex, El Paso, 78; Toys Designed by Artists, Ark Art Ctr, 79-80. *Pos:* Owner-dir, Two-Twenty-Two Gallery, El Paso, 63-; fine art appraiser, 63- *Bibliog:* Betty Chamberlain (auth), Professional page, Am Artist, 11/74. *Mem:* Charter mem Visual Artists & Galleries Asn; Appraisers Asn Am; founder Valuors Consortium, Houston; sr mem Am Soc Appraisers; La Watercolor Soc. *Media:* Watercolor, Acrylic. *Specialty:* Nineteenth and twentieth century painting, print and sculpture. *Publ:* Coauth, The Status Game, Avalon Hill, 82. *Mailing Add:* 6109 Pinehurst El Paso TX 79912

SCHUSTER, EUGENE IVAN
DEALER, HISTORIAN
b St Louis, Mo, Dec 8, 36. *Study:* Wayne State Univ, BA & MA; Univ Mich, Ann Arbor, 59-62; Univ London, Warburg Inst, Fulbright scholar with E H Gombrich & Courtauld Inst, 62-65; London Sch Econ, 62-65. *Pos:* Dir, London Arts Gallery. *Teaching:* Lectr art hist, Wayne State Univ, 59-62; lectr art hist, Eastern Mich Univ, 60; lectr art hist, Rackham Exten, Univ Mich, 61; lectr art hist, Nat Gallery, London, 62-65. *Mem:* Founders Soc, Detroit Inst Arts; Detroit Art Dealers Asn; Appraisers Asn Am. *Res:* Quattrocento in Florence, especially formative changes caused by humanistic studies and leading to the Renaissance. *Specialty:* Old and modern master graphics;

western painting and sculpture from the 15th to the 20th centuries. *Publ:* Auth, Les Peintres Maudits: A Study of the Cultural Relationship of the Jewish Artists of Paris, 60; auth, Sir Charles Locke Eastlake, Plymouth Art Mus, Eng. *Mailing Add:* 321 Fisher Bldg Detroit MI 48202

SCHUTTE, THOMAS FREDERICK
ADMINISTRATOR
b Rochester, NY, Dec 19, 35. *Study:* Valparaiso Univ, Ind, AB, 57; Ind Univ, Bloomington, MBA, 58; Univ Colo, Boulder, DBA, 63. *Pos:* Asst dean, Wharton Sch, Univ Pa, Philadelphia, 73-75; pres, Philadelphia Col Art, 75-83; dir, Union Independent Cols Art, 75-; pres, RI Sch Design, 83- *Interests:* American 18th and 19th century decorative arts. *Publ:* Auth, Is the antiques dealer aware of his economic position in the market place?, 1-5/63 & A salesmanship model for the antiques dealer, 4/64, Antiques Dealer; ed, An Uneasy Coalition: Design & Corporate America, Univ Pa, 75. *Mailing Add:* 405 Mulberry Lane Haverford PA 19041

SCHUTZ, ESTELLE
PAINTER, PRINTMAKER
b New York, NY, Oct 10, 07. *Study:* Cooper Union, cert; Pratt Graphic Ctr. *Work:* Philadelphia Mus of Art; Brooklyn Mus, NY; McAllen Int Mus, Tex. *Exhib:* Brooklyn Mus, NY; Pa Acad Fine Arts, Philadelphia; Philadelphia Mus of Art; Boston Printmakers Exhib, Mass; one-woman shows, Kans State Univ, Manhattan, Western Mich Univ, Kalamazoo, Fla State Univ, Tallahassee & Hofstra Univ, Hempstead, NY; and others. *Awards:* John Taylor Arms Award/Printmaking, Audubon Ann, New York; Burndy Corp Award/Painting, Silvermine Ann, New Canaan, Conn; John Carl Georgio/ Walter Giger Mem Award/Printmaking, Nat Asn Women Artists Ann, New York. *Mem:* Soc Am Graphic Artists; Nat Asn Women Artists; Prof Artists Guild. *Media:* Acrylics; Etching. *Mailing Add:* 7076 Catalpa Rd Frederick MD 21701

SCHUTZ, PRESCOTT DIETRICH
DEALER
b New York, NY, Feb 19, 48. *Study:* Sorbonne, Ecole du Louvre, Paris; Columbia Univ, BA(art hist). *Pos:* Dir contemp art, Hirschl & Adler Galleries, 73-81, dir sales & exhibs, 81- *Mem:* Drawing Ctr, New York. *Specialty:* American art; contemporary American realism. *Mailing Add:* c/o Hirschl & Adler Galleries 21 E 70th St New York NY 10021

SCHWABACHER, ETHEL K
PAINTER, HISTORIAN
b New York, NY, May 20, 03. *Study:* With Max Weber, 28; in Europe, 28-33; with Arshile Gorky, 35-36. *Work:* Whitney Mus Am Art, New York; Albright-Knox Gallery, Buffalo; Rockefeller Univ; Syracuse Univ; Wichita State Univ. *Exhib:* Whitney Mus Am Art Ann, 52-65; Mexico City Biennale, 60; Walker Art Ctr, 60; Carnegie Inst Int, 61; Brooklyn Mus Watercolor Int, 61-62; Abstract Expressionism: First & Second Generation, 72; and many others. *Media:* Mixed. *Publ:* Auth, Arshile Gorky, Whitney Mus Am Art & Macmillan, 57 & Arte Visivi, Rome, 62; auth, John Ford, Nadelstein Press, 74. *Mailing Add:* 1192 Park Ave New York NY 10128

SCHWACHA, GEORGE
PAINTER
b Newark, NJ, Oct 2, 08. *Study:* With Arthur W Woelfle & John Grabach. *Work:* Newark Mus; Mint Mus Art; Montclair Mus; Birmingham Art Mus; Butler Art Inst; plus many others. *Exhib:* Corcoran Gallery Art; Currier Gallery Art; Denver Art Mus; Elgin Acad Art; Delgado Mus Art; plus many others. *Awards:* Award, Meriden Arts & Crafts, 52; Award, Fla Southern Col, 52; Gold Medal, Audubon Artists, 61; plus others. *Mem:* Am Watercolor Soc; Nat Soc Painters in Casein; Philadelphia Watercolor Club; Audubon Artists. *Mailing Add:* 273 Glenwood Ave Bloomfield NJ 07003

SCHWALB, SUSAN
INSTRUCTOR, PAINTER
b New York, NY, Feb 26, 44. *Study:* Carnegie-Mellon Univ, BFA, 65; Fel, Va Ctr Creative Arts, 73, MacDowell Colony, 74 & 75. *Work:* Pilathea Art Mus Mod Art, Ont; MacDowell Colony, Peterborough, NH; Yaddo, Saratoga Springs, NY; Va Ctr for Creative Arts, Sweet Briar; Fogg Art Mus, Harvard Univ. *Exhib:* Works on Paper, Brooklyn Mus, 75; Silverpoint Drawings, US Embassy Small Exhib Prog, 78-82; Art on Paper, Weatherspoon Art Gallery, Univ NC, Greensboro, 78 & 82; Am Drawings III, Smithsonian Traveling Exhib, 80-82; Jewish Themes/Contemp Am Artists, Jewish Mus, New York, 82; Sacred Artifacts, Objects of Devotion, Alternative Mus, 82-83; Am Ctr, Belgrade, Yugoslavia, 83; and others. *Pos:* Art dir, Aphra, Literary Mag, 74-75 & Women Artist News, 75-77. *Teaching:* Instr, Kean Col of NJ, 78-79, City Univ New York, 79-82 & Parsons Sch Art, 82; assoc prof, Mass Col Art, 82- *Awards:* Comt for the Visual Arts Grant, New York, 77; Int Communications Agency Travel Grant, 81. *Bibliog:* Lynn Miller & Salley Swenson (auths), Lives & Works, Talks with Women Artists, Scarecrow Press, 82; Grace Glueck (auth), article, New York Times, 82; Theodore F Wolff (auth), article, Christian Sci Monitor, 82. *Mem:* Artists Equity of New York; Coalition of Women's Art Orgn (exec comt, 77-78); Women's Caucus for Art (bd mem, 78-79). *Media:* Mixed. *Publ:* Illusr, Illustrated Issue of Aphra, 73; contribr, Crafting with Plastics, Chilton Bk Co, 75; contribr, Women Artist News, Mid-March Assoc, 75-77; auth, Notes From Houston, Womanart, 78. *Mailing Add:* 10 Winsor Ave Watertown MA 02172

SCHWALBACH, MARY JO
PAINTER, SCULPTOR
b Milwaukee, Wis, July 8, 39. *Study:* Pine Manor Jr Col, AA; Univ Wis, BS; NY Univ Inst Fine Arts; Sch Visual Arts; also in Paris & Rome. *Work:* Univ Calif Mus, Berkeley; Jazz Mus, New York; Kellogg State Bank, Green Bay, Wis; Nat Hockey League, New York; Whitney Publ, New York. *Comn:* Sculpture, 1st Fed Savings & Loan, Menomonee Falls, 69; three hockey sculptures, Philadelphia Flyers, The Spectrum, Philadelphia, 70; sculpture of Mario Andretti, Clipper Mag, New York, 72; sculpture, Computer TV Gulf & Western Bldg, New York, 72; 1st Nat City Bank, Buffalo, 72. *Exhib:* One-man shows, Dannenberg, New York, 72 & Spectrum Gallery, New York, 79; retrospective, Bergstrom Mus, Neenah, Wis, 70; Beyond Realism, Upstairs Gallery, East Hampton, NY, 72. *Pos:* Mem staff, Mus Mod Art, 62-67. *Teaching:* Asst instr printmaking, Mus Mod Art Sch, New York, 65. *Bibliog:* Article, Clipper Mag, 8/72; S Fischler (auth), Mary Jo Schwalbach-sports action, Sports Hockey, 72; article, Goal Mag, 78. *Media:* Mixed Media. *Publ:* Illusr, Down Beat, 65-72 & Prestige Record Jackets, 66-69; art reproduced in New Yorker, 70; 55 drawings, Goal Mag & Jazz Mag. *Mailing Add:* 14 E 80th St New York NY 10021

SCHWARCZ, JUNE THERESA
CRAFTSMAN, ENAMELIST
b Denver, Colo, June 10, 18. *Study:* Univ Colo, 36-38; Univ Chicago, 38-39; Pratt Inst, 39-41; Inst Design, Chicago, with Moholy Nagy. *Work:* Lannan Found, Palm Beach, Fla; Johnson Wax Collection; Kunstgewerbemuseums, Zurich, Switzerland; Nat Collection Fine Arts, Smithsonian Inst, Washington, DC; Mus Contemp Craft, New York; and others. *Comn:* Enameled bowl with technique demonstration bowls, Mus Contemp Crafts, 58; three piece panel, Cent Nat Bank, Enid, Okla, 62. *Exhib:* New Talent USA, Art in Am, 60; Objects USA, Johnson Wax Collection & Exhib, 69; one-man shows, Mus Bellerive (Kunstgewerbermuseum), Zurich, Switz, 71, Schmuckmuseum, Pforzheim, Ger, 72 & Mus Contemp Crafts, New York; two-man show, de Young Mus, San Francisco. *Awards:* Ceramic Nat Purchase Award, Everson Mus, Syracuse, 60; First Calif Craftsmen's Biennial, Oakland Mus, 61; Goldsmith 70, Minn Mus Art, 70. *Bibliog:* Ventura (auth), June Schwarcz: Electroforming, Crafts Horizons, 11/65; Hammel (auth), June Schwarcz: Enamelist, Am Craft Mag, 10/81; Bennett (auth), article, Metalsmith, 83. *Mem:* Am Crafts Coun. *Media:* Enamel, Copper. *Publ:* Contribr, Craftmen's World, 59 & Research in Crafts, 61, Am Crafts Coun; auth, The arts turn to plating, J Electroplaters Soc, 11/67. *Mailing Add:* 18 Wray Ave Sausalito CA 94965

SCHWARTZ, ADRIENNE CLAIRE See Mim, Adrienne C

SCHWARTZ, AUBREY E
PRINTMAKER, SCULPTOR
b New York, NY, Jan 13, 28. *Study:* Art Students League; Brooklyn Mus Art Sch. *Work:* Nat Gallery Art, Washington, DC; Brooklyn Mus Art; Philadelphia Mus Art; Libr Cong, Washington, DC; Art Inst Chicago. *Comn:* Ed lithographs, Predatory Birds, Gehenna Press, 58, Midget & Dwarf, Tamarind Workshop, 60 & Bestiary, Kanthos Press, 61. *Exhib:* Young Am, Whitney Mus Am Art, 57; Print Coun Am Show, 57; one-man show, Grippi Gallery, New York, 58; Art USA, New York Coliseum, 59; Contemp Graphic Art, US State Dept, 59. *Teaching:* Prof art, State Univ NY, Binghamton, currently. *Awards:* Guggenheim Found Fel Creative Printmaking, 58-60; Tamarind Fel Creative Lithography, 60; First Prize Graphic Art, Boston Arts Festival, 60. *Mailing Add:* Harpur College State Univ NY Binghamton NY 13901

SCHWARTZ, BARBARA ANN
PAINTER, WRITER
b Philadelphia, Pa, Aug 23, 48. *Study:* Carnegie-Mellon Univ, BFA, 70. *Exhib:* Brooklyn Mus, 74; Whitney Biennial Exhib Contemp Am Art, 75 & 79; Artpark, Lewiston, NY, 76; Willard Gallery, New York, 76, 78 & 79; Art in Pub Spaces, New York, 77; Contemp Arts Ctr, Cincinnati, 78; Dart Gallery, Chicago, 79 & 80; Three Dimensional Painting, Mus Contemp Art, Chicago, 80; and others. *Teaching:* Instr drawing, Brooklyn Mus Art Sch, 74-75; instr drawing & sculpture, Sch Visual Arts, New York. *Awards:* Creative Artists Pub Serv Prog, 82-83. *Bibliog:* Jeanne Siege (auth), articles, Art Am, 75, 77 & 81. *Publ:* Ed, Art News, 71-72; auth, Young New York artists, 72 & auth, New York sculpture (column), 72-75; Craft Horizons; auth, SoHo, an interview with a neighborhood, Bolaffi Arte, 74. *Dealer:* Willard Gallery New York NY; Hirschl & Adler Modern New York NY. *Mailing Add:* 87 Crosby St New York NY 10012

SCHWARTZ, BELLA
PAINTER, ASSEMBLAGE ARTIST
b New York, NY. *Study:* George Washington Univ, Washington, DC, BA, MA; Am Univ, Washington, DC. *Exhib:* Corcoran Gallery Art, Washington, DC, 56-57; Philadelphia Mus Art, 70; Washington Artists Equity, traveling, 72-73; Works on Paper Traveling Exhib, Kuumba Learning Ctr, 80. *Mem:* Washington Water Color Asn (pres, 72-74); Artists Equity Asn (pres, Washington area chap, 77-79); Women's Caucus Art; Washington Women's Art Ctr. *Media:* Mixed. *Dealer:* Gallery 10 Ltd 1519 Connecticut Ave NW Washington DC 20036. *Mailing Add:* 2122 Massachusetts Ave NW Washington DC 20008

SCHWARTZ, CARL E
PAINTER, PRINTMAKER
b Detroit, Mich, Sept 21, 35. *Study:* Art Inst Chicago, BFA; Univ Chicago, BFA. *Work:* Art Inst Chicago; Libr Cong & Smithsonian Inst, Washington, DC; Brit Mus; Brooklyn Mus Art; and many others. *Exhib:* Am Painting Exhib, Smithsonian Inst, Washington, DC & Tour, 72; 18th Nat Print Exhib, Brooklyn Mus, 72-73; Calif Palace of Legion of Honor, San Francisco, 73; Eight State Painting Exhib, J B Speed Mus Art, 75; one-man exhibs, Ill State Mus, 77, Ill Inst Technol, 77, Gallery 4, Alexandria, Va, 78, Peter Miller Gallery, Chicago, 79, Harmon Gallery, Naples, Fla, 81 & Art Inst Chicago, 82; and many others. *Teaching:* Instr figure painting & drawing, NShore Art League, 58-, Suburban Fine Arts Ctr, 60- & Deerpath Art League, Wake Forest, Ill, currently. *Awards:* Purchase Awards, J B Speed Mus Art, 73, Ill State Mus, 74 & Dickinson State Univ, 76. *Bibliog:* Allan Davidson (auth), article, Art League News, 67; Thomas Carbol (auth), The Printmaker in Illinois, Ill Art Educ Asn, 72. *Mem:* NShore Art League. *Media:* Acrylic. *Mailing Add:* 2911 N Halsted Chicago IL 60657

SCHWARTZ, ELLEN JUDITH
CURATOR, MUSEUM DIRECTOR
b Washington, DC, Nov 3, 49. *Study:* Yale Univ, BA(A Conger Goodyear Award & Marshall-Allison Fel), 71; Inst Fine Arts, NY Univ, MA, 79. *Collections Arranged:* Images of Experience (auth, catalog), 82, The Art of Notation (auth, catalog), 82, Partitions, 82, The Destroyed Print (auth, catalog), 82, Exceptions, 83, Bridges (auth, catalog), 83 & Contemporary Third World Architecture (auth, catalog), 83, Pratt Inst; and others. *Pos:* Paris corresp, Art Int Mag, Lugano, Switz, 71-72; admin asst, Hirshhorn Mus & Sculpture Garden, 76; ed, Harry N Abrams, New York, 76-79; contrib ed, Art News Mag, New York, 77-; cur exhibs, Pratt Inst, Manhattan & Brooklyn, 79-82; chmn bd trustees, Rotunda Gallery, Brooklyn Borough Hall, 81-; dir exhibs, Pratt Inst, 83- *Teaching:* Vis asst prof, Pratt Inst, 81- *Mem:* Am Asn Mus; Col Art Asn; Women's Caucus, New York Chap; NE Mus Conf; Asn Col & Univ Mus & Galleries (NE coordr, 82-). *Publ:* Ed, The Mechanism of Meaning (Arakawa/Gins), Harry N Abrams, 79; auth, Vito Acconci, 81, Artists, the critics are watching, 81, At the Whitney and the Guggenheim: No surprises, 81, Dennis Oppenheim, 82 & others, Art News. *Mailing Add:* 40 Harrison St Apt 29-G New York NY 10013

SCHWARTZ, EUGENE M
COLLECTOR, PATRON
b Butte, Mont, Mar 18, 27. *Study:* New Sch Social Res; NY Univ; Columbia Univ; Univ Wash. *Pos:* Acquisitions comt, Whitney Mus Am Art, 67-79; mem, 20th Century Comt, Metrop Mus Art, 75- *Collection:* Contemporary American art since World War II, chiefly of the sixties: parts of the collection shown as a group at Jewish Museum, Everson Museum of Art and the Albany Institute; also individual pieces exhibited at Metropolitan Museum of Art, Museum of Modern Art, Whitney Museum, New York, Los Angeles County Museum and Tate Gallery. *Mailing Add:* 1160 Park Ave New York NY 10028

SCHWARTZ, HENRY
PAINTER, INSTRUCTOR
b Winthrop, Mass, Oct 27, 27. *Study:* Sch Mus Fine Arts, Boston, dipl(traveling fel), 53; Akad Bildendekunst, Salzburg, Austria, with Oskar Kokoschka, dipl. *Work:* Mus Fine Arts, Boston; Wheaton Col, Mass; DeCordova Mus. *Exhib:* Five one-man shows, Boris Mirski Gallery, 56-68; Carnegie Inst Int, 61; Harvard Univ, 75; Boston Atheneum, 80; Newton Arts Ctr, 81. *Teaching:* Instr painting, Sch Mus Fine Arts, 56- *Awards:* Mus Sch Fel, 53; Ford Found Grant, 80. *Media:* Oil. *Publ:* Illusr, filmstrip, United Churches of Christ, 61; illusr, Boston Mag, 64-65. *Dealer:* Gallery Naga 67 Newbury St Boston MA 02116. *Mailing Add:* 8 Garrison St Boston MA 02116

SCHWARTZ, LILLIAN (FELDMAN)
FILMMAKER, SCULPTOR
b Cincinnati, Ohio, July 13, 27. *Study:* Univ Cincinnati. *Work:* Mus Mod Art, New York; Moderna Museet, Stockholm, Sweden; Stedlijk Mus Art, Amsterdam, Holland; Los Angeles Co Mus Art; Newark Mus Art, NJ. *Comn:* Painting/collage, Columbia Univ, New York, 67; murals, Int Bus Machines, Zurich, Switz, 72, sculpture, Miami, Fla, 77; New York Philharmonic, 76; mural, Am Telephone & Telegraph, Basking Ridge, NJ, 76. *Exhib:* Mus Mod Art, New York, 68-69; Metrop Mus, New York, 72 & 73; Whitney Mus Am Art, New York, 73; 25th Int Film Festival, Cannes, France, 74; Hirshhorn Mus, Washington, DC, 75; Albright-Knox Art Gallery, Buffalo, NY, 76; Huntsville Mus, Ala, 78; Venice Biennial, 80; Grand Palais, Paris, 80; and others. *Teaching:* Prof, Univ Md, 77-; adj prof, Kean Univ, Union, NJ, 81-, Rutgers Univ. *Awards:* Red Ribbon, Brooklyn Arts & Cult Asn, Nat Acad Television Arts & Sci, 73; Int Women's Art Festival, Walker Art Inst, Minneapolis, 76; Spec Merit, Video Expos, Victor Co, Japan, 80. *Bibliog:* McCauley (auth), Computers and Creativity, Praeger, 75; Keating Productions, The Artist and the Computer (film), Am Telephone & Telegraph, 76. *Mem:* Artists Equity Asn (NY & NJ); Artists League Cent NJ; Nat Acad Television Arts & Sci; Soc Motion Pictures & Television Engineers; Independent Cinema Artists & Producers. *Media:* Computer, Microphotography; Plastic, Electronics. *Publ:* Contribr, Art and the Future, Praeger, 72; contribr, Plastics, Shilton, 74; contribr, Computer Animation, Hastings House, 74; contribr, The Artist and the Computer, Harmony, 76; auth, Filmmaking with computer interdisciplinary science, Rev Spectrum, 79; and others. *Dealer:* Belle Shuller Gallery 972 Hempstead Cincinnati OH 45231; Belle Shuller Gallery 825 SW Early Terrace Port Charlotte FL 33952. *Mailing Add:* 524 Ridge Rd Watchung NJ 07060

SCHWARTZ, MARVIN D
HISTORIAN
b New York, NY, Feb 15, 26. *Study:* City Col New York, BS, 46; Inst Fine Arts, NY Univ, 47-51; Univ Del, MA, 54. *Pos:* Jr cur, Detroit Inst Arts, 51-52; cur decorative arts & indust design lab, Brooklyn Mus, 54-68, ed publ, 59-60; adv dept design, Sears, Roebuck & Co, 64-72; auth, weekly antiques column, New York Times, 66-72; lectr & consult, Metrop Mus Art, 68-; trustee, Jerome Levy Found; NY ed, Antique Monthly, 74- *Teaching:* Lectr, City Col New York, 48-51 & 56-64; lectr, State Univ NY Col Purchase, 69-82. *Awards:* Stipend, Belg-Am Educ Found. *Mem:* Soc Archit Historians; Col Art Asn Am; fel H F DuPont Winterthur Mus. *Publ:* Auth, Collectors Guide to American Clocks, 75; auth, Collectors Guide to American Silver, 75; plus many others. *Mailing Add:* Off Community Educ Metrop Mus of Art New York NY 10028

SCHWARTZ, SING-SI
PHOTOGRAPHER
b New York, NY, Oct 20, 54. *Study:* New Sch for Social Res, advan photo printing with George Tice; psychol portraiture with Phillippe Halsman, 73; Rochester Inst Technol, AAS, 75, BS, 77. *Comn:* Photograph, Burma Airline & posters, Burma Govt, 71; photograph, Vt Bi-Centennial Comn, 75; photographic mural, Wool Bur, Chicago Hq, 81. *Exhib:* One-man shows, Pen & Brush Club, New York, 77, Rochester Inst Technol, NY, 77, Dawson Gristmill Gallery, Vt, 77 & Portchester Libr, NY, 78. *Pos:* Mem staff, Villager Newspaper, New York, 68-74; photogr/correspondent, Cosmorama Pictorial, Hong Kong, 70- *Teaching:* Instr, Int Ctr Photog, New York, 81. *Awards:* Elected as one of 100 outstanding Chinese abroad for accomplishments in photography, Chinese Govt, Taiwan, 71-77. *Bibliog:* Beautiful girls of Hong Kong seen through the eyes of photographer Sing-Si Schwartz, Ming-Pao Weekly, Hong Kong, 8/15/71; article, Interior Design, 10/81. *Mem:* Nat Arts Club; Am Soc Mag Photogr; assoc Allied Artists Am; Overseas Press Club. *Publ:* Photogr, Creating with Card Weaving, Crown Publ Inc, 73; photogr, The How and Why of Chinese Painting, Van Nostrand, 74; contribr, 40 American Watercolorists & How They Work, Watson-Guptill, 77; photogr, Joan Whitney Payson Gallery of Art, Westbrook Col, Maine, 77; photogr, A guide to flowers and flower painting, North Light, 80. *Mailing Add:* Nat Arts Club 15 Gramercy Park S New York NY 10003

SCHWARTZ, THERESE
PAINTER, WRITER
b New York, NY. *Study:* Corcoran Sch Art, Washington, DC; Am Univ; Brooklyn Mus Art Sch. *Work:* Corcoran Gallery Art; Nelson/Atkins Mus, Kansas City, Mo; Fred C Olsen Found; Ciba-Geigy Corp; Brooklyn Mus, New York. *Exhib:* Phillips Mem Gallery, 54; Mus Art Mod, Paris, 56; Univ NC, 69; Stanford Mus, Conn, 72; Suffolk Co Mus, 72; plus others. *Pos:* Ed, New York Element, 68-72; contrib ed, Feminist Art J; mem bd dirs, Princeton Arts J. *Teaching:* Instr fine arts, Fairleigh Dickinson Univ, currently. *Awards:* Second Prize for Oils, Corcoran Gallery Art Regional Show, 52; New Talent USA Award, Art Am, 62; Women Artists Year Three, Mabel Smith Douglass Libr, Rutgers Univ, 73. *Bibliog:* G Brown (auth), article, Arts, 9/69; P Scheldjahl, New York, Art Int, 10/69; David Knaus (auth), Therese Schwartz taking the square, Helicon Nine, No 8, 83. *Publ:* Auth, Plastic Sculpture and Collage, Hearthside, 69; auth, The political scene, column in Arts Mag, 70-71; auth, The politicalization of the avant-garde (ser), Art in Am, 11/71, 3/72, 3/73 & 1/74. *Dealer:* GHJ Graphics 157 E 57th St New York NY 10022. *Mailing Add:* Apt 9A 161 W 75th St New York NY 10023

SCHWARZ, FELIX CONRAD
PAINTER, EDUCATOR
b New York, NY, Apr 13, 06. *Study:* Corcoran Sch Art; George Washington Univ; Columbia Univ; also study in Eng, France, Belg, Italy, Holland, Switz & Spain. *Work:* George Washington Univ. *Comn:* Many portraits for pvt comns. *Exhib:* One-man shows, Birmingham Mus Art, 68, Montgomery Mus Fine Arts, 68, Spring Hill Col, 69, Thor Gallery, Louisville, Ky, 69 & Sheridan Gallery, St Petersburg, 75; plus many others. *Pos:* Ed, Advanced Sch Digest, formerly. *Teaching:* Prof fine arts at the State Univs of Va, NC, Minn & Wis over a period of 40 yrs; lectr hist & art appreciation, Inst of Lifetime Learning. *Bibliog:* Rev articles in La Rev Mod, Art News, New York Times, New York Herald Tribune & others. *Media:* Oil, Watercolor. *Publ:* Auth, Your life, Education, Virginia J & New York Times. *Mailing Add:* 1500 North Dakota Ave NE St Petersburg FL 33703

SCHWARZ, KURT L
DEALER, HISTORIAN
b Vienna, Austria, Apr 5, 09; US citizen. *Study:* Inst for Art Hist, Univ Vienna, PhD. *Pos:* Owner, Antiquarian & Art Books, 47- *Mem:* Antiquarian Booksellers Asn of Am (chap chmn, 63-65); Antiquarian Booksellers Asn Int, Eng; Art Libr Soc NAm. *Specialty:* Rare books on the arts, prints. *Mailing Add:* 738 S Bristol Ave Los Angeles CA 90049

SCHWARZ, MYRTLE COOPER
DESIGNER, MOSAIC ARTIST
b Breckenridge Co, Ky, Dec 10, 1900. *Study:* Western Ky State Univ, AB; Col William & Mary, MA; Columbia Univ, MA, PhD. *Exhib:* One-man shows, Col William & Mary, Okla State Univ & Univ Wis; Art Club & Art Ctr, St Petersburg, Fla; Gulf Coast Art Ctr, Clearwater, Fla; and numerous nat & regional shows. *Pos:* Chmn math & pres art sect, Va Educ Asn; mem comt, Seven Coop Univs Teacher Training; chmn Lang Arts Develop, Va State Curriculum; mem comt, Prof Standards & Develop, Nat Educ Asn; dir, Community Art Ctr, Enid, Okla. *Teaching:* Instr, Exten Serv, Univ Ky; prof educ, Col William & Mary; prin high sch & supt schs, Va & Ky; prof art educ

& dir, Community Ctr, Phillips Univ; prof educ & dir art educ, Okla State Univ; vis prof, Monticello Col; prof Eng, Wis State Univ; instr creative crafts, Continuing Educ, Inst for Lifetime Learning. *Mem:* Enid Artists League; Univ Women's Serv Club; Nat Art Educ Asn (chmn Div Higher Educ & Teacher Training). *Media:* Mixed. *Publ:* Auth, articles in Va J Educ, Ky & Okla J Educ. *Mailing Add:* 1500 North Dakota Ave NE St Petersburg FL 33703

SCHWEBEL, RENATA MANASSE
SCULPTOR

b Zwickau, Germany, Mar 6, 30; US citizen. *Study:* Antioch Col, BA, 53; Columbia Univ, MFA, 61; Art Students League, 68. *Work:* Columbia Univ, New York; Antioch Col, Ohio; Colt Industries, New York; Southwest Bell, Houston; Heinrichgruber House, Berlin. *Exhib:* Silvermine Guild New England Ann, Conn; Hudson River Mus Competitions, NY; Wadsworth Atheneum; New Britain Mus; one-woman show, Sculpture Ctr, New York. *Awards:* Chaim Gross Found Award, 80; Medal of Honor, Nat Asn Women Artists, 81; Medal of Honor, Audubon Artists, 82. *Bibliog:* Padavano (auth), The Process of Sculpture, Doubleday, 81. *Mem:* Sculptors Guild (pres, 80-83); Audubon Artists; Nat Asn Women Artists; Conn Acad Fine Arts. *Media:* Welded Metal, Ceramic Clay. *Dealer:* Sculpture Center 167 E 69th St New York NY 10021. *Mailing Add:* 36 Silver Birch Dr New Rochelle NY 10804

SCHWEISS, RUTH KELLER
SCULPTOR, DESIGNER

US citizen. *Study:* Washington Univ, St Louis, fine arts cert; Cranbrook Art Acad, Bloomfield Hills, Mich, three yr int fel, sculpture with Carl Milles. *Work:* Many private collections. *Comn:* Bear for pool garden, comn by J A Baer, II, St Louis, 70; Blachette (bronze), Founder Monument, St Charles, Mo, 72; Children in the Rain, Ger Coun, Hamm, Ger, 73; Sons of Founders (bronze reliefs), Stix, Baer & Fuller, St Louis, 75; bronze memorial, Leif Sverdrup, St Louis, 79. *Exhib:* Nat Acad Design, New York, 43; Detroit Art Mus Regional Show, Mich, 43; Pacific Show, Hawaiian Art Mus, Honolulu, 44; Int Art Show, Rotunda Gallery, London, 73; Ars Longa Gallery, Houston, 74. *Awards:* Mus Purchase Prize, Cranbrook Art Mus, 42; Ruth Renfrow Sculpture Prize, St Louis Art Mus, 45; Thalinger Sculpture Prize, St Louis Artists Guild, 50. *Bibliog:* Ruth Keller Schweiss, Gonterman Assoc, 65; The World of Ruth Keller Schweiss (film), Rick Noel, 74; picture story, St Louis Home / Garden, 79. *Mem:* Acad Prof Artists (exec dir, 68-83); Nat Soc Arts & Lett (corresp secy, 69-71; treas, 75-); Media Nine; St Louis Artists Guild (secy & mem bd, 65-67). *Media:* Bronze Castings of Limited Editions from Any Carved or Modeled Medium. *Mailing Add:* 4 Daniel Rd St Louis MO 63124

SCHWEITZER, GERTRUDE
PAINTER, SCULPTOR

b New York, NY. *Study:* Pratt Inst; Nat Acad Design, New York; Acad Julian, Paris; Pratt Inst, hon DFA. *Work:* Metrop Mus Art, New York; Art Inst Chicago; Toledo Mus Art; Brooklyn Mus; Whitney Mus Am Art, New York; plus many others. *Exhib:* One-man exhibs, Norton Gallery Art, West Palm Beach, 47 & 66, Galerie Charpentier, Paris, 48, 54 & 61, Hanover Gallery, London, 53, Philadelphia Art Alliance, 69 & Hokin Gallery, Palm Beach, 71; and others. *Pos:* Chmn arts & skill corps, Am Red Cross, 42-45. *Awards:* Am Watercolor Soc Medal, 34; Soc Four Arts Awards in Watercolor, 48 & 59 & Awards in Oils, 50 & 51; NJ State Exhib First Prize as Best Woman Painter, Montclair Art Mus, 52; plus many others. *Bibliog:* Rene Barotte (auth), G Schweitzer, Peintures et Dessins, Ed Chene, Paris, 65. *Mem:* Nat Acad Design; Audubon Artists; Am Artists Prof League; Am Watercolor Soc. *Mailing Add:* Stone Hill Farm Colts Neck NJ 07722

SCHWEITZER, M R
DEALER, GALLERY DIRECTOR

b Sept 7, 11. *Collections Arranged:* Waters, Salt & Sweet (with catalog), 59; Americans at Home & Abroad from 1850's (with catalog), 67. *Pos:* Owner, Schweitzer Gallery, NC. *Mem:* Charter mem, Am Soc Appraisers. *Res:* American painting. *Specialty:* American painting, 1830-1930; European painting, 16th to 19th centuries. *Collection:* American and English 19th century; Catalan, Spanish and Italian 17th century; French, Scandinavian, Russian. *Mailing Add:* 958 Madison Ave New York NY 10021

SCHWEIZER, PAUL DOUGLAS
MUSEUM DIRECTOR, HISTORIAN

b Brooklyn, NY, Nov 26, 46. *Study:* Marietta Col, Ohio, BA, 68; Univ Del, MA, 74, PhD, 79. *Collections Arranged:* Avant-Garde Painting & Sculpture in America: 1910-25 (collab effort, co-auth, catalog), Del Art Mus, spring 75; Edward Moran, Del Art Mus, 79; North Country Folk Art, 82 & Coles Court and Empire, 83, Munson-Williams-Proctor Inst, Utica, NY. *Pos:* Consult, Choptank Collection, Middletown, Del, 76-77; cur collections, St Lawrence Univ, Canton, NY, 77-78, dir, Richard F Brush Art Gallery, 78-80; dir, Mus Art, Munson-Williams-Proctor Inst, Utica, NY, 80-; bd mem, Williamstown Regional Art Consevation Lab, 81- *Teaching:* Instr art hist, Univ Del, Wilmington, 76; instr art hist, St Lawrence Univ, 77-78, asst prof fine arts, 78-80. *Awards:* Unidel Fel, Univ Del, 72-76. *Mem:* Col Art Asn; Asn Art Mus Dirs. *Res:* John Constable and the Rainbow; American painting & sculpture of the late 19th century. *Publ:* Auth, Genteel taste at the National Academy of Design, Am Art Rev, 75; auth, Edward Moran: American Marine Painter, Del Art Mus; auth, John Constible, rainbow science and English color theory, Art Bulletin, 82; auth, Literary sauce for Coles voyage and Life, Am Art J, 83. *Mailing Add:* Munson-Williams-Proctor Inst 310 Genesee St Utica NY 13502

SCHWENINGER, ANN ROZZELLE
ILLUSTRATOR

b Boulder, Colo, Aug 1, 51. *Study:* Univ Colo, 69-72; Calif Inst Arts, BFA, 73-75; also with Uri Shulevitz and Peter Hopkins, 75- *Awards:* Notable Bk Award, Am Libr Asn, 82. *Media:* Watercolor, Pencil. *Publ:* Illusr, ABC Cat, Harper & Row, 83; illusr, Tales of Amanda Pig, Dial Press, 83; illusr, The Musicians of Bremen, 83 & illusr, Silent Night, 83, Western Publ; auth & illusr, Christmas Secrets, Viking Press, 84; and many others. *Mailing Add:* 319 E 24th St New York NY 10010

SCHWIDDER, ERNST CARL
SCULPTOR, DESIGNER

b St Louis, Mo, Nov 9, 31. *Study:* Univ Wash, BA, 53 & MFA, 55. *Comn:* Wood sculpture & carved wood furniture, St Joseph Cath Church, Chicago, 72; St Matthew Lutheran Church, Portland, Ore, 75 & Lutheran Church, Palo Alto, Calif, 81; bronze sculpture & stone furniture, Our Savior Lutheran Church, Everett, Wash, 69; wood sculpture, Hope Lutheran Church, Bradenton, Fla, 74; and others. *Exhib:* Eight Washington Artists, Portland Art Mus, 55; Mus Mod Art Int Biennial, Sao Paulo, Brazil, 55; Pacific Coast Art, San Francisco Mus Art, 56; Artists West of the Mississippi, Colorado Springs Art Ctr, 57; Cult Exchange Expos, Moscow, USSR, 59. *Pos:* Owner, Ernst Schwidder Assoc. *Teaching:* Chmn sculpture & design, Valparaiso Univ, Ind, 58-61 & Seattle Pac Univ, 63-67; chmn sculpture & design, Pac Lutheran Univ, Tacoma, 67-, prof, 75- *Media:* Multimedia. *Mailing Add:* Dept Art Pac Lutheran Univ 12102 Park Ave S Tacoma WA 98447

SCHWIEGER, C ROBERT
PRINTMAKER, EDUCATOR

b Scottsbluff, Nebr, Dec 5, 36. *Study:* Nebr Western Col, AA; Chadron State Col, BFA(educ); Univ Northern Colo, MA; Univ Denver, MFA. *Work:* Ohio State Univ; Miss Art Asn; Ga Inst Technol; Olivet Col, Mich; Oklahoma Art Ctr, Oklahoma City. *Comn:* Gilded gold and mixed media on glass mural, Univ Northern Colo, 66. *Exhib:* 12th Midwest Biennial, Joslyn Art Mus, Omaha, 72; Printmaking Invitational, Univ Wis, Oshkosh; Recent Trends & New Directions in Printmaking, Northern Ill Univ; Am Printmakers Invitational, Univ SDak; St Cloud State Univ; Univ Dallas; and others. *Teaching:* Assoc prof, Minot State Col, 67-81, coordr art, 67-83, prof, 81- *Awards:* Purchase Award, Univ Tex, Austin; Northwest Printmakers Int Jury Commendation, Seattle Art Mus, 71; 16th Nat Print & Drawing Exhib Jury Commendation, Okla Art Ctr, 74. *Mailing Add:* 706 25th St NW Minot ND 58701

SCHWIERING, CONRAD
PAINTER

b Boulder, Colo, Aug 8, 16. *Study:* Univ Wyo, BA; Art Students League; Grand Cent Sch Art, New York; Am Mus Nat Hist, New York; study with Bert Phillips, Taos, NMex, Charles S Chapman, New York & George B Bridgman, New York. *Work:* Nat Cowboy Hall of Fame, Oklahoma City; Whitney Gallery Western Art, Cody, Wyo; Genesee Country Mus, Rochester; Wyo State Mus, Cheyenne; Mont Hist Soc, Helena; and others. *Exhib:* One-man show, Nat Cowboy Hall Fame, Oklahoma City, 81; Whitney Gallery Western Art, Cody, Wyo; Artists Am, Denver, Colo; and others. *Teaching:* Instr fine art, Univ Wyo, Laramie, 49; instr mountain landscape, Teton Artists Asn, Jackson Hole, 57-64. *Awards:* Best of Show, Springville Nat Art Show, 66; Trustees Gold Medal, Nat Cowboy Hall Fame, 81. *Bibliog:* Dean Krakel (auth), Painter of the Tetons, Persimmon Hill Mag; Documentary profiles in Am Art Video Ventures, Oklahoma City; Dean Krakel (auth), Painting on the Square, Powder River Book Co. *Mem:* Soc Western Artists; Nat Acad Western Art. *Media:* Oil. *Publ:* Contribr, Cowboy in Art, 68; contribr, Western Painting Today, 75. *Dealer:* Grand Cent Art Galleries 50 E 50th St New York NY 10017; Trailside Galleries 7330 Scottsdale Mall Scottsdale AZ 85251. *Mailing Add:* Star Rte Box 223 Jackson Hole WY 83001

SCOTT, ARDEN
SCULPTOR

b Port Chester, NY, Oct 21, 38. *Comn:* Nassau Co Mus Fine Arts, NY, 77; pub sculpture, Riverhead, NY, 81; Atlanta Arts Festival, 83. *Exhib:* Whitney Mus Biennial, 73; one-person show, 112 Green Gallery, NY, 74; O K Harris Gallery, New York, 75 & 80; Forms in Focus, Coop City Gallery, 77; Elvehjem Mus Art, Madison, Wis, 80; 55 Mercer Gallery, 82; and others. *Teaching:* Prof sculpture, Bard Col, 75- & Parsons Sch Design, 78. *Awards:* Guggenheim Fel, 81. *Bibliog:* Marcia Tucker (auth), Making it big, MS Mag, 4/74. *Media:* Wood, Stone. *Dealer:* O K Harris Gallery 340 West Broadway New York NY 10013. *Mailing Add:* 73 Leonard St New York NY 10013

SCOTT, C(HARLES) A(RTHUR)
SCULPTOR

b San Diego, Calif, Dec 2, 40. *Study:* San Diego State Univ, BA, 68; Univ Calif, Santa Barbara, MFA, 70. *Work:* San Diego State Univ, Calif; Univ Calif, Santa Barbara; Western Wash Univ & Whatcom Mus Hist & Art, Bellingham, Wash; Favell Mus Western Art & Artifacts, Klamath Falls, Ore. *Exhib:* 58th Ann NW Artists, Seattle Art Mus, 72; Gov's Ann, State Capitol Mus, Olympia, Wash, 72 & 73; Western Gallery, Bellingham, Wash, 72, 73 & 74; Santa Barbara Mus Art, Calif, 74; Whatcom Mus Hist & Art, Bellingham, Wash, 80; 8th Ann Western Art Asn Exhib, Ellensburg, Wash, 80; and others. *Pos:* Vis artist, Fonderiaversillia, Pietrasanta, Italy, 77; asst to Mark di Suvero, For Handel (sculpture), Bellingham, Wash, 73-74. *Teaching:* Instr, Western Wash Univ, Bellingham, 70-77. *Awards:* Purchase Prizes, 9th & 10th Ann Small Sculpture, Western Gallery, Bellingham, Wash, 72 & 73; 1st Prize, Design Competition, Seattle Water Dept, 74. *Bibliog:* Barry Kahn (auth),

Things are seldom what they seem, Bellingham Herald, 11/28/80. *Mem:* Western Art Asn; Nat Cowboy Hall Fame. *Media:* Bronze. *Dealer:* Shidoni Gallery and Artists Studio Tesuque NM. *Mailing Add:* 3100-1/2 St Clair Bellingham WA 98226

SCOTT, CAMPBELL
PRINTMAKER, SCULPTOR
b Milngavie, Scotland, Oct 5, 30; Can citizen. *Study:* Studied with S W Hayter, Paris; Glasgow Sch Art, Scotland. *Work:* British Mus, London; Bibliot Nat, Paris; Scottish Nat Gallery Mod Art; Montreal Mus Art; Victoria & Albert Mus. *Comn:* Bronze sculpture, Pub Libr, Niagara Falls, Can; wood sculpture, Pub Libr, St Catharines, Can. *Exhib:* FAAP Gravura, Sao Paulo, Brazil, 68; 1st British Int Print Biennale, Gt Brit, 69; Traveling Exhib, Nat Gallery Can, Ottawa, 69; 4th Am Biennial Engraving, Santiago, Chile, 70; Exhib Can Graphics, Can Embassy, Washington, DC, 71 & Pratt Inst, New York, 71. *Mem:* Can Graphic Arts Soc. *Mailing Add:* 89 Byron Niagara on the Lake ON L0S 1J0 Canada

SCOTT, DAVID WINFIELD
ADMINISTRATOR
b Fall River, Mass, July 10, 16. *Study:* Art Students League; Harvard Col, AB; Claremont Grad Sch, MA & MFA; Univ Calif, Berkeley, PhD. *Pos:* From lectr art to prof, Scripps Col, 46-63; dir, Nat Collection Fine Arts, Washington, DC, 64-69; consult, Nat Gallery Art, Washington, DC, 69- *Mailing Add:* 3016 Cortland Pl NW Washington DC 20008

SCOTT, HENRY E, JR
PAINTER, EDUCATOR
b Cambridge, Mass, Aug 22, 1900. *Study:* Harvard Univ, Sachs fel, 25, Bacon art scholar, 26-28, BA & MA; Art Students League; also with Edward Forbes, Italy. *Work:* Fogg Art Mus, Cambridge; Univ Kans Med Ctr & Univ Mo, Kansas City; Amherst Col; Regency House, Kansas City. *Comn:* Originated & directed stage production of Giotto's Frescoes of the Nativity, Pittsburgh, 32-33, Amherst Col, 35-; stage designs for Amherst Masquers, 35-36; stage designs for Univ Kansas City Playhouse, 49-50; also many portraits. *Exhib:* Amherst Col, 41; Springfield, Mass, 42; Boston & Cambridge, Mass, 47; four shows, Martha's Vineyard, 47-63; Kansas City, Mo, 50-69; and others. *Collections Arranged:* Eight exhibs yearly, Univ Mo-Kansas City, 48-65. *Pos:* Asst to dir, Mem Art Gallery, Univ Rochester, 28-29; cur art, Amherst Col, 42-43; mem, Munic Art Comn, Kansas City, Mo, 54-69. *Teaching:* Lectr & asst head tutor, Div Fine Arts, Harvard Univ & Radcliffe Col, 23-26; instr art, Univ Rochester, 28-29; asst prof, Univ Pittsburgh, 29-34; assoc prof, Amherst Col, 35-43; assoc prof, Univ Mo, Kansas City, 47-59, chmn dept art, 47-64, prof, 59-70, emer prof, 70- *Awards:* Prize, Rochester Art Asn, 28. *Mem:* Col Art Asn Am; Am Asn Univ Prof. *Media:* Watercolor, Oil; Fresco. *Publ:* Auth, Historical Outline of the Fine Arts, 36. *Mailing Add:* Univ Mo Art Dept 5100 Rockhill Rd Kansas City MO 64110

SCOTT, JOHN
ILLUSTRATOR, PAINTER
b Camden, NJ, Dec 1, 07. *Study:* La France Art Inst, Philadelphia, illus with Joseph Clement, 28. *Work:* Mus Am Illus, New Britain, Conn; Hist Arch US Army, Washington, DC. *Comn:* Biblical subjects, Mormon Church, Salt Lake City, 68 & 78, Independence, Mo, 71 & Washington, DC, 73; painting, Permian Oil Mus, Midland, Tex, 70. *Pos:* Ed, Sports Afield Mag, Hearst Publ, 48-75. *Bibliog:* Zack Taylor (auth), article, Sports Afield, 8/79; Jack Hines (auth), article, Art West, 7/81. *Mem:* Soc Illusr, New York. *Media:* Oil, Gouache. *Dealer:* Settlers West Gallery 6420 N Campbell Tucson AZ 85718. *Mailing Add:* 478 N Salem Rd Ridgefield CT 06877

SCOTT, JOHN
PAINTER
b Windsor, Ont, 50. *Study:* Ont Col Art, Toronto, AOCA, 76; Univ Toronto; Centennial Col, Toronto. *Work:* Nat Gallery Can, Can Coun Art Bank, Ottawa; Art Gallery Ont, Toronto; London Regional Art Gallery, England; Art Gallery Stratford, Ont. *Exhib:* Solo exhibs, Carmen Lamanna Gallery, Toronto, 81 & 83; Fragments, Content, Scale, 49th Parallel Gallery, New York, 83; Modern Times: The Artist as Social Critic, The Gallery, Stratford, Ont, 83; Attitude, Can Nat Exhib, Toronto, 83; Chromaliving, ChromoZone Gallery, Toronto, 83. *Awards:* Can Coun Grants, 77-81; Floyd S Chalmers Fund Award, Ont Arts Coun, 82. *Bibliog:* John Bentley Mays (auth), Scott's obsession still compelling, Globe and Mail, 11/28/81; Charlotte Townsend-Gualt & Terrence Heath (auth), Visions: Contemporary Art in Canada, Douglas & McIntyre, Vancouver, 83. *Mailing Add:* c/o Carmen Lamanna Gallery 840 Yonge St Toronto ON M4W 2H1 Canada

SCOTT, JOHN BELDON
HISTORIAN, EDUCATOR
b Scottsburg, Ind, Aug 3, 46. *Study:* Ind Univ, BA, 68; Rutgers Univ, MA, 75, PhD(Am Acad Rome Prize Fel, Delmas Found Fel), 83. *Pos:* Ed, Rutgers Art Rev, 78-79. *Teaching:* Instr, Rutgers Univ, 77-79; lectr, Univ Pa, 81-82; asst prof, Univ Iowa, 82- *Mem:* Col Art Asn; Soc Archit Historians. *Res:* Italian Renaissance and Baroque; northern Baroque. *Publ:* Auth, The catafalques of Philip II in Saragossa, In: Studies in Iconography, 79; auth, S Ivo Alla Sapienza and Borromini's symbolic language, J Soc Archit Historians, 82; auth, Urban VIII, Bernini and the Contess Matilda, 83. *Mailing Add:* Sch Art & Art Hist Univ Iowa Iowa City IA 52242

SCOTT, JOHN FREDRIK
HISTORIAN, EDUCATOR
b Westfield, NJ, May 14, 36. *Study:* Princeton Univ, AB, 58; Johns Hopkins Univ, MAT, 62; Columbia Univ, PhD, 71. *Collections Arranged:* Before Cortes (auth, catalog), Metrop Mus Art, 70; Rice Art Collection, Sewall Art Gallery, 77; South American Art, Mus Fine Arts, Houston, 80; Ecuadorian Art (auth, catalog), Johnson Mus Art, 82. *Pos:* Research assoc, Metrop Mus Art, New York, 68-71; adj cur, Mus Fine Arts, Houston, 78-80. *Teaching:* Asst prof primitive art, Cornell Univ, Ithaca, NY, 71-77; asst prof primitive art, Rice Univ, Houston, 77-81; assoc prof Latin Am art, Univ Fla, Gainesville, 81- *Awards:* Nat Endowment Humanities Grant, 74-75; Foreign Area Fel, 66-68. *Mem:* Col Art Asn Am; Archaeology Inst Am (vpres Houston soc, 80-81, pres Gainesville soc, 83-); Asn Latin Am Art (vpres Precolumbian, 83-); Soc Am Archaeol. *Res:* Pre-Columbian art, especially sculpture. *Publ:* Auth, El Meson, Veracruz & Its Monolithic Reliefs, Baessler Archives, 77; auth, Danzantes of Monte Alban, Dumbarton Oaks, 78; auth, Pre-Columbian Art & Architecture, Acad Am Encycl, 80; auth, Post-Olmec Art in Veracruz, Antrop Americanista, 80; auth, Monuments of Los Idolos, Veracruz, J New World Archeol, 82. *Mailing Add:* 1501 NW 46th Terr Gainesville FL 32605

SCOTT, JOHN TARRELL
PRINTMAKER, SCULPTOR
b New Orleans, La, June 30, 40. *Study:* Xavier Univ La, BA, 62; Mich State Univ, MFA, 65. *Work:* Johnson Publ Co, Chicago, Ill; Golden State Mutual Life Insurance Co, Los Angeles, Calif; Pan American Life, New Orleans, La; One Canal Place, New Orleans, La. *Comn:* Relief wall sculpture, Civic Ctr, Naples Co, Fla, 60-61; bronze pieta, Edgewood United Church, Lansing, Mich, 64; Madonna & St Joseph, St Angela Marici Church, Metaire, La, 68; steel figure, Mt Carmel High Sch, New Orleans, 76. *Exhib:* Black Am Artists Nat, Ill Bell Tel Co, Chicago, 70; Fiske Univ, Nashville, Tenn, 73; The Classic Revival, Ill Bell Tel Co, 75; Migrations, Colombia, SAm, 76; Mitchell Mus, Mt Vernon, Ill, 76. *Pos:* Mem visual arts comt, Contemp Arts Ctr, currently. *Teaching:* Prof printmaking & sculpture, Xavier Univ of La, New Orleans, 65- *Awards:* Hand Hollow Found, 83; United Negro Col Fund Grant, 83. *Mem:* New Orleans Arts Coun (bd dirs, currently); Congo Square Arts Collective (asst dir, currently). *Media:* Mixed. *Mailing Add:* Dept of Art Palmetto & Pine Sts New Orleans LA 70125

SCOTT, JONATHAN
PAINTER
b Bath, Eng, Oct 30, 14. *Study:* Heatherly Sch, London; Mauritz Heymann Sch, Munich; The Accad, Florence. *Work:* Laguna Mus Art, Calif; Santa Fe, NMex; Lindsay Art Asn, Calif; Carmel, Calif; G G de Silva Collection, Los Angeles. *Comn:* Paintings, USN Art Prog, 63-64; also portrait comns. *Exhib:* Occidental Col, Los Angeles, 76; Butler Inst Am Art, Youngstown, Ohio; Ringling Mus, Sarasota, Fla; Mus Maritime, Paris, France; Kramer Gallery, Los Angeles; Stables Gallery, Taos, NMex; plus others. *Teaching:* Instr drawing & painting, Univ Southern Calif, 46, Pasadena Art Mus, 47-48, Riverside Art Asn, 62-63; instr watercolor, workshops, Taos, 82-83. *Awards:* Awards, Calif Watercolor Soc, 55, Laguna Beach Art Asn, 61 & NMex Watercolor Soc, 74. *Mem:* Nat Watercolor Soc; Taos Art Asn. *Media:* Oil, Watercolor. *Dealer:* Total Arts Gallery Taos NM 87571. *Mailing Add:* PO Box 1154 Taos NM 87571

SCOTT, MARIAN (DALE)
PAINTER
b Montreal, Que, June 26, 06. *Study:* Montreal Art Asn, scholar, 17-20; Monument Nat, with Dionnet, 18-20; Ecole Beaux Arts, Montreal, 23-25; Slade Sch, London. *Work:* Nat Gallery Can, Ottawa; McGill Univ Art Collection, Montreal; Montreal Mus Fine Arts; Edmonton Art Gallery; Dept External Affairs, Ottawa, Mus Art Contemporain, Montreal; and others. *Comn:* Oils, McGill Univ, 43 & Montreal Gen Hosp Chapel, 58. *Exhib:* New York World's Fair, 39; Panorama, Peinture du Quebec, Mus Art Contemporain, 40-66; Biennale, Sao Paulo, Brazil, 51-53; 50 Years of Canadian Painting, Nat Gallery Can; Expos Createurs Quebec, 71. *Teaching:* Instr painting, St George's Sch, Montreal, 37-39; instr painting, Montreal Mus Fine Arts, 42-45. *Awards:* First Prize for Painting, Can Group Painters, 66; Purchase Award, Thomas More Inst, Montreal, 67; Baxter Purchase Award, Ont Soc Artists. *Mem:* Soc Artists Visual Arts Que; Can Acad Arts. *Media:* Acrylic. *Mailing Add:* 451 Clarke Ave Montreal PQ H3Y 3C5 Canada

SCOTT, ROBERT MONTGOMERY
PATRON, ADMINISTRATOR
b May 22, 29; US citizen. *Study:* Harvard Col, AB, 51; Univ Pa Law Sch, LLB, 54. *Pos:* Trustee, Pa Mus Art, 65-, pres, 80-, chief exec officer, 82- *Awards:* Superior Hon Award, US State Dept, 73. *Mem:* Greater Philadelphia Cult Alliance; Am Asn Mus. *Mailing Add:* Benjamin Franklin Parkway Box 7646 Philadelphia PA 19101

SCOTT, SAM
PAINTER, EDUCATOR
b Chicago, Ill, Apr 7, 40. *Study:* Univ Mich, BFA, 65; Md Inst Col Art, MFA, 69; also with Grace Hartigan, David Hare, Joseph Goto, Zubel Kachadoorian. *Work:* NMex Fine Arts Mus, Santa Fe; Phoenix Fine Arts Mus; Colorado Springs Fine Arts Mus; Denver Fine Arts Mus; AT&T Corp, NY. *Comn:* Mural painting, Westinghouse Elec Corp Bldg, Norman, Okla, 72; mural, Jelco Corp Bldg, Minneapolis, Minn, 72. *Exhib:* Corcoran Mus Ann, Washington, DC, 67; Richard Demarco Edinburgh Festival Show, Scotland, 73; one-man shows, Mus NMex, Santa Fe, 74 & Scottsdale Art Ctr, 78; Biennial Contemp Am Art, Whitney Mus Am Art, New York, 75; 10 Take

10 (retrospective), Colorado Springs Fine Arts Mus, 77; Phoenix Art Mus, 79-80. *Pos:* Artist in residence, Sun Valley Ctr Arts & Humanities, Idaho, 75 & 76; resident artist, Sch Prog, City Santa Fe, NMex, 77-78; panel coord mem, Tucson Vis Artists Consortium, 78-80. *Teaching:* Instr painting, Md Inst Col Art, 67-69; instr painting, St Johns Col, Santa Fe, 71; asst prof art, Univ Ariz, 78- *Awards:* Walters Fine Arts Mus Traveling Grant, Baltimore, 67; Weatherhead Found Purchase Prize, Cleveland, Ohio, 70; NMex Arts Comn Prize, 73. *Bibliog:* V G Kirby (auth), Sam Scott, another universe, Southwest Gallery Mag, 72; Arthur Sussman (auth), Paintings of Sam Scott, The aesthetic end, KOAT TV, Albuquerque, 5/19/74. *Media:* Oil on Canvas. *Publ:* Contrib, NMex Mag, 71. *Dealer:* Watson de Nagy Gallery 1106 Berthea Houston TX 77006; Sebastian Moore Gallery Denver CO. *Mailing Add:* Dept Art Univ Ariz Tucson AZ 85721

SCOTT, SANDY (SANDRA LYNN)
PRINTMAKER, ILLUSTRATOR
b Dubuque, Iowa, July 24, 43. *Study:* Kansas City Art Inst. *Work:* Wildlife World Mus, Monument, Colo; El Paso Zoo, Tex. *Comn:* Rodeo Events (etchings), Nat Cowboy Hall Fame, Oklahoma City, 78; Grand Slam, 79 & Bears of North America, 80, Nat Sporting Fraternity Ltd, New York; Kodiak Bears, WesTex Oil Co, El Paso, 80; Wood Ducks, Albuquerque, NMex, 81. *Exhib:* Am Artists Prof League, New York, 82 & 83; Catharine Lorillard Wolfe Art Club, New York, 82 & 83; Salmagundi Open Sculpture Exhib, New York, 83; New York Pen & Brush, 83; Ann Soc Am Impressionists Show, 84; more than fifty one-woman shows at galleries throughout the country. *Pos:* Background artist, Calvin Motion Pictures, Kansas City, Mo, 62-65. *Awards:* New York Pen & Brush Award, Ann Sculpture Exhib, 83; Medal Hon Sculpture, Catharine Lorillard Wolfe Art Club, 83; Barett-Colea Award & Salmagundi Club Cert Merit, Salmagundi Club Open Sculpture Exhib, 83. *Bibliog:* Sandy Scott: Etchings, Prints Mag, 7-8/81; Carrol Nelson (auth), Sandy Scott, In: Masters of Western Art, Watson-Guptill, 82; article, Artists of the Rockies, spring 83. *Mem:* Soc Animal Artists. *Media:* Etching, Stone Lithograph. *Publ:* Illusr, The Ultimate Fishing Book, Houghton-Mifflin, 81. *Mailing Add:* 2901 Piedmont El Paso TX 79902

SCOTT, WALTER
PAINTER, ARCHITECT
b Pittsburgh, Pa, May 24, 19. *Study:* Carnegie Inst Technol, with Sam Rosenberg, Kindred McCleary & Camille Grapin, BArch, 41. *Exhib:* One-man shows, Mamaronek Artists Guild, NY, 72 & Briarcliff Col, 75; Nat Soc of Painters in Casein & Acrylic Ann, New York, 72-82; NJ Painters & Sculptors Soc Ann, Nat Arts Club, New York, 76; Hudson River Open, Hudson River Mus, Yonkers, NY, 76-79; and others. *Pos:* Architect, Harrison & Abramovitz, Architects, New York, 48- *Awards:* Silvermine Guild Award, 72 & Koenig Art, 74, New Eng Exhib; Hyplar Award, Nat Soc Painters Casein & Acrylic Ann, Grumbacher, 72; and others. *Mem:* Silvermine Guild Artists; Nat Soc Painters Casein & Acrylic (bd dir, 77-78); Hudson River Contemp Artists; Artists Equity Asn; Am Inst of Architects. *Media:* Multimedia. *Dealer:* Silvermine Guild of Artists New Canaan CT 06840. *Mailing Add:* 266 Pennsylvania Ave Yonkers NY 10707

SCOTT, WILLIAM P(OWELL)
PAINTER, WRITER
b Bryn Mawr, Pa, May 16, 56. *Study:* Pa Acad Fine Arts, Phladelphia, cert, 78, special commendation, Cresson Traveling scholar, 78 & J Henry Schiedt Mem scholar, 79. *Exhib:* Solo exhib, Gross McCleaf Gallery, Philadelphia, 80; Philadelphia Painting Exhib, Southern Allaghenies Mus Art, Loretto, Pa, 82; Five Artists/Recent Work, Gross McCleaf Gallery, Philadelphia, 82; Tcn Young Artists, Woodmere Art Gallery, Philadelphia, 79; and others. *Pos:* Asst dir, Gross McCleaf Gallery, Philadelphia, 81- *Awards:* Woodmere Endowment Fund Mem Prize, Woodmere Art Gallery, 79. *Media:* Oil. *Res:* Berthe Morisot (French, 1841-1895). *Publ:* Auth, Continuity anc change: Conversations with Jane Piper, 78, Martha Armstrong: Abstracted landscapes, 80, Watercolors of Susan Van Campen, 80, The mystery of ordinary objects, 82 & Nora Speyer, 84, Am Artist; auth, Harry Soviak's Watercolors, Philadelphia Arts Exchange, 78. *Mailing Add:* Gross McCleaf Gallery 1713 Walnut St Philadelphia PA 19103

SCOVILLE, JONATHAN ARMSTRONG
PAINTER, PRINTMAKER
b New York, NY, Nov 13, 37. *Study:* Art Students League, 56-57 & 64-65; NY Univ, 60-62. *Work:* Metrop Mus Art, New York; Boston Pub Libr Wiggin Collection; Butler Inst Am Art; Nat Collection Fine Art, Smithsonian Inst; Tufts New England Med Ctr, Boston. *Comn:* Landscapes, Berkshire Life Insurance Co, Pittsfield, Mass, 82 & Sohio Petroleum Co, Houston, 82. *Exhib:* One-man shows, Inst Contemp Art, Boston, 70, Houston Fine Arts Ctr, Denver, 72, Slater Mem Mus, Norwich, Conn, 79, Mattatuck Mus, Waterbury, Conn, 80 & Old State House, Hartford, Conn, 82; Wadsworth Atheneum Ann Exhib, 70s & 80s; Berkshire Mus Ann Exhib, Pittsfield, Conn, 70s & 80s. *Pos:* Assoc dir, Terry Dintenfass Gallery, New York, 62-64; dir, Dorsky Gallery, New York, 65-67. *Teaching:* Artist in residence, Colo Womens Col, 72- *Awards:* Residence fels, Yaddo, 67 & MacDowell Colony, 69-71 & 75-80; Conn Comn Arts Grants, 76 & 79. *Mem:* Art Students League; Berkshire Art Asn. *Media:* Oil, Pastel; Etching. *Dealer:* Condeso-Lawler Gallery 76 Greene St New York NY 10012. *Mailing Add:* Old Town Rd West Cornwall CT 06796

SCRIBNER, CHARLES, III
HISTORIAN, LECTURER
b Washington, DC, May 24, 51. *Study:* Princeton Univ, AB, 73, MFA, 75, PhD, 77. *Pos:* Exec vpres, Charles Scribner's Sons, 83- *Teaching:* Instr

Baroque art, Princeton Univ, 76-77, mem adv coun, Dept Art & Archaeol, 83- *Res:* Baroque art, especially religious art of Rubens, Bernini and Caravaggio--cultural world of the Counter-Reformation. *Publ:* Auth, Sacred architecture: Rubens' Eucharist tapestries, Art Bulletin, 75; auth, Daniel Hopfer's Venus and Amor, Princeton Univ Art Mus Rec, 76; auth, In Alia Effigie: Caravaggio's London Supper at Emmaus, Art Bulletin, 77; auth, The Triumph of the Eucharist: Tapestries by Rubens, UMI Res Press, 82; auth, Rubens and Bernini, Ringling Mus J, 83. *Mailing Add:* 215 E 68 St New York NY 10021

SCRIVER, (BOB) ROBERT MACFIE
SCULPTOR
b Browning, Mont, Aug 15, 14. *Study:* Carroll Col, Helena, Mont, Hon PhD(art), 76. *Work:* Glenbow Found, Calgary, Alta; Whitney Gallery Western Art, Cody, Wyo; Mont Hist Soc, Helena; Panhandle Plains Mus, Canyon, Tex. *Comn:* Statue (bison), Great Falls High Sch, Mont, 67; Bill Linderman (statue), Rodeo Cowboy Asn, Cowboy Hall Fame, Oklahoma City, 68; Rustler (statue), C M Russell High Sch, Great Falls, 68. *Exhib:* Acad Western Art, Cowboy Hall Fame, Oklahoma City, 73; Allied Art Ctr, Calgary, Alta, 73; solo exhib, Stremmel Galleries, Security Nat Bank, Reno, 75; Rodeo in Bronze Ser, Wells Fargo Bank, San Francisco, 76; Grand Cent Art Gallery, New York, 76. *Awards:* Gold Medals, 69-71 & Silver Medal, 72, Cowboy Hall Fame; Silver Medal, Nat Acad Western Art, 73. *Bibliog:* Article, Am Artist Mag, 63; article, Rev Mod, 64. *Mem:* Salmagundi Club; Nat Sculpture Soc; Cowboy Artists Am; Nat Acad Western Art. *Media:* Bronze. *Publ:* Auth, An Honest Try, 75. *Mailing Add:* Box 172 Browning MT 59417

SCUCCHI, ROBIE (PETER), JR
EDUCATOR, PAINTER
b Lake Village, Ark, Apr 10, 44. *Study:* Ark State Univ, with Dan F Howard, BS(painting), 67; Southern Ill Univ, Edwardsville, painting with John Richardson, 70-71; Inst Allende, Univ Guanajuato, Mex, with James Pinto & Fred Samuelson, MFA(painting), 71. *Work:* Claypool-Young Art Gallery, Morehead State Univ, Ky; Matrix Art Gallery, Ind Univ, Bloomington; Grinstead Art Gallery, Cent Mo State Univ, Warrensburg; Jackson Hall Art Gallery, Ky State Univ, Frankfort; Gallery Fine Arts, Univ Ark, Little Rock. *Exhib:* Washington & Jefferson Col Gallery, Washington, Pa, 73 & 79; Birmingham Mus Art, Ala, 74; one-man shows, Jackson Hall Art Gallery, Ky State Univ, Frankfort, 81, Claypool-Young Art Gallery, Morehead State Univ, Ky, 81 & Matrix Art Gallery, Ind Univ, Bloomington, 82; and others. *Teaching:* Instr & head painting, drawing & design, NW High Sch, House Springs, Mo, 67-71; assoc prof art, Miss State Univ, Starkville, 71- *Awards:* Best Show Awards, St Charles Art Guild 4th Ann, 76 & Ark Bicentennial, 76; 2nd Place Purchase, Am Inst Architects, 72. *Mem:* Nat Soc Painters Casein & Acrylic; Col Art Asn Am; SE Col Arts Conf; Miss Mus Art Asn; Nat & Miss Art Educ Asn (state assemblyman, 78-79, state vpres, 78-80). *Media:* Charcoal, Acrylic. *Mailing Add:* 2402 Maple Dr Starkville MS 39759

SEABERG, STEVE (STEVENS)
ASSEMBLAGE ARTIST, PERFORMANCE ARTIST
b Evanston, Ill, Sept 30, 30. *Study:* Northwestern Univ, BS, 52, MA, 61; Academie Grande Chaumiere, Paris, 56. *Work:* Art Bus Collection, State Ga, Atlanta; Cable Atlanta, Pub Access Channel 16. *Comn:* Mural, comn by Ted Berrigan, New York, 66; mural, comn by Melvin Wildberger, Brooklyn, NY, 67; Lex et Domus (mural), The Law Office, Atlanta, 76; The Black Arts (mural), Nat Endowment Arts, Atlanta, 78; Living Sculpture (monument), City of Atlanta, 83. *Exhib:* Chicago and Vicinity, 60, Biennial Print & Drawing Exhib, Art Inst Chicago, 62; solo exhibs, Here Come de Judgement!, Clocktower Gallery, New York, 79 & Ancestors, Malmö Konsthall, Sweden, 81; Artists in Georgia, High Mus Art, Atlanta, 82; Collage & Assemblage, Miss Mus Art, Jackson, 82; Leisure America, Tampa Mus Art, Fla, 83; Birmingham Biennial, Birmingham Mus Art, Ala, 83. *Pos:* Artist & artist preparator, Field Mus Natural Hist, Chicago, 67-65; painter in residence, Neighborhood Art Ctr, Atlanta, 76-79; program dir, Arts Interface, Atlanta, 80-83. *Teaching:* Vis lectr art hist, Northwestern Univ, 61-64; lectr & asst prof studio & art hist, Rutgers Univ, 67-70; instr humanities, Clark Col, Ga, 70-73. *Awards:* Nat Endowment Arts Visual Artist Fel, 78; Site Work Grants, Arts Festival Atlanta, 79-81; Third Prize, Birmingham Biennial, Birmingham Art Asn, 83. *Bibliog:* Öyvind Fahlström (dir, film), Sweden's TV, 68; Ann Livet (auth), Steve Seaberg's skeletons, Art Papers, 6/79; Tom Patterson (auth), Who is Steve Seaberg?, Brown's Guide to Ga, 8/82. *Publ:* Contrib, Chapters in the prehistory of Eastern Ariz, Field Mus Natural Hist, 64; auth, Sunlight in Jungleland, private publ, 65; coauth, Guds Ansikte, Raben & Sjögran, 65; illusr, Om Baddräkter, Författerförlaget, 77; Song of Atlanta, Ali Baba, 81. *Mailing Add:* 683 Queen St SW Atlanta GA 30310

SEABOURN, BERT DAIL
PAINTER
b Iraan, Tex, July 9, 31. *Study:* Oklahoma City Univ, cert(art); Famous Artists Schs, Westport, Conn, cert(art); Okla Cent State Univ; Okla Univ. *Work:* Okla Art Ctr, Oklahoma City; Five Civilized Tribes Mus, Muskogee, Okla; Heard Mus, Phoenix; Vatican Mus Mod Religious Art, Italy; Pac Northwest Indian Ctr, Gonzaga Univ. *Exhib:* Kennedy Ctr Performing Arts, 76 & 83; New Britain Mus Am Art, Conn, 79; Pintura Amerinda Contemp/EUA, 80; Kimball Art Ctr, Park City, Utah, 80; Denver Mus Natural Hist, Colo, 80; Native Am Ctr Living Arts, Niagara Falls, NY, 81; Mus Natural Hist, Smithsonian Inst, Washington, DC, 83; and others. *Pos:* Artist & journalist, USN, 51-55; art dir & artist, Okla Gas & Elec Co, Oklahoma City, 55-77. *Awards:* Grand Award, Five Civilized Tribes Mus, 73; Grand Award, Red Cloud Indian Ann, 74; Gov Art Award, Okla, 81. *Bibliog:* Dick Frontain (auth), Cherokee artist Bert D Seabourn, Prairie Hawk, 79; Gary L Roberts

(auth), The spiritual paintings of Bert Seabourn, Art Voices South, 80; Tricia Hurst (auth), Bert Seabourn common ties, Southwest Art, 81. *Mem:* Artists Okla Inc (pres, 69); Art Dirs Club Oklahoma City (pres, 70); Okla Art Guild (pres, 70); Southwest Watercolor Asn; Oklahoma City Advert Club. *Media:* Watercolor, Acrylic; Etching, Monotype. *Publ:* Auth & illusr, Indian Gallery, 72; auth & illusr, Master Artists of the Five Civilized Tribes, 76. *Mailing Add:* 6105 Covington Lane Oklahoma City OK 73132

SEACE, BARRY WILLIAM
PRINTMAKER, EDUCATOR
b Harrisburg, Pa, Oct 10, 46. *Study:* Kutztown State Col, with Frederick Keller, BS(art educ), 68; Univ Tenn, with Byron McKeeby, MFA(printmaking), 72. *Work:* Montgomery Mus Fine Art, Ala; Northern Ill Univ Ctr Gallery, DeKalb; Tenn State Mus, Nashville; Libr Cong Print Collection, Washington, DC; Calif Col Arts & Crafts, San Francisco. *Exhib:* Boston Printmakers 25th Anniversary Exhib, 73; New Orleans Int Exhib, 74; Nat Drawing Exhib, Southern Ill Univ, DeKalb, 75; Springfield 56th Nat Exhib, Mus Fine Art, Mass, 75; one-man show, Montreal Mus Fine Arts, Que, 76; and others. *Teaching:* Teaching asst drawing, Univ Tenn, Knoxville, 70-72; asst prof printmaking, Mt Holyoke Col, 72- *Awards:* Purchase Award, 4th Ann Nat Graphics Exhib, DeKalb, 71; Purchase Award, 8th Ann Nat Print & Drawing Competition, Dulin Gallery, 73; Merit Award, Springfield 56th Nat, Mus Fine Art, Mass, 75. *Mem:* Col Art Asn Am; Graphics Soc, Hollis, NH; Springfield Art League; Friends of Art, Mt Holyoke Col. *Media:* Mixed. *Mailing Add:* Holyoke Community Col Dept Art 303 Homestead Ave Holyoke MA 01040

SEAMAN, DRAKE F
PAINTER
US citizen. *Study:* Kachina Art Sch, with Jay Datus, 59-63; also murals with Ray Strong, 70. *Comn:* Landscape mural, Seventh Day Adventist Church, Santa Barbara, Calif; Prodigal Son (mural), St Joseph's Catholic Church, Williams, Ariz, 83. *Exhib:* Palace Arts & Sci, San Francisco, 70; Santa Barbara Mus Art, 70; O'Brien's Art Emporium, Scottsdale, Ariz, 70-71; Troys Cowboy Art Gallery, Scottsdale, 71-72; Jamison Gallery, Tucson, Ariz, 72; El Prado Gallery, Sedona, Ariz, 74-78; Am Painters in Paris, France, 75; plus others. *Bibliog:* Bob Austin (auth), Reflections on Oil, Austin Gallery, 70; article in SW Art, 4/76. *Media:* Oil. *Publ:* Auth (autobiog), Modern Veterinary Practice, 74 & Animal Cavalcade, 74. *Mailing Add:* PO Box 23 Williams AZ 86046

SEAMANS, BEVERLY BENSON
SCULPTOR
b Boston, Mass, Oct 31, 27. *Study:* Mus Sch Fine Arts, Boston, 48-50; with George Demetrios, 66-70; also with Peter Abate, 68- *Work:* Essex Inst & Peabody Mus, Salem, Mass. *Comn:* Bronze, First Nat Bank Boston, Mass, 69; bronze, Salem Hospital, Mass, 76; bronze, Mass Inst Technol, 80; bronze, Camp Kieve, Nobleboro, Maine, 81; and other pvt collections. *Exhib:* Nat Sculpture Soc, New York, 73, 76-80; one-person shows, Essex Inst, Salem, 74, Mus Sci, Boston, 76, Pingrees Sch, Hamilton, 75 & 77 & Peabody Mus, Salem, 79-80; and other group & one-person shows. *Awards:* First Prize, Marblehead Arts Asn, 77 & 80; Silver Medal, Nat Sculpture Soc, 78; Third Prize, Marblehead Arts Asn, 83. *Bibliog:* Sharron King (auth), Woman 75, Channel 4, Boston, 75. *Mem:* Nat Sculpture Soc; New Eng Sculptors Asn; Copley Soc; Cambridge Arts; Marblehead Arts. *Media:* Bronze, Marble. *Mailing Add:* 5 Harbor View Marblehead MA 01945

SEAMES, CLARANN
PAINTER, ILLUSTRATOR
b Buffalo, NY. *Study:* Albright Art Sch, cert(with honors); Univ Buffalo, BFA(with honors); Syracuse Univ, MFA; also with Charles Burchfield. *Work:* Albright/Knox Gallery, Buffalo, NY; Munson-Williams-Proctor Inst, Utica, NY; Utica Col; Syracuse Univ; Gallery on the Park, Troy. *Exhib:* Cooperstown Nat, NY, 75; Western NY Regional Exhib, Albright-Knox Gallery; Cent NY Artists Ann, Munson-Williams-Proctor Inst; Young Am Gallery, St Louis, Mo; Robertson Mem Ann, Binghamton. *Pos:* Head fashion illusr, L L Berger, Buffalo, NY, 55-59; all art advertising, Casual MS, 61-70; art dir, Syracuse Mag, 63-65. *Teaching:* Instr painting, Albright Art Sch, 55-58; instr figure drawing, Univ Buffalo, 55-59; prof fashion illusr, Syracuse Univ, 61- *Bibliog:* Art rev in Buffalo Eve News & Courier, Syracuse Herald J & many others. *Media:* Multimedia. *Mailing Add:* 101 Janet Dr Syracuse NY 13224

SEARLES, CHARLES
PAINTER, SCULPTOR
b Philadelphia, Pa. *Study:* Pa Acad Fine Arts, four-year cert, 73. *Work:* First Pa Bank, Philadelphia; Hrlem State Bldg, New York; Smithsonian Inst; Howard Univ. *Comn:* Celebration (mural), Gen Serv Admin, Philadelphia, 76; Playtime (mural), City Philadelphia, 78. *Exhib:* Black Artist in America, Whitney Mus Am Art, 71; Invisible Artist, Philadelphia Mus Art, 73; Jubilee, Boston Mus Fine Arts, 75; Afro-American Abstract, PS1 Gallery, New York, 81; one-person shows, Landmark Gallery, New York, 81, Peale Gallery, Pa Acad Fine Arts, 82 & Sande Webster, Philadelphia, 83. *Teaching:* Lectr drawing, Philadelphia Col Art, 73- *Awards:* Cresson Award, Sr Show, Pa Acad Fine Arts, 71; Nat Endowment Fel Arts, 78; Creative Artists Pub Serv Fel, 80. *Media:* Acrylic; Painted Wood Sculpture. *Dealer:* Sande Webster 2018 Locust St Philadelphia PA. *Mailing Add:* 640 Broadway New York NY 10012

SEARLES, STEPHEN
SCULPTOR
b Leonia, NJ. *Study:* Art Students League, with George Bridgman, Frank V DuMond & Reginald Marsh; Grand Cent Sch Art, New York, with Georg Lober & Harvey Dunn; Gloucester with Emile Gruppel also with Gelin, Fontainebleau, France. *Comn:* Our Lady of Good Voyage Statue, Church of Our Lady of Good Voyage, Gloucester, Mass; portrait busts, Norman Rockwell & Arthur Fiedler; and many others. *Exhib:* Sculpture, Grassy Gallery, Biarritz, France, 46, Guild of Boston Artists, 72 & Rockport Art Asn, 72. *Teaching:* Instr drawing & sculpture, Biarritz Am Univ, 45-46; instr life drawing & sculpture, Newark Sch Fine & Indust Art, 50-53; instr life drawing, Vesper George Sch Art, Boston, 62- *Awards:* Sculpture Awards, Salmagundi Club, 52, Am Artists Prof League, 76 & 77 & Rockport Art Asn, 77 & 78. *Mem:* Nat Sculpture Soc; Am Artists Prof League; Am Vet Soc Artists; Nat Arts Club; life mem Art Students League. *Media:* Bronze, Stone. *Dealer:* Guild of Boston Artists 162 Newbury St Boston MA 02116. *Mailing Add:* 44 Flint St Boston MA 02145

SEARS, STANTON GRAY
PAINTER, SCULPTOR
b Bethlehem, Pa, Oct 22, 50. *Study:* RI Sch Design, BFA, 73; Pa State Univ, MFA, 76. *Comn:* Sculptures, NH Art Asn, Manchester, 79 & 80; sculptures, Phillips Exeter Acad, NH, 81. *Exhib:* Stedman Art Gallery, Rutgers Univ, Camden, NJ, 79; Lee Hall Gallery, Northern Mich Univ, Marquette, 79; Allentown Art Mus, Pa, 79; De Cordova Mus, Lincoln, Mass, 79; Currier Gallery Art, Manchester, NH, 81; solo show, Plymouth State Col Art Gallery, Plymouth, NH, 81; Silvermine Guild Artists, New Canaan, Conn, 81; and others. *Teaching:* Instr, Pa State Univ, State Col, 75-78; instr, Univ NH, Durham, 80-81; instr, Manchester Inst Arts & Sci, NH, 81- *Awards:* Drawing Award, Educ Ctr Arts, New Haven, Conn, 78; Currier Award, NH Art Asn 34th Ann, Currier Gallery, 80; Award for Advanc Am Art, Arts Coun Holyoke, Mass, 81. *Bibliog:* David Elliot (auth), What are those stripes in the ravine, Univ NH Newspaper, 81; Laura Holland (auth), Sears' high overhead, Valley Advocate, 81; John Wharton (auth), David Fullam, Stanton Sears, Art New Eng, 81. *Mem:* Col Art Asn Am; NH Art Asn. *Media:* Graphite, Pastel; Welded Aluminum. *Dealer:* Boston Art Work 2345 Washington St Newton Lower Falls MA 02162. *Mailing Add:* 24 West Bridge St Manchester NH 03101

SEAWELL, THOMAS ROBERT
PRINTMAKER, PAINTER
b Baltimore, Md, Mar 17, 36. *Study:* Washington Univ, BFA, 58; Tex Christian Univ, MFA, 60. *Work:* Pushkin Mus, Moscow; Brit Mus, London; Libr Cong, Washington, DC; Mem Art Gallery, Rochester, NY; Brooklyn Mus, NY. *Exhib:* Prints & Posters from USA, seven mus in Israel, 69; Boston Printmakers Nat Exhibs, 70-79; Prints USA 1974, UP Gallery, Univ Pittsburgh; 2nd Miami Graphics Biennial, Metrop Mus & Art Ctr, 75; 30 Yrs of Am Printmaking Including 20th Nat Print Exhib, Brooklyn Mus, 76; Colorprint USA, 77-80; Int Biennial, Philadelphia Print Club, 79. *Pos:* Vis artist, numerous schs art, 77-83, ETex State Univ, spring 83. *Teaching:* Prof drawing & printmaking, State Univ NY Col Oswego, 63- *Awards:* State Univ NY Res Found Printmaking Fels, 67, 70 & 74. *Bibliog:* The Complete Collagraph, Romano & Ross, The Free Press, Macmillan, 80; 30 Years of American Printmaking including the 20th National Exhibition, Brooklyn Mus, 76. *Mem:* Boston Printmakers; Philadelphia Print Club; Soc NJ Painters & Sculptors; Soc Am Graphic Artists; Philadelphia Watercolor Club. *Dealer:* Associate American Artists 663 5th Ave New York NY 10022 & 1614 Latimer St Philadelphia PA 19103; Miriam Perlman Inc 505 N Lakeshore Dr Suite 5410 Chicago IL 60611. *Mailing Add:* RD 1 Box 235 Sterling NY 13156

SEAWRIGHT, JAMES L, JR
SCULPTOR, EDUCATOR
b Jackson, Miss, May 22, 36. *Study:* Univ Miss, BA, 57; Art Students League, NY, 61-62. *Work:* Mus Mod Art, Whitney Mus Am Art & Solomon R Guggenheim Mus, New York; Larry Aldrich Mus, Ridgefield, Conn; Brandeis Univ Rose Art Mus, Waltham, Mass. *Comn:* Electronic Environ, Seattle-Tacoma Int Airport, 73; outdoor sculpture, NJ State Mus, Trenton, 76. *Exhib:* Whitney Ann, Whitney Mus Am Art, 67; The Sixties, Mus Mod Art, 67; Focus on Light, NJ State Mus, Trenton, 68; Magic Theater, Nelson Gallery Performing Arts Found, Kansas City, Mo, 68; Cybernetic Serendipity, Inst Contemp Art, London, 69; Theodoron Awards Show, Solomon R Guggenheim Mus, New York, 69; Works for New Spaces, Walker Art Ctr, Minneapolis, 71; Art of the Space Age, Huntsville Mus Art, Ala, 78. *Pos:* Dir visual arts prog, Princeton Univ, 74- *Teaching:* Teacher sculpture, Sch Visual Arts, New York, 67-69; lectr sculpture, Princeton Univ, 69- *Awards:* Theodoron Found Award, Guggenheim Mus, 69; fel Graham Found Walker Art Ctr, 70-71; Nat Endowment Arts Comn, NJ State Mus, 76. *Bibliog:* Article in Life Mag, 4/67; Douglas Davis (auth), interview, Art in Am, 1-2/68; Ralph T Coe (auth), The Magic Theater, Circle Press, 70. *Publ:* Contribr, On the Future of Art, Viking, NY, 70. *Mailing Add:* 155 Wooster St New York NY 10012

SEBASTIAN (ENRIQUE CARBAJAL G)
SCULPTOR
b Chihuahua, Mexico, Nov 16, 47. *Study:* Nat Sch Plastic Arts, Univ Mex, 69; Res Fel, Nat Univ Mex, 79- *Work:* Mus Mod Art, Mexico City, Jerusalem, Rio de Janeiro & Caracas; Schubladen Mus, Bern, Switzerland. *Comn:* Construccion (mural), Col Civil Engineers, Mexico City, 74; Trono de Netzahaulcoyotl, gift from Govt Mex to Vancouver, Can, 78; Glorieta (sculpture), Gucadigose, Villahermosa, Mexico, 76; Tlaloc (sculpture) & Ctr Sculptural Space, Nat Univ Mex, Mexico City, 79. *Exhib:* One-man shows,

Palace Fine Arts, Mexico, 74, Mus Mod Art, Mexico, 76, Loeb Gallery, Bern, Switzerland, 80; Graphic Arts Biennial, Florence, Italy, 74; Mus Mod Art, Paris, 77, Rio de Janeiro, 78 & Caracas, Venezuela, 78; The Rutherford Barnes Collection, Denver, 79. *Collections Arranged:* Arte Correro (auth, catalog), Carrillo Gil Mus, 79; Mex Sculptors in Can, Capilano Col Art Gallery, Vancouver, Can, 80. *Teaching:* Instr urban sculpture, Escuela Nac de Arte Plastico, Mexico City, 70-78; instr painting, La Esmeralda, Mexico City, 75-77; prof res, Univ Nac Autonoma Metrop, Mexico City, 78-81. *Awards:* First Prize, I Biennial Art, Mexico, 74. *Bibliog:* Roberto Pontual (auth), Geometric sensivel, Edicones J Brasil, 78; Frank J Malina (auth), Visual Art, Mathematics & Computers, Pergamon Press, 79; Louis G Redstone (auth), Public Art-New Directions, McGraw-Hill, 81. *Mem:* Mex Asn Visual Artists (pres, 81-). *Media:* Steel, Aluminum. *Publ:* Auth, My Transformable Structures Based on the Mobius Strip, Leonardo, Vol 8, Pergamon Press, 75; co-auth, Extructura y Biografia de un Objeto, Nat Univ Mex, 79. *Dealer:* Rutherford Barnes Collection 1415 Larimer Sq Denver CO 80202. *Mailing Add:* CDA Protasio Tagle 42 Mexico 18 DF Mexico

SECKEL, PAUL BERNHARD
PAINTER, PRINTMAKER
b Osnabrueck, Ger, July 18, 18; US citizen. *Study:* London Cent Sch Arts & Crafts; Univ Buffalo, BFA; Yale Univ, MFA. *Exhib:* Recent Drawings, USA, Mus Mod Art, New York, 56; Drawings by Invitation, Flint Inst Art, 57; Exhib of Paintings Eligible for Purchase, Am Acad Arts & Lett, 63; Audubon Artists Ann. *Awards:* Emily Lowe Award, 63. *Mem:* New York Artists Equity Asn. *Media:* Acrylic, Oil. *Publ:* Auth, How to Make Original Color Lithographs--A Manual for Professional Artists, 70. *Mailing Add:* 12 Van Etten Blvd New Rochelle NY 10804

SECKLER, DOROTHY GEES
CRITIC, PAINTER
b Baltimore, Md, July 9, 10. *Study:* Teachers Col, Columbia Univ, BS(art educ); Md Inst Art, dipl traveling scholar, 31; NY Univ; also in Europe. *Exhib:* One-woman show, Leonore Ross Gallery, Provincetown, Mass, 80; Provincetown Mus, 80-81; two-woman show, Outermost Gallery, Provincetown, Mass, 82. *Pos:* Assoc ed, Art News & Art News Ann, 50-55; gallery ed, Art in Am, 55-61, contrib ed, 61-68; spec contribr fine arts, MD (Med News Mag), 57-73. *Teaching:* Lectr mod art; lectr, Mus Mod Art, 45-49; part-time instr, NY Univ, 47-52; lectr & instr, City Col New York, 57-60; lectr & instr, Pratt Inst, 60-61. *Awards:* Am Fedn Arts Award for Art Criticism, 54. *Bibliog:* Archives Am Art, Smithsonian Inst, Washington, DC. *Publ:* Coauth, The questioning public, Mus Mod Art Bulletin, 49; coauth, Figure Drawing Comes to Life, 57; contribr, Encycl World Art, 59; auth, Provincetown Painters, Everson Mus, Syracuse, NY, 77; contribr numerous articles, Arts, Art Am & Art News; also rev on exhibs & monogr. *Mailing Add:* 64 Sagamore Rd Bronxville NY 10708

SECUNDA, (HOLLAND) ARTHUR
PAINTER, COLLAGE ARTIST
b Jersey City, NJ, Nov 12, 27. *Study:* NY Univ; Art Students League; Acad Grande Chaumiere; Acad Julian; with Zadkine & L'hote, Paris, 48-50; Inst Meschini, Rome; also study in Mex. *Work:* Smithsonian Inst, Washington, DC; Nat Collection Fine Arts, Washington, DC; Mus Mod Art, New York; Art Inst Chicago; Brooklyn Mus; plus many others in US, Sweden, Belg & Switz. *Exhib:* One-man shows, La Jolla Art Mus, Calif, 66, Galerie Richard Foncke, Gent, Belg, 68, Konstsalongen Kavaletten, Uppsala, Sweden, 71, Galerie Leger, Malmo, Sweden & Arras Gallery, New York, 75; plus many others. *Awards:* Tamarind Fel, Calif, 70 & NMex, 72. *Dealer:* Galerie P Cramer Chantepoulet 13 Geneva Switz; Owl Gallery 1074 Broadway Woodmere NY 11598. *Mailing Add:* 1659 11th Street Santa Monica CA 90404

SEDERS, FRANCINE LAVINAL
DEALER
b Paris, France, Dec 12, 32; US citizen. *Study:* Univ Paris Law Sch, MLaws; Univ Wash, MCS. *Pos:* Mgr, Otto Seligman Gallery, Seattle, Wash, 65-66, mgr & owner, 66-70; mgr & owner, Francine Seders Gallery, Seattle, 70- *Specialty:* Contemporary paintings, sculpture and graphics. *Mailing Add:* 6701 Greenwood Ave N Seattle WA 98103

SEED, SUZANNE LIDDELL
PHOTOGRAPHER, WRITER
b Gary, Ind, Mar 8, 40. *Study:* Yale Univ Summer Sch Music Art, 61; Ind Univ, with Henry Holmes Smith, BA, 63; Art Inst Chicago, MFA, 82. *Work:* Chrysler Mus; Chase Manhatten Bank, NY; Exchange Nat Bank, Chicago. *Exhib:* Los Angeles Inst Contemp Art's Photog, Downey Mus Art, 80; Chicago Contemp Photog, Los Angeles Ctr Photographic Studies, Calif, 81; Women/Image/Nature, Tyler Sch Art, Philadelphia, Pa & Rochester Inst Technol, NY, 81; and others. *Mem:* Soc Photogrs Communications; Soc Photogrs Educ; Writers' Guild. *Publ:* Auth & illusr, Saturday's Child, J Philip O'Hara, 73; contribr, Women See Men, McGraw Hill, 77; contribr, Women Photograph Men, Morrow, 77; auth & illusr, Fine Trades, Follett, 79. *Dealer:* Marjorie Neikrug 224 East 68th St New York NY 10021. *Mailing Add:* 175 E Delaware Chicago IL 60611

SEEMAN, HELENE ZUCKER
WRITER, CURATOR
b New York, NY, Apr 20, 50. *Study:* Boston Univ, BA; Queens Col, NY, MLS. *Collections Arranged:* Photorealism Traveling Exhibition, NZ mus, 75-76; Audrey Flack, Univ Bridgeport, Conn, 75; Look Again, Taft Mus, Cincinnati, Ohio, 76; Rothmans of Pall Mall Traveling Exhibition, 77-78;

New Realism, Jacksonville Mus, Fla, 77; Off the Beaten Path, Brainerd Gallery, State Univ NY Col, Potsdam, 77. *Pos:* Cur, Prudential Ins Co, NJ, 80- *Teaching:* Lectr, New Sch, NY, 80 & 83, Avila Col, 81, Scripts Col, 82, Walker Art Ctr, 83. *Bibliog:* Randy Rosen (auth), Corporate collecting at a crossroads, Nat Arts Guide, 11-12/80; Connoisseur's corner, Wall St Transcript, 6/28/82; Keepers of corporate art, Fortune, 3/21/83. *Mem:* Art Libr Soc NAm. *Interests:* Organization, research and published documentation of artists and special exhibitions. *Publ:* Coauth, SoHo, Neal Schuman, 79; coauth, The PhotoRealists, Abrams, 79; contrib, Alternative Careers for Librarians, Neal Schuman, 79. *Mailing Add:* 176 Broadway 4D New York NY 10038

SEGAL, GEORGE
SCULPTOR
b New York, NY, Nov 26, 24. *Study:* NY Univ, BS(art educ); 50; Rutgers Univ, MFA, 63. *Work:* Mus Mod Art, New York; Mus Mod Art, Stockholm, Sweden; Art Gallery Ont, Toronto; Nat Gallery Can, Ottawa, Ont; Art Inst Chicago; and others. *Comn:* The Holocaust, Lincoln Park, San Francisco, 83. *Exhib:* Retrospective, Walker Art Ctr, 78-79; Whitney Mus Am Art, 78; Amherst Univ Art Mus, 80; Galerie Kornfeld, Zurich, 80; Whitney Mus Am Art, 80; Wenkenpark Riehen, Basle, Switz, 80; Nassau Co Mus Fine Art, Roslyn, NY, 80; Sidney Janis Gallery, New York, 80; Galerie Speyer, Paris, 69; Expo 70, Osaka, Japan; Walker Art Ctr, Minneapolis, 70-71; NJ State Mus, Trenton, 71; Art Inst Chicago, 71; Munson-Williams-Proctor Inst, Utica, NY, 72; Detroit Inst Art, 73; plus many other group & one-man shows. *Awards:* Walter K Gutman Found Award, 62; First Prize, Art Inst Chicago, 66. *Bibliog:* George Segal, Artsmag, 12/74; Ellen Zeiffer (auth), George Segal: sculptural environments, Am Artist, 1/75; Robert Pincus Witten (auth), Reviews: George Segal, Artforum, 1/75; plus others. *Dealer:* Sidney Janis Gallery 6 W 57th St New York NY 10019. *Mailing Add:* Davidsons Mill Rd New Brunswick NJ 08901

SEGAL, TAMA & DAVID
DEALER, DIRECTOR
Tama, b Brooklyn, NY, Feb 13, 49, David, b Bronx, NY, Aug 31, 40. *Study:* Tama, Brooklyn Mus; Pratt Inst; New Sch; David, City Col, New Sch Social Res, BFA, 64. *Pos:* Owners, Segal Gallery, 77- *Mem:* Munic Art Soc New York; Santa Fe Festival Arts. *Mailing Add:* Segal Gallery 63 E 57th St New York NY 10022

SEGALOVE, ILENE JUDY
VIDEO ARTIST, PHOTOGRAPHER
b Los Angeles, Calif, Nov 24, 50. *Study:* Univ Calif, Santa Barbara, BFA; Loyola Univ, MA(commun arts). *Exhib:* Artists Choice, Los Angeles Co Mus Art, 75; Southland Video, Long Beach Mus Mod Art, 75; Documentary Tapes, Mus Mod Art, New York, 75; Whitney Biennial, New York, 75 & 77; Los Angeles Inst Contemp Art, Calif, 76; Long Beach Mus Art, Calif, 77; one-person show, Univ Calif, Irvine, 78; Mus Contemp Art, Chicago, 80; Paris Biennele, 81; Contemp Mus Art, Houston, 82; Media Art Ctr, NY, 82; Inst Contmep Art, Boston, 83; and others. *Awards:* Nat Endowment Arts Grant, 76, 79 & 83; Am Film Inst, 80; James D Phelan Award in Video, Rocky Mountain Film, 83. *Bibliog:* Interview, KCET Public TV, 83. *Mailing Add:* 2238 Walnut Ave Venice CA 90291

SEGAN, KENNETH AKIVA
DRAFTSMAN, PRINTMAKER
b New York, NY, Feb 19, 50. *Study:* Southern Ill Univ, BA, 77; Univ Mo, MFA, 80. *Work:* Smithsonian Inst, Washington, DC; Nelson Gallery-Atkins Mus, Kansas City, Mo; Musee des Beaux-Arts, Budapest, Hungary; Prints Division, New York Pub Libr; NJ State Mus, Trenton; and many others. *Exhib:* West 82-Art and the Law, Landmark Ctr, St Paul, 82; Boston Printmakers 34th National, DeCordova Mus, 82; Recent Acquisitions: Works on Paper, Portland Art Mus, Ore, 83; 60th Soc Am Graphic Artists, New York, 83; Am Inst Archits, Seattle, 83; Sept Competition, Alexandria Mus, La, 83; and others. *Awards:* Purchase Prize, West 80-Art and the Law, West Publ Co, 80. *Bibliog:* Article, Kansas City Star, 2/10/80; article, Weekly, Seattle, 3/11/81; article, Oregonian, Portland, 9/25/82. *Media:* Etching, Drypoint; Mixed Media Drawings. *Dealer:* Equivalents Gallery 1822 Broadway Seattle WA 98122; Ainsworth Gallery 42 Bromfield St Boston MA 02108. *Mailing Add:* Studio 701 909 4th Ave Seattle WA 98104

SEGGER, MARTIN JOSEPH
HISTORIAN, MUSEUM DIRECTOR
b Felixtowe, Eng, Nov 22, 46; Can citizen. *Study:* Univ Victoria, BA, 69, with Alan Gowans, dipl, 70; Warburg Inst, Univ London, with E H Gombrich, MPhil, 73. *Collections Arranged:* Arts of the Forgotten Pioneers (with catalog), Maltwood Mus, 71; Samuel Maclure-Architect, 74 & House Beautiful, An Exhibit of Decorative Arts 1860-1920 (with catalog), 75, BC Prov Mus; Colonial Painters of British Columbia, 79; The Victoria Portrait, 81. *Pos:* Dir, Maltwood Mus, Victoria, 71-, BC Heritage Trust, Provincial Heritage Adv Bd, Heritage Can & Int Coun Monuments & Sites Can; consult mus training, Egypt/UNESCO, 83; consult, Heritas Inc, 83. *Teaching:* Lectr art hist & mus studies, Univ Victoria, BC, 71- *Awards:* Am Asn State & Local Hist & Commun Award, Heritage Can Found. *Mem:* Soc Archit Historians; Can Mus Asn (nat exec mem, 75-77); Victorian Soc, UK; Soc Study Archit Can (dir, currently); and others. *Publ:* Auth, Area Heritage Preservation Report-City of Victoria, 75, ed, Canadian Antiques Collector, BC Issue, 75; auth, Victoria: A Primer for Regional History in Architecture, 79; auth, The British Columbia Parliament Buildings, 79; auth, Heritage of Canada, 81; auth, Museum Operations Manual, 83. *Mailing Add:* 1035 Sutlej St Victoria BC V8V 2V9 Canada

SEGUR, ELEANOR CORINNE
PAINTER, INSTRUCTOR
b Toledo, Ohio, Aug 2, 23. *Study:* Buffalo Univ; Pratt Inst, illus, Sch Visual Arts, New York, advert; Art Students League; also with Edgar Whitney, Rex Brandt, George Post & Carl Molno. *Work:* Smithsonian Inst & Pentagon Bldg, DC; Craft Students League, New York. *Exhib:* Artist of the Month, Brunswick, NJ, 70; Nat Arts Club, 15 Gramercy Pk, New York, 70-80; solo exhib, Art Asn Padukah, Ky, 75; Brooklyn Watercolor Soc, Brooklyn Mus, NY, 76 & Metrop Mus Art, New York, 77; NJ Watercolor Soc, Morristown, NJ Mus, 77-79; Princeton Art Asn, McCarter Theatre, NJ, 80. *Pos:* Draftsman & sr artist, Ford Instrument Co, New York, 60-63; demonstr & lectr, Nat Arts Club, 72, 74 & 78, Metrop Mus Art, New York, 72-80 & Catharine Lorillard Wolfe Art Club Inc, 74. *Teaching:* Lectr landscapes & portraits, Craft Students League, New York, 69-80; demonstr design, figures & flowers, Nat Art League New York, 71-80; instr watercolors, New York Botanica Gardens, 72-77. *Awards:* Seven Scholarships, Washington Sq Outdoor Art Show, 65-69; Four First Prizes, Jackson Heights Art Club, New York, 68-71. *Mem:* Catharine Lorillard Wolfe Art Club (co-chmn, 66-70); Nat Art League NY; Artists Equity; Brooklyn Watercolor Soc; Island Art Guild; and others. *Media:* Watercolor, Pen & Ink. *Publ:* Auth & illusr, Watercolor Workbook (manual), Va Graphics, 74 & 76. *Mailing Add:* 42-42 80 St Apt 7P Elmhurst NY 11373

SEGY, LADISLAS
DEALER, COLLECTOR
b Budapest, Hungary, Feb 10, 04. *US citizen. Study:* Cent State Univ, hon DLitt, 53. *Pos:* Dir & owner, Segy Gallery. *Teaching:* Lectr, African Sculpture & Its Background & African Sculpture & Mod Art, US. *Specialty:* African sculpture. *Collection:* African art; French and American modern painting and sculpture; Peruvian textiles; Mexican Mascala sculptures; prehistoric axes. *Publ:* Auth, African Sculpture, 58 & Masks of Black Africa, 75, Dover; auth, African Sculpture Speaks, Da Capo, 4th ed, 75; over 50 papers in scholarly mag in eight countries; plus others. *Mailing Add:* 50 W 57th St New York NY 10019

SEHRING, ADOLF
PAINTER, SCULPTOR
b Urupino, Russia, June 8, 30; US citizen. *Study:* Berlin Acad Art, 46-49. *Work:* Chrysler Mus, Norfolk; Bayly Mus, Va; St Mary's Inst, Mich; US Dept State Embassy, Rome & London; Mellon Collection, Pa. *Comn:* Portrait of Pope John Paul II, St Mary's Inst Eastern Art (Now in the Vatican Collection, Rome), 78. *Exhib:* Youth Paints, Victoria & Albert Mus, London, Eng, 47; Qualite dela Vie, Grandpalais Salon, Paris, 75; Virginia Scene, Bayly Mus, Charlottesville, 78; Adolf Sehring, St Mary's Collection Mus, Mich, 78; Bi-Annual Exhib, Va Mus Art, Richmond, 81; Chrysler Mus, 83. *Pos:* Lectr, Lehigh Valley Art Groups, 75; lectr, Varied Civic Groups, 72-81. *Awards:* First Prize of Germany, Rias, Berlin, 46. *Bibliog:* Levin Houston (auth), Adolf Sehring and Realism, Kembel Publ, 77; S Bullard (auth), Sehring Paints, Daily Progress, 78; Rome Accepts Papal Portrait by Sehring, Associated Press, 78. *Mem:* NY Artist's Equity Asn. *Media:* Oil, Watercolor; Bronze. *Dealer:* Emery Samet Box 363 Cliffside Park NJ 07010. *Mailing Add:* 101 W Locust St Box 363 Culpepper VA 22701

SEIDE, PAUL A
SCULPTOR
b New York, NY, Feb 15, 49. *Study:* Egani Neon Glassblowing Sch, cert, 71; Univ Wis, BS(art), 74. *Work:* Nat Mus Mod Art, Kyoto, Japan; Corning Mus Glass, NY; Chrysler Mus Art, Norfolk, WVa; Wheaton Mus Glass, NJ; Lannan Found Mus, Palm Beach, Fla; and others. *Exhib:* Okla Art Ctr, Oklahoma City, 78; Corning Mus Glass, NY, 78-79; Leigh Yawkey Woodson Art Mus, Wausau, Wis, 79 & 81; Hokkaido Mus Mod Art, Sapporo, Japan, 82; Kohler Art Ctr, Sheboygan, Wis, 82; Gallandet Col, Washington, DC, 82; Tucson Mus Art, Ariz, 83; and others. *Pos:* Design dir & vpres, Milropa Studios, New York, 75- *Teaching:* Instr, Milropa Studios, New York, 75-76 & New Sch Social Res, New York, 76-77. *Awards:* Res Grant, Union Molycorp, Los Angeles, 82. *Bibliog:* Judy Spurgin (auth), article, Art Craft Mag, 10-11/80. *Mem:* Glass Art Soc. *Dealer:* Heller Gallery 965 Madison Ave New York NY 10021; Kurland Summers Gallery 8742A Melrose Ave Los Angeles CA 90069. *Mailing Add:* 62-82 Saunders St Rego Park NY 11374

SEIDEN, ARTHUR
PAINTER, ILLUSTRATOR
b Brooklyn, NY. *Study:* Queens Col, BA(cum laude), 74; Art Students League, 8 yrs study with Will Barnet, S Dickinson, Charles Alston & Mario Cooper; New Sch, with Stuart Davis. *Work:* Kerlan Collection, Univ Minn; Philip Morris Corp & Kennedy Gallery, New York; Rutgers Univ, New Brunswick, NJ. *Exhib:* Am Watercolor Soc, Nat Acad Design, New York, 64, 67 & 68; one-man show, Lotos Club, New York, 74, group shows, Lotos Club, 75 & Union Carbide Bldg Gallery. *Teaching:* Guest instr, New York City Community Col. *Awards:* Bk Awards, 54, 57 & 61. *Mem:* Am Watercolor Soc; life mem Lotos Club; life mem Art Students League; Artist's Equity NY Inc; Soc Illusr. *Media:* Transparent Watercolor. *Publ:* Illusr, Train to Timbuctoo, Golden Bks, 51; illusr, Greek Gods and Heroes, 61, Big Treasure Book of Fairy Tales, 64 & Big Book of Kittens, 68, Grosset & Dunlap; illusr, Doc stops a war, Reader's Digest. *Mailing Add:* 380 Howard Ave Woodmere NY 11598

SEIDL, CLAIRE
PAINTER
b Greenwich, Conn, May 17, 51. *Study:* London Polytech, Sir John Cass Col Art, 72; Syracuse Univ, Col Visual & Performing Arts, BFA(cum laude), 73;

City Univ New York, Hunter Col, MFA, 82. *Work:* Albright Col, Pa; Aldrich Mus, Conn; Gen Instrument Corp, New York; Richardson-Vicks Corp, Conn; Mobil Oil Corp, New York; and others. *Exhib:* Silvermine Guild, Conn, 77; Aldrich Mus, Conn, 81; solo shows, Hunter Gallery, New York, 82 & John Davis Gallery, Akron, Ohio, 83; Columbus Mus, Ohio, 83; New Work--New York, Newcastle Polytech, England, 83; Juxtapositions, Stephen Rosenberg Gallery, 83; and others. *Collections Arranged:* Ten Downtown, 11th Ann Open Studios of NY Artists, 78; Color/Gestures with Mary Abbott, Freedman Gallery, 79; Summer Selections, Haber Theodore Gallery, New York, 81; and others. *Pos:* Bd of dirs, 22 Wooster, New York, 79- *Teaching:* Instr painting & design, Col New Rochelle, NY, 78-79; instr, painting & drawing, Fairleigh Dickenson Univ, NJ, 80. *Awards:* Nancy Ashton Mem Fund Prize, 82; William Graf Fel, 82; Fel, Cummington Community of the Arts, 83. *Bibliog:* Valentin Tatransky (auth), Ten downtown, Arts Mag, 9/78; Jacqueline Moss (auth), The symphonic interplay of looking at the '60's and '70's, 3/21/82; Marina Vaizey in Berlin: New work--New York, London Sunday Times, 10/30/83. *Mem:* 22 Wooster (treas, 79-80). *Media:* Oils. *Dealer:* John Davis Gallery 61 S Main St Akron OH 44308; Stephen Rosenberg Gallery 115 Wooster St New York NY 10012. *Mailing Add:* 140 W Broadway New York NY 10013

SEIDLER, DORIS
PAINTER, PRINTMAKER
b London, Eng. *Study:* Atelier 17, New York, with Stanley William Hayter. *Work:* Smithsonian Inst, Washington, DC; Philadelphia Mus Art; Brooklyn Mus; Seattle Mus Art; Whitney Mus Am Art, New York. *Exhib:* Vancouver Int Print Exhib; First & Second Hawaii Nat Print Exhib, Honolulu Acad Arts; Pa Acad Fine Arts, Philadelphia; Soc Am Graphic Artists, Kennedy Gallery, 71; Jewish Mus, New York; Atelier 17, Brooklyn Mus, 78; Whitney Mus Am Art; Libr Cong, Washington, DC; Nassau Co Mus Fine Art, NY. *Awards:* MacDowell Artists Colony Fel, 66 & 75; Purchase Award, Brooklyn Mus, 68; Medal for Creative Graphics, Audubon Artists, 72. *Mem:* Soc Am Graphic Artists (rec secy, 64-71, vpres, 81). *Publ:* Auth, articles in Artist Proof. *Dealer:* Assoc Am Artists Gallery 663 Fifth Ave New York NY 10019. *Mailing Add:* 14 Stoner Ave Great Neck NY 11021

SEKIMACHI, KAY
WEAVER, INSTRUCTOR
b San Francisco, Calif, Sept 30, 26. *Study:* Calif Col Arts & Crafts, with Trude Guermonprez; Haystack Mountain Sch of Crafts, with Jack Lenor Larsen. *Work:* Bonaventure Hotel, Los Angeles, Calif; Matthews Ctr, Ariz State Univ, Tempe; Mus Contemp Crafts, New York; Smithsonian Inst, Washington, DC; The Royal Scottish Mus, Edinburgh. *Comn:* Rm Dividers, Japan Air Lines Lounge, Terminal Bldg, San Francisco Int Airport. *Exhib:* Mod Am Wall Hangings, Victoria & Albert Mus, London, 62; Wall Hangings, Mus Mod Art, New York, 68; Woven Structures, Camden Arts Ctr, London, Eng, 72; 6th Biennale Int de la Tapisserie, Lausanne, Switz, 73; Govett-Brewster Art Gallery, New Plymouth, NZ, 74; 2nd Int Exhib of Miniature Textiles, Brit Crafts Ctr, London, Eng, 76; Fiberworks: Americas & Japan, Nat Mus Mod Art, Kyoto, Japan, 77. *Teaching:* Instr weaving, Adult Div, San Francisco Community Col, 65-; workshop instr, US & Hawaii. *Awards:* Textile Award, Fiber/Clay & Metal, St Paul, Minn, 53; Designer/Craftsman USA Award, Brooklyn Mus, NY, 53; Nat Endowment Arts Craftmen's Fel, 74. *Bibliog:* Lee Nordness (auth), Objects, USA, Viking, 70; Jack L Larsen & Mildred Constantine (coauths), Beyond Craft: The Art Fabric, Van Nostrand, Reinhold, 73; Irene Waller (auth), Textile Sculpture, Studio Vista, London, 77. *Mem:* Am Crafts Coun. *Mailing Add:* 2145 Oregon St Berkeley CA 94705

SELCHOW, ROGER HOFFMAN
PAINTER, SCULPTOR
b Greenwich, Conn, Feb 13, 11. *Study:* Grand Cent Sch Art, New York; Columbia Univ; also with Dong Kingman; Acad Grande Chaumiere, Paris; also with Andre Lhote & Fernand Leger, Paris; Inst Statale d'Arte, Florence, Italy. *Work:* Mus Beaux-Arts, Liege, Belg; Wadsworth Atheneum; NY Univ; Brooklyn Mus; Metrop Mus Art, New York; plus others. *Exhib:* Groupe Espace Paris, Vaison-la-Romaine, France, 59; Vingt-Ans d'APIAW, Mus Beaux Arts, Liege, Belg, 65; retrospective, Bruce Mus, Greenwich, Conn, 69; Images Gallery, New York, 83; Isoa Gallery Group, Grennwich, Conn, 83. *Pos:* Dir, Atelier Vieux Vaison, Vaison-la-Romaine, France, 53-60. *Awards:* Two First Place Medals, Grand Cent Sch Art, 33; First Prize, Greenwich Soc Artists, 54. *Bibliog:* Robert Vrinat (auth), Portrait d'Artiste--Selchow, Actualite Artistique Paris, 4/53; Gilbert Chaboud (auth), Un Americain Vaisonnais: Selchow, Le Meridionale-La France Orange, 3/55. *Media:* Oil, Watercolor; Electro-Wire. *Dealer:* Raydon Gallery 1091 Madison Ave New York NY 10028; Isoa Gallery 143 Lower Cross Rd Greenwich CT 06830. *Mailing Add:* London Terrace Gardens Apt 9-F 415 W 23rd St New York NY 10011

SELETZ, EMIL
SCULPTOR
b Chicago, Ill, Feb 12, 09. *Study:* Short training periods with Jo Davidson & George Gray Barnard. *Comn:* Dr Robert Gordon Sproul (bronze bust), Univ Calif; Einstein (heroic bronze), Albert Einstein Col Med, New York; Sir William Osler (bronze), Temple Med Sch, Philadelphia; Heroic Bust of Lincoln, San Jose Court House, Calif & Law Sch, Philadelphia; Franklin Roosevelt (heroic bust), President L B Johnson Libr, Tex. *Exhib:* Ann Exhib, Painters & Sculptors Club, 52-68; Calif Art Club, 55-68; Show Case 21, 62-77; one-man show, Beverly Hills Women's Club, 67; Univ Southern Calif, 68. *Awards:* Gold Medal, Artist of the SW, 52 & 68; First in Sculpture, Painters & Sculptors Club of Calif, 70; First in Sculpture, Show Case 21, 76. *Mem:* Show Case 21, Calif Art Club; Artists of the SW (pres, 60-67); Painters & Sculptors Club Calif. *Media:* Bronze. *Mailing Add:* 9201 Sunset Blvd Los Angeles CA 90069

SELIG, J DANIEL
MUSEUM DIRECTOR, CURATOR
b Philadelphia, Pa, Apr 12, 38. *Study:* Univ Pa, BA, 59; Harvard Univ, MA, 60; Yale Univ, MA, 62. *Collections Arranged:* John Quidor: Painter of American Legend (coauth, catalog), Wichita Art Mus, 73; The Lyric Landscape of Leonid (auth, catalog), 74, Graphic Art of Bernard Kohn, 74 & Colonial Spanish Art of the Americas (coauth, catalog), 75, Reading Pub Mus, Pa; Architecture on Paper, AIA Gallery, Philadelphia, 74. *Pos:* Cur & asst to dir, Wichita Art Mus, Kans, 72-73; dir, Reading Pub Mus, Pa, 73-76; dir, Trenton City Mus, 77-79; dir, Vanderbilt Mus, Huntington, NY, 79-80; dir, Giles Gallery, 80- *Teaching:* Lectr, Div Educ, Boston Mus Fine Arts, Mass, 62-67; asst prof art hist, Univ Notre Dame, South Bend, Ind, 69-71; vis lectr art hist, Univ Ill, Chicago, 71-72. *Bibliog:* The Spires of Jersey City, New York Times, 9/17/82. *Mem:* Victorian Soc Am, Metrop Chapter; Soc Archit Historians. *Publ:* Auth, Traditional Boston architecture, Cult Resources Boston, 65; auth, The reality of realism: Hopper's sunlight on brownstones, Wichita Art Mus Bull, winter, 73; auth, Architecture on paper (catalog), Reading Pub Mus, 73; auth, The Reading Museum--The American Collection, Am Art Rev, 1-2 & 3-4/74; auth, A voice for small museums, Museologist, 76. *Mailing Add:* 251 Fifth St Jersey City NJ 07302

SELIG, (MR & MRS) MANFRED
COLLECTORS, PATRONS
Collection: Old and modern paintings; graphic art. *Mailing Add:* Empire Children's Wear Co 88 Vine St Seattle WA 98121

SELIGER, CHARLES
PAINTER
b New York, NY, June 3, 26. *Work:* Metrop Mus Art, Mus Mod Art, Solomon R Guggenheim Mus & Whitney Mus Am Art, New York; Hirshhorn Mus, Washington, DC. *Exhib:* Abstract & Surrealist American Art, Art Inst Chicago, 47 & 65th Am Exhib, 62; Abstract Art in America, Mus Mod Art, New York, 51; Art of Organic Forms, Smithsonian Inst, Washington, DC, 68; one-man shows, Andrew Crispo Gallery, New York, 74-81 & Makler Gallery, Philadelphia, 79; Art 77: A Selection of Works by Contemp Artists from New York Galleries, 77 & This is Today: An Exhib of Works by Living Artists, 77, Root Art Ctr, Hamilton Col, Clinton, NY; Albright-Knox Art Gallery, Buffalo, NY, 77-78; Miami-Dade Community Col, 81; Jacksonville Art Mus, 81; and others. *Bibliog:* Addison Parks (auth), Through the keyhole: some meaning and method to Charles Seliger, Arts Mag, 6/80. *Media:* Oil, Acrylic. *Dealer:* Andrew Crispo Gallery 41 E 57th St New York NY 10022. *Mailing Add:* 10 Lenox Ave Mt Vernon NY 10552

SELIGMAN, THOMAS KNOWLES
CURATOR, ADMINISTRATOR
b Santa Barbara, Calif, Jan 1, 44. *Study:* Stanford Univ, BA, 65; Acad of Art Col, San Francisco, BFA, 67; Sch of Visual Arts, New York, MFA, 68. *Collections Arranged:* Eskimo Art from the Toronto-Dominion Bank, 72, Man and Animals in Pre-Columbian Mesoamerica, 73, Australian Aboriginal Art from the Louis Allen Collection, 74, African and Ancient Mexican Art--The Loran Collection (coauth, catalog), 74-75, Fire, Earth and Water--Sculpture from the Land Collection of Mesoamerican Art (ed, catalog), Honolulu Acad of Arts & Seattle Art Mus, 75 & Masterpieces of Primitive Art from the Museum of Primitive Art in New York, 77, San Francisco Mus Fine Arts; Form and Freedom, Rice Inst Arts; The Art of Being Huichol, Field Mus, Chicago & Am Mus Natural Hist, New York; Treasures of Ancient Nigeria, co-organized with Detroit Inst Arts & Metrop Mus Art, 78-80; Bay Area Collects (coauth, catalog); Spirits, Gods and Kings. *Pos:* Dir, Africana Mus, Liberia, 69-71; deputy dir educ & exhibs, Fine Arts Mus of San Francisco, 72- *Teaching:* Asst prof African art hist, Cuttington Col, Liberia, Africa, 69-71. *Awards:* Aid to Mus Prof Award, Nat Endowment for the Arts, 75. *Mem:* Art Mus Asn (trustee, currently); Am Anthrop Asn; Am Asn Mus; Friends of Ethnic Arts (dir, 74-); Am Fedn Arts. *Res:* African aesthetics; art in context in Liberia, Sierra Leone and Ivory Coast. *Publ:* Auth, African art at the M H de Young Memorial Museum, African Arts, Univ Calif, Los Angeles, Vol 7 (4); auth, Educational use of an anthropology collection in an art museum, Curator, fall 74; auth, An indigenous concept of fakes--authentic African art?, African Arts, Univ Calif, Los Angeles, Vol 9 (3). *Mailing Add:* Fine Arts Mus of San Francisco Golden Gate Park San Francisco CA 94118

SELIGMANN, HERBERT J
WRITER
b New York, NY Nov 13, 1891. *Study:* Harvard Col, BA (cum laude), 12. *Pos:* Commentator, Georgia O'Keeffe (film), TV Pub Broadcasting System, 77. *Publ:* Ed, Letters of John Marin, An Am Place, 31; auth, Essays on John Marin, Marsden Hartley, 55, auth, The Zorachs of Robinhood Cove, 58 & auth, Vincent Hartgen, 60, Down East Mag; auth, Alfred Stieglitz Talking, Yale Univ Libr, 66. *Mailing Add:* 10 E 70th St New York NY 10021

SELLA, ALVIN CONRAD
PAINTER, EDUCATOR
b Union City, NJ, Aug 30, 24. *Study:* Yale Univ Sch Art; Art Students League, with Brackman & Bridgman; Columbia Univ, with Machau; Col Fine Arts, Syracuse Univ; Univ NMex; also in Mex. *Work:* Bristol Iron & Steel Co; Collectors of Am Art; Sullins Col. *Exhib:* Am Fedn Arts Traveling Exhib, 61-62; one-man exhibs, Centenary Col, Lauren Rogers Mus Art, Laurel, Miss, Munic Art Gallery, Jackson, Miss & Birmingham Mus Art, Ala, 69 & Dick Jemison Gallery, Birmingham, 76; Birmingham Mus Art, 76, Watercolor Soc Ala, 76; plus many others. *Teaching:* Head, Dept Art, Sullins Col, 48-61; prof art, Univ Ala, 61-; vis prof, Spring Workshops, Miss Art Colony, 62-64; vis prof, Shreveport Art Colony, 64-68; artist in residence, Summer Sch Arts,

Univ SC, 68. *Awards:* First Award, 54th Ann Miss Exhib; Third Prize, 7th Mobile Art Exhib, 72; 32nd Ann Watercolor Exhib First & Second Prize, Birmingham Mus Art, 72. *Mem:* Art Students League; Am Asn Univ Prof; Col Art Asn Am; fel Int Inst Arts & Lett. *Mailing Add:* Dept of Art Univ of Ala University AL 35486

SELLERS, JOHN LEWIS
EDUCATOR, DESIGNER
b Alexander City, Ala, Aug 28, 34. *Study:* Auburn Univ, BAA; Peabody Col, MA; also with Maltby Sykes for printmaking & Harry Lowe for painting. *Pos:* Art dir, Motive Mag, Nashville, Tenn, 65-67; assoc creative designer, McDonald & Saussy Agency, Inc, Nashville, 65-68; partner & creative dir, Les Hart Agency, Inc, Nashville, 68-70. *Teaching:* Prof, Col Visual & Performing Arts, Syracuse Univ, 73-, chmn dept visual commun, 78- *Awards:* Magazine of the Year Award Runner Up, Mag Publ Asn, Mag Ed Asn & Columbia Univ Sch Journalism, 67; Best US Travel Brochure, Int Asn Travel Agents, 68. *Bibliog:* Don Barron (auth), Syracuse U: Preparation for the big world, Art Direction, 10/76; Jo Yanow (auth), John Sellers: The professional as educator, Graphics Today, Spring, 77; Paul Palange (auth), A teacher first, Syracuse Alumni Mag, Fall 77. *Mem:* Art Dirs Club New York. *Mailing Add:* 117 Circle Rd Syracuse NY 13210

SELLERS, WILLIAM FREEMAN
SCULPTOR
b Bay City, Mich, June 1, 29. *Study:* Univ Mich, BArch, 54, MFA, 62. *Work:* Suspension, Six Cubes & Converging Cubes, Mem Art Gallery, Rochester, NY. *Comn:* Four Squares (painted steel), Student Asn, State Univ New York, Cortland, 69. *Exhib:* Sculpture & Prints Ann, Whitney Mus Am Art, New York, 66, Contemp Am Sculpture Ann, 68; Plus by Minus: Today's Half-Century, Albright-Knox Art Gallery, Buffalo, 68; American Sculpture of the Sixties, Grand Rapids Art Mus, Mich, 69; Painting and Sculpture Today, Indianapolis Mus Art, 70; Carleton Col, 81; Contemporary Sculpture, State Univ NY, 83; and others. *Teaching:* Instr design, Rochester Inst Technol, 62-65; asst prof sculpture, Univ Rochester, 66-70; asst prof art, Lehman Col, 70-, chmn dept art, 75-77; artist-teacher, Carleton Col, 81- *Awards:* Jurors' Show Award, Mem Art Gallery, 66. *Media:* Metal, Wood. *Dealer:* Max Hutchinson Gallery 138 Greene St New York NY 10012. *Mailing Add:* RD 1 Box 345 Salt Point Turnpike Salt Point NY 12578

SELLIN, DAVID
HISTORIAN, CURATOR
b Philadelphia, Pa, Apr 13, 30. *Study:* Skolds Atelier, Stockholm, Sweden, 46-47; Univ Pa, BA, 52; Royal Acad Art, Stockholm, painting, 52-53; Univ Pa, MA, 56, PhD, 68; Univ Rome, Italy, 56-57; Univ Cologne, 67-68. *Collections Arranged:* Eakins Collection, Philadelphia Mus Art, 61; African Art and the School of Paris (auth, catalog), Colgate Univ Art Ctr, 66; Fred and Florence Olsen Collection, Davison Art Ctr, Wesleyan Univ, 70-72; American Art in the Making (auth catalog), Smithsonian Inst & circulated to nine mus, 76; Eakins, MacDowell and Kenton (consult & auth catalog), Northcross, Roanoke, Va, 77; Art and Architecture of the US Capitol, Washington, DC, 80; American Artists in Brittany and Normandy (auth, catalog), traveling to Pa Acad & Amon-Carter Mus, Ft Worth, Tex, Phoenix Art Mus, Ariz & Nat Mus Am Art, Washington, DC, 82-83. *Pos:* Asst cur, Philadelphia Mus Art, 58-60; dir schs, Pa Acad Fine Arts, 60-62; gallery dir, Colgate Univ, 63-67 & Wesleyan Univ, 70-72; cur, Off Archit, US Capitol, Washington, DC, 76-80; guest cur, Phoenix Art Mus, 80-83. *Teaching:* Assoc prof art hist, Colgate Univ, Hamilton, NY, 63-67 & Wesleyan Univ, Middletown, Conn, 68-72; guest prof art hist, Newcomb Col, Tulane Univ, New Orleans, 67-68; distinguished vis prof, Univ Tex, Austin, 79; adj prof, Am Univ, DC, 79; vis prof, Univ Mass, Amherst, 83. *Awards:* King Gustav V Fel, 52; Fulbright-Hays Fel, Rome, 56; Smithsonian Inst Fel, 72. *Mem:* Victorian Soc Am; Columbia Hist Soc (bd mem, currently); Soc Arch Historians. *Res:* North Italian art circa 1400 and the international Gothic style; nineteenth century American art and its sources. *Publ:* Auth, Michelino da Besozzo, Univ Pa, 68; auth, Essays on: Centennial Sculpture, Remington, Fremiet, in Sculpture of a City, Walker, 74; auth, The First Pose: Eakins, Roberts, and a Century of... Nudes, Norton, 76; auth, Thomas Eakins' Gross Clinic, Norton (in prep). *Mailing Add:* 1834 16th St NW Washington DC 20009

SELSER, CHRISTOPHER
DEALER
b Omaha, Nebr, Sept 15, 50. *Study:* Univ Ariz, BA, 77. *Collections Arranged:* 1000 Years Southwest Ceramic Art (auth, catalog), ACA Gallery, 81. *Pos:* Owner, Selser Gallery, Tucson; owner & dir, ACA Am Ind Arts, New York, currently. *Specialty:* American Indian Art. *Mailing Add:* 15 Park Ave New York NY 10028

SELTZER, JOANNE LYNN
PAINTER, PHOTOGRAPHER
b Philadelphia, Pa, June 21, 46. *Study:* Northwestern Univ, cert, 63; Univ Mich, BFA(painting & ceramics), 69; NY Univ, MA(photog), 79; New Sch Social Res, 73; Pratt Inst, 74; Pratt Graphics Ctr, 74. *Work:* Ripley Mus, WVa; Soc Friends Mus Contemp Art, Ghent, Belg; Brooklyn Mus; Toledo Mus Art, Ohio; Readers Digest Found, Pleasantville, NY. *Exhib:* Painting and Sculpture Today, Indianapolis Mus Art, 78; Art About the Strange Nature of Money, Städtische Kunsthalle, Ger, 78, Van Abbe Mus, Holland, 78 & Ctr Georges Pompidou, Paris, 79; Typisch Frau, Bonner Kunstverein, Bonn & Städtisches Mus, Regensburg, Ger, 81; Heresied Benefit, Grey Art Gallery, NY Univ, 81; Mapped Art, Charts, Roots, Regions Traveling Exhib, 81-83; Hundreds of Drawings, Artists Space, New York, 83. *Teaching:* Guest lectr, Univ Iowa, 79, Univ Va, 79, Koninklijke Akad Bosch, Holland, 80 & 82, NY

Univ, 81 & Drew Univ, 81. *Bibliog:* Peter Frank (auth), article, Art News, 9/76; Lucy Lippard (auth), From the Center, E P Dutton, 77; Jos Knaepen (auth), article, Bulletin, Belg, 1/22/82. *Publ:* Contribr, Kunstlerinnen Int, 77 & Flash Art, 77. *Dealer:* Gallerie Yaki Kornblit Willemsparkweg 69 Amsterdam 1071 GS Holland. *Mailing Add:* 210 Centre St New York NY 10013

SELTZER, PHYLLIS
PRINTMAKER, PAINTER
b Detroit, Mich, May 17, 28. *Study:* Univ Iowa, BFA & MFA; Lasansky's Workshop, sr study hist of technol, with M Kranzberg. *Work:* Brooklyn Art Mus; Cleveland Mus Art; Minn Mus Art, Minneapolis; Nat Gallery Art, Ottawa, Ont; Butler Mus, Youngstown, Ohio. *Comn:* Bicentennial print, Cleveland Area Arts Coun, 75; ed of 25, Exodus print, Cleveland Health Dept. *Exhib:* 19th Nat Print Exhib, Brooklyn Mus, 74; Social Commentary/ Printmaking, Georgetown Col, Ky; Recent Trends in Printmaking, Mitchell Mus, Ill, 79; one-woman show, Playhouse, Cleveland, Ohio, 81; New Gallery, Cleveland, Ohio, 81; Vixseboxse Gallery, 83; and others. *Pos:* Coordr fine arts, Cleveland Col, Case Western Reserve Univ, 66-70; interior designer, Dalton, Van Dijk, Johnson, Cleveland, 72-74. *Teaching:* Lectr art hist & printmaking, Lake Erie Col, Painesville, Ohio, 70-72; lectr art fund, Cleveland State Univ, 71- *Awards:* Tiffany Fel, 52; Painting Award, Walker Mus, 61; Purchase Award, Brooklyn Mus 19th Nat, 75. *Bibliog:* Elizabeth McClelland (auth), article in WCLV Guide, Cleveland, 73; Dorothy Hall (auth), Art & artists, Park East, New York, 5/29/75; Helen Cullinan (auth), Prints at JCU, Plain Dealer, Cleveland, 6/75. *Mem:* New Orgn Visual Arts (secy, 73, vpres, 74); Am Soc Aesthet; Print Club Cleveland (pres, 83). *Media:* Ozalid, Pochoir; Oil. *Dealer:* Associated American Artists 663 5th Ave New York NY; Vixseboxse Gallery Cleveland OH. *Mailing Add:* 11225 Harborview Dr Cleveland OH 44102

SELVIG, FORREST HALL
HISTORIAN, WRITER
b Tacoma, Wash, Jan 3, 24. *Study:* Harvard Col, AB, 49; Univ Calif, Berkeley, 53-56. *Collections Arranged:* Selections From Richard Brown Baker Collection, 60; The Nabis, 61; Pavel Tchelitchew, 64; Jean Helion, 65; Charles Demuth (with catalog), 68; and others. *Pos:* Asst dir, Minneapolis Art Inst, Minn, 61-63; asst dir, Gallery Mod Art, New York, 63-65; dir, Akron Art Inst, 66-68; ed, New York Graphic Soc, Greenwich, Conn, 68-71. *Bibliog:* Ben Shahn Talks with Forrest Selvig, Arch Am Art J, Vol 17, 77. *Mem:* Am Asn Mus. *Res:* Late 19th century French painting, especially the Nabis and the Symbolists. *Publ:* Auth, The Nabis and Their Circle, 62; auth, American Collections, 63; ed, 19th Century Landscape Painting, 71; ed, Mosaic Deterioration and Preservation, 80; ed & trans, Views of Florence in 120 Paintings by Fabio Borbottoni, Firenze Perduta, 82. *Mailing Add:* Via Capodistria 7 00198 Rome Italy

SELVIN, NANCY
CERAMIST, SCULPTOR
b Los Angeles, Calif, 1943. *Study:* Univ Calif, Berkeley, BA, 69, with Voulkos & Ron Nagle, MA, 70. *Work:* Kohler Art Gallery, Sheboygan, Wis; Pruto Gallery, Mills Col, Oakland, Calif; Hokkoku Shimbun, Tokyo; Ariz State Univ Art Gallery, Tempe; Calif Crafts Mus, Palo Alto. *Exhib:* Mus Contemp Crafts, New York, 76; San Francisco Mus, 77; Reality and Illusion, traveling, 79-80; Calif Crafts Mus, Palo Alto, 82; Scripps Col Gallery, Claremont, Calif, 82; Oxford Gallery, Eng, 83; and others. *Teaching:* Instr ceramics, State Univ NY, Albany, 70-72; instr, Laney Col, Oakland, Calif, 73- *Awards:* Merit Award, Monterey Peninsula Mus Art, 78; Purchase Award, Shimpo-Am Corp, 80; Craftsman Fel, Nat Endowment Arts, 80. *Bibliog:* Suanne Muchnic (auth), article, Los Angeles Times, 12/18/81; Elaine Levin (auth), Ceramic metaphors, Artweek, 12/23/81; Melinda Levine (auth), Parallel views, Am Craft, 4/82. *Mem:* Am Craft Coun; Inst Ceramic Hist. *Media:* Mixed. *Dealer:* Jacqueline Anhalt 748 1/2 LaCienega Los Angeles CA 90069; Meyer Breier Weiss San Francisco. *Mailing Add:* 982 Cragmont Berkeley CA 94708

SELWITZ, RUTH F
PAINTER, SCULPTOR
b Pittsburgh, Pa. *Study:* Carnegie Inst Technol; Art Inst Pittsburgh; Samuel Rosenberg's Workshop for Prof Artists. *Work:* Butler Inst Am Art, Youngstown, Ohio; Springfield Art Mus, Mo; Westmoreland Co Mus Art, Greensburg, Pa; Mellon Nat Bank, Pittsburgh; Westinghouse Corp; and many others. *Exhib:* Butler Inst Art Nat Mid-Yr Show, Youngstown, Ohio, 63-67; Appalacian Corridors Exhib, Charleston, WVa, 68; Westmoreland Co Mus Art, Greensburg, Pa, 68-78; Pittsburgh Plan Art, 71, 72 & 76; Panoras Gallery, New York, 73; Gallery Space, 82; and many others. *Awards:* Purchase Prize, Midyear Nat Show, Butler Inst Am Art, 64; Patrons Fund Prize, Assoc Artists Pittsburgh, 65 & 67; First Prize, Watercolor USA, Springfield Art Mus, 67. *Bibliog:* Donald Miller (auth), Three woman art show winds down, Pittsburgh Post-Gazette, 5/75; Helen Kaiser (auth), Spray art makes splash in Monroeville, Pittsburgh Press, 11/76; Jody Knott (auth), Artist enjoys her experiments, Daily Tribune, 1/82. *Mem:* Pacific Palisades Art Asn; Los Angeles Art Asn. *Media:* Mixed Media; Acrylic, Hand Cast Paper. *Mailing Add:* 33 Monte Trigio Dr Pacific Palisades CA 90272

SELZ, PETER H
HISTORIAN, CURATOR
b Munich, Ger, Mar 27, 19. *Study:* Univ Chicago, fel, 46-49, MA & PhD; Univ Paris, Fulbright Award, 49-50; Calif Col Arts & Crafts, hon DFA, 67. *Collections Arranged:* Directions In Kinetic Sculpture (catalog), 65; Funk (catalog), 67; Richard Lindner, 69; Pol Bury, 70; Excellence, 70; Harold Paris (catalog), 72; Ferdinand Hodler (catalog), 72; The American Presidency in

Political Cartoons (coauth, catalog), 76; German and Austrian Expressionism (catalog), 78; Two Decades of American Painting: 1920-1940 (catalog), Dusseldorf, Zurich & Brussels, 79; and many others. *Pos:* Head art educ prog, Inst Design, Ill Inst Technol, 53-55; chmn dept art & dir art gallery, Pomona Col, 55-58; cur painting & sculpture exhibs, Mus Mod Art, 58-65; dir, Univ Art Mus, Univ Calif, Berkeley, 65-73; ed, Art Am; mem consult comt, Art Quart; proj dir, Christo's Running Fence Project, Calif, 74-76. *Teaching:* Asst prof art hist, Inst Design, Univ Chicago, 53-54; prof art hist, Univ Calif, Berkeley, 65- *Awards:* Belg-Am Educ Found Fel, 53; Order of Merit, Fed Ger Repub, 63; Sr Fel, Nat Endowment Humanities, 72; and others. *Mem:* Col Art Asn Am (dir, 59-68). *Publ:* Auth, The Work of Jean Dubuffet, 62; auth, Emil Nolde, 63; auth, Max Beckman, 64; auth, Art in Our Times, 81; auth, Sam Francis, second ed 82; and others. *Mailing Add:* Dept of Art Hist Univ of Calif Berkeley CA 94720

SEMAK, MICHAEL
PHOTOGRAPHER, EDUCATOR
b Welland, Ont, Jan 9, 34. *Study:* Ryerson Polytech Inst, Toronto, cert archit technol, 59. *Work:* Nat Gallery Can, Pub Arch, Ottawa; George Eastman House, Rochester, NY; Mus Mod Art, New York. *Comn:* Photographing Canada, Nat Film Bd, Ottawa, 64, 66, 67, 72 & 74; Photographing Tunisia, Nat Geog Soc, Washington, DC, 67; Photographing WVa, Time-Life Bks, New York, 68; Photographing Italy, Can Coun, Ottawa, 71; Photographing USSR, York Univ, Toronto, 75. *Exhib:* Ghana Image 4, Nat Film Bd, Ottawa, 69; Ghetto, New Sch Social Res, New York, 70; Mixed Subjects, Image Gallery, New York, 71; Italy 1971, Il Diaframma Gallery, Milan, 73; Mixed Subjects, Deja Vue Gallery, Toronto, 75. *Pos:* Toronto chmn interarts, Canada-USSR Asn, 73- *Teaching:* Lectr photog, Visual Arts Dept, Fac Fine Arts, York Univ, Toronto, 71-73, asst prof, 73-76, assoc prof, 77- *Awards:* Gold Medal for Photog Excellence for Ghana Show, Nat Film Bd, 69; Award of Excellence in Photo-Jour, Pravda Newspaper, Moscow, 70 & 72; Excellence Int Fedn Photog Arts Dipl, Switz, 72. *Bibliog:* Don Long (auth), Tell a story, Can Photo Ann, 75. *Mem:* Royal Can Acad Art. *Publ:* Ed, Concerned photographer, Popular Photog, 70; Semak portfolio, Creative Camera, 70 & 73, Camera Can, 71 & Nuova Fotografia, 73; coauth, Michael Semak monograph, Impressions Mag, 74; and others. *Mailing Add:* 1796 Spruce Hill Rd Pickering ON L1V 1S4 Canada

SEMANS, JAMES HUSTEAD
PATRON
b Uniontown, Pa, May 30, 10. *Study:* Princeton Univ, AB; Johns Hopkins Univ, MD. *Pos:* Chmn bd trustees, NC Sch Arts, 64-81; bd mem, Mary Duke Biddle Found. *Publ:* Auth, Siena-Six Summers of Music, 74. *Mailing Add:* 1415 Bivins St Durham NC 27707

SEMCHISHEN, OREST M
PHOTOGRAPHER
b Mundare, Alta, Jan 9, 32. *Study:* Goldeye Workshops, Nordegg, Alta, with Hubert Hohn, 75-76; Friends Photog Workshop, Tucson, Ariz, 77. *Work:* Nat Film Bd, Can Coun Art Bank, Pub Archives, Ottawa; Edmonton Art Gallery, Alta; Nickle Art Mus, Calgary. *Comn:* Photog proj, Alta 75th Anniversary Comn, 80. *Exhib:* Byzantine Churches of Alta, Edmonton Art Gallery, 76; Confedn Art Gallery, Charlottetown, PEI, 77; Prov Mus, Edmonton, 81, and others; Banff Purchase, Glenbow Mus, Calgary, 79; Points of View: Photos of Architecture, Vancouver Art Gallery, BC, 81 & Mus de Beaux Arts, Montreal, 81. *Bibliog:* James Adams (auth), World through a radiologist's camera, Edmonton J, 81; Terry Fenton (auth), 4 Photographers, Update, Edmonton Art Gallery, 82. *Mem:* Royal Can Acad Arts; Can Artists Representation; Nat Asn Photog Art; Friends Photog. *Publ:* Contribr, Byzantine Churches of Alberta, Edmonton Art Gallery, 76; contribr, The Banff Purchase, Banff Ctr, 79; contribr, Keepsake, Western Emerging Arts, 81. *Mailing Add:* 4208 - 109A St Edmonton AB T6J 2R8 Canada

SEMMEL, JOAN
PAINTER
b New York, NY, Oct 19, 32. *Study:* Cooper Union, dipl, 52; Art Students League, with Morris Kantor, 58-59; Pratt Inst, BFA, 63, MFA, 72. *Work:* Mus Contemp Art, Houston; Aldrich Mus, Ridgefield; Michener Collection, Mus Univ Tex, Austin; Newport Beach Mus; Chysler Mus; and others. *Exhib:* One-person shows, Lerner-Heller Gallery, New York, 75, 77, 78, 79 & 81; Pelham von Stoffler Gallery, Houston, 77; Meyers Gallery, State Univ NY, Plattsburgh, 80; Franklin & Marshall Col, 80 & Douglass Women's Series, New Brunswick, NJ, 81; Nothing But Nudes, Downtown Whitney, New York, 77; Contemporary Women: Consiousness & Content (cur), Brooklyn Mus, 77; and others. *Teaching:* Assoc prof painting, Mason Gross Sch Art, Rutgers Univ. *Awards:* Off Educ EPDA Fel, 70-72; Creative Artists Pub Serv Prog Award, NY State Coun on Arts, 75-76; Nat Endowment Arts Grant, 80. *Bibliog:* Vivien Raynor (auth), article, New York Times, 4/22/78; Donald Kuspit (auth), article, Art Am, 3/80; Charlotte Streiier Rubinstein (auth), American Women Artists, Avon Paperback, 82. *Mem:* Women in the Arts; Womens Ad Hoc Comt. *Media:* Oil. *Mailing Add:* 109 Spring St New York NY 10012

SENDAK, MAURICE BERNARD
WRITER, ILLUSTRATOR
b Brooklyn, NY, June 10, 28. *Study:* Art Students League, 49-51. *Exhib:* One-man show, Gallery Sch, Visual Arts, New York, 64; Ashmolean Mus, Oxford, Eng, 75. *Pos:* Writer & illusr children's bks, 51- *Awards:* Caldecott Award for Where the Wild Things Are, 63; Hans Christian Andersen Illusr Award, 70. *Publ:* Auth & illusr, Maurice Sendak's Really Rosie: Starring the Nutshell Kids, Harper & Row, 75; illusr, Some Swell Pup, Farrar, Straus & Giroux, 76; ed, The Disney Poster Book, Crown, 77; auth & illusr, Seven Little Monsters, 77 & Outside Over There, 81, Harper & Row; and others. *Mailing Add:* 200 Chestnut Hill Rd Ridgefield CT 06877

SENNEMA, DAVID C
MUSEUM DIRECTOR, ADMINISTRATOR
b Grand Rapids, Mich, July 6, 34. *Study:* Albion Col, Mich, BA, 56. *Pos:* Dir, Columbia Nusic Fest Asn, SC, 64-67; exec dir, SC Arts Comn, Columbia, 67-70; asst dir, Fed & State Prog Nat Endowment Arts, Washington, DC, 71-73; dir, SC State Mus, 76- *Teaching:* Prof, arts adminr & dir community arts mgt, Sangamon State Univ, Springfield, Ill, 73-76. *Mem:* Am Asn Mus; Am Asn State & Local Hist; Carolina Coliseum Adv Comt; Southeastern Mus Conference; SC Federation Mus. *Publ:* Auth, Building a Foundation for Community Arts Activity, 74; auth, Euphoria State Arts Agency--A Simulation, 74; Video Tapes on Arts Administration, 75. *Mailing Add:* SC Mus Comn PO Box 11296 Columbia SC 29211

SEPLOWIN, CHARLES JOSEPH
SCULPTOR
b New York, NY, July 19, 45. *Study:* Univ NH, BA(art); RI Sch Design, MFA(sculpture). *Work:* Municipal Fire House Ctr, New York; Titan Steel Corp, New York; Montclair State Col; Univ NH. *Exhib:* Aldrich Mus, 75; one-man show, Elizabeth Weiner Gallery, New York, 80; Drawing Ctr New York, 82; Sculpture Ctr, New York, 83; Cheltenham Art Ctr, Philadelphia, 83; Mus Mod Art Latin Am, Washington, DC, 83; and others. *Teaching:* Instr sculpture, Montclair State Col, 74- *Bibliog:* Articles in Craft Horizons, 8/74 & Arts Mag, 9/74. *Mailing Add:* 463 West St New York NY 10014

SEPPA, HEIKKI MARKUS
METALSMITH, EDUCATOR
b Sakkijarvi, Finland, Mar 8, 27; US citizen. *Study:* Georg Jensen Silversmiths, Copenhagen, 48-49; Cranbrook Acad Art, 60-61; Goldsmith Sch Helsinki, Cent Sch Indust Arts, Finland, Master Silversmith, 63. *Work:* Evansville Mus Sci & Art, Ind; Steinberg Gallery Art, Washington Univ, St Louis, Mo; Tex Tech Univ, Lubbock; State Univ, El Paso, Tex; Univ Ill, Normal. *Comn:* Over 200 pvt collections, St Louis area patrons, 65-78; The Search, W G Elliot Soc of Washington Univ, 69; Menorah Shaare Emeth Temple, St Louis, Mo, 80. *Exhib:* Reprice, Mus of Cranbrook Acad Art, Bloomfield Hills, Mich, 75; Krannert Art Mus, Univ Ill, Champaign, 76; The Metalsmith, Phoenix Art Mus, Ariz, 77; 3-Exhib, Burnaby Art Gallery, BC, 77; Goldsmiths Hall, London, 78; Schmuck Mus Pforzheim, Ger, 79; and others. *Teaching:* Assoc prof metalsmithing, Washington Univ, St Louis, 65-79, prof art, 79- *Awards:* Craftsman Fel, Nat Endowment for the Arts, 75; dipl for lifetime work in profession, Precious Metal Indust League of Finland. *Bibliog:* Izabel Blase (auth), He made his toy's, Goldsmith J, Soc NAm Goldsmiths, 77; Excellence, Am Craft Mag, 8/79; article, Forum Mag, Seoul, Korea, 80. *Mem:* Soc NAm Goldsmiths. *Media:* Gold, Silver. *Publ:* Auth, Form Emphasis for Metalsmiths, Kent State Univ Press, 78. *Mailing Add:* #8 Price Court St Louis MO 63132

SEPYO, JAMES (JAMES H CAMERON)
PAINTER, PRINTMAKER
b Hudson Co, NJ, June 29, 33. *Study:* Weusi Acad African Arts & Studies, MA, 70; Bob Blackburn's Sch Printmaking, New York, 72. *Work:* Studio Mus in Harlem, NY; Hagg Gallery, Atlanta, Ga; Origem Gallery, St Thomas, VI; Phelican Village, Barbados, WI; NY State Bldg, New York. *Comn:* Murals in Mt Morris Park Recreation Ctr, New York City Dept Cultural Affairs, 73. *Exhib:* The Leon Thomas Show, Sculpture Garden Mus Mod Art, New York, 69; Expression from the Roots, NY State Bldg Gallery, New York, 77; Spiritual Realism, Brooklyn Restoration Gallery, NY, 78; At the Cork Gallery, Lincoln Ctr, New York, 78; Int Award Winning Show, Gables Gallery, Coral Gables, Fla, 81; Brooklyn Mus, 81. *Pos:* Art dir, NY Dept Recreation, 70-81; bd dirs, Weusi Acad Nat Arts Consortium, 75-79; dir master of skills in printmaking, Washington Heights Int Gallery, 81- *Awards:* Murals Award, Mt Morris Park Ctr, NY Dept Cultural Affairs, 73; Award for Graphics, Roosevelt Public Libr, 75. *Bibliog:* Obaleygwa Abileye (auth), Tropical impulses, Daily News Charlotte Amalie, St Thomas, VI, 11/14/74; John Felder (auth), Artist in motion, Amsterdam News, New York, 3/26/77. *Media:* Mixed. *Publ:* Contribr, A walk through the studio museum, Essence Mag, 71; contribr, Salute to Minority Artists, United Mutual Life Insurance, 81. *Dealer:* Cedrie McClester Creative Assoc Network 888 Seventh Ave Suite 400 New York NY 10019. *Mailing Add:* 20 Henry St 20 Henry Brooklyn NY 11201

SERGER, HELEN
ART DEALER
b Skoczow, Poland, Feb 1, 01; US citizen. *Mem:* Art Dealers Asn Am. *Specialty:* Paintings, drawings and graphics by German and Austrian expressionists; 20th century masters; Dada, Bauhaus, constructivist and surrealist artists. *Mailing Add:* 9 E 82nd St New York NY 10028

SERISAWA, IKUO
DEALER
US citizen. *Study:* Art Inst Chicago, 43-47. *Pos:* Owner & dir, I Serisawa Gallery, currently. *Specialty:* Contemporary paintings and graphics, antique Japanese prints and modern Oriental graphics. *Mailing Add:* 8320 Melrose Ave Suite 103 Los Angeles CA 90069

SERISAWA, SUEO
PAINTER
b Yokohama, Japan, Apr 10, 10; US citizen. *Study:* Study with Yoichi Serisawa (father) & George Barker; Otis Art Inst. *Work:* Metrop Mus Art, New York; Los Angeles Co Mus Art; Santa Barbara Mus Art; Smithsonian Inst, Washington, DC; San Diego Fine Arts Gallery; and others. *Exhib:* Carnegie Inst Int, Pittsburgh, 52; Tokyo Int, Japan, 52; Sao Paulo Biennale,

Brazil, 55; Whitney Mus Am Art, New York, 60; Pacific Heritage, US State Dept, Berlin, Ger, 65; plus others. *Teaching:* Instr painting, Kann Inst Art, 48-51; instr painting, Scripps Col, 49-50 & Univ Southern Calif, Idyllwild Campus, 75- *Awards:* Carol H Beck Gold Medal, Pa Acad Fine Arts, 47; Purchase Award, Metrop Mus Art, 50; Purchase Award, Los Angeles Co Mus, 50, 56 & 57. *Bibliog:* Arthur Millier (auth), Inner development of artist, Am Artist, 50; Ed Biberman (auth), 20 Artists (film), Los Angeles Mus & Univ Calif, Los Angeles, 70; Joe Mugnaini (auth), Oil Painting Techniques and Materials, 69 & Logics of Drawing, 73, Reinholt; plus others. *Media:* Sumi Ink, Woodcut. *Dealer:* I Serisawa Gallery 8320 Melrose Ave Los Angeles CA 90069. *Mailing Add:* 3033 Warren Lane Costa Mesa CA 92626

SERNIAK, REGINA (STEWART)
PAINTER, WRITER
b Passaic, NJ. *Study:* Cooper Union; Hunter Col. *Work:* Columbia Mus of Art, SC; Greenville Co Mus, SC; Comune de Urbino, Italy; Aldrich Mus of Contemp Art, Ridgefield, Conn. *Exhib:* Collegeo Raffaello, Urbino, Italy, 73; Art Exhib, Beth Elohim, New York, 74; ACA Gallery, New York, 74; Contemp Reflections, Aldrich Mus of Contemp Art, 76; Soho Ctr for Visual Artists, New York, 77. *Pos:* Designer scenery & costumes, Paterson Lyric Opera Theatre, NJ, 65-74; promotion for art & antiques, Channel 13 TV Sta, New York, 76; consult, Oriental art, 70-; co-owner, Stewart Studio, 76- *Teaching:* Instr painting & drawing, NY Univ, New York, 76- *Awards:* First Prize/Painting, Ann John Roebling Exhib, John Roebling Found, 60. *Bibliog:* Notable Americans, Hist Preserv Am, 76. *Media:* Acrylic. *Publ:* Auth, The Golden Handbook of Collectibles, Western Publ, 76; auth, American Woodworking Tools, E P Dutton, 77. *Mailing Add:* 31 E Seventh St New York NY 10003

SERRA, RICHARD
SCULPTOR
b San Francisco, Calif, Nov 2, 39. *Study:* Univ Calif, Berkeley; Univ Calif, Santa Barbara, BA; Yale Univ, BA & MFA. *Exhib:* Whitney Mus Am Art, 75-77; solo exhib, Mus Mod Art, New York, 78, Richard Hines Gallery, Seattle, 79, Univ Calif, Berkeley, 79, KOH Gallery, Tokyo, 79 & Galerie Schmela, Dusseldorf, 79; PS1, Long Island City, 79. *Awards:* Skohegan Sch Medal, 75. *Mailing Add:* PO Box 645 Canal St Sta New York NY 10013

SERRA, RUDY
SCULPTOR
b San Francisco, Calif, Apr 9, 48. *Study:* City Col San Francisco, AA; San Francisco State Col, BA; Univ Calif, Berkeley, MA & MFA. *Exhib:* San Francisco Art Inst, 73 & 76; 1975 Whitney Biennial, New York, 75; San Francisco Mus Mod Art, 77; Faculty Exhib, Univ Conn, 80-82; one-person shows, Univ Houston, 80, Baruch Col, 82 & Marianne Deson Gallery, 83; Oakland Mus, 82; and others. *Teaching:* Vis asst prof sculpture, Calif State Univ, Chico, 75; asst prof, Am River Col, Sacramento, 76-77; vis asst prof sculpture, Univ Calif, Davis, fall 78; asst prof sculpture & drawing, Univ Conn, Storrs, 79- *Awards:* Nat Endowment Arts Grant, 76 & 78. *Bibliog:* Roberta Smith (auth), Biennial review, Artforum, 5/75; Amy Goldin (auth), The new Whitney Biennial, Art Am, 5-6/75; Judith Dunham (auth), Introduction 75, Artweek, 7/75. *Media:* Wood, Steel. *Mailing Add:* 108 Franklin St New York NY 10013

SERRA-BADUE, DANIEL
PAINTER, EDUCATOR
b Santiago de Cuba, Sept 8, 14. *Study:* Escuela Munic Bellas Artes, Santiago de Cuba, 24-26; Borrell-Nicolau & Luis Muntane, Escuela Bellas Artes, Barcelona, 32-36; Art Students League, Nat Acad Design & Columbia Univ, 38-40; Escuela Nac Bellas Artes, Havana, 43; Pratt Graphic Art Ctr, 64; Art Critics Workshop, Am Fedn Arts, 67. *Work:* Museo Municipal, Santiago de Cuba; Museo Nac, La Habana; Inst Cult Hispanica, Madrid; Mus Contemp Latin Am Art, Washington, DC; Metrop Mus Art, New York. *Exhib:* Am Soc Contemp Artists Ann, New York, 74 & 79; Six Cuban Painters Working in New York, Ctr Inter-Am Relations, New York, 75; 149th Ann Exhib, Royal Scottish Acad, Edinburgh, 75; 57th Nat Print Exhib, Soc Am Graphic Artists, Parsons Gallery, New York, 79; Ibizagrafica 80, Mus Art, Ibiza; and others. *Teaching:* Prof, Sch Plastic Arts, Santiago de Cuba, 45-60; instr art, Univ Oriente, Cuba, summers 48 & 50; prof design, Sch Journalism, Santiago de Cuba, 54-59; prof, Nat Sch Fine Arts, Havana, 60-62; lectr painting, Columbia Univ, 62-63; instr drawing & painting, Brooklyn Mus Art Sch, 62-; asst prof art hist, St Peter's Col, NJ, 67-70, chmn dept, 67-77, assoc prof, 70-77, prof, 77- *Awards:* Guggenheim Fel, 38-39; Oscar B Cintas Found Fel, 63 & 64; First Prize Painting, Am Soc Contemp Artists, 74; plus others. *Bibliog:* Al Brunelle (auth), Daniel Serra-Badue, Art News, 2/73; Rafael Santos Torroella (auth), Serra-Badue, El Noticiero Universal, Barcelona, 6/5/73; Alberto del Castillo (auth), Daniel Serra-Badue, Goya, Madrid, 7-8/73. *Mem:* Am Soc Contemp Artists; Col Art Asn Am; Soc Am Graphic Artists; Soc Archit Historians; Artists Equity New York. *Publ:* Auth, weekly articles in Diario de la Marina, Havana, 46-47; auth, weekly articles in Diario de Cuba, Santiago de Cuba, 57-58. *Mailing Add:* 15 W 72nd St #10T New York NY 10023

SERWAZI, ALBERT B
PAINTER
b Philadelphia, Pa, Aug 20, 05. *Study:* Pa Acad Fine Arts. *Work:* Butler Art Inst, Youngstown, Ohio; Corcoran Gallery Art, Washington, DC; Whitney Mus Am Art, NY; Reading Pub Mus & Art Gallery, Pa; Springville Mus of Art, Utah; and others. *Exhib:* Ann, Pa Acad Fine Arts, 34-64; Painting in the United States, Carnegie Inst, 39-45; Artist for Victory, Metrop Mus Art, 43; Ann, Nat Acad Design, 47, 52, 58, 70-75 & 76-78. *Awards:* J Henry Scheidt Memorial Prize Oil, Pa Acad Fine Arts, 41; Gold Medal, Philadelphia Sketch

Club, 44; First Award, Chester Co Art Asn, 83. *Mem:* Academician Nat Acad Design; fel Pa Acad Fine Arts; Chester Co Art Asn, Pa; Philadelphia Watercolor Club. *Media:* Oil, Watercolor. *Mailing Add:* PO Box 430 3725 Gradyville Rd Newtown Square PA 19073

SETH, LAUREL
DEALER

b Santa Fe, NMex, Mar 15, 53. *Specialty:* Traditional and contemporary paintings; sculpture, primarily regional. *Mailing Add:* Canyon Rd Art Gallery 710 Canyon Rd Santa Fe NM 87501

SEVERSON, WILLIAM CONRAD
SCULPTOR

b Madison, Wis, Nov 22, 24. *Study:* Univ Wis, Madison, BS, AA, 47; Syracuse Univ, with Ivan Mestrovic, MFA(sculpture), 49. *Work:* Nat Cathedral Washington DC; Concordia Seminary, St Louis, Mo; St Louis Sculptors' Gallery, Mo; Cheltenham Art Asn, Philadelphia, Pa; Morris Arboretum, Philadelphia, Pa. *Comn:* Ciborium, Shrine Our Lady of Snows, Belleville, Ill, 64; Connectors, Blue Cross/Blue Shield, Chapel Hill, NC, 74; Solaris (bronze, solar), Tampa Electric Co, Fla, 80; Protein Cube, Ralston Purina, St Louis, Mo, 72; Primogenesis, Friends Mus Sci Nat Hist, St Louis, Mo, 81. *Exhib:* NY World's Fair, Mo Pavilion, New York, 65; Chillicothe, Mo State Council Arts, 65; Casa D'Artes, Taos, NMex, 70; Sculpture in Archit Concept, Fordham/Lincoln Ctr, New York, 76; 7th Ann, Shidonaa, Santa Fe, NMex, 81. *Pos:* Pres, St Louis Sculptors' Gallery, 64-68. *Awards:* First Place, Univ Wis, Green Bay, 77; Purchase Prize, Philip & Muriel Berman, 79. *Bibliog:* Thelma R Newman (auth), Plastics as Art Form, Chilton, 64; Theodore F Wolff (auth) Something for all to share, Christian Sci Monitor, 80; Louis G Redstone (auth), Public Art--New Directions, McGraw-Hill, 81. *Mem:* Int Sculpture Conf; Ecumenical Coun Drama & Art. *Media:* Steel, Bronze. *Mailing Add:* 18350 Chesterfield Airport Road Chesterfield MO 63017

SEVIGNY, MAURICE JOSEPH, II
EDUCATOR, ADMINISTRATOR

b Amesbury, Mass, July 24, 43. *Study:* Mass Col Art, BSEd, 65; Ohio State Univ, MA, 69, PhD, 77. *Teaching:* Asst prof art educ, Western Ky Univ, 69-76; teaching assoc, Ohio State Univ, 76-78; assoc prof art, chair, Div Art Educ, Bowling Green State Univ, Ohio, 78-81, dir, Sch Art, 79, prof, 81- *Awards:* Award Excellence Dissertation Res, Rev Res Visual Arts Educ, 79; Ann Hollis Moore Award Distinguished Serv, Bowling Green State Univ Student Union, 82. *Mem:* Nat Coun Policy Studies Art Educ; Ohio Art Educ Asn (adv coun rep, 78, chmn Higher Educ, 79); Nat Art Educ Asn; Nat Coun Art Adminr; Nat Soc Schs Art & Design. *Res:* Studio learning and performance; assessment at the university level from the triangulated perspective of teacher, student, classroom ethnographer; gender differences in non-verbal communication. *Publ:* Auth, Triangulation and descriptive research, Rev Res Visual Arts, 5/78; auth, Utilizing recorded materials for the clinical component of teacher training, In: Human Relations and the Clinical Component, Ohio Dept Educ, 80; auth, Triangulate inquiry: A methodology for the analysis of classroom interaction, In: Analysis of Discourse: Ethnographic Approaches, Ablex Publ, 81. *Mailing Add:* Sch of Art Bowling Green State Univ Bowling Green OH 43403

SEVY, BARBARA SNETSINGER
LIBRARIAN

b Montpelier, Vt, June 4, 26. *Study:* Univ Vt, BS; Drexel Univ, MSLS. *Pos:* Librn, Philadelphia Mus Art, 68- *Mem:* Art Libr Soc NAm (secy, 81-83); Am Libr Asn (chmn art sect, 74); Spec Libr Asn (secy mus div, 68-69). *Mailing Add:* 26th St & Benjamin Franklin Pkwy Philadelphia PA 19101

SEWELL, DARREL L
CURATOR, HISTORIAN

b Cushing, Okla, Dec 21, 39. *Study:* Univ Chicago, BA, 62, MA, 62. *Collections Arranged:* Philadelphia: Three Centuries of American Art (auth, catalog), 76; Installation of American Collections, 77; Copley from Boston (auth, catalog), 80; Thomas Eakins: Artists of Philadelphia (auth, catalog), 81-82; One Hundred Years of Acquisitions (auth, catalog), 83. *Pos:* Intern, Conservation Dept, Art Inst Chicago, 65; cur educ, Nat Collection Fine Arts, 70-73; cur, Am Art, Philadelphia Mus Art, 73- *Teaching:* Asst prof art hist, Ohio State Univ, Columbus, 66-67 & Univ Ill, Chicago Circle, 68-70. *Publ:* Auth, What you see is what you get: An approach to the use of museums for education, Art Educ, 12/71. *Mailing Add:* Philadelphia Mus Art PO Box 7646 Philadelphia PA 19101

SEWELL, JACK VINCENT
MUSEUM CURATOR

b Dearborn, Mo, June 11, 23. *Study:* St Joseph Jr Col, Mo, 41-43; City Col New York, 43-44; Univ Chicago, MFA, 50; Harvard Univ, 51-53. *Collections Arranged:* Complete reinstallation of Oriental Collections, Art Inst Chicago, 58. *Pos:* Mem staff, Oriental dept, Art Inst Chicago, 50-56, assoc cur Oriental art, 56-58, cur, 58- *Mem:* Far Eastern Ceramic Group; Japan-Am Soc Chicago; The Cliff Dwellers; Arts Club Chicago. *Res:* Indian and Far Eastern art; arts of China; strength in delicacy--archaic Chinese bronzes and sculptures of Gandhara. *Publ:* Contribr, Archaeol & Chicago Art Inst Quart. *Mailing Add:* 1350 N Lake Shore Dr Chicago IL 60610

SEWELL, RICHARD GEORGE
PRINTMAKER, PAINTER

b St Louis, Mo, Aug 22, 42; Can citizen. *Study:* Univ Nac Autonoma de Mexico, 65; Kansas City Art Inst, Mo, 66; Univ Mo, Kansas City, BA, 67. *Work:* Can Coun, Ottawa; The Gallery, Stratford, Ont; Nova Scotia Art Gallery, Halifax; Owens Art Gallery, Mt Allison, NB; Winnipeg Art Gallery, Man. *Exhib:* Invitational Print Editions, Winnipeg Art Gallery, 81; The Drint Suite, The Gallery, Stratford, Ont, 81; Brit Int Biennale of Prints, Bradford, England, 78, 80 & 82; Printmakers, Art Gallery Ont, Toronto, 82; Canadian Contemporary Prints, Bronx Mus, 82. *Teaching:* Co-founder & dir, Open Studio Print Workshop, Toronto, 70-82; instr printmaking, Sheridan Col Applied Arts, 82- *Bibliog:* William J S Boyle (auth), The Drint Suite, pvt publ, 81. *Media:* All; Acrylic, Oil. *Publ:* Contribr, Open Studio-ten years, Open Studio, 80; contribr, Anthology on contemporary issues in printmaking, Univ Alberta, 83. *Dealer:* Mira Godard Gallery 22 Hazelton Ave Toronto Ont Canada M5S 2E2. *Mailing Add:* 49 Appleton Ave Toronto ON M6E 3A4 Canada

SEXAUER, DONALD RICHARD
PRINTMAKER, EDUCATOR

b Erie, Pa. *Study:* Col William & Mary; Edinboro State Col, BS; Kent State Univ, MA. *Work:* Butler Inst Am Art, Youngstown, Ohio; New York Pub Libr; Mint Mus Art, Charlotte, NC; Montgomery Mus Fine Arts, Ala; Franklin Mint, Pa; and others. *Comn:* Print eds, Woman, Assoc Am Artists, Int Graphic Art Soc, 66, To Fly, To Fly, 66; Vietnam Fragments (folio), Off, Chief Mil Hist, Washington, DC, 71; Mecklenburg Bicentennial Comn (folio). *Exhib:* Soc Am Graphic Artists, 64-; New Talent In Printmaking, New York, 66; 140th Ann, Nat Acad Design, 66; San Diego Print Exhib, 71; 16th Hunterdon Nat, Clinton, NJ, 72. *Teaching:* Prof printmaking, Sch Art, E Carolina Univ, 60- *Awards:* Print Prize, Nat Acad Design 140th Ann, 66; Purchase Awards, Piedmont Print Ann, Mint Mus, 69-74; Purchase Award, Bradley Print Show, Peoria. *Mem:* Soc Am Graphic Artists; Acad Artists Asn. *Media:* Intaglio. *Publ:* Illusr, Red clay reader number 5, Southern Lit Rev, 68. *Dealer:* Foliograph Tyson's Corner Ctr McLean VA 22101. *Mailing Add:* 109 Greenbriar Dr Greenville NC 27834

SEXTON, JOHN (WILLIAM)
PHOTOGRAPHER

b Maywood, Calif, May 22, 53. *Study:* Photog workshops with Ansel Adams, Wynn Bullock, Paul Caponigro & Brett Weston, 73-74. *Work:* Univ Ariz Ctr Creative Photog, Tucson; Polaroid Corp Collection, Clarence Kennedy Gallery, Cambridge, Mass; Newport Harbor Art Mus, Newport Beach, Calif; Monterey Peninsula Mus Art, Calif; China Photogrs Asn, Bening, Chica. *Exhib:* One-man exhib, Chapman Col, Orange, Calif, 76; Bell Gallery, Brown Univ, Providence, RI, 80; New Landscapes, Friends Photog Gallery, Carmel, Calif, 80; Message From The West Coast, Photo Gallery Int, Tokyo, 81; Focus Gallery, San Francisco, 81; and others. *Pos:* Co-dir & instr, Owens Valley Photog Workshops, Agoura, Calif, 76-; tech consult to Ansel Adams, Carmel, Calif, 79-82. *Teaching:* Instr, Cypress Col, Calif, 77-79; instr, Univ Calif, Santa Cruz, 80-81; instr, Ansel Adams Yosemite Workshops, 80- *Awards:* Imogen Cunningham Award, Focus Gallery, San Francisco, 81. *Bibliog:* Ron Eggers (auth), Working with the masters, Rangefinder, 80. *Mem:* Friends Photog; Soc Photog Educ. *Publ:* Contribr, Photo-Image Mag, Lodestar Press, 76; contribr, Darkroom Photog Mag, Sheptow Publ, 79; contrib, The negative, New York Graphic Soc, 81; contrib, Zoom Mag, Joel Laroche-France, 81. *Dealer:* Weston Gallery PO Box 655 Carmel CA 93921. *Mailing Add:* 24700 Crewtview Circle Carmel CA 92923

SEYLE, ROBERT HARLEY
SCULPTOR, DESIGNER

b National City, Calif, Oct 9, 37. *Study:* La Sierra Col, Riverside, Calif; Otis Art Inst, Los Angeles, BFA, MFA. *Work:* Storm King Art Mus, Corning, NY; Palm Springs Desert Mus, Calif; Beneficial Ins Group, Los Angeles; Metro Media Studios, Hollywood, Calif. *Comn:* Nail sculpture 11, Henry J Ittleson, Jr, Palm Springs, 67; nail sculpture 89, Julian Brody, Des Moines, Iowa, 72; nail sculpture 110, Dr Alonzo Proctor, Lodi, Calif, 74; nail sculpture 125, Arthur Elrod Interiors, Palm Springs, 75; nail sculpture 154, Steve Chase, Palm Springs, Calif, 81. *Exhib:* One-man show, Palm Springs Desert Mus, 74; group show, Calif State Capitol Bldg, Sacramento, 75; Ankrum Gallery, Los Angeles, 78; Riverside Art Ctr, Calif, 78; San Bernardino Co Mus, 78; and others. *Bibliog:* Ray Faulkner & Edwin Ziegfeld (auths), Art Today, Holt, Rinehart & Winston Inc; Bernard Morris (auth), California people, Eyewitness News, ABC-TV, 74; Noonday WVa, Channel 12, Clarksburg, WVa, 80. *Mailing Add:* c/o Ankrum Gallery 657 N La Cienega Blvd Los Angeles CA 90069

SEYLER, DAVID W
CRAFTSMAN, EDUCATOR

Study: Art Acad Cincinnati, dipl; Art Inst Chicago; Univ Chicago, BFA; Univ Wis, MS. *Work:* Syracuse Univ, NY; Univ Chicago; Cincinnati Art Mus; Sheldon Mem Art Gallery, Lincoln, Nebr. *Comn:* Mural, USN Great Lakes Training Sta, 43; stained glass & altar, Holy Trinity Episcopal Church, Lincoln, 62-72; mural, KOLN-TV, Lincoln, 68-69; designer & sculptor, Nebr State Centennial Medal & Univ Nebr Centennial Medal; tapestry, Grace United Methodist Church, Lincoln, 79-80. *Teaching:* Prof sculpture & head crafts dept, Univ Nebr, Lincoln, 48-82, prof emer, 82. *Awards:* Woods Found Travel Grant, Italy, 59-60; Univ Nebr Found Grant, Eng, 71-72. *Bibliog:* Warren E Cox (auth), Pottery & Porcelain & Herbert Peck (auth), The Book of Rookwood Pottery, Crown; Paul Evans (auth), American Art Pottery, Scribner, 75; Kovel (auth), Collector's Guide to American Art Pottery, Crown, 76. *Mem:* Nebr Arts Coun; Nebr Craft Coun; Nebr Art Asn; Col Art Asn Am; fel Int Soc Arts & Lett. *Media:* Multimedia. *Dealer:* Lakewood Arts Studio Lincoln NE 68508. *Mailing Add:* 3434 S 28th St Lincoln NE 68502

SHACKELFORD, BUD (LYNE T)
PAINTER, INSTRUCTOR

b Washington DC, Nov 15, 18. *Study:* Univ Ala; Chouinard Sch Art, Los Angeles, Calif; Art Students League. *Exhib:* Am Watercolor Soc, 68-78, Ann, 78 & Audubon Artists, 73, Nat Acad, New York; Watercolor USA, Springfield Art Mus, Mo, 68-72; Butler Art Inst Ann, Youngstown, Ohio, 71-72; Watercolor West, Riverside Art Mus, Calif, 75-77. *Pos:* Animator, Walt Disney Studios, 39-40; art dir, Phillips Ramsey Advert Co, 51-61; pres, Art Assocs Inc, San Diego, Calif, 61-66. *Teaching:* Instr watercolor, San Diego Art Inst, 70-72, Hewitt Painting Workshops, 70-77 & Painting Holidays, 78-79. *Awards:* Over 200 awards. *Bibliog:* Watercolor Page, Shackelford advocates strong design, Am Artist Mag, 3/67; Marlene Schiller (auth), Artists as demonstrators, Am Artist Mag, 2/79; Linda Lewis (auth), Life and excitement--Bud Shackelford, Southwest Art Mag, 5/73. *Mem:* Am Watercolor Soc; Nat Watercolor Soc; Nat Soc Art Directors; San Diego Watercolor Soc (pres 68-69); San Diego Art Guild (dir 71-72). *Media:* Watercolor, Acrylic. *Publ:* Auth, As I See It, Alfred Knopf, 45; auth, Fun with Watercolor, pvt publ, 73; auth, Experimental Watercolor Techniques, Watson-Guptill, 80. *Mailing Add:* 11532 Rolling Hills Dr El Cajon CA 92020

SHACKELFORD, SHELBY
PAINTER

b Halifax, Va, Sept 27, 1899. *Study:* Md Inst Art, Baltimore, with Marguerite & William Zorach, Othon Friesz & Fernand Leger, grad. *Work:* Baltimore Mus Art; New York Pub Libr; Morgan State Col; Provincetown Art Asn; Nat Bank Chicago; and others. *Exhib:* Corcoran Gallery, Washington, DC, 65; Notre Dame Col, 72; Jewish Community Ctr, Baltimore, 72; Fells Point Gallery, 75; Cherry Stone Gallery, 76 & 77; retrospective, Provincetown Art Asn, 82; Lyle Evan Gallery, Lexington, Mass, 83; and others. *Teaching:* Head dept art, St Timothy's Sch, Stevenson, Md, 44-62; instr painting, Baltimore Mus Art, 50-65. *Awards:* Purchase Prizes, 50-54 & First Prize Painting, 59, Baltimore Mus Art; Prize for Drawing, Eastern Art Asn; Prize, Jewish Community Ctr, 72. *Media:* Casein, Soot. *Publ:* Auth & illusr, Now for Creatures, 34; auth & illusr, Electric Eel Calling, 40. *Dealer:* Lyle Evan Gallery Lexington MA. *Mailing Add:* Box 517 Wellfleet MA 02667

SHADBOLT, JACK LEONARD
PAINTER

b Shoeburyness, England, Feb 4, 09. *Study:* Euston Rd Group, London, Eng; with Andre L'Hote, Paris; Art Students League; hon degrees from Univ BC, Victoria Univ & Simon Fraser Univ. *Work:* Art Gallery Toronto, Ont; Nat Gallery Can; Montreal Mus Fine Arts; Seattle Art Mus, Wash; Vancouver Art Gallery; and others. *Comn:* Murals, Edmonton Int Airport & Charlottetown Mem Ctr; other comn in pvt collections. *Exhib:* Sao Paulo, Brazil; Caracas, Venezuela; Carnegie Inst; Seattle World's Fair, 62; Retrospectives, Nat Gallery Can & touring, 69 & Vancouver Art Gallery, 78; and others. *Teaching:* Head drawing & painting sect, Vancouver Sch Art, formerly. *Awards:* Order of Can, 73; Molson Award, Can Section, 78; OSA Award. *Bibliog:* Joan Lourdes (auth), Jack Skadbolt Retrospective Catalog, Nat Gallery Can, 69; Jack Skadbolt, Seven Years: Retrospective Catalog, Vanguard, 81. *Publ:* Auth, In Search of Form, 69, Mind's I, 73 & Act of Art, 81, McClelland & Stewart. *Dealer:* Bau-Xi Gallery 3045 Granville Vancouver BC Can. *Mailing Add:* 5121 Harborview Rd N Burnaby BC V5B 1C9 Canada

SHADDLE, ALICE
SCULPTOR, COLLAGE ARTIST

b Hinsdale, Ill, Dec 21, 28. *Study:* Oberlin Col; Univ Chicago, Ill; Sch of Art Inst Chicago, BFA & MFA. *Work:* Smithsonian Inst, Washington, DC. *Comn:* Portrait of Franz Liszt (three-dimensional collage), Mercury Rec Mfg Co, 66. *Exhib:* Made With Paper, 67 & Chicago Needs Famous Artists, 69, Mus Contemp Art, Chicago; Soc for Contemp Art, 69, Exhib by Artist in Chicago & Vicinity, 75, Vision, 76 & Prizewinners, 79, Art Inst Chicago; Indianapolis Mus Art, Ind, 76; 26th Ill Invitational, Ill State Mus, Springfield, 76; Nat Drawing Show, Kohler Arts Ctr, Sheboygan, Wis, 76; Ill Traveling Sculpture Exhib II, 78-79. *Teaching:* Instr printmaking & drawing, Roosevelt Univ, Chicago, 64-66; childrens painting teacher, Hyde Park Ctr, Chicago, 55-78; childrens painting teacher, Triangle Art Ctr, Chicago, 78-79. *Awards:* Logan Medal, 75th Exhib by Artist of Chicago & Vicinity, Art Inst Chicago, 75; Ill Arts Coun Grant, 79; Nat Endowment for Arts Grant, 79. *Bibliog:* Meilach & Ten Hoor (auth), Collage & Assemblage, Crown, 73; C L Morrison (auth, rev), Artforum, 76 & 78; article in Art in Am, 78 & 79. *Mem:* Artemisia Gallery & Fund (treas, 77-79); Hyde Park Art Ctr (scholar chmn). *Media:* Paper, Latex, Heavy Wrapping Paper; Oil & Canvas, Watercolor on folded Paper. *Publ:* Contribr, Art: Choosing & Expressing, Benefic Press, 77, Leonardo, Vol II, Pergamon Press, 78. *Dealer:* Artemisia Gallery 9 W Hubbard Chicago IL 60610. *Mailing Add:* 4858 S Kenwood Chicago IL 60615

SHADRACH, JEAN H
PAINTER, DEALER

b La Junta, Colo. *Study:* Univ NMex; Sumie, Okinawa; Constantine & Roman Chatov Studio, Atlanta, Ga; Alaska Methodist Univ; Anchorage Community Col. *Work:* Anchorage Fine Arts Mus; Alyeska Pipeline Co, Anchorage; Jewelmont, Inc, Minneapolis; Standard Oil Co Calif; Murray, Bradley & Rockney; and others. *Exhib:* All Alaska Art Exhib, Anchorage, 68-72; Northwestern Watercolor Soc Ann, Seattle, 70; Design I, Anchorage, 71; Artists of Alaska, traveling, 71-; Frye Mus, Seattle; and others. *Pos:* Co-owner, Artique, Ltd, Fine Art Gallery, Anchorage, 71- *Awards:* Best Show, Elmendorf AFB, 69; Drawing Award, All Alaska Art Exhib, 70; Gov Award, Alaska, 70. *Mcm:* Alaska Artist Guild (pres, 70-71); Artists Equity Asn. *Media:* Acrylic. *Specialty:* Alaskan artists' work. *Publ:* Auth, Okinawa Sketchbook, 62. *Mailing Add:* Artique Ltd 314 G St Anchorage AK 99501

SHAFFER, RICHARD
PAINTER, PRINTMAKER

b Fresno, Calif, Mar 17, 47. *Study:* Univ Calif, Santa Cruz, BA(philos), 69; New Sch Social Res, New York, grad study philos; San Francisco Art Inst, BFA(painting), 73; Stanford Univ, Palo Alto, Calif, MFA(painting), 75. *Work:* Equitable Life, New York; Roswell Mus & Art Ctr, NMex; ARCO Visual Arts Ctr, Los Angeles; Dallas Mus Fine Arts, Tex; Nova Corp, Canada. *Exhib:* Directions in Contemporary American Realism, San Antonio Mus, Tex, 81; Am Acad & Inst Arts & Lett, New York, 81; Dallas Mus, Tex, 81; Nat Mus Am Art, Washington, DC, 82; Kimbell Art Mus, Fort Worth, Tex, 83; and others. *Pos:* Artist-in-residence, Roswell Mus, 75-76, MacDowell Colony, Peterborough, NH, fall 77, Yaddo, Saratoga Springs, NY, spring 78, Ossabaw Found, Savannah, Ga, spring 79; vis artist, Univ Iowa, Iowa City, fall, 81; artist in residence, Bellagio Study & Conference Ctr, Lake Como, Italy, 83. *Teaching:* Instr printmaking, Univ Calif, Santa Cruz, summer 75; assoc prof painting & drawing, Univ Tex, Arlington, 78- *Awards:* Fulbright fel, Fulbright-Hays Exchange Act, 76-77; Nat Endowment Arts, painting, 81; Award, Am Visual Artists, 82. *Bibliog:* Real, really real, super real, San Antonio Mus, 81; Ned Rifkin (auth), Response (catalog), Tyler Mus, 80; Harry Rand (auth), Awards in the Visual Arts I, Southeastern Ctr Contemp Art, 82. *Mem:* MacDowell Colony Fellows. *Publ:* Auth, Andenken, L A Louver Publications Inc, 82. *Dealer:* L A Louver Galleries 55 N Venice Blvd Venice CA 90291. *Mailing Add:* 2616 Brentwood Circle Arlington TX 76013

SHAHLY, JEHAN
PAINTER

b Detroit, Mich, Dec 12, 28. *Study:* Mich State Univ, BA; Art Students League; New Sch Social Res; Hunter Col, MA. *Work:* San Francisco Mus Art; Univ Southern Ill; Univ Mass; Geigy Collection; Bradford Jr Col. *Exhib:* Grand Central Mods Gallery, New York, 62 & 63; Six Painters, Kansas City Mus, 63; one-woman shows, Green Mountain Gallery, New York, 73, Ulster Co Community Col, 76 & Landmark Gallery, New York, 78; and others. *Pos:* Lectr, Guggenheim Mus. *Awards:* Purchase Prizes, San Francisco Mus Art, 56 & Wichita Mus, Kans, 57; Creative Artists Pub Serv Grant, 76. *Bibliog:* Lawrence Campbell (auth), article, Art News Mag, 11/73; April Kinsley (auth), article, Art Int, 1/74; Robbie Ehrlich (auth), article, Arts Mag, 12/78. *Media:* Oil. *Mailing Add:* 799 Greenwich St New York NY 10014

SHALIT, MITZI (MILDRED M)
CONSULTANT, DEALER

b New York, NY, Apr 5, 23. *Study:* Pratt Inst, Brooklyn, NY; Art Students League; Fleisher Art Mem, Philadelphia, Pa. *Pos:* Pvt dealer & art consult specializing in corp art collections and cataloging of same. *Mailing Add:* 41 Conshohocken State Rd 302 Bala-Cynwyd PA 19004

SHALKOP, ROBERT LEROY
MUSEUM DIRECTOR, HISTORIAN

b Milford, Conn, July 30, 22. *Study:* Maryville Col, Tenn, 40-42; Univ Chicago, 46-50, MA, 49; Sorbonne, Univ Paris, 51-52. *Collections Arranged:* Arroyo Hondo, the Folk Art of a New Mexican Village (with catalog); Reflections of Spain: a Comparative View of Spanish Colonial Sculpture (with catalog), 68; Reflections of Spain II: Spanish Colonial Painting (with catalog), 69; 100 Years of Painting in the Pike's Peak Region (with catalog); Russian Orthodox Art in Alaska (with catalog), 73; Sydney Laurence, an Alaskan Impressionist (with catalog), 75; Eustace Ziegler (with catalog), 77; Contemporary Native Art of Alaska (with catalog), 79; Henry Wood Elliot (with catalog), 82. *Pos:* Dir, Rahr Civic Ctr, Manitowoc, Wis, 53-56; dir, Everhart Mus, Scranton, Pa, 56-62; dir, Brooks Mem Art Gallery, Memphis, Tenn, 62-64; assoc dir, Colorado Springs Fine Arts Ctr & cur, Taylor Mus, 64-71; dir, Anchorage Hist & Fine Arts Mus, 72- *Mem:* Asn Art Mus Dirs; Am Asn Mus; Art Mus Asn. *Publ:* Auth, Wooden Saints, the Santos of New Mexico, 67; auth, Sydney Laurence, His Life and Work, 82. *Mailing Add:* Anchorage Hist & Fine Arts Mus 121 W Seventh Ave Anchorage AK 99501

SHAMAN, SANFORD SIVITZ
MUSEUM DIRECTOR, CURATOR

b Pittsburgh, Pa, July 11, 46. *Study:* Ohio Univ, Athens, BFA, 68; State Univ NY Binghamton, 70-71; Villa Schifanoia Grad Sch Fine Arts, Florence, Italy, MFA, 74. *Collections Arranged:* Harris K Prior Memorial Exhibition, Mem Art Gallery, Rochester, NY, 76; Contemporary Chicago Painters (auth, catalog), Ohio State Univ, Fla State Univ, Univ SFla & Univ Northern Iowa Gallery Art, 77-78; De Kooning 1969-1978 (auth, catalog), Univ Northern Iowa Gallery Art, St Louis Art Mus, Contemp Arts Ctr, Cincinnati & Akron Art Inst, 78-79; Standards by Allan Kaprow (auth, catalog), Univ Northern Iowa Gallery Art; The Contemporary American Potter (ed & contribr, catalog), 80-82 & Noritake Art Deco Porcelains: Collection of Howard Kottler (auth, catalog), 82-84, Smithsonian Inst Traveling Exhibs; Philip Pearlstein: Painting to Watercolors Traveling Show (auth, catalog), 83-84. *Pos:* Cur, Huntington Galleries, WVa, 74-75; asst cur, Mem Art Gallery, Rochester, NY, 75-77; dir, Gallery of Art, Univ Northern Iowa, Cedar Falls, 77-80; dir, Museum Art, Wash State Univ, Pullman, 80- *Teaching:* Vis lectr, WVa State Col, 75; adj faculty, Univ Northern Iowa, 78. *Awards:* Villa Schifanoia Grad Sch Fine Arts Scholar, Florence, 72; Univ Northern Iowa Fac Res Award, 79-80; Nat Endowment Arts Fel, 83. *Mem:* Am Asn Mus; Eastern Wash State Hist Soc (trustee, currently); Asn Col & Univ Mus & Galleries (pres, currently); and others. *Publ:* Auth, Willem de Kooning, abstract expressionist, See Mag, 9-10/78; auth, foreword, Contemporary Metals: Focus on Idea, Wash State Univ & Western Asn Mus, 81; auth, Foreword, Swords of the Samurai, Wash State Univ, 81; auth, Introduction, American Potters, Watson-Guptill, 81; contribr, Arts Voice, Atlanta Art Papers & New Art Examiner, 83. *Mailing Add:* Museum Art Washington State Univ Pullman WA 99164

SHANE, FREDERICK E
PAINTER
b Feb 2, 06; US citizen. *Study:* Kansas City Art Inst, 23-24; also with Randall Davey, Santa Fe, NMex, 24; Braodmoor Art Acad, summers 25 & 26. *Work:* City Art Mus, St Louis, Mo; Mus Art & Archaeol, Univ Mo-Columbia; Springfield Mus Art, Mo; State Univ NY Col, Oswego; IBM Corp Collection; and many others. *Comn:* Paintings of Army Medicine, War Dept, Abbott Collection, Washington, DC; portrait of James M Wood, Stephens Col; mural, US Post Off, Eldon, Mo; Scruggs-Vandervoort-Barney Collection, Univ Mo; Jefferson City Jr Col. *Exhib:* Art Inst Chicago; Corcoran Gallery Art, Washington, DC; Pa Acad Fine Arts, Philadelphia; Carnegie Inst Int, Pittsburgh; New York World's Fair, 39-40 & 64-65; Watercolor USA, 76; retrospective, Art Mus Univ Mo, Columbia & State Hist Soc, 82; and many others. *Pos:* Artist corresp, Army Med Corps, 44. *Teaching:* Prof art, Univ Mo, 38-71, chmn dept, 58-67, emer prof fine arts, 71- *Awards:* Second Painting Prize, Davenport Mus Art, Iowa, 50; Popular Painting Prize, Columbia Art League, 60; Byler Award for Achievement in Art & Teaching, 71; and many others. *Bibliog:* Archives Am Art, Smithsonian Inst, Washington, DC. *Media:* Oil, Casein. *Publ:* Auth, Fred Shane Drawings, Univ Mo. *Mailing Add:* 633 N Foothill Rd Beverly Hills CA 90210

SHANER, (GEORGE) DAVID
CERAMIST, CRAFTSMAN
b Pottstown, Penn, Nov 11, 34. *Study:* State Col, Kutztown, Penn, BS(art ed), 56; NY State Col Ceramics, Alfred Univ, MA(ceramic design), 59. *Work:* Royal Ont Mus, Toronto; Mus Contemp Crafts, New York; Everson Mus Art, Syracuse, NY; Nat Arts Collection, Smithsonian Inst, Washington, DC; Kansas City Art Inst, Mo. *Exhib:* Everson Mus Art, New York, 66 & 79; Craftsman USA, Mus Contemp Crafts, New York, 66; US Info Agency Exhib, Far East, Middle East, South Am & Africa, 74; Smithsonian Inst, Washington, DC, 79; Potters Dozen-NCECA, Univ Mich, Ann Arbor, 80; 8th Chunichi Int Exhib Ceramic Arts, Nagoya, Tokyo & Kanazawa, Japan, 80. *Pos:* Asst prof art, Univ Ill, Urbana, 59-63; res potter & dir, Archie Bray Found, Helena, Mont, 63-70; self-employed studio potter, Bigfork, Mont, 70- *Awards:* Louis Comfort Tiffany Scholar Award, 63; Nat Endowment Arts craftsman fel, 73 & 78. *Bibliog:* Garth Clark (auth), A Century of American Ceramics: 1878-1978, 79; Peter Sabin (auth), David Shaner: Montana Conversation, Studio Potter Vol 8, No 1, Daniel Clark Found, 79; Harrington (auth), Northwest Ceramics, Univ Wash Press, 79. *Mem:* Archie Bray Found (trustee, 70-, chmn 76-); Mont Arts Coun (vchmn, 77-). *Mailing Add:* 7135 Montana Hwy 35 Bigfork MT 59911

SHANGRAW, CLARENCE FRANK
HISTORIAN, CURATOR
b Burlington, Vt, Aug 9, 35. *Study:* Inst Far Eastern Lang, Yale Univ, cert; Univ Calif, Berkeley, AB(with high honors), MA(Oriental lang & lit). *Collections Arranged:* Avery Brundage Collection of Asian Art Permanent Collection, 65-; Chinese Treasures from the Avery Brundage Collection, 69; Paintings from the Abe Collection, Osaka, 70; Chinese Gold, Silver & White Porcelain from the Carl Kempe Collection, 71; Ancient Indonesian Art of the Central & Eastern Japanese Periods, 71; Rarities of the Musee Guimet: Asian Art from a French Museum, winter 75; Exhibition of Archeological Finds of the People's Republic of China, summer 75; 5,000 Years of Korean Art (contribr, catalog), 79; Chinese Blue-and-White Porcelain from Drake's Bay, 79; Treasures form the Shanghai Museum--6,000 Years of Chinese Art (contribr & translr, catalog), Asian Art Mus, 83. *Pos:* Res asst, De Young Mus, San Francisco, 65-66, asst cur, 66-67; cur, Asian Art Mus, San Francisco, 69-71, sr cur, 72- *Teaching:* Adj prof, John F Kennedy Univ, Sch Museum Studies, 79- *Mem:* Col Art Asn Am; Asn Asian Studies; Oriental Ceramics Soc, London; Am Asn Mus; Archaeol Inst Am. *Res:* Early Chinese ceramics, prehistoric to the Han; Chinese Buddhist sculpture; archaeology in China. *Publ:* Auth, A Cross-section of Chinese Blue and White Porcelains in the Asian Art Museum, 7/80 & auth, Chinese Cloissone and Painted Enamels in the 18th Century, 7/80, Apollo; auth, Korean art in western collections: The Asian Art Museum of San Francisco, Arts of Asia, 11/82; coauth, The Drake and Cermeno Expeditions' Chinese Porcelains at Drakes Bay, California, 82; auth, Archaeological treasures from Shanghai, Archaeol, 5/83; and others. *Mailing Add:* Asian Art Mus Golden Gate Park San Francisco CA 94118

SHANNON, CHARLES
PAINTER
b Montgomery, Ala, June 22, 14. *Study:* Emory Univ, 30-32; Cleveland Sch Art, dipl(cum laude), 36. *Work:* War Dept Collection Combat Paintings, Washington, DC. *Exhib:* Nat Gallery, 44; Metropolitan Mus Art, New York, 50; retrospective, Southeastern Ctr Contemp Art, Winston-Salem, NC, Hunter Mus Art & others, 81-82; Southern Works on Paper, 1900-1940, 81-82 & Southern Drawings and Prints, 83-84, Southern Arts Fedn; Painting in the South, 1546-1980, Va Mus, 83-84; West 83--Art and the Law Traveling Exhib, 83-84. *Pos:* Picture ed & illusr, Army Info & Educ Div, New York, 42-46. *Teaching:* Artist in residence, WGa Col, 40-42; instr, Univ Ala Exten Ctr, Montgomery, 58-68; prof art & dept head, Auburn Univ, Montgomery, 69-79. *Awards:* First Award Figure Composition, Cleveland Mus Art Ann May Show, 36; Third Prize Int Div, Golden Gate Exposition, San Francisco, 39; Purchase Award, West 83--Art and the Law, West Publ Co, 83. *Mailing Add:* 128 Early St Montgomery AL 36104

SHANNONHOUSE, SANDRA LYNNE RIDDELL
SCULPTURE
b Petaluma, Calif, May 19, 47. *Study:* Univ Calif, Davis, BS, 69, MFA(dramatic art), 73; studied with Robert Arneson. *Work:* Utah Mus Fine Arts, Salt Lake City. *Exhib:* A Decade of Ceramic Art 1962-1972, San Francisco Mus Mod Art, Calif, 73; R Joseph Monson Collection, Seattle Mus Art, Wash, 74; one-man shows, Quay Gallery, San Francisco, 75, 78 & 80; Birthday Show, Mus Contemp Crafts, New York, 76; Calif Clay I & II, Braunstein/Quay Gallery, New York, 76 & 77; An Exhib of Bay Area Ceramics, Fine Arts Mus, San Francisco, 77; Northern California Clay Routes: Sculpture Now, San Francisco Mus Mod Art, 79; Clay Attitudes, Queens Mus, New York, 79; and others. *Teaching:* Lectr form in theatre, Univ Calif, Davis, 74; instr ceramics & drawings, Am River Col, Sacramento, Calif, 75-76; guest artist, Otis Art Inst, Los Angeles, Calif, 76-78; artist-in-residence ceramics, Oxbow Summer Sch Art, Saugatuck, Mich, 76. *Bibliog:* Suzanne Foley (auth), A Decade of Ceramic Art, San Francisco Mus Art, 72; Sandy Ballatore (auth), The California clay rush, Art in Am, 76; Mac McCloud (auth), Dealer's choice, Images & Issues, 9-10/83. *Media:* Bronze, Clay. *Dealer:* Stephen Wirtz Gallery 345 Sutter St San Francisco CA 94108. *Mailing Add:* 110 East E St Benicia CA 94510

SHAPERO, ESTHER GELLER See Geller, Esther

SHAPIRO, ADRIAN MICHAEL
DEALER, WRITER
b Galveston, Tex, April 13, 50. *Study:* Univ Tex, Austin, BA(cum laude), 72, MA, 73; Ind Univ, Bloomington, PhD, 77. *Collections Arranged:* Slavko Kopac--Recent Work (coauth, catalog), 82; Claude Bellegarde--Homage to Color, 82. *Pos:* Managing partner, FAME Gallery, Houston, 80-; dir, Post Oak Fine Art Distribr, Houston, 81- *Mem:* Houston Art Dealers Asn; Mid-Am Appraisers Asn; Int Fine Arts Asn Inc. *Specialty:* Twentieth century paintings, prints and sculpture by internationally recognized artists. *Publ:* Auth, Fine art: Looking for ... aesthetic investments, Houston Bus J, 79; contribr, Old art making new bucks, Houston Chronicle, 79; auth, The origin of print collecting, Art Happenings Mag, 81; auth, The search for original prints, Southwest Art Mag, 82; auth, Corporate art collections, Art Happenings Mag, 83. *Mailing Add:* 1980 Post Oak Blvd Suite J Houston TX 77056

SHAPIRO, BABE
PAINTER
b Irvington, NJ, May 4, 37. *Study:* NJ State Teachers Col, Newark, BS; Hunter Col, with Robert Motherwell, MA. *Work:* Newark Mus; Andrew Dickson White Mus, Cornell Univ; Albright-Knox Art Gallery, Buffalo; Corcoran Gallery Art, Washington, DC; Scottish Nat Gallery of Mod Art, Edinburgh. *Exhib:* Biennial Exhib Contemp Am Painting, Univ Ill, 63; New York World's Fair, 65; Cincinnati Art Mus, 66; Indianapolis Mus Art, 70; New Am Acquisitions, Colorado Springs Fine Arts Mus, 72; plus others. *Pos:* Dir, Mount Royal Grad Sch Painting, Md Inst Col Art, Baltimore, currently. *Teaching:* Artist in residence, Quincy Art Club, 66. *Awards:* Newark Mus Triennial Purchase Prize Award, 58 & 61; First Prize in Painting, Monmouth Col, NJ, 63. *Media:* Acrylic. *Dealer:* A M Sachs Gallery 29 W 57th St New York NY 10019; Gertrude Kasle Gallery 310 Fisher Bldg Detroit MI 48202. *Mailing Add:* 31 Walker St New York NY 10013

SHAPIRO, DAISY VIERTEL
COLLECTOR, PATRON
b New York, NY, July 8, 92. *Study:* Painting with Louise Pollet & Alex Redein. *Mem:* Solomon R Guggenheim Mus; Archit Am Art; fel Morgan Libr; Am Fedn Arts; Mus City of New York; plus others. *Collection:* Contemporary American painting and sculpture; donations of many works of art to museums and colleges including Dartmouth College. *Mailing Add:* 200 East End Ave New York NY 10028

SHAPIRO, DAVID
PAINTER
b Brooklyn, NY, June 26, 44. *Study:* Skowhegan Sch Art, Maine, 65; Pratt Inst, BFA, 66; Ind Univ, Bloomington, MFA, 68. *Work:* Ind Univ Art Mus, Bloomington; San Francisco Mus Mod Art, Calif; Guggenheim Mus, New York; Westinghouse Corp, Pittsburgh; Mus Mod Art, New York. *Exhib:* Gertrude Kasle Gallery, Detroit, 70 & 73; Poindexter Gallery, New York, 71, 73, 74 & 77; William Sawyer Gallery, San Francisco, 73; Alexander Milliken Gallery, New York, 78; Roy Boyd Gallery, Chicago, 78. *Teaching:* Instr, Pratt Inst, 69-71; vis artist, Barnard Col, 72; guest artist, Kansas City Art Inst, 73; instr, Parsons Sch Design, 74-80. *Bibliog:* M L Thompson (auth), Cosmos and chaos, Arts Mag, 10/80. *Dealer:* Alexander Milliken Gallery 90 Prince St New York NY 10012. *Mailing Add:* 315 Riverside Dr New York NY 10025

SHAPIRO, DAVID
PAINTER, PRINTMAKER
b New York, NY, Aug 28, 16. *Study:* Educ Alliance Art Sch, 33-35; Am Artists Sch, 36-39. *Work:* Metrop Mus Art, New York; Brooklyn Mus, NY; Philadelphia Mus Art; Nat Mus Am Art; Libr Cong, Washington, DC; and others. *Comn:* Black & white intaglios, Assoc Am Artists Gallery, New York, 70-75; color lithographs, Litografie Int, Milan, Italy, 70; stained glass windows, Garden Jewish Ctr, Flushing, NY, 70; black & white intaglio, Ferdinand Roten Galleries, 77; original print, Collectors Group, 76, 77 & 82. *Exhib:* Pa Acad Ann, Philadelphia, 47; Whitney Ann, New York, 52; Brooklyn Mus Print Ann, 53; Libr Cong Print Ann, 53; Corcoran Biennial, Washington, DC, 59. *Pos:* Art ed, Hofstra Rev, Hofstra Univ, 65-70. *Teaching:* Instr studio art, Smith Col, 46-47; asst prof studio art & art hist, Univ BC, 47-49; prof studio art & art hist, Hofstra Univ, Hempstead, NY, 61-81, prof emer, 81-; artist in residence & prof am art, Univ Belgrade, 81. *Awards:* Fulbright Fel, 51-53 & 81; Purchase Awards, Brooklyn Mus Print Ann, 46, Libr Cong Print Ann, 50 & Mus Fine Arts, Springfield, Mass, 57. *Mem:* Soc Am Graphic Artists (pres, 68-70, exec coun, 70-); Col Art Asn Am.

Res: American art with emphasis on art of the 30's. *Publ:* Auth, Stanley William Hayter, expression of the unconscious (catalog essay), 4/70; contribr, 19th century American painting, New York Hist Soc Quart, 1/72; auth, Social Realism: Art as a Weapon, Frederick Ungar Publ Co, 73; contribr, Search for an American image, Am Art Rev, 5-6/74; contribr, Abstract expressionism: the politics of apolitical painting, Prospects, 77. *Dealer:* Assoc Am Artists Gallery 663 Fifth Ave New York NY 10022; Kennedy Galleries 40 W 57th St New York NY 10019. *Mailing Add:* RFD 77 Cavendish VT 05142

SHAPIRO, DEE
PAINTER, LECTURER
b Brooklyn, NY, Nov 30, 36. *Study:* Univ Mex, 56; Queens Col, BA, 58, MS, 60. *Work:* Newark Mus; Oklahoma Art Mus, Oklahoma City; Herbert F Johnson Mus, Ithaca, NY; NY Univ; Dayton Art Inst, Ohio. *Exhib:* Solo exhibs, Nassau Co Mus Fine Arts, Roslyn, NY, 74 & 83, Andre Zarre Gallery, NY, 76-78, 80, 81 & 83, Everson Mus, Syracuse, Ny, 81, Dubins Gallery, La, 82 & Ana Sklar Gallery, Fla, 83; Brooklyn Mus, 75; Albright-Knox Mus, Buffalo, NY, 80; Suzanne Brown Gallery, Scottsdale, Ariz, 81. *Pos:* Gallery dir & cur, North Shore Community Arts Ctr, 79-81. *Teaching:* Instr, Adelphi Univ, 81-, Empire State Col, 83. *Awards:* Award, Nat Asn Women Artists, 73; Award Excellence, Heckscher Mus, 74. *Bibliog:* Judith Tannenbaum (auth), Dee Shapiro, Arts Mag, 78; Barbara Flug Colin (auth), The pattern of a painter, New York Arts J, 81. *Mem:* Col Art Asn. *Dealer:* Andre Zarre 41 East 57th St New York NY 10022. *Mailing Add:* 28 Clover Dr Great Neck NY 11021

SHAPIRO, IRVING
PAINTER, INSTRUCTOR
b Chicago, Ill, Mar 28, 27. *Study:* Art Inst Chicago; Chicago Acad Fine Art; Am Acad Art, Chicago. *Work:* Univ Vt; Columbus Mus Art, Ga; Lakeview Mus Art, Peoria, Ill; Ill State Mus, Springfield; Macon Mus Art, Ga. *Exhib:* Am Watercolor Soc Ann, Nat Acad Design Gallery, 58-72; Union League Club Chicago, 55, 57 & 59; Butler Inst Am Art, Youngstown, Ohio, 62; Art Inst Chicago Sales & Rental Galleries, 66-68. *Teaching:* Instr watercolors, Am Acad Art, 45-, dir, 71- *Awards:* Am Watercolor Soc Award, 81; Grumbacher Silver Medal, 81; Winsor & Newton Bronze Medal, 82. *Mem:* Am Watercolor Soc; Midwest Watercolor Soc. *Media:* Watercolor. *Publ:* Auth & illusr, article, Am Artist, 59 & 79; auth & illusr, Watercolor Techniques, 70; auth & illusr, Acrylic Watercolor, 71; auth & illusr, Palette Talks, 72 & 79. *Dealer:* Gallery of the Ravens Estes Park CO 80517; R H Love Galleries, Chicago IL. *Mailing Add:* 1335 Astor #14A Chicago IL 60610

SHAPIRO, JOEL (ELIAS)
SCULPTOR
b New York, NY, Sept 27, 41. *Study:* NY Univ, BA & MA. *Work:* Fogg Art Mus; Metrop Mus Mod Art, New York; Whitney Mus Am Art, New York; Albright-Knox Art Gallery, Buffalo; Stedelijk Mus, Amsterdam. *Exhib:* One-man shows, Mus Contemp Art, Chicago, 76, Albright-Knox Art Gallery, Buffalo, NY, 77, Akron Art Inst, Ohio, 79, Contemp Arts Ctr, Cincinnati, 81, Whitney Mus Am Art, 82 & Dallas Mus Fine Art, 82; Drawings/Sculptures, Inst Contemp Art, Boston, 80; Am Drawing in Black and White, Brooklyn Mus, NY, 80; Whitney Biennial, Whitney Mus Am Art, NY, 81; New Dimensions in Drawing, Aldrich Mus Contemp Art, Conn, 81; Drawings from Georgia Collections, 19th & 20th Centuries, High Mus Art, Atlanta, 81; New Acquisitions, Whitney Mus Am Art, NY, 81; Akron Art Mus, Ohio, 81; and others. *Bibliog:* Jeremy Gilbert-Rolfe (auth), Joel Shapiro: works in progress, 12/73 & Marc Field (auth), On Joel Shapiro's sculptures and drawings, summer 78, Artforum; Carter Ratcliff (auth), Joel Shapiro's drawings, Print Collector's Newlett, 3-4/78. *Mailing Add:* c/o Paula Cooper 155 Wooster St New York NY 10012

SHAPSHAK, RENE
SCULPTOR
b Paris, France; US citizen. *Study:* Ecole des Beaux Arts, Paris; Ecole des Beaux Arts, Bruxelles; Art Sch, London, Eng. *Work:* Philathea Col Mus Mod Art, London, Ont; Butler Inst Am Art, Youngstown, Ohio; Munic Mus, Paris; Cecil Rhodes Mus, Bishop-Stortford, Eng; Pinakotheki, Athens, Greece; and others. *Comn:* Marble bas-relief, 42 & granite bas-relief, 42, New Gen Post Off, Capetown, SAfrica; metal sculptures, SAfrican Broadcasting Corp, 50 & munition factory, Pretoria, 54; fountain, City of New York, 72; and others. *Exhib:* One-man exhib, UN, 55; Palais des Beaux Arts, Paris, 55; Whitney Mus Art, New York, 56; Mus Art Mod, Paris, 71-72; Willimantic State Col, Conn; plus others. *Pos:* Dir, Rene Shapshak Mus Mod Art, London, Ont, Canada. *Awards:* Comdr, Order of St Dennis of Zante, Greece, 75; Acad Palms Gold Medal, Int Am Inst, Washington, DC, 80; Grand Croix, St Georges & Constantine, Cannes, France, 81. *Mem:* Am Fedn Arts; Fr Art Theatre; patron Syndicate African Artists; fel Royal Soc Arts; fel Nat Soc Lit & Arts. *Mailing Add:* Hotel Chelsea 222 W 23rd St New York NY 10011

SHARITS, PAUL JEFFREY
FILM ARTIST, PAINTER
b Denver, Colo, Feb 7, 43. *Study:* Univ Denver, BFA(painting), 64; Ind Univ, MFA(visual design), 66. *Work:* Mus Mod Art, New York & Paris; Wallraf-Richartz Mus, Cologne, Ger; Albright-Knox Art Gallery, Buffalo, NY; Ga Mus Art, Athens; Arco Ctr Visual Arts, Los Angeles. *Comn:* Four-screen film environment, Contemp Arts Mus, Houston, 71; four-screen film environment, Artpark, State of NY, Lewiston, 75. *Exhib:* One-man shows, Albright Knox Art Gallery (film), Buffalo, 76, Cirrus Gallery (painting), Los Angeles, Calif, 81 & Nina Freudenheim Gallery (painting), Buffalo, NY, 83; Projected Images, Walker Art Ctr, Minneapolis, 74; Hist of the Am Avant-Garde Cinema, Mus Mod Art, New York, 76; Open to New Ideas: A Collection of

New Art for Jimmy Carter, Ga Mus Art, Univ Ga, Athens, 76; Illusion & Reality (traveling exhib), Australia, 77; Film Retrospective, Centre Nat d'Art et de Cult Georges-Pompidou, Paris, 77; Film Installation, Whitney Biennial, 81; and many others. *Teaching:* Instr film, Md Art Inst, Baltimore, 67-70; asst prof film, Antioch Col, Yellow Springs, Ohio, 70-73 & State Univ NY, Buffalo, 73- *Awards:* Film Making Grant, Creative Artists Pub Serv Prog, New York, 75; Bicentennial Film Proj Grant, Nat Endowment for the Arts & NY State Coun on the Arts, 76; Nat Endowment Arts Grant for film, 79 & 83. *Bibliog:* Regina Cornwell (auth), Sharits: Object & illusion, 9/71 & Rosalind Krauss (auth), Sharits: Stop time, 4/73, Artforum; Annette Michelson (auth), Sharits & the critique of illusionism, Projected Images, 74. *Mem:* Col Art Asn Am. *Media:* Film. *Publ:* Auth, Red, blue, Godard, Film Quart, summer 66; auth, Notes on film, Film Cult, summer 69; auth, Words per page, Afterimage, Cambridge, Eng, fall 72; auth, Blank deflections: Golden cinema, Film Cult, winter-spring 70; coauth, Eight interviews/statements, Art in Am, 7-8/75. *Dealer:* Cirrus Gallery 542 S Alameda St Los Angeles CA 90013; Galerie Ricke Friesenplatz 23 Cologne WGer. *Mailing Add:* Ctr for Media Study State Univ NY Buffalo NY 14214

SHARP, ANNE
PAINTER, PRINTMAKER
b Red Bank, NJ, Nov 1, 43. *Study:* Pratt Inst, Brooklyn, NY, BFA, 65, with Richard Lindner; Brooklyn Col, MFA, with Lee Bontecou. *Work:* Smithsonian Inst, Nat Air & Space Mus, Washington, DC; Albright-Knox Art Gallery, Buffalo, NY; St Vincent's Hospital, New York; Philip Morris, Inc, New York; New York Life Insurance Co Am. *Exhib:* Community Gallery, Brooklyn Mus, 73; MOMA Bookstore, Mus Mod Art, New York, 75-76; Nat Arts Club Print Show, New York, 79; Arteder 82, Bibao, Spain, 82; Cabo Frio Biennale 83 & Int Print Show, 83, Cabo Frio, Brazil. *Teaching:* Instr, NY Univ, 78, Sch Visual Arts, 78-, Pratt Manhattan Ctr, 82-, State Univ NY, Purchase, 83. *Awards:* Teaching fel, Artist's Show, Brooklyn, NY, 72; artist sponsor, Great Lakes Col Asn Apprenticeship Prog, 73-76; resident artist, Artist Open House, Va Ctr for Creative Art, 75; Artist in Residence Grant, Artpark, 80. *Bibliog:* Peter Frank (auth), Prints, Art News, 2/75; Grace Glueck (auth), They create a new art scene, New York Sunday Times, 5/75; Jerry Tallmer (auth), Moving in the space of stars, New York Post, 8/79. *Mem:* Artists Equity Asn; Nat Trust Historic Preservation, 11/4/81; Women's Caucus on Art; Women; and others. *Media:* Oil, Acrylic; Silkscreen. *Publ:* Illusr, Terminal Placebos, 75 & Planting Beeches, 75, New Rivers Press; auth, Women artists and the business of art, 78; auth, Charles Schucker at Max Hutchinson Gallery, Arts Mag, 78. *Dealer:* Arlene Levien 45 E 82nd St New York NY 10028. *Mailing Add:* 20 Waterside Plaza New York NY 10010

SHARP, HAROLD
ILLUSTRATOR, CARTOONIST
b New York, NY, Mar 2, 19. *Study:* Nat Acad Design, 37-41; Columbia Univ, BA; Hunter Col, MA. *Pos:* Advert illusr for Texaco, Schering, Upjohn & Alcoa, formerly; illusr, L W Frolich Agency & Gray Agency, currently. *Awards:* Ashton Award, Hunter Col. *Media:* Mixed. *Publ:* Cartoons publ in Esquire, New York Times, This Week Mag, Ladies Home J, J Am Med Asn, Parade Mag & others; cartoons publ in Sat Rev in Lit, Esquire, NY Times & Ladies Home J. *Mailing Add:* 3973 Saxon Ave New York NY 10463

SHARP, LEWIS INMAN
CURATOR, ADMINISTRATOR
b New York, NY, Dec 22, 41. *Study:* Lewis & Clark, Col, Portland, Ore, BA, 65; Univ Del, MA, 68 & PhD, 80. *Pos:* Asst cur Am paintings & sculpture, Metrop Mus Art, New York, 72-75, assoc cur Am paintings & sculpture, 75-82, adminr Am wing, 80-83, curator, 82-83. *Publ:* Auth, John Quincy Adams Ward: History & contemporary influences, The Am Art J IV, 11/72; auth, The Smith Memorial, Sculptures of a City: Philadelphia's Treasures in Bronze & Stone, Walker Publ Co, 74; auth, New York Public Sculpture by 19th Century American Artists, Metrop Mus Art, 74. *Mailing Add:* 40 West 74th St New York NY 10023

SHARP, WILLOUGHBY
VIDEO ARTIST, CONSULTANT
b New York, NY, Jan 23, 36. *Study:* Brown Univ, BA; Univ Paris; Univ Lausanne; Columbia Univ, MA. *Work:* Guggenheim Mus & Mus Mod Art, New York; Boston Mus Fine Arts; Mus Conceptual Art, San Francisco; plus others. *Exhib:* Information, Mus Mod Art, New York, 70; Earth, Air, Fire, Water: Elements of Art, Boston Mus Fine Art, 71; Circuit: A Video Invitational, Everson Mus Art, Syracuse, NY, Henry Gallery, Univ Wash, Cranbrook Acad, Bloomfield & Los Angeles Co Mus, plus others, 73-74; Kunst Bleibt Kunst: Project, 74, Cologne, Ger, 74. *Pos:* Dir, Kineticism Press, 68-; pres, Avalanche Video, 70-; vpres, Ctr New Art Activities, Inc, (Sharpcom), 74-; dir, Franklin Street Arts Ctr, New York, 76-82; dir, Worldpool, Toronto, 79. *Awards:* Rockefeller Found Grant, 71; Kaplan Fund Grant, 71; Nat Endowment Arts Grant, 72 & 80; and others. *Bibliog:* Robert E Dallos (auth), Sculpture, New York Times, 8/30/67; Anthony Bannon (auth), Sharp puts himself into his art literally, Buffalo Eve News, 3/17/75; Douglas David (auth), Art, Newsweek, 7/21/75. *Dealer:* Electronic Arts Intermix Inc 84 Fifth Ave New York NY 10011. *Mailing Add:* 112 Franklin St New York NY 10013

SHARPE, (NORMAN) BLAIR
PAINTER
b Montreal, Que, Can, July 25, 54. *Study:* Kent Sch, West Germany, A level, 72; Ottawa Sch Art, 73-74. *Work:* Can Coun Art Bank, Ottawa, Ont; Esso Resources Can--Petro Plaza Collection, Calgary, Alta. *Exhib:* Regional Exhib,

Agnes Etherington Art Ctr, Kingston, Ont, 81; Paint: The Expressive Touch, Gallery III, Univ Manitoba, Winnipeg & Gairloch Gallery, Oakville, Ont, 81; SAW Gallery, Ottawa, Ont; Cedar Ridge Gallery, Scarborough, Ont, 82; and others. *Awards:* Post A Award, British Forces Educ, 73; Project Grant, Ont Arts Coun, 76, 77 & 80. *Bibliog:* David Burnett (auth), article, Artscanada, 5-6/77; Anna Babinska (auth), article, Artmag, Can, 2-3/80; Doris Finta (auth), Sharpe, Durr & Mello, Artmag, Can, 11/81. *Mem:* Canadian Artists' Representation, Ottawa (chmn, 81-82); Visual Arts Ont. *Media:* Acrylic, Watercolor. *Dealer:* Wells Gallery 459 Sussex Dr Ottawa ON Can K1N 6Z4. *Mailing Add:* 32 Lewis Street Ottawa ON K2P 0S3 Canada

SHARPE, DAVID FLEMMING
PAINTER, PRINTMAKER

b Owensboro, Ky, June 7, 44. *Study:* Art Inst of Chicago, BFA, 66, MFA, 68. *Work:* Art Inst of Chicago; Everson Mus, Syracuse, NY; Okla Art Ctr, Oklahoma City; Owens-Corning Corp Collections; Am Tel & Tel Collection. *Exhib:* Artists Under 30, 68, Soc of Contemp Art, 69 & 71, Recent Acquisitions, 70 & Distinguished Alumni 1945 to Present, 76, Art Inst of Chicago; Chicago Painting in the 1960s (touring major mus of Can), 71-72; Outside City Limits (touring NY state), 77-78; Masterpieces of Chicago Art, Chicago Cult Ctr, 77; Soho Ctr for Visual Arts, New York, 77; New Work-New York (traveling USA & Europe), 77-78; Larry Aldrich Mus Contemp Art, Ridgefield, Conn, 78. *Media:* Oil, Watercolor; Drawing. *Dealer:* Sonia Zaks 620 N Michigan Ave Chicago IL 60611. *Mailing Add:* 114 W Houston New York NY 10012

SHARROW, SHEBA
PAINTER, EDUCATOR

b Brooklyn, NY, Apr 28, 26. *Study:* Art Inst Chicago, BFA, 48; Pa Acad Fine Art, 52; Tyler Sch Art, Temple Univ, MFA, 68. *Work:* Millersville State Col, Lancaster, Pa; Citibank, New York; Va Ctr Creative Arts, Sweet Briar, Va. *Exhib:* Art Inst Chicago, 48-51; State Mus Ill, Springfield, 49; Pa Acad Fine Art, Philadelphia, 52 & 64; Butler Inst Am Art, Youngstown, Ohio, 68; Nat Acad Design, New York, 69 & 79; Philadelphia Art Alliance, 63, 65, 69 & 70; William Penn Mem Mus, Harrisburg, Pa, 71, 75 & 78-80. *Teaching:* Assoc prof, Millersville State Col, Pa, 68- *Awards:* Resident Fels, Va Ctr Creative Arts, 78 & 79. *Mem:* Artists Equity Asn; Col Art Asn; Women's Caucus Art. *Media:* Acrylic. *Publ:* Contribr, chap, Women's Studies and the Arts, Hacker Art Books, 79. *Dealer:* Rosenfield Gallery Philadelphia PA. *Mailing Add:* 915 Virginia Ave Lancaster PA 17603

SHATALOW, VLADIMIR MIHAILOVICH
PAINTER

b Belgorod, Russia, July 20, 17; US citizen. *Study:* Inst Art, Kharkov, 34-36 & Inst Art, Kiev, USSR, 38-41. *Work:* Nat Acad of Design, New York; Mint Mus of Art, Charlotte, NC; Woodmere Art Gallery, Philadelphia; San Diego Fine Arts Gallery; Sun Co Collection, Randor, Pa. *Exhib:* Butler Inst Am Art, Youngstown, Ohio, 68; Watercolor Show, Pa Acad Fine Arts, Philadelphia, 69; Am Watercolor Soc Ann, New York, 70; Wichita Centennial Watercolor Competition, Kans, 71; Watercolor USA Nat, Springfield, Mo, 72; Marietta Col, Ohio. *Awards:* Gold Medal, Allied Artists Am, 65-66; Grand Award Plaque, Nat Competition, Kans, 70; Gold Medal of Honor, Am Watercolor Soc, 81; and others. *Mem:* Assoc mem Nat Acad Design; Allied Artists Am; Audubon Artists; Philadelphia Watercolor Club; Am Watercolor Soc. *Media:* Oil, Tempera. *Mailing Add:* 2104 Poplar St Philadelphia PA 19130

SHATTER, SUSAN LOUISE
PAINTER

b New York, NY, Jan 17, 43. *Study:* Pratt Inst, BFA, 65; Skowhegan Sch Painting & Sculpture, summer 65; Boston Univ, MFA, 72. *Work:* Boston Mus of Fine Arts; Univ Utah Mus, Salt Lake City; Chase Manhattan Bank, New York; Philadelphia Mus of Art; Fed Reserve Bank of Boston. *Comn:* Colorado River in Utah (4ft x 8ft painting), America 1976, US Dept Interior, 75; Panorama of Manhattan Island (3 1/2ft x 12 1/2ft), Am Tel & Tel Co, New York, 77. *Exhib:* New Talent Knoedler Gallery, New York, 71; one-woman shows, Fischbach Gallery, New York, 73, 75, 78, 80 & 82; Boston Watercolor Today, Mus of Fine Arts, Boston, 76; America 1976 (traveling shows), Corcoran Gallery of Art, Washington, DC, 77; New York Now, Phoenix Mus, Ariz, 79; Am Realism since 1960, Pa Acad, 81-83; Gund Collection, Mus Fine Arts, Boston, 82; Realist Watercolors, Fla Int Univ, 83; and others. *Pos:* bd govs, Skowhegan Sch Photog; instr, Sch Visual Arts, 83. *Teaching:* Vis artist, Univ Pa, Philadelphia, 74-75 & 79, acting chmn, 83-84; mem fac painting, Skowhegan Sch Painting, Maine, summers 77 & 79 & Benninton Col, 79. *Awards:* Radcliffe Inst Fel, Boston, 75; Ingram-Merrill Found Grand, New York, 76; Nat Endowment, 80. *Bibliog:* John Ashbery (auth), Review of Fischbach show, New York Mag, 3/80; Ken Baker (auth), American watercolor today, Portfolio, 9-10/82; Donald Kuspit (auth), Review of Fischbach show, Art Am, 10/82. *Media:* Watercolor; Oil. *Publ:* illusr, Am Watercolors & Drawings (auth, John Arthur), Graphics Soc, NY, 80. *Dealer:* Fischbach Gallery 29 W 57th St New York NY 10019; Harcus Gallery Seven Newbury St Boston MA 02116. *Mailing Add:* 26 W 20th St New York NY 10011

SHAW, COURTNEY ANN
LIBRARIAN, HISTORIAN

b Hagerstown, Md, Feb 10, 46. *Study:* Univ Wis-Madison, BA; Case Western Res Univ, MSLS; Ariz State Univ; also weaving, Atelier, France. *Pos:* Asst librn, Yavapai Jr Col, Prescott, Ariz; art librn, Ariz State Univ; head fine arts libr, Lake Placid Sch Art; head art libr & expert Medieval & Renaissance tapestries studies, Univ Md. *Teaching:* Teacher art hist, Lake Placid, NY. *Mem:* Art Libr Soc; Conservation Guild; Art Libr Soc NAm; Washington Art Libr Resource Comt. *Mailing Add:* Art-Sociology Bldg Univ of Md College Park MD 20742

SHAW, DONALD EDWARD
PAINTER, SCULPTOR

b Boston, Mass, Aug 24, 34. *Study:* Boston Mus Sch Fine Arts. *Exhib:* Videotape: Sky Drawings, Tex Gallery, Houston, 76; Inauguration, San Angelo State Univ Mus, Tex, 76; Tex 30, Nave Mus, Victoria, Tex, 77; Kornblatt Gallery, Baltimore, Md, 77; one-man show, Moody Gallery, Houston, Tex, 78 & 79; and others. *Awards:* Travel Grant to Arg, Casa De'Arg, 77. *Bibliog:* Ann Holmes (auth), Fantastic artists, Southwest Art Gallery Mag, 2/72; N Laliberte & A Mogelon (auths), Art in Boxes, Van Nostrand, Reinhold Co, 74. *Media:* Mixed. *Publ:* Contribr, Agencia Noticias Mex, 69 & cover illus, Southwest Art Gallery Mag, 72. *Mailing Add:* c/o Moody Gallery 2015J W Gray Houston TX 77019

SHAW, ELSIE BABBITT
SCULPTOR, PAINTER

b Charlotte, NC, Dec 6, 29. *Study:* Salem Acad, 48; Mt Vernon Jr Col, 49; Rollins Col, BA, 51; study with Jerry Farnsworth, 60, Hilton Leech, 60 & Syd Solomon, 65; Atlantic Ctr Arts, New Smyrna Beach, Fla, with Duane Hansen, 82. *Work:* Greenville Mus Art, SC; Tyler Mus Art, Tex; Am Nat Bank, Chattanooga, Tenn; Univ NC. *Comn:* Citrus Grove (copper & bronze), comn by Frank Hubbard, Orlando & Art Sources, Jacksonville, for Citrus Club, Orlando, Fla, 73. *Exhib:* Nat Acad Design, New York, 63, 67 & 71; Isaac Delgado, New Orleans, La, 64; Columbia Mus Art, SC, 65; Butler Inst Art, Youngstown, Ohio, 66-68; Greenville Mus Art, NC, 85. *Teaching:* Artist in residence basic & metal sculpture, Maitland Art Ctr, Fla, summer 75. *Awards:* Piedmont Purchase Award, Mint Mus Art, Charlotte, NC, 64; Mr & Mrs R E Holley Award, Arts Nat, Tyler Mus Art, Tex, 69; Salmagundi Club Prize, Nat Acad Design, 71. *Bibliog:* Mary Lou Norwood (auth), Exploring Florida waterways in a houseboat, Am Artist Mag, 4/69; Sound on Art & Artists (TV doc), Channel 24 TV, Orlando, 73; Dona Z Meilach (auth), Small Environments, Box Art, Crown Publ, 75. *Mem:* Allied Artists Am. *Dealer:* Art Sources Gulf Life Tower Jacksonville FL 32207; G S McKenna Galleries Charlotte NC 28207. *Mailing Add:* PO Box 1060 De Land FL 32720

SHAW, ERNEST CARL
SCULPTOR

b New York, NY, Apr 17, 42. *Work:* Aldrich Mus Contemp Art, Ridgefield, Conn; Indianapolis Mus; Nelson Rockefeller; Wichita Art Mus, Kans; and others. *Comn:* Orlando Int Airport, Reading, Pa. *Exhib:* Storm King Art Ctr, Mountainville, NY, 77; Contemp Reflections, Aldrich Mus Contemp Art, 77; one-man shows, Storm King Art Ctr, 78, Hamilton Gallery Contemp Art, 78, Allentown Art Mus, 81, Wichita Art Mus, 81, Huntington Galleries, WVa, 81; one-man shows, Sculpture Now, New York, 78; three-man show, Hamilton Gallery Contemp Art, 78; A M Sachs Gallery, 80; and other group and one-man shows. *Media:* Steel. *Mailing Add:* 2 Wawarsing Rd New Paltz NY 12561

SHAW, JOSEPH WINTERBOTHAM
HISTORIAN, EDUCATOR

b Chicago, Ill, July 6, 35. *Study:* Brown Univ, BA, 57; Wesleyan Univ, MA, 59; Univ Pa, PhD, 70. *Teaching:* Asst prof, Univ Toronto, 70-73, assoc prof, 73-77, prof, 77- *Awards:* Various research grants for Aegean Bronze Age architecture and archaeology. *Mem:* Can Mediterranean Inst; Am Sch Classical Studies; Archaeological Inst Am (pres, Toronto chap, 79-82). *Res:* Bronze Age Aegean art. *Publ:* Auth, Minoan Architecture: Materials and Techniques, Inst Poligraphico, Rome, 73; coauth, Kenchreai, Vol 1, Brill, 78; auth, Consideration of the Site of Akrotiri as a Minoan Settlement, Thera & Aegean World, 78; auth, Evidence for the Tripartite Shrine, Am J Art, 78; auth, Excavation at Kommos, Crete, Hesperia, 76-82. *Mailing Add:* Fine Art/Grad Dept Hist Art Univ Toronto Toronto ON M5S 1A1 Canada

SHAW, KAREN
PAINTER

b Bronx, NY, Oct 25, 41. *Study:* Hunter Col, City Univ New York, BFA, 65; grad work Hunter Col & C W Post, 70-71. *Work:* The Herbert F Johnson Mus Art, Ithaca, NY; The Israel Mus, Jerusalem; City Univ Grand Ctr, New York; Best Products, Richmond, Va. *Comn:* 11 large paintings, Mall, City Univ Grad Ctr, New York, 80. *Exhib:* Book Works, Albright Knox Art Gallery, Buffalo, NY, 77; Words at Liberty, Mus Contemp Art, Chicago, Ill, 77; one woman shows, Forum Stadtpark, Graz, Austria, 78 & Int Cultureel Centrum, Antwerp, Belgium, 80; Matrix 53, Wadsworth Atheneum, Hartford, Conn, 79-80; Am Women Artists, Museu de Arte Contemporanea, Sao Paulo, Brazil, 80; Artists Books, Walker Arts Ctr, Minneapolis, Minn, 81; Artists Books, Frankfurter Kunstverein, WGermany, 81. *Awards:* First Prize Graphics, Nassau Co Art Asn, 75; Nat Endowment Arts, US Govt, 78-79. *Bibliog:* Lenore Malen (auth), Karen Shaw: the reckoner, Arts Mag, 4/79. *Media:* Oil, Acrylic. *Publ:* Contribr, A Big Jewish Book, Anchor Press Doubleday, 78; auth, Market Research, Univ Akron, Ohio, 78. *Dealer:* Bertha Urdang Gallery 23 East 74 Street New York NY 10021. *Mailing Add:* 712 Lakeside Drive Baldwin NY 11510

SHAW, (GEORGE) KENDALL
PAINTER

b New Orleans, La, Mar 30, 24. *Study:* Ga Inst Technol, 44-46; Tulane Univ, BS, 49, MFA, 59; La State Univ, 50; New Sch Social Res, 50-52; Brooklyn Mus Art Sch, 53; also with Edward Corbett, Ralston Crawford, Stuart Davis, O Louis Guglielmi, George Rickey & Mark Rothko. *Work:* Albright-Knox Art Gallery, Buffalo, NY; Mus Contemp Art, Nagaoka, Japan; NY Univ; Chase Manhattan Bank, NY; and others. *Exhib:* One-man exhibs, John Bernard Myers Gallery, New York, 72, Alessandra Gallery, New York, 77 & Lerner-Heller Gallery, 79, 81 & 82; Contemporary Painting, Mus Contemp

Art, Nagaoka, 65; Modular Painting, Albright-Knox Art Gallery, 70; Sets for The First Reader by Gertrude Stein, Mus Mod Art & Metrop Mus Art, New York, 70-71; Pattern Painting, PS1, New York, 77; and others. *Teaching:* Instr painting, Parsons Sch Design, 66- *Bibliog:* Articles, Arts Mag, 1/77 & Art News, summer 82. *Mem:* Col Art Asn Am; Art Workers Coalition. *Mailing Add:* 916 President St Brooklyn NY 11215

SHAW, MARY TODD
SCULPTOR, PAINTER

b Gadsden, Ala. *Study:* Atlanta Col Art, cert, 41; Univ NC, Charlotte, BCA, 74. *Work:* Columbia Mus, SC; Mint Mus Art; Gibbs Gallery Art, Charleston, NC; Hickory Mus Art, NC; Birmingham Mus Art. *Comn:* Monotypes, Art Coalition Charlotte, NC, 82. *Exhib:* Nat Asn Women Artists Exhib, Nat Acad, New York & Royal Scottish Acad, Edinburgh; Piedmont Exhib, Mint Mus Art; State Dept Show, Mus Bella Artes, Buenos Aires; Hunter Mus Art Ann; Allied Artists Exhib, Nat Arts Club, New York; Exhib Va Artists, Va Mus Fine Arts; Southeastern, High Mus Art. *Teaching:* Instr drawing & painting, Mint Mus Art, 64-74; instr painting, Spirit Sq, 76- & Cent Piedmont Col, 79-80. *Awards:* Best in Show, Arts & Sci Exhib, Charlotte, NC; Best of Show, Roanoke Va Ann Outdoor Exhib; Henri Bendel Award, Nat Asn Women Artists Exhib. *Bibliog:* Charlene Whisnant (auth), Red Clay Reader, Vol 1, 67, Vol 4, 68 & Vol 7, 70; Jeff Huberman (auth), 43-68, 68; Donaz Meilach & Evieten Hoor (auths), Collage & Assemblages, Crown Publ, 73. *Mem:* Southern Graphics Asn; Tri-State Sculptors; Int Sculptors; Nat Asn Women Artists; NC Print & Drawing Soc. *Media:* Boxes. *Mailing Add:* 6611 Burlwood Rd Charlotte NC 28211

SHAW, NANCY (RIVARD)
CURATOR, HISTORIAN

b Saginaw, Mich. *Study:* Oakland Univ, Mich, BA(studio art), 69; Wayne State Univ, Mich, MA(art hist), 73; Attingham Summer Inst, England, 77. *Collections Arranged:* Heritage & Horizon: American Painting 1776-1976 (with catalog), Detroit Inst Art, 76; Daniel Chester French: An American Sculptor, Detroit Inst Art, 77; John Singer Sargent and the Edwardian Age, Detroit Inst Art, 79. *Pos:* Asst cur Am art, Detroit Inst Arts, 72-76, cur Am art, 77- *Bibliog:* Cotopaxi, Detroit Inst Arts Bulletin, 78. *Mem:* Decorative Art Chap, Soc Archit Hist. *Res:* Late nineteenth and early twentieth century painting and sculpture with a particular emphasis on turn-of-the-century Beaux-Art, and arts and crafts movements. *Publ:* Contribr, American paintings acquired during the last decade, Detroit Inst Arts Bulletin, 77; auth, Curatorial notes on the collection: Cotopaxi, Detroit Inst Arts Bulletin, 78; auth, American paintings at The Detroit Institute of Arts, Antiques Mag, 11/78; auth, The Quest for Unity: American Art Between World's Fairs, 1876-1893 (exhib catalog), 83. *Mailing Add:* The Detroit Inst of Arts 5200 Woodward Ave Detroit MI 48202

SHAW, PAUL JEFFERSON
CALLIGRAPHER, GRAPHIC ARTIST

b Ann Arbor, Mich, Sept 28, 54. *Study:* Reed Col, BA, 76; Columbia Univ, MA, 78, MPhil, 80. *Exhib:* Writing, Illuminating & Lettering, Calligraphy Space 2001, New York, 78; Words & Images, Folger Libr, Washington, DC, 82; Brooklyn Art Mus, 83. *Collections Arranged:* Calligraphy in the Graphic Arts, 81-83. *Teaching:* Prof calligraphy, Sch Visual Arts, 79- & Long Island Univ, 81-; prof lettering design, New York Inst Technol, 81- *Awards:* Fels, Newberry Libr, 80 & Smithsonian Inst, 80. *Mem:* Soc Scribes Ltd (bd gov, 78-83). *Media:* Ink, Gouache and Paper; Collage. *Publ:* Auth, Black Letter Primer, Pentalic Corp, 80; auth, Constant surprises: The calligraphy of George Salter, Scripsit, 81; auth, Wad as Lettering Artist: Pattern and Motion, private publ, 83; auth, The letter g, Visible Language, 83. *Mailing Add:* 110 Morningside Dr New York NY 10027

SHAW, RENATA VITZTHUM
LIBRARIAN

b Mänttä, Finland, July 21, 26; US citizen. *Study:* Univ Chicago, MA(art hist), 49; Univ Helsinki, Finland, MPhilos(art hist), 51; Ecole de Louvre, Paris, dipl(museology), 52; Catholic Univ Am, MS(libr sci), 62. *Pos:* Reference librn art, Prints & Photog Div, Libr Congress, Washington, DC, 62-67; supervisory librn art, 67-71; bibliog specialist art, 71-81; asst chief prints & photog div, 82, actg chief prints & photog div, 83. *Teaching:* Lectures in the Library of Congress on visual resources. *Mem:* Art Librn North Am; Spec Libr Asn; Am Libr Asn. *Res:* Art bibliography; collection development; visual librarianship; organization of visual collections; automation of library holdings, visual resources, production of videodisk of visual resources and retrieval of visual information. *Interests:* Development of a research collection in the field of art history encompassing all periods, present holdings 296,738 volumes. *Publ:* Auth, Handbook of Latin American Studies: Book Annotations, Univ Fla, 74; auth, Quarterly Journal of the Library of Congress: Essays, Libr Cong, 75; auth, Encyclopedia of Library & Information Science, Marcel Dekker, 77; auth, Graphic Sampler: A Century of Photographs, 1846-1946, Libr Cong Collection, 80. *Mailing Add:* 4850 Langdrum Lane Chevy Chase MD 20015

SHAW, RICHARD BLAKE
SCULPTOR

b Hollywood, Calif, Sept 12, 41. *Study:* Orange Coast Col, 61-63; San Francisco Art Inst, BFA(Agnus Brandenstein Fel), 65; Alfred Univ, 65; Univ Calif, Davis, MA, 68. *Work:* Oakland Mus, Calif; San Francisco Mus; Nat Mus Art, Tokyo; Stedelijk Mus, Amsterdam, Holland; Whitney Mus Am Art, New York. *Exhib:* One-man shows, San Francisco Mus Art, 73 & Braunstein Gallery, 81; Whitney Mus Am Art, New York, 70 & 81; International Ceramics, 1972, Victoria & Albert Mus, London, 72; American Crafts--A Contemporary View, Mus Contemp Art, Chicago, 76; Renwick Gallery,

Smithsonian Inst, Washington, DC, 76 & 79; The Chosen Object: Europ & Am Still Life, Joslyn Art Mus, Omaha, Nebr, 77; Newport Harbor Art Mus, Calif, 81; San Jose Mus Art, Calif, 81; Boise Gallery Art, Idaho, 81; Greenberg Gallery, St Louis, 81. *Teaching:* Chmn ceramics dept, San Francisco Art Inst, 65-; mem fac, Univ Wis-Madison, summer 71. *Awards:* Nat Endowment Arts Grant, 70; Nat Endowment Arts Crafts Grant, 74. *Bibliog:* Articles in Viking Press, 69 & Arts Can, summer 71. *Mem:* Order Golden Brush; Int Soc Ceramists. *Media:* Ceramics, Mixed Media. *Mailing Add:* c/o Braunstein Gallery 254 Sutter St San Francisco CA 94108

SHEA, JUDITH
SCULPTOR

b Philadelphia, Pa, Nov 13, 48. *Study:* Parsons Sch Design, 69; Parsons/New Sch, BFA, 75. *Work:* Neuberger Mus, State Univ New York Col, Purchase; Chase Manhattan Bank, New York; Dallas Mus Fine Art. *Exhib:* Clothing Constructions, Los Angeles Inst Contemp Art, 79; Material Pleasures, Contemp Art Mus, Chicago, 80; 7 Artists, Neuberger Mus, Purchase, NY, 80; Biennial Whitney Mus Am Art, New York, 81; The Soft Land, Palazzo Farnese, Ortona, Italy, 81; one-person show, New York Univ Gallery, 81; Milwaukee Art Ctr, 83; Directions 83, Hirshhorn Mus, 83; Sculpture Now, Va Mus Contemp Art, 83; and others. *Teaching:* Instr, Parsons Sch Design, New York, 79-; instr, New York Univ, 80- *Bibliog:* John Ashberry (auth), An exhilarating mess, Newsweek, 1/81; Lisa Liebman (auth), Judith Shea at Willard, Artforum, 9/83; Richard Flood (auth), The Sixth Day: New Figure Sculpture, Renaissance Soc Chicago, 9/83; and others. *Media:* Cloth, Bronze. *Publ:* Auth, Beyond fashion: Mariano Fortuny, Art Am, 11/82; auth, Valentino, Artforum, 12/82. *Dealer:* Willard Gallery 29 E 72nd St New York NY 10028. *Mailing Add:* 124 Chambers St New York NY 10007

SHEAD, S RAY
PAINTER, PRINTMAKER

b Cartersville, Ga, Nov 27, 38. *Study:* Atlanta Art Inst, BFA, 60; Art Ctr Col Design, BPA, 63; Ga State Univ, MVA; Inst Allende, Mex; also with John Rodgers & Loser Fiedelson, Los Angeles. *Work:* Columbus Mus, Ga; Montgomery Mus, Ala; Opelika Art League, Ala; Atlanta High Mus, Ga; Southwest Ga Art Mus, Albany. *Comn:* Painting, Chrysler Corp, Atlanta, 60; sculpture, Dibco-Wayne Corp, Atlanta, 68; painting, Callaway Gardens, Ga, 70. *Exhib:* Dixie Ann, Montgomery, Ala, 60; 6th Ann Callaway Gardens Exhib, Ga, 69; 49th Shreveport Art Exhib, La, 70; Ga Artists Exhib I & II, Atlanta, 71-72; SC Artists, 74. *Pos:* Art dir, Compton Advert, New York, 63-67; art dir, Marschalk Co, Atlanta, 67. *Teaching:* Assoc prof art & head dept, LaGrange Col, 68-73; head dept art, Presby Col, 73- *Awards:* Second Dixie Ann Award, 60; Southern Contemp Award, 69; 6th Ann Columbus Exhib Award, 70. *Mem:* Col Art Asn Am. *Media:* Acrylic, Epoxy. *Dealer:* Beverly Singlee Atlanta GA 30034. *Mailing Add:* 2933 Cocklebor Trail Decatur GA 30034

SHEAKS, BARCLAY
PAINTER, WRITER

b East Chicago, Ind. *Study:* Va Commonwealth Univ, BFA; Col William & Mary, teaching cert. *Work:* Va Mus Fine Arts, Richmond; Butler Inst Am Art, Youngstown, Ohio; Columbia Mus Fine Arts, SC; Mobile Mus, Ala; Chrysler Mus, Norfolk, Va. *Comn:* Portrait of USS Enterprise, comn by off of ship, 65; portrait of USS John F Kennedy, City of Newport News, 69; painting series, Exec Suite, Tenneco Corp, Newport News Shipyard, 72; space paintings, NASA, Langley Res Ctr, Hampton, Va; painting depicting surface of Mars, US Bicentennial Expo on Sci & Technol, Kennedy Space Ctr, 76; and others. *Exhib:* Nat Drawing Biennial (drawing selected for Smithsonian Inst Nat Traveling Exhib), Norfolk Mus, Va, 65; Butler Inst Art Mid-Year Show Am Painting, 65, 66 & 67; 99 Exhibition, Am Watercolor Soc, Nat Acad Design, New York, 66; Juried Art Exhib, Corcoran Gallery Art, Washington, DC, 67; Ten Top Realists SE, Gallery Contemp Art, Winston-Salem, NC, 69-70. *Pos:* Art consult, Hunt Mfg Co, Philadelphia, 65; lectr, Va Mus, Richmond, 70; artist in residence, Richmond Humanities Ctr, 71 & Va Mus, Richmond, 78. *Teaching:* Head art dept, Newport News Pub Schs, 49-69; assoc prof art, Va Wesleyan Col, 69- *Awards:* Va Comn Arts & Humanities Top Award, 79. *Bibliog:* Russel Woody (auth), chap, In: Painting in Synthetic Media & Complete Guide to Polymer Paintings, Van Nostrand Reinhold. *Mem:* Tidewater Artists Asn. *Media:* Acrylic, Polymer. *Publ:* Auth, Painting with Acrylics from Start to Finish, 72, Drawing and Painting the Natural Environment, 74 & Painting with Oils, Davis; auth, Painting with Oils, Davis. *Dealer:* Chester Smith Seaside Art Gallery PO Box 1 Nags Head NC 27959. *Mailing Add:* 51 Hopkins St Newport News VA 23601

SHEARD, WENDY STEDMAN
HISTORIAN, EDUCATOR

b New Haven, Conn, July 24, 35. *Study:* Vassar Col, BA, 57; Yale Univ, with Charles Seymour Jr, MA, 65, PhD, 71. *Collections Arranged:* Antiquity in the Renaissance (auth, catalog), Smith Col Mus Art, 78. *Teaching:* Asst prof art hist, Mt Holyoke Col, 78-79; vis asst prof, Univ Hartford, 79-80 & Boston Univ, 83-84. *Mem:* Col Art Asn; Asn Independent Art Historians. *Publ:* Ed, Collaboration in Italian Renaissance Art, Yale Univ Press, 78; auth, Asa adorna: The prehistory of the Vendramin Tomb, Jahrbuch Berliner Mus, Vol 20, 78; auth, Giorgione and Tullio Lombardo in Giorgione, Convegno Int Studi, Castelfranco, Italy, 79. *Mailing Add:* 693 Leetes Island Rd Stony Creek CT 06405

SHECHTER, BEN-ZION
DRAFTSMAN, ILLUSTRATOR

b Tel Aviv, Israel, Aug 7, 40; US & Israel citizen. *Study:* Bezalel Sch Art, Jerusalem, BFA, 66; Sch Visual Arts, New York, 67-69. *Work:* Whitney Mus

Am Art & New York Publ Libr, New York; Mus Fine Art, Boston; Brooklyn Mus; Houghton Libr, Harvard Univ, Cambridge, Mass; Univ Iowa Mus. *Exhib:* West '80 Art & The Law, Minn Mus Art, St Paul, 80; Interiors/Exteriors: Figurative Artist, Brooklyn Mus, 80; Tweed Mus, 80; solo show, Wuster Mus, Racine, Wis, 82; Univ Iowa Mus, 83; American Book Art Now, Elvehjem Mus, Madison, 83; Cayuga Community Col, Auburn, NY, 83; and others. *Awards:* Purchase Award, West Publ, 80. *Bibliog:* Lawrence Alloway (auth), Park Slope: The urban subject, Brooklyn Mus, 80; Susan Paul (auth), Interiors/Exteriors, Phoenix, Brooklyn, 80; N Scott Marraday (auth), Recent press book, Fine Print, 81. *Media:* Silverpoint, Pencil; Pen & Ink, Watercolor. *Publ:* Illusr, Common Ground, Bieler Press, 80. *Dealer:* Martin Sumers Graphics 50 W 57th St New York NY. *Mailing Add:* 429 4th St Brooklyn NY 11215

SHECHTER, LAURA J
PAINTER, DRAFTSMAN
b Brooklyn, NY, Aug 26, 44. *Study:* Brooklyn Col, BA, 65. *Work:* Boston Mus Fine Arts, Mass; Brooklyn Mus, NY; Carnegie Inst, Pittsburgh, Pa; Indianapolis Mus Art, Ind; Albright-Knox Art Gallery. *Exhib:* One-man shows, Suffolk Mus, Stony Brook, NY, 71, Wuster Mus, Wis, 82 & Greenville Co Mus Art, SC, 82; Contemp Realist, Akron Art Inst, Ohio, 74; The New American Still Life, Westmoreland Co Mus Art, Greenburg, Pa, 79; Am Drawing in Black & White, Brooklyn Mus, NY, 80 & 81; Still Life, Albright-Knox Art Gallery, Buffalo, NY, 81; West 81/Art & The Law, Minn Mus Art, St Paul, 81; Contemporary Art-Gund Collection, Boston Mus, 82; Perspectives on Contemporary Realism, Pa Acad Fine Art, 82 & Art Inst Chicago, 83. *Collections Arranged:* 15 Still Painters, a New Sensibility, Forum Gallery, New York, Brevard Art Ctr, Melborn, Fla, 78; Interior/Exterior: Figurative, Brooklyn Mus, 80; Artists of Park Slope, Brooklyn Mus. *Awards:* Creative Artists Pub Serv Prog Grant, 81-82. *Bibliog:* Ruth Bass (auth), Reviews New York, Art News, 80; Ralph Poweroy (auth), Laura Shechter, Arts Mag, 81; Eric Widing (auth), Laura Shechter, Am Artist, 83. *Mem:* Womens Caucus Art; Artists Equity. *Media:* Oil, Watercolor; Pencil, Silverpoint. *Dealer:* Tatist Cheff & Co 50 W 57th St New York NY; Van Straagn Gallery 361 W Superior Chicago IL. *Mailing Add:* 429 4th St Brooklyn NY 11215

SHECHTMAN, GEORGE HENOCH
DEALER
b Paterson, NJ, Dec 8, 41. *Study:* Rutgers Univ, BA(art hist), 64. *Pos:* Dir, Gallery Henoch, New York, currently. *Specialty:* Contemporary American paintings. *Mailing Add:* c/o Gallery Henoch 80 Wooster St New York NY 10012

SHECTER, MARK
PAINTER, MURALIST
b Baltimore, Md, Apr 18, 43. *Study:* Philadelphia Col Fine Arts; Boston Univ; Leicester Col; Am Univ, Washington, DC; Univ Miami, Coral Gables, Fla, BA. *Work:* Corcoran Mus Art, Washington, DC; Lowe Mus Art, Univ Miami, Fla; Rose Mus Art, Brandeis Univ, Boston; Jewish Theological Seminary Mus, Cincinnati, Ohio; Hagerstown Mus Fine Art, Md. *Comn:* Adam (monument), Beth Tfiloh Synagogue, Baltimore, 68; Moses, Jewish Mus, Baltimore, 68; Art in Embassies Prog, US State Dept, 70; Dr Soloman Schechter, Theological Seminary, New York, 74; Colorama (yellow still life), Jewish Community Ctr, Baltimore, 77. *Exhib:* Chrysler Mus Art, Norfolk, Va, 68; Int Art Exhib, Coliseum, New York, 69; Johns Hopkins Univ Art Exhib, Baltimore, 70; Am Painters in Paris Exhib, Vendome Art Gallery, France, 75. *Dealer:* Globe Gallery 1800 N Charles St Baltimore MD 21201. *Mailing Add:* 1800 N Charles St Baltimore MD 21201

SHECTER, PEARL S
PAINTER
b New York, NY, Dec 17, 10. *Study:* Hunter Col, BFA; Columbia Univ, MFA; Hans Hofmann Sch Painting; Archipenko Sch Art, New York; New Bauhaus Sch Design, with Moholy-Nagy; Acad Grande Chaumiere, Paris. *Work:* NY Univ; John F Kennedy Libr; Miami Univ, Ohio; Int Rels Found, New York; also in many pvt collections. *Exhib:* Walker Art Ctr, Minn, 63; Mfs Hanover Trust Bank, 70 & 71; Union Carbide Gallery, New York, 72, 75 & 78; Bankers Trust Gallery, 80-81; Warner Communications Gallery, New York, 82; Bankers Trust Gallery, 83; and others. *Pos:* Art dir, Elisabeth Irwin High Sch, 75. *Teaching:* Lectr studio courses, NY Univ, 58-69; instr studio courses, Newton-Harvard Creative Art Ctr, 63. *Awards:* Carnegie Found Grant, 50; Gold Medal, Patronato Scholastico Arti, Italy, 63; Gold Medal, Academia Italia, 81. *Bibliog:* Artists New York (tape), Voice of Am, 72. *Mem:* Int Asn Art Bull UNESCO; Artists New York (pres, 72-76); NY Soc Women Artists; Nat Soc Lit & Art. *Media:* Acrylic, Gold Leaf; Collage. *Publ:* Contribr, Art News, Art Digest & Art Now, 63-70, Park East, 80. *Mailing Add:* 60 E Ninth St New York NY 10003

SHEEHAN, EVELYN
PAINTER
b Hymera, Ind, Dec 27, 19. *Study:* Scripps Col, with Jean Ames; also study with Phil Dike & Rex Brandt. *Work:* Lytton Collection, Los Angeles; Calif Bank, San Francisco; Mus Art, Univ Ore, Eugene; Tacoma Bank, Wash. *Exhib:* Spokane Ann Art Exhib, Cheney-Cowles Mus Art, Wash, 69; Watercolor USA, Springfield Art Mus, Mo, 70; 32nd Ann Northwest Exhib, Seattle Art Mus, Wash, 71; Dimensional Construction Exhib, Portland Contemp Craft Gallery, 77; Exhib of Paintings, Governor's Ceremonial Chambers, Salem, 77; one-man show, Mus Art, Univ Ore, Eugene, 71. *Awards:* Lytton Purchase Award, Watercolor USA, 67; Mo Award, 32nd Ann Nat Watercolor Soc, 71; Cash Award, 62nd Ann Nat Watercolor Soc, 82. *Mem:* Nat Soc Painters in Casein; Nat Watercolor Soc; Portland Art Asn. *Media:* Water Media, Collage. *Mailing Add:* 3935 SW Corbett Ave Portland OR 97201

SHEEHE, LILLIAN CAROLYN
PAINTER, ENAMELIST
b Conemaugh, Pa, Oct 16, 15. *Study:* Indiana Univ Pa, BS(art); ceramics & sculpture with Sheldone Grumbling, majolica with Hugh Geise & painting & sculpture with George Ream. *Comn:* Golf mural, comn by J Cover, Johnstown, Pa, 44; designed & printed Christmas cards, Pa Rehab Ctr & Bur Voc Rehab, 59-71; emblem design, Lee Hosp Rehab Med Dept, 66; fired glass picture, Pepsi Cola Co, Washington, DC, 78; 30 fired glass pictures, Pepsi Cola Co, Johnstown, Pa, 79. *Exhib:* All Allied Artists Shows, 36-; Pittsylvania Ceramic Guild All-Pa Competition, 64-71; Three Rivers Arts Festival, 65 & 66; Allied Artists Graphic Arts Show, 70; Sheraton '75. *Teaching:* Art supvr, East Conemaugh Schs, 36-42; instr art & world hist, Westmont High Sch, 44-45 & 53-54; instr art & art supvr, Ferndale-Dale Grade & High Schs, 55-59; instr arts & crafts, Pa Voc Rehab Ctr, 59-75. *Awards:* Phoebe Jerema Award, Pittsylvania Ceramic Guild, 71; David Glosser Libr Craft Award, 73; A B Crichton Award, Allied Artists Ann Show. *Bibliog:* George Mengelson (producer), Art Exhibit (two TV shows on glass work), 69; article, Johnstown Tribune-Democrat, 7/76; Catholic Register, Altoona, Pa, 5/76. *Mem:* Allied Artists (pres, 70-72); Area Arts Coun (pres, 75-77); Arts Assocs; Cult Affairs Comt. *Media:* Mixed. *Res:* Experimented twenty-years on uses of fired glass and its combinations for pictorial work. *Publ:* Auth & illusr, Allied Artists Fall Show Catalog (also cover design), 58; auth, Useless to useful, Leather Craftsman Mag, 61; auth & illusr, Antiquity in a day, Ceramics Arts & Crafts, 64 & Textbook on Photo--Tinting--Color--Oils, Bur Voc Rehab, 65; auth, I Dreamed in Glass, Antique Trader, 7/77; and others. *Mailing Add:* 1333 Christopher St Johnstown PA 15905

SHEERIN, JERRY
PAINTER, ARCHITECT
b Chicago, Ill, May 24, 33. *Study:* Art Inst Chicago, 44-45; Univ Ill, Urbana, BA(archit), 60; Univ Tokyo, with Kenzo Tange, 65. *Work:* Mus Espanol Arte Contemp, Madrid; Mus 20th Century Art, Alicante; Mus Abstract Art, Cuenca; Mus Contemp Art, Skopje, Yugoslavia; Mus Contemp Art, Pamames; and many others. *Exhib:* Solo exhibs, Mus Fine Arts, Santander, 79, Fundacion Joan Miro, Barcelona, 80 & Galeria Ciento, Barcelona, 80; Ibiza Biennial, Mus Art Contemp, 76; Galeria Kreisler Dos, Madrid, 80; Galeria Ciento, Barcelona, 80; and many other group and one-man exhibs. *Pos:* Art critic, var newspapers & mag, 77-; Spain corresp, Int Herald Tribune, Paris, 77-79. *Teaching:* Prof, Univ Calif, Berkeley, 66-67. *Bibliog:* Felix Guisasola (auth), El Silencio de las Formas, Jerry Sheerin, El Pais, Madrid, 7/80; Angel Apetia (auth), Jerry Sheerin, Heraldo de Aragon, Zaragoza, 12/80; M T Casanelles (auth), Jerry Sheerin, El Europeo, 12/80. *Dealer:* Galeria Aele Claudio Coello 28 Madrid Spain. *Mailing Add:* Plaza Camorritos 5 Madrid 27 Spain

SHEETS, MILLARD OWEN
DESIGNER, PAINTER
b Pomona, Calif, June 24, 07. *Study:* Chouinard Art Inst, 28; Otis Art Inst, Hon MFA, 63; Univ Notre Dame, Hon LLD, 64. *Work:* Metrop Mus Art & Whitney Mus Art, New York; Art Inst Chicago; Los Angeles Mus Art; Nat Mus Am Art; Smithsonian Inst; and many others. *Comn:* Libr tower granite mosaic, Univ Notre Dame, South Bend, Ind; mosaic dome & chapel, Nat Shrine, Washington, DC; mosaic facade, Detroit Pub Libr; mural, Rainbow Tower, Hilton Hotel, Honolulu; two large murals, Los Angeles City Hall E, Los Angeles; numerous banks & savings & loan bldgs & murals in Calif & Tex. *Exhib:* Art Inst Chicago; San Francisco Mod Mus Art; Sao Paulo, Brazil; Arthur Tooth Galleries, London, Eng; and many others. *Pos:* Artist, Life Mag, Burma-India Front, 43-44; US State Dept Specialist Prog to Turkey & Russia, 60-61; trustee, Scripps Col, 66-82; trustee, Calif Inst Arts, 68-76; trustee, Art Ctr Sch of Design. *Teaching:* Chouinard Art Inst, 28-35; prof art, Scripps Col, 31-, head dept art, 32-55; dir, Otis Art Inst, 53-59. *Awards:* Prizes, Art Inst Chicago, Nat Watercolor Soc & Philadelphia Watercolor Soc; and many others. *Mem:* Nat Acad Design; Nat Watercolor Soc; Am Watercolor Soc; Econ Round Table, Los Angeles. *Dealer:* Kennedy Galleries 40 W 57th St New York NY 10019. *Mailing Add:* 34800 S Hwy One Barking Rocks Gualala CA 95445

SHEIRR, OLGA (KROLIK)
PAINTER
b New York, NY, June 7, 31. *Study:* Art Students League, with Reginald Marsh, 48-50; Brooklyn Col, with Rothko, Reinhardt, Still & Ernst, BA, 53; Pratt Graphic Ctr, with Michael Ponce de Leon, 65-70. *Work:* Mus City New York; St Vincents Hosp, New York; Greenville Co Mus, SC; NY Univ Hosp. *Comn:* Serigraph eds, Art Resources and Treasures, New York, 79 & Summit Fine Arts, New York, 79. *Exhib:* Soc Am Graphic Artists 46th Print Exhib, AAA Gallery, New York, 65; 27th New England Exhib Painting and Sculpture, Silvermine Guild Artists, 66 & 76; Noho Gallery, 75-; 59th Ann Nat April Salon, Springville Mus Art, Utah, 81 & 83; First Int Contemp Painting Exhib in Arab World, Riyadh, Saudi Arabia, 82; Six Artists, Edward Williams Gallery, Fairleigh Dickinson Univ, 83. *Collections Arranged:* Noho Gallery Exhib, New York, 76; Twenty Three Artists at Ten Studios (auth, catalog), New York, 77; Six at the Arsenal (auth, catalog), New York, 78. *Bibliog:* William Pellicone (auth), article, Art Speak, 4/82; James T McCartin (auth), article, Arts Mag, 5/82; Marilu Knode (auth), article, Manhattan Arts, 11/83. *Mem:* Women in Arts; Coalition Womens Art Orgn; New York Artists Equity; Womens Caucus Art. *Dealer:* Noho Gallery 168 Mercer St New York NY 10012; Edward Western Gallery 168 Mercer St New York NY 10012. *Mailing Add:* 360 First Ave Apt 11G New York NY 10010

SHELTON, PETER T
SCULPTOR
b Troy, Ohio, Jan 18, 51. *Study:* Pomona Col, BA(fine arts), 73; Hobart Sch Welding Technol, cert, 74; Univ Calif, Los Angeles, MFA, 79. *Work:* State Wash; Artpark, Lewiston, NY. *Comn:* Artpark, Lewiston, NY; Exposition Park, Los Angeles. *Exhib:* Solo exhibs, Chapman Col, Orange, Calif, 80 & Malinda Wyatt Gallery, Los Angeles, 81; Los Angeles Co Mus Art, 81; Open Space Gallery, Victoria, Can, 82; Artists Space, New York, 82; Mus D'Art Mod, Paris, 82; Ctr Contemp Art, Seattle, 83; Portland Ctr Visual Arts, 84; and others. *Teaching:* Lectr sculpture, Otis/Parsons Sch Art & Design, 80-; lectr sculpture, Claremont Grad Sch, 81- *Awards:* Purchase Award, State Wash, 77; Fel, Nat Endowment Arts, 80. *Bibliog:* Christopher Knight (auth), Your place or Shelton's, Los Angeles Herald Examiner, 81; Merle Schipper (auth), Peter Shelton's places and spaces, Images & Issues, 81; Melinda Wortz (auth), Peter Shelton at the Santa Barbara Contemporary Arts Forum, Artnews, 83. *Media:* Multi-Media. *Publ:* Contribr, Neckwall, Footscreen, Sleeper, Dreamworks, Human Sci Press, 82. *Dealer:* Malinda Wyatt Gallery 76 Market St Venice CA 90291. *Mailing Add:* 5571 West Pico Blvd Los Angeles CA 90019

SHELTON, ROBERT LEE
DESIGNER, EDUCATOR
b Memphis, Tenn, Apr 8, 39. *Study:* Memphis State Univ, BFA; Univ Ala, MA. *Work:* South Central Bell, Regional Off, Birmingham, Ala; First Nat Bank, Montgomery, Ala; Ambassadors Off, Fed Repub Ger. *Exhib:* Nat Small Painting Biennial, Purdue Univ, 66; Nat Black & White Prints, Kans State Univ, 66; Mid-South Ann, Memphis, Tenn, 69; Hunter Gallery Ann, Chattanooga, Tenn, 69; Graphics USA, Dubuque, Iowa, 70. *Teaching:* Asst prof drawing & design, Auburn Univ, Ala, 64-68; prof printmaking & design, Birmingham-Southern Col, Ala, 68- *Awards:* First Prize, Macon Mus, 68; First Purchase Award, Columbus Mus Art, 69 & 72; First Purchase Award, Montgomery Mus Art, 70. *Bibliog:* Martin Hames (auth), Robert Shelton, 1975 Birmingham Festival of Arts Bull, 3/75. *Mem:* Birmingham Art Asn (bd mem, 74-75, pres, 81-); Tenn Valley Art Asn. *Media:* Crayon, Oil . *Publ:* Auth, Contemporary printmaking in the US, Birmingham Festival Bulletin, 73. *Dealer:* Courtyard Gallery 2800 Sixth Ave S Birmingham AL 35208. *Mailing Add:* Birmingham Southern Col Art Ctr Box A21 35254 Birmingham AL 35208

SHEMESH, LORRAINE R
PAINTER
b Jersey City, NJ, Mar 27, 49. *Study:* Boston Univ, BFA(magna cum laude), 71; Tyler Sch Art, Rome, 71-72; Tyler Sch Art, with John Moore, MFA(painting fel), 73. *Work:* DeCordova Mus, Lincoln, Mass; Mus RI Sch Design, Providence; Am Tel & Tel, Chicago. *Exhib:* Collectors Collect Contemporary, Inst Contemp Art, Boston, 77; Art at Amherst, Mead Art Mus, Mass, 81; Staempfli Gallery, New York, 81; AIR Gallery, New York, 81 & 82; Paintings, Drawings & Quilts, Allan Stone Gallery, New York, 83; and others. *Teaching:* Asst prof painting & drawing, RI Sch Design, 73-80 & Amherst Col, 80-81. *Awards:* RI State Coun Arts Grant, 79; Yaddo Fel, 81 & 83. *Mem:* Col Art Asn Am. *Media:* Oil. *Dealer:* Allan Stone Gallery 48 East 86th St New York NY 10028; Alpha Gallery 121 Newbury St Boston MA 02116. *Mailing Add:* 548 East 82nd St Apt 2A New York NY 10028

SHEON, AARON
HISTORIAN, ADMINISTRATOR
b Toledo, Ohio, Oct 7, 37. *Study:* Univ Mich, AB, MA, 60; Inst d'Art et d'Archeolgie, Paris, 62; Princeton Univ, MFA, PhD, 66. *Pos:* Assoc prof, Univ Pittsburgh, Pa, 66-78, prof, 78- *Awards:* Ford Found Grant, Univ Pittsburgh, 67; Bowman Fac Award, Univ Pittsburgh, 76; Hon Award, Pa Soc Architects, 82. *Mem:* Col Art Asn; Soc Fr Art Hist. *Res:* French 19th and 20th century art history; art and scientific thought; educational role of the museum. *Publ:* Auth, Multistable perception in romantic caricatures, Studies in Romanticism, 77; auth, Organic Vision: The Architecture of Peter Berndston, 80; auth, Octave Tassaert's Le Suicide, Arts, 81; auth, Courbet, French realism and discovery of unconscious, Arts, 81; auth, 1913: Forgotten cubist exhibitions in America, Arts, 83. *Mailing Add:* Dept of Fine Arts Univ Pittsburgh Pittsburgh PA 15260

SHEPARD, LEWIS ALBERT
DEALER, HISTORIAN
b East Orange, NJ, May 24, 45. *Study:* Rutgers Univ, New Brunswick, BA, 67; Ind Univ, Bloomington, MA, 70. *Collections Arranged:* Cowboys, Indians, Trappers & Traders (with catalogue), Mead Art Gallery, Amherst Col, 73 & Am Painters of the Arctic (with catalogue), 75. *Pos:* Trainee catalogue & dept head, Sotheby Parke Bernet, New York, 70-72; cur, Mead Art Gallery, Amherst Col, 72-77; proprietor, dealer & appraiser, pvt pract, Worcester, Mass, 77- *Teaching:* Asst instr mod art, Ind Univ, Bloomington, 69-70; instr Am art, Amherst Col, 73-76 & Clark Univ, 80 & 84. *Mem:* Col Art Asn; Worcester Heritage Preserv Soc (bd dirs, 79-). *Res:* American 19th and 20th century painting; Western Americana; Arctic exploration; arts and crafts movement. *Specialty:* American and European 19th and 20th century art. *Collection:* American drawings 1830-1930. *Publ:* Auth, Willard Metcalf Exhibition--a Review, Am Art Rev, 77; auth, American Art at Amherst College--a Summary Catalogue, Amherst Col, 78. *Mailing Add:* 2 Congress St Worcester MA 01609

SHEPHERD, DON (DONALD ALLEN)
DESIGNER, GLASS ARTIST
b Eureka, Calif, Oct 9, 30. *Study:* Calif Sch Fine Arts, San Francisco, 49-50; Catan-Rose Inst Art, Jamaica, NY, cert(fine art), 57. *Work:* Corning Glass Ctr, NY; Huntington Galleries Mus, WVa; Philadelphia Mus Art, Pa; Ohio Univ, Athens; New York Public Libr. *Comn:* Vatican Pavillion, NY World's Fair, Archdiocese New York, 65; bronze relief (exterior entrance), Fromkes Law Bldg, St Johns Univ, Jamaica, NY, 75; stained glass mosaic, Visitors Ctr, Rikers Island Prison, Art Comn, New York, 76. *Exhib:* New Glass--A World Wide Survey, Corning Glass Ctr, NY, 79; one-man show, Heller Gallery, New York, 81; New Glass-Focus Glass Art Soc, Huntington Galleries Mus, WVa, 80; Habatat Gallery 9th Nat Invitational, Lathrop Village, Mich, 81; Glass Routes, DeCordova Mus, Lincoln, Mass, 81; Beyond Tradition, 25th Anniv Exhib, Am Craft Mus, New York, 81. *Pos:* Co-dir, Jonynas & Shepherd Art Studio Inc, Hollis, NY, 57-76; new product designer/consult, Libey Glass Co, Toledo, Ohio, 74-77; design dir/designer, Blenko Glass Co Inc, Milton, WVa, 75-; design dir, DAS Designs, Stamford, Conn, 76-; designer interior & graphics, St Mary's Hospital, Brooklyn, NY, 77 & 79. *Awards:* Bertha Von Moschzisker Mem Purchase Prize, Philadelphia Mus Art, 57; Purchase Award, Wesley and Westminster Found, 60; Honor Award--Architectural Excellence, Md Soc Am Inst Architects, 78. *Bibliog:* Robert H Mutrux (auth), Post-vatican perspective, Progressive Architecture, 12/71; Vincent O'Brien (auth), Techniques of Stained Glass, Van Nostrand Reinhold, 77; Paul Holister (auth), Contrast in Styles, New York Times, 7/2/81. *Mem:* Glass Art Soc; Options, art for the environment. *Media:* Mixed. *Dealer:* Heller Gallery 965 Madison Ave New York NY 10021. *Mailing Add:* 49 Old North Stamford Rd Stamford CT 06905

SHEPHERD, REGINALD
PAINTER, PRINTMAKER
b Portugal Cove, Nfld, Can, Mar 28, 24. *Study:* Ont Col Art, Toronto, AOCA, 49. *Work:* Mem Univ Gallery, St John's, Nfld, Can; Univ Ore, Corvallis; Art Gallery London, Ont; Dalhousie Art Gallery, Halifax, NS; Mt Allison Univ Gallery, Sackville, NB. *Comn:* Reredos, St Patricks Roman Cath Church, St John's, Nfld, 62; painting for calendar, Royal Trust Co, Toronto, 69; 12 watercolors, City of St John's, Nfld, 73; oil mural in Atlantic Pl, Crosbie & Co, St John's, Nfld, 75. *Exhib:* First Biennial Exhib, Nat Gallery Can, Ottawa, 55; Survey 64, Montreal Mus; solo exhibs, Mem Univ Gallery, St John's, Nfld, 72, Canada House Gallery, London, England, 83, Univ Leeds Gallery, England, 83 & Piazza Cardelli, Rome, Italy, 83-84; Traveling Print Exhib, Univ Ore, Corvallis, 76. *Teaching:* dir & instr drawing & painting, Nfld Acad Art, 49-61; vis lectr art educ, Mem Univ, St John's, 51-61; specialist fine arts, Prince Wales Col, 62-80. *Awards:* Can Govt Fel for study in Holland, Royal Soc Can, 56-57. *Bibliog:* Rex Murphy (dir), Here & Now (film), Can Broadcasting Corp TV, 76; Neil Murray (auth), Profile, Nfld Herald, 79; Colleen Lynch (auth), Watercolours reflect human values, Nfld Daily News, 1/84. *Mem:* Royal Can Acad Arts (provincial vpres, 78-83); fel Int Inst Arts & Lett. *Media:* Watercolor, Serigraphy. *Dealer:* The Gallery 284 Duckworth St St John's Nfld Can A1C 5M9. *Mailing Add:* 26 Oxen Pond Rd St John's NF A1B 3J3 Canada

SHEPHERD, WILLIAM FRITZ
PAINTER
b Casper, Wyo, April 1, 43. *Study:* Univ Wyo, BA, MFA, 72. *Work:* Amoco Oil Co, Houston; Univ Wyo Art Mus, Laramie; Int Tel & Tel, Basking Ridge, NJ; Denver Nat Bank; pvt collection of Mrs Joseph Hirshhorn, Washington, DC. *Exhib:* Wyo State Arch Art Gallery, Cheyenne, 77; Washington & Jefferson Col Nat, 78; New Works New Mexico, Blaffer Gallery, Univ Houston, 81; Rosalind Constable Selects, Sweeney Ctr, Santa Fe, 81; Best of Decade, Hills Gallery, Santa Fe, 81. *Awards:* Spec Jurors Prize, Washington & Jefferson Col, 74. *Bibliog:* Harold Olejarz (auth), article, Arts Mag, 1/79; William Peterson (auth), Smoke rings, Shinto shrines, Doktor Thrill and the Snake Lady, Art News, 12/80; Carol Everingham (auth), Bi-lateral--bi-literal rocks, Artspace, spring 83. *Media:* Oil on Canvas. *Mailing Add:* 105 Lugar De Oro Santa Fe NM 87501

SHEPP, ALAN
SCULPTOR
b Cleveland, Ohio, Nov 11, 35. *Study:* Bowling Green State Univ, BA, 57; Cleveland Inst Art, BFA, 58; Univ Wash, Seattle, MFA, 63. *Work:* London Co Coun, England; Seattle Art Mus; Walker Art Ctr; Univ Wis, Menomie; Cleveland Mus Art. *Comn:* Marble relief, Mill Valley City Hall, Calif, 82; slate relief, Bank Am, San Francisco, 83. *Exhib:* Toledo Mus Art, 57; May Show, Cleveland Mus Art, 58; Seattle Art Mus, 63; Contemp Mus Art, Chicago, 70; Aesthetics of Graffiti, San Francisco Mus Mod Art, 78. *Awards:* Fulbright Fel to Italy, 63-64; Calif State Univ Res Grant, 74; Nat Endowment Arts Fel, 79. *Bibliog:* Robert McDonald (auth), Manifestations of graffiti, Artweek, 78; Robert Yaskowitz (auth), article, Arts Mag, 79; Joanne Burstein (auth), Sculpture 82, Artweek, 82. *Media:* Slate. *Mailing Add:* c/o Stephen Wirtz Gallery 345 Sutter St San Francisco CA 94108

SHEPPARD, CARL DUNKLE
HISTORIAN
b Washington, DC, Jan 11, 16. *Study:* Amherst Col, BA; Harvard Univ, MA, 42, PhD, 47. *Teaching:* Instr, Univ Mich, Ann Arbor, 46-49; from asst prof to prof, Univ Calif, Los Angeles, 50-64; prof art hist & chmn dept, Univ Minn, Minneapolis, 64-83, prof emer, 83- *Awards:* Del Amo Found Grant, Spain, 57; McMillan Travel Grant, Italy, 68; Kress Found Grant, 83. *Mem:* Col Art Asn Am (mem bd dirs, 70-); Soc Archit Historians; Int Ctr Medieval Art; Medieval Acad; Int Cong Art Historians. *Publ:* Auth, Carbon 14 dating & Santa Sophia, Dumbarton Oaks Papers, Istanbul, 65; auth, Byzantine carved marble slabs, Art Bulletin, 3/69; auth, Classicism in Tuscan Romanesque sculpture, 77, A note on the date of Taq-i-bustan, 81 & auth, Pre-Romanesque sculpture: Evidence for the cultural evolution of the people of the Dalmation Coast, 84, Gesta; and others. *Mailing Add:* Dept of Art Hist 108 Jones Hall Univ of Minn Minneapolis MN 55455

SHEPPARD, JOSEPH SHERLY
PAINTER, SCULPTOR
b Owings Mills, Md, Dec 20, 30. *Study:* Md Inst Col Art, cert (fine art); also with Jacques Maroger. *Work:* Butler Inst Am Art; Fine Arts Mus, Mobile, Ala; Baltimore Mus Art; Carnegie Inst; Centro per l'Arte Contemp di Firenze, Italy; and others. *Comn:* Murals, Police Dept Hq Bldg, Baltimore; mural, Equitable Trust Co, Baltimore; bronze bas-relief, Baltimore Fire Dept; Fox Hunt (mural), Yorkridge Fed, Baltimore; Allegheny Beverage Co, Baltimore. *Exhib:* One-man shows, Butler Inst Am Art, 64 & 72, Westmoreland Co Mus, 66, 72 & 82 & Davenport Munic Art Gallery, Iowa, 67 & 83; consecutive shows, Florence, Italy, 77-; and others. *Pos:* Owner studio, Florence, Italy. *Teaching:* Instr painting & artist-in-residence, Dickinson Col, 56-57; instr drawing, painting & anat, Md Inst Col Art, 60-75. *Awards:* Prize for Figure Painting, Allied Artists, 63; John J McDonough Prize, Butler Inst Am Art, 67; Gov Prize, Md Artists Exhib, Baltimore Mus, 71; and others. *Mem:* Allied Artists Am; Nat Sculpture Soc; Soc Animal Artists. *Publ:* Auth, Anatomy, 75, Drawing the Female Figure, 75, Drawing the Male Figure, 76 & Learning From the Masters, 79, Watson-Guptill; auth, Keeping Christmas, Stemmer House, 81. *Dealer:* Grand Cent Galleries 40 Vanderbilt Ave New York NY 10017; Jerry Gildens Gallery 303 Reisterstown Rd Baltimore MD 21208. *Mailing Add:* PO Box 276 Camden DE 19934

SHEPPARD, NINA AKAMU See Akamu, Nina

SHER, ELIZABETH
VIDEO ARTIST, PRINTMAKER
b Washington, DC, Feb 13, 43. *Study:* Smith Col, Mass, 60-62; Univ Calif, Berkeley, BA, 64, MA, 67; San Francisco Art Inst, 65-66. *Work:* US Info Agency, Washington, DC; Oakland Mus; Calif Palace Legion Hon; Sierra Mus Art; Carnegie Mellon Univ. *Exhib:* Fifty-Seven Calif Printmakers, Calif Palace Legion Hon; San Francisco Int Film Festival, 82 & 83; Athens Int Film & Video Festival, Mich, 83; AFI Women in Film III, John F Kennedy Ctr, Washington, DC, 83; Ann Arbor Film Festival, Mich, 83; Milan Festival Am Independent Cinema, Italy, 83. *Collections Arranged:* Guest cur, Mixed Media on Paper, Berkeley Art Ctr, 78. *Pos:* Dir, IV Studios, Berkeley, Calif, 82- *Teaching:* Assoc prof, Calif Col Arts & Crafts, 77- *Awards:* Purchase Award, Seventh Nevada Ann, 82; Union of Independent Art Col Fac Grant, 82. *Bibliog:* Articles, San Diego Mag, 81 & Artweek Mag, 82; Video, Ego Mag, 82. *Mem:* Film Arts Found; Calif Soc Printmakers; Bay Area Video Coalition; Women's Caucus Art. *Publ:* Illusr, A Child's Library of Dreams, Celestial Arts, 78. *Mailing Add:* IV Studios 985 Regal Rd Berkeley CA 94708

SHERBELL, RHODA
SCULPTOR, CONSULTANT
b Brooklyn, NY. *Study:* Art Students League, with William Zorach & Reginald Marsh; Brooklyn Mus Art Sch, with Hugo Robies; study in Italy & France. *Work:* Nat Art Mus Sport, Conn; Colby Col Art Mus, Waterville, Maine; New York Pub Libr; Queens Mus, NY; Smithsonian Inst. *Comn:* Marguerite & William Zorach Bronze, Nat Arts Collection, Smithsonian Inst, Washington, DC, 64; bronzes of Aaron Copland & Yogi Berra, Montclair Art Mus; Casey Stengel, Country Art Gallery Long Island, Baseball Hall of Fame, Cooperstown, NY; Yogi Berra, comn by Percy Uris. *Exhib:* Pa Acad Fine Arts, 60; Brooklyn Mus Art Award Winners Exhib, 65; Nat Acad Design, 67, 72, 80 & 82; Nat Asn Women Artists, 75-82; Salmagundi Club, 80-82; solo exhibs, Bergan Mus Art & Sci, NJ & Bronx Mus Art, New York; and many more. *Pos:* Dir sculpture, Allied Artists, currently; dir pub rels, Audubon Artists, currently. *Awards:* Nat Acad Design Award, 79; Chaim Gross Found Prize, Audubon Artists, 79-81; Nat Asn of Women Artists, 79 & 80; and many others. *Bibliog:* Articles, Mus Mag, 4/82 & McCall's Mag, 8/82; Woman in Bronze (film), PBS TV, Channel 21; and many others. *Mem:* Allied Artists Am; Audubon Artists; life mem Art Students League; Nat Asn Women Artists; assoc mem Am Watercolor Soc; and many more. *Media:* Bronze. *Collection:* Contemporary American realistic work, including M Soyer, W Zorach, Marguerite Zorach, Mervin Honig, Harry Sternberg, John Koch, Agostine, H Jackson, Margit Beck and others. *Dealer:* Frank Rehn Inc 655 Madison Ave New York NY 10021. *Mailing Add:* 64 Jane Ct Westbury NY 11590

SHERE, CHARLES EVERETT
CRITIC
b Berkeley, Calif, Aug 20, 35. *Study:* Univ Calif, Berkeley, AB(hons), 61. *Pos:* Writer & producer art-oriented TV progs, KQED-TV, San Francisco, 67-75; writer rev & essays, Oakland Tribune, 73- *Teaching:* Mills Col, Oakland, 73- *Awards:* Art Critics Fel, Nat Endowment Arts, 78. *Res:* Extensive personal research into art of the early 20th century, especially Marcel Duchamp, and current California art. *Publ:* Auth catalog essay, New Deal Art in California, Univ Santa Clara, 76; auth catalog essay, Thomas Akawie exhib, San Jose Mus Art, 77; auth introd, The David Lance Goines Poster Book, Harmony Books, 78; auth catalog essays, Nell Sinton Retrospective, 80 & Joan Brown Exhib, 83, Mills Col; auth catalog essay, Cheryl Bowers Exhib, Kirk de Gooyer Gallery, Los Angeles, 83. *Mailing Add:* 1824 Curtis St Berkeley CA 94702

SHERIDAN, HELEN ADLER
LIBRARIAN, CURATOR
b Kansas City, Mo. *Study:* Ohio State Univ; Univ Kans, BA; Univ Calif Los Angeles, MA; Western Mich Univ, MLS. *Collections Arranged:* German Expressionist Art in Western Michigan Collections, (ed, catalog), 78; Kalamazoo Collects Photography, (ed, catalog), 79; Super Realism from the Morton G Neumann Family Collection, (ed, catalog), 81; Dwayne Lowder: In A Southern Tradition (ed, catalog), 82; New Image/Pattern & Decoration from the Morton G Neumann Family Collection (ed, catalog), 83. *Pos:* Head librn & cur collections, Kalamazoo Inst Arts, Mich, 75-82, asst to dir collections & exhibs, 83- *Teaching:* Instr arts of the 20th century, Western Mich Univ, 66-75. *Mem:* Col Art Asn; Art Libr Soc NAm (vchmn, Mich Chap, 76-77, chmn, 77-78). *Res:* Regionalist artists and western Michigan area artists; documentation of local artists and art collections. *Interests:* American arts of the twentieth century; regionalist art and photography. *Publ:* Co-ed, The Vagaries of Invention, 81. *Mailing Add:* 314 S Park St Kalamazoo MI 49006

SHERIDAN, SONIA LANDY
MEDIA ARTIST
b Newark, Ohio, Apr 10, 25. *Study:* Hunter Col, AB, 45; Columbia Univ, 46-48; Taiwan She Da Univ, 58; Yoshida Studio, Tokyo, 59; with Nathan Oliveira, 60; Calif Col Arts & Crafts, MFA, 60. *Work:* Art Inst Chicago; Mus Sci & Indust, Chicago; San Francisco Mus Art; George Eastman House, Rochester, NY; Nat Gallery, Ottawa, Can. *Exhib:* Projects (two-person show), Mus Mod Art, New York, 74; Women of Photog, San Francisco Mus Art, 75; retrospective, Univ Iowa Mus Art, 76; Illusion & Reality, six maj Australian mus, 77-78; one-man show, Energized Art Sci: Patterns in Motion, Mus Sci & Indust, Chicago, 78 & Art Sci (permanent exhib), 79; Electroworks, Eastman House & traveling, 79-81; Erweiterte Fotografie, Wiener Secession, 81. *Collections Arranged:* Traveling exhib, The Inner Landscape and the Machine (assembled, cataloged), Visual Studies Workshop, Rochester, 72- *Teaching:* Instr art educ & design, Calif Col Arts & Crafts, 60-61; founder, prof & area head generative systems, Sch Art Inst Chicago, 61-80, prof emer, 80- *Awards:* Union Independent Cols Art Grant, 75; Pub Media Grant, 76 & Artists Grant, 81-82, Nat Endowment Arts. *Bibliog:* Raymond Synard (ed), Color Theory and Imaging Systems, Soc Photog Scientists & Engrs, 73; Diane Kirkpatrick (auth), Chicago the City and Its Artists, Univ Mich, 78; Richard Wickstrom (auth), NMex State Univ, Art Science, 78. *Media:* Still Imaging. *Publ:* Auth, Energized Artscience: Sonia Landy Sheridan, Mus Sci & Indust & 3M, 78; auth, Generative Systems: Personal Report, Afterimage-Visual Studies Workshop, 79; auth, Tools and the artist, Afterimage, 6/81; auth, Generative systems versus copy art, Leonardo, Vol 16, No 2; auth, Altering our experiences and perceptions, Electra, Mus Mod Art, Paris, 83. *Dealer:* Visual Studies Workshop 31 Prince St Rochester NY 14607; Photo Researchers Inc New York NY 10022. *Mailing Add:* 718 Noyes Evanston IL 60201

SHERMAN, CLAIRE RICHTER
HISTORIAN, EDUCATOR
b Boston, Mass, Feb 11, 30. *Study:* Radcliffe Col, BA(Fulbright Scholar), 51; Univ Mich, with Marvin J Eisenberg, MA(Am Univ Women Fel), 58; Johns Hopkins Univ, with Adolf Katzenellenbogen, PhD, 64. *Pos:* Sr fel, Ctr Advan Study Visual Arts, Nat Gallery Art, 81-82; consult, J Paul Getty Trust, 83. *Teaching:* Instr art hist, Univ Mich, 58-59; lectr art hist, Am Univ, 66-72; vis assoc prof of art, McIntire Dept of Art, Univ of Va, 76. *Awards:* Grant in Aid, Am Coun Learned Socs, 75 & 82. *Mem:* Col Art Asn Am; Southeastern Medieval Asn; Women's Caucus Art. *Res:* Illustrations of Aristotle's Ethics & Politics in fourteenth and fifteenth century manuscripts; women scholars in the arts. *Publ:* Auth, The Portraits of Charles V of France (1338-80), 69; auth, Representations of Charles V of France as a Wise Ruler, 71; auth, The Queen in Charles V's Coronation Book, Viator, Medieval & Renaissance Studies, Vol 8, 77; auth, Some visual definitions of the illustrations of Aristotle's Nichomachean Ethics and Politics in the French translation of Nicole Oresme, Art Bulletin, Vol 59, 77; ed & contribr, Women as Interpreters of the Visual Arts, 1820-1979, 81; and many others. *Mailing Add:* 4516 Que Lane NW Washington DC 20007

SHERMAN, IRA D
GOLDSMITH, JEWELER
b Chicago, Ill, April 15, 50. *Study:* Upper Iowa Col; Univ Northern Iowa; Univ Colo. *Exhib:* All Colo Art Exhib, Denver Art Mus, 74, 75 & 76; Contemporary Crafts of the Americas, Smithsonian Inst, 75 & traveling; Marietta Crafts Nat, Marietta Col, 77 & 80; Southwest Metalsmithing Exhib, Eau-Claire, Wis, 80; All Colo Artist Invitational, Denver Art Mus, 81; Int Gold Corp Gold Competition, New York, 83 & traveling; Colorado Artists in the Nations Capital, Seraph Gallery, Washington, DC. *Teaching:* Instr jewelry design, Arapahoe Community Col, 75-79 & Metrop State Col, 77-80. *Awards:* First Place, All Colo Art Exhib, 76; Cert Merit, Int Gold Corp Gold Competition, 83. *Bibliog:* Articles, Rocky Mountain News, 9/81, West Coast Goldsmith Mag, 8/83 & Jewelers Circular Keystone Mag, 9/83. *Mem:* Soc NAm Goldsmiths; Colo Artists Craftsmen; Am Crafts Coun; Colo Crafts Advocacy Group. *Media:* Gold. *Publ:* Contribr, Jewelry, Contemporary Design and Technique, Davis Co; contribr, Contemporary Crafts of the Americas, Regnery Co. *Dealer:* Cohen Gallery 665 S Pearl Denver CO. *Mailing Add:* Alva Studio 316 E Louisiana Denver CO 80210

SHERMAN, LENORE (WALTON)
PAINTER, WRITER
b New York, NY, May 11, 20. *Study:* With Leon Franks, Hayward Veal, Orrin A White & Sergei Bongart, watercolor with James Couper Wright & portrait with Eignar Hansen. *Work:* San Diego Law Libr; var banks. *Exhib:* Southern Calif Expos, Del Mar, 70-72; Calif Fedn Women's Club Fine Arts Festival, 71; Southern NMex State Fair, 81 & 82; and others. *Teaching:* Instr oil painting, San Diego Art Inst, 60-67, Foothills Art Asn, La Mesa, Calif, summer 72 & Las Cruces Arts & Crafts Asn, NMex, 80-81. *Awards:* First Award Oils, 82 & Best in Show, 82, NMex State Fair; and others. *Bibliog:* Ed Ainsworth (auth), The Cowboy in Art, World Publ, 68; articles in San Diego Union, 60-72; articles, Las Cruces Sun News, NMex, 80-81. *Media:* Oil. *Publ:* Auth, Creative Painting, 75 & Experimental Painting, 80, Foster Art Bks. *Mailing Add:* 1425 Country Club Circle Las Cruces NM 88001

SHERMAN, SARAI
PAINTER, SCULPTOR

b Philadelphia, Pa. *Study:* Tyler Sch Art, Temple Univ, BFA, BS(educ); Barnes Found; Univ Iowa, MFA. *Work:* Whitney Mus Am Art & Mus Mod Art, New York; Hirshhorn Collection, Smithsonian Inst, Washington, DC; Uffizi Gallery Print Collection, Florence, Italy; Collection Mod Art, Southwestern Methodist Univ, Dallas; Univ Nebr, Lincoln. *Exhib:* Recent Painting USA: The Figure, Traveling Show, Mus Mod Art, New York, 62-63; Premio Marzotto, Milan, Paris, Hamburg, London & Belgrade, 67-68; Venice Biennial, Int Graphics: USA, Italy, 72; Childe Hassam Acquisition Fund, 75; 30 Years--Painting, Sculpture, Drawing, Palazzo Acad, Tod, Italy, 83. *Awards:* Award for Painting, Nat Inst Arts & Lett, 64; Europ Community Prize, Premio Marzotto, 67; Ann Painting Award, Repub San Marino, 75. *Bibliog:* Bryant (auth) & Venturoli (auth), Painting of Sarai Sherman (monogr), Galleria Penelope, Rome, 63. *Media:* Oil, Graphics. *Dealer:* Galleria Giula Via Giula 148 Rome Italy. *Mailing Add:* 17 W Ninth St New York NY 10011

SHERMAN, Z CHARLOTTE
PAINTER

b Los Angeles, Calif, June 18, 24. *Study:* Univ Calif, Los Angeles; Kann Art Inst; Otis Art Inst, scholar. *Work:* Munic Art Gallery, Los Angeles; Palm Springs Mus, Calif; Glass Container Corp Am; Winthrop Rockefeller Found, Ark; Laguna Art Mus. *Exhib:* Los Angeles Co Mus Art, 56 & 58; Heritage Gallery, Los Angeles, 63-83; Grand Prix Int de Deauville, Paris, 72; Prix de Rome Palais des Beaux Artes, Rome, 73; Palm Springs Mus, 76, 77, 80 & 81; Laguna Art Mus, 80; and others. *Awards:* Phelan Found Award, 61; Pasadena Mus Ann Award, 61; All City Exhib Award, Barnsdale, Los Angeles, 63 & 65; and others. *Bibliog:* Joseph Mugnaini (auth), Oil Painting Techniques, Van Nostrand, 63; Bertrand Sorlot (auth), article, La Rev Mod, Paris, 74; Don Rothenberg (producer), Z Charlotte Sherman, Portrait of a Woman Artist (film), 77. *Mem:* Nat Watercolor Soc. *Media:* Oil, Watercolor. *Dealer:* Heritage Gallery 718 N La Cienega Blvd Los Angeles CA 90069. *Mailing Add:* 1300 Chautauqua Blvd Pacific Palisades CA 90272

SHERR, RONALD NORMAN
PAINTER

b Plainfield, NJ, July 17, 52. *Study:* DuCret Sch Art, Plainfield, NJ; Nat Acad Design Sch Fine Art; also with Burton Silverman. *Work:* Phoenix Mus Art, Ariz; Nat Portrait Gallery, Washington, DC. *Exhib:* Ann Exhib, Nat Acad Design, New York, 78; Hassam Fund Exhib, Inst Arts & Letters, New York, 78; Painting & Sculpture Today, Indianapolis Art Mus, Ind, 78; Drawing Exhib, Univ NH, 79; A Heritage Renewed: Representational Drawing Today Traveling Exhib, 83. *Teaching:* Instr painting, Nat Acad Sch Fine Art, New York. *Awards:* John F & Anna Lee Stacey Found Grant, Quemado, NMex, 76; Benjamin Altman Figure Prize, $1500, Nat Acad Design, New York, 78; Award for Excellence, Int Ed Design Competition, 83. *Mem:* Salmagundi Club, New York; Artists Equity, New York. *Media:* Oil, Drawing. *Mailing Add:* 159 2nd Ave Apt 7 New York NY 10003

SHERROD, PHILIP LAWRENCE
PAINTER, POET

b Pauls Valley, Okla, Oct 12, 35. *Study:* Okla State Univ, BS, 57, BA(etching, pottery & drawing), 59; Art Students League, Am Fed Arts & Lett Scholar, 63. *Work:* Tulane Univ Mus, Women's Col, New Orleans, La; Everhart Mus, Scranton, Pa; Almsford House, Anderson Fine Arts Ctr, Ind; Rose Art Mus, Brandeis Univ, Waltham, Mass. *Exhib:* Inside Out, Joslyn Art Mus, 81; Am Acad Art & Letters Inst Awards Exhib, New York, 83; Street Painters, Arbitrage Gallery & Art Student's League, New York, 83; Painting New York, Mus City New York, 83; Bodies & Souls, Artist's Choice Mus, 83; and others. *Pos:* Pres & founder, Street Painters, New York. *Teaching:* Instr color & design, Okla State Univ, 59; instr painting, Taos, NMex, 59; asst painting, Art Students League, New York, 60; instr, Morristown Art Asn, NJ, 73-74; instr, Summit Art Ctr, NJ, 77-81. *Awards:* Creative Artists Pub Serv Prog Grant, 80; Adolphe/Ester Gottlieb Found Grant, 81; Nat Endowment Arts Grant, 82. *Bibliog:* Barry Schwartz (auth), Arts in Society (Humanist Alternative), Univ Wis, 4/73 & New Humanism: Art in a Time of Change, Praeger, 74. *Media:* Oil, Etching. *Publ:* Auth, 30 Mentaltalia (poems & paintings), Merging Media Publ, 80. *Dealer:* Allan Stone Gallery 48 E 86th St New York NY 10028. *Mailing Add:* 41 W 24th St New York NY 10010

SHERRY, WILLIAM GRANT
PAINTER

b Amagansett, NY, Dec 7, 14. *Study:* Acad Julian, Paris, cert, with Pierre Jerome; Heatherly Sch Art, London, with Ian McNab. *Work:* Farnsworth Mus, Rockland, Maine; Zellerbach Collection, San Francisco; Wintersteen Collection, Philadelphia; Mod Mus Art, Ft Lauderdale, Fla; Springfield Mus Fine Art, Mass; and others. *Exhib:* De Young Mus, San Francisco; Colby Col, Maine; Ringling Mus, Sarasota, Fla, 49; Boston Arts Festival, 56; Art USA, Madison Square Garden, New York, 58. *Teaching:* Chief instr painting & art dir, Fla Gulf Coast Art Ctr, Belleair, Fla, 57-64; art instr, Hamilton AFB, Ignacio, Calif, 65-67. *Awards:* Laguna Beach Festival Arts, Nat Painting Contest, 51; Mr & Mrs Chauncey A Steiger Purchase Prize, Springfield Mus, 57. *Media:* Oil. *Dealer:* Galerie de Tours 701 Sutter St San Francisco CA. *Mailing Add:* 51 Park Terr Mill Valley CA 94941

SHERWOOD, A (FRANCES ANN CRANE)
SCULPTOR, DESIGNER

b Birmingham, Ala, Sept 12, 32. *Study:* Univ Fla; Hampton Inst; Wesley Col; Del State Col; Univ Phillipines; Okaloosa Walton Col, Niceville, Fla; Univ W Fla, Pensacola. *Work:* Lilliputian Found, Washington, DC; Acad Art, Easton, Md; US Navy; US Air Force; Mobile Art Gallery, Ala. *Comn:* Oil paintings, Phillips Sch, Hampton, Va, 66. *Exhib:* Norfolk Mus, Va, 66 & 67; Va Mus Fine Arts, Richmond, 67; Audubon Soc, Washington, DC, 69; Royal Art Gallery, Manila, Philippines, 72; Meat Packers Gallery, Pensacola, 74; Bicentennial Show, US Embassy, Manila, Philippines, 76. *Teaching:* Instr art, Pope AFB, NC, 61-63; instr art, Alexander Graham Bell Jr High Sch, Fayetteville, NC, 62-63; instr art, Max Bruner Jr High Sch, Ft Walton, Fla, 74-75; instr art, Dept of Defense, PI, 76-78. *Awards:* Atlantic City Nat Art Show, NJ, 68 & 69; Mobile Art Fair, Ala, 73 & 74; Billy Bowlegs Art Festival, Ft Walton Beach, Fla, 73, 74 & 75. *Bibliog:* S Sternberger (auth), Art is where she finds it, Eve J, Del, 70; Sharon Demarko (auth), Finding art wherever she looks, Pensacola News J, 73; Capt Karen Miller (auth), article in Ladycom Mag, 8/75. *Collection:* Pre-Columbian pottery; Central American stone ware; Chinese celadon; Sung, Ming and Ching porcelain; brass from Asia; ethnic artifacts of the Philippines. *Publ:* Illusr, Flavet News, Gainesville, Fla, 58-60; illusr var bulletins, Gainesville, Fla, 58-60; illusr, Agr News & Univ Fla, 59. *Mailing Add:* 6665 W Sixth Ave Hialeah FL 33012

SHERWOOD, LEONA
PAINTER, INSTRUCTOR

b New York, NY. *Study:* Studied with John Chetcuti, New York, 46-48; Philip Hicken, Mass, 58; Robert Gelinas, Fla, 65; Ringling Sch Art, 81. *Work:* Hickory Mus Art, NC; Edison Col, Fort Myers, Fla; Collegiate Sch Boys, New York; Diamond Shamrock Co, Cleveland, Ohio; Barnet Bank, Bradenton, Fla. *Comn:* Paintings, Strathmore Co, Sarasota, Fla, 67-; painting, Lido Ambassador, Sarasota, Fla, 71; painting, Thru Hang-Up Gallery, Sarasota, Fla, 81; and others. *Exhib:* one-person show, Hickory Mus Art, NC, 79; Florida Women in Art, Edison Col, Ft Myers, 82; Tampa Mus, 82; Lagrange VIII, Ga, 83; Third Women in Art, Springfield, Ill, 83; and others. *Teaching:* Instr contemp painting & drawing, Longboat Key Art Ctr, Fla, 69- & Art League Manatee, Bradenton, Fla, 74-; instr painting & drawing, Art League Manatee, Bradenton, Fla, 74- *Awards:* Best of Show, South Fla Mus, 70; First Painting, Nat League Pen Women State Biennial, 77-78 & First Award, 79. *Bibliog:* Dorothy Stockbridge (auth), Artist likes contest with canvas, Sarasota J, 77; Sheila Scotter (auth), An artist, cook & gardener, Australian Women's Weekly & Tatler, London, Eng, 79. *Mem:* Fla Artist Group; Nat League Am Pen Women; Fla Watercolor Soc; Sarasota Art Asn; Art League Manatee. *Media:* Multimedia. *Publ:* Auth, Learn to really see, not just look, Islander, 81. *Dealer:* The Hang-Up Gallery S Osprey Ave Sarasota FL 33548; Tallulah Gallery Tallulah Falls GA. *Mailing Add:* 615 Buttonwood Dr Longboat Key FL 33548

SHERWOOD, RICHARD E
PATRON, COLLECTOR

b Los Angeles, Calif, July 24, 28. *Study:* Yale Univ, BA; Harvard Univ, LLB. *Pos:* Trustee, Los Angeles Co Mus Art, 65-, pres, 74-78, chmn, 78-82; mem, Overseers Comt to Visit the Harvard Art Mus, 75-; mem, Int Coun, Mus Mod Art, 78- *Teaching:* Vis lectr, Yale Law Sch, 81-82. *Mem:* Ctr Theatre Group Los Angeles (pres, 82-); Performing Arts Council, Los Angeles Music Ctr (gov, 82-). *Mailing Add:* 400 S Hope St Los Angeles CA 90071

SHESTACK, ALAN
MUSEUM DIRECTOR, HISTORIAN

b New York, NY, June 23, 38. *Study:* Wesleyan Univ, Middletown, Conn, BA, 60; Harvard Univ, Cambridge, Mass, MA; Zentralinstitut Fur Kunstgeschichte, Munich, 63-64; Wesleyan Univ, DFA, 78. *Collections Arranged:* Master E S (auth catalog), Philadelphia Mus Art, 67; Fifteenth-century Engravings (auth catalog), Nat Gallery Art, Washington, DC, 67-68; Graphic Art of the Danube School (with catalog), Yale Art Gallery, St Louis Art Mus, Philadelphia Mus Art, 68-69; The Danube School (auth catalog), Yale Univ Art Gallery, 71; Hans Baldung Grien (auth, catalog), Nat Gallery Art, Washington, DC, 81. *Pos:* Mus cur graphic art, Nat Gallery, 65-67; cur prints & drawings, Yale Univ Art Gallery, New Haven, Conn, 68-71, dir, 71-; bd dir, Am Fedn Art, 81-; indemnification panel, Nat Endowment Arts Artifacts, 80- *Teaching:* Adj prof hist art, Yale Univ, 71- *Awards:* Woodrow Wilson Fel, 61-62; David E Finley Fel, Nat Gallery, 63-65; Ctr Advan Studies Visual Arts Sr Fel, 84. *Mem:* Col Art Asn Am (bd dirs, 73-76); Am Asn Mus; Art Mus Dirs (pres, 83-84); Print Coun Am. *Res:* Fifteenth and sixteenth century printmaking in Europe; German art of 15th and 16th centuries. *Publ:* Auth, The Complete Engravings of Martin Schongauer, 68 & Master LCz & Master WB, 71; auth, Mastery LCz and Master WB, Collector's Editions, 71; coauth, Hans Baldung Grien: Prints and Drawings, Univ Chicago Press, 81. *Mailing Add:* Box 2006 Yale Sta New Haven CT 06520

SHEYA (SHEYA NEWMAN LEDERMAN)
PAINTER, INSTRUCTOR

b Brooklyn, NY. *Study:* Hunter Col, BA(fine arts), 42; Grand Cent Art Sch, with Harvey Dunn, 44-45; Wayne State Univ, 59-62. *Work:* Educ Exhibitors Traveling Show in Schs, Long Island, NY. *Exhib:* Birmingham Artists Ann, Cranbrook Mus, Mich, 60; Landscape Artists, Smithsonian Inst, Washington, DC, 64; Fifty New York Artists, Harness House Gallery, New York, 78; Reflections of Winter, Town Hall, Manhasset, NY, 78-79; one-person show, US Customs House Exhib Hall, New York, 79; Cranbrook Mus, Birmingham, Mich, 60; NY State Prebiennial, Lever House, 83; Long Beach Mus, 83. *Pos:* Dir art, Rose-Martin, New York, 44-46; Hayes-Endler, New York, 46-80; Luckoff & Wayburn, Detroit, 53-56 & Hecht Co, Washington, DC, 63-64. *Teaching:* Instr, Detroit Continuing Educ, 55-59; instr, Port Washington Adult Educ, Long Island, NY, 65-81; instr, pvt art classes, 66- *Mem:* Nat League Am Pen Women (NY art chmn & pres, 82-84); Artists Equity Asn; Audubon Artists; Hempstead Harbour Artists Asn. *Media:* Oil, Watercolor. *Mailing Add:* 44 Jayson Ave Great Neck NY 11021

SHIBLEY, GERTRUDE
PAINTER
b Brooklyn, NY. *Study:* Brooklyn Col, BA; with Francis Criss, 42; Hans Hofmann Sch Fine Arts, 52-53. *Work:* Wichita State Univ Mus Collection, Kans; Philadelphia Mus Fine Arts Rental Collection; Univ Ala, Birmingham; Provincetown Art Asn & Mus, Mass. *Exhib:* Nat Asn Women Painters, Nat Acad Design Gallery, 51-52; Prizewinners Village Art Ctr, Whitney Mus Am Art, New York, 54; New York WPA Artists, Then & Now, Parsons Sch of Design, 77; Tenth St Days--the Co-ops of the 50s, New York, 77; Abraham Rattner Ctr Arts, Sag Harbor, NY, 79-80; Provincetown Art Asn & Mus, Mass, 80-81; plus others. *Pos:* Ceramist, Design Technics, 44-48. *Teaching:* Instr painting, Halloran Hosp, Staten Island, 42-44; instr painting, Ruth Ettinger Sch, New York, 55-56. *Awards:* Prize for One-man Show, Village Art Ctr, 49; Hon Mention, Terry Art Award, Miami, Fla, 52. *Mem:* Guild Hall; Provincetown Art Asn. *Media:* Acrylic; Oil. *Mailing Add:* 351 W 24th St New York NY 10011

SHIELDS, ALAN J
DESIGNER, PAINTER
b Lost Springs, Kans, Feb 4, 44. *Study:* Kans State Univ; Univ Maine. *Work:* Mus Mod Art, Whitney Mus Am Art, Guggenheim Mus, New York; Akron Art Inst, Ohio; Hirshhorn Mus, Washington, DC. *Exhib:* Whitney Mus Am Art, 69 & 72; Art Inst Chicago, 70, 72 & 73; Corcoran Gallery Art, Washington, DC, 71; Guggenheim Mus, New York, 71; Seattle Art Mus, Wash, 73; Mus Mod Art, New York, 74; American Painting in the 70's, Albright-Knox Art Gallery, 78; one-man shows, Andre Emmerich Gallery, Zurich, 79 & Williams Col, Mass, 79; Allen Mem Art Mus, Oberlin, Ohio, 80; Heath Gallery, Atlanta, 81; Dorry Gates Gallery, Kansas City, Mo, 81. *Awards:* Guggenheim Fel, 73. *Bibliog:* Howardena Pindell (auth), Tales of brave Ulysses, Print Collectors Newslett, 1/75; John Ashbery (auth), Emblazoned Shields, New York Mag, 6/78. *Dealer:* Paula Cooper 155 Wooster St New York NY 10012. *Mailing Add:* PO Box 1554 Shelter Island NY 11964

SHIH, JOAN FAI
PAINTER, INSTRUCTOR
b Swatow, China. *Study:* Studied Chinese painting & calligraphy in Hong Kong, 49-52; Art Students League New York, 53; Kansas City Art Inst, BFA, 56, MFA, 61; Pa Acad Fine Arts, 57-59, 61-63. *Exhib:* Pa Acad Fine Arts Mus Galleries, Philadelphia, 62, 63, 69 & 72; Philadelphia Art Alliance, 66, 68, 79 & 83; Mus Philadelphia Civic Ctr, 70, 74, 79, 80 & 82; Nat Asn Women Artists Traveling Exhib, 78-; Nat Asn Women Artists Ann, Fed Bldg, New York, 79-83; Peale House Galleries, Pa Acad Fine Arts, 82; Bergen Mus, Paramus, NJ, 83; and others. *Teaching:* Instr, Kansas City Art Inst, Mo, 59-61; instr, Converse Col, Spartanburg, SC, 66-67; lectr, Rosemont Col, Pa, 69- *Awards:* First Prize & Purchase Award, D W Newcomer's Sons Ann, Kansas City, 60; Elizabeth Erlanger Mem Prize, Nat Asn Women Artists 91st Ann, New York, 80. *Mem:* Nat Asn Women Artists; Philadelphia Watercolor Club; Hong Kong Art Club; Coalition Women's Art Orgns; fel Pa Acad Fine Arts. *Media:* Watercolor, Oil. *Dealer:* Plum Gallery 625 Baron DeKalb Rd Wayne PA 19087. *Mailing Add:* 2013 Locust St Philadelphia PA 19103

SHIKLER, AARON
PAINTER
b Brooklyn, NY, Mar 18, 22. *Study:* Tyler Sch Fine Arts, Temple Univ, BFA, BSEd & MFA; Barnes Found; Hans Hofmann Sch. *Work:* Metrop Mus Art, New York; Mint Mus Art, Charlotte, NC; Sheldon Mus Art, Lincoln, Nebr; New Britain Mus Am Art, Conn; Charleston Art Gallery of Sunrise, WVa. *Comn:* Portraits of President & Mrs John F Kennedy for White House. *Exhib:* New Britain Mus Art, Conn, 64; Gallery Mod Art, New York, 65; Nat Acad Design, 65; Brooklyn Mus, 71; Calif Palace Legion Honor, San Francisco, 71; and others. *Awards:* Thomas B Clarke Prize, 61; US Dept State Traveling Grant, 76; Benjamin Figure Prize, Nat Acad Design, 76; and others. *Bibliog:* articles, Am Artist, 9/71 & Current Biog, 12/71. *Mem:* Nat Acad Design; Century Asn. *Publ:* Contrib two chaps, In: Pastel Painting, 68. *Dealer:* Davis & Long Co 746 Madison Ave New York NY 10021. *Mailing Add:* 44 W 77th St New York NY 10024

SHILLEA, THOMAS JOHN
PHOTOGRAPHER, EDUCATOR
b Peckville, Pa, May 7, 47. *Study:* Kutztown State Col, BS(art educ), 69; Rochester Inst Technol, MFA(photog), 79. *Work:* Rochester Inst Technol Arch. *Exhib:* Pratt Inst, Brooklyn, 79; Daniel Wolf Gallery, New York, 80-81; Pennsylvania Photographers, Governors Mansion, Harrisburg, 81; Tyler Sch Art, 82; Lowe Fine Arts Gallery, Syracuse Univ, 83; Platinum Prints, New Orleans Mus Art, 83. *Teaching:* Instr photog, Art Inst Philadelphia, 81-83 & Rochester Inst Technol, 83- *Mem:* Am Soc Mag Photogr; Friends Photog; Visual Studies Workshop; Soc Photog Educ. *Publ:* Coauth, The Platinum Print, Graphic Arts Res Ctr, Rochester Inst Technol, 79; contribr, Time-Life Photography Year 1982; contribr, The Portrait, 83 & The Human Figure, 83, D'Ai Nippon Inc. *Dealer:* Harold Simon 20 Church St Montclair NJ 07042. *Mailing Add:* PO Box 11 Mumford NY 14511

SHIMIZU, YOSHIAKI
HISTORIAN, CURATOR
b Tokyo, Japan, Feb 27, 36. *Study:* Harvard Col, BA, 63; Univ Kans, MA, 68; Princeton Univ, MFA, 71, PhD, 74. *Pos:* Cur Japanese art, Freer Gallery Art, Smithsonian Inst, Washington, DC, 79- *Teaching:* Asst prof art & archaeol, Princeton Univ, NJ, 73-75, vis lectr & prof, 81-; asst prof oriental art, Univ Calif, Berkeley, 75-78, assoc prof art hist, 78-79. *Res:* Primarily in Japanese art of the medieval period with reference to Chinese art. *Publ:* Auth,

Reconstruction Problems of Kokawa-dera Engi (in Japanese), Ars Buddhica, Mainichi Press, Tokyo, 72; coauth, Japanese Ink Paintings, Princeton Univ Press, 76; contribr, Zaigai Nihonno Shiho (Japanese art treasures abroad), Mainichi Press, 79; Six Narrative Paintings of Yin T'o-lo: Their Symbolic Content, Arch Asian Art, XXXIII, 80 & Workshop Management of the Early Kano Painters, 1530-1600, XXXIV, 81, Asia House, New York; Seasons and Places in Yamato Landscape and Poetry, Ars Orientalis, Vol 12, Ann Arbor, Mich, 81. *Mailing Add:* 534 Ninth St SE Washington DC 20003

SHIMODA, OSAMU
SCULPTOR
b Manchuria, June 4, 24. *Study:* St Paul Univ, Tokyo; Acad Grande Chaumiere, Paris. *Work:* St Paul Univ, Tokyo; Syracuse Mus; Nat Mus Mod Art, Tokyo. *Comn:* Murals, Hawaii CofC & Indust, 59; outdoor monumental sculpture, Embassy of Japan, Ottawa, Can, 78. *Exhib:* Granite Gallery, New York, 66; Nat Mus Mod Art Ann, Tokyo, 67; Suzanne Kohen Gallery, Minneapolis, 70; Bertha Schaefer Gallery, 70; Sculptors Guild, 71 & 72. *Mem:* Sculptors Guild (bd mem, currently). *Media:* Iron. *Dealer:* New Bertha Schaefer Gallery 983 Park Ave New York NY 10022. *Mailing Add:* 300 Seventh St Brooklyn NY 11215

SHIMOMURA, ROGER YUTAKA
PAINTER, EDUCATOR
b Seattle, Wash, June 26, 39. *Study:* Univ Wash, BA(graphic design), 61; Syracuse Univ, MFA(painting), 69. *Work:* Seattle Art Mus; Metrop Mus & Art Ctr, Miami, Fla; Ill Bell Tel Co, Chicago; Denver Art Mus; Birmingham Art Mus, Ala. *Comn:* Tryptych (72in x 144in), Seattle Opera House, Wash, 77. *Exhib:* Pyramid Galleries Ltd, Washington, DC, 76; Tacoma Art Mus, Wash, 77; Morgan Gallery, Kansas City, Kans, 77, 79; Dobrick Gallery, Chicago, 77, 80; Elaine Horwitch Gallery; and many others. *Teaching:* Asst instr painting & drawing, Univ Wash, Seattle, 65-66 & Syracuse Univ, NY, 67-69; prof art, Univ Kans, Lawrence, 69- *Awards:* Japan Found Grant, 75; Nat Endowment for the Arts Grant, 77; eight gen res grants, Univ Kans; and numerous others. *Bibliog:* Harold Haydon (auth), An unexpected sensation, Chicago Sun-Times, 5/17/74; JoAnn Lewis (auth), The American ethic, Washington Post, 6/3/76; David L Shirley (auth), Twitting the Samurai style, New York Sunday Times, 11/23/76. *Media:* Acrylic on Canvas. *Dealer:* Dobrick Gallery 161 E Erie Chicago IL 60611; Woodside/Braseth 1101 E Howell Seattle WA. *Mailing Add:* 1019 Delaware Lawrence KS 66044

SHIPLEY, JAMES R
EDUCATOR, DESIGNER
b Marion, Ohio, Dec 26, 10. *Study:* Cleveland Inst Art, dipl, 35, with Viktor Schreckengost; Western Reserve Univ, BS, 36; Univ Southern Calif; Inst Design, Chicago; Univ Ill, AM, 48. *Exhib:* May Show, Cleveland Mus Art, 35; Mich Artists Ann, Detroit Inst Art, 37; Central Ill Invitational, Milliken Univ, 44; Ill State Fair, 78. *Pos:* Commercial artist, J H Maish Advert Agency, Marion, Ohio, 29-31; designer, Gen Motors Corp, Detroit, 36-38; consult, State of Ind Comn Higher Educ, 76. *Teaching:* Prof art, Dept Art & Design, Univ Ill, Champaign, 39-78, head dept, 55-77; instr prod design, Inst Design, Chicago, summer 48; acad dir design, Advan Studies for Designers, Inst Contemp Art, Boston, summer 58; prof & actg head dept art, Pa State Univ, 78-79. *Awards:* Univ Ill Res Bd Grant Visual Pollution, 70-72. *Mem:* Fel Nat Asn Schs Art (vpres, 60-61, pres, 61-63); Midwest Col Art Asn (vpres, 60-61, pres, 61-62); Indust Designer Soc Am; Ill Arts Coun. *Publ:* Auth, Programs in art in the state universities, Print, 1-2/60; auth, Interior Design, Small Homes Coun, rev ed, 69; coauth, The new artist, In: Contemporary American Painting & Sculpture, 1969, Univ Ill, 69; contribr, Graduate Education in the Humanities & the Arts, State Ill Bd Higher Educ, 70. *Mailing Add:* 27 Greencroft Champaign IL 61820

SHIPLEY, ROGER DOUGLAS
SCULPTOR, EDUCATOR
b Cleveland Heights, Ohio, Dec 27, 41. *Study:* Am Sch Fontainebleau, France, with Monsieur Goetz, cert(painting), 62; Otterbein Col, Ohio, BA, 64; Cleveland Inst Art, 64-65; Cranbrook Acad Art, Mich, painting with Louis Bosa & sculpture with William McVey, MFA, 67. *Work:* Nat City Bank, Cleveland, Ohio; Kalamazoo Inst of Arts, Mich; Cranbrook Acad of Art; Lock Haven State Col, Pa; Otterbein Col, Westerville, Ohio. *Exhib:* 31st Ann Mid-Year Show, Butler Inst of Am Art, Youngstown, Ohio, 66; A Plastic Presence, Milwaukee Art Ctr, Wis & San Francisco Mus of Art, 69-70; one-man show, Lock Haven State Col, Pa, 76; Soft & Light Exhib, Taft Mus, Cincinnati, Ohio, 73; 30th Ann Ohio Ceramic, Sculpture & Crafts Show, Butler Inst of Am Art, Youngstown, Ohio, 78; Out of the Woods, Cheltenham Art Ctr, Pa, 80; Henri Gallery, Washington, DC, 80; and many others. *Teaching:* Assoc prof painting, drawing, printmaking & two-dimensional design, Lycoming Col, 67- *Awards:* Purchase Prize, Bald Eagle Regional Art Exhib III, Williamsport, Pa, 79; Second Place Sculpture Award & Charlie Gohn Sculpture Award, William Penn Mus, Harrisburg, Pa, 83; Sixth Prize, 5th Regional Art Exhib, Williamsport, Pa, 83. *Bibliog:* Thomas Willis (auth), Bringing the art of plastics into focus, Chicago Tribune, 2/70; Owen Findsen (auth), The brightness of lesser lights, Cincinnati Enquirer, 10/73; Edward J Sozanski (auth), Penns landing sculpture show, in doors and out, Philadelphia Inquirer, 8/83; and others. *Mem:* Bald Eagle Art League; Greater Williamsport Community Arts Coun. *Media:* Multimedia. *Dealer:* Island Art Gallery Box 265 Manteo NC 27954; Langman Gallery Inc 218 Old York Rd Jenkintown PA 19046. *Mailing Add:* 3000 Inwood Rd Williamsport PA 17701

SHIPPEN, ZOË (ZOË SHIPPEN VARNUM)
PAINTER
b Boston, Mass, Nov 12, 02. *Study:* Detroit Sch Fine Arts; Boston Mus Sch; Mary C Wheeler Sch, Providence, RI; Ecole des Beaux Arts Americaine, Fontainbleau, France; Kunst Acad, Vienna, Austria; Art Students League. *Work:* Parrish Mus, Southampton, NY. *Comn:* Many portraits including the two children of the late President John F Kennedy. *Exhib:* Washington Gallery, Miami Beach, Fla, 44-47; Worth Ave Gallery, Palm Beach, Fla, 44-61; Arthur U Newton Gallery, New York, 46; El Lyceum, Havana, Cuba, 47; James Hunt Barker Gallery, Palm Beach, 73. *Media:* Pastel, Oil. *Dealer:* Portraits Inc 41 E 57th St New York NY 10022; James Hunt Barker Galleries 345 Worth Ave Palm Beach FL 33480. *Mailing Add:* 220 Fairview Rd Palm Beach FL 33480

SHIRE, PETER
b Los Angeles, Calif, Dec 27, 47. *Study:* Chouinard Art Inst, BA, 70. *Work:* Mus Mod Art, Lodz, Poland. *Exhib:* Art For Use, 80 & Art For Tabletop, 80, Am Crafts Mus, New York; Patterns, Downer Art Mus, Downey, Calif, 80; Pacific Current Ceramics, San Jose Mus Art, Calif, 82; three-person exhib, Mus Mod Art, Paris, 82 & Mus Mod Art, Lodz, Poland, 82; On and Off the Wall: Shaped and Colored, Oakland Art Mus, 83. *Teaching:* Guest instr ceramics, Calif State Univ, Los Angeles, spring 81, Univ Calif, Los Angeles Exten, spring 82, Hochschule Angewandte Kunst, Vienna, spring 83 & Otis Parsons Sch Design, Los Angeles, fall 83. *Awards:* Purchase Prize, Cerritos Col, 74. *Bibliog:* Article, Casa Vogue, 4/80; Luckman Glasoon (auth), article, Ceramics Month, 12/80. *Media:* Ceramic; Steel, Aluminum. *Publ:* Auth, Teatypes, Tea Garden Press, 80. *Dealer:* Janus Gallery 8000 Melrose Ave Los Angeles CA 90046. *Mailing Add:* 1930 Echo Park Ave Los Angeles CA 90026

SHISHIM, FRANCIS See Bob & Bob

SHIVES, ARNOLD EDWARD
PAINTER, PRINTMAKER
b Vancouver, BC, Dec 27, 43. *Study:* Univ BC, 62-64; San Francisco Art Inst, BFA, 66; Stanford Univ, MA, 68. *Work:* San Francisco Mus Mod Art; Stanford Univ; Can Coun Art Bank, Ottawa; Art Gallery Greater Victoria, BC; Nickle Arts Mus, Calgary, Alta. *Exhib:* Art For Business Sake, Art Gallery Ont, 75; Four Canadian Artists, Galerija Mod Ljubljana, Yugoslavia, 76-77; From This Point of View, Vancouver Art Gallery, 77; World Print Competition, San Francisco Mus Mod Art, 77-79; Printmakers 82, Art Gallery Ont, Toronto, 82; New Acquisitions, Nickle Arts Mus, Calgary, Alta, 83; Arnold Shives: Prints, Art Gallery Greater Victoria, BC, 83; Vancouver: Art and Artists 1931-1983, Vancouver Art Gallery, BC, 83. *Awards:* Carnegie Corp New York Fel, 66 & 68; Can Coun Arts Grant, 76 & 77. *Bibliog:* Kay Kritzwizer (auth), Culiner, Shives form plausible bridge, Globe & Mail, Toronto, 10/25/76; John Grande (auth), Linocuts, monotypes, etchings, Arts West Mag, 10/82; Nancy Tousley (auth), Artist shows skill in various print media, Calgary Herald, 1/12/84. *Publ:* Illusr, A Climber's Guide to the Coastal Ranges of British Columbia, Alpine Club Can, 64. *Dealer:* Paul Kuhn Fine Arts 722 11th Ave SW Calgary AB T2R 0E4. *Mailing Add:* 763 Kilkeel Pl North Vancouver BC V7N 2X2 Canada

SHLIEN, HELEN S
DEALER
b Kansas City, Mo. *Study:* Sarah Lawrence Col, BA, 41; Univ Chicago, MA, 64. *Pos:* Owner, Contemp Prints & Drawings Gallery, Chicago, 65-67; cur, Inst Contemp Art, Boston, Mass, 69-72; gallery dir, Boston Visual Artists Union, 74-75; owner, Helen Shlien Gallery, Boston, 78- *Awards:* Nat Endowment Arts Grant, 77. *Mem:* Col Art Asn. *Specialty:* Contemporary painting and sculpture. *Publ:* Auth, Artists' Associations in the USA, A Descriptive Directory, pvt publ, 77. *Mailing Add:* 14 Newbury St Boston MA 02116

SHOEMAKER, PETER
PAINTER, EDUCATOR
b Newport, RI, Jan 9, 20. *Study:* Calif Sch Fine Arts, San Francisco, with Clyfford Still, Clay Spohn & Elmer Bischoff, cert, 50; Univ Calif, Berkeley, BA, 51. *Work:* Calif Palace of Legion of Honor, San Francisco; Richmond Art Ctr, Calif; Oakland Mus, Calif. *Exhib:* Corcoran Biennial, Washington, DC, 57; Pacemakers, Contemp Arts Mus, Houston, 57; Carnegie Int, Pittsburgh, 58; Bay Area: Painting Invitational, 79, Three Calif Artists, 80 & 30th Painting Ann, 83, Richmond Art Ctr, Calif. *Teaching:* Prof painting, Calif Col Arts & Crafts, Oakland, 60- *Awards:* 27th Ann Painting Prize, Richmond Art Ctr, 80. *Bibliog:* Mary Fuller (auth), Was there a San Francisco school?, Artforum, 1/71. *Mem:* San Francisco Art Inst. *Mailing Add:* 622 Panoramic Way Berkeley CA 94704

SHOEMAKER, VAUGHN
EDITORIAL CARTOONIST, PAINTER
b Chicago, Ill, Aug 11, 02. *Study:* Chicago Art Inst; Chicago Acad Fine Arts, Ill. *Work:* Huntington Libr, San Marino, Calif; Syracuse Univ, NY; Wheaton Col, Ill. *Exhib:* Obrien Galleries, Chicago, 35 & 36; Marshall Field Galleries, Chicago, 38; El Prado Gallery, Sedona, Ariz. *Pos:* Cartoonist, Chicago Daily News, 22-25, chief ed cartoonist, 25-52; ed cartoonist, New York Herald Tribune, 56-61; chief ed cartoonist, Chicago Am-Chicago Today, 61-72. *Teaching:* Instr ed cartooning, Chicago Acad Fine Arts, 27-42; instr ed cartooning, Studio Sch Art, Chicago, 43-45. *Awards:* Pulitzer Prizes, Columbia Univ, 38 & 47; Headliners Award, Atlantic City, 43. *Bibliog:* Gerald W Johnson (auth), The Lines are Drawn, Lippincott, 58. *Mem:* Hon mem Palette & Chisel Acad Fine Arts, Chicago; Sigma Delta Chi; Soc Western Artists, San Francisco; hon mem Ridge Art Asn, Chicago. *Publ:* Auth, '38 A D, '39 A D, '40 A D, '41-42 A D, '43-44 A D & '45-46 A D; plus others. *Mailing Add:* Drawer V Carmel CA 93921

SHOOK, GEORG
PAINTER
b Miss, May 24, 34. *Study:* Univ Fla; Ringling Inst Art, Sarasota, Fla; with Bernard Robinson, Orlando, Fla. *Work:* Ellen J Martin & T H B Dunnegan Collections, Springfield, Mo; City of Springfield Collection & Watercolor USA Collection, Springfield Art Mus; Lloyd O Angell Collection, Golden, Colo; Nat Bank of Com; Artists Registry, Memphis Brooks Mus Art, Tenn. *Exhib:* 9th-13th Tenn All-State Artists Ann, Nashville, 69-73; 14th-18th Mid-South Ann, Brooks Art Gallery, Memphis, 69-73; Watercolor USA, Springfield Art Mus, 70-73; Cent South Ann, Parthenon Galleries, Nashville, 70-73; 105th, 106th, 109th & 110th Ann Am Watercolor Soc, New York, 72, 73, 76 & 77; plus others. *Pos:* Art dir, Memphis Publ Co, 61- *Teaching:* Demonstrations and workshops. *Awards:* Four consecutive Purchase Awards, Watercolor USA, Springfield, Mo; ten consecutive Awards, Tenn Watercolor Soc; CFS Award, Am Watercolor Soc, New York; over 100 major awards. *Bibliog:* Cover & feature article, Art Voices S Mag, 3/78; Sharp Focus Watercolor Painting, 81 & Painting Creative Watercolors from Photographs, Watson-Guptill. *Mem:* Am Watercolor Soc; Art Dirs Club, Memphis (pres, 70-72); Memphis Watercolor Soc (co-founder & dir, 69-); Tenn Watercolor Soc (pres, 71-72); Southern Watercolor Soc (pres, 77-78). *Media:* Watercolor, Mixed Media. *Mailing Add:* 41 Union Ave #3 Memphis TN 38103

SHOOTER, TOM
PAINTER
b Williamsport, Pa, Aug 18, 41. *Study:* Lycoming Col, 59-61; Sch Mus Fine Arts, Boston, cert, 65 & grad cert, 66; with Jan Cox, Boston, 66; Tufts Univ, BFA, 71. *Work:* Tufts Univ Collection; Sch Mus Fine Arts Collection, Boston; Spaulding & Sly Corp Collection, Boston; Tufts New Eng Med Ctr Collection, Boston; Commercial Union Assurance Co Collection, Boston. *Exhib:* Works on Paper, Fogg Mus, Harvard Univ, 74; Corporations Collect, De Cordova Mus, Lincoln, Mass, 74; Painting Invitational, Brockton Art Ctr, Mass, 75; Painted in Boston, Inst Contemp Art, 75; Boston 78, Brockton Art Ctr, 78; Art of the State, Rose Mus, Brandeis Univ, 79; New Paintings, Sunne Savage Gallery, Boston, 79. *Teaching:* Instr painting, Sch Mus Fine Arts, Boston, 65-66; instr painting, Tufts Univ, Naples, Italy, 68-69; instr painting & drawing, Cambridge Ctr Adult Educ, 70-78; instr painting, Sch Mus Fine Arts, Boston, 76-78. *Awards:* 34th James William Paige Fel, Boston Mus Fine Arts, 66; Nat Endowment Arts & Humanities Grant, 66; Mass Found Arts & Humanities Grant, 79. *Bibliog:* Kay Larson (auth), Boston, identity crisis, Art News & The flowering of Boston art, 2/75; Jane Holtz-Kay (auth), article, 2/76 & On view in Boston, summer 76, Artnews. *Dealer:* Sunne Savage Gallery 105 Newbury St Boston MA 02116. *Mailing Add:* 540 W 29th St New York NY 10001

SHOR, BERNICE ABRAMOWITZ
EDITOR
b Newark, NJ, July 11, 45. *Study:* Conn Col, BA. *Pos:* Managing ed, Art Now Gallery Guide, 74- *Mailing Add:* Art Now 144 N 14th St Kenilworth NJ 07033

SHORE, MARY (MCGARRITY)
PAINTER
b Philadelphia, Pa, Mar 19, 12. *Study:* Cooper Union Art Sch, scholar; Art Inst Chicago. *Work:* Addison Gallery Am Art, Andover, Mass; Fitchburg Art Mus, Mass; Baltimore Art Mus. *Exhib:* One-man shows, Boris Mirski Gallery, Boston, 60 & 64, Fitchburg Art Mus, 65, Stockbridge Sch Gallery, 72 & Horizon Gallery, 75-82; Traveling Assemblage Exhib, Mus Mod Art, US & Can, 63; Montserrat Gallery, Beverly, Mass, 77. *Awards:* Blanche E Colman Art Found Award, 66. *Mem:* Artists Equity Asn (past pres New Eng Chap & nat dir). *Mailing Add:* Way Rd Gloucester MA 01930

SHORE, STEPHEN
PHOTOGRAPHER
b New York, NY Oct 8, 47. *Work:* Metrop Mus Art, Mus Mod Art, New York; Int Mus Photog, Rochester, NY; Mus Fine Arts, Boston; Art Inst Chicago. *Exhib:* Solo exhib, Metrop Mus Art, New York, 71, Mus Mod Art, New York, 76, Kunsthalle, Dusseldorf, Ger, 76 & Ringling Mus, Sarasota, Fla; New Topographics, Int Mus Photog, Rochester, NY, 75; Counterparts, Metrop Mus Art, New York. *Teaching:* Asst prof photog, Bard Col, 82- *Bibliog:* Max Kozloff (auth), The framing of Stephen Shore, Am Photog, 2/79. *Publ:* Auth, Uncommon places, 82 & The gardens at Giverny, 83, Aperture. *Dealer:* Pace-MacGill E 57th St New York NY. *Mailing Add:* 5075 Jackson Creek Rd Bozeman MT 59715

SHORES, (JAMES) FRANKLIN
PAINTER
b Hampton, Va, Nov 9, 42. *Study:* Pa Acad Fine Arts, Cresson Europ Traveling Scholar, Eakins Figure Painting Prize. *Work:* Pa Acad Fine Arts, Philadelphia; Camden Pub Libr, Maine. *Exhib:* Pa Acad Fine Arts Ann, 67 & 69; Philadelphia Watercolor Club Exhibs, 68- *Pos:* Instr art, Pa Acad Fine Arts, 65- *Awards:* Harry Deitch Mem Prize, Philadelphia Watercolor Club, 78. *Mem:* Philadelphia Watercolor Club (pres, currently). *Media:* Watercolor, Oil. *Mailing Add:* 612 S Ninth St Philadelphia PA 19147

SHORNEY, MARGO KAY (MCIVER)
DEALER, SCULPTOR
b Great Falls, Mont, July 5, 30. *Study:* Col Educ, Great Falls, Mont, with Sister Mary Trinitas, 49-51; Univ Denver, with Clarence Van Duzer & Mrion Buckan, 51-53. *Work:* Great Falls Pub Lib, Mont; Cooper West Insurance Agency, Elk City, Okla; John Thompson Movie Service, Oklahoma City; Dr R G Williams Medical Offices, Tulsa, Okla; Country Club Pub, Oklahoma

City. *Comn:* Christmas mural, Lake View Country Club, Oklahoma City, 69; Oil Depicting Old & New, Delta Gamma Society, Norman, Okla, 79. *Exhib:* Eleventh Mem Ann, 77 & 17th Ann Artists Salon, 78, Okla Mus Art; Okla Spring Gala, N Park Mall, Oklahoma City, 81; Okla Sculpture Soc, Kirpatrick Ctr, Oklahoma City, 81; First Ann Women's Invitational, Quail Springs Mall, Oklahoma City, 81. *Collections Arranged:* Okla Art Guild Spring Regional, 78; 25th Anniversary, Okla Art Guild, 79. *Pos:* Owner & dir, Shorney Gallery, 76- *Teaching:* Lectr, Okla Art Guild & S Oklahoma City Assoc, 82-83. *Mem:* Charter mem Okla Sculpture Soc; Okla Art Gallery Owners Asn (pres, 81-82); Okla Art Guild (bd dirs, 79-82); Great Falls Mont Inst Arts (pres, 52-54). *Specialty:* Oklahoma native and resident artists featuring a variety of media including graphics, sculpture, oils, watercolors, acrylics, pastels, pottery, weaving & jewelry. *Mailing Add:* 6616 N Olie Oklahoma City OK 73116

SHORTER, EDWARD SWIFT
PAINTER, COLLECTOR
b Columbus, Ga, July 2, 02. *Study:* Mercer Univ, AB & LLD; Corcoran Sch Art; Fontainbleu, Paris, with Andre L'Hote, Wayman Adams & Hugh Breckenridge; Boston Mus Sch Art. *Work:* Corcoran Gallery Art; Atlanta Art Asn; Wesleyan Col, Mercer Univ, Macon, Ga. *Comn:* Portrait, Mercer Univ; paintings, Housing Authority Columbus, Tift Col & St Francis Hosp. *Exhib:* Pa Acad Fine Arts; Corcoran Gallery Art; Southern States Art League; Soc Washington Artists; Southeastern Art Ann; Fifty Years of Painting (retrospective), Columbus Mus Arts & Sci, 78. *Collections Arranged:* Am Traditionalists of Twentieth Century; Special Exhibition Old Master Drawings & Graphics; Contemporary Exhibition Georgia Artists. *Pos:* Actg dir, Columbus Mus Arts & Crafts, 53-55, dir, 55-68, emer dir, 68- *Awards:* Gari Melcher Award, Artists Fel; Algenon Sydney Sullivan Award, Mercer Univ. *Mem:* Am Asn Mus; Artists Equity Asn; Am Artists Prof League; Salmagundi Club; Soc Washington Artists. *Media:* Oil. *Collection:* American paintings; European porcelains; Oriental ivories and rugs. *Mailing Add:* 6001 Green Island Dr Columbus GA 31904

SHOSTAK, EDWIN BENNETT
SCULPTOR
b New York, NY, Aug 23, 41. *Study:* Ohio Univ, 59-60; Cooper Union, 60-61. *Work:* Phillip Johnson Collection, New Canaan, Conn; Sydney Lewis Collection, Richmond, Va; Mr & Mrs Horace Solomon Collection, New York; Mr & Mrs Stephen Garrison Collection, New York; Mr & Mrs Moses Taylor Pyne Collection, New York & Bombay, India. *Exhib:* Am Exhib of Am Sculpture, Whitney Mus of Am Art, New York, 70 & Biennial, 73; 76 Jefferson St, Mus of Mod Art, New York, 75; Selections for New & Old Collections, Art Mus of STex, Corpus Christi, 76; Non-Collectible Art from the Collection of Horace & Holly Solomon, Sarah Lawrence Col, Bronxville, NY, 77; A Collection, A Collector, Norman Fisher Collection, Jacksonville Art Mus, 79. *Awards:* Creative Artists Pub Serv Award, 73; Guggenheim Fel, 74-75. *Bibliog:* Robert Hughes (auth), In search of the new; pursuit of the old, Time Mag, 1/71; Le Salon des Artists Independents, Grand Palais, Paris, France, 80; Decorative Sculpture, Sculpture Ctr, New York, 81; plus numerous others. *Media:* Wood, Metals. *Mailing Add:* 303 E Houston St New York NY 10002

SHOULBERG, HARRY
PAINTER, PRINTMAKER
b Philadelphia, Pa, Oct 25, 03. *Study:* Am Artists Sch; also with Carl Holty & Sol Wilson. *Work:* Metrop Mus Art, New York; Carnegie Inst, Pittsburgh; Norfolk Mus Arts & Sci, Va; Denver Mus, Colo; Butler Inst Am Art. *Exhib:* American Oil Painting, Corcoran Gallery Art, Washington, DC, 41; Print & Watercolor Exhib, Pa Acad Fine Arts, Philadelphia, 46; Libr of Cong Print Exhib, Washington, DC, 47; Audubon Artists 28th Ann, New York, 70; Nat Acad Design 146th Ann, New York, 71; League of Present Day Artists, New York, 75; Nat Soc of Painters in Casein & Acrylic at the Nat Acad of Design, New York, 76 & 77; Summit Gallery, New York, 77; one-man show, Harbor Gallery, Cold Spring Harbor, NY, 80. *Awards:* M J Kaplan Mem Award, Am Soc Contemp Artists, 66; Pearl Award, Painters & Sculptors Soc NJ, 79; Erlanger Mem Award, Am Soc Contemp Artists, 80. *Bibliog:* H Shokler (auth), Artists manual for silk screen printmaking, 46 & A Reese (auth), American prize prints of the 20th century, 49, Am Artists Group. *Mem:* Audubon Artists; Am Soc Contemp Artists; NJ Soc Painters & Sculptors; Artists Equity Asn; Nat Soc Painters Casein & Acrylic. *Media:* Oil. *Dealer:* Belanthi Gallery 142 Court St Brooklyn NY 11201. *Mailing Add:* 112-114 W 14th St New York NY 10011

SHOWELL, KENNETH L
PAINTER
b Huron, SDak, Oct 22, 39. *Study:* Kansas City Art Inst, BFA, 63; Ind Univ, MFA, 65. *Work:* Art Inst Chicago; Whitney Mus Am Art, New York; Michener Collection, Univ Tex, Austin; Akron Mus, Ohio. *Exhib:* Whitney Mus Am Art Ann, 67-69; Highlights of the 1969-1970 Art Season, Aldrich Mus, Ridgefield, Conn; Lyrical Abstraction, Whitney Mus Am Art, New York, 71; Spray, Santa Barbara Mus Art, 71; Painting & Sculpture Today 1972, Indianapolis Mus Art, Ind, 72. *Bibliog:* R Pincus-Witten (auth), New York, Artforum, 1/70; C Ratcliff (auth), The new informalists, 2/70 & J Weissman (auth), Showdown in Soho, 11/74, Art News. *Media:* Acrylic, Oil. *Mailing Add:* 82 Forsyth New York NY 10002

SHRADY, FREDERICK
SCULPTOR
b Eastview, NY, Oct 22, 07. *Study:* Oxford Univ; Art Students League; painting with Yashuti Takaka, Paris; study in Florence, Italy; Holy Cross Col,

Hon DFA, 69. *Work:* Metrop Mus Art, New York; Holy Cross Col; Fordham Univ, New York; Vatican Mus, Vatican State; pvt collection of Pope Paul. *Comn:* Dionysis & Appolo, Univ Bridgeport, Conn, 74; St Eliza Seton Shrine, St Patrick's Cathedral, New York, 75; bronze, FBI Bldg, Washington, DC, 79; bronze Christ, Rosary Hill Hosp, Hawthorne, NY, 81; bronze Madonna, Vatican Gardens, Vatican City, 83; and others. *Awards:* Legion of Honor & Palme D'Acadamie, 37, French Govt. *Media:* Bronze, Metal. *Dealer:* Weintraub Gallery 992 Madison Ave New York NY 10021. *Mailing Add:* Maple Rd Easton CT 06612

SHUBIN, MORRIS JACK
PAINTER, LECTURER
b Mansfield, Wash, Feb 25, 20. *Work:* Laguna Beach Mus Art, Calif; Utah State Univ, Logan; Las Vegas Art Mus, Nev; Home Savings & Loan, Calif; City La Mirada, Calif; and others. *Exhib:* Nat Watercolor Competition, Wichita, Kans, 70; Nat Watercolor Soc Ann, Palm Springs Art Mus, Calif, 81; Art and the Law, Atlanta, 83; Utah State Univ, Logan, 83; and others. *Teaching:* Instr watercolor workshops, Fla, Tex, NMex, Ore, Colo, Mo & Mex, 74-84. *Awards:* First Award, San Bernardino Co Fine Art Mus, Redlands, Calif, 83; Addeso Franklin Page Award, Owensboro Mus, Ky, 83. *Bibliog:* Gerald Brommer (auth), Transparent Watercolor, Davis, 73. *Mem:* Am Watercolor Soc; Nat Watercolor Soc (treas, 70-72, vpres, 72-73); WCoast Watercolor Soc; Pasadena Soc Artists. *Media:* Multimedia. *Publ:* Auth, Watercolor page, Am Artists, 8/74. *Dealer:* Fireside Gallery PO Box 3374 Carmel CA 93921; Sandra Zahn Oreck Gallery 529 Wilkinson Row New Orleans LA 70130. *Mailing Add:* 313 N 12th St Montebello CA 90640

SHUCK, KENNETH MENAUGH
MUSEUM DIRECTOR, PAINTER
b Harrodsburg, Ky, May 21, 21. *Study:* Ohio State Univ, BS(art educ) & MA(art hist); Univ Chile, Inst Int Educ scholar, 50. *Exhib:* Denver Art Mus Ann; Watercolor USA & 10 State Regional, Springfield, Mo. *Collections Arranged:* 10 State Regional Exhib, 51-75; Watercolor USA, 61-75. *Pos:* Dir, Springfield Art Mus, Mo, 51-76; dir, Fine Arts Dept, Mo State Fair, 67-71; arts consult, painter (watercolor) & craftsman, 51- *Mem:* Midwest Mus Conf (pres, 63); Mo State Coun Arts (chmn visual arts, 66-68); Am Asn Mus; Am Fedn Arts. *Media:* Watercolor, Acrylic. *Mailing Add:* 938 E Elm Springfield MO 65806

SHUEBROOK, RON (RONALD LEE)
PAINTER, EDUCATOR
b Ft Munroe, Va, July 29, 43. *Study:* Haystack Mountain Sch, Maine, 65 & 67; Kutztown State Col, Pa, BS, 65, MEd, 69; Kent State Univ, Ohio, MFA, 72. *Work:* Can Coun Art Bank, Ottawa, Ont; NS Art Bank & Art Gallery NS, Halifax; Hamilton Art Mus, Ont; Art Inst Chicago; Art Gallery Ont, Toronto. *Exhib:* Edmonton Art Gallery, Alta, 77; Art Gallery NS, Halifax, 81; Art Gallery Harbour Front, Toronto, 81; Secession Mus, Vienna, 81; Canadian Drawings, Saidye Bronfman Ctr, Montreal, Que, & traveling, 83-84; and others. *Collections Arranged:* John Clark (auth, catalog), Southern Alta Art Gallery, Lethbridge, 82. *Teaching:* Instr & coordr summer sch, Univ Sask, Saskatoon, 72-73; asst prof, Acadia Univ, Wolfville, NS, 73-77; assoc prof, York Univ, Toronto, 77-79; chmn studio div, NS Col Art & Design, Halifax, 79-83, assoc prof painting & area coordr, 83- *Awards:* Fels, Fine Art Work Ctr, Provincetown, Mass, 69-70 & MacDowell Colony, Peterborough, NH, 81; Project Grants, Can Coun, 80, 81 & 83. *Bibliog:* Liz Wylie (auth), article, Art Mag, Toronto, 12/80; Gemey Kelly (auth), Ron Shuebrook, Southern Alberta Art Gallery, Lethbridge, 83; Joan Murray (auth), article, Arts Atlantic, summer 83. *Mem:* Univ Art Asn Can; Can Asn Univ Teachers; Visual Arts NS (found exec, 75-77). *Publ:* Auth, The maritimes, Artscanada, Toronto, 3/75; auth, William Tucker at Sable-Castelli, Artmag, Toronto, 6/78; auth, Myron Stout, Arts Mag, New York, 4/80; auth, Empathetic Witness: Halifax, NS, Vanguard, Vancouver Art Gallery, 2/81; auth, William Tucker, Artscribe, London, 8/82. *Dealer:* Olga Korper 80 Spadina Ave Toronto ON M5V 2J3 Canada. *Mailing Add:* Studio Div NS Col Art & Design 5163 Duke St Halifax NS B3J 3J6 Canada

SHUFF, LILY (LILLIAN SHIR)
PAINTER, PRINTMAKER
b New York, NY. *Study:* Hunter Col, BA & MA; Columbia Univ; Brooklyn Acad Fine Art; Art Students League, with Morris Kantor; also with Adja Junkers & Jerry Farnsworth. *Work:* Metrop Mus Art, New York; Libr of Cong, Washington, DC; Yale Univ Art Gallery, New Haven, Conn; Butler Inst Am Art, Youngstown, Ohio; Ga Mus Am Art; Archives Am Art, Smithsonian Inst, Washington, DC; plus 33 other nat mus collections. *Exhib:* Ten Years of American Prints 1947-1956, Brooklyn Mus, NY, 56; Munic Mus Art, Uneo Park, Tokyo, 60; Mus Nac Bellas Artes, Buenos Aires, 63; Royal Scottish Acad, Edinburgh, Scotland, 63; Int Cult Ctr, New Delhi, India, 66; and 30 one-man shows in US mus. *Awards:* Elizabeth Rungius Fulda Prize for Oil, Nat Asn Women Artists, 69, 70, 76 & 77; Silver Medal for Creative Painting, Audubon Artists, 79; Allied Artist Am, Nat Casein Soc, 63, 65, 69, 73, 76, 77, 81 & 83. *Bibliog:* Article in Think, 59; Alfred Khouri Collection, Norfolk Mus, 63; Archives of American Art, Smithsonian Inst, Washington, DC. *Mem:* Nat Asn Women Artists (chmn mem jury, 56-58 & 64-66, bd dirs, 58-67); Nat Soc Painters Casein (rec secy, 57-64 & corr secy, 68-83); New York Soc Women Artists (bd gov, 56-71); Audubon Artists (graphics dir, 70-72); NJ Painters & Sculptors (admis jury, 71). *Media:* Oil, Watercolor. Interest: Slides of paintings circulated in universities and colleges in US by Georgia Museum of Fine Art, Athens. *Publ:* Contribr, Art Collector's Almanac, 65; contribr, Today's Art, 70, 74 & 77; contribr, How to Paint a Prize Winner, 70. *Dealer:* East Side Gallery 307 E 37th St New York NY 10016. *Mailing Add:* 155 W 68th St New York NY 10023

SHULER, THOMAS H, JR
PHOTOGRAPHER, EDUCATOR
b Detroit, Mich, Apr 15, 49. *Study:* Princeton Univ, BA, 71; Univ Del, MA, 78. *Work:* Corcoran Gallery Art; Mus Francais Photog, Bievres, France; Bibliot Nat, Paris; Libr Cong, Washington, DC. *Exhib:* Recent Acquisitions, 77 & Still Life, 78, Corcoran Gallery Art; Focus Gallery, San Francisco, 79; MFA Gallery-The Platinotype, Rochester Inst Technol, 79; Photographer's Gallery, London, England, 79; Nuages, Bibliot Nat, Paris, 80; Invisible Light, Harvard Univ, 81; and others. *Teaching:* Instr photog, Smithsonian Inst, 75-76; chmn, asst prof & prog head photog, Northern Va Community Col, 76- *Awards:* Medaille Verrieres Buisson, Mus Francais Photog, 78. *Bibliog:* Ben Forgey (auth), A sense of the moment when everything's right, Washington Star, 5/5/78; Time-Life Photo Annual, 79; Hafey & Shillea (auth), The Platinum Print, Graphic Arts Res Ctr, Rochester Inst Technol, 80; and others. *Mem:* Soc Photog Educ. *Publ:* Ed, Places, Infrared Photographs 1976-1978, pvt publ, 78. *Mailing Add:* 3626 Windom Pl NW Washington DC 20008

SHULL, CARL EDWIN
PAINTER, EDUCATOR
b Greenup, Ill, Dec 8, 12. *Study:* Eastern Ill Univ, BA(educ), 39; Peabody Col, MA, 40; Chicago Art Inst, advan work, 40-42; Ohio State Univ, PhD, 54. *Work:* Canton Art Inst, Ohio; Sheldon Swope Art Gallery, Terre Haute, Ind; Lakeview Ctr Arts & Sci, Ill; Eastern Ill Univ collection; Evansville Mus Arts & Sci, Ind. *Comn:* Murals, US Navy, South Pac Area, 44-45; Space Flight, pvt comn, Terre Haute, Ind, 71; Sports in Art (35 paintings on sports), Field House, Lakeland Col, Mattoon, Ill, 74; oil painting, Wabash Col Art Ctr, Mt Carmel, Ill, 83. *Exhib:* One-man shows, Univ Ill, 62, Evansville Mus Arts & Sci, 71 & Univ Wis, Platteville, 74; Mid Year Am Painting Exhib, Butler Inst Am Art, Youngstown, Ohio, 53 & 63; Nat Painting Show, Sheldon Swope Art Gallery, Terre Haute, Ind, 67; Tarble Art Ctr, Eastern Ill Univ, Charleston, 82 & 83. *Pos:* Commercial artist, Graham & Hugent Studios, Chicago, Ill, 41-42. *Teaching:* Instr arts & crafts, Univ Mo, 46-47; prof painting & drawing, Eastern Ill Univ, Charleston, 47-; retired. *Awards:* Purchase Awards, Wabash Valley Exhib, Sheldon Swope Art Gallery, Terre Haute, Ind, 68 & 71; Tri-State Exhib, Evansville Mus Art & Sci, Ind, 71 & Wabash Col Brubeck Gallery, 83. *Bibliog:* Shull & Wiseman (auth), Approaches in Life Drawing (film), Eastern Ill Univ, 70; Willis Waltman (auth), Shull's Life Class Relates Work to Other Art Areas, Eastern Ill Univ, 77. *Media:* Oil, Watercolor. *Publ:* Auth-illusr, Techniques in Life Drawing, 74, Elements in Landscape Painting, 74, Heads, Heads, Heads, 75, Lore and Design of Nature's Harvest, 76 & Lore and Legend of Birds in Design, 77, Eastern Ill Univ. *Mailing Add:* RR4 Charleston IL 61920

SHUMACKER, ELIZABETH WIGHT
PAINTER, INSTRUCTOR
b Chattanooga, Tenn, Sept 25, 12. *Study:* Univ Chattanooga, BA, postgrad work in painting & graphics; spec drawing classes, Hunter Mus, Chattanooga, Tenn. *Work:* High Mus Art, Atlanta, Ga; Brooks Mem Gallery, Memphis, Tenn; Inst Cult Mexicano-Norteamericano, Guadalajara, Mex; Hunter Mus, Chattanooga; Tenn Arts Comn. *Exhib:* High Mus, Atlanta, 53-58 & 61; Butler Inst Am Art, Youngstown, Ohio, 55 & 62; Brooks Mem Art Gallery, Memphis, Tenn, 56-69; Smithsonian Inst, Washington, DC, 60 & 81; Springfield Art Mus, Mo, 62; Heal's Art Gallery, London, 78-79; Salon Nations, Paris, 83; 31 one-man shows including six Mex cities. *Teaching:* Instr beginning, intermediate & advan painting, Hunter Gallery Art, Chattanooga, Tenn, 55-75; vis instr advan painting, Univ Chattanooga, spring 69 & Univ Tenn, Chattanooga, 75. *Awards:* First Prize Water Color, Southeastern Ann, Atlanta, 57 & Mid-South Exhib, Brooks Mem Gallery, Memphis, Tenn, 57; First Prize & Best in Show, 2nd Nat Small Painting Exhib, Gallery North, Mt Clemens, Mich, 74. *Mem:* Tenn Water Color Soc. *Media:* Acrylic, Collage. *Mailing Add:* 1400 Riverview Rd Chattanooga TN 37405

SHUTE, BEN E
PAINTER
b Altoona, Wis, July 13, 05. *Study:* Art Inst Chicago; Chicago Acad Fine Arts. *Work:* High Mus Art, Atlanta; Columbus Mus Arts & Crafts, Ga; Ga Inst Technol, Atlanta; Emory Univ, Atlanta; Mus Art, Columbia, SC; and others. *Exhib:* Calif Palace of Legion of Honor, San Francisco; Pasadena Art Inst; Butler Inst Am Art, Youngstown, Ohio; Telfair Acad Art; Brooklyn Mus; and others. *Pos:* Chmn, Southeastern Ann Exhib, 16 yrs; mem bd, Ga Art Asn. *Teaching:* Lectr contemp Am painting; instr art, Atlanta Art Inst, 28-43, head fine arts dept, 43-70. *Awards:* Atlanta Watercolor Club, 60; Mead Paper Co Award, 61; Southeastern Ann, 61; and others. *Mem:* Asn Ga Artists; Nat Soc Painters Casein. *Mailing Add:* 1002 Cardova Dr NE Atlanta GA 30324

SHUTE, ROBERTA E
SCULPTOR, PAINTER
b Saskatoon, Sask. *Study:* Corcoran Mus Art Sch, 49-52; Am Univ, 52-53; study with Hans Hofmann, 53. *Comn:* Environ sculpture (with Maxine Cable), Noche Crist, engrs & technicians, Allied Chem, New York, 70; maj installation, Wolf Trap, summer 71; happening for Summers in the Park Prog, Nat Park Serv, Washington, DC, 72; installations, Textile Mus, DC, summer 74. *Exhib:* Baltimore Mus, 53; Corcoran Mus, 53, 54, 56, 59, 65 & 67; Pa Acad, 54; Art: USA Nat, New York, 58; Nat Acad Sci, 72; and others. *Teaching:* Painting, Corcoran Mus Sch, 51-52; guest lectr plastic sculpture, Am Univ, 72; sculpture, Glen Echo Creative Educ Prog, 73. *Awards:* Nathan Goodman Estate Award, 51; Second Prize, Washington Soc Artists, 62; First Prize, Art & Religion, 63. *Mem:* Artists Equity Asn; Washington Women's Art Ctr. *Media:* Miscellaneous Media, Fabric. *Dealer:* Gallery Ten Ltd 1519 Connecticut Ave NW Washington DC 20036. *Mailing Add:* 3536 Edmunds St NW Washington DC 20007

SIBERELL, ANNE HICKS
PRINTMAKER, ILLUSTRATOR
b Los Angeles, Calif. *Study:* Univ Calif, 2 yrs; Chouinard Art Inst, BFA; Silvermine Col Art, New Canaan, Conn, painting with John Wheat & Richard Lytle; Rowayton Art Ctr, Conn, printmaking with Antonio Frasconi; Col San Mateo, Calif, etching. *Work:* Kerlan Collection, Walter Libr, Univ Minn, Minneapolis; Rep Bank New York; Oakland Mus; Bankers Trust Collection, San Francisco; DeGrummond Collection, Univ Southern Miss. *Comn:* Ed 100 woodcuts, Silvermine Guild Art, Silvermine Col Art, 66. *Exhib:* International Artist's Book Show, Art Inst Chicago, 81; solo shows, Montalvo Ctr Arts, Saratoga, Calif, 81 & San Francisco Conservatory Music, 82; Breaking the Bindings/American Book Art Now, Elvehjem Mus Art, Madison, Wis, 83; From Coast to Coast, State Univ NY, Purchase, 83; Books at Hvidovre Art Library, Odder, Denmark, 83; and many others. *Pos:* Asst art ed, Walt Disney Prods, Inc, 56-59; ed filmstrip prep from children's lit, Weston Woods Studios, Conn, 60. *Teaching:* Art for Children, Silvermine Col Art, 66-68 & Martin Luther King Jr Ctr, San Mateo, 68-70; woodblock printmaking, San Mateo Adult Educ, 70; illus children's lit, 74-75 & teaching, 76-78; guest lectr, Bakersfield Col, Calif, 77 & Univ Ky, 80. *Awards:* Award for Color Woodcut, Conn Mus Show, Hartford, 68; Rounce & Coffin Award for Bk Design & Illus, 73; San Francisco Art Festival Award, Palo Alto Cult Ctr, 77. *Bibliog:* Design without Clients, Fortune Mag, 75; TV interview, Festival of the Arts, San Carlos, Calif, 75. *Mem:* Los Angeles Printmaking Soc; Calif Soc Printmakers; Appeltree Etchers, Inc (bd dirs, 72-74); Soc Children's Bk Writers. *Media:* Oil Based Paint and Ink; Collage and Metals. *Publ:* Coauth, Feast of Thanksgiving, 74 & Martin Luther King, Jr, Story of a Dream, 78, Childrens Press; auth & illusr, Houses, Shelters from Prehistoric Times to Today, Holt, Rinehart & Winston, 79; illusr, Emanuel Thayer's, Climbing Sun--The Story of a Hopi Indian Boy, Dodd, Mead, 80; auth & illusr, Whale in the Sky, E P Dutton, 82. *Mailing Add:* 1041 La Cuesta Rd Hillsborough CA 94010

SIBLEY, CHARLES KENNETH
PAINTER, EDUCATOR
b Huntington, WVa, Dec 20, 21. *Study:* Ohio State Univ, BS; Art Inst Chicago; Columbia Univ, MA; State Univ Iowa, MFA. *Work:* Metrop Mus Art, New York; NC Mus, Raleigh; Va Mus, Richmond; Rochester Mem Mus, NY; Chrysler Mus, Norfolk, Va; and others. *Comn:* Panels, USS Kennedy, 71; Virginia Landscape (oil), Gov Mansion, Richmond, 72; mural, Old Dom Univ Libr, Norfolk, Va, 77. *Exhib:* Carnegie Inst, Pittsburgh, 57; Whitney Mus Am Art Bi-Annual, New York, 57-59; Nat Soc Arts & Lett, 59; Nat Acad Design, 61; 50 Artists--50 States, Am Fedn Arts, 68. *Pos:* Mem bd dirs, Norfolk Va Children's Art Ctr. *Teaching:* Instr painting & design, Duke Univ, 50-51 & Tex State Univ, 52-54; prof painting & design, Old Dom Univ, 55-82, chmn dept, 55-70, prof emer, 82- *Awards:* Louis Comfort Tiffany Grant, 55; Stern Medal, Nat Acad Design, 61; Irene Leache Mem First Prize, Norfolk Mus, 71. *Media:* Mixed. *Mailing Add:* c/o Old Dominion Univ Norfolk VA 23508

SICA
PRINTMAKER, SCULPTOR
b New York, NY, May 21, 32. *Study:* Art Students League, 49-50; Pratt Graphic Ctr, 69-70. *Work:* Mus Mod Art, Paris, France; Victoria & Albert Mus, London, Eng; Montreal Mus Fine Arts, Can; Brooklyn Mus, NY; Los Angeles Mus, Calif. *Comn:* Edition 30 Prints, Yugoslav Consal, Montenegro, 80. *Exhib:* British Biennial, Bradford Mus, Eng, 72-79; Shiedam Mus, Rotterdam, 73; 1st Miami Graphic Biennial, Miami Mus, Fla, 73; New Graphics, New Berger Mus, Purchase, NY, 76; US Graphics, Tokyo Central Mus, Japan, 79. *Awards:* NJ State Mus Graphics, 76. *Media:* Collage, Clay. *Dealer:* Langman Editions 218 Old York Rd Jenkintown PA 19046. *Mailing Add:* 158 West 13th St New York NY 10011

SICKMAN, JESSALEE BANE
PAINTER, INSTRUCTOR
b Denver, Colo, Aug 17, 05. *Study:* Univ Colo; Goucher Col; Corcoran Sch Art, Washington, DC; also with Richard Lahey & Eugen Weisz. *Work:* Corcoran Gallery Art. *Comn:* Portrait, comn by Mr Pach, Cleveland, Ohio, 51; Pigeons, comn by Mrs Bruton, Alexandria, Va, 55; Figure Study, comn by Mrs Woods, San Diego, Calif, 71; figure study & still life, comn by Mr & Mrs Ira Glackens, Shepherdstown, WVa. *Exhib:* One-man Watercolor Show, Pub Libr, Washington, DC, 42; Corcoran Gallery Art Biennial Exhibs, 42-50; Colony Club, Washington, DC, 58 & 62; Soc Washington Artists, Smithsonian Inst, 68 & Arts Club. *Teaching:* Instr still life, Warrentown Country Sch, Va, 40; instr life portrait, Corcoran Sch Art, 40-63; instr portrait & still life, Sickman Studios, Washington, DC, 64- *Awards:* Landscape Award, Corcoran Sch Art, 37; Alice Barney Mem Portrait Award, 38. *Mem:* Artists Equity Asn; Soc Washington Artists. *Media:* Oil. *Mailing Add:* 1215 Eye St NW Washington DC 20015

SICKMAN, LAURENCE CHALFANT STEVENS
ADMINISTRATOR, HISTORIAN
b Denver, Colo, Aug 27, 06. *Study:* Harvard Univ, AB(cum laude), 30, Harvard-Yenching Fel, Peking, China, 30-35, resident fel, Fogg Art Mus, 37-39; Rockhurst Col, Hon DFA, 72; Baker Univ, Baldwin, Kans, LHD, 73; Mo Univ, Hon DLit, 74; Kansas City Art Inst, Hon DFA, 75; Columbia Univ, LHD, 77. *Pos:* Cur Oriental art, Nelson Gallery Art, Kansas City, Mo, 35-45, from vdir to dir, 46-77, ed, Arch Asian Art, 66-74, emer dir & consult to trustees 77- *Teaching:* Lectr hist art, Univ Kans, 70-; lectr hist art, Univ Mo-Kansas City, 70-77. *Awards:* Knight Order of the Pole Star, H M King of Sweden, 68; Charles Land Freer Medal, 73. *Mem:* Asn Art Mus Dirs (pres, 64); Am Asn Mus (coun mem, 63-69); Col Art Asn Am (bd dirs, 63-68); Chinese Art Soc Am (bd gov, 48-, ed, Arch, 48-66); Am Coun Learned Socs.

Res: Far Eastern art, especially Chinese paintings and sculpture. *Publ:* Ed, The university prints, Oriental Art, Series O, Early Chinese Art, 38; coauth, The art & architecture of China, Pelican History of Art, 56; ed & contrib, Chinese Calligraphy & Painting in the Collection of John M Crawford, Jr, 62. *Mailing Add:* Nelson Gallery, Atkins Mus 4525 Oak St Kansas City MO 64111

SIDEN, FRANKLIN
DEALER, LECTURER
b Highland Park, Mich, Nov 16, 22. *Study:* Soc Arts & Crafts, 32-36; Meinzinger Art Sch, 40; Univ Ill, BS, 47; Wayne State Univ, MA(art hist), 77. *Pos:* Owner, Franklin Siden Gallery, Detroit, Mich, 64-72 & West Bloomfield, Mich, 72- *Teaching:* Lectr art, Bloomfield Birmingham Art Asn, 74 & 76-77; lectr art & collecting prints, Univ Courses in Adult Educ, 78. *Bibliog:* Six Detroit dealers who are serving a growing art market, The Art Gallery, 66; Kick out the jams: Detroit's cass corridor 1963-1977, Detroit Inst Arts, 80. *Mem:* Founders Soc, Detroit Inst Arts; Friends of Mod Art, Detroit Inst Arts; Mus Mod Art, New York; Cranbrook Acad Arts, Bloomfield Hills. *Specialty:* Modern and contemporary paintings, sculptures and prints. *Mailing Add:* 3649 Quail Hollow 6024 Brook Lane Bloomfield Hills MI 48013

SIDER, DENO
PAINTER, SCULPTOR
b Norwich, Conn. *Study:* Norwich Acad, dipl; also with Leon Franks. *Work:* Mattatuck Mus, Conn. *Comn:* Map of US & decor, Aldo, Hollywood, 56; side panels & fish murals (mixed media), Aquarium, Tarzana, 66. *Exhib:* Int Madonna Festival, Los Angeles, 58-61 & 63-64; Calif State Show, Sacramento, 62 & 66; Los Angeles Co Art Show, Los Angeles, 66; Hollywood Bowl Art Festival, Los Angeles, 68-69. *Pos:* Partner, Leedes Art Gallery, 64-71, owner, 71-; illus, Epicurean Mag, 69-70; illus & ed, Prospector News, 71-; illus & supv, Polygems, 77- *Teaching:* Instr art & oils & owner, Sider Art Sch, Hollywood, 54-64; instr art & oils, Leedes Art Sch, Encino, Calif, 64- *Awards:* Madonna Festival Award, Methodist Church, Los Angeles, 63 & 64; Hollywood Bowl Best of Show, 68 & 69; Tuaca Purchase Award, 70. *Mem:* Life mem San Fernando Valley Art Club; Calif Art Club; Valley Artist Guild; Burbank Art Asn. *Media:* Oil, Clay, Ink, Charcoal. *Mailing Add:* 19319 Van Owen Reseda CA 91335

SIEBER, ROY
EDUCATOR, HISTORIAN
b Shawano, Wis, Apr 28, 23. *Study:* New Sch Social Res, BA, 49; Univ Iowa, MA, 51, PhD, 57. *Pos:* Mem foreign area fel prog, Africa Screening Comt, 59-63; cur primitive art, Ind Univ Fine Arts Mus, 62-; mem primitive art adv comt, Metrop Mus Art; mem joint comt Africa, Am Coun Learned Socs-Social Sci Res Coun, 62-70; trustee, Mus African Art. *Teaching:* From instr to asst prof art hist, Univ Iowa, 50-62; mem fac, Ind Univ, 62-64, prof art hist, 64-74, chmn fine arts dept, 67-70, Rudy Prof Fine Arts, 74-; vis prof, Univ Ghana, 64 & 67; vis prof, Univ Ife, Nigeria, 71; Benedict Distinguished Vis Prof, Carleton Col, 76-77. *Awards:* African-Am Univ Grant, 64; Ind Univ Int Studies Grant, 64 & 67; Nat Endowment for Humanities Sr Fel, 70-71 & 80-81; plus others. *Mem:* African Studies Asn; Col Art Asn Am; Am Asn Univ Prof; Midwest Art Asn (secy, 63). *Res:* African art. *Publ:* Auth, Sculpture of Northern Nigeria, Mus Primitive Art, NY, 61; co-auth, Sculpture of Black Africa, Los Angeles Co Mus Art, 68; auth, African Textiles & Decorative Arts, Mus Mod Art, NY, 72; auth, African Furniture and Household Objects, Am Fedn of Arts, 80. *Mailing Add:* Dept Fine Arts Ind Univ Bloomington IN 47401

SIEBNER, HERBERT
PAINTER, MURALIST
b Stettin, Ger, Apr 16, 25; Can citizen. *Study:* Atelier Max Richter, Stettin, 41-43; Berlin Acad, under Carl Hofer, with Kaus & Schumacher, 46-49. *Work:* Seattle Art Mus; Confedn Art Mus, PEI; Nat Gallery Ottawa; City of West Berlin; Victoria Art Gallery. *Comn:* Sgraffito, Crown House, Victoria, BC, 60; sgraffito-encaustic, Univ Victoria, 65; planetary hist, Mus Victoria, 68; life-frieze, Govt BC, 75. *Exhib:* Int Graphic Expos, Lugano, Switz, 58, Lubljana, Yugoslavia, 59; Can Biennial, Ottawa, 58 & 62; Int Triennial of Xylographia, Carpy, Italy, 69; Int Graphic Exhib, Spain, 71, Italy, 72; retrospective show, Univ Victoria, 79. *Teaching:* Vis prof painting, Univ Wash, 63 & Univ BC, 64, Univ Alta, 65; lectr painting, Univ Victoria, 67 & 69. *Awards:* Can Coun Sr Grant, 62; Guest of Hon, Berlin Acad, 63; Hon Citizen, City of Victoria, BC, 73. *Bibliog:* Anthony Emery (auth), Art of Herbert Siebner, Can Art Mag, 58; Robin Skelton (auth), The man & the vision, Malahat Rev, Univ BC, 71; Creative Canada, Univ Toronto, 72. *Mem:* Union Prof Artists, Ger; Can Group Painters; Soc BC Artists; Royal Can Acad; The Limners. *Media:* Sgraffito, Acrylic & Lithography. *Publ:* Illus, Inscriptions, 67 & Muse Book, 72; auth, Colour, Line & Form, 70; auth, H Siebner, 25 years: Monograph, Univ Victoria, 79; auth, 30 Years of BC Art, Victoria Art Gallery, 84. *Mailing Add:* 270 Meadow Brook Rd Victoria BC V8X 3X3 Canada

SIEG, ROBERT LAWRENCE
SCULPTOR, ENAMELIST
b Cement, Okla. *Study:* Cent State Univ, Okla, BA, 63; Inst Allende, Univ de Guanajuato, MFA, 68. *Work:* Ark Arts Ctr, Little Rock; Okla Art Ctr, Oklahoma City; Mus Art, Univ Okla, Norman; Okla Arts & Humanities Coun Collection, Oklahoma City. *Exhib:* Past Jurors Invitational, Okla Art Ctr, 69; Eight-State Exhib Painting & Sculpture, Okla Art Ctr, 73; Goddard Arts Ctr, Okla, 78; Inter-D Exhib, McAllen Int Mus, Tex; Midwest Biennial Joslyn Art Mus, Omaha, Nebr; Monroe Ann, Masur Mus Art, La; Delta Art Exhib, Ark Art Ctr; Werkstatt Menschen, Okla State Univ, 84. *Teaching:* Asst prof art, ECent Okla State Univ, 66-81. *Awards:* Sculpture Award, 15th Mid-Am,

Nelson Gallery Art, Kansas City, 65; Inter-Am Craft Alliance Award, McAllen Int Mus, Tex, 70; AAC Purchase Awards, Toys Designed by Artists, Ark Art Ctr, 74. *Bibliog:* B J Smith (auth), Features artist, Cimarron Rev, 4/73. *Mem:* Okla Designer Craftsman. *Media:* Wood, Metal. *Mailing Add:* 1017 E Central Blvd Ada OK 74820

SIEGEL, (LEO) DINK
ILLUSTRATOR, CARTOONIST
b Birmingham, Ala. *Study:* Nat Acad Design; Art Students League; Am Sch Art; also with Robert Brackman. *Mem:* Soc Illusr. *Media:* Watercolor, Ink. *Publ:* Illusr, Redbook, Cosmopolitan, Saturday Evening Post, Field & Stream Mag, Good Housekeeping, New Yorker & Playboy. *Mailing Add:* 100 W 57th St New York NY 10019

SIEGMANN, NAOMI RITA
SCULPTOR
b New York, NY, Oct 12, 33. *Study:* Sculpture with Tosis, 63-68; also with Enrique Miralda, 68-70. *Work:* Aldrich Mus Contemp Art, Ridgefield, Conn; Olin F Featherstone Mus, Roswell, NMex; Museo de Arte Moderno, Mexico; Yad Vashem Mem Mus, Jerusalem, Israel; Rotunda Illustrious Men, Panteon Dolores, Mexico. *Comn:* Candelabras, Beth Israel Community Ctr, Mexico, 73; Fuente, bronze, Corp Mexicana de Valores Bursatiles, Mexico, 79; sculpted panel and candelabras, Cuban-Hebrew Community Ctr, Miami, 83; and others. *Exhib:* Aldrich Mus Contemp Art, Ridgefield, 76; Mus Carillo Gil, Mexico, 77; Mus Tecnologia, Mexico, 77; one-man show, Mus Arte Mod, Mexico City, 79; Inst Nacional Belles Artes, 82; Int Exposition Itinerant Traveling Show, 83; and others. *Bibliog:* Berta Taracena (auth), Arte-mundo plural, Tiempo, 8/29/77; Graciela Kartofel (auth), article, Vogue, Mexico, 7/82; article, Los Angeles Times, 11/13/82. *Media:* Wood, Stone. *Mailing Add:* Risco 217 Pedregal de San Angel Delegacion Alvaro Obregon 01900 Mexico 01900 DF Mexico

SIEGRIEST, LUNDY
PAINTER
b Oakland, Calif, Apr 4, 25. *Study:* Calif Col Arts & Crafts, Oakland, cert. *Work:* Whitney Mus Am Art, New York; Denver Art Mus, Colo; Libr Cong, Washington, DC; Oakland Mus. *Exhib:* Third Biennale Sao Paulo, Brazil, 55; Carnegie Inst Int, Pittsburgh, 55; Young Americans Under 35, 58 & Contemporary American Painting, 60, Whitney Mus Am Art; 17 American Painters, Brussels World's Fair, 58. *Teaching:* Instr painting, Acad Art, San Francisco, 51-64, Jr Ctr Art, Oakland, 53-71 & Civic Arts, Walnut Creek, Calif, 64. *Awards:* Albert M Bender Grant, 52; Purchase Awards, Calif Palace of Legion of Honor, 52 & Santa Barbara Mus, 55. *Bibliog:* New talent, Art USA, Art in Am, 57; Contemporary American Painting, Univ Ill, 63. *Media:* Mixed. *Mailing Add:* 479 Cavour St Oakland CA 94618

SIGISMUND, VIOLET M
PAINTER, PRINTMAKER
b New York, NY. *Study:* Art Students League; also with Sidney Laufman & George Grosz. *Exhib:* Butler Inst Am Art, Youngstown, Ohio, 62; group print shows, Albany Inst Arts, 71, Washington Co Mus, Md, 71-73 & Cayuga Mus, 73; one-woman show, Paul Kessler, Provincetown, Mass, 73; Nat Asn Women Artists Traveling Group Oil Show, US, 75-77; Israel & Egypt, 81-82 & Traveling Group Print Show, 79-81; and others. *Awards:* Silver Medal, Knickerbocker Artists, 52; Friend's Award, Silvermine Guild, 60; Sargent Prize, Nat Asn Women Artists, 63. *Mem:* Knickerbocker Artists; Nat Asn Women Artists; Provincetown Art Asn; Artists' Equity Asn (chmn mem, 60-73, mem bd dirs, 81-82). *Media:* Oil, Watercolor; Woodblock, Lithography. *Dealer:* Clinton Seeley Rye Beach NH 03871; Waverly Gallery 103 Waverly Pl New York NY 10011. *Mailing Add:* One Sheridan Sq New York NY 10014

SIGNATURE, CYNTHIA See Schmuckal, Janet Bell

SIHVONEN, OLI
PAINTER
b Brooklyn, NY, Jan 31, 21. *Study:* Art Students League; Black Mt Col, NC. *Work:* Mus Mod Art, Whitney Mus Am Art, New York; Roswell Mus & Art Ctr; Art Inst Chicago; and others. *Comn:* Lobby wall painting, State Agency Bldg, S Mall, Albany, NY, 68; painting, Northwestern Univ, Evanston, Ill, 69. *Exhib:* Geometric Abstraction in America, 62 & Whitney Ann, 63, 65 & 67, Whitney Mus Am Art; The Responsive Eye, Mus Mod Art, New York, 65; 30th Biennial Am Painting, Corcoran Gallery Art, 67; Plus X Minus Today's Half Century, Albright-Knox, Buffalo, NY, 68. *Awards:* Nat Endowment Arts Grants, 67 & 76; Purchase Award, Corcoran Biennial, 67. *Media:* Acrylic, Oil. *Mailing Add:* 245 Grand St New York NY 10002

SIKORA, ZDZISLAW R
PRINTMAKER
b Mannheim, WGer, Sept 10, 52; US citizen. *Study:* Univ Ill, Chicago, BA, 75; Univ Wis, Madison, MFA, 78. *Work:* Mus Grabado, Buenos Aires, Argentina; Honolulu Acad Art; Mus Arts & Sci, Macon, Ga; R J Reynolds Indust, Winston-Salem, NC; Dulin Gallery Art. *Exhib:* Southeast Graphics Invitational, Mint Mus Art, 81; solo exhib, Spirit Sq Art Ctr, Charlotte, NC, 83 & Int Images Ltd, Pittsburgh, Pa, 84; Printmakers in the South 1860-Present, Southern Arts Found, Atlanta, 83-84; three-person exhib, Jane Haslem Gallery, Washington, DC, 84; New Americna Graphics Three, US Info Agency, 84-85. *Collections Arranged:* Wesleyan Int Exhib Prints & Drawings Traveling Exhib, Wesleyan Col, Ga, 80-82. *Teaching:* From instr to asst prof prints & design, Wesleyan Col, Ga, 79-82; asst prof printmaking, Montgomery Col, Md, 82- *Awards:* Purchase Prizes, Fifth Ann Eastern US

Print Exhib, 81, 12th Nat Print & Drawing Exhib, 83 & Sixth Hawaii Nat Print Exhib, 83. *Bibliog:* Tom Dewey II (auth), Gallery Paper, Univ Ala, 81. *Mem:* Col Art Asn; Southern Graphics Coun (treas, 80-82, pres, 82-84); World Print Coun; Los Angeles Printmaking Soc; Philadelphia Print Club. *Media:* Etching. *Dealer:* Jane Haslem Gallery 406 Seventh St NW Washington DC. *Mailing Add:* Art Dept 51 Mannakee St Montgomery Community Col Rockville MD 20850

SILBER, MAURICE
PAINTER, ILLUSTRATOR
b Brooklyn, NY, Apr 12, 22. *Study:* Cooper Union; Art Students League; Empire State Col, Saratoga Springs, NY, 80; Pratt Inst, indust design with Donald Dohner; study with Ed Whitney, Robert E Wood, Tom Hill & John Pike; New York Univ, MA, 83. *Work:* USAF Art Collection & USN Combat Art Collection, Washington, DC; Nat Park Serv, Washington, DC; Marine Mus, Amagansett, NY; Alliance Francaise, Costa Rica; Teatro Nacional, Costa Rica. *Comn:* Philadelphia Naval Shipyard, NACAL Assignment, 72-74 & 80; Eglin AFB, USAF, Fla, 72; San Antonio, Tex, USAF, 73; US Dept Interior, Nat Park Serv, 75; USAF NORAD & USAF Acad, Colorado Springs, 76. *Exhib:* Salmagundi Club, New York, 71-83; Teatro Nacional, San Jose, Costa Rica, 77-83; Knickerbocker Artists Ann, 78-83; Gallery 80, 83; St Johns Univ, 83; and many others. *Awards:* First Prize & Spec Award, Am Inst, Westinghouse, New York World's Fair, 39; Anco Award, Knickerbocker Artists, 79; and others. *Bibliog:* Air Force Art, Bolling Beam, Morkap Pub Co, 10/73; Air Force Art, Seacoast Flyer, Star Press, Maine, 9/74; AFSA, US Air Force, Impressions at Eglin, 12/74. *Mem:* Salmagundi Club (chmn admis, 72-74); Soc Illusrs; Nat Art League; Artists Equity of New York; Knickerbocker Artists of NY. *Media:* Watercolor; All Media. *Publ:* Auth & illusr, The Water Color Page, Am Artist, 6/72. *Mailing Add:* 183-07 69th Ave Fresh Meadows NY 11365

SILBERMAN, ARTHUR
LIBRARY DIRECTOR, WRITER
b Antwerp, Belgium, Jan 8, 29; US citizen. *Collections Arranged:* From Pictographs to Jerome Tiger Traveling Educ Exhib, 68-72, American Indian Painting Traveling Educ Exhib, 72-75 & 100 Years Native American Painting (auth, catalog), 78, Okla Mus Art, Oklahoma City. *Pos:* Dir, Native Am Painting Ref Libr, Oklahoma City, 75-; hon cur, Native Am Painting, Okla Hist Soc Mus, Oklahoma City, 76-; guest cur, Okla Mus Art, Oklahoma City, 78; consult, Okla TV Authority, 78, WABC-TV, New York, 79, Am Indian Inst, Univ Okla, Norman, 80 & Mus Am Indian, New York, 81. *Awards:* Oklahoma City Univ Distinguished Native Am Arts Award, 81. *Res:* All phases of history and development of Native American painting. *Interests:* To increase the appreciation of Native American painting by making reference material available to educators, writers, publishers and museums; to increase public awareness through lectures,, publications and exhibits. *Publ:* Auth, Tiger, 71 & Early Kiowa Art, 73, Okla Today Mag; auth, Animals in Indian Art (sound slides), State Okla Dept Libr, 73. *Mailing Add:* Box 32434 Oklahoma City OK 73123

SILBERSTEIN-STORFER, MURIEL ROSOFF
INSTRUCTOR, PAINTER
b Brooklyn, NY. *Study:* Carnegie Inst Technol, BFA; Philadelphia Mus Art, with Hobson Pitman; Inst Mod Art, with Victor D'Amico, Donald Stacy & Jane Bland. *Comn:* Prog drawings, Philadelphia Symphony Orch Children's Concerts, 49; murals & other projs, Mt Sinai Hosp & Philadelphia Psychiat Hosp. *Exhib:* Jewish Community Ctr Group Show, 71-72; one-woman shows, Panoras Gallery, New York, 72, Pacem in Terris Gallery, New York, 75 & Gallery 84, 78 & 83; Pacem in Terris Gallery, New York, 76-77. *Pos:* Assoc tech dir & scene designer, Pittsburgh Playhouse, 44-46; interior display designer, var Pittsburgh Dept Stores, 46-47; art educ consult, Staten Island Ment Health Schs, Head Start, Staten Island Community Col & others. *Teaching:* Instr, Inst Mod Art, Mus Mod Art, New York, 63; Int Playgroups Art Workshops, New York, 70-; Staten Island Community Col, 70-, Metrop Mus Art, currently & Napeague Inst Art, currently; guest lectr art educ, var cols & community groups, New York, 67- *Awards:* Woman of Achievement, Staten Island Advan, 67; Achievement Award, Lambda Kappa Mu Sorority. *Mem:* New York Art Comn (comnr, 70-); Metrop Mus Art (trustee, 71-77 & emer trustee, 77-); Staten Island Coun Arts; Art Comn City New York (vpres, currently); Snug Harbor Cult Ctr (trustee); and others. *Media:* Assemblage, Collage. *Res:* Art education; community arts projects. *Publ:* Auth, pamphlet for parent-child workshops, Metrop Mus Art, New York; auth, Doing Art Together, Simon & Schuster, 82. *Mailing Add:* 1200 Broadway New York NY 10001

SILER, TODD (LAEL)
PAINTER, SCULPTOR
b Long Island, NY, Aug 21, 53. *Study:* Smith Col, with Leonard Baskin, 73-74; Bowdoin Col, BA(cum laude), 75; Mass Inst Technol, with Otto Piene, MS(visual studies), 80. *Work:* Denver Art Mus. *Comn:* Mural & sculptures, comn by Larry Merchant, New York & Los Angeles, 73; sculpture, comn by Ralph Peterson, St Peters Lutheran Church, New York, 74. *Exhib:* Reality of Illusion, Denver Art Mus & traveling, 79-81; Schemes: A Decade of Installation Drawings, Mus D'Art Contemp, Montreal & traveling, 81; solo exhibs, Inquiries Into the Biomirror, 81 & Thoughts, Thought Assemblies, 83, Ronald Feldman Fine Arts, New York; Revolutions Per Minute (The Art Record), Tate Gallery & traveling, 82; Alea(s), Mus D'Art Mod, Paris, 82. *Pos:* Res fel, Ctr Adv Visual Studies, 81-; co-pres & consult, United Sciences & Arts, 83- *Teaching:* Instr visual design, Mass Inst Technol, 82-83. *Awards:* Thomas J Watson Fel to Paris, IBM, 75-76; Coun Arts Award, Mass Inst Technol, 79 & 83. *Bibliog:* Matha Fleming (auth), Todd Siler, Galerie France

Morin, Vanguard Mag, 12/81-1/82; Michael Schrage (auth), Cerebreactors, Omni Mag, 10/82; Ellen Handy (auth), article, Arts Mag, 11/83. *Media:* All. *Publ:* Auth, Cerebreactors, private publ, 81; illusr, Gates of freedom: A Passover Haggadah, New Star Press, 82; auth, The Biomirror, pvt publ, 83. *Dealer:* Ronald Feldman Fine Arts Inc 31 Mercer St New York NY 10013. *Mailing Add:* Ctr Advan Visual Studies Mass Inst Technol Cambridge MA 02139

SILINS, JANIS
PAINTER, HISTORIAN
b Riga, Latvia, June 1, 1896; US citizen. *Study:* Univ Moscow; Riga Univ, MA & PhD; Univ Stockholm; Univ Marburg; Art Sch Ilya Mashkov, Moscow; Art Sch Kazan. *Work:* Art Mus Jelgava, Latvia; and others. *Exhib:* One-man shows, Würzburg, Ger, 46 & Yonkers, NY, 68 & 69; Exhib Artists in Exile, Stuttgart, Ger, 48; Latvian Exhib Arts & Crafts, Boston, 64; Latvian Artist Group New York, 67; and others. *Collections Arranged:* Hugh Gowan Miller Collection Paintings, Norfolk Mus, Va, 55; Arts of Norway, Morse Art Gallery, Winter Park, Fla & Tour, 58; plus many others. *Pos:* Dir art mus, Riga Univ, 41-44; art consult, Norfolk Mus, 55-; exec dir, Morse Gallery Art, 56-60. *Teaching:* Instr art hist, Riga Univ & Latvian Acad Art, 31-44, Univ Wurzburg, 46-51 & Rollins Col, 56-63. *Awards:* Order of Three Stars, Govt Latvia, 36; Kristian Baron Award, Riga Univ, 37; Award, Cult Found Am Latvian Asn, 80. *Bibliog:* L Liberts (auth), article, 46 & A Annus (auth), Seeking for beauty & truth, 66, Laiks; article, Latvian Art Mag, 4/78 & 1/79; and others. *Mem:* Latvian Artist Group New York; Sarasota Art Asn; Latvian Humanities & Social Sci Asn, New York; Latvian-Am Asn Univ Prof & Instrs; Am Asn Univ Prof. *Media:* Oil, Watercolor. *Res:* Basic problems of art philosophy, especially ontology of art; principles of modern art; Latvian art. *Publ:* Auth, Laudolf Liberts, Painter & Stage Designer, 42; auth, Janis Gailis, a Latvian Landscape Painter, 48; auth, article, Images & Ideas, 64; auth, Latvian Art, 1800-1914, 2 Vols, 80; auth, Martin Krumins, A landscape painter, 81; and others. *Mailing Add:* 426 15th Ave NE St Petersburg FL 33704

SILKOTCH, MARY ELLEN
PAINTER
b New York, NY, Sept 12, 11. *Study:* Van Emburgh Sch Art; also with Jonas Lie, Sigismund Ivanowski & Dudley Gloyne, summers. *Work:* In pvt collections. *Exhib:* Nat Acad Women Artists; Montclair Art Mus, NJ; Am Artists Prof League; Atlantic City Art Ctr; Irvington Mus & Art Asn; and others. *Pos:* Vpres, Trailside Mus Arts Ctr, NJ, 66-67; vpres, Academic Artists, 67-69. *Teaching:* Instr art, Van Emburgh Sch, Plainfield, 44-64; instr art, Adult Educ, Dunellen, NJ, 48-57; instr art, Bound Brook Adult Educ, 50-57; instr art, North Plainfield, 51-54. *Awards:* Prizes, Am Artists Prof League, Plainfield Art Asn & East Orange, NJ; and others. *Mem:* Nat Asn Women Artists; Plainfield Art Asn; Am Artist Prof League; Artists Equity Asn; Westfield Art Asn. *Dealer:* Jaro Art Gallery 955 Madison Ave New York NY 10021. *Mailing Add:* 60780 Coyote Canyon Box 237C Star Route Anza CA 92306

SILLS, THOMAS ALBERT
PAINTER
b Castalia, NC, Aug 20, 14. *Work:* Whitney Mus Am Art, Metrop Mus Art, Mus Mod Art & Chase Manhattan Collection, New York; Sheldon Mem Gallery, Lincoln, Nebr; and many others. *Exhib:* Wilson Col, Chambersberg, Pa, 68; Student Ctr Art Gallery, Brooklyn Col, NY, 69; New American Painting & Sculpture, The First Generation, Mus Mod Art, New York, 69; Afro-Am Artists Exhib, Mus Philadelphia Civic Ctr, Pa, 69; Mt Holyoke Col, South Hadley, Mass, 69; and other group & one-man exhibs. *Awards:* William & Norma Copley Found Award, 57. *Mailing Add:* 240 W 11th St New York NY 10014

SILVER, LARRY ARNOLD
CURATOR, HISTORIAN
b Los Angeles, Calif, Oct 14, 47. *Study:* Univ Chicago, BA, 69; Harvard Univ, MA, 71, PhD, 74. *Pos:* vis cur, St Louis Art Mus, 81-82; vis res cur, Art Inst Chicago, 81-84. *Teaching:* Asst prof Medieval and Renaissance art, Univ Calif, Berkeley, 74-79; assoc prof Medieval, Renaissance & Baroque art & chmn dept, Northwestern Univ, 79- *Awards:* Porter Prize, Col Art Asn, 75. *Mem:* Col Art Asn; Renaissance Soc Am; Soc Values in Higher Educ. *Res:* Painting and graphics in northern Europe, 15th and 16th century. *Publ:* Auth, The Sin of Moses: Comments on the early Reformation ... by Lucas van Leyden, Art Bulletin, 73; coauth, Carnal Knowledge: Late engravings of Lucas van Leyden, Nederlands Kunst, 78; coauth, Flemish and Dutch Paintings (catalog), Ringling Mus, 80; auth, Early Northern European Paintings (catalog), St Louis Art Mus, 82; auth, Forest primeval: Albrecht Altdorfer and ... landscape, Simiolus, 83. *Mailing Add:* Dept Art Hist 254 Kresge Hall Northwestern Univ Evanston IL 60201

SILVER, PAT
DRAFTSMAN, ILLUSTRATOR
b San Francisco, Calif, June 6, 22. *Work:* Town Los Altos Hills; City Menlo Park, Calif. *Comn:* Illus poetry bk, St Mary's Col Press, Winona, Wis, 73. *Exhib:* 5th & 8th Ann Hortt Mem Exhib, 63 & 66 & 3rd Ann Drawing Exhib, 67, Ft Lauderdale Mus Art, Fla; Helen Euphrat De Anza Col Graphics Regional Exhib, Cupertino, Calif, 72; 5th & 7th Ann Pastel Exhib, Pastel Soc Am, Nat Arts Club, Gramercy Park, NY. *Pos:* Owner, Viewpoints Art Gallery, Los Altos, 73-80. *Awards:* First Award Drawing, 37th Ann, Fla Fedn Art, 63; Cert Award, Graphics Arts Awards Competition, Printing Indust Am, 74; First Award, Soc Western Artists, 76. *Mem:* Pastel Soc Am; Soc Western Artists; Palo Alto Art Club. *Media:* Charcoal, Pastel; Etching, Drypoint. *Mailing Add:* 657 Knoll Dr San Carlos CA 94070

SILVER, RAWLEY A
EDUCATOR, PAINTER

b New York, NY. *Study:* Cornell Univ, BA, 39; Art Students League, with George Grosz, 48, 50; Columbia Univ, MA(fine arts educ), 64, EdD(fine arts educ), 66. *Exhib:* Solo & group, Mamaroneck Artists Guild Ann, NY, 55-; Hudson River Mus Invitational, Yonkers, NY, 76. *Collections Arranged:* Shout in Silence (auth, catalog), 69-77 & Art as Language (auth, catalog), 79-82, Smithsonian Inst Traveling Exhib. *Teaching:* Art, 61-73; adj assoc res prof art therapy, Col New Rochelle Grad Sch, 74-81. *Awards:* Biennial Award Res, Am Art Therapy Asn, 76 & 80; Res Grants, US Off Educ, Nat Inst Educ & NY State Dept Educ. *Bibliog:* Martin Engel (auth), Review of the month, Rehabilitation Lit, 10/79; Felice W Cohen (auth), article, Arts in Psychotherapy, Vol 7, No 3, 80; Kristen Vilstrup (auth), article, Am J Art Therapy, Vol 22, No 2, 83. *Mem:* Hon life mem Am Art Therapy Asn; Nat Asn Women Artists; Mamaroneck Artists Guild; Artists Equity. *Media:* Watercolor, Oils. *Res:* Developing and assessing cognitive and creative skills nonverbally through drawing. *Publ:* Auth, Demonstration Project in Art Education for Deaf, US Off Educ, Dept Health, Educ & Welfare, 67; auth, Cognitive Skills Development Through Art Experiences, Urban Educ Proj Report, New York, 73; auth, Developing Cognitive and Creative Skills Through Art, Univ Park Press, 78; auth, Stimulus Drawings and Techniques in Therapy, Development, and Assessment, Trillium Bks, 82; auth, Silver Drawing Test of Cognitive and Creative Skills, Spec Child Publ, 83. *Mailing Add:* 1600 Harrison Ave Suite 105A Mamaroneck NY 10543

SILVER, THOMAS C
SCULPTOR, EDUCATOR

b Salem, Ore, May 27, 42. *Study:* San Francisco Art Inst, with Joan Brown, 60-61; Calif State Col, Long Beach, BA, 66; Univ Kans, with Elden Tefft, MFA. *Work:* De Witt Gallery, Hope Col, Holland, Mich; Anderson Gallery, Richmond, Va; Va Mus of Fine Arts, Richmond. *Exhib:* Traveling Exhib of the Americas, Oakland Mus, Calif, 63-65 & 65-67; A, Craftsmen Coun, Mus West, 65; New Sculpture, Corcoran Gallery of Art, Washington, DC, 70; Traveling Sculpture Exhib, Va Mus of Fine Arts, 71-73; Henri Gallery, Washington, DC, 71; Va Mus of Fine Arts, 72; May Show, Cleveland Mus of Art, Ohio, 72-77; Contemp Relig Imagery in Am Art, Ringling Mus of Art, Sarasota, Fla, 74. *Teaching:* Instr sculpture, Va Commonwealth Univ, 65-72; assoc prof sculpture, Cleveland State Univ, Ohio, 72-82. *Awards:* Century 21 Ctr Merit Award, 63; three First Prizes, Kans Designers & Craftsmen Exhib, 67; Cert of Distinction, Va Artists Show, Va Mus Fine Arts, 69 & 71. *Bibliog:* Alan R Meisec (auth), Exhibitions, Craft Horizon, 63; La Mar Harrington (auth), First annual Western Craft Council, Craft Horizon, 64. *Mem:* New Organization Visual Arts, Cleveland. *Media:* Bronze. *Mailing Add:* 3270 Hyde Park Cleveland Heights OH 44118

SILVERBERG, ELLEN RUTH
PAINTER, DEALER

b New York, NY, Mar 7, 47. *Study:* Art Students League; Cooper Union, BFA, 67. *Pos:* Dir, Art Gallery Studio 53 Ltd, New York, currently. *Specialty:* Contemporary limited edition graphics and oils, specializing in Simbari, Delacroix, Rockwell, Boulanger, Gorman, Wyeth & Erte. *Mailing Add:* c/o Studio 53 424 Park Ave New York NY 10022

SILVERMAN, BURTON PHILIP
PAINTER, ILLUSTRATOR

b Brooklyn, NY, June 11, 28. *Study:* Pratt Inst; Art Students League, 46-49; Columbia Univ, BA, 49. *Work:* Brooklyn Mus; Philadelphia Mus Art; Anchorage Mus Art, Alaska; Nat Mus Am Art; Parrish Mus Art, Southampton, NY. *Exhib:* Pa Acad Art Ann, Philadelphia, 49; Butler Inst Am Art Ann, Ohio, 54-70, 71, 74, 76, 79 & 82; Nat Acad Design, 59-83; Pa State Mus of Art, 76; Portsmouth Mus of Art, WVa, 76, 78, 80 & 82; Am Watercolor Soc, 78-80; Artists of America, Colo Hist Soc, Denver, 81 & 82. *Teaching:* Instr drawing & painting, Sch Visual Arts, New York, 64-67. *Awards:* Benjamin Altman Figure Prize, Nat Acad Design, New York, 69; Purchase Prize, Am Drawings II, Portsmouth, WVa, 79 & 83; Gold Medal, Am Watercolor Soc, 79; and others. *Bibliog:* Fredrick Whitaker (auth), Four realists, 10/64, Elizabeth Case (auth), Burton Silverman captures the moment, 6/71 & Pat Van Gelder (auth), Drawing the human figure, an interview with Burt Silverman, 7/81, Am Artist Mag; and others. *Mem:* Am Watercolor Soc; academician Nat Acad Design; Graphic Artists Guild. *Media:* Multimedia. *Publ:* Auth, Homage to Thomas Eakins, 67 & Art for Pablo Picasso's Sake, 68, Book World; auth, A Portfolio of Drawings, 68; auth, Painting People, Watson-Guptill, 77; auth, Breaking the Rules of Watercolor, Watson-Guptill, 83; and others. *Dealer:* Sindin Galleries 1035 Madison Ave New York NY 10021; Capricorn Galleries 4849 Rugby Ave Bethesda MD 20014. *Mailing Add:* 324 W 71st St New York NY 10023

SILVERMAN, RONALD H
EDUCATOR, WRITER

b Cleveland, Ohio, Aug 2, 26. *Study:* Univ Calif, Los Angeles, BA, 52; Los Angeles State Col, MA, 55; Stanford Univ, EdD, 62. *Pos:* Consult, Nat Assessment Educ Progress Art; assoc dir, Getty Inst Educators Visual Arts. *Teaching:* Prof art, Calif State Univ, Los Angeles, 55- *Awards:* Outstanding Prof Award, Calif State Univ, Los Angeles, 78; Award, Nat Art Educ Asn, 81. *Mem:* Nat Art Educ Asn; Am Educ Res Asn; Calif Art Educ Asn; and others. *Publ:* Auth, Spectrum of Music, Macmillan, 74; auth, Goals and roles in art education of children, In: The Arts, Human Development and Education, McCutchan, 76; auth, A comprehensive model for teaching art, In: Report of the NAEA Commission on Art Education, Nat Art Educ Asn, 77; ed, Art, Education and the World of Work, Nat Art Educ Asn, 80; auth, Learning About Art, Romar, 82. *Mailing Add:* Art Dept Calif State Univ Los Angeles CA 90032

SILVERMAN, SHERLEY C
PAINTER, SCULPTOR

b Maywood, Ill, Jan 20, 09. *Study:* Univ Ill; Chicago Acad Fine Arts; Frederick Grant; worked in Pietrasanta, Italy, 63-65; also with John Kearney & Ralph Bormacher. *Work:* B'nai B'rith Exhib Hall, Washington, DC; also in many nat & int collections, as well as in numerous pvt collections, notably that of Mr & Mrs Harold Green, Palm Springs, Calif. *Comn:* Welded steel sculpture, comn by Hon Philip Klutznick; Ode to Eleanor (painting), comn by Mrs Nelson Hartstone, Palm Beach; Mother & Child, comn by Mr & Mrs Richard Tucker. *Exhib:* Patronat Premi Int, DiBuix Joan Miro, Barcelona, Spain; UNESCO; Int Biennale Della Regioni, Italy; Tournoi Int Des Beaux Arts, France; Int Contemp Exhib, Rome, Italy; among many others. *Pos:* Hon past pres, Mid-Am Art Asn, Chicago, 68-70. *Teaching:* Pvt art classes, 60- *Awards:* Gold Medal of Recognition & Bronze Plaque, La Scala Gallery, Florence, Italy; Int Medal of Honor, Int Centro Studi E Scambi; Honoris Causa Silver Medal, Acad Int, Tommaso, Campanella. *Mem:* US Commite Int Centro Studi E Scambi; Int Arts Guild (comdr); Acad Int Leonardo Da Vinci; Acad Int, Tommaso, Campanella. *Mailing Add:* 9240 W Bay Harbor Dr Bay Harbor Islands FL 33154

SILVERTOOTH, DENNIS CARL
SCULPTOR

b Killeen, Tex, Aug 20, 57. *Study:* Corpus Christi Community Art Ctr, with Maurice Schmidt & Ann Armstrong, 74. *Exhib:* American Cowboy: Fact & Fiction, Eastman Kodak, New York, 75; Tex Art Classic, Tarrant Co Convention Ctr, Ft Worth, 76-79; Shidoni Summer Sculpture Show, Shidoni Foundry & Gallery, Santa Fe, NMex, 77-81; Philbrook Presents Sculpture, Philbrook Mus, Tulsa, Okla, 78; Midland Col Sculpture Show, Tex, 78-81; and others. *Awards:* Best Sculpture, Art About Town, Dallas Crippled Childrens Soc, 77; Best Sculpture, 34th Ann American Indian Artist Exhib, Philbrook Mus, Okla, 79; Artist of the Year, Santa Fean Mag, 80. *Bibliog:* Donn Puca (auth), A young artist working magic, Southwest Art Collector, 12/79; Marion Love (auth), article, Santa Fean Mag, 8/80; Joseph Cain (auth), article, Art Voices/South, 9-10/80. *Media:* Bronze, Plaster. *Mailing Add:* 3014 Pimlico Corpus Christi TX 78418

SIMEL, ELAINE
PRINTMAKER, PAINTER

b New York, NY. *Study:* High Sch Music & Art, New York; Black Mountain Col, NC; Syracuse Univ, NY, BFA; studied with Josef Albers, Robert Motherwell, Harry Sternberg & Ruth Leaf. *Work:* De Cordova & Dana Mus, Lincoln, Mass; Publ Clearing House, Port Washington, NY; Hunt Inst Botanical Doc, Pittsburgh; Reader's Digest, New York. *Exhib:* Huntington Twp Art League, Heckscher Mus, NY, 77; Soc Am Graphic Artists, Am Art Asn Gallery, New York, 77; Boston Printmakers 29th Nat Exhib, De Cordova & Dana Mus, 77; Audubon Artists 35th Ann Exhib, Nat Acad Galleries, New York, 77; and many others. *Awards:* John Carl Georgi Mem Prize, Nat Asn Women Artists, 76. *Bibliog:* Malcolm Preston (auth), Newsday, 4/75; David Shirey (auth), Artistic Cooperation, NY Times, 3/76; Malcolm Preston (auth), article, Newsday, 7/77. *Mem:* Nat Asn Women Artists; Graphic Arts Coun NY; Soc of Am Graphic Artists. *Media:* Etching; Oil. *Publ:* Contribr, Ruth Leaf's Printmaking Techniques, Watson-Guptill, 76. *Dealer:* Assoc Am Artists 663 Fifth Ave New York NY 10022. *Mailing Add:* 49 Pond Rd Great Neck NY 11024

SIMKIN, PHILLIPS M
SCULPTOR

b Philadelphia, Pa, Jan 19, 44. *Study:* Tyler Art Sch, Temple Univ, BFA; Cornell Univ, MFA; Univ Pa, post grad fel. *Comn:* Sculpture, Pub Ctr for Collection & Dissemination of Secrets, Inst Contemp Art, Univ Pa, 73; Displacement Proj I (with Doris Olafson), Inst Contemp Art, Boston, 74; Displacement Proj II (with Doris Olafson), Philadelphia Mus Art, 74; Artpark (with Thom Farmer), Lewiston State Arts Park, New York, 75. *Exhib:* Displacement Proj II-a Public Event, Philadelphia, 74; Commodity Exchange, Human Puzzle, Lewiston, NY, 75; Choices Maze, Inst Art & Urban Resources, PS1, New York, 76; Project Looking Glass, Three Centuries of Am Art exhib, Philadelphia Mus of Art, 76; Proj--Is There Anything Else You Want to Tell Me?, Brooklyn Mus, 77; solo proj, Pa Acad of Fine Arts, Philadelphia, 78; Sculpture Performance Comn, Nat Fine Arts Comt, XIII Winter Olympics, Lake Placid, NY, 80; and others. *Pos:* Art dir, Earthweek Inc, Philadelphia, 71-73; co-dir (with John Formicola), The Luncheonette Inc Artist Ctr, Philadelphia, 75; adv bd mem, Dept Community Programs, Philadelphia Art Mus, 77-82. *Teaching:* Assoc prof studio fine arts, York Col, City Univ New York, 73-; adj asst prof studio fine arts, Moore Col Art, Philadelphia, 73-; artist-in-residence, Brooklyn Mus, 77. *Awards:* Nat Endowment Arts Artist Fel, 75-76; Creative Artists Pub Serv Sculpture Grant, New York, 76; Artist Fel Grant, Pa State Coun Arts, 80. *Mailing Add:* c/o Marian Locks Gallery 1524 Walnut St Philadelphia PA 19105

SIMMONS, CLEDA MARIE
PAINTER, GRAPHIC ARTIST

b Douglas, Wyo, June 24, 27. *Study:* Univ NMex, Albuquerque, with Ralph Douglas & Raymond Jonson; studied seven yrs in Madrid, Spain. *Work:* Pan Am Gallery, San Antonio, Tex. *Exhib:* US Info Serv Traveling Show, Mus Mod Art, Paris & Madrid, 53; two-woman show, Jonson Gallery, Univ NMex, 56; Detroit Art Inst, 64; Denver Mus, 70; EQUUS, Denver, Colo, 77; RI Sch Design, Providence, 81; and others. *Pos:* Graphic artist, ESA Women Int, Loveland, Colo, 69-70, art ed, 70-73, art dir, 73-77, ed Jonquil Mag, assoc ed & art dir, 77-78. *Awards:* Purchase Award, Ateneo de Belles Artes, Madrid, Spain, 54. *Bibliog:* Mary Hagen (auth), The challenge of art, Southwest Art Mag, 1/77; article in Int Soc Artists Communicator, 7-8/78. *Mem:* Boston

Visual Arts Union; Copley Soc Boston; and others. *Media:* Mixed. *Publ:* Illusr, Our Government, 69; coauth, Art of Editorship, ESA Women Int, 72; illusr, Beneath the Peaks, ESA Women Int, 73; illusr, This is Loveland, League of Women Voters, 76. *Dealer:* Gay D'Amaro 21 Maplewood Medfield MA 02052. *Mailing Add:* 20939 De Mina St Woodland Hills CA 91367

SIMMONS, JOHN HERBERT
EDUCATOR, HISTORIAN
b Springfield, Mo, Mar 23, 38. *Study:* Drury Col, BA, 60; Univ Ark, MA, 73; Univ Rome, DA, 78. *Collections Arranged:* All cataloged, Ernest Trova, Work by Contemp Sculptor, 71, Classical Greek Ceramics, Early Movement Through Gallo Rome, 75, Sung Dynasty Ceramics, Chinese Ceramics, 75, Egyptian Art, Works from the Duncan Collection, 78, Chinese Art, Neolithic Through Ching Dynasty, 79 & Alice Neel, 80. *Pos:* Chmn bd trustees, Springfield Art Mus, Mo, 79-80. *Teaching:* Prof & chmn art dept, Drury Col, 69- *Mem:* Col Art Asn; Am Inst Archaeol; assoc Am Inst Archit. *Res:* Chinese art with papers published and read on Ku kai chih; also early printing in Europe. *Interests:* Chinese art, especially ceramics, and early European printed books. *Publ:* Auth, Ku kai chih, an Early Chinese Printer, 73, Ching-te-Chan, 74 & The Loud Brothers of Philadelphia, 75, Gallery. *Mailing Add:* Tunis/Peace Corp Dept State Washington DC 20520

SIMMONS, JULIE LUTZ
PAINTER, COLLAGE ARTIST
b San Diego, Calif. *Study:* Murray State Univ, BS, 64; with Miles Batt, Ed Betts, Virginia Corb, Maxine Masterfield, Barbara Nechic & Charles Reid; Southeast Mo State Univ. *Work:* Eye Ctr Fla, Ft Myers; Commerce Bank, Poplar Bluff, Mo; Tri-Co Bank, Sikeston, Mo; Med Assoc, Memphis; Hickman Painting Co, Dallas. *Comn:* Watercolors, comn by Gerald A Bowie, West Point, Ga, 82, Fred Brauchle, Charlotte, Tex, 82, Edwin Noffel, Cape Girardeau, Mo, 83, John Virant, Chesterfield, Mo, 83 & Elmer K Oberhellman Inc, St Louis, 84. *Exhib:* Watercolor Oklahoma, House Gallery, Oklahoma City, 80, 81 & 83; Kans Watercolor Soc, Wichita Art Mus, 82 & 83; Midwest Watercolor Soc Seventh Ann Exhib, Davenport Art Gallery, Iowa, 83; Rocky Mountain Nat Watermedia Exhib, Foothills Art Ctr, Golden, Colo, 83; Ga Watercolor Soc Fourth Exhib, Mem Arts Ctr, Atlanta, 83 & 84. *Teaching:* Studio workshops watercolor, Charleston, Mo, 70- *Awards:* House of Bamboo Award, Cent South Art Exhib, 81; Gallery Ellington, Kans Watercolor Soc, 82; First Prize, Midwest Watercolor Soc Seventh Ann Exhib, 83. *Mem:* Assoc, Watercolor Soc, Am & Nat; Watercolor Soc, Midwest, Southern & Ky. *Media:* Watercolor; Collage. *Mailing Add:* Rt 1 Box 10 Charleston MO 63834

SIMMONS, LAURIE
PHOTOGRAPHER
b New York, NY, Oct 3, 49. *Study:* Tyler Sch Art, Temple Univ, BFA, 71. *Exhib:* Invented Images, Univ Calif Art Mus, Santa Barbara, 80; Color Photog Five New Views, Marlborough Gallery, New York, 81; Figures, Forms, Expressions, Albright-Knox Art Gallery, Buffalo, NY, 81; Body Language-- Figurative Aspects of Recent Art, Hayden Gallery, Mass Inst Technol, Boston, 81; Five Int Biennale, Wiener Secession, Vienna, Austria, 81; and others. *Bibliog:* Andy Grundberg (auth), Water buoyed, Soho News, 5/81; Michael R Klein (auth), article, Arts Mag, 5/81; Abigail Solomon Gadeau (auth), Conventional Pictures, Print Collectors Newsletter, 11/81. *Dealer:* Metro Pictures 169 Mercer New York NY 10012. *Mailing Add:* 547 Broadway New York NY 10012

SIMMONS, PERCY SLOTSKY
COLLECTOR
b London, Eng, Dec 27, 06; US citizen. *Study:* City of London Col, 27-29. *Collections Arranged:* Prints and Master Drawings, Indianapolis Collectors, Indianapolis Mus Art, 79. *Pos:* Mem exec bd, Eureka Col Art Coun, Ill, currently; co-founder, Print & Drawing Soc, Indianapolis Mus Art, Ind. *Mem:* Col Art Asn Am; Master Drawings Asn. *Collection:* Old master drawings and prints, etchings of seventeenth and eighteenth centuries and Chiascuro prints of sixteenth, seventeenth and eighteenth centuries. *Mailing Add:* 5602 Central Ave Indianapolis IN 46220

SIMON, BERNARD
SCULPTOR, INSTRUCTOR
b Russia, Jan 6, 1896. *Study:* Educ Alliance & Art Workshop, New York. *Work:* Everson Mus, Syracuse, NY; Heritage Mus, Provincetown, Mass; Fogg Mus, Boston; Hirshhorn Collection; Fairleigh Dickenson Univ; also in pvt collections. *Exhib:* Silvermine Guild Art; Hyannis Art Asn; Am Soc Contemp Artists; plus others; Barnum & Bailey Mus, Sarasota, Fla; Knickerbocker Artists, New York; Sculptors League, New York. *Teaching:* Instr, Mus Mod Art, New York, New Sch Social Res & Bayonne Art Ctr, currently. *Awards:* Knickerbocker Artists Prize; Am Soc Contemp Artists Prize; Silvermine Guild Artists Prize. *Mem:* Silvermine Guild Arts; Brooklyn Soc Artists; Knickerbocker Artists; Audubon Artists; Artist Equity. *Media:* Marble, Wood. *Dealer:* Naples Gallery Naples FL; Rauschbach Gallery 1007 Kane Concourse Miami FL 33154. *Mailing Add:* 490 West End Ave New York NY 10024

SIMON, DAVID L
HISTORIAN, EDUCATOR
b Lawrence, Mass, June 14, 46. *Study:* Boston Univ, BA, 69, MA, 71; Courtauld Inst Art, Univ London, PhD, 77. *Teaching:* Asst & assoc prof art, State Univ NY Col, Cortland, 74-81; chmn & Ellerton M Jette prof art, Colby Col, 81- *Awards:* Am Coun Learned Soc Travel Grant, 78; US-Spanish Comt Educ & Cult Affairs Res Fel, 78-79; Mellon Found Fel, Metrop Mus Art,

80-81. *Mem:* Col Art Asn; Int Ctr Medieval Art. *Res:* Romanesque sculpture. *Publ:* Auth, Daniel and Habakkuk in Aragon, J Brit Archaeol Asn, 75; auth, Roland, the Moor and the Pilgrim and Spanish Romanesque sculpture, Acta, 75; auth, Still more by the Cabestany master, Burlington Mag, 79; auth, Le Sarcophage de Dona Sanch a Jaca, 79 & L'Art Roman, Source de L'Art Roman, 80, Cahiers St-Michel Cuxa. *Mailing Add:* Art Dept Colby Col Waterville ME 04901

SIMON, HELENE
SCULPTOR
b Bagdad, Iraq; US citizen. *Study:* Bedford Col, London; Am Univ, Beirut, Lebanon; Islamic Art with Mary Devonshire, Cairo, Egypt; painting with Anthony Toney & Jacob Lawrence; New Sch, sculpture with Lorrie Goulet. *Work:* Phoenix Art Mus, Ariz; Jewish Mus, New York; Hirshhorn Mus, Washington, DC; NY Univ Art Collection, New York; Fordham Univ Art Collection, Bronx; and others. *Exhib:* One-man shows, Bodley Gallery, New York, 71 & 73, Fordham Univ, 75 & Haber Theodore Gallery, 80; Sculptors 9, Caravan House, New York, 71; Stable Gallery, Scottsdale, Ariz, 73; Habib Anavian Gallery, 81-83. *Bibliog:* Andrea Mikotajuk (auth), In the galleries, 12/71 & 1/72 & Gordon Brown (auth), In the galleries, 12/73, Arts Mag. *Media:* Marble, Bronze. *Mailing Add:* 200 E 74th St New York NY 10021

SIMON, HERBERT BERNHEIMER
SCULPTOR, COLLAGE ARTIST
b Nashville, Tenn, Sept 20, 27. *Study:* Brooklyn Mus Art Sch; Hans Hofmann Studio, NY; Colorado Springs Fine Art Ctr; Hunter Col, study with Robert Motherwell; NY Univ, BA & MA, study with Philip Guston. *Work:* Everhart Mus, Scranton, Pa; Lehigh Univ, Bethlehem, Pa. *Comn:* Two Modules (sculpture), Coal St Park, Wilkes-Barre, Pa, 77; Facets (aluminum relief), Wilkes Col, Wilkes-Barre, Pa, 77. *Exhib:* Drawings USA, Mus Mod Art, New York, 55; one-man shows, Phoenix Gallery, NY, 64 & 66 & Sordoni Art Gallery, Wilkes-Barre, Pa, 74-80; William Penn Mus, Harrisburg, Pa, 72 & 80; Regional Exhib, Everhart Mus, Scranton, Pa, 76; Fed Hall, New York, 82; and others. *Teaching:* Instr painting & drawing, Sch Design, NC State Col, Raleigh, 56-58; assoc prof sculpture & 3-D design, Wilkes Col, Wilkes-Barre, Pa, 69- *Awards:* Fel, MacDowell Colony, Peterborough, NH, 63. *Bibliog:* William Sterling (auth), Herbert Simon: Metal Sculpture 1976-1980, Wilkes Col, Wilkes-Barre, Pa, 80. *Media:* Steel, Aluminum. *Mailing Add:* c/o Art Dept/Wilkes Col 170 South Franklin St Wilkes-Barre PA 18766

SIMON, JEWEL WOODARD
PAINTER, SCULPTOR
b Houston, Tex, July 28, 11. *Study:* Atlanta Univ, AB(summa cum laude), 31, painting with Hale Woodruff, 46; pvt study with B L Hellman, 34; sculpture with Alice Dunbar, 47; Atlanta Col Art, BFA, 67; Art Instr Inc, cert grad, 62; Tamarind Inst, lithography, 81. *Work:* Educ Dept, Ringling Mus, Sarasota, Fla; Atlanta Univ Gallery; Du Sable Mus, Chicago; Carver Mus, Tuskegee, Ala; Kiah Mus, Savannah, Ga; and others. *Comn:* Portrait of Frankie Adams, Atlanta Sch Social Work, 70; portrait of A F Herndon, founder, Atlanta Life Insurance Co, 70; oil landscapes, cover design, The Vision, Atlanta Life Ins Co, Atlanta, Memphis & Dallas, 73; plus others. *Exhib:* One-woman shows, Clark Col, 73 & Carver Mus, Tuskegee, Ala, 74; Huntsville Mus, 79; Int Soc Artists, New York, 79; and many other group & one-man shows. *Collections Arranged:* South Eastern, 50, End of Year Show, 64-67, Show of Georgia Artists, 71 & Highlights of Atlanta University Collection Touring Show, 73, High Mus Art, Atlanta. *Pos:* Slice lectures and exhibs, various cols & univs; career consult, High Schs & Elem Schs. *Awards:* Arts Serv Award, Phoenix Arts & Theater Co, 78; Golden Dove Heritage Award, Kappa Omega Chap, A K A Sorority, 79; Bronze Jubilee Award, 81; and others. *Bibliog:* Samella S Lewis & Ruth C Waddy (auths), Black Artists on Art, 69; Marion Brown (auth), The Negro in the Fine Arts, Negro Heritage Libr, Vol 2, 70; Women Artists in America, II, Art Dept, Univ Tenn, Chattanooga. *Mem:* Nat Conf Artists (co-founder & nat treas, 58-73); Graphic Soc; Black Artists Atlanta (treas, 73-75); Ga Arts Coun; High Mus Collectors. *Media:* Oil, Watercolor; Multimedia. *Publ:* Contribr, Prints by American Negro Artists, Cult Exchange Ctr, 64, Black Dimensions in Art, Carnation Co, 70 & American Printmakers, Graphic Group, Arcadia, Calif, 74. *Mailing Add:* 67 Ashby St SW Atlanta GA 30314

SIMON, LEONARD RONALD
ADMINISTRATOR, WRITER
b Norristown, Pa, Dec 9, 36. *Study:* Ohio State Univ. *Collections Arranged:* Two Centuries of Black American Art (coauth, catalog), 75. *Pos:* Registr, Stanford Mus, 65-69; deputy dir, Calif Arts Coun, 77-80. *Teaching:* Instr Black Am art, Univ Calif, Riverside, 76-77 & 80- *Mem:* Col Art Asn. *Res:* Black American artists. *Publ:* Auth, The American presence of the Black artist, Am Art Rev, 76; auth, The sound of people, Arts in Soc, Vol 12, No 1. *Mailing Add:* 360 S Mills Ave Claremont CA 91711

SIMON, MICHAEL A
PHOTOGRAPHER
b Budapest, Hungary, June 20, 36; US citizen. *Study:* Budapest Tech Univ, 54-56; Pa State Univ, 57-58; Wis Arts Bd photog fel, 80. *Work:* Mus Mod Art, New York; George Eastman House, Rochester, NY; Univ Kans, Lawrence; Minneapolis Inst Arts, Minn; Sheldon Mem Art Gallery, Lincoln, Nebr. *Exhib:* Contemp Photog VII, George Eastman House, Rochester, NY, 72; Midwest Invitational, Walker Art Ctr, Minneapolis, 73; one-man shows, Wright Art Ctr, 77, 78 & 80 & Minneapolis Inst Arts, Minn, 79; Recent Aquisitions, Minneapolis Inst Arts, Minn, 76; Madison Art Ctr, Wis, 83; Aspen Ctr Visual Arts, Colo, 83; and others. *Pos:* Cur photog, Wright Art Ctr, Beloit Col, currently. *Teaching:* Assoc prof photog, Beloit Col, Wis, 69-; artist-

in-residence photog, Univ Del, 74; vis artist photog, Art Inst Chicago, 78; artist in residence, Avila Col, Kansas City, Mo, 81. *Awards:* Nat Endowment Arts Photog Survey Grant, 80; Nat Endowment Arts Exhib Grant, 81; grant, Wis Humanities Comt, 81. *Bibliog:* Diaframma Italiana, Milan, Italy, 1-2/75. *Mem:* Soc Photog Educ (nat bd mem, 76-84, chmn nat bd dir, 79-81, chmn reg affairs comt, 81-83). *Res:* Mellon Foundation grant for the research of the history of photography in Hungary (76-80). *Publ:* Auth, Helyzetkep az Egyesult Allamokbol (on American photography), Fotomuveszet, Hungary, 4/77; coauth, First Lessons in Black and White Photography, Holt, Rinehart & Wi, 78; auth, The evolution of photographic styles: a case study, Exposure 16:4, 79; auth, Massachusetts Review of Photography, Vol 2, No 3, 81; auth, Camera Lucida, Vol 1, No 4, 81. *Mailing Add:* 925 Church St Beloit WI 53511

SIMON, NORTON
COLLECTOR
b Portland, Ore, Feb 5, 07. *Pos:* Pres, Norton Simon Mus, Pasadena, Calif; pres, Norton Simon Found & Norton Simon Inc Found. *Collection:* Old Master European paintings from the Renaissance through the mid-20th century, including paintings by Renoir, Cezanne, van Gogh and others; complete bronze modeles by Degas; sculpture by Maillol, Moore, Rodin, Giacometti and others; graphic works by Rembrandt, Goya and Picasso; Indian and Southeast Asian bronze and stone sculpture. *Mailing Add:* 411 W Colorado Blvd Pasadena CA 91105

SIMON, ROBERT BARRY
CURATOR, HISTORIAN
b New York, NY, Nov 27, 52. *Study:* Columbia Col, BA, 73; Columbia Univ, MA, 75, MPhil, 76, PhD, 82. *Collections Arranged:* Sixteenth Century Portraits (auth, catalog), Soprintendevza, Florence, Italy, 80-82; US Info Agency Permanent Collection (auth, catalog), 82. *Pos:* Chester Dale Fel, Metrop Mus Art, New York, 76-78; dir, Fine Arts Group Crosson Dannis, 82- *Teaching:* Lectr Ital renaissance art, Juilliard Sch, 82- *Mem:* Col Art Asn; Renaissance Soc Am; Am Asn Mus; Int Coun Mus; Unione Amici Cane & Gatto, Italy. *Res:* Florentine painting of the sixteenth century; Bronzino, Crivelli, Opie & Smetham; problems of portraiture. *Publ:* Auth, Poussin, Marino and the interpretation of mythology, Art Bulletin, 78; auth, From Leonardo to Titian, Arts, 79; auth, Bronzino's portrait of Cosimo I De'Medici, Burlington Mag, 83; translr, The Vatican Collections, Metrop Mus, 83; contribr, Art Museums of the World, Greenwood Press, 84. *Mailing Add:* 315 E 72nd St New York NY 10021

SIMON, SIDNEY
SCULPTOR, PAINTER
b Pittsburgh, Pa, May 21, 17. *Study:* Carnegie Inst Technol; Pa Acad Fine Arts, Emlen Cresson fel, 40 & Edwin Austin Abbey fel, 40-41, BFA, with George Harding; Univ Pa, BA; Barnes Found. *Work:* Metrop Mus Art, New York; Corcoran Gallery; Am Embassy, Paris; Cornell Univ Med Ctr, Kramer Col, Ithaca, NY; Colby Col, Waterville, Maine; and others. *Comn:* Crucifix & St John, Our Lady of Angels, Glenmont, NY; bronze grill, State Univ NY Downstate Med Ctr Entrance Hall; wall design, Walt Whitman High Sch, Yonkers, NY; The Circus (mobile), Woodland House, Hartford, Conn; entrance sculpture, 747 Bldg, New York, 72. *Exhib:* Pa Acad Fine Arts Ann, 48-52 & 62-72; Am Painting, Metrop Mus Art, 50; 20 one-man shows, Whitney Mus Am Art Ann, 50-; Mus Mod Art Assemblage Exhib, 62; L'Aquarelle Contemporaine aux Etats Units, State Dept, 63; Sculpture Retrospective, Int Sculpture Ctr, New York, 81. *Pos:* Mem, New York City Art Comn, 75-78. *Teaching:* Instr & founding dir, Skowhegan Sch Painting & Sculpture, Maine, 45-58 & 75-76, acad dir, 81-; Artist in residence, Am Acad Rome, 69-70; vis sculptor, Sarah Lawrence Col, 71-72; vis prof, Salzburg Sem Am Studies, 71; instr, Art Students League, 73-; vis artist, Univ Pa, 77 & 80. *Awards:* Gold Medal, 81 & Greer Prize, 83, Nat Acad Design; Award, Acad Arts & Letters, 81; Silver Medal, Nat Arts Club, 82. *Bibliog:* Richard McLanathan (auth), Sidney Simon, Grippi Gallery, 75; Barbara Kafka (auth), article in Craft Horizon, 67; J Place (auth), article in Am Artist, 11/79. *Mem:* Artists Equity Asn; Skowhegan Sch Painting & Sculpture; Provincetown Art Asn; Truro Ctr for Arts (vpres); Sculpture's Guild (vpres). *Media:* Wood, Bronze. *Mailing Add:* 95 Bedford St New York NY 10014

SIMONDS, CHARLES FREDERICK
SCULPTOR, ARCHITECT
b New York, NY, Nov 14, 45. *Study:* Univ Calif, Berkeley, BA, 67; Rutgers Univ, Douglass Col, New Brunswick, NJ, MFA, 67. *Work:* Mus Mod Art, New York; Walker Art Ctr, Minneapolis; Guggenheim Mus; Whitney Mus; Mus Contemp Art, Chicago; and others. *Comn:* Dwellings, over 300 works constructed in the streets of New York for an imaginary civilization of little people migrating through the city, 70-; Project Uphill-La Placita (park playlot sculpture), Lower East Side Coalition for Human Housing, 74; full scale Dwellings, 74 & Growth House, 75, Art Park. *Exhib:* Biennial of Paris, 73 & 75; Whitney Biennial, 75 & 77; Small Scale, Art Inst Chicago, 75; Scale & the Environment, Walker Art Ctr, Minneapolis, 77; Made by Sculptors, Stedelijk Mus, Amsterdam, Neth, 78; Contemp Sculpture, Selections from the Collection of the Mus Mod Art, New York, 79; one-man shows, Projects: Picaresque Landscape, Mus Mod Art, New York, 76 & 77, Temenos, Albright-Knox Art Gallery, Buffalo, NY, 77, Floating Cities & Other Archit, Westfalischer Kunstverein, Munster, 78 & Mus Sables D'olonne, France, 79; Circles & Towers Growing, traveling exhib, Mus Contemp Art, Chicago, Los Angeles Co Mus Art, Ft Worth Art Mus & Contemp Arts Mus, Houston, Tex; and many others. *Pos:* Mem bd, Lower East Side Coalition for Human Housing, 74- *Awards:* Artist in Residence Grant, 74 & Young Artists Grant, Nat Endowment for the Arts, 74-75; Nat Endowment Arts, 80. *Bibliog:* John Beardsley (auth), Charles Simonds: Extending the metaphor, Art Int, Vol 22,

No 9, 2/79; Mark Stevens (auth), The dizzy decade, Newsweek, 3/26/79; Kate Linker (auth), Charles Simonds' emblematic architecture, Artforum, 3/79; and many others. *Publ:* Auth, Microcosm to macrocosm, 2/74 & auth, Three peoples, 75, Art Forum. *Mailing Add:* 26 E 22nd St New York NY 10010

SIMONE (MILDRED SIMONSON)
SCULPTOR, PAINTER
b New York, NY. *Study:* Art Students League, with Yasuo Kuniyoshi & Louis Bosa, 45-47; Rockport Art Sch, Provincetown, with Hans Hoffman, 46; New Sch Social Res, with Louis Bosa, 50; Brooklyn Mus, with Xavier Gonzales & Vincent Glinsky, 50; Hunter Col, with Ba BA, 28. *Work:* Brooklyn Mus. *Exhib:* Mother's Day Bouquet, Brooklyn Mus, 47; San Miguel de Allende, Whitney Mus, 50; Mother and Child, Nat Acad, New York, 53; Chiquita, Smithsonian Inst, 58; To Market, Riverside Mus, New York, 59; various works, Assoc Am Artists, New York, 59-62; David & Saul, Calif Legion Honor, San Francisco, 60; Motherhood, Miami Beach Publ Libr, 77. *Awards:* Second Prize, Whither Thou Goest, Brooklyn Mus, 47; article, New York Times, 4/27/52; America discovers art, New York Post, 10/58. *Mem:* Charter mem Artists Equity; Brooklyn Soc Artists. *Media:* Bronze, Marble; Oil. *Publ:* Illusr & compiler, In the Beginning Cookbook, Progressive Synagogue, 69. *Dealer:* Lincoln Mall Gallery Miami Beach FL; Cambi Gallery Bay Harbor Island FL. *Mailing Add:* 50 E Tenth St Apt 7B New York NY 10003

SIMONI, JOHN PETER
PAINTER, EDUCATOR
b Denver, Colo, Apr 12, 11. *Study:* Colo State Col Educ, BA & MA; Nat Univ Mex; Kansas City Art Inst, with Thomas Hart Benton; Univ Colo, with Max Beckmann; Ohio State Univ, PhD; Mass Inst Technol; also in Trentino, Italy; Int Univ Art, Florence, Italy, cert specialization (museology, conserv & restoration), 79. *Work:* Colo Friends Art Collection. *Comn:* Mural paintings, The Kerr McGee Ctr, Oklahoma City, Okla, 75, The Mid-Kans Savings & Loan Bank of Wichita, 76, Reading & Bates Petroleum Ctr of Tulsa, Okla, 76 & Sheplers of Wichita, Kans, 76; and others. *Exhib:* Mulvane Mus Art; Wichita Art Mus; Colo State Univ; Birger Sandzen Mem Gallery, Lindsborg, Kans; Univ Wichita. *Pos:* Gallery dir, Baker Univ, 37-55; dir univ galleries, Univ Wichita, 57-63; designer, John Coultis Interiors, 57-76; color consult, Western Lithograph Co, Wichita, Kans & Houston, Tex, 61-63; co-dir univ gallery, Wichita State Univ, 64-65. *Teaching:* Head dept art, Baker Univ, 37-55; prof art, Univ Wichita, 55-57, chmn dept art, 57-63; prof art, Wichita State Univ, 64-78; retired. *Awards:* Decorated Knight Order of Crown, Italy, 47; Knight Officer, Order of Merit, Repub Italy, 66; Academician of Italy with Gold Medal, Accademia Italia Arti Lavoro, 80. *Mem:* Am Soc Aesthet; Col Art Asn Am; Kans Fedn Art; Southwestern Col Art Conf (pres, 62-64); fel Int Inst Arts & Lett; and others. *Publ:* Columnist, Wichita Eagle; columnist, Baldwin Ledger, 65-68; columnist, Estes Park Trail Gazette, 60-; columnist, Art in the Bluestream, El Dorado Times, 76- *Mailing Add:* PO Box 1154 Estes Park CO 80517

SIMPER, FREDERICK
PAINTER
b Mishawaka, Ind, July 31, 14. *Study:* Self-taught. *Work:* Detroit Inst Arts; South Bend Art Mus, Ind; US Embassies Collection. *Exhib:* Detroit Inst Arts, 38-68; Art Inst Chicago, 48; Watercolor USA, Springfield, Mo, 65; Butler Inst Art, Youngstown, Ohio; Pa Acad Fine Arts, Philadelphia. *Pos:* Art dir, D'Arcy, Macmanus Int, 49-80. *Teaching:* Instr watercolor, Soc Arts & Crafts, Detroit, 48-51; instr watercolor, Bloomfield Art Asn, Birmingham, Mich, 68-70. *Awards:* Detroit Inst Arts Founders Soc Award, 42; Baltimore Sun Award for Black & White Drawing, 45; Mich Watercolor Soc Award, 72. *Mem:* Mich Watercolor Soc. *Media:* Watercolor. *Mailing Add:* 3075 Spring Ct West Bloomfield MI 48033

SIMPSON, DAVID
PAINTER, EDUCATOR
b Pasadena, Calif, Jan 20, 28. *Study:* Calif Sch Fine Arts, with Clifford Still & others, BFA, 56; San Francisco State Col, MA, 58. *Work:* San Francisco Mus Art; Oakland Art Mus, Calif; Mus Mod Art, New York; Philadelphia Mus Art; Baltimore Mus Art. *Exhib:* Carnegie Inst Int, Pittsburgh, 61 & 64; Americans 1963, Mus Mod Art, New York, 63; Calif Painters & Sculptors: The Mod Era, San Francisco & Washington, DC, 76; Retrospective, Oakland Mus, Calif, 78; plus others. *Teaching:* Prof art, Univ Calif, Berkeley, 65- *Media:* Acrylic. *Dealer:* Modernism Inc 236 Eighth St San Francisco CA 94108. *Mailing Add:* 565 Vistamont Berkeley CA 94708

SIMPSON, LEE
PAINTER
b Cisco, Tex, Oct 9, 23. *Study:* Columbia Univ, with Arnold Leondar; also with Louise Nevelson & Elaine DeKooning, New York. *Work:* Empire Savings & Loan, Denver; Midland Fed Savings & Loan, Denver; Am Express, Denver; Int Bus Machines, Dallas; Beech Aircraft, Wichita; and others. *Comn:* Mural, Perryton Nat Bank, Tex, 69; lithograph, PBS TV, Denver, 78. *Exhib:* Spec Group Show, Panhandle-Plains Hist Mus, Canyon, Tex, 69; 9th & 10th Ann Awards Show, Taos Art Asn, 71 & 72; Southwest Fine Arts Biennial, Mus NMex, Santa Fe, 72; one-man show, WTex State Univ, Canyon, 68. *Pos:* Owner & instr oil painting, Simpson Gallery & Studio, Amarillo, 62-70. *Teaching:* Guest lectr oil painting, WTex State Univ, 69; guest instr oil painting, Amarillo Jr Col, 69-70. *Awards:* Juror's Citation Award, State Citation Show, Tex Fine Arts Asn, 68 & 69; First Award, 9th Ann Awards Show, Taos Art Asn, 72. *Bibliog:* Whitney Meeckum (auth), The man is the medium, Southwest Art Mag, 4/70. *Media:* Oil, Pastel. *Dealer:* Ledoux Gallery PO Box 2418 Taos NM 87571; Adelle M Fine Art 3317 McKinney Ave Dallas TX 75204. *Mailing Add:* c/o Ledoux Gallery PO Box 2418 Taos NM 87571

SIMPSON, MARIANNA SHREVE
HISTORIAN, EDUCATOR
b Washington, DC, Nov 17, 49. *Study:* Univ Pa, BA, 70; Johns Hopkins Univ, 71-72; Harvard Univ, PhD, 78. *Pos:* From asst to actg registr, Baltimore Mus Art, 71-72; res assoc, Freer Gallery Art, Smithsonian Inst, 79-80; asst dean, Ctr Advan Study Visual Arts, Nat Gallery Art, Washington, DC, 80-*Teaching:* Lectr, Harvard Univ, Cambridge, Mass, 78 & Georgetown Univ, Washington, DC, 80-; vis asst prof, Univ Calif, Los Angeles, 80. *Awards:* Mus Intern Fel, Nat Endowment Arts & Fogg Art Mus, Harvard Univ, 76-77; Pre-Doctoral Fel, Smithsonian Inst, 77-78; Grant-in-aid, Am Coun Learned Soc, 79. *Mem:* Middle East Studies Asn; Col Art Asn. *Res:* Medieval Islamic art, with focus on problems in illustrated manuscript studies of fourteenth through sixteenth centuries. *Publ:* Auth, Arab and Persian Painting in the Fogg Art Mus, Fogg Art Mus, 80; auth, The Illustration of an Epic: The Earliest Shahnama Manuscripts, Garland, 79; auth, The narrative structure of a medieval Iranian beaker, 81 & The production and patronage of the Haft Aurang by Jami in the Freer Gallery of Art, 82, Art Orientalis; auth, The role of Baghdad in the formation of Persian painting, In: Art et Societe Dans le Monde Iranien, Paris, 82. *Mailing Add:* 512 G Street SE Washington DC 20013

SIMPSON, MARILYN JEAN
PAINTER, INSTRUCTOR
b Birmingham, Ala. *Study:* Univ Ala; Art Students League; Inst Allende, San Miguel Allende, Mex; Madison Art Sch, Conn; with Robert Brackman; Am Univ Avignon, France; Rome & Florence, Italy. *Exhib:* Nat Arts Club, Gramercy Park; Grand Nat Exhib, NY; Am Arts Prof League; Kottler Gallery; Smithsonian Inst, Washington, DC. *Teaching:* Dir & instr, Acad Fine Arts, Ft Walton Beach, Fla. *Awards:* Gold Medal, Acad Rome. *Mem:* Am Artists Prof League. *Media:* Pastel, Oil. *Mailing Add:* Rte 1 Box 43-C Mary Esther FL 32569

SIMPSON, MERTON D
PAINTER, DEALER
b Charleston, SC, Sept 20, 28. *Study:* NY Univ; Cooper Union Art Sch, with Robert Motherwell & Baziotes; also with William Halsey. *Work:* James J Sweeney Collection, Guggenheim Mus; Howard Univ, Washington, DC; Scott Field Mus, Chicago; Atlanta Univ; Gibbs Art Gallery. *Exhib:* Guggenheim Mus & Metrop Mus Art, New York; Brooklyn Mus, NY; Nat Gallery, Paris; Nat Mus Japan. *Pos:* Owner, Merton D Simpson Gallery, New York. *Awards:* Red Cross Exchange Exhib Award, Tokyo & Paris, 50; Awards, Atlanta Univ, 50, 51 & 56 & Oakland Art Mus, 52. *Specialty:* Primitive art, especially African. *Mailing Add:* 1063 Madison Ave New York NY 10028

SIMPSON, WILLIAM KELLY
HISTORIAN, EDUCATOR
b New York, NY, Jan 3, 28. *Study:* Yale Univ, BA, 47, MA, 48, PhD, 54; Ecole Practique Hautes Etudes, Paris. *Collections Arranged:* The Pennsylvania-Yale Expedition to Nubia, Peabody Mus, Yale Univ, New Haven, Conn, 63; Recent Accessions in Egyptian & Ancient Near Eastern Art & The Horace L Mayer Collection, 72, Mus Fine Arts, Boston; Metrop Mus, New York; Univ Pa Mus, Philadelphia. *Pos:* Cur Egyptian art, Mus Fine Arts, Boston, 70- *Teaching:* Prof Egyptol, Yale Univ, 56-; vis prof Egyptol, Univ Pa. *Awards:* Guggenheim Found Fel, 65. *Mem:* Archaeol Inst Am; Am Oriental Soc; Am Res Ctr in Egypt; Int Coun Mus Mod Art, New York; and others. *Res:* Art, history, and literature of ancient Egypt. *Publ:* Auth, Papyrus Reisner I-Records of a Building Project, 63; auth, Papyrus Reisner II-Accounts of the Dockyard Workshop, 65; auth, Papyrus Reisner III-Records of a Building Project in the Early Twelfth Dynasty, 69; coauth, The Ancient Near East: A History, 71; coauth, The Literature of Ancient Egypt, 72; auth, The Mastaba of Queen Mersyankh III, 74. *Mailing Add:* Katonah's Wood Rd Katonah NY 10536

SIMS, LOWERY STOKES
HISTORIAN, CURATOR
b Washington, DC, Feb 13, 49. *Study:* Queens Col, City Univ New York, BA, 70; Johns Hopkins Univ, MA, 72. *Collections Arranged:* Portraits of Helena Rubenstein (auth, catalog), Metrop Mus, New York, 75; Low Cost Housing (auth, catalog), Studio Mus, Harlem, 77; Robert Hale: Tribute to a Curator, Metrop Mus, New York, 78; Hans Hofmann: The Renate Series, Metrop Mus, New York, 80; Carnival (auth, catalog), Visual Arts Resource and Research Ctr, 80; John Marin: Selection Works from Mus, Metrop Mus, New York, 81. *Pos:* Asst mus educ, Metrop Mus Art, New York, 72-75; assoc cur 20th century art, 75- *Teaching:* Adj lectr survey art, Queens Col, City Univ New York, 73-76; adj lectr African art, 75; lectr found art hist & curatorship, Sch Visual Arts, 75-76 & 82-84. *Mem:* Col Art Asn; Int Asn Art Critics; New York Comn Status Women; Art Table (mem bd, 81-). *Res:* 20th century painting, sculpture and architecture especially of the last 30 years, with special interest in Afro-American artists. *Mailing Add:* Metrop Mus Art Fifth Ave at 82nd St New York NY 10028

SIMS, PATTERSON
CURATOR
b Nov 17, 47. *Study:* Chestnut Hill Acad, Philadelphia, Pa; Darrow Sch, New Lebanon, NY; Trinity Col, Hartford, Conn; New Sch Social Res, New York, BA. *Collections Arranged:* Seven Decades of MacDowell Colony Artists, James Yu Gallery, 76; On Canvas, 76, 30 Years of American Art, 77, Whitney Biennial Exhibition, 77, American Art 1900-1950, 77, Selections from the Promised Gift of Mrs Percy Uris, 77 & American Art 1920-1945, 77-78, Whitney Mus Am Art, New York; American Art 1900-1950, Seattle Art Mus,

77; School of Visual Arts 1977 End of the Year Show, 77. *Pos:* Asst dir, O K Harris Works of Art, New York, 69-76; assoc cur permanent collection, Whitney Mus Am Art, 76- *Teaching:* Part-time instr, Sch Continuing Educ, NY Univ, currently. *Publ:* Auth, Alan Shields, Moore Col Art, Pa; auth, Jan Matulka: A Life in Art, Smithsonian Press. *Mailing Add:* c/o Whitney Mus Am Art 945 Madison Ave at 75th St New York NY 10021

SIMSON, BEVLYN A
PAINTER, PRINTMAKER
b Columbus, Ohio, Sept 9, 17. *Study:* Ohio State Univ, BFA & MFA; mus in Europe & Japan. *Work:* Chase Manhattan Bank, New York; Kresge Collection, Detroit; Columbus Mus Art; J B Speed Mus, Louisville, Ky; Tyler Mus, Tex; and others. *Comn:* Nine paintings, Lobby, Ohio State Nisonger Ctr; three-panel paintings, First Investment Co, 69 & First Community Bank, 81. *Exhib:* One-person shows, J B Speed Mus, Louisville, Ky, 70, Capital Univ, 77, Springfield Art Mus, 80, Franklin Univ, 81 & Collectors Gallery, Columbus Mus Art, 83; 37th Nat Painting Show, Butler Inst Am Art, Youngstown, Ohio, 73; Contemp Prints for Collectors, Columbus Mus Art, 74 & 75; Ohio Women Artists: Past & Present, Butler Inst Am Art, 76; and others. *Awards:* Columbus Mus Art Painting Award, 69, 71, 73 & 79; Best of Show, Schumacher Gallery, Capital Univ, 81; Dipl di Merito, Univ della Arte, Acad Ital, 82. *Bibliog:* Jacqueline Hall (auth), Bevlyn Simson displays works internationally, Columbus Dispatch, 4/9/75; Mary Bridgman (auth), Bevlyn Simson rhymes colors & shapes, Columbus Dispatch, 12/11/77; Tricia & Mat Herban (auths), Bevlyn Simson neo-geometrics show a technique of modern art, Columbus Citizen-J, 5/16/83. *Mem:* Am Fedn Arts; Nat League Am Pen Women; Bexley Area Art Guild; Columbus Art League (past pres). *Media:* Acrylic; Lithograph, Silkscreen. *Publ:* Auth, Prints & Poetry, 69. *Mailing Add:* Bevlyn Simson Gallery 289 S Roosevelt Ave Columbus OH 43209

SINA, ALEJANDRO
KINETIC ARTIST, SCULPTOR
b Santiago, Chile, May 10, 45. *Study:* Univ Chile, MBA, 73; Ctr Advan Visual Studies, Mass Inst Technol, with Gyorgy Kepes & Otto Piene, fel, 73-79. *Work:* Mus Sci & Indust, Chicago; Nat Mus Fine Arts, Santiago; Nat Sci Mus, Veno Park, Tokyo; Saitama Childrens Mus, Higashi-Matsuyama, Japan; Worcester Sci Ctr, Mass. *Comn:* Neon Rainbow, Creative Times, New York, 76; neon mobile, comn by Graham Gund, Hyatt Regency, Cambridge, Mass, 77; neon cluster, Spaulding & Slye, Burlington, Mass, 77; participatory kinetic lightworks, Art Pub Space, Rye, NY, 78-80, 82 & 83; kinetic light sculpture, Cambridge Arts Coun, Mass, 82-84. *Exhib:* Gaslight Phenomena, Inst Contemp Art, Boston, 77; Five Artists, Five Technologies, Grand Rapids Art Mus, Mich, 79; Fourth Bienal Arte, Medellin, Colombia, 81; 16th Bienal Arte, Sao Paulo, Brazil, 81; Art in Light and Illusion, Isetan Mus Art, Tokyo, 82; Light: Recent Issues in Illumination, Morris Mus, Morristown, NJ, 82. *Teaching:* Instr, Ctr Advan Visual Studies, Mass Inst Technol, 73-77. *Awards:* Fulbright Fel, 73-75; Nat Endowment Arts Grant, 76-77. *Bibliog:* Milan Ivelic & Gaspar Galaz (auths), La Pintura en Chile, Univ Catolica, Valparaiso, 82; Sixto Escobar (producer), The Art of Alejandro Sina, La Plaza Prog, TV Channel 7, Boston, 83; Michael Webb (auth), The Magic of Neon, Gibbs M Smith Inc, 83. *Media:* Glass; Gas, Electricity. *Mailing Add:* 21 Andem Pl #1 Brookline MA 02146

SINAIKO, ARLIE
SCULPTOR, COLLECTOR
b Kapule, Russia, Oct 1, 02; US citizen. *Study:* Univ Wis, BS; Northwestern Univ, MD; Art Inst Chicago; Sculpture Ctr, New York; Art Students League; Atelier, with Archipenko, Lassaw & Harkavy. *Work:* Harry Lynde Bradley Collection, Milwaukee; Ringling Mus, Sarasota, Fla; Phoenix Art Mus, Ariz; Witte Mem Mus, San Antonio, Tex; Delgado Mus, New Orleans; and others. *Exhib:* Pa Acad Fine Arts; Detroit Inst Art; Riverside Mus, NY; Art USA, 1959; Provincetown Art Asn, Mass. *Awards:* Purchase Prize, Pa Acad Fine Arts, 61; Hon Mention for Sculpture, Audubon Artists, 68; Kellner Award for Sculpture, Am Soc Contemp Artists, 71. *Mem:* Am Soc Contemp Artists; Artists Equity Asn; Audubon Artists; Provincetown Art Asn; Sculptors League. *Collection:* Renoir sculpture; Klee drawing; also work of Derain, Dufy, Fujita and many contemporary artists and many lithographs and etchings of Picasso, Braque, Matisse, Rouault and Miro; early American primitive painters. *Mailing Add:* 115 Central Park W New York NY 10023

SINCLAIR, ROBERT (W)
PAINTER, SCULPTOR
b Saltcoats, Sask, Can, Feb 9, 39. *Study:* Univ Manitoba Sch Art, BFA, 61; Univ Iowa, MA, 65, MFA, 67. *Work:* Art Gallery, Windsor, Ont; Agnes Etherington Art Gallery, Queens Univ, Kingston, Ont; Confederation Art Gallery, Charlottetown, PEI; Glenbow Mus, Calgary, Alta; Edmonton Art Gallery, Alta. *Comn:* Foyer painting (acrylic stain), Oxford Develop Group, Royal Trust Tower, Edmonton, Alta, 79. *Exhib:* A Prairie Sweet, Glenbow Mus, Calgary, Alta, 73; A Response to the Environment, Rutgers Univ Gallery, NJ, 75; Changing Visions, Art Gallery Ont, Toronto, 76-77; one-man shows, Gallery/Stratford, Ont, 76 & Edmonton Art Gallery, Alta, 82-83; Pertaining to Space, Art Gallery Ont, Toronto, 76-77. *Teaching:* Prof art painting & drawing, Dept Art & Design, Univ Alta, 65-; vis artist, Univ Iowa, 73 & Banff Sch Fine Art, 76. *Mem:* Royal Canadian Acad Arts; Can Soc Painters Watercolour. *Media:* Acrylic Stain, Watercolor. *Dealer:* Aggregation Gallery 83 Front St East Toronto ON Can M5E 1B8. *Mailing Add:* 1-18-RR 2 Winterburn AB T0E 2N0 Canada

SINGER, ARTHUR B
ILLUSTRATOR, PAINTER
b Manhattan, NY, Dec 4, 17. *Study:* Cooper Union Art Sch, painting & design with Mr & Mrs Wallace Harrison, painting with Guy Pene Dubois & painting & illus with Lewis Daniel & Howard Willard, cert; Art Students League. *Work:* Buckingham Palace, London, Eng. *Comn:* Birds of Fla (map), Nat Geographic Soc, 73; Madagascar's Birds, Defenders of Wildlife, 75. *Exhib:* The Bird in Art, Univ Ariz Art Gallery, Tucson, 65 & Ark Arts Ctr, Little Rock, 65; Nature in Art, Newark Mus, NJ, 72; Audubon Artists, Graham Gallery, New York, 73; Animals in Art, Royal Ont Mus, Toronto, 75; and others. *Awards:* First Recipient of Augustus St Gaudens Medal, Cooper Union, 62. *Bibliog:* Dick Kirkpatrick (auth), National Wildlife visits Arthur Singer, Nat Wildlife Mag, 12-1/70; Barbara Delatiner (auth), Art that's all in the family, New York Times, 7/77; Oliver L Austin Jr (auth), Arthur Singer, The Fla Naturalist, 7/66. *Mem:* Soc Animal Artists; Cornell Lab of Ornithology; Am Ornithologists Union; Linnaran Soc of New York. *Media:* Watercolor, Oil, Acrylic. *Collection:* Japanese prints of artists like Hirshige, Holsusic and Utamsio; Southwest Indian pottery, Peruvian weaving, African sculpture, Audubon's Elephant folio prints and Fine old bird books. *Publ:* Auth & illus, A Guide to Field Identification Birds of North America, Golden Press, 66; illus, Zoo Animals, Golden Press, 67; illusr, The Hamlyn Guide to Birds of Britain and Europe, Hamlyn Publ, 70; illusr, The Life of the Hummingbird, Crown Publ, 73; illus, Oceanic Bird of Antarctica, 73, Parrots, 74 & Cranes of the World, 78, Audubon Soc Mag. *Dealer:* Hammer Galleries Inc 33 W 57th St New York NY 10019. *Mailing Add:* 30 Hightop Lane Jericho NY 11753

SINGER, CLIFFORD
PAINTER, PRINTMAKER
b Great Neck, NY, May 19, 55. *Study:* Alfred Univ, BFA, 77; Empire State, 77; Hunter Col, 77-79. *Work:* Aldrich Mus Contemp Art, Ridgefield, Conn; Chemical Bank; Texaco Inc; Best Products Corp; Gen Instrument Corp; and others. *Comn:* Lemma III (three paintings), Mobil Oil Corp Hq, New York, 83. *Exhib:* Aldrich Mus Contemp Art, 80 & 81; Branchville Soho Gallery, Ridgefield, Conn, 82; Gallery 212, Paris, 82; Small Works, 80 Washington Sq E Galleries, 83; Sotheby Parke Bernet Thirteen Collection Exhib, TV Auction, NY, 83. *Bibliog:* Article, Aspen Times, 1/29/81; article, New York Times, 2/15/81. *Media:* Acrylic; Silkscreen. *Mailing Add:* 510 Broome St New York NY 10012

SINGER, CLYDE J
PAINTER
b Malvern, Ohio, Oct 20, 08. *Study:* Columbus Art Sch, Ohio; Art Students League, with Kenneth Hayes Miller, John Steuart Curry & Thomas Hart Benton. *Work:* Pa Acad Fine Arts, Philadelphia; Wadsworth Atheneum, Hartford, Conn; Thomas Gilcrease Inst Hist & Art, Tulsa, Okla; Butler Inst Am Art, Youngstown, Ohio; Canton Art Inst, Ohio. *Comn:* Skaters (mural), Post Off, New Concord, Ohio, 40. *Exhib:* Over 40 exhibs in maj mus, 35-58, incl Carnegie Mus Int, Pittsburgh, Pa, 36-39; Corcoran Gallery Art Biennial, Washington, DC, 37; Golden Gate Int Expos, San Francisco, 39; Whitney Mus Am Art Painting & Sculpture Biennial, 41; Artists for Victory, Rockefeller Ctr, New York, 45; The Neglected Generation of American Realist Painters, 1930-1948, Wichita Art Mus, Kans, 81. *Pos:* Art critic, Vindicator, Youngstown, 40-; asst dir, Butler Inst Am Art, 40- *Awards:* Norman Wait Harris Silver Medal, Art Inst Chicago, 35; First Hallgarten Prize, Nat Acad Design, 38; Pagasus Award, Ohioana Libr Asn, 72. *Bibliog:* Roger Bonham (auth), Clyde Singer: Ohio painter, Am Artist, 2/69; Paul Chew (auth), Singer Retrospective 1932-1972, Westmoreland Co Mus Art, 3/72. *Media:* Oil. *Mailing Add:* 210 Forest Park Dr Youngstown OH 44512

SINGER, ESTHER FORMAN
PAINTER, CRITIC
b New York, NY. *Study:* Art Students League, 39-41; Temple Univ, 41-44; NY Univ, 47-49; New Sch Social Res, 68-70; Fairleigh Dickinson Univ, pvt study with Hans Hoffman, Brackman, George Gross & Tosun Bayrak; Univ Arte Contemp, Parma, hon degree, 82. *Work:* NJ State Mus, Trenton; Finch Mus Contemp Art, New York; Library of Congress, Washington, DC; Morris Mus Arts & Sciences, Morristown, NJ; Newark Mus, NJ. *Exhib:* 1978 Invitational, Morris Mus, 78; Rutgers Univ, New Brunswick, NJ, 81; Key Gallery, NY, 81; one-woman shows, NJ Inst Technol, 82 & Royal Palm Art Gallery, Palm Beach, Fla, 83; and others. *Pos:* Guest panelist, Art Forms, WOR-TV, 67-68; ed, Newark News, 70-74; art critic, Am Artist Mag, 72- & Worrall Press, 74-; adv, NJ Mag, 83- *Teaching:* Instr elementary art, Baird Community Ctr, South Orange, NJ, currently. *Bibliog:* Smith (auth), Feature story & cover photo, NJ Music & Art Mag, 10/65; Nancye Kallis (auth), rev in Art Rev Mag, 4/66; Carlotte Winslow (auth), article in NJ Suburban Life Mag, 3/70. *Mem:* Am Vet Soc Artists; Int Platform Asn; Nat Soc Painters & Sculptors; Miniature Artists Asn NJ; Nat Soc Lit & Arts. *Media:* Mixed Media, Collage. *Dealer:* Rauchback Galleries 1007 Kane Concourse Bay Harbor Miami FL 33154; Key Gallery 130 Green St New York NY. *Mailing Add:* 15 Lawrence Way Cedar Grove NJ 07009

SINGER, JOEL
FILMMAKER, PHOTOGRAPHER
b Montreal, Que, Nov 29, 48. *Study:* San Francisco Art Inst, MFA, 76. *Work:* Mus Mod Art, New York; San Francisco Art Inst, Calif. *Exhib:* Mus Mod Art, New York, 77 & 83; Cinematheque, San Francisco, Calif, 77-81; Millennium Film Mus, New York, 81; Carnegie Mus, Pittsburgh, 81; Boston Film & Video Found, Mass, 81. *Pos:* Mem bd dirs, Eye Music Filmworks, 76- & Canyon Cinema Cooperative, 80- *Awards:* First Prize, San Francisco Art Inst Film Festival, 77; Second Prize, Bellevue Int Film Festival, 78; Cash Award, Ann

Arbor Int Film Festival, 81. *Bibliog:* Richard Bartone (auth), International Avant-Garde structural film, Millennium Film J, 78; P Adams Sitney (auth), Visionary Film, Oxford Univ Press, 79; Jerry Tartaglia (auth), Politics & landscape, Millennium Film J, 79. *Mailing Add:* PO Box 183 Mill Valley CA 94942

SINGER, NANCY BARKHOUSE
DEALER
b St Louis, Mo, Oct 5, 12. *Study:* Univ Wis, BA, 33; Wash Univ, St Louis. *Collections Arranged:* Laumeier Int Sculpture Park, St Louis, Mo; Univ Mo, St Louis; First St Forum, St Louis; Wichita Col Art Gallery. *Pos:* Dir, Nancy Singer Gallery, currently. *Mem:* First St Forum; Contemp Art Soc; Print & Drawing Soc. *Specialty:* Contemporary master prints. *Mailing Add:* 31 Crestwood Dr St Louis MO 63105

SING HOO
SCULPTOR, PAINTER
b Canton, China, May 15, 08; Can citizen. *Study:* Toronto Col Art; Ont Col Art, with A Barnes & Emmannual Hahn, AA; Slade Sch, Univ London, with Turner. *Work:* London Mus, Eng; Nat Gallery Ottawa; Royal Ont Mus, Toronto. *Comn:* Sun Dial & bronze figures of daughter & gardener, Parks, Toronto. *Exhib:* Ont Soc Artists, 32-68; Can Nat Exhib, 32-68; Royal Can Acad Art, 36-72; Sculptor's Soc Can, 40-67. *Pos:* Asst, Paleont Dept, Royal Ont Mus, 34-40. *Teaching:* Lectr Oriental & Western art, Chinese Sch, 36-40. *Mem:* Royal Can Acad Arts. *Media:* Bronze, Marble. *Mailing Add:* 139 Livingstone Ave Toronto ON M6E 2L9 Canada

SINGLETARY, ROBERT EUGENE
DRAFTSMAN, PAINTER
b Bloomington, Ill, Dec 4, 45. *Study:* Ill State Univ, with Walter Bock & Harold Boyd; Corcoran Gallery Art, Washington, DC. *Work:* Philadelphia Mus Art; Nat Mus Am Art, Washington, DC; State Dept, Washington, DC; Univ Ark, Little Rock; Philip Morris, USA, Richmond, Va. *Exhib:* 4th Biennial of Drawings USA, St Paul, Minn, 69; Nat Drawing Exhib, San Francisco Mus, 70; Drawing Soc Nat Exhib, Corcoran Gallery Art, 70; one-man show, Fendrick Gallery, Washington, DC, 72 & 80; Brooklyn Mus Art, New York, 81. *Awards:* Purchase Award, Philadelphia Mus Art, 70. *Bibliog:* Drawing Society's 1970 National Exhibition, Am Fedn Art, 70; Cornelia Noland (auth), The Singletary style, Washingtonian, 8/71; Joanna Eagle (auth), Washington, DC, Art Gallery Mag, 4/72. *Media:* Graphite Lead, Acrylic. *Dealer:* Fendrick Gallery 3059 M St Washington DC 20007. *Mailing Add:* Apt 5 511 Prince St Alexandria VA 22314

SINGLETON, ROBERT ELLISON
PAINTER, PRINTMAKER
b Jacksonville, NC, Dec 13, 37. *Study:* Col William & Mary; Richmond Prof Inst; Smithsonian Inst, Washington, DC. *Work:* Mint Mus Art, Charlotte, NC; Loch Haven Art Ctr, Orlando, Fla; City Baltimore, Md; Jacksonville Art Mus, Fla; Greenville Co Mus, SC; and many others. *Comn:* Murals & paintings, Sentinel Star Co, Orlando, Fla, 68 & 71; paintings, Koger Properties, San Antonio, Tex & Jacksonville & Orlando, Fla, 69 & 71; paintings, George Barley Inc, 70-72; painting, Tupperware Int, Orlando, Fla, 72; paintings, Bank East Orange, Orlando, 72; and others. *Exhib:* One-man shows, Mus Arts & Sci, Daytona Beach, Fla, 68 & Loch Haven Art Ctr, Orlando, 70; Piedmont Graphics, Mint Mus Art, Charlotte, NC, 71 & 72; John F Kennedy Ctr, Washington, DC, 76; Hunter Mus, Chattanooga, Tenn, 77; Vorpal Galleries, New York, 79 & 82; and others. *Pos:* Art dir, WXEX-TV, Richmond, Va, 61-62; cur exhibs, Jamestown Found, Va, 62-63. *Teaching:* Instr painting, Loch Haven Art Ctr, Orlando, 65-73; artist-in-residence, Grant Co, WVa, 81-82. *Awards:* First Place, Int Winter Park Sidewalk Art Festival, 67-69; MacDowell Colony Grant, 71-73; Purchase Awards, Exhib 280, Huntington Galleries, WVa, 81; and others. *Bibliog:* Film documentary, WFIA-TV, Tampa, 71; series of interviews (videotape), WMFE-TV, Orlando, 72-73; 20 American Landscape Painters and How They Work, Watson-Guptill, 77. *Dealer:* Vorpal Galleries 465 West Broadway New York NY 10012. *Mailing Add:* PO Box 1 Baker WV 26801

SINNARD, ELAINE (JANICE)
PAINTER, SCULPTOR
b Ft Collins, Colo, Feb 14, 26. *Study:* Art Students League, 48-49, with Reginald Marsh; NY Univ, 51, with Samuel Adler; also with Robert D Kaufmann, 51; Sculpture Ctr, 55, with Dorothea Denslow; Acad Grande Chaumiere, Paris, 56. *Comn:* Five wall hangings (with Mrs Cris Darlington, Marlin Studios), Scandinavian Airline, New York, 61; three oil paintings, Basker Bldg Corp 5660, Miami Beach, Fla, 70. *Exhib:* One-woman shows, Ward Eggleston Galleries, New York, 59, Fairleigh Dickinson Univ, NJ, 60 & Lord & Taylor Art Gallery, 63-78; Sinnard Art Studio, New York; Chevy Chase Gallery, Washington, DC. *Bibliog:* Article in Art News, 54; James E Duffy (auth), article in World Telegram, 59; Fran Hepperle (auth), article in Times Herald Rec, 72-83. *Media:* Oil. *Dealer:* Bergdorf Goodman c/o Nena's Choice Gallery Fifth Ave at 57th St New York NY 10019; Corp Art Dirs Inc 41 E 57th St New York NY 10002. *Mailing Add:* Box 304 New Hampton NY 10958

SINTON, NELL (WALTER)
PAINTER, EDUCATOR
b San Francisco, Calif. *Study:* San Francisco Art Inst, with Maurice Sterne; Inst Creative & Artistic Develop. *Work:* San Francisco Mus Art; Oakland Mus Art, Calif; Chase Manhattan Bank, New York; Am Tel & Tel Co, NJ; Mills Col, Oakland; and others. *Exhib:* San Francisco Mus Art, 57, 63 & 70; Staempfli Gallery, New York, 60; Am Acad Arts & Lett, New York, 67; Univ

Calif, Berkeley, 72; The Modern Era, Smithsonian Inst, DC, 77; 30 yr retrospective, Mills Col, 81; and others. *Pos:* Artist mem, San Francisco Art Comn, City & Co, 58-63. *Teaching:* Instr drawing, San Francisco Art Inst, 70-71; lectr symp, Mt Holyoke Col, Mass, 76; artist-in-residence, La State Univ, 77 & Univ of Ill, Urbana, 78; instr drawing & painting, Col Marin, 80- *Awards:* San Francisco Art Inst Award, De Young Mus, 56; Oakland Mus Art Awards, 58 & 61. *Bibliog:* M Tapie (auth), Morphologie autre, 60; F Martin (auth), Review San Francisco, Art Int, 63 & Artforum, 63 & 67. *Media:* Acrylic, Oil. *Dealer:* Braunstein Gallery 254 Sutter St San Francisco CA 94108. *Mailing Add:* 1020 Francisco St San Francisco CA 94109

SIPIORA, LEONARD PAUL
MUSEUM DIRECTOR, MUSEOLOGIST
b Lawrence, Mass, Sept 1, 34. *Study:* Vanderbilt Univ; Univ Mich, Ann Arbor, AB(cum laude), 55, MA, 56. *Collections Arranged:* Ann Nat Sun Carnival Exhib; Biennial, Int Designer Craftsmen; W S Horton Retrospective, 70; Tom Lea Retrospective, 71; Walter Griffin Retrospective, 71. *Pos:* Co-founder & pres, El Paso Arts Coun, 69-70, dir, 71-; dir, El Paso Mus Art, 67- *Mem:* Tex Asn Mus (pres, 77-79); Am Asn Mus; Am Fedn Arts; Am Platform Asn; Asn Art Mus Dir. *Res:* Nineteenth and twentieth century American painting. *Collection:* American paintings and graphics. *Publ:* Auth, The Universality of Tom Lea (catalog), 71; auth, A community oriented art museum, Southwest Gallery Art Mag, 71; auth foreword, Biography of John Enneking, 72. *Mailing Add:* 1211 Montana St El Paso TX 79902

SIRENA (CONTESSA ANTONIA MASTROCRISTINO FANARA)
PAINTER, COLLECTOR
b White Plains, NY. *Work:* Mus Campidoglio, Mus Mod Art, Rome, Italy; Mus Castello Sforzesco, Milano, Italy; Regione Fruili Venezia Giulia, Regione Siciliana; Regione Sarda. *Comn:* Paintings for Federico Fellini, Frankie Laine, Gina Lollobrigida, Vittorio de Sica, The Vatican & Pope Paul XI. *Exhib:* One-woman shows, Gallerie Andre Weil, Paris, 68, Mike Douglas TV Show Exhib, 68, Palazzo delle Esposizioni, Comune di Roma, Rome, 69 & State Gallery in Teatro Massimo, Palermo, Sicily, 70; C W Post Univ Gallery, 77; and many others. *Pos:* Dir, Sirena Art Studios, New York, formerly. *Awards:* Gold Medal of Pres of Senate, Italy & Mayor of Rome, 72; Gold Medal Award, Accad of Paestum; Artist of the Year Award, Int Beaux Arts, 81; and many others. *Bibliog:* Guilio Bolaffi (auth), Bolaffi on modern art, Torino, Italy, 70 & 72; Giovanni Quattrucci (auth), Sirena, Europe Ed, 72; 3 paintings in Family Bible Encycl, Vol 19-20, Curtis Books & Copylab, 72. *Mem:* Accad of Paestum; Accad dei 500; Accad Tiberina; Int Comt Cult, Rome; Metrop Mus Art. *Publ:* Illusr & auth, autobiography, MPH Publ, 76. *Mailing Add:* 1035 Fifth Ave New York NY 10028

SIRKIS, NANCY
PHOTOGRAPHER, EDUCATOR
b New York, NY, Aug 22, 36. *Study:* RI Sch Design, BFA, 58; Hunter Col, New York, MA, 82. *Work:* Skidmore Col Art Gallery, Saratoga, NY. *Exhib:* Solo shows, Witkin Gallery, 70, Jewish Mus, 71 & AIR Gallery, 81, New York; Addison Gallery, Andover, Mass, 72; Douglass Col, New Brunswick, NJ, 74; and others. *Teaching:* Staff instr, Int Ctr Photog, 76-; instr photog, Marymount Manhattan Col, 78- *Mem:* Col Art Asn. *Publ:* Auth, Newport: Pleasures and Palaces, 63, auth, Boston, 65, auth, Reflections of 1776: The Colonies Revisited, 74 & auth, Massachusetts: From the Berkshires to the Cape, 77, Viking Press; auth, One Family, Little Brown & Co, 70. *Mailing Add:* 310 Riverside Dr New York NY 10025

SIRUGO, SAL (SALVATORE)
PAINTER
b Pozzallo, Italy; US citizen. *Study:* Art Students League, 48-49; Brooklyn Mus Art Sch, NY, 50-51. *Work:* NY Univ; Pace Univ, New York; Southern Ill Univ, Carbondale; Dillard Univ, New Orleans, La; Ciba-Geigy Corp, Harrison, NY; and others. *Exhib:* Whitney Mus Am Art Ann, New York, 52; Pa Acad Fine Arts Ann, Philadelphia, 53; one-man exhibs, Tanager Gallery, 61, K Gallery, 63, Great Jones Gallery, 66 & Landmark Gallery, 76, 78 & 81, Gallery Asn New York, Traveling Exhib, 78-80; and others. *Awards:* Woodstock Found Award, Woodstock Artists Asn, 52; Longview Found Award, 62; Creative Artists Pub Serv Prog Fel, 79-80. *Bibliog:* Corinne Robins (auth), Sal Sirugo, Arts, 1/77; Joellen Bard (auth), Sal Sirugo, Arts, 12/78; Tram Combs (auth), Sirugo's miniature sublime, Woodstock Times, 2/19/81. *Mem:* Life mem Art Students League; Artists' Club. *Media:* Acrylic, Inks. *Dealer:* Landmark Gallery 469 Broome St New York NY 10013. *Mailing Add:* 321 W 24th St New York NY 10011

SISCHY, INGRID B
EDITOR, CURATOR
b Johannesburg, SAfrica, Mar 2, 52; Brit citizen. *Study:* Sarah Lawrence Col, BA, 73. *Exhib:* In the Twenties: Portraits from Photog Collection, Mus Mod Art, New York, 79 & 80. *Pos:* Asst ed, Print Collector's Newslett, 75-76 & assoc ed, 76-77; curatorial intern, Dept Photog, Mus Mod Art, New York, 78-79; dir, Printed Matter Inc, 78-80; ed, Artforum, 80- *Mailing Add:* c/o Art Forum Mag 205 Mulberry St New York NY 10012

SISLER, REBECCA
SCULPTOR, WRITER
b Mt Forest, Ont, Oct 16, 32. *Study:* Ont Col of Art; Royal Danish Acad Fine Arts. *Work:* Art Gallery of Ont, Toronto; Hamilton Teacher's Col, Ont; Peel Art Gallery; Univ Guelph. *Comn:* Stone fountain group, Centennial Park, St Thomas, Ont, 66; peace mem, Town of Markham, 67; The Knight (stone figure), comn by pvt donor for Peel Art Gallery, Brampton, 74; wooden cross, St Paul's Cathedral, London, Ont, 68. *Exhib:* Royal Can Acad; Art Gallery

Ont, Toronto; Nat Gallery Can, Ottawa, Ont; Artist's Choice, Can Nat Exhib, 68; Ont Soc Artists 100 Yrs, Art Gallery Ont, 72; Toronto-Dominion Sculpture Exhib, Toronto-Dominion Ctr, Toronto, 72; Ann Show of Ont Soc Artists & Sculptors, Soc Can, Art Gallery Ont. *Pos:* Educ dir, McMichael Can Collection, 69-70; dir, Sisler Gallery, 74-77; exec dir, Royal Can Acad Arts, 78-82; cult attache to Gov Gen Can, 82- *Awards:* Sculpture Award, Art Gallery of Toronto, Can Coun, 58 & Can Nat Exhib Artist's Choice, 68. *Bibliog:* Pearl McCarthy (auth), Art & artists, 58, Kay Kritzwiser (auth), Sisler, an industrious sculptor, 64 & Art, 73, Globe & Mail, Toronto. *Mem:* Royal Can Acad Arts (coun, 76-77); Sculptor's Soc Can; Ont Soc Artists. *Media:* Multimedia. *Publ:* Auth, The Girls, A Biography of Frances Loring & Florence Wyle, Clarke-Irwin, 72; auth, Frances Loring, Monograph & Florence Wyle, Monograph, Dundurn Press, 77; auth, Passionate Spirits: A History of the Royal Canadian Academy of Arts 1880-1980, Clarke-Irwin, 80; and others. *Mailing Add:* Box 135 Old Chelsea PQ J0X 2N0 Canada

SISSOM, EVELYN JANELLE See Lee-Sissom, E

SISSON, LAURENCE P
PAINTER
b Boston, Mass, Apr 27, 28. *Study:* Worcester Mus Sch, grad, 49; Yale Univ, summer sch, scholar, 48-49. *Work:* Mus Fine Arts, Boston; Portland Mus, Maine; Dartmouth Col; DeCordova Mus, Mass; Worcester Mus, Mass. *Comn:* Four murals, Boston Five Cent Saving Bank Br Offs, 55-67; mural, Worcester Polytech Inst, 66; mural, Carrick Agency, Whitinsville, Mass, 72. *Exhib:* Hallmark Int Exhib, 49; Ill Art Festival, 51; Am Watercolor Soc, 55-60; one-man shows, Gallery Mod Art, New York, 69 & Brockton Art Ctr, Mass, 72. *Pos:* Corporator, Worcester Art Mus, 72- *Teaching:* Teacher & dir, Portland Art Mus Sch, Maine, 54-58. *Awards:* Fourth Am Prize, Hallmark Int Show, 49; First Prize, Boston Arts Festival, 56 & 64 & Boston Watercolor Soc, 57. *Bibliog:* Maine Harvesters of the Sea (film), Film Group, 69; W Caldwell (auth), The man and the artist, Down E Mag, 68. *Media:* Oil, Watercolor. *Publ:* Auth, Along Time River, 75. *Dealer:* Gerald Peters 439 Camino del Monte Sol Santa Fe NM 87501; O'Brien's Art Emporium Inc 7122 Stetson Dr Scottsdale AZ 85251. *Mailing Add:* Rte 1 Box 170 Santa Fe NM 87501

SISTI, (TONY) ANTHONY J
COLLECTOR, PAINTER
b New York, NY, Apr 21, 01. *Study:* Albright Art Sch, Buffalo; Royal Acad, Florence, Italy; with Felice Carena; Acad Julian, Paris, France; Royal Acad, Munich. *Comn:* Portrait, Hon Frank A Sedita, Mayor of Buffalo, Fedn Ital Socs of Buffalo, 70. *Exhib:* One-man & group exhibs, Mus Mod Art, Mus of City of New York & Riverside Mus, New York; one-man show, Carl Battaglia Gallery Ltd, New York, 78; Calif Palace of Legion of Honor, San Francisco; Howard Univ, Washington, DC; Albright-Knox Art Gallery; plus others. *Awards:* Prize, Patteran Soc, 43; Prize, Western NY Exhib, Buffalo, 47; Prize, Buffalo Soc Artists, 47; and others. *Collection:* Old masters, impressionists, modern art. *Mailing Add:* 469 Franklin St Buffalo NY 14203

SITTON, JOHN M
PAINTER, LECTURER
b Forsyth, Ga, Jan 9, 07. *Study:* Yale Univ, BFA, 29; Am Acad Rome, fel painting, 29-32; with Eugene Savage & Barry Faulkner. *Work:* Addison Gallery Am Art, Andover, Mass; Mint Mus, Charlotte, NC; Lubbock Art Mus, Tex. *Comn:* Mural painting, Bd Room, Fed Res Bldg, Atlanta, Ga, 37; mural, Riverside Mem Chapel, New York, 38. *Exhib:* One-man exhib, Grand Cent Art Galleries, New York, 33; High Art Mus, Atlanta, 39, Light House Gallery, Tequesta, Fla, 71 & Parker Playhouse, Ft Lauderdale, Fla, 71; American Painters in Paris, 76; plus others. *Pos:* Dir, Finch Summer Sch Painting, 38; dir life drawing, NY Sch Appl Design Women, 38-41. *Teaching:* Instr art anat, NY Univ, 32; instr watercolor, Columbia Univ, 36-37; asst prof painting & art hist, Cornell Univ, 40-44. *Awards:* Prix de Rome, Am Acad Rome, 29; Nat Mural Competition, Riverside Mem Chapel, 38; First Award Portraiture (oil), Broward Art Guild, Ft Lauderdale, 75; Water Color Prize, Fla Tri-Co Award Ann Exhib, 78. *Mem:* Life mem Century Asn; life mem Allied Artists Am; Alumni Asn Am Acad Rome; Boca Raton Art Ctr; Artist Equity Asn. *Media:* Oil, Watercolor. *Publ:* Auth, An adventure in painting, 38 & Painting of my silk decorations, 38, Art Instr Mag. *Mailing Add:* 1241 SE 14th St Deerfield Beach FL 33441

SIVARD, ROBERT PAUL
PAINTER
b New York, NY, Dec 7, 14. *Study:* Pratt Inst; Nat Acad Design; Acad Julian, Paris. *Work:* NJ State Mus Art; Gibbs Art Gallery, Charleston, SC; Libr Cong, Washington, DC; US Info Agency, Dept State. *Comn:* Murals (with Frank Schwartz), Ore State Capitol, 39; commemorative postage stamp, The American Woman, 60. *Exhib:* 15 One-man shows, Midtown Gallery, New York, 54-80; Mus Art Mod, Paris, 54; US Embassy, Paris, 55 & 71; Carnegie Int, 57; Galerie Charpentier, 59; Philadelphia Mus, 60; Dallas Mus, 65. *Collections Arranged:* US Nat Exhib, Moscow, 59; Off US Exhibs, Sao Paulo Bienales, 59, 61, 63 & 65 & Venice Bienales, 62 & 64. *Pos:* Dir visual & art serv, US Embassy, Paris, 50-55; chief exhibs div, US Info Agency, 58-65; agency art dir, 66-75. *Awards:* Gold Medal, Art Dirs Club, 58; Butler Mus Purchase Prize, 70; Purchase Prize, Am Inst & Acad, 80. *Bibliog:* Articles, Medicine de France, No 222, 71, Chicago Tribune Mag, 6/2/74 & Smithsonian Mag, 12/76. *Media:* Casein, Oil. *Dealer:* Midtown Gallery 11 E 57th St New York NY 10022. *Mailing Add:* 3013 Dumbarton Ave NW Washington DC 20007

SKALAGARD, HANS
MARINE PAINTER, LECTURER
b Skuo, Faroe Islands, Europe, Feb 7, 24; nat US. *Study:* Royal Acad Art, Copenhagen; with marine artist Anton Otto Fisher, New York. *Work:* Constitution, Dudley Knox Libr & War of 1812 Constitution & Guerriere, Hermann Hall, Naval Post Grad Sch, Monterey, Calif; Casco, Reid Hall, Robert Louis Stevenson Sch, Pebble Beach, Calif; Frigate Ship United States, Salvation Army Hq & Savannah US Frigate, Allen Knight Maritime Mus, Monterey; and others. *Comn:* Olivebank Deck View, comn by Dr Wm Rustad, Sea Cliff, San Francisco, 68; USN BB Maine, comn by Hal Whitten, Dean Witter & Assoc, San Mateo, Calif, 73; Anna Maerske, comn by Capt Olsen, Port Capt Maersk Line, San Francisco, 75; and other pvt collections. *Exhib:* Calif Palace of the Legion of Honor, 60; Lucein Labaudt Art Gallery, San Francisco, 60; Robert Louis Stevenson Sch, 67, 68 & 69; Galerie De Tours, San Francisco, 72; Gallerie Vallombreuse, Biarritz, France, 75; New Los Angeles Maritime Mus, 80; Skaalegaard's Square-Rigger Art Gallery, Carmel, Calif, 81; and others. *Pos:* Dir, Skaalegaard's Square-Rigger Art Gallery, Carmel, 66-; Calif hist librn, Mayo Hayes O'Donnel Libr, Monterey Hist & Art Asn, 72 & 73; dir bd, Allen Knight Maritime Mus, 72-76; cult dir, Sons of Norway, Monterey, 74-76. *Awards:* Silver Medal & Hon Dipl, 70; Gold Medal & Title Master Painter, Tommaso Campanella Acad Arts, Lett & Sci, Rome, 72; Gold Medal, Academia Italia Delle Arti e Del Honoro, Parma, 80. *Bibliog:* Judith A Eisner (auth), Carmel closeup, Pine Cone, Carmel, 9/14/72; and others. *Mem:* Life hon Academia Italia Delle Arti e Del Honoro. *Media:* Multimedia. *Mailing Add:* Los Cortes Bldg PO Box 6611 Carmel CA 93921

SKELLEY, ROBERT CHARLES
EDUCATOR, PRINTMAKER
b Bellevue, Ohio, Jan 15, 34. *Study:* Ind Univ, AB & MFA. *Work:* Libr of Cong, Washington, DC; Mint Mus, Charlotte, NC; Montgomery Mus Art, Ala; Springfield Col, Mass; Southern Ill Univ, Carbondale. *Exhib:* Dixie Ann Graphic Exhib, Montgomery Mus Art; Boston Printmakers, Mass; Mint Mus Ann Graphics; Libr Cong Print Ann; American Graphics, Col of Pac, Stockton, Calif. *Teaching:* Prof graphic design, Univ Fla, Gainesville, 61-81. *Awards:* Dixie Ann Best in Show Purchase, Montgomery Mus Art; Boston Printmakers Hon Mention, Boston Mus Art; Libr of Cong Purchase Award. *Bibliog:* Graphic rev in La Rev Mod, 1/65 & Art Rev Mag, 4/66; Norman Kent (auth), Robert Skelley wood cuts, Am Artist Mag, 1/71; Lanny Sommesse (auth), Robert Skelley Woodcuts, Novum Gebrauchs Graphik, 10/76. *Mem:* Soc Am Graphic Artists; Southern Graphic Artist Circle. *Mailing Add:* Dept of Art Univ Fla Gainesville FL 32607

SKEMP, ROBERT OLIVER
PAINTER
b Scottdale, Pa, Aug 22, 10. *Study:* Art Students League, with Thomas Hart Benton, George Bridgman, George Luks, Frank DuMond & Robert Laurent, 28-29; Grand Cent Sch Art, 29-30; in France & Spain; also with Charles Baskerville & J Cummings Chase, 30-32. *Work:* Rayburn Bldg, US Coast Guard, Anderson House, Pentagon, Washington, DC; Gov's Mansion, Raleigh, NC; New York Pub Libr; Ackland Gallery, Univ NC, Chapel Hill; Springfield Art Mus, Ill. *Comn:* Man's Search for Happiness, Church of Jesus Christ of Latter-Day Saints, World's Fair, New York, 64 & Osaka, Japan, 69; portrait, Gen Armistead Maupin for Order of the Cincinnati, Washington, DC, 74; portrait, J Paul Getty, Getty Oil Corp, Delaware City, Del, 78; portrait, Mr & Mrs Lowell Thomas, Pawling, NY; portrait, Secy Treasury Donald Regan, Pace Univ, NY; and others. *Exhib:* Am Soc Marine Artists, World Trade Ctr, 79; Int Maritime Art Awards Show, The Gallery, Mystic, Conn, 80-81; Contemp Marine Art, Peabody Mus, Salem, Mass, 81. *Awards:* Gold Medal, 51, two Gold Medals, 52 & Second & Third Places, 53, Art Dirs Club Chicago. *Bibliog:* Howard Munce (auth), Portrait painting, Northlight Mag, winter 70. *Mem:* Fel Am Soc Marine Artists (dir, 79-83). *Media:* Oil. *Dealer:* Portraits Inc 985 Park Ave New York NY 10028; Grand Cent Art Gallery 50 E 50th St New York NY. *Mailing Add:* 32 Hyde Lane Westport CT 06880

SKINNER, ELSA KELLS
ILLUSTRATOR, PAINTER
b Syracuse, NY. *Study:* Syracuse Univ, BFA; Univ NMex, with Randall Davey & Kenneth Adams; also with Rex Brant, Milford Zornes, Robert E Wood, Jr, Bud Biggs & George Post. *Work:* Albuquerque City Hall; Bernalillo Co Health Bldg, Albuquerque; NMex Bank & Trust Co, Hobbs; Miccosukee Indian Learning Ctr, Fla. *Comn:* Oil portrait of Onate, NMex Hist Soc, NMex State Univ, Las Cruces. *Exhib:* Nat Asn Am Pen Women Nat, Smithsonian Inst, Washington, DC, 60; Mus NMex Biennial, Santa Fe, 63; Southwestern Regional, Oklahoma City, 64; El Paso Sun Carnival Nat, Tex, 67; Albuquerque I, Mus of Albuquerque, NMex, 69; Watercolor Oklahoma, Oklahoma City Mus, 75. *Pos:* Painter & designer, Charles Hall, New York, 32-33; freelance bookjacket designer, Thomas Nelson & Sons, 34-35; designer, Decorative Utilities Corp, Newark, NJ, 34-40; freelance illusr & designer, Berland Printing Co, New York, 35-39. *Awards:* three First Prizes, NMex State Fair; Old Mine at Golden, First Purchase Award, City of Albuquerque, 68. *Media:* Watercolor. *Dealer:* NMex Art League's Ken Roberts Gallery 3401 Juan Tabo Blvd Albuquerque NM. *Mailing Add:* 2245 Inez Dr Albuquerque NM 87110

SKINNER, ORIN ENSIGN
DESIGNER
b Sweden Valley, Pa, Nov 5, 1892. *Study:* Rochester Atheneum Art Sch, NY, with Herman J Butler, dipl, 15; also res in France & Eng, 23-25. *Comn:* Stained glass windows, Princeton Univ Chapel, 30, St John the Divine Cathedral, New York, 32, Heinz Mem Chapel, Univ Pittsburgh, 38, St Patrick's Cathedral, New York, 56 & Grace Cathedral, San Francisco, 66. *Pos:* Designer, Charles A Baker, Rochester, 12-16; designer, R Toland Wright, Cleveland, 17-19; mgr, treas & pres, Charles J Connick Assocs, 20-; ed, Stained Glass, 30-48. *Awards:* Master Craftsman, Boston Soc Arts & Crafts, 40. *Mem:* Fel Int Inst Arts & Lett; fel Stained Glass Asn Am (pres, 48-49). *Media:* Stained Glass. *Res:* Restoration of Great Western Rose Window of Rheims Cathedral. *Publ:* Contribr, Am Architect, 27, Liturgical Arts, 37, Am Fabricks, 50 & Holy Cross Mag, 67. *Mailing Add:* 37 Walden St Newtonville MA 02160

SKLAR, DOROTHY
PAINTER
b New York, NY. *Study:* Univ Calif, Los Angeles, BE; Chouinard Art Ctr Sch, Los Angeles; also with S Macdonald Wright & Millard Sheets. *Work:* Los Angeles Munic Art Comn, Los Angeles City Hall; Baptist Univ, Shawnee, Okla; Westside Jewish Community Ctr, Los Angeles. *Exhib:* Pa Acad Fine Arts, 53, 54 & 57; Los Angeles Co Mus Art, 55; Butler Inst Am Art, Youngstown, Ohio, 63-68; Frye Mus, Seattle, Wash, 66; Calif State Fair, Sacramento, 66; Nat Soc Painters in Casein & Acrylic, 77. *Teaching:* Instr art, Santa Monica City Schs, 43. *Awards:* Awad in Oil, Laguna MusArt, 60; Ida M Holiday Mem Award, Nat Asn Women Artists, 60; Childe Hassam Award, Frye Mus, 66. *Mem:* Nat Watercolor Soc (treas, 61, vpres, 62); Artists Equity Asn (treas, Southern Calif Chap, 51); Nat Soc Painters Casein; Nat Asn Women Artists; Artists for Econ Action (vpres, 77-); and others. *Media:* Watercolor, Acrylic. *Mailing Add:* 6612 Colgate Los Angeles CA 90048

SKLAR-WEINSTEIN, ARLENE (JOYCE)
PAINTER, PRINTMAKER
b Detroit, Mich, Oct 25, 31. *Study:* Parsons Sch Design; Mus Mod Art, New York, scholar & with Bernard Pfreim; Albright Art Sch; NY Univ, with Hale Woodruff, BA, 52, MS(art educ), 55; Pratt Graphics Ctr, with Andrew Stasik; Ctr for Understanding Media, film making, 74; College of New Rochelle, 75, 81. *Work:* Mus Mod Art, New York; New York Pub Libr Permanent Print Collection; Grace Gallery, New York City Community Col, Brooklyn; Hudson River Mus Permanent Collection, Yonkers, NY; Metrop Mus Art, Slide Libr; and others. *Exhib:* Regional graphics, Albright-Knox Gallery, Buffalo, NY, 52; Yonkers Art Asn Regional, Hudson River Mus, 70 & 71; Nat Asn Women Artists Nat, Lever House, New York, 72; one-man shows, Evolutions, Hudson River Mus, 71 & West Broadway Gallery, 72, 73, 75, 76, 78 & 80; Wool Bureau, New York, 83. *Pos:* Visual arts coordr, Coun Arts Westchester, White Plains, NY, 69-70. *Teaching:* Art specialist, Hillside Sch, Hastings-on-Hudson, NY, 73-81; lower sch art specialist, Marymount Sch NY, 81- *Awards:* Geigy Award for Painting, Ciba-Geigy Corp, 69; First Prize, Hudson River Mus Regional, Yonkers Art Asn, 71; Print Competition Award, Gestetner Corp, 71. *Bibliog:* Masters & Houston (auths), Psychedelic Art, Grove, 68; H H Arnason (auth), History of Modern Art, Abrams, 69. *Mem:* Yonkers Art Asn, Hudson River Mus (pres, 70-72); Women in Art (rotating leadership, 72); The Abraxas Group, Westchester; Mamaroneck Artist Guild; Hastings Creative Arts Coun (bd mem, 73-). *Media:* Acrylic, Serigraph; Fiber. *Dealer:* West Broadway Gallery 431 W Broadway New York NY 10013. *Mailing Add:* 18 Harvard Lane Hastings-on-Hudson NY 10706

SKOFF, GAIL LYNN
PHOTOGRAPHER
b Los Angeles, Calif. *Study:* Univ Calif, Berkeley, 67-69; San Francisco Art Inst, BFA, 72, MFA, 79. *Work:* Nat Mus Am Art, Smithsonian Inst; Bibliot Nat, Paris; Oakland Mus, Calif; Ctr Creative Photog, Tucson, Ariz; Smith Col Art Gallery. *Exhib:* Exchange, Ft Worth Mus Art & San Francisco Mus Mod Art, 75-76; Attitudes: Photography in the '70's, Santa Barbara Mus Art; Soc Encouragement Contemp Art Photog Invitational, San Francisco Mus Mod Art, 80; Contemporary Hand-Colored Photographs, DeSaisset Mus, Univ Santa Clara, 81; American Photographers and the National Parks, traveling to New York Pub Libr, Los Angeles Co Mus, Amon Carter Mus, Corcoran Gallery, and others; In Color: Ten California Photographers, Oakland Mus, 83. *Teaching:* Instr photog and hand-colored photog, Univ Calif Extension, San Francisco, 76-; instr photog, Univ Calif, Berkeley, summer 80. *Awards:* Nat Endowment Arts Photogr Fel, 76. *Bibliog:* Hal Fisher (auth), article, Artforum, 80; Contemporary hand-colored photography, Picture Mag, 81; Dana Asbury (auth), Gail Skoff/Judy Dater, Popular Photog, 83. *Mailing Add:* 1718 Jaynes St Berkeley CA 94703

SKOGLUND, SANDRA LOUISE
PHOTOGRAPHER, SCULPTOR
b Boston, Mass, Sept 11, 46. *Study:* Smith Col, BA, 68; Univ Iowa, MFA, 72. *Work:* Metrop Mus Art, New York; St Louis Mus Art, Mo; Dallas Mus Art, Tex; Addison Mus Am Art, Mass; Univ Mass Gallery Art, Amherst. *Exhib:* Contemporary Photographs, Fogg Art Mus, Harvard Univ, Boston, 80; Installation: Radioactive Cats, Addison Mus Am Art, Mass, 80; Installation: Revenge of the Goldfish, Ft Worth Art Mus, Tex, 81; Whitney Biennale, Whitney Mus Am Art, New York, 81; New American Color Photography, Inst Contemp Art, England, 81; The New Color, Int Ctr Photog, New York, 81. *Awards:* Emerging Artist, Nat Endowment Arts, 80. *Bibliog:* Carol DiGrappa (auth), article, Camera Arts Mag, 5/6/81. *Dealer:* Castelli Graphics 4 E 77th St New York NY 10021. *Mailing Add:* 253 Elizabeth St New York NY 10012

SKY, ALISON
ENVIRONMENTAL ARTIST
b New York, NY, Aug 1, 46. *Study:* Columbia Univ, 62; Adelphi Univ, with Peter Lipman-Wulf, BA(fine arts), 67; Art Students League, with Jose de

Creeft & John Hovannes, scholar, 67-69. *Work:* Smithsonian Inst, Washington, DC; Mus Mod Art, New York; and others. *Comn:* Best Products Co Inc, Richmond, Va, 78; Nat Shopping Ctrs Inc, 77-78; WilliWear Ltd, 82; McDonald Corp, 83; Formica Corp, 83; and others. *Exhib:* Louvre, Paris, 75; Cooper Hewitt Mus, New York, 78; America Now, traveling, Hudson River Mus, New York & Wadsworth Atheneum, Hartford, Conn, 79; Mus Mod Art, New York, 79; and others. *Pos:* Vpres & co-founder principal, SITE Projects Inc, 78- *Awards:* Int Design, Am Soc Interior Designers, 79; Award, Progressive Archit, 80; Ward for Showroom Design, Interiors Mag, 83. *Mem:* Fel Am Acad Rome. *Media:* Multi-Media. *Publ:* Auth, Sky Book, Profile Press, 72; ed, On SITE On Energy, SITE/Scribners, 74; coauth, Unbuilt America, McGraw-Hill, 76; coauth, SITE: Projects and Theories 1969-1978, Dedalo Libri, 78; coauth, SITE: Architecture as Art, Acad Ed & St Martins Press, 81. *Dealer:* Ronald Feldman Fine Arts 31-33 Mercer St New York NY 10012. *Mailing Add:* 83 Spring St New York NY 10012

SLADE, ROY
PAINTER, GALLERY DIRECTOR
b Cardiff, Wales, July 14, 33. *Study:* Cardiff Col Art, NDD, 54; Univ Wales, ATD, 54. *Work:* Arts Coun Gt Brit; Contemp Art Soc; Nuffield Found; Westinghouse Corp; Brit Overseas Airways Corp. *Exhib:* One-man shows, Jefferson Pl Gallery, Washington, DC, 68, 70 & 72; Washington Art, State Univ NY Col, Potsdam & State Univ NY, Albany, 71; Nat Print Club, Nat Col Fine Art, Washington, DC, 72; Pyramid Gallery, Washington DC, 76 & 77; Robert Kidd Gallery, Birmingham, Mich, 81; and others. *Pos:* Vchmn, Comt Art in Pub Places, State of Mich, 83-; comnr, Comn on Inst Higher Educ, NCentral Asn Col & Sch, 83- *Teaching:* Sr lectr post-grad studies, Leeds Col Art, Eng, 64-69; prof painting, Corcoran Sch Art, Washington, DC, 67-68, dean, 70-77, dir, Gallery, 72-; pres, Cranbrook Acad of Art, Bloomfield Hills, Mich, 77- *Awards:* Fulbright-Hays Scholar, 67; Welsh Soc of Philadelphia Award. *Mem:* Nat Soc of Lit & Arts; Nat Coun Art Admin (chmn, 81-). *Publ:* Auth, Report from Washington, Studio Int, 1/72; Studio Int; auth, A new cultural centre, Yorkshire Post, 2/69; auth, Artist in America, Contemp Rev, 5/69; The Temple Flourishes, Nat Council of Art Administrators Publ, 80; auth, Toward understanding and collaboration, Nat Asn Sch Art & Design Publ & Asn Art Mus Dir Publ, 82. *Dealer:* Pyramid Galleries Ltd 2121 P NW Washington DC 20037; Robert Kidd Gallery 107 Townsend Birmingham MI 48011. *Mailing Add:* c/o Cranbrook Acad of Art 500 Lone Pine Rd PO Box 801 Bloomfield Hills MI 48013

SLATE, JOSEPH FRANK
PAINTER, WRITER
b Holliday's Cove, WVa, Jan 19, 28. *Study:* Univ Wash, BA, 51; printmaking, Tokyo, Japan, 57; Yale Univ Sch Art & Archit, Alumni fel & BFA, 60; study of sumi-e painting, Kyoto, Japan, 75. *Work:* Drawings, Yale Univ; Poems & Prints (bk), Newberry Collection of Rare Bks, Univ Chicago. *Exhib:* 12th Nat Print Show, Brooklyn Mus, 60; Artist in Residence Exhib, Milton Col, Univ Wis, 63; Whitney Mus, New York, 74; Cent Ohio Watercolor Soc, Schumacher Gallery, Columbus, 75; Hopkins Hall Gallery, Columbus, Ohio, 76; Mus Art, Port Huron, Mich, 78; Colburn Gallery, Kenyon Col, 83. *Pos:* Consult, studies on aesthet & perception, Yale Univ Dept Psychol, 60-65; mem exec comt, Kress Found Consortium Art Hist, 65-69; consult, Nat Endowment for the Arts, 77-78. *Teaching:* Chmn dept, Kenyon Col, 64-72 & 81-82, prof art, 62-, chmn fine arts div, 67-69. *Awards:* Yale Alumni Fel, 60; Painting Award, Ohio Expo, 62; Outstanding Educator of Am, 73. *Bibliog:* Janice Prindle (auth), Before we sleep, Village Voice, 10/82; Wash Alumnus, fall 82; article, Publishers Weekly, 9/16/83. *Mem:* Soc Children's Book Writers; Authors Guild; and others. *Publ:* Auth, Those Old Italians, 62 & Respect, 64, New Yorker; auth, The Star Rocker, Harper & Row, 82; auth, How Little Porcupine Played Christmas, Crowell, 82; auth, The Mean, Clean, Giant Canoe Machine, Crowell, 83; and others. *Mailing Add:* Box A Gambier OH 43022

SLATER, GARY LEE
SCULPTOR
b Montevideo, Minn, Oct 27, 47. *Study:* Univ Minn, BFA, 70; Ariz State Univ, MFA, 73. *Work:* Sky Harbor Int Airport, Phoenix, Ariz; Mus Fine Arts, NMex; City Monterey Park, Calif; City Palo Alto, Calif; Tucson Mus Art, Ariz. *Comn:* Sculpture, Mohave Savings and Loan, Kingman, Ariz, 80; sculpture, Westridge Mall, Phoenix, Ariz, 81; sculpture, City Casa Grande, Ariz, 81; sculpture, WTTW TV, Chicago, 82; Charles Goddard Ctr Arts, Ardmore, Okla. *Exhib:* Two-man show, Corten Steel: Contemp Sculpture, Bowers Mus, Santa Ana, Calif, 74; SW Fine Arts Biennial, Santa Fe, NMex, 76; Summer Outdoor Sculpture Exhib, Palo Alto, Calif, 77; Ariz Biennial, Tucson Mus Art, 80; NAm Sculpture Exhib, Golden, Colo, 83; and others. *Awards:* Nat Endowment Arts Grant, 73-74; Purchase Awards, 9th Ann Drawing & Sculpture Show, Del Mar Col, Corpus Christi, Tex, 75 & Ariz Outlook 76, Tucson Mus of Art, 76. *Media:* Metal. *Dealer:* Elaine Horwitch Gallery 4200 N Marshall Way Scottsdale AZ 85251. *Mailing Add:* 2037 W Camino Cir Mesa AZ 85201

SLATER, VAN E
PRINTMAKER, EDUCATOR
b Magnolia, Ark, June 14, 37. *Study:* Univ Calif, Los Angeles, BA & MA. *Work:* Oakland Mus, Calif; in pvt collection of Bill Cosby; Golden State Mutual Life Insurance, Los Angeles; and many other pub & pvt collections. *Exhib:* Oakland Mus; Emerald Gallery, Diplomat Hotel, Hollywood Beach, Fla; Long Beach Mus, Calif; Carnegie Inst, Pittsburgh; Huntsville Mus, Ala; plus many others. *Collections Arranged:* Community Art Exhibition, 73; Elementary Schools of Compton, Calif, 73; Dr Samella Lewis Art Exhibition & Lecture, 73; Art West Associated, Inc Art Exhibition, 74; Bernie Casey Art

Exhibition & Lecture, 74; plus many others. *Teaching:* Assoc prof art, Compton Col, Calif, 66-; drawing instr, Santa Monica City Col, 65-66; drawing instr, Los Angeles City Col, 69-70; lectr, many orgns; nat art consult. *Awards:* Hale Woodruff Award, Carnegie Inst, Pittsburgh, 71; Watts Festival Purchase Award, Calif, 71; and others. *Bibliog:* Dr Samella Lewis (auth), Art: African-American, 78. *Mem:* Artists Equity. *Res:* Afro-American and American art. *Publ:* Printmaking: Four Artists (film), Four Media, Babette Eddelston, 68; auth, Local Black Artists of Southern California, 69, 70 & 71; Black Art Black Artists (film), Univ Calif Exten, Los Angeles, 71; auth, Black Artists of Southern California, 72. *Mailing Add:* Compton Community Col 1111 E Artesia Blvd Compton CA 90221

SLATKES, LEONARD J
HISTORIAN
b Hartford, Conn, Jan 11, 30. *Study:* Syracuse Univ, BFA, 52; Oberlin Col, MA, 54; Inst Fine Arts, NY Univ, 56-58; Columbia Univ, 58-60; Univ Utrecht, Fulbright Fels, US Educ Found, PhD, 62, Sr Fulbright Scholar, 79-80. *Teaching:* Asst prof art hist, Univ Chicago, 62-64 & Univ Pittsburgh, 64-66; assoc prof art hist, Queens Col, City Univ New York, 66-81, prof, 81- *Awards:* Grant-in-Aid, Am Coun Learned Soc, 66; Research Grants, City Univ New York, 69, 78 & 81. *Mem:* Col Art Asn. *Res:* Northern Renaissance art; Northern mannerism; Italian and Northern Baroque art; history of graphic arts. *Publ:* Auth, Dirck van Baburen: A Dutch Artist in Utrecht and Rome, 65; auth, Hendrick Terbrugghen in America, 65-66; auth, The Netherlandish Artists, Vol I, 79; auth, Rembrandt, 80; auth, Vermeer and His Contemporaries, 81. *Mailing Add:* Dept of Art Queens Col Flushing NY 11367

SLATKIN, WENDY
HISTORIAN
b New York, NY, June 20, 50. *Study:* Barnard Col, Columbia Univ, with Barbara Novak, BA, 70; Villa Schifanoia Grad Sch Fine Arts, Florence, Italy, MA, 71; Univ Pa, with John McCoubrey, PhD, 76. *Teaching:* Asst prof art hist, survey & post-renaissance, Camden Col Arts & Sci, Rutgers Univ, 76-83; vis lectr, Univ Calif, Riverside, 83- *Publ:* Auth, The genesis of Maillol's la Mediterranee, Art J, spring, 79; auth, The early sculpture of Maillol, Gazette des Beaux Arts, 10/80; auth, Reminiscences of Maillol: A conversation with Dina Vierny, Arts Mag, 2/80; auth, Maternity and sexuality in the 1890's, Woman's Art J, spring 80; auth, Women Artists in History, Prentice-Hall, 84. *Mailing Add:* Art Hist Dept Univ Calif Riverside CA 92521

SLAUGHTER, LURLINE EDDY
PAINTER
b Heidelberg, Miss, June 19, 19. *Study:* Miss State Col Women, Columbus, grad; Miss Art Colony Workshops, with Alvin Sella, Fred Mitchell, Ida Kohlmeyer, Howard Goodson, Frank Engel, Andrew Bucci, Alex Russo & Bob Gelinas; pvt study with Marie Hull & Malcolm Norwood. *Work:* Pine Bluff Arts Ctr, Ark; Miss State Col Women; Univ of the South, Sewanee, Tenn; Miss State Univ, Starkville; Univ Southeastern La. *Exhib:* Six Nat Oil Painting Exhibs, Jackson, Miss, 60-69; Hunter Gallery Ann, Chattanooga, Tenn, 65; Cent South Ann, Parthenon Mus, Nashville, Tenn, 66; Masur Mus Ann, Monroe, La, 66; Fine Arts Registry, Brooks Mem Mus, Memphis, Tenn, 70; one-man shows, TV, Miss, Tenn & Ark. *Awards:* Outstanding Artist Award, Fine Arts Registry, 66; Best in Show Awards, Holiday Arts Festival, McComb, Miss, 67 & 75 & Miss Art Colony, 74; Best in Show, Acapulco Ann Invitational, 79. *Mem:* Miss Art Colony. *Media:* Acrylic, Oil. *Mailing Add:* Seldom Seen Plantation Silver City MS 39166

SLAVIN, ARLENE
PAINTER, MURALIST
b New York, NY, Oct 26, 42. *Study:* Cooper Union, BFA, 64; Pratt Inst, MFA, 67. *Work:* Brooklyn Mus, NY; Metrop Mus Art, New York; Fogg Art Mus, Cambridge, Mass; Allen Mem Art Mus, Oberlin, Ohio; Chase Manhattan, New York. *Comn:* Greeting card, Mus Mod Art, New York, 80; mural, Univ Colo, Colorado Springs, 81; mural, Pratt Inst, Brooklyn, 81; Albert Einstein Hosp, New York; NY Aquarium, Brooklyn; Pub Art Fund, New York; Hudson River Mus, Yonkers, NY. *Exhib:* Whitney Biennial Contemp Art, 73 & Am Drawings 1967-1973, Whitney Mus; one-woman shows, Alexander F Milliken Gallery, New York, 79-83 & Pratt Inst Gallery, 81; Six Decades of Collecting, Heckscher Mus, Huntington, NY, 81; Useable Art, Queens Mus, Flushing, NY, 81; Ornamentalism, Hudson River Mus, Yonkers, NY. *Teaching:* Instr painting, Hofstra Univ, Long Island, NY, 71-72, Pratt Inst, 74 & Skowhegan Art Sch, Maine, 75 & 76; vis critic, Grad Sch, Univ Pa, 77; vis artist, Syracuse Univ, NY, 79. *Awards:* Printmaking grant, Nat Endowment for the Arts, 77. *Bibliog:* Alexander Anderson (auth), Arlene Slavin folding screens, 5/80 & Susan Putterman (auth), Arlene Slavin aquarium, 11/81, Arts Mag; Robert Jensen & Patricia Conway (auths), Ornamentalism, Clarkson Potter, 82. *Media:* Mixed; Aquatints. *Dealer:* Alexander F Milliken Gallery 98 Prince St New York NY 10012; 724 Prints 93 Mercer St New York NY 10012. *Mailing Add:* 119 E 18th St New York NY 10003

SLAVIN, NEAL
PHOTOGRAPHER
b New York, NY, Aug 19, 41. *Study:* Scholar, Lincoln, Col, Oxford Univ, Eng, 61; Cooper Union, BFA, 63. *Work:* Metrop Mus Art, Mus Mod Art, Photog Arch, Int Ctr Photog, New York; Int Mus Photog, George Eastman House, Rochester, NY. *Exhib:* Rooms, Mus Mod Art, New York, 76; Documenta, Kassel, West Germany, 77; Venezia, The History of Polaroid, Venice, Italy, 79; The Official Cabinet Portraits of the Carter Administration, Nat Portrait Gallery, Washington, DC, 80; Aspects of Am Photog, Galerie

Spectrum, Hannover, West Germany, 81; The New Color, Int Ctr Photog, New York, 81; Color as Form: A History of Color Photog, Int Mus Photog & George Eastman House, Rochester, NY, 81; and others. *Pos:* Lectr, Cooper Union Forum, New York, 75, Int Mus Photog, Rochester, NY, 75, Int Ctr Photog, New York, 77, Univ Calif, Los Angeles, 77, Milan workshops, Italy, 78, Ansel Adams Workshop, Yosemite, Calif, 77 & 80 & Smithsonian Inst, Washington, DC, 81. *Awards:* Fulbright Fel Photog, Portugal, 68; Nat Endowment Arts Grant, 72; Creative Artist Pub Serv Prog Award, 77. *Bibliog:* Amerika 76, D U Mag, Switz, 1/76; The ten toughest photographs of 1975, Esquire, 2/76; New frontiers in color, Newsweek, 4/76. *Publ:* Auth, Portugal, Lustrum Press, 71; auth, When Two or More Are Gathered Together, Farrar, Straus & Giroux, 76; auth, Annie, Abbeville Press, New York, 81. *Mailing Add:* 62 Greene St New York NY 10012

SLAWINSKI, JOSEPH
MURALIST, CONSERVATOR
b Warsaw, Poland, Nov 27, 05; US citizen. *Study:* With S Kalinowski & W Drapiewski, Poland; Munic Sch Dec Arts & Painting, Warsaw, dipl; Acad Fine Arts, Warsaw, dipl; also studied in Italy, France, Belg & Holland. *Comn:* Ten hist paintings (sgraffito), Resurrection Mausoleum, Chicago, Ill, 67; Baptism of Mieszko (4 1/2ft x 7ft, hist copper), St Joseph's Cathedral, Cath Diocese of Buffalo, NY, 66; Cantacle to the Sun (sgraffito, 10ft x 6ft), Daemen Col, Snyder, NY, 68; Commodore Perry (sgraffito alfresco mural, 24 1/2ft x 9ft), Buffalo Bd of Educ, W Hertel Mid Sch, Buffalo, NY, 69; Peace (sgraffito mural, 22ft x 7 1/2ft), Barnabite Fathers, Our Lady of Fatima Basilica, 75. *Exhib:* Nat Mus, Warsaw, 54. *Pos:* Owner, Niagara Falls Gallery & Studio Sgraffito. *Teaching:* Prof mural techniques & conserv of works of art, Munic Sch Dec Arts & Painting & Acad Fine Arts, Warsaw, 37-47. *Awards:* Monetary Award, Nat Mus, Warsaw, 56; Polonia Restituta for Artistic Work & Lect, Poland, 46. *Media:* Sgraffito; Alfresco-Tempera. *Res:* Special study of Giotto's fresco technique in Assisi, Italy. *Specialty:* Mural art; sketches, drawings, work cartoons adapted to specific mural techniques; examples of mural techniques. *Mailing Add:* 125 Buffalo Ave Niagara Falls NY 14303

SLAYMAKER, MARTHA
PAINTER, PRINTMAKER
b Saratoga, Ind. *Study:* Edinboro Col, Pa; Ohio State Univ, Columbus; John Herron Sch Art, Ind Univ, with William Crutchfield, 60-62. *Work:* Indianapolis Mus Art, Ind; Albuquerque Mus Art, Hist & Sci, NMex; NMex Mus Fine Arts, Santa Fe; Nat Mus Jos, Nigeria; Univ Northern Ariz, Flagstaff; and others. *Comn:* Relief sculpture, Noblesville Public Libr, Ind, 72; relief sculpture, Lutheran Church, Indianapolis, Ind, 73; 2 relief sculptures, comn by Harrison Eiteljorg, Indianapolis, Ind, 78; art awards, Indiana Arts Commission, Indianapolis, 79. *Exhib:* Contemp Western Am, Indianpolis Mus Art, Ind, 79; one-woman shows, Univ NMex, 75 & 77, Galerie Motte, Geneva, Switzerland, 80, Novotel Galleries, Paris, 82 & La Commanderie, Poet LaVal, France, 83; Sante fe Festival of the Arts, NMex, 79, 81 & 82; and others. *Bibliog:* Mary Carroll Nelson (auth), Mixed media mixes with archaeology, Today's Art & Graphics, 12/81; Daniel Gibson (auth), Time and the shard, Artlines, 9/83; Mary Carroll Nelson (auth), Martha Slaymaker printmaker, Am Artist, (in prep); and others. *Mailing Add:* 451 Gavilan Pl NW Albuquerque NM 87107

SLEIGH, SYLVIA
PAINTER, INSTRUCTOR
b Llandudno, Wales. *Study:* Brighton Sch Art, Eng. *Exhib:* One-artist shows, Bennington Col, Vt, 63, Soho 20 Gallery, 73, Fine Arts Ctr, Univ RI Kingston, 74 & AIR Gallery, 74, 76 & 78; Tokyo Int Biennial: New Image in Painting, 74; G W Einstein Co, Inc, 80 & 83. *Pos:* Selection Comt, Women Choose Women, New York Cult Ctr, 73. *Teaching:* Instr life painting, New Sch Social Res, 74-80; Kreeger Wolf Distinguished Prof, Northwestern Univ, 77. *Awards:* Nat Endowment Arts Visual Artists Fel Grant, 82. *Bibliog:* John Russell (auth), Sylvia Sleigh, Lerner-Heller Gallery, New York, 72; Linda Nochlin (auth), Some women realists, Arts, 74; John Perreault (auth), Male nudes, Village Voice, New York, 10/18/73. *Media:* Oil on Canvas. *Publ:* Contribr, Anonymous was a Woman, 74 & Art: A Woman's Sensibility, 75, Feminist Art Prog, Calif Inst of the Arts. *Dealer:* Soho 20 Gallery 99 Spring St New York NY 10012; G W Einstein Co Inc. *Mailing Add:* 330 W 20th St New York NY 10011

SLES, STEVEN LAWRENCE
PAINTER, STAINED GLASS ARTIST
b Jersey City, NJ, June 16, 40. *Study:* Inst de San Miguel de Allende, Mex, 58; Bard Col, 58-60; Univ Madrid, summer, 59; Swarthmore Col, BA(English lit), 62; Mexico City Univ, 61; Art Students League, New York, 62; also with Hans Hofmann & Sol Wilson. *Work:* HRH Princess Anne, Buckingham Palace, Eng; Bertrand Russell House, Sussex, Eng; plus many pvt collections. *Exhib:* Wrigley's Mansion, Phoenix, Ariz, 81; Ross Gallery, Scottsdale, Ariz, 81; Scottsdale Ctr Arts, 81; and many others. *Pos:* Life mem, Vereinigung der Mund und Fussmalenden Künstler in aller Welt, Vaduz, Lichtenstein; founder, Arts for All Inc, Tucson, Ariz. *Awards:* Charles Prize, Pearson T Bainbridge Award, Jersey City, 70; First & Second Prizes, Kenny Inst Int Mus Art Show, Minn, 71; Royal Soc for Encouragement of Arts, Manufactures & Commerce fel, London, Eng, 78; plus others. *Bibliog:* Sheer Determination (film), Vereinigung Der Mund und Fussmalenden Kunstler in Aller Welt Gallery, 64-83; article, Ariz Republic, 10/81; article, New Times, 10/81; and others. *Mem:* Fel Royal Soc Arts; Nat Soc Lit & Arts; and others. *Media:* Multimedia. *Publ:* Auth, Eliminating Society's Barriers, Creatively, 77, auth, Whispers of Eternity, 78, auth, Arts for All Gallery-Museum: Founding Papers, 79 & auth, A Host of Reveries, 79, privately publ; and others. *Mailing Add:* 5371 E Fourth St Tucson AZ 85711

SLETTEHAUGH, THOMAS CHESTER
PRINTMAKER, EDUCATOR
b Minneapolis, Minn, May 8, 25. *Study:* Univ Minn, BS, 49, MEd, 50, with Walter Quint, Peter Lupori, Malcolm Myers & John Rood; Pa State Univ, DEd, 56, with Viktor Lowenfeld & Kenneth Beittel; spec study, Williams Col, Univ SC, Univ Ga & Syracuse Univ. *Work:* Bucharest Univ, Romania; Cult Ctr, Budapest, Hungary; Univ Belgrade, Yugoslavia. *Comn:* Symbol of Excellence, Miss Univ Women, 70; Miss Univ Women Crest for Apollo 14, Alumni Asn, 71. *Exhib:* Carnegie Mus Regional, Pittsburgh, 70; Heidelberg Univ Gallery, 75; Serigraphs, Cambridge Univ, Eng & Centro de Altos Estudios, Madrid, Spain, 76; Serigraph Techniques, Nat Gallery, Budapest, Hungary, 77; Klienen Gallery, Vienna, Austria, 78; Univ Ctr, Dubrovnik, Yugoslavia, 80. *Collections Arranged:* Max Klager--Printmaker, Heidelberg Univ, WGer; John Jackson--Drawings, Cambridge Univ, Eng; Charlotte Strobele Graphics, Univ Vienna, Austria; Zheng Sheng Tian Paintings, Hangzhov, PRC. *Teaching:* Prof fine arts, Miss Univ Women, 68-70; assoc prof grad studies art educ, Univ Minn, 70- *Awards:* Psychoaesthetics Develop Award, Col Educ, Univ Minn, 71. *Bibliog:* Hans Stumbauer (auth), Art education in Austria, Art Sch Linz, 71; Paul Cornel Chitic (auth), articles in Tribune & Art Rev, Bucharest, Romania, 72. *Mem:* Int Soc Educ in Art; Int Soc Aesthet; Int Soc Art Hist; Int Soc Empirical Aesthet; Int Union Architects. *Publ:* Auth, Psychoaesthetics-The creative intellect, Int Union Architects, 75; auth, The analysis & synthesis of psychoaesthetics, Cambridge Univ, 75; auth, Southern Hemisphere Research, Aboriginals in Australia and Maori in New Zealand, 78 & Oriental Seminar in People's Republic of China, Hong Kong, Japan and Philippines, Int Soc for Educ through Art, United Nations Educ, Sci & Cult Orgn, 79 & 81. *Mailing Add:* 135 Wulling Hall Univ of Minn Minneapolis MN 55455

SLETTEN, BYRON K
PAINTER, PRINTMAKER
b Minneapolis, Minn, Oct 18, 52. *Study:* Univ Nebr, BFA, 74; Univ Fla, MFA, 76. *Work:* Yale Univ Art Gallery, New Haven, Conn; Dade Co Fla, Miami; Fla House of Representatives, Tallahassee; Dept Natural Resources Bldg, Tallahassee, Fla; Univ Fla, Gainesville. *Exhib:* 4th Ann Eastern US Print Exhib, Charlotte Printmakers, NC, 80; Faculty Exhib, Krannert Art Mus, Champaign, Ill, 81; Artspace, Miami, Fla, 82; Mus Fine Arts, St Petersburg, Fla, 82; Univ Hong Kong, 82. *Teaching:* Asst prof painting, Univ Ill, Champaign, 81- *Awards:* Purchase Awards, Univ Fla Gallery, 76 & Charlotte Printmakers Soc, 81; Individual Artist Fel Award, Division Cultural Affairs, Fla Arts Council, 81-82. *Mem:* Col Art Asn; Southern Graphics Council. *Media:* Acrylic; Intaglio. *Dealer:* Virginia Miller Gallery 169 Madeira Miami FL 33134; Peter Rose Gallery 200 E 58th St New York NY 10022. *Mailing Add:* Univ Ill 408 East Peabody Champaign IL 61820

SLIDER, DORLA DEAN
PAINTER
b Tampa, Fla, Sept 9, 29. *Study:* Study with Dr Walter Emerson Baum, 40-48. *Work:* Hartford Ins Group, Conn; Del Art Mus; Reading Art Mus, Pa; Allentown Art Mus, Pa; Plymouth Meeting Mall Asn, Pa; Philco Corp, Pa. *Exhib:* Allied Artists of Am, Nat Acad Design, 67-75; Pa Acad Fine Arts, Philadelphia, 69; William Penn Mus, Harrisburg, Pa, 75; Watercolor USA, Springfield, Ohio; Butler Inst of Am Art, Ohio. *Awards:* Herb Olsen Award, Am Watercolor Soc, New York, 72; Gold Medal, Knickerbocker Artists New York, 77; Doris Kennedy Mem Award, Audubon Artists, New York, 79; plus others. *Bibliog:* Henry C Pitz (auth), Brandywine Tradition, Houghton Mifflin Co, Boston, 69; articles in Brandywine Bugle, Trade Mag, Pa, 71-74. *Mem:* Am Watercolor Soc; Nat Soc Painters in Casein & Acrylic; Knickerbocker Artists; Artists Equity Asn; Audubon Artists; plus others. *Media:* Oil, Watercolor. *Dealer:* Chadds Ford Gallery Inc Rte 1 & 100 Chadds Ford PA 19317. *Mailing Add:* 500 79th St Ocean Marathon FL 33050

SLIPPER, GARY PETER
PAINTER, PRINTMAKER
b Calgary, Alta, Can, Apr 27, 34. *Study:* With Prof Zobali, Florence, Italy, 54. *Work:* Can Coun Collection, Nat Gallery Can, Ottawa; Sir George Williams Univ, Montreal; Vancouver Art Gallery, BC; Queens Univ, Kingston, Ont. *Exhib:* Courtney Exhib, Fairleigh Dickinson Univ, 63; 80th Spring Exhib, Mus Fine Arts, Montreal, 63; Nat Exhib Graphics, Wesleyan Col, 64; Five Realists, Montreal Mus, 66; Drawing Biennial, Nat Gallery Can, Ottawa, 66; 51st Ann Exhib, Conn Acad Fine Arts, Hartford, 81. *Awards:* Visual Arts Award, Can Coun Grant, 68. *Mem:* Royal Can Acad. *Media:* Oil. *Dealer:* Eduard Nakhamkin Fine Arts 1070 Madison Ave New York NY 10028. *Mailing Add:* 313 W 29th St New York NY 10001

SLIVE, SEYMOUR
HISTORIAN, MUSEUM DIRECTOR
b Chicago, Ill, Sept 15, 20. *Study:* Univ Chicago, AB, 43, PhD, 52. *Pos:* Dir, Fogg Art Mus, Harvard Univ, 75-82; Elizabeth & John Moors Cabot dir, Harvard Art Mus, emer. *Teaching:* Instr fine arts, Oberlin Col, Ohio, 50-51; asst prof art & chmn dept, Pomona Col, Calif, 52-54; from asst prof to prof fine arts, Harvard Univ, 54-73, Gleason prof fine arts, 73- *Awards:* Officer of Order of House of Orange-Nassau, 62; Charles Rufus Morey Prize, Col Art Asn Am, 70; Award for Achievement in Art Hist, Art Dealers' Asn Am, 79. *Mem:* Fel Am Acad Arts & Sci; hon mem Karel van Mander Soc; Col Art Asn (dir, 58-62 & 65-69); Renaissance Soc; foreign mem Dutch Soc Sci. *Res:* Baroque art. *Publ:* Auth, Rembrandt and His Critics, 1630-1730, Martinus Nijhoff, The Hague, 53; auth, Drawings of Rembrandt, 2 vols, Dover Publ, New York, 65; coauth, Dutch Art and Architecture: 1600-1800, Penguin Bks, Baltimore, 66; auth, Frans Hals, 3 vols, Phaidon Press, London, 70-74; auth, Jacob van Ruisdael, Abbeville Press, New York, 81; and others. *Mailing Add:* Fogg Art Mus Harvard Univ Cambridge MA 02138

SLIVKA, DAVID
SCULPTOR

b Chicago, Ill. *Study:* Calif Sch Fine Arts. *Work:* Univ Pa, Philadelphia; Baltimore Mus; Rutgers Univ, Camden, NJ; Everson Mus, Syracuse, NY; Brooklyn Mus, NY. *Exhib:* Mus Mod Art, 62; Hirshhorn Collection Mod Sculpture, Guggenheim Mus, 62-63; Mus Fine Arts, Boston, 68; Selections from Chase Manhattan Bank Collection, 71; Albright-Knox Art Gallery, Buffalo, NY, 74; one-man shows, Southern Ill Univ, Carbondale, 68, Everson Mus, Syracuse, NY, 74 & Univ Pa, Philadelphia, 75. *Teaching:* Prof sculpture, Univ Mass, Amherst, 64-67; artist in residence, Southern Ill Univ, Carbondale, 67-68; instr, Queens Col, NY, 71-73; prof, Pa Acad Fine Arts, Philadelphia, 72-82. *Awards:* Brandeis Univ Creative Arts Award for Am Sculpture, 62; Louis Comfort Tiffany Award-Sculpture, 77. *Bibliog:* Harvey Arnason (auth), Modern Sculpture from the Joseph Hirshhorn Collection, Guggenheim Mus, 62; Georgine Oeri (auth), The sculpture of David Slivka, Quadrum, 63; Harold Rosenberg (auth), The anxious object, Illus, 65. *Media:* Miscellaneous. *Mailing Add:* 549 W 52nd New York NY 10019

SLOAN, JEANETTE
PAINTER, PRINTMAKER

b Chicago, Ill, Mar 18, 46. *Study:* Marymount Col, Tarrytown, NY, BFA, 67; Art Inst of Chicago; Univ Chicago, MFA, 69, with Joshua Taylor & Max Kahn. *Work:* Nat Mus Am Art, Smithsonian Inst, Washington, DC; Cleveland Mus Fine Arts; Art Inst Chicago; Minneapolis Inst Art; Yale Univ Art Gallery; and others. *Exhib:* Hapatat Gallery, Dearborn, Mich, 78; Hackley Art Mus, Muskegon, Mich, 78; Madison Art Ctr, Wis, 78; one-person shows, Frumkin & Struve Gallery, Chicago, 81 & Ill State Mus, Springfield, 81; and many others. *Awards:* Purchase Award, Ill State Mus, 76; Galex Award, 11th Ann Galex Competition, Galesburg Civic Art Ctr, Ill, 77; Watson F Blair Prize, Prints & Multiples, Art Inst Chicago, 81; and others. *Bibliog:* Gerrit Henry (auth), rev in Art News, 1/78; Anne I Lockhart (auth), Jeanette Pasin Sloan, Arts, New York, 4/79; Michele Vishney (auth), Still-Life and the Art of Jeanette Pasin Sloan, Arts, 3/83. *Media:* Acrylic, Colored Pencils; Lithography. *Dealer:* G W Einstein Co Inc New York NY; Frumkin & Struve Gallery Chicago IL. *Mailing Add:* 535 Keystone River Forest IL 60305

SLOAN, RICHARD
PAINTER, ILLUSTRATOR

b Chicago, Ill, Dec 11, 35. *Study:* Am Acad of Art, Chicago, Ill; Famous Artists Sch, Westport, Conn. *Work:* Smithsonian Inst, Washington, DC; Denver Mus Natural Hist, Colo; Miss State Wildlife Mus, Jackson; Ga Mus Sci & Indust, Atlanta. *Comn:* stamp & print, Raptor Fund Inc, Ill, 81; stamp & print, La Wild Turkey Fedn, 82; stamp & print, Nebr Wildlife Fedn, 83. *Exhib:* Cincinnati Mus Natural Hist, Ohio, 82; Soc Animal Artists, Acad Natural Scis, Philadelphia, 82; Royal Scottish Acad, Edinburg, Scotland, 82; British Mus Natural Hist, London, Eng, 82; Carnegie Mus Natural Hist, Pittsburgh, Pa, 82; and many others. *Pos:* Staff artist, Lincoln Park Zoo, Chicago, 62-65. *Mem:* Soc Animal Artists, New York. *Media:* Acrylic, Gesso Panel. *Publ:* Illusr (cover painting), La Conservationist, La Wildlife & Fish Comn, 74; illusr, Nat Wildlife, Nat Wildlife Fed, 76; illusr (cover painting), Turkey Call, Nat Wild Turkey Fedn, 78; illusr, Audubon's birds of America, Roger Tory & Virginia Marie Peterson, 81; and others. *Dealer:* Artists Union 31 S Willson Bozeman MT 59715. *Mailing Add:* PO Box 17988 Fountain Hills Scottsdale AZ 85268

SLOAN, ROBERT SMULLYAN
PAINTER

b New York, NY, Dec 5, 15. *Study:* City Col New York, AB, 36; Inst Fine Arts, NY Univ, 37-39. *Work:* IBM Collection; Bradford Jr Col, Haverhill, Mass; Herbert F Johnson Mus, Ithaca, NY; Nat Portrait Gallery, Washington, DC. *Comn:* Many covers & spec features, Time, Coronet & Colliers, 41-50; posters, Russian War Relief, 43 & Doing All You Can, Brother, US Treas, 43; paintings, Herbert F Johnson Mus Art, 78. *Exhib:* Corcoran Biennial, 49; Portraits of Year, Portraits, Inc, 49; Am Watercolor Soc Exhib, Nat Acad Design Gallery, 56; one-man shows, Leger Galleries, White Plains, NY, 55, Herbert F Johnson Mus, Cornell Univ, 74 & Capricorn Galleries, Bethesda, Md, 75; Time Salutes Pennsylvania, Hist Soc Pa, 82. *Awards:* Citation for Distinguished Serv, US Treas, 43; Watercolor Div Award, Nat Soldier Art Show, USA, 45. *Bibliog:* George Wiswell (auth), Discovery of a Copley portrait, Am Heritage Mag, 60. *Mem:* Appraisers Asn Am; Mamaroneck Artists Guild (pres, 54). *Media:* Oil. *Publ:* Illusr, Army Educ Prog & other mags. *Mailing Add:* 1412 Arlington St Mamaroneck NY 10543

SLOANE, JOSEPH CURTIS
HISTORIAN

b Pottstown, Pa, Aug 8, 09. *Study:* Princeton Univ, AB, 31, MFA, 34, PhD(Hodder fel), 49. *Teaching:* Instr art hist, Princeton Univ, 35-37; asst prof art hist & chmn dept art, Rutgers Univ, 37-38; from assoc prof art hist to prof & chmn dept art, Bryn Mawr Col, 38-58; prof art hist & chmn dept art, Univ NC, Chapel Hill, 58-78, dir, William Hayes Ackland Art Ctr, currently. *Awards:* Fulbright Sr Res Grant, 52; NC Award (Arts), 76; Morrison Award, Roanoke Island Hist Asn, 82. *Mem:* Col Art Asn Am (past pres); NC Art Soc (past pres); hon life mem Asn Art Mus Dirs. *Res:* Nineteenth and twentieth century art, especially painting. *Publ:* Auth, French Painting Between the Past & the Present, Princeton Univ, 51; auth, Paul Marc Joseph Chenavard, Univ NC, 62; auth, The American Situation, Univ NC Publ, 76; auth, articles in Art Bulletin, Art Quart, Gazette Beaux-Arts, Art J & others. *Mailing Add:* 3117 Carol Woods Chapel Hill NC 27514

SLOANE, PHYLLIS LESTER
PAINTER, PRINTMAKER

b Worcester, Mass. *Study:* Carnegie-Mellon Univ, BFA. *Work:* Cleveland Mus of Art, Ohio; Philadelphia Mus of Art, Pa; Massillon Mus, Ohio; Canton Art Ctr, Ohio; Hunterdon Art Ctr, Clinton, NJ; and others. *Comn:* Mural (on bldg side), Cleveland Area Arts Coun, Am Inst of Architects & NOVA, 74; ed of print La Nue, Univ Print Club, Cleveland, 77; 4 print eds, Transworld Art Corp, 79; presentation print, Cleveland Print Club, 83; portfolio, Image Resource Ctr, NOVA, Cleveland, 83. *Exhib:* Ohio Women Artists: Past & Present, Butler Inst of Am Art, Youngstown, 76; Hunterdon Nat Print Exhib, 78, 79 & 81; Boston Printmakers Exhib, 79-81; Janus Gallery, Santa Fe, 81; Cleveland House Gallery, 83; Univ Mus, Indiana, Pa, 83; and others. *Awards:* Graphics Awards, Cleveland Mus Art May Show, 78 & 79 & Oklahoma Ann Nat Print Exhib, 81; Cleveland Visual Arts Award, 82. *Mem:* New Orgn for Visual Arts (bd trustees, 73-). *Media:* Acrylic; Silkscreen. *Publ:* Auth, articles, Printworld, 82 & 83. *Dealer:* New Gallery 11427 Bellflower Rd Cleveland OH 44106; Munson Gallery 653 Canyon Rd Sante Fe NM 87501. *Mailing Add:* 2558 Fairmount Blvd Cleveland OH 44106

SLONE, SANDI
PAINTER, INSTRUCTOR

b Boston, Mass, Oct 1, 39. *Study:* Wheaton Col, 57-59; Mus Fine Arts, Boston, 70-73; Wellesley Col, BA, 74. *Exhib:* Corcoran Biennial, 77; New Acquisitions, Young Am Painters, Boston Mus Fine Arts, 77; Boston Mus Fine Arts Bicentennial, 77; New Abstract Painters, Edmonton Art Gallery, Alta, 77; one-person show, Inst Contemp Art, Boston, 77. *Teaching:* Instr painting, Sch of Mus Fine Arts, Boston, 71-; instr painting, Boston Col, 73-76 & Brandeis Univ, 76-77. *Bibliog:* Kenworth Moffett (auth), Sandi Slone: Recent Paintings, Inst Contemp Art, Boston, 77; Paul Richards (auth), Corcoran biennial, Washington Post, 2/77; Carter Ratcliffe (auth), New York roundup, Art Int, 7-8/77. *Media:* Acrylic. *Dealer:* Acquavella Contemp Art 18 E 79th St New York NY 10021; Harcus Krakow 7 Newbury St Boston MA 02116. *Mailing Add:* 30 Bowker St Brookline MA 02146

SLONEM, HUNT
PAINTER, MURALIST

b Portsmouth, NH. *Study:* Skowhegan Sch Painting & Sculpture, 72; Tulane Univ, BA, 73. *Work:* Metrop Mus Art, New York; Grey Gallery, NY Univ; New Orleans Mus Art, La; Okla Art Ctr; Everson Mus. *Comn:* Fan Dance (mural), World Trade Port Authority Ctr, New York, 80. *Exhib:* Painting & Sculpture Today, Indianapolis Mus, 78; Soc Artistes Independants, L'Am Aux Independants, Gran Palais, Paris, 80; solo exhib, Hunter Mus, Chattanooga, Tenn, 81; Works on Paper, Weatherspoon Mus, Greensboro, NC, 81. *Awards:* Greenshields Found Grant for Painting, 76; Millay Colony Arts, 82; MacDowell Colony Fel, 83. *Bibliog:* David Bourdon (auth), Made in USA, Portfolio Mag, 80; John Yau (auth), article, Arts Mag, 83; Gerrit Henry (auth), article, Art in Am, 83. *Media:* Oil on Canvas. *Dealer:* Harm Bouckaert Gallery 100 Hudson St New York NY 10013. *Mailing Add:* 87 E Houston New York NY 10012

SLOSHBERG, LEAH PHYFER
MUSEUM DIRECTOR

b New Albany, Miss, Feb 21, 37. *Study:* Miss State Col Women, BFA, 59; Tulane Univ, La, MA, 61. *Pos:* Cur arts, NJ State Mus, Trenton, asst dir, 69-71, dir, 71- *Mem:* Am Asn Mus; Conserv Ctr Art & Artifacts (bd mem, 79-); Northeast Mus Conf. *Res:* American art; museum management. *Mailing Add:* New Jersey State Mus 205 W State St Trenton NJ 08625

SLOTNICK, MORTIMER H
PAINTER, EDUCATOR

b New York, NY, Nov 7, 20. *Study:* City Col New York; Columbia Univ. *Work:* In pvt collections of Mrs Harry S Truman, Mrs Cordell Hull and others; New Brit Mus Am Art, Conn; Nat Mus Am Art, Smithsonian Inst; Johnson Art Mus, Cornell Univ; Nat Archives; and others. *Exhib:* Whitney Mus Am Art, Riverside Mus, Hudson River Mus, New York Pub Libr, Nat Acad Design, New York; and others. *Teaching:* Prof art & art educ, City Col New York; supvr arts & humanities, City Sch Dist, New Rochelle, NY; prof art educ, Col New Rochelle. *Mem:* Allied Artists Am; Am Artists Prof League; Artists Equity, NY; Am Vet Soc Artists. *Publ:* Works publ by Am Artists Group, Donald Art Co, Bernard Picture Co & Scafa-Tornabene Art Publ. *Mailing Add:* 43 Amherst Dr New Rochelle NY 10804

SLUSKY, JOSEPH
SCULPTOR, LECTURER

b Philadelphia, Pa, June 7, 42. *Study:* Univ Calif, Berkeley, BArch, MA(art), study with James Prestini, Ibram Lassaw, James Melchert, Wilfred Zogbaum, Sidney Gordin, Harold Paris, Richard O'Hanlon, William King & Robert Hudson. *Work:* Hayward Area Festival of the Arts, Calif; City San Francisco; San Francisco Dept Water. *Comn:* Outdoor sculpture, City Berkeley, 81; interior lobby sculpture, San Francisco Dept Water, 84. *Exhib:* Bay Area Artists Exhib, Oakland Mus, 77-79; Painted Sculpture, Palo Alto Cult Ctr, 80; Sculptural Sights at Syntex, Syntex Corp, Palo Alto, 80; Brook House Sculpture, Kaiser Ctr, Oakland, 82; Sculpture 82, A Contemporary Survey, Sonoma State Univ, Rohnert Park, Calif, 82; Drawings and Sculpture, San Jose Inst Contemp Art, San Jose, 83; and others; Spaces, Walnut Creek Civic Arts Gallery, Calif, 79; Sculptural Sights at Syntex, Syntex Corp, Palo Alto, Calif, 79-80; Painted Sculptue, Palo Alto Cultural Ctr, Calif, 80; and others. *Teaching:* Lectr sculpture & visual studies, Univ Calif, Berkeley, 69-70, summer 73 & 78-; instr sculpture & drawing, Ohlone Col, Fremont, Calif, 72- *Awards:* Eisner Award for Creative Achievement, Univ Calif, Berkeley, 66; Purchase Award, Hayward Festival of the Arts, 75 & 79. *Bibliog:* Janice Ross (auth), Peninsula exhibits join into spirit of sculpture conference, Oakland Tribune, 8/82; Karen Oliphant (auth), Sculpture unifies life, Argus, 8/82; Sandy Ballatore (auth), Sculpture by the bay dominate or integrate, Images & Issues, 11-12/82. *Media:* Metal, Acrylic. *Dealer:* Smith Andersen Gallery 200 Homer Palo Alto CA 94301; Brook House Box 1177 Orinda CA 94563. *Mailing Add:* 5537 Claremont Ave Apt 4 Oakland CA 94618

SMALL, NEAL
SCULPTOR, DESIGNER
b New York, NY, Aug 4, 37. *Study:* Mus Mod Art Sch; Tex A & M Sch Archit, 54-56; WVa Wesleyan, 56-58. *Work:* Mus Mod Art, New York; Brooklyn Mus; Philadelphia Mus Art; Albright-Knox Art Gallery, Buffalo, NY; Dallas Mus Fine Arts. *Comn:* Bk of drawings, comn by Mrs Fred Howard, New York, 77, collage, 78. *Exhib:* Excellence in Design, 67, 68 & 69, Brooklyn Mus, 67, Smithsonian Inst, DC, 68 & Mus Sci & Indust, Chicago, 69; Flint Invitational, Flint Inst Art, De Waters Art Ctr, Flint, Mich, 71; one-man show, Mus Univ SFla, 71; AIR Gallery, 81. *Collections Arranged:* Environment, St Louis Mus, 70; US Info Agency Show, Zagreb, Yugoslavia, 71, Bucharest, Romania, 72. *Pos:* Pres, Neal Small Designs, New York, 66-73; pres, Squire & Small, 74-79; dir, AIR Gallery, formerly. *Awards:* Awards for excellence of design, Ann Design Revs, Indust Design, 68, 69 & 70. *Media:* Acrylic, Bronze and Collage. *Dealer:* Charles Byron 25 E 83rd St New York NY 10028. *Mailing Add:* 178 Fifth Ave New York NY 10010

SMALLEY, DAVID ALLAN
SCULPTOR
b New London, Conn, Dec 17, 40. *Study:* RI Sch Design, 58-60; Univ Conn, with Antony Padovano, BFA, 63; Ind Univ, MFA, 65. *Work:* Lyman Allyn Mus & Conn Col, New London. *Comn:* Warlock III (cor-ten steel), Conn Commission Arts, New London, 73. *Exhib:* Conn Painting, Drawing & Sculpture, Univ Bridgeport, New Britain Mus & Conn Col, 79; Penwith Gallery, Cornwall, Eng, 79; Krausaar Galleries, New York, 80-81; one-man show, Lyman Allyn Mus, New London, Conn, 81 & Kraushaar Galleries, New York, 84. *Pos:* Bd dirs, Art Resources Conn, 75-80. *Teaching:* Prof sculpture, Conn Col, 65- *Awards:* Ingram Merrill Found Grant, 69; Research Grant, Dana Found, 80. *Bibliog:* Barbara Zabel (auth), Profile, Art Voices, 7-8/81. *Mem:* Mystic Art Asn. *Media:* Stainless Steel, Brass. *Dealer:* Kraushaar Galleries 724 5th Ave New York NY. *Mailing Add:* Five N Ridge Rd New London CT 06320

SMALLEY, STEPHEN FRANCIS
EDUCATOR, PAINTER
b Rockville, Conn, Apr 14, 41. *Study:* Mass Col Art, BS, 63; State Col, Boston, MEd, 65; Pa State Univ, DEd, 70. *Work:* Bridgewater State Col, Mass; Mansfield State Col, Pa. *Exhib:* Sixty-third Ann, Newport Art Asn, RI, 74; 27th New England Exhib, Silvermine Guild Artists, New Canaan, Conn, 76; Mass Exhib, Worcester Art Mus, 77; Boston 78, Brockton Art Mus, Mass, 78; one-man show, Norman, Boston Gallery, Mass, 78. *Teaching:* Fac art, Rindge Technical High Sch, Cambridge, Mass, 63-65; teaching asst design & printmaking, Pa State Univ, 65-67; assoc prof & chmn, Dept Art Educ, Tyler Sch Art, 67-72; prof & chmn dept art, Art Dept, Bridgewater State Col, Mass, 72- *Awards:* Summer Res Award, Tyler Sch Art, 71; Prof Develop Award, Bridgewater State Col, Mass, 81. *Mem:* Nat Art Educ Asn; Mass Art Educ Asn (coun mem, 79-81). *Media:* Acrylics, Pen & Ink. *Mailing Add:* 144 Atkinson Dr Bridgewater MA 02324

SMART, MARY-LEIGH
CONSULTANT, PATRON
b Springfield, Ill, Feb 27, 17. *Study:* Oxford Univ, dipl Extra Mural Delegacy, 35; Wellesley Col, BA, 37; Columbia Univ, MA, 39; also with Bernard Karfiol, 38-39. *Collections Arranged:* Art: Ogunquit, A National Exhibition of Artists Who Have Worked in Ogunquit (auth, catalog), 67, Peggy Bacon, A Celebration (auth, catalog), 79 & three photography exhibitions each season, 80-, Barn Gallery, Ogunquit, Maine. *Pos:* Founding secy & prog dir, Barn Gallery Assocs, Ogunquit, Maine, 58-78, cur, Hamilton Easter Field Art Found Collection, 66-79, pres, 69-70 & 82-, hon dir, 71-78, cur exhibs, 79-; founding mem bd adv, Univ Art Galleries, Univ NH, 73-, mem bd overseers, 75-, vpres, 75-81, pres, 81- *Bibliog:* Article, Arch Am Art J, Vol 18, 1/26/78 & 4/26/78; Mary Snell (auth), Mary-Leigh Smart: A Life Devoted to Art, Maine Sunday Tel, 4/24/83. *Mem:* Nat Comt Friends Art, Wellesley Col. *Interests:* Contemporary art and organizations promoting it; Christopher C Cook. *Collection:* Twentieth century New England painting and sculpture; American, European and Asian contemporary graphics; photography. *Publ:* Auth, Hamilton Easter Field Art Foundation Collection (catalog), 66. *Mailing Add:* RFD2 Box 381 York ME 03909

SMART, WINI
PAINTER, DEALER
b Neptune, NJ, Mar 17, 32. *Study:* Philadelphia Mus Col Art; Fleisher Art Mem, Philadelphia; Art Students League. *Work:* Northeast Harbor Libr, Maine; Boro Hall, Red Bank, NJ; Town Hall, Dover Twp, Toms River, NJ; Point Pleasant Beach Libr, NJ. *Comn:* Battle of Monmouth (mural), NJ Nat Gas Co, Freehold, 64; hist mural, NJ Nat Gas Co, Red Bank, 65; two hist murals, First Nat Bank, Toms River, 68; mural & bas-relief, First Presby Church, Freehold, 70; hist mural, Boro of Freehold, 76. *Exhib:* NJ Watercolor Soc Ann, Monmouth Mus, 68, 72 & 74-79; Knickerbocker Artist Ann, Nat Arts Club, New York, 73, 74, 75 & 76; Franklin Mint Marine Art Competition, 74; Nat Acad of Design, New York, 75; one-artist show, Union League, Philadelphia, 76. *Pos:* Dir, Smart Studio, Northeast Harbor. *Awards:* Winsor & Newton Award, NJ Watercolor Soc, 68 & 75; Purchase Awards, Monmouth Art Festival, Red Bank, 66 & 68; Best in Show, Freehold Art Soc

Ann, 74 & 75. *Mem:* Manasquan River Group of Artists, Spring Lake, NJ (pres, 54-56); Freehold Art Soc (pres, 60-62, 68-70); Catherine Lorillard Wolfe Art Club, New York; Guild of Art, Shrewsbury, NJ; NJ Watercolor Soc (officer, 78-80). *Media:* Watercolor, Oil. *Specialty:* Watercolors of Maine. *Publ:* Illusr, Early History of Toms River & Dover Township, 67 & Cooks & Artists, 58. *Dealer:* Anchor & Palette Gallery 43 Mount Bay Head NJ 08742; Tatler Gallery 301 Market Pl Hilton Head SC 29928. *Mailing Add:* 18 Fairview Ave Brick NJ 08723

SMEDLEY, GEOFFREY
EDUCATOR, SCULPTOR
b London, Eng, Feb 24, 27. *Study:* Camberwell Sch Art, London; Slade Sch Fine Arts, London, 54. *Work:* Victoria & Albert Mus & Arts Coun Gr Brit, London. *Comn:* Sculpture Garden, Commune Pirano, Istria, Yugoslavia, 72; Southern Arts Asn Eng, Portsmouth, 74. *Exhib:* Whitechapel Art Gallery, 72; Arts Coun, traveling, 73 & 76; Agnes Etherington Art Ctr, Queen's Univ, Kingston, Ont, 78; Nature as Material, traveling, Eng, 80-81; solo exhib, Vancouver Art Gallery, BC, 82. *Teaching:* Prof fine arts, Univ BC, 78- *Bibliog:* Scott Watson (auth), article, Vanguard, 2/82; Douglas & McIntyre (auths), Contemporary Art in Canada, Visions, 83. *Publ:* Auth, My sculptural array at Forma Viva, Leonardo, 75. *Mailing Add:* Dept Fine Arts Univ BC Vancouver BC V6T 1W5 Canada

SMIGOCKI, STEPHEN VINCENT
PAINTER, PRINTMAKER
b Washington, DC, Nov 20, 42. *Study:* Univ Md, BA(fine arts), 64, MA(drawing), 68; Univ SFla, Tampa; Fla State Univ, painting with Karl Zerbe, PhD(art educ). *Work:* Ringling Mus, Sarasota, Fla; Huntington Gallery, WVa; WVa Sci & Cult Complex, Sunrise Gallery, Charleston. *Exhib:* Dallas Summer Arts Festival Nat Competition, Tex, 71; Biennial I Six-State Painting Competition, Va Commonwealth Univ, 73; Drawings '74 Nat Exhib, Wheaton Col, Norton, Mass, 74; Thirteen State Regional Exhib, Appalachian Corridors, Charleston, WVa, 75; All WVa Exhib, Charleston, 79 & 81. *Pos:* Graphic artist, Univ Md Ctr Adult Educ, 64-66. *Teaching:* Coordr & prof art, Fairmont State Col, WVa, 72- *Awards:* Purchase Awards, Huntington Galleries Exhib 280, WVa, 72 & Appalachian Corridors, 75. *Media:* Watercolor. *Publ:* Contribr, Echo Without Sound, Northwoods Press, 80. *Dealer:* Louis Andre/Wolfe St Gallery 420 S Washington Alexandria VA 22314. *Mailing Add:* 35 Park Dr Fairmont WV 26554

SMITH, ALBERT
COMIC ARTIST, EDITOR
b Brooklyn, NY, Mar 21, 02. *Pos:* Artist, ed, Syndicate Dept, New York World, 20-30; comic artist, United Features Syndicate, 30-32; artist, Bell Syndicate, 32-; artist, Mutt & Jeff Comic Strip, 32-; head, Smith Serv, 50, feature ed, Smith Serv Div, Am Press Asn; writer, comic artist, Rural Delivery, Remember When, 50-; artist, Life in the Suburbs, Cicero's Cat. *Mem:* Nat Cartoonists Soc (pres); Am Newspaper Comic Coun, Inc. *Mailing Add:* c/o McNaught Syndicate 60 E 42nd St New York NY 10017

SMITH, ALBERT E
PAINTER, DEALER
b San Francisco, Calif. *Exhib:* One-man shows, DeSaisset Gallery, Univ Santa Clara, John Bolles Gallery, San Francisco, Calif State Univ, Modesto, William Sawyer Gallery, San Francisco, Calif State Univ, Hayward; Univ Calif Exten Gallery, San Francisco, 74; Off the Stretcher Show, Col Marin, 75; one-man shows, William Sawyer Gallery & John Boles Gallery, San Francisco, Tokyo, Japan, 82; and many other group & one-man shows. *Pos:* Owner, Atherton Gallery, Menlo Park, Calif. *Specialty:* American and English artists. *Dealer:* Asher/Faure Gallery Los Angeles CA. *Mailing Add:* 1616 El Camino Real Menlo Park CA 94025

SMITH, ALEXIS (PATRICIA ANNE)
CONCEPTUAL ARTIST
b Los Angeles, Calif, Aug 24, 49. *Study:* Univ Calif, Irvine, 66-70, BA(art), 70; study with Robert Irwin & Ed Moses. *Comn:* The Grand, Keeler Grand Foyer, DeVos Hall, Grand Rapids, Mich, 83. *Exhib:* Lowe, Munger, Smith, Wilson, Los Angeles Co Mus Art, 72; Four Los Angeles Artists, Corcoran Gallery Am Art, Washington, DC, 75; Whitney Biennial, Whitney Mus Am Art, New York, 75, 79 & 81; solo exhibs, Whitney Mus Am Art, 75, Rosamund Felsen Gallery, 78 & 80 & De Appel, Amsterdam, 79; Am Narrative/Story Art, Contemp Art Mus, Houston, Tex, 77; Narration, Inst Contemp Art, Boston, 78; Holly Solomon Gallery, 77, 78, 79 & 81; Univ Calif, Los Angeles, 79-82; Museum as Site, Los Angeles Co Mus Art, 81; New Directions, Hirshhorn Mus & Sculpture Garden, 83; and many others. *Teaching:* Univ Calif, Los Angeles, 79-82. *Awards:* New Talent Award, Contemp Arts Coun, Los Angeles Co Mus Art, 74; Nat Endowment Arts Fel Grant, 76-77. *Bibliog:* Nancy Marmer (auth), Alexis Smith: The narrative act, Artforum, 12/76; Alexis Smith: Scheherezade the storyteller, Flash Art, 11-12/77; Leo Rubinfien, Through western eyes, Art in Am, 9-10/78. *Media:* Multimedia. *Publ:* Contribr centerfold, Avalanche, fall 75; auth, Alone, 77; contribr, Italics, Paris Rev, spring 79; contribr, Shanghai Express, Los Angeles Herald-Examiner, 11/81. *Dealer:* Rosamund Felsen Gallery 669 N LaGenaga Blvd Los Angeles CA 90069; Holly Solomon Gallery 392 W Broadway New York NY 10012. *Mailing Add:* 1907 Lincoln Blvd Venice CA 90291

SMITH, ARTHUR HALL
PAINTER, EDUCATOR
b Norfolk, Va, Mar 23, 29. *Study:* Ill Wesleyan Univ, BFA, 51; Ecole Beaux-Arts, Paris, Fulbright fel, 51; Atelier 17, Paris, with S W Hayter, 52; grad study, Univ Wash, 55; also with Mark Tobey, Seattle, Wash, 55-57. *Work:*

Chrysler Mus, Norfolk; Corcoran Gallery Art, Washington, DC; Phillips Collection, Washington, DC; Baltimore Mus Art, Md; Seattle Art Mus. *Comn:* Centennial murals, Mem Ctr, Ill Wesleyan Univ, Bloomington, 50; Mammals in World Art, Mammal Hall, US Mus Natural Hist, Smithsonian Inst, Washington, DC, 58; Truckee Storage Triptych, Bur Water Reclamation, US Dept Interior, Washington, DC, 72. *Exhib:* Va Artists Ann, Va Mus Fine Arts, Richmond, 51; The American Artist and Water Reclamation, Nat Gallery Art, Washington, DC, 72; 25 Yr Retrospective, Exhib Hall, Cathedral St John the Divine, New York, NY & Dimock Gallery, Washington, DC, 76; Grafik aus den USA, Bawag Found, Vienna, Austria, 76; one-man shows, Washington Artists Series, Corcoran Gallery Art, 61 & Editions of One, Fine Arts Pavilion, Montgomery Jr Col, Takoma Park, Md, 77; and others. *Teaching:* Asst prof painting, George Washington Univ, 74-81, assoc prof, 81- *Awards:* Merwin Medal for Painting, Bloomington Art Asn, 48; Painting Prize, 15th Area Exhib, Corcoran Gallery Art, 62; Hereward Lester Cooke Found Grant, 83-84. *Bibliog:* Benjamin Forgey (auth), article, Art News, 4/76; Larry Marscher (auth), Washington in ruins, Times, Vol 9, No 5, 10/81. *Media:* Mixed. *Publ:* Auth introductory essay, Mark Tobey Exhib, St Alban's Sch, Washington, DC, 59; auth intro, Drawings of Kevin MacDonald Exhib, Phillips Collection, Washington, DC, 77; auth catalog essay, James McLaughlin, A Retrospective: In Memoriam, Phillips Collection, Washington, DC, 82; auth, An appreciation, introductory essay to The Phillips Collection: The Intimate Scale, Dimock Gallery, Washington, DC, 83. *Dealer:* Franz Bader Gallery 2124 Pennsylvania Ave NW Washington DC 20037. *Mailing Add:* Apt 23 2131 Florida Ave NW Washington DC 20008

SMITH, B J
MUSEUM DIRECTOR, INSTRUCTOR
b Beaver, Okla, Aug 22, 31. *Study:* Okla State Univ, Stillwater, BFA, 55; Univ Okla, Norman, MFA, 59. *Work:* Mus Art, Univ Okla, Norman; State Collection of Okla Artists & craftsmen, Oklahoma City. *Exhib:* Okla Artists Ann, Philbrook Art Ctr, Tulsa, 58, 64-68 & 73; Ann Eight State Exhib, 63, 64, 68, 70 & 74, 13 Artists You Should Collect, 65, Okla Art Ctr, Oklahoma City; Ninth Midwest Biennial, Joslyn Art Mus, Omaha, 66; Springfield Ann, Springfield Art Mus, Mo, 66, 70 & 71; Okla in Washington, John F Kennedy Ctr for the Performing Arts, Washington, DC, 76; solo exhib, WNebr Arts Ctr, Scottsbluff, 83; Pioneer Mus & Arts Ctr, Woodward, Okla, 83. *Pos:* Asst to dir, Okla Art Ctr, Oklahoma City, 61-65; dir, Gardiner Art Gallery, Okla State Univ, 65- *Teaching:* Asst prof drawing, color & design, Okla State Univ, 65-81, assoc prof, 81- *Awards:* Purchase Awards, Ninth Midwest Biennial, Joslyn Art Mus, Omaha, 66; Okla Biennial, Okla Art Ctr, Oklahoma City, 67 & Okla Artists Ann, Philbrook Art Ctr, Tulsa, 68. *Media:* Acrylic, Masonite. *Mailing Add:* 2132 W Sunset Dr Stillwater OK 74074

SMITH, BARBARA TURNER
INSTRUCTOR, VIDEO ARTIST
b Pasadena, Calif, July 6, 31. *Study:* Pomona Col, BA, 53; Chouinard Art Inst, 65; workshops with Alex Hay, 68 & Steve Paxton, 69; Univ Calif, Irvine, with Bob Irwin, Larry Bell & Emerson Woelfer, MFA, 71. *Work:* Newport Harbor Art Mus, Newport Beach, Calif. *Exhib:* People Who Should Be Seen, Los Angeles Co Art Mus, Los Angeles, 65; All Night Sculptures, Mus Conceptual Art, San Francisco, 73; Performance Conf, Womanspace & Woman's Bldg, 73, 75 & 77; Retrospective (auth, catalog), Univ Calif, San Diego, 74; Irvine Milieu, La Jolla Mus Contemp Art, Calif, 75; Tortue Gallery, Los Angeles, Calif, 81. *Pos:* Co-founder, F-Space Gallery, Santa Ana, Calif, 70-72; founding mem, Grandview I & II Gallery, Los Angeles, 73-75; organizer, New Dimensions in Sci series, Los Angeles Inst Contemp Art, 75. *Teaching:* Fac fel art, Univ Redlands, Calif, 75-; vis performance artist, Univ Calif, San Diego, 77; vis artist, San Francisco Art Inst, 78; lectr, Univ Calif, Los Angeles, 79-82. *Awards:* Nat Endowment Arts Grants, 74 & 79. *Bibliog:* G S Lischka, (ed), die Lowin, Switz, 12/75; Nancy Buchanan (auth), Barbara Smith: Communication/communion, Portrait Rev, Vol V, 76; Emily Hicks (auth), Performing sex as ritual, Artweek, 9/81. *Media:* Body and Video. *Publ:* Auth, Rope, pvt publ, 71; auth, Burden case tried, dismissed, Artweek, 73; auth, Women in industry, Los Angeles Inst of Contemp Art J, 74; contribr, Buddha mind performance, In: Vision, Crown, 75; auth, Rachel Rosenthal performs Charm, Artweek, 2/77. *Mailing Add:* 240 S Broadway Los Angeles CA 90012

SMITH, (MRS) BERTRAM
COLLECTOR, PATRON
b Dallas, Tex. *Study:* New York Inst Fine Arts. *Pos:* Patron, trustee, mem painting & sculpture acquisitions comt & secy int coun, Mus Mod Art, currently. *Collection:* Post-impressionist, School of Paris paintings, drawings and sculpture. *Mailing Add:* 907 Fifth Ave New York NY 10021

SMITH, CECIL ALDEN
PAINTER, SCULPTOR
b Salt Lake City, Utah, Feb 12, 10. *Study:* Pvt study with Jack Sears, 28-32; Univ Utah; Brigham Young Univ. *Work:* Corcoran Gallery Art, Washington, DC; Cuban Mus, Daytona Beach, Fla; Denver Art Mus, Colo; and others; Peggy & Harold Samuels traveling collection, Locust Valley, NY. *Comn:* Mural, State Bur Mines, Boise, Idaho, 31; murals, Brigham Young Univ, 66-67; mural, Uatah Idaho Sugar Co, Salt Lake City, 68; murals, Veltex Corp, Utah & Tex, 69-70. *Exhib:* Corcoran Gallery Art, Washington, DC, 37; Western Heritage Art Fair, Littleton, Colo, 76 & 77; Mt Oyster Club Ann Exhib, Tucson, Ariz, 78; Western Horseman Gallery Art, Colorado Springs, 79; Prof Rodeo Cowboy Asn Hall of Fame, Colorado Springs, 79; Kalamunda Mus Art, Somers, Mont, 80. *Pos:* Scenic artist, Old Salt Lake Theatre, Utah, 28-29; book illusr, Caxton Printers, 40-50; art dir, Agnew Advert Agency, Lewiston, Idaho, 59-60; asst art dir, Brigham Young Univ Motion Picture Dept, Provo, Utah, 66-70. *Teaching:* Instr anat & life drawing, Art Ctr, Salt

Lake City, Utah, 37-38; pvt instr, 70-80. *Awards:* Western Award, Paris Expos, France, US Govt, 37; Award, Accademico Italy, 80; Award, Accademico Nations, Italy, 83. *Bibliog:* David Oliveria (auth), A rare breed of artists, Southwest Art Mag, 2/78; Royal B Hasserick (auth), Western Painting Today, Watson-Guptill, 75; M V Weedon (auth), Last of the rare breed, Western Horseman Mag, 77. *Mem:* Accademica Italia, Italy; Buckaroo Artists Am. *Media:* Multimedia. *Publ:* Auth & illusr, Ride 'em Cowboy, Newspaper Enterprises Am, 37-38; illusr, Forged in Strong Fires, Hoogles and Alexander, Singing Sails and others, Caxton Printers, 40-50; illusr, Blue Book, McCalls Corp, 41; illusr, Western Horseman, 52-77; illusr, Bullets West, Lancer Publ, 71. *Dealer:* Kalamunda Mus Western Art Box 325 Somer MT 59932. *Mailing Add:* 1485 Montana 82 Somers MT 59932

SMITH, DAVID LOEFFLER
PAINTER, EDUCATOR
b New York, NY, May 1, 28. *Study:* Bard Col, BA; Cranbrook Acad Art, MFA; also with Hans Hofmann & Raphael Soyer. *Exhib:* Carnegie Inst, 60 & 61; Seligman Gallery, New York; one-man shows, First St Gallery, New York, 72, 76, 79 & 81. *Teaching:* Prof painting, Swain Sch Design, New Bedford, Mass, currently; actg chmn dept art, Chatham Col; vis critic, Md Art Inst, Queens Col, State Univ New York, Parson's Sch Design. *Awards:* Henry Posner Prize, Carnegie Inst, 61. *Media:* Oil. *Publ:* Auth, articles, Am Artist, 59-62, Antiques Mag, 11/67, Arts Mag, 3/68 & Art & Artists, 1/70 & 5/71. *Dealer:* First St Gallery 386 W Broadway New York NY 10012. *Mailing Add:* 122 Hawthorn St New Bedford MA 02740

SMITH, DINAH MAXWELL
PAINTER, PHOTOGRAPHER
b New York, NY, May 30, 41. *Study:* L'Academie Julian, 58; RI Sch Design, BFA(painting), 63. *Work:* Bridgeport Mus, Conn; RI Sch Design, Providence; Galerie Liliane Francois, Paris; Chemical Bank. *Exhib:* Still-Life Paintings and Drawings by East End Artists, Parrish Art Mus, Southampton, NY, 81; one-woman show, Tower Gallery, Southampton, NY, 81 & Sarah Y Rentschler Gallery 81 & 82; Smith & Smith, Sarah Y Rentschler Gallery, New York, 83; Adam F Gimbel Gallery, New York, 83; Guild Hall Members, East Hampton, 83; and others. *Awards:* Nat Arts Club Graphics Prize, 72; Nat Arts Club Special Award, 74; Honorable Mention, 5 Towns M & A Found, 81. *Bibliog:* New York Reviews, Artnews, 5/82; James R Genovese (auth), Light at the end of the island, 5/28/83 & Phyllis Braff (auth), From the studio, 9/22/83, Hamptons Newspaper Mag. *Media:* Oils, Watercolor. *Mailing Add:* 300 E 51st St New York NY 10022

SMITH, DOLPH
PAINTER, EDUCATOR
b Memphis, Tenn, July 26, 33. *Study:* Memphis State Univ; Memphis Acad Arts, BFA, 60. *Work:* Ark State Univ, Jonesboro; Brooks Mem Art Gallery, Memphis, Tenn; Southwestern at Memphis; Tenn Arts Comn, State of Tenn, Nashville; NC Nat Bank, Charlotte. *Comn:* Paintings for various locations nationwide, Holiday Inns Am, 65-72; painting for Tenn Exec Mansion Christmas Card, comn by Gov & Mrs Winfield Dunn, 71; painting for Sen Albert Gore, Democratic Party, Shelby Co, Tenn, 71. *Exhib:* One-man shows, Brooks Mem Art Gallery, 65, Charles Bowers Mem Mus, Santa Ana, Calif, 67 & Cheekwood, Nashville, Tenn, 73; Brooks Mem Art Gallery, 69; Vanderbilt Univ Fac Club, Nashville, Tenn, 70; Memphis Acad Arts, Tenn, 72 & 77; and others. *Pos:* Art dir, Ward Archer Assoc, Memphis, 64-67. *Teaching:* Asst prof painting & drawing, Memphis Acad Arts, 64-81, prof, 81-; vis instr painting, Southwestern Col, 66-68. *Awards:* First Prize for Watercolor, Mid-South Exhib, 64 & Grand Award 76, Brooks Mem Art Gallery; Purchase Prize, Tenn Bicentennial Art Competition, 76. *Bibliog:* Jo Potter (auth), The Real World of Dolph Smith, WKNO TV, 65; William Thomas (auth), Dolph Smith's Mid-South, Mid-South Mag, 2/9/69. *Media:* Watercolor. *Publ:* Illusr, Delta Rev Mag, 10/67, 11-12/69 & fall 70; illusr, Mid-South Mag, 12/71. *Dealer:* Memphis Academy Arts Overton Park Memphis TN 38104. *Mailing Add:* 1458 Vinton Memphis TN 38104

SMITH, ELIZABETH JEAN
LIBRARIAN
b Indiana, Pa, Apr 25, 30. *Study:* Va Commonwealth Univ, BFA, 52; Rutgers Univ, MLS, 61. *Exhib:* Va Show, Va Mus Art, Richmond, 53. *Pos:* Asst art librn, Smith Col, Northampton, Mass, 61-64; arts & Archit librn, Pa State Univ, University Park, 64- *Mem:* Art Libr Soc NAm; Col Art Asn. *Publ:* Article, Linton Park, Pennsylvania painter, Antiques, 11/81. *Mailing Add:* E409 Pattee Libr Pa State Univ University Park PA 16802

SMITH, EMILY GUTHRIE
PAINTER
b Ft Worth, Tex, July 8, 09. *Study:* Tex Woman's Univ; Art Students League; Univ Okla; also with Mitchell Jamieson & Frederic Taubes. *Work:* Ft Worth Art Mus; Dallas Mus Fine Arts, Tex; WTex Mus Fine Arts, Lubbock; Univ Tex, Arlington; Longview Mus Fine Arts, Tex. *Exhib:* Am Watercolor Soc, New York; one-man retrospective, Ft Worth Art Mus; one-man show, 20th Century Texas Painters, Wichita Falls Mus Fine Arts; Pastel Soc of Am, 76 & 77; Mainstreams 77, Marietta, Ohio, 77. *Teaching:* Instr portrait painting, mosaics & drawing, Ft Worth Art Ctr Mus, 55-70; instr, Taos, NMex & Las Vegas, NMex, summers 60-69. *Awards:* Top Award, 6th & 7th Ann Pastel Soc of Am, Floral award 8th Ann. *Media:* Pastel, Oil, Mosaic, Murals. *Collection:* Contemporary painting. *Publ:* Contrib, Texas Hill Country, Thirteen Artists by Texas, A & M Press. *Dealer:* L & L Gallery 1107 N Fourth Longview TX 75601; Carlin Galleries 417 Montgomery Fort Worth TX. *Mailing Add:* 408 Crestwood Dr Ft Worth TX 76107

SMITH, ERNEST JOHN
ARCHITECT, DESIGNER

b Winnipeg, Man, Dec 17, 19. *Study:* Univ Man, BArch(with honors), 44; Mass Inst Technol, MArch(fel), 47; Banff Sch Advan Mgt, 68. *Work:* Nat Gallery Ottawa Royal Can Acad Collection; Sch Archit, Univ Man. *Comn:* Centennial Centre, Centennial Bd, Winnipeg, Man, 65; Lombard Place Complex, Winnipeg, 68; Winnipeg Sq Develop, Trizec Corp, Winnipeg, 74; Great West Life Centre, Winnipeg, 78; Simons, Texada Development, Vancouver, BC, 81; and others. *Exhib:* Residence, East Kildonan, Man, 61; Sch Archit, Univ Man, 61; Man Asn Archit, Winnipeg & Montreal, 68; Kiwanis Ctr Deaf, Winnipeg, 75. *Teaching:* Sr design critic, Univ Man, 3 yrs. *Awards:* Can Gold Medal, Royal Archit Inst Can, 44. *Bibliog:* George Derksen (auth), Smith Carter Parkin prepares for the future, Man Bus J, 6/70; Deanna Waters (auth), Interview with the professionals, Opportunity, 74; and others. *Mem:* Fel Royal Archit Inst Can (dean, 72-75, chancellor, 79-82); academician Royal Can Acad Arts (mem coun, 74); Man Asn Archit (pres, 53-54, 58-61, mem exec comt, 49-54); Ont Asn Archit; Nat Joint Comt Construction Materials (chmn, 63-65); and others. *Publ:* Contribr, Can Archit. *Mailing Add:* 1601 Buffalo Pl Winnipeg MB R3T 3K7 Canada

SMITH, FRANCES KATHLEEN
CURATOR, HISTORIAN

b Bolton, Eng, Nov 19, 13; Can citizen. *Study:* London Univ, Eng; Queen's Univ, Kingston, Ont, BA, 56; Oxford Univ, Eng, with Pope Hennessey, Italian sculpture, 56-57. *Collections Arranged:* Andre Bieler: 50 Years (auth, catalog), Retrospective, traveled, Can, 70-71; Heritage Kingston (contribr, catalog), 73; Painting Now 1976/77 (auth, catalog); Henry Moore, Sculpture, Prints, Drawings, 78; Daniel Fowler of Amherst Island, (auth, catalog), traveled, Can, 79; The Brave New World of Fritz Brandtner Traveling Show (coauth, catalog), 81-82; Kathleen Moir Morris (auth, catalog), 83. *Pos:* Cur, Agnes Etherington Art Centre, Kingston, Ont, Can, 57-79, cur emer, 79- *Awards:* Merit Award, Ont Asn Art Galleries, 80; Merit Award, Can Mus Asn, 81. *Mem:* Can Mus Asn (nominating comt, 78); Ont Asn Art Galleries (secy, 68-69). *Res:* Canadian artists: Daniel Fowler, Andre Bieler & Fritz Brandtner and other Canadian artists. *Publ:* Coauth, A Permanent Collection of the Agnes Etherington Art Centre, 68; auth, George Harlow White 1817-1887, 75 & Daniel Fowler of Amherst Island, 79, Art Ctr, Queens Univ, Kingston, Ont; auth, Andre Bieler: An Artist's Life and Times, Merritt Publ Co, Toronto, 80. *Mailing Add:* RR#1 Bateau Channel Kingston ON K7L 4V1 Canada

SMITH, FRANK ANTHONY
PAINTER

b Salt Lake City, Utah, Aug 4, 39. *Study:* Univ Utah, BFA, 62, MFA, 64. *Work:* Univ Utah Mus Fine Art; Utah State Univ; Salt Lake Art Ctr; Nat Gallery, Washington, DC. *Comn:* design (dance pieces), Repertory Dance Theatre, 66, 71 & 73; stimuli sensory environ for children, Salt Lake Art Ctr, 70; mural, Univ Utah Biol Bldg, 72. *Exhib:* Look Again, Illusionist Painting, Taft Mus, Cincinnati, 76; Reality of Illusion, Univ Southern Calif, 79; Four Corners Biennial, Phoenix, Ariz, 81; Illusions, Faire Int D'art Contemp, Grand Palais, Paris, 82; solo exhib, Suellen Haber Gallery, New York, 82; and others. *Pos:* Illusr, Star Trek: The Movie, 77. *Teaching:* Prof painting & drawing, Univ Utah, 68- *Awards:* San Francisco Art Dirs Gold Medal, 64; Purchase Award, 3rd Intermountain Biennial, 68. *Media:* Acrylic. *Dealer:* Osuna Gallery Washington DC; Yares Gallery Scottsdale AZ. *Mailing Add:* Dept of Art Univ of Utah Salt Lake City UT 84112

SMITH, GARY DOUGLAS
PRINTMAKER, PAINTER

b San Francisco, Calif, July 29, 48. *Study:* Calif Col Arts & Crafts, BFA, 71; extensive study in Mexico; Atelier 17, Paris; etching with S W Hayter, also engraving with George Ball. *Work:* Palm Springs Mus Art, Calif; Achenbach Found Graphic Arts, San Franicisco. *Exhib:* San Francisco Mus Mod Art, 70 & 77; Anchorage Hist & Fine Arts Mus, Alaska, 77; El Paso Mus Art, Tex, 77; World Print Competition & Traveling Show, 79; Krannert Art Mus, Ill, 79; Toledo Mus Art, Ohio, 79; Achenbach Found Graphic Arts, San Francisco, 83. *Bibliog:* Thomas Albright (auth), Landscapes in translation, San Francisco Chronicle, 7/7/71; John Marlowe (auth), interview, Currant Art Mag, 76; Carol A Hayes (auth), Profile of an artist, Bay Views Mag, 9/81. *Mem:* Graphic Arts Coun; World Print Coun. *Media:* Prismacolor Pencil, Silverpoint. *Mailing Add:* c/o Vorpal Gallery 393 Grove St San Francisco CA 94102

SMITH, GORDON
PAINTER

b Brighton, Eng, June 18, 19. *Study:* Winnipeg Sch Art; Vancouver Sch Art; Calif Sch Fine Arts; Harvard Univ Summer Sch; Simon Fraser Univ, LLD, 74. *Work:* Nat Gallery Can; Mus Mod Art, New York; Victoria & Albert Mus, London; Albright-Knox Art Mus, Buffalo, NY; Art Gallery Ont; and others. *Exhib:* Can Biennial, 63; Seattle World's Fair, 63; New Design Gallery, Vancouver, BC, 64; Graphic Biennials, Yugoslavia, Ger, Norway & New York; one-man shows, Toronto, Montreal, New York & Vancouver. *Teaching:* Assoc prof art, Univ BC, formerly. *Awards:* Can Biennial, 56; Can Coun Sr Fel for Study Abroad, 60-61. *Mem:* BC Soc Art; Can Soc Painter-Etchers & Engravers; assoc Royal Can Acad Arts; Can Group Painters. *Media:* Acrylic on Canvas, Graphic Media. *Mailing Add:* 5030 The Byway West Vancouver BC V7W 1L7 Canada

SMITH, GRAHAM
HISTORIAN, EDUCATOR

b Banff, Scotland, May 30, 42. *Study:* St Andrews Univ, Scotland, MA(with hon), 64; Edinburgh Univ, Scotland, dipl(hist art), 65; Princeton Univ, MFA, 68, PhD, 71. *Teaching:* Asst prof hist art, Univ BC, 69-72; assoc prof, Univ Mich, 75-83, prof, 83- *Mem:* Col Art Asn Am; Midwest Art Hist Soc (mem bd dirs, 83-). *Res:* Sixteenth century Florentine painting; 19th century British photography. *Publ:* Auth, The Casino of Pius IV, Princeton Univ Press, 77; auth, Jealousy, pleasure and pain in Agnolo Bronzino's Allegory of Venus and Cupid, Pantheon, 81; auth, Cosimo I and the Joseph Tapestries for the Palazzo Vecchio, Renaissance & Reformation, 82. *Mailing Add:* Dept Hist Art Univ Mich Ann Arbor MI 48109

SMITH, GRIFFIN (MARY-GRIFFIN SMITH HOEVELER)
CRITIC

b Augusta, Ga, Apr 23, 30. *Study:* Wellesley Col, AB(art hist), 51; Harvard-Fogg Mus, with Sydney J Freedberg; Univ Florence. *Pos:* Registrar-cur, Lowe Mus, Univ Miami, 65-69; art ed & critic, Miami Herald, 69-77; US corresp, Art News, New York, 74- *Teaching:* Lectr museology, Univ Miami, 68-69; vis prof art hist, Miami-Dade Community Col, 70-71. *Publ:* Auth, 33 Miami artists, 11/71 & Portrait of the black arts, Haiti, 8/72, Tropic Mag. *Mailing Add:* 1317 Alhambra Circle Coral Gables FL 33134

SMITH, HARRY WILLIAM
MINIATURIST, ILLUSTRATOR

b Chicago, Ill, July 12, 37. *Study:* Wash Univ, St Louis; Command Mgt Art Sch, Ft Belvoir, Va; Chicago Acad Fine Arts. *Work:* Yorktown Mus, NY; Farnsworth Mus, Rockland, Maine. *Comn:* Federal Parlor of Maine (miniature), Colby Col Art Mus, 76. *Exhib:* Mid-States Exhib, Evansville Mus Art, 70; Int Exhib Paintings, Marshall Fields Gallery, Chicago, 70 & 71; solo exhib, Brown Co Art Gallery, Nashville, Ind, 71; Maine Forms of American Architecture, Colby Mus Art, Maine, 76; Copley Soc Boston, 77-78; Maine State Mus, Augusta, 83. *Teaching:* Instr advan art, Camden Sch, Maine, 77- *Bibliog:* Rosner & Beckerman (auths), Inside World of Miniatures, McKay, 76; Joyce Uezia (auth), article, Assoc Press, 83; Nancy McKeon & Corky Pollan (auth), Let it be wee, New York Mag, 83. *Mem:* Copley Soc; Brown Co Art Gallery Asn (bd dirs, 70-71). *Publ:* Auth & illusr, ABCs of Maine, Down East Books, 80; auth & illusr, The Art of Making Furniture in Miniature, E P Dutton, 82; auth & illusr, Windjammers of the Maine Coast, 82, ABCs of Vermont, 83 & ABCs of New Hampshire, 84, Down East Books. *Dealer:* Coe Kerr Gallery 49 E 82nd New York NY. *Mailing Add:* 50 Harden Ave Camden ME 04843

SMITH, HASSEL W, JR
PAINTER

b Sturgis, Mich. *Study:* Northwestern Univ, BS(cum laude), 36; Calif Sch Fine Arts. *Work:* Whitney Mus; Tate Gallery, London; Albright-Knox Gallery; Dallas Mus Contemp Art; Phillips Gallery. *Exhib:* Solo exhibs, Calif Palace Legion Hon, 48 & 53, Galleria del Ariete, Milan, Italy, 62, Bristol Art Gallery, England, 72, Gallery Paule Anglim, San Francisco, 77, 81 & 82, Oakland Mus, 81 & San Jose Mus Art, Calif, 83; retrospectives, Pasadena Art Mus, Calif, 61 & San Francisco Mus Mod Art, 75. *Teaching:* Lectr painting, San Francisco Art Inst, 78-79, vis artist, 81; vis lectr painting, Bristol Polytechnic, England, 78-81. *Awards:* Rosenberg Fel for Independent Study in Painting, 41-42. *Media:* Oil on Canvas. *Mailing Add:* c/o Gallery Paule Anglim 14 Geary St San Francisco CA 94111

SMITH, HELEN M
ILLUSTRATOR, PAINTER

b Canton, Ohio, Oct 19, 17. *Study:* Univ Melbourne, Australia, 42-43; Wash Univ, BFA, 53, MA, 58; Art Instr, Inc, cert; St Louis Univ. *Work:* Permanent Collection, Mo State Gallery. *Exhib:* St Louis Artists Guild; Ann Mo Exhib; Liturgical Art, Seattle; Cath Art Exhib, Calif; Springfield Art Mus, Mo; and others. *Pos:* Med illusr, St Louis Univ Med Ctr, 61-65; dir med illus, Dept Ophthal, Wash Univ, 64-68; consult, Am Col Radiol, 64-; pres, Mericom-Syrmeco, Inc, 75- *Teaching:* Instr art, Villa Duchesne, St Louis, 53-56; instr art & head dept, Maryville Col, 58-60; asst prof art & archaeol, 60-68, dir art dept, 60-61, dir art & archaeol depts, 61-68; lectr, Harvard Univ & Oriental Inst Archaeol, Yale Univ, 60; asst prof art hist & dir instr graphics, Southern Ill Univ, 68. *Awards:* Ruth Kelso Renfrow Art Club Award, 55; First, Second & Third Prizes, Soc Tech Writers & Publ Exhib. *Mem:* St Louis Artists Guild; Archaeol Soc Am; Oriental Archaeol Soc; fel Int Inst Arts & Lett; Ill Art Educ Asn. *Publ:* Illusr, Aghios Kosmos, 59; illusr many med jour & bks. *Mailing Add:* 11447 Clayton Rd St Louis MO 63131

SMITH, HENRY HOLMES
PHOTOGRAPHER, EDUCATOR

b Bloomington, Ill, Oct 23, 09. *Study:* Ill State Univ; Art Inst Chicago; Ohio State Univ; New Bauhaus, Chicago Sch Design; Ind Univ; also with L Moholy-Nagy, Gyorgy Kepes, Hin Bredendieck, Alexander Archipenko; Maryland Inst Col Art, Hon DFA, 68; Indiana Univ, Hon DFA, 82; Philadelphia Col Art, Hon DFA, 83. *Work:* Mus Mod Art, New York; Eastman House, Rochester, NY; Mus Fine Arts, St Petersburg, Fla; Univ Nebr Mus Art, Lincoln; Art Inst Chicago Mus; and others. *Exhib:* Abstract Photography, Mus Mod Art, New York, 51, Sense of Abstraction, 60; Photography at Mid-Century, Eastman House, 59, Twentieth Century Photographers, 66; Photographers Choice, Art Gallery, Ind Univ, Bloomington, 59, 50th Anniversary, Mus Art, 73; and others. *Teaching:* Instr photog, New Bauhuas, Chicago, 37-38; prof photog, Ind Univ, Bloomington, 47-77, emer prof, 77- *Mem:* Found mem Soc Photog Educ. *Res:* Esthetics of photography. *Publ:* Auth, New figures in a classic tradition, In: Aaron Siskind

Photographer, 65; auth, Photography in our time, In: Photographers on Photography, 66; auth, Traumas of fair women, In: Women & Other Visions, 75; auth, Across Atlantic & out of woods, In: Photography of Moholy-Nagy, 75; auth, Models for critics, In: Photographic History, 75; and others. *Dealer:* The Gallery N Grant St Bloomington IN 47401. *Mailing Add:* Dorian Way San Rafael CA 94901

SMITH, JAMES MORTON
MUSEUM DIRECTOR, HISTORIAN
b Bernie, Mo, May 28, 19. *Study:* Southern Ill Univ, BEd, 41; Univ Okla, MA, 46; Cornell Univ, PhD, 51. *Pos:* Ed, Inst Early Am Hist & Cult, 55-66; dir, State Hist Soc Wis, 70-76; dir, Winterthur Mus, 76- *Teaching:* Prof hist, Cornell Univ, 66-70; prof hist, Univ Wis, 70-76; prof hist, Univ Del, 76- *Mem:* Asn Art Mus Dirs; Am Hist Asn; Orgn Historians; Am Asn Mus. *Res:* Early American history and culture. *Mailing Add:* Winterthur Mus Winterthur DE 19735

SMITH, JO-AN
DESIGNER, JEWELER
b Eugene, Ore, Apr 8, 33. *Study:* Ind Univ, 65; pvt studies in Buenos Aires, Arg, 66; San Salvador, El Salvador, 67; Univ Tex, El Paso, BA, 71, NMex State Univ, MA, 75. *Work:* Tex A&M Univ; Smithsonian Inst, Washington, DC; plus others. *Exhib:* Update: Body Ornament, Am Craft Coun, Winston-Salem, NC, 77; Marietta Col Craft Nat, Ohio, 77; Am Goldsmith Now, St Louis, Mo, Santa Fe Festival Arts, 78; Gold, Las Cruces, NMex, 79; and others. *Pos:* Custom designer, Glenn Cutter Jewelers, Las Cruces, NMex, 75- *Teaching:* Instr, NMex State Univ, 75-81. *Awards:* Second Place Purchase Prize in Crafts, Llano Estacado Art Asn, 74; First Place in Show, Las Cruces Chap, NMex Designer Craftsmen, 74; Hon Mention, The Metalsmith, Phoenix & Seattle, 76-77. *Mem:* Soc NAm Goldsmiths; Dona Ana Arts Coun. *Media:* Drawings; Precious Metals. *Publ:* Contribr, Bead J, Craftsman's Gallery, Design, Golddust, Goldsmith's J & Working Craftsman. *Dealer:* Glenn Cutter Jewelers 1374 Mesilla Valley Mall Las Cruces NM 88001. *Mailing Add:* Box 1681 Las Cruces NM 88001

SMITH, JOHN IVOR
SCULPTOR, EDUCATOR
b London, England, Jan 28, 27; Can citizen. *Study:* McGill Univ, BSc, 48; Montreal Mus Fine Arts; study with Arthur Lismer, Jacques de Tonnancour & Eldon Grier. *Work:* Art Gallery Ont, Toronto; Provincial Mus Que, Quebec City; Winnipeg Art Gallery, Manitoba; London Pub Art Mus, Ont; Edmonton Art Gallery, Alta. *Comn:* 20' Fiberglas chimeric figure, Expo '67, Montreal, 67; 9' Fiberglas female figure, Can Govt Exhib Comn, Ottawa, 67. *Exhib:* Nat Outdoor Sculpture Show, Ottawa, Ont, 60; Can Sculpture, Dorothy Cameron Gallery, Toronto, Ont, 64; Sculpture '67, City Hall, Nat Gallery Can, Toronto, 67; Expo '67, Montreal; Can Sculpture, Rodin Gallery, Paris, France, 70. *Teaching:* Assoc prof sculpture, Concordia Univ, Montreal, 66- *Awards:* First Prizes, Winnipeg Art Gallery, 59-61; Grand Centennial Award, Montreal Mus Fine Arts, 60; Senior Art Awards, Can Coun, 67, 69 & 73. *Mem:* Royal Can Acad. *Media:* Fiberglas, Automotive Enamels. *Dealer:* Isaacs Gallery 832 Yonge St Toronto ON Can. *Mailing Add:* RR2 Belvedere Cr Duncan BC V9L 1N9 Canada

SMITH, JOSEPH A(NTHONY)
PAINTER, ILLUSTRATOR
b Bellefonte, Pa, Sept 5, 36. *Study:* Pa State Univ, with Hobson Pittman, 55-57 & 60; Pratt Inst, BFA. *Work:* Pa Acad Fine Arts, Philadelphia; Bloomsburg State Col, Pa; Rutgers Univ. *Exhib:* Pa Acad Fine Arts, 61, 67 & 69; one-man exhib paintings, drawings & sculpture, Staten Island Inst Arts & Sci, 66; Nat Acad Arts & Lett, New York, 68; Am Drawings: The Last Decade, Katonah Gallery, New York, 71; Bethel Gallery, Conn, 78; Newhouse Gallery, 82; and others. *Pos:* Design consult, Brooks Bros, 70-75; exhib designer & consult, Staten Island Inst Arts & Sci, 70-75; mem bd dirs, Staten Island Coun Arts, 71-76. *Teaching:* Assoc prof fine art, Pratt Inst, 61-; asst prof fine art, Pa State Univ, University Park, summers 69-73. *Awards:* Mary S Litt Award for Watercolor, 100th Ann Am Watercolor Soc, 67; First Prize Juror's Choice, 3rd Ann Arts Festival, Pa State Univ, University Park, 71; Award Merit, Soc Illusr, 73, 74, 79 & 82. *Bibliog:* Jane Cottingham (auth), The imaginary drawings of Joseph A Smith, Am Artist, 7/81. *Media:* Oil, Wax. *Publ:* Illusr, Sierra Club Survival Songbook, 71; illusr, Witches, Abrams, 80; illusr, Harper's Mag, Newsweek & Time Mag. *Mailing Add:* 59 John St Sixth Floor New York NY 10038

SMITH, KATHERINE (CHAFEE)
CRITIC
b Huntington, NY, June 5, 45. *Study:* Marymount Col, Tarrytown, NY, BFA, 67; Hunter Col, City Univ New York, MA, 71. *Pos:* Colo ed, Artspace: Southwestern Contemp Arts Quart, 77-82. *Teaching:* Instr art, Colo Women's Col, Denver, 79-81. *Mem:* Col Art Asn; Asn Prof Art Adv. *Res:* Contemporary art, photography and crafts with emphasis on the American West; nineteenth century art. *Publ:* Auth, Western states biennial, Art News, 79; auth, Visions of the West, Rocky Mountain, 81; auth, Contemporary Indian painting, Portfolio, 82; auth, A Western Vision of Art, History and Work (catalog), 82. *Mailing Add:* 936 Detroit St Denver CO 80206

SMITH, KEITH A
PHOTOGRAPHER, PRINTMAKER
b Tipton, Ind, May 20, 38. *Study:* Art Inst of Chicago, BAE, with Aatis Lillstrom, Ken Josephson, Vera Berdich & Sonia Sheridan; Inst Design, Ill Inst Technol, MS(photog), with Aaron Siskind, Arthur Siegel & Misch Kohn; Guggenheim Fel in Photog, 72 & 80. *Work:* Mus Mod Art, New York; Art Inst of Chicago; Int Mus Photog, George Eastman House, Rochester, NY; Nat Gallery of Can, Ottawa, Ont; Houghton Rare Books Libr, Harvard Univ. *Exhib:* Solo exhibs, Light Gallery, New York, 76, Chicago Ctr Contemp Photog, 78 & Stuart Wilber Inc, Chicago, 78, 79 & 80; Mirrors and Windows: American Photography Since 1960, Mus Mod Art, 78 & traveling, 78-80; American Photography of the Seventies, Art Inst Chicago, 79; Cliche Verre: 1939 to the Present, Detroit Inst Arts, 80; Hand-Colored Photographs, Philadelphia Col Art, 80; and others. *Teaching:* Instr photog, Univ Calif, Los Angeles, 70; instr photog generative systems, Sch of Art Inst Chicago, 71-74; coordr of printmaking, Visula Studies Workshop, Rochester, 74- *Awards:* Guggenheim Fel, 72 & 80; Nat Endowment Arts Grant, 78. *Media:* Photography; Etching with Photoetching. *Publ:* Auth, When I Was Two, Visual Studies Workshop, 77; auth, Book 91, 82 & Book 89 Patterned Apart, 83, Space Heater Multiples; coauth (with Jonathan Williams), Lexinton Nocturne, A Poem by Jonathan Williams as Interpreted by Keith Smith, private publ, 83; auth, Book 95 Structure of the Visual Book, Visual Studies Workshop Press, 83. *Mailing Add:* 22 Cayuga St Rochester NY 14620

SMITH, KENT ALVIN
SCULPTOR
b White Earth Indian Reservation, Minn, Dec 23, 43. *Study:* Univ Minn, Minneapolis, with Katherine Nash, BA(sculpture), 71, MFA(sculpture), 75. *Work:* General Mills Inc, Univ Minn Galleries, Fed Reserve Bank, Minneapolis; Bemidji State Univ, Minn. *Comn:* Outdoor sculpture, Portfolio Management Corp, Minneapolis, 75. *Exhib:* Bois Fort Gallery, Ely, Minn, 74 & 75; Ojibwe Exhib, Bemidji State Univ & Minn State Hist Soc, St Paul, 74 & 75; Flatland Sculpture, Drake Univ, Des Moines, Iowa, 75; Drawing Show, Univ Minn, 75. *Pos:* Res asst, Ceramic Shell, Univ Minn, 68-69; sculpture asst to Katherine Nash, Minneapolis, 68-69; gallery technician, Univ Minn Galleries, 69-73. *Teaching:* Artist in residence, Bemidji State Univ, 74-75, instr contemp Am Indian sculpture & painting, 74-82. *Bibliog:* Gerald Vizenor (auth), The Everlasting Sky, Collier-Macmillan, 70; Brian Anderson (auth), The present: Is there Indian art, Minneapolis Tribune, 10/22/72; Don Morrison (auth), Ojibwe art 1974, Minneapolis Star, 6/74. *Mem:* Col Art Asn; Ojibwe Art Asn. *Media:* Cast Metal, Wood. *Dealer:* Art Lending Gallery 2500 Groveland Terrace Minneapolis MN 55403. *Mailing Add:* Dept of Art Bemidji State Univ Bemidji MN 56601

SMITH, LAWRENCE BEALL
PAINTER, SCULPTOR
b Washington, DC, Oct 2, 09. *Study:* Art Inst Chicago, Univ Chicago, PhB, 31; with Ernest Thurn, Gloucester, Mass; also with Charles Hopkinson & Harold Zimmerman, Boston. *Work:* Fogg Mus, Cambridge, Mass; Libr Cong, Washington, DC; Metrop Mus Art, New York; Addison Gallery, Andover, Mass; Wichita Art Mus, Kans; and others. *Comn:* Normandy Invasion, Abbott Labs, Washington, DC, 44; Paintings of Mo, Scruggs-Vandervort-Barney, Univ Mo, 46; portraits of Robert Hutchins, Univ Chicago, 52 & Harold Swift, 60 & Charles Merrill, Jr, Boston, 65. *Exhib:* Carnegie Inst, Pittsburgh, 41; Whitney Mus, New York, 60; Norfolk Mus Drawing Biennial, 67; Nat Acad Design Ann, New York, 74 & 75. *Pos:* Mem adv bd, Katonah Gallery, NY, 54-75. *Awards:* Cert of Excellence, Am Inst Graphic Arts, 53; Purchase Prize, Norfolk Mus, 67; Ellen C Speyer Prize, Nat Acad Design, 76. *Bibliog:* Harry Salperer (auth), The shorthand caricaturist, Esquire Mag, 42. *Media:* Oil; Stone. *Publ:* Illusr, Robin Hood, Grossett, 54; illusr, Ogden Nash's Girls Are Silly, Watts, 62; illusr, Henry Fielding's Tom Jones, Bk Month Club, 64; illusr, Henry James's Washington Square, 71 & illusr, Edith Wharton's Age of Innocence, 73, Ltd Ed Club. *Dealer:* Assoc Am Artists 663 Fifth Ave New York NY 10021. *Mailing Add:* Rte 121 Cross River NY 10518

SMITH, LAWSON WENTWORTH
SCULPTOR, EDUCATOR
b Havana, Cuba, Apr 20, 47; US citizen. *Study:* Okla State Univ, BFA, 70; Univ Nebr, MFA, 74. *Work:* Ctr Visual Arts Gallery, Ill State Univ, Bloomington & Normal. *Exhib:* One-man shows, Contemp Arts Found, Oklahoma City, 71; Henri Gallery, Washington, DC, 75, 77, 79 & 82 & Rockefeller Art Ctr, Fredonia, NY, 81; Eight State Exhib, Okla Art Ctr, 76; Arena '78 Nat, Binghamton, NY, 78; Rutgers Nat Drawing Exhib, 79 & 81; plus others. *Teaching:* Instr sculpture, Wichita State Univ, Kans, 74-75; asst prof studio art, Syracuse Univ, NY, 76- *Awards:* Purchase Award, Ball State Univ, 76; Purchase Award, 35th Ann Exhib, Sioux City Art Ctr, Iowa, 73; Sculpture Award, Fingerlakes Regional, Mem Art Gallery, Rochester, NY, 80; and others. *Media:* Wood, Thread. *Dealer:* Henri Gallery 21st & P St NW Washington DC 20036. *Mailing Add:* 111 Euclid Dr Fayetteville NY 13066

SMITH, LEON POLK
PAINTER, COLLAGE ARTIST
b Chickasha, Okla, May 20, 06. *Study:* ECent State Col, BA, 34; Columbia Univ, MA, 38. *Work:* Guggenheim Mus; Metrop Mus Art; Mus Mod Art; Hirshhorn Mus, Washington, DC; Whitney Mus Art. *Exhib:* One-man shows, Ace Gallery, Vancouver, Can & Venice, Calif, 79; retrospective, San Francisco Mus & Rose Mus, 68; Paris-New York, Musee Nat d'Art Mod, Georges Pompidou (Beaubourg), Paris, France;; Nat Mus Berlin, 84; Nat Gallery, Washington, DC, 84. *Teaching:* Lectr, Brandeis Univ, 68; resident artist, Univ Calif, Davis, 72; lectr, State Univ NY, Old Westbury, 78, Ace Gallery, Vancouver, Can & Venice, Calif, 79. *Awards:* Grants, Nat Coun Arts, 67 & Tamarind, 68; Hassum/Speicher Fund Purchase Exhib, Am Acad Arts Inst Arts & Lett, NY, 79; and others. *Mailing Add:* 31 Union Sq W Studio 14E New York NY 10003

SMITH, LOWELL ELLSWORTH
PAINTER

b Canton, Ohio, Nov 20, 24. *Study:* Miami Univ, Ohio, BFA, 48; Famous Artists Schs, dipl, 55. *Work:* Canton Art Mus, Ohio; Akron Art Mus; Frye Mus, Seattle; Cowboy Hall Fame, Ohlahoma City. *Comn:* Painting, Canton Hist Soc, Ohio, 60. *Exhib:* Nat Acad Western Art, Cowboy Hall Fame, Ohlahoma City, 78 & 81-83; The Oaxaca Experience, Frye Mus, Seattle, 80; Western Heritage Show, Houston, 81-83; Artists of American, Colo Hist Soc, Denver, 82-83; Am Watercolor Soc Exhib, Nat Acad, New York. *Pos:* Illusr, Canton Art Serv, Ohio, 48-54 & Manning Studio, Cleveland, 54-60. *Teaching:* Instr landscape & figure painting, privately, 60- *Awards:* Gold Medal Watercolor, Nat Acad Western Art, 82 & 83; Prix West, Nat Acad Western Art Show, Cowboy Hall Fame, 83. *Bibliog:* Don Blanchard (producer), The Mood, the Moment (TV film), Metrop Libr, Oklahoma City, 82; Mary Bowman (auth), article, Artists of Rockies, 82; Susan Dodd Whelan (auth), Light washed shadows, Southwest Art Mag, 83. *Mem:* Ohio Watercolor Soc; Am Watercolor Soc; Nat Acad Western Art; Soc Am Impressionists. *Media:* Watercolor. *Dealer:* Seth Canyon Rd Gallery 710 Canyon Rd Santa Fe NM 87501; Shriver Gallery Taos NM. *Mailing Add:* 152 Elm St Hudson OH 44236

SMITH, LUTHER A
PHOTOGRAPHER

b Tishomingo, Miss, Mar 16, 50. *Study:* Univ Ill, Urbana, with Art Singabaugh & Bart Parker, BA, 72; RI Sch Design, with Harry Callahan & Aaron Siskind, MFA(photog), 74. *Work:* Portland Mus Art, Maine; Mass Inst Technol; Ark Arts Ctr, Little Rock; Monmouth Col, Ill; La Grange Col, Ga. *Exhib:* Photography, Kansas City Art Inst, Mo, 78; Black & White & Color, Mass Inst Technol, 79; Contacts, Western Heritage Mus, Omaha, Nebr, 80; Invisible Light, Smithsonian Inst Traveling Exhib, 80-83; Second Sight, Carpenter Ctr, Harvard Univ, 81. *Teaching:* Vis lectr, Univ Ill, Urbana, 74-75; instr art, 75-78, asst prof, 78-81, assoc prof, 81- *Awards:* Purchase Prizes, Allied Arts Asn, 79, Chattahoochi Art Asn, 80 & Ark Art Ctr, 80. *Mem:* Soc Photographic Educ. *Publ:* Illusr, Camera, 75; illusr, Chicago Mag, 78; illusr, Darkroom Dynamics, 78; Electronic Flash Photography, 80 & Photographing Indoors With Your Automatic Camera, 81, Curtin-London. *Mailing Add:* PO Box 2961 Champaign IL 61820

SMITH, MICHAEL A
PHOTOGRAPHER

b Philadelphia, Pa, Feb 16, 42. *Study:* Self-taught. *Work:* Mus Mod Art, Metrop Mus Art, New York; Art Inst Chicago; Mus Fine Arts, Boston; Philadelphia Mus Art. *Exhib:* Solo exhibs, Sheldon Mem Art Gallery, 76, Del Art Mus, 78 & Ringling Mus Art, 80; Landscapes 75-79, Stanford Univ Mus Art, 81, Toledo Mus Art, 81 & Norton Gallery Fine Art, West Palm Beach, Fla, 82. *Awards:* Photogr Fel, Nat Endowment Arts, 77; Best Photog Bk of Yr, Le Grand Prix DuLivre, Recontres Int dela Photog, Arles, France, 81; Second Prize for Photog, 59th Int Competition, The Print Club, Philadelphia, 82. *Bibliog:* Estelle Jussim (auth), A dead straight picture: The landscapes of Michael A Smith, Boston Rev, 2/77; James Enyeart (auth), Intro to Landscapes 1975-1979, Ludima Press, 81; Richard Trenner (auth), A portrait of the artist, Ont Rev, fall-winter 82-83. *Mem:* Soc Photog Educ. *Publ:* Auth & illusr, Twelve Photographs 67-69, pvt publ, 70; auth, On teaching photography, Exposure, J Soc Photog Educ, 76; auth & illusr, Landscapes 1975-1979 (exhib catalog), Lehigh Univ, 81; auth & illusr, Landscapes 1975-1979 (monogr), Lodima Press, 81; auth & illusr, Eight Landscape Photographs, Regnis Press, 83. *Mailing Add:* Bunker Hill Rd Box 400 Ottsville PA 18942

SMITH, MOISHE
PRINTMAKER

b Chicago, Ill, Jan 10, 29. *Study:* New Sch Social Res, BA, 50; Univ Iowa, with Lasansky, MFA, 53; Skowhegan Sch Painting & Sculpture; Acad Florence; also with Giorgio Morandi. *Work:* Mus Mod Art, New York; Kestner Mus, Hannover; Galleria Degli Uffizi, Florence; Metrop Mus Art, New York; Nat Gallery Art, Washington, DC; and others. *Exhib:* Print Coun Am Traveling Exhib, 59 & 62; Int Prints, Cincinnati Mus, Ohio, 62; Salon de Mai, Paris, 65; Libr Cong, 69, 71 & 73; Cracow Int, 78 & 80; Ljubljana Int, 81. *Teaching:* Vis artist printmaking, Univ Wis, 66-67; vis artist printmaking, Ohio State Univ, spring 71; vis artist, Univ Iowa, autumn 71; assoc prof, Univ Wis-Parkside, 72-77; prof, Utah State Univ, Logan, 77- *Awards:* Four Seasons Res Grant, Southern Ill Univ, 57; Eastern Europe Res Grant, Univ Wis-Parkside, 76; Mountain Landscape & Nat Monuments REs Grants, Utah State Univ, 83; and others. *Mem:* Boston Printmakers; Print Club; Nat Acad Design; Soc Am Graphic Artists. *Media:* Intaglio. *Mailing Add:* Dept of Art Utah State Univ Logan UT 84322

SMITH, NAN S(HELLEY)
SCULPTOR, CERAMIST

b Philadelphia, Pa, Nov 10, 52. *Study:* Tyler Sch Art, Temple Univ, Philadelphia, BFA, 74; Ohio State Univ, Columbus, MFA, 77; Univ Ill, Japan House, with Shozo Sato, 79. *Exhib:* Twenty-third Ann Drawing & Small Sculpture Show, Ball State Univ, 77; Fac Exhib, Krannert Art Mus, Champaign, Ill, 77 & 78; Sculpture & Ceramic, Festival Gallery, Krannert Ctr Performing Arts, Urbana, Ill, 78; Selections, Calif Polytechnic Univ, 78; one-woman show, Univ Gallery, Univ Fla, 81, Stetson Univ, 83 & Gulf Coast Art Ctr, 83; and others. *Teaching:* Vis instr design & ceramics, Univ Ill, Champaign-Urbana, 77-79; asst prof ceramics, Univ Fla, Gainesville, 79- *Awards:* Ford Found Grant, Univ Ill, 77 & 78; Individual Artists fel, Div Cult Affairs, Dept State, Fine Arts Coun Fla & Nat Endowment Arts, 80-81; Grad Fac Res Grant, Grad Sch Sponsored Res, Univ Fla, 81. *Bibliog:* Alan Saperstein (dir), You Gotta Have A Dream (film), WUFT Public TV, 81; Interview with Alan S Smith (videotape), Stetson Univ, 83. *Mem:* Col Art Asn; Nat Coun Educ Ceramic Arts. *Media:* Wood, Clay; Plaster. *Mailing Add:* 4409 NW 27th Terrace Gainesville FL 32605

SMITH, PAUL J
MUSEUM DIRECTOR

b Sept 8, 31. *Study:* Art Inst Buffalo; Sch Am Craftsmen. *Pos:* Vpres, Louis Comfort Tiffany Found, currently; mem bd trustees, Haystack Mountain Sch Crafts, Deer Isle, Maine, currently; mem bd, Opportunity Resources of Arts, Inc, formerly; dir, Am Craft Mus, currently. *Mailing Add:* 1349 Lexington Ave New York NY 10028

SMITH, PAUL ROLAND
PAINTER, EDUCATOR

b Colony, Kans, Sept 12, 16. *Study:* Pittsburg State Col, BS; Univ Iowa, MFA. *Work:* Des Moines Art Ctr, Iowa; Wright Mus, Beloit, Wis; Univ Iowa, Iowa City; Sioux City Art Ctr, Iowa; St Cloud Mus, St Cloud State Col, Minn. *Exhib:* One-man shows, Assoc Am Artists Gallery, New York, 54 & Krasner Gallery, New York, 73-77. *Pos:* Mem bd dirs, Minn Mus Art, 71- *Teaching:* Prof painting & drawing, Univ Northern Iowa, 51-65; prof painting & drawing & chmn dept art, Hamline Univ, 65-75. *Awards:* First Awards, Des Moines Art Ctr, 57, Minn Centennial State Fair, 58 & Sioux City Art Ctr, 59. *Mem:* Artists Equity Asn (pres, 64-67); Midwest Col Art Asn (prog dir, 69); Col Art Asn Am; Walker Art Ctr; Minn State Arts Coun. *Media:* Oil, Watercolor. *Publ:* Auth, Adult Nursery Rhymes, Waverly Publ, 72. *Mailing Add:* Box 352 Nisswa MN 56468

SMITH, RALPH ALEXANDER
WRITER, EDUCATOR

b Ellwood City, Pa, June 12, 29. *Study:* Columbia Univ, AB, Teachers Col, MA & EdD. *Pos:* Exec secy, Coun for Policy Studies Art Educ, 78- *Teaching:* Instr art hist & art educ, Kent State Univ, 59-61; asst prof art hist & art educ & chmn dept art, Wis State Univ-Oshkosh, 61-63; asst prof art hist & art educ, State Univ NY Col New Paltz, 63-64; asst prof aesthet educ, Univ Ill, Urbana, 64-67, assoc prof, 67-71, prof cultural and educ policy, 71- *Awards:* First Barkan Mem Award. *Mem:* Am Soc Aesthet; Philos Educ Soc; Nat Art Educ Asn. *Res:* Theoretical foundations of aesthetic and humanistic education. *Publ:* Ed, Aesthetics and criticism in art education, Rand, 66; auth, Aesthetic education: A role for the humanities program, Teachers Col Rec, 1/68; ed, Aesthetic concepts and education, 70 & Aesthetics and problems of education, 71, Univ Ill Press; Regaining Educational Leadership, Wiley, 75. *Mailing Add:* 1310 S Sixth St Univ Ill Champaign IL 61820

SMITH, ROBERT ALAN
PAINTER, DESIGNER

b Pasadena, Calif. *Study:* Chouinard Art Inst, Los Angeles, 46; Inst Allende, San Miguel de Allende, Mex, 48; painting with David Alfaro Siqueiros, Mex; Chouinard Art Inst, 53. *Work:* Libr of Cong, Washington, DC; Nat Collection, Smithsonian Inst, Washington, DC; Metrop Mus Art, New York; Philadelphia Mus, Pa; Pasadena Art Mus, Calif. *Exhib:* Ann Print Exhib, Libr Cong, 59 & 60; 50 American Printmakers, De Cordova Mus, Mass, 61; Santa Barbara Mus Art, Calif, 64; American Art Today, New York World's Fair, 65; White House, Washington, DC, 67. *Teaching:* Instr painting, Calif Inst Arts, Los Angeles, 65; instr, Ventura Col, 65-78. *Awards:* Purchase Awards, Libr of Cong, 60 & Pasadena Art Mus, 62; James D Phelan Award for Calif Painters, 61. *Bibliog:* Langsner (auth), Art news from Los Angeles, Art News Mag, 2/59 & 2/60 & Los Angeles letter, Art Int, 3/62; Seldis (auth), Art, Los Angeles Times, 10/61. *Interests:* Graphic design concepts in motion picture film. *Publ:* Contribr, Western Serigraph Inst Bulletin, 61 & Ventura Fine Arts Mag, 62; illusr, Long Ago Elf, 68 & Crocodiles Have Big Teeth All Day, 70, Follett. *Mailing Add:* 1309 Gregory St Ojai CA 93023

SMITH, ROBERT CHARLES
DESIGNER, EDUCATOR

b Buffalo, NY, Jan 21, 26. *Study:* Albright Art Sch, Univ Buffalo, BFA, 50; Univ Cincinnati. *Work:* Ball State Univ Gallery, Muncie, Ind; Butler Inst Am Art, Youngstown, Ohio; Morton D May Collection, St Louis, Mo. *Comn:* Fountain, Pub Libr Hamilton Co, Cincinnati, Ohio, 60; fountain, Temple Ark & Eternal Light, Glen Manor Temple, Cincinnati, 64; fountain, Munic Opera Asn Forest Park, St Louis, Mo, 74; fountain, Boone Co Nat Bank, Columbia, Mo, 75. *Exhib:* Print Ann, Brooklyn Mus, NY, 50, 51 & 52; Fountains '69, Taft Mus, Cincinnati, 69; TFAA-1979, Laguna Gloria Art Mus, Austin, Tex, 79; Multiples '80, Contemp Arts Ctr, New Orleans, La, 80; one-man shows, Univ City Pub Libr, 81 & Martin Schweig Gallery, St Louis, 81. *Pos:* Art dir, Writer's Dig, Cincinnati, 54-69; art dir, Environ Mag, St Louis, Mo, 65-70; graphics consult, City of University City, Mo, 77-80; graphics consult, City Bridgeton, Mo, 80-81. *Teaching:* Instr design, Albright Art Sch, 50-52; instr design & drawing, Art Acad Cincinnati, 52-65; prof design, Sch Fine Arts, Wash Univ, 65- *Awards:* Purchase Prize, Ann Sculpture Exhib, Butler Inst, 61; Community Arts Award, Community Arts Prog, US Dept of Housing & Urban Develop, 73; Purchase Award, Ann Drawing Show, Ball State Univ Art Gallery, 74. *Bibliog:* A Darack (auth), Fountains of Cincinnati, Cincinnati Enquirer, 63; K Hanna (auth), Fountains '69, Taft Mus, 69; S Pollack (auth), R C Smith--Waterworks, New Art Examiner, 81. *Mem:* Arts Coord Coun St Louis Area; Col Art Asn. *Media:* Graphics; Fountains. *Mailing Add:* 6316 Washington Ave St Louis MO 63130

SMITH, ROBERT LEWIS
MUSEUM DIRECTOR, EDUCATOR

b Salem, Ohio, Aug 5, 40. *Study:* Univ Southern Calif; Univ Calif, Los Angeles, BA, 63, MFA, 66. *Collections Arranged:* Three Photographers--Bullock, Sommer, Teske, 68; P Lodato, 70; Jud Fine, 72; Foundations in Clay, 77; Narrative Themes: Audio Works, 78; Sound, 79; Leroy Neiman-Andy Warhol, 81; Changing Trends: Content and Style, 82. *Pos:* Gallery dir, Calif State Univ, Northridge, 66-70 & Brand Lib Art Ctr, Glendale, Calif, 70-73; dir & founder, Los Angeles Inst Contemp Art, 74- *Teaching:* Prof exhib & design, Calif State Univ, Northridge, 66- *Bibliog:* Michael Auping (auth), Interview with Bob Smith, La Mamelle, Berkeley, Calif, 75. *Publ:* Auth & designer numerous exhib catalogs. *Mailing Add:* 2020 S Robertson Blvd Los Angeles CA 90034

SMITH, RUTH REININGHAUS See   Reininghaus,   Ruth

SMITH, SAM
PAINTER, EDUCATOR

b Thorndale, Tex, Feb 11, 18. *Study:* With Randall Davey, Jack Levine, Ben Turner & Carl von Hassler. *Work:* War Dept Hist Properties Sect; Santa Fe Mus; Univ NMex; NMex State Fair Collection; Panhandle Mus Fine Art. *Comn:* Mural, Camp Barkley, Tex, War Dept, 42; paintings, Infantry Weapons, Camp Barkley, 42. *Exhib:* One-man show, Corcoran Gallery Art, Washington, DC, 48; Santa Fe Mus Fine Art, NMex, 49; Botts Mus Art, Albuquerque, NMex, 64; Panhandle-Plains Hist Mus, Canyon, Tex, 64; Roswell Mus Art, NMex, 65. *Teaching:* Prof art, Univ NMex, 56- *Awards:* Questa, NMex Purchase Prize, 62 & First Prize for Watercolor, 62, NMex State Fair; First Prize for Watercolor, Ouray Alpine Show, Colo, 64. *Bibliog:* Robert Ruark (auth), Sam Smith, artist, Assoc Press, 48. *Mem:* Life mem NMex Art League; Artists Equity Asn. *Media:* Watercolor, Oil. *Dealer:* Brandywine Galleries Ltd Albuquerque NM 87108. *Mailing Add:* 213 Utah NE Albuquerque NM 87108

SMITH, SHERRI
WEAVER, EDUCATOR

b Chicago, Ill, Mar 21, 43. *Study:* Stanford Univ, Calif, BA, 65; Cranbrook Acad Art, Bloomfield Hills, Mich, MFA, 67. *Work:* Art Inst Chicago; Hackley Art Mus, Muskegon, Mich, Am Tel & Tel Co; Borg Warner Corp; Colorado Springs Fine Arts Ctr, Colo. *Comn:* Wall hangings, Detroit Plaza Hotel, 77; Fed Bldg, Ann Arbor, 78; Du Page Co Hosp, Ill, 78; Int Business Machines, Atlanta. *Exhib:* Mus Mod Art, New York, 69; Biennale of Tapestry, Lausanne, Switz, 71-77; Three-Dimensional Fibers, Govett-Brewster Art Gallery, New Plymouth, NZ, 74; Am Crafts 76, Mus Contemp Art, Chicago, 76; Fiberworks, Cleveland Mus Art, Ohio, 77; one-person show, Hadler Gallery, New York, 78; Mainstream, the Art Fabric Traveling Exhib; and others. *Teaching:* Instr weaving & textile design, Colo State Univ, Ft Collins, 71-75; prof weaving & textile design, Sch Art, Univ Mich, Ann Arbor, 75- *Bibliog:* Larson & Constantine, Beyond Crafts, The Art Fabric, Van Nostrand, 75; Kuenzi (auth), La nouvelle tapisserie, Bonvent, 75; Waller (auth), Textile sculptures, Studio Vista, 77. *Dealer:* Jacques Baruch Gallery 900 N Michigan Ave Chicago IL 60611; Modern Masters Tapestries 11 E 57th New York NY 10022. *Mailing Add:* 1733 Jackson Ave Ann Arbor MI 48103

SMITH, SHIRLEY ANN
PAINTER

b Wichita, Kans. *Study:* Kans State Univ, BFA; Provincetown Workshop Art Sch, Mass; Art Students League. *Work:* Whitney Mus Am Art, New York; Univ Calif Art Mus, Berkeley; Aldrich Mus Contemp Art, Ridgefield, Conn; Phoenix Art Mus, Ariz; Everson Mus, Syracuse, NY; and others. *Exhib:* American Painting 1970, Va Mus, Richmond; Lyrical Abstraction, Aldrich Mus Contemp Art, 70; Recent Acquisitions & Lyrical Abstraction, Whitney Mus Am Art, New York, 71; From the Museum Collection Art by Women, Univ Calif Art Mus, Berkeley, 73; Abstract Works from Collection, Ulrich Mus, Wichita, Kans, 75; Auditorium Installation Exhib, Everson Mus, Syracuse, NY, 76-79; UN OIA Exhib, US Mission, New York, 78; Views by Women Artists, Women's Caucus Art, 82; and others. *Awards:* Grumbacher Artists Mat Co Award Mixed Media, New Eng Exhib, Silvermine, 67. *Bibliog:* Lawrence Campbell (auth), article, Art News, 2/73; April Kingsley (auth), article, Art Int, 3/73; Rosemary Mayer (auth), article, Arts, 2/73. *Mailing Add:* 141 Wooster St New York NY 10012

SMITH, SUSAN CARLTON
PAINTER, SCULPTOR

b Athens, Ga, June 30, 23. *Study:* Univ Ga, Athens, BS, MFA; Univ Va. *Work:* Ga Mus Art & Univ Ga, Athens; Duke Univ Mus Art; Trent Collection, Duke Univ Med Ctr Libr, Durham; Health Affairs Libr, Univ NC. *Comn:* Portrait, Venus Flytrap (watercolor), Hunt Botanical Libr, Carnegie-Mellon Univ, Pittsburgh, Pa; watercolor portraits, Sch Med, Univ Ga, Athens; Phallus Impudicans (watercolor), Duke Univ Mus Art, Durham, NC; Hand puppets, comn by Ga State Dept Educ. *Exhib:* NC Wildlife Artists Show, State Mus Natural Hist, Raleigh, 69; Nature Interpretations: Watercolors & Sculptures, Duke Univ Mus Art, 71-; Int Exhib of Botanical Art, Johannesburgh, SAfrica, 73; Boston Mus Sci, Mass, 74; NC Botanical Garden, 76; Int Mycological Cong, Fla, 77; Traveling Exhib of NC Artists, 78; and many others. *Pos:* Asst cur, Trent Collection, Med Ctr Libr, Duke Univ, 67- *Teaching:* Adj instr dept art, Duke Univ, currently. *Awards:* Best Children's Bk Illus for Ladybug, Ladybug, Am Inst Graphic Arts, 69; Printing Indust Am Award for Illus for Hey Bug & Other Poems About Little Things, 72. *Bibliog:* Meg McGriff (auth), Watercolors & nature sculptures, Athens

Banner Herald, 77. *Media:* Watercolor; Natural Materials. *Publ:* Illusr, Wildflowers of North Carolina, Univ NC Press, 68; illusr & contribr, Ladybug, Ladybug, 69 & illusr, Hey Bug! & Other Poems About Little Things, 72, Am Heritage Press, New York; illusr, A Child's Book of Flowers, Doubleday Publ Co, 76. *Dealer:* Paul R Reynolds 12 E 41st St New York NY 10017. *Mailing Add:* Duke Univ Med Ctr Libr Durham NC 27710

SMITH, THELMA DEGOEDE
PAINTER, EDUCATOR

b Los Angeles, Calif, May 5, 15. *Study:* Calif State Univ, Los Angeles, BA(with hons); Calif State Univ, Fullerton, MA. *Work:* Long Beach Mus Art, Calif; Downey Mus Art, Calif; Ill State Univ; Nat Orange Show Hq, San Bernardino, Calif; Hunt Foods Inc Collection, Fullerton; and others. *Exhib:* Calif Hawaii Regional, San Diego Mus Art Fine Arts Gallery, 71, 72 & 74; one-woman show, Loma Linda Univ, 71 & Palos Verdes Mus Art, 74; All Calif Exhib, Palos Verdes Mus Art, 73-74; American Painters in Paris, New Conv Ctr, 76; and others. *Teaching:* Instr oil painting, N Orange Co Community Col Dist, Fullerton, 67- *Awards:* Best of Show, First Award & Purchase Prize, 13th Ann Art Unlimited, Downey Mus Art, 70; Purchase Award, 16th All Calif Competition, Laguna Beach Mus Art, 70; First Purchase Prize, Nat Orange Show, San Bernardino, 71 & 74. *Bibliog:* TV interview & presentation of paintings, Channel 10, Brea, Calif, 73. *Mem:* Los Angeles Art Asn; Orange Co Art Asn (dir, 70-75); Laguna Beach Art Asn. *Media:* Acrylic. *Mailing Add:* 2916 Hillcrest Ave Orange CA 92667

SMITH, TONY
SCULPTOR

b South Orange, NJ, 1912. *Study:* Art Students League, 34-35; New Bauhaus, Chicago, 37-38; archit apprentice of Frank Lloyd Wright, 38-40. *Work:* Mus Mod Art, New York; Corcoran Gallery Art, Washington, DC; Wadsworth Atheneum, Hartford, Conn; NJ State Mus, Trenton; Detroit Inst Art, Mich. *Exhib:* Wadsworth Atheneum, Hartford, Conn, 64, 67 & 74; Philadelphia Inst Contemp Art, 67; Whitney Mus Am Art Ann, 70-73; Metrop Mus Art, New York, 70; Los Angeles Co Mus Art, Los Angeles, 71; San Francisco Mus Art, 71; Seattle Art Mus Pavilion, Wash, 73; Cleveland Mus Art, 74; Painting & Sculpture Today 1974, Indianapolis Mus Art, Ind & Contemp Arts Ctr, Cincinnati, 74; Art Inst Chicago, 74; Walker Art Ctr, Minneapolis, 74; New Orleans Mus Art, La, 76; Meadow Brook Art Gallery, Oakland Univ, Rochester, Mich, 77; and others. *Mailing Add:* c/o The Pace Gallery 32 E 57th St New York NY 10022

SMITH, VICTOR JOACHIM
PAINTER, EDUCATOR

b Grand Island, Nebr, Apr 3, 29. *Study:* Chouinard Art Inst, Los Angeles; Calif State Univ, Long Beach, BA, MA. *Work:* San Francisco Mus Art, Calif; Long Beach Mus Art; Newport Harbor Art Mus, Newport Beach, Calif; Laguna Beach Mus Art, Calif; La Jolla Mus Contemp Art, Calif; plus others. *Exhib:* Mus Mod Art, Turin, Italy, 62; Mus-Manifeste (traveling exhib), Austria, WGer & Italy, 64-65; one-man shows, Long Beach Mus Art, 60, Santa Barbara Mus Art, Calif, 62, Pasadena Art Mus, Calif, 63, Los Angeles Munic Art Gallery, 68, Los Angeles Co Mus Art, Los Angeles, 72 & Newport Harbor Art Mus, 75; plus others. *Teaching:* Prof drawing & painting, Calif State Univ, Fullerton, 62-80, chmn art dept, 76-77, vchmn art dept, 77-80, prof emer, 81. *Awards:* Over seventy-five awards for painting in Calif. *Bibliog:* Michele Tapie (auth), Morphologic autre, Int Inst Aesthetic Res, Turin, 60; article in Artforum, Vol 1 (1962); Allan S Weller (auth), Contemporary American painting & sculpture, Univ Ill Press, 67. *Media:* Mixed. *Publ:* Auth, Morris Graves, 63 & The Pacific Coast invitational, 63, Artforum. *Mailing Add:* Dept of Art Calif State Univ Fullerton CA 92634

SMITH, VINCENT D
PAINTER, PRINTMAKER

b Brooklyn, NY, Dec 12, 29. *Study:* Art Students League New York with Reginald Marsh, 53; Brooklyn Mus, NY, 54-56; Skowhegan Sch Painting & Sculpture, Maine, studied with Sidney Simon & Ben Shann, 55; Bub Blackburn Printmaking Workshop, New York, with Krisna Reddy & Bob Cale, 71. *Work:* Mus Mod Art, New York; Columbus Gallery Fine Art, Ohio; Newark Mus Asn, NJ; Brooklyn Mus, NY; Ackland Art Mus. *Comn:* Four Murals on Canvas, Boys & Girls High Sch, Brooklyn Bd Educ, New York, 76; Mural, Crotona Social Serv Ctr Human Resources Admin, New York, 80. *Exhib:* Contemp Black Am Artist, Whitney Mus Am Art, New York; People & Places, Whitney Mus Downtown, New York; one-man shows, Kibo Art Gallery, Mt Kilimanjaro, Tanzania, 73, Reading Pub Mus, Pa, 74, Portland Art Mus Maine, 74, Erie Art Ctr, Pa, 77 & Larcada Gallery, New York, 67, 68, 70, 73, 75 & 77. *Teaching:* Instr painting & printmaking, Whitney Mus Am Art, New York, 67-76; artist-in-residence, Cite des Arts' Int, Paris, France, summer 78. *Awards:* Nat Endowment Arts Travel Grant, 73; Childe Hassam Fund Purchase Award, Am Acad Arts & Letters, 73-74; Thomas B Clarke Award, 149th Ann Exhib, Nat Acad Design, 74. *Bibliog:* The Pulse of Afro-American Culture, 30 minute film on Vincent Smith, his work and influence, WTVG; Peter Mark (auth), African influences in contemporary Black American painting, Art Voices, 1-2/81; Judith Wilson (auth), Afro-American artists in the 20th century, Art America, 80. *Media:* Painting and Printmaking. *Publ:* Contribr, Atticia Book, Custom Commun Systs, 73; illusr, Folklore Stories from Africa, Garrard Publ, 75. *Mailing Add:* 264 E Broadway New York NY 10002

SMITH, WILLIAM ARTHUR
PAINTER, PRINTMAKER

b Toledo, Ohio, Apr 19, 18. *Study:* Keane's Art Sch, Toledo; Art Students League; Grand Cent Art Sch, New York; Ecole Beaux Arts, Paris; Acad

Grande Chaumiere, Paris; Univ Toledo, MA. *Work:* Metrop Mus Art, New York; Los Angeles Co Mus, Calif; Libr Cong, Washington, DC; Nat Acad Design, New York. *Comn:* Mural of hist Md, State of Md, Md House, Aberdeen, 68; design of ten postage stamps, US Postal Serv. *Exhib:* Contemp Arts US, Los Angeles, 56; 200 Yrs Watercolor Painting Am, Metrop Mus Art, 66-67; 27 one-man exhibs, major cities Europe, Asia & US. *Teaching:* Lectr, var univs & art schs, Europe, Asia & US. *Awards:* Nat Acad Design Awards, 49 & 51; Nat Acad Design Prize for Oil Painting, Adolf & Clara Obrig, 51; Two Grand Prizes & Gold Medals, Am Watercolor Soc, 56 & 65. *Mem:* Nat Acad Design (rec secy, 54-55); Am Watercolor Soc (pres, 56-57, hon pres, 57-); Int Asn Art (vpres, 66-69, pres, US comt, 70-, int pres, 73-76 & life hon pres, 76-); Audubon Artists; Nat Soc Mural Painters. *Media:* Oil, Watercolor; Lithography, Intaglio. *Publ:* Auth & illusr, Art behind the iron curtain, 2/60 & Changing art of the Orient, 8/65, Harpers Bazaar; auth, Ben Shahn, In: Ben Shahn, Osaka Shiritsu Bijutsukan-Mainichi Shimbun, Japan, 70. *Mailing Add:* Windy Bush Rd Pineville PA 18946

SMITHER, EDWARD MURRAY
DEALER, CONSULTANT

b Huntsville, Tex, July 23, 37. *Study:* Sam Houston State Univ, BS, 58; Dallas Mus Fine Arts Sch, 59. *Pos:* Dir, Cranfill Gallery, Dallas, 70-72; owner & dir, Smither Gallery, Dallas, 72-74; co-owner, Delahunty Gallery, Dallas, 74-82; pvt dealer & consult, 83-; advisor, Gihon-McMunay Found, Dallas & Assemblage Club, Dallas, currently. *Mem:* Art Pub Places Fine Arts Comt Dallas. *Mailing Add:* 1934 Kessler Pkwy Dallas TX 75208

SMONGESKI, JOSEPH LEON
PAINTER, DESIGNER

b Two Rivers, Wis, Feb 6, 14. *Study:* Art Inst Chicago; Univ Chicago; Univ Wis-Madison. *Work:* St Ann's, Wollaston, Mass; Boston Mus Fine Arts; Thomas Mann Publ Libr, Two Rivers; Copley Soc, Boston; Chicago Art Inst. *Exhib:* Art Inst Chicago, 39; Layton Art Ctr, Milwaukee, 39; Copley Soc Boston, Boston Mus Fine Arts, 58 & 71-75; Parrish Mus, Long Island, NY, 64; S Shore Art Ctr, Cohasset, Mass, 64, 65 & 66; Oshkosh Pub Mus, Wis, 82; Art Complex Mus, Duxbury, Mass, 84. *Pos:* Color consult, Western Publ Co, New York, 41-46; designer, D C Heath & Co, Boston, 46-65; art dir, D C Heath & Raytheon, Lexington, Mass, 65-77. *Teaching:* Instr painting, S Shore Art Ctr; instr painting, Milton Adult Educ Ctr, Mass. *Awards:* New Eng Book Show Award, Bookbuilders of Boston, 73. *Bibliog:* Articles in Quincy Patriot Ledger, 74, Boston Globe, 74-75. *Mem:* Copley Soc Boston; Milton Art Asn; Salmagundi Club New York; and others. *Media:* Watercolor, Oil. *Dealer:* Chapellier Gallery 815 Park Ave New York NY 10021; Arvest Galleries 77 Newbury St Boston MA 02116. *Mailing Add:* 42 Brook Wollaston MA 02170

SMYTH, CRAIG HUGH
ADMINISTRATOR, HISTORIAN

b New York, NY, July 28, 15. *Study:* Princeton Univ, AB, 38, MFA, 41, PhD, 56; Harvard Univ, Hon MA, 75. *Pos:* Res asst & sr mus aide, Nat Gallery Art, Washington, DC, 41-42; dir, Harvard Univ Ctr for Ital Renaissance Studies, Florence, 73- *Teaching:* Lectr, Frick Collection, New York, 46-50; from asst prof to prof, Inst Fine Arts, NY Univ, 50-73, actg dir & actg head dept fine arts, 51-53, dir & head grad dept fine arts, 53-73; prof fine arts, Harvard Univ, 73- *Mem:* Col Art Asn Am (dir, 53-57, secy, 56); Comite Int Hist Art (alt US mem, 70-); US Nat Comt Hist Art; Metrop Mus Art (hon trustee, 68-). *Res:* 16th century Italian painting and drawing; 16th century Italian architecture. *Publ:* Auth, Venice and the emergence of the high renaissance in Florence: observations and questions, In: S Bertelli, N Rubinstein & C Smyth, ed, Florence and Venice: Comparisons and Relations, 79; auth, Sunken courts of the Villa Giula & the Villa Imperiale, In: Essays in Memory of Karl Lehmann, 63; coauth, Michelangelo & St Peter's--I: The attic as originally built on the south hemicycle, Burlington Mag, 69; auth, Bronzino as draughtsman, 71; co-auth, Michelangelo & St Peter's--II: Observations on the interior of the Apses, a model of the Apse vault, and related drawings, Romisches Jahrbuch Fur Kunstgeschichte, 75; and others. *Mailing Add:* Villa I Tatti Via di Vincigliata 26 Florence Italy

SMYTH, DAVID RICHARD
SCULPTOR

b Washington, DC, Dec 2, 43. *Study:* Corcoran Sch Art, Washington, DC, 62-64; Art Inst Chicago, BFA, 67, MFA, 69. *Work:* Whitney Mus Am Art, New York; Brooklyn Mus. *Comn:* Relief painting, Blue Cross-Blue Shield, C F Murphy Archit, Chicago, 69. *Exhib:* Solo exhibs, Whitney Mus Am Art, New York, 72, Ithaca House Gallery, 80 & Herbert Johnson Mus, Ithaca, NY, 82; Mus Contemp Art, Chicago, 72; Brooklyn Mus, 74; Nat Gallery, Washington, DC, 76; Art Inst Chicago, 77 & 78; Krannert Art Mus, 80; Marianne Deson Gallery, Chicago, 81; and others. *Awards:* Richard Rice Jenkins Award, Art Inst Chicago, 70; Tamarind Inst Fel, Albuquerque, NMex, 72; NY State Coun Art Fel, 78. *Bibliog:* Articles, Arts Mag, 11/75 & Art News, 11/75 & 4/76; and others. *Mailing Add:* 209 N Aurora St Ithaca NY 14850

SMYTH, ED
ILLUSTRATOR, PAINTER

b New York, NY, May 21, 16. *Study:* Pratt Inst; Columbia Univ with Mario Cooper; Wash Univ with Gustav Goetsch & Fred Carpenter. *Exhib:* Wyo State Art Mus, Cheyenne, 75; Royal Watercolor Soc, Nat Cowboy Hall of Fame, Oklahoma City, 76; Wyo Image, State Capitol, Cheyenne, 77. *Bibliog:* Archie L Nash (auth), Ed Smyth, Artist with brush & camera, Western Horseman Mag, 9/67; Jack Rice (auth), Artist with camera is drawn to horses, St Louis Post-Dispatch Mag, 10/67; Diane Simmons (auth), article, Art West, 8-9/82. *Mem:* Wyo Artists' Asn. *Media:* Watercolor; Pen & Ink, Conte. *Publ:*

Auth & illusr, Born to buck, Western Horseman, 10/67; auth & illusr, Hooked by the Wily Trout, 9/72; illusr, Murchison's moose, Saturday Evening Post, fall 74; auth & illusr, Big Horn art bonanza-Bradford Brinton Mem, Art West, Fall 1977. *Mailing Add:* The Line Camp Gallery Box 308 Story WY 82842

SNEED, PATRICIA M
DEALER, COLLECTOR

b Spencer, Iowa, Oct 24, 22. *Study:* Drake Univ, 40-42; Univ Cincinnati, 45-46. *Collections Arranged:* Fifty Artists for Fifty States (nat art exhib), 65-; Art in Other Media, 70. *Pos:* Founder & mem women's bd, Burpee Art Mus, currently; owner & dir, Sneed Gallery, 35 & 58- *Mem:* Am Fedn Arts. *Specialty:* Contemporary American art. *Collection:* Contemporary American art. *Mailing Add:* 2024 Harlem Blvd Rockford IL 61103

SNELSON, KENNETH D
SCULPTOR, PAINTER

b Pendleton, Ore, June 29, 27. *Study:* Black Mountain Col, NC, 48-49; with Fernand Leger, Paris, 50. *Work:* Whitney Mus Am Art & Mus Mod Art, New York; Staedelijk Mus, Amsterdam, Holland; City Buffalo, NY; Storm King Art Ctr. *Comn:* Japan Iron & Steel Fedn, Expo '70, Osaka, Japan, 70; Baltimore Inner Harbor, Md, 80; Albright-Knox Art Gallery, 82; Stanford Univ, Calif, 82. *Exhib:* Int Sculpture Symp, Osaka, Japan, 69; one-man shows, Ger, 71, Wilhelm Lehmbruck Mus, Ger & Berlin Nationalgalerie, 77, Hirshhorn Mus, 81 & Albright-Knox Art Gallery, 81; Portrait of an Atom Traveling Exhib, 79-83. *Awards:* Deutscher Akad Austauschdienst for Berlin Kunstlerprogram, 76; Am Inst Archit Medal, 81. *Bibliog:* Articles, Artforum, 5/77 & Art News, 2/81. *Media:* Mixed. *Publ:* Auth, A design for the atom, Indust Design, 2/63; auth, Continuous Tension, Discontinuous Compression Structures, 65 & A Model for Atomic Forms, 66 & 78, US Patent Off. *Mailing Add:* 140 Sullivan St New York NY 10012

SNIDOW, GORDON E
PAINTER, SCULPTOR

b Paris, Mo, Sept 30, 36. *Study:* Art Ctr Col Design, BA. *Work:* Nat Cowboy Hall Fame, Oklahoma City; Phoenix Mus, Ariz; Gilcrease Mus, Tulsa, Okla; Mont Hist Soc, Helena; W B Davis Mus, Duncan, Okla. *Exhib:* Cowboy Artist Am Ann Exhib, Nat Cowboy Hall Fame & Phoenix Art Mus, 65-75 & 78; two-man show, Nat Cowboy Hall Fame, 70; one-man show, C M Russell Gallery, Mont Hist Soc, 73. *Awards:* Silver Medal for Watercolor, Cowboy Artist of Am, 74, Mem Award, 78; Best of Show Award, Western Art Assocs, Phoenix Art Mus, 78. *Bibliog:* Meigs (auth), The Cowboy in American Prints, Sage Swallow, 72; Broder (auth), Bronzes of the American West, Abrams, 74; Hassrick (auth), American Painting Today, Watson-Guptill, 75. *Mem:* Cowboy Artist Am (secy-treas, 67-68, vpres, 68-69, pres, 70-71 & 78-79). *Media:* Oil, Watercolor; Charcoal. *Publ:* Contribr, Persimmon Hill, 70; auth, Gordon Snidow, Chronicler of the Contemporary West, 73. *Mailing Add:* PO Box 2496 Ruidoso NM 88345

SNODGRASS, JEANNE OWENS (MRS M EUGENE KING)
MUSEOLOGIST, HISTORIAN

b Muskogee, Okla, Sept 12, 27. *Study:* Art Instr, Inc; Northeastern State Col; Okla Univ. *Collections Arranged:* 214 exhibs of Indian art & artifacts, Philbrook Art Ctr, 55-68; Am Indian Artists Nat Competition Ann, Philbrook Art Ctr, 55-68. *Pos:* Asst to dir & cur Am Indian Art, Philbrook Art Ctr, 55-68; admin asst to pres, Educ Dimensions, Inc, 69-71; registr, Gilcrease Mus, 73-; assoc, Am Indian Affairs & mem Arts & Crafts Adv Comt; juror, many nat & regional Indian Art Exhibs. *Teaching:* Lectr, American Indian painting. *Awards:* Outstanding Contrib to Indian Art Award, US Dept Interior, 67. *Mem:* Okla Mus Asn (charter secy); Tulsa Hist Soc; Am Asn Mus. *Publ:* Ed, American Indian Basketry, 64; auth, American Indian Painters: A Biographical Directory, Heye Found, 68; American Indian Painting, Amarillo Art Ctr, Tex, 81; contribr, Oscar Howe, A Retrospective Exhibition, 82; auth, articles, Southwestern Art Mag, 82-83. *Mailing Add:* 3931 S Madison Tulsa OK 74105

SNOW, CYNTHIA REEVES
PAINTER

b Laurel Springs, NC, Oct 2, 07. *Study:* Univ NC, Greensboro, AB; Peabody Col, Nashville, Tenn, MA; NY Univ; Univ Minn; Walter Art Ctr. *Work:* Thaw (oil), New Britain Mus Am Art, Conn; watercolors, SDak Mem Art Ctr, Benton Mus Art, Storrs, Conn & Eastern Conn Col, Willimantic. *Exhib:* Gallery on the Green, Canton, Conn, 71; Sharon Arts Festival, Conn, 71; Slater Mem Mus, Norwich, Conn, 71; Nat Conf-Aesthet, Fairfield Univ, 73; Eastern Connecticut Artists, Slater Mem Mus, 73; and many others. *Teaching:* Instr, Fla State Univ, Tallahassee, 40-47; prof, Univ Conn, Storrs, 48-78, emer prof, 78- *Awards:* Watercolor Prize for Landscape Theme-9b, New Eng Ann, Mystic, Conn, 73; John Slade Ely Award, Nat Soc Women Artists, 74; First Prize, Conn Watercolor Soc, 77; and others. *Mem:* San Diego Independent Scholars; San Diego Art Guild; Nat Soc Women Painters; Mystic Art Asn; Conn Acad Fine Arts. *Media:* Watercolor, Oil. *Mailing Add:* 13663 Mar Scenic Dr Del Mar CA 92014

SNOW, JOHN
PRINTMAKER, PAINTER

b Vancouver, BC, Dec 12, 11. *Work:* Victoria & Albert Mus, London, Eng; Nat Gallery Can; Univ Toronto; Can Coun. *Exhib:* Premiere Expos Bienale Int Gravure, Tokyo & Osaka, Japan, 57; 5th Int Biennial Color Lithography, Cincinnati, 58; Royal Acad Arts, London, 63; Cardiff Commonwealth Arts Festival, Cardiff & Brit Isles, 65; Salon Beaux Arts, Paris, 69. *Awards:* C W Jeffrey's Award, Can Soc Graphic Art, 61; Jessie Dow Award, Montreal Mus Fine Arts, 62. *Bibliog:* Ken Jones (dir), The Sad Phoenician and Friends (film), Clopton Films. *Mem:* Can Soc Graphic Art; Royal Can Acad Arts. *Mailing Add:* 915 18th Ave SW Calgary AB T2T 0H2 Canada

SNOW, LEE ERLIN
PAINTER, INSTRUCTOR
b Buffalo, NY, Jan 2, 24. *Study:* Univ Buffalo, BA, 47; Otis Art Inst, with Joseph Young, scholar; Univ Calif, Los Angeles, with Neda Al-Hilali. *Work:* Skirball Mus, Los Angeles; Halls Crown Ctr, Kansas City; Jewish Fedn, Los Angeles; Craft & Folk Art Mus, Los Angeles. *Comn:* Mosaic portrait Bess Hawes, Folk Music Classes Univ Calif, Los Angeles. *Exhib:* Art Rental Gallery, Los Angeles Co Mus of Art, 76-80; solo shows, Southwest Craft Ctr Gallery, San Antonio, 75; Front Rm, Dallas, Tex, 76 & Galeria del Sol, Santa Barbara, Calif, 76; Jewish Fedn Craft Show, Los Angeles, 83; Los Angeles Art Asn Exhib, Craft & Folk Art Mus. *Pos:* Interviewer, Starship Earth, KHJ Radio, Los Angeles. *Teaching:* Instr multimedia fibre, Barnsdall Arts & Crafts Ctr, Los Angeles, 72-76; workshop leader non-loom weaving, World Crafts Conf, Toronto, Ont, 74; instr multimedia fibre, Los Angeles Co Mus Art, Los Angeles, 75. *Awards:* Third Prize Painting & Award Study, Westwood Art Asn, 63. *Bibliog:* Film interview, Theta Cable TV, Los Angeles, 73; Lois McAfee (auth), Oh, what a tangled web, Sun-Tel, San Bernardino, 1/75; article, Los Angeles Times Home Mag, 12/17/78. *Mem:* Southern Calif Designer Craftsmen (sr adv, 78-80); Santa Barbara Weavers Guild; Los Angeles Art Asn; Am Crafts Coun; Southern Calif Weavers Guild. *Media:* Oil. *Publ:* Coauth, Weaving Off-Loom, 73 & contribr, Creating Art From Fibers and Fabrics, 74, Regnery; contribr, How to Create Your Own Designs, Doubleday, 75; contribr, Exotic Needlework, 78 & Ethnic Jewelry, 81, Crown. *Mailing Add:* 333 Old Mill Rd #318 Santa Barbara CA 93110

SNOW, MICHAEL
PAINTER, FILMMAKER
b Toronto, Ont, Dec 10, 29. *Study:* Ont Col Art, Toronto. *Work:* Mus Mod Art & Anthology Film Arch, New York; Art Gallery Toronto; Montreal Mus Fine Arts; Nat Gallery Can, Ottawa; Centre Pompidou, Paris. *Exhib:* Solo exhibs, Walker Art Ctr, 74, Mus Mod Art, New York, 76, Centre Georges Pompidou, 77, 78 & Issacs Gallery, Toronto, 79 & Frederick S Wright Gallery, Univ Calif, Los Angelos, 83; Re-Visions: Projects & Proposals in Film & Video, Whitney Mus American Art, 79; and others; and others. *Awards:* Grand Prize, 4th Int Exp Film Festival, Brussels, Belg, 68; Guggenheim Fel, 72. *Mem:* Royal Can Acad Arts. *Dealer:* Isaacs Gallery 832 Yonge St Toronto ON Can. *Mailing Add:* 137 Summerhill Ave Toronto ON M4T 1B1 Canada

SNYDER, DAN
SCULPTOR
b Philadelphia, Pa, July 23, 48. *Study:* Pa State Univ, BFA, 70; Univ Calif, Davis, MFA, 72. *Work:* Oakland Mus, Calif; E B Crocker Art Mus, Sacramento; Am Acad, Rome, Italy; Univ Calif, Davis. *Comn:* Welcome Wall (sculpture), Art Comm San Francisco, 83. *Exhib:* Oakland Mus, Calif, 73; Am Acad, Rome, 75; Allrich Gallery, San Francisco, 77, 79, 81 & 82; San Francisco Mus Mod Art, 79; Monterey Peninsula Mus Art, 83; and others. *Teaching:* Instr sculpture, Pa State Univ, 75-76. *Awards:* Spec proj grant, Nat Endowment Arts, 73; Fel, Prix de Rome, 73-75. *Media:* Ceramics, Mixed Media. *Dealer:* Allrich Gallery 251 Post St San Francisco CA 94108. *Mailing Add:* 170 Vernon Terr Oakland CA 94610

SNYDER, JOAN
PAINTER
b Highland Park, NJ, Apr 16, 40. *Study:* Douglas Col, BA, 62; Rutgers Univ, MFA, 66. *Work:* Metrop Mus Art, Mus Mod Art & Whitney Mus Am Art, New York; Dallas Mus Fine Arts, Tex; Neuberger Mus, Purchase, NY; and others. *Exhib:* Retrospective, Neuberger Mus, Purchase, NY, 78; one-woman shows, traveling, San Francisco Art Inst, Grand Rapids Mus Art, Renaissance Soc, Chicago & Va Commonwealth Univ, Richmond, 79-80; New Works on Paper, Mus Modern Art, New York, 81; 1981 Biennial exhib, Whitney Mus Contemporary Art, New York, 81; American Abstraction Now, Istitute Contemporary Art, Virginia Mus, 82; and others. *Awards:* Nat Endowment for Arts grant, 74. *Bibliog:* Gerrit Henry (auth), article, Art in America, summer 82; Ronney Cohen (auth), article, Artforum, 9/82; Deborah C Phillips (auth), article, Artnews, 9/82; and others. *Media:* Oil, Acrylic. *Dealer:* Hamilton Gallery 20 W 57th St New York NY 10019. *Mailing Add:* 105 Mulberry St New York NY 10013

SNYDER, KIM LAWRENCE
CURATOR, PAINTER
b Ft Washakie, Wyo, June 5, 42. *Study:* Cent Wyo Col, Riverton, AA, 70; Idaho State Univ, BA, 74; Univ Idaho, MFA, 76; Boise State Univ, 82. *Work:* Idaho Hist Soc, Boise; Cent Wyo Col, Riverton; Shoshone Indian Ctr, Ft Washakie. *Exhib:* Transition Art Gallery, Pocatello, Idaho, 73; Columbia Basin Col, Pasco, Wash, 75; one-man shows, Mus of the Plains Indian, 75, Wyo Hist Soc Mus, Cheyenne, 78, Cent Wyo Mus of Art, Casper, 78 & Idaho State Libr, Boise, 80; Univ Art Gallery, Moscow, Idaho, 76; Idaho State Capitol, Boise, 76; Idaho Mus Natural Hist, Pocatello, 81. *Collections Arranged:* Chippewa-Cree Crafts, 76-77, Paintings by Frank Day (ed, catalogue), 77, Metalwork by Gail Larson (ed, catalogue), 77, Fashions by Jewel Gilham (ed, catalogue), 77, Shoshone Arts & Crafts (ed, catalogue), 77 & Indian Tipi Exhib, 77, Mus Plains Indian. *Pos:* Mus cur, Idaho State Hist Mus, 76- *Teaching:* Instr painting, Univ Idaho, Moscow, 75-76. *Awards:* First Prize Sculpture, Wind River Artists Nat Exhib, Wind River Valley Artist Guild, 75; Second Prize Painting, Western Idaho Fair. *Bibliog:* Norma Ashbee (auth), Today in Montana, KRTV, Great Falls, Mont, 77; George Horse Capture (auth), Indian Country, KFBB-TV, Great Falls, 77; Allen Bell (auth), Rocky Mountain Mix, KUID-TV, Moscow, Idaho, 76. *Mem:* Wind River Valley Artists Guild. *Media:* Oil, Acrylic Lacquer. *Publ:* Contribr, Paintings and Sculpture by Kim Snyder, Artcraft Printers, 75. *Mailing Add:* PO Box 5021 Boise ID 83705

SNYDER, RUTH (COZEN)
ENVIRONMENTAL ARTIST, SCULPTOR
b Montreal, Can; US citizen. *Study:* Univ Calif, Los Angeles; Otis Art Inst. *Work:* Laguna Beach Mus Art, Calif; Cedars-Sinai Med Ctr, Crocker Nat Bank, Los Angeles; Coos Art Mus, Coos Bay, Ore; US Embassy, Lisbon; and others. *Exhib:* Watercolor West, Riverside Art Ctr & Mus, Calif, 77, Butler Mus Am Art, 77 & 78 & San Bernardino Co Mus, Calif, 78 & 79; Coos Art Mus, Coos Bay, Ore; Riverside Art Ctr & Mus, Calif, 82 & 83; Brigham Young Univ, 83; Gallery Arcadia, Paris, 83; and others. *Collections Arranged:* Nat Watercolor Soc 57th Ann Exhib, Western Asn Art Mus, Oakland, Calif; Inst Mus Serv, DC, 79; Invitational, San Bernardino Mus Art, Calif; Ann Watercolor Soc, Laguna Beach Mus, 79 & 80; Los Angeles 9, Palm Springs Desert Mus (auth, catalog), 80. *Pos:* Exec bd mem, Watercolor West, Riverside, Calif, 77-80. *Teaching:* Lectr oil painting, Los Angeles Art Asn, 78; lectr & videotape demonstrator acrylic painting, Long Beach Art Asn, Calif, 80. *Awards:* Annenberg Award, Nat Watercolor Soc, 78; First Prize Painting, San Bernardino Co Mus, 79; 1st Place, Nat Watercolor Soc Exhib, 81; and others. *Bibliog:* Neil Menzies (auth), article, Artweek, 11/80; Hazel Simon (auth), article, Riverside Press, 82-83; article, Herald, Provo, Utah, 10/83. *Mem:* Artists for Econ Action, Los Angeles; Am Watercolor Soc, New York; Nat Watercolor Soc; Women Painters West. *Media:* Multimedia. *Publ:* Contribr, Ctr Mag for Democratic Studies, Santa Barbara, 5-6/76; contribr, Creative Seascape Painting by Edward Betts, Watson-Guptill; and others. *Mailing Add:* 2200 Main St Santa Monica CA 90405

SNYDER, WILLIAM B
PAINTER, EDUCATOR
b San Francisco, Calif, Sept 26, 26. *Study:* Chouinard's Art Inst, 43; San Francisco State Col; Stanford Univ, fel, 61-62. *Work:* Oakland Art Mus, Calif; City Chico, Calif; Haggin Mus, Stockton, Calif; Richmond Art Ctr, Fairfield, Calif; and others. *Exhib:* Art: USA 58, New York, 58; Church Art USA: 58, Grace Cathedral, San Francisco, 58; 4th & 5th Winter Invitational, Palace Legion Honor, San Francisco, 63 & 64; Phelan Award Biennial DeYoung Mus, 65; Christmas Show, San Francisco Mus Mod Art, 70; Collector's Exhib, Oakland Art Mus, 78; one-man shows, Wooster Col, Ohio, 74, Sacramento State Univ, Calif, 77 & San Francisco Art Comn, 78. *Pos:* Set illusr, MGM Picture Studio, Culver City, Calif, 46-47. *Teaching:* Instr drawing, Stanford Univ, 61-62; instr art, Foothills Jr Col, 62-63; instr drawing & painting, Laney Col, Oakland, Calif, 64- *Awards:* First Prize, San Joaquin Valley Regional Fall Arts Festival, Stockton Art League, Calif, 58; Purchase Award, Chico Savings & Loan, 66; Purchase Award, Fairfield Art Comn, 74. *Bibliog:* Tom Albright (auth), $5,000: Study for nightwatch, Art Gallery Mag, 3/73 & Interview: William Snyder, Currant Art Mag, 8/75; Ralph Pomeroy (auth), Triumph of Disneyanity, Art & Artists, London, 8/74. *Media:* Oil, Watercolor. *Publ:* Illusr, Monterey Advocate, Panadero, 66-68. *Dealer:* Joseph Chowning Gallery 1717 17th St San Francisco CA 94103. *Mailing Add:* PO Box 563 Woodacre CA 94973

SOBOTIK, KENT
CURATOR, HISTORIAN
b Hallettsville, Tex, Dec 13, 40. *Study:* Univ Vienna, Austria, 63; Baylor Univ, BA, 64; Boston Univ, MA, 70. *Collections Arranged:* 100 Paintings from the Boston Museum (auth, catalog), Metrop Mus Art, New York, 70; The Bick Collection of Italian Drawings (co-auth, catalog), Ringling Mus, Fla, 70; Central Europe 1600-1800 (auth, catalog), Ringling Mus, Fla, 72. *Pos:* Lectr & research asst, Paintings Dept, Mus Fine Arts, Boston, Mass, 67-70; asst cur, Ringling Mus Art, Fla, 70-73; chief cur, Mus Fine Arts, Houston, Tex, 73-78; chief cur, Dayton Art Inst, Ohio, 79- *Teaching:* Instr art hist, Boston Univ, 68-70. *Mem:* Am Asn Mus; Asn Studies Central European Art (treas, 78-). *Res:* Late 16th-18th century paintings, sculpture & drawings, central European. *Publ:* Auth, 100 Paintings from the Boston Museum, New York Graphic Society, 70; contribr, The Museum of Fine Arts, Houston: A Guide to the Collection MFA, Colish, 81. *Mailing Add:* PO Box 941 Dayton OH 45401

SOFFER, SASSON
ENVIRONMENTAL ARTIST, CONCEPTUAL ARTIST
b Baghdad, Iraq, June 1, 25; US citizen. *Study:* Brooklyn Col, with Mark Rothko & others, 50-54. *Work:* Indianapolis Mus Fine Art; Albright-Knox Gallery, Buffalo; Rockefeller Inst, New York; Butler Inst Am Art, Youngstown, Ohio. *Exhib:* Whitney Mus Am Art, New York; one-man shows, Betty Parsons Gallery, New York, 61-63, Corpus Christi Mus, Tex, 64, Portland Mus, Maine, 66, Montclair State Col, NJ, 74 & Battery Park, New York, 75 & 76; and others. *Pos:* Ford Found artist in residence, Portland Mus, 66. *Awards:* Ford Found Purchase Award, Whitney Mus Am Art, 62 & North Jersey Cult Coun, 74. *Mailing Add:* 78 Grand New York NY 10013

SOKOL, DAVID MARTIN
HISTORIAN, CURATOR
b New York, NY, Nov 3, 42. *Study:* Hunter Col, AB, 63; Inst for Fine Arts, NY Univ, MA, 66, PhD, 70. *Pos:* Chmn acquisitions comt, Frank L Wright Home & Studio Found, 75-77; cur, Terra Mus Am Art, 81- *Teaching:* Instr art hist, Kingsborough Community Col, Brooklyn, NY, 66-68; asst prof art hist, Western Ill Univ, Macomb, 68-71; assoc prof art & archit hist, Univ Ill, Chicago, 71-82, chmn dept, 76-, prof, 82- *Mem:* Col Art Asn (placement comt, 77); Am Studies Asn (nat coun, 76-78); Am Asn Univ Prof (comt T, 75-78); Asn Historians Am Art (treas, 79-). *Res:* American painting and decorative arts, relations between American and European art. *Publ:* Auth, John Quider: Painter of American Legend, Wichita Art Mus, 73; auth, American Architecture & Art, 76 & American Decorative Arts & Old World Influences, 79, Gale; coauth, History of American Art, Abrams, 79; auth, Otto Neumann, 82 & Heidelberger Kunstverein, Solitude, 82, Terra Mus Am Art. *Mailing Add:* 330 S Taylor Ave Oak Park IL 60302

SOKOLE, MIRON
PAINTER

b Odessa, Russia; US citizen. *Study:* Cooper Union, cert; Nat Acad Art, with Ivan Olinsky. *Work:* Butler Inst Am Art, Youngstown, Ohio; Mus Tel Aviv, Israel; Univ Minn, Minneapolis; IBM Collection; Upjohn Collection. *Exhib:* Metrop Mus Art, New York, 42, 44 & 52; Int Expos, Mus Art Mod, Paris, 46; Watercolors Show, Whitney Mus Am Art, New York, 53 & 54; Dallas Mus, 56; Corcoran Gallery Art Biennial, Washington, DC, 58; Collectors Gallery, 63 & 68; 21st Ann, Norfolk Mus, Va, 65; Fashion Inst of Technol, 71; Woodstock Art Asn, 73; WPA Then & Now Show, 77; plus others. *Teaching:* Instr painting & drawing, Am Artists Sch, New York, 38-41; resident artist, Kansas City Art Inst, Mo, 47-51; prof art, Fashion Inst Technol, New York, 62- *Bibliog:* Salpeter (auth), Miron Sokole, Esquire, 9/45; A Guskin (auth), Painting in USA, 54; Martha Cheney (auth), Modern art in America, Tudor. *Mem:* Woodstock Artists Asn; Exp Art & Technol; Artists Equity Asn (nat dir, 52). *Media:* Oil, Acrylic. *Dealer:* Art Collectors Place 51 E 73rd St New York NY 10021. *Mailing Add:* 250 W 22nd St New York NY 10011

SOKOLOWSKI, LINDA ROBINSON
PRINTMAKER, PAINTER

b Utica, NY, May 20, 43. *Study:* RI Sch Design, BFA(painting), 65; State Univ NY, Potsdam; Univ Iowa, with Mauricio Lasansky & James Lechay, MA, 70 & MFA, 71. *Work:* State Univ NY, Potsdam; Stout State Univ, Menomonie, Wis. *Exhib:* One-man shows, Kraushaar Galleries, New York, 76 & 79; Ball State Univ Drawing & Small Sculpture Nat Exhib, Muncie, Ind, 77; Int Miniature Print Competition, Pratt Graphic Ctr, 77; The Graphic Works 1972-1977, State Univ NY, Binghamton, 78; 43rd & 44th Ann Painting Exhib, Butler Am Art; The Realist Tradition in Central New York, Munson-Williams-Proctor Inst; More Than Land or Sky: Art of Appalachia, Nat Mus Am Art, Smithsonian Inst, 81. *Teaching:* From instr to assoc prof art, State Univ NY, Binghamton, 71- *Publ:* Auth, The Original Prints and Restrikes from the Plates of Kaethe Kollwitz, Univ Iowa Press, 70; illusr, Boundary 2 J, State Univ NY, Binghamton, fall, 76. *Dealer:* Kraushaar Galleries 724 Fifth Ave New York NY 10028. *Mailing Add:* RFD 1 Box 194 Swan Lake NY 12783

SOLBERG, MORTEN EDWARD
PAINTER

b Cleveland, Ohio, Nov 8, 35. *Study:* Cleveland Inst Art. *Work:* Nat Gallery Art, Washington, DC; Cleveland Mus Art; Am Bicentennial Gallery, Huntington Beach, Calif; Nat Acad Design, New York. *Comn:* Painting of hist fountain, Marriott Hotels, Newport Beach, Calif, 75; painting of hist settings, Irvine Co, Newport Beach, 75. *Exhib:* Nat Acad Design, New York, 66 & 76; Watercolor USA, Springfield, Mo, 67; Soc Painters in Casein & Acrylic, New York, 67; Am Watercolor Soc, New York, 68 & 74-76; Nat Watercolor Soc, Los Angeles, 70-75. *Pos:* Art dir, Am Greeting Corp, Cleveland, 58-68; art dir, Buzza Cardoza Corp, Anaheim, Calif, 68-71; pres, Calif Graphics, Design Studio, Orange, 71-73. *Awards:* Paul B Remey Mem Award, Am Watercolor Soc, 68; Soc Animal Artists Medal; San Bernardino Co Mus Award; and others. *Bibliog:* Angie McCance (auth), Morten Solberg, Artist Register, 74; Janell Gregg (auth), Contributing artist, Orange Co Illus, 75; Ray Merchant (auth), article in Am Artist Mag, 10/76; and others. *Mem:* Soc Animal Artists, NY; Nat Watercolor Soc (ad hoc bd mem, 74, first vpres, 75); Am Watercolor Soc. *Media:* Mixed. *Dealer:* Carson Gallery Denver CO; The Greenwich Workshop Trumbull CT. *Mailing Add:* 59 El Arco Santa Barbara CA 93105

SOLDNER, PAUL EDMUND
SCULPTOR, CERAMIST

b Summerfield, Ill, Apr 24, 21. *Study:* Bluffton Col, BA; Univ Colo, MA; County Art Inst, Los Angeles, MFA. *Work:* Victoria & Albert Mus, London; San Francisco Mus Art; Oakland Art Mus, Calif; Emerson Mus, Syracuse, NY; Smithsonian Mus, Washington, DC; and others. *Comn:* Ceramic mural, Home Savings & Loan Asn Los Angeles, 56; 40 large planters, Scripps Col, 61; three major pieces, Objects USA for circulating exhib, US & Europe, Johnson Wax Collection, 69. *Exhib:* Ostend Int Exhib, Belg, 59; Ceramic Int, Prague, Czech, 62; Triennali, Venice, Italy, 64; Contemporary Ceramic Art, Nat Mus Mod Art, Kyoto, Japan, 71; Int Ceramics, Victoria & Albert Mus, London, Eng, 72; World Craft Exhib, Toronto, Can, 74; Masters in Ceramic Art, Everson Mus, Syracuse, NY, 75; and others. *Teaching:* Prof ceramics, Scripps Col & Claremont Grad Sch, Calif, 55-66 & 70-; vis prof ceramics, Univ Colo, Boulder, 66-67; prof ceramics, Univ Iowa, 67-68. *Awards:* Louis Comfort Tiffany Found Grant, 66 & 72; Purchase Award, Victoria & Albert Mus, 72; Craftsmen's Fel Grant, Nat Endowment Arts, 76. *Bibliog:* Daniel Wilson (auth), With These Hands, ABC-TV, Johnson Wax Sponsor, 71; John W Conrad (auth), Contemporary Ceramics, Prentice-Hall, 77; Donald Campbell (auth), Using the Potter's Wheel, Van Nostrand Reinhold, 77; and others. *Mem:* Am Craft Coun; Nat Coun Educ Ceramic Arts. *Media:* Clay. *Mailing Add:* Art Dept Claremont Grad Sch Harper-East 15 Claremont CA 91711

SOLEM, (ELMO) JOHN
PRINTMAKER, EDUCATOR

b St Paul, Minn, Aug 10, 33. *Study:* Minn Sch Art, 51-53; Wartburg Col, Waverly, Iowa, BA, 59; Univ Calif, Los Angeles, MA, 62. *Work:* Santa Barbara Mus Art, Calif; Atlantic Richfield Corp Art Collection, Los Angeles; US Embassy, Oslo, Norway; Los Angeles Printmaking Soc; Tex Tech Univ, Lubbock. *Exhib:* Ann Exhib, Artists of Los Angeles, Los Angeles Co Mus Art, 61; Northwest Printmakers' 34th Int Exhib, Seattle Art Mus, 63; 19th Nat Exhib Prints, Libr Congress, DC, 63; 14th Nat Print Exhib, Brooklyn Mus,

64; Arts of Southern Calif XVI: Prints, Long Beach Mus Art, Calif, 65; Prints Calif, Oakland Mus, Calif, 75; Artists/Teachers in Southern Calif, Santa Barbara Mus Art, Calif, 75; Early Sixties, Univ Calif, Los Angeles, Frederick Wight Gallery, Univ Calif, Los Angeles, 78; Los Angeles Bicentennial Exhib, Mus Sci & Industry, 81. *Teaching:* Extension instr art, Univ Calif, Los Angeles, 63-76; assoc prof art, printmaking, drawing & painting, Calif Lutheran Col, Thousand Oaks, 67- *Awards:* Tiffany Found grant, Graphics, 63; Purchase Awards, 5th Ann Colorprint, USA, Tex Tech Univ, 74 & Los Angeles Printmaking Soc 2nd Nat Exhib, 74. *Bibliog:* Louis Newman (auth), Recent works on paper, Monograph, 78; Betts Kimball (auth), John Solem: a portrait of the artist, Westlake Mag, 79. *Media:* Etching, Intaglio. *Dealer:* Louis Newman Galleries 322 N Beverly Drive Beverly Hills CA 90210. *Mailing Add:* PO Box 296 Topanga CA 90290

SOLERI, PAOLO
ARCHITECT, SCULPTOR

b Torino, Italy, 1919. *Study:* Polytech Torino, Frank Lloyd Wright fel. *Work:* Mus Mod Art, New York. *Comn:* Il Donnone (sculpture), Phoenix Civic Ctr, Ariz, 72. *Exhib:* Corcoran Gallery Art, Washington, DC, 70; Whitney Mus Am Art, New York, 70; Mus Contemp Art, Chicago, 70; Nat Conf Ctr, Ottawa, Can, 71; Univ Art Mus, Berkeley, Calif, 71; Two Suns Arcology Exhib, Xerox Corp-sponsored, 76; and others. *Teaching:* Distinguished vis lectr, Ariz State Univ, Sch Archit, currently. *Awards:* Graham Found, 62; Guggenheim Found, 64 & 67; Gold Medal, World Biennale Archit, Sofia, Bulgaria, 81. *Publ:* Auth, Arcology: The City in the Image of Man, 69 & The Sketchbooks of Paolo Soleri, 71, Mass Inst Technol; auth, The Bridge Between Matter & Spirit is Matter Becoming Spirit, Doubleday, 73; auth, Fragments, Harper & Row; auth, Omega Seed, Doubleday. *Mailing Add:* Cosanti Found 6433 Doubletree Ranch Rd Paradise Valley AZ 85253

SOLINGER, DAVID M
COLLECTOR, PATRON

Pos: Mem bd trustees, Am Fedn Arts, 54-; pres, Whitney Mus Am Art, 66-74, chmn, 74-77, hon pres, 77-; chmn mus coun, Cornell Univ. *Collection:* 20th century paintings and sculpture. *Mailing Add:* 33 East 70th St New York NY 10021

SOLLEY, THOMAS TREAT
MUSEUM DIRECTOR

b New York, NY, Sept 4, 24. *Study:* Yale Univ, BA, 50; Ind Univ, MA, 66. *Collections Arranged:* The American Scene, 1900-1970, 70; Noguchi & Richey & Smith, 70; Hungarian Art, The Twentieth Century Avant-Garde, 72. *Pos:* Archit proj engr, Eli Lilly Co, Indianapolis, 51-61; pvt architect, Indianapolis, 61-64; asst dir, Art Mus, Ind Univ, Bloomington, 68-71, dir, 71- *Mem:* Childrens Mus Indianapolis (adv trustee); Asn of Art Mus Dirs. *Mailing Add:* Art Mus Ind Univ Bloomington IN 47401

SOLMAN, JOSEPH
PAINTER

b Vitebsk, Russia, Jan 25, 09; US citizen. *Study:* Nat Acad Design, New York, 26-29; Art Students League, 29-30. *Work:* Whitney Mus Am Art, New York; Phillips Gallery, Washington, DC; Fogg Mus, Cambridge, Mass; Butler Inst Am Art, Youngstown, Ohio; Los Angeles Co Mus. *Exhib:* ACA Galleries, New York, NY, 30-; Whitney Mus Am Art Ann, 52, 53 & 55; Int Asn Plastic Arts Europ Traveling Show Am Art, 56; 2nd Expos Contemp Art, Inst Brasil-Estados Unidos, Rio de Janeiro, 60. *Pos:* Treas, Nat Acad Design, 79- *Teaching:* Instr oil painting, Mus Mod Art, 52-54; instr oil painting, New Sch Social Res, 64-66; instr oil painting, City Col New York, 67-75. *Awards:* Nat Inst Arts & Lett Award for Painting, 61; Isaac N Maynard Prize for Portrait, 69 & Saltus Gold Medal for Merit, 71, Nat Acad Design. *Bibliog:* D Seckler (auth), Solman paints a picture, Art News, summer 51; S Burrey (auth), Joseph Solman: the growth of conviction, Arts, 10/55; Una E Johnson (auth introd), The Monotypes of Joseph Solman, Da Capo Press, 77. *Mem:* Fedn Mod Painters & Sculptors (pres, 65-67, vpres, 67-). *Media:* Monotype; Oil, Gouache. *Publ:* Auth, Joseph Solman, Crown, 66. *Dealer:* ACA Galleries 21 E 67th St New York NY 10021. *Mailing Add:* 156 Second Ave New York NY 10003

SOLMSSEN, PETER
ADMINISTRATOR

b Berlin, Ger, Nov 1, 31; US citizen. *Study:* Harvard Col, AB, 52; Univ Pa Law Sch, JD, 59. *Exhib:* One-man photog exhib, Mus Art, Sao Paulo, Brazil, 70. *Pos:* US cult attache, Sao Paulo, 67-70; adv on the Arts, US Dept State, 74-80; pres, Arts Int, 81-83; pres, Philadelphia Col Art, 83- *Publ:* Auth & illusr, Sao Paulo, 70. *Mailing Add:* Philadelphia College of Art Broad & Pine Sts Philadelphia PA 19102

SOLODKIN, JUDITH
LITHOGRAPHER, PUBLISHER

b New York, NY, Apr 7, 45. *Study:* Brooklyn Col, BA, 65; Fulbright Hays Scholar alternate, France & Prix de Rome, Italy, 66-67; Columbia Univ, MFA(cum laude), 67; Tamarind Inst, Ford Found Grant, Tamarind Master Printer, 74. *Work:* Art Mus, Univ NMex; Tamarind Inst Collection, NMex; Pratt Graphics Ctr, Printmaking Workshop, New York. *Exhib:* Dallas Mus Fine Arts, 72; one-person shows, Douglass Col, Rutgers Univ & Elizabeth Pub Libr, NJ, 76; Razor Gallery, 77; Grey Gallery, ECarolina Univ 78 & Walters Art Gallery, Rutgers Univ, 79; and others. *Pos:* Master printer, Petersburg Press & SOLO Press, 74-78; partic artist apprenticeship prog, Great Lakes Col Asn, 76 & 78 & Parsons-New Sch, 77; proprietor & master printer, SOLO Press, 78. *Teaching:* Instr lithography, Univ Ind, Bloomington, 74; instr lithography, Pratt Graphics Ctr, 74-, Sch Visual Arts, 75- & Douglass Col,

Rutgers Univ, 77-79. *Awards:* Louis Comfort Tiffany grant to SOLO Press Apprenticeship Prog, 77. *Bibliog:* Lisa Weinberg (auth), Judith Solodkin on SOLO Press, Woman Artists Newsletter, 77; Amy Goldin (auth), Patterern and print, Print Collectors Newslett, 3-4/78. *Mem:* Nat Print Asn; Graphics Art Coun NY; Artists Equity Asn. *Dealer:* Kathryn Markel Fine Arts 50 W 57th St New York NY 10019. *Mailing Add:* 461 Park Ave S New York NY 10016

SOLOMON, BERNARD ALAN
PRINTMAKER, EDUCATOR

b Chicago, Ill, June 21, 46. *Study:* Art Inst Chicago, with Raymond Martin & Adrian Troy, BFA, 68; Inst Design, Ill Inst Technol, with Misch Kohn, MSVD, 70. *Work:* McDonald Corp, Pittsburgh, Pa; Nat Collection Fine Arts, Washington, DC; Skirball Mus Judaica, Los Angeles; High Mus, Atlanta, Ga; Huntsville Mus Art, Ala; and others. *Exhib:* Twenty-three int, nat & regional juried exhibs, 20 group exhibs & invitationals, 35 one-man & maj exhibs. *Pos:* Co-dir, First Nat Color Blend Print Exhib, 78-80, Comparisons & Contrasts, 80-82, World Fest Yid Spirit, 81, Celebration of Jewish Cult, 81 & Prints Today: Holland/USA, 82-84. *Teaching:* Instr printmaking, Mercyhurst Col, Erie, Pa, 69-71; instr, Ga Southern Col, Statesboro, 71-74, asst prof, 74-77, assoc prof, 77-. *Awards:* Third Prize, Mus Purchase, Greenville Co Mus, 76; Edinboro Print Competition Award, 79; Bronze Medal Illus, Int Bk Design Exhib, Leipzig, 82. *Mem:* Southern Graphics Coun (secy, 78-80); Nat Print Coun; World Print Coun (consult). *Media:* Wood Engraving, Etching. *Publ:* Illus, Yevtuchenko's Babi Yar, 67; illusr, The Zaddick Christ, Attic Press, 74; illusr, Charles Levendosky's Small Town America, 74; auth & illusr, Modes of Death, 75 & auth & illusr, Song of Songs, 83, Boxwood Press. *Dealer:* Elena Kornetchuk Russian Images Int Art Sewickley PA; Lyle Evan Gallery Lexington MA. *Mailing Add:* c/o Boxwood Press PO Box 2362 Statesboro GA 30458

SOLOMON, DANIEL
PAINTER

b Topeka, Kans, July 13, 45. *Study:* Univ Ore, BSc. *Comn:* Outdoor mural, Benson & Hedges Tobacco Co, 71. *Exhib:* Can Artists, Art Gallery Ont, 68; Survey 69, Montreal Mus Fine Arts, 69; one-man shows, Isaacs Gallery, 70, 71, 73 & 74, Mirvish Gallery, 77, Klonaridis, 80 & others; 14 Canadians: A Critic's Choice, Hirshhorn Mus & Sculpture Garden, DC, 77; New Abstract Art, Edmonton Art Gallery, Alta, 77; Six from Toronto, Watson/de Nagy, Houston, Tex, 77. *Teaching:* Instr painting, Ont Col Art, Toronto, 70-80. *Awards:* Can Coun Bursary for Painting, 70, 72 & 75. *Bibliog:* L Lippard (auth), rev, 2/69 & M Greenwood (auth), rev, 8-9/71, Arts Mag; D Dellamora (auth), rev, Arts Mag, 5/81. *Media:* Acrylic. *Mailing Add:* c/o Klonaridis Inc 144 Front St W Suite 600 Toronto ON M5J 2L7 Canada

SOLOMON, GERALD
DEALER

b May 31, 34. *Pos:* Pres-dir, Solomon & Co Fine Art, New York, currently. *Specialty:* 20th century American and European paintings, graphics, drawing and sculpture. *Mailing Add:* Solomon & Co Fine Art 959 Madison Ave New York NY 10021

SOLOMON, HOLLY
DEALER, COLLECTOR

b Fairfield, Conn. *Study:* Vassar Col; Sarah Lawrence Col, BA. *Pos:* Dir, Holly Solomon Gallery Inc, New York. *Teaching:* Instr art hist, Fashion Inst Am, 73-75. *Awards:* Award for Film, Edinborough Film Festival, 73. *Bibliog:* Andy Worhol (auth), 50 Best Friends, 65. *Specialty:* Avant garde American. *Collection:* Pop art, conceptual art, narrative art, performing art & decorative art. *Mailing Add:* 724 Fifth Ave New York NY 10019

SOLOMON, HYDE
PAINTER

b May 3, 11; US citizen. *Study:* Art Students League. *Work:* Whitney Mus Am Art, New York; Wadsworth Atheneum, Hartford, Conn; Munson-Williams-Proctor Inst, Utica, NY; Art Mus Princeton Univ, NJ; Brandeis Univ Mus, Mass. *Exhib:* Corcoran Gallery Biennials, Washington, DC, 57 & 59; Va Mus of Fine Arts, Richmond; Carnegie Inst Int, Pittsburgh, 57-59; 60 American Painters, Walker Art Ctr, Minneapolis, 60; Nature in Abstraction, Whitney Mus Am Art, New York, 60; 157th Ann, Pa Acad Fine Arts, 62; Five Am Painters, Knoedler Gallery, New York, NY, 63; Autumn Invitational, Roswell Mus, NMex, 77; 156th & 157th Painting Annuals, Nat Acad of Design, New York, NY, 77 & 78; solo exhibs, Ledoux Gallery, Taos, 79 & Stables Gallery, Taos, 80. *Teaching:* Artist in residence, Princeton Univ, 59-62. *Awards:* Childe Hassam Fund Purchase Award, Acad Arts & Lett, 70; Mark Rothko Found Grant, 73; Gottlieb Found Grant, 78. *Bibliog:* Thomas B Hess (auth), US painting: Some recent directions, Art News Ann, 56; Martica Sawin (auth), Profile of Hyde Solomon, Arts Mag, 11/58. *Media:* Oil. *Mailing Add:* c/o Gerard Solomon 1 Pilgrim Dr Succasunna NJ 07876

SOLOMON, RICHARD H
PUBLISHER, COLLECTOR

b Boston, Mass, May 12, 34. *Study:* Harvard Col, AB, 56; Harvard Bus Sch, MBA, 58. *Pos:* Pres, Pace Editions Inc/Pace Primitive & Ancient Art, New York, currently; chmn, Pace/MacGill Int 20th Century Photography Gallery, currently; chmn Overseers Visiting Comt, Visual & Environmental Studies Dept, Harvard Col, currently. *Mem:* Art Dealers Asn Am; Primitive Art Dealers Asn Am; Am Asn Mus; Mus Shop Asn. *Specialty:* Contemporary graphics (prints, multiples, tapestries, posters), African, Oceanic and American Indian art. *Collection:* Contemporary art and Primitive art. *Mailing Add:* c/o Pace Editions Inc 32 East 57th St New York NY 10022

SOLOMON, RUTH B
ADMINISTRATOR, CONSULTANT

b New York, NY, June 8, 21. *Study:* Hofstra Univ, BS, 67, MA(fel), 68. *Collections Arranged:* Artists of Suffolk Co Exhibs (auth, catalog), 70-78, Windows and Doors (auth, catalog), 72, Mistaken Identity (auth, catalog), 73 & The Drama of the Sea (auth, catalog), 75, Heckscher Mus, Huntington, NY. *Pos:* Asst dir, Heckscher Mus, 68-80; dir, Art Connections Unlimited, 81- *Mem:* Am Asn Mus; Int Coun Mus; Long Island Mus Asn (chmn, 78). *Res:* Long Island artists register; active biographical and slide file of approximately eight hundred Nassau and Suffolk county artists. *Publ:* Auth, Teachers Guide to Heckscher Museum Collection, 68; and others. *Mailing Add:* 37 Highwood Rd East Norwich NY 11732

SOLOMON, (MRS) SIDNEY L
COLLECTOR

b Boston, Mass, May 15, 09. *Study:* Radcliffe Col, AB; Simmons Col, BS. *Collection:* Sculpture of the twentieth century to contemporary, including Giacometti, Lipschitz, Marini, Nevelson, Dubuffet, Arp, Chadwick, Calder, Schmidt, Doris Cassar & Trova; painting collection includes Sargent, Vuillard, Tomayo, Leger, Giacometti, Monet and Matta; drawings of Maillol, Archipenko, Degas, Lachaise & many others; watercolors of Nolde & Marini; also a collection of pop art. *Mailing Add:* 834 Fifth Ave New York NY 10021

SOLOMON, SYD
PAINTER

b Uniontown, Pa, July 12, 17. *Study:* Art Inst Chicago, 35; Acad Beaux Arts, Paris, 45. *Work:* Whitney Mus Am Art & Solomon R Guggenheim Mus, New York; Philadelphia Mus Art; Wadsworth Atheneum, Hartford, Conn; Joseph H Hirshhorn Mus, Washington, DC; and many others. *Exhib:* Nat & int exhibs incl, Univ Ill, Corcoran, Biennial, Whitney Mus, Corcoran Gallery Art, Washington, DC; Guggenheim Mus; Art Inst Chicago, Nat Acad, New York; Retrospective, Ringling Mus, Sarasota, Fla & New York Cultural Ctr, 74; Ft Lauderdale Mus, 75; St Petersburg Mus, 79; and many others. *Pos:* Camouflage designer, Engrs Bd, Washington, DC, 42; dir fac, Famous Artists Sch, 53-73. *Teaching:* Instr, Art Inst Pittsburgh, 47; Ringling Sch Art, 48-50; Famous Artists Sch Inc, 54-67 & Sarasota Sch Art, 50 & 55; prof art, New Col, Sarasota, Fla, 64-65 & 67-69; instr painting, Univ Ill, 68, Robertson Ctr Arts & Sci, Binghamton, NY, 69, Tampa Bay Art Ctgr, 72, Univ Calif, 76 & Boca Raton Ctr Art, 77. *Awards:* Int Hallmark Exhib Award, New York, 52; Purchase Award, Hassam & Speicher Fund, 79; plus others. *Mem:* Nat Soc Lit & Arts. *Dealer:* Phoenix Gallery Washington DC; Art Sources 2101 Gulf Life Tower Jacksonville FL 32207. *Mailing Add:* 9210 Blind Pass Rd Sarasota FL 33581

SOLOMON, VITA PETROSKY
PAINTER, PRINTMAKER

b 1916. *Study:* Moore Col Art, dipl, 37; Tyler Sch Fine Arts, Temple Univ, BFA, BS(educ), 58, MFA, 60. *Work:* Philadelphia Mus Art; City Hall, Philadelphia; Nat Portrait Gallery, Smithsonian Inst, DC; US Court House, Philadelphia, Pa; Univ Pa, Philadelphia. *Comn:* Portraits, Pearl S Buck, Pearl S Buck Found, Smithsonian Inst, Washington, DC, 67, Judge Raymond Pace Alexander, Philadelphia Bar Asn, Law Libr, 70, Alfred Williams, Governor, Fed Reserve Bank, Philadelphia, 75, Keith Doms, dir, Free Libr Philadelphia, 79 & Chief Judge Joseph S Lord III, US District Court, 81. *Exhib:* Am Watercolor Soc, Metrop Mus, New York; Ann Juried, Royal Acad Arts, London, Eng; Ann Juried, Paris Salon, Paris, France; Pa Acad Fine Art, Philadelphia; Invitational, Philadelphia Mus Art; Invitational, Nat Acad, New York; Ann Invited, Detroit Inst Art; Ann Exhib, Royal Inst, London, Eng. *Teaching:* Instr art hist & coordr art dept, Cheltenham High Sch, 67-82. *Awards:* Silver Medal, Paris Salon, Paris, France, 66; Jane Peterson Medal, Audubon Artists, New York, 75; Eugenia Atwood Prize, Philadelphia Print Club, Philadelphia Mus Art, 75. *Bibliog:* Leon Witconis (auth), Portrait Pros, Focus, Business Weekly, 74; Ralph Fabri (auth), Vita P Solomon paints a portrait, Today's Art, 75. *Mem:* Am Watercolor Soc; Allied Artists Am; Artists' Equity Asn; Cheltenham Art Ctr Print Guild; Philadelphia Watercolor Soc. *Media:* Watercolor, Oil; Lithography, Pastel. *Mailing Add:* 1500 Locust St 3716 Philadelphia PA 19102

SOLOWAY, RETA
PAINTER

b Washington, DC. *Study:* Corcoran Sch Art; Parsons Sch; Philadelphia Mus Sch Art, 31-35; Philadelphia Graphic Sketch; Nat Acad Sch, 69; New Sch Social Res, 71; Sarah Lawrence Col, 75; Hofstra Univ, 76-79; and with Umberto Romano, Thornton Oakley, Henry Pitz, Joseph Stefanelli, Eric Isenburger & Mario Cooper. *Work:* Gregory Mus, Hicksville, NY. *Comn:* Portraits, Maj Gen Arthur Gaines, Denver, Colo, 70 & Dean Emer Charles Smythe, Pennington Prep Sch, 71. *Exhib:* Nat Art League, 65-80; Malverne Artists Long Island, 65-80; Allied Artists Am, 69-80; Catharine Lorillard Wolfe Art Club, 75-80. *Teaching:* Demonstr, Nat Acad, 66-75 & 77, Nat Arts Club, 73-77, Malverne Libr, 70-80 & IPA Nat Conv, Washington, DC, 72- *Awards:* Pen & Brush Club Award, 80; Pen & Brush Watercolor Award, 80; Grumbacher Watercolor Award, 81; and others. *Mem:* Allied Artists Am (corresp secy, 79-81; pres, 81-); Artists Equity Asn NY; Nat Soc Painters Cascin & Acrylic; Catharine Lorillard Wolfe Art Club; Am Artists Prof League. *Media:* Oil, Watercolor. *Publ:* Contribr, Portrait in Occupational Therapy, 46 & Portrait of the World, 65. *Mailing Add:* 145 Lexington Ave Franklin Square NY 11010

SOLTESZ, FRANK JOSEPH
PAINTER
b Derry, Pa, June 14, 12. *Study:* Art Inst Pittsburgh, scholar, oil painting with Samuel Rosenberg; Carnegie Inst Technol, scholar; also with Charles Kinghan. *Work:* Frye Mus, Seattle, Wash. *Comn:* Paintings, The Fine Am Art Calendar, 74-80; painting, Graymoor Friars, 75. *Exhib:* Assoc Artists Exhib, Pittsburgh, 39; Am Watercolor Soc, New York, 62-77; Hudson Valley Art Asn, White Plains, NY, 62-80; Acad Artists, Springfield, Mass, 63-78; Am Artists Prof League, New York, 69-80. *Teaching:* Pvt classes in watercolor, Ridgefield, Conn, 64-80. *Awards:* Gold Medal of Honor, Hudson Valley Art Asn, 65; Gold Medal of Honor, Am Artists Prof League, 68 & 72; Presidents Award, Am Artists Professional League, 80. *Mem:* Am Watercolor Soc; Am Artists Prof League; Hudson Valley Art Asn (dir, 67-72); Acad Artists Asn; Providence Art Club. *Media:* Watercolor, Oil. *Mailing Add:* Star Rt One, Box 38A-2A Spring Branch TX 78070

SOLWAY, CARL E
DEALER
b Chicago, Ill, Jan 12, 35. *Pos:* Dir, Carl Solway Gallery, Cincinnati. *Mem:* Art Dealers Asn Am. *Specialty:* 20th century American and European painting, sculpture and graphics; urban environment and wall projects; publisher of graphic works by John Cage, Buckminster Fuller, Richard Hamilton, Nancy Graves & Nam June Paik. *Mailing Add:* 314 W Fourth St Cincinnati OH 45202

SOMBERG, EMILIJA O K
PAINTER
b Utena, Lithuania, Feb 20, 24; US citizen. *Study:* Univ Hamburg, BA, 49; Southern Conn State Col, MS, 62; NY Univ, 64. *Work:* Tweed Mus; Lithuanian Embassy, Washington, DC; Southern Conn State Col; Univ Minn, Minneapolis; Libr Cong. *Exhib:* Green Ross Gallery, New York, 65; retrospective, Normandale Community Col, 78, Nobles Co Art Ctr, Worthington, Mich, 78, Custer Co Arts Ctr, Miles City, Mont, 81 & Tweed Mus, 81; Minneapolis Inst Art, 79; Minn Mus Art, 80. *Teaching:* Instr art, pub schs, New York, Conn & NJ, 64-74. *Bibliog:* Martin Keller (auth), Somberg achieves liberation through art, Insight, 9/78; Somberg's retrospective, Univ Minn Rev, 3/79; Mary Scarvalone (auth), Somberg's art, Minn Daily, 5/79. *Media:* Oil. *Mailing Add:* 1131 Monroe St NE Minneapolis MN 55413

SOMERS, H(ARRY W)
PAINTER, PRINTMAKER
b Zweibruecken, Ger, May 28, 22; US citizen. *Study:* Dookie Col, Australia; City Col New York, cert; Art Students League; Brisbane Art Ctr, Australia; also with Joseph Schwartz & S Greene. *Work:* Dookie Col, Victoria, Australia; Stadtmuseum Zweibruecken, Ger; Lowe Art Mus, Coral Gables, Fla; Metrop Mus & Art Ctr, Miami, Fla; Nat Art Gallery, Wellington, NZ; and others. *Exhib:* One-man shows, Galerie Felix Vercel, New York, 70-75 & Hilde Gerst Gallery, Palm Beach, Fla, 73-78; Hollywood Art Mus, Fla, 76; Mayer Gallery, Ft Lauderdale, 76-79; Klein Gallery, Beverly Hills, 78-79; and others in US & abroad. *Bibliog:* Charles Z Offin (auth), article, 70, 71 &72 & Beatrice Dain (auth), article, 3/74, Pictures on Exhibit; Lawrence Dame (auth), Somers the impressionist, Palm Beach Post, 1/78. *Mem:* Am Artists Prof League; Artists Equity Asn. *Media:* Oil, Graphic. *Publ:* Auth, The Art of Collecting, 63. *Dealer:* D Treff Box 8223 Coral Springs FL 33065 *Mailing Add:* 1600 Riverwood Lane Coral Springs FL 33065

SOMERVILLE, ROMAINE STEC
ADMINISTRATOR
b Scranton, Pa, May 24, 30. *Study:* Marymount Col, BA, 51; Columbia Univ, MA, 53; Yale Univ, 58-60. *Collections Arranged:* The Peale Collection of the Maryland Historical Society, 75 & Life in Maryland in the 18th Century, Bicentennial Exhib, 76, Md Hist Soc. *Pos:* Bd mem, Baltimore Heritage, Inc, 68-, Baltimore City Comt, Md Hist Trust, 71- & Soc for Preserv of Md Antiq, 75-77; asst dir & chief cur, Md Hist Soc, 72-78, dir, 79- *Teaching:* Lectr art hist, Marywood Col, Scranton, Pa, 54-58; lectr Am decorative arts, Johns Hopkins Univ Evening Sch, 78- *Res:* Nineteenth century American architecture, decorative arts and painting. *Publ:* Coauth, Four Generations of Commissions: The Peale Collection of the Maryland Historical Society, 75 & contribr, Maryland Heritage, Five Baltimore Institutions Celebrate the American Bicentennial, 76, Md Hist Soc. *Mailing Add:* 118 W Lafayette Ave Baltimore MD 21217

SOMMER, FRANK H, III
LIBRARIAN, ARCHEOLOGIST
b Newark, NJ, July 30, 22. *Study:* Yale Col; Yale Grad Sch; Corpus Christi Col, Cambridge Univ, Henry Fel, 47-48; Art Students League. *Work:* New Univ Art Gallery; Peabody Mus, Yale Univ; Brooklyn Mus, NY; Mus of Mod Art, New York; Winterthur Mus, Del. *Collections Arranged:* Pennsylvanian German Folk Art, 62; Recent Accessions, Winterthur Libr, 63-78 & Winterthur Mus. *Teaching:* Teaching asst, Yale Univ, 46-48; from instr to prof anthrop & art hist, Univ Del, 48- Pos, Coordr, Winterthur Prog, Univ Del, 51-53; keeper of folk art, Winterthur Mus, 58-63, head librs, 63- *Mem:* Col Art Asn; Art Libr Soc NAm; Grolier Club. *Res:* Design books, trade catalogues, architectural books; Anglo-American classicism and United States folk art. *Publ:* Coauth, Excavations, Yale Univ, 49; auth, Triumph of Neptune, Warburg, 61; auth, Thomas Jefferson's First Plan, Friends Independence Hall Nat Park, 76; auth, Metamorphoses of Britannia, Yale Univ, 76; auth, Arts of the Pennsylvania Germans, Winterthur Mus, 83. *Mailing Add:* c/o Winterthur Mus Winterthur DE 19735

SOMMER, FREDERICK
PHOTOGRAPHER, LANDSCAPE ARTIST
b Angri, Italy, Sept 7, 05; US citizen. *Study:* Cornell Univ, Ithaca, NY, MA(landscape archit), 27; Univ Ariz, Hon DFA, 79. *Work:* Ctr Creative Photog, Univ Ariz, Tucson. *Exhib:* One-man shows, Photogs, Paintings & Drawings, Inst Design, Ill Inst Technol, Chicago, 57, Art Inst Chicago, 63, Drawings & Objects, Washington Gallery Mod Art, Washington, DC, Pasadena Art Mus, 65, Philadelphia Col Art, Pa, 68 & Light Gallery, New York, 72; and others. *Pos:* Coordr, Fine Arts Studies, Prescott Col, Ariz, 66-71. *Awards:* Distinguished Career in Photography, Friends Photog, 82. *Bibliog:* Cynthia Jaffee McCabe (auth), The Golden Door, Artist-Immigrants of America, 1876-1976, Hirshhorn Mus & Sculpture Garden, Smithsonian Inst, Washington, DC, 76. *Publ:* Auth, The Poetic Logic of Art & Aesthetics, 72. *Mailing Add:* PO Box 262 Prescott AZ 86302

SOMMERS, JOHN
PRINTMAKER, EDUCATOR
b Cassopolis, Mich, May 31, 27. *Study:* Albion Col, BA, 52, 66-68; Univ NMex, 68, 70-72; cert (Tamarind Master Printer fel), 69. *Work:* Tamarind Collection, Univ NMex; Amon Carter Mus Western Art; Mus Mod Art, New York; Grunwald Graphic Arts Found, Univ Calif, Los Angeles; Hartford Asr Sch Collection; and others. *Exhib:* Univ Dallas Graphics Invitational, Irving, Tex, 74 & 79; Lithographs, Heistand Gallery, Miami Univ, Ohio, 78; 11th Printmaking West Exhib, Utah State Univ, Logan, 79; 21st Nat Print Exhib, Brooklyn Mus, 79; 4th Miami Int Print Biennial, Fla, 80; Univ Hawaii, 82. *Pos:* Studio mgr, Tamarind Inst, Univ NMex, 70-75, tech dir, 75-82, dir res & printer training, 82-83; contrib ed, Tamarind Papers, 76- *Teaching:* Lectr in art, Univ NMex, 75-; lithography workshops, Tamarind Inst, Univ NMex, 74-78 & throughout US, 74- *Awards:* Purchase Prize, Northern Ill Univ, 68; Purchase Prize, Univ Dallas, 74 & 79; Cash Award-First, NMex State Univ, 75. *Mem:* Los Angeles Printmaking Soc; World Print Coun; Albuquerque United Artists. *Media:* Lithography. *Publ:* Auth, Tamarind today, Graphics Mag, 3-4/79. *Dealer:* Nimbus Gallery Dallas TX 75202; New Trends Gallery Sante Fe 87501. *Mailing Add:* 8414 San Juan Rd NE Albuquerque NM 87108

SOMMESE, LANNY BEAL
EDUCATOR, DESIGNER
b East Moline, Ill, May 14, 43. *Study:* Univ Fla, Gainesville, BD(graphics), 65, BFA(painting), 66; Univ Ill, Urbana, MFA(graphic design), 70. *Work:* Libr Cong; Zachata Art Gallery, Warsaw, Poland; Lahti Art Mus, Finland; Colo State Collection, Ft Collins; Moravian Gallery, Brno, Czech. *Comn:* Drawing, Dantes Rest Inc, State College, Pa, 81; posters, IBM Typewriter Div, Lexington, Ky, 82 & Herman Miller Seating, Holland, Mich, 83. *Exhib:* Warsaw Poster Biennale, Poland, 74, 76, 78 & 80; New York Art Dirs Club, 76 & 82; Colo State Biennale, Ft Collins, 79, 81 & 83; Lahti Poster Biennale, Finland, 79, 81 & 83; Brno Graphic Design Biennale, Czech, 80 & 82. *Teaching:* Instr, Univ Ill, Urbana, 70; from instr to prof & head graphic design, Pa State Univ, 70- *Awards:* Merit Award, New York Art Dirs Club, 76, 79 & 82; Gold Medal, Univ & Col Design Asn, 79. *Bibliog:* Gibbons & Kinser (auths), article, Graphis 202, 78; Fukuda (auth), article, Idea 176, 83; Neumeier (auth), article, Communication Arts, 5-6/83. *Mem:* Am Inst Graphic Arts. *Publ:* Auth, James McMullan, Graphis 213, 82; auth, Tom Carnase, Ligature, 82; auth, McRay Magleby, Print, 82; auth, Design and technology, 7/83 & coauth, Design training USA, 9/83, Novum Gebrauchgraphlk. *Mailing Add:* 481 Glenn Rd State College PA 16801

SONDAY, MILTON FRANKLIN, JR
CURATOR
b Hamburg, Pa, Dec 18, 39. *Study:* Wyomissing Inst Fine Arts, Pa, 55-61; Carnegie-Mellon Univ, Pittsburgh, Pa, 57-61, BFA(painting & design), 61; Penland Sch Crafts, NC, summer 66; ETenn State Univ (Penland Sch), summer 67; US Dept Agr Grad Sch, Washington, DC, fall 67; The Textile Mus (seminar), 67; The New Sch, New York, 68; Ctr Int d'Etude des Textiles Anciens, Lyon, France, 69. *Exhib:* Student Exhib, Carnegie Inst of Technol, 57-61; Reading Pub Mus & Art Gallery, Pa, 63; Gallery Mod Art, Fredricksburg, Va, 63. *Pos:* Mus asst & staff artist, Textile Mus, Washington, DC, 62-65, keeper of rugs, 65-67; asst cur textiles, Cooper Union Mus, New York, 67-68; cur textiles, Cooper-Hewitt Mus Design, Smithsonian Mus, New York, 68- *Awards:* New York Home Fashion League Art Award, 72. *Mem:* Ctr Int d'Etudes des Textiles Anciens, Lyon, France. *Publ:* Illusr, Tiahnuaco Tapestry Design, 63 & Principles of Textile Conservation Science, 63-64, The Textile Mus ; auth, Counterchange & New Color, Handweaver and Craftsman, summer, 69; coauth, with N Kajitani, A Type of Mughal Sash, 70 & A Second Type of Mughal Sash, 71, The Textile Mus J. *Mailing Add:* c/o Cooper-Hewitt Mus 2 East 90 St New York NY 10028

SONENBERG, JACK
PAINTER, SCULPTOR
b Toronto, Ont, Dec 28, 25; US citizen. *Study:* Ont Col Art, Toronto; NY Univ; Washington Univ, BFA. *Work:* Guggenheim Mus, Whitney Mus Am Art & Metrop Mus Art, New York; Nat Gallery Can, Ottawa. *Exhib:* Whitney Mus Am Art, 67 & 73; Whitney Mus Am Art Biennial, 73; Cut, Folded & Torn, Mus Mod Art, New York, 74; Painting & Sculpture Today, Indianapolis Mus Contemp Art Ctr, 74; Small Scale in Contemp Art, Chicago Art Inst, 75; New Ways with Paper, Nat Collection, Smithsonian Inst, 77; Between Object and Illusion, Rutgers Univ, 80; Sitesights 1980, Pratt Inst; Contemporary American Prints and Drawings 1940-80, Nat Gallery, Washington, DC, 81. *Pos:* Ford Found & Am Fedn Arts Artist in resident grant, Hampton Inst, 66. *Teaching:* Instr painting & printmaking, Pratt Inst, 68- *Awards:* First Prize for Painting, 13th New Eng Ann, 62; NY State Coun Creative Artist Serv Prog Grant, 73 & 76; Guggenheim Found Grant, 73. *Media:* Multimedia. *Mailing Add:* 217 E 23rd St New York NY 10010

SONFIST, ALAN
ENVIRONMENTAL ARTIST
b New York NY, Mar 26, 46. *Work:* Mus Mod Art, New York; Boston Mus Fine Art; Oberlin Art Mus, Ohio; Wallarf-Richartz Mux, Koln, Ger; Power Inst, Sydney, Australia. *Exhib:* One-man shows, Thelen Galerie, Koln, Ger, 75, Neue Galerie, Aachen, Ger, 75, Smithsonian Inst, 78 & High Mus Art, Atlanta, 79; Boston Mus Fine Arts, 71 & 77; Stedelijk Mus, Holland, 71; Nature of Things, Harcus Karkow, Boston, 71; Interaction with the Environment, Whitney Mus Am Art, 78; Hudson River Artists, Vassar Col Art Mus, 79; and others. *Awards:* Creative Artists Pub Serv Grant, 77; Nat Endowment Arts Grant, 78. *Bibliog:* R Horvitz (auth), Nature as artifact, Artforum, 10/73; Grace Glueck (auth), Art people, New York Times, 3/10/78; Clyde Burnett (auth), Sonfist's monument, Atlanta Jour & Const, 3/25/79. *Mailing Add:* 205 Mulberry St New York NY 10012

SONNABEND, JOAN
DEALER, COLLECTOR
b Boston, Mass, July 9, 28. *Study:* Sarah Lawrence Col, BA, 50. *Specialty:* Contemporary American and European prints, drawings, paintings, and sculpture. *Mailing Add:* 72 Mt Vernon St Boston MA 02108

SONNEMAN, EVE
PHOTOGRAPHER, FILMMAKER
b Chicago, Ill, Jan 14, 46. *Study:* Univ Ill, Urbana-Champaign, BFA, 67; Univ NMex, Albuquerque, MA, 69. *Work:* Mus Mod Art, New York; Mus Fine Arts, Houston; Art Inst Chicago; Minneapolis Inst Art; Menil Found, Houston. *Exhib:* One-man shows, Art Resources Ctr, Whitney Mus, New York, 73, Galerie Farideh Cadot, Paris, France, 77 & 80, Castelli Gallery, New York, 77, 78, 80 & 82, Cirrus Gallery, Los Angeles, 81 & Tucson Mus Art, Ariz, 81; Mus Mod Art, New York, 78-80; Ctr Beabourg, Paris, 80; Venice Biennale, 79 & 81; and others. *Teaching:* Vis artist photog, Rice Univ, 71-72; vis instr photog, Sch Visual Arts, New York, 75-; vis instr art, Cooper Union Col Art & Architecture, 75- *Awards:* Photography grants, Nat Endowment Arts, 71-72 & 78. *Bibliog:* Group Portrait: 3 New York Photographers (film), Cable Arts, NY State Coun Arts, 75; Real Time, Printed Matter Press, New York, NY; Carter Ratcliff (auth), article, Art Am, Vol 65, No 6. *Dealer:* Castelli Gallery 4 E 77th St New York NY 10021. *Mailing Add:* 98 Bowery New York NY 10013

SONNENBERG, FRANCES
SCULPTOR
b Brooklyn, NY. *Study:* With Prof Alfred Van Loen. *Comn:* Five ft carved acrylic sculpture, Aquarius, Fla, 75. *Exhib:* One-woman shows, Stephan Gallery, New York, Buyways Gallery, Fla, Shelter Rock Gallery, NY, Cedar Crest Col, Pa & Adelphi Univ, NY; and others. *Teaching:* Sculpture classes in own studio, 72- *Mem:* Nat Asn Women Artists; NY Soc Women Artists (secy, 73-74; rec secy, 74-); Metrop Painters & Sculptors (rec secy, 73-, secy, 74-); Am Soc Contemp Artists; Artist Craftsman. *Media:* Acrylic. *Mailing Add:* Rockhill Rd Roslyn Heights NY 11577

SONNENSCHEIN, HUGO
PATRON, HISTORIAN
b Chicago, Ill, Feb 22, 17. *Study:* Swarthmore Col; Lake Forest Col, BA; Univ Va, LLB & JD; John Marshall Law Sch, Chicago, LLM. *Pos:* Ed, Chicago Bar Rec, 50-66; trustee, Lake Forest Col, 69- *Mem:* Gov life mem & fel, Art Inst Chicago; Mus Mod Art; Soc Contemp Art; Asn Art Historians. *Res:* Prints and drawings; legal art. *Interests:* Donor, Sonnenschein Gallery and collections to Lake Forest Col, Lake Forest Acad & Univ Mich. *Mailing Add:* 115 S La Salle St Chicago Il 60603

SOORIKIAN, DIANA TASHJIAN
PAINTER
b Philadelphia, Pa, Sept 16, 28. *Study:* Philadelphia Col Art, BFA, 50; Columbia Univ, with Jack Tworkov, MFA, 73. *Work:* NJ State Mus, Trenton; Columbia Univ; Becton Dickinson Co, Paramus, NJ. *Exhib:* Pa Acad Fine Arts Ann Exhib, 57 & 67; Silvermine Guild Artists Exhib, 72, 73 & 74; Trenton State Mus Ann Exhib Painting & Sculpture, 73 & 74; NJ Artists Third Biennial, Newark Mus, 81-82; Bergen Co Artists, Bergen Community Mus, Paramus, NJ, 82-83. *Pos:* Asst art dir, Johnstone Inc, New York, 58-62; graphics designer, Market Signs, New York, 81- *Awards:* Eloise Egan Mem Award, 23rd New England Exhib, 72; Purchase Prize, Trenton State Mus Ann Exhib Painting & Sculpture, 74; NJ State Coun Arts Grant, 83. *Bibliog:* David Spengler (auth), The self got lost, Bergen Rec, 7/4/74; Piri Halasz (auth), Jersey artists saluted, New York Times, 6/9/75. *Media:* Oil Pastel, Graphite. *Mailing Add:* Paulin Blvd Leonia NJ 07605

SORBY, J RICHARD
PAINTER, DESIGNER
b Duluth, Minn, Dec 21, 11. *Study:* Univ Minn; Univ Northern Colo, AB, 37, MA, 51; Art Inst Chicago; Univ of the Am, Mexico City; Univ Calif, Los Angeles, with John Ferren; Univ Colo, with Jimmy Ernst. *Work:* William Rockhill Nelson Gallery, Kansas City, Mo; Brigham Young Univ. *Comn:* Spaulding Mem, Univ Northern Colo, Greeley, 58. *Exhib:* Denver Art Mus Ann Western Artists, 40-59; Nat Watercolor Competition, Nat Gallery Art, Washington, DC, 41; Mid-Am Ann Exhibs, Nelson Gallery Art, Kansas City, Mo; Nat Rocky Mountain Watermedia Exhib, Boulder, Colo, 79; Calif State Fair Exhib; Whitney Mus Am Art, New York; Pa Acad Fine Arts, Philadelphia; Oakland Art Mus, Calif; Crocker Art Gallery, Sacramento; San Diego Art Mus, solo exhib, Joslyn Mem Gallery, Omaha & San Jose Mus Art, Calif; and others. *Teaching:* Instr art, Univ Nebr, Lincoln, 40-42; assoc prof painting, Sch Art, Univ Denver, 47-59; prof painting & design, Calif State

Univ, San Jose, 59-72, emer prof, 72- *Awards:* Purchase Award, 4th Biennial 10 State Exhib, Joslyn Mem Mus, 56 & Ann Metro Exhib, Denver Art Mus, 64; First Prize for Non-objective Painting, Univ Santa Clara, 66. *Bibliog:* Arneil (auth), Work of Richard Sorby, Empire Mag, Denver Post, 11/58; M L Stribling (auth), Painting in Found Materials, 71. *Media:* Acrylic, Watercolor; Mixed Media. *Publ:* Illusr, Lincoln-Mercury Times, 54, Ford Times, 56 & Empire Mag, Denver Post, 58. *Mailing Add:* Morningsun Studio Glen Haven CO 80532

SOREFF, HELEN
PAINTER
b New York, NY. *Study:* Atlanta Art Inst, BFA(High Mus Art Scholar, Beaux Arts Scholar), 52; Art Students League, Grand Concours, 53; NY Univ; C W Post Col, Long Island Univ, MA, 76. *Comn:* Painting, Big Thing Show, Seattle Wash Art Comt, 69; painting, Inter-Disciplinary Jour, Queens Col, NY, 72. *Exhib:* Corcoran Mus Lending Libr, Washington, DC, 64-66; Albright-Knox Mus, Buffalo, NY, 65-66; Seattle Art Mus, 69; Grey Gallery, New York, 81; Sidney Lewis Collection, 82; Sculpture Sites, East Hampton, NY, 82-83; Ronald Feldman, Franklin Furnace, New York, 82-83; Condesa-Lawler Gallery, New York, 83; and others. *Teaching:* Instr basic art, Univ Wash, Seattle, 69; lectr contemp art, Spec Progs, Hofstra Univ, Hempstead, NY, 71-72; Friends Seminary, 80-81. *Bibliog:* Articles, Artforum, 9/78, Art News, 9/78 & Arts Mag, 10/78. *Mem:* Women Arts. *Media:* Acrylic. *Dealer:* Condesa-Lawler Gallery 76 Greene St New York NY 10012; Bertha Urdang Gallery 23 E 74th St New York NY. *Mailing Add:* 79 Mercer St New York NY 10012

SOREL, EDWARD
ILLUSTRATOR, WRITER
b New York, NY, Mar 26, 29. *Study:* Cooper Union, dipl, 51. *Exhib:* One-man shows, Graham Gallery, New York, 73 & New Sch Social Res, 74; Push Pin Style, Mus des Arts Decoratifs, Paris, 70; Univ Ky, 75. *Pos:* Co-founder, Push-Pin Studios, New York, 53-56; art dir, CBS Promotion Art, New York, 56-57; syndicated cartoonist, King Features, 69-71; contribr, Atlantic Mag, 69-; contrib ed, New York Mag, 72-; cartoonist, Village Voice, 74- *Awards:* New York Herald Tribune Book Award for Illustration, 62; St Gauden's Medal, Cooper Union, 73. *Bibliog:* Carlos C Drake (auth), Edward Sorel, Graphis, No 105, 63; Jerome Snyder (auth), Edward Sorel, Graphis, No 154, 71-72. *Mem:* Am Inst Graphic Arts; Illusr Guild; Alliance Graphique. *Media:* Pen & Ink, Watercolor. *Publ:* Illusr, Word People, 70; illusr, Magical Storybook, 72; auth & illusr, Moon Missing, 72; auth & illusr, Making the World Safe for Hypocrisy, 72; auth & illusr, Superpen, 78. *Mailing Add:* Rte 301 Carmel NY 10512

SORELL, VICTOR ALEXANDER
HISTORIAN, ADMINISTRATOR
b Mexico City, Mex, Oct 31, 44. *Study:* Shimer Col, BA; Univ Chicago, with Joshua C Taylor and John Rewald, MA; Univ Chicago. *Collections Arranged:* Mexposicion I (with catalog in Eng & Span), 75 & Mexposicion II: Photographic Images of the Mex Revolution by Agustin Victor Casasola, 76, A Montgomery Ward Gallery, Univ Ill, Chicago Circle; Hispanic American Art in Chicago & Chilean Arpilleras, Univ Galleries, Chicago State Univ, 80. *Pos:* Co-ed, Abrazo (Embrace) J, 76-; prog adminr, Park Forest Art Ctr, 78 & 79; coordr, Hispanic Am Cult Enrichment Progs, Chicago State Univ, 79-80 & 83; fac fel art hist & sr prog officer, Nat Endowment Humanities, 80-83. *Teaching:* Chmn art dept, Chicago State Univ, 75-80 & 83. *Awards:* Fac Scholar, Inst Bilingual Educ, Educ Prof Develop Act, 75; Grant, Ill Humanities Coun, 76; Grants, Ill Arts & Humanities Coun, 80. *Mem:* Col Art Asn Am; el Movimiento Artistico Chicano (chmn, 79). *Res:* Documentary investigation of modern (1900-present) Canadian, Mexican & US mural art; Chilean arpilleras and subject of human rights as reflected in visual arts. *Publ:* Auth, Barrio murals in Chicago: Painting the Hispanic-American experience on our community walls, In: Revista Chicano--Riquena, Ind Univ-Northwest, 75; co-reviewer articles in American studies sect, Am Quart, 69-73; translr, Jose David Alfaro Siqueiros (auth), Como se Pinta un Mural (How to Paint a Mural), 78; ed, Guide to Chicago Murals: Yesterday and Today, 1st ed, 78, 2nd ed, 79; auth, Hispanic American Art in Chicago (catalog), 80. *Mailing Add:* 10601 S Parkside Ave Apt 2-A Chicago Ridge IL 60415

SORGE, WALTER
PAINTER, PRINTMAKER
b Forestberg, Alta, Oct 25, 31. *Study:* Univ Calif, Los Angeles, BA, 54, MA, 55; Columbia Univ, EDD, 64; also with Stanley William Hayter, Paris, 61-62 & 68. *Work:* Victoria & Albert Mus, London, Eng; J B Speed Mus, Louisville, Ky; Sheldon Swope Art Gallery, Terre Haute, Ind. *Exhib:* One-man show, Inst Mex NAm Relationes Cult, Mexico City, 71; Sheldon Swope Art Gallery, Terre Haute, Ind, 71, Am Embassies, Ankara, Izmir & Istanbul, Turkey, 74-75; Second Can Biennial, 57 & Canadian Watercolors, Drawings & Prints, 66, Nat Gallery Can; Smithsonian Inst Traveling Exhib, Washington, DC, 67; and others. *Pos:* Chmn dept painting, drawing & printmaking, Ky Southern Col, 64-69 & Hardin-Simmons Univ, Tex, 69-70; chmn dept, Eastern Ill Univ, Charleston, 70-75, prof art, 75-; exchange prof, Portsmouth Polytech Inst, England, 77. *Awards:* C W Jefferys Award, 26th Ann Exhib, Can Soc Graphic Art, 59; Jr League Purchase Award, Mid-States Art Exhib, Evansville Mus Arts & Sci, Ind, 67; Helen Van Aken Purchase Award, Fifth Ann Gulf Coast Exhib, Mobile Art Gallery, 70. *Media:* Watercolor, Mixed Media; Intaglio. *Mailing Add:* 715 Lincoln Charleston IL 61920

SORMAN, STEVEN
PAINTER, PRINTMAKER

b Minneapolis, Minn, June 14, 48. *Study:* Univ Minn, BFA, 71. *Work:* Mus Mod Art, New York; Whitney Mus Am Art, New York; Art Inst Chicago; Des Moines Art Ctr, Iowa; Walker Art Ctr, Minn. *Exhib:* Printmakers Midwest Invitational, Walker Art Ctr, Minn, 73; Corcoran Biennial, Corcoran Gallery Art, Washington, DC, 75; Paper as Medium, Smithsonian Inst, Washington, DC, 78; Painting and Sculpture Today, Indianapolis Mus Art, Ind, 78; 21st Nat Print Exhib, Brooklyn Mus, New York, 78; 13th Int Biennial Graphic Art, Ljubljana, Yugoslavia, 79; Artist and Printer, Walker Art Ctr, Minn, 80; Bienal Americana de Artes Graficas, Museo de Arte Moderno La Tertulia, Colombia, 81; 23rd Nat Print Exhib, Brooklyn Mus, 83. *Awards:* Bush Found Artist's Fel, 79; Minn State Arts Bd Fel, 79; Merit Award, San Francisco Mus Mod Art, 80. *Bibliog:* Ronny H Cohen (auth), Three artists--three arguments, The Print Collector's Newsletter, 5-6/80; Madeleine Deschamps (auth), La Peinture Americaine, Paris, 81; Richard Field (auth), Prints: History of an Art, Contemporary Trends, Geneva, 81. *Mailing Add:* Box 149 Marine On St Croix MN 55047

SOROKA, MARGERY
PAINTER

b New York, NY, May 30, 20. *Study:* Hunter Col; Art Students League; Sch Visual Arts; with Edgar A Whitney & Rex Brandt. *Work:* Va State Col; Northland State Jr Col, Thief River Falls, Minn; E R Squibb Sci Info Libr, New Brunswick, NJ; Forbes, Inc, New York; Old Queen Gallery, New Brunswick, NJ. *Exhib:* Am Watercolor Soc, var times, 64-81; Watercolor USA, 68; Audubon Artists, 68-81; Central Ontario Art Asn, 81. *Pos:* Art dir, Planned Parenthood Fedn of Am Inc, New York, 73-80. *Awards:* Lena Newcastle Award, Am Watercolor Soc, 68; Gold Medal, Nat Art League, 82; Solo Award, Pen & Brush Inc, 83. *Bibliog:* Rex Brandt (auth), The Artist's Sketchbook, 67; Barbara Nechis (auth), Watercolor the Creative Experience, 79; Frank Webb (auth), Watercolor Energies, 83. *Mem:* Am Watercolor Soc; Audubon Artists; Knickerbocker Artists; Salmagundi Art Club; Nat Asn Women Artists. *Media:* Watercolors. *Publ:* Contribr, The Watercolor Page, Am Artist Mag, 2/71. *Mailing Add:* 200 E 16th St New York NY 10003

SOROKIN, MAXINE ANN
PAINTER, EDUCATOR

b Brooklyn, NY, Dec 15, 48. *Study:* Kingsborough Community Col, AA, 67; Brooklyn Col, with Philip Pearlstein, Jimmy Ernst, Robert Wolff & Samuel Gelber, BA(cum laude), 70, MFA, 72. *Comn:* Window & portal paintings, Congregation of Kehillath Jacobs Synagogue, Newton, Mass, 73; paintings, Solomon Schechter Day Sch, Newton, Mass. *Exhib:* Invitational, Newton City Hall, Mass, 73-76; Meetinghouse Gallery, Boston, 73; Boston Visual Artists Union, 74 & 75; two-person exhibs, Goethe Inst, Boston & Jewish Community Ctr Southern NJ, Cherry Hill, 80. *Teaching:* Fel & grad asst painting, Brooklyn Col, 71-72; lectr art, Univ Mass, Boston, 72-73; instr art, Art Inst Boston, 73-; instr, W Rox Community High Sch, 75- & Jewish Community Ctr Brookline, Brighton-Newton, Mass, currently. *Awards:* Eisler Award Painting Excellence, City Univ New York, 70. *Bibliog:* Lisa Taylor (producer), Woman 76, WBZ Television, 76. *Mem:* Boston Visual Artists Union; West Roxbury Artists Asn (vpres, 77-78); West Roxbury Hist Soc; Victorian Soc. *Media:* Oil, Pen & Ink. *Dealer:* Boston Fine Arts 420 Boylston St Boston MA; Crieger Art Assocs 801 Water Street Framingham MA 01701. *Mailing Add:* 61 Perham St West Roxbury MA 02132

SOSHANA (SUSANNE AFROYIM)
PAINTER

b Vienna, Austria, Sept 1, 27. *Study:* Art Students League, New York; Art Acad, Vienna. *Work:* Mus d'Art Mod, Paris; Mus d'Art Mod, Rome; Jewish Mus, New York; Mus Mod Art, Sao Paulo, Brazil; Mus Mod Art, Mexico. *Exhib:* Grands et des Jeunes, 64; one-person exhibs, Ruth White Gallery, New York, 67, Essen, 68, Moos Gallery, Montreal, 69, Toronto, 70, Gallery Seiler-Statte, Vienna, 70; and many others. *Mem:* Am Asn Artists; Archit League. *Mailing Add:* 8 Barstow Rd Apt 7G Great Neck NY 11021

SOSNOWITZ, HENRY ABRAM
COLLECTOR, PATRON

b Warsaw, Poland, July 13, 40; US citizen. *Study:* Lublin Univs, Warsaw, BA; also with Henryk Sienkiewicz. *Work:* Sosnowitz collection of artist Kenneth Hari in Vatican, Rome, Trenton State Mus, NJ, Lincoln Ctr Libr & Mus Collection, Sport Mus & Metrop Mus Art, New York. *Interests:* American art to create a renaissance in the US. *Collection:* Picasso, Kenneth Hari, G'Miglio, J A Whistler, Mary Cassett, F Leyendecker & Larry Rivers. *Mailing Add:* Box 243 Keasbey NJ 08832

SOTERAS, JAIME
SCULPTOR

b Santiago de Cuba, Cuba, May 26, 22; US citizen. *Study:* Nat Sch Fine Arts, San Alejandro, Havana, Cuba, Master, 44; Oriente Univ, Santiago de Cuba, 49. *Work:* Don Emilio Bacardi Mus, Santiago de Cuba; Colon Wax Mus, Madrid, Spain. *Comn:* Frieze sculpture, Ctr Spanish Colony, Santiago de Cuba, 56; Cathedral St Peter & Paul, Philadelphia, Rambush Assoc, New York, 82. *Exhib:* Spanish Am Painter & Sculptors, Metrop Mus Art, New York, 76; 36th Exhib, Audubon Artists, New York, 78; Re-Encuentro Cubano, Miami, Fla, 78; Art from the Other Americas, Jamaica Art Ctr, New York, 78; A Tribute to J J Sicre, Kromex Gallery, New York, 78; and others. *Pos:* Vpres, Galleria Artes Plasticas, 57-59. *Teaching:* Prof life modeling, Sch Fine Arts, Santiago de Cuba, 45-60, 62-70, dir, 59-60; prof life modeling, Nat Sch Fine Arts, San Alejandro, Havana, 60-62. *Awards:* Gold Medals for Sculpture, Assoc Art Teachers, Cuba, 49 & Galeria Artes Plasticas, Cuba, 53.

Bibliog: Pedro R Monge (auth), Pedro Monge presenta a Jaime Soteras, Despertar, 10/76. *Mem:* Allied Artists Am, New York; Am Medallic Sculpture Asn. *Media:* All. *Mailing Add:* 39-25 51st St Apt 1-F Woodside NY 11377

SOTTUNG, GEORGE (K)
PAINTER, ILLUSTRATOR

b Chicago, Ill. *Study:* Art Inst Chicago, grad; DePaul Univ; Brooklyn Mus Art, apprentice to Haddon H Sundblom. *Work:* US Naval Acad Mus, Annapolis, Md; Bethesda Naval Hosp Rotunda, Washington, DC; Princeton Univ, NJ; US Naval War Col, Newport, RI; US Military Acad, West Point. *Comn:* First Atlantic Crossing, 75, The Forrestal, 76, Capt Healy, 78 & Invasion of Normandy, 79-80, US Govt; portraits, Grolier Inc, Washington, 76- *Exhib:* Grumbacher Exhib, Scott-Fanton Mus, Danbury, Conn, 66; Allied Artists Am Exhib, Nat Acad Galleries, New York, 75 & Am Watercolor Soc Exhib, annually; Am Painters in Paris Exhib, Palais des Cong, France, 75 & 76; solo shows, Union League Club, Chicago, 80 & Univ Club, Chicago, 80; Art Inst Chicago; Smithsonian Inst; Fogg Mus; and others. *Collections Arranged:* Allied Artists Am Exhib (auth, catalog), 75; Hudson Valley Art Asn Ann Show, 76; Am Watercolor Soc 112th Ann Exhib, 79; Ann Exhib Watercolor, 79 & Ann Exhib Oil Paintings, 80, Salmagundi Club, New York. *Pos:* Illusr, Chicago Tribune Co, 54-62, Charles E Cooper Studios, New York, 62-64, Good Housekeeping, 70-82 & Readers Digest, 73-76. *Awards:* Allied Artists Am Watercolor Award, 75; Seley Gold Medal, Salmagundi Club, 75; President's Show Silver Medal, 80. *Bibliog:* US Navy Artists (film), US Govt, 74; Ellen Anderson (auth), Meet George Sottung, North Light/Fletcher Art Serv, 76. *Mem:* Salmagundi Club; Am Watercolor Soc; Soc Illusr; Berkshire Art Asn; Chicago Press Club. *Media:* Oil, Acrylic; Watercolor. *Mailing Add:* 111 Tower Rd Brookfield Center CT 06805

SOULT, JAMES THOMAS
GRAPHIC ARTIST

b Beloit, Wis, Mar 12, 35. *Study:* Col San Mateo; Hayward State Univ, with Mel Ramos, BA; San Jose State Univ, also with Al Barela, MA. *Work:* Richmond Art Ctr, Calif; City of Fremont, Calif; Alameda Co Art Comn, Alameda. *Exhib:* New York Int, NY Coliseum, New York, 70; Washington & Jefferson 4th Nat Painting Show, Ball State Univ, 72; Trading Co, Univ Calif, San Francisco, 74; one-man show, Xergo Gallery, Oakland, Calif, 74. *Collections Arranged:* Richmond Area Artists, 73; Battenberg-Beaseley Sculpture Exhib, 74; Artes Plasticas de Mexico (with catalog under NEA grant), 74-75. *Pos:* Activ coordr, Olive Hyde Art Ctr, Fremont, 68-72; cur, Richmond Art Ctr, Calif, 72-78. *Teaching:* Instr drawing, Ohlone Col, Fremont, Calif, 70-73. *Awards:* Cal-Expo, State of Calif, Sacramento, 71; 10th Ann Benedictine Awards, Julius Wiles & Sons Inc, 72; Zellerbach Gallery Exhib, KQED-TV, 73. *Bibliog:* 3 Bay Area artists on KQED-TV, 73; Dona Meilach (auth), Soft Sculpture, Crown, 74; Thomas Albright (auth), The Trading Company San Francisco Chronicle, 75. *Mem:* Western Asn Art Mus; Am Asn Mus. *Media:* Colored Pencil & Other Media on Paper; Silverpoint on Canvas. *Mailing Add:* c/o Graphics Gallery 2140 Bush St San Francisco CA 94115

SOUTHEY, TREVOR J T
PAINTER, SCULPTOR

b Gatooma, Rhodesia, Jan 12, 40; US citizen. *Study:* Brighton Col Art, Eng, cert, 59; Natal Technical Col, Durban, SAfrica, dipl, 60; Brigham Young Univ, Provo, Utah, BFA, 67, MA, 69. *Work:* Utah State Mus, Salt Lake City & Springville Mus Art, Utah; Rhodes Nat, Zimbabwe; Brigham Young Univ; Mormon Mus, Salt Lake City. *Comn:* Painting, Decision Making Information, Santa Ana, Calif, 71; painting, Brigham Young Univ, Provo, Utah, 75; sculpture, Church Jesus Christ LDS, Fayette, NY, 78; mural, Salt Lake Int Airport, 81; life size sculpture, Univ Utah Medical Ctr, Salt Lake City, 81; and others. *Exhib:* Utah State Mus, Salt Lake City, 79 & Ill Ctr, Chicago, 79; Twenty Utah Printmakers, traveling show, Utah Arts Coun, 82; and others. *Teaching:* Asst prof drawing & painting, Brigham Young Univ, Provo, 69-76. *Bibliog:* Trevor Southey/Stephen Doherty, Images and Ideas, American Artist, 80; Steven P Sondrup (auth), Trevor Southey--the art and the man, Artists of the Rockies and the Golden West, summer 82. *Mem:* North Mountain Artists Cooperative; Alpine Community Arts (chmn, 78-). *Media:* Oil, Etchings; Bronzes. *Publ:* Illusr, The Search, 69, Doubleday; illusr, The Growing Season, Bookcraft, 75; illusr, Marriage and Divorce, Deseret Book, 76; illusr, The Sex Book, Pelton, 78; illusr, A Widening View, Bookcraft, 83; and others. *Dealer:* Andreas Galleries 8545 Leesburg Pike Vienna VA 22180; Old Town Gallery Box 2521 Park City UT 84060. *Mailing Add:* 1474 S 800 E Salt Lake City UT 84105

SOUZA, AL (ALFRED FRANCIS)
PHOTOGRAPHER, EDUCATOR

b Plymouth, Mass, Apr 22, 44. *Study:* Art Students League, New York, 67-70; Univ Mass, Amherst, BSCE, 67, MFA, 72. *Work:* Bibliot Nat, Paris, France; Mus Mod Art, Belgrade, Yugoslavia; Mus Fine Arts, Houston, Tex; Can Coun Art Bank, Ottawa; Dartmouth Col, Hanover, NH. *Exhib:* One-man shows, Dobrick Gallery, Chicago, 78, Dartmouth Col, Univ Mass, Brown Univ, traveling, 79-80 & Delahunty Gallery, Dallas, 80; and others. *Teaching:* Asst prof studio art, Smith Col, Northampton, Mass, 73-79; instr photog, Amherst Col, Mass, 74-77. *Awards:* Nat Endowment Arts Photogr Fel, 78. *Bibliog:* Max Kozloff (auth), article, Artforum, 75; David Corey (auth), article, Arts Mag, 78. *Mem:* Col Art Asn. *Dealer:* O K Harris Gallery 383 W Broadway New York NY 10012. *Mailing Add:* 415 Meadow St Amherst MA 01002

SOUZA, PAUL MARCIEL
PAINTER, INSTRUCTOR
b Honomu, Hawaii, Jan 16, 18. *Study:* Honolulu Acad Arts; Univ Hawaii; Art Ctr Col Design. *Work:* Lytton Savings & Loan, Canoga Park, Calif; Pac Savings & Loan, Downey, Calif; Univ Hawaii; Ahmanson Collection, Los Angeles. *Comn:* Exterior ceramic mural, Long Beach Harbor Admin Bldg; paintings for Gunsmoke (TV prog), Columbia Broadcasting Syst. *Exhib:* One-man shows, Emerson Gallery, Encino, Calif, 65; Challis Galleries, Laguna Beach, Calif, 74 & Goteborg, Sweden, 75; Am Watercolor Soc, New York; 1979 Exhibs, Stockholm, Norkoping & Kristiansand, Sweden. *Teaching:* Instr painting & drawing, Art Ctr Col Design, Los Angeles, 46- *Awards:* Sanders Purchase Award, 70 & Ahmanson Award, 73, Nat Watercolor Soc; Nat Aquamedia Award, Golden, Colo. *Bibliog:* Henry J Seldis, Souza creates refreshing debut, Los Angeles Times Calendar, 7/29/62. *Mem:* Am Watercolor Soc; Nat Watercolor Soc (vpres, 64-65 & 70-71). *Media:* Watercolor, Oil. *Mailing Add:* 2828 Oak Point Dr Hollywood CA 90068

SOVARY, LILLY
PAINTER, DESIGNER
b Sovar, Hungary; US citizen. *Study:* Calif State Univ, San Francisco, with Alexander Nepote; Calif State Univ, San Jose, with Dr Tansey; Univ Idaho, with John Davis & Ray Obermyer. *Exhib:* San Francisco Univ Art Dept Exhib, 53-54, Univ Idaho Archit & Art Dept, 56-59 & 81st Ann Painting Exhib, San Francisco Mus Art, 62; and others. *Teaching:* Guest lectr, Univ Idaho, 56-59 & organic art & lang arts, Calif Col Arts & Crafts, 71 & Langley-Porter Clin, 73. *Bibliog:* Dana Atchley & William Farley (auths), Sovary: The Contemporary Artist (film), Calif Col Arts & Crafts & Dana Atchley's Space Atlas & Notebook, 72-73. *Media:* Watercolor, Oil; Crayon, Driftwood. *Res:* Comparison of contemporary architectural styles. *Mailing Add:* 1276 Second Ave San Francisco CA 94122

SOVIAK, HARRY
PAINTER, SCULPTOR
b Lorain, Ohio, May 25, 35. *Study:* Bowling Green State Univ; Cranbrook Acad Art, with Fred Mitchell & Zoltan Sepeshy, BFA, MFA. *Work:* Philadelphia Mus of Art; New Orleans Mus Art; NJ State Mus; Chase Manhattan Bank; Chemical Bank, New York. *Exhib:* Albright-Knox Art Gallery, Buffalo, NY, 63; San Francisco Mus of Art, 65; Mus of Mod Art, New York, 66; Philadelphia Mus of Art, 70; NJ State Mus, Trenton, 70; one-man shows, Marian Locks Gallery, Philadelphia, 70, 73, 76, 78 & 81; Arthur Roger Gallery, New Orleans, 80 & 81; Weatherspoon Art Gallery, NC, 82; Pam Adler Gallery, New York, 82 & 83; Twentieth Century American Watercolor Traveling Exhib, Gallery Asn NY, 83. *Teaching:* Prof painting & drawing, Philadelphia Col Art, 63- *Awards:* Buenos Aires Convention Fel, 58-59. *Bibliog:* J Patrice Marandel (auth), article, Art Int, 11/70; Ralph Pomeroy (auth), article, Arts Mag, 9/82; Ronny H Cohen (auth), article, Art in Am, 1/83. *Media:* Watercolor, Graphics; Painter Metal. *Dealer:* Pam Adler Gallery 37 W 57th St New York NY 10019; Arthur Roger Gallery 3005 Magazine St New Orleans LA 70115. *Mailing Add:* 181 St John's Pl Brooklyn NY 11217

SOWERS, MIRIAM R
PAINTER
b Bluffton, Ohio, Oct 4, 22. *Study:* Miami Univ; Art Inst Chicago; Univ NMex. *Work:* Tex A&I Univ; Mus of NMex Art Gallery; Lovelace Clin, Albuquerque; New York World's Fair; Nat Arch, Washington, DC. *Exhib:* Butler Inst Am Art; IPA Nat, Washington, DC; All-Albuquerque Show, NMex; Jonson Gallery, Univ NMex; one-man show, Am Bible Soc Gallery, New York; plus other group & one-man shows. *Pos:* Owner, Symbol Gallery Art, 61-79; owner, Sowers Symbolic art Studios, currently. *Awards:* Prizes, Toledo Mus Art, Ouray Colo Nat & NMex State Fair; plus others. *Bibliog:* Mary Carroll Nelson (auth), article, in Southwest Art Mag; articles in Albuquerque J & Tribune & The Santa Fe New Mexican; Mary Carroll Nelson (auth), Miriam Sowers, Art Voices, 9-10/81. *Media:* Oil. *Specialty:* Oils on gold leaf; silver and copper; symbolism of man and nature. *Publ:* Auth, Parables from Paradise, Branden Press; Auth, The suns of man, Symbol, 81. *Dealer:* Cliffrose Gallery 1st Plaza Galeria Albuquerque NM; Artisans Gallery Ruidoso NM. *Mailing Add:* c/o Symbolic Art Studio 3020 Glenwood Dr NW Albuquerque NM 87107

SOWINSKI, STANISLAUS JOSEPH
PAINTER, ICONOGRAPHER
b Milwaukee, Wis, May 7, 27. *Study:* San Diego Sch Arts, 48-49; San Diego State Univ, with Jeane Charlot, Jean Swiggett & Everett G Jackson, BA, 52. *Work:* Dept Defense, Pentagon; Univ Calif, Sacramento; San Diego State Univ; Escondido Hist Soc, Calif. *Comn:* Paintings (salvage opers), Oahu, Hawaii, 61 & nautical mural, Adak, Alaska, 62, Navy Dept; promotional paintings, First Fed Savings & Loan, San Diego, 81-83; 21 major icons, Sts Constantine & Helen Churches, Solana Beach, Calif, 82-83; hist painting, City Escondido, Calif, 83. *Exhib:* Am Artists League, Corcoran Gallery, 65; solo exhibs, US Embassy, London, 67 & Escondido Hist Mus, Calif, 83; Royal Soc Brit Artists, London, 67; Royal Acad, London, 67; Calif State Fair, Sacramento, 71; Calif-Hawaii Competition, San Diego Mus Art, 72. *Pos:* Demonr watercolor, Grumbacher Inc, New York, 76-79 & Inveresk Paper Co, Bath, UK, 79-83. *Teaching:* Instr watercolor workshops, Calif, Ore & SDak, 71-; instr watercolor painting, San Diego Art Inst, 76-77. *Awards:* First in Watercolor, Southern Calif Expo, San Diego, 59; Best in Show, Hawaii State Fair, 62 & Allied Artists Am, 65. *Mem:* San Diego Art Inst; San Diego Watercolor Soc. *Media:* Watercolor, Oil; Acrylic, Pen & Ink. *Publ:* Illusr, Amphibious Operations, Navy Dept, 60; illusr, Brand Book IV, 76 & Brand Book V, 77, Westerners; illusr, Christmas in Arizona, 83. *Dealer:* O'Brien's Art Emporium 7122 Stetson Dr Scottsdale AZ 85251. *Mailing Add:* 814 Minor Dr Escondido CA 92025

SOYER, RAPHAEL
PAINTER
b Russia, Dec 25, 1899; US citizen. *Study:* Cooper Union; Nat Acad Design; Art Students League. *Work:* Whitney Mus Am Art, Mus Mod Art, Metrop Mus Art, New York; Addison Mus Art, Andover, Mass; Philadelphia Mus Art, Pa. *Exhib:* Pa Mus Fine Arts, 34; Art Inst Chicago, 40; Whitney Mus Am Art, 43 & 46; Brooklyn Mus, 44; Dallas Mus Fine Arts, 45; Calif Palace Legion Hon, 46; Mus Mod Art, New York, 46; Nat Collection of Fine Arts, Washington, DC, 77; Albert Leob Gallery, Paris, 79; Hirshhorn Mus, Washington, DC, 80; 65 year retrospective, Smithsonian Travelling Exhib, 83. *Teaching:* Instr painting, Art Students League; instr painting, Am Art Sch; instr painting, New Sch Social Res. *Awards:* Joseph H Temple Gold Medal, Pa Acad Fine Arts, 43; Walter Lippincott Prize, 46; Award of Merit, Acad Arts & Lett, 77. *Bibliog:* Lloyd Goodrich (auth), Raphael Soyer, Praeger, 67; Sylvan Cole (auth), 50 Years of Printmaking, Da Capo, 67; Lloyd Goodrich (auth), Raphael Soyer, Abrams, 72; and others. *Mem:* Nat Acad Design; Am Acad Arts & Lett. *Media:* Oil, Graphic. *Publ:* Auth & illusr, A Painter's Pilgrimmage, 62; auth & illusr, Homage to Thomas Eakins, 66; auth & illusr, Self Revealment, 69; auth, Diary of an Artist, New Repub Bk Co, 77. *Dealer:* Forum Gallery 1018 Madison Ave New York NY 10021. *Mailing Add:* 88 Central Park W New York NY 10023

SPAETH, ELOISE O'MARA
COLLECTOR, WRITER
b Decatur, Ill, June 19, 04. *Study:* Millikin Univ. *Pos:* Trustee, Dayton Art Inst, 38-44, dir, Mod Gallery, 40-44; trustee, Am Fedn Arts, 45-, chmn exten serv, 47-59; trustee, Guild Hall Mus, 50-, chmn acquisitions comt, 62-; trustee, Arch Am Art, 59, chmn, currently; mem, Smithsonian Fine Art Comn. *Awards:* Smithson Medal, Smithsonian Inst, 79. *Mem:* Am Asn Mus; Col Art Asn Am; Art Collectors Club. *Collection:* Contemporary religious art; antiquities; contemporary American and European art. *Publ:* Auth, American Art Museums and Galleries, 60, 66 & 69; auth, Collecting Art, 68; contribr to art & relig publ. *Mailing Add:* 65 E 76th St New York NY 10021

SPAFFORD, MICHAEL CHARLES
EDUCATOR, PAINTER
b Palm Springs, Calif, Nov 6, 35. *Study:* Pomona Co, BA, 59; Harvard Univ, MA(art hist), 60. *Work:* Seattle Art Mus, Wash; Galeria de Inst Mexicano-Norte Americano, Mexico City; Undergrad Libr, Univ Wash; Pac NW Bell, Seattle. *Comn:* Mural, Kingdome, Seattle, Wash, 79; murals, House Chambers State Capitol Bldg, Olympia, Wash, 81. *Exhib:* Art Across America, Knoedler Gallery, New York (travel), 65-67; Drawing Society 1970, Am Fedn Arts, New York (travel), 70-71; 73rd Western Ann Invitational, Denver Art Mus, 71; Art of the Pacific Northwest from 1930s to the Present, Smithsonian Inst, 75; one-man shows, Labors of Hercules & Other Works, Utah Mus Fine Arts, 75, Am Acad & Inst Arts & Letters Awards Selection Show, New York, 80 & 83 & Seattle Art Mus, 82. *Teaching:* Instr painting, Mexico City Col, 61-62; assoc prof painting-drawing, Univ Wash, 63-78, prof, 78- *Awards:* Louis Comfort Tiffany Found Grant Painting, 66; Prix de Rome, Am Acad Rome, 67-69; Award in Painting, Am Acad & Inst Arts & Lett, 83. *Media:* Oil on Canvas. *Dealer:* Francine Seders Gallery 6701 Greenwood Ave N Seattle WA 98103. *Mailing Add:* 2418 E Interlaken Blvd Seattle WA 98112

SPAGNOLO, KATHLEEN MARY
PRINTMAKER, ILLUSTRATOR
b London, Eng, Sept 12, 19. *Study:* Bromley Art Sch; Royal Col Art, London, Royal scholar & Princess of Wales scholar, 39-42; Sch Design, with E W Tristram; Am Univ, with Robert Gates & Krishna Reddy. *Work:* Dept of Interior, Washington, DC; Univ Va, Charlottesville; George Washington Univ; Libr Cong, Washington, DC. *Comn:* Rendering (bench), Index Am Design, Nat Gallery Art, Washington, DC, 69. *Exhib:* Corcoran Gallery Art, Washington, DC, 62; Philadelphia Print Club, 63; Silvermine Guild Artists, 63; Soc Washington Printmakers, 69-75; one-man exhib, Va Mus Fine Arts, 78; All Hallows by the Tower, London, 82. *Mem:* Soc Washington Printmakers; Washington Watercolor Asn; Washington Print Club; Artist's Equity Asn. *Media:* Graphics. *Dealer:* Gallery 4 115 S Columbus Alexandria VA 22314. *Mailing Add:* 7401 Recard Lane Alexandria VA 22307

SPAMPINATO, CLEMENTE
SCULPTOR
b Italy, Jan 10, 12; US citizen. *Study:* Acad Fine Arts, Rome, Italy; Fr Acad Nude, Rome; Sch Governatorate, Rome; Royal Sch Medal, Rome. *Work:* Nat Mus Sport, New Madison Square Garden, New York; Rockwell Gallery Western Art, Corning, NY; Isaac Delgado Mus Art, New Orleans, La; Notre Dame Univ, Ind; Okla Art Ctr, Oklahoma City. *Comn:* Archit reliefs, Bd Educ & Dept Pub Works, New York, 57-75; three different bronze statues of Columbus, Huntington, NY, 64, Mineola, NY, 65 & Bridgeport, Conn, 71; two limestone bas reliefs, Brooklyn Heights Br Libr, NY, 60; Fox Chase (bronze statue), St Charles, Chicago, 73; Bobby Jones (sculpture), World Golf Hall Fame, Pinehurst, NC, 74; and others. *Exhib:* Sport Sculpture Nat, Rome, 40-48; Allied Artists Am, New York, 46-51; Am Artists Prof Art League, New York, 51; Nat Sculpture Soc, New York, 52-78; Nat Acad Design, New York, 64-76; and others. *Awards:* First Prize, Nat Competition Sport Figure, Rome, 39; First Prize, Nat Competition Ski Trophy Olympic Games, Rome, 40; Gold Medal, Grand Award Munic Art League, Chicago, 70. *Mem:* Fel Nat Sculpture Soc; Circolo Artistico Int; Int Fine Arts Coun; Int Am Inst. *Media:* Bronze, Marble. *Dealer:* Campanile Galleries Inc 200 S Michigan Ave Chicago IL 60604; Regency Auction Gallery Inc 1050 Second Ave at 56th St New York NY 10022. *Mailing Add:* 36 Littleworth Ln Sea Cliff NY 11579

SPANDORFER, MERLE SUE
PAINTER, PRINTMAKER

b Baltimore, Md, Sept 4, 34. *Study:* Syracuse Univ, 52-54; Univ Md, BS, 56. *Work:* Metrop Mus Art, Mus Mod Art, New York; Pa Acad Fine Arts; Libr Cong, DC. *Comn:* Fifty-four graphics, Inland Steel Corp, Alexandria, Va, 75; graphics, Thiokol Corp, Newtown, Pa, 76. *Exhib:* Print Exhib, Brooklyn Mus Art, NY, 73; World Print Competition, San Francisco Mus Art, 73; Md Regional, Baltimore Mus Art, 74; 9th Int Encounter on Video, Mus Alvar y Carmen Carrillo Gil, Mexico City, 77; group exhib, Delaware Mus Art, Wilmington, 78; 15 one-man shows including RI Sch Design, Providence, 79 & Yoseido Gallery, Tokyo, Japan, 81; Marian Locks Gallery, Philadelphia, 82. *Pos:* Dir educ, Cheltenham Sch Fine Arts, 75- *Teaching:* Instr painting, Cheltenham Sch Fine Arts, 65-; instr printmaking, Tyler Sch Art, Philadelphia, 79- *Awards:* Governor's Prize & Purchase Award, Baltimore Mus Art, 70; Md Inst Art Award, 71; Purchase Award, Cheltenham Sch Fine Arts, 77. *Bibliog:* Gerrit Henry (auth), article, Art News, 5/70; Lea Vergine (auth), Dall' Informale Alla, Body Art, 76; Peter Frank (auth), Outside, inside, all around the town, Village Voice, 11/78. *Mem:* Artists Equity; Am Color Print Soc. *Media:* Permanent Pigment, Gum Arabic and Ammonium Dichromate. *Dealer:* Ericson Gallery 23 E 74th St New York NY 10021; Marian Locks Gallery 1524 Walnut St Philadelphia PA 19102. *Mailing Add:* 8012 Ellen Lane Cheltenham PA 19012

SPARK, VICTOR DAVID
DEALER

b Brooklyn, NY, May 16, 1898. *Study:* NY Univ, BS, 21. *Pos:* Dir, Victor D Spark Art Gallery. *Specialty:* American and foreign paintings, drawings and other works of art; appraisals of fine art. *Mailing Add:* 1000 Park Ave New York NY 10028

SPARKS, JOHN EDWIN
PRINTMAKER, INSTRUCTOR

b Washington, DC, Sept 14, 42. *Study:* Richmond Prof Inst; Yale-Norfolk Summer Sch Art & Music; Md Inst Col Art, BFA; Univ Ill, Urbana, MFA. *Work:* Libr of Cong, Washington, DC. *Exhib:* 36th Int Exhib, Northwest Printmakers, Seattle, 65; Libr of Cong Print Exhib, Washington, DC, 66; 47th Exhib, Soc Am Graphic Artists, New York, 66; 3rd Print Show, Eastern Mich Univ, Ypsilanti, 70; 10th Nat Print Exhib, Silvermine Guild Artists, Conn, 74. *Pos:* Cataloger, George A Lucas Print Collection, Union of Independent Cols Art, 69; dir first restrike ed, Rodolphe Bresdin's etching Flight into Egypt, 70; art adv, Md Arts Coun, 70-71. *Teaching:* Instr lithography & intaglio, Md Inst Col Art, 66-, chmn, Printmaking Dept; instr intaglio & lithography, Lake Placid Summer Workshop, 71-75; instr intaglio, NS Col of Art & Design, 77. *Awards:* Printmaking Grant, Louis Comfort Tiffany Found, 67. *Media:* Intaglio, Lithography. *Mailing Add:* c/o Md Inst Col Art 1300 West Mt Royal Ave Baltimore MD 21217

SPAULDING, D(ONALD CLIFFORD)
ILLUSTRATOR, PAINTER

b Brooklyn, NY, Aug 8, 26. *Study:* Art Students League with DuMond, McNulty & Hale; also with Norman Rockwell, 47-50. *Work:* West Point Mus, US Military Acad, New York. *Exhib:* American Cavalry in West, West Point Mus, NY, 79; 1st Ann SIDS Show, Denver, 81; Experience the West Show, Mus Rockies, Bozeman, Mont, 81. *Awards:* Peoples Choice Award, SIDS Art Show, 81. *Bibliog:* Jim Marks (auth), No Hollywood cliches for Don Spaulding, Art West Mag, 81; Susan E Meyer (auth), Norman Rockwell's People, Abrams, 81. *Mem:* Soc Am Hist Artists (secy, 80-81). *Media:* Oil, Charcoal; Gouache, Pen & Ink. *Publ:* Illusr, Random House Dictionary of the English Language, 66; illusr, New Book of Knowledge, Grolier, 68; illusr, Great Indian Tribes, Hamond, 70. *Mailing Add:* c/o Grizzly Tree Gallery Mt Crested Butte CO 81230

SPAULDING, WARREN DAN
PAINTER, LECTURER

b Boston, Mass, Oct 7, 16. *Study:* Mass Sch Art, cert(painting), 37; Sch Fine Art, Yale Univ, BFA(Alice K English Fel), MFA, 49. *Work:* Univ Maine, Orono; Joslyn Art Mus, Omaha; US Sect Fine Arts, Marine Hosp, Carville, La; Branford Col, Yale Univ; St Louis Artists Guild, Mo. *Exhib:* Cincinnati Art Mus Am Art Ann, 40; Am Watercolors, Nat Gallery Art, Washington, DC, 40; Pa Acad Fine Arts Painting & Sculpture Ann, 51 & 54; Midwest Biennial, Joslyn Art Mus, 56 & 58; Maine Art Gallery Ann, 61-79; one-man show, Parsonage Gallery, Durham, NH, 77. *Teaching:* Instr painting, Sch Fine Arts, Yale Univ, 49-50; art dir, Taft Sch, Watertown, Conn, 50-51; prof compos, Sch Fine Arts, Washington Univ, 51-61; instr art, Farnsworth Art Mus, 73-74. *Awards:* Nat Watercolor Competition Purchase Award, US Sect Fine Art, 40; First Prize for Oil & Sculpture Exhib, St Louis Artists Guild, 51; Purchase Prize, Midwest Biennial, Joslyn Art Mus, 58. *Bibliog:* Edward Betts (auth), Creative Seascape, 81. *Media:* All. *Mailing Add:* Star Route 32 Box 272 Owl's Head ME 04854

SPEAR, LAURINDA HOPE
ARCHITECT

b Rochester, Minn, Aug 23, 50. *Study:* Brown Univ, BA, 72; Columbia Univ, MArch, 75; Mass Inst Technol, currently. *Comn:* Babylon, Pacific Developers, Miami, Fla, 77; The Atlantis, Stonecrest Development, Miami, Fla, 78; The Palace, Helmsley Enterprises, Miami, Fla, 78; Imperial at Brickell, Harlon Group, Miami, Fla, 79; Overseas Tower, Overseas Finance Corp, Miami, Fla, 80. *Exhib:* New Americans, Inst Archit & Urban Studies, 79 & Pa State Univ, 80; Work of Arquitectonica, Fla AIA, Orlando, 79; Young Architects, Yale Univ, New Haven, Conn, 80; Work of Arquitectonica, Univ Va, 81. *Pos:* Principal, Arquitectonica, Coral Gables,

Fla, 77- *Awards:* Design Award, NY Soc Architects, 75; Rome Prize in Architecture, Am Acad, Rome, 78; Citation--1980, 1978, 1975, Progressive Archit, 80. *Mem:* Archit Club Miami; Dade Co Historic Preservation Bd. *Mailing Add:* 4215 Ponce de Leon Blvd Coral Gables FL 33146

SPEAR, RICHARD EDMUND
EDUCATOR

b Michigan City, Ind, Feb 3, 40. *Study:* Univ Chicago, BA(art hist); Princeton Univ, MFA(art hist) & PhD(art hist). *Pos:* Dir, Allen Mem Art Mus, Oberlin Col, 72-83; pres, Intermuseum Conserv Asn, 75-77. *Teaching:* Mildred C Jay prof art hist, Oberlin Col, 64-; distinguished vis prof, George Washington Univ, 83-84. *Awards:* Premio Daria Borghese Gold Medal, Rome, 72. *Mem:* Col Art Asn. *Res:* Seventeenth century painting. *Publ:* Auth, Caravaggio and His Followers, Cleveland Mus Art, 71 & Harper & Row, rev ed 75; auth, Renaissance and Baroque Paintings from the Sciarra and Fiano Collections, Pa State Univ Press & Ugo Bozzi, Rome, 72; auth, Domenichino, Yale Univ Press, 82. *Mailing Add:* Dept Art Oberlin Col Oberlin OH 44074

SPECTOR, BUZZ (FRANKLIN MAC SPECTOR)
CONCEPTUAL ARTIST, EDITOR

Chicago, Ill, Mar 13, 48. *Study:* Southern Ill Univ, Carbondale, BA(studio art), 72; Univ Chicago, MFA, 78. *Work:* Mus Contemp Art, Chicago; Ind Mus Art; Ctr Visual Arts Gallery, Ill State Univ, Normal; Ill State Mus, Springfield; Univ Alberta Art Mus, Edmonton. *Exhib:* Artists Books from the Permanent Collection, Mus Contemp Art, Chicago, 81; 33rd Ill Invitational, Ill State Mus, Springfield, 81; 79th Chicago & Vicinity Show, Art Inst Chicago, 81-83; Breaking the Bindings: American Book Art Now, Elvehjem Art Mus, Madison, Wis, 83; EarthArt, Mus Contemp Art, Chicago, 83-84; Prints O Multiples, traveling to Nat Acad Design, New York, Nat Mus Am Art, Smithsonian Inst & Portland Art Ctr, Ore. *Pos:* Ed, WhiteWalls, 78- *Teaching:* Instr graphic design, Columbia Col, Chicago, 82-83; vis artist advan studio, Univ Ill, Chicago, 82-83; vis lectr artists books, Art Inst Chicago, 83. *Awards:* Fel for Drawing & Artists Books, Nat Endowment Arts, 82-83. *Bibliog:* Dan Graham (auth), Signs, Artforum, 4/81; Christopher Lyon (auth), article, Images & Issues, 9-10/82; Karla Kruggel Powell (auth), Book art, Reader, Chicago, 7/22/83. *Mem:* Renaissance Soc, Univ Chicago (bd mem, 80-). *Publ:* Auth, Objects and Logotypes: Relationships Between Minimalist Art and Corporate Design (exhib catalog), Renaissance Soc, 80; coauth, Words as Images (exhib catalog), WhiteWalls, 81; ed, The Flue, Quart J Franklin Furnace, New York, Vol 3, No 1; ed, Exposure, Quart J Soc Photog Educ, Vol 21, No 3. *Dealer:* Roy Boyd Gallery 215 W Superior St Chicago Ill 60610 & Los Angeles. *Mailing Add:* 7002 N Clark St Chicago IL 60626

SPECTOR, JACK J
HISTORIAN, EDUCATOR

b Bayonne, NJ, Oct 2, 25. *Study:* City Col New York, BS, 56; Columbia Univ, MA, 59, PhD, 64; Fulbright Fel, Paris, 60-61. *Teaching:* Prof art hist, Rutgers Univ, 62-79; vis prof Romanticism, City Univ New York Grad Ctr, 79. *Awards:* Am Coun Learned Socs Grant, 70. *Mem:* Col Art Asn; Am Soc for Aesthetics. *Res:* Nineteenth century French Romanticism, chiefly Eugene Delacroix; psychoanalytic approaches to 19th and 20th century art. *Publ:* Auth, The Murals of Eugene Delacroix at Saint-Sulpice, Col Art Asn, 67; contribr, The method of Morelli and its relation to Freudian psychoanalysis, Diogenes, Paris, 69; auth, The Aesthetics of Freud, Penguin, 72, Praeger, 73, Kindler, 74, Mursia, 77 & Monte Avila, Venezuela, 79; auth, Delacroix's Death of Sardanapalus, Penguin, 75; contribr, The Vierge du Sacre-Coeur: Religious politics & personal expression in an early Delacroix, Burlington Mag, 4/81. *Mailing Add:* 28 Spring St Somerset NJ 08873

SPECTOR, NAOMI
WRITER

b Lynn, Mass, Mar 6, 39. *Study:* Brandeis Univ, BA, 60; NY Univ, MA, 66. *Pos:* Asst dir, Byron Gallery, New York, 63-64; mgr, Fischbach Gallery, New York, 67-70; dir, John Weber Gallery, New York, 73-75. *Res:* Contemporary art. *Specialty:* Minimal-conceptual. *Publ:* Auth, Dorothea Rockburne (catalog essay), Contemp Art Ctr, Cincinnati, 75; auth, Dorothea Rockburne: New Color Work (catalog essay), John Weber Gallery, New York, 76; auth, Robert Ryman: Six Aquatints, The Print Collector's Newsletter, 3-4/77; auth, Robert Ryman (catalog), Whitechapel Art Gallery, London, Eng, 77; and others. *Mailing Add:* 435 W Broadway New York NY 10012

SPEED, (ULYSSES) GRANT
SCULPTOR

b San Angelo, Tex, Jan 6, 30. *Study:* Brigham Young Univ, BS; also with Soloman Aranda. *Work:* Whitney Mus, Cody, Wyo; Diamond M Mus, Snyder, Tex; Devonian Found, Calgary, Alta; Repub Nat Bank, Dallas. *Comn:* Sculpture, Brigham Young Univ Animal Sci Dept, 75-76, 76-77 & 77-78; monuments, Charlie Goodnight, Mesa Petrolium, Amarillo, Tex, 79, Buddy Holly, city of Lubbock, Tex, 79 & John Wayne, comn by Ron Chamnis, Dallas, 80. *Exhib:* Ann Preview Exhib, Tex Art Gallery, 71-78; Phoenix Art Mus, 73-75; two-man show, Tex Art Gallery, Dallas, 75; Spec Exhib, Whitney Mus, Cody, 75; Montrail Galleries, Scottsdale, Ariz, 77. *Awards:* Achievement Award Art, Brigham Young Univ Animal Sci Dept, 72; Purchase Award, Men's Art Coun Phoenix, 73; Gold Medal Award/ Sculpture, Cowboy Artists of Am Ann, 76. *Bibliog:* Ed Ainsworth (auth), Cowboy in Art, World, 68; Pat Broder (auth), Bronzes of the American West, Abrams, 74; Don Hedgpeth (auth), From Broncs to Bronzes, 79. *Mem:* Cowboy Artists Am (pres, 72-73, bd dirs, 73-74 & 76-78). *Media:* Bronze. *Publ:* Auth, Hooked on cowboyin', Western Horseman, 70. *Dealer:* Tex Art Gallery 1408 Main St Dallas TX 75202; Main Trail Galleries Jackson WY 83001. *Mailing Add:* 139 S 400 East Lindon UT 84062

SPEERS, TERYL TOWNSEND
PAINTER, EDUCATOR
b Coronado, Calif, May 9, 38. *Study:* Ray Froman Sch Art, Univ Tex, study with Millard Sheets, Chen Chi, Charles Reid, Edgar Whitney & Carl Molno. *Work:* Foothills Art Ctr, Golden, Colo; US Navy. *Comn:* Painting, USN, US Bristol County, 68; painting, Grumman Int Corp Off, 76; painting, Rawson Int Corp Off. *Exhib:* Mus Albuquerque Western Fedn Group Show, 75; Watercolor Soc Group Show, Brimingham Mus Art, Ala, 76; Western Fedn Group Show, Tucson Mus Art, Ariz, 76; Butler Inst Am Art Mid-Yr Ann, Youngstown, Ohio, 77; Watercolor USA Ann, Springfield, Ill, 77; Checkwood Art Ctr, Southern Watercolor Soc Group Show, Tenn, 77; one-man show, Stephen F Austin State Univ, Tex, 78; and others. *Pos:* Art experience facilitator, Tex Inst Child Psychiat, 75-76. *Teaching:* Instr water media painting, Canary Hill Galleries, Houston, Tex, 74-77, Tex Art Supply Inc, Houston, 75-77 & pvt studio, Houston, 78- *Awards:* Director's Award, Southern Watercolor Ann Exhib, 77; Art League Houston Dimension Award, 82; Southwestern Watercolor Soc Award, 83. *Bibliog:* Pat Lasher (auth), Seeing the ordinary in a special way, Southwest Art Mag, 9/77; Naomi Brotherton (auth), Spotlight on the artist, The Scene, Southwestern Watercolor Soc, 1/78; Watercolor Energies, Frank Webb, 82. *Mem:* Watercolor Art Soc, Houston (vpres, 74-75, pres, 75-76); Southwestern Watercolor Soc (vpres, Houston Chap, 74); Southern Watercolor Soc; Art League Houston; Rocky Mountain Nat Watermedia Soc. *Media:* Watermedia. *Dealer:* Gallery Gemini Worth Ave Palm Beach FL; South Wharf Gallery Nantucket MA. *Mailing Add:* 3763 Westerman Houston TX 77005

SPEIGHT, FRANCIS
PAINTER, EDUCATOR
b Windsor, NC, Sept 11, 1896. *Study:* Wake Forest Col; Corcoran Gallery Art; Pa Acad Fine Arts; Wake Forest Univ, DHL, 62; Col Holy Cross, DFA, 64. *Work:* NC Mus Art; Toronto Gallery Art; Pa Acad Fine Arts; Rochester Mem Gallery; Butler Inst Am Art; and many others. *Exhib:* Retrospective, NC Mus Art, Raleigh, 61 & Pa State Univ, 74; Pa Acad Fine Arts, Peale House, 79. *Teaching:* Instr, Pa Acad Fine Arts, 26-61 & summers 30-79; prof art & artist in residence, ECarolina Univ, 61-76, emer prof, 76- *Awards:* Prize, Pa Nat Exhib, Ligonier Valley, 61; Gold Medal Achievement Art, State NC, 64; Carnegie Prize, Nat Acad Design, 81; plus many others. *Mem:* Nat Acad Design; Nat Inst Arts & Lett; NC Art Soc. *Mailing Add:* 508 E Ninth St Greenville NC 27834

SPEIGHT, JERRY BROOKS
EDUCATOR, WRITER
b Murray, Ky, Nov 27, 42. *Study:* Murray State Univ, Ky, BS, 64, MA, 68; Memphis State Univ. *Comn:* YMCA Supergraphic, City of Somerset, Ky, 75. *Exhib:* Mid-States Art Exhib, Evansville Mus Arts & Sci, Ind, 70 & Mid-States Craft Exhib, 70 & 73; All Ky Drawing Competition, Univ Ky, Lexington, 78; one-man show, Owensboro Mus Arts & Sci, Ky, 79. *Pos:* Regional corresp for Art Voices South Mag, Art Voices Publ Co, West Palm Beach, Fla, 78- *Teaching:* Art dept chmn, Brescia Col, Owensboro, Ky, 70-74; instr art educ, Univ Ky, Lexington, 74-75 & Murray State Univ, Ky, 75- *Awards:* Merit Award, All Ky Drawing Competition, 78; Ky Art Educator of Year, 80. *Mem:* Ky Art Educ Asn (vpres, 77-78); Nat Art Educ Asn. *Media:* Watercolor, Graphite. *Res:* Artists' work from a technical and conceptual standpoint. *Publ:* Auth, John Thomas Bensing, Sch Arts, 11/80; auth, Wear an original painting, Fiberarts, 1/81; auth, Richard Abrams, Art Voices, 4-5/81; auth, Basic photography experiences, Sch Arts, 5/81; auth, A shoe recall, Sch Arts, 10/81; and many others. *Mailing Add:* 1803 College Farm Rd Murray KY 42071

SPEIGHT, SARAH BLAKESLEE See Blakeslee, Sarah

SPEISER, STUART M
COLLECTOR, PATRON
b New York, NY, June 4, 23. *Exhib:* Stuart M Speiser Collection of Photorealism, shown at 20 museums, including, Addison Gallery Am Art, Andover, Mass, 74, Allentown Art Mus, Pa, 74, Witte Mem Mus, San Antonio, Tex, 74, Brooks Mem Mus, Memphis, Tenn, 75 & Krannert Mus, Champaign, Ill, 75; donated to Smithsonian Inst, 78. *Awards:* James Smithson Medal, Smithsonian Art Inst, 79. *Bibliog:* Judy Beardsall (auth), Stuart M Speiser Photo-Realist Collection, Art Gallery Mag, 10/73; Phyllis Derfner (auth), New York letter, Art Int Lugano Rev, 11/73; Gregory Battcock (auth), New York, Art & Artists, London, 3/74. *Interests:* Promoting new art movements and pioneering in law as it pertains to artists, in capacity as an attorney. *Collection:* Photorealism. *Mailing Add:* 200 Park Ave New York NY 10166

SPELMAN, JILL SULLIVAN
PAINTER
b Chicago, Ill, Feb 17, 37. *Study:* Hilton Leech Art Sch, Sarasota, Fla, 55-57; and with Paul Ninas, New Orleans, 56-58. *Work:* Univ Mass, Amherst. *Exhib:* Watercolor USA, Springfield Art Mus, Mo, 67; Mainstreams '70, Marietta Col, Ohio, 70; Salon 72, Ward Nasse Gallery, New York, 72; one-man shows, Phoenix Gallery, New York, 73, 75 & 77 & Ward-Nasse Gallery, New York, 77; and others. *Pos:* Pres, Phoenix Coop Gallery, 72-74; assoc ed, Artists Rev Art, 77-78. *Teaching:* Lectr, Ringling Mus Art, Sarasota, 58-60. *Awards:* Sarasota Art Asn First Prize, Art Student Exhib, 57; Hamel Prize, Sarasota Art Asn Ann, 58; Grumbacher Oil Prize, Knickerbocker Artists Ann, 70. *Mem:* Asn Artist-Run Galleries. *Media:* Acrylic. *Dealer:* Rhodd Sande Gallery 61 E 57th St New York NY. *Mailing Add:* 22 W 96th St New York NY 10025

SPENCE, ANDREW
PAINTER
b Bryn Mawr, Pa, Oct 4, 47. *Study:* Tyler Sch Art, Temple Univ, Philadelphia, BFA, 69; Univ Calif, Santa Barbara, MFA, 71. *Exhib:* One-man show, Nicholas Wilder Gallery, Los Angeles, 74 & 76 & Barbara Toll Fine Art, New York, 82 & 83; Biennial Contemp Art, Whitney Mus Am Art, 75; Four Californians, La Jolla Mus Contemp Art, 77; Nine Critical Perspectives, PS1, Long Island City, 82; Painting and Sculpture Today, Indianapolis Mus Art, 82; and others. *Bibliog:* Timothy App (auth), Six approaches to formalist abstraction, Artweek, 3/5/77; Suzanne Muchnic (auth), Four abstractions-- Krebs, Spence, Therrien & Georgesco, Artweek, 5/26/77; Katherine Howe (auth), Andy Spence at Barbara Toll Fine Arts, Images & Issues, summer 82. *Mailing Add:* 6 Varick St New York NY 10013

SPENCE, ROBERT
HISTORIAN
b Greensboro, Md, Aug 20, 25. *Study:* Univ Md, College Park, BA & MA; Univ Wis-Madison, PhD; also study with John Summerson & Anthony Blunt. *Pos:* Fel, Ctr Great Plains Studies, 79. *Teaching:* Prof Am & mod art hist, Univ Pittsburgh, 62-66; prof Am & mod art hist, Univ Nebr, Lincoln, 66-, chmn dept art, 70-74. *Mem:* Col Art Asn Am; Nat Coun Art Adminr; Soc Archit Hist. *Res:* American authors and the visual arts; art in Nebraska. *Publ:* Coauth, Kress Study Collection of Italian Renaissance Art at University of Wisconsin, 61; auth, Leonard Baskin: the Artist as Counter-Decadent, 63; auth, Misch Kohn: a Critical Study of His Printmaking, 65; coauth, The Etchings of J Alden Weir, 68, auth, James A Eisentrager: Painter From the Plains, 82. *Mailing Add:* Dept of Art Univ Nebr Lincoln NE 68588

SPENCER, HAROLD EDWIN
HISTORIAN, PAINTER
b Corning, NY, Oct 1, 20. *Study:* Art Students League, 41-42; Univ of Calif, BA(highest honors in art), 48 & James Phelan scholar, MA, 49; Harvard Univ (summer scholar), 58, Fac of Arts & Sci Fel, 60-61 & Frank Knox Fel, 64, PhD, 68. *Exhib:* Mo Exhib, St Louis Art Mus, 52, 55, 59 & 61; Ann Drawing and Print Exhib, San Francisco Art Mus, 55-56; Washington Printmakers Soc, Smithsonian Inst, Washington, DC, 57 & 62; Conn Acad of Art Ann, Wadsworth Atheneum, Hartford, Conn, 76; Monotypes Today I-VII, 77-83; Nine Conn Artists Slater Mus, Norwich, Conn, 83. *Pos:* Chmn art dept, Blackburn Col, Carlinville, Ill, 49-62; assoc prof, Occidental Col, Los Angeles, Calif, 62-68, chmn art dept, 63-68; assoc prof, Univ Conn, Storrs, 68-69, prof, 69-, assoc dept head, 77-79. *Awards:* Ruth Kelso Renfrow Prize, 17th Mo Exhib, St Louis Art Mus, 59; Jr League Prize, 18th Mo Exhib, St Louis Art Mus, 61; Roberts Prize, Conn Acad Art Ann, 82. *Bibliog:* Roberta Capers (auth), Reviews of Readings in Art Hist, Art Bull, 71; Henri Dorra (auth), article in Art J, summer 78. *Mem:* Col Art Asn; Conn Acad of Arts & Sci. *Media:* Oil; Monotype. *Res:* Nineteenth Century European Painting and American Art. *Publ:* Auth, The Image Maker: Man and His Art, Scribner's, 75; auth, Criehaven: A Bellows Pastoral, William Benton Mus Art, Bulletin, 77; ed, American Art: Readings from the Colonial Era to the Present, Scribner's, 80; auth, Reflections on Impressionism, Its Genesis and American Phase, catalog, William Benton Mus Art, 80; ed, Readings in Art History, Scribner's 82 & 83. *Mailing Add:* RR 1 Box 56 Ashford CT 06278

SPENCER, HOWARD DALEE
CURATOR, PRINTMAKER
b Dayton, Ohio, Mar 23, 50. *Study:* Studied with Howard E Wooden, 69-74; Ind State Univ, BS(art educ), 72, MFA, 76. *Collections Arranged:* Through the Looking Glass: Works by Grandma Layton, 80; The Neglected Generation of American Realist Painters: 1930-1948, 81; Ernest Shaw: Sculptures, Paintings & Drawings, 81; The Legendary Wichita Bill: A Retrospective Exhibition of Paintings by John Noble (auth, catalog), Wichita Art Mus, 82. *Pos:* Preparator & interim dir, Sheldon Swope Art Gallery, Terre Haute, Ind, 78; cur collections & exhibs, Wichita Art Mus, Kans, 79- *Mem:* Am Asn Mus. *Res:* American art & architecture. *Mailing Add:* 619 Stackman Dr Wichita KS 67203

SPENCER, JOHN R
HISTORIAN, ADMINISTRATOR
b Moline, Ill, Sept 20, 23. *Study:* Grinnell Col, BA, 47; Yale Univ, MA, 51, PhD, 53; also with Charles Seymour, Jr; Grinnell Col, Hon DFA, 72. *Pos:* Dir mus, Oberlin Col, 62-72; dir mus prog, Nat Endowment Arts, 72-78. *Teaching:* Instr & asst prof art, Yale Univ, 52-58; assoc prof art & actg chmn dept, Univ Fla, 58-62; prof hist art, Oberlin Col, 62-72; prof & chmn art dept, Duke Univ, 78- *Mem:* Col Art Asn (secy, 67, vpres, 71); Am Asn Mus; Asn Art Mus Dir; Instituto per la Storia dell'arte lombarda; Am Fedn Arts. *Res:* 15th century Italian art, with emphasis on painting and theoretical writings. *Publ:* Auth, L B Alberti, on painting, 55 & 67; auth, Filarete's treatise on architecture, 65. *Mailing Add:* Dept of Art Duke Univ Durham NC 27708

SPERAKIS, NICHOLAS GEORGE
PAINTER, PRINTMAKER
b New York, NY, June 8, 43. *Study:* Pratt Inst, 60; Nat Acad Design Sch Fine Art, New York; Art Students League, 63; Pratt Graphic Art Ctr. *Work:* Brooklyn Mus, Mus Mod Art, New York; Philadelphia Mus Art; Chrysler Mus Permanent Collection, Provincetown, Mass; Midwest Mus Am Art, Ind; Exeter Acad, Conn; and others. *Exhib:* Brooklyn Mus Biennials, 64, 66 & 70; Ann Print Exhib, Honolulu Acad Fine Arts, Hawaii, 71; Reading & Bucks Co Collect, Reading Mus Art, Pa, 77; Friends of Corcoran, Corcoran Gallery Art, 81; Ann Acquisition Exhib, Midwest Mus Am Art, Elkart, Ind, 81; one-man exhibs, Washington Irving Gallery, New York, 82, Galerie Taub, Philadelphia, 82-83, Arbitrage Gallery, New York, 83 & Retrospective of

Woodcuts, Museo Universitario Del Chopo, Mexico City, 84; and others. *Teaching:* Instr painting, New Sch Social Res, New York, 72-; teacher, Fashion Inst Technol, New York, 72- *Awards:* Lawrence & Hinda Rosenthal Fel, Am Acad Arts & Lett & Nat Inst Arts & Lett, 69; J S Guggenheim Mem Found Fel Graphics, 70; MacDowell Colony Summer Residency, 76. *Bibliog:* Robert Henkes (auth), The crucifixion as depicted by contemporary artists, Nazarine Col, 72; Barry Shwarts (auth), 20th Century Humanist Art, Praeger, 73; articles, Arts Mag, 75-78 & 80. *Mem:* Am Fedn Modern Painters & Sculptors; Rhino Horn Orgn Humanist Art. *Dealer:* Paul Kessler Gallery 108 Commercial St Provincetown MA 02657. *Mailing Add:* 245 W 29th St 12A New York NY 10001

SPERO, NANCY
PAINTER, COLLAGE ARTIST

b Cleveland, Ohio, Aug, 24, 26. *Study:* Art Inst Chicago, BFA, 49; Atelier Andre L'Hote; Ecole des Beaux Arts, 49-50. *Work:* Mass Inst Technol; Judson Mem Church, New York; First Nat Bank, Chicago; Ramapo Col, NJ. *Exhib:* Words & Images, Philadelphia Col Art, 79; Art of Conscience: The Art of the Last Decade, Wright State Univ, 80; Issue Social Strategies by Women Artists, Inst Contemp Art, London, 80; Crimes of Compassion, Chrysler Mus, Norfolk, Va, 81; Art & Ecological Issues, Hunter Col, New York, 81; other exhibs & one-woman shows. *Teaching:* Vis artist, State Univ New York Col Purchase, 81. *Awards:* NY State Coun for the Arts Creative Artists Pub Serv Prog fel, 76-77; Nat Endowment for Arts grant, 77-78. *Bibliog:* Donald B Kuspit (auth), Spero's Apocalypse, Artforum, Apr,80; Peter Schjeldahl (auth), Opposites attract, Village Voice, 4/15/81; Lucy Lippard (auth), Nancy Speros's 30 years ward, Village Voice, 4/19/83. *Media:* Collage on Paper. *Publ:* Auth, The Whitney Museum and women, Art Gallery Mag, 1/71; contribr, Women's speakout, NY Element, 2-3/72; co-ed, Rip-off file, Ad Hoc Comt Women Artists, 73; contribr, Art: A woman's sensibility, Calif Inst Fine Arts, 75; auth, Ende, women's studies, Gordon & Breach Sci Publ Ltd, Great Britain, Vol 6, 78. *Dealer:* AIR Gallery 63 Crosby St New York NY 10012; Willard Gallery 29 E 72nd St New York NY 10021. *Mailing Add:* 530 La Guardia Pl New York NY 10012

SPERRY, ROBERT
CERAMIST, FILMMAKER

b Bushnell, Ill, Mar 12, 27. *Study:* Univ Sask, BA, 50; Art Inst Chicago, BFA, 54; Univ Wash, MFA, 55. *Work:* Smithsonian Inst; Everson Art Mus, Syracuse; Lannon Found, Palm Springs, Fla; Johnson Wax Collection; and others. *Exhib:* Ceramic Nat, Syracuse, 54-64; Young Americans, New York, 55-56; Int Ceramic Exhib, Ostend, Belg, 59; Third Int Exhib Contemp Ceramics, Prague, 62; Am Studio Potter, Victoria & Albert Mus, Eng, 66. *Teaching:* Prof ceramics, Univ Wash, 55- *Awards:* Tiffany Grant, 57; Ctr Asian Arts Award, 63; Japan Soc Award, 66. *Bibliog:* Painterly ceramic exploration, Artweek, 10/31/81. *Media:* Clay. *Publ:* Producer, The Village Potters of Onda (film), 66; producer, Profiles Cast Long Shadows (film), 68. *Mailing Add:* 1404 E Lynn Seattle WA 98112

SPEYER, A JAMES
CURATOR, ARCHITECT

b Pittsburgh, Pa. *Study:* Carnegie Inst Technol, BS; Chelsea Polytechnique, London, Eng; Sorbonne; Ill Inst Technol, with Mies van der Rohe, MA. *Pos:* Pvt architect, 46-57; Chicago corresp, Art News Mag, 55-57; cur contemp art, Art Inst Chicago, 61- *Teaching:* Prof advan archit, Ill Inst Technol, 46-61; vis prof archit, Nat Univ Athens, 57-60; instr mod art, Ford Found Sem, Art Inst Chicago, currently. *Mailing Add:* Art Inst Chicago Michigan Ave & Adams St Chicago IL 60603

SPICER, JEAN (DORIS) UHL
PAINTER, INSTRUCTOR

b Philadelphia, Pa, Nov 5, 35. *Study:* Philadelphia Col Art, dipl, 57; also with Domenic DiStefano, 71. *Work:* Widner Col, Chester, Philadelphia; Fred Clark Mus, Bucks Co, Pa. *Comn:* Exhibitor/Flower Show, Philadelphia, 80; paintings, Havertown Sch Dist, Pa, 83. *Exhib:* Philadelphia Mus Art, 73; Bicentennial Cult Exchange Show, Wales, Gr Brit, 76; Art Alliance, Philadelphia, 77; Fidelity Bank, Philadelphia, 77 & 79; Salmagundi Club, New York, 79; Artists Equity Asn, traveling, Philadelphia, 80. *Teaching:* Instr, Lower Merion Sr High Sch, Philadelphia, 75-; instr, Studio II Art Gallery, Radnor, Pa, 78-80; instr, Creutzberg Art Ctr, Radnor, Pa, 78- *Awards:* Silver Medal, Art Dirs Club, 82; Gold Medal, Rittenhouse Sq, 83. *Bibliog:* Sally Kistler (auth), Local artist joins Rittenhouse Show, News Delaware Co, 76; Gen Tully (auth), Art news, Suburban & Wayne Times, 77; Joseph Dempsey (auth), Dynamic duo, Living Mag, 78. *Mem:* Am Watercolor Soc; Philadelphia Watercolor Club; Artists Equity Asn; assoc Am Watercolor Soc. *Media:* Watercolor. *Mailing Add:* No 11 Tenby Rd Havertown PA 19083

SPICKETT, RONALD JOHN, SR
PAINTER, INSTRUCTOR

b Regina, Sask, Apr 11, 26. *Study:* Alta Col Art, Calgary, dipl; Ont Col Art, Toronto; Inst Allende Mex, scholar, 55. *Work:* Nat Gallery Ottawa; Dept External Affairs, Can Govt; London Art Gallery, Ont; Art Gallery Toronto; Edmonton Art Gallery; plus others. *Comn:* Sculpture, Med Arts Bldg, Calgary, 60; sculpture, Bank of Montreal, Edmonton, 62; mural painting, Bowlen Bldg, Govt Alta, Calgary, 68-69. *Exhib:* Environment, Calgary, 61-77; Nat Gallery Can Biennial; Mem Univ Gallery, Nfld, 70; Banff Festival Arts, Alta, 71; Alt Art Found Japan tour, 79 & Paris, photos, 79. *Teaching:* Instr painting & drawing, Univ Calgary, 69- *Awards:* Can Coun Award, Govt Can, 63, 69 & 76. *Bibliog:* Articles in Can Art & 300 Yrs of Can Art. *Mem:* Royal Can Acad Art. *Media:* Oil. *Mailing Add:* c/o April Rain 3427 Elbow Dr Calgary AB T2S 2J5 Canada

SPIEGEL, SAM
COLLECTOR

b Austria, Nov 11, 04. *Study:* Univ Vienna. *Mem:* Art Collectors Club. *Collection:* Modern impressionist art. *Mailing Add:* 711 Fifth Ave New York NY 10022

SPIEGELMAN, LON HOWARD
PAINTER, ASSEMBLAGE ARTIST

b Los Angeles, Calif, Nov 25, 41. *Study:* San Jose State Univ, BA, 65. *Work:* Univ Md, Catorsville; Gallery Laraviney, Paris, France; Galleria D'Arte Nuova 13, Alessandra, Italy; Univ Sidney, Australia; Syracuse Univ, NY. *Exhib:* Omaha Flow Systems, Joslyn Art Mus, Omaha, Nebr, 73; 16th Ann Art Unlimited, Downey Mus Art, Calif, 74; Mial Art Archive Wein, Univ Wein, Austria, 78; First Int New Dada, Univ Lund, Sweden, 79; Poste-Restant Show, Liverpool Acad Arts, England, 79; Nuove Cartoline, Mus del Folklore, Rome, Italy, 80. *Teaching:* Instr phototype, Santa Monica Col, Calif, 78-81; instr mail art, Otis Art Inst, Los Angeles, 80-81 & Los Angeles Co Art Mus, Calif, 81. *Awards:* First Place, Westwood Art Asn, 73, Los Angeles Art Asn, 76 & Civic Fine Arts Asn, 80. *Bibliog:* Nancy Howell-Kochler (auth), Photo Art Processes, Davis Publ, 80; Randy Hardson (auth), SWAK, Workman Publ, 81; Linda Burnham (auth), High performance, Astro Arts, 81. *Media:* Mixed. *Publ:* Auth, The Fence is Always Browner on the Other Side, 70; The Sayings of Poor Lon, 75, Lee's Alphabet, 78 & Penelope, 78, pvt publ; contribr, Umbrella, Astro Arts, 80-81. *Mailing Add:* 1556 Elevado St Los Angeles CA 90026

SPIER, PETER EDWARD
ILLUSTRATOR, WRITER

b Amsterdam, Neth, June 6, 27; nat US. *Study:* Ryks Acad Voor Beeldende Kunsten, Amsterdam, 45-47. *Pos:* Jr ed, Elsevier's Weekly, Amsterdam, 50-51 & Elsevier Publ Co, Houston, 52; free-lance auth & illusr, New York, 52-; speaker & lectr, schs & libr. *Awards:* Caldecott Medal, 78; Christopher Award, 70 & 78; NY Times Award, 77. *Publ:* Auth & illusr, Noah's Ark, 77, Oh, Were They Ever Happy!, 78, Bored, Nothing to Do, 78, The Legend of New Amsterdam, 79 & People, 80; illusr, over 150 bks; contribr illus, many nat mags. *Mailing Add:* Wardencliff Rd Shoreham NY 11786

SPIKE, JOHN THOMAS
HISTORIAN, CRITIC

b New York, NY, Nov 8, 51. *Study:* Wesleyan Univ, Conn, BA, 73; Harvard Univ, AM, 74, PhD, 79. *Collections Arranged:* Five by Five: Selections from the Permanent Collection, Solomon R Guggenheim Mus, New York, 73; Postwar Paintings: From the Solomon R Guggenheim Mus, Regional Arts Ctr, Danville, Ky, 73-74; Prints and Drawings in Italy Circa 1600, Fogg Art Mus, Harvard Univ, 74; Italian Baroque Paintings from New York Private Collections (auth, catalog), Art Mus, Princeton Univ, 80; Italian Still Life Paintings from Three Centuries Traveling Exhib (auth, catalog), 83. *Pos:* New York correspondent, Burlington Mag, London, Eng, 78-; guest cur, Art Mus, Princeton Univ, 79-80; Nat Acad Design, 81-82; Ringling Mus Art, 82-85; Kimbell Art Mus, 83-86. *Mem:* Int Asn Art Critics; Col Art Asn; Touring Club Italiano; Drawing Soc. *Res:* Italian Renaissance and Baroque; paintings by Mattia Preti; still life paintings. *Publ:* Auth, Mattia Preti's passage to Malta, Burlington Mag, 78; auth, Documents for the Chapel of France, Storia dell Arte, 79; auth, Mattia Preti, the Feast of Absalom, Nat Gallery Can, Ann Bull, 79; ed, The Illustrated Bartsch, Vol XIX, Parts 1-3, Abaris Books, 82. *Mailing Add:* 85 East End Ave New York NY 10028

SPINK, FRANK HENRY, JR
WRITER, PAINTER

b Chicago, Ill, Sept 23, 35. *Study:* Univ Ill, Urbana, BArch, 58; Univ Wash, MUP, 64. *Work:* Chung Cheng Art Gallery, St John's Univ, Jamaica, NY. *Exhib:* Jack London Square, Oakland, Calif, 65; Fremont Fall Art Fair, Calif, 66; Soc Western Artists, DeYoung Mus, San Francisco, 67; Palace Fine Arts Dedication Festival, San Francisco, 67; 12th, 13th, 14th & 15th Ann Sumie Soc, New York, 75, 76, 77 & 78. *Pos:* dir of publ, Urban Land Inst, 72. *Awards:* Summer Sketch Prize, Univ Ill, 55. *Mem:* Sumee Soc Am; Fremont Art Asn (pres, 66-67). *Res:* Adaptive reuse of existing building for the National Trust for Historic Preservation. *Publ:* Ed, Community Builders Handbook Series, 75; contribr, Storm Water Management-Objectives, Principles & Design Considerations, 73; contribr, Shopping Center Development Handbook, 77; contribr, Residential Development Handbook, 78; contribr, Downtown Develop Handbook, 80. *Mailing Add:* 5158 Piedmont Pl Annandale VA 22003

SPINK, WALTER M
EDUCATOR, ADMINISTRATOR

b Worcester, Mass, Feb 16, 28. *Study:* Amherst Col, BA(summa cum laude), 49; Harvard Univ, MA(art hist), 50, PhD, 54; Fulbright grant, Dept Anthrop, Indian Mus, Calcutta 52-53. *Pos:* Cur, Brandeis Univ Art Collection, 56-61, acting chmn, Dept Fine Art, 59-60; dir, Asian Art Arch, Univ Mich, Ann Arbor, 62; dir, Photog Exped to India, 64-68. *Teaching:* Instr, Dept Fine Arts, Brandeis Univ, 56-61, assoc prof, 61-68; vis lectr, Dept Art, Brown Univ, 60; from assoc prof to prof art histd, Univ Mich, Ann Arbor, formerly; vis lectr, Dept S Asian Studies, Univ Chicago, summer 72. *Mem:* Am Inst Indian Studies (trustee, 62-65 & 72-73); Asn Asian Studies; Col Art Asn; Am Comt S Asian Art (pres, 72-76, dir color slide proj, 74-). *Publ:* Auth, Ajanta to Ellora, 67, Krishnamandala, 71, Ctr & Southeast Asian Studies, Univ Mich; auth, The Axis of Eros, Schocken, 73 & Penguin, 75; auth, Jogeswari, J Indian Soc of Oriental Art, 77; auth, The Great Cave at Elephanta, with a study of sources, In: The Gupta Period, 77. *Mailing Add:* Dept Art Hist Tappan Hall Univ Mich Ann Arbor MI 48104

SPINOSA, GARY PAUL
SCULPTOR

b Memphis, Tenn, Dec, 26, 47. *Study:* Yale Univ Summer Sch Art & Music, 70; Cleveland Inst Art, BFA(Agnes Gund Mem Traveling Scholar), 72. *Work:* Southern Alleghenies Mus Art, Pa; Cleveland Art Asn, Ohio; Butler Inst Am Art. *Comn:* Public sculpture, Ohio Arts Coun, 78. *Exhib:* May Show, Cleveland Mus Art, 71-82; Eight State Ann, Speed Mus Art, Louisville, 74; Butler Inst Am Art, 74-75; European Triannual Sculpture Exhib, Paris, 78; one-man shows, Kent State Univ, 80, Ashland Col, 81 & Sandusky Cult Ctr, 82. *Awards:* Fel Grant, Ohio Arts Coun, 79; First Place for Sculpture, May Show, Cleveland Mus Art, 81. *Media:* Clay. *Dealer:* Dodd Co 1025 Huron Rd Cleveland OH 44115. *Mailing Add:* RD 1 Venango PA 16440

SPINSKI, VICTOR
SCULPTOR, EDUCATOR

b Newton, Kans, Oct 10, 40. *Study:* Kans State Teachers Col, BSE, 63; Ind Univ, Bloomington, MFA, 67. *Work:* State Univ NY Potsdam; Haystack Mountain Sch Crafts, Deer Isle, Maine; Elmira Col, NY; Del Art Mus, Wilmington. *Exhib:* Coffee, Tea & Other Cups, Mus Contemp Crafts, New York, 71; Int Exhib Ceramics, Victoria & Albert Mus, London, Eng, 72; Soup Tureens, Campbell Mus, Camden, NJ, 76; Century of Ceramics in US, Everson Mus Art, Syracuse, NY, 79; Clay Attitudes, Queen's Mus, New York; 11th Regional Sculpture Exhib, Mus Philadelphia Civic Ctr, Pa; Ten East Coast Potters, Brooklyn Mus Art Sch, NY; Ind Crafts, Herron Mus Art, Indianapolis. *Teaching:* Grad teaching asst, Ind Univ, 67; prof ceramics, Univ Del, 67-; summer fac, Haystack Mountain Sch Crafts, 68 & 70, Brooklyn Mus Art Sch, 70 & Council Grove Craft Sch, Missoula, Mont, 74-76. *Bibliog:* Judith Schwartz (auth), Victor Spinski, Currant, 76; Lisa Hammel (auth), She wants her gallery to shake people up--and it does, New York Times, 76; Clark & Hughto (auth), Century of Ceramics in the United States, E P Dutton, 79. *Mem:* Nat Coun Ceramic Arts; Am Crafts Coun; Int Acad Ceramics. *Media:* Ceramics; Photography. *Publ:* Auth, Ceramic Photosilkscreening, Nat Coun Educ Ceramic Arts, 70. *Dealer:* Theo Portnoy Gallery 56 W 57th St New York NY 10019. *Mailing Add:* 340 W Chesnut Hill Rd Newark DE 19713

SPITZ, BARBARA S
PRINTMAKER

b Chicago, Ill, Jan 8, 26. *Study:* Art Inst Chicago; RI Sch Design; Brown Univ, AB. *Work:* Art Inst Chicago; Philadelphia Mus Art; Smart Gallery, Univ Chicago; De Cordova Mus, Lincoln, Mass; Los Angeles Co Mus, Calif. *Comn:* First Ill Print Comn Prog, 73. *Exhib:* Art Inst Chicago 71st Ann, 68; Soc Am Graphic Artists Ann, Kennedy Galleries, New York, 71 & 79; Smithsonian Traveling Exhibs, 73 & 74; Libr Cong & Nat Collection Fine Arts, 73 & 74; Tokyo Cent Mus, 77; Nat Acad Design, New York, 77; Pratt Graphic Ctr, New York, 77. *Awards:* Childe Hassam Purchase Award, Am Acad of Arts & Lett, 73; First Prize, 77 & Purchase Award, 78, Ill Regional Print Show; Stuart M Egnal Prize, Int Biennial Print Exhib, Print Club, Philadelphia, 77. *Bibliog:* Article, Printmaker in Illinois, Ill Educ Asn, 72, Illinois Printmakers I Proj, Ill Arts Coun, 74 & others. *Mem:* Artist Equity Asn; Chicago Soc Artists; Los Angeles Printmaking Soc; Boston Printmakers; Soc Am Graphic Artists. *Media:* Intaglio. *Mailing Add:* 1106 Somerset Lane Newport Beach CA 92660

SPOERER, DALE RAYMOND
COLLECTOR, EDUCATOR

b Monterey Park, Calif, Nov 23, 29. *Study:* Bakersfield Col, AA, 46; San Francisco State Univ, BA, 55; Univ San Francisco, MA, 71. *Pos:* Exec bd, Eureka Col Arts Coun, Ill. *Teaching:* Prof, City Col San Francisco, 70- *Mem:* Mus Soc San Francisco; Graphic Arts Coun, Calif Palace Legion Honor. *Interests:* West coast artists; educational television art auction; collection development. *Collection:* Kip Stewart, Noal Betts, Dennis Argent, Yin Ling Miao Chan; Japanese brush masters (contemporary); ethnic Tapa prints of Western Samoa. *Mailing Add:* 16 Sussex St San Francisco CA 94131

SPOHN, FRANZ FREDERICK
SCULPTOR, PRINTMAKER

b Columbus, Ohio, June 6, 50. *Study:* Ohio State Univ, BFA, 73, MFA, 75. *Work:* Glenbow Mus, Calgary, Alta; Ohio State Univ. *Exhib:* Portrait of the Artist, Fendrick Gallery, Washington, DC, 81; Candy Collages, Ringhouse Gallery, Edmonton, Alta, 81; one-man show, Glenbow Mus, Calgary, Alta, 81; Collage & Assemblage Traveling Exhib, Miss Mus Art, Jackson, 81-83; Feast Your Eyes, Philadelphia Mus Art, 82; Material Illusions, Unlikely Materials, Taft Mus, Cincinnati, 83; and others. *Collections Arranged:* Eighteen Buys Twenty, Portico Gallery, Philadelphia, 83. *Bibliog:* Nancy Tousley (auth), Artist sweetens his biting satire, Calgary Herald, 2/12/81; Keith Morrison (auth), Realistic self portraits, New Art Examiner, 4/81; Jo Ann Lewis (auth), Artistic couples, Wash Post, 5/31/81. *Mem:* Col Art Asn; Print Club Philadelphia. *Media:* Mixed. *Dealer:* Marian Locks Gallery 1524 Walnut St Philadelphia PA 19107. *Mailing Add:* 915 E Passyunk Ave Philadelphia PA 19147

SPOHN, KATHRYN JO
PAINTER, EDUCATOR

b Ft Lee, Va, Oct 28, 50. *Study:* Ohio State Univ, BA, 73, BFA, 73, MFA, 75. *Work:* Rutgers Univ, Camden, NJ; Viterbo Col, La Crosse, Wis; Ohio State Univ, Columbus; Batelle Mem Inst, Columbus, Ohio. *Exhib:* Animals: Celebration & Communion, San Jose Mus Art, Calif, 81; Woman Artists in Philadelphia, Philadelphia Mus Art; Everhardt Mus Art, Scranton, Pa; Philadelphia Invitational Exhib, Southern Alleghenies Mus Art, Loretto, Pa. *Teaching:* Instr printmaking, Cleveland State Univ, 75-76; asst prof printmaking, Washington State Univ, 78-79 & Rutgers Univ, 79- *Bibliog:*

Joann Lewis (auth), Artistic couples, Washington Post, 5/31/80; Keith Morrison (auth), Realistic self portraits, New Art Examiner, 4/81; Wendy Slatkin (auth), Rutgers national 81, Arts Mag, 82. *Mem:* Col Art Asn; Print Club. *Media:* Acrylic, Oil. *Mailing Add:* Art Dept Rutgers Univ Camden NJ 08102

SPONENBURGH, MARK
HISTORIAN, SCULPTOR

b Cadillac, Mich, June 15, 16. *Study:* Cranbrook Acad Art, scholar, 40; Wayne Univ; Ecole Beaux-Arts, Paris, France; Univ London; Univ Cairo; Hon DFA, 70. *Work:* Detroit Inst Art; Portland Art Mus; Univ Ore; Mus Mod Art, Egypt; Pakistan; plus others. *Comn:* Architectural sculpture, MacGruder Veterinary Hosp, 80. *Exhib:* Pa Acad Fine Arts; Durand-Ruel & Paris Salon, France; Inst Fine Arts Cairo; Nat Gallery, Pakistan; 30 one-man exhibs, sculpture; plus others. *Pos:* Consult, Nat Col of Art, Pakistan, Moukhtar Mus, Cairo, Egypt & Marine Sci Ctr, Newport, Ore. *Teaching:* Assoc prof, Univ Ore, 46-56; vis prof, Royal Col Arts, 56-57; prof & dean, Nat Col Arts, Pakistan, 58-61; prof, Ore State Univ, 61-, chmn art dept, 82- *Awards:* Distinguished Lecturer, Phi Kappa Phi, 82; Fulbright Found fel, 51-53. *Mem:* Int Asn Egyptologists; Royal Soc Arts; Royal Soc Antiquaries; Inst Asn Art Historians; Am Res Ctr in Egypt. *Media:* Wood, Stone. *Res:* Stylistic Analogies in Coptic & Celtic; Sculpture of the Early Medieval Period. *Publ:* Contribr, Arts Quart, J Inst Egypte, Rev Caire, Near E Bull & J Near E Studies; Royal Soc Antiquaries. *Mailing Add:* Dept Art Ore State Univ Corvallis OR 97331

SPRAGUE, MARK ANDERSON
PAINTER, EDUCATOR

b Champaign, Ill, Jan 5, 20. *Study:* Univ Ill, BFA, 46, MFA, 49. *Work:* Ill State Univ Mus, Bloomington. *Comn:* Painting for Great Ideas of Western Man, Container Corp Am, Chicago, Ill. *Exhib:* Am Fedn Arts Circulating Exhib, Washington, DC, 49; Art Inst Chicago 60th Am Ann, 51; Western Art Ann, Denver, Colo, 51-52; Corcoran Gallery Art Biennial, Washington, DC, 51-53; Nat Acad Design Ann, New York, 58-62. *Teaching:* Prof art, Univ Ill, Champaign, 46- *Media:* Oil, Polymer. *Mailing Add:* 912 Devonshire Dr Champaign IL 61820

SPRAGUE, PAUL EDWARD
HISTORIAN, CONSULTANT

b Cumberland, Md, Feb 28, 33. *Study:* Rutgers Univ, BA, 54; Oberlin Col; Princeton Univ, MA, 63, PhD, 69. *Pos:* Consult, Hist Preserv Serv, 74- *Teaching:* Asst prof archit hist, Univ Notre Dame, 64-68; asst prof art hist, Univ Chicago, 68-74; assoc prof archit hist, Univ Wis, Milwaukee, 78- *Mem:* Soc Archit Hist (mem bd dirs, 73-75 & 82-); Victorian Soc Am (mem bd dirs, 75-81); Int Coun Monuments & Sites (mem bd dirs, 75-78); Asn Col Schs Archit; Midwest Art Hist Soc. *Res:* Louis Sullivan, Frank Lloyd Wright and their students and colleagues. *Publ:* Coauth, The Hasbrouck-Sprague Survey of Historic Architecture in Oak Park, Illinois, 74 & auth, Frank Lloyd Wright and the Prairie School in Oak Park, 76, Village Oak Park; auth, Drawings of Louis Sullivan, Princeton Univ Press, 79; auth, Origin of balloon framing, Soc Archit Historians J, 82; auth, Louis Sullivan, In: Macmillan Encyclopedia of Architecture, Free Press, 82. *Mailing Add:* 37835 Atkins Knoll Oconomowoc WI 53066

SPRANG, ELIZABETH (LEWIS)
PAINTER, LITHOGRAPHER

b Capitol View, Md. *Study:* Univ Calif, Los Angeles, 3 yrs; studied painting with F Tolles Chamberlain, lithography with Lynton Kistler & Richard Haines, Calif; Naropa Inst, Colo, studied American & Meso-American art & symbolism with Jose Arguelles & Tibetan thangka painting with Glen Eddy. *Exhib:* Los Angeles Co Mus Art, Los Angeles, 50; Libr Cong Ann Print Show, 52-55; Oakland Art Mus, Calif, 53; Calif State Fair, Sacramento, 53-55; Pa Acad of Fine Arts, 55; Northwest Printmakers Ann, Seattle Art Mus, 55; one-woman show, Heard Mus, Phoenix, Ariz, 66. *Mem:* Artists Equity Asn, Santa Fe Chap (treas, 73-74). *Media:* Mixed. *Publ:* Illusr, Conspicuous California Plants, San Pasqual Press, 38; auth & illusr, Art, beauty and country life in Utah, Dialogue Mag, 70; auth & illusr, Good-bye River, Mojave Books, 79. *Dealer:* Los Llanos Gallery of Contemp Art Santa Fe NM 87501 & Denver CO. *Mailing Add:* Rte 4 Box 16-B Santa Fe NM 87501

SPRINGER, LYNN ELISE
CURATOR

b San Diego, Calif, Apr 9, 43. *Study:* Washington Univ, BA(art hist), 65, museology, 67; Winterthur Mus/Univ Del, Summer Inst, 69; Attingham Park/Brit Nat Trust Summer Sch, Eng Country House, 70-71, 73 & 75. *Pos:* Asst cur decorative arts, St Louis Art Mus, 72-74, assoc cur Am & European decorative arts, 75-76, cur Am & European decorative arts, 77-81; cur European Decorative Arts, Art Inst Chicago, 81- *Mem:* Fel Am Friends of Attingham; Decorative Arts Chap, Soc of Archit Historians (pres, 79-81); Nat Trust for Hist Preserv; Victorian Soc in Am; Am Ceramic Circle; and others. *Publ:* Auth, A collection of Biblical pictures, Antiques, 72; auth, The Rediscovered work of William J Hinchey (catalog), 74, coauth, Currents of Expansion: Painting in the Midwest, 1820-1940 (catalog), 77 & St Louis Silversmiths, 80, St Louis Art Mus. *Mailing Add:* Art Inst Chicago Mich Ave at Adams St Chicago IL 60603

SPROAT, CHRISTOPHER TOWNSEND
SCULPTOR

b Boston, Mass, Sept 23, 45. *Study:* Skowhegan Sch Painting & Sculpture; Boston Univ; Boston Mus Sch Fine Arts; also with George Aarons. *Exhib:* One-man show, Inst Contemp Art, Boston, 70; Elements of Art, Mus Fine

Arts, Boston, 71-72 & Rohm/Sproat, 74; Whitney Mus Am Art Biennial, New York, 73; Hayden Gallery, Mass Inst of Technol, Cambridge, Mass; Marian Goodman Gallery, New York, 80; and other group & one-man shows. *Awards:* Mass Arts & Humanities Found Fel, 75 & 78; Nat Endowment for Arts Grant, 75-76 & 80-81; and others. *Bibliog:* Kenneth Baker (auth), Sproat & Samaras, Boston Rev Arts, 4/72; Carl Belz (auth), Deliberating with color, drawing with light, Art in Am, 5-6/72; and others. *Mem:* Inst Contemp Art. *Dealer:* Bette Stoler Gallery 13 White St New York NY 10013. *Mailing Add:* 7 Mercer St New York NY 10013

SPROUL, ANN STEPHENSON
PAINTER
b DeWitt, Mo, Aug 9, 07. *Study:* Cent Mo State Univ; also with William B Schimmel, Ariz, John Pike & Edgar Whitney, New York & John Pellew, Conn. *Work:* Pvt galleries in Chile, Switzerland, Czechoslovakia, England & Canada. *Comn:* Mural of Frontier Town, Silver Spur Saloon & Restaurant, Cave Creek, Ariz; Christmas card designs, Mr & Mrs Dow Patterson, Phoenix, 73-74 & Cave Creek Community Schs, 74; illus Christmas letter, Armstrong Congoleum, Cecil Armstrong, Carefree, Ariz, 74. *Exhib:* Plaza Art Fair, Kansas City, Mo, 63-69; Greater Kansas City Art Asn, Kansas City Mus, 64; Ararat Temple Beaux Arts, Ararat Temple Auditorium, Kansas City, 64; one-man show, Am Asn Univ Women, Sophian Plaza, Kansas City, 65; Discovery of Art Mag Exhib, Kansas City, 68. *Pos:* Owner & demonstr watercolor & brush tech, Washboard Watercolor Gallery, Frontier Town, Cave Creek, 72- *Teaching:* High Sch teacher art & art supvr, Carrollton Pub Schs, Mo, 59-69; teacher watercolor, Community Sch, Cave Creek, 74- *Awards:* First in Watercolor, Greater Kansas City Art Asn, 64 & Mo Div, Nat League Am Pen Women, 65; Publisher's Award, Discovery of Arts Mag, 68. *Bibliog:* Article in Ariz Desert Foothills, Mesa, Ariz, 75; Watercolor Techniques by Ann Sproul (film of tech demonstrations for schs), Outdoor Pictures, Anacortes, Wash, 75. *Mem:* Nat League Am Pen Women. *Media:* Watercolor, Pencil. *Publ:* Auth, The Art of Poster Making, Kappa Delta Pi Scroll, 28; illusr, Of Time & Space (poems), 74. *Dealer:* Grapevine Gallery Box 132 Oklahoma City OK 73101; Beach Front Gallery Box 1028 Cambria CA 93428. *Mailing Add:* 5924 East Carriage Dr PO Box 93 Cave Creek AZ 85331

SPROUT, FRANCIS
PAINTER, EDUCATOR
b Tucson, Ariz, Mar 5, 40. *Study:* Univ Ariz, BFA; Univ Calif, San Diego, MFA(Ford Found Fel). *Work:* Univ Calif Exten Off, La Jolla; Johnson Publ Co, Chicago; Johns-Manville Corp, Atlanta, Ga; Exeter Co, Denver; Mountain Bell, Denver; and others. *Comn:* Cover design, Jour Umoja, Univ Colo, Boulder, 75. *Exhib:* Los Angeles 1972: A Panorama of Black Artists, Los Angeles Co Mus Art, 72; Emerging Southern California Artists, Pollock Gallery, Art Mus, Southern Methodist Univ, Dallas, 72; 74th Western Ann, 73 & 2nd, 3rd, 5th & 6th All-Colo, 74-80, Denver Art Mus; Colo-Nebr Exchange, Joslyn Mus Art, Omaha, 73; Remnant Transpositions, Fine Arts Ctr, Univ Colo, Boulder, 79; East Meets West, Harriet Tubman Gallery, Boston, Mass, 81; and others. *Teaching:* Asst prof painting, Univ Denver, 72-75; instr Afro-Am art hist, Univ Colo, Boulder, 74-81; assoc prof painting, Metrop State Col, Denver, 81. *Awards:* African Inst Fel, Hamline Univ, summer 78. *Bibliog:* Rena Andrews (auth), The fine arts, Denver Post, 12/31/73; and others. *Mem:* Col Art Asn Am; and others. *Media:* Acrylic, Metal. *Mailing Add:* 1535 Platte St Denver CO 80202

SPRUCE, EVERETT FRANKLIN
PAINTER, PRINTMAKER
b Faulkner Co, Ark, Dec 25, 08. *Study:* Dallas Art Inst, 25-29; pvt study with Olin H Travis & Thomas M Stell. *Work:* Whitney Mus Am Art, Metrop Mus, New York; Dallas Mus Fine Arts, Tex; Walker Art Ctr, Minneapolis, Minn; and many others. *Exhib:* Carnegie Inst, Pittsburgh; Corcoran Gallery Art, Washington, DC; Brussels, Belg & Bordhighera, Italy; Ford Found Retrospective, circulated nationally by Am Fedn Arts; Pan-Am Union, Washington, DC; Dallas Mus Fine Arts; one-man show, Paintings & Drawings, 1950-1979, Huntington Gallery, Univ Tex, Austin, 79; and others. *Pos:* Gallery asst, Dallas Mus Fine Arts, 31-34, registrar, 35, asst dir, 35-40. *Teaching:* Instr, Dallas Mus Sch, 36-40; instr art, Univ Tex, Austin, 40-44, asst prof, 44-47, chmn dept art, 48-50, prof art & mem grad fac, 54-74, emer prof, 75- *Awards:* Bordighera, Italy, 54; D D Feldman Award, Tex State Fair, 55; Dallas Mus Fine Arts Prize, 55; and others. *Bibliog:* Portfolio of Paintings, Vol I, In: Blaffer Series, Univ Tex. *Mailing Add:* 15 Peak Rd Austin TX 78746

SPRUYT, E LEE
PAINTER, PRINTMAKER
b Lisbon, Port, Feb 10, 31; US citizen. *Study:* Apprentice (at 14) to Pachita Crespi; Pratt Inst; Art Students League; Carnegie Inst Technol, three yrs, scholar; Ateneum Sch, Finland; study with Roger Anliker, Robert Rabinowitz & Samuel Rosenberg. *Comn:* Three pen & ink drawings, Metrop Opera Bd Rm, 73; pen & ink drawings, Opera News Yearbk for 74-75 season, 74; 250 edition signed prints, Metrop Opera 90th Anniversary Poster, 75; poster/drawings for Carnegie Hall, Brooklyn Acad Music, 80-82; opera poster, New York City Opera, 81; and others. *Exhib:* Traveling Exhib, Mus Performing Arts, Lincoln Ctr, 72-73; Tribute to Rudolph Bing, Robert Tobin Foundation, Marion Koogler McNay Art Inst, San Antonio, Tex, 73; John F Kennedy Ctr Performing Arts, Texico Grant, Washington, DC, 74; Art in Embassies Prog, Washington, DC, with work in Bolivia, Uruguay, Jordan, Paris, Quebec, Equador, Belgium & State Dept, Washington, DC; and others. *Teaching:* Instr drawing, Carnegie-Mellon Univ; instr art, Boys Club, RI. *Bibliog:* Articles, NY Times, 10/72; Metrop Opera Prog, 11/72 & Am Artist, 9/73. *Media:* Mixed. *Mailing Add:* 419 E 91st St New York NY 10028

SPURGEON, SARAH (EDNA M)
PAINTER, EDUCATOR
b Harlan, Iowa, Oct 30, 03. *Study:* Univ Iowa, BA & MA; Harvard Univ; Grand Cent Sch Art; also with Grant Wood, Paul Sachs & others. *Work:* Iowa Mem Union, Iowa City; Seattle Art Mus, Wash; Ginkgo Mus, Vantage, Wash; Henry Gallery, Univ Wash, Seattle. *Comn:* Mural, Univ Experimental Sch, Iowa City. *Exhib:* Kansas City Art Inst; Joslyn Mus; Des Moines Art Salon; Seattle Art Mus; Gumps, San Francisco; and others. *Teaching:* From assoc prof to prof art, Cent Wash Univ, 39-71, emer prof, 71- *Awards:* Carnegie Fel, 29-30; Prizes, Iowa Art Salon, 30 & 31; Prizes, Univ Iowa, 31; Sarah Spurgeon Art Gallery, Randal Art Bldg, Cent Wash Univ, dedicated 77. *Mem:* Nat Educ Asn; Am Asn Univ Prof; Wash Educ Asn; Women Painters Wash. *Publ:* Contribr, Design & Childhood Educ Mag. *Mailing Add:* 204 E Ninth St Ellensburg WA 98926

SPURGIN, JOHN EDWIN
ADMINISTRATOR, PAINTER
b Indianapolis, Ind, Dec 17, 32. *Study:* Ind State Univ, BS & MA; Mich State Univ, with Angelo Ippolito; Univ Cincinnati, with Robert Knipschild, MFA. *Work:* Mich Educ Asn, East Lansing; Hubbard Milling Co, Mankato, Minn; Bemidji State Univ, Minn; Southwest State Univ, Marshall, Minn; Univ Cincinnati, Ohio. *Exhib:* Biennial of Painting & Sculpture, Walker Art Ctr, Minneapolis, 66; Okla Art Ctr, Oklahoma City, 67; Minn Mus, St Paul, 70; Miami Univ, Oxford, Ohio, 72; Northeast La Univ, Monroe, 74; one-man shows, Univ Wis, Marshfield, 75, Southwest State Univ, Marshall, 77 & Art Ctr Minn, 83; Pillsbury Competitive Exhib, Minneapolis, 81; and others. *Collections Arranged:* American National Bank Collection Exhibition, St Paul, Minn, 74; Mankato Clinic, Ltd, Minn, 81. *Pos:* Gallery dir, Gallery Five Hundred, Fine Arts, Inc, Mankato, 69-72 & Nichols Gallery, Mankato State Univ, 73-75. *Teaching:* Instr art educ, Flint Inst Art, Mich, 60-64; prof design, painting & printmaking, Mankato State Univ, 65-, chmn art dept, 75- *Awards:* First Prize Painting, Rochester Area Artists, Rochester Art Ctr, Minn, 66; Best-in-Show, Southern Minn Art Exhib, Mankato Free Press, 67 & 72; Minn State Individual Artists Grant, 77-78. *Media:* Mixed Media. *Mailing Add:* 2629 E Main St Mankato MN 56001

SPURLING, NORINE M
GRAPHIC ARTIST, EDUCATOR
b Bermuda Islands, Jan 16, 30. *Study:* Moore Col Art, Philadelphia; Pa Acad Fine Art, Philadelphia; State Univ NY, Buffalo, MFA, 75. *Work:* Mem Art Gallery, Rochester, NY; Charles Rand Penney Upstate NY Collection, Lockport; Hyatt Regency Hotel, Buffalo, NY. *Exhib:* West '80 Art & the Law, Minn Mus Art, St Paul, 80; solo exhibs, Deland Mus, Fla, 77, Shelia Nussbaum Gallery, Millburn, NJ, 83 & Access to the Arts, Dunkirk, NY, 84; Printed by Women, Port History Mus, Philadelphia, 83; Nat Drawing, Trenton, NJ, 83; Col Mainland Nat Exhib, Texas City, 83; 27th Nat Print Exhib, Clinton, NJ, 83; plus many others. *Pos:* Exhib coordr, AAO Gallery, Buffalo, 76; gallery dir, AC Gallery, Buffalo, 77-79. *Teaching:* Instr drawing, Black Mountain Col II & State Univ at Buffalo, NY, 77- *Bibliog:* Bryce Kanbara (auth), Norine Spurling: Drawings, the Blue Hush, Hamilton Artists Inc, 82. *Mem:* Buffalo Soc Artists (pres, 75-76); Col Art Asn; Womens Caucus Art. *Media:* Pastel, Charcoal. *Publ:* Illusr, Lightworks: A Handbook of Photographic Alternatives by J Arnow, Van Nostrand Reinhold, 80; illusr, Western NY Women Artists Calendar, 83; ed, Western NY Artists (catalog), AAO Gallery, 83. *Dealer:* Jerel Gallery 4555 Main St Williamsville NY 14211; Shelia Nussbaum Gallery 358 Millburn Ave Millburn NJ 07041. *Mailing Add:* 163 Millbrook Dr Williamsville NY 14221

SPURLOCK, WILLIAM HENRY, II
HISTORIAN, CRITIC
b Chicago, Ill, Oct 23, 45. *Study:* Trinity Univ, San Antonio, Tex, BA; Univ NMex, Albuquerque, MA; Union Grad Sch, PhD. *Collections Arranged:* Vito Acconci (auth, catalog), Wright State Univ Art Gallery, 76; Barry Le Va (auth, catalog), Dennis Oppenheim, 77; Larry Bell (auth, catalog), Siah Armajani, 76; Photo-Realist Photography in Calif (auth, catalog), Santa Barbara Mus Art, 80; Herbert Bayer: Sited Sculpture and the Environment (auth, catalog), Roland Reiss, Sam Richardson, 81; and others. *Pos:* From asst to fine art consult, Atlantic Richfield Co, Los Angeles, 79-; cur exhibs & contemp art, Santa Barbara Mus Art, 78-81. *Teaching:* Asst dir educ in art hist & admin, Des Moines Art Ctr, Iowa, 72-74; asst prof arts admin & art hist, Wright State Univ, Dayton, Ohio, 74-78. *Mem:* Int Asn Art Critics; Col Art Asn; Am Asn Mus; Int Coun Mus; Am Fedn Arts. *Res:* Modern and contemporary art forms; environmental arts; criticism & theory. *Publ:* Auth, Social & Ecological Issues in Contemporary Art, National Arts Guide, 3-4/80; auth, Cecile Abish, 78; auth, Richard Fisher, Current Charts: Chosen Lands, 78; auth, Federal Art Patronage in the State of New Mexico: 1933-1943 (catalog), Mus NMex, 78; auth, Dialogue/Discourse/Research: Eleanor Antin, Helen and Newton Harrison, Fred Lonidier, Barbara Strasen, Santa Barbara Mus Art, 79; auth, numerous articles & essays on contemp art & artists. *Mailing Add:* Santa Barbara Mus Art 1130 State St Santa Barbara CA 93101

SQUADRA, JOHN
PAINTER, COLLAGE ARTIST
b New York, NY, June 25, 32. *Study:* RI Sch Design, BFA, 53. *Work:* San Francisco Mus Mod Art. *Exhib:* Artist's Showcase, Mus of Art, Bridgeport, Conn, 78; one-man shows, Nonson Gallery, Soho, NY, 79, Miner's Gallery, Boulder, Colo, 79 & Gallery-Musee des Duncan, Paris, 80; Vered Int Art Gallery, East Hampton, New York, 80; People 81, Hudson River Mus, Yonkers, New York. *Teaching:* Teacher oils, acrylics, watercolor, Rowayton Arts Ctr, Conn, 74- *Awards:* Top Ten, Irene Leache Mem, Norfolk Mus, Va,

55; Third Prize, Darien Art Show, 77; First Prize, Rowayton Arts Ctr, 78. *Bibliog:* Article, Le Nouveau J, Paris, 11/80; article, Playboy Mag, 2/81; Hudson River Museum Show, New York Times, 10/81; rev, Playboy Mag, 2/81; rev, Hudson River Mus Show, 10/81; and others. *Media:* Oil, Acrylic. *Publ:* Illusr, Songs From Silences, 76; auth & illusr, Dr Miraculous, 81. *Dealer:* Yolanda Kelly Lake Point Tower Suite 809 505 Lake Shore Dr Chicago IL 60611. *Mailing Add:* 151 Highland Ave Rowayton CT 06853

SQUIER, JACK LESLIE
SCULPTOR, EDUCATOR
b Feb 27, 27; US citizen. *Study:* Ind Univ, BS, 50; Cornell Univ, MFA, 52. *Work:* Mus Mod Art & Whitney Mus Am Art, New York; Hirshhorn Mus, Washington, DC; Everson Mus, Syracuse, NY; Johnson Mus, Cornell Univ; Stanford Univ Mus. *Comn:* Disc (fiber glass & aluminum leaf sculpture), Ithaca Col, 68. *Exhib:* Carnegie Int, Pittsburgh; Brussels World's Fair; Recent Sculpture USA, Mus Mod Art; 30 Americans Under 35, Whitney Mus Am Art, 57; Hirshhorn Mus, Washington, DC; Mus Fine Arts, Boston; Art Inst Chicago; Denver Art Mus; Abright-Knox Art Gallery, Buffalo, NY. *Teaching:* Prof sculpture, Cornell Univ, 58- *Bibliog:* William Lipke (auth), Disc, by Jack Squier, Cornell Univ, 68. *Mem:* Int Asn Art (deputy vpres, 72-); Sculptors Guild. *Media:* Resin, Fiberglass. *Mailing Add:* 211 Berkshire Rd Ithaca NY 14850

SQUIRES, GERALD LEOPOLD
PAINTER, EDUCATOR
b Nfld, Can, Nov 17, 37. *Study:* Danforth Tech, Toronto; Ont Col Art, Toronto; mainly self-taught. *Work:* Breakwater Bk Publ Co, Nfld; Montreal Mus Fine Arts; Mem Univ Nfld; Univ Toronto; Saidye & Samuel Bronfman Collection, Montreal. *Comn:* Can Permanent Trust, St John's, Nfld, 72; Dept Pub Works, Paradise, Nfld, 77; painting, comn by Can Cath Conf Asn for New Can Sunday Mass Bk, Ottawa, 76; The Matthew (aluminum sculpture), Bonavista High Sch, Nfld, 78; Ferryland Head (acrylic mural), Village Shopping Ctr, St John's, Nfld, 78. *Exhib:* Black Expo, 75 & Boatman Series (traveling exhib), 76-78, Mem Univ Art Gallery; 50 Can Drawings (traveling exhib), 77; Other Realities, the Legacy of Surrealism in Can Art, Agnes Etherington Art Centre, Kingston, Ont, 78; Can House, London, Eng, Paris, France & Brussels, Belg, 79; one-man shows, Portraits, Mem Univ Nfld Art Gallery & other arts & cult ctrs in Nfld, 78 & Ferryland Downs, traveling Can, 79-81. plus others. *Teaching:* Instr art, Mem Univ Nfld, 70-73, exten artist in residence, 72. *Awards:* First & Second Prize, Great Northern AUK Workshop Conceptual Partic Painting & Sculpture, Nfld Arts & Lett Competition, 72. *Bibliog:* Kat Kritzweiser (auth), From a modern squires an old monk's dream, Globe & Mail Toronto; Robert Percival (auth), Sculpture Review, Art Mag, 75; Peter Bell (auth), The visual arts in Newfoundland, Arts Atlantic, Vol 1 (fall, 77). *Mem:* Great Northern AUK Workshop; founding mem Oshawa Art Gallery. *Media:* Acrylic, Steel. *Dealer:* The Gallery 284 Duckworth St St John's NF A1C 1H3 Can; Mem Univ Nfld Art Gallery Elizabeth Ave St John's NF A1C 5S7 Can. *Mailing Add:* Ferryland NF A0A 2H0 Canada

SQUIRES, NORMA-JEAN
SCULPTOR, PAINTER
b Toronto, Ont; US citizen. *Study:* Art Students League; Cooper Univ, BFA, 61; also spec studies with James Rosati; Calif State Univ, Northridge, scholar. *Work:* Sterling Forest Gardens, Long Island, NY; Galeria Vandres, Madrid, Spain; Warner Brothers, Burbank, Calif; Security Pacific Bank, Calif. *Exhib:* Recent Trends in American Art, Westmoreland Co Mus Art, Greensburg, Pa, 69; 4x4 plus 4x8, Newport Harbor Mus, 75; Many Arts of Sci, Calif Inst of Technol, Pasadena, 76; Current Media Art, Collector's Choice Gallery, Laguna Beach, Calif, 79; one-woman show, Brand Libr Art Galleries, Glendale, Calif, 79; and many others. *Teaching:* Instr sculpture, Lucinda Art Sch, Tenafly, NJ, 67-69. *Awards:* Sarah Cooper Hewitt Award Advan Sci & Art, Cooper Union, 61. *Bibliog:* Shirley Fischler (auth), article, Toronto Daily Star, 4/68; Burton Wasserman (auth), Modern Painting--The Movements, The Artists, Their Work, Davis Publ, 70. *Mem:* Women's Caucus Art; Artists Equity. *Media:* Mixed. *Publ:* Illusr, three children's bks, Addie Ripple Co, 78. *Dealer:* David Stuart Los Angeles CA. *Mailing Add:* 2764 Woodwardia Dr Los Angeles CA 90077

SRAGOW, ELLEN
GALLERY DIRECTOR
b New York, NY. *Study:* Hofstra Univ, BA, 64; New York Univ, MA, 66. *Pos:* Registrar & asst cur, New York Univ Art Collection, 67-71; dir, Prints on Prince St Gallery, 74-76; dir, Ellen Sragow Gallery, 76- *Specialty:* Contemporary prints, drawings, works on paper and paintings; American prints, drawings, paintings form the 1930's-early 1940's, including the WPA period. *Mailing Add:* c/o Ellen Sragow Gallery 80 Fifth Ave New York NY 10011

STACK, FRANK HUNTINGTON
PAINTER, PRINTMAKER
b Houston, Tex, Oct 31, 37. *Study:* Univ Tex, Austin, BFA; Art Inst Chicago; Univ Wyo, Laramie, MFA; Acad Grande Chaumiere, Paris. *Work:* Minneapolis Inst of Art, Minn; Sheldon Mem Gallery, Univ of Nebr; Madison Art Ctr, Wis; Ga Mus of Art, Athens; Kalamazoo Art Inst, Mich. *Exhib:* Ten Missouri Painters, 69; Living Am Artists & the Figure, Pa State Univ Art Mus, 74; one-man shows, Etchings by Frank Stack, US Info Serv, US Embassy, Turkey & Prints by Frank Stack, Kalamazoo Art Inst, Mich, 76; and others. *Pos:* Asst fine arts ed, Houston Chronicle, Tex, 59-60. *Teaching:* Instr, asst prof, assoc prof & prof art, Univ Mo-Columbia, 63- *Awards:* Summer Res Fel, 68, 74 & 76 & Foreign Study Grant, 70, Univ Mo Res Coun. *Bibliog:* Etchings by Frank Stack, Sunday Clothes, winter 72; Donald Hoffman (auth), Artists

at the Center, Kansas City Star, 7/29/73; Sidney Larson (auth), Etchings and Lithographs by Frank Stack, Singing Wind Publ, 76; exhib catalog, Watercolors by Frank Stack, Mo Arts Coun, 77. *Mem:* Col Art Asn Am; Mo Arts Coun; and others. *Media:* Oil, Watercolor, Etching, Lithography. *Publ:* Contribr, Motive Mag, 58, 69 & 70; co-auth, A selection of etchings by John Sloan, Univ Mo, 68; auth, A metal plate sketchbook, Am Artist, 10/75; illusr, Hog Killin' Time & Other Poems, Trilobite Press, Denton, Tex, 75; illusr, Duplicate Keys--Poems by Jon Bracker Thorpe Springs Press, Berkeley, 78. *Dealer:* The Lakeside Studio 150 S Lakeshore Rd Lakeside MI 49116; Harco Gallery Rt 2 Box 34A Columbia MO 65201. *Mailing Add:* 409 Thilly Ave Columbia MO 65201

STACK, GAEL Z
PAINTER, EDUCATOR
b Chicago, Ill, Apr 28, 41. *Study:* Univ Ill, Champaign, BFA; Southern Ill Univ, MFA. *Work:* Mus Fine Art, Houston; Solomon R Guggenheim Mus, New York. *Exhib:* Prints 79, Galveston Art Ctr, 79; Tex Artists Invitational, Contemp Arts Ctr, New Orleans, La, 80; Emergent Americans, Guggenheim Mus, New York, 81; Four Painters, Contemp Arts Mus, Houston, Tex, 81; Works by Women, travelling exhib, 81-82; Texas on Paper, Contemp Arts Mus, Houston, 82; Art from Houston in Norway, Stavanger Mus, 82; New Art from a New City, Frankfurter Kunstverein, Ger, 82; New Orleans Triennale, New Orleans Mus Art, 83; Southern Fictions, Contemp Arts Mus, Houston, 83; and others. *Teaching:* Instr, Univ Wis, La Crosse, 72-73; asst prof, Univ Houston, 74-81, assoc prof, 81- *Awards:* Res Enabling Travel Grant, Univ Houston, Tex; Nat Endowment Arts Grant, 82. *Bibliog:* Peter Schjeldahl (auth), Stock options, Village Voice; Charlotte Moser (auth), Artists the critics are watching, Art News, 5/81; Grace Glueck (auth), How emerging artists really emerge, Art News, 5/81. *Dealer:* Janie C Lee Gallery 2304 Bissonnet Houston TX 77005. *Mailing Add:* 2015 W Main Houston TX 77098

STACK, MICHAEL
PAINTER
b Chicago, Ill, Oct 30, 41. *Study:* Univ Ill, BFA, 64; Univ Fla, MFA, 66. *Work:* Okla Art Ctr; Olivet Univ; Nelson-Atkins Mus Art; Ill State Univ, Bloomington; Univ Fla, Gainesville. *Comn:* Garden of Earthly Delights (painting), KCRF Inc, Hayworth, Ill, 69; painting, MLLJN Inc, Bloomington, Ill, 73; tensegrity structure, Metrop Life Insurance, Overland Park, Kans, 83; Dancin' (serigraph), Kansas City Arts Coun & Crown Ctr Redevelopment Corp, Kansas City, Mo, 83. *Exhib:* Ultimate Concerns, Ohio Univ, Athens, 65; Art Across American, Knoedler Gallery, New York & traveling, 65-66; Fla State Fair Fine Art Exhib, Tampa, 65 & 66; 72nd Chicago & Vicinity Exhib, Art Inst Chicago, 69; Nat Print & Drawing Exhib, Western Ill Univ, 70; Mid-Four Painting Exhib, Nelson-Atkins Mus Art, 80; Three Painters, Mulvane Art Ctr, Topeka, Kans, 83. *Teaching:* Instr painting, Ill State Univ, 67-70; vis artist, NS Col Fine Arts, 69 & Kansas City Art Inst, 76. *Awards:* Third Prize, Chicago Fine Arts Exhib, 63; Merit Award, Fla State Fair, 65; Third Prize, Mid-Four Painting Exhib, 80. *Bibliog:* Mary King (auth), Fishbowl taxicab, Stack-ed deck, St Louis Post Dispatch, 4/11/80; Mary Sprague (auth), article, New Art Examiner, 7/80; Donald Hoffmann (auth), Contrast of theme ..., Kansas City Star, 10/9/83. *Mem:* Col Art Asn; Kansas City Artists Coalition. *Media:* Acrylic, Oil. *Dealer:* Batz Gallery 4116 Pennsylvania Kansas City MO 64111. *Mailing Add:* 3513 Gillham Rd Kansas City MO 64111

STACKS, WILLIAM LEON
PAINTER, RESTORER
b Charlotte, NC, Apr 25, 28. *Study:* With Alice Steadman, W Lester Stevens & William J Potter. *Work:* New York State Mus; SC State Mus; St John's Mus Art, Wilmington, NC; Greenville Mus SC; Telfair Acad, Ga; and others. *Comn:* Restoration comns, pvt & corporate collections, govt bldgs & univs, incl Davidson Col, Univ SC, Univ NC, Wake Forest Univ & Clemson Univ. *Exhib:* Washington Soc Miniature Painters, 71-83; Nat Soc Painters Casein & Acrylic, New York, 72 & 80; Am Artists Prof League, 73-81; Am Watercolor Soc, 77; Hudson Valley Art Asn, 77; Knickerbocker Artists, 80-81; and others. *Collections Arranged:* Assisted, Elliott Daingerfield Retrospective (with catalog), Mint Mus, Charlotte & NC State Mus, Raleigh, 71. *Pos:* Bd mem, NC Arts Coun, 72-75. *Teaching:* Pvt instruction. *Awards:* Minor S Jamieson Award, Founder's Award & others, Washington Soc Miniature Painters & Gravers, 77-82; Member's Award, Rockport Art Asn, 79; Metrop Mus Award, Nat Arts Club, 79; and others. *Mem:* Rockport Art Asn; Salmagundi Club; Nat Arts Club; Am Artists Prof League; Allied Artists Am. *Dealer:* St John's Museum Wilmington NC; Connoisseur Gallery Bernardsville NJ. *Mailing Add:* One Mallard Rd Hilton Head Island SC 29928

STACY, DONALD L
PAINTER, EDUCATOR
b West Paterson, NJ, Sept 3, 25. *Study:* Newark Sch Fine Art; Art Students League; Univ Paris Sch Art & Archeol; Univ Aix-Marseille; Pratt Graphic Art Ctr; New Sch Social Res. *Work:* Print Dept, Mus Mod Art; Birla Acad Art, Calcutta. *Comn:* Three decorative wall panels, US Plywood. *Exhib:* Documenta II, Kassel, Ger; Kyoto Gallery, Japan; Grenchen, Switz; Philadelphia Print Club; Knoedlers, York; George Wittenborn, Art Books, New York. *Teaching:* Mem fac, Dept Art, Inst Mod Art, Mus Mod Art, 57-69, Dept Art, Sch Visual Arts, New York, 69-70 & Dept Art, New Sch Social Res, 67- *Awards:* Fulbright Grant, 53-55. *Mem:* Am Inst for Conserv of Hist & Artistic Works; Engadiner Kollegium, Zurich. *Media:* Acrylic, Oil. *Publ:* Auth, The Runaway Dot: a Concept Book for Children, Bobbs, 69; contribr, articles in: Main Currents in Mod Thought, 69-74; contribr, Emergent Man, Gordon & Breach, 73; auth, Experiments in Art, Scholastic, 75; auth, Drawing and Painting from Imagination, Stravon Press, 80. *Mailing Add:* 17 E 16th St New York NY 10003

STACY, JOHN RUSSELL
ILLUSTRATOR, JEWELER
b Denver, Colo, Mar 18, 19. *Study:* Denver Art Inst, dipl, 39; Univ Wash, 47. *Work:* Boy Scouts Am Hq, Cimarron, NMex; Yellowstone & Grand Teton Nat Parks, Wyo; Libr Congress, Washington, DC. *Comn:* Painting, Izaac Walton League Am, Denver, Colo, 39; illus, Colo Sch Mines, Golden, 60-70; illus, Geological Soc Am, Boulder, Colo, 60-70. *Pos:* Illusr, US Geological Survey, Denver, Colo, 50-74; dir & illusr, Rocky Mountain Nature Asn, Estes Park, Colo, 74. *Awards:* First Place, Federal Ed Asn, 65; Meritorious Serv Award, Stewart Udall, Secy Interior, 68; Two International Faceters Fair Awards, 83. *Mem:* Life Santa Cruz Art League (bd dirs, 81-82). *Media:* Watercolor, Charcoal. *Publ:* Auth & illusr, Terrain Diagrams in Isometric Projection--Simplified, Annals Asn Am Geographers, 58; illusr, Philmont Country, Professional Paper 505, 64, Geologic Story of Yellowstone National Park, 73, Geologic Story of Canyonlands National Park, 74 & Geologic Story of Arches National Park, 75, US Geological Survey. *Mailing Add:* c/o Tadco 552-194 Bean Creek Rd Scotts Valley CA 95066

STADLER, ALBERT
PAINTER
b New York, NY, Aug 12, 23. *Study:* Univ Pa; Univ Fla. *Exhib:* Corcoran Gallery Art, Washington, DC; Dayton Art Inst, Ohio; Los Angeles Co Mus Art, Calif; Walker Art Ctr, Minneapolis, Minn; Art Gallery Toronto, Ont; 20th Nat Print Exhib, Brooklyn Mus, NY, 77; and many others. *Media:* Acrylic. *Interests:* Color, in all its changing hues, chromas and lights. *Mailing Add:* 54 Beach St New York NY 10013

STAEMPFLI, GEORGE W
DEALER, PAINTER
b Bern, Switz, Dec 6, 10; US citizen. *Study:* Univ Erlangen, PhD, 35. *Exhib:* One-man shows, M Knoedler & Co, New York, 41 & 47, Forum Gallery, New York, 78, Aberbach Gallery, London, Eng, 78, Levy Gallery, Hamburg, Germany, 79 & Capricorn Gallery, Washington, DC, 80 & 83. *Pos:* Cur, Mus Fine Arts, Houston, Tex, 55-57; coordr fine arts, Am Pavilion, Brussels Expo, 57-58; pres, Staempfli Gallery, 69- *Specialty:* Contemporary European and American painting and sculpture. *Mailing Add:* 47 E 77th St New York NY 10021

STAFFEL, DORIS
PAINTER, EDUCATOR
b New York, NY, 1921. *Study:* Tyler Sch Art, 39-44; Iowa Univ, MA, 45; Hans Hoffman Sch, 45-47. *Work:* Iowa Univ; Tylor Woodruff, London, Eng. *Exhib:* One-woman shows, Chatham Col, Pittsburgh, Pa, 65, Tyler Abroad, Rome Gallery, Italy, 68 & Gross McCleaf Gallery, Philadelphia, Pa, 79 & 82; Broad Spectrum, Allentown Art Mus, Pa, 81; Ann Drawing Exhib, Beaver Col, Glenside, Pa, 81. *Teaching:* Assoc prof painting, Philadelphia Col Art, 61- *Awards:* Purchase Prize, Beaver Col, 78. *Media:* Oil, Watercolor. *Mailing Add:* c/o Gross McCleaf Gallery 1713 Walnut Street Philadelphia PA 19103

STAFFEL, RUDOLF HARRY
CERAMIST, INSTRUCTOR
b San Antonio, Tex, June 15, 11. *Study:* Chicago Art Inst, Ill; Escuela Para Maestros, San Juan Teotihuacan, Mex; pvt study with Jose Arpa & Xavier Gonzalez, San Antonio. *Work:* Mus of Contemp Crafts, New York; Philadelphia Mus Art; Smithsonian Inst, Washington, DC; Dartmouth Col Galleries & Collections, Hopkins Ctr, Hanover, NH; Everson Mus, Syracuse, NY. *Exhib:* Twenty-Five Years of Art in Clay USA, Lang Art Gallery, Scripps Col, 69; Objects USA, Johnson Collection Exhib, Smithsonian Inst, Washington, DC, 69; Ceramics 70 Plus Woven Forms, Everson Mus Art, Syracuse, NY, 70; Thirty Ceramists USA, Victoria & Albert Mus, London, Eng, 72; Contemp Clay--Ten Approaches, Dartmouth Col Galleries, Hanover, 76; 300 Years of American Art, Philadelphia Mus Art, 76; Tureens 1976, Campbell Mus, Camden, NJ, 76; one-man show, Helen Drutt Gallery, Philadelphia, 76. *Teaching:* Prof ceramics, Tyler Sch Art, Temple Univ, 40-82. *Awards:* Lindbach Award, Excellence in Teaching, Temple Univ, 66; Merit Award, Ceramic Arts--USA--1966, Int Mineral and Chemicals Corp, 66; Craftsman Fel, Nat Endowment Arts, Washington, DC, 77. *Bibliog:* Richard B Petterson (auth), Ceramic Art in America, Prof Publ Inc, 69; Roger D Bonham (auth), Full Cover, Ceramic Monthly, 2/75; Robert & Paula Winokur (auth), The Light of Rudolf Staffel, Craft Horizons, 4/77. *Mem:* Nat Coun for Educ Ceramic Arts; Am Asn Col Prof. *Media:* Ceramic Clay. *Dealer:* Helen Drutt Gallery 1625 Spruce St Philadelphia PA 19103. *Mailing Add:* 3835 Cresson Philadelphia PA 19127

STAHL, BEN (ALBERT)
PAINTER, WRITER
b Chicago, Ill, Sept 7, 10. *Work:* New Britain Mus Am Art; Albion Col; Adelphi Col; Duke Univ. *Comn:* Fourteen stations of cross for Cath Bible & Cath Press, Chicago, 55. *Exhib:* Art Inst Chicago; Nat Acad Design; Audubon Mus; one-man show, Fenn Galleries, Ltd, 78; Macleo Gallery, 81; and others. *Pos:* Founder & vpres, Mus of Cross, Sarasota, Fla, 65- *Teaching:* Instr, Art Inst Chicago, 41 & Am Acad Art, Chicago, 42; mem founding fac, Famous Artists Schs, Westport, Conn, 49- *Awards:* Saltus Gold Medal, Nat Acad, 49; Art Dirs Clubs, New York, 52; Soc Illusrs Hall of Fame, 79; and 47 others. *Mem:* Am Art Found (bd adv, currently). *Publ:* Auth, The Secret of Red Skull, Houghton Mifflin, 71; auth & host, Journey into Art with Ben Stahl, SC ETV Network, 77; illusr, Saturday Evening Post, Am Artist Mag, Northlight Mag & others; illusr, Gone With the Wind, 81 & Little Women, 81, Franklin Mint; illusr, Little Women, Franklin Mint, 81. *Mailing Add:* Apdo 421 GTO San Miguel de Allende Mexico

STALLER, ERIC P
PHOTOGRAPHER
b Mineola, NY, Sept 14, 47. *Study:* Univ of Mich, BArch, 71. *Work:* Mus Mod Art, New York; Everson Mus, Syracuse; Int Mus Photog, Rochester. *Comn:* Lighting installations, Int Ctr of Photog, New York, 79, City Univ New York, 79 & Md Inst Col Art, Baltimore, 79. *Exhib:* Biennials, Indianapolis Mus, 76 & Taft Mus, Cincinnati, 76; Wagstaff Collection, Corcoran Gallery, Washington, DC, 78; Nat Acad Scis, Washington DC, 81. *Awards:* Creative Arts Pub Serv Prog Grant, 77; Nat Endowment Arts Grant, 78. *Bibliog:* Owen Edwards (auth), Tripping the light fantastic, Am Photog Mag, 4/78. *Media:* Light. *Mailing Add:* 31 Walker St 383 W Broadway New York NY 10013

STALLWITZ, CAROLYN
PAINTER, PHOTOGRAPHER
b Abilene, Tex, Apr 27, 36. *Study:* WTex State Univ, with Clarence Kincaid, Jr, BS(art); also with Emilio Caballero, Stefan Kramer & Lee Simpson. *Work:* Pioneer Natural Gas Co, Amarillo, Tex; First Nat Bank, Dumas, Tex; First State Bank, Dumas, Tex; Kracke-Gober Corp, Houston; Cliff Dwellers, Los Alamos, NMex. *Exhib:* Tex Watercolor Soc Exhib, 70; Wichita Centennial Nat Art Exhib, 70; Best of Southwest, 71; Amarillo Fine Art Asn Citation Show, 73; Denver Audubon Wildlife Art Show, 77. *Teaching:* Instr drawing, Amarillo Art Ctr, 73-74, instr watercolor, 74- *Mem:* Moore Co Arts Asn (pres, 69-70); Tex Arts Alliance; Amarillo Fine Art Asn; Tex Fine Art Asn; Tex Watercolor Soc. *Media:* Watercolor, Pencil. *Publ:* Window on the Prairie, Feather Press, 81. *Dealer:* Colony Art & Frame Shop 2604 Wolflin Ave Amarillo TX 79109; The Cliff Dwellers Los Alamos NM 87544. *Mailing Add:* Box 1225 Dumas TX 79029

STAMATS, PETER OWEN
COLLECTOR, PATRON
b Cedar Rapids, Iowa, July 20, 29. *Study:* Dartmouth Col, BA, 51. *Pos:* Mem, Iowa State Arts Coun, 66-70. *Mem:* Cedar Rapids Art Asn (dir, 58-, pres, 59-60, trustee, 78-). *Interests:* Support of Cedar Rapids Museum of Art. *Collection:* Fifteenth century to 20th century prints; Pre-Columbian textiles; vintage American photography; 19th century Aymara weavings. *Mailing Add:* 427 Sixth Ave SE Cedar Rapids IA 52406

STAMELOS, ELECTRA GEORGIA MOUSMOULES
PAINTER, GRAPHIC ARTIST
b Jersey City, NJ. *Study:* Corcoran Mus Sch, study with Aurelius Battaglia & Heinz Warneke, 43-45; Nat Art Sch, 45-48; Magda Sch Design, Am Univ, Washington, DC, 46; work with Margaret Cramer, 61-63; Univ Mich, study with Guy Palazola, 64; Ctr Creative Studies, 65-68; Wayne State Univ, BA(painting), 70; Eastern Mich Univ, MFA(watercolor), 76. *Work:* Nat Watercolor Soc, Calif; Northwest Br, YWCA, Detroit; State Farm Ins Co, Dearborn, Mich; Brown, Lund & Fitzgerald, Washington, DC; Eastern Ill Univ; and others. *Comn:* Hardedge acrylic, Northwest Br, YWCA, Detroit, 70. *Exhib:* Butler Inst Am Art, Youngstown, Ohio, 76, 77, 79 & 80; Source Detroit, Cranbrook Art Mus, Birmingham, Mich, 76; Watercolor USA 77 & 79, Springfield Art Mus, 77 & 80; Nat Watercolor Soc, Fine Arts Gallery, Calif State Univ, Northridge, 77-81; Detroit Realist, Oakland Univ, 79. *Teaching:* Instr drawing & painting, Nat Art Sch, Washington, DC, 45-48; instr drawing & painting, Northwest Br, YWCA, Detroit, 68-72; instr watercolor, Ann Arbor Asn, Mich, 77-78; lectr, Birmingham Bloomfield Art Asn, 79-, Applied Arts, Univ Mich, Dearborn, 80- *Awards:* Purchase Award, Mich Watercolor Soc, 76; Purchase Award, 7 for 76, Eastern Ill Univ, 76; Purchase Award, 57th Ann, Nat Watercolor Soc, 77. *Mem:* Nat Watercolor Soc, Calif; Mich Watercolor Soc; Mid-W Watercolor Soc; Birmingham-Bloomfield Art Asn; Ann Arbor Art Asn. *Media:* Watercolor, Acrylic; Pencil, Pastel. *Publ:* Auth, Bibliography of Georgia O'Keefe, J Nat Art Educ Asn, 76; illusr, The Tree House (24 drawings), 76; illusr, SE Michigan Calendar, 82. *Dealer:* Cantor/Lemberg Gallery 538 N Woodward Ave Birmingham MI 48011; Freeman Gallery 3046 Lake Lansing Rd East Lansing MI 48823. *Mailing Add:* 4450 Fenton Rd Hartland MI 48029

STAMM, GEOFFREY EATON
ADMINISTRATOR, HISTORIAN
b Washington, DC, July 30, 43. *Study:* Univ Paris, CPLF cert, 64; Hamilton Col, AB, 65; Am Univ, Washington, DC; Corcoran Sch Art, Washington, DC; Inst Art Admin, Harvard Univ, cert, 74. *Pos:* Coordr spec proj, Indian Arts & Crafts Bd, Washington, DC, 69-74; asst to gen mgr, 74-78, asst gen mgr, 78-; mem, Fed Interagency Crafts Comt, Washington DC, 76- *Mem:* Am Crafts Coun; World Crafts Coun; Am Asn Mus; Int Coun Mus. *Res:* Twentieth century American Indian, Eskimo and Aleut fine arts and handcrafts. *Publ:* Contribr & illusr, Institute of American Indian Arts, 68, illusr, Future Directions in Native American Art, 73 & ed, Protection for Native American Artists and Craftsmen, 74, US Dept Interior; contribr, Authentic Indian Jewelry, Gro-Pub, 75; auth, The Federal Agency as Mentor: Developing Native American Arts, US Dept Interior, 80; and others. *Mailing Add:* 2475 Virginia Ave NW Washington DC 20037

STAMM, TED
PAINTER
b Brooklyn, NY, Aug 30, 44. *Study:* Hofstra Univ, BFA, 67. *Work:* Aldrich Mus, Ridgefield, Conn; Phoenix Mus, Ariz; Prudential Insurance Co, Boston; Commodities Corp, Princeton, NJ; Chase Manhattan, New York; and others. *Exhib:* Contemp Reflections 1971-72, Aldrich Mus Contemp Art, Ridgefield, Conn & Selections from the Collection, 78; Book Objects, Albright-Knox Art Gallery, Buffalo, NY; Poets Painters, Denver Art Mus, 79; one-man shows, Roy Boyd, Chicago, 80, Tony Birckhead Gallery, Cincinnati, 80, Clocktower, New York, 81 & Harm Bouckaert, New York, 82; Contemp Art Ctr,

Cincinnati, 83. *Pos:* Guest lectr, Hofstra Univ, 71, 75 & 78; Pratt Inst, Brooklyn, 76, 78 & 79; Univ Rochester, 78; Munson-Williams-Proctor Inst, Utica, NY, 79; guest lectr, C W Post, 79-81. *Teaching:* Instr contemp art, Brooklyn Mus Art Sch, 71-77; adj prof painting & drawing, C W Post Ctr, Long Island Univ, Greenvale, 77-83, Hofstra Univ, 78; adj prof hist contemp art, Jersey City State Col, 77-78; instr, Sch Visual Arts, 80-84. *Awards:* Nat Endowment Arts, 81-82; Guggenheim Fel, 83-84. *Bibliog:* Robert Pincus-Witten (auth), Entries: styles of artists and critics, Arts Mag, 11/79; William Zimmer (auth), Surely Temple Black, Soho News, 2/81; Tiffany Bell (auth), Ted Stamm, Arts Mag, 5/81. *Publ:* Contribr, Special Execution Tags, Art-Rite 4, 73 & Statement Regarding Artists Books, Art-Rite 14, 76. *Mailing Add:* 101 Wooster St New York NY 10012

STAMOS, THEODOROS (S)
PAINTER
b New York, NY, Dec 31, 22. *Study:* Am Artists Sch. *Work:* Mus Mod Art, New York; Metrop Mus Art, New York; Whitney Mus Am Art, New York; Univ Calif Mus, Berkeley; NJ State Mus, Trenton; and others. *Comn:* Oil mural, SS Arg, Moore McCormack Lines, 46, tapestry, New York, 71; two murals, Buro Klaus Hoebeck, Cologne, 83. *Exhib:* Documenta, Kassel, Ger; Abstr Expressionists & Imagists, Guggenheim Mus, New York; Dada, Surrealism & Their Inheritors, Mus Mod Art; Corcoran Gallery Art, Washington, DC; Whitney Mus Am Art, New York; Metrop Mus Art, New York; Santa Barbara Mus, 70; Charles E Slatkin Gallery, New York, 72; Joslyn Art Mus, Omaha, Nebr, 73; Mus Knoedler, Zurich, 83. *Teaching:* Instr art, Art Students League; lectr art, Columbia Univ; prof art, Brandeis Univ. *Awards:* Brandies Univ Creative Arts Award, Tiffany Found Fel; Nat Arts Grant. *Bibliog:* K Sawyer (auth), Stamos, Mus Poche Paris, 60; R Pomeroy (auth), Theodoros Stamos, Abrams, 73. *Mem:* Life fel Metrop Mus Art. *Publ:* Illusr, Sorrows of Cold Stone, Dodd. *Mailing Add:* 37 W 83rd St New York NY 10024

STAMPER, WILLSON YOUNG
PAINTER
b New York, NY, Jan 5, 12. *Study:* Art Students League; Cincinnati Art Acad; US Navy Photog Sch; US Navy Advanced Motion Picture Sch; also pvt study with Kimon Nicolaides & Rico Lebrun. *Work:* Mus Mod Art, New York; Cincinnati Art Mus; Cincinnati Mod Art Soc; Honolulu Acad Arts; Advertiser Art Found, Honolulu. *Comn:* Two Ceramic Murals, Int Airport, Honolulu, 75; Portrait of Famous Chanter, State Found for Cult & Arts, Honolulu, 75; Portrait of Chief Justice William Richardson. *Exhib:* One-man shows, Cincinnati Art Mus, 37, Honolulu Acad Art, 46, 50 & 54; San Francisco Worlds Fair, 39; Albright-Knox Art Gallery, Buffalo, 51; Carnegie Inst Int, Pittsburgh, 52. *Pos:* Conservator of art, Cincinnati Art Mus & Taft Mus, 36-43; conservator art, Honolulu Acad Art, 45-62. *Teaching:* Instr drawing & painting, Cincinnati Art Acad, 37-43; dir, Sch of Honolulu Acad Arts, 45-62. *Awards:* First Prize Artist of Greater Cincinnati, Cincinnati Art Mus, 42; Purchase Award, Watamull Found, 45, 48, 49 & 58; First Prize Honolulu Ann, Honolulu Acad Arts, 47-49 & 52, 55. *Bibliog:* Madge Tennent (auth), Miracle in art, Paradise Pac Mag, 58; Art in Hawaii, House Beautiful Mag, 58; article, Artists of Hawaii, Vol 1, State Found Cult & the Arts, Univ Press of Hawaii, 74. *Mem:* Hawaii Painter & Sculptors League; Int Inst Conservation Hist & Artistic Works. *Media:* Oil, Watercolor. *Publ:* Contribr, George B Bridgeman's One Hundred Best Heads, Bridgeman Publ, 33; contribr, K Nicolaides' Natural Way to Draw, Houghton Mifflin, 41; illusr & coauth, Cultural Considerations for Planning in Micronesia, Trust Territory Planning, US State Dept, 68. *Mailing Add:* 224 N Kalaheo Ave Kailua HI 96734

STAMPFLE, FELICE
CURATOR, WRITER
b Kansas City, Mo, July 25, 12. *Study:* Washington Univ, AB & AM; Radcliffe Col. *Pos:* Cur drawings & prints, Pierpont Morgan Libr, 45-83, cur emer, 84; ed, Master Drawings, 63-83. *Res:* Drawings, especially 17th century Dutch and Flemish & 18th century Italian. *Publ:* Auth, var articles, reviews & exhib catalogs. *Mailing Add:* c/o Pierpont Morgan Libr 29 E 36th St New York NY 10016

STAMSTA, JEAN
FIBER ARTIST
b Sheboygan, Wis, Nov 2, 36. *Study:* Univ Wis, Milwaukee, BS, 58; Haystack Mountain Sch Crafts, 66; Fiberworks Ctr Textile Research, 81. *Work:* Cleveland Mus Art, Ohio; Am Craft Mus, New York; Milwaukee Art Mus, Wis; Mus Fine Arts, Columbus; US Vice President's House, Washington, DC. *Comn:* Wall hanging, First National Bank, Amarillo, Tex, 77; woven panels, Bank of Commerce, Milwaukee, 78; wall hanging, Sentry Insurance, Wis, 78; wall hangings, Miller Brewing Co, Milwaukee, 79. *Exhib:* 5th Biennial Tapestry, Lausanne, Switzerland, 71; one-man shows, Am Craft Mus, New York, 71 & Mem Union Gallery, Univ Wis, Madison, 82; 2nd Int Exhib Miniature Textiles, British Crafts Ctr, London, 77; Fiberworks, Cleveland Mus Art, Ohio, 77; Wisconsin Direction II, Milwaukee Art Mus, 78; Clay, Fiber, Metal: By Women, Bronx Mus, NY, 78; Fiber 81, Rochester Art Ctr, Minn, 81. *Teaching:* Instr weaving, Mt Mary Col, Milwaukee, Wis, 70-73; instr weaving, Univ Northern Mich, summer 77; instr weaving, Rochester Inst Technol, New York, summer, 80. *Awards:* Purchase Award, Columbus Mus Fine Arts, 72; First Prize, Marietta Col Crafts Nat, 74; Nat Endowment Arts Craftsman Fel, 74. *Mem:* Am Crafts Coun; Surface Design Asn. *Dealer:* Hadler/Rodriguez Gallery 38 East 57th St New York NY 10022; David Barnett Gallery 2101 W Wisconsin Ave Milwaukee WI 53233. *Mailing Add:* W 299 N 9313 Hwy F Ctr Oak Rd Hartland WI 53029

STAN, CYNTHIA (CYNTHIA STAN MELLOW)
PRINTMAKER, COLLAGE ARTIST
b Wilmington, Del, July 17, 53. *Study:* Inst European Studies, Vienna, 74; Colo State Univ, Ft Collins, BFA, 75; Pa State Univ, MFA, 78. *Work:* Security Pac Bank, Los Angeles; Hercules Inc, Wilmington, Del; Brevard Art Ctr & Mus, Melbourne, Fla; Marywood Col, Scranton, Pa. *Exhib:* Small Works, Philadelphia Print Club, 82; solo exhib, Brevard Art Ctr & Mus, Melbourne, Fla, 82; Spacescapes, Sch Visual Arts Mus, New York, 82; Her Own Space, Muse Gallery, Philadelphia, 83; 67th Del Exhib, Del Art Mus, Wilmington, 83-84. *Teaching:* Asst printmaking, Pa State Univ, 76-78; instr art, Wilmington Friends Sch, Del, 78-; instr printmaking, Univ Del, Newark, 81. *Awards:* Del State Arts Coun Grants, 81 & 82-83. *Bibliog:* Joan Gabriel (auth), Show at Bacam, Today, Melbourne, Fla, 10/31/82; Penelope Bass Cope (auth), Boxed creativity, Sunday News J, Wilmington, Del, 10/2/83. *Mem:* Philadelphia Print Club; Los Angeles Printmaking Soc. *Media:* Intaglio; Handmade Paper. *Mailing Add:* 14 Lower Snuff Mill Row Yorklyn DE 19736

STANCIL, KIMSEY
HISTORIAN, ADMINISTRATOR
b Augusta, Ga, Nov 30, 43. *Study:* Univ Fla, Gainesville, 61-63; Univ Calif, Los Angeles, BA(art hist, cum laude), 77. *Collections Arranged:* The Naifs (auth, catalog), Exhib European & Am naif painters, 79. *Pos:* Admin asst, Serendipity Gallery, Inc, Brentwood, Calif, 77-80; dir arch, Galerie Michael, Century City, Calif, 81- *Res:* Wrote monographs on Larry Gray, Seymour Meyer, Hiromichi Yamagata, David Lampson, Catherine Eaton, Glenda Vaughn, Bruce Bomberger, Leonard Creo, Victor Santoyo and Gary Hinte; interrelationships between art and religion through the ages. *Publ:* Ed, Fine Arts Monthly, Serendipity Gallery, 79. *Mailing Add:* 6550 Hazeltine Van Nuys CA 91401

STANCZAK, JULIAN
PAINTER, INSTRUCTOR
b Borownica, Poland, Nov 5, 28; US citizen. *Study:* Uganda, Africa & London, Eng; Cleveland Inst Art, BFA, 54; Yale Univ, with Albers & Marca-Relli, MFA, 56. *Work:* Dayton Art Inst, Ohio; Albright-Knox Art Gallery, Buffalo; Larry Aldrich Mus, Ridgefield, Conn; Des Moines Art Ctr, Iowa; Libr Cong, Washington, DC; plus others. *Exhib:* Albright-Knox Art Gallery, 68; Univ Ill, 69; Herron Mus Art, Indianapolis, Ind, 69; Butler Art Inst, Youngstown, Ohio, 73; Indianapolis Mus Art, 76; Brooklyn Mus Art, NY, 76; Larry Aldrich Mus; Pa Acad Fine Arts, Philadelphia; Corcoran Gallery Art, Washington, DC; Nat Gallery Art, Washington, DC; one-man exhibs, Ohio State Univ, 76, Miller Gallery, Cincinnati, 78, ASA Gallery, Oak Ridge, 78, Kauffman Fine Arts, Houston, 78, Int Monetary Fund, Washington, DC, 78 & Butler Inst Am Art, 80; and others. *Teaching:* Instr, Art Acad Cincinnati, 57-64; instr painting & drawing, Cleveland Inst Art, 64-82; instr design, currently; artist in residence, Dartmouth Col, 68. *Awards:* Cleveland Fine Arts Award, 70; Outstanding Educ Am, 70; Ohio Arts Coun Award, 72. *Bibliog:* George Rickey (auth), Constructivism: Origins and Evolution, Braziller, 67; Udo Kultermann (auth), Neue Formen des Bildes, Verlag Ernst Wasmuth, Tubingen, 69; Kenneth F Bates (auth), Basic Design, World Publ, 70; and many others. *Mem:* Am Abstract Artists; Am Int Platform Asn. *Res:* Pioneer in optical art. *Dealer:* Martha Jackson Gallery 32 E 69th St New York NY 10021. *Mailing Add:* 6229 Cabrini Ln Cleveland OH 44131

STANDEN, EDITH APPLETON
HISTORIAN
b Halifax, NS, Feb 21, 05; US citizen. *Study:* Oxford Univ, BA. *Pos:* Art secy, Joseph Widener Collection, Elkins Park, Pa, 29-42; assoc cur, Metrop Mus Art, New York, 49-70, consult, 70- *Mem:* Col Art Assn Am. *Res:* European post-medieval tapestries. *Publ:* Auth, var articles in Metrop Mus Bulletin, Metrop Mus J & Art Bulletin, and others, 51-77; coauth, Art Treasures of the Metropolitan, 52; coauth, Decorative Art from the Samuel H Kress Collection, 64. *Mailing Add:* Metrop Mus of Art Fifth Ave & 82nd St New York NY 10028

STANFORTH, MELVIN SIDNEY
EDUCATOR, PRINTMAKER
b Tuscaloosa, Ala, Sept 22, 37. *Study:* Univ Ala, BFA; Wayne State Univ, MFA. *Work:* Weatherspoon Gallery, Univ NC, Greensboro; Louisburg Col, NC; Greenville Art Ctr, NC; NC Nat Bank Corp Hq, Charlotte; Duke Univ Med Ctr. *Exhib:* Regional Painting Exhib, 73-76 & Regional Drawing & Prints Exhib, 73-77, Southeastern Ctr Contemp Arts, Winston-Salem, NC; Ball State Univ Nat Drawing Exhib, Muncie, Ind, 74; Potsdam Nat Drawing Exhib, NY, 75; Piedmont Graphics, Greenville Co Mus, Greenville, SC, 77-78; Award Winners Exhib, NC Mus of Art, Raleigh, 79. *Teaching:* Prof drawing & design, E Carolina Univ, Greenville, NC, 69- *Awards:* Second Purchase Award, NC Artists Exhib, NC Arts Coun, 71; Purchase Awards, Regional Painting Exhib, 73 & Regional Drawing & Prints Exhib, 73, Southeastern Ctr Contemp Arts, Winston-Salem, NC. *Media:* Lithography. *Mailing Add:* 2205 E Fifth St Greenville NC 27834

STANLEY, BOB
PAINTER, PHOTOGRAPHER
b Yonkers, NY, Jan 3, 32. *Study:* Oglethorpe Univ, BA; High Mus Art, Atlanta, 52; Columbia Univ; Art Students League; Brooklyn Mus Art Sch, Max Beckman painting scholar, 55 & 56. *Work:* Whitney Mus Am Art, New York; Milwaukee Art Ctr, Wis; Fogg Art Mus, Cambridge, Mass; Corcoran Gallery Art; Metrop Mus Art, New York; and others. *Exhib:* Whitney Mus Am Art Painting Ann, 67, 69 & 72 & 73 Biennial; two-man show (with Bart Wasserman), PS1, Long Island City, NJ, 77; one-man shows, Hal Bromm Gallery, Elizabeth Weiner Gallery, New York, 78 & Holly Keenberg,

Winnipeg, Man, Can, 80; Worchester Art Mus, Mass, 81; Am Acad & Inst Arts & Letters, 82. *Teaching:* Instr, Sch Visual Arts, New York, 70-72; vis artist, La State Univ, Baton Rouge, 76, Syracuse Univ, 78 & Princeton Univ, 79-80. *Awards:* Cassandra Found Award, 69. *Bibliog:* Carter Ratcliff (auth), Bob Stanley & Bart Wasserman at PS1, Art in Am, 1-2/78; Mario Amaya & Naomi Spector (auth), Monograph: Bob Stanley's Louisiana Sweet, publ by artist & Siena Studios, New York, 78; Michael Floresco (auth), article, Arts Mag, 11/80. *Media:* Oil, Acrylic. *Mailing Add:* 3 Crosby St New York NY 10013

STANLEY, CHARLES EDWARD
DEALER, ADMINISTRATOR

b Kings Mountain, NC, Apr 4, 40. *Study:* Young Harris Col, AA, 60; Greensboro Col, 62; Royal Shakespeare Inst, cert, 64. *Collections Arranged:* Drawings of Ed Dodd (auth, catalog), Handshake Gallery Art, 78; Innersights I & II (for the blind & visually impaired), Handshake Gallery Art, 79-80. *Pos:* Dir & cur, Handshake Gallery Art, Atlanta, Ga, 74-80; bd mem, Metrop Atlanta Rapid Transit Authority, Arts Adv Coun, 77-80; co-dir & co-owner, Stanley & Schenck, Inc, Dealers in Fine Contemp Art, 80- *Mem:* Ga Asn Mus Galleries (vpres, 79, pres, 80); Fulton Coun Arts Comn (bd dirs, 80-83). *Specialty:* Contemporary paintings; sculpture by southern Am artists. *Mailing Add:* Glendale Terrace, Unit A-4 Atlanta GA 30309

STANLEY, M LOUISE
PAINTER, INSTRUCTOR

b Charleston, WVa, Aug 28, 42. *Study:* La Verne Col, BA, 64; Calif Col Arts & Crafts, BFA, 67, MFA, 69. *Work:* De Saisset Mus, Univ Santa Clara, Calif. *Exhib:* One-man shows, Univ Art Mus, Univ Calif, Berkeley, 78, PS1, Queens, NY, 78 & Quay Gallery, San Francisco, 83; The Work Show, Downtown Ctr Fine Arts Mus, San Francisco, Calif, 78; Events, The New Mus, New York, 80; Humor, Los Angeles Inst Contemp Art, Calif, 81; Drawings by Painters, Long Beach Mus Art, Calif, 82. *Teaching:* Instr painting & drawing, San Francisco State Univ, Calif, 77-78; asst prof painting, drawing & watercolor, La State Univ, Baton Rouge, 78-79; instr painting, San Francisco Art Inst, Calif, 82-; vis artist, Univ NC, Chapel Hill, 84. *Awards:* Nat Endowment Arts Grant, 83. *Bibliog:* Richard Martin (auth), Dr Spock's generation: a crystal palace of childhood, Art J, 80; David Winter (auth), Louise Stanleys' work merits three stars, Peninsula Times Tribune, 10/28/81. *Mem:* Charter mem Calif Fedn Art Teachers Local 1. *Media:* Watercolor, Oil. *Mailing Add:* c/o Quay Gallery 254 Sutter St San Francisco CA 94108

STAPEN, NANCY
CRITIC, WRITER

b New York, NY, Dec, 3, 50. *Study:* Brandeis Univ, BA(fine art, magna cum laude), 72. *Collections Arranged:* Robert Henry Logan Retrospective, 84. *Pos:* Asst dir, Clark Gallery, Lincoln, Mass, 81-; coordr, Museum Goers Month, var Boston mus, 83. *Teaching:* Chmn fine arts, Belvoir Terrace Fine Arts, Lenox, Mass, summers 76-78; instr sculpture, Concord-Carlisle High Sch, Mass, 79-80; instr learning through art, De Cordova Mus, 81-83. *Mem:* Am Asn Art Critics; Women's Caucus Art. *Res:* Visual arts; specializing in contemporary art. *Publ:* Auth, A conversation with Robert Morris, Boston Phoenix, 82; auth, Doug Anderson, Artforum, 83; auth, Art deco (collecting in Boston), Boston Mag, 83; auth, Lois Torf on collecting, Art New England, 83; auth, Bonnie Biggs, Artforum, 83. *Mailing Add:* 40 Linnaean St Cambridge MA 02138

STAPLETON, JOSEPH F
LECTURER, PAINTER

b Brooklyn, NY, Mar 20, 21. *Study:* St John's Univ, Brooklyn, NY, BS(summa cum laude); Brooklyn Col; Columbia Univ; Art Students League, with Vytlacil, Dumond, Kantor, Olitsky, Holty & Barnet. *Work:* Birla Inst, Calcutta, India; Art Students League; Pratt Inst, New York. *Exhib:* Am Painting Today, Metrop Mus Art, New York, 50; Ann Invitational, Pa Acad Art, Philadelphia, 52; one-man show, Hofstra Col, Long Island, 56; Ten-Yr Retrospective, Avant Garde Gallery, New York, 57; Charles Egan Gallery, New York, 63-64. *Teaching:* Instr painting, Metrop Mus Art, New York, 57-59; instr painting & drawing, Pratt Inst, 70-, adj asst prof, currently; instr painting & drawing, Art Students League, New York, 73- *Bibliog:* Russell Arnold (auth), Portfolio of drawings--Joseph Stapleton, Crucible, Atlantic Christian Col, fall 68. *Media:* Oil, Ink. *Publ:* Auth & illusr, Leaflets in Japanese for psychological warfare, US Govt, 44-45; illusr, Who Wrote the Classics?, John Day Co, 68. *Mailing Add:* 24 E 20th St New York NY 10003

STAPP, RAY VERYL
PAINTER, PRINTMAKER

b Norton, Kans, July 10, 13. *Study:* Bethany Col, Kans, with Birger Sandzen, BFA; Kansas City Art Inst, with Thomas Hart Benton; Art Students League, with Dumond, Reilly & Trafton; Teachers Col, Columbia Univ, with Ziegfield, MA; Pa State Univ, with Lowenfeld, EdD. *Work:* Painting, Lowenfeld Mem Collection, Pa State Univ. *Exhib:* Ninth Colorprint USA 1980, Lubbock, Tex; Rocky Mountain Regional Print Show, 81. *Pos:* Engraver & lithographer, Hallmark Card Co, 37-39; advert artist, Armstrong Cork Co, 48-49; prod illusr, Boeing Airplane Co, 56-57. *Teaching:* From instr to asst prof design & art educ, Bethany Col, 49-56; from asst prof to assoc prof art, Edinboro State Col, 57-64; from assoc prof to prof design & art educ, Eastern Ill Univ, 79; retired. *Media:* Oil; Serigraph, Ceramics. *Res:* Relationships of measures of creativity, general intelligence and memory; extension of research used as criteria for evaluating children in grades 4-8. *Publ:* Auth, Planning an art lesson, Arts & Activities, 67; auth, Lettering can be easy, Sch Arts, 72; auth, Evaluation of one humanities course, Humanities J, 75; auth, Some things to think about, Arts & Activities, 77; auth, Ceramic glazes with Kansas volcanic ash, 80. *Mailing Add:* 1200 S Monaco Pkwy #16 Denver CO 80224

STAPP, WILLIAM F
CURATOR

b McKinney, Tex, Mar 2, 45. *Study:* Tulane Univ, BA, 67; Univ Pa, MA, 70; Goddard Col, MA, 76; Princeton Univ, with Peter Bunnell. *Collections Arranged:* Survey of the Photographic Collection, Princeton Univ, 74-76. *Pos:* Res asst, Princeton Univ Art Mus, 75-76; cur, Nat Portrait Gallery, 76- *Teaching:* Instr mus collections, Philadelphia Mus Art, 71-76; instr hist photog, Moore Col Art, Philadelphia, 75-76 & Philadelphia Col Art, 75-76. *Mem:* Soc for Photog Educ; Photog Hist Soc of NY. *Res:* History of photography; nineteenth century and portrait photography. *Publ:* Auth, Early attempts to improve the daguerreotype, Image, 76; contribr, Philadelphia: Three Centuries of American Art, Philadelphia Mus Art, 76. *Mailing Add:* Nat Portrait Gallery Eighth & F Sts NW Washington DC 20007

STAPRANS, RAIMONDS
PAINTER, SCULPTOR

b Riga, Latvia, Oct 13, 26; US citizen. *Study:* Sch Art, Esslinger, Stuttgart, 46; Univ Wash, BA, 52; Univ Calif, MA, 55; also with Archipenko. *Work:* Calif Palace Legion Hon, San Francisco; Oakland Mus, Calif; Santa Barbara Mus, Calif; Los Angeles Co Mus; Phoenix Art Mus. *Exhib:* Portland Art Mus, Ore, 56 & 57; Oakland Art Mus, 57; Calif Palace Legion Hon Winter Invitational, 57, 59 & 60; Litton Industs, 62; Am Acad Arts & Lett, New York, 70; and many one-man shows, in US, Can & Europe. *Teaching:* Instr, Univ Alaska, 78 & 81. *Awards:* San Francisco Art Festival. *Bibliog:* California Canvas (film), KRON, San Francisco, 66; Artists Eye (film), Motion Media, 67. *Media:* Oil; Plastic. *Dealer:* Maxwell Galleries 551 Sutter San Francisco CA 94102. *Mailing Add:* 2052 20th St San Francisco CA 94107

STARK, BRUCE GUNSTEN
CARTOONIST, ILLUSTRATOR

b Queens, NY, Feb 17, 33. *Study:* Sch Visual Arts, New York, 55-58. *Work:* Everett Dirksen Libr; L B Johnson Libr; Baseball Hall of Fame; Cooperstown, NY; Basketball Hall of Fame, Mass. *Exhib:* One-man shows, Art Inst Pittsburgh, 68, Univ Kutztown, Pa, 70 & NY Bank for Savings, New York, 71; Nat Art Mus Sport, New York, 71. *Pos:* Artist, cartoonist, New York Daily News, 61- *Awards:* Page One Award for Best Sports Cartoon, 70 & 73. *Mailing Add:* 161 Chestnut St Emerson NJ 07630

STARK, GEORGE KING
EDUCATOR, SCULPTOR

b Schenectady, NY, June 14, 23. *Study:* State Univ NY Col Buffalo, BS(art educ); Teachers Col, Columbia Univ, MA; State Univ NY Buffalo, EdD; and with Dorothy Denslow. *Work:* IBM Collection; Lowe Art Mus, Univ Miami, Fla; Am Art Clay Co; State Univ NY Col Buffalo; State Univ NY Col Oswego; also in pvt collections. *Comn:* Sculptured light fixtures, Savoy Hilton Hotel, New York, 59; space modulator, Sheraton-Palace Hotel, San Francisco, 60; divider screen, Park-Sheraton Hotel, New York, 60; wall relief sculpture, Prudential Steamship Lines, New York, 61; sculptured fountain, comn by Robert E Maytag, Newton, Iowa, 71. *Exhib:* 17th & 19th Ceramic Nat, 52 & 56 & Ceramic Int Exhib, 58, Syracuse Mus Fine Arts; Western NY Ann, Albright-Knox Gallery, Buffalo, 57 & 60; one-man show, Lowe Art Mus, 67. *Teaching:* Prof art, State Univ NY Col Oswego, 64- *Awards:* Shared First Prize for Ceramic Sculpture, 19th Ceramic Nat, 56; Am Inst Architects Sculpture Award, Albright-Knox Gallery, 57 & 60. *Res:* Analysis of artist-teacher's statements on their creativity. *Publ:* Auth, Silent images, 11/63 & Mass communication and faculty/student dialogue, 4/69, Art Educ J; auth, On sculpture, Sch Arts, 3/64; auth, Games theory in education, Sch & Soc, fall 67; auth, Think stream, S & W, fall & winter 69-70. *Mailing Add:* 229 E Seventh St Oswego NY 13126

STARK, MELVILLE F
PAINTER, EDUCATOR

b Honesdale, Pa, Sept 29, 03. *Study:* East Stroudsburg State Col; Univ Pa, MS; Mus Col Fine Arts, Philadelphia; Syracuse Univ, with Cullan Yates & W E Baum; also in Eng & France. *Work:* In 22 US Embassies; Lehigh Co Ct House, Allentown, Pa; Allentown City Hall; Reading Art Mus, Pa; plus many others. *Exhib:* Am Watercolor Soc; Pa Acad Fine Arts; Nat Soc Painters Casein; Mus Fine Arts, Springfield, Mass; Allied Artists Exhib, Butler Art Inst; Philadelphia Watercolor Club. *Pos:* Dir, Allentown Art Mus, 54-60. *Teaching:* Head dept painting, Baum Art Sch Allentown Art Mus, 31-62, dir, Sch, 56-62; head dept painting, Cedar Crest Col, 40-55; head dept art hist, Muhlenberg Col, 55-60. *Awards:* First Myers Mem Award, Nat Soc Painters Casein; First Prize for Landscape, Manatee Art League, Bradenton, Fla; Hon Mention, Mus Fine Arts, Springfield; First Prize, Sarasota Art Asn; First Prize, Longboat Key Art Asn. *Mem:* Mus Fine Arts, Springfield; Rockport Art Asn; NShore Art Asn; Sarasota Art Asn; Salmagundi Club. *Media:* Oil, Watercolor, Pastel, Acrylic. *Mailing Add:* RD 1 Zionsville PA 18092

STARK, SHIRLEY
SCULPTOR, PRINTMAKER

b New York, NY, May 27, 27. *Study:* Univ Detroit; Wayne State Univ. *Work:* Wurlitzer Found, Taos, NMex; Mus NMex, Santa Fe; Jerome Found, St Paul; Printmaking Workshop, New York; Roswell Mus, NMex. *Comn:* Sudario (basalt), comn by Lou Criss, Ranchos de Taos, NMex, 72; Sun-Rite (basalt), 73 & Shakti (basalt), 74, comn by William Bomar, Taos; logo, Balck Heritage Reference Ctr, Langston Hughes Libr, Corona, NY, 83. *Exhib:* Ohio Ceramic & Sculpture Show, Butler Inst Am Art, 62 & 68; 65th Ann Exhib, Mus Art, Carnegie Inst, 75; Historical Roots, Detroit Hist Mus, 80; Forever Free: An Exhibit of African-American Women 1862-1980, 81-82; Third New World Festival of the African Diaspora, Paramaribo, Suriname, 82; Cayman Gallery, New York, 83. *Collections Arranged:* Adaptation-Innovation: Black Women

Artists (auth, catalog), New York, 84. *Teaching:* Vis Andrew Mellon prof sculpture, Carnegie-Mellon Univ, 75. *Awards:* Sculpture Fel, MacDowell Colony, 68; Sculpture Grant, Wurlitzer Found, Taos, 69, 71 & 74. *Mem:* Int Asn Art; Artists Equity. *Mailing Add:* 112-50 Northern Blvd #6F Flushing NY 11368

STARKWEATHER-NELSON, CYNTHIA LOUISE
PAINTER, COLLAGE ARTIST

b Moline, Ill, July 29, 50. *Study:* Northern Ill Univ, BFA, 72; Univ Minn, Minneapolis, MFA, 76. *Work:* Gen Mills, New York; Bank Am, San Francisco; Prudential Insurance Co, Northwestern Life Insurance, Faegre & Benson Law Firm, Minneapolis. *Exhib:* One-woman show, Am Gallery, Bern, Switz, 81; Drawing, Minneapolis Inst Arts, 81; Works on Paper, Davis-McClain Gallery, St Louis, 82; Of, On, Or About Paper, USA Today, Arlington, Va, 82; New American Paperworks, US & Far East, 82-84; and others. *Pos:* Printer, Vermillion Ed Ltd, Minneapolis, 76-79. *Awards:* Minn State Arts Bd Grants, 78 & 80. *Bibliog:* Mary A Martin (auth), Landscape portraiture, Twin Cities Mag, 80. *Mem:* St Paul Arts Collective. *Dealer:* Peter M David Gallery 430 Oak Grove Minneapolis MN. *Mailing Add:* 2129 Berkeley St Paul MN 55105

STARRS, MILDRED
PAINTER

b Brooklyn, NY. *Study:* Maxwell Training Sch Teachers; Pratt Inst; NY Univ, with J Haney, cert. *Work:* Meadowbrook Hosp, Long Island; John F Kennedy Bldg Art Gallery; George Washington Univ Law Sch, Washington, DC; Nat Gallery Sports, New York; Nassau Co Mus Fine Arts, 81. *Comn:* Sta Basket & Home, comn by Mr & Mrs Dick Waters, Conn; Dogwood, comn by Mr & Mrs John Robinson, NY; Arrangement in White Vase, comn by Mrs Harry Schroeder, Fla; Winter, comn by Mr & Mrs Noel Ehrler, 83; Dunes, comn by Mr & Mrs Thomas Smyth, 83; and others. *Exhib:* Catharine Lorillard Wolfe Art Club, Nat Gallery, 67; Hudson Valley Art Asn, Co Ctr, White Plains, NY, 69-77; Allied Artists Am, Nat Gallery, New York, 71 & 76; Am Watercolor Soc, Nat Gallery, New York, 77; Am Artists Prof League, Grand Cent Gallery, New York, 77; World Trade Ctr, 79; Claddaugh Gallery, Queens, NY, 80 & 81; Salmagundi Club, 83. *Teaching:* Instr art, Bd Educ, New York, 27-61, chmn art, 46-61. *Awards:* First Prize, St Luke Art Guild, 63 & 64; Best in Show, Catharine Lorillard Wolfe Art Club, 67; Spec Awards, Nat Art League, 70 & 79; Gold Medal & Best Watercolor in Show, Nat Art Club, 76. *Mem:* Am Artists Prof League; Art League Nassau Co; Nat Art League (vpres, 62-75); Catharine Lorillard Wolfe Art Club (mem bd dirs & treas, 66-81); Hudson Valley Art Asn; and others. *Media:* Watercolor, Pastel. *Mailing Add:* 301 Park Lane Douglaston NY 11363

STARS, WILLIAM KENNETH
EDUCATOR, MUSEUM DIRECTOR

b DePauw, Ind, Mar 13, 21. *Study:* Duke Univ, BA, 48; Dept Art, Univ NC, MA(art hist), 50; Dept Art Educ, NY Univ, 54-67. *Exhib:* Nat Collegiate Press Cartooning, 48; Ala Water Color Soc, 53-66; NC Mus Art, 53-66; High Mus, 53-66; Loeb Student Ctr, 53-66. *Collections Arranged:* All collections of the Duke Univ Mus Art, 67-83. *Pos:* Conservator & restorer, Duke Univ Mus Art, 67-73, actg dir, 73-74, dir, 74-83. *Teaching:* Instr sculpture & drawing, Durham High Sch, Duke Univ, 50-66; asst prof art educ, ceramics, Duke Univ, 69-75, assoc prof, 75-, dir arts & crafts workshop, 69- *Awards:* Nat Collegiate Press Cartooning Award, 48; Outstanding Prof, Duke Univ, 66. *Mem:* Int Inst Conserv; Southeastern Col Art Conf; Nat Art Educ Asn; Am Asn Univ Prof. *Media:* Egg Tempera. *Publ:* Auth, Richard Miller (catalog), Duke Univ Art Dept, 67; auth, DeGrazia of Arizona (catalog), Raimondo Puccinelli (catalog), 74 & Italian Paintings from the Mary & Harry L Dalton Collection, 74, Duke Univ Mus Art. *Mailing Add:* 2543 Sevier St Durham NC 27705

STASACK, EDWARD ARMEN
PAINTER, PRINTMAKER

b Chicago, Ill, Oct 1, 29. *Study:* Univ Ill, BFA & MFA. *Work:* Libr Cong, Washington, DC; Honolulu Acad Arts; Philadelphia Mus Art; Metrop Mus Art, New York; Art Inst Chicago. *Comn:* Precast concrete murals, City Honolulu, Fort St Mall, 68 & Honolulu Community Col, 72; Captain Cook Series (print portfolio), Hawaii State Found Cult & Arts; outdoor sculpture & wall sculpture, Hawaii State Intake Serv Ctr, Honolulu. *Exhib:* Krakow Print Biennial, Poland, 70; one-man show, Honolulu Acad Arts, Hawaii, 76; Cleveland Inst Art, 76; Amfac Exhib Room, Honolulu, 77; Ryan Gallery, Kailua, Hawaii, 81. *Teaching:* Prof art, Univ Hawaii, 69-, chmn dept, 69-72. *Awards:* Rockefeller Found Fel, 59; MacDowall Colony Found Fels, 71 & 75; Award, Exhib of Last Days of Capt Cook, Hawaii State & US Bicentennial Comn, 76. *Bibliog:* George Tahara (dir), Drawing-Painting-Stasack (film), 67; Neogy & Haar (auth), Artists of Hawaii, 74. *Mem:* Soc Am Graphic Artists; Honolulu Printmakers (pres, 59-61); Hawaii Artists League; Hawaii Arts Coun. *Media:* Acrylic, Oil; Collagraph. *Publ:* Auth, Hawaiian petroglyphs, Malamalama Mag, 67; auth, reviews, Honolulu Star-Bull, 68 & 74; coauth, Hawaiian petroglyphs, Bishop Mus, 70. *Mailing Add:* 2535 The Mall Univ Hawaii Honolulu HI 96822

STASIK, ANDREW J
PRINTMAKER, GALLERY DIRECTOR

b New Brunswick, NJ, Mar 16, 32. *Study:* NY Univ; Columbia Univ, BFA, 54; Univ Iowa; Ohio Univ, MFA, 56. *Work:* Mus Fine Arts, Budapest, Hungary; Nat Mus, Krakow, Poland; Metrop Mus Art, New York; Libr Cong, Nat Collection Fine Arts, Washington, DC; and many others. *Exhib:* Int Biennale Graphics, Krakow, Poland, 66, 68, 70 & 72; 4th Am Biennale Santiago, Chile, 70; one-man exhibs, Molloy Col, 71 & Jacques Baruch Gallery, 73; two-man exhib, Montclair State Col, 74; and others. *Pos:* Dir, Pratt Graphics Ctr, currently. *Teaching:* Vis assoc prof, Pratt Graphics Ctr, currently. *Awards:* Purchase Award, Okla Art Ctr, 70; Purchase Prize, Multiples Exhib, Western Mich Univ, 70; President's Award in Graphics, Audubon Artists Ann, 70; and many others. *Publ:* Auth & illusr, Prints & poems (folio), 63; ed, Printmaking in Eastern Europe, Abrams, 71; ed, Honore Daumier: A Centenary Tribute, 80. *Mailing Add:* Pratt Graphics Ctr 160 Lexington Ave New York NY 10016

STATMAN, JAN B
PAINTER, INSTRUCTOR

b New York, NY. *Study:* Hunter Col, with William Baziotes, Bernard Klonis & Richard Lippold, AB. *Work:* Mus Mod Art Alto Aragon, Huesca, Spain; Civic Mus Contemp Art, Sasso Ferrato, Italy; Longview Bank & Trust Co, Tex; Southland Savings Asn, Tex; plus others. *Exhib:* Solo exhibs, Barnwell Art Ctr, Shreveport, La, Craft Alliance, Shreveport, La, 83 & Longview Mus & Arts Ctr, Tex, 84; Ann Southwest Art Exhib, Mus Southwest, Midland, Tex, 81; Nat Sun Carnival Exhib, El Paso Mus Art, 82. *Pos:* Auth, Art Notes (weekly column), Longview News, 65-70, Artists World (weekly column), Gtr Longview Post, 70-77 & Final Word (weekly column), Dallas Morning News, 81-82; auth, Artists World (weekly column), Gtr Longview Post, 70-77. *Teaching:* Instr painting, Longview Mus & Arts Ctr, Tex, 72- & Kilgore Col, 82-; instr pvt workshops. *Awards:* First Prize Painting, 33rd Ann Cedar City Nat Art Exhib, Utah, 73; Best of Show & First Prize Oil & Acrylic Painting, 3rd Ann NMex Art League Small Painting Exhib, 73; Jr League Purchase Award, 25th Ann Exhib, Longview Mus & Arts Ctr, 83; plus others. *Bibliog:* Ruthe Winegarten (auth), A New York Yankee in Longview Texas, Equal Times, Dallas, Tex, 76; Donna Berliner (auth), Jan B Statman, Art Voices-South, 12/78; Rebecca Pflugefelder (auth), Artist's quest, Longview Morning J, 79. *Mem:* Artists Equity Asn; Tex Press Women; Nat Fedn Press Women. *Media:* Acrylic, Watercolor. *Mailing Add:* 27 Country Pl Longview TX 75601

STAUFFER, RICHARD L
SCULPTOR, EDUCATOR

b New Cambria, Kans, Apr 1, 32. *Study:* Kans State Teachers Col, with Norma Eppink, BSE, 55; Kans Univ, with Rueschoff & Timmerman, MS, 63; Wichita State Univ, MA, 69. *Work:* Jewish Community Ctr, Kansas City, Kans; Joslyn Art Mus, Omaha, Nebr; Hays Art Coun, Kans; Hutchinson Art Asn, Kans; Birger Sandzen Gallery, Lindsborg, Kans. *Comn:* Concretes, Friends of Art, Emporia, Kans, 72; wood assemblage, Lueatke, Los Angeles, 74; welded steel, Rock Springs Camp, Junction City, Kans, 78. *Exhib:* Western Arts, Walker Art Ctr, Minneapolis, Minn, 64; 7th Nat Crafts, Jackson, Miss, 71; Objects Mid-Am, Sheldon Mem Art Gallery, Lincoln, Nebr, 73; Glass Now, Joslyn Art Mus, Omaha, Nebr, 78; Business & Arts, Wichita Art Mus, Kans, 79; Hot & Cold Glass, Nebr Arts, Omaha, 79; Salina Art Ctr, Kans, 82 & 83. *Pos:* Treas & mem, Western Arts & Kans Artist Crafts, 71-77; area ed, Kans Art Educ Asn, 78-; dir, Kans High Sch Art Festival, 78-; newsletter ed, Kans Art Educ Asn, 80- *Teaching:* Asst prof art educ, Kans State Teachers Col, Emporia, 59-63; assoc prof sculpture, glassblowing & art educ, Emporia Kans State Univ, 63- *Awards:* Purchase Award, Smoky Hill Art Exhib, Norman Jeter, 76; Jurors' Pick, Crafts I, Ferguson, 77; Purchase Award, Salina Art Ctr, 83. *Bibliog:* Hoffaman (auth), Kansas designer crafts, Kansas City Star, 74; Kwolek-Holland (auth), article, Manhattan Mercury, 82. *Mem:* Kans Artist Craftsman Asn (treas, 77); Kans Art Educ Asn; Western Arts Asn; Community Arts Inc (pres, 72); Kans Sculptor Asn. *Media:* Glass. *Mailing Add:* 2001 Lincoln Emporia KS 66801

STAVANS, ISAAC
PAINTER

b Tampico, Mex, Aug 25, 31. *Study:* Mexico City Col, BA, 52; Brooklyn Col, MA, 53; apprentice to Arnold Belkin, 56-60. *Work:* Pedagogical Mus, Mex Inst Cult Relations, Mexico City. *Exhib:* International Week of the Plastic Arts, Mus City Mexico, 77; solo exhib, Artists House, Jerusalem, 77, Univ Ariz, 81 & Mus Art & Hist, Ciudad Juarez, Mex, 83; Recent Works, Misrachi Gallery, Mexico City, 79. *Teaching:* Instr painting, CDI Art Sch, 65-74, Hispanic-Mex Univ, 65-74 & privately, 74- *Bibliog:* Alfonso de Neuvillate (auth), Stavans: Reminiscences and evolations, Novedades Newspaper, 2/5/76; Berta Taracena (auth), Art: Recent shows, Tiempo Mag, 7/19/76; Bryan Johnstone (auth), Stavans inner landscapes, Ariz Daily Wildcat Newspaper, 1/23/81. *Mem:* Mex Soc Visual Artists. *Media:* Oil, Mixed Techniques. *Dealer:* Misrachi Gallery Genova No 20 Mexico 6 DF Mex 06600. *Mailing Add:* Bosque Minas 55B Apt 1104 Bosques Herradura Estado Mexico 53920 Mexico

STAVEN, LELAND CARROLL
PRINTMAKER, PAINTER

b Milwaukee, Wis, Dec 17, 33. *Study:* Univ Wis-Milwaukee, BFA, 56; Layton Sch Art, 57; Calif Col Arts & Crafts, MFA, 60; Ill Inst Technol, 63. *Work:* Univ Ga Art Mus; Ga Tech Univ Art Gallery; South DeKalb Col; LaGrange Col. *Exhib:* 18th Southeastern Ann Exhib, Atlanta, Ga, 63; Contemp Southern Art Exhib, 64; 1st Cent S Exhib, Nashville, Tenn, 66; 1st Ann Greater Birmingham Arts Alliance Exhib, Ala, 75; 2nd Ann Nat Dogwood Festival Art Show, Atlanta, 75. *Pos:* Vchmn, Ga Comn Arts, Atlanta, 67-72. *Teaching:* Chmn dept painting, drawing & printmaking, Berry Col, 60-68 & Mercer Univ Atlanta, 68-69; assoc prof painting, drawing & printmaking & cur, Dalton Galleries, Agnes Scott Col, 70- *Awards:* Purchase Awards, Asn Ga Artists, 61 & Fourth Ann Callaway Gardens Art Exhib, 67; Achievement Award, Appalachian Corridors: Exhib I, 68. *Mem:* Southeastern Col Art Conf. *Media:* Acrylic, Oil. *Dealer:* Ann Jacob Gallery Peachtree Ctr 231 Peachtree St NE Atlanta GA 30303. *Mailing Add:* 1553 Springbrook Dr Decatur GA 30033

STAYTON, JANET
PAINTER
b Natchez, Miss, Sept 2, 39. *Study:* Tex Christian Univ, BFA, 61; Tulane Univ, MFA, 63. *Work:* MacArthur Arts Ctr, Little Rock, Ark; Brooklyn Mus Fine Arts; Chase Manhattan Bank Collection, New York; Prudential Insurance Co, Newark, NJ; Lehman, Kuhn & Loeb, New York; and others. *Exhib:* One-woman exhibs, Hamilton Gallery, New York, 77, 79 & 80, Van Straaten Gallery, Chicago, 81 & Galerie Nord, Randers, Denmark, 82; Midyear Ann, Butler Inst Art, Youngstown, Ohio, 77; Painting & Sculpture Today, Indianapolis Mus Art, 78; Out of the House, Whitney Downtown Mus Art, 78; Expressions of Self, Douglass Art Gallery, Rutgers Univ, 79; 100 New Acquisitions, Brooklyn Mus, 81; Protagonisti, Il Ponte, Rome, 82. *Bibliog:* Hilton Kramer (auth), One-person show, Hamilton Gallery, New York Times, 11/77; Donna Stein (auth), New editions, Print Rev 10, fall 79. *Media:* Oil. *Dealer:* Michael Klein Inc 250 W 104 St New York 10025; Van Straaten Gallery 361 W Superior Chicago IL 60610. *Mailing Add:* 216 Lafayette St New York NY 10012

STEAD, REXFORD ARTHUR
ADMINISTRATOR, HISTORIAN
b Recife, Pernambuco, Brazil, Jan 24, 23; US citizen. *Study:* Brown Univ; Asia Inst, MA; also with Arthur Upham Pope & Robert von Heine-Geldern. *Collections Arranged:* Pre-Hispanic Art of Mexico, 65; Cocle Ceramics, 66; Art of Ancient Iran, 66; Sculpture of Ancient WMex, 70; Art of Black Africa, 73; Age of the Pharaohs, 74; Two Centuries of Black Am Art, 76; Heeramaneck Collection of Ancient Near Eastern & Cent Asian Art, 77-78. *Pos:* Dir, Mus Fine Arts, St Petersburg, Fla, 62-67, hon trustee, 68-; deputy dir, Los Angeles Co Mus Art, 67-79. *Mem:* Am Asn Mus; Calif Confederation of the Arts; Nat Schs Alumni Coun. *Res:* Ancient art with emphasis on pre-Islamic Iran, also Safavid period court carpets. *Publ:* Contribr, A Survey of Persian Art, A U Pope Mem Vol, 72; auth, The Ardabil Carpets, 74. *Mailing Add:* 1688 Marmont Ave Los Angeles CA 90069

STEADMAN, DAVID WILTON
MUSEUM DIRECTOR
b Honolulu, Hawaii, Oct 24, 36. *Study:* Harvard Col, BA(magna cum laude), 60; Harvard Univ, MAT, 61; Univ Calif, Berkeley, MA(art hist), 66; Princeton Univ, PhD, 74. *Collections Arranged:* P P Rubens before 1620 (with catalog), Princeton Art Mus, 71; Selections from the Norton Simon, Inc Mus Art (with catalog), 73; Graphic Art of Francisco Goya (with catalog), Galleries of Claremont Cols, 75, 18th Century Drawing from California Collections (with catalog), 76 & Works on Paper 1900-1960 from Southern Calif Collections (with catalog), 77. *Pos:* Lectr, Frick Collection, New York, 70-71; asst dir, Art Mus, Princeton Univ, 71-72, actg dir, 72-73, assoc dir, 73; dir, Galleries of Claremont Cols, 74-80; res cur, Norton Simon Mus, Pasadena, Calif, 77-80. *Teaching:* Asst prof 17th & 18th centuries art, Pomona Col, 74-78, assoc prof, 78-80. *Awards:* Nat Defense Educ Act fel, 66-69; Chester Dale Fel, Nat Gallery Art, 69-70. *Mem:* Am Asn Mus Dirs; Col Art Asn; Art Mus Assoc (trustee). *Res:* 17th and 18th century drawings. *Publ:* Auth, Abraham van Dipenbeeck, UMI Res Press, 82. *Mailing Add:* Chrysler Museum Olney Rd & Mowbray Arch Norfolk VA 23510

STEARNS, ROBERT
CURATOR, ADMINISTRATOR
b Los Angeles, Calif, Aug 28, 47. *Study:* Calif State Univ, San Luis Obispo, 68; Univ Calif, San Diego, BFA, 70. *Collections Arranged:* Dimensions of Black (auth, catalog), La Jolla Mus, 70; Kes Zapkus: Paintings 1968-78 (auth, catalog), 78, Robert Wilson: From A Theater of Images (auth, catalog), 80, Alex Katz: Paintings and Drawings 1959-79, 81 & Dynamix and The New Art of Energy (auth, catalog), 82, Contemp Arts Ctr, Cincinnati; Tableaux, 82, Scott Burton Chairs, 83 & Word Works (auth, catalog), Walker Art Ctr, Minneapolis. *Pos:* Asst dir, Paula Cooper Gallery, New York, 70-72; dir, The Kitchen Ctr for Video & Music, New York, 72-78; founding dir & pres, Artists Television Network, New York, 76-77; dir, Contemp Arts Ctr, Cincinnati, 78-82; dir performing arts, Walker Art Ctr, Minneapolis, 82- *Teaching:* Lectr performance art & alternative media, var US cols & univs. *Mem:* Col Art Asn; New Music Alliance Inc; Ohio Found Arts Inc (bd trustees, 81-82); Minn Independent Choreographer's Alliance (bd trustees, currently). *Publ:* Ed, The Kitchen Center Annual, Haleakala Inc, 75 & 76; contribr, Video Art: An Anthology, Harcourt Brace, 76. *Mailing Add:* Walker Art Ctr Vineland Place Minneapolis MN 55403

STEARNS, THOMAS ROBERT
SCULPTOR, EDUCATOR
b Oklahoma City, Okla, Sept 4, 36. *Study:* Memphis Acad Art, Tenn, 55-57; Cranbrook Acad Art, 57-60; Acad Belli Arti, Venice, Italy, 60-61. *Work:* Minn Mus Art, St Paul; Venini Mus, Venice, Italy; Mus Art, Iowa City, Iowa; Ringling Mus, Sarasota, Fla. *Exhib:* Seattle World's Fair, Wash, 61; Brussels Int, Belgium, 61; Venice Biennale, Venice, Italy, 62; Glass: Czechoslovakia & Italy, Mus Contemp Crafts, New York, 64; Am Oil Painting & Sculpture, Pa Acad Fine Arts Mus, 66; Johnson Collection, Objects, Smithsonian Inst, Washington, DC, 69; Drawing USA, Minn Mus, St Paul, 71; Pacemakers and Trendsetters, Detroit Inst Art, Mich, 73; Venini Retrospective Renwick, Nat Mus Am Art, Washington, DC, 81. *Pos:* Guest research designer, Venini Glass, Venice, Italy, 60-62. *Teaching:* Assoc prof sculpture & painting, Philadelphia Col Art, 70- *Awards:* Italian Govt Award Fel, 60-61; John Simon Guggenheim Fel, 65-66; Nat Inst Arts & Letters Grant, 65-66. *Bibliog:* Domas (auth), Thomas Stearns per Venini, Domasmagazine, Italy, 62; New York Commentary, Thomas Stearns, Willard Gallery, Studio Int, 64. *Media:* Mixed, Charcoal. *Mailing Add:* 2121 Walnut St (Van Pelt Entrance) Philadelphia PA 19103

STEBBINS, THEODORE ELLIS, JR
HISTORIAN, ADMINISTRATOR
b New York, NY, Aug 11, 38. *Study:* Yale Univ, BA, 60; Harvard Univ Law Sch, JD, 64, Harvard Univ, PhD, 71. *Collections Arranged:* Luminous Landscape, Fogg Art Mus, 66; Martin Johnson Heade, Whitney Mus Am Art, 69; New Haven Scene, New Haven Colony Hist Soc, 70; Richard Brown Baker Collects, Yale Univ, 75; Am Landscapes at the Wadsworth Atheneum, Hudson River Sch, 76; Am Master Drawings, Whitney Mus, 76. *Pos:* Assoc cur, Garvan Collections, Yale Univ Art Gallery, 68-77, cur Am painting & sculpture, 71-77; cur Am painting, Mus of Fine Arts, Boston, Mass, 77- *Teaching:* Instr hist art, Smith Col, 67; asst prof hist art, Yale Univ, 69-75, Morse fel, 72, assoc prof, 75-77; vis prof, Boston Univ, 78, prof art hist, 82- *Awards:* Chester Dale Fel, Nat Gallery Art, Washington, DC, 66. *Mem:* Col Art Asn Am; Am Fedn Arts. *Res:* American landscape painting of the nineteenth century; history of American drawings and watercolors. *Collection:* Nineteenth and twentieth century American art. *Publ:* Auth, Alice Kaplan, collector, 5-6/82 & American masters, 9-10/83, Portfolio; co-ed, American Paintings at Yale University, Yale Univ Art Gallery, 82; coauth, The Lane Collection: 20th Century Paintings in the American Tradition, 83 & A New World: Masterpieces of American Painting, 1760-1910, 83, Mus Fine Arts, Boston Univ; and others. *Mailing Add:* Mus of Fine Arts Boston MA 02115

STECKEL, ANITA
COLLAGE ARTIST, PAINTER
b New York, NY. *Study:* Cooper Union; Art Students League, with Edwin Dickenson. *Work:* Patrick Lannan Mus, Palm Beach, Fla. *Exhib:* Whitney Mus, 69; Bronx Mus, 76; Brooklyn Mus, 77; Krannert Mus, Ill, 77; Biennial, Columbia, SAm, 81; Documenta Seven, Kassel, Ger, 82; Patrick Lannan Mus, Palm Beach, Fla, 82. *Teaching:* Art, Parsons Sch Design, 79- *Awards:* Nat Endowment Arts Grant Painting, 83. *Bibliog:* Dorothy Seiberling (auth), article, New York Mag; Lawrence Campbell (auth), article, Art News; Maryse Holder (auth), article, Changes. *Media:* Collage, Oil. *Publ:* Auth, The Art of New York, Abrams, 83; auth, The Male Nude, Paddington Press. *Dealer:* Alex Rosenberg 20 W 57th St New York NY. *Mailing Add:* 463 West St New York NY 10014

STECKEL, HARRIET JEANNE See Yaffa Yael Stec-El

STECKLER, STUART JAY
DEALER, COLLECTOR
b New York, NY, Sept 29, 31. *Pos:* Owner, Ex Libris Art Books, Scottsdale, Ariz, currently. *Collection:* Contemporary American art; New York school; abstract illusionism; photorealism; contemporary American Indian sculpture. *Mailing Add:* 5024 North 45th Pl Phoenix AZ 85018

STECZYNSKI, JOHN MYRON
DRAFTSMAN, EDUCATOR
b Chicago, Ill, June 22, 36. *Study:* Art Inst Chicago; Craft Ctr, Worcester, Mass; Univ Notre Dame, BFA, 58; Yale Univ, Woodrow Wilson fel, 58, MFA, 61; Acad Fine Arts, Polish Govt grant, 60, Warsaw; and with Umberto Romano. *Comn:* Wood relief panels, Ursuline Provincialate, Kirkwood, Mo, 57-58; wood sculpture, Moreau Sem, Notre Dame, Ind, 58, Jossals for Easter, 71, Christmas, 71, Lent, 73 & Penticost, 75, Univ Lutheran Church, Cambridge, Mass; drawing, James de Normandie, 80; drawing, Boston Col, 83; and others. *Exhib:* Dom Akademicki, Warsaw, Poland, 61; Stone Church, Lincoln, Mass, 80; Helen Shlien Gallery, Boston, 80; Univ Luthern Church, 81; Boston Col Gallery, 81 & 84; and others. *Teaching:* Prof art, Worcester Art Mus Sch, 61-64; instr art hist, Boston Mus Fine Arts Sch, 64-67 & Tufts in Italy, Naples, 67-68; asst prof & chmn dept art, Newton Col Sacred Heart, 68-75; asst prof, Boston Col, 75-79, assoc prof, 79-, asst chmn dept fine arts, 77- *Awards:* Polish Arts Club Chicago Prize, 59; Chopin Fine Arts Club Award, Butler Inst Am Art, 61. *Media:* Pen & Ink; Miscellaneous Media. *Mailing Add:* Dept Art Boston Col Chestnut Hill MA 02167

STEEL, RHYS CAPARN See Caparn, Rhys

STEEL, VIRGINIA OBERLIN
GALLERY DIRECTOR, CURATOR
b Pa, Sept 27, 50. *Study:* Carnegie-Mellon Univ; Univ Hartford, BA, 73; Univ Mass-Amherst, MA, 75. *Collections Arranged:* Rutgers National Works on Paper Competition, 77, 79, 81 & 83; Contemp Artists Exhibs, 77, 78 & 82. *Pos:* Dir, Stedman Art Gallery, Rutgers Univ, Camden, NJ, 76- *Teaching:* Mus Studies Prog, Rutgers Univ, Camden, NJ, 79- *Mem:* Am Asn Mus; Col Art Asn. *Mailing Add:* Stedman Art Gallery Rutgers Univ Camden NJ 08102

STEELE, BENJAMIN CHARLES
PAINTER, EDUCATOR
b Roundup, Mont, Nov 17, 17. *Study:* Cleveland Inst Art, dipl; Kent State Univ, BS; Denver Univ, MA; Univ Ore; Ill State Univ; Mont State Univ. *Comn:* Arts of the West (mural), Denver Univ; Indoor and Outdoor Sports (mural), Eastern Mont Col; and pvt collections. *Exhib:* Fedn Rocky Mountain States, 68; Yellowstone Art Ctr Auction Shows, 68-; Billings Arts Asn Verbal-Visual Shows, 74-; Mont Arts & Crafts Exhib, Senate Caucus Room, Washington, DC; Mont Inst Arts Little Festival, 75- *Teaching:* Art teacher, New London, Ohio High Sch, 51-52; crafts dir, Fort Riley, Kans, 53-54; staff crafts dir, Mil District Wash, 54-56 & Fort MacPherson, Ga, 54-59; prof art & head dept, Eastern Mont Col, Billings, 59-82, prof emer, 82- *Awards:* Teacher of the Year, Mont Art Educ Asn, 64; Teaching Merit Award, Eastern Mont Col, 77; Distinguished Prof Award, Eastern Mont Col, 80. *Bibliog:*

Dorothy Larsen (auth), Man of gentle fiber & Nancy Olson (auth), Briefly biographical, Mont Arts Mag; also feature art in Washington Post, Altanta Const, Kansas City Star & many others. *Mem:* Nat Art Educ Asn; Am Asn Univ Professors; Billings Art Asn; Mont Inst Arts; Yellowstone Art Ctr; and others. *Publ:* Auth, Craft Directors Handbook, 55; illusr, Code of the US fighting man, Army Digest, 66; illusr, cover design, Mont Arts, 73; illusr, cover designs, Horizons O'er the Musselshell, Along the Zimmerman Trail, 74 & Tracking Billings' Past. *Mailing Add:* 2425 Cascade Ave Billings MT 59102

STEELE, LISA
VIDEO ARTIST
b Kansas City, Mo, Sept 22, 47. *Study:* Univ Mo, Kansas City, 65-68. *Work:* Art Gallery of Ont, Toronto; The Kitchen, New York; Western Front, Vancouver, BC. *Exhib:* A Response to the Environment, Rutgers Univ Art Gallery, New Brunswick, NJ, 75; Video Int, Aarhus Mus of Art, Denmark, 76; Videotapes, Mus of Mod Art, New York, 77; Southland Video Anthology, Part 4, Long Beach Mus of Art, Calif, 77; Kunsthalle, Basel, Switz, 78; Venice Biennale, 80; and others. *Pos:* Video coordr, A Space Gallery, Toronto, 72-74. *Bibliog:* Peggy Gale (auth), Lisa Steele: Looking very closely, Parachute, Montreal, 1-3/76; Eric Cameron (auth), Structural videotape in Canada, In: Video Art, Harcourt, Brace & Jovanovich, 76; Peggy Gale, Video art in Canada: Four worlds, Studio Int, London, 5-6/76. *Media:* Videotape. *Mailing Add:* c/o Art Metropole 217 Richmond St W 2nd Floor Toronto ON M5V 1W2 Canada

STEEN, CAROL J
SCULPTOR, PAINTER
Highland Park, Mich, Nov 6, 43. *Study:* Mich State Univ, BA, 65; Cranbrook Acad Art, MFA, 71. *Work:* Printmaking Workshop, New York; Smithsonian Archives Am Art; Am Craft Mus, New York. *Exhib:* Damon Brandt Gallery, New York, 83; Personal Expressions, Valencia Col, Fla, 83; Newcastle Invitational, Newcastle Polytechnic Gallery, England, 83; two-person exhib, Univ Calif, Berkeley, 83; 12 Years, 55 Mercer Street Gallery, New York, 83; and many others. *Teaching:* Ford Found vis lectr studio art, Univ Mich, 75; asst prof studio art, William Paterson Col, 77-82 & Touro Col, 83- *Awards:* Founders Soc Purchase Prize, 22nd Artist Craftsman Exhib, Detroit Inst Art, 71; Fel, MacDowell Colony, Peterborough, NH, 80; Grant, Printmaking Workshop, New York, 82. *Bibliog:* Joy Hakanson Colby (auth), 3 artists in New York City, Detroit News Mag, 9/77; Vered Lieb (auth), Artists on art, Re-View Mag, 79; Jon Friedman (auth), article, Arts Mag, 12/82. *Mem:* Col Art Asn, New York; 55 Mercer St Gallery, New York (pres, 82-, bd dirs, 83-). *Media:* Metal; Tar. *Dealer:* Damon Brandt Gallery 45 Bond St New York NY 10012. *Mailing Add:* 163 Bowery New York NY 10002

STEFAN, ROSS
PAINTER
b Milwaukee, Wis, June 13, 34. *Study:* Primarily self-taught; collab with Dan Muller, Milwaukee, Dale Nichols, Antigua, Guatemala & Frederic Whitaker, La Jolla, Calif. *Work:* Ford Motor Co; Milwaukee Jour; Harmsen's Western Americana, Denver; Gilcrease Inst Am Hist & Art, Tulsa; Amerind Found, Dragoon, Ariz. *Exhib:* One-man shows, Rosequist Galleries, Tucson, 70-82; Our Western Heritage, Univ Ariz, 62; Grand Central Art Galleries, New York, 72; 34th Ann Ariz Exhib, Rosequist Galleries, 82; and others. *Awards:* Artist of the Yr, Tucson Festival Soc Award, 78. *Bibliog:* Sen Barry Goldwater (auth), Ross Stefan 1975, Wollheims' Rosequist Galleries; John K Goodman (auth), Ross Stefan: An Impressionistic Painter of the Contemporary Southwest, Northland Press, 77; Jon Stefan (auth), article, Artists of the Rockies, fall 79. *Media:* Oil on Canvas. *Res:* Painters of the Southwest as it is today; since 1948, Southern Arizona, Navajo and Hopi country, the Rio Grande North to Santa Fe and Taos, New Mexico. *Mailing Add:* c/o Rosequist Galleries 2843 N Campbell Ave Tucson AZ 85719

STEFANELLI, JOE
PAINTER
b Philadelphia, Pa, Mar 20, 21. *Study:* Philadelphia Mus Col Art, 38-40; Pa Acad Fine Arts, 40-41; New Sch Social Res, New York, 49-50; Art Students League, 50-51; Hans Hofmann Sch Painting, New York, 51-52. *Work:* Whitney Mus Am Art; Walker Art Ctr; Norfolk Art Mus; Baltimore Mus; NY Univ; and others. *Comn:* Mural, Brooklyn Bd Educ, 71. *Exhib:* Whitney Mus Am Art; Mus Mod Art, New York; Pa Acad Fine Arts; Walker Art Ctr, Minneapolis; Corcoran Gallery Art; Carnegie Inst Int; Art Inst Chicago; one-man shows, Westbeth Galleries, 71, New Sch Social Res, 72 & Ingber Gallery, 84; and others. *Teaching:* Instr, Univ Calif, Berkeley, summers 60 & 63; vis critic, Cornell Univ; artist in residence, Princeton Univ, 63-66; vis critic, Univ Ark; instr, Columbia Univ, 66-74; instr, New Sch Social Res, 66- *Awards:* Fulbright Award for Rome, 58-59; Am Res Ctr Egypt Fel, 66-67; NY State Coun Arts Award, 71; and others. *Mem:* Fel Am Research Ctr Egypt. *Dealer:* Ingber Gallery 460 W Broadway New York NU 10012. *Mailing Add:* 463 West St D1006 New York NY 10014

STEFANOTTI, ROBERT ALAN
ADMINISTRATOR
b Arlington, NJ, Feb 1, 47. *Study:* Bowland Col, Univ Lancaster, Eng, AB(with hons); Bryn Mawr Grad Sch. *Pos:* Chief consult, Rollins Found, currently. *Mailing Add:* 70 Greenwich #517 New York NY 10011

STEFFLER, ALVA W
EDUCATOR, CURATOR
b Philadelphia, Pa, June 22, 34. *Study:* Pa Art Acad; Ind Univ, MAT; Northern Ill Univ, MFA. *Pos:* Cur & dir Am art collection, Wheaton Col, Ill; 71- *Teaching:* Asst prof art hist, painting & sculpture, Grace Col, Winona Lake, Ind, 67-69; assoc prof studio & art hist, Wheaton Col, Ill, 69- *Res:* American art history and museology. *Mailing Add:* 318 E Madison Wheaton IL 60187

STEG, J L
PRINTMAKER, PAINTER
b Alexandria, Va. *Study:* Rochester Inst Technol, cert; State Univ Iowa, BFA & MFA. *Work:* Libr Cong, Washington, DC; Smithsonian Nat Collection, Washington, DC; Brooklyn Mus, NY; Mus Mod Art, New York; Fogg Mus, Cambridge, Mass. *Exhib:* One-man shows, Weyhe Gallery, 45 & Assoc Am Artists, 64, New York; Big Prints USA, State Univ NY Col New Paltz, 68; USIS Cult Ctr, Ankara, Turkey, 75; 30 Year Retrospective Traveling Exhib, New Orleans Mus Art, 78; and others. *Teaching:* Instr drawing & painting, Cornell Univ, 49-51; prof drawing & printing, Tulane Univ La, 51- *Awards:* Charles Lea Prize, Philadelphia Print Club, 50-64; Purchase Prize, Eighth Int Print & Drawing Exhib, Lugano, 64; Purchase Prizes, State Univ NY Col Potsdam Print Exhib, 64-68. *Mem:* Am Color Print Soc. *Publ:* Auth, article, Artists Proof, 66. *Dealer:* Assoc Am Artists 663 Fifth Ave New York NY 10022. *Mailing Add:* Newcomb Col Dept of Art Tulane Univ New Orleans LA 70118

STEGEMAN, CHARLES
PAINTER, EDUCATOR
b Ede, Netherlands, June 5, 24; Can citizen. *Study:* Acad Beeldende Kunst, The Hague; Acad Royale Beaux Arts, Brussels; Inst Nat Superieur Beaux-Arts, Antwerp. *Work:* Nat Gallery Can; Ont Art Gallery; Vancouver Art Gallery; Art Gallery Gtr Victoria; Univ BC. *Exhib:* Western Art Circuit, Western Can, 52-53; Toronto Art Gallery, 61; Winnipeg Biannual, 61; Montreal Mus Fine Arts, 62; Chicago Centennial Exhib, Ill, 63. *Teaching:* Prof painting, Art Inst Chicago, 62-69; prof painting & chmn dept fine arts, Haverford Col, 69- *Awards:* Humanities Fel, Medical Col Pa, 81- *Media:* Oil, Acrylic. *Mailing Add:* 2 College Circle Haverford PA 19041

STEGMAN, PATRICIA
PAINTER
b San Antonio, Tex, Nov 27, 29. *Study:* Kansas City Univ, Mo, 48-49; Kansas City Art Inst, Mo, BFA, 52; Art Students League, study with Reginald Marsh, Will Barnet, Vaclav Vytlacil & Morris Kantor, 54-57. *Exhib:* Life Drawings, Atlantic Gallery, Brooklyn, NY, 77; Tenth St Now, Landmark Gallery, New York, NY, 77; Tenth St Days--Retrospective of Art of the 50s, Fourteen Sculptors Gallery, New York, 77; one-artist shows, Brata Gallery, New York, 61 & 63 & Gallery 91, Brooklyn, 75 & 76; and others. *Pos:* Scenic artist/designer, Circle Repertory Co, New York, 74 & Big Apple Theatre Co, Brooklyn, 74 & 75; staff writer, Artists Review Art, New York & Phoenix (newspaper), Brooklyn, 76- *Teaching:* Instr painting & drawing, Kansas City Art Inst, 52. *Mem:* Art Students League. *Media:* Oil, Watercolor. *Dealer:* Atlantic Gallery 458 W Broadway New York NY 10012. *Mailing Add:* 245 Dean St Brooklyn NY 11217

STEIDER, DORIS (MRS C B MCCAMPBELL)
PAINTER, SCULPTOR
b Decatur, Ill, Apr 10, 24. *Study:* Purdue Univ, BS(appl design), 45; Kirksville Col Osteopathy, Cert Lab Technician, 49; Univ NMex, with Kenneth Adams, MA(fine art), 65. *Work:* WTex Mus, Lubbock; NMex Governor's Collection, Santa Fe; Holt, Rinehart & Winston; NMex State Fair Collection, Albuquerque Pub Libr Print Collection. *Comn:* Sixteen wall panels (collaborated with Betty Sabo), St Joseph's Hosp, Albuquerque, 66. *Exhib:* Nat League Am Pen Women, Smithsonian Inst, DC, 63; Army Traveling Print Shows, US Army, 63-64; Ann Competition by Invitation, Witte Mus Western Art, San Antonio, Tex & Mont State Hist Soc Mus, Helena, 65; one-man exhib, Triton Mus, San Jose, Calif, 68; Ft Sill Int Show, Okla, 74; Spring Panarama Art, Baker Gallery Fine Art, Lubbock, Tex, 81; plus many others. *Awards:* Special Award for Traditional Oils, Nat League Am Pen Women, 65; First Sculpture, 13th Ann Nat Art Show, La Junta, Colo, 81. *Bibliog:* Mary Carroll Nelson (auth), Doris Steider chose egg tempera, Am Artist Mag, 78; Mary Carroll Nelson (auth), Doris Steider, Art Voices South, 9-10/80. *Mem:* Nat League Am Pen Women (nat bd mem, 75); Artist's Equity. *Media:* Egg Tempera; Bronze. *Dealer:* Baker Gallery of Fine Art 13th & Ave L Lubbock TX 79408. *Mailing Add:* Rt 5 Box 5235 Apt 23-C Albuquerque NM 87123

STEIG, WILLIAM
CARTOONIST, SCULPTOR
b New York, NY, Nov 14, 07. *Study:* City Col New York, 23-25; Nat Acad Design, 25-29. *Work:* Wood sculpture, RI Mus Art & Smith Col; paintings, Brooklyn Mus. *Exhib:* One-man exhib, Downtown Gallery, New York, 39; Smith Col, 40; and others. *Awards:* Caldecott Medal, 70; William Allen White Award, 75; Christopher Award for Dominic, 73. *Media:* Wood. *Publ:* Auth & illusr, The Real Thief, 73, Dominic, 72, Abel's Island, 76, The Amazing Bone, 76 & Caleb & Kate, 77; contribr, New Yorker & other leading mags. *Mailing Add:* RD 1 Box KH2 Kent CT 06757

STEIGER, FREDERIC
PAINTER, INSTRUCTOR
b Solwutz, Rumania; Can citizen. *Study:* Self taught. *Work:* Contemporary Art Western Hemisphere, Int Bus Machine Corp; Hallmark Collection Can Art, Toronto; Toronto Pub Libr; Mem Univ Nfld. *Comn:* Portraits of speakers & prime ministers including Premier J R Smallwood of Nfld, 51, Premier William G Davis of Ont, 76 & John C Crosbie, 83; painting for Imperial Oil Bldg, St John's, Nfld; Hallmark Cards, 62-74; painting, Lt Col Keiller MacKay, former Lt Gov Ont, 65. *Exhib:* Eaton Fine Art Gallery, Toronto,

73-79; Can Opera Festival, O'Keefe Centre Gallery, Toronto, 74; Royal Can Acad; Ont Soc Artists; Mem Univ, St John's; Montreal Mus Fine Arts; Vancouver Art Gallery. *Teaching:* Teacher, Summer Sch Teachers, Woodstock, Ont & pvt studio. *Awards:* Bronze Medal for Courage; Contemporary Art of Western Hemisphere, IBM Corp. *Bibliog:* Articles in La Rev Mod, Paris & Oesterreichische Kunst, Vienna. *Media:* Oil. *Dealer:* Galerie Lyson Cumberland Square Toronto ON. *Mailing Add:* 406 Bloor St E Toronto ON M4W 1H4 Canada

STEIGMAN, MARGOT See Robinson, Margot

STEIN, CLAIRE A
ADMINISTRATOR
b New York, NY, Sept 19, 23. *Study:* Art Students League; Adelphi Col, BA; sculpture with Robert Cronbach. *Collections Arranged:* Nat Sculpture Soc Ann, 68-80; North Shore Community Art Ctr Exhib, 60s. *Pos:* Bd dir, North Shore Community Art Ctr, 57-62; exec dir, Nat Sculpture Soc, 67- *Publ:* Contribr, Nat Sculpture Rev, fall 73, winter 74 & 75 & spring 75; contribr sculpture suppl, Grolier Encyclopedia, 70-73. *Mailing Add:* c/o Nat Sculpture Soc 15 E 26th St New York NY 10010

STEIN, DONNA MICHELE
CURATOR, CRITIC
b Los Angeles, Calif, Oct 2, 42. *Study:* Univ Calif, Los Angeles, BA, 63; NY Univ Inst Fine Arts, MA, 65. *Collections Arranged:* Selected Prints from the Private Collection of Farah Pahlavi, Her Imperial Majesty, the Shahbanou of Iran (cataloged), Negarestan Mus, Tehran, 76; Drawings by 14 Young American Artists (cataloged), Galerie Litho, Tehran, 76; Nature: 12 Americans (cataloged), Iran-Am Soc, Tehran, 78; and others. *Pos:* Registr, Pasadena Art Mus, 64; asst cur dept prints & illus bks, Mus Mod Art, 66-72; cur, RCA Corp Collection, 73-75; consult mod art & mus, Spec Bureau of Her Imperial Majesty, the Shahbanou of Iran, 75-77; consult/archivist, l Universal Ltd Art Ed, West Ilsip, NY, 78-81. *Teaching:* Adj fac hist of prints, New Sch Social Res, New York, 73-75; fac contemp art, NY Univ, 74-75. *Awards:* Nat Endowment Art Fel, 72-73; French Govt Grant, summer 80; Nat Endowment Arts Design Arts, 83. *Mem:* Col Art Asn; Art Table. *Res:* Late 19th and 20th century art, architecture, prints and photography. *Publ:* Auth, L'Estampe Originale, a Catalogue Raisonne, Mus Graphic Art, 70; auth, Thomas Wilfred: Lumia, Corcoran Gallery Art, DC, 71; auth, The PepsiCo Sculpture Collection, PepsiCo, Purchase, NY, 80; auth, The cubist print, Art Mus, Univ Calif, Santa Barbara, 81; auth, Cubist Prints/Cubist Books, Franklin Furnace, NY, 83; and others. *Mailing Add:* 41 W 72nd St New York NY 10023

STEIN, FRITZ HENRY
DEALER
b New York, NY, July 25, 32. *Study:* Univ RI, BA; New York Sch Interior Design; also with Harve Stein & Murray Kupferman. *Pos:* Art dir, G Fox Co, Hartford, Conn, 55-60; co-owner, Constitution Galleries, West Hartford, Conn & Gloucester, Mass, 60-63; interior designer, Silberman's of Norwich, Conn, 63-71; owner, Stone Ledge Studio Art Galleries, Noank, Conn, 71- *Mem:* Noank Hist Soc, Conn (dir); Mystic Art Asn, Conn (dir & pres, 83-84). *Specialty:* Eighteenth and nineteenth century collectors gallery; contemp Am artists. *Mailing Add:* Box 237 59 High St Noank CT 06340

STEIN, HARVE
PAINTER, RESTORER
b Chicago, Ill, Apr 23, 04. *Study:* Art Inst Chicago, 22-26; Julian Acad, Paris, France, 27; Art Students League, 30-33; and with Harvey Dunn & Jacques Maroger. *Work:* US State Dept; Univ Minn; Brown Univ; Pub Arch, Toronto; Montclair Art Mus, NJ; and others. *Exhib:* Nat Watercolor Exhibs throughout US. *Pos:* Restorer, Stone Ledge Studio Art Galleries, Noank, Conn, 63- *Teaching:* Prof fine art, RI Sch Design, 44-69, emer prof, 69-; instr painting, Conn Col, 46, 47 & 51; instr, New London Art Students League, 48-59; Mitchell Col, summer sessions, 55-56. *Awards:* Providence Watercolor Club Award, 56; New Haven Paint & Clay Club, 57; Providence Art Club, 63; plus others. *Mem:* Hon life mem Soc Illustrators; life mem Am Watercolor Soc; Audubon Artists; Artists Fel; Appraisers Asn Am; and others. *Media:* Watercolor. *Publ:* Illusr, many bks; contribr, nat mags; auth, Illustrator explains, Am Artist Mag, 58. *Mailing Add:* PO Box 237 Noank CT 06340

STEIN, JUDITH ELLEN
HISTORIAN, CURATOR
b New York, NY, June 27, 43. *Study:* Barnard Col, Columbia Univ, BA(art hist), 65; Univ Pa, MA(art hist), 67, PhD(art hist), 81. *Pos:* Staff lectr, Philadelphia Mus Art, 66-71; arts reviewer, Art in Am, 74-82 & Nat Pub Radio, Philadelphia, 79-; coordr, Morris Gallery, Pa Acad Fine Arts, 81-; asst cur, Pa Acad Fine Arts, 83- *Teaching:* Instr, Tyler Sch Art, Philadelphia, 71-78. *Mem:* Col Art Asn; Int Art Critics Asn (nat adv bd, 79-81). *Res:* Iconography during the late 18th and 19th centuries, and the education and careers of 19th century women artists. *Publ:* Auth, Dating the Bardi St Francis Master Dossal: Text and Image, Franciscan Studies, 76; auth, Portrait: Philadelphia, Portfolio, 80; auth, American Realism, Connoisseur, 81; auth, The Artists' New Clothes, Portfolio, 83. *Mailing Add:* 2400 Waverly Philadelphia PA 19146

STEIN, LUDWIG K
EDUCATOR, PAINTER
b Wyoming, Del, Mar 20, 38. *Study:* Kutztown State Col, BFA, 64; Tyler Sch Art, with Steve Green, David Pease & Charles Schmitt, MFA, 69. *Work:* Sheldon Mem Gallery Art, Univ Nebr, Lincoln; Everson Mus Art, Syracuse, NY; Philadelphia Mus Art; Univ Belfast, Ireland; Long Beach Art Found, NJ.

Exhib: One-man shows, Newport Harbor Art Mus, Calif, 77, Newcastle-Upon-Tyne, Eng, 77, Lubin House, New York, 78, Richard Demarco Gallery, Edinburgh, Scotland, 78 & St Martins Col Art, London, 78; and many others. *Teaching:* Instr, Wis State Univ, Eau Claire, 69-71; instr, Univ Calif, Northridge, 71-72; assoc prof, Syracuse Univ, NY, 72- *Awards:* Best Show, Waterloo Regional, Iowa, 71; Jurors Award, Tyler Alumni, 76; Grant, Northern British Arts Coun, 77. *Mem:* Col Art Asn. *Media:* Acrylic, Watercolor. *Mailing Add:* c/o Marian Locks Gallery 1524 Walnut St Philadelphia PA 19102

STEIN, ROGER BREED
HISTORIAN, EDUCATOR
b Orange, NJ, Mar 29, 32. *Study:* Harvard Univ, AB, 54, AM, 58, PhD, 60. *Collections Arranged:* The View & the Vision (with catalog), Henry Art Gallery, Univ Wash, 68; Seascape & the American Imagination (with catalog), Whitney Mus Am Art, 75. *Teaching:* Assoc prof Eng & Am art hist, Univ Wash, Seattle, 67-70; assoc prof, State Univ NY, Binghamton, 70- *Awards:* Prize in Humanities, Am Acad Arts & Sci, 60; Guggenheim Fel, 68-69; Smithsonian Fel, Nat Collection Fine Arts, 77-78. *Mem:* Am Studies Asn; Orgn Am Historians; Mod Lang Asn; Col Art Asn Am. *Publ:* Auth, John Ruskin & American Aesthetic Thought, 1840-1900, 67; auth, Introduction, American Naval Prints, Int Exhibs Found, Washington, DC, 76-77; auth, Structure as meaning: Towards a cultural interpretation of American painting, Am Art Rev III, 76; auth, Copley's Watson and the Shark and aesthetics in the 1770's, Discoveries & Considerations, State Univ NY Press, 76. *Mailing Add:* Dept of Art & Art Hist State Univ NY Binghamton NY 13901

STEIN, RONALD JAY
SCULPTOR
b New York, NY, Sept 15, 30. *Study:* Cooper Union, cert fine art, with Will Barnet; Yale Univ, with Joseph Albers, BFA; Rutgers Univ, MFA. *Work:* Carnegie Inst, Pittsburgh, Pa; Guggenheim Mus, New York; Joseph H Hirshhorn Collection, DC; Wadsworth Atheneum, Hartford, Conn; Finch Col Mus, New York. *Comn:* Mosaic murals (with Lee Krasner Pollock), Uris Bros, New York, 58; plaster sculpture, Playboy Mag. *Exhib:* Carnegie Int, 57; Inst Contemp Art, Boston, 58; Art Inst Chicago Int, 60; one-man shows, Marlborough Gallery, London, Eng, 67, Irving Gallery, Milwaukee, 71 & Hokin Gallery, Palm Beach, Fla, 73; Art in the Mirror, Mus Mod Art, New York, 70; Bologna & Landi Gallery, East Hampton, NY, 83. *Media:* All Media. *Dealer:* Marlborough Gallery 40 West 57th St New York NY 10022. *Mailing Add:* 836 Fireplace Rd East Hampton NY 11937

STEIN, WALTER
PAINTER
b New York, NY, Nov 30, 24. *Study:* Art Students League; Cooper Union; NY Univ; New Sch Social Res; Acad Belle Arti, Florence. *Work:* Phillips Collection, Washington, DC; Indianapolis Mus Art; Fogg Art Mus, Cambridge, Mass; Mus Mod Art & Metrop Mus Art, New York. *Teaching:* Instr painting, Scarsdale Art Ctr, NY, 68-69; instr drawing, Cooper Union, 69-70; instr painting, Five Towns Art Ctr, NY, 70-71; instr, Parsons Sch Design, 74- *Media:* Oil, Watercolor. *Publ:* Ed & illusr, Common Botany, 53; illusr, Histoires Naturelles, Harvard Univ, 60; ed & illusr, Tichborne's Elegy, 68; illusr, For Love of Her, Clarkson Potter, 74 & 78. *Mailing Add:* c/o Parsons Sch Design 66 West 12th St New York NY 10011

STEINBAUM, BERNICE
DEALER
b Flushing, NY, Jan 3, 41. *Study:* Queens Col, BA, 61; Hofstra Univ, MA, 69. *Pos:* Pres, BFM Gallery, New York, 77-81; pres, P M & Stein Gallery, New York, 81- *Teaching:* Instr fine arts, Hofstra Univ, 69-71 & Farmingdale Univ, 71-77. *Specialty:* American contemporary painters and sculptures. *Mailing Add:* P M & Stein Gallery Ltd 903 Madison Ave New York NY 10021

STEINBERG, LEO
EDUCATOR, HISTORIAN
b Moscow, USSR, July 9, 20; US citizen. *Study:* Slade Sch Art, Univ London, dipl(fine arts), 40; Inst Fine Arts, NY Univ, PhD, 60; Philadelphia Col Art, Hon Dr, 81. *Teaching:* Prof art hist, Hunter Col & Grad Ctr City Univ New York, 61-75, Univ Pa, 75- *Awards:* Am Acad Arts & Sci fel, 78; Univ Col fel, London, 79. *Publ:* Auth, Michelangelo's last judgment as merciful heresy, Art in Am, 11-12/75; auth, Resisting Cezanne: Picasso's three women, Art in Am, 11-12/78; auth, The Line of Fate in Michelangelo's Painting, Critical Inquiry 6, spring 80; auth, A Corner of the Last Judgment, Daedalus, spring 80; auth, The sexuality of Christ, Renaissance Art, 84 & Mod Oblivion, 84. *Mailing Add:* Dept of Art Hist Univ Pa Philadelphia PA 19174

STEINBERG, SAUL
CARTOONIST
b Ramnicul-Sarat, Bucharest, Rumania, June 15, 14, US citizen. *Study:* Univ Bucharest, 32; Univ Milan, archit, 32. *Work:* Metrop Mus Art, Mus Mod Art, New York; Albright-Knox Art Gallery, Buffalo, NY; Fogg Mus, Harvard Univ, Cambridge, Mass; Victoria & Albert Mus, London. *Comn:* Mural, Terrace Plaza Hotel, Cincinnati, Ohio, 48. *Exhib:* Fourteen Americans, Mus Mod Art, New York, 46; Art Inst, Chicago, 49; Roy & Marie Neuberger Collection (traveling), Whitney Mus, New York, 55; one-man shows, Kunsthalle, Hamburg, 68 & Kunstverein, Cologne (traveling, W Ger & Austria), 74; retrospective, Kolnischer Kunstverein, Cologne, Ger, 74-75; Contemp Images in Watercolor, Akron Art Inst, 76; Documenta 6, Kassel, Ger, 77; The Object as Poet, Renwick Gallery, Washington, DC, 77; American Drawings 1927-1977, Minneapolis Inst Art, 77; and others. *Pos:* Cartoons, Bertoldo, Milan, 36-39; staff, New Yorker, formerly. *Bibliog:* John

Ashbery (auth), Saul--The stamp of genius, Art News, New York, 11/69 & Saul Steinberg: Calligraphy, Art News Ann, New York, 70; Grace Glueck (auth), The artist speaks: Saul Steinberg, Art in Am, New York, 11-12/70. *Publ:* Illusr, Cartoons published in Sombra, Brazil, Cascabel, Argentina & Settebello, Italy; auth, All in Line, The Art of Living & The Passport, New York, 45; auth, Steinberg Dessins, Paris, 55; coauth, Anti-Photographer Masks, In: Creative Camera, London, 2/69. *Dealer:* Sidney Janis Gallery 6 W 57 St New York NY 10019. *Mailing Add:* c/o The New Yorker 25 W 43rd St New York NY 10036

STEINER, MICHAEL
SCULPTOR, PRINTMAKER
b New York, NY, 1945. *Work:* Storm King Art Ctr; Boston Mus Fine Arts; Mus Mod Art. *Exhib:* Whitney Mus Am Art, 70 & 72; Edmonton Art Gallery, Alta, 72; solo exhib, Andre Emmerich Galleries, 75-79, Kunst und Museumsverein, Wuppertal, 78, Am House, Berlin, 79, Am Haus, Hannover, 79 & Gallery Ninety-Nine, Bay Harbor Islands, Fla, 80; Everson Mus Art, 76 & 79. *Teaching:* Instr, Emma Lake Workshop, Univ Sask, Regina, 69; vis artist, Cranbrook Art Inst, Bloomfield Heights, Mich, 69. *Awards:* Guggenheim Award, 71. *Bibliog:* Terry Fenton (auth), article, Art Int, 70; Kenworth Moffett (auth), Olitski: New sculpture, Art Int, 3/78; Noel Frackman (auth), article, Arts Mag, 4/78. *Media:* Steel, Aluminum. *Mailing Add:* 704 Broadway New York NY 10003

STEINER, PAUL
WRITER, CRITIC
b Ger; US citizen. *Study:* NY Univ, BS. *Pos:* Assoc ed, Esquire, Inc, 47-52; feature writer & columnist, NAm Newspaper Alliance, Women's News Serv, 60-80; writer, Pop Scene Serv (syndicated rev of New York mus exhibs), 67-; contrib ed, Nat Jeweller, 76, 77 & 78; columnist, Murray Hill News, 77-79, NY Entertainer & TGIF Entertainment Guide, 79-; corresp, New York Post, 77-, New York Mag, Nat Star, US Mag, 78-, People Mag, New York Daily News, 81, Omni, 81- & Globe, 81-; contrib ed, Show Illus, 81-; columnist, Stagebill, 81-, Artspeak, 81-, TV Today, 82-, Jewish J, 83- & Reuters, 83-. *Awards:* Columnist Award, 69 & Press Award, 70, Beaux Arts Soc NY; Int Press Award, New York, 81. *Mailing Add:* 161 West 54th St New York NY 10019

STEINFELS, MELVILLE P
PAINTER, DESIGNER
b Salt Lake City, Utah, Nov 3, 10. *Study:* Art Inst Chicago; Chicago Sch Design. *Work:* Murals (buon fresco, fresco secco, mosaic, ceramic tile), Church of the Epiphany, Chicago, Loyola Univ, Chicago, Our Lady of Sorrows Church, Farmington, Mich, Newman Club, Ann Arbor, Mich, St Mary Magdalen Church, Melvindale, Mich & many others. *Comn:* Murals, All Saints Mausoleum, Des Plaines, Ill, Resurrection Mausoleum, Justice, Ill & Queen of Heaven Mausoleum, Hillside, Ill; ceramic tile, Crucifixion Mausoleum, Hillside, Ill, 81. *Teaching:* Resident artist, Siena Heights Col, 45-50; instr drawing, painting & design. *Publ:* Illusr, Monthly Missalette (covers), J S Paluch Co Inc, 81-84. *Mailing Add:* 332 Talcott Pl Park Ridge IL 60068

STEINHARDT, ALICE
PAINTER, PHOTOGRAPHER
b New York, NY Feb 9, 50. *Study:* Univ Miami, Coral Gables, BA, 72; Int Ctr Photog, New York, 75. *Work:* Ctr Creative Photog, Tucson; Corcoran Gallery Art; Los Angeles Co Mus Art. *Exhib:* Recent Acquisitions, Corcoran Gallery Art, 80; solo exhib, G Ray Hawkins Gallery, Los Angeles, 80 & 84, Photog Gallery, La Jolla, 82 & Light Gallery, New York, 84; California Colour, Photogr Gallery, London, 81; Color Photography, Brown Univ Mus, 84. *Awards:* Purchase Prize, LaGrange III, 77. *Bibliog:* Article, Photo Bulletin, 80. *Mem:* Friends Photog; Los Angeles Ctr Photog Studies. *Media:* Oil on Silver Print. *Dealer:* G Ray Hawkins Gallery 7224 Melrose Ave Los Angeles CA 90046. *Mailing Add:* 404 E Third St Long Beach CA 90802

STEINHOUSE, TOBIE (THELMA)
PAINTER, PRINTMAKER
b Montreal, Que. *Study:* Sir George Williams Univ; Art Students League, with Morris Kantor & Harry Sternberg, 46-47; Ecole Beaux-Arts, Paris; Atelier 17, Paris, France, with W S Hayter, 61-62. *Work:* Nat Gallery Can, Ottawa; Montreal Mus Fine Arts, PQ; Confederation Art Gallery, Charlottetown, PEI; Ministry of External Affairs of Can, Moscow Embassy, USSR; McMichael Conserv Collection, Kleinburg, Ont. *Exhib:* One-man show, Galerie Lara Vincy, France, 57; Montreal Mus Fine Arts, 59 & 63; 2nd Int Biennial Engraving, Santiago, Chile, 65; 1st & 3rd Brit Int Print Biennial, Bradford, Eng, 68 & 72; 9th Int Biennial Art, Menton, France, 72; and others. *Awards:* Sterling Trust Award, Soc Can Painter-Etchers & Engravers, 63; Jessie Dow First Prize Award, Montreal Mus Fine Arts, 63; Govt Can Centennial Medal of Honor, 67; and others. *Bibliog:* Guy Viau (auth), La Peinture Moderne au Canada Francais, Ministere Affaires Cult, PQ, 64; Guy Robert (auth), Ecole de Montreal, Collection Artistes Can, 65; V Nixon (auth), Tobie Steinhouse-artist, Vie des Arts Mag, summer 72; and others. *Mem:* Royal Can Acad Arts; Can Group Painters (pres, 66-68); L'Atelier Libre Recherches Graphique; Soc Can Painter-Etchers & Engravers; Can Soc Graphic Art; and others. *Dealer:* La Guilde Graphique 9 St Paul St W Montreal PQ H2Y 1Y6 Can; Galerie Les Deux B St Antoine-sur-Richelieu PQ Can. *Mailing Add:* 208 Cote St Antoine Rd Montreal PQ H3Y 2J3 Canada

STEINKE, BETTINA
PAINTER
b Biddeford, Maine, June 25, 13. *Study:* Fawcett Art Inst, Newark, NJ; Cooper Union, New York; Phoenix Art Inst, New York. *Work:* Nat Cowboy Hall of Fame & Western Heritage, Oklahoma City; Ft Worth Mus, Tex; Gilcrease Mus, Tulsa, Okla; Philbrook Mus, Tulsa, Okla; also in pvt collections in US & abroad. *Exhib:* One-man shows, Well Known Personalities, Eskimo, Winnipeg, 56, Portraits Around US, Oklahoma City, 68 & Palm Springs Desert Mus, 78; Watercolor Show, Curacao, Neth, 78; two-man show, O'Brien's Art Emporium, Scottsdale, Ariz, 75; and others. *Awards:* Silver Medals for Drawing, 74 & 76 & Prix de West, 78, Nat Acad Western Art; Artist of Year Award, Tucson Festival Soc, Ariz, 80. *Bibliog:* Fred Whitaker (auth), Painter of people, Am Artist, 1/71; Don Hedgpeth (auth), Bettina, Portraying Life in Art, Northland Press, 78; and many others. *Mem:* Pastel Soc Am; Soc Illusr; Nat Acad Western Art. *Media:* Oil, Pastel. *Publ:* Illusr, NBC Symphony Orch, 37; illusr, articles, Lamp, 50-53; also illusr for var mags & bks. *Mailing Add:* PO Box 2342 Santa Fe NM 87501

STEINMETZ, GRACE ERNST TITUS
PAINTER
b Lancaster, Pa. *Study:* Pa Acad Fine Arts; Barnes Found; Millersville State Col, BS; Univ Pa, MS. *Work:* Univ Southern Fla, Lakeland; Franklin & Marshall Col; Elizabethtown Col, Pa; Millersville State Col, Pa; Lancaster Co Art Asn, Pa. *Exhib:* Knickerbocker Soc, 70; Moore Col Art, 70; Nat Soc Painters Casein & Acrylic, 81; Audubon Artists, 81; Allied Artists Am, 81. *Teaching:* Assoc prof art hist, Elizabethtown Col, 64-65; adj prof oil painting, 69 & 73-74. *Awards:* Best of Show, Lancaster Co Art Asn, 67 & 75; Award for Nontraditional Watercolor, Painters & Sculptors Soc NJ, 68; Grumbacher First Prize, Nat Soc Painters Casein & Acrylic, 69. *Mem:* Nat Soc Painters Casein & Acrylic; Echo Valley Art Group; fel Royal Soc Arts. *Media:* All. *Mailing Add:* Box 340 RD 7 Manheim PA 17545

STEIR, PAT
PAINTER
b Newark, NJ, 1938. *Study:* Boston Univ, 60; Pratt Inst, 62. *Work:* Whitney Mus Am Art, New York; Ciba-Geigy Corp, New York. *Exhib:* Drawings, Mus Mod Art, New York, 64; Landscapes, Mus Mod Art, New York, 72; Paintings on Paper, Larry Aldrich Mus Contemp Art, Ridgefield, Conn, 72; Drawing Exhib, Corcoran Gallery, Washington, DC, 72; Annual, Whitney Mus Am Art, 72; American Drawings, 1963-1973, Whitney Mus Am Art, New York, 73; Mus Mod Art, 73; Recent Acquisitions, Whitney Mus Am Art, 73; Private Notations: Artist's Sketchbooks II, Philadelphia Col Art, 76; Drawings of the 70's, Art Inst Chicago, 77; one-woman show, Douglas Col, Rutgers Univ, New Brunswick, NJ, 72; Corcoran Gallery Art, Washington, DC, 73; Ball State Univ, Muncie, Ind, 73; Univ Md, 76; White Gallery, Portland State Univ, Ore, 76; and others. *Awards:* Nat Endowment Arts, 74. *Bibliog:* Jonathan Crary (auth), Pat Steir, Arts Mag, 6/76; Michael Andre (auth), Pat Steir, Art News, spec prints ed, 9/76; Paul Brach (auth), Pat Steir (rev), Artforum, 10/76. *Mailing Add:* 105 Mulberry New York NY 10013

STELL, H KENYON
PRINTMAKER, HISTORIAN
b Adams, NY, Jan 22, 10. *Study:* Syracuse Univ, BFA(illus) & cert art educ; NY Univ, MA(educ admin); Syracuse Univ, doctoral study. *Work:* Marine Midland Bank, Cortland, NY. *Exhib:* Nassau-Suffolk Art League, Garden City, NY, 46; Assoc Artists Syracuse, Mus Fine Art, 48; State Univ Art Faculties Exhib, 54-60; Print Show, Key Bank, Watertown, NY, 83. *Pos:* Consult, Marine Bank Art Collection, 69. *Teaching:* Art supvr, Toaz Jr High Sch & Huntington High Sch, Huntington, NY, 39-47; prof art & chmn dept, State Univ NY Col Cortland, 47-66, prof art hist, 66-74, emer prof, 74-; vis prof art, Univ Maine, Orono, summer 51. *Awards:* 15 Yr Citation, Nat Art Educ Asn, 60. *Mem:* State Univ NY Col Fac Asn. *Media:* Woodcut; Acrylic, Oil. *Res:* John Trumbull. *Mailing Add:* 921 Spanish Circle Apt E-434 Delray Beach FL 33444

STELLA, FRANK
PAINTER
b Malden, Mass, May, 1936. *Study:* Phillips Acad, with Patrick Morgan; Princeton Univ, with William Seitz & Stephen Greene. *Work:* Mus Mod Art; Whitney Mus Am Art; San Francisco Mus Art; Albright-Knox Art Gallery, Buffalo, NY; Walker Art Ctr, Minneapolis, Minn; and many others. *Exhib:* Corcoran Gallery Art, Washington, DC, 67; The Art of the Real, Mus Mod Art, 68, Retrospective, 70; Philadelphia Mus Art, 68; Whitney Mus Am Art Ann, 69 & 72; Mus Mod Art, New York, 69-70; Mus Contemp Arts, Chicago, 70; Contemp Arts Ctr, Cincinnati, 70; Carnegie Inst Int, 71; Whitney Mus Am Art, 71; High Mus, Atlanta, Ga, 72; Art Mus STex, Corpus Christi, 72; Mus Fine Arts, Houston, 74; Univ Miami, 74; Va Mus Fine Art, Richmond, 74; Walker Art Ctr, Minneapolis, 74. *Awards:* First Prize, Int Biennial Exhib Paintings, Tokyo, 67. *Bibliog:* Lawrence Alloway (auth), Systemic Painting, Guggenheim Mus, 66; Oto Bihalji-Merin (auth), Adventures of Modern Art, Abrams, 66; Gregory Battcock (ed), Minimal Art: A Critical Anthology, Dutton, 68; plus many others. *Dealer:* Lawrence Rubin Gallery 49 W 57th St New York NY 10019. *Mailing Add:* 17 Jones St New York NY 10021

STELZER, MICHAEL NORMAN
SCULPTOR, INSTRUCTOR
b Brooklyn, NY, Jan 6, 38. *Study:* Pratt Inst, 56; Art Students League, 60-62; Nat Acad Sch Fine Arts, Edward Mooney traveling scholar, 66 & Nat Sculpture Soc Joseph Nicolosi grant, 67; and with Nathaniel Choate, 64, Michael Lantz, 64-67 & Donald DeLue, 68 & 69. *Comn:* 12 ft relief, Worchester Polytech Inst, 64. *Exhib:* Am Artists Prof League Grand Nat, 63,

76 & 77; Nat Arts Club, 63-64; Nat Acad Design, 64-67, 70-71 & 74-77; Allied Artists Am, 67 & 71-81; Nat Sculpture Soc Ann Exhib, 68-81. *Teaching:* Instr sculpture, Fashion Inst Technol, New York, 79. *Awards:* Helen Foster Barnett Prize, Nat Acad Design, 66; Gold Medal, Hudson Valley Art Asn, 76; Gold Medal, Grand Nat Exhib, Am Artists Pro Prof League, 76. *Bibliog:* Article in, Pen & Brush, 66; Opportunities offered the young sculptor, 67 & Interpreting the human figure, 68, Nat Sculpture Rev. *Mem:* Nat Sculpture Soc; Hudson Valley Art Asn; Allied Artists Am; Am Artists Prof League. *Mailing Add:* 8 Everit St Brooklyn NY 11201

STENZLER, ERNA J
SCULPTOR, INSTRUCTOR
b Reading, Pa. *Study:* Carnegie Inst Technol, 38; Tyler Sch Fine Arts, BS, BFA, MFA, 44. *Work:* Swarthmore Sr High Sch, Pa; Cheltenham Sr High Sch & Cheltenham Twp Comnr, Pa. *Exhib:* Metrop Mus Art, New York, 45; Philadelphia Mus Art, 59, 62 & 72; Pa Acad Fine Arts, 47, 48 & 52; Philadelphia Art Alliance, 56; Nat Acad Design, New York, 60 & 77; solo shows, Philadelphia Art Alliance, 60, 66 & 74, William Penn Mus, Harrisburg, Pa, 74 & Hahn Gallery, Philadelphia, 76 & 80; Moore Inst Art, 62-64, 66 & 68; Allied Artists Am, New York, 76; and others. *Teaching:* Instr, pvt lessons, 54-; instr sculpture, Cheltenham Sch Fine Arts, 56- *Awards:* Benjamin Bernstein Purchase Award, Philadelphia Art Alliance, 57; Charles K Smith Award, Woodmere Art Gallery, Philadelphia, 58; Fel, Tyler Sch Fine Arts, 64. *Bibliog:* Dorothy Grafly (auth), article, Art Focus; articles, Philadelphia Inquirer, 56, 68 & 72 & Philadelphia Evening Bulletin, 64 & 74. *Mem:* Artists Equity Asn. *Media:* Wood. *Dealer:* Hahn Gallery 8439 Germantown Ave Philadelphia PA 19118. *Mailing Add:* 8310 Roberts Rd Elkins Park PA 19117

STEPHANY, JAROMIR
PHOTOGRAPHER, EDUCATOR
b Rochester, NY, Mar 23, 30. *Study:* Rochester Inst Technol, AAS, 56, with Ralph Hattersley, Miner White & B Newhall, BFA, 58; Ind Univ, with Henry Holmes Smith, MFA, 60. *Work:* George Eastman House; Univ Md, Baltimore Co; Detroit Inst Arts; Mus Fine Arts St Petersburg, Fla; Baltimore Mus Fine Arts. *Exhib:* Mus Mod Art, New York, 60; Smithsonian Inst, Washington, DC, 69; Baltimore Mus Art, 70; Addison Gallery Am Art, 75; one-man shows, Dundalk Community Col, Md, 77, Mus Without Walls, Md, 75-76, Catskills Ctr Photog, 79, Int Ctr Photog, 80 & Dalsheimer Gallery, 81; and others. *Pos:* Series writer, Developing Image, Extended Learning Inst, Channel 53-TV, Va. *Teaching:* Lectr hist photog, Md Inst Col Art, 66-77; assoc prof, Dept Visual Arts, Univ Md, Baltimore Co, 72- *Awards:* Univ Md Baltimore Co Summer Fel, 83. *Mem:* Soc Photog Educ (chmn & ed newsletter, Mid-Atlantic Region, 74-80). *Dealer:* G H Dalsheimer Gallery 519 N Charles St Baltimore MD 21201. *Mailing Add:* 786 Creekview Rd Severna Park MD 21146

STEPHEN, FRANCIS B
JEWELER, SCULPTOR
b Dublin, Tex, Mar 7, 16. *Study:* Fine Art Ctr, Colorado Springs, Colo; Univ Okla, study with Jean Charlot & Robert von Neumann, MFA. *Work:* Witte Mem Mus, San Antonio, Tex; Okla Art Ctr; Hallmark Collection, Mo. *Exhib:* The Patron Church, Mus Contemp Crafts, New York, 61; 11th Mid-Am Exhib, Nelson Gallery, Kansas City, Mo, 61; Craft Exhib, Dallas Mus Fine Arts, 71-74 & 78; South Central States Crafts Exhib, Denver Art Mus, Colo, 73; Contemporary Crafts of The Americas, Denver Art Mus, 74; Lake Superior Int Crafts Exhib, Tweed Mus Art, Univ Minn, Duluth, 74-75; The Metalsmith, Phoenix Art Mus, Ariz, 77; one-man show, Mus of Art, Okla Univ, 79; and others. *Teaching:* Asst prof jewelry & sculpture, North Tex State Univ, Denton, 64-67; prof jewelry, Tex Tech Univ, Lubbock, 67- *Awards:* Swarovski Award, Great Designs in Jewelry, Swarovski & Co, 67; Grand Award, 15th Tex Crafts Exhib, 71; Purchase Award, Miniature Works, Tex Tech Mus Art, 75. *Mem:* Soc of NAm Goldsmiths. *Media:* Metal; Bronze, Clay. *Mailing Add:* 4610 29th Lubbock TX 79410

STEPHENS, CURTIS
DESIGNER, PHOTOGRAPHER
b Athens, Ga, Dec 13, 32. *Study:* Univ Ga, MFA. *Work:* Objects USA, Johnson's Wax Collection; Ill State Mus, Springfield. *Exhib:* Designed for Production, Mus Contemp Crafts, 64; Objects USA, Johnson's Wax Collection, Smithsonian Inst, 69; 24th & 25th Ill Exhib, Ill State Mus, 71 & 72. *Pos:* Designer, Callaway Mills, LaGrange, Ga, 63-66; photogr, 1960 Pandora (Popular Photog Award-Winning Yearbk, Univ Ga). *Teaching:* Asst prof art, LaGrange Col, 61-63; asst prof art, Univ Northern Mich, 66-68; assoc prof art & design, Univ Ill, Champaign-Urbana, 68-, assoc dir sch, 75- *Bibliog:* Lee Nordness (auth), Objects: USA, Viking Press, 70; Jay Hartley Newman & Lee Scott Newman (auth), Plastics for the Craftsman, Crown, 72. *Media:* Plastics. *Mailing Add:* Sch of Art & Design Univ of Ill Champaign IL 61820

STEPHENS, RICHARD ALAN
ADMINISTRATOR, PAINTER
b San Francisco, Calif, Apr 13, 25. *Study:* Menlo Col, AA; Stanford Univ, BA, MA. *Work:* Alfred Marion Collection. *Teaching:* Prof art hist & advert, Acad Art Col, 51-54, pres, 51-, chmn bd, currently. *Mem:* Nat Asn Trade & Tech Schs; Soc Communicative Arts. *Media:* Oil, Watercolor. *Mailing Add:* 625 Sutter San Francisco CA 94102

STEPHENS, WILLIAM BLAKELY
EDUCATOR, PAINTER
b Corpus Christi, Tex, June 8, 30. *Study:* Univ Tex, BFA, 56, with Hiram Williams, MEd, 57, MFA, 66; Univ Fla, EdD, 72. *Exhib:* 23rd Ann Tex Painting & Sculpture, Dallas Mus Fine Arts, 61; 4th Ann Southwest States

Exhib, Roswell, NMex, 62; Art on Paper, Weatherspoon Gallery, Greensboro, NC, 67; Appalachian Corridors Exhib, Charleston, WVa, 68; Super Graphics, Brooks Mem Art Mus, Memphis, Tenn, 74; one-man show, Emerging Figures, Univ Texas at Tyler, 82. *Pos:* Art ed, New Voices in Educ, 71-72. *Teaching:* Asst occup ther, Univ Fla, 70-71; assoc prof art educ, Memphis State Univ, 72-76; prof & chmn dept art, Univ Tex at Tyler, currently. *Awards:* Univ Texas at Tyler Faculty Research Grants, 78 & 80. *Mem:* Life mem Tex Fine Arts Asn; Asn Teacher Educators; Nat & Tenn Art Educ Asns. *Media:* Acrylic. *Res:* Artists' personality types. *Publ:* Auth, Blue Ridge Studies, Fac Publ, Appalachian State Univ, 5/69; auth, On creativity and teaching: talk with Hiram Williams, Art J, summer 71; auth, Relationship between selected personality characteristics ..., Studies in Art Educ, spring 73; auth, University art departments and academies of art: The artists' psychological types to their specialties and interests, Bull of Res in Psychological Type, summer 77; Hiram Williams, Memphis State Univ, 78. *Mailing Add:* Dept of Art Univ of Tex Tyler TX 75701

STEPHENSON, JOHN H
SCULPTOR, EDUCATOR
b Waterloo, Iowa, Oct 27, 29. *Study:* Univ Northern Iowa, BA; Cranbrook Acad Art, MFA. *Work:* Int Mus Ceramics Faenza, Italy; Everson Mus, Syracuse, NY; Portland Art Mus; Parrish Art Mus, South Hampton, NY; St Paul Art Ctr. *Comn:* The Wall (ceramic mural), Arbor A, Int Mkt, Ann Arbor, Mich, 71; Champion No 3 (sculpture), Mich Mall, Battle Creek, Mich, 76. *Exhib:* 1977 Ceramic Conjunction, Long Beach Mus of Art, Calif, 77; Contemp Ceramic Sculpture, Univ of NC, Chapel Hill, 77; one-man show, Gallery 7, Fisher Bldg, Detroit, 78; Century of Ceramics in the United States, Everson Mus, Syracuse, 79-80; Clay Attitudes, Queens Mus, Flushing, 80. *Teaching:* Instr ceramics, Cleveland Inst Art, 58-59; prof ceramics, Univ Mich, Ann Arbor, 59- *Awards:* Rackham Res Grants, Japan, Univ Mich, 62; Medagla Oro Della Citta Faenza, 65; Mixed Media Prize, Univ Mich, 69. *Mailing Add:* 4380 Waters Rd Ann Arbor MI 48103

STEPHENSON, SUSANNE G
CERAMIST, EDUCATOR
b Canton, Ohio, Nov 5, 35. *Study:* Carnegie-Mellon Univ, BFA; Cranbrook Acad of Fine Art, Bloomfield Hills, Mich, MFA. *Work:* Mus of Contemp Crafts, New York; Butler Inst of Am Art, Youngstown, Ohio; Univ Mich Mus of Art, Ann Arbor; Columbus Gallery of Fine Arts, Ohio; El Paso Mus Art. *Comn:* Ceramic Planters, Burroughs Corp, Detroit, Mich, 70, Grosse Pointe Br, Nat Bank of Detroit, 72 & Harper Hosp, Detroit, 72; Liturgical Vessels, Lutheran Chapel, Eastern Mich Univ, Ypsilanti, 72. *Exhib:* Works in Fiber, Metal, Clay by Women, Bronx Mus, NY, 78; Century of Ceramics, USA, 1878-1979, Everson Mus Art, Syracuse, Renwick Gallery, DC & Cooper-Hewitt Mus, 79; one person show, Robert Kidd Gallery, Birmingham, Mich, 81, and others; Contemporary American Potter, Univ North Iowa, Smithsonian Traveling Exhibition, 80-81; and many others. *Teaching:* Instr ceramics, Univ Mich, Ann Arbor, 60-61; prof ceramics, Eastern Mich Univ, 63- *Awards:* Award, Artisan's, 69; Best in Ceramics, Beaux Arts Designer Craftsmen Exhib, Columbus, Ohio; Purchase Award, Downey Mus Art, Calif, 82. *Bibliog:* Garth Clark & Margie Hughto (coauths), Century of Ceramics, E P Dutton, 79; Garth Clark (auth), American Potters, Watson Guptill, 81; Janet Koplos (auth), Alternations--the ceramics of Susanne Stephenson, Am Crafts, 1/83. *Mem:* Am Craftsmen's Coun; Mich Potters Asn; Nat Coun Educ for Ceramic Arts; Am Asn Univ Prof. *Media:* Porcelain, Stoneware. *Dealer:* Detroit Gallery of Contemp Crafts 301 Fisher Bldg Detroit MI 48202; Robert Kidd Gallery 107 Townsend St Birmingham MI 48011. *Mailing Add:* 4380 Waters Rd Ann Arbor MI 48103

STERMER, DUGALD ROBERT
ILLUSTRATOR, DESIGNER
b Los Angeles, Calif, Dec 17, 36. *Study:* Univ Calif, Los Angeles, BA, 60; printmaking with John Paul Jones. *Exhib:* One-man show, Andre's, San Francisco, 69; group show, Greengrass Gallery, 78. *Pos:* Consult ed, Communication Arts, Palo Alto, Calif, 74-; art dir & designer, Oceans, San Francisco, 77-; design dir, Flowers, Los Angeles, 79-, design consult, Sierra, San Francisco, 82- *Teaching:* Lectr advan design, Acad Art, San Francisco, 78; instr illus, Artists in Print, San Francisco, 78-79. *Awards:* Award of Excellence, Ann Exhibs, Soc Illustrators; Art Ann, Communication Arts, 76-78; plus others. *Bibliog:* Martin Fox (auth), The graphics of dissent, Print, 66; Richard Coyne (auth), Dugald Stermer, Communication Arts, 72; 50 Important US Designers, Idea, 78. *Mem:* Am Inst Graphic Design; Soc Publ Designers; San Francisco Soc Communicating Arts. *Media:* Watercolor, Acrylics. *Publ:* Auth, The Art of Revolution, McGraw-Hill, 71; ed, The enviroment, Richard Coyne, 72 & ed & illusr, Vanishing creatures, 80, Communication Arts; auth & illusr, Vanishing Creatures, Lancaster-Miller, 80; auth & illusr, Vanishing Plants & Flowers, Overlook Press, 84. *Mailing Add:* 1844 Union St San Francisco CA 94123

STERN, (MR & MRS) ARTHUR LEWIS
COLLECTORS
Mr Stern, b Rochester, NY, Apr 11, 11; Mrs Stern, b New York, NY, Apr 21, 13. *Study:* Mr Stern, Yale Univ, BA; Harvard Law Sch, JD; Mrs Stern, Goucher Col, BA; Rochester Inst Technol. *Pos:* Mr Stern, mem bd dirs, Mem Art Gallery, Rochester, 60-, pres, 67-69; Mrs Stern, chmn art selection comt, Mem Art Gallery, Rochester, 64- *Mem:* Am Fedn Art; Mus Mod Art. *Collection:* Modern painting and sculpture; Greek, Asian and European artifacts. *Mailing Add:* 14 Elmwood Hill Ln Rochester NY 14610

STERN, H PETER
COLLECTOR
Study: Harvard Univ, AB(magna cum laude), 50; Columbia Univ, MA, 52; Yale Univ Law Sch, LLB, 54. *Pos:* Pres, Ralph E Ogden Found, Mountainville, NY; vchmn, Mid-Hudson Pattern for Prog, 68-; pres, Storm King Art Ctr, vchmn, Int Fund for Monuments, DC; hon dir, Friends of Vassar Art Gallery, Poughkeepsie; pres, Star Expansion Indust Corp, Mountainville. *Collection:* Contemporary paintings, graphics and sculpture. *Mailing Add:* Otterville Rd Mountainville NY 10953

STERN, IRENE MONAT
PAINTER
b Nov 20, 32; US citizen. *Study:* New Sch Social Res; classes at Mus Mod Art & Whitney Mus; mainly self-taught. *Work:* Nat Collection of Fine Arts, Smithsonian Inst, Gen Elec World Hq, Joseph H Hirshhorn Mus, First Nat City Bank, Int Off, Washington, DC; and others. *Comn:* Am Broadcasting Co Western Hq; Atlantic Richfield Collection; Pac Mutual Life Ins Co Exec Hq. *Exhib:* Esther Robles Gallery, Los Angeles, 73; Color-73, Brand Mus & Libr; Am Acad Arts & Lett, 74; Downtown Gallery, Honolulu, 74; Source Gallery, San Francisco, 75; and others. *Bibliog:* Articles in Life Mag, 4/24/72, Interiors, 74 & Artweek, 5/31/75. *Media:* Acrylic. *Mailing Add:* PO Box 1972 Santa Monica CA 90406

STERN, JAN PETER
SCULPTOR
b Nov 14, 26; US citizen. *Study:* Syracuse Univ Col Fine Arts, BID; New Sch Social Res. *Work:* Hirshhorn Mus, Nat Collection Smithsonian Inst, Capitol Mall, Washington, DC; Pasadena Art Mus; Univ Mich Inst Sci & Technol; and others. *Comn:* Monumental sculptures, Prudential Ctr, Boston, 66; Maritime Plaza, Golden Gateway Ctr, San Francisco, 67, Alcoa Hq, Chicago, 68, Cardinal Spellman Retreat House, New York, 69 & Los Angeles City Hall Mall, 72. *Exhib:* Phoenix Art Mus, 67; Mus Contemp Art, 68; St Louis Art Mus, 68; San Francisco Mus Art, 70; Marlborough Gallery, New York, 70; and other group & one-man shows. *Bibliog:* Monumental sculpture show, Artforum, 2/68; Louis Redstone (auth), Art in Architecture, 68 & Garrett Eckbo (auth), Landscape We See, 69, McGraw, documented by Nat Educ TV; and others. *Media:* Stainless Steel, Metals. *Mailing Add:* PO Box 1972 Santa Monica CA 90406

STERN, JEAN
HISTORIAN, DEALER
b Casablanca, Morocco, Mar 28, 46; US citizen. *Study:* Calif State Univ, San Diego, MA(art hist), 72; Univ Calif, Los Angeles, Am art with E Maurice Bloch. *Collections Arranged:* The Paintings of Franz A Bischoff, Petersen Galleries, 3/80; The Paintings of Sam Hyde Harris, Petersen Galleries, 10/80; Western Masters, Petersen Galleries, 10/81. *Pos:* Consult in Pre-Hispanic Art, Fine Arts Gallery of San Diego, 76; dir, Petersen Art Galleries, Beverly Hills, Calif, 80- *Teaching:* Instr art hist, San Diego Mesa Col, 76-77. *Mem:* Appraisers Asn Am. *Res:* Early 20th century American art; pre-Hispanic art (iconography of western Mexico). *Publ:* Auth, Robert Henri & the 1915 San Diego Exposition, Am Art Rev, 9-10/75; ed, The Cross & The Sword: Art of the Spanish Southwest (exhib catalog), Fine Arts Gallery of San Diego, 76; co-ed, Pre-Hispanic Art History, Peek Publ, 77; auth, Franz A Bischoff, Arts & Antiques, 5-6/81; auth, Alson S Clark, 83; and others. *Mailing Add:* c/o Petersen Galleries 270 North Rodeo Drive Beverly Hills CA 90210

STERN, LOUIS
DEALER, CONSULTANT
b Jan 7, 45; US citizen. *Study:* Calif State Univ, Northridge, BA. *Pos:* Pres, Wally Findlay Galleries, Beverly Hills, Calif, 80-82; pres, Louis Stern Galleries, Beverly Hills, Calif, currently. *Mem:* Am Art Coun. *Specialty:* Impressionist, post-impressionist, Pont-Aven and 20th century American and European painting. *Mailing Add:* 13206 Addison St Sherman Oaks CA 91423

STERNBERG, HARRY
PAINTER, GRAPHIC ARTIST
b New York, NY, July 9, 04. *Study:* Art Students League; and graphics with Harry Wickey. *Work:* Mus Mod Art & Metrop Mus Art, New York; Walker Art Ctr, Minneapolis; Whitney Mus; Victoria & Albert Mus, London; Brooklyn Mus; and others. *Comn:* Murals, US Treas Dept, Sellersville, Pa, 36 & Chicago, Ill, 38. *Exhib:* Whitney Mus Am Art Ann, New York, 48-50; Timber Gallery, Idyllwild, Calif, 81; one-man shows, Galeria Palomas, PR, 81 & 82, San Diego Print Club, 82 & Deicas Gallery, La Jolla, 82; Idyllwild Sch Music & Art, 82; and others. *Teaching:* Instr painting & graphics, Art Students League, 34-68; instr graphics, New Sch Social Res, 42-45; head dept art, Idyllwild Sch Music & Art, Univ Southern Calif, 59-69, instr, 80-84; instr, Palm Springs Desert Mus, 80-83. *Awards:* J S Guggenheim Mem Found Fel, 63; Purchase Award, Am Acad Arts & Lett, 72. *Media:* Mixed Media. *Publ:* Auth, Silk screen color printing & Modern methods and materials of etching, McGraw; auth, Composition, Woodcut & Abstract-realist Drawing, Pitman; director & producer, The Many Worlds of Art (film); auth, Catalogue de raissone Sternberg Graphics, Wichita State Univ, 76. *Dealer:* ACA Gallery 25 E 73rd St New York NY 10021. *Mailing Add:* 1606 Conway Dr Escondido CA 92027

STERNE, DAHLI
PAINTER, SCULPTOR
b Stettin, Ger, Jan 3, 01; US citizen. *Study:* Kaiserin Auguste Victoria Acad, BA; and with Albert Pels, Ludolf Liberts & Josef Shilhavy, US. *Work:* Oklahoma City Art Ctr; Evanston Mus Art; Fla Southern Col; Seton Hall Univ; Gracie Mansion, New York; plus others. *Exhib:* Nat Arts Club, 53-58;

Allied Artists Am, 55; 50 Am Artists, 55-58; Col Mt St Vincent, New York; Allied Artists Am; Metrop Mus, New York, 80; and others. *Pos:* Art dir, Nat Coun Jewish Women. *Awards:* Citation, Okla Art Asn, 54; Award, Am Artists Prof League, 55; Gold Medal, Ogunquit Art Ctr, 57. *Mem:* Am Artists Prof League; Catharine Lorillard Wolfe Art Club; Artists Equity Asn; fel Royal Soc Arts, Eng; Nat Soc Arts & Lett (vpres, 71-72). *Media:* Oil. *Mailing Add:* 315 W 70th St New York NY 10023

STERNE, HEDDA
PAINTER
b Bucharest, Romania, Aug 4, 16; US citizen. *Study:* Pvt study in Paris, Bucharest & Vienna. *Work:* Univ Ill; Metrop Mus Art; Mus Mod Art; Univ Nebr; Art Inst Chicago; and others. *Exhib:* Painting & Sculpture Today, Art Asn Indianapolis, 65-66; The Visual Assault, Univ Ga, 67-68 & Barnard Col, 68; Phillips Collection, Westmoreland Mus, 69; Lee Ault & Co, New York, 75; Retrospective Show, Montclair Mus Art, 77; and others. *Teaching:* Instr art hist, Carbondale Col, 64; conducted workshop for art teachers, NY State Coun Arts, 68. *Awards:* Fulbright Fel to Venice, 63; First Prize, Art Inst Newport Ann, 67; Tamarind Fel, 67; Childe Hassam Purchasing Award, Acad Arts & Lett; and others. *Bibliog:* Robert Motherwell & Reinhardt (ed), Modern Artists in America, Wittenborn, 51; Nathaniel Pousette-Dart (ed), American Painting Today, Hastings, 56; Herbert Read (auth), The Quest and the Quarry, Rome-New York Art Found Inc, 61; and others. *Mailing Add:* 179 E 71st ST 24 W 57th St New York NY 10021

STETSON, DANIEL EVERETT
GALLERY DIRECTOR, CURATOR
b Oneida, NY, Jan 3, 56. *Study:* State Univ NY Col Potsdam, BA, 78; Syracuse Univ, NY, MFA(grad asst), 81. *Collections Arranged:* Twentieth Anniversary of Vogel Collection, Philip Pearlstein: Painting to Watercolors (auth, catalog), Jose de Creeft (1884-1982) (auth, catalog), Reuben Nakian: Leda and the Swan (auth, catalog), Leonard Baskin: Woodcuts and Etchings (auth, catalog), Art Nouveau Glass & Pottery (auth, catalog) & Jacob Landau: The Graphic Work, A Retrospective, Gallery Art, Univ Northern Iowa. *Pos:* Actg dir, Picker Art Gallery, Colgate Univ, Hamilton, NY, 80-81; dir, Gallery Art & cataloger, Permanent Collection, Univ Northern Iowa, Cedar Falls, 81- *Teaching:* Museology, Colgate Univ, 80-81; adv, Univ Northern Iowa, 80- *Awards:* Fel, Northeast Mus Conf, 79. *Mem:* Am Asn Mus; Iowa Mus Asn; Cedar Arts Forum; Arts Alive, Cedar Falls; and others. *Mailing Add:* Gallery Art Univ Northern Iowa Cedar Falls IA 50613

STETTNER, LOUIS
PHOTOGRAPHER
b New York, NY, Nov 7, 22. *Study:* Princeton Univ, 42-44; Inst Hautes Etudes Cinematographiques, BA, 49. *Work:* Victoria & Albert Mus, London; Bibliotheque Nat, Paris; Mus Mod Art, New York; Nat Mus Am Art; Int Ctr Photog, New York. *Exhib:* Bibliotheque Nat, Paris, 49; Photography in the Fine Arts, Chicago Inst Art, 61 & traveling exhib; Photo League, Int Ctr Photography, New York, 81; Critics Choice, Victoria & Albert Mus, London, 83; Subjective Photography, San Francisco Mus Mod Art, 84. *Awards:* Photog Fel, Yaddo, 56; Creative Photog Grant, NY State Coun Arts, 73 & Nat Endowment Arts, 74. *Bibliog:* Norman Hall (auth), The Indestructable Image, Brit Photog, 67; Alan Porter (auth), monograph, Swiss Camera, 72; Ken Poli (auth), Delights of the Quiet Eye, Popular Photog, 83. *Media:* Black and White. *Publ:* Auth, Paris Street Scenes, Two Cities Publ, 49; auth, Weegee the Famous, Knopf Publ, 78; auth, Sur Le Tas, Cercle D'Art, 79; auth, Streetwork, Symbax Inc, 81. *Dealer:* George Aptecker 235 S Harrison St East Orange NJ 07018. *Mailing Add:* 172 W 79th St New York NY 10024

STEVANOV, ZORAN
PAINTER, SCULPTOR
b Novi Sad, Yugoslavia, June 25, 45; US citizen. *Study:* Fla Atlantic Univ, Boca Raton, BA, 68; Wichita State Univ, Kans, MFA, 70. *Work:* Wichita State Univ; Emporia State Univ, Kans; Ft Hays State Univ, Kans. *Comn:* Sculpture fountain, State Kans, Emporia State Univ Libr, 71-73. *Exhib:* Nat Exhib Drawing & Sculpture, Muncie, Ind, 67; Nat Ann Exhib, Monroe, La, 71; Kans Biennial Art Exhib, Lindsborg, 72; Eight State Ann Exhib, Oklahoma City, 74; three-man show, Lynn Kottler Gallery, New York, 75. *Teaching:* Instr sculpture & design, Emporia State Univ, 70-73; assoc prof design, Ft Hays State Univ, 73-, assoc prof art, currently. *Awards:* Second Prize Ann State Exhib, Fort Lauderdale, Fla, 67; First Prize Ann State Exhib, Hollywood, Fla, 68; Third Prize Nat Art Exhib, Winter Park, Fla, 68; and others. *Mem:* Col Art Asn. *Dealer:* Paula Insel Gallery 987 Third Ave New York NY 10022. *Mailing Add:* 1208 Donald Hays KS 67601

STEVENS, EDWARD JOHN, JR
PAINTER, DIRECTOR
b Jersey City, NJ, Feb 4, 23. *Study:* NJ State Teachers Col, Newark, BA, 43; Columbia Univ Teachers Col, with Henry Varnum Poor & George Picken, MA, 44, Art Exten, 44-47. *Work:* Whitney Mus Am Art, New York; NJ State Mus, Trenton; Art Inst Chicago, Ill; Pa Acad Fine Arts; Honolulu Acad Arts, Hawaii. *Exhib:* 24 one-man exhibs, Weyhe Gallery, New York, 44-77; Whitney Mus Am Art Ann, 54; Brooklyn Mus Int Watercolor Exhib, 55; Pa Acad Fine Arts Ann, 63; Newark Mus NJ Triennial, 64. *Teaching:* Instr painting, Newark Sch Fine & Indust Art, 47-59, coord dir, 59- *Awards:* Artist of Yr, Hudson Artists, 54; Bronze Medal, NJ Tercentenary, 64; Henry Ward Ranger Fund Purchase Award, Nat Acad Design, 68. *Mem:* Philadelphia Watercolor Club; Audubon Artists. *Media:* Gouache. *Dealer:* E Weyhe 794 Lexington Ave New York NY 10021. *Mailing Add:* 362D Hackensack St Wood-Ridge NJ 07075

STEVENS, ELISABETH GOSS
WRITER, CRITIC
b Rome, NY, Aug 11, 29. *Study:* Wellesley Col, BA, 51; Columbia Univ, MA(high hons), 56. *Pos:* Ed assoc, Art News, 64-65; art critic, Washington Post, 65; free lance art critic & writer, 65-78; columnist, The Gallery, Wall St J, 69-71; Sunday art columnist, Trenton Times, 74-77; art & archit critic, Baltimore Sun, 78- *Awards:* Citation for Critical Writing, Baltimore Washington Newspaper Guild, 80; MacDowell Colony, 81; Fel, Va Ctr Creative Arts, 82. *Mem:* Soc Archit Historians; Col Art Asn; Am Studies Asn. *Publ:* Auth, The urban museum crisis (sr), Washington Post, 6-7/72; contribr, Black Arts Ctr Mus News, 3/75; auth, Howard Russell Butler (exhib catalog), E R Squibb & Sons, 77; auth, Elisabeth Stevens' Guide to Baltimore's Inner Harbor, Stemmer House, 81; auth, Fire & Water: Six Stories, Perivale Press, 83; and others. *Mailing Add:* 6604 Walnutwood Circle Baltimore MD 21212

STEVENS, JACQUIE (JAQUELINE LAUREN)
CERAMIST, INSTRUCTOR
b Omaha, Nebr, April 3, 49. *Study:* Univ Colo; Inst Am Indian Arts, Santa Fe, AFA, 78; Col Santa Fe, BA, 81. *Work:* Inst Am Indian Arts Mus, Santa Fe. *Exhib:* Fifteenth Ann NAm Arts Show, Heard Mus, Phoenix, 82; One With the Earth, Smithsonian Inst, 83; The Clay Sings, Wheelwright Mus, Santa Fe, 83; Ceramics, Gallery Mack, New York, 83; Exhibit of New Work, Magic Mountain Gallery, Taos, NMex, 83; Recent Works, Robert Dean Gallery, Scottsdale, Ariz, 84. *Teaching:* Instr pottery & ceramics, Armand Hammer United World Col Am West, Montezuma, NMex, 83- *Awards:* Blue Ribbon Contemp Pottery, Heard Mus, Phoenix, 82; Southwest Am Indian Artists Fel, 83; Blue Ribbon, 62nd Indian Market, Santa Fe, 83. *Bibliog:* American Indian Art, Am Indian Art Mag, 83; Carolyn Meyer (auth), Art Scene, Channel 6, Santa Fe, 83. *Media:* Ceramics. *Dealer:* Wheelwright Mus Box 5153 Santa Fe NM 87502. *Mailing Add:* 3304 James St Santa Fe NM 87501

STEVENS, MARJORIE
COLLAGE ARTIST, PAINTER
b Terre Haute, Ind, Mar 8, 02. *Study:* Largely self-taught; instr from George Post & Dong Kingman; Univ Calif Exten; Acad Advert Arts. *Exhib:* Calif State Fair, annually since 52; one-woman shows, De Young Mem Mus, San Francisco, 55, Emma Frye Mus, Seattle, 60 & Rosicrucian Mus, San Jose, Calif, 77; Am Watercolor Soc, 63, 65, 66, 69, 70, 74, 75 & 77; West Coast Watercolor Soc, annually since 63. *Teaching:* Watercolor classes, Daly City Adult Classes, Calif, 67 & 68; watercolor painting, pvt classes, 75-81. *Awards:* Klumpkey Mem, 68; Larry Quackenbush Mem, Am Watercolor Soc, 72; Jade for Asilomar Award for Best Watercolor, Soc Western Artists, 77-80. *Bibliog:* Frederick Whitaker (auth), Watercolor in California, Mag Am Artists, 5/68; and others. *Mem:* Am Watercolor Soc; Soc Western Artists (bd dirs, 52-81, bd trustees, 70-81); charter mem West Coast Watercolor Soc. *Media:* Watercolor, Transparent and Opaque. *Mailing Add:* 1550 Haight St San Francisco CA 94117

STEVENS, MAY
PAINTER
b Boston, Mass, June 9, 24. *Study:* Mass Col Art, BFA, 46; Art Students League, 48; Acad Julian, Paris, 48. *Work:* Whitney Mus Am Art; Brooklyn Mus; Herbert F Johnson Mus, Cornell Univ; San Francisco Mus Art; Ohio State Univ; and others. *Exhib:* Recent Acquisitions & Women Artists From Permanent Collection, Whitney Mus Am Art, 70; Johnson Mus, Cornell Univ, 73; Everson Mus, Syracuse, NY, 76; Int Feminist Exhib, Gemeente Mus, Neth, 79-80; Int Exhib of Women's Polit Art, Inst Contemp Art, London, 80; Art of Conscience: The Last Decade, Wright State Univ, Dayton, Ohio; and many others. *Teaching:* Instr painting, Sch Visual Arts, 62-; adj lectr art, Queens Col, New York, 64-75; vis artist, Cornell Univ, 73. *Awards:* MacDowell Colony fels, 70-73; Creative Artists Pub Serv Grant, 74; Nat Endowment Arts Grant for Painting, 83. *Bibliog:* Moira Roth (auth), Visions and re-visions, Artforum, 11/80; Peter Selz (auth), Art In Our Times, Abrams, 81; Lisa Tickner (auth), May Stevens, Block 5, 81; and others. *Mem:* Artists Equity Asn; Col Art Asn. *Media:* Oil, Acrylic. *Publ:* Auth, Working It Out, Pantheon, 77; auth, Between Women, Beacon Press, 84. *Mailing Add:* 97 Wooster St New York NY 10012

STEVENS, MICHAEL KEITH
SCULPTOR
b Gilroy, Calif, July 14, 45. *Study:* Am River Col, 63-65; Calif State Univ, Sacramento, BA, 65, MA, 70; Univ Guadalajara, Mex, 66. *Work:* Univ NMex, Albuquerque; Israel Mus, Jerusalem. *Exhib:* The Animal Image: Contemporary Objects & the Beast, Renwick Gallery, 81; Sculpture Invitational, Alaska Arts Coun, Anchorage, Fairbanks & Juneau, 81; Humor in Art, Los Angeles Inst Contemp Art, 81; Works in Wood, Morgan Gallery, Shawnee Mission, Kans, 81; Bay Area Figurative Sculpture, Transamerica Pyramid Gallery, San Francisco, 82; Northern California: Focus on the Figure, Brentwood Gallery, St Louis, 82. *Awards:* Phelan Award Art for Sculpture, San Francisco Found, 82. *Bibliog:* Dona Z Meilach (auth), Woodworking: The New Wave, Crown Publ, 81; Peggy Bagley (auth), Artists profile, Art Voices, 1-2/82. *Dealer:* Betsy Rosenfield Gallery 212 W Superior St Chicago IL 60610; Braunstein Gallery 254 Sutter St San Francisco CA 94102. *Mailing Add:* 3977 Rosemary Circle Sacramento CA 95821

STEVENS, NELSON L
PAINTER, EDUCATOR
b Brooklyn, NY, Apr 26, 38. *Study:* Ohio Univ, BFA, 62; Kent State Univ, 69. *Comn:* Work to Unify African People, United Community Construct Worker, Roxbury, Mass, 73; I am a Black Woman, Univ Year for Action,

Springfield, Mass, 74; United Community, Ctr Exp Educ & M Jackson, Springfield, 75. *Exhib:* Afri-Cobra I, II & III & Afri-Cobra 77, Philadelphia, Pa; one-man show, Studio Mus in Harlem, NY; Levels & Degrees, Fisk Univ, Nashville, Tenn; FESTAC 77, Lagos, Nigeria & Janet Carter Gallery, New York, 77. *Teaching:* Instr, Cleveland Pub Sch Syst, 62-66 & Cleveland Mus Art, 66-68; asst prof art, Northern Ill Univ, DeKalb, 69-72; assoc prof art, Dept Afro-Am Studies, Univ Mass, Amherst, 72- *Mem:* Col Art Asn Am; Nat Conf Artists; Afri-Cobra. *Media:* Acrylic, Acrylic Spray. *Publ:* Illusr, The Cry of My People, Archie Shepp Album, ABC Dunhill, 72; illusr, There is a Trumpet in My Soul, Archie Shepp Album, Artista, 75; illusr cover, Mass Rev, Univ Mass. *Mailing Add:* Dept of Art Univ Mass Amherst MA 01002

STEVENS, RICHARD CLIVE
PAINTER, ILLUSTRATOR
b Springfield, Mass, Jan 4, 17. *Work:* Springfield Mus Fine Arts, Mass; Wistariahurst Mus, Holyoke, Mass; Univ Mass, Amherst; Western New Eng Col, Springfield, Mass. *Exhib:* one-man exhibs, Rand Mus, Westfield Athenaeum, Mass, 73, Am Int Col, Springfield, 79 & Western New Eng Col, 79; Springfield Art League 55th Nat Exhib, Walter Vincent Smith Mus, 74; Acad Artists Asn 26th Ann Nat Exhib Art, Mus Fine Arts, Springfield, 75. *Pos:* Consult, Strathmore Paper Co, currently. *Awards:* Muriel Alvord Award, Acad Artists Asn Nat Exhib, 65; Best Watercolor, West Springfield Art Festival, 74; Best Watercolor, Agawam Art Festival, 75. *Mem:* Acad Artists Asn (pres, 74 & 75); Springfield Art League; Am Artists Prof League. *Media:* Mixed. *Mailing Add:* 463 Ridge Rd Wilbraham MA 01095

STEVENS, WILLIAM ANSEL, SR
PAINTER, CARTOONIST
b Akron, Ohio, Sept 6, 19. *Study:* Kent State Univ; NMex State Univ; also with E Ladislaw Novotny, Fredric Taubes, Gerry Pierce, Kenneth Barrack & Ramon Froman. *Work:* US Naval Air Station Corpus Christi, Tex Hist Collection; White Sands Missile Range, NMex; US Forest Serv; White Sands Nat Monument; CofC, Alamogordo. *Comn:* Various oil portraits & landscapes in the US, Ger, Japan, Hawaii & Alaska. *Exhib:* NMex State Fair, Albuquerque, 65; Llano Estacado Art Exhib, Hobbs, NMex, 67-68; Sun Carnival Art Exhib, El Paso, Tex, 68-69; Nat Wild Turkey Fedn Show, 78; Law West Exhib, 78. *Pos:* Owner, Art Enterprises, Alamogordo, 60-; ed cartoons for three newspapers, 67-69; ed & illusr, Mgt Digest, 74-75. *Awards:* Grand Champion Art Award, Otero Co Fair, Alamogordo CofC, 62; Grand Champion Art Award, US Forest Serv, White Sands, NMex, 64 & 71; First Place Art Award, CofC Banquet, Alamogordo, 71. *Bibliog:* B Schwartz (auth), Sun dial, El Paso Times Sunday Mag, 5/75; J Baldwin (auth), article in art sect, Alamogordo Daily News; E White (auth), article in art sect, Missile Ranger, White Sands Missile Range, Dept Defense Publ. *Mem:* Black Range Artists Inc; NMex Desert Arts League (pres, 69-70). *Media:* Oil, Watercolor, Pen & Ink. *Publ:* Illusr, Capabilities of the White Sands Complex, 75 & 77; auth, Dear Smudge (weekly art column), 79-80; auth & illusr, Al n' Mo (comic strip), 83- *Mailing Add:* 1416 Taft Ave Alamogordo NM 88310

STEVENSON, A BROCKIE
PAINTER, EDUCATOR
b Montgomery Co, Pa, Sept 24, 19. *Study:* Pa Acad Fine Arts, Philadelphia; Barnes Found, Merion, Pa; Skowhegan Sch Painting & Sculpture, Maine. *Work:* Corcoran Gallery Art & Nat Collection Fine Arts, Washington, DC; Pa Acad Fine Arts; State Univ NY Potsdam; Woodward Found, Washington, DC. *Exhib:* Eight Washington Artists, Columbia Mus Art, SC, 71; Pyramid Galleries, Washington, DC, 73; Our Land, Our Sky, Our Water, Spokane World's Fair, 74; retrospective, Northern Va Community Col, Annandale, 74; Images of the '70s: Nine Washington Artists, Corcoran Gallery Art, DC, 80; one-man show, Fendrick Gallery, Washington, DC, 78. *Pos:* War artist corresp, European Theater Operations Southern Base Sect, USA, Eng, 43-44 & Off Chief Eng, France, 44-45. *Teaching:* Instr compos, Sch Fine Arts, Washington Univ, 60-62; from assoc prof to prof design, drawing & painting, Corcoran Sch Art, Washington, DC, 65- *Bibliog:* Paul Richard (auth), article, Washington Post, 4/29/78; Benjamin Forgey (auth), article, Washington Star-News, 5/7/78; David Tannous (auth), article, Art Am, 9-10/78; among others. *Media:* Acrylic. *Dealer:* Fendrick Gallery 3059 M St Washington DC 20007. *Mailing Add:* Corcoran Sch of Art 17th & New York Ave NW Washington DC 20006

STEVENSON, BRANSON GRAVES
PAINTER, PRINTMAKER
b Franklin Co, Ga, Apr 5, 01. *Study:* Inst Nac, Panama; Col Great Falls, Mont; and with Margarite Wildenhain, Bernard Leach & Shoji Hamada. *Work:* Mont Inst Arts, Helena; C M Russell Gallery, Great Falls, Mont; Mont Hist Soc, Helena; Univ Ore, Eugene. *Comn:* Fresco mural, Great Falls, 45; Story of Paper (glass mural), Great Falls Pub Libr, 68; doc TV film, Jr League Great Falls, 71; 138 proofs of lithographs, First Nat Bank, Great Falls, 71-72. *Exhib:* Retrospective, Russell Gallery, 70; one-man show, Yellowstone Art Ctr, Billings, Mont, 72; Mont Hist Soc, 72; Northern Mont Col, 72; Ore Arts Comn, Eugene, 72. *Pos:* Founder, dir, secy & trustee, Archie Bray Found, Helena, 51-; dir, C M Russell Mus, 53- *Teaching:* Lectr humanities, Col Great Falls, 63- *Awards:* Purchase Prize for Rhubarb (lithograph), Univ Ore; Awards for Emulsion Wax Watercolors, Etching, Drawings & Lithographs, Mont State Fair. *Bibliog:* Kathleen Cronin (auth), article in, Mobil World, 71; Ray Steele (auth), Branson G Stevenson, the man & his works, KRTV, 72; Herb Anderson, Jr (auth), The Life, the Times and the Art of Branson Graves Stevenson, 79. *Mem:* Life mem Mont Hist Soc & Art Gallery; life mem & fel Mont Inst Arts. *Media:* Graphics. *Collection:* Etchings and graphics, including etchings by Goya, Rembrandt and Seymore Haden, sculpture by C M Russell and painting by Florencio Molino Campos. *Publ:* Contribr, Craft Horizons, Ceramic Indust, Mont Arts & others. *Dealer:* Import Depot Great Falls, Russell Mus Great Falls, MT 59401. *Mailing Add:* 715 Fourth Ave N Great Falls MT 59401

STEVENSON, HAROLD
PAINTER
b Idabel, Okla, Mar 11, 29. *Study:* Univ Okla, Norman; Univ Mex, Mexico City; Art Students League, New York. *Work:* Whitney Mus, New York; Ctr George Pompidou, Paris. *Exhib:* Ann Exhib, Whitney Mus, New York, 62; Galleria La Medusa, Rome, 73; one-man shows: Okla Art Ctr, Univ Okla, Oklahoma City, 49 & Galerie Iris Clert, Paris, 79; Americans in Paris, Mus Nat Art Mod, 79; Stevenson, Musee Girodet, Montargis, France; La Famille des Portraits, Louvre Mus Portrait of Francois de Menil, 79-80; and many others. *Teaching:* Artist-in-residence, Austin Col, Sherman, Tex, formerly. *Bibliog:* Andy Warhol (dir), Harold (film), New York, 64; Lucy Lippard (auth), Pop Art, New York, 66. *Dealer:* Galerie Iris Clert 3 rue Duphot Paris 75001 France; Alexander Iolas Gallery 15 E 55th St New York NY 10022. *Mailing Add:* 302 S East Adams Idabel OK 74745

STEVENSON, RUTH CARTER
COLLECTOR, PATRON
b Ft Worth, Tex, Oct 19, 23. *Study:* Sarah Lawrence Col, BA, 45. *Pos:* Chmn bd, Amon Carter Mus Western Art; emer trustee, Ft Worth Art Mus; founder, Ft Worth Art Coun; vpres, Int Coun Mus Mod Art, 67-72; trustee, Nat Trust Hist Preservation, 68-74; nat chmn collector's comt, Nat Gallery of Art, 74-79; mem vis comt, Fogg Mus, Cambridge, Mass, 77-; trustee, Nat Gallery Art, 79-; pres, Amor G Carter Found, currently. *Mem:* Nat Endowment of the Arts; Ft Worth City Art Comn (chmn, George Rickey Sculpture Comt, 74-75). *Collection:* French 19th century; European and American sculpture and graphics. *Mailing Add:* 1200 Broad Ave Ft Worth TX 76107

STEVENSON, RUTH ROLSTON
PAINTER, INSTRUCTOR
b Brooklyn, NY, May 27, 1897. *Study:* Pratt Inst, dipl-BFA, 20; Art Students League, with John Sloan, 37. *Work:* Huntington Mus, WVa; Norfolk Mus Arts & Sci, Va. *Comn:* Two murals, Pratt Inst, Brooklyn, 20; Celebrated Musicians Collection, Nat Art Club, New York, 67 & 72. *Exhib:* Nat Asn Women Artists Travel Exhib, Europe, 54-59; Witte Mus, San Antonio, Tex, 59, Ill State Mus, Springfield, 60 & Nat Acad, New York, 64 & 73; Invitational, Southern Vt Art Asn & Hudson Valley Art Asn, 60; Catherine Lorillard Wolfe, Nat Acad, New York, 59; Am Watercolor Soc Travel Exhib, Europe, 67; retrospective exhib, Grand Central Gallery, New York, 81. *Teaching:* Instr drawing & painting, Pratt Inst, Brooklyn, NY, 20-24 & Newark Pub Sch Fine & Indust Arts, NJ, 27-36. *Awards:* Gold Medal, Nat Arts Club, 57; First Prize Watercolor, Nat Asn Women Artists, 60; Am Watercolor Soc Award, 67. *Mem:* Am Watercolor Soc; Nat Arts Club; Pen & Brush Club; Nat Asn Women Artists; Am Artists Prof League. *Media:* Watercolor, Oil. *Mailing Add:* 26 W Ninth St New York NY 10011

STEVOVICH, ANDREW VLASTIMIR
PAINTER, PRINTMAKER
b Salzburg, Austria, July 2, 48; US citizen. *Study:* RI Sch Design, BFA(painting); Sydney Richmond Burley Award; Presidential Fel Travel in Europe), 70; Mass Col Art, MFA(painting), 80. *Work:* Brockton Art Mus, Mass; Danforth Mus, Framingham, Mass; New Britain Mus Am Art, Conn. *Exhib:* Triennial, Brockton Art Mus, 78 & 81; one-man shows, Clark Univ Art Gallery, 80 & Coe Kerr Gallery, New York, 83; 20th Anniversary Exhib, Corcoran Gallery Art, 81; Boston Artists Work on Paper, Boston Univ Art Gallery, 81; Realistic Directions, Pa State Univ, University Park, 83. *Media:* Oil, Pastel; Etchings. *Dealer:* Coe Kerr Gallery 49 E 82nd St New York NY 10028. *Mailing Add:* 120 Sewall Ave Brookline MA 02146

STEWARD, DONN HORATIO
PRINTMAKER, PUBLISHER
b Moose Jaw, Sask, Can, Nov 26, 21; US citizen. *Study:* Univ Iowa, Iowa City, with Mauricio Lasansky, BA, 42, MA, 48; Ecole des Beaux-Arts, Paris, Fulbright scholar, 52-53; Tamarind Litho Inst, printer fel, 65-66. *Work:* Brooklyn Mus; British Fine Arts Coun, London; Des Moines Art Ctr, Iowa; Northwest Printmakers, Seattle, Wash; San Francisco Mus Art; and many others. *Exhib:* Northwest Printmakers Ann Int, Seattle, 48-57; Des Moines Art Ctr, 49-54; Brooklyn Mus Nat Print Ann, 51, 53 & 54; Artists of Suffolk Co, Part VI, Prints, Heckscher Mus, Huntington, NY, 72; one-man show, Heckscher Mus, 75; Prints by 4 New York Painters, Frankenthaler, Motherwell, Newman & Johns, Metrop Mus Art, 70; A la Pintura, Motherwell, Alberti, Metrop Mus Art & Univ Iowa Mus Art, 72. *Pos:* Printer's asst, Mauricio Lasansky, Iowa City, 47-52; master printer, Universal Ltd Art Ed, West Islip, NY, 66-74; master printer-publ, Donn H Steward, Halesite, NY, 74- *Teaching:* Instr printmaking, Univ Iowa, 48-54; asst prof, Fla State Univ, Tallahassee, 54-57; vis lectr, Washington Univ, St Louis, Mo, 57-58; vis artist, Univ Iowa, 78-79; instr, Pratt Graphics Ctr, 81; instr printmaking workshop, Huntington Twp Art League, 75- *Bibliog:* Amei Wallach (auth), Donn Steward, Printer, Sun Newsday, Long Island, 2/9/75; Richard S Field (auth), Recent American Etching (catalogue), Nat Collection of Fine Arts, Washington, DC, 10/75; Stephanie Terenzio (auth), The Painter and the Printer, Am Fedn Arts, 80; and others. *Mem:* Long Island Printmakers Soc. *Media:* Intaglio. *Mailing Add:* One Noyes Lane Apt 7 Halesite NY 11743

STEWART, ARTHUR
PAINTER
b Marion, Ala, July 29, 15. *Study:* Auburn Univ; Art Inst Chicago; and with Kelly Fitzpatrick. *Work:* Birmingham Mus Art, Ala; Montgomery Mus Art, Ala; Atlanta Art Asn, Ga; also in collection of Queen Elizabeth II, England. *Comn:* Four murals (with Kelly Fitzpatrick), Bank of Tallassee, Ala. *Exhib:* Art in War Traveling Exhib, Life Mag, 41-42; four Southeastern Ann, 49-59; Norfolk Mus Arts & Sci Traveling Exhib, 64; Ala Watercolor Soc, 69-70; Palm Beach Gallery, 79. *Teaching:* Instr drawing, Birmingham Mus Art, formerly; pvt instr. *Awards:* Purchase Award for Spanish Bouquet, Norfolk Mus Arts & Sci, 64; Award for Early Light, Meade Co, 64; Harriete Murray Award for Rosalie, Birmingham Centennial Exhib, 72; and others. *Bibliog:* Alfred Frankfurter (auth), Parisian scenes, San Francisco Chronicle, 49; Richard Howard (auth), Arthur Stewart florals, Crescenzi Gallery, 67. *Mem:* Birmingham Art Asn (vpres, 65-66); Ala Watercolor Soc (pres, 65-67); Ala Art League; Ala Art Asn. *Media:* Watercolor, Oil, Acrylic. *Dealer:* Elizabeth Agee 1915 11th Ave S Birmingham AL 35205. *Mailing Add:* 2969 Pump House Rd Birmingham AL 35243

STEWART, BILL
SCULPTOR, CERAMIST
b Plattsburgh, NY, June 21, 41. *Study:* State Univ NY Col, Buffalo, BS(art educ), 63; Ohio Univ, MFA, 66. *Work:* Burchfield Ctr, Buffalo; Mus Contemp Crafts, New York; Campbell Mus, Camden, NJ; Mem Art Gallery, Rochester; Univ Iowa Mus Art. *Exhib:* Clayworks--20 Americans, Mus Contemp Crafts, New York, 71; Figure and Fantasy, Renwick Gallery, 74; Clay, Whitney Mus, 74; Clay USA, Fendrick Gallery, Washington, DC, 75; Sculptureens USA, Campbell Mus, Camden, NJ, 76; Contemporary Ceramic Sculpture, Achland Mem Art Ctr, Univ NC, Chapel Hill, 77; Tribute to Josiah Wedgewood, Philadelphia Mus Art, 80; Ancient Inspirations--Contemporary Interpretations, Roberson Ctr, Binghamton, NY, 82. *Teaching:* Prof art, State Univ NY, Brockport, 66- *Awards:* Nat Endowment Arts Res Grant, 76; Lillian Fairchild Award, Univ Rochester, 79; Chancellor's Award Excellence in Teaching, State Univ NY, 82. *Media:* Ceramics. *Dealer:* Theo Portnoy Gallery 162 W 56th Suite 207 New York NY 10019. *Mailing Add:* 2489 Roosevelt Hwy Hamlin NY 14464

STEWART, DOROTHY S
PAINTER, PRINTMAKER
b Brooklyn, NY. *Study:* Art Students League; Nat Acad Sch Fine Art, New York; NY Univ. *Comn:* In pvt collections. *Exhib:* Allied Artists Am 56-68th Ann, 69-81; Catharine Lorillard Wolfe Art Club 68-87th Ann, 65-83; Salmagundi Club, 74-77; Mus Art, Sci & Industry, 80 & 82; Knickerbocker Artists, 80-82. *Teaching:* Instr art, Malverne Sr High Sch, NY, 65-66. *Awards:* Salmagundi Club Prize, 76; Catharine Lorillard Wolfe Art Club Award, 74, 79 & 83; Kent Art Assoc Awards, 74, 78 & 80; and others. *Mem:* Catharine Lorillard Wolfe Art Club (dir, 70, 2nd vpres, 71-74); Allied Artists Am (asst corresp secy, 78-79); Am Artists Prof League; Kent Art Asn (pres, 77-78); life mem Art Students League; among others. *Publ:* Contribr, Prize-winning art book 7, Allied Publ, Inc, Ft Lauderdale, Fla, 67. *Mailing Add:* 14 Club Dr Candlewood Trails New Milford CT 06776

STEWART, F CLARK
PAINTER, EDUCATOR
b Evansville, Ind, July 18, 42. *Study:* Univ Redlands, Calif, BA(art), 64; Claremont Grad Sch & Univ Ctr, Calif, MFA(painting), 66. *Work:* Mint Mus Art, Charlotte, NC; Tenn State Mus, Nashville; Dulin Gallery Art, Knoxville; Miss Art Asn Collection, Jackson; Carroll Reece Mus, Johnson City, Tenn; and others. *Exhib:* 34th Semi-Ann Southeastern Exhib, Gallery Contemp Art, Winston-Salem, NC, 71; 17th Ann Drawing & Small Sculpture Show, Ball State Univ Art Gallery, Muncie, Ind, 72; Drawings USA, Minn Mus Art, St Paul, 73; Southeast Graphics Invitational, Mint Mus, Charlotte, NC, 79-81; More Than Earth & Sky, Nat Mus Am Art, Washington, DC, 81; solo shows, Univ EKy, Richmond, 82 & Hunter Mus, Chatanooga, Tenn, 82; and others. *Pos:* Adv bd mem, Contemp Artists Southeast, Atlanta, 76-79; visual arts panel founding comt, Knoxville Arts Coun. *Teaching:* Prof drawing, Univ Tenn, Knoxville, 66- *Awards:* Purchase Prize, Mint Mus, 72; Purchase Prize, Tenn Asn Mus, 76; Puchase Award, Marietta Nat Print & Drawing Show, 81. *Bibliog:* Dr Frederick C Moffatt (auth), Painting, Sculpture & Photography, In: Heart of the Valley, 76; Christine Maddox (auth), Interviews with Regional Artists (film), E Tenn Dept Continuing Educ, 78. *Mem:* Col Art Asn. *Media:* Acrylic, Mixed-Media. *Publ:* Illusr, The Marriage of Heaven and Hell, Darkpool Press, Tenn, 72. *Dealer:* Gemart Inc 3039 Kingston Pike Knoxville TN 37919; Gallery 23 Patten Parkway Chattanooga TN 37403. *Mailing Add:* 702 Forest Hills Blvd Knoxville TN 37919

STEWART, JACK
PAINTER, EDUCATOR
b Atlanta, Ga, Jan 27, 26. *Study:* With Steffen Thomas, Atlanta; Yale Univ Sch Fine Arts, under Albers & deKooning, BFA; Columbia Univ Sch Archit; NY Univ, MA. *Work:* Yale Univ Art Gallery; Columbia, SC Mus Fine Arts; Greenville Mus, SC. *Comn:* Mural on facade of Versailles Hotel, Miami Beach, Fla, 55; six mosaic murals on SS Santa Paula, Grace Lines, 57; mural on facade of Hotel Aruba Caribbean, Netherlands Antilles, 58; two mosaic murals in Pub Sch 28, Manhattan, NY, 58; stained glass, Cinerama, Inc, New York, 60. *Exhib:* Pa Acad Fine Arts, Philadelphia, 53; Col Raffaello, Urbino, Italy, 73; NY Univ, 75; one-man shows, Washington Sq East Galleries, New York, 75 & Woods Gerry Gallery, Providence, RI, 76. *Teaching:* Lectr art & archit, New Sch Social Res, 53-58; instr design, Pratt Inst, 55-61; lectr drawing & painting, Columbia Univ, 67-76; instr drawing & painting, Cooper Union Sch Art & Archit, 60-71, assoc prof & chmn dept, 71-74; instr graphics & drawing, Queens Col, New York, 74-76; instr painting & drawing, New York Univ, 74-76; provost & vpres acad affairs, RI Sch Design, 76-77; prof art & chmn dept, Ind State Univ, Terre Haute, 78-80. *Publ:* Contribr, Mosaic Art Today, 59; ed, Modern Mosaic Techniques, Watson Guptill, 67; auth, short articles on drawing & mosaic, In: Jefferson Encycl, World, 69; contribr, Art of Mosaic, 69. *Mailing Add:* 31 E Seventh St New York NY 10003

STEWART, JEFFREY
DEALER, GALLERY DIRECTOR
b Spokane, Wash, June 7, 47. *Pos:* Dir, Wortsman Stewart Galleries, San Francisco, 73-83; pres, Stewart Am Art, San Francisco, 83- *Specialty:* Nineteenth and early twentieth century American paintings, watercolors, pastels and drawings; selected realistic contemporary work, especially work by California artists. *Publ:* Auth, The Art of Emil Carlsen (1853-1932), Rubicon-Wortsman Rowe, 75; auth, The art of Emil Carlsen, Southwest Art Mag, 75. *Mailing Add:* Stewart Am Art 500 Sutter St Suite 204 San Francisco CA 94102

STEWART, JOHN (JOHN STEWART HOUSTON)
DEALER
b Orange, NJ, Dec 24, 45. *Study:* Miami Univ, BA, 68. *Collections Arranged:* Works by Van Selm, Barnwell Art Ctr, Shreveport, La, 78; Sculpture of Russell Jacques, Abilene Fine Arts Mus, 79; Watercolors by Jo Taylor, El Dorado Art Ctr, Ark, 80; Figurative Works by Charles Campbell, Univ Tex, Dallas, 81; Mardi Gras by Arie Van Selm, Dallas City Hall, 81; Int House, New Orleans, 81 & touring in Europe; Nathan Jones Touring Exhib, Randall Gallery, New York, 81, Fed Reserve Bank, Cleveland, 81, Fed Reserve Bank, Cincinnati, 81, Univ Tex, Arlington, 81, Univ Calif, Los Angeles, 82 & Fisk Univ, 82; Landscapes by Jeff Tabor, Tex Womens Univ, 82; Artists from the Stewart Gallery, Abilene Christian Univ, 83; Black Heritage Today, Longview Mus, Tex, 83; Landscapes by Four American Artists, Coninck Gallery, Holland. *Pos:* Designer & planner, Galleria des Bellas Artes, Phoenix, 71 & White Gallery, Westlake Village, Calif, 80; founder & dir, Stewart Gallery, Dallas, 72-; dir & mgr, Artists Courtyard, 76-; partner, Jones-Houston Graphics, currently. *Specialty:* Art by young, contemporary artists. *Mailing Add:* 7139 Azalea Dallas TX 75230

STEWART, JOHN DOUGLAS
HISTORIAN
b Kingston, Ont, Jan 28, 34. *Study:* Queen's Univ, Kingston, Ont, BA(hons), 55; McGill Univ, BLS, 56; Courtauld Inst, Univ London, PhD, 68. *Teaching:* Lectr art hist, Univ Toronto, 64-65; asst prof art hist, Queen's Univ, Kingston, Ont, 65-70, assoc prof, 70-80, prof, 80- *Awards:* Best Local Hist Award, Can Hist Asn, 74; Leave Fels, Can Coun, 74-75 & 81-82. *Res:* 17th century English painting, sculpture and architecture; 19th century Canadian architecture. *Publ:* Auth, Sir Godfrey Kneller, Nat Portrait Gallery, 71; coauth, Heritage Kingston, Agnes Etherington Art Ctr, 73; coauth, English Portraits of the Seventeenth and Eighteenth Centuries, W A Clark Mem Libr, 74; auth, Sir Godfrey Kneller and the English Baroque Portrait, Oxford Univ Press, 83. *Mailing Add:* Dept Art Queen's Univ Kingston ON K7L 3N6 Canada

STEWART, JOHN LINCOLN
EDUCATOR, WRITER
b Alton, Ill, Jan 24, 17. *Study:* Denison Univ, AB, 38; Ohio State Univ, MA, 39, PhD, 47; Denison Univ, hon DA, 64. *Pos:* Assoc dir, Hopkins Art Ctr, Dartmouth Col, 62-64; dir, Mandeville Ctr for Arts, Univ Calif, San Diego, 75-76. *Teaching:* From asst prof to prof, Dartmouth Col, 49-54; prof Am lit & provost, John Muir Col, Univ Calif, San Diego, 64- *Awards:* Howard Found Fel, 53-54; Dartmouth Fac Fel, 62-63. *Res:* Contemporary American and British literature. *Publ:* Auth, John Crowe Ransom, Univ Minn, 62; auth, Burden of Time, the Fugitives and Agrarians, Princeton Univ, 65; co-auth, Horizons Circled, Univ Calif, 74; plus others. *Mailing Add:* John Muir Col Univ of Calif at San Diego La Jolla CA 92037

STEWART, JOHN P
PAINTER, PRINTMAKER
b Ft Leavenworth, Kans, Mar 11, 45. *Study:* Univ Colo, with Roland Reiss & Wendel Black, BFA, 67; Univ Calif, Santa Barbara, MFA, 69. *Work:* Corcoran Gallery Art, Washington, DC; Whitney Mus Am Art, New York; Ponce Mus, PR; New Orleans Mus of Art, La; Mint Mus, NC. *Exhib:* Recent Acquisitions, Whitney Mus, New York, 72; Contemp Art Ctr, Cincinnati, Ohio, 76; Ohio Selection, Dayton Art Inst, 79; The Reality of Illusion, Denver Art Mus & traveling, 79-80; A J Wood Gallery, Pa, 80; Osuna Gallery, Washington DC, 81 & 82; and others. *Teaching:* Assoc prof, Univ Cincinnati, 73- *Awards:* Individual Artist Grant, Ohio Arts Coun, 78 & 82. *Dealer:* Osuna Gallery 406 7th St NW Washington DC 20001. *Mailing Add:* 2510 Moorman Ave Cincinnati OH 45206

STEWART, PAUL LEROY
PRINTMAKER, EDUCATOR
b Cleveland, Ohio, June 28, 28. *Study:* Cleveland Inst Art, 46-48; Albion Col, BA, 53; Univ Mich, Ann Arbor, MA, 59. *Work:* Detroit Inst Art; Libr Cong; Ga Mus Art, Athens; Minneapolis Inst Art; Art Mus City Sacramento. *Comn:* Bicentennial print, Mich Workshop Fine Prints, Detroit, 75. *Exhib:* Solo exhib, DeWaters Art Ctr, Flint, Mich, 79; New American Graphics II Travelling Exhib, Univ Wis, Madison, 82; 66th Ann Nat Exhib, Nat Collection Fine Arts, Smithsonian Inst; Northwest Printmakers Int Exhib, Univ Wash, Seattle; Boston Printmakers Nat Exhib; 6th Int Miniature Print Exhib, Pratt Inst, New York & travelling. *Teaching:* Assoc prof art, Albion Col, 59-72; prof, Univ Mich, Ann Arbor, 73-; guest instr lithography, Univ NMex, Albuquerque, summer 79. *Awards:* Hal H Smith Mem Award, Detroit Inst Art Ann Exhib Mich Artists, 66; Purchase Award, Nat Print Exhib, Univ Dallas, 77; Landfall Press Award, Ill Regional Print Exhib, 78. *Bibliog:* C Overvoorte (auth), article, For the Time Being Fine Arts Mag, Vol II, No 2, 73. *Mem:* Mich Asn Printmakers. *Media:* Lithography. *Dealer:* Dais Annis 7402 Azalea Ct West Bloomfield MI 48033. *Mailing Add:* 2281 Ayrshire Rd Ann Arbor MI 48105

STEWART, REGINA See Serniak, Regina

STEWART, ROBERT GORDON
CURATOR, HISTORIAN
b Baltimore, Md, Mar 5, 31. *Study:* Univ Pa, BFA, 54. *Collections Arranged:* Nucleus for a National Collection, 1st Exhib Nat Portrait Gallery, Smithsonian Inst, 65, Recent Acquisitions, 66; National Gallery of 19th Century Distinguished Americans (with catalog), 69; Henry Benbridge (with catalog), 71; Robert Edge Pine (with catalog), 79. *Pos:* Architect & cur, Jefferson Barracks Hist Park, St Louis, Mo, 58-61; dir properties, Nat Trust Hist Preservation, 61-64; cur collection, Nat Portrait Gallery, Smithsonian Inst, 64- *Teaching:* Vis lectr museology, George Washington Univ, 67-70. *Res:* American portraiture from 18th century to present. *Publ:* Contribr, In the Minds and the Hearts of the People, 74; contribr, The Dye is Now Cast, 75; contribr, Abroad in America, 76. *Mailing Add:* 4104 46th St NW Washington DC 20016

STEWART, WILLIAM
PAINTER
b Waco, Tex, Aug 18, 38. *Study:* Univ Tex, BFA, 60, MFA, 62. *Work:* Fordham Univ, Bronx, NY; Fairleigh Dickinson Univ, Madison, NJ. *Exhib:* One-man shows, O K Harris Gallery, New York, 69, Rudolf Zwirner Gallery, Cologne, Ger, 70, Pergola Gallery, San Miguel de Allende, 78, Regional Mus, Oaxaca, Mex, 79 & Il Balcone Gallery, San Francisco, 79; and many others. *Teaching:* Asst dir educ dept & instr, San Francisco Mus Art, Calif, 63-64; art instr, Fairleigh Dickinson Univ, 68-70 & City Col New York, 71-72; instr educ dept, Newark Mus, 73-74; instr painting & drawing, Instituto Allende, San Miguel de Allende, Guanajuato, Mex, 77-; vis artist, Univ Iowa, 81. *Bibliog:* Colin Naylor (ed), Contemporary Artists, St James Press Ltd, London, Eng, 77. *Media:* Oil, Watercolor. *Mailing Add:* Inst Allende San Miguel de Allende Guanajuato Mexico

STICKER, ROBERT EDWARD
PAINTER
b Jersey City, NJ, Dec 26, 22. *Study:* Art Students League, with Frank Reilly. *Work:* Vesuvius Crucible Co, Pittsburgh; IBM Corp, Union Carbide Corp, Am Tel & Tel & Nat Distillers, New York. *Exhib:* Franklin Mint Marine Competition, 74; Ann Am Soc Marine Artists, Grand Cent Galleries, New York, 80. *Pos:* Mem bd control, Art Students League, 59- *Awards:* Gold Medal, Franklin Mint Nat Marine Competition, 74. *Mem:* Fel Am Soc Marine Artists; Hudson Valley Art Asn; Am Artists Prof League. *Media:* Acrylic, Oil. *Publ:* Illusr, Famous small boat voyages, 69-72 & Classical work boats of America, 73- (ser of paintings), Yachting Mag. *Mailing Add:* c/o Grant Central Art Gallery 24 W 57th St New York NY 10019

STIEBEL, ERIC
DEALER
b Frankfurt, Ger, July 22, 11; US citizen. *Study:* Univ Frankfurt, 29-30; Univ Munich, 30-31; Univ Berlin, 31-32. *Pos:* Pres, Rosenberg & Stiebel, currently. *Mem:* Nat Antique & Art Dealers Asn Am; Art & Antique Dealers League Am; Art Dealers Asn Am; Int Confedn Dealer in Works Art; Syndicat Nat des Antiquaires. *Specialty:* Old master paintings and drawings; important French 18th century furniture; Renaissance bronzes. *Mailing Add:* 912 Fifth Ave New York NY 10021

STIEBEL, GERALD GUSTAVE
DEALER
b New York, NY, Sept 28, 44. *Study:* C W Post Col, BA, 65; Courtauld Inst, London, 65-66; Study Centre Fine & Decorative Arts, London, dipl, 66; Columbia Univ, MA(art hist), 67. *Collections Arranged:* Grand Gallery Exhib, Metrop Mus Art, New York, 74-75; Experts Choice, Va Mus Art, 83. *Pos:* Treas, Rosenberg & Stiebel Inc, 68-71, vpres, 71- *Teaching:* Lectr, numerous univs & mus incl Guggenheim Mus & Metrop Mus Art, New York. *Mem:* La Confederation Int Negociants Oeuvres d'Art (bd dirs, 80-, pres, 81-); Int Confederation Art Dealers (pres, 81-84); Art Dealers Asn Am (bd dirs, 80-); Art & Antique Dealers League Am; Nat Antique & Art Dealers Asn Am (secy, 71-73, vpres, 73-77, pres, 77-79, bd dirs, 79-). *Specialty:* Old master paintings and drawings; important French 18th century furniture; Renaissance bronzes. *Publ:* Auth, The Passionate Collector, Designer Mag, 72; auth, Collector's Handbook, Cincinnati Art Mus, 78. *Mailing Add:* 32 E 57th St New York NY 10022

STIEBEL, PENELOPE HUNTER See Hunter-Stiebel, Penelope

STIEGELMEYER, NORMAN EARL
PAINTER, SCULPTOR
b Denver, Colo, Oct 28, 37. *Study:* San Francisco Art Inst, BFA & MFA; Acad Art, Nuremburg, Ger. *Work:* San Francisco Mus Mod Art; Oakland Mus Art, Calif; City San Francisco. *Exhib:* Painting Ann, 68 & Human Concern & Personal Torment, 69, Whitney Mus Am Art, New York; one-man show, Calif Palace Legion Hon, 69; Just Yesterday, San Francisco Mus of Art, 69; West Coast Artists (touring show), Fla State Mus, 69; Recent Acquisitions, Oakland Mus of Art, 75; Painting & Sculpture in Calif--The Mod Era, San Francisco Mus of Art & Nat Collection of Fine Arts, Washington, DC, 77; Bay Area Update, Huntsville Mus of Art, Ala, 77; San Francisco Mus Art, 81; Visionary Art, Walnut Creek Civic Arts Gallery, 81; and others. *Pos:* Guest cur, San Francisco Art Festival, 68-69, San Francisco Art Inst Art Gallery, 71 & Walnut Creek Art Ctr, 75 & 81. *Teaching:* Prof drawing & painting, Univ Calif Extension, San Francisco; prof drawing & painting, Diablo Valley Col, Pleasant Hill, 75- *Awards:* Painting Award, San Francisco Art Inst, James J Schwabacher, 64; Fulbright Scholar & Ger Govt Acad Exchange Serv Grant, WGer, 65; One-Man Show Award, Calif Palace

Legion Hon, 69. *Bibliog:* Carter Ratcliff (auth), Art in California, Art in Am, 77; Palmer French (auth), article, Artweek, 81; Tom Albright (auth), article, Art News, 81; and others. *Mem:* Walnut Creek Art Ctr. *Media:* Multimedia. *Publ:* Auth, Omnibus-Exstasis-et-Celestialis, 70 & The Silver Book of Drawings, 71, Cumberland Press. *Mailing Add:* 146 Oakvale Rd Walnut Creek CA 94596

STIEGLER, ROBERT WILLIAM
PHOTOGRAPHER, FILMMAKER
b Chicago, Ill, July 30, 38. *Study:* Inst Design, Ill Inst Technol, BS, 60, MS, 70. *Work:* Int Mus Photography, Rochester, NY; Mus Contemp Art, Chicago; Art Inst Chicago. *Exhib:* Summer Light, Light Gallery, New York, 82; one-person exhib, Chicago Ctr Contemp Photog, 83; Portrait of America, Smithsonian Inst; US Eye, Nat Fine Arts Comt, Lake Placid, NY; Form as Content, Visual Studies Workshop, Rochester, NY; The Photographer in the City, Mus Contemp Art, Chicago. *Teaching:* Assoc prof photog, Univ Ill, Chicago, 66- *Awards:* Nat Endowment Arts Fel, 80; Ill Arts Coun Grant, 83. *Bibliog:* Allen Porter (auth), article, Camera, C J Bucher Ltd, Switz, 76. *Mem:* Soc Photog Educ. *Mailing Add:* 1245 Carmen Chicago IL 60640

STILES, HELEN
PAINTER, PRINTMAKER
b New York, NY. *Study:* New Sch Social Res, with R Gwathmey & C Egas; Brooklyn Mus Art Sch, with Reuben Tam; Educ Alliance Art Sch, with Chaim Gross; Pratt Graphics Ctr, with M Lovejoy & D Finkbinder. *Exhib:* Nat Soc Painters Casein & Acrylics Travelling Exhib, 79-80 & 81-82; Audubon Artists 37th Ann, Nat Acad Galleries, 79 & 38th Ann, Nat Arts Club, New York, 80; Pratt Graphics Ctr Ann Competition, 80; First Ann Prize Competition, Provincetown Art Asn Mus, Mass, 83; Bergen Mus Art & Sci Exhib, Paramus, NJ, 83; and others. *Teaching:* Art, Lewis Carroll Pub Elementary Sch, Fresh Meadows, NY, 65-74. *Awards:* First in Oil, Caton Rose Art Inst Exhib, 62; Lillian Cotton Mem Prize, Nat Asn Women Artists Ann Exhib, 76; Doris Kreindler Mem Award, 25th Ann Exhib, Nat Soc Painters in Casein & Acrylic, 78. *Bibliog:* Joan Nash (auth), Art thrives on Long Island, Long Island Daily Press & Star J, 3/8/62. *Mem:* Nat Asn Women Artists; Artists Equity New York. *Media:* Oil, Acrylic; Intaglio, Screenprint. *Mailing Add:* 189-04 64th Ave Flushing NY 11365

STILLMAN, DAMIE
HISTORIAN, EDUCATOR
b Dallas, Tex, July 27, 33. *Study:* Northwestern Univ, BS, 54; Univ Del, MA, 56; Columbia Univ, PhD, 61. *Collections Arranged:* Architecture & Ornament in Late 19th Century America (ed, catalog), 81. *Teaching:* Asst prof art hist, Oakland Univ, 61-65; assoc prof, Univ Wis, Milwaukee, 65-67, prof, 67-77; prof, Univ Del, 77-, chmn dept, 81- *Awards:* Nat Endowment Humanities Fel, 70-71; Founders Award, Soc Archit Historians, 75. *Mem:* Col Art Asn Am; Soc Archit Historians (mem bd dirs, 75-78, second vpres, 78-80, first vpres, 80-82, pres, 82-84). *Res:* American and British architecture and decorative arts with special emphasis on neo-classicism. *Publ:* Co-ed, American Colonial Painting, Harvard Univ Press, 59; auth, New York City Hall: Competition and execution, J Soc Archit Historians, 64; auth, The Decorative Work of Robert Adam, Tiranti, 67; ed, Architecture & Ornament in Late 19th Century America, Univ Del, 81; auth, English Neo-classical Architecture, Zwemmer (in prep). *Mailing Add:* Dept Art Hist Univ Del Newark DE 19716

STILLMAN, E CLARK
COLLECTOR
b Eureka, Utah, Oct 24, 07. *Study:* Univ Mich, AB & AM. *Res:* African sculpture; medieval and modern book illumination and illustration. *Collection:* Traditional Congolese sculpture; manuscript and printed Books of Hours. *Mailing Add:* 24 Gramercy Park New York NY 10003

STILLMAN, GEORGE
ADMINISTRATOR, PAINTER
b Laramie, Wyo, Feb 25, 21. *Study:* Calif Sch Fine Arts, cert, 49; Ariz State Univ, BFA, MFA, 70. *Work:* Oakland Mus Art, Calif; High Mus Art, Atlanta, Ga; Seattle Art Comn; San Francisco Mus Art; Ariz State Univ Collections, Tempe. *Comn:* Murals, comn by Wash Art Comn, Olympia, La Cross, 78, Medical Lake, 78, Omak, 80, Naches, 80, Burbank, 80 & others. *Exhib:* 2nd Ann Int Drawing & Painting Show, Calif Palace of the Legion of Honor, San Francisco, 47; San Francisco Mus Art 69th Ann, 49; two-man show, Lucien Labaudt Gallery, San Francisco, 49; one-man shows, Galeria Arte Mod, Mexico City, 51 & Columbus Mus, Ga, 72; Nat Juried Show, Cape Coral, Fla, 77; Gov Invitational, Wash Statewide, 79, 80 & 81; and others. *Teaching:* Prof & chmn, Dept Art, Columbus Col, Ga, 70-72 & Cent Wash Univ, 72- *Awards:* Bender Award, San Francisco Art Asn, 49; Ann Bremer Award San Francisco Mus Art, 49; Tex Fine Art Asn Drawing Award, La Gloria Mus, 77. *Bibliog:* A Frankenstein (auth), var rev in San Francisco Chronicle, 48-51; articles in Diebenkorn Catalog: Published Lithographs, Mill Valley, Calif, 49. *Mem:* Col Art Asn. *Media:* All. *Dealer:* Foster-White Gallery Seattle WA. *Mailing Add:* 1127 Franklin Ave Ellensburg WA 98926

STILLMAN-MYERS, JOYCE
PAINTER
b New York, NY, Jan 19, 43. *Study:* Art Students League, 71; Pratt Inst, 72; Long Island Univ, MFA, 75. *Work:* Aldrich Mus Contemp Art; Nat Gallery, Canberra, Australia; Tomasolo Gallery, Union Col; Byers Mus, Chicago; C W Post Col, Long Island Univ, Greenvale, NY. *Exhib:* Out of the House, Whitney Mus Am Art, 78; Selections of Photo Realism, Southern Alleghenies Mus, St Francis Col, 79; Still-Life, Kent State Univ, 80; solo exhib, Heckscher

Mus, Huntington, NY, 80; Creative Artists Pub Serv Prog at State Mus, NY, 81; Homework, Women's Hall of Fame, Lowe Gallery, Syracuse Univ, 81; and others. *Teaching:* Vis artist painting, Towson Univ, spring 82. *Awards:* Creative Artists Pub Serv Prog, New York, 79; Distinctive Merit, 58th Exhib, Art Dir's Club, 79. *Bibliog:* Ellen Schwartz (auth), Review & illustration, Art News, 77; Katherine Lochridge (auth), Four, Heckscher Mus, 80; Harmony Hammond (auth), Homework, Creative Artists Pub Serv Prog, 81. *Media:* All. *Dealer:* Louis K Meisel Gallery 141 Prince St New York NY 10012. *Mailing Add:* 684 Broadway New York NY 10012

STINSMUEHLEN, SUSAN DODDS
GLASS COLLAGE ARTIST, PAINTER
b Baltimore, Md, Nov 5, 48. *Study:* Hood Col, Ind Univ; Univ Tex; also with Narcissus Quagliata & Paul Marioni, 72. *Work:* Leigh Yaukey Woodson Mus, Wausau, Wis; Wagga Wagga City Art Gallery, New South Wales, Australia; Pilchuck Galss Ctr, Stanwood, Wash; Corning Mus Glass. *Comn:* Etched glass, Gov Mansion, Austin, Tex, 79; wall & window installation, comn by Chan, Austin, Tex, 81; glass entrance, comn by Yovens, Houston, 82; glass facade, comn by Sammy Ford, Blanco, Tex, 82; glass wall mural, Veterans Admin Med Ctr, Dallas, 83. *Exhib:* Texas Crafts, Dallas Mus Fine Arts, 81; Americans in Glass, Leigh Yawkey Woodson Mus, Wis, Cooper Hewitt Mus, New York & Krannert Mus, Ill, 81; International Directions in Glass Art, Wagga Wagga City Art Mus, Australia, 81-82; New Works, Laguna Gloria Art Mus, Austin, Tex, 82; Ornamentalism, Hudson River Mus, New York & Huntington Gallery, Tex, 82-83; Sculptural Glass, Tucson Mus Art, 83. *Teaching:* Guest artist & instr glass collage, RI Sch Design, 80, Mass Col Art, 80 & Pilchuck Glass Ctr, summers 80-83. *Awards:* Nat Endowment Arts Grant, 82. *Bibliog:* William Warmus (auth), The glass telescope, Neus Glas, 81; Robert Jensen (auth), Ornamentalism, Crown Publ, 82; Michael Ennis (auth), The cutting edge, Tex Mo, 3/83. *Mem:* Glass Art Soc (bd dirs, 82-84); Tex Glass Artists Asn; Austin Contemp Visual Artists Asn. *Media:* Glass Wall Panels, Collage. *Dealer:* Mattingly Baker 3000 McKinney Dallas TX 75204. *Mailing Add:* 1003 W 34th Austin TX 78705

STIPE, WILLIAM S
COLLAGE ARTIST
b 1916. *Study:* Univ Iowa, BA & MA, 36; Mus Sch, Boston, with Karl Zerbe, 40; Inst Design, Chicago, 47. *Work:* Springfield Art Mus, Mo; Ohio Univ, Athens; Northern Trust Co, Chicago; Int Minerals & Chem Corp, Skokie, Ill; Kans State Univ. *Comn:* Wall painting, Evanston CofC, Davis L Bus Stop, 71. *Exhib:* Denver Art Mus, Colo; Nat Mus Fine Arts, Boston, Mass; Butler Inst Am Art, Youngstown, Ohio; Columbia Mus Art, SC; one-man shows, Culver-Stockton Col, Canton, Mo & Ill Arts Coun Gallery, Chicago, 72; and many other group & one-man shows. *Teaching:* Mem fac, Northwestern Univ, 48. *Awards:* Second Prize, Washington, DC Watercolor Club, 49; Pauline Palmer Second Prize, 59th Ann Chicago Show, Art Inst, 56; First Prize, Old Orchard Art Fair, Skokie, Ill, 70. *Interests:* Handmade paper art. *Mailing Add:* 1216 W Jarvis Chicago IL 60626

STITT, SUSAN (MARGARET)
MUSEUM DIRECTOR
b East Liverpool, Ohio, Jan 24, 42. *Study:* Col William & Mary, AB; Univ Pa, MA. *Pos:* Asst to dir, Hist Soc Pa; dir, Mus Albemarle; adminr, Mus Early Southern Decorative Arts; asst to dir, Brooklyn Mus; proj dir surv placement & training, Old Sturbridge Village, Mass; dir, Mus at Stony Brook, currently. *Mem:* Am Asn Mus; Long Island Mus Asn; NE Mus Conf; New York State Asn Mus (coun mem); and others. *Publ:* Auth, The will of Stephen Charlton & Hungars Parish, Va Mag Hist & Biog, 7/69; auth, Museum of Early Southern Decorative Arts, 70; auth, Today's labor practices, the search for equality, Mus News, 9-10/75; auth, Trustee orientation: A sound investment, Mus News, 5-6/81; and others. *Mailing Add:* Mus at Stony Brook 1208 Route 25a Stony Brook NY 11790

STODDARD, DONNA MELISSA
ADMINISTRATOR, GALLERY DIRECTOR
b St Petersburg, Fla, July 1, 16. *Study:* Fla Southern Col, BS, 37; Pittsburgh Art Inst; Pa State Col, MEd, 42; New York Sch Interior Design, 53; Univ Tampa, 59; Univ Fla, 60; Philathea Col, hon DHL, 68. *Collections Arranged:* Directed Fla Int Art Exhib, 52; organized & installed permanent contemp art collection, Fla Southern Col. *Pos:* Coordr dept art, Fla Southern Col, 40-83, dir, Melvin Gallery, formerly, prof art emer, 83- *Awards:* Am Cult Award, 52; Grumbacher Award, 53; Miami Women's Club Gold Medal, 53; and others. *Mem:* Am Asn Univ Women; Col Art Asn Am; fel Royal Soc Art, London; Nat Coun Art Adminr; Kappa Pi; and others. *Publ:* Contribr, Design Mag. *Mailing Add:* 925 Lexington Fla Southern Col Lakeland FL 33801

STOESSEL, HENRY KURT
PAINTER, DESIGNER
b Chemnitz, Ger, Apr 17, 09; US citizen. *Study:* Chicago Art Inst, 25-28; Ray Schs, Chicago, 25-27; Grand Central Sch Art, New York, 28-30; New Sch Social Res, 38-39; also with Eric Pape, 30-31. *Work:* US Navy Combat Artists Collection; USAF Mus Collection (21 paintings), Washington, DC; US Pentagon Traveling Shows. *Exhib:* Guest show, Woodstock Artist Asn, 50; 2nd Ann Nat Soc of Painters in Casein, 56; 47th Ann Hudson Valley Art Asn Exhib, 75. *Pos:* Art dir, Arnold Hoffman Studios, New York, 31-38; owner & pres, Stoessel Studios, Inc, New York, 38- & Stoessel Graphics, Inc, New York, 60-74. *Teaching:* Pvt classes; painting, Jackson High Sch Art Club. *Awards:* Salmagundi Prizes, 74-79; Oil Award, Knickerbocker Artists, 80; plus 61 graphic design awards. *Bibliog:* G Byrnes (auth), Complete Guide to Drawing, Illustrating & Painting, Simon & Schuster, 48. *Mem:* Am Artists Prof League; Salmagundi Club (Jury of Awards, 74-75); Soc of Illusrs (chmn, Warwick Students projects, 62-64, chmn mem, 66). *Media:* Oil, Acrylic. *Mailing Add:* 625 Pearl St Boulder CO 80302

STOEVEKEN, ANTHONY CHARLES
PRINTMAKER, EDUCATOR
b Milwaukee, Wis, Oct 28, 38. *Study:* Univ Wis-Milwaukee, BS(art educ), 60, MS(art), 66; Tamarind Lithography Workshop, Los Angeles, Master Printer(Ford Found Fel), 68. *Work:* Mus Mod Art, New York; Gruenwald Graphic Arts Found, Univ Calif, Los Angeles; Los Angeles Co Mus Art, Los Angeles; Pasadena Art Mus, Calif; Purdue Univ Art Mus, West Lafayette, Ind. *Comn:* Ed of prints, Edgewood Orchard Galleries, Fish Creek, Wis, 74; exterior mural, John Michael Kohler Art Ctr, Sheboygan, Wis, 77. *Exhib:* Northwest Printmakers 41st Int Exhib, Seattle Art Mus, & Portland Art Mus, Ore, 70; 42nd Ann Seattle Print Int, Seattle Art Mus, 71; IX Salon de Grabado, Inst Cult Peruano--Norte Americano, Lima, Peru, 73; 74th Exhib by Artists of Chicago & 77th Exhib, Works on Paper, Chicago Art Inst, 73 & 78; Wis Directions Two, Milwaukee Art Ctr, 78; two-man show, John Michael Kohler Art Ctr, Sheboygan, Wis, 79 & Bradley Gallery, Milwaukee, 80. *Pos:* Asst studio mgr, Tamarind Lithography Workshop, Los Angeles, 68; tech dir, Graphic studio, Univ Fla Tampa, 68-70. *Teaching:* Asst prof art, lithography, Univ SFla, Tampa, 68-70; assoc prof art, lithography, Univ Wis-Milwaukee, 70- *Awards:* Univ Wis-Milwaukee grad sch grant, aluminum plate & lithography, 75; Wis Arts Bd res grant, Chine-Colle, 79. *Bibliog:* Donald Key (auth), Graphic by University of Wisconsin-Milwaukee teacher, Milwaukee J, 72; Barbara Manger (auth), Tuchocke and Stoeveken at the Kohler Art Center, Mid-West Art, Gary Pizarick, 76; James Auer (auth), Fantasy in the family, Milwaukee Journal, 80. *Mem:* Col Art Asn; Mid-America Col Art Asn (pres, 81). *Media:* Lithography, Drawing. *Dealer:* Hank Baum Gallery 633 Battery St San Francisco CA 94111. *Mailing Add:* 5074 N Hollywood Ave Milwaukee WI 53217

STOEVEKEN, CHRISTEL E See Tucholke, Christel-Anthony

STOFFLET, MARY
CRITIC, HISTORIAN
b Long Branch, NJ, Dec 23, 42. *Study:* Skidmore Col, BA, 64; NY Univ, MA, 69; M H de Young Mem Mus, San Francisco, Rockefeller/Nat Endowment Arts Fel Mus Educ, 75-76. *Collections Arranged:* International Rubber Stamp Art Exhibition, La Mamelle Arts Ctr, San Francisco, 76; Cityscapes, 77 & Yosemite, 79, Fine Arts Mus of San Francisco, Downtown Ctr. *Pos:* Newsletter ed, Western Asn of Art Mus, Oakland, 74-77; contrib ed, Artweek, 74-81; assoc ed, La Mamelle, 75-77; ed, Front, 76-; coordr intern prog, M H de Young Mem Mus, 77-80; contrib ed, Images & Issues, 80-; asst cur, San Francisco Int Airport, 82- *Teaching:* Instr art hist, Oakland Mus, Calif, 77-; lectr art hist, San Francisco State Univ, 77 & 81. *Awards:* Critic's Fel, Nat Endowment Arts, 81. *Mem:* Col Art Asn; Media Alliance; Helicon Video & Visuals (adv bd, 81); Northern Calif Art Writers Guild (steering comt, 82-). *Publ:* Auth & ed, Three Bay Area Artists (catalog), Univ Calif, Riverside, 76; auth, American Women Artists: 20th Century, Slides & Notes, 78 & Women Artists: Sculptors/Photographers, Slides & Notes, 79, Harper & Row; ed, Correspondence Art: Sourcebook for the Network of International Postal Art Activity, Contemp Arts Press, 83. *Mailing Add:* PO Box 14397 San Francisco CA 94114

STOIANOVICH, MARCELLE
PAINTER, LITHOGRAPHER
Study: Col d'Art Applique a l'Industrie, Paris, France. *Work:* Work in pvt collections. *Comn:* Window display, Guerlain, Paris; book jacket designs for Doubleday & Co. *Exhib:* Salon des Artistes Francais, Paris, France; Galerie Pierre Hautot, Paris; Assoc Am Artists, New York; Mitsukoshi Galerie, Paris, France; FAR Galleries & Weyhe Gallery, New York; Venable Gallery, Washington, DC; and others. *Awards:* Hon Mention for Watercolor, Beaux-Arts, Paris, 50; Selected Film Credits, Festival Am Films, Deauville, France, 75. *Bibliog:* Lithographies by Original Print Collectors Group (USA), Rombaldi, Paris, France, Collier Art Co, Perspective Et de Vaduz, Union des Arts et Traditions Lithographiques, Paris, France. *Media:* Watercolor. *Mailing Add:* 9 Rue Campagne Premiere Paris 14 France

STOKES, LOUIS (WALTER)
SCULPTOR
New York, NY, June 23, 41. *Study:* Duquesne Univ, BA, 63; Hollins Col, MA, 65; Univ Calif, Berkeley, PhD, 68. *Work:* Can Coun Art Bank, Ottawa: Robert McLaughlin Gallery, Oshawa, Ont. *Comn:* Fiberglass water fountain sculpture, McMaster Univ, Hamilton, Ont, 72; outdoor wood wall relief, Metrop Toronto Zoo, 74; laminated wood wall sculpture, Ont Govt, Newmarket, 80; environmental steel sculpture, Nat Capital Comn, Ottawa, 80; ann award sculpture (bronze), Acad Can Cinema, Toronto, 81. *Exhib:* Solo exhibs, Alchemy Spirals, Dalhousie Art Gallery, Halifax, NS, 80, Wood Sculptures 1976-1982, Art Gallery Windsor, Ont, 82, Sacred Trees, Toronto City Sculpture Garden, 82-83 & Sculpture In the Park, Can Nat Exhib, Toronto, 83; Contemp Outdoor Sculpture at the Guild, Toronto, 82; and others. *Bibliog:* Peter Such (auth), Contemporary outdoor sculpture at the Guild, Artmag, 9-10/82; Dale McConathy (auth), Architecture as imagination of the future: Sculpture as speculation on the past, Artscanada, 11/82; Ted Fraser (auth), Louis Stokes: Sculpture 1976-1982, Artmagazine, spring 83. *Mem:* Royal Can Acad Arts. *Media:* All. *Mailing Add:* RR 1 Locust Hill ON L0H 1J0 Canada

STOKES, THOMAS PHELPS
PAINTER
b New York, NY, Mar 15, 34. *Exhib:* Collectors Exhib, Cleveland Mus, 64; Members Gallery, Albright-Knox Art Gallery, Buffalo, 66; Phillips Collection, Washington, DC, 69; Gift of Time, Mus NMex, Santa Fe, 70; Univ

Art Gallery, Va Polytech Inst & State Univ, 71; Avco Ctr for Visual Art, 77; Ruth Schaftner Gallery, Los Angeles, Calif; and others. *Bibliog:* John Canaday (auth), articles, New York Times, 5/4/68 & 9/27/69; Anita Feldman (auth), articles, summer 68 & fall 69, Arts Mag; C Ratcliff (auth), article, Art Int, 11/69. *Media:* Oil. *Mailing Add:* 443 S San Pedro Los Angeles CA 90013

STOKSTAD, MARILYN
HISTORIAN, EDUCATOR
b Lansing, Mich, Feb 16, 29. *Study:* Carleton Col, BA, 50; Mich State Univ, MA, 53; Univ Mich, PhD, 57. *Pos:* Res cur medieval art, Nelson Gallery, Kansas City, 69- *Teaching:* Prof hist art, Univ Kans, 58-, chmn dept, 61-72, dir, Mus Art, 61-67, assoc dean, Col Arts & Sci, 72-76. *Awards:* Humanities Inst Fel, 76-77; Univ Distinguished Prof of Art Hist, 79; Dumbarton Oaks Fel, 81-82; and others. *Mem:* Col Art Asn Am (pres, 78-80); Midwest Col Art Conf (pres, 64-65); Int Ctr Medieval Art; Am Asn Univ Prof; Soc Archit Historians; and others. *Res:* Medieval art; art of the British Isles and Scandinavia; Spanish art. *Publ:* Auth, Renaissance art outside Italy, Art Horizons, 68; ed & auth, Hortus Imaginum: Studies in Western Art, Humanistic Series 45, Univ Kans, 74; auth, Santiago de Compostela in the Age of the Pilgrimages, Okla Univ, 79; auth, Scottish Culture, Abrams, 81; ed & auth, Museums, Humanities and the Educated Eye, Univ Kans, 82; and others. *Mailing Add:* 2603 Stratford Lawrence KS 66044

STOLL, (MRS) BERRY VINCENT
COLLECTOR
b Louisville, Ky, Feb 2, 06. *Study:* Bryn Mawr Col; Louisville Art Sch. *Pos:* Vpres, J B Speed Art Mus, Louisville, currently. *Collection:* Paintings and antiques. *Mailing Add:* 3905 Lime Kiln Ln Louisville KY 40222

STOLLER, JOHN CHAPMAN
DEALER
b Minneapolis, Minn, Feb 7, 40. *Study:* Univ Minn, BA(art hist). *Pos:* Owner, John C Stoller & Co, presently. *Specialty:* Contemporary American and European paintings, drawings, sculpture and graphics. *Mailing Add:* John C Stoller & Co 400 Marquette Ave Minneapolis MN 55403

STOLOFF, CAROLYN
PAINTER
b New York, NY. *Study:* Univ Ill; Columbia Univ, BS; Art Students League; Atelier 17; with Xavier Gonzalez, Eric Isenburger & Hans Hofmann. *Exhib:* Whitney Mus Am Art; Pa Acad Fine Arts; Audubon Artists; Nat Asn Women Artists; Oakland Art Mus; one-person shows, Dubin Gallery, Manhattanville Col, New York, NY; and others. *Teaching:* Asst prof painting & drawing, Manhattanville Col, 57-74, chmn dept art, 60-65, lectr, Art & Eng, 69-74; vis writer, Stephens Col, 75. *Awards:* Silver Anniversary Medal, Audubon Artists, 67; Award, Nat Coun Arts, 68; MacDowell Grants, 61, 62, 70 & 76; and others. *Mem:* Artists Equity Asn; Authors Guild; Poetry Soc Am; Audubon Artists. *Publ:* Auth, Stepping Out, Unicorn Press, 71; auth, Dying to Survive, Doubleday & Co, 73; auth, Swiftly Now, Ohio Univ Press, 82; auth, A Spool of Blue: New and Selected Poems, Scarecrow Press, 82; and others. *Mailing Add:* 24 W Eighth St New York NY 10011

STOLOFF, IRMA
SCULPTOR
b New York, NY. *Study:* Art Students League, with Alexander Stirling Calder, Boardman Robinson, Howard Giles, Yasuo Kuniyoshi & Alexander Archipenko. *Work:* Butler Inst Am Art, Youngstown, Ohio; Rose Art Mus, Brandeis Univ; Norfolk Mus, Va; Wichita Art Mus, Kans. *Comn:* Portraits, bas-reliefs & figure compositions, pub & pvt comns. *Exhib:* Allied Artists Am, Nat Acad Design Galleries, 66; New York Soc Women Artists, 70; Audubon Artists, 72; Nat Asn Women Artists, 72; and others. *Teaching:* Pvt instr, currently. *Awards:* Barstow Prize for Sculpture, Nat Asn Women Artists, 53; Excalibur Award for Sculpture, Catharine Lorillard Wolfe Art Club, 69; Mr & Mrs Michael J Solomone Prize for Sculpture, Audubon Artists, 71. *Bibliog:* Datos biograficos de Irma Stoloff, Espacios, Mexico City, 11/53; Irma Stoloff y la escultura abstracta, La Presna, 11/53; Cornelia Justice (auth), The artists outpouring, Ledger Star, 68; and others. *Mem:* Audubon Artists (exec bd, 65-70); Nat Asn Women Artists; Silvermine Guild Artists; New York Soc Women Artists; Artists Equity Asn. *Mailing Add:* 46 E 91st St New York NY 10128

STOLOW, NATHAN
CONSERVATOR, CONSULTANT
b Montreal, Que, May 4, 28. *Study:* McGill Univ, Montreal, BS, 49; Univ Toronto, MA, 52; Courtauld Inst Art, Univ London, PhD, 56. *Collections Arranged:* Progress in Conservation, Nat Gallery Can, traveling, 72-74. *Pos:* Dir & sci consult, Nat Conserv Res Lab, Nat Gallery of Can, 57-72; dir, Can Conserv Inst, Nat Mus Can, Ottawa, 72-76; spec adv, Nat Mus Can, Ottawa, 76-79; conservat, Proj Australian Nat Gallery, 82-84. *Teaching:* Lectr art conserv, Univ Ottawa, Can, 76-78, Ctr for Restoration & Museology, Mex, 78- & Univ Victoria, 79-81. *Awards:* Can Centennial Medal, Recognition of Conserv Contribs, Govt Can, 78; Fel, Can Mus Asn, 79. *Mem:* Int Coun of Mus (coordr comt for conserv, 58-, mem exec coun, 72-74); fel Am Inst Conserv; Int Inst for Conserv, London (coun mem, 72-78). *Res:* Consultant on conservation of works of art and collections; scientific research on old masters and materials. *Publ:* Auth, Controlled Environment for Works of Art in Transit, UNESCO, Rome Ctr, 66; auth, The Canadian Art Fraud Case, Can Art, 64; coauth, On Picture Varnishes and Their Solvents, Case Western Reserve Univ & Oberlin Col, 71; ed, Progress in Conservation (catalog), Nat Gallery of Can, 72; auth, Conservation Standards Exhibitions, UNESCO, Paris, 80. *Mailing Add:* PO Box 2542 Sta D Ottawa ON K1P 5W6 Canada

STOLPE, DANIEL OWEN
PRINTMAKER, SCULPTOR
b Los Angeles, Calif, Nov 14, 39. *Study:* Pasadena City Col, AA, 60; Los Angeles Co Art Inst, 59-60; apprentice with Don La Viere Turner, 61-62 & Joe Funk, 65-66. *Work:* Portland Art Mus; Fogg Art Mus; Boston Pub Libr; Univ Tex Humanities Res Ctr, Austin; Grunwald Ctr Graphic Arts, Univ Calif, Los Angeles. *Comn:* Ser silkscreens, Scollon Studios, Vancouver, 70-71; Endangered Wildlife Drawings, World Wildlife Fund Asn, San Clemente, Calif, 71. *Exhib:* Solo exhib, Univ Calif, Santa Cruz McHenry Libr, 78, Univ Utah, Salt Lake City, 80, Coos Bay Art Mus, Ore, 80 & Calif State Univ Smith Mus, 81; 24th Nat Exhib Am Art, Chautauqua Art Asn Galleries, 81; Cabo Frio Int Print Biennial, Brazil, 83; and others. *Teaching:* Artist in residence mythology, Univ Calif, Santa Cruz, 78; master printer, Native Images Inc, 81- *Awards:* Spec Proj Grant, Calif Arts Coun, 78. *Bibliog:* Vickie Ware (auth), Trickster, Art Business News, 81; Marilyn Hanson & Daniel Stolpe (auths), Myths and Images, Coyote Suites I & II, Aptos Press, 82; Eric Mathes (producer & dir), Mythic Imagery of Daniel O Stolpe, Ampersind Video Arts, 83. *Publ:* Illusr, Atlantic Monthly, 72 & Smithsonian Mag, 72; illusr, On the Way Home, Houghton-Mifflin, 73; illusr, Native American Series, Univ Calif, Los Angeles, 78; illusr, Raise the stakes, Planet Drum Mag, 83. *Dealer:* Walton-Gilbert Galleries 420 Sutter St San Francisco CA 94108. *Mailing Add:* 2593 Mission St Santa Cruz CA 95060

STOLTENBERG, DONALD HUGO
PAINTER, PRINTMAKER
b Milwaukee, Wis, Oct 15, 27. *Study:* Inst Design, Ill Inst Technol, BS(visual design). *Work:* Boston Mus Fine Art; Addison Gallery Am Art, Andover, Mass; DeCordova Mus, Lincoln, Mass; Portland Mus Art. *Exhib:* Venice Observed, Fogg Mus, Cambridge, Mass, 56; Boston Arts Festival, 56-61; Corcoran Gallery Art Exhib, Washington, DC, 63; Landscape, DeCordova Mus, 71; Am Art Exhib, Art Inst Chicago; Mass Open, Worcester Art Mus, 77. *Teaching:* Instr painting & printmaking, DeCordova Mus Sch; vis critic, RI Sch Design. *Awards:* Grand Prize, Boston Arts Festival, 57, First Prize in Painting, 59; First Purchase Prize, Portland Mus Arts Festival. *Mem:* Boston Printmakers; Boston Watercolor Soc; Am Soc Marine Artists. *Media:* Oil, Watercolor. *Publ:* Auth, Collagraph Printmaking, 75 & The Artist and the Built Environment, 80, Davis. *Mailing Add:* 947 Satucket Rd RD 1 Brewster MA 02631

STOMPS, WALTER E, JR
PAINTER, PRINTMAKER
b Hamilton, Ohio, July 13, 29. *Study:* Miami Univ, BFA; Art Inst Chicago, with Boris Anisfeld, Paul Weighardt, Isabelle MacKinnon & Edgar Pillet, MFA; Syracuse Univ. *Work:* Cleveland Mus Art; Miami Univ. *Comn:* Ctr City Murals Proj, Nat Endowment Arts, Dayton, 72; Gen Motors (Frigidaire), Dayton; Bicentennial Poster Proj, Dayton. *Exhib:* Mid-States Exhib, Evansville, Ind, 77, 79 & 80; Cent S Exhib, Nashville, Tenn, 77; 1st Ann Mid-Am Exhib Art, Owensboro Mus Art, Ky, 79; Eight States Exhib, Speed Mus Art, Louisville; Print Invitational, Univ Kans, Lawrence, 80; and others. *Teaching:* Prof painting & drawing, Western Ky Univ, 75- *Awards:* James Nelson Raymond Award, Art Inst Chicago, 59; Purchase Awards, Dayton Art Inst, 66 & 68 & Owensboro Mus Art, Ky, 79; and others. *Media:* Acrylic. *Publ:* Illusr, Dayton USA, 72. *Mailing Add:* 729A Lynwood Dr Bowling Green KY 42101

STONE, DON
PAINTER
b Council Bluffs, Iowa, Mar 27, 29. *Study:* Vesper George Sch Art, Boston, 51. *Work:* Marietta Col, Ohio; Mobile Art Mus, Ala; Charles Greenshield Collection, Montreal; Peabody Maritime Mus, Salem, Mass. *Comn:* Large egg tempera, Univ NH, Durham, 79. *Exhib:* Nat Acad Design & Am Watercolor Soc, New York; Boston Soc Watercolor Painters, Boston Mus Fine Art, 71; Winter, 77 & New England Painters, 78, DeCordova Mus, Lincoln, Mass. *Teaching:* Instr art, Vesper George Sch Art, Boston, 60-65; instr, New Eng Sch Art, Boston, 60-65; Monhegan Island Workshop, Maine. *Awards:* Gold Medals, Franklin Mint, 74 & 75 & Hudson Valley Art Asn, 80. *Mem:* Assoc Nat Acad Design; Am Watercolor Soc; Guild Boston Artists; New Eng Watercolor Soc; Hudson Valley Art Asn. *Media:* Egg Tempera, Watercolor. *Publ:* Auth, Watercolor page, Am Artist, 62. *Dealer:* Whistlers Daughter Art Gallery 88 S Finley Ave Basking Ridge NJ 07920. *Mailing Add:* 11 Fairway Dr Kennebunk ME 04043

STONE, GWEN
PRINTMAKER, ASSEMBLAGE ARTIST
b New York, NY, Feb 1, 13. *Study:* Col Marin, Kentfield, Calif; San Francisco Art Inst, Calif; Univ Calif, Berkeley, teaching cert; also with Walt Kuhlman. *Work:* Monterey Peninsula Mus Art, Calif; Clorox Corp, Oakland, Calif; Bank Am World Hq, San Francisco; Int Bus Machines Corp, Palo Alto, Calif; Standard Oil, Saudi Arabia. *Exhib:* San Francisco Mus Mod Art Ann, 59; Okla Nat Drawing & Watercolor Exhib, Okla Art Ctr, Oklahoma City, 65; one-person shows, Calif Palace Legion Honor, San Francisco, 66 & 67 & The Pillowbook Series (collage), Redding Mus, 83; Works on Paper by Women Nat, Woman's Bldg, Los Angeles, Calif, 77; Pratt Inst Print Show, 80; Print Show, Univ Mich, Flint, 81; Four Views (collage), Shasta Col Art Gallery, Calif, 83. *Pos:* Guest instr, Mendocino Art Ctr, Calif, summer 1970. *Teaching:* Instr life drawing, Col Marin, Kentfield, 67-69, instr design, 67-70, instr collage & assemblage, 75-77; vis instr, Mendocino Art Ctr, Calif, summer 70; instr collage, Art Sch, Belvedere, 77-79. *Awards:* Purchase Awards, San Francisco Art Festival, San Francisco Art Comn, 65 & Painting & Print Exhib, Palo Alto Civic Ctr, Calif, 75; Kingley Ann, Crocker Art Gallery, 79. *Bibliog:* E M Polley (auth), East Bay, 65 & Marilyn Hagberg (auth), San

Diego, 65, Artforum; Lynn Grant (auth), article, Visual Dialog, Vol 2 (1976). *Mem:* Ctr Visual Arts, Oakland, Calif; Calif Soc Printmakers, Berkeley. *Media:* Silkscreen; Handmade Paper. *Publ:* Auth, Conversation with Robert Arneson, 76, Eleanor Bender talks with Gwen Stone, 76, Women Artists: Realities, 77 & Conversation with Wayne Thiebaud, 77, Visual Dialog. *Mailing Add:* 17530 Pilar Rd Montague CA 96064

STONE, JEFFREY INGRAM
PAINTER, PRINTMAKER
b Richmond, Va, Mar 14, 45. *Study:* Univ Calif, Northridge, BA, 67; Pratt Inst, MFA, 69. *Work:* Mus Mod Art, New York. *Exhib:* Eighteenth Nat Print Exhib, Brooklyn Mus, 73; Fourth Ann Nat Print Exhib, Atlanta Art Mus, 73; Second Ann Int Norwegian Biannale, Norway Nat Arts Mus, 74; Premio Int Biella Per I'Incisione, Biella's Art Mus, Italy, 80. *Teaching:* Adj asst prof printmaking, Pratt Inst, Brooklyn, NY, 70-; guest instr, Brooklyn Col, NY, 73-76 & Yale Univ, 74-75. *Awards:* Purchase Award, Fourth Ann Nat Print Exhib, Ga, 73. *Bibliog:* Fletcher Kastner (auth), Jeffrey Ingram Stone Graphics, Galaxy Press, 79. *Mem:* Artist Equity NY. *Media:* Oil, Watercolor. *Publ:* Illusr, The psychiatric holocaust, Penthouse Mag, 79; illusr, Sweet songs of spring, New York Mag, 78. *Dealer:* Associated American Artist 663 5th Ave New York NY. *Mailing Add:* 106 5th Ave New York NY 10011

STONE, JEREMY
DEALER
b Boston, Mass, Nov 15, 57. *Study:* Cooper Union, 74-75; NY Univ, 76; Goddard Col, 76-77. *Pos:* Spec activities coordr, Commonwealth Cult Preservation Trust, Boston, 79; art consult, Mass Gen Hosp, Boston, 79-80; proj magr, Ann Kohs & Assoc, San Francisco, 81-82; pres, owner & dir, Jeremy Stone Gallery, San Francisco, 82- *Bibliog:* Dwight Chapin (auth), Color her artfully, San Francisco Examiner, 4/19/83; Sandy Nelson (auth), Gallery history, Images & Issues, 11-12/83. *Specialty:* Twentieth century American drawings and paintings. *Mailing Add:* Jeremy Stone Gallery 126 Post St San Francisco CA 94108

STONE, JIM (JAMES J)
PHOTOGRAPHER, EDUCATOR
b Los Angeles, Calif, Dec 2, 47. *Study:* Mass Inst Technol, with Minor White, SB, 70; RI Sch Design, with Harry Callahan & Aaron Siskind, MFA, 75. *Work:* Corcoran Gallery Art, DC; Fogg Art Mus, Harvard Univ, Cambridge, Mass; Int Mus Photog, Rochester, NY; Lehigh Univ, Bethlehem, Pa; Polaroid Collection (Europa), Amsterdam, Neth. *Exhib:* Photovision, Boston Ctr Arts, 72; New Eng Experience, De Cordova Mus, Lincoln, Mass, 72; Photog Unlimited, Fogg Art Mus, Harvard Univ, 74 & Contemp Photog, 76; Still Life, Corcoran Gallery Art, DC, 79; Venezia '79, Venice, Italy, 79. *Teaching:* Instr, Boston Col, 73-; instr, RI Sch Design, 75-78; artist in residence, Alaska State Con Arts, 77. *Awards:* Mass Arts & Humanities Found photog fel, 76; Nat Endowment Arts Grant, 80. *Bibliog:* Channing (ed), Art of the State/State of the Art, Addison House, 78; Shamlian (auth), article in Philadelphia Photo Rev, 78; Hughes (ed), 1980 Annual, Popular Photog, 80. *Mem:* Visual Studies Workshop; Boston Photog Resource Ctr; Soc Photog Educ. *Media:* Black and White Gelatin-Silver Prints; Platinotype. *Publ:* Ed, Darkroom Dynamics: a Guide to Creative Darkroom Techniques, Van Nostrand, 79. *Dealer:* Carl Siembab Gallery 162 Newbury St Boston MA 02116. *Mailing Add:* 124 Ashmont St Dorchester MA 02124

STONE, M LEE
DEALER
b Chicago, Ill, Apr 11, 37. *Study:* Univ Ill, BS, 58; Univ Ill Col Med, MD, 62. *Specialty:* Nineteenth and twentieth century works of art on paper; American artists, 1900-1960; exclusive dealer for Gerald Geerlings. *Mailing Add:* 2101 Forest Ave Suite 130 San Jose CA 95128

STONE, SYLVIA
SCULPTOR
b Toronto, Ont; US citizen. *Study:* Pvt study in Can; Art Students League. *Work:* Walker Art Ctr, Minneapolis; Whitney Mus Am Art, New York; Hartford Atheneum, Conn; Xerox Corp, New York; Larry Aldrich Mus, Ridgefield, Conn. *Comn:* Xerox Corp, New York, 69; Sunrise Mall, Massapequa, NY, 72; Gen Serv Agency, Fed Court House, Ft Lauderdale, Fla, 79. *Exhib:* One-woman shows, Andre Emmerich Gallery, 72, 75, 77 & 79 & Bennington Col, 77; 14 Sculptors--Industrial Edge, Walker Art Ctr, Minneapolis, 69; Whitney Mus Am Art Sculpture Ann, New York, 69, 71 & 73; Plastic Presence, Jewish Mus, Milwaukee Art Ctr & San Francisco, 70; 200 Yrs Am Sculpture, Whitney Mus Am Art, New York, 75; Hayward Gallery, London, Eng, 75; 3rd Biennalle Small Sculpture, Budapest, Hungary, 75; Perspective 1976, Albright Col, 76; and others. *Teaching:* Instr, Brooklyn Col, 68- *Awards:* Creative Artist Pub Serv Award, NY State, 71; Nat Endowment for the Arts, 76. *Bibliog:* Irv Sandler (auth), Sylvia Stone at Emmerich, Art in Am, 72 & Sylvia Stone's Egyptian gardens, Arts Mag, 4/77; Corrinne Robbins (auth), The edges of illusion, Art Spectrum, 75. *Media:* Aluminum; Plexiglas. *Dealer:* Andre Emmerich Gallery 41 E 57th St New York NY 10022. *Mailing Add:* 519 Broadway New York NY 10012

STONE, WILLARD
DESIGNER, SCULPTOR
b Oktaha, Okla, Feb 29, 16. *Study:* Bacone Col, Muskogee, Okla; spec studies under Acee Blue Eagle and Woodrow Crumbo. *Work:* Gilcrease Mus, Tulsa, Okla; Nat Cowboy Hall of Fame, Oklahoma City; Okla State Univ; Okla Hist Bldg, Oklahoma City. *Comn:* Sequoyah the Teacher, 65 & Alice Brown Davis (chief of the Seminoles), 67, Okla Hist Soc; bust of Henry Bellmon, Gov Okla, 66; The Good Earth (mural), pvt collection, 71; Chiefs of the Five Civilized

Tribes, Five Civilized Tribes Mus, currently. *Exhib:* One-man shows, Kennedy Galleries, New York, Gilcrease Mus, Tulsa, Philbrook Art Ctr, Tulsa, El Paso Mus Art, Tex, Tex Tech Univ & Will Rogers Mem Mus. *Pos:* Artist in residence, Thomas Gilcrease Mus, 46-49; pattern maker designer, Ernest Ornamental Iron Works, 48-50; tool designer, die maker, Douglas Aircraft, 50-59. *Awards:* Waite Phillips Trophy Grand Award, Philbrook Art Ctr, 72; Grand Awards, Five Civilized Tribes Mus, 73 & 78, Masters Grand Award, 74, Heritage Award, 82 & First Award Sculpture, 83. *Mem:* Green Country Artists Asn; Ozark Arts-Crafts Asn. *Media:* Sculpture in Wood & Bronze. *Res:* Bronze busts of old Indian chiefs, years 1800-1860. *Mailing Add:* Star Rte E Box 6 Locust Grove OK 74352

STONEBARGER, VIRGINIA
PAINTER, EDUCATOR
b Ann Arbor, Mich, Mar 9, 26. *Study:* Antioch Col, BA, 50; Colorado Springs Fine Arts Ctr, 50-51; Art Students League, 51-52; Hans Hofmann Sch, 54; NY Univ, 54 & 56; Univ Wis-Milwaukee, MS, 72. *Exhib:* Univ Wis, 59; Milwaukee Art Ctr, 59-61; one-woman shows, Lakeland Col, 69, Univ Wis, 71, Jewish Community Ctr, Milwaukee, 78 & Galleria Simon, 79; plus many others. *Teaching:* Instr art, Univ Lake Sch, Hartland, Wis, 59-62; instr art, Waukesha Co Tech Inst, 70-72; instr, Milwaukee Area Tech Col, Com Art Inst, 73-77; instr painting, Univ Wis, Milwaukee Exten, 82-; lectr art, Univ Ariz, 83. *Awards:* Prize, Milwaukee Art Ctr, 60; Danforth Found Fel, 69; plus others. *Dealer:* David Barnett Gallery 2101 W Wisconsin Ave Milwaukee WI 53233. *Mailing Add:* 805 South 5th St Milwaukee WI 53204

STONEHAM, JOHN
LIBRARIAN
b Eng, Oct 1, 29; US citizen. *Pos:* Co-ed, The Lively Arts, Baltimore, 59-61; head librn, Md Inst, 65- *Teaching:* Teacher lit, Md Inst. *Mem:* Founding mem Worst Verse Conspiracy Baltimore; Art Libr Soc NAm. *Res:* Bad verse; military costume; curiosa; Chaucer; Malory. *Mailing Add:* Md Inst Col of Art 1400 Cathedral St Baltimore MD 21201

STONER, JOYCE HILL
CONSERVATOR, EDUCATOR
b Washington, DC, Oct 9, 46. *Study:* Col William & Mary, BA(fine arts); summa cum laude); NY Univ, Inst Fine Arts, Conserv Ctr, MA(fine arts) & dipl conserv, spec grad study with Bernard Rabin. *Work:* Freer Gallery Art; Winterthur Mus, Del; Va Mus Fine Arts, Richmond; Del Art Mus; and others. *Comn:* Wilmington murals, New York Pub Libr. *Collections Arranged:* Know What You See, a traveling exhib organized by Louis Pomerantz, Found Am Inst Conserv & Smithsonian Inst Traveling Exhib Serv, 76; Flaking, Foxing and Fine Works, conserv exhib, Del Art Mus, 77. *Pos:* Managing ed, Art & Archaeol Tech Abstracts, 69-; consult conserv paintings, Freer Gallery Art, 75-76; exec dir, Found Am Inst Conserv, 75-79; paintings conservator, Winterthur Mus, Del, 76-82; supv conserv section, 81-82; vis scholar painting conserv, Metrop Mus Art, 80. *Teaching:* Assoc prof intro art conserv, Va Commonwealth Univ, 75-76; asst prof paintings conserv, Univ Del, 76-79; assoc prof, 79-; assoc dir, Art Conserv Prog, 80-82, dir, Art Conserv Prog, 82- *Mem:* Fel Int Inst Conserv Historic & Artistic Works; fel Am Inst Conserv Historic & Artistic Works; Found Am Inst Conserv (exec dir, 75-79); Fac Energy Conserv Workshops, Am Asn Mus; Int Coun Mus. *Res:* History of art conservation in America. *Publ:* Ed, Annotated Bibliography of the Care of Collections During an Energy Crisis, Am Asn Mus Energy Workshop Planning Comt, 78; auth, Pioneers in American Museums--George L Stout, 78 & William Suhr, 81, Mus News; auth, John Brealey's trained and sympathetic eye, Mus News, 81; auth, The gentle art of painting conservation, Art & Antiques, 82; and others. *Mailing Add:* 303 Old College Univ Del Newark DE 19711

STONES, MARGARET ALISON
EDUCATOR, HISTORIAN
b England, Mar 11, 42. *Study:* Univ London, BA, 64, PhD(hist art), 70. *Teaching:* Assoc prof Medieval art, Univ Minn, 69-81, prof, 81-83; vis prof, Univ Reading, 75; prof, Univ Pittsburgh, 84- *Mem:* Medieval Acad Am; Brit Archaeol Asn; Int Arthurian Soc; Int Ctr Medieval Art. *Res:* Manuscript illumination. *Publ:* Contribr, The Earliest illustrated prose Lancelot, Miss, Reading Medieval Studies III, 77; auth, The Minnesota Vincent of Beauvais from Cambron, James Ford Bell Libr, Univ Minn, 77; coauth, Medieval Illumination, Glass and Sculpture in Minnesota Collections (catalog), Univ Minn, 78; auth, Four illustrated Jacobus manuscripts, In: The Vanishing Past, Studies of Medieval Art, Liturgy and Metrology Presented to Christopher Hohler, BAR Int Ser III, 81; auth, Notes on three illuminated Alexander manuscripts, In: The Medieval Alexander Legend and Romance Epic, Essays in Honour of David J A Ross, Millwood/London/Nendeln, 82. *Mailing Add:* Dept of Fine Arts Univ of Pittsburgh Pittsburgh PA 15260

STORER, FRANCES NELL
PAINTER, INSTRUCTOR
b Central City, Ky, June 17, 17. *Study:* Cincinnati Conserv Music, Ohio, 37-39; Rex Brandt Summer Sch, Corona del Mar, Calif, 56-75, with Joan Irving Brandt, George Post, Jae Carmickell & Elliot O'Hara; plus many others. *Work:* Citizens Fidelity Bank & Trust; United Ky Bank Inc. *Exhib:* Am Watercolor Soc, New York, 63-64, 65-68, traveling exhib, 65 & 100th Ann Show, 67; Brooks Mus, Memphis, Tenn, 64; Corp Collection Exhib, J B Speed Mus, Louisville, 77; one-person show, Owensboro Mus, Ky, 79 & Ky Watercolor Soc, United Ky Bank Inc, 80; Harpeth Hall Sch, Nashville, Tenn, 81; Paducah Art Asn, Ky, 82; plus others. *Pos:* Operator, Storer Gallery, 60-65. *Teaching:* Taught classes in own studio & Storer Gallery, Central City, Ky, 58-65; pvt classes, Louisville, Ky. *Awards:* Woman of the Yr, Times

Argus, Central City, Ky, 62. *Mem:* Am Watercolor Soc; Art Ctr Asn & Arts Club, Louisville; Ky Watercolor Soc. *Media:* Watercolor. *Dealer:* J B Speed Art Mus Belknap Campus Louisville KY 40208. *Mailing Add:* 8405 Nottingham Pkwy Louisville KY 40222

STORER, INEZ MARY
COLLAGE ARTIST, SCULPTOR
b Santa Monica, Calif, Oct 11, 33. *Study:* Univ Calif, Berkeley, 54-55; San Francisco Art Inst, with Nathan Oliviera, 55; Los Angeles Art Ctr, with Lorser Feitleson, 56; Dominican Col, BA, 70; San Francisco State Univ, MA, 71. *Work:* Oakland Art Mus, Calif; Dallas Art Mus; United Gas & Pipeline, Houston; Container Corp Am; Ammex Corp, Ga. *Exhib:* San Francisco Art Inst Ann 77; Bay Area Artists Exhib, Oakland Art Mus, 77; one-man show, San Francisco Mus Mod Art, Calif, 78; Univ Calif, Davis, 80; San Francisco Mus Art, 80; Richard Demarco Gallery, Edinburgh, Scotland, 80. *Pos:* Dir, Lester Gallery of Contemp Art, 73-; invited artist, Int Inst Experimental Printmaking, San Francisco, 75- *Teaching:* Prof painting, Col Marin, Kentfield, 69-78; lectr, San Francisco State Univ, 70-72; prof painting, Calif State Col, Sonoma, 76-82 & Univ Calif, Santa Cruz, 76. *Bibliog:* Roberta Loach (critic/ed), Visual Dialogue, Winter 1976 & Greece, 77, Art Mag. *Mem:* San Francisco Art Dealers Asn (mem bd dirs, 75-). *Media:* Collage; Assemblage. *Publ:* Illusr, Laura N Baker's O Children of the Wind and Pines, Lippincott, 67; illusr, Floating Island: Collection of Poetry, Michael Sikes, 77. *Dealer:* Smith Anderson 200 Homer St Palo Alto CA 94301. *Mailing Add:* PO Box 117 Inverness CA 94937

STORM, HOWARD
PAINTER, SCULPTOR
b Newton, Mass, Oct 26, 46. *Study:* Denison Univ; J Ferguson Stained Glass Studio, Weston, Mass, apprenticeship; San Francisco Art Inst, BFA, 69; Univ Calif, Berkeley, MA, 70, MFA, 72. *Work:* Roswell Mus, NMex; Denison Univ; Mt St Joseph Col, Ohio; Ky Arts Comn, Frankfort; Baylor Univ. *Exhib:* One-man shows, Berkeley Mus, 72 & Baylor Univ, 73; Huntington Galleries, 72-74; Univ Cincinnati, 74; Cincinnati Art Mus, 75; plus others. *Pos:* Artist in residence, Roswell Mus, 71-74 *Teaching:* Assoc prof art, Northern Ky Univ, 72- *Awards:* Eisner Prize, Univ Calif, Berkeley, 72; Purchase Award, Preview '73; Purchase Award, Huntington Galleries. *Mem:* Col Art Asn Am; Mid-West Art Asn. *Media:* Acrylic, Oil; Wood. *Mailing Add:* 90 Hawthorne Ft Thomas KY 41075

STORM, LARUE
PAINTER, SCULPTOR
b Pittsburgh, Pa. *Study:* Univ Miami, AB & MA; Art Students League, Woodstock; also printmaking with Calvaert Brun, Paris & study in Los Angeles & Mich. *Work:* Lowe Mus, Coral Gables, Fla; Columbia Mus Art, Ga; Norton Gallery Art, West Palm Beach, Fla; Peabody Col, Nashville, Tenn. *Exhib:* Corcoran Gallery Art Biennial, Washington, DC, 57; Butler Inst Am Art, Youngstown, Ohio, 58-60; Miami Six, El Paso Mus, 65; Fla Creates, var mus Fla, 71-; one-man show, Lowe Mus Art, Norton Gallery Art & Columbia Mus Art; and others. *Teaching:* Adj asst prof drawing & design, Univ Miami, 67-82. *Publ:* Auth, Jose Guadalupe Posada: Guerrilla Fighter of the Throwaways, Carrell, 70. *Mailing Add:* 3737 Justison Rd Coconut Grove Miami FL 33133

STORM, MARK (KENNEDY)
PAINTER, SCULPTOR
b Valdez, Alaska, Sept 4, 11. *Study:* Univ Tex Archit Sch, 30-34. *Work:* Mus Natural Sci, Houston; Am Gen Insurance Co, Houston. *Comn:* Oil painting, Int Ropes Ltd, Eng, 69; oil paintings, Houston Livestock Show & Rodeo, 73; oil paintings, Melacres Charolais Ranch, Chapel Hill, Tex, 74 & Pearce Indust Inc, Houston, 77. *Exhib:* Ann Tex Cowboy Artists Asn Shows, Tex, 73-; When You Say Cowboy, Amarillo Art Ctr, Tex, 74; Tex Cowboy Artists, Phippen-O'Brien Gallery, Scottsdale, Ariz, 74; Tex Cowboy Artists, Stamford Art Found, Tex, 74. *Awards:* Best of Show, Tex Cowboy Artists Show, 76. *Bibliog:* Jim Scarbrough (auth), Mark Storm, Quarter Horse J, 71; Leon Hale (auth), Cowboy artist..., Houston Post, 74. *Mem:* Tex Cowboy Artists Asn (pres, 75-76). *Media:* Oil, Pen and Ink. *Publ:* Illusr, Picture Tales from Mexico, 41; illusr, Marsmen in Burma, 49; illusr, Texas Brags, 50; auth & illusr, Gruyo of the Flying H, 56; contribr, XIT--The American Cowboy, Oxmoor. *Dealer:* Southwest Galleries 5825 Kirby Dr Houston TX 77005. *Mailing Add:* 2256 Shakespeare Houston TX 77030

STORY, WILLIAM EASTON
PAINTER, MUSEUM DIRECTOR
b Valley City, NDak, Feb 13, 25. *Study:* Art Inst Chicago, BFA; Ball State Teachers Col, MA; also with Stanley William Hayter. *Work:* Butler Inst Am Art, Youngstown, Ohio; Ball State Univ Art Gallery. *Exhib:* Whitney Mus Am Art Ann, 57; Corcoran Gallery 25th Biennial, Washington, DC, 57; Cincinnati Art Mus 2nd Interior Valley Competition, 58; Artistas Brasileiros E Am, Mus Art Mos, Sao Paulo, Brazil, 60; Collages by American Artists, Ball State Univ Art Gallery, 72. *Pos:* Asst dir, Am Mus in Brit, Bath, Eng, 66-68; dir, Parrish Art Mus, Southampton, 68-69; dir, Ella Sharp Mus, Jackson, Mich, 69-72; dir, Ball State Univ Art Gallery, 72-; dir, Saginaw Art Mus, 82- *Teaching:* Asst prof art & supvr art gallery, Ball State Univ, 56-66. *Mem:* Am Asn Mus; Midwest Mus Asn; Mich Mus Asn. *Publ:* Contribr, America in Britain, 67 & 68. *Mailing Add:* Art Gallery Ball State Univ Muncie IN 47306

STOTT, DEBORAH
HISTORIAN
b Minneapolis, Minn, June 11, 42. *Study:* Wellesley Col, BA, 64; Columbia Univ, MA, 66, PhD, 75. *Teaching:* Instr art hist, Wheaton Col, Mass, 70-75;

asst prof, Intercollegiate Ctr Classical Studies, Rome, 75-76; assoc prof, Univ Tex, Dallas, 76- *Awards:* Am Acad Rome Fel, 80-81; Delmas Found Grant, 80 & 82; Bunting Inst Fel, Radcliffe Col, 82-83. *Mem:* Col Art Asn Am. *Res:* Style and theory in Italian renaissance reliefs. *Publ:* Auth, Jacques Lipchitz and Cubism, Garland Publ, 78; auth, Jacopo Sansovino's Bronze Reliefs and Venetian Colorism, Hofstra Univ, 82; auth, Fatte a sembianza di pittura: Jacopo Sansovino's bronze reliefs in San Marco, Art Bulletin, spring 82. *Mailing Add:* 906 S Glasgow Dallas TX 75223

STOUMEN, LOU
FILMMAKER, PHOTOGRAPHER
b Springtown, Pa, July 15, 17. *Study:* Lehigh Univ, BA(fine arts), 39; Univ Southern Calif, 49; Lehigh Univ, LHD, 72. *Work:* Mus Mod Art & Int Ctr Photog, New York; Nat Gallery Art, Ottawa, Can; Ctr Creative Photog, Tucson, Ariz; Univ Calif, Los Angeles. *Exhib:* Family of Man, Mus Mod Art, New York, 55; solo exhibs, Photographs, Friends of Photog, Carmel, Calif, 77, Ordinary Miracles, Univ Calif Los Angeles Art Gallery, 81, Photographs, Photo Gallery Int, Tokyo, Japan, 82 & Forty Years on Times Square, Int Ctr Photog, New York, 83. *Teaching:* Prof motion pictures & TV, Univ Calif, Los Angeles, 66- *Awards:* Academy Awards for True Story of Civil War, 56 & Black Fox, 64; First Prize, The Naked Eye, Venice Film Festival, 57. *Bibliog:* James L Enyeart (auth), Photography of Lou Stoumen (monograph), Friends of Photog, 77; Janis Bultman (auth), Masters of photography, Darkroom Mag, 81; Suzanne Muchnic (auth), Champion of camera art, Los Angeles Times, 81. *Mem:* Los Angeles Ctr Photog Studies (bd dirs, 81-82, bd trustees, 82-83); Acad Motion Picture Arts & Sci; Soc Photog Educ; PEN. *Collection:* Photographs, films, illustrated books. *Publ:* Auth, Can't Argue with Sunrise, Celestial Arts, 75; auth, Ordinary Miracles, Hand Press, 81; auth, Times Square/1940 Till Now, Aperture, 84. *Dealer:* Ledel Gallery New York NY; Weston Gallery Carmel CA. *Mailing Add:* 12015 Coyne St Los Angeles CA 90049

STOUT, MYRON STEDMAN
PAINTER
b Denton, Tex, Dec 5, 08. *Work:* Nat Gallery Art, Washington, DC; Carnegie Mus, Pittsburgh; Guggenheim Mus, Mus Mod Art & Whitney Mus Am Art, New York. *Exhib:* Whitney Mus Am Art, 58, 64, 73 & 80; Mus Mod Art, 59 & 75-77; Jewish Knox, 63; Guggenheim Mus, 64-65 & 69; Albright-Knox Gallery, 68; Corcoran Biennial, 69; Contemp Arts Mus, Houston, 77. *Awards:* Nat Endowment for Arts, 67; Guggenheim Fel, 69 Merit Award, Am Acad & Inst Arts & Letters, 82. *Dealer:* Richard Bellamy Oil & Steel Gallery 57 Chambers St New York NY 10007. *Mailing Add:* 4 Brewster St Provincetown MA 02657

STOUT, RICHARD GORDON
PAINTER
b Beaumont, Tex, Aug 21, 34. *Study:* Cincinnati Art Acad, 52-53; Sch Art Inst Chicago, BFA, 57; Univ Tex, MFA, 69. *Work:* Mus Fine Arts, Houston; Dallas Mus Fine Arts; Marion Koogler McNay Art Inst, San Antonio; Rice Univ; Univ Houston. *Exhib:* Momentum Mid Continental Exhib, Chicago, 56-57; One Hundred Contemporary American Draftsmen, Univ Mich, 63; Marion Koogler McNay Art Inst, 64 & 71; Contemporary Arts Mus, Houston, 75; Jurgen Schweinebroden, Berlin, 80. *Pos:* Mem adv bd, Mus Fine Arts, Houston, 73- *Teaching:* Instr painting, Mus Fine Arts, Houston, 58-67; assoc prof drawing & painting, Univ Houston, 67- *Awards:* Longview Purchase Prize, Jr Serv League, 65 & 72; Tex Fine Arts Asn Awards, 66 & 71; Houston Area Exhib First Prize, Blaffer Gallery, Univ Houston, 75; and others. *Media:* Acrylic. *Dealer:* Houston Galleries 2323 San Felipe Houston TX 77019; Touchstone Gallery Ltd 118 E 64th St New York NY. *Mailing Add:* 1213 Bonnie Brae Houston TX 77006

STOVALL, LUTHER MCKINLEY (LOU)
PRINTMAKER
b Athens, Ga, Jan 1, 37. *Study:* RI Sch Design; Howard Univ, BFA. *Work:* Washington Post Co, Corcoran Gallery Art, Nat Collection Fine Arts, Smithsonian Inst, Washington, DC; Ringling Mus. *Comn:* Poster, Houston Mus Fine Arts, 70; posters, Corcoran Gallery Art, Washington, DC, 70 & 71; Bikes Have Equal Rights (poster), DC Dept Motor Vehicles, Washington Ecol Ctr, 70-72; print, Equal Employment Opportunity Comn Portfolio, Washington, DC, 73; A Sense of Amity, AFL-CIO, 76. *Exhib:* Prints & Posters, Corcoran Gallery Art, Du Pont Ctr, Washington, DC, 69-71; Johns Hopkins Ctr Advan Inst Study, Washington, DC, 70-71; Atlantic Christian Col, NC, 72; Traveling Exhib Prints & Posters, Baltimore Mus Art, Md, 72-73; two-man show, Fendrick Gallery, Washington, DC, 74; 'Tis Mindful of Sweetness, Fendrick Gallery, Washington, DC, 77. *Pos:* Dir, Workshop, Inc, 68- *Teaching:* Master printmaking & silkscreen, Workshop, Corcoran Gallery Art, 69-72. *Awards:* Stern Grant, 68-72; Individual Artist Grant, 72 & Workshop Grant, 72-76, Nat Endowment Arts. *Bibliog:* Jay Jacobs (auth), We have to like the way you look, Art Gallery, 3/70; Paul Richard (auth), The community art spirit, 3/73 & Art & energy, 11/13/74, Washington Post. *Mailing Add:* Workshop Inc 3145 Newark St NW Washington DC 20008

STOVER, DONALD LEWIS
CURATOR
b Staunton, Va, Jan 8, 43. *Study:* Va Polytechnic Inst Col Archit, 61-65; St Marys Univ, BA, 72; Univ Del Winterthur Prog, 75-77. *Collections Arranged:* Early Texas Furniture and Decortive Arts (auth, catalog), 72 & Tischlermeister Jahn (auth, catalog), 75, San Antonio Mus Asn; Art of Louis C Tiffany (auth, catalog), 81, American Sculpture (auth, catalog), 82 & Pennsylvania German, 83, Fine Arts Mus San Francisco. *Pos:* Cur furniture, San Antonio Mus Asn, 72-75; cur in charge, Decorative Arts & Sculpture,

Fine Arts Mus San Francisco, 81-83, cur in charge, Am Decorative Arts & Sculpture, 83- *Mem:* Soc Winterthur Grads; Decorative Arts Trust; Am Decorative Arts Forum Northern Calif; Western Region Arch Am Art (chmn, currently). *Res:* Nineteenth century Texas cabinetmakers; mid-19th century emmigrant cabinetmakers, New York; Louis Comfort Tiffany; American sculpture. *Publ:* Coauth, Early Texas Furniture, Trinity Press, 74; auth, American decorative arts: Recent acquisitions, Apollo Mag, 80. *Mailing Add:* 2286 Jackson St San Francisco CA 94115

STOWMAN, ANNETTE BURR
PAINTER, INSTRUCTOR
b Paris, France, Jan 21, 09; US citizen. *Study:* Vassar Col, AB, 29; Art Students League, 56-58. *Work:* Hickory Art Mus, NC; Greenville Mus Art, SC; Tamahassee DAR Sch, SC; Riveredge Found Collection, Can. *Exhib:* New York City Ctr Gallery, 61; Nat Artists Club Exhib, 62; Colorama Gallery, New York World's Fair, 65; Volusia Co, Fla Regional Show, 68; Metrop Mus, 78; Goldsboro Art Mus, NC, 78. *Teaching:* Instr art, Daytona Community Col Div Continuing Educ, 70- *Awards:* First Prize, Daytona Art League, 71, Second Prize, 74; Artists Choice, New Smyrna Beach Artists Workshop, 72; Second Prize, New Smyrna Beach Art Fiesta, 72. *Mem:* Burr Artists; life mem Art Students League; New Smyrna Beach Artists Workshop; Daytona Art League; artist mem Nat League Am Pen Women. *Media:* Oil, Acrylic. *Dealer:* Burr Artists 15 Gramercy Park S New York NY 10003. *Mailing Add:* PO Box 278 Edgewater FL 32032

STRAIGHT, ELSIE H
LIBRARIAN, SCULPTOR
b Cumberland, England. *Study:* Art Inst Pittsburgh, dipl(illus), 39; New York Sch of Applied Design for Women, with Kimon Nicholaides, dipl(des), 41; Roger Williams Col, BA, 66; Univ RI, MLS, 72. *Pos:* Librn, Ringling Sch Art Libr, 74-82, retired. *Mem:* Art Libr Soc NAm, Southeastern Region; Sch Libr Asn (secy, 70). *Media:* Stone, Clay. *Res:* John Simmons Collection of French Revolutionary Statesmen and military leaders; 17th century prints. *Interests:* Portrait artists, painters and sculptors; Pre-Columbian art. *Mailing Add:* 435 Edwards Dr Sarasota FL 33580

STRASEN, BARBARA ELAINE
PAINTER, CONCEPTUAL ARTIST
b Brooklyn, NY, Aug 12, 42. *Study:* Yale Univ Sch Art, summer 62; Carnegie-Mellon Univ, BFA, 63; Univ Calif, Berkeley, MA, 64. *Exhib:* Biennial Contemp Art, Whitney Mus Am Art, New York, 75; Santa Barbara Mus Art, 79; PS1, New York, 79 & 80; San Diego State Univ, 82; San Diego Natural Hist Mus, 82; AIR Gallery, New York, 83; and others. *Teaching:* Instr visual arts, Southwestern Col, Calif, 71-73; asst prof visual arts, Univ Calif, San Diego, 73-78. *Awards:* Individual Artists Fel, Nat Endowment Arts, 75-76; Creative Arts Grant, Regents of Univ of Calif, 76; res proj grants, Univ Calif, San Diego, 76 & 77. *Bibliog:* Noel Frackman (auth), rev in Arts Mag, 6/75; David Bourdon (auth), rev of show at Parsons-Dreyfuss Gallery, Village Voice, 6/13/77. *Media:* Acrylic. *Publ:* Auth, Immigrants, J Los Angeles Inst Contemp Arts, 2/75; auth, Desert Notes, Santa Barbara Mus Art, 79. *Dealer:* Parsons-Dreyfuss Gallery 54 W 57th St New York NY 10019. *Mailing Add:* 353 Ocean View Ave Encinitas CA 92024

STRASSBERG, ROY I
CERAMIST, SCULPTOR
b Brooklyn, NY, Sept 18, 50. *Study:* State Univ NY Col, Oswego, BA, 72; Univ Mich, MFA, 74. *Work:* Tenn State Mus, Nashville; SDak Mem Art Ctr, Brookings; Mint Mus Art, Charlotte, NC; Sourwood Regional Art Ctr, Jonesboro, Tenn. *Exhib:* J B Speed Mus, Louisville, Ky, 76; Mint Mus Art, Charlotte, NC, 76; Mus Contemp Crafts, New York, 78; Ft Wayne Mus Art, Ind, 80; Wichita Mus Art, Kans, 81; Plains Art Mus, Moorehead, Minn, 81; and others. *Teaching:* Fel ceramics, Univ Mich, 73-74; instr, Memphis State Univ, 74-76; asst prof, Mankato State Univ, 76- *Awards:* Grand Prize, Miss River Crafts, Brooks Mem Art Gallery, 75; Second Prize, Midwest Craft Exhib, Rochester Art Ctr, Minn, 77; Purchase Award, Plains Art Mus, 79. *Mem:* Nat Coun Educ Ceramic Arts. *Media:* Clay. *Publ:* Contribr, Ceramics Monthly, 5/76-5/80 & Am Craft Mag, 8/76-12/81. *Dealer:* Cooper/Lynn Gallery 54 Seventh Ave S New York NY 10014; Robert L Kidd & Assocs 107 Townsend St Birmingham MI 48011. *Mailing Add:* 505 North Fourth St Mankato MN 56001

STRATER, HENRY
PAINTER
b Louisville, Ky, Jan 21, 1896. *Study:* Acad Julien, Paris; Art Students League; Pa Acad Fine Arts, with Arthur Carles & Charles Grafly; Acad San Fernando; Acad Grande Chaumiere, Paris; Ecole M Denis, with Edouard Vuillard; also with Ignacio Zuloaga, Spain. *Work:* Philadelphia Mus Art; Art Mus Princeton Univ; Detroit Inst Arts; City Art Mus St Louis; Butler Inst Am Art, Youngstown, Ohio. *Exhib:* Salon Automne, Paris, 22; Whitney Studio Club Portrait Exhib, 26; Brooklyn Mus Watercolor Ann, 26; Corcoran Gallery Art Biennial, Washington, DC, 32; IBM Gallery Sci & Art, Golden Gate Expos, San Francisco, 39-40; Mus Art Ogunquit, 81. *Pos:* Contribr, Living Am Art, 35-37; dir, secy & trustee, Mus Art Ogunquit, Maine, 52- *Awards:* Second Prize, Golden Gate Expos, IBM Fine Arts Collection, 39; Third Prize for Oil, Soc Four Arts, 47; First Prize for Drawing, Norton Gallery Art, 60. *Bibliog:* Betty Chamberlain (auth), Henry Strater: Form and adventure through color, Am Artists, 5/72; Henry Strater (film), Jane Morrison Prod, 75; article, Boston Globe, 8/81; and others. *Mem:* Ogunquit Art Asn (pres, 46-48); The Players, New York; Arts Club, Louisville; Soc Four Arts; Palm Beach Art Inst. *Media:* Oil. *Publ:* Illusr, 14 Cantos, Ezra Pound, Three Mts Press, Paris, 23; auth, 24 Drawings by Henry Strater, Anthoenson, 58; ed, Henry Strater, 62; ed, Henry Strater, New Paintings, Frank Rehn Gallery, 67. *Dealer:* Frank Rehn Gallery 655 Madison Ave New York NY 10021. *Mailing Add:* Mus of Art Ogunquit Ogunquit ME 03907

STRATTON, DOROTHY (MRS WILLIAM A KING)
PAINTER, PRINTMAKER

b Worcester, Mass, Dec 21, 08. *Study:* Pratt Inst, cert, 42; Brooklyn Mus Sch, 42-43; Academie Grande Chaumiere, with Andre Chote, Paris, 48-49; Univ Calif, with Rico Lebrun, 56-57; Univ Calif, Los Angeles, 61; Univ Calif, San Diego, 66-67. *Work:* Long Beach Mus Art; Tunisian Ministry Cult Affairs, Tunis; Los Angeles Munic Art Collection, City Hall; Art in Embassies, Dept of State, Washington, DC; Southwestern Col (Calif). *Exhib:* One-woman shows, Pasadena Art Mus, 59, La Jolla Mus Contemp Art, 62, Univ San Diego, 73 & 30 Yr Retrospective 80, San Diego State Univ, 79; Art in embassies Prog, 65-83; Calif Soc Printmakers Nat Traveling Shows, 72 & 82-84; Pratt Graphics Ctr, New York, 80-83. *Pos:* Miniature set decorator, Paramount, George Pal Prod, 45-47; gallery receptionist & ed publicity, Munic Art Dept, Los Angeles, 52-61; registr & mem secy, La Jolla Mus Art, 64-65, vol art libr, 66-74; mem, Contemp Art Comt, San Diego Mus Art, 72-82. *Teaching:* Instr seminars printmaking, 73-75. *Bibliog:* Isabelle Wasserman (auth), Tribute to 30 Yrs, San Diego Union-Tribune, 10/21/80; The urban eye, San Diego Mag, 10/80; Martin Petersen (auth), Applause, San Diego Mag arts, 10/80. *Mem:* Artists Equity Asn; life mem Westwood Art Asn (pres, 56-57); Arts Coun, Univ Calif, Los Angeles; Calif Soc Printmakers; San Diego Mus Artists Guild. *Mailing Add:* 1647 Strine Dr McLean VA 22101

STRAUSER, STERLING BOYD
PAINTER

b Bloomsburg, Pa, Aug 15, 07. *Study:* Bloomsburg State Col, with George Keller, BA. *Work:* Cheekwood Mus, Nashville, Tenn; Everhart Mus, Scranton, Pa; Lehigh Univ; Vanderbilt Univ; E Stroudsburg State Col. *Exhib:* Art: USA, 58, New York, 58; Sports & Recreation Panorama, Munic Art Gallery, Davenport, Iowa, 59; one-man show, Lehigh Univ, 61, Lyzon Gallery, Nashville, 65- & William Penn Mus, Harrisburg, Pa, 73; retrospective, Haas Gallery Art, Bloomsburg Univ, 82. *Awards:* Top Award Regional Art Exhib, Everhart Mus, 58. *Bibliog:* Lee Nordness (auth), The great momentalist, 6/58 & David Burliuk (auth), American momentalist, 6/61, Color & Rhyme. *Media:* Oil. *Publ:* Illusr, Mademoiselle, 6/56. *Dealer:* Lyzon Gallery 411 Thompson Lane Nashville TN 37211. *Mailing Add:* 150 Analomink St East Stroudsburg PA 18301

STRAUTMANIS, EDVINS
PAINTER, SCULPTOR

b Liepaja, Latvia, Oct 27, 33. *Study:* Art Inst of Chicago, dipl, 56; Univ Chicago, 58-59. *Work:* Housotonic Mus Art, Bridgeport, Conn; Sydney and Frances Lewis Found; Herbert Distel's Mus Drawers, Kunsthaus, Zurich, Switz; and many pvt collections. *Comn:* Steel outdoor sculpture, Governors State Univ, 69. *Exhib:* Soc Contemp Art, Art Inst Chicago, 65, 66 & 70; Sculpture Ann, Whitney Mus of Am Art, New York, 68; Painting & Sculpture Today, Indianapolis Mus of Art, 70 & 74 & Contemp Art Ctr & Taft Mus, Cincinnati, 74; LoGiudice Gallery, 70 & 73; Walter Kelly Gallery, 73 & 79; Allan Stone Gallery, 82; Grayson Gallery, 83; and others. *Bibliog:* Dennis Adrian (auth), Art panorama, Chicago Daily News, 3/73 & Arts Mag, 9/77; Herman Cherry (auth), article, Arts Mag, 11/82; and others. *Dealer:* Allan Stone Gallery 48 E 86th St New York NY 10028 *Mailing Add:* 69 Greene St New York NY 10012

STRAWN, JARRETT W (JASON)
SCULPTOR, EDUCATOR

b Decatur, Ala, June 28, 43. *Study:* Middle Tenn State Univ, Murfreesboro, BS(art), 67; Univ SFla, Tampa, MFA(sculpture & multi-media), 73; New York Studio Sch; Teachers Col, Columbia Univ; New Sch; Univ Tenn, Arrowmont. *Work:* Tenn Arts & Crafts Comn, Nashville; Rudy Farms Collection, Nashville, Tenn; Atlanta Festival Arts; Wright Art Ctr, Beloit, Wis; Wustum Mus, Racine, Wis; and others. *Comn:* Jermy, Jeremy, Jeremey Set, comn by Larry Manness, Rome, Italy, 69; Mem for Kent State, St Leo Col, Fla, 70; Tower-Steps, Manuel Alum Dance Co, New York, 73-74; Flyer, Lar Lubovitch, New York, 74; Handles, Warner Brake & Elec, Beloit, Wis, 79-80. *Exhib:* One-man show, Sculpture, Wright Art Ctr, Beloit, Wis, 77; Nat Sculpture Traveling Show, 77; Wis Biennial Exhib, Madison Art Ctr, Wis, 78; Wis Sculpture 1979, Wustum Mus, Racine, Wis, 79; Rockford Ann, Burpee Mus, Rockford Ill, 79; and others. *Pos:* Chmn dept art, Beloit Col, Wis, 77-; nat liaison & mem design comt, Off City Planning, Beloit, Wis, 78-; proj co-dir, Nat Endowment for Arts residency, 80, dir, 80-; owner-mgr, Southouse, Inc, New York & Tenn. *Teaching:* Vis instr, St Leo Col, Fla, 69-70; instr ceramics, Ridgewood Sch Art, NJ, 73-74; instr design, Parsons Sch Design, New York, 76-77. *Awards:* Merit & Purchase Award, Atlanta Festival Arts, 71; Second Award, Nat Sculpture, '76, 76. *Bibliog:* Martin (auth), Beds and cars, Tampa Mag-Tribune, 69; Auer (auth), Thinking big in Beloit, 78 & Salsini (auth), Wisconsin in the 80's, 80, Milwaukee J. *Mem:* Col Art Asn; Nat Asn Schs Art; Tenn Artist-Craftsmen Asn; Art Squad; Mid-Am Col Art Asn. *Media:* Wood, Steel. *Publ:* Ed, The child, In: An Anthology of Poetry, Middle Tenn State Univ, 66-67; auth, Vertical furnishings, In: The Encyclopedia of Crafts and ..., Time-Life Books & Plenary Press, 75-76; coauth, Refinishing, Popular Mechanics, 76; auth, Fine arts in College: A proposal for redesigning the curriculum, Am Artist, 77. *Mailing Add:* 723 Church St Beloit WI 53511

STRAWN, MELVIN NICHOLAS
PAINTER, SCULPTOR

b Boise, Idaho, Aug 5, 29. *Study:* Chouinard Art Inst; Los Angeles Co Art Inst; Jepson Art Inst; Calif Col Arts & Crafts, BFA & MFA. *Work:* Oakland Art Mus; Antioch Col; Colo State Univ. *Comn:* Environ design (sculpture), Ottawa Col, Kans, 72. *Exhib:* Colo State Univ Centennial Exhib, 70; Cedar City Nat, Utah, 72; I-25 Artists Alliance, Colorado Springs Fine Arts Ctr, 72; Colorado Springs Biennial, Colorado Springs Fine Arts Ctr, 81; and others. *Teaching:* Instr art, Midwestern Univ, Mich State Univ, Antioch Col & Univ Denver, 56-72; chmn dept art, Antioch Col, 66-69; prof & dir, Sch Art, Univ Denver, 69- *Awards:* First Purchase Award, Colo State Univ Centennial, 70. *Media:* Oil. *Mailing Add:* 7 S Lane Cherry Hills Village CO 80110

STREETER, TAL
SCULPTOR, EDUCATOR

b Oklahoma City, Okla, Aug 1, 34. *Study:* Univ Kans, BFA & MFA; Colorado Springs Fine Arts Ctr, with Robert Motherwell; Colo Col; with Seymour Lipton, 3 yrs. *Work:* Mus Mod Art, New York; San Francisco Mus Art; Wadsworth Atheneum, Hartford, Conn; Corcoran Gallery; Storm King Art Ctr, NY; and others. *Comn:* Large-scale sculpture, Ark Art Ctr, Little Rock; High Mus Art, Mem Arts Ctr, Atlanta, Ga; Sculpture in Environment, New York City Parks Dept; large scale sculpture, Co Col Morris, 80; Libr for the Blind, Trenton, NJ, 81-83. *Exhib:* Cool Art & Highlights of the Season, Aldrich Mus, 70; Del Art Mus, 77; Drawings by Sculptors, Corcoran Gallery, 78; Sky Art, Mass Inst Technol, 80 & 81; Ars Electronica, Linz, Austria, 82; Univ of Ky Mus Art, 82; Kunst and Technik, Munich, Ger, 83; and others. *Teaching:* Vis artist, Fairleigh Dickinson Univ, 62; vis artist in residence, Dartmouth Col, 63; vis artist, Univ NC, Greensboro, 70 & 72-73 & Penland Sch Crafts, NC, 74-76; Fulbright prof, Seoul, Korea, 71; vis lectr, US Info Serv, Japan, 72; adj prof, Queen's Col, 73; prof & chmn III-D/media area, prof, State Univ NY Col Purchase, 73- *Awards:* State Univ NY Int Studies Grant, Japan, 69; NY State Coun Arts Grant, 76; and others. *Bibliog:* G A Ruda (auth), Kitesmanship: Tal Streeter, Craft Horizons, 74; Donald Ritchie (auth), Kite crazy, Natural Hist, 75; Carter Ratcliff (auth), Tal Streeter: Beyond absolutes, Arts Mag, 77; article, Sky painting, Newsweek, 8/80; and others. *Media:* Multimedia. *Publ:* Auth, Seymour Lipton, the Sculptor's Way, 61, Univ Kans Mus Art; auth, The Art of the Japanese Kite, Weatherhill/Lippincott, 74 & 82; Heavenly humors: The modern kite, Am Craft, 79; and others. *Dealer:* RedLine Construction Co Inc Old Verbank Rd Milbrook NY 12545; Lippincott Large-Scale Sculpture 400 Sackett Point Rd North Haven CT 06473. *Mailing Add:* Old Verbank Sch Millbrook NY 12545

STREETMAN, JOHN WILLIAM, III
ADMINISTRATOR

b Marion, NC, Jan 19, 41. *Study:* Western Carolina Univ, AB; Lincoln Col, Oxford Univ, cert. *Collections Arranged:* Indonesia, Jewel of the East Indies, 71; Two American Realists: William Bailey and DeWitt Hardy, 73 & 74. *Pos:* Founding dir, Jewett Creative Arts Ctr, South Berwick, Maine, 66-70; exec dir, Polk Pub Mus, Lakeland, Fla, 70-75; dir, Mus Arts & Sci, Evansville, Ind, 75- *Mem:* Fla Art Mus Dirs Asn; Fla League Arts (bd dirs & trustee, currently); Am Asn Mus; Midwestern Mus Conf. *Mailing Add:* 411 SE Riverside Dr Evansville IN 47713

STREETT, TYLDEN WESTCOTT
SCULPTOR, EDUCATOR

b Baltimore, Md, Nov 28, 22. *Study:* Johns Hopkins Univ; St John's Col; Md Inst Col Art, with Sidney Waugh & Cecil Howard, BFA & MFA; also asst to Lee Lawrie. *Comn:* Archit sculpture, West Point, NY, 58 & 61; archit sculpture, Kuwait Embassy, Washington, DC, 65; John O'Donnell (bronze portrait statue), O'Donnell Sq, Baltimore, 79; archit sculpture (relief on facade), Waverly Sch, Baltimore, 82; Former Presidents of Seafarers International Union (bronze portraits), Washington, DC & Piney Point, Md, 83. *Exhib:* Corcoran Gallery Art, Washington, DC, 60; Baltimore Mus Art, 69. *Teaching:* Instr sculpture, Md Inst Col Art, Baltimore, 59-, dir, Grad Studies, 66-72; instr sculpture, Jewish Community Ctr, Baltimore, 63-65. *Awards:* John Gregory Award, 62; Union Independent Col Art Grant, 71; Ford Found Grant, 80; and others. *Mem:* Nat Sculpture Soc; Artists Equity Asn. *Publ:* Auth, Plaster Casting Using a Waste Mold (film), 70. *Mailing Add:* 4622 Keswick Rd Baltimore MD 21210

STRICKLAND, THOMAS J
PAINTER

b Keyport, NJ, Dec 28, 32. *Study:* Newark Sch Fine & Indust Arts, NJ; Am Art Sch & Nat Acad Fine Arts, New York, with Robert Philipp & Gordon Samstag. *Work:* Elliott Mus, Stuart, Fla; Hollywood Art Mus, Fla; St Hugh Catholic Church; Salem Col; St Vincent Col; and others. *Exhib:* Butler Inst Am Art Fine Arts Festival, Youngstown, Ohio, 63; 7th Grand Prix Int Peinture Cote d'Azur, Cannes, France, 71; Hollywood Art Mus, 72, 75 & 76; Cape Coral Nat Art Show, Fla, 73; Martin Co Hist Soc, Elliott Mus, Fla, 74; Am Painters in Paris, 75; and others. *Awards:* First Prize, Hollywood Arts & Crafts Guild Ann Mems Art Exhib, 72; First Prize, Hollywood Art Mus Ann Regional Show, Fla, 73; Charles Hawthorne Mem Award, Nat Arts Club, 77; plus others. *Bibliog:* Ann D Browne (auth), Personality of the month, Directions, 12/73; Lawrence T Mahoney (auth), The 2703 faces of Tom Strickland, Tropic, 8/15/76. *Mem:* Blue Dome Art Fellowship; Miami Palette Club; Pastel Soc of Am; Fla Pastel Asn; and others. *Media:* Oil, Pastel. *Publ:* Auth, A painting demonstration by Thomas J Strickland, Directions, 5/74 & 7/74; auth, The impressionistic pastels of Thomas J Strickland, 5/76, Painting self-portraits, 7/76 & How Thomas Strickland paints a still life, 3/77, Today's Art. *Mailing Add:* 2598 Taluga Dr Miami FL 33133

STRICKLER, SUSAN ELIZABETH
CURATOR, HISTORIAN

b Baltimore, Md, Jan 23, 52. *Study:* Ecole du Louvre, Paris, 1st yr cert, 72; Mt Holyoke Col, BA, 73; Univ Del, MA, 77. *Collections Arranged:* Four Delaware Valley Primitives (auth, catalog), 73; John Ritto Penniman 1782-1841: An Ingenious New England Artist, 82. *Pos:* Res assoc, Toledo Mus Art,

Ohio, 78-79; spec proj dir, Va Mus, Richmond, 79-80; cur Am art, Worcester Art Mus, Mass, 81- *Mem:* Col Art Asn; Am Asn Mus; New Eng Mus Asn; Decorative Arts Chap, Soc Archit Historians. *Res:* American painting, especially eighteenth and nineteenth centuries. *Publ:* Contribr, American painting and sculpture (catalog), Del Art Mus, 75; auth, American paintings (catalog), Toledo Mus Art, 79. *Mailing Add:* 55 Salisbury St Worcester MA 01608

STRIDER, MARJORIE VIRGINIA
SCULPTOR
b Guthrie, Okla. *Study:* Kansas City Art Inst, Mo; Okla Univ, BFA. *Work:* Albright Knox Mus, Buffalo, NY; Storm King Art Ctr, NY; Wadsworth Atheneum, Hartford, Conn; Larry Aldrich Contemp Art Mus, Conn; Hirshhorn Mus, Washington, DC; and others. *Exhib:* Whitney Sculpture Ann, Whitney Mus Am Art, NY, 70; one-woman shows, Hoffman Gallery, New York, 73 & 74, The Clocktower, New-york, 77, Grad Ctr, City Univ New York, 77 & Bernice Steinbaum Gallery, New York, 83; 10 Years Work Traveling Exhib, C W Post Ctr, Long Island Univ, Sculpture Ctr, New York, Joslyn Art Mus, Omaha, McNay Art Inst, San Antonio & elsewhere, 82-85; and others. *Teaching:* Prof sculpture, Sch Visual Arts, New York, 68-; prof sculpture, Univ Iowa, summer 70 & Univ Ga, summer 72; also lectr var univ & col throughout US. *Awards:* Longview Found Grant, 73; Nat Endowment Arts Grant, 74 & 80-81. *Bibliog:* Lucy Lippard (auth), Six Years, Praeger, 73; Lawrence Alloway (auth), Great Drawings of the Western World, Shorewood Publ, 80; Robert Pincus-Witten (auth), Post Minimalism, Out of London Press, London, 80; plus others. *Media:* Painted Bronze and Aluminum. *Publ:* Auth, Moving out-moving up, Art News, 1/71; auth, Radical scale, Art & Artists, 1/72; illusr & contribr, Modern American Painting & Sculpture, Abrams, 72. *Mailing Add:* 7 Worth St New York NY 10013

STRIKER, CECIL L
HISTORIAN, EDUCATOR
b July 15, 32. *Study:* Oberlin Col, AB, 56; Inst Fine Arts, NY Univ, MA, 60, PhD, 68; Univ Pa, Hon MA, 73. *Pos:* Field archeologist, Dumbarton Oaks Ctr Byzantine Studies, 66- *Teaching:* From instr to asst prof medieval art, Vassar Col, 62-68; from assoc prof to prof Byzantine & Medieval art & arch & chmn dept art hist, Univ Pa, 68- *Mem:* Col Art Asn Am ; Archeol Inst Am; Asn Field Archeol; Am Res Inst Turkey (pres, 78-); Coun Am Overseas Res Ctrs (chmn, 81-). *Res:* Byzantine architecture and archeology; medieval architecture. *Publ:* Coauth, Work at Kalenderhane Camii in Istanbul: Preliminary reports, Dumberton Oaks Papers, 67-74; auth, The Myrelaion (Bodrum Camii) in Istanbul, Princeton Univ Press, 82; auth, Tree ring dating in the Aegean & neighboring regions, J Field Archeol, 84. *Mailing Add:* Dept Art Hist Univ Pa Philadelphia PA 19104

STRINGER, JOHN NORRIS
GALLERY DIRECTOR
b Melbourne, Australia, Oct 2, 37. *Study:* Caulfield Inst Technol, Melbourne, Cert Art, 56; Royal Melbourne Inst Technol, Dipl Art, 59; Univ Melbourne, Fine Arts, 59. *Collections Arranged:* Illusion and Reality, 76, The Chinese Exhibition (recent archeol discoveries from Peoples' Repub China), 76 & El Dorado: Colombian Gold, 77, toured to major Australian state art mus; 25 Anos Despues (auth, catalog), Mus Arte Mod, Bogota, Colombia, 79. *Pos:* Asst dir, Int Prog, Mus Mod Art, New York, 70-75; exhib coordr, Visual Arts Bd, Australia Coun, New York, 75-76; exec dir, Australian Art Exhibs Corp, 76-77; dir visual arts, Ctr for Inter-Am Relations, 79- *Mem:* Int Coun Mus; Art Galleries Asn Australia. *Publ:* Auth, The Field, Nat Gallery Victoria, Melbourne, 68; auth, Illusion and Reality, Australian Gallery Dirs Coun, 76. *Mailing Add:* Ctr for Inter-American Relations 680 Park Ave New York NY 10021

STRINGER, MARY EVELYN
EDUCATOR, HISTORIAN
b Huntsville, Mo, July 31, 21. *Study:* Univ Mo, AB; Univ NC, AM; Harvard Univ, univ traveling fel, 66-67, with Ernst Kitzinger, PhD, 73. *Teaching:* Prof art, Miss Univ Women, 47- *Awards:* Fulbright Scholar, 55-56; Danforth Found Grant, 59-60 & 64-65. *Mem:* Col Art Asn Am; Medieval Acad; Int Ctr Medieval Art; Southeastern Col Art Conf; and others. *Res:* stained glass windows in America. *Publ:* Auth, Review of Andrew Martindale, Gothic Art, 69; auth, Composite nativity-adoration of English medieval alabasters, NC Mus Art Bulletin, 70; auth, Three Faces of A-T-AH: Artist-Teacher-Art Historian, Southeastern Col Art Conf Rev, 80. *Mailing Add:* W Box 1109 MVW Columbus MS 39701

STRISIK, PAUL
PAINTER
b Brooklyn, NY, Apr 21, 18. *Study:* Art Students League, with Frank Vincent Dumond. *Work:* Parrish Mus Art, Southampton, NY; Percy H Whitney Mus, Fairhope, Ala; Mattatuck Mus, Conn; Utah State Univ; and many prominent corp collections. *Exhib:* Allied Artists Am Ann; one-man shows, Grand Cent Art Gallery, New York, 60-70, Rockport Art Asn, 69-75, Gordan Col, Mass, 72 & Johnson-Welch Gallery, Kansas City, Mo, 78; and others. *Awards:* Gold Medal, Hudson Valley Art Asn, 70; Best in Show, Am Artists Prof League Grant Nat, 72; Gold Medal, Nat Acad Western Art, Okla, 81; Over 130 awards, including 13 gold medals. *Mem:* Nat Acad Western Art; assoc Nat Acad Design; Am Watercolor Soc; Allied Artists Am; Knickerbocker Artists. *Media:* Multimedia. *Publ:* Auth, Watercolor page, Am Artists, 4/70; auth, article, Am Artists, 79; auth, article, SW Art Mag, 3/81; auth, Art W Mag, 1/83; auth, The Art of Landscape Painting, Watson-Gutpil Publ, 83. *Mailing Add:* 123 Marmion Way Rockport MA 01966

STROESSNER, ROBERT JOSEPH
CURATOR, HISTORIAN
b Denver, Colo, Dec 12, 42. *Study:* Univ Denver, BFA, 64; Univ Colo, grad studies, 70. *Exhib:* Hispanic Am Heritage, Denver Art Mus, Colo, 68, Treasures from the Permanent Collection, 69, The Mother & Child, 75 & The Inca of Peru, 77; touring exhibs, Ancient Art of Costa Rica, 78, Moche Art of Peru, 79 & Spain & New Spain, 79. *Collections Arranged:* New World Collection, Denver Art Mus, 68-79; Ancient Art of Costa Rica, Jan & Frederick R Mayer Collection, 77 & The Misco United Collection, 79; Pre-Columbian Collection & Mitch Miller Collection, Wichita Art Mus, 78. *Pos:* Asst cur native arts, Denver Art Mus, 68-71, cur new world dept, 71-83. *Teaching:* Instr Meso-Am art hist, Univ Colo, Denver Ctr, 73 & 75. *Awards:* Order of the Brilliant Star (cravat), Repub of China, 77. *Bibliog:* Grace Glueek (auth), Experts guide to the experts, Art News, 78. *Res:* Spanish Colonial arts of Latin America. *Publ:* Coauth, Santos of the Southwest, Denver Art Mus, 71; coauth, Traditional Folkarts of Hispano New Mexico, Mus San Diego, 76; contribr, How to Know American Folkart, Dutton, 77; auth, Pre-Columbian Art from Costa Rica, F R Mayer Collection, Colo State Univ, 77; auth, Ancient Art from Costa Rica, Mid-Am Indian Ctr, Wichita, 78. *Mailing Add:* 811 Downing St Denver CO 80209

STROH, CHARLES
PRINTMAKER, EDUCATOR
b Aberdeen, SDak, Feb 20, 43. *Study:* Minneapolis Sch Art, with Eugene Larkin, BFA, 65; Univ Wis, Milwaukee, with T Stoeveken, R Burkert & J Ernst, MS, MFA, 72; US Peace Corps, Kabul, Afghanistan; Northern State Col. *Work:* Milwaukee Art Mus, Wis; Washington Co Mus Fine Arts, Md; Roanoke Mus Fine Arts, Va; Weinstein Collection, Va; Coe Col Collection, Cedar Rapids, Iowa. *Exhib:* Southeastern Ctr Contemp Arts, Winston-Salem, NC, 74; Va Mus, Richmond, 76; Spiva Art Ctr, Joplin, Mo, 77; Des Moines Art Ctr, Iowa, 77; Davenport Munic Gallery, 78; Blanden Mus, Ft Dodge, Iowa, 78; and others. *Collections Arranged:* The Hand-Printed Lithograph (auth, catalog), traveling, Iowa Arts Coun, 80-81; Prints from Kans State Univ Permanent Collection, 81 & Gordon Parks: Photographer (auth, catalog), Kans State Univ, 81; Gordon Parks: Photographer, Miami-Dade Community Col, 82. *Teaching:* Instr, Manhattan Arts Coun, 80- *Pos:* Bd dirs, Northern Mich Univ, Marquette, 72-73; asst prof, Roanoke Col, Salem, Va, 73-76; assoc prof & chmn dept, Coe Col, Cedar Rapids, Iowa, 76-80; prof & head dept, Kans State Univ, Manhattan, 80- *Awards:* Cert Distinction, Roanoke Area Exhib, Va, 75; Drawing Award, Quad Cities Fine Arts Exhib, Ill, 77; Best Graphic, Mid-Miss Ann Exhib, Ill, 78. *Mem:* Col Art Asn; Found Art: Theory & Educ; Nat Coun Art Adminrs. *Media:* Lithography, Screenprinting. *Publ:* Auth, Art in the general curriculum: Emphasis on the cognitive, 74 & auth, More on sins of omission, 81, Art Educ; auth, art articles, Cedar Rapids Gazette, Iowa, 78-80; illusr, still photographs for animated film, United Way & Three Arts Advert Agency, Cedar Rapids, Iowa, 80; auth, Artists and art educators: Are we really half-brained, MACAA, Milwaukee, 81. *Mailing Add:* 331 North 14th St Manhattan KS 66502

STRONG, BEVERLY JEAN
DEALER, COLLECTOR
b Eugene, Ore, Oct 1, 27. *Pos:* Owner, Gallery Tiqua, currently. *Specialty:* Contemporary paintings; antique folk art; American Indian art; tribal rugs. *Collection:* Spanish colonial painting and sculpture. *Mailing Add:* Gallery Tiqua 7077 Main St #6 Scottsdale AZ 85251

STRONG, CHARLES RALPH
PAINTER, EDUCATOR
b Greeley, Colo, Dec 25, 38. *Study:* Coronado Sch Fine Art, 57; San Francisco Art Inst, BFA, 62, MFA, 63; also with Elmer Bischoff, Jack Jefferson, Frank Lobdell & James Weeks. *Work:* De Saisset Art Gallery, Univ Santa Clara; Oakland Mus, Calif; San Francisco Art Inst. *Exhib:* Three-artist show, Painted Images, Oakland Mus, 71; Linda Farris Gallery, Seattle, 74; Eastern Wash Hist Soc Traveling Exhib, Western US & Can, 74-76; Works on/of Paper, Zara Gallery, San Francisco, 77; Smith-Andersen Gallery, Palo Alto, 78; and others. *Teaching:* Instr painting & drawing, San Francisco State Col, 65-68; lectr painting & drawing, Stanford Univ, summers 70, 71 & 74; from assoc prof art to prof, Col Notre Dame, Calif, 70-, gallery dir, 76- *Awards:* Fulbright Fel to Eng, 64. *Bibliog:* Work in The Paper Revolution, Am Artist, 8/77; Jules Heller (auth), Paper--the white art, 78; article, Visual Dialogue Mag, 78. *Mailing Add:* c/o Smith-Anderson Gallery 200 Homer Ave Palo Alto CA 94301

STRONGHILOS, CAROL
PAINTER
b New York, NY. *Study:* Hunter Col, MA; Art Students League; Brooklyn Mus Art Sch, study with Reuben Tam. *Exhib:* NJ State Mus, 72; Monmouth Col, 72; Brooklyn Mus, 74; Larry Aldrich Mus, 75; Women in the Arts, 76 & 77; Newark Mus, 77; Art in Pub Bldg, NY Orgn of Independent Artists, World Trade Ctr, 77; Women 78, Women's Caucus for the Arts, City Univ New York, 78; one-woman shows, Brooklyn Mus, 71 & Whitney Mus, 75. *Pos:* Founder, NY Feminist Art Inst, New York; consult, Am the Beautiful Fund, 76-77; dir, Art Sch-Mid Westchester, 83. *Teaching:* Instr painting, Brooklyn Mus Art Sch, 71-77 & Brooklyn House of Detention, 74-77; instr painting & drawing, Five Towns Music & Art Ctr, 74-76, Feminist Art Inst, 79-80. *Awards:* Fac & Alumni First Prize, Brooklyn Mus, 70. *Mem:* Women in the Arts; Woman's Caucus for Art, Col Art Asn. *Media:* Acrylic, Oil. *Dealer:* Bernice Steinbaum Gallery 903 Madison Ave New York NY. *Mailing Add:* 15 Laight St New York NY 10013

STROSAHL, WILLIAM
PAINTER
b Brooklyn, NY, June 11, 10. *Study:* Self-taught; Dolphin Fel. *Exhib:* Royal Watercolor Soc, London, Eng, 62; 200 Yrs Watercolor, Metrop Mus Art, New York, 64; Am Watercolor Soc (traveling show), Mus Fine Arts, St Petersburg, Fla, 76 & Fry Mus, Seattle, Wash, 77. *Pos:* Art dir, J Walter Thompson, New York, 30-41; art dir, William Esty Co, New York, 42-55, creative dir, 55-69. *Awards:* Gold Medal, Allied Artists Am, 58; Medal, Audubon Artists, 80; Walter Biggs Award, Nat Acad Design, 80; and others. *Bibliog:* Wendon Blake (auth), Acrylic Painting, 72 & Norman Kent (auth), 25 Watercolorists, 75, Watson-Guptill; Sue Myers (auth), Fairfield group, Am Artist Mag, 74. *Mem:* Am Watercolor Soc (vpres); Nat Soc Painters in Casein & Acrylic (dir); Assoc Nat Acad Design; Audubon Artists. *Media:* Watercolor; Acrylic. *Mailing Add:* 301 Haviland Rd Stamford CT 06903

STROTHER, JOSEPH WILLIS
ADMINISTRATOR, PAINTER
b New Orleans, La, Dec 14, 33. *Study:* La Col, BA; Univ Ga, MA & EdD. *Work:* Rapides Nat Bank Collection; NC Nat Bank Collection; Wachovia Bank State Collection; Ga Mus; Dillard Collection, Weatherspoon Gallery, Univ NC, Greensboro. *Exhib:* Mead Painting of Year, Atlanta, 61; four shows, Nat Art on Paper, Greensboro, 64-69; NC Artist Ann, 71-74; Ga Artist Ann, 72-74; Tex Ann, 74. *Teaching:* Art supvr, Marietta City Schs, Ga, 57-61; instr art, Montgomery Jr Col, Md, 61-64; instr art, Univ NC, Greensboro, 64-66; assoc prof art, Univ Ga, 66-76; prof art & dir, Sch of Art/Archit, La Tech Univ, 76- *Awards:* Award, Ocala Jr Col, 69; Purchase Award, NC Sch Ment Health Exten, Chapel Hill, 71; Purchase Awards, Alexandria, La, 77 & 80. *Mem:* Nat Asn Schs Art & Design; Col Art Asn Am. *Media:* Acrylic, Encaustic Monoprints. *Mailing Add:* Sch of Art/Archit La Tech Univ Ruston LA 71272

STROTHER, VIRGINIA VAUGHN
PAINTER
b Ft Worth, Tex, July 19, 20. *Study:* Tex Christian Univ, BFA(with hons), Spec Div Courses printmaking; watercolor with Barse Miller. *Work:* Tex Fine Arts Asn Permanent Collection, Austin; Univ Tex, Arlington; Sci Dept, Tex Christian Univ; Woman's Club Ft Worth Permanent Collection; and many others. *Exhib:* Tex Fine Arts Asn Nat Ann, Laguna Gloria Mus, Austin, 72 & 75; Delta Seven State Exhib, Ark Art Ctr, Little Rock, 72; El Paso Mus Nat Exhibs, 72 & 76; Eight State Exhib Painting & Sculpture, Okla Art Ctr, Oklahoma City, 74; Monroe Nat Ann, Masur Mus Art, La, 73; Southwestern Watercolor, 82; and ten one-person exhibs. *Teaching:* Dir preparatory workshop art, Tex Christian Univ, 50-54. *Awards:* Citations & Travel Awards, Tex Fine Arts Asn, 69, 70, 72, 75 & 78; Award of Merit, NMex Art League, Albuquerque, 71; Award, Ft Worth Art Mus, 73. *Mem:* Southwestern & Tex Watercolor Socs; Tex Fine Arts Asn (state adv bd, 68-75); Nat League Am Pen Women (pres, Ft Worth Br, 70-72). *Media:* Oil, Watercolor. *Dealer:* Contemp Fine Arts Gallery 2425 Cedar Springs Dallas TX 75201. *Mailing Add:* 4109 Shannon Dr Ft Worth TX 76116

STROUD, PETER ANTHONY
PAINTER, EDUCATOR
b London, Eng, May 23, 21. *Study:* Teacher Training Col, London Univ, Central Hammersmith Schs Art, 48-53. *Work:* Tate Gallery, London; Guggenheim Mus, New York; Los Angeles Co Mus, Detroit Inst Fine Arts; Pasadena Art Mus. *Comn:* Mural, Int Union Archit Congress Bldg, London, 61; mural, State Sch Leverkusen, Ger, 63; mural, Mfrs Hanover Trust Co, New York, 69. *Exhib:* Carnegie Inst Int, Pittsburgh, 61 & 64; Guggenheim Mus Int, 64; The Responsive Eye, Mus Mod Art, New York, 65; Mus Mod Art, Oxford, Eng, 69; Nat Gallery Victoria, Melbourne, Australia, 70; Univ Calif, Santa Barbara, 70; Ulster Mus, Belfast, Northern Ireland, 71; Finch Col, New York, 72; and others. *Teaching:* Prof visual studies, Bennington Col, 63-68; prof painting, Grad Sch, Rutgers Univ, New Brunswick, 68- *Awards:* Pasadena Mus Fel, 64. *Bibliog:* Dore Ashton (auth), Peter Stroud's relief-paintings, Studio Int, 66; John Coplans (auth), Interview with Peter Stroud, Artforum, 66. *Media:* Acrylic. *Mailing Add:* One Lincoln Pl Apt 11-I New Brunswick NJ 08902

STRUPPECK, JULES
SCULPTOR, EDUCATOR
b Grangeville, La, May 29, 15. *Study:* Univ Okla, BFA; La State Univ, MA. *Exhib:* Am Fedn Arts Traveling Exhib, 41; Bertha Schaefer Gallery, 53; Whitney Mus Am Art, 54; Archit League, 54; San Francisco Mus Art, 66. *Teaching:* Prof sculpture, Newcomb Col, Tulane Univ La, presently. *Awards:* Prizes, Gallery Art, Miami, Bertha Schaefer Gallery & Marine Hosp, New Orleans, La; plus others. *Publ:* Auth, The Creation of Sculpture, Holt, Reinhart & Winston, 52; contribr, Design Mag. *Mailing Add:* Dept of Art Newcomb Col Tulane Univ New Orleans LA 70118

STRUVE, WILLIAM WALTER
DEALER
b Wilkes-Barre, Pa, Dec 16, 36. *Study:* Mich State Univ; Northwestern Univ, BA, 60. *Pos:* Dir, Allan Frumkin Gallery, Chicago, Ill, 60-70; pvt dealer, East Haddam, Conn, 70-79; dir/partner, Frumkin & Struve Gallery, Chicago, Ill, 79- *Mem:* Chicago Art Dealers Asn. *Specialty:* Contemporary American painting, sculpture, drawings and prints. *Mailing Add:* Frumkin & Struve Gallery 309 N Superior St Chicago IL 60610

STUART, DAVID
DEALER
b Scotland, SDak. *Study:* Otis Art Inst, Los Angeles. *Pos:* Dir, David Stuart Galleries. *Mem:* Art Dealers Asn Am. *Specialty:* Contemporary painting and sculpture; pre-Columbian and African arts. *Mailing Add:* 748 N La Cienega Blvd Penthouse Los Angeles CA 90069

STUART, DONALD ALEXANDER
DESIGNER, CRAFTSMAN
b Toronto, Ont, Aug 25, 44. *Study:* Ont Col Art; Sch Am Craftsmen, Rochester Inst Technol, MFA. *Work:* Massey Found, Nat Mus Can; Jean A Chalmers Nat Craft Collection, Can Crafts Coun; Chalmers Collection, Ont Crafts Coun. *Comn:* sterling silver coffee serv, Royal Philatelic Soc, Toronto, 78; Cadillac Fairview Corp, Denver, 78; tapestry, Can Life Assurance, Toronto, 79; Sun Life Assurance, Boston, 80; Elmwood Club, Toronto, 82; plus many other tapestries & jewelry, pvt comns, 69-82. *Exhib:* 100 Years, The Evolution of the Ontario College of Art, Art Gallery Ont, 76-77; Lake Superior 77, Duluth, Minn, 77; Objects '79, Colo; solo exhibs, Brampton Art Gallery, 81 & Craft Gallery, Toronto, 82; and others. *Pos:* Mgr, Weaving indust in Pangnirting, Baffin Island, for Eskimo women, 69-72. *Teaching:* Teaching master weaving, jewelry & design, Georgian Col, Barrie, Ont, 72- *Awards:* Visual Artist Award, Ont Arts Coun, 81; Gold Award, 82 & Silver Award, 83, Can Jewellery Design. *Bibliog:* The Craftsman's Way, Univ Toronto Press, 81; G Hook (auth), Don Stuart, Weaver and metalsmith, Crafts Can, 80 & Donald Stuart, Metalsmith, Soc NAm Goldsmiths, 82. *Mem:* Ont Crafts Coun (dir, 74-78, pres, 83-84); Craft Collab (pres, 77-81); Metal Arts Guild; Can Crafts Coun; Am Crafts Coun. *Media:* Jewelry. *Publ:* Contribr, The wonderful world of crafts, Toronto Star, 76; contribr, Donald Stuart's international distinction, Craftsnews, Ont Crafts Coun, 76; contribr, The OCA Revisited Canada Crafts, Page Publ, 77; auth, Teaching contracts, Craftsnews, 77; The technique of inlay, Craftsman, Ont Crafts Coun, 81. *Dealer:* Creiger Sesen Assoc Ltd Ten PO Sq Boston MA 02109; Ont Crafts Coun 346 Dundas St W Toronto M5T 1G5. *Mailing Add:* 4 Maple Crescent RR3 Barrie ON L4M 4S5 Canada

STUART, JOSEPH MARTIN
PAINTER, MUSEUM DIRECTOR
b Seminole, Okla, Nov 9, 32. *Study:* Univ NMex, BFA, 59, MA, 62. *Work:* Art Mus, Univ NMex, Albuquerque; Salt Lake Art Ctr, Salt Lake City; Col of Idaho, Caldwell; Sioux City Art Ctr, Iowa. *Exhib:* Northwest Artists 50th & 52nd Ann, Seattle Art Mus, 64 & 66; Midwest Biennial, Joslyn Art Mus, Omaha 74 & 76; Drawings USA, Minn Mus of Art, St Paul, 77; Nat Drawings, Rutgers Univ, Camden, NJ, 77; plus others. *Collections Arranged:* Jannis Spyropoulos: Paintings, Roswell Mus & Art Ctr, NMex, 62; Edward Kienholz: Sculpture, Boise Gallery Art, Idaho, 67; Art of South Dakota, 74, The Calligraphic Statement, 77 & Berry Collection of Asian Arts & Crafts, 79, Ben Reifel Collection, 82, SDak Mem Art Ctr, Brookings. *Pos:* Cur, Mus Art, Univ Ore, 62-63; dir, Boise Gallery Art, 64-68; dir, Salt Lake Art Ctr, 68-71; dir, SDak Mem Art Ctr, 71- *Teaching:* Lectr art, Univ Utah, 69; prof art hist, SDak State Univ, 71- *Awards:* First Prize in Painting, Cheney Cowles Mem Mus, Spokane, 65; Salt Lake Art Ctr Purchase Award, 67; Purchase Award, Sioux City Art Ctr, 73. *Mem:* Col Art Asn; Am Asn Mus; Artists Equity Asn. *Media:* Acrylic. *Publ:* Auth, An interview with Billy Apple, Boise Art Asn Bull, 66; auth, Stimuli, Utah Archit, fall 69; auth, Art of South Dakota, SDak State Univ, 74; auth, Architecture of Harold Spitznagel, 75, Oscar Howe Paintings, 80 & SDak Mem Art Ctr, Brookings. *Mailing Add:* 719 Eighth St Brookings SD 57006

STUART, KENNETH JAMES
DIRECTOR, ILLUSTRATOR
b Milwaukee, Wis. *Study:* Pa Acad Fine Arts, with Arthur B Carles; also in Paris, France. *Work:* Hitler, Libr Cong, Washington, DC. *Pos:* Mag & bk illusr & painter, 44; art ed, Sat Eve Post, Philadelphia, 44-62; art dir, Reader's Digest, New York, 62-77; develop lit & graphic work, 77-79; graphics dir, Am Hist & Cult Soc, Washington, DC, 75- *Teaching:* Head dept illus, Moore Col Art, Philadelphia, 39-44, bd managers, 44-56. *Awards:* Salmagundi Gold Medal, 60; Typographic Excellence Award, Type Dir Club New York, 62; Show Award for Outstanding Work in Mag Illus, Soc Illustrators, 66; and many others. *Mem:* Salmagundi Club. *Media:* Watercolor. *Mailing Add:* 295 Ridgefield Rd Wilton CT 06897

STUART, MICHELLE
PAINTER, SCULPTOR
b Los Angeles, Calif, Feb 10, 19. *Study:* Chouinard Art Inst, Los Angeles; apprenticed to Diego Rivera, Mex; New Sch Social Res. *Work:* Allen Mem Art Mus, Oberlin Col; Aldrich Mus Contemp Art, Ridgefield, Conn; Power Inst Mus, Sydney, Australia; Mus Art, Univ NMex; Landesmuseum, Graz, Austria; and others. *Exhib:* Mus Mod Art, 76; Drawings of the Seventies, Art Inst Chicago, 77; one-man shows, Gallery Fine Arts, State Univ NY Stonybrook, 76, Mass Inst Technol, 77, Univ NMex Art Gallery, 78 & Ehrensperger Gallery, Zurich, Switz, 79; Albright-Knox Art Gallery, Buffalo, NY, 80; Hirshhorn Mus & Sculpture Garden, Washington, DC, 81; Joslyn Art Mus, Omaha, Nebr, 81; Walker Art Ctr, Minneapolis, 81; and many other group & one-man shows. *Awards:* Nat Endowment for Arts Fel for Individual Artists, 74, 77 & 80; NY State Creative Artists Pub Serv Grant, 75; Guggenheim Mem Found Fel, 75. *Bibliog:* Corrine Robbins (auth), Michelle Stuart: The mapping of myth and time, Arts, 12/76; Ellen Lubell (auth), Michelle Stuart, Icons from the archives of time, Arts, Vol 53, No 10, 79; and others. *Media:* Mixed. *Publ:* Illusr, In, On, Or, About the Premises, Cape-Goliard, London, 68. *Dealer:* Susan Caldwell Gallery 383 W Broadway New York NY 10012. *Mailing Add:* 152 Wooster St New York NY 10012

STUART, SIGNE NELSON See Nelson, Signe

STUBBLEBINE, JAMES HARVEY
HISTORIAN
b New York, NY, Dec 28, 20. *Study:* Harvard Col, BA, 42, NY Univ, MA, 54, PhD, 58. *Teaching:* Mem fac, Wellesley Col, 54-56; prof art hist, Rutgers

Univ, 57- *Awards:* Fels, Kress Found, 69-70 & Nat Endowment Humanities, 75-76; Lindback Award, Rutgers Univ, 79. *Mem:* Col Art Asn. *Res:* Early Italian painting. *Publ:* Auth, Guido da Siena, Princeton Univ Press, 64; ed, Giotto: The Arena Chapel Frescoes, W W Norton, 69; auth, Duccio di Buoninsegna and His School, Princeton Univ Press, 79; auth, Dugento Painting, An Annotated Bibliography, G K Hall, 83. *Mailing Add:* Dept Art Hist Rutgers Univ New Brunswick NJ 08903

STUCKEY, CHARLES F
HISTORIAN, CURATOR
b Teaneck, NJ, Mar 14, 45. *Study:* Yale Univ, BA, 67; Univ Pa, MA & PhD, 72. *Collections Arranged:* Toulouse-Lautrec: Paintings (auth, catalog), 79; Scott Burton: Chairs (auth, catalog), 83. *Pos:* res assoc, Broida Mus, 83- *Teaching:* Asst prof art hist, The Johns Hopkins Univ, Baltimore, 72-77. *Mem:* The Turner Soc. *Res:* 19th and 20th century European and American art. *Publ:* Reading Rauschenberg, 77, Blossoms and Blunders: Monet and the State, 79, Bill deKooning and Joe Christmas, 80, What's Wrong with this Picture, 81 & Manet Revised: Whodunnit, 83, Art Am. *Mailing Add:* 9 East Broadway New York NY 10038

STUHL, MICHELLE
SCULPTOR, ENVIRONMENTAL ARTIST
b Toledo, Ohio. *Study:* Univ Wis-Madison, BS, 78; RI Sch Design, MFA, 82. *Work:* Corning Glass Ctr, NY. *Exhib:* New Glass Traveling Exhib, Corning Glass Ctr, Metrop Mus Art, New York, Smithsonian Inst, De Young Mem Mus, Victoria & Albert Mus, and others, 79; Mass Col Art, Boston, 80; List Art Ctr, Brown Univ, 81; Mus Fine Art, Providence, 82; Sculpture Invitational, Barrington Col, RI, 82. *Mailing Add:* Old Route 28 Mt Tremper NY 12457

STULER, JACK
PHOTOGRAPHER, EDUCATOR
b Homestead, Pa, Aug 30, 32. *Study:* Phoenix Col, 57; Ariz State Univ, BA, 60, with Van Deren Coke, MFA, 63; workshop with Ansel Adams, 66. *Work:* George Eastman House, Rochester, NY; Gen Aniline Films, New York; Univ Collections, Ariz State Univ, Tempe; Yuma Art Ctr, Ariz; Phoenix Col. *Exhib:* George Eastman House, 63; Photog In Twentieth Century, Nat Gallery Can, 67; Am Photog: The Sixties, Sheldon Mem Art Gallery, Univ Nebr, Lincoln, 66; Photog USA, DeCordova Mus, Lincoln, Mass, 68; Celebrations, Hayden Gallery, Mass Inst Technol, 74; Ariz Arts Showcase, John F Kennedy Ctr for the Performing Arts, Washington, DC, 74; First Light, Focus Gallery, San Francisco, Calif, 75; one-man show, Univ of Ore, Eugene, 76. *Teaching:* Asst prof photog art, Ariz State Univ, 66-72, assoc prof, 73-75, prof, 75-, currently. *Awards:* First Award Biennial Photog, Phoenix Art Mus, 67; Southwestern Art Best of Show, Yuma Fine Arts Asn, 68; Summer Fel, Ariz State Univ, 68. *Bibliog:* Nathan Lyons (auth), The younger generation, Art Am, 12/63. *Mem:* Soc Photog Educ; Inst Cult Exchange Through Photog (mem adv bd, 66-). *Publ:* Contribr, Photography in the Twentieth Century, Horizon, 67; contribr, Photog Ann, 69; contribr, Being without clothes, Aperture, 15:3, 70; contribr, Camera, Lucerne, Switz, 11/71. *Mailing Add:* 400 West Baseline Rd Sp 52 Tempe AZ 85283

STULL, JEAN HIMROD
PAINTER, INSTRUCTOR
b Waterford, Pa, Jan 30, 29. *Study:* Edinboro State Col, BS(art educ); Pa State Univ. *Work:* Mus Fine Arts, Springfield, Mass; Frye Mus, Seattle; First Nat Bank of Pa, Erie; Edinboro Univ; Midwestern Intermediate Unit III Traveling Collection, Pa; and others. *Exhib:* Audubon Artists, New York, 66, 68 & 81; Watercolor USA, Springfield, Mo, 66-68 & 75; Pa Soc of Watercolor Painters Annual, 80 & 81; Pa Artists, Capitol Bldg, Harrisburg, 81-82; Invitational for Pa Govs Mansion, Harrisburg, 81-82; plus many others. *Teaching:* Teacher art, Bessemer Sch Dist, Pa, 49-51 & Ft LeBoeuf Sch Dist, Waterford, Pa, 56- *Awards:* Lena Newcastle Mem Award, Am Watercolor Soc, 66; Awards of Excellence, Mainstreams, Marietta Col, 70 & 74; Rocky Mountain Nat Watermedia Award, 75 & 81; Best of Show, Cincinnati Mus Nat Hist, 82; and others. *Bibliog:* Meyer (auth), Forty Watercolorists and How They Work, Watson-Guptill, 76. *Mem:* Am Watercolor Soc; Northwestern Pa Artists Asn. *Media:* Watercolor. *Publ:* Auth & illusr, untitled weekly column in Erie Dispatch, 56; contribr & illusr, The Sandpiper, 56-64; auth & illusr, untitled weekly column in Erie Times-News, 57 & 58; auth & illusr, Finding Birds on Presque Isle, 65; auth, The Watercolor Page, Am Artist, 1/75. *Mailing Add:* 661 Benson Rd Waterford PA 16441

STULL, ROBERT J
SCULPTOR, ADMINISTRATOR
b Springfield, Ohio, Nov 4, 35. *Study:* Ohio State Univ, BS, 62, MA, 63; NY Univ Japanese Language Sch, 64-65; Fulbright Res Scholar Ceramics, Japan, 65-67. *Work:* Smithsonian Inst; Cent State Univ, Ohio; Kyoto Col Fine Arts, Japan. *Comn:* Ceramic sculpture, First Nat Bank, Chicago, 69; Martin Luther King Libr, Columbus, Ohio, 72, SAI Archit & Assoc, Boston, 73 & Gallery Seven, Detroit, Mich, 77; mural painting, St John's Parrish Ctr, Columbus, Ohio, 75. *Exhib:* Brooklyn Mus, 66; Everson Mus, Syracuse, NY, 68; Mus Contemp Crafts, New York, 70; Detroit Inst Art, 71; Mus Art Mod, Paris, 72; Eastern Mich Univ, Ypsilanti, 72-80; L'Domo et L'Arte, Milan, Italy, 73. *Pos:* Founder & gen partner, JDS Assoc, Columbus, 74- *Teaching:* Assoc prof ceramics, Univ Mich, 68-72; prof ceramics & visual commun, Ohio State Univ, 72-, chmn art dept, 75-79, assoc dean, Col Arts, 79- *Awards:* Outstanding Achievement Award, African Studies Ctr, Univ Mich, 75; Elizabeth Catlett Moro Award & Virginia Kiah Award, Nat Conf Artists, 78. *Bibliog:* Cover, Ceramics Mo Mag, 65; Four Artists, Ind Univ Press, 69; Lee Nordness (auth), Objects USA, Viking Press, 70. *Mem:* Col Art Asn; Nat

Conf Artists (bd dirs, 76-, chmn, 78); Kuumba Theatre, Chicago. *Media:* Ceramic, Acrylic. *Collection:* African art; Japanese, Chinese and Korean ceramics. *Publ:* Producer & dir, TV tapes, Nat Guard Bur, Washington, DC, 77. *Dealer:* Gallery Seven/Charles McGee Gallery Fisher Bldg Detroit MI. *Mailing Add:* 2287 Brookwood Rd Columbus OH 43209

STUMP, JEANNE
EDUCATOR, HISTORIAN
b Indianapolis, Ind, Sept 30, 22. *Study:* Univ Ill, BA, 47; Univ Kans, MA, 66, PhD, 72. *Collections Arranged:* Les Mardis-Stephane Mallarme and the Artists of His Circle (auth, catalog), 65; Women Artists 77 (ed & contribr, catalog), 77; Ritual and Reality: Prints of the Nabis (auth, catalog), 79. *Pos:* Ed, The Register, Univ Kans Mus Art, 66-68. *Teaching:* Assoc prof, Univ Kans, 72-, chmn, Art Hist Dept, 78- *Awards:* Kans Univ Distinguished Teaching Award, Standard Oil Ind Found, 69; Mortar Board Teaching Award, Univ Kans, 76. *Mem:* Col Art Asn Am; Midwest Art Hist Soc (bd mem, 79-82). *Res:* Nineteenth century art; French symbolist art; women artists. *Publ:* Contribr, Varieties of Symbolism, 65 & Maillolin the 1890's, The Register, 71, Univ Kans Mus Art; auth, Maillol in the 1890's, The Register, Mus Art Univ Kans, 71. *Mailing Add:* Dept Art Hist Univ Kans Lawrence KS 66044

STURGEON, JOHN FLOYD
VIDEO ARTIST, SCULPTOR
b Springfield, Ill, Jan 6, 46. *Study:* Yale Univ, Yale-Norfolk fel, 67; Univ Ill, BFA, 68; Cornell Univ, MFA, 70. *Work:* Mus Mod Art, New York; Los Angeles Co Mus Art; Long Beach Mus Art; Kunstmuseum, Bonn, WGer; Biennale Venice, Italy; and others. *Comn:* Video/performance, Conf Univ Iowa, 82; No Earth/No Earth Station (video/performance), Los Angeles Mus Art, 83. *Exhib:* Long Beach Mus Art, 75 & 76; Whitney Mus Am Art, 75; San Francisco Mod Art, 76; one-man shows, Mus Mod Art, New York, 78, Los Angeles Inst Contemp Art, 78 & Inst Contemp Art, Boston, 83; Mus Mod Art, New York, 79, 80, 82 & 83; Los Angeles Co Mus Art, 83; and others. *Pos:* Video artist, Los Angeles Inst Contemp Art, 78-79; vis artist, Sch Art Inst Chicago, 80. *Teaching:* Instr, Univ Calif, Los Angeles, 79-80; vis artist fac, Claremont Grad Sch, Calif, 80, Art Inst Chicago, 80, 82 & 83; asst prof, Rensselaer Polytechnic Inst, 83- *Awards:* Individual Artists Fels, Nat Endowment Arts, 75, 77 & 80; Guggenheim Found Fel, 81; Western States Regional Media Arts Fel, Nat Educ Arts, 82; and others. *Bibliog:* Louise Lewis (auth), Art as alchemy, Artwwek, 7/28/79; Barbara London (auth), Independent Video: The first fifteen years, Artforum, 9/80; Michael Nash (auth), Present tense rights of passage, Art-Com, fall 83; Louise Lewis (auth), Art as Alchemy, Art Wk, Vol 10, No 25, 7/28/79; Barbara London (auth), Independent video: The first 15 years, Artforum, 9/80. *Publ:* Contribr, Video Art, Harcourt Brace Jovanovich, 76; contribr, Two Video Installations, Long Beach Mus Art, 78; auth, Spinning dream, Dreamworks, fall 80; auth, US Film & Video Festival (catalog), 83; auth, Polulism--Report from the Field, Art-Com, spring 83; and others. *Dealer:* L A Louver Gallery 55 North Venice Blvd Venice CA 90291. *Mailing Add:* Arts Dept Rensselaer Polytechnic Inst Troy NY 12181

STURGEON, MARY C
HISTORIAN
b Los Angeles, Calif, Dec 6, 43. *Study:* Univ Minn, BA(summa cum laude), 65; Bryn Mawr Col, MA, 68, PhD(classical archaeol & Greek), 71; Am Sch Class Studies in Athens, 68-70 & 70-71. *Teaching:* Asst prof Greek & Roman Art, Oberlin Col, 72-77; assoc prof Greek art, Univ NC, Chapel Hill, 77- *Mem:* Archaeol Inst Am; Col Art Asn; Am Sch Classical Studies in Athens. *Res:* Greek sculpture. *Publ:* Auth, A new group of sculptures from ancient Cornith, Hesperia, 75; auth, A Hellenistic lion-bull group in Oberlin, 75 & A bronze statuette of Hercules, 76, Allen Mem Art Mus Bulletin; auth, The reliefs of the Theatre of Dionysus in Athens, Am J Archaeol, 77; auth, Corinth IX 2: Sculpture, The reliefs from the theater, Princeton-Am Sch, 77. *Mailing Add:* Dept of Art Ackland 003A Univ of NC Chapel Hill NC 27514

STURGES, HOLLISTER
CURATOR, HISTORIAN
b Kingston, NY. *Study:* Cornell Univ, BA, 62; Univ Calif, Berkeley, MA, 69. *Pos:* Dir, Univ Mo Art Gallery, Kansas City, 76-78; cur European art, Joslyn Art Mus, 80- *Teaching:* Instr, Univ Mo, Kansas City, 72-80; lectr, Univ Nebr, Lincoln, 83. *Mem:* Col Art Asn. *Res:* 18th and 19th century French printing with emphasis on social themes; contemporary American. *Publ:* Auth, Christo's aesthetics of manipulation; Kansas City's wrapped walkways, New Art Examiner, 78; auth, Chicago abstractionists: Romanticized structures, Univ Mo, Kansas City, 78; auth, Angels and urchins: Images of children at the Joslyn, 80, I-80 series: Mario Merz, 81 & Jules Breton and the French Rural Tradition, 82, Joslyn Art Mus. *Mailing Add:* Joslyn Art Mus 2200 Dodge St Omaha NE 68102

STURMAN, EUGENE
PAINTER, SCULPTOR
b New York, NY, Jan 28, 45. *Study:* Alfred Univ, BA, 67; Univ NMex, MA, 69; Tamarind Lithograph Workshop, 70. *Work:* Metro Media Studios, Hollywood, Calif; Warner Bros Records, Universal City, Calif; Los Angeles Co Mus; Newport Harbor Mus. *Exhib:* LA Six 74, Los Angeles Co Mus, 74; 24 from Los Angeles, Barnsdall Munic Gallery, Los Angeles, 74; Basle Art Fair, Switz, 74 & 75; Whitney Mus Am Art Biennial, 75; Chicago Art Fair, 82; Los Angeles Co Mus, 83. *Teaching:* Instr printmaking, Long Beach State Univ, 72-74; lectr printmaking, painting & drawing, Univ Calif, Los Angeles, 74- *Awards:* Michael Levins Award, Alfred Univ, 66; New Talent Award, Los Angeles Co Mus, 74; Nat Endowment Arts Grant, 75. *Media:* Copper, Lead,. *Dealer:* Koplin Gallery 8225 1/2 Santa Monica Blvd Los Angeles Ca 90046. *Mailing Add:* 1108 W Washington Blvd Venice CA 90291

STUSSY, JAN
PAINTER, EDUCATOR
b Benton Co, Mo, Aug 13, 21. *Study:* Univ Calif, Los Angeles, AB, 44; Univ Southern Calif, MFA, 53; also with Stanton MacDonald-Wright, 44-72. *Work:* San Francisco Mus Art; Los Angeles Mus Art; Mus Mod Art, New York; Santa Barbara Mus Art; Fine Arts Gallery, Univ NMex. *Comn:* Painting on Masonite, Container Corp Am, New York, 66; painting, Automatic Retailers Am, Los Angeles, 66; silk screen, Metromedia, Los Angeles, 67. *Exhib:* Galeria Schneider, Rome, Italy, 59; The Human Figure, Mus Mod Art, 62; Ann Nat Exhib, Krannert Art Mus, Ill, 65; Int Exchange Exhib, Munic Gallery, Oslo, Norway, 74. *Teaching:* Prof art, Univ Calif, Los Angeles, 46- *Awards:* Critics Award for Best One-Man Show of Year, Newspaper Critics, Santiago, Chile, 68; Univ Calif, Los Angeles Fine Arts Coun Award, 70. *Bibliog:* A house stamped with its owner talents, Living for Young Homemakers, 6/54; Mayo Mohs (auth), Man in a box, Time, 10/6/67; Leslie Wenger (auth), Man is a devout acrobat, Currant, 4-5/75. *Mem:* Los Angeles Printmakers Soc; Westwood Inst Arts. *Media:* Oil, Acrylic. *Publ:* Auth, Equipment for landscape painting, 51 & Will you be on our jury?, 52, Am Artist. *Mailing Add:* 12444 Rochedale Lane Los Angeles CA 90049

STUSSY, MAXINE KIM
SCULPTOR
b Los Angeles, Calif, Nov 11, 23. *Study:* Univ Southern Calif, art scholar, 43; Univ Calif, Los Angeles, AB, 47; also res & pvt study in Rome, Eng, Ger, 59 & 63. *Comn:* Bob Hope Award Trophy, Bob Hope Athletic Award Comn, 60; Bob Hope New Talent Award, Universal Studios, 61; Wall Sculptures in Wood, Neuropsychiatric Hosp Lobby, Univ Calif, Los Angeles, 68; Wood Sculpture, St Martin of Tours Church, Brentwood, 72. *Exhib:* Los Angeles Co Mus, Los Angeles, 54, 58, 59, 61; Galleria Schneider, Rome, Italy, 59; Denver Art Mus, 60; 25 Calif Women of Art, Lytton Ctr of Visual Arts, Los Angeles, 68; Bednarz Gallery, Los Angeles, 76; Zara Gallery, San Francisco, 77; and others. *Awards:* First Prize, Sculpture, Bronze, Los Angeles Co Art Mus, 61. *Bibliog:* Bea Miller (auth), The anatomy of an artist, Home Mag, Los Angeles Times, 70; Beverly Edna Johnson (auth), Sculptures evolved from wood, Home Mag, Los Angeles Times, 75; Kathleen Reinoehl (auth), The many faces of Maxine Kim Stussy, Am Artist Mag, 7/75. *Media:* Multimedia. *Dealer:* Pavilion Gallery 7150 Main St Scottsdale AZ; Zara Gallery San Francisco CA. *Mailing Add:* 12444 Rochedale Lane W Los Angeles CA 90049

SUBA, SUSANNE
PAINTER, ILLUSTRATOR
b Budapest, Hungary. *Study:* Pratt Inst, grad. *Work:* Metrop Mus Art, New York; Brooklyn Mus, NY; Art Inst Chicago; Mus City of New York; Kalamazoo Inst Art, Mich. *Exhib:* Ansdell Gallery, London, Eng; Hammer Gallery, New York; Kalamazoo Inst Art; Art Inst Chicago; Mus Mod Art, New York. *Awards:* Awards, Am Inst Graphic Art, Art Dirs Club New York & Art Dirs Club Chicago. *Mailing Add:* 470 West 24th St New York NY 10011

SUBLETT, CARL C
PAINTER
b Johnson Co, Ky, Feb 4, 19. *Study:* Western Ky Univ; Univ Study Ctr, Florence, Italy; Univ Tenn. *Work:* Nat Acad Design, New York; Hunter Gallery Art, Chattanooga, Tenn; Mint Mus, Charlotte, NC; Stephens Col, Springfield, Mo; Tenn Arts Comn, Nashville, Tenn. *Exhib:* Southeastern Art Ann, Atlanta, Ga; Paintings of Yr, Atlanta; New Painters of South, Birmingham, Ala; Watercolor USA, Springfield, Mo, 64-72; Am Watercolor Soc, New York, 72. *Teaching:* Former prof art, Univ Tenn, retired. *Awards:* Rudolph Lesch Award, Am Watercolor Soc, 72; Purchase Award, Am Collection, Hunter Gallery Art, 72; Purchase Award, Collection Tenn Art League & Parthenon, Nashville, 72. *Mem:* Nat Acad Design; Knoxville Watercolor Soc; Tenn Watercolor Soc; Port Clyde Arts & Crafts Soc, Maine. *Media:* Watercolor, Oil. *Dealer:* Collectors Gallery Nashville TN. *Mailing Add:* 2104 Lake Ave Knoxville TN 37916

SUDLOW, ROBERT N
PAINTER
b Holton, Kans, Feb 25, 20. *Study:* Univ Kans, BFA; Univ Calif, Berkeley; Calif Col Arts & Crafts, Oakland, MFA; Acad Grande Chaumiere, Paris; Acad Andre L'Hote, Paris. *Work:* City Art Mus, St Louis, Mo; Yellow Freight Collection, Kansas City, Mo; Joslyn Art Mus, Omaha; Sheldon Art Mus, Lincoln, Nebr; Menninger Found, Topeka, Kans. *Exhib:* Summer Invitational, Nelson Art Mus, 78-79 & 83; Wichita Art Mus, 79; one-man show, Beauchamp Gallery, Topeka, 83. *Teaching:* Prof art, Univ Kans, 47- *Awards:* Gov Artist, 76. *Media:* Oil, Watercolor. *Dealer:* Am Legacy Gallery 5911 Maine Kansas City MO 66103; Pickard Gallery Oklahoma City OK 73118. *Mailing Add:* Dept Art Univ Kans Lawrence KS 66045

SUGARMAN, GEORGE
SCULPTOR, PAINTER
b New York, NY, May 11, 12. *Study:* City Col New York, BA; Atelier Zadkine, Paris, 51. *Work:* Walker Art Ctr, Minneapolis; Kunstmuseum, Zurich, Switz; Mus Mod Art, New York; Whitney Mus Am Art, New York; Chicago Art Inst. *Comn:* Metal sculptures, First Nat Bank, St Paul, Minn, 71; Fed Courthouse, Baltimore, 75-77; Miami Int Airport, Fla, 77 & Detroit Gen Hosp, 80 & Wills Eye Hospital, Philadelphia, Pa, 81. *Exhib:* Whitney Mus Am Art Sculpture Ann, 60-; Carnegie Inst Int, Pittsburgh, 61; Sao Paulo Biennal, Brazil, 63; Sculpture of the Sixties, Los Angeles Co Mus Art, 67; Int Pavilion, Venice Biennal, 69; Retrospective, Stedelijk Mus, Amsterdam, Holland, 69-70; 200 Yrs Am Sculpture, Whitney Mus Am Art, New York, 76;

Retrospective, Joslyn Art Mus, Omaha, Nebr, 81; and others. *Teaching:* Assoc prof sculpture, Hunter Col, 60-70; vis prof sculpture, Grad Sch Art & Archit, Yale Univ, 67-68. *Awards:* Second Prize for Sculpture, Pittsburgh Int, 61-62; Longview Found Grants, 61-63; Nat Art Coun Award, 66. *Bibliog:* I Sandler (auth), Sugarman-Sculptural Complex, First Nat Bank St Paul, 71; Sam Hunter (auth), American Art of the 20th Century, 72; Holliday T Day (auth), The Shape of Space: The Sculpture of George Sugarman, 81; and others. *Media:* Metal, Acrylic. *Dealer:* Robert Miller 724 Madison Ave New York NY 10021. *Mailing Add:* 21 Bond St New York NY 10012

SUGIMOTO, HENRY Y
PAINTER
US citizen. *Study:* Calif Col Arts & Crafts, BFA; Calif Sch Fine Arts; Acad Colarossi, Paris. *Work:* Wakayama City Mus, Japan; Calif Palace Legion of Honor, San Francisco; Tokyo Nat Art Mus, Japan; Wakayama Mod Art Mus, Japan; Hiroshima Peace Mem Hall, Japan. *Comn:* NY Japanese Consulate General's Residence, 73; murals, Lobby, Wakayama City Hall, Japan, 77; mural, Japanese American United Church. *Exhib:* Rine Art Exhib, San Francisco World Expos, 39; US Exhib, Mod World Exhib, Tokyo, Japan, 50; Salon Artistes Francais, Paris, 63; Doc Painting Traveling Exhibs, 72 & 80; one-man exhib, Interchurch Ctr Gallery, 78; one-man shows, Documentary paintings, Tokyo, Osaka, Wakayama & Hiroshima, Japan. *Pos:* Art consult, War Relocation Authority, 43-45. *Teaching:* Instr art, Denson High Sch, Ark, 43-44. *Awards:* Medal from Emperor of Japan, Sixth Order of Rising Sun, 82; Silver Medal, Japanese Govt, 82; Gold Medal, Wakayama City, Japan, 82. *Bibliog:* New America, Life & War Relocation Authority, 46; Fuji Television, Japan, 79; Iwanami Bunko Movie, Japan, 81. *Mem:* Washington Printmaker Soc; Nika-kai Art Asn, Tokyo. *Media:* Oil, Watercolor. *Res:* Documentary painting of the War Relocation Centers of Japanese during World War II. *Publ:* Illusr, Toshio and Tama, 49 & New Friends for Susan, 51; contribr, Beauty Behind Barbed Wire, 52, Nisei, 69 & Compilation of Documentary War Relocation Camp Scenes, World War II, 81. *Dealer:* Wiener Gallery 963 Madison Ave New York NY 10021. *Mailing Add:* 600 W 146th St New York NY 10031

SUJO, CLARA DIAMENT
GALLERY DIRECTOR, DEALER
b Argentina. *Pos:* Mem bd dirs, Mus Bellas Artes Caracas, 58-63; dir, Estudio Actual, Caracas, 68- & CDS Gallery, New York, 81- *Teaching:* Prof art hist & fine Arts, Cristobal Rojas Sch Fine Arts, Caracas, 58-65; teacher, Neumann Found Inst Design, 67-70. *Mem:* Int Asn Art Critics; Art Table Inc. *Specialty:* International contemporary art. *Publ:* Auth, Art in Latin America Today, Panamerican Union, 62; coauth, Joseph Albers, Kellar Velag, 67; contribr, The Emergent Decade, Cornell Univ, 65. *Mailing Add:* 13 E 75 St New York NY 10021

SULLINS, ROBERT M
PAINTER
b Los Angeles, Calif, Aug 31, 26. *Study:* Univ Ill, 47-48; Univ Wyo, BA(art), 50, MA(art), 58; Inst Allende, San Miguel, Mex, MFA, 66. *Work:* Norfolk Mus Arts & Sci, Va; Northern Ill Univ, DeKalb; Civic Ctr, Scottsdale, Ariz; Inst Int Educ, New York. *Comn:* Crucifixion (mural), St Joseph's Cath Church, Rawlins, Wyo, 61; Upstatescape (painting), State Univ NY, Col Oswego, 66; mural, The Flame Room, Rawlins, 67; Kinetic machine, Mirrors, Motors & Motion Show, Rochester Mus, NY, 70. *Exhib:* One-man shows, Rutgers Univ, 77, Univ Rochester, 78; and others; Childe Hassam Exhib, Am Acad Arts & Lett, 69; Kinetic Art Show, Albright-Knox Art Gallery, Buffalo, NY, 70; Am Drawing Biennial, XXIV, Norfolk Mus Arts & Sci, 71; Xerox Show, Rochester, NY. *Pos:* Supvr art, Pub Schs Rawlins, Wyo, 55-59. *Teaching:* Prof art, State Univ NY, Col Oswego, 60- *Awards:* Fulbright Fel, 59-60; Robert Ahl Mem Grant, 60; State NY Res Fel, 71. *Media:* Acrylics, All Media. *Dealer:* Abe-Rothstein-Horizon Galleries 10345 W Olympic Blvd Los Angeles CA 90064 & 43 Glendale Rd Newton Ctr MA 02159; Village Art Gallery, Hannibal, NY. *Mailing Add:* 51 W Eighth St Oswego NY 13126

SULLIVAN, BILL
PAINTER, PRINTMAKER
b New Haven, Conn, Sept 10, 42. *Study:* Silvermine Col Art, 60-65; Univ Pa Grad Sch Fine Arts, MFA, 68. *Work:* Cleveland Mus Art, Ohio; Mus de Arte Mod, Bogota, Colombia; Reading Mus, Pa; Mus de Bellas Artes, Maracaibo, Venezuela; Chase Manhattan Bank, New York. *Exhib:* Salon des Independents, Grand Palais, France, 80; solo exhibs, Siegal Contemp Art, New York, 81 & David Findlay Jr Gallery, New York, 84; Painted Light, Artists Choice Mus Traveling Exhib, 83; New Vistas: Contemporary American Landscapes, Hudson River Mus, Yonkers, NY, 84. *Collections Arranged:* Painterly Realism, Am Fedn Arts Traveling Exhib (auth, catalog), 70. *Awards:* Premio Quirama, Inst de Integracion Cult, Medelin, Colombia, 79; Ingram Merrill Found Fel, 81. *Bibliog:* William Zimmer (auth), article, Soho News, 5/28/80; Gerrit Henry (auth), Painterly realism and the modern landscape, Art in Am, 9/81; Ruth Bass (auth), article, Art News, 2/82. *Media:* Oil on Canvas. *Dealer:* David Findlay Jr 41 E 57th St New York NY 10022; Orion Editions 835 Madison Ave New York NY 10021. *Mailing Add:* 687 Eighth Ave New York NY 10036

SULLIVAN, DAVID FRANCIS
PAINTER, PRINTMAKER
b Stoughton, Mass, Apr 13, 41. *Study:* Univ NH, 57-61; Chouinard Sch Fine Arts, Los Angeles, Calif; Boston Mus Fine Arts Sch. *Work:* Addison Gallery Am Art, Andover, Mass; Philadelphia Mus Art, Pa; Cleveland Mus, Ohio; Minn Mus Art, St Paul. *Exhib:* Twenty-fifth Nat Exhib Prints, Smithsonian Inst, 77; Art in Transition, Mus Fine Arts, Boston, 77; Nat Print Exhib,

Trenton State Col, NJ, 78; Art of the State, Hayden Gallery, Mass Inst Technol, Cambridge, 78; Printmaking Biennial, Brooklyn Mus, NY, 78; Recent Trends in Am Printmaking, Mitchell Mus, 79; New Am Still Life, Westmoreland Co Mus Art, Greensburg, Pa, 79. *Awards:* Purchase Awards, De Cordova Mus, 76 & Trenton State Col, 78; Stuart M Egnal Prize, Philadelphia Mus Art, 77. *Media:* Oils; Prints, Silkscreens. *Mailing Add:* 94 N Main St Andover MA 01810

SULLIVAN, JIM
PAINTER
b Providence, RI, Apr 1, 39. *Study:* RI Sch Design, Providence, Fulbright scholar & BFA, 61; Stanford Univ, 62-63. *Work:* Whitney Mus Am Art, New York; Worcester Art Mus, Mass; Albany State Mus; Wadsworth Atheneum, Hartford, Conn. *Exhib:* Whitney Mus Am Art Ann, 67, 69 & 72; Lyrical Abstraction, Larry Aldrich Mus, Conn & Whitney Mus Am Art, 70-71; Small Works Group Show, Mus Mod Art, New York, 71; Ind Mus Art, Indianapolis, 72; McNay Mus, San Antonio, Tex, 81; American Still Life 1945-1983, Contemp Arts Mus, Houston, 83; New York Painting Today, Three Rivers Festival, Pittsburgh, 83; Folker Skulima Gallery, Berlin, 83; Dart Gallery, Chicago, 84. *Teaching:* Prof painting, Bard Col, 65- *Awards:* Guggenheim Found Grant, 72; Nat Endowment Arts Grant, 83. *Bibliog:* Kay Larson (auth), article, New York Mag, 1/19/81; Vivian Raynor (auth), article, New York Times, 1/9/81; Judith Wilson (auth), article, Village Voice, 1/14/81; and others. *Dealer:* Nancy Hoffman 429 W Broadway New York NY 10012. *Mailing Add:* 59 Wooster St New York NY 10013

SULLIVAN, MAX WILLIAM
MUSEUM DIRECTOR
b Fremont, Mich, Sept 27, 09. *Study:* Western Mich Univ, AB, 32; Harvard Univ, AM, 41; Providence Col, LLD, 50. *Pos:* Dir Exhib New Eng handicrafts, Worcester Mus Art, 42-43; consult, Metrop Mus Art, 43-44; dean sch, RI Sch Design, 45-47, pres corp, 47-55; dir, Portland Art Mus, Portland Art Asn & Mus Art Sch, 56-60, secy bd trustees, 56-60; dir, Everson Mus Art, Syracuse, NY, 61-71; prog dir, Kimbell Art Mus, Ft Worth, Tex, 71-74, dir admin serv, 74-76; dir, Univ Art Gallery, Univ of Tex at Arlington, 76- *Teaching:* Instr, Cranbrook Sch, 33-35; instr arts & crafts, Middlesex Sch, Concord, Mass, 35-38; head art dept, Groton Sch, Mass, 38-42; consult art educ, Harvard Sch Educ, 40-42; dir educ, RI Sch Design, 44-45. *Mem:* Am Inst Architects. *Res:* Contemporary architecture and contemporary sculpture; classical studies, especially Magna Graecia, Central Italy & Renaissance. *Publ:* Auth & ed, Contemporary New England Handicrafts, Worcester Art Mus, Mass, 43; contrib & ed, Calligraphy: The Golden Age & Its Modern Revival, Portland Art Mus, 58; contribr, Everson Dedication Portfolio, 69 & American Ship Portraits & Marine Painting, 70, Everson Mus; contribr, Catalogue of the Collection, Kimbell Art Mus, 72. *Mailing Add:* PO Box 19089 Univ Tex Art Gallery Arlington TX 76019

SULLIVAN, RONALD DEE
SCULPTOR, EDUCATOR
b Norman, Okla, Feb 6, 39. *Study:* Univ Okla, BFA, 63; Calif State Univ, Sacramento, MA, 69; ETex State Univ, postgrad. *Comn:* Wall mounted sculpture, Calif State Univ, Sacramento, 62; archit steel sculpture, comn by Kenneth Owen, Corpus Christi, Tex, 76; sculptured trophies, World Championship Quarterton Sailboat Races, Corpus Christi, 76; wall mounted sculpture, comn by Dr T P O'Brien, Medical Plaza Bldg, Corpus Christi, 77; three drawings, Corpus Christi Nat Bank, Tex, 83. *Exhib:* Art Mus STex, Corpus Christi, 76; one-man shows, Temple Univ, Philadelphia, 72 & ETex State Univ, Commerce, 78; Nat Exhib, Oscar Howe Cult Ctr, Mitchell, SDak, 75; Celebration of Texas Sculpture, Sam Houston State Sculpture Ctr, Huntsville, 82. *Pos:* Mem bd dirs, Tex Asn Sch Art, 80-83. *Teaching:* Prof drawing, design & sculpture, Del Mar Col, Corpus Christi, 70- *Awards:* First Prize Art Found Award, Art Mus STex, 71; Second Prize, Univ SDak, 75. *Bibliog:* Linda Lewis (auth), Artlook, SW Art, 10/74; Mystery & Magic of Glass, KEDTV Channel 16, Corpus Christi, 75; Joseph A Cain (auth), Profiling the artists and their works, Art Voices S, 3/80. *Media:* Mixed. *Mailing Add:* 2845 Topeka Corpus Christi TX 78404

SULLIVAN, RUTH WILKINS
HISTORIAN, CURATOR
b Boston, Mass, Nov 20, 26. *Study:* Wellesley Col, AB. *Collections Arranged:* Chinese Export Porcelain, 65; American Painting from 1830 (with catalog), 65; Chinese Art from the Cloud Wampler Collection (with catalog), 68; American Ship Portraits & Marine Painting (with catalog), 70. *Pos:* Admin asst, Everson Mus Art, 58-60, registr, 60-62, ed publ, 63-70, cur collections, 66-70; consult, Mus Am China Trade, 71; cur educ, Kimbell Art Mus, 71-82, res cur, 83- *Awards:* Woman Achievement Arts, Post Stand, 68. *Mem:* Col Art Asn Am; Archaeol Inst of Am. *Res:* Chinese gold and silver from the T'ang Dynasty; Chinese export silver for the Anglo-American market; Duccio's Maesta; iconographic studies. *Collection:* American silver of the Colonial period. *Publ:* Contribr, Kimbell Collection Catalogue, 72; coauth, Chinese Export Silver: 1785-1885, 75; auth, The Art Museum as Educator, 78; auth, Kimbell Handbook, 81; and others. *Mailing Add:* 4500 Westridge Ave Unit 1 Ft Worth TX 76116

SULTAN, ALTOON
PAINTER
b Brooklyn, NY, Sept 29, 48. *Study:* Brooklyn Col, BA, 69, MFA, 71, study with Phillip Pearlstein; Boston Univ at Tanglewood, 69; Skowhegan Sch Painting & Sculpture, study with Gabriel Laderman, 70. *Work:* NJ State Mus, Trenton; Boston Mus Fine Arts, Mass; Madison Fine Arts Ctr, Wis; Princeton Univ Libr; Hunter Mus, Chattanooga, Tenn. *Exhib:* Artists Salute

Skowhegan, Kennedy Gallery, New York, 77; one-woman shows, Marlborough Gallery, 77, 79 & 81; New York Showcase, Oklahoma Art Ctr, 81; Collectors Gallery, Columbus Mus Art, 81; A Private Vision: Contemporary Art from the Graham Gund Collection, Boston Mus Fine Arts, Mass, 82; Lower Manhattan from Street to Sky, Whitney Mus Am Art, 82; Small Pictures, New Britain Mus Am Art, 82; Painted Light, Reading Pub Mus, Butler Inst Am Art, 83; and others. *Awards:* MacDowell Colony Fel, 72 & 74; Yaddo Fel, 75 & 76; Nat Endowment Arts Fel Grant, 83. *Bibliog:* Carolyn B Aron (auth), Porches, NJ Monthly, 6/80; June Cutler (auth), article, Am Artist, 5/83. *Media:* Oil; Drypoint. *Dealer:* Marlborough Gallery 40 W 57th St New York NY 10019. *Mailing Add:* 131 Allen St New York NY 10002

SULTAN, DONALD K
PAINTER, PRINTMAKER
b Asheville, NC, May 5, 51. *Study:* Univ NC, Chapel Hill, BFA, 73; Art Inst Chicago, MFA, 75. *Work:* High Mus Art; Dallas Mus Fine Arts; Albright-Knox Art Gallery; Mus Mod Art, New York; La Jolla Mus, Calif. *Exhib:* Solo exhib, Hans Strelow Gallery, Düsseldorf, WGer, 82, Blum-Helman Gallery, New York, 82 & Akira Ikeda Gallery, Japan, 83; Prints from Blocks--Gaugin to Now, Mus Mod Art, New York, 83; Boston Mus Fine Arts, 83; Tendencias en Nueva York, Palacio Vela'zquez, Madrid, Spain, 83. *Awards:* Creative Artists Pub Serv Grant, 78-79; Nat Endowment Arts Grant, 80. *Bibliog:* John Russell (auth), article, New York Times, 4/30/82; Kay Larson (auth), Urban renewal, New York Mag, 5/3/82. *Dealer:* Blum-Helman Gallery 20 W 57th St New York NY 10019. *Mailing Add:* 54 N Moore St New York NY 10013

SULTAN, LARRY A
PHOTOGRAPHER
b July 13, 46. *Study:* Univ Calif, BA, 68; San Francisco Art Inst, MFA, 73. *Work:* Mus Mod Art, New York; Ctr Creative Photog, Univ Ariz; Fogg Art Mus; Univ Alaska, Fairbanks; Bibliot Nat, Paris. *Comn:* Plexiglas map, Atlantic Richfield Co, Los Angeles, 79. *Exhib:* Contemporary Photographs, Fogg Art Mus, 76; Evidence, San Francisco Mus Mod Art, 77 & Chicago Mus Contemp Art, 79; Beyond Color, San Francisco Mus Mod Art, 80; Attitudes: Photography in 1970s, Santa Barbara Mus Art, 80; Photographs From the Museum of Modern Art, Seibu Art Mus, Tokyo, 82; Color as Form, Corcoran Gallery, 82; Newsroom, Univ Art Mus, Berkeley, 83. *Teaching:* Instr photog, Univ Calif, Berkeley, 73-78 & San Francisco Art Inst, 78-; asst prof art, Lone Mountain Col, 74-78. *Awards:* Grant, 76 & fel, 80, Nat Endowment Arts; Guggenheim Found Fel, 83. *Bibliog:* Ben Lifson (auth), Modern dreams, Village Voice, 9/77; Douglas Davis (auth), Harvards challenging evidence, Newsweek, 6/8/78; Kathryn Livingston (auth), article, Am Photogr, 8/80. *Dealer:* Stephan Wirtz Gallery 345 Sutter St San Francisco CA 94108. *Mailing Add:* 119 Boardwalk Greenbrae CA 94904

SUMM, HELMUT
PAINTER, EDUCATOR
b Hamburg, Ger, Mar 10, 08; US citizen. *Study:* Univ Wis, grad, 30; Marquette Univ, MEd, 46; also with Umberto Romano, Carl Peters & Robert Von Neumann. *Work:* Milwaukee Art Ctr, Milwaukee J Gallery, Milwaukee; Milwaukee J Gallery Wis Art; Univ Wis-Green Bay Contemp Art Collection; Lakeland Col Collection Wis Art. *Comn:* Mural, St John's Lutheran Sch, Glendale, Wis, 56; mural, Home for Aged Lutherans, Milwaukee, 57. *Exhib:* Milwaukee Art Mus Friends of Art, 64-; Wis Watercolor Soc, 74; Retrospective Exhib, Fine Arts Galleries, Univ Wis, Milwaukee, 78; Artist in Full Maturity, Charles Allis Art Libr; Bergstrom Art Ctr, Neenah, Wis, 79. *Teaching:* Instr art, Milwaukee Pub Schs, 31-48; dir dept art, Univ Wis-Milwaukee Exten, 48-56, prof art & art educ, Univ Wis-Milwaukee & Exten, 56-78, emer prof, 78- *Awards:* Purchase Award for Oil, Beloit & Vicinity Exhib, 64; Watercolor Award, Wis Salon, 65; Purchase Award, Milwaukee Art Commission, Ozaukee Co Exhib, Wis Watercolor Soc. *Bibliog:* Don Key (auth), Review of Theodore's Gallery, 65 & Violet Dewey (auth), What's new in art, 67, Milwaukee J. *Mem:* Wis Watercolor Soc; Wis Painters & Sculptors (pres, 63); Delta Phi Delta. *Media:* Oil, Watercolor. *Publ:* Auth, University of Wisconsin Extension Art Programs, WTMJ. *Dealer:* Friends of Art Milwaukee Art Mus 750 N Lincoln Memorial Dr Milwaukee WI 53202. *Mailing Add:* 6183 N Lake Dr Milwaukee WI 53217

SUMMER, (EMILY) EUGENIA
PAINTER
b Newton, Miss, June 13, 23. *Study:* Miss Univ for Women, BS; Columbia Univ, MA; Art Inst Chicago; Calif Col Arts & Crafts; Penland Sch Crafts, NC; Seattle Univ. *Work:* Miss Mus Art, Jackson; First Nat Bank Collection, Jackson; Nat Bank Commerce Collection, Columbus, Miss; First Nat Bank, Laurel, Miss; First Miss Nat Bank, Hattiesburg. *Exhib:* Am Fedn Arts Circulating Exhib, 61-62; Art in Embassies Prog, US State Dept, Rio de Janeiro, Brazil, 66-67; Mid-South Exhibs, Brooks Mem Art Gallery, Memphis, Tenn; Eighth Decade: Painters Choice, Ga Col Milledgeville, 71; 5th Greater New Orleans Int Art Exhib, 75; Nat Asn Painters Acrylic & Casein, Nat Arts Club, New York, 80. *Teaching:* Prof art, Miss Univ Women, 50-, head div fine & performing arts, 82- *Awards:* Dumas Milner Purchase Award, Nat Watercolor Exhib, Jackson, 62, Jurors Award, 68; Purchase Prizes, Lauren Rogers Mus Exhib & Miss Southern Univ Exhib; Award of Merit, Miss Mus Art, 83. *Mem:* Col Art Asn Am; Miss Art Asn; Southeastern Col Art Asn; Kappa Pi. *Mailing Add:* 915 Fifth Ave S Columbus MS 39701

SUMMERFORD, BEN LONG
PAINTER, EDUCATOR
b Montgomery, Ala, Feb 3, 24. *Study:* Am Univ, BA & MA; Ecole Beaux-Arts, Paris; also with Karl Knaths & Jack Tworkov. *Work:* Corcoran Gallery

Art, Washington, DC; Phillips Gallery, Washington, DC; Fort Wayne Mus Art, Ind; Nat Collection Fine Arts, Washington, DC. *Exhib:* Fulbright Painters, Whitney Mus Am Art, 59; one-man shows, Jefferson Pl Gallery, Washington, DC, 64 & 67 & Franz Bader Gallery, 75 & 81; Phillips Collection Retrospective, 82. *Teaching:* Prof painting, Am Univ, 50-, chmn, Dept Art, 57- *Awards:* Fulbright Fel, France, 49-50. *Media:* Oil. *Mailing Add:* 10216 Brown's Mill Rd Vienna VA 22180

SUMMERS, CAROL
PRINTMAKER
b Kingston, NY, Dec 26, 25. *Study:* Bard Col, BA, 51, PhD, 75. *Work:* Corcoran Gallery Art, Libr Cong, Nat Gallery, Washington, DC; Metrop Mus Art, New York; Kunstmuseum, Malmö, Sweden. *Exhib:* One-person shows, Mus Mod Art, New York, 64-66, AAA Gallery, New York, 67 & Bard Col, 68; Retrospective, San Francisco Mus Art, Calif, 67; 20th Nat Print Exhib, Brooklyn Mus, 77; ADI Gallery, 77; plus others. *Teaching:* Instr, Brooklyn Mus Sch Art, 54, Pratt Graphic Art Ctr, 62, Hunter Col, 63, Sch Visual Arts, New York, 65, Pa State Univ, 68, Columbia Univ, New York, 69 & San Francisco Art Inst, 73; US Info Serv tour of India, 74 & 79. *Awards:* Ital Govt Grant, Italy, 55; Louis Comfort Tiffany Found Fels, 55 & 61; Guggenheim Found Fel, 59. *Mem:* Print Coun Am (artist adv bd); Print Club Philadelphia. *Media:* Wood. *Mailing Add:* 133 Prospect Ct Santa Cruz CA 95065

SUMMY, ANNE TUNIS
PAINTER, PRINTMAKER
b Baltimore, Md. *Study:* Pa Acad Fine Arts. *Work:* William Penn Mem Mus Contemp Collection, Harrisburg; Franklin & Marshall Col; Millersville State Col, Pa; Edison Community Col, Fla. *Exhib:* Butler Inst Am Art Midyear Show, Youngstown, Ohio, 68; Pa Acad Fine Arts Fel Shows, 69-70; Soc Four Arts, Palm Beach, 74 & 78; Md Biennial, Baltimore Mus Art, 74; Arvida, Sarasota, 79 & 82; Millersville State Col, Pa, 80; Major Fla Artists, Sarasota, 81, 82 & 83; one-man show, Bradley Gallery, Naples, 82. *Awards:* Newman Medal, Nat Soc Painters in Casein & Acrylic, 68; Hon Mention, 13th Maj Fla Artists, Harman Gallery, Naples, Fla, 76; Hamel Award, Fla Artists Group, Sarasota, 80. *Bibliog:* Article, Naples Now, 83. *Mem:* Fla Artists Group. *Media:* Acrylic; Engraving. *Dealer:* Foster Harmon Gallery Am Art 1415 Main St Sarasota FL 33577. *Mailing Add:* 2885 Gulf Shore Blvd N Naples FL 33940

SUNDBERG, CARL GUSTAVE
ENAMELIST, DIRECTOR
b Erie, Pa, June 23, 28. *Study:* Albright Art Sch, Univ Buffalo, grad; study with Joseph Plaucan, Virginia Cuthbert, Albert Blaustien, Letterio Calipia & Robert Bruce. *Work:* Butler Inst Am Art, Youngstown, Ohio; Tyler Mus Art, Tex; Erie Pub Mus; Erie Art Mus; Albright-Knox Rental Art Gallery. *Comn:* Six porcelain panels (mod motif with coins), Union Bank, Erie, 69; three porcelain enamel panels, Gannon Resource Ctr, Erie, 73; three enclosure set (Plexiglas-enamel), St Vincent Hosp, Erie, 74. *Exhib:* Midyear Shows, Butler Inst Am Art, Youngstown, 68 & 70-82; Washington & Jefferson Col Nat Exhib, 69, 72 & 74; Miss Nat Arts Festival, 70; Audubon Artists, New York, 71; two-man show, Thiel Col, Greenville, Pa, 77; Pa Woodwinds, traveling exhib, 81; and others. *Pos:* Art dir, Erie Ceramic Arts Co, 53-; dir, Galerie 8, Erie, 67-74. *Teaching:* Instr painting, Erie Art Ctr, 64-78. *Awards:* Purchase Prize & Hon Mention, Butler Inst Am Art Mid Year Show, 70 & 81; Purchase Prize, Tyler Mus Art 7th Nat Exhib, 70; Prize for Non-Traditional, Chautauqua Exhib, 72 & 76. *Bibliog:* Clyde Singer (auth), article, Youngstown Vindicator, 6/28/70; Ada C Tanner (auth), article, Chautauqua Daily, 8/17/70; Peggy Krider (auth), Art Demonstration (film), Villa Maria Col, 70. *Mem:* Erie Art Ctr (pres, 67-69); Erie Arts Coun (vpres, 70-71); Chautauqua Art Asn; Northwestern Pa Artist Asn (co-dir); Artist Equity, Philadelphia. *Media:* Porcelain Enamel, Graphic. *Mailing Add:* 5518 Bondy Dr Erie PA 16509

SUNDBERG, WILDA (REGELMAN)
PAINTER, INSTRUCTOR
b Erie, Pa, Oct 5, 30. *Study:* Albright Art Sch, Univ Buffalo, 49-51; Gannon col, 64-66; Mercyhurst Col, Pa, 78-79. *Work:* Thiel Col, Greenville, Pa; Erie Pub Libr; Erie Art Mus. *Exhib:* Albright-Knox Mem Gallery, Buffalo, 71 & 81; Butler Inst Am Art, Ohio; one-woman shows, Waterford Community Ctr, Pa, 76, Thiel Col, Pa, 77 & Erie Art Mus, 84; Counterpoint II, Pittsburgh, Pa, 81; Pa Gov Mansion, Harrisburg, 81-82; and others. *Teaching:* Instr art, Erie Art Mus, 64-83; instr drawing & painting, Mercyhurst Col, 79-83. *Awards:* Chautauqua Nat Watercolor Award, Chautauqua Art Asn, 70. *Mem:* Pittsburgh Watercolor Soc; NW Pa Artist Asn; Artists Equity, Philadelphia Chap, Pa; Erie Arts Coun. *Media:* Transparent Watercolor. *Mailing Add:* 5518 Bondy Dr Erie PA 16509

SUNDERLAND, NITA KATHLEEN
EDUCATOR, SCULPTOR
b Olney, Ill, Nov 9, 27. *Study:* Duke Univ; Bradley Univ, BFA & MA. *Comn:* Archit sculpture, Bradley Univ Bookstore, 64; monumental sculpture, Williams Hall Mall, 67; archit sculpture, St John's Cath Church, Woodhull, Ill, 69; monument bronze sculpture, City Beautiful Comt, City Peoria, Fulton Street Mall, 75. *Exhib:* Chicago Mus Without Walls, 78; 31st Illinois Invitational, 79; Selections from the Collection of George M Irwin, 80; 30 Years of Pub Sculpture in Ill, 81; Eighteen Ill Sculptors, 83. *Teaching:* Prof sculpture, Bradley Univ, 56- *Bibliog:* Three Illinois Artists (film), Ill Arts Coun, WCBV-TV, Peoria, 79. *Media:* Mixed. *Dealer:* Roy Boyd Gallery 215 W Superior Chicago IL 60610. *Mailing Add:* Grosenbach Rd, RR 1 Washington IL 61571

SUNDIN, ADELAIDE TOOMBS
CERAMIST, SCULPTOR
b Boston, Mass, May 8, 15. *Study:* Mass Col Art, with Cyrus Dallin & Raymond Porter, BS(educ), 38; Mass Inst Technol, 42-47. *Work:* Mass Inst Technol. *Comn:* Bronze bas-relief, comn by family of Dr Otis, Otis Airfield, Mass, 36. *Exhib:* Pa Acad Fine Arts Ann, 41 & 42; Corcoran Gallery Art Ann Exhib, 42; solo exhib, Centerville Gallery, Wilmington, 77 & Hudiksvall Mus, Sweden, 80; Women at MIT, Boston Athenaeum, 77 & Mass Inst Technol, 81; Am Medallic Sculpture Asn, Am Numismatic Soc, New York, 83. *Bibliog:* Jane Guernsey (auth), An ancient art revived, Philadelphia Inquirer, 79. *Mem:* Copley Soc Boston; Portraits Inc New York; Am Medallic Sculpture Asn. *Media:* Parian Porcelain. *Mailing Add:* 132 Hedge Apple Lane Wilmington DE 19807

SUNKEL, ROBERT CLEVELAND
HISTORIAN, ADMINISTRATOR
b Clarksville, Tex, Jan 19, 33. *Study:* Kilgore Col, Tex, AA; Tex Christian Univ, BFA & MFA; Herron Sch Art, Ind Univ; Temple Univ; Northern Ill Univ. *Pos:* Cur, Percival DeLuce Mem Collection, Northwest Mo State Univ, 74-78. *Teaching:* Instr art, Henderson State Col, 58-60; from instr to asst prof art, Northwest Mo State Univ, 60-74, actg chmn dept, 63-71, assoc prof, 74-, chmn dept, 76-78, head div fine arts, 78- *Mem:* Soc Archit Historians; Am Asn Univ Prof; Col Art Asn Am; Mid-Am Col Art Conf; Midwest Art Hist Soc. *Res:* English Baroque and Palladian architecture, particularly the work of Wren, Gibbs and Hawksmoor. *Mailing Add:* PO Box 75 Maryville MO 64468

SURGALSKI, PATRICK J
PAINTER, PRINTMAKER
b Detroit, Mich, Mar 17, 53. *Study:* San Jose State Univ, BFA, 79; Cranbrook Acad Art, MFA, 81. *Work:* Brooklyn Mus, New York; Cranbrook Mus, Bloomfield Hills, Mich. *Exhib:* Bay Area Printmakers, Santa Rosa Col, Calif, 79; Mich Asn Printmakers, Kalamazoo Art Inst, 80; Summer Invitational, Cranbrook Mus, Bloomfield Hills, Mich, 81. *Pos:* Dir, Mantissa Press, Northville, Mich, 79-82; artist-in-residence, Cranbrook Acad Art, 81. *Media:* Oil; Monotype, Lithography. *Dealer:* Sixth Street Gallery Royal Oak MI. *Mailing Add:* 43454 Reservoir Plymouth MI 48170

SURLS, JAMES
SCULPTOR, EDUCATOR
b Terrell, Tex, 1943. *Study:* Sam Houston State Col, BS, 66; Cranbrook Acad Art, MFA, 69. *Work:* Bendix Corp, Dearborn, Mich; Solomon R Guggenheim Mus & Am Tel & Tel, New York; Liquid Paper Corp, Dallas; Ft Worth Art Mus, Tex. *Comn:* Sea Flower, New Fed Bldg, New Bedford, Mass, 78; The Buford Proj, collabr with Ed Blackburn, Vernon Fisher & Jim Malone, Buford TV, Tyler, Tex, 78; work in progress, One Dallas Ctr, through Delahunty Gallery, Dallas, 80. *Exhib:* Artists Make Toys, Art Mus STex, Corpus Christi, 75; Exchange DFW/SFO, Ft Worth Art Mus & San Francisco Mus Mod Art, 75-76; Tex/Lax: Tex in LA, Union Gallery, Calif State Univ, Los Angeles, 76; 9 Artists Theodoran Awards, Solomon R Guggenheim Mus, New York, 77; Whitney Mus Am Art Biennial, New York, 79; Fire, Contemp Arts Mus, Houston, Tex, 79; Response, Tyler Mus Art, Tex, 80. *Teaching:* Instr sculpture, Southern Methodist Univ, Dallas, 70-75; assoc prof, Univ Houston, 75- *Awards:* Nat Endowment Arts Fel, 79. *Media:* Wood. *Dealer:* Delahunty Gallery 2611 Cedar Springs Dallas TX 75202. *Mailing Add:* PO Box 9 Splendora TX 77372

SURREY, MILT
PAINTER
b New York, NY, Mar 18, 22. *Work:* Cincinnati Art Mus; Columbia Mus Art, SC; Detroit Inst Arts; Evansville Mus Art, Ind; Miami Mus Mod Art; and many others. *Exhib:* Soc Four Arts, Palm Beach, 69; Nat Arts Club, New York, 69; Cape Coral Nat Art Show, 70; George Walter Vincent Smith Art Mus, Springfield, Mass, 70; Parrish Art Mus, Southampton, NY, 70. *Awards:* John Knecht Mem Award, Berwick Arts Festival, 69. *Media:* Oil. *Mailing Add:* 62 E 55th St New York NY 10022

SURREY, PHILIP HENRY
PAINTER
b Calgary, Alta, Oct 8, 10. *Study:* Winnipeg Sch Art, with LeMoine FitzGerald; Vancouver Sch Art, with Frederick Varley & Jock Macdonald; Art Students League, with Alexander Abels; Concordia Univ, LLD(hon), 81. *Work:* Nat Gallery Can, Ottawa; Montreal Mus Fine Arts; Mus Quebec, Quebec City; Art Gallery Hamilton, Ont; Art Gallery Winnipeg, Man; and others. *Exhib:* Hamilton Art Gallery Winter Exhibs, 58-71; 25 Quebec Painters, Montreal Mus Fine Arts, 61; Master Can Painters & Sculptors, London, 63; one-man retrospective, Peintre Dans La Ville, Mus Art Contemp, Montreal, 71 & Ctr Cult Can, Paris, 72. *Teaching:* Former instr drawing, Concordia Univ. *Awards:* First Prize, Montreal Spring Show, 53; Second Prize, Winnipeg Show, 60. *Bibliog:* J De Roussan (auth), Le peintre des reflets de la ville, Vie Arts, 63 & Philip Surrey, Ed Lidec, Montreal, 68; Paul Duval (auth), Four Decades, Clarke, Irwin, Toronto; and others. *Mem:* Royal Can Acad Arts. *Media:* Acrylic, Oil. *Dealer:* Galerie Gilles Corbeil 2165 Crescent St Montreal PQ Can. *Mailing Add:* 478 Grosvenor Ave Montreal PQ H3Y 2S4 Canada

SUSSMAN, ARTHUR
PAINTER
b Brooklyn, NY, Mar 30, 27. *Study:* Syracuse Univ, BFA; Brooklyn Mus Sch Art. *Work:* NMex Mus Fine Art, Santa Fe; Okla Art Ctr; Skirball Mus; Univ NMex; Albuquerque Public Sch. *Exhib:* One-man shows, Miami Mus Mod

Art, 64, Artists House, Haifa, Israel, 64, Bernard Black Gallery, NY, 65 & 67, Jonson Gallery, Univ NMex, 67 & 77 & Newman Fine Arts, Scottsdale, Ariz, 78; plus many others. *Pos:* Art & film ed, KOAT TV, Albuquerque, formerly; pub TV film critic, indust art consult & courtroom sketch artist, currently; owner, A Sussman Gallery, currently. *Teaching:* Artist in residence, Univ Albuquerque, formerly. *Awards:* Oriental Studies Found Grant, 62. *Mem:* Nat Mural Painters Soc. *Media:* Oil, Mixed. *Mailing Add:* c/o Arthur Sussman Gallery PO Box 13493 Albuquerque NM 87192

SUSSMAN, BONNIE K
DEALER, GALLERY DIRECTOR
b Minneapolis, Minn. *Study:* Univ Minn, BS. *Pos:* Dir-owner, Peter M David Gallery, Minneapolis, 70- *Mem:* Metrop Art Dealers Asn, Twin Cities of Minnesota (pres, 78-). *Specialty:* Contemporary American and English paintings, prints, drawings, watercolor, photography; artists' books; handmade paper. *Mailing Add:* 430 Oak Grove St No 101 Minneapolis MN 55403

SUSSMAN, ELISABETH SACKS
CURATOR
b Baltimore, Md, July 16, 39. *Study:* Simmons Col, BS, 60; Boston Univ, MA(art hist), 64. *Pos:* Spec asst, Mus Fine Arts, Boston, 72-75; cur, Inst Contemp Art, Boston, 76- *Teaching:* Museology, Tufts Univ, 75- *Mem:* New Eng Coun, Am Asn Mus. *Publ:* Coauth, San Francisco's shingle-style architects: Fitting a house to the land, Sat Rev, 72; coauth, Building with nature: Roots of the San Francisco Bay Tradition, Peregrin-Smith, 74; contribr, Frontier America: The Far West, Mus Fine Arts, Boston, 75; Florine Steltheimer: Still Lifes, Portraits, Panoramas, Inst Contemp Art, 80. *Mailing Add:* 45 Crescent St Cambridge MA 02138

SUTER, SHERWOOD EUGENE
EDUCATOR, PAINTER
b Bluffton, Ohio, Sept 22, 28. *Study:* Western Mich Univ, BS(art), 50; Columbia Univ, MFA & Fine Arts Educ, 56. *Work:* Abilene Savings Asn, Tex; First State Bank, Abilene. *Exhib:* State-wide Show of Paintings, Abilene Fine Arts Mus, Kendall Art Mus, San Angelo, Tex, Women's Art Forum, Wichita Falls & Howard Payne Col, Brownwood, 70-71; one-man show, Abilene Chamber of Commerce, 76. *Collections Arranged:* American Watercolor Society Annual Show, McMurry Col, Abilene. *Teaching:* Assoc prof & chmn art dept, McMurry Col, 57-; instr painting, Abilene Fine Arts Mus, 74- *Awards:* Top Award/Watercolor, 70 & Top Award/Oil, 71, Abilene Fine Arts Mus, Abilene Savings Asn. *Media:* Watercolor; Oil. *Mailing Add:* c/o Art Dept Box 8 McMurry Col Abilene TX 79697

SUTHERLAND, SANDY
PAINTER
b Cincinnati, Ohio, Apr 10, 02. *Study:* Art Students League; Mech Inst, NY. *Work:* Nat Arts Club. *Exhib:* Metrop Mus Art Exhib Am Watercolors, 52; Am Watercolor Soc, 70; Allied Artists Am, 71; Grand Cent Art Galleries, 72; Nat Arts Club, 72. *Awards:* Am Watercolor Soc Prize for Non-Mem, 51; Hoe Medal for Free Hand Drawing, Mech Inst, 55; First Award of Merit for Painting, Kenneth Taylor Gallery, 58. *Mem:* Allied Artists Am; life mem Am Watercolor Soc; life mem Art Students League; Nat Arts Club. *Media:* Oil, Watercolor. *Publ:* Auth, Figure sketching in watercolor, 63 & Painting in oil on paper, 68, Am Artist. *Mailing Add:* 6740 Gulfport Blvd St Petersburg FL 33707

SUTTER, JAMES STEWART
SCULPTOR, EDUCATOR
b Milwaukee, Wis, Feb 12, 40. *Study:* Univ Wis, BA(art educ), 64; Univ Iowa, MA(sculpture), 65; Univ Mass, univ fels, 65-67, MFA(sculpture), 67. *Work:* St Lawrence Univ, Canton, NY; Roland Gibson Art Found Inc, Concord, NH; Mus Fine Arts, Springfield, Mass; Lutheran Brotherhood Ins Co, Minneapolis; State Univ Iowa, Iowa City; plus others. *Exhib:* 164th Ann Nat Drawing, Watercolor & Sculpture Show, Philadelphia Mus Fine Arts, 69; one-man shows, Hansen Galleries, 75 & 80 & Fredric Remington Mus, 81, New York; 26th & 27th Ann Drawing & Sculpture Show, Ball State Univ, 80 & 81; R K Parker Gallery, New York, 82 & 83; Int Sculpture Ctr, Washington, DC, 83; and others. *Teaching:* Drawing asst, Univ Mass, 66-67; assoc prof sculpture, State Univ NY Col Potsdam, NY, 67-79, prof art, 79-; guest prof sculpture & drawing, Skidmore Col, Saratoga Springs, 79-83. *Awards:* First Prize, 5th Ann Arena Nat, Binghamton, NY, 78; Chmn Award Sculpture, Third Ann Nat Art Exhib, Laramie, Wyo, 78; Prize, 26th Ann Drawing & Sculpture Show, Ball State Univ, Ind, 80; and others. *Mem:* Col Art Asn. *Media:* Bronze, Aluminum. *Publ:* Coauth, with Dr Frank Seiberling, The Role of Sculpture in Modern Architecture, Univ Iowa, 65. *Dealer:* R K Parker 157 Spring St New York NY; Judith Posner Associates Milwaukee WI. *Mailing Add:* 11 New St Norwood NY 13668

SUTTMAN, PAUL
SCULPTOR
b NMex, July 16, 33. *Study:* Univ NMex, BFA, 56; Cranbrook Acad Art, MFA, 58. *Work:* Joseph H Hirshhorn Mus, Washington, DC; Mus Mod Art, New York; Art Mus, Macomb Col, Mich; Kalamazoo Art Ctr; Roswell Art Ctr. *Comn:* Two figures, Eastland Shopping Ctr, Detroit, 65; figure, Martha Cooke Bldg, Univ Mich, 68. *Exhib:* Sculpture From Hirshhorn Collection, Guggenheim Mus, 62; Biennale Sculpture Contemp, Rodin Mus, Paris, 68 & 70; US Info Serv Traveling Exhib, Istanbul & Ankara, Turkey, 72; After Surrrealism, Metaphors & Similes, Ringling Art Mus, Sarasota, Fla, 72; Los Angeles Mus, 77; Jodi Scurry Gallery, 77; Mus of Albuquerque, 78. *Teaching:* Instr sculpture, Univ Mich, Ann Arbor, 58-62; artist in residence, Dartmouth

Col, spring 73; vis prof art, Univ NMex, 76- *Awards:* Rackham Found Res Grant, Italy, 60; Fulbright Fel Paris, Inst Int Educ, 63; Prix de Rome Fel, Am Acad Rome, 65-68. *Bibliog:* The Bronze Man, Nat Educ TV, 60. *Media:* Bronze, Marble. *Dealer:* Donald Morris Gallery 20082 Livernois Detroit MI 48221; Mekler Gallery Los Angeles CA. *Mailing Add:* Terry Dintenfass Inc 50 W 57th St New York NY 10021

SUTTON, CAROL (LORRAINE)
PAINTER
Norfolk, Va, Sept 3, 45. *Study:* Richmond Prof Inst, BFA, 67; Univ NC, MFA. *Work:* Mus Fine Arts, Boston; Nat Collection Fine Art, Smithsonian Inst; Weatherspoon Art Gallery, Greensboro, NC; Edmonton Art Gallery, Alta; Agnes Etherington Art Gallery, Kingston, Ont. *Exhib:* Certain Traditions: Recent British & Canadian Art, Edmonton Art Gallery, Alta & traveling through Canada, England & Wales, 78; The New Generation: A Critic's Choice, Andre Emmerich Gallery, New York & traveling to Berlin, Ger & Am Cult Ctr, Paris, 80; Edmonton Art Gallery, Alta, 81; Viewpoint 29 x 9, Art Gallery Hamilton, Ont, 81; Heritage of Jack Bush, Robert McLaughlin Gallery & traveling in Canada, 81. *Bibliog:* James Clark (auth), The Problem of Fundamental Ontology Book, Limits Bk Co, 81; Karen Wilkin (auth), Toronto: Fans, flickers & penny arcades, Art News, 2/82. *Media:* Acrylic on Canvas. *Dealer:* Salander O'Reilly New York NY; Gallery One Toronto ON Canada. *Mailing Add:* 27 Davies Ave Toronto ON M4M 2A9 Canada

SUTTON, PATRICIA
PAINTER
b New York, NY, Sept 9, 41. *Study:* Cornell Univ, 59-63, BFA; Hunter Col, 64-68, MA. *Work:* Hirshhorn Mus & Sculpture Garden; Whitney Mus Am Art, New York; San Francisco Mus Fine Arts; Walker Art Ctr; Herbert F Johnson Mus; and others. *Exhib:* Lyrical Abstraction, Aldrich Mus of Contemp Art, 70 & Whitney Mus Am Art, 71; Highlights 1969-1970, 70 & Ten Years, 74, Aldrich Mus Contemp Art; one-woman shows, Fairleigh Dickinson Univ, Rutherford, NJ, 68; four shows, Andre Emmerich Gallery, 70-75, Everson Mus, 70, Medici-Berenson Gallery, Fla, 72, 74 & 75 & Deutcher O'Reilly Gallery, 76; and others. *Teaching:* Instr, Fairleigh Dickinson Univ, 68 & Hunter Col, 72; vis artist, San Francisco Art Inst, 74; instr, State Univ NY, Purchase, 79-80; asst prof, Hartford Art Sch, Univ Hartford, 83- *Awards:* First Prize, Scholastic Art Award, 59; NY State Coun on the Arts Grant & Am the Beautiful Fund Grant, Hoosick Falls Art Ctr, 71. *Bibliog:* Larry Aldrich (auth), Young Lyrical Painters, Art in Am, 11-12/69; Hilton Kramer (auth), Art: Two interesting talents make debut, New York Times, 6/13/70 & Review, 10/29/76; Noel Frackman (auth), Pat Lipsky Sutton, Arts Mag, 1/76; and others. *Mailing Add:* 11 Riverside Dr New York NY 10023

SUZUKI, JAMES HIROSHI
PAINTER
b Yokohama, Japan, Sept 19, 33. *Study:* Sch of Fine & Appl Art, Portland, Maine, 52; Corcoran Sch Art, 53-54; privately with Yoshio Markino. *Work:* Corcoran Gallery of Art, Washington, DC; Wadsworth Atheneum, Hartford, Conn; Rockefeller Inst, New York; Nat Mus Mod Art, Tokyo, Japan; Toledo Mus Art, Ohio. *Exhib:* Corcoran Gallery Art, 56, 58 & 60; Whitney Mus Am Art; Baltimore Mus Art, Md; Contemp Painters of Japanese Origin in Am, Inst Contemp Art, Boston; Everson Mus Art, Syracuse, NY, 58; Wadsworth Atheneum, 59; Waning Moon and Rising Sun, Mus Fine Arts of Houston, 59; San Francisco Mus Art, 63 & 64; solo exhibs, Quay Gallery, 73, Braustein Quay Gallery, 76 & 78 & Sacramento State Univ, 78; Aesthetics of Graffiti, San Francisco Mus Mod Art, 78. *Teaching:* Instr, Univ Calif, Berkeley, 62-63 & Univ Ky, 66-68; assoc prof art, Sacramento State Univ, currently. *Awards:* Eugene Weiss Scholar, Corcoran Gallery Art, 54; John Hay Whitney Fel, 58; Larry Aldrich Prize, Silvermine Guild, 59. *Dealer:* Braunstein Quay Gallery 254 Sutter St San Francisco CA 94108. *Mailing Add:* 2021 E 29th St Oakland CA 94606

SUZUKI, KATSKO (KATSKO SUZUKI KANNEGIETER)
DEALER
b Nagoya, Japan. *Study:* Kinjyo Female Col, Nagoya; Bunka Gakuin, Tokyo, Japan. *Pos:* Dir & pres, Suzuki Graphics Inc, New York, 70- *Bibliog:* E Stern (auth), article, NY Work Mag, 6/13/77; N Sano (auth), article, The Mainichi Graph, 4/9/78; S Sawyer & B Fasciani (auths), article, The Executive Female, 3-4/81. *Specialty:* Mainly specialized in graphics; many gallery artists are international; extended for small paintings, sculptures and other media at Suzuki Gallery (subsidiary). *Publ:* Auth, articles in Hanga Geijyutsu (Arts in Graphics), 74-75. *Mailing Add:* 38 E 57th St New York NY 10022

SUZUKI, SAKARI
PAINTER
b Iwateken, Japan; US citizen. *Study:* Calif Sch Fine Arts, San Francisco; Art Students League, NY Metrop Scholar, 34. *Work:* High Mus Art, Atlanta, Ga; Dept Labor, Washington, DC. *Comn:* Mural, Willard Parker Hosp, New York, 37. *Exhib:* Corcoran Gallery Art, Washington, DC, 34; one-man shows, ACA Gallery, New York, 36, Artists Gallery, New York, 48 & 51 & Mandel Bros Art Gallery, Chicago, 55; Pa Acad Fine Arts, Philadelphia, 52. *Pos:* Scenic artist, Munic Opera, St Louis, Mo, 53-55, Starlight Theatre, Kansas City, Mo, 56-69, Gen Motors Futurama, 62-64 & Lyric Opera, Chicago, 65-70. *Teaching:* Instr painting, Am Artists Sch, New York, 38-40. *Awards:* Am Artists Cong Prize, 36. *Mem:* United Scenic Artists Am. *Media:* Oil. *Mailing Add:* 5040 Marine Dr Apt B8 Chicago IL 60640

SVENDSEN, LOUISE AVERILL
CURATOR

b Old Town, Maine, Nov 22, 15. *Study:* Wellesley Col, BA; Yale Univ, MA & PhD. *Pos:* Assoc cur, Solomon R Guggenheim Mus, 62-66, cur, 66-78, sr cur, 78- *Teaching:* Instr hist of art, Duke Univ, Durham, NC, 43-45; asst prof, Goucher Col, Baltimore, Md, 45-50 & Am Univ, Washington, DC, 51-52; lectr, Solomon R Guggenheim Mus, New York, 54-62. *Publ:* Auth, Rousseau, Redon and Fantasy, 68, Ilya Bolotowsky, 74 & Frank Lloyd Wright, Architect, 75, Guggenheim Mus; Alberto Giacometti, Sculptor and Draftsman, Am Fedn Arts, 77. *Mailing Add:* 16 Park Ave New York NY 10016

SVENSON, JOHN EDWARD
SCULPTOR

b Los Angeles, Calif, May 10, 23. *Study:* Claremont Grad Sch, Calif; sculpture with Albert Stewart. *Work:* Alaska State Mus, Juneau; Ahmandson Ctr, Los Angeles; San Bernardino City Mus. *Comn:* Two hist panels, San Gabriel Mission Chapel, Calif, 58; bldg facade & sculpture, Purex Corp, Lakewood, Calif, 60; bronze Alaska Tlingit Medal, Soc Medalists Ann Issue, 72; medallion & sculpture, Alyeska Pipeline Serv, Anchorage; bas-relief, Alaska Mutual, Anchorage; plus others. *Exhib:* Lang Galleries, Scripps Col, Claremont, 61; Los Angeles Co Mus Art, 62; Newman Galleries, Philadelphia, 71; Kennedy Galleries, New York, 72; Alaska State Mus; Green Galleries, Anchorage; plus others. *Pos:* Trustee, Alaska Indian Arts, Inc, Port Chilkoot, 67- Teaching: Pvt instr, currently. *Awards:* Awards for Excellence in Sculpture, Am Inst Archit, 57 & 61; First Prize, Laguna Art Festival, 61; and others. *Mem:* Fel Nat Sculpture Soc; Soc Medalists, New York. *Media:* Wood, Bronze. *Mailing Add:* 2480 Vista Dr Upland CA 91786

SVERDLOVE, ZOLITA
PAINTER, PRINTMAKER

b New York, NY, Feb 21, 36. *Study:* Art Students League, 49-52; Cooper Union Art Sch, cert, 56, BFA, 77; San Francisco State Univ, 59-60; Calif Sch Fine Arts, 60; Pratt Graphic Arts Ctr, 67; Southern Methodist Univ, 70-74. *Work:* Owens-Corning Collection, Toledo Mus, Ohio; Dallas Mus Fine Arts, Tex; Purdue Univ, Ind; Marymount Col, New York; Mr & Mrs Charles V Hooks, Hooks-Epstein Gallery, Houston; plus many others. *Comn:* Grand Hotel, Houston, 79; Fluor Corp, Los Angeles. *Exhib:* Art Festival, 60-63 & Ann Flower Show, 64, Oakland Mus, Calif; Western Artists Ann, De Young Mem Mus, 65; Ann New Eng Painting & Sculpture Show, Silvermine Guild of Artists, 67; Tex Painting & Sculpture Ann, Dallas Mus Fine Arts, 71, 1st Tex Invitational, 72 & 75 Yrs at Dallas Mus Fine Arts, 78; 1st Tex Invitational, Beaumont Mus, 74; Owens-Corning Collection Show, 77; one-person shows, Hooks-Epstein Gallery, Houston, 78 & Longview Mus, Tex, 79; Brand Libr & Art Gallery, Glendale, Calif, 82; and many others. *Awards:* Purchase Prize, Purdue Univ, 70; Top Prize, Dallas Mus Fine Arts, 72; Nat Endowment Arts Grant, 73-74; and others. *Bibliog:* Joy Patty (auth), article, Houston Mus Fine Arts, 4/76; article, Dallas Moring News, 11/77; review & photograph, by Glenna Parks, Art Wk, 11/4/78. *Mem:* Los Angeles Printmakers Soc; Women's Coalition for Arts; Los Angeles County Mus Graphic Arts Coun. *Media:* Painting and Prints. *Publ:* Designed & publ five booklets for Nat Endowment for Arts grant, 73-74; contribr, Mundus Artium, Univ Tex, Dallas, 76. *Dealer:* Allan Stone 48 East 86th New York NY; Valley House Gallery 6616 Spring Valley Rd Dallas TX. *Mailing Add:* 1445 Indiana Ave South Pasadena CA 91030

SWAIN, ROBERT
PAINTER

b Austin, Tex, Dec 7, 40. *Study:* Am Univ, Washington, DC, BA. *Work:* Corcoran Gallery of Art, Washington, DC; Walker Art Ctr, Minneapolis; Denver Art Mus, Colo; Albright-Knox Mus, Buffalo, NY; Everson Art Mus, Syracuse, NY. *Comn:* Painting (8 1/2ft x 20ft), Schering Labs, Bloomfield, NJ, comn by Skidmore, Owings & Merrill, New York, 70; painting (5ft x 10ft), Phillip Mallis of Kahn & Mallis Assocs, New York, 72; painting (4ft x 27ft), IBM, Charlotte, NC, 81; painting (5ft x 9ft), Tupperware World Headquarters, Kissimmee, Fla, 81. *Exhib:* The Art of the Real, Mus of Mod Art, New York, 68; one-man shows, Susan Caldwell Gallery, 74, 76, 78 & 81, Everson Art Mus, Syracuse, 74 & Columbus Gallery of Fine Arts, Ohio, 76; 31st Biennial, Corcoran Gallery of Art, 69; The Structure of Color, Whitney Mus of Am Art, 71; Painting & Sculpture Today, Indianapolis Mus of Art, Ind, 74; Color as Language (traveling exhib, Latin Am), Mus of Mod Art, New York, 74-75; Nina Freudenheim Galley, Buffalo, NY, 78; Toni Birckhead Gallery, Cincinnati, Ohio, 80. *Teaching:* Prof fine arts, Hunter Col, New York. *Awards:* Guggenheim Fel, 69; Nat Endowment for Arts Grant, 76. *Bibliog:* Scott Burton (auth), Light, from Aten to Laser, MacMillan Co, 69; B Wasserman (auth), Modern Painting, Davis Publ, 70; Roberta Smith (auth), Artforum, 76. *Media:* Acrylic. *Mailing Add:* 57 Leonard St New York NY 10013

SWAIN, ROBERT FRANCIS
GALLERY DIRECTOR

b Halifax, NS, Oct 25, 42. *Study:* Carleton Univ, BA. *Collections Arranged:* Joan Frick, 74; Robert Sinclair, 76; Made Glorious: 25 Years of Stratford Design, 76; A History of Children's Book Illustrations, 77; Fantastic Shakespeare; Coasts: The Sea and Canadian Art. *Pos:* Dir, Agnes Etherington Art Ctr, Kingston, Ont. *Mem:* Int Comt Mus; Ont Asn Art Galleries (dir); and others. *Publ:* Auth, many exhib catalogs. *Mailing Add:* c/o Agnes Etherington Art Ctr Queen's Univ Kingston ON K7L 3N6 Canada

SWAN, BARBARA
PAINTER

b Newton, Mass, June 23, 22. *Study:* Wellesley Col, BA; Boston Mus Sch. *Work:* Philadelphia Mus Art; Boston Mus Art; Worcester Mus; Fogg Art Mus; Boston Pub Libr. *Exhib:* Carnegie Ann, 49; Contemporary American Painting, Univ Ill, 50; View 1960, Inst Contemp Arts, Boston, 60; Brooklyn Mus Biennial Print Exhib, 65; New Eng Women, De Cordova Mus, 75; Eight New Eng Artists, Works on Paper, Boston Mus Fine Arts, 77; New England Realists, Danforth Mus, 80. *Teaching:* Instr painting, Wellesley Col, 46-49; instr art, Milton Acad, 51-54; instr painting & drawing, Boston Univ, 60-65. *Awards:* Albert Whitin Traveling Fel, Boston Mus Art, 48; Assoc Scholar, Inst Independent Study, Radcliffe Col, 61-63; George Roth Prize, Philadelphia Print Club, 65. *Media:* Oil. *Dealer:* Alpha Gallery 122 Newbury St Boston MA 02116. *Mailing Add:* 808 Washington St Brookline MA 02146

SWANSON, J N
PAINTER, SCULPTOR

b Duluth, Minn, Feb 4, 27. *Study:* Col Arts & Crafts, Oakland, Calif; Carmel Art Inst; also with Donald Teague & Armin Hansen. *Work:* Cowboy Hall Fame, Oklahoma City; BMA Collection, Kansas City; Read Mullin Collection, Phoenix; Sunset Mag Collection Art; Leaning Tree Mus, Boulder, Colo; Diamond M Mus, Tex. *Comn:* Pvt comn only. *Exhib:* Monterey Co Fair Prof Div, Calif, 67; Springville Regional Show, Utah; Cowboy Artists Ann Show, Hall Fame, Okla, 70-75; Soc Western Artists, De Young Mus, San Francisco, 71. *Awards:* San Francisco Best of Show Award, Monterey Co Fair, 67; Soc Western Artists Atelier Award, De Young Mus, 71. *Bibliog:* Ainsworth (auth), Cowboy in Art, World, 68; Paul Weaver (ed), Cowboy Artists Ann Exhib Bks, Northland, 69-75; Broder (auth), Bronzes of the American West, Abrams, 74. *Mem:* Cowboy Artists Am (vpres, 70). *Media:* Oil; Plastilene Clay. *Res:* Complete Western library for research into historical Western painting; first hand knowledge of the cowboy subject of present day. *Mailing Add:* Star Rte Box 120 Carmel Valley CA 93924

SWANSON, RAY V
PAINTER

b Alcester, SDak, Oct 4, 37. *Study:* Northrop Inst, BS, 60. *Work:* Indianapolis Mus Art; Riverside Art Collection Mus, Calif. *Exhib:* Wichita Nat Art Exhib, Kans, 70; Franklin Mint Gallery Am Art, 73-74; Capitol Bldg, Phoenix, Ariz, 75; Nat Acad Western Art, Cowboy Hall of Fame, 76. *Awards:* Gold Medal, Nat Acad Western Art, Cowboy Hall of Fame, 75; Silver Medal, Royal Western Watercolor, Cowboy Hall of Fame, 75; Gold Medal, Franklin Mint Gallery, 75-76. *Bibliog:* J & J Ward (auth), Renaissance of Western Art, Franklin Mint Gallery, 74; Tom Cooper (auth), The Best of Arizona Highways, Ariz Hwys, 75; Royal B Hassrick (auth), Western Painting Today, Watson-Guptill Publ, 77. *Mem:* Prescott Fine Arts Asn. *Media:* Oil; Watercolor. *Publ:* Contribr, Artist of the Rockies, Colo Publ, 75; contribr, Illuminator, Grand Cent Publ, 75. *Dealer:* Husberg Fine Arts Gallery 330 Hwy 179 Sedona AZ 86336. *Mailing Add:* 15 Perkins Dr Prescott AZ 86301

SWANSON, VERN GROSVENOR
MUSEUM DIRECTOR, HISTORIAN

b Central Point, Ore, Feb 4, 45. *Study:* Brigham Young Univ, Provo, Utah, BA, 69; Univ Utah, Salt Lake City, MA(art hist), 75; Univ London, Courtauld Inst Art, PhD(art hist), 82. *Collections Arranged:* The Work of Eugene Higgins (auth, catalog), 75 & An Exhibition of British and American Paintings (auth, catalog), 76, Auburn Univ; The Unknown Alma-Tadema (auth, catalog), Brigham Young Univ, Utah, 79; Permanent Collection (auth, catalog), 81 & 57th National April Salon (auth, catalog), 81, Springville Mus Art; over 25 other temporary exhibs at the Springville Mus. *Pos:* Mus aide supervisor, National Gallery Art, Washington DC, 69-70; gallery dir, House Fine Arts, Provo, Utah, 70-71; art consult British classical art, major auction houses, 73-; mus dir, Springville Mus Art, Utah, 80- Teaching: Asst prof art hist, Auburn Univ, Ala, 73-76. *Mem:* Am Asn Mus; Victorian Soc Am; Western Asn Art Mus. *Res:* Development of the cultural arts among the Mormons in Utah. *Publ:* Coauth, The Apodyterium and the Voice of Spring, The Other Nineteenth Century, 78; auth, Alma Tadema: The Painter of The Victorian of The Ancient World, C Scribner's, 77; auth, Valoy Eaton: Seeing beyond the superficial, Southwest Art, 80; auth, The Fantasy Art of James C Christensen, Press Publishing, 81; auth, The master's touch: Arnold Frieberg illusr, Southwest Art, 81. *Mailing Add:* 1540 Hobble Creek Dr Springville UT 84663

SWARTZ, BETH AMES
PAINTER

b New York, NY, Feb 5, 36. *Study:* Art Students League; Cornell Univ, BS, 57; NY Univ, MA, 60. *Work:* Jewish Mus, New York; Tucson Art Mus; Nat Mus Am Art, Washington, DC; Phoenix Art Mus; Brooklyn Mus. *Exhib:* Whitney Counterweight, New York, 77; one-person shows, Frank Marino Gallery, New York, 79 & 81, Elaine Horwitch Gallery, Scottsdale, Ariz, 80 & 82, Israel Revisited Touring Show, 81-83; Paper: Surface and Image, Rutgers Univ, touring, 81-82; Artists in the American Desert Touring Show, 81-82; and others. *Teaching:* Assoc, Exten Dept, Ariz State Univ, 63-74. *Awards:* Nat Endowment Arts Grant, 75; Ariz Comn Arts & Humanities Educ Grant, 77. *Bibliog:* Anna Katherine (auth), Exploration of elemental forces, Artlines, 10/83; Carol Donnell-Kotrozo (auth), Review of Beth Ames Swartz, Elaine Horwitch Galleries, Artforum, 11/83; Mary Carroll Nelson (auth), Connecting--The Art of Beth Ames Swartz, Northland Press, 84; and others. *Mem:* Nat & Ariz Art Educ Asns. *Media:* Fire on Paper; Mixed-Media. *Publ:* Are we stifling our children's creativity?, Point West Mag, 63; Help your child create, Art Handbook for Parents, 65; auth, Inquiry into fire, Ariz Artist, fall 77. *Dealer:* Elaine Horwitch Gallery 4211 N Marshall Way Scottsdale AZ 85251. *Mailing Add:* 5346 E Sapphire Lane Scottsdale AZ 85253

SWARTZ, PHILLIP SCOTT
PAINTER, COLLECTOR
b Robinson, Ill, May 20, 36. *Study:* Eastern Ill Univ, BS, 58, MS, 63; Miami Univ, Ohio. *Work:* J B Speed Mus, Louisville, Ky. *Exhib:* Viewpoint 75, Cincinnati Art Club, Ohio, 75; Miniature Painters, Sculptors & Gravers, Washington Arts Club, DC, 75, 76 & 77; Nat Small Painting Exhib Biennial, Gallery North, Mt Clemons, Mich, 76; Am Nat Miniature Exhib, Laramie Art Guild, Wyo, 76-77; Contemp Miniature (traveling exhib), Univ Mich, Ann Arbor, 77. *Collections Arranged:* Hamilton Campus, Miami Univ, Ohio. *Pos:* Coordr, Artist Ser, Miami Univ, 76-80. *Awards:* Second Prize, Am Nat Miniature Exhib, Laramie Art Guild, 77; First Prize, Fla Nat Miniature Exhib, Clearwater, 78; Fifth Prize, Ky State Fair, 79. *Mem:* Am Soc Artists; Fine Arts Coun, Hamilton, Ohio. *Media:* Acrylic, Oil. *Collection:* Contemporary prints. *Publ:* Coauth, The Scientific Interest of Robert W Gibbes, SC Mag of Hist, 65. *Mailing Add:* 408 St Petersburg Robinson IL 62454

SWARTZMAN, ROSLYN
PRINTMAKER, SCULPTOR
b Montreal, Que, Aug 17, 31. *Study:* Montreal Artists Sch; Montreal Mus Fine Arts; Ecole des Beaux Arts, with Albert Dumouchez. *Work:* Nat Gallery Can, Ottawa, Ont; Montreal Mus Fine Arts, Que; DeCordova Mus, Boston; Brooklyn Mus, NY; New York Pub Libr. *Exhib:* 2nd Int Graphics Biennial, Miami, 75; Jewish Experience in the 20th Century, Mt St Vincent Univ, Halifax, NS; Can Landscape through Drawings & Prints, Mus Fine Arts, Montreal; Boston Printmakers, 78; one-man show, Burnaby Art Gallery, BC, 80 & Saidye Bronfman Ctr, 81; and others. *Teaching:* Teacher & dir graphics dept, Sayde Bronfman Ctr, Montreal, 71- *Awards:* G A Reid Award Etching, Soc Can Painter, Etchers & Engravers, 65; two patron selection awards, Boston Printmakers 30th Exhib; Thomas Moore Purchase Award, Montreal, 80; and others. *Mem:* Royal Can Acad; Graphic Arts Coun Can; Print & Drawing Coun Can; Graphics Soc NH. *Media:* Intaglio; Bas-Relief. *Dealer:* Gallery Pascal Graphics 334 Dundas St W Toronto ON Can. *Mailing Add:* 4174 Oxford St Montreal PQ H4A 2Y4 Canada

SWAY, ALBERT
PAINTER, ETCHER
b Cincinnati, Ohio, Aug 6, 13. *Study:* Cincinnati Art Acad; Art Students League. *Work:* Metrop Mus Art, New York; New York Pub Libr; Carnegie Inst; Cincinnati Art Mus; Libr of Cong, DC. *Exhib:* Libr Cong, 43-45; Albright-Knox Art Gallery, 51; Soc Am Graphic Artists, 51-; Royal Soc Painters, Etchers & Engravers, London, Eng, 54; Am-Japan Contemp Print Exhib, Tokyo, 67; one-man show, Garden State Watercolor Soc 14th Ann Exhib, NJ, 83; and others. *Teaching:* Instr drawing & painting, New York Hosp League, 63-64. *Awards:* First Prize in Graphics, Cincinnati Mus Asn, 39. *Mem:* Soc Am Graphic Artists; Garden State Watercolor Soc. *Publ:* Illusr filmstrips on New York State history, produced by Our York State, NY, 50-; med illusr, A Syllabus for Health Visitors, Navajo Tribal Coun, Ariz, 60; med illusr, Respiratory diseases, Nat Tuberculosis Asn, 61; med illusr, Hepatic Excretory Function (ser filmstrips); Am Gastroenterol Asn, 72; med illusr, Congenital Malformations of the Heart, Grune & Stratton, 75; plus med illus in sci jour. *Mailing Add:* PO Box 43 Kendall Park NJ 08824

SWEENEY, J GRAY
HISTORIAN, CURATOR
b Jacksonville, Fla, Nov 20, 43. *Study:* Univ NMex, BA, 66; Ind Univ, MA, 69, PhD, 75. *Collections Arranged:* Themes in American Painting (auth, catalog), Grand Rapids Art Mus, 77; The Agrarian Landscape in American and French Painting (auth, catalog), Tweed Mus Art, 77; Mathias Allen (auth, catalog), Grand Rapids, 79; Artists of Grand Rapids: 1840-1980 (auth, catalog), 81; Great Lakes Marine Painting of the 19th Century (auth, catalog), Muskegon Mus Art, 83. *Pos:* Cur, Themes in Am Painting, Grand Rapids Art Mus, 71-77; cur, Hackley Art Mus, 77-, Tweed Mus, 80, Grand Rapids Art Mus, Mich, 81 & Muskegon Mus Art, 83. *Teaching:* Asst prof 19th & 20th century Am painting, Grand Valley State Col, 71-78, assoc prof, 78-83, prof, 84- *Awards:* Fels, Carnegie Found, 67 & 70 & Samuel H Kress Found, 70-71. *Mem:* Col Art Asn; Midwest Art Hist Soc; Assn Hist Am Art; Am Asn Mus. *Res:* Nineteenth century American landscape painting; influence of Thomas Cole. *Publ:* Auth, American Paintings, Hackley Art Mus; auth, American paintings, Tweed Mus, Univ Minn, 82; auth, Anthropomorphism: Its Role in Shaping Western Values in Nature and in the Environment, Am Acad Arts & Sci; auth, To the memory of Cole: A recently discovered memorial painting by Frederic E Church, In: Hudson River Perspective, Yale Univ Press, 84. *Mailing Add:* 335 Garfield NW Grand Rapids MI 49504

SWEENEY, JAMES JOHNSON
ADMINISTRATOR, LECTURER
b Brooklyn, NY, May 30, 00. *Study:* Georgetown Univ, AB, 22; Jesus Col, Cambridge Univ, 22-24; Sorbonne, Paris, 25; Univ Siena, 26; Hon DFA, Grinnell Col, 57, Univ Mich, 60, Univ Notre Dame, 61 & Univ Buffalo, 62; Hon LHD, Rollins Col, 60, Col of the Holy Cross, 60, Georgetown Univ, 63 & Univ Miami, 68; Ripon Col, Hon ArtsD, 60. *Collections Arranged:* Many exhibs, Univ Chicago, Mus Mod Art, New York, Art Gallery Toronto, Va Mus Fine Arts, Mass Inst Technol, Mus Art Mod, Paris, Tate Gallery, London & Honolulu Acad Arts. *Pos:* Dir painting & sculpture, Mus Mod Art, New York, 45-46 & Guggenheim Mus, 52-60; dir, Mus Fine Arts, Houston, 61-68, consult dir, 68-; gallery consult, Nat Capital Develop Comn, Canberra, Australia, 68-; art adv, Israel Mus, 72- *Teaching:* Lectr, many univs & mus, US, 35- *Awards:* Chevalier, Legion d'Honneur, France, 55; Officier, Ordre des Arts et des Lett, Paris, 59; Art Am Award, 63. *Mem:* Asn Int Art les Moyens Audio-Visuels; hon mem Arts Club Chicago; hon mem Buffalo Fine Arts Acad; hon mem Int Coun Mus Mod Art; hon mem Am Inst Interior Designers; and many others. *Publ:* Auth, Vision & Image, 68, African Sculpture, 70, Joan Miro, 70, Alexander Calder, 71 & Pierre Soulages, 72; and many other bks, articles & films. *Mailing Add:* 120 East End Ave New York NY 10028

SWEET, MARY (FRENCH)
PAINTER
b Cincinnati, Ohio, Oct 10, 37. *Study:* Stanford Univ, with Daniel Mendelowitz, AB(art), 59, MA(art), 60. *Comn:* Painting, USS Barb Submarine, 63. *Exhib:* Oakland Art Asn Ann, Oakland Art Mus, 68; Watercolor New Mexico, Mus NMex, Santa Fe, 74; El Paso Sun Carnival, El Paso Mus Art, 74; Watercolor Perspectives, 74, Introductions, 76 & Watercolor New Mexico, 81, Mus Albuquerque. *Awards:* Best of Show & Purchase Award, La Junta, Colo Ninth Ann Nat Show, 77 & Carlsbad, NMex 14th Ann, 77; Jurors Award Excellence, Santa Fe Festival Arts, 79. *Bibliog:* Mary Carroll Nelson (auth), Wilderness landscapes by Mary Sweet, Am Artist, 9/82; Ed Martafield (auth), Women artists & writers of the Southwest, New Am, Vol 4, No 3, 82; Joseph Traugott (auth), Abstract form, vivid colors typify works, Albuquerque J, 10/30/83. *Mem:* NMex Watercolor Soc. *Media:* Acrylics, Mixed Media. *Dealer:* Meridian Gallery 220 Central SW Albuquerque NM 87102; Gekas-Nicholas Gallery 6538 E Tanque Verde Rd Tucson AZ 85715. *Mailing Add:* PO Box 280 Tijeras NM 87059

SWEET, STEVE (STEVEN MARK)
COLLAGE ARTIST, SCULPTOR
b Boston, Mass, Mar 13, 52. *Study:* Antioch Col, with Paul Sharits, Allan Jones & Tony Conrad, BA(visual arts), 74. *Work:* Pan-Am Life Insurance Corp, New Orleans; United Media Enterprises, New York. *Comn:* Mini-mural, New Orleans Arts Coun, 79; Pictures of My Life (monument photogs), 80 & Zilch Symphony (sculpture), 81, Contemp Arts Ctr, New Orleans; The Appliance Giant Mural, comn by Tony Campo, New Orleans, 83. *Exhib:* Louisiana Major Works, Contemp Arts Ctr, New Orleans, 79; New Orleans Triennial, New Orleans Mus Art, 80; Focus, Ft Worth Art Mus, 81; Services to the Field, 81 & My Cousin the Saint, 83, Contemp Arts Ctr, New Orleans; Network-Southeast Artist Invitational, Nexus, Atlanta, 83; New Music America 83, Hirshhorn Mus & Sculpture Garden, 83. *Awards:* Project Grant, Money from Nancy, La State Arts Coun, 79; Services to the Field, Contemp Arts Ctr & Nat Endowment Arts, 80; Nat Endowment Arts Fel, 81. *Bibliog:* Robert Raczka (auth), Comics in relief, Art Week, 5/16/81; Roger Green (auth), Flattened people: Portraits in depth, Times Picyunne-States Item, 1/83; Jeff Zeldman (auth), Picture perfect, City Papers, Washington, DC, 10/14/83. *Mem:* Contemp Arts Ctr; Int Soc Copier Artists. *Dealer:* Aaron-Hastings Gallery 1130 St Charles Ave New Orleans LA 70130. *Mailing Add:* 727 Hidalgo St New Orleans LA 70124

SWENEY, FRED
ILLUSTRATOR, PAINTER
b Holidaysburg, Pa, June 5, 12. *Study:* Cleveland Sch Art. *Work:* In pvt collections; Am Mus Wildlife Art, Lake City, Minn. *Pos:* Supvr, Leece-Neville Co; artist-illusr, Brown & Bigelow, 49- *Teaching:* Instr, Ringling Sch Art, 49-78. *Awards:* Lithographic Award, 61 & Graphic Arts Award, 62; Award for Wild Wings, 79; and others. *Media:* Oil. *Publ:* Auth & illusr, Techniques of Drawing and Painting Wildlife, 59, Drawing and Painting Birds, 61 & Painting the American Scene in Watercolor, 64; illusr & contribr, Sports Afield Mag & Field & Stream; auth & illusr, The Art of Painting Animals, Prentice-Hall, 83. *Mailing Add:* 25314 SE 31st Pl Issaquah WA 98027

SWENSON, ANNE (BEATRICE)
PAINTER, INSTRUCTOR
b Stafford Springs, Conn. *Study:* Art Students League; also with W Fisher, V Drennan, P Giambertone & T Kochi; City Univ New York, BA(art hist, summa cum laude), 80; NY State Teachers Cert(art), 81. *Work:* St Peter's Rectory, Staten Island, NY; and pvt collections in Italy & England. *Exhib:* Metrop Mus Art, 75 & 77; Snug Harbor Cult Ctr, Staten Island, NY, 76-83; Artists Equity Asn Exhib, 77; Goldsboro Art Ctr, NC, 77; Dawson Grist Mill Gallery, Vt, 79; Salmagundi Club, New York, 81. *Teaching:* Lectr & demonstr mosaics, Staten Island Mus, 59; teacher oil, St Peters Elem Sch, 60-63, S B Wagner High Sch, 74 & Our Lady Good Counsel & Immaculate Conception Elem Schs, 80-; pvt instr art, currently; Our Lady Good Coun & Immaculate Conception Elementary Schs, 80- *Awards:* Anna B Morse Gold Medal, Gotham Painters, 66; Art Achievement Award, Centennial Comt 7th Regiment, Armory, NY, 80. *Bibliog:* With photos of work, Staten Island Advan, 59, 60 & 69. *Mem:* Burr Artists (dir, 67-81); Gotham Painters (treas, 74-); Artists' Fedn Snug Harbor; New York Artists Equity Asn; gold medal mem Accad delle Arti del Lavoro, Parma, Italy. *Media:* Oil, Watercolor. *Publ:* Illusr, Indian Asn Am; auth, Rugs through the ages, New Bulletin Staten Island Mus, Vol 9, No 3. *Mailing Add:* 10 Phelps Pl Staten Island NY 10301

SWENSON, (JEAN) MARY JEANETTE HAMILTON
PAINTER, PRINTMAKER
b Laurens, SC, June 25, 10. *Study:* Columbia Univ, with Hans Mueller, BS, 56, with Arthur Young, MA(graphic arts), 60; Fine Arts Sch for Am, Fountainbleau, France, with Lucien Fontanerosa; Ariz State Univ, with Arthur Hahn, 5 summers. *Work:* Metrop Mus Art, New York; Nat Graphic Arts Collection, Smithsonian Inst, Washington, DC; Graphic Arts Collection, New York Pub Libr; Laurens Pub Libr, SC. *Exhib:* Soc Western Artists, M H de Young Mus, San Francisco, 64; Nat Art Roundup, Las Vegas, Nev, 65; Fine Arts Bldg, Colo State Fair, Pueblo, 65; Duncan Gallery, Paris, 74; Co Fed Svgs & Loan Asn, Denver, Colo, 78. *Awards:* Honorable Mention for Drawing, Soc Western Artists, 64; Duncan Gallery Prix de Paris, 74. *Mem:* Delta Phi Delta; Am Mensa Ltd. *Mailing Add:* 684 W 99th Ave Denver CO 80221

SWERGOLD, MARCELLE M
SCULPTOR
b Antwerp, Belgium, Sept 6, 27; US citizen. *Study:* NY Univ, painting with Aaron Berkman & Henry Kallem; Art Students League, with John Hovanes & Jose deCreft; wax with Harold Caster. *Work:* New Britain Mus Am Art, Conn; Int Treasury Fine Art, Plain View, NY. *Exhib:* Fairleigh Dickinson Univ, Teaneck, NJ, 72; Cork Gallery, Philharmonic Hall, Lincoln Ctr, New York; Allied Artists, Nat Acad Gallerie, New York; Audubon Artist Ann, New York, 78; New Britain Mus Am Art, Conn, 80; and others. *Bibliog:* Museum collection grows again, Herald, Conn, 12/80; International New York city, Park East Weekly, 12/80; Palmer Poroner (auth), Off season crop of quality shows, 12/80. *Mem:* New York Soc Women Artists (corresp secy, 77-79, pres, 79-81, exec vpres, 81-); Artists Equity Asn, New York; Contemp Artist Guild. *Media:* Bronze, Stone. *Dealer:* Robert U Schwalbe 146 Maple St Englewood NJ 07631. *Mailing Add:* 2231 Broadway New York NY 10024

SWICK, LINDA ANN
SCULPTOR
b Bedford, Ohio, Sept 9, 48. *Study:* Kent State Univ, BA, 70; Fla State Univ, MFA, 77. *Exhib:* Solo show, Washington Proj Arts, Washington, DC, 78; Rutgers Univ, Camden, NJ, 79; Laguna Gloria Art Mus, Austin, 80; Middendorf Lane, Washington, DC, 80; Corcoran Gallery, Washington, DC, 81; Lawndale, Univ Houston, 82. *Pos:* Set designer for animated films, Broadcast Arts, Washington, DC, 80- *Awards:* Fel, City Washington, DC, 82. *Bibliog:* Sylvia Shauck (auth), interview, Art & Craft Mag, 6/80; Charlotte Moser (auth), Washington art, Art News, 10/81. *Media:* Wood. *Dealer:* Gallery K 2032 P St Washington DC. *Mailing Add:* 1717 S St NW Washington DC 20009

SWIGART, LYNN S
PHOTOGRAPHER
b Kansas City, Mo, Aug 22, 30. *Study:* Bradley Univ, Peoria, Ill, BS(psychol, philos); also photog with Minor White & George Tice. *Work:* Carpenter Ctr for the Visual Arts, Harvard Univ, Cambridge, Mass; Stanford Univ. *Exhib:* One-man shows, Williams Benton Mus, Univ Conn, 77; Stanford Univ, 78, Univ Iowa, 78; Ill State Mus, 78; Cape Ann Historical Asn, Mass, 81. *Teaching:* Instr photog, Multi-Media Arts Inst, Bradley Univ, summer 73 & 74. *Mem:* Lakeview Ctr for Arts; Peoria Art Guild. *Publ:* Contrib, Olson's Gloucester, LSU Press, 80 & Boundry, 2/76. *Dealer:* Peoria Art Guild 1831 N Knoxville Peoria IL 61604. *Mailing Add:* 1624 W Parkside Dr Peoria IL 61606

SWIGGETT, JEAN DONALD
GRAPHIC ARTIST, PAINTER
b Franklin, Ind, Jan 6, 10. *Study:* Chouinard Inst Fine Art, Los Angeles, 30-31; San Diego State Univ, AB, 34; Univ Southern Calif, MFA, 39; Claremont Grad Sch, 50-52. *Work:* Long Beach Mus Art; San Diego Mus Art. *Comn:* Mural, Post Off, Franklin, Ind, 39; murals, SS President Jackson & SS President Adams, 40-41; illus, Psychol Today, 75. *Exhib:* Southern Calif Regional Drawing & Print Show, 73-77 & 81; Varieties of Visual Reality, Northern Ariz Univ, 75; one-man shows, Southwestern Col, 75; Palomar Col, 76 & San Diego Mus Art, 80; and others. *Teaching:* Teaching asst drawing, Univ Southern Calif, 40-41; instr painting, Wash State Col, 41-42; prof painting & drawing, San Diego State Univ, 46-77, emer prof, 77- *Awards:* San Diego Art Inst Ann, 71 & 81; Calif-Hawaii Regional Award, San Diego Mus Art, 72; Jewish Community Ctr Award, San Diego, 73 & 79; and others. *Mem:* Art Guild Fine Art Soc, San Diego (pres, 53-54, secy, 77-78). *Media:* Oil, Colored Pencil. *Res:* Romanesque architecture and sculpture. *Mailing Add:* 8635 7th Ave, Apt 9E San Diego CA 92103

SWINTON, GEORGE
PAINTER, WRITER
b Vienna, Austria, Apr 17, 17; Can citizen. *Study:* McGill Univ, BA, 46; Montreal Sch Art & Design, 46-47; Art Students League, New York, 49-50. *Work:* Nat Gallery Can; Vancouver Art Gallery; Winnipeg Art Gallery; Hamilton Art Gallery; Confederation Art Ctr, Charlottetown. *Exhib:* 2 retrospectives, Winnipeg Art Gallery; 4 Can Biennials; 3 Montreal Spring Exhibs; 11 Winnipeg Shows; many one-man shows. *Teaching:* Lectr art, Smith Col, 50-53; prof art, Univ Man, 54-74, adj prof anthrop, 70-74; prof art hist, Carleton Univ, 74- *Awards:* Donner Can Found Grant, 74-76; mem, Order Can, 80; Social Sci & Humanities Res Coun Grant, 80; and others. *Media:* Oil, Watercolor. *Res:* Prehistoric and contemporary Eskimo art. *Publ:* Auth, Changing traditions in Eskimo art, Arts Rev, London, 10/72; auth, Eskimo art: survival of a great tradition, Asn Can Studies in US Newslett, DC, autumn 72; auth, Eskimo art: beyond the mythologized past, Art News, New York, 1/78; auth, The Inuit phenomenon: Eskimo sculpture or Canadian art? Art Mag, 6/78; auth, Touch and the real: Contemporary Inuit aesthetics, theory, usage and relevance, In: Art in Society, London, 78; and others. *Mailing Add:* c/o Terramor Farms White Lake ON K0A 3L0 Canada

SYKES, (WILLIAM) MALTBY
PAINTER, PRINTMAKER
b Aberdeen, Miss, Dec 13, 11. *Study:* With Wayman Adams, John Sloan, Diego Rivera, Andre Lhote, Fernand Leger & Stanley William Hayter. *Work:* Mus Mod Art, New York; Stedlijk Mus, Amsterdam; Metrop Mus Art, New York; Boston Mus Fine Arts; Philadelphia Mus Art. *Comn:* Color engravings ed 210 prints, Trellis, Int Graphic Arts Soc, 55; Cathedral Interior, 58 & Floating Still Life, 62. *Exhib:* Salon d'Automne, Paris, 51; Int Biennial Contemp Color Lithography, Cincinnati Art Mus, 52; Am Watercolors, Drawings & Prints, Metrop Mus Art, New York, 52; Curator's Choice Exhib, Philadelphia Print Club, 56; Contemp Am Graphic Art, US Info Agency &

Tour Abroad, 61. *Teaching:* Prof art, Auburn Univ, 42-77, artist in residence, 68-77, emer prof, 77- *Awards:* Albany Inst Hist & Art Purchase Award, Print Club, Albany, 63; Philip & Esther Klein Award, Am Color Print Soc, 65; Sabbatical Award, Nat Endowment Arts, 67-68. *Mem:* Soc Am Graphic Artists. *Media:* Oil, Acrylic; Etching, Lithograph. *Publ:* Auth, The Multimetal lithography process, Artists Proof, 68; contrib, Printmaking Today, Holt, Rinehart & Winston, rev ed, 72; contrib, The Print, Abrams, 75. *Mailing Add:* 712 Brenda Ave Auburn AL 36830

SYLVESTRE, GUY
CRITIC, WRITER
b Sorel, Que, May 17, 18. *Study:* Col Ste Marie, Montreal; Univ Ottawa, MA. *Pos:* Ed, Gants du Ciel, 43-46; nat librn, Nat Libr, presently. *Mem:* Soc Ecrivains Can; Can Libr Asn; Royal Soc Can Acad Can Francaise. *Publ:* Auth, Anthologie de la Poesie Canadienne-Francaise, Beauchemin, 64 & 74; auth, Panorama des Lettres Canadiennes Francaises, 64 & Literature in French Canada, 67, EOQ; auth, Ecrivains Canadiens, HMH, 64 & McGraw, 67; auth, Structures Sociales du Canada Francais, Laval, 66; and many others. *Mailing Add:* 1870 Rideau Garden Ottawa ON K1S 1G5 Canada

SZABO, STEPHEN LEE
PHOTOGRAPHER
b Berwick, Pa, July 17, 40. *Study:* Art Ctr Col Design, Los Angeles, Calif; Pa State Univ. *Work:* Int Ctr Photog, Mus Mod Art, New York; Corcoran Gallery Art, Libr Cong, Washington, DC; Int Mus Photog, George Eastman House, Rochester, NY. *Exhib:* Old Techniques by Young Photographers, Eastern Shore, Phillips Collection, Washington, DC, 73, Springfield Art Mus, Mo, 77, Hunter Mus Art, Chattanooga, Tenn, 77, Int Ctr Photog, NY, 77, Fine Arts Mus of the South, Mobile, Ala, 77 & Baltimore Mus Art, Md, 77. *Bibliog:* Paul Richard (auth), Of time and the photograph, Washington Post, 72; A dialogue with the present to document the past, Camera, 76; Mark Power (auth), Washington photographs and the contact print, Wash Rev Arts, 77. *Publ:* Illusr, Where We Live, Fed Home Loan Mortgage Corp, 73; auth-illusr, The Eastern Shore, Addison House, 76. *Dealer:* Kathleen Ewing Gallery 3020 K St NW Washington DC 20007. *Mailing Add:* Quindacqua Ltd 3243 P St NW Washington DC 20007

SZABO, ZOLTAN
PAINTER, WRITER
b Belapatfalva, Hungary, July 9, 28; Can citizen. *Study:* Hungarian Nat Acad Indust Art, 47-48; Famous Artists, 55-56. *Work:* Hungarian Nat Art Gallery, Budapest; Hawaii State Found, Honolulu; Art Gallery of Algoma, Sault Ste Marie, Ont, Can; Manitowoc Marine Mus, Wis; Rock Springs Mus, Wyo. *Comn:* Watercolor painting, comn by Sault Col for Prime Minister Pierre Elliot Trudeau, 73; watercolor portrait of Pres Lawson Sault Col Appl Arts & Technol, Sault Ste Marie, Ont, 75; winter watercolor, City of Sault Ste Marie, 75. *Exhib:* One-man show, Watercolors, York Fine Art Gallery, Aurora, 79; Algoma Fall Festival Exhib, Sault Ste Marie Pub Libr, Ont, 75; Demonstration & Exhib, Salmagundi Club, New York, 78; Retrospect Watercolors, Mississauga Pub Libr, Ont, 79; Am Landscapes, Challis Gallery, Laguna Beach, Calif, 80; and other group & one-man shows. *Pos:* Visual art dir, Algoma Fall Festival, Sault Ste Marie, 74-75. *Teaching:* Resident artist, fac mem & coordr, Sault Col Appl Arts & Technol, Sault Ste Marie, 70-76; travel workshops watercolor, Art Clubs, US, 76- *Bibliog:* Watercolor page, Am Artist, 1/73; Susan Meyer (auth), 40 Watercolorists and How They Work, Watson-Guptill, 75; Pat Lambrecht (auth), Zoltan Szabo: Artist and teacher, Art West Mag, Vol II, Issue 4, 79. *Mem:* Midwest Watercolor Soc (bd mem, 75-79); lifetime hon mem Southwest Watercolor Soc. *Media:* Watercolor, Tempera. *Publ:* Auth, Landscape Painting in Watercolor, 72, Creative Watercolor Techniques, 74, Zoltan Szabo Paints Landscapes: Advanced Techniques in Watercolor, 77 & Zoltan Szabo: Artist at Work, 79, Watson-Guptill. *Dealer:* Pivan Gallery 1911 Eleventh St Boulder CO 80302. *Mailing Add:* PO Box 736 Sault St Marie MI 49783

SZARAMA, JUDITH LAYNE
DRAFTSMAN, ILLUSTRATOR
b Stamford, Conn, Aug 12, 40. *Study:* Swain Sch Design, New Bedford, Mass, BFA. *Work:* Montclair Art Mus, NJ; Miami Art Ctr, Fla; Miami Pub Libr Lending Print Collection. *Exhib:* One-man show, Prints & Drawings, Baker Gallery, Coconut Grove, Fla, 67 & 68; 33 Miami Artists, Miami Art Ctr, 71; 9th Nat Biennial Print Exhib, Silvermine Guild Artists, New Canaan, Conn, 72; Drawings, Ft Lauderdale Mus Arts, Fla, 72; RI Sch Design Fac Exhib, Mus Art, 79; and others. *Pos:* Tech illusr, Eastern Air Lines, Miami, 67-70; asst to chmn grad studies, RI Sch Design, 73-75, dir exhib, 75-, dir continuing educ, 78, dean grad & continuing educ, 79; independent designer & producer, Audio Visual Work, New York, 79- *Teaching:* Instr anat, figure drawing, etching & painting, Miami Art Ctr; instr drawing, Div Archit Studies, RI Sch Design, 75, instr drawing & composition, Summer Workshop Prog, 75. *Awards:* Mint Mus Purchase Award, 70; Outstanding Educator Am, 75; Woman Yr, State RI, 75. *Bibliog:* Frank Laurent (auth), Art, 68 & Bob Watters (auth), Where to let your art hang out, 71, Village Post, Coconut Grove. *Media:* Pencil, Graphic. *Publ:* Auth, Thinking Creatively, Billboard Publ Inc, 8/80. *Mailing Add:* 1276 Lexington Ave New York NY 10028

SZESKO, JUDITH CLARANN See Jaidinger, Judith C

SZESKO, LENORE RUNDLE
PAINTER, PRINTMAKER
b Galesburg, Ill, Mar 13, 33. *Study:* Art Inst Chicago, BFA(drawing, painting, illus), 61, MFA(painting), 66; wood engraving with Adrian Troy. *Work:*

Standard Oil Co, Chicago; NJ State Mus; Jayell Publ House, Miami, Fla; Springfield Col; Kemper Ins Co Collection, Long Grove, Ill. *Exhib:* Conn Acad Fine Arts 62nd Ann, Wadsworth Atheneum, Hartford, Conn, 72; Cedar City Ann Fine Art Exhib, Utah, 72-75; Contemp Am Graphics, Old Bergen Art Guild, Bayonne, NJ (traveling exhib), 72-80; Soc Am Graphic Artists 52nd Nat Print Exhib, New York & Chicago, 73; NH Print Club 1st & 2nd Int, Nashua, 73-74. *Awards:* James R Marsh Mem Purchase Prize, Hunterdon Art Ctr 16th Print, Clinton, NJ, 72; Muth Award, Miniature Painters, Sculptors & Gravers Soc of Washington, DC, 73; Award Highest Merit/Drawing, Miniature Art Soc of Fla Nat Exhib, 76; and others. *Mem:* Audubon Artists, Inc, New York; Painters & Sculptors Soc NJ; Boston Printmakers, Mass; Miniature Art Soc NJ; La Watercolor Soc. *Media:* Multimedia. *Collection:* American Indian and Pre-Columbian, some African art; antique furniture and dolls. *Mailing Add:* 835 S Ridgeland Ave Oak Park IL 60304

SZILVASY, LINDA MARKULY
PAINTER, WRITER
b Granite City, Ill, Oct, 7, 40. *Study:* Lindenwood Col Women, St Charles, Mo, BA, 61; George Peabody Col, Nashville, Tenn, MA, 62. *Work:* Eden Theol Sem, Webster Groves, Mo; US Army Chaplain Mus, Ft Hamilton, NY; Lindenwood Col Women; George Peabody Col. *Comn:* Paintings used for official Christmas cards, First Cavalry Div, Ft Hood, Tex, 72; III Corps, Ft Hood, 73 & 75 & Officer Wives Club, Ft Leonard Wood, Mo, 75; jeweled ostrich shells painted symbols of longevity, comn by Charlene Franz for Premier Sun Yun-hsuan & Pres Chiang Ching-kuo, Taiwan, 78. *Exhib:* One-woman show, Petite Pigalle Gallery, St Louis, Mo, 62; Invitational, Lindenwood Col Women Gallery, St Charles, Mo, 67 & Jeweled Eggs, 77; Ann Show, Women's Club Gallery, Houston, 72; 10th Ann Arts & Crafts Festival, Killeen, Tex, 73; jeweled eggs, Galeria de las Artes, Las Cruces, NMex, 80. *Teaching:* Art instr, Omaha Pub Sch System, Nebr, 63-66, Killeen Independent Sch Dist, Tex, 72-73 & var eggs-ibits, Dallas, Mich & Md, 75- *Awards:* Sweepstakes Winner, 10th Ann Arts & Crafts Festival, Killeen, Tex, 73; Best in Show Eggs-ibits: Dallas, 75, New Carrollton, Md, 75 & 76 & Oklahoma City, Okla, 76. *Bibliog:* Barbara Brabec (auth), The jeweled egg, Artisan Crafts, 4/75; ed staff, The egg and leather, Make It With Leather Mag, 1/77; ed staff, Eggs, $250 a dozen and up, El Paso Today Mag, 4/80. *Mem:* Am Crafts Coun; Artists' Equity Asn. *Media:* Jeweled Egg Shells, Paintings and Sculptures Inside; Paintings on Canvas. *Publ:* Illusr, Around the World in 99 Beds, by Dottie Miller, Eden Publ House, 73; contribr, A bit of the woods, Creative Craft Mag, 6/75; auth, The Jeweled Egg: A Handbook for Beginning and Advanced Craftsmen, Asn Press, 76; contribr, Creative Cash: How to Sell Your Crafts, by Barbara Brabec, Countryside Bks, 79; contribr, Almost Everything About Heirloom Eggs, by Aline Becker, privately publ, 80. *Mailing Add:* 9006 Belk St El Paso TX 79904

SZNAJDERMAN, MARIUS S
PAINTER, PRINTMAKER
b Paris, France, July 18, 26; US citizen. *Study:* Sch Plastic Arts, Caracas, Venezuela, with Rafael Monasterios, Ramon Martin Durban & Ventrillon-Horber, 47-48; Columbia Univ, BS, with printmaker Hans Mueller, BS, 53; T C Colombia, MFA, 58. *Work:* Cincinnati Art Mus, Ohio; Mus Mod Art, New York; Rayo Mus, Roldanillo, Colombia; Yad Washem Mus, Jerusalem, Israel; Printmakers Workshop, New York; and others. *Exhib:* Bienal of Venezuelan Art, Fine Arts Mus, Caracas, 81; Bienal of Latin Am Prints, San Juan, PR, 81; one-man shows, Estevez Vilas Gallery, Cincinnati, 82; Rayo Mus, Colombia, 82 & Galeria Borkas, Lima, 82; and many others. *Pos:* Dir, Galeria Venezuela, New York, 74-83. *Teaching:* Instr art hist & painting, Sch Visual Arts, New York, 65-71; lectr, Fairleigh Dickinson Univ, Madison, NJ, 69-73; artist-in-residence, AIM Prog, NJ Pub Sch, 74- *Bibliog:* Hispanic Culture in New Jersey (film), NJ Pub TV, 78. *Mem:* Mod Artists Guild of NJ (pres, 64-65). *Media:* All. *Mailing Add:* 242 Summit Ave Hackensack NJ 07601

SZOKE, JOHN
DEALER, PUBLISHER
US citizen. *Study:* NY Univ, BS, 72; Grad Sch Bus Admin, MBA, 73. *Pos:* Owner, John Szoke Graphics, New York. *Teaching:* Asst prof, Baruch Col, City Univ New York, 75-79. *Mailing Add:* 144 East 57th New York NY 10022

T

TABACHNICK, ANNE
PAINTER
b Derby, Conn, July 28, 37. *Study:* Hans Hofmann Sch, scholar, three yrs; Hunter Col, BA(anthrop); Univ Calif, Berkeley; NY Univ. *Work:* Hyde Collection, Glens Falls, NY; Mus of Univ Calif, Berkeley; Mus Of Univ Mass, Amherst; Metrop Mus Art; Dayton Art Inst, Ohio. *Exhib:* Many one-woman shows in New York & other cities, 51-75; Mus Mod Art Traveling Show-Hofmann & His Students, 62; one-woman shows, Dayton Art Inst, 65, La State Univ Gallery, 75 & Hyde Collection, 76. *Pos:* Reviewer, Art News, 66-67. *Teaching:* Instr art, Dayton Art Inst, 65-67; instr art, Harvard Univ, 68-69; prof painting, Md Inst Col Art, 70-; vis artist, La State Univ, Baton Rouge, 75, 78 & 81. *Awards:* Creative Artists Pub Serv Fel, NY State Coun on Arts, 74 & 78; Adolph & Esther Gottlieb Grant, 82; Guggenheim Grant, 83. *Bibliog:* D Cochrane (auth), Hans Hofmann's students, 3/74 & Tabachnick-lyrical expressionist, 6/74, Am Artist; George Nelson Preston (auth), Against the grain: The paintings of Anne Tabachnick, Arts, 1/79. *Media:* Acrylic, Watercolor. *Dealer:* Ingber Gallery 460 W Roadway New York NY. *Mailing Add:* 463 West St New York NY 10014

TABACK, SIMMS
ILLUSTRATOR, DESIGNER
b New York, NY, Feb 13, 32. *Study:* Cooper Union, BFA; Sch Visual Arts. *Exhib:* Soc Illusr Ann Exhib, 63-78; Art Dir Club Show; Am Inst Graphic Arts; Soc Publ Designers; Type Dir Club. *Teaching:* Instr illus & design, Sch Visual Arts, New York, 67-78. *Awards:* Cert of Merit, Soc Illusr Show & Ten Best Illus Children's Books, New York Times, 67. *Mem:* Soc Illusr; Graphic Artists Guild (pres, 79-80); Illusr Guild (pres, 75-76). *Media:* Pen & Ink; Watercolor. *Publ:* Illusr, Please Share That Peanut, Harcourt-Brace, 67; illusr, Too Much Noise, Houghton-Mifflin, 68; illusr, Euphonia and the Flood, Parent's Mag Press, 76; illusr, Laughing Together, Four Winds Press, 77; auth-illusr, Joseph Had a Little Overcoat, Random House, 77. *Dealer:* Milton Newborn 135 E 54th St New York NY 10022. *Mailing Add:* 38 E 21st St New York NY 10010

TABAK, CHAIM
PAINTER, SCULPTOR
b Nov 13, 46; US citizen. *Study:* Brooklyn Col, 70-71; Art Students League New York, cert, 75. *Work:* Brooklyn Mus; Wichita Art Mus, Kans. *Exhib:* On Radioactive Waste, Harvard Univ, 81 & Yale Univ, 81; International Printmakers, Snug Harbor Cult Ctr, Staten Island, NY, 82; Artists Protest, Pratt Graphics Ctr, New York, 82; Art and the Law, Landmark Ctr, Minneapolis, 82; HRCA 67th Ann, Hudson River Mus, Yonkers, NY, 82. *Bibliog:* Anthony S Maulucci (auth), Radioactive waste as a subject of art, New Haven Register, 2/5/78; John D Klein (reporter), Pollution art, WNEW-TV, New York, 9/81. *Mem:* 41 Union Sq Art Group, New York (dir, 82-84). *Dealer:* Dorsky Galleries Ltd 58 W 58th St New York NY 10019. *Mailing Add:* 41 Union Sq W #825 New York NY 10003

TABASCO, EVANGELINE (SAM WIENER) See Wiener, Sam

TACHA, ATHENA
SCULPTOR, EDUCATOR
b Larrissa, Greece, Apr 23, 36; nat US. *Study:* Nat Acad Fine Arts, Athens, MA(sculpture), 59; Oberlin Col, Ohio, MA(art hist), 61; Univ Paris, PhD(aesthetics), 63. *Comn:* Tide Park, Main St, Smithtown, NY, 77; Ripples, Federal Bldg, Norfolk, Va, 79; Curving Arcades, Univ Ariz, Tucson, 81; crossings, Int Airport, Columbus, Ohio, 82; Blair Fountain, Arkansas River, Tulsa, 83; and others. *Exhib:* One-woman shows, Zabriskie Gallery, New York, 79 & 81; many other exhibs throughout the world, 66- *Teaching:* Prof art, Oberlin Col, Ohio, 73- *Awards:* First Prize (sculpture), May Show, Cleveland Mus Art, 68, 71 & 79; Artists Grantee, Nat Endowment Arts, 75; Fel, Ctr Advanced Visual Studies, Mass Inst Technol, 74. *Bibliog:* Articles, Landscape Architecture, 5/78, Artforum, 1/81; Athena Tacha: Public Sculpture, 82. *Mem:* Artists Equity Asn; Col Art Asn Am (dir, 73-76). *Publ:* Auth, Rodin Sculpture, Cleveland Mus Art, 67; auth, Brancusi's Birds, 69; ed, Art in the Mind, 70. *Mailing Add:* 291 Forest St Oberlin OH 44074

TAFT, FRANCES PRINDLE
HISTORIAN, LECTURER
b New Haven, Conn, Dec 12, 21. *Study:* Vassar Col; Yale Univ, grad sch, with George Heard Hamilton, George Kubler & Sumner McKnight Crosby. *Pos:* Actg dean, Cleveland Inst Art, 73-74. *Teaching:* Chmn liberal arts & instr art survey, 19th & 20th century art, pre-Columbian art, Cleveland Inst Art, 52-; instr, Cleveland Col, Case Western Reserve Univ. *Mem:* Col Art Asn Am; Western Reserve Archit Historians (pres, 71-72); Art Asn Cleveland; Cleveland Mus Art (prog chmn, 72, trustee, 72-). *Res:* Pre-Columbian art in Mesoamerica & Peru. *Collection:* Small pre-Columbian collection and collection of painting, sculpture & prints with a focus on Cleveland artists. *Mailing Add:* 6 Pepper Ridge Rd Cleveland OH 44124

TAGGART, WILLIAM JOHN
PAINTER, SCULPTOR
b Buffalo, NY, Aug 8, 40. *Study:* Art Inst Chicago, BFA; Univ NMex, MFA. *Work:* Int Arrivals Bldg, JFK Airport, New York; Installation, Pub Sch 3, New York; Univ NMex, Albuquerque; Art in the Embassies Prog, Bonn, Ger & New Delhi, India; Mus Contemp Art, Chicago. *Comn:* Sculpture, Port Authority, New York, 73. *Exhib:* Whitney Mus Am Art, New York, 74; Off the Wall, Pace Univ, New York, 74; Hokin Gallery, Chicago, 80; Nina Freudenheim Gallery, Buffalo, NY, 81; Betty Parsons Gallery, New York, 81; Appalachian State Univ, Boone, NC, 82; and others. *Pos:* Vis artist, Sch Art Inst Chicago, 78- *Teaching:* Instr printmaking, Cooper Union, New York, 68-71; instr visual fundamentals, York Community Col, 75; instr, Montclair State Col, NJ, 77- *Mailing Add:* 429 Broome New York NY 10013

TAHEDL, ERNESTINE
STAINED GLASS ARTIST, PAINTER
b Vienna, Austria, Oct 10, 40; Can citizen. *Study:* Acad for Appl Arts, Vienna, Austria, with Franz Herbert, MA in Graphic Arts, 61; with Prof Heinrich Tahedl, coliab in design & execution of stained glass works, 61-63. *Work:* Paintings represented in pub galleries in Vienna, San Salvador, Montpellier, France, London, Ont & Mus du Que, Can. *Comn:* Stained glass murals, Medel Art Gallery, Saskatoon, Sask, 70, Red Revenue Bldg, Quebec, Que, 71, Bibliotheque Varennes, Quebec, 81, Grrenfield Park Libr, Quebec, 82 & Ctr D'Accueil, St Bruno, 82. *Exhib:* one-woman shows, Lefebvre Gallery, Edmonton, Alta, 77-78 & 80-83; McDowell Gallery, Toronto, 82 & Tudor Collection, Montreal, 83; Musee des Arts Decoratifs, Paris, 80; Third & Fourth Int Print Biennale, Korea, 81 & 83; and others. *Awards:* Bronze Medal, Vienna Int Exhib of Painting, 63; Allied Arts Medal, Royal Archit Inst of Can, 66; Can Coun Arts Award, 67. *Bibliog:* Article, Canadian Interiors, Vol 17,

80; Rebecca Sisler (auth), Passionate Spirits, Clarke Irwin, Toronto, 80. *Mem:* Royal Can Acad Arts; Conseil Gravure Que; Soc Artistes Arts Visuels Que. *Publ:* Ltd ed portfolio etchings, Circle of Energy, Art World Int, 81. *Dealer:* Shayne Gallery 5471 Royalmount Montreal PQ Can; Lefevbre Gallery 10238 123rd St Edmonton AB Can. *Mailing Add:* 79 Collard Dr RR One King City ON L0F 1K0 Canada

TAHIR, ABE M, JR
DEALER
b Greenwood, Miss, Feb 18, 31. *Study:* Univ Miss, BBA; George Washington Univ, MBA. *Pos:* Dir, Tahir Gallery, currently. *Specialty:* Original prints. *Publ:* Auth, Hnizdovsky Woodcuts, 76. *Mailing Add:* 823 Chartres St New Orleans LA 70116

TAI, JANE S
ADMINISTRATOR
b Poughkeepsie, NY, May 14, 44. *Study:* Syracuse Univ, BA, 67. *Pos:* Exhib coordr, Everson Mus Art, Syracuse, NY, 67-69; exhib coordr, Am Fedn Arts, New York, 70-75, asst dir, exhib dir, 75-78, assoc dir prog, 78-83, assoc dir & exhib prog dir, 83- *Mailing Add:* American Fedn of Arts 41 E 65th St New York NY 10021

TAICHER, RICHARD
PAINTER
b Philadelphia, Pa, Dec 6, 29. *Study:* Temple Univ, BFA, 52, BS(educ), 53. *Work:* Philadelphia Col Textiles & Sci, Temple Univ & Woodmere Art Gallery, Philadelphia, Pa. *Exhib:* Ann Award Exhib, Civic Ctr, Philadelphia, Pa, 78-80; Pa Acad Fine Arts, Philadelphia; Allied Artists, Nat Acad Design, NY; Butler Inst Am Art, Youngstown, Ohio; Chattaugua Ann, NY; Silvermine Show, New Canaan, Conn; Art USA, Madison Square Garden, NY. *Pos:* Bd dirs, Tyler Sch Fine Arts. *Awards:* Purchase Prizes, Mus Fine Arts, Springfield, Mass, Mus Natural Hist Art, Holyhoke, Mass & Temple Univ. *Mem:* Artists Equity; Am Soc Interior Designers. *Media:* Oil, Pastel. *Dealer:* Pearl Fox Gallery 103 Windsor Ave Melrose Park PA 19176. *Mailing Add:* 613 Passyunk Ave Philadelphia PA 19147

TAIRA, FRANK
PAINTER, SCULPTOR
b San Francisco, Calif, Aug 21, 13. *Study:* Calif Sch Fine Arts; Art Students League; Columbia Univ. *Exhib:* San Francisco Mus Arts, 40; one-man shows, Hudson Guild Gallery, 67 & Caravan House Galleries, 80; Knickerbocker Artists, 68; Nat Arts Club, 68; Far Gallery, 69; Nat Acad of Design, New York, 76; Allied Artists of Am, 76. *Teaching:* Instr painting & drawing, Topaz Art Sch, Utah, 42-43. *Awards:* Nat Arts Club Award, 68. *Media:* Oil, Watercolor; Bronze. *Mailing Add:* 760-67th Street Brooklyn NY 11220

TAIT, CORNELIA DAMIAN
PAINTER, WRITER
b Philadelphia, Pa. *Study:* Temple Univ, scholar, BS; Tyler Sch Fine Arts, BFA(hon), MFA. *Work:* Temple Univ; murals, Tyler Art Sch, Philadelphia, Pa; Asociatia Romania, Bucharest; Nara Philos Study Ctr, Duncannon, Pa; and others. *Comn:* Murals, comn by Morris Rotenberg, Philadelphia, 46; and others. *Exhib:* Philadelphia Art Alliance, 65; Pa Acad Fine Arts, 66; retrospectives, Woodmere Art Gallery, Chestnut Hill, Philadelphia, 66, traveling exhib, Romania, 73 & Romanian Libr, New York, 74; American Painters in Paris, Palais de Congres, 75-76; and others. *Teaching:* Instr art & supvr, Buckingham Friends Sch, 50-53; supvr art, Abington Twp Cult Ctr, 63; lectr, Violet Oakley Mem Found, Philadelphia, 73; lectr Romanian Libr, New York, 74. *Awards:* Painting Award, Phillips Mill Asn, New Hope, 65; Winner, Nat & Int Housing & Urban Develop Art Competition, 72-73; Gold Medal Academician of Italy, 79-80; plus others. *Bibliog:* Interview, Voice of Am, 73, 74 & 76. *Mem:* Artists Equity Asn; Philadelphia Redevelop Authority Artists; Int Platform Asn; Violet Oakley Mem Found; and others. *Media:* Oil, Tempera. *Res:* Byzantine architecture; folk and contemporary art of Romania; folk arts of the American Indians. *Mailing Add:* 10 Armour Rd Hatboro PA 19040

TAJIRI, SHINKICHI
SCULPTOR, EDUCATOR
b Los Angeles, Calif, Dec 7, 23. *Study:* Art Inst Chicago, with Ossip Zadkine; with F Leger, Paris; Acad Grande Chaumiere, Paris. *Work:* Stedelijk Mus, Amsterdam; Mus Mod Art, New York; Louisiana, Copenhagen; Roysman Mus, Rotterdam; CNAC, Paris. *Comn:* AKU fountain, 60; Overhand Knot, Schiphol Airport, Amsterdam. *Exhib:* Stedelijk Mus, 60-67; Venice Biennial, 62; Andre Emmerich Gallery, New York, 65; Kunsthalle, Basel, Switz, 69; Kunsthalle Lund, Sweden, 71. *Teaching:* Guest prof sculpture, Minneapolis Col Art & Design, 64-65; prof sculpture, Hochschule der Kunste, West Berrlin, Ger, 69- *Awards:* Golden Lion, 8th Int Festival Amateur Films, Cannes, France, 55; Mainichi Shibum Prize for Sculpture, Mainichi Newspapers, Tokyo, 63; Grand Prix, The Wet Dream Film Festival, Amsterdam, 70. *Bibliog:* L Freed (auth), Seltsame Spiele, Barmieyer & Nikel, 69. *Publ:* Auth, The Wall, 70; auth, Mayday, 70; auth, Land Mine, 70; ed, Portrait, Self-portrait & Measurements, 72; ed, The Vanishing Island, 74; and others. *Dealer:* Cort Gallery Ostergade 24 Copenhagen Denmark. *Mailing Add:* Castle Scheres Baarlo Netherlands

TAKACH, MARY H
MUSEUM DIRECTOR, HISTORIAN
b New York, NY. *Study:* State Univ NY Binghamton, BA(art hist & humanities), MA(art hist), 73. *Pos:* Cur, asst prof, asst dir, Joe & Emily Lowe Art Gallery, Syracuse Univ, NY, 74-77; dir special exhib, House on Admin

Comt, US House of Representatives, 78; consult humanities adminr, Nat Endowment for Humanities, DC, 78; dir, Pensacola Mus Art, Fla, currently. *Teaching:* Asst prof art hist survey & grad mus studies prog, Syracuse Univ, NY, 74-77. *Awards:* Jennie F Snapp scholar, 70; Ruth Fraizer res scholar, Eng Delta-Kappa Gama Hon Teaching Soc, 74. *Mem:* Col Art Asn; Am Asn Mus. *Res:* Transcribe, annotate and index letters of Benjamin West (1738-1820); catalog raisonne of works by Thomas Douelty (1793-1856). *Publ:* Auth, Still life painting, Sch Arts Mag, 12/65; contribr, Strictly Academic, a Study of Life Drawing in fle 19th Century, 74 & contribr, Binghamton Collects (exhib catalog), 75, Univ Art Gallery, State Univ NY Binghamton. *Mailing Add:* PO Bos 641 Pensacola FL 32593

TAKAI, TEIJI
PAINTER
b Osaka, Japan, Feb 5, 11. *Study:* Shinano Bashi Art Inst, Osaka. *Work:* Corcoran Gallery, Washington, DC; Mod Art Mus, Tokyo, Japan; Columbia Mus, SC; Uniontown Art Club, Pa; Wakayama Mod Art Mus, Japan. *Exhib:* Several one-man shows, Poindexter Gallery, 59-72; Whitney Mus Am Art Ann, New York, 59 & 61; Corcoran Biennial, 61-62; Carnegie Int, Pittsburgh, 61-62; Retrospective, Takashimaya Tokyo, 67. *Teaching:* Vis prof art, Winthrop Col, fall 70 & 72. *Awards:* Okada Prize, 40; Fukushima Prize, 64. *Mem:* Niki Art Asn; Int Artist Asn. *Media:* Oil. *Mailing Add:* c/o Poindexter Gallery 1160 Fifth Ave New York NY 10029

TAKAL, PETER
PAINTER, PRINTMAKER
b Bucharest, Romania, Dec 8, 05; US citizen. *Study:* Paris, France. *Work:* Mus Mod Art, New York; Metrop Mus Art, New York; Whitney Mus Am Art, New York; Cleveland Mus Art; Los Angeles Co Mus Art; and in over 100 mus collections in US & abroad. *Comn:* City Roofs (print), 56, Trees & Fields (print), 57, Print Club Cleveland; four prints, Int Graphic Arts Soc, New York, 56-65; Meditation (print), Assoc Am Artists, New York, 58; Of Man, Of Nature (suite of 20 lithographs), Tamarind Lithography Workshop, Los Angeles, 64; two prints, Hollander Workshop, New York, 69; and others. *Exhib:* Pa Acad Fine Arts, 53-69; Whitney Mus Am Art Ann, 55-69; Recent Drawings USA, Mus Mod Art, New York, 56; one-man show, Cleveland Mus Art, 59 & Smithsonian Inst, 59-60; American Prints Today Traveling Exhib, Print Coun Am, 59, 62 & 63; White House, Washington, DC, 66 & 70; and more than 50 one-man shows in US & abroad, 32-77. *Teaching:* Lectr art, Cleveland Mus Art, 58; artist in residence, Beloit Col Mus, 65; lectr art, Cent Col, 68. *Awards:* Fel, Yaddo Found, 61; Purchase Award, 3rd Nat Print Exhib, Pasadena Art Mus, 62; Ford Fel, Tamarind Lithography Workshop, 63-64; and others. *Bibliog:* Pierre Mornand (auth), Takal portraitiste lineaire evocateur de l'insaisissable, Le Courrier Graphique, 37; Norman Kent (auth), What is good drawing, Am Artist Mag, 45; Leona E Prasse & Louise Richards (auth), Recent Works of Peter Takal, Cleveland Mus Art, 58; and others. *Mem:* Artists Equity Asn New York; Soc Am Graphic Artists; and others. *Media:* Intaglio, Lithography; Drawing. *Publ:* Auth, Selected Works of Peter Takal, Drawings & Poems, Int Univ, 45; auth & illusr, Drawings by Peter Takal, New York Art Libr, 58; auth, Artist's Proof, Vol 1, No 2; illusr, Mother & Child in Modern Art, Duell, 64; auth, About the Invisible in Art, Wright Art Ctr, Beloit Col, 65; and others. *Dealer:* Weyhe Gallery 794 Lexington Ave New York NY 10021; Gallery Weber 13 rue de Monthoux CH1201 Geneva Switzerland. *Mailing Add:* 40 Rue du Mole CH1201 Geneva Switzerland

TAKASHIMA, SHIZUYE VIOLET
ILLUSTRATOR, PAINTER
b Vancouver, BC, Can, June 12, 28. *Study:* Ont Col Art, BA, 53; Fine Arts Inst, San Miguel, Mex (weaving), 65; Pratt Art Ctr Graphic Arts, New York, 66. *Work:* Nat Gallery, Ottawa, Can; Imperial Oil; Can Titanium Pigments Ltd, Montreal; Montreal Standard Publ Co, Montreal; Midland Computer Bldg, Syracuse, NY. *Comn:* Four Posters, Midwestern Regional Libr, Kitchener, Ont, 78. *Exhib:* Hamilton Art Gallery, Ont, 61; Hart House, Univ Toronto, 61; VI Biennial Exhib, Nat Gallery Ottawa, 65; Mystic Circle Traveling Show, Burnaby Art Gallery, 74; five-man show, Montreal Mus Fine Arts, 65; four-man show, Art Gallery Ont, Toronto, 60; one-man shows, Burnaby Art Gallery, BC, 65 & 78 & Japanese Can Cult Ctr, Toronto, 74. *Pos:* Assoc ed, Rika Mag, 76-79; Inner City Angels, Toronto, 79- *Teaching:* Instr drawing & painting, Forest Hill Learning Resources, 71 & Ont Col Art, Toronto, 76- *Awards:* Can Coun Grant, 71 & 73; Bronze Award, Can Asn Children's Libr Asn, 72; Sankai Shinbun Ann Literary Award, Tokyo, 74. *Bibliog:* Robin Mathews (auth), Young Artists, Can Forum, 61; David P Silcox (auth), Young Artists, Can Art Mag, 62. *Media:* Oils, Watercolor. *Dealer:* Barbara Wells Gallery 13 Kaymar Dr Ottawa ON K1J 7C8 Can; Gallery House Sol Georgetown ON Can. *Mailing Add:* 21 Raglan Ave Toronto ON M6C 2K7 Canada

TAKEMOTO, HENRY TADAAKI
CRAFTSMAN, SCULPTOR
b Honolulu, Hawaii, July 23, 30. *Study:* Univ Hawaii, BFA; Los Angeles Co Art Inst, MFA. *Work:* Smithsonian Inst. *Exhib:* Int Exhib Contemp Ceramics, Ostend, Belg, 59; 3rd Int Exhib Contemp Ceramics, Prague, Czech, 62; Studio Potter Exhib, Victoria & Albert Mus, London, Eng, 66-70; Objects: USA, Johnson Wax Collection Contemp Crafts, Smithsonian Inst, Washington, DC, 70-73; Contemp Ceramic Art, US, Can, Mex, Japan, 71-72. *Pos:* Designer & glaze chemist, Wedgewood of Eng, 69- *Teaching:* Instr ceramics, Calif Sch Fine Arts, San Francisco, formerly; instr ceramics, Scripps Col, 65-69; instr ceramics, Otis Art Inst, formerly. *Awards:* Double Purchase Prize, Wichita Art Asn, 59; Silver Medal for Sculpture, Ostend, Belg, 59; Bronze Medal, Mus Contemp Crafts, NY, 60; and others. *Media:* Ceramics. *Mailing Add:* 3209 Landa St Los Angeles CA 90039

TALABA, L (LINDA TALABA CUMMENS)
SCULPTOR, PRINTMAKER
b Detroit, Mich, July 15, 43. *Study:* Detroit Inst Technol, with Maxwell Wright; pvt instr With Lois Pety; Ill Wesleyan Univ, with Fred Brian, BFA; Southern Ill Univ, with David Folkman, Tom Walsh & Lewis Brent Kington, MFA. *Work:* Henry Ford Found Print Collection, Detroit; J B Speed Mus Traveling Print Collection, Tenn; Albion Univ Print Collection; Leopold Schepp Found Collection, New York; Detroit Art Inst Rental Gallery & Collection; and others. *Comn:* Painting, Waterford Twp Bd Educ, 61; painting, Isaac E Crary, Jr High Sch, 63; painting, Burton Title & Abstract Co, Detroit, 67; bronze door ornaments, Little Grassy Mus, Southern Ill Univ, 70; bronze sculpture, Dir & Bur Budget, State of Ill, Springfield, 75; and other comn by individuals. *Exhib:* Libr of Cong Print Show, 65; one-man show, Renee Gallery, Detroit, 68 & Lewis Towers Gallery, Loyola Univ, 75; Ball State Nat Drawing & Small Sculpture; Western Ill Univ, Macomb, 79; North Shore Art, 80; and others. *Teaching:* Guest artist sculpture, Springfield Art Asn, 74-78; guest artist sculpture, Sangamon State Univ, 75-78; guest artist, Lake Co Extension, 80- & Suburban Fine Art Ctr, Highland Park, Ill, 83- *Awards:* Ill State Mus Craftsmans Award, 75; Ball State Univ Nat Award for Sculpture, 75. *Mem:* Delta Phi Delta (treas Bloomington chap, 63-64); Womens Caucus for Art; Am Asn Univ Women; Chicago Art Inst; and others. *Media:* Bronze, Plexiglas; Graphics, Intaglio. *Publ:* Illusr, Lakeland's Paradise, Bd Educ Oakland Co, Pontiac, Mich, 61; art ed, The Argus Newspaper, 62 & illusr, The Black Book (literary mag), 63-65, Ill Wesleyan Univ; illusr, Experimental Math Books, Cent Mid-Western Regional Educ Labs, 70, and others. *Dealer:* Arthur Rubin Gallery Central & Greenbay Rd Highland Park IL 60035. *Mailing Add:* 1316 Oxford Rd Deerfield IL 60015

TALBOT, JAROLD DEAN
MUSEUM DIRECTOR, EDUCATOR
b Solano, NMex, Aug 28, 07. *Study:* Cumming Sch of Art, Des Moines, Iowa; Grand Cent Sch of Art, New York; studied with Edmund Greacen, Ivan Olinsky, Keith Shaw Williams; Millikin Univ, AB, 51. *Exhib:* Audubon Artists, New York, 48; Ohio Valley Oil & Water Color Show, Cincinnati, 54; Interior Valley Show, Cincinnati Art Mus, 58; Ann Exhib, Ill State Mus, Springfield, 59; 14th Ann Exhib, N Miss Valley Artists, 60. *Collections Arranged:* Ann Exhib Cent Ill Artists, 48-60; Tri-State Exhib of Painting & Sculpture, 60-63 & Nat WVa Centennial Exhib of Painting & Sculpture, 63, Huntington Galleries; Ann Exhib New Mexico Artists, Mus of Fine Arts, Santa Fe, 63; Photo Show, Orange Co, New York Hist Churches, 66-67. *Pos:* Dir, Decatur Art Ctr, Ill, 47-60, Huntington Galleries, WVa, 60-63, Fine Arts Gallery, Mus Fine Art, Santa Fe, NMex, 63 & Smith Clove Mus Folk-life, Monroe, NY, 64-71; cur, Hill-Stead Mus, Farmington, Conn, 72-82, retired. *Teaching:* Instr art, Bradley Univ, Peoria, Ill, 46; asst prof art, Millikin Univ, Decatur, Ill, 46-60. *Mem:* Am Asn Mus; Nat Trust Hist Preserv. *Mailing Add:* 24 Main St PO Box 374 Monson MA 01057

TALBOT, JONATHAN
PAINTER, COLLAGE ARTIST
b New York, NY, Nov 14, 39. *Study:* Brandeis Univ; New Sch Social Res; San Francisco Acad Art. *Work:* Smith Col Mus, Northampton, Mass; Byer Mus Arts, Evanston, Ill; Fairleigh Dickinson Univ, Madison, NJ; Toronto Central Libr, Ont; and many other pub & pvt collections. *Exhib:* Mus Managerie, Mus Mod Art, New York, 76; Mohawk Hudson Regional, Albany Inst Hist & Art, 81; Eastern US Print Exhib, Charlotte, NC, 81; Nat Acad Ann, New York, 81 & 82; Boston Printmaker's 34th Nat Exhib, De Cordova Mus, 82; Seventh Ann Small Works Exhib, NY Univ, 83; and many other group and solo shows. *Awards:* Ranger Fund Purchase Award, Nat Acad, 82; Audubon Artists Award, 41st Ann Exhib, Nat Arts Club, 83; C R Gibson Award, Art of Northeast USA, 83; and others. *Publ:* Illusr (frontpiece), A Portrait of the Artist as a Young Man, Easton Press, 77. *Mailing Add:* RD 2, Box 245 Warwick NY 10990

TALLEY, DAN R
WRITER, VIDEO ARTIST
b Hogansville, Ga, Jan 6, 51. *Study:* Atlanta Col Art, BFA, 73; Univ Hartford, MFA(art), 76. *Work:* McKissick Mus, Univ SC, Columbia. *Comn:* Temporary installations, Bennington Col, Vt, 76, Berry Col, Mt Berry, Ga, 78 & collab with Michelangelo Pistoletto, City of Atlanta, Ga, 79. *Exhib:* Expressions: Video Art in Conn, WHTC, Hartford, Conn, 76; Magnetic Image, High Mus Art, Atlanta, Ga & Avant-Garde: 12 in Atlanta, 79; Southeastern Video Sampling, McKissick Mus, Columbia, SC, 78. *Pos:* Asst ed, Contemp Art/Southeast, Atlanta, 76-77; ed, Art Papers, 79-82. *Teaching:* Contemp issues, Atlanta Col Art, 81- *Bibliog:* C W Burnett (auth), Talley at Heath, Atlanta J, spring 77; Sherry Baker (auth), Back to school, Artnews, 2/78; Anne Livet (auth), Creative collaborations, Contemp/Southeast, spring 79. *Mem:* Atlanta Art Workers Coalition (pres, 77-80). *Media:* Film Video. *Publ:* Contribr, Oppenheim interview, Atlanta Art Workers Coalition Newspaper, 9/79; contribr, Duane Hanson: interview, Art Papers, 3-4/81; contribr, Linda Armstrong at Chastain Gallery, Art Papers, 1/83; contribr, Benny Andrews at Madison Morgan Cult Ctr, Art Papers, 1/83; contribr, I used to be a Conceptual interview, Red Hand Bk III, 7/83; and others. *Mailing Add:* 28 16th St NW Atlanta GA 30309

TAM, REUBEN
PAINTER, EDUCATOR
b Kapaa, Hawaii, Jan 17, 16. *Study:* Univ Hawaii, BA, 37, fifth yr cert, 38; Calif Sch Fine Arts; Columbia Univ, with Meyer Schapiro; New Sch Social Res. *Work:* Mus Mod Art, New York; Metrop Mus Art, New York; Whitney Mus Am Art, New York; Brooklyn Mus; Nat Collection Fine Arts, Smithsonian Inst, Washington, DC. *Exhib:* Contemp Am Painting, Whitney Mus Am Art, New York, 41-65; Am Painting, Metrop Mus Art, New York, 53; one-man exhibs, Calif Palace Legion Hon, 40, Portland Art Mus, Ore, 61, Ore State Univ, 66, Wichita Art Asn, Kans, 71, Sheldon Mem Art Gallery, Univ Nebr, 76 & El Paso Mus, Tex, 78; and others. *Teaching:* Instr advan painting, Brooklyn Mus Art Sch, 46-75; prof painting, Ore State Univ, summer 66; vis artist, Ore State Syst Higher Educ, summer 71; vis prof art, Queens Col, New York, 73. *Awards:* Guggenheim Fel, 48; First Prize, Nat Acad of Design Ann, 74 & 77; Award, Am Acad & Inst Arts & Letters, 78; and others. *Bibliog:* Nordness & Weller (auth), Art USA Now, Viking, 62; Gussow (auth), A sense of place: The artist & the American land, Sat Rev, 72; Sawin (auth), Reuben Tam: Island paintings, Arts, 12/75. *Media:* Oil, Acrylic. *Dealer:* Coe Kerr Gallery Inc 49 E 82nd St New York NY 10028. *Mailing Add:* PO Box 831 Kapaa HI 96746

TAMASAUSKAS, OTIS KAZYS
PRINTMAKER
b Terschenreuth, Ger, July 11, 47. *Can citizen. Study:* Univ Windsor, BA(fine arts), 74. *Work:* Windsor Art Gallery, Ont; McDonald Stewart Art Ctr, Guelph, Ont; Art Bank, Ottawa; Agnes Etherington Gallery. *Comn:* Olympic Portfolio, York Univ, Toronto, 76. *Exhib:* International Works on Paper, London Regional Art Gallery, Ont, 81; It Can't Be Done On Canvas, Miriam Pearlman Gallery, Chicago, 82; The Big Print, Harbourfront Art Gallery, Toronto, 82; Can Contemp Print Show, Fine Line Gallery, Bronx Mus, 82; Premio Int Biella, Unione Indust Biellese, Torino, Italy, 83; World Print Four, World Print & Drawing Coun, San Francisco, 83. *Pos:* Co-dir lithography, Open Studio, 76-79; dir etching, 79-80; dir lithography, Three Schools Art, 77-78. *Teaching:* Asst prof printmaking, Univ McMaster, 78-80 & Queens Univ, Kingston, 80-82 & 84; lectr, Scarborough Col, Univ Toronto, 78- *Awards:* Purchase Award, Southwest 32, St Clair Col, Windsor, 74; Ont Arts Coun Grant, 77; Purchase Award, Int Print Biennale, Cartwright Hall, England, 82. *Bibliog:* Kay Woods (auth), Exploring innovations, Arts West, 7/81; Greg Burliuk (auth), Printmaking: The Art of Creating Effects, Whig-Standard, 81; James Elliot (auth), Unequivocably talented, Windsor Star, 82. *Mem:* Ont Soc Artists (exec mem, 78 & 83); Visual Arts Ont (dir, 78); Royal Can Acad Arts. *Media:* Lithography, Intaglio. *Dealer:* Mira Godard Gallery Hazelton Ave Toronto ON. *Mailing Add:* Gen Delivery Priceville ON N0C 1K0 Canada

TAMAYO, RUFINO
PAINTER
b Oaxaca, Mex, 99. *Work:* Mus Mod Art, New York; Mus Art Mod, Paris, France; Mus Arte Mod, Rome, Italy; Mus Royale, Brussels, Belg; Phillips Mem Gallery, Washington, DC. *Comn:* Murals, Govt Mex, Palace Fine Arts, Mexico City, 52, Mus Nac Antropologia, Mexico City, 64 & UN, New York, 72; mural, Dallas Mus Fine Arts, 53; mural, UNESCO Bldg, Paris, 58. *Exhib:* One-man show, San Francisco Mus Art, 53; Nat Mus Mod Art, Tokyo, Japan, 76; Mus Bellas Artes, Caracas, Venezuela, 77; retrospectives, Phillips Col, Washington, DC, 78 & Marion Koogler McNay Art Inst, San Antonio, 79; Guggenheim Mus, 79; Marlborough Gallery, New York, 79 & 81. *Awards:* Oficiel Legion d'Honeur, France; Carnegie Inst, 52 & 55; Guggenheim Int Found Award, 60. *Mem:* Hon mem Acad Arts & Lett; Acad Arte, Buenos Aires, Arg; Acad Diseno, Florence, Italy. *Mailing Add:* Callejon del Santisimo 12 San Angel Mexico DF Mexico

TAMBELLINI, ALDO
VIDEO ARTIST, SCULPTOR
b Syracuse, NY, Apr 29, 30. *Study:* Art Inst, Lucca, Italy, 41-46; Syracuse Univ, NY, BFA, 54; Grad Sch Archit & Allied Arts, Univ Ore, 55-56; Univ Notre Dame, with Ivan Mestrovic, MFA, 59. *Work:* Mus Mod Art, New York; Everson Mus Art, Syracuse, NY. *Comn:* Black Gate Cologne (1st video broadcast by artists, with Otto Piene), WDR-TV, Cologne, Ger, 68; The Media is the Media, WGBH, Boston, Mass, 69. *Exhib:* Some New Beginnings E A T, Brooklyn Mus, New York, 68; one-man shows, Cineprobe, Mus Mod Art, New York, 71 & Everson Mus Art, Syracuse, 78; Television as a Creative Media, Howard Wise Gallery, New York, 69; Spec Video Show, Whitney Mus Am Art, New York, 71; Project '74, Kolinslen Kunstverein, Cologne, Ger, 74; Centerbeam group proj, Doc 6 with Ctr Advan Visual Studies, Mass Inst Technol, Kassel, Ger, 77; Int Biennial Exhib Graphic & Visual Art, Vienna, Austria, 79; Sky Art Conference, Ctr Advan Visual Studies, Mass Inst Technol, 81, Linz, Austria, 82 & Munich, Ger, 83. *Collections Arranged:* Group Center '62 Outdoor Sculpture Show, St Mark's Church in the Bowery, New York. *Pos:* Founder, Black Gate, Pilot Electromedia Ctr in New York, 67; dir, Pilot Proj Video, Div Humanities & Art Inst Chicago, 77. *Teaching:* Fel/instr, Ctr Advan Visual Studies, Mass Inst Technol, Cambridge, 76- *Awards:* NY State Coun Arts Media Award, 69 & 73; Int Grand Prix, Oberhausen Film Festival, 69; Mass Inst Technol Coun Arts Grant, 79 & 81. *Bibliog:* Gene Youngblood (auth), In: Expanded Cinema, Dutton, New York, 70; Doug Davis (auth), Art and the Future, Praeger Publ, New York, 73; Video Art, Dumont Press, Cologne, Ger, 83. *Media:* Video; Film. *Mailing Add:* Ctr for Advan Visual Studies 40 Massachusetts Ave Cambridge MA 02139

TAMBURINE, JEAN
SCULPTOR, PAINTER
b Meriden, Conn, Feb 20, 30. *Study:* Traphagen Sch, New York, 48-49; Art Students League, New York, with Jon Corbino & John Groth, 48-50; also with Elizabeth Gordon Chandler. *Work:* Middletown Pub Libr & State Libr, Middletown, Conn; Nashville Pub Libr, Tenn; Strong Sch, Hartford, Conn; and others. *Exhib:* Town & Country Club Exhib, West Hartford, Conn, 66; George Walter Vincent Smith Art Mus, Springfield, Mass; one-woman show, L'Heure Joyeux, Paris, France, 69; Pearl S Buck Found Exhib, Meriden Pub

Libr, 72; Ellsworth Gallery, Simsbury, Conn, 76; and others. *Pos:* Comnr, Conn Comn on Arts, State Conn, 63-65; chmn & organizer, Cult Comn for Art Appointments to Pub Bldg, 66-70. *Awards:* Founders Prize, Pen & Brush, New York, 81; Assoc Members Prize, Academic Artists Assoc, Inc, Springfield, Mass, 81; Martha Moore Mem Award for Excellence in Portrait, Rockport Art Asn, 83. *Mem:* North Shore Arts Asn; Allied Artists Am; Rockport Art Asn, Mass; Am Artists Prof League; Salmagundi Club. *Publ:* Auth & illusr, How Now, Brown Cow, Abington Press, 67; illusr, It's Nice To Be Little, Rand-McNally, 65; illusr, The Complete Peddlers Pack, Univ Tenn Press, 67; illusr, Something Was Missing, Follett, 69; illusr, Five Busy Bears, Rand-McNally, 69; and others. *Mailing Add:* c/o The Bertolli Studio 73 Reynolds Dr Meriden CT 06450

TANCOCK, JOHN LEON
ADMINISTRATOR, HISTORIAN
b London, Eng, June 11, 42. *Study:* Downing Col, Cambridge Univ, Eng, MA, 63; Courtauld Inst Art, Univ London, PhD, 77. *Collections Arranged:* Multiples the First Decade (auth, catalog), Philadelphia Mus Art, 71. *Pos:* Assoc cur, Philadelphia Mus Art, 67-73; head dept contemp art, Sotheby Parke Bernet, 73-76, head dept impressionist & mod painting, 76- *Publ:* Auth, The influence of Marcel Duchamp, In: Marcel Duchamp, Philadelphia Mus Art & Mus Mod Art, New York, 73-74; auth, The Sculpture of Auguste Rodin, Philadelphia Mus Art & David Godine, 76. *Mailing Add:* c/o Sotheby Parke Bernet 980 Madison Ave New York NY 10021

TANGER, SUSANNA
PAINTER, WRITER
b Boston, Mass, June 9, 42. *Study:* Boston Mus Sch; Univ Colo; Univ Calif, Berkeley. *Exhib:* Post Washington NY Cent Hall Gallery, 75; City of Paris Mus Mod Art, 75; PS 1, New York, 76; Hal Bromm Gallery, New York, 76; Galerie Rencontres, Paris, France, 76; Moore Col of Art Gallery, Philadelphia, 77; and others. *Mailing Add:* 141 Wooster St New York NY 10012

TANGREDI, VINCENT
SCULPTOR
b Compobasso, Italy, May 15, 50. *Study:* Ont Col Art, Toronto, AOCA, 73. *Work:* Can Coun Art Bank, Ottawa; Art Gallery Ont; Nat Gallery Can; York Univ, Downsview, Ont. *Exhib:* Information and Perception, Art Gallery Ont, 72; solo exhibs, Carmen Lamanna Gallery, Toronto, 75-80 & 82 & 49th Parallel Gallery, New York, 84; Transparent Things, Vancouver Art Gallery, 76; Nine Canadian Artists, Kunsthalle, Basel, Switz, 78; Proj Studios One, New York, 84. *Awards:* Grants, Ont Art Coun, 74-78 & Can Coun, 76, 78, 79 & 83. *Bibliog:* Walter Klepac (auth), article, Artscanada, 75. *Publ:* Contrib ed, Impulse Mag, Vol 5, No 3, 77. *Mailing Add:* c/o Carmen Lamanna Gallery 840 Yonge St Toronto ON M4W 2H1 Canada

TANKSLEY, ANN
PAINTER
b Pittsburgh, Pa, Jan 25, 34. *Study:* Carnegie Inst Technol, with Samuel Rosenberg & Balcomb Green, BFA; Art Students League, with Norman Lewis; New Sch Social Res, with Robert Conover; Bob Blackburn Printmaking Workshop. *Work:* Johnson Publ Co, Chicago; Studio Mus In Harlem, New York. *Exhib:* Solo exhibs, Black Hist Mus, 72, Acts of Art, New York, 73-74 & Spectrum IV Gallery, New York, 82; Forever Free, Joslyn Art Mus, 81; Cinque Womens Exhib, New York, 83. *Teaching:* Adj art instr, Suffolk Co Community Col, 73-76. *Awards:* Harlem Cult Coun Grant, 81. *Bibliog:* Elton C Fax (auth), Black Artists of the New Generation, Dodd, Mead & Co, 77; Grace Glueck (auth), Women artists 80, Art News, 10/80; Palmer & Poroner (auths), Art to illustrate man's kinship to nature, Art Speak, 5/27/82. *Mem:* Artist Equity Asn. *Media:* Oil, Charcoal. *Dealer:* Cinque Gallery 20 W 72nd St New York NY 10023. *Mailing Add:* 18 Carlton Rd Great Neck NY 11021

TANNENBAUM, JUDITH E
CURATOR, CRITIC
b Bronx, NY, Oct 26, 44. *Study:* Douglass Col, Rutgers Univ, New Brunswick, NJ, BA(Eng), 66; Hunter Col, City Univ New York, MA(art hist), 73. *Collections Arranged:* Concept, Narrative, Document: Recent Photographic Works from the Morton Neumann Family Collection & Three Dimensional Painting, Mus Contemp Art, Chicago; Landscape in Sculpture, Day In/Day Out: Ordinary Life as a Source for Art & Harry Koursaros, Paintings 1955-1980 (auth, catalog), 81, Freedman Gallery, Albright Col. *Pos:* Ed-in-chief, Noyes Art Books, New York, 75-77; acting cur, Mus Contemp Art, Chicago, 78-79; contrib ed, Arts Mag, New York, 73-81; dir, Freedman Gallery, Albright Col, Reading, Pa, 81- *Teaching:* Instr art hist, Albright Col, Reading, Pa, 81- *Mem:* Col Art Asn Am. *Res:* European and American modern and contemporary art. *Publ:* Auth, Ilya Bolotowsky, 74, Arts Mag; auth, Blythe Bohnen: The kinesthetic of form, 77, Arts Mag; ed, New York Art Yearbook, Noyes Art Books, 76; contribr, Handbook of the Guggenheim Museum Collection, S R Guggenheim Mus, New York, 80. *Mailing Add:* 220 E 78th St New York NY 10021

TANNER, JAMES L
CRAFTSMAN
b Jacksonville, Fla, July 22, 41. *Study:* Fla A&M Univ, BA, 64; Aspen Sch Contemp Art, summer 64; Univ Wis-Madison, MS, 66, MFA, 67; also studied with Harvey Littleton, Donald Reitz, Hal Lotterman & Amos White. *Work:* Del Mus Art, Wilmington; Ill State Univ, Normal; Ray & Lee Grover Antiques, Inc, Cleveland, Ohio; North Hennepin State Jr Col, Minneapolis; Mus Contemp Crafts, New York. *Exhib:* Objects USA, circulated by Smithsonian Inst, 69-70; Glass 2000 BC-1971 AD, John Michael Kohler Art Ctr, Sheboygan, Wis, 71; Reflections on Glass, Long Beach Mus Art, 71-72; Brooks Mem Art Gallery, Memphis, Tenn, 79; Black Artist South, Huntsville Mus Art, Ala, 79; Clayworks, Univ SDak, 80. *Teaching:* Prof art ceramics, Mankato State Univ, Minn, 68- *Awards:* Individual Artist Grant, 80-81; President's Fac Res Award, Mankato State Univ, 77. *Bibliog:* Lee Nordness (auth), Objects USA, 70; Ray Grover & Lee Grover (coauth), Contemporary Art Glass, Crown Publ Co, Inc, 75; Paul Donhauser (auth), The History of American Ceramics--Studio Potter, W C Brown, Kendall/Hunt Publ, 78. *Mem:* Nat Coun Educ Ceramic Arts; Am Craftsman Coun; Minn Craftsman Coun (bd dirs, 72-77). *Media:* Ceramics. *Mailing Add:* Rte 3 Box 189 Janesville MN 56048

TANNER, JOAN ELIZABETH
PAINTER, COLLAGE ARTIST
b Indianapolis, Ind, Nov 25, 35. *Study:* Univ Wis, BA, 57, teachers cert, 58. *Work:* Santa Barbara Mus Art. *Exhib:* Nine West, San Diego Mus Art, 69; Surrealism is Alive & Well in the West, Calif Inst Technol, 72; Abstraction: Alive-Well, State Univ NY Col Potsdam, 75; '79 Collage, Baum/Silverman Gallery, Los Angeles, 79; New Paintings/Paperworks, 1120 Artist's Space, Santa Barbara Mus Art, 79; and others. *Pos:* Pres, Santa Barbara Contemp Arts Forum, presently. *Mem:* Los Angeles Inst Contemp Art. *Mailing Add:* 624 Olive Rd Santa Barbara CA 93108

TANNER, WARREN
PAINTER, ADMINISTRATOR
b Brooklyn, NY, Sept 24, 42. *Study:* Hunter Col, BFA & MA(fine arts). *Work:* Am Telephone & Telegraph; Gen Instrument Corp; Aldrich Mus; Best Products; Needham, Harper & Steers. *Exhib:* Artists Who Make Prints, Orgn Independent Artists, Fordham Univ, 80; Geometric Abstraction, Brooklyn Law Sch, 80; Soho Ctr Arts, New York, 81; Just Above Midtown New York, 81; Aldrich Mus, Ridgefield, Conn, 82; MOA Gallery, New York, 82; Spring Exhib, Am Acad, Rome, 83. *Pos:* Founder, Orgn of Independent Artists, 76-, dir, 77-; panelist, First Nat Conf, Alternative Visual Arts Orgn, Santa Monica, Calif, 78. *Teaching:* Vis lectr art & govt, Pratt Inst, Grad Div, 77; panelist art or polit, Artists Talk on Art, SoHo Ctr for Visual Arts, New York, 78. *Awards:* William Graff Scholar, Hunter Col, 64; Artist-in-Residence, Helen Wurlitzer Found, Taos, NMex, 76; Rome Prize Fel, Am Acad Rome, 82-83. *Bibliog:* Grace Glueck (auth), Art People/Weekend, New York Times, 6/10/77; Citiscope Morris Hirshfield, Channel 31 TV, New York, 12/77. *Mem:* Int Asn Art; Arts Consortia Educ; Downtown, Lower Manhattan Cult Coun. *Publ:* Forum: Charging fees for exhibiting work, Am Artist, 7/78. *Mailing Add:* 118 Prince St New York NY 10012

TAPER, GERI
PAINTER
b Pittsburgh, Pa, Dec 5, 29. *Study:* Univ Pittsburgh, BS, 51; Carnegie Mus Sch; Carnegie-Mellon Grad Studies, 70-72. *Work:* Allentown Mus Art, Pa; Carnegie Mus Art, Pittsburgh; Chase Manhattan Bank, Citibank NAm, New York. *Comn:* The Seasons, Pittsburgh Nat Bank, 73; Trptch (acrylic), Carnegie Libr, Pittsburgh, 74; Learning Environment, Minsky Sch Girls, Pittsburgh, 75; North Corp, Philadelphia, 77; Language (acrylic), Ressler, Ressler & Ressler, New York, 81. *Exhib:* Westmoreland Mus, Greensburg, Pa, 73-75; William Penn Mem Mus, Harrisburg, Pa, 75; Springfield Art Mus, Mo, 75; solo exhib, Carnegie Mus Art, Pittsburgh, 76; Nancy Poole Gallery, Toronto, 79; Grey Art Gallery, NY Univ, 81; and others. *Teaching:* Instr adult educ, Univ Pittsburgh, 69-70; instr, Duquesne Univ, 71-72; instr, Laroche Col, 72-73. *Awards:* Juror's Award, Carnegie Mus Art, 76. *Mem:* Found Community Artists New York. *Media:* Acrylic. *Mailing Add:* c/o A M Sachs Gallery 29 West 57th St New York NY 10019

TARBELL, ROBERTA KUPFRIAN
HISTORIAN, CURATOR
b Mineola, NY, Jan 6, 44. *Study:* Cornell Univ, Ithaca, NY, BS, 65; Univ Del, Newark, MA, 68, PhD, 70. *Collections Arranged:* Early Paintings by Marguerite Zorach (auth, catalog), Smithsonian Inst, 73; Peggy Bacon: Personalities and Places (auth, catalog), Smithsonian Inst, 75; Chaim Gross (auth, catalog), 77; Vanguard American Sculpture (coauth, catalog), Rutgers Univ Art Gallery, 79; Figurative Tradition (coauth, catalog), Whitney Mus Am Art, 80; Hugo Robus (auth, catalog), Smithsonian Inst, 80. *Pos:* Research assoc, Nat Mus Am Art, Smithsonian Inst, 74-80; guest cur, Jewish Mus, 76-77; guest cur, Whitney Mus Am Art, Rutgers Univ Art Gallery & Farnsworth Art Gallery, 79-80; guest cur, Univ Del Gallery, 80-82. *Teaching:* Instr art hist, Univ Del, 67-69, asst prof Am art, 76, vis assoc prof Am & modern art, 79-83. *Awards:* Unidel Grad Fel, Univ Del, 69-72; Smithsonian Inst Pre-Doctoral Fel, 72-74; John Sloan Mem Res Grant, 83. *Mem:* Col Art Asn; Soc Archit Historians. *Res:* Twentieth century American art; modern sculpture. *Mailing Add:* Rd 2 Box 347 Hockessin DE 19707

TARDO, (MANUEL) RODULFO
SCULPTOR
b Matanzas, Cuba, Feb 18, 19; US citizen. *Study:* Nat Fine Arts Sch, Havana, Cuba, prof(sculpture & drawing); Clay Club & Art Students League, scholar. *Work:* Nat Mus Cuba; Sch Archit, Havana; Sch Pedagogy, Havana Univ; Art Gallery Matanzas; Cathedral of St John the Divine, New York. *Comn:* Eagles, Califano Mansion, Glen Cove, NY, 70; bust, Mother Cabrini Park, Newark, NJ, 75; image, Nat Shrine of Immaculate Conception, Washington, DC, 75-76; outdoor bronze sculpture, Church Immaculad Corazon de Maria, Elizabeth, NJ; indoor sculptures, Church Immaculad Corazon de Maria, Newark, NJ, 83. *Exhib:* Philadelphia Mus Art, 49; Mus Nat D'Art Mod, Paris, France, 51; Bienal Hispanoamericana de Arte, Madrid, Spain, 52;

Brooklyn Mus, NY, 73; Metrop Mus Art, New York, NY, 76; one-man shows, Galerie Int, New York, 71, Cisnero Gallery, New York, 73 & Horizon Galleries, New York, 82. *Pos:* Dir, Art Mag, Matanzas, 50-52. *Teaching:* Prof drawing, Sch Plastic Arts, Matanzas, 41-51, dir, 44-49, prof sculpture, 51-61. *Awards:* Gold Medals, Tampa Univ, 52 & Accad Italia Delle, 80. *Bibliog:* Articles, Art News, 2/70 & Arts Mag, 11/70; Jeanne Paris (auth), Rodulfo Tardo, Long Island Press, 71. *Mem:* Artisti Contemp Accad Italia. *Publ:* Auth, Tendenze e Testimonianze dell Arte Contemporanea, Nicole Panepinto & Calogero Panepinto, 83. *Dealer:* Raydon Gallery 1091 Madison Ave New York NY 10023. *Mailing Add:* 50-12 41st St Long Island City NY 11104

TARGAN, JUDY
PRINTMAKER, DESIGNER
b New York, NY, Oct 12, 31. *Study:* Smith Col, BA(magna cum laude), 53; Rutgers Univ, 55; Fairleigh Dickinson Univ, 56-59. *Work:* State Mus, Trenton, NJ; Newark Mus, NJ; Libr Cong, Washington, DC; Univ Pa, Philadelphia; and many others. *Comn:* Women's Div, Jewish Community Fedn, Metropolitan, NJ, 80; Nat Women's Div, Albert Einstein Col Medicine, NJ, 81. *Exhib:* Nat Print, Hunterdon Art Ctr, NJ, 78; State Mus, Trenton, NJ, 78; Boston Mus Fine Arts, Mass, 78; Newark Mus, NJ, 79; Outstanding Women Artists of NJ, YMHA & YWHA, 79; Art for the Table, Philadelphia Art Alliance, Pa, 80. *Awards:* Roth Award, Nat Asn Women Artists, 77; Purchase Award, Irvington Art Asn, NJ, 78; First Prize, Summit Art Ctr Regional Show, 79. *Mem:* Artists Equity; Printmaking Coun NJ; Nat Asn Women Artists. *Mailing Add:* 40 Glenside Rd South Orange NJ 07079

TARIN, GILBERTO A
PAINTER, PRINTMAKER
b San Antonio, Tex, Feb 19, 43. *Study:* Univ of Americas, Puebla, Mex, with Victor Cuevas & Fernando Belain; Our Lady of Lake Univ, San Antonio, Tex. *Work:* San Antonio Art League; SW Craft Ctr, San Antonio. *Exhib:* One-man shows, Galeria Rewi, Mexico City, 71 & Galeria Agustin Arrieta, Puebla, 72; Okla Art Mus, Oklahoma City, 74; Walker & Guthrie Art Ctr, Minneapolis, Minn, 74; McNay Art Inst, San Antonio, 77; and others. *Awards:* Purchase Prize, Tex Watercolor Soc, 74; Cash Award, 26th Ann Tex Watercolor Soc, James K Naylor Mem, 75; First Prize, 47th Ann San Antonio Artists Exhib, Julian Onderdonk Mem, 77. *Mem:* Tex Watercolor Soc. *Media:* Pen & Ink, Gouache; Lithography. *Dealer:* Maggie L Reed 2222 Nacogdoches St San Antonio TX 78209. *Mailing Add:* 927 SW 38th San Antonio TX 78237

TARSHIS, JEROME
WRITER
b New York, NY, June 27, 36. *Study:* Columbia Col, AB, 57. *Awards:* Nat Endowment Arts Art Critic's Fel, 79. *Res:* History of modernism and postmodernism in art and literature. *Publ:* Contribr, Smithsonian, Portfolio, American Heritage, Atlantic Monthly, Art in Am. *Mailing Add:* 1315 Polk St San Francisco CA 94109

TASCONA, ANTONIO TONY
PAINTER, SCULPTOR
b St Boniface, Man, Mar 16, 26. *Study:* Winnipeg Sch Art, dipl; Univ Man Sch Fine Arts. *Work:* Winnipeg Art Gallery, Man; Confederation Art Gallery & Mus Charlottetown, PEI; Art Gallery Ont, Toronto; Nat Gallery Can, Ottawa; Can Coun Collection, Ottawa. *Comn:* Aluminum bas relief, Man Centennial Art Ctr, 67-68; lacquer painting on aluminum, Winnipeg YWCA, 68; sculpture, Fletcher Argue Bldg, Univ Man, 69; epoxy resin disks, in steel rings, Fed Dept Pub Works for Freshwater Inst, Univ Man, 72. *Exhib:* Walker Art Ctr Biennial, Minneapolis, 58; Nat Gallery Can Traveling Exhib Australia, 67; one-man shows, Damjkar Galleries, Ribe, Denmark, 75, Windsor Pub Art Gallery, Ont, 78; Winnipeg Print Show, Can Cult Ctr, Paris, France, 76-77; Winnipeg Centennial Pub Libr Sculpture Competition, Man; Tony Tascona Permanent Exhib, Univ Man, 78; and others. *Teaching:* Univ Man, Sch Architecture. *Awards:* Can Coun Arts Award Fel, 72; Can Silver Jubilee Medal, by Her Majesty, the Queen; Gold Medal, Accademia Italia, 80; and others. *Bibliog:* Rene Ostiguey (auth), Western Canadian art, Vie Arts Montreal, 66; P Fry (auth), Tony Tascona, Artscanada, 72; plus others. *Mem:* Winnipeg Art Gallery; Can Conf Artists; Can Artist Representation; Royal Can Acad Arts. *Mailing Add:* 151 Tache Ave St Boniface MB R2H I2Y Canada

TASENDE, JOSE MARIA
GALLERY DIRECTOR, DEALER
b Bilbao, Spain, 1932; US citizen. *Study:* Inst Bilbao, Basque Country, BA, 48. *Collections Arranged:* Francisco Zuniga: Exhibit of Drawings & Sculpture, Fine Arts Gallery San Diego, 71 & Everson Mus, 77; Jose Luis Cuevas: An Exhibition of Recent Works, Phoenix Art Mus, 75 & Calif Palace Legion Hon, 75; Jose Luis Cuevas Drawings, Brigham Young Univ, 77; Giacomo Manzu: Exhibition of Sculptures & Drawings, Springfield Mus Art, Mo, 78; Roberto Matta: Paintings & Drawings, Metrop Mus, Coral Gables, Fla, 81; Henry Moore Sculptures & Drawings, Blanden Mem Art Gallery, Ft Dodge, Iowa, 82. *Mem:* Art Mus Asn Am. *Mailing Add:* Tasende Gallery 820 Prospect St La Jolla CA 92037

TASGAL-KLIEGMAN, G
CALLIGRAPHER, INSTRUCTOR
b New York, NY. *Study:* Hunter Col; study with Oronzo Maldarelli; Hans Hofmann Sch Fine Arts, Scholar, study with Hans Hofmann; Graphic Arts Ctr, with Shiko Munakato. *Work:* US Educ Found, India. *Exhib:* Whitney Mus, New York; Mus NMex, Santa Fe; Massilon Mus, Ohio; Joslyn Mem Art Mus, Omaha, Nebr; Riverside Mus, New York; plus numerous others. *Teaching:* Studio instruction. *Awards:* First Prize for Sculpture,

Knickerbocker Artists, 74. *Bibliog:* Rave reviews of work in New York Times & New York World-Telegram; plus others. *Mem:* Nat Asn Women Artists (prog comt); Knickerbocker Artists (exec bd); Artists Equity Asn NY; Allied Artists Am; Exp in Art & Technol. *Media:* Multimedia. *Mailing Add:* 430 W 116th St New York NY 10027

TASSE, M JEANNE
EDUCATOR, CALLIGRAPHER
b Worcester, Mass. *Study:* Anna Maria Col, AB, 55; Univ Notre Dame, MA, 62; Boston Univ, PhD, 72. *Teaching:* Prof art & music, Anna Maria Col, 55-75; prof art, Marietta Col, 75- *Mem:* Col Art Asn; Int Ctr Medieval Art; Nat Soc Arts & Lett (vpres Ohio Valley chap, 82-84, pres-elect, 84-); founding mem Marietta Calligraphy Soc (pres, 81-). *Media:* Pen and Ink. *Res:* Iconographic source study of the circular illustrations in the Beatus manuscripts; medieval sculpture. *Collection:* Medieval manuscript folios; miniature prints and paintings. *Mailing Add:* 100 Becker Lane Marietta OH 45750

TATA, SAM BEJAN
PHOTOGRAPHER
b Shanghai, China, Sept 30, 11; Can citizen. *Study:* Self-taught. *Work:* Nat Gallery Can, Pub Arch Can & Nat Film Bd Can, Ottawa; Mus Mod Art, New York. *Exhib:* Phoenix Art Ctr, Ariz, 57; George Eastman House, Rochester, NY, 58; Nat Film Bd, Ottawa, 71; Nat Gallery Can, Ottawa, 81. *Awards:* Gold Medal, Photog Soc India, 47, Bronze Medal, 48; Silver Medal, Bombay Art Soc, 48. *Bibliog:* Norman Hall (auth), Sam Tata's rebellion, Photog, London, 56; John Linder (auth), review, Photoage, Montreal, 62; Hugh Hood (auth), article, Can Fiction Mag, 79. *Mem:* Royal Photog Soc, London; Royal Can Acad Arts. *Publ:* Illusr, Frank Lowe's Montreal, McClelland & Stewart, 63; illusr, Expos 67 Sculpture, Tundra Bks, 67; illusr, Marcel Braitstein, Sculpteur, 70. *Mailing Add:* 1750 Crevier Apt 7 St Laurent Montreal PQ H4L 2X5 Canada

TATE, GAYLE BLAIR
DEALER, PAINTER
b Abilene, Tex, Apr 3, 44. *Study:* Univ Wyo, Laramie, 62-64; Fla State Univ, Tallahassee, BS, 67; Loch Haven Art Ctr, Orlando, Fla, 71-72. *Pos:* Pres, Tate Gallery, Tallahassee, 72-; pres, Interarts Inc/Tate Galleries, Tampa, 73- *Teaching:* Lectr art & Christianity, Univ Tampa, 82. *Mem:* Southeast Prof Art Dealers Asn (pres, 82-). *Media:* Oil. *Specialty:* Nineteenth and early twentieth century European and American works in painting and sculpture. *Collection:* Many works directly from artists and 19th and early 20th century artists. *Publ:* Auth, Miro, The Early Works, Interarts Inc, 78; auth, Art Heart Series, Antique Press, 82-83. *Dealer:* Ray Ketchem Gallerry Atlanta GA. *Mailing Add:* PO Box 333 Black Mountain NC 28711

TATHAM, DAVID FREDERIC
HISTORIAN
b Wellesley, Mass, Nov 29, 32. *Study:* Univ Mass, AB; Syracuse Univ, MA & PhD. *Teaching:* Prof hist art, Syracuse Univ, 68- *Mem:* Col Art Asn; Am Antiq Soc. *Res:* American painting and graphic arts of the nineteenth century. *Publ:* Auth, The Lure of the Striped Pig, Imprint Soc, 74; auth, John Henry Bufford, American Lithographer, Univ Press Va, 76; auth, Winslow Homer's Drawings, Lowe Art Gallery, 79; auth, Winslow Homer in the 1880's, Everson Mus, 83; and others. *Mailing Add:* Dept of Fine Arts Syracuse Univ Syracuse NY 13210

TATISTCHEFF, PETER ALEXIS
DEALER, GALLERY DIRECTOR
b New York, NY, Dec 12, 38. *Study:* Yale Univ, New Haven, Conn. *Collections Arranged:* New Images, Figuration in American Painting, Queens Mus, NY, 74, New Figurative Painting Tour, 77, First Charleston Ann Tour, 77. *Pos:* Pres & dir, Tatistcheff & Co Inc, New York. *Specialty:* Contemporary American painting, drawing. *Mailing Add:* 50 W 57th St 38 E 57th St New York NY 10019

TATOSSIAN, ARMAND
PAINTER
b Alexandria, Egypt, Sept 26, 48; Can citizen. *Study:* Painting with Adam Sherrif Scott, 66-69; McGill Univ, 67-69; Cararra Acad, Bergamo, Italy, mural techniques with Langarette, 70; also painting & lithography with Carzou, Paris, 71. *Work:* Nat Gallery Can, Ottawa; Nat Gallery Athens, Greece; Mus Fine Arts Soviet Armenia; Quebec Mus; Joliette Art Mus. *Comn:* Fight for Liberation (painting), Ecole Polytechnique, Athens, Greece, 74; paintings, Bank Can Nat, Montreal, 74. *Exhib:* Solo exhibs, Kaspar Gallery, Toronto, 79; Pub Arch Can, Ottawa, 80, Linchrist Gallery, Ontario, 80 & Galerie Bernard Desroches, Montreal, 81 & 83; Fed Reserve Bank Gallery, Boston, 81. *Teaching:* Prof, Art Educ, Concordia Univ, 71-74. *Bibliog:* Jean Trepanier (auth), Cent peintres du Quebec, 80; Guy Robert (auth), Art au Quebec, 83 & Art au Quebec depuis trois siecles, 83. *Mem:* Assoc Royal Can Acad Art; res mem Arts Club Montreal; Arts & Lett Club Toronto; Conseil peinture Quebec. *Media:* Oil, Acrylic. *Dealer:* Galerie Bernard Desroches 1444 Sherbrooke St W Montreal PQ Can. *Mailing Add:* 201 Metcalfe Ave Apt 811 Westmount PQ H3Z 2H7 Canada

TATRO, RONALD EDWARD
SCULPTOR, INSTRUCTOR
b Kankakee, Ill, Jan 12, 43. *Study:* Southern Ill Univ, BA & MFA. *Work:* Southern Ill Univ, Carbondale; Southwestern Col. *Exhib:* Fourteenth Ann Purchase Prize Competition, Riverside Art Ctr & Mus, Calif, 76; 22nd Ann All-Calif Show, Laguna Beach Mus Art, Calif, 76; Nat Small Sculpture Exhib,

Cypress Col, Calif, 76; 15th Ann La Mirada Fiesta de Artes, Calif, 76; Crafts-Sculpture-Painting-Graphics, Orange Co Art Asn, Fullerton, Calif, 76; and others. *Teaching:* Instr basic art, Southern Ill Univ, Carbondale, 66-67; asst prof art, Va State Col, 67-68; instr sculpture, Grossmont Col, 68- *Awards:* Third Prize in Sculpture, San Diego Art Inst, 75; Juror's Award, Crafts-Sculpture-Painting-Graphics, Orange Co Art Asn, 76. *Media:* Steel. *Mailing Add:* 210 Highline Trail El Cajon CA 92021

TATTI, BENEDICT MICHAEL
SCULPTOR, PAINTER
b New York, NY, May 1, 17. *Study:* Masters Inst Roerich Mus, with L Slobodkin; Da Vinci Art Sch, with A Piccirilli; State Univ NY; Art Students League, with William Zorach & O Zadkine; Hans Hofmann Sch Art. *Work:* In pvt collections of Mr & Mrs Cass Canfield, New York, Mr & Mrs Zero Mostel, New York & Mr & Mrs Sam Golden, NJ. *Comn:* Sundial, comn by R W Bliss for Dumbarton Oaks, Washington, DC, 52; Bison, comn by E Taylor for Tokyo Park, Japan, 60; D'Aragon Mem, comn by A D'Aragon, Hartsdale, NY, 69; medallions of D Sarnoff, D Eisenhower & Mark Twain, Newell & Lennon, New York. *Exhib:* Artists for Victory, Metrop Mus Art, New York, 42; Pa Acad Fine Arts, Philadelphia, 50-54; Mus Mod Art, New York, 60; Claude Bernard Gallery, Paris, France, 60; Roko Gallery, New York, 67. *Pos:* Consult restoration, Alexanders Sculpture Studio, 46-72; sculptor-designer, Loewry-Smith Assocs, 52-65; artist in residence, Nat Ctr Experiments TV, San Francisco, 69. *Teaching:* Instr sculpture & head dept, H S Art & Design, formerly; instr sculpture, Craft Students League, 66-67. *Awards:* Creative Arts Prog Grant, NY State Coun Arts, 72; Medal of Honor for Sculpture, Painters & Sculptors Soc NJ, 72. *Mem:* Am Soc Contemp Artists; Sculptors League, New York; Painters & Sculptors Soc NJ. *Dealer:* Alexander Gallery 117 E 39th St New York NY 10016. *Mailing Add:* 214 E 39th St New York NY 10016

TAUCH, WALDINE AMANDA
SCULPTOR, COLLECTOR
b Schulenburg, Tex. *Study:* With Pompeo Coppini. *Work:* Witte Mem Mus, San Antonio, Tex; Pan Handle Plains Hist Mus, Campos, Tex; Wesleyan Mus, Ga. *Comn:* Heroic monument to Bedford, Ind, State Ind, 22; The Doughboy Statue, Am Legion, Austin, Tex, 31; Moses Austin Monument, State Tex, 41; Higher Education, comn by Mr & Mrs Andrew Casoles for Trinity Univ (Tex), 68; Gen Douglas MacArthur, Howard Payne Col, Brownwood, Tex, 69. *Exhib:* Nat Sculpture Soc Traveling Show, 31; Women Painters & Sculptors, New York, 32; Coppini Acad Fine Arts, 54-; Witte Mem Mus; Nat Acad Design, New York; and others. *Bibliog:* Shaffer (auth), Making the Texas Ranger of to-day, San Antonio Express, 61; John Field (auth), Unveiling of Gen Douglas MacArthur. *Mem:* Coppini Acad Fine Arts (sponsor, 57-, emer pres, 60-); Nat Sculpture Soc; Am Acad Arts & Lett; Panhandle Plains Hist Soc & Mus (dir arts, 72-73); fel Am Artists Prof League. *Collection:* Paintings by Van iest, Rolla Taylor, Harold Roney & Frank Garvari. *Mailing Add:* 115 Melrose Pl San Antonio TX 78212

TAVENNER, PATRICIA (PAT)
COLLAGE ARTIST, PHOTOGRAPHER
b Doster, Mich, Mar 22, 41. *Study:* Mich State Univ, BA; Calif Col Arts & Crafts, Oakland, MFA. *Work:* San Francisco Mus Art; Oakland Mus Art, Calif; Mills Col; Kansas City Art Inst, Mo. *Comn:* Facade, Mus Contemp Crafts, New York, 71; sect of wall, Can Nat Res Libr, Ottawa, 73. *Exhib:* Small Formatt, Los Angeles Co Mus Art, Los Angeles, 69; Photo Media, Mus Contemp Crafts, New York, 71; Books by Artists, Moore Col, Philadelphia; Inst Environ, Paris, France, 74; one-woman show, Mills Col, Oakland, 74. *Teaching:* Instr, Univ Calif, Berkeley Exten, 67-82; asst prof art, Calif State Univ, San Jose, 72-73 & Calif State Univ, San Francisco, 72-73. *Bibliog:* Donna Meilach (auth), Collage and Assemblage, Crown, 73. *Mem:* Womens Caucus for Art. *Media:* Montage. *Publ:* Contribr, Art et Communication Marginale, 74; contribr, Women See Women, 75; contribr, Art: A Womans Sensibility, 75; contribr, Rubber Stamp Art, 78. *Mailing Add:* 687 Fairmont Ave Oakland CA 94611

TAWNEY, LENORE
WEAVER, ASSEMBLAGE ARTIST
b Lorain, Ohio. *Study:* Univ Ill, 43-45; Inst Design, Ill, with Archipenko, 46-47; also with Martta Taipale, Finland, 54. *Work:* Mus Contemp Crafts, New York; Mus Mod Art, New York; Kunstegwerbe Mus, Zurich; Art Inst Chicago; Brooklyn Mus; and others. *Exhib:* Art Inst Chicago, 79; one-person show, Tacoma Art Mus, Wash, 81; Fiber 82, Hunterdon Art Ctr, Clinton, NJ, 82; Katonah Gallery, NY, 82; Port Hist Mus, Philadelphia, 83; 11th Int Bienniale Tapestry Exhib, Lausanne, Switzerland, 83; and others. *Media:* Linen, Collages. *Mailing Add:* c/o Willard Gallery 29 E 72nd St New York NY 10021

TAYLOR, ANN
PAINTER
b Rochester, NY, Mar 23, 41. *Study:* Vassar Col; New Sch Soc Res, BA, 62; self-taught painter. *Work:* Bank Am, Houston; Bausch & Lomb Inc, Rochester; Centurion Petroleum Corp, Houston; Honeywell Inc, Minneapolis; Xerox, Rochester; and others. *Exhib:* Butler Inst Am Art, Youngstown, Ohio, 66; Gallery Mod Art, New York, 67; Saginaw Art Mus, 68 & 84; Mem Art Gallery, Univ Rochester, 70; Scottsdale Ctr Arts, Ariz, 82 & 84; Rochester Mus & Sci Ctr, 84. *Bibliog:* Donna Marxer (auth), Painting the Very Air, Southwest Art, 2/78; Carol Kotrozo (auth), Ann Taylor, Artspace, 4/81; Donald Locke (auth), Ann Taylor, Arts Mag, 2/83. *Media:* Oil, Lithographs. *Dealer:* C G Rein Galleries 4235 North Marshall Way Scottsdale AZ 85251; Gallery Henoch 80 Wooster St New York NY. *Mailing Add:* 7209 East McDonald Dr No 31 Scottsdale AZ 85253

TAYLOR, BILL (WILLIAM BRADLEY)
SCULPTOR, INSTRUCTOR
b Atlantic City, NJ, Jan 1, 26. *Study:* Inst Contemp Arts, DC, with Alexander Giampietro, cert, 51. *Work:* Talladega Col Mus, Ala; Miami Dade Co Pub Libr Exhib, Miami, Fla. *Exhib:* 200 Yrs of Black Am Art, Los Angeles Co Mus Art; High Mus Art, Atlanta, Ga, 77; Mus Fine Arts, Dallas, 77; Brooklyn Mus Art, 77. *Teaching:* Instr sculpture, Corcoran Sch Art, DC, 65-68; asst prof sculpture, Univ DC, 68-83. *Awards:* Sargent Johnson Award, Nat Exhib Black Artists, Smith Mason Gallery, DC, 71. *Bibliog:* Carol L Myers (auth), Black Power in the Arts, Flint, Mich, 70. *Media:* Stone (Granite Field Stones); Welded Steel. *Mailing Add:* Univ DC Dept of Art 916 G St Washington DC 20001

TAYLOR, BRIE (BENJAMIN DE BRIE)
EDUCATOR, PAINTER
b Paris, France, Mar 5, 23; US citizen. *Study:* Harvard Univ, BS, 47; Art Students League New York, dipl, 55. *Work:* Johnson Mus, Cornell Univ; Mus Mod Art Miami, Fla. *Exhib:* Butler Inst Biennial, 57; American Artists, Dallas Mus Fine Arts, 57; Brooklyn and Long Island Artists, Brooklyn Mus, 58 & 60-62; solo exhib, Mus Mod Art Miami, Fla, 59; Contemporary American Painting, Whitney Mus, 60; Corcoran Gallery Biennial, 61; West Side Artists, Riverside Mus, New York, 66; Indiana Artists, Indianapolis Mus Art, 71. *Pos:* Dean, Parsons Sch Design, 68-70 & Herron Sch Art, Ind Univ, 70-73; dir, Inst Design, Ill Inst Technol, 73-75. *Teaching:* Instr painting & drawing, Pratt Inst, 60-68; instr drawing & visual communications, Parsons Sch Design, 67-70; prof drawing & art hist, Inst Design, Ill Inst Technol, 73- *Awards:* Fels, MacDowell Colony, 62 & Yaddo, 62. *Bibliog:* James R Mellow (auth), In the galleries, Arts Mag, 10/58; Dore Ashton (auth), Art, New York Times, 10/3/58; Henry Butler (auth), New Herron dean, Indianapolis News, 10/30/70. *Mem:* Col Art Asn; Art Students League New York; Figurative Art League Evanston, Ill; Am Asn Univ Prof. *Media:* Oil, Watercolors. *Res:* Art and natural history. *Publ:* Auth, Towards a plastic revolution, Art News, 64; auth, A problem in painting, Sch Arts, 67; auth, John Heliker, Arts Mag, 68; auth, articles, In: Art, Crowell-Collier, 70; auth, Design Lessons From Nature, Watson-Guptill, 74. *Mailing Add:* 1900 W Bradley Pl Chicago IL 60613

TAYLOR, FREDERICK BOURCHIER
PAINTER, SCULPTOR
b Ottawa, Ont, July 27, 06. *Study:* McGill Univ, BArch, 30; Univ London Goldsmiths Col Art, with Stanley Anderson; London Co Coun Sch Arts & Crafts; Byam Shaw Sch Painting, with Ernest Jackson. *Work:* Nat Gallery Can, Ottawa; Pub Archives Can, Ottawa; Art Gallery Ont, Toronto; Montreal Mus Fine Arts; Can War Art Collection; and many others. *Comn:* Etching, Govt Can, Ottawa, 32; etchings & painting for corps in Can & USA, 32-72; portraits, McGill Univ, 41-66; series of paintings, Algoma Steel Corp, Saulte Ste Marie, Ont, 46-47; and many other pvt comn. *Exhib:* Ont Soc Artists, Toronto, 31-; Royal Can Acad Arts, Toronto, 31-72; many group & int traveling exhibs, Can, US & Mex, 31-78; Royal Inst Painters, London, 36. *Pos:* Chmn Que region, Fed Can Artists, 44-45, nat vpres, 45-46. *Teaching:* Instr & lectr drawing & modeling, McGill Univ Sch Archit, 40-43. *Mem:* Royal Can Acad Arts; Print & Drawing Coun Can. *Media:* Oil. *Dealer:* Walter Klinkhoff Gallery 1200 Sherbrooke St W Montreal PQ Can; Roberts Gallery 641 Yonge St Toronto ON Can. *Mailing Add:* Apartado Postal 101 San Miguel de Allende Gto 37700 Mexico

TAYLOR, GAGE
PAINTER
b Ft Worth, Tex, Jan 20, 42. *Study:* Univ of Tex, BFA, 65; Mich State Univ, MFA, 67. *Work:* Pioneer Mus, Stockton, Calif. *Exhib:* Divergent Representation, Smithsonian Inst, Washington, DC, 71; Extraordinary Realities, Whitney Mus of Am Art, New York, 73; Our Land, Our Sky, Our Water, Expo 74, Spokane, Wash, 74; Baja, San Francisco Mus of Art, Calif, 75; Paris Biennale, Mus of Mod Art, Paris, 75; Alternative Realities, Mus of Contemp Art, Chicago, Ill, 76; Calif Painting & Sculpture, Mus of Mod Art, San Francisco, 76 & Nat Collection of Fine Arts, Washington, DC, 77; plus others. *Teaching:* Instr landscape painting, San Francisco Art Inst, 71; instr painting & drawing, pvt studio, 72- *Bibliog:* Thomas Albright (auth), Visuals, Rolling Stone, 9/71; Mary Rourke (auth), Fantastic voyages, Newsweek, 7/77; Walter Hopps (auth Introd), Visions I, Pomegranate, 77. *Media:* Oil, Gouache. *Dealer:* Joseph Chowning Gallery 1717 17th St San Francisco CA; Illuminarium Gallery Larkspur Landing Larkspur CA. *Mailing Add:* Box 383 Woodacre CA 94973

TAYLOR, GRACE MARTIN
PAINTER, EDUCATOR
b Morgantown, WVa. *Study:* Pa Acad Fine Arts; WVa Univ, AB & MA; Ohio Univ; Art Inst Chicago; Art Students League; Bisttram Sch Art; Hans Hofmann Sch Fine Arts. *Work:* Am Color Print Soc; Hallmark Co; Charleston Art Gallery, WVa; and others. *Exhib:* Nat Acad Design, New York, 44 & 48; Am Watercolor Soc, New York, 58 & 59; Am Drawing Biennial, Norfolk Mus, 65; Contemp Gallery, Palm Beach, 67; one-man shows, Artist of the Yr, WVa Univ, 58 & 67 & WVa Univ Creative Arts Ctr, 74. *Pos:* Dean, Mason Col Music & Fine Arts, 50-55, pres, 55-56. *Teaching:* Assoc prof art & head dept, Mason Col Music & Fine Arts, 34-56; assoc prof art, Morris Harvey Col, 56-68; lectr, WVa Univ Div Exten Credit, 67-71. *Awards:* First Prize for Prints, Seven State Exhib, Va Intermont Col, 48; Three State Ann First Prize & Jurors Award, Huntington Galleries, 54 & 64; Citizen of the Yr in Art in WVa, WVa Rhododendron Arts Festival, 71 & First Prize Drawing, 74; Purchase Award Drawing, Allied Artists of WVa, WVa Arts Coun, 73. *Bibliog:* Haas & Packer (auth), Instruction in Audio-Visual Aids, 50 & Morris Davidson (auth), Painting with Purpose, 64, Prentice-Hall. *Mem:* Provincetown Art Asn; Allied Artists WVa (pres, 35-36); Am Asn Univ Prof. *Media:* Oil, Casein. *Mailing Add:* 1604 Virginia St E Charleston WV 25311

TAYLOR, HARRY GEORGE
PRINTMAKER, PHOTOGRAPHER

b Detroit, Mich, Aug 17, 18. *Study:* Sch, Art Inst, Chicago, MFA, 49, studied with Boris Anisfeld, S W Hayter & Moise Smith. *Work:* Utah State Fine Arts, Capitol, Salt Lake City, Utah; Ogden Bd Educ Sch Mus, Utah; Co Sch Mus, Pleasant View, Utah. *Comn:* Eight ft wooden cross, 67 & 12ft wooden sculpture, 68, St James Church, Ogden, Utah; Mini-Show of Graphics, Ogden City Rd Educ, 70. *Exhib:* M H De Young Mem Mus Nat Exhib, San Francisco, Calif, 60; one-man show, Salt Lake Art Ctr, Salt Lake City, Utah, 65-73; Soc Am Graphic Artists Ann Nat Print & Drawing Exhib, Chicago, Ill, 62; Calif Soc Printmakers Traveling Show, Vt, NY, Maine, Ohio, Mass, Pa, Iowa, Wis & others, 75-77; Utah Statewide Competition, 77. *Pos:* Art dir, Meridian Publ Co, Ogden, Utah, 60-77. *Teaching:* Instr painting & drawing, St Bonaventure-Olean, NY, summer, 47; instr oil & watercolor, Weber State Col, Ogden, Utah, 59. *Awards:* Purchase Awards, Chicago Veterans, US Army, 49 & Capital Show, State of Utah, 52; First Place Graphics, 18th Ann Exhib, Ogden Palette Club, 77. *Bibliog:* James L Haseltine (auth), Catalog, Meridian Pub Co, 65; Bob Halliday (auth), 70 & Charlotte, 72, Salt Lake Tribune. *Mem:* Calif Soc Printmakers; Sch of the Art Inst Alumni Asn; Ogden Palette Club (vpres, 67); Venice Int. *Media:* Etching; Woodcut. *Publ:* Illusr, Improvement Era, Norman Press, 60; illusr, How to make a woodcut, Your Home, Meridian, 70; illusr, Hill Air Force Guide, US Air Force, 74; illusr, Exhibit for the Blind, Weber Col, 76; illusr, A Book of Korean Recipes, Twink Lee-Miller, 77. *Mailing Add:* 905 Rancho Blvd Ogden UT 84404

TAYLOR, HUGH HOLLOWAY
HISTORIAN, EDUCATOR

b Charlottesville, Va, July 18, 41. *Study:* Col of William & Mary, Williamsburg, Va, AB(art hist), 63; George Washington Univ, MA(art hist & theory), 65, with Lawrence Leite. *Collections Arranged:* Dir cataloging of collection of Washington Co Hist Soc, Pa, 76-77. *Teaching:* Prof art hist, Washington & Jefferson Col, Washington, Pa, 65-, Edith M Kelso Chair Art Hist, currently. *Mem:* Soc Archit Historians; Nat Trust Hist Preserv; Washington Co (Pa) Hist & Landmarks. *Res:* Nineteenth century architecture of western Pennsylvania. *Mailing Add:* 123 Christman Ave Washington PA 15301

TAYLOR, JOHN C E
PAINTER, EDUCATOR

b New Haven, Conn, Oct 22, 02. *Study:* Acad Julian, Paris, France, 26-28; also with Walter Griffin, France, 26-28; Yale Univ, MA, 40. *Work:* Mus Am Art, New Britain, Conn. *Comn:* Designs for wood carvings, 57-68 & crypt chapel doors, 72, Trinity Col Chapel, Conn; Westover award tablet, Westover Sch, Middlebury, Conn, 58; design for wood carvings, St James Church, Glastonbury, Conn, 62 & St Mary's by the Sea, Fenwick, Conn. *Exhib:* Spring Salon, Paris, 28; Corcoran Gallery Art Biennial, 35 & 39; Artists for Victory Traveling Exhib, 45-46; one-man retrospective, Trinity Col, Conn, 70. *Teaching:* Mem fac art, Lawrenceville Sch, NJ, 36-41; mem fac art, Trinity Col, Conn, 41-56, head dept fine arts, 45-64, prof art hist, 56-70, emer prof fine arts, 70-; instr art hist, Loomis Sch, 55-72, scholar in residence, 70-72. *Awards:* Cooper Prize, Conn Acad Fine Arts, 35; Second Prize, New Orleans Art Asn, 46; Black & White Prize, Rockport Art Asn, 55. *Bibliog:* E A Jewell (auth), Exploring realism & abstraction, New York Times, 31; F Berkman (auth), Much avant-garde art profanation of nature, Hartford Times, 70; J Goldenthal (auth), Taylor work in retrospect, Hartford Courant, 70. *Mem:* Conn Acad Fine Arts; Rockport Art Asn; North Shore Arts Asn; Washington Arts Asn, Conn. *Media:* Oil, Pencil. *Mailing Add:* 30 Four Mile Rd West Hartford CT 06107

TAYLOR, JOHN FRANK ADAMS
WRITER

b Dallas, Tex, Oct 8, 15. *Study:* Princeton Univ, AB(philos), 36, PhD, 40; Lewis & Clark Col, Hon LHD, 68. *Comn:* The Masks of Society (bk), Guggenheim Found, 63-64. *Pos:* Dir, Humanities Res Ctr, Col Arts & Lett, Mich State Univ, 65-67. *Teaching:* Fel art & archaeol, Princeton Univ, 41-42; prof & head dept lit & fine arts, Mich State Univ, 46-52, prof philos, 52- *Awards:* Distinguished Fac Award, Mich State Univ, 61. *Res:* Aesthetics, philosophy of art, theory of form and expression in the visual arts. *Publ:* Auth, The American artist: An essay on the uses of freedom, Centennial Rev Arts & Sci, 63; auth, The humanities in land grant universities, Sat Rev, 64; auth, Design & Expression in the Visual Arts, Dover, 64; auth, The art of encounter, Arts in Soc, 65; auth, The Public Commission of the University, NY Univ Press, 81; and others. *Mailing Add:* 4539 Nakoma Dr Okemos MI 48864

TAYLOR, JOHN LLOYD
MUSEUM DIRECTOR, CONSULTANT

b Muskegon, Mich, May 24, 35. *Study:* Muskegon Community Col, Mich, AA; Southern Ill Univ, BA & MA; Courtauld Inst Art, London Univ; Univ Denver. *Collections Arranged:* Options, 68; A Plastic Presence, 69; Giacometti: Complete Graphics, 70; Picasso in Milwaukee, 71; Eight Artists, 71; The Private World of George Segal, 73; Mr & Mrs Sidney Kohl Collection (auth, catalog), 73-75; German Expressionism, 79; New York Sch Painting, 81; Contemporary American Painting and Sculpture, 82; and others. *Pos:* Dir, Madison Art Ctr, Wis, 65-67; dir exhib & collections, Milwaukee Art Mus, 67-72; dir, Art Hist Galleries, Univ Wis-Milwaukee, 72-74, dir, Fine Arts Galleries, 76- *Teaching:* Asst prof, Univ Wis-Milwaukee, 72-74 & 76- *Awards:* Nat Endowment Arts Fel Mus Prof, 72 & 74. *Mem:* Col Art Asn Am; Int Coun Mus; Am Asn Mus; Arch Am Art; Int Inst Conserv. *Res:* Abstract expressionism. *Publ:* Auth, DeWain Valentine, 73 & Bob Stanley, 74, Art Int; auth, George Sugarman, Art in Am, 74; auth, Wisconsin printmaking workshops, Art News, 75; and others. *Mailing Add:* 2425 West McKinley Ave Milwaukee WI 53205

TAYLOR, JOSEPH RICHARD
SCULPTOR

b Wilbur, Wash, Feb 1, 07. *Study:* Univ Wash, BFA, 31, MFA(cum laude), 32; Univ Okla; Columbia Univ, 40. *Work:* Western Hemisphere Collection, IBM; De Golyer Collection, Univ Okla Libr; Philbrook Mus, Tulsa. *Comn:* W B Bizzell Mem Statue, Univ Okla, 50. *Exhib:* Kansas City Art Inst Ann Midwest Exhib, 33-40; New York World's Fair, 38-39; San Francisco World's Fair, 40; Mus Mod Art, New York, 40; Univ Okla Art Mus; plus others. *Pos:* Lectr & art judge, art clubs & festivals, 69-; actg dir, Art Sch, Univ Okla. *Teaching:* Prof art & head dept sculpture, Fine Arts Col, Univ Okla, 32-63, David Ross Boyd prof, 63-71, emer prof, 71- *Awards:* Okla Hall of Fame, 60; Distinguished Serv Citation, Okla Univ, 77; Distinguished Lifetime Serv in Arts Governor's Award, 78; Best of Show, Okla Sculpture Soc, 81; and others. *Bibliog:* Article, Fortune Mag, 4/61 & fall 69; article, Nat Sculpture Rev Mag, fall 70 & summer 71. *Mem:* Okla Sculpture Soc; Okla Artists Asn. *Media:* All Media. *Mailing Add:* 701 W Brooks St Norman OK 73069

TAYLOR, KENDALL FRANCES
ADMINISTRATOR, HISTORIAN

b New York, NY. *Study:* Univ Oslo, Norway, cert achievement, 60; Fairleigh Dickinson Univ, Rutherford, NJ, BA(lit), 62; Vanderbilt Univ, Nashville, Tenn, MA(lit), 63, MAT(lit), 64; Syracuse Univ, MA(art hist), 75, PhD(interdisciplinary humanities), 79. *Collections Arranged:* Philip Evergood in the Hirshhorn Mus Collection (auth, catalog), Smithsonian Inst, Washington, DC, 78; Political Comment in Contemporary Art (auth, catalog), Brainerd Gallery, 79 & Black and White: Two Views of New York City During the Depression (auth, catalog), 79; The Benefactors: 20th Century Patronage of the Arts (auth, catalog), 80. *Pos:* Chairperson coun, State Univ NY Gallery & Exhib Dirs, 79-80; dir, Brainerd Art Gallery, State Univ NY Col Potsdam, 79-80; dir traveling exhibs, Libr Cong, Washington, DC, 81- *Teaching:* Lectr Brit & Am lit, Univ Md, Europ Div, 65-69; instr mus studies, State Univ NY Col Potsdam, 79-80; instr mus studies, George Washington Univ, Washington, DC, 81- *Awards:* Fels, Ford, 63 & Smithsonian, 77-79. *Mem:* Am Asn Mus; Col Art Asn; Univs Art Asn Can; Writers Guild Am. *Res:* Twentieth century American art and cultural history. *Publ:* Auth, The Poetry of Alberto Marasi, Md Abroad, Univ Md, winter 66; auth, Craft and Art in Los Angeles, Wollstonecraft Press, 74; auth, Philip Evergood and the humanist intention, Am Art Rev, Vol 18, No 3, 78; auth, The Philip Evergood papers, Arch Am Art J, 79; auth, Three men and their museums, Mus Mag, Vol 2, No 6, 82; and others. *Mailing Add:* 1841 Columbia Rd NW Washington DC 20009

TAYLOR, LISA
MUSEUM DIRECTOR

b New York, NY, Jan 8, 33. *Study:* Johns Hopkins Univ, 56-58; Georgetown Univ, 58-62; Corcoran Sch Art, 58-65; Parsons Sch Design, Hon DFA, 77. *Comn:* A Living Mus (film), Smithsonian Inst, 68. *Pos:* Admin asst, President's Fine Arts Comt, 58-62; membership dir, Corcoran Gallery Art, Washington DC, 62-66; prog dir, Smithsonian Inst, Washington, DC, 66-69; dir, Cooper-Hewitt Mus, New York, 69-; mem vis comt, Bank St Col & Fashion Inst Technol, currently; mem, Mayor's Adv Coun Design, New York, currently; adv bd, Art Deco Soc, currently. *Awards:* Exceptional Serv Award, Smithsonian Inst, 69; Bronze Apple Award, Indust Design Soc Am, 76; Thomas Jefferson Award, Am Soc Interior Designers, 76. *Bibliog:* Barbara Dubivsky (auth), Focus on: the Bazaar Woman, Harper's Bazaar, 5/73; Robert Mehlman (auth), Design comes to life, Indust Design, 9-10/76; Barbaralee Diamonstein (auth), The Cooper-Hewitt goes public, Art News, 9/76. *Mem:* Am Crafts Coun; Archit League; Mus Coun New York City; Mus Coun NY State; Art Mus Dirs Asn. *Publ:* Ed, Urban Open Spaces, 79; ed, Cities, 82; ed, The Phenomenon of Change, 84. *Mailing Add:* c/o Cooper-Hewitt Mus Two East 91st New York NY 10028

TAYLOR, MARIE
SCULPTOR

b St Louis, Mo, Feb 22, 04. *Study:* Art Students League; Wash Univ Sch Art, 23-24. *Work:* St Louis Art Mus; also in many pvt collections. *Comn:* Main altar, St Paul's Church, Peoria, Ill, 60; Jefferson Mem Nat Expansion, St Louis Riverfront, for Mansion House, St Louis, 67. *Exhib:* Joslyn Mus Art; Kansas City Art Inst; Southern Ill Univ, Carbondale, 52; Brooks Mem Art Gallery, Memphis, Tenn, 55; Sculpture 1969, Span Int Pavillion, 69; and others. *Awards:* Prizes, Cleveland Art Mus, St Louis Art Guild & Nat Asn Women Artists; and others. *Bibliog:* M King (auth), Christmas exhibits at St Louis galleries, St Louis Post Dispatch, 12/12/69; Dona Z Meilach (auth), Creative carving, Turtle, 69 & Contemporary stone sculpture, Oracle, 70; and many others. *Mem:* Sculptors Guild, NY. *Mailing Add:* 4607 Maryland Ave St Louis MO 63108

TAYLOR, MARY CAZORT
CURATOR, HISTORIAN

b Little Rock, Ark. *Study:* Washington Univ, St Louis, Mo, BFA, 53; Univ Mich, Ann Arbor, MA, 61, PhD, 70. *Pos:* Cur drawings, Nat Gallery Can, Ottawa, 70-, head printing & drawing dept, currently. *Teaching:* Adj prof art hist, Carleton Univ, Ottawa, 77- *Mem:* Keepers of Pub Graphic Collections. *Res:* European drawings, concentration in North Italian, particularly Bolognese, late eighteenth century. *Publ:* Coauth & ed, European Drawings from the National Gallery of Canada, Toronto, 69; auth, The pen and wash drawings of the Brothers Gandolfi, Master Drawings, Vol 14 (1976), 159-65. *Mailing Add:* Dept of Prints & Drawings Nat Gallery of Can Ottawa ON K1A 0M8 Canada

TAYLOR, MICHAEL (ESTES)
GLASS BLOWER, SCULPTOR
b Lewisburg, Tenn, May 10, 44. *Study:* Middle Tenn State Univ, BS; ETenn State Univ, MA & MFA; Penland Sch Arts & Crafts; Univ Wis; Univ Utah. *Work:* Corning Mus of Glass, NY; Lannon Found, Palm Beach, Fla; Tenn State Mus, Nashville; Mus fur Kunsthandiwerk, Frankfurt, WGer; Vanderbuilt Univ, Nashville; and others. *Comn:* Sculptural glass panel Venderbilt Univ, Nashville, 73; two clear glass sculptures, Standard Oil Corp, Chicago, 75. *Exhib:* one-man show, Univ SC, Columbia, 73; Glass: Am, Europe & Japan, Mus fur Kunsthandiwerk, Frankfurt, WGer, 74; Contemp World Glass, Kunsthaus am Mus, Koln, WGer, 75; Contemp Art Glass Group Exhib, Lever House, New York, 76; Am Contemp Glass, Huntington Galleries, WVa, 76; and other group & one-man shows. *Pos:* Chmn arts fac, George Peabody Col, 76- *Teaching:* Instr glass sculpture, Vanderbilt Univ, Nashville, 72-; vis artist, glass, Konfax Skolen, Stockholm, Sweden, 74 & Gerrit Rietuield Akad, Amsterdam, Holland, 74; chmn art dept, Col Idaho, 79-81; chmn glass dept, Rochester Inst Technol, 81- *Awards:* Lewis Comfort Tiffany grant, Tiffany Found, 69; Thord Gray Fel, Am-Scand Found, 74; Fulbright-Hayes Scholar, 74. *Bibliog:* Richard Skull (auth), Michael Taylor: Glass (film), producer, Micki Colman, 68; Rusty Chapman (dir), Glass Craft (film). *Mem:* Tenn Artists-Craftsmen Asn (pres, 70-71); Am Crafts Coun; Glass Art Soc. *Media:* Glass. *Mailing Add:* Glass Dept Rochester Inst Technol Rochester NY 14623

TAYLOR, MICHELE F
PAINTER
b Nov 1, 46; US citizen. *Study:* Ore State Univ, BA(fine arts), 68; Chounard Art Inst, BS, 70. *Work:* Postland Art Mus, Ore; Univ Ore Mus; Ga Pac, Atlanta; Payne-Webber, Portland, Ore. *Exhib:* All Ore Art Exhib, Salem, 81; Portland Art Mus, 82; Northwest Watercolor, Bellevue Art Mus, Wash, 82; Ore Printmakers Invitational, Gresham, 83; Art About Agriculture, Ore State Univ, Corvallis, 84; Summer Images, Seattle Art Mus, 84. *Awards:* State Ore Grant, 79; First Award, Garden Invitational, Salem Art Mus, 79; Cash Award, Art in Agriculture, Ore State Univ, 83. *Bibliog:* Julie Tripp (auth), article, Oregonian News, 2/27/83; article, Ore Mag, 9/83. *Media:* Oil. *Mailing Add:* 421 Middlecrest Rd Lake Oswego OR 97034

TAYLOR, PRENTISS (HOTTEL)
PAINTER, LITHOGRAPHER
b Washington, DC, Dec 13, 07. *Study:* Painting with Charles W Hawthorne; Art Students League, with Charles Locke, Eugene Fitsch & Anne Goldwaite. *Work:* Mus Mod Art, New York; Phillips Collection, Washington, DC; Art Inst Chicago; Nat Collection Fine Arts; and others. *Comn:* Mural in tempera of Bath, Eng, comn by Mr & Mrs R F Flint, New Haven, Conn, 40; mural in oil, Christian Sci Hq, Washington, DC, 49. *Exhib:* Chicago Int Watercolors & Prints, Art Inst Chicago, 30's; Nat Print Exhib, Libr of Cong, Washington, DC, 43-; Painting Watercolor Graphics Ann, Whitney Mus Am Art, New York, 45; Painting in the US, 1946-1949, Carnegie Inst, Pittsburgh; Am Drawing Biennials, Norfolk Mus, Va, 60's; plus many others. *Pos:* Art therapist, St Elizabeth Hosp, Washington, DC, 43-54; art therapist, Chestnut Lodge, Rockville, Md, 58-78. *Teaching:* Prof lectr painting, Am Univ, 55-75. *Awards:* Nat Print Exhib Purchase Awards, Libr of Cong, Washington, DC, 43-; Va Artists Purchase Awards in Watercolors, Va Mus Fine Arts, 43; Cannon Prize in Graphic Arts, Nat Acad Design, 54, Cert of Merit, 77. *Bibliog:* H Salpeter (auth), Prentiss Taylor, Coronet, 4/39; A Cohen (auth), Prentiss Taylor, DC Gazette, 70; Carl Zigrosser (auth), Prints & Their Creators, 74; plus others. *Mem:* Soc Am Graphic Artists; Philadelphia Water Color Club; Artists Equity Asn (bd mem, 71); Soc Washington Printmakers (pres, 43-77). *Media:* Watercolor, Graphic. *Res:* Art as psychotherapy; how art may reintegrate the disordered mind; talent/status vs expectancy/achievement. *Publ:* Illusr, Negro Mother, 31; illusr, Scottsboro Limited, 32; illusr, Why Birds Sing, 33; illusr, American Herb Calendar, 37. *Dealer:* Bethesda Art Gallery 7950 Norfolk Ave Bethesda MD 20014; Franz Bader 2124 Pennsylvania Ave NW Washington DC 20037. *Mailing Add:* 4520 Yuma St NW Washington DC 20016

TAYLOR, RENE CLAUDE
MUSEUM DIRECTOR, HISTORIAN
b London, Eng, Dec 9, 16. *Pos:* Dir, Museo de Arte de Ponce, PR, 62- *Mailing Add:* Museo de Arte de Ponce Ave Las Americas PO Box 1492 Ponce PR 00731

TAYLOR, ROBERT
CRITIC, WRITER
b Newton, Mass, Jan 19, 25. *Study:* Colgate Univ, AB, 47; Brown Univ Grad Sch, 48. *Pos:* Art critic, Boston Herald, 52-67; Boston corresp, Pictures on Exhibit, 54-59; mem staff, Boston Globe Mag, 68-72; art critic, 72-, arts ed, 73- *Teaching:* Prof Eng, Wheaton Col, 60-; lectr art hist, Boston Univ, 72-74. *Publ:* Auth, In Red Weather, 61; ed, publs, Inst Contemp Art, Boston, 67. *Mailing Add:* c/o Boston Globe Mag 135 Morrissey Blvd Boston MA 02107

TAYLOR, ROD ALLEN
ADMINISTRATOR, SCULPTOR
b Feb 29, 32; US citizen. *Study:* Va State Col, BS, 58; Ala State Univ, MEd, 72; Pa State Univ, PhD(art educ), 74. *Work:* Ghent Gallery, Norfolk, Va; Gallery One, Portsmouth, Va; Smith-Mason Art Int, Washington, DC; Bonbonniere Gallery, Managua, Nicaragua; The Little Art Gallery, Raleigh, NC. *Exhib:* Twenty-sixth Ann Metrop Exhib, 63 & Creative Crafts Exhib, 64, Smithsonian Inst, Washington, DC; NY State Expo, Syracuse, 64; President's Park Art Fair, White House Park, Washington, DC, 65; 17th Area Exhib, Corcoran Gallery of Art, Washington, DC, 65; Tidewater Ann Outdoor Exhib, Norfolk, Va, 75. *Pos:* Educ consult, Univ S Ala, Mobile, 70-72; chmn fine arts dept, Norfolk State Col, Va, 74-80. *Teaching:* Instr art educ, Ala State Univ, Montgomery, 68-70 & Pa State Univ, 72 & 74. *Bibliog:* Samella Lewis (ed), Black Artists on Art, Ward Ritchie Press, 71. *Mem:* Nat Art Educ Asn; Nat Conf Artists; Southern Sculptors Soc. *Media:* Stone, Bronze. *Publ:* Auth, The Relationship of Art and Personality, 74. *Mailing Add:* 432 Longdale Crescent Chesapeake VA 23325

TAYLOR, ROSEMARY
CERAMIST, SCULPTOR
b Joseph, Ore. *Study:* Cleveland Inst Art; NY Univ; Greenwich House; Arrowmount Col. *Exhib:* Mansfield Art Ctr, Ohio, 79; Little Art Gallery, NC, 80-81; Art Gallery, Key West, Fla, 81; Taylor Gallery, Baltimore, 81; Hudson River Gallery, New York, 81; and many others. *Pos:* Juror, Fulbright Award & Grants, 81-82. *Teaching:* Instr, Rahway Art Ctr, 50-60. *Mem:* NJ Designer-Craftsman; Am Craft Coun. *Media:* Stoneware. *Publ:* Contribr, McCall's Needlework, Craft Mag & Craft Report; and others. *Mailing Add:* Box 46 River Rd Lumberville PA 18933

TAYLOR, SANDRA ORTIZ
PAINTER, PRINTMAKER
b Los Angeles, Calif, Apr 27, 36. *Study:* Univ Calif, with William Brice & Sam Amato, BA; Iowa State Univ, with Byron Burford, MA. *Work:* Univ Iowa; Macy's Corp, New York; Univ Calif Res Libr, Los Angeles; Oakland Mus. *Exhib:* Prints California, Oakland Mus & Contemp Graphics Ctr, Santa Barbara Mus, 75; 15th Nat Print Show, Bradley Univ, 75; Bicentennial Landscape Exhib, San Francisco Art Comn Gallery, 76; World Print Coun, San Francisco, 81 & 82; San Francisco-Tokyo Exchange Show, Tokyo City Mus, 84; and others. *Pos:* Gallery asst, John Bolles Gallery, 70-71. *Teaching:* Instr, San Francisco Community Col, 66- & Indian Valley Col, Marin, Calif, 74. *Bibliog:* Dwight Johnson (auth), article, Palo Alto Times, 74; Lois Fishman (auth), article, Artweek, 74; Alfred Frankenstein (auth), article in San Francisco Chronicle, 74; and others. *Mem:* Col Art Asn Am; Women's Caucus Art; Artists Equity; and others. *Media:* Multimedia. *Mailing Add:* 31 Coleridge San Francisco CA 94110

TAYSOM, WAYNE PENDELTON
SCULPTOR, EDUCATOR
b Afton, Wyo, Oct 10, 25. *Study:* Univ Wyo; Columbia Univ; Univ Utah, BFA, 48; Ecole Beaux-Arts, Paris; Teachers Col, Columbia Univ, MA, 50; Cranbrook Acad Art. *Work:* Ore State Univ Mem Union; Corvallis Clin, Ore; Univ Ore Erb Mem Union; US Nat Bank Ore, Portland. *Comn:* Archit sculpture, Lane Co Courthouse, Eugene; Corvallis Br, US Nat Bank Ore; fountain & doors, Ore State Univ Libr; coun chamber doors, Salem Civic Ctr, Ore; St Mary's Cath Church, Corvallis; and others. *Exhib:* One-man show, Portland Art Mus, 54; Paper Works, 72; Seattle World's Fair, 62; Am Crafts Coun, Western Craftsmen, 64; Hunnicutt Art Gallery, Hawaii, 67; and others. *Teaching:* Instr sculpture, Univ Ore, 51-52; prof sculpture, Ore State Univ, 53- *Awards:* Purchase Prize, Portland Art Mus, 56. *Mem:* Portland Art Asn; Corvallis Art Asn. *Mailing Add:* Dept of Art Ore State Univ Corvallis OR 97331

TEAGUE, DONALD
PAINTER
b Brooklyn, NY, Nov 27, 1897. *Study:* Art Students League; studied with Norman Wilkinson, London. *Work:* Metrop Mus Art, New York; Brooklyn Mus; Art Inst Chicago; Nat Cowboy Hall Fame, Oklahoma City. *Exhib:* Art Inst Chicago; Royal Watercolor Soc, London; Kyoto Mus, Japan; Calif Statewide Exhib, Santa Cruz, 55; Int Exhibs, Marietta Col, 68 & 72. *Awards:* Silver Medal Watercolor, Nat Acad Western Art, 77; Gold Medal Watercolor, 77 & Silver Medal Mixed-Media, 78, Cowboy Artists Am. *Bibliog:* Ernest Watson (auth), Donald Teague, illustrator, Am Artist, 44. *Mem:* Hon mem Am Watercolor Soc; Nat Acad Design; Salmagundi Club. *Media:* Watercolor. *Mailing Add:* PO Box 745 Carmel CA 93921

TECZAR, STEVEN W
PAINTER, EDUCATOR
b St Joseph, Mo, Aug 8, 48. *Study:* Univ Mo, Columbia, BA, 70, MA, 72. *Work:* Greenville Co Mus Art, SC; Southeastern Ctr Contemp Art, Winston-Salem, NC; Va Mus Fine Arts, Richmond. *Comn:* Screening Center Design, Am Acad Periodontology, Chicago, 74; play structure, Va Commonwealth Univ Child Care Corp, Richmond, 75; Sculpture (wood), Southern Bankshares Inc, Richmond, 75 & Richmond, Fredericksburg & Potomac Railroad Co, 76; play structure, Ethical Soc Nursery Sch, St Louis, 81. *Exhib:* Twelfth Dulin National Print and Drawing Competition, Dulin Gallery Art, Knoxville, Tenn, 78; one-man show, Louis D Beaumont Gallery, St Louis, 80; Paper as Art-Art as Paper, Bixby Gallery, St Louis, 80; 1940-80 Fellowship Recipients, Va Mus, Richmond, 80; Recent Work, Messing Gallery, St Louis, 82; Third Annual Paper in Particular, Art Ctr Gallery, Columbia, Mo, 82; Realism Today, Evansville Mus, Ind, 83; The Next Show, Va Mus, Richmond, 83; DeKalb Nat Print & Drawing Competition, Swen Parson Gallery, Northern Ill Univ, 84. *Teaching:* Grad teaching asst design, Univ Mo, Columbia, 72; asst prof drawing & design, Va Commonwealth Univ, Richmond, 72-79; assoc prof & art div chmn, Maryville Col, St Louis, 79- *Awards:* WVa Arts & Humanities Coun Purchase Award, Charleston Art Gallery Sunrise, 74; Va Mus Purchase Award, 75; Purchase Award, 46th Southeastern Competition, Southern Ctr Contemp Art, 78. *Bibliog:* Nancy N Rice (auth), Kathleen Forecki, Jacquelyn Ruttinger, Steven Teczar, New Art Examiner, 12/82; Patricia Degener (auth), Anniversary Show at Univ Mo, St Louis, St Louis Post-Dispatch, 10/18/83. *Mem:* Col Art Asn Am; Mid-Am Col Art Asn; Nat Coun Art Adminrs. *Media:* Ink, Acrylic. *Publ:* Auth

TEN EYCK / 925

Research and development/design of a wood construction for the Pollak Building, In: A Survey of Faculty and Graduate Research in Interior Design, Interior Design Educators Coun, 74. *Mailing Add:* 518 Cornelia Avenue St Louis MO 63119

TEFFT, ELDEN CECIL
SCULPTOR, EDUCATOR
b Hartford, Kans, Dec 22, 19. *Study:* Univ Kans, BFA, 49, MFA, 50; Cranbrook Acad Art, 51-52; with Bernard Frazier, William McVey. *Comn:* Quest of Space (bronze, aluminum), Fairfax Sch, Kans City, 59; St Francis (bronze), St Benedict's Col, Atchison, Kans, 59; Flight Forms (certrock), Fidelity State Bank, Topeka, Kans, 67; Franklin D Murphy (bronze), Sculpture Garden, Univ Calif, Los Angeles, 69; Moses (bronze), Kans Sch Religion, Lawrence, Kans, 81. *Exhib:* One-man show, Philbrook Art Ctr, Tulsa, Okla, 48; San Francisco Mus Art, Calif, 50; Carnegie Mus, Philadelphia, Pa, 50; The Midwest Show, Joslyn Art Mus, Nebr, 52; 58th Ann Exhib for Western Artists, Denver Art Mus, Colo, 53; Mid-Am Invitational, William Rockhill Nelson Gallery Art, Kans City, Mo, 55; Missouri Show, St Louis Art Mus, 59. *Pos:* Chmn, Nat/Int Sculpture Conferences, 60-78; dir, Nat Sculpture Ctr, Lawrence, Kans, 67-77, Int Sculpture Ctr, Lawrence, Kans, 77-80 & Sculpture Research Ctr, Univ Kans, Lawrence, 80-; dir, Int Sculpture Ctr Inc, Washington, DC. *Teaching:* Prof sculpture, Univ Kans, Lawrence, 50-, Univ Philippines, Quezon City, Univ Ore, Eugene, 64 & Univ de Costa Rica, San Jose, 71. *Awards:* First Award, Wichita Art Asn, 57; Award, City Art Mus St Louis, Mo, 59. *Bibliog:* Dennis Kowal & D Meilach (auths), Sculpture Casting, Crown Publ, Inc, NY, 72; Robert Rose (auth), Moses, The Creation of a Heroic Sculpture, Centron Inc, Lawrence, Kans (in prep). *Media:* Bronze, Stone. *Res:* World sculpture founding techniques and their effect on the creative process. *Publ:* Auth, Bronze Casting of Sculpture (film), Int Film Bureau, Chicago, 60; contribr & ed, Proceedings of the Biennial Nat/Int Sculpture Conferences, Int Sculpture Ctr, 60-78; auth, Craft Horizons The Primitive Foundry, 65; auth, Lost Wax Sculpture Foundry Equipment: Recommendation & Sources, 77 & Lost Wax Sculpture Foundry: Design, 79, Int Sculpture Ctr. *Mailing Add:* 1315 Naismith Dr Lawrence KS 66044

TEILHET-FISK, JEHANNE HILDEGARDE
HISTORIAN, EDUCATOR
b Palo Alto, Calif, May 16, 39. *Study:* Univ Calif, Los Angeles, BA, 62, MA, 67 & PhD(art hist), 75. *Collections Arranged:* Arts of East Africa, Los Angeles Mus Sci & Indust, 67; Dimensions of Black (auth, catalog), La Jolla Mus Art, 70; Dimensions of Polynesia (auth, catalog), San Diego Fine Arts Gallery, 73; Gaugin: Polynesian Sources, Mus A Gauguin, Tahiti, 81. *Pos:* Asst cur, Jos Mus, Nigeria, 67-68; consult ed, Tofua Press, San Diego, Calif, 75-77; filmmaker, Tapa Production in Tonga, 76- *Teaching:* Assoc prof non-Western art hist, Dept Visual Arts, Univ Calif, San Diego, 68- *Awards:* Rockefeller Found Award, Dimensions of Black, 69-70; Kress Found & Nat Endowment Arts Awards, Dimensions of Polynesia, 73. *Res:* Focus on non-Western arts of Oceania, Nepal & Afro-Am with special interests in masking complexes, woman's art forms & folk art. *Publ:* Auth, The Equivocal Nature of the Masking Tradition in Polynesia, Univ Hawaii, 79; auth, The Equivocal Role of Women Artists in Non-Literate Cultures, Heresies, 78; auth, Te Tamari No Atua, Arts Mag, 79; auth, The Role of Women Artists in Polynesia and Melanesia, Dunmore Press, 83; auth, Paradise Review: An Interpretation of Gauguin's Polynesian Symbolism, UMI Press, 83; and others. *Mailing Add:* 12744 Via Donada Del Mar CA 92014

TEITZ, RICHARD STUART
MUSEUM DIRECTOR, HISTORIAN
b Fall River, Mass, July 18, 42. *Study:* Yale Univ, AB; Harvard Univ, MA. *Collections Arranged:* Etruscan Art, 67; Victoran Art, 69; Am Contemp Art, 69; Toulouse-Lautrec, 71; Marisol, 71; Escher, 71. *Pos:* Dir, Wichita Art Mus, Kans, 67-69; assoc dir, Worcester Art Mus, Mass, 69-70, dir, 70-81; dir, Hood Mus Art, Dartmouth Col, Hanover, NH, 81- *Teaching:* Instr archit hist, Boston Archit Ctr, 63-66; instr art hist, Clark Univ, 66-67; prof art, Dartmouth Col, 81- *Mem:* Col Art Asn Am; Asn Art Mus Dirs; Int Coun Mus; Am Asn Mus. *Res:* Classical and Renaissance art. *Collection:* Old master drawings. *Publ:* Auth, Masterpieces of Etruscan Art, 67; auth, Masterpieces of Religious Art, 67; auth, American Victoriana, 69. *Mailing Add:* Hood Mus Art Dartmouth College Hanover NH 03755

TELBERG, VAL
PHOTOGRAPHER, PAINTER
b Moscow, Russia, Feb 14, 10; US citizen. *Study:* Wittenberg Col, BA, 32; Art Students League, 42-56. *Work:* Mus Mod Art, New York; Santa Barbara Mus Art; San Francisco Mus Mod Art; Princeton Univ Art Mus; Minn Inst Art. *Exhib:* Solo exhib, Brooklyn Mus Art, 48, Smithsonian Inst, 51, Parrish Mus Art, Southampton, NY, 65, Hudson River Mus, Yonkers, NY, 66, Guild Hall Mus, East Hampton, NY, 82, New Orleans Mus Art, 82 & San Francisco Mus Mod Art, 83. *Teaching:* Instr photog, Southampton Col, summer 66; co-dir, Youth Theatre Workshop, Guild Hall, East Hampton, NY, 71-76. *Awards:* Yaddo Fels, 53 & 54; Huntington Hartford Fel, 54. *Bibliog:* Deschin (auth), Say It With Your Camera, McGraw-Hill, 50; D Anderson (auth), Elements of Design, Holt, Rinehart & Winston, 61; Helen Harrison (auth), 16 feet of dreamlike imagery, New York Times, 8/15/82. *Mem:* Art Students League. *Media:* Photomontage. *Publ:* Illusr, House of Incest, Swallow Press, 58. *Dealer:* Laurence Miller 30 Christopher St New York NY 10014. *Mailing Add:* PO Box 920 Sag Harbor NY 11963

TELLER, DOUGLAS H
PRINTMAKER, EDUCATOR
b Battle Creek, Mich, June 1, 33. *Study:* Western Mich Univ, BA, 56; Mich State Univ, George Washington Univ, MFA, 62. *Work:* Corcoran Gallery Art, State Dept, George Washington Univ, Smithsonian Inst & Libr of Cong, Washington, DC. *Exhib:* Corcoran Gallery Touring Show, 59 & 60; Relig Arts Show, Smithsonian Inst, DC, 61; Provincetown Art Asn, Chrysler Mus, Mass, 63; Soc Washington Printmakers Int Show, Nat Collection Fine Arts, DC, 64; one-man show, Corcoran Gallery Art, 65; Massilon Mus Invitational, Ohio, 69; two-man show, Dimock Gallery, George Washington Univ, DC, 79; George Washington Univ, 80-83; and others. *Teaching:* Prof graphics & design, George Washington Univ, DC, 63- *Awards:* Third Graphics Award, Arts Club Washington, 61; Third Relig Art Show Award, Smithsonian Inst, 61; First & Purchase Award, Corcoran Gallery Art, 65. *Media:* Serigraphy. *Publ:* Auth, Art and Design, George Washington Univ, 60. *Mailing Add:* Dept Art George Washington Univ Washington DC 20052

TELLER, JANE (SIMON)
SCULPTOR
b Rochester, NY. *Study:* Rochester Inst Technol; Skidmore Col; Barnard Col, BA; also with Ibram Lassaw. *Work:* Newark Mus, NJ; Skidmore Col, Saratoga Springs, NY; Princeton Univ; Dresden Mus, East Germany; Rockefeller Univ, New York; NJ State Mus; and others. *Comn:* Menorah (iron & Plexiglas) & Eternal Light (iron & Plexiglas), Temple Judea, Doylestown, Pa; Wood Sculpture, Unitarian Church, Princeton, NJ; sculpture, NJ State Council on the Arts. *Exhib:* Whitney Mus, 62; NJ State Mus, Trenton, 65-77; Mus Mod Art, New York; Am Embassy, Tokyo, 75; Montclair Art Mus; Philadelphia Art Mus; Queens Col Gallery, NY. *Awards:* Purchase Award, NJ State Mus, 71; Purchase Prize, Trenton State Col, NJ, 72-79; 50th Anniversary Exhib Prize, Philadelphia Art Alliance. *Bibliog:* Donald Willcox (auth), Wood Design, Watson-Guptill, 68; Woodcraft, Golden Press, 76; Dona Z Meilach (auth), Woodworking--The New Wave, Crown. *Mem:* Sculptors Guild; Artists Equity Asn. *Media:* Wood, Graphic. *Mailing Add:* 200 Prospect Ave Princeton NJ 08540

TEMES, MORTIMER (ROBERT)
CARTOONIST, DESIGNER
b Jersey City, NJ, Apr 15, 28. *Study:* Art Students League, with William McNulty, Jon Corbino, Frank Reilly & Robert B Hale, 47-49; NY Univ, BA, 53. *Pos:* Prof free lance cartoonist, 50-; dir spec serv, NJ Inst Technol, 58- *Mem:* Nat Cartoonists Soc; Cartoonists Guild. *Media:* Pen, Ink; Pencil, Watercolor. *Publ:* Illusr, Engineers & Engineering--Some Definitions, 68; illusr, Making Tomorrow Happen, 70; cartoons have appeared in many nat mags & cartoon anthologies. *Mailing Add:* 10 Sycamore Dr Hazlet NJ 07730

TEMPLETON, ROBERT CLARK
PAINTER
b Red Oak, Iowa, May 11, 29. *Study:* Kansas City Art Inst, 46-49; Art Students League, 50-52; Mannheim Acad, Ger, 56. *Work:* Nat Portrait Gallery, Smithsonian Inst; New Sam Rayburn House Off Bldg, House of Rep Collection; Chief of Staff Portrait Collection, Pentagon; Lyndon B Johnson Presidential Libr, Austin, Tex; Emory Univ Ralph E McGill Rm, Atlanta. *Comn:* Presidential portrait James Earl Carter, Ga State Senate, Atlanta, 79; portrait Secretary Treasury Donald Regan, Merrill Lynch, New York; portrait Pres World Bank A W Clausen, Bank Am, San Francisco. *Exhib:* Audubon Artists Exhib, Nat Acad, New York, 59; Ann Iowa Artists Exhib, Des Moines Art Ctr, 64; 14th Mid-Am Ann, William Rockhill Nelson Gallery, Kansas City, 64; If Elected, Nat Portrait Gallery, 72. *Pos:* Mem adv coun, Conn Mattatuck Community Col, Waterbury, 76- *Bibliog:* Gordon Brown (auth), Art for the underground house, Art Voices, 65; John Brod Peters (auth), Portrait of a portraitist, St Louis Globe-Democrat, 1/11/76; Strokes of genius, Saturday Evening Post, 1/79. *Media:* Oil, Pastel. *Mailing Add:* 197 Carmel Hill Rd Woodbury CT 06798

TEN (JAN TEN BROEKE)
PAINTER
b Marienberg, Netherlands, June 8, 30. *Exhib:* Newark Mus, 61; one-man show, Flemington Studio Arts, NJ, 71, Upstairs Gallery, Somerville, NJ, 71 & Papermill Playhouse, Milburn, NJ, 72; Plainfield Regional Art Mus, NJ, 79; and others. *Awards:* Wally's Award, Plainfield Art Asn, 66, First Prize in Oils, 69; Tracy Long Mem Award, Summit Art Ctr, 66. *Bibliog:* Doris Brown (auth), Surrealist's exhibit opens, 5/3/70, Franklin artist, 8/8/71 & Dutch-born artist, 6/25/72, Sunday Home News. *Mem:* Hunterdon Co Art Ctr; NJ Print Coun; Artists Equity. *Media:* Oil. *Dealer:* Geist Mill Studio Mill St Califon NJ 07830. *Mailing Add:* Box 158 RD 1 Somerset NJ 08873

TEN EYCK, CATRYNA (CATRYNA TEN EYCK SEYMOUR)
PAINTER, PRINTMAKER
b New York, NY, June 30, 31. *Study:* Smith Col; Art Students League. *Work:* Nat Collection Fine Arts, Smithsonian Inst, Washington, DC; Calif Palace Legion Hon, San Francisco; Denver Art Mus; Honolulu Acad Arts; Munson-Williams-Proctor Inst, Utica, NY. *Exhib:* 60th Am Ann Exhib, Art Asn Newport, RI, 71; one-man show, New Sch Social Res, New York, 73; Ann Juried Exhib, Sahron Creative Arts Found, Conn, 74. *Awards:* First Prize for Graphics, Springfield Art League, 71; First Prize, Tanglewood Poster Design Competition, Berkshire Art Asn, 75. *Mem:* Cooperstown Art Asn. *Media:* Graphic, Acrylic. *Publ:* Auth, Enjoying the Southwest, Lippincott, 73. *Dealer:* Jean Lumbard Fine Arts 38 E 57th St New York NY 10022; Betsy Marden Fine Arts 1 Astor Place New York NY 10003. *Mailing Add:* Box 363 Salisbury CT 06068

TENNANT, DONNA KAY
GALLERY DIRECTOR, CRITIC
b Waynesburg, Pa, Nov 28, 49. *Study:* Univ Rochester, NY, BA(art hist), 71; Univ NMex, Albuquerque, MA(art hist), 79; also with Beaumont Newhall. *Pos:* Art critic, Houston Chronicle, Tex, 79-81; contrib ed, Artspace Mag, Albuquerque, 79-81; contribr, Artweek Mag, Oakland, Calif, 81-82; registr, Jeremy Stone Gallery, San Francisco, 82- *Mem:* Women's Caucus Art, San Francisco; Am Asn Mus; Media Alliance, San Francisco. *Res:* Second generation abstract expressionism; 19th & 20th century art, history of photography. *Publ:* Auth, Michael Tracy, Artspace, 79; auth, catalog, Amy Freeman Lee, Incarnate Word Col, 81; auth, James Surls, Artweek, 81; auth, John Alexander, Ultra Mag, 81; auth, Magical collages, San Francisco Chronicle, 5/15/82. *Mailing Add:* 2603 Parana Houston TX 77080

TENZER, (DR & MRS) JONATHAN A
COLLECTORS
Dr Tenzer, b New York, NY, May 21, 40. *Study:* Dr Tenzer, Univ Vt, BA, 62; Univ Pa, DMD, 66. *Collection:* A Wyeth, Moses (Anna Robertson), Rockwell; and others. *Mailing Add:* River Bend Rd RD 2 Allentown PA 18103

TERAOKA, MASAMI
PAINTER, SCULPTOR
b Onomichi, Japan, Jan 13, 36. *Study:* Kwansei Gwakuin Univ, Kobe, Japan, BA(esthetics), 59; Otis Art Inst, BA, MFA, 68. *Work:* Oakland Mus; Achenbach Found Graphic Arts, Fine Arts Mus San Francisco; Los Angeles Co Mus Art; Newport Harbor Art Mus, Newport Beach, Calif; Minneapolis Inst Arts. *Exhib:* LA 8, Los Angeles Co Mus Art, 76; one-person exhibs, Whitney Mus Am Art, 79; Newport Harbor Art Mus, Newport Beach, Calif, 80, Fine Arts Mus San Francisco, 80, Honolulu Acad Arts, 80, Santa Barbara Mus Art, 81 & Oakland Mus, 83; 38th Corcoran Biennial Am Painting & Second Western States Exhib, 82. *Media:* Watercolor. *Mailing Add:* c/o Space 6015 Santa Monica Blvd Los Angeles CA 90038

TERKEN, JOHN
SCULPTOR
b Rochester, NY, Jan 11, 12. *Study:* Beaux Arts Inst Design, with Chester Beach, Lee Lawrie & Paul Manship; NY Sch Fine & Indust Arts; Columbia Sch Fine Arts; also Europ art ctrs. *Work:* Roswell Mus, NMex; Gregory Mus, Hicksville, NY. *Comn:* Eagle Fountain, Salisbury Park, East Meadow, NY, 61; New Horizons, Hempstead Town Plaza, 69; Richard Henry Dana Monument, San Juan Capistrano Hist Soc, Calif, 72; Colonial Lad (bicentennial figure), East Meadow, Pub Libr, NY, 77; Three Metaphysical Pioneers, comn by Phineas Parkhurst Quimby, Emma Curtis Hopkins & Ernest Holmes, 79; and others. *Exhib:* Nat Acad Design, New York, 68; Nat Arts Club, New York, 70; Hudson Valley Art Asn, Westchester, NY, 71; Acad Artists Asn, Springfield, Mass, 71; Nat Sculpture Soc, New York, 72. *Pos:* Advert mgr, Nat Sculpture Rev, 49-65, mem ed bd, 70-, mem, Bd Coop Educ Serv, Long Island Dist, 69-, deleg to Fine Arts Fedn New York, 70- *Teaching:* Lectr sculpture, East Meadow High Sch. *Awards:* Louis Comfort Tiffany Found Award, 49; Lindsey Morris Mem Prize, Nat Sculpture Soc, 65; Coun Am Artists Award, Am Artists Prof League, 72. *Mem:* Fel Nat Sculpture Soc (mem coun, 62-, secy, 68-70, first vpres, 77-78 & 78-79); fel Hudson Valley Art Asn; assoc Int Inst Conservators; Acad Artists Asn; Art League Nassau Co; and others. *Media:* Bronze. *Mailing Add:* 386 Chambers Ave East Meadow NY 11554

TERMES (DICK A TERMES)
PAINTER, PHOTOGRAPHER
b San Diego, Calif, Nov 7, 41. *Study:* Black Hills State Col, BS, 64; Univ Wyo, Laramie, MA(art), 69; Otis Art Inst, Los Angeles, MFA, 71. *Work:* Denver Art Mus; Otis Art Inst, Los Angeles; Civic Fine Arts Ctr, Sioux Falls, SDak; Chamberlain Libr, SDak; High Plain Heritage Ctr, Spearfish, SDak. *Comn:* Muses Greek Mythology, comn by Jeanette Lusk, Huron, SDak, 83; murals, SDak Arts Coun, Sioux Falls, 73-80; spheres, comn by Bernice Pink, Chicago, 82 & High Plain Heritage Soc, Spearfish, SDak, 83. *Exhib:* Pillsbury Am Art Exhib, Tenn, 81; Spherical Thinking and Total Photos, Col Archit Gallery, Ariz State Univ, 82 & Univ Ky, Lexington, 83; Chicago Design Fest, Barb Pearman Gallery, 83; solo exhib, Gallery 72, Omaha, Nebr & Calif State Polytech. *Teaching:* Instr art, Henley High Sch, Klamath Falls, Ore, 64-66, Sheridan High Sch, 66-68 & Black Hills State Col, 71-72. *Awards:* SDak Arts Coun Fel, 76 & 80. *Bibliog:* Susan O'Neill (auth), Six point perspective--the total view, Denver Post, 77; David Miller (auth), Total photographer has whole world in his hands, 80, Mod Photog, 80; Daralice Boles (auth), Termes total photo, Progressive Archit, 83. *Media:* Lexan Plastic Globe Canvas, Acrylic. *Mailing Add:* Rte 2 Box 435B Spearfish SD 57783

TERMINI, CHRISTINE
PAINTER, SCULPTOR
b Brooklyn, NY, Sept 30, 47. *Study:* Pratt Inst, BFA, study with Phillip Pearlstein; Hunter Col, MFA, study with Tony Smith & Robert Walker. *Exhib:* Long Beach Mus, NY, 81; Nat Soc Painters Casein & Acrylic, 81; one-woman show, Univ Pa, 82; Art Views, East Hampton, 83; Sound Shore Gallery Inc, Portchester, 83; and others. *Pos:* Art dir, Circle Galleries, New York, 76-77; Jack Gallerie, New York, 76-77; Gallerie La Grande Illusion, New York, 77, Neill Gallery, New York, 78-79; Atelier Royce Ltd, 81, Hanover Fine Arts, Mass, 83. *Teaching:* Lectr galleries, New Sch, Sch Visual Arts, New York, 77-78. *Bibliog:* Chris Jones (auth), The 24 Hour Room, Am Home Mag, 5/77; Current Exhibitions, Women in the Arts Newsletter, 8/77. *Mem:* Women in the Arts; Artists Equity Asn of New York; Found for the Community of Artists; Audubon Artists; Nat Soc Painters in Casein & Acrylic. *Media:* Acrylic; Oil; Clay. *Mailing Add:* 243 E 78th St New York NY 10021

TERRA, DANIEL J
COLLECTOR, PATRON
b Philadelphia, Pa, June 8, 11. *Study:* Pa State Univ, BS, 31; Lehigh Univ, Columbia Univ & Northwestern Univ, 31-36; MacMurray Col, JD, 73; Nat Col Educ, hon DFA, 80. *Pos:* Founder, sponsor & pres, Terra Mus Am Art, Evanston, Ill, currently; US ambassador at large for cult affairs, 81- *Mem:* Nat Arts Club, New York. *Collection:* Early John Singleton Copley portrait; Samuel F B Morse's Gallery of the Louvre and George Caleb Bingham's The Jolly Flatboatmen; a growing number of important Luminist and other nineteenth century paintings; strong representation of American Impressionist works; Maurice Predergast oils, watercolors and monotypes; and many other select works up to and including paintings by Andrew Wyeth and Kenneth Noland. *Mailing Add:* c/o Lawter Int Inc 990 Skokie Blvd Northbrook IL 60062

TERRELL, ALLEN TOWNSEND
SCULPTOR
b Riverhead, NY, Nov 2, 1897. *Study:* Columbia Univ Sch Archit, cert proficiency, 21; Art Students League, with Edward McCartan; Pa Acad Fine Arts, with Albert Laessle; Ecoles Am Fontainebleau, France; Acad Julien, Paris, France; also with Charles Despiau. *Work:* Suffolk Co Hist Soc, Riverhead; Metrop Mus Art, New York & Mus City New York; Archives of Am Art, Smithsonian Inst, Washington, DC; Brooklyn Mus, NY. *Comn:* childrens playrm, 39 & cabin in class lounge (with John Marsman), 46, SS America, US Lines. *Exhib:* Nat Arts Club, 59; Allied Artists Am, 65; Nat Acad Design, 72; one-man show sculpture, Nat Arts Club, 75. *Teaching:* Instr watercolor & still life, Parsons Sch Design, 34-35. *Awards:* Bronze Medal of Hon for Sculpture, Nat Arts Club, 59; Dessie Greer Prize for Sculpture, Nat Acad Design, 72; Bronze Medal, Hort Soc NY; and others. *Mem:* Fel Nat Sculpture Soc; Allied Artists Am; Am Watercolor Soc; Nat Arts Club; Pastel Soc Am. *Media:* High Fire Stoneware, Iron. *Interests:* Antique architectural drawings; drawings collections. *Publ:* Auth, Drawing for sculpture, Nat Sculpture rev, summer 74. *Mailing Add:* 42 Stuyvesant St New York NY 10003

TERRIS, ALBERT
SCULPTOR, CALLIGRAPHER
b New York, NY, Nov 10, 16. *Study:* With Aaron J Goodelman, 33; Works Progress Admin Art Sch, New York; Beaux Arts Inst Design, New York 33-34; City Col New York, with George W Eggers, BSS, 39; Inst Fine Arts, New York Univ, with Walter Friedlander, Richard Krautheimer & A Phillip McMahon, 39-42. *Pos:* Signature piece (with Jimmy Ernst), for Pontiac Hour, Television, Playwrights 56, comn by Nat Broadcasting Co, 56; Sun (for Wide, Wide World), comn by Abe Liss of Electra Films, 58; Words: Strong, Weak, Argonne Nat Lab, Downers Grove, Ill, comn by Dr Ted Novy, 62. *Exhib:* One-man shows, Artist Space, 75 & Gloria Cortella Gallery, New York, 77; Mus Art, Carnegie Inst, Pittsburgh, 58, 61; Brooklyn Mus Biennale, NY, 60; Sculpture Show, Mus Mod Art, New York, 62; Bundy Int Sculpture Exhib, Waitsfield, Vt, 63; Treasures of 20th Century Art, Maremont Collection, Washington Gallery Mod Art, Washington, DC, 64; Critics Choice, Sculpture Ctr New York, 72; and others. *Pos:* Deputy chmn in charge of Dept Art, Sch Gen Studies, Brooklyn Col, NY, 58-70. *Teaching:* Prof sculpture & theory of art, Dept Art, Brooklyn Col, NY, 54- *Awards:* First Prize, Brooklyn Mus Biennial, 60. *Bibliog:* Sidney Geist (auth), Month in review, Arts Mag, 1/58; Michel Seuphor (auth), The Sculpture of this Century, George Brazillier, 60; James Schinneller (auth), Art, Experience & Self Discovery, Int Text Bk Co, Scranton, Pa, 2nd ed, 68. *Media:* Mixed; Acrylic. *Publ:* Contribr, Artists on the current scene, Arts Ann (4), 60; contribr, The Private Myth, Tanager Gallery, 60; auth, Retrospective 1950, 1975, metal sculpture, Freeport Mem Libr, 77. *Mailing Add:* 280 S Ocean Ave Freeport NY 11520

TERRY, DUNCAN NILES
STAINED GLASS ARTIST, CRAFTSMAN
b Bath Maine, Nov 6, 09. *Study:* Sch Mus Fine Arts, Boston; Cent Sch Arts & Crafts, London; also with Ferdnand Leger, Paris. *Comn:* Carved glass, Riverside Church, New York, The White House, Washington, DC & St Mary's Church, Kittanning, Pa; stained glass & carved glass, St James Church, Long Branch, NJ & Trinity Cathedral, Trenton, NJ; work in 30 states, England & Japan. *Media:* Glass. *Mailing Add:* 1213 Lancaster Ave Rosemont PA 19010

TERRY, HILDA (HILDA TERRY D'ALESSIO)
CARTOONIST
b Newburyport, Mass, June 25, 14. *Study:* Art Students League; Nat Acad Design; NY Univ. *Comn:* Fulton Fish Market (acrylics), comn by Sam Marg, New York, 71. *Pos:* Dir, Hilda Terry Gallery, New York; computer animator for electronic score boards; pres & dir, Computered Scoreboard Graphics Exchange Inc; dir archs, Reeder & Terry Ltd. *Teaching:* Instr cartooning, New Sch Social Res, 68; instr cartooning, New York Phoenix Sch Art & Design, 69-71. *Awards:* Wohelo Award, Camp Fire Girls; Best Waste-Not Cartoon, New York Times, 42; NCS Outstanding Animations Cartoonist, 79. *Mem:* Nat Cartoonists Soc. *Specialty:* Computer art and science. *Publ:* Auth, Teena (comic strip), 41-64; auth, Teena (comic bks), 46-49; auth, Originality in Art, 54; assoc ed, Art Collectors Almanac, 65. *Mailing Add:* 8 Henderson Pl New York NY 10028

TERRY, MARION (E)
PAINTER, INSTRUCTOR
b Evansville, Ind, June 4, 11. *Study:* Albright Art Sch; Univ Buffalo; also with Xavier Gonzalez. *Work:* New York Hosp Soc; Univ Bank, Coral Gables;

Abbott Labs, Chicago; Ford Motor Co, Dearborn; Honeywell Mfg Co, Philadelphia. *Comn:* Living War Memorial (476 portraits of every Dade Co serviceman who lost his life in World War II); seven paintings, Com Bank, Winter Park, Fla; four paintings, First Nat Bank, Winter Park; City Nat Bank, Clearwater, Fla. *Exhib:* Southeastern Ann; Ford Motor Co Traveling Exhibs, 55, 57-58; Ft Worth, Tex, 58; Fla Gulf Coast Art, Clearwater, 71 & 73; St Petersburg Art Club; and many others in Miami and Palm Beach, Fla. *Pos:* Art critic, Gulf Beach J. *Teaching:* Instr painting, Craft Village, St Petersburg, 44-69; instr painting, C of C, Madeira Beach, Fla, 69-72; instr pvt classes, Treasure Island Recreation, 74- *Awards:* Award for Pennsylvania Town, 71, First Prize for Landscape in B Minor, 74 & Two Ctr Exhib, 80, Art Guild, Treasure Island, Fla; plus others. *Mem:* Fla Art Group; Fla Fedn Arts; Art Guild, Treasure Island. *Media:* Oil, Acrylic. *Publ:* Illusr, cover for 50th anniversary & auth, articles in St Petersburg Times. *Mailing Add:* 14080 N Bayshore Dr Madeira Beach FL 33708

TESKE, EDMUND RUDOLPH
PHOTOGRAPHER
b Chicago, Ill, Mar 7, 11. *Study:* Huettle Art Sch, Chicago; Art Inst Chicago; Univ Chicago. *Work:* Mus Mod Art, New York; Chicago Art Inst; San Francisco Mus Mod Art; George Eastman House, Rochester, NY; Frederick Wight Gallery, Univ Calif Los Angeles. *Exhib:* Photog 1974, Los Angeles Co Mus Art, 74; one-man shows, San Francisco Mus Art, 63, Art Inst Chicago, 70, Friends of Photog, Carmel, Calif, 75, Revision Gallery, Santa Monica, 75, Susan Spiritus Gallery, Newport Beach, Calif, 76 & Visual Studies Workshop, Rochester, NY, 77; Witkin Gallery, New York, 79. *Pos:* Fel, Taliesin Fel, Frank Lloyd Wright, Spring Green, Wis, 36-37. *Teaching:* Instr, New Bauhaus Inst Design, Chicago, 37-38 & Fed Arts Proj, Chicago, 39-40; asst prof art, Chouinard Art Inst, Los Angeles, 62-64; vis prof photog, Col Fine Arts, Univ Calif Los Angeles, 65-70 & 79 & Immaculate Heart Col, Los Angeles, 74. *Awards:* Grants, Frank Lloyd Wright, 36 & Nat Endowment Arts, 75. *Bibliog:* Wright & Brownell (auth), Architecture & Modern Life, Harper & Bros, 37; Hitchcock (auth), In the Nature of Materials, Duell, Sloan & Pearce, 42; Life-the Art of Photography, Time-Life Books, 71. *Publ:* Auth, Edmund Teske, pvt pub, 74. *Dealer:* Lee Witkin Witkin Gallery 41 E 57th St New York NY 10022. *Mailing Add:* 1652 N Harvard Blvd Los Angeles CA 90027

TETTLETON, ROBERT LYNN
PAINTER, EDUCATOR
b Ruston, La, Dec 23, 29. *Study:* La Polytech Inst, BA, 50; La State Univ, Baton Rouge, MEd, 53. *Exhib:* Mid-South Art Show, Brooks Mem Art Gallery, Memphis, Tenn, 69; one-man shows, Little Theater, Monroe, La, 54, Mary Buie Mus, Oxford, Miss, 70, Sardis Pub Libr, Miss, 79, Univ Gallerie, University, Miss, 81; Teacher's Touch, Miss Mus Art, Jackson; plus others. *Teaching:* Instr art, Northeast La State Col, 55-56; asst prof art, Univ Fla, 61-65; prof art, Univ Miss, 65-, chmn art dept, 65-76. *Mem:* Nat Art Educ Asn; Southeastern Col Art Asn; Col Art Asn; Am Asn Univ Prof; Miss Art Educ Asn (pres, 79-82); and others. *Media:* Oil, Acrylic. *Mailing Add:* 137 Leighton Rd Oxford MS 38677

TEWI, THEA
SCULPTOR
US citizen. *Study:* Art Students League; Greenwich House; New Sch Social Res. *Work:* Nat Collection Fine Arts, Smithsonian Inst, Washington, DC; Cincinnati Art Mus; Chrysler Mus, Norfolk, Va; Univ Notre Dame; Am Ins Co Corp Collection, Galveston, Tex; plus many others. *Exhib:* One-person shows, Hallway Gallery, Washington, DC, 76 & 80 & Randall Gallery, New York, 77, 79, 81 & 83; 18th-20th Ann New Eng Exhib, Silvermine Guild Artists, 65 & 67-69; Nat Arts Club Exhib Relig Art, 66; Erie Summer Festival Arts, Pa State Univ, 68; 6th Biennial of Sculpture, Carrara, Italy, 69; and many others. *Awards:* First Prize for Sculpture, Am Soc Contemp Artists, 71, 75, 76 & 79; Nat Arts Club Medal of Merit, 74 & 75; Sculpture Prize, Nat Asn Women Artists, 75 & 76; and others. *Bibliog:* D Meilach (auth), Contemporary Stone Sculpture, Crown, 70. *Mem:* Am Soc Contemp Artists; Sculptors League (pres, 71-); Nat Asn Women Artist; Am Soc Contemp Artists. *Media:* Stone. *Mailing Add:* 100-30 67th Dr Forest Hills NY 11375

TEXOON, JASMINE
PAINTER, INSTRUCTOR
b New York, NY, Sept 19, 24. *Study:* Nat Acad Design, with Gilford Beal, H Hildebrandt & Charles Hinton, 4 yrs with honors; Brooklyn Mus Art Sch, with Bocour; Art Students League, with Byron Browne. *Work:* Christ the King (mural), St Lawrence Sem, Mt Calvery, Wis; relig mural, Monastery St Lazarro Mus, Venice, Italy; painting, Col Armeno Permanent Collection, Venice; relig paintings, St Mary's Convent, Yonkers & Church Holy Cross Sch, New York; Sacrifice (painting), Ovar Mus, Portugal; and others. *Comn:* Painting of home, comn by Mr & Mrs Zambetti, Sr, New York, 50; painting of boy & his dog, comn by Mr & Mrs Russell, New York, 54; three landscapes, comn by Mr & Mrs Alexander Walker, Yonkers, 67; portrait of a little girl, comn by Donata Pellegrini, Yonkers, 68; relig painting, pvt comn, 80. *Exhib:* Raymond Duncan Gallery, Paris, France, 62, 65 & 68-69; Lynn Kotler Gallery, New York, 63; Int Exhib Drawings, Florence, Italy, 71; one-man shows, Manhattan Col, New York, 55 & Burr Gallery, New York, 59; and others. *Pos:* Occup therapist for deaf patients, Rockland State Hospital, 64- *Teaching:* Instr pvt classes, 49-61 & 71- *Awards:* Honors for Art Work, Nat Acad Design Sch, 47; Prix de Paris, Ligoa Duncan Gallery, 62, 65, 68, 69 & 80. *Bibliog:* Article, J Am, 59-; Leonardo da Vinci, Cahiers d'Art, 70; Enciclopedia Internazionale Degli Artisti, Bugatti, 70. *Mem:* Life mem Art Students League; Burr Artists; Centro Studi E Scambi Internazionale Rome, Italy. *Media:* Oil, Pastel. *Mailing Add:* 3523 Riverdale Ave New York NY 10463

TEYRAL, JOHN
PAINTER, INSTRUCTOR
b Yaroslav, Russia, June 10, 12. *Study:* Cleveland Inst Art; Boston Mus Fine Arts Sch; Grande Chaumiere, Paris; Accad Belli Arti, Florence, Italy. *Work:* Cleveland Mus Art; City of Cleveland, Ohio; Butler Inst Am Art; Pepsi Cola Collection; Montclair Mus Art, NJ. *Comn:* Mural, President Garfield Mem, Cleveland; Many portraits of prominent persons. *Exhib:* Carnegie Inst Int; Metrop Mus Art; Va Mus Fine Arts; Corcoran Gallery Art; Univ Nebr; and others. *Teaching:* Instr drawing, Boston Mus Sch Fine Arts, 36-37; instr painting & drawing, Cleveland Inst Art, 39-77; retired. *Awards:* Prizes, Cleveland Mus Art, 41-61 & Butler Inst Am Art, 44; Fulbright Grant to Italy, 49-50; and others. *Publ:* Auth, Encaustic--the hot wax medium, In: Portraits in the Making, Phoebe Flory Walker, G P Putnam's Sons, 48. *Dealer:* Harmon Gallery Naples FL 33940. *Mailing Add:* 2540 Overlook Rd Cleveland Heights OH 44106

THACHER, ANITA
ENVIRONMENTAL ARTIST, FILMMAKER
b New York, NY, April 4, 36. *Study:* Antioch Col; New Sch Social Res, BA, 64; New York Studio Sch Drawing, Painting & Sculpture, 65-66. *Work:* Metrop Mus Art, New York; Chicago Art Inst; Neuberger Mus, State Univ NY, Purchase; SC Art Inst, Columbia; Inst Arts, Rice Univ Mus. *Exhib:* New Directors--New Films, Mus Mod Art, New York, 75; New American Filmmakers, Whitney Mus, 75; Int Festival Jeune Cinema Hyeres, France, 79; Film as Installation, Clocktower, New York, 80 & 83; Schemes: A Decade of Installation Drawings Traveling Show, 81; 19th New York Film Festival, Lincoln Ctr, 81; Film Installation, PS1 Inst Art & Urban Res, New York, 81; Directions 83, Hirshhorn Mus & Sculpture Garden, 83. *Awards:* Cine Golden Eagle, 75; French Minister Cult Award, Huy Festival, 76; Golden Athena, Athens Int Festival, 79. *Bibliog:* Ann Wooster (auth), Transformational grammar, Afterimage, 12/81; Tony Pipolo (auth), Anita Thacher's sea travels, Millenium Film J, fall-winter 82-83; Ann Wooster (auth), Manhattan short cuts, Afterimage, summer 83. *Mem:* New York Women in Film; Asn Independent Video Filmmakers; MacDowell Colony (mem bd dirs, 80-83). *Media:* Film, Video. *Publ:* Contribr, Frames, 78, Cover Mag, summer 80, Idiolects J, 83 & Film as Installation Catalog, 83. *Mailing Add:* 33 Second Ave New York NY 10003

THALACKER, DONALD WILLIAM
ADMINISTRATOR, ARCHITECT
b Detroit, Mich, July 29, 39. *Study:* Washington & Lee Univ, Lexington, Va, BA, 61; Univ Calif, Berkeley, BA(archit), 67. *Collections Arranged:* Louise Nevelson, George Segal, Mark di Suvero, Dan Flavin, Sam Francis, Robert Hudson, Louise Bourgeois, Isamu Noguchi, Jack Heal, Richard Hunt, Stephen Antonakos, Tony Smith, Al Held, Claes Oldenburg, Beverly Pepper, George Rickey, Leonard Baskin, Richard Serra, art-in-archit exhib, Fed Bldg, US Gen Serv Admin, 73-83. *Pos:* Dir, Art-in-Archit Prog, Gen Serv Admin, Washington, DC, 73-; mem, New York Public Art Preservation Comt, 79- *Teaching:* Lectr, New Sch Art Community Inst, New York, 78, 9th, 10th & 11th Int Sculpture Conf, New Orleans, 76, Toronto, 78 & Washington, DC, 80; lectr, World Art Mkt, New York, 80 Nat Coun Art Adminrs, Washington, DC, 81 & Cornell Univ, 82. *Awards:* Exceptional Service Award, Gen Serv Admin, 79. *Bibliog:* Article, Washington Post, 10/28/79; Don Hawthorne (auth), Does the public want public sculpture, Art News, 5/82; Fraser Baron (auth), article, New Art Examiner, 2/83. *Mem:* Am Inst Archit. *Publ:* Auth, The Art-in-Architecture Program of the US General Services Administration, Oakland Univ Press, Rochester, Mich; The Place of Art in the World of Architecture, Bowker, 80. *Mailing Add:* 18th & F St NW Washington DC 20405

THAMES, EMMITT EUGENE
PAINTER
b Brookhaven, Miss, Oct 28, 33. *Study:* Self taught. *Work:* Lauren Rogers Mus Art, Laurel, Miss; Deposit Guaranty Nat Bank, Jackson, Miss; Miss Power Co, Gulfport, Miss. *Exhib:* Solo exhibs, Miss Art Asn, Jackson, Miss, 76, Lauren Rodgers Mus Art, Laurel, Miss, 78 & R W Norton Art Gallery, Shreveport, La, 84; The Return to Realism, 77 & America the Beautiful, 17 Points of View, 79, Merrill Chase Galleries, Chicago. *Awards:* First Place Watercolor, Edgewater Tri-State, Edgewater Merchants Asn, 66 & Tri-State Exhib, Biloxi Art Asn, 70; Purchase Award, Watercolor USA, Mellers Photo Lab, 71. *Bibliog:* A conversation with Emmitt Thames (film), Miss Educ TV, 75; Marda Kaiser Burton (auth), Emmitt Thames, more feeling than formula, Southwest Art, 1/81; Carter Hillyer (auth), An interview with Emmitt Thames, Miss Mag, 11-12/83. *Mem:* Gulf Coast Arts Coun; Mobile Art Asn. *Media:* Watercolor, Egg Tempera. *Dealer:* James L Brown 3011 N State St Jackson MS 39216. *Mailing Add:* 100 45th St Gulfport MS 39501

THAW, EUGENE VICTOR
DEALER, COLLECTOR
b New York, NY, Oct 27, 27. *Study:* St John's Col, BA, 47; Columbia Univ (art hist), 47-49. *Exhib:* Pvt collection, Pierpont Morgan Libr, Cleveland Mus, Art Inst Chicago & Nat Gallery Can, 75-76. *Pos:* Writer, Spectator, London, 76-77 & Times, London, 77-78; art dealer & pres, E V Thaw & Co, Inc, 50-; vchmn, Artemis, S A, 76- *Teaching:* Lectr fine arts, St John's Col, 73, Mus Fine Arts, Boston, 83 & Nat Gallery, Washington, DC, 83. *Mem:* Art Dealers' Asn Am (bd dir, 64-, secy & treas, 66-68, vpres, 68-70 & pres, 70-72). *Collection:* Master drawings. *Publ:* Coauth, Jackson Pollock: A Catalogue Raisonne, Yale Univ Press, 78; auth, articles, New York Review of Books, 80, New Criterion, 83 & New Republic, 83. *Mailing Add:* 726 Park Ave New York NY 10021

THEK, PAUL
SCULPTOR

b Brooklyn, NY, Nov 2, 33. *Study:* Cooper Union, New York; Art Students League, New York; Pratt Inst, New York, 51-54. *Work:* Stedelijk Mus, Amsterdam; Ctr Nat Art & Cult, Paris; Smithsonian Inst, DC; Moderna Museet, Stockholm. *Comn:* Sets & costumes for the ballet Arena, comn by Glen Tetley, Nederlands Dans Theater, 69; sets, Louis Falco Co, New York, 78. *Exhib:* Galerie 20, Amsterdam, 69; Documenta 5, Kassel, W Ger, 72; one-man shows, Mod Mus, Stockholm, 69 & 72, Kunstmus, Lucerne, Switz, 73 & Philadelphia Inst Contemp Art, 77; and others. *Awards:* Fulbright Fel, 67; Nat Endowment Arts, 77. *Bibliog:* Mary Stewart (auth), In the Galleries: Paul Thek, Art Mag, New York, 11/67; B Caroir (auth), Individuelle Mythologien, Kunstwerk, Baden-Baden, 3/74; Paul Thek: Entretien avec Harald Szeeman, article, Chroniques de l'Art Vivant, Paris 4/74. *Publ:* Auth, A Document Made by Paul Thek and Edwin Klein, Amsterdam/Stockholm, 69. *Dealer:* Galerie M E Thelen Lindenstrasse 20 5 Cologne Germany. *Mailing Add:* 58 E Third St New York NY 10003

THELIN, VALFRED P
PAINTER, LECTURER

b Waterbury, Conn, Jan 8, 34. *Study:* Layton Sch Art; Art Inst Chicago; Int Design Conf Ctr, Insel Mainau, WGer; art seminars in six European countries & Mex. *Work:* Reading Mus, Pa; Ft Wayne Mus, Ind; Butler Inst Am Art, Youngstown, Ohio; Corcoran Gallery Art; Inst Cult Rels, Mexico City. *Exhib:* Watercolor USA, Springfield Mus, Mo, 63-72; Am Watercolor Soc, Nat Acad Galleries, New York, 63-72; Art in the Embassies, sponsored by Smithsonian Inst, Washington, DC, 68-73; Landscape 1 & Art Expo '72, De Cordova Mus, Lincoln, Mass, 70 & 72; Six by Eight, Philbrook Art Mus, Tulsa, Okla, 71; Smithsonian Inst, 78 & 79. *Awards:* John Singer Sargeant Award, Watercolor USA, Springfield Mus, 68; Henry Ward Ranger Award, Audubon Artists, Nat Acad Design, 69; Barse Miller Mem Award, Am Watercolor Soc, 74. *Bibliog:* Joshua Kind (auth), Chicago, Art News, 2/66; Safer (auth), New York reviews, Arts Mag, 4/68; B Sheaks (auth), Painting with acrylics, Davis, 6/72. *Mem:* Ogunquit Art Asn (pres, 71-72); life mem Rockport Art Asn; Pa Acad Fine Arts; Sarasota Art Asn; Philadelphia Watercolor Soc. *Media:* Watercolor, Acrylic. *Publ:* Contribr, Art in Am, 3/67, 68 & 72 & The Art Gallery, 71 & 72; auth, Watercolor page, Am Artist, 12/74; auth, Master Class in Watercolor, Watson-Guptill, 75. *Mailing Add:* Box 473 Shore Rd Ogunquit ME 03907

THEOFILES, GEORGE
HISTORIAN, DEALER

b Reading, Pa, July 28, 47. *Study:* Md Inst Col Art, BFA(graphics), 69. *Pos:* Owner, catalog publ & seller, Miscellaneous Man, Vintage Graphics, New Freedom, Pa, 70- *Awards:* Gold Medal Poster Design, Baltimore Md Art Dir Club, 70- *Mem:* Co Military Historians; Int & New England Antique Appraiser's Asn. *Specialty:* American and European poster art and communication graphics, 1850-1950. *Publ:* Publ, Catalog of Original Poster Art and Graphics (tri-ann), 71-; auth, American Posters of World War I, Dafran House, 72. *Mailing Add:* Box 1776 New Freedom PA 17349

THIBAULT, CLAUDE
CURATOR

b Riviere Ouelle, Que, May 5, 48. *Study:* Laval Univ, Licence es Lettres, 72. *Collections Arranged:* Tresors des Communautes Religieuses de La Ville de Quebec (with catalog), 73; Le Diocese de Quebec, 1674-1974 (with catalog), 74; Francois Baillairge et son Oeuvre, 1759-1830 (with catalog), 75; L'Art du Quebec au lendemain de la Conquete 1760-1790 (with catalog), 77; L'Art du Paysage au Quebec 1800-1940 (with catalog), 79. *Pos:* Conserv ancient art Quebec, Mus Quebec, 72- *Mem:* Int Asn Art Critics; Am Can Mus; Int Coun Mus. *Res:* Ancient art of Quebec. *Publ:* Ed, La fin d'une epoque, Joseph-Pierre Ouellet, Architecte, 73; A la Decouverte du Patrimoine avec Gerard Morisset, Que, Mus de Que, 81. *Mailing Add:* Mus Quebec Parc des Champs de Bataille Quebec PQ G1S 1C8 Canada

THIBERT, PATRICK A
SCULPTOR, INSTRUCTOR

b Windsor, Ont, Feb 25, 43. *Study:* Univ Windsor, Ont, BFA, 72; Fla State Univ, Tallahassee, MFA, 74. *Work:* McIntosh Art Gallery, Univ Western Ont, London; Can Coun Art Bank, Ottawa; Laurentian Univ Mus & Art Ctr, Sudbury, Ont. *Exhib:* Solo shows, Olga Korper Gallery, Toronto, 77, 79, 81 & 83, Trajectory Gallery, London, Ont, 77 & 83 & Harbourfront Art Gallery 79 & 83; Contemporary Sculpture, Guildwood Hall, Toronto, 82; Sculpture Tour, Univ Tenn, Knoxville, 83-84; and others. *Teaching:* Grad teaching asst, Fla State Univ, Tallahassee, 73-74; instr, St Clair Col Applied Art & Technol, Windsor, Ont, 74-75; teacher master, Fanshawe Col Applied Art & Technol, London, Ont, 75- *Awards:* Ont Arts Coun Material Grants, 75-83; *Bibliog:* Jim Tiley (auth), Patrick Thibert: New sculpture at Gallery O, 2-3/80 & Badana Zack (auth), Pat Thibert at Gallery O and Factory 77, 81/82, Artmag. *Media:* Metal, Wood. *Dealer:* Olga Korper Gallery 80 Spadina Ave Fourth Floor Toronto ON. *Mailing Add:* RR 2 Lambeth ON N0L 1S0 Canada

THIEBAUD, (MORTON) WAYNE
PAINTER, EDUCATOR

b Mesa, Ariz, Nov 15, 20. *Study:* Sacramento State Col, BA, 51 & MA, 52; Calif Sch Arts & Crafts, Hon Dr, 73; Dickenson Col, Hon DFA, 83. *Work:* Mus Mod Art; Whitney Mus Am Art; Libr Cong; Albright-Knox Art Gallery; Washington Gallery Mod Art; plus many others. *Comn:* Fountain mobile structure, Calif State Fair, 52; mosaic mural, Munic Utility Dist Bldg, Sacramento, 59; producer 11 educ motion pictures, Bailey Films, Hollywood, Calif. *Exhib:* One-man shows, De Young Mem Mus, 62 & Whitney Mus Am Art, 71; Environments USA 1957-1967, Sao Paulo Bienal, Brazil, 67; Int Contemp Art, Houston, Tex; San Francisco Mus Art; Kompas 4-West Coast USA, Stedelijk Abbemuseum, Eindhoven, Neth, 69; Documenta 5: Inquiry into Reality--Today's Image, Kassel, Ger, 72; Los Angeles Munic Mus, Calif, 73; Delphian Gallery, Sheridan, Ore, 77; plus many other group & one-man shows. *Teaching:* Chmn art dept, Sacramento City Col, 51; guest instr, San Francisco Art Inst, 58; prof art, Univ Calif, Davis, 60-; prof art & artist in residence, Cornell Univ, 66; artist in residence, Yale Univ, 74 & Rice Univ, 75. *Awards:* Creative Res Found Grant, 61; DFA(hon), Calif Col Arts & Crafts, 74; Citation Most Distinguished Art Studio Teacher of Year, Col Art Asn Am, 81. *Bibliog:* Sam Hunter (ed), New Art Around the World: Painting and Sculpture, Abrams, 66; Lucy R Lippard (auth), Pop Art, Praeger, 66; Allen S Weller (auth), The Joys and Sorrows of Recent American Art, Univ Ill Press, 68. *Publ:* Auth, American Rediscovered, 63 & Delights, 65. *Mailing Add:* Dept Art Univ Calif Davis CA 95616

THIELE, ROBERT RANSOM
PAINTER, SCULPTOR

b Milwaukee, Wis, July 12, 41. *Study:* Northland Col; Kent State Univ, BFA & MFA. *Work:* Ft Lauderdale Mus Arts, Fla Int Univ. *Comn:* Mural-sized painting, Fla Bd Mus Dir for House of Rep Bldg, Tallahassee, 73-74. *Exhib:* Hortt Memorial Competition, Ft Lauderdale Mus, 72-75 & 77; O K Harris Gallery, New York, 73 & one-man show, 78; Fla Creates Traveling Exhib, 73-74; Biennial Am Painting, Whitney Mus, New York, 75; Nat Drawing Invitational, Emporia Kans State Univ, 77 & 78; Sculpture 1980, Md Art Inst. *Teaching:* Assoc prof art, Miami Dade Community Col, 69- *Awards:* Best in Show, Hortt Mem Competition, 72 & 77; Best in Show, Fla Creates Exhib, 73 & 74. *Bibliog:* Articles, Arts Mag, 5/78, Art Now, 10/78 & Art News, 12/79. *Mailing Add:* Art Dept 11380 NW 27th Ave Miami FL 33167

THIELEN, GREG GLEN
CURATOR

b St Peter, Minn, Sept 21, 40. *Study:* Southwest Mo State Univ, BA(cum laude), 70, MA, 80. *Collections Arranged:* Five Centuries of Printmaking, 74; Body Language: the Figure as Subject and Statement, 75; A Space of One's Own (auth, catalog), Springfield Art Mus, 77, John Careggio: Paintings and Drawings (auth, catalog), 78 & The Etchings of Anders Zorn (auth, catalog), 79; Fish, Fowl and Other Fauna, 81. *Pos:* Art reference librn & registr, Springfield Art Mus, Mo, 71-76; cur of collections, 77- *Publ:* Coauth, Selections from the Springfield Art Mus Permanent Collection, 80; auth, Japanese painted porcelain, Glaze, 2/81; auth, Profile-Anthony Rice, Art Voices, 3-4/81; auth, Fruit crate art, Art Voices, 1-2/82; coauth, Harry Truman in Caricature and Cartoon, Univ Iowa Press, 84. *Mailing Add:* 1131 S Hillcrest Springfield MO 65807

THIERY, THOMAS ALLEN
PAINTER

b St John, Ind, Oct 16, 39. *Study:* Art Inst Chicago; Ind Univ; Taylor Univ; Moody Bible Inst; Western Mich Univ, BA; Eastern Mich Univ, MA. *Work:* Ferris State Col Collection Contemp Am Artists; Clark Equipment Co, Buchanan, Mich; Warning House, Elkhart, Ind; Dana Corp, Todedo. *Exhib:* Nat Arts Club Painting Exhib, 70; Mainstreams, 71-74; NMex Art League Nat Painting Exhib, 72-74; Toledo Mus Art Fedn Exhib, 72-75; Watercolor USA, 74; and others. *Awards:* Best in Show, Toledo Art Mus Fedn; Mainstreams '73 Award; Taylor Univ Fel, 80; and others. *Bibliog:* Watercolor page, Am Artist, 75. *Mem:* Charter mem Rocky Mountain Watermedia Soc. *Media:* Watercolor, Oil. *Mailing Add:* Box 54 Onsted MI 49265

THIES, CHARLES HERMAN
PAINTER, PRINTMAKER

b Poplar Bluff, Mo, Aug 22, 40. *Study:* SE Mo State Univ, BS(fine arts educ), 63; Kans State Univ, MA(drawing & painting), 70. *Work:* Nelson Gallery-Atkins Mus, Kansas City, Mo; Springfield Art Mus, Mo; St Louis Art Mus; Wichita Art Mus, Kans; Minn Mus of Art, St Paul; and others. *Comn:* Exterior mural, Ford Found Sponsored Prog at Kans State Univ, 69. *Exhib:* 43rd Ann Exhib, Springfield Art Mus, Mo, 75; Thirty Miles of Art, Nelson Gallery-Atkins Mus, Kansas City, Mo, 76; Western Ann Nat Drawing Exhib, Western Ill Univ, 76; Drawings/USA, Minn Art Mus, St Paul, 77; Joslyn Biennial, Joslyn Art Mus, Omaha, Nebr, 78. *Pos:* Asst dir of admis, Kansas City Art Inst, Mo, 76-77. *Teaching:* Instr drawing, design & figure drawing, Florissant Valley Community Col, St Louis, Mo, 69-76 & 3-D design, Johnson Co Comunity Col, Overland Parks, Kans, 76. *Awards:* Painting Award, Exhib 70, St Louis, N Co Art Asn, 70; Drawing Award, Quincy Ill Fine Arts Asn, 71; Purchase, Drawings/USA 1977, Minn Mus of Art. *Media:* Litho, Etching; Oil. *Publ:* Lithographs and Etchings, Am Design, Ltd. *Mailing Add:* 16073 E Hamilton Place Aurora CO 80013

THIRY, PAUL (ALBERT)
ARCHITECT, COLLECTOR

b Nome, Alaska, Sept 11, 04. *Study:* Ecole des Beaux Arts, Fontainebleau, dipl, 27; Univ Wash, BArchit, 28; St Martins Col, DFA, 70; Lewis & Clark Col, Arts D(hon), 79. *Comn:* State Libr, Capitol Comt, State Wash, Olympia, 58; Embassy, US Dept State, Santiago, Chile, 60; Seattle Ctr Coliseum, City Seattle, 64; Contemp Arts Pavilion, Seattle Art Mus, 64; World War II Monument, US 4th Inf Div, permanently located at Utah Beach, France, 68. *Exhib:* Salon d'Art Sacre, Mus Mod Art, Paris, 54; Nat Gold Medal Exhib, Archit League, New York, 56; Architectura Actual de Am, Madrid, 65; Ann Exhib, Nat Acad Design, New York, 68; New Am Archit, US Info Agency, New Delhi, India, 73. *Pos:* Mem & vchmn, Hist Am Bldg Surv, 56-61; prin architect, Century 21 Expos, Seattle, 57-62; mem, President's Coun for Pennsylvania Ave, 62-65; prof adv, Int Sculpture Competition Treaty Tower,

Libby Dam, Mont, 74-75. *Awards:* Officier d'Acad, Repub France, 50; Distinguished Citizen in the Arts, City Seattle, 62; Herbert Adams Mem Medal, Nat Sculpture Soc, 74 & Henry Hering Medal, 76. *Bibliog:* Monogr, Nuestra Arquitectura, Arg, 7/49; Robert Koehler (auth), monogr, Pac Architect & Builder, Seattle, 2/61; Esther McCoy (auth), monogr, Arts & Archit, Los Angeles, 1/65. *Mem:* Hon mem Am Inst Interior Design; fel Am Inst Architects (chancellor, 62-64); hon mem Nat Sculpture Soc; academician Nat Acad Design; life mem Soc Archit Historians (dir, 67-70). *Collection:* Primitive arts of the Alaskan Eskimo and the Indians of the Northwest Coastal Areas. *Publ:* Coauth, Churches & Temples, Reinhold, 53; ed, Washington in transition, 1/63 & auth, Planning of Washington as a Capital, 4/74, Am Inst Architects J; auth, Architectural treatment of dams, Arts & Archit, 8/67; coauth (with Mary Thiry), Eskimo Artifacts, Designed for Use, Super Publ Co, Seattle, Wash, 78. *Mailing Add:* 800 Columbia St Seattle WA 98104

THOLLANDER, EARL
ILLUSTRATOR, GRAPHIC ARTIST
b Kingsburg, Calif, Apr 13, 22. *Study:* Univ Calif, BA. *Bibliog:* Earl Thollander Discusses Painting, 4/54 & Artist reporter on tour, Am Artist Mag, 3/60; Adrian Wilson (auth), The Design of Books, Reinhold Studio Vista, 67; Diana Klemin (auth), The Illustrated Book, Clarkson N Potter, 70. *Media:* Pen Drawing, Acrylic, Watercolor. *Publ:* Auth & illusr, Back Roads of Arizona, Northland Press, 78; auth & illusr, Back Roads of Oregon, Potter, 79; auth & illusr, Back Roads of Texas, Northland Press, 80; auth & illusr, Back Roads of Washington, Potter, 81; auth & illusr, Earl Thollander's Back Roads of California, Potter, 82. *Dealer:* Depot Gallery Vintage 1870 Yountville CA 94599. *Mailing Add:* House in the Woods Murray Hill Calistoga CA 94515

THOMAS, BYRON
PAINTER
b Baltimore, Md, 1902. *Study:* Md Inst Art; Martinet Sch Art; Art Students League, Tiffany Found fel. *Work:* Pastime Bowling Alley, Mus Mod Art; Pine Trees, Pa Acad Fine Arts; Maples, Springfield Art Mus; US Dept Army; plus numerous pvt collections. *Exhib:* Numerous one-man and group shows in US & abroad. *Pos:* War artist, Life Mag, Europe, 43-44. *Teaching:* Teacher painting, Cooper Union, 31-50. *Awards:* Many prizes & awards. *Mailing Add:* 48 Elm St Woodstock VT 05091

THOMAS, C DAVID
PRINTMAKER
b July 15, 46. *Study:* Portland Sch Art, Maine, dipl, 68; Tufts Univ, BFA, 72; RI Sch Design, MFA, 74. *Work:* Brooklyn Mus; Mus Fine Art, Boston; DeCordova Mus, Lincoln, Mass; Philadelphia Mus Art; Portland Mus, Maine. *Exhib:* Thirty Years of American Printmaking, Brooklyn Mus, 78; Recent Prints, Gallery Nat Asn Graphic Artists, Boston, 83. *Teaching:* Asst prof art, Emmanuel Col, 78- *Awards:* Bort Award, Boston Mus Sch, 72; Emmanuel Col Fac Develop Grant, 83. *Mem:* Boston Printmakers (exec bd, 79-); Philadelphia Print Club; Los Angeles Print Soc; Nat Asn Graphic Artists (chair, 80-). *Media:* Lithography. *Dealer:* Gallery Nat Asn Graphic Artists 67 Newbury St Boston MA 02116. *Mailing Add:* 1727 Beacon St Waban MA 02168

THOMAS, ELAINE FREEMAN
EDUCATOR, ADMINISTRATOR
b Cleveland, Ohio, July 21, 23. *Study:* Northwestern Univ, Evanston, 44; Tuskegee Inst, BS(magna cum laude), 45; Black Mountain Col, 45, with Josef Albers & Robert Motherwell; NY Univ, Bodden fel, MA, 49, with Hale Woodruff; Mexico City Col, 56; Berea Col, 61; Univ Paris, 66; Southern Univ Workshop; Columbia Univ, 70. *Collections Arranged:* One-man exhib, Winston-Salem State Univ, 70; Discovery 70, Univ Cincinnati; George Washington Carver Exhib, White House, 71; Ala Black Artists Exhib, Birmingham Festival Art, 72; plus others. *Teaching:* Ast prof art & chmn dept, Tuskegee Inst, 45- *Awards:* Distinguished Participation, Am Artists Prof League, 68; Beaux Arts Festival Award. *Mem:* Am Asn Mus; Col Art Asn Am; Nat Art Educ Asn; Nat Conf Artists; Ala Art League. *Mailing Add:* Chmn Dept of Arts Tuskegee Inst Tuskegee AL 36088

THOMAS, HELEN (DOANE)
PAINTER, WRITER
b Portland, Ore. *Study:* Philadelphia Col Art; Art Students League, New York. *Work:* Chase Manhattan Bank, New York; Mus Univ Wichita, Kans; Finch Mus, New York; Univ Ala, Birmingham; New Eng Ctr Contemp Art, Brooklyn, Conn. *Exhib:* East Hampton Gallery, New York, 70; Albright-Knox Art Gallery, Buffalo, NY, 70-72; Philadelphia Mus Gallery, Pa, 72-75; Phoenix Gallery, New York, 73, 75, 77 & 80; Maison de la Cult, Cluses & Annemasse, France, 76; Ga Inst Technol, Atlanta, 76; Univ Ala, Birmingham, 76. *Pos:* Treas, Phoenix Gallery, New York, 72-74; pres, 74-79; art critic, Arts Mag, 77-79. *Bibliog:* Article, Arts Mag, 10/77. *Mem:* Nat Asn Women Artists. *Media:* Oil on Canvas. *Publ:* Auth, The application of the Ostwald System in my painting, Leonardo Mag, winter 79. *Mailing Add:* 241 University Dr Coral Gables FL 33134

THOMAS, JOHN
PAINTER, PRINTMAKER
b Bessemer, Ala, Feb 4, 27. *Study:* Univ Ga, 46-48; New Sch Social Res, New York, BA, 51; NY Univ, with William Baziotes, MA, 54; Univ Stranieri, Perugia, Italy, 54. *Work:* Hirshhorn Collection, Smithsonian Inst; Hawaii State Found Cult & Arts Collection, Capitol Bldg, Honolulu; Hawaii Community Col, Hilo; Honoka'a State Off Bldg; Contemp Art Ctr of Hawaii, Honolulu. *Exhib:* Second Pac Coast Biennial, Seattle Art Mus, Portland Art Mus, Santa Barbara Mus & San Francisco Legion of Honor, 57-58; Whitney Ann Am Art, New York, 59; Contemp Am Painting & Sculpture Biennial, Univ Ill, Champaign-Urbana, 61-65; Artists of Hawaii Ann Exhib, Honolulu Acad Arts, 65-; American Painting, 1966, Va Mus Fine Arts, Richmond, 66; Contemp Art Ctr of Hawaii, Honolulu, 76-79; Biblioteca Americana, Bucharest, Romania, 77; Watercolor Traveling Exhib, Honolulu Acad Arts, 78-79 & Fifth Hawaii Nat Print Exhib, 80. *Teaching:* Vis prof life drawing, State Univ Iowa, 62-63; prof art, Univ Hawaii, Manoa & Hilo, 65-67 & 70-74; vis artist painting, Univ Wash, 68-69. *Awards:* Nat Endowment Arts Grant, 77; Hawaii State Senate Congratulations (for Boy with Goldfish), 77; Hawaii Artists League Juror's Award, Ann Exhib, Honolulu, 78. *Bibliog:* Betje Howell (auth), article, Am Artist, 2/78; Tanner Thomas & Elliott Siu (coauths), Boy with Goldfish, multi-arts concept, Prem Honolulu Symphony Orchestra, 76; Harvey Hess (auth), article, Aloha Mag, 1/80. *Mem:* Hawaii Artists League; Komohana Artists Asn, Kailua-Kona (founding pres, 73-74). *Media:* Oil, Watercolor. *Publ:* Auth, Orchid Art and the Orchid Isle, Malama Arts Inc, 82. *Dealer:* Malama Arts Inc PO Box 1761 Honolulu HI 96806. *Mailing Add:* PO Box 1478 Kailua Kona HI 96740

THOMAS, LEW
PHOTOGRAPHER, WRITER
b San Francisco, Calif, Dec 19, 32. *Study:* Univ of San Francisco, BA, 60. *Work:* de Saisset Art Gallery, Univ of Santa Clara, Calif; La Mamelle's Art Ctr, San Francisco; Mus Mod Art, New York; Mus Fine Arts, Houston. *Exhib:* Rhinoceros, A Demonstration of Visual & Audial Poetic Experimentation, M H de Young Mem Mus, 75; Exchange, SFO/DFW, San Francisco Mus Mod Art, 76; West Coast Conceptual Photog, 76 & Photog & Lang, 76, La Mamelle's Arts Ctr; Mirrors and Windows, Mus Mod Art, New York, 78; Attitudes of the 70's, Santa Barbara Mus, 79; one-man shows, Washington Proj Arts, 79, Lawson deCelle Gallery, San Francisco, 79 & Ohio State Univ, Columbus, 80; Target III: In Sequence, Mus Fine Arts, Houston, 82; Big Pictures by Contemp Photogrs, Mus Mod Art, New York, 83; Photography in California: 1945-Present, San Francisco Mus Mod Art, 84; and others. *Collections Arranged:* 8 x 10 (auth, catalog), Mills Col Art Gallery, Oakland, Calif, 75; Photog & Lang (ed, catalog), 76 & West Coast Conceptual Photog (ed, catalog), 76, La Mamelle's Arts Ctr. *Teaching:* Vis artist, San Francisco Art Inst, 77; instr photogr, San Francisco Art Inst, 81, City Col Art Inst, 82-83; lectr, San Francisco State Univ, 83, Ctr Experimental and Interdisciplinary Arts, 83, Univ Ariz, 83-84. *Awards:* Photographer Fels, Nat Endowment for the Arts, 75 & 79 & Ilo Liston Mem Publ Award, Mills Col, 75; Artist Fel, Nat Endowment for the Arts, 79-80. *Mem:* Col Art Asn Am; Soc Photgraphic Educ. *Media:* Images & text. *Res:* Theoretical. *Publ:* Auth, The Thinker, Fine Arts Mus San Francisco, 74; ed, Photography & ideology, Dumb Ox, 5/77; auth, Structural(ism) and Photography, 79 & Bibliography(s), 80, NFS Press; auth, Still Photography: The Problematic Model, NFS Press, 81; auth, The Extravagant Depression: John Gutmann's Photographs of the Thirties, Harry N Abrams, 83. *Mailing Add:* 243 Grand View Ave San Francisco CA 94114

THOMAS, LIONEL ARTHUR JOHN
PAINTER
b Toronto, Ont, Can, Apr 3, 15. *Study:* John Russell Acad, Toronto; Ont Col Art, Toronto; Calif Sch Fine Art, San Francisco; also with Hans Hofmann, Provincetown, Mass. *Work:* Fla State Col, Lakeland; Nat Gallery, Ottawa; Art Gallery Toronto; Vancouver Art Gallery; Univ Victoria, BC. *Comn:* Bronze fountain, Edmonton City Hall, Alta, 58; Vancouver Pub Libr, 61; enamel doors, St Thomas More Col, Saskatoon, Sask, 62; BC Prov Govt Mus, Victoria, 68; oil on panels (with L & P Thomas), Student Union Bldg, Univ BC, 69. *Exhib:* Fine Arts Fac Exhib, Univ BC, 76, Myths, Legends & Science in Astrology & Astronomy, 77; one-man show, Vancouver Planetarium & Mus, 77; Fleischmann Atmospherium Planetarium, Univ Nev, Reno, 78 & 79; Reading Mus & Art Gallery, Pa, 79. *Pos:* Chmn, Comt Appl Design, BC Govt, Victoria, 65-68. *Teaching:* Assoc prof design, Sch Archit, 50-64 & Univ BC, 64- *Awards:* Allied Arts Medal, Royal Archit Inst Can, 56. *Bibliog:* Stephen Franklin (auth), Artist and a briefcase, Weekend Mag, 58; article, BC Beautiful, spring 70; Mate Laoonsen (auth), Centauran, Vancouver Mag, 10/76; and others. *Mem:* Royal Can Acad; Am Craftsmen Coun; Am Soc Archeologists; Can Fedn Artists; Ont Crafts Found; and others. *Mailing Add:* 3351 Craigend Rd Univ BC West Vancouver BC V6V 3G1 Canada

THOMAS, REYNOLDS
PAINTER, ILLUSTRATOR
b Wilmington, Del, Jan 21, 27. *Study:* Univ Fine Arts, Mex, 50-51; Pa Acad Fine Arts, 52-56, scholar, 54. *Work:* William A Farnsworth Mus Fine Art, Rockland, Maine; Del Art Mus, Wilmington; Northern Ind Art Mus, Hammond; Wilmington Trust Co, Del; Northern Trust Co, Chicago; and many others. *Comn:* Portraits of Princess Grace de Monaco, Palace in Monaco, 71-72; two portraits of Pope Paul VI, Vatican, Rome, 72; two altar murals, St Paul's Catholic Church, Delaware City, Del; and many others. *Exhib:* One-man shows, William A Farnsworth Mus, Rockland, Maine, 66, Kennedy Galleries, New York, 67 & 69, Country Art Gallery, Locust Valley, NY; Int Art Ctr, Milan, Italy, 72; Maison-Sur-Mer Art Gallery, Myrtle Beach, SC, 76; and many others. *Teaching:* Professorship art, Acad Tiberina, Univ Rome, Italy, formerly. *Awards:* Prizes, Del Art Ctr, 56; Grand Prix of Rome, 71; Int Grand Prize & Trophy for Painting, La Stanza Letteraria, Rome, 72; and others. *Bibliog:* Peter Boggia (auth), Reynolds Thomas: A painter in love with Italy, Ital New J, 5/8/71; Mario Portalupo (auth), article, Nat Art Mag, Italy, 4/5/73; and others. *Mem:* Am Fedn Arts; Int Art Guild, Monte Carlo. *Media:* Mixed. *Mailing Add:* PO Box 236 Tenants Harbor ME 04860

THOMAS, ROBERT CHESTER
SCULPTOR
b Wichita, Kans, Apr 19, 24. *Study:* With David Green, Pasadena, Calif, 46-47 & Ossip Zadkine, Paris, 48-49; Univ Calif, Santa Barbara, BA, 51; Calif Col Arts & Crafts, MFA, 52. *Work:* Santa Barbara Mus Art, Calif; Whatcom Mus Hist & Art, Bellingham, Wash; Univ Calif, Santa Barbara; Joseph H Hirshhorn Collection, Washington, DC; Ariz State Univ. *Comn:* Painted wood sculpture, J Magnin, Century City, Calif, 66; bronze figure, Class of 1967, Univ Calif, Santa Barbara, 67; ceramic fountain, comn by Phyllis Plous, Santa Barbara, 68. *Exhib:* San Francisco Mus Art, 52, 53, 56 & 57; one-man shows, Santa Barbara Mus Art, 55, La Jolla Art Ctr, Calif, 60 & Adele Bednarz Galleries, Los Angeles, 70-72 & 74; Retrospective, Univ Calif, Santa Barbara, 66; Whatcom Mus Hist & Art, Bellingham, Wash, 78; and others. *Teaching:* Prof sculpture, Univ Calif, Santa Barbara, 54- *Awards:* Bronze Medal for sculpture, City of Los Angeles, 49; Silver Medal for sculpture, Calif State Fair, 54; Purchase Prize for sculpture, Santa Barbara Mus Art, 59. *Media:* Stone, Wood. *Mailing Add:* 38 San Mateo Ave Goleta CA 93117

THOMAS, STEFFEN WOLFGANG
SCULPTOR, PAINTER
b Fürth, Ger, Jan 7, 06; US citizen. *Study:* Sch Appl Arts, Nürnberg, Ger; Acad Fine Arts, Munich, Ger, with Herman Hahn, Bernhart Bleeker & Josef Wakerle. *Work:* High Mus, Atlanta, Ga; St John's Mus, Wilmington, NC; State Capitol, Atlanta; Am Col Surg, Chicago; Univ Edinborough, Scotland. *Comn:* Bronze monument of Gov Eugene Talmadge, Talmadge Mem Comt, State Capitol Grounds, Atlanta, 49; Ala Confederate bronze monument, State of Ala, Vicksburg Nat Mil Park, Miss, 51; aluminum bas relief murals, Fulton Nat Bank, Atlanta, 54; Mother and Child (9ft marble monument), Fulton County Ct House Garden, Atlanta; Trilon (9ft hammered copper fountain), Atlanta Colony Square at 15th St. *Exhib:* Southeastern Art Show, Atlanta Art Asn, 49-51; Nat Soc Miniature Arts, Smithsonian Inst, Washington DC, 52; one-man shows, High Mus, 36, St John's Gallery, Wilmington, NC, 79 & 83 & W C Hill Gallery, Atlanta, 79; Kraskin Galleries, Atlanta & DC, 80; Bryant Galleries, New Orleans & Jackson, Miss, 80. *Pos:* Art dir Ga, Nat Youth Admin, 39-42. *Awards:* First & Purchase Prize for Head of Youth, City of Fürth, 25; hon mention, Fine Arts Acad, Munich, 28. *Bibliog:* Katerine Barnwell (auth), Artist's studio or lion's den, Atlanta J-Constitution Mag, 3/62; Ann Carter (auth), Reaching higher, Sun Atlanta J-Constitution, 2/69, Ethel Kerlin & staff (auth), Mr Steffen Thomas, WETV, 69. *Media:* Bronze; Painting, Graphics. *Publ:* Auth, Charcoal Drawings; Chronicle of a Georgia Working Artist 1930-1977. *Mailing Add:* 848 Mentelle Dr NE Atlanta GA 30308

THOMAS, TAMARA B
CONSULTANT
b Calif. *Study:* Univ Calif, Berkeley, BA(art hist). *Collections Arranged:* Security Pacific Nat Bank, 70; United Bank Denver; Taubman Co Inc; Investment Mortgage Int, San Francisco; plus many others. *Pos:* Pres, Fine Arts Services Inc, Los Angeles, 70-; dean's coun, Univ Calif, Los Angeles Grad Sch Archit & Urban Planning, currently; bd mem, Asn Professional Art Advisors, New York; trustee, Inst Art & Urban Resources, New York, currently. *Mem:* Friends of Whitney Mus, New York; Mod & Contemp Art Coun, Los Angeles Mus of Art. *Res:* Explanatory material on works acquired, bridging gap between public and contemporary art. *Specialty:* Consultation to major private collectors, corporations, and real estate developers, architects and interior design firms on art acquisitions, display and integration. *Mailing Add:* Fine Arts Services Inc 107 S Irving Blvd Los Angeles CA 90004

THOMAS, WILLIAM RADFORD
EDUCATOR, PAINTER
b Waco, Tex, Nov 4, 30. *Study:* Univ Tex, Austin, BFA & PhD; NMex Highlands Univ, MA. *Work:* Israel Mus, Jerusalem; Dallas Mus Fine Arts, Tex; Oakland Mus, Calif; Laguna Gloria Art Mus, Austin, Tex; Simon Fraser Univ, Burnaby, BC. *Comn:* Altar, Holy Trinity Episcopal Church, Austin, 56; sculpture (welded steel), Bank of the Southwest, Houston, 63; sculpture (welded steel), Mercantile Bank of Houston, 64. *Exhib:* 19th Nat Print Exhib, Libr of Cong, Washington, DC, 62; Simcoe Co Mus, Minesing, Ont, 77; Nat Exhib Leather, Leaf Rapids, Man, 77; Grace Campbell Gallery, Prince Albert, Sask, 77; Rockefeller Arts Ctr, State Univ NY, 81; Berry Col, Mt Berry, Ga, 82; Pensacola Nat Watermedia, Fla, 82; and many others. *Collections Arranged:* Sculpture of Frank Gallo, 72, American Drawing, 73, Documents & Images, 73 & Environmental Communication--Graphic Arts of Signage & Display in Our Environment, 73, Eastern Wash State Col; Charles Easley Photographs, Rockefeller Arts Ctr, State Univ NY, 81. *Pos:* Dir, Eastern Wash Gallery Art, 70-74. *Teaching:* Instr drawing-painting, San Antonio Art Inst, Tex, 58-61; chmn dept art-photog, Amarillo Col, 64-67; asst prof design-prints, NTex State Univ, 67-68; admin asst dean fine arts, Univ Tex, Austin, 68-70; chmn dept, Eastern Wash State Col, 70-74; chmn dept, ETenn State Univ, 74-80; dir, Rockefeller Arts Ctr, State Univ NY, 80-82. *Awards:* Purchase Awards, Tex Ann Painting & Sculpture, Dallas Mus Fine Arts, 59 & 29th Ann, Witte Mem Mus, San Antonio, 59; Award, Tex Watercolor Soc, 58. *Bibliog:* Richard Byrne (auth), In the guise of paintings, Phoenix, Austin, 68; Alfred Frankenstein (auth), Our land, our sky, our water, Expos 74, Spokane, 74; Ken Friedman (auth), Radford Thomas, Ecart Publ, Geneva, 75; plus others. *Mem:* Col Art Asn Am; Nat Asn Schs Art; life mem Tex Fine Arts Asn. *Media:* Ink; Water Soluble Media. *Publ:* Contribr, The Visual Arts, Telecourse, KSPA-TV, Spokane, Wash, 71; coauth, A Conceptual Design Statement..., US Army Corps Engineers, 72; ed, Ken Friedman: Sightings, E Wash State Univ, 74; auth, Development of a museum for Southwestern Univ, Georgetown, Texas, 74. *Dealer:* Image South Gallery 1931 Peachtree Rd NE Atlanta GA 30309. *Mailing Add:* 203 S St Mary's St San Antonio TX 78205

THOMAS, YVONNE
PAINTER
b Nice, France. *Study:* Cooper Union; Art Students League; studied with Hans Hoffman, Amedee Ozenfant, B Neurman & Robert Motherwell. *Work:* Guggenheim Mus; Corcoran Gallery; Atlantic Richfield, Los Angeles; Brandeis Univ; Loeb Ctr, NY Univ. *Exhib:* American Abstract Artists, 48; Eleven Americans, Riverside Mus, New York, 55; Women in the Arts, New York Cult Ctr, 73; Hudson River Mus Ivitational, Yonkers, NY, 76; Brooklyn Mus, 75; The Magic Circle, Bronx Mus, 77; Acad & Inst Arts & Lett, New York, 82. *Teaching:* Instr painting & drawing, Colo Mountain Col, summers 67-72 & La State Univ, 73. *Media:* Oil, Acrylic. *Mailing Add:* 147 W 15th St New York NY 10011

THOMASON, MICHAEL VINCENT
PHOTOGRAPHER, CURATOR
b West Palm Beach, Fla, June 20, 42. *Study:* Univ South, Sewanee, Tenn, BA, 64; Duke Univ, MA, 66, PhD, 68. *Exhib:* Work & Leisure in Turn Century Mobile, Fine Arts Mus South, Mobile, 80; Allied Arts Competition, 77, Mobile, 77; The Image of Progress: Alabama Photographs 1877-1917, Birmingham Mus Art, Ala, 81; Buildings Reborn: Adaptive Re-use Proposals, traveling exhib, Ala, 80. *Collections Arranged:* Work & Leisure Turn Century Mobile (auth, catalog), 80; The Image of Progress (auth, catalog), Birmingham, Ala, 81; Mobile's Black Heritage in Photographs, 83; Mardi Gras from the Gay Nineties to the Great Depression, 83. *Pos:* Dir, Photo Archives, Univ South Ala, Mobile, 78- *Teaching:* Prof, Univ S Ala, 78- *Awards:* First Prize, Allied Arts Competition, 77. *Media:* Black & White. *Res:* Uses of photography in history; the photography as a historical source. *Publ:* Coauth, Mobile: American River City, Easter, Mobile, 75; coauth, Mobile: The Life and Times of a Great Southern Seaport, Windsor, Calif, 81. *Mailing Add:* Photog Arch, Brookley 2001 Univ S Ala Mobile AL 36688

THOMASON, TOM WILLIAM
JEWELER, GOLDSMITH
b Shawnee, Okla, Oct 28, 34. *Study:* Univ NMex, BFA, 62. *Work:* Am Inst Architects, Albuquerque, NMex. *Comn:* Bronze Sculpture, Arlene Vanderbilt Webb, New York, 67; Cross & Collection Plates, St Mark's Episcopal Church, Albuquerque, 68; Archit Awards, Am Inst Architects, Albuquerque, 69; Archit Medals, Univ NMex, 70; Desk Award Plaques, NMex Coun Exceptional Children, 77-79. *Exhib:* Young Americans, Mus Contemp Crafts, New York, 62; 1st Survey Contemp Am Crafts, Univ Tex Art Mus, Austin, 67; one-man shows, Art Ministry, Tananarive, Madagascar, 67 & Wichita Art Asn Mus, Kans, 80; Southwestrn Craftsmen, Dallas Mus of Fine Arts, Tex, 68; Silver & Gold, Corcoran Gallery Art, Washington, DC, 72; Contemp Crafts Biennial 1st, Folk Art Mus, Santa Fe, NMex, 76. *Collections Arranged:* Contemporary Crafts Exhibition, New Mexico Pavilion, World's Fair, New York, 64; Santeros of New Mexico, Studio Gallery, Albuquerque, 68. *Pos:* Owner & mgr, Studio Gallery, Albuquerque, 63-; design & sales adv, Zuni Arts & Crafts Coop, NMex, 68. *Teaching:* Guest artist design, Univ Madagascar, Tananarive, 67. *Awards:* Purchase Award, NMex Contemp Crafts, Am Inst Architects, Albuquerque, 70; First Prize, Metal, NMex Contemp Crafts, NMex State Fair, 73; First, Third & Fourth Prizes, Metal, Tulsa Gallery of Fine Arts, Okla, 73. *Bibliog:* Lois E Franke (auth), Handwrought Jewelry, McKnight & McKnight, 67. *Mem:* NMex Designer Craftsmen (vpres 62-65, pres, 65-66); Albuquerque Designer Craftsmen (vpres, 62-65); Corrales Art Asn (vpres, 64 & 66); Albuquerque Gallery Asn (pres, 78); World Crafts Coun. *Media:* Bronze; Silver, Gold. *Specialty:* Contemporary art in painting, sculpture and art crafts. *Publ:* Contribr, Marcilla Chamberlain, auth, Making Metal Jewelry, Watson-Guptill, US & Pitman Ltd, Eng, 77. *Mailing Add:* 615 16th St NW Albuquerque NM 87104

THOMPSON, BRADBURY
DESIGNER, DIRECTOR
b Topeka, Kans, Mar 25, 11. *Study:* Washburn Univ, AB, 34 & DFA, 65; RI Sch Design, DFA, 83. *Comn:* Book design for ann of advert art, 43 & 54, graphic arts prod yearbk, 48 & 50, Westvaco Inspirations & Am Classics, 39, Homage to the book, 68 & The quality of life, 68; Designer, 45 US Stamps, 58-81; plus many others. *Exhib:* Int Exhib Graphic Art, Paris, 55, London, 56, Milan, Italy, 61, Amsterdam, 62 & Hamburg, Ger, 64; traveling one-man exhib, Am Inst Graphic Art, 58 & 75. *Pos:* Art dir, Capper Publ, 34-38, Rogers, Kellogg, Stillson, Inc, 38-41, Off War Info, 42-45 & Mademoiselle, 45-59; publ art dir, Street & Smith Publ, 45-59; consult, Westvaco Corp, 45-83; design dir, Art News & Art News Ann, 45-72; art dir, Living for Young Homemakers, 47-49; consult, Famous Artists Sch, 59-72, McGraw Hill Publ, 60-78, Time-Life Bks, 64-70, Harvard Bus Rev, 64-67, Field Enterprises Educ Corp, 64-78, Cornell Univ, 65-75, Menninger Found, 77-; designer, Smithsonian Mag, 69, Washburn Col Bible, 69-80; bd trustees, Washburn Univ, 70-; mem citizens stamp adv comt, Fed Design Prog Panel, 69- *Teaching:* Vis prof, Sch Art & Archit, Yale Univ, 56-; bd gov, Philadelphia Col Art, 56-59. *Awards:* Gold T-Square Award, Nat Soc Art Dirs, 50; Am Inst Graphic Arts Medal, 75; Art Dirs Club Hall of Fame, 77. *Bibliog:* Articles in Smithsonian, 6/79, Town & Country, 12/79 & Communication Arts, 1-2/80. *Mem:* Art Dirs Club (first vpres, exec comt); Soc Illusr; Am Inst Graphic Arts (bd dirs); Alliance Graphique Int; Nat Soc Art Dirs; plus others. *Publ:* Auth, The Monalphabet, 45 & Alphabet 26, 50; plus others. *Mailing Add:* Jones Park Riverside CT 06878

THOMPSON, DAVID ELBRIDGE See Hompson, Davi Det

THOMPSON, DONALD ROY
PAINTER, EDUCATOR
b Fowler, Calif, Mar 2, 36. *Study:* Calif State Univ, Sacramento, BA, 60, MA, 62. *Work:* Oakland Mus, Calif; Seattle First Nat Bank; Calif State Univ, Sacramento; IBM Santa Teresa Lab, San Jose, Calif; Art Mus Santa Cruz Co, Calif. *Exhib:* One-man shows, Cabrillo Col, Aptos, Calif, 80, The Gallery, Santa Cruz Main Libr, Calif, 80 & Foster Goldstrom Fine Arts, San Francisco 82; West '81/Art and the Law, Minn Mus Art, St Paul; Museum Collection, Art Mus Santa Cruz Co, Calif, 83; Leila Taghinia-Milani, New York, 83; Foster Goldstrom Fine Arts, San Francisco, 83. *Teaching:* Instr art, Cabrillo Col, 71- *Awards:* Purchase Award, West Publ Co, 81. *Bibliog:* Charles Johnson (auth), Color is form and subject, Sacramento Bee, 1/26/75; Mark Levy (auth), Vital fabrications, Artweek, 12/18/82; Claude Lesuer (auth), Rare summer pleasures, Artspeak, 6/23/83. *Dealer:* Foster Goldstrom Fine Arts 228 Grant Ave San Francisco CA 94108. *Mailing Add:* 225 Union St Santa Cruz CA 95060

THOMPSON, DOROTHY BURR
EDUCATOR, LECTURER
b Delhi, NY, Aug 19, 1900. *Study:* Bryn Mawr Col, AB, 23, European fel, 23, AM, PhD, 31; Wooster Col, Hon DFA, 72. *Collections Arranged:* Comment in Clay, Royal Ont Mus, 47. *Pos:* Actg dir, Royal Ont Mus, 46-47. *Teaching:* Lectr archaeol for circuit, Archaeol Inst Am, 40-; lectr class archaeol, Univ Toronto, 43-47; prof class archaeol, Univ Pa, 54 & 68; vis lectr archaeol, Oberlin Col, 68; prof class archaeol, Princeton Univ, 69-70; vis lectr, Univ Sydney, 72. *Awards:* Order of Phoenix, Govt Greece, 56. *Mem:* Archaeol Inst Am (exec comt, 48-52); Deutsches Archäologisches Inst. *Res:* Classical Greek subjects such as figurines, garden art and private life. *Publ:* Auth, Terracottas from Myrina in Museum of Fine Arts, Boston, privately publ, 34; auth, Swans and Amber (transl of Greek lyrics), Univ Toronto Press, 49; auth, Troy, the Terracotta Figurines of the Hellenistic Period, Princeton Univ Press, 63; auth, Ptolemaic Oinochoai and Portraits in Faience, Oxford Press, 73; contribr var jour. *Mailing Add:* Inst for Advan Study Princeton NJ 08540

THOMPSON, ERNEST THORNE
EDUCATOR, PAINTER
b St John, NB; US citizen. *Study:* Mass Sch Art, Boston; Mus Fine Art, Boston; independent European study; Col New Rochelle, NY, DFA(hon), 80. *Work:* Bibliot Nat, Paris; Nat Mus, Washington, DC; Univ Notre Dame; Col of New Rochelle; Farnsworth Mus, Rockland, Maine. *Comn:* Stations of the Cross, 24 & Football Championship Mem, 24, Univ Notre Dame; The Sacred Heart (mural), St Patrick's Church, McHenry, Ill, 25; Adventures of Don Quixote (murals), Oliver Hotel, South Bend, Ind, 26; Landmarks of New York (watercolor ser), Simpson, Thatcher & Bartlett, New York, 56. *Exhib:* Exhibs of Am Prints, Tate Gallery London, 27 & Bibliot Nat, Paris, 28; Fifty Prints of the Year, New York, 28; Ann exhibs, Am Watercolor Soc & Allied Artists of Am, New York, 49-74; Exchange Exhib, Royal Watercolor Soc, London, Am Watercolor Soc, 60. *Pos:* Vpres, Pemaquid Group of Artists, Bristol, Maine, 60-75; mem bd dirs, Maine Gallery, Wiscasset, 60-, dir, 62-75. *Teaching:* Prof art & dir sch fine art, Univ Notre Dame, 22-29; prof art & chmn dept fine art, Col of New Rochelle, 29-67; dir, Huguenot Sch Art, New Rochelle, NY, 47-51. *Awards:* Rudolf Lesch Award & Medal, 56 & Lily Saportas Award, 64, Am Watercolor Soc; Charles L Fox Award, Farnsworth Mus, Rockland, Maine, 74. *Mem:* Allied Artists of Am (pres, 65-67, hon life pres, 83-); hon mem Am Watercolor Soc (bd dirs, 62-64, 66-68); Chicago Soc Etchers; New Rochelle Art Asn (bd dirs, 40-45). *Media:* Watercolor, Oil. *Publ:* Auth, New England--Twelve Woodcuts, Univ Wash, 28; auth, Technique of the Modern Woodcut, Pencil Points Press, New York, 28. *Dealer:* Grand Cent Art Galleries New York NY 10017. *Mailing Add:* Muscongus Point Medomak ME 04551

THOMPSON, ERNEST THORNE, JR
SILVERSMITH, DESIGNER
b South Bend, Ind, Nov 9, 28. *Study:* Huguenot Sch Art, with Courtney Allen, Charles R Kingnan, Ernest T Thompson, Sr, dipl; Sch Mus Fine Arts, Boston, with Joseph L Sharrock, Sr & Hazel Olsen Brown, dipl. *Work:* Mus Sci, Boston, Mass; US Air Force Chapel, Bien Hoe, Vietnam; Corp Plate, Boston, Gt Brit. *Comn:* Industrial comns & pvt collections; chapel & altar pieces, Miles Mem Hosp Chapel. *Pos:* Trustee, Soc Arts & Crafts, 61-64; juror, Sterling Silver Design Competition, 75; owner & partner, Thompsons Studio Inc. *Teaching:* Dept head jewelry & silversmith, Boston Mus Sch, 61-70 & Portland Sch Art, 69- *Bibliog:* Bill Cauldwell (auth), Stop, silversmith at work, Ford Times Mag, 10/69; Richard Stilwell (auth), Ernest Thompson unselfish in silver, Maine Guide Dir, 74; article in House Beautiful Mag, 2/80. *Media:* Gold, Silver; Bronze, Pewter. *Mailing Add:* Back Meadow Rd Damariscotta ME 04543

THOMPSON, JEAN DANFORTH
TAPESTRY ARTIST, PAINTER
b Baltimore, Md, May 3, 33. *Study:* Md Inst Art, 50; Univ Md, BA, 54; Wright State Univ, MA, 72. *Work:* Univ Md; Am Embassy, Bonn, WGer; US Cent Intelligence Agency, McLean, Va. *Comn:* Fiber murals, Xerox, Arlington, Va, 80, Nat Rural Electric Coop Asn, Washington, DC, 80, McDonalds Corp, Fairfax, Va, 81, Wintergreen, Va, 82 & Am Apparel Asn, Rosslyn, Va, 83. *Exhib:* Am Craft Coun Exhib, Textile Mus, Washington, DC, 79; Am Textile Exhib, Folger Mus Gallery, Washington, DC, 80; Art USA, Textural Art Gallery, London, 80; solo exhib, Geilsdorfer Gallerie, Cologne, WGer, 82-83; Gayle Wilson Gallery, South Hampton, NY, 83. *Collections Arranged:* Art USA, London, 80. *Mem:* Torpedo Factory Artists Asn (pres, 79-80, bd mem, 79-83); Fiber Workshop; Artists Equity. *Media:* Fiber, Collage. *Mailing Add:* Studio 16 Torpedo Factory Art Ctr 105 N Union St Alexandria VA 22314

THOMPSON, JOHN MAURICE See DeVegatales, Jugo

THOMPSON, JUDITH KAY
PAINTER
b Kansas City, Kans, May 28, 40. *Study:* William Jewell Col, Liberty, Mo, 58-60; Kansas City Art Inst, Mo, 62-65, BFA(painting), study with Wilbur Niewald & Harold Bruder; Univ Cincinnati & Art Acad, Ohio, 65-67, MFA(painting); Aspen Sch Contemp Art, Colo, 68. *Exhib:* 16th Nat Art Round-up, Lorenzi Park Gallery, Las Vegas, Nev, 72; Works on Paper-Women Artists, Brooklyn Mus, NY, 75; Nat Asn Women Artists Spring Ann, Nat Acad Galleries, New York, 76; Artists Choice, Women in the Arts, traveling to New York, Penn, & Va, 76-77; Women Artists 77, Univ Mo Kansas City, 77; Marietta Nat, Ohio, 78; and other group & one-person shows. *Pos:* Lectr Women Painters in History, 74-77. *Teaching:* Instr painting & drawing, Benedicta Arts Ctr, 69; instr drawing, 2-D design & 3-D design, St Cloud State Univ, 69. *Awards:* Goldie Paley Award Oil Painting, Nat Asn Women Artists Spring Ann, 76. *Mem:* Nat Asn Women Artists. *Media:* Oil. *Mailing Add:* 5920 Bisonnet Apt 71 Houston TX 77081

THOMPSON, KENNETH WEBSTER
ILLUSTRATOR, PAINTER
b New York, NY, Apr 26, 07. *Study:* Grand Cent Sch Art; also with George Pierce Ennis. *Work:* Wartime illus, Libr Cong, Washington, DC. *Exhib:* Am Watercolor Soc Ann; Soc Illusr; Nantucket Artists Ann; Nat Arts Club; Cerberus Gallery. *Awards:* Thirteen awards, Chicago Art Dir Club; three awards, Am Inst Graphic Arts; seven awards, incl three medals, NY Art Dir Club; and others. *Mem:* Life mem Soc Illusr; life mem Am Watercolor Soc; Nantucket Artists Asn; Artists Guild. *Media:* Gouache, Watercolor. *Publ:* Illusr, The continent we live on (series), 62-68; illusr, The sea, 66. *Mailing Add:* 20 W 11th St New York NY 10011

THOMPSON, LOCKWOOD
COLLECTOR
b Cleveland, Ohio, 01. *Study:* Williams Col, AB, 23; Harvard Law Sch, LLB, 26. *Pos:* Mem adv coun, Cleveland Mus Art, 49, chmn 81-83; co-organizer & 1st pres, Cleveland Soc for Contemp Art, 61; mem, Int Coun Mus Mod Art, New York, 63-; legal coun & pub mem comn accreditation, Nat Asn Schs Art; mem adv bd, Cleveland Inst Art & Friends of the Tate Gallery, London. *Mem:* New Orgn Visual Arts (adv bd). *Collection:* Contemporary art. *Mailing Add:* 1010 Euclid Ave Apt 401 Cleveland OH 44115

THOMPSON, LYNN P
PAINTER, PHOTOGRAPHER
b Plainfield, NJ, July 22, 22. *Study:* Bennett Jr Col, 39-40; Douglas Col, BA, 43; Cornell Med Col, MD, 46; Nat Acad Design; Art Students League. *Work:* New York Hosp; Khanbegian Gallery, Sonogee, Bar Harbor, Maine; Inglemoor, Englewood, NJ. *Comn:* El Molino (oil), comn by George Moore, Sotogrande, Spain, 80; seascape, comn by Dr Eibl, Vienna, 80; Maine seascape, Drawing Room, Pennsula, Ohio, 81; painting (oil), New York Hosp, 83. *Exhib:* Solo exhib, Bergen Mus, Paramus, NJ, 74 & El Molino, Spain, 79; Federated Art Asn, NJ State Mus, Trenton, 75; New York Physicians Art Asn Ann, Union Carbide, 76; New York Physicians Art Exhib, New York Acad Med, 76-79. *Pos:* Dir, New York Hosp Art Comn, 66-74 & 77-80 & Child Life Ctr, New York, 82-; dir & adv, Rotating Art Cart Prog, NJ, Maine, NY & San Francisco, 79-; coordr, Hosp Audiences, New York, 82- *Teaching:* Instr watercolor, Sonogee, Bar Harbor, Maine, 79- *Awards:* Prix Etats-Unis, Duncan Gallery, New York & Paris, 75; First & Second Awards, New York Physicians Art Asn Ann, 76-79; Bocour Award, Orange Art Asn, 78. *Bibliog:* New York Physicians Art Association Winners, Cornell Alumni News, 81; J Scott Orr (auth), Art Cart brightens life of Bergen Pines patients, Sunday Star-Ledger, NJ, 8/22/82; Benjamin Hamowitz (auth), Rotating art at New York Hospital, Cornell-New York Hosp Alumni News, 83-84. *Mem:* Salmagundi Club; Catharine Lorillard Wolfe Club; Allied Artists Am; New York Physicians Art Asn (dir, 78-); Bergen Co Artists Guild. *Media:* Watercolor, Oil. *Publ:* Contribr, Cornell Med Col Alumni News, 81 & 84. *Dealer:* Upper Gallery 34B-435 E 70th St New York NY 10021. *Mailing Add:* 11 Creston Ave Tenafly NJ 07670

THOMPSON, MALCOLM BARTON
PAINTER
b Coraopolis, Pa, Dec 25, 16. *Study:* Pratt Inst, grad; Art Students League; also illus with Nicholas Riley. *Comn:* US Army in Action Ser, Pentagon, 49. *Exhib:* Soc Casein Artists, New York, 70; Slater Mem Mus, Norwich, Conn, 71; Conn Watercolor Soc, Hartford, Conn, 71; Mainstreams '71, Marietta, Ohio, 71; Am Watercolor Soc Traveling Exhibs, 72 & 73. *Teaching:* Instr watercolor & anat, McLane Art Inst, New York, 38-40. *Awards:* Marjorie Salembier Award, Conn Classic Arts, 68; First Prize, New Canaan Art Show, 70; Grumbacher Acrylic Award, Am Artists Prof League, 71 & 75. *Mem:* Am & Conn Watercolor Soc; Silvermine Guild Artists. *Media:* Acrylic, Watercolor. *Dealer:* Newman Galleries 1625 Walnut St Philadelphia PA 19103; Settlers West Galleries 6420 N Campbell Ave Tucson AZ 85718. *Mailing Add:* 40 Honey Hill Rd Georgetown CT 06829

THOMPSON, NANCY KUNKLE
GOLDSMITH, EDUCATOR
b Marion, Ind, Dec 30, 41. *Study:* Ball State Teachers Col, BS(art), 63; Ind Univ, MFA(jewelry design & metalsmithing), 68. *Work:* Ind Univ Mus Art, Bloomington; Greenville Co Mus Art, SC. *Exhib:* For Men Only, Lee Nordness Gallery, New York, 71; Extraordinary Vehicles, J M Kohler Arts Ctr, Sheboygan, Wis, 74; Southeastern Crafts, Greenville Co Mus Art, SC, 74; Bicentennial Craft Invitational, Ind Univ Art Mus, 76; Wearables, Renwick Gallery, DC, 79. *Teaching:* Asst prof jewelry & metalwork, Va Commonwealth Univ, 73- *Awards:* Exp Metalwork, Carnegie Found, 68;

Slide Doc of Hist Jewelry-Ornamental Devices, Va Commonwealth Univ, 71, Fac Grant-in-Aid, 76. *Bibliog:* Geff Reed (auth), Thompson/Kerrigan, Craft Horizons, 72. *Mem:* Am Crafts Coun; Col Art Asn; Soc NAm Goldsmiths. *Media:* Precious Metals, Nonmetallic Materials. *Mailing Add:* PO Box 7035 Richmond VA 23221

THOMPSON, RICHARD CRAIG
PAINTER, SCULPTOR

b McMinnville, Ore, June 27, 45. *Study:* Ore State Univ, 63-65; Univ NMex, BFA, 67, MA, 72; painting with John Kacere; also lithography with Garo Antresian. *Comn:* Twenty Sculpture Pieces, Univ Md, 69; Impermanent Sculpture, Mich Arts Coun, Detroit, 74; Cowboy Nights, Warehouse Living Arts Ctr, Corsicana, Tex. *Exhib:* Oregon Artists Under Thirty-Five, Portland Art Mus, Ore, 74; Biennial of Contemp Am Art, Whitney Mus, New York, 75 & 81; one-man shows, Strohl Gallery, Memphis, 80 & Monique Knowlton Gallery, New York, 81-; Hill's Gallery, Santa Fe, NMex, 75-78; Scottish Arts Festival, Edinburgh, Scotland, 80; and others. *Teaching:* Lectr painting & drawing, Univ Albuquerque, 72-75; vis lectr color, Wayne State Univ, spring 74; instr design-color, Univ NMex, 75-78. *Awards:* Juror's Prize, Phoenix Art Mus, Ariz; Nat Endowment for the Arts Fel, 78; artist-in-residence grant, Roswell Mus, NMex. *Bibliog:* Charlotte Moser, New Mexico, open land and psychic elbow room, Artnews, 12/77; article in New America, Univ NMex, 79; Portfolio, Paris Review, Summer 79. *Media:* Mixed Media. *Dealer:* Monique Knowlton Gallery 19 East 71st New York NY. *Mailing Add:* 12106 Kirkholm Houston TX 77089

THOMPSON, RICHARD E, JR
DEALER, COLLECTOR

b Oak Park, Ill, Dec 30, 39. *Study:* Univ Wis. *Collections Arranged:* Richard Thompson, Sr, 77. *Pos:* Dir, Richard Thompson Gallery, San Francisco, 77-. *Mem:* Mus Soc San Francisco. *Specialty:* Twentieth century American impressionists. *Collection:* American Impressionists. *Publ:* Auth, Richard Thompson American Impressionist, privately publ, 77. *Mailing Add:* 80 Maiden Lane San Francisco CA 94108

THOMPSON, RICHARD EARL, SR
PAINTER

b Oak Park, Ill, Sept 26, 14. *Study:* Chicago Acad of Fine Arts, 30-31; Am Acad of Art, Chicago, 32-33; Art Inst of Chicago, 44. *Work:* New Britain Mus Am Art, Conn; Marquette Univ Collection, Milwaukee, Wis; Naval Art Collection, Pentagon, Washington, DC; R W Norton Art Mus, Shreveport, La; Milwaukee Art Mus, Wis; and others. *Comn:* Landscape, comn by Joseph Uehline, Schlitz Brewing, Co, Milwaukee, Wis, 75; portrait, comn by John Forester, Wausau, Wis for Yawkey-Woodson Mus, 76; Wis Mem Park, Milwaukee. *Exhib:* Bergstrom Art Ctr, Neenah, Wis, 65; Vincent Price Collection of Fine Art, USA, 65; Knickerbocker Artists, New York, 77; Leigh Yawkey Woodson Art Mus, Wausau, Wis, 79. *Pos:* Painting mem, Pallette & Chisel Club, Chicago, 39-41. *Teaching:* Instr oil painting, Am Acad of Art, Chicago, 35-37; artist-in-residence, Univ Wis, Rhinelander. *Awards:* Nat High Sch Poster Contest, 32; George Washington Poster Contest, 32. *Bibliog:* Patricia Jobe Pierce (auth), Richard Earl Thompson, American Impressionist, a Prophetic Odyssey in Paint, 82. *Mem:* Salmagundi Club; Soc Am Impressionists. *Media:* Oil on Canvas, Pastel and Charcoal. *Publ:* Contribr, Milwaukee J, 68-74 & ed cover story, 7/22/79; contribr (cover), Yankee Mag, 5/76, 10/76, 7/78, 8/79, 5/80, 2/81 & 10/83; ed profile, Southwest Art Mag, 10/78, 5/81 & 10/82; ed feature, Country Gentleman Mag, fall 79. *Mailing Add:* 80 Maiden Lane San Francisco CA 94108

THOMPSON, ROBERT CHARLES
PAINTER, EDUCATOR

b Conroe, Tex, Nov 5, 36. *Study:* Univ Tex, BFA; Stephen F Austin State Univ, MA & MFA. *Work:* Southeast Ark Arts & Sci Ctr, Pine Bluff; First Nat Bank, Conway; Witte Mus, San Antonio, Tex; Pulaski Fed Savings & Loan Asn, Little Rock. *Exhib:* Young Artists Am, Xavier Univ, 60; Miniature Painter, Sculptors & Gravers Nat, Washington, DC, 68; Small Painting Nat Exhib, Univ Pac, 70; 4th Ann Nat Print & Drawing, Northern Ill Univ, 71; Ann Mid-South Exhib, Brooks Gallery, Memphis, Tenn, 71. *Teaching:* Asst prof art & art hist, Univ Cent Ark, 68-78, assoc prof, 78- *Awards:* Tex Watercolor Soc Purchase Award, 65; Invitational Exhib Award, 70 & First Place Oils & Acrylics, 73, Ann Ark Festival Arts. *Media:* Oil, Acrylic. *Mailing Add:* Rte 6 Box 138 Conway AR 72032

THOMPSON, TAMARA (BRYANT)
ASSEMBLAGE ARTIST, COLLAGE ARTIST

b Anderson, Ind, Apr 8, 35. *Study:* Univ Ky, BA(art); Ind Univ, MFA; study with Leon Golub, Creighton Gilbert & Rudy Pozzatti. *Work:* Ind Univ, Bloomington; Colgate Univ; Univ Ky; Syracuse Univ; Univ NMex. *Exhib:* One-man show, Picker Art Gallery, Colgate Univ, 78; 17 Connecticut Artists, Wadsworth Atheneum, Hartford, 60; Arts of Cent New York 36th & 38th Ann, Munson-Williams-Proctor Inst, Utica, 73 & 75; Explorations in Color Xerography, Picker Art Gallery, Colgate Univ, 79; Electroworks, Int Mus of Photog, George Eastman House, Rochester, 79-80; Multiples '80, Contemp Arts Ctr, New Orleans, 80; Photogenesis, Albuquerque, 81; and others. *Pos:* Dir art classes, Wadsworth Atheneum, 59-61; vis artist in residence, Univ Ky, 65, Everson Mus, Syracuse, 79 & Int Mus Photog, George Eastman House, Rochester, 80. *Teaching:* Instr art, Univ Ky, 65-66; instr fine arts, Colgate Univ, 72-80, asst prof fine arts, 80-83. *Awards:* First Prize, Hartford Soc Women Painters, 60 & 61; Colgate Univ Fac Develop Fund Grant, 77-78, Res Coun Grant, 79-81. *Bibliog:* Catherine Lord (auth), Women and photography, Afterimage, 1/80 & Modern photography, 9/80; and others. *Mem:* Col Art Asn Am; Albuquerque United Artists. *Media:* Multimedia. *Dealer:* Hoshour Gallery Albuquerque NM. *Mailing Add:* 1400 Marron Circle NE Albuquerque NM 87112

THOMPSON, WADE
PAINTER, EDUCATOR

b Moorhead, Minn, July 30, 46. *Study:* Macalester Col, with Jerry Rudquist, BA, 68; Bowling Green State Univ, with Robert Mazur, MA, MFA, 72. *Work:* Macalester Col; Bowling Green State Univ; Provincetown Art Asn, Mass; Sch Law, Temple Univ. *Exhib:* One-man shows, Hansen Galleries, New York, 77, Alnico Gallery, New York, 77 & Nat Art Ctr, New York, 80; NDak Nat Print & Drawing Ann, Univ NDak, Grand Forks, 81 & 83; Second Ann Art Competition Spoleto, Marble Arch Gallery, Charleston, SC, 83; and many others. *Pos:* Designer, Assoc Design, St Paul, Minn, 70-71. *Teaching:* Asst prof art, Tyler Sch Art, Temple Univ, 75-79; assoc prof art, Southwest Mo State Univ, 79- *Awards:* First Prize Merit in Painting, Arena '74 Nat Exhib, 74; Best of Show, Nat Cape Coral Art Exhib, Fla, 76; Purchase Award, Nat Graphics Competition, Provincetown Art Asn, Mass, 76. *Bibliog:* Arena '74, WBNG-TV, Binghamton, NY, 74; Judith Hemphill (auth), People, Elmira Today, NY, 75; Madeleine Burnside (auth), rev in E Side Express, New York, 77. *Mem:* Artists Coalition Kansas City; and others. *Media:* Multimedia. *Publ:* Illusr, Prospectus, Minn Educ Asn, 70; illusr, Governor's Conference on Environmental Education, St Cloud, Minn, 70. *Mailing Add:* 2361 S Fort Ave Springfield MO 65807

THOMPSON, WILLIAM JOSEPH
EDUCATOR, SCULPTOR

b Denver, Colo, Apr 19, 26. *Study:* RI Sch Desgin, with Vladimir Raemaesch; Cranbrook Acad Art, with William McVey; Art Students League, Woodstock, NY, with Kuniyoshi. *Work:* Columbus Mus Fine Arts, Ohio; Ga Art Comn, Atlanta; Ga Mus, Atlanta; Pembroke State Col; Ga Power Co. *Comn:* Limestone relief, comn by architect for St Christopher's Church, Columbus, Ohio, 62; four portal high relief, First Congregational Church, Columbus, 64; portrait figure of J F Kennedy, Univ Dayton, 64; bronze portrait figure (14 ft) of R B Russell, State of Ga, 73-75; bronze group, Gov Comt for Ga Prisoner of War Mem, Americus, Ga, 73-76. *Exhib:* Southeastern Ann Exhibs, High Mus, Atlanta, 65, 66 & 67; one-man exhib, Grand Cent Mod, New York, 66; Southern Sculpture 67; Smithsonian Inst Traveling Exhib, 69-70; Ga Artists Exhib, High Mus, Atlanta, 72 & 74. *Teaching:* From instr to asst prof sculpture, Ohio State Univ, 54-64; from assoc prof to prof sculpture & drawing, Univ Ga, 64-, mem grad fac, 66- *Awards:* First Prize in Sculpture, Columbus Mus Fine Arts, 56; Columbus Chap, Am Inst Architects Award for Comn: St Andrew, 60; First Prize, Southern Sculpture 67. *Bibliog:* Articles, La Rev Mod, Paris, 68 & Atlanta Mag, Inc, 74. *Mem:* Nat Acad Design. *Media:* Bronze. *Mailing Add:* 120 Cedar Circle Athens GA 30601

THOMSEN, MITCH (NANCY MITCHELL)
PAINTER

b Terrace Park, Ohio, Oct 22, 50. *Study:* Cincinnati Art Mus, 60-63; Loretto Heights Col, 70-72; Colo State Univ, BA, 74; Denver Univ, 75; Palm Beach Jr Col, with Jim Houser, 81-82. *Work:* Veterans Admin Hosp, Denver; Quinlan Art Ctr, Space Servs Int Collection, Gainesville, Ga; Kimberly-Clark Collection, Atlanta; Gee & Jenson Engineers, Architects Inc, West Palm Beach. *Exhib:* Watercolor Soc Ala Ann Nat, Birmingham Mus Art, 80-81; 32nd Knickerbocker Artists, Salmagundi Club, New York, 82; Soc Four Arts 44th Ann, Palm Beach, 82; Nat Watercolor Soc 62nd Ann, Laguna Beach Mus Art, 83; Audubon Artists 41st Ann, Nat Arts Club, New York, 83; San Diego Watercolor Soc Int, Atrium Imperial, 83. *Awards:* Verna Lammi Award, Norton Gallery Ann, 81; First Place Watercolor, Middletown Am Ann, Middletown Fine Arts Ctr, 82; Arches Paper Award, Nat Watercolor Soc 62nd, 83. *Mem:* Nat Watercolor Soc; Southern Watercolor Soc; Fla Artists Group; Gainesville Art Asn; Allied Artists. *Media:* Watercolor. *Dealer:* Abstein Gallery Art 1139 Spring St NW Atlanta GA 30309. *Mailing Add:* 2002 N Lakeside Dr Lake Worth FL 33460

THOMSON, CARL L
PAINTER, APPRAISER

b Brooklyn, NY, Mar 6, 13. *Study:* Pratt Inst. *Work:* Salmagundi Club; Burr Artists Group. *Exhib:* Salmagundi Club Ann Watercolor & Oil Shows, 59-72. *Pos:* Advert designer, C Thomson Assoc, 47-59; art dir, Am Home Prod Corp, 59-70; owner, Thomson Gallery; pres, Equitable Appraisal Co, Inc, New York, 70- *Teaching:* Instr drawing, Salmagundi Club, 61-63. *Awards:* Graphic Arts Award, Printing Industs Am, 69; Cert Spec Merit, Printing Industs Metrop New York, 70. *Mem:* Salmagundi Club (pres, 81-83). *Media:* Watercolor, Oil. *Mailing Add:* 19 E 75th St New York NY 10021

THON, WILLIAM
PAINTER

b New York, NY, Aug 8, 06. *Study:* Art Students League, 24-25; Bates Col, Hon DFA, 57. *Work:* Metrop Mus Art; Butler Inst Am Art; Brooklyn Mus; Calif Palace Legion Honor, San Francisco; Whitney Mus; and over 45 maj US mus. *Exhib:* Corcoran Gallery Art, Washington, DC; Pa Acad Fine Arts, Philadelphia; Va Mus Fine Arts, Richmond; Art Inst Chicago; Whitney Mus Am Art, New York; and many others. *Pos:* Trustee, Am Acad in Rome. *Awards:* Dawson Medal, Philadelphia Watercolor Club, 68; Altman Prize, Nat Acad Design, 69; Gold Medal of Honor, Am Watercolor Soc, 70; plus many others. *Bibliog:* Alan Gruskin (auth), William Thon--The Artist and His Technique, Viking Press, 64. *Mem:* Am Watercolor Soc; Dolphin Soc; Am Inst Arts & Lett; Nat Acad Arts & Lett. *Dealer:* Midtown Galleries 11 E 57th St New York NY 10022. *Mailing Add:* Port Clyde ME 04855

THORNDIKE, (CHUCK) CHARLES JESSE
CARTOONIST

b Seattle, Wash, Jan 20, 1897. *Study:* Univ Wash; Seattle Art Sch; Calif Sch Fine Arts; also with Lee F Randolph, Rudolph Schaefer, Harold Von Schmidt

& Johonnot. *Work:* Smithsonian Inst, Washington, DC; Mus Natural Hist, New York; Mus Arts & Sci, Miami; Cartoonists Exchange, Pleasant Hill, Ohio; Washington Sch Art, DC. *Exhib:* Cartoon Mus, Orlando, Fla Travelling Exhib US Army, Europe; Celebrity Caricatures, Jockey Club, Miami, 73-76. *Pos:* Art dir, Gen Motors Acceptance Corp, New York, 28-31; art dir, US Navy, 41-46; cartoonist, Miami Choice & Winner's Circle Magazines, 72-80. *Teaching:* Instr cartooning & com art, Com Art Sch, 34-35, New York Sch Design, 35-36, Terry Art Sch, Miami, Fla, 49-51 & Univ Miami, 51- *Mem:* Jockey Club, Miami. *Publ:* Auth & illusr, The secrets of cartooning, 35, The art of cartooning, 36, The art and use of the poster, 37, Arts and crafts for children, 38 & Oddities of nature (syndicated newspaper feature), 48, House Little Bks. *Mailing Add:* 11660 Canal Dr North Miami FL 33161

THORNE-THOMSEN, RUTH T
PHOTOGRAPHER, EDUCATOR
b New York, NY, May 13, 43. *Study:* Southern Ill Univ, Carbondale, BFA(painting), 70; Columbia Col, Chicago, BA(photog), 73; Art Inst Chicago, MFA(photog, John Quincy Adams fel), 76. *Work:* Mus Contemp Art & Art Inst, Chicago; San Francisco Mus Mod Art; Santa Barbara Mus Art, Calif; Walker Art Ctr, Minneapolis. *Exhib:* The Photographer and the City, Mus Contemp Art, Chicago, 77; Attitudes: Photography in the 70's, Santa Barbara Mus Art, Calif, 79; Crisscurrents: Additions to the Permanent Collection of Photography During 1979, San Francisco Mus Mod Art, 80; Chicago/Chicago: An Exhibition of Recent Painting, Drawing, Photography and Video, Contemp Arts Ctr, Cincinnati, 80; Landscape Images: Recent Photographs by L Conner, J Fishkin & R Thorne-Thomsen, La Jolla Mus Contemp Art, Calif, 80; Photographic Reflections of the World of Illusion and Fantasy, San Francisco Mus Mod Art, 81; Midwest Photography, Walker Art Ctr, Minneapolis, 81; solo exhib, Art Inst Chicago, 81 & Marcuse Pfeifer Gallery, New York, 83. *Teaching:* Instr photog, Columbia Col, Chicago, 74-83; asst prof, Univ Colo, Denver, 83- *Awards:* Nat Endowment Humanities Fel, summer sem, Paris, 79; Nat Endowment Arts Fel, 82. *Bibliog:* Discoveries, In: Photography Year 1980, Time-Life Bks, 80; Jno Cook, The marvelous journey: Photographs of Ruth Thorne-Thomsen, Nits & Wits Mag, 3-4/82; Scully, Grundberg, Milliard & Miles (auth), Landscape: Image & idea, Mod Photog Mag, 9/82. *Mem:* Soc Photog Educ. *Mailing Add:* 930 W Fourth Ave Denver CO 80223

THORNS, JOHN CYRIL, JR
DESIGNER, PAINTER
b Denver, Colo, Apr 14, 26. *Study:* Ft Hays State Univ, BA; Ind Univ, with Henry Hope & George Rickey, MA(art hist); Univ Iowa, with John Schulze & Lester Longman, MFA(archit design). *Work:* Hastings Col, Nebr; Friends of Art Collection, Kans State Univ; Marian Col, Wis; Hansen Mus, Logan, Kans. *Comn:* Bldg design, First Presby Church, Hays, Kans, 74; campanile design, Campus, Ft Hays State Univ, 75. *Exhib:* Nat Decoration Arts Show, Wichita Art Asn Gallery, 58 & Kans Watercolor Soc, 72-83; Am Craftsman Coun Exhib, Mus Contemp Crafts, New York, 62 & 63; Watercolor USA, Springfield Art Mus, Mo, 63 & 64; Hansen Mus, 83. *Pos:* Pres, Hays Arts Coun, Kans, 72-74. *Teaching:* Mem fac, Ft Hays State Univ, 54-72, prof art hist & design & chmn dept art, 72- *Awards:* Award Winner, Exhib Brochure Ser, Mid-Am Dist, Am Col Pub Rels Asn, 63; Cent State Bank Purchase Award for Collage Undergrowth, Kans Watercolor Soc Show, 74-80. *Mem:* Col Art Asn Am; Delta Phi Delta (pres, 70-73); Kans Watercolor Soc; Kans Art Educ Asn; Nat Coun Art Adminr. *Media:* Collage; Acrylic, Watercolor. *Publ:* Illusr, Frontier Mag, 57-62; contribr, Ft Hays Studies, Ser 1 & 2, Ft Hays State Univ, 60 & 66; ed, The Palette, spring 66-70 & 73. *Mailing Add:* Coronado Estates 500 W 36th Hays KS 67601

THORNTON, JIM (JAMES HOWARD)
PAINTER, EDUCATOR
b St Stephen, NB, Apr 12, 37. *Study:* Sir George Williams Univ, BA, 66; Inst Allende, MFA, 67. *Work:* IBM Corp, Columbus, Ohio; Ohio State Univ Art Gallery. *Exhib:* Gallery Contemp Art, Winston-Salem, NC; Traveling Exhib, Ohio Wesleyan Univ, Univ Waterloo & Gallery O, Toronto, 78-80; Bau-XI Gallery, 81-83; and others. *Pos:* Dir, Gallery Sch, Art Gallery Ont, 78-; guest speaker, Art Gallery Windsor, 79. *Teaching:* Instr studio art, Southern Seminary Jr Col, 67-69; guest lectr, Pembroke State Univ, 68 & Washington & Lee Univ, 69; asst prof fine arts, Columbus Col Art & Design, 71-78; guest lectr & vis artist, Univ Notre Dame, 73 & Columbus Gallery Fine Arts, 76-77; lectr art hist, Franklin Univ, 73 & 74. *Awards:* Grant, Ohio Arts Coun, 78. *Bibliog:* Knockabout ponk from a bubblegum palette, 10/14/78 & Peter White (auth), Zap! Take that expressionism, 5/2/80, Toronto Globe & Mail; John Bentley Mays (auth), article, Arts Mag, 9-10/80. *Dealer:* Bau-XI Gallery Ltd 340 Dundas St W Toronto Ont Can M5T 1G5. *Mailing Add:* Art Gallery Ont 317 Dundas St W Toronto ON M5T 1G4 Canada

THORNTON, RICHARD SAMUEL
EDUCATOR, ADMINISTRATOR
b Columbia, Mo, Aug 5, 34. *Study:* Univ Mo, BA, 56; Cranbrook Acad Art, MFA, 57. *Teaching:* Prof graphic design, Wash State Univ, 60-77, chmn art dept, 72-76; prof graphic design & head art dept, Univ Conn, Storrs, 77- *Mem:* Nat Asn Schs Art; Danforth Assoc. *Publ:* Auth, Washington State University The Hill, Wash State Alumni, 63 & 66; auth, Japanese graphic design, Commun Arts, 68; auth, Education of the Japanese Designer, Graphis, 69; auth, Dutch graphic design, Print Mag, 76; auth, West Coast designer, Graphic Design, Japan, 79. *Mailing Add:* Dept of Art Univ Conn Storrs CT 06268

THORPE, HILDA (SHAPIRO)
PAINTER, SCULPTOR
b Baltimore, Md, Dec 1, 19. *Study:* Am Univ. *Work:* Nat Mus Am Art; Phillips Collection; Corcoran Gallery Art; US Info Agency, Smithsonian Inst, Pakistan; Dept Health, Educ & Welfare, Washington, DC. *Exhib:* 28th Biennial Exhib, Corcoran Gallery Art, 63; North American Artists Traveling Exhib, 64; Small Sculpture Int Prog, Smithsonian Inst, Pakistan, 70; solo exhib, 75 & American Art, 76, Phillips Collection; New Ways With Paper, Nat Collection Fine Arts, 77; The Collage Medium, Pensacola Mus Art, Fla, 81. *Teaching:* Adj prof, Am Univ, 71- *Bibliog:* Ben Forgey (auth), Art, Washington Star, 9/30/79; David Tannous (auth), Sculpture shows in Washington, Aura, winter 80; Jo Ann Lewis (auth), The nation, Washington, DC, Art News, 12/80. *Mem:* Artists Equity. *Media:* Handmade Paper and Painted Canvas. *Dealer:* Addison-Ripley Gallery 9 Hillyer Ct Washington DC 20008. *Mailing Add:* 200 King St Alexandria VA 22314

THRALL, ARTHUR
PRINTMAKER, EDUCATOR
b Milwaukee, Wis, Mar 18, 26. *Study:* Univ Wis, Milwaukee, BS & MS; Univ Wis, Madison; Univ Ill, Urbana; Ohio State Univ. *Work:* Brit Mus, London, Eng; Libr Cong, Washington, DC; Art Inst Chicago; Brooklyn Mus, NY; Tate Gallery, London, Eng. *Comn:* 100 print ed, New York Hilton Hotel, 62. *Exhib:* Carnegie Inst Int Print Exhib, Pittsburgh, 51; Young American Printmakers, Mus Mod Art, New York, 53; one-man show, Smithsonian Inst, 60; 160th Ann, Pa Acad Art, Philadelphia, 64; 143rd Ann, Nat Acad Design, New York, 67. *Teaching:* Assoc prof art, Milwaukee-Downer Col, 56-64; prof art, Lawrence Univ, 64-, chairperson, Art Dept, 81-; vis prof art, Univ Wis-Madison, 66-67. *Awards:* Louis Comfort Tiffany Found Fel Graphics, 63; Purchase Award, Brooklyn Mus 14th Ann, 63; Cannon Prize, Nat Acad Design 143rd Ann, 67. *Bibliog:* M Fish (auth), Arthur Thrall, Wis Architect, 65; D Anderson (auth), The Art of Written Forms, Holt Rinehart & Winston, 69. *Mem:* Soc Am Graphic Artists; Boston Printmakers; Audubon Artists. *Media:* Intaglio; Oil and Watercolor. *Dealer:* Associated American Artists 663 Fifth Ave New York NY 10022; Benjamin--Beattie Gallery Chicago IL. *Mailing Add:* 59 Bellaire Ct Appleton WI 54911

THRELKELD, DALE
PAINTER, SCULPTOR
b Mo, Apr 11, 44. *Study:* Northeast Mo State Col, BS, 66; Ball State Univ, MA, 70; Southern Ill Univ, Edwardsville, MFA, 75. *Work:* Brooklyn Mus of Art, NY; St Lawrence Univ; and others. *Exhib:* New Talent Exhib, Gimpel & Weitzenhoffer Gallery, New York, 74; Los Angeles Print Soc Nat Print Exhib, 74; 28th Ann Ill Invitational, Ill State Mus, 75; Unique Works on Paper, van Straaten Gallery, Chicago, 75; Arco Collection, Los Angeles; and others. *Teaching:* Art instr drawing, Belleville Area Col, Ill, 75- *Awards:* Purchase Awards, Dulin Gallery Art, 70, Ark Arts Ctr, 71 & Ill State Mus, 75. *Media:* Mixed. *Dealer:* Frank Marino New York NY; van Straaten Gallery 646 N Michigan Ave Chicago IL 60611. *Mailing Add:* 24 Hilldale Dr Belleville IL 62223

THURMAN, CHRISTA CHARLOTTE MAYER
CURATOR
b Darmstadt, Ger, Dec 12, 34; US citizen. *Study:* Finch Col, NY, BA, 58; NY Univ Inst Fine Arts, MA, 66. *Collections Arranged:* Masterpieces of Western Textiles: A Handbook on the Art Institute of Chicago's Western Textile Collection (auth, catalog), Art Inst Chicago, 69; Coverlets: a Handbook on the Collection of Woven Coverlets in the Art Institute of Chicago (coauth, catalog), 73, Raiment for the Lord's Service: a Thousand Years of Western Vestments (auth, catalog), 76 & Claire Zeisler: a Retrospective (auth, catalog), 79; Ancient Textiles from Nubia (coauth, catalog), Art Inst Chicago & Univ Chicago, 79. *Pos:* Conserv apprentice, New York, 59-61; asst cur dept textiles, Cooper Union Mus, New York, 61-67; assoc cur dept textiles, Art Inst Chicago, 67-68 & cur, 68-82. *Teaching:* Vis asst prof hist archit & art, Univ Ill, Chicago Circle, 74. *Bibliog:* Alan G Artner (auth), The department of textiles, 1/16/78 & Peter Gorner (auth), Nubian textiles, 5/24/79, Chicago Tribune. *Mem:* Fel Am Inst Conserv Hist & Artistic Works; Centre Int d'Etude Textiles Anciens; Am Asn Mus; Int Comt Mus & Collections Costumes & Textiles; Costume Soc Am. *Mailing Add:* The Art Inst of Chicago Michigan Ave at Adams St Chicago IL 60603

THURSTON, JACQUELINE BEVERLY
PHOTOGRAPHER, EDUCATOR
b Cincinnati, Ohio, Jan 27, 39. *Study:* Carnegie-Mellon Univ, BFA(painting), 61; Stanford Univ, MA(painting), 62. *Work:* Libr Cong; San Francisco Mus Mod Art; Oakland Mus, Calif; St Louis Mus Art; Henry Gallery, Univ Washington, Seattle; and other pub & pvt collections. *Exhib:* Observations/Translations--Four Photogr, Oakland Mus, Calif, 72; Two Photogr, Oakland Mus, 75; Photography 2, Jack Glenn Gallery, Newport Beach, Calif, 75; Am Photogr: Past into Present, Seattle Mus of Art, Wash, 76; Graham Nash Collection, Univ Santa Clara, Calif, 79, San Francisco Mus Mod Art, 80; one-person show, Susan Spiritus Gallery, Newport Beach, 77 & 80. *Teaching:* Prof design & printmaking, San Jose State Univ, Calif, 75- *Awards:* Nat Endowment Arts Photogr Fel, 76 & 78. *Mem:* Soc Photog Educators. *Publ:* Coauth (with Ronald Carraherr), Optical Illusions and the Visual Arts, Van Nostrand Reinhold, 66. *Mailing Add:* 1688 Woodhaven Way Oakland CA 94611

THWAITES, CHARLES WINSTANLEY
PAINTER, MURALIST
b Milwaukee, Wis, Mar 12, 04. *Study:* Univ Wis; Layton Sch Art. *Work:* Univ Wis; Gimbel Collection; Edgar Kaufman Collection; Cottonwood Hist Soc

Mus, Windom, Minn; Milwaukee Art Ctr. *Comn:* Murals, US Post Off, Greenville, Mich, Plymouth & Chilton, Wis & Windom, Minn; portraits, pres of St John's Col, Annapolis, Md & Santa Fe, NMex; mural designs for fed bldgs, Pub Bldgs Admin. *Exhib:* Chicago Art Inst; Corcoran Biennials, Washington, DC; Pa Acad Fine Arts; Metrop Mus Art, New York; Whitney Mus Am Art, New York; Nat Acad Design, New York; Walker Art Ctr, Minneapolis; Calif Palace Legion Honor, San Francisco; Nelson-Atkins Gallery, Kansas City; Colorado Springs Fine Arts Ctr, Colo; Mus NMex, Santa Fe; Univ Minn Traveling Exhib of Govt Art 1930-1940, 77-78; and others. *Pos:* Artist in residence, St John's Col, Santa Fe, NMex, 73-74. *Awards:* Forty-eight State Mural Competition Prize, 39; Prizes & Medal, Calif Palace Legion Honor, 46. *Bibliog:* Article, The Studio, London, Eng, Vol 131, No 634; Dr Francis V O'Connor (auth), Federal art patronage, Univ Md, 66; Forbes Watson (auth), American painting today, Am Fedn Arts. *Mailing Add:* Box 4454 Santa Fe NM 87502

TIBBS, THOMAS S
EDUCATOR, MUSEUM DIRECTOR
b Indianapolis, Ind, Aug 30, 17. *Study:* Univ Rochester, AB & MFA; Columbia Univ. *Exhib:* Craftsmanship in a Changing World, 56; Louis Comfort Tiffany Retrospective, 58; Six Decades of American Painting, 61; Affect & Effect, 68; Jose de Rivera Forty Year Retrospective, 72. *Pos:* Assoc dir educ, Rochester Mem Art Gallery, 47-52; dir, Huntington Galleries, WVa, 52-56; dir, Mus Contemp Crafts, New York, 56-60; dir, Des Moines Art Ctr, Iowa, 60-68; dir, La Jolla Mus Contemp Art, 68-73. *Teaching:* Lectr art hist, Calif State Univ, San Diego, 69- *Mem:* Am Asn Mus; Asn Art Mus Dir; fel Royal Soc Art, London. *Mailing Add:* Dept of Art San Diego State Univ San Diego CA 92182

TICE, GEORGE ANDREW
PHOTOGRAPHER, AUTHOR
b Newark, NJ, Oct 13, 38. *Study:* Newark Vocational & Tech High Sch, NJ, 55. *Work:* Metrop Mus of Art, New York; Mus of Mod Art, New York; Art Inst of Chicago; Bibliot Nat, Paris, France; Victoria & Albert Mus, London, Eng. *Comn:* Two 55ft photog murals, Field Mus of Natural Hist, Chicago, 75. *Exhib:* One-man shows, Metrop Mus Art, New York, 72, NJ State Mus, 76, Mus Mod Art, New York, 79, Witkin Gallery, New York, 81 & Photo Gallery Int, Tokyo, 82; Photpgraphy in America, Whitney Mus, 74; Mirrors & Windows, Mus ModArt, 79; and others. *Teaching:* Instr master class photog, The New Sch, New York, 70- *Awards:* Grand Prix, Festival d'Arles, France, 73; Nat Endowment for Arts Fel, 73; Guggenheim fel, 73-74. *Bibliog:* Gerry Badger (auth), Recent books, British J Photog, 3/77; Barbara Lobron, Romantic notions, Camera Arts, 6/83; Peggy Sealfon (auth), Meet the masters, Peterson's Photographic, 10/83. *Publ:* Auth, Paterson, 72, Urban Landscapes, 75 & Lincoln, 84, Rutgers; auth, Artie Van Blarcum, Addison House, 77; auth, Urban Romantic, The Photographs of George Tice, Godine, 82; and others. *Dealer:* The Witkin Gallery 41 E 57th St New York NY 10022. *Mailing Add:* 323 Gill Lane 9B Iselin NJ 08830

TIEGREEN, ALAN F
PAINTER, ILLUSTRATOR
b Boise, Idaho, July 6, 35. *Study:* Univ Southern Miss, AB, 57; Art Ctr Col Design, 61. *Work:* High Mus Art, Atlanta, Ga. *Comn:* Painting, Atlanta Bur Cult Affairs, Ga, 75; mural, Simmons Corp, Atlanta, 76; paintings, Hilton Hotels, Knoxville, Tenn, 81. *Exhib:* Nat Drawing Exhib, High Mus, Atlanta, 65; Prof Art Am, Smithsonian Inst, Washington, DC, 66; SEastern Ann Exhib, 67 & Ga Artists Exhib, 68, High Mus, Atlanta; SEastern Regional, Columbus, Ga, 70. *Teaching:* Prof, Ga State Univ, 65- *Awards:* First Award, Nat Drawing Soc, 65; Purchase Prize, Atlanta Arts Festival, Ga, 68; 1st Award, Decatur Sesquicentennial, Ga, 72. *Bibliog:* Clyde Burnette (auth), Charcoal drawings, Atlanta Newspapers, 2/80; article, Art Voices, 7/81; article, American Illustrators, Dell, 81. *Media:* Acrylic; Ink, Charcoal. *Publ:* Illusr, Doodle & the Go-Cart, Viking, 72; illusr, Ramona the Brave, Morrow, 75; illusr, Silver Woven in my Hair, Atheneum, 77; illusr, Kelly's Creek, Crowell, 77; illusr, Ramona Age 8, Morrow, 81. *Dealer:* Artists Assocs Gallery 3261 Roswell Rd Atlanta GA 30305. *Mailing Add:* 315 Drexel Ave Decatur GA 30030

TIERNEY, PATRICK LENNOX
HISTORIAN, EDUCATOR
b Weston, WVa, Jan 28, 14. *Study:* Univ Calif, Los Angeles, EdB(cum laude), 36; Columbia Univ, New York, MA, 44; Sogetsu-Ryu, Tokyo, Japan, Seizan I, 52. *Pos:* Cur, Asian Art, San Diego Mus Art, 74-82; mem & trustee, Mingei Mus, San Diego, 77- *Teaching:* Chmn arts fac, Pasadena City Col, Calif, 46-71; lectr, Univ of Calif, Los Angeles & San Diego, 52-71; assoc dean col fine arts & prof hist Oriental art, Univ Utah, 71- *Awards:* Emmy, Acad Television Arts & Sci, 67; Honors Citation, Resolution of Bd of Trustees, Pasadena City Col, Calif, 71. *Mem:* Royal Asiatic Soc, Seoul, Korea; Pacificulture Found, Pasadena, Calif (dir, mus div, 61-70, mem bd dir, Asian Mus, 61-); Acad Television Arts & Sci; Salt Lake Art Ctr (mem bd dir, 71-); Japan-Am Soc, Southern Calif (dir, 72-); and others. *Res:* Folk art of Japan. *Publ:* Coauth, Japan, Int Publ, 58; coauth, Chanoyu, as a form of non literary art criticism, Chanoyu J, Kyoto, 76; coauth, Cambodia, Khmer Remains, 79. *Mailing Add:* 3758 Adonis Dr Salt Lake City UT 84117

TIFFANY, MARGUERITE BRISTOL
PAINTER, LECTURER
b Syracuse, NY. *Study:* Syracuse Univ, BS; Columbia Univ, MA; Newark Sch Fine & Appl Arts, cert; Parsons Sch, New York, cert; NY Univ; also with Emile Walters, Iceland & William Zoroch, New York. *Exhib:* NJ State Ann, Montclair Mus, 33, 34, 35 & 37; Ogunquit Art Ctr Ann, Maine, 41-70; Am Artistic Prof League Ann, Spring Lake, NJ, 41-71; Newark Mus, 72 & 76; Gotham Painters, New York, 74-78; and others. *Teaching:* Prof art, Rutgers Univ, 25-40, William Paterson Col, 29-56 & Fairleigh Dickinson Univ, 56-65. *Awards:* Bronze Profile, William Paterson Col Art Bldg, 78; Tiffany Art Scholar, 78. *Mem:* Am Artists Prof League, NJ Chap; Paterson Art League; Eastern Arts Asn; Gotham Painters; Int Miniature Soc. *Media:* Oil, Watercolor. *Publ:* Auth, Art and picture study, NJ Dept Educ, 30; auth, article, Educ Mag (art issue), 2/46; contribr, Art education in principle and practice, 33; auth, Art room planning guide, Dept Educ, Trenton, NJ, 60-63; illusr, two articles, Newark Sunday News, 4/12/70 & 4/14/70. *Mailing Add:* 330 E 33rd St Paterson NJ 07504

TIFT, MARY LOUISE
PRINTMAKER
b Seattle, Wash, Jan 2, 13. *Study:* Univ Wash, BFA(cum laude); Art Ctr Col Design; San Francisco State Univ. *Work:* Philadelphia Mus Art, Pa; US Embassies, Paris & Athens; Achenbach Print Collection, San Francisco Palace Legion Hon; Brooklyn Mus; Libr Cong, Washington, DC. *Exhib:* First Int Print Biennale, Segovia, Spain, 74; US Mission to UN, Geneva, Switz, 74; World Print II, San Francisco Mus Mod Art, 77; one-man show, Gumps' Gallery, San Francisco, Calif, 77; Brooklyn Mus, NY, 78; retrospective, Ore State Univ, 81; Utah State Univ, 83. *Pos:* Coordr design, San Francisco Art Inst, 57-60. *Teaching:* Asst prof design, Calif Col Arts & Crafts, Oakland, 49-57. *Awards:* Purchase Awards, Northwest Printmakers Int, 69, Nat Exhib Prints, Nat Gallery, Washington, DC, 73 & Hawaii Nat Print Exhib, 78. *Bibliog:* Leonard Edmonson (auth), Etching, Reinhold. *Mem:* Calif Soc Printmakers; Print Club Philadelphia. *Media:* Etching, Silkscreen. *Dealer:* Gump's Gallery San Francisco CA. *Mailing Add:* 607 Chapman Dr Corte Madera CA 94925

TIGERMAN, STANLEY
PAINTER, ARCHITECT
b Chicago, Ill, Sept, 20, 30. *Study:* Mass Inst Technol, 48-49; Inst Design, 49-50; Yale Univ, BArch, 60 & MArch, 61. *Comn:* Modular structure, Metrop Structures, Chicago, 71. *Exhib:* Soc Contemp Artists Show, Art Inst Chicago, 65; Eight Chicago Artists, Walker Art Ctr, Minneapolis, Minn, 65; one-man shows, Evanston Art Ctr, Ill, 69, Art Res Ctr, Kansas City, Mo, 69 & Springfield Arts Asn, Ill, 70. *Pos:* Prin, Stanley Tigerman & Assocs, Chicago, 62- *Teaching:* Prof archit & art, Univ Ill, Chicago Circle, 65-71; archit-in-residence, Am Acad in Rome, 80. *Awards:* Graham Found Fel advan study fine arts, 65; Honor Awards, Nat Am Inst Architects & Housing & Urban Develop, 70 & Chicago Chap Am Inst Architects, 71. *Bibliog:* R A M Stern (auth), New Directions in American Architecture, Braziller, 69; Faulkner & Ziegfield (auth), Art Today, Holt, Rinehart & Winston, 69; Dahinden (auth), Urban Structures of the Future, Praeger, 72. *Mem:* Am Inst Architects; Yale Art Asn; Ill Arts Coun; Yale Club NY; Arts Club Chicago. *Media:* Acrylic. *Publ:* Contribr, Young architects in America, Zodiac Int, 64; contribr, Instant city, Archit J Hui, 66; contribr, City shape 21, Toshi Jutaku, Tokyo, 68; auth, Formal generators of structure, Leonardo Mag, 68. *Mailing Add:* 920 N Michigan Ave Chicago IL 60611

TILLENIUS, CLARENCE (INGWALL)
PAINTER, WRITER
b Sandridge, Man, Aug 31, 13. *Study:* Teulon Col, with A J Musgrove; Univ Winnipeg, hon LLD, 70. *Comn:* Collection of wildlife painting, Monarch Life Assurance Co, Winnipeg, 54-80; dioramas, habitat groups, Nat Mus Can, Ottawa, Ont, 60-72, BC Mus, Victoria, 65-70 & Mus Alta, Edmonton, 72-74; dioramas, paintings, Man Mus Man & Nature, Winnipeg, 69-79. *Exhib:* Two one-man shows, London Art Gallery, London Shute Inst, 54; one-man exhib, Monarch Life Bldg, 62, Whitney Gallery Western Art, Cody, Wyo, 64, Man Mus Man & Nature, 74 & Glenbow-Alta Inst, 75. *Pos:* Diorama dir, Nat Mus Can, Ottawa, 62-72. *Teaching:* Lectr art appreciation, Man, 50-52; lectr wildlife painters, Glenbow Inst, 70; dir wildlife drawings, Okanagan Summer Sch Arts, Penticton, BC, 73- *Awards:* Man Centennial Medal Honor, Gov Gen, Prov Man, 72. *Bibliog:* Peter Kelly & Paul Guyot (coauth), Tillenius on the Prairies (film), Can Broadcasting Corp, 63; Eric Mitchell (auth), Clarence Tillenius, Nature Can Mag, 73; Richard Savage (auth), Tokens of Myself--Tillenius, the Man and the Art (film), Wilderness Trail Motion Picture Co, 78. *Mem:* Explorers Club, New York; Soc Animal Artists; life mem Man Naturalist Soc. *Media:* Oil, Watercolor. *Res:* Lifetime study of wild animals, wilderness travels across North America into Yukon and the arctic. *Publ:* Illusr, Little Giant, 51; illusr & auth, Fur Bearers of Canada, 51; illusr & auth, Monarchs of the Canadian Wilds, 54-75; auth, Sketchpad Out of Doors, 56 & 62; illusr, Orphan of the North, 58. *Dealer:* Sportsmans Edge Galleries 136 E 74th New York NY 10021; Loch Art Gallery 306 St Marys Rd Winnipeg MB Can. *Mailing Add:* 441 Dominion St Winnipeg MB R3G 2M8 Canada

TILLEY, LEWIS LEE
PAINTER, FILMMAKER
b Parrott, Ga, May 17, 21. *Study:* High Mus Sch Art, 37-39; Emory Univ, 37-39; Univ Ga, BFA, 42; Colorado Springs Fine Arts Ctr, with Boardman Robinson, Adolph Dehn & John Held, 42-45; Inst Allende, Mex, MFA, 68. *Work:* Post Card No 2, Colorado Springs Fine Arts Ctr, Colo; Ga Art Asn; Southern States Art League. *Comn:* Mural, Broadmoor Cheyenne Mountain Zoo, Colorado Springs, 58; dragon wall mural, Victor Hornbein House, Denver, 59; mural, First Nat Bank, Colorado Springs, 59; four polyester resin sculptures, Colorado Springs Eye Clin, 60; exterior wall mural, Horace Mann Jr High Sch, Colorado Springs, 62. *Exhib:* Am Fedn Arts; Graphic Arts Chicago; Denver Ann & Biennial; Artists West of Mississippi; Washington Cathedral Relig Exhib. *Pos:* Producer & dir, Alexander Film Co, 58-62; communications media adv, US Agency Int Develop, Ind Univ, 62-64.

Teaching: Instr painting, life drawing & design, Colorado Springs Fine Arts Ctr, 45-51; prof art, painting, graphic design & drawing, Southern Colo State Col, 65- *Awards:* First Purchase Award for oil, Canon City Blossom Festival, 69; First Purchase Award for oil, Colo State Fair, 70. *Bibliog:* Discovery No 49, Mod Photog, 58. *Media:* Oil, Acrylic. *Publ:* Auth, History of writing and painting, 63; illusr, English with the twins, 63; illusr, History of medicine, 63; ed, The story of Nok culture, 63. *Mailing Add:* 30 Mesa Rd Colorado Springs CO 80903

TILLIM, SIDNEY
PAINTER, INSTRUCTOR
b Brooklyn, NY, June 16, 25. *Study:* Syracuse Univ, BFA, 50. *Work:* NJ State Mus, Trenton; St Louis Art Mus; Edmonton Art Gallery, Alberta; Joseph H Hirshhorn Mus & Sculpture Garden; Univ Tex, Austin; and others. *Exhib:* Contemporary Realism in Figure & Landscape, Wadsworth Atheneum, Hartford, Conn, 64; J B Speed Art Mus, Louisville, Ky, 65; Aspects of New Realism, Milwaukee Art Ctr, 69; 22 Realists, 70 & Ann, 72, Whitney Mus Am Art; 30th Ann, Chicago Art Inst, 70; one-man shows, Robert Schoelkopf Gallery, New York, 65 & 67, Noah Goldowsky Gallery, New York, 69 & 74, Edmonton Art Gallery, Alta, 73 & 76, Tibor de Nagy Gallery, New York, 77 & Meredith Long Contemp, New York, 79; Realism in American Art Since 1960, Pa Acad Fine Arts, Philadelphia, 81; Contemp Arts Mus, Houston, 83. *Pos:* Contrib ed, Arts, 59-65; contrib ed, Artforum, 65-69. *Teaching:* Instr art hist & drawing, Pratt Inst, 64-68; instr art hist & painting, Bennington Col, 66- *Awards:* Painting Grants, Nat Endowment Arts, 74 & Ingram-Merrill Found, 76. *Media:* Acrylic. *Publ:* Auth, The new avant garde, Arts, 2/64; auth, Gothic parallels, 1/67, Walker Evans· Photography as representation, 3/67, Scale and the future of Modernism, 10/67 & Earthworks and the new picturesque, 12/68, Artforum. *Mailing Add:* 17 Bleecker St New York NY 10012

TILLOTSON, ROBBIE
PAINTER
Study: Appalachian State Univ, BA, 72; Univ NC, Greensboro, MFA, 74. *Work:* R J Reynolds Nat Hq, Winston-Salem, NC; Va Ctr Arts, Sweet Briar; Equitable Life Insurance, Mobil Found, New York; Washington & Lee Univ. *Exhib:* Weatherspoon Art Gallery, Greensboro, NC, 81; Southeastern Ctr Arts, Winston-Salem, NC, 82; Univ Essex, Colchester, England, 82; US Embassy, The Hague, Netherlands, 82; Nat Arts Club, New York, 83. *Pos:* Dir, New York Campus, Appalachian State Univ, 74-79. *Awards:* Yaddo Fel, 79 & 83; Micheal Karolyi Painting Grant to France, 81; Ludwig Vogelstein Grant, 83. *Bibliog:* Bob Calcello (auth), article, Interview Mag, 75; William Zimmer (auth), articles, Arts Mag, 77 & Soho Weekly News, 79. *Mem:* New York Artists Equitable. *Media:* Acrylic, Oil Pastel on Paper. *Publ:* Coauth, Zelda Fitzgerald still lives, Feminist Art J, 75. *Dealer:* Jean Lumbard Gallery 38 E 57th St New York NY 10019. *Mailing Add:* N Main Denton NC 27239

TIMMAS, OSVALD
PAINTER, LECTURER
b Estonia, Sept 17, 19; Can citizen. *Study:* Tartu State Univ; Atelier Sch Tartu & Tallinn, Estonia, with Nicholas Kummits & Gunther Reindorff. *Work:* London Art Mus, Ont; Art Gallery Hamilton; Art Gallery Windsor; Rodman Hall Art Ctr, St Catharines, Ont; Erie Art Ctr, Pa. *Exhib:* Can Watercolors, Drawings & Prints, Nat Gallery Can, Ottawa, 66; Audubon Artists, 66-69, Am Watercolor Soc, 66, 67 & 69 & Nat Acad Design, 67, 68 & 71, New York; Royal Can Acad Arts, Nat Gallery Can, 70; OSA Image (circulating show), Ont Pub Galleries, 75-77 & 79; Watercolour Painting in Canada, A Survey, Univ Waterloo, 79; and one-man shows. *Awards:* Medal & Award for creative aquarelle, Audubon Artists, 67 & 68; Major Award for watercolor painting, Coutts-Hallmark Co Can, 69 & 70; Lacana Grant, 79. *Bibliog:* Anthony Ferry (auth), A floating world, 2/20/65 & It's now time for Timmas, 11/11/65, Toronto Star; Stevens (auth), Osvald Timmas, La Rev Mod, 11/66. *Mem:* Royal Can Acad Arts; Am Watercolor Soc; Can Soc Painters Watercolor; Ont Soc Artists (vpres, 71-75). *Media:* Watercolor, Acrylic. *Dealer:* Gustafsson Galleries 303 Main St N Brampton ON L6X 1N5 Can. *Mailing Add:* 776 Marlee Ave Toronto ON M6B 3J9 Canada

TIMMINS, WILLIAM FREDERICK
PAINTER
b Chicago, Ill. *Study:* Am Acad Art, Chicago; Art Students League, with George Bridgman; Grand Cent Art Sch, New York, with Harvey Dunn & Mario Cooper. *Work:* Longyear Found Mus, Boston; House of Four Winds, Calif Hist Bldg, Monterey; US Coast Guard Acad, New London, Conn, 80. *Comn:* Mural, Allstate Savings & Loan Asn, Salinas, Calif, 72; painting, J M Smucker Co, Orrville, Ohio, 81; also many comns for pvt portraits and paintings. *Exhib:* Salinas Rodeo Western Art Show, Calif, 82 & 83; Esther Wells Collection, Calabasas, Calif, 83; Festvial of the American West, Logan, Utah, 83; one-man show, Who's Who Gallery, Carmel, Calif, 83; Gallery Select, Seattle, 83; and others. *Mem:* Soc Int Artists; Soc Western Artists; Portrait Soc of Am. *Media:* Watercolor, Oil. *Dealer:* Esther Wells Collection 23548 Old Calabasas Rd Calabasas CA; Wickenburg Gallery Wickenburg AZ 85358. *Mailing Add:* PO Box 5685 Carmel CA 93921

TIMMS, PETER ROWLAND
MUSEUM DIRECTOR
b Philadelphia, Pa, Aug 26, 42. *Study:* Brown Univ, Providence, RI, BA, 64; Harvard Univ, MA, 69 & PhD(anthrop), 76. *Pos:* Dir, Fitchburg Art Mus, Mass. *Publ:* Auth, Flint Implements of the Old Stone Age, Shire, United Kingdom, 74. *Mailing Add:* 70 Prichard St Fitchburg MA 01420

TIMOTHY, GROVER See Whiten, Tim

TIMPSON, MICHAEL G
SCULPTOR
b Athy, Co Kildare, Ireland, Feb 15, 51. *Study:* Univ Col Dublin, 72-73; Mass Col Art, BFA, 79; Mass Inst Technol, currently. *Work:* DeCordova Mus, Lincoln, Mass. *Comn:* Installation, DeCordova Mus, Lincoln, Mass, 81; outdoor sculpture, Mass Arts & Humanities Found, Boston, 82; installation, Danforth Mus, 83; outdoor sculpture monument, Task Force Bench Lawyers, Boston, 84. *Exhib:* New England Sculptors, Copley Soc, Boston, 78; Exchange, Univ Colo, Denver, 79; New Works Installations, DeCordova Mus, 82; New Works, Danforth Mus, Framingham, Mass, 83; Brockton Art Mus Triennial, Mass, 83. *Awards:* New Works Award, Mass Arts & Humanities, 82 & 83. *Bibliog:* Christine Temin (auth), article, Boston Globe, 83; Sarah MacFadden (auth), Report from Boston, Art in Am, 83. *Dealer:* Helen Shlien Gallery 14 Newbury St Boston MA 02116. *Mailing Add:* 172 Fayerweather St Cambridge MA 02138

TING, WALASSE
PAINTER
b Shanghai, China, Oct 13, 29. *Work:* Mus Mod Art, New York; Guggenheim Mus, New York; Carnegie Inst, Pittsburgh; Stedelijk Mus, Amsterdam, Holland; Israel Nat Mus, Jerusalem. *Exhib:* Paul Facchetti, Paris, France, 54; Martha Jackson Gallery, 60; Carnegie Inst Int, 61, 64, 67 & 70; Galerie Birch, 63; Galerie France, 68; Lefebre Gallery, 71. *Awards:* Guggenheim Fel, 70. *Dealer:* Lefebre Gallery 47 E 77th St New York NY 10028. *Mailing Add:* 463 W St New York NY 10014

TINNING, GEORGE CAMPBELL
PAINTER
b Saskatoon, Sask, Feb 25, 10. *Study:* Elliot O'Hara Sch, Maine; Art Students League. *Work:* Nat Gallery Art, Ottawa, Ont; Nat War Mus, Ottawa, Ont; Montreal Mus Fine Arts, McGill Univ, Montreal; Charlottetown Art Mus, PEI; Univ Manitoba, Winnipeg. *Comn:* Mural, Jenkins Valve Co, Lachine, Que, 60; mural, Bank Montreal, 61; Legends of Quebec (drawing), Baie Comeau Hotel, Que. *Pos:* War artist, Hist Sect, Can Army, 43-46. *Teaching:* Pvt classes. *Awards:* Dow Awards for watercolor, 42 & 48, Montreal Mus Fine Arts. *Mem:* Academician Royal Can Acad Art; Can Soc Painters Watercolor. *Media:* Watercolor, Acrylic. *Publ:* Auth, Can Art, spring, 49; auth & illusr, Lincoln Mercury Times, 50-59. *Dealer:* Continental Galleries Inc Drummond St Montreal PQ Can. *Mailing Add:* Apt 52 1509 Sherbrooke St W Montreal PQ H3G 1M7 Canada

TOBEY, ALTON S
PAINTER, LECTURER
b Middletown, Conn, Nov 5, 14. *Study:* Yale Univ Sch Fine Arts, BFA, 37, MFA, 47. *Work:* Smithsonian Inst; King Feisel Naval Base, Saudi Arabia; Am Bur Shipping, New York; Wadsworth Atheneum, Hartford, Conn; Evyan Perfumes, New York. *Comn:* mural, East Hartford Post Off, 38; Life of Gen MacArthur (six murals), Edwin Abbey Mural Fund for MacArthur Mem, 65; two murals on anthrop, Smithsonian Mus Natural Hist, 67; 14 murals on Am hist, comn by dir of Proj 400, Chadds Ford, Pa, 70; mural, Am Bur Shipping, New York; and others. *Exhib:* one-man shows, Burliuk Gallery, New York, 53, Trinity Col, Hartford, Conn, 70, Katonah Gallery, NY, 73, Galerie Alliance, Copenhagen, Denmark, 74, Am Ctr, Stockholm, Sweden, 75 & Portrait Gallery, Westport, Conn, 76; Sarah Lawrence Col, Bronxville, NY; Silvermine Guild, New Canaan, Conn; Univ Pa Art Mus, Philadelphia; Hudson River Mus, Yonkers, NY; Albany Mus, NY. *Teaching:* Instr & lectr styles, techniques & hist art, Yale Sch Fine Arts, 45-49; lectr hist art, City Col New York, 50-51. *Mem:* Abraxas; Silvermine Artists Guild; Artists Equity New York (dir, 70-79, pres emer, 79-); Nat Soc Mural Painters (vpres, 72-); Mamaroneck Art Guild. *Media:* Oil, Acrylic. *Publ:* Contribr, Man & Power, Golden Bks; contribr, Epic of Man, Life Bks. *Mailing Add:* 296 Murray Ave Larchmont NY 10538

TOBIAS, ABRAHAM JOEL
PAINTER, SCULPTOR
b Rochester, NY, Nov 21, 13. *Study:* Cooper Union Art Sch, 30-31; Art Students League, 31-33; Fed Art Proj, New York, 38-40. *Work:* Brooklyn Mus, NY; Los Angeles Co Mus Art; New York Pub Libr; Rochester Pub Libr, NY. *Comn:* The Student (fresco mural), Howard Univ, Washington, DC, 45; two war mem fresco panels, James Madison High Sch, Brooklyn, acrylic mural, Domestic Rels Ctr, Dept Pub Works, New York, 56; two Plexiglas panels for entrance, Polytech Inst Brooklyn, 58; mosaic & terrazzo mural, Henrietta Szold Sch, New York Bd Educ, 60. *Exhib:* Mus Mod Art, New York; San Francisco Mus; Brooklyn Mus; Adelphia Col; Archit League New York; and others. *Pos:* Art dir, Intelligence Div, US Air Forces, Washington, DC, 43-44; graphic designer, Off Strategic Serv, Washington, DC, 44-45. *Teaching:* Lectr mural painting, Howard Univ, 45; artist in residence, Adelphi Univ, 47-57; lectr mural painting, Asn Am Cols Prog, 52 & 55; inst artist, Polytech Inst Brooklyn, 70- *Awards:* Award for Mural Painting, Archit League New York, 52. *Bibliog:* Joseph L Young (auth), Mosaics: Principles & Practice, Reinhold, 64; Lawrence N Jensen (auth), Synthetic Painting Media, Prentice Hall, 64; Louis Botto (auth), In the know, Look Mag, 69. *Media:* Multimedia. *Publ:* Auth, Mural painting, 2/57 & auth, A mural painting for science & technology, 3/69, Am Artist Mag. *Mailing Add:* 98-51 65th Ave Rego Park Flushing NY 11374

TOBIAS, JULIUS
SCULPTOR, INSTRUCTOR
b New York, NY, Aug 27, 15. *Study:* Atelier Fernand Leger, Paris, 49-52. *Exhib:* Pa Acad Fine Arts, Philadelphia, 58; Mus Mod Art Traveling Exhib, Tokyo, 59; New Eng Exhib, Silvermine, Conn, 60; Whitney Mus Am Art

Sculpture Ann, 68; Indianapolis Mus Art, Ind, 70. *Teaching:* Instr painting, New York Inst Technol, 66-71; instr sculpture, Queens Col (NY), 71-74; vis artist, Ind Univ, Bloomington, 74-75, Univ Minn, Minneapolis, 77, Univ NC, Chapel Hill, 78, Univ Calif, Los Angeles, 83. *Awards:* Guggenheim Mem Found Fels, 72-73 & 78; Nat Endowment Arts Grant, 75-76; Adolf & Esther Gottlieb Found Grant, 80. *Bibliog:* James R Mellow (auth), Two sculptors worlds apart, 1/31/71 & Peter Schjeldahl (auth), A journey well worth making, 1/20/74, New York Times; Corinne Robins (auth), Julius Tobias: a decade of spatial dialogue, Arts Mag, 3/77; Judith Lopes Cardozo (auth), article, Artforum Mag, 12/77. *Media:* All Media. *Dealer:* Fifty-five Mercer Street Gallery 55 Mercer St New York NY 10013. *Mailing Add:* 9 Great Jones St New York NY 10012

TOBIAS, ROBERT PAUL
PAINTER, SCULPTOR
b Reading, Pa, Dec 14, 33. *Study:* Ariz State Univ, BS(appl arts, ceramics), 64, MFA(sculpture), 69. *Work:* Matthews Ctr, Ariz State Univ, Tempe; Univ Ariz Mus Art, Tucson; Univ Western Col, Yuma; Phoenix Art Mus, Ariz. *Comn:* Monumental sculpture, La Placita, City of Tucson, 74. *Exhib:* Painting, 1973 Four Corners Exhib, Phoenix & 1974 Mainstreams, Marietta Col, Ohio; sculpture, Nelson Art Mus, Kansas City, Mo, 70, Yuma Invitational, 73 & Arizona's Outlook '74, Tucson Art Ctr. *Teaching:* Instr design, Univ Kans, Lawrence, 69-71; assoc prof sculpture & design, Univ Ariz, Tucson, 71- *Awards:* Sculpture Purchase Award, Wis State Univ, Platteville, 67; Painting Award, 1972 Yuma Invitational, Ariz Western Col; Sculpture Exhib Award, Tucson Art Mus, 74. *Bibliog:* Tobias show in Lawrence, Kansas City Star, 3/22/70; Darrell Dobraus (auth), Artists review, Desert Silhouette, Tucson, 10/75. *Dealer:* Gekas/Nicholas Gallery 6538 East Tangue Verde Rd Tucson AZ 85715. *Mailing Add:* Dept of Art Univ Arizona Tucson AZ 85721

TOBIN, JOHN EDWARD, JR
SCULPTOR, EDUCATOR
b Brooklyn, NY, Apr 22, 47. *Study:* Allan Hancock Col, Santa Maria, Calif, AA, 70; Old Dominion Univ, Norfolk, Va, BFA, 75. *Work:* Chrysler Mus, Norfolk, Va. *Comn:* Clay sculpture for visually handicapped, Va Mus Fine Art, Richmond, 80. *Exhib:* Biennial Exhib Va Craftsmen, Va Mus, Richmond, 77; Biennial Exhib Piedmont Crafts, Mint Mus, Charlotte, NC, 78; Toys Designed by Artists, Ark Art Ctr, Little Rock, 78-79; Whimsy, Mint Mus Art, Charlotte, NC, 79-80; Fantasies, Va Mus Fine Art, Richmond, Va, 80. *Pos:* Mus asst, Portsmouth Community Arts Ctr, Va, 78-79. *Teaching:* Art instr ceramics, Portsmouth Community Arts Ctr, Va, 79-81; artist-in-residence, Norfolk City Public Schs, Norfolk, Va, 81-82. *Awards:* Certificate of Distinction, Va Mus, 76; Best in Show/First Place, Sculpture Hampton Fair Day, Va, 79; Best in Show Crafts, Portsmouth Nat Seawall Art Show, 81. *Bibliog:* Bob Trotter (auth), Portfolio of regional artists, Art Voices, 11-12/81. *Mem:* Va Crafts Coun; Ceramic Designers Asn (pres, 80); Tidewater Artists Asn; Tidewater Craft Guild. *Dealer:* Va Mus Crafts Gallery Boulevard & Grove Ave Richmond VA 23221. *Mailing Add:* 226 Chesapeake Ave Portsmouth VA 23704

TODD, MICHAEL CULLEN
SCULPTOR, PAINTER
b Omaha, Nebr, June 20, 35. *Study:* Univ Notre Dame, BFA, 57; Univ Calif, Los Angeles, MA, 59; Woodrow Wilson Fel, 59; Fulbright Fel, France, 61. *Work:* Whitney Mus Am Art, New York; Los Angeles Co Mus Art; Oakland Mus; Hirshhorn Mus & Sculpture Garden, Washington, DC. *Exhib:* Whitney Mus Am Art Sculpture Ann, 64-70; Sculpture of 60's, Los Angeles Co Mus Art, 65 & Philadelphia Mus, 66; Living Am Art, Maeght Found, France, 71; Exhibs Large Scale Sculpture, Lippincott Corp; Charles Cowles Gallery, New York, 81; and others. *Teaching:* Instr sculpture, Bennington Col, 66-68; asst prof sculpture, Univ Calif, San Diego, 68-76. *Media:* Steel, Aluminum. *Dealer:* Paule Anglim Gallery 710 Montgomery St San Francisco CA 94111; Charles Cowles Gallery 420 W Broadway New York NY 10012. *Mailing Add:* 2817 Clearwater Los Angeles CA 90039

TOIGO, DANIEL JOSEPH
PAINTER
b Albia, Iowa, May 20, 12. *Study:* Apprenticeship with Herb Olsen, Dale Nichols & Ben Stahl; Chouinard Art Inst, with William Moore. *Work:* Paintings, State Capitol Bldg, Sacramento, San Diego Art Inst, Santa Paula CofC & Ahmanson Collection, Los Angeles, Calif. *Exhib:* Frye Mus, Seattle, Wash, 68; Santa Paula Ann Art Exhib, 68-71; Am Artists Prof League Grand Nat, 68-72; Calif State Fair, Sacramento, 70-71; Ft Hayes State Univ, Kans; and others. *Teaching:* Pvt instr landscape, 45- *Awards:* Los Angeles All City Purchase Award, Howard Ahmanson, 68 & 69; San Diego Art Inst Award, Walter Scott, 68; Am Artists Prof League Award, 71 & 75. *Bibliog:* Artist--Dan Toigo (film), Chico State Col, 70; article, Am Artist Mag, 7/76. *Mem:* Fel Am Artists Prof League; Calif Art Club; San Gabriel Fine Arts Asn (dir, 67-). *Media:* Oil, Watercolor. *Mailing Add:* 5278 Ellenwood Dr Los Angeles CA 90041

TOKER, FRANKLIN K B
HISTORIAN
b Montreal, Que, Apr 29, 44; US citizen. *Study:* McGill Univ, BA, 64; Oberlin Col, AM, 66; Harvard Univ, PhD, 73. *Collections Arranged:* Poussin en detail, Fogg Art Mus, Harvard Univ, 67. *Pos:* Archeol dir excavations, Cathedral of Florence, Italy, 69-74 & 80. *Teaching:* A W Mellon vis prof fine arts, Carnegie-Mellon Univ, Pittsburgh, 74-76, assoc prof, 76-80; assoc prof, Dept Fine Arts, Univ Pittsburgh, 80- *Awards:* A D Hitchcock Award, Soc Archit Historians, 71; Guggenheim Fel, 79; A K Porter Prize, Col Art Asn Am, 80. *Bibliog:* Ada Louise Huxtable (auth), The current age of rediscovery,

New York Times, 11/27/77 & Henry Tanner (auth), Florence cathedral credited to sculptor, 5/7/80. *Mem:* Life mem Col Art Asn Am; Soc Archit Historians; Int Ctr Medieval Art; Arch Inst. *Res:* Medieval art; American and 19th century architecture and urban design. *Publ:* Auth, The Church of Notre-Dame in Montreal, McGill/Queen's Univ Press, 70, rev ed, L'Eglise Notre-Dame de Montreal, HMH-Hurtubise, 81; coauth, S Reparata: L'Antica Cattedrale Fiorentina, Bonechi, Florence, Italy, 74; auth, Florence cathedral: The design stage, Art Bull, 78; auth, Arnolfo's S Maria del Fiore, J Soc Archit Hist, 78; and others. *Mailing Add:* Dept Fine Arts Univ Pittsburgh Pittsburgh PA 15260

TOLL, BARBARA ELIZABETH
DEALER, CURATOR
b Philadelphia, Pa, June 8, 45. *Study:* Goucher Col, Towson, Md, AB, 67; Radcliffe Col, 67; Pratt Inst, New York, MFA, 69. *Pos:* Dir, Hundred Acres Gallery, New York, 70-77; freelance cur & dealer, 77-81; dir, Barbara Toll Fine Arts, New York, 81- *Specialty:* Young artists; eccentric representation and abstract art. *Mailing Add:* 138 Prince St New York NY 10012

TOLLES, BRYANT FRANKLIN, JR
MUSEUM DIRECTOR, HISTORIAN
b Hartford, Conn, Mar 14, 39. *Study:* Yale Univ, BA, 61 & MAT, 62; Boston Univ, PhD(hist), 70. *Pos:* Asst dir & libr, NH Hist Soc, Concord, 72-74; dir & librn, Essex Inst, Salem, Mass, 74- *Teaching:* Asst dean & instr hist, Tufts Univ, Medford, Mass 65-71. *Mem:* Am Hist Asn; Orgn Am Historians; Soc Archit Historians; Nat Trust for Hist Preserv; Am Asn Mus. *Res:* New England architectural history, late 18th and 19th century. *Interests:* American architectural history. *Publ:* Auth, Textile Mill Architecture in East Central New England, Essex Inst Hist Collection, 71; auth, College architecture in New England in printed & sketched views, Antiques, 73; auth, Gridley J F Bryant and the first building for Tufts College, Old-Time New England, 73; auth, New Hampshire Architecture: A Guide, Univ Press of New Eng, 79; auth, Architecture in Salem: An Illustrated Guide, Essex Inst, 83. *Mailing Add:* 13 Washington Sq Salem MA 01970

TOLMIE, KENNETH DONALD
PAINTER
b Halifax, NS, Sept 18, 41. *Study:* Mt Allison Univ, Sackville, NB, BFA(honors). *Work:* Nat Gallery Can, Ottawa, Ont; Montreal Mus Fine Arts, Que; Hirshhorn Collection, Washington, DC; Art Gallery NS, Halifax; Confederation Mus, Charlottetown, PEI; and others. *Exhib:* Nat Gallery Can, Ottawa, 64 & 66; Art Gallery NS, Halifax, 81; West Bend Gallery, Wis, 82; Ken Tolmie: The Bridgetown Series Traveling Show, 82-84; Beckett Gallery, Hamilton, 83; Lunenburg Pub Art Gallery, NS, 83; and others; 40th Ann Exhib, Can Soc of Graphic Art, Univ Western Ont, 73; Annapolis Valley Seven, Art Gallery NS, 80; Kent Tolmie: Social Realist, Carriage Gallery, Wolfville, NS, 81; Owens Gallery Mt Allison Univ & Confederation Mus traveling exhib, 81-83; and many others. *Awards:* Purchase Prizes, Burnaby Art Gallery, 73, McIntosh Gallery, Univ Western Ont, 73 & Contemp Can Graphics, Carleton Univ, 74. *Bibliog:* F Redgrave (auth), Ken Tolmie: The Bridgetown series, Arts Atlantic, summer 82; Visions (film), TV-Ontario, 82-83; W Elliot (auth), The art of Ken Tolmie, Arts W, 12/83; and others. *Media:* Oil, Watercolor. *Dealer:* Beckett Gallery 142 James St S Hamilton ON Can L8P 3A2; Zwickers Gallery 5415 Doyle St Halifax NS Can. *Mailing Add:* 6229 Regina Terrace Halifax NS B3H 1N4 Canada

TOMASINI, WALLACE J
ADMINISTRATOR, HISTORIAN
b Brooklyn, NY, Oct 19, 26. *Study:* Univ Mich, AB, 49, AM, 50, PhD, 53; Univ Florence, Fulbright grant, 51-52; NY Univ Inst Fine Arts, 54-57. *Teaching:* Instr hist of art, Finch Col, 54-57; asst prof art hist, Univ Iowa, 57-61, assoc prof, 61-64, prof, 64-, dir, Sch Art & Art Hist, 72- *Awards:* Am Numismatic Soc Grant, 57; Am Philos Soc Grant, 58. *Mem:* Am Numismatic Soc; Mid-Am Col Art Conf; Int Exchange Scholars; Sixteenth Century Studies; Midwest Art Hist Soc; and others. *Res:* Social and economic determinants of Italian Renaissance art; Late Imperial and Barbaric numismatics. *Publ:* Auth, Report on Visigothic Numismatic Research, 62; auth, Exhibition Catalogue: Drawing & the Human Figure 1400-1964, 64; auth, The Barbaric Tremissis in Spain & Southern France, Anastasius to Leovigild (numismatic notes & monogr 152), 64; contribr, 17th Century Art Essay (CIC Exhib Catalogue), 73. *Mailing Add:* 729 N Linn St Iowa City IA 52240

TOMCHUK, MARJORIE
PRINTMAKER
b Manitoba, Can, Oct 16, 33; US citizen. *Study:* Univ Mich, BA, 57, MA, 61; Long Beach State Col, 62; Sophia Univ, Japan; Pratt Graphics Ctr, NY. *Work:* Nat Air & Space Mus, Smithsonian Inst, Inst, DC; DeCordova Mus, Mass; Butler Inst of Am Art, Youngstown, Ohio; Mus of Native Am Cult, Spokane, Wash; Nelson Gallery, Kansas City, Mo; and others. *Exhib:* Nat Print Exhib, Brooklyn Mus, 70; World Art Exposition, Boston, 79; one-man shows, Art Expo New York, 79, 80 & 81, Prints, Los Angeles, 80, Art Washington, 79, 80 & 81 & Art Expo Calif, 81; Prints '80, Los Angeles. *Awards:* Boston Nat Print Show, Purchase Prizes, DeCordova Mus, 71 & 73; Nat Arts Club Award, New York, 72; Stamford Art Club First Prize, 73. *Mem:* Silvermine Guild Artists (bd mem, 73-78); Philadelphia Print Club; Pratt Graphics Ctr. *Media:* Etching, Embossing. *Publ:* Contribr, article, J Print World, Vol 5, No 4; contribr, article, Prints, 7-8/82. *Mailing Add:* 44 Horton Lane New Canaan CT 06840

TOMES, MARGOT LADD
ILLUSTRATOR
b Yonkers, NY. *Study:* Pratt Inst, Brooklyn, NY. *Work:* Kerlan Col, Univ Minn, Minneapolis; Hunter Col, New York; Univ Ala. *Pos:* Illusr of Children's Books, Coward, McCann & Geoghegan, Seabury Press, Holiday House, G P Putnam's Sons, J P Lippencott, Thomas Y Crowell, New York & Bowmar Inc, Calif, 67- *Awards:* One of Ten Best Books of the Year, New York Times, 77. *Media:* Gouache, Pen & Ink. *Publ:* Illusr, King George's Head was Made of Lead, Coward, McCann & Geoghegan, 74, Little Sister and the Month Brothers, Seabury Press, 76, Phoebe and the General, Coward, McCann & Geoghegan, 77, Jack and the Wonder Beans, G P Putnam's Sons, 77 & Giant Poems, Holiday House, 78. *Mailing Add:* 172 E 80 New York NY 10021

TOMKINS, CALVIN
WRITER
b Orange, NJ, Dec 17, 25. *Study:* Princeton Univ, BA. *Pos:* Staff writer, The New Yorker, Mag, 61- *Publ:* Auth, The Bride and the Bachelors, Viking Press, 65; auth, Merchants and Masterpieces: The Story of the Metropolitan Museum of Art, E P Dutton, 70; auth, Living Well Is the Best Revenge, 71 & auth, The Scene: Reports on Post-Modern Art, 76, Viking Press; auth, Off the Wall: Robert Rauschenberg and the Art World of Our Time, Doubleday & Co, Inc, 80. *Mailing Add:* c/o The New Yorker 25 W 43rd St New York NY 10036

TOMKO, GEORGE PETER
HISTORIAN, CURATOR
b Cleveland, Ohio, Mar 17, 36. *Study:* Case Western Reserve Univ, Cleveland, Ohio, BA, 57, 57-63 & 65. *Collections Arranged:* Paintings from Midwestern University Collections, 73; Arts Symposium: Exhibit of work by guest speakers Philip Pearlstein, Robert Smithson, Peter Blake & Otto Muehl, 74; John Silk Deckard Retrospective, 74; The Way West: Artist Explorers of the Frontier, 79; Masters of American Watercolor (auth catalog), 80; Painterly Realism, 81; Stuart Davis: The Formative Years 1910-1930, 82. *Pos:* Cur collections, Wichita Art Mus, 70-72; gallery dir, Ohio State Univ, 72-74; dir, Parrish Art Mus, 75; cur Western collections, Joslyn Art Mus, Omaha, Nebr, 77-80; cur, Rahr-West Mus, 80- *Teaching:* Instr art hist, Dickinson Col, Carlisle, Pa, 63-64; asst prof art hist, Ohio Univ, Athens, 65-67; asst prof art hist, Transylvania Col, Lexington, Ky, 67-68. *Mem:* Col Art Asn; Am Asn of Mus. *Res:* Nineteenth and twentieth century American painting and sculpture. *Publ:* Auth, Roland P Murdock Collection, Wichita Art Mus, 72; contribr, The Frederick W Schumacher Collection, Columbus Gallery Fine Arts, 76; contribr, Permanent Collection of the Springfield (Mo) Mus Art, 82; contribr, Prints of the American West, 83. *Mailing Add:* Rahr-West Mus Manitowoc WI 54220

TOMPKINS, ALAN
PAINTER
b New Rochelle, NY, Oct 29, 07. *Study:* Columbia Univ, BA; Yale Univ, BFA. *Comn:* Mural paintings comn by US Treas Dept for post off at Indianapolis, Ind, 36, Martinsville, Ind, 37 & Boone, NC, 40; mural painting, Gen Elec Co, Bridgeport, Conn, 44; mural painting, cent Baptist Church, Hartford, Conn, 58. *Exhib:* Ind Artists Ann, 37-38; Art Inst Chicago Ann, 38; Conn Acad Ann, 52-81. *Pos:* Dir, Hartford Art Sch, Univ Hartford, 57-69, vchancellor, 60-74; comnr, Fine Arts Comn, Hartford, 59-69. *Teaching:* Instr painting, Cooper Union Art Sch, 38-43; lectr painting, Columbia Univ, 46-51; prof painting & art hist, Univ Hartford, 51-74, retired. *Awards:* First Prize for painting, Conn Acad, 68-70 & 73; Painting Awards, Beth-El Regional Exhib, 72 & 79 & Canton Open Show, 77, 80 & 81. *Mem:* Conn Acad (vpres, 70-72). *Media:* Oil. *Res:* 20th century art. *Mailing Add:* 11 Milburn Dr Bloomfield CT 06002

TOMPKINS, BETTY (I)
PAINTER, PRINTMAKER
b Washington, DC, June 20, 45. *Study:* Syracuse Univ, BFA, 66; Central Wash State Col, BEd, 69, MA, 69. *Exhib:* Contemporary Reflections, Aldrich Mus, Conn, 77; On Paper, 80 & Ikon/Logos, 81, Alternative Mus, New York, 80; one-person exhib, Bernice Steinbaum Gallery, New York, 83; New Talent: Printmaking, Castelli Graphics, New York, 83; Printmaking Studios, Zimmerli Art Mus, New Brunswick, NJ, 83. *Collections Arranged:* Animals in the Arsenal (auth, catalog), Central Park Zoo, 81; New York on Paper, Central Wash Univ, 84. *Pos:* Contrib ed, Appearances Mag, 79- *Awards:* Fel, Ossabow Island Proj, 79; Fel, MacDowell Colony, 82 & 83; Creative Artists Pub Serv Prog Grant, NY State Coun Arts, 83. *Bibliog:* Joanne Barkan & Jon Friedman (auth), The beast in question, Arts Mag, 81; Sande Zorn (auth), Cows in the gallery, Holstein World, 82. *Media:* Acrylic, Watercolor; Etching. *Dealer:* Bernice Steinbaum Gallery 903 Madison Ave New York NY 10021. *Mailing Add:* 101 Prince St New York NY 10012

TONELLI, EDITH ANN
MUSEUM DIRECTOR, HISTORIAN
b Westfield, Mass, May 20, 49. *Study:* Vassar Col, NY, BA, 71, Helen Squier Townsend Fel, 71; Hunter Col, City Univ New York, with Vicent Longo & Robert Morris, MA(creative arts), 74; Boston Univ, Doctoral Fel, 74-79, with Patricia Hills, PhD, 81. *Collections Arranged:* Homer to Hopper: 60 Years of American Watercolor (auth, catalog), 76; By the People, For the People: New England (auth, catalog), 77; African Art: The Spirit Manifest, 78; Non Conformists: Contemporary Commentary from the Soviet Union (auth, catalog), 80; Louis Faurer: Photographs of Philadelphia & New York, 1937-1973 (auth, catalog), 81; Ralston Crawford: Photographs/Art and Process (auth, catalog), 82. *Pos:* Cur, DeCordova Mus, Mass, 76-78; dir, Univ Md Art

Gallery, 79-; dir, Frederick S Wight Art Gallery, Univ Calif, Los Angeles, 82- *Teaching:* Instr Am material culture, Boston Univ, Mass, 76; asst prof, Univ Md, College Park, 80-82; adj asst prof, Univ Calif, Los Angeles, 82- *Awards:* Smithsonian Fel, 79. *Bibliog:* Jane Holtz Kay (auth), Boston, Art News, 12/77. *Mem:* Am Asn Mus; Col Art Asn; Art Mus Asn; Am Asn Col Univ Mus Galleries; Asn Art Mus Dirs. *Res:* Twentieth century American art; American prints. *Publ:* Auth, The Avant-Garde in Boston: The WPA's federal art project, Archives Am Art J, 80; contribr, Frank Mechau, Aspen Ctr Visual Arts, 81. *Mailing Add:* S Wight Art Gallery Univ Calif, Los Angeles Los Angeles CA 90024

TONEY, ANTHONY
PAINTER, EDUCATOR
b Gloversville, NY, June 28, 13. *Study:* Syracuse Univ, BFA; Teachers Col, Columbia Univ, MA & EdD. *Work:* Whitney Mus Am Art, Nat Acad Design & Syracuse Univ, NY; Univ Ill, Urbana; Teachers Col, Columbia Univ; and others. *Comn:* Murals, Bowne Hall, 68 & six panels, Brockway Cafeteria, St Mary's Dorm, Syracuse, NY, 71; and many others. *Exhib:* Whitney Mus Am Art Ann, 50-60; Audubon Artists Ann, 55-83; Nat Acad Design Ann, 60-83; one-man shows, Amphora Gallery, La Jolla, Calif, 79, Mid-Hudson Arts & Sci Ctr, Poughkeepsie, NY, 79 & ACA Gallery, New York, 83; Concoran Gallery Art, Washington, DC; Brooklyn Mus; Los Angeles Co Mus; Metrop Mus; and others. *Teaching:* Instr creative art, Hofstra Univ, 52-55; instr creative painting, New Sch Social Res, 52-; instr creative painting, Five Towns Music & Art Found, 52-78; instr, Rockland Ctr Arts, 74-76 & North Westchester Ctr Arts, 80- *Awards:* Medals of Honor, Audubon Artists, 68 & 75; Benjamin Altman Prize, Nat Acad, 75-80; Emily Lowe Award, Audubon Artists, 83. *Mem:* Nat Acad Design (asst secy & mem coun, 79-); Audubon Artists (mem bd, 75-, vpres, 81-82); Nat Soc Mural Painters (treas, 73-76); Artists Equity Asn (mem bd dirs, 71-72); Int Inst Arts & Lett. *Media:* Oil. *Publ:* Auth, article, Leonardo, 10/77; auth, Painting and Drawing--Discovering Your Own Visual Language, Prentice-Hall, NJ, 78; contribr, An Appreciation, The Palette and the Flame, Posters of the Spanish Civil War, Int Publ, 79; contribr, Drawing, In: Funk & Wagnalls Encycl, 80; contribr, Drawing as exploration, Syracuse Scholar, fall 81. *Dealer:* ACA Gallery 21 E 67th St New York NY 10021. *Mailing Add:* 16 Hampton Pl Katonah NY 10536

TOOKER, GEORGE
PAINTER, PRINTMAKER
b Brooklyn, NY, Aug 5, 20. *Study:* Phillips Acad, grad, 38; Harvard Univ, AB, 42; Art Students League, with Reginald Marsh, Kenneth Hayes Miller & Harry Sternberg, 43-44. *Work:* Whitney Mus Am Art, Metrop Mus Art, Mus Mod Art, New York; Walker Art Ctr, Minneapolis; Nat Collection Fine Arts, Smithsonian Inst, Washington, DC. *Exhib:* Art Inst Chicago; 28th Venice Biennial; Mus Mod Art, New York; Metrop Mus Art, New York; Corcoran Gallery Art; retrospective, Jaffee-Friede Gallery, Hopkins Ctr, Dartmouth Col, Hanover, NH, 67, Fine Arts Mus San Francisco, Calif Palace Legion Honor, Mus Contemp Art, Chicago, Whitney Mus Am Art, New York & Indianapolis Mus Art, Ind, 74-75. *Teaching:* Instr, Art Students League, 65-68 & Hirshhorn Mus & Sculpture Garden, 84. *Awards:* Nat Inst Arts & Lett Grant, 60; Gov Award Excellence Arts, Montpelier, Vt. *Mem:* Nat Acad Design, New York; Inst Arts & Lett. *Mailing Add:* c/o Marisa del Rc Gallery 41 E 57th St New York NY 10022

TOPERZER, THOMAS RAYMOND
EDUCATOR, PAINTER
b Homestead, Pa, Aug 12, 39. *Study:* Sterling Col, 59-61; Southwestern Col (Kans), BA, 63; Univ Nebr-Lincoln, Woods fel, 69-70, MFA, 70. *Work:* Des Moines Art Ctr, Iowa; Springfield Art Mus, Mo; Rochester Art Ctr, Minn; Blanden Art Mus, Iowa; Ill State Univ. *Exhib:* Iowa Artists, Des Moines Art Ctr; New Horizons, Chicago; Nat Drawing, San Francisco Mus Art; Nat Prints & Drawings, Okla Art Ctr, Mid-America, Kansas City-St Louis, 74. *Pos:* Dir, Blanden Art Mus, 70-71; dir, Rochester Art Ctr, 71-72; asst dir, Mus & Galleries, Ill State Univ, 72, dir, Univ Galleries, Ctr Visual Arts Gallery, 73-82, ed, Univ Mus Newslett, 75-76. *Teaching:* Assoc prof photog & chmn, Bethel Col, currently. *Mem:* Am Asn Mus; Col Art Asn; Art Mus Asn. *Mailing Add:* Coord Fine Arts/Bethel Col 3900 Bethel Dr St Paul MN 55112

TOPOL, ROBERT MARTIN
COLLECTOR
b New York, NY, Mar 9, 25. *Collection:* Frescos, oils and sculptures. *Mailing Add:* 825 Orienta Ave Mamaroneck NY 10543

TOPPER, DAVID R
EDUCATOR, HISTORIAN
b Pittsburgh, Pa, Jan 1, 43. *Study:* Duquesne Univ, BS, 64; Case Inst Technol, MS, 66 & MA, 68; Case Western Reserve Univ, PhD, 70. *Teaching:* Prof art hist, Univ Winnipeg, Man, 70- *Mem:* Int Soc Arts, Sci & Technol; Am Soc Aesthet; Univ Art Asn Can. *Res:* Historical perspectives on visual perception of images. *Publ:* Auth, Gombrich on what a picture is not, Can Rev Art Educ Res, 80/81; auth, The Perception of Visual Art: A Bibliography, Vance, 81; coauth, Depth perception in linear and inverse perspective pictures, Perception, 81; auth, Historical perspectives on the visual arts, science and technology, Leonardo, 82; auth, Art in the realist ontology of J J Gibson, Synthese, 83. *Mailing Add:* Hist Dept Univ Winnipeg Winnipeg MB #R3B 2E9 Canada

TORBERT, DONALD ROBERT
EDUCATOR, HISTORIAN
b Bluerock, Ohio, Dec 21, 10. *Study:* Ohio State Univ, BA, MA; Univ Minn, PhD; also with Boardman Robinson & Sol Wilson. *Collections Arranged:* State Centennial Exhib of Architecture, Minneapolis Inst Arts, 58. *Pos:* Mem, Comt on Urban Environment, 68-78 & Heritage Preserv Comn, 72-78, City Minneapolis; mem state rev comt, Nat Roster Hist Places, State Minn, 70-78. *Teaching:* Instr design & watercolor, Ohio State Univ, 34-36; instr design, Univ La, summer 39 & Univ Syracuse, NY, summer 40; prof art hist, Univ Minn, 36-78. *Awards:* Post-doctoral Fulbright, Paris, 59-60. *Mem:* Col Art Asn; Soc Archit Historians. *Res:* Scandinavian sources of wood-framed architecture in United States. *Publ:* Auth, A Century of Art & Architecture, Univ Minn, 58; auth, A Century of Minnesota Architecture, Minneapolis Inst Arts, 58; auth, Significant Architecture in the History of Minneapolis, City Planning Comn & Minneapolis Chap of Am Inst Architects, 69-73. *Mailing Add:* 420 Foxen Dr Santa Barbara CA 93105

TORBERT, STEPHANIE BIRCH
PHOTOGRAPHER, EDUCATOR
b Wichita Falls, Tex, May 31, 45. *Study:* Univ NMex, BFA, 68; Sch for Am Craftsman, Rochester Inst Technol, NY, 68; Visual Studies Workshop, State Univ NY, Buffalo, MFA, 71. *Work:* Univ Minn Art Gallery, Minneapolis Inst Arts, Minneapolis; Int Mus Photography, George Eastman House, Rochester; Ctr for Creative Photog, Tucson, Ariz; Mus NMex, Santa Fe. *Exhib:* Minn Survey: Six Photogrs, Minneapolis Inst Arts & Nat Endowment Arts, 78; one-person shows, Minneapolis Inst Arts, 70, Walker Art Ctr, Minneapolis, 73, Int Mus Photog, George Eastman House, Rochester, NY, 78 & Friends Photog, Carmel, Calif, 79; and others. *Pos:* Visual arts panel, Minn State Arts Bd, 76- *Teaching:* Instr photog, N Hennepin Community Col, Minneapolis, 74-75 & Minneapolis Col Art & Design, 77-82. *Awards:* Minn State Arts Bd Artists Fel, 74; Bush Found Artists Fel, Minneapolis, 76-77; Nat Endowment Arts Grant, Minn Survey: Six Photogr, 77; and others. *Mem:* Soc Photog Educ. *Media:* Cibachrome, Non-Silver Process. *Mailing Add:* 3824 Harriet Ave S Minneapolis MN 55409

TORFFIELD, MARVIN
SCULPTOR
b Brooklyn, NY, July 25, 43. *Study:* Pratt Inst, BFA; Skowhegan Sch Painting & Sculpture, 66; Yale Univ Sch Art & Architecture, MFA, 70. *Comn:* Sculpture, The Great Lawn, Cent Park, New York Pub Art Fund, 80. *Exhib:* Jewish Mus, New York, 69; Seagram Bldg, Seagram Plaza, New York, 73; Whitney Mus, New York, 74; Artists Space, New York, 75; Paula Cooper Gallery, New York, 77; Leo Castelli Gallery, 83; and others. *Teaching:* Fellow visual & environ studies, Harvard Univ, 71-72. *Awards:* Nat Endowment Arts Grant, 70-71; Creative Artists Pub Serv Fel, 75-76; Guggenheim Fel, 75-76. *Mailing Add:* 50 Greene St New York NY 10013

TORLAKSON, JAMES DANIEL
PAINTER, PRINTMAKER
b San Francisco, Calif, Feb 19, 51. *Study:* Calif Col Arts & Crafts, BFA, 73; San Francisco State Univ, MA, 74. *Work:* San Francisco Mus Mod Art; Oakland Mus, Calif; Brooklyn Mus; Del Art Mus, Wilmington; Detroit Art Inst. *Exhib:* Variations on the Camera's Eye, Smithsonian Inst & SAm, 74; Twenty Yrs of Am Printmaking, Brooklyn Mus, 76 & Eight West Coast Printmakers, 78; one-man shows, Calif Palace Legion of Hon, Achenbach Found, San Francisco, 76 & San Jose Mus Art, Calif, 79; VX Inst Sao Paul Biennial, Int Communications Agency, SAm, 79; Recent Trends in Am Printmaking, Mitchell Mus, Mt Vernon, Ill, 79; and others. *Teaching:* Calif Col Arts & Crafts. *Awards:* Airport Purchase Award, San Francisco Int Airport Painting Competition, 77; purchase awards, 17th Nat Print & Drawing Exhib, Bradley Univ, 79 & Boston Printmakers 31st Nat Exhib, 79. *Bibliog:* Peter Frank (auth), New York Reviews, Artnews, 10/75. *Mem:* Calif Soc Printmakers. *Media:* Watercolor; Aquatint Etching. *Dealer:* John Berggruen 228 Grant Ave San Francisco CA 94108; Getler/Pall 50 W 57th St New York NY 10019. *Mailing Add:* 433 Rockaway Beach Ave Pacifica CA 94044

TORLEN, MICHAEL ARNOLD
PAINTER, EDUCATOR
b San Diego, Calif, Feb 28, 40. *Study:* Cranbrook Acad Art, Bloomfield Hills, Mich, BFA, 62; Ohio State Univ, Columbus, fel 63-64, with Hoyt Sherman, MFA, 65. *Work:* Aldrich Mus, Ridgefield, Conn; Neuberger Mus & Roy Neuberger Collection, Purchase, NY; Prudential Insurance Co, Newark, NJ. *Comn:* Symbolic portraits, Arlene Sarapa, Wingafe Paine & Buford Pippin, New York, 76; Meditation Mandala, Growth Ctr, New York, 77 & Goldleaf Omega Cross, 78. *Exhib:* Weatherspoon Ann, Univ NC, Greensboro, 67, 69 & 83; Aldrich Mus, Ridgefield, Conn, 72 & 73; one-man shows, Neuberger Mus, Purchase, NY, 79 & Cathedral St John the Divine, NY, 83; Artists Space, New York, 83; Luise Ross Fine Art, New York, 83; and others. *Teaching:* Asst prof painting & drawing, Univ Ga, 65-70; assoc prof & dept head painting & drawing, State Univ NY Col, Purchase, 72- *Awards:* Purchase Award, Ga Comn Arts, 69; State Univ NY Res Fel & Grant, 78; Visiting Artist Traveling Grant, Vis Arts Bd, Australia Coun, 82. *Bibliog:* Robert Yoskowitz (auth), article, Arts Mag, 9/81. *Mem:* Col Art Asn; Lindisfarne Asn. *Dealer:* Luise Ross 162 56th St New York NY. *Mailing Add:* Div of Visual Arts State Univ NY Col Purchase NY 10577

TORN, JERRY (GERALD J)
DRAFTSMAN, PHOTOGRAPHER
b Burlington, Iowa, Mar 16, 33. *Study:* Univ Iowa, studied printmaking with Mauricio Lasansky, BA(fine arts), 58. *Work:* Art Inst Chicago, First Nat Bank Chicago, Ill; Ill State Mus, Springfield; Portland Art Mus, Ore; Kemper Insurance Co, Long Grove, Ill. *Comn:* Drawings for exec dining room, First Nat Bank Chicago, London Branch, 81; Lithograph Suite, Plucked Chicken Press, Chicago, 83. *Exhib:* New Figurative Work, Univ Ind, Gary, 80; Drawings of David, Univ Wis, Marshfield, 81; 62nd Ann Exhib, Arts Club Chicago, 82; Dancers, Univ Wis, Marinette, 82, Art Guild, Burlington, Iowa, 82 & Fairweather Hardin Gallery, Chicago, 82. *Pos:* Assoc dir, Fairweather Hardin Gallery, Chicago, 74- *Teaching:* Instr design, Loyola Univ, Chicago, 70-71. *Bibliog:* Sandra Conn (auth), Julie Schnieder and Jerry Torn, Reader, 4/2/80; Alan Artner (auth), Jerry Torn, Chicago Tribune, 7/25/80; Margaret Hawkins (auth), Jerry Torn, New Art Examiner, 11/80. *Mem:* Arts Club Chicago. *Media:* Graphite. *Dealer:* Fairweather Hardin Gallery 101 E Ontario St Chicago IL 60611. *Mailing Add:* 1318 W Cornelia Chicago IL 60657

TORNHEIM, NORMAN
SCULPTOR
b Chicago, Ill, Sept 16, 42. *Study:* Art Ctr Col Design, BS, 66; Calif State Univ, San Diego, MA, 75. *Work:* Las Vegas Art Mus, Nev; Marietta Col, Ohio; Smith Col, Northampton, Mass; Ind Univ. *Comn:* Sculpture, comn by Mr & Mrs Stern, Calif, 76; sculpture, comn by Mr & Mrs Lewis, Calif, 77; sculpture, comn by Dr I Mori, Calif, 77. *Exhib:* Mainstreams 76, Marietta Col, Ohio, 76; Calif Craftsmen, Monterey Mus Art, Calif, 76; Designer-Craftsmen 76, Richmond Art Ctr, Calif, 76; Nat Competition 77, Dahl Fine Arts Ctr, 77; Calif Craftsmen, E B Crocker Art Mus, Sacramento, 77; Goldsmiths USA, Univ Wash, Seattle, 77; Musical Instruments, The Smithsonian Inst, Washington, DC, 78-80. *Collections Arranged:* Golden West Col Invitational, 78. *Teaching:* Instr wood, metal & leather, San Diego State Univ, Calif, 72-75; instr wood, metal, leather & clay, Golden West Col, Huntington Beach, Calif, 75- *Awards:* Jurors Award, Las Vegas Art Mus, 75; Purchase Award, Ark Art Ctr, 76; Merit Award, Nat Competition 77, Dahl Fine Arts Ctr, 77. *Bibliog:* Dona Z Meilach (auth), Wood Objects as Functional Sculpture, Crown, 76. *Media:* Clay, Porcelain. *Publ:* Contribr, Artweek, 76-77. *Mailing Add:* Golden West Col 15744 Goldenwest Huntington Beach CA 92647

TORREANO, JOHN FRANCIS
PAINTER, LECTURER
b Flint, Mich, Aug 17, 41. *Study:* Cranbrook Acad Art, BFA, 63; Ohio State Univ, MFA, 67; also with Robert King & Hoyt L Sherman. *Work:* Whitney Mus Am Art, New York; Aldrich Mus Contemp Art, Ridgefield, Conn; Michener Collection, Univ Tex; Chase Manhattan Bank; Mus Art, RI Sch Design, Providence. *Exhib:* One-man shows, John Doyle Gallery, Chicago, Susan Caldwell Gallery & Artists Space, New York; Texas Gallery, Houston; Hamilton Gallery Contemp Art, New York; and others. *Teaching:* Asst prof painting, Univ SDak, 67-68; instr painting, Sch Visual Arts, 69-70, State Univ NY, Purchase & Goddard Col, 73-75; vis artist, Art Inst Chicago, 72, NS Col Art & Design, Halifax, 75, Univ NMex, Las Cruces, 76-80 & RI Sch Design, 82-83; vis lectr, Ohio State Univ, Columbus, 75. *Awards:* Nat Endowment Arts Grant & Creative Artists Pub Serv Grant, 78-79; Nat Endowment Arts Fel, 82-83. *Bibliog:* Jeff Perone (auth), Approaching the decorative, 12/76, Artforum; Thomas Lawson (auth), Painting in New York, Flash Art, 10-11/79; Carrie Rickey (auth), rev, Flash Art, 1-2/80; and others. *Media:* Acrylic. *Mailing Add:* 103 Franklin St New York NY 10013

TOSCHIK, LARRY
PAINTER, WRITER
b Milwaukee, Wis, July 17, 22. *Study:* Wis Art Acad, scholar; Layton Art Sch, Milwaukee. *Work:* Col Bus Admin Ariz State Univ; Riveredge Found, Calgary; US House of Rep. *Comn:* Battlefield monument, 361st Inf 91st Div Mil Cemetery, Florence, Italy, 44; 30 paintings (wildlife), Hallmark Permanent Collection, 69-71; 20 silver medallions, Ducks Unlimited Inc, Chicago, 74; four wildlife lithographs, Franklin Mint; ltd ed porcelain plates, Artists of the World. *Exhib:* Nat Cowboy Hall of Fame, Oklahoma City, Okla, 73; Waterfowl Festival, Easton, Md, 73; Pac Flyway Show, Santa Rosa, Calif, 75; Retrospective, Scottsdale Ctr for Arts, 78; Austin Gallery, 82 & 83; and others. *Awards:* 3M Co Design Award, 62; Ducks Unlimited Inc Artist of the Year, 75-76; two awards, Printing Indust of Am, 77. *Mem:* Audubon Soc. *Media:* Oil, Watercolor. *Publ:* Auth & illusr, Whispering skies of Arizona, 73, Shadowed trails, 76, Prowlers of the clouds, 79 & Shorebirds, 82, Ariz Highways Mag; illusr, Wildlife Techniques Manual. *Dealer:* Austin Gallery 7103 Main St Scottsdale AZ 85251. *Mailing Add:* Box 305 Pine AZ 85544

TOTH, CARL WAYNE
PHOTOGRAPHER
b Cleveland, Ohio, Dec 7, 47. *Study:* Rochester Inst Technol, AAS, 68; State Univ NY, Buffalo, with Donald Blumberg, BA, 70, MFA, 72. *Work:* Int Mus Photog at George Eastman House, Rochester, NY; Visual Studies Workshop, Rochester; Mus Mod Art, New York; Australian Nat Gallery, Canberra; San Francisco Mus Mod Art, Calif. *Exhib:* Photography Unlimited, William Hayes Fogg Art Mus, Cambridge, Mass, 74; Young American Photographers, Kalamazoo Inst Arts, 75; Recent Acquisitions, Detroit Inst Art, 77; Santa Barbara Mus Art, Calif, 79; New Mus, New York, 79; San Francisco Mus Art, Calif, 79; and others. *Teaching:* Head dept photog, Cranbrook Acad of Art, Bloomfield Hills, Mich, 72- *Awards:* Photogr Fel, Nat Endowment Arts, 75 & 79. *Bibliog:* Photography Year, Time Life Books, 73; Exhibition Review, Artforum, 1/75. *Mem:* Soc Photog Educ. *Dealer:* Light Gallery 724 Fifth Ave New York NY 10019. *Mailing Add:* Cranbrook Acad of Art PO Box 801 Bloomfield Hills MI 48013

TOULIS, VASILIOS (APOSTOLOS)
PRINTMAKER, EDUCATOR
b Clewiston, Fla, Mar 24, 31. *Study:* Univ Fla, with Fletcher Martin & Carl Holty, BDes; Pratt Inst, with Richard Lindner, Fritz Eichenberg, Jacob Landau & Walter Rogalski, BFA. *Work:* US State Dept, Washington, DC; Mus Arte Mod, Mexico City, Mex; Caravan House, New York. *Comn:* Portfolio of prints, Ctr for Contemp Printmaking, 68. *Exhib:* Brooklyn Mus, NY, 66; Fleishcer Mem, Philadelphia, 66; Mus Arte Mod, Mexico City, 67; Int Miniature Print Exhib, 68; New Paltz Nat Print Exhib, 68; and others. *Teaching:* Lectr serigraphic printmaking, Univ RI, 67 & Pratt Inst Seminar, 69; head graphic workshops, Pratt Inst, 66-, instr printmaking, 69-71, assoc prof & head undergrad printmaking, 71-; dir silk screen workshops, The Artists Collective, Hartford, Conn, 73- *Awards:* Tiffany Found Grant in Printmaking, 67. *Mem:* Am Asn Univ Prof; United Fedn Col Teachers; Screen Printers Asn. *Mailing Add:* RFD 3 Putnam Valley NY 10579

TOUSIGNANT, CLAUDE
PAINTER, SCULPTOR
b Montreal, PQ, Dec 23, 32. *Study:* Sch Art & Design, Montreal; Acad Ranson, Paris. *Work:* Nat Gallery Can; Phoenix Art Mus, Ariz; Larry Aldrich Mus, Ridgefield, Conn; York Univ; Mus Contemp Art, Montreal & Quebec; and others. *Exhib:* Solomon R Guggenheim Mus, New York, 65; Can Art, Paris, Rome & Brussels; Lausanne, Switz, 68; Mass Inst Technol, Cambridge; Washington Gallery Mod Art; Retrospective, Nat Gallery Can, 73-75; and many other group exhibs & more than 20 one-man shows. *Pos:* Pres, Claude Tousignant, Inc. *Teaching:* Instr design, Sch Art & Design, Montreal. *Awards:* Prize, Salon de la Jeune Peinture, 62 & Centennial Exhib, 67; Rome Prize, 73. *Mem:* Artistes Prof de Montreal; Royal Can Acad Arts. *Mailing Add:* 4678 St Andre Montreal PQ H2J 3A1 Canada

TOVISH, HAROLD
SCULPTOR, EDUCATOR
b New York, NY, July 31, 21. *Study:* Columbia Univ, 40-43; Ossip Zadkine Sch Sculpture, Paris, 49-50; Acad Grande Chaumiere, Paris, 50-51. *Work:* Whitney Mus Am Art & Mus Mod Art, New York; Philadelphia Mus Art; Hirshhorn Mus, DC; Boston Mus Fine Art, Mass. *Comn:* Epitaph (sculpture), State of Hawaii, 70. *Exhib:* Twenty-Eighth Venice Biennial, Italy, 56; Carnegie Inst Int, 58; Recent Sculpture: USA, Mus Mod Art, New York, 59; Whitney Mus Am Art Ann, 66; retrospective, Watson Gallery, Wheaton Col, 67; solo exhib, Guggenheim Mus, 68 & Boston Univ Art Gallery, 80; Int Award Exhib, Guggenheim Mus, 68; Inst Contemp Art, Boston, 76 & 77; Boston Mus Fine Art, 77. *Teaching:* Asst prof sculpture & drawing, Univ Minn, 51-54; vis prof sculpture, Univ Hawaii, 64-70; prof art, Boston Univ, 71- *Awards:* Am Inst Arts & Lett Grant, 60 & 71; Guggenheim Fel, 67; Fel, Ctr Advanced Visual Studies, Mass Inst Technol, 68. *Bibliog:* H Harvard Arneson (auth), New talent, Art in Am, 54. *Mem:* Boston Visual Artists Union. *Media:* Bronze. *Dealer:* Terry Dintenfass Inc 50 W 57th St New York NY 10019; Alpha Gallery 119 Newbury St Boston MA 02116. *Mailing Add:* 380 Marlborough St Boston MA 02115

TOWN, HAROLD BARLING
PAINTER, WRITER
b Toronto, Ont, June 13, 24. *Study:* Ont Col Art, grad, 44; York Univ, hon LHD, 66. *Work:* Tate Gallery, London; Mus Mod Art, New York; Stedelijk Mus, Amsterdam, Holland; Solomon R Guggenheim Mus, New York; Nat Gallery Can. *Comn:* Mural on canvas, Ont Hydro Comn, St Lawrence Seaway Power Proj, 57; decorative exterior enamel frieze, North York Pub Libr, Toronto, 59; two-part mural & sculptural screen, Toronto Int Airport, Malton, Can Govt, 62; mural on canvas, Queens Park Proj, Ont Govt, 69. *Exhib:* Cezanne & Structure in Modern Painting, Guggenheim Mus, 63; Documenta, Kassel, Ger, 64; Can Govt Pavilion, Expo '67 & Expo '70, Osaka, Japan; one-man shows, Venice Biennial, Italy, 56, 64 & 72; retrospective, Art Gallery Windsor, 75. *Pos:* Mem bd gov, Ont Art Col, 71. *Awards:* Officer, Order Can, 68; hon fel, Founders Col, York Univ; Medal of Merit, City Toronto, 79. *Bibliog:* David Silcox (auth), The First Exhibition of New Work, 1969/73, 73; Visions, Contemporary Art in Canada, Douglas & McIntyre, Vancouver & Toronto, 83; Contemporary Canadian Art, Hurtig Publ, 83. *Mem:* Royal Can Acad. *Publ:* Auth, Enigmas, 64; coauth, Drawings of Harold Town, 69; auth, Silent stars, sound stars, film stars, 71; auth, Albert Franck: Keeper of the Lanes, McClelland & Stewart, 74; coauth, Tom Thomson: The Silence and the Storm, McClelland & Stewart, 77. *Dealer:* Waddington Galleries 33 Hazelton Ave Toronto ON Can. *Mailing Add:* 9 Castle Frank Crescent Toronto ON M4W 3A2 Canada

TOWNLEY, HUGH
SCULPTOR, PRINTMAKER
b Lafayette, Ind, Feb 6, 23. *Study:* Univ Wis, 46-48; also with Ossip Zadkine, Paris, 48-49; London Co Coun Arts & Crafts, 49-50. *Work:* Mus Mod Art; Whitney Mus Am Art; Boston Mus Fine Arts; Fogg Mus Art, Harvard Univ; Los Angeles Co Mus Art. *Comn:* Cast concrete reliefs & archit walls, Old Stone Bank, Bristol, RI, 65; wood relief, Bristol Hosp, Conn, 69; three concrete pieces, Class of 65, Brown Univ, Providence, RI, 70; three concrete pieces, State of Ky Comprehensive Training Ctr, Somerset, Ky, 72; designed 14 benches for City of Providence, RI, 79. *Exhib:* New Talent Show, Mus Mod Art, 55; Ann Drawings & Sculpture, Whitney Mus Am Art, 62 & 63; 65th Am Painting & Sculpture Exhib, Art Inst Chicago, 64; Dartmouth Col, 75; Keene State Univ, NH, 76; Wingspread Gallery, Northeast Harbour, Maine, 77; Inst Contemp Art, Boston, 77; solo exhib, Western Carolina Univ, 78 & Worcester Art Mus, Mass, 80. *Teaching:* Instr sculpture & drawing, Layton Sch Art, Milwaukee, 51-56; asst prof sculpture, Beloit Col, 56-57; asst prof sculpture & drawing, Boston Univ, 57-61; prof art, Brown Univ, 61-; vis

prof, Univ Calif, Berkeley, 61, Santa Barbara, 68; vis lectr, Harvard Univ, 67. *Awards:* Grant for Creative Work in Art, Nat Inst Arts & Lett, 67; Gov Award, State of RI Coun Arts, 72; Ore Sculpture Symposium, Eugene, 74. *Media:* Wood, Concrete; Lithography. *Mailing Add:* 1 Resolute Ln Bristol RI 02809

TOWNSEND, J BENJAMIN
CRITIC, HISTORIAN
b Stillwater, NY, Feb 17, 18. *Study:* Princeton Univ, BA, 40; Harvard Univ, MA, 42; Yale Univ, PhD, 51. *Collections Arranged:* This New Man: A Discourse in Portraits (with catalog), 68 & Presidential Portraits (with catalog), 68, Nat Portrait Gallery, Smithsonian Inst; Martha Visser 't Hooft: Paintings & Drawings, 1950-1973 (with catalog), 73, Six Corporate Collectors (with catalog), 75 & Works by Charles E Burchfield (with catalog), 79, Burchfield Art Ctr. *Pos:* Asst dir, Nat Portrait Gallery, Smithsonian Inst, 67-68. *Teaching:* Prof art & lit, State Univ NY Buffalo, 57-83, chmn master arts humanities, 60-66, chmn dept art & art hist, 69-71, prof emer, 83. *Res:* Journals of Charles Burchfield. *Publ:* Auth, John Davidson, Poet of Armageddon, Yale, 61, reprint, 78, auth, 100: The Buffalo Fine Arts Academy, 1862-1962, Albright-Knox Art Gallery, 62. *Mailing Add:* 879 W Ferry St Buffalo NY 14209

TOWNSEND, JOHN F
SCULPTOR, PAINTER
b La Crosse, Wis. *Study:* Carroll Col, Waukesha, Wis, BS, 51; Minneapolis Sch of Art, 53-55; Univ of Minn Grad Sch, MFA, 59. *Work:* Mus Fine Art, Boston, Mass; Rose Mus, Brandeis Univ, Waltham, Mass; Allentown Art Mus, Pa; Chase Manhattan Bank, New York; World Bank, Washington, DC. *Exhib:* Art for US Embassies, Inst Contemp Art, Boston, 66; Optical Art Traveling Exhib, Mus Mod Art, New York, 66-68; Small Paintings for Mus Collections, Am Fedn of Art Traveling Exhib, 67-68; one-man shows, Eleanor Rigelhaupt Gallery, Boston, 67, Ward-Nasse Gallery, Boston, 70, Danco Gallery, Florence, Mass, 79 & Berkshire Artisans, Pittsfield, Mass, 81; and others. *Pos:* Dir art exhibs, 60-64 & dir grad art prog, 71-74, Univ Mass, Amherst. *Teaching:* Instr sculpture & painting, Eastern NMex Univ, Portales, 59-60; from instr to full prof sculpture, drawing & design, Univ of Mass, Amherst, 60-; part-time instr painting, Mt Holyoke Col, South Hadley, Mass, 61-62. *Awards:* First Award Sculpture, Second Ann Univ Arts Faculty Exhib, Argus Gallery, Madison, NJ, 63; Crane Co Award, 17th Ann Exhib of Painting & Drawing, 68 & 15th Spring Exhib, Berkshire Mus, Pittsfield, Mass. *Bibliog:* Dona Z Meilach (auth), Contemporary Art with Wood, Crown Publ Inc, New York, 68. *Media:* Acrylic; Wood. *Mailing Add:* 118 Aubinwood Rd Amherst MA 01002

TOWNSEND, MARVIN J
CARTOONIST, ILLUSTRATOR
b Kansas City, Mo, July 2, 15. *Study:* Kansas City Art Inst; Col Com Art Sch. *Work:* Syracuse Univ. *Awards:* Earl Temple Award. *Media:* Ink. *Publ:* Strips, gag cartoons & illus for trade, bus & prof mags, 41-; auth, Robo (cartoon strip), Nat Safety News, 58-; auth, Moontoons Jokes and Riddles, 70; auth, Ghostly Ghastly Cartoons, 71; auth, Campgroans (Mo cartoon feature), Woodall's Campground Mgt; and others. *Mailing Add:* 631 W 88th St Kansas City MO 64114

TOWNSEND, (ALVIN) NEAL
EDUCATOR, CRAFTSMAN
b Rock Island, Tex, Oct 26, 34. *Study:* Univ NMex, BFA, 61, MA(grad asst), 62; with Kenneth Adams, Elaine De Kooning, Keith Monroe & Robert Mallary. *Work:* Roswell Mus & Art Ctr, NMex; Art Mus, Fine Arts Ctr & Jonson Gallery of Univ NMex & Mus Albuquerque. *Exhib:* Young Americans, Mus Contemp Crafts, New York, 62; South West States Biennial, Mus Fine Arts, Santa Fe, NMex, 64; Southwestern Craftsmen, Dallas Mus, Tex, 68; 3rd Biennial Int Craft, Tweed Mus Art, Duluth, Minn, 75; 11th Biennial Des Crafts, El Paso Mus Art, Tex, 79; Fletcher Brownbuilt Pottery Award Exhib, Auckland, NZ, 82; Salzbrand 83, Handwerkskammer Koblenz, WGer, 83. *Pos:* Post crafts dir, Dept Defense, Sandia Base, NMex, 62-68; post crafts dir, Dept Army, Ft Belvoir, Va, 69-70; dir, Art Educ Gallery, Univ NMex, 82-83. *Teaching:* Instr art, North East La State Col, Monroe, 62; from asst prof to prof art educ, Univ NMex, 70-; instr ceramics, Vancouver Sch Art, Can, 80-. *Awards:* First Place Ceramics, Mus Int Folk Art, 63; First Place, NMex Arts & Crafts Fair, 67; Merit Award, Southwestern Arts & Crafts Festival, 78. *Bibliog:* Flo Wilks (auth), Neal Townsend profile, Artcraft Mag, 80; Crafts Horizons, Am Crafts Coun, NY, 64. *Mem:* Albuquerque United Artists; NMex Potters Asn. *Media:* Clay. *Dealer:* Mariposa Gallery 113 Romero NW Albuquerque NM 87104. *Mailing Add:* 2583 Ramirez Rd SW Albuquerque NM 87105

TOWNSEND, STANLEY DALE
PAINTER, INSTRUCTOR
b Princeton, Ind, Sept 6, 47. *Study:* ETenn State Univ, BFA(Brightly scholar), 72. *Work:* Tenn State Mus, Nashville; Waverly Hotel, Atlanta; Am Asn Col & Univ, DC; ETenn State Univ, Johnson City; and others. *Comn:* Murals, Ga Coun Arts, Dalton, 74 & Chattanooga City Sch System, 75; oil painting, Kayo Oil Corp, Chattanooga, 80. *Exhib:* Ann Area Art Exhib, 67-71, Ann Competition, 68-70, Hunter Gallery Art, Chattanooga; one-man shows, Hunter Gallery Art, 78, Carroll Reece Mus, Johnson City, Tenn, 79 & Image South Gallery, Atlanta, 79; Southeastern Graphics Invitational, Mint Mus Art, Charlotte, NC, 79; Graphics Invitational, Gibbes Art Gallery, Charleston, SC, 80; Nat Mus Am Art, Smithsonian Inst, Washington DC, 81; Sawtooth Gallery, Winston-Salem, NC, 82; Birmingham Mus Art, Ala; Southern Ohio Mus & Cult Ctr, Portsmouth; Miss Mus Art, Jackson; and

other group and one-man shows. *Pos:* Asst dir, Slocumb Gallery, ETenn State Univ, Johnson City, 70-72; asst dir, Hunter Mus Art, Chattanooga, 73-74; artist-in-residence, Ga Coun Art & Nat Endowment Arts, Dalton, Ga, 74-75 & Hunter Mus Sch Art, Chattanooga, 75-78. *Teaching:* Instr drawing, painting & printmaking, Hunter Mus Sch Art, 70-78. *Awards:* Art Honors Award, ETenn State Univ, Johnson City, 69; Purchase Award, Southeastern Graphics Invitational, NC Nat Bank, Charlotte, 79. *Media:* Oil. *Dealer:* Margaret Townsend Gallery 406 High St Chattanooga TN 37403; Art South Inc 613 Felder Ave Montgomery AL 36106. *Mailing Add:* 406 High St Chattanooga TN 37403

TOWNSEND, STORM D
SCULPTOR

b London, Eng, Aug 31, 37. *Study:* London Univ, NDD, ATC, Goldsmiths' Col Art, 6 yrs, with Harold Parker & Ivor Roberts Jones. *Work:* Fine Arts Mus NMex, Santa Fe; Genesee Co Mus, Rochester. *Comn:* Life-size portrait in bronze, comn by David Cargo, Gov NMex, 67; hon portrait plaque & life-size bronze, NMex Glorietta Conv Ctr. *Exhib:* One-person shows, Gallery Marquis, Denver, Colo, 75, & Gallery Eleven, Lubbock, Tex, 77; Survey of Contemp NMex Sculpture, NMex Mus Fine Art, Santa Fe, 76; Santa Fe Festival Arts, 79; Great Garden Exhib, Sculptural Arts Mus, Atlanta, 82. *Teaching:* Instr sculpture, Pojoaque Art Ctr, Santa Fe, 65-66, Col of Santa Fe, 73-75 & Univ Albuquerque, NMex, currently. *Awards:* Jajasan Siswa Lokantara Resident Fel to study the arts in Indonesia, 60-61; Resident Fels, Huntington Hartford Found, Calif, 63 & Helene Wurlitzer Found, Taos, NMex, 64. *Bibliog:* Robert M Powers (auth), NMex Mag, 78; Mary Carrol Nelson (auth), articles, Am Artist, 79 & Art Voices S, 80. *Media:* Cast Bronze, Clay. *Mailing Add:* PO Box 1165 Corrales NM 87048

TOWNSEND, VERA B
EDUCATOR, HISTORIAN

b Savannah, Ga, June 14, 23. *Study:* Univ Ga, Athens, BA, 45, MA, 50; Emory Univ, PhD, 68. *Collections Arranged:* Vis assoc cur, Laurence McKinin: A Retrospective (auth, catalog), Univ Mo, 83. *Teaching:* Instr humanities, Oglethorpe Univ, Atlanta, 48-49; instr classics, Emory Univ, Atlanta, 58-61; assoc prof art hist, Univ Mo, Columbia, 68-, chmn dept art hist & archaeol, 82- *Mem:* Mo Coun Fine Arts; Midwest Art Historians; Col Art Asn. *Res:* Poetry and painting in France, 1850-1914; beginnings of non-objective art; contemporary criticism. *Publ:* Auth, Douglas Freed, Arts Mag, 80; auth, Ut Poesis Pictura, Muse, 81. *Mailing Add:* Dept Art Hist & Archaeol 109 Pickard Hall Univ Mo Columbia MO 65211

TRACHTENBERG, GLORIA P
PAINTER, GRAPHIC ARTIST

b Brooklyn, NY. *Study:* Brooklyn Col, BA(art), 71; NY Univ, MA(art), 73; Brooklyn Mus Art Sch, with Reuben Tam; Art Students League, with Robert Brachman. *Work:* NY Univ Med Ctr; Brooklyn Col; Mt Sinai Hosp, Anchor Engraving Corp, Forest Paper Corp, New York. *Comn:* Series (paintings of children), Donald Art Corp, New York, 61; series (flower paintings), 70 & series (country scenes), 72, Arthur Kaplan & Co, New York; landscapes, BLD Art Publ, New York, 73 & Graphic Arts Unlimited, New York, 79. *Exhib:* Salmagundi Club, New York, 70; Metrop Mus Art, New York, 77; Brooklyn Artists, Brooklyn Mus, 79; Brooklyn Col, 79; Long Beach Mus Art, 82; New England Ann, Westenhook Gallery, Sheffield, Mass, 82; Am Soc Contemp Artists, State Univ NY, Alfred, 83. *Teaching:* Instr drawing, Sch Visual Arts, 79-80 & Kingsborough Community Col, 80- *Awards:* Am Artist Mag Drawing Prize, 70; First Prize Oil, Long Beach Art Asn, 72; Andrews Nelson Whitehead Award, Greenwich Art, Conn, 79. *Bibliog:* Dorothy Hall (auth), Art & artists, Park East, 3/14/71; Craig Bailey (auth), Watercolor show follows form, Staten Island Advance, 4/28/81; Renee Phillips (auth), Memories, dreams, reflections in Soho, Manhattan Arts, 8/31/83. *Mem:* Artists Equity; Am Soc Contemp Artists; Nat League Am Penwomen; Long Beach Art Asn; Brooklyn Watercolor Soc. *Media:* Oil, Watercolor. *Dealer:* Best in Art 1916 Ave K Brooklyn NY. *Mailing Add:* 1768 Ocean Ave Brooklyn NY 11230

TRACHTMAN, ARNOLD S
PAINTER

b Lynn, Mass, Oct 5, 30. *Study:* Mass Sch of Art, BFA; Sch of the Art Inst of Chicago, MFA. *Work:* Fogg Art Mus, Harvard Univ, Cambridge, Mass; Addison Gallery of Am Art, Andover Mass; Wiggin Collection, Boston Pub Libr, Mass; Boston Mus of Fine Arts. *Exhib:* Brockton Art Ctr, Mass, 79; Watergate Galerie Borjeson, Malmo, Sweden, 74; one-man shows, Inst Contemp Art, Boston, 70 & Addison Gallery Am Art, Andover Mass, 76; AAMARP Gallery, Boston, 81; Bradford Col, Mass, 82; Staatliche Kunsthalle, Berlin, WGer, 83; and others. *Teaching:* Instr art, Lynnfield High Sch, Mass, 71-80, Cambridge Sch, Weston, 80-81, Mass Col Art, 81- *Mem:* Boston Visual Artist Union. *Media:* Acrylic, Watercolor. *Mailing Add:* 27 Dana St Cambridge MA 02138

TRACY, BERRY BRYSON
CURATOR, ADMINISTRATOR

b Hampton, Iowa, Sept 4, 33. *Study:* Parson's Sch Design, with Robert J Castle, 52; Univ Iowa, BA(Am studies), 55; Attingham Park Adult Col, Shropshire, Eng, with George Trevelyan, 55; Newark Mus, mus philos & techniques with Katherine Coffey, 60. *Comn:* Criteria & proposals, Chicago Hist Soc, 60; restoration, Boscobel Restoration Inc, 75. *Collections Arranged:* Classical America, 1815-1845 (with catalog), Newark Mus, 63; 19th Century America, Furniture & Other Decorative Arts (with catalog), 70, New American Wing, 80, Metrop Mus Art. *Pos:* Historical technician, Dept Conservation, State Ill, 57-60; adv for restoration and furnishing, 57-75; cur decorative arts, Newark Mus, 60-64; asst cur, Metrop Mus Art, New York, 64-65, assoc cur, 65-68, cur, 68-72, cur in chg Am Wing, 73-; mem, Spec Fine Arts Comt, US Dept of State, Washington, DC, 71-77 & 77-; pres, Berry Tracy Inc, 81- *Bibliog:* John Canaday (auth), Good show in Newark, New York Times, 6/2/63; Marvin D Schwartz (auth), Classical America 1815-1845, Art Quart, summer 63; Jay Cantor (auth), Critic's view of 19th century America, Winterthur Portfolio, 72. *Mem:* Friends Attingham (bd dir, 70-74); Nat Asn Arts & Lit; Nat Trust Hist Preservation; Newark Mus. *Publ:* Auth, 19th Century American Furniture in the Collection of the Newark Museum, 61 & auth, English Pottery in the Collection of the Newark Museum, 62, Newark Mus; auth, Late classical styles in American silver, 1810-1830, Antiques Mag, 12/64; auth, Catalogue of Collections at Boscobel Restoration, Inc, 80. *Mailing Add:* PO Box 633 Goshen NY 10924

TRACY, LOIS BARTLETT
PAINTER, WRITER

b Jackson, Mich. *Study:* Rollins Col, 29; with Hans Hofmann, 45-46; Mich State Univ, MA, 58; New Col Workshop, 65, with Balcomb Greene, Afro, James Brooks, Marca-Relli & Sid Solomon. *Work:* Air & Space Mus, Smithsonian Inst, Washington, DC; Norton Gallery Art, Palm Beach, Fla; Univ Va; Hugh McKean, Morse Gallery of Art, Winter Park, Fla; Univ NC; and others. *Exhib:* Southeastern Shows, Atlanta, Ga; Four Arts Soc, Palm Beach, Fla, 77; Harmon Gallery, Naples, Fla, 78; Major Fla Artists, 79; Retrospect, Melvin Gallery, Lakeland, Fla, 80; plus others. *Teaching:* Instr, Univ Va Exten, 52-58 & 64-65; head dept art, Clinch Valley Col, 56-57; head dept art, Southeastern Col, Univ Ky, 64-66; head dept art, Edison Jr Col, Ft Myers, Fla, 68- *Awards:* First Award, Fla Artists Group, 68; Watercolor Award, Southeastern Ann, High Mus Art; Gold Medal, New York World's Fair, State of Fla; plus others. *Bibliog:* Cosmic artist, Yankee, 7/49; Bartlett Tracy, NH Profiles, 4/52. *Mem:* Am Asn Univ Prof; Fla Artists Group; Sarasota Art Asn; Galerie Int New York; Nat Asn Women Artists. *Media:* Acrylic, Oil. *Publ:* Auth, Painting Principles and Practices, 65, 67, 69 & 71; auth, Adventuring in Art, in press. *Dealer:* Center St Gallery Winter Park FL 32789. *Mailing Add:* 580 Artist Ave Englewood FL 33533

TRACY, MICHAEL
SCULPTOR, PAINTER

b Bellevue, Ohio, Sept 30, 43. *Study:* St Edward's Univ, Austin, BA, 64; Cleveland Inst Art, 64-67; Univ Tex, Austin, MFA, 69. *Work:* Art Mus STex, Corpus Christi; San Antonio Art Mus & McNay Art Inst, San Antonio, Tex; Mus Fine Art, Houston. *Exhib:* Art Mus STex, Corpus Christi; Marion Koogler McNay Art Inst, San Antonio, 71; Contemp Arts Mus, Houston, 74; Off the Wall, Art Mus San Antonio, 80; New Art at the Tate, Tate Gallery, London, 83. *Bibliog:* Suzie Kalil (auth), Michael Tracy's metaphysics, Artweek, 2/28/80; Donna Tennant (auth), article, Artspace, winter 80. *Media:* Multimedia. *Dealer:* Dela Hunty 2701 Canton Dallas TX; Dela Hunty 291 Church New York NY. *Mailing Add:* San Ygnacio TX 78067

TRAGER, PHILIP
PHOTOGRAPHER

b Bridgeport, Conn, Feb 27, 35. *Study:* Wesleyan Univ, BA, 56; Columbia Univ Sch Law, JD, 60. *Work:* Mus Mod Art, Metrop Mus Art, New York; Corcoran Gallery Art; Bibliot Nat, Paris; Smithsonian Inst. *Comn:* Photog study Wesleyan Univ, Bd Trustees, 80. *Exhib:* Two-person exhib, San Francisco Mus Mod Art, 74; solo exhib, Baltimore Mus Art, 77, Mus City New York, 80 & Am Inst Architects, Washington, DC, 82; New Acquisitions, Corcoran Gallery Am Art, 81; Five Years at the Creative Photography Gallery, Mass Inst Technol, 82; Manhattan Observed: Fourteen Photographers Look at New York 1972-1981, New York Hist Soc & New York State Mus, Albany, 82; Ranchos de Taos, A Photographic History, Mus Fine Art, Colorado Springs Fine Arts Ctr & Amon Carter Mus Western Art, Ft Worth; and others. *Teaching:* Instr masterclasses & workshops, Int Ctr Photog & Maine Photog Workshop. *Awards:* Conn Soc Architects Lay Person Award, 80. *Bibliog:* Lee D Witkin & Barbara London (auths), The Photograph Collector's Guide, New York Graphics Soc, 79; Hilton Kramer (auth), article, New York Times Book Rev, 80; Lynne Enten (auth), article, Art in Am, 81. *Media:* Silver Photographs. *Publ:* Auth, Echoes of Silence, 72, Photographs of Architecture, 77, Philip Trager: New York, 80 & Wesleyan Photographs, 82, Wesleyan Univ Press. *Mailing Add:* 20 Rolling Ridge Rd Fairfield CT 06430

TRAHER, WILLIAM HENRY
PAINTER, MURALIST

b Rock Springs, Wyo, Apr 6, 08. *Study:* Nat Acad Design, 30-33; Yale Univ Sch Fine Art, 38-39. *Work:* Diorama backgrounds, Denver Mus Natural Hist. *Comn:* De Witt Ark Post Off, US Treas Dept, 41; cloud recognition mural, Williams Air Force Field, Ariz, 43; wilderness murals, Columbia Savings & Loan, Pueblo, Colo, 68; four landscape murals, St Louis Arch, Nat Park Serv, 70. *Exhib:* 5th Int Exhib Lithography & Wood Engraving, Art Inst Chicago, 36; New Horizons in American Art, Mus Mod Art, New York, 36; 2nd Nat Exhib Am Art, Munic Art Comt, New York, 37; Fine Art in Advertising, Art Dir Club, New York, 50; Surrealism, Mus Mod Art, Denver Art Mus, 62. *Pos:* Art dir, Philip H Gray Advert Agency, 45-47; artist & researcher, Jeppesen Map Co, Denver, 52-53; tech illusr, Lowry AFB, Denver, 53-54; chief artist, Denver Mus Natural Hist, 54- *Awards:* Purchase Prize, Penny Art Fund, Colo Fedn Woman's Clubs, 36; Beaux Arts Inst Design Award, 38; medal for originality, 6th Southwest Int Exhib, 55. *Bibliog:* J Devran (auth), Studio in a cigarette case, Rocky Mountain Life, 1/48; D Evans (auth), A maker of visions, Denver Mag, 6/65; J Jellico (auth), Giant in the museum, Am Artist, 4/74. *Media:* Acrylic. *Publ:* Illusr, Stars and Men, Bobbs, New York & Arnolds, London, 39; illusr, Wyoming design, state series, Container Corp, 49; illusr, Index of American design, Christensen, 54; illusr, US Golf Asn Ann, 60; auth, The artist cornered, Photog Soc Am J, 65. *Mailing Add:* 2331 Niagara St Denver CO 80207

TRAKAS, GEORGE
SCULPTOR

b Quebec, Que, May 11, 44. *Study:* Brooklyn Mus Art Sch; Hunter Col, New York Univ, BS. *Work:* Solomon R Guggenheim Mus. *Comn:* Omaha Opportunities Industrialization Ctr, 80; Nat Oceanic and Atmospheric Admin, Seattle, 83. *Exhib:* Projects: Pier 18, Mus Mod Art, New York, 71; Ten Young Artists: Theodoron Awards, Guggenheim Mus, New York, 71; one-man show, City Univ Grad Ctr, New York, 75; Projects in Nature, Far Hills, NJ, 75; Artpark, Lewiston, NY, 76; Documenta 6, Kassel, WGer, 77; Venice Biennale, 80; Fattoria Di Celle, Santomato, Italy, 82. *Teaching:* Lectr, Boston Mus, 72; lectr, Cooper Union, 78; lectr, Yale Univ, 80. *Awards:* Nat Endowment Arts Fel, 79; Guggenheim Fel, 83. *Bibliog:* Paul Stimson (auth), article, Art Am, 9-10/75; Kate Linker (auth), George Trakas & the syntax of space, Arts Mag, 1/76. *Media:* Steel, Wood. *Publ:* Contribr, Outcrops, Avalanche, fall 71; contribr (catalogue essays), Projects in Nature, 75 & Artpark, 76. *Mailing Add:* PO Box 395 New York NY 10013

TRAKIS, LOUIS
SCULPTOR, EDUCATOR

b New York, NY, June 22, 27. *Study:* Cooper Union, BFA; Columbia Univ; Art Students League; Politechneion, Athens, Greece; Fulbright grants, Acad Fine Arts, Rome, Italy, 59-60 & 60-61. *Exhib:* Pa Acad, Philadelphia; Metrop Mus of Art, Tokyo; Appunto Gallery, Rome; Galleria re Magi, Milan, Italy; Corcoran Gallery, Washington, DC; Brooklyn Mus, NY; Feingarten Gallery, NY; Benson Gallery, Bridgehampton, LI, NY. *Teaching:* Instr sculpture, Philadelphia Col of Art, Columbia Univ, New Sch for Social Res & Southhampton Col, prof art, Manhattanville Col, 65- *Awards:* Louis Comfort Tiffany Found Award/Sculpture, 61 & 63. *Mem:* Artists Equity, New York; Am Asn Univ Profs. *Mailing Add:* 532 16th St Brooklyn NY 11215

TRANK, LYNN EDGAR
EDUCATOR, PAINTER

b Cook, Nebr, Feb 24, 18. *Study:* Univ of Nebr, BFA; Washington Univ, BFA; Univ of Iowa, MFA; Ohio State Univ, PhD; study with Alfredo Zalce, Mexico. *Work:* Joslyn Art Mus, Omaha; Des Moines Art Ctr, Iowa; Evansville Mus of Art, Ind; Philadelphia Library Print Collection, Pa; Sheldon Swope Art Gallery, Terre Haute, Ind. *Exhib:* 57th Ann Am Exhib (watercolor & drawings), Art Inst of Chicago, 46; 1st Biennial Painting and Prints, Walker Art Ctr, 47; Drawing & Small Sculptures Nat, Muncie, Ind, 55, 56, 58, 59; Nat Print Show, Wichita, Kans, 56; Craft Exhib Invitational 59, Art Gallery, Muncie, 58; Watercolor USA, Springfield, Mo, 63-64; Wabash Valley Exhib, Sheldon Swope Gallery, Terre Haute, 70-72; and others. *Teaching:* Prof drawing, painting & printmaking, Eastern Ill Univ, Charleston, 52- *Awards:* Graphic Arts Award, Tri-State Exhib, 55, 56; Wabash Valley Labor Coun Prize, Wabash Valley Exhib, Terre Haute, 70. *Mem:* Col Art Asn. *Media:* Collagraph, Watercolor on Canvas. *Publ:* Illusr, Febold Feboldson, Univ Nebr Press, 48; contribr, The Print, Creative Graphics, New York, 59. *Mailing Add:* c/o Dept Art Eastern Ill Univ Charleston IL 61920

TRAPP, FRANK ANDERSON
MUSEUM DIRECTOR, HISTORIAN

b Pittsburgh, Pa, June 13, 22. *Study:* Carnegie Inst Technol, BA, 43; Harvard Univ, MA, 47, PhD(Fulbright Scholar), 52. *Pos:* Dir, Mead Art Gallery, Amherst Col, 65- *Teaching:* From instr to asst prof art hist, Williams Col, 51-56; from asst prof to prof art hist, Amherst Col, Mass, 56-, chmn dept fine arts, 63-75 & 76-78; Andrew W Mellon vis prof, Univ Pittsburgh, 79-80. *Awards:* Nat Endowment Humanities Sr Fel, 71-72. *Mem:* Col Art Asn; Century Asn; Asn Art Mus Dir. *Publ:* Auth, Attainment of Delacroix, Johns Hopkins Press, 70; auth, Aged lion returns: Jean-Leon Gerome, Burlington Mag, 5/73; auth, South Kensington Exhibition of 1874, Connoisseur, 12/74; ed, The Classical Collection at Amherst College, 79; auth & ed, The Temptation of St Anthony by Odilon Redon, Amherst Col, 80; and others. *Mailing Add:* 71 Spring St Amherst MA 01002

TRAUB, CHARLES H
EDUCATOR, PHOTOGRAPHER

b Louisville, Ky, Apr 6, 45. *Study:* Univ of Ill, Champaign, BA, 67; Inst of Design, Ill Inst of Technol, MS(photog), 71, with Aaron Siskind. *Work:* Int Ctr Photog, New York; Mus of Mod Art, New York; Art Inst of Chicago, Ill; Fogg Mus, Harvard Univ, Cambridge, Mass; Int Mus of Photog, Rochester, NY; and others. *Exhib:* Photographs of Charles Traub, Art Inst of Chicago, 75; The City, Mus of Contemp Art, Chicago, 77; one-man shows, Light Gallery, New York, 77 & Hudson River Mus, 81; Contemp Photog, Fogg Mus, 77; Five Photogr, Halstead 831 Gallery, Birmingham, Mich, 77. *Pos:* Free lance photogr, 69-; pres, Photog Adv Group, Chicago, Ill, 75-77; dir, Light Gallery, New York, 78-; sr ed, Matrix Publ. *Teaching:* Vis artist, Franconia Col, NH, 73-74; prof photog & chmn dept, Columbia Col, Chicago, Ill, 71-; vis artist, Tyler Sch Art, Philadelphia, Pa, 81. *Mem:* Soc of Photog Educ; Col Art Asn. *Dealer:* Light Gallery 724 Fifth Ave New York NY 10019; Marcus Pfeiffer New York NY. *Mailing Add:* 39 E Tenth St New York NY 10003

TRAUERMAN, MARGY ANN
PAINTER, INSTRUCTOR

b Sioux Falls, SDak. *Study:* Univ Iowa, Iowa City, BFA; Am Acad Art, Chicago; Art Students League, New York; Los Angeles City Col. *Exhib:* Am Watercolor Soc Ann, 53-68; NY Figurative Painting & Traveling Exhib, 71; one-man shows, Chatham Col, Pittsburgh, 61, First Street Gallery, New York, 72, 74, 77, 79, 82 & 84 & Landmark Gallery, McAllen, Tex, 75. *Teaching:* Instr art, Art & Design High Sch, New York, 52-77; instr art, Queens Col, New York, spring 75. *Bibliog:* David Loeffler Smith (auth), Celebrated

women artists, 1/62 & Heritage of the thirties, 10/62, Am Artist; Watercolor page, Am Artist, 7/74. *Mem:* Am Watercolor Soc. *Media:* Watercolor. *Dealer:* First Street Gallery 386 West Broadway New York NY 10012. *Mailing Add:* 2 W 67th St New York NY 10023

TRAUSCH, THOMAS V
PAINTER

b Chicago, Ill, Sept 4, 43. *Study:* Univ Ill, BFA, 66; Am Acad Art, with Irving Shapiro, 74-77. *Work:* Parker Pen Co, Janesville, Wis; Elmhurst Fine Arts Mus, Ill; Smith-Barney, Chicago. *Comn:* History of Communication (mural), Huwen-Davies Advertising, Chicago, Ill, 75; paintings, Ashwell & Co, Chicago, Ill, 81-82. *Exhib:* Nat Arts Club Watercolor Open, New York, 82; Davenport Art Gallery, Iowa, 83; Watercolor Soc Alabama, Birmingham Mus Art, 83; Audubon Artists Ann, Nat Arts Club, New York, 83; Seventh Nat Watercolor Exhib, Springfield Art Asn Gallery, Ill, 83; and others. *Teaching:* Pvt instr watercolor, currently. *Awards:* Completion Grant, Historical Landmarks, Ill Arts Coun, 77; Purchase Award, Elmhurst Fine Arts Festival, Elmhurst Fine Arts Found, 81; Watercolor Award, Okla Watercolor Asn, 82. *Bibliog:* Craig Schreiner (auth), Trausch takes life as free spirit, Daily Sentinel, 82. *Mem:* Assoc Am Watercolor Soc; Mid-West Watercolor Soc; Watercolor Soc Ala. *Media:* Watercolor. *Mailing Add:* 507 W Third St Woodstock IL 60098

TRAVANTI, LEON EMIDIO
PAINTER, DESIGNER

b Kenosha, Wis, Aug 5, 36. *Study:* Cranbrook Acad of Arts, MFA, 60; Layton Sch of Art, BFA, 59. *Work:* Milwaukee Art Ctr; Bergstrom Mus, Neenah, Wis; Rahr Art Ctr, La Crosse, Wis; Univ Mo; Univ Wis. *Comn:* Paintings & drawings, Ansul Int, Brussels, Belgium, 74, Lane Ltd, Sydney, Australia, 74-75 & Malaysia Ancom, Quala Lumpour, Malaysia, 75; painting, First Wis Nat Bank, 76; Marine Nat Bank, Milwaukee. *Exhib:* Walker Art Ctr Biennial, Minneapolis, Minn, 56; Butler Inst of Am Art, Youngstown, Ohio, 56; Chicago Art Inst, 56 & 58; Detroit Inst of Art, 60; Columbia Col, Mo, 78; Fitzsimmons, New York, 78; Pillsbury Nat, 81-82; West Art & the Law Nat, 83; one-man show, Charles Allis Art Mus, Milwaukee, 83; and others. *Pos:* Art dir, Wis Archit & Milwaukee Mag, Schmidt Publ, 60-64; dir graphic design, Sch Fine Arts, Univ Wis, 64-74. *Teaching:* Prof art & design, Univ Wis, Milwaukee, 64-; vis prof art, Univ Mo, Columbia, 77-78; vis lectr graphic design, Parsons Sch of Design, summer 77 & 79; vis lectr, Pratt Inst, Manhattan Campus, 78-79. *Awards:* Purchase Prizes, Milwaukee Renaissance, 60, Wis Invitational, 65 & Pillsbury Co, Minneapolis; and others. *Bibliog:* Walter Herdig (ed), Ann report paintings, Graphis Ann, 66-67 & 75-76; Paintings in reports, Print Mag, 76 & Current Am Paintings, La Revue Moderne, Paris, 60. *Mem:* Milwaukee Advert Club; Am Inst Graphic Arts; Graphic Arts Guild; Soc of Typographic Arts; and others. *Media:* Multimedia. *Dealer:* Andro Crispo Corp Collections 41 E 57th St New York NY 10022; Judy Posner Gallery Milwaukee WI. *Mailing Add:* 2847 N Farwell Ave Milwaukee WI 53211

TRAVERS-SMITH, BRIAN JOHN
PAINTER, INSTRUCTOR

b Tangshan, North China, June 26, 31; US & Can citizen. *Study:* Ont Col Art, Toronto, 49-50; self-taught in watercolor. *Work:* Art Gallery Greater Victoria, BC; Provincial Collection BC; Dofasco Collection, Hamilton, Ont; Chevron Standard Collection, Calgary, Alta; Hiram Walker Collection, Kelowna, BC. *Exhib:* One-man show, Art Gallery Greater Victoria, BC, 62; Allied Artists Am, New York, 69, 71, 72 & 81; Am Watercolor Soc, ann & traveling, 71, 76, 77 & 81; Can Soc Painters Watercolour, Toronto, 76 & 77; BC Through the Eyes of Its Artists, Govt BC, traveling Europe, 79. *Pos:* Bd dirs, Art Gallery Greater Victoria, BC, 63-70, pres, bd dirs, 69-70; bd dirs, Emily Carr Col Art & Design, 80-82. *Teaching:* Instr, Studios in Victoria, BC, 65-75. *Awards:* First Prize, Vancouver Island Ann, 62. *Bibliog:* Margaret Harold (auth), Brian Travers-Smith, Prize-Winning Watercolors, 63; R Ashwell (auth), Brian Travers-Smith, Westworld Mag, 4/78. *Mem:* Am Watercolor Soc; Allied Artists Am; Can Soc Painters Watercolor; Fedn Can Artists; NW Watercolor Soc (past vpres). *Media:* Watercolor. *Mailing Add:* c/o Travers-Smith Galleries Ltd 590 Transit Rd Victoria BC V8S 4Z5 Canada

TRAVIS, DAVID B
CURATOR, HISTORIAN

b Omaha, Nebr, Jan 31, 48. *Study:* Univ of Chicago, BA(art hist), Smithsonian Inst, res fel, 72. *Collections Arranged:* Exhibitions of photography, Art Inst of Chicago, 73-; Starting with Atget (auth, catalog), 77; Photographs from the Andre Jammes Collection: Niepce to Atget (ed, catalog), 77; Photography Rediscovered: American Photographs 1900-1930 (auth, catalog), 79; Photographs in Chicago Collections (auth, catalog), 82. *Pos:* Asst cur photog, Art Inst of Chicago, 74-77, assoc cur photog, 77-78, cur photog, 79- *Teaching:* Lectr hist of photog, Sch of the Art Inst of Chicago, 74. *Mailing Add:* The Art Inst of Chicago Mich Ave at Adams St Chicago IL 60603

TREASTER, RICHARD A
PAINTER, EDUCATOR

b Lorain, Ohio, July 14, 32. *Study:* Cleveland Inst Art, BFA. *Work:* Butler Inst Am Art; Nat Acad Design, New York; Cleveland Mus of Art, Ohio; Southern Alleghenies Mus of Art, Loretto, Pa; Wittenberg Univ, Springfield, Ohio. *Exhib:* 200 Years Am Watercolor, Metrop Mus Art, 66; Cleveland Inst Art, 68 & 75; Watercolor USA, 72; one-man shows, Charleston Art Gallery, WVa & Southern Alleghenies Mus of Art, Loretto, Pa, 77; Lyman Allyn Mus, New London, Conn, 80. *Teaching:* Instr painting, Cooper Sch Art, Cleveland, 66-67; assoc prof, Cleveland Inst Art, 66-80; adj prof, Ursuline Col, 76-81. *Awards:* Mainstreams Award of Excellence, Marietta Col, 69; Emily

Goldsmith Award, Am Watercolor Soc, 69; Third Butler Medal, Butler Inst Am Art, 76. *Bibliog:* Ralph Fabri (auth), Medal of merit, Today's art, 8/66; Norman Kent (auth), Richard Treaster--American artist, Am Artist, 1/72. *Mem:* Am Watercolor Soc. *Media:* Watercolor, Egg Tempera. *Publ:* Auth, John Singer Sargent: the great Gatsby of art, Cleveland Plain Dealer Mag, 9/23/79; auth, Influence of other artists, Am Artist, 7/83. *Dealer:* A B Closson Jr Co 400 Race St Cincinnati OH 45202. *Mailing Add:* 1228 Virginia Ave Lakewood OH 44107

TRECHSEL, GAIL ANDREWS
CURATOR
b Washington, DC, Nov 4, 53. *Study:* Col William & Mary, Va, BA, 74; Cooperstown Grad Prog, NY, MA(mus studies), 76; Winterthur Summer Inst, 77; Attingham Summer Sch, 81. *Collections Arranged:* Wedgwood Boulton: Artists of Industry, 78, By Hammer and Hand: Irish Decorative Arts, 80, Sewn in the South: Southern Quilts in Southern Collections, 80 & John Graham Collection, 82, Birmingham Mus Art. *Pos:* Nat Endowment Humanities Intern, Colonial Williamsburg, Va, 75-76; cur decorative arts, Birmingham Mus Art, Ala, 76-82, asst dir, 83- *Teaching:* Adj prof, Univ Ala, Birmingham, currently. *Mem:* Wedgwood Int Seminar (bd mem, 78-, treas, 80-); Am Ceramics Circle; Eng Ceramics Circle; Women's Caucus Art (bd mem, 80-); Birmingham Art Asn (pres, 78-79). *Publ:* Coauth, Index to American Coverlet Weavers, Univ Va Press, 78; auth, Frances Oliver Collection of European Porcelain, 80 & auth, Alabama Quilts, 80, Birmingham Mus Art; auth, Lamprecht collection of cast iron art, 2/83 & auth, Beeson collection of wedgwood in Birmingham Museum of Art, 6/83, Mag Antiques. *Mailing Add:* 3406 Altamont Way Birmingham AL 35205

TRECKER, STANLEY MATTHEW
SCULPTOR, PHOTOGRAPHER
b Manning, Iowa, July 15, 44. *Study:* Ind Univ, Bloomington, MBA, 68; Columbia Col, Chicago, BA, 75; Sch Art Inst Chicago, MFA, 78. *Work:* Art Inst Chicago; George Eastman House. *Exhib:* Arles Festival, France, 75; Calif Inst Fine Arts, Valencia, 77; Moming Gallery, Chicago, 78; ARC Gallery, Chicago, 78; Art Inst Chicago, 78; Artist Coop, Toronto, Can, 79. *Pos:* Cur, Moming Gallery, Chicago, 77-80; dir, Photog Resource Ctr, Boston, 80-83. *Teaching:* Instr photog, Columbia Col, Chicago, 78-80. *Awards:* Ill Art Coun Grant, 79; Artists' Found Project Grant, 83. *Mem:* Soc Photog Educators (bd dirs, 83-); Col Art Asn. *Mailing Add:* 50 Bloomfield Rd Boston MA 02124

TREDENNICK, DOROTHY W
EDUCATOR, LECTURER
b Bristol, Conn, Oct 5, 14. *Study:* Norwich Art Sch, 32-34; Berea Col, AB(hist), 46, AB(polit sci), 46; Univ Mich, Gen Educ Bd fel, 50-51, MA(art hist), 51. *Pos:* Assoc dir, Slater Mem Mus, 39-43. *Teaching:* Instr art, Norwich Art Sch, 33-34; prof art hist & humanities, Berea Col, 46-70, Morris Belknap prof art, 70-, co-chmn dept art, 54-70; lectr, US & Asia. *Awards:* Seabury Award for Excellence in Teaching, Berea Col, 62; Fulbright Award Chinese Civilization, 63; Nat Endowment Humanities Grant, Univ Calif, 77; and others. *Mem:* Col Art Asn; Southern Humanities Conf; Phi Kappa Phi; Asn Gen & Liberal Studies. *Publ:* Coauth, This is Our Best, 55; coauth, Kress Study Collection, 61; auth, Living by Design, 63; auth, Art & Protestant Church Today, 66; auth, Design for Living, 68. *Mailing Add:* Box 1834 Berea Col Berea KY 40404

TREESE, WILLIAM R
LIBRARIAN, PAINTER
b Burlington, Wash, Dec 7, 32. *Study:* Art Inst Chicago, BFA, 60; Stanford Univ, MA, 61; Drexel Univ, Philadelphia, MLS, 64. *Pos:* Art librn, Free Libr, Philadelphia, 61-64; art librn, Univ Calif, 66- *Mem:* Art Libr Soc NAm. *Publ:* Coauth, Computerized approach to art exhibition catalogues, Libr Trends, 1/75; ed, Catalogs of the Art Exhibition Catalog Collection of the Arts Library, University of California, Santa Barbara, Somerset House, 77; auth, Rephotographing microforms, Microform Rev, summer 83. *Mailing Add:* Arts Library Univ Calif Santa Barbara CA 93106

TREIMAN, JOYCE WAHL
PAINTER
b Evanston, Ill, May 29, 22. *Study:* Univ Iowa, BFA. *Work:* Whitney Mus Am Art, New York; Art Inst Chicago; Denver Art Mus, Colo; Metrop Mus Art, New York; Portland Mus, Ore. *Exhib:* American Painting, Art Inst Chicago, 46-60; Whitney Mus Am Art, New York, 51-53, 57 & 58; Recent Painting: The Figure, Mus Mod Art, New York, 62; Am Acad of Arts & Lett, 74-76; San Francisco Art Inst Ann, Calif, 77; Retrospective 1947-1977, Munic Art Gallery, Los Angeles; Contemp Am Monotypes Travelling Exhib, 78-80 & Am Portrait Drawing, 79, Smithsonian Inst. *Teaching:* Vis prof painting, Art Ctr Col Design, summer 68 & San Fernando Valley State Col, 68-69; vis lectr painting, Univ Calif, Los Angeles, 69-70. *Awards:* Tiffany Fel, 47; Logan Prize, Art Inst Chicago, 51; Tamarind Lithography Fel, Ford Found, 62. *Media:* Oil. *Dealer:* Fairweather-Hardin Gallery 101 E Ontario St Chicago IL 60611; Tortue Gallery 2917 Santa Monica Blvd Santa Monica CA 90404. *Mailing Add:* 712 Amalfi Dr Pacific Palisades CA 90272

TREISTER, KENNETH
PAINTER, SCULPTOR
b New York, NY, Mar 5, 30. *Study:* Univ Miami; Univ Fla, BArch, 53. *Work:* Norton Gallery, Palm Beach, Fla; Miami Mus Mod Art, Fla; Fla Supreme Ct, Tallahassee. *Comn:* Family of God (limited ed bronze menoras), 69 & six bronze plaques depicting hist of Jews, United Jewish Appeal; ten paintings depicting 4,000 yr hist of Jews, Temple Israel, Miami. *Exhib:* Greenwich Gallery, New York; Mus Fine Arts, Columbus, Ga; Lowe Art Gallery, Coral Gables, Fla; Contemp Art Mus, Houston, Tex; High Mus, Atlanta, Ga; and several one-man shows. *Teaching:* Guest lectr art & archit, Mass Inst Technol, Univ Syracuse, Univ Pa, Fla Atlantic Univ, Dade Jr Col/South Campus, Univ Miami, Univ Fla & Jewish Fedn. *Awards:* First Prize for Four Conversations (sculpture), Nat Ceramic Exhib, Lowe Art Gallery, 53. *Mem:* Blue Dome Soc, Miami; Fla Sculptural Soc; Southern Asn Sculptors. *Mailing Add:* 2699 S Bayshore Dr Coconut Grove FL 33133

TRENTHAM, GARY LYNN
EDUCATOR, FIBER ARTIST
b Gleason, Tenn, Dec 7, 39. *Study:* Murray State Univ, BA, 61, MA, 65; Ind Univ, Bloomington, with Budd Stalnaker & Joan Sterrenberg, MFA, 72. *Work:* Steuben Glass, New York; Ind Univ, Bloomington; Collection of Vpres of Corning Glass, NY; Auburn Univ, Ala. *Exhib:* Piedmont Crafts Exhib, Mint Mus of Art, Charlotte, NC, 73-74 & 76; 7th Int Biennial of Tapestry, Centre Int de la Tapisserie Ancienne et Mod, Lausanne, Switz, 75; Fiber Structures, Carnegie Inst, Pittsburgh, 76; 2nd Int Exhib of Miniature Textiles, Brit Craft Centre, London, 76; Source Detroit, Cranbrook Acad of Art, Bloomfield Hills, Mich, 76; Exhib of Contemp & Hist Baskets, Peabody Mus of Harvard, Worcester, Mass, 76; Textiles: Past & Prologue, Greenville Co Mus of Arts, SC, 76; Basket Invitational, Florence Duhl Gallery, New York, 77; and others. *Teaching:* Assoc instr textiles, Ind Univ, Bloomington, 69-72; from assoc prof to prof textile design, Auburn Univ, 72- *Awards:* Fiber Prize, Marietta Col Crafts Regional, Ohio, 73; Res & Exhib Expense Awards, Auburn Univ, 74-77; First Prize Fiber, El Paso Designer Craftsmen, Tex, 77. *Mem:* Am Crafts Coun; World Crafts Coun; Ala Crafts Coun. *Publ:* Contribr, Modern Approach to Basketry, Crown, 74; contribr, articles, Craft Horizons, 74 & 76; contribr, articles, Rev Design, Japan, 75; contribr, The New Basketry, Van Nostrand, 76; contribr, Decorative Art & Modern Interiors, Studio Vista, London, 77. *Dealer:* Florence Duhl Gallery 33 W 54th New York NY 10019. *Mailing Add:* Spidle Hall Auburn Univ Auburn AL 36830

TRENTON, PATRICIA JEAN
HISTORIAN
b Los Angeles, Calif, May 14, 27. *Study:* Univ Calif, Berkeley & Los Angeles, BA, MA(art hist), PhD, 80. *Collections Arranged:* Colorado Collects Historic Western Art: The Nostalgia of the Vanishing West (auth, catalog), 73, Paintings from the Philip Anschutz Collection, 73, Picturesque Images from Taos and Santa Fe (auth, catalog), 74 & Robert Rockwell Foundation, Mini-Exhibition of the West, Denver Art Mus, 74. *Pos:* Cur Am art, Denver Art Mus, Colo, 69-74. *Awards:* Nat Award by Graphics Art Industry for Am Art, Denver Art Mus Collection, 69; Bicentennial-Centennial Comnr's Seal for Scholarship for book, Harvey Otis Young, 75; Rockefeller Fel, Univ Calif Los Angeles, 77. *Mem:* Col Art Asn. *Res:* Landscapists in the West during the nineteenth century. *Publ:* Coauth, American Art from the Denver Art Museum Collection, 69 & auth, Harvey Otis Young, 1840-1901: The Lost Genius, 75, Denver Art Mus; coauth, The Rocky Mountains: A Vision for the Artists of the Nineteenth Century, Clarkson Potter, New York, (in prep). *Mailing Add:* Anchorage West 1401 S Knoll Ave Pasadena CA 91109

TRIANO, ANTHONY THOMAS
PAINTER, EDUCATOR
b Newark, NJ, Aug 25, 28. *Study:* Newark Sch Fine & Indust Art, 46-50; with Reuben Nakian, 47-52; also with Samuel Brecher. *Work:* Lowe Mus, Coral Gables, Fla; Paterson State Col, Wayne, NJ; Hartford Art Found, Conn; Seton Hall Univ, South Orange, NJ; and others. *Exhib:* Gallery Selections, J L Hudson Gallery, Detroit, 64; New Jersey & the Artist, NJ State Mus, Trenton, 65; Boochever Art Collection, Paterson State Col, 68; Images of James Joyce, Montclair Mus, NJ, 75; Time, Life & Hope, Univ of Ala, Huntsville, Ala, 78; and others. *Teaching:* Artist in residence & asst prof art, Seton Hall Univ, 70- *Awards:* Twenty-fifth Ann NJ State Art Award, Montclair Mus, 57; Purchase Award, Newark Mus, 59. *Bibliog:* Mike Berg (auth), The Life & World of Triano, Seton Hall Univ, 68; William Sheppard (auth), Inside the Arts (film), Brooklyn Col, 70; D Simon (auth), Profiles (film), Seton Hall Univ, 71. *Media:* Oil, Acrylic. *Publ:* Illusr, Exploring Nature's Rhythms, 60 & illusr, Duck Fever, 61, Abbott Labs; contribr, H & G colors for your personal bed & bath, 56 & contribr, House of color, 67, House & Garden; illusr, Courbet's unpainted pictures, Arts Mag, 80. *Mailing Add:* Art Dept Seton Hall Univ South Orange NJ 07079

TRIEFF, SELINA
PAINTER, INSTRUCTOR
b Brooklyn, NY, Jan 7, 34. *Study:* Art Students League, study with Morris Kantor; Hans Hofmann Sch, study with Hofmann; Brooklyn Col, BA, study with Rothko & Reinhardt, 55. *Work:* Brooklyn Mus; New York Pub Libr; Inst for Human Develop; Prudential Life Insurance Co; Bayonne Jewish Ctr. *Exhib:* Contemp Am Figure Painting, Wadsworth Atheneum, 64; Work on Paper, Brooklyn Mus, 75; Butler Inst Ann, 77; Galleri Anna, Gothenborg, Sweden, 79; Contemp Figure Painting, Hera Gallery, Wakefield, RI, 79; Manhattan Civic Col, 82; Douglass Col, 83; Prince St Gallery, 84. *Teaching:* Instr drawing, New York Inst of Technol, 75-; vis artist painting, Notre Dame Univ, Ind, 76; instr painting, New York Studio Sch, currently. *Awards:* Second Prize, Goddard Col Ann, 76; Purchase Prize, View from the Ctr, Bayonne Community Ctr, 78; Thomas B Clarke Prize, Nat Acad Design, 79; and others. *Bibliog:* Corinne Robins (auth), Selina Trieff, Arts, 78; Hilton Kramer (auth), article, New York Times, 82. *Mem:* Women in the Arts; Womens Caucus Art; Col Art Asn. *Media:* Oil, Charcoal. *Mailing Add:* c/o Prince Street Gallery 121 Wooster St New York NY 10012

TRIMM, H WAYNE
ILLUSTRATOR, PAINTER
b Albany, NY, Aug 16, 22. *Study:* Cornell Univ, 40; Augustana Col, BS, 48; Kans State Univ, 49; Col Forestry, Syracuse Univ, MS, 53. *Comn:* Dioramas, Springfield Mus Art; three ecol dioramas, Augustana Col, 67; movie for Audubon Screen Tour, 68-69; diorama, Good Samaritan Ctr, Clear Lake, SDak, 74; mural, Gilboa-Blenheim Mus, 74; and others. *Exhib:* Am Bird Artists Traveling Exhib, Audubon Artists; Joslyn Mus Art; Buffalo Mus Sci; San Jose State Univ; New York Coliseum Sportsman's Show; and others. *Pos:* Art dir, Conservationist Mag, Div Educ Serv, NY State Dept Environ Conserv, 53-, sr ed, 53-73; ed, Outdoor Communicator Mag, currently. *Teaching:* Lectr conserv & wildlife painting, currently; instr nature & sci illus, State Univ NY, Albany & Col St Rose, Nat Wildlife Fedn Summits, currently. *Mem:* Columbia Co Arts & Crafts; Soc Animal Artists; hon mem Tuscarora Indian Tribe; Am Ornithologists Union; Guild Nat Sci Illusr. *Media:* Watercolor; Oil; Marble, Wood. *Publ:* Illusr, The Mammals of California and Its Coastal Waters, 54; illusr, Collier's Encycl, 60-61; illusr, The Birds of Tikal, 64; illusr, The Birds of Colorado, 66; illusr, Audubon Mag, NY State Conservationist, Time-Life Nature Bks, Nat Wildlife Mag & others. *Mailing Add:* RD #1 Box 83 Ravena NY 12143

TRIPLETT, MARGARET L
PAINTER
b Vermillion, SDak, Dec 30, 05. *Study:* Univ Iowa, BA; Boston Mus Fine Arts Sch; Yale Univ, MA; also with Grant Wood. *Work:* Munson-Williams-Proctor Inst, Utica, NY; Slater Mem Mus, Norwich, Conn; Univ Conn, Health Ctr. *Exhib:* Conn Watercolor Soc; De Cordova & Dana Mus; Slater Mus Art; Lyman Allyn Mus; Art in Transition: A Century of the Mus Sch, Mus of Fine Arts, Boston, 77; plus others. *Pos:* Trustee, Hartford Art Sch, Univ Hartford, 62-70; dir, Innovation I, Eastern Conn State Col, Willimantic, 75. *Teaching:* Instr art, Norwich Art Sch, 29-43, dir, 43-70; retired. *Awards:* Jesse Smith Noyes Found Grant, 69; Second Prize, Mystic Art Asn Juried Show, 77. *Mem:* Conn Art Asn; Conn Watercolor Soc; Mystic Art Asn (bd dirs, 72); life mem Nat Educ Asn; plus others. *Publ:* Coauth, The Norwich Art School, A Study of the Directors, In Combination with An On-going Study of Former Students, 71. *Mailing Add:* 1 Prunier Ct Norwich CT 06360

TRISSEL, JAMES NEVIN
PAINTER, PRINTMAKER
b Davenport, Iowa, Nov 7, 30. *Study:* State Univ Iowa, BA; Colo State Col, MA; State Univ Iowa, MFA. *Work:* Univ Wis; Beloit Col; Colo Col; Colorado Springs Fine Arts Ctr. *Exhib:* One-man show, Beloit Col, 57, & Colorado Springs Fine Arts Ctr, 66 & 72, Ankrum Gallery, Los Angeles, 76; Wis Salon, 58; El Paso Biennial, 64 & 66. *Pos:* Actg dir, Wright Art Ctr, Beloit Col, 58-59; dir, Univ Exten Prog in Art, Univ Calif, Los Angeles, 62-64; proprietor, The Press, Colo Col, 78- *Teaching:* Instr art, Beloit Col, 58-60; asst prof art & art theory, Univ Calif, Los Angeles, 60-64; assoc prof art & art hist, Colo Col, 64-70, prof art, 70-, chmn dept art, 71-77. *Media:* Oil. *Dealer:* Carlin Galleries 710 Montgomery Ft Worth TX 76107; Ankrum Gallery 657 N La Cienega Blvd Los Angeles CA 90069. *Mailing Add:* 422 N Custer Ave Colorado Springs CO 80903

TRIVIGNO, PAT
PAINTER, EDUCATOR
b New York, NY, Mar 13, 22. *Study:* Tyler Sch Art; NY Univ; Columbia Univ, BA & MA. *Work:* Solomon R Guggenheim Mus, New York; Brooklyn Mus, NY; Everson Mus, Syracuse, NY; New York Times; Gen Elec Corp. *Comn:* Murals, Lykes Steamship Lines & Cook Conv Ctr, Memphis. *Exhib:* Whitney Mus Am Art Ann; Art Inst Chicago; Pa Acad Fine Arts; Am Acad Arts & Lett; Univ Ill Biennial; and others. *Teaching:* Prof art, Tulane Univ La, 50-, chmn art dept. *Bibliog:* Articles in New York Times, 10/8/50 & 1/10/60; R Pearson (auth), Modern Renaissance in American Art, Harper. *Media:* Acrylic, Oil. *Mailing Add:* 1831 Marengo St New Orleans LA 70115

TRONCALE, FRANK THOMAS
DEALER, COLLECTOR
b Birmingham, Ala, Aug 11, 41. *Study:* Birmingham Southern Col, BA, 65. *Pos:* Docent (tour guide), John & Mable Ringling Mus Art, 77-79. *Specialty:* Contemporary graphics. *Collection:* Contemporary graphics of Dali, Nierman, Nieman, Paul Maxwell, Picasso, Rothe, Calder and Peter Max. *Mailing Add:* The Hang-up Inc 3850 S Osprey Ave Sarasota FL 33579

TROP-BLUMBERG, SANDRA (SANDRA TROP BLUMBERG)
ADMINISTRATOR
b Brooklyn, NY. *Study:* NY Univ, BS(cum laude); Everson Mus Art; Inst Arts Admin; Harvard Univ. *Pos:* Cur traveling exhibs, Everson Mus Art, Syracuse, NY, 72, asst to dir, 73, actg dir, 74, asst dir, 74- *Mem:* Int Coun Mus (int comt mus & collections mod art); Am Asn Mus. *Mailing Add:* Everson Mus Art 401 Harrison St Syracuse NY 13202

TROSKY, HELENE ROTH
PRINTMAKER, PAPERMAKER
b Monticello, NY. *Study:* New Sch Social Res, with Kuniyoshi Egas; Manhattanville Col, BA, with Al Blaustein, John Ross & Garner Tullis. *Work:* Wichita Mus of Art; Sheldon Swope Mus of Art, Terre Haute, Ind; Staten Island Mus; Hudson River Mus. *Exhib:* Conn Acad Fine Arts, 67 & 68; Silvermine Guild, 68-70; one-person shows, Hudson River Mus, Yonkers, NY, 69, Wichita Mus Art, Kans, 77; Alan Brown Gallery, Hartsdale, NY, 80; Westchester Community Col, 81. *Pos:* Columnist, Muse Roundup, Harrison Independent Greenburgh Rec & Yonkers Rec, 60-76; art consult, Westchester

Libr Syst, 65-70; dir, Second Regional Plan, New York, 65- *Teaching:* Art dir, Westchester Co Music & Art Camp, 65, 66, 71 & 72; lectr art hist, Brandeis Univ Women, 66-; instr printmaking, Manhattanville Col, 71-76; lect art hist, Westchester Community Col, 81-83. *Awards:* Westchester Art Soc Award, 67; Northern Westchester Award, 68; Nat Asn Women Artists Award, 69 & 82. *Mem:* Silvermine Guild; Conn Acad Fine Arts; Westchester Art Soc (exec dir & chmn bd, 60-); Artists Equity New York; Nat Asn Women Artists; and others. *Publ:* Auth, art columns & revs for Westchester Women's News, Harrison Independent & North Castle News, 82-83. *Dealer:* Raydon Gallery 1091 Madison Ave New York NY 10028; Alan Brown Gallery Hartsdale NY. *Mailing Add:* Yarmouth Rd Purchase NY 10577

TROTT, HELEN
PAINTER, INSTRUCTOR
b New York, NY, May 25, 36. *Study:* Hunter Col, BA, 58; City Col New York, MA, 65. *Exhib:* Nat Soc Painters Casein & Acrylic, Nat Acad Galleries, New York, 76 & 78 & Nat Arts Club, 80; Audubon Artists, Nat Acad Galleries, New York, 79; Painters & Sculptors Soc NJ, Bergen Community Mus, 81. *Teaching:* Instr art, Paul Dunbar Junior High Sch, Bronx, NY, 61-64; instr art, Christopher Columbus High Sch, Bronx, NY, 64-67. *Awards:* Gold Key Award, Senior Scholastic Art Exhib, Macy's, 53; Patron of the Arts Award, Painters & Sculptors Soc NJ, 80 & Honorable Mention, 81; Beaux Art Award, Westchester Co Fed Woman's Clubs, 82. *Bibliog:* Dina Weintraub (auth), The studio, Westchester Woman, 79. *Mem:* Nat Soc Painters Casein & Acrylic; Painters & Sculptors Soc NJ; Artists Equity. *Media:* Acrylic, Watercolor. *Mailing Add:* 2305 Sultana Dr Yorktown Heights NY 10598

TROVA, ERNEST TINO
SCULPTOR, PAINTER
b St Louis, Mo, Feb 19, 27. *Work:* Hirshhorn Mus, Washington, DC; Guggenheim Mus, Mus Mod Art & Whitney Mus Am Art, New York; Aldrich Contemp Art Mus, Ridgefield, Conn. *Exhib:* Los Angeles Co Mus Art; Solomon R Guggenheim Mus; Hirshhorn Mus, 74; New West, Albuquerque, 78; Mus & Inst Am Indian Arts, Sante Fe, 79; Cody Gallery, Sante Fe, 80; Warner Roberts Gallery, Palo Alto, Calif, 81; and others. *Bibliog:* Donald Miller (auth), Ernest Trova as neo-surrealist, Art Inst, 9/70; David Zack (auth), Trova, Esquire, 10/73; Jean Lipman & Helen M Franc (auth), Bright Stars: American Painting & Sculpture Since 1776, New York, 76. *Dealer:* Pace Gallery 32 E 57th St New York NY 10022. *Mailing Add:* 6 Layton Terr St Louis MO 63124

TRUBNER, HENRY
ADMINISTRATOR, CURATOR
b Munich, Ger, June 10, 20; US citizen. *Study:* Fogg Art Mus, Harvard Univ, BA & MA. *Collections Arranged:* Ceramic Art Japan: 100 Masterpieces from Japanese Collections (auth, catalog), Seattle Art Mus, 72-73; Int Symp on Japanese Ceramics, 72 & Int Symp on Chinese Ceramics, 77, Seattle Art Mus; Chinese Cermics from Japanese Collections (auth, catalog), Seaattle Art Mus, 77-78; Song of the Brush (auth, catalog), Seattle Art Mus, 79-80; Okyo and the Maruyama Shijo School of Japanese Painting (auth, catalog), St Louis Art Mus and Agency for Cultural Affairs, Tokyo, 80; Treasures of Asian Art from the Idemitsu Collection (auth, catalog), Seattle Art Mus, Kimbell Art Mus, Japan House Gallery & Denver Art Mus, 81-82. *Pos:* Cur Oriental art, Los Angeles Co Mus Art, 47-58; cur Far Eastern dept, Royal Ont Mus, Toronto, 58-68; cur dept Asian art, Seattle Art Mus, Wash, 68-, assoc dir, 75- *Teaching:* Assoc prof Asian art, Univ Toronto, 58-68. *Mem:* Asia Soc (mem adv comt); Japan Soc (adv comt on arts); Am Asn Mus; Oriental Ceramic Soc, London; Japan Am Soc, Seattle (bd dir); and others. *Res:* Japanese and Chinese ceramics. *Publ:* Coauth, Art treasures from Japan, 65-66; coauth, Asiatic art in the Seattle Art Museum, Kodansha Int, Tokyo, 73. *Mailing Add:* Seattle Art Mus Volunteer Park Seattle WA 98112

TRUBY, BETSY KIRBY
PAINTER, ILLUSTRATOR
b Winchester, Va, Nov 8, 26. *Study:* Hiram Col; Cleveland Sch Art; NMex Inst Mining & Technol; Univ NMex; also with David Moneypenny, Oden Hullenkramer & Joe Morello. *Work:* Int Moral Re-Armament Ctr, Mackinaw Island, Mich; Cancer Res & Treatment Ctr, Albuquerque; Geronimo Springs Art Mus, Truth or Consequences, NMex; Aldridge Fine Art Gallery, Old Town, Albuquerque; La Quinta Mus, Albuquerque. *Comn:* Portraits, Lillian Hutchinson, 65-68; Indian child portrait, NMex Easter Seal Soc, 69; paintings, First Presby Church, Albuquerque, 72-73; historical portrait, Synod Southwest, Presby Church, 75; paintings, Cystic Fibrosis Found, NMex, 76 & 77. *Exhib:* Fine Arts Gallery, Carnegie Inst, Pittsburgh, 46; NMex Fiesta Biennial, State Mus, Santa Fe, 64 & 68; Nat Alpine Holiday Exhib, Ouray, Colo, 68; Nat Art Show, Lawton, Okla, 74; Nat League Am Pen Women Mid-Ad Cong, Phoenix, Ariz, 75. *Teaching:* Instr ceramics, US Pub Health Hosp, 48-49; instr ceramics, Ohio Pub Sch Syst, 49-50. *Awards:* Second Prize Oil Portrait, Southern Regional, Nat League Am Pen Women, Boulder, Colo, 65 & First Premium Pastel Portrait, Nat Mid-Ad, Salt Lake City, 73; Second Premium Pastel, 73 & First Premium, 76, NMex State Fair. *Bibliog:* Flo Wilkes (auth), B Truby-retrospect, Albuquerque J, 67; Vivian Woods (auth), Arts & artists, Nevadan, 72; J Bonnette (auth), The Creative Process, KNME TV, Univ NMex, 73. *Mem:* Nat League Am Pen Women; Artists Equity; NMex Art League. *Media:* Pastel, Tempera. *Publ:* Cover illusr, Flags, 73 & Let Our Light Shine, 74. *Mailing Add:* 6609 Loftus Ave NE Albuquerque NM 87109

TRUDEAU, GARRY B
CARTOONIST
b New York, NY, 1948. *Study:* Yale Univ, dipl, Sch Art & Archit, dipl. *Pos:* Creator, Doonesbury (comic strip). *Awards:* Pulitzer Prize, 75. *Publ:* Auth, Adjectives Will Cost You Extra, 82, Gotta Run, My Government is Collapsing, 82 & Cartoons from In Search of Reagan's Brain, 82, Fawcett; auth, Ask for May, Settle for June, 82 & Unfortunately, She Was Also Wired for Sound, 82, Holt, Rinehart & Winston. *Mailing Add:* c/o Universal Press Syndicate 4400 Johnson Dr Shawnee Mission KS 66205

TRUDEAU, YVES
SCULPTOR
b Montreal, Que, Dec 3, 30. *Study:* Ecole Beaux Arts Montreal, sr matriculant with Marie Mediatrice. *Work:* Mus Quebec; Galerie Nat Can; Mus Art Contemp Montreal; Mus Art Prague, Czech; Mus Plein Air D'Ostrava, Czech; and others. *Comn:* Phare Du Cosmos, Expo 67, Universe Plaza, 67; large sculpture, Nat Capitol Comn, Ottawa, 78; large work, Transport Can, Can Seaway Building, St Catherine, Ont, 79; bronze relief & doors, Teleglobe Can, Montreal, 81; aluminium relief doors, Place Acad, Montreal, 83; and others. *Exhib:* Int Symp Sculpture, Ostrava, 69; Biennale Middleheim, Anvers, Belg, 71; Premiere Biennale Petite Sculpture, Budapest, Hungary, 71; one-man show, Mus Quebec, 70, Contemp Mus Montreal, 78; and others. *Teaching:* Prof sculpture, Ecole Beaux-Arts Montreal, 67-69; prof sculpture concept & metal, Univ Que, Montreal, dir, visual art dept, 79-81. *Awards:* Can Coun Awards, 63 & 69; Ministere Educ Quebec Award, 70-71. *Bibliog:* Robert Guy (auth), Yves Trudeau, sculpteur, Asn Sculpteurs Quebec, 71. *Mem:* Royal Can Acad Arts (vpres, 75-83); Can Conf Arts (vpres, 82-83); Asn Sculpterus Quebec (pres, 60-66); Int Conf Mus; Int Asn Plastic Art. *Media:* Multimedia. *Publ:* Auth, article in Metiers D'Arts Quebec, 63; coauth, Catalogue, Galerie Nat Can, 66; auth, Confrontation 67 (catalog), 67. *Mailing Add:* 5429 Ave Durocher Outremont Montreal PQ H2V 3X9 Canada

TRUETTNER, WILLIAM
ADMINISTRATOR
Pos: Cur eighteenth and nineteenth century painting & sculpture, Nat Collection Fine Arts, currently. *Mailing Add:* Nat Collection Fine Art 8th & G St NW Washington DC 20560

TRUEX, DUANE PHILIP
MUSEUM DIRECTOR, CONSULTANT
b Syracuse, NY, Aug 30, 47. *Study:* Ithaca Col Sch Music, BFA, 69; Okla State Univ; State Univ NY, Binghamton. *Collections Arranged:* Treasure House: Museums of the Empire State (catalog), 79, Charles Eldred: Drawing and Sculpture (catalog), 80 & Emil Holzhauer: 75 Years Retrospective Exhibition (catalog), 80, Roberson Ctr Arts & Sci; Susquehanna: Images of The Settled Landscape (catalog), 81; Ancient Inspirations, Contemporary Interpretations (catalog), 83-84. *Pos:* Dir pub rels, Kansas City Philharmonic, 72-73; exec dir, Baton Rouge Symphony, La, 73-76, Arts & Humanities Coun Greater Baton Rouge, 73-78 & Roberson Ctr Arts & Sci, Binghamton, NY, 78-83. *Teaching:* Vis lectr, Russell Sage Col, NY, formerly. *Mem:* Am Coun on Arts; Nat Asn Community Arts Agencies; Am Asn Mus; NY State Asn Mus. *Publ:* Contribr, Financial Accountability for community arts agencies, 75 & Common services of the community arts council, 78, Am Coun Arts; auth, Planning: Challenges, Opportunities, Paradoxes, Roberson Ctr Arts & Sci, 79; auth, A review of energy management in museums and historical agencies, Mus News, 8/83; and others. *Mailing Add:* Roberson Ctr for Arts & Sci 30 Front St Binghamton NY 13905

TRUEX, VAN DAY
PAINTER, DESIGNER
b Delphos, Kans, Mar 5, 04. *Study:* Parsons Sch Design, New York; Kans Wesleyan, DFA. *Work:* Calif Palace Legion of Honor, San Francisco; Mus Kans State Univ, Manhattan; Nelson Rockhill Mus, Kansas City, Mo; Philadelphia Mus Art, Pa; Metrop Mus Art, New York. *Pos:* Designer, Yale & Towne Mfg Co, 51-53; designer, Tiffany & Co, 51- *Teaching:* Pres, Parsons Sch Design, 41-51. *Awards:* Chevalier, Legion d'honneur, France, 51. *Dealer:* Graham Gallery 1014 Madison Ave New York NY 10021. *Mailing Add:* 84560 Menerbes France

TRUITT, ANNE (DEAN)
SCULPTOR
b Baltimore, Md, Mar 16, 21. *Study:* Bryn Mawr Col, BA, 43; Inst Contemp Art, Washington, DC, 48-49; Dallas Mus Fine Arts, 50. *Work:* Nat Collection Fine Arts & Nat Gallery Art, Washington, DC; Mus Mod Art; Whitney Mus Am Art; Walker Art Ctr. *Exhib:* One-woman shows, Andre Emmerich Gallery, 63, 65, 69, 75 & 80, Baltimore Mus Art, 69 & 74, Pyramid Gallery, 71-73, 75-77 & 79, Whitney Mus Am Art, 74, Corcoran Gallery Art, 74 & Osuna Gallery, Washington, DC, 81. *Teaching:* Prof, Univ Md. *Awards:* Guggenheim Fel, 71; Nat Endowment Arts Fel, 72 & 77; Australia Arts Coun Grant, 81. *Bibliog:* Gregory Battcock (auth), Minimal Art, A Critical Anthology, Dutton, 68; Clement Greenberg (auth), Anne Truitt: American artist, Vogue, 68; Eleanor Munro (auth), Originals: American Women Artists, Simon & Schuster, 79; and others. *Media:* Wood, Acrylic. *Publ:* Auth, Daybook: The Journal of an Artist, Pantheon Bks, 82 & Penguin Bks, 84. *Dealer:* Andre Emmerich 41 E 57th St New York NY 10022; Osuna Gallery 406 7th St NW Washington DC 20004. *Mailing Add:* 3506 35th St NW Washington DC 20016

TSAI, HSIAO HSIA
PAINTER, SCULPTOR
b China; US citizen. *Study:* Nat Col Art China, BFA; Univ Okla, MFA(scholar); Hamilton State Univ, Hon PhD, 78. *Exhib:* White Mus, San Antonio, 65, 66 & 80; Jess Besser Mus, Pensacola Art Ctr, 75; Everhart Mus, Pa, 75; Dallas Mus Fine Arts, 76; Brick Stone Mus, 77; Corpus Christi Mus, 78-81; and many others. *Awards:* Watercolor Abstract Art Ctr, Tex, 74, 76 & 77; Nat Asn Women Artists, New York, 83; Gold Medal, Italy Competition, 83; and many others. *Mem:* Hon mem Int Asn Art. *Mailing Add:* Hsiao-Hsia Tsai Gallery Fine Art 1437 Casa Verde Dr Corpus Christi TX 78411

TSAI, WEN-YING
SCULPTOR, PAINTER
b Amoy, China, Oct 13, 28; US citizen. *Study:* Univ Mich, ME, 53; Art Students League, 53-57; grad fac polit & social sci, New Sch Social Res, 56-58. *Work:* Tate Gallery, London; Centre Nat d'Art Contemporain, Paris; Kaiser Wilhem Mus, Krefeld, Ger; Albright-Knox Art Gallery, Buffalo, NY; Whitney Mus Am Art, New York. *Comn:* Gloucester Tower (cybernetic water sculpture), Palmer & Turner Archits, Hong Kong, 80; Raffles Tower Fountain, Singapore Land Pte Ltd, Singapore, 82; Dancing Menorah with Lotus, Israel Mus, Jerusalem, 82. *Exhib:* One-man shows, Hayden Gallery, Mass Inst of Technol, Cambridge, Corcoran Gallery of Art, Washington, DC, Musee d'Art Contemporain, Montreal, Que, Hong Kong Mus Art, 79 & Isetan Mus, Tokyo, 80; group shows, The Responsive Eye, 65 & The Machine Show, 68, Mus Mod Art, New York; Cybernetic Serendipity, Inst Contemp Arts, London, 68; 3rd Salon Int Galeries Pilotes, Mus Cantonal Beaux Arts, Lausanne, Switz, 70; Pittsburgh Int, Carnegie Inst Mus Art, 70; Electra-1983, Musee D'Art Moderne, Paris, 83. *Pos:* Proj engr, Guy B Panero, Engineers, New York, 56-60; proj mgr, Cosentini Assocs, Engineers, New York, 62-63. *Awards:* Whitney Fel, 63; Ctr Advan Visual Studies Fel, Mass Inst Technol, 69-71; design in steel award, Am Iron & Steel Inst, 71. *Bibliog:* Art for tomorrow-the 21st century, produced on CBS-TV, 69; Jonathan Benthall (auth), Cybernetic sculpture of Tsai, Studio Int, 3/69; Fred Barzyk (auth), Video variations (with Boston Symphony Orchestra), produced on WGBH-TV, 71. *Media:* Water, Fiber Optics, Fiberglass and Stainless Steel. *Dealer:* Galerie Denise Rene Paris. *Mailing Add:* 565 Broadway New York NY 10012

TSCHACBASOV, NAHUM
PAINTER, PRINTMAKER
b Baku, Russia, Aug 30, 1899; US citizen. *Study:* Lewis Inst, Chicago; Armour Inst Technol; Columbia Univ; also in Paris, France. *Work:* Metrop Mus Art & Whitney Mus Am Art, New York; State Dept, Washington, DC; Tel-Aviv Mus, Israel; Philadelphia Mus Art; and many others. *Exhib:* Carnegie Inst Int, Pittsburgh; Art Inst Chicago; Corcoran Gallery Art, Washington, DC; Va Mus Fine Arts, Richmond; Univ Tex, Austin; and many other group & one-man shows in the US & Europe. *Pos:* Owner, Tschacbasov Fine Arts; pres, Am Arch World Art, Inc. *Teaching:* Former instr, Am Artists Sch & Art Students League. *Awards:* Pepsi-Cola Award, 47. *Publ:* Publ, two portfolios of etchings, 47; auth & publ, The American library compendium and index of world art, 61 & An illustrated survey of western art; contribr, articles to Art Students League Quart & Numero. *Mailing Add:* 222 W 23rd St New York NY 10011

TSE, STEPHEN
PAINTER, EDUCATOR
b Hong Kong, Oct 20, 38; US citizen. *Study:* Washburn Univ, Topeka, Kans, BFA; Univ Idaho, MFA; also with Jack Tworkov. *Work:* Wenatchee Valley Col, Wash; Yakima Valley Col, Wash; Spokane Falls Community Col, Wash; Rainier Nat Bank, Olympia, Wash; First Nat Bank Idaho, Boise; and many others. *Comn:* Sculpture panels with painting, Student Union, Univ Idaho, 65. *Exhib:* One-man shows, Gallery-76, Wenatchee Valley Col, Wash, 78 & Kirsten Gallery, Seattle, 77, 78, 80 & 82; Nat Painting Exhib, Grover M Hermann Fine Art Ctr, Marietta Col, Ohio, 79; Nat Small Painting Purchase Exhib, Western Ill Univ, Macomb, 79; Compton Gallery, Wash State Univ, Pullman, 83; and many others. *Teaching:* Chmn art dept, Big Bend Community Col, 66- *Awards:* First Award Painting, Wing Luke Invitational Art Exhib, 79 & Wing Luke Mus, Seattle, 79; Second Award, Ann Art Exhib, Carnegie Ctr, Walla Walla, Wash, 79; Best of Show, Wing Luke Art Exhib, Wing Luke Mus, Seattle, 83; and others. *Mem:* Wash Art Asn; Oriental Ceramic Soc, London. *Media:* Oil and Watercolor; Clay. *Dealer:* Kirsten Gallery 5320 Roosevelt Way NE Seattle WA 98105. *Mailing Add:* 957 S Garden Dr Moses Lake WA 98837

TSELOS, DIMITRI THEODORE
HISTORIAN, WRITER
b Kerasea, Greece, Apr 10, 1900; US citizen. *Study:* Univ Chicago, PhB, 26, MA, 28; Princeton Univ, Carnegie Found Scholar, 28-32, MA, 29, MFA, 31, PhD, 33; Inst Fine Arts, NY Univ, with Richard Offner & Walter Cook, 29-30; also with Charles R Morey. *Teaching:* From instr medieval & mod art to assoc prof, Inst Fine Arts, NY Univ, 31-49; lectr mod art, Swarthmore Col, 37-41, Univ Southern Calif, summers 37-41 & Vassar Col, 42-43; vis prof, Bryn Mawr Col, 44-46; prof art, Univ Minn, 49-71, prof emer & consult, 71-; distinguished vis prof, Northwestern Univ, 77. *Awards:* Fulbright Res Grants, Greece, 55-56 & 63-64. *Mem:* Col Art Asn Am; Archaeol Inst Am; Soc Archit Historians; Am Asn Univ Prof; Minn Hist Soc. *Res:* Medieval painting; modern architecture; modern Greek art. *Publ:* Auth, Exotic influences in the architecture of F L Wright, Mag Art, 53; auth, The sources of the Utrecht psalter miniatures, 55; auth, Modern illustrated books, 59; auth, Defensive addenda on the origins of the Utrecht psalter, Art Bull, 67; auth, F L Wright and world architecture, J Archit Historians, 69. *Mailing Add:* 1494 Branston St St Paul MN 55108

TSENG YU-HO (BETTY TSENG YU-HO ECKE)
PAINTER, HISTORIAN
b Peking, China, Nov 29, 24; US citizen. *Study:* Fu-jen Univ, Peking, BA, 42; Univ Hawaii, MA, 66; Inst Fine Arts, NY Univ, PhD, 72. *Work:* Honolulu Acad Arts, Hawaii; Walker Art Ctr, Minneapolis; Nat Mus Mod Art, Stockholm, Sweden; Mus Cernuschi, Paris, France; Stanford Art Gallery, Calif. *Comn:* Mural, St Katherine's Church, Kaui, Hawaii, 57; mural, Manoa Chinese Pavilion, Honolulu, 68; mural, Golden West Savings & Loan, San Francisco, Calif, 64; wall painting, Castle & Cooke Co, Ltd, Honolulu, 68; wall painting, Honolulu Int Airport, 72. *Exhib:* Contemporary American Painting & Sculpture, Univ Ill, Urbana, 58, 61 & 65; Carnegie Inst Painting & Sculpture Int, Pittsburgh, Pa, 61 & 65; Kunstverein, Munich & Frankfurt, Ger; Walker Art Ctr; San Francisco Mus Art, Calif; and others. *Teaching:* Instr studio art, Honolulu Acad Art, 50-63, consult Chinese art, 53-; assoc prof Chinese art hist, Univ Hawaii, 63-66; prog chmn art hist, Univ Hawaii, 71-, prof art, 73-. *Awards:* Am Artists of the Western States Award, Stanford Art Gallery; NY Univ Founders Day Award for Outstanding Scholarship, 72. *Bibliog:* Article, Time Mag, 1/19/62; Seldis (auth), Pacific heritage, Art in Am, 65. *Mem:* Am Col Art Asn; Asian Soc; Asian & Pacific Art Asn Hawaii (organizer, 72). *Media:* Watercolor, Collage. *Res:* Chinese art; the Art of Chinese folding fan; folk art. *Publ:* Contribr, four articles, Studies of 16th Century Chinese Artists, 54-63; contribr, Encyclopedia World Art, Rome, 64; auth, Some Contemporary Elements on Chinese Classic Pictorial Art, 65 & 71; illusr, The Analects of Confucious, 70. *Mailing Add:* 3460 Kaohinani Dr Honolulu HI 96817

TSEU, ROSITA IISU
ADMINISTRATOR, INSTRUCTOR
b Peking, People's Republic of China, Jan 6, 16; US citizen. *Study:* Col Municipal Francaise, Shanghai, 30-36; Ecole des Beaux Arts, Paris; Sochow Art Acad, Shanghai; Otis Art Inst, Los Angeles; Brit Com Inst, 47; Univ Calif Los Angeles, teaching cert(art), 82. *Comn:* Portraits, Adm Jarret, USA Navy, retired, 52; portraits, Mme Chang Hsueh Liang, 62, Rabbi Willner, 63 & Anna Chennault, 70. *Exhib:* One-person show, San Gabriel Fine Arts Gallery, 77-80; Invitational Exhib, Nat Mus Hist, Taipei, Taiwan, 79; Ambassador Col Gallery, Pasadena, Calif, 81. *Pos:* Managing dir, Sergie Bongart Sch of Art, 72-75. *Teaching:* Portrait classes in own studio, 70- *Awards:* Over 200 awards including numerous gold medals; Premio Centura D'Oro Award, Florence, Italy, 82. *Mem:* Calif Art Club; San Gabriel Fine Arts Asn; Los Angeles Chinese Art Asn. *Media:* Multimedia. *Dealer:* Katona Gallery 11971 San Vincenti Blvd Brentwood CA 90049; China Culture Center Inc 210 Mandarine Plaza 970 N Broadway Los Angeles CA 90012. *Mailing Add:* 6869 Pacific View Dr Hollywood CA 90068

TSUTAKAWA, GEORGE
SCULPTOR, PAINTER
b Seattle, Wash, Feb 22, 10. *Study:* With Alexander Archipenko, 36; Univ Wash Sch Art, BFA, 37, MFA, 50. *Work:* Seattle Art Mus, Wash; Denver Art Mus, Colo; Santa Barbara Mus Art; Henry Art Gallery, Univ Wash, Seattle. *Comn:* Aluminum fountain sculpture, Expo 74, Spokane, Wash; hanging fountain sculpture, KING Broadcasting Corp, Seattle, Wash, 81; fountain sculpture, Tsutsujigaoka Park, Sendai, Japan, 81; Ohkura Park, Setagaya, Tokyo, Japan, 82; Govt Ctr, Toledo, Ohio, 83; and others. *Exhib:* 3rd Biennial, Sao Paulo, Brazil, 55; San Francisco Painting & Sculpture Ann, San Francisco Mus Art, 55, 58 & 60; Int Art Festival, Amerika Haus, Berlin, EGer, 66; Pacific NW Artists; Japan Nat Mus, Osaka, Japan, 82; and others. *Teaching:* Prof art, Univ Wash, 46-80, emer prof art, 80- *Awards:* Awards for Obos No 9 (wood), San Francisco Mus Art & Denver Art Mus, 60; Cultural Award Rising Sun, Emperor Japan, 81; Centennial Hall Honor Award, State Washington, 81; and others. *Bibliog:* Charles Cowles & Martha Kingsbury (auths), Northwest Tradition, Seattle Art Mus, 78; Gerald Nordland (auth), Franklin D Murphy Sculpture Garden, Univ Calif, Los Angeles, 78; Masayoshi Homma (auth), Exhib of Tsutakawa Fountain Sculptures, Sendai, Japan, 81; and others. *Media:* Bronze, Watercolor. *Mailing Add:* 3116 S Irving St Seattle WA 98144

TUBIS, SEYMOUR
PAINTER, PRINTMAKER
b Philadelphia, Pa, Sept 20, 19. *Study:* Temple Univ; Philadelphia Mus Sch; Art Students League; with Georges Braque; Acad Grande Chaumiere, Paris; Inst d'Arte, Florence, Italy; also with Hans Hofmann. *Work:* Metrop Mus Art, New York; Libr Cong, Washington, DC; Soc Am Graphic Artists, New York; Univ Calgary, Alta; US Dept of State, Washington, DC & Embassies in Asia, Europe & Africa. *Exhib:* Nat Exhib Prints, Drawings & Watercolors, Metrop Mus Art, 52; Int Exhib Graphics, Seattle Art Mus, 68; Dallas Mus of Art, 70; Seattle Art Mus, 71; Mediterranea Paintings, Prints & Sculpture, Discovery Gallery, Santa Fe, 75; The New West, Albuquerque, NMex, 78; Inst Am Indian Arts, Santa Fe, NMex, 79; The Cody Gallery, Santa Fe, NMex, 80; Warner Roberts Gallery, Palo Alto, Calif, 81. *Pos:* Artist-designer, New York Times, 59-62. *Teaching:* Instr painting, design & graphic arts, Inst Am Indian Arts, 62-, chmn dept fine arts, 65-80. *Awards:* Fourth Purchase Award in painting, Joe & Emily Lowe Found, 54; First Prize in watercolor, Mus NMex, 75; Nat Endowment Arts, 80. *Bibliog:* Michelle Seiuere (auth), Les exposition Seymour Tubis, Opera, 7/26/50; John MacGregor (auth), Seymour Tubis experiments with printmaking, Pasatiempo, 8/27/67; Martha Buddeke (auth), Seymour Tubis takes two directions, J Arts, Albuquerque J, 11/21/71. *Mem:* Life mem Art Students League; Soc Am Graphic Artists; Col Art Asn Am; Santa Fe Designer/Craftsmen. *Media:* Oil, Intaglio, Bronze, Wood, Bone. *Publ:* Contribr, 72nd ann, Royal Soc Painters, Etchers & Engravers, 54; contribr, Western review, Western NMex Univ, 66; illusr, Yerma, Santa Fe NMex, 71; contribr, Indian painters and white patrons, El Palacio, 71. *Dealer:* Warner Roberts 533 Ramona St Palo Alto CA 94301; Bethesda Gallery Bethesda MD 20014. *Mailing Add:* c/o Nina L Tubis 1151 S Birch St Apt 407 Denver CO 80222

TUCHMAN, ELLEN FRANCES
PAINTER
b Los Angeles, Calif, Oct 16, 54. *Study:* Univ Calif, Los Angeles, 72-74; Calif Col Arts & Crafts, BFA, 76. *Work:* Metrop Mus Art, New York; Southeast Banking Corp, Miami; Container Corp, Chicago; Prudential Life Insurance Co, Newark, NJ; Gen Electric Corp, Conn. *Exhib:* Gold, Mus Mod Art, 78; Other Media, Fla Int Univ, 80; Starry Night, Kathryn Mancel Gallery, New York, 81; Elegant Night, Security Pac Bank, Los Angeles, 81; Graphics Plus, Johnson Mus, 81; Interpretations of the Feminine, Occidental Col, Los Angeles, 83. *Pos:* Asst, Art Lending Dept, Mus Mod Art, 77-78, Painting & Sculpture Dept, 78-80. *Awards:* NY State Coun Arts Grant Graphics, 81; Ariana Found Arts Grant Mixed Media, 82. *Bibliog:* Susan Putterman (auth), article, Arts Mag, 5/81; Suzanne Munchnic (auth), Galleries, Los Angeles Times, 10/30/82; Sandy Ballatore-Nelson (auth), 1982 best exhibitions in LA, Images & Issues, 1-2/83. *Media:* Acrylic, Watercolor. *Dealer:* Kathryn Markel 50 W 57 St New York NY 10019. *Mailing Add:* 501 W 113 St New York NY 10025

TUCHMAN, MAURICE
MUSEUM CURATOR
b Jacksonville, Fla, Nov 30, 36. *Study:* Nat Univ Mex; City Col New York, BA, 57; Columbia Univ, MA, 59. *Collections Arranged:* Five Younger Calif Artists, 65; Edward Kienholz, 66; Irwin-Price, 66; John Mason, 66; Am Sculpture of 60's (with catalog), 67; Soutine (with catalog), 68; Art & Technol (with catalog), 71; European Paintings in the 70's (with catalog), 75; Richard Diebenkorn: Paintings and Drawings, 77. *Pos:* Art ed mod art sect, Columbia Encycl, 62; mem curatorial & lect staff, Guggenheim Mus, 62-64, organizer, summer 64; sr cur mod art, Los Angeles Co Mus Art, 64- *Awards:* Fulbright Scholar, 60-61. *Mailing Add:* Los Angeles Co Mus Art 5905 Wilshire Blvd Los Angeles CA 90036

TUCHMAN, PHYLLIS
HISTORIAN, CRITIC
b Passaic, NJ, Jan 4, 47. *Study:* Sarah Lawrence Col Summer Session in Florence, 67; Boston Univ, BA(distinction in fine arts), 68; Inst of Fine Arts, NY Univ, MA, 73, with Robert Rosenblum & Robert S Rubin. *Collections Arranged:* Six in Bronze, Williams Col Mus Art, 84. *Pos:* Mem ed bd, Marsyas, New York, 71-74. *Teaching:* Instr art hist, Sch of Visual Arts, New York, 72-75; adj lectr art hist, Hunter Col, 76-79; vis lectr art, Williams Col, 81-83. *Awards:* Nat Endowment for Arts art critic's grant, 78-79; Nat Endowment Humanities fel, 80. *Mem:* AICA; Art Table; Col Art Asn. *Res:* 19th and 20th century European and American art, particularly sculpture. *Publ:* Auth, George Segal, Abbeyville Press, 83; ed, Sculptors Writings 1945-1970, G K Hall, 84. *Mailing Add:* 340 E 80th St New York NY 10021

TUCHOLKE, CHRISTEL-ANTHONY (CHRISTEL E STOEVEKEN)
PAINTER
b Poland, March 2, 41; US citizen. *Study:* Univ Wis, Milwaukee, BS, 64 & MS, 65; Tamarind Lithography Workshop, Los Angeles, 68. *Work:* Milwaukee Art Mus, Wis; Miller Brewing Company Headquarters, Milwaukee, Wis; Wis Telephone Headquarters, Milwaukee; Bradley Univ, Peoria, Ill; Wright Art Ctr, Beloit, Wis. *Comn:* Exterior Mural, John Michael Kohler Art Ctr, Sheboygan, Wis, 77; four paintings, Northwestern Mutual Life Insurance Company, Milwaukee, Wis, 79; Telephone Book Cover, Wis Telephone Company, 81. *Exhib:* Drawings USA, Minn Mus Art, St Paul, 75; 76th & 77th Exhibs by Artists of Chicago & Vicinity, Art Inst, Ill, 77 & 78; Wis Directions Two, Milwaukee Art Mus, 78; Wis Artists Make Toys, Milwaukee Art Mus, 79; Wis Biennale, Madison Art Ctr, 80 & 82; State of the Art: Wisconsin Painting and Drawing, J Michael Kohler Art Ctr, Sheboygan, Wis, 82; and others. *Awards:* Top Award, Madison Art Ctr, 80; Purchase Award, Wright Art Ctr, 80; Purchase Award, Bradley Univ, 81. *Media:* Acrylic, Pastel. *Dealer:* Bradley Galleries 2565 N Downer Ave Milwaukee WI 53211; Edgewood Orchard Galleries Fish Creek WI 54212. *Mailing Add:* 5074 North Hollywood Ave Whitefish Bay WI 53217

TUCKER, ANNE WILKES
CURATOR, HISTORIAN
b Baton Rouge, La, Oct 18, 45. *Study:* Randolph-Macon Women's Col, Lynchburg Va, BA(art hist), 67; Rochester Inst of Technol, AAS(photog), 68; Visual Studies Workshop, MFA, photo hist and mus procedure with Nathan Lyons and Beaumont Newhall, 70. *Collections Arranged:* Photographs of Women, Mus of Mod Art, New York, 71; The Target Collection of American Photography (ed, catalog), traveling, Mus Fine Arts, Houston, 77; Target II: Five American Photographers (auth, catalog), traveling & Anthony G Cronin Mem Collection (auth, catalog), 79; Photographic Crossroads: The PhotoLeague (auth, catalog), touring, Ottawa, 78; George Krause: Photographs, Mus of Fine Arts, 78; Suzanne Bloom and Ed Hill: Research and Collaboration (ed, catalog), Mus Fine Arts, Houston, 80; Sidney Grossman: Photographs (auth, catalog), traveling, Mus Fine Arts, Houston, 81. *Pos:* Res asst, George Eastman House, Rochester, NY, 68-70; curatorial intern, Photog dept, Mus of Mod Art, 70-71; cur, Mus of Fine Arts, 76- *Teaching:* Vis lectr photographic hist, Cooper Union, New York, 72-75; affiliate artist in photographic hist, Univ of Houston, 76-79. *Awards:* Guggenheim Fel, 83. *Mem:* Soc Photog Educ (secy, 77-79); Col Art Asn. *Res:* Concentrated on 20th century American photographs. *Interests:* Absences and gaps in current photographic history. *Publ:* Auth & ed, The Woman's Eye, Alfred A Knopf, New York, 73; auth, Photography in America: Problems of a Show and Catalogue, Afterimage, 75; coauth, Lee Witkin, Rare Books and Photographs (catalog one), Witkin Gallery, 71; ed, Eliot Porter: Intimate Landscapes, 1950-1977, Crain Group, 83. *Mailing Add:* Mus of Fine Arts 1001 Bissonnet Houston TX 77005

TUCKER, CHARLES CLEMENT
PAINTER

b SC, Sept 13, 13. *Study:* Art Students League, scholar & with Frank Vincent DuMond, Ivan G Olinsky & George B Bridgman. *Work:* Univ NC, Chapel Hill; Duke Univ; Mint Mus, Charlotte, NC; 4th Circuit Ct Appeals, Richmond Fed Bldg, Va; plus many others. *Exhib:* Metrop Mus Art, 42, Nat Acad Design, 50, Coun Am Artist Socs, 66, Hudson Valley Art Asn, 68-72 & Allied Artist Am, 71-72. *Awards:* First Award, NC Nat Exhib, 58 & 59; Dirs Award, Coun Am Artist Soc, 66; Artist of Year, Charlotte-Mecklenburg Bi-Centennial, 68. *Bibliog:* Legette Blythe (auth), Miracle in the Hills, McGraw, 53 & Call Down the Storm, Holt, 58; Works of Art, US Capitol. *Mem:* Allied Artist Am; Hudson Valley Art Asn; life mem Art Students League; Am Artist Prof League. *Mailing Add:* 3621 Arborway Dr Charlotte NC 28211

TUCKER, CURTIS (DEE)
CERAMIST, LECTURER

b Austin, Tex, Sept 26, 39. *Study:* Los Angeles City Col, 57-58; Calif Western Univ, 58-59; Univ Zaragoza, Spain, 62-63; Otis Art Inst, with Michael Frimkess & Bob Glover, 66-68. *Work:* Evans-Tibbs Collection, Vt Ave Gallery, Washington, DC; Tenn State Univ, Nashville; Albany State Univ; Ala State Univ, Montgomery. *Exhib:* Contemporary African-American Crafts, Brooks Mem Art Mus, 79; Power Objects: Ancient to the Future, Howard Univ Art Gallery, 80; Dimensions and Directions: Black Artists of the South, Miss Art Mus, Jackson, 80; Traditional Crafts, Mus Nat Ctr Afro-Am Artists, Boston, 82; Magic of Clay, Calif Mus Afro-Am Hist & Cult, Los Angeles, 82; Surrealism and the Afro-American Artist, Evans-Tibbs Collection, Washington, DC, 83; and others. *Collections Arranged:* First Ann Miami-Dade Community Art Show, Miami-Dade Community Col, 72. *Teaching:* Instr ceramics, Miami-Dade Community Col, 68-71 & Haystock Mountain Sch Crafts, Deer Isle, Maine, summer 74; dir ceramic workshops, Fla A&M Univ, 73-75. *Awards:* Best of Show, Black Artists of Florida, Lowe Art Gallery, Univ Miami, 70; Best Use of Clay, Southeast Florida Craftsmen, Hollywood Mus Art, 72. *Bibliog:* Ellen Ashdown (auth), The ceramics of Yvonne & Curtis Tucker, Art-Craft, 2-3/80 & Afro-Raku: The ceramics of Yvonne & Curtis Tucker, Black Art: Int Quart, winter 80. *Mem:* Fla Arts Coun Afro-Am Affairs; Kuumba Artists Asn Fla; Nat Conf Artists. *Media:* Clay, Raku. *Publ:* Auth, Black art, Theatre Afro Arts Mag, 70; contribr, African, Indian & Oriental Influences in the Aesthetics of Two Contemporary Craftspeople: First National African-American Crafts Conference: Select Writings, Shelby State Community Col, 80. *Dealer:* Evans-Tibbs Gallery 1910 Vermont Ave Washington DC 20001. *Mailing Add:* 3007 Kevin St Tallahassee FL 32301

TUCKER, GLENN F
CRITIC, COLLECTOR

b Tullahoma, Tenn, May 28, 36. *Study:* Univ Tenn, BFA, 58, MA, 59; All Souls Col, with A L Ronse; also in Eng. *Pos:* Art critic, San Antonio Light, 63- *Awards:* Journalist of the Year, Incarnate Word Col, 65. *Collection:* Elizabethan sketches, stage designs, original prints and graphics. *Publ:* Auth, Behind the flower portrait, Harvard Quart, 67; auth, Shakespeare and painting, 69 & auth, The man in the Grafton portrait, 71, Sewanee Rev; auth, What is an original print, Southwestern Art, 73. *Mailing Add:* 911 E Contour Dr San Antonio TX 78212

TUCKER, JAMES EWING
CURATOR, PAINTER

b Rule, Tex, Aug 13, 30. *Study:* Midwestern Univ; Univ Tex, Austin, BFA; Univ Iowa, MFA. *Work:* NC State Univ, Raleigh; Weatherspoon Art Gallery; Miller Brewing Co; Pine Bluff Art Ctr, Ark; Witte Mus, San Antonio. *Collections Arranged:* Art on Paper, Cone Collection & Dillard Collection, Weatherspoon Art Gallery, 65- *Pos:* Cur, Weatherspoon Art Gallery, 59-, ed, Bulletin, 65- *Media:* Mixed. *Dealer:* Ingber Gallery 460 West Broadway New York NY 10012. *Mailing Add:* 632 Scott Ave Greensboro NC 27403

TUCKER, LEATRICE YVONNE See Edwards-Tucker, Yvonne

TUCKER, MARCIA
MUSEUM DIRECTOR, CURATOR

b New York, NY, Apr 11, 40. *Study:* Ecole du Louvre & Acad Grande Chaumiere, Paris, France, 59-60; Conn Col, BA(fine arts), 61; NY Univ Inst Fine Arts, MA, 69; San Francisco Art Inst, Hon Dr, 5/83. *Collections Arranged:* Anti-Illusion: Procedures/Materials, 69, Robert Morris, 70 (with catalog), The Structure of Color, 71, James Rosenquist & Bruce Nauman (with catalog), Retrospective Exhibs, 72 & 73, Lee Krasner, Joan Mitchell & Al Held; John Baldessai 1980, Not Just For Laughs: The Art of Subversion, 81. *Pos:* Cur, William N Copley Collection, 63-66; ed assoc, Art News, 65-69; assoc cur, Whitney Mus Am Art, 69-76; founder & dir, The New Mus, New York, 76- *Teaching:* Instr art, Univ RI, 66-68; instr art, City Univ New York, 67-68; instr art, Sch Visual Arts, 69-73; guest lectr, cols, univs & inst. *Awards:* Arts Manager of the Year, Arts Mgt Mag, 83. *Publ:* Auth, PreNaumanology, 70 & The anatomy of a brush stroke: Recent paintings by Joan Snyder, 71, Artforum; auth, Bad Painting, 78 & Barry LeVa, 79 (exhib catalogs), The New Mus; auth, Terry Allan (on everything), Artforum, 80; and others. *Mailing Add:* New Mus Contemp Art 583 Broadway New York NY 10012

TUCKER, PERI
WRITER, ILLUSTRATOR

b Kashau, Austria-Hungary, July 25, 11; US citizen. *Study:* Columbus Sch Fine Arts; also with E C Van Swearingen. *Exhib:* one-man show, Fla Gulf

Coast Art Ctr, Belleair, Fla, 67; Whiskey Painters of Am Nat Shows (travelling exhib), Akron Art Inst, Ohio, 73, 26 E Art Ctr, Tulsa, Okla, 75, De Colores Gallery, Denver, Colo, 76; Cuyahoga Valley Art Ctr, Cuyahoga Falls, Ohio, 81. *Pos:* Illusr, children's books, Saalfield Publ Co, 38-51; writer & artist, Akron Beacon J, 42-51; writer & artist, St Petersburg Times, 52-66; free-lance writer & artist, 67- *Media:* Watercolor, Ink. *Mailing Add:* 201 Driftwood Lane Harbor Bluffs Largo FL 33540

TUCKER, TOBA PATO
PHOTOGRAPHER, INSTRUCTOR

b Bronx, NY, July 1, 35. *Study:* Self-taught photographer. *Work:* Mus Am Indian, Mus Mod Art & Mus City New York, NY; Mus Francais de la Photographie, Bievres, France. *Exhib:* Phot Univers 1978, Mus Fracais de la Photographie, France, 78; Am Vision, Nat Artists Alliance, New York, 79; Creative Artist Public Service Program, State Mus, Albany, NY, 81; Navajo Portraits, Mus Am Indian, New York, 82; Mus City New York. *Teaching:* Instr photog, Int Ctr Photog, New York, 78-81. *Awards:* First Prize, Mus Francais de la Photographie, 78; Creative Artist Public Service Grant, 79; Nat Endowment Arts Fel, 81. *Bibliog:* Carol deGrappa (auth), Survivors, Camera Arts, 5/81; Navajo Portaits, Popular Photog, 82. *Mailing Add:* 476 Broome St New York NY 10013

TUCKER, WILLIAM G
SCULPTOR

b Cairo, Egypt, Feb 28, 35. *Study:* Oxford Univ, BA(mod hist), 58; Cent Sch Art & St Martin's Sch Art, London, 59-61. *Work:* Tate Gallery, London; Guggenheim Mus, Metrop Mus, Mus Mod Art, New York; Kroller-Muller Mus, Holland; and others. *Comn:* Angel (sculpture), Livingston Develop Corp, Lanark, Scotland, 76. *Exhib:* London, The New Scene, Walker Art Ctr, Minneapolis, 66; Guggenheim Int Sculpture, Solomon R Guggenheim Mus, New York, 67; Dokumenta 6, Kassel, Ger, 68; Brit Sculptors, 72, Royal Acad, London, 72; The Condition of Sculpture, Hayward Gallery, London, 75; Robert Elkon Gallery, New York, 79, 80 & 82; New Work on Paper, Mus Mod Art, New York, 81; Bernard Jacobson Gallery, New York, 82; and many others. *Awards:* Guggenheim Fel, 80-81. *Bibliog:* Hilton Kramer (auth), article, New York Times, 5/25/79; Dore Ashton (auth), article, Arts Mag, 6/79. *Media:* Mixed. *Publ:* Auth, Early Modern Sculpture, Oxford Univ Press, 74; articles in Studio Int, Art in Am, Tracks, and others. *Mailing Add:* 99 Commercial St Brooklyn NY 11222

TUCKERMAN, JANE BAYARD
PHOTOGRAPHER, EDUCATOR

b Boston, Mass, June 11, 47. *Study:* Art Inst Boston, 68-71; RI Sch Design, MFA, 73-75. *Work:* Metrop Mus Art & Mus Mod Art, New York; Minneapolis Inst Art, Minn; Detroit Inst Arts; Boston Mus Fine Arts. *Comn:* New Work's Portfolio, Boston Photog Resource Soc, 81. *Exhib:* Solo exhibs, Addison Gallery Am Art, 76 & Photogalerie Pennings, Eindhoven, Holland, 81; Venezia 79, Int Mus, Venice, Italy; Invisible Light, Smithsonian Inst Traveling Exhib, 80-84; Alternative Image, Kohler Arts Ctr, Sheboygan, Wis, 82; Photography Plus, Mus Univ Mo, St Louis, 83. *Collections Arranged:* Second Sight: Exhib of Infrared Photog (auth, catalog), traveling in US, Canada & Europe, 81-84. *Teaching:* Asst prof photog, Wellesley Col, 76-77; assoc prof & dir photog prog, Harvard Univ, 78-; guest instr & lectr, Maine Photog Workshop, Rockport, 78-80 & Factory Visual Arts, Seattle, 79. *Awards:* Polaroid Exhib Grant for Second Sight, 81; New Works Fel, Traveling Exhib in New England, Mass Coun Arts & Boston Photog Soc, 81-82; Individual Artists Fel, Nat Endowment Arts, 82-83. *Bibliog:* Allen Porter (auth), Camera Mag, 74, 80 & 81; Pamela Allara (auth), The scope of Boston art is much broader than it would appear, Art News, 11/81; Photography Year 1982, Time/Life Bks, 82. *Mem:* Soc Photog Educ. *Publ:* Contribr, Self Portrayal, Friends Photog, 78; contribr, Darkroom Dynamics, Curtain & London, 79; contribr & illusr, American photographer, CBS Publ, 82; contribr, Aperture Mag, 83. *Dealer:* Equivalents Gallery 1822 Broadway Seattle WA 98122; Pierce St Gallery 217 Pierce St Suite 206 Birmingham MI 48011. *Mailing Add:* Main St Box 399 Dublin NH 03444

TUFTS, ELEANOR M
HISTORIAN, EDUCATOR

b Exeter, NH. *Study:* Simmons Col, Span with Edith F Helman, BS; Radcliffe Col, Renaissance with Millard Meiss, also Rembrandt with Jakob Rosenberg, MA; NY Univ Inst Fine Arts, Span painting with Jose Lopez-Rey, PhD. *Teaching:* Asst prof art hist, Univ Bridgeport, 66-68; assoc prof Baroque art, Southern Conn State Col, 68-74; prof women artists, Span & baroque art, Southern Methodist Univ, 74-, chairperson div fine arts, 74-78. *Awards:* Nat Endowment for Humanities Summer Res Grant, 74. *Mem:* Col Art Asn Am (mem bd). *Res:* Monograph on Luis Melendez; women artists of the past. *Publ:* Auth, Albertinellis rediscovered at Yale, 68 & auth, Bellows & Goya, 71, Art J; auth, Luis Melendez: Documents on his life & work, 72 & auth, A second self-portrait by Luis Melendez, 74, Art Bulletin; auth, Our Hidden Heritage: Five Centuries of Women Artists, 74. *Mailing Add:* Div of Fine Arts Southern Methodist Univ Dallas TX 75275

TULK, ALFRED JAMES
PAINTER, MURALIST

b London, Eng, Oct 3, 1899; US citizen. *Study:* Oberlin Col; Nat Acad Design, cert; Art Students League, cert; Yale Univ Sch Art, BFA, 23; Inst Bellas Artes, Guanajuato, Mex, MFA, 63. *Work:* Birmingham Mus Art, Ala; Orlando Pub Libr, Fla; Univ Conn, Storrs. *Comn:* Stained glass window, Col WAfrica, Monrovia, Liberia, 40; murals, Salvation Army Hosp, Flushing, NY, 48; Iconastasis, Franciscan Monastery, New Canaan, Conn, 52; mural, D A Long Co Bldg, Hamden, Conn, 59; three murals, Picuris Indian Pueblo,

Penasco, NMex, 63. *Exhib:* Burnett Gallery, Amherst, Mass, 74; Post Col, Waterbury, Conn, 75; Albertus Magnus Col, New Haven, 77; Yale Univ, 78; Eli Whitney Mus, 79; and many others. *Pos:* Dir dept mural painting, Rambusch Decorating Co, New York, 26-46; gen designer, Karl Hackert Studios, Chicago, 46-72; assoc designer, Studios of George Payne, Paterson, NJ, 48-52. *Teaching:* Instr drawing & painting, Dept Adult Educ, City Stamford, 54-58; instr drawing & painting, Art Guild North Haven, 65-70. *Awards:* Drawing Prize, Yale Art Sch, 21; Bronze Medal, Beaux Arts Inst Design, 22; First Prize Oil Painting, Greenwich Art Soc, 58. *Mem:* Nat Soc Mural Painters; New Haven Arts Coun; North Haven Art Guild. *Media:* Oil, Watercolor. *Mailing Add:* 210 Upper State St North Haven CT 06473

TULLIS, GARNER H
PAINTER, PRINTMAKER
b Cincinnati, Ohio, Dec 12, 39. *Study:* Univ Pa, BFA, 64; Accademia Di Belli Arte, Italy, Fulbright Scholar, 64-65; Stanford Univ, MA(Carnegie Fel), 67. *Work:* Cleveland Mus Art, Ohio; Philadelphia Mus Art, Pa; San Francisco Mus Mod Art, Calif; Mus Mod Art, New York; Brooklyn Mus Art, NY. *Exhib:* Ann Invitational, Pa Acad Fine Arts, 64; 49th Ann, Cleveland Mus Art, Ohio, 65; Nat Ann, San Francisco Mus Mod Art, Calif, 66; Albright-Knox Gallery, Buffalo, NY, 72; one-man show, Cleveland Art Inst, Ohio, 75; Works in handmade paper, Mus Mod Art, New York, 76; 30 Yrs, 30 Printmakers, Nat Collection Fine Arts, Washington, DC, 78; Paper as Medium Traveling Exhib, Smithsonian, 78-82. *Pos:* Dir, Inst Experimental Printmaking, 73- *Teaching:* Foundry supervisor sculpture, Univ Calif, Berkeley, 67-69; artist-in-residence papermaking, Bennington Col, 76; assoc prof printmaking, Univ Calif, Davis, 76- *Awards:* Nat Endowment Arts Grant, 76. *Bibliog:* Jules Heller (auth), Papermaking Today, Watson-Guptill, 78; Paper: Art & Technology, World Print Council, 79; Patricia Newman (auth), Experimental workshop of Garner Tullis, Smithsonian Mag, 8/80. *Mem:* Life mem, The Print Club, Philadelphia; Calif Soc Printmakers; Col Art Asn. *Dealer:* Pace Edition Inc 32 E 57th St New York NY 10022. *Mailing Add:* 1 Vista Del Orinda Orinda CA 94563

TULLSEN, REX
PAINTER, INSTRUCTOR
b Pine Ridge, SDak, June 19, 07. *Study:* Fed Sch Illus, Minneapolis (correspondence), 33-34; Bloomfield Art Asn, Birmingham, Mich (part-time), 62-66; Inst Allende, San Miguel Allende, Mex, 68. *Pos:* Layout artist & illusr, Gen Motors Corp, Detroit, Mich, 35-67. *Teaching:* Instr oil painting, Sun City Recreation Asn, Ariz, 1 74-78, instr drawing, 77-80. *Media:* Oil and Line Drawing, Watercolor. *Mailing Add:* 10314 Brookside Dr Sun City AZ 85351

TULUMELLO, PETER M
ADMINISTRATOR, EDUCATOR
b Welland, Ont, Can, Apr 15, 54. *Study:* Daemen Col, 73-74; Univ Waterloo, Ont, BA(fine arts, hon), 78; Univ Regina, Sask, MFA, 80. *Work:* Univ Waterloo, Ont; Univ Regina. *Pos:* Dir & cur, Estevan Nat Exhib Ctr, 81-83 & Mus Northern Hist, Ont, 84- *Teaching:* Lectr, Univ Regina, 79- *Awards:* Proj Cost Grant, Can Coun Award, 82. *Mem:* Asn Cult Execs; Western Can Art Asn; Sask Mus Asn; Can Mus Asn. *Mailing Add:* 66 State St Welland ON L3B 4K5 Canada

TULVING, RUTH
PAINTER, PRINTMAKER
b Estonia; Can citizen. *Study:* Ont Col Art, 62. *Teaching:* Instr painting & printmaking, Ont Col Art, Toronto. *Mem:* Royal Can Acad Art; Ont Soc Artists (pres, currently). *Media:* Acrylic; Embossing, Etching. *Mailing Add:* 45 Baby Point Crescent Toronto ON M6S 2B7 Canada

TUNICK, DAVID
DEALER, BOOK DEALER
b Greenwich, Conn, Nov 17, 43. *Study:* Williams Col, BA(art hist), 66. *Pos:* Pres, David Tunick, Inc, New York, 66- *Mem:* Art Dealers Asn Am; Antiqn Booksellers' Asn Am; Int League Antiqn Booksellers; Chambre Syndicale de l'Estampe, Paris. *Publ:* Auth, Old Master & Modern Prints (ser of ann catalogs), 71-80; auth, Twenty-One Prints by Tissot (catalog), 72; auth, Viscount Downe collection of Rembrandt etchings, an auction review, 73 & auth, Anatomy of an auction: The Kornfeld sale of Old Masters, 74, Print Collector's Newsletter; coauth, Sixty-Five Prints by James McNeill Whistler (catalog), 75. *Mailing Add:* 12 E 81st St New York NY 10028

TUNIS, ROSLYN
CURATOR
b Montreal, Que; US citizen. *Study:* State Univ NY, Binghamton, BA(studio art & art hist), 72; MA(art hist & anthrop), 80. *Collections Arranged:* Festival of Mexico (auth, catalog), 73; The Fine Art of Craftsmanship (auth, catalog), 74; William Bingham: America a Good Investment (auth, catalog), 75; Artistic Spirit of the North American Indian (auth, catalog), 76; Treasure House: Museums of the Empire State (auth, catalog), 79; Charles Eldred: Sculpture and Drawing (auth, catalog), 80. *Pos:* Cur art, Roberson Ctr for Arts & Sci, Binghamton, NY, 72- *Mem:* Am Crafts Coun; NY State Craftsmen; Am Asn Mus. *Res:* Art of the Iroquois. *Mailing Add:* 624 Valley View Dr Endwell NY 13760

TURANO, DON
SCULPTOR, MEDALIST
b New York, NY, Mar 9, 30. *Study:* Sch Indust Art, with Albino Cavalido; Corcoran Sch Art, with Heinz Warneke; Skowhegan Sch Painting & Sculpture, with H Tovish; Rinehart Sch Sculpture, with R Puccinelli. *Comn:* Silver & wood mace, Am Col Physicians, Philadelphia, 64; carved oak panels,

First Presby Church, Royal Oak, Mich, 65; limestone figures, Cathedral of St Peter & St Paul, Washington, DC, 65; four arks (locust wood), Temple Micah, Washington, DC, 71; Silver Medallion, Univ Notre Dame, Ind, 72. *Exhib:* Pa Acad Fine Arts, Philadelphia, 63; St Louis Mus, Mo, 64; Univ Colo, Boulder, 65; Audubon Ann, Nat Acad Design Galleries, 66; Xerox Corp, Rochester, NY, 71. *Teaching:* Instr sculpture, George Washington Univ, 61-65; instr sculpture, Corcoran Sch Art, 61-65. *Awards:* First Prize, Corcoran Gallery Art, 66; First Prize, Festival Relig Art, 67; First Prize, George Washington Univ, 68. *Mem:* Nat Sculpture Soc; assoc Washington Relig Art Comn. *Media:* Bronze, Wood. *Mailing Add:* 2810 27th St Washington DC 20008

TURK, RUDY H
MUSEUM DIRECTOR, WRITER
b Sheboygan, Wis, June 24, 27. *Study:* Univ Wis; Univ Tenn; Ind Univ; Univ Paris, Fulbright Scholar, 56-57. *Collections Arranged:* The Works of John Roeder, Richmond Art Ctr, Calif, 61-62; Contemporary Glass, San Diego Mus Fine Arts, 67; The World of David Gilhooly, Ariz State Univ, 69 & Enamels by June Schwarcz, 70; Henry Strater Retrospective, 79; The World of Viola Frey, 82; Found & Assembled, 82. *Pos:* Art historian & dir art gallery, Univ Mont, 57-60; dir, Richmond Art Ctr, 60-65 & Univ Art Collections, Ariz State Univ, 67-; asst dir, San Diego Mus Fine Arts, 65-67. *Teaching:* Prof art, Ariz State Univ, 67-77. *Awards:* Golden Crate Award, Western Asn Art Mus, 74; Ariz Designer Craftsmen Honorary Merit Award, 75; City Scottsdale Award, 82. *Mem:* Asn Am Mus; Col Art Asn Am; Ariz Arts Comn. *Res:* Contemporary art; 18th century French art; humanities; American ceramics. *Collection:* Eighteenth century French prints; contemporary American art. *Publ:* Auth, I L Udell, Univ Art Collections, 71; coauth, Scholder/Indians, Northland, 72; coauth, The Search for Personal Freedom, William C Brown, Vols I & II, 4th ed 72, 5th ed 77, 6th ed 81; auth, Monumental Landscapes of Merrill Mahaffey, Northland, 79; plus critical studies, art catalogues & art reviews. *Mailing Add:* Univ Art Collections Ariz State Univ Tempe AZ 85282

TURNBULL, BETTY
CURATOR, DEALER
b Hollywood, Calif, Aug 4, 24. *Study:* Los Angeles Valley Col (art hist, design, drawing & painting), 56-59. *Collections Arranged:* Art of the Northwest Indian & Alaska Eskimo, Fine Arts Patrons of Newport Harbor, 68; Directly Seen; New Realism, 70 & Art of the Indian Southwest, 71, Newport Harbor Art Mus & Pasadena Mus Art; Mary Cassatt (auth, catalog), 74; The Flute and the Brush: Indian Miniature Paintings, 76; The Last Time I Saw Ferus (auth, catalog), 76; David Park Retrospective (auth, catalog), 77; The Prometheus Archives-A Retrospective of the Work of George Herms, 79; Via Celmins Survey (intro catalog), 79; California, The State of Landscape 1827-1981 (auth, catalog), Newport Harbor Art Mus, 81; and others. *Pos:* Cur art, Newport Harbor Art Mus, Calif, 69-72 & 73-77, actg dir, 72-73; cur exhibs & collections, 77-81; dir, Turnbull, Lutjeans, Kogan (TLK) Gallery, 81- *Specialty:* Contemporary painting, sculpture & graphics. *Mailing Add:* 1419 Bonnie Doone Terrace Corona Del Mar CA 92625

TURNER, A RICHARD
HISTORIAN, EDUCATOR
b New Bedford, Mass, July 28, 32. *Study:* Princeton Univ, PhD, 59. *Pos:* Chairperson, Inst Fine Arts, New York, 79- *Teaching:* Prof Renaissance art, Princeton Univ, 60-68; prof & chmn Renaissance art, Middlebury Col, Vt, 68-75; pres & prof art, Grinnell Col, 75-79. *Mem:* Col Art Asn Am. *Res:* Historiography and criticism of Renaissance art. *Publ:* Auth, The Vision of Landscape in Renaissance Italy, Princeton, 66 & 73. *Mailing Add:* Inst Fine Arts 1 E 78th St New York NY 10021

TURNER, ALAN
PAINTER, PRINTMAKER
b New York, NY, July 6, 43. *Study:* City Col New York, BA, 65; Univ Calif, Berkeley, MA(painting), 67. *Comn:* Lithograph, Kunstvereine, Hamburg, Ger, 71. *Exhib:* Whitney Mus Am Art Biennial Exhib, 75; Am Acad & Inst Arts & Letts, New York, 78; Nobe Gallery, New York, 78; Edward Thorp Gallery, New York, 79; Minneapolis Inst Art, 79; one-man show, Edward Thorp Gallery, New York, 79. *Awards:* Univ Calif Alumni Asn Traveling Fel, 67; Eisner Award for Painting, Univ Calif, 67; Nat Endowment Arts Individual Fel Grant, 77. *Bibliog:* Ellen Edwards (auth), Tracing trends in narrative images, Miami Herald, 12/29/78. *Media:* Oil. *Publ:* Auth, Etchings, Parasol Press, 78. *Mailing Add:* c/o Brooke Alexander 20 W 57th St New York NY 10019

TURNER, (CHARLES) ARTHUR
PAINTER, INSTRUCTOR
b Houston, Tex, Nov 17, 40. *Study:* NTex State Univ, BA, 62; Cranbrook Acad Art, Bloomfield Hills, Mich, MFA, 66, with Zoltan Shepeshy. *Work:* Mus Fine Arts, Houston; McNay Art Inst, San Antonio; The Galleries, Cranbrook Acad Art; Beaumont Art Mus, Tex; Am Tel & Tel Co, New York; and others. *Exhib:* Dallas Mus Fine Art, 71; one-man show, Moody Gallery, Houston, 78 & Patricia Moore Gallery, Aspen, 83; Recent Acquisitions, Mus Fine Arts, Houston, 78; Five Artists from Texas, George Belcher Gallery, San Francisco, 79; Moody Gallery Exhib, Linda Durham Gallery, Santa Fe, NMex, 81; Houston Artists Exhib, Stavanger Mus, Norway, 82; and others. *Teaching:* Asst prof painting, Madison Col (Va), 66-68; instr painting, Sch Art, Mus Fine Arts, Houston, 69-; guest instr, Univ Houston, 73. *Awards:* Second Award, Southwestern Watercolor Soc 7th Ann, 71; First Purchase Award, Beaumont Art Mus 20th Ann, 71; First Award, Art Found Ann, Art Mus South Tex, 73. *Bibliog:* Richard Hutchens (auth), Arthur Turner--painter, Forum, summer 68; Arthur Turner, Facets, 6/69; Edwy B Lee (auth), Arthur Turner, drawings, Art Voices/South, 3/78. *Mem:* Tex Fine Arts Asn; Tex Watercolor Soc; Col Art Asn Am. *Media:* Colored Pencil, Watercolor. *Dealer:* Moody Gallery 2015 W Gray Houston TX 77019. *Mailing Add:* 2419 Julian Houston TX 77009

TURNER, BRUCE BACKMAN
PAINTER
b Worcester, Mass, Oct 28, 41. *Work:* Sloan-Kettering Cancer Ctr, New York; Cheshire Pub Libr, Conn; also pvt collections throughout the US. *Exhib:* North Shore Arts Asn Ann, East Gloucester, Mass, 72; 2nd Greater New Orleans Nat Exhib, La, 72; Attleboro Mus Ann, Mass, 75; Am Fortnight Exhib, Hong Kong, China, 75; Mainstreams, Marietta Col, Ohio, 76; and many others. *Teaching:* Pvt classes oil painting, Rockport, Mass, 71-72. *Awards:* Shumaker Award, Rockport Art Asn, Mass, 76; Seley Purchase Prize, 76 & Arthur T Hill Mem, 79, Salmagundi Club, New York; plus many others. *Mem:* Am Artists Prof League; Rockport Art Asn; North Shore Arts Asn; Acad Artists Asn; Salmagundi Club. *Media:* Oil. *Mailing Add:* 4 Story St Rockport MA 01966

TURNER, DAVID
MUSEUM DIRECTOR, EDUCATOR
b Houston, Tex, Dec 1, 48. *Study:* Southern Methodist Univ, Dallas, BBA, 71; Univ Ore, Eugene, MA, 74. *Collections Arranged:* Approaches to Photography (auth, catalog), 79; Amarillo Earthworks, 81; Native American Paintings, 81; Touring the World (auth, catalog), 81; Early French Moderns, (auth, catalog), 82. *Pos:* Asst registrar, Mus Fine Arts, Houston, Tex, 71-72; cur educ, Amarillo Art Ctr, Tex, 77-80, dir, 80- *Teaching:* Instr art hist & photog, Umpqua Community Col, Roseburg, Ore, 74-77. *Mem:* Am Asn Mus; Tex Asn Mus; Soc Photog Educ. *Publ:* Auth & ed, American Images (video tape), 79 & auth, Amarillo Landmarks, 81, Amarillo Art Ctr; auth, Jack Boynton, Artspace, 81. *Mailing Add:* PO Box 447 Amarillo TX 79178

TURNER, EVAN HOPKINS
MUSEUM DIRECTOR
b Orono, Maine, Nov 8, 27. *Study:* Harvard Univ, AB, MA & PhD; Sir George Williams Univ, hon LHD, 65; Swarthmore Col, hon LHD, 67; Temple Univ, hon DL, 74. *Pos:* Lectr & res asst, Frick Collection, New York, 53-56; gen cur & asst dir, Wadsworth Atheneum, Hartford, Conn, 55-59; dir, Mont Mus Fine Arts, 59-64; dir, Philadelphia Mus Art, 64-77; dir, Ackland Art Mus, 78- *Teaching:* Adj prof art hist, Univ Pa, 70-78; adj prof art hist, Univ NC, Chapel Hill, 78- *Mem:* Am Asn Mus; Asn Art Mus Dirs ((pres, 75-76); Benjamin Franklin fel Royal Soc Arts; Am Fedn Arts (bd mem). *Res:* Thomas Eakins; 19th century American sculpture. *Mailing Add:* 103 E Queen St Hillsborough NC 27278

TURNER, JAMES THOMAS, SR
SCULPTOR, PAINTER
b Denver, Colo, Mar 15, 33. *Study:* Famous Artist Course; Western Brass & Foundry; also sculpture with Edgar Britton & Fritz White. *Work:* White House; Crawford State Bank, Nebr; Can Bank Seattle; in pvt collection of John Wayne & Sen Fred Harris, Okla. *Comn:* Seven Days of Creation (wood carved door), Cath Church, Fairplay, Colo, 71; Four Horsemen of the Apocalypse (door), Four Horsemen Art Gallery, Fairplay, 72; Bronze busts of founders, Pro-Rodeo Hall of Fame, Colorado Springs, 79-80; Rose Mem Hosp, Denver, 82; Kellogg Corp Headquarters, Denver, 84. *Exhib:* Pacific Northwest Indian Ctr, Spokane, Wash, 73; Death Valley Days, Calif, 74; C M Russell Art Auction & Sale, Great Falls, Mont, 74; Miniature Painters, Engravers & Sculptors Soc, 74; Calif Int Artist of the Year, 74; Golden West Art Show, Merchandise Mart, Denver, 80; Festivals of the Masters, Orlando, Fla, 82. *Bibliog:* Steve Cady (auth), A Casting for the President, Channel 7 TV, Denver, 71-72; 100 Years of Western Art, Channel 6, Denver; Patricia Janis Broder (auth), Bronzes of the American West, Abrams, 74. *Mem:* Denver Art Mus; Am Fedn Arts; Artists Equity. *Dealer:* Gallery A Taos NM 87571; Byran & Scott Jewelers Ltd 112 N Tejon Colorado Springs CO 80903. *Mailing Add:* 5930 Coal Mine Rd Littleton CO 80123

TURNER, JANET E
PRINTMAKER, EDUCATOR
b Kansas City, Mo, Apr 7, 14. *Study:* Stanford Univ, AB, 36; Kansas City Art Inst, with Thomas H Benton, dipl, 41; Claremont Col, with Millard Sheets & Henry McFee, MFA, 47; Columbia Univ, EdD, 60. *Work:* Metrop Mus Art, New York; Philadelphia Mus Art, Pa; Victoria & Albert Mus, London; US Info Serv; Libr of Cong & Smithsonian Inst, Washington, DC. *Exhib:* American Painting Today, 50 & Watercolors & Prints, 52, Metrop Mus Art, New York; Ninth Nat Exhib, Libr of Cong, Washington, DC, 51; Nat Acad Design, New York, 61; 4th Int Bordighera Biennale, Italy; 7th Int Print Biennale, Cracow, Poland. *Teaching:* Instr art, Girl's Collegiate Sch, 42-47; asst prof art, Stephen F Austin State Col, 47- 56; from asst prof to prof art, Calif State Univ, Chico, 59-80, prof emer, 80- *Awards:* Guggenheim Fel, 53; Cannon Prize, Nat Acad Design, 61; Outstanding Prof Award, Calif State Univ & Col System, 75. *Mem:* Academician Nat Acad Design; Soc Am Graphic Artists; Nat Asn Women Artists; Am Color Print Soc; Nat Serigraph Soc (pres, 57-59, vpres, 59-62). *Media:* Intaglio, Serigraph. *Dealer:* Gump's 250 Post San Francisco CA 94108; Assoc Am Artists Inc 663 5th Ave New York NY 10022. *Mailing Add:* 567 E Lassen Sp 701 Chico CA 95926

TURNER, JANICE KAY
DEALER
b Muskegon, Mich, May 8, 38. *Study:* Ray-Vogue Sch Design; Otis Art Inst; also painting with Mitsumi Kanemitsu & drawing with Charles White. *Pos:* Co-owner, Janus Gallery, currently. *Teaching:* Instr gallery practices, Univ Southern Calif, 81-83. *Bibliog:* Laurie Gottlieb (auth), article, Home Mag, Los Angeles Times, 1/75. *Mem:* Artists Equity; Friends Fine Art, Univ Southern Calif; Mod & Contemp Arts Coun. *Specialty:* Contemporary paintings, sculpture & artists furniture. *Mailing Add:* Janus Gallery 8000 Melrose Los Angeles CA 90046

TURNER, NORMAN HUNTINGTON
PAINTER, WRITER
b Storm Lake, Iowa, July 11, 39. *Study:* Univ Colo, 57-58; Univ Iowa, 58-60; New York Studio Sch, 64-65; Empire State Col, BA, 79; Painting Fel, NJ State Coun Arts, 80. *Exhib:* Drawing Each Other, Brooklyn Mus, 71; one-man shows, Green Mountain Gallery, 72-75 & Ingber Gallery, 77 & 79, New York; New Paintings from the Del Water Gap, Hopper House Nyak, 77; Younger Artists' Choice Mus, 83; Painted Light Artists' Choice Mus, 83; and others. *Pos:* Critic, Arts Mag, 77- *Teaching:* Instr painting & drawing, Artists Environment Found, 78-79, artist-in-residence, 78-; adj lectr, Queens Col, spring 82 & 83; instr painting, New York Studio Sch, 82- *Bibliog:* Lawrence Campbell (auth), rev in Art News, 11/72; Laura Schwartz (auth), rev, 2/73, Ellen Lubell (auth), rev, 4/75 & Allen Ellenzweig (auth), rev, 4/77, Arts Mag; Jed Perl (auth), rev, Art in Am, 5-6/77. *Media:* Oil on Canvas, Drawing. *Publ:* Auth, Subjective curvature in late Cezanne, Art Bulletin, 12/81; auth, Painterly landscape, Arts, 4/82. *Mailing Add:* 1012 Park Ave Hoboken NJ 07030

TURNER, RALPH JAMES
SCULPTOR, GRAPHIC ARTIST
b Ashland, Ore, Oct 24, 35. *Study:* Reed Col, with calligrapher, Lloyd Reynolds, BA, 58; Portland Art Mus Sch, with painter, Louis Bunce, dipl, 58; Portland State Col, 59; Univ Ore, with Jan Zach & Gerald di Guisto, MFA(sculpture), 62; Univ Ariz, 65, 72 & 73. *Work:* Catalina Observatory, Univ Ariz, Tucson; Flandrau Planetarium, Tucson; Hayden Planetarium, New York; Nat Aeronautical & Space Admin-Ames, San Francisco; Phoenix (five ft limestone), Syracuse Univ, NY, 66. *Comn:* Jupiter (two planetary models), NASA/Ames, Mt View, Calif, 74 & 76; Dr Gerard Kuiper (bronze bust), Univ Ariz, 75; Phobos (planetary model), Smithsonian Inst, 78; Seer (marble carving), M & J Shapiro, Beverly Hills, Calif, 80; mural of athletes, Multnomah Athletic Club, Portland, Ore, 81; four northwest Indian motif wood carvings, Myland Hills Ctr, Beaverton, Ore, 82; and others. *Exhib:* Ralph J Turner, Sculpture, Tucson Art Ctr, 63 & Univ Ariz, Tucson, 64; three-man exhib, Space & Art, Rainbow Gallery, Cannon Beach, Ore, 76; Planets & Progs: A Retrospective, Delphian Found, Sheridan, Ore, 77 & Willamette Sci & Technol Ctr, Eugene, 77; Hexagon Galaxies, Delphian Found, 80; Electro Arts Gallery, San Francisco, 81. *Pos:* Res assoc planetary models, Lunar & Planetary Lab, Univ Ariz, Tucson, 64-73; co-dir/designer, Rock Creek Experimental Sta, 73- *Teaching:* Instr sculpture, Univ Ariz, Tucson, 62-65; asst prof design & drawing, Syracuse Univ, NY, 66-69; art coordr graphics, humanities & sculpture, Pima Col, Tucson, 70-72. *Awards:* Nat Endowment Humanities Fel, 72-73. *Bibliog:* Sculpture by Ralph J Turner, NW Rev, Univ Ore, 63; Alexander Schmeckebier (auth), Murals & sculpture on the campus of Syracuse University, Syracuse Univ Art Mus, 68; Fred Crafts (auth), Is it art or science, Eugene Register Guard, 77. *Media:* Stone, Wood; Acrylic on Plexiglas. *Publ:* Auth, The Northeast Rim of Tycho, Lunar & Planetary Commun, 70; auth, Extraterrestrial landscapes through the eyes of a sculptor, Leonardo, 72; auth, A model of the eastern portion of Schroter's Valley, Lunar & Planetary Commun, 73; auth, A model of Phobos, Icarus, Cornell Univ, 78; auth, Modeling and mapping Phobos, Sky & telescope, 77-78. *Mailing Add:* Rte 2 Box 167 Sheridan OR 97378

TURNER, RAYMOND
SCULPTOR
b Milwaukee, Wis, May 25, 03. *Study:* Milwaukee Art Inst; Layton Sch Art; Wis State Univ; Beaux Arts Inst, New York. *Work:* Ft Wadsworth, Staten Island, NY; Smithsonian Inst, Washington, DC; Baseball Hall of Fame, Cooperstown, NY. *Comn:* Commemorative coins of Fats Waller, Am Negro Commemorative Soc, 70, Theodore Roosevelt, Int Fraternal Commemorative Soc, 70, Emily Dickinson, Soc Commemorative Femmes Celebres, 70, Eddie Rickenbacker, Nat Commemorative Soc, 73 & Evacuation of Boston by British, American Bicentennial Commemorative Soc, 76; and others. *Exhib:* Detroit Art Inst, 27; Salon Aulomne, Paris, 28; Pa Acad Fine Arts, Philadelphia, 40; Nat Acad Design, New York, 67; Nat Sculpture Soc, New York, 72; Sports of the Olympics, Nat Art Mus of Sport, New York, 72; New York City WPA Art Exhib, Parsons Sch of Design, 77. *Awards:* August Helbig Prize, Detroit Art Inst, 27; Guggenheim Found Fel, 28; Pauline Law Prize, Allied Artists Am, 66. *Mem:* Fel Nat Sculpture Soc. *Media:* Wood, Bronze. *Mailing Add:* 51 Seventh Ave S New York NY 10014

TURNER, ROBERT CHAPMAN
CERAMIST, EDUCATOR
b Port Washington, NY, July 22, 13. *Study:* Swarthmore Col, BA; Pa Acad Fine Arts; State Univ NY Col Ceramics, Alfred Univ, MFA. *Work:* Dienst Beeldende Kunst, Hertogenbusch, Netherlands; St Louis Mus Art; Smithsonian Inst, Washington, DC; Los Angeles Co Fair Asn; Philadelphia Mus Art. *Exhib:* Nat Mus Art, Buenos Aires, Arg, 63; Victoria & Albert Mus, London, Eng, 72; Boston Mus Fine Arts, 74; one-man exhibs, Alta Col Art, Calgary, 74; Florence Duhl Gallery, New York, NY, 78, Helen Drutt Gallery, Philadelphia, 80 & Okun-Thomas Gallery, St Louis, 81; Exhib A, Chicago, 79 & 82. *Teaching:* Instr ceramics, Black Mountain Col, 49-51; prof ceramic art, State Univ NY Col Ceramics, Alfred Univ, 58-79, actg head div art & design, 74-76. *Awards:* Int Exhib Ceramics Silver Medal, Cannes, France, 54; Silver Medal, Third Int Cong Contemp Ceramics, Prague, Czech, 62; Ceramic Art USA Award, 66; State Univ NY Chancellor's Award for excellence in teaching, 74. *Bibliog:* Daniel Rhodes (auth), Robert Turner, 57 & Howard Yana Shapiro (auth), Bob Turner, 72, Craft Horizons. *Mem:* Hon mem Nat Coun Educ Ceramic Arts; fel Am Crafts Coun; Int Acad Ceramics, Geneva, Switz. *Media:* Clay. *Publ:* Auth, Born remembering, Studio Potter, 6/82. *Dealer:* Exhibit A 361 W Superior Chicago IL 60610. *Mailing Add:* Cook Rd Box 121 Alfred Station NY 14803

TURNER, THEODORE ROY
PAINTER, EDUCATOR

b Frederick Hall, Va, Jan 10, 22. *Study:* Richmond Prof Inst, Col William & Mary, BFA, 43; New Sch Social Res, New York, painting with Abraham Rattner & printmaking with Louis Shanker, 46-50; NY Univ Inst Fine Arts, MA, 50. *Work:* New York Pub Libr Print Collection; Va Mus Fine Arts, Richmond; Miss Art Asn, Jackson; Dartmouth Col, Hanover, NH; Univ Va, Charlottesville. *Exhib:* Brooklyn Mus Print Ann, 51 & 55; Am Fedn Arts Traveling Exhib Prints, 55; Va Mus Biennials, 59, 67 & 71; Watercolor USA, Springfield, Mo, 64; one-man shows, Babcock Galleries, New York, 68 & 69. *Teaching:* Instr medieval archit, Dartmouth Col, 50-52; assoc prof painting, Univ Va, 52-, actg chmn, McIntire Dept Fine Arts, 62-67; vis artists, Roanoke Fine Arts Ctr, Va, 71. *Awards:* Cert Distinction & Purchase Award, Va Mus Fine Arts, 59; Purchase Award, 20th Watercolor Nat, Miss Art Asn, 61; Painting Award, 18th Irene Leache Mem, Norfolk Mus, 66. *Bibliog:* Sue Dickinson (auth), Theodore Turner, Richmond Times-Dispatch, 6/23/68; Theodore Turner article, New York Mag, 6/24/68; Larry Campbell (auth), Theodore Turner's watercolors, Art News, 12/69. *Mem:* Va Ctr Creative Arts (adv bd, 71-72). *Media:* Watercolor, Oil. *Dealer:* Babcock Galleries 20 East 67th St New York NY 10021. *Mailing Add:* 916 Old Farm Rd Charlottesville VA 22903

TURNER, WILLIAM EUGENE
PAINTER, EDUCATOR

b Dallas, Tex, Oct 15, 28. *Study:* Southern Methodist Univ, BA, 52; Univ NMex, summer 53; La State Univ, MA, 54. *Work:* Portsmouth Arts Ctr, Va; Arkansas Arts Ctr, Little Rock; Atlantic Richfield Corp, Dallas, Tex & Anchorage, Alaska. *Comn:* Hallway murals for Dallas Middle & High Sch (with Bill Hendricks, archit), comn by STB Archit & Planners, Tex, 77. *Exhib:* Drawing Invitational, Emporia State Univ, Kans, 82; Smithsonian Inst traveling exhib, 82-83; Art in the Metroplex, Tex Christian Univ, Ft Worth, 83; Delta States Art Ann, Ark Art Ctr, Little Rock, 83; Works on Paper, SW Tex State Univ, San Marcos, 83; Works on Paper, Rutgers Univ, Camden, NJ, 83. *Teaching:* Prof painting & design, Univ Tex, Arlington, 1959- *Awards:* Purchase Awards, Works on Paper, Portsmouth Art Ctr, 82 & Delta States Exhib, Ark Art Ctr, 83. *Mem:* Col Art Asn. *Media:* Oil, Pencil. *Mailing Add:* 1116 Mockingbird Lane Arlington TX 76013

TURNURE, JAMES HARVEY
EDUCATOR, HISTORIAN

b Yonkers, NY, July 8, 24. *Study:* Princeton Univ, AB, MFA(art hist), PhD. *Teaching:* Instr, Cornell Univ, Ithaca, NY, 53-58, asst prof, 58-64, assoc prof, 64-68; prof, Bucknell Univ, Lewisburg, Pa, 69-, Samuel H Kress Prof art hist, 74- *Mem:* Col Art Asn Am; Archcol Inst Am; Ist per la Storia Dell'arte Lombarda. *Res:* Interpretation of evidence in archaeology and art history. *Publ:* Auth, Statuette of Imhotep, Rec of Art Mus, 52 & Princeton's enigmatic relief, 63, Princeton Univ; auth, Late style of Ambrogio Figino, Art Bulletin, 65; auth, Etruscan ritual armor..., Am J Archaeol, 65; contribr, Il Duomo di Milano, Edizioni La Rete, 69. *Mailing Add:* RD 1 Box 398A Lewisburg PA 17837

TUROFF, MURIEL PARGH
SCULPTOR, PAINTER

b Odessa, Russia, Mar 1, 04; US citizen. *Study:* Art Students League; Pratt Inst; Univ Colo. *Work:* Smithsonian Inst Portrait Gallery, Washington, DC; Jewish Mus, New York. *Comn:* Enamel on copper artifacts, St James Lutheran Church, Coral Gables, Fla, 74. *Exhib:* Mus Natural Hist, New York, 58; Cooper Union Mus, New York, 60; Lowe Mus Beaux Arts, Miami, Fla, 68; YM-YWHA, Miami, Fla, 71; Bacardi Gallery, Miami, 76. *Teaching:* Instr art & ceramics, Riverdale Neighborhood House, New York, 43-47; instr ceramics in occupational therapy, Vet Hosp, Bronx, 45-46; instr basic design, Westchester Co Ctr, NY, 59-61; instr enamelling, Miami Art Ctr, 70-75. *Awards:* Blue Ribbon for best in show, Blue Dome Art Fel, 66 & 73; Second Prize, YM-YWHA, 71. *Mem:* Artists Equity Asn; Fla Sculptors; Blue Dome Art Fel (treas, 64-68); Fla Craftsmen. *Media:* Metal, Enamel. *Publ:* Auth, How to Make Pottery, Crown, 49. *Mailing Add:* 517 Gerona Ave Coral Gables FL 33146

TURRELL, JAMES ARCHIE
ENVIRONMENTAL ARTIST, SCULPTOR

b Los Angeles, Calif, May 6, 43. *Study:* Pomona Col, BA, 65; Univ Calif, Irvine, 65-66; Claremont Grad Sch, MA, 73. *Work:* Stedelijk Mus, Amsterdam, Holland; Villa Panza, Varese, Italy; Chase Manhattan Bank, New York. *Comn:* Roden Crater, Ariz, Dia Art Found, New York. *Exhib:* Lichtprojecties En Lichtruimten, Stedelijk Mus, Amsterdam, 76; Light Space, Arco Ctr for Visual Art, Los Angeles, 76; one-man shows, Pasadena Art Mus, 67 & Stedelijk Mus, 76; Light Installation, Mus Art, Univ Ariz, Tucson, 80; Light and Space, Whitney Mus, New York, 80; and others. *Awards:* Nat Endowment for the Arts, 68; Guggenheim, 74. *Bibliog:* Calvin Tomkins (auth), The talk of the town-light, New Yorker, 12/15/80; Robert Hughes (auth), Poetry out of emptiness, Time Mag, 1/5/81; Nancy Marmer (auth), James Turrell: The art of deception, Art in Am, 5/81; and others. *Dealer:* Flow Ace Gallery 185 Windward Ave Venice CA 90291. *Mailing Add:* Box 725 Flagstaff AZ 86002

TUTTLE, RICHARD
PAINTER

b Rahway, NJ. *Study:* Trinity Col, Conn; Cooper Union. *Work:* James A Michener Found; Nat Gallery, Can; Corcoran Gallery Art, Washington, DC; Kaiser-Wilhelm Mus, Ger; plus other pub & pvt collections. *Exhib:* One-man shows, Galeria Schmela, Dusseldorf, 68, Nicholas Wilder Gallery, Los Angeles, 69, Albright-Knox Art Gallery, Buffalo, 70, Mus Fine Art, Dallas, 71 & Mus Mod Art, New York, 72; Anti Illusion: Procedures/Materials, Whitney Mus Am Art, 69; Corcoran Gallery Art 31st Biennial, 69; Soft Art, NJ State Mus, 69; Am Paintings of 60's, Am Fedn Arts, 69; Documenta, Kassel, WGer, 72; retrospective, Whitney Mus Am Art, 75; and others. *Bibliog:* The avant garde: subtle, cerebral, elusive, Time, 11/2/68; This is the loose paint generation, Nat Observer, 8/4/69; Robert Pincus-Witten (auth), The art of Richard Tuttle, Artforum, 2/70; and many others. *Publ:* Contribr, Art Int. *Mailing Add:* c/o Jack Tilton Gallery 24 W 57th St New York NY 10019

TWARDOWICZ, STANLEY JAN
PAINTER, PHOTOGRAPHER

b Detroit, Mich, July 8, 17. *Study:* Meinzinger Art Sch, Detroit, 40-44; Skowhegan Sch Painting & Sculpture, Maine, summers 46 & 47. *Work:* Mus Mod Art, New York; Los Angeles Co Mus Art; NY Univ; Fogg Art Mus; Vassar Col Art Gallery. *Exhib:* Art Inst Chicago, 54, 55 & 61; five exhibs, Mus Mod Art, 57-69; Mus Fine Arts, Boston, 66; one-man shows, Peridot Gallery, New York, 56-70; retrospective, Heckscher Mus, Huntington, NY, 74; 30 Yr Retrospective Photog, Emily Lowe Gallery, Hempstead, NY, 79. *Teaching:* Instr art, Ohio State Univ, 46-51; assoc prof art, Hofstra Univ, 65- *Awards:* Guggenheim Found Fel, 56-57. *Mailing Add:* 57 Main St Northport NY 11768

TWAROGOWSKI, LEROY ANDREW
DRAFTSMAN, EDUCATOR

b Chicago, Ill, Sept 12, 37. *Study:* Art Inst Chicago, 55-59; Univ Kans, Lawrence, BFA, 61, MFA, 65. *Work:* Denver Art Mus, Colo; Ft Hays State Univ, Hays, Kans; Hastings Col, Nebr; US Nat Bank, Omaha, Nebr; Mountain Bell Corp, Denver, Colo. *Comn:* Colo Coun Arts & Humanities, 78. *Exhib:* Second All-Colo Competitive Exhib, Denver Art Mus, 74; 2nd Brit Int Drawing Biennale, Middlesbrough, Eng, 75; Drawings USA/75 Biennale, Minn Mus of Art, St Paul, 75; Spree/Colo Celebration of the Arts, Denver, 76; Rocky Mountain Drawing & Painting Exhib, Aspen Found for the Arts, Colo, 77; Denver Art Mus, 78. *Teaching:* Prof drawing, Colo State Univ, 67- *Media:* Graphite. *Dealer:* Frumkin & Struve Chicago IL. *Mailing Add:* 1501 Welch St Ft Collins CO 80521

TWIGGS, LEO FRANKLIN
PAINTER, EDUCATOR

b St Stephen, SC, Feb 13, 34. *Study:* Claflin Col, Orangeburg, SC; Art Inst Chicago; NY Univ, with Jason Seley & Hale Woodruff; Univ Ga, with Sam Adler. *Work:* Johnson Publ Co, Chicago; Spring Mills, New York; Wachovia Bank & Trust Co, NC; City of Atlanta, Ga; Herbert F Johnson Mus, Cornell Univ. *Exhib:* Sch Art & Archit, Univ Cincinnati, 70; Nat Exhib Black Artists, Washington, DC, 71; Artists USA, Carnegie Inst Int, Pittsburgh, 71; Salute to Black Artists, NJ State Mus, Trenton, 72; Directions in Afro-American Art, Cornell Univ, 74; Studio Mus, New York, NY. *Pos:* Exec dir, Stanback Mus & Planetarium. *Teaching:* Prof art, SC State Col, Orangeburg, currently. *Awards:* Award of Distinction, Smith Mason Gallery, 71; Merit Prize, Guild SC Artists, 75; Governor's Trophy, 80. *Bibliog:* Thomas W Leavitt (auth), Directions in Afro-American art, Cornell Univ, 75; E Fax (auth), Black Artists of the New Generation, 78; M Carnell (auth), article in Art Craft Mag, 79; and others. *Mem:* Col Art Asn Am; Nat Art Educ Asn; Nat Conf Artists (chmn, educ div, 72); Guild SC Artists (vpres, 72); SC Mus Comn. *Publ:* Auth, articles in Explor Educ, 70, Design Mag, 72, Negro Educ Rev, 72, Sch Arts, 72 & Mus News, 72. *Mailing Add:* PO Box 1691 SC State Col Orangeburg SC 29117

TWIGGS, RUSSELL GOULD
PAINTER

b Sandusky, Ohio, Apr 29, 1898. *Study:* Carnegie-Mellon Univ. *Work:* Whitney Mus Am Art, New York; Wadsworth Atheneum, Hartford, Conn; Mus Art, Carnegie Inst Int, Pittsburgh; Brooklyn Mus, NY; Westmoreland Co Mus Art, Greensburg, Pa. *Exhib:* Abstract & Surrealist Painting, Art Inst Chicago, 47; Whitney Mus Am Art Ann, 55; five Carnegie Inst Int, 55-67; Mus Mod Art Drawing Show, 56; Corcoran Gallery Art, Washington, DC, 57. *Pos:* Massier, Carnegie-Mellon Univ, 24- *Awards:* Carnegie Inst Group Prize, Assoc Artists Pittsburgh, 49; Second Prize Painting, Cincinnati Art Mus, 55; Mrs Henry J Heinz, II Award, 62. *Bibliog:* Paul Lancaster (auth), The artist, Wall St J, 57; Connie Kienzle (auth), Russell Twiggs, Roto-Pittsburgh Press, 71. *Mem:* Pittsburgh Plan Art. *Media:* Acrylic. *Dealer:* Pittsburgh Plan for Art 1251 N Negley Ave Pittsburgh PA 15206. *Mailing Add:* 652 Maryland Ave Pittsburgh PA 15232

TWITTY, JAMES (WATSON)
PAINTER, PRINTMAKER

b Mt Vernon, NY, Apr 13, 16. *Study:* Art Students League, with Edwin Dickenson, Stephen Greene & Morris Kantor; Univ Miami, with Xavier Gonzalez & Eliot O'Hara. *Work:* Nat Gallery Art & Corcoran Gallery Art, Washington, DC; Brooklyn Mus, NY; Baltimore Mus Art, Md; Mus Fine Art, Dallas; plus others. *Exhib:* One-man shows, Corcoran Gallery Art, 66, David Findlay Galleries, New York, 71, 73-74, 76, 78 & 81, George Washington Univ, 75, Hokin Gallery, Chicago, 76, Bettina Gallery, Zurich & Pollock Gallery, Ont, Can, 81; plus others. *Teaching:* Assoc prof painting, Corcoran Sch Art, 64-74; lectr fine arts, George Washington Univ, 64-74; exchange prof painting, Leeds Col Art, Eng, 67-68; vis prof painting, Miami Art Ctr, Fla, 70; vis prof painting, San Antonio Art Inst, Tex, 72. *Awards:* Allied Artists Am Award, 61; Soc Wash Art Award, 65; First Ann Exhib Award, Miami, 66. *Bibliog:* Frank Getlein (auth), A Washington artist in a New York setting, Washington DC Star-News, 73. *Mem:* Life mem Art Students League; Am Soc Painters & Sculptors. *Media:* Acrylic, Silkscreen. *Dealer:* David Findlay Jr Galleries 41 E 57 New York NY 10022. *Mailing Add:* 1600 South Eads St Apt 1234-S Arlington VA 22202

TWOMBLY, CY
PAINTER
b Lexington, Va, Apr 25, 28. *Study:* Boston Mus Sch Fine Arts, 48-49; Washington & Lee Univ, 50; Art Students League, 51; Black Mountain Col, with Frank Kline & Robert Motherwell, 52. *Work:* RI Sch Design; Mus Mod Art, Whitney Mus Am Art, New York; also pvt collections in New York, Chicago, Washington, DC & Europe. *Exhib:* Whitney Mus Am Art Ann, New York, 67; Herron Inst Art, Indianapolis, 69; Guggenheim Mus, New York, 76; Mus Mod Art, 76; Galerie Klewan, Munich, 78; Heiner Friedrich Inc, New York, 78; Lucio Amerilio Gallery, Naples, 79; Galleriet Lund, 79; Galerie Karsten Greve, Cologne, 79; and others. *Teaching:* Head dept art, Southern Sem & Jr Col, Buena Vista, Va, 55-56. *Awards:* Va Mus Fine Arts Fel for Travel in Europe & Africa, 52-53. *Bibliog:* Pierre Restany (auth), Lyrisme et Abstraction, Edizioni Apollinairi, Milan, 60. *Mailing Add:* c/o Leo Castelli Gallery 420 W Broadway New York NY 10013

TYKIE (SYLVIA SQUIRES GANZ)
PAINTER
b Southampton, Long Island, NY, Oct 8, 32. *Study:* Cortland State Univ, 51-53; also with Helen A Del Grosso, 70-71. *Comn:* Paintings, First Federal Savings Loan, Delray Beach, Fla, 79 & 81. *Exhib:* Henry Morrison Flagler Mus, Palm Beach, Fla, 76; Nat Miniature Art Exhib, Nutley Savings & Loan Asn, NJ, 77-81; Nat Miniature Art Soc Fla Exhib, Kapok Tree, Clearwater, 77-81; Nat Painters, Sculptors & Gravers Soc, Arts Club, Washington, DC, 78-81; Nat Ann Miniature Art Exhib, Gallery La Luz, NMex, 79-81; Smithsonian Inst. *Awards:* Founders Award for Best Painting, 45th Ann Exhib Miniature Painters, Sculptors & Gravers Soc, Washington, DC, 78; First Acrylic, Nat Miniature Show, La Luz, NMex, 80; Best in Show, Del Ray Art League, 81. *Mem:* Assoc Miniature Painters, Sculptors & Gravers Soc, Washington, DC; Miniature Art Soc NJ; Miniature Art Soc Fla; Del Ray Art League. *Media:* Acrylic. *Mailing Add:* 10290 Seagrape Way Palm Beach Gardens FL 33410

TYLER, KENNETH EUGENE
PRINT PUBLISHER, PRINTMAKER
b East Chicago, Ind, Dec 13, 31. *Study:* Art Inst Chicago, 49-52, BAE, 57; Ind Univ, 51-52; Chicago Univ, 55-57; John Herron Sch Art, MAE, 63. *Work:* Mus of Mod Art, New York; Los Angeles Co Mus of Art, Los Angeles; San Diego Mus; Walker Art Ctr; Nat Mus of Australia, Camberra. *Pos:* Tech dir, Tamarind Lithography Workshop, 64-65; dir, Gemini GEL, 66-73; dir, Tyler Graphics Ltd, 74- *Teaching:* Teacher art & theatre & scene shop dir, Evanston Township High Sch, 57-58. *Awards:* Ford Grant, 63; grant, Nat Coun on Visual Arts for Res & Develop Work in Lithography, 67. *Bibliog:* Gemini GEL, Mus of Mod Art, New York, 70; Reaching Out: Master Printer Kenneth Tyler (16mm color film, 35 minutes), Avery/Tirce Productions, 74; Judith Goldman (auth), Art Off the Picture Press--Tyler Graphics Ltd, Hofstra Univ, 77. *Mailing Add:* PO Box 294 Bedford NY 10506

TYLER, RON C
CURATOR, HISTORIAN
b Temple, Tex, Dec 29, 41. *Study:* Abilene Christian Col, BS(educ), 64; Tex Christian Univ MA, 66, PhD, 68. *Collections Arranged:* The Wild West, Amon Carter Mus Western Art, 70; The Big Bend (auth, catalog), 75; The Image of America in Caricature & Cartoon (auth, catalog), 75; Posada's Mexico (ed, catalog), 79; Alfred Jacob Miller: Artist on the Oregon Trail (ed, catalog), 82. *Pos:* Asst dir collections & prog, Amon Carter Mus Western Art, 69- *Res:* 19th century American art and photography; Mexican art and printmakers. *Publ:* Auth, The Mexican War: A Lithographic Record, Tex State Hist Asn, 73; auth, The Rodeo Photographs of John A Stryker, Encino Press, 78; auth, Visions of America: Pioneer Artists in a New Land, Thames & Hudson, 83. *Mailing Add:* c/o Amon Carter Mus Western Art PO Box 2365 Ft Worth TX 76113

TYLER, VALTON
PRINTMAKER, PAINTER
b Texas City, Tex, Mar 30, 44. *Study:* Dallas Art Inst, Tex, 67. *Work:* Tyler Mus Art, Tex. *Exhib:* First Fifty Prints, Pollock Galleries, Southern Methodist Univ, Dallas & Tyler Mus Art, 72; 8th Ann New Talent in Printmaking, Assoc Am Artists, New York, 72; one-man shows, Galerie Claude Jongen, Brussels, Belg, 77 & Vallery House Gallery, Dallas, 79. *Bibliog:* Reynolds (auth), The fifty prints--Valton Tyler, Southern Methodist Univ Press, 72. *Media:* Aquatint; Oil on Canvas. *Publ:* Auth, Jalons et Actualites des Arts, 1/77; auth, Un Artiste de 33 Ans, Hebdomadaire, 2/24/77; auth, Ultra, 12/81. *Mailing Add:* 3525 Granada Ave Dallas TX 75205

TYSON, MARY (MRS KENNETH THOMPSON)
PAINTER
b Sewanee, Tenn, Nov 2, 09. *Study:* Grand Cent Art Sch, with George P Ennis, Howard Hildebrandt & Wayman Adams; New Sch Social Res, with Julian Levi. *Work:* Artists Asn Nantucket Permanent Collection; Guild Hall Collection; Monterey Peninsula Mus, Carmel, Calif. *Exhib:* Int Exhib, Brooklyn Mus, 35 & 37; Am Watercolor Soc Ann; Nat Arts Club Watercolor Exhib, 68-81; Addison Gallery, Andover; one-woman shows, Bruce Mus, Greenwich, Conn, St Louis Mus, Bodley Gallery, New York; and others. *Awards:* Solo Award, 69; Elizabeth Morse Genius Mem Award, 70; Award, Guild Hall, East Hampton, 77; and others. *Mem:* Life mem Am Watercolor Soc; Pen & Brush Club; Easthampton Guild Hall; Nat Arts Club. *Media:* Watercolor. *Mailing Add:* 20 W 11th St New York NY 10011

TYSON, RAE JULIAN
ADMINISTRATOR, SCULPTOR
b Lockport, NY, Jan 3, 44. *Study:* Ball State Univ; Niagara Univ; Univ of Buffalo, Parsons Col, BA, 67. *Work:* H F Johnson Mus, Ithaca, NY. *Exhib:* Nat Gallery Can, Ottawa, 77; Artwords and Bookworks, Los Angeles Inst of Contemp Art, Calif, 78; Artist Books, Chicago Art Inst, 78; one-man shows, Vehicule Gallery, Montreal, 76; Hallwalls Gallery, Buffalo, 77; Marion Locks Gallery, Philadelphia, 78 & 55 Mercer Gallery, New York, 79; and others. *Pos:* Visual arts dir, Artpark, Lewiston, NY, 74-78. *Teaching:* Guest lectr contemp art, Cranbrook, RI Sch of Design, Chicago Art Inst, Walker Art Ctr, NS Col of Art & Design, plus many others, 74- *Bibliog:* Lucy R Lippard (auth), A is for Artpark, Art in Am, 74; Barbara Baracks (auth), Artpark: The New Aesthetic Playground, Artform, 76; Michael Blackwood (auth), Artpark People (film), Blackwood Productions, 77. *Mem:* Am Crafts Coun; Can Crafts Coun; Northeast Mus Asn; Col Art Asn. *Media:* Multimedia. *Publ:* Auth, Rae Tyson: Drawings, 76 & Drawings II, 78, Journeyman Press. *Mailing Add:* 511 Lake St Wilson NY 14172

TYTELL, LOUIS
PAINTER
b New York, NY, Jan 8, 13. *Study:* City Col New York, BS, 34; Columbia Univ, MA, 35; Skowhegan Sch Painting & Sculpture; New Sch Social Res. *Work:* Newark Mus; Corcoran Gallery of Art; Wickersham Gallery, Univ NC, Raleigh; Libr of Cong Print Collection, Washington, DC. *Exhib:* 110 American Painters, Walker Art Ctr, 44; Pa Acad Fine Arts Ann, 49 & 66; Nat Acad Design Ann, 62, 66 & 68; Nat Inst Arts & Lett, 67; Mus Mod Art Lending Serv Gallery, 73-78; Edward Hopper House, Nyack, NY, 78. *Teaching:* Chmn dept art, High Sch Music & Art, New York, 61-67 & 69-75; assoc prof art, City Col New York, 67-69. *Awards:* Tiffany Fel, 62; Am Inst Arts & Lett Grant, 67. *Media:* Oil, Pastel. *Dealer:* Roko Gallery 816 Broadway New York NY 10003. *Mailing Add:* 107 Green Rd West Nyack NY 10994

TYZACK, MICHAEL
PAINTER, EDUCATOR
b Sheffield, Eng, Aug 3, 33. *Study:* Sheffield Col Art & Crafts, Eng MEd(arts & crafts), 52; Slade Sch Fine Art, Univ Col, London, with Victor Pasmore, William Townsend & Anthony Gross, DFA, 55. *Work:* Tate Gallery, London, Eng; Victoria & Albert Mus, London; Sao Paulo Mus, Brazil; Peau de Lion Collection, Zurich, Switz; Indianapolis Mus Art. *Comn:* Multiple, Documenta Found, Kassell, WGer, 68; mural scale paintings, Univ Hospital Wales, Cardiff, 71; designs for proposed mural, comn by Albert Simons, Ctr for Fine Arts, Charleston, SC, 77; design for wall hanging, SC State Ports Authority, Charleston, 79. *Exhib:* New Shapes of Color, Stedelijk Mus, Amsterdam, 66-67; Documenta 4, Kassell, WGer; Troisieme Salon Int des Galeries Pilotes, Mus Cantonal des Beaux Arts, Lausanne, Switz & Mus Art Mod, Paris, France, 70; 56-Group-Wales, a 20 Yr Retrospective, Nat Mus Wales, Cardiff, 76; Art-Patron-Art, Southeast Ctr for Contemp Art, Winston Salem, NC, 79-80; and others. *Pos:* Consult, News & Courier, Charleston, SC, 79- *Teaching:* Assoc prof painting, Univ Iowa, 71-76; prof fine arts, Col Charleston, SC, 76- *Awards:* French Govt Fine Art Scholar, 56; First Prize, John Moores Liverpool Exhib 5, 65; Comn Award, Arts Coun Great Britain, 69. *Bibliog:* Edward Lucie Smith & Patricia White (auth), Art in Britain, 1969-1970, Dent, London, 71; Anthony F Janson (auth), Profile-Michael Tyzack, Art Voices South, 80. *Mem:* Artists Int Asn, London (vchmn), 64-66, exec comt, 64-68); Col Art Asn Am. *Dealer:* Frances Aronson Gallery 107 W Paces Ferry Rd NW Atlanta GA 30305. *Mailing Add:* 930 Lakeview Dr Mt Pleasant SC 29464

U

UBANS, JURIS K
PAINTER, EDUCATOR
b Riga, Latvia, July 12, 38; US citizen. *Study:* Yale Univ, with William Bailey & Bernard Chaet, 65; Syracuse Univ, BFA, 66, with Ainslee Burke & Frederick Hauck; Pa State Univ, MFA, 68, with Enrique Montenegro & Eugenio Battisti. *Work:* Yale Univ; Syracuse Univ; Pa State Univ; Univ Southern Maine; and pvt collections. *Comn:* A Season in Hell (ballet visuals), Syracuse Univ, NY, 66; Good Woman of Setzuan (teater visuals), Univ Maine, Portland-Gorham, 72; Renascence (planetarium visuals), 75 & From Morn Till Midnight (theater visuals), 76; Photography Maine 1973 (poster, catalogue & cert design), Maine State Comn on Arts & Humanities, 73. *Exhib:* Everson Mus Art, Syracuse, 66; Nat Exhib Prints & Drawings, Okla Art Ctr, Okla, 69-70; Statements in Media, Haystack Traveling Exhib, 72-73; solo shows, Univ Maine, Augusta, 74 & Univ of the South, Sewanee, Tenn, 78; First Light Traveling Show, Calif, 75-76; Grand Valley State Col, Allendale, Mich, 79; and others. *Collections Arranged:* As It Was (auth, ed, catalogue), 74, Ben Shahn-Photographs (auth & ed, catalogue), 76 & Walker-Evans-Photographs, 78, Univ Southern Maine. *Pos:* Dir art gallery, Univ Southern Maine, 68-, chmn art dept, 74-; pres bd dir, Film Study Ctr, Portland, 72- *Teaching:* From asst prof to prof painting, film, photog & drawing, Univ Southern Maine, 68-; coordr Soleri sem, Haystack Mountain Sch, Deer Isle, Maine, summer 71. *Awards:* Helen B Stoeckel Fel, Yale Univ, 66; Hiram Gee Fel, Lowe Art Ctr, Syracuse, NY, 65; Greogry Batcock Prize, Independent Filmmakers, 68. *Mem:* Col Art Asn; Nat Asn Sch Art; Am Film Inst; and others. *Media:* Oil, Mixed Media. *Mailing Add:* Dept of Art Univ of Southern Maine Gorham ME 04038

UBERTALLI, HECTOR
PAINTER, SCULPTOR
b Arg, Mar 28, 28; US citizen. *Study:* Acad Fine Arts, Buenos Aires; also with Juan Hohmann, Ana Weiss Rossi, Felix Aranguren & Carlos Alonso, Buenos Aires. *Exhib:* Palm Beach Galleries, 65-78; Hammer Galleries, New York, 75; Retrospectives, Lorenzutti Found, Buenos Aires, 79 & Norton Mus, WPalm Beach, Fla, 79; Seaview Gallery, Palm Beach, 81; and many others. *Teaching:* Pvt instr. *Bibliog:* H Adams (auth), article, Palm Beach Life, 1/72; article, Palm Beach Daily News, 4/28/74; Barbara Thoren (auth), article, Japan Times, 5/80; and others. *Mem:* Soc Four Arts; Fla Artists Group. *Media:* Acrylic. *Mailing Add:* 2919 N Dixie Hwy West Palm Beach FL 33407

UCCELLO, VINCENZA AGATHA
PAINTER, EDUCATOR
b Hartford, Conn. *Study:* St Joseph Col, BS, 56; Wesleyan Univ, Conn, MALS, 61; Villa Schifanoia, Pius XII Inst, Florence, Italy, MFA, 63; Corcoran Sch Art, with Gene Davis; State Univ Iowa, with Byron Burford. *Exhib:* Connecticut Women Artists Inc, New Britain Mus Am Art, 66; 12th Ann Drawing & Small Sculpture Exhib, Ball State Univ, 66; solo exhib, St Joseph Col, Conn, 81; Paperworks--Twelve New England Artists, Worcester Craft Ctr, Mass, 83; Sculptural Paper, Brookfield Craft Ctr, Conn, 83. *Collections Arranged:* A Collectors Choice Mem Exhib, 67, Women in Art (By Women, About Women), 69, Childe Hassam, Impressionist Printmaker, 81, American Paintings of the 1920s & 1930s, 82 & American Prints 1850-1950, 83 (auth, catalogs), St Joseph Col, Conn. *Teaching:* Instr art, Glastonbury, Conn High Sch, 57-61; assoc prof, St Joseph Col, Conn, 64-, chairperson fine arts dept & acting cur mus, 78- *Awards:* Alexander Harper Mem Award, 40th Ann Painting Exhib, Conn Women Artists Inc, 66; Yale Univ Vis Fac Fel, Mellon Found, 80; Judges Choice, Mem Exhib, Canton Artists Guild, 83. *Mem:* Col Art Asn Am; Am Craft Coun; Ctr Book Arts; Canton Artists Guild; Conn Women Artists Inc (pres, 74-76). *Media:* Miscellaneous, Handmade Paper. *Mailing Add:* 219 Penn Dr West Hartford CT 06119

UCHIMA, ANSEI
PRINTMAKER, PAINTER
b Stockton, Calif, May 1, 21. *Work:* Art Inst Chicago; Rijks Mus, Amsterdam; Libr of Cong, Washington, DC; Philadelphia Mus, Pa; Metrop Mus Art, New York. *Exhib:* Tokyo Int Print Biennials, 57 & 60; Grenchen Int Print Triennials, 58, 61 & 70; 5th Sao Paulo Int Biennial, 59; Vancouver Int Print Exhib, 67; 35th Venice Int Biennial, 70; and over 50 one-man shows in the US, Japan & Europe. *Teaching:* Mem fac printmaking, Sarah Lawrence Col, 62-; lectr printmaking, Columbia Univ, 68- *Awards:* Guggenheim Fel, 62-63 & 70-71. *Mem:* Soc Am Graphic Artists; Japan Print Asn. *Mailing Add:* 652 W 163rd St New York NY 10032

UCHIMA, TOSHIKO
PAINTER, ASSEMBLAGE ARTIST
b Manchuria, China; Japanese citizen. *Study:* Kobe Col, Japan, BA; and with Ryohei Koiso. *Work:* Art Inst Chicago; Hampton Inst, Va; Brooklyn Mus; Striped House Mus, Tokyo, Japan. *Exhib:* Grenchen Int Print Triennial, Switz, 58; Art Inst Chicago, 60. *Publ:* Contribr, Sphynx (portfolio prints & poems), 54. *Mailing Add:* 652 W 163rd St New York NY 10032

UDINOTTI, AGNESE
SCULPTOR, PAINTER
b Athens, Greece, Jan 9, 40; US citizen. *Study:* Ariz State Univ, BA & MA. *Work:* Phoenix Art Mus, Ariz; Univ Utah; Am Collections, Ariz State Univ; Glendale Community Col; Western Col Yuma. *Comn:* Steel doors, Wilson Jones & Assocs, Scottsdale, Ariz, 70 & Imagineering, Tucson, Ariz, 72; relief, comn by Mrs M Ehrlich, Phoenix, 70; steel diptych, comn by Har Oude Jans, Amsterdam, Holland, 72; outdoor sculpture, comn by Glendale Community Col, 74; outdoor sculpture, comn by Harold Hart, Okemos, Mich. *Exhib:* One-man shows, Vorpal Galleries, San Francisco, 68, 71 & 75, Laguna Beach, 79, Art Forms Gallery, Athens, 69, 71, 75, 77 & 81; Vorpal, NY, 76, 79 & 81; Pasquale Ianetti Gallery, San Francisco, 83. *Teaching:* Workshop leader welded sculpture, Orme Sch Fine Arts Prog, Mayer, Ariz, 71 & 72; Univ Southern Calif, summer 72. *Awards:* Hellenic Am Union Sculpture Award, 68; Sculpture Prize, Phoenix Art Mus 1st Biennial, 71; Solomos Prize for sculpture, Panos Nikoli Tselepi, Athens, 71. *Bibliog:* Seiden Meilach (auth), Creating Art from Anything, Reilly & Lee, 68; Cortright (auth), Agnese Udinotti; A study in armor, Phoenix Mag, 1/78; An independent, unopressive artist, Southwest Art Mag, 4/77. *Media:* Steel, Oil. *Publ:* Udinotti, Northland Press & Macabre love songs and aphorisms, Greek Publ, Kedros; My Udinotti J, Vol 1, Amaranth Press, 77, Vol 2, Udinotti Publ, 79. *Mailing Add:* c/o 4215 N Marshall Way Scottsdale AZ 85251

UDVARDY, JOHN WARREN
SCULPTOR, ADMINISTRATOR
b Elyria, Ohio. *Study:* Skowhegan Sch Painting & Sculpture, scholar, summer 57; Cleveland Inst Art, scholar, 55-58, BFA, 63; Yale Univ, scholar, 64-65, MFA, 65. *Work:* Cleveland Inst Art; Betty Parsons Gallery, New York; Columbia Broadcasting System, New York; Fogg Mus, Cambridge, Mass; Princeton Univ, NJ. *Comn:* Design of symbol & emblem for Ecol Action RI, 70. *Exhib:* Young New Eng Painters, Sarasota, Fla, Portland, Maine & Manchester, NH, 69; Smith Col, Northampton, Mass, 77; Touchstone Gallery, New York, 78 & 79; and others; and others. *Teaching:* Instr drawing, Cleveland Inst Art, 62-63; asst printmaking, Yale Univ, 64-65; asst prof painting & design, Brown Univ, 65-73; chmn, Freshman Found Div, RI Sch Design, 73-77 & 79-82, prof design, 78-79. *Awards:* Mary C Page Europe Traveling Scholar, Cleveland Inst Art, 60-61. *Mem:* Mass Archaeol Soc; Nat

Audubon Soc. *Media:* Wood. *Publ:* Illusr, Los, fall 68 & spring 70, Art J, winter 73, Art in Am, 3-4/75, Mich Quart Rev, spring 79. *Dealer:* The Touchstone Gallery 29 W 57th St New York NY 10019. *Mailing Add:* 900 Hope Bristol RI 02809

UELSMANN, JERRY
PHOTOGRAPHER
b Detroit, Mich, June 11, 34. *Study:* Rochester Inst Technol, BFA, 57; Ind Univ, MS, 58, MFA, 60; Guggenheim Fel, 67; Photog Fel, Nat Endowment Arts, 73. *Work:* Mus Mod Art, New York; Philadelphia Mus Art; Art Inst Chicago; Nat Gallery Can, Ottawa; Int Mus Photog, George Eastman House, Rochester, NY. *Exhib:* Photography in America 1850-1965, Yale Univ Art Gallery, 65; Photography in the Twentieth Century, George Eastman House in collab with Nat Gallery Can, 67; one-man shows, Mus Mod Art, New York, 67, Philadelphia Mus Art, 70 & Art Inst Chicago, 72; Witkin Gallery, New York, 75 & 78; San Francisco Mus of Mod Art, 77. *Teaching:* Prof photog, Univ Fla, 60-, Grad res prof art, 74- *Awards:* Grant, Univ Fla, 70. *Bibliog:* Jerry N Uelsmann (monograph), Aperture, 71; Silver Meditations (monogr), Morgan & Morgan, 75; James L Enyeart (auth), Jerry N Uelsmann Twenty-five Years: A Retrospective, New York Graphic Soc, 82. *Mem:* Founding mem Soc Photog Educ; fel Royal Photog Soc Gt Brit. *Publ:* Contribr, Contemp Photog, 64, Camera, 67, Aperture, 67, 68 & 70, Life, 69 & Infinity. *Dealer:* Witkin Gallery 41 E 57th St New York NY 10022. *Mailing Add:* 5701 SW 17th Dr Gainesville FL 32608

UHRMAN, CELIA
PAINTER, WRITER
b New London, Conn, May 14, 27. *Study:* Brooklyn Col, BA & MA, 53; Brooklyn Mus Art Sch, 56-57; Teachers Col, Columbia Univ, 61; City Univ New York, 66; Univ Danzig, PhD, 77. *Work:* Brooklyn Col; Ovar Mus; govt bldgs in Spain & Portugal. *Exhib:* 2nd All New England Drawing, Lyman Allyn Mus, New London, Conn, 60; 26th Ann Contemp Am Paintings, Soc Four Arts, Palm Beach, Fla, 64; Premi Int Dibeaux, Joan Miro, Barcelona, Spain, 70; 26th Expos Int d'Art Contemporain, Luxembourg, 74; Des Beaux-Arts Exhib, Monaco, Monte-Carlo, 69, 70 & 72. *Teaching:* Teacher art & spec talent classes, Lefferts Jr High Sch, Brooklyn, NY, 58-59. *Awards:* Academic Laurel, 27th Int Exhib Contemp Art, Moka Club, Paris, 74; Cert of Appreciation, New York Bd Educ, 82; Cert Koret Living Lib, Fromm Inst, Univ San Francisco. *Bibliog:* Jim Burns Talk Show (interview), WECT-TV, Wilmington, NC, 7/10/73; Rev in Int News, Int Arts Bull, 75; Div Gen Educ, NY Univ, Part IV (film), 58. *Mem:* Centro Studi E Scambi Int, Rome (hon US rep, 70- & mem int exec comt); Int Arts Guild, Monte-Carlo (commandeur mem arts & lett, 66); New York Artists Equity. *Media:* Oil, Watercolor. *Publ:* Auth, A Pause for Poetry for Children, 73; auth, The Chimps are Coming (novel), 75; and others. *Mailing Add:* 1655 Flatbush Ave Brooklyn NY 11210

UHRMAN, ESTHER
PAINTER, WRITER
b New London, Conn, July 7, 21. *Study:* Traphagan Sch Fashion, (design & illus), 55; New York City Community Col, AA, 74; Cornell Univ, 77; Col New Rochelle; Danzig Univ, PhD, 77. *Work:* Ovar Mus, Portugal; var pub bldgs in Spain. *Exhib:* Washington Watercolor Soc 65th Ann, Smithsonian Inst, 62; Tribute to Southeastern Connecticut, Mohican Hotel, New London, 62; Uhrman Show of Water Colors, Rivoli, Brooklyn, 63; Premi Int Dibuix Joan Miro, Barcelona, Spain, 70; 26th Expos Int Art Contemp, Luxembourg, 74. *Awards:* Silver Medal Olympic Design, Ital Govt, 68; Golden Windmill Radio Drama Award, Holland, 71; Dipl of Honor Palme, Int Arts Guild, Monaco, 72. *Bibliog:* Charles Richman (auth), articles in Brooklyn Rec, 57-; article in Flatbusha, 60; articles in Int Arts Bull, 72- *Mem:* Centro Studi e Scambi Int, Rome (hon US rep, 74-); Int Arts Guild, Monte Carlo (commandeur mem arts & lett, 66-). *Media:* Oil, Watercolor. *Publ:* Auth, Cover Your Walls, Diet Indust, 57; auth, Gypsy Logic, 70 & Mocking Ghost, Life is Tremendous, 72; auth, Brotherhood, Pub Employee Press, 74; auth, From Canvase to Masada, 78. *Mailing Add:* 1655 Flatbush Ave Apt C106 Brooklyn NY 11210

ULBRICHT, JOHN
PAINTER
b Havana, Cuba, Nov 6, 26; US citizen. *Study:* Art Inst Chicago, dipl, 50. *Work:* Europ Parliament, Strasbourg; Nat Portrait Gallery, London; State Univ NY, Buffalo; Pasadena Art Mus; Treasury Ministry, Madrid, Spain; and others. *Comn:* Portrait of Mrs Betty Ford, comn by Pres Gerald Ford, 75; portrait of Chief Judge David Bazelon, US Fed Court House, Washington, DC, 76. *Exhib:* Kunstcentrum, Worpswede (Bremen), Ger, 79; one-man shows, 12 Spanish Portraits, Pavilion of Spain, New York World's Fair, 65; Richard DeMarco Gallery, Edinburgh, 69 & Iolas-Velasco Gallery, Madrid, 72; plus others in the US & Europe. *Pos:* Asst dir, Denver Art Mus, 52-53. *Awards:* John Quincy Adams Foreign Travel Fel, Art Inst Chicago, 50. *Bibliog:* Camilo Cela (auth), John Ulbricht: 12 Spanish Portraits, Papeles de Son Armadans, 65; Josep Melia (auth), John Ulbricht, Ed Rayuela, Madrid, 74; Janer Manila (auth), John Ulbricht, Palma, 81; and others. *Media:* Oil. *Dealer:* Sala Pelaires Gallery Pelaires 23 Palma de Mallorca Spain. *Mailing Add:* Es Clapes 85 Galilea Mallorca Spain

ULLBERG, KENT
SCULPTOR
Goteborg, Sweden, July 15, 45. *Study:* Swedish State Sch Art, cert(drawing & sculpture); Swedish Mus Natural Hist, anat, 4 yrs; Mus Des Sci Naturelles, Orleans, France. *Work:* Swedish Mus Natural Hist, Gothenburg; Exhib Palace, Peking, China; Corpus Christi Mus, Tex; Los Angeles Co Mus; Denver Mus Natural Hist. *Comn:* Monumental sculptures, Corpus Christi

Nat Bank, Tex, 81, City Corpus Christi, 83, Corp Plaza, Boca Raton, Fla, 83, Lywam Art Mus, Wausau, Wis, 83 & Genesee Mus, Rochester, NY, 84; monumental sculpture, Corpus Christi Nat Bank, Tex, 81. *Exhib:* Ann Exhib, Nat Acad Design, New York, 75-81; Nat Sculpture Soc Ann Exhib, New York, 77-81; Nat Cowboy Hall of Fame, Oklahoma City, Okla, 77-81; Salon D'Automne, Paris, France, 78; Artists of Am, Colo Heritage Ctr Mus, 81. *Pos:* Cur, Nat Mus & Art Gallery, Botswana, Africa, 71-74; cur/consult, Denver Mus Natural Hist, 74-76. *Awards:* Merit Awards, Soc Animal Artists, New York, 78-82; Gold Medal Sculpture, Nat Acad Western Art, Oklahoma City, 81-82; Gold Medal, Nat Sculpture Soc, New York 83. *Bibliog:* Article, Southwest Art, 5/76; article, Colo Outdoors, 7/77; article, Artists of the Rockies, winter 83. *Mem:* Nat Sculpture Soc; Nat Acad Western Art; Cowboy Hall Fame; assoc mem Nat Acad Design, New York; Soc Animal Artists, New York. *Media:* Bronze, Steel. *Dealer:* Grand Central Gallery 50 East 50th St New York NY 10022; Trailside Gallery 7330 Scottsdale Mall Scottsdale AZ 85251. *Mailing Add:* 14337 Aquarius St Padre Island Corpus Christi TX 78418

ULLMAN, (MRS) GEORGE W
COLLECTOR
Mem: Costume Soc Am; Am Fedn Arts; Ariz Costume Inst. *Collection:* French furniture and paintings, Louis XV and Louis XVI periods; Haitian paintings; contemporary paintings of Philip Curtis; Spanish paintings, seventeenth and eighteenth century on painted furniture & glass. *Mailing Add:* 4642 N 56th St Phoenix AZ 85018

ULLRICH-ZUCKERMAN, B
PAINTER, PHOTOGRAPHER
b Evanston, Ill. *Study:* Northwestern Univ, BA, 30; Art Inst Chicago, BFA, 34; with Boris Anisfeld & Francis Chapin; also with Edward Weston, 42; Univ Chicago, MA, 48. *Work:* New Orleans Mus Art; Univ Ariz Collection Am Painting, Tucson; photog in Hall of Justice, San Francisco, Calif; Midwest Color Slide Art Collection, Chicago Main Pub Libr, Ill; plus in many pvt collections throughout USA. *Exhib:* San Francisco Mus Mod Art, 39, 41 & 70; one-person shows, San Francisco Mus Mod Art, 40, Univ Pac, Stockton, Calif, 76, Photog Ctr, San Francisco, 77 & Univ Calif, San Francisco, 83; De Young Mus, San Francisco, 43 & 70; Calif Expo, Sacramento, 77; One Market Plaza Gallery, San Francisco, 77; and others. *Teaching:* Instr pvt classes, 46-; vis lectr, Univ Pac, 76 & Ctr Learning in Retirement, Univ Calif Exten, San Francisco, 83. *Mem:* Artists Equity Asn (secy Chicago chap, 55-56); San Francisco Women Artists (secy artists coun, 74-75). *Publ:* Contribr, Am Heritage, 2/65; contribr (photog), Imogen's Sign, In: Imogen Cunningham, an Interview (film), shown 75-; contribr (photog), Free Our Sisters, reproduced in Visual Dialog Mag, fall 78; contribr, Imogen After Ninety (radio broadcast article), 78. *Mailing Add:* 2254 42nd Ave San Francisco CA 94116

ULRICH, EDWIN ABEL
MUSEUM DIRECTOR
b Brooklyn, NY, Dec 23, 97. *Collections Arranged:* Three Generations of the American Family of Painters....Waugh, 1814-1973, 77. *Pos:* Dir, Edwin A Ulrich Mus, Hyde Park, 56- *Collection:* American art, specializing in Frederick J Waugh, 1861-1940; has given Frederick J Waugh Collection to Wichita State Univ and donated a trust to support the collection; in recognition, Bd of Regents named the new univ mus, Edwin A Ulrich Mus of Art; also loaned paintings to Smithsonian Inst for traveling exhib, 69-71; paintings have been exhibited in various cities and mus. *Mailing Add:* Edwin A Ulrich Mus Albany Post Rd PO Box 400 Hyde Park NY 12538

UMLAUF, CHARLES
SCULPTOR
b Mich, July 17, 11. *Study:* Art Inst Chicago, with Albin Polasek; Chicago Sch Sculpture, with Viola Norman. *Work:* Krannert Art Mus, Univ Ill, Urbana; Des Moines Art Ctr, Iowa; Metrop Mus Art, New York; Okla Art Ctr; Mus Fine Arts, Houston, Tex; and nine other Tex mus. *Comn:* Marble reredos relief, St Michael & All Angels Church, Dallas, Tex, 61; Spirit of Flight (bronze fountain sculpture), Lovefield Airport, Dallas, 61; Torch Bearers (bronze), Univ Tex, Austin, 63; Icarus (bronze), Space Technol Ctr, Univ Kans, Lawrence, 64; Family Group (three figural bronze), Houston Mus Natural Sci, Tex, 72. *Exhib:* American Sculpture, Metrop Mus Art, New York, 51; Int Relig Biennial, Salzburg, Austria, Ger, Spain & Eng, 58-59; 20th Ceramic Int, Everson Mus, Syracuse, NY & tour, 59-60; 161st Ann, Pa Acad Fine Arts, Philadelphia, 66; three retrospectives, Valley House Gallery, Dallas, 59 & Univ Tex Art Mus, Austin, 67 & 80; and 30 solo exhibs including New York & Italy. *Teaching:* Prof sculpture, Univ Tex, Austin, 52-81, Leslie Waggener Prof Fine Arts, 80-81, prof emer, 81- *Awards:* Guggenheim Grant, 49-50; Univ Tex Grant, 66; Ford Found Grant, 79. *Bibliog:* Donald B Goodall (auth), Charles Umlauf, Sculptor, Univ Tex Press, 67; Earl Miller (dir), Bronze Sculpture in the Making (film), produced by Univ Tex, 69; Gibson A Danes (auth), The Sculpture and Drawing of Charles Umlauf, Univ Tex Press, 80. *Media:* Bronze, Marble. *Dealer:* Bryant Galleries 1855 Lakeland Drive Jackson MS 39216; Sol del Rio Gallery 1020 Townsend San Antonio TX 78209. *Mailing Add:* 506 Barton Blvd Austin TX 78704

UMLAUF, KARL A
PAINTER, SCULPTOR
b Chicago, Ill, May 16, 39. *Study:* Univ Tex, Austin, BFA, 57-61; Yale Univ, fel, summer 60; Cornell Univ, MFA. *Work:* New Orleans Mus Art, La; Everson Mus, Syracuse, NY; Joslyn Art Mus, Omaha; Silvermine Guild Artists; Dallas Mus Art; and others. *Exhib:* Fourteenth & 22nd Ann Delta Exhib, Ark Art Ctr, Little Rock, 72 & 79; Project South, Southwest Ft Worth

Art Ctr, 72; Potsdam Nat Print & Drawing Exhib, State Univ NY Potsdam, 72; Artist Biennial, New Orleans Mus, 73 & 77; 16th Nat Exhib Prints & Drawings, Oklahoma Art Ctr, 75; Ann Nat Painting & Sculpture Exhib, Longview Mus, Tex, 76; Works on Paper Southwest '78, Dallas Mus Art; The First 20 Years, Tyler Mus Art, Tex, 83. *Teaching:* Vis prof art, Ind Univ, Bloomington, 74-75; prof & dept head, ETex State Univ, Commerce, 81- *Awards:* First Prize, Okla Art Ctr, 70; First Prize, Evansville Mus Art, 75; Purchase Prize, Delta Ann, Ark Art Ctr, 80; and others. *Media:* Cast Paper, Mixed Media on Canvas. *Dealer:* Gallery One Fort Worth TX; Watson De Nagy & Co Houston TX. *Mailing Add:* 109 Royal Ln Commerce TX 75428

UMLAUF, LYNN (CHARLOTTE)
PAINTER, COLLAGE ARTIST
b Austin, Tex, Jan 8, 42. *Study:* Art Students League, 61-62; Acad Fine Arts, Florence, 65-66; Univ Tex, Austin, MFA, 68. *Exhib:* Whitney Mus Am Art Biennial Exhib, 75; A Month of Sundays, 76 & A Painting Show, 77, PS1; Painting and Sculpture Today, Indianapolis Mus Art, 78; solo exhibs, Hal Bromm Gallery, New York, 78, 79 & 80 & Young Hoffman Gallery, Chicago, 83; Drawings of a Different Nature, Portland Ctr Visual Arts, 80; One Plus One Equals Two, Bernice Steinbaum Gallery, New York, 84. *Teaching:* Instr, Fairleigh-Dickenson Univ, 71-72, Philadelphia Col Art, 79, Kutztown State Col, 80-81 & Sch Visual Arts, 81- *Bibliog:* Nancy Grove (auth), article, Artforum, 10/79; Valentin Tatranski (auth), article, Arts Mag, 2/81; Tiffany Bell (auth), Responses to Neo-Expressionism, Flash Art Int, 5/83. *Media:* Acrylic, Pastel. *Dealer:* Rhona Hoffman 215 W Superior St Chicago IL 60610. *Mailing Add:* 222 Bowery New York NY 10012

UNGER, MARY ANN
SCULPTOR
b New York, NY, May 10, 45. *Study:* Mt Holyoke Col, BA(magna cum laude), 67; Univ of Calif, Berkeley, with Voulkas, B Hudson & R Melchert, 68; Columbia Univ, with Bladen, Sugarman & T Harrison, MFA, 75. *Exhib:* Seventh Ann Contemp Reflections, Aldrich Mus Contemp Art, 78; solo exhibs, 10 Downtown, New York, 77, Paradise as a Garden, City Univ New York Grad Ctr, 82 & Waterfalls, 55 Mercer, New York, 83; Painted Sculpture, Sculpture Ctr, New York, 82; The Curve of a Plane, 22 Wooster Gallery, New York, 83; and others. *Pos:* Rockefeller Found vis artist, NC Sch Arts, Winston-Salem, 81. *Teaching:* Instr printmaking and drawing, Montclair State Col; instr sculpture, Kutztown State Col, Pa, 79; instr adult degree prog, Goddard Col, 79-80; vis lectr, Bronx Mus, 79 & Landmark Gallery, New York, 80. *Awards:* Creative Artists Pub Serv Grant Sculpture, 79; Yaddo Residence Fels, 78 & 80. *Bibliog:* Barbara Talbot (auth), article, Ocular, Vol 4, No 2, 79; Gerald Marzaroti (auth), Art picks, Soho Weekly News, 1/19/82; Grace Glueck (auth), article, New York Times, 1/31/82. *Mailing Add:* 5 East Third St New York NY 10003

UNTERSEHER, CHRIS CHRISTIAN
SCULPTOR
b Portland, Ore, May 14, 43. *Study:* San Francisco State Col, BA, 65; Univ Calif, Davis, MA, 67. *Work:* Objects USA, Johnson Wax Collection, Racine, Wis; Allan Stone Galleries Collection, New York; Jim Newman Found, San Francisco, Calif; Oakland Mus, Calif. *Exhib:* Objects USA, Johnson Wax Collection, in traveling show, 69-73; 20 Americans, Mus Contemp Crafts, New York, 71; one-man shows, Hansen-Fuller Gallery, San Francisco, 67-70 & De Young Mus, San Francisco, Calif, 68 & 77; Clay, Whitney Mus, New York, 74; Quay Ceramics Gallery, San Francisco, 75 & 77. *Teaching:* Instr ceramics, Univ Calif, Davis, 68-69; instr ceramics, Univ Cincinnati, 69-70; chmn ceramics dept, Univ Nev, Reno, 70-, assoc prof art, 78- *Awards:* Purchase Award, Mem Union Art Gallery, Univ Calif, Davis, 68. *Bibliog:* David Zack (auth), Art news: Nut art in quake time, 70; Nordness (auth), Objects: USA, Viking, 70; Lowell Darling (auth), Clay without tears, Art Ctr World, 71. *Mem:* Am Crafts Coun. *Dealer:* Quay Ceramics Gallery 560 Sutter St San Francisco CA 94102. *Mailing Add:* Dept of Art Univ of Nev Reno NV 89507

UPRIGHT, DIANE W
EDUCATOR, WRITER
b Cleveland, Ohio. *Study:* Wellesley Col, 65-67; Univ Pittsburgh, BA, 69; Univ Mich, MA, 74, PhD, 76. *Collections Arranged:* Morris Louis: The Veil Cycle (auth, catalog), Walker Art Ctr & traveling, 77; Abstract Expressionism, Fogg Art Mus, Harvard Univ, 78; The Drawings of Morris Louis (auth, catalog), Nat Collection of Fine Arts & traveling, 79; Contemporary Painting & Sculpture, 79 & David Smith: Sculpture, Drawings & Paintings, 79, Fogg Art Mus, Harvard Univ. *Teaching:* Asst prof mod art hist, Univ Va, Charlottesville, 76-78; asst prof, Harvard Univ, 78-81, assoc prof, 81-83. *Mem:* Col Art Asn. *Publ:* Auth, Morris Louis: Disposing the diagonal, Arts Mag, 4/76; auth, In addition to the veils, Art in Am, 1-2/78; auth, The informal paintings of Philippe Hosiasson, Arts Mag, 12/78; auth, Sam Francis: The paintings of the 1950s, The Phillips Collection, 80; auth, Morris Louis: A Catalogue Raisonne of the Paintings, Harry N Abrams, 84. *Mailing Add:* 45 E 89th St New York NY 10128

UPTON, JOHN DAVID
EDUCATOR, CURATOR
b Des Moines, Iowa, May 4, 32. *Study:* Calif Sch Fine Arts; Univ Rochester, with Minor White & Beaumont Newhall; Univ Calif, Berkeley; Calif State Univ Long Beach, BA & grad study art hist. *Work:* Mass Inst Technol Creative Photog Collection, Cambridge; Fine Arts Collection, Metrop Mus Art. *Exhib:* 15 American Photographers, Houston Mus Contemp Art, 64; one-man shows, Mass Inst Technol Creative Photography Gallery, Cambridge, 65 & Camerawork Gallery, Costa Mesa, Calif, 68; Light 7, Mass Inst Technol Art

Gallery, Cambridge, 68. *Collections Arranged:* The Photograph as: Metaphor, Object & Document of Concept (auth, catalog), 74 & The Photograph as Artifice (auth, catalog), 78, Calif State Univ Long Beach; Color as Form: A History of Color Photography, Corcoran Gallery Art, Washington, DC, 82. *Pos:* Chmn dept of photog & asst chmn div of fine arts, Orange Coast Col, Costa Mesa, Calif, 63-; vis cur, Int Mus Photog, George Eastman House, Rochester, NY, 79-82. *Teaching:* Prof hist of photog & creative photog, Orange Coast Col, Costa Mesa, Calif, 63-; vis lectr hist photog, Univ Calif Los Angeles, 75; Calif Inst Arts, Valencia, Ca, 83- *Bibliog:* Minor White (auth), Photographers northwest, Aperture, Vol 11, No 3, 64; Robert Routh (auth), An Educator's Educator, Petersen's Photog, 12/75. *Mem:* Soc for Photog Educ (mem bd trustees, 75-79); Friends Photog (mem bd trustees, 74-80). *Res:* History of photography since 1900, especially Alfred Steiglitz, Minor White & Edward Neston. *Publ:* Contribr, New Vision of the 70's, Photographers Choice, Addison House, 75; coauth, Photography, Little, Brown & Co, 76, revised, 84. *Mailing Add:* c/o Orange Coast Col 2701 Fairview Costa Mesa CA 92626

UPTON, RICHARD THOMAS
PAINTER, PRINTMAKER

b Hartford, Conn. *Study:* Univ Conn, BFA; Ind Univ, MFA; Ecole des Beaux Arts. *Work:* Nat Collection of Fine Arts, Smithsonian Inst, Washington, DC; Mus Mod Art, New York; Victoria & Albert, Mus, London, Eng; Bibliot Nat, Paris, France; Montreal Mus Fine Art, Can. *Comn:* Eros Thanatos Suite (German poem & woodcuts), Interlaken Corp, Providence, RI, 67; Salamovka Poster (limited ed silkscreen), Okla Art Ctr, Oklahoma City, 74; River Road Suite (lithographs), 76 & Robert Lowell at 66 (suite of drawings), 77, Salmagundi Mag for the Humanities. *Exhib:* Sept Graveures un Sculpteur de Medailles, Musee Denon, Chalon-Sur Saome, France, 73; Brit Int Print Biennale, US Sect touring Eng, 73; Recent Acquisitions 1969-1973, Bibliot Nat, Paris, France, 74; The Delaware Water Gap, Corcoran Gallery Art, Washington, DC, 75; Everson Mus Art, Syracuse, NY, 75; Nat Collection Prints & Poetry, Libr of Cong, Washington, DC, 76-77; Retrospective of prints from Elvehjem Art Mus, Atelier 17, France, 77; Okla Art Ctr, 77; Tweed Mus Art, Duluth, Minn, 77; Weatherspoon Art Gallery, Greensboro, NC, 77. *Collections Arranged:* Salamovka Series and Other New Paintings (auth, catalog), Oklahoma Art Ctr, Oklahoma City, 74. *Pos:* Dir, Erebus Press, Saratoga, NY. *Awards:* Fulbright Fel; Nat Educ Asn grant, Artists for Environ; Interlaken Corp Designer Award, Providence, RI, 67. *Bibliog:* James Kiehl (auth), Richard Upton's Credo, Salmagundi Mag for the Humanities; Laurence Schmeckebier (auth), Richard Upton: 1960-1970, Syracuse Univ, 70; Harry Gaugh (auth), Richard Upton New Paintings-Prints, Hartwick Col. *Media:* Oil, Water Based Media; Lithography, Intaglio. *Publ:* Auth, Impressions--A Paris Suite, 64, coauth, Credo, 68 & coauth, Eros Thanatos, 68, Interlaken Corp; coauth & illustr, Models, 75 & River Road (with Stanley Kunitz), 75, Erebus Press. *Dealer:* Weyne Gallery Lexington Ave New York NY; Townhouse Galleries 2400 E Las Olas Blvd Ft Lauderdale FL 33301. *Mailing Add:* 113 Regent St Saratoga Springs NY 12866

URBAN, REVA
PAINTER, SCULPTOR

b Brooklyn, NY, Oct 15, 25. *Study:* Art Students League, Carnegie scholar, 43-45. *Work:* Mus Mod Art, New York; Art Inst Chicago; Univ Mus, Berkeley; Finch Col Mus, New York; Averthorp Gallery, Jenkintown, Pa. *Exhib:* Pittsburgh Int, 58; 1st Biennale Chrislicher Kunst der Gegenwart, Salzburg, Austria, 58; Continuity & Change, Wadsworth Atheneum, Hartford, Conn, 62; Documenta III, Kassel, Ger, 64; Seven Decades-Crosscurrents in Modern Art 1895-1965; seven one-person shows, New York, Washington, DC, Chicago & Ger. *Awards:* Tamarind Fel. *Bibliog:* Sam Wagstaff, Jr (auth), Reva, Am Abstract Painters & Sculptors, 62; Peter Selz (auth), Reva Urban, Univ Art Collections, 66. *Media:* Oil, Pastel Crayon. *Mailing Add:* PO Box 659 Radio City Sta New York NY 10101

URQUHART, TONY (ANTHONY MORSE)
SCULPTOR, PAINTER

b Niagara Falls, Ont, Apr 9, 34. *Study:* Yale Univ, Norfolk, Conn, 55; Albright Art Sch, Buffalo, dipl, 56; Univ Buffalo, NY, BFA, 58. *Work:* Nat Gallery Can, Ottawa; Art Gallery Ont, Toronto; Mus Mod Art, New York; Victoria & Albert Mus, London; and others. *Comn:* Mural, Govt Ont, 68, bas-relief, 78. *Exhib:* Carnegie Int, Philadelphia, 58; Guggenheim Int, New York, 59; solo shows, Winnipeg Art Gallery, Man, 59 & Walker Art Ctr, Minneapolis, 60; Am Acad Arts & Lett, New York, 60; Nat Gallery Can, Ottawa, 75; Mus Mod Art, Paris, 76; retrospective, Kitchener-Waterlou Gallery, traveling, 78-80. *Pos:* Artist-in-residence, Univ Western Ont, 60-65; artist-in-residence, Kitchener-Waterloo Art Gallery, 81-83. *Teaching:* From asst prof to assoc prof, Univ Western Ont, London, 67-72; prof, Univ Waterloo, 72-, chmn, 77-79, 82- *Awards:* First Prize, Albright-Knox Art Gallery, 58; Baxter Award, Art Gallery Ont, 60; Fel, Can Coun Sr Arts, 79-80. *Bibliog:* Dorothy Cameron (auth), Tony Urquhart: Reunion, 71, J Vastokas (auth), Archtypal imagery in the work of Tony Urquhart, 74 & Joe Bodelai (auth), Tony Urquhart: The story so far, 76, Artscan. *Mem:* foun mem Can Artists Rep/Front Artists Can (nat secy, 67-71); Jack Chambers Mem Found (chmn bd govs, 78-); Can Conf Arts (vpres, 71-72). *Media:* Oil; Mixed Media, Oil. *Publ:* Auth, The Urquhart Sketchbook, Isaacs Gallery, Toronto, 62; ed, The Broken Ark: Book of Beasts, Oberon Press, Ont, 69, reprinted 78; ed, I Am Walking in the Garden of Your Imaginary Palace, AYA Press, Toronto, 82. *Dealer:* Bau-Xi 340 Dundas St W Toronto ON Can; Bau-Xi 3045 Granville St Vancouver BC Can. *Mailing Add:* 24 Water St Wellesley ON N0B 2T0 Canada

USHER, ELIZABETH REUTER
LIBRARIAN, LECTURER

b Seward, Nebr. *Study:* Concordia Teachers Col, Seward, dipl, DLitt(hon), 81; Univ Nebr, BScEd; Univ Ill, LSc; Cranbrook Acad of Art, Bloomfield Hills, Mich; NY Univ. *Pos:* Librn, Cranbrook Acad of Art, Bloomfield Hills, 45-48; catalog/reference librn, Metrop Mus of Art, New York, 48-53, head cataloguer, 53-54, actg head of libr, 54-57, chief, Art Reference Libr, 57-68, chief librn, 68-80; chief librn emer, Thomas J Watson Libr, 81- *Awards:* Special, Librn Asn Hall Fame, 80. *Mem:* Spec Libr Asn; Col Art Asn; NY Libr Club; Art Libr Soc/NAm; Archons Colophon. *Res:* Art librarianship; bibliography. *Interests:* Modern art history. *Publ:* Auth, Rare Books and the Art Museum Library, Spec Libr, 1/61; auth, Continuing Bibliography for the Fine Arts in the United States, Colloques Int, Paris, 3/69; auth, The Metropolitan Museum of Art Library (Research and Reference) (Memorial Name: The Thomas J Watson Library), In: Allen Kent & Harold Lancour, ed, Encyclopedia of Library & Information Science Vol XVII, Dekker, 76. *Mailing Add:* 557A Heritage Village Southbury CT 06488

USUI, KIICHI
CURATOR

b Tokyo, Japan, Dec 2, 31. *Study:* Tokyo Univ Arts, BFA; Art Students League with Morris Kantor; Univ Mich, MA(Oriental art hist). *Collections Arranged:* Meadow Brook Invitational I: Outdoor Sculpture, 81 & II: Painting, 83; Nat Sculpture Competition Phoenix Ctr, Pontiac, Mich, 82. *Pos:* Cur, Meadow Brook Art Gallery, Oakland Univ, 71- *Bibliog:* Auth, Art in architecture, Space Design, 6/78. *Mem:* Mich Mus Asn; Am Asn Mus; Detroit Inst Art; Meadow Brook Gallery Assoc. *Mailing Add:* Meadow Brook Art Gallery Oakland Univ Rochester MI 48063

UTTECH, THOMAS MARTIN
PAINTER, EDUCATOR

b Merrill, Wis, Oct 27, 42. *Study:* Layton Sch Art, BFA; Univ Cincinnati, MFA. *Work:* Milwaukee Art Ctr; Univ Wis-Madison. *Exhib:* Directions, Milwaukee Art Ctr, 75; Artists of Chicago & Vicinity, 75; Whitney Mus Am Art Ann, New York, 75; Beauty of the Beast, Images of Animals in Am Art & The Human Image in Am Art of the 70s, John Michael Kohler Art Ctr, 77; Regenbogen fur eine bessere Wuttembergishe Kunstverein, Stuttgart, Ger, 77; two-man exhib (with Jerome Krause), Visions from the Northwoods, Milwaukee Art Ctr, 77. *Teaching:* Assoc prof painting, drawing & photog, Univ Wis-Milwaukee, 68- *Awards:* Top Exhib Award, Wis Painters & Sculptors, Milwaukee Art Ctr, 73; Peninsula Sch Art Grant, Fish Creek, Wis, 73; Univ Wis Res Grant, 75 & 79. *Bibliog:* C Kohlman (auth), article in Midwest Art; Claudia Strohm (auth), Door County Creations (30 min interview), Channel 10, Milwaukee, 7/75; Amy Goldin (auth), New Whitney Biennial: pattern emerging, Art Am, 5-6/75. *Mem:* Wis Painters & Sculptors (pres, 73-76). *Media:* Oil, Photographs. *Publ:* Illusr, A roadless area revisited, Audubon Mag, 75; illusr, Earth Care, Sierra Club & Audubon Soc, 75. *Dealer:* Dorthy Bradley Milwaukee WI; David Swanson Saint Paul MN. *Mailing Add:* 2582 N Cramer St Milwaukee WI 53211

UTZ, THORNTON
PAINTER, SCULPTOR

b Memphis, Tenn, Nov 15, 14. *Study:* Am Acad Art, Chicago. *Work:* Milwaukee Art Mus; Air & Space Mus, Washington, DC; First Lady Collection, Smithsonian Inst; Port of Hist, Philadelphia; Palace, Monaco. *Comn:* Giraffe (stainless steel & concrete), Lindsey Hopkins Comn, Atlanta, 75; seven paintings, Jimmy Carter Collection, Plains, Ga, 75-76; sculpture (concrete & steel), First Presby Church, Sarasota, Fla, 78; portrait, Sonja Bernadotte & children, 83; seven paintings (landscapes), Pan Am Banks, Sarasota, Fla & Gen Tel & Tel, Sarasota, Fla, 83. *Pos:* Bd mem, Ringling Art Sch, 64- *Awards:* Black & White Illus Award, Art Inst Chicago, 44; Citation Merit, Soc Illusr Ann, 59. *Bibliog:* Richard Thruelsen (auth), Men at work--Thornton Utz, Saturday Evening Post, 12/3/49; Ernest Watson (auth), article, Am Artist, 52; John Diffily (auth), article, Southwest Art Mag, 7/81. *Mem:* Soc Illusr; Chicago Artists Guild; Am Portrait Soc. *Media:* Mixed. *Mailing Add:* 123 Island Circle Sarasota FL 33581

V

VACCARINO, ROBIN
SCULPTOR, PAINTER

b Seattle, Wash, Aug 14, 28. *Study:* Univ Calif, Los Angeles; Otis Art Inst, MFA(magna cum laude), 66. *Work:* Los Angeles Co Mus; Santa Barbara Mus; Library of Congress, Washington, DC; DeCordova Mus; and others. *Comn:* Latham & Watkins, Atlantic Richfield Plaza, 72; Credit Lyonnais Int, Los Angeles, 75; Hyatt Regency, Dallas, Tex, 78; Progressive Savings & Loan, Beverly Hills; Security Pac Nat Bank, Los Angeles; and others. *Exhib:* Long Beach Mus of Art, Ann New Artist, Calif 69; Otis Mus 50th Anniv Exhib, Los Angeles, 69; Library of Congress Nat Print Exhib, Washington, DC, 69; Univ of Calif, Santa Cruz, 77; Santa Barbara Mus, 80; Los Angeles Municipal Gallery, Barsdale Park; Los Angeles Bicentennial, 81; and others. *Teaching:* Instr painting, Otis Art Inst, Parsons Sch Design, Los Angeles & Paris, currently. *Awards:* Calif Arts Coun Grant, 79; Nat Endowment Arts Individual fel, 80-81; and others. *Bibliog:* Joseph Mugaini (auth), Drawing, A Search for Form, Reinholt, 66; Innovative printmakers in southern Calif, Southwest Art Mag, 73; article in Artweek, 74. *Media:* Aluminum; Oil, Acrylic. *Mailing Add:* 3593 Berry Dr Studio City CA 91604

VACCARO, LUELLA GRACE
CERAMIST, PAINTER
b Miles City, Mont, June 2, 34. *Study:* Univ Wash, Seattle; Univ Calif, Berkeley; workshops with Peter Voulkas. *Work:* Antonio Prieto Collection, Mills Col, Oakland, Calif; Ceramics Monthly Collection, Columbus, Ohio. *Exhib:* 32nd & 33rd Int Print Exhib, Seattle Art Mus, Wash, 61-62; Latitude 53 Gallery, Edmonton, Alta, 79; Mail Art Expo '80, Santa Cruz, Calif, 79; one-artist shows, Univ of Kans, 66 (125 pieces) & Lawrence City Libr, 67 (40 pieces); Kellas Gallery, Lawrence, Kans, 81 & 82; and many others. *Awards:* Laguna Gloria Award, Tex Fine Arts Asn, Austin, 61; Kans Designer Craftsman Award, Kans Univ Art Mus, Lawrence, 68; Ceramic Monthly Award, Ceramics Monthly, Columbus, Ohio, 71. *Bibliog:* Luella Vaccaro and Her Pottery, Sunflower Cablevision interview, 79. *Media:* Oil; Stoneware, Clay. *Dealer:* Kellas Gallery 7 E 7th St Lawrence KS 66044. *Mailing Add:* 535 Kansas St Lawrence KS 66044

VACCARO, NICK DANTE
PAINTER, EDUCATOR
b Youngstown, Ohio, Apr 09, 31. *Study:* Univ Wash, BA, 58; Univ Calif, Berkeley, MA, 60; with David Park. *Work:* San Francisco Art Asn; Univ Calif, Berkeley; Youngstown Univ, Ohio. *Comn:* Mosaic, Pac Coast Paper Mills, Seattle, 57. *Exhib:* Libr Cong, Washington, DC, 60; Okla Art Ctr, Oklahoma City, 60, 61, 64-66 & 76; Calif Palace Legion Honor, San Francisco, 61; one-man shows, Univ Tex, Austin, 61, Wichita Univ, Kans, 67, Univ Okla, Norman, 72 & Univ Kans, Lawrence, 73 & 82; DeYoung Mus, San Francisco, 62; Houston Mus of Fine Arts, Tex, 63; Mid-Am, Nelson Gallery, Kansas City, 64-66 & 70; Kellas Gallery, Lawrence, Kans, 77 & 81; and many others. *Teaching:* Instr drawing & painting, Dept Art, Univ Tex, 60-61, asst prof drawing color, Sch Archit, 61-63; prof drawing & painting, Univ Kans, 63-, chmn dept art, 63-67; vis artist, Pa State Univ, 70. *Awards:* Purchase Awards, San Francisco Mus Art, 58, Dallas Mus Fine Arts, 61 & Montgomery Mus Fine Art, 62. *Media:* Mixed Media. *Publ:* Illusr, Tex Quart, Vol 5, No 1; illusr, Image, Univ Tex, Austin, 63; auth, Gorky's debt, Art J, 63. *Mailing Add:* 535 Kansas St Lawrence KS 66044

VACCARO, (PATT) PATRICK FRANK
PRINTMAKER, PAINTER
b New Rochelle, NY. *Study:* Ohio State Univ. *Work:* US Govt for Am Foreign Embassies; Butler Inst Am Art, Youngstown, Ohio; St Peter's Col, Jersey City, NJ; Farnsworth Mus, Wellesley Col, Mass; Ann Arbor Art Asn, Mich. *Comn:* Presentation Print, Friends Am Art, Youngstown, 69; Honor Print commemorating first solar church, St Paul's, Ore, 80. *Exhib:* William Penn Mus, Pa; Boston Libr Tour Italy, 55-59; Boston Printmakers Ann, Boston Mus Fine Arts, 55-; Am Colorprint Soc Ann, Philadelphia, 59-; Butler Inst Am Art Midyears, Youngstown, 62-67; Cleveland Mus Art Nat US Tour, 67; Print Club Ann,, Philadelphia, 76-80. *Awards:* First Watercolor Awards, Aurora Art Ctr, Ill, 64; Quaker Storage Award, Am Colorprint Soc, 69; Graphics Awards, Butler Inst Am Art. *Mem:* Boston Printmakers; Am Colorprint Soc. *Media:* Watercolor & Acrylics; Serigraphy. *Publ:* Illusr, Christian Herald; illusr, Together, Methodist Monthly, 69; illusr, Presby-Westminster Press, 71-72. *Mailing Add:* 7078 Oak Dr Poland OH 44514

VALENSTEIN, ALICE
PAINTER, COLLECTOR
b New York, NY, Feb 12, 04. *Study:* Teachers Col, Columbia Univ, study with Winold Reiss, Morris Davidson, Victor Candell & Leo Manso. *Work:* Staten Island Mus, NY; Emily Lowe Mus, Coral Gables, Fla; Hofstra Univ, NY; Miami Mus Mod Art, Fla; Mills Col, Oakland, Calif. *Exhib:* One-woman shows, Krasner Gallery, NY, Carus Gallery, NY, Katonah Gallery, NY, Miami Mus Mod Art & Alonzo Gallery, NY, Brunswick Sch, Conn. *Pos:* Interior decorator, Alice Starr Interior Decorator, 27- *Awards:* Scarsdale Art Asn; Westchester Arts; Brandeis Univ. *Mem:* Nat Asn Women Artists. *Collection:* Contemporary fellow artists. *Dealer:* Jack Alonzo 30 W 57th St New York NY 10021. *Mailing Add:* 20 Heathcote Rd Scarsdale NY 10583

VALENSTEIN, SUZANNE GEBHART
CURATOR
b Baltimore, Md, July 17, 28. *Pos:* Assoc cur Far Eastern art, Metrop Mus Art, New York, presently. *Teaching:* Vis lectr Chinese ceramics, Princeton Univ, NJ, fall 76. *Mem:* Oriental Ceramic Soc London; Oriental Ceramic Soc Hong Kong; Asia Soc. *Publ:* Auth, Ming Porcelains: a Retrospective, China Inst in Am, 70; auth, A Handbook of Chinese Ceramics, 75 & Highlights of Chinese Ceramics, 75, Metrop Mus Art; coauth, Oriental Ceramics: The World's Great Collections, Vol XII, The Metropolitain Museum, Kodansha Int, 77; auth, Chinese celadons reclaimed from the sea, Oriental Art Mag, spring 79. *Mailing Add:* Metrop Mus Art Fifth Ave at 82nd St New York NY 10028

VALENTIN, JEAN-PIERRE
DEALER
b France, Jan 31, 49; Can citizen. *Study:* Paris Business Sch, MBA(int trade), 71. *Bibliog:* A Gascon (auth), J P Valentin et sa Galerie, Le Collectionneur, 78; G Robinson (auth), L' Art Francais Montreal, Can Art Investor's Guide, 80. *Mem:* Prof Art Dealers' Asn Can (pres, 81-). *Specialty:* Prominent Quebec artists and Canadian artists; works by European masters of the 20th century. *Mailing Add:* Galerie L' Art Francais 370 W Laurier Montreal PQ H2V 2K7 Canada

VALENTINE, DEWAIN
SCULPTOR
b Ft Collins, Colo, Aug 27, 36. *Study:* Univ Colo, BFA, 58, MFA, 60; Yale-Norfolk Art Sch, Yale Univ Fel, 58. *Work:* Whitney Mus Am Art, New York; Los Angeles Co Mus Art; Atlantic Richfield Corp, Washington, DC; Milwaukee Art Ctr; Stanford Univ Art Mus. *Exhib:* Los Angeles Co Mus Art, 79; Six Los Angeles Sculptors, Federal Reserve Bank, Washington, DC, 80; California Innovations, Calif State Univ, Fullerton; Palm Springs Desert Mus, 81; Southern California Art, 1940-1980, Laguna Beach Mus Art, Calif, 81; and many others. *Teaching:* Instr design & drawing, Univ Colo, 58-61 & 64-65; instr plastics, Univ Calif, Los Angeles, 65-67. *Awards:* John Simon Guggenheim Fel, 80; Nat Endowment Arts Grant, 81. *Bibliog:* Nory Hastings (auth), cover article, Western Plastics, 11/74; Fran Preisman (auth), De Wain Valentine, Seizing light, Artweek, 7/75; Joan Hugo (auth), The behavior of materials, Artweek, 10/79. *Media:* Glass. *Mailing Add:* 69 Market St Venice CA 90291

VALERIO, JAMES ROBERT
PAINTER, EDUCATOR
b Chicago, Ill, Dec 2, 38. *Study:* Art Inst Chicago, BFA, 66, & MFA(Anne Louis Raymond Fel), 68; spec study with Seymour Rosofsky. *Work:* Ill Bell Telephone Co; Univ Iowa Mus Art; Prudential Insurance Co; Albuquerque Mus Art. *Exhib:* One-man shows, Michael Walls Gallery, New York, 74 & John Berggruen Gallery, San Francisco, 77; Current Concerns, Part 2, Los Angeles Inst of Contemp Art, Calif, 75; Painting & Sculpture in California: The Mod Era, Nat Col of Fine Arts of the Smithsonian Inst, Washington, DC & San Francisco Mus of Art, 76-77; Uncommon Visions, Mem Art Gallery, Univ Rochester, NY, 79; Reflections of Realism, Albuquerque Mus Art, NMex, 79; Real, Really Real, Super Real, San Antonio Mus Art, Tex, 81; Contemp Am Realism Since 1960, Pa Acad Fine Arts, 81. *Teaching:* Asst prof art, Rock Valley Col, Rockford, Ill, 68-70; assoc prof art, Univ Calif, Los Angeles, 70-79; assoc prof, Cornell Univ, 79-82. *Awards:* Purchase Award, Long Beach Mus of Art, 70; Creative Arts Award Fel, Univ Calif, Los Angeles, 76. *Bibliog:* T Brewster (auth), Every picture tells a story, Horizon Mag, 11/81. *Dealer:* Allan Frumkin Gallery 50 W 57th St New York NY. *Mailing Add:* Highgate Circle Ithaca NY 14850

VALESCO, FRANCES
MURALIST, PRINTMAKER
b Los Angeles, Calif, Aug 3, 41. *Study:* Univ Calif, Los Angeles, BA, 64; Sacramento State Univ, 64-65; Calif State Univ, Long Beach, MA, 72. *Comn:* Grazing Cow Mural, 76, Women's Mural, 78-79 & Playland and the Movies Mural, 79, San Francisco Neighborhood Arts Prog; Desert Mural, 82 & Buffalo Sky Mural, 82, Dept Housing & Urban Develop, Off Community Develop, San Francisco. *Exhib:* 162nd Ann Exhib, Pa Acad Fine Arts, 67; Artist's Proof: The Multiple Image, Fine Arts Mus, San Francisco, 76; Gallery 612, Tokyo, Japan, 82; Sun Gallery, Hayward, Calif, 82; Fine Arts Faculty Exhib, San Francisco Acad Art Gallery, 83; Print Show, Diablo Valley Col, 83; Galeria Museo, Mission Cult Ctr, San Francisco, 83. *Pos:* Community artist, San Francisco Art Comn, 75-80; artist in residence in the community, Calif State Arts Coun, 80-83. *Teaching:* Lectr etching & screen printing, Univ Calif, Berkeley, 75-76 & 79; lectr screen printing, drawing & mural painting, Sonoma State Univ, 77-80; instr printmaking, San Francisco Acad Art, 82- *Awards:* Arts Coun Award, Univ Calif, Los Angeles, 63; Purchase Prize, Kingsley Ann, Crocker Mus, Sacramento, 64; Print Purchase for Embassies, Beirut, Lebanon & Kuala Lumpur, Malasia, US Info Agency, 67. *Bibliog:* John C Oglesby (auth), article, Sacramento Bee, 64; Elizabeth Pomada (auth), The city's art brigade, San Francisco Mag, 76, Judith Anderson (auth), San Francisco's splashy outdoor art, San Francisco Chronicle, 82. *Mem:* Calif Soc Printmakers (historian, 78-80). *Media:* Mixed. *Publ:* Ed & illusr, Media Mixed, Joined Arts, 67; illusr, Music of the Whole Earth, Scribners, 76; contribr & illusr, Cenizas, Univ Calif, Santa Cruz, 83; coauth, Combining color xerography with the technique of silk screen and intaglio, Leonardo, 84. *Mailing Add:* 135 Jersey St San Francisco CA 94114

VALLANCE, JEFFREY K R
SCULPTOR, PAINTER
b Torrance, Calif, Jan 25, 55. *Study:* Calif State Univ, Northridge, BA, 79; Otis Inst Parsons Sch Design, MFA, 81. *Work:* Australian Nat Gallery, Canberra. *Comn:* Man and Dog (mural), Fallbrook Sq Mall, Woodland Hills, Calif, 73; Dinosaurs (mural), Powelle Butte Grocery, Ore, 77; Space (mural), Crippled Childrens Soc, Woodland Hills, Calif, 77; Blinky (gravestone), Los Angeles Pet Cemetery, Calabasas, Calif, 78. *Exhib:* Solo exhibs, Washington Proj Arts, 78, Daniel Sorano Hall Nat Treasure, Dakar, Senegal, 80, Univ Art Mus, Santa Barbara, 82 & Mus Contemp Art, Chicago, 83; Critical Perspectives, PS1, Long Island, 82; Five From Los Angeles, Mandeville Art Gallery, Univ Calif, San Diego, 82. *Pos:* Art dir, Crippled Childrens Soc, Woodland Hills, Calif, 76-77; host, Cutting Edge, MTV, Los Angeles, 83. *Bibliog:* Peter Schjeldahl (auth), Los Angeles demystified, Village Voice, 81; Howard Singerman (auth), article, 81 & Bob Pincus (auth), article, 84, Artforum. *Media:* Enamel, Electronics. *Res:* Polynesian myth of Tiki. *Publ:* Auth, Blinky the Friendly Hen, private publ, 79. *Dealer:* Rosamund Felsen Gallery 669 N La Cienega Los Angeles CA 90069. *Mailing Add:* 20764 Stephanie Dr Canoga Park CA 91306

VALLEE, WILLIAM OSCAR
PAINTER, GRAPHIC ARTIST
b South Paris, Maine, June 18, 34. *Study:* Univ Alaska. *Work:* Many in pvt collections. *Exhib:* Anchorage Fur Rendezvous, 63; Easter Arts Festival, 63; Alaska Festival Music & Art, 63 & 64; one-man shows, Anchorage Petrol Club, 63 & Anchor Galleries, 63. *Pos:* Instituted (in coop with Am Artists Prof League), Am Art Wk, 63; treas, Soc Alaskan Arts, 63; co-founder, Alaska-Int Cult Arts Ctr; bd dirs & co-founder, Anchorage Community Art Ctr, currently; pres & chmn bd, Alaska Map Serv, Inc, currently. *Awards:* Anchorage Fur Rendezvous, 63; Easter Art Festival, 63; Artist of the Month, Alaska Art Guild, 64. *Mem:* Alaska Art Guild (pres & chmn, 64); Alaska Watercolor Soc (pres, 63); Am Soc Photogrammetry; Am Artist Prof League. *Media:* Watercolor. *Mailing Add:* 4118 Irene Dr Anchorage AK 99501

VALLILA, MARJA R
SCULPTOR
b Prague, Czech, Oct 20, 50; US citizen. *Study:* Hampshire Col, BA, 72; Cornell Univ, MFA, 75. *Work:* Johnson Mus; Everson Mus; Kennedy Airport, McCory Corp, New York; Gen Mills Corp, Minneapolis. *Exhib:* Solo exhib, Zabriskie Gallery, New York, 77 & 80, Mus Fine Arts, Springfield, Mass, 79 & Tulane Univ, 81; A Study in Materials, Storm King Art Ctr, 78; Architectural Sculpture, Los Angeles Inst Contemp Art, 80; View From Upstate, AIR Gallery, New York, 82. *Teaching:* Asst prof sculpture, Cornell Univ, 79-80, mem adv coun, 81-; asst prof, Bard Col, 80 & State Univ NY, Albany, 81- *Awards:* State Univ NY Res Grant, 83. *Bibliog:* David L Shirley (auth), article, New York Times, 7/14/77; Sally Jessup (auth), article, Art World, 5/21/80. *Mem:* Col Art Asn. *Media:* Welded Steel, Cast Iron. *Dealer:* Zabriskie Gallery 724 Fifth Ave New York NY 10019. *Mailing Add:* Box 167 Cottekill NY 12419

VALTMAN, EDMUND
CARTOONIST
b Tallinn, Estonia, May 31, 14; US citizen. *Study:* Pvt studios, 36-39; Tallinn Art & Appl Art Sch, 42-44. *Work:* Lyndon Johnson Libr, Austin, Tex; Univ Southern Miss Libr; Univ Cincinnati Libr; State Hist Soc Mo, Columbia; Wichita State Univ Libr, Kans. *Exhib:* World Cartoon Festival, Knokke-Heist, Belg, 71; one-man cartoon exhibs, Estonian House, New York, 72, Toronto, 73, Baltimore Mem Hall, 76 & West Hartford Art League, 79; Gallery on the Green, Canton, Conn, 81. *Pos:* Editorial cartoonist, Hartford Times, 51-75. *Awards:* Pub Interest Award, Nat Safety Coun, 58; Pulitzer Prize for Cartooning, Columbia Univ, 62; Frank Tripp Award, Gannett Newspapers, 63. *Mem:* Asn Am Ed Cartoonists; Nat Cartoonists Soc; Conn Acad Fine Arts; Canton Artists Guild; West Hartford Art League. *Media:* India Ink. *Collection:* Editorial cartoons. *Publ:* Cartoon, In: The Ungentlemanly Art, McMillan, rev ed 75; cartoon, In: Avain Aikamme Maailman, Werner Söderström, Helsinki, Finland, 83. *Mailing Add:* 41 Foothills Way Bloomfield CT 06002

VAN AALTEN, JACQUES
PAINTER, SCULPTOR
b Antwerp, Belg, Apr 12, 07. *Study:* Nat Acad Design, 26-30, grad; Art Students League, 32-34; Acad Grande Chaumiere, Paris, 55; Tulane Univ La, 70-71. *Work:* Portrait of Pope Pius XII, Vatican Mus Permanent Collection, Rome; Relig Ministry Bldg, Jerusalem; Truman Libr, Independence, Mo; La State Art Collection, New Capitol Bldg, Baton Rouge; Rockport Art Asn, Mass; plus many others in pvt collections in USA & abroad. *Exhib:* Whitney Mus, 40; Detroit Inst Art Mus, Mich, 46; Isaac Delgado Mus Art, New Orleans, 58-59; Rockport Art Asn, Mass, 62-81; Mus-Norton Gallery, Palm Beach, Fla, 63; La Artists Group, La Art Comn Gallery, Old Capitol Bldg, Baton Rouge; plus many other group & one-man shows. *Teaching:* Instr art, Nassau Conserv Art, Long Island, NY, 40; instr art, van Aalten Studio Sch, Detroit, 44-47; instr art, Deerfield Beach & Boca Raton, Fla, 74-81. *Awards:* Suydam Medal, 30; Tiffany Scholar, 30; Silver Pontifical Medal, received from Pope Pius XII, Vatican City, Rome, Italy, 56. *Mem:* Life mem Rockport Art Asn; life mem Art Students League; Nat Soc Mural Painters; Isaac Delgado Mus Art Asn. *Mailing Add:* Lyndhurst K-1043 Deerfield Beach FL 33441

VAN ALSTINE, JOHN RICHARD
SCULPTOR
b Johnstown, NY, Aug 14, 52. *Study:* St Lawrence Univ, 70-72; Kent State Univ, BFA, 74; Cornell Univ Sch Art & Archit, MFA, 76. *Work:* Nat Mus Am Art, Smithsonian Inst; Hirshhorn Mus & Sculpture Garden; Denver Mus; Carnegie Inst Mus Art; McKissick Mus, Univ SC, Columbia. *Comn:* Outdoor public sculptures, Am Linen Co & Burlington Northern Railroad, Billings, Mont, 82 & Luck Stone Corp, Richmond, Va, 83. *Exhib:* Solo exhibs, Johnson Mus, Ithaca, NY, 76 & Southeastern Ctr Contemp Art, Winston-Salem, NC, 84; Directions 79, Hirshhorn Mus, 79; Western States Biennial, Denver Mus, San Francisco Mus Mod Art, Nat Collection Fine Arts & Seattle Mus Art, 79. *Teaching:* Asst, Cornell Univ, 74-76; asst prof, Univ Wyo, Laramie, 76-80 & Univ Md, College Park, 80- *Awards:* Tiffany Found Fel, 80; Washington, DC Comn Arts Fel, 82; Creative & Performing Arts Award, Univ Md, 83. *Bibliog:* Color--five new views, Art Forum, 10/81; David Tannous (auth), article, Art in Am, 12/81; Paul Richard (auth), article, Washington Post, 5/83. *Media:* Stone, Steel. *Dealer:* Diane Brown Gallery 100 Green St New York NY 10012. *Mailing Add:* 218 1/2 Bright St Jersey City NJ 07302

VANASSE, LOUIS RAYMOND
COLLECTOR, INSTRUCTOR
b Northampton, Mass, Jan 22, 31. *Study:* St Michael's Col, AB(Eng); Univ of Mass, MA(Eng). *Teaching:* Instr humanities, Northampton Sch System, Mass, 60- *Awards:* John Hay Fel, Studies in the Humanities, Williams Col, 62; Fulbright-Hays Grant, study in Ghana, W Africa, African Art, Univ Mass, 74. *Collection:* Twentieth century American Artists. *Mailing Add:* 17 Aubinwood Rd Amherst MA 01002

VAN BRUNT, PHILIP G
DIRECTOR, ASSEMBLAGE ARTIST
b Kobe, Japan, Mar 31, 35; US citizen. *Study:* Chaffey Col, Ontario, Calif, AA; Otis Art Inst, Los Angeles, MFA, 60; also with Arthur Ames. *Work:* Santa Barbara Mus Art, Calif; Salk Inst, La Jolla; Lyman Allyn Mus, New London, Conn; Presidente Mus, Guadalajara, Mex; Carnegie Inst, Pittsburgh, Pa. *Comn:* Processional Cross, St Mark's Episcopal Church, Upland, Calif, 64; oil painting, Gen Foods Corp, Calif, 65; enamel mural, pvt residence, Los Angeles, 69; mural, collage, Clinton Nat Bank, Conn, 74. *Exhib:* Enamels',

Mus Contemp Crafts, New York, 59; Los Angeles Co Mus Art, Calif, 59-61; 17 Conn Artists, Slater Mem Mus, Norwich, Conn, 72; one-man show, La Jolla Art Mus, 68 & Lyman Allyn Mus, New London, Conn, 74. *Pos:* Asst dir, Downey Mus Art, Calif, 60-65. *Teaching:* Instr painting, Lyman Allyn Mus, summers; instr, Westridge Sch, Pasadena, Calif, 63-64; dir art, Williams Sch, New London, Conn, 72-73. *Awards:* Gold Medal, Nat Orange Show, San Bernardino, Calif, 58. *Bibliog:* Jean Yoder (auth), Titanic epilogue, Commutator J. *Mem:* Otis Art Assoc, Los Angeles. *Media:* Found Objects, Collage. *Publ:* Contribr, Joseph Mugnaini (auth), Oil Painting, 72; illusr, Choristers guild letters, 74-75. *Dealer:* Henri Gallery 1500 21st St NW Washington DC 20036. *Mailing Add:* 110 Hempstead St New London CT 06320

VAN BUREN, RAEBURN
ILLUSTRATOR, CARTOONIST
b Pueblo, Colo, Jan 12, 91. *Study:* Art Students League, 13. *Work:* Boston Univ Mus; Syracuse Univ. *Pos:* Creator of United Feature Syndicated Comic Strip Abbie & Slats. *Awards:* Cartoonist of the Year, B'nai B'rith, Philadelphia, 58; Gold Key to Hall of Fame, Nat Cartoonist Soc, 79. *Mem:* Charter mem Nat Cartoonists Soc; life mem Soc Illusr; Artists & Writers Soc. *Publ:* Contribr illus, Sat Eve Post, Collier's, Redbook, New Yorker, McClure Syndicate & King Features Syndicate, and others. *Mailing Add:* 21 Clover Dr Great Neck NY 11021

VAN BUREN, RICHARD
SCULPTOR
b Syracuse, NY, 1937. *Study:* Mexico City Col; Univ Mex; San Francisco State Col. *Work:* Mus Mod Art, New York; Walker Art Ctr, Minneapolis; Nat Gallery Australia, Canberra; Art Mus STex, Corpus Christi. *Comn:* Three-unit wall sculpture, Walker Art Ctr, 71. *Exhib:* Whitney Sculpture Ann, Whitney Mus Am Art, New York, 68 & 70; Milwaukee Art Mus, 69 & 71; Art Inst Chicago, 69 & 72; Walker Art Ctr, Minneapolis, 71; Albright-Knox Art Gallery, Buffalo, NY, 71; Contemp Art Mus, Houston, 72; Harvard Univ, 73; Contemp Arts Ctr, Cincinnati, 73; Indianapolis Mus Art, Ind, 74; Va Mus Fine Arts, Richmond, 74; New York Cult Ctr, 74; one-man exhib, City Univ New York, 75; and others. *Bibliog:* Phyllis Tuchman (auth), An interview with Richard Van Buren, 12/69 & Susan Heineman (auth), Richard Van Buren, 4/75, Artforum; Carter Ratcliff (auth), Solid color, Art News, 5/72. *Mailing Add:* Paula Cooper Gallery 155 Wooster St New York NY 10012

VANCO, JOHN LEROY
ADMINISTRATOR, PHOTOGRAPHER
b Erie, Pa, Aug 21, 45. *Study:* Allegheny Col, BA(art hist); Whitney Mus Am Art. *Pos:* Exec dir, Erie Art Ctr, 68- *Awards:* Best Prof, ESFA Photog Exhib, 72. *Publ:* Auth, What Ever Happened to Louis Eilshemius?, 67; contribr, American Art & Western Wildlife, 72; illusr, Roger Misiewicz: Wolfman of the Blues, 72. *Mailing Add:* 1317 Parade St Erie PA 16503

VAN DE BOVENKAMP, HANS
SCULPTOR
b Barneveld, Holland, June 1, 38. *Study:* Archit Sch Amsterdam, 57; Univ Mich, Ann Arbor, BScDes, 61. *Exhib:* Berenson-Medici Gallery, Miami, Fla, 69-78; Benson Gallery, Bridgehampton, NY, 69, 75 & 78; Lever House, New York, 69 & 73-83; Storm King Art Ctr, Cornwall, NY, 73-74; Aquarius Int, Caracas, Venezuela, 74-75; Am Inst of Arts & Lett, New York, 76; Arnot Art Mus, Elmira, NY, 76; Nat Acad of Design, New York, 77; and others. *Pos:* Exec bd, New York Sculptors Guild. *Awards:* Emily Lowe Award, 64; I-80 Nebr Award, 75. *Media:* Aluminum, Stainless Steel. *Dealer:* Arras Gallery 29 W 57th St New York NY. *Mailing Add:* Box 837 Tillson NY 12486

VANDENBERGE, PETER WILLEM
SCULPTOR, MURALIST
b Voorburg, Zuid-Holland, Neth, Oct 16, 35; US citizen. *Study:* Art Acad, The Hague, Neth; Calif State Univ, Sacramento, BA; Univ Calif, Davis, MA. *Work:* Henry Gallery, Univ Wash, Seattle; Mus Contemp Crafts, New York; Johnson Collection Am Crafts, Racine, Wis; Crocker Art Mus, Sacramento; Burpee Art Mus, Rockford, Ill. *Comn:* Three glazed relief tile murals, San Francisco City Col, 71; pub murals, San Francisco Arts Comn, City of San Francisco; glazed tile relief, Contra Costa Jr Col Dist Off, John F Gordon Educ Ctr, Martinez, Calif, 75; tile mural, Sacramento Metrop Arts Comn, 79. *Exhib:* Clay Works, Mus Contemp Crafts, 71; Int Ceramic Exhib, Victoria & Albert Mus, London, 72; Four Ceramic Sculptors from California, Alan Frumkin Gallery, New York, 73, Calif Ceramic Sculptors I & II, 74, Five Ceramic Sculptors from Calif, Chicago, 75; Clay, Whitney Mus Am Art, New York, 74; Fendrick's Gallery, Washington, DC, 76; Campbell Mus Contemp Crafts, Cranbrook Acad Art, Bloomfield Hills, Mich, 76; A Century of Ceramics in the United States, Everson Mus Art, Syracuse, NY, 79; and others. *Teaching:* Asst prof ceramics & sculpture, San Francisco State Univ, 66-73; assoc prof ceramics & sculpture, Calif State Univ, Sacramento, 73- *Awards:* Madeleine Cortese Williams Found Award, 63 & 66; Purchase Award for Sculpture, Home Savings & Loan Assoc, Los Angeles, 73. *Bibliog:* D Zack (auth), Mythology, California ceramics, Art & Artist Mag, London, 9/69, Nut art in quake time, Art News, 70 & Laugh in clay, Craft Horizon Mag, 71. *Media:* Stoneware, Porcelain; Clay, Terra Cotta. *Dealer:* Quay Ceramics Gallery 254 Sutter St San Francisco CA 94108; Allan Frumkin 41 57th St New York NY 10022. *Mailing Add:* 713 37th St Sacramento CA 95819

VAN DER BEEK, EDWARD STANLEY
FILMMAKER, VIDEO ARTIST
b New York, NY, Jan 6, 27. *Study:* Cooper Union, 52-53; Black Mountain Col, NC, 56-57, Cooper Union, Hon Dr, 72. *Work:* Films in various public libraries & film collection in various museums. *Exhib:* Lincoln Ctr, NY Film Festival, New York, 65 & 79; Inst Contemp Art, Houston, 67; Metrop Mus Art, New York, 69; Vancouver Art Mus, Can, 71; Art Inst Chicago, 75; Whitney Mus Am Art, New York, 79; Mus Mod Art, New York, 79; Kennedy Ctr, DC, 79. *Teaching:* Artist fel, Ctr Advan Visual Studies, Mass Inst Technol, Boston, 69-72; assoc prof art, Univ S Fla, Tampa, 72-75; prof art, Univ Md, Baltimore Co, 75- *Awards:* Computer Film Award, Expo '67, Montreal, Can; Experimental Film Award, Washington Area Film League, 78; Short Films Award, NY Film Festival Lincoln Ctr, 79; and others. *Bibliog:* CBS Camera Three, Van Der Beekiana, 68; David Curtis (auth), Experimental Cinema, London, Eng, 71; Gene Youngblood (auth), Expanded Cinema, 74. *Media:* Film, Video. *Dealer:* Electronic Arts Intermix 84 Fifth Ave New York NY 10011. *Mailing Add:* 5112 South Rolling Rd Relay Baltimore MD 21227

VANDERLIP, DIANNE PERRY
GALLERY DIRECTOR, EDUCATOR
b Toledo, Ohio, Apr 20, 41. *Study:* Ohio Univ, BFA; NY Univ; Pratt Inst. *Collections Arranged:* Recorded Activities (with catalog), 70; Artists Books (with catalog), 73; N, E, W, S & Middle (with catalog), 75; Alphons Schilling Stereoptics, 75; John Sloan/Robert Henri: Their Philadelphia Yrs, 76; Alan Shields' Environments, 77; Robert Hudson, 77; Poets & Painters, 79; Lucas Samaras Pastels, 81. *Pos:* Dir, Vanderlip Gallery, Philadelphia, 66-68; dir, Moore Col Art Gallery, 68-78; cur & consult, Dechert, Price & Rhoads, Philadelphia, 74-; panelist & consult, Nat Endowments Arts, Washington, DC, 74-; cur of contemp art, Denver Art Mus, 78- *Teaching:* Prof aesthetics, Moore Col Art, 68- *Awards:* Award of Excellence, Philadelphia Art Dir Club, 71. *Bibliog:* Dore Ashton (auth), Beyond literalism, Art Mag, 69; Lucy Lippard (auth), Dematerialization of Art, Praeger, 73; Dianne Kelder (auth), Artists books, Art in Am, 74. *Mem:* Am Asn Mus; Am Fedn Arts; Soc Arts & Lett. *Collection:* Contemporary paintings and drawings by American artists. *Publ:* Ed, More Ray Gun Poems by Claes Oldenburg, 74; ed, Hopi Kachina Dolls, 75. *Mailing Add:* Denver Art Mus 100 W 14 Ave Pkwy Denver CO 80204

VAN DER MARCK, JAN
DIRECTOR
b Roermond, Netherlands, Aug 19, 29. *Study:* Univ Nijmegen, BA, MA & PhD(hist art), 56; Univ Utrecht; Columbia Univ. *Collections Arranged:* Charles Biederman, 65 & Lucio Fontana, 66, Walker Art Ctr, Minneapolis; Pictures to be Read/Poetry to be Seen, 67; Christo: Wrap in Wrap Out, 69; Moholy-Nagy, 69 & Art by Telephone, 69, Mus Contemp Art, Chicago; American Art: Third Quarter Century, 73, Seattle Art Mus; Arman, Mus Contemp Art, La Jolla, Calif, 74; Herbert Bayer, 77, Lucio Pozzi, 77 & Alain Kirili, 78. *Pos:* Cur, Gemeentemuseum, Arnhem, Netherlands, 59-61; deputy dir fine arts, Seattle World's Fair, 61-62; cur, Walker Art Ctr, Minneapolis, 63-67; dir, Mus Contemp Art, Chicago, 67-70, Valley Curtain Corp, 71-72, Dartmouth Col Mus & Galleries, 74-80 & Dade Co Ctr Fine Arts, Miami, 80- *Teaching:* Assoc prof art hist, Univ Wash, Seattle, 72-74. *Awards:* Fel, Netherlands Orgn Pure Res, 54-55; fel, Rockefeller Found, 57-59. *Mem:* Am Fedn Arts; Am Asn Mus Dir. *Publ:* Auth, Romantische Boekillustratie in Belgie, Romen, 56; auth, Lucio Fontana, Connaissance, 74; auth, George Segal, Abrams, 75; also articles in Artforum, Art in Am & other journals. *Mailing Add:* Dade Co Ctr Fine Arts 101 W Flagler St Miami FL 33130

VAN DER MEULEN, JAN
HISTORIAN, EDUCATOR
b Adelaide, South Africa, Oct 10, 29; US. *Study:* Univ Cape Town, B(arch), 52; Univ Marburg, Fed Republic Ger, DPhil, 62. *Pos:* Tech supv, Lichtbeelden Inst, Amsterdam, Holland, 55-56; free assoc, Archit Walter Freiwald, Marburg, WGer, 56-59; dir, South African Mus, 63-64. *Teaching:* Prof medieval art hist, Pa State Univ, 68-74; prof, Cleveland State Univ, 74-82; chmn dept, 74-82; vis prof, Univ Bonn, WGer, 82-83. *Awards:* Stipendiary, Alexander Von Humboldt-Stiftung, 66-68; Fulbright Prof, Univ Frankfurt, 78-79; Richard Merton Chair, Deutsche Forschunasgemeinschaft, 82-83. *Res:* Chartres Cathedral; late antique origins of Christianity in Gaul. *Publ:* Auth, A logos creator at Chartres, J Warburg & Courtauld Inst, London, 66; auth, Nortre Dame de Chartres Die Vorromanische Ostanlage, Mann, Berlin, 75; coauth, The West Portals of Chartres Cathedral, Vol 1, Am Univ Press, 81; ed, Sanctuaries of the Gallic Frankish Church, Lang, Frankfurt, 81-83; auth, Romanische Kultstätten, In: Palast und Hütte, Zabern, Mainz, 82. *Mailing Add:* 4201 Franklin Blvd Cleveland OH 44113

VANDERSALL, AMY L
HISTORIAN, EDUCATOR
b West Newton, Pa, Oct 9, 33. *Study:* Col Wooster, Ohio, BA, 55; Mt Holyoke Col, South Hadley, Mass, MA, 58; Yale Univ, MA, 62, PhD, 65. *Teaching:* Asst prof medieval art hist, Smith Col, 66-72; assoc prof, Univ Colo, 73-81, prof, 81- *Mem:* Int Ctr Medieval Art (bd of dirs, 75-78); Col Art Asn; Medieval Acad Am. *Res:* Carolingian ivory carving, Anglo-Saxon art and Romanesque sculpture. *Publ:* Auth, Two Caroloingian ivories in the Metropolitan Museum of Art, New York, Metrop Mus J, 72; auth, Date and provenance of the Franks casket, Gesta, 73; auth, Homeric myth in early medieval England: The lid of the Franks casket, Studies Iconography, 75; auth, Relationship of sculptors and painters at the court of Charles the Bald, 76 & Romanesque sculpture in American museums: The west, 80, Gesta. *Mailing Add:* Dept of Fine Arts Box 318 Univ of Colo Boulder CO 80309

VANDER SLUIS, GEORGE J
PAINTER, EDUCATOR
b Cleveland, Ohio, Dec 18, 15. *Study:* Cleveland Inst Art; Colorado Springs Fine Arts Ctr; Fulbright scholar, Italy, 51-52. *Work:* Rochester Mem Art Gallery, NY; Everson Mus Art, Syracuse, NY; Munson-Williams-Proctor Inst, Utica, NY; State Univ NY Albany; Colorado Springs Fine Arts Ctr; and others. *Comn:* Mural, US Govt Sect Fine Arts, Wyo, 41; Barn Door decorations in NY State, NY State Coun Arts grant, 66; wall painting, Hotel Syracuse, City Walls New York & NY State Coun Arts, 71; designed two US airmail stamps, 71; mural, Rena Dankovich Mem Chapel, Syracuse Univ, 81; and others. *Exhib:* The Door, Mus Contemp Crafts, New York, 68; one-man shows, J Seligmann Gallery, New York, 59; Royal Marks Gallery, New York, 62, 63 & 64; Krasner Gallery, New York, 68, 69 & 71, Everson Mus of Art, Syracuse, NY, 77 & Syracuse Univ Lubin House, New York, 78; and others. *Teaching:* Instr painting & drawing, Colo Fine Arts Ctr, 40-42 & 45-47; prof painting & drawing, Syracuse Univ, 47-82, assoc dean, Sch Art, 70-71; prof emer, 82. *Awards:* Jurors' Award, Rochester Mem Art Gallery, 58 & 69. *Bibliog:* J Albino (auth), Barn door painting, Dodge News, 11/67; article, New York Times, 4/7/67; article, Record, 12/8/77. *Media:* Acrylic. *Mailing Add:* 4132 Onondaga Blvd Grad Div Syracuse Univ Camillus NY 13031

VAN DOMMELEN, DAVID B
WRITER, FIBER ARTIST
b Grand Rapids, Mich, Aug 21, 29. *Study:* Harrington Interior Design Inst, cert; Mich State Univ, BA & MA; also with Abraham Rattner & Mariska Karasz. *Work:* Mich State Univ Mus of Art, East Lansing; Arrowmont Sch of Crafts, Gatlinburg, Tenn; Am Home Econ Asn Collection, Washington, DC; Marshall Field Permanent Collection, Chicago; Portland Mus of Fine Arts, Maine. *Exhib:* Group Traveling Show, Smithsonian Inst, Washington, DC, 57-58; Invention with Thread, Montclair Art Mus, NJ, 61; one-man shows, Portland Mus of Art, Maine, 63, Kalamazoo Art Ctr Mus, Mich, 66, Univ Iowa, Iowa City, 67 & WVa State Univ Mus, Institute, 75; and many others. *Collections Arranged:* Retrospective 1956-1968, Pa State Univ, 68. *Teaching:* Prof art educ, Pa State Univ, 59-; summer instr, Haystack Sch of Crafts, 62, 63 & 74; guest prof, Univ Iowa, 66-69; summer instr, Arrowmont Schs Crafts, 70-81. *Awards:* Fishburn Award, Int Understanding, Educ Press Am, 73. *Bibliog:* John Peter (auth), Sewing machine art, Look Mag, 8/61; Ruth Bunker (auth), David Van Dommelen, Cross-Country Craftsman, 10/62. *Mem:* Nat Art Educ Asn; Nat Craftsman's Asn. *Media:* Fiber. *Publ:* Auth, Decorative Wall Hangings, 62 & Walls: Enrichment and Ornamentation, 65, Funk & Wagnalls; auth, Designing and Decorating Interiors, John Wiley, 65; auth, New Uses for Old Cannonballs, Funk & Wagnalls, 66; auth, Doughboy Letters, VDI Press, 77. *Mailing Add:* 1981 Highland Dr State College PA 16801

VAN DUINWYK, GEORGE PAUL
GOLDSMITH, EDUCATOR
b New York, NY, Sept 30, 41. *Study:* Calif State Univ, Northridge, with Frederick Lauritzen, BA, 64; Calif State Univ, Long Beach, with Alvin A Pine, MA, 71; RI Sch of Design, with John A Prip, MFA, 72. *Work:* Oakland Mus, Calif. *Exhib:* Mod Am Metalsmithing & Jewelry, Corcoran Gallery of Art, Washington, DC, 72; Jewelry Invitational, Albright-Knox Mus, Buffalo, NY, 74; World Silver Fair, Mexico City, Mex, 74; Univ Colo, 74; 275 Yrs of Am Metalsmithing, Mus of Contemp Crafts, New York, 75; Goldsmiths 77, Phoenix Art Mus, Ariz, 77; Profiles of US Jewelry, Tex Tech Univ, Lubbock, 77; and others. *Pos:* Craftsman-in-residence, RI State Coun on the Arts, 76-77; dir tech resources, Jewelry Inst, Providence, RI, 77-79. *Teaching:* Assoc prof metalsmithing, Calif State Univ, Long Beach, 72-73; adj prof metalsmithing, RI Sch of Design, 73-74; asst prof, Kent State Univ, 79-82. *Awards:* Purchase Award, The Metal Experience, Oakland Mus, 71; Design Award, Designer/Craftsman 77, Richmond Art Ctr, Calif, 76; Nat Endowment for the Arts Grant, Slide Jury Proj, 77. *Bibliog:* Ralph Turner (auth), Modern Jewelry, Eng publ, 76; Thelma Newman (auth), The Container Book, Chilton, 77; Oppi Untracht (auth), Jewelry Techniques, Doubleday 77. *Mem:* Ohio Designer Craftsmen; Soc NAm Goldsmiths; Am Crafts Coun. *Media:* Precious & Nonprecious Metals. *Dealer:* Art Wear 409 W Broadway New York NY 10013. *Mailing Add:* 43 Farwell Newport RI 02840

VANESS, MARGARET HELEN
PAINTER, PRINTMAKER
b Seattle, Wash, Nov 6, 19. *Study:* Univ Wash, BFA(printmaking), BFA(painting) & MFA; Drexel Univ; spec study with Francis Cellentano & Glen Alps. *Work:* US Embassies in Athens, Bogata, Bierut, Caracas, Copenhagen, Seoul, Managua, Lima, Lagos, Dar es Salaam & Tanzania; Cheney-Cowles Mus, Spokane, Wash; Pratt-Manhatten Ctr Gallery, New York; World Print Orgn, San Francisco, Calif; Evergreen State Col Libr Collection, Olympia, Wash; and others. *Comn:* Two ed of ten prints each, US Info Agency, 73; mural, Med Ctr, Boeing Co, Philadelphia, Pa, 74. *Exhib:* Wash State Capitol Mus, Olympia, 64; Northwest Ann, Seattle Art Mus, Wash, 65 & 67; Pacific-Northwest Arts & Crafts Print Invitational, 70; Judkin Mem Art Mus, Bath, Eng, Pratt Manhatten, New York, 72-74; 60th Ann, Del Art Mus, Wilmington, 74; Philadelphia Art Alliance, Pa, 75; one-person show, Greenhill-Lower Merion, Philadelphia, Pa, 76; Nat Print Exhib, Cheney-Cowles Mus, Spokane Wash, 77; Gov Invitational, Olympia, Wash, 78; and others. *Collections Arranged:* Group Exhibs, Burien Arts Asn Festival of Arts, 66-69; King Co Arts Comn, Seattle Arts Comn Touring Exhib, 71, Exhib of Prints, 72. *Pos:* Illusr, Boeing Co, Seattle, Wash, 72-73 & 78 & Philadelphia, Pa, 74-75; illusr, Du Pont Co, Wilmington, Del, 73-74. *Teaching:* Instr painting & drawing, Burien Arts Gallery Sch, Seattle, Wash, 68-69; asst printmaking Univ Wash, Seattle, 71-73. *Awards:* First Award

Painting, Boeing Co, 68 & 74; First Awards Print, Pac Northwest Arts & Crafts Asn, 70 & 71; and others. *Bibliog:* Carolyn Wright (auth), Thesis exhibit at Henry Gallery, Univ Washington Daily, 6/73; Andrew Seraphin (auth), Four printmakers in Gallery F, Art Alliance Bulletin, 4/75. *Mem:* Col Art Asn, New York; Philadelphia Print Club; charter mem Burien Arts Asn (trustee, 65-69). *Media:* Acrylic, Mixed Media; Collagraph, Serigraphy. *Mailing Add:* 17128 Second Southwest Seattle WA 98166

VAN GINKEL, BLANCHE LEMCO
ARCHITECT, ADMINISTRATOR
b Can. *Study:* McGill Univ, BArch; Harvard Univ, MCP. *Exhib:* Plan for Old Montreal, Place Ville Marie, Montreal, Que, 63; Midtown Manhattan Plan Exhib, Art Dir Club & New York Cult Ctr, New York, 72; Work of van Ginkel Assoc, Columbia Univ, New York, 73; Spectrum Can, Royal Can Acad of Arts, Montreal, 76; and others. *Pos:* Rep to Can Conf of Arts, Ottawa, Royal Archit Inst of Can, 71-74; mem adv comt on design, Nat Capital Planning Comn, 77-82; chmn, Massey Awards, Ottawa, Ont, 77- *Teaching:* Asst prof archit, Univ Pa, Philadelphia, 51-57; vis prof, Harvard; dean, Sch Archit, Univ Toronto, Ont, 77-82, prof arch, 77- *Awards:* Massey Medal, 64; Grand Prix for Film, Int Fedn Housing & Planning, 56. *Bibliog:* New patterns for a metropolis, Archit Forum, 10/71; Les effets Reels...,Archit Concept, 5/73. *Mem:* Royal Can Acad of Arts; fel Royal Archit Inst of Can. *Publ:* Auth, The form of the core, J Am Inst Planner, 2/61; ed & contribr, Automobile Issue of Can Art, 62; contribr, Phenomenon of Pollution, Harvest House, 68; ed & contribr, Expo 67 Architectural Design, 67; contribr, Aesthetic considerations, In: Urban Problems, Holt Rinehart & Winston, 71. *Mailing Add:* Sch of Archit Univ Toronto 230 College St Toronto ON M5S 1A1 Canada

VAN HAAFTEN, JULIA
CURATOR, WRITER
b Lancaster, Pa, Nov 3, 46. *Study:* Barnard Col, BA, 68; Columbia Univ, MLS, 70. *Collections Arranged:* Original Sun Pictures (with catalog), 77 & 96 Images: Talbot to Stieglitz (with catalog), 81, New York Pub Libr Collection; 96 Images: Talbot to Stieglitz (with catalog), New York Pub Libr Col, 81. *Pos:* Contribr, Libr J, Portfolio Mag, Hist Photog, 73-; dir photog collections, New York Pub Libr, 79- *Bibliog:* Article, AB Bookmen's Weekly, 1/12/82, Darkroom Photogr, 1/83 & Photography Year, Time-Life, 82. *Mem:* Am Inst Conserv/Photo Materials Group. *Res:* Nineteenth century photography; illustrated books, albums, other forms of publications of photographs. *Publ:* Contribr, Guide to the literature of art history, Am Libr Asn, 81; joint auth, Egypt and the Holy Land: 77 Views by Francis Frith, Dover, 81. *Mailing Add:* c/o New York Pub Libr Fifth Ave at 42nd St New York NY 10018

VAN HOESEN, BETH (MRS MARK ADAMS)
PRINTMAKER
b Boise, Idaho, June 27, 26. *Study:* With Escuela Esmaralda, Mexico City, 45; San Francisco Art Inst, 46-47 & 51-52; Stanford Univ, BA, 48; Ecole Arts, Fontainbleau, 48-51; Acad Julian, Paris, 48-51; Acad Grande Chaumier, Paris, 48-51; San Francisco State Univ, 57-58. *Work:* Brooklyn Mus & Mus Mod Art, New York; San Francisco Mus Mod Art; Victoria & Albert Mus, London; Chicago Art Inst; and others. *Exhib:* Calif State Fair, Sacramento, 51; Libr Cong, 56 & 57; San Francisco Mus Mod Art, 56, 59, 61 & 70; Boston Mus Fine Arts, 59, 60 & 62; Philadelphia Acad Fine Arts, 59, 61, 63 & 65; solo exhibs, De Young Mus, San Francisco, 59, Achenbach Found, Calif Palace Legion Honor, 61 & 74, Santa Barbara Mus, 63, 74 & 76, E B Crocker Art Gallery, Sacramento, 66, Hansen/Fuller/Goldeen Gallery, San Francisco, 66, 77 & 80 & Oakland Mus, 80; Brooklyn Mus, 62, 66, 68 & 77; Continuing Am Graphics, Osaka, Japan, 70; Hawaii Nat Print Exhib, Honolulu, 71 & 80; Oakland Mus, 75; Fine Arts Mus San Francisco, 81. *Mem:* San Francisco Women Artists; Calif Soc Printmakers. *Publ:* Auth, A Collection of Wonderful Things, Scrimshaw, 72. *Dealer:* John Berggruen Gallery 228 Grant San Francisco CA 94108. *Mailing Add:* 3816 22nd St San Francisco CA 94114

VAN HOOK, DAVID H
PAINTER, ADMINISTRATOR
b Danville, Va, Dec 25, 23. *Study:* Univ SC, with Edmund Yaghijian. *Work:* Jacksonville Mus Art, Fla; Greenville Co Mus, SC; C & S Nat Bank, Columbia, SC; murals, Caughman Rd Sch, Columbia; Columbia Mus Art. *Exhib:* Mint Mus, Charlotte, NC, 66; Columbia Mus Art, 67; C & S Nat Bank Exhib, 68; Pfeiffer Col, Misenheimer, NC, 69; Contemp Artist of SC Tricentennial Exhib, Columbia, Greenville & Charleston, SC, 70; and many other group & one-man shows. *Collections Arranged:* Jasper Johns Print Traveling Exhibit, 71; Eight Washington Artists, 71. *Pos:* Registr, Columbia Mus Art, 51-58, asst to dir, 58-60, cur exhibs, 61-79. *Awards:* Rose Talbert Award, 54; Hon Award, Columbia Mus Art, 59; Purchase Prize, Guild SC Artists, 61. *Mem:* Guild SC Artists; Am Asn Mus; Southeastern Mus Conf. *Mailing Add:* 939 Brantley Columbia SC 29210

VAN LAAR, TIMOTHY JON
PAINTER, PRINTMAKER
b Ann Arbor, Mich, Mar 7, 51. *Study:* Calvin Col, BA, 73; Wayne State Univ, MFA, 75. *Work:* Detroit Inst Art; Southeast Banking Corp, Miami; Herman Miller Inc, Zeeland, Mich; Best Products Inc, Richmond, Va; Steelcase Inc, Grand Rapids, Mich. *Exhib:* Houston Mus Fine Arts, Tex, 80; Drawings by Mich Artists, Six Mich Art Mus, 81-82; Contemp Cliche-Verre Prints, Five Mich Art Mus, 81-82; Univ Ill Painting, Nat Mus, Taipei, Taiwan, 81; two-person exhib, Race St Gallery, Grand Rapids, 82; solo exhib, Asbury Col, Wilmore, Ky, 83; and others. *Pos:* Printer lithography, Mich Workshop Fine Prints, Detroit, 74-76; resident artist, Urban Inst Contemp Art, Grand Rapids,

Mich, 78. *Teaching:* Instr painting & printmaking, Calvin Col, 77-81; asst prof painting, Univ Ill, Urbana-Champaign, 81- *Awards:* Mich Coun Arts Artist Consultancy Grants, 78 & 79; Univ Ill Research Bd Grant, 82. *Media:* All Media; Lithograph, Intaglio. *Publ:* Auth, Printmaking: Editions as artworks, J Aesthetic Educ, 80; ed, Syro-Palestinian Folk Art from the DeVries Collection, Calvin Col, 80. *Dealer:* Cantor/Lemberg Gallery 538 N Woodward Birmingham MI; Virginia Miller Galleries 169 Madeira Coral Gables FL. *Mailing Add:* 408 E Peabody Dr Champaign IL 61820

VAN LEER, W LEICESTER
COLLECTOR
b Warwick, NY, Jan 29, 05. *Study:* Smith Col; also with Mary Turlay Robinson. *Collection:* Includes works by Delacroix, Matisse, Boudin, Dufy, Burchfield, Wyeth, Prendergast, Davies, Bishop, Homer, Segonzac, Marin, Cropsey, Utrillo, Beal, Andrew Wyeth & others. *Mailing Add:* 12 E 73rd St New York NY 10017

VAN LEUNEN, ALICE LOUISE
TEXTILE ARTIST, INSTRUCTOR
b Evansville, Ind, Feb 7, 43. *Study:* Smith Col, BA, 65; Ind Univ, 66-67. *Comn:* Textile panels, Playboy Club, Chicago, 78; woven textile hanging, Ore State Revenue Bldg, Salem, 81; woven wall hangings, Multnomah County, Ore, 83. *Exhib:* Works in Fabric, Renshaw Gallery, Linfield Col, Ore, 79; three-women exhib, Seattle Pac Univ, 79; Duo Exhib, Univ Ore Mus of Art, 78; one-woman shows, Contemp Crafts Gallery, Portland, 79 & The Lawrence Gallery Salishan, Gleneden Beach, Ore, 80; Smithsonian Inst, Washington DC, 80. *Pos:* Asst dir, Delphian Gallery-Delphian Found, 77; exhib asst, Contemp Crafts Gallery, Portland, 78-79. *Teaching:* Seminar instr, Dept Fine Arts, Univ Ore, 78-; lectr textiles, Portland State Univ, 80- *Awards:* Cash Award, 76 Traveling Exhib Competition, Univ Ore Mus of Art, 6/76; Honorable Mention, 6th Ann Exhib, Corvallis Art Ctr, 11/76. *Bibliog:* Northwest Designer-Craftsmen, NW Designer-Craftsmen Mag, Seattle, 76; The state of the crafts--a visual review, Frank Petock & Assoc, 1980, Interweave Mag, summer 80. *Mem:* Artists Equity; NW Designer Craftsmen, Inc, Seattle; Am Crafts Coun, NW Region. *Media:* Fiber and Paper. *Dealer:* Lawrence Gallery PO Box 148 Gleneden Beach OR 97388; Gallery West 4836 SW Scholls Ferry Rd Portland OR 97225. *Mailing Add:* PO Box 408 Lake Oswego OR 97034

VAN LOEN, ALFRED
SCULPTOR, EDUCATOR
b Oberhausen-Osterfeld, Ger, Sept 11, 24; US citizen. *Study:* Royal Acad Art, Amsterdam, Holland, 41-46. *Work:* Metrop Mus Art & Mus Mod Art, New York; Brooklyn Mus, NY; Nat Mus, Jerusalem, Israel. *Comn:* Brass fountain, James White Community Ctr, Salt Lake City, Utah, 58; Peace Window, Community Church, New York, 63; Jacob's Dream (brass), Little Neck Jewish Ctr, NY, 70; bronze & acrylic symbolic portrait of Guy Lombardo, Hall of Fame, Stony Brook, NY, 72. *Exhib:* Whitney Mus Am Art Ann, New York, 67; Emil Walters Gallery, New York, 68; Stony Brook Mus, 68; Heckscher Mus, Huntington, NY, 71 & 74; Nassau Community Col, NY, 72; C W Post Col, 65, 68, 72, 80 & 81. *Pos:* Art dir, South Huntington Pub Libr. *Teaching:* Instr, Hunter Col, 53-54 & NShore Community Art Ctr, NY, 55-61; prof sculpture, C W Post Col, Long Island Univ, 62- *Awards:* First Prize, Village Art Ctr, 49; Louissa Robbins Award, Silvermine Guild Artists, 56; First Prize Sculpture, Am Soc Contemp Artists, 64. *Bibliog:* Paul Mocsanyi (auth), Alfred Van Loen, Channel Press, 60; Mark Smith (auth), Alfred Van Loen, portrait, Long Island Mag, 64; Sculptured emotion of A V L, Mod Castings, 65. *Mem:* Am Soc Contemp Artists; Long Island Univ Pioneer Club. *Media:* Mixed. *Publ:* Auth, Simple Methods of Sculpture, Channel Press, 58; auth, Instructions to Sculpture, C W Post Col, 66; auth, Origin of Structure & Design, Hamilton Press, 67; auth, Drawings by Alfred Van Loen, Harbor Gallery Press, 69; auth, The Dancing Line, Harbor Gallery Press, 81. *Mailing Add:* 221 Beverly Rd Huntington Station NY 11746

VANN, LOLI (MRS LILIAN VAN YOUNG)
PAINTER
b Chicago, Ill, Jan 7, 13. *Study:* Art Inst Chicago; also with Sam Ostrowsky. *Work:* Chaffey Col, Ontario, Calif; Hollenbeck High Sch, Los Angeles. *Exhib:* Exhib Am Paintings, Carnegie Inst, Pittsburgh; Am Painting, Metrop Mus Art, New York; Corcoran Gallery Art Biennial, Washington, DC; Am Paintings & Int Watercolor Exhibs, Art Inst Chicago. *Awards:* Purchase Prize, Chaffey Community Art Asn; Hon Mention, Calif Watercolor Soc; Second Prize, Los Angeles Co Mus Art. *Media:* Multimedia. *Dealer:* Copenhagen Gallery Solvang CA 93463. *Mailing Add:* 2293 Panorama Terr Los Angeles CA 90039

VANN, SAMUEL LE ROY
PAINTER
b Ithaca, NY, Sept 16, 52. *Study:* Ft Lewis Col, BA, 73. *Work:* Everson Mus Art; Menninger Fund, Topeka, Kans. *Exhib:* Watercolors USA, Springfield Art Mus, Mo, 77; Chautauqua 20th Nat Show, CAA Gallery, NY, 78; Second International All on Paper Show, Assoc Art Orgn Western NY, Buffalo, 80; Rivers, Gorges, Canyons Traveling Exhib, 82-82; Midwest Watercolor Soc First 100 Exhib, Tweed Mus Art; Golden Sands Int Show, El Centro, Calif. *Teaching:* Asst dir painting, Chautauqua Inst Ctr Arts, 79-80. *Awards:* First Prize Graphics, Twelfth Ann Western Art Show, 77 & Third Ann Nat Miniature Show, 77; First Prize Painting, Second Int All on Paper Show, 80. *Media:* Watercolors. *Dealer:* Bishop Gallery 7164 Main Scottsdale AZ 85251. *Mailing Add:* 84 E Main St Trumansburg NY 14886

VAN OORDT, PETER
PAINTER, GRAPHIC ARTIST

b Rotterdam, Neth, Apr 4, 03; US citizen. *Study:* Acad Rotterdam, Neth; Sch Appl Arts, Utrecht; Royal Acad, Amsterdam; Grosvenor Sch Arts, London. *Work:* Art Mus Honolulu, Hawaii; Santa Barbara Mus Fine Arts, Calif. *Exhib:* Inst of Fine Arts, Peking, China, 36 & 40; Honolulu Acad Arts, Hawaii, 40; Los Angeles Co Mus Art, 48; Santa Barbara Mus Fine Art, Calif, 51; Duncan Galleries, Paris, 74. *Pos:* Travel poster artist, Brit Railways, Ralph & Brown Studios, 32-39; background artist for cartoon films, Warner Bros, Hollywood, 47-49; designer, Lamb Studios (ecclesiastical arts), Northvale, NJ, 55-73. *Mailing Add:* 217 Hungry Hollow Rd Spring Valley NY 10977

VAN RIPER, PETER
PRINTMAKER, CONCEPTUAL ARTIST

b Detroit, Mich, July 8, 42. *Study:* Univ NC, BA(art hist, Far Eastern hist); Univ Tokyo, MA(Far Eastern art hist); Univ Mich. *Work:* Everson Mus Art, Syracuse, NY; Mus Mod Art, New York; Los Angeles Inst Contemp Art; Mus Mod Art, Oxford, Eng; Stedelijk Mus, Amsterdam. *Exhib:* One-man shows, US Info Serv Japan Performance Tour, 74, Video & Graphics Exhib, Everson Mus, 75 & Washington Proj Arts, 79; Kunst Bleibt Kunst, Kunstverein Art Mus, Cologne, Ger, 74; Holography 75 First Decade, Int Ctr Photog, New York. *Teaching:* Teacher multi-media art, Calif Inst of Arts, Valencia, 70-73. *Awards:* Traveling Exhib Award, Western Asn of Art Mus, 74. *Mem:* Editions/Sch of Holography, Ann Arbor, Mich & San Francisco (pres); Fluxus, New York. *Publ:* Auth, It, 75. *Dealer:* Upstairs Gallery 1457 Grant Ave San Francisco CA 94133. *Mailing Add:* 537 Broadway New York NY 10012

VAN ROEKENS, PAULETTE (MRS ARTHUR MELTZER)
PAINTER

b France, Jan 1, 96; US citizen. *Study:* Philadelphia Sch Design for Women; Pa Acad Fine Arts, Philadelphia; Graphic Sketch Club; also with Henry Snell, Joseph Pierson & Leopold Seyfeert; Moore Col Art, LHD, 61. *Work:* Pa Acad Fine Arts, Philadelphia; Reading Mus, Pa; Woodmere Art Gallery, Philadelphia; Sch Design for Women Alumnae, Philadelphia; Allentown Mus, Pa. *Exhib:* Corcoran Gallery Art, Washington, DC; Pa Acad Fine Arts, Philadelphia; Art Inst Chicago; Carnegie Inst, Pittsburgh; Nat Acad Design, New York; 14 solo shows. *Teaching:* Instr, Graphic Sketch Club, 20-27; asst prof painting & drawing, Moore Col Art, 23-61. *Awards:* Bronze Medal First Prize, Philadelphia Sketch Club; Gold Medal First Prize, Plastic Club; Mary T Mason Prize, Woodmere Art Gallery, 65. *Media:* Oil, Pastel. *Mailing Add:* 1521 Welsh Rd Huntingdon Valley PA 19006

VAN SANT, TOM R
SCULPTOR, PAINTER

b Los Angeles, Calif, Feb 26, 31. *Study:* Stanford Univ, BA, 53; Otis Art Inst Los Angeles Co, MFA, 57; also studied with Herb Jepson, Peter Voulkos & Millard Sheets. *Work:* Davies Pac Ctr, Honolulu; Pac Design Ctr, Los Angeles; Libr Cong; Smithsonian Inst; Inst Contemp Art, London. *Comn:* Sculptured concrete walls, Irvine Co, Newport Beach, Calif, 68; sculptured concrete mural, Honolulu Int Airport, 73, mural, Taipei Int Airport, Taiwan, 74; fountain sculpture, City of Los Angeles, 75; bronze sculpture, Warmington Co, Newport Beach, Calif, 82. *Exhib:* One-man exhibs, Inst Contemp Art, London, 76, Myer Galleries, Melbourne & Sydney, Australia, 77, Stedelijk Mus, Amsterdam, Holland, 77, Honolulu Hale, City Hall, 77 & Pac Design Ctr, Los Angeles, 80. *Teaching:* Instr design & drawing, Otis Art Inst Los Angeles Co, 60-66; instr creativity, Omega Sem, Fall City, Wash, 66-68; fel, Ctr Advan Visual Studies, Mass Inst Technol, 81- *Awards:* Art in Architecture Award, Am Inst Archit, 56, 61 & 68; Award of Merit, First Ann Exhib Illus West, 59; Purchase Award, Int Sculpture Symposium, Calif State Univ, Long Beach, 74. *Bibliog:* Fundaburk (auth), Art in Public Places in the US, Popular Press, 75; Piene (auth), Sky Art Conf, Ctr Advan Visual Studies, Mass Inst Technol, 81-83. *Publ:* Co-dir, Flight Forms (film), Ed Spiegel Co, 76. *Mailing Add:* 5698 Tryon Rd Los Angeles CA 90068

VAN SCHAACK, ERIC
HISTORIAN, ADMINISTRATOR

b Evanston, Ill, June 10, 31. *Study:* Dartmouth Col, AB, 53; Columbia Univ, PhD, 69. *Teaching:* Lectr & research asst, The Frick Collection, New York, 60-62; from asst prof to prof, Goucher Col, Baltimore, 64-76, chmn, Dept Visual Arts, 73-76; prof & chmn, Fine Arts Dept, Colgate Univ, 77- *Awards:* Italian Govt Grant & Fulbright Travel Grant, 62-63; Ford Found Grant Humanities, 72-73; Colgate Univ Humanities Fac Development Fund Grant, 79-80. *Mem:* Col Art Asn Am; Soc Archit Historians; Nat Trust Hist Preserv; Preserv League, New York. *Res:* Italian Renaissance & Baroque art; American architecture. *Publ:* Auth, Master Drawings in Private Collections, Lambert-Spector, 62; auth, An unpublished letter by Francesco Albani, Art Bulletin, 69; coauth, The music in Van Dyck's Rinaldo and Armida, Baltimore Mus Art Ann III, 69; contrib, Italian Paintings: Baltimore Mus Art, 81; contrib, Francesco Albani's Guida di Bologna, Acts of the 24th International Congress of the History of Art, Bologna, 82. *Mailing Add:* Dept Fine Arts Colgate Univ Hamilton NY 13346

VAN SUCHTELEN, ADRIAN
PRINTMAKER, EDUCATOR

b Semarang, Indonesia, June 18, 41; US citizen. *Study:* El Camino Col, Calif; Otis Art Inst, Los Angeles, BFA, MFA, 66. *Work:* Indianapolis Mus Art; De Cordova Mus, Lincoln, Mass; Cleveland Mus Art; Riverside Mus, Calif; Milwaukee Art Ctr; and others. *Comn:* Art work on film Young Lovers, Samuel Goldwyn Studios, Los Angeles, 64. *Exhib:* Drawing Soc Nat Exhib, Am Fedn Arts, NY, 70-72; Colorprint USA, Tex, 74; Davidson Nat Print &

Drawing Exhib, NC, 75; Pratt Graphics Ctr Int Print Exhib, NY, 75; one-man show, Northern State Col, SDak, 83; and others. *Teaching:* Prof drawing & grad dir, Utah State Univ, 67- *Awards:* Purchase Award, NMex State Univ, 71; Ben & Abbey Grey Found Purchase Award, Salt Lake Art Ctr, 72; Purchase Prize, Boston Printmakers, 81. *Mem:* Graphics Soc; Boston Printmakers Soc. *Publ:* Contrib, Drawing A Search for Form, 65; auth & illusr, Lifetime Career Schools, Correspondence Art Course, 67; contrib, Oil Painting, Techniques and Materials, 69; The Hidden Elements of Drawing, 73. *Dealer:* Sylvesters Art Studio 61 E 320 S Salt Lake City UT 84111. *Mailing Add:* 655 East 1800 N Logan UT 84321

VAN TONGEREN, HERK
SCULPTOR

b Holland, Mich, Aug 19, 43. *Study:* Studied in Europe, 62-64; Univ Colo, BA, 69, MFA, 70. *Work:* Yale Univ Art Gallery; Nat Mus Am Art, Smithsonian Inst; Nelson Atkins Mus, Kansas City, Mo; Denver Art Mus; Oakland Mus, Calif. *Comn:* Sculpture (bronze), State Conn, New Haven, 83; Branch Found, Ft Pierce, Fla (in progress). *Exhib:* Alan Stone Gallery, New York, 80; Hamilton Gallery, New York, 81; one-man exhib, Cordier & Ekstrom, New York, 81 & 83 & NJ State Mus, 83; A Survey of Cast Metal Sculpture in the 80s, Fuller Goldeen Gallery, San Francisco, 82; Bronze Sculpture in the Landscape, Wave Hill, Bronx, NY; and others. *Pos:* Exec dir, Johnson Atelier, Princeton, NJ, 77-; ed, Sculptor's News Exchange, Arlington, Va, 77-80. *Teaching:* Instr sculpture design, Univ NC, Greensboro, 71-74; asst prof sculpture design, San Diego State Univ, Calif, 75-77; lectr, Univ Calif, Berkeley, 80. *Awards:* Honorable Mention, Calif Small Images, Calif State Univ, Los Angeles, 76. *Bibliog:* Matthew Light (auth), article, Art, 4/83; Ronny Cohen (auth), article, Art News, 5/83; Kay Larson (auth), article, New York, 8/22/83. *Media:* Mixed. *Dealer:* Cordier & Ekstrom 417 East 75th St New York NY 10021. *Mailing Add:* 53 Railroad Pl Rosedale Rd Hopewell NJ 08525

VAN VEEN, STUYVESANT
PAINTER

b New York, NY, Sept 12, 10. *Study:* City Col New York; Pa Acad Fine Arts; Nat Acad Design; Art Students League; New York Sch Indust Art; also with Daniel Garber, Thomas Benton & David Karfunkel. *Work:* Columbia Univ Anthopology Archs; Newark Mus, NJ; Fairleigh Dickinson Univ, NJ; Smithsonian Inst, Washington, DC; New York Hist Soc; and others. *Comn:* Pittsburgh Panorama (mural), Pittsburgh Post Off, Courthouse, comn by US Treas Dept, 37; The Story of Pharmacy (mural), New York World's Fair, World's Fair Corp, 38; Synthesis (mural) & Security (mural), for courtrooms in Philadelphia Munic Ct Bldg, Philadelphia Art Comn; Bridge of Wings (mural), Wright-Patterson AFB, Ohio Hq Bldg, USAF, 45; Dodgers Victories (murals), for seven lobbies at Ebbets Field Apts, Brooklyn, NY, HFH Corp, 63. *Exhib:* Carnegie Int, Pittsburgh, 29 & 43; Am Ann, Art Inst Chicago Century Progress, six from 33-46; Cincinnati Mus Ann, five from 36-49; Whitney Mus Am Art Ann, 39-40; Nat Acad Design Ann, 65-69; Mid Hudson Ctr Arts & Sci, 81; and many others. *Pos:* Res assoc, Dept Anthrop, Columbia Univ, 35-38; art dir, Cincinnati Ord Dist, War Dept, 42-43; cofounder & set designer, Stage Inc, Cincinnati Civic Theater, 48-49; art mural consult, Int Fair Consult, 62-64. *Teaching:* Pvt art classes, 30-41, instr & supvr painting & drawing, Cincinnati Art Acad, 46-49; assoc prof art, City Col New York, 49-75; retired. *Awards:* Nelson Whitehead Prize, 66 & Award, 79, Am Soc Contemp Artists; Prize, New Eng Ann, Silvermine Guild Artists, 68; Silver Medal, Audubon Artist, 82; and others. *Mem:* Am Acad & Inst Arts & Letters; Nat Soc Painters Casein (bd dirs, 53); Artists Equity Asn (pres, 58-59); Audubon Soc of Artists; Am Soc Contemp Artists; and others. *Media:* Oil, Aqueous Media. *Publ:* Illusr, Gesture & Environment, Kings Crown, 41; illusr, The Rebel Mail Runner, Holiday, 54; illusr, Garibaldi, Random, 57; illusr, The Art of Making the Dance, Rinehart, 60; illusr & comment, Gesture, Race & Culture, Mouton, 72. *Dealer:* ACA Gallery 21 E 67th St New York NY 10021; Mary Ryan Gallery 452 Columbus Ave New York NY 10024. *Mailing Add:* 320 Central Park W New York NY 10025

VAN VLIET, CLAIRE
PRINTMAKER, PUBLISHER

b Ottawa, Ont, Can, Aug 9, 33. *Study:* San Diego State Univ, AB, 52; Claremont Grad Sch, MFA, 54. *Work:* Nat Gallery, Washington, DC; Philadelphia Mus Art; Montreal Mus Fine Arts; Cleveland Mus Art; Victoria & Albert Mus, London. *Exhib:* Kunst zu Kafka Traveling Exhib, WGer, 75; Claire Van Vliet & The Janus Press, Wiggin Gallery, Boston Pub Libr, 77; Rutgers Univ Art Gallery, 78; Paper as Medium, Smithsonian Traveling Exhib, 78-80; NEFA Traveling Exhib, 82-83; The Janus Press 1975-80, Fleming Mus Traveling Exhib, 82-84. *Pos:* Proprietor, Janus Press, 55- *Teaching:* Asst prof printmaking, Philadelphia Col Art, 59-65; vis lectr, Univ Wis, 65-66; Univ Vt, 74-75; Univ Ala, 83. *Awards:* VCA Grant, 75-77; Nat Endowment Arts Grants, 76, 78 & 80. *Mem:* Soc Printers Boston; The Print Club, Philadelphia. *Media:* Relief, Lithography and Paper. *Publ:* Illusr & ed, Sky and Earth-Variable Landscape, Janus Press, 70; auth & illusr, Satellite, Mus Mod Art, 71; illusr & ed, The Tower of Babel-an Anthology, Janus Press, 75. *Dealer:* Mickelson Gallery 707 G St NW Washington DC 20001; AAA 1614 Latimer St Philadelphia Pa 19103. *Mailing Add:* RD 1 West Burke VT 05871

VAN VRANKEN, ROSE (ROSE VAN VRANKEN HICKEY)
SCULPTOR, PRINTMAKER

b Passaic, NJ, May 15, 19. *Study:* Pomona Col, BA(art, with hon), 39; Art Students League, with William Zorach & Robert Laurent, 39-42; NY Univ Grad Inst Fine Arts, one year; Univ Iowa, sculpture with Humbert Albrizio & printmaking with Mauricio Lasansky, MA(sculpture), 43; Ricker Col,

Maine, Hon DFA, 76. *Work:* Tex Fine Arts Asn, Laguna Gloria Mus, Austin; Des Moines Art Ctr, Iowa; Houston Pub Libr, Tex; Coventry Cathedral, Eng; Tex Commerce Bank, Houston, 80. *Comn:* Theotokis (bronze), St Cyril Alexandria Church, Houston, Tex, 81; Finial Investment Corp, Houston, Tex. *Exhib:* Nat Asn of Women Artists Ann, Nat Acad, New York, 51-79; Nat Asn of Women Artists Traveling Show, Stedelijk Mus, Amsterdam, 56-57; Audubon Artists Nat Ann, Nat Acad, New York, 65 & 80; Salmagundi Club Ann, New York, 78-83. *Teaching:* Research asst art hist, Univ Iowa, 42-43; instr sculpture & mem bd dir, Madison Art Ctr Mus, Wis, 65-68; instr sculpture, Jewish Community Ctr, Houston, 69-70, Art League of Houston, 70-74 & Continuing Educ Prog, Rice Univ, 75-78. *Awards:* Acad Artists Asn Award for Sculpture, 79 & 80; Nat Assoc Women Artists, New York, 80; Second Prize for Sculpture, 80 & First Prize for Sculpture, 82, Salmagundi Club, New York. *Bibliog:* Archives Am Art, Smithsonian Inst, Washington, DC; Art Voices South Mag, 11-12/78; Houston Chronicle Mag, 10/77. *Mem:* Salmagundi Club; Tex Soc Sculptors (vpres, 74-75, pres Gulf Coast Chap, 75-76); Nat Asn Women Artists; Acad Artists Asn; International Platform Asn. *Media:* Mixed. *Dealer:* Hobe Sound Galleries 11900 SE Dixie Hwy Hobe Sound FL 33455; Sol del Rio Gallery 1020 Townsend St San Antonio TX 78209. *Mailing Add:* 435 Tallowood Houston TX 77024

VAN WINKELEN, BARBARA
PAINTER, ILLUSTRATOR
b Waban, Mass. *Study:* Yale Univ Sch Fine Arts, BFA, 43. *Exhib:* Ellsworth Gallery Int, Simsbury, Conn, 77 & 78; 59th Ann, Springfield Mus, Mass, 78; 82nd Ann, Catharine Lorillard Wolfe Art Club, New York, 78; Conn Watercolor Soc, 78 & 80 & Conn Acad, 80, Wadsworth Atheneum, Hartford, Conn; Slater Mem Mus, Norwich, Conn, 78-81; Conn Acad Fine Arts, Olde State House, Hartford, Conn, 81. *Pos:* Staff asst, Mus Mod Art, New York, 43-44; tech illusr, United Technol, 53-71. *Teaching:* Children art, Wadsworth Atheneum, Hartford, Conn, 48-50. *Awards:* First Prizes, Essex Art Asn, 77 & Nantucket Artists Asn, 79-83; Best in Show, Conn Women Artists, 83. *Bibliog:* Maureen O'Sullivan (auth), Nantucket Artist Barbara van Winkelen (film), 79. *Mem:* Conn Acad Fine Arts; Conn Watercolor Soc; Conn Women Artists (bd dirs, 80-82); Nantucket Artists Asn. *Media:* Egg Tempera; All Media. *Dealer:* Portobello 98 Main St Nantucket MA 02554; Ainsworth Gallery 42 Bromfield St Boston MA 02108. *Mailing Add:* 1864 Poquonock Ave Poquonock CT 06064

VAN WINKLE, LESTER G
SCULPTOR, EDUCATOR
b Greenville, Tex, Jan 11, 44. *Study:* ETex State Univ, BS; Univ Ky, MA; also sculpture with Michael D Hall. *Work:* Arrowmont Sch Arts & Crafts, Gatlinburg, Tenn; Dade Co Jr Col, Miami. *Exhib:* Sculpt 70, Corcoran Gallery Art, Washington, DC, 70; Whitney Biennial of Painting & Sculpture, Whitney Mus, New York, 73; one-man shows, Henry Gallery, Washington, 73-75 & Webb Parsons Gallery, Bedford, NY, 74-75; Waves Exhib, Cranbrook Acad Art Galleries, 74. *Teaching:* From asst prof to assoc prof sculpture, Va Commonwealth Univ, 69- *Dealer:* Henri Gallery 1500 21st St NW Washington DC 20036. *Mailing Add:* Dept of Art Va Commonwealth Univ Richmond VA 23284

VAN WYK, HELEN
PAINTER, LECTURER
b Fair Lawn, NJ. *Study:* Art Students League; New Sch Social Res; also with Maximilian Aureal Rasko. *Work:* Norfolk Mus Arts & Sci, Va; Bergen Co Mus, NJ; St Vincent's Col, Latrobe, Pa; Minneapolis Club; Livonia Sch Syst, Mich. *Comn:* Mural, comn by Joseph Grumbacher, Exec Off, M Grumbacker, Inc, New York, 63; portraits, comn by Pamela Charles, Cindy Adams, Paolo Pansa & others. *Exhib:* Acad Artists, Springfield, Mass, 53 & 57; Audubon Artists, New York, 54, 55 & 63; Nat Acad Design, New York, 54, 55 & 64; Silvermine Guild Artists, Conn, 59. *Pos:* Ed, Palette Talk, Grumbacher, Inc, 67- *Awards:* John C Pierson Prize, Ogunquit Art Ctr, Maine, 49; First Prize for Still Life, Catharine Lorillard Wolfe Art Club, 55; Curtis Mem Award, Rockport Art Asn, 72 & 73. *Bibliog:* Walter Brooks (auth), Art of Acrylic Painting, Grumbacher, 69; Herb Rogoff (auth), Each demonstration a challenge, Am Artist Mag, 69. *Media:* Oil. *Publ:* Coauth, Casselwyk Book on Oil Painting, pvt publ, 61; auth, Acrylic Portrait Painting, Watson-Guptill, 70; auth, Helen Van Wyk's Successful Color Mixtures, 73 & Painting Flowers the Van Wyk Way, 81, Art Instr Assocs. *Mailing Add:* 2 Briarstone Rd Rockport MA 01966

VAN YOUNG, OSCAR
PAINTER
b Vienna, Austria; US citizen. *Study:* Art Acad, Odessa, Russia; with Sam Ostrowsky, Paris & Chicago; Calif State Univ, Los Angeles, BA & MA. *Work:* Los Angeles Co Mus Art, Calif; Chaffey Col, Ontario, Calif; Frye Mus, Seattle; Ill State Mus; Smithsonian Inst; and others. *Exhib:* Am Paintings & Int Watercolor Shows, Art Inst Chicago; Calif Palace of Legion of Honor; Pa Acad; Va Mus Biennial; Corcoran Gallery Art Biennial, Washington, DC; one-man shows, Art Inst of Chicago, Los Angeles Co Mus of Art, Los Angeles, Palm Springs Desert Mus, San Francisco Mus of Art, Santa Barbara Mus, Calif, James Vigeveno Galleries, Westwood, Calif & Cowie Galleries, Los Angeles; Retrospective, San Bernardino Valley Col Gallery of Art; Zantman Galleries, Palm Desert, Calif, 83. *Teaching:* Instr advan painting, Otis Art Inst, 54-56; instr design, painting & drawing, Pasadena City Col, 59-73; asst prof advan painting, Los Angeles State Univ, 61-63. *Awards:* Bartels Prize, Art Inst Chicago; Purchase Prize, Chaffey Col; Purchase Award, Frye Mus; and others. *Bibliog:* Ronald D Scofield (auth), California painter turns against early realism, Santa Barbara; Joseph Mugnaini (auth), Oil Painting Techniques & Materials, Van Nostrand Reinhold Co, 69; Janice Lovoos (auth), Painting for the joy of it, SW Art, 7/77. *Media:* Oil. *Dealer:* Copenhagen Galleri Solvang CA 93463; Zantman Galleries Carmel CA. *Mailing Add:* 2293 Panorama Terr Los Angeles CA 90039

VARGA, FERENC
SCULPTOR
b Szekesfehervar, Hungary; US citizen. *Study:* Acad Fine Arts, Budapest, Hungary, with Prof Eugene Broy & Prof Francis Sidlo; govt scholar, Italy, 38 & France, 42. *Work:* Nat Art Gallery, Budapest; Mus Fine Arts, Budapest; Vatican Mus, Rome, Italy; Mus Zurich, Switz. *Comn:* Portrait, VRegent of Hungary, Budapest, 42; monument, City of Windsor, Ont, Can, 50; group of statues, Ft Lincoln Mem, Washington, DC, 55 & 8ft bronze statue of Patrick Henry, 78; monument, City of Detroit, Mich, 66; and others. *Exhib:* Nat Art Gallery, Budapest, 42; Exhib Ecclesiastical Arts Guild, Detroit, 52; Nat Sculpture Soc, New York, 59; one-man show, Masters' Gallery, Toronto, Ont, 64; Eszterhazy Gallery, Palm Beach, Fla, 71. *Teaching:* Assoc prof sculpturing, Acad Fine Arts, Budapest, 28-40. *Awards:* Lord Rotheremere Ward, 28; Medal of Bethlehem Distinction, Fine Arts & Sci Soc of Church of Hungary, 47. *Bibliog:* Dr E Schwartz (auth), Ferenc Varga, Ons Volk, Brussels, 49 & Last uns nach Bethlehem eilen, Am-Ung Verlag, Cologne, 59; J P Danglade (auth), Magnificent statue of the Christ by sculptor, Varga, The Cemeterian, Columbus, 62. *Mem:* Fine Arts & Sci Soc of Church of Hungary, Budapest; Acad Cath Hungarica Sci Atrib Prov, Vatican City; Nat Sculpture Soc. *Media:* Multimedia. *Mailing Add:* 296 NE Sixth Ave Delray Beach FL 33444

VARGA, MARGIT
PAINTER, WRITER
b New York, NY, May 5, 08. *Study:* Art Students League, with Boardman Robinson & Robert Laurent. *Work:* Metrop Mus Art; Springfield Mus Fine Arts, Mass; Univ Ariz, Tucson; IBM Collection; Pa Acad Fine Arts. *Comn:* Mural for lobby, Kidder, Meade & Co, Paramus, NJ. *Exhib:* Whitney Mus Am Art, 51; Univ Ill, 51; Art Inst Chicago; Carnegie Inst; Corcoran Gallery Art; one-man show, Wichita Mus, 83. *Pos:* Art ed, Life Mag, 36-56, asst art dir, 56-60; art consult, Time, Inc, 60-70. *Media:* Oil. *Dealer:* Midtown Galleries 11 E 57th St New York NY 10022. *Mailing Add:* Box 784 Hildreth Lane Bridgehampton NY 11932

VARGO, JOHN
EDUCATOR, PAINTER
b Cleveland, Ohio, Aug 9, 29. *Study:* Cleveland Inst Art, with Paul Riba & Louis Bosa. *Work:* Cleveland Mus Art; Syracuse Univ; Munson-Williams-Proctor Inst, Utica, NY; LeMoyne Col, Syracuse. *Comn:* The Erie Canal (mural), First Fed Savings Syracuse, 60. *Exhib:* Cooperstown 35th Ann Exhib, NY, 70; Rochester Finger Lakes Exhib, NY, 71; Artist as a Journalist, Soc Illusr, 77; one-man shows, LeMoyne Col, 71 & Everson Mus, 78; and others. *Pos:* Illusr, Advance Art, Cleveland, 51-58. *Teaching:* Prof illus & serigraph, Syracuse Univ, 58- *Awards:* Eagan Pres Plaza Award & Popular Prize, 64, NY State Fair; First Prize for Portrait Painting, Cooperstown Art Asn, 70; Award for Painting, Mem Art Gallery, Univ Rochester, 71. *Media:* Tempera, Watercolor. *Publ:* Illusr, covers, Michael Brown's Laying Waste, 11/80 & Roger Shattuck's The Forebidden Experiment, 1/81, Washington Sq Press; illusr, cover, Daoma Winston's The Lotteries, Pocket, 4/81; illusr, Jacobo Timmerman's Prisoner Without a Name, Cell Without a Number, Reader's Digest, 11/81. *Mailing Add:* 6319 Danbury Dr Jamesville NY 13078

VARNEDOE, JOHN KIRK TRAIN
HISTORIAN
b Savannah, Ga, Jan 18, 46. *Study:* Williams Col, BA; Stanford Univ, MA & PhD. *Teaching:* Asst prof, Stanford Univ, Calif, 73-74 & Columbia Univ, New York, 74-80; assoc prof, Inst Fine Arts, New York Univ, 80- *Awards:* David E Finley Fel, Nat Gallery Art, Washington, DC, 70-72; Nat Endowment Arts Grant, 77-78. *Res:* Articles and lectures on work of Rodin, especially drawings, and Gustave Caillebotte, plus other modern art topics; history of photography. *Publ:* Coauth, The Drawings of Rodin, 71; ed, Modern Portraits: The Self and Others, 76; ed & co-auth, Gustave Caillebotte: A Retrospective Exhibition, 76; coauth (with Elizabeth Streicher), Graphic Works of Max Klinger, 77; auth, Northern Light: Realism and Symbolism in Scandanavian Painting, 1880-1910, 82. *Mailing Add:* 1 E 78th St New York NY 10021

VARNELIS, KAZYS
EDUCATOR, PAINTER
b Alsedziai, Lithuania, Feb 25, 17; US citizen. *Study:* Inst Fine Arts, Kaunas, Lithuania, MA, 41; Acad Fine Arts, Vienna, Austria, 45. *Work:* Art Inst Chicago; Mus Contemp Art, Chicago; Guggenheim Mus, New York; Akron Art Inst, Ohio; Milwaukee Art Ctr, Wis. *Exhib:* Biennial Chicago & Vicinity Show, Art Inst Chicago, 67-74; one-man shows, Mus Contemp Art, Chicago, 70, Milwaukee Art Ctr, Wis, 74 & Mus Art, Univ Iowa, Iowa City, 75; Ill Painters Traveling Exhib, Ill Arts Coun, Chicago, 71; 12 Lithuanian Artists in Am, Corcoran Gallery Art, DC, 73; Abstract Art in Chicago, Mus Contemp Art, Chicago, 76; Reality of Illusion, traveling exhib to Denver Art Mus, Univ Calif, Los Angeles, Honolulu Acad Art, among others, 79-80. *Pos:* Dir, Mus Ecclesiastical Art, Kaunas, Lithuania, 41-45. *Teaching:* Prof art, City Col Chicago, 68-82. *Awards:* Vielehr Award, Art Inst Chicago, 69 & 74; Nat Endowment Arts fel grant, 75. *Bibliog:* Jan Van der Marck (auth), The modulated monochromes of Kazys Varnelis, ArtsCanada, 71; Heinz Ohff (auth), Galerie der neuen Kuenste, Bertelsmann Kunstverlag, WGer, 71; I Michael Danoff (auth), Kazys Varnelis Paintings, Milwaukee Art Ctr, 74. *Media:* Acrylic. *Dealer:* Image Gallery Main St Stockbridge MA 01262. *Mailing Add:* Ice Glen Rd Stockbridge MA 01262

VARNEY, EDWIN
PRINTMAKER, EDITOR
b New Rochelle, NY, Oct 16, 44. *Study:* Syracuse Univ, BA, 65, MA, 66; Univ Vancouver, PhD, 76. *Work:* Vancouver Art Gallery, BC; Smith Col Art Gallery, Northampton, Mass; Alta Col Art, Calgary; Rotterdam Acad, Holland; Univ Colo, Boulder. *Comn:* Wood sculpture, Burnaby Art Coun, BC, 71; concrete sculpture, BC Sculptor's Soc, 77. *Exhib:* Space Window, RI Sch Design, Providence, 78; Artists' Stamps, Mus Art & Hist, Geneva, Switz, 79; Mail Etc, Univ Colo, Boulder, Tyler Sch Art, Philadelphia & Fla State Univ, Tallahassee, 79; and others. *Pos:* Artist/poet-in-residence, Intermedia Press, Vancouver, BC, 71-73, publ, ed & designer, 73- *Mem:* Cent Visual Arts Asn (bd dirs, 79-80); Can Artists Rep. *Media:* Lithography; Mixed Media. *Publ:* Openings, 69, Human Nature, 74, ed, First, Second and Third International Artists' Stamp Edition, 76, 78 & 80, ed, Four Canadian Poets, 78 & ed, Contemporary Surrealist Prose, 79, Intermedia Press. *Mailing Add:* Intermedia Press Box 3294 Vancouver BC V6B 3X9 Canada

VARNUM, ZOË SHIPPEN See Shippen, Zoe

VAUX, RICHARD
PAINTER, PRINTMAKER
b Greensburg, Pa, Sept 15, 40. *Study:* Miami Univ, BFA, 63; Northern Ill Univ, MFA, 69. *Work:* Heckscher Mus Art, Huntington, NY; Northern Ill Univ; NY; C W Post Col, Greenvale, NY; Univ Mass, Amherst; and others. *Exhib:* Butler Inst Am Art, Youngstown, Ohio, 68; Stamford Mus, Conn, 70; Minn Mus Art, St Paul, 71; Guild Hall Mus, Easthampton, NY, 78; Long Beach Mus Art, 79; Hudson River Mus, 79; Silvermine Guild, Conn, 80; and others. *Teaching:* Prof art, Adelphi Univ, 83. *Media:* Acrylic, Oil, Graphics. *Mailing Add:* Lloyd Lane Huntington NY 11743

VAZQUEZ, PAUL
PAINTER
b Brooklyn, NY, Sept 19, 33. *Study:* Ohio Wesleyan Univ, BFA, 56; Univ Ill, MFA(Kate Neal Kinley Fel), 57. *Work:* Univ Ill, Urbana; Ball State Teachers Col, Muncie, Ind. *Exhib:* One-man shows, Paley & Lowe Gallery, 71, 72 & 73, shows in Koln Ger & Vienna, Austria, 75; David Findlay Gallery, New York, 76, 78, 79 & 80 & Gallery 99, Miami Beach, Fla, 77; American Painting, Chicago Inst Am Art, 72; and others. *Teaching:* Instr art hist, Bennett Col, 63-66; asst prof humanities, Western Conn State Col, 66-69; prof drawing & painting, Univ Bridgeport, 69- *Awards:* Purchase Award, Butler Inst Am Art, 58; Conn Comn Arts Grant for Painting, 74. *Bibliog:* Virginia Mann (auth), article, Arts Mag, 2/78; Robert Sievert (auth), article, Arts Mag, 2/80. *Dealer:* David Findlay Gallery 984 Madison Ave New York NY 10021. *Mailing Add:* 205 Savoy St Bridgeport CT 06606

VEGA, EDWARD
SCULPTOR, EDUCATOR
b Deming, NMex, Oct 13, 38. *Study:* NMex State Univ, Las Cruces, BFA, 68; Univ NMex, Albuquerque, MA, 70; lithog with Garo Antreasian; drawing with Ilya Bolotowsky; sculpture with Charlie Mattox. *Exhib:* Graphics '73, Western NMex Univ, Silver City; 50th Regional Art Exhib, Shreveport, La, 73; Gov Gallery, Santa Fe, NMex, 78; Roswell Mus, 79; Santa Fe Festival of the Arts, 79; and others. *Pos:* NMex Arts Comn chmn, 79. *Teaching:* Asst prof sculpture, drawing, Univ Albuquerque, 76- *Awards:* Third Place Purchase Award Sculpture, Univ NMex, 75; Res Grant Sculpture, NMex State Univ, 75; Artist in Residence Fel, Roswell Art Ctr; and others. *Media:* Steel, Wood. *Mailing Add:* Dept of Art Univ of Albuquerque Albuquerque NM 87140

VELASQUEZ, OSCAR
PAINTER, ILLUSTRATOR
b Pharr, Tex, Apr 5, 45. *Study:* Cooper Sch Art, AA, 65. *Work:* Joslyn Art Mus, Omaha; Nat Acad Design-Henry Ward Ranger, New York; Erskine Col, Due West, SC; Opera House, Abbeville, SC. *Exhib:* Ga Watercolor Soc, High Mus, Atlanta, 79; SC Watercolor Soc, Greenville Mus Art; Am Watercolor Soc, Columbia Mus Art, SC, 79; Camden Art Mus, SC, 83; Sumter Art Mus, SC, 83; Cannon Bldg, Capitol, Washington, DC, 83; and others. *Awards:* High Winds Medal, 75 & Silver Medal of Honor, 77, Am Watercolor Soc; Georgia Gold Award, Watercolor Soc, 81. *Mem:* Am Watercolor Soc; SC Watercolor Soc; Southern Watercolor Asn; Ga Watercolor Soc. *Media:* Watercolor, Acrylic; Oils. *Mailing Add:* Rte 1 Box 127 Abbeville SC 29620

VELICK, BRUCE
GALLERY DIRECTOR
b Los Angeles, Calif, Jan 29, 49. *Study:* Univ Calif, Davis, BA(design), 71. *Pos:* Dir, Bruce Velick Gallery, San Francisco, currently. *Specialty:* Contemporary art with emphasis on emerging artists in northern California. *Mailing Add:* 55 Grant Ave San Francisco CA 94108

VELICK, PAUL See Bob & Bob

VENEGAS, HAYDEE E
MUSEUM DIRECTOR, HISTORIAN
b Arecibo, PR, Mar 4, 50. *Study:* Univ PR, BA(art hist), 73; Fla State Univ, MA(mod art), 78. *Collections Arranged:* One Hundred Fifty Years of the Tapia Teatre, 76, Egyptian Art, 79 & Toys Made by Children, 79, Mud Fundacion Arqueologica; Miguel Pou Centenary, 80; Julie Roadodil Valle, 82; Francisco Oller: A Realist Impressionist. *Pos:* Dir, Mus Fundacion Arqueologica, 76-79; asst dir, Ponce Art Mus, 80- *Teaching:* Vis prof Puertorican art, Inter-Am Univ, summer 75. *Bibliog:* Connie Underhill (auth), The museum as a place, San Juan Star, Sunday Mag, 12/30/79. *Mem:* Am Asn Mus; Int Comt Mus; Col Art Asn; Asn of Latin-Am Historians. *Res:* Puerto Rican art; Francisco Oller, 19th century painter. *Publ:* Contribr, Juan Ramon Valazquez, El Mundo, 78; contribr, El Velorio: Propuesta para una reinterpretacion, Plastica, 79; auth, Francisco Oller: Profile of a Puerto Rican Painter, Mus Art Ponce, 83. *Mailing Add:* 1708 Segre St Rio Piedras PR 00926

VENET, BERNAR P
SCULPTOR, CONCEPTUAL ARTIST
b France, April 20, 41. *Study:* Sch Villa Thiole, Nice, France, 57-58. *Work:* Mus Mod Art, New York; Guggenheim Mus; Mus Nat Art Mod, Ctr Georges Pompidou, Paris; Neue Galerie Alten Kurhaus, Aachen, WGer; La Jolla Mus Contemp Art. *Comn:* Painting, Atlantic Richfield Co, Los Angeles, 81; sculpture, Mus Art Contemp, Dunkerque, 83. *Exhib:* Solo exhibs, La Jolla Mus Contemp Art, 76 & Mus Art & Indust, St Etienne, 77; Biennale de Paris: Une anthologie 1959-1967, 77; Documenta VI, Kassel, 77; Biennale Venize, 78; and others. *Bibliog:* Catherine Millet (auth), Bernar Venet, Chene, France & Pre, Italy, 75; J Pierre Mirouze (producer), film, WDR, WGer, 75; Seth Schneidman (producer), film, Seven Hills Productions, 83. *Media:* Wood Reliefs, Corten Steel. *Mailing Add:* 533 Canal New York NY 10013

VENEZIA, MICHAEL
PAINTER
b Brooklyn, NY, July 23, 35. *Study:* State Univ NY Col, Buffalo, BS, 63; Univ Mich, Ann Arbor, MFA, 68. *Work:* Mus Mod Art, New York; Nat Gallery Can, Ottawa; Kunsthaus, Zurich, Switz; Mem Art Gallery Univ Rochester, NY; Detroit Inst Arts; and others. *Exhib:* Works on Paper, Mus Mod Art, New York, 74; one-man shows, Paintings, Bykert Gallery, New York, 73 & Sperone Westwater Fischer, Inc, New York, 79; Two Artists: Dan Hill & Michael Venezia, Whitney Mus Art, New York, 77; Artists & Friends: Dan Flavin & Michael Venezia, Contemp Arts Ctr, Cincinnati, Ohio, 77; Drawings About Drawing Today, Acklund Art Mus, Chapel Hill, NC, 79; Selected Paintings 1969-1980, Detroit Inst Arts, 80; Carol Tylor Art Dallas, Tex, 81; and others. *Teaching:* Vis lectr fine arts, Guildford Col, Surrey, Eng, 66-67, London Col Printing, 66-67; assoc prof fine arts, Univ Rochester, NY, 68- *Awards:* Creative Artists Pub Serv Award, NY Coun Arts, State Univ NY Col, Fredonia, 75; Tiffany Found Award for Painting, 79; Artist Fel Painting, Nat Endowment Arts, 81. *Bibliog:* Judith Lopes Cardozo (auth), article, Artforum, 12/77; article, Art Am, 80. *Media:* Powdered Metals, Glass and Pigments on Canvas and Paper. *Mailing Add:* c/o Sperone Westwater Fisher Inc 142 Green St New York NY 10012

VENTIMIGLIA, JOHN THOMAS
SCULPTOR, INSTRUCTOR
b Augusta, Maine, Jan 12, 43. *Study:* Sch Art, Syracuse Univ, BFA, 65; Rinehart Sch, Md Inst Art, MFA(sculpture), 67; with N Carlberg, G Hartigan, D Hare, R Engman. *Exhib:* Maine Sculpture 76, Univ of Maine, 76; Barn Gallery, Ogunquit, Maine, 77; Maine Coast Artists, Rockport; Payson Gallery of Art, Portland; Barridoff Galleries, 79-82; and many others. *Pos:* Asst to Piotr Kowlaski, Int Sculpture Symp, Calif State Univ, Long Beach, 65; dir, Portland Sch Art, Outdoor Sculpture Exhib Series, 73-78. *Teaching:* Instr sculpture, design & drawing, Portland Sch Art, Maine, 72- *Awards:* Scholar, Showhegan Sch Painting & Sculpture, 64; First Prize, 3rd Ann Bridgeton Arts Festival, Maine, 73. *Bibliog:* 76 Maine Artists (exhib catalog), Maine State Bicentennial Comn, 76. *Media:* Steel, Bronze. *Mailing Add:* 31 Pine St Portland ME 04102

VENTURI, ROBERT
ARCHITECT
b Philadelphia, Pa, June 25, 25. *Study:* Princeton Univ, AB, 47, MFA, 50; Rome Prize Fel, Am Acad in Rome, 54-56; Oberlin Col, Hon DFA, 77; Yale Univ, Hon DFA, 79; Univ Pa, Hon DFA, 80; Princeton Univ, Hon DFA, 83. *Hon Degrees:* DFA, Oberlin Col, 77 & Yale Univ, 79. *Comn:* Guild House, in assoc with Cope & Lippincott, Philadelphia, 63; addition & renovation of Allen Mem Art Mus, Oberlin Col, Ohio, 76; Franklin Court, Nat Park Serv, Philadelphia, 76. *Exhib:* Work of Venturi & Rauch, Whitney Mus Am Art, New York, 71 & Pa Acad Fine Arts, Philadelphia, 75; Invisible Artist, Philadelphia Mus Art, 74; 200 Yrs of Am Archit Drawing, Cooper-Hewitt Mus, New York, 77; Drawings for a More Mod Archit, The Drawing Ctr, New York, 77; Archit 1: An Exhib, Leo Castelli Gallery, New York, 77; Roma Interrota, Incontri Int d'Arte, Rome, 77-78; The Work of Venturi and Rauch, Kunstgewerke Mus, Zurich; and others. *Pos:* Partner, Venturi & Rauch Architects & Planning, Philadelphia, 64-; architect-in-residence, Am Acad in Rome, Italy, 66, trustee, 69-74. *Teaching:* From asst to assoc prof archit, Univ Pa, 51-65; Davenport Prof archit, Yale Univ, 66-70; mem panel of visitors archit, Univ Calif, Los Angeles, 66-68. *Awards:* Medal for Complexity & Contradiction in Archit, Am Inst Archit, 78; Thomas Jefferson Mem Found Medal, Univ Va, 83; Louis Sullivan Award & Prize, Int Union Bricklayers & Allied Craftsmen, 83. *Bibliog:* Vincent Scully (auth), American Architecture & Urbanism, Praeger, 69; Robert A M Stern (auth), New Directions in American Architecture, Braziller, 69; Yukio Futagawa, Global Architecture, EDITA, Tokyo, 76. *Mem:* Pa Soc Architects; Am Inst Archit. *Publ:* Coauth, Learning from Las Vegas, MIT Press, 72; auth, Complexity and Contradiction in Architecture, Mus Mod Art, 66. *Mailing Add:* Venturi Rauch & Scott 4236 Main Philadelphia PA 19127

VERMES, MADELAINE
CRAFTSMAN
b Hungary, Sept 15, 15. *Study:* Alfred Univ; Craft Students League; Greenwich House Potters. *Work:* Cooper Union Mus; Mus Int delle Ceramiche, Faenza, Italy. *Exhib:* Coliseum, New York, 57; Art League Long

Island, NY, 58; Int Ceramic Arts, Smithsonian Inst, Washington, DC; Philadelphia Art Alliance, Pa; one-man show, Brentano's Gallery, New York, 57; and many others. *Mem:* Artist-Craftsmen New York; Nat League Am Pen Women; York State Craftsmen. *Mailing Add:* Isabella House 525 Audubon Ave Rm 1501 New York NY 10040

VERMEULE, CORNELIUS CLARKSON, III
HISTORIAN, WRITER
b On Atlantic Ocean, Aug 10, 25; US citizen. *Study:* Harvard Univ, AB, 47, MA, 51; Univ Col, Univ London, PhD, 53. *Work:* Mus Fine Arts, Boston; Nat Mus, Pylos, Hellas; Morphou-Omorfo Mus, Cyprus. *Collections Arranged:* Many exhibs, Fogg Mus Art, 50-72; Sir John Soane's Mus, London; Mus Fine Arts, Boston; Art Ctr Plainfield, Mass. *Pos:* Asst, Sir John Soane's Mus, 51-53; cur classical art, Mus Fine Arts, Boston, 57-, actg dir, 72-73; cur coins, Mass Hist Soc, Boston, 69- *Teaching:* Asst prof fine arts, Univ Mich, Ann Arbor, 53-55; asst prof archaeol, Bryn Mawr Col, 55-57; prof classics, Yale Univ, 72-73; prof fine arts, Boston Col, 78- *Awards:* Boston Col US Bicentenial Medal, 81- *Mem:* Life mem Col Art Asn Am; fel Royal Numismatic Soc; life fel Am Numismatic Soc (mem coun, 60-78); life mem Archaeol Inst Am; life mem Hellenic & Roman Soc. *Res:* European painting, Greek and Roman art; Renaissance sculpture. *Interests:* Classical and Neo-classical style, Greek sculpture technique. *Publ:* Auth, Numismatic Art in America, 71; coauth, Greek, Etruscan & Roman Art, 72; auth, Greek Sculpture & Roman Taste, 77; auth, Art of Antiquity, Greek and Roman Art, Vols II-V, 79-83; auth, Greek and Roman Sculpture in America, 82. *Mailing Add:* Mus of Fine Arts Boston MA 02115

VEROSTKO, ROMAN JOSEPH
EDUCATOR, HISTORIAN
b Tarrs, Pa, Sept 12, 29. *Study:* Art Inst of Pittsburgh, dipl; St Vincent Col & Seminary, Latrobe, Pa, BA, 55; Pratt Inst, MFA, 61; New York Univ; Columbia Univ; Atelier 17, Paris. *Pos:* Staff ed art & archit, New Catholic Encyclo, Catholic Univ, Washington, 64-68; acad dean, Minneapolis Col Art & Design, 75-78. *Teaching:* Prof art hist, Minneapolis Col Art & Design, Minn, 68- *Bibliog:* C J McNaspy (auth), Art & the New Catholic Encyclo, Am, 3/67; F Debuyst (auth), Sculptures de Ciment, Roman Verostko, Art D'Eglise, 68. *Mem:* Col Art Asn; Am Asn Univ Prof; World Future Soc. *Res:* Changing roles of the artist in our society. *Publ:* Auth, Abstract Art and the Liturgy, Liturgical Arts, 62; auth, Abstract Art and the Church, New Catholic Encyclo, 68; auth, Experience in Community: The New Art, Liturgical Arts, 72; auth, Le Sacre et la Profane, Art D'Eglise, 75; auth, A futures outlook on the role of artists and designers, Futurics, 80; and others. *Mailing Add:* 5535 Clinton Ave S Minneapolis MN 55419

VERSHBOW, (MR & MRS) ARTHUR
COLLECTORS
Mr Vershbow, b Boston, Mass, Mar 22, 22; Mrs Vershbow, b Boston, Mass, June 12, 24. *Study:* Mr Vershbow, Mass Inst Technol, BS & MS; Mrs Vershbow, Radcliffe Col, AB. *Collection:* Prints, particularly works by Redon, Piranesi and Callot; illustrated books, especially 15th to 17th centuries. *Mailing Add:* Box 32 Boston MA 02125

VERZYL, JUNE CAROL
DEALER, COLLECTOR
b Huntington, NY, Feb 5, 28. *Study:* Parsons Sch of Design. *Pos:* Co-dir, Verzyl Gallery, 66- *Bibliog:* Jane Margold (auth), Galleries struggle with an image, Newsday, 3/31/67; Kevin Hayes (auth), Gallery almost set to re-open, Northport Observer, 10/29/81. *Mem:* Northport Hist Soc. *Specialty:* Contemporary American painting, graphics and sculpture. *Collection:* Contemporary American work, including Filmus, Refregier, Benda, Twardowicz, Clawson and Christopher; also a large collection of New England gravestone rubbings. *Mailing Add:* 25 Bevin Rd Northport NY 11768

VERZYL, KENNETH H
DEALER, DRAFTSMAN
b Long Island City, NY, Sept 18, 22. *Study:* NY State Agr & Tech Inst, grad, 42. *Work:* Nicholas Roerich Mus, New York; East Northport Pub Libr, New York. *Exhib:* One-man shows, Recent Drawings, Performing Arts Found Gallery, Huntington Sta, NY, 72, Drawings of Poets & Authors, Syosset Pub Libr, NY, 72, Drawings by Kenneth H Verzyl, Nicolas Roerich Mus, New York, 73, Berkshire Mus, Pittsfield, Mass, 74 & Hilson Gallery, Deerfield Acad, Mass. *Pos:* Dir, Verzyl Gallery, Northport, NY, 66- *Bibliog:* Malcom Preston (auth), Power of the pen, Newsday, Garden City, NY, 72; Martin Curry (auth), New art display has psychological impact, Observer, Northport, NY, 72. *Mem:* Guild Hall, Easthampton, NY; Am Fedn Arts, New York. *Media:* Steel Pen and India Ink on Vellum Paper. *Specialty:* Contemporary American paintings, sculpture and graphics. *Dealer:* Studio II New York Ave Huntington NY 11743. *Mailing Add:* 25 Bevin Rd Northport NY 11768

VESTAL, DAVID
PHOTOGRAPHER
b Menlo Park, Calif, Mar 21, 24. *Study:* Art Inst Chicago, 41-44; studied photography with Sid Grossman, 47-55. *Work:* Mus Mod Art, New York; Art Inst Chicago; George Eastman House, Rochester; Mus NM, Santa Fe; High Mus Art, Atlanta. *Exhib:* Solo exhib, Witkin Gallery, New York, 71; East Street Gallery, Grinnell, Iowa, 75 & MFA Gallery, Rochester Inst Technol, 79; Photographic Crossroads: The Photo League, Nat Gallery Can, Ottawa, Int Ctr Photog, New York Mus Fine Arts, Houston & Minneapolis Inst Arts, 78; The Great West: Real/Ideal, Univ Colo, Boulder, 79 & Smithsonian Inst Travelling Exhib. *Pos:* Contrib ed, Popular Photog, 75- *Teaching:* Private instr

photog, 56-; vis artist, Art Inst Chicago, 72-73. *Awards:* Guggenheim Fel, 66 & 73-74. *Bibliog:* David Vestal, Photog Ann, 62; Vision and Expression, 69; David Vestal, Photog Ann, 76. *Media:* Black and White. *Res:* Craft, history and esthetics of black and white photography. *Publ:* Articles in Popular Photog, Camera 35, Infinity & others, 62-; ed, US Camera Annual 1971, 70; ed, Leica Manual, 72; auth, The Craft of Photography, Harper & Row, 75. *Mailing Add:* PO Box 309 Bethlehem CT 06751

VEVERS, TONY
PAINTER, EDUCATOR
b London, Eng, May 20, 26; US citizen. *Study:* Yale Univ, BA, 50; Accad Belle Arti, Florence, Italy, 50; Hans Hofmann Sch, New York, 52-53. *Work:* Isaac Delgado Mus, New Orleans; Univ Mass, Amherst; Purdue Univ, Lafayette, Ind; Chrysler Mus, Norfolk, Va; J H Hirshhorn Mus, Washington DC. *Exhib:* Pa Acad Fine Arts Ann, 66; Provincetown Painters, Everson Mus, Syracuse, NY, 77; one-man shows, Roko Gallery, New York, 65; Babcock Galleries, New York, 69; Artist's Space Gallery, New York, NY, 76 & Long Point Gallery, Provincetown, Mass, 78, 80 & 81. *Teaching:* Lectr painting, Univ NC, Greensboro, 63-64; prof painting & art hist, Purdue Univ, Lafayette, 64-; vis staff, Fine Arts Work Ctr, Provincetown, Mass, 70-71, consult, 71-76. *Awards:* Grants, Nat Endowment Arts, 66 & Purdue Univ, 70; New England Painting & Sculpture Prize, 71. *Mem:* Col Art Asn; Art Asn Provincetown (vpres, 71-). *Publ:* Auth, The Sun Gallery, Provincetown Art Asn, 7/81. *Dealer:* Long Point Gallery Provincetown MA 02657. *Mailing Add:* 484 Maple St Lafayette IN 47906

VIAN, ORFEO
EDUCATOR, PRINTMAKER
b Portogruaro, Prov, Venice, Italy, Dec 10, 24; US citizen. *Study:* John Herron Art Sch, BFA; Ind Univ, Bloomington, MFA. *Work:* The Print Club of Albany, NY; St John's Univ, Jamaica, NY; Butler Univ, Indianapolis, Ind; Calif Col of Arts & Crafts, Oakland. *Comn:* One edition of original prints for portfolios by six outstanding printmakers alumni of Herron Art Sch Garo Antreasian, John Bernhardt, Edwin Fulwider, Misch Kohn, George Jo Mess & Orfeo Vian, comn by Alumni Asn of John Herron Art Sch, Indianapolis, 49. *Exhib:* 3rd Nat Print Ann Exhib, Brooklyn Mus, New York, 49; 46th Ann Watercolor and Print Exhib, Pa Acad of Fine Arts, 48; 3rd Biennial Open Nat Print Exhib, Print Club of Albany, NY, 49; 7 Artisti USA, Academia di Belle Arti, Perugia, Italy, 71; Three New York Artists, Northern Ill Univ, DeKalb, 72; two-man show, Ind Central Univ, Indianapolis, 65 & 71; one-man shows, St John's Univ, Jamaica, NY, 76 & Bellarmine Col, Louisville, Ky, 65. *Teaching:* Vis prof printmaking, Notre Dame, Ind, summer 60; prof printmaking & hist of art, St John's Univ, Jamaica, 65-; exchange prof, Nat Taiwan Normal Univ, Taipei, 79. *Awards:* Purchase Prize, 3rd Biennial Open Nat Print Exhib, Print Club of Albany, NY, 49. *Mem:* The Graphics Soc; Col Art Asn of Am. *Media:* Woodcut & Silkscreen. *Mailing Add:* 6 Horseshoe Lane Commack NY 11725

VICENTE, ESTEBAN
PAINTER
b Turegano, Spain, Jan 20, 03; US citizen. *Study:* Acad Belles Artes, Madrid, Spain. *Work:* Whitney Mus Am Art, Mus Mod Art & Metrop Mus Art, New York; Nat Collection Fine Arts, Smithsonian Inst, Washington, DC; San Francisco Mus Fine Arts; Los Angeles Co Mus Art; Tate Gallery, London. *Exhib:* Eighth St Art Show, 49; Mus Mod Art, New York; Guggenheim Mus, New York; Art Inst Chicago; Inst Contemp Art, Boston; Carnegie Int, Pittsburgh; Whitney Mus Am Art Biennial, 50-64; plus many others. *Teaching:* Instr art, Black Mountain Col, 48; instr art, Univ Calif, Berkeley, 54 & 58, NY Univ, 59-69, Yale Univ, 60-61 & Univ Calif, Los Angeles, 62; artist in residence, Des Moines Art Ctr, Princeton Univ, 65-66 & 69-72 & Honolulu Acad Fine Arts, 69; instr, New York Studio Sch, 65-83. *Awards:* Purchase Awards, 60 & 61 & Tamarind Fel, 62, Ford Found; Childe Hassam Purchase Award, Am Acad Arts & Lett, 71; Altman Landscape Award, Nat Acad Design. *Bibliog:* Elaine De Kooning (auth), Vicente paints a collage, Art News, 52; John Ashberry (auth), article in Art News, 5/72; Theodore Woolf (auth), article, Christian Sci Monitor, 5/83. *Media:* Oil, Collage. *Dealer:* Gruenebaum Gallery 38 E 57th St New York NY 10022; Yares Gallery Bishop Lane Scottsdale AZ. *Mailing Add:* Main St Bridgehampton NY 11932

VICKERY, CHARLES BRIDGEMAN
PAINTER
b Hinsdale, Ill, July 16, 13. *Study:* Art Inst Chicago; Am Acad Fine Art, Chicago; also with Ben Stahl. *Work:* Univ Club, Chicago; Union League Club, Chicago; prints, Royal Acad, London. *Exhib:* Rockport Art Asn, Mass; Union League Club; Ackerman Gallery, London; Springfield Mus, Ill; Pallette & Chisel Acad, Chicago. *Awards:* Diamond Medal Award, Pallette & Chisel Acad, 68; Waters of the World Prize, NShore Art Asn, Gloucester, 70; Union League Club Prize, 72. *Bibliog:* Eleanor Jewett (auth), article, Chicago Tribune, 45; C J Bulliet (auth), article, Chicago Daily News, 8/51. *Mem:* Palette & Chisel Acad (dir, 67-69); Rockport Art Asn; NShore Art Asn. *Media:* Oil, Acrylic. *Dealer:* W Russell Button Gallery 955 Center St Douglas MI 49406; Mystic Mus Marine Gallery Mystic Conn. *Mailing Add:* 4533 Wolf Rd Western Springs IL 60558

VICKREY, ROBERT REMSEN
PAINTER
b New York, NY, Aug 20, 26. *Study:* Yale Univ, BA; Art Students League; Yale Sch Fine Arts, BFA; also with Kenneth Hayes Miller & Reginald Marsh. *Work:* Nat Mus Am Art, Corcoran Gallery Art, Washington, DC; Metrop Mus Art, Whitney Mus Am Art, New York; Butler Inst Am Art; and 50 others. *Comn:* Covers for Time Mag; also portraits & bk jackets. *Exhib:*

Whitney Mus Am Art; Mus Mod Art, New York; Santa Barbara Mus, Calif; Mus Fine Arts, Houston; Neuberger Mus, Purchase, NY; Chrysler Mus, Norfolk, Va; Lyrical Realist Traveling Exhib, 82-83. *Awards:* Am Audubon Artists; Int Hallmark Competition, Windsor; Newton Mem Award. *Mem:* Am Watercolor Soc; Audubon Artists; Nat Acad Design. *Media:* Tempera. *Publ:* Coauth, New Techniques in Egg Tempera & auth, Robert Vickery--Artis at Work, Watson-Guptill. *Dealer:* ACA Galleries 21 E 67th St New York NY 10021. *Mailing Add:* Box 445 Orleans MA 02653

VICTOR, MARY O'NEILL
MUSEUM DIRECTOR
b Boston, Mass, Dec 27, 24. *Study:* Boston Univ, 43-47. *Collections Arranged:* American Watercolors 1850-1972, 72; Art of Ancient Orthodoxy, 72; Where the Action Is (sports in art), 73; Art of the Old West, 74; Chop Art: American Motorcycle Design, 75; Cleveland Woodward: Painter by God's Good Light, 76; Southern Antiques and Folk Art, 76; Jewish Art: A Continuing Heritage, 77; Wildlife Art: American Sculpture, 77; The Ripening of American Art: Duveneck and Chase, 79; Five Thousand Years of Dynasty Art, 80; The Art of Peter Carl Faberge, 81; Holography 82: 5000 Years of Art, 82. *Pos:* Registr, Mus Fine Arts, Boston, 64-69; dir, Fine Arts Mus of the South, Mobile, 69- *Mem:* Am Asn Mus; Am Fedn Arts. *Collection:* Nineteenth and twentieth century American paintings, sculpture and graphics; contemporary crafts; Miller collection of Oriental & European art. *Mailing Add:* Fine Arts Mus of the South Mobile AL 36608

VIDAL, HAHN
PAINTER
b Hamburg, Ger, Mar 11, 19; US citizen. *Study:* With Eduardo Couce Vidal. *Work:* Eduardo Sivori, Mus Artes Plasticas, Buenos Aires, Arg; Juan B Castagnino, Mus Cuidad Rosario, Arg; Mus Seattle, Wash; Mus Mobile, Ala; Hist Mus Taiwan, China; and others. *Comn:* Hahn Vidal Rm, Boca Raton Hotel & Club, Fla, 69. *Exhib:* Okla Mus Art, Oklahoma City, 70 & 72; Grand Cent Art Gallery, 70 & 73; Dayton, Ohio, 70 & 73; Arvest, Boston, 74 & 77; Valencia, Spain, 75, 77 & 79; Wichita Art Asn, Kans, 78; Castellon, Spain, 78; Charles & Emma Frye Art Mus, Seattle, Wash; and others. *Mem:* Salmagundi Club; Soc Illusr. *Media:* Oil. *Dealer:* Grand Cent Art Gallery Inc 40 Vanderbilt Ave New York NY 10019. *Mailing Add:* 345 W 58th St New York NY 10019

VIELEHR, WILLIAM RALPH
SCULPTOR
b Chicago, Ill, Jan 6, 45. *Study:* Univ Colo, 63-66; Colo State Univ, BFA, 69. *Work:* Crossroads Mall, Boulder, Colo; Chicago Mus Contemp Art; Prudentiat Bache, Boulder, Colo; Northern Ill Univ; Cherry Creek Plaza, Denver. *Exhib:* Joslyn Art Mus, Omaha, Nebr, 72 & 74; Denver Art Mus, 72; Allrich Gallery, San Francisco, 75; Attitudes Gallery, Denver, 75; Sebastian Moore Gallery, Denver, 77; and others. *Pos:* Dir, Form Inc, 81- *Teaching:* Vis artist sculpture workshop, Jefferson Co Schs, 71-72 & Colo State Univ, 73. *Awards:* Purchase Prize, Designer Craftsmen Asn, 72; City Arts Grant, Boulder, Colo, 80. *Bibliog:* Boulder Sculpture Symposium, 82; Sculpture in the Gardens, Denver Botanic Gardens, 83. *Media:* Cast Bronze & Aluminum. *Dealer:* Form Inc 2888 Bluff St Boulder CO 80301. *Mailing Add:* PO Box 4351 Boulder CO 80306

VIERA, CHARLES DAVID
EDUCATOR, PAINTER
b Dartmouth, Mass, Feb 21, 50. *Study:* Swain Sch Design, BFA, 72; Skowhegan Sch Painting & Sculpture; Brooklyn Col Grad Sch, with Phillip Pearlstein, MFA, 74. *Work:* Pvt collection of A Hess, New York. *Comn:* Murals, Am Renaissance Festival, Brooklyn Mus, 79. *Exhib:* Brooklyn 1976, Brooklyn Mus; Facing Time, Nat Arts Club, New York, 77; 153 Ann, Nat Acad, New York, 78; solo shows, Animal Drawings, Long Island Univ, 80 & Paintings, Nassau Co Mus, 81; retrospective, Charles Viera 1972-1982, Brooklyn Mus Art Sch, 82; Works on Paper, Adam Gimbel Gallery, New York, 83. *Teaching:* Instr painting & drawing, Brooklyn Mus Art Sch, 75- & Parsons Sch Design, 79-; assoc prof, Long Island Univ, 79- *Bibliog:* Show of contrast, Phoenix, New York, 76; Inmates try art, 76 & Performers recreate art, 79, New York Times. *Media:* Mixed. *Mailing Add:* c/o Adam Gimbel Gallery 15 E 49th St New York NY 10022

VIERA, RICARDO
PAINTER, PRINTMAKER
b Ciego de Avila, Cuba, Dec 15, 45; US citizen. *Study:* Sch of the Mus of Fine Arts, Boston, dipl, 72; Tufts Univ, BFA, 73; RI Sch of Design, Providence, MFA, 74. *Work:* Allentown Art Mus, Pa; Tel Aviv Mus, Israel; Canton Art Inst, Ohio; Cleveland Mus; Fed Soc Arts & Humanities, Lagos, Nigeria; and others. *Exhib:* One-man shows, Inst Contemp Art, Boston, 73 & Canton Art Inst, Ohio, 80; Transitions in Art, Boston Mus of Fine Arts, 77; The Kadishman Connection, Israel Mus, Jerusalem, 79; Instituto de Cultura Puertorriquena, San Juan, 81; Alfred O Deshong Mus, Chester, Pa, 82; and many others. *Collections Arranged:* American Figure Drawing, Lehigh Univ & Victorian Col of Art, Melbourne, Australia, 79; Intentions & Techniques (auth, catalog), 79, 26th Ann Contemp Am Art Exhib (auth, catalog), traveling, 81 & Computer Art (auth, catalog), 82, Wilson Gallery, Lehigh Univ, Bethlehem, Pa; Michael Smith, Landscape Photography (auth, catalog), traveling, 81; and others. *Pos:* dir & cur, Lehigh Univ Art Galleries, 74-, chmn pro-tempore, 77-78; community arts coordr & discussion leader, Baum Sch Art, Allentown, Pa, 79-; consult, Cuban Mus Art & Cult, Miami, 81-; bd dirs, Pa Citizens Arts, 79-, ARTS, Washington, DC; bd dirs, Valley Art Coun. *Teaching:* Instr, Lehigh Univ, 74-78, assoc prof, 78. *Awards:* Elizabeth H Bartol Scholarship, Boston Mus of Fine Arts Sch, 71-72; Cintas fel, Cintas

Found, Inst of Int Educ, 74-75; Mellon Found Grant, 78-80; and others. *Bibliog:* Ricardo Viera/Illustraciones Enlace, Nueva Revista Hispanoamericana, 76; Keith Schneider (auth), Capturing the intensity of life, Times Leader, Wilkes-Barre, Pa, 9/13/79; Norma Niurka (auth), A box of surprises, Miami Herald, 10/7/81. *Mem:* Print Club Philadelphia; Am Asn of Mus; Am Asn Mus/NEastern Conf. *Media:* Oil, Acrylic; Enamel Spray, Oil Crayon. *Publ:* Illusr, Dr Fernando Ortiz, auth, Los Negros Brujos, Ed Universal, Miami, Fla, 73; illusr, Libro Quinto de Lectura Gramatica y Ortografia, Leal & Sanchez Boudy, Miami, 75; illusr, Introduccion al Estudio de la Civilizacion Espanola, Barroso, Miami, 76; auth, Arte Visual en la Palabra de Lydia Cabrera, Festschriften/Ed Universal, 77; auth, From Limestones to aluminum plate lithography, RI Sch of Design Bull, 77. *Dealer:* Forma Hispanic Arts Dealers 305 Alcazar Coral Gables FL 33134. *Mailing Add:* 6945 Weaversville Rd Northampton PA 18067

VIESULAS, ROMAS
PRINTMAKER, EDUCATOR
b Lithuania, Sept 11, 18; US citizen. *Study:* Ecole des Arts et Metiers, Ger, grad; Ecole des Beaux Arts, Paris. *Work:* Mus Mod Art, New York; Mus Mod Art, Kamakura, Japan; Vatican Mus, Vatican City, Rome, Italy; Art Gallery, NSW, Sydney, Australia; Nat Gallery Art, Washington, DC; and others. *Comn:* Spring (ed), Print Club, Philadelphia, 65; Up-on (100 prints), Int Graphic Arts Soc, New York, 68. *Exhib:* Whitney Mus Am Art Ann, 66; Two Decades of American Prints 1947-1968, Brooklyn Mus, 69; Int Graphic, Kunsthalle Bremen, Bremen, WGer, 76; Int Graphic, Stockholm Nationalmuseum, Stockholm, Sweden, 76; 30 Yrs of Am Printmaking, Brooklyn Mus, NY, 76-77; Pintores de los Paises Balticos, Mus Contemp Art Caracas, Venezuela, 77; Am Prints of the 20th Century, Philadelphia Mus Art, Pa, 77-78; Oxford Gallery, Eng, 78; Am Acad in Rome, Italy, 79; and many others. *Teaching:* Prof printmaking, Tyler Sch Art, Temple Univ, 60- *Awards:* Guggenheim Fels, 58, 64 & 69; Tamarind Fel, 60; Medal, Biennial Graphic Arts, Krakow, 70. *Bibliog:* Jules Heller (auth), Printmaking Today, Holt, Rinehart & Winston, 72; Fritz Echenberg (auth), The Art of the Print, Abrams, 76; On making and displaying inkless embossed prints on dyed paper, Leonardo, Vol 12, 79. *Mem:* Print Club Philadelphia; Soc Am Graphic Artists. *Media:* Intaglio. *Mailing Add:* Dept of Printmaking Tyler Sch Arts Temple Univ Philadelphia PA 19126

VIGIL, VELOY JOSEPH
PAINTER, PRINTMAKER
b Denver, Colo, Mar 5, 31. *Study:* Colo Inst Art, Denver Art Acad, Denver. *Work:* Colorado Springs Fine Arts Ctr, Colo; Heard Mus, Phoenix, Ariz; Armour Dial Res Ctr, Scottsdale, Ariz; Phoenix Art Mus; Am Greetings Corp, Cleveland, Ohio. *Comn:* Posters, Art Wagon Gallery, Scottsdale & Hall Gallery, Ft Worth, 77. *Exhib:* Nat Watercolor Soc Ann, Laguna Beach Art Mus, Calif, 67; Am Watercolor Soc, Nat Acad Galleries, New York, 68; Indian Arts & Crafts Exhib, Heard Mus, Phoenix, Ariz, 76; one-man exhibs, Segal Gallery, New York, 79, 81 & 83; Smithsonian Inst, 82; and others. *Collections Arranged:* Nat Watercolor Soc Travel Show, Embassy of Switz, 72 & Va Mus Fine Arts, Richmond, 73-74; Contemporary Indian Artist, Smithsonian Inst, 82. *Awards:* Winslow Homer Award, Springfield Art Mus, Mo, 70; Franklin Murphy Award, Ankrum Gallery, Los Angeles, Calif, 72; Avery Mem Award, Heard Mus Guild, Phoenix, 76. *Bibliog:* Lisa Sherman (auth), article, Arts Mag, 9/83; Don H Jones (auth), article, Artist, Santa Fean Mag, 9/83; Patricia Black (auth), Breaking Free, Collectors Mart, 9/83. *Media:* Watercolor, Acrylic. *Mailing Add:* 110 Morada Lane PO Box 2934 Taos NM 87571

VIGTEL, GUDMUND
ADMINISTRATOR
b July 9, 25; US citizen. *Study:* Isaac Grunewald's Sch Art, Stockholm, 43-44; Univ Ga, BFA, 52, MFA, 53. *Collections Arranged:* The New Tradition, 63; An Anthology of Modern American Art, 64; The Beckoning Land, 71; The Modern Image, 72; The Düsseldorf Academy & the Americans, 73; and numerous others. *Pos:* Admin asst, Corcoran Gallery Art, 54-57, asst to dir, 57-61, asst dir, 61-63; dir, High Mus Art, 63- *Mem:* Am Asn Mus; Asn Art Mus Dirs. *Mailing Add:* High Mus Art 1280 Peachtree St NE Atlanta GA 30309

VILLA, CARLOS
PAINTER
b Dec 11, 36. *Study:* San Francisco Art Inst, BFA, 61; Mills Col, MFA, 63. *Exhib:* de Young Mus, San Francisco, 72; Whitney Mus Am Art Ann, New York, 72; San Francisco Mus, 74; San Francisco Art Inst, 76; Calif Show: The Mod Era, San Francisco Mus, Calif & Nat Collection Fine Arts, Washington, DC, 76-77; Calif Bay Area Art--Update, Huntsville Mus Art, Ala, 77; New in the Seventies, Univ Tex, Austin, 77; and many others. *Teaching:* Asst, Mills Col, 61-63; asst, Studio 1, Oakland, Calif, 61-63; instr, Tel Hill Neighborhood Ctr, Urban Arts, San Francisco, 69-70; chmn interdept studies, San Francisco Art Inst, currently; asst prof art, Calif State Univ, Sacramento, currently. *Awards:* Nat Endowment Arts Grant, 73; Adeline Kent Award, San Francisco Art Inst, 73. *Bibliog:* Article, 12/70 & Emily Wasserman (auth), article, 1/71, Artforum. *Mailing Add:* 1664 Grove St San Francisco CA 94117

VILLENEUVE, JOSEPH ARTHUR
PAINTER
b Chicoutimi, Que, Jan 4, 10. *Study:* Nil-Autoidate. *Work:* Mus Beaux Arts Montreal; Mus Quebec; Nat Gallery Can, Ottawa; Mus Contemp Art, Montreal; and others. *Exhib:* Mus Quebec; Vancouver Art Gallery; Mus Beaux Arts, Montreal; Galerie Morency, Montreal; Galerie Waddington,

Montreal. *Awards:* Chevalier Membre de l'Orde du Canada. *Bibliog:* Arthur Villeneuve's Quebec Chronicles (exhib catalog), Montreal Mus Fine Arts. *Dealer:* Galerie Morency 1564 St Denis Montreal PQ Can; Muss-De-Liartiste Chicoutimi. *Mailing Add:* 669 Rue Tache Chicoutimi PQ G7J 3H3 Canada

VINCENT, CLARE
CURATOR, HISTORIAN

b Jersey City, NJ, Aug 30, 35. *Study:* Col William & Mary, AB, 58; Inst Fine Arts, NY Univ, MA, 62; Inst Fine Arts & Metropolitan Mus Art, cert, 62. *Collections Arranged:* A Sure Reckoning, 68, Northern European Clocks in New York Collections, 72, Nineteenth Century French Sculpture, 80 & Rodin: The Gates of Hell, 82, Metropolitan Mus Art, New York. *Pos:* Asst to cur decorative arts, Cooper Union Mus, 60-61; curatorial asst western European arts, Metropolitan Mus Art, New York, 62-67, asst cur, 67-72, assoc cur European sculpture & decorative arts, 72- *Mem:* Col Art Asn; Furniture Hist Soc; Antiquarian Horological Soc (vpres Am sect, 77-). *Res:* European clocks and timekeeping instruments; European metalwork; 19th century European sculpture. *Publ:* Auth, In search of a likeness: Some European portrait sculpture, Metropolitan Mus Art Bulletin, 4/66; auth, John Henry Belter's patent parlour furniture, Furniture Hist, Vol III, 67; auth, John Henry Belter: Manufacturer of all kinds of fine furniture, In: Technological Innovation and the Decorative Arts, Univ Va, 74; coauth, To finance a clock: An example of patronage in the 16th century, In: The Clockwork Universe, Neil Watson, 80; auth, Rodin at the Metropolitan Museum of Art: A History of the Collection, Metropolitan Mus Art, 81. *Mailing Add:* 326 E 85th St New York NY 10028

VINELLA, RAY (RAIMONDO JOHN)
PAINTER

b Bari, Italy, April 6, 33. *Study:* Art Ctr Col Design, with Lorsor Fietleson, Harry Carmean & John Lagatta, BPA, 59, BFA, 68. *Work:* Diamond M Found Mus, Snyder, Tex; Mus Native Am Cult, Spokane, Wash. *Exhib:* First Exhib Southwest Art, Peoples Republic China, 81; Mus Native Am Cult, Spokane, Wash, 82. *Teaching:* Instr painting, Taos Acad Fine Art, 71-72 & Taos Art Workshops, 82-; fac dean, Taos Sch Fine Art, 77-78. *Awards:* B Altman Award, 51; Prof Award, Painting Competition, Mex State Fair, 71 & 73. *Bibliog:* Tricia Hurst (auth), The Taos six, Southwest Art, 10/74; Peggy Ridgway (auth), article, Art Gallery, 2/83. *Mem:* Soc Am Impressionists; Monac Art Soc. *Media:* Oil, Egg Tempera. *Mailing Add:* c/o Taos Art Gallery E Kit Carson Rd Taos NM 87571

VIRET, MARGARET MARY (MRS FRANK IVO)
PAINTER, INSTRUCTOR

b New York, NY, Apr 18, 13. *Study:* Terry Art Sch; Miami Art Sch; Miami Art Ctr; Univ Miami; also with Dong Kingman, Eliot O'Hara, Xavier Gonzalez, Eugene Massin, Georges Sellier & Jack Amoroso; plus many other prominent instrs. *Work:* Norton Gallery; Lowe Art Gallery. *Comn:* Cuba Home Scene, Miami Woman's Club, 63; ballet scenes, Pauline Hill Co, Miami, 65; Spring Flowers (watercolors), Fla C of C, 69; Florida Everglades Scene for Wall, Capt Gene, 70; Florida Flowers for Wall, Laura, Pompano Beach, Fla. *Exhib:* Tampa Art Mus, 55; Fla Fedn Art, 55-56; Bass Art Mus, Miami Beach, 55-57, 62 & 63; Lowe Art Gallery, 60, 62 & 70; American Contemporary, Four Arts Soc, 65; plus others. *Pos:* Chmn, Dade Co Art, 56-58; art dir, Fla Fedn Women's Clubs, 56-63; pres, Laramore Rader Poetry Group, Miami, 70-72; art dir, Miami Women's Club, 67-, dir fine arts, 77-78. *Teaching:* Instr art, Miami Art League, 55-56; instr art adult classes, YWCA & YMCA, Miami, 63-68 & Dade Co Schs, 68- *Awards:* Best Watercolor for Flowers, Fla Fedn Women's Clubs, 61; Best Watercolor for Marine, Bass Art Mus, 62; Best Watercolor for Flowers, Burdines Coral Gables Art Club, 63. *Bibliog:* Irene Gramling (auth), Sphinx, Franklin Press, 65 & 66; Edna Chauser (auth), Cultural Alliance, Chase, 71; featured in Her Story--Julia's Daughters, 80. *Mem:* Fla Fedn Art (vpres, 56-58); hon mem Hibiscus Fine Arts Guild; hon mem Allied Arts NMiami; life mem Miami Palette Club; trustee Miami Art League; and others. *Media:* Multimedia. *Mailing Add:* 294 NE 55th Terr Miami FL 33137

VIRGONA, HANK (HENRY P)
PRINTMAKER, PAINTER

b Brooklyn, NY, Oct 24, 29. *Study:* Pratt Inst Evening Sch, 54. *Work:* Metrop Mus Art, Pub Libr, New York; Arch Am Art, Smithsonian Inst; Slater Mem Mus; Sioux City Art Ctr, Iowa. *Exhib:* Two Hundred Years of American Drawing, Far Gallery, New York, 76; New American Still Life, Westmoreland Co Mus, Pa, 79; The Presidency: Relevant & Irrelevant Traveling Exhib, 80; West and the Law Traveling Exhib, 80-82; Prints USA, Pratt Inst, New York, 82. *Pos:* Co-founder, 41 Union Sq Open Studios, 80. *Teaching:* Instr etching, pvt lessons, 82- *Awards:* Gold Medal, Soc Illusr, 70; Purchase Prizes, Nat Acad Art, 79 & Prints USA, Pratt Inst, 82. *Bibliog:* Ellyn Bloom (auth), Hank Virgona: The art of social satire, Am Artist Mag, 73. *Mem:* Artists Equity, New York. *Media:* Etching; Watercolor. *Publ:* Auth, The System Works! The Etchings and Random Notes of Hank Virgona, Da Capo Press, 77; illusr, Ivan the Terrible, Ivan the Fool, G Putnam Sons, 80. *Dealer:* Washington Irving Gallery 117 E 17th St New York NY 10003. *Mailing Add:* 41 Union Sq W New York NY 10003

VISCO, ANTHONY SALVATORE
EDUCATOR, SCULPTOR

b Philadelphia, Pa, Sept 13, 48. *Study:* Fleischer Art Mem, Philadelphia; Philadelphia Col of Art; Accad delle Belle Art, Florence, Italy; Skowhegan Sch of Painting & Sculpture, Maine. *Comn:* Bronze crucifix & bronze baptismal fount lid, Church of St Anastasia, Newtown Sq, Pa, 76. *Exhib:* Ann Student Exhib, Philadelphia Col of Art, 66-70; Invitational, Acad of Mus,

Philadelphia, 75; Kenmore Gallery, Philadelphia, 75; 41st Eucharistic Cong, Exhib of Liturgical Arts, Civic Ctr, Philadelphia, 76. *Pos:* Art instr, Recreation Ctr for Older People, Philadelphia, summer, 68; apprentice, Waler Erlbacher, Elkins Park, Pa, summer, 70; sculpture technician, Skowhegan Sch, Maine, summer, 75. *Teaching:* Instr sculpture, Philadelphia Col of Art, 76-, Creuzberg Ctr, Radnor, Pa, 76- *Awards:* State scholar, Philadelphia Col of Art, 66-70; Fulbright-Hayes Scholar, Florence, Italy, 70-71; Greenshields Award, Pvt Studio Work, Can, 75-76. *Media:* Wax, Bronze. *Mailing Add:* 4229 Cheltenham Ave Philadelphia PA 19124

VISSER'T HOOFT, MARTHA
PAINTER

b Buffalo, NY, May 25, 06. *Work:* Albright-Knox Art Gallery, Buffalo; Whitney Mus Am Art, New York; Rollins Col Mus Art; Munson-Williams-Proctor Inst, Utica, NY. *Exhib:* American Painting Today, Metrop Mus Art, New York, 50; Carnegie Inst Int, Pittsburgh, 52; Art Inst Chicago, 56; Artistas Brasileros Americanos, Mus Mod Art, Sao Paulo, Brazil; one-man show, Charles Burchfield Ctr, State Univ NY Col Buffalo, 73; In Western NY, Albright-Knox Gallery, 79. *Awards:* Purchase Award, Columbia Mus Art, 59; Second Prize in Oil, Chautauqua Inst Art, 64; NY State Univ Buffalo Community Coun Award, 75; plus others. *Bibliog:* J Benjamin Townsend (auth), Martha Visser't Hooft Paintings & Drawings, 1950-1973, State Univ NY Col Buffalo Alumni Found, 73. *Mem:* Hon mem Buffalo Fine Art Acad, Albright-Knox Gallery; Charles Burchfield Ctr, State Univ NY Col Buffalo. *Dealer:* More-Rubin Gallery Buffalo NY; Charles Burchfield Ctr, State Univ Col Buffalo, NY. *Mailing Add:* 800 W Ferry St Apt 6B Buffalo NY 14222

VITALE, LYDIA MODI
MUSEUM DIRECTOR, CURATOR

b New York, NY. *Study:* Scholar Award, Art Students League, New York; apprentice of Hans Hoffman, New York; internship, Museo Nac de Hist, 45-46 & Museo Nac de Antropologia, 58, Mexico City; studies in art conserv & restoration, Univ Calif, Davis, 70. *Collections Arranged:* Art Nouveau, 68, Fish-Fox-Kos: Concept Art, 71, Westward Ho: Russell, Remington, Price, Hansen, 76, New Deal Art: California (ed, catalog), 76 & Graham Nash Collection, 78, de Saisset Art Gallery & Mus, Univ Santa Clara; Graham Nash Collection, 78, de Saisset Art Gallery & Mus, Univ Santa Clara. *Pos:* Display dir, Prince Matchabelli, Inc, New York; art dir & set/costume designer, Actor's Workshop, San Francisco, 56-57; dir, cur & art instr, Triton Mus of Art, San Jose, Calif, 65-67; dir, de Saisset Art Gallery & Mus, Univ Santa Clara, 67-79, consult, 79- *Awards:* Adolph's Found Grant, 74, Calif Arts Comn Grant, 74 & Nat Endowment for the Humanities Grant & exten, 74 & 75, New Deal Art, California. *Mem:* Western Asn of Am Mus (exec secy, 69-71); Am Asn Art Mus; Bay Area Lawyers for the Arts; Archeoclub d'Italia (bd dirs, currently). *Publ:* Ed catalogues, Twenty Color Photographs: Light Abstractions, Wynn Bullock, 72, Fletcher Benton: Selected Works 1964-74, 74 & Scholder Collects Scholder 1965-75 Retrospective, 75, de Saisset Art Gallery & Mus; co-ed, James W McManus: Survey of Selected Works 1967-77, de Saisset Art Gallery & Mus, 77. *Mailing Add:* 100 Font Blvd Apt 3E San Francisco CA 94132

VIVENZA, FRANCESCA
GRAPHIC ARTIST, PAINTER

b Rome, Italy, May 4, 41; Can citizen. *Study:* High Sch Fine Art, Milan, Italy; Acad Belle Arti Brera, Milan; frescos with Gianfilippo Usellini. *Comn:* Geology & Metamorphosis of Sci (drawings), Univ Toronto Mining Bldg, 74; mural, Toronto Peace Convention, 76. *Exhib:* One-man shows, Albert White Gallery, Toronto, 72, 74, 76, 78 & 81; Pub Libr, Cambridge, Ont, 77 & Galleria D'Azeglio, Bologna, 78; Olga Korper Gallery, 82; Harbor Front Gallery, Toronto, 83. *Teaching:* Prof hist art, Secondary Schs, Milan & Como, Italy, 67-69; guest artist, Humber Col, fall 74; artist-in-residence, Scarborough Col, Ont, 78, York Univ. *Bibliog:* C Morgan (auth), Artist of outside-inside, Mosaico, 75; J Purdie (auth), article in Globe & Mail, 1/31/76; article, Toronto Star, 11/27/82; and others. *Mem:* Canadian Artist's Representation. *Media:* Mixed Media. *Publ:* Auth, Geranimal, Daddy Lion & Other Stories, Groundwood, 78. *Dealer:* Olga Korper Gallery 80 Spadina Fourth Floor Toronto ON Can. *Mailing Add:* 73 Ellerbeck St Toronto ON M4K 2V2 Canada

VIVOT, LEA (LEA DRAHOMIRA VIVOT-FISHMAN)
SCULPTOR

b Czechoslovakia; Can citizen. *Study:* Art Sch Stage Design, Prague, with Svoboda, 64-68; Acad Brera, Milan, 68; Ont Col Art, Toronto, with Erick Freifeld, 69-73. *Work:* Univ Guelph, Ont; Hosp for Sick Children, Toronto; St Joseph's Health Ctr, Toronto. *Exhib:* Solo exhib, Kar Gallery, Toronto, 79; Summer Exhib, Royal Acad Arts, London, 79; Sculpture of the 1980s, McMichael Collections, Kleinburg, Ont, 80; Sculptor's Soc Can, Pt Claire, Que, 82; Toronto Waldorf Sch, 82; Whitten Gallery, King City, Ont, 83; and others. *Teaching:* Creative artist in sch, Kleinburg Pub Sch, Ont, 79. *Bibliog:* Sculpture Bronzing (film), City TV, Toronto, 12/6/82; Barbara McLeod (interviewer), Romance Factor/Sculpture (film), Can Broadcasting Corp, 12/14/82; The endless bench, Toronto Star 3/22/83. *Mem:* Sculpture Soc Can; Royal Acad Arts; Ont Col Art, Toronto; Art Students League. *Media:* Bronze. *Mailing Add:* RR 1 Kleinburg ON L0J 1C0 Canada

VODICKA, RUTH KESSLER
SCULPTOR

b New York, NY. *Study:* City Col New York; with O'Connor Barrett; Sculpture Ctr, New York; Art Students League, 56-57 & 59; New Sch Social Res, 65; NY Univ, 69; Empire State Col Prog, 75- *Work:* Norfolk Mus, Va; Montclair State Col, NJ; Grayson Co State Bank, Sherman, Tex. *Comn:*

Eternal Light (bronze sculpture), Temple of Jewish Community Ctr, Harrison, NJ, 65. *Exhib:* Whitney Mus Ann, New York, 52-57; Am Fedn Arts Traveling Exhib, 57-58; Galerie Claude Bernard, Paris, 60; Walk-Through-Dance-Through-Sculpture, New York Cult Arts Festival, Bryant Park, 67; Sculpture for the Dance, Hudson River Mus, Yonkers, NY, 73; and others. *Teaching:* Instr sculpture, Queens Youth Ctr, Bayside, 53-56; instr sculpture, Emanuel Midtown YM & WHA, New York, 66-69; instr sculpture, Great Neck Arrandale Sch, 69-70; vis artist, Hillside Sch, Hastings-on-Hudson, 73-74. *Awards:* Joseph W Beatman Award for Best Work in Any Medium & First Prize, Silvermine Guild Artists, 57; Medal of Honor, Painters & Sculptors Soc NJ, 62; Julia Ford Pew Prize, Nat Asn Woman Artists, 66; and others. *Bibliog:* Louis Calta (auth), Multi-purpose sculpture on view in Bryant Park, New York Times, 10/67; Environmental happening, Journal News, Mt Kisco, 9/73; They Choreograph to sculpture (cover), Patent Trader, 10/73. *Mem:* Am Soc Contemp Artists; Audubon Artists; Nat Asn Women Artists; Sculptors Guild (exec bd, 75); Women in Arts. *Media:* Bronze, Brass. *Publ:* Contribr, Feminist Art J, 72, Women & Art, 72, Artworkers Newslett, 73-75. *Mailing Add:* 97 Wooster St New York NY 10012

VO-DINH, MAI
PAINTER, PRINTMAKER
b Hue, Vietnam, Nov 14, 33; US citizen. *Study:* Sorbonne, Fac Lett, 56; Acad Grande Chaumiere, 57; Ecole Nat Superieure Beaux-Arts, 59. *Work:* Musee d'Art Moderne Delaville de Paris; Mus Rouen; Schiedam Mus, Holland; Nashville Mus, Tenn; Wash Co Mus Fine Arts, Md. *Exhib:* One-man shows, Washington Co Mus Fine Arts, Md, 78 & Univ Md, 80; Arts Club Washington, Touchstone Gallery & Paul Rosen Graphics, Washington, DC, 83; and others. *Awards:* Christopher Award, Christopher Found, New York, NY, 75. *Bibliog:* Sidney Fields (auth), A Voice for Vietnam, New York Daily News, 2/71; Libbie Powell (auth), International Recognized Artist, The Daily Mail, Hagerstown, Md, 11/74; Henry Scarupa (auth), An artist's odyssey, Baltimore Sun, 7/80. *Mem:* Artists Equity Asn New York; Int Asn Artists. *Media:* Oil, Acrylic; Woodblock. *Publ:* Auth & illusr, Xu Sam Set, La Boi Press, Paris, 80; transr & illusr, Fragrance of Zen, Buddah Cult Ctr, 81; illusr, The Happy Funeral, Harper & Row, 82; illusr, The Gift, Knopf, 83; illusr, Angel Child, Dragon Child, Raintree Publishers, 83; illusr, Fragrance of Zen, Buddhist Cultural Center, Los Angeles, 81. *Dealer:* Phoenix II Int Square Washington DC. *Mailing Add:* Stonevale Burkittsville MD 21718

VOELKER, ELIZABETH
PAINTER, COLLAGE ARTIST
b Pittsburgh, Pa, 1931. *Study:* Carnegie-Mellon Univ, BFA, 53. *Work:* Phillips Collection, Nat Collection Fine Arts, Washington, DC; Art Mus, Carnegie Inst, Pittsburgh, Pa; San Francisco Mus Mod Art; Calif Palace Legion Hon; Santa Barbara Mus Art. *Exhib:* Pittsburgh Artists from the Permanent Collection, Mus Art, Carnegie Inst, Pittsburgh, Pa, 77; Recent Acquisitions, Nat Collection Fine Arts, Washington, DC, 78, Calif Palace Legion Hon, 78 & Santa Barbara Mus Art, 83; solo exhibs, San Jose Mus Art, 82 & Santa Barbara Mus Art, 82; Allport Gallery, 83 & 84. *Teaching:* Lectr, Univ Calif Exten, San Francisco, 72. *Awards:* MacDowell Colony Grant, 76; Hereward Lester Cooke Found Grant, 77; Va Ctr Creative Arts Grant, 82-84. *Bibliog:* David Burdon (auth), There's a new kid in town, Village Voice, 77; Judith Weiner (auth), Oriental ideas enrich paintings, collages, Oakland Press, 81; Andrea Liss (auth), A deceptive simplicity, Artweek, 83. *Media:* Oil, Oil Pastel; Collage. *Dealer:* Allport Gallery 126 Post St San Francisco CA 94108; Fendrick Gallery 3059 M St NW Washington DC 20007. *Mailing Add:* 872 Clayton St San Francisco CA 94117

VOELKER, JOHN
PAINTER, DESIGNER
b Givens, Ohio. *Study:* Columbus Col Art & Design, Ohio, 53-57; design workshop with Canzani; advan painting with Kuehn. *Work:* Columbus Gallery Fine Arts, Ohio; Abilene Mus Fine Arts, Tex. *Comn:* Posters, Cerebral Palsy Found, 56; Tex Fine Arts Asn, Dallas, 71 & Logo Design Bicentennial with Tex Fine Arts Asn, 75. *Exhib:* Ultimate Concerns, Prints & Drawings, Ohio Univ, 63 & 64; Artists of Gulf States & Tex, Delgado Mus, New Orleans, 64 & 66; Chautauqua Exhib Am Art, NY, 67; 11th Ann Prints & Drawings, Okla Art Ctr, Oklahoma City, 69; Southwest Painting Ann, Albuquerque, NMex, 70. *Pos:* Art coordr, Coronet Packaging, Dallas, 61-75. *Awards:* Permanent Collection Choice, Ultimate Concerns, Ohio Univ, 63; Haydon Calhoun Gallery Award, Painting & Sculpture Ann, Dallas Mus Fine Arts, 64; Best of Show, Tex Fine Arts Asn, 72. *Bibliog:* Article, Columbus Sunday Mag, Dispatch, 3/56; article, Dallas Times Herald, 10/76. *Mem:* Artists Equity, Dallas; Tex Fine Arts Asn; Artists Coalition of Tex. *Dealer:* Adelle Taylor 3317 McKinney Dallas TX. *Mailing Add:* 4135 University Dallas TX 75205

VOGEL, DONALD
PRINTMAKER, INSTRUCTOR
b Poland, Dec 24, 02; US citizen. *Study:* Parson Sch Design; Columbia Univ, BS & MA. *Work:* Seattle Art Mus; Pa State Univ; Metrop Mus Art, New York; Munson-Williams-Proctor Inst; Soc Am Graphic Artists; and others. *Exhib:* Brooklyn Mus, 50; Am Fedn Arts Traveling Exhib, 50; Royal Soc Painters, Etchers & Engravers, 54; Calif Western Univ, San Diego, 60; Pratt Graphic Art Ctr, 64; and others. *Teaching:* Instr art, High Sch Art & Design, New York. *Awards:* Munson-Williams-Proctor Inst, 43; Northwest Printmakers, 43 & 46; Libr of Cong, 50. *Mem:* Soc Am Graphic Artists. *Publ:* Contribr, Print Collector's Quart, La Rev Mod & others. *Mailing Add:* 415 East 52nd St New York NY 10022

VOGEL, DONALD S
PAINTER, DEALER
b Milwaukee, Wis, Oct 21, 17. *Study:* Corcoran Gallery Art, Washington, DC; Art Inst Chicago; Work Prog Admin Easel Proj, Chicago. *Work:* Ft Worth Art Ctr, Tex; Dallas Mus Fine Arts; Beaumont Mus Art, Tex; Mobile Art Ctr, Ala; Philbrook Art Ctr, Tulsa, Okla. *Exhib:* One-man shows, Philbrook Mus Art, Tulsa, 69, Beaumont Art Mus, Tex, 70, Charles B Goddard Ctr, Ardmore, Okla, 81 & San Jacinto Tower, Dallas, 83; and many others. *Collections Arranged:* Clara McDonald Williamson, 66 & Velox Ward (with catalog), 72, Amon Carter Mus Art, Ft Worth; Valton Tyler (with catalog), Southern Methodist Univ, 72. *Pos:* Dir, Valley House Gallery Inc. *Awards:* Bronze Medal, Am Acad Rome, 42; Dallas Allied Arts Ann Awards, Dallas Mus Fine Arts, 44-46; 8th Tex Gen Exhib Award, Houston Mus Fine Arts, 46. *Mem:* Art Dealers Asn Am; Am Fedn Arts; Dallas Mus Fine Arts. *Specialty:* Paintings and sculpture of the nineteenth and twentieth centuries. *Publ:* Coauth & ed, Passion: Georges Rouault (catalog), 62; coauth, Aunt Clara, 66; ed, The Paintings of Hugh H Breckenridge (catalog), 67. *Mailing Add:* Valley House Gallery, Inc 6616 Spring Valley Rd Dallas TX 75240

VOGEL, (MR & MRS) HERBERT
COLLECTORS
Mr Vogel b New York, NY, Aug 16, 22; Mrs Dorothy Vogel b Elmira, NY, May 14, 35. *Study:* Mr Vogel, NY Univ Inst Fine Arts, with Erwin Panofsky, Alfred Salmony, Richard Offner & Walter Friedlaender; Mrs Vogel, Syracuse Univ, BA, 57; Univ Denver, MA, 58. *Exhib:* Selections from the Collection of Dorothy & Herbert Vogel, Clocktower, New York, 75; Works from the Collection of Dorothy & Herbert Vogel, Univ of Mich Mus of Art, 77; From the Vogel Collection, Ben Shahn Gallery, William Patterson Col, 81; Twentieth Anniversary Exhib-Vogel Collection, Brainerd Art Gallery, State Univ Co Arts & Sci, Potsdam, NY, 82; Gallery Art, Univ Northern Iowa, Cedar Falls, 83; and others. *Bibliog:* Anthony Haden-Guest (auth), A new art-world legend, NY Mag, 4/28/75; Grace Glueck (auth), Art Notes: The in couple, New York Times, 5/4/75; Paul Gardner (auth), Look! it's the Vogels!, Art News, 3/79. *Collection:* Contemporary drawing, sculpture and painting. *Mailing Add:* 305 E 86th St New York NY 10028

VOGEL, JOSEPH
PAINTER, PRINTMAKER
b Poland, April 22, 11; US citizen. *Study:* Nat Acad Design Art, New York, 29-32; Students League, Grande Chaumiere, Paris, 33; Acad Julien, Leger Studio, with Andre L'Hote, 48-53. *Work:* Metrop Mus Art, New York; Nat Collection Am Art, Washington, DC; Philadelphia Mus Art; Baltimore Mus Art; St Louis Art Mus. *Exhib:* One-man exhibs, Inst Am Contemp Art, Los Angeles, 42, Abraxas Gallery, Laguna Beach & Newport Beach, 79, 80 & 81 & Walter Wiggins Gallery, Roswell, NMex, 83; Whitney Mus Art Invitationals, 33-38; Ryder Gallery, Los Angeles, 62-64; Newport Harbor Art Mus Invitational, 63; Prints for the People--Works Proj Admin Graphics, Nat Collection Fine Arts, Washington, DC, 79. *Teaching:* Instr painting, Chouinard Art Inst, 61-63; instr drawing & painting, Beverly Hills High Sch, 63-65 & Culver City High Sch, 63-66. *Media:* Oil, Tempera. *Dealer:* Walter Wiggins Gallery 209 W First St Roswell NM 88201; Freidenrich Contemp Art Inc Newport Beach CA. *Mailing Add:* 508 W 13th St Roswell NM 88201

VOGL, DON GEORGE
PAINTER, PRINTMAKER
b Milwaukee, Wis, July 22, 29. *Study:* Art Inst Chicago & Univ Chicago, BAE, 57; Univ Wis, Milwaukee, MS(art educ), 58. *Work:* Art Gallery, Univ Notre Dame, Ind; Alverno Col, Mt Mary Col & Cardinal Stritch, Milwaukee. *Comn:* Immaculate Conception Church, Hartford, Mich, 69; St Mark's Church, Niles, Mich, 70; Notre Dame Univ Law Libr, 75; Methodist Church, Stevenville, Mich; Railroad Bridge over Michigan Ave, South Bend, Ind. *Exhib:* Chicago Vicinity Show, 65; Watercolor USA, Springfield, Mo, 68; Tri-State Graphics, Louisville, Ky, 74; Indianapolis Painters & Sculptors, 75; one-man show, Quincey Col, Ill; and others. *Pos:* Vpres, Visual Improvement Prog, South Bend, 74-75. *Teaching:* Instr art, Marygrove Col, Detroit, 61-63; assoc prof, Univ Notre Dame, 63- *Awards:* First Award Painting, Wis State Fair, 58; La Vera Pohl Award, Wis Painters & Sculptors, 60; Second Award Graphics, Salamonie Art Show, Warren, Ind, 74. *Bibliog:* Rudy Pozatti (auth), Indiana printmakers, Ind Art Educ Asn, 12/74. *Mem:* Am Col Art Asn. *Media:* Lithography; Acrylic, Oil. *Dealer:* Deson-Zaks 226 East Ontario St Chicago IL 60611; William van Straaten Gallery 646 N Michigan Chicago IL. *Mailing Add:* Art Dept Univ Notre Dame Notre Dame IN 46556

VOLID, RUTH
DEALER, CONSULTANT
b Chicago, Ill. *Study:* Art Inst of Chicago; Chouinard Art Sch, Los Angeles; Otis Art Inst; Univ of Chicago. *Pos:* Pres, Ruth Volid Gallery Ltd, 70- *Bibliog:* Barbara Varro (auth), A New Start at Midlife, Sun Times, 10/77. *Mem:* Mus of Contemp Art, Chicago (bd affil, 76-); Arch of Am Art; life mem Print & Drawing Club, Art Inst Chicago; Arts Club Chicago; Am Soc Interior Designers (bd mem, currently). *Publ:* Art/an added dimension, Designer, 10/79. *Mailing Add:* 225 W Illinois St Chicago IL 60610

VOLKERDING, LAURA
PHOTOGRAPHER
b Louisville, Ky, 1939. *Study:* Univ Louisville, BS, 61; Inst Design, MS, 65. *Work:* Art Inst Chicago; Libr Cong; Smithsonian Inst Nt Collection Fine Arts; Can Ctr Archit, Montreal; Stanford Art Mus. *Exhib:* Stanford Art Mus, 81-82; Soc Encouragement Contemp Art Invitational, San Francisco, 82; New Landscapes, Friends Photog, Carmel, Calif; Panoramas, Renaissance Soc, Chicago; The Panoramic Photograph, Grey Gallery, New York. *Mailing Add:* 148 Bertita San Francisco CA 94112

VOLKIN, HILDA APPEL
PRINTMAKER, PAINTER

b Boston, Mass, Sept 24, 33. *Study:* Mass Col Art, BS, 54; Radcliffe Col, MA, 56. *Work:* Cleveland Mus Art, Ohio; Univ NMex, Albuquerque; Albuquerque Mus Art; Los Alamos Nat Lab, NMex. *Exhib:* Governor's Gallery, NMex State Capitol, Santa Fe, 80; Here and Now: 35 Artists in New Mexico, Mus Albuquerque, 80; Santa Fe Festival Arts, 81 & 82; Paper--The Continuous Thread, Cleveland Mus Art, Ohio, 82; Bergen Community Mus, Paramus, NJ, 83; and others. *Pos:* Dir, Fuller Lodge Art Ctr, 77-80. *Teaching:* Instr painting, Univ NMex, Los Alamos, 74- *Awards:* Purchase Award for Watercolor, Massillon Mus, 66; Graphics Awards, Cleveland Mus Art, 74 & Nat Asn Women Artists, 79. *Mem:* Nat Asn Women Artists. *Dealer:* Gallery A Taos NM; Munson Gallery Santa Fe NM. *Mailing Add:* 8421 Aztec Rd NE Albuquerque NM 87111

VOLPE, ROBERT
PAINTER, LECTURER

b New York, NY, Dec 13, 42. *Study:* Sch Art & Design, New York; New Sch Social Res; Parsons Sch Design, New York; Art Students League New York. *Work:* South Street Seaport Mus, New York; State Univ NY Downstate Med Ctr Collection; Antietam Nat Mus, Md. *Exhib:* One-man shows, Kottler Galleries, New York, 70, South Street Seaport Mus, 74, Nahas Gallery, New York, 75-80 & Salmagundi Club, New York, 76-83; NY Tel Co Exhib, 79; Knickerbocker Artists Exhib, 80 & 83. *Pos:* Cur, Antietam Nat Mus, Sharpsburg, Md, 72-80; mem bd dirs, Found Community Artist, New York, 72-75; dir, Art Identification Unit, City New York, 72-78; dir, Volpe Orgn Art Consults, 83; dir, Volpe-Winfield Assocs, Art Consult *Teaching:* Lectr, Harvard Law Sch, 74, Avila Col, Mo, 77 & Columbia Univ, 83. *Awards:* Graphic Awards, Guggenheim Mus, 77, Sch Visual Art, New York, 77 & 80 & Metrop Mus Art, 79. *Bibliog:* Articles, Wall St J, 78 & Life Mag, 79; article, Mus Mag, 2/82. *Mem:* Salmagundi Club; Knickerbocker Artists; Artist Fel Found; Off Naval Combat Artist Group. *Media:* Oil, Watercolor. *Publ:* Auth, The Italian Experience in Arts and Literature, The Metamorphosis Continues, Ctr Migration Studies, Ital Embassy, Washington, DC, 83. *Mailing Add:* c/o Salmagundi Club 47 Fifth Ave New York NY 10003

VON DEM BUSSCHE, WOLF
PAINTER, PHOTOGRAPHER

b Ger; US citizen. *Study:* Columbia Col, 56-62; Columbia Univ Sch Painting & Sculpture, 59-62; Art Students League, 61-62; self-taught in photog. *Work:* San Francisco Mus Mod Art; Mus Mod Art, Int Ctr Photog, Metrop Mus, New York; George Eastman House, Rochester, NY. *Exhib:* Vision & Expression, George Eastman House, Rochester, NY, 69; Soc Encouragement Contemp Art Award Exhib, San Francisco Mus Mod Art, 80; Int Triennial Exhib Photog, Musee d'art et d'hist, Fribourg, Switz, 81; Counterparts, Metrop Mus, New York 82; Space Framed, Harvard Univ Sch Design, 82; Urban Landscape, 82 & California Sharp School, 83, San Francisco Mus Mod Art; The Pet and the Beast: Portraits of Animals, Tisch Sch Arts, NY Univ, 83; three-person show, Phoenix Art Mus, 83. *Bibliog:* Carole Kismaric (auth), monograph, Camera, No 10, 71; Jerome Tarshis (auth), article, Art in Am, 1/81; Thomas Albright (auth), article, Art News, 4/82. *Publ:* Illusr, Canyons & Mesas, Time-Life Books, 74. *Mailing Add:* 7144 Norfolk Rd Berkeley CA 94705

VON GUNTEN, ROGER
PAINTER, DRAFTSMAN

b Zurich, Switz, Mar 29, 33. *Study:* Kunstgewerbeschule Zurich, 48-53; Iberoamerican Univ, Mex, 59-60. *Work:* Mus Arte Mod, Mexico City; Univ Oaxaca, Mex; Mus Univ Veracruzana, Xalapa, Mex; Centro Arte Mod, Guadalajara, Mex. *Comn:* Paintings, Mex Pavilions, Expo 67, Montreal & Hemisfair, San Antonio, 68; murals, Mex Pavilion, Expo 67, Osaka, Japan, 69 & Centro Arte Mod, Guadalajara, Mex, 70. *Exhib:* Fifteen Mexican Painters, Nat Mus Mod Art, Tokyo, 74; 12 Latin American Artists, Univ Tex, Austin, 75; Bienal Latinoamericana de Sao Paulo, Brazil, 78; Mexique d'Hier et Aujourd hui, Petit Palais, Paris, 81; Pintura Contemporanea de Mexico, Banco Exterior Easpana, Madrid, 83; and others. *Teaching:* Instr drawing, Univ Iberamericana, Mexico City, 63-64; instr engraving, Mexico City Col, 63-64. *Awards:* First Prize, II Festival Pictorico de Acapulco, Mexico, 64. *Bibliog:* J Garcia Ponce (auth), Nueve pintores, Mexicanos, Ed Era, Mex, 68; Damian Bayon (auth), Aventura plastica Hispanoamericana, Ed Fondo Cult Economica, Mex, 74; Tomi Garcia Ascot (auth), Roger von Gunten, Ed Univ Autonoma Mex, 79. *Media:* Oil, Acrylic. *Mailing Add:* c/o Galeria Juan Martin Amberes 17 Mexico City Mexico

VON MEYER, MICHAEL
SCULPTOR

b Russia, June 10, 1894; US citizen. *Study:* Calif Sch Fine Arts, San Francisco. *Work:* Daily Californian Newspaper Bldg, Salinas; House Off Bldg, Washington, DC; US Post Off, Santa Clara, Calif; Church of Transfiguration, Denver, Colo; Marina Heights, Vallejo, Calif. *Comn:* St Innocent Eastern Orthodox Church, Encino, Calif; St Therese's Shrine, Fresno, Calif; Russian Orthodox Holy Trinity Cathedral, San Francisco; Russian Cath Ctr; Beach Chalet, San Francisco. *Exhib:* San Francisco Mus Art; Corcoran Gallery Art, Washington, DC; Oakland Art Gallery, 36; Pomeroy Galleries, San Francisco, 66; Monterey Peninsula Mus Art, 69. *Awards:* Winner, Woman's Art Asn San Francisco, 26; Bronze Medal, Oakland Art Gallery 4th Ann Sculpture, 34. *Bibliog:* E M Polley (auth), Art & artists, Sun Times Herald, Vallejo, Calif; Robert Hagan (auth), The walls they left behind, San Francisco Mag, 64; Ann Gold (auth), Shades of Imperial Russia, San Francisco Sunday Examiner & Chronicle, 11/20/77. *Mailing Add:* c/o Hoover Gallery 710 Sansome St San Francisco CA 94111

VON REBHAN, ELINOR ANNE
SLIDE LIBRARIAN

b Northampton, Mass, Oct 10, 45. *Study:* Sweet Briar Col, BA(art hist), 67. *Pos:* Slide librn, Nat Gallery of Art, 68-81, chief slide librn, 81- *Mailing Add:* Nat Gallery of Art Washington DC 20565

VON RINGELHEIM, PAUL HELMUT
SCULPTOR

b Vienna, Austria. *Study:* Brooklyn Col, BS, 56; Fairleigh Dickinson Univ, MA, 58; Art Students League, 58-59; Acad Fine Arts, Munich, 60-61. *Work:* Welton Becket Assoc; Mus Mod Art, New York; Mus Mod Art, Tel Aviv; Mus Mod Art, Tokyo; Whitney Mus Am Art. *Comn:* World Peace Monument, US Pavilion, Worlds Fair, 64; fulcrum, Westinghouse Nuclear Ctr, Pittsburgh, 72; Interstate 80 Bicentennial Sculpture Project, Houston Ctr, Tex Eastern Corp. *Exhib:* Whitney Mus Am Art, 63 & 65; Mus Mod Art, New York, 64, 67 & 69; Jewish Mus, New York, 66 & 68; Cleveland Mus, 66; Albright-Knox Gallery, 67; Frick Mus, Pittsburgh, 68; solo exhib, O K Harris Gallery, New York, 71-73, 76, 78, 80 & 82. *Teaching:* Instr printmaking, Brooklyn Mus Sch, 57-58; prof sculpture, Sch Visual Arts, New York, 67-71. *Awards:* Fulbright Scholar, 74-75. *Mem:* Archit League City New York. *Mailing Add:* 9 Great Jones St New York NY 10012

VON RYDINGSVARD, URSULA
SCULPTOR

b Deensen, Germany, July 26, 42. *Study:* Univ Miami, Coral Gables, Fla, BA, 64, MA, 65; Univ Calif, Berkeley, 69-70; Columbia Univ, New York, MFA, 75. *Work:* Newberger Mus, Purchase, NY; Aldrich Mus Contemp Art, Ridgefield, Conn; City Dayton; Big Six Towers, Woodside, New York. *Exhib:* Corcoran Gallery, Washington, DC, 75; one-woman shows, 55 Mercer Gallery, New York, 77, 79 & 80 & Rosa Esman Gallery, New York, 81 & 82; Indoor-Outdoor Sculptures, PS 1, Long Island, NY, 78; Song of a Saint, Artpark, Lewiston, NY, 79; Art on the Beach, Battery Park City Landfill, New York, 80. *Pos:* Asst prof sculpture, Pratt Inst, Brooklyn, NY, 77-82, Fordham Univ, 80-82, Sch Visual Arts, New York, 81-82, Yale Univ, 82- *Awards:* Nat Endowment Arts, 79; Creative Artists Public Service Program, 80; Guggenheim Fel, 83. *Bibliog:* Grace Glueck (auth), articles, New York Times, 4/18/80 & 11/5/82; John Russell (auth), articles, New York Times, 8/79, 6/80 & 4/81. *Media:* Wood. *Dealer:* Bette Stoler Gallery 13 White St New York NY 10013. *Mailing Add:* 210 Spring St New York NY 10012

VON SCHLEGELL, DAVID
SCULPTOR

b St Louis, Mo, May 25, 20. *Study:* Univ Mich, 40-42; Art Students League, 46-48. *Work:* Whitney Mus Am Art, New York; Hirshhorn Mus, Washington, DC; Carnegie Inst, Pittsburgh; Yale Art Gallery, New Haven, Conn; H F Johnson Mus, Cornell Univ, Ithaca, NY. *Comn:* Sculptures, R W Godard Mem, Worcester, Mass, 79, Ind Univ, Indianapolis, 79, Yeatmans Cove, Cincinnati, 80, One Oxford Ctr, Pittsburgh, 82 & Tulsa Int Airport, 83; and others. *Exhib:* Whitney Ann, 60-68 & Lipman Found, 69, Whitney Mus Am Art, New York; Primary Structures, Jewish Mus, New York, 67; Carnegie Int, Pittsburgh, 70; Sculpture for New Spaces, Walker Art Ctr, Minneapolis, 71; Middleheim Biennial, Belg, 71; Univ Wash, 71; plus many other group & one-man shows. *Teaching:* Vis lectr sculpture, Univ Calif, Santa Barbara, 68; instr painting, Sch Visual Arts, 68-69; vis instr sculpture, Cornell Univ, 69-70; dir studies sculpture, Yale Univ, 71- *Awards:* Purchase Prize, Carnegie Int, 67; Nat Found Arts, 69 & Guggenheim, 74. *Bibliog:* Jacobs (auth), The artist speaks: D V S, Art in Am, 5-6/68; 2 outdoor pieces, Dus Arts, 5-6/73. *Mailing Add:* 190 Dromara Rd Guilford CT 06437

VON SCHLIPPE, ALEXEY
PAINTER, EDUCATOR

b Moscow, Russia, Sept 12, 15; US citizen. *Study:* Acad Fine Arts, Berlin, Ger; pvt studies in Rome, Italy; Royal Art Mus, Brussels, Belg, with Prof Phillipot. *Work:* West Berlin Gallery, Ger; Munich Gallery; Slater Mus, Norwich, Conn; Benton Mus, Storrs, Conn; T Vitney Col, New York. *Exhib:* New England Artists, Boston, 67; New Haven Art Festival, 68-73; Munich Int Europ Summer Show, Ger, 72-78; one-man shows, Sotheby Parke Bernet, Munich, WGer, 79 & Am House, Munich, WGer. *Teaching:* Asst prof art, art appreciation & hist, Univ Conn, 63-68, assoc prof design, 68-, prof art, art appreciation & hist & design, 77-83, prof emer, 83. *Awards:* First Prize, Norwich Free Acad, 62; Second Prize, Hartford Atheneum, 64. *Bibliog:* Articles, Art Rev, 67 & Univ Conn Chronicle, 2/73. *Mem:* Am Soc Psychopathology of Expression, US chapter. *Media:* Oil over Egg Tempera; Watercolor. *Mailing Add:* 18 Caulkins Rd Norwich CT 06360

VON WEISE, WENDA FRAKER
PRINTMAKER, TAPESTRY ARTIST

b Summit, NJ, May 15, 41. *Study:* Cleveland Inst Art, BFA, 75; Cranbrook Acad Art, MFA, 78. *Work:* Cleveland Mus Natural Hist, Ohio; Banc Ohio, Columbus. *Comn:* Photo screen printed quilted tapestries, Gund Found, Cleveland, 79, Ga Power Co, Atlanta, 81 & Mildred Andrews Fund for Cleveland Mus Natural Hist, 81. *Exhib:* Quilt Nat, Dairy Barn, Athens, Ohio, 79, 81 & 83; Art for Use, Am Craft Mus, New York, 80; Surface Design Exhib, Fashion Inst Technol, New York, 80; Ohio Quilts, Canton Art Inst, Ohio, 82; The Cleveland Inst of Art: 100 Years, Cleveland Mus Art, 83. *Teaching:* Instr printmaking, Cleveland State Univ, 79; artist in residence, Notre Dame Univ, South Bend, 80; assoc prof surface design, Cleveland Inst Art, 80- *Awards:* Jury Award, May Show, Cleveland Mus Art, 79; Individual Artist Fel Grant, Ohio Arts Coun, 80-81. *Bibliog:* Beth Gutchen (auth), Quilt national, Fiber Arts, 9/79 & Art for use, Am Crafts, 4/80; Dennis Dooley (auth), Here they come, Northern Ohio Live, 10/81. *Mem:* Surface Design Asn; Cleveland Soc

Contemp Art (secy, 81-83); Textile Arts Club, Cleveland Mus Art (trustee, 81-84); New Orgn Visual Arts, Cleveland (trustee, 79-82). *Media:* Fabric; Screen Printing. *Dealer:* Novart 1375 Euclid Ave Cleveland OH 44115; The New Gallery 11427 Bellflower Rd Cleveland OH 44106. *Mailing Add:* 2875 Coleridge Rd Cleveland Heights OH 44118

VON ZUR MUEHLEN, BERNIS SUSAN
PHOTOGRAPHER
b Philadelphia, Pa, Apr 10, 42. *Study:* Univ Pa, BA(lit), 63. *Work:* Corcoran Gallery Art, DC; Baltimore Mus Art, Md; Int Ctr Photog, New York. *Exhib:* Va Mus Fine Arts, Richmond, 75 & Va Photogr, 75 & 78; Nation's Capital Photogr, Corcoran Gallery Art, DC, 76 & Recent Acquisitions, 79; one-woman shows, Photographs, Baltimore Mus Art, Md, 78 & Del Art Mus, 81; Int Art Fair, Bologna, Italy, 78; Osuna Gallery, Washington, DC, 81; Second Street Gallery, Charlottesville, Va, 83. *Awards:* Three Judges' Awards, Womansphere, Glen Echo, Md, 75; Purchase Award, Corcoran Gallery Art, 76. *Bibliog:* David Tannos (auth), Report from Washington, Art in Am, 7-8/79. *Dealer:* Osuna Gallery 406 7th St NW Washington DC 20004. *Mailing Add:* 3096 Cobb Hill Ln Oakton VA 22124

VON ZUR MUEHLEN, PETER
PHOTOGRAPHER
b Berlin, Ger, Mar 10, 39; US citizen. *Study:* Washington Univ, St Louis, BA, 61; Princeton Univ, PhD, 72. *Work:* Corcoran Gallery. *Exhib:* Virginia Photographers, Va Mus Fine Arts, 75 & 78; Nations Capital Photographers, Corcoran Gallery Art, 76; one-person exhib, Va Mus Fine Arts, 76 & Bailey Art Mus, Charlottesville, Va, 79; One of a Kind, Franklin Inst, Philadelphia, 78, Denver Art Mus, 81; Houston Mus Fine Arts, Carpenter Ctr, Mass Inst Technol & Corcoran Gallery Art; Still Life in Photography, 78 & Recent Acquisitions, 81 & 83, Corcoran Gallery Art. *Awards:* Cert Distinction, Va Photographers, Va Mus Fine Arts, 75. *Bibliog:* David Tannous (auth), article, 7/78 & Capital art: In the major leagues?, 7/79, Art in Am. *Mailing Add:* 3096 Cobb Hill Lane Oakton VA 22124

VOORHEES, DONALD EDWARD
PAINTER, LITHOGRAPHER
b Neptune, NJ, May 6, 26. *Study:* Acad Arts, Newark, NJ; Art Students League, New York. *Work:* Bethlehem Steel, Tulsa, Okla; Citibank, New York; Metrop Life, New York; Pfizer Chem Co, New York; Sun Oil Co, Tulsa, Okla; and many others. *Exhib:* Frye Mus, Seattle, Wash; Edward Dean Mus, Cherry Valley, Calif; Cent Mus Wyo; Martello Mus, Key West, Fla; plus others. *Awards:* Hudson Valley Art Asn Award; NJ Watercolor Soc Award; Salmagundi Club Award. *Mem:* NJ Watercolor Soc (pres, 75-76); Artists Fel; Salmagundi Club. *Media:* Watercolor. *Publ:* Articles in Prints Mag, winter 79 & Graphics Mag, 6/79. *Dealer:* Donald Voorhees Gallery 325 Hwy 35 Red Bank NJ 07701. *Mailing Add:* 10 Ocean Blvd Atlantic Highlands NJ 07716

VOOS, WILLIAM JOHN
ADMINISTRATOR, PAINTER
b St Louis, Mo, July 2, 30. *Study:* Wash Univ Sch Fine Arts, BFA, 52; Univ Kans, MFA, 53; NY Univ, US Arts & Humanities Art Admin fel, 67. *Work:* Rend Lake Col Collection, Mt Vernon, Ill; Mus Contemp Art, Recife, Brazil; Ga Coun Arts. *Comn:* Mural, Army Educ Ctr, Ft Bragg, NC, 54; playground mural, Ferguson Park Comn, Mo, 60. *Exhib:* One-man show, Lafayette Art Ctr, Ind, 66 & Northern State Col, 74; Fac Shows, Steinberg Hall, Wash Univ, 68-72; Atlanta Col Art Fac Show, High Mus Art, 75; Mus Contemp Art, Recife, Brazil, 75. *Teaching:* Assoc prof art & chmn humanities div, Florissant Valley Community Col, 64-68; assoc prof art & assoc dean sch fine arts, Wash Univ, 68-73; dean, Atlanta Col Art, 73-75, pres, 75- *Mem:* Atlanta Pub Libr Art Adv Coun; Nat Coun Art Adminrs; Nat Asn Sch Art (exec bd mem, 70-73); Union Independent Col Art (chairperson, 81-83); Metrop Atlanta Rapid Transit Authority Coun Arts. *Media:* Acrylic, Watercolor. *Mailing Add:* 3229 Wendwood Dr Marietta GA 30062

VORIS, ANNA MAYBELLE
CURATOR
b Mt Rainier, Md, Aug 5, 20. *Study:* George Washington Univ, BA; Cath Univ Am, MA; Johns Hopkins Univ. *Pos:* Cur Spanish painting, Nat Gallery Art, Washington, DC, 71-80, consult, 80- *Mailing Add:* 1228 Pebble Beach Blvd Sun City Center FL 33570

VORWERK, E CHARLSIE
PAINTER, ILLUSTRATOR
b Tennga, Ga, Jan 28, 34. *Study:* Ga State Col Women, AB; com art study, 2 yrs. *Work:* Mamie Padgett Collection, Ga Col. *Comn:* Bicentennial mural, Fine Arts Coun, Summerville, SC, 75; designs for altar kneelers, St Paul's Episcopal Church, 75; official city flag, City Coun & YWCO, Summerville, 75; plus other individuals & companies. *Exhib:* Ann Exhib Miniature Painters, Sculptors & Gravers Soc, Washington, DC, 70-75; Miniature Art Soc NJ, Paramus, 71-75; 23rd & 24th Gran Prix Int Peinture de Deauville, France, 72 & 73; 9th & 10th Gran Prix Peinture de la Cote D'Azur, Cannes, France, 73 & 74; Miniature Art Soc Int Exhib, 80; and others. *Pos:* Billboard designer, Vanesco Poster, Chattanooga, Tenn; fashion illustrator, Lovemans; cartographic draftsman, Tenn Valley Authority; free lance com artist. *Teaching:* Pvt group art classes for children & adults. *Awards:* Gold Medal, Italian Acad Art, 80; Golden Centaur Award, Ital Acad Art, 83; Statue Victory World Cult Prize, 84. *Bibliog:* Articles, Rev Mod, Paris, 71, 73 & 74 & Il Giornale D'Italia & Iltempo, 73. *Mem:* League Charleston Artists (secy, 75, 76 & 77); Summerville Artist Guild; Charleston Artists Guild; Ital Acad Art; Miniature Art Soc Fla. *Media:* Multimedia. *Publ:* Illusr, low country tourists brochures, for various orgns & Episcopal church periodicals and

brochures; illusr, Tales and Taradiddles, 76, Epitaphs of St Paul's Cemetery 1858-1978, 77, Captain Tom, 80 & The St Paul's Sampler, 83. *Dealer:* Chester Smith Seaside Art Gallery PO Box 1 Nags Head NC 27959. *Mailing Add:* 315 W Carolina Ave Summerville SC 29483

VOSE, ROBERT CHURCHILL, JR
DEALER
b Boston, Mass, Mar 30, 11. *Study:* Harvard. *Pos:* Treas, Vose Galleries of Boston, 53-76, pres, 76-80, chmn, 81- *Bibliog:* J Post (auth), The Old Family Business, Yankee Mag, 73; William N Banks (auth), New England's reigning antique dealers, Country J Mag, 12/78. *Mem:* Copley Soc, Boston. *Res:* Alvan Fisher, 1792-1863; Ralph Blakelock, 1847-1919. *Specialty:* Eighteenth, nineteenth and early twentieth century American paintings; to a lesser degree, eighteenth and nineteenth century English and nineteenth century French paintings. *Publ:* Auth, Alvan Fisher, American Pioneer in Landscape and Genre, Conn Hist Soc, 62. *Mailing Add:* Vose Galleries of Boston Inc 238 Newbury St Boston MA 02116

VOULKOS, PETER
SCULPTOR, EDUCATOR
b Bozeman, Mont, Jan 29, 24. *Study:* Mont State Univ, BS, 68; Calif Col Arts & Crafts, MFA; Mont State Univ, LHD, 68. *Work:* Baltimore Mus Art, Md; Denver Art Mus; Smithsonian Inst, Washington, DC; Japanese Craft Mus; San Francisco Mus Art; and others. *Exhib:* Brussels World's Fair, 58; Int Sculpture Exhib, Battersea Park, London, 63; Los Angeles State Col, 64; Univ Calif, Irving, 66; Whitney Mus Am Art, 70; one-man shows, San Francisco Mus Art, 72, Kansas City Art Inst, 75 & Detroit Inst Art, 76; plus many others. *Teaching:* Instr, Archie Bray Found, Black Mountain Col, Los Angeles Co Art Inst, Mont State Univ, Greenwich House Potter & Teachers Col, Columbia Univ; prof art & design, Univ Calif, Berkeley, 59- *Awards:* Silver Medal, Int Ceramic Exhib, Ostend, Belg, 54; Gold Medal, Int Ceramic Exhib, Cannes, France; Rodin Mus Prize in Sculpture, I Paris Biennial, 59; and others. *Bibliog:* Lee Nordness (auth), Objects: USA, London, 70; M Leopold (auth), Los Angeles letter, Art Int, summer 73. *Mailing Add:* 1306 Third St Berkeley CA 94710

VOURVOULIAS, JOYCE BUSH See De Guatemala, Joyce

VRANA, ALBERT S
SCULPTOR
b Cliffside Park, NJ, Jan 25, 21. *Study:* Univ Miami. *Work:* Captive (cast bronze), Atlanta Mem Art Ctr, Ga; War Flower (bronze), Lowe Art Gallery, Univ Miami, Fla. *Comn:* Cast stone relief from styrofoam molds, US Govt for Fed Off Bldg, Jacksonville, Fla, 66; free-standing monument (ferro cement & bronze), Arlen House, Miami Beach, 69; monumental mural (ferro cement & hammered bronze), State of Fla for Fla Int Univ, Miami, 72; Glorious Cross (bronze & carved Lucite), Holy Trinity Church, Georgetown, 79; cast stone relief, Johnson City Pub Libr, Tenn, 80; and others. *Teaching:* Instr sculpture, Miami-Dade Jr Col, 66-67; instr & consult sculpture, Penland Sch, summers 68- *Awards:* Tiffany Grant, 63; Nat Endowment for the Arts, 78. *Bibliog:* VRANA (film), Portland Cememt Asn & Dan Bailey, 66; Le beton sculpte par moulage, Batir Mag, Paris, 67; Harry Forgeron (auth), Sculptured structures molded in plastic foam, New York Times, 67. *Media:* Cast Bronze, Architectural Concrete. *Publ:* Contrib, Sculpture from Plastics, 67; contribr, Spiel mit Form und Struktur, 68; contribr, Contemporary Art with Wood, 68; contribr, Plastics as an Art Form, 69; contribr, Contemporary Stone Sculpture, 70. *Dealer:* IFA Galleries Inc 2623 Connecticut Ave Washington DC 20008. *Mailing Add:* Rte 3 Box 330C Bakersville NC 28705

VYTLACIL, VACLAV
PAINTER, EDUCATOR
b New York, NY, Nov 1, 1892. *Study:* Art Inst Chicago; Art Students League; Bavarian Royal Acad Art, Munich, Ger; Hans Hofmann Sch Art, Munich. *Work:* Metrop Mus Art, Whitney Mus Am Art, New York; Pa Acad Fine Arts, Philadelphia; Duncan Philips Mus Art, Washington, DC; Rochester Mus Art, NY. *Exhib:* Whitney Mus Am Art, New York, 40-62; Artists for Victory, Metrop Mus Art, New York, 44; Pa Acad Fine Arts, Philadelphia, 52; Duncan Philips Mus Art, Washington, DC, 55; Southern Vt Art Ctr, Manchester & Univ Notre Dame, 75; Retrospective, Montclair Art Mus, NJ, 75; one-man exhib, Martin Diamond Gallery, New York, 79; and others. *Teaching:* Instr art, Minneapolis Sch Art, 17-21; lectr mod art & artist in residence, Univ Calif, Berkeley, 28-29; instr art, Calif Col Arts & Crafts, summers 36 & 37; lectr hist art & chmn dept art, Queen's Col, 42-45; instr art, Colorado Springs Fine Art Ctr, 51-53 & Univ Ga, 68; instr painting & lectr hist mod art, Art Students League, formerly. *Awards:* William M R French Gold Medal, 36. *Mem:* Fedn Mod Painters & Sculptors; Am Abstract Artists; Art Students League. *Media:* Oil, Acrylic, Tempera. *Mailing Add:* Old Kings Hwy Sparkill NY 10976

W

WAALAND, JAMES BREARLEY, II
DEALER, GALLERY DIRECTOR
b Findlay, Ohio, May 15, 53. *Study:* Bowling Green State Univ, BA, 75. *Pos:* Owner & dir, Waaland Gallery Antique Art, 76- *Specialty:* Nineteenth and early twentieth century American and European paintings; Chinese ceramics of the 18th and 19th centuries; vintage photographic images. *Mailing Add:* 2801 Western Ave Findlay OH 45840

WACHS, ETHEL
EDUCATOR, COLLECTOR
b New York, NY, Dec 26, 23. *Study:* Brooklyn Col, with Philip Pearlstein, A D Reinhardt & Jimmy Ernst, BS, MA & MS. *Exhib:* Nat Asn Women Artists, Federal Bldg, New York, 80-83; Nat Acad Design, New York, 80 & 82; Am Soc Contemp Artists, US Custom House, New York, 80; Audubon Artists, Nat Arts Club, New York 81 & 82; Bergen Community Mus, Paramus, NJ, 83. *Teaching:* Teacher fine arts, M D Bacon High Sch, New York, 58-; instr adult educ, Brooklyn Col, New York, 68- *Awards:* Lone Star Industries, Silvermine Guild, 76; Binney & Smith, Knickerbocker Artists, 80; Audubon Medal Honor, 82. *Mem:* NY Artists Equity; NY Soc Women Artists; Nat Asn Women Artists; Audubon Artists; Am Soc Contemp Artists. *Media:* Watercolor. *Collection:* Contemporary American art. *Dealer:* Voltaire's Route 2 New Milford CT 06776. *Mailing Add:* 20 E 9th St New York NY 10003

WACHSTETER, GEORGE
ILLUSTRATOR
b Hartford, Conn, Mar 12, 11. *Work:* New York Pub Libr Theatre Collection; US Steel Collection; NBC Collection; plus works in pvt collections. *Exhib:* One-man traveling exhib for NBC Book of Stars, 58. *Pos:* Illusr for major advert agencies, theatrical & motion picture productions, 36-; illusr for CBS, ABC, NBC radio & TV networks, 37-; weekly contrib illus & caricature to drama pages, New York Herald Tribune, 41-50; contrib illus & caricature drama & political pages, New York Times, 38-50, TV artist, 50-51; caricaturist for Theatre Guild on the Air, produced by US Steel, 45-63; drama artist, New York J-Am, 56-63, TV mag cover artist, 58-63; drama artist, New York World Tel, 64-66; syndicated feature illusr for Hallmark TV Drama Series, 64-69. *Media:* Ink, Watercolor. *Publ:* Illusr, NBC Book of Stars, Simon & Schuster, 57. *Mailing Add:* 85-05 Elmhurst Ave Elmhurst NY 11373

WADDELL, EUGENE
PAINTER
b Charlottesville, Va, Oct 7, 25. *Study:* Duquesne Univ; Univ Pittsburgh, BS; Carnegie Inst Technol, murals with Claude Hurd; Cooper Union; NY Univ; also with A Raymond Katz, Buell Mullen, Ludwig Deschenek & others. *Work:* NY Tel Bldg, White Plains; IBM, Armonk, NY & Stamford; Dexter Corp, Windsor Locks, Conn; Am Can Co, Greenwich, Conn; plus others. *Comn:* City scene murals, Ayer/Jorgenson/MacDonald, Los Angeles, 67; typography mural, Matrotype Co, Ltd, Eng, 68; still life mural, Bass & Ullman, New York, 69; Exuberance (mural), Wheelabrater-Frye, New York, 70; abstract murals, Humbert & Jones, New York, 71. *Exhib:* Berkshire Mus, Pittsfield, Mass, 66; Mayan II Gallery, Watch Hill, RI, 69; Nationwide Art Gallery, Fairfield, Conn, 70; Automation House Gallery, New York, 74; Mus Mod Art, New York; plus many others. *Teaching:* Instr art, Stormville Art Sch, 50-52; instr new methods of painting, River House, Pawling, NY & Dover Jr High Sch, 71; guest instr art, Holiday Hills, Pawling, 73 & 74. *Awards:* First Prize, Art League Hudson Valley, 73. *Mem:* Life fel Royal Soc Art, London, Eng; Archit League New York; Nat Coun Arts & Govt; Inst Contemp Arts, London; Allied Artists Am. *Mailing Add:* 32 Ridgeview Ave White Plains NY 10606

WADDELL, JOHN HENRY
SCULPTOR, PAINTER
b Des Moines, Iowa, Feb 14, 21. *Study:* Art Inst Chicago, BFA, MFA, BAE & MAE; Nat Col Educ, Evanston, Ill, Hon DFA, 79. *Work:* Phoenix Art Mus, Ariz; Univ Ariz, Tucson; Scottsdale Civic Ctr, Ariz; Kenyon Col; Nat Col Educ, Evanston, Ill. *Comn:* Dance Mother, Phoenix Art Mus, 59-62; That Which Might Have Been, Unitarian Church, Phoenix, 63-64; The Family, Maricopa Co Complex, 65-67; Dance, Phoenix Civic Ctr, 70-74; I Am That I Am, Temple Beth Israel, Phoenix, 82. *Exhib:* One-man shows, Unitarian Church, Phoenix, 77; Verde Valley Artists Asn, Jerome, Ariz, 77; Nat Col Educ, Evanston, Ill, 79, Sedona Art Ctr, Ariz, 80 & many others; Scottsdale Ctr Arts, Ariz, 84. *Teaching:* Asst prof art, Inst Design, Chicago, 55-57; prof art, Ariz State Univ, 57-61 & 64; Master Apprentice Prog, Waddell Sculpture Fel, 72- *Awards:* Man of Yr, Valley of Sun Chap, Nat Soc Arts & Lett, 75; Artist of Yr Ariz, Youth Month, 81; Alumni Award Merit, Eureka Col, Ill, 82. *Bibliog:* Harry Wood (auth), Soul, 67; Man of Bronze (film), 75. *Media:* Bronze; Oil, Watercolor. *Mailing Add:* Oak Creek Valley Rd HC 66 Box 2273 Cornville AZ 86325

WADDINGHAM, JOHN ALFRED
PAINTER, PRINTMAKER
b London, Eng, July 9, 15; US citizen. *Study:* Coronado Sch Fine Arts, Calif, 53-54; Portland Art Mus, 40-45; Univ Portland, 46-47; also with Rex Brandt, Eliot O'Hara & George Post. *Work:* Portland Art Mus; Bush House, Salem, Ore; Univ Ore Mus; Vincent Price Collection; Ford Times Collection. *Comn:* Genesis (mural), St Barnabas Episcopal Church, Portland, 60. *Pos:* Promotion art dir, Ore J, Portland, 46-59; mem staff, Oregonian, Portland, 59, ed art dir, 59-80; proprietor, John Waddingham Hand Prints, 65- *Teaching:* Instr watercolor, Ore Soc Artists, 54-56; instr, Mittleman Jewish Community Ctr, 80-81; Portland Community Col, 81; instr, Ore Sch Arts & Crafts, 81- *Awards:* Gold Medals, Italy, 76, 77 & 80; Award for Newspaper Illus, 76. *Bibliog:* Featured artist, Am Artist, 5/67. *Mem:* Portland Art Dirs Club (past pres); Watercolor Soc Ore; NW Watercolor Soc. *Dealer:* Portland Art Mus Rental Sales Gallery 1219 SW Park Ave Portland OR 97205; Univ Ore Mus Art Eugene OR 97403. *Mailing Add:* 955 SW Westwood Dr Portland OR 97201

WADE, JANE
DEALER
b Dallas, Tex, June 30, 25. *Study:* Univ Ariz; in Europe; Curt Valentin Gallery, New York; Otto Gerson Gallery, New York. *Collections Arranged:* Drawings by Sculptors, Smithsonian Inst & US Tour. *Pos:* Secy & asst, Curt Valentin Gallery, 48-56; secy & assoc, Otto Gerson Gallery, 56-63; vpres, Marlborough-Gerson Gallery, 63-64; owner & dir, Jane Wade Ltd. *Bibliog:* Jay Jacobs (auth), By appointment only, Art in Am, 7-8/67; By appointment only, Newsweek, 9/4/67; By appointment only, Time, 8/3/70. *Mem:* Art Dealers Asn Am. *Specialty:* Twentieth century painting and sculpture. *Mailing Add:* 467 Mariscal Rd Palm Springs CA 92262

WADE, ROBERT SCHROPE
PHOTOGRAPHER, SCULPTOR
b Austin, Tex, Jan 6, 43. *Study:* Univ Tex, Austin, BFA, 65; Univ Calif, Berkeley, MA, 66. *Work:* Witte Mus, San Antonio, Tex; Groningen Mus, Holland; Beaubourg Mus, Paris, France; Chicago Telephone Co; Chase Manhattan Bank, New York. *Comn:* Map of the United States (300 ft-outdoor), for Bicentennial '76, Northwood Contemp Coun & Nat Endowment, near Dallas; Biggest Cowboy Boots, Washington Art Site, DC, 79. *Exhib:* Whitney Contemp Ann, Whitney Mus Am Art, New York, 69 & 73; one-man shows, Kornblee Gallery, New York, 71 & 74 & Janus Gallery, Los Angeles, 78; Contemp Arts Mus, Houston, 75; San Francisco Mus Mod Art, 76; Kunsthaus, Zurich, Switz, 77; Maps, Mus Mod Art, New York, 77; Paris Biennale, Mus Mod Art, Paris; Art Mus of STex, Corpus Christi, 79; Showdown, Alternative Mus, New York, 83; Six Frogs Over Greenville, Tango, Dallas, Tex, 83; 4th Ann Tex Sculpture Symposium Exhib, Austin, 83; 2nd Wild West Show, Calgary, Can, 83; Projected Photo Works (solo exhib), Cult Activities Ctr, Temple, Tex, 84. *Teaching:* Instr, McLennan Col, 66-70; artist in residence, Northwood Inst, 70-72, dir, Northwood Exp Art Inst, Dallas, 72-77; asst prof, NTex State Univ, Denton, 73-77. *Awards:* Nat Endowment Grants, 73 & 74. *Bibliog:* Robert Pincus-Witten (auth), New York, Artforum, 12/71; Roberta Smith (auth), article in Art in Am, 7/76; Jo Ann Lewis (auth), article in Art News, 12/79. *Dealer:* Segal Gallery 63 E 57th New York NY 10022; Elaine Horwich Gallerry 129 W Palace Ave Santa Fe 87501. *Mailing Add:* 2701 Cantor St Dallas TX 75226

WAGNER, CHARLES H
ADMINISTRATOR, INSTRUCTOR
b Baltimore, Md. *Study:* Md Inst Col Art, BFA; Johns Hopkins Univ; Yale Univ, MFA. *Work:* Md Inst Col Art; Western Md Col, Westminster. *Exhib:* Baltimore Watercolor Club, Md, 73-75; Western Md Col, 75; Lindwood Gallery, 83; Rehobeth Art League, 83; Revelations Gallery, Baltimore, 83. *Pos:* Dir, Md Inst, Towson Sch, Md, 60-; supvr art instr, Howard Co Pub Sch, Columbia, Md, 70- *Teaching:* Instr drawing & painting, Md Inst Col Art, Baltimore, 50-; dept chmn sec art, Baltimore Co Pub Schs, Md, 55-70; instr design, Towson State Univ, Md, 72-73; instr drawing, Howard Community Col, 82- *Awards:* Bronze Medal Figure Painting, Md Inst, 55; John Hay Fel, Yale Univ, 60-61; First Prize Design, Nat Educ Asn, 65. *Mem:* Nat Art Educ Asn; Md Art Asn; Baltimore Watercolor Club. *Publ:* Illusr, Baltimore County Serves the Nation, 59; auth, Classroom Discipline, 60; auth, Team Teaching in Art, 74; contribr, art curric guides, 82. *Mailing Add:* Regwood Rd Hydes MD 21082

WAGNER, G NOBLE
PAINTER, SCULPTOR
b Pa, Nov 20, 07. *Study:* Temple Univ Tyler Sch Art, BFA, MFA, 59. *Work:* Philadelphia Art Mus; Albright-Knox Art Gallery, Buffalo, NY; Chemical Bank, NY; City Philadelphia; Jefferson Univ Alumni Collector. *Exhib:* Nat Print & Watercolor Exhib, Pa Acad Fine Arts, 69; Cheltenham Art Centre Ann Regional Sculpture Exhib, Philadelphia Civic Ctr, 71-78; Philadelphia Art Mus, 72; one-man shows, Hartley Gallery, New York, 73 & Marian Locks Gallery, Philadelphia, Pa, 71-78. *Pos:* Co-founder & dir educ, Cheltenham Sch Fine Arts, Cheltenham Twp Art Centre, 40-, pres, 41-42, chmn bd gov, 42-43, established Aegean Sch Fine Arts, Greece. *Teaching:* Instr art & philos, 51-56; instr art, Oak Lane Co Day Sch, Temple Univ, 59-60, instr art educ, Univ, 60-65, instr art educ, Elem Educ Teachers for State Cert, 62-63; instr philos art educ, Cheltenham Twp Art Centre, 61-, instr painting & sculpture, 62- *Awards:* Twenty-Second Ann Award Exhib, 69 & Print Exhib Award, 71, cheltenham Art Centre; Distinguished Alumni Award, Tyler Sch Art, Temple Univ, 79. *Mem:* Pa Art Educ Asn (mem coun, 69); Philadelphia Print Club; Philadelphia Art Alliance. *Res:* The nature of a meaningful art education course for elementary education student teachers; art education for adults. *Mailing Add:* 7955 Waltham Rd Cheltenham PA 19012

WAGNER, GORDON PARSONS
ASSEMBLAGE ARTIST, ENVIRONMENTAL ARTIST
b Redondo Beach, Calif, Apr 13, 15. *Study:* Univ Calif, Los Angeles; Chouinard Art Inst, Los Angeles. *Work:* Downey Mus Art; Standard Oil Co Chicago; Sodertalje Konsthall, Stockholm, Sweden. *Exhib:* Corcoran Gallery Biennial, Washington, DC, 57-61; one-man shows, Master Works, Downey Mus, Calif, 77 & Calif State Univ, Fresno, 80; Palos Verdes Art Mus, Calif, 81; Miniature 82, Triton Mus, Santa Clara, Calif, 82; 3-D Imagery, Univ Calif, Riverside, 83; and many others. *Awards:* Purchase Awards, Ahmanson Collection, Los Angeles, 56 & Denver Mus Art, 59; Award, Nat Watercolor Soc, 67. *Bibliog:* Michael Leopold (auth), Art of the 70's, Art Int Mag, summer 74; Betje Howell (auth), Gordon Wagner, Art Voices Mag, 81; Judith Hoffberg (auth), Gordon Wagner: Magician and myth maker, Los Angeles Inst Contemp Art J, 9-10/83. *Mem:* Los Angeles Inst Contemp Art. *Mailing Add:* 441 N Holliston Ave Pasadena CA 91106

WAGNER, MERRILL
PAINTER
b Seattle, Wash, June 12, 35. *Study:* Sarah Lawrence Col, BA, 57; Art Students League, New York, with Edwin Dickenson, George Grosz & Julian Levy, 59-63. *Comn:* Permanent Installation, Project Studio One Inst for Art & Urban Resources, 78. *Exhib:* 26 Contemporary Women Artists, Aldrich Mus, Ridgefield, Conn, 71; Christmas Show, Art Lending Service, Penthouse, Mus of Mod Art, 71; one-person shows, The Clocktower, Inst Art & Urban Resources, New York, 79, Hal Bromm Gallery, New York, 79 & 81, David Bellman Gallery, Toronto, 81 & Watson DeNagy Gallery, Houston, 82; Surfaces/Textures, Mus Mod Art, 81; Harm Bouckaert Gallery, 82; and others. *Bibliog:* Tiffany Bell (auth), article, Arts Mag, 2/78; Ross Skoggard (auth), article, Art in Am, 5/81; Grace Glueck (auth), article, New York Times, 12/82. *Mem:* Am Abstract Artists (pres, 82-85). *Media:* Multimedia. *Dealer:* Hal Bromm Gallery 90 W Broadway New York NY 10007. *Mailing Add:* 17 W 16 New York NY 10011

WAGNER, RICHARD ELLIS
PAINTER
b Trotwood, Ohio, June 18, 23. *Study:* Antioch Col; Dayton Art Inst, Ohio; Univ Colo, BFA & MFA. *Work:* Denver Art Mus, Colo; Libr of Cong, Washington, DC; Dartmouth Col, Hanover, NH; DeCordova Mus, Lincoln, Mass; Rochester Mus, NY. *Comn:* Murals, Horizon House, Naples, Fla, 71. *Exhib:* Recent Drawings USA, Mus Mod Art, New York, 56; Art USA, Madison Sq Garden, 58; Boston Arts Festival, Mass, 58, 60 & 62; Jefferson Arts Festival, New Orleans, 69; Youngstown Art Festival, Butler Inst Am Art, 70; and 52 one-man shows, 53- *Teaching:* Assoc prof art, Dartmouth Col, 53-66. *Awards:* Purchase Prizes, Denver Art Mus, 50 & Libr of Cong, 52; City of Manchester Award, Currier Gallery, Manchester, NH, 56. *Media:* Acrylic, Oil. *Publ:* Illusr, Ford Times, 58-70; illusr, Sketches in San Juans, 76; illusr, Sketches in Southwest Seasons, 82. *Dealer:* Telluride Art Gallery Telluride CO; Saks Gallery Denver CO. *Mailing Add:* 13980 Co Rd 29 Dolores CO 81323

WAGONER, ROBERT B
PAINTER, SCULPTOR
b Marion, Ohio, July 13, 28. *Study:* With Burt Procter & Olaf Weighorst. *Work:* Leanin' Tree Publ Mus, Boulder, Colo; Winthrop Rockefeller Collection. *Exhib:* Death Valley 49ers, Calif, 61; two-man shows, Scottsdale, Ariz, 72 & 73 & three-man show, 74; Mont Hist Soc, Helena, 74; Previews, Tex Gallery, Dallas, 75-79. *Pos:* Dir, Death Valley 49ers, 69- *Awards:* First Award & Top Artists Award, Death Valley 49ers, 72 & 73 & First Award, 74, 75 & 76. *Bibliog:* James Serven (auth), Cattle, guns and cowboys, Ariz Hwys Mag, 70; Robert Wolenik (auth), Colorful west of Robert Wagoner, Westerner, 1-2/73; Portrait of a Westerner, Sierra Life Mag, 81. *Media:* Oil, Watercolor; Canvas, Masonite. *Dealer:* Texas Art Gallery Dallas TX; Saddleback Western Art Gallery Santa Ana CA. *Mailing Add:* 2710 Highland Dr Bishop CA 93514

WAHLING, JON B
SCULPTOR, WEAVER
b Council Bluffs, Iowa, Apr 14, 38. *Study:* Kansas City Art Inst & Sch Design, BFA, 62; Haystack Mountain Sch Crafts, Deer Isle, Maine, summers 63-65; Cranbrook Acad Art, MFA, 64; also with Maija Grotell & Glen Kauffman. *Work:* Columbus Mus of Art, Ohio; Massillon Mus, Ohio; Yager Gallery, Hartwick College; Univ Art Mus, Univ Tex, Austin. *Comn:* Fibre sculpture hanging, Merchants & Mechanics Fed Loan & Savings Bank, Springfield, Ohio, 79. *Exhib:* Two-person exhib, Nationwide Insurance Co, Columbus, Ohio, 82; Fiber Directions, Grunnier Gallery & Mus, Iowa State Univ, Ames, 82; 20th Ann Exhib, Ohio Designer Craftsmen, touring, 83; In the Round, Southern Ohio Mus & Cult Ctr, Portsmouth, 83; The Works, Statewide Touring Exhib, Ohio Found Arts, 83-84. *Teaching:* Instr weaving, Columbus Cult Arts Ctr, Columbus Recreation & Parks Dept, Ohio, 64-, art dir & asst, 79-; instr weaving, Penland Sch Crafts, NC, summers 66, 67 & 71. *Awards:* Craftsmen USA Nat Merit Award, Mus Contemp Crafts, New York, 66; Ten Outstanding Young Men Award, Columbus Jaycees, 72; Bordens Award for Outstanding Design in Fibre, 7th Beaux Arts Designer/Craftsmen Exhib, 73. *Mem:* Am Crafts Coun; Ohio Designer Craftsmen (trustee, 73-74 & 78-79); hon mem Cent Ohio Weavers Guild; Ohio Designer Craftsmen; Ohio Designer Craftsmen (secy, 82-83). *Media:* Fibre, Metal. *Dealer:* Ed Miller Assoc 112 Mercer New York NY 10012. *Mailing Add:* 44 Stimmel St Columbus OH 43206

WAHLMAN, MAUDE SOUTHWELL
HISTORIAN, EDUCATOR
b New York, NY. *Study:* Colo Col, BA(art), 69; Northwestern Univ, MA, 69; Yale Univ, PhD(art hist, teaching fel), 80. *Collections Arranged:* Contemp African Arts, 73-75; Contemporary African Fabrics, Mus Contemp Art, Chicago, 75; Ten Afro-American Quilters, 82- *Pos:* Consult African ethnology, Field Mus Nat Hist, Chicago, 71-74. *Teaching:* Asst prof art hist & southern studies, Univ Miss, 80- *Awards:* Wenner-Gren Found Fel for mus res, Field Mus, 71; Nat Endowment Arts Grant, 82; Res Grant for southern folk arts, Nat Endowment Humanities, 81-84. *Mem:* African Studies Asn; Am Studies Asn; Soc Folk Arts Preservation; Women's Caucus Art. *Res:* The historical and ethnic roots of American folk arts. *Publ:* Auth, Contemporary African Arts, Field Mus, 74; auth, Ceremonial Art of West Africa, Mich State Univ, 79; auth, Traditional Art of West Africa, Colby Col, 80; co-ed, Spirit of Africa, Memphis State Univ, 82; auth, Afro-American Quiltmaking, Ind Univ (in prep). *Mailing Add:* Art Dept Univ Miss University MS 38677

WAHRHAFTIG, ALMA LAVENSON See Lavenson, Alma

WAID, JIM (JAMES E)
PAINTER
b Elgin, Okla, Nov 2, 42. *Study:* Univ NMex, with Morris Kantor & John Kacere, BFA, 65; Univ Ariz, MFA, 71. *Work:* Superior Court Art Trust, Washington, DC; Phoenix Art Mus; Univ Ariz Mus Art. *Comn:* Santa Cruz (mural), Tucson Pub Libr, 77. *Exhib:* LA #1, Mus Sci & Industry, Los Angeles, 75; 35th Biennial, Corcoran Gallery Art, 77; Southwestern Biennial, Mus NMex, Santa Fe, 78; First Western States Biennial, Nat Collection Art, Washington, DC, 79-80; Four Corners States Biennial Exhib, Phoenix Art Mus, 81. *Teaching:* Instr art, Pima Community Col, 71-80. *Awards:* Purchase Prizes, Arizona's Outlook, Tucson Mus Art, 80 & 14th Southwestern Invitational, Yuma Art Ctr, Ariz, 80. *Mem:* Artists Equity; Dinnerware Artists Coop (treas, 79-82). *Dealer:* Yares Gallery 3625 Bishop Lane Scottsdale AZ 85251. *Mailing Add:* 1133 W Alameda Tucson AZ 85745

WAINWRIGHT, ROBERT BARRY
PAINTER, PRINTMAKER
b Chilliwack, BC, June 29, 35. *Study:* Vancouver Sch Art, dipl, 62; Atelier 17, Paris, with S W Hayter, Emily Carr Travel Study Scholar, 62. *Work:* Nat Gallery Can; Art Gallery Ont; Mus Fine Arts, Mus Art Contemp, Montreal; Can Indust Ltd, Toronto. *Exhib:* Premio Int Biella L'Incisione, Italy, 71, 73 & 76; solo exhib, Galerie Martal, Montreal, 72, Concordia Univ, Montreal, 76 & 80 & Mazelow Gallery, Toronto, 77; Galerie Elca London, Montreal, 84. *Teaching:* Assoc prof printmaking, Concordia Univ, Montreal, 66- *Awards:* Can Coun Grants, 63-64 & 67-68; Erindale Col Purchase Prize, Int Exhib Graphics, Montreal, 71. *Bibliog:* Catherine Bates (auth), ... An artist to watch ..., Montreal Star, 73. *Mem:* Royal Can Acad Arts; Can Artists Rep. *Dealer:* Galerie Elca London 1616 Sherbrooke St W Montreal PQ H3H 1C9. *Mailing Add:* 4248 Hampton Ave Montreal PQ H4A 2K9 Canada

WAITE, ELIN JANE
DESIGNER, EDUCATOR
b Redondo Beach, Calif, June 21, 33. *Study:* Chouinard Art Inst, Los Angeles, 52-56; Calif Inst Arts, Chouinard Campus, 62; Calif State Univ, Long Beach, 80. *Work:* Corcoran Gallery, Smithsonian Collection & Libr Cong, Washington, DC. *Comn:* USAF Doc Art Proj Collection (hist), The Pentagon, Washington, DC, 60-80; Patriotic Hall (mural), Dept Mil & Vet Affairs Bicentennial Proj, Los Angeles Co Bd Supvr, 76. *Exhib:* Western Serigraph Soc Exhib, Libr Cong, Washington, DC, 54; Competition, Calif State Fair Fine Art Pavilion, Sacramento, 56; Olympic Art Guild, Los Angeles Guild Artists, 58-61; Art on Loan, Los Angeles Co Art Mus, 60-62; USAF Doc Exhib, Smithsonian Air Space Mus, Washington, DC, 78. *Collections Arranged:* Westways Magazine 1907-1980 Collection of Paintings, Westways Art Collection, Los Angeles, 80. *Pos:* Art dir, Westways Mag, Automobile Club of Southern Calif, 69- *Teaching:* Instr graphic design, Calif Inst Arts, Chouinard Campus, 69-71; prof illus, Calif State Univ, Long Beach, 74-78; instr illus, Art Ctr Col Design, Pasadena, 76-77; prof graphic design, Calif State Univ, Northridge, 76-79, prof illus, 79-; prof, Otis Parsons Sch Design, 79- *Awards:* Life Achievement Award, Soc Illusr Los Angeles, 78. *Bibliog:* Mike Shenon (auth), Westways: A publication of the Automobile Club of Southern California, Commun Arts Mag, 1-2/79; Ren Wicks (auth), Illus W Ann, USAF. *Mem:* Soc Illusr Los Angeles (pres, 68-69); Commun Arts Soc Los Angeles (head scholar comt); Los Angeles Printing Craftsmen Asn; Women's Bldg Los Angeles (adv bd, 79-80); Woodbury Univ, Los Angeles (adv bd, 79-80). *Interests:* Historical, western United States, and current trends; modern artists. *Publ:* Contribr, Commun Arts Mag, 1-2/79; contribr, Graphics Today, 80. *Dealer:* c/o Westways Mag 1741 Ivar Ave Los Angeles CA 90051. *Mailing Add:* 12124 Viewcrest Rd Studio City CA 91604

WAITZKIN, STELLA
SCULPTOR, PAINTER
b New York, NY. *Study:* NY Univ; Columbia Univ; also with Meyer Shapiro & Hans Hofmann. *Work:* Nat Gallery Fine Arts; Patrick Lanon Col, Fla; Walker Art Ctr; Tel-Aviv Mus, Israel; Everson Mus, Syracuse. *Exhib:* one-woman show, Serious Literature, Calhoun Col, Yale Univ, 74; Potsdam Plastics, NY Univ, 75; Contemp Am Sculpture, Va Mus Downtown Gallery, 75; James Yu Exhib, 75; Renwick Gallery, Smithsonian Inst, Washington, DC; Nat Collection Fine Arts, Washington, DC; Selected Work, 1973-1983, Everson Mus, Syracuse, 83; Terminal Invitational, NY, 83; and others. *Pos:* lectr, New York Univ. *Teaching:* Guest lectr, Columbia Univ Grad Sch, 73. *Awards:* Yaddo Found Fels, 73-76; MacDowell Found Fels, 74-83; Louis Comfort Tiffany Grant, 77. *Bibliog:* Taylor Mead, Studio Art (film); D Holmes (auth), article in Arch Am Art, 71; articles in Arts Mag, 73 & 74. *Media:* Sandstone, Polyester Resin. *Publ:* Reproductions & articles in art publs; film work. *Dealer:* Fendrick Gallery 3059 M St NW Washington DC 20007; Peter David Gallery 430 Oak Grove Minneapolis MN 55403. *Mailing Add:* 222 W 23rd St New York NY 10011

WAKSBERG, NAOMI
PAINTER, PRINTMAKER
b Germany, July 16, 47; US citizen. *Study:* Ohio State Univ, Columbus, BFA & BSci, 69; Md Inst Art, Baltimore, 70; Rutgers Univ, New Brunswick, NJ, MA & MFA, 72. *Work:* Ohio State Univ, Columbus; Continental Life Insurance Co, New York; Continental Group Investors, New Haven, Conn; First Nat Bank, Chicago; Japanese Embassy, Washington, DC; and others. *Exhib:* One-person show, Lehigh Univ, Bethlehem, Pa, 80; Artists Books, Philadelphia Art Alliance, 81; Rutgers Invitational, State Mus, Trenton, NJ, 82; Alternative Mus, New York, 82; Condeso/Lawler, New York, 82; Muse Found, Philadelphia, 83; and others. *Pos:* Coordr & cur, Women Artists Series, Douglass Col Libr, 72-76; project dir, Her Own Space, Muse Foud, 82. *Teaching:* Instr art hist, Trenton State Univ, NJ, 80-81. *Awards:* Bea Camhi

Award, Hudson River Mus, 80; NJ Arts Fel, 82-83. *Bibliog:* Kay Larson (auth), Small talk, Village Voice, 2/11/80; Victoria Donahue (auth), rev, Philadelphia Inquirer, 5/81; Judith Stein (auth), article, Art Express, 11-12/81. *Mem:* Muse Found, Philadelphia (bd dirs, 80-); Women's Caucus Art (steering comt, 79-81); Col Art Asn. *Media:* Acrylic, Oil Pastel. *Publ:* Contribr, Lehigh University Fall Collections, Lehigh Univ, 80. *Dealer:* Condeso/Lawler 119 West 25th St New York NY; Van Straaten Gallery 646 N Michigan Ave Chicago IL. *Mailing Add:* 137 Greene St New York NY 10012

WALBURG, GERALD
SCULPTOR, EDUCATOR
b Berkeley, Calif, May 5, 36. *Study:* Calif Col Arts & Crafts, 54-56; Calif State Univ, San Francisco, BA, 65; Univ Calif, Davis, MFA, 67. *Work:* Storm King Art Ctr, Mountainville, NY; San Francisco Mus Art, Calif; Oakland Mus; Stanford Mus, Stanford Univ; City of San Francisco. *Exhib:* One-person shows, San Francisco Mus Art, 67 & 69 & Crocker Art Gallery, Sacramento, 73; Joslyn Art Mus, Omaha, Nebr, 70; Oakland Mus, Calif, 71 & 74; Storm King Art Ctr, Mountainville, NY, 73-74; Baltimore Mus Art, Md, 73; Soc of the Four Arts, Palm Beach, Fla, 74; New York Cult Ctr, 75; and others. *Teaching:* Assoc prof art, Calif State Univ, Sacramento, 68-80. *Bibliog:* Kurt Von Meier (auth), Bay area, Arts Mag, 3/71; John Fitzgibbon (auth), Sacramento, Art in Am, 12/71. *Mailing Add:* 1734 34th St Sacramento CA 95816

WALCH, JOHN LEO
PAINTER, SCULPTOR
b Oklahoma City, Okla, Jan 14, 18. *Study:* Loyola Univ, Chicago, BA, 39; Sch of the Chicago Art Inst, 35-41; studied sculpture with Bernard Frazier, painting with Herny Hensche, Robert E Wood, Edgar Whitney, John Pike, Mel Crawford & Milford Zornes & graphic art with Emilio Amero. *Work:* Fogg Mus of Art, Cambridge, Mass; Philbrook Art Ctr, Tulsa, Okla; Mabee-Gerrer Mus, Shawnee; Okla Mus Art, Oklahoma City; and others. *Comn:* Stations of the Cross, sculpture & liturgical design, Church of Christ The King, Oklahoma City, 64; two murals, Church of St James, Oklahoma City, 71 & 77; mural & bronze sculpture, St Francis Hosp, Tulsa, Okla, 79; sculpture, St Anthony Hosp, Oklahoma City, 79; sculpture, St Charles Borromeo Church, Oklahoma City, 79. *Exhib:* Int Exposition of Mod Sacred Art, Vatican City, Rome, Italy, 50; one-man shows, Okla Art Ctr, Oklahoma City, 50, 63 & 68, Philbrook Art Ctr, Tulsa, 57 & Southern Plains Indian Mus, Anadarko, 62, Okla; Eight-State Exhib, 58 & 72 & Nat Print & Drawing Exhib, 71, Okla Art Ctr, Oklahoma City; Contemp Christian Arts Gallery, New York, 61; Birger Sandzein Mus, Linsberg, Kans, 63; Mabee-Gerrer Mus, Shawnee, Okla, 81; and others. *Pos:* Dir, Mabee-Gerrer Mus, Shawnee, 82- *Teaching:* Vis instr figure drawing & painting, Briar Cliff Col, Sioux City, Iowa, 65-66; numerous workshops figure & portrait drawing, Okla Art Guild, Oklahoma City, 70- *Awards:* Purchase Award, Okla Ann Exhib, Philbrook Art Ctr, Tulsa, 61; and others. *Bibliog:* Articles in Okla Today Mag & Orbit Mag. *Mem:* Okla Art Guild (bd dir, 65-). *Media:* Oil, Acrylic; Bronze, Hydracal. *Publ:* Illusr, Roman Missal, Cath Bk Publ Co, NY, 64; illusr, Catholic Art Calendar, Cath Church Extension Soc, Chicago, 67-71. *Dealer:* St Thomas More Book Store & Gallery 1745 NW 16th Oklahoma City OK 73106; Shorney Gallery 6616 N Olie Oklahoma City OK 73116. *Mailing Add:* 317 N Blackwelder Oklahoma City OK 73106

WALD, PALMER B
ADMINISTRATOR
b Newport, RI, Nov 5, 30. *Study:* RI Col, Providence, BEd, 53; New York Univ, Grad Sch Arts & Sci; Brooklyn Law Sch, LLB, 66. *Pos:* Administrator/secy, Whitney Mus Am Art, 74-82; asst attorney general, Trusts and Estates Bureau, Dept of Law, New York, 68-74. *Publ:* Auth, In the public interest, Mus News, 6/74. *Mailing Add:* One Nevada Plaza New York NY 10021

WALD, SYLVIA
PAINTER, SCULPTOR
b Philadelphia, Pa. *Study:* Moore Inst Art, Philadelphia. *Work:* Mus Mod Art, Metrop Mus Art & Whitney Mus Am Art, New York; Guggenheim Mus; Nat Gallery Art, Washington, DC; Brooklyn Mus, NY; plus others. *Exhib:* Curator's Choice, Smithsonian Inst & Tour US, 54; 50 Yrs Am Art, Mus Mod Art & Tour Europe, 55; Women Choose Women, NY Cult Ctr, 73; one-woman shows, Knoll Int, Munich, 79 & Contruction & Sculpture, Aaron Berman Gallery, New York, 81; Beyond the Wall, Berman Gallery, 83; Contemporaries, Sid Deutsch, 83; and others. *Bibliog:* Harvey Daniels (auth), Printmaking, 72; Zigrosser (auth), Prints and Their Creators--A World History, 74; Una E Johnson (auth), American Prints and Printmakers, 80. *Mem:* Am Fedn Arts. *Mailing Add:* 417 Lafayette St New York NY 10003

WALDMAN, PAUL
PAINTER
b Erie, Pa, 1936. *Study:* Brooklyn Mus Art Sch; Pratt Inst. *Work:* Mus Mod Art, New York; Smithsonian Inst, Washington, DC; Brooklyn Mus, NY; Los Angeles Co Mus Mod Art, Los Angeles; Hirshhorn Mus, Washington, DC; and many others. *Exhib:* Knoedler Gallery, 71; Hirshhorn Mus, 74; Castelli Gallery, 73, 75, 78, 81 & 84; Blum Hellman, 78; Kunsthalle Tranegarden, Copenhagen, 81; and others. *Pos:* Ford Found Grant, 65. *Teaching:* Instr, Greenwich Art Ctr, spring 63; instr, New York Community Col, 63-64; instr, Brooklyn Mus Art Sch, 63-67; vis artist, Ohio State Univ, 66; vis prof, Univ Calif, Davis, spring 66; instr, Sch Visual Arts, 66- *Mailing Add:* 38 W 26th St 420 W Broadway New York NY 10010

WALINSKA, ANNA
PAINTER, LECTURER
b London, Eng, Sept 8, 16. *Study:* Nat Acad Design, New York; Art Students League; Acad Andre L'Hote, Paris. *Work:* Helena Rubinstein Mus, Tel-Aviv, Israel; Wichita State Univ Mus; Norfolk Mus Arts & Sci; Jewish Mus & Mus Cathedral of St John The Divine, NY; and others. *Comn:* Prime Minister UNU-cil, Government Burma, Rangoon, Burma, 55; Mrs Eleanor Roosevelt, New York, 59; Gov H H Lehman, State of Israel Bonds, New York, 59; Pres F D Roosevelt, New York, 68. *Exhib:* Pa Acad, 36; Picture of the Year Exhib, Metrop Mus Art, New York, 43 & 45; Drawing Exhib, Mus Mod Art, New York, 56; retrospectives, Jewish Mus, New York, 57, Cathedral of St John The Divine, New York, 79, War Mem Bldg, Baltimore, Md, 80, Hebrew Union Col Mus, New York, 80 & Mercy Col, Detroit, Mich, 80; Gres Gallery, Baltimore Mus, Md, 59; one-woman shows, Community Col Mus, Delaware, Pa, 75 & Grimaldis Gallery, Baltimore, Md, 80; and others. *Pos:* Established dir, Guild Art Gallery 35-37; asst to dir, Contemp Art Pavilion, New York World's Fair, 40. *Teaching:* Instr art, Master Inst United Arts, New York, 57-71; artist-in-residence, Mercy Col, Detroit, Mich, 80 & Misericordia Col, Dallas, Pa, 81. *Awards:* First Prize in Casein, Silvermine Guild, 57; First Prize in Oil, 59 & Watercolors, 60, Am Soc Contemp Artists. *Bibliog:* Hla Shain (auth), The middle way, The Guardian, 2/55; Richard Mann (auth), Anna Walinska: Holocaust, Alex London, 12/79. *Mem:* Am Soc Contemp Artists; Nat Asn Women Artists; Audubon Soc; Casein Soc; Federation Modern Painters & Sculptors. *Publ:* Illusr, The Merry Communist, Pilgrim House, 35; illusr, The Gate Breakers, Herzl Press, 63. *Mailing Add:* 875 West End Ave New York NY 10025

WALKER, BERTA
DEALER
b Forest Hills, NY. *Study:* Univ Colo, 59-61; Burdett Col Bus, AA, 64. *Pos:* Dir mus progs, Opportunity Resources Arts, New York, 76-79; corp relations/spec events, Whitney Mus Am Art, New York, 79-81; assoc dir, Marisa del Re Gallery, New York, 81-83; dir, Contemp Dept, Graham Gallery, New York, 84- *Mem:* Fine Arts Work Ctr Artists Colony, Provincetown, Mass (chmn bd, currently); Art Table; Am Fedn Arts. *Specialty:* Contemporary American art. *Mailing Add:* c/o Marisa del Re Gallery 41 East 57th St New York NY 10021

WALKER, CLAY E
PRINTMAKER, SCULPTOR
b Middlesboro, Ky, July 28, 24. *Study:* Ecole Beaux Arts, Amsterdam, with Gertrude Stein, 45-46; Univ Toledo, BA, 50; Kent State Univ, MA, 60. *Work:* Libr Cong; Houston Mus Fine Arts; Detroit Inst Art; Butler Inst Am Art; San Francisco Mus Fine Arts. *Comn:* Murals, US Army, Lurgan, Ireland, 43 & Fecamp, France, 45; houses, Design & Construction, Oberlin, Ohio, 58-60, Costa Mesa, Calif, 67, Escondido, Calif, 70 & Vista, Calif, 80. *Exhib:* American Printmakers Travelling Exhib, US & Norway, 55-56; Ten Years of American Prints, Brooklyn Mus, 56; Mid-Year Exhib Am Paintings, Butler Inst Am Art, 60; Exhibitions American Art, US Info Serv, Europe; one-man shows, Toledo Mus Art, Witte Mem Mus Art, San Antonio, Tex, Howard Wise Gallery, Cleveland & many others. *Pos:* Dir, San Antonio Art Inst, 61-63. *Teaching:* Instr, Calif Inst Art, Los Angeles, 67-69. *Awards:* Fifty-three awards in regional & nat exhibs. *Media:* Woodcuts. *Mailing Add:* 11660 Torner Heights Dr Escondido CA 92025

WALKER, EDWARD D (RUSTY)
PAINTER
b Danville, Ill, Oct 31, 46. *Study:* Queensland Inst Technol, Brisbane, Australia, BA, 66. *Work:* Pres Gerald R Ford, Rancho Mirage, Calif; San Francisco Mus Mod Art; Charles & Emma Frye Art Mus, Seattle; Bender Room, Special Collections, Stanford Univ, Calif; Harcourt Brace Jovanovich Publ, New York; plus many others. *Comn:* Portraits for Col J Ladd, Comdr, Offutt Air Force Base, Hq Strategic Air Command, US Air Force, Bellevue, Nebr, 67-71; John Steinbeck (portrait), comn by Maurice Dunbar, Cupertino, Calif, 72; bkcover & illustrations, Hermes Publ, Seattle, 76 & Bk Nest Publ, Los Altos, Calif, 79; bk illustrations, Davis Publ, Worster, Mass, 80; Robert L Montgomery (portrait), Alta Bates Hospital, Berkeley, Calif, 83. *Exhib:* Crocker Kingsley Ann, E B Crocker Art Mus, Sacramento, 76; Westcoast Watercolor Soc, Frye Mus, Seattle & Rosicrucian Mus, San Jose, Calif, plus others, 76-80; Am Watercolor Soc, Nat Acad Design, New York, 77; Exhib of Watercolors by Renowned Am Watercolorists, A Huney Gallery, San Diego, Calif, 78-79. *Pos:* Artist, US Air Force, Strategic Air Command Hq, Offutt Air Force Base, Bellevue, Nebr, 67-71; juror of awards, various art asns, including Calif State Fair, 73-; instr oil & watercolor, many regional & nat asns, 73- *Teaching:* Instr watercolor, Asilomar Watercolor Workshops, Monterey, Calif, 77-80, Hewitt Workshops, San Miguel De Allende, Mexico, 83; instr oils & watercolor, Fresno Watercolor Workshop, 77; instr watercolor, Asilomar Watercolor Workshops, Monterey, Calif, 77-80; plus others. *Awards:* First Award, Laguna Gloria Mus, Austin, Tex, 76; Emily Lowe Mem Award, Am Watercolor Soc, Nat Acad NY, 77; First Award, A Huney Gallery Nat Invitational Western Art Show, San Diego, 79. *Bibliog:* Cover & feature article in Southwest Art, 6/80; feature article in Am Artist Mag, 10/80; and others. *Mem:* Nat Watercolor Soc; Westcoast Watercolor Soc (vpres, 80). *Media:* Watercolor, Oils, Pen and Ink. *Publ:* Illusr, Fine Art Prints, Yosemite & The Steinbeck Cat, James Int Art, 76; illusr, Christmas Cards for Nat Asn for Visually Handicapped, 78-80; illusr, Calendar, Morning Fog, Bankers Life Nebr, 79; illusr, Calendar, Pueblo Blankets, Bay View Fed Savings, 80. *Dealer:* Scott Gallery 107 Orinda Way Orinda CA 94563; John Pence Gallery 550 Sutter St San Francisco CA 94108. *Mailing Add:* 5724 Panama Ave Richmond CA 94804

WALKER, HERBERT BROOKS
SCULPTOR, MUSEUM DIRECTOR

b Brooklyn, NY, Nov 30, 27. *Study:* Art Students League, with Harry Sternberg & Robert B Hale, 43; Yale Sch Fine Arts, BFA, with R Eberhardt, R Zallinger, Graziani, R Albers & De Konning. *Work:* Photographs of Antonio Gaudis Work, Mus Mod Art, New York; Barbados Mus, BWI; Walker Mus. *Comn:* Paintings, movie, photographs, Gahagan Dredging, Orinoco River, Venezuela, 53-54; paintings & photographs, US Steel, Cerro Bolivar, Venezuela; earth sculpture, Walker Mus, 60. *Exhib:* One-man shows, Stony Brook Mus, Long Island, NY, 52, Barbados Mus 54 & IORC, Abadan, Iran, 58; Walker Mus, 60-; Rodin Mus, 70. *Collections Arranged:* Oil Exhibs, IORC, Abadan, Iran, 58 & 59; spec exhibs for pub schs, 60-72 & Walker Mus, Fairlee, Vt, 60- *Pos:* Materials prod head, IROC, Abadan, Iran, 58-59; dir, Walker Mus, 59- *Teaching:* Instr art, Thetford Acad, 64-66. *Bibliog:* H Brooks Walker, 1951, Eye Mag, Yale Univ, 67. *Mem:* Life mem Art Students League; Yale Arts Alumni Asn. *Media:* Sheet Metal, Bronze. *Publ:* Illusr, Gaudi, Mus Mod Art, 57. *Mailing Add:* Lake Morey Fairlee VT 05045

WALKER, JAMES ADAMS
PAINTER, PRINTMAKER

b Connersville, Ind, Jan 24, 21. *Study:* Western Mich Univ, BS, 46; Univ Mich, 47-48; Teachers Col, Columbia Univ, MA, 49, prof dipl, 58; E Carolina Univ, 49-56; Claremont Grad Sch, 59; Mich State Univ, MFA, 61. *Work:* Dullin Gallery Art, Knoxville, Tenn; Flint Inst Arts, Mich; Mercyhurst Col, Erie, Pa; Western Mich Univ, Kalamazoo; Butler Inst Am Art, Youngstown, Ohio. *Exhib:* 19th Nat Competition Prints, Libr of Cong, Washington, DC, 63; 14th & 15th Nat Brooklyn Mus Print Exhib, 64 & 66; 32nd Nat Graphic Arts Drawing Exhib, Wichita Art Asn, Kans, 65; 11th Nat Biennial Print Exhib, Print Club Albany, NY, 66. *Teaching:* Art supvr & critic instr, E Carolina Univ, 49-56; art instr, Northern Community High Sch, Flint, 56-63; art instr, Nat Music Camp, Interlochen, Mich, summer 63; assoc prof art, Kent State Univ, Warren, Ohio, 66- *Awards:* Purchase Award, 25th Ann Mich Acad Sci, Arts & Lett, 66; Hugh J Baker Mem Prize for Prints, 43rd Ann Hoosier Salon, Indianapolis, 67; First Print Purchase Award, Butler Inst Am Art, 68 & 77. *Bibliog:* Arne W Randall (auth), Murals for schools, Davis, Mass, 56; Charles E Meyer (auth), Papers of the Michigan Academy of Science, Arts & Letters, Univ Mich, 62; Eleanor Nelson (auth), Faculty Focus, Kent State Univ, 71. *Mem:* Mich Acad Sci, Arts & Lett (chmn fine arts sect, 65-67); Trumbull Art Guild (bd dirs & bd trustees, 69-75). *Media:* Watercolor; Serigraph. *Publ:* Auth, Newsprint, paste & chicken wire, 50, Let's scribble a mural, 53 & Buttermilk & chalk drawing, 54, Sch Arts Mag; auth, Cypress knees, Indust Arts Mag, 59. *Mailing Add:* 8778 Gull Rd Richland MI 49083

WALKER, JOY
PAINTER, PRINTMAKER

b Tacoma, Wash, July 17, 42. *Study:* Univ Paris, Sorbonne, 62-63; Univ Ore, BA(with hon), 64; Columbia Univ, 65; New York Studio Sch, 65-67. *Work:* Art Gallery of Ont, Toronto; Can Coun Art Bank, Ottawa; Dept of External Affairs, Ottawa; Robert McLaughlin Gallery, Oshawa, Ont; Mint Mus Art, Charlotte, NC. *Exhib:* One-man shows, Andre Zarre Gallery, New York, 77-78, 81 & 83; Abstractions (traveling exhib), Montreal, Paris, London & Stratford, Ont, 76-77; Southern Alta Art Gallery, Lethbridge, 80; Project Studio I, Queens, NY, 80; Fashion Moda, New York, 83. *Teaching:* Instr painting, Banff Ctr, Alta, Can, summer 75 & 78, York Univ, Ont, 76-78 & Univ Ill, Champaign, 79; vis artist, Emily Carr Col Art, Vancouver, BC, 80. *Awards:* Print Winner, Editions I, Ont Arts Coun, 74; Arts Grants, Prov of Ont, 74, 76 & 78-79 & Can Coun, 75. *Media:* Oil, Silkscreen. *Mailing Add:* c/o Andre Zarre Gallery 41 East 57th St New York NY 10022 M5V 2B6

WALKER, LARRY
PAINTER, EDUCATOR

b Franklin, Ga, Oct 22, 35. *Study:* High Sch Music & Art, New York; Wayne State Univ, Detroit. *Work:* Haggin Art Mus, City Hall & San Joaquin Delta Col, Stockton, Calif; Univ of the Pac, Stockton; Oakland Mus, Calif; City Atlanta; and others. *Comn:* Mural, Univ of the Pac, 65; Mural, comn by Benjamin Holt Found for San Joaquin Delta Col, 74; and others. *Exhib:* West Coast 74: The Black Image, E B Crocker Mus, Sacramento & Los Angeles Munic Art Gallery, 74; Northern Calif Arts Ann, Exposition Gallery, Sacramento, 76; Festac (2nd World Black & African Festival of Arts & Cult, Lagos, Nigeria, 77; Black Artists South, Hunstville Mus, Ala; and others. *Teaching:* Prof painting, drawing & art educ, Univ of the Pac, 64-, chmn art dept, 73-80; prof & chmn dept art, Ga State Univ, currently. *Awards:* First Award/Painting, Stockton Art League 26th Ann, Dr & Mrs Spracher, 76; Calif Expo Award; Stockton Art League Award. *Bibliog:* Samella Lewis & Ruth Waddy (auths), The Black Artist on Art, Vol I, Contemp Crafts Publ, 69. *Mem:* Nat Coun of Art Adminrs (mem bd dirs, 76-80, chmn, 77-79); Stockton Arts Comn (vchairperson, 76-78, chmn, 78-80). *Media:* Multimedia. *Publ:* Auth, The state of the arts in San Joaquin County, 3/81; auth, article, San Joaquin Co Arts Coun, 3/82; and others. *Dealer:* Collectors Gallery Oakland Mus 1000 Oak St Oakland CA 94607; Michael Himovitz Enterprises Inc Box 216 Carmichael CA 95608. *Mailing Add:* Dept Art Ga State Univ, Univ Plaza Atlanta GA 30303

WALKER, MARIE SHEEHY
PAINTER

b Glen Cove, NY, May 23, 52. *Study:* Rosemont Col, BFA, 74; Art Students League, with Robert Brackman, 74-77. *Work:* Rosemont Col. *Comn:* Heffernan Hall (watercolor), Rosemont Col, 74. *Exhib:* Nat Acad Design Ann Exhib, New York, 82; Pastel Soc Am Ann Exhib Pastels Only, Nat Arts Club, New York, 82 & 83; Nassau Co Mus Ann Show, Roslyn, NY, 82 & 83; Nat

Asn Women Artists Exhib, Bergen Community Mus, Paramus, NJ, 83; Nat Asn Women Artists Traveling Painting Exhib, 83-85. *Awards:* Pastel Soc Am Award, Salmagundi Show, 80; Charlotte Winston Mem Award, Nat Asn Women Artists Exhib, 83; Gold Medal Oil Painting, Nat Art League, 83. *Mem:* Pastel Soc Am; Nat Asn Women Artists; Art Students League; Salmagundi Club; Nat Art League. *Media:* Pastel, Oil. *Mailing Add:* 4 Homestead Path Huntington NY 11743

WALKER, MARY CAROLYN
CRAFTSMAN, JEWELER

b Lancaster, Pa, Oct 24, 38. *Study:* Pa State Univ, BS(home art); Rochester Inst of Technol Sch for Am Craftsmen, with Don Drumm & Eleanor Moty. *Exhib:* Marietta Col Crafts Regional, Ohio, 72; Southern Tier Arts & Crafts Show, Corning, NY, 73; First World Silver Fair, Mexico, 74; Spec Exhib for Nat Gov Conf, 76; one-person show, Pa Designer Craftsmen Gallery, Bushkill, 82; and others. *Pos:* Partner, Tamcraft Products Co, Neffsville, Pa, 60- *Teaching:* Instr jewelry, Cumberland Valley High Sch Adult Educ. *Awards:* First Prize Metals, Harrisburg Arts Festival, 72; Best in Show, 73 & First Prize Jewlery, 76, Pa Guild of Craftsman; and others. *Bibliog:* R Stevens (auth), Arts decoratifs, La Revue Mod des Arts et de la vie, France, 12/72. *Mem:* Am Crafts Coun (secy, NE Region, 71-74); Pa Guild of Craftsman (treas, 70-71, pres, 72, vpres, 73); Harrisburg Craftsmen (pres, 70, secy, 72, treas, 73); Doshi Ctr Contmep Art (bd dirs, 82-83). *Media:* Sterling Silver. *Mailing Add:* 22 Conway Dr Mechanicsburg PA 17055

WALKER, MORT
CARTOONIST

b El Dorado, Kans, Sept 3, 23. *Study:* Univ Mo, BA; Wm Penn Col, Hon LLD, 81. *Work:* Bird Libr, Syracuse Univ; Boston Univ Libr; Kans State Univ; Montreal Humor Pavilion; Smithsonian Inst. *Exhib:* Metrop Mus Art, New York, 52; Brussels World's Fair, 64; Mus Louvre, Paris, 65; New York World's Fair, 67; Expo, Montreal, 69. *Pos:* Creator of Beetle Bailey, King Features Syndicate, 50-, Hi & Lois, 54-, Sam's Strip, 61-63, Boner's Ark, 68- & Sam & Silo, 77; pres, Mus Cartoon Art, Port Chester, NY, currently; chmn bd, Comicana Corp, currently. *Awards:* Am Legion Fourth Estate Award, 78; Newspaper Comics Coun Award, 79; Inkpot Award, 79. *Mem:* Nat Cartoonists Soc (pres, 60); Newspaper Comics Coun; Artists & Writers Asn; Cartoonists Guild. *Media:* Ink. *Publ:* Ed, Nat Cartoonists Soc Album, 61, 65 & 72; auth, Most, 71; auth, Land of Lost Things, 72; auth & illusr, Backstage at the Strips, 76 & Lexicon of Comicana, 81. *Dealer:* Mus of Cartoon Art Port Chester NY 10573; Graham Gallery 1014 Madison Ave New York NY 10021. *Mailing Add:* c/o King Features 235 E 45th St New York NY 10017

WALKER, SANDRA RADCLIFFE
PAINTER

b Milton, Pa, Aug 25, 37. *Comn:* Design, Simon Weisenthal Congressional Medal, 80. *Exhib:* Biennial, Corcoran Gallery Art, Washington, DC, 74 & 81; Va Mus Biennial, Richmond, 79; USICA Exhib, Galeria Arte, Honduras, 79; one-woman shows, Gallery 4, Alexandria, Va, 80 & Franz Bader Gallery, Washington, DC, 84; Watercolor USA, Springfield Art Mus, Mo, 83; Allied Artists Am, New York, 83; and others. *Awards:* H Lester Cooke Found Grant, Washington, DC, 77. *Bibliog:* Anon (auth), The Watercolor Page-- Sandra Walker, Am Artist Mag, 2/77. *Mem:* Nat Watercolor Soc; Washington Watercolor Soc. *Media:* Watercolor. *Dealer:* Franz Bader Gallery 20th & I St NW Washington DC. *Mailing Add:* 3770 Bel Pre Rd Apt 1 Silver Spring MD 20906

WALKER, WILLIAM BOND
ADMINISTRATOR, LIBRARIAN

b Brownsville, Tenn, Apr 13, 30. *Study:* Bisttram Sch Fine Art, Taos, NMex & Los Angeles Calif, with Emil Bisttram, 48-49; State Univ Iowa, Iowa City, with Mauricio Lasansky, Howard Warshaw, James Lechay & Stuart Edie, BA, 53; Rutgers Univ Grad Sch of Libr Serv, MSLS, 58. *Pos:* Cataloger & reference librn, Libr Metrop Mus Art, New York, 57-59; chief librn, Art Reference Libr, Brooklyn Mus, 59-64, Libr Nat Collection Fine Arts & Nat Portrait Gallery, Smithsonian Inst, 64-80 & Thomas J Watson Libr, Metrop Mus Art, New York, 80- *Mem:* Am Libr Asn; Art Libr Soc of NAm (nat chmn, 75); Spec Libr Asn Mus Div (nat chmn, 61-62); Grolier Club, New York. *Res:* American sculpture of eighteenth to twentieth century; art library classification at Library of Congress. *Interests:* Twentieth century American prints. *Publ:* Auth, Art books & periodicals: Dewey and LC (classification), Libr Trends, Vol 23, 1/75; auth, The development of national and international cooperation between art libraries, Art Libr J, spring 78; auth, Art libraries, Spec Libr, 12/78; auth, Bibliography on American Sculpture, Eighteenth to Twentieth Century, Washington, DC, Smithsonian Inst Press, 80. *Mailing Add:* Metrop Mus Art 5th Ave at 82nd St New York NY 10028

WALKEY, FREDERICK P
MUSEUM DIRECTOR

b Belmont, Mass, May 29, 22. *Study:* Duke Univ; Boston Mus Fine Arts Sch; Tufts Col, BSEd. *Pos:* Exec dir, De Cordova Mus, Lincoln, Mass, formerly; dir, Newport Art Mus & Art Asn, currently. *Mem:* New Eng Conf; Am Asn Mus; Am Fedn Arts. *Mailing Add:* Newport Art Mus & Art Asn 76 Bellevue Ave Newport RI 02840

WALKINGSTICK, KAY
PAINTER

b Syracuse, NY, Mar 2, 35. *Study:* Beaver Col, Glenside, Pa, BFA, 59; Pratt Inst, Brooklyn, MFA, 75. *Work:* Newark Mus, NJ; Southern Plains Indian Mus, Anadarko, Okla; Israel Mus, Jerusalem; Albright-Knox Art Gallery, Buffalo; San Diego Mus Fine Art. *Exhib:* Newark & NJ State, Trenton, 66-68,

70-71 & 81; Aldrich Mus, Ridgefield, Conn, 75; Bronx Mus, 80; Southern Plains Indian Mus, Anadarko, Okla, 80; Pratt Inst Gallery, NY, 81; Jersey City Mus, NJ, 81-82; and others. *Teaching:* Instr painting, Williams Col & Dickinson Univ, 70-73; instr, Upsala Col, East Orange, NJ, 75-79. *Awards:* NJ Coun Arts Fel, 81; Nat Endowment Arts Grant, 83; Residency, William Flanasan Mem Creative Person's Ctr, 83; and others. *Bibliog:* Ida K Rigby (auth), Psychological fields, Artweek, 10/13/79; Vivien Raynor (auth), article, New York Times, 6/19/81; Deborah C Phillips (auth), article, Art News, 6/81. *Media:* Acrylic, Wax. *Dealer:* Bertha Urdang 23 East 74th St New York NY; Wenger Gallery 4683 Cass St San Diego CA. *Mailing Add:* 279 Tenafly Rd Englewood NJ 07631

WALL, BRIAN
SCULPTOR
b London, Eng, Sept 5, 31; US citizen. *Study:* Luton Col Art, Eng; with Barbara Hepworth, 54-58. *Work:* Tate Gallery, London; Nat Gallery, Dublin; Art Gallery NSW, Sidney; Oakland Mus; Univ Art Mus, Berkeley. *Comn:* Thornaby (sculpture), New Town Ctr, Thornaby, Eng, 68; Ali (sculpture), Univ Houston, Tex, 78. *Exhib:* 2nd Paris Biennale, Mus Mod Art, 61; Sculpture of the Sixties, Tate Gallery, 65; Queen's Silver Jubilee Exhib, London, 77; Max Hutchinson Gallery, New York, 77, 78 & 81; Int Sculpture Conf, Washington DC, 80; one-man shows, Seattle Art Mus, 82, San Francisco Mus Mod Art, 83 & John Berggruen Gallery, San Francisco, 83; and others. *Teaching:* Chmn sculpture dept, Cent Sch Art & Design, London, 64-72; prof sculpture, Univ Calif, Berkeley, 69- *Bibliog:* Charles Spencer (auth), Brian Wall, sculptor of simplicity, Studio Int, 3/66; G S Whittet (auth), Question and artist: Brian Wall, Studio Int, 10/69; Hilton Kramer (auth), article in New York Times, 5/13/77. *Media:* Steel. *Dealer:* Max Hutchinson Gallery 138 Greene St New York NY 10012; John Berggruen Gallery 228 Grant Ave San Francisco CA 94108. *Mailing Add:* 1824 Grant Ave San Francisco CA 94133

WALL, RALPH ALAN
PAINTER
b Hobart, Ind, Aug 1, 32. *Study:* Univ Okla; Oklahoma City Univ, BS. *Work:* Bimson Collection, Valley Nat Bank, Phoenix, Ariz; Fidelity Bank Collection, Oklahoma City; Mountain Oyster Club, Tucson, Ariz; Big Chief Collection, Ardmore, Okla; Frost Bank, San Antonio. *Comn:* Southland Corp, Dallas; and others. *Exhib:* One-man shows, Goddard Ctr, Ardmore, Okla & Ponca City Art Ctr, Okla, 72; Mus of the SW, Midland, Tex, 76; group shows, O S Ranch Show, Post, Tex, 79 & 81; Western Heritage Horse, Cattle & Art Auction, Houston, Tex, 79. *Teaching:* Instr acrylics & oil, private classes & workshops, currently. *Awards:* Am Inst Graphic Art Award (packaging), 67; Gold Medal, 1974 Portfolio Western Art, Franklin Mint, 74; Gold Award, Texas Ranger Hall of Fame, 79. *Bibliog:* Freddie Steve (auth), Franklin Mint paint, Paint Horse J, 11/74; Susan Hallsten McGarry (auth), This life is but a shadow, Southwest Art Mag, 10/81; Gretchen Schmitz (auth), The artist, Ralph Wall, Prints Mag, 7-8/82; and others. *Mem:* Hon mem Mountain Oyster Club, Tucson. *Media:* Multimedia. *Publ:* Illusr, American Horseman, 9/73; Paint Horse J (cover), 1/75 & 11/75; illusr, Leanin Tree Greeting Card Series, 77, 78 & 82 & Okla Today, summer 76 & spring 79; illusr, Dean Krakel's Adventures in Western Art, 77; illusr, Quarterhorse J (cover), 1/80. *Dealer:* Folger Gallery PO Box 3214 Midland TX 79701; Settler's West Galleries 6420 N Campbell Ave Tucson AZ 85718. *Mailing Add:* Rte 8 Box 63H New Braunfels TX 78130

WALL, SUE
PAINTER, PRINTMAKER
b Cleveland, Ohio, Feb 18, 50. *Study:* Ohio Univ, BFA, 71, MFA, 73. *Work:* Cleveland Mus Art; Canton Art Inst Mus, Ohio; Butler Inst Am Art, Youngstown, Ohio; Univ Iowa Mus Art; Kenneth Beck Ctr Cult Arts, Cleveland. *Exhib:* Butler Ann Mid-Year Show, Youngstown, 75-77; one-person shows, Zanesville Art Ctr, Ohio, 75, Hamilton Gallery, Des Moines, Iowa, 75, Strong's Gallery, Cleveland, 75, 77 & 79, Canton Art Inst, Ohio, 76, Gallery 200, Columbus, 76 & Piccolo Mondo, Palm Beach, Fla, 76 & 78; and many others. *Awards:* Grumbacher Cash Award, 79th Ann Catharine Lorillard Wolfe, 75; Truman Award, 150th Ann Nat Acad Exhib, 75; First Prize, Am Nat Miniature Show, Laramie Art Guild, 76. *Bibliog:* Rhoda Levinsohn (auth), article, Sunday Plain Dealer, Cleveland, 75 & Art Look 102, Apple Publ, S Africa, 9/76; Millie Wolff (auth), article, Palm Beach Daily News, 2/78. *Mem:* New Organization Visual Arts; Audubon Artists; Nat Soc Painters Casein & Acrylic; Miniature Art Soc NJ; Artists Equity, New York. *Media:* Acrylic. *Mailing Add:* Apt 76 230 W End Ave New York NY 10023

WALLACE, DAVID HAROLD
HISTORIAN, MUSEOLOGIST
b Baltimore, Md, Dec 24, 26. *Study:* Lebanon Valley Col, BA; Columbia Univ, MA & PhD. *Pos:* Asst ed, NY Hist Soc, New York, 52-56; mus cur, Independence Nat Hist Park, Philadelphia, 58-68; asst chief, Br Mus Opers, Nat Park Serv, 68-71, chief, 71-73, chief Br Reference Serv, 74-80, emeritus, 80- *Res:* American artist biographies. *Publ:* Coauth, Dictionary of artists in America, 1564-1860, NY Hist Soc, 57; auth, John Rogers, the People's Sculptor, 67. *Mailing Add:* 9 W Third St Frederick MD 21701

WALLACE, ELIZABETH S
ADMINISTRATOR, SCULPTOR
b Mankato, Kans. *Study:* Washburn Univ, AB; Univ Nebr, BFA, MFA; also with Thomas Sheffield. *Work:* Elder Gallery, Lincoln, Nebr. *Exhib:* One-person shows, Nebr Wesleyan Univ, Lincoln, 66, Haymarket Art Gallery, 70 & Elder Gallery, 74 & 79, Midland Col, 78. *Pos:* Dir, Elder Gallery, Lincoln, 76- & Univ Place Art Ctr & Wesleyan Lab Gallery, 77-

Teaching: Asst prof ceramics, Nebr Wesleyan Univ, 72-, asst prof sculpture & art hist & head dept art, 76- *Mem:* Nebr Art Asn (bd trustees, 76-); Lincoln Arts Coun (bd trustees, 77-); Wesleyan Arts Coun (pres, 75-76); Nebr Crafts Coun; Am Crafts Coun. *Mailing Add:* 420 Lakewood Lincoln NE 68510

WALLACE, GAEL LYNN
PAINTER
b Ft Worth, Tex, Aug 5, 41. *Study:* Okla State Univ, with Dale McKinney & David Allende, BA, 64; independent study with Don Fusco & Tom Owen. *Comn:* Old west storefront murals, Graden Elementary Sch, Kansas City, Mo, 78. *Exhib:* The Heritage, Kansas City Mus of Hist & Sci, Mo; Colo State Fair, Pueblo, 80; 60th Ann Nat Watercolor Soc, Laguna Beach Mus Art, Calif, 80 & 82; Rocky Mountain Nat Aquamedia, 82; Colorado 83 Biennial, Colorado Springs Fine Art Mus, 83. *Awards:* Second Place, Black Forest Int Painting & Sculpture Exhib, 79-80; Honorable Mention, Colo State Fair, 80; Purchase Award, Nat Watercolor Soc, 80. *Bibliog:* Diane Wengler (auth), The Beauty of nature, Gazette Telegraph, 12/13/80. *Mem:* Nat Watercolor Soc; Professional Artists Colo. *Media:* Acrylic. *Mailing Add:* 23 Kris Ln Manitou Springs CO 80829

WALLACE, JOHN EDWARD
PAINTER
b St Louis, Mo, Dec 29, 29. *Study:* Washington Univ, with Paul Burlin & Carl Holty, BFA; Ind Univ, MFA; Skowhegan Sch Painting & Sculpture, with Henry Varnum Poor. *Work:* St Louis Art Mus; Detroit Inst Arts. *Comn:* Mural in true fresco, South Solon Meeting House, Maine, 54; sculpture panel in bronze, Aquatic House, St Louis Zool Gardens, 59. *Exhib:* Pa Acad Fine Arts, 52; Ann Nat Print Exhib, Brooklyn Mus, 53; Artist in Residence Exhib, Roswell Mus, NMex, 68; Bertrand Russell Centenary, Nottingham, Eng, 73; Provincetown Art Asn, Mass, 78; Green Mountain Gallery, New York, 79; plus many others. *Pos:* Chmn, New Directions for Studio Teaching, 59th Ann Col Art Asn Am, 71. *Teaching:* Prof painting & drawing, Prairie State Col, Chicago Heights, Ill, 68-79 & chmn art dept, 71-74; vis artist, Truro Ctr Arts, 76-80, Silvermine Guild Art, 82, Stamford Mus, 82; instr drawing & silk screen, Western Conn State Col, 81- *Awards:* Resident Fel in Painting, Huntington Hartford Found, Calif, 60; Artist-in-residence grant, Roswell Mus, NMex, 68. *Mem:* Col Art Asn Am. *Media:* Acrylic, Watercolor. *Mailing Add:* 25 Tauton Lake Rd Rt 3 Newtown CT 06470

WALLACE, KENNETH WILLIAM
PAINTER, EDUCATOR
b Penticton, BC, July 7, 45. *Study:* Calgary Col Art, Alta, cert, 71; Vancouver Sch Art, BC, cert, 73; Banff Sch Fine Arts, 73. *Work:* Nat Art Gallery, Ottawa; Art Gallery Ont, Toronto; Vancouver Art Gallery, BC; Winnipeg Art Gallery, Man; Burnaby Art Gallery, BC. *Exhib:* Nine one-man shows, Bau-zi Art Gallery, Toronto & Vancouver, 75-80 & Burnaby Art Gallery, BC, 80; Three Directions Painting, Univ BC Fine Arts, Vancouver, 76; New Abstract Art Am, Edmonton Art Gallery, Alta, 77; Affinities, Vancouver Art Gallery, 79. *Collections Arranged:* Images of Women (auth, catalog), Winnipeg Art Gallery, 75; Canadian Painters in Watercolor (auth, catalog), Glenbow Inst, Alta, 76; Olympic Exhibition of British Columbian Artists (auth, catalog), Montreal, Que, 76; West Coast on Canvas (auth, catalog), Birmingham Art Gallery, Ala, 79. *Teaching:* Instr painting & drawing, Univ BC, 76-78, instr painting, Dept Fine Arts, 77-80. *Awards:* Int Critics Award, Annecy Film Festival, France, 75; Can Coun Art Awards, 75-79. *Bibliog:* Mary Fox (auth), Images from the inside outside, Western Living, 76; Pat Fleisher (auth), interview in Arts Mag, Toronto, Ont, 76; Karen Wilken (auth), Vancouver scene, Art News, New York, 79. *Dealer:* Bau-xi Galleries Ltd 3045 Granville St Vancouver BC V6H 3J9 Can. *Mailing Add:* 2724 W 13th Ave Vancouver BC V6K 2T4 Canada

WALLACE, LYSBETH (MAI)
WEAVER, EDUCATOR
b Hopkinsville, Ky. *Study:* Univ Ky; Kansas City Art Inst; Cranbrook Acad of Art, Bloomfield Hills, Mich with Maija Grotell & Marianne Strengell. *Work:* Evansville Mus of Arts & Sci, Ind; Berea Col, Ky. *Comn:* Woven tapestries, Production Credit Asn Bldg, Glasgow, Ky, 76; woven inlay tapestry, Town & Country Garden Club for Pub Libr, Hopkinsville, 77; tapestry, Pub Libr, Hopkinsville, 77. *Exhib:* Alumni Show, Cranbrook Acad of Art, 54; Designer/Craftsmen Show, Univ Kans, 63; Int Craft Show, Calif State Univ, Northridge, 63; Evansville Mus Art & Sci, Ind, 63-81; Capitol Arts Ctr, Bowling Green, Ky, 81; and others. *Pos:* Handweaving expert, UN Tech Assistance Admin, Manila, Philippines, 51-53. *Teaching:* Instr design, Washburn Univ, Topeka, Kans, 46-48; from instr to asst prof weaving, Southern Ill Univ, Carbondale, 55-60; asst prof weaving, Ill State Univ, Normal, 61-65; from asst prof to prof weaving & design, Western Ky Univ, 65- *Awards:* Anonymous Award, Designer/Craftsman, Univ Kans, 63; Purchase Award, Mid-State Craft Show, Malcom Koch, 67; Purchase Award, Berea Biennial, Berea Col, 70. *Bibliog:* Betty Pepies (auth), New fibers for old forms, Living for Young Homemakers, 52; Patricia K Brooks (auth), Experiment in the Philippines, Craft Horizons, 54. *Mem:* Col Art Asn; Am Craftsmen Coun; KY Guild of Artist & Craftsmen. *Publ:* Auth, Handweaving in the Philippines, UN, 53; auth, Tapestry weaver in the mid-west, 60 & Lysbeth Wallace teaches weaving, 61, Handweaver & Craftsman; illusr, Lucile Van Cleve Wallace's Recollections & Recipes, Circulation Serv, Kansas City, Nov 77. *Dealer:* Swearingen-Haynie Gallery Brownsboro Ctr Brownsboro Rd Louisville KY 40207. *Mailing Add:* Fine Arts Dept Western Ky Univ Col Heights Bowling Green KY 42101

WALLACE, RICHARD WILLIAM
EDUCATOR, HISTORIAN
b Rochester, NY, Oct 4, 33. *Study:* Williams Col, BA, 55; Princeton Univ, MFA, 61, PhD, 64. *Teaching:* Instr art hist, Princeton Univ, 60-61; from asst prof to prof, Wellesley Col, 64- *Awards:* Fulbright Fel, 62-64; Nat Endowment Arts Summer Stipend, 67; Am Coun Learned Soc Fel, 69. *Res:* Italian baroque art. *Publ:* Contribr, Salvator Rosa (exhib catalog), Arts Coun Gr Brit, 73; auth, The Etchings of Salvator Rosa, Princeton Press, 79; Salvator Rosa in America (exhib catalog), Wellesley Col, 79; contribr, The Illustrated Bartsch, Abaris Books, 82. *Mailing Add:* Dept Art Wellesley Col Wellesley MA 02181

WALLACE, ROBERT DAN
EDUCATOR, HISTORIAN
b Los Angeles, Calif, Jan 15, 23. *Study:* Stanford Univ, BA, 47, MA, 48; Univ Geneva, LittD, 53. *Teaching:* Prof art, San Diego State Univ, 57-82. *Mem:* Col Art Asn; Art Historians Southern Calif; Archit Historians Southern Calif; Soc Archit Historians. *Res:* Medieval art. *Publ:* Auth, L'Influence de la France Gothique sur deux des Precurseurs de la Renaissance Italienne: Nicolo et Giovanni Pisano, Libr E Droz, Geneva, 53. *Mailing Add:* 750 Bangor San Diego CA 92106

WALLACE, SONI
PAINTER
b London, Eng, Apr 18, 31; US citizen. *Study:* Silvermine Art Guild, New Canaan, Conn; Mus Mod Art, with Zolten Hecht; Pratt Graphics, New York. *Work:* Gibbes Art Mus, Charleston, SC; Univ Ala Mus. *Comn:* Three covers for mag, Distinguished Resorts, 68, 70 & 71. *Exhib:* Conn Watercolor Soc 31st Ann, Fairfield Univ, 69; Love/Peace, Am Greetings Gallery, NY, 69; Northwest Printmakers 41st Int Exhib, Seattle Art Mus, 70; solo shows, Pacem-in-Terris Gallery, New York, 70, Danbury Libr Gallery, Conn, 71 & Phoenix Gallery, New York, 75. *Awards:* Max Granick Award, Am Soc Contemp Artists, NY, 71; Award, Washington Art Asn, Conn, 72; Am Soc Contemp Artists Ann, 74. *Mem:* Nat Asn Women Artists; Am Soc Contemp Artists; Silvermine Guild Artists; Washington Art Asn; Women in the Arts. *Media:* Acrylic, Watercolor. *Mailing Add:* 150 E 77th St New York NY 10021

WALLACH, ALAN
CRITIC, HISTORIAN
b Brooklyn, NY, June 8, 42. *Study:* Columbia Col, BA, 63; Columbia Univ, PhD, 73. *Teaching:* Assoc prof art hist, Kean Col NJ, Union, 74- *Mem:* Col Art Asn Am; Am Studies Asn; Caucus Marxism & Art; Art Historians Asn (Great Britain). *Res:* Nineteenth century American art; history of museums; criticism of 20th century art. *Publ:* Auth, The voyage of life as popular art, Art Bull, 77; coauth, The museum of modern art as late capitalist ritual, Marxist Perspectives, 78; coauth, The universal survey museum, Art Hist, 80; auth, The avant garde of the eighties, Art Criticism, 81; auth, Thomas Cole and the aristocracy, Arts, 81. *Mailing Add:* 22 Park Ave 1 Hoboken NJ 07030

WALLER, AARON BRET
MUSEUM DIRECTOR, HISTORIAN
b Liberal, Kans, Dec 7, 35. *Study:* Univ Kans, Lawrence; Kansas City Art Inst & Sch of Design, BFA, 57; Univ Kans, Lawrence, MFA, 58; Univ Oslo, Norway. *Collections Arranged:* School for Scandal: Thomas Rowlandson's London (coauth, catalog), 67 & The Waning Middle Ages (ed, catalog), 69, Univ Kans; Images of Love & Death in Late Medieval and Renaissance Art (ed, catalog), 75 & Works from the Collection of Dorothy & Herbert Vogel (auth, catalog), 77, Univ Mich. *Pos:* Dir, Mus of Art, Univ Kans, Lawrence, 68-70; head, Dept Pub Educ, Metrop Mus of Art, New York, 70-73; dir, Mus of Art, Univ Mich, 73-80; dir, Mem Art Gallery, Rochester, New York, 80- *Teaching:* Asst prof art hist, Univ Kans, Lawrence, 64-70; assoc prof art hist, Univ Mich, Ann Arbor, 73-80; adj assoc prof art hist, Univ Rochester, New York, 80- *Awards:* Grant, Nat Educ Asn Prof Dept, 80-81; and others. *Mem:* Asn Art Mus Dirs; Intermuseum Conserv Asn (pres, 77-78); Am Asn of Mus; Col Art Asn. *Res:* Graphic arts; 20th century art. *Mailing Add:* Univ Mich Mus of Art Ann Arbor MI 48109

WALLIN, LELAND DEAN
PAINTER, EDUCATOR
b Sioux Falls, SD, Oct 14, 42. *Study:* Columbus Col Art & Design, Ohio, 61; Kans City Art Inst, Mo, BFA, 65; Univ Cincinnati Art Acad, Ohio, MFA fel, 67; Aspen Sch Contemp Art, Colo, 68; Sabbatical Study, Philip Pearlstein's Studio, NY, 76. *Exhib:* One-man shows, Minneapolis Col Art & Design, Minn, 77 & Harold Reed Gallery, New York, 83; Brooklyn 79, Brooklyn Mus, New York, 79; Ten Realist Views, Rutgers Univ, Robeson Gallery, Newark, NJ, 81; Realism: A Close Look, Pensacola Jr Col, Fla, 81; Selected 20th Century Am Nudes, Univ NC, Greensboro, 81. *Collections Arranged:* New Realism 70 (auth, catalog), St Cloud State Univ, Minn, 70. *Teaching:* Prof fine arts, St Cloud State Univ, Minn, formerly. *Awards:* Fac travel res grants, 73-74. *Bibliog:* Vivien Raynor (auth), Realism at the Robeson Gallery, New York Times, 8/81; Ralph Pomeroy (auth), article, Arts Mag, New York, 4/83; Gerrit Henry (auth), exhib catalog, Harold Reed Gallery, 83. *Mem:* Col Art Asn. *Media:* Mixed. *Publ:* The Evolution of Philip Pearlstein, Art Int Mag, Part I, summer 79, Part II, fall 79. *Dealer:* Harold Reed Gallery 120 E 78th St New York NY 10021. *Mailing Add:* 151 West 28th Street New York NY 10001

WALLIS, HELEN V
PHOTOGRAPHER
b Alhambra, Calif, Jan 21, 36. *Study:* Univ Calif, Berkeley, BA, 57; Stanford Univ, with Jerry Uelsmann, MA, 58; Univ Fla, Gainesville, MFA, 68. *Work:* Int Ctr Photog, New York. *Exhib:* One-person shows, Images Gallery, New Orleans, La, 77; Focus Gallery, San Francisco, Calif, 78 & Film-makers Gallery, Pittsburgh, Pa, 80; Electroworks, George Eastman House, Rochester, NY, 79-81. *Pos:* Gallery owner, Gallery 115, Santa Cruz, Calif, 73-75. *Teaching:* Instr, Univ Calif, Santa Cruz, 73-77; instr, Cornell Univ Summer Sch, Ithaca, NY, 77 & 78; instr, Friends of Photog & Ansel Adams Workshops, Carmel, Calif, 77. *Awards:* Purchase Award, Humboldt State Univ, 77. *Mem:* Soc Photographic Educ. *Media:* Color, Black & White. *Mailing Add:* 759 Seacliff Drive Aptos CA 95003

WALMSLEY, WILLIAM AUBREY
LITHOGRAPHER, COLLECTOR
b Tuscumbia, Ala, Oct 9, 23. *Study:* Univ Ala, BFA, 51 & MA, 53; Art Students League; Acad Julian, Paris; Tamarind Lithography Workshop, Los Angeles. *Work:* Mus Mod Art, New York; Libr Cong, Washington, DC; Tate Gallery, London, Eng; Hawaii Acad Art, Honolulu; Ohio State Univ, Columbus. *Exhib:* Nat Print Exhib, Honolulu Acad Art, Hawaii, 74; Davidson Print Exhib, NC, 74; Philadelphia Print Club Int, Pa, 75; Libr Cong, Print Exhib, Washington, DC, 75; Soc Am Graphic Artist Print Exhib, New York, 75. *Teaching:* Prof lithography, Fla State Univ, Tallahassee, 62; vis artist lithography, Northern Ill Univ, Dekalb, summer 73; vis artist lithography, Penland Sch Crafts, Spruce Pine, NC, summer 75 & 77. *Awards:* Purchase Awards, Colorprint USA, Tex Tech, Lubbock, 72 & Potsdam Prints, NY, 72; Second Purchase Award, 12th Ann Calgary Graphic, Alta, 72. *Bibliog:* Emil Weddige (auth), Lithography, Int Textbk Co, 66; Clare Romano & John Ross (coauths), Complete Screenprint & Lithography, Freepress, Macmillan, 74. *Mem:* Southeastern Graphic Coun (pres, 76-78); Southeastern Col Art Conf (bd dir, 77-80); Soc Am Graphic Arts; Boston Printmakers; Southern Graphics Coun. *Collection:* Prints by Goya, Picasso, Callot, Ernst, Beckman, Matisse & Piranesi. *Mailing Add:* 1536 Christobal Dr Tallahassee FL 32303

WALSH, J(OHN) MICHAEL
DEALER, PRINTMAKER
b Peoria, Ill, July 16, 53. *Study:* Univ Iowa, printmaking with M Lazansky & U Meyers, BFA, 77; Bradley Univ, with W A S Hatch, MA, 80. *Exhib:* Davenport Munic Gallery, Iowa, 78; Minot State Col Mus, NDak, 79 & 81; Univ SDak Mus, Vermillion, traveling, 79 & 80; Dulin Gallery Art, Knoxville, Tenn, 80; Okla Arts Ctr, Oklahoma City, 81; Bradley Nat Exhib, Peoria, Ill, 83. *Pos:* Asst dir, Tower Park Gallery, Peoria, Ill, 78-; cur exhibs, Peoria Art Guild, Ill, 80-82; dir, Walsh Fine Arts, 83- *Teaching:* Instr papermaking workshop, Peoria Art Guild, 81- *Awards:* Purchase Award, Univ SDak, Vermillion, 80; First Place, Junction City Arts, Peoria, Ill, 82. *Mem:* Col Art Asn; World Print Coun. *Dealer:* Van Stratten Gallery 361 W Superior St Chicago IL 60610; Tower Park Gallery 4709 Prospect Peoria IL 61614. *Mailing Add:* c/o Walsh Fine Arts 1827 Winnebago Peoria IL 61614

WALSH, JANET BARBARA
PAINTER, ADMINISTRATOR
b Philadelphia, Pa, Aug 11, 39. *Study:* Art Students League, with Mario Cooper, Daniel Greene & Dale Meyers, cert, 69; Sch Visual Arts, with Francis Criss, Robert Frankenberg, cert; Silvermine Guild Artists, with Charles Reid, 79-81; also with Robert Wood, Pensacola, Fla, 81. *Exhib:* Nat Acad Design, New York; Edward Dean Mus, Cherry Valley, Calif; Charles & Emma Frye Art Mus, Seattle; Marietta Col, Ohio; Panhandle Plains, Canyon, Tex; Grants Pass Mus Art, Ore, 80. *Pos:* Studio coordr, Avon Products, 79- *Awards:* Catharine Lorillard Wolfe Award, Metrop Mus; T H Saunders Award, Artists Watercolor, 79; Gallery Award, Ky Watercolor Show, Framehouse Gallery. *Mem:* Am Watercolor Soc (corresp secy, 79-); Allied Artists; Catharine Lorillard Wolfe Art Club; Art Students League. *Media:* Watercolor. *Mailing Add:* 130 West 80th St New York NY 10024

WALSH, JOHN, JR
MUSEUM DIRECTOR
b Mason City, Wash, Dec 9, 37. *Study:* Yale Univ, BA; Univ Leiden, Netherlands; Columbia Univ, MA, PhD. *Pos:* Lectr & curatorial asst, Frick Collection, New York, 66-68; from assoc for higher educ to assoc cur of Europ paintings to cur dept of Europ paintings, Metrop Mus Art, New York, 68-75; Mrs R W Baker cur paintings, Boston Mus Fine Arts, 77-, formerly; vis prof fine arts, Harvard Univ, 79; dir, J Paul Getty Mus & Arts Int Inc, currently. *Teaching:* From adj assoc prof to prof art hist, Barnard Col & Columbia Univ, 70-77. *Mem:* Yale Univ Art Gallery Governing Bd; Col Art Asn; Am Asn Mus. *Mailing Add:* J Paul Getty Mus PO Box 2112 Santa Monica CA 90406

WALSH, PATRICIA RUTH
PAINTER
b Cleveland, Ohio. *Study:* Col Mt St Joseph, Cincinnati, BA; Art Students League; Syracuse Univ, NY, MFA. *Exhib:* Northwest Printmakers Int, Seattle Art Mus, 65; Pollution Show, Oakland Mus, 70; Three Watercolorists, San Jose Civic Art Ctr, 73; Spaces & Places, Palo Alto Cult Ctr, 75; Walnut Creek Civic Arts Ctr, 80. *Pos:* Liturgical designer, Holy Names Col, Oakland, Calif & St Clement's Church, Hayward, Calif; consult, St Francis de Sales Cathedral, Oakland. *Teaching:* Asst prof fine arts, Nazareth Col, Rochester, NY, 57-65; prof fine arts, Calif Col Arts & Crafts, 65- *Media:* Oil, Watercolor. *Mailing Add:* c/o Calif Col Arts & Crafts 5212 Broadway St Oakland CA 94618

WALTER, MAY E
COLLECTOR, PATRON

Pos: Mem art adv coun, Snite Mus Art, Notre Dame Univ; secy, trustee & mem exec comt, Am Craftsman's Coun, 62-77, hon trustee, 77- *Interests:* Patron, New York Univ Art Collection & Snite Museum of Art, Notre Dame University. *Collection:* Twentieth century masters, including Cubists and Futurists. *Mailing Add:* 923 Fifth Ave New York NY 10021

WALTER, PAUL F
COLLECTOR, PATRON

b Mt Vernon, NY, July 29, 35. *Study:* Oberlin Col, Ohio; Columbia Univ, New York. *Collections Arranged:* Indian Paintings, Morgan Libr; Indian Drawings from Paul Walter Collection, Los Angeles Co Mus. *Pos:* Trustee, Walter Found, Princeton, NJ, Byrd Hoffman Found, New York; mem photog comt, Mus Mod Art, New York, 79, Metrop Mus Art; chmn, Kitchen Ctr, New York, 67-, Friends Morgan Libr, New York, currently. *Interests:* Art education, avant garde theatre music and dance. *Collection:* Collection of Indian art; avant garde paintings, drawings and sculpture; photographs; Whistler prints and Japanese prints. *Mailing Add:* 450 East 52nd St New York NY 10022

WALTER, VALERIE HARRISSE
SCULPTOR

b Baltimore, Md, Feb 15, 92. *Study:* Md Inst, Baltimore; Art Students League; apprentice to Augustus Lukeman; Hunter Col; Col Notre Dame, Md; McCoy Col, Johns Hopkins Univ. *Work:* Gen Umberto Nobile, Aeronaut Ministry, Rome, Italy; Gorilla, John Daniel II & Bamboo (life-size bronze gorillas), Baltimore Zoo; three sculptures of gorillas, Dept Anthrop, Johns Hopkins Univ. *Comn:* Geheimrat Carl van Noorden (marble bust), Frankfurt, Ger & Vienna, 34; Charlotte (bronze head), comn by Dr Mason Faulkner Lord, Baltimore, 57; bronze bas-relief, Dr & Mrs W Waldemar W Argow, Unitarian Church, Baltimore, 62; Toni (bronze), comn by Mrs Richard O'Brien; Nathalie (bronze bust), comn by Mr J Sawyer Wilson. *Exhib:* Corcoran Gallery Art, Washington, DC; Pa Acad Fine Arts, Philadelphia; Paris Salon; San Francisco Mus Art; Hispanic Mus, New York. *Awards:* First Prize for Sculpture, Soc Washington Artists Ann. *Media:* Marble, Teak. *Mailing Add:* B-305 700 W 40th St Baltimore MD 21211

WALTERS, BILLIE
CERAMIST

b Colman, Tex, Mar 12, 27. *Study:* Univ Colo; Univ NMex, BFA, 79, MA, 81. *Work:* Univ Calgary; Ariz State Univ; Southern Conn State Col; Western NMex Univ. *Exhib:* Ceramics Int, Calgary, Alta, 73; Mus Albuquerque, 79; Los Angeles Folk Art Mus, 79; Lange Gallery, Scripps Col, Claremont, Calif; and others. *Pos:* Crafts Rep, Bd NMex Arts & Crafts Fair, 74-; Southwest cur, Women's Caucus for Art Exhib, Bronx Mus, NY, 78. *Teaching:* Instr ceramics, Univ NMex, 79-81. *Awards:* Purchase Awards, Ceramics Int, 73 & Mus Albuquerque, NMex, 79. *Bibliog:* W R Mitchell (auth), Ceramic Art of the World 1973, Govt Can, Alta, 73; Elsbeth Woody (auth), Handbuilding Ceramic Forms, Farrar Straus Giroux, New York, 79. *Mem:* Albuquerque United Artists; NMex Potters Asn; Albuquerque Designer-Craftsman. *Mailing Add:* 3835 Rio Grande Blvd NW Albuquerque NM 87107

WALTERS, ERNEST
PAINTER

b Elizabethtown, Ky, Nov 11, 27. *Study:* Univ Louisville; Univ Miami; French Studio Schs. *Work:* Mus Mod Art, New York; Israel Mus, Jerusalem; Frankfurt Mus, Ger; Albertina, Vienna, Austria; Mus d'Art Mod, Brussels, Belg. *Exhib:* IFA Galleries, Washington, DC; Galerie Richter, Wiesbaden, Ger; Siemens, Overbeck Gallery, Lubeck; Galerie Kumar, Vienna, Austria; Daedal Fine Arts, Baltimore; and others. *Media:* Oil. *Publ:* Auth, Wiener Schwarzweiss, 68; auth, An Astonished Survivor, 73. *Dealer:* IFA Galleries 2623 Connecticut Ave NW Washington DC 20008; Daedal Fine Arts Fallston Mall Fallston MD 21047. *Mailing Add:* 257 Foster Knoll Dr Joppa MD 21085

WALTERS, SYLVIA SOLOCHEK
PRINTMAKER, EDUCATOR

b Milwaukee, Wis, Aug 24, 38. *Study:* Univ Wis, Madison, BS, MS, MFA. *Work:* Elvejhem Collection, Madison; St Louis Art Mus; Francis McCray Gallery, Western NMex Univ; Seven-Up Co, St Louis; First Nat Bank of Boston. *Exhib:* Eight State Prints, J B Speed Mus, 73, 81; 3rd Hawaii Nat Prints, Honolulu Acad, 75; 3rd Graphics Biennial Metrop Mus & Art Ctr, Miami, 77, 80; Univ Utah Mus, 77; 57th Print Club, Int Competition, 81; and others. *Pos:* Graphic & book designer, Univ Wis Press, 64-67; dir Gallery 210, Univ Mo, 74-; chmn dept art, Univ Mo, 77- *Teaching:* Instr printmaking, Layton Sch of Art, 63-64; instr drawing, Doane Col, 67-68 & St Louis Univ, 68-69; prof drawing, Univ Mo, St Louis, 69-, chmn art dept, 77-81. *Awards:* Purchase Awards, Colorprint USA, 79, Vermillion, 79, 4th Miama Int Print Biennial, 80; and others. *Bibliog:* Donald Anderson (auth), The Art of Written Forms, Holt, Rinehart, Winston, 69; Nancy Rice (auth), Sylvia Solochek Walters, The St Louis Seen, fall 77; Marlene Schiller (auth), article Am Artist 10/79. *Mem:* Col Art Asn; Women's Caucus for Art; Boston Printmakers, Print Club. *Media:* Woodcut and Relief Prints, Lithography. *Publ:* Auth, American Women Printmakers, Gallery 210, Univ Mo, St Louis, 75; auth, Art on the Mississippi, 4/76 & Place, Race & Rights in St Louis, summer 76, Women Artist News. *Dealer:* Assoc Am Artists 663 Fifth Ave New York NY 10022; Nancy Singer Gallery 31 Crestwood St Louis MO 63105. *Mailing Add:* 7452 University Dr St Louis MO 63130

WALTNER, BEVERLY RULAND
PAINTER

b Kansas City, Mo. *Study:* Yale Univ, with Joseph Albers; Univ Miami, BA, 55; Kent State Univ, Blossom Kent Art Prog with Richard Anuszkiewicz, 68; Northern Ill Univ, MFA, 68. *Work:* Northern Ill Univ, De Kalb; also numerous pvt collections. *Exhib:* Tenth Mid-Western Biennial, Joslyn Art Mus, Omaha, Nebr, 68; Chautauqua Exhib Am Art, Chautauqua Art Asn, NY, 68-73 & 78; Ann Exhib, Nat Soc Painters Casein & Acrylics, New York, 69, 70, 72 & 73; 35th Ann Mid Yr Show, Butler Inst Am Art, Youngstown, Ohio, 70; Ark Nat Art Exhib, Univ Ark, Little Rock, 70; Ann Exhib Am Painting, Soc Four Arts, Palm Beach, Fla, 71 & 74. *Teaching:* Instr art, Barry Col, Miami Shores, Fla, 69-70. *Awards:* Top Award, New Horizons in Painting, N Shore Art League, 66; First Place, 68 & Louis E Seldon Mem Award, 72, Chautauqua Art Asn. *Bibliog:* Donald L Hoffman (auth), The color image, Kansas City Star, 1/19/69; Bill van Mauer (auth), Colors get her vivid messages across, Miami News, 2/8/72. *Mem:* Chautauqua Art Asn; Prof Artist Guild (treas, Miami area, 77-78, vpres, 78); Artists Equity Asn; Visual Arts Coalition. *Media:* Acrylic, Oil. *Mailing Add:* 7500 Almansa Coral Gables FL 33143

WALTON, DONALD WILLIAM
WRITER, LECTURER

b Cleveland, Ohio. *Study:* Western Reserve Univ, BA; John Huntington Art Sch. *Pos:* Dir fine arts, Franklin Mint, 69-74, managing dir, Franklin Gallery, 74-77, sr design mgr, Hallmark, 77-82. *Awards:* Doc on Norman Rockwell, Int Film Festival & NY Film Festival, 74. *Mem:* Am Fedn Arts; Nelson-Atkins Gallery. *Publ:* Auth, Art is to Enjoy, 63; auth, A Rockwell Portrait: An Intimate Biography, 78. *Mailing Add:* 330 E Bridlespur Dr Kansas City MO 64114

WALTON, FLORENCE GOODSTEIN (F GOODSTEIN-SHAPIRO)
PAINTER, HISTORIAN

b New York, NY, July 22, 31. *Study:* Cooper Union, 50-51; City Col New York, BS(art educ), 52; Hans Hofmann Sch Fine Arts, 56-57; Univ Minn, MA(art hist), 73. *Work:* Bonython Gallery, Sydney, Australia; Martin Luther King Collection, Atlanta, Ga; Augsburg Col Collection, Minneapolis; Juana Mordo Gallery, Madrid, Spain. *Exhib:* Am Watercolor Soc, Smithsonian Inst, Washington, DC, 63; Cooper Union Gallery, New York, 67; Los Angeles Co Mus Art, 69; Boynthon Art Gallery, Sydney, 69; Tweed Gallery, Univ Minn, Duluth, 71; Hamline Univ, St Paul, Minn, 76; St Cloud State Univ, Minn, 83; Peter M David Gallery, 83. *Pos:* Art prog dir, Emanuel-Midtown Y Community Ctr, 63-65; secy & pub rels dir, Aspects Gallery, New York, 64-66; dir, Artists Against War Exhib, New York, 67-68. *Teaching:* Instr art hist, Lakewood State Jr Col, 71- *Awards:* STA Award for Excellence, Art Inst Chicago, 54. *Bibliog:* New voices, Village Voice, 3/64; Artist paints death, Australian, 9/30/69; Shades of whispering glades, Sydney Morning-Herald, 9/30/69. *Mem:* Col Art Asn Am; Am Inst Archaeol; Exp Art & Technol. *Media:* Oil, Charcoal. *Res:* Pre-Hellenic Greek ware; Goya's black paintings; Indian Gupta architecture. *Publ:* Auth, Lumen room, Technol & Environ, 70. *Mailing Add:* 8066 Ruth St NE Minneapolis MN 55432

WALTON, GUY E
WRITER, EDUCATOR

b New York, NY, Oct 18, 35. *Study:* Wesleyan Univ, BA, 57; NY Univ, MA, 62, PhD, 67. *Teaching:* Assoc prof Baroque art & archit, NY Univ, 72- *Mem:* Col Art Asn; Soc Archit Historians; Soc l'Hist l'Art Francais. *Res:* Seventeenth century French and Italian sculpture; architecture and decor of palaces. *Publ:* Auth, Pierre Puget in Rome: 1662, Burlington Mag, 69; auth, L'enveloppe de Versailles ..., Bulletin Soc l'Hist l'Art Francais, 77; auth, Lievin Cruyl, In: Essays for H W Hanson, Abrams, 81; auth, The abduction of Helen, a 17th century French bronze, Bulletin Detroit Mus, 83; auth, Louis XIV's Versailles, Penguin Books (in press). *Mailing Add:* 100 Bleecker St New York NY 10012

WALTON, HARRY A, JR
COLLECTOR

b Covington, Va, Sept 24, 18. *Study:* Univ Va, 37; Columbia Univ, 39; Lynchburg Col, AB, 39. *Exhib:* Works have been exhibited in libraries at: Trinity Col, Washington, DC, Col William & Mary, Norfolk Mus Art & Sci, Univ Va & Lynchburg Col. *Mem:* Fel Pierpont-Morgan Libr, NY; Univ Va Bibliog Soc. *Collection:* Early books and manuscripts, Bibles, fine binding, Aldinae and first editions. *Mailing Add:* White Oak Dairy Box 790 Covington VA 24426

WALTON, MARION (MARION WALTON PUTNAM)
SCULPTOR

b New Rochelle, NY, Nov 19, 1899. *Study:* Bryn Mawr Col; Art Students League; Acad Grande Chaumiere, Paris, with Antoine Bourdelle. *Work:* Lincoln Mus, Nebr; Mus Winter Park, Fla; and many pvt collections in US, France, Eng, Italy & Sweden. *Comn:* World's Fair, US Govt, 39; Post Off mural, US Govt; and many pvt comn. *Exhib:* Whitney Mus Am Art, New York; Metrop Mus Art, New York; Art Inst Chicago; La Jeune Sculpture, Rodin Mus, Paris, France; Pa Acad Fine Arts; Philadelphia Mus Art; Triennale Europ de Sculpture, Palais Royal, Paris; Bienalle Int, Ravenna, Italy, 79; and many others. *Teaching:* Prof sculpture, Sarah Lawrence Col, 50-51; pvt lessons, currently. *Awards:* Gold Medal, Bicnalle Int, Ravenna, Italy, 79. *Bibliog:* Mag Art, Am Fedn Art, 7/40; M Seuphor (auth), La Sculpture de ce Siecle, 59. *Mem:* Sculptors Guild; Artists Equity Asn. *Media:* Mixed. *Mailing Add:* 49 Irving Pl New York NY 10003

WALTZER, STEWART PAUL
DEALER, PAINTER
b New York, NY, Mar 17, 48. *Study:* NY Univ, BA, 69, MA, 70; Columbia Univ; New York Studio Sch; also with Irving Sandler, Audrey Flack, Chuck Close & Kenneth Noland. *Exhib:* City Univ New York; Sarah Y Rentschler Gallery, 79; Martin Gerard, 80; Gallery Don Stewart, 84. *Pos:* Dir, Andre Emmerich Gallery Downtown, 72-74, Tibor de Nagy Gallery, 74-77 & Meredith Long Contemp, 77-79; pres, Waltzer & Assocs, 79- *Awards:* Gallery Don Stewart 1460 Sherbrooke St W Montreal Canada. *Specialty:* American 20th. *Dealer:* Galeria Joan Prats 29 W 57th St New York NY. *Mailing Add:* Waltzer & Co 262 Bowery New York NY 10019

WANDS, ALFRED JAMES
PAINTER
b Cleveland, Ohio, Feb 19, 04. *Study:* Cleveland Art Inst, BFA; Western Reserve Univ, BS; Univ Colo; Acad Julien, Paris; John Huntington Inst. *Work:* Cleveland Art Mus; Brooklyn Mus Arts & Sci; Calif Palace of Legion of Honor, San Francisco; Denver Art Mus; Colo Springs Fine Arts Ctr. *Comn:* Five Colorado landscapes, Denver Pub Schs, 46; Christ in the Temple (mural), Grant Ave Methodist Church, Denver, 47; mural of Rocky Mountains, YMCA of the Rockies, Denver, 67; elk (mural), Rocky Mountain Nat Park, Estes Park, Colo, 75; two oils, Colorado Springs Fine Arts Ctr, 78. *Exhib:* Carnegie Inst Int, Pittsburgh; Corcoran Art Gallery Biennial, Washington, DC; Art Inst Chicago Am Ann; Kansas City Art Inst Midwestern Ann, Mo; Denver Art Mus Ann. *Pos:* Chmn, Denver Art Comn, 45-61. *Teaching:* Instr painting, Cleveland Art Inst, 26-30; prof painting & drawing, Colo Women's Col, Denver, 30-47; instr painting, Univ Colo, Denver, 47-50. *Awards:* Silver Medal, Kansas City Art Inst, 42; Best in Show & First Painting, Denver Artists Guild Ann Exhib, 81; and others. *Mem:* Denver Artists Guild (pres, 32, 41 & 63); Carmel Art Asn; Col Art Asn Am (secy, Colo Chap, 36-42). *Media:* Oil, Watercolor. *Publ:* Auth, How to Paint Mountains, 75. *Dealer:* Studio Art Gallery San Carlos & Ocean Carmel CA 93921. *Mailing Add:* 2065 Ivanhoe St Denver CO 80207

WANDS, ROBERT JAMES
EDUCATOR, PAINTER
b Denver, Colo, June 24, 39. *Study:* With Alfred Wands, 56-60; Univ Denver, BFA, 61, MA, 63; Cleveland Art Inst; Western Reserve Univ. *Work:* Univ Denver; Colo Womens Col; Western Colo Ctr Arts, Grand Junction; Univ Southern Colo. *Comn:* Painting, Fine Am Art Calendar, Cleveland, 70; murals, Cleopatra Health Spa, Pueblo, Colo, 76 & YMCA, Estes Park, Colo, 77; paintings, United Bank, Pueblo, Colo, 78 & Republic Bank, Pueblo, Colo, 79. *Exhib:* Own Your Own Art Shows, Sangre Cristo Art Ctr, Pueblo, Colo, 63-83; S S Hope Invitational, Butler Inst Am Art, 70; Colo Biennial, Denver Art Mus, 72; I-25 Artist Alliance, Colorado Springs Fine Arts Ctr, 72 & Dangre Cristo Art Ctr, Pueblo, Colo, 73; solo exhib, Sangre Cristo Art Ctr, Pueblo, Colo, 73, Western Colo Ctr Arts, Grand Junction, 74 & Univ Southern Colo, 81. *Pos:* Artist in residence, Asn Camp, Estes Park, Colo, summers 74-78. *Teaching:* Instr painting, Univ Denver, 63; assoc prof, Univ Southern Colo, 63- *Awards:* Purchase Prize, 65 & Meritorious Award, 72, Colo State Fair; Best of Show, Own Your Own Art Show, Sangre Cristo Art Ctr, 79. *Media:* Acrylic, Oil. *Dealer:* Off Broadway Art Galleries 119 Broadway Pueblo CO 81004. *Mailing Add:* 1306 W Abriendo Pueblo CO 81004

WANG, CHI-CHIEN
PAINTER
b Soochow, China, Feb 14, 07. *Study:* Soochow Univ, grad. *Work:* Brooklyn Mus Art, NY; Art Mus, Princeton Univ, NJ; Bank of Am, San Francisco; Fogg Mus, Boston. *Exhib:* The New Chinese Landscape, Six Contemporary Chinese Artists, 66; De Young Mem Mus, San Francisco, 68; Indianapolis Mus Art, 72; Fogg Mus, Harvard Univ, 73; Watercolor Soc, Nat Acad Art & Design, New York, 74. *Teaching:* Prof art, Shanghai Acad Art, 33-34; vis lectr, Columbia Univ, New York, 51-52 & Univ Calif, Berkeley, 68-69; chmn art dept, Chinese Univ, Hong Kong, 62-64. *Mem:* China Inst. *Mailing Add:* 150 E 69th St New York NY 10021

WANG, SAM
PHOTOGRAPHER
b Peking, China, Apr 4, 39; US citizen. *Study:* Augustana Col, Sioux Falls, BA, 64; Univ Iowa, MFA, 66. *Work:* Greenville Co Mus Art, SC; Metrop Mus Art, NY; Mint Mus Art, Charlotte, NC; Herbert F Johnson Mus Art, Ithaca, NY; Chase Manhattan Collection; and others. *Comn:* E R photo-serigraph, Piedmont Mortgage and Loan, Greenville, 74. *Exhib:* Contemp Directions, Addison Gallery Am Art, 75; Silver & Silk, Mus of Hist & Technol, Smithsonian Inst, 75-77; Translations: Photography in New Forms, Herbert F Johnson Mus, 79; one-man shows, Photoserigraphs, Mint Mus Art, 70, Greenville Co Mus Art, 72, 77 & 81 & Light Factory, 79, RI Sch Design Photog Gallery, 79 & Fay Gold Gallery, 83; Counterparts, Metrop Mus Art, San Francisco Mus Mod Art & Corcoran Gallery Art, 83. *Pos:* Mem bd dir, Soc Photog Educ, New York, 73-77; chmn, State Art Collections Comm, SC, 77-78. *Teaching:* Prof photog & printmaking, Clemson Univ, SC, 66-; vis artist photog & graphics, Penland Sch of Crafts, NC, summers 70, 74, 79 & 81; vis artist printmaking workshop, Univ Notre Dame, 79. *Awards:* Unicolor Artist Support Award, 83. *Bibliog:* David Featherstone (auth), Art Week, 73; Joe Earle (auth), Artist collects photgraphy as his raw material, Greenville-Piedmont, 77. *Mem:* Soc Photog Educ (bd dirs, 73-77); Guild SC Artists; Southeastern Col Art Conf. *Media:* Photoserigraphy; Photography. *Publ:* Illusr, South Carolina Architecture 1670-1970, SC Tricentennial Comn, 70; illusr, New Am Nudes, Morgan & Morgan, 81. *Mailing Add:* 108 Poole Lane Clemson SC 29631

WANLASS, STANLEY GLEN
SCULPTOR, PAINTER
b American Fork, Utah, Apr 3, 41. *Study:* Brigham Young Univ, BFA, 66, MA, 68. *Work:* Fr Clatsop Nat Mem, Ore; Springville Art Mus, Utah; Hutchings Mus, Lehi, Utah; Mus Western Expansion, St Louis, Mo. *Comn:* Portrait of founder John Hutchings, Hutchings Mus, Lehi, Utah, 66; mural, Wash Nat Life Insurance Co, Tacoma, 66; Surf II (sculpture), Wash State Arts Comn, Everett, 76; corp image, symbol & box design, Magic Mill Inc, Salt Lake City, Utah, 78; bronze statue, Nat Park Serv, 83. *Exhib:* Cour de Maison, Univ Grenoble Ecole de Beau Arts, Gallerie Vieux-Temple, Grenoble, France, 70; Des Arts Graphiques, Palais des Cong, Paris, France, 76; Pageant Arts, Utah, 81; Squibb Gallery, Princeton, NJ, 83; Hermitage Plantation, Sandwich, Mass, 83; and others. *Teaching:* Instr painting, drawing & design, Brigham Young Univ, Provo, Utah, 65-70; instr drawing, Europ Art Acad, Paris, summer 66; prof painting, drawing, design & art hist, Univ Grenoble, France, 69-70; prof drawing & design, Medicine Hat Col, Univ Calgary, Alta, summers 70 & 71; prof painting, drawing & design, Clatsop Col, Astoria, Ore, 71- *Awards:* Merrill/Brockbank Awards, 65 & Brigham Young Univ, 66; Bicentennial Medal Design, State Ore, Franklin Mint, Pa, 72; Silver Medal, Springville Art Mus, Utah, 81. *Bibliog:* Bicentennial by design, Am Artist Mag, 3/73; Peggy & Harold Samuels (auth), Contemporary Western Artists, SW Art Publ Co, 82; Gorodn Chism (auth), article, SW Art Mag, 82; and others. *Media:* Bronze, Cor-Ten Steel; Acrylic, Oil. *Publ:* Contribr, ser of running articles on lost wax casting, In: Bronze Casting: An Art in Itself, Lehi Free Press, 78. *Dealer:* Grand Cent Art Galleries Inc 43rd & Madison Ave New York NY 10017. *Mailing Add:* 907 Fifth St Astoria OR 97103

WARASHINA, M PATRICIA
CERAMIST, EDUCATOR
b Spokane, Wash. *Study:* Univ Wash, Seattle, BFA, MFA. *Work:* Everson Art Mus, Syracuse, NY; Nelson Gallery of Art, Kansas City, Mo; Detroit Art Inst, Mich; Henry Art Gallery, Seattle, Wash; John Michael Kohler Arts Ctr, Sheboygan, Wis. *Exhib:* Int Exhib of Ceramics, Victoria & Albert Mus, London, Eng, 72; Sensible Cup Int Exhib, Sea of Japan Expos, Kanazawa, Japan, 73; Clay, Whitney Mus of Am Art, New York, 74; 1st World Crafts Exhib, Ont Sci Ctr, Toronto, 74; The Collector, Mus of Contemp Crafts, New York, 74; NW 77 Exhib, Mod Art Pavilion, Seattle Ctr, Wash, 77. *Teaching:* Instr art, Wis State Univ, Platteville, 64-65; instr art, Eastern Mich Univ, Ypsilanti, 66-68; prof art, Univ Wash, Seattle, 70- *Media:* Clay. *Dealer:* Foster/White Art Gallery 311 1/2 Occidental Ave S Seattle WA 98104. *Mailing Add:* 1404 E Lynn Seattle WA 98112

WARBURG, STEPHANIE WENNER
PAINTER, INSTRUCTOR
b Kalamazoo, Mich, Dec 29, 41. *Study:* Univ Mich Col Archit & Design, BS(drawing & design); and with Guy Palazzola, Milton Cohen & Mildred Fairchild; Columbia Univ Teachers Col, MA(fine arts & fine arts educ). *Exhib:* Mystic Art Mus Regional Show, Conn, 68; Slater Mus, Norwich, Conn, 69; Gilman Gallery, Chicago, 72; Lord & Taylor Gallery, New York, 72; Flora & Fauna of Madeira, Funchal, Madeira, Portugal, 73. *Pos:* Artistic consult, New Eng Conserv Music, Boston, 74- *Teaching:* Chmn, Dept Art, Latin Sch Chicago, 70-72; instr watercolor & freehand drawing, Chamberlayne Jr Col, Boston, 75- *Awards:* Am Cancer Soc Art Awards, 67 & 68; Lyme Art Asn Second Prize for Painting, 68. *Bibliog:* Susan Croce Kelly (auth), It's all in the family: Sister artists display work here, St Louis Globe Dem, 70; On exhibit, Where Mag, 12/72. *Media:* Impasto, Oil Wash. *Dealer:* Paine Furniture Co Boston MA 02116. *Mailing Add:* 360 Beacon St Boston MA 02116

WARD, EVELYN SVEC
TAPESTRY ARTIST, COLLAGE ARTIST
b Solon, Ohio. *Study:* Otterbein Col, BA; Sorbonne, Paris. *Work:* Cleveland Mus Art; Otterbein Col, Cleveland. *Exhib:* Fibre Structures, Mus of Art, Carnegie Inst, Pittsburgh, Pa, 76; one-person shows, Ross Widen Gallery, 77 & 81 & Otterbein Col, Westerville, Ohio, 83; Miniature Fiber Arts (nat exhib), Armory of Arts, Santa Fe, NMex, 79; Beaux Arts Designer/Craftsmen '79, Columbus Mus Art, Ohio, 79; Int Biennale Exhib of Lace, Palais Congres, Brussels, Belgium, 83; and others. *Collections Arranged:* Fiberworks, Cleveland Mus of Art (auth, catalog), 77. *Pos:* Textile asst, Cleveland Mus of Art, 50-55. *Awards:* Juror mention, May Show, Cleveland Mus of Art, 57 & 67; Distinguished Alumni Award for Spec Achievement Fine Arts, Otterbein Col, 79. *Bibliog:* D Z Meilach (auth), Art from Fibres and Fabrics, 72 & Virginia C Bath (auth), Lace, 74, Henry Regnery Co; Mildred Constantine & Jack Larsen (co-auth), The art fabric: Mainstream, Van Nostrand Reinhold, 81. *Mem:* Textile Arts Club (pres, 64-66); Women's Comt, Cleveland Inst of Art; Am Crafts Coun; Ohio Designer Craftsmen; Cleveland Soc for Contemp Art. *Dealer:* Ross Widen Gallery 5120 Mayfield Rd Cleveland OH 44124. *Mailing Add:* 27045 Solon Rd Solon OH 44139

WARD, JOHN LAWRENCE
HISTORIAN, PAINTER
b East Orange, NJ, Feb 6, 38. *Study:* Hamilton Col, BA; Yale Univ, MA(art hist); Univ NMex, MFA(painting). *Work:* Univ NMex; Miss Mus Art, Jackson. *Exhib:* One-man shows, Fla Tech Univ, Orlando, 76 & Univ of Fla, Gainesville, 76; The Human Presence, Jacksonville Art Mus, Fla, 74; Southeastern Ctr for Contemp Art, Winston-Salem, NC, 79; Southern Realism, Miss Mus Art & traveling, 79; plus others. *Teaching:* Assoc prof art hist, Univ Fla, 62-64 & 66- *Mem:* Col Art Asn. *Media:* Oil. *Res:* Flemish painting, pictorial space construction and perception; criticism of photography. *Publ:* Auth, A new look at the Friedsam Annunciation, Vol L, 68, Art Bulletin; auth, The criticism of photography as art: The photographs

of Jerry Uelsmann, 70; auth, A proposed reconstruction of an altarpiece by Rogier Van der Weyden, Vol LIII, 71 & Hidden symbolism in Jan Van Eyck's Annunciations, Vol LVII, 75, Art Bulletin; auth, The Perspective of Pictorial Space in Perspective Pictures, Vol IX, Leonardo, 76. *Mailing Add:* Art Dept AFA Univ of Fla Gainesville FL 32611

WARD, LYLE EDWARD
PAINTER, EDUCATOR

b Topeka, Kans, Feb 4, 22. *Study:* Stevens Point State Teachers Col, Wis, 43; Kansas City Univ, 50; Kansas City Art Inst, BFA, 51, MFA, 52; also with Miron Sokole, New York, 46-52. *Work:* Brooklyn Mus, NY; Corcoran Gallery, Washington, DC; Butler Inst Am Art, Youngstown, Ohio; Mus Art, Univ Okla, Norman; Mulvane Art Mus, Topeka. *Exhib:* One-man shows, Kansas City Art Inst, 60, Superior St Gallery, Chicago, 60 & Univ Miss, Oxford, 72; Avanti Galleries, New York, 75; Treishman Gallery, Hendrix Col, Conway, Ark, 76. *Teaching:* Prof art & chmn dept, Col of the Ozarks, Clarksville, Ark, 56- *Awards:* Arts Festival Award, Worthen Bank, Little Rock, 60 & 62; First Prize, Delta Exhib, Ark Arts Ctr, 63, 65 & 67; 18th Arts Festival Award, Ft Smith Festival Bd, Ark, 68. *Bibliog:* Gordon Brown (auth), article, Arts Mag, 75; Ed Albin (auth), cover story & rev, Art Voices/S, 79; Lyle Ward (auth), article, Art Voices/S Ark, 79. *Mem:* Col Art Asn Am; Mid-Am Art Asn; Southeast Art Conf. *Media:* Oil. *Publ:* Auth, articles, Southwest Times, 68, Ark Gazette, 74, Arts Mag, 75, Art Voices, 79. *Dealer:* Avanti Galleries 145 E 72nd St New York NY 10021. *Mailing Add:* 610 Johnson St Clarksville AR 72830

WARD, LYND (KENDALL)
ILLUSTRATOR, WRITER

b Chicago, Ill, June 26, 05. *Study:* Teachers Col, Columbia Univ, BS, 26; Staatliche Akad Graphische Kunst, Leipzig, Ger, 26-27. *Work:* Libr Cong; New York World's Fair, 39; Nat Acad Design; Newark Mus; Metrop Mus Art; and others. *Exhib:* Am Art Cong; New York World's Fair, 39; Nat Acad Design; John Herron Art Inst. *Awards:* Prize, Nat Acad Design, 49, John Taylor Arms Mem Prize, 62; Samuel F B Morse Gold Medal, 66; Rutgers Medal, 69; and others. *Mem:* Academician Nat Acad Design; Soc Am Graphic Artists (pres, 53-59); Soc Illusr. *Publ:* Auth & illusr (novels in woodcuts), God's Man, 29, Madman's Drum, 30, Song Without Words, 36 & Vertigo, 37; auth & illusr, Nic of the Woods, 65; and others. *Mailing Add:* 11-782 Indian Ridge Rd Reston VA 22091

WARD, PHILLIP A
CERAMIST, EDUCATOR

b Melrose, Mass, April 10, 27. *Study:* Sch Mus Fine Arts, Boston, dipl(hon), 50; Tulane Univ, MFA, 59. *Work:* Mus Fine Arts, Boston; Univ Fla Gallery, Gainesville; Stetson Univ; Johnson Wax Collection, Racine, Wis. *Comn:* Altar wall tiles, Cathedral in the Pines, Tample, NH, 75; Abode II (wall relief), comn by G Leonard Emmel, Gainesville, 64; Abode III (wall relief), comn by Michael Schoeffel, Gainesville, 69; Presentation Urns, Nat Asn Ceramic Engineers, Gainesville, 75; atrium pool & fountain, comn by Harvey Sharron, Gainesville, 78. *Exhib:* Syracuse Ceramic Nat, Everson Mus, 55 & 66; Piedmont Crafts Exhib, 64-72 & Regional Sculpture Invitational, 72, Mint Mus; Coastal States Invitational, Jacksonville Mus, Jax, Fla, 73; Southeast Invitational, Greenville Co Mus, SC, 74; one-man show, Stetson Univ, 77 & Ctr Mod Art, Micanopy, Fla, 78; Fla Fac Invitational, Fla Int Univ, 78; and others. *Teaching:* Fel ceramics, Tulane Univ, 58; prof art, Univ Fla, Gainesville, 59- *Awards:* Purchase Award, Piedmont Craft Exhib, Mint Mus Art, 70, Fla Craftsmen Exhib, Walter Heller Corp, 71 & Middle Tenn State Univ, 72. *Bibliog:* Jack Nicholson (auth), Phillip & Jacqueline Ward, Craft Horizons, 5-6/68; article, Ceramics Monthly, 68; article, Craft Horizons, 1-2/70. *Mem:* Am Crafts Coun (pres southeast region, 65-67); Fla Craftsmen (pres, 67 & 68). *Media:* Ceramics. *Mailing Add:* 3624 SW 18th St Gainesville FL 32608

WARD, WILLIAM EDWARD
DESIGNER, PAINTER

b Cleveland, Ohio, Apr 4, 22. *Study:* Western Reserve Univ, BS, 47, MA, 48; Cleveland Inst Art, dipl, 47; Columbia Univ, 50. *Work:* Cleveland Mus Art; Akron Art Inst, Ohio; Cleveland Art Asn; Cleveland Trust Bank. *Comn:* Firemen's Memorial (sculpture), Cleveland Fire Dept, 68; official seal for Sch of Med & Case Western Reserve Univ, 69; traveling exhib for George Gund Collection Western Art, New York, 72; mural, Harris Corp, Cleveland, 75; installation design, Am Ceramic Soc Mus, 81. *Exhib:* One-man shows, Painting & Photography, Cleveland Inst Art, 48 & Acrylics & Watercolors, Ross Widen Gallery, Cleveland, 73, 78 & 80; Cleveland Inst Art Fac Exhib, 60-; Wheaton Col, Ill, 69; Ohio Fine Arts Exhib, Massilon Mus Art, Ohio, 75. *Collections Arranged:* All special exhibition and permanent collection installations, Cleveland Mus Art, 58- *Pos:* Educ & Oriental Depts asst, Cleveland Mus Art, 47-57, designer, 57- *Teaching:* Prof calligraphy, Cleveland Inst Art, 60-, instr watercolor, 67-69. *Awards:* First Prize in Textile Design, Cleveland Mus Art May Show, 57; City Canvas Competition Comn Award, Cleveland Area Arts Coun, 75; Design Award, Champion Int Order Roundtable, 78. *Mem:* Int Design Conf; City of Cleveland Fine Arts Adv Comt; Cleveland Soc Contemp Art; Print Club Cleveland; The Rowfant Club. *Media:* Watercolor, Acrylic. *Collection:* Folk art of Oaxaca, Mexico area and Kalighat paintings from the Calcutta region, India. *Dealer:* Ross Widen Gallery 5120 Mayfield Rd Cleveland OH 44124. *Mailing Add:* 27045 Solon Rd Solon OH 44139

WARDER, WILLIAM
PAINTER, WRITER

b Guadalupita, NMex, July 23, 20. *Study:* Univ NMex, with Raymond Jonson, Kenneth Adams & Randall Davey, BFA; Art Students League, with Louis Bouche & Morris Kantor; Univ Calif, Los Angeles. *Work:* Art Mus NMex, Santa Fe; NMex State Fair Collection, Albuquerque; Mus Albuquerque; Raton Mus, NMex. *Comn:* Tom Sawyer & Huck, Works Progress Admin Proj, 36; mural Army life, Ft Warren, Wyo, 43; NMex hist murals, Int State Bank, Raton, 70. *Exhib:* Am Watercolor Soc, Nat Acad, New York, 48; Audubon Artists Exhib, 48; New York World's Fair Ford Pavillion Nat Exhib, 64; Watercolor USA, Springfield, Mo, 64 & 73; Southwest Fine Arts Biennial, Mus NMex, 74. *Pos:* Writer/producer, Educ TV, KNME, Channel 5, Albuquerque, NMex; mural painter, Albuquerque Pub Schs. *Teaching:* Artist-in-sch, Las Vegas, NMex, 71-73 & Espanola, 74-75, Albuquerque, 74-; lectr & workshops on creative process in pub schs in Southwest. *Awards:* Nat Endowment Arts Grants, 71-75; Gold Medal, Int Platform Assocs Art, 78; Writer/Producer/Talent Award for How to be an Artist (educ television prog series), 79; and others. *Bibliog:* Senator Peter Domenici (auth), speech entered into US Cong Dirs, 6/25/73; Artist-in-schools, NMex Sch Rev, Spring 74 & Falls 77-78. *Media:* Watercolor, Oil. *Res:* Distinguishing the self and person as two entities in the individual that relate to intrinsic creativity and the extrinsic social productivity as bases for educational orientations. *Publ:* Auth, Alternative Approach in Education Using Art as the Medium, 74. *Dealer:* Brandywine Galleries 120 Morningside Dr SE Albuquerque NM 87108. *Mailing Add:* Box 201 DD Tijeras NM 87059

WARDLAW, GEORGE MELVIN
PAINTER, SCULPTOR

b Baldwyn, Miss, Apr 9, 27. *Study:* Memphis Acad Arts, BFA, 51; Univ Miss, with David Smith & Jack Tworkov, MFA, 55. *Work:* DeCordova Mus, Lincoln, Mass; Mus Fine Arts, Springfield, Mass. *Comn:* Wall relief sculpture, 76 & sculpture, 76, Mt Sinai Med Ctr. *Exhib:* Abstract Paintings, 71 & solo exhib, 78-79, DeCordova Mus, Lincoln, Mass; Chicago Art Inst; Metrop Mus Art, New York; Nat Gallery; Portland Mus Art, Maine. *Teaching:* Asst prof art, State Univ NY Col, New Paltz, 56-63; assoc prof painting & exec off, Yale Univ, 64-68; prof painting & chmn dept, Univ Mass, Amherst, 68- *Awards:* Miss Inst Arts & Lett Award, 83; Univ Mass Fac Res Fel, 83. *Media:* Acrylic; Metal. *Dealer:* Stux Gallery Boston MA. *Mailing Add:* 47 Morgan Circle Amherst MA 01002

WARDWELL, ALLEN
MUSEUM DIRECTOR

b New York, NY, Jan 18, 35. *Study:* Yale Univ, BA, 57; NY Univ, MA, 60. *Collections Arranged:* Yakutat South Indian Art of the Northwest Coast (auth, catalogue), 64, The Sculpture of Polynesia (auth, catalogue), 67 & The Art of the Sepik River (auth, catalogue), 71, Art Inst of Chicago; Gold of Ancient America (auth, catalogue), Mus of Fine Arts, Boston, 68; Objects of Bright Pride, Northwest Coast Indian Art from the American Museum of Natural History (auth, catalogue), Am Fedn Arts, 78. *Pos:* Asst cur of primitive art, Art Inst of Chicago, 60-63, cur primitive art, 63-73, actg cur of decorative arts, 64-70 & asst dir mus serv, 70-72; dir, Asia Soc Gallery, 74- *Mem:* Yale Univ Art Gallery; Asn of Am Mus Dirs; Indo-US Subcomn on Educ & Cult. *Publ:* Contribr, Bibliography Northwest Coast Indian Art, Mus of Primitive Art, Art Inst of Chicago, 70. *Mailing Add:* 725 Park Avenue New York NY 10021

WARHOL, ANDY
PAINTER, FILMMAKER

b Cleveland, Ohio, Aug 8, 31. *Study:* Carnegie Inst Technol, 45-49. *Work:* Albright-Knox Art Gallery, Buffalo; Los Angeles Co Mus Art; Whitney Mus Am Art, Mus Mod Art, New York; Walker Art Ctr, Minneapolis; and others. *Exhib:* The 1960's, Mus Mod Art, 67; Baltimore Mus Art, 75; Art Inst Chicago, 75; Whitney Mus Am Art, 74 & 80; Mus Mod Art, New York, 80; New Orleans Mus, La, 80; Portland Ctr Visual Arts, Ore, 80; Mus Fine Arts, St Petersburg, Fla, 80; Chrysler Mus, Norfolk, Va, 80; Castelli Graphics, New York, 81; Ronald Feldman Fine Arts, New York, 81; and others. *Awards:* Sixth Film Cult Award, 64; Los Angeles Film Festival Award, 64. *Bibliog:* Peter Gidal (auth), Andy Warhol: Films and Paintings, 71; Daniela Palazzoli (auth), L'Arte nella Societa: Fotografia, Cinema, Videotape, 76; John Szarkowski (auth), Mirrors and Windows: American Photography since 1960, 78. *Mem:* Film Co-op. *Publ:* Auth, The Philosophy of Andy Warhol: From A to B and Back Again, 75; auth, Andy Warhol's Exposures, 79; auth, Andy Warhol: Portraits of the Seventies, 79; coauth, Popism: The Warhol Sixties, 80. *Dealer:* Leo Castelli Gallery 420 W Broadway New York NY 10013. *Mailing Add:* Andy Warhol Enterprises 860 Broadway New York NY 10003

WARK, ROBERT RODGER
ADMINISTRATOR, HISTORIAN

b Edmonton, Alta, Oct 7, 24; US citizen. *Study:* Univ Alta, BA & MA; Harvard Univ, MA & PhD. *Pos:* Cur art, Huntington Libr & Art Gallery, 56- *Teaching:* Instr art, Harvard Univ, 52-54; instr art, Yale Univ, 54-56; lectr art, Calif Inst Technol, 60-; lectr art, Univ Calif, Los Angeles, 65- *Mem:* Col Art Asn Am; Asn Art Mus Dirs. *Res:* English art of the Georgian period. *Publ:* Ed, Sir Joshua Reynolds, Discourses on Art, 59; auth, Early British Drawings in the Huntington Collection 1700-1750, 69; auth, Drawings by John Flaxman in the Huntington Collection, 70; auth, Ten British Pictures 1740-1840, auth, Drawings by Thomas Rowlandson in the Huntington Collection, 75; plus others. *Mailing Add:* Henry E Huntington Libr & Art Gallery 1151 Oxford Rd San Marino CA 91108

WARKOV, ESTHER
PAINTER
b Winnipeg, Man, Oct 12, 41. *Study:* Winnipeg Sch Art, 58-61. *Work:* Nat Gallery, Ottawa; Mus Fine Arts, Montreal; Vancouver Art Gallery; Winnipeg Art Gallery; Beaver Brook Art Gallery, Fredricton, NB. *Exhib:* Expo '67, Montreal; Marlborough Godard Exhib, 73; Mus Mod Art, Paris, 73; Albright Knox Art Gallery, Buffalo, 74. *Awards:* Can Coun Bursaries, 67-72; Can Coun Grant, 73-74. *Bibliog:* Esther Warkov, Can Broadcasting Corp, 73. *Mem:* Royal Can Acad Arts. *Media:* Oil. *Dealer:* Marlborough Godard Ltd 1490 Sherbrooke W Montreal PQ Can. *Mailing Add:* 341 Matheson Ave Winnipeg MB R2W 0C9 Canada

WARNER, BOYD, JR
PAINTER
b Kaibeto, Ariz, May 26, 37. *Work:* In the pvt collections of James T Bialec, Phoenix, Ariz; Dick Van Dyke, Cave Creek, Ariz; Alan Alda, Senator & Mrs Barry Goldwater, Ariz; James Buchanan, Okla; Dr Gentile, Mesa, Ariz; Glenn Ford and others. *Exhib:* Heard Mus Indian Art Show, Phoenix, 69-71; Ariz State Fair, Phoenix, 69-71; 27th Indian Art Show, Philbrook Art Ctr, Tulsa, Okla, 72; one-man shows, Garelick's Gallery, Scottsdale, Ariz, 77 & Birmingham Gallery Inc, Mich, 77; and others. *Awards:* Grand Award for portrait of A Smiling Indian, Scottsdale Nat Indian Art Show, 75; First Award for painting Shalako, NMex State Fair, 74; First & Second Award, NMex State Fair, 76; and others. *Mailing Add:* 3734 W Dunlap #C-4 Phoenix AZ 85021

WARNER, DOUGLAS WARFIELD
PAINTER, EDUCATOR
b Tulsa, Okla, June 8, 30. *Study:* Okla State Univ, BFA, 53; Univ Wis, MS(art), 57. *Work:* Brit Mus, London; Smithsonian Inst & Libr Cong, Washington, DC; Cleveland Mus Art, Ohio; Calif Palace Legion Honor, San Francisco. *Comn:* Nine Sculptures, Flint Bd Educ, Mich, 75; Public Canvas I (billboard), Michelob Lite, Flint, Mich, 81; painting, Perfusions Services Inc, Brighton, Mich. *Exhib:* 154th Ann Drawing Exhib, Pa Acad Fine Arts, Philadelphia, 59; Mich Artists' Ann, Detroit Inst Art, 59, 60, 61 & 65; Drawing USA, St Paul Art Ctr, Minn, 63; Am Sculpture 1900-1965, Flint Inst Arts, Mich, 65; 19th Exhib Prints & Drawings, Okla Art Ctr, Oklahoma City, 77; Six Printmakers, Univ Nev, Reno, 79; Mich Watercolor Soc, 80 & 81; Denver Mus Art; plus others. *Teaching:* Instr drawing & design, C S Mott Community Col, Flint, Mich, 57-, chmn dept art, 63-67. *Awards:* Purchase Awards, Philbrook Art Ctr, 53, Okla Art Ctr, 77 & Mich Coun Arts, 78. *Bibliog:* S Gordon Gapper (auth), Flint profile, Flint J, 4/3/66. *Mem:* Mich Watercolor Soc; Mich Asn Printmakers. *Media:* Pencil and Paint on Paper. *Dealer:* Xochipilli Gallery 568 N Woodward Ave Birmingham MI 48063. *Mailing Add:* 619 Commonwealth Ave Flint MI 48503

WARNER, HERBERT KELII, JR
INSTRUCTOR, PRINTMAKER
b Honolulu, Hawaii, July 29, 43. *Study:* Univ Hawaii, BFA, 67; Pratt Inst, MFA, 72. *Work:* Rutgers Univ, Camden, NJ. *Exhib:* Purdue Univ, West Lafayette, Ind, 77; Okla Nat Drawing & Prints, Oklahoma City, 77; Asn Am Artists, New York, 77; Libr Cong, Washington, DC, 77; Trenton State Mus, NJ, 80. *Teaching:* Asst prof, Rutgers Univ, Camden, NJ, 72-79; teacher design, Art Inst Philadelphia, 80-82. *Awards:* Purchase Awards, Purdue Univ, 77 & Honolulu Acad Arts, 77; Fel, State NJ, 78. *Mem:* Print Coun NJ; Artists Equity Asn; Pratt Graphic Soc. *Media:* Etching, Lithography. *Mailing Add:* 5425 Walker St Philadelphia PA 19124

WARNER, JO
PAINTER
b Clayton, NMex, Apr 30, 31. *Study:* Univ Colo, Boulder, BFA; Skowhegan Sch Painting & Sculpture, Maine, with Jack Levine & Henry V Poor; Art Students League, with Morris Kantor & Byron Brown. *Exhib:* Recent American Painting & Sculpture, Mus Mod Art Circulating Exhib, 61-63; West Side Artists-New York City, Riverside Mus, 64; Kutztown State Col Mus, Pa, 75; Tenth St Days--The Co-ops of the 50s, New York, NY, 77; solo exhibs, Univ Wis-Eau Claire Mus, 64 & 79 & Phoenix Gallery, New York, 72 & 76. *Awards:* Award & Ganeles Prize Sculpture, Nat Asn Women Artists, 74. *Mem:* Women in Arts. *Media:* Oil, Collage. *Dealer:* Phoenix Gallery 30 W 57th St New York NY 10019. *Mailing Add:* 142 West End Ave New York NY 10023

WARREN, BETTY
PAINTER, INSTRUCTOR
b New York, NY. *Study:* Nat Acad Design; Cape Sch Art, with Henry Hensche. *Work:* Albany Inst Hist & Art, NY; State Univ NY, Albany; Albany Law Sch, NY; Univ Wis, Madison; NY State Supreme Court, Albany; and others. *Exhib:* Allied Artists Am, New York, 65 & 67; Am Watercolor Soc, New York, 66; Nat Arts Club Nat, New York, 69-71; Knickerbocker Artists, New York; Pastel Soc Am; and others. *Pos:* Owner & dir, Malden Bridge Sch Art, NY, 65- *Teaching:* Instr painting & drawing, Albany Inst Hist & Art, 59-75. *Awards:* Purchase Prizes, Albany Inst Hist & Art, 50 & 64; Gold Medal, Catharine Lorillard Wolfe Art Club; Giffuni Award Portrait, Pastel Soc Am, 83. *Bibliog:* Norman Kent (auth), The paintings of Betty Warren, Am Artist, 67. *Mem:* Grand Cent Art Galleries; Nat Arts Club; Am Artists Prof League; Pastel Soc Am. *Media:* Oil, Pastel. *Dealer:* Bridge Ed Malden Bridge NY 12115; Portraits Inc 41 E 57th St New York NY 10022. *Mailing Add:* 76 Western Ave Albany NY 12203

WARREN, DAVID BOARDMAN
CURATOR
b Baltimore, Md, Mar 11, 37. *Study:* Princeton Univ, AB(cum laude), 59; Univ Del, MA, 65. *Collections Arranged:* Bayou Bend Collection (auth, catalog), Mus Fine Arts, Houston, 65-; Southern Silver (auth, catalog), Mus Fine Arts, Houston, 68; Gothic Revival Style in America 1830-1870 (auth, catalog), Mus Fine Arts, Houston, 76; An American Sampler 1700-1875, Charles Bybee Mem Collections, 81; Nineteenth Century American Landscape: Selections from the Thyssen-Bornemisza Collection (auth, catalog), Mus Fine Arts, Houston, 82. *Pos:* Cur, Bayou Bend Collection, Mus Fine Arts, Houston, 65-, assoc dir, 75- *Teaching:* Lectr, Am Decorative Arts, Rice Univ, 66-73. *Publ:* Coauth, Texas Furniture: The Cabinetmakers and Their Work 1840-1870, Univ Tex Press, 75; contribr, A Guide to the Collections, Mus Fine Arts, Houston, 81. *Mailing Add:* 1001 Bissonnet St Houston TX 77005

WARREN, FERDINAND EARL
PAINTER, ADMINISTRATOR
b Independence, Mo, Aug 1, 1899. *Study:* Kansas City Art Inst. *Work:* Metrop Mus Art, New York; Brooklyn Mus Art, NY; Rochester Mem Gallery, Youngstown, Ohio; Currier Gallery Art, Springfield, NH; NASA Permanent Collection, Nat Gallery Art, Washington, DC. *Comn:* Two war bond posters, US Treas Dept, 43; History of the Printed Word (mural), Foote & Davies, Atlanta, 57; Robert Frost (portrait from life), Agnes Scott Col, Decatur, Ga, 58; copper enamel cross, St Agnes Episcopal Church, Atlanta, 63; Apollo 14 (painting), NASA, Washington, DC, 71. *Exhib:* Richmond Va Ann, 48-49; Corcoran Gallery Art, Washington, DC, 49; Art in the Embassies, US Dept State, 66-70; Nat Acad Design Ann, New York; Carnegie Int, Pittsburgh. *Pos:* Artist in residence, Univ Ga, 50-51; chmn dept art, Agnes Scott Col, 52-69. *Awards:* Silver Medal, Am Watercolor Soc, 50; Purchase Prize, Butler Inst Am Art, 54; Edwin Palmer Prize, Nat Acad Design, 61. *Bibliog:* Forbes Watson (auth), Painting Today; Ernest Watson (auth), Composition in Landscape. *Mem:* Nat Acad Design. *Media:* Oil. *Mailing Add:* 227 E Hancock St Decatur GA 30030

WARREN, JACQUELINE LOUISE
PAINTER, EDUCATOR
b National City, Calif, Nov 3, 46. *Study:* Southwest Mo State Univ, BS, 67; Ariz State Univ, MFA, 71. *Work:* Sch Ozarks, Branson, Mo; Ariz State Univ, Tempe. *Exhib:* Ariz State Fair, 70; Intent 77, Bruce Gallery, Edinborough, Pa, 78; Invitational, Campus Gallery, Monroe, La, 79; Works of Paper Nat Competition, Alice Lloyd Col, Pippa Pass, Ky, 80; Paper Nat Competitive, Columbia Col, Mo, 81. *Collections Arranged:* Art on Paper, Cox Gallery, Drury Col, 81. *Teaching:* Prof painting & drawing, Southwest Mo State Univ, Springfield, 75-79; prof design, Drury Col, 79- *Awards:* First Prize, Ariz State Fair, 70; Best of Show, Spiva Mus, Joplin, Mo, 78; First Prize, Sch Ozarks, Branson, Mo, 79. *Bibliog:* Edgar Albin (auth), Artist profile, Art Voices South Mag, 81. *Mem:* Col Art Asn. *Media:* Mixed. *Dealer:* Tall Grass Gallery Kansas City KS; Metro Gallery Springfield MO. *Mailing Add:* Drury College 900 N Benton Springfield MO 65802

WARREN, JULIANNE BUSSERT BAKER
PHOTOGRAPHER
b Lima, Ohio, May 8, 16. *Work:* Pub Libr Cincinnati & Hamilton Co; Truman Libr & Johnson Libr, Austin, Tex; Smithsonian Inst. *Comn:* Photographs of seven US Presidents; Prime Minister Wilson, London; Princess Margaret. *Exhib:* Cincinnati Art Mus, 59; Shillito's Dept Store, Cincinnati, 61; Jewish Community Ctr, Cincinnati, 70; Cincinnati Woman's Club, 74; one-man shows, Pub Libr Cincinnati & Hamilton Co, 67 & Exhib of Collection, 78. *Pos:* Mgr, Photo-finishing Co, Cincinnati, 41-48; Photogr radio station, 50-52; news photogr, Cincinnati Post, 52-68. *Awards:* First Prize, Nat Heirloom Contest, 59; First Prize, Newspaper Guild's Page-One Ball, 61; two prizes, Best Women's Page Photography, Univ Mo, 65. *Mem:* Asn Am Edit Cartoonists (historian, 71-). *Publ:* Contribr & illusr, Press Photography, MacMillan, , 61; co-auth, Cincinnati in Color, Hastings House, 78. *Mailing Add:* 1815 William Howard Taft Rd Apt 203 Cincinnati OH 45206

WARREN, L D
CARTOONIST
b Wilmington, Del, Dec 27, 06. *Work:* Cincinnati Art Mus, Eden Park, Ohio; Harry S Truman Libr; Libr Commun & Graphic Arts, Ohio State Univ, Columbus; Lyndon B Johnson Libr, Austin, Tex; Mus Cartoon Art, Greenwich, Conn. *Comn:* Numerous cartoon illus for bks, mag & brochures over a period of many yrs. *Exhib:* Cartoon Exhib, Metrop Mus Art, New York, 54; Int Salon of Cartoons, Int Pavillon of Humor, Montreal, 68-74; Asn Am Ed Cartoonist Exhib, World Cartoon Gallery, Skopje, Yugoslavia, 69 & 71 & Nat Portrait Gallery, London, 70; Editorial Cartoons by L D Warren, Cincinnati Art Mus, 74; Ohio State Univ, 83. *Pos:* Staff artist, Camden Courier-Post, NJ, 25-27; cartoonist, Philadelphia Rec, 27-47; ed cartoonist, Cincinnati Equirer, 47-78; retired. *Teaching:* Guest instr cartooning, Art Acad Cincinnati, 57. *Awards:* Freedoms Found Awards, 49-73; Nat Headliners Club Award, 61; Best Cartoon of the Sixties, Nat Found Hwy Safety, 71; Martha Kinney Cooper Ohioana Bk Award (Social Hist & Journalism Graphics), Columbus, Ohio, 77. *Bibliog:* Joseph Eble (auth), As L D sees the world, Pictorial Mag, Cincinnati Enquirer, 66; Judge John W Peck (auth), Federal judge talks about comics, The Cartoonist, 67. *Mem:* Asn Am Ed Cartoonists (vpres, 60 & 75); Nat Cartoonists Soc; Cincinnati Art Mus. *Media:* Ink, Crayon. *Publ:* Illusr, Penny Penguin (informative comic bk for children), Stern & Co, 35; illusr, Terry and Bunky Play Football (in Japanese, 49) & Terry and Bunky Play Basketball (series of children's sports bks), Putnam, 45-51; auth, Want to be a cartoonist?, Cartoonist Profiles, 69; coauth (with Walter C Langsam), The World and Warren's Cartoons, Exposition Press, 77. *Mailing Add:* 1815 William Howard Taft Rd Apt 203 Cincinnati OH 45206

WARREN, PETER WHITSON See Whitson

WARREN, WIN (W WINTON)
PAINTER, LECTURER
b Jakin, Ga, Nov 13, 14. *Study:* Univ Ga, LLB & JD; US Dept Agr Grad Sch, 67; Cath Univ Am, 68 & 69; Univ Md Grad Sch, with Nicholas Krushenick, Jerry Clapsaddle, Helen Van Wyk & Joseph Kelly, 77-82. *Comn:* Equestrian portraits of George Washington & Lafayette, Johnston & Lemon Brokerage Firm, Washington, DC, 76; mural for community ctr, with Alice Plaster, Md-Nat Capital Park & Planning Comn, Mt Ranier, 79. *Exhib:* Univ Md, College Park, 79; Artists Today Exhib, Md-Nat Capital Park & Planning Comn, 79; one-man show, Montpelier Cultural Arts Ctr, Laurel, 80; Int Platform Art Show, 83; Art Barn Asn-Nat Park Serv Exhib, 83. *Pos:* Lect & tours Am Art, Educ Dept, Nat Mus Am Art, Smithsonian Inst, Washington DC, 79- *Mem:* Artists' Equity Asn; Col Art Asn; Olney Art Asn; Cult Alliance Greater Washington; Montpelier Cult Arts Ctr (adv bd, currently). *Media:* Acrylic, Oils. *Mailing Add:* 6917 Oakridge Rd Hyattsville MD 20782

WARRINER, LAURA B
PAINTER
b Tulsa, Okla, Jan 18, 43. *Study:* Okla Baptist Univ; Oklahoma City Univ. *Exhib:* Nat Watercolor Soc 54th Ann, Laguna Beach Mus, Calif, 74; Watercolor USA, Springfield Art Ctr, Mo, 74; Nat Acad Design, 149th Ann Exhib, 107th Ann Exhib Am Watercolor Soc & Allied Artists Am 60th Ann Exhib, Nat Acad Design Galleries, New York 74-78. *Awards:* Award for Watercolor, Allied Artists Am 60th Ann Exhib, 74, Barbara Vassilieff Award for Flowers-Still Life, Allied Artists Am 61st Ann Exhib, 75; Century Award of Merit, Rocky Mountain Nat Watermedia Exhib, 75. *Bibliog:* Ralph Fabri (auth), Flower painting in all media, 2/74 & Can you succeed in art without really trying, 9/74, Today's Art; Barbara Nechis (auth), Watercolor the Creative Experience, Northlight. *Mem:* Am Watercolor Soc; Nat Watercolor Soc; Okla Watercolor Asn; Southwestern Watercolor Soc (pres, 73-74). *Media:* Multimedia. *Mailing Add:* 1700 NW 39th St Oklahoma City OK 73118

WARSINSKE, NORMAN GEORGE, JR
SCULPTOR, PAINTER
b Wichita, Kans, Mar 4, 29. *Study:* Univ Mont, BA; Kunstwerkschule, Darmstadt, Ger; Univ Wash, BA. *Comn:* Bronze fountain, Theodora Retirement Home, Seattle, 66; brass & steel screen, Yellowstone Boy's Ranch, Billings, Mont, 69; gold leaf steel stabile, IBM Bldg Lobby, Seattle, 71; stainless stabile, Seattle First Nat Bank, Bellevue, 75; bronze & plexiglas fountain, J Hughes Home, Mauna Kea, Hawaii, 79; and others. *Exhib:* Northwest Ann, Seattle Art Mus, 59-65; Santa Barbara Invitational, Calif, 63; Sculpture, Los Angeles Co Mus Art, 64; Woodside Seattle, 73. *Teaching:* Asst instr drawing, Univ Wash, 58-59. *Awards:* First Prize for Sculpture, Bellevue Art Festival, 60; Best of All Categories, Henry Art Gallery, 66. *Bibliog:* Louis Redstone (auth), Art in Architecture, McGraw, 68; M R Heinley (auth), Norman Warsinske--metal artistry, Designers W, 6/70. *Mem:* Seattle Munic Art Comn (vpres, 65-69); Northwest Craft Ctr (pres, 65-70). *Media:* Bronze, Steel; Acrylic. *Publ:* Illusr cover, Am Inst Architects J, 8/71. *Dealer:* Miller-Pollard Inc 4538 University Way NE Seattle WA 98105. *Mailing Add:* 3823 94th NE Bellevue WA 98004

WASEY, JANE
SCULPTOR
b Chicago, Ill, June 28, 12. *Study:* With Paul Landowski, Paris; Simon Moselsio, New York; also with John Flanagan & Heinz Warneke. *Work:* Ariz State Univ, Tempe; Univ Colo; Dartmouth Col; Pa Acad Fine Arts; Whitney Mus Am Art, New York; plus others. *Comn:* Andre the Seal (sculpture), Marine Park, Rockport, Maine, 78. *Exhib:* Art Inst Chicago; Brooklyn Mus; Univ Chicago; Detroit Inst Arts; one-man shows, Philbrook Art Ctr, 49; Weathervanes Contemp, New York, 54 & Kraushaar Galleries, 56 & 71; and others. *Teaching:* Instr sculpture, Bennington Col, 48-49; pvt art classes, 50-60. *Awards:* First Prizes for Sculpture, Parrish Art Mus & Guild Hall, NY; Mrs John Henry Hammond Award, Nat Asn Women Artists, 51; Phillips Mem Prize, Archit League, 55; and others. *Bibliog:* Brumme (auth), Contemporary American Sculpture; Anton Henze (auth), Contemporary Church Art; Design for learning, Town & Country, 10/49; and others. *Mem:* Sculptor's Guild; Nat Asn Women Artists; Nat Sculpture Soc; Audubon Artists. *Media:* Stone, Wood. *Dealer:* Kraushaar Galleries 724 Fifth Ave New York NY 10019. *Mailing Add:* Lincolnville ME 04849

WASHBURN, GORDON BAILEY
MUSEUM DIRECTOR
b Wellesley Hills, Mass, Nov 7, 04. *Study:* Deerfield Acad; Williams Col, AB, 28; Fogg Mus Art, Harvard Univ; Williams Col, Hon MFA, 38; Allegheny Col, Hon DFA, 59; Univ Buffalo, Hon DFA, 62; Washington & Jefferson Col, Hon DFA, 68, LHD, 74. *Collections Arranged:* Pittsburgh International (triennially); French Painting 1100-1900 & Pictures of Everyday Life-Genre Painting in Europe, 1500-1900, Carnegie Inst; American Painting in the 1950's, Am Fedn Arts, 68; three exhibs per yr, Asia House Gallery, 61-74. *Pos:* Dir, Albright Art Gallery, Buffalo, NY, 31-42; dir, Mus Art, RI Sch Design, 42-49; dir dept fine arts, Carnegie Inst, Pittsburgh, 50-62; dir, Asia House Gallery, New York, 61-74; emer dir, 74- *Awards:* Guggenheim Fel, 49-50; Chevalier, Legion of Honor, 52; Comdr, Royal Order NStar, Sweden, 73. *Mem:* Col Art Asn Am; Asn Art Mus Dirs; Am Asn Mus. *Mailing Add:* 420 E 80th St New York NY 10021

WASHBURN, JOAN T
DEALER, GALLERY DIRECTOR
b New York, NY, Dec 26, 29. *Study:* Middlebury Col, BA. *Collections Arranged:* and others. *Pos:* Dir, Washburn Gallery, New York, currently. *Specialty:* Nineteenth and twentieth century American painting and sculpture. *Mailing Add:* Washburn Gallery 42 E 57th St New York NY 10022

WASHBURN, STAN
PRINTMAKER, PAINTER
b New York, NY, Jan 2, 43. *Study:* Calif Col Arts & Crafts, Oakland, BFA, 67 & MFA, 68. *Work:* Chicago Art Inst; Brooklyn Mus, New York; Calif Palace of Legion of Honor, San Francisco; Libr Cong, Washington DC; Mus Fine Arts, Boston. *Exhib:* Davidson Nat Print & Drawing Competition, NC, 73-75; Prints Calif, Oakland Mus Art, 75; Int Miniature Print Competition, Pratt Graphics Ctr, New York, 75 & 77; 24th Nat Exhib Prints, Libr Cong, Washington, DC, 75; Hassam Fund Purchase Prize Exhib, Am Acad of Arts & Lett, New York, 75 & 76; one-man show, Achenbach Found for Graphic Arts, Calif Palace of Legion of Honor, 77; and others. *Awards:* Pennell Fund Purchase, Libr 75; Purchase Award, Int Miniature Print Collection, Pratt Graphics Ctr, New York, 77. *Bibliog:* One-half hour spec, KQED-TV, San Francisco, 75. *Mem:* Calif Soc Printmakers. *Media:* Etching; Oil. *Publ:* Auth & illusr, True History of the Death by Violence of George's Dragon, 74, illusr, Schinocephalic Waif, 75; illusr, Great Wheadle Tragedy, Godine, 75. *Dealer:* Pucker/Safrai 171 Newbury St Boston MA 02116. *Mailing Add:* 2010 Virginia St Berkeley CA 94709

WASHINGTON, JAMES W, JR
SCULPTOR, PAINTER
b Gloster, Miss. *Study:* Nat Landscape Inst; also with Mark Tobey; Grad Theological Union Ctr Urban Black Studies, Berkeley, Calif, Hon DFA, 75. *Work:* Seattle Art Mus, Wash; San Francisco Art Mus. *Comn:* The Creation (series 6), Seattle Pub Libr, 67; The Creation (series 7-10), Seattle First Nat Bank Main Br, 68; busts of hist men, Progress Plaza, Philadelphia, 69; The Creation (series 5), Meany Jr High Sch, Seattle, 70; Woodchuck Sunning (sculpture), Frankfurt, WGer, 74; and others. *Exhib:* Expo '70, Osaka, Japan, 70; Art of the Pac Northwest, Nat Collection of Fine Arts, Washington, DC, 74; one-man exhibs, Foster/White Gallery, Seattle, Wash, 68, 78 & 80 & Mus Hist & Indust, Seattle, 80; retrospective, Frye Art Mus, Seattle, 80; Festival Sundiata, Seattle, 80; Portopia 81, Kobe, Japan, 81; and others. *Pos:* Secy, Seattle Chap, Artists Equity Asn, 49-53, pres, 60-62; mem gov coun art, State of Wash, 59-60, state art comnr, 61-66. *Awards:* Award for Bird Hatching, Oakland Munic Art Mus, 57; Award for Wounded Bird, Seattle World's Fair, 62; Gov Sculpture Award, 70. *Bibliog:* Ann Faber (auth), James Washington's stone sculpture excellence, Seattle Post Intelligence, 56; Pauline Johnson (auth), James Washington speaks, Art Educ J, 68; Arch Am Art, Smithsonian Inst, 83. *Mem:* Int Platform Asn. *Media:* Oil, Tempera; Granite, Marble. *Mailing Add:* 1816 26th Ave Seattle WA 98122

WASSER, PAULA KLOSTER
EDUCATOR, PAINTER
b Hatton, NDak. *Study:* Univ Minn; Minneapolis Sch Art; Univ NDak, BS, 26; Stanford Univ, MA, 31, 48; Univ Mex, 33; Univ Southern Calif, 39; also study var art schs. *Exhib:* Tucson Fine Arts Festival; Ariz Art Guild; Ariz State Fair; Univ Nev, Reno; one-man shows, Phoenix & Scottsdale, Ariz; and others. *Teaching:* Instr art, Grand Forks Jr High Sch, NDak, 23-25; supvr student art, State Teachers Col, Valley City, NDak, 26-27; actg head dept art, Ariz State Univ, 27-33, head dept, 33-54, prof art, 49-64, cur Am collection, 50-64, emer prof art, 65- *Mem:* Hon life mem & fel Int Inst Arts & Lett; Delta Phi Delta; Col Art Asn Am; Am Asn Mus; Nat Art Educ Asn. *Media:* Multimedia. *Publ:* Compiled brochures of College Collection, 50-52, 55-56 & 59-63; auth, The Arizona State College Collection of American Art, 54; contribr, Am Homes Mag & Design; and others. *Mailing Add:* 181 Lassen Circle Vacaville CA 95688

WASSERMAN, ALBERT
PAINTER, DESIGNER
b New York, NY, Aug 22, 20. *Study:* Art Students League, with Charles Chapman, 37-39; Nat Acad Design, Pulitzer Prize scholar, 38-40; with Sidney Dickinson; US Army Univ, France. *Work:* Traphagen Collection, Ariz; Aimee Ornstein Mem Libr, Adelphi Univ, NY, 83. *Comn:* Many private portrait commissions. *Exhib:* Nat Acad Design, New York, 40 & 41; Allied Artists Am, New York, 41-; NJ Painters & Sculptors Soc, 41-; Am Watercolor Soc, New York, 53-69; Audubon Artists, New York, 60. *Pos:* Graphic design consult, var agencies, 48- *Teaching:* Instr & lectr, Jackson Heights Art Asn, 55- & Nat Art League, 67-69; instr & lectr, Nat Art League, 67-69. *Awards:* Obrig Prize, 41, Nat Acad Design; Friedrichs Prize, Allied Artists Am, 41. *Bibliog:* Ethel Traphagen (auth), article, Fashion Digest, 54. *Mem:* Salmagundi Club; Allied Artists Am; NJ Painters & Sculptors Soc; assoc Am Watercolor Soc; Nat Art League; and others. *Media:* Oil. *Mailing Add:* 34-24 82nd St New York NY 11372

WASSERMAN, BURTON
PAINTER, PRINTMAKER
b Brooklyn, NY, Mar 10, 29. *Study:* Brooklyn Col, with Burgoyne Diller & Ad Reinhardt, BA; Columbia Univ, MA & EdD. *Work:* Philadelphia Mus Art, Pa; Munson-Williams-Proctor Inst, Utica, NY; Del Art Ctr, Wilmington; Montreal Mus Fine Arts; NJ State Mus, Trenton; and others. *Comn:* Relief triptych, Mr & Mrs Herbert Kurtz, Melrose Park, Pa, 71; var indust & residential relief construction projs, Philadelphia area, 74-79. *Exhib:* 21st Am Drawing Biennial, Norfolk Mus Arts & Sci, 65; Art Alliance, Philadelphia, 66-80; USA Pavilion, Int Expos, Osaka, Japan, 70; Color Prints of the

Americas, NJ State Mus, 70; Int Graphics Exhib, Montreal Mus Art, 71; Silkscreen: History of a Medium, Philadelphia Mus Art, 71-72; Benjamin Mangel Gallery, Philadelphia, Pa, 72-82; and others. *Teaching:* Prof art, Glassboro State Col, 60- *Awards:* Brickhouse Drawing Prize, 21st Am Drawing Biennial, Norfolk Mus Arts & Sci, 65; Ryan Purchase Prize, Art from NJ Ann Exhib, NJ State Mus, 67; Esther-Philip Klein Award, Am Color Print Soc Ann, 70; and others. *Mem:* Artists Equity Asn (nat pres, 71-73); Am Color Print Soc (mem exec coun, 65-81). *Media:* Oil, Silkscreen, Spray Enamels. *Publ:* Auth articles in Leonardo, Am Artist, Art Educ, Sch Arts, & many more, 59-72; auth, Modern Painting: the Movements, the Artists, Their Work, 70 & co-auth, Basic Silkscreen Printmaking, 71, Davis, Mass; auth, Bridges of Vision: the Art of Prints & the Craft of Printmaking, NJ State Mus, 70; auth, Exploring the Visual Arts, Davis, Mass, 76. *Dealer:* Benjamin Mangel Gallery 1604 Locust St Philadelphia PA 19103. *Mailing Add:* 204 Dubois Rd Glassboro NJ 08028

WASSERMAN, CARY (ROBERT)
PHOTOGRAPHER, CONCEPTUAL ARTIST
b Los Angeles, Calif, Nov 27, 39. *Study:* Univ Calif, Los Angeles, BA, 61, MA, 63; Ind Univ, with Henry Holmes Smith, 67-70. *Work:* Mus Fine Arts, Boston; Smith Col Mus Art; Wellesley Col Mus Art; Portland Mus Art, Maine; Polaroid Collection. *Comn:* Charlestown: In Progress, Polaroid Corp, Cambridge, Mass, 74; A Call To Arts, Cambridge Arts Coun, Mass, 75; Large Totem (sculpture), WBZ-TV, Boston, 81. *Exhib:* Photographs: 1969-1971, Addison Gallery Am Art, 72; Points of View, Inst Contemp Art, Boston, 72; Photographs: 1970-1974, Portland Mus Art, Maine, 74; Private Realities, Mus Fine Arts, Boston, 74; Color Photography Now!, Wellesley Col Mus Art, 75; Color Photography Retrospective, Williams Col Mus, 78; Aspects of the 70s, DeCordova Mus, 80; Polaroid Photographs in Historic Perspective, Brown Univ, 80. *Collections Arranged:* Color in Photography, Soc Photog Educ, 75; Art Month, Clarence Kennedy Gallery, 76; Photo-Media, BVAU Gallery, 77; Color Photography: National Exhibit (auth, catalog), 81 & Seven Artists, 83, Boston Visual Artists Union. *Pos:* Creative dir, Art Consults Group, Cambridge, Mass, 74- *Teaching:* Instr filmmaking, Phillips Acad Summer Session, 73 & 79; instr photog, Univ Maine, 76-77; vis lectr, Univ Lowell, 77-79 & 82-83. *Awards:* Cambridge Arts Coun Award, Cambridge City Hall Open Competition, 76; Blanche E Coleman Award, 82. *Bibliog:* Kelly Wise (auth), Wasserman at large, Boston Globe, 83. *Mem:* Boston Visual Artists Union (secy-gen, 78-80). *Publ:* Contrib, Private Realities: Recent American Photography, New York Graphic, 74; contrib, The Photographers Choice, Addison House, 75; auth, SX-70 manipulation, Petersens Photog, 76; conribr, Creative Camera International Yearbook, 77; auth, SX-70 image manipulation, Darkroom Tech, 83. *Dealer:* Lopoukhine Gallery 10 Newbury St Boston MA 02116. *Mailing Add:* Art Consults Group Six Porter Rd Cambridge MA 02140

WASSERMAN, JACK
EDUCATOR
b New York, NY, Apr 27, 21. *Study:* Washington Sq Col, NY Univ, BA; NY Univ Inst Fine Arts, with Karl Lehmann & Richard Krautheimer, MA & PhD. *Teaching:* Instr art, Univ Conn, 53-60; asst prof art, Ind Univ, Bloomington, 60-62; prof Renaissance art, Univ Wis-Milwaukee, 62-75; dean, Tyler Sch Art, Temple Univ, Philadelphia, 75-77; prof art hist, 75- *Awards:* Am Coun Learned Soc Grant, 70; Am Philos Soc Grant, 71; Kress Found Grant, 75. *Mem:* Col Art Asn Am; Soc Archit Historians (bd dirs, 70-); Royal Soc Arts; Amici de Brera; Soc per la Storia dell'Arte Lombarda, Milan, Italy (mem bd councellors, 82-). *Publ:* Auth, The dating & patronage of Leonardo's Burlington House cartoon, Art Bulletin, 71; auth, Michelangelo's Virgin & Child with St Anne at Oxford, Burlington Mag, 69; auth, Leonardo da Vinci, Abrams, 75; auth, The Genesis of Raphael's Alba Madonna, Studies in History of Art, Nat Gallery Art, Washington, 78; auth, Reflections on Leonardo's Last Supper, Arte Lombarda, 83; and others. *Mailing Add:* Dept of Art Hist Temple Univ Philadelphia PA 19122

WATANABE, RYO
PAINTER, PRINTMAKER
b Tokyo, Japan, Sept 12, 36. *Study:* Art Sch, Bunka-Gakuin Col, Tokyo, 58-61; Art Students League, 65-67; Pratt Inst, New York, 68-70. *Work:* Brooklyn Mus & Mus Mod Art, New York; White House, Washington, DC; Philadelphia Mus Art; Wadsworth Atheneum, Hartford, Conn; and others. *Exhib:* 19th Print Biennial, Brooklyn Mus, NY, 74; Philadelphia Biennial Int, Philadelphia Mus, Pa, 77; one-man shows, J Field Gallery, New York, 80, Galerie Saison, Tokyo, 82 & Sande Webster Gallery, 82; Seventh Int Print Biennial, Bradford, Eng, 81; 15th Int Biennial of Graphic Art, Ljubljana, Yugoslavia, 83; and others. *Teaching:* Instr, Graphics Ctr, Pratt Inst, New York, 75-; instr, Rutgers Univ, Newark, NJ, 76-78 & 81-82. *Awards:* Philadelphia Int William H Walker Prize, Print Club, 77. *Media:* Lithography, Oil. *Mailing Add:* 117 Hester St New York NY 10002

WATERHOUSE, CHARLES HOWARD
ILLUSTRATOR, PAINTER
b Columbus, Ga, Sept 22, 24. *Study:* Newark Sch Fine & Indust Art; also with Steven R Kidd. *Work:* USMC Mus, US Navy Combat Art Collection & USAAF Collections, Washington, DC; Rutgers Univ, New Brunswick, NJ; NJ Bell Tel Co, Newark. *Comn:* Marines in the Revolution, 74, Vietnam Refugees, 75 & Marines in Mexican War, USMC, 75-76; Hamilton's Battery, Class of 24, Rutgers Univ, 74; Tarawa Beach Head, L P H Tarawa, US Navy, 75. *Exhib:* One-man shows, NJ State Mus, Trenton, US Naval Acad, Annapolis, Md, Los Angeles Mus Nat Hist, San Francisco City Hall & Soc Illusrs, New York, 75. *Pos:* Staff artist, Prudential Ins Co, 50-55; free-lance illusr, Nat Publ & Books, 55-73; artist in residence, USMC, 73. *Teaching:*

Instr, lectr & demonstr illus, Newark Sch Fine & Indust Art, 55-73. *Bibliog:* Norman Kent (auth), Vietnam drawings, Am Artist, 68; Ed Fleming (auth), Vietnam Sketchbook, AP News Features, 68; F B Nihart (auth), Paintings by Charles Waterhouse, Marine Corps Publ, 75. *Mem:* Soc Illusr; Salmagundi Club; Nat Soc Mural Painters; USMC Combat Corresp; Naval Air Cooperation & Liason Comt Artists. *Media:* Acrylic, Ink. *Publ:* Illusr, Outdoor Life, Argosy, Saga, Reader's Digest & others, 55-; illusr, Grosset, Dunlap, Viking, Am, & Rutgers Press, 55-; auth & illusr, Vietnam Sketchbook from Delta to DMZ, 68; auth & illusr, Vietnam War Drawings, Air, Land & Sea, 70; illusr, Marines in the Revolution, 75. *Mailing Add:* 67 Dartmouth St Edison NJ 08817

WATERHOUSE, RUSSELL RUTLEDGE
PAINTER
b El Paso, Tex, Aug 11, 28. *Study:* Tex A&M Univ, BS, 50; Art Ctr Col Design, Pasadena, Calif, 54-56. *Work:* Tex Tech Univ Mus Art, Lubbock; El Paso Mus Art; Tex A&M Univ, College Station; Univ Tex, El Paso. *Exhib:* One-man shows, Wichita Falls Tex Cult Ctr & Mus Art, 72, Tex A&M Univ, 77, Dallas Safari Club, 83 & Americana Mus, El Paso, 84; Game Conservation Int, San Antonio, 83. *Pos:* Mem, Tex Comn Arts & Humanities, 70-75. *Media:* Watercolor, Acrylic. *Publ:* Illusr, Goodbye to a River, Knopf, 60; illusr, The Legal Heritage of El Paso, 63 & Pass of the North, 68, Tex Western Press. *Mailing Add:* 5500 Westside Dr El Paso TX 79932

WATERS, HERBERT (OGDEN)
PRINTMAKER, EDUCATOR
b Swatow, China, Nov 15, 03; US citizen. *Study:* Denison Univ, PhB; Pa Sch Indust Art; Art Inst Chicago; Harvard Univ Grad Sch Fine Art. *Work:* Metrop Mus Art, New York; Libr Cong, Washington, DC; Boston Mus Fine Art; Boston Pub Libr; Springfield Art Mus, Mass. *Comn:* Membership print, Rochester Print Club, NY, 52; baptistry mural, Campton Baptist Church, NH, 54; mem bookplates, Denison Univ Libr, 59 & 72. *Exhib:* New York World's Fair Art Exhib, 39; Am Watercolors Prints & Drawings, Metrop Mus Art, New York, 52; Boston Print Makers Exhib, 52-; Soc Am Graphic Artists, 60-; Appalachian Corridors I & II, Charleston, WVa, 68 & 70. *Teaching:* Vis prof graphic art, art hist & painting, Univ NH, summers 46-59; teacher studio & art hist, Holderness Sch, Plymouth, NH, 46-60; asst prof, Alderson-Broaddus Col, 61-80. *Awards:* John Taylor Arms Purchase Award Graphic Art, Soc Am Graphic Artists, 54; Prize in Watercolor, WVa Centennial, 63; Award Graphic Art, Appalachian Corridors I & II, 68 & 70. *Mem:* Nat Acad Design; Soc Am Graphic Artists; Boston Print Makers Soc; NH Art Asn (pres, 60). *Media:* Wood Engravings. *Publ:* Illusr, New England Year, 40; illusr, New England Days, 41; contrib, New Hampshire art calendar, 74. *Mailing Add:* Upper Mad River Rd Campton NH 03223

WATERS, TERRANCE
ARCHITECT
b El Centro, Calif, Nov 6, 20. *Study:* Los Angeles City Col, 38-40; Univ Calif, Los Angeles, 46-48; Am Inst Architects, apprentice to John Lautner, 49-51. *Exhib:* Spec exhibs houses on tours, Sacramento, Calif, 54-65; Steel Framed Home, Bethlehem Steel Corp Traveling Exhib, entire western US, 58-60; ten exhibs archit works & inventions, Los Angeles, 58-80 & Washington, DC, 70; one-man show, Bldg Ctr, Los Angeles, 63; Future World 83, Los Angeles Convention Ctr, 83. *Pos:* Architect & consult, pvt firm, 48- *Res:* Hyperbolic building system. *Publ:* Uniformity, discontinuity and the only solution, Arts & Archit, 5/64; auth, The Tungsten Conspiracy, 67. *Mailing Add:* 33560 Mulholland Hwy Malibu CA 90265

WATERSTON, HARRY CLEMENT
PAINTER
b New York, NY, Mar 15, 09. *Study:* NY Sch Fine & Appl Art; Art Students League; NY Univ Sch Educ, BS(art educ); also studied watercolor with Eliot O'Hara, Edgar Whitney & Mario Cooper. *Work:* Slater Mus, Norwich, Conn; lithograph, Smithsonian Inst, Washington, DC; Winsor & Newton Collection, Secaucus, NJ; Butler Inst Am Art, Youngstown, Ohio; and others. *Exhib:* Grand Nat, Am Artists Prof League, 62, 74, 75, 76 & 79; Watercolor Show, Nat Arts Club, 63; Hudson Valley Art Asn; Cross-section Show, Artists Equity Asn, 75, 77, 78 & 81; Bronx Mus, 76 & 77; Audubon Artists, 77 & 80. *Teaching:* Teacher art, New York High Schs, 30-37. *Awards:* Anne G Morse Medal, Gotham Painters Show, 62. *Mem:* Fel Am Artists Prof League; NY Artists Equity Asn (bd mem, 75, pres, 79-81); Nat Coun Art Jewish Life (hon pres, 83); Am Soc Contemp Art, Metrop Painters & Sculptors (vpres, 79-). *Media:* Watercolor. *Publ:* Contrib, Sketches of Riverdale, Riverdale Press, 66- *Dealer:* Continental Art Gallery 72-21 Austin St Forest Hills NY 11375; Lexington Art Gallery 968 Lexington Ave New York NY. *Mailing Add:* 80 Knolls Crescent Bronx NY 10463

WATERSTREET, KEN (JAMES KENT)
PAINTER, INSTRUCTOR
b Ogden, Utah, July 18, 40. *Study:* Calif State Univ, Sacramento, BA, 63, MA, 69. *Work:* E B Crocker Art Mus, Sacramento; Southern Ill Univ; Stuart M Speiser Collection, Smithsonian Inst; San Francisco Mus Mod Art; Oakland Mus, Calif. *Exhib:* Human Concern/Personal Torment, Whitney Mus of Am Art, New York, 69; one-man shows, Louis K Meisel Gallery, New York, 74 & 77 & Zara Gallery, San Francisco, 79; Hue & Far Cry of Color, Ft Wayne Mus, Ind, 76; E B Crocker Art Mus, Sacramento, 80; Joseph Chowning Gallery, San Francisco, 81 & 83; and others. *Pos:* Comnr, Sacramento Metrop Arts Comn, 77 & 78. *Mem:* Visual Artists & Galleries Asn. *Media:* Oil on Canvas. *Dealer:* Hansen Galleries 561 Broadway New York NY 10012; Joseph Chowning Gallery 1717 17th St San Francisco CA 91403. *Mailing Add:* 3218 Tobari Ct Sacramento CA 95821

WATHALL, BETTIE GERALDINE See Becker, Bettie

WATIA, TARMO
PAINTER, EDUCATOR

b Detroit, Mich, May 11, 38. *Study:* Univ Mich, BS(design), 60 & MFA, 62. *Work:* Boise Art Gallery, Idaho; Boise Cascade Bldg, Idaho; Harrett Mus, Twin Falls, Idaho. *Exhib:* Graphics 71, Nat Print & Drawing Exhib, Silver City, NMex, 71; 38th Ann Idaho, Boise Art Gallery, 74; 16th Ann Prints & Drawings, Okla Art Ctr, Oklahoma City, 74; Watercolor USA, Springfield, Mo, 75; 53rd Ann Nat Art Exhib, Springville Mus of Art, Utah, 77; 2nd Biennial Idaho Artists, Boise, 81. *Teaching:* Instr art, Southern Ore Col, Ashland, 66-69; assoc prof art, Boise State Univ, Idaho, 69- *Awards:* Second Place Award, Rock Springs, Wyo, 72; Purchase Award, Boise Art Gallery, Idaho, 74; Cash Award/Painting, Ninth Ann Arts & Crafts Festival, Coeur D'Alene, Idaho; and others. *Media:* Oil, Gouache. *Mailing Add:* 1015 N Tenth St Boise ID 83702

WATKINS, EILEEN FRANCES
CRITIC

b Long Island, NY, Nov 22, 50. *Study:* Marywood Col, BA. *Pos:* Art ed, Newark Star-Ledger, currently. *Mem:* NJ Press Women. *Mailing Add:* Star-Ledger Star-Ledger Plaza Newark NJ 07101

WATKINS, LEWIS
SCULPTOR, PAINTER

b Beckley, WVa, July 24, 45. *Study:* WVa State Col, BS(art educ), 78; Univ Southern Fla, MA, 82; St Leo Col, Fla, hon degree, 83. *Work:* Fla State Mus, Gainesville; WVa Fine Arts & Cult Ctr, Charleston; Vatican Mus, Rome, Italy; Leslie Stephens Fine Arts Ctr, Birmingham, Ala; Hyatt Regency Hotel, Atlanta, Ga. *Comn:* Limestone sculpture, Hernando Co, Brooksville, Fla, 81; Solidarity (steel sculpture), Brandon, Fla, 82; Crosses of Life (steel sculpture), City Atlanta, Ga, 83; Youth of Today (stone sculpture), Hernando Co, Fla, 83; St Leo (steel sculpture), St Leo Col, Fla, 83. *Exhib:* Tools of Life, John W Davis Fine Art Gallery, Institute, WVa, 81; Leslie Stephens Fine Art Ctr, Samford Univ, Birmingham, Ala, 82; and others. *Teaching:* Vis artist series, Samford Univ, Birmingham, Ala, 82; vis artist, St Leo Col, Fla, 82, Univ Tampa, Fla, 83 & Univ SFla, Tampa, 83. *Awards:* Distinguished Serv Art Award, Atlanta, Ga, 83; Cert Recognition Art, State Ga, 83; Pub Serv Cult Award, Hernando Co, Fla, 83. *Bibliog:* Terry Misfeldt (auth), article, Future Mag, 6/83; Tom Kuennen (auth), article, Rock Products Mag, 6/83; John Levine (auth), article, Pit & Quarry Mag, 9/83. *Media:* Watercolor, Acrylic; Marble, Steel. *Publ:* Coauth, Creating a year book, Instructor Mag, 80. *Mailing Add:* 1039 S Mildred Ave Brooksville FL 33512

WATKINS, RAGLAND TOLK
CURATOR, DEALER

b San Francisco, Calif, Oct 31, 48. *Study:* Lake Forest Col, BA, 72; NY Univ, MA, 82. *Collections Arranged:* Bochner, Le Va, Rockburne, Tuttle (ed & contribr, catalog) Contemp Arts Ctr, Cincinnati, 75. *Pos:* Field rep, New York State Coun Arts, 76-77; assoc dir exhibs, Artists Space, New York, 77-81; dir, Concord Contemp Art, New York, 81- *Mailing Add:* 169 Sullivan St New York NY 10022

WATKINS, WILLIAM MYERS III See Gold Star

WATROUS, JAMES SCALES
PAINTER, HISTORIAN

b Winfield, Kans, Aug 3, 08. *Study:* Univ Wis, BS, MA & PhD. *Work:* Lawrence Univ; Kans State Univ. *Comn:* Symbols of Printing (mural), Webcrafters Press, Madison, Wis, 52; Justice (aluminum), Wis Bar Ctr, Madison, 58; The Conjurer (mosaic mural), Wash Univ, St Louis, Mo, 59; Man: Creator of Order & Disorder, 64, Symbols of Communication, 72 & Mem Libr, 77 (mosaics), Univ Wis. *Pos:* Bd dir, Wis Found Arts, 75-; bd dir, Midwest Art Hist Soc, 74-75. *Teaching:* Prof art hist, Univ Wis-Madison, 41-76, Hagen Prof art hist, 64-76, chmn dept art hist, 52-61. *Awards:* Inst Advan Educ Fac Fel, Italy, 54; Award of Merit, Wis Chap Am Inst Architects, 62; Wis Gov Award in Arts, 69. *Mem:* Mid-Am Col Art Asn (pres, 59); Col Art Asn Am (pres, 62-64); hon fel Wis Acad Scis, Arts & Letters, 82. *Res:* Technical studies in the fine arts. *Publ:* Auth, The Craft of Old-Master Drawings, Univ Wis, 57. *Mailing Add:* 2809 Sylvan Ave Madison WI 53705

WATSON, ALDREN A
DESIGNER, ILLUSTRATOR

b Brooklyn, NY, May 10, 17. *Study:* Yale Univ, 35; Art Students League, with George Bridgman, Charles Chapman, Robert Brackman, William Auerbach-Levy & others. *Work:* Illus bks in libr, US, Can, Europe & pvt collections. *Comn:* Mural, SS Pres Hayes, Thomas Crowell Co Off, 64. *Exhib:* Fifty Bks Shows, Soc Illusr Ann; New Eng Textbk Shows. *Pos:* Textbk designer, D C Heath & Co, Boston, 65-66; chief ed curric oriented mat, Silver Burdett Co, Morristown NJ, 66-68; official NASA artist, Apollo 8, 68; consult art dir, Houghton Mifflin, Boston, 68-72. *Teaching:* Pvt instr, hand bookbinding. *Awards:* Prize, Domesday Bk Illus Competition, 45. *Bibliog:* Chap in Forty Illustrators & How They Work. *Mem:* Author's Guild. *Publ:* Auth & illusr, My Garden Grows, 62 & Maple Tree Begins, 70, Viking; auth & illusr, Hand Bookbinding, 63, 68 & 75; auth & illusr, Hand Tools: Their Ways and Workings, Norton, 82; coauth, Furniture Making Plain & Simple, Norton, 84; and others. *Mailing Add:* PO Box 482 Brattleboro VT 05301

WATSON, CLARISSA H
DEALER, WRITER

b Ashland, Wis. *Study:* Layton Art Sch, Milwaukee; Univ Wis-Milwaukee; Milwaukee-Downer Col, BA; Country Art Sch, with Harry Sternberg. *Collections Arranged:* Long Island Artists Washington, DC, 67; The Collectors' Collections, Adelphi Univ, Garden City, Long Island, 68; Gabriel Spat (1890-1967) Retrospective, Fine Arts Asn Willoughby, Cleveland, Ohio, 70; Nobility of the Horse in Art--to Save America's Wild Horses, Washington, DC, 71. *Pos:* Dir-founder, Country Art Sch, Westbury, Long Island, 53 & co-founder, Country Art Gallery, Locust Valley, Long Island, 53-; art consult, Adelphi Univ, 67-69; dir film festivals, 7 Village Arts Coun, Locust Valley, 69-71; dir-producer, Mediaeval Christmas Festival, Locust Valley, 70-73; trustee, Nassau Co Mus Fine Arts, 77- *Specialty:* Nineteenth and twentieth century American realism and American and European naifs. *Publ:* Auth, The art virus, This Wk Mag, 64; ed, The Artists' Cookbook, Stevenson, 71; auth, Fourth Stage of Gainsborough Brown, McKay, 77; The Bishop in the Back Seat, Atheneum, 80. *Mailing Add:* Country Art Gallery 113 Forest Ave Locust Valley NY 11560

WATSON, DARLIENE KEENEY
PAINTER

b Amarillo, Tex, Mar 16, 29. *Study:* Univ Colo, BFA; Art Inst Chicago; Malden Bridge Sch Art, NY; also with Dick Goetz, Oklahoma City & New York; Lui-Sang Wong, San Francisco & Ho Nien Au, Taiwan. *Work:* St John's Univ, Jamaica, NY. *Exhib:* Art Barn, Artists Equity & Nat Parks, 74; Art League Northern Va; Fairfax County Coun Arts; Potomac Valley Watercolor Soc; Southern Watercolor Soc; var local & regional shows in East & Southwest US. *Teaching:* Instr, Oriental brush painting, Northern Va Community Col, Manassas, 80-81. *Awards:* First Prize, Sumie Soc Am, 73 & 75; Third Prize, St Peter's 5th Ann Exhib, 75; Equal Merit Award, Potomac Valley Watercolor Soc, 77. *Bibliog:* Widening Horizons in Creative Arts, Ada King Wallis, 61. *Mem:* Sumie Soc Am (chap pres, 75-77); Fairfax County Coun Arts; Potomac Valley Watercolor Soc; Washington Women's Arts Ctr; Va Watercolor Soc; and others. *Media:* Watercolor, Acrylic. *Publ:* Contribr, Anima (an experimental journal), Vol VII, No 1. *Mailing Add:* 9617 Jomar Dr Fairfax VA 22032

WATSON, HELEN RICHTER
MURALIST, SCULPTOR

b Laredo, Tex, May 10, 26. *Study:* Scripps Col, Calif, BA, 47; Clarement Grad Sch & Univ Ctr, MFA, 59; spec work with Bernard Leach, 50; Swed Govt grant, Stockholm, Sweden, 52-53; spec work with Marguerite Wildenhain, 60; Alfred Univ, NY, 66. *Work:* Wichita Art Asn, Kans; Pitzer Col, Claremont, Calif; Pasadena Mus of Art, Calif. *Comn:* Murals, Lobby, Laredo Nat Bank, Tex, 58; stairwell, grill units & off dividers, Tyler Bank & Trust Co, Tex, 59; ceramic units, comn by Millard Sheets, Scottish Rite Masonic Temple, Los Angeles, 62; sculpture, Bicentennial Comt Corpus Christi, Nueces Co Courthouse, 76; sculpture, Enterprise Develop Assocs, Mall de Norte, Laredo, Tex, 77. *Exhib:* Media Explored, Laguna Beach Mus, Calif, 67; Artist as Craftsman--Craftsman as Artist, Long Beach Mus of Art, 67; 25 Yrs of Ceramic Art, Scripps Col, 69; one-woman show, Okla Art Ctr, Oklahoma City, 72; 1st Ann Exhib of Ceramic Art Women's Bldg, Los Angeles, 74; retrospective & doc exhib, Nuevo Santander Mus, Laredo, Tex, 79; and other group & one-man shows. *Teaching:* Instr ceramics, Chaffey Col, Ontario, Calif, 50-52, Mt San Antonio Col, Walnut, Calif, 55-57, Otis Art Inst, Los Angeles, 58-; artist in residence, Claremont Men's Col, Calif, 77-78. *Awards:* Frost Bros Award & Estill Gray Purchase Award, Witte Mem Mus, 51. *Bibliog:* Beverly Johnson (auth), From established artists come exciting new forms, Home Mag, Los Angeles Times, 2/72; Kim Blair (auth), Potter's career is shaping up, Los Angeles Times, 3/72; John P Simoni (auth), Excellent shows around the state, Wichita Eagle, 3/72. *Mem:* Southern Calif Designer Craftsmen; Design Div, Am Ceramic Soc; Artists Equity; Calif Design; Laredo Art Asn. *Publ:* Contribr, Twenty-five years of ceramic art, Ceramic Monthly, 70; contribr, Ceramics: A Potter's Handbook, Holt, Rinehart, Winston, 3rd ed, 71; contribr, Claywork: Form and Idea in Ceramic Design, Davis Publ, 75. *Dealer:* Barbara Beretich Gallery 8 Bonita & Harvard Rd Claremont CA 91711. *Mailing Add:* 520 E Sixth St Claremont CA 91711

WATSON, HOWARD N(OEL)
PAINTER, PRINTMAKER

b Pottsville, Pa, May 19, 29. *Study:* Pa State Univ, 47-49; Tyler Sch Fine Arts, 53-55; Mus Col Art, dipl, 60. *Work:* White House, Art in Embassies, Washington, DC; Temple Univ; private collections of Richard Manogian & Walter Mondale. *Comn:* Logan Square (mural), Archdiocese Philadelphia, 75; Betsy Ross Making Flag, Upholsterer Int Union NAm, Philadelphia, 76. *Exhib:* Pa Acad Fine Arts, 62-68; Denver's Artists of America, 81-82; Audubon Artist Show, New York; Am Watercolor Soc Exhibs, New York; Allied Artists Am Exhibs, New York; Knickerbocker Artists Exhibs, New York; Nat Acad, New York; Philadelphia Watercolor Club Shows. *Teaching:* Instr watercolor, Hussian Sch Fine Arts, 61-63, Philadelphia Col Art, 63-70 & Abington Art Ctr, 71- *Awards:* Super Achiever Award Art, Juvenile Diabetes Found, 78; Distinguished Pennsylvanians Award Art, State Pa, 80. *Bibliog:* Article, Forbes Mag, 80. *Mem:* Philadelphia Watercolor Club (pres, 82-83); Am Watercolor Soc; Allied Artists Am; Knickerbocker Artists. *Media:* Watercolor. *Publ:* Philadelphia Watercolors, Barre Publ, 70; Old Philadelphia Impressions, Heritage Publ, 76; Proud Past, 77. *Dealer:* Newman Art Gallery 1625 Walnut St Philadelphia PA. *Mailing Add:* Sedgley Commons Apt Z 844 N 29th St Philadelphia PA 19130

WATSON, KATHARINE JOHNSON
MUSEUM DIRECTOR, HISTORIAN

b Providence, RI, Nov 11, 42. *Study:* Duke Univ, BA, 64; Univ Pa, MA(art hist), 67, PhD(art hist), 73. *Pos:* Instr & cur of exhibs, Univ Pittsburgh, Pa, 69-70; cur art before 1800, Oberlin Col, 73-77; co-ed, Allen Mem Art Mus Bulletin, 74-77; dir, Bowdoin Col Mus Art, Brunswick, Maine, 77-; trustee,

Williamstown Regional Art Conserv Laboratory Inc & Mus Art, Ogunquit, currently; mem accreditation comn, Am Asn Mus, 83- *Teaching:* Instr Ital sculpture & Europ Baroque art, Univ Pittsburgh, 69-70; lectr mus sem, Oberlin Col, Ohio, 73-79; mus dir mus sem, Bowdoin Col, 78- *Awards:* Kress Found fel, Univ Pa, 67-68; Chester Dale fel, Nat Gallery Art, 70-71; Am Coun Learned Socs fel, 77-78; and others. *Mem:* Asn Art Mus Dirs; Col Art Asn; Am Asn Mus; New Eng Mus Asn. *Res:* Sixteenth and seventeenth century Italian sculpture; art patronage in eighteenth and nineteenth century America. *Publ:* Auth, A Bronze Mercury after Giambologna, Allen Art Mus Bulletin, 75-76; auth, Sculpture in the Allen Art Museum, Hellenistic to the Twentieth Century, Apollo, 76; auth, Sugar sculpture for grand ducal weddings from the Giambologna Workshop, The Connoisseur, 78; contribr, Giambologna 1527-1608: Sculptor to the Media, Arts Coun Gt Brit, 78; auth, Pietro Tacra, Garland Press, 83. *Mailing Add:* Bowdoin Col Mus of Art Brunswick ME 04011

WATSON, RONALD G
PAINTER, EDUCATOR
b Grand Island, Neb, Oct 9, 41. *Study:* Univ Neb, Lincoln, BFA, 64, MFA(Woods Painting Fel), 67. *Work:* Grand Rapids Art Mus, Mich; Nat Collection Fine Arts, Washington, DC. *Comn:* Outdoor steel sculpture, City of Grand Rapids, Mich, 74; sculpture garden, Veterans Admin, Washington, DC, 81. *Exhib:* One-man exhibs, Grand Rapids Art Mus, Mich, 73, Ohio State Univ Art Gallery, 78 & Dobrick Gallery, Chicago, 82; Works on Paper, San Jose Inst Contemp Art, Calif, 82; Delta Ann, Ark Art Ctr, Little Rock, 83. *Teaching:* Prof drawing & painting, Aquinas Col, Grand Rapids, Mich, 68-82 & Tex Christian Univ, 82- *Awards:* Artist Fel, Nat Endowment Arts, 75. *Bibliog:* Margaret Robinette (auth), Outdoor Sculpture, Watson-Guptill, 76; Fay L Hendry (auth), Outdoor Sculpture in Grand Rapids, Michigan, Iota Press, 74; Donald Thalacker (auth), Art in World of Architecture, Chelsea House, 80. *Mem:* Col Art Asn. *Publ:* Auth, The challenge of public sculpture, Mich Art J, 76; Art in public places, Ferris State Col, 79. *Dealer:* Ft Worth Gallery 901 Boland Ft Worth TX 76104. *Mailing Add:* 1015 Arch Adams #220 Ft Worth TX 76107

WATSON, ROSS
HISTORIAN
b Bangor, NIreland, July 29, 34. *Study:* Pembroke Col, Cambridge, BA(hist with hon), 56, MA, 59; Courtauld Inst Art, London, dipl (hist art, with distinction), 63. *Collections Arranged:* Brit Coun Exhib 18th Century English Watercolors (auth, catalog), Rijks Mus, Amsterdam, Albertina, Vienna, 66; J M W Turner from Mellon Collection, Nat Gallery Art, Washington, DC, 69; John Constable from Mellon Collection, 69; Joseph Wright Derby, from Mellon Collection, 69-70; William Hogarth from Mellon Collection, 70-71; Eye of Thomas Jefferson, Bicentennial Exhib, 76. *Pos:* Asst keeper, City Mus & Art Gallery, Birmingham, Eng, 63-66; asst cur, Paul Mellon Collection, Washington, DC, 66; cur, Nat Gallery Art, Washington, DC, 66-77. *Mem:* Walpole Soc; Asn Irish Art Hist. *Res:* Eighteenth century European, particularly British painting. *Publ:* Coauth, Renaissance furniture, Antiques Int, 66; auth, Guardi and the visit of Pius VI to Venice in 1782, Nat Gallery Art Report & Studies Hist Art, 67; auth, Irish portraits in American Collections, Irish Georgian Soc Bull, 69; auth, National Gallery of Art, Washington, DC, 79. *Mailing Add:* 5414 Cathedral Ave NW Washington DC 20016

WATSON-ABBOTT, LYNDA
JEWELER, SILVERSMITH
b Orange, Calif. *Study:* Orange Coast Col, AA; Rochester Inst of Technol; Chapman Col; Calif State Univ, Long Beach, BA, MA & MFA. *Work:* Objects USA, Johnson's Wax Co; Mus of Contemp Crafts, New York. *Exhib:* Art in Crafts, Bronx Mus, 77; Landscape, New Views, Cornell Univ, 78; Soc NAm Goldsmiths Europ Exhib, 79; Metals-Focus on Idea, Wash State Univ Traveling Exhib, 80-; Metalsmith's Exhib, Univ Kans, 81; and others. *Pos:* Designer/Production artist, Buzza Cardoza Greeting Card Co, 61-65; designer, Hencury Head Workshop, 65-69 & Signature V Collection, Reed and Barton Silversmiths, 76-78. *Teaching:* Instr jewelry metal, Calif State Univ, Los Angeles, 69, Cabrillo Col, 70- & Colo Mountain Col, summers 74-77 & 79. *Awards:* Nat Endowment Arts Craftsman's Grant, 77-78. *Bibliog:* Ralph Turner (auth), Contemporary Jewelry, Van Nostrand, Reinhold, 75; Olivia Emery (auth), Craftsman Lifestyle, Calif Design, 77; Analee Gold (auth), Crafts in Industry, Craft Horizons, 8/77. *Mem:* Am Crafts Coun; World Crafts Coun; Soc NAm Goldsmiths. *Media:* Silver; Copper, Brass. *Publ:* Contribr, Jewelry Techniques, Craft Horizons, Calif Design, Objects USA & Contemporary Jewelry, 78. *Mailing Add:* 418 Darwin St Santa Cruz CA 95062

WATTENMAKER, RICHARD J
MUSEUM DIRECTOR, HISTORIAN
b Philadelphia, Pa, Feb 22, 41. *Study:* Univ Pa, BA; New York Univ, Inst Fine Arts, MA, PhD. *Collections Arranged:* The Art of William Glackens (with catalog), 67; The Art of Charles Pendergast (with catalog), 68; The Art of Jean Hugo (with catalog), 73; The Fauves (with catalog), 75; Puvis de Chavannes and The Modern Tradition (with catalog), 75; The Dutch Cityscape in the 17th Century and its Sources (with catalog), 77; European Tools from the 17th to the 19th Century (with catalog), 81. *Pos:* Dir, Rutgers Univ Art Gallery, 66-69; chief cur, Art Gallery Ont, Toronto, 72-78; dir, Chrysler Mus, 79-80; dir, Flint Inst Arts, 80-, assoc art mus dir & trustee, Intermus Conserv Asn, Oberlin, currently. *Mem:* Col Art Asn; Am Asn Mus; Artist Blacksmith Asn NAm. *Res:* 19th and 20th century European painting; Renaissance and Post-Renaissance European painting; American painting and decorative art. *Publ:* Auth, Art Gallery of Ontario (illus handbook/catalog), Art Gallery Ont, 74. *Mailing Add:* Flint Inst Arts 1120 East Kearsley St Flint MI 48503

WATTS, ROBERT M
CONCEPTUAL ARTIST, DESIGNER
b US, June 14, 23. *Study:* Univ Louisville, BME, 44; Art Students League, 46-48; Columbia Univ, AM, 51. *Work:* Mod Museet, Stockholm; Houston Art Mus; Albright-Knox Art Mus, Buffalo; Art Inst Chicago. *Exhib:* New Media, New Forms II, Martha Jackson Gallery, New York, 60; Assemblage, 61 & The Machine, 68, Mus Mod Art; Whitney Mus Am Art Ann Contemp Am Sculpture, 65; Happening & Fluxus, Koelnischer Kunstverein, Koln, Ger, 71. *Teaching:* Prof film & mixed media, Rutgers Univ, New Brunswick, 52-, univ res coun grant for film & mixed media, 64-71; Carnegie Corp vis artist & consult, Univ Calif, Santa Cruz, 68. *Awards:* Exp Workshop Award, Carnegie Corp, 64. *Bibliog:* Max Kosloff (auth), Pop culture & the new vulgarians, Art Int, 62; Brian O'Dougherty (auth), Art: machines in revolt, 62 & Grace Glueck (auth), If its art you want...., 67, New York Times. *Mem:* Life mem Art Students League. *Media:* Mixed Media. *Publ:* Coauth, Newspaper, 63; auth, Fluxus, assorted events & objects, 64-72; auth, Postage stamps, fluxpost, 65; contribr, The Arts on Campus: the Necessity for Change, 70; coauth, Proposals for Art Education, 70. *Mailing Add:* RD 3 Bangor PA 18013

WAUFLE, ALAN DUANE
MUSEUM DIRECTOR
b Hornell, NY, Feb 11, 51. *Study:* Col William & Mary, BA; Duke Univ, MA. *Collections Arranged:* Antique Quilts & Coverlets of Gaston County, 77, Textile History of Gaston County, 78, Frank Creach: Retrospective, 78, The Christmas Doll, 79, Wheels & Runners: 18th Century America on the Move, 83, Gaston Co Mus Art & Hist. *Pos:* Dir, Gaston Co Mus Art & Hist, Dallas, NC, 76- *Mem:* NC Mus Coun; Am Asn State & Local Hist; Am Asn Mus; SE Mus Conf. *Res:* Iconography of works celebrating the 1571 Battle of Lepanto. *Mailing Add:* Gaston Co Mus Art & Hist PO Box 429 Dallas NC 28034

WAWRYTKO, M(ARY) F(RANCES)
ENAMELIST, SCULPTOR
b Sandusky, Ohio, Apr 28, 50. *Study:* Bowling Green State Univ, 70-73; Cleveland Inst Art, BFA, 77; Studio Foundry, lost wax casting, with Ron Dewey, 76-79. *Work:* Bowling Green State Univ Firelands Campus, Huron, Ohio. *Comn:* Grace Episcopal Church, Sandusky, Ohio, 77; Christ Episcopal Church, Huron, Ohio, 77 & 80; Calvary Episcopal Church, Sandusky, Ohio, 79-80. *Exhib:* Butler Inst Am Art, Youngstown, Ohio, 77 & 78; Massillon Mus, Ohio, 78; Equitable Gallery, Cleveland, 78; Wichita Art Asn, Kans, 79; Sandusky Area Cult Ctr, Ohio, 79; and others. *Awards:* Applied Arts Award, Ohio State Fair, 75; Purchase Prize, Butler Inst Am Art, 77 & 78; Sculpture Prize, Ohio Artists & Craftsmen Show, Massillon, Ohio, 78. *Bibliog:* Patricia Olson (auth), Precious creatures exhibited, Sandusky Register, 12/1/77; Edris Eckhardt (auth), Finding a future in the past, Nova News, 4/78; Helen Cullinan (auth), Rekindle lost techniques, Plain Dealer, 11/23/78. *Mem:* New Orgn Visual Arts; Natural Hist Mus Arts Soc; Ohio Designer Craftsmen; Am Crafts Coun; Artists Equity Asn. *Media:* Clay, Bronze. *Dealer:* Gallery Yolanda Inc 148 East Ontario Chicago IL 60611. *Mailing Add:* 1945 Columbus Rd Cleveland OH 44113

WAYNE, JUNE
PAINTER
b Chicago, Ill. *Work:* Bibliot Nat, France; Bibliot Royale Bruxelles; Mus Mod Art, New York; San Diego Mus Art; Art Inst Chicago; and others. *Exhib:* Tidal Waves & Visas: Tapestries & Lithography, June Wayne La Demeure, Paris, 75; From Lurcat to Today: Masterpieces of Tapestry, La Royale Belge, Bruxelles, Belg; Tapisseries, Lithographies, traveling, 76-79; The Dorothy Series, traveling, Western Asn Art Mus, 80-; and others. *Pos:* Founder & dir, Tamarind Lithography Workshop, 60-70; mem bd dirs, Grunwald Graphic Arts Found, Univ Calif, Los Angeles, 65-75, adv to Arts Mgt Prog, Grad Sch Admin, 69-; mem overseers comt, Sch Visual & Environ Arts, Harvard Univ, 74-76. *Awards:* For film, Golden Eagle, Cine, Academy Award Nomination, 74; Nat Endowment Arts Visual Arts Fel, 80; LULU Award, 83. *Bibliog:* Baskett (auth), The Art of June Wayne, Abrams, 68; Dominique De Santi (auth), Les Tempetes de June Wayne, Le Monde, Paris; Bernard Kester (auth), The tapestries of June Wayne, Craft Horizons, 74; plus others. *Mem:* Art Table; Women Film; Severance Soc; Artists Equity. *Publ:* Auth, The creative process: Artists, carpenters and the flat earth soc, Craft Horizons, 76. *Dealer:* Armstrong Gallery 50 W 57th St New York Ny 10019; Peter Plone Assocs 1108 N Tamarind Ave Los Angeles CA 90038. *Mailing Add:* 1108 N Tamarind Ave Los Angeles CA 90038

WEARE, SHANE
PRINTMAKER
b England, Aug 29, 36. *Study:* Royal Col Art, London, Eng, ARCA(printmaking), 63; Univ Iowa, asst etching, 63-64. *Work:* Brit Mus, London; Lib Libr Cong, Washington, DC; Brooklyn Mus, NY; Art Inst Chicago; San Francisco Mus Art. *Exhib:* Int Exhib Graphic Art, Ljubliana, Yugoslavia, 66; Brit Int Print Biennale, 68; 22nd Ann Print Exhib, Boston Mus, 70; World Print Competition, San Francisco Mus Art, 73; one-man show, Calif Palace of Legion of Honor, City of San Francisco, 73; 20th Nat Print Exhib, Brooklyn Mus, New York, 77. *Awards:* Purchase Awards, Los Angeles Soc Printmakers, 68-74, City of San Francisco, 72, City of Palo Alto, 74 & Univ Colo, 74; Spaces Between Prog Award, KQED-TV, San Francisco, 75. *Bibliog:* John Brunsden (auth), Technique of Etching & Engraving, Batsford, 66. *Mem:* Calif Soc Printmakers (vchmn, 72-73). *Media:* Pastel. *Dealer:* Soker-Kaseman Gallery 1457 Grant Ave San Francisco CA 94133. *Mailing Add:* 6449 Harwood Ave Oakland CA 94618

WEAVER, JAMES D
MUSEUM DIRECTOR
b Houston, Tex, Oct 13, 49. *Study:* Univ Houston, BA(art hist), 75; Syracuse Univ, MFA(museology), 78. *Collections Arranged:* Charles Jones: Vietnam Suite (auth, catalog), Tyler Mus Art, Tex, 82; Springfield Art Museum's Permanent Collection (coauth, catalog), 81; Recent Works from East Tex (auth, catalog), 82, Paintings and Prints from Tyler Collections: Part I (auth, catalog), 82, Depictions of the Advent in Early European Art, 83, Karl Umlauf: The First Twenty Years (auth, catalog), 83 & Midnight Air: Don Beason (auth, catalog), 83, Tyler Mus Art, Tex. *Pos:* Cur educ, Springfield Art Mus, Mo, 79-81; dir, Tyler Mus Art, Tex, 81- *Teaching:* Guest prof, Univ Tex, Tyler, 82- *Mailing Add:* 1300 S Mahon Ave Tyler TX 75701

WEAVER, JOHN BARNEY
SCULPTOR
b Anaconda, Mont, Mar 28, 20. *Study:* Art Inst Chicago, dipl(Albert Kuppenhiemer Scholar), 46; monumental sculpture with Albin Polasek, Emil Zettler, Edward Chasang & Egon Weiner. *Work:* Bronzes, Charles Russell, Statuary Hall, Washington, DC, Double Equestrian, Fort Walsh, Sask, Archaic Indian, NY State Mus, Albany & Govt House, Edmonton, Alta; Astokimake (portrait bust), Rideau Hall, Ottawa; heads & figures, Anthrop Hall, Smithsonian Inst. *Comn:* The Stake & The Pronghorns (bronze), Prov Mus & Arch, Alta, 67; Madonna of the Wheat, Edmonton, Alta, 81; Arthur Henry Griesbach, Edmonton, Alta, 81; Deerfoot, Calgary, Alta, 82; Indian Archer and Geese (aluminum cast friczc), Edmonton, Alta, 83. *Exhib:* Chicago & Vicinity, Art Inst Chicago, 47; 68th Exhib Soc Washington Artists, Natural Hist Bldg, Washington, DC, 61; Steel to the West (bronze), US, Toronto, London, Paris & Brussels, 78; Media Ctr, Robson Sq, Vancouver, BC, 80; Salon Nations, Paris, 83. *Pos:* Sculptor, Mont Hist Soc, 55-60, Smithsonian Inst, 61-66 & Provincial Mus & Archives, Alta, 66-71. *Teaching:* Instr life drawing, Layton Sch Art, Milwaukee, 46-51; instr life drawing & sculpture, Grant McEwan Community Col, Edmonton, Alta, 72-76. *Awards:* Alta Achievement Award for Excellence in Sculpture, 77; Diploma Merit, Univ Arts, Parma, Italy, 81; Gold Medal, Int Parliament Security & Peace, 82. *Bibliog:* Ruth Bowen (auth), Alberta art in bronze, My Golden West, 70; Mario Monteverdi & Calogero Panepinto (auth), The history of international art, Univ Arts, Parma, Italy, 82. *Mem:* Italian Acad Art, Parma; Acad Europe; Acad Nations; life mem Univ Mont Mus Rockies; life mem Mont State Hist Soc. *Media:* Bronze. *Dealer:* Studio West Ltd Fine Art Bronze Foundry PO Box 550 Cochrane AB T0L 0W0 Can. *Mailing Add:* PO Box 1723 Hope BC V0X 1L0 Canada

WEAVER, (JOHN) ROBERT
PAINTER, PRINTMAKER
b Stillwell, Kans, Sept 9, 35. *Study:* Kansas City Art Inst, BFA, 65; Univ NMex, Tamarind Found printer fel, 66; Univ Nebr, MFA, 68. *Work:* Albrecht Art Gallery, St Joseph, Mo; Sheldon Mem Art Gallery, Lincoln, Nebr; Ill State Univ, Bloomington-Normal; Okla Art Ctr, Oklahoma City; Univ Wis-Green Bay. *Exhib:* One-man shows, Albrecht Art Gallery, St Joseph, Mo, 69, Sheldon Mem Art Gallery, Lincoln, Nebr, 72, Canton Art Inst, Ohio, 73, Slippery Rock State Col, Pa, 73 & Landfall Press, Chicago, 79; Invitational Nebr '75, Joslyn Art Mus, Omaha, 75. *Awards:* William Vreeland Award, Univ Nebr, 67; Governor's Arts Award, 78. *Media:* Oil; Printmaking. *Mailing Add:* 1219 McCarty Jefferson City MO 65101

WEBB, FRANK (FRANCIS H)
PAINTER, INSTRUCTOR
b North Versailles, Pa, Sept 14, 27. *Study:* Art Inst Pittsburgh, with Edgar A Whitney. *Work:* Butler Inst Am Art, Youngstown, Ohio; PPG Found, Pittsburgh; Tweed Art Mus, Duluth, Mich; Ford Times Collection, Detroit. *Exhib:* Am Watercolor Soc Ann, Nat Acad, New York, 71-80; Nat Arts Club, New York, 71-81; Butler Inst Am Art, Youngstown, Ohio, 73; Audubon Artists, Nat Arts Club, New York, 73-83; Allied Artists, Nat Arts Club, New York, 73-80; Nat Acad Ann, New York, 77; Midwest Watercolor Soc Ann, Rawr-West Mus, Manitowac, Wis, 79-83; and many others. *Pos:* Pres, Phillips Studio, Pittsburgh, 57-80. *Teaching:* Guest lectr painting throughout US and Canada, 73- *Awards:* Sizek Award, Butler Midyear Ann, Butler Inst Am Art, Youngstown, Ohio, 73; Bronze Medal of Honor, Am Watercolor Soc, 76; Aquamedia Award, Rocky Mountain Nat, 75. *Bibliog:* Barbara Nechis (auth), Watercolor the creative experience, North Light, 79; Edward Betts (auth), Creative Seascape Painting, Watson-Guptill, 81. *Mem:* Am Watercolor Soc; Rocky Mountain Nat Watermedia Asn; Allied Artists of Am; Audubon Artists. *Media:* Watercolor. *Publ:* Illusr, Watercolor Energies, North Light Publ, 83. *Mailing Add:* 108 Washington St Pittsburgh PA 15218

WEBB, TODD
PHOTOGRAPHER, HISTORIAN
b Detroit, Mich, Sept 15, 05. *Work:* Mus City New York, Mus Mod Art, New York; Worcester Art Mus, Mass; NMex Fine Arts Mus, Santa Fe. *Exhib:* I See a City (prints), Mus City New York, 46; Diogenes With a Camera, Mus Mod Art, 53; solo exhibs, Chicago Art Inst, 56, Amon Carter Mus, Ft Worth, 65 & NMex Mus, Santa Fe, 71; Ideas & Images, Am Found Arts, New York, 62-64. *Awards:* Guggenheim Fel, 55 & 56; Nat Endowment Arts Grant, 79. *Publ:* Auth, Gold Strikes and Ghost Towns, 61 & The Gold Rush Trail and the Road to Oregon, 63, Doubleday; illusr, 19th Century Texas Homes, 65 & 19th Century Public Buildings, 74, Univ Tex Press. *Mailing Add:* 120 North St Bath ME 04530

WEBBER, HELEN
TAPESTRY ARTIST, PAINTER
b New York, NY, June 18, 28. *Study:* Queens Col, BA, 51; RI Sch Design, with Norman LaLiberte, MA, 62. *Work:* Fluor Corp Hq Collection, Irvine, Calif. *Comn:* Tapestries & mosaic columns, Bay Area Rapid Transit Hq, San Francisco & Oakland, 72; tapestries, Carnival Cruise Lines, Miami, 81; tapestry, St Patrick's Hosp, Lake Charles, La, 83; tapestry, Radisson Plaza Hotel, Lexington, Ky; tapestry, Liberty Bank, Houston; and others. *Exhib:* Brooklyn Mus, 63; solo exhibs, Gallerie Int, New York, 64, & Jones Gallery, La Jolla, 78 & Burlington House, New York, 80; Mus Contemp Crafts, New York, 65; Ctr Arts, Scottsdale, Ariz, 81. *Pos:* Founder, Women Design, Aspen, 77; pres, Women Design Int, 83- *Teaching:* Instr, Calif Col Arts & Crafts, Oakland, 73-74. *Awards:* First in Watercolor, RI Arts Festival, 59; Outstanding Contribution Design, Women Design Int, 80. *Bibliog:* Art and Fabric: Helen Webber, Today's Art & Graphics, 4/81; A profile of the artist, Interiors Mag, 12/81; Bestiary tapestry/Am Artist Series, Readers Digest, 5/81. *Media:* Fabric Collage. *Publ:* Auth & illusr, The Sea is My Blanket, Astor Bks, 65; illusr, What is Sweet, What is Sour, Holt, Rinehart, 67; illusr, Miranda's Music, Thomas Crowell Co, 68; illusr, The Frog's Saddlehorse and Other Tales, J B Lippincott, 71; auth, Art in Public Places in the US, Bowling Green Univ Press, 75. *Mailing Add:* Heron Int Studios 410 Townsend St San Francisco CA 94107

WEBER, ALBERT JACOB
PAINTER, EDUCATOR
b Chicago, Ill, July 10, 19. *Study:* Art Inst Chicago, BFA; Mexico City Col, MAA. *Exhib:* Pa Acad Fine Arts, 50, 52, 59 & 60; five shows, Univ Mich, 56-69; Soc Washington Printmakers, 57 & 60; Detroit Inst Art, 57, 60 & 66; Am Fedn Arts Traveling Exhibs, 58-60; plus many other group & one-man shows. *Teaching:* Instr, Mexico City Col; prof art, Univ Mich, Ann Arbor, 55- *Awards:* Prize, Grand Rapids Art Gallery, 58; Purchase Prizes, Butler Inst Am Art, 59-61; Purchase Prize, Graphic Art & Drawing Exhib, Olivet Col, Mich, 62; H Rackham Grant for Travel and Painting, 80-81; plus others. *Mailing Add:* 554 Elizabeth Apt 4 Ann Arbor MI 48104

WEBER, IDELLE
PAINTER
b Chicago, Ill. *Study:* Scripps Col; Univ Calif, Los Angeles, BA & MA. *Work:* Nat Collection Fine Arts, Washington, DC; Va Mus, Richmond; Worcester Art Mus, Mass; Albright-Knox Art Gallery, Buffalo, NY; Yale Univ Art Gallery, New Haven, Conn; and others. *Exhib:* Guggenheim Mus, New York, 64; Wadsworth Atheneum, Hartford, Conn, 66 & 74; Whitney Downtown, New York, 75; Realismus und Realitat, Darmstadt, WGer, 75; Nat Collection Fine Arts, 76; McNay Art Inst, San Antonio, 76; O K Harris Gallery, 77 & 79; City Univ New York, 78; Contemp Am Realism Since 1960, Pa Acad Fine Arts, 81; Larry Aldrich Ctr Contemp Arts, 81; and many others. *Teaching:* Adj asst prof, Grad Div, NY Univ. *Awards:* Nat Scholastic Art Awards, Scripps Col. *Bibliog:* Alwynne Mackie (auth), New realism and the photographic look, Am Art Review, 78; Charlotte S Rubinstein (auth), American Women Artists: From Early Indian Times to Present, G K Hall/Avon, 82; and others. *Mem:* Col Art Asn; Women's Caucus Art. *Media:* Oil, Watercolor. *Mailing Add:* c/o Siegel Contemporary Art 24 W 57th St New York NY 10019

WEBER, JAN
PAINTER
b Lafayette, Ind. *Study:* Univ NMex; pvt instructors. *Work:* Gov Mansion, Santa Fe, NMex; Bataan Mem Hosp, Albuquerque, NMex. *Exhib:* NMex Biennial, Santa Fe; El Paso Sun Carnival, Tex; travel exhib, Hoosier Art Salon, Indianapolis, Ind; Southern Colo State Col, Pueblo; NMex Arts & Crafts, Albuquerque. *Teaching:* Instr painting & drawing, Art Ctr Sch, Albuquerque, 66-69; instr painting & drawing, Kirtland AFB, 67-72; instr painting & drawing, Sandia Base, Albuquerque, 67-74. *Mem:* Artists Equity; Nat League Am Pen Women; NMex Arts & Crafts (bd mem, 74-75). *Media:* Oil, Acrylic. *Dealer:* Kachina Gallery 114 Old Santa Fe Trail Santa Fe NM 87501. *Mailing Add:* 7133 Kiowa Ave NE Albuquerque NM 87110

WEBER, JEAN M
MUSEUM DIRECTOR, ADMINISTRATOR
b Boston, Mass, Apr 2, 33. *Study:* Brown Univ, BA; RI Sch Design; Edinburgh Univ; State Univ Iowa. *Collections Arranged:* The Summer Place, 70; American Impressions, 70; Commedia dell'Arte, 71; Objects & Images, 71; Tantric Art of Tibet, 72; Ceramic Arts of China, 74; Viewpoints: The American Land, 76; Fairfield Porter's Maine, 77. *Pos:* Dir, J B Speed Art Gallery, Louisville, Ky, 66-69; Dir, Parrish Art Mus, Southampton, NY, 69-79; vpres, NE Mus Conf, 78-79, pres, 79-80; dir, Rochester Mus, Rochester Mus & Sci Ctr, 79-81; dir, Mus NMex, 81-; co-dir, Mus Mangement Inst, Univ Calif, Berkeley, 81; adv coun, Nat Mus Act, Washington, DC, 81-82; State Dept Cultural Exchange, China Delegation, 81; trustee, Interpueblo Cult Ctr, 81-82, Brown Univ, 83- *Teaching:* Adj assoc prof, Southampton Col, 70-79. *Awards:* Danforth Found Fel, 54-55; Int Mus Sem Award, NY State Coun Art, Metrop Mus, 72. *Mem:* Am Asn Mus; Int Coun Mus; NY State Asn Mus. *Publ:* Auth, articles in Am Art Rev, Museologist & Mus News. *Mailing Add:* c/o Mus NMex PO Box 2087 Santa Fe NM 87503

WEBER, JOHN
DEALER
Pos: Assoc cur, Dayton Art Inst, Ohio, 58-60; dir, Martha Jackson Gallery, New York, 60-62; dir, Dwan Gallery, Los Angeles & New York, 62-71; pres, John Weber Gallery, New York, 71- *Mem:* Art Dealers Am. *Specialty:* Contemporary art. *Mailing Add:* 142 Greene New York NY 10012

WEBER, JOHN PITMAN
MURALIST, EDUCATOR

b Washington, DC, Dec 6, 42. *Study:* Harvard Col, BA(cum laude), 64; Atelier 17, Paris, with S Hayter & Jean Helion, Fulbright-Hayes Scholar, 64-66; Ecole des Beaux Arts; Art Inst Chicago, with Yoshida & Halsted, MFA(painting), 68. *Comn:* Wall of Choices, Nat Endowment Arts, Christopher House Settlement, Chicago, 70; The Builders (with Celia Radek), Nat Endowment Arts, A to Z Equip, Chicago, 75; Profecy (mural), comn by Hillard Weiss, Chicago, 77; For the People of the Future (mural, with Lynn Takata), Human Serv, Chicago, 80; Circulo Vivo (mural, with Lynn Takata), Youth Servs, Chicago, 81. *Exhib:* Murals for the People, Mus of Contemp Art, Chicago, 71; Radical Attitudes Toward the Gallery, Art Net, London, Eng, 77; Mural Art USA, Royal Mus, Bruxelles, Belguim, 78; L'art Public, Caen, France, 81; solo exhibs, Gallery 345, New York, 83 & 84; and others. *Pos:* Dir & founding mem, Chicago Mural Group, Chicago, 70- *Teaching:* Assoc prof studio art & art hist, Elmhurst Col, Ill, 68-; adj asst prof mural art, Art Inst Chicago, 73-75; vis artist mural workshop, Univ NDak, Grand Forks, 75 & Dartington Col Art, Eng, 80. *Awards:* Sheffield & Barry Mural, 72, Wilton/Diversey Mural, 73 & Haas Park Mural, 76. *Mem:* Nat Art Educ Asn; Alliance Cult Democracy. *Media:* Assemblage, Etching. *Publ:* Auth, Murals as people's art, In: Les Etats Unis en Movement, DeNoel, Paris, 72; coauth, A critical context for community murals, El Gallo Illus, 77; coauth, Toward a People's Art, The Contemporary Mural Movement, Dutton, 77; auth, Murals, an update, New Art Examiner, 5/78; auth, Community Sculpture, Art & Artists, 2/83. *Mailing Add:* 4830 N Springfield Chicago IL 60625

WEBSTER, LARRY
PAINTER, PRINTMAKER

b Arlington, Mass, Mar 18, 30. *Study:* Mass Col Art, BFA; Boston Univ, MS. *Work:* DeCordova Mus, Lincoln, Mass; Grand Rapids Art Mus, Mich; Munic Gallery, Davenport, Iowa; Springfield Art Mus, Mo; Art Mus, Colby Col, Waterville, Maine; and others. *Exhib:* Nat Acad Design, New York, 66-81; Allied Artists Am, 64-81; Am Watercolor Soc, New York, 61-79; Watercolor USA; Rocky Mountain Nat Watermedia Exhib, 78-81. *Pos:* Package designer, Union Bag & Paper Corp, 53-54; illusr, USA, 54-56; graphic designer, vpres & dir, Thomas Todd Co, Boston, 56-78. *Teaching:* Asst prof typographic design, hist type & watercolor painting, Mass Col Art, 64-65. *Awards:* Golden Award, Rocky Mountain Nat Watermedia Exhib, 78 & 79; Fetzer Mem Award, Rocky Mountain Nat Watermedia Exhib, 81; High Winds Medal, Am Watercolor Soc, 82; and others. *Mem:* Nat Acad Design; Am Watercolor Soc; Allied Artists Am; Soc Printers, Boston; Boston Watercolor Soc. *Media:* Watercolor, Acrylic; Intaglio, Mixed Media. *Mailing Add:* 116 Perkins Row Topsfield MA 01983

WEBSTER, SALLY (SARA B)
HISTORIAN

b Hammond, Ind, May 24, 38. *Study:* Barnard Col, BA, 59; Harvard-Radcliffe Prog in Business Admin, cert, 60; Univ Cincinnati, MA, 74; Grad Ctr, City Univ New York, PhD(Am art). *Pos:* Dir educ, Taft Mus, Cincinnati, Ohio, 74-75; dir, AIR Gallery, New York, 79-81; partner, Rose Web Proj, New York. *Teaching:* Instr hist art, Col Staten Island, fall 83. *Mem:* Heresies Collective, New York; Col Art Asn; Soc Archit Historians; Arch Am Art; Asn Historians Am Art. *Publ:* Auth, In der Kunst der Frau provoziert die Frage nach, Frauen in Amerika, 78; auth, Thomas Anshutz: the Philadelphia connection, Arts, 79; auth, Mary Cassatt's Allegory of Modern Woman, Helicon Nine, 79; auth, A Report: Alternative Spaces and the Crisis Threatening Their Survival, Nat Endowment Arts, spring 82; auth, Collaboration: Patsy Norvell & Robert Zakanitch, Norton Gallery & Sch Art, 83. *Mailing Add:* 158 W 94th St New York NY 10025

WEBSTER, STOKELY
PAINTER, PRINTMAKER

b Evanston, Ill, Aug 23, 12. *Study:* With Lawton Parker, Paris, 22; Art Students League; Nat Acad Design; Yale Univ Sch Fine Arts, with Wayman Adams. *Work:* Mus of City New York; Phillips Collection, DC; Nat Collection Am Art, Washington, DC; Indianapolis Mus Art; Newark Mus, NJ; and others. *Comn:* Many portrait comn. *Exhib:* Nat Acad Design, New York, 45-; Salon des Artiste Francais, Paris, 70-73; Salon d'Automne, Paris, 73-74; Chicago Art Inst; one-man shows, Eric Gallery, New York, 75. *Teaching:* Instr, Winter Park Artists Workshop, Stetson Univ. *Awards:* First Halgarten Prize, Nat Acad Design. *Media:* Oil; Graphic, Etching. *Mailing Add:* 255 Ocean Palm Dr Flagler Beach FL 32036

WECHSLER, JUDITH GLATZER
HISTORIAN, FILMMAKER

b Chicago, Ill, Dec 28, 40. *Study:* Brandeis Univ, BA, 62; Columbia Univ, MA, 67; Univ Calif, Los Angeles, PhD, 72. *Comn:* Daumier, Paris, and the Spectator (film), 77; Cezanne the Late Work (film), 78; Pissarro, At the Heart of Impressionism (film), 81; Edouard Manet: Painter of Modern Life (film), 83. *Collections Arranged:* Robert Moskowitz (cataloged), Mass Inst Technol Hayden Gallery, 71; Daumier: Parisian Types, Brandeis Univ, 79. *Pos:* Asst ed, Schocken Books Inc, NY, 63-65; consult, off of Charles and Ray Eames, Venice, Calif, 76-78; res fel, Ctr for Advanced Visual Studies, Mass Inst Technol, 77-79. *Teaching:* Vis lectr, Brown Univ, 70; asst prof to assoc prof 19th & 20th century art, Mass Inst Technol, 70-77; vis assoc prof 19th & 20th century art, Tufts Univ, Medford, Mass, 79-81; lectr, Harvard Univ, 81-82; assoc prof, RI Sch Design, 81- *Awards:* Nat Endowment for Humanities fel grants, summer 73 & 75; Nat Endowment Arts, 81; Nat Endowment Humanities Grant, 83-84. *Mem:* Col Art Asn. *Res:* 19th and 20th century art; film series on Western post-Renaissance art. *Publ:* Ed introd, Cezanne in Perspective, Prentice-Hall Inc, 75; auth, Gyorgy Kepes, 78 & ed introd, On Aesthetics in Science, 78, MIT Press; auth, The Interpretation of Cezanne, UMI Res Press, 81; auth, A Human Comedy: Physiognomy and Caricature in 19th Century Paris, Thames and Hudson Ltd, Univ Chicago Press, 82. *Mailing Add:* 68 Fuller St Brookline MA 02146

WECHSLER, SUSAN
CURATOR, WRITER

b Neptune, NJ, Sept 15, 43. *Study:* Douglass Col, Rutgers Univ, BA, 65; Teachers Col, Columbia Univ. *Exhib:* Marietta Crafts Nat, 75; solo exhib, Queens Mus, NY, 76; Object: Color and Craft, Brockton Art Ctr, Mass, 77; Women Artists: Clay, Fiber and Metal, Bronx Mus, 78 & traveling. *Collections Arranged:* The Raw Edge: Ceramic of the Eighties (with catalog), Hillwood Art Gallery, C W Post Col, 83. *Pos:* Coordr, Arch Ceramic Art, Alfred Univ, 82- *Teaching:* Adj ceramic hist, Parsons Sch Design, 83. *Awards:* Artpark Fel, Nat Heritage Trust, 77; Nat Endowment Arts Award, 81. *Mem:* Nat Oral Hist Asn; Nat Coun Educ Ceramic Arts; Am Craft Coun; Int Asn Art Critics. *Res:* Contemporary American ceramics. *Publ:* Auth, Low-Fire Ceramics: A New Direction in American Clay, Watson-Guptill, 81; contribr, Who's Afraid of American Pottery (catalog), Dienst Beeldende Kunst, 82; auth, Ron Nagle: An interview, Vol 1, No 1, 82 & Celestial bodies, Vol 2, No 2, 83, Am Ceramics. *Mailing Add:* 420 West End Ave New York NY 10024

WECHTER, VIVIENNE THAUL
EDUCATOR, PAINTER

b New York, NY. *Study:* Jamaica Teachers Col, with Hunter, BP; Columbia Univ; NY Univ; Pratt Inst; Sculpture Ctr, New York; Art Students League; with Robert Beverly Hale & de Creeft; Morris Davidson Sch Mod Art; Union Grad Sch, NY, PhD. *Work:* Corcoran Gallery Art, Washington, DC; Everson Mus, Syracuse, NY; Johnson Mus, Cornell Univ, Ithaca, NY; Notre Dame Mus, South Bend, Ind; Mus Fine Art, Houston & Ft Worth, Tex. *Comn:* The Emerging Sun (sculpture), Manhattan Psychiatric Ctr, New York, 79; Leap into Faith (sculpture), George Meany Ctr Labor Studies, Washington, DC, 81; The Tradition of Caring (250 bronzes), Miami Jewish Home for Aged & Hosp & Gerontology Inst; colored lithographs, comn by Atelier Eleanor Ettinger. *Exhib:* Mus Mod Art, New York; Works on Paper, Pavilion D'Exposition, Paris, 75; Invitational Biennale, Mus Mod Art, Rijeka, Yugoslavia, 76, 78 & 80; solo shows, Franklin & Marshall Col, Pa, 79 & Kornblatt Gallery, Baltimore, Md, 80; Regional Invitational, City Univ New York Grad Ctr; Contemp Issues Women, traveling throughout US; Everson Mus, 80; and many others. *Pos:* Moderator weekly broadcast arts & humanities, Today's World, formerly; vpres, IAA-US Comt, UNESCO, currently. *Teaching:* Artist in residence, Fordham Univ, 64-, chmn acquisitions & exhibs, 64-, prof inter-arts, 67-; vis artist, Kansas City Art Inst, Marist Col, Md Inst Col Art & others. *Awards:* Am Soc Artists; Jersey City Mus; Am Acad Arts & Letts. *Bibliog:* G Brown (auth), article, 68, R Gurin (auth), article, 68 & Ronald Kuchta (auth), article, 81, Arts Mag. *Mem:* Col Art Asn Am; Fedn Mod Painters & Sculptors (vpres, currently); Am Soc Artists; Kappa Pi. *Publ:* Illusr, The Park of Jonas, 67; ed, Five Museums Come to Fordham, 68; ed, Visual Fordham, 69 & 70; auth, A View From the Ark, Barlenmir House, 75; auth, Philosophical Aspects of Thanatology, Arno Press. *Mailing Add:* Fac Mem Hall Fordham Univ Bronx NY 10458

WECKER, CHRISTOPH ULRICH
GALLERY DIRECTOR

b Heilbronn, WGer, Dec 9, 21. *Study:* Tubingen, Ger, PhD(law & econ). *Pos:* Dir, Goethe House New York, 75- *Mailing Add:* 1014 Fifth Ave New York NY 10028

WEDDIGE, EMIL
LITHOGRAPHER, EDUCATOR

b Sandwich, Ont, Dec 23, 07; US citizen. *Study:* Eastern Mich Univ, BS; Univ Mich, MDes; also with Emil Ganse, Morris Kantor & E Desjobert, France. *Work:* Metrop Mus Art, New York; Cape Kennedy, Fla; Libr Cong, Washington, DC; Philadelphia Mus Art; Detroit Art Inst. *Comn:* Lithography in color, Chrysler Motor Car Co, 55; suite of lithographs in color, Parke, Davis & Co, 56; History of Paper (suite), Dow Chem Co, 57; portrait of a city, Detroit Edison Co, 58; Sesquicentennial Suite, Univ Mich, 66. *Exhib:* Joseph Pennel Exhib, 34-68; Am Color Print Soc, 48-71; Print Club, 48-71; Biennial Color Print Exhib, 52 & 54; Van Gogh Mem Exhib, Pontoise, France, 60. *Teaching:* Instr art, Eastern Mich Univ, 36-37; prof art, Univ Mich, Ann Arbor, 38-73, emer prof, 73- *Awards:* Founders Prize, Detroit Inst Arts, 42; Best Print Award, Am Color Print Soc, 56; James Cleating Print Prize, Michigan Exhib, 64. *Bibliog:* Article, Statesman, India, 60; Joy Hakanson (auth), Art, Detroit News, 69; William Tall (auth), Art, Detroit Freepress, 69. *Mem:* Am Fedn Arts; Am Color Print Soc; Print Club; Print Coun Am. *Publ:* Auth, Lithography, 66. *Dealer:* Gallery Renaissance 400 Renaissance Ctr Suite 282 Detroit MI 48243; Cares Gallery 111 E Oak Chicago IL 60611. *Mailing Add:* 870 Stein Rd Ann Arbor MI 48103

WEDIN, WINSLOW ELLIOTT
ARCHITECT, EDUCATOR

b Minneapolis, Minn, Sept 30, 33. *Study:* Univ Minn, BA(art) & BA(archit); St Paul Sch Art; Auburn Univ; Fla State Univ, MA, also with Ralph Rapson, Edward Young, Christian Schmidt & Elof Wedin. *Comn:* Ensculptic III (environ sculpture in plastic), comn by Mr & Mrs James Littlejohn, 66; mural around hall, Knights of Columbus, Crystal City, Minn; testing lab on I-75, State of Fla, 74. *Exhib:* Minn State Fair, St Paul, 56-64; Lutheran Brotherhood Exhib, 58; Collector's Gallery, Minneapolis, 62; Univ Women's Club, St Paul, 63 & 64; one-man show, Ramsey Jr Col, St Paul, 68. *Pos:* Free lance architect, 60-; design consult, Int Design Ctr, Minneapolis, 66-69. *Teaching:* Asst prof archit, Auburn Univ, 68-70; asst prof educ facilities, Fla State Univ, 71-73, asst prof housing design, 73-; vis assoc prof archit, Univ Petroleum & Minerals, Dhahran, Saudi Arabia, 76-79; vis critic, Univ NC, Charlotte, 81. *Awards:* Second Prize for Jewelry, Minn State Fair, 59; First Prize for Sculpture, Soc Minn Sculptors, 62; Fla Solar Energy Ctr, 80. *Bibliog:* House made from spray foam, Life Mag, 3/70; Cindy Miller (auth), Condo living, Tallahassee Democrat, 75; Futurist architect in Saudi Arabia, Futurist, 81. *Mem:* Soc Minn Sculptors (vpres, 66-68); Lemoyne Art Found, Tallahassee; Walker Art Found, Minneapolis; World Futures Soc, Tallahassee (pres, 74-76 & 80-81); co-founder Ctr Aesthet Exploration, Washington, DC. *Media:* Wood, Concrete. *Publ:* Contribr, Educational Environments for Latin America, Fla State Univ, 71; coauth, The Open Media Center, Drexel Univ, 72; coauth, The Responsive House, Mass Inst Technol, 74; auth, The Copper Bannana, Elixir Inst Tallahassee, 75. *Mailing Add:* 220-5 North Belmont Rd Tallahassee FL 32301

WEEBER, GRETCHEN
PAINTER
b Albany, NY. *Study:* Albany Inst Hist & Art; Inst Allende, San Miguel de Allende, Mex; also with Betty Warren. *Work:* Rensselaer Co Hist Soc, Troy, NY; Home Savings Bank, Albany; NY State Conf Mayors, Albany; First Lutheran Church, Albany; Hadwen House, Satler Mus, Nantucket, Mass; plus others in pvt collections. *Exhib:* Greater Schenectady Exhib, NY, 60-66; NY State Expos, Syracuse, 62 & 64; Berkshire Ann, Pittsfield, Mass, 64, 67 & 68; Artists Asn Nantucket, Kenneth Taylor Galleries, Mass, 69-; Artists of the Upper Hudson, Albany Inst Hist & Art, 70; and many other group & one-man shows. *Awards:* Raymond Scofield Prize for Best Watercolor, Albany Artists Group, 64; First Prize, Rensselaer Co Hist Soc, 68; Georgie Walling Award for Nantucket Subjects, Artists Asn Nantucket, 76. *Mem:* Artists Asn Nantucket (bd mem, 72-73). *Media:* Watercolor. *Mailing Add:* 11 N Liberty St Nantucket MA 02554

WEEDMAN, KENNETH RUSSELL
SCULPTOR, PRINTMAKER
b Little Rock, Ark, Sept 26, 39. *Study:* Memphis Acad Art; Univ Tulsa, BA & MA. *Work:* Cincinnati Mus Art, Ohio; Masur Mus Art, Monroe, La; Univ Tulsa; Baldwin-Wallace Art & Drama Ctr, Berea, Ohio. *Exhib:* Conn Acad, Wadsworth Atheneum Mus, 66; Artist of Southeast & Tex Biennials, New Orleans City Art Mus, 66, 71 & 75; Past Jurors, Okla Art Ctr, Oklahoma City, 69; one-man shows, Bienville Gallery, New Orleans, 71 & Art & Drama Ctr Galleries, Baldwin-Wallace Col, 73; Prints: Made in Kentucky, Louisville Art Gallery, 83. *Collections Arranged:* Old Master Prints, 81 & English Graphics, 84, Cumberland Col Gallery. *Pos:* Ed, Sculpture Quart, Southern Asn Sculptures, 74-75; cur, Cumberland Col, 81- *Teaching:* Instr sculpture, Sul Ross State Col, Alpine, Tex, 65-66; vis artist, Nicholls State Univ, Thibodaux, La, 70-71; asst prof sculpture, Cumberland Col, Williamsburg, Ky, 68- *Awards:* Purchase Award, 6th Delta Exhib, Ark Arts Ctr, 63; Award of Merit for Sculpture, Univ Tulsa, 64 & Nebr Wesleyan Univ, 66; Andrew Mellon Found Grant, 81. *Bibliog:* Harold D Cole (auth), Kenneth Weedman, Baldwin-Wallace Col, 73; Dona Z Meilach (auth), Soft Sculpture, Crown Publ, 74. *Mem:* Col Art Asn of Am. *Media:* Plastic, Steel; Etching, Lithography. *Publ:* Contribr, Sculpture Quart, 74 & 75. *Mailing Add:* PO Box 790 CC Sta Williamsburg KY 40769

WEEDY, THERESA
PHOTOGRAPHER, CURATOR
b Los Angeles, Calif, Nov 15, 50. *Study:* Calif State Univ, Fullerton, 72-74, BA(art), 72; Univ Calif, San Francisco Exten, 75-79; San Francisco Art Inst, MFA(photog), 81. *Exhib:* San Francisco-Chicago Art Exchange, Art Inst Chicago, 81; Foto-Vision 81, Foto Gallery, New York, 81; Alliance for Survival: Benefit Auction for the Nuclear Freeze Initiative, Jack Rutberg Gallery, Los Angeles, 82; New Images: Photographs of the Los Angeles Basin and the San Francisco Bay Area, 82; Am Inst Graphic Arts Awards Traveling Exhib, San Francisco, Los Angeles, New York & Europe, 82; Photography: A Contemporary Collection, Falkirk Cult Ctr, San Rafael, Calif, 83; and others. *Collections Arranged:* Earl Dotter: American Labor (with catalog), 83, Joseph Czarnecki: Inside Poland and Solidarity (with catalog), 83 & Cynthia Gano Lewis & Tamarra Kaida (with catalog), 84, San Francisco Camerawork Inc. *Pos:* Freelance photog & artist, 76-; bd dir, San Francisco Camerawork Inc, 77-, bookstore mgr, 78-81, asst dir, 81- *Teaching:* Instr photog workshop, Assoc Students Univ Calif, Berkeley, 75-76. *Awards:* Merit Awards, Floating Found Photog, New York, 76 & Fourth Ann Magic Silver Show, 78; two Am Inst Graphic Arts Awards for album covers, 82. *Bibliog:* Theresa Weedy, Zoom, French ed, Vol 94, 82; Thomas Albright (auth), Landscapes & figures: Distant from reality, San Francisco Chronicle, 7/17/83; Donna-Lee Phillips (auth), Labor's struggle, Artweek, 10/1/83. *Mem:* Media Alliance, San Francisco; Friends of Photog, Carmel, Calif; Soc Photog Educ. *Res:* Censorship and freedom of vision. *Publ:* Auth, Reflections, 80, Nada Dura Para Simpre, 81 & White Dog/Black Dog, 81; ed, Issues and views: Photographic exploitation and the right of privacy, Camerawork Newsletter, San Francisco Camerawork Inc, 83

WEEGE, WILLIAM
PRINTMAKER, EDUCATOR
b Milwaukee, Wis. *Study:* Univ Wis-Milwaukee; Univ Wis-Madison, MA, 67, MFA, 68. *Work:* Akron Art Inst; Brooklyn Mus; Art Inst Chicago; Frankfurt Libr, Ger; Mus Mod Art, New York; plus many others. *Exhib:* Mechanics in Printmaking, 70 & Artist as Adversary, 70, Mus Mod Art, New York; Large Print Show, Whitney Mus Am Art, 71; Works on Paper, Alice Simsar Gallery, Ann Arbor, Mich, 79, Inst for Experimental Printmaking, San Francisco, 79 & Circle Campus, Chicago, 79; Artrain, Mich Arts Coun, 79; Jones Road Print Shop, University of Mich, Kalamazoo, Mich, 79; Paper as Medium, Smithsonian Inst, 79-80; and many others. *Teaching:* From instr lettering to assoc prof art, Univ Wis-Madison, 67-80. *Bibliog:* Article, Arts, 1/78; article, Art News, 2/78. *Mailing Add:* PO Box 185 Barneveld WI 53507

WEEKES, SHIRLEY MARIE
PAINTER
b Buffalo, NY, May 9, 17. *Study:* Detroit Art Acad; Detroit Soc Arts & Crafts; Burnley Sch Prof Art, Seattle, Wash; Univ Wash with Fred Anderson; also with Sergei Bongart (award of scholar); Master Painter Prog with Carl Morris, Port Townsend, Wash. *Work:* Charles & Emma Frye Mus, Seattle; Washington Mutual Bank Collection; Craftsman Press Collection; Laguna Beach Mus Art, Va; Steele Scott Collection. *Exhib:* One-woman shows, Frye Mus, Seattle, 67 & 72, Challis Galleries, Laguna Beach, Calif, 70, 72 & 74 & Haines Gallery, Seattle, 73 & 75; Frye Mus, Seattle, 65-69 & 71-75; Okla Mus of Art, 77; Laguna Beach Mus Art, 80; and others. *Awards:* Craftsman Press Award, Craftsman Press, 65; 7th Ann Puget Sound Show, Frye Mus, Seattle, 65 & West Coast Oil Show, 68; Northwest Watercolor Show, Northwest Watercolor Soc, 72. *Mem:* Soc Western Artists; Northwest Watercolor Soc; San Diego Watercolor Soc. *Media:* Acrylic, Watercolor. *Dealer:* Challis Galleries 1390 S Coast Hwy Laguna Beach CA 92653. *Mailing Add:* 40451 Calle Fiesta Rancho California Temecula CA 92390

WEEKS, EDWARD F
HISTORIAN, MUSEOLOGIST
b Boston, Mass. *Study:* Goethe Inst, Graffing, Ger, cert, 61; Columbia Univ, BS(art hist), 62; Inst Fine Arts, NY Univ, MA, 70, with Robert Goldwater & Colin Eisler; Inst Arts Admin, Harvard Univ, cert, 73. *Pos:* Asst dir, Cummer Gallery Art, Jacksonville, Fla, 62-65; exec asst to dir, Albright-Knox Art Gallery, Buffalo, NY, 67-69; selector, Am Fedn Arts Mus Purchase Fund Collection, 68; cur, High Mus Art, Atlanta, Ga, 69-70; cur, Birmingham Mus Art, Ala, 70-; guest art critic, Birmingham News, 70-; art consult, Downtown Club Collection, 73-, Eye Found Hosp, 73- & Birmingham Civic Ctr, 74- *Teaching:* Instr mod sculpture, Univ Ala, Birmingham, spring 75. *Mem:* Nat Inst Arts & Lett; Am Asn Mus; Southeastern Mus Asn; Col Art Asn Am; Birmingham Festival Arts. *Res:* Western paintings and sculpture since 1400; twentieth century sculpture and painting; Flemish and Dutch painting, 1500-1630. *Interests:* Organizing major Old Master exhibits from American collections. *Collection:* American paintings, watercolors, prints and photography, nineteenth and twentieth centuries; Pre-Columbian art. *Mailing Add:* 201 Mountain Ave Birmingham AL 35213

WEEKS, JAMES (DARRELL NORTHRUP)
PAINTER, EDUCATOR
b Oakland, Calif, Dec 1, 22. *Study:* Calif Sch Fine Arts, 40-42 & 46-48; Hartwell Sch Design, 47; Escuela Pintura, Mexico City. *Work:* Corcoran Gallery Art, Washington, DC; San Francisco Mus Art; Am Fedn Art, New York; Howard Univ, Washington, DC; Oakland Mus. *Comn:* America 76 (painting), US Dept of the Interior traveling exhib, 76; painting, Boston 200 Bicentennial Exhib, 76. *Exhib:* Corcoran Gallery, 63; Carnegie Int, Pittsburgh, 64; one-man shows, San Francisco Mus Art, 65 & Boston Univ Art Gallery, 71; Expo '70, Osaka, Japan; Calif Painting & Sculpture--The Mod Era, San Francisco Mus of Art & Corcoran Gallery, Washington, DC, 76; James Weeks 30 Yr Retrospective--Paintings & Drawings, Brandeis Univ & Oakland Mus, 78. *Teaching:* At San Francisco Art Inst, 58-67 & Univ Calif, Los Angeles, 67-70; assoc prof grad painting, Boston Univ, 70-81, prof, 81-; vis artist, Yale Univ, 79 & 81. *Awards:* Nat Endowment Arts grant/painting, 77-78; Purchase Award, Am Inst Arts & Letters, 80. *Bibliog:* A Ventura (auth), James Weeks: The plain path, Arts Mag, 2/64; James Weeks, paintings, Felix Landau Gallery, 64. *Dealer:* Hirschl & Adler Gallery 21 E 70th St New York NY 10021; Charles Campbell Gallery 647 Chestnut St San Francisco CA 94133. *Mailing Add:* 11 Notre Dame Rd Bedford MA 01730

WEEMS, KATHARINE LANE
SCULPTOR
b Boston, Mass. *Study:* May Sch, Boston; Sch Mus Fine Arts, Boston; also with Anna Hyatt Huntington, Brenda Putnam, Charles Grafly & George Demetrios. *Work:* Mus Fine Arts, Boston; Mus Sci, Boston; Colby Col Art Mus, Maine; Glenbow Found Mus, Alta; Brookgreen Gardens, SC. *Comn:* Brick carvings of animals, Biol Labs, Harvard Univ; Lotta Fountain, Esplanade, Boston; US Legion of Merit & Medal for Merit, US Govt; Goodwin Medal, Mass Inst Technol, Cambridge, Mass; Dolphins of the Sea (12ft bronze group), New England Aquarium, Boston. *Exhib:* Nat Acad Design; Nat Sculpture Soc Exhib, 81. *Awards:* Widener Gold Medal, Philadelphia Acad Fine Arts, 27; Speyer Prize, 31, 63, 73 & 75 & Saltus Gold Medal for Merit, 60, Nat Acad Design; Kalos Kagathos Found Sculpture Prize, 81. *Mem:* Nat Acad Design; Nat Sculpture Soc; Nat Inst Arts & Lett; Guild Boston Artists; Archit League New York. *Dealer:* Guild of Boston Artists 162 Newbury St Boston MA 02116. *Mailing Add:* Box 126 Manchester MA 01944

WEESE, MYRTLE A
PAINTER
b Roslyn, Wash, Oct 30, 03. *Study:* Los Angeles Co Art Inst; also with George Flower & Ejnar Hansen. *Work:* Paintings & portraits in pvt collections. *Exhib:* Bowers Mem Mus, Santa Anna, Sierra Madre City Hall, Los Angeles City Hall, Descanso Gardens, 61 & Sierra Madre, 67; plus others. *Awards:* Prizes, Brea Women's Club, 61 & Las Artistas, 61, Gold Medal, Greek Theatre, Los Angeles, 61. *Mem:* Scand-Am Soc; Am Inst Fine Arts; Las Artistas Art Club; Prof Artists Los Angeles. *Media:* Oil. *Mailing Add:* 12821 Fourth St 18 Yucaipa CA 92399

WEGMAN, WILLIAM
PAINTER, VIDEO ARTIST
b Holyoke, Mass, Dec 2, 43. *Study:* Mass Col Art, Boston, BFA, 65; Univ Ill, Urbana-Champaign, MFA, 67. *Work:* Whitney Mus Am Art, New York; Mus

Mod Art, New York & Paris; Los Angeles Co Mus Art; Int Mus Photog, Rochester, NY. *Comn:* Semi-buffet color video tape, WGBH, Boston, 74-75; video tape rev, Channel 13, WNET, New York, 75. *Exhib:* William Wegman: Selected Works 1970-1979, Univ Colo Art Gallery, Boulder, 80; Penthouse Exhib, Mus Mod Art, New York, 80; Pier and Ocean, Hayward Gallery, London, Eng, 80; Out of New York, Root Art Ctr, Hamilton Col, Clinton, New York, 81; Whitney Biennial, Whitney Mus Am Art, 81; Morton C Newmann Family Collection, Art Inst Chicago, 81; Audrey Strohl Gallery, Memphis, Tenn, 81; Staged Shots, Delahunty Gallery, Dallas, Tex, 81; and many others. *Teaching:* Univ Wis, 68-70; Cal State Univ, Long Beach, 70. *Awards:* Guggenheim Fel, 75; Nat Endowment Arts Grant, 75-76 & 82. *Bibliog:* Jane Livingston (auth), William Wegman, Los Angeles Co Mus Art, 73; Liza Bear (auth), interview, Avalanche, winter/spring 73; Maud Lauin (auth), Notes on William Wegman, Artforum, 3/75. *Publ:* Auth, Pathetic readings, Avalanche Mag, 74; contribr, Paris Rev, fall 74; coauth, Man's Best Friend, Abrams, 82. *Dealer:* Holly Solomon Gallery 724 Fifth Ave New York NY 10019. *Mailing Add:* 431 E 6th St New York NY 10009

WEGNER, NADENE R
GOLDSMITH, EDUCATOR

b Sheboygan, Wis, Feb 18, 50. *Study:* Univ Wis-Milwaukee, BFA, 72; Tyler Sch Art, Temple Univ, MFA, 75. *Work:* Tyler Sch Art, Temple Univ, Philadelphia, Pa. *Exhib:* Craftwork 76, Metrop Mus & Art Ctr, Miami, Fla, 76; Intent: Jewelry/Metal, Edinboro, Pa, 76; Women's Art Symp, Terre Haute, Ind, 77; Copper, Brass & Bronze Competition, Tucson, Ariz, 77; Profiles of US Jewelry, Lubbock, Tex, 77; and others. *Teaching:* Asst prof metalsmithing & Jewelry, Louisville Sch Art, Ky, 75- *Awards:* First Prize, Second & Third Nat Ring Show, Athens, Ga; Award, Copper II Exhib, 80; and others. *Bibliog:* Metalsmithing USA, 75 & New York Metal, 76, Craft Horizons; Marcia Chamberlain (auth), Metal Jewelry Techniques, Watson-Guptill, 76. *Mem:* Am Crafts Coun; distinguished mem Soc NAm Goldsmiths. *Media:* Precious Metals, Precious Woods. *Mailing Add:* 3003 Aubert Ave Louisville KY 40206

WEHR, WESLEY CONRAD
PAINTER, CONSULTANT

b Everett, Wash, Apr 17, 29. *Study:* Univ Wash, BA & MA; also with Mark Tobey. *Work:* Munic Gallery Mod Art, Dublin, Ireland; Boymans-Van Beuningen Mus, Rotterdam; Nat Mus Am Art, Smithsonian Inst; Baltimore Mus; Minneapolis Inst Arts. *Exhib:* Shepherd Gallery, New York, 73; Gallerie Rosenau, Bern, Switz, 76; Belcher Gallery, San Francisco, 79; one-man show, Expo 8, Basel, Switz, 77; retrospective, Art Gallery of Greater Victoria, BC, 80. *Pos:* Res assoc paleontology, Wash State Mus, Univ Wash, Seattle. *Media:* Mixed Media. *Publ:* Conversations with Mark Tobey, Northwest Arts, 76-79; Elizabeth Bishop: Conversations and Classnotes, The Antioch Review, summer 81; Ernest Bloch, Northwest Arts, 80. *Mailing Add:* Wash State Mus Univ of Wash Seattle WA 98195

WEIDENAAR, REYNOLD HENRY
ETCHER, PAINTER

b Grand Rapids, Mich, Nov 17, 15. *Study:* Kendall Sch Design, 35-36; Kansas City Art Inst, scholar, 38-40. *Work:* Libr Cong, Washington, DC; Detroit Inst Arts, Mich; Nat Gallery SWales, Liverpool, Eng; Honolulu Acad Fine Arts, Hawaii; Hackley Art Gallery, Muskegon, Mich. *Comn:* Murals, church hist, La Grave Ave Christian Reformed Church, 65 & Urban Renewal, Mich Consol Gas Co, Grand Rapids. *Exhib:* Regular exhibitor, Nat Acad Design, Detroit Inst Arts & Libr Cong. *Teaching:* Instr life drawing & painting, Kendall Sch Design, 56-74. *Awards:* Guggenheim Found Award, 44; Tiffany Found Scholar, 48. *Mem:* Nat Acad Design; Soc Am Graphic Artists; Am Watercolor Soc. *Media:* Watercolor, Resin-Oil. *Publ:* Auth, Our Changing Landscape, Baker-Brook House, 70; Michigan Sketchbook, Baker Book House, 80. *Dealer:* East June 1 Gallery Fine Art Bellamy Lane Bethlehem CT 06751; Hefner Galleries 1450 Wealthy St SE Grand Rapids MI. *Mailing Add:* 4041 Pointe o' Woods Ct SE Apt 108 Grand Rapids MI 49508

WEIDMAN, JEFFREY
LIBRARIAN, HISTORIAN

b New York, NY, Feb 17, 45. *Study:* Hamilton Col, Clinton, NY, AB, 67; Ind Univ, Bloomington, with Albert Elsen & John Jacobus, MA(art hist), 69, with Louis Hawes, PhD(art hist, Samuel H Kress Fel), 82, MLS, 82. *Exhib:* H P Lovecraft, Lilly Libr, Indiana Univ, Bloomington, 82. *Pos:* Art librn, Clarence Ward Art Libr, Oberlin Col, Ohio, 83- *Teaching:* Assoc instr art hist, Ind Univ, Bloomington, 68, 72-74 & 76. *Awards:* Gerd Muehsam Award, Art Libr Soc NAm, 83. *Bibliog:* Milo M Naeve (auth), A picture and sculpture by William Rimmer, Bulletin Art Inst Chicago, 77; Lewis Shepard (auth), American Art at Amherst, Wesleyan Univ Press, 78; Brockton's Artistic Heritage, Brockton Art Mus, 81. *Mem:* Acad Libr Asn, Ohio; Am Libr Asn; Art Libr Soc NAm; Col Art Asn. *Res:* Nineteenth century American art, especially the work of William Rimmer. *Interests:* Classical, Baroque, British and American eighteenth to twentieth century art, especially American painting and sculpture of the nineteenth century; art reference materials. *Publ:* Ed, The First College Bowl Question Book, Random House, 61; auth, Reclassification of the Hamilton College portraits, Hamilton Col, 67; contribr, Seymour Lipton, Harry Abrams, 70; contribr, The Art Institute of Chicago Centennial Lectures, Contemp Bks, 83. *Mailing Add:* c/o Clarence Ward Art Libr Allen Art Bldg, Oberlin Col Oberlin OH 44074

WEIDNER, MARILYN KEMP
CONSERVATOR, LECTURER

b Floral Park, NY, Jan 10, 28. *Study:* Pratt Inst; Hofstra Univ, BA; Univ Pa; Metrop Mus Art, with Minna Horowitz Nagel; Freer Gallery Art, with Takashi Sugiura. *Pos:* Asst registrar, Mus Mod Art, New York, 51-56; registrar, Brooklyn Mus, 56-58; conservator, pvt practice, Philadelphia, 58-78; dir, Conserv Ctr Art & Hist Artifacts, Philadelphia, 78- *Teaching:* Adj prof conserv art on paper, NY State Univ, Cooperstown Grad Progs, 71-74. *Awards:* Certified Conservator of Historic & Artistic Works on Paper, 75. *Mem:* Fel Int Inst Conserv Art & Hist Artifacts; Am Inst Conserv Art & Hist Artifacts; Peale Club; Pa Acad Fine Arts; Inst Paper Conserv, London. *Publ:* Contribr, Damage and deterioration of art on paper, In: Studies in Conservation, Int Inst Conserv Art & Hist Artifacts, 67; contribr, A vacuum table of use in paper conservation, Am Inst Conserv Art & Hist Artifacts Bulletin, 74; contribr, Repair of Wall Charts from Cloister Edhrata, Pa Conserv & Restoration of Pictorial Art, Butterworth's, 76. *Mailing Add:* 612 Spruce St Philadelphia PA 19106

WEIDNER, MARY ELIZABETH
PAINTER, EDUCATOR

b St Louis, Mo, June 10, 50. *Study:* Sch Fine Arts, Washington Univ, St Louis, Mo, BFA(fel), 72, MFA, 75. *Work:* Papercraft Corp, F B Foster Corp & Carnegie-Mellon Univ, Pittsburgh. *Exhib:* Butler Inst Am Art, Youngstown, Ohio, 77, 79 & 80; William Penn Mem Mus, Harrisburg, Pa, 80; Broussard Mem Galleries, Baton Rouge, La, 80; Carnegie Inst Mus Art, Pittsburgh, 81; Coos Mus Art, Coos Bay, Ore, 81; Herman Fine Arts Ctr, Marietta, Ohio, 81; and many others. *Teaching:* Lectr, Grinnell Col, Iowa, 75-76; instr, Carnegie-Mellon Univ, Pittsburgh, 76-78, asst prof, 78- *Bibliog:* The Art of Drawing, Purdue Univ, 79. *Mem:* Col Art Asn; Women's Caucus Art; Assoc Artists Pittsburgh. *Media:* Oil, Colored Pencil. *Dealer:* Wiebe Gallery 927 Penn Ave Pittsburgh PA 15222; Baker Gallery 828 Prospect St La Jolla CA 92037. *Mailing Add:* 1222 Palo Alto Pittsburgh PA 15212

WEIDNER, ROSWELL THEODORE
PAINTER, INSTRUCTOR

b Reading, Pa, Sept 18, 11. *Study:* Pa Acad Fine Arts, Cresson Foreign Traveling Scholar, 35; Barnes Found, Merion, Pa. *Work:* Pa Acad Fine Arts; Philadelphia Mus Art; Pa State Univ; Metrop Mus Art, New York; Libr Cong, Washington, DC. *Comn:* Portraits, of Herman Beerman, Univ, Pa, 68, Robert C Sale, Conn State Libr, Hartford, 69 & Clair R McCollough, Nat Asn Broadcasters, Washington, DC, 70, Hahnemann Hospital, Philadelphia, 81. *Exhib:* Pa Acad Fine Arts Ann, Philadelphia, 36-70; Directions in Painting, Carnegie Inst, Pittsburgh, Pa, 43; Drawing Soc Second Eastern Cent Exhib, Philadelphia Mus Art, 70; 24th Am Drawing Biennial, Norfolk Mus Arts & Sci, Va & Smithsonian Traveling Exhib, 71; one-man exhib, Newman Galleries, Philadelphia, 78 & Marian Locks Gallery, Philadelphia, 81. *Teaching:* Sr instr painting, Pa Acad Fine Arts, 38-; instr painting, Philadelphia Col Art, 49-51. *Awards:* Fel prize, Pa Acad Fine Arts Ann, 43; Dawson Mem Medal, Philadelphia Watercolor Club, 64, 72 & 76; Percy Owens Award, 75. *Bibliog:* William P Scott (auth), Roswell Weidner: Painting in the Pine Barrens, Am Artist, 12/80. *Mem:* Fel Pa Acad Fine Arts (pres, 54-67, vpres, 67-72); Philadelphia Watercolor Club (bd dirs, 65-72); Artists Equity Asn. *Media:* Oil, Charcoal. *Mailing Add:* 612 Spruce St Philadelphia PA 19106

WEIL, LISL
ILLUSTRATOR, WRITER

b Vienna, Austria; US citizen. *Pos:* Auth & illusr of over 100 children's books; concert illusr with major symphony orchestras, US; concert illus on nationwide TV specials, movie films & schools. *Mailing Add:* 25 Central Park W New York NY 10023

WEIL, ROSE R
EDITOR, ADMINISTRATOR

b Suffern, NY, Mar 4, 31. *Study:* Hunter Col, BA, 52; Columbia Univ, 52-53. *Pos:* Ed, Col Art Asn Newspaper, 76-; managing ed, Art J, New York, 80-, bk rev & mus news ed, 81- *Mem:* Col Art Asn (exec secy, 73-); Artists Environment Found; Art & Community Inst. *Mailing Add:* 580 W End Ave New York NY 10024

WEIL, STEPHEN E
MUSEUM EXECUTIVE, LECTURER

b New York, NY, June 24, 28. *Study:* Brown Univ, AB, 49; Columbia Univ, LLB, 56. *Pos:* Vpres & gen mgr, Marlborough-Gerson Gallery, New York, 63-67; adminr, Whitney Mus Am Art, New York, 67-74; deputy dir, Hirshhorn Mus & Sculpture Garden, Smithsonian Inst, 74- *Teaching:* Co-dir & fac mem, Mus Mgt Inst, Berkeley, Calif, 79- *Awards:* Golden Crate Award, Western Asn Art Mus, 80. *Mem:* Am Asn Mus (coun mem & treas, 75-79, vpres, 79-82); Art Mus Asn Am (mem bd, 82-); Int Found Art Research (mem bd, 79-); Volunteer Lawyers Arts, NY (mem adv bd, 75-); Opportunity Resources Arts (mem adv bd, 74-). *Publ:* Auth var articles in Art News, Art in Am, Law Libr J, Mus News & Print Collectors Newsletter, 70-83; co-ed, Legal & Business Problems of Artists, Art Galleries & Museums, 73 & coauth, Art Works: Law, Policy, Practice, 74, Practising Law Inst; auth, Beauty and the Beasts, Smithsonian Inst Press, 83. *Mailing Add:* Hirshhorn Mus Smithsonian Inst Washington DC 20560

WEILER, MELODY M
PRINTMAKER, EDUCATOR

b Santa Monica, Calif, Mar 4, 47. *Study:* State Univ NY, Buffalo, BFA; Ohio Univ, MFA; also with Harvey Breverman, Seymour Drumlevitch, Donald Roberts & Harvey Daniels. *Work:* Ohio Univ, Athens; Kemper Gallery, Kansas City, Mo. *Comn:* Ceramic & screened mural, Ohio Univ, Athens, 70-71; cover design, Glass Eye Productions, Los Angeles, 76; posters, Hollins Col, Va & Murray State Univ, Ky, 76-77. *Exhib:* Western NY Art Exhib,

Albright-Knox Art Gallery, Buffalo, 69; Nelson-Atkins Art Mus, Kansas City, Mo, 74; Huber Gallery, Washington, DC, 79; Lake Placid Sch Art, NY, 79; Imagery Gallery, Jacksonville, Fla, 79; Southeastern Ctr for Contemp Art, Winston-Salem, NC, 79; Appalachian Ctr for Crafts, Cookeville, Tenn, 80; and others. *Teaching:* Instr printmaking/design, Atlanta Sch of Art, Ga, 71-72; instr found design, Kansas City Art Inst, Mo, 72-73; asst prof printmaking, Murray State Univ, 75-78, assoc prof, 78- *Awards:* Res grant, Hand Papermaking, Murray State Univ, 76-77 & 77-78; Nat Endowment Arts Grants, 77 & 78. *Mem:* Col Art Asn; Ctr for the Bk Arts; World Print Coun; Int Paper Historians. *Media:* Papermaking; Serigraphy. *Publ:* Contribr, Exploring Printmaking for Young People, Van Nostrand Reinhold, 72; photogr, The Painted Vega, 75 & illusr, cover design, Southern Exposure, 76, Glass Eye Productions; contribr, Washingtonian Mag, 78 & Art Craft, 2-3/80. *Mailing Add:* Dept of Art Murray State Univ Murray KY 42071

WEILL, ERNA
SCULPTOR, INSTRUCTOR
b Frankfurt am Main, Ger; US citizen. *Study:* Univ Frankfurt, with Helene von Beckerath; also with John Hovannes, New York. *Work:* Ga Mus Art, Athens; Birmingham Mus, Ala; Jewish Mus, New York; Hyde Park Libr, New York; Israel Mus, Hebrew Univ, Jerusalem; and others. *Comn:* Bronze portrait sculptures, Linus Pauling, Portola Valley, Calif, Martin Buber, Hebrew Univ, Leonard Bernstein, Dr Martin Luther King & Elie Wiesel; and others. *Exhib:* New York World's Fair; NJ State Mus, Trenton; Brooklyn Mus; Montclair Mus; Newark Mus; and others. *Teaching:* Instr sculpture, Brooklyn Mus, Forest Hills Pub Schs, Forest Hills Jewish Ctr & Teaneck Jewish Ctr; instr sculpture, Adult Educ Prog, Ft Lee, NJ; pvt instr, sculpture; lectr, Fairleigh Dickinson Univ; lectr, var clubs & temples, NJ. *Awards:* Mem Found Jewish Cult grant for relig sculpture; Best in Sculpture, Artist-Craftsman, New York, 75. *Bibliog:* Bernard Buranelli (auth), World of Erna Weill, Rec Mag, 64; Avram Kampf (auth), Contemporary synagogue art, Union Am Hebrew Congregations, 65. *Mem:* Artists Equity Asn New York; New York Soc Artists Craftsmen; Mod Artists Guild, NJ; Sculptors Affil Art Ctr. *Media:* Miscellaneous Media. *Publ:* Auth, Any child can model in clay, Design; coauth, article, Crisis, 10/65; contribr, Libr J & NJ Educ Rev. *Mailing Add:* 886 Alpine Dr Teaneck NJ 07666

WEIN, ALBERT W
SCULPTOR, PAINTER
b New York, NY, July 27, 15. *Study:* Md Inst, 27-29; Nat Acad Design; Grand Cent Sch Art; Beaux Arts Inst, with Hans Hofmann. *Work:* Vatican Mus Numismatic Collection, Vatican City; NY Univ Hall of Fame; Jewish Mus, New York; Brookgreen Gardens, SC; Palm Springs Desert Mus, Calif. *Comn:* Exterior sculptures, Hillside Mem Park, Los Angeles, 60-68; exterior, St Michael's Episcopal Church, Anaheim, Calif, 67; bas-relief panels, Univ Wyo Phys Sci Ctr, 68; 25th Anniversary Medal, UN, 70; granite bas-relief, Libby Dam Treaty Tower & designer medal for Libby Dam Dedication, Libby, Mont, 75. *Exhib:* Whitney Mus Am Art Ann, New York, 50; Am Sculpture, Metrop Mus Art, New York, 51; San Francisco Mus Art Ann, 57; one-man shows, Jewish Mus, 58 & Grand Cent Art Galleries, New York, 83; 30 yr retrospective, Palm Springs Desert Mus, 69. *Teaching:* Vis prof sculpture, Univ Wyo, 65-67; mem fac, Nat Acad of Design, 77-78; adj prof art, Pace Univ, 79. *Awards:* Artists Fund Prize, 76 & 80 & Gold Medal for Sculpture, 79, Nat Acad Design; Cert Merit, Nat Acad Design, 78 & 83. *Bibliog:* J Lovoos (auth), Art of Albert Wein, Am Artist, 1/63 & article, Christian Sci Monitor, 4/67. *Mem:* Fel Am Acad Rome; fel Nat Acad of Design; fel Int Inst Arts & Lett; fel Huntington Hartford Found; fel Nat Sculpture Soc. *Media:* Bronze, Marble. *Mailing Add:* 30 Quakerbridge Rd Ossining NY 10562

WEINBAUM, JEAN
PAINTER, SCULPTOR
b Zurich, Switz, 26. *Study:* Zurich Sch Fine Arts, 42-46; Acad Grande Chaumiere; Ecole Paul Colin; Acad Andre L'Hote, 47-48. *Work:* Mus Mod Art, Paris, France; Nat Collection Fine Arts, Washington, DC; Univ Art Mus, Berkeley, Calif; Stanford Univ Mus, Calif; Calif Palace Legion Honor, San Francisco. *Comn:* Eleven stained glass windows, Chapelle de Mosloy, 51; rosette stained glass, Berne sur Oise, 55; 22 stained glass windows, St Pierre du Regard, 57; Wall of Light (monumental stained glass window), Escherange, 62; eight windows, Lycee de Jeunes Filles, Bayonne, France, 66. *Exhib:* Mus Mod Art, Paris, 62, 63 & 65; one-man shows, Galerie Smith-Andersen, Palo Alto, Calif, 70-73, 76 & 79, Calif Palace Legion Honor, 71, Musee Arts Decoratifs, Lausanne, Switz, 72, Bildungszentrum, Gelsenkirchen, Ger, 72 & San Francisco Mus Mod Art, 81; and others. *Bibliog:* Francois Mathey & others (auth), Vitrail Francais, In: Tendances Modernes, Ed Deux Mondes, Paris, 58; Robert Sowers (auth), Stained Glass: an Architectural Art, Universe Bks, New York, 65; Shuji Takashina (auth), Stained glass works by Jean Weinbaum, Space Design, Tokyo, 9/67. *Media:* Watercolor, Oil, Stained Glass. *Dealer:* Van Doren Associates. *Mailing Add:* PO Box 40291 San Francisco CA 94140

WEINBERG, BELLA REBECCA
PAINTER, WRITER
b New York, NY, Aug 30, 12. *Study:* Washington Workshop, DC, drawing, 50; Md Sch Art-Design, figure drawing, 60; basically self-taught. *Work:* pvt collections, US & Abroad. *Exhib:* Austrian Traveling Art Show, US State Dept, DC, 67; Art-in-Embassy Exhib, US State Dept, Bermuda, Cent African Repub & Switz, 67; Miniature Painters Sculptors, Smithsonian Inst, 68; Art Barn Exhib, Nat Park Serv, 72-78; one-woman shows, Springtime Paintings, Cosmos Club, 75 & Paintings, Drawings, Sculpture, Rockville Civic Mansion, Md, 78; plus others. *Pos:* Dir-owner, Chevy Chase Galerie, Inc, Bethesda,

Md, 63-69; art buyer, W J Sloane, DC, 69-71; dir, Fine Arts Gallery, JCC of Greater Washington, Rockville, Md, 71-77; free-lance writer, 78- *Teaching:* Lectr art, Montgomery Co Libr System, 78-79 & Nat League Pen Women, 80. *Awards:* Am Artist Prof League Award, 58; Achievement Award, Montgomery Co Arts Asn, 69; Painting & Sculpture Awards, Nat League Pen Women, 76-79. *Bibliog:* Ed Nikki Burr (auth), Gallery hopping, Art Scene, fall 71. *Mem:* Artists' Equity Asn; Nat League Pen Women; Washington Independent Writers; Writer's League of Washington. *Res:* Geneological lines of art through the centuries and into 20th century art. *Publ:* Auth, The David Lloyd Kreegers, collectors of distinction, 79, John Safer, sculptor, the curved line, 79 & Rosilind Miller, painter, 80, Art Voices S; auth, Lunda Hoyle Gill, ethnographic portraits, Prints, spring 80; auth, Cultural diplomacy in action, Embassy News, 80; plus others. *Dealer:* Town Ctr Gallery Bethesda MD 20814. *Mailing Add:* 10401 Grosvenor Pl Rockville MD 20852

WEINBERG, ELBERT
SCULPTOR, EDUCATOR
b Hartford, Conn, May 27, 28. *Study:* Hartford Art Sch, with Henry Kreis; RI Sch Design, with Waldemar Raemisch; Yale Univ Sch Fine Arts. *Work:* Whitney Mus Am Art, Mus Mod Art, New York; Phillips Acad, Andover; Boston Mus Fine Arts, Mass; Wadsworth Athenaeum, Hartford. *Comn:* Bronze procession (sculpture), Mr & Mrs Albert List, Jewish Mus, 59; Jacob Wrestling with Angel (sculpture), Brandeis Univ, Waltham, Mass, 64; Shofar (bronze), Rockdale Temple, Cincinnati, Ohio, 69; Justice (bronze), Boston Univ Law Sch Lobby, 74; Bronze Procession 2, Beth El Temple, West Hartford, Conn, 75. *Exhib:* Whitney Mus Am Art, New York, 57, 58, 60 & 64; Carnegie Inst, Pittsburgh, Pa, 58 & 61; Sculpture USA, Mus Mod Art, New York, 59; 64 Americans Exhib, Art Inst Chicago, Ill, 61; Hirshhorn Collection, Guggenheim Mus, New York, 62. *Teaching:* Instr sculpture, Cooper Union, 56-59; vis prof sculpture, Boston Univ, 70- & Tyler Sch Art, Temple Abroad; artist-in-residence, Union Col, Schenectady, NY, 76- *Awards:* Prix de Rome, Am Acad Rome, 51-53; Guggenheim Fel, 59; Sculpture Award, Am Inst Arts & Lett, 69. *Bibliog:* Articles & photographs in several bks. *Mem:* Sculptors Guild, New York. *Dealer:* Alpha Gallery 121 Newbury St Boston MA 02116. *Mailing Add:* c/o Grace Borgenicht Gallery 724 Fifth Ave New York NY 10019

WEINBERG, EPHRAIM
ADMINISTRATOR, EDUCATOR
b Philadelphia, Pa, Apr 28, 38. *Study:* Philadelphia Col Art; Univ Pa. *Pos:* Dean, Pa Acad Fine Arts, 77-82, dir, Schs, 82- *Teaching:* Lectr, Bournemouth Col Art, Eng, 64-65; prof, Bucks Co Community Col, Newton, Pa, 67-68; prof, Philadelphia Col Art, 69-71; prof, Art Inst Chicago, 71-77. *Mem:* Nat Asn Arts Adminr; Philadelphia Art Alliance (vpres, currently); Nat Asn Sch Art & Design (treas, currently); Nat Mus Am Jewish Hist (vpres, currently); Nexus: Found Today's Art (bd mem, currently). *Publ:* Auth, Who teaches art, In: Art Education: Junior High School, Nat Art Educ Asn, 73; coauth (with Donald J Irving), The master of fine arts program, In: The Status of the Arts in Higher Education, 76 & auth, Venerable institutions in an age of conservation, In: The Visual Arts in the Ninth Decade, 80, Nat Coun Arts Adminr; auth, The school of the Pennsylvania Academy of the Fine Arts, Antiques, 3/81; auth, School and Museum: The Pennsylvania Academy of the Fine Arts: A Case Study, Asn Art Mus Dirs, 82. *Mailing Add:* Pa Acad of Fine Arts Broad & Cherry Sts Philadelphia PA 19102

WEINBERG, H BARBARA
HISTORIAN, CONSULTANT
b New York, NY. *Study:* Barnard Col, BA; Columbia Univ, MA, PhD(art hist, archaeol). *Teaching:* Assoc prof art hist, Queens Col, City Univ of New York & Grad Sch, 72- *Mem:* Col Art Asn of Am; Victorian Soc in Am. *Res:* Nineteenth century American painting. *Publ:* Auth, The Decorative Work of John La Farge, Garland, 77. *Mailing Add:* Dept Art Queens Col City Univ NY Flushing NY 11367

WEINER, ABE
PAINTER, INSTRUCTOR
b Pittsburgh, Pa, Nov 5, 17. *Study:* Carnegie Inst Technol, cert painting & design, 41, with Robert Gwathmey & Samuel Rosenberg. *Work:* Hillman Libr, Univ Pittsburgh. *Comn:* Painting & mosaic on aluminum, Alcoa Co Pittsburgh; painting, PPG Industs. *Exhib:* Assoc Artists Pittsburgh, 40-72 & Shows, 46-49, Carnegie Inst; Carnegie Inst Int, Pittsburgh, 50; Contemp Soc Exhib, Art Inst Chicago, 52; 50 Most Promising Artists US, Metrop Mus Art, 53; one-man show, Univ Pittsburgh, 81. *Teaching:* Instr painting, Arts & Crafts Ctr, 57-60; instr painting & drawing & asst dir, Ivy Sch Prof Art, 61-; instr painting, Irene Kaufman Ctr, 65- *Awards:* First Prize & Second Prize, 41 & 45, Judge's Prize, 59 & Purchase Award, 74 & 75, Assoc Artists Pittsburgh; and others. *Mem:* Assoc Artists Pittsburgh. *Media:* Acrylic, Dry Pigment. *Mailing Add:* 1636 Denniston Ave Pittsburgh PA 15217

WEINER, EGON
SCULPTOR
b Vienna, Austria, July 24, 06; US citizen. *Study:* Sch Arts Crafts, Acad Fine Arts, Vienna. *Work:* Syracuse Mus Fine Arts; Augsburg Col, Minneapolis; Augustana Col, Rock Island, Ill; and others. *Comn:* Portrait bust of Dr Eric Oldberg (bronze), Med Ctr, Chicago, 72; bronze busts of Nobel Prize Winner Willy Brandt, Harvard Univ, 72 & Ernest Hemingway, Oak Park Libr, Ill, 74; heads of Secy of State Henry Kissinger, 77 & Diana, daughter of Apollo 8 Astronaut Anders, 77; and others. *Exhib:* Art Inst Chicago, 60-71; Art Inst Oslo Ann Exhib, 71, 73 & 75-76; US Info Serv Libr, Am Embassy, Oslo, 72-73; and many others. *Pos:* Educ consult, Film of Del Prado Mus, Madrid, Spain, 69; educ consult, Int Film Bur, Chicago, formerly. *Teaching:* Lectr, US

& abroad; prof sculpture & life drawing, Art Inst Chicago, 45-71, emer prof, 71-; vis prof art, Augustana Col, 56. *Awards:* Gold Medals, Munic Art League, Chicago, 69 & Soc Arts & Lett, 70; Gold Medal, Soc Arts & Lett, 70; Austrian Cross of Honor First Class for Sci & Art, 77; plus others. *Mem:* Life fel Int Inst Arts & Lett; Munic Art League, Chicago (dir, 61-64); Nat Inst Arts & Lett; and others. *Media:* Stone, Wood, Steel and Bronze. *Mailing Add:* 835 Michigan Ave Evanston IL 60202

WEINER, LAWRENCE CHARLES
SCULPTOR
b Bronx, NY, Feb 10, 40. *Work:* Mus Mod Art, New York; Vanabbe Mus, Eindhoven, Netherlands; Sttisches Mus Munchengladbach, WGer; Centre Georges Pompidou, Paris; Nat Gallery of Australia, Canberra; and others. *Exhib:* Information, Mus of Mod Art, New York, 70; Idea & Image in Recent Art, Art Inst Chicago, Ill, 74; one-man shows, Laguna Gloria Mus, Austin, Tex, 77, Renaissance Soc, Chicago, 78, NS Col Art & Design, Halifax, 79, Mus Contemp Art, Chicago, 80 & Leo Castelli Gallery, New York, 81; and many other group & one-man shows. *Awards:* Deutscher Akademischer Austauschdienst Fel, 75; Nat Endowment Arts Fel, 76-77. *Publ:* Auth, Statements, Siegelaub, New York, 68; auth, A Primer, Documenta Five, 72; auth, Within Forward Motion, Kabinet Fur Aktuelle Kunst, 73; auth, Various Manners with Various Things, Inst Contemp Art, London, 76; auth, Works, Printed Matter, 77. *Mailing Add:* 13 Bleecker St 420 W Broadway New York NY 10012

WEINER, TESS MANILLA See Manilla, Tess

WEINGARTEN, HILDE (KEVESS)
PAINTER, PRINTMAKER
b Berlin, Ger; US citizen. *Study:* Art Students League; Cooper Union Art Sch, with Morris Kantor, Robert Gwathmey & Will Barnet, cert, 47, BFA, 76; Pratt Graphics Ctr. *Work:* Brooklyn Mus; Herbert F Johnson Mus, Cornell Univ; Israel Mus, Jerusalem; New York Pub Libr Print Collection; Fogg Art Mus, Harvard Univ; and others. *Exhib:* Albright Art Gallery, Buffalo, 55; Dallas Mus of Fine Art, 56; Brooklyn Mus, 58, 63, 71, 74, 76, 77 & 80; New York World's Fair, 65; Graphics 71 Print Exhib, Western NMex Univ, Silver City, 71; Audubon Artists, Nat Acad Design, New York, 71, 73, 75, 77 & 78-82; Palazzo Vecchio, Florence & Pompeiian Pavilion, Naples, Italy, 72; Pratt Graphics Ctr Annuals, 72-79; plus many other group & six one-artist shows. *Awards:* Akston Found Prize, Nat Asn Women Artists, 80; Silver Medal Creative Graphics, Audubon Artists, 81; and others. *Mem:* Artists Equity Asn, New York (bd dirs, 64-72); Nat Asn Women Artists; Am Soc Contemp Artists; Painters & Sculptors Soc NJ; Audubon Artists. *Media:* Oil, Acrylic; Intaglio, Collagraph. *Publ:* Illusr, Tune of the calliope, 58 & German folksongs, 68. *Mailing Add:* 140 Cadman Plaza W Brooklyn NY 11201

WEINHARDT, CARL JOSEPH, JR
MUSEUM DIRECTOR, HISTORIAN
b Indianapolis, Ind, Sept 22, 27. *Study:* Harvard Univ, AB(magna cum laude), 48, MA, 49, MFA, 55; Christian Theol Sem, Indianapolis, HHD, 67; Ind State Univ, HHD, 71. *Collections Arranged:* Five Centuries German Prints, Metrop Mus Art, 56, 18th Century Design, 60; Four Centuries American Art, Minneapolis Inst Arts, 63; Pavel Tchelitchew, Gallery Mod Art, 64, Lovis Corinth, 65; Treasures From Metrop, Indianapolis Mus Art, 70; and others. *Pos:* Staff mem, Metrop Mus Art, 55-58, assoc cur prints & drawings, 58-60; dir, Minneapolis Inst Arts, 60-62; dir, Gallery Mod Art, New York, 62-65; dir, Indianapolis Mus Art, 65-75; dir, Villa Vizcaya & Gardens, Miami, Fla, 76; mem steering comt, Miami Downtown Develop Auth; coordr, Metrop Dade Co Ctr Fine Arts, 77-79; actg dir, Bass Mus, 79-80. *Teaching:* Lectr archit, Boston Archit Ctr, 54-55; lectr fine art, Columbia Univ, 58-60. *Bibliog:* A Challenge Accepted, Time-Life Broadcasts, 71. *Mem:* Am Asn Mus; Nat Soc Arts & Lett; Drawing Soc; Olana Preserv (trustee); Miami Design Preserv League. *Publ:* Auth, The Etchings of Canaletto, Metrop Mus Art, 56; auth, Beacon Hill, Bostonian Soc, 58; auth, The James Ford Bell American Wing, Minneapolis Inst Art, 63; auth, Newport preserved, Art Am, 65; auth, A Catalogue of European Paintings in the Indianapolis Museum of Art, 71; and others. *Mailing Add:* 3725 Frante Rd Miami FL 32907

WEINMAN, ROBERT ALEXANDER
SCULPTOR
b New York, NY, Mar 19, 15. *Study:* Nat Acad Design; Art Students League; Hobart Sculptor's Welding Course; also sculpture with A A Weinman, Lee Lawrie, Paul Manship, E McCartan, C Jennewein & J E Fraser. *Work:* Brookgreen Gardens, SC. *Comn:* Limestone tympana, Our Lady Queen of Martyrs Church, Forest Hills, NY, 39; bronze elk, Elks, Walla Walla, Wash, 48; bronze doors, Armstrong Libr, Baylor Univ, Waco, Tex, 51; athletic medals, Nat Collegiate Athletic Asn, 52; Morning Mission (bronze), Tulsa, Okla, 62. *Exhib:* Nat Acad Design Ann, 37, 38, 49 & 53; Pa Acad Fine Art Ann, 38 & 39; Allied Artists Am, 46; Sculpture Int, Philadelphia, 49; Sculpture Ann, Nat Acad Design, 83. *Awards:* Mrs Louis Bennett Prize, Nat Sculpture Soc, 52; J S Saltus Medal, 64 & Sculptor Yr Gold Medal Award, 75, Am Numismatic Soc; and others. *Mem:* Academician Nat Acad Design; fel Nat Sculpture Soc (secy, 62-65, first vpres, 65-68 & 70-73, pres, 73-76); Collectors Art Medals (charter dir, 71). *Media:* Clay, Plaster. *Publ:* Contribr, Nat Sculpture Rev, 62-75. *Mailing Add:* Cross River Rd RD 3 Bedford NY 10506

WEINSTEIN, FLORENCE
PAINTER, SCULPTOR
b New York, NY, June 5, 1895. *Study:* Adelphi Col, BA, 16; Subjects Artist Sch, New York, 48-49; Black Mountain Col, NC, 48-; study with Motherwell,

49-50; Hofmann Sch, Provincetown, Mass, 52. *Work:* Edwin A Ulrich Mus Art, Wichita, Kans; New Paltz Univ Mus, New York; Norfolk Mus Arts & Sci, Va; Picker Art Gallery, Colgate Univ, NY; Skidmore Col Mus; and others. *Exhib:* Art US, New York, 58; Int Carnegie Inst, Pittsburgh, Pa, 58-59; 40 Yrs Am Collage, Buecker & Harpsichords, New York, 74; Tenth St Days, Soho, New York, 77; Work of Art Gallery Saugerties, NY, 81;and many others. *Awards:* Best Painting in Show, Woodstock Art Asn, 82. *Mem:* Woodstock Art Asn; Artists Club, New York. *Mailing Add:* 246 E 46th St New York NY 10017

WEINSTEIN, JOYCE
PAINTER
b New York, NY, June 7, 31. *Study:* City Col New York, 48-50; Art Students League, 48-50. *Work:* Mus Mod Art, New York; Pa Acad Fine Arts; Edmonton Art Gallery, Alta; NJ State Mus, Trenton; Weatherspoon Mus, Greensboro, NC. *Exhib:* Works on Paper, Women Artists, Brooklyn Mus, 75; New Abstract Art, Edmonton Art Gallery Mus, 77; New Acquisitions, Mus Mod Art, New York, 81; solo exhibs, Martin Gerard Gallery, Edmonton, Alta, 81-82, Gallerie Wentzel, Cologne, WGer, 82, Gallery One, Toronto, 83 & Haber Theodore Gallery, New York, 83; Recent Acquisitions, Edmonton Art Gallery Mus, 83. *Awards:* Lambert Fund Award, Pa Acad Fine Arts, 53. *Bibliog:* Grace Glueck (auth), article, New York Times, 12/14/79; Lelde Muehlenbachs (auth), Edmonton, Joyce Weinstein at Martin Gerard Gallery, Artmagazine 55, Toronto, 9-10/81; Valentin Tatransky (auth), Joyce Weinstein at Haber Theodore Gallery, Arts Mag, 5/83. *Mem:* Women Arts Found Inc (bd mem, 71-83, exec coordr, 78-82). *Media:* Oil on Canvas, Miscellaneous. *Dealer:* Haber Theodore Gallery 24 W 57 St New York NY 10019; Gallery One 121 Scollard St Toronto Ontario Canada M5R 164. *Mailing Add:* 37 E 18 St New York NY 10003

WEINTRAUB, ANNETTE
PAINTER, EDUCATOR
b New York, NY, July 2, 46. *Study:* Cooper Union, BFA, 67; Univ Pa Grad Sch Fine Arts, MFA, 70. *Work:* Aldrich Mus Contemp Art, Ridgefield, Conn; Prudential Insurance Co; Best Products Co, Ashland, Va; WTex Mus Asn; Wichita Art Mus. *Exhib:* Contemp Reflections, 1975-76, Aldrich Mus Contemp Art, 76; New Talent, A M Sachs Gallery, New York, 79; Art on Paper, Weatherspoon Art Gallery, Greensboro, NC, 79; group exhib, Members' Gallery, Albright-Knox Art Gallery, Columbus Art Mus, Ohio, 80, & Lisa Dubins Gallery, Los Angeles, 80; Woman--Inside and Out, Gallery Yves Arman, 83. *Teaching:* Adj lectr painting, drawing & design, York Col, 71-81, asst prof advert design, City Col, 83-, City Univ New York. *Awards:* Resident Fel, Yaddo, Saratoga Springs, NY, 79. *Bibliog:* Ellen Lubell (auth), Manhattan (and Hoboken), Soho Weekly News, 5/24/79. *Mem:* Women's Caucus Art (adv bd New York chap, 79-80). *Media:* Colored Pencil and Wax Varnish on Canvas, Colored Pencil on Paper. *Mailing Add:* 2 Bond St New York NY 10012

WEISBERG, GABRIEL P
HISTORIAN, EDUCATOR
b New York, NY, May 4, 42. *Study:* New York Univ, BA, 63; Johns Hopkins Univ, MA, PhD, 67. *Pos:* Cur art hist, Cleveland Mus Art, 73-81; asst dir, Nat Endowment Humanities, 83- *Teaching:* Asst prof art hist, Univ NMex, 67-69; assoc prof art hist, Univ Cincinnati, 69-73; Mellon prof art hist, Univ Pittsburgh, 81- *Awards:* Nat Endowment Arts Fel, 77; Robert C Smith Award, Decorative Art Soc, 80. *Mem:* Print Coun Am; Decorative Arts Soc; Col Art Asn Am (bd dirs, 80-). *Res:* Study of 19th century realism, Japonisme and art nouveau as a formalistic concern and as an example of social history. *Publ:* Auth, The Etching Renaissance in France 1850-1880, Univ Utah, 71; coauth, Japonisme: Japanese Influence on French Art, Cleveland Mus Art, 75; auth, Francois Bonvin Life and Work, Geoffroy-Dechaume, 79; auth, The Realist Tradition: French Painting and Drawing, Cleveland Mus Art, 80; ed, The European Realist Tradition, 83. *Mailing Add:* Asst Dir Nat Endowment Humanities Washington DC 20506

WEISBERG, RUTH ELLEN
PRINTMAKER, EDUCATOR
b Chicago, Ill, July 31, 42. *Study:* Accad di Belli Arte, Perugia, Italy, Laurea; Univ Mich, BS & MA; Atelier 17, Paris, with S W Hayter. *Work:* Bibliot Nat, France; Chicago Art Inst; Los Angeles Co Mus of Art; New York Pub Libr; Norwegian Nat Collection. *Comn:* Together Again (ed of 150 lithographs), Midwest Regional Orgn for Rehabilitation & Training, 75; The Gift (ed of 60 lithographs), Univ Synagogue, Los Angeles, 75; Interlude, Los Angeles Co Mus of Art, 75. *Exhib:* Artist's Proof: The Multiple Image, Fine Arts Mus of San Francisco, 76; two-person shows, Union Gallery, Ariz State Univ, 76, Palos Verdes Art Gallery, Los Angeles, 76 & Santa Barbara Community Col, 78; Works by Women on Paper, Nat Invitational, Women's Bldg, Los Angeles, 77; solo exhib, Judah Magnes Mus, Berkeley, 81; and others. *Pos:* Assoc dean, Univ Southern Calif, 74-75 & 76-77. *Teaching:* Asst prof fine arts, Eastern Mich Univ, Ypsilanti, 66-67; assoc prof fine arts, Univ Southern Calif, Los Angeles, 70- *Awards:* Purchase Award, Los Angeles Printmaking Soc, Griffin Press, 76. *Bibliog:* V Thorson (auth), Sensory visions of Ruth Weisberg, Womanspace J, 8/73. *Mem:* Los Angeles Printmaking Soc (pres, 74-76); Graphic Arts Coun, Los Angeles Co Mus (mem bd, 76-77); Women's Caucus for Art (mem nat adv bd, 77-80); Artist for Econ Action; Malaspina Printmakers Soc. *Media:* Lithography. *Publ:* Illusr, Tom O'Bedlam's Song, 69 & auth & illusr, The Shtetl, A Journey and A Memorial, 72, Kelyn Press. *Mailing Add:* 2421 Third St Santa Monica CA 90405

WEISMAN, MARCIA SIMON
COLLECTOR, LECTURER
b Portland, Ore, Aug 22, 18. *Study:* Mills Col, Oakland, Calif. *Exhib:* Calif Artists in Washington, Calif Sen Off, 74; Collector's Choice, Los Angeles Inst Contemp Art, 75; Los Angeles Artists, State Capitol Bldg, Sacramento, 77; Prints from Gemini GEL, Cedars-Sinai Med Ctr, 79. *Collections Arranged:* Portion of Corporate Collection of California Art, (cataloged), Calif State Univ, Long Beach, 78. *Pos:* Art consult; founding mem, Contemp Art Coun & mem, Far Eastern Art Coun, Los Angeles Co Mus Art; mem collectors comt, Nat Gallery Art, DC, 75-; chairperson adv coun for arts, Cedars-Sinai Med Ctr, 76-; mem bd trustees, San Francisco Mus Mod Art, 77-; mem, Calif Arts Coun, 80-81; founding trustee, Mus Contemp Art, Los Angeles, currently. *Teaching:* Instr, Univ Calif, Los Angeles Exten, 2 yrs; lectr, Los Angeles Co Mus Art, La Jolla Mus Contemp Art, Calif State Univ, Long Beach, Detroit Mus, Cedars-Sinai Med Ctr, Los Angeles & Univ Calif, Los Angeles; adj prof art, Calif State Univ, Long Beach, 77- *Mem:* Founding mem Fel Contemp Art; President's Adv Comt Arts. *Collection:* 20th century contemporary art; modern art. *Mailing Add:* 1140 Angelo Dr Beverly Hills CA 90210

WEISMANN, DONALD LEROY
EDUCATOR, PAINTER
b Milwaukee, Wis, Oct 12, 14. *Study:* Univ Wis-Milwaukee, BS; Univ Minn; Univ Wis-Madison, PhM; St Louis Univ; Harvard Univ, Carnegie Corp scholar, 41; Ohio State Univ, PhD. *Work:* Butler Inst Am Art, Youngstown, Ohio; Chrysler Mus, Provincetown, Mass; Columbia Mus Art, SC; D D Feldman Collection, Humanities Res Ctr, Univ Tex, Austin; Witte Mus, San Antonio, Tex. *Comn:* Mural, Ill Centennial Bldg, Springfield, 41; TV videotape ser, Mirror of Western Art, Nat Educ TV, 60 & Visual Arts, Ford Found & US Off Educ, 61; films, Terlingua, 71 & Station X, 75, Pub Broadcast Corp; Azimuth, 76. *Exhib:* Ann Exhib Am Art, 40-41 & Int Watercolor Exhib, 42, Art Inst Chicago, Ill; Ann Exhib Art US & Territories, Butler Inst Am Art, 57-58; Gulf-Caribbean Exhib, Houston Mus Fine Arts, Tex, 58; World's Fair, New York, 64-65; Colorado Springs Fine Arts Ctr, Colo; Cincinnati Mus of Art, Ohio; Corcoran Gallery of Art, Washington, DC; Dallas Mus of Fine Arts, Tex; Inst of Contemp Arts, Boston, Mass; Toledo Mus of Art, Ohio. *Collections Arranged:* Ulfert Wilke Retrospective, 53 & Victor Hammer Retrospective, 54, Univ Ky, Lexington. *Teaching:* Assoc prof, NTex State Univ, summer 40; asst prof art & art hist, Ill State Univ, 40-42 & 46-48; asst prof art hist, Wayne State Univ, 49-51; prof art & head dept, Univ Ky, 51-54; prof art, Univ Tex, Austin, 54-, chmn dept, 54-58, grad prof art hist, 58-, univ prof in arts, 64-, chmn comp studies, 67-72. *Awards:* Purchase Award for Painting, Butler Inst Am Art, 57; Bromberg Award for Excellence in Teaching, Univ Tex, Austin, 65; Lett of Commendation for Enhancement of Arts in Am, President of US, 72. *Mem:* Nat Coun Arts; Nat Humanities Fac. *Media:* Collage, Film. *Res:* Creative process in art and science; language and visual form. *Publ:* auth, Visual Arts as Human Experience, 70; auth & illusr, Why Draw?, 74; auth, The 12 Cadavers of Joe Mariner, 77; auth, Follow the Bus with the Greek License Plates, 81; auth, Duncan Phyfe and Drum, 84. *Dealer:* Carlin Galleries 710 Montgomery St Ft Worth TX 76107. *Mailing Add:* 405 Buckeye Trail Austin TX 78746

WEISS, HARVEY
SCULPTOR
b New York, NY, Apr 10, 22. *Study:* Nat Acad Design; Art Students League; and with Ossipe Zadkine, Paris. *Work:* Albright-Knox Art Gallery; Krannert Mus; Silvermine Guild Collection; Nelson Rockefeller Collection; Joseph H Hirshhorn Collection; plus others. *Comn:* Menorah, Temple B'nai Zion, Shreveport, La, 67; relief, Mt Vernon Synagogue, NY, 69; relief, Conn Off Bldg, Westport, 71. *Exhib:* Five one-man shows, Paul Rosenberg & Co, 59-70; one-man show, Silvermine Guild, 68 & 83; retrospective, Fairfield Univ, 70; Am Inst Arts & Lett, 70; Sculptor's Guild Ann Shows. *Teaching:* Assoc prof sculpture, Adelphi Univ, Garden City, NY, currently. *Awards:* Three Ford Found Purchase Awards; Olivetti Award, New Eng Ann Exhib, 69; Nat Inst Arts & Lett Grant, 70. *Mem:* Sculptors Guild (pres, 70-71); Silvermine Guild Artists (bd trustees, 68-70); Auth Guild. *Media:* Bronze, Welded Brass. *Publ:* Auth & illusr, Paint Brush & Palette, 66, Collage & Construction, 70, Gadget Book, 71, Lens & Shutter, 71 & Machines & How They Work, 83; and others. *Mailing Add:* 42 Maple Lane Greens Farms CT 06436

WEISS, JEFF
PHOTOGRAPHER, EDUCATOR
b Bronx, NY, Nov 6, 42. *Study:* Univ Mich, BS, 64; with Paul Caponigro, 68 & Minor White, 69. *Work:* Fogg Art Mus; Nat Collection Fine Art; Art Inst Chicago. *Exhib:* Jeff Weiss--Roland Freeman, Nat Collection Fine Art, Washington, DC, 71; Photography, Fogg Art Mus, 76 & 77; Altered States, Univ Ill, Urbana, 82; Visual Cataloging and Mapping, Visual Studies Workshop, Rochester, NY, 82; Television Show, Robert Friedus Gallery, New York, 83. *Pos:* Mem bd dirs, Photog Resource Ctr, Boston, 79- *Teaching:* Mem fac photog, Goddard Col, 70-81; vis artist, Art Inst Chicago, 81-; vis fac mem art, Univ Iowa, Iowa City, 83. *Awards:* Vt Coun Arts Individual Artist Grant Photog, 75; Nat Endowment Arts Major Artists Fel Photog, 81. *Bibliog:* S D Peters (auth), Gallery, City Paper, 2/4/82; C Squires (auth), Photography, Village Voice, 2/8/83. *Mem:* Soc Photog Educ. *Mailing Add:* c/o H F Manes Gallery 177 Prince St New York NY 10012

WEISS, JOHN JOSEPH
PHOTOGRAPHER, EDITOR
b Philadelphia, Pa, Jan 31, 41. *Study:* Temple Univ, BS, 63; Mass Inst Technol, 69-73; RI Sch Design, MFA, 73. *Work:* Mus Mod Art, New York; Addison Gallery Am Art, Andover, Mass; Princeton Univ, NJ; Del Art Mus;

Wilmington; Photog Place, Philadelphia. *Exhib:* Addison Gallery Am Art, Andover, Mass, 73; Mass Inst Technol Creative Photog Gallery, Cambridge, 76; Photopia, Philadelphia, 79; Triad Gallery, Porland, Maine, 81; G H Dalsheimer Gallery, Baltimore, 83; The Photographers' Gallery, London, 83. *Pos:* Coordr photog, Mass Inst Technol, 76- *Teaching:* Instr photog, Mass Inst Technol, 69-73; asst prof photog, Univ Del, Newark, 75-79, assoc prof, 79- *Publ:* Contribr, Portraits, Mod Photog, 77; auth, A darkroom philosophy, Camera 35, 77; ed, Venus, Jupiter and Mars--The Photographs of Frederick Sommer, Del Art Mus, 80; Philadelphia Photog Rev, 81; auth, biography of Frederick Sommer, Collier's Encycl. *Mailing Add:* Dept of Art Univ Del Newark DE 19711

WEISS, LEE (ELYSE C WEISS)
PAINTER
b Inglewood, Calif, May 22, 28. *Study:* Calif Col Arts & Crafts, 46-47; also with N Eric Oback, 57 & Alexander Nepote, 58. *Work:* Nat Mus Am Art; Nat Acad Design, New York; Phillips Collection, Washington, DC; Exec Residence, State Wis; Springfield Mus Art, Mo; and many others. *Comn:* Am Artist & Water Resources, one of 40 Am artists chosen for Bur Reclamation Art Proj, US Dept Interior, 71; artist for space shuttle launch, NASA, 84. *Exhib:* Am Watercolor Soc, New York, 65-; Pa Acad Fine Arts, Philadelphia, 65 & 68; Landscape as Interpreted by Twenty-two Artists, Minneapolis Inst Fine Arts, Minn, 66; American Artist & Water Reclamation, Nat Gallery Art, Washington, DC, 72; San Jose Mus Art, Calif, 74; Nat Air & Space Mus, Smithsonian Inst, Washington, DC, 78; Canton Art Inst, 79; plus many other group & one-man shows. *Awards:* Century Award of Merit, 78 & Jeffco Award, 79, Rocky Mountain Nat Watermedia Exhib; Cert of Merit, Nat Acad Design; many others; High Winds Medal, Am Watercolor Soc, 78; First Award, Nat Watercolor Soc, 82. *Bibliog:* cover story in North Light Mag, 77; Lawrence C Goldsmith (auth), Watercolor Bold & Free, Watson-Guptill, 80; Frank Getlein & Jo Ann Lewis (coauths), The Washington DC Art Review, Vanguard Press, 80. *Mem:* Am Watercolor Soc; Nat Watercolor Soc; Wis Painters & Sculptors; Wis Watercolor Soc. *Media:* Watercolor. *Publ:* Coauth, Lee Weiss watercolors, Col Printing & Publ, 71; auth, article in, Watercolor Page, Am Artist Mag, 9/72; auth, Lee Weiss, Watercolors II, the Seventies, Am Printing & Publ Co, 81. *Dealer:* Franz Bader Gallery 2124 Pennsylvania Ave NW Washington DC 20037; Louis Newman Galleries 322 N Beverly Dr Beverly Hills CA 90210. *Mailing Add:* 106 Vaughn Ct Madison WI 53705

WEISS, LINDA (LINDA MARGARET WEISS-EDWARDS)
SILVERSMITH, GOLDSMITH
b Detroit, Mich, Dec 6, 51. *Study:* Cent Mich Univ, BFA, 73; Univ Wash, BFA, 75; Cranbrook Acad Art, travel grant to Eng, 76 & 78, MFA, 77. *Comn:* Cloisonne enamel & rosewood, Wiseway Corp, Chicago, 78; 18 karat gold neck piece, comn by Mr & Mrs Norman Stewart, Birmingham, Mich, 78; jewelry, comn by Mr & Mrs Douglas Steakley, Carmel, Calif, 80; sterling silver & 14 karat gold kiddush cup, comn by Congregation Shir Hadash, Los Gatos, Calif, 80; Bronze holloware, comn by Mark Bloome Enterprises, Los Angeles, Calif, 83; and others. *Exhib:* Int Crafts, Tweed Mus Art, Duluth, Minn, 77; Calif Craftsmen, Monterey Mus Art, Calif, 78; Objects '79, Western Colo Ctr Arts, Grand Junction, 79; Young Americans-Metal 1980, Am Crafts Mus, New York, 80; Nat Metalsmiths Invitational, Ctr Visual Arts, Anchorage, Alaska; Metalsmith '81, Soc NAm Goldsmiths, Lawrence, Kans, 81; and others. *Collections Arranged:* National Metalsmiths Invitational, New Haven, Conn, 77; California Metals Invitational, Long Beach, 78; Designer-Craftsmen Exhibs, Richmond Art Ctr, Calif, 78 & 81; Pensacola Nat Crafts, Fla, 79; Current Directions--Metal Arts of the '80's, Monterey Mus Art, Calif, 83; Continuing Traditions in Silver, Argentium Gallery, San Francisco, 83; and others. *Pos:* Bd dirs, Mich Silversmiths Guild, 76-78; designer, goldsmith & mgr, McLean & Co, Goldsmiths, Sausalito, Calif, 78-81; partner, Weiss/Edwards Designs, Sausalito, Calif, 79-; jewelry design consult, Boring & Co, San Francisco, currently. *Teaching:* Vis artist metalsmithing & jewelry design, Univ Mich, Ann Arbor, 77; vis artist silversmithing & metalsmithing, Calif Col Arts & Crafts, Oakland, 79-80; prof, Acad Art Col, San Francisco, 81. *Awards:* Merit Award, Monterey Mus Art, 78; Hazel Salmi Award, Soroptimist Int, Richmond Art Ctr, 81; Award for Excellence, Merlins Found, Fairfax, Calif, 83. *Bibliog:* Laurie Haig Glass (auth), Designer-craftsmen '78, Artweek, 11/18/78; Murray Bovin (auth), Jewelry Making for Schools, Tradesmen, Craftsmen, Bovin Publ, New York, 79; The Goodfellow Catalog of Wonderful Things No 3, Goodfellow Catalog Press, Berkeley, 81; and others. *Mem:* Soc NAm Goldsmiths; Am Crafts Coun; Col Art Asn. *Media:* Metals. *Publ:* Auth, Health hazards in the field of goldsmithing, Goldsmiths J, Soc NAm Goldsmiths, 78; auth, Health column, Metalsmith Mag. *Dealer:* Concepts Gallery PO Box 301 Carmel CA 93921; Union St Goldsmiths San Francisco CA. *Mailing Add:* PO Box 1032 Sausalito CA 94965

WEISS, PEG
HISTORIAN, CURATOR
Study: Syracuse Univ, BA, 54, PhD, 73; Univ Munich & Syracuse Univ, MA, 60. *Collections Arranged:* Art Deco Environment, 76 & Animal Kingdom in American Art, 77, Everson Mus; Kandinsky in Munich, Guggenheim Mus, 82. *Pos:* Publ cur, Everson Mus, Syracuse, NY, 74, cur collections, 75-79, chief cur, 79-; guest cur, Solomon R Guggenheim Mus, New York, 79-82. *Teaching:* Vis asst prof art hist, Columbia Univ, 74-75; adj prof art hist, Syracuse Univ, 74- *Awards:* Fulbright Scholar, 67-68; Millard Meiss Publ Fund Award, 77; Nat Endowment Humanities Fel for Independent Study & Research, 81-82. *Mem:* Col Art Asn Am; Int Comt Mus; Am Asn Mus; Am Soc Aesthetics. *Publ:* Auth, Kandinsky & the Jugendstil Arts & Crafts Movement, Burlington Mag, 5/75; auth, Kandinsky the utopian focus, Arts Mag, 4/77; auth, Kandinsky: Symbolist Poetics & Theater in Munich, Pantheon, 77; auth, Kandinsky in Munich--The Formative Jugendstil Years, Princeton Univ, 79; auth, Galka Scheyer and The Blue Four, Univ Calif. *Mailing Add:* 238 Scottholm Terr Syracuse NY 13224

WEISS, RACHEL
SCULPTOR, HOLOGRAPHER
b Paterson, NJ, Sept 22, 54. *Study:* Marlboro Col, BA, 76; Mass Col Art, MFA, 80. *Work:* Ctr Georges Pompidou, Paris; Nat Mus Sci & Technol, Ottawa, Ont. *Exhib:* Ctr Advan Visual Studies, Cambridge, Mass, 81; Helen Shlien Gallery, Boston, 81 & 83; Nat Mus Sci Technol, Ottawa, Ont, 82; Ctr Georges Pompidou, Paris, 82; BMW Mus, Munich, WGer, 83; and others. *Pos:* Producer, Art Assault, 80- *Teaching:* Asst instr holography, Mass Col Art, Boston, 79-80, spec prog asst, 78-81; asst instr holography, Brown Univ, Providence, RI, 80-81. *Bibliog:* Jamey Gambrell (auth), Salon for the South Pole, Artforum, 12/81. *Mem:* Boston Performance Artists. *Mailing Add:* 108 Winthrop Rd Brookline MA 02146

WEISSMAN, JULIAN PAUL
WRITER, DEALER
b New York, NY, June 28, 43. *Study:* Hobart Col, Geneva, NY, BA. *Pos:* Art Critic, The Press, 73-77; ed assoc, writer & reviewer, Art New Mag, New York, 74-; mgr, Susan Caldwell Gallery Inc, New York, 74-75; mgr, Gloria Cortella Inc (gallery), New York, 76-77; dir, Alexander F Milliken Inc (gallery), New York, 78-79; dir, Gruenebaum Gallery Inc, New York, 79- *Res:* Impressionism; German expressionism; the Bauhaus; 20th century sculpture; contemporary art and artists who live and work in New York. *Specialty:* Contemporary art gallery, primarily devoted to showing first and second generation abstract expressionists. *Publ:* Auth, Standoff in Soho, Art News Mag, 74; auth, What's wrong at the Whitney?, The Press, Vol 3, No 3, 75; auth, Master Atget ... & Portraits of the Artists, Art News Mag, 76; auth, Here comes the taxman, Soho Weekly News, 76; auth, Dazzling drawings are redefining the art, The Press, Vol 4, No 1, 76. *Mailing Add:* 26 Beaver St New York NY 10004

WEISSMAN, WALTER
SCULPTOR, WRITER
b Brooklyn, NY, Dec 9, 47. *Study:* Kingsborough Community Col, with Gregory Battcock, AA, 67; Brooklyn Col, with Harry Holtzman, BA(hon; arts), 70; Hunter Col, with Robert Morris, MA(fine arts), 75. *Exhib:* Contemporary Reflections No 4, Aldrich Mus Contemp Art, 75; Open Studios at PS1, Queens, NY, 77; Benefit for Chile Committee--Memoralto Letelier, Cayman Gallery, New York, 77; Centennial Exhib Sculpture, NJ Inst Technol, Newark, 81; AIR Gallery Ann, New York, 83; solo exhib, Structures and Shelters, 14 Sculptors Gallery, New York, 83. *Collections Arranged:* Drawings, Models and Sculpture: A Re-Opening: Season's Premier, 14 Sculptors Gallery, 82. *Pos:* Sr ed, Art & Artists, New York, 78-; vpres, 14 Sculptors Gallery, currently. *Teaching:* Asst instr photog, Yale Univ, 68; instr painting & drawing, Brooklyn Col, 71. *Bibliog:* Robbie Ehrlich (auth), article, Arts Mag, 6/80; Eileen Watkins (auth), article, Newark Star-Ledger, 5/81. *Mem:* Artists Meeting Cult Change (secy, 76-78); Found Community Arts (pres, 80-). *Specialty:* Contemporary experimental sculpture. *Publ:* Coauth, An Anti-Catalog, Artists Meeting Cult Change, 77; auth, Interview with John Perreault, 4/80, Automata and autonomy: Sculpture now, 11/81 & ed, Special Supplement, 11/81, Artworkers News; ed, Special Supplement, Art & Artists, 82. *Mailing Add:* 463 West St New York NY 10014

WEITZENHOFFER, A MAX
DEALER
b Oklahoma City, Okla, Oct 30, 39. *Study:* Univ Okla, BFA. *Pos:* Dir, Gimpel & Weitzenhoffer Ltd. *Mem:* Art Dealers Asn Am. *Specialty:* 20th century American and European paintings and sculpture. *Mailing Add:* 1040 Madison Ave New York NY 10021

WEITZMANN, KURT
EDUCATOR, HISTORIAN
b Almerode, Ger, Mar 7, 04; US citizen. *Study:* Univ Munster; Univ Wurzburg; Univ Vienna; Univ Berlin, PhD, 29; Univ Heidelberg, Hon Dr, 67; Univ Chicago, Hon Dr, 68; Univ Berlin, Hon Dr, 82. *Pos:* Stipend, Ger Archaeol Inst, Greece, 31 & Berlin, 32-34; permanent mem, Inst Advan Study, 35-72; consult cur, Metrop Mus Art, 72-82. *Teaching:* Assoc prof art & archaeol, Princeton Univ, 45-50, prof art & archaeol, 50-72, emer prof, 72-; vis lectr art & archaeol, Yale Univ, 54-55; vis prof art & archaeol, Univ Alexandria, 60; guest prof art & archaeol, Univ Bonn, 62; vis scholar, Dumbarton Oaks, Washington, DC. *Awards:* Prix Gustave Schlumberger, Acad Inscriptions & Belles Lett, Paris, France, 69. *Mem:* Fel Medieval Acad Am; Ger Archaeol Inst; Am Philos Soc; Col Art Asn Am; Archaeol Inst Am. *Res:* Late classical, Byzantine and medieval art; expeditions to Mt Athos & Mt Sinai. *Publ:* Auth, Byzantine Book Illumination and Ivorien, 80; auth, Byzantine Liturgical Prayers and Gospels, 80; auth, Classical Heritage and Near Eastern Art, 81; auth, The Medieval West and Its Contacts with Byzantium, 82; auth, Studies in the Arts at Sinai, 82. *Mailing Add:* 30 Nassau St Princeton NJ 08540

WELCH, CHARLES D See Cracker Jack Kid

WELCH, JAMES WYMORE
PAINTER, MURALIST
b Omaha, Nebr, June 7, 28. *Study:* George Washington Univ, BA; Univ Omaha, study with Anna C Myers; Acad Fine Arts, Tokyo, Japan, with Shiguru Yamamoto; Keio Univ, Hiyoshi, Japan, study with Daisuke Sakai; Sch of Fine Arts, Seoul, Korea, study with Kim Il Han; study with Mark Rothko. *Work:* Nat Mus, Seoul; Joslyn Mem Mus, Omaha; Nat Mus Mod Art, Tokyo; Fed Reserve Bank, Richmond, Va; Philip Morris USA, Richmond. *Comn:* Poster panel designs, US State Dept Arts Abroad Prog,

Washington, DC, 63; acrylic mural, Univ Panama, Repub Panama, 59; acrylic painting, McDonald's Corp, New York, 79; acrylic paintings, IBM Corp, New York, 81; acrylic paintings, Xerox Corp, New York, 82. *Exhib:* Oriental Art Trends for Today, Fine Arts Pavillion, Osaka, Japan, 50; Ann Invitational, Palacio de Fine Arts, Panama City, Republic Panama, 59-60; Presidential Fine Arts Show, Duk-Soo Palace, Seoul, 63; 13th Biennial Show, Valentine Mus, Richmond, 74; Corcoran Gallery Art Biennial, DC; Minimal Arts of the 70's, Hirshhorn Mus, Washington, DC, 79; and others. *Pos:* Pres, Metrop Artists Asn, Richmond, Va. *Teaching:* Guest instr abstract painting, Univ Panama, 58-60; guest lectr Western US art, US State Dept/Korean Govt, Seoul, 63-64. *Awards:* Presidential Award, Presidential Fine Arts Show, Seoul, 63; Purchase Award, Shockoe Slip Art Fair, Xerox Corp, 76; Purchase Award, Federated Arts Show, Richmond, 82. *Bibliog:* Pam Sampsell (auth), Painting is third career for banker, Richmond News Leader, 78; B Green (auth), Artists works have deceptively simple sophistication, Richmond News Leader, 81; B Green (auth), Minimal art recieves critical acclaim, Richmond News Leader, 82. *Mem:* Metrop Artists Asn, Richmond; Federated Arts Coun, Richmond; Accademia Italia Delle Arti E Del Lavoro. *Media:* Oil, Acrylic. *Dealer:* Welch Studio 1500 Park Ave Richmond VA 23220. *Mailing Add:* 1500 Park Ave Richmond VA 23220

WELCH, (MR & MRS) ROBERT G
COLLECTORS
Mr Welch b Kewanee, Ill, July 9, 15. *Study:* Stanford Univ, AB, 37. *Teaching:* Guest lectr at many univs. *Mem:* Cleveland Mus Art; Mus Mod Art, New York (Cleveland growth bd); Cleveland Soc Contemp Art. *Collection:* Contemporary metal sculpture. *Mailing Add:* 16800 S Woodland Rd Cleveland OH 44120

WELCH, ROGER
SCULPTOR, PHOTOGRAPHER
b Westfield, NJ, Feb 10, 46. *Study:* Miami Univ, Ohio, BFA, 69; Whitney Mus Independent Study Prog, 70-71; Art Inst Chicago, MFA, 71. *Work:* Georgia Mus of Art, Athens; Rufino Tamayo Mus, Mexico City; Mus Mod Art, New York; Mus Bellas Artes, Caracas, Venezuela; Wallraf Richartz Mus, Cologne, Ger; and others. *Comn:* The O J Simpson Project (multi-media work), Albright-Knox Art Gallery, 77. *Exhib:* One-man shows, Milwaukee Art Ctr, 74, Albright-Knox Art Gallery, 77, Mus Nac, Havana, 81, Mus Bellas Artes, Caracas, Venezuela, 81 & Whitney Mus Am Art, 82; Words, Whitney Mus Am Art, 77; Alternatives in Retrospect-An Historical Overview 1969-1975, New Mus, New York, 81; Four Artists and the Map, Spencer Mus Art, Kans, 81; Urban Pulses, Pittsburgh Plan Art, 83; and others. *Collections Arranged:* The Solomon Collection, Sarah Lawrence Col, 76; Collection for Jimmy Carter, Ga Mus Art, 77. *Teaching:* Guest lectr many univs, 76-81. *Awards:* Creative Artists Pub Serv Grant, 73 & 76; Nat Endowment Arts Grants, 74 & 80. *Bibliog:* Douglas Davis (auth), After photography, Village Voice, Vol 26, No 14, 81; David Sterritt (auth), Merged media, Christian Sci Monitor, 11/4/82; William Zimmer (auth), Remembering memory lane, New York Times, 2/27/83. *Publ:* Contribr, Tracks J, spring 75; contribr, Unbuilt America, McGraw-Hill, 76; contribr, The Individual in a Social World, Addison-Wesley, 77; contribr, The Big Jewish Book, Doubleday, 78. *Dealer:* Sonnabend Gallery 420 W Broadway New York NY 10012. *Mailing Add:* 87 E Houston St New York NY 10012

WELCH, STUART CARY
CURATOR, HISTORIAN
b Buffalo, NY, Apr 2, 28. *Study:* Harvard Col, AB, 50. *Pos:* Cur, Near Eastern & Indian Art, Fogg Art Mus, Harvard Univ, cur manuscripts, Harvard Col Libr; consult Islamic art dept, Metrop Mus Art, New York. *Teaching:* Lectr, Near Eastern & Indian Art, Harvard Univ. *Res:* Safavid painting (Iran); Mughal and Rajput painting (India). *Publ:* Coauth, Gods, Thrones and Peacocks: Northern Indian Painting from Two Traditions, Asia Soc, 65; auth, A King's Book of Kings: The Shahnameh of Shah Tahmasp, Metrop Mus Art, New York, 72; auth, Room for Wonder: Indian Painting under the British Raj, Am Fedn Arts, 78; coauth, The Houghton Shahnameh, Harvard Univ Press, 80; auth, Annemarie Schimmel: A Pocketbook for Akbar, Metrop Mus Art, 83. *Mailing Add:* Fogg Art Mus 32 Quincy St Cambridge MA 02138

WELDON, BARBARA MALTBY
PAINTER, PRINTMAKER
b Yuma, Ariz. *Study:* San Diego State Univ, 50-52; Univ Calif, San Diego, 70-73. *Work:* Bank Am World Hq, San Francisco; San Diego Mus Art, Calif; Copley Mem Libr & Salk Inst, La Jolla, Calif; Security Pac Bank. *Comn:* Many comns in pvt collections. *Exhib:* Nat Acad Design, New York, 79; solo exhibs, Thomas Babeor Gallery, La Jolla, Calif, 80-83 & Ivory Kimpton Gallery, San Francisco, 82-83; Newport Harbor Art Mus, Newport Beach, Calif, 81; Contemporary Californians, Laguna Beach Mus Art, Calif, 84; and others. *Awards:* First Award, Nat Watercolor Soc, 74; Second Prize, San Diego Mus Art, 75; William A Paton Prize, Nat Acad Design, 79. *Bibliog:* Robert McDonald (auth), Musical inspirations, 1/81 & Andree Marechal-Workman (auth), Translucent and lyrical, 1/82, Artweek; Richard Reilly (auth), Barbara Weldon lights up Babeor Gallery with subtle colors, San Diego Union, 11/82. *Media:* Watercolor, Acrylic. *Dealer:* Ivory/Kimpton Gallery 55 Grant Ave San Francisco CA; Thomas Babeor Gallery 7470 Girard Ave La Jolla CA. *Mailing Add:* 6131 Romany Dr San Diego CA 92120

WELLER, ALLEN STUART
EDUCATOR, HISTORIAN
b Chicago, Ill, Feb 1, 07. *Study:* Univ Chicago, PhB, 27, PhD, 42; Princeton Univ, MA, 29; Ind Cent Col, Hon LLD, 65; Univ Fla, Hon DFA, 77. *Collections Arranged:* Contemporary American Painting & Sculpture,

Krannert Art Mus, 48-53, biennially, 55-74. *Pos:* Guest cur, Mitchell Mus, Mt Vernon, Ill, 78, 79, 80 & 83. *Teaching:* Prof hist art, Univ Mo-Columbia, 29-47; prof hist art, head dept, dean col fine & appl arts & dir mus, Univ Ill, 47-75; vis prof, Univ Minn, Univ Colo, Univ Calif, Univ RI & Ore State Univ. *Mem:* Fel Royal Soc Arts London; fel Nat Asn Schs Art; Col Art Asn Am (bd dirs, currently); Soc Archit Historians; Nat Asn Schs Art (bd dirs, currently). *Res:* Italian Renaissance; contemporary American painting and sculpture. *Publ:* Auth, Francesco de Giorgio, 1439-1501, 42; auth, Abraham Rattner, 56; auth, Art USA Now, 62; auth, Joys and Sorrows of Recent American Art, 68; auth, Lorado in Paris, 84. *Mailing Add:* 412 W Iowa St Urbana IL 61801

WELLINGTON, DUKE
PAINTER
b Kans, Aug 9, 1896. *Study:* Kans State Col; Los Angeles Art Ctr; Art Students League; and with Eliot O'Hara, Edgar A Whitney, Hayward Veal, Doel Reed, Alice Harold Murphy, Reed Schmickle & Joseph Fleck. *Work:* Graphica, NY; Hoover Mus, Joplin; in many pvt collections, incl Maurice Chevalier, Paris, Irving Berlin, NY & Gustav S Eyssell, NY. *Exhib:* Kansas City Mo Art Asn, Kansas City Mus, 57; Kans Painters Show, Kans State Col Pittsburg, 58; Ozark Artist Guild, Joplin, Mo, 58; Spiva Art Ctr, Joplin, 59; Wichita Art Mus, 68. *Pos:* Art dir, Tex Theatre, San Antonio, 24-26, Paramount Theatres, New York, 27-36 & Nat Screen Serv, Los Angeles, Calif, 46-56; demonstr art, NBC/KOAM Educ TV, Pittsburg, 66-67. *Awards:* Ozark Artist Guild Award for Clown Lou Jacobs, 58; Spiva Art Ctr Award for Hens, 59; Kans Painters Show Award for Finitude, 59. *Bibliog:* Robert Kelly (auth) San Antonio boy promoted, San Antonio Eve News, 5/25/28; George Britt (auth), Lure movie fans, NY World Telegram, 10/7/32; R E Brenner (auth), Duke, artist deluxe, Signs of the Times, Cincinnati, Ohio, 2/32. *Mem:* Spiva Art Ctr; life mem Scene & Pictorial Painters Int; Wichita Art Mus. *Media:* Oil. *Publ:* Auth, Theory and practice of poster art, Signs of Times Publ Co, 34. *Mailing Add:* c/o Talisman Gallery 115 East 12th St Bartlesville OK 74003

WELLIVER, NEIL G
PAINTER
b Millville, Pa, July 22, 29. *Study:* Philadelphia Mus Col Art, BFA, 53; Yale Sch Art, MFA, 55. *Work:* Metrop Mus Art, Mus Mod Art, Whitney Mus Am Art; Pa Acad Fine Arts, Philadelphia; Hirshhorn Mus, Washington, DC. *Comn:* Portrait, Bishop of Portland, Maine, 76; 41st Int Eucharist Cong, Philadelphia, 76. *Exhib:* Pa Acad Fine Arts, 65 & 77; Whitney Mus Am Art, New York, 72 & 73; Contemp Landscape Painting, Okla Art Ctr, Tulsa, 75; Art Inst Chicago, 75; Am 76 Traveling Exhib, US Dept Interior, 76-78; Univ Mo, Kansas City, 77; NC Mus Art, Raleigh, 77; Am Realism, William & Mary Col, Va, 78; one-person exhibs, Brooke Alexander Gallery, New York, 78-80; Butler Inst Am Art, 79; retrospective (travelling), 83; and others. *Pos:* Critic painting, Cooper Union Art Sch, 54-57; critic painting, Yale Univ, Univ Pa & Md Inst Col Art. *Teaching:* Instr, Cooper Union, 53-57, Yale Univ, 55-65, Swarthmore Col, 66 & Univ Pa, 66-77. *Awards:* Morse Fel, 60-61; Skowhegan Award, 75; Guggenheim Fel, 83. *Bibliog:* Robert M Doty (auth), The Imagery of Neil Welliver, Art International 9-10/82; Donald Kuspit (auth), Terrestrial Truth: Neil Welliver, Art In America, 4/83; Edgar Allen Beem (auth), article, Maine Times, 7/22/83. *Publ:* Contribr, Bicentennial Exhib Catalogue, US Dept Interior, 75; contribr, Art News, Craft Horizons & Perspecta. *Dealer:* Fischbach Gallery 29 W 57th St New York NY 10019; Brooke Alexander 20 W 57th St New York NY 10019. *Mailing Add:* RD 2 Lincolnville ME 04849

WELLS, ALISA
PHOTOGRAPHER
b Erie, Pa. *Study:* Ansel Adam Workshop, 61; Nathan Lyons Workshop, Rochester, NY, 61-62 & 65-66. *Work:* Int Mus Photog, George Eastman House, Rochester; Krannert Art Mus, Univ Ill, Champaign; Pasadena Art Mus, Calif; NMex Fine Arts Mus; Visual Studies Workshop. *Exhib:* one-person shows, State Univ NY, Buffalo, 72, Mus NMex, Santa Fe, 73 & Stables Gallery, Taos, NMex, 77; Gli Americani, Fotografi Oggi, Italy, 73; Light & Lens, Hudson River Mus, 73; An Inquiry into the Aesthetics of Photog, Nat Gallery of Can, 74; Women of Photog, San Francisco Mus Art & Seattle Art Mus, 75; Exhib Women Artists, Berlin, WGer, 77; and many others. *Pos:* Assoc cur, Int Mus Photog, George Eastman House, 62-69; asst to dir, Visual Studies Workshop, Rochester, 69-72; free lance photogr, Santa Fe, NMex, 72- *Awards:* Creative Artists Pub Serv Grant, NY, 72; Nat Endowment for the Arts Fel, 72; Western State Art Found Grant, 75. *Bibliog:* Mike Weaver (auth), New American Photography, Form, 68; Anne Tucker (auth), The Women's Eye, Knopf, 73; Women of Photography, San Francisco Mus of Photog, 75. *Publ:* Contribr, Photography in the 20th century, Horizon Press, 67; contribr, The Figure in the Landscape, Int Mus Photog, George Eastman House, 70; contribr, The Art of Photography, Life Series, 71; contribr, New Mexico Portfolio, Ctr of the Eye, 76. *Mailing Add:* 124 E Lupita Santa Fe NM 87501

WELLS, BETTY CHILDS
ILLUSTRATOR, PAINTER
b Baltimore, Md, Dec 7, 26. *Study:* Johns Hopkins Univ, 46; Md Inst Art, grad, 48, scholar, 49. *Work:* Peale Mus, Baltimore; White House & Supreme Court, Washington, DC; Univ Md Sch Law; Toronto Pub Libr. *Comn:* Interior murals (plaster & mosaic), Taylor Manor Psychiat Ctr, Ellicott City, Md, 69; interior murals (mosaic), Lake Clifton Sch, Baltimore, 71; exterior mural (bas relief in stone), Violetville Recreation Ctr, Baltimore, 72; exterior mural (mosaic), Templeton Sch, Baltimore, 73; Chief Justice Warren E Burger (portrait sketch), 76; Mrs Warren E Burger (portrait), Col William & Mary, 83. *Exhib:* Audubon Artists Ann, Nat Acad Art, New York, 65; one-woman

shows, Int Gallery, Baltimore, 66 & Baltimore Mus Art, 74; Syracuse Univ, NY, 76; US Supreme Court, Washington, DC, 78-79; Florida State Univ, 80; and others. *Pos:* Freelance courtroom illusr, Washington Post, 72-77 & WTOP, Washington, DC, 73-74; courtroom illusr, NBC, 74- *Teaching:* Instr basic drawing, Md Inst Art, 46-48. *Awards:* Best in Show, Easton Acad Arts, Md, 66; Two Emmies, 78; Am Bar Asn Gavel Award, 79. *Bibliog:* Larry Lewis (auth), Quick on the draw, Md Living, News Am Mag, 70; Robert Leslie (auth), Walls designed by Betty Wells, Idea, Japan, Vol 23, No 130; cover story, Am Bar Asn J, 7/79. *Mem:* Artists Equity Asn (pres, Md Chap, 66-68); Broadcast Designer Asn; Nat Acad TV Arts & Sci. *Media:* Multimedia. *Publ:* Contribr, Designing and Making Mosaics, Davis, 71; contribr, Arts for Architecture, Dept Housing & Urban Develop, 73; illusr, Supreme Court on Nixon Tapes, New York Times, US News & World Report, 74 & Newsweek, 10/77 & 12/77; illusr (covers), Am Bar Asn J, 3/77 & Litigation, winter 76; cover design & illusr, Bryson B Rash's Footnote Washington, EPM Publ Inc, 83. *Mailing Add:* 2180 Rosewell Drive Virginia Beach VA 23454

WELLS, LYNTON
PAINTER
b Baltimore, Md, Oct 21, 40. *Study:* RI Sch Design, BFA, 62; Cranbrook Acad Art, MFA, 65. *Work:* Mus Mod Art, New York; Dallas Mus Fine Art, Tex. *Exhib:* One-man shows, Andre Emmerich Gallery, New York, 75, Clair Copley, Los Angeles, 76, Droll/Kolbert Gallery, 78 & Univ Wis-Eau Claire, 79; retrospective, Princeton Univ Art Mus, 79; and others. *Awards:* Nat Endowment Arts Grant, 75. *Bibliog:* Bruce Boice (auth), article, Artforum, 5/73. *Dealer:* Holly Solomon Gallery 724 Fifth Ave New York NY 10019. *Mailing Add:* c/o Holly Solomon Gallery 392 W Broadway New York NY 10012

WELLS, MAC
PAINTER
b Cleveland, Ohio, Feb 3, 25. *Study:* Oberlin Col, BA, 48; Cooper Union, 48-49; also with Nahum Tschacbasov & Yasuo Kuniyoshi. *Work:* Michener Collection, Univ Tex, Austin; Aldrich Mus, Ridgefield, Conn; Herron Mus Art, Indianapolis, Ind; Purdue Univ, West Lafayette; Univ Mass, Amherst; and others. *Comn:* Three-dimensional card, Mus Mod Art, New York, NY, 65. *Exhib:* One-man shows, A M Sachs Gallery, New York, 65 & 67, Max Hutchinson Gallery, New York, 70 & 72, Susan Caldwell Gallery, New York, 75, Landmark Gallery, 79 & 55 Mercer Gallery, New York, 81; and others. *Teaching:* Asst prof, gen studio, Hunter Col, 66-81, assoc prof, 81-; instr painting & design, Moore Col Art, Philadelphia, 66-72; instr painting, Skowhegan Sch Painting & Sculpture, Maine, 69. *Awards:* Yaddo fel, 64 & 65. *Bibliog:* New Talent, Art in Am, 7-8/65; Lucy Lippard (auth), New York letter, Art Int, 11/20/65. *Mem:* Am Abstract Artists. *Media:* Multimedia. *Mailing Add:* 64 Grand St New York NY 10013

WELLS, THOMAS (WINCHESTER)
PAINTER
b Chicago, Ill, Oct 20, 16. *Study:* Yale Univ Sch Fine Arts, BFA, 42. *Work:* Seattle Art Mus, Safeco Insurance Co & Pacific Car & Foundry, Seattle, Wash; Wash State Capitol Mural Design, Olympia; Matson Navigation Co, San Francisco, Calif. *Comn:* NW Indian Design (mural), Bellingham Hotel, Wash, 50; Theotokos (mosaic), St Demetrios Church, Seattle, Wash, 65; Maritime Lumber (mural), Wash Mutual Bank, Seattle, Wash, 68; Jetfoil (mural), Boeing Aircraft Co, Seattle, Wash, 72. *Exhib:* Seven Northwest Annuals, Seattle Art Mus, Wash, 50-60; one-man shows, Zantman Art Galleries, 74-79, Haines Gallery, Seattle, 74, 76 & 78 & Foster White Gallery, Seattle, 81; Three Marine Exhibs, Mystic Seaport Mus, Conn, 78, 79 & 80; Marine Artist Shows, Grand Central Galleries, New York, 79 & 80; One Marine Exhib, Peabody Mus, Salem, Mass, 80; Retrospective Exhib, Frye Art Mus, 81. *Awards:* 3 First Place Best of Show, Mus Sci & Industry, Seattle, 55, 56 & 57. *Bibliog:* Peter Stanford (auth), Sea History Mag, Nat Maritime Trust, 80. *Mem:* Fel Am Soc Marine Artist; Puget Sound Group of NW Painters Seattle. *Media:* Oil, Watercolor. *Dealer:* Foster White Gallery 311 1/2 Occidental Seattle WA 98104; Zantman Art Galleries Ltd 6th & Massion Carmel CA 93921. *Mailing Add:* 8514 Paisley Dr NE Seattle WA 98115

WELPOTT, JACK WARREN
PHOTOGRAPHER, EDUCATOR
b Kansas City, Kans, Apr 27, 23. *Study:* Ind Univ, BS, 49, MS, 55, MFA, 59. *Work:* Mus Mod Art, New York; Bibliot Nat, Paris; Eastman House, Rochester, NY; Ctr Creative Photog, Tucson, Ariz; San Francisco Mus Art. *Exhib:* One-man shows, Eastman House, 66, Art Inst Chicago, 72, San Francisco Mus Art, 76, Univ Southern Calif, Los Angeles, 77, Univ Ore, 79 & Ctr Creative Photog, 79; group show, Metrop Mus Art, New York. *Collections Arranged:* Artist as Teacher/Teacher as Artist, San Francisco Mus Art, 76. *Teaching:* Prof photog, San Francisco State Univ, 59-; vis prof, Univ Ariz, Tucson, 77. *Awards:* Nat Endowment for Arts fel, 79. *Bibliog:* Arthur Ollman (auth), Jack Welpott: Photographer, Vidio, 74. *Mem:* Friends Photog. *Publ:* Co-auth, Women and Other Visions, Morgan & Morgan, 75. *Dealer:* Witkin Gallery 41 E 57th St New York NY 10022. *Mailing Add:* 28 1/2 Precita Ave San Francisco CA 94110

WENGER, JANE (B)
PHOTOGRAPHER, EDUCATOR
b New York, NY, Jan 24, 44. *Study:* Alfred Univ, NY, BFA, 66; Ill Inst Technol, Chicago, 69; Univ Ill, Circle Campus, Chicago, MFA, 80. *Work:* Mus Mod Art, New York; Mus Contemp Art, Chicago, Ill; Milwaukee Art Mus, Wis; Lehigh Univ, Bethelehem, Pa; Southern Ill Univ, Edwardsville. *Exhib:* One-woman shows, Artemisia Gallery, Chicago, Ill, 76, Foto Gallery, New York, 78 & 80, Allen Fromkin Photographs, Chicago, Ill, 80, Mus

Contemp Art, Chicago, Ill, 81, Milwaukee Art Mus, Wis, 81 & PS 1, New York, 82. *Teaching:* Instr photog, Univ Ill, Circle Campus, 75- *Awards:* Project Completion Grants, Ill Arts Coub, 79-83. *Bibliog:* Carole Harme (auth), The dialectics of sexuality, New Art Examiner, 79; Lynne Warren (auth), Jane Wenger, Art Mag, 3/81; Mary Jane Jacob (auth), Options 7, Jane Wenger: An Environmental Installation, Mus Contemp Art, 81. *Mem:* Soc Photog Educ. *Mailing Add:* 1509 N Wicker Pk Chicago IL 60622

WENGER, MURIEL
DEALER, COLLECTOR
b Brooklyn, NY, June 11, 15. *Study:* Brooklyn Col, BA; La Jolla Mus Contemp Art. *Collections Arranged:* Mex Govt Exhib, Colonial Art of the 18th Century, San Diego Mus Art, 69 & Phoenix Art Mus, 69. *Pos:* Assoc dir, Galerias Carlota, Tijuana & Mexico City, Mex, 64-71; co-dir, Wenger Gallery, La Jolla & San Diego, 69- *Specialty:* Contemporary art. *Mailing Add:* PO Box 3100 La Jolla CA 92038

WENGER, SIGMUND
DEALER, CONSULTANT
b Brooklyn, NY, Nov 20, 10. *Study:* NY Univ, BA. *Collections Arranged:* Francisco Icaza, La Jolla Mus Contemp Art, 66, Phoenix Art Mus, 67, Long Beach Mus, 68 & Ariz State Univ, 68; Antonio Rodriquez Luna, San Diego Mus Art, 67; Marta Palau, San Diego Mus Art, 69, Univ Tex, 70, Long Beach Mus, 70 & Ariz State Univ, 70; Marta Pan, Univ Southern Calif, 72. *Pos:* Dir, Galerias Carlota, Tijuana & Mexico City, Mex, 63-72; co-dir, Wenger Gallery, La Jolla & San Diego, 69- *Specialty:* Contemporary art. *Mailing Add:* PO Box 3100 La Jolla CA 92038

WENNER, L JOHN G
EDUCATOR, PAINTER
b Allentown, Pa, Sept 16, 12. *Study:* Muhlenberg Col, BPhil; NY Univ, MA(art educ); Univ Lausanne, Switz & Corcoran Art Sch, art; Pa Acad Fine Arts, Philadelphia, scholar, with Walter Emerson Baum; also with, Baroness Hilla Rebay & Peggy Bacon; Yale Univ, NY Univ & Boston Univ, grad study. *Work:* Guggenheim Mus, New York; Corcoran Gallery Art; Nat Gallery Art; Wadsworth Atheneum, Hartford, Conn; Silvermine Guild Artists, New Canaan, Conn; and others. *Exhib:* One-man shows, Arts Club; Allentown Art Mus, Pa; Lehigh Univ Gallery, Pa; Wiley Gallery, Hartford, Conn; Kalarson Gallery, New York; and others. *Pos:* Color consult for John Ford; designer, Metrop Opera Co; designer, US govt seals (War Dept, Navy Dept etc). *Teaching:* In charge art educ, Irvington, NJ schs; teacher, Hamilton High Sch, Trenton, NJ, Allentown Prep Sch, Pa, NY Univ & Muhlenberg Col; art consult & spec art teacher, elem lab schs, Cent Conn State Col, coordr fine arts & assoc prof art, emer assoc prof art, currently. *Mem:* Art League New Britain; Conn Watercolor Soc; Conn Acad Fine Arts; Conn Art Educ Asn; Artists' Equity Asn (vpres, Conn Chap); and others. *Mailing Add:* 54 Seneca St New Britain CT 06053

WENSLEY, WILLIAM CHARLES
PAINTER, INSTRUCTOR
b Suffern, NY. *Exhib:* 102nd, 103rd, 105th & 106th Ann Exhib, Am Watercolor Soc, New York, 69, 70, 72 & 73; Watercolor USA, Springfield Art Mus, Mo, 71; 151st Ann Exhib, Nat Acad Design, New York, 76; Fla Watercolor Soc, Maitland & Longboat Key, 80 & 83. *Teaching:* Inst watercolor, Mus Fine Art, Syracuse, NY, 49-55; instr watercolor, Fla Gulf Coast Art Ctr, 60-75; instr watercolor landscape, Wensley Watercolor Classes, 75-80. *Awards:* Helen Gapen Oehler Award, Am Watercolor Soc, 75; Award of Distinction, Fla Watercolor Soc, 79; John Pike Mem Award, Am Watercolor Soc, 80. *Mem:* Am Watercolor Soc; Fla Watercolor Soc. *Media:* Watercolor. *Publ:* Auth, Watercolor page--William Wensley, Am Artist, 80. *Mailing Add:* 2100 Nursery Rd Apt J1 Clearwater FL 33546

WENTWORTH, MURRAY JACKSON
PAINTER, INSTRUCTOR
b Boston, Mass, Jan 18, 27. *Study:* Art Inst Boston. *Work:* Farnsworth Mus Art, Rockland, Maine; Springfield Mus Art, Mo; First Nat Bank, Boston; DeCordova Mus, Lincoln, Mass; Utah State Univ, Logan. *Exhib:* Metrop Mus Art, New York, 66; Butler Inst Am Art, Youngstown, Ohio, 69; Brockton Fuller Mem Mus, Mass, 70; DeCordova Mus, Mass, 77; one-man shows, Farnsworth Mus, 72 & Guild of Boston Artists, 77 & 80; Rocky Mountain Nat Watercolor Exhib, 82. *Teaching:* Instr watercolor, pvt & watercolor workshops, 77- *Awards:* Ranger Fund Purchase Prize, Nat Acad Design, 65; Nat Arts Club Bronze Medal Hon, 68; Am Watercolor Soc Bronze Medal Hon, 69. *Mem:* Am Watercolor Soc; Allied Artists Am; New England Watercolor Soc (vpres, 71-); Guild Boston Artists; assoc Nat Acad Design. *Media:* Watercolor. *Publ:* Contribr, watercolor page, Am Artist Mag, 70. *Mailing Add:* 132 Central St Norwell MA 02061

WERNER, (CHARLES GEORGE)
EDITORIAL CARTOONIST
b Marshfield, Wis, Mar 23, 09. *Study:* Oklahoma City Univ; Northwestern Univ. *Work:* Mo State Hist Soc; Syracuse Univ, NY; Wis State Hist Soc, Madison; Addison Gallery Am Art, Andover, Mass. *Exhib:* Asn Am Ed Cartoonists travel tour. *Pos:* Ed cartoonist, Daily Oklahoman, 35-41; chief ed cartoonist, Chicago Sun, 41-47; ed cartoonist, Indianapolis Star, 47- *Awards:* Pulitzer Prize, 38; First Place Award, Nat Found Highway Safety, 71; Award for Caricature, Int Salon Art, Montreal, 73; and others. *Mem:* New York Cartoonists Soc; Asn Am Ed Cartoonists (pres, 69). *Mailing Add:* 4445 Brown Rd Indianapolis IN 46226

WERNER, DONALD (LEWIS)
PAINTER, PHOTOGRAPHER
b Fresno, Calif, Feb 2, 29. *Study:* Fresno State Col, BA, with Adolf & Ella Odorfer & Jane Gale; Chouinard Art Inst, Los Angeles; also costuming with Majorie Best. *Work:* Murals, Dan River Mills, Wellington Sears & Martex, New York; Fresno Art Ctr, Calif; Hudson River Mus, Yonkers, NY. *Comn:* Collage murals, New York World's Fair; The Ancestors: Native Artisans of the Americas (exhib & graphic design), US Custom House, New York, 79. *Exhib:* Solo exhibs, Gallery 84, New York, 59-75, 79 & 82, Painting & Photog, Fresno Art Gallery, 67 & 79, Photog, Focus Gallery, San Francisco, 68, Painting & Photog, Hudson River Mus, 69 & 72 & Photog, St Paul Civic Ctr, Minn, 70. *Collections Arranged:* Art in Westchester, 66, African Art, 71, Light, Motion, Sound, 71, Sky, Sand & Spirits, 72, 20th Century Sculpture, 72 & Light & Lens-Methods of Photography (with catalog), 73, Hudson River Mus; Mus of the Am Indian, New York, NY, 78; Echoes of the Drums, Customs House, New York, NY, 78; The Ancestors, Peking, China, 81-82; Star Gods, Am Mus Natural Hist, New York, 82-83. *Pos:* Display designer, Seventeen Mag, 11 yrs; store designer & displayer, Gimbels, 68-69; mus artist & designer, Hudson River Mus, 68-75. *Awards:* First Prize for Watercolor, Fresno Art Ctr, 60. *Bibliog:* Beeching (auth), Theatrical displays and display techniques (film), Scope Prod, 69. *Media:* Watercolor; Collage Photography. *Publ:* Auth, photogr & designer, Reflections of Winter: Summer Comes Too Fast, Holt, Rinehart & Winston, 78; bk designer, The Peaceable Kingdom, Macmillan, 79; designer, With Eagle Glance, Mus Am Indian, 82; designer, Americans in Venice, Coe Kerr, 83. *Dealer:* Gallery 84 1046 Madison Ave New York NY 10016. *Mailing Add:* 65 W 92nd St New York NY 10025

WERNER, FRITZ
PAINTER
b Vienna, Austria; US citizen. *Study:* Acad Fine Arts, Vienna, Munich & Paris. *Work:* Cincinnati Art Mus; Oklahoma City Art Mus; Christ Hosp, Cincinnati; St John's Hosp, Kansas City, Mo; Am Univ. *Comn:* Portrait comns of William Howard Taft, Pres of US; Sen Robert Taft; Warren Austin, former US Ambassador to UN; William S Knudsen, former pres Gen Motors Corp; Achmed Ziwar Pascha, former pres Egypt. *Exhib:* two one-man shows, Wildenstein Art Gallery, New York; Nat Acad Design, New York; Stendahl Art Gallery, Los Angeles; Courvoisier Art Gallery, San Francisco; Galleria Whitcomb, Buenos Aires, Arg; and others. *Awards:* Gundel Portrait Prize, State of Austria; Scholarship, Acad Fine Arts, Vienna, Austria. *Media:* Oil, Pastel. *Mailing Add:* Apt 9-D 1001 Genter St La Jolla CA 92037

WERNER, HOWARD
SCULPTOR
b Neptune, NJ, July 27, 51. *Study:* Rochester Inst Technol, BFA, 77; Sch Am Craftsmen. *Work:* Sch Am Craftsmen, Rochester, NY. *Exhib:* Carnegie Mus Art, 79; Richard Kagan Gallery, Philadelphia, 78-83; Elements Gallery, New York, 78-80; Vladimir Kagan Gallery, New York, 82-83; Woodworks of the Northeast, Wooster Crafts Ctr, Mass, 83; Synderman Gallery, Philadelphia, 83. *Pos:* Resident, Art Park, Lewiston, NY, 75-77; traveling residency, NY State Parks & Recreation Cultural Program, 76; vis artist, Nat Endowment Arts Omni Int, Atlanta, Ga, 77; resident, Peters Valley, Layton, NJ, 77-78; bd adv, Robert Meadows Sch Hand Woodworking, 81- *Teaching:* Instr sculpture & furniture design, Peters Valley, Layton, NJ, 77-82; instr sculpture, Haywood Tech Inst, NC, 78; instr sculpture, Keane Col, NJ, 81; instr workshop, State Univ NY, New Paltz, 83. *Bibliog:* Review, Craft Horizons, 78; John Kelsey (auth), New Handmade Furniture, Fine Woodworking, 79; Michael Stone (auth), review, New York Times, 10/81. *Mem:* Am Craft Coun; Peters Valley. *Media:* Wood. *Publ:* Coauth, Carving, Fine Woodworking, 77. *Mailing Add:* Route 28 Mt Tremper NY 12457

WERNER, NAT
SCULPTOR
b New York, NY, Dec 8, 08. *Study:* City Col New York, BA; Columbia Univ, MA; Art Students League, with Robert Laurent. *Work:* Whitney Mus Am Art, New York; Lyman Allen Mus, New London, Conn; Mt Sinai Hosp, Detroit; Tel Aviv Mus, Israel; Howard Univ Gallery, Washington, DC. *Comn:* Bas-relief, Fowler Post Off, Ind; sculptures, New York World's Fair, 39, Argus Res, New York, bronze, New York Eng Soc & wood, James Madison High Sch, New York & Howard Univ, Washington, DC. *Exhib:* Whitney Mus Am Art Ann, 36-63; Pa Acad Fine Arts, 39-56; Brussels Int, 46; Fairmount Int, Philadelphia, 50; Art USA, New York, 58-59; one-man shows, Benson Gallery, Bridgehampton, NY, 73, 75 & 78, Guildhall, Easthampton, 78 & Sculpture Ctr, New York, 80. *Teaching:* Instr sculpture, Stuyvesant Adult Ctr, 60- *Awards:* First Prize, Guildhall Easthampton, 53-54; Purchase Award, Southampton Col, Long Island, 76. *Mem:* Sculptors Guild (pres, 63-65). *Dealer:* Benson Gallery, Bridgehampton NY 11932; ACA Galleries 25 E 73rd St New York NY 10021. *Mailing Add:* 225 E 21st St New York NY 10010

WERNER VAUGHN, SALLE
PAINTER, ILLUMINATOR
b Tex. *Work:* San Francisco Mus of Mod Art, Calif; Akron Art Inst, Ohio; Lomas-Nettleton Co, Dallas, Tex; Am Tel & Tel, New York; Bridwell Mus, Southern Methodist Univ, Dallas; and others. *Exhib:* Biennial Exhib Painting & Sculpture Show, Whitney Mus, New York, 73; Contemporary Watercolors, Akron Art Inst, Ohio, Indianapolis, Ind & Rochester, NY, 76; Helen Serger, La Boetie Inc, New York, 77; Carus Gallery, New York, 79; one-man show, Tyler Mus of Art, Tex, 73. *Teaching:* Founder experimental art, Art Involvement & Motivation, 70- *Bibliog:* Patsy Swank (auth), Salle Werner (film), Dallas Educ TV, 72; Arch Am Art, Smithsonian Inst. *Media:* Watercolor, Oil; Tempera. *Dealer:* La Boetie Inc 9 E 82nd New York NY 10028. *Mailing Add:* 2235 Brentwood Houston TX 77019

WERNESS, HOPE B
HISTORIAN
b Del Rio, Tex, Feb 10, 43. *Study:* Univ Calif, Santa Barbara, BA, 65, PhD, 72; Tulane Univ, MA. 68. *Teaching:* Vis lectr art hist, San Jose State Univ, Calif, 76-77; asst prof art hist, Calif State Col, Stanislaus, Turlock, Calif, 77-81, assoc prof & acting chair, 81- *Awards:* Nat Endowment Humanities Summer Seminar, 80. *Mem:* Col Art Asn. *Res:* Nineteenth century art history, specializing in Van Gogh, twentieth century art history; pre-Columbian and primitive art. *Mailing Add:* 3201 N Olive Ave Turlock CA 95380

WERT, NED OLIVER
EDUCATOR, PAINTER
b Millersburg, Pa, May 26, 36. *Study:* Ind Univ Pa, BA(art educ), 58; Pa State Univ, MEd(art), 64; Kent State Univ, with Alex Katz, Jim Melchert & Jack Tworkov, 70. *Work:* Southern Alleghenies Mus Art, Loretto, Pa; Pittsburgh Plate Glass Corp, Gulf Oil Corp, Alcoa Corp, Pittsburgh, Pa; Am Int Sch, Dusseldorf, WGer. *Exhib:* Assoc Artists Pittsburgh, Carnegie Mus Art, 72-83; Butler Inst Art Ann Nat Exhib, 75; Three Rivers Festival, Pittsburgh, Pa, 80; La Mostra CAS, Camera Commercio, Lucca, Italy, 82; Triennial Invitational, Southern Alleghenies Mus Art, Loretto, Pa, 82; Five Ind Univ Pa Artists, Noho Gallery, New York, 83; and others. *Teaching:* Art, Elizabethtown Area Sch Dist, Pa, 58-70; prof painting, Ind Univ Pa, 70- *Awards:* Equibank Award, Aqueous 78 Nat Exhib, 78; Best of Show, Fourth Ann Exhib, Westmoreland Mus, 82; Jurors Award, Assoc Artists Pittsburgh, Carnegie Mus Art, Pittsburgh, Pa, 82. *Mem:* Assoc Artists Pittsburgh; Nat Art Educ Asn; Pa Art Educ Asn (pres, 82-84); Allied Artists Johnstown; Pittsburgh Soc Artists. *Media:* Acrylic. *Publ:* Coauth, Multiple image and sound: Motivation for creative activity, Art Teacher Mag, fall 74; coauth, Colored light and shadow: A stimulus for creative movement, Pa J Physical Educ, winter 74; coauth, Multi-media: Motivation for the arts and basic education, Learning Resources Mag, 4/75; coauth, Readings: Developing arts programs for handicapped students, Pa Dept Educ, 82. *Dealer:* Bird in the Hand Gallery 427 Broad St Sewickley PA 15143. *Mailing Add:* Box 1 Brush Valley PA 15720

WESCHLER, ANITA
SCULPTOR, PAINTER
b New York, NY. *Study:* Le Grand Verger, Lausanne, Sitzerland; Parsons Sch Design, grad; Nat Acad Design; Pa Acad Fine Arts, with Albert Laessle; Art Students League, with William Zorach; Columbia Univ; Barnes Found. *Work:* Whitney Mus Am Art, Amherst Univ; Brandeis Univ; Metrop Mus Art; Yale Univ; plus other pub & pvt collections. *Comn:* Sculpture, US Treas Dept, US Post Off, Elkin, NC; ten life-size portrait heads (bronze), Inst for Achievement of Human Potential, Philadelphia. *Exhib:* Group shows, Whitney Mus Am Art, Nat Inst Arts & Lett, Metrop Mus Art, Philadelphia Mus Art, Mus Mod Art, and others; also over 30 one-man shows nationwide. *Pos:* Deleg to US Comt Int Asn Art; deleg, Fine Arts Fedn New York. *Awards:* Prizes, Corcoran Gallery Art, Montclair Art Mus & San Francisco Mus Art; Audubon Artists Medal of Honor; MacDowell Colony & Yaddo Fels. *Mem:* Archit League; Fedn Mod Painters & Sculptors; Nat Asn Women Artists; Sculptor's Guild (mem exec bd); Artist Craftsmen NY. *Media:* Multimedia. *Publ:* Auth, Nightshade, Colony Press; auth, Sculptor's Summary. *Dealer:* Coryell Gallery Lambertville NJ; Roads Art 400 E 57th St New York NY. *Mailing Add:* 136 Waverly Pl New York NY 10014

WESLEY, JOHN
PAINTER
b Los Angeles, Calif, Nov 25, 28. *Work:* Albright-Knox Art Gallery, Buffalo, NY; Hirshhorn Mus and Sculpture Garden, Smithsonian Inst, Washington, DC; Mus Mod Art; Univ Rochester; Univ Tex. *Exhib:* The Figure Int, Am Fedn of Arts, New York, 67-68; 1968, Whitney Mus Art, 69; Indianapolis Mus Art, Ind, 69; Documenta V, Kassel, Ger, 72; one-man shows, (13) Robert Elkon Gallery, New York, 63-80 & Univ Rochester, 74; Indianapolis Mus Art, 76; Another Aspect of Pop Art, Long Island City, 78; Art about Art, Whitney Mus Am Art, 78; and others. *Teaching:* Instr, Sch Visual Arts, New York, 70-73. *Awards:* Guggenheim Fel, 76. *Bibliog:* Hannah Green (auth), A Journal in Praise of the Art of John Wesley, In: The Unmuzzled Ox, spring 74. *Dealer:* Robert Elkon Gallery 1063 Madison Ave New York NY 10028. *Mailing Add:* 52 Barrow St New York NY 10014

WESLING, WILLIAM ARNOLD
PAINTER, ILLUSTRATOR
b Sharon, Pa, Sept 26, 24. *Study:* Univ Pittsburgh, 45; Art Inst Pittsburgh, 48. *Work:* Art Inst Pittsburgh, Pa; Trident Technical Col, Charleston, SC; Jacksonville Sci Mus, Fla; Fla Univ, Gainesville. *Comn:* Paintings, Jax Zoological Soc, Jacksonville, Fla; Amelia Island Co. *Exhib:* Jacksonville Sci Mus, Fla; Golden Eagle Gallery, Cody, Wyo; Buffalo Bill Mus, Cody, Wyo; Whitney Gallery Western Art, Cody, Wyo; and others. *Pos:* Art dir, State Fla Development Comn, 60-67. *Awards:* Over 50 show awards nationally. *Mem:* Audubon Soc; Nat & Fla Wildlife Fedn; Nat Wild Turkey Asn; Ducks Unlimited. *Media:* Oil, Watercolor; Mixed Media. *Mailing Add:* Rt 2 Box 1078 Ft McCoy FL 32637

WESSEL, HENRY, JR
PHOTOGRAPHER
b Teaneck, NJ, July 28, 42. *Study:* Pa State Univ, BA, 66; State Univ NY, Buffalo, Visual Studies Workshop, MFA, 72. *Work:* Mus Mod Art, New York; Nat Gallery Can, Ottawa; Int Mus Photog, George Eastman House, Rochester, NY; Sheldon Art Gallery, Univ Nebr, Lincoln; Philadelphia Mus Art. *Exhib:* Mus Mod Art, New York; Nat Gallery Can, Ottawa; Contemporary Photography V, 70 & New Topographics, 75; George Eastman House Traveling Exhibs; one-man shows, Mus Mod Art, New York, 73, Pa

State Univ, 74, Fraenkel Gallery, San Francisco, 81 & Charles Cowles Gallery, New York, 81; and many others. *Teaching:* Instr, Pa State Univ, 67-69, Ctr Eye, Aspen, Colo, 73, Univ Calif, Berkeley, 73 & San Francisco Art Inst, 73-; asst prof, San Francisco State Univ, Calif, 74; vis artist, Univ Calif, Davis, 77; vis lectr, Calif Col Arts & Crafts, 77. *Awards:* Guggenheim Fel, 71 & 78; Nat Endowment Arts Grant, 74 & 76. *Bibliog:* ARticles, Art News, 9/73, Camera, Lucerne, Switz, 5/74 & Art in Am, 1/76. *Publ:* Contribr, Mirrors and windows, Mus Mod Art, New York, 79; contribr, Nude, Harper & Row, 80. *Dealer:* Fraenkel Gallery 55 Grant Ave San Francisco CA 94108; Charles Cowles Gallery 420 W Broadway New York NY 10012. *Mailing Add:* Box 475 Point Richmond CA 94807

WESSELMANN, TOM
PAINTER, SCULPTURE
b Cincinnati, Ohio, Feb 23, 31. *Study:* Hiram Col; Univ Cincinnati, BA; Art Acad Cincinnati; Cooper Union Art Sch, cert. *Work:* Albright-Knox Art Gallery, Buffalo, NY; Mus Mod Art & Whitney Mus Am Art, New York; Suermondt Mus, Aachen, Ger; Atkins Mus Fine Arts, Kansas City, Mo; and others. *Exhib:* One-man shows, Green Gallery, 62, 64 & 65, Sidney Janis Gallery, New York, 66, 68, 70, 72, 74, 76, 79, 80 & 82 & Ehrlich Gallery, 79; Mus Contemp Art, Chicago, Ill, 69; DeCordova Mus, Lincoln, Mass, 69; and many other group & one-man shows. *Media:* Oil; Painted Steel & Aluminum. *Dealer:* Sidney Janis Gallery 6 W 57th St New York NY 10019. *Mailing Add:* RD 1 Box 36 Long Eddy NY 12760

WEST, CLARA FAYE JOHNSON
PAINTER, CONSERVATOR
b Coffeeville, Miss, May 8, 23. *Study:* Corcoran Sch Art, Washington, DC, with Eugen Weisz, Nicolai Cikovsky & Heinz Warneke; also with Jaska Shaffran. *Work:* Miss Univ for Women; Miss State Univ; Piney Woods Country Life Sch, Miss; Wood Jr Col, Miss; St Paul Episcopal Church, Chattanooga, Tenn. *Comn:* Portrait, US Sen John C Stennis, comn by Class of 23, Miss State Univ; portrait plaques of three univ pres & 14 trustees for State Bd Inst Higher Learning, comn by Res & Develop Ctr, Jackson, Miss, 75-81; six portraits of univ pres & six portrait drawings, Jackson State Univ, Miss, 77; Harvey Cromwell portrait, comn by Mrs Cromwell, Cromwell Commun Ctr, Miss Univ Women, 77; and over 400 portraits and over 300 restorations in pub & pvt collections. *Exhib:* Mary Buie Mus, Oxford, Miss, 49; Mid-South Exhib, Brooks Mem Gallery, Memphis, 59; one-man shows, West Memphis Libr, Ark, 59; Miss State Univ, 65-67 & 72 & Hogarth Student Ctr, Miss Univ Women, 70-77. *Teaching:* Guest instr portrait painting, Miss Univ Women, 69-73. *Awards:* First Prize for Seeds for Britain (poster), Brit War Relief Soc, 43. *Mem:* Am Inst Conservators Hist & Artistic Works; Art Asn Columbus (pres, 72-73). *Media:* Oil, Acrylic. *Mailing Add:* 410 Tenth St S Columbus MS 39701

WEST, E GORDON
ADMINISTRATOR, PAINTER
b Salt Lake City, Utah, June 1, 33. *Study:* Art Inst Chicago; Univ Louisville, BS(Allen Hite scholar), 54. *Comn:* San Antonio, Southwestern Bell Tel Co, 72; wildlife series of drawings, Arts Limited Ltd, San Antonio, 74; painting, San Antonio Chap, Geol Soc Am, 75; and others. *Exhib:* Tex Watercolor Ann, San Antonio, 63-79; Tex Fine Arts Ann, Austin, 65, 67 & 68; Southwestern Watercolor, Dallas, 69; Southern Watercolor Soc Ann Exhib, 80; Western Federation Ann Exhib, 80. *Pos:* Post arts & crafts dir, Ft Leonard Wood, Mo, 57-60; dir arts & crafts prog, Fifth US Army Hq, 61-73; chief arts & crafts prog, US Air Force Hq, 73-77, chief, Recreation Serv, 77- *Awards:* Tex Watercolor Ann Awards, var times, 66-82; Southwestern Watercolor Regional Award, 69; and others. *Mem:* Tex Watercolor Soc (pres, 66-67); San Antonio Art League (vpres, 65); San Antonio Watercolor Group. *Media:* Watercolor. *Publ:* Auth, Tex Hill Country & Pecos to Rio Grande, Texas A & M Press; auth, articles, Am Artist. *Dealer:* Hope Kaplan c/o Odyssey Art Gallery 5800 Broadway San Antonio TX 78209. *Mailing Add:* 8610 Norwich Dr San Antonio TX 78217

WEST, RICHARD VINCENT
MUSEUM DIRECTOR, HISTORIAN
b Prague, Czech, Nov 26, 34; US citizen. *Study:* Univ Calif, Santa Barbara, BA(with highest honors), 61; Akad Bildenden Kuenste, Vienna, with Wotruba, 61-62; Univ Calif, Berkeley, MA(art hist), 65; Mus Mgt Inst, 81. *Collections Arranged:* Section d'Or (auth, catalog), 67-68; Language of the Print (auth, catalog), 68-69; Rockwell Kent: The Early Years (auth, catalog), 69; Pre-Rembrandtists (auth, catalog), 74; Munich & Am Realism (auth, catalog), 76. *Pos:* Cur & dir, Bowdoin Col Mus Art, 67-72; dir, Crocker Art Mus, 73-83; dir, Santa Barbara Mus Art, 83- *Teaching:* Lectr, Bowdoin Col, Univ Calif, Davis & Calif State Univ, Sacramento. *Awards:* Ford Fel, 65-67; Smithsonian Fel, 71. *Mem:* Asn Art Mus Dir; Am Asn Mus; Art Mus Asn Am (pres, 75-77); Calif Asn Mus; Col Art Asn. *Publ:* Auth, Painters of the Secton d'Or, 67; coauth, Language of the Print, Random House, 68; Walker Art Building Murals, 72; Rockwell Kent reconsidered, Am Art Rev, 12/77. *Mailing Add:* Santa Barbara Mus Art 1130 State St Santa Barbara CA 93101

WEST, VIRGINIA M
FIBER ARTIST, WRITER
b Boston, Mass. *Study:* Goucher Col; Philadelphia Col Textiles; Md Inst Col Art. *Work:* Baltimore Mus Art; Del Art Mus; Hilton Hotel, Baltimore, Md; Goucher Col Kraushaar Gallery, Baltimore; Peterson Howell & Heather, Hunt Valley, Md. *Comn:* Ark curtain, Shaarei Zion Synagogue, Baltimore, Md, 68; Tapestry, The Center Club, Baltimore, 80; fiber artwork, Community Ctr, Baltimore, 80; Fiber Murals, Lucayan Beach Hotel, Freeport, The Bahamas, 82. *Exhib:* Contemp Crafts Exhib, Del Art Mus, Wilmington,

70-75; Md Artists Exhib, Baltimore, 70 & 75; Fibre Art American Artists, Ball State Univ, 72; Mus Contemp Crafts, New York, 72; Galleria d'Assisi, Italy, 79. *Teaching:* Weaving, fiber sculpture & basketry as a textile art, Md Inst Col Art, 69-; instr sem & workshops, US, Can, New Zealand & Australia. *Awards:* Baltimore Outdoor Art Festival, 68; First Award, Creative Crafts Biennial, 68; Purchase Award, Baltimore Mus Art, 70. *Mem:* Am Crafts Coun (secy, 69-72); Md Crafts Coun (pres, 62-64); Baltimore Weavers Guild (pres, 59-61). *Media:* Fiber. *Res:* Basketry styles and techniques. *Publ:* Auth, feature article, Shuttle, Spindle & Dyepot, 72, 73 & 79, Fiber Arts, 78-81 & Handwoven, 80 & 81; auth, Weavers Wearables, 79; auth, Fabulous Fabrics, 84. *Mailing Add:* Grasty Rd RFD 7 Baltimore MD 21208

WEST, W RICHARD (DICK)
SCULPTOR, PAINTER
b Darlington, Okla, Sept 8, 12. *Study:* Haskell Inst; Bacone Col; Univ Okla, BFA & MFA; Univ Redlands; also with Olaf Nordmark; Baker Univ, Baldwin City, Kans, Hon DFA, 76. *Work:* Smithsonian Inst, Washington, DC; Joslyn Mem Art Mus, Omaha, Nebr; Philbrook Art Ctr, Tulsa, Okla; Gilcrease Mus, Tulsa; Bacone Col, Okla. *Comn:* Post off mural, Okemah, Okla, 41; bas-relief panels, Univ Redlands, Calif, 60's; Crucifixion (sculpture), NAm Indian Ctr, Chicago, 60's. *Exhib:* Kansas City Mus Hist & Sci, Mo, 71; one-man show, Southern Plains Mus, Anadarko, Okla, 80; Cult Ctr Am Indian, Houston, 81; Turtle, Niagara Indian Art & Cult Ctr, Niagara Falls, NY; Santa Fe Festival Arts, 81; and others. *Pos:* Comnr, Indian Arts & Crafts Bd, Dept Interior, 79- *Teaching:* Dir oil painting & perspective, Bacone Col, 47-70, artist-in-residence, 80, prof emer art, 80-; dir Indian art & sculpture, Haskell Indian Jr Col. *Awards:* Citation of Indian Arts & Crafts, 60; First Place for Sculpture, Philbrook Art Ctr Nat Show, 60; Waite Phillips Award, 64. *Bibliog:* Ed Shaw (auth), Another Face of Jesus (film), Am Baptist Films, 69; Charles Waugaman (auth), Cheyenne Artist, Friendship Press, 70; Dorothy Elliot (auth), Dick West Artist, Kansas, 71; and others. *Res:* Indian art & sculpture. *Mailing Add:* RR 1 Box 447 Ft Gibson OK 74434

WESTCOAST, WANDA
SCULPTOR, EDUCATOR
b Seattle, Wash, Oct 31, 37. *Study:* Univ Wash, BA & MFA(painting); and with Spencer Mosely, Alden Mason, Wendell Brazeau & Walter Isaacs. *Exhib:* Centennial Exhib, San Francisco Art Inst, 71; Henry Gallery, Seattle, Wash, 60, 61 & 72; Invisible-Visible, Long Beach Mus Art, Calif, 72; Los Angeles Co Mus Art, 72, 73 & 75; Whitney Mus Am Art Biennial, 75; Los Angeles Inst Contemp Art, Calif. *Pos:* Guest cur, Calif State Univ, Los Angeles, 64. *Teaching:* Asst prof, Univ Wash, 59-60; assoc prof, Calif State Univ, Los Angeles, 61-, chairperson art dept, 67-68; instr, Santa Monica City Col, 66; chairperson dept humanities, Otis Art Inst, Parsons Sch Design, Los Angeles, 74- *Awards:* Northwest Craft Awards, Univ Wash, 59 & 60; artist in residence, Summer Sch Arts, Port Townsend, Wash & Alaska State Art Comn, 6/75; Leadership Award, YWCA Ann, Los Angeles, 77. *Bibliog:* Lucy Lippard (auth), article, Artforum, 12/30/70 & Women's imagery, Ms Mag, 3/73; J Dematrakas (auth), Womanspace (film), 74. *Mem:* Founder Womanspace, Los Angeles. *Media:* Plastic. *Publ:* Auth, Art Series, Educ TV, Seattle, 60 & Los Angeles, 63 & 64. *Mailing Add:* Dept Humanities Otis Art Inst Los Angeles CA 90057

WESTERLUND ROOSEN, MIA (MARIA ELUDIA)
SCULPTOR
b New York, NY, Sept 20, 42. *Study:* Nat Acad Fine Art, New York; Art Students League; Manhattanville Col. *Work:* Nat Gallery Can; Art Gallery Ont; Yale Univ Art Gallery; Albright-Knox Art Gallery; Vancouver Art Gallery. *Exhib:* Material Matters, Norton Gallery, Palm Beach, Fla, 80; Sculptural Death, Visual Arts Mus, New York, 81; American Abstraction Now, ICA Richmond, Va, 82; Castelli and His Artists, La Jolla Mus, Calif, 82; Painting and Sculpture Candidates, Am Acad Arts & Lett, New York, 83. *Media:* Concrete, Steel. *Mailing Add:* c/o Leo Castelli Gallery 420 W Broadway New York NY 10012

WESTERMANN, H C
SCULPTOR, PAINTER
b Los Angeles, Calif, Dec 11, 22. *Study:* Art Inst Chicago, BFA, 54, Hon DFA, 79. *Work:* Mus Contemp Art, Chicago; Whitney Mus Am Art; San Diego Mus Art; Seattle Art Mus; Des Moines Art Ctr. *Exhib:* New Images of Man, Mus Mod Art, New York, 59; Painting & Sculpture of a Decade, Tate Gallery, London, 64; solo exhibs, Los Angeles Co Mus, 69, Whitney Mus Am Art, 78, Des Moines Art Ctr, 78 & San Francisco Mus Mod Art, 79; Ten Independents, Guggenheim Mus, 72. *Awards:* Awards, Nat Arts Coun, 67 & Sao Paulo Biennial, 72. *Bibliog:* Dennis Adrian (auth), Some notes on H C Westermann, Art Int, 63; Franz Schulze (auth), Fantastic Images, Follett Publ, 72. *Mem:* Artists Equity. *Media:* Wood, Metal; Watercolor. *Dealer:* Xavier Fourcade 36 E 57th St New York NY 10021. *Mailing Add:* Box 28 Brookfield Center CT 06805

WESTERMEIER, CLIFFORD PETER
PAINTER, EDUCATOR
b Buffalo, NY, Mar 4, 10. *Study:* Buffalo Sch Fine Arts; Pratt Inst Art Sch; New York Sch Fine & Appl Arts; Univ Buffalo, BS; Univ Colo, PhD. *Work:* Albright-Knox Art Gallery; Nat Cowboy Hall of Fame & Western Heritage, Oklahoma City, Okla. *Comn:* Many pvt portrait commissions. *Exhib:* Albright-Knox Art Gallery; Am Watercolor Soc; Syracuse Mus Fine Art; Boulder, Colo; one-man show, Tucson, Ariz; and others. *Teaching:* Instr art, Buffalo Sch Fine Art, 35-44; instr art, Univ Buffalo, 35-44; instr hist, Univ Colo, 44-46; asst prof, St Louis Univ & Maryville Col, 46-52; prof, Univ Ark, Fayetteville, 52-64; guest lectr, Univ Tex, 54; guest lectr, Univ Colo, Boulder,

57 & 59, prof, 64-78, emer prof, 78- *Awards:* Patteran Award, 39 & 40. *Publ:* Auth, Man, Beast, Dust: The Story of Rodeo, 47; auth & illusr, Trailing the Cowboy, 55 & Who Rush to Glory, 58; auth, Colorado's First Portrait, Univ NMex, 70; contribr, Britannica Jr & Encycl Britannica. *Mailing Add:* 1703 Columbine Ave Boulder CO 80302

WESTERVELT, ROBERT F
HISTORIAN, CERAMIST
b New York, NY, Apr 6, 28. *Study:* Williams Col, AB; Claremont Grad Sch, MFA; Emory Univ, PhD. *Work:* Delgado Mus, New Orleans; High Mus of Atlanta, Ga; Frank Wingate Collection of Contemp Am Ceramics, Syracuse Univ; Scripps Col Collection, Claremont, Calif. *Comn:* Ceramic decoration (with Joseph Amisano, archit), Visual Arts Bldg, Univ Ga, 59. *Exhib:* Georgia Artists, Smithsonian, Washington, DC, 64; Scripps Col Invitational, Claremont, 69. *Pos:* Consult, Ctr Study Southern Cult, Univ Miss, 81- *Teaching:* Assoc prof hist Am art, Agnes Scott Col, Decatur, Ga, 57-81; prof art, Gainesville Jr Col, Ga, 83- *Awards:* Cash grant, Atlanta Arts Festival, 64; Purchase Awards, Delgado Mus & Arts Festival of Atlanta; Ga Coun Arts Grant, 81-82. *Mem:* Ga Designer Craftsman; Southeastern Col Art Asn; Ga Mountain Crafts. *Media:* Stoneware, Porcelain. *Publ:* Auth, The whig painter of Missouri, Am Art J, Kennedy Gallery, 70. *Mailing Add:* 5450 Pine Forest Rd Gainesville GA 30501

WESTFALL, CAROL D
SCULPTOR, EDUCATOR
b Everett, Pa, Sept 7, 38. *Study:* RI Sch of Design, BFA; Maryland Inst, Col of Art, MFA. *Work:* Goucher Col Collection, Towson, Md; Del Mus of Art, Wilmington; NJ State Mus, Trenton; Polylok Corp Collection, New York; PD 100, Architects, Mexico City. *Comn:* Nine batiks, R F Kennedy Family Collection, 70 & three batiks, L B Johnson Family Collection, 70, Washington Gallery of Art, DC. *Exhib:* Washington Co Mus, Hagerstown, Md, 72; Del Mus of Art, Wilmington, 73; Baltimore Mus of Art, Md, 74; 7th Biennial of Tapestry, Mus Contonal des Beaux Arts, Lausanne, Switz, 75; Auditorium Gallery, NJ State Mus, Trenton, 75; Mus of Art, Carnegie Inst Int, Pittsburgh, Pa, 76; Mus of Contemp Crafts, New York, 76; and other group & one-woman shows. *Teaching:* Instr fibers & fabrics, Md Inst, Baltimore, 68-73; asst prof fibres & fabrics, Montclair State Col, NJ, 73-81, assoc prof, 81-; guest instr, Teachers Col, Columbia Univ, New York, 77- & Sch Am Craftsmen, Rochester Inst Technol, 77. *Awards:* Morton & Sophie Macht Found Award, Baltimore Mus of Art, 72; Levi Sculpture Award, Baltimore Mus of Art, 74; Governor's Purchase Award, NJ Biennial, State of NJ, 75; Indo-Am Fel, 80-81. *Bibliog:* Articles in Crafts Horizons, 69-77. *Mem:* Handweavers Guild of Am; Am Crafts Coun; NJ State Coun on the Arts, Artists in Schs Prog; World Crafts Coun. *Media:* Mixed Media. *Publ:* Coauth, Plaiting Step by Step, Watson-Guptill, 76. *Mailing Add:* 162 Whitford Ave Nutley NJ 07110

WESTIN, ROBERT H
HISTORIAN
b St Paul, Minn, Jan 11, 46. *Study:* Univ Minn, BA, 68; Pa State Univ, MA, 70, PhD, 78; Birbeck Col, Univ London, with Sir Nikolas Pevsner & Sir John Summerson. *Collections Arranged:* Figurative Drawings from Windsor Castle of the Roman Baroque; Collection of Her Majesty the Queen; Carlo Maratti and His Contemporaries (coauth, catalog), Mus of Art, Pa State Univ, 75. *Teaching:* Asst prof Renaissance-Baroque art hist, Ariz State Univ, Tempe, 73-78; assoc prof art, Univ Fla, Gainesville, 78- *Awards:* Nat defense Educ Art Title IV, US Govt, 71-72; Ariz State Univ Fac Fel, 74. *Mem:* Col Art Asn; Mid-Am Col Art; Nat Coun Art Adminr; SE Col Art Conf; Southeastern Am Soc Eighteenth Century Studies. *Res:* Collections of Metropolitan Museum of New York, Philadelphia Museum of Art and the collection of Janos Scholz, Cooper-Hewitt Union; Roman Baroque sculpture and Michelangelo. *Publ:* Auth, Antonio Raggi's Death of St Cecilia, Art Bulletin, 74; coauth, Contributions to the late chronology of Giuseppe Mazzuoli, Burlington Mag, 74; auth, Ars Mohendi tradition and the visualization of death in Seventeenth Century Roman Baroque sculpture, Int J Death Educ, 80; coauth, Carlo Maratti and Camillo Rusconi: Two new portrait medallions, Burlington Mag, 80. *Mailing Add:* 6101 NW 54th Way Gainesville FL 32601

WESTLUND, HARRY E
PUBLISHER, DEALER
b Chicago, Ill, Nov 20, 41. *Study:* Calif State Col, Long Beach, BA, 67; Tamarind Inst, Albuquerque, Master Printer, 70. *Work:* Pasadena Mus, Calif; Gruenwald Found, Univ Calif, Los Angeles; Mus of Mod Art, New York, Los Angeles Co Mus of Art, Los Angeles; Tamarind Inst Collection, Univ NMex. *Exhib:* Eight Tamarind Printers, Motel Gallery, Albuquerque, Nmex; New Multiples, San Diego; Art of the Master Printer, Robinson Galleries, Houston, Tex; Collectors Exhib, Starline Gallery, Albuquerque, 78; Bramante Gallery, Walla Walla, Wash, 80. *Pos:* Shop mgr, Lakeside Studios, Mich, 71; mgr, Tamarind Publ, Tamarind Inst, 72-75; litho/silkscreen staff printer, Cirrue Ed, Hollywood, Calif, 75-76; dir, Serigraphics Custom Silkscreen Workshop, Albuquerque, 76- *Specialty:* Publishing, custom printing, silkscreen process. *Collection:* Contemporary; Old Master. *Publ:* Auth, Polymer Reversal Technique as Applied to Zinc Plates, Tamarind, 71. *Mailing Add:* 502 Mullen Rd NW Albuquerque NM 87107

WESTWATER, ANGELA KING
DEALER, EDITOR
b Columbus, Ohio, July 6, 42. *Study:* Smith Col, BA; NY Univ, MA. *Pos:* Asst dir, Ctr Int Studies, NY Univ, 67-69; res assoc, Inst Govt & ed, Ga Govt Rev, Univ Ga, 69-71; managing ed, Artforum, 72-75; trustee, Louis Comfort Tiffany Found, pres, 80-; partner, Sperone, Westwater, Fischer Inc, New York, 75- *Mem:* Art Dealers Asn Am. *Specialty:* Contemporary painting and sculpture. *Mailing Add:* Sperone Westwater Fischer Inc 142 Greene St New York NY 10012

WETHEY, HAROLD EDWIN
HISTORIAN
b Port Byron, NY, Apr 10, 02. *Study:* Cornell Univ, AB; Harvard Univ, MA, PhD. *Pos:* Contribr ed, Handbk of Latin-Am Studies, 46-59. *Teaching:* From instr to asst prof art hist, Bryn Mawr Col, 34-38; asst prof, Washington Univ, 38-40; assoc prof, Univ Mich, Ann Arbor, 40-46, prof, 46-72; vis prof art, Univ Tucuman, Arg, 43; US State Dept vis prof art, Univ Mex, summer 60. *Awards:* Fel, Am Coun Learned Soc, 36 & 63-64; Russel lectureship, Univ Mich, Ann Arbor, 64-65; Guggenheim Fel, 71-72; and others. *Bibliog:* Hortus Imaginum: Essays in Western Art, 75. *Mem:* Col Art Asn Am; Hispanic Soc Am; Acad de S Fernando; Soc Peruana Historia; and others. *Res:* Drawings by Titian, Giorgione and some close contemporaries; Alonso Cano. *Interests:* Spanish art; Italian Renaissance and Baroque art. *Publ:* Auth, Alonso Cano, Painter, Sculptor & Architect, 55; auth, El Greco & His School, 62; auth, Titian, the Religious Paintings, 69; auth, Titian, Vol II, The Portraits, 71; auth, Titian, Vol III, Mythological & Historical Paintings, 75; and many others including contribr to leading encyclopedias & mags. *Mailing Add:* 1510 Cambridge Rd Ann Arbor MI 48104

WETHINGTON, WILMA ZELLA
PAINTER, INSTRUCTOR
b Clinton, Iowa, Apr 15, 18. *Study:* Marshall Univ, Huntington, WVa; Wichita State Univ; also with Mario Cooper, John Pike, Charles R Kinghan, Tom Hill, Clayton Henri Staples, Robert Wood & others. *Work:* Univ Wyo, Laramie; Wichita State Univ, Kans; Episcopal Diocese Kans, Topeka; Briarcroft Savings & Loan Asn, Lubbock, Tex; Wesley Hospital, Wichita, Kans. *Comn:* Life-sized portrait of Miss America, comn by Gov Wm Avery, 66; portrait of Pres Emory Lindquist, comn by Wichita State Univ, 70; portrait of Bishop Edward Turner, comn by Episcopal Diocese, Kans, 74. *Exhib:* Am Watercolor Soc, New York, 72; Hudson Valley Art Asn, New York, 72-74; Southwestern Watercolor Soc, Dallas, Tex, 73, 74; New Orleans Int Art Mart, 74; Nat Soc Painters in Casein & Acrylic, New York, 75. *Teaching:* Pvt art instr, Wichita, Kans, 50-; instr painting, McConnell Air Base, Wichita, spring 73; instr painting, portraiture & drawing, Wichita Art Asn, 81- *Awards:* First Prize, 8th West Biennial, Grand Junction Art Mus, Colo, 70; Best of Show, North Platte Artists Guild, Nebr, 73; First Award in Watercolor, Okla Mus Art, 75. *Mem:* Am Watercolor Soc; Hudson Valley Art Asn; Kans Watercolor Soc; Southern Watercolor Soc; Okla Watercolor Asn. *Media:* Oil, Pastel. *Dealer:* Ellington Gallery 550 N Rock Rd Wichita KS; Wichita Gallery Fine Art Fourth Financial Ctr Wichita KS. *Mailing Add:* 2 Linden Dr Wichita KS 67206

WETHLI, MARK
PAINTER, EDUCATOR
b Westfield, NY, Nov 9, 49. *Study:* Univ Miami, Fla, BFA, 71, MFA, 73. *Exhib:* Ten American Realists, DM Gallery, London, Eng, 75; Biennial, Whitney Mus Am Art, New York, 75; Summer Invitational, Nancy Hoffman Gallery, New York, 77; solo exhib, Art Space, Los Angeles, 80; American Drawings in Black & White, Brooklyn Mus Art, NY, 80; West Coast Realism (catalog), Laguna Beach Mus Art, Calif, 83; California Drawing, Modernism, San Francisco, 84. *Teaching:* Instr painting, Barry Col, Fla, 74; asst prof, Univ Northern Iowa, Cedar Falls, 76-78 & Calif State Univ, Long Beach, 78- *Awards:* Fels, Nat Endowment Arts, 74; MacDowell Colony, 83 & Millay Colony, 83. *Bibliog:* Suzanne Muchnic (auth), The galleries, Los Angeles Times, 2/22/80; Hilton Kramer (auth), American drawings, New York Times, 11/28/80. *Media:* Oil, Graphite. *Mailing Add:* 404 E Third St Long Beach CA 90802

WEXLER, CLAIRE THYRA See Davidson, Thyra

WEXLER, GEORGE
PAINTER, EDUCATOR
b Brooklyn, NY, Jan 18, 25. *Study:* Cooper Union Sch Art; NY Univ, BA; Mich State Univ, MA. *Work:* Mitsubishi Corp; Kemper Collection; Chemical Bank NY; Manufacturers Hanover; Allied Bank Tex; and others. *Comn:* Murals, Detroit, Mich, 55 & Milwaukee, Wis, 56, Victor Gruen Assocs. *Exhib:* Landscape in America, New Sch Social Res, 63; one-man shows, Angeleski Gallery, New York, 61, Albany Inst Art, NY, 66, First St Gallery, New York, 72, 75 & 78 & Schenectady Mus Art, NY, 72. *Teaching:* Asst prof design, Mich State Univ, 50-57; prof painting, State Univ NY Col New Paltz, 57- *Awards:* Hon mention, Michiana, South Bend, Ind, 54; hon mention, Ball State Ann Drawing Exhib, Ind, 62; Painting Prize, Mid-Hudson Ann, Albany Inst Art, 63-65. *Bibliog:* Gussow (auth), Sense of Place, Sat Rev, 72; Agar (auth), American Artist Mag, 5/81. *Media:* Oil. *Dealer:* Fischbach Gallery 29 W 57th St New York NY. *Mailing Add:* 359 Springtown Rd New Paltz NY 12561

WEXLER, JEROME LEROY
PHOTOGRAPHER, CHILDREN'S BOOK ILLUSTRATOR
b New York, NY, Feb 6, 23. *Study:* Self-taught. *Work:* Nat Mus Natural Hist, Smithsonian Inst. *Awards:* Eight Outstanding Sci Books Children awards, Nat Sci Teachers Asn & Childrens Book Coun, Joint Comt. *Publ:* 31 books published to date. *Mailing Add:* 13 Langshire Dr Madison CT 06443

WEYHE, ARTHUR
SCULPTOR
b New York, NY. *Work:* Everson Mus Art, Syracuse, NY; Herbert F Johnson Mus Art, Cornell Univ; Neuberger Mus, Purchase, NY; William Benton Mus of Art, Storrs, Conn; Storm King Art Ctr, Mountainville, NY. *Exhib:* NY Sculpture Selected by Ivan Karp, William Patterson Col, Wayne, NJ, 74; 55 Mercer Gallery, New York, 75 & 77; O K Harris Gallery, New York, 76; Waterside Plaza, New York, 78; PS1, Long Island City, 79; and others. *Mailing Add:* 140 Sullivan St New York NY 10012

WEYNEROWSKI, HANKA See Kali

WHARTON, DAVID W
PRINTMAKER, LECTURER
b Wichita Falls, Tex, Nov 19, 51. *Study:* Cranbrook Acad Art, MFA, 78; Univ Okla, BFA, 79. *Work:* Pacific Nat Bank, Guadelope, WI; Levi Strauss Corp, San Francisco, Calif; Cranbrook Acad Art, Bloomfield Hills, Mich; Col Southern Idaho, Caldwell; Univ Lethbridge, Alta. *Comn:* Rocky Mountain Mag, comn by Leslie Sielko, Boulder, Colo, 79. *Exhib:* Los Angeles Printmaking Soc, Los Angeles Co Mus, Calif, 80; Regional Printmakers, Blue Door Too, Denver, Colo, 80; Cranbrook Printmakers, St Mary's Col, Notre Dame, 81; Denver Art Mus, Colo, 81; Northwest Prinmakers, Mont State Univ, Bozevian, 81; Recent Decents, Colo Mountain Co, Breckenridge, 81. *Pos:* Dir printmaker, Sun Valley Ctr Art, 78-81. *Teaching:* Prof printmaking, Univ Washington, 81; prof printmaking, Humboldt State Univ, 81. *Awards:* Litzier Award, Sch Art, Univ Okla, 74; Western States Arts Found Fel, 79; Art Pub Places Award, Wash State, 83. *Bibliog:* Leslie Silka (auth), Storyteller, Rocky Mountain Mag, 79; James Mills (auth), Printmakers, Denver Post, 80; What's western about western art, Milkweed Chronicle, 80. *Mem:* Col Art Asn. *Dealer:* Robischon Gallery 1122 E 17th Ave Denver CO 80218. *Mailing Add:* Box 957 Ketchum ID 83340

WHEELER, MARK
PAINTER, CARTOONIST
b Bellingham, Wash, Sept 26, 43. *Study:* Burnley Sch of Professional Art, dipl, Seattle, Wash; Western Wash State Univ (graphic arts); seminar in Marketing Arts, Calvin Goodman, Los Angeles, 77-78. *Work:* Japan Mus of Art, Tatayama. *Comn:* Serigraph series, Northern Commercial Co, Anchorage, Alaska, 74; indust illus, Ketchikan Pulp Co, 75; watercolors, Division of Marine Transportation, State of Alaska, 75; watercolors, Princess Cruises, 75; five murals, Nat Bank Alaska, Ketchikan Br, 76. *Exhib:* All Alaska Shows, Anchorage, 74-76; Advert Fedn Alaska Ann Invitational Auction, 75 & 76; one-man shows, Art Ctr Mus, Anchorage, Alaska, 72-77 & The Gallery (Alaska Watercolor Soc), Anchorage, 76. *Pos:* Owner, Mark Wheeler Publishing, Ketchikan, 58-; staff artist, The Seattle Times, Wash, 65-66; art dir, Pacific Standard Life Insurance Co, Burlingame, Calif, 67 & Sterling Theatres, Seattle, 68. *Teaching:* Instr watercolor, Northern Commercial Co, Anchorage, 73-74 & Wrangell Arts Coun, Alaska, 78- *Bibliog:* Stanton H Patty (auth), A Spoof on All Things Alaskan, The Seattle Times, 9/17/72; Rod Cardwell (auth), Faces and Places, Tacoma New Tribune, 2/4/73; Richard Foley (auth), Mark Wheeler--Alaskan Artist, The Southeastern Log, No 10. *Mem:* Charter mem Alaska Watercolor Soc; Anchorage Arts Coun; The Alaska Press Club; The Advert Found of Alaska. *Media:* Watercolor, Acrylic; Pen & Ink. *Publ:* Auth & illusr, Half Baked Alaska, Mark Wheeler Publ, 72; illusr, Country Station and Country Scene, Haddad's Fine Arts Inc, 73, A Portfolio of Twelve Alaskan Watercolors, Northern Commercial Co, 74 & A Sunny Day in Ketchikan, Alaska Fed Savings & Loan, 78; cover illus, Ketchikan Phone Bk, 79. *Mailing Add:* 320 Bawden St No 701 Ketchikan AK 99901

WHEELER, ORSON SHOREY
SCULPTOR, LECTURER
b Barnston, PQ, Sept 17, 02. *Study:* Bishop's Univ, BA & hon DCL, 76; Royal Can Acad, Montreal; Cooper Union; Beaux Arts inst Design; Nat Acad Design; also study in Europe. *Comn:* Bust, Can Pac Railways; bust, Court House, Montreal, PQ; Supreme Court, Ottawa; Robinson Residence for Retired Teachers, Cowansville, PQ; sculpture, Dow Chem Can, Ltd; plus many others including many in pvt Collections in US & Can. *Exhib:* Nat Acad Design, New York, 40; Smith Col, 45; Ottawa, 50; Quebec City, PQ, 51 & 60; Montreal Mus Fine Arts, 52-57; plus many others. *Pos:* Chmn permanent collection, Can Handicrafts Guild, 44-64, co-chmn, 64-68. *Teaching:* Lectr fine arts, Sir George William Univ; seasonal lectr archit, McGill Univ. *Awards:* Dominican Govt Centennial Medal, 67. *Bibliog:* Quebec Arts '58, film produced by CBC, Madones et Abstractions (Fr version), shown at Brussels World's Fair, 58. *Mem:* Sculpture Soc Can (treas, '52-67); Royal Can Acad Art. *Interests:* Made over 200 scale models of world famous buildings to illustrate the history of architecture, models exhibited at Montreal Museum Fine Arts, 55. *Mailing Add:* 1435 Drummond St Montreal PQ H3G 1W4 Canada

WHEELOCK, ARTHUR KINGSLAND, JR
CURATOR, EDUCATOR
b Worcester, Mass, May 13, 43. *Study:* Williams Col, BA, 65; Harvard Univ, PhD, 73. *Pos:* Cur Dutch & Flemish painting, Nat Gallery of Art, Washington, DC, 76- *Teaching:* Asst prof Northern Baroque art, Univ Md, College Park, 74- *Awards:* David E Finley Fel, Nat Gallery Art, 71-74; Nat Endowment Arts Grant, 79-80; Cur Fel, Nat Gallery Art, 83-84. *Mem:* Col Art Asn. *Res:* Dutch and Flemish art of the seventeenth century, primarily Vermeer and Rembrandt; artists' techniques; problems of optics and perspective. *Publ:* Auth, Perspective, Optice & Delft Artists Around 1650, Garland Press, 77; auth, Constantijn Huygens & early attitudes towards the camera obscura, Hist of Photog, 77; auth, De geschiedenis en bekoring van 'De Molen, De Kroniek van het Rembrandthuis, 77; coauth, Gods, Saints & Heroes: Dutch Painting in the Age of Rembrandt, Nat Gallery Art, 80; auth, Jan Vermeer, Abrams, 81; and others. *Mailing Add:* Nat Gallery of Art Washington DC 20565

WHIDDEN, CONNI
PAINTER, INSTRUCTOR
b Cambridge, Mass. *Study:* Boston Mus Sch Fine Arts, 32-38, Sturdivant Traveling Fel Europe, 38-39; also with Hans Hofmann & Ferdinand Leger. *Work:* US Embassy, Brussels; St George's Gallery, London; Boston Mus Fine Arts; Smithsonian Inst; Honolulu Acad Art. *Exhib:* One-woman shows,

Reflections of Hawaii, Honolulu Acad Art Mus, 70, Pontiac Art Ctr, 78 & Wilson Mus, Castine, Maine, 82; Selection Paintings, Detroit Inst Arts, 76; 50s Show, NoHo Gallery, New York, 77-78; Now Show, Landmark Gallery, New York, 77-78; 50s, Gallery Asn NY State Traveling Show, two yrs; two-person show, Cranbrook Acad Art Mus, 79; and others. *Pos:* Artist mem, Bank St Col Art Educ Eval Comt, Ford Found, 68; artist lectr, Princeton Univ Art Mus, 69; vis artist, Ind Univ, 71; artist lectr, Cranbrook Acad Art, 72-75. *Teaching:* Instr painting, Chelsea Studios, London, 45-47; instr drawing & painting, Cranbrook Acad Art Mus, 72- *Awards:* Nat Scholar Art Educ, Harvard Univ, 39; Purchase Award, Anglo-French Ctr, London, 47. *Mem:* Mich Watercolor Soc; Birmingham Soc Painters; Arch Am Art, Detroit Inst Art. *Media:* Acrylic, Oil. *Dealer:* Birmingham Gallery Inc Haynes Birmingham MI 48011. *Mailing Add:* Castine ME 04421

WHIPPLE, BARBARA
PRINTMAKER, WRITER
b San Francisco, Calif. *Study:* Swarthmore Col, BA, 43; Rochester Inst Technol, BS, 56; Tyler Sch, Temple Univ, MFA, 61. *Work:* Newark Pub Libr, NJ; Elizabethtown Col, Pa; Lancaster Country Day Sch, Pa; Washington Co Mus, Md. *Comn:* Woodcut prints, Jr League & Lancaster Pub Libr, Pa. *Exhib:* One-man shows, Elizabethtown Col, Pa, 71 & Lebanon Valley Col, Annville, Pa, 73; Centenary Col, NJ, 74; Foothills Art Ctr, Colo, 80 & 83; Adams State Col, Alamosa, Colo, 82; WNebr Art Ctr, 83; and others. *Pos:* Contrib ed, Am Artist, currently. *Teaching:* Instr art, Mem Art Gallery, Univ Rochester, 55-58; instr art, Rochester Sch Deaf, 56-58; asst prof art, Geneseo State Teachers Col, 58-59; instr printmaking, Elizabethtown Col, 74-76; instr drawing, Franklin & Marshall Col, 74. *Awards:* First Prize, Lancaster Open Award, Pa, 68; Juror's Award, Reading Regional, Pa, 69; First Prize Drawing, Philadelphia Watercolor Club, 79. *Bibliog:* Barbara Whipple, printmaker, La Rev Mod, 1/66; featured in Colo Outdoors, 1/80; Jane Larson (auth), The many traditions of Barbara Whipple, Am Artist, 5/80. *Mem:* Philadelphia Watercolor Club; Artists Equity Asn; Colo Artists Asn. *Publ:* Coauth, Water-Media Techniques, Watson-Guptill, 83. *Mailing Add:* Box 609 Buena Vista CO 81211

WHIPPLE, ENEZ MARY
ADMINISTRATOR
b Syracuse, NY. *Study:* Syracuse Univ, BS; Southampton Col Long Island Univ, Hon DFA, 81. *Pos:* Exec dir, Guild Hall East Hampton Inc, NY, 48- *Teaching:* Adj prof humanities, Southampton Col, Long Island Univ, 71. *Mem:* Am Fedn Arts; Long Island Mus Asn; Am Asn Mus; NY State Asn Mus. *Mailing Add:* Guild Hall of East Hampton 158 Main St East Hampton NY 11937

WHITAKER, EILEEN MONAGHAN
PAINTER
b Holyoke Mass, Nov 22, 11. *Study:* Mass Col Art, Boston. *Work:* Atlanta Art Mus, Ga; Charles & Emma Frye Mus, Seattle, Wash; Hispanic Mus, New York; Nat Acad Design, New York; Okla Art Mus, Okla City. *Exhib:* Harvest Time Extramadura, Nat Acad Design, New York, 58; Harvest Rite, Royal Watercolour Soc, London, Eng, 62; Mayan Motif, Am Acad Arts & Letters, New York, 63; Mayan Warrior, Museo de Acuarela, Mex, 68; Tender Message, M H De Young Mem Mus, San Francisco, 69; Ceremonial Preparations, Phoenix Art Mus, Ariz, 72; Mayan Girls at the Temple, Nat Acad Design, New York, 80. *Awards:* Ranger Fund Purchase, 58; Silver Medal, Am Watercolor Soc, 65; Western Subject, Santa Fe Federal Savings & Loan, 78. *Bibliog:* Weldon Blake (auth), Acrylic Watercolor Painting, Watson-Guptill, 70; Gerald F Brommer (auth), Transparent Watercolor, Davis Publ; Royal B Hassrick (auth), Western Painting Today, Watson-Guptill, 75. *Mem:* Academician, Nat Acad Design; Am Watercolor Soc; hon mem Watercolor West; hon mem Providence Watercolor Club; hon mem San Diego Watercolor Soc. *Media:* Transparent Watercolor. *Publ:* Auth, My Concept of Watercolor, The Artist, London, 59; contribr, 100 Watercolor Techniques, 68 & Watercolorists at Work, 72, Watson-Guptill. *Dealer:* Jones Gallery 1264 Prospect St La Jolla CA 92037. *Mailing Add:* 1579 Alta La Jolla Dr La Jolla CA 92037

WHITAKER, IRWIN A
EDUCATOR, CRAFTSMAN
b Wirt, Okla, Oct 19, 19. *Study:* San Jose State Col, BA; Claremont Col, MFA, with Richard Pettersen. *Work:* Detroit Art Inst; Kresge Art Ctr, Mich State Univ; Univ Nebr Art Mus; Los Angeles Co Mus Art. *Exhib:* Many nat & regional exhibs. *Teaching:* Instr ceramics, Southern Ore Col, 49-50; prof ceramics, Mich State Univ, 50-81, prof emer, 81- *Awards:* First Award for Ceramics, Calif State Fair, 49; Purchase Award for Ceramics, Univ Nebr, 59; Purchase Award for Enamel, Detroit Inst Art, 62. *Bibliog:* Paul S Donhauser (auth), History of American Cermaics, 78. *Media:* Ceramics, Enamels. *Publ:* Auth, Crafts and craftsmen, 67; coauth (with Emily Whitaker), A Potter's Mexico, 78. *Mailing Add:* 1104 Paseo Contento Nogales AZ 85621

WHITAKER, WILLIAM
PAINTER, ILLUSTRATOR
b Chicago, Ill, Mar 5, 43. *Study:* Univ Utah, BA; Otis Art Inst. *Work:* Brigham Young Univ; Weber State Col; Nat Cowboy Hall of Fame. *Comn:* Many portraits, 67-83. *Exhib:* Utah Inst Arts, 72-73 & 76; Nat Acad Western Art, Oklahoma City, 75-83; Am Western Art Exhib, Beijing, China, 81; Artists Am, Denver, 80-83. *Pos:* Advert mgr, Capital Records Inc, Hollywood, Calif, 68-69. *Teaching:* Assoc prof art & design, Brigham Young Univ, 69-80. *Awards:* Gold Medal, 76 & Silver Medal, 77, Nat Acad Western Art; Press Award, Western Rendezvous Art, 82. *Bibliog:* Articles, Ariz Hwy, 4/74 & 7/75; article, SW Art, 3/82; Profiles in American Art: William Whitaker, PBS-TV, 83. *Mem:* Nat Acad Western Art. *Media:* Oil, Pastel. *Dealer:* Jenny Whitaker 2846 Marrerest Circle W Provo UT 84604. *Mailing Add:* 2846 Marrcrest Circle W Provo UT 84604

WHITCOMB, KAY
ENAMELIST, MURALIST
b Arlington, Mass, May 20, 21. *Study:* RI Sch Design, 39-42; Cambridge Sch Art, 40-41; apprentice in enameling to Doris Hall, 46-47. *Comn:* Gosselies (enamel on steel), Hotel Ville, Gosselies, Belg, 74; Creche (needlepoint), Better Homes & Gardens, Des Moines, 75; San Diego Bicentennial Quilt, San Diego Hist Soc, 76; Infinite Wisdom (enamel on steel), Univ Hosp, San Diego, 76; Arab Transportation, Int Airport, Dubai, United Arab Emirates, 81. *Exhib:* Int Kunsthandwerk, Industrial Arts Mus, Stuttgart, Ger, 69; Int Festival Enamel, Laguna Beach Mus Art, Calif, 76; Int Biennale, Art Enamel, Limoges, France, 78; Focus, San Diego Mus Art, 80; Int Shippo, Cent Mus, Tokyo, 81; Enamels 50-80, New England, 81. *Teaching:* Instr design & enameling, San Diego Community Col, 74-81. *Awards:* Prix Syndicat d'Initiative, Int Biennale, Art Enamel, Limoges, France, 78; Int Shippo Prize, Tokyo, 81. *Bibliog:* Martin Peterson (auth), On view, Applause, 12/79; Wayne Endicott (auth), Artist turns enameling paste into art, Ceramic Industry, 10/81. *Mem:* Founding mem NAm Comt Enamel Creators (pres, 83); Cloisonne Collectors Club; founding mem Enamel Guild: West (pres, 76-78); Allied Craftsmen San Diego (vpres, 72-73); San Diego Art Guild (chmn, 68-69). *Media:* Enamel. *Res:* Turn of century golden era enameling. *Publ:* Auth, Germany Stuttgart: International handcraft, Craft Horizons, 71; auth, Shippo Yaki excursion--enamel tour of Japan, 78, First international Shippo exhibition May 1978, Tokyo Japan, 78 & Multi techniques of enamel, 78, Goldsmith J. *Dealer:* Knowles Gallery Girard St La Jolla CA 92037. *Mailing Add:* 1631 Mimulus Way La Jolla CA 92037

WHITCOMB, THERESE TRUITT
HISTORIAN, INSTRUCTOR
b Evanston, Ill, Sept 19, 30. *Study:* Rosemont Col; San Diego Col for Women, BA, 53; San Diego State Univ, MA, 69. *Comn:* Interior: San Diego Mission, Diocese of San Diego, 71; Casa del Prado Ct, Comt of 100, San Diego, 77; Mission San Luis Rey Mus (designed & executed), Franciscan Friars, 79; Sacred Heart Church, Coronado, Calif, 82; St Agnes Church, San Diego, 83. *Collections Arranged:* Contemporary Primitives, 76, Founder's Gallery Univ San Diego, Carousel Animals as Sculpture, 77, California Chair, 79 & The Naive Eye Now, 79; San Luis Rey Museum, 79. *Pos:* Dir, Founder's Gallery, Univ San Diego, 71-; trustee, San Diego Mus Art, 75-82. *Teaching:* Prof art hist, Univ San Diego, 68-, coord/chmn of art dept, 70- *Awards:* Outstanding Teacher, Univ San Diego, 77. *Bibliog:* Elise Miller (auth), San Diego art, Los Angeles Times; George Maher (auth), Twilight of Splendor, Little Brown & Co, 76; Zenia Cleigh (auth), Mission as art, San Diego Mag, 79. *Mem:* Asn Archit Historians; Southern Calif Art Historians; Western Asn Art Mus; Col Art Asn. *Res:* California missions, 19th and 20th century California architecture, American primitive art. *Publ:* Contribr, Sword and the Cross, San Diego Mus, 76; contribr, California's Catholic Heritage, Penguin Press, 76. *Mailing Add:* 3407 Angwin Dr San Diego CA 92123

WHITE, ALBERT
DEALER, COLLECTOR
b Toronto, Ont. *Pos:* Pres, Albert White Gallery, currently. *Mem:* Prof Art Dealers Asn of Can. *Specialty:* Modern art, Moore, Picasso, Miro, Chagall; primitive art, Africa, New Guinea, Pre-Columbian. *Collection:* Primitive art. *Publ:* Auth, Albert White on art investment, Toronto Life, 4/74. *Mailing Add:* 25 Prince Arthur Ave Toronto ON M5R 1B2 Canada

WHITE, AMOS, IV
CERAMIST, PHOTOGRAPHER
b Montgomery, Ala. *Study:* Ala State Univ, BS, 58; Sculpture Studio, with Isaac S Hathaway, 58; Univ Southern Calif, MFA, 61; Long Island Univ, 66; Univ Md, PhD, 82. *Work:* Quinn Gallery, Univ Southern Calif; Lemoyne Art Found, Tallahassee, Fla. *Exhib:* Designer-Craftsmen USA, 60 & Young Americans, 62, Mus Contemp Crafts, New York; Am Fedn Arts Traveling Exhib, 63; 18th Nat Decorative Arts & Ceramics Exhib, Wichita, 64; Outstanding Atlantic Seaboard Artists, Jacksonville, Fla, 73; Black Artists South, Huntsville Mus Art, 79; plus many others. *Pos:* Md Conf pres, Am Asn Univ Prof, 78-79. *Teaching:* Assoc prof ceramics, Fla A&M Univ, Tallahassee, 61-69; prof & chmn art dept, Bowie State Col, Md, 69-, prof photog, 70-, chmn dept fine & performing arts, 83- *Awards:* Design West, Los Angeles Mus Sci & Indust, 60; Merit Award, Am Craftsmen's Coun, 61; Ceramic Award, Fla State Fair Fine Arts Comn, 65. *Bibliog:* Lewis & Waddy (auth), Black artists/art, Contemp Crafts, 69; J W Chase (auth), Afro-American Art & Crafts, Von Nostrand-Reinhold, 71. *Mem:* Fla Craftsmen (pres, 69); Am Craftsmen's Coun, New York (Fla state councilman, 68-69); Md Fedn Art; Nat Coun Art Adminr; Col Art Asn Am. *Media:* Clay. *Mailing Add:* 12307 Rockledge Dr Bowie MD 20715

WHITE, B J (BEVERLY JO)
PAINTER
b Hobart, Okla, Dec 12, 46. *Study:* Okla City Univ, BS, 69; Phillips Univ, 74-76; La Tech Univ, 80 & 82. *Work:* Presby Hosp, Baptist Hosp, Moak, Hunsacker, Rouse, Thomas & Co, Amerex Inc, South Community Hosp, Oklahoma City. *Exhib:* Okla Mus Art Members Ann, 78-81; Am Watercolor Soc, Nat Acad Galleries, New York, 82; Midwest Watercolor Soc, West Bend Gallery, Wis, 82 & Davenport Art Gallery, Iowa, 83; Southwestern Watercolor Soc, Brookhaven Col, Tex, 83; Aqueous, Pittsburgh Ctr Arts, Pa, 83. *Awards:* Merit Award, Burleson Ann Art Exhib, 81 & 82; Cash Award, Kans Watercolor Soc Tri-State Competition, 82 & Okla Watercolor Asn, 83. *Bibliog:* Marcia Lionberger (auth), The nature of her art, Art Gallery, 5-6/83. *Mem:* Okla Watercolor Asn (first vpres, 79-80, pres, 80-81); assoc Am Watercolor Soc; Southwestern Watercolor Soc; Southern Watercolor Soc; Edmond Art Asn. *Media:* Watercolor. *Dealer:* Chummings Gallery 100 N Broadway Suite F Edmond OK 73034. *Mailing Add:* 13 Pleasant Oaks Dr Edmond OK 73034

WHITE, BRUCE HILDING
SCULPTOR
b Bay Shore, NY, July 11, 33. *Study:* Univ Md, BA; Columbia Univ, MA & EdD. *Work:* Univ Ill, Champaign; Ill State Mus, Springfield; Indianapolis Mus Art, Ind; Rogers Libr & Mus Art, Laurel, Miss. *Comn:* Sculpture, Quail Spring Mall, Oklahoma City, 80, City Chicago, 80, Col Hills Mall, Normal, Ill, 81, Atlantic Richfield Corp, Rolling Meadows, 82 & Ill Revenue Bldg, Springfield, 83. *Exhib:* Chicago & Vicinity Artists 72nd & 73rd Ann, Art Inst Chicago, 69 & 71; Painting and Sculpture Today, Indianapolis Mus Art, Ind, 78 & 80; Art 1981, Chicago Int Art Expo, Navy Pier, 81; 30 Years of Public Sculpture in Illinois, Lakeview Mus, Peoria, 81; one-person show, Brea Civic Ctr, Calif, 82; Mayor Byrne's Mile of Sculpture, Navy Pier, Chicago, 82; Mile II, Chicago Sculpure Int, 83; and others. *Teaching:* Prof sculpture, Northern Ill Univ, 68- *Media:* Sheet Metal, Cast Metal. *Mailing Add:* c/o Dept Art Northern Ill Univ De Kalb IL 60115

WHITE, DEBORAH
DEALER
b Toronto, Can. *Study:* Univ Toronto, BA; Univ Florence, spec cert. *Pos:* Dir, Albert White Gallery, currently. *Mem:* Can Prof Art Dealers Asn. *Specialty:* Modern art, international artists, Moore, Chagall, Picasso, Leger, Miro, Lichtenstein, and others; primitive and pre-Columbian art. *Mailing Add:* 25 Prince Arthur Toronto ON M5R 1B2 Canada

WHITE, DORIS A
PAINTER
b Eau Claire, Wis. *Study:* Art Inst Chicago. *Exhib:* Butler Inst Am Art, Youngstown, Ohio; Am Watercolor Soc, New York; Art Alliance, Philadelphia; Inst Arte Mex; Ill Mus, Springfield; and many others. *Awards:* Ranger Fund Purchase Award, Nat Acad Design; RCA Victor Purchase Award, Lowe Gallery; Assoc Mem Award, Allied Artists Am; and others. *Mem:* Nat Acad Design; Am Watercolor Soc; Wis Watercolor Soc. *Mailing Add:* 2750 Church Rd Jackson WI 53037

WHITE, FRANKLIN
PAINTER, DRAFTSMAN
b Richmond, Va, 1943. *Study:* Skowhegan Sch Painting & Sculpture, Maine, 66; Brooklyn Mus Art Sch, 67-68; Nat Collection Fine Arts Internship, 69-70; Howard Univ, BFA, 69, MFA, 71. *Work:* Woodward Found, Washington, DC; Am Fedn Arts; Stern Found, Washington, DC; Washington Post; Corcoran Gallery Art. *Comn:* Three multi-color serigraphs, The Workshop, Washington, DC, 72 & 78. *Exhib:* Contemp Black Artists in Am, Whitney Mus Am Art, New York, 71; 2nd Ann Exhib Washington Artists, Phillips Collection, 72; Corcoran Mus Art, 72 & 75; Directions in Afro-Am Art, Johnson Mus, Cornell Univ, Ithaca, NY, 74; 77 Artists, Wash Project for the Arts, 77; one-man shows, Corcoran Gallery, Washington, DC, 72, Jefferson Pl Gallery, 72 & 74 & Gallery Rebecca Cooper, Washington, DC, 75 & 77; and others. *Pos:* Info guide intern, Nat Collection Fine Arts, 69-70. *Teaching:* Instr painting & drawing, Georgetown Univ & Md Sch of Arts & Design; artist-in-residence, DC Pub Sch & DC Comn on the Arts, 70-71; instr, Corcoran Gallery Art Sch, 75- *Awards:* Painting Award, Skowhegan Sch Arts & Design; Nat Endowment Arts Grant, 70-71. *Bibliog:* Roberta Smith (auth), Directions in Afro-American art, Artforum, 75; Henri Ghent (auth), article, Art in Am, 1-2/75; Benjamin Forgery (auth), Washington DC round-up, Artnews, 2/75. *Mailing Add:* c/o Corcoran Sch Art 17th St & NY Ave NW Washington DC 20006

WHITE, IAN MCKIBBIN
MUSEUM ADMINISTRATOR
b Honolulu, Hawaii, May 10, 29. *Study:* Harvard Col, BA(archit), 51, Harvard Univ Grad Sch Design, 51-52; Univ Calif, Los Angeles, 57-58; Bowdoin Col, Maine, DFA, 77. *Comn:* Designed, Frieda Shiff Warburg Sculpture Garden, Brooklyn Mus, New York, 66; designed, Peary-McMillan Arctic Mus, Bowdoin Col, Brunswick, Maine, 67. *Pos:* Supt, Brooklyn Mus, New York, 61-63, asst dir, 64-67; dir, Calif Palace Legion of Honor, San Francisco, 68- & dir mus, Calif M H deYoung Mem Mus, San Francisco, 70-; mem adv mus panel, Nat Endowment Arts, 73-76; trustee, The Corning Mus of Glass, Corning, NY, 77- *Awards:* Order of the Republic, Egypt, 79. *Mem:* Int Coun Mus; Am Asn Mus; Am Asn Mus Dir (vpres, 75-76, pres, 76-77); Victorian Soc Am; Am Fedn Arts (trustee, 71-). *Mailing Add:* c/o Calif Palace of Legion of Honor Lincoln Park San Francisco CA 94121

WHITE, JAMES RICHARD
SCULPTOR, EDUCATOR
b Dayton, Ohio, Jan 14, 50. *Study:* Ohio Univ, BFA(painting), 72, MFA(sculpture), 74. *Work:* USAF, Dayton, Ohio. *Comn:* Murray State Univ, Ky. *Exhib:* One-man shows, Wright State Univ, Dayton, Ohio, 79 & SE Mo State Univ, Cape Girardeau, 79; Evansville Mus Arts & Sci, Ind, 79 & 80. *Teaching:* Asst prof, Murray State Univ, Ky, 74-81; assoc prof, Ariz State Univ, Tempe, 81- *Awards:* Ind Found Arts & Sci Award, 80. *Bibliog:* Jerry Speight (auth), Shelter skelter, Ky Art Educ J, 12/79, Air city, free air, air fair affair, School Arts/Davis, 9/80 & James R White, sculptor, Art Voices S/Davis, 7/80. *Mem:* Col Art Asn. *Media:* Metal, Wood. *Mailing Add:* Art Dept Ariz State Univ Tempe AZ 85281

WHITE, JOHN M
PAINTER, CONCEPTUAL ARTIST
b San Francisco, Calif, May 10, 37. *Study:* Patri Sch of Art Fundamentals, San Francisco, 62-65; Otis Art Inst, Los Angeles, MFA, 69. *Work:* Los Angeles Co Art Mus, Los Angeles; Smithsonian Arch Am Art; Newport-Harbor Art Mus, Newport Beach, Calif; Solomon R Guggenheim Mus, New York; St

Louis Art Mus, Mo; and others. *Exhib:* New Work, New Talent, Los Angeles Co Art Mus, 74; Drawing Show, Newport Harbor Art Mus, 75; one-man shows, Barbara Okun Gallery, St Louis, 77, Baum-Silverman Gallery, Los Angeles, 78 & 81 & Roy Boyd Gallery, Chicago, 81; performances, Vancouver Art Gallery, BC, 75, Miami-Dade Community Col, Fla, 75, St Louis Mus Contemp Art, 77 & Chicago Art Inst, 78; Solomon R Guggenheim Mus, 81; and many others. *Teaching:* Vis artist performance workshop, Claremont Grad Sch, 77- & Otis Art Inst, 77-79. *Awards:* New Talent Award, Los Angeles Co Art Mus, 72; Nat Endowment Arts Grants, 76-77 & 78-79; CETA Grant Artist in Residence, 78-79. *Media:* Mixed. *Mailing Add:* 2141 Glencoe Ave Venice CA 90291

WHITE, NORMAN TRIPLETT
SCULPTOR
b San Antonio, Tex, Jan 7, 38. *Study:* Harvard Col, with T Lux Feininger, 55-59, BA(biol), 59. *Work:* Nat Gallery Can, Ottawa, Art Bank, Ottawa. *Comn:* Light mural, CBC Bldg, Vancouver, BC, 75. *Exhib:* Some More Beginnings, Exp in Art & Technol Show, Brooklyn Mus, New York, 68; Norm White at the Electric Gallery, Toronto, 71; Le Musee Electrique, Mus Contemp Art, Montreal, 74; retrospective, Vancouver Art Gallery, BC, 75; New Directions, Nat Gallery of Can, 77; Sound at PS-1, Clocktower, New York, 78; Buffalo Media Study, New York, 81. *Teaching:* Ont Col Art, Toronto, 78-84. *Awards:* Can Coun Bursaries, 69-71 & 76-82; Ont Arts coun, 82-83. *Media:* Multimedia. *Mailing Add:* 373 Montrose Ave Toronto ON M6G 3H2 Canada

WHITE, PHILIP BUTLER
PAINTER, COLLECTOR
b Chicago, Ill, Jan 23, 35. *Study:* Univ Southern Calif, BFA(painting). *Exhib:* Butler Inst Am Art, Youngstown, Ohio, 62-64; Ill State Mus, Springfield, 63, 65, 67, 69 & 70; Am Watercolor Soc, New York, 70-71; Union League Club, Chicago, 74-78; Nat Acad Design, New York, 75-76. *Awards:* First Prizes, Ill State Fair, 60 & 65 & Union League, Chicago, 63 & 67; Thomas B Clark Awards, Nat Acad Design, 65, 68 & 70. *Bibliog:* Cover story, Am Artist, 8/78. *Media:* Oil, Egg Tempera. *Collection:* Contemporary realistic art. *Mailing Add:* 710 Clinton Pl River Forest IL 60305

WHITE, RALPH
PAINTER, EDUCATOR
b Minneapolis, Minn, Jan 3, 21. *Study:* Minneapolis Col Art & Design, cert, 42; Pratt Inst, cert, 46. *Work:* Everson Mus, Syracuse, NY; Mem Mus, Corpus Christi, Tex; Wright State Univ, Dayton, Ohio; St Mary's Col of Md. *Exhib:* Denver Art Mus 59th Western Art Ann, 53; Butler Inst Am Art 22nd Ann Midyear Show, 57; Tex Contemp Artists Knoedler Gallery, New York (circulated nationally); Watercolor USA, Springfield Art Mus, Mo, 71 & 77; Ralph White Acrylics, Palacio de Bellas Artes, Mexico City, 72-73. *Teaching:* Prof studio art, Univ Tex, Austin, 46-82, actg chmn dept art, 67-73, prof emer, 82. *Awards:* Vanderlip Fel, Minn Sch Art, 42; Purchase Award, Minneapolis Inst Art, 42; Onderdonk Purchase Award, Tex Paint & Sculpture Ann, Witte Mus, 49. *Bibliog:* Richard Teller Hirsch (auth), Tale Painting Tells, Alcalde, Univ Tex, 12/70; Eleanor Freed (auth), 2 views of space, Houston Post, 2/6/72; Margaret T Dry (auth), Laguna Gloria spotlights Ralph White, Austin Am Statesman, 1/5/75. *Mem:* Tex Watercolor Soc; Tex Asn Fine Arts (adv bd, 73-76); Dallas Ft Worth Soc Visual Commun; Austin Prof Artists (pres, 59). *Media:* Acrylic, Watercolor. *Mailing Add:* 4701 Agarita Rd Austin TX 78734

WHITE, ROBERT (WINTHROP)
SCULPTOR, EDUCATOR
b New York, NY, Sept 19, 21. *Study:* With Joseph Weisz, Munich, 32-34; also with John Howard Benson & Waldemar Raemisch, RI Sch Design. *Work:* Brooklyn Mus, NY; RI Sch Design Mus, Providence; Springfield Mus, Mass. *Comn:* Bronze, St Anthony of Padua Sch, Northport, NY, 59; A E Verrill Silver Medal, Peabody Mus Natural Hist, Yale Univ, 60; three wooden & metal figures, Mrs Hester Pickman, St Michael's Roman Cath Church, Bedford, Mass, 60-66; bronze relief portrait of Joseph Wilson, Xerox Corp, Stamford, Conn, 72; Pershing Monument, Pershing Square, Washington, DC, 83; and others. *Exhib:* Pa Acad Ann, Philadelphia, 50; Int Exhib Relig Art, Stazione Marittima, Trieste, Italy, 58; Continuing Tradition of Realism in American Art, Hirschl & Adler Galleries, New York, 62; Eight Americans, Amsterdam, Breda, Nymegen, Holland, 69; Representational Spirit, Univ Art Gallery, Albany, NY, 70; The Figure, Pratt Inst, traveling exhib, 80-81; and many other group & one-man exhibs. *Pos:* Resident sculptor, Am Acad Rome, Italy, 69-70 & Skowhegan Sch of Painting & Sculpture, 74; guest lectr, MFA Prog, Parson's Sch Design, 81. *Teaching:* Instr life drawing, Parsons Sch Design, New York, 49-52; assoc prof art, State Univ NY, Stony Brook, 62- *Awards:* Am Acad Rome Fel, 52-55; Nat Acad Design Proctor Mem Prize, 62; Farfield Found Grant, 69. *Bibliog:* Article, Arts Mag, 9/80. *Media:* Multimedia. *Publ:* Illusr, Enchanted, Pantheon, 51 & Confessions of Nat Turner, Harper's Mag, 67. *Dealer:* James Graham & Sons 1014 Madison Ave New York NY 10021. *Mailing Add:* Moriches Rd St James NY 11780

WHITE, RUTH
DEALER, COLLECTOR
b New York, NY. *Study:* With Kurt Seligmann. *Pos:* Owner, Ruth White Gallery. *Specialty:* Contemporary paintings, sculpture and graphics. *Collection:* Kurt Seligmann; Ozenfant; paintings and sculpture by various young American artists. *Mailing Add:* Shadybrook Village 8405 Byron Lane Sarasota FL 33580

WHITE, STUART JAMES
SCULPTOR, ASSEMBLAGE ARTIST
b Salisbury, Md, May 31, 44. *Study:* Carnegie-Mellon Univ, BFA, 68, MFA, 70, DA, 78. *Work:* Newark Mus, NJ; NJ State Mus, Trenton. *Comn:* Construction (wallpiece), Tanners Coun Am, Washington, DC, 79. *Exhib:* Carnegie Inst Ann, 72-76; Appalachian Nat, Mint Mus, 78; Art in Boxes, Philadelphia Art Alliance, 79; constructions, 55 Mercer Gallery, New York, 81; solo exhib, NJ Biennial, Newark Mus, 82 & figurative work, NJ State Mus, Trenton, 83. *Pos:* Dir, Robeson Gallery, Rutgers Univ, Newark, 79- *Teaching:* Intern drawing, Carnegie-Mellon Univ, 72-73; asst prof art hist, Mt Union Col, 74-78; dept head resins, Johnson Atelier, Princeton, 78-79; vis specialist, Montclair State Col, 79-; asst prof sculpture, Rutgers Univ, Newark, 79- *Awards:* Grant, Newark: Genesis of a City, NJ Comt Humanities, 80; Purchase Award, Lebau Ctr Ann, Union, NJ, 81; Sculpture Fel, NJ State Coun Arts, 83. *Bibliog:* Hildreth York (auth), Stuart White: The Figurative Work, NJ State Mus, 83. *Mem:* Col Art Asn Am. *Publ:* Auth, Calvin Albert, 78 & Dennis Oppenheim, 79, Sculpture News Exchange; coauth, Stalking the post office mural: An artful odyssey, New York Sunday Times, 80. *Mailing Add:* 72 Alpine Pl Kearney NJ 07032

WHITE, SUSAN CHRYSLER
PAINTER
b Chico, Calif, June 12, 54. *Study:* Univ Calif, Berkeley, BA, 77; Univ Calif, Davis, with Wayne Thiebaud, Roy DeForest, Robert Arneson, Ellen Lanyon & Manuel Neri, MFA, 80. *Work:* Worcester Art Mus, Mass; Prudential Insurance Co, Newark, NJ; Rutgers Univ; Meniscus Med Communications, Philadelphia. *Exhib:* Challenge Exhib 82, Fleisher Art Mem, Philadelphia, 82; Four Emerging Expressionists, Peter Miller Gallery, Chicago, 82; Philadelphia Artists, Philadelphia Mus Art, 82-83; An Invitational: Six Artists, Philadelphia Art Alliance, 83; one-person show, Peter Miller Gallery, Chicago, 83-84 & Janet Fleisher Gallery, Philadelphia, 84; and others. *Teaching:* Instr & vis artist, La State Univ, 80; vis lectr, Tyler Sch Art, 81 & Rutgers Univ, 82. *Awards:* Ann Bremmar Award, Berkeley Mus, 77; Purchase Award, Rutgers Univ Nat, 82; Philadelphia Mus Art Purchase Award, Cheltenham Art Ctr 41st Ann Painting Exhib, 82. *Media:* Oil, Oil Pastels. *Dealer:* Peter Miller Gallery Huron St Chicago IL; Janet Fleisher Gallery 17th St Philadelphia PA. *Mailing Add:* 939-A N Second St Philadelphia PA 19123

WHITEHILL, FLORENCE (FITCH)
PAINTER
b Hillsdale, NY. *Study:* Mass Col Art, Boston; Grand Cent Sch Art, New York. *Work:* New York Hist Soc; East Hampton Soc, NY; Tamassee Daughters Am Revolution Sch, SC. *Exhib:* Catharine Lorillard Wolfe Art Club Ann, 49-81; Acad Artists Asn, Fine Arts Mus, Springfield, Mass, 56-58, 64 & 67; Nat League Am Pen Women Biennial, Smithsonian Inst, Washington, DC, 58; Hudson Valley Artists, 77-79; Knickerbocker Artists, 78-81; Salmagundi Club, 78-81; and others. *Awards:* Best Watercolor, Catherine Lorillard Wolfe Art Club, 68; Award of Honor for Watercolor, Nat League Am Pen Women, 58; Knickerbocker Artist Award, 79; and others. *Bibliog:* Mary Barbara Reinmuth (auth), Pen woman, New York Br, Nat League Am Pen Women, winter 57-58. *Mem:* Catharine Lorillard Wolfe Art Club (pres, 53-56, corresp secy, 59-71); Am Artists Prof League; Acad Artists Asn; Nat League Am Pen Women (state art chmn, 64-66, NY br treas, 72-81); life fel Royal Soc Arts, London; and others. *Media:* Watercolor. *Mailing Add:* 7 Peter Cooper Rd New York NY 10010

WHITEMAN, EDWARD RUSSELL
PAINTER
b Buffalo, NY, Dec 16, 38. *Study:* Univ Buffalo Albright Art Sch, AA. *Work:* Nat Collection Fine Arts, Washington, DC; Albright-Knox Art Gallery, Buffalo; New Orleans Mus Art, La; Montgomery Mus Fine Arts, Ala; Crysler Mus Art, Mass. *Exhib:* Whitney Biennial Contemp Am Art, New York, 75; Eight State Exhib Paintings & Sculpture, Okla Art Ctr, 75; Pratt Graphic Ctr, 75; Corcoran Gallery of Art, DC; La Jolla Mus Contemp Art, Calif, 79; Columbia Mus Art, SC; Paper Making & Paper Using, Southeastern Ctr Contemp Art, Winston-Salem, NC; Edward Whiteman: Works on Treated Paper, 1975-1982, Mus Art, Carnegie Inst, 82. *Awards:* Purchase Award, New Orleans Mus Art, 75; Artist Fels, Nat Endowment for the Arts & Southeastern Ctr Contemp Art, 78-79; Ford Found Grant, 80. *Bibliog:* Jean Nathan (auth), Newswatch Art, Channel 6 News, 75; Terrington, Calas (auth), Edward Whiteman and the unlovely metaphor, Arts Quarterly New Orleans, Vol 4, No 3, 82. *Media:* Liquitex, Pastel. *Dealer:* Arthur Roger Gallery 3005 Magazine Street New Orleans LA 70115. *Mailing Add:* c/o Arthur Roger Gallery 3005 Magazine St New Orleans LA 70115

WHITEN, COLETTE
SCULPTOR, INSTRUCTOR
b Birmingham, Eng, Feb 7, 45. Can citizen. *Study:* Ont Col of Art, AOCA. *Work:* Nat Gallery of Can, Ottawa; Art Gallery of Ont, Toronto; Art Bank, Ottawa. *Comn:* Sculpture, Art Gallery Ont, 72; Gov Can Bldg, North York, Ont, 76; sculpture, Dept Pub Works, 77; sculpture, Mental Health Ctr, Toronto, 78; Sudbury & District Chamber Commerce Centennial Proj, 83. *Exhib:* 8th Biennale de Paris, Mus d'Art Mod de la Ville de Paris, France, 73; Carmen Lamanna Gallery at Owens Art Gallery, Sackville, 75; Some Canadian Women Artists, Nat Gallery Can, Ottawa, 75; Celebration of the Body, Etherington Art Ctr, 76; Ont Now, A Survey of Contemp Art, Kitchener-Waterloo Gallery, Art Gallery of Hamilton, 76; one-person shows, London Art Gallery, Ont, 78 & Carmen Lamanna Gallery, 73-75 & 77-80); The 1st Australian Sculpture Triennial, Melbourne, 81. *Teaching:* Instr concept develop, Ont Col of Art, Toronto, 74-; resident artist, Univ Western

Ont, London, 78-79. *Awards:* Eaton Traveling Scholar, 72; Can Arts Coun Bursary, 73 & 76. *Bibliog:* John Bentley Mays (auth), Friends are Cast as Artworks in Colette Whiten's Sculptures, Globe & Mail, 4/12/80; David Burnett & Marilyn Schiff, Contemporary Canadian Art, Hurtig Publ, Edmonton, 83. *Media:* Plaster, Wood. *Publ:* Contribr, Carmen Lamanna Gallery at Owens Art Gallery, Owens Art Gallery, Sackville, NB, 75. *Mailing Add:* c/o Carmen Lamanna Gallery 840 Yonge St Toronto ON M4W 2H1 Canada

WHITEN, TIM (GROVER TIMOTHY)
SCULPTOR, ENVIRONMENTAL ARTIST
b Inkster, Mich, Aug 13, 41. *Study:* Cent Mich Univ, BS, 64; Univ Ore, creative arts grant, 65, MFA, 66. *Work:* Nat Gallery Can, Can Coun Art Bank & Ministry External Affairs, Ottawa, Ont, Can; Art Gallery Ont, Toronto. *Comn:* Cast concrete walls, Dept Parks & Recreation, Jasper, Ore, 64; monumental sculpture, Lane Co Parks Comn, Orchard Lake, Eugene, Ore, 66; Earth Work Ritual Installation, Art Park, Lewiston, NY, 77; Ritual Installation, Central Park, Art Across the Park, New York, 82. *Exhib:* Supplement '66, Fountain Gallery, Portland, Ore, 66; Works Mostly on Paper, Inst Contemp Art, Boston, Mass, 70; Present Co-In Pursuit of Recent Art in Ont, Art Gallery of Ont, Toronto, 74; Lect on the Weather, Albright Knox Art Gallery, Buffalo, NY, 76; Morada, Art Park, Lewiston, NY, 77; Markings, Auspices of Ministry of External Affairs, traveling exhib to Chicago, Boston, Atlanta & DC, 78; Voler/Vole, York Univ Fine Arts Markham Gallery, Toronto, 79; 5th Ann Dalhousie Drawing Exhib, 80; and others. *Teaching:* Assoc prof fine arts, York Univ, Downsview, Ont, 68-; vis lectr, univs & arts schs, Can, 70- *Awards:* O'Connell Purchase Award, 63. *Bibliog:* John Chandler (auth), Notes towards a new aesthetics, 10-11/72, Dale McConathy (auth), To collect drawing, 4-5/77 & Joan Vastokas (auth), The roots of abstraction, 5-6/78, Arts Can. *Media:* Human Skulls, Mud; Found Objects, Paper. *Res:* Investigation of consciousness as it manifests in a variety of cultures, historically and contemporarily. *Dealer:* Bau-Xi Gallery Ltd 3045 Granville St Vancouver BC V6H 3J9 Can; Bau-Xi Gallery Ltd 340 Dundas St W Toronto ON M5T 1G5 Can. *Mailing Add:* 70 Pinewood Ave Toronto ON M6C 2V1 Canada

WHITESELL, JOHN D
PRINTMAKER
b Hamilton, Ohio, Dec 1, 42. *Study:* Earlham Col, Richmond, Ind, BA; Miami Univ, Ohio, with Robert Wolfe, Jr; Ind Univ with Rudy Pozzatti & Marvin Lowe, MFA. *Work:* Bradford City Art Gallery, Yorkshire, Eng; Libr Cong, Washington, DC; Miami Art Ctr, Fla; US Info Agency, Prints in Embassies Prog. *Comn:* Vermillion Seven (suite of prints), comn & publ by Univ SDak, 75. *Exhib:* Nat Print, Libr Cong, 71 & 73; 5th Ann Nat Exhib Prints, San Diego, Calif, 72; 1st Int Graphics Biennial, Miami, Fla, 73; Nat Print Los Angeles, 73; Bradley Nat Print Show, Peoria, Ill, 75. *Teaching:* Assoc prof printmaking, Univ Louisville, Ky, 73- *Awards:* Third Award, Miami Print Int, 73; Purchase Awards, Libr Cong, 73 & Bradley Univ, 75. *Media:* Silkscreen; Lithographs. *Mailing Add:* Dept of Art Univ of Louisville Louisville KY 40208

WHITESIDE, WILLIAM ALBERT, II
PAINTER, EDUCATOR
b Bradenton, Fla, Aug 1, 25. *Study:* Ringling Sch Art, 48-51; Fla State Univ, Tallahassee, with Karl Zerbe & Arthur Deshales, BS(art educ), 58, MFA(painting), 66. *Work:* Fla State Univ, Tallahassee; Rosenberg Mem Libr, First Hutchings-Sealy Nat Bank, Galveston, Tex; First Nat Bank, Sweetwater, Tex. *Comn:* Portrait-riverscape, Burt Reynolds, 81. *Exhib:* Third Monroe Ann, Masur Mus Art, La, 66; Midyear Show, Butler Inst Am Art, 66 & 67; Seventh Ann Nat Western Art Show, San Antonio, Tex, 69; solo exhib, Asheville Mus Art, NC, 72; 30th Ann Painting Exhib, Abilene Fine Arts Mus, Tex, 73; NC Watercolor Soc, Asheville Art Mus, NC, 76; and others. *Teaching:* Instr art, Fla State Univ, 64-65; instr painting, NTex State Univ, 66-68 & Western Carolina Univ, 73-75; artist in residence, High Hampton Inn & Country Club, 69-75. *Awards:* Transparent Watercolor Award, 73 & Purchase Award, 74; Tex Watercolor Soc; NC Watercolor Soc Purchase Award, 76. *Media:* Watercolor, Egg Tempera. *Mailing Add:* PO Box 522 Cashiers NC 28717

WHITLOCK, JOHN JOSEPH
MUSEUM DIRECTOR, EDUCATOR
b South Bend, Ind, Jan 7, 35. *Study:* Ball State Univ, BS, 57, MA, 63; Ind Univ, EdD, 71. *Work:* Ball State Univ, Muncie, Ind; Hanover Col, Ind. *Exhib:* One-man shows, Franklin Col, Ind, 69, Westminister Presby Church Gallery, 71, Unitarian Church Gallery, 71, Rockford, Ill, Grace St Luke's Festival Arts in Relig, 76 & Unitarian Fel, 83; and others. *Collections Arranged:* Senufo Door/A Study of its Iconography, 70; Ghana Door/A Study of its Origin, 70; Return to Humanism, 71; Carroll Cloar, 76; Japanese Woodblock Prints, 77; Bill Eggleston Photographs, 77; Richard Hunt Sculpture, 77; Recent Media, 77. *Pos:* Dir & cur, Burpee Art Mus, Rockford, Ill, 70-72; dir, Brooks Mem Art Gallery, Memphis, Tenn, 72-78; dir, Univ Mus, Southern Ill Univ, Carbondale, 78- *Teaching:* Art teacher & supvr, Union City, Ind, 57-59; art dir & teacher, Madison, Ind, 59-64; instr educ, Hanover Col, 64-66, asst prof art, 66-69; teaching assoc art educ, Ind Univ, Bloomington, 69-70; prof arts & humanities, Elgin Community Col, 70-72; prof, Mus Studies Prog, Southwestern at Memphis, 73-78; prof museology, Memphis State Univ, 76-78; prof mus studies, Southern Ill Univ, Carbondale, 78- *Awards:* Ball State Univ Fine Arts Purchase Award, 57. *Mem:* Am Asn Mus; Midwest Asn of Mus; Int Coul of Mus; Asn Art Mus Dirs. *Publ:* Auth, Art in the small college, Midwest Art Educ Conf, Houston, Tex, 65; auth, Reproduction was better than the painting, Art Educ, 71; auth, Return to Alexandria, Viewpoints, Ind Univ, 76; auth, articles, Mus Studies & Mus Scope, 76; contribr, Who pours the tea?, Art J, fall 81. *Mailing Add:* c/o Univ Mus Southern Ill Univ Carbondale IL 62901

WHITMORE, LENORE K
PAINTER
b Lemont, Pa, Aug 9, 20. *Study:* Pa State Univ, BS; Herron Sch Art; Provincetown Workshop; and with Garo Antresian, Will Barnet, Edward Manetta, Victor Candell & Leo Manso. *Work:* John Calvert Collection; G D Sickert Collection; Indianapolis Found; DePauw Univ, Jerone Picker Collection. *Exhib:* Eastern Mich Nat Polymer Exhib, 68; Audubon Artists Exhibs; Int de Femme, 69; Painters & Sculptors Soc NJ; traveling exhib, US, 75. *Pos:* Pres, Indianapolis Art League Found, 59-64. *Teaching:* Instr lit & painting, Ridgewood Sch Art, 69 & 70. *Awards:* Motorola Nat Art Exhib Awards, 61 & 62; Mark A Brown Award in Composition, Hoosier Salon, 63; Permanent Pigments Award, Painters & Sculptors Soc NJ, 68. *Mem:* Nat Asn Women Artists; Pen & Brush Club; Mod Artists Guild; Indianapolis Art League; Ind Artists Club. *Media:* Mixed Media. *Mailing Add:* Box 802 203 Oak St Ridgewood NJ 07450

WHITNEY, CHARLOTTE ARMIDE
PAINTER, JEWELER
b New York, NY, Dec 13, 23. *Study:* Corcoran Sch Art, George Washington Univ, with Eugen Weiscz & Peggy Bacon, BFA, 45; Cranbrook Acad Art, with Zoltan Sepeshy, MFA, 46. *Work:* Series of 24 wild plant water colors & series of 32 tree flower water colors, Kingman Mus, Battle Creek, Mich. *Exhib:* Miniature Painters, Sculptors & Engravers Soc, Washington, DC 20th exhib, Smithsonian Inst, 53; jewelry & metal work, Sioux City Art Ctr, 55; Drawings of Florence Traveling Exhib, Univ Calif, Davis, Ball State Univ & Battle Creek Art Ctr, Mich, 74-75; Exhib Water Colors, Kingman Mus, Battle Creek, Mich, 75 & 77; Battle Creek Artists Guild show, Battle Creek Art Ctr, Mich, 80. *Pos:* Co-dir, Whitney Galleries, Birmingham, Mich, 50-59; dir traveling exhib Olivet Restoration Drawings, Mich Coun Arts & Olivet, Mich City Hall, 74-75. *Teaching:* Art, Roeper City & Country Sch, Bloomfield Hills, Mich, 50-59, Olivet Col, Mich, 65-70 & Olivet Schs, Mich, 72-. *Awards:* Olivet Downtown Storefronts Restoration Award, Keep Mich Beautiful, 73. *Bibliog:* Joy Hakansen (auth), House is home and gallery, Detroit News, 3/54; Virginia Gust (auth), Olivet woman sketches youth into old buildings, Enquirer & News, Battle Creek, Mich, 2/4/73. *Mem:* Battle Creek Artists Guild (secy, 78-79, treas, 82-); Soc Archit Historians. *Media:* Watercolor, Technical Pen Drawing; Metalcraft. *Publ:* Auth, Children's Art, Olivet Col Press, 65. *Mailing Add:* 614 Summer St Olivet MI 49076

WHITNEY, EDGAR ALBERT
PAINTER, INSTRUCTOR
b New York, NY, Apr 16, 91. *Study:* Cooper Union; Art Students League; Nat Acad Design; Columbia Univ; Grand Cent Sch Art; also with Jay Comaway, Eliot O'Hara & Charles W Hawthorne; Cincinnati Art Col, hon MFA, 81. *Work:* Farnsworth Mus, Rockland, Maine; Nat Acad Design, NY; Art Club St Petersburg; Lake Worth Art Asn, Fla; pvt collection of Lawrence Rockefeller. *Exhib:* Am Watercolor Soc; Nat Art League; Nat Acad Design, 71 & 72. *Pos:* Art dir, McCann Erickson, New York; contrib ed, Am Artist Mag. *Teaching:* Instr watercolor & compos, Pratt Inst, 38-52; instr, NY Bot Gardens; creator-instr, Whitney Watercolor Tours. *Awards:* Audubon Artists Award, 58; Nat Art League Award, 52-58; Nat Acad Ranger Fund Purchase Prize, 69. *Bibliog:* David Clark (auth), Watercolor Holiday, Universal Films, Hollywood, Calif. *Mem:* Am Watercolor Soc (treas, 54-60); Philadelphia Watercolor Club; life mem Art Students League; hon life mem Southwestern Watercolor Socs; hon life mem La Watercolor Socs. *Media:* Watercolor. *Publ:* Auth, Watercolor: The Hows and Whys, 58 & Complete Guide to Watercolor, 65, Watson-Guptill; auth, Watercolor & casein articles, In: Grolier Encycl; and others. *Dealer:* Downtown Gallery 532 Chartres New Orleans LA 70130; Schramm Galleries 1507 E Las Olas Blvd Ft Lauderdale FL 33301. *Mailing Add:* 19-70 81st St Jackson Heights NY 11370

WHITNEY, MAYNARD MERLE
SCULPTOR, EDUCATOR
b Cedar Rapids, Iowa, Dec 18, 31. *Study:* Iowa Wesleyan Col, BA, 58; Univ Calif, Los Angeles, 60; Univ Iowa, 61; Univ Ore, MFA(sculptor), 65. *Work:* Joslyn Art Mus, Omaha, Nebr; Sheldon Art Gallery, Lincoln, Nebr; Denver Art Mus, Colo; Elder Art Gallery, Nebr Wesleyan Univ, Lincoln; Omaha Nat Bank, Nebr. *Comn:* Hanging Plexiglas sculpture, Ford-Warren Libr, Denver Pub Libr, 75. *Exhib:* Artrain (toured nine western states), 73; 13th Midwest Biennial, Joslyn Art Mus, Omaha, 74; 14th Ann Own Your Own Show, Pueblo Art Ctr, Colo, 74; one-man show, Sheldon Art Gallery, Lincoln, 70 & Kansas State Univ, Manhattan, 71; and others. *Teaching:* Chmn dept art, Nebr Wesleyan Univ, Lincoln, 65-72 & Colo Women's Col, Denver, 72-81. *Awards:* Creative Teaching Award, Nebr Wesleyan Univ, 67; Mus Purchase, 11th Midwest Biennial, Joslyn Art Mus, Omaha, 70; Purchase Award, 6th Ann Midland Exhib, Omaha Nat Bank, 70. *Media:* Multimedia, Stone. *Mailing Add:* 17668 E Loyola Dr F Aurora CO 80013

WHITNEY, RICHARD WHEELER
PAINTER
b Burlington, Vt, Jan 22, 46. *Study:* Univ NH, Durham, BA, 68; with Sidney F Willis, Bennington, NH, 65; with R H Ives Gammell, Boston, 66-71. *Work:* New Hampshire State House, Concord; Univ Chicago; Mass State House Collection & Suffolk Univ Collection, Boston; Anderson House Mus, Washington, DC; and others. *Comn:* Portrait, Former Undersecy Educ, Tehran, 77; Mercersburg Acad, Pa, 81; Lee Co Pub Libr, Sanford, NC, 81; Alaska Scenic Collection, Little Susitna Co, Anchorage, 83; Boston Univ Sch Medicine, 83; and others. *Exhib:* Allied Artists Am Nat Exhibs, New York, 76, 77, 80, 81 & 83; solo exhibs, Guild Boston Artists, 80 & 82; Maryhill Mus, Wash; Springfield Mus, Utah; Amarillo Art Ctr, Tex, 83; and others. *Collections Arranged:* Allied Artists Am, New Eng Exhib, 82. *Teaching:* Instr painting, Sharon Arts Ctr, NH, 71-77; instr art, Cushing Acad, Ashburnham, 71-80. *Awards:* Am Artists Nat Art Competition, New York, 78; Crescent Gallery Award, Allied Artists, New York, 80; Medal of Honor, Am Artist Prof League, 83. *Bibliog:* Eric Maloney (auth), Richard W Whitney, Art Voices Mag, 81; Charles Movalli (auth), A conversation with Richard Whitney, Am Artist Mag, 82. *Mem:* Allied Artists Am; Portraits Inc; Guild Boston Artists; Nat Arts Club; Am Portrait Soc. *Media:* Oil. *Publ:* Auth, Principles of Visual Impressionism, Checkerberry Hill Press, 79; auth, Return to Excellence, Profile, fall 83. *Dealer:* Vose Galleries Boston Inc 238 Newbury St Boston MA 02116. *Mailing Add:* 40 Mechanic St Keene NH 03431

WHITNEY, SUSAN GILLIAN
DEALER, GALLERY DIRECTOR
b Dublin, Ireland, Mar 31, 51; Can citizen. *Study:* Sir George Williams Univ, Montreal, 69; Univ Regina, 70. *Collections Arranged:* David Thauberger: 49th Parallel, New York, 81; Made in Saskatchewan (folk art), 82; Wilf Perreault, 83; and others. *Pos:* Dir, Kesik Gallery, Regina, Sask, 78-79; dir, Susan Whitney Gallery, Regina, 79- *Specialty:* Contemporary prairie artists, folk art and funky ceramic artists, including Joe Fafard, David Gilhooly, Vic Cicansky, David Thauberger, Russ Yuristy & Wilf Perreault. *Mailing Add:* 1627 Victoria Ave Regina SK S4P 0P8 Canada

WHITNEY, WILLIAM KUEBLER
PAINTER, HISTORIAN
b New Orleans, La, July 6, 21. *Study:* Corcoran Sch Art, Washington, DC, 40-42, with still life painter, N Cikovsky, Sr; Wayne State Univ, Detroit, 56-57; Cranbrook Acad Art, Bloomfield Hills, Mich, with Zoltan Sepeshy, BFA, 49, MFA, 58. *Work:* Mus of Cranbrook Acad of Art; Battle Creek Civic Art Ctr. *Comn:* Four murals, New Eaton Country Court House, Charlotte, Mich, 75. *Exhib:* Soc of Washington Artists Ann, 42 & Corcoran Biennial of Am Art, 45, Corcoran Gallery of Art, Washington, DC; Honolulu Artists Ann, Honolulu Acad of Art, 44; Mich Artists Ann, 47 & Works in Progress in Mich, 48-49, Detroit Inst Art; one-man show, Drawings of 19th Century Mid-Mich Bldgs, Octagon House, Am Inst of Archit, Washington, DC, 72, Drawings of Florence, Univ Calif, Davis, Ball State Univ, Muncie, Ind & Battle Creek Art Ctr, Mich, 74-75; Battle Creek 100, Battle Creek Art Ctr, 77; plus others. *Collections Arranged:* 22 Michigan Artists at Olivet, 73, Paintings by Irving Althage, 74 & Paintings by Michael Cassino, 76, Armstrong Mus, Olivet Col, Mich. *Pos:* Co-dir, Whitney Galleries, Birmingham, Mich, 50-59. *Teaching:* From instr to prof art hist, painting & drawing, Olivet Col, 59-79, head art dept, 60-75, dir, Armstrong Mus, 72-79. *Awards:* Bronze Medal Still Life, Soc Washington Artists, DC, 42; Award of Merit, Mich Acad of Sci, Arts & Lett, 50. *Bibliog:* Joy Hakanson (auth), House is home and gallery, Detroit News, 3/54; Nancy Crawley (auth), Paving the way to innovative art, Battle Creek Enquirer & News, 4/77. *Mem:* Soc of Archit Historians; Battle Creek Artists' Guild; Am Asn of Univ Prof. *Media:* Acrylic, Technical Pen Drawing. *Res:* Bronze doors of St Zeno, Vernoa, Italy; 19th century American houses in the midwest. *Collection:* Nineteenth and twentieth century paintings, prints and drawings. *Publ:* Illusr, Drawings of Florence, Olivet Col, 71. *Mailing Add:* 614 Summer St Olivet MI 49076

WHITSON (PETER WHITSON WARREN)
DRAFTSMAN, COLLAGE ARTIST
b Concord, Mass, Sept 7, 41. *Study:* Univ NH, BA, 63; Univ Iowa, MFA, 67; Eastern Montana Col. *Work:* Univ NH; Univ Iowa; Kansas City Art Inst; Mod Museet, Stockholm, Sweden; Galeria Teatru Studio, Warsaw, Poland. *Exhib:* One-man shows, SLUJ Int, 74 & 75, State Univ NY, Fredonia, 75; and others; Mod Museet, Stockholm; Nat Art Gallery, Wellington, NZ; Color Collages, Yellowstone Art Ctr, Billings, Mont, 80; and others. *Pos:* Pres, founder, Western Dakota Junk Co, Billings, Mont, 69-; founder & pres, Acad Neodada, 74-79; pres, Nat Acad Conceptualists, 79-80; ed & publr, SLUJ Press, 75-; gallery dir, Eastern Mont Col, 78-79, slide librn, 79-80; art ed, Alkali Flats Mag, 81. *Teaching:* Asst drawing, Univ Iowa, 65-67; from instr to assoc prof drawing, design & art hist, Eastern Mont Col, 67-80. *Mem:* United SLUJ Workers; Mont Miniature Art Soc; and others. *Publ:* Auth, Al's Ham 'n' Egger & Body Shop Again, Basilisk Press, 74; The SLUJ Book, 76, Lost in the Mail, 78, Umbrella, 79 & Autoroticism, 80, SLUJ Press; auth & contribr to many other corresp art publs, 69- *Mailing Add:* Western Dakota Junk Co 902 24th St W Billings MT 59102

WHITSON, ANGIE
SCULPTOR, PAINTER
b San Jose, Calif, July 13, 32. *Study:* Pasadena Mus Art, with Thomas Larsen, 74; Art League, Los Angeles, Calif, with Hal Reed, 74-78; Northridge Univ, Calif, with David Elder, 75-76. *Work:* Pierce Col, Conoga Park, Calif; Ore Hist Soc; Xerox Corp. *Comn:* Sculptures, Golden Nugget, Atlantic City, NJ, McDonald's, Greenville, NC, Bernhardt Iron Works, Harbor City, Calif, Lozano, Mexico City & Gassaway, Nev. *Exhib:* Art-A-Fair, Ann Festival Laguna, Laguna Beach, Calif, 77-83; Miniature Soc NJ, Nutley Gallery, NJ, 79; Miniature Soc Washington, DC, Archit Inst, 79; Cody Art Gallery, Wyo, 79; La Luz, NMex, 83; Saddleback Art Gallery, Anaheim, Calif, 82-83. *Teaching:* Instr sculpture, Pierce Col, Conoga Park, Calif, 78-80. *Awards:* First Place, El Centro Int, San Pilot Club, 79; Gold Medals, San Gabriel Fine Art Asn, 79, 80 & 81; Sculpture Award, 79 & eight Gold Medals, 81-83, Miniature Soc Washington DC. *Bibliog:* Article, Nevada Sun, Las Vegas, 82. *Mem:* San Gabriel Fine Arts Asn (bd mem, 78-81). *Media:* Oil, Acrylic. *Mailing Add:* 5105 Tendilla Ave Woodland Hills CA 91364

WHITTOME, IRENE DIANNE
SCULPTOR, PAINTER
b Mar 5, 42; Can citizen. *Study:* Vancouver Sch Art, BFA, 63. *Work:* Nat Gallery Can; Montreal Mus Fine Arts; Bibliot Nat, Paris; Mus Art Mod, Buenos Aires; Munic Mus, Birmingham, England. *Comn:* Print, Art Bank Can, 78; installation, Can Coun, New York, 79; sculpture, Hakone Open-Air Mus, Tokyo, 84. *Exhib:* Int Grafik-Bienale, Frenchen, Ger, 72; Paperworks, Nat Gallery Can, 78; solo exhibs, Montreal Mus Fine Arts, 80, Vancouver Art Gallery, 81, Winnnipeg Art Gallery, 81 & Hamilton Art Gallery, 81. *Collections Arranged:* The Second Dalhousie Drawing Exhibition (auth, catalog), Dalhousie Art Gallery, Halifax, NS, 77. *Teaching:* Assoc prof art, Concordia Univ, Montreal, 68- *Awards:* Medal Hon, Int Grafik-Biennale, Frechen, Ger, 72. *Bibliog:* N Laliberte Mogelon (auth), Art in Boxes, Van Nostrand-Reinhold, 74. *Mem:* Royal Can Acad Arts; Jack Chambers Found. *Publ:* Auth, Book of Insects, Vancouver Art Gallery, 63. *Dealer:* Yajima Galerie Fine Arts 307 Ste Catherine Ouest Suite 515 Montreal PQ H2X 2A3. *Mailing Add:* 18 Rue Laurier Ouest Montreal PQ H2T 2N3 Canada

WHITTY-JOHNSON, PATRICIA
PAINTER
b New Orleans, La, Mar 28, 43. *Study:* Newcomb Art Sch, Tulane Univ, BFA, with Ida Kohlmeyer; Washington Univ, St Louis, Mo, MFA, with Arthur Osver; Rome, Italy, 68-69. *Work:* Miss Mus Art; State of La; Ctr, Oklahoma City. *Exhib:* Drawing & Small Sculpture Show, Ball State Univ, Muncie, Ind, 65, 70 & 71; Tex Painting & Sculpture Exhib, Dallas Mus Fine Arts, 71; one-person shows, Loft-on-Strand Gallery, Galveston, Tex, 77; 13th & 14th Ann Okla Exhib of Painting, Okla Art Ctr, 71-72; 12th Midwest Biennial, Joslyn Mus of Art, Omaha, Nebr, 72; two-person show, Vincent Mann Gallery, New Orleans, 74; Southern Realism, Miss Mus Art, 79; Browsard Gallery, La State Capitol Bldg, 79. *Pos:* Co-dir, Johnson-Whitty Gallery, New Orleans, 75-80; co-chmn & founder, Vis Artists Prog, Newcomb Art Sch, Tulane Univ, 76-80; co-proj dir, La: Maj Works, 80. *Teaching:* Vis artist, St Louis Community Col, 78. *Awards:* Molly Palfrey Mem, Second Prize, SW Graphics, San Antonio, Tex, 72; Triennial Cash Award, Contemp Arts Ctr, New Orleans, 79; La State Arts Coun grants, 79 & 80. *Bibliog:* Alberta Collier (auth), The world of art, Times Picayune, 1/74; Suzanne Fosberg (auth), Johnson-Whitty's artists for the 70s, Courier, 5/76; George E Jordan (auth), Local artists reveal images of themselves, Times Picayune, 10/77. *Mem:* Artists Equity. *Media:* Acrylic, Oil. *Mailing Add:* c/o Galerie Simonne Stern 2727 Prytania St New Orleans LA 70130

WHYTE, BRUCE LINCOLN
DEALER, PUBLISHER
b New York, NY, Mar 13, 41. *Study:* Fordham Univ, BS, 62; NY Univ, MS, 63. *Pos:* Founder & chmn, Original Print Collectors Group, Ltd, 72-; gov, Nat Arts Club, 73-76, chmn graphic arts, 73- *Awards:* Best in Art Catalogs USA, Maxwell Sroge Publ. *Bibliog:* Leo Lloyd (auth), Graphic art by mail, United Press Int, 6/4/79; Sandra Salmans (auth), Good buys in fine art, New York Times, 1/25/81. *Mem:* Soc Am Graphic Artists; Fine Arts Publ Asn. *Specialty:* Contemporary original prints and fine old master prints. *Mailing Add:* c/o Original Print Collectors Group 215 Lexington Ave New York NY 10016

WHYTE, RAYMOND A
PAINTER
b Canmore, Alta, Aug 3, 23; US citizen. *Study:* Art Students League, scholar, with Edwin Dickinson; Venice, Paris & Madrid; Univ Toronto. *Work:* Crocker Art Mus, Sacramento, Calif; Mills Col; Stevensons Col; De Beers Mus SAfrica. *Comn:* Mural, Austral Oil Co, Houston, Tex, 65; triptych, Gerald B Kara, New York, 68; memorabilia (oil), Bernard G Cantor, Beverly Hills, Calif, 70; Orson Bean, Calif; large triptych, B Gerald Cantor, New York, 77; plus many other portrait & painting comns. *Exhib:* Nat Acad, 49-; one-man shows, Galerie DeTours, San Francisco, 62-83 & Crocker Art Mus, Sacramento, 67; Family Portraits 1730-1976, Philadelphia Mus of Art; Tweed Gallery, NJ, 82; Trompe L'Oiel Gallery, New York, 83; and others. *Bibliog:* Kevin Sanders (auth), Contemporary surrealists, ABC TV Art Rev, 2/3/72; John Angelini (auth), Profile in Whyte, NJ Music & Arts, 6/77; article, Univ Colo Quart, 78; and others. *Media:* Oil. *Dealer:* Galerie DeTours 701 Sutter St San Francisco CA 94109; Trompe L'Oiel Gallery 24 E 81st St New York NY 10028. *Mailing Add:* 30 Fayson Lakes Rd Kinnelon NJ 07405

WICKISER, RALPH LEWANDA
ADMINISTRATOR, PAINTER
b Greenup, Ill, Mar 20, 10. *Study:* Art Inst Chicago, 28-31; Eastern Ill Univ, BA, 34, hon PhD, 56; Vanderbilt & Peabody, Tiffany fel, 34-35, MA, 35, PhD, 38. *Work:* Delgado Mus, New Orleans, La; Lehigh Univ, Bethlehem, Pa; La Art Comn, Baton Rouge; Mint Mus, Charlotte, NC; High Mus, Atlanta, Ga; and others. *Exhib:* Libr Cong Ann Print Exhib, 48; Whitney Mus Am Art Ann, 53-; United Nations, New York, 75; Lotus Gallery, New York, 76 & 77; Savage Gallery, Boston, 77; Mikelson Gallery, Washington, DC, 77; Newman Gallery, Philadelphia, 77; Esta Robison Gallery, New York, 82; and others. *Teaching:* From instr to prof painting & chmn dept, La State Univ, 37-56; prof painting & dir div art educ, State Univ NY Col New Paltz, 56-59; prof painting, Pratt Inst, 59-, chmn art educ dept, 59-65, chmn grad art, 65-75. *Awards:* Grant for One Yr Painting & Study, 52; and others. *Bibliog:* Artist as a teacher, Col Art J, winter 51-52. *Mem:* Col Art Asn Am. *Media:* Oil. *Publ:* Auth, Introduction to Art Activities, 47; contribr, Education of the Artist, 51; contribr, Contemporary Painter's Attitude Toward Tradition, 55; auth, Introduction to Art Education, 57; co-auth, Higher Education & the Arts. *Mailing Add:* Box 263 Bearsville NY 12409

WICKS, EUGENE CLAUDE
PAINTER, EDUCATOR
b Coleharbor, NDak, Oct 7, 31. *Study:* Univ Colo, BFA, MFA, 59. *Work:* Art Inst Chicago, Ill; Philadelphia Print Club, Pa; Lakeview Art Ctr, Peoria, Ill; Decatur Art Ctr, Ill; Am Fedn Arts Overseas Collection. *Exhib:* Libr Cong, Washington, DC, 59; Brooklyn Mus Print Exhib, 60, 62 & 64; Northwest Printmakers Ann Exhib, 60-68; 1st Biennial Exhibs of Prints, Art Inst Chicago, 62; Philadelphia Acad 185th Ann, 63; one-man show, Edinburgh Col of Art, Scotland, 64 & Western Mich Univ, Kalamazoo, 75, plus others. *Pos:* Vis artist, Dept Art, Univ Colo, summer 63; dir, Nat Asn of Schs of Art, 75- *Teaching:* Prof painting, Univ Ill, Urbana, 59-; dir, Nat Sch Art & Design, 77- *Awards:* Purchase Awards, 1st Biennial, Art Inst Chicago, 62, Print Exhib, 62 & 24th Ann, Decatur Art Ctr, 68. *Mem:* Nat Asn Schs Art & Design; Nat Coun Art Adminr; Col Art Asn. *Mailing Add:* 2121 Gunn Dr Champaign IL 61820

WIDMER, GWEN ELLEN
PHOTOGRAPHER, EDUCATOR
b Chicago, Ill, Mar 10, 45. *Study:* Goshen Col, Ind, BA, 67; Art Inst Chicago, MFA, 73. *Work:* J B Speed Art Mus, Louisville, Ky; Madison Art Ctr, Wis; Kalamazoo Inst Arts, Mich. *Exhib:* Photogr Midwest, Walker Art Ctr, Minneapolis, 73; The Invented Landscape, New Mus, New York, 79; The Hand Colored Photograph, Philadelphia Col Art, Pa, 79; Attitudes: Photog in the 1970's, Santa Barbara Mus Art, Calif, 79; Color in Question, The Catskill Ctr Photog, Woodstock, NY, 79; one-person show, Camerawork Gallery, San Francisco, Calif, 80; and many others. *Teaching:* Instr photog, Univ Ill, Urbana/Champaign, 72-74; instr photog, Univ Northern Iowa, Cedar Falls, 76- *Awards:* Photog Fel, Nat Endowment Arts, 75 & 80; Third Prize, Bicentennial Exhib of Photog, Andromeda Gallery, Buffalo, NY, 77; Purchase Award, Light II, Humboldt State Univ, 77. *Mem:* Soc for Photog Educ. *Publ:* Contribr, Popular Photography, Vol 75 (2), Ziff-Davis, 74; contribr, Self--Portrayal, Friends of Photog, Carmel, Calif, 78; Darkroom Dynamics, Curtin & London, Marblehead, Mass, 79; contribr, Color, Life Libr of Photography, Time-Life Bks, 80; and others. *Mailing Add:* 4840 Southern SE Albuquerque NM 87108

WIDSTROM, EDWARD FREDERICK
SCULPTOR
b Wallingford, Conn, Nov 1, 03. *Study:* Detroit Sch Art; Art Students League. *Work:* New Haven Paint & Clay, Inc, Conn; Brookgreen Gardens, SC; Benton Col, Conn; Meriden Art & Crafts Asn, Conn; also in pvt collections. *Comn:* 36 Presidents of US, Int Silver Co, Meriden, 39-70; portrait reliefs, St Stevens Sch, Bridgeport, Conn, 50, Munic Bldg, Meriden, 66 & Marionist Sch, Thompson, Conn, 68. *Exhib:* Nat Acad Design, New York, 40-75; Nat Sculpture Soc, New York, 60-81; Hudson Valley Art Asn, White Plains, NY, 60-80; Am Artists Prof League, New York, 69-71; Coun Am Artists, New York. *Awards:* Silver Medal, 72, John Spring Award, 73 & C P Dietsch Award, 75, Nat Sculpture Soc. *Mem:* Nat Sculpture Soc; Am Artists Prof League; Hudson Valley Art Asn; Conn Acad Fine Arts; Meriden Arts & Crafts Asn. *Media:* Bronze, Metal. *Mailing Add:* 21 Lydale Pl Meriden CT 06450

WIEBE, CHARLES M
DEALER, HISTORIAN
b Morgantown, WVa, Oct 8, 49. *Study:* WVa Univ, Morgantown, BA(painting), 72; Univ Florence, Italy, with Eugenio Battisti, 74-75; Pa State Univ, MA(art hist), 79. *Pos:* Gallery rep, Marson Ltd, Baltimore, 78-80; owner & dir, Wiebe Gallery, Pittsburgh, 80- *Teaching:* Lectr, Vatican Mus, Rome, 75; lectr Japanese prints, Univ Pittsburgh, 84- *Mem:* Col Art Asn Am. *Res:* Italian Renaissance art. *Specialty:* Japanese woodblock prints; old master prints; contemporary paintings and sculpture. *Mailing Add:* Wiebe & Bonwell Galleries 705 Liberty Ave Pittsburgh PA 15222

WIEDENHOEFT, RENATE
PHOTOGRAPHER
b Berlin, Ger, Nov 23, 42. *Study:* Univ Wis, Madison; Autodidact; also with Dr Ron Wiedenhoeft. *Pos:* Co-founder, partner & pres, Saskai Cult Doc, 66- *Mem:* Col Art Asn; Art Libr Soc. *Res:* Western European art and architecture from the Renaissance to early 20th century. *Interests:* Photography of art and architecture, the cataloging of images and the distribution of color transparencies to museums and universities throughout the world. *Publ:* Auth, Saskia Cultural Documentation, pvt publ, 77. *Mailing Add:* Saskia Ltd 6931 S Yukon Way Littleton CO 80123

WIEGAND, ROBERT
PAINTER, VIDEO ARTIST
b Mineola, NY, May 15, 34. *Study:* Albright Art Sch, Buffalo, NY; State Univ NY Buffalo, BS(art educ); NY Univ. *Work:* New York Dept Parks; Lever Bros Co, New York; Reliance Savings Bank, New York; Mus Mod Art, New York; New York Univ, New York. *Exhib:* Mus Mod Art, 69; one-man shows, Everson Mus, 79, Film Anthology Arch, 80, Kitchen Ctr, 80, Global Village, 81, The Mudd Club, 81 & Jeda Gallery, 83; plus many others. *Pos:* Artist, Comprehensive Employment Training Act, 79-80. *Awards:* New York Bd Trade Award, 70; Rockefeller Found Travelling Artist's fel, 77. *Bibliog:* Soichi Furita (ed), Graphics in the Environment, Graphic Design of the World, Kodansha Pub, Japan, 74; Ira Schneider & Beryl Korot (ed), Video Art, Harcourt Brace, 74; New American Art, Compton's Yrbk, Encycl Britannica, 75. *Mailing Add:* 16 Greene St New York NY 10013

WIEGHORST, OLAF
PAINTER
b Denmark, Apr 30, 1899. *Work:* Nat Cowboy Hall Fame, Oklahoma City; Whitney Mus, Cody, Wyo. *Exhib:* One-man shows, Cowboy Hall Fame, Oklahoma City, 74, San Diego Fine Art, Calif, 80, Tucson Mus Art, Ariz, 81 & Gilcrease, Tulsa, Okla, 82. *Bibliog:* William Reed (auth), Olaf Wieghorst, Northland Press, 72. *Media:* Oil. *Mailing Add:* 5037 Bluff Pl El Cajon CA 92020

WIELAND, JOYCE
PAINTER, FILMMAKER
b Toronto, Ont, 1931. *Study:* Cent Tech Sch, grad. *Work:* Nat Gallery Can; Montreal Mus Fine Arts, Can; Philadelphia Mus Art; Mus Mod Art Film Archives, New York; Royal Belg Film Archives; and others. *Comn:* Toronto Transit Comn, Spadina Line, 77; Laidlaw Found, 81-82. *Exhib:* The Wall-Art for Architecture Traveling Exhib, Art Gallery Ont, 69 & Rothmans Art Gallery, Stratford, Ont, 70; Oberhausen Film Festival, Austria, 69; Survey '70-Realism(e)s, Montreal Mus Fine Arts & Art Gallery Ont, 70; Eight Artists from Canada, Tel Aviv Mus, Israel, 70; Directors' Fortnight, Cannes Film Festival, France, 70; Isaacs Gallery, Toronto, 83; New Perceptions: Portraits, Art Gallery at Harbourfront, 83. *Teaching:* Instr, Nova Scotia Col Art, 71, Arts Sake Inc, Toronto, 79-82. *Awards:* Can Coun Grants, 66, 68 & 72; Officer of the Order of Canada, 72; Three Canadian Film Awards, 77. *Mem:* Royal Can Acad Arts. *Dealer:* Isaacs Gallery 832 Yonge St Toronto ON Can; Yajima Gallery Montreal PQ Can. *Mailing Add:* 497 Queen St E Toronto ON M5A 1V1 Canada

WIENER, DANIEL
SCULPTOR
b Cambridge, Mass, Dec 30, 54. *Study:* Univ Calif, Berkeley, AB, 77. *Work:* Int Paper Co, New York; Atlantic Richfield Co, Los Angeles; La Jolla Mus Contemp Art, Calif. *Exhib:* Santa Barbara Mus, Calif, 79; Mus Mod Art, Kyoto & Tokyo, Japan, 81; Exhib Ctr MRO, Kanazawa, Japan, 82; Visual Arts Ctr Anchorage, 82; Oakland Mus, Calif, 82; Brown Univ Art Gallery, 83; and others. *Awards:* Exhib Award, Nat Small Format Show, Newspace Gallery, Corvallis, Ore, 79. *Bibliog:* Kyoto Mus, Glass in the Modern World, Tankosha Publ, 81; Suzaan Boettger (auth), From the sunny side..., Artforum, 1/83; Kenneth Baker (auth), Space invaders, Boston Phoenix, 1/18/83; and others. *Media:* Glass, Wood. *Mailing Add:* c/o Wirtz Gallery 345 Sutter St San Francisco CA 94108

WIENER, PHYLLIS AMES
PAINTER
b Iowa City, Iowa, Sept 17, 21. *Study:* Univ Minn, 52, 54 & 56, with Cameron Booth; Inst Allende, San Miguel, Mex, with Pinto, 61. *Work:* Minneapolis Art Inst; Walker Art Ctr, Minneapolis; J Patrick Lannon Collection, Chicago; Am Asn Univ Women; Pillsbury Collection, Minneapolis; and others. *Comn:* Three dimensional painting, Norwest Bank Rochester, Minn, 82; diptych, Cathedral St Mark, Minneapolis, 83. *Exhib:* Walker Biennial, 52-64; US State Dept Traveling Show, 62; Pa Acad Fine Arts, Philadelphia, 64; Butler Inst Art, Youngstown, Ohio, 65; one-man show, Minneapolis Art Inst, 67; retrospective, Univ Minn, 81; Phyllis Needlman Gallery, Chicago, 80 & 82; Pindar Gallery, New York, 84; and others. *Teaching:* Instr oil painting, Walker Art Ctr, 60-66; instr composition, Univ Minn Exten Div, 62-72; instr, Art Ctr Minn, 60-83. *Awards:* Walker Art Ctr Biennial Awards, 54, 58 & 62; Minneapolis Inst Art Awards, 55, 58 & 62; Individual Artist's grant, Minn State Arts Bd, 80. *Bibliog:* G Brush (auth), Phyllis Wiener at Needlman Gallery, New Art Examiner, 2/81. *Mem:* Minn State Arts Bd; Womens Art Registry Minn. *Media:* Watercolor, Acrylic. *Dealer:* Warm Gallery 414 First Ave N Minneapolis MN 55401; Barbara Callaway One SW First Ave Rochester MN 55901. *Mailing Add:* 1225 La Salle Apt 801 Minneapolis MN 55403

WIENER, SAM (EVANGELINE TABASCO)
SCULPTOR, INSTRUCTOR
b Shreveport, La, Mar 24, 28. *Study:* Yale Sch Fine Arts, BFA, 51; Univ Mich. *Work:* Va Mus Fine Arts, Richmond; Univ; Mus Fine Arts, Columbia, SC. *Comn:* Glazed tile murals, Am Airlines Terminal, Kennedy Airport, New York, 60; stained glass windows, Agudath Sholom Congregation, Stamford, Conn, 67; glazed tile murals, Abraham and Straus, Smithtown, NY, 68; lobby wall hangings, ITT Am Bldg, New York, 70; modular sculptures, Vest Pocket Park Proj, New York, 71. *Exhib:* Archit Art, Mus Contemp Crafts, New York, 62; Objects USA, Smithsonian Inst & traveling, 69-71; NY Correspondence Sch, Whitney Mus Am Art, 70; Am Painting & Sculpture Today, Indianapolis Mus, 77; Five Artists in Glass, San Jose Mus, Calif, 77; solo exhibs, The Supermarket of Art, Anderson Gallery, Va Commonwealth Univ, 81; Sam Wiener & Evangeline Tabasco, Herbert Johnson Mus, 81 & Splendors of the Sohites, Aspen Ctr Fine Arts, Lowe Mus, Miami, Fla & seven others, 82-83. *Teaching:* Adj asst prof design & drawing, Columbia Univ Archit Sch, 60; instr visual commun, Cooper Union Art Sch, 67-68; instr drawing & compos, Parsons Sch Art, 82- *Bibliog:* Noel Frackman (auth), article, Arts Mag, 4/78; Peter Frank (auth), article, Village Voice, 4/78; Mark Stevens (auth), The splendors of ancient Soho, Newsweek, 10/6/80. *Media:* All. *Dealer:* O K Harris 383 W Broadway New York NY 10012. *Mailing Add:* 451 W Broadway New York NY 10012

WIESENDANGER, MARGARET HARRIS
CONSERVATOR, PAINTER
b Westport, Conn, Nov 12, 08. *Study:* Pa Mus Sch Indust Art, grad, 32; Columbia Univ, summer art classes, 32 & 37; Syracuse Univ, summer art classes, 33. *Exhib:* Am Watercolor Soc Show, Whitney Mus Am Art, New York, 35; Okla Ann, Philbrook Art Ctr, Tulsa, 43-68; joint show, Univ of South Art Gallery, Sewanee, Tenn, 69; one-man show, Spiva Art Ctr, Joplin, Mo, 73. *Collections Arranged:* Cases in Egyptian Gallery, Opening of Mabee-Gerrer Mus, Shawnee, Okla, 79; Opening Exhibit & Paintings by Floyd Gates, Tulsa Co Hist Soc Mus. *Pos:* Conservator, W E Groves Collection, 68-72; conservator, Mabee-Gerrer Mus, Shawnee, Okla, 74-, bd mem, 79- *Teaching:* Teacher, Norwich Art Sch, Conn, 33-37 & Philbrook Art Ctr, Tulsa, Okla, 42-52. *Awards:* Hon Mention, Philbrook Art Ctr, Tulsa, Okla, 48. *Bibliog:* Janet Keene (auth), Like a dome of many colors, Tulsalite, 11/13/67; news item, Exhibit by Tulsa artist scheduled at Art Center, Joplin Globe, Mo, 10/3/73; M De Vinna (auth), Art column, Tulsa Sunday World, 10/7/73 & 12/9/73. *Media:* Oil, Watercolor. *Collection:* Restorable important paintings & prints; African & Pacific sculpture. *Publ:* Coauth, Louisiana Painters and Paintings in the Collection of W E Groves, W E Groves Gallery, 71; auth, Commentary miscellany, 80. *Dealer:* Cremer Gallery 8575 E 31st Pl Tulsa OK 74145. *Mailing Add:* PO Box 27063 Tulsa OK 74149

WIESENDANGER, MARTIN WOLFGANG
HISTORIAN, CONSERVATOR
b Ger, Feb 13, 08; US & Swiss citizen. *Study:* Columbia Univ, 26-29; Murray Pease's Lab, Metrop Mus Art, conserv tech, 29-35. *Exhib:* Okla Ann, Philbrook Art Ctr, Tulsa, 44-46; Univ of South Art Gallery, Sewanee, Tenn. 69. *Collections Arranged:* Assisted Thomas Gilcrease in assembling his collection, Gilcrease Mus Hist & Art, Tulsa, 39-47; Paintings from the W E Groves Collection (auth, catalog), W E Groves Gallery, 69; History of the Color Print, Philbrook Art Ctr, Tulsa, 79. *Pos:* First dir, Thomas Gilcrease Mus, Tulsa, 42-47; mem arts & exhib comt, Philbrook Art Ctr, Tulsa, 43-68 & 77-; conservator, Mabee-Gerrer Mus, Shawnee, Okla, 74-, bd mem, 79-81, bd chmn, 81-83. *Teaching:* Instr, Univ Tulsa, Okla, 42-50; teacher & movie film producer, Childrens Classes, Philbrook Art Ctr, Tulsa, 57 & 58. *Awards:* First Place Graphics, Philbrook Art Ctr, 50. *Bibliog:* Janet Keene (auth), Like a dome of many colors, Tulsalite, 11/13/67; David Milsten (auth), chap I, In: Biography of Thomas Gilcrease, Bk 4, Naylor Co, 69; Dean Krakel (auth), Adventures in Western Art, Lovell Press, 77. *Mem:* Int Inst Conserv; fel Am Inst Conserv. *Media:* Metal Sculpture; Graphics. *Res:* Pre-Columbian art and archaeology of Yucatan in movies and slides. *Collection:* Restorable important paintings & prints; African & Pacific sculpture. *Publ:* Auth, An Indian foundation, Southwest Rev, autumn 46; illusr, Indian drawings of Cimarron County by W D Hartley, Ford Times, 54; coauth, Louisiana Painters and Paintings in the Collection of W E Groves, W E Groves Gallery, 71; auth & illusr, Beneath optima earth, Okla Today, 75; auth, Montgomery, the corn painter, Newslett Tulsa Co Hist Soc, 76; and others. *Mailing Add:* PO Box 27063 Tulsa OK 74149

WIESENFELD, PAUL
PAINTER
b Los Angeles, Calif, Apr 1, 42. *Study:* Chouinard Art Inst, Los Angeles, Calif, BFA, 59; Kunstakademie, Munich, Germany, 66; Ind Univ, MFA, 68. *Work:* Whitney Mus Art, New York; Va Mus Fine Arts, Richmond; Stadtische Galerie im Lenbachhaus, Munich, Germany; Albright Knox Art Gallery, Buffalo, NY; Vienna Mus Moderner Kunst, Austria. *Exhib:* Twenty-Two Realists, Whitney Mus Am Art, New York, 70; Albright Knox Art Gallery, Buffalo, NY, 73; New Images in Am Figurative Painting, Queens Mus, NY, 74; 7 Realists, Yale Univ Art Gallery, New Haven, Conn, 74; one-man shows, Neue Galerie, Aachen Mus, 76 & Lenbacchaus, Munich, West Germany, 80; Contemp Naturalism, Nassau Co Mus Fine Art, Roslyn, NY, 80; Contemp Am Realism since 1960, Pa Acad Fine Arts, Philadelphia. *Teaching:* Asst prof fine arts, State Univ NY, Buffalo, 69-73. *Awards:* Tiffany Found Grant, 63; First Julius Hallgarten Prize, Nat Acad Design, 72; Nat Endowment Arts Award, 76. *Bibliog:* Pincus-Witten (auth), 22 realists, Artforum, 4/70; Ruth Bass (auth), Paul Wiesenfeld, Art News, 11/81; Hilton Kramer (auth), Paul Wiesenfeld, New York Times, 5/8/81. *Media:* Oil. *Mailing Add:* c/o Robert Schoelkopf Gallery 825 Madison Ave New York NY 10021

WIGGINS, BILL
PAINTER
b Roswell, NMex, Sept 24, 17. *Study:* NMex Mil Inst, Roswell; Abilene Christian Univ, Eng, with Francis Speight; Fed Art Proj, Work Proj Admin, Roswell. *Work:* Roswell Mus & Art Ctr. *Exhib:* Newport 43rd Ann, RI, 54; Low Ruins Nat, Tubac, Ariz, 65; 5th Arts Nat, Tyler, Tex, 68; Mainstreams 68, Marietta Col, Ohio; Ark State Univ Nat, Jonesboro, 70. *Teaching:* Instr art, Roswell Mus & Art Ctr, 55-63. *Bibliog:* Elena Montes (auth), Bill Wiggins of Roswell, NMex Mag, 10/65; United States art, La Rev Mod, Paris, 12/65; Walt Wiggins (auth), Wiggins: A Thirty-Year Retrospective, 82. *Mem:* Artists Equity Asn. *Media:* Oil. *Mailing Add:* 711 W Eighth St Roswell NM 88201

WIGGINS, WALTON WRAY
WRITER, PHOTOGRAPHER
b Roswell, NMex, May 13, 24. *Study:* Signal Corps Motion Picture Cameraman Sch, 45. *Exhib:* Solo exhibs, Dallas Mus Fine Art, 43 & Roswell Mus & Art Ctr, NMex, 55 & 58. *Collections Arranged:* Pioneer Savings & Trust permanent collection (auth, catalog), 80. *Pos:* Photo-journalist, Argosy, True & Sports Illus, New York, 50-59; publ, Speedhorse Publ, Norman, Okla, 78; publ, Pintores Press, Roswell, NMex, 79-81. *Awards:* Detroit Art Dir Award, Gen Motors, 55. *Bibliog:* Cowboy photographer, US Camera, New York, 45; Toughest assignment, Popular Photog, 58; Janet Marshall (auth), Action photography, Rangefinder, Los Angeles, 60. *Publ:* Auth, Alfred Morang, A Neglected Master, 79, Ernest Berke, Paintings and Sculptures of the Old West, 80, Juan Dell, First Lady of Western Bronze, 81 & Bill Wiggins, A Thirty Year Retrospective, 82, Pintores Press. *Mailing Add:* 6 El Arco Iris Roswell NM 88201

WIGHT, FREDERICK S
PAINTER, ADMINISTRATOR
b New York, NY, June 1, 02. *Study:* Univ Va, BA; Harvard Univ, MA. *Work:* Los Angeles Co Mus Art, Los Angeles; Roswell Art Mus, NMex; Palm Springs Desert Mus, Calif. *Exhib:* One-man shows, M H de Young Mem Mus, San Francisco, Calif, 56, Esther Robles Gallery, Los Angeles, Calif 60 & Long Beach Mus Art, Calif, 61 & Palm Springs Desert Mus, Calif, 69 & 78; Los Angeles Municipal Art Gallery, 81; Newspace Gallery, Los Angeles, Calif, 82; and others. *Collections Arranged:* Jacques Lipchitz Retrospective, 63, Kurt Schwitters, 65, Henri Matisse Retrospective, 66, Negro in American Art, 66, Jean Arp Memorial, 68 & Gerhard Marcks Retrospective, 69; and many others. *Pos:* Assoc dir, Inst Contemp Art, Boston, Mass, formerly; dir, Frederick S Wight Galleries, Univ Calif, Los Angeles, 53-73. *Teaching:* Instr art hist, Univ Mich, 50 & Harvard Univ, 51; prof 20th century art, Univ Calif, Los Angeles, 53-73, chmn dept art, 63-66. *Awards:* Nat Endowment Arts Grant, 73; 25th Anniversary Award & Medal, Nat Gallery. *Mem:* Int Asn Art Critics; Univ Calif Los Angeles Art Coun. *Media:* Oil, Wood. *Publ:* Auth, Hans Hofmann, 57, Arthur G Dove, 58, Richard Neutra, 58 & Modigliani, 61; auth, Potent Images, Macmillan, 76; and many others. *Mailing Add:* 405 Hilgard Ave Los Angeles CA 90024

WIITASALO, SHIRLEY
PAINTER
b Toronto, Ont, Can, 1949. *Study:* Ont Col Art, Toronto, 67-78. *Work:* Can Coun Art Bank, Ottawa; Nat Gallery of Can, Ottawa; Owens Art Gallery, Mt Allison Univ, Sackville, NB; Mem Univ Art Gallery, St John's Nfld; Art Gallery Ont, Toronto. *Exhib:* Solo exhibs, Carmen Lamanna Gallery, 74, 76, 78, 80 & 81; Contemp Ont Art, Art Gallery Ont, Toronto, 74; Carmen Lamanna at Owens Art Gallery, Mt Allison Univ, Sackville, NB, 75; Some Canadian Women Artists, Nat Gallery Can, Ottawa, 75; Ont Now-A Survey of Contemp Art, Kitchener-Waterloo Gallery, Art Gallery of Hamilton, Ont, 76; 17 Canadian Artists-A Protean View, Vancouver Art Gallery, BC, 76; Kanadische Künstler Kunsthalle, Basel, Switz, 78; 20th Century Can Painting, Nat Gallery Can, 81; Canadian Horizon, Can Coun, 82; Fiction, Art Gallery Ont, 82; and others. *Awards:* Can Coun Grants, 69, 70, 72 & 73; Ont Arts Coun Grant, 75-76; Can Coun Sr Grant, Can Coun, 82. *Media:* Oil on Canvas. *Mailing Add:* 840 Yonge St Toronto ON M4W 1H1 Canada

WILBERT, ROBERT JOHN
PAINTER, EDUCATOR
b Chicago, Ill, Oct 9, 29. *Study:* Univ Ill, BFA, 51, MFA, 54. *Work:* Saginaw Mus, Mich; South Bend Art Ctr, Ind; Kresge Art Ctr, Mich State Univ; Detroit Inst Arts; Wayne State Univ, Detroit. *Exhib:* American Watercolors, Drawings & Prints, Metrop Mus Art, 52; Butler Inst Am Art Midyear Ann, 60, 62, 63 & 68; Pa Acad Fine Arts Ann, 61 & 63; one-man show, Wayne State Univ, Mich; J B Speed Art Mus, Louisville, Ky, 65 & 75; Eastern Mich Univ, Ypsilanti, 72; Cranbrook Acad Art Gallery, Bloomfield Hills, Mich, 72 & 79; Kalamazoo Art Ctr, Mich, 73; Slusser Art Ctr, Univ Mich, Ann Arbor, 74 & 76; Detroit Inst Arts, 76. *Teaching:* Instr painting, Flint Inst Arts, Mich, 54-56; prof painting, Wayne State Univ, 56- *Awards:* 57th Exhib Mich Artists Werbe Award, Detroit Inst Arts, 69; Nat Endowment Arts Fel, 77; Mich Found Arts Award, 80. *Media:* Oil, Watercolor. *Dealer:* Donald Morris Gallery 105 Townsend Birmingham MI; Donald Morris Gallery 20082 Livernois Detroit MI 48221. *Mailing Add:* Dept of Art & Art Hist Wayne State Univ Detroit MI 48202

WILBUR, LAWRENCE NELSON
PAINTER, PRINTMAKER
b Whitman, Mass, Dec 21, 97. *Study:* Mass Normal Sch, 17; Grand Cent Sch Art, with Harvey Dunn, N C Wyeth & Pruette Carter, 26-27. *Work:* Nat Collection Fine Art & Nat Galleries Art, Washington, DC; Metrop Mus Art, New York; Boston Mus Fine Art; Philadelphia Mus Fine Art; Libr Congress; and others. *Exhib:* Watercolor & Prints, Metrop Mus Art, New York, 52; Audubon Artists; Etchings by Invitation, Royal Soc Brit Painters/Etchers & Engravers, Gt Brit; Watercolors, Montclair Mus, NJ; NJ Soc Am Graphic Artists; Nat Acad Design; and others. *Awards:* Silver Medal Watercolor, Am Watercolor Soc, 51; Bronze Medals, Allied Artists Am, 52 & Audubon Artists, Am Artists Mag, 57. *Bibliog:* Frederick Whitaker (auth), From dark to light, Am Artists Mag, 58. *Mem:* Audubon Artists Inc (bd gov); Soc Am Graphic Artists; Am Watercolor Soc; Allied Artists of Am (rec secy). *Media:* Oil, Watercolor; Etching, Wood Engraving. *Mailing Add:* 125 W 96th St New York NY 10025

WILCOX, GORDON CUMNOCK
PAINTER, ILLUSTRATOR
b Boston, Mass, Aug 12, 34. *Study:* Sch Practical Art, Boston; Art Students League, with Olinsky & Dickinson; Nat Acad Design. *Work:* Barclay's Bank of New York; The Wall St Group Inc. *Exhib:* Panhandle-Plains Hist Mus, Canyon, Tex, 65; Expos Intercontinentale, France, 67 & Monaco, 68; one-man shows, Wickersham Gallery, New York, 68 & Southampton Gallery, NY, 76; Wichita Centennial Nat Art Exhib, Kans, 70; Gallery Cutler, Palm Beach, 78. *Awards:* John Duck Award, Parrish Art Mus, Southampton, NY, 71. *Mem:* Visual Artists & Galleries Asn, Inc; Am Soc Marine Artists; Artists Equity Asn New York; Coast Guard Art Prog Artists. *Media:* Watercolor. *Mailing Add:* 400 E 88th St New York NY 10018

WILCOX, JARVIS GEER, JR
PAINTER
b Houston, Tex, July 18, 42. *Study:* Yale Univ, BA, 64; with Arthur Stern, 64-65. *Work:* Mus City New York; Staten Island Mus, New York; Chrysler Mus, Va; Acad Arts, Md. *Exhib:* American Painters in Paris, 75; Silvermine

Guild Artists, Conn, 78; Audubon Artists Show, New York, 78; American Artists Professional League Show, New York, 77-81. *Awards:* A Congor Goodyear Prize for Excellence in Art History, Yale Univ, 64. *Bibliog:* Cecile Corona (auth), Jarvis Wilcox, palette knife mosaics, Am Artist, 8/81. *Mem:* Salmagundi Club, New York. *Media:* Oil, Conte. *Dealer:* Audrey Leeds 12 East 87th St New York NY 10028. *Mailing Add:* 412 W 110th St New York NY 10025

WILDE, JOHN
PAINTER
b Milwaukee, Wis, Dec 12, 19. *Study:* Univ Wis, BS & MS. *Work:* Whitney Mus Am Art, New York; Pa Acad Fine Arts, Philadelphia; Art Inst Chicago; Detroit Inst Art; Wadsworth Atheneum, Hartford, Conn. *Exhib:* Whitney Mus Am Art, 52-68; 52 Americans Under 36, Metrop Mus Art, 54; Contemp Drawing USA, Mus Mod Art, 58; Three Centuries of the Nude in American Art 1675-1975, New York Cult Ctr, 75 & Minneapolis Inst of Arts, 76; Am Master Drawings & Watercolors (From Colonial Times to the Present), Minneapolis Inst of Arts, 76, Whitney Mus of Am Art, New York, 76 & San Francisco Fine Arts Mus, 77; Contemp Am Drawing, Fine Arts Gallery, San Diego, 77; and many others. *Teaching:* Alfred Sessler Distinguished Prof Art, Univ Wis-Madison, 69-82, prof emer, 82- *Awards:* Lambert Purchase Award, Pa Acad Fine Art, 63; Childe Hassam Purchase Award, Nat Acad Design, 65 & 80; Purchase Award, Butler Inst Am Art, 68. *Bibliog:* Lee Nordness (ed), Art USA Now, Viking Press, 63; Una E Johnson (auth), 20th Century Modern Drawings, Shorewood, 67; Theodore Stebbins, Jr (auth), American Master Drawings & Watercolors, Harper & Row, 76. *Media:* Oil, Pencil. *Dealer:* The Bradley Galleries 2565 N Downer Ave Milwaukee WI 53211; David Findlay Jr Gallery E 57th St New York NY 10022. *Mailing Add:* RFD 1 Evansville WI 53536

WILEY, WILLIAM T
PAINTER
b Bedford, Ind, Oct 21, 37. *Study:* San Francisco Art Inst, BFA, 60, MFA, 62. *Work:* San Francisco Mus Art; Mus Mod Art, New York; Los Angeles Co Mus Art; Oakland Mus, Calif; and many others. *Exhib:* Looking West, Joslyn Art Mus, Omaha, Nebr, 70; retrospective, Univ Calif, Berkeley, 71 & Walker Art Ctr, 79; one-man shows, Studio Marconi, Milan, Italy, 71, Art Inst Chicago, 72, Corcoran Gallery Art, Washington, DC, 72, Mus Mod Art, New York, 75 & 76, Galerie Paul Fachetti, Paris, 77, Landfall Press Gallery, Chicago, 78 & Delahunty Gallery, Dallas, 78; Albright-Knox Art Gallery, Buffalo, NY, 72; Whitney Mus Am Art, New York, 73; Corcoran Gallery Art, Washington, DC, 75; Mus Contemp Art, Houston, 77; Inst Contemp rt, Boston, 78; Albright-Knox Art Mus, 78; Sixth Int Drawings, Rijeka, 78; Denver Art Mus Biennial, 79; Dallas Mus, 81. *Teaching:* Assoc prof art, Univ Calif, Davis, 62- *Awards:* Purchase Prize, Whitney Mus Am Art, 68; Nealie Sullivan Award, San Francisco Art Inst, 68; Traveling Grant, Australian Arts Coun, 80; and others. *Bibliog:* James R Mellow (auth), Realist William Wiley, New York Times, 10/11/70; John Perrault (auth), Toward a new metaphysics, Village Voice, 10/15/70; Cecile McCann (auth), Probing the western ethic, Artweek, 5/15/71. *Publ:* Coauth, The Great Blondino (film), shown Belg Film Festival, 67; contribr, Over Evident Falls (theater event), Sacramento State Col, 68; auth, Man's Nature (film), shown Hansen Fuller Gallery, 71. *Dealer:* Hansen Fuller Goldeen 228 Grant Ave San Francisco CA 94108; Allan Frumkin Gallery New York NY. *Mailing Add:* c/o Wanda Hansen 615 Main St Sausalito CA 94965

WILHELMI, WILLIAM MERLE
CERAMIST, CRAFTSMAN
b Garwin, Iowa, Feb 4, 39. *Study:* San Diego State Col, BA, 60; Univ Calif, Los Angeles, MFA, 69. *Work:* Long Beach Mus Art, Calif; Everson Art Mus, Syracuse, NY; Tweed Mus Art, Duluth, Minn; Libr Congress; Renwick Gallery, Smithsonian Inst, Washington, DC; and others. *Comn:* Tile mural postal symbol, US Postal Dept, Laredo, Tex, 76; tile mural, Whataburger Nat Hq, Corpus Christi, 79; planters & tile murals, Corpus Christi State Univ, 79; Corpus Christi Nat Bank, 82. *Exhib:* Baroque '74, Mus Contemp Crafts, New York, 74; Renwick Gallery, Washington, DC, 76, 80 & 82; 20th Century Ornament, Cooper-Hewitt Mus, New York, 78; Contemp Am, STex Art Mobile, Corpus Christi, 79; Hill's Gallery, Santa Fe, 81; Marilyn Butler Gallery, Scottsdale, Ariz, 81; Libr Congress, 83; and others. *Pos:* Resident potter, Richard Colley, architect, Corpus Christi, 69-76 & Kaffie Gallery, Corpus Christi, 76-; bd trustees, Art Mus STex, 80-82. *Awards:* Two Purchase Awards, San Mateo Col, 69; First Place & One-Man Show Art Found Award, Art Mus STex, 73; Tex Arts Comn, 81. *Bibliog:* People in Particular, KEDT-TV, Judy Brin, 77. *Mem:* Am Crafts Coun; Tex Designer Craftsmen; Tex Potters Guild; Art Found. *Publ:* Contribr, Claywork-Form and Idea in Ceramic Design, Davis Publ Inc, 75; contribr, Contemporary Ceramic Techniques, Prentice-Hall, 77; contribr, Decorative Art in Modern Interiors, Cassell & Co Ltd, 77 & 78; contribr, Studio Potter, Daniel Clark Found, 78; Tex Monthly, 12/80. *Mailing Add:* 1129 Ocean Dr Corpus Christi TX 78404

WILKE, HANNAH
SCULPTOR, INSTRUCTOR
b New York, NY, Mar 7, 40. *Study:* Temple Univ, BFA, 61, BS, 62. *Work:* Albright-Knox Art Gallery, Buffalo, NY; Allen Art Mus, Oberlin, Ohio; Brooklyn Mus, NY; Power Inst, Sydney, Australia; Metro-Media, Channel 5, New York. *Comn:* Mural (latex), comn by Carl Solway Gallery for Ponderosa Systs, Dayton, Ohio, 74; greeting card, Mus Mod Art, New York, 77. *Exhib:* Drawing & Sculpture Show, Albright-Knox Art Gallery, 77; Whitney Mus Biennial, New York, 73; Brooklyn Mus, NY, 74; Albright-Knox Art Gallery, 75; Whitney Mus Am Art, New York, 77; Washington Proj Arts, 79; Mus de Arte de Sao Paulo, Brazil, 80; New York State Mus, Albany, 81; Leo Castelli

Gallery, New York, 81; New Mus, New York, 83; and many others. *Pos:* Cur, Store Days, 70-77. *Teaching:* Instr sculpture, Sch Visual Arts, NY, 74- *Awards:* Nat Endowment for the Arts, 76, 79 & 80; Award, Alaska Coun Arts, 80; Guggenheim Fel, 82. *Bibliog:* Mark Savitt (auth), Hannah Wilke, the pleasure principle, Arts, 9/75; Ruth Iskin (auth), Conversation with Hannah Wilke, Visual Dialogue, Vol 2, 77; Ernst (auth), Hannah Wilke talks, Oasis d'Neon, 78-79; plus others. *Media:* Multimedia. *Publ:* Contribr, Woman's sensibility, art, 75; contribr, Flash Art, 5/75; auth, My Father's Brother's Wife's Mother, Heresies, 78. *Mailing Add:* 62 Greene St New York NY 10012

WILKE, ULFERT S
PAINTER, ADMINISTRATOR
b Bad Tolz, Ger, July 14, 07; US citizen. *Study:* With Willy Jaeckel, 23; Arts & Crafts Sch, Brunswick, 24-25; Acad Grande Chaumiere, 27-28; Acad Ranson, Paris, 27-28; Harvard Univ, 40-41; State Univ Iowa, MA, 47. *Work:* Philadelphia Mus, Pa; Guggenheim Mus, New York; Cleveland Mus Art, Ohio; Whitney Mus Am Art, New York; Mus Tel Aviv, Israel. *Exhib:* Solomon R Guggenheim Mus, 54; Lettering by Mod Artists, Mus Mod Art, New York, 64; Ulfert Wilke, Recent Works, Joslyn Art Mus; Zero Through Nine (portfolio), Tamarind Inst, 78; Mekler Gallery, Los Angeles, 78; Calligraphies: Content Without Words (portfolio), Tamarind Inst, 80; Viking Ships, Honolulu Acad Arts, 81; and others. *Collections Arranged:* Oscar Kokoschka, Kalamazoo Inst Arts, 40; As Found, Inst Contemp Art, Boston, 66; Very Small Paintings, Objects & Works on Paper, Univ Iowa Mus Art, 72. *Pos:* Head dept art & dir, Kalamazoo Col & Inst Arts, Mich, 40-42; art & educ dir, Springfield Art Asn, Ill, 46-47; dir, Univ Iowa Mus Art, 68-75. *Teaching:* Asst prof art, Univ Louisville, 48-55; vis grad prof painting, Univ Ga, 55-56; assoc prof art, Rutgers Univ, New Brunswick, 62-68. *Awards:* Albrecht Durer Prize, Ger, 27; Guggenheim Found Fels Study in Europe, 59-60 & 60-61; Am Acad & Inst Arts & Letts, 78. *Bibliog:* J Langsner (auth), Art, 11/61 & G Nordland (auth), Calligraphy & the art of Ulfert Wilke, 4/71, Art Int; G Nordland (auth), Ulfert Wilke: A Retrospective, 83. *Mem:* Asn Am Mus Dirs. *Media:* Oil, Acrylic. *Publ:* Illusr, portfolios, Music to Be Seen, 56; Fragments From Nowhere, 58 & One, Two & More, 60; auth, An Artist Collects-Ulfert Wilke Selections from Five Continents, 75; illusr, Without Words, Tamarind Inst, 77. *Mailing Add:* Box 211 Rte 3 Solon IA 52333

WILKIN, KAREN
CURATOR, CRITIC
b New York, NY. *Study:* Barnard Col, BA(cum laude), 62; Columbia Univ, MFA(Woodrow Wilson Fel), 63. *Collections Arranged:* Sculpture in Steel: Gonzalez, Caro, Steiner & Scott (with catalog), 74; The Collective Unconscious: US/Canada 1940s (with catalog), 75; Adolph Gottlieb: The Pictographs Touring Exhib (with catalog), 77-78; Certain Traditions: Recent British & Canadian Art (with catalog), 78-80; David Smith: The Formative Years Touring Exhib (with catalog), 81-82. *Pos:* Chief cur, Edmonton Art Gallery, Alta, 71-78; cur, Westburne Collection, Montreal, 76- *Teaching:* Lectr art hist, Univ Alta, Edmonton, 67-70; adj prof, Trent Univ, Peterborough, Ont, 79- *Awards:* Fulbright Fel, Rome, 64-65; Can Coun Sr Arts Grant, 81. *Mem:* Int Asn Art Critics; Asn Prof Art Adv. *Res:* Contemporary art, with particular emphasis on sculpture; US art from 1930s to present. *Publ:* Auth, Anthony Caro and Bernini, 76 & Adolph Gottlieb: Pictographs, 77, Art Int; coauth, Modern Painting in Canada, Hurtig, 78; auth, David Smith, Abbeville Press, 84. *Mailing Add:* 356 College St Toronto ON M5T 1S6 Canada

WILKINS, DAVID GEORGE
HISTORIAN, GALLERY DIRECTOR
b Battle Creek, Mich, Sept 12, 39. *Study:* Oberlin Col, BA, 61; Univ Mich, MA, 63 & PhD, 69. *Pos:* Dir, Univ Art Gallery, Univ Pittsburgh, 76- *Teaching:* Prof art hist, Dept Fine Arts, Univ Pittsburgh, 67- *Mem:* Col Art Asn; Soc of Archit Historians; Renaissance Soc of Am. *Res:* Florentine painting and sculpture; American painting. *Publ:* Auth, Giotto's Madonna, 70 & Florentine frescoes, 78, Art Quart; contribr, Art in nineteenth century Pittsburgh, Univ Art Gallery, 77; auth, Donatello's Dovizia, 83 & coauth, Donatello, 84, Art Bulletin. *Mailing Add:* Univ Art Gallery Univ Pittsburgh Pittsburgh PA 15260

WILKINSON, KIRK COOK
DEALER, PAINTER
b New York, NY, Nov 23, 09. *Study:* Parson's Sch Design; watercolor painting with Felice Waldo Howell. *Work:* Scarborough Art Gallery, NY; Pocker Art Gallery, New York; Kendall Art Gallery, Wellfleet, Mass. *Exhib:* Art Dir Club New York, 34-; Art Dir Club Philadelphia, 54 & 56; Jr League Westchester Ann, 66-69; Westchester Art Asn Ann, 69; Cape Cod Art Asn Ann, 70-72; plus others. *Pos:* Art dir, Country Life, Am Home Mag, NY, 35-36; art dir, House Beautiful Mag, New York, 36-37; art dir, Conde Nast, New York, 37-39; art dir, Women's Day Mag, New York, 38-70; pres & organizer, Parson's Sch Design Alumni Coun, 44; owner, Kendall Art Gallery, currently. *Teaching:* Instr graphics & ann lectr, Parson's Sch Design, 31-52. *Awards:* Gold Medal, New York Art Dir Club, 54; Gold Medal, Philadelphia Art Dir Club; Second Prize Watercolor, Jr League Westchester Show, 69; plus others. *Bibliog:* Charles Coiner (auth), Commentary on the art & layout of Women's Day, Art Direction Mag, 4/54. *Mem:* Am Fedn Arts; Soc Illusr; Century Asn; Dutch Treat Club; Provincetown Art Asn; plus others. *Media:* Watercolor, Casein, Acrylic. *Specialty:* Contemporary art, sculpture and ceramics. *Publ:* Auth, Let's talk about your pictures, Popular Photog, 4/54; auth, Lighting is the news, 10/59 & New thinking man, 2/62, Art Direction. *Dealer:* Kendall Art Gallery Inc Wellfleet MA 02667. *Mailing Add:* c/o Kendall Art Gallery Box 742 Wellfleet MA 02667

WILL, JOHN A
PRINTMAKER, PAINTER
b Waterloo, Iowa, June 30, 39. *Study:* Univ Iowa, MFA, 64; Rijsacadamie von Beeldende Kunston, Amsterdam, 64-65; Tamarind, Albuquerque, NMex. *Work:* New York Pub Libr; Art Inst Chicago; Libr Cong; Mus NMex, Santa Fe; Glenbow Art Gallery, Calgary. *Exhib:* Libr Cong Nat Print Exhib, 73; Int Triennial Original Color Graphics, Grenchen, Switz, 73; Brit Int Print Biennial, Bradford, Yorkshire, 74; 2nd Miami Graphics Int Biennial, Fla, 75; 11th Int Biennial Graphic Art, Ljubljana, Yugoslavia, 75; and others. *Teaching:* Asst prof drawing, Univ Wis-Stout, 65-70; resident artist, Yale Univ, summer 66 & Peninsula Sch Art, Fish Creek, Wis, summer 68; prof lithography, Univ Calgary, 71-; instr, Nova Scotia Col Art & Design, summers 73-75, 77 & 79; instr, Baniff Ctr, summers 80 & 81. *Awards:* Fulbright Fel, Holland, 64-65; Ford Found Grant, 70-71. *Media:* Graphics, Painting; Video. *Mailing Add:* Dept of Art Univ of Calgary Calgary AB T2N 1N4 Canada

WILLENBECHER, JOHN
SCULPTOR, PAINTER
b Macungie, Pa, May 5, 36. *Study:* Brown Univ, BA, 58; NY Univ Inst Fine Arts, 58-61. *Work:* Whitney Mus Am Art, New York; Albright-Knox Art Gallery, Buffalo, NY; James A Michener Found Collection, Univ Tex, Austin; Hirshhorn Mus & Sculpture Garden, Washington, DC; Solomon R Guggenheim Mus, New York. *Comn:* US Fed Bldg & Court House, Providence, RI, 82; Republicbank, Houston, 83. *Exhib:* Mixed Media & Pop Art, Albright-Knox Art Gallery, Buffalo, 63; Young Americans, Whitney Mus Am Art, New York, 65; Kunst-Lucht-Kunst, Stedelijk Mus, Eindhoven, Holland, 66; John Willenbecher, Everson Mus Art, Syracuse, NY, 75; Arts Club, Chicago, Ill, 76; Allentown Art Mus, Pa, 79; Neuberger Mus, Purchase, NY, 79. *Teaching:* Lectr painting, Philadelphia Col Art, 72-73; artist in residence, Dartmouth Col, 77 & Univ Wis, Milwaukee, 83. *Awards:* Nat Endowment Arts Fel, 76. *Bibliog:* Joseph McElroy (auth), Through the labyrinth: The art of John Willenbecher, Art Int, 3/75; William Wilson (auth), John Willenbecher: Pyramids, spheres & labyrinths, 3/75 & Daniel Cameron (auth), John Willenbecher and the riddle of Grangeur, 9/83, Arts Mag. *Mem:* Art Comn New York. *Mailing Add:* 145 W Broadway New York NY 10013

WILLIAMS, BENJAMIN FORREST
CURATOR, HISTORIAN
b Lumberton, NC, Dec 24, 25. *Study:* Corcoran Sch Art, with Eugene Weisz; George Washington Univ, AA; Univ NC, AB; Columbia Univ, Paris Exten; Ecole du Louvre; Netherlands Inst Art Hist; Art Students League New York. *Work:* Atlanta Art Asn; NC Mus Art; Duke Univ; Greenville Civic Art Gallery, NC; Knoll Assoc, New York. *Exhib:* Va Intermont, Bristol; Weatherspoon Gallery, Greensboro; Person Hall Gallery, Chapel Hill, NC; Asheville Art Mus; Am Fedn Arts traveling exhibs; and others. *Collections Arranged:* Retrospectives for Josef Albers, Hobson Pittman, Jacob Marling, Victor Hammer, Fedor Zakharov, Henry Pearson & the collections of the NC Mus Art; and others. *Pos:* In charge of Ann NC Artists' Exhib; principal investor, Black Mountain Col Res Proj; first cur art, NC State Univ, 79-81; independent art consult, 81- *Awards:* Ronsheim Mem Award, Corcoran Sch Art, 46; Washington Soc Arts, 47; Prizes, Southeastern Ann, 47. *Mem:* Am Asn Mus; Southeastern Mus Conf; Col Art Asn Am. *Publ:* Contribr articles on 19th century American painting & sculpture to NC Mus Art Bull & NC Hist Rev. *Mailing Add:* 2813 Mayview Rd Raleigh NC 27607

WILLIAMS, CASEY
PHOTOGRAPHER
b Houston, Tex, 1947. *Study:* Univ Tex, Austin, BFA, 70; San Francisco Art Inst, MFA, 76. *Work:* Mus Fine Arts, Houston; Mus Mod Art, New York. *Exhib:* Solo exhibs, Tex Christian Univ, 78 & Media Ctr, Rice Univ, 79; Emerging Texas Photographers, Laguna Gloria Art Mus, Austin, 80; The New Photography, Contemp Arts Mus, Houston, 81; Texas Photo Sampler, Washington Proj Arts, 81; New Orleans Triennial, New Orleans Mus Art, 83; Big Pictures by Contemporary Photographers, Mus Mod Art, New York, 83; Singular Points of View, Art Mus STex, 84. *Teaching:* Instr photog, Glassell Sch Art, Houston, 79- *Bibliog:* Susie Kalil (auth), Photography--rooted in ambiguity, Houston Post, 6/19/82; Kay Larson (auth), Beyond pure photography, New York Mag, 5/2/83; Patricia Johnson (auth), Developing camera-derie, Houston Chronicle, 7/24/83. *Mailing Add:* c/o Tex Gallery 2012 Peden Houston TX 77019

WILLIAMS, CHESTER LEE
SCULPTOR
b Durham, NC, July 24, 44. *Study:* NC Cent Univ, BA, 68; Univ Mich, MFA, 71. *Work:* Student Union Gallery, NC Cent Univ, Durham, Voorhees Col Libr, Denmark, SC; Art Dept Gallery, Univ Mich, Ann Arbor; Univ Gallery, Appalachian State Univ, Boone, NC; Black Arch Mus & Res Ctr, Fla A&M Univ, Tallahassee; and others. *Comn:* Sculpture, bronze casting, comn by Dr Oscar Cole, New York, 71 & Dr & Mrs Robert Zakarin, Tallahassee, 77; painting & sculpture, Fla A&M Univ, 77-78; bronze bust of Johnathan Gibbs, Fine Arts Coun of Fla, Div Cult Affairs, State of Fla, Tallahassee, 77-78; plus many others. *Exhib:* Appalachian State Univ, 75; Howard Univ Galleries, Washington, DC, 76; Ala State Univ, Montgomery, 77; Huntsville Mus Art, Ala, 79; LeMoyne Art Found, Tallahassee, 79; plus many others. *Collections Arranged:* Richard Hunt Print's Show, Fla A&M Univ Gallery, 75. *Pos:* Illusr, Nat Air Pollution Control Ctr, Durham, NC, 69-70; Bd mem, LeMoyne Art Found, Tallahassee, FL. *Teaching:* Instr creative woodwork, Sch Design, Durham, NC, 68-69; asst prof sculpture & art appreciation, Voorhess Col, Denmark, SC, 71-74; assoc prof sculpture & painting, Fla A&M Univ, 74- *Awards:* Fine Arts Coun Fla Grant, 77-78; Sculpture Award, Harmon Gallery, Naples, Fla, 80; Purchase Award, Summer of 80 Fine Art

Exhib, Naples, Fla, 80. *Bibliog:* Neil Weiss (auth), Survival tactics an artist's forum, Contemp Art/Southeast, 79; Betty Rubenstein (auth), Nuclear fear translated in bronze: Chester L Williams, Tallahassee Democrat, 4/30/79; Ellen A Ashdown (auth), Black sculptor in the south: Chester L Williams, Crisis, 4/79; and many others. *Mem:* Col Art Asn of Am; Nat Conf Aritsts. *Media:* Bronze Casting. *Dealer:* LeMoyne Art Foundation Tallahassee FL; Image South Gallery Atlanta GA. *Mailing Add:* 950 Richardson Rd Tallahassee FL 32301

WILLIAMS, DAVE HARRELL
COLLECTOR, PATRON
b Beaumont, Tex, Oct 5, 32. *Mem:* Print Selection Comt, Whitney Mus Am Art; Assoc Dept Prints, Mus Mod Art. *Collection:* American prints beginning with Winslow Homer up to and including contemporary artists, emphasis 1910-1940. *Mailing Add:* 510 Park Ave New York NY 10022

WILLIAMS, GERALD
POTTER, EDITOR
b Asansol, India, Jan 5, 26; US citizen. *Study:* Cornell Col; Notre Dame Col, NH, Hon DFA, 71. *Work:* Fitchburg Art Mus, Mass; Syracuse Univ, NY; Objects USA, Johnson Collection; Currier Gallery Art, NH. *Comn:* Ceramic mural, Sunapee & resin mural, Laconia, State of NH; resin mural, Int Paper Box Machine Co, Nashua, NH; ceramic mural, Sheen, Finney, Bass & Green Law Off, Manchester. *Exhib:* Am Studio Pottery, Victoria & Albert Mus, London, Eng, 67, Ceramic Int, 72; Syracuse Ceramic Nat, 70; one-man shows, Contemp Crafts Mus, New York, 69 & Currier Gallery Art, Manchester, 70. *Pos:* Trustee, Haystack Sch, Maine; founder & co-dir, Phoenix Workshops; ed, Studio Potter Mag; pres, Nat Coun Apprenticeship Art & Craft. *Teaching:* Instr sculpture, Currier Gallery Sch Art, 52-72; instr ceramics, Dartmouth Col, 64-65; instr ceramics, Haystack Sch Crafts. *Awards:* Fel, Am Craft Coun, 80; Ceramic Symposium Award, 81. *Bibliog:* Nordness (auth), Objects: USA, 70. *Mem:* NH Art Asn; League NH Craftsmen; Nat Coun Educ Ceramic Arts. *Media:* Clay. *Res:* Wet-firing process; photo-resist process. *Publ:* Auth, Textiles of Oaxaca, 64; ed, The Studio Potter, 72; ed, Apprenticeship in Craft, 81. *Mailing Add:* RFD 1 Goffstown NH 03045

WILLIAMS, HIRAM DRAPER
PAINTER
b Indianapolis, Ind, Feb 11, 17. *Study:* Williamsport Sketch Club, with George Eddinger; Pa State Univ, BS, with Victor Lowenfeld & MEd, with Hobson Pittman & Lowenfeld. *Work:* Mus Mod Art & Whitney Mus Am Art, New York; Milwaukee Art Ctr; Nat Art Collection & Corcoran Gallery Art, Washington, DC; and others. *Exhib:* Art USA: Painting, Mus Mod Art, 61; Art USA II; Carnegie Inst Int, Pittsburgh, 64; Art Across Am, 65; Art: USA: Now, 66. *Teaching:* Asst prof art educ, Univ Southern Calif, 53-54; asst prof art educ, Univ Tex, Austin, 54-60, res grant, 58; prof painting, Univ Fla, 60- *Awards:* D D Feldman Award, 58; Guggenheim Found Fel, 63; Distinguished Professorof Art, Univ Fla, 81. *Bibliog:* Donald Weisman (auth), Recent paintings of Hiram Williams, Univ Tex Quart, 59; William B Stephens (auth), On creating & teaching, Col Art J, summer 71 & Hiram Williams: Exploring the Sources of His Creation, William B Stephens, Memphis State Univ Press, 78. *Media:* Oil. *Publ:* Coauth, Forms, Univ Tex, 69; auth, Notes for a Young Painter, Prentice-Hall, 84. *Mailing Add:* 2804 NW 30th Terr Gainesville FL 32605

WILLIAMS, IDAHERMA See Idaherma

WILLIAMS, JOHN ALDEN
HISTORIAN
b Ft Smith, Ark, Sept 6, 28. *Study:* Am Univ Beirut, 50-51; Univ Munich, with Hans Sedlmayer, 51-52; Univ Ark, BA(hist & philos), 53; Princeton Univ, MA & PhD, 53-57; further work under Sir K A C Creswell in Cairo on hist of Islamic art & archit, 57-59. *Pos:* Asst field dir, Am Ctr for Res in Egypt, 57-59; sr res fel, Ctr Middle East Studies, Harvard Univ, 71-72. *Teaching:* Asst & assoc prof Islamic studies, McGill Univ, Montreal, Que, Can, 59-66; dir & prof, Ctr for Arabic Studies, Am Univ Cairo, 66/69; prof art hist & Middle East studies, Prof Ctr for Arabic Studies, Univ Cairo, 69-72; prof art hist & Islamic study, Univ Tex, Austin & Univ Cairo, alternate yrs, 72- *Mem:* Col Art Asn Am. *Res:* History of Islamic art and architecture. *Publ:* Coauth, Architecture of Muslim India (400 slides with commentary), Art and Architecture of Ancient Egypt (400 slides with commentary) & Timurid Monuments of Central Asia (40 slides with commentary), Visual Educ Inc, 77; auth, Veiling in Egypt as a political and social phenomenon, In: Islam & Development, Syracuse Univ Press, 80; auth, The Khanqah of Siryaqus, In: Towards an Islamic Humanism, Cairo, 83; and others. *Mailing Add:* c/o Ctr for Middle East Studies Univ Tex Austin TX 78712

WILLIAMS, JOHN WESLEY
HISTORIAN, EDUCATOR
b Memphis, Tenn, Feb 25, 28. *Study:* Duke Univ; Yale Univ, BA; Univ Mich, PhD. *Teaching:* From instr to assoc prof Medieval art, Swarthmore Col, Pa, 60-72, chmn fine arts dept, 71-72; prof, Univ Pittsburgh, 72-, chmn fine arts dept, 79- *Awards:* Fulbright-Hays Res Grant, Spain, 64 & 69; Nat Endowment Humanities Project Grant, 71-73. *Mem:* Col Art Asn Am; Int Ctr Medieval Art. *Res:* Spanish Medieval art. *Publ:* Auth, Romanesque Bible of San Millan, JWCI, 65; auth, Valeranica and the Scribe Florentus, Madrider Mitteilungen, 70; auth, San Isidoro: Evidence for a new history, Art Bulletin, 73; auth, Early Spanish Manuscript Illumination, George Braziller, 77; ed, Actas del Simposio sobre Beato de Liebana, Vol II, Madrid, 80; and others. *Mailing Add:* 749 S Linden Ave Pittsburgh PA 15208

WILLIAMS, JOYCE
PAINTER, INSTRUCTOR
b Lynch, Ky. *Study:* Va Intermont Col, Bristol, 50; Univ Ky, AB, 52; studied with John Pike, Edmund Fitzgerald & Milford Zornes. *Work:* Tex Tech Univ Mus, Lubbock; Wausau Insurance Co, Wis; Am Nat Bank, Austin, Tex; Pittsburgh Plate Glass, Pa; Huntington Galleries, WVa. *Exhib:* Southern Watercolor Soc, 77-83; Knickerbocker Artists, 79-83; Tweed Mus Art, Duluth, Minn, 80; Salmagundi Club, 80-83; Am Watercolor Soc and traveling, 81-83; San Diego Watercolor Soc, 81 & 83; Nat Watercolor Soc, 83; and many others. *Teaching:* Instr, workshops in Ky, WVa & Ohio, currently. *Awards:* Katherine Brugger Award, Watercolor West, 83; Grumbacher Silver Medallion, 83; Robert McCollum Award, Salmagundi Club, 83; over 100 awards since 1965. *Bibliog:* Stephen Doherty (auth), Joyce Williams, North Light Mag, 7/79; Maryann Davis (auth), article, Beaux Arts Mag, 12/80. *Mem:* Salmagundi Club; Knickerbocker Artists; Artists Fel; Rocky Mountain Watercolor Soc; San Diego Watercolor Soc; and many others. *Media:* Watercolor, Oils. *Dealer:* Hobe Sound North Gallery Portland ME; PS Galleries Ogunquit ME & Dallas TX. *Mailing Add:* 2722 Auburn Ave Ashland KY 41101

WILLIAMS, LEWIS W, II
HISTORIAN, EDUCATOR
b Champaign, Ill, Apr 24, 18. *Study:* Univ Ill, BFA, 46, MFA, 48; Univ Chicago, PhD, 58. *Pos:* Dir, Assoc Cols Midwest Arts London & Florence, Florence, Italy, 71-72. *Teaching:* Instr art hist, Univ Mo-Columbia, 48-50; asst art hist, Northwestern Univ, Evanston, 53-55; prof art hist, Beloit Col, 55- *Awards:* Teacher of Yr, Beloit Col, 66. *Mem:* Col Art Asn Am; Am Asn Univ Prof. *Res:* American sculpture. *Mailing Add:* Dept of Art Beloit Col Beloit WI 53511

WILLIAMS, MARY FRANCES
CURATOR, EDUCATOR
b Providence, RI, Apr 26, 05. *Study:* Radcliffe Col, BA, MA & PhD. *Collections Arranged:* 41st-61st Ann Loan Exhibitions of American Art, Randolph-Macon Woman's Col. *Pos:* Mem, Va State Art Comn, 56-70. *Teaching:* Asst prof art, Hollins Col, 36-39; asst prof art, Mt Holyoke Col, 39-42; prof art hist & cur, Randolph-Macon Woman's Col, 52-73; retired. *Awards:* Jonathan Fay Prize, Radcliffe Col, 27; Gillie A Larew Distinguished Teaching Award, 72; Mary Frances Williams Professorship in Humanitites, Randolph-Macon Woman's Col, 80. *Mem:* Nat League Am Pen Women; Lynchburg Fine Arts Ctr; Phi Beta Kappa; Archaeol Inst Am; Alliance Francaise. *Publ:* Auth, Catalogue of the collection of American art at Randolph-Macon Woman's College, 65 & 2nd ed, 77. *Mailing Add:* 239 Westmoreland St Lynchburg VA 24503

WILLIAMS, MARYLOU LORD STUDY
CONSULTANT, COLLAGE ARTIST
b Neodesha, Kans. *Study:* Beloit Col, Ba, 62; Univ Wis, Madison, MA(art), 65; NY Univ & Inst Mod Art, Mus Mod Art, New York, with Victor D'Amico. *Work:* NY Univ Art Collection; Wright Mus Art, Beloit Col; Janesville Art League Gallery, Wis; Hawaii State Found Cult & Arts, Honolulu; Contemp Arts Ctr-Hawaii Gallery, Honolulu; and others. *Comn:* Series of five charcoal drawings, General Motors Assembly Div Plant, Janesville, 54; oil painting, First Nat Bank, Janesville, 65; assemblage for lanai, Ossipoff, Snyder, Roland & Getz Architects, Honolulu, 72. *Exhib:* One-man show, Collages--Marylou Williams, Foundry Gallery, Honolulu, 71 & 73; Burpee Art Mus, Rockford, 77; Art for the Out-of-Doors, Paul Waggoner Gallery, Chicago, Ill, 77; Downtown Gallery, Honolulu, Hawaii, 79; Wis Painters & Sculptors, Milwaukee Inst Design, 81; and others. *Collections Arranged:* Georgia O'Keeffe (with catalog), Daland Fine Arts Ctr, Kohler Gallery, Milton Col, Wis, 65; Festival of Far Eastern Art (with catalog), Wright Art Ctr, 80; Wis Painters & Printmakers Traveling Exhib, Wis mus, 83. *Pos:* Dir & owner, Devlin Gallery, Janesville, 60-65; dir & cur, Theodore Lyman Wright Mus Art, Beloit Col, Wis, 75-83; art consult/cur, 83- *Teaching:* Chmn & asst prof art hist, design & gallery dir, Milton Col, Wis, 64-67; art coordr, elementary through community col, Dept Educ, Pago Pago, Am Samoa, 76-71; instr mus sch, Honolulu Acad Arts, summer 70, 71 & 73; instr mus sch, Bernice P Bishop Mus, Honolulu, 71-72. *Awards:* First Award, Beloit & Vicinity Exhib, Art League Beloit, 61; First Award, Rockford & Vicinity Exhib, Rockford Art Asn, 65; First of Top Ten Award, Wis Painters, Sculptors, Milwaukee Art Ctr, Wis, 66. *Bibliog:* James Auer (auth), article, Milwaukee J, 5/9/76, 6/12/77 & 8/21/83; and others. *Mem:* Am Asn Mus; Wis Citizens Arts; Wis Painters & Sculptors League; Hawaii Artists League; Wis Acad Scis, Arts & Letters. *Res:* Study in depth of Polynesian bark cloth (tapa). *Dealer:* Paul Waggoner Gallery 2269 N Lincoln Chicago IL; Bradley Galleries Milwaukee WI. *Mailing Add:* 2528 Riverview Dr Janesville WI 53545

WILLIAMS, NEIL
PAINTER
b Bluff, Utah, Aug 19, 34. *Study:* Calif Sch Fine Arts, BFA, 59. *Work:* Whitney Mus Am Art, New York; Richmond Mus, Calif; Mass Inst Technol, Cambridge; Weatherspoon Gallery, Univ NC; Continental Arts Soc, London. *Exhib:* One-man exhibs, Dwan Gallery, 66, Andre Emmerich Gallery, New York, 66 & 68 & Logiudice Gallery, 72; Walter Kelly Gallery, 73; Luisastrina Gallery, Sao Paulo, 81. *Awards:* Nat Arts Coun Grant, 66; Guggenheim Fel, 68; Athena Found Grant, 81. *Bibliog:* Richard Hirsch (auth), Private affinities & public users, Arts Mag, Vol 40, No 7; John Perreault (auth), Systematic painting, Artforum, 11/66; Lucy Lippard (auth), Perverse perspectives, Art Int, 3/67. *Mailing Add:* PO Box 114 Sagaponack NY 11962

WILLIAMS, RANDALPH ANDREW
SCULPTOR, PAINTER

b New York, NY, Apr 30, 47. *Study:* New York Univ, BS(art educ), 70; Concordia Col, Sir George Williams Univ, Montreal, Que, Can, MA(art educ), 72. *Work:* New York State Off Bldg, Harlem; City of New York Art Collection. *Comn:* Dance sculpture, comn by Rika Burnham for Helen Adams, Shelia Kaminisky & Danie Co, 77; sculpture, El Museo del Barrio, New York, 79. *Exhib:* Whitney Counterweight, James Yu Gallery, Soho, NY, 77; one-man shows, Just Above Midtown Gallery, 75-78 & Studio Mus, Harlem, NY, 77; The Emily Lowe Gallery, Long Island, NY, 79; Creative Times Exhib, Am Acad, Rome; and others. *Teaching:* Instr fel sculpture, Sir George Williams Univ, Montreal, 70-71; art educ, art hist, educ & assoc mus educator, Metrop Mus Art, New York, 72- *Awards:* Workspace for Artists, Painting/Installation, New York Art & Urban Resource Ctr, 77-78; Nat Endowment Arts Fel. *Bibliog:* Hilton Kramer (auth), Rev, New York Times, 4/8/77; Linda Bryant & Mary Phillips (auths), Contextures, Just Above Midtown Inc, 3/78; Barbara Cavaliere (auth), Rev, Arts Mag, 2/79. *Media:* Acrylic. *Publ:* Ed, Black Creations (inst for Afro-Am Affairs), New York Univ, 72-75. *Mailing Add:* 219 Bowery New York NY 10002

WILLIAMS, RAYMOND LESTER
PAINTER, INSTRUCTOR

b Lenoir City, Tenn, Nov 10, 26. *Study:* Chicago Acad Fine Arts, study with Edgar Whitney, John Pellew, Edmound Fitzgerald & Zolton Zabo, cert. *Work:* United Tel Co, Bristol, Tenn; Dobyns-Bennett High Sch & Tenn Eastman Co, Kingsport; Carrol Reese Mus & Tipton-Haynes Mus, Johnson City, Tenn. *Comn:* Hist Landmark paintings, Merchants Asn, Tenn, 76; Highlands of Roan, Southern Appalachian Highlands Conservancy, 77; Church Circle, City of Kingsport, Tenn, 79; Kingsport Chamber Commerce, Tenn, 81; and others. *Exhib:* Tenn State Mus, Nashville, 73; Ann Arbor State Street Art Show, Mich, 74-81; Coconut Grove Art Festival, Miami, Fla, 79; Lenox Square Fine Art, Atlanta, 80; Wilkes Art Gallery, North Wilkesboro, NC, 83; and many others. *Pos:* Graphic artist, Tenn Eastman Co, 50-74; painter & gallery owner, 74- *Awards:* Best of Show, Jonesboro Days, Jonesboro, Tenn, 75 & 81; Award, Tenn Watercolor Soc, 79; Best of Show, Dunwoody Fine Arts Asn, Atlanta, Ga, 83; and others. *Mem:* Tenn Watercolor Soc (dist dir, 74-75); Tenn Artists; Kingsport Art Guild (pres, 75-76). *Media:* Watercolor, Oils. *Mailing Add:* 3322 Roller Dr Kingsport TN 37663

WILLIAMS, TODD
SCULPTOR, PAINTER

b Savannah, Ga, Jan 6, 39. *Study:* City Col New York; Sch Visual Arts, New York, cert & scholar, 64. *Work:* Smithsonian Inst, Washington, DC. *Comn:* sculpture, Mary Bethune Towers, New York, 70; wall painting, New York Parks Dept, Livingston & Bond Sts, Brooklyn, 70; sculptures, New York Bd Educ, I S 167, Bronx, 73 & Boys & Girls High Sch, Brooklyn, 75; 83rd Precenct Station House, New York Police Dept, 83. *Exhib:* Colored Sculpture, Oakland Art Mus, 65; Witte Mem Mus, Madison, Wis, 66; Cranbrook Acad of Art, Bloomfield Hills, Mich, 66; Books, Boxes & Things, Jewish Mus, New York, 69; Contemp Black Artists, Whitney Mus Am Art, New York, 71; Banners, Nat Mus, Singapore, 76 & Hirshhorn Mus, Washington, DC, 76. *Collections Arranged:* Colored Sculpture, Am Fedn Art, 65; Ten Negro Artists from the United States Dakar, Senegal, US State Dept, 65; Small Sculpture from the United States, 71 & Bicentennial Banners, 76, Smithsonian Inst. *Pos:* Bd mem, City Walls Inc, New York. *Teaching:* Adj instr sculpture, Brooklyn Col, NY, 73-76; asst prof sculpture, Columbia Univ, New York, 76- *Awards:* John Hay Whitney Found Fel, 65; J Clawson Mills Fel, Archit League of New York, 66. *Media:* Mixed-Media. *Mailing Add:* 310 Atlantic Ave Brooklyn NY 11201

WILLIAMS, WALTER (HENRY)
PAINTER, PRINTMAKER

b Brooklyn, NY, Aug 11, 20. *Study:* Brooklyn Mus Art Sch, 51-55; Skowhegan Sch Painting & Sculpture, summer 53; also with Ben Shahn, spring 52. *Work:* Metrop Mus Art, Whitney Mus Am Art, New York; Brooklyn Mus; Nat Gallery Arts, Washington, DC; Riverside Mus, New York. *Exhib:* Whitney Mus Ann, 53-63; Int Watercolor Biennial, Brooklyn Mus, 63; Corner, Charlottenborg, Copenhagen, Denmark, 63; Pa Acad Ann, 66; Nat Acad Design 147th Ann, 72. *Teaching:* Artist in residence, Fisk Univ, 68-69. *Awards:* John Hay Whitney Found Fel, 55; Nat Inst Arts & Lett Grant, 60; Adolph & Clara Obrig Prize, Nat Acad Design, 72. *Bibliog:* Cedric Dover (auth), American Negro art, Studio, London, 58; Janet Erickson & Adelaide Sproul (auth), Printmaking Without a Press, Reinhold, 67. *Mem:* Billed Kunstnernes Forbund, Denmark. *Mailing Add:* c/o Terry Dintenfass Inc 50 W 57th St New York NY 10019

WILLIAMS, WAYNE FRANCIS
SCULPTOR

b Newark, NY, July 22, 37. *Study:* Syracuse Univ, BFA(Chaloner Found Fel), 58, MFA, 62. *Work:* Ministry Pub Educ Collections, Brussels, Belg; Murdock Collection, Wichita Mus, Kans; Whitney Found Collection, Cornell Univ; Nebr Art Asn, Univ Nebr-Lincoln; NY State Univ Col Albany. *Comn:* Life size welded sculpture, North Rose Wolcott Sch, NY, 72. *Exhib:* Belg Salon des Beaux Arts, Mus voor Schone Kunsten, Ghent, Belg, 60; one-man shows, Maynard Walker Gallery, 61 & 64 & Frank Rehn Gallery, New York, 74; New York Art Dealers Exhib, Park Bernet Gallery, New York, 64. *Teaching:* Instr drawing, Syracuse Univ, 60-63; prof drawing & sculpture, Community Col Finger Lakes, 68- *Awards:* Louis Comfort Tiffany Found Award for Sculpture, 64. *Bibliog:* John Canaday (auth), Wayne Williams-Maynard-Walker, New York Times, 10/64; Dorothy Hall (auth), Williams at Rehn,

Park East, New York, 4/74; Roberta Olson (auth), Wayne Williams-Rehn, Arts Mag, 6/74. *Media:* Metals. *Publ:* Auth, The art program at Community College of Finger Lakes, NY State Art Teachers Mag, 5/74. *Dealer:* John Clancy c/o Frank Rehn Gallery 655 Madison Ave New York NY 10021. *Mailing Add:* RD 3 364 Gardner Rd Newark NY 14513

WILLIAMS, WILLIAM THOMAS
PAINTER, EDUCATOR

b Cross Creek, NC, July 17, 42. *Study:* Skowhegan Sch Painting & Sculpture, summer 65; Pratt Inst, BFA, 66; Yale Univ, MFA, 68. *Work:* Mus Mod Art & Whitney Mus Am Art, New York; Yale Univ, New Haven, Conn; Wadsworth Atheneum, Hartford, Conn; Johnson Mus, Cornell Univ, Ithaca, NY. *Comn:* Print, Jewish Mus, New York, 70; environ sculpture, Menil Found, Houston, 70; environ murals, Gottesmans Plaza, New York, 70; print portfolio, HKL Ltd Publ, New York, 71; print, LD Group Int, New York, 78. *Exhib:* Whitney Ann, Whitney Mus Am Art, 69 & Struct of Color, 71; L'Art Vivant Aux Estats-Unis, Found Maeght, St Paul, France, 70; DeLuxe Show, Menil Found, Houston, 71; Acquisitions, Mus Mod Art, New York, 72; Painting & Sculpture Today, Indianapolis Mus Art, 72; Extensions, Wadsworth Atheneum, Hartford, Conn, 74; Festac, Nat Mus & Theatre, Lagos, Nigeria, 77. *Teaching:* Prof art, City Univ New York, Brooklyn Col, 70- *Awards:* Nat Endowment for Arts & Humanities traveling grant, 65 & artist fels, 70. *Mailing Add:* 654 Broadway New York NY 10012

WILLIAMSON, GAIL McKENNIS
PRINTMAKER, PAINTER

b Wilmington, NC, May 12, 39. *Study:* Richmond Prof Inst, Va Commonwealth Univ, BFA & MFA; Royal Col Art; Visual Studies Workshop. *Work:* Victoria & Albert Mus, London; Southern Regional Arts Asn, Eng; NC Mus Art; Mint Mus Art, Charlotte, NC; Dillard Collection, Univ NC, Greensboro. *Exhib:* 3rd & 4th Brit Int Print Biennales, Bradford, Eng, 72 & 74; 4th Int Print Biennale, Cracow, Poland, 72; Mod Prints, Bethnal Green Mus, London; Paperworks, Washington Gallery Art, 74; one-person show, Va Mus Fine Arts, 68. *Pos:* Gallery dir, Scott-McKennis Fine Art, Richmond, Va, 75-80; co-founder & co-dir, Richmond Printmaking Workshop, Inc, 77-80. *Teaching:* Instr painting, printmaking & drawing, Va Commonwealth Univ, 65-69; instr printmaking & drawing, Univ NC, Wilmington, 69-71; instr silkscreen, Univ Reading, Eng, 72-73; asst prof art, Roberts Wesleyan Col, Rochester, NY, 74-75. *Awards:* Va Mus Fine Arts Biennial Exhib Awards, 67 & 69; Purchase Award, 3rd Brit Int Print Biennale, 72; Purchase Award, Gallery Contemp Art, Winston-Salem, 73. *Media:* Mixed; Oil, Acrylic. *Mailing Add:* 5109 Downy Lane 102 Richmond VA 23228

WILLIAMSON, JASON H
PAINTER, DEALER

b Bristol, Va, Mar 20, 26. *Study:* Emory & Henry Col, Va; Vesper George Sch of Art, Boston, Mass, cert. *Comn:* Signed and numbered reproduction color prints, comn by Grey Stone Press, Nashville, Tenn. *Exhib:* Am Watercolor Soc, 65, 74-77 & 80; Watercolor USA, Springfield, Mo, 63, 72 & 74; one-man shows, East Tenn State Univ, Johnson City, 54, Memphis Acad of Arts, Tenn, 60, 67, Emory and Henry Col, Va, 67, Tenn Tech Univ, 73 & Ark Arts Ctr, Pine Bluff, 74 and many others; and others. *Pos:* Art dir, S E Massengill Co, Bristol, Tenn, 49-56 & Plough Inc, Memphis, 56-58; free lance advert art, Memphis, 58-62; advert art studio head, Williamson--Parker, 62-75; gallery owner, Golden Fleece Art Gallery, Memphis, 70-75 & Carefree, Ariz, 76-83. *Teaching:* Dept head advert art, The Memphis Acad of Art, Tenn, 60-69; nat competition judge, pvt classes and workshops, artist watercolor & oil. *Awards:* John Young Hunter, Am Watercolor Soc, 74; Annenberg Fund Award, Nat Watercolor Soc, 76; Colo Watermedia Award, Rocky Mountain Nat, 77. *Bibliog:* Watercolor Page, Am Artist Mag, 6/78; Southwest Art, 10/79. *Mem:* Am Watercolor Soc; Nat Watercolor Soc; 22 x 30 Watercolor Group Ariz; Tenn Watercolor Soc (hon lifetime); Memphis Watercolor Group (hon lifetime). *Media:* Watercolor, Oil. *Specialty:* Watercolor and oil. *Interest:* Support many worthwhile art organizations. *Dealer:* Golden Fleece Art Gallery 42 Easy St Carefree AZ 85331. *Mailing Add:* PO Box 1943 Cave Creek AZ 85331

WILLIAMSON, MARGARET THOMPSON See Patch, Peggie

WILLIG, NANCY TOBIN
CRITIC, WRITER

b New York, NY, Aug 31, 43. *Study:* Syracuse Univ Sch Art, BFA, 65. *Pos:* Art dir, Buffalo Mag, 65-75, asst ed, 65-69; art critic, Courier Express, Buffalo, 71-77, ed, Sunday Mag, 78-81; freelance writer, Art News, New York Times & Progressive Archit, currently; News art dir, Buffalo Courier Express, currently. *Awards:* Awards for Ed Content & Visual Content for Buffalo Mag, Am Asn Com Publ, 66-71; Merit Award for Criticism, Am Newspaper Guild, 75; 1st & 2nd Place Awards, newspaper design & headline writing, Am Newspaper Guild. *Mailing Add:* 308 Highland Ave 787 Main St Buffalo NY 14240

WILLIS, ELIZABETH BAYLEY
HISTORIAN, COLLECTOR

b Somerville, Mass. *Study:* Univ Wash, AB, with Lyonel Feininger, Mark Tobey & Morris Graves. *Pos:* Assoc, Willard Gallery, New York, 43-46; cur, Henry Gallery, Univ Wash, 46-48; cur, San Francisco Mus Art, 48-50; actg asst dir, Calif Palace Legion of Honor, 50-51; consult decorative arts, prod & mkt, Mingei Kan, Tokyo, 51-52; expert mem UN Tech Asst Bd for Taiwan, Vietnam, India & Morocco, 52-59; consult textile export, India, 55-57. *Res:*

Tribes of India's northeast frontier (1959-1964), especially their arts and textiles; textile arts of India; folk arts of Japan. *Collection:* Artifacts, pottery and textiles from Tibet, Bhutan, Japan & Morocco, now in the Permanent Collection of the Smithsonian Institution; costumes and textiles from the same countries now in Permanent Collections of the University of Washington and the Washington State Museum; Ming and Ch'ing paintings in a private collection. *Mailing Add:* PO Box 10126 Bainbridge Island WA 98110

WILLIS, JAY STEWART
SCULPTOR, EDUCATOR

b Fort Wayne, Ind, Oct 22, 40. *Study:* Univ Ill, Urbana, study with Frank Gallo & Roger Majorweiz, BFA(sculpture), 61; Univ Calif, Berkeley, study with Donald Haskin, Harold Paris, Jacques Schnier & Peter Voulkos, MA(sculpture), 66. *Work:* Moore Col Art; Del Mar Col, Corpus Christi, Tex; Am Tel & Tel, Chicago; Metrop Mus Art, New York; Calif State Univ, Fullerton. *Comn:* Multiple Structures, Cirus Ed, 73; sculpture comn by Terry Inch, Los Angeles, 74; sculpture (with Bob Smith), ABC Century City, Los Angeles, 75; sculpture (with Don Brewer), ALCOA, Univ Southern Calif sculpture garden, Los Angeles, 78; sculpture, comn by Ernesto W Hahn & Charles Kober Assocs, Pasadena, Calif, 80. *Exhib:* Current Concerns ... 100 plus Current Directions in Southern Calif Art, Los Angeles Inst of Contemp Art, 75 & 77; one-man shows, Fisher Gallery, Univ Southern Calif, Los Angeles, 78, Del Mar Col, Corpus Christie, Tex, Cirrus Gallery Ltd, Los Angeles, 72-75, 78 & 81; Aspects of Abstract: Recent West Coast Abstract Painting & Sculpture, Crocker Art Mus, Sacramento, Calif, 79; Painter Sculpture, Municipal Art Mus, Los Angeles, Calif; plus others. *Teaching:* Instr sculpture, Univ Ariz, Tucson, 66-69; assoc prof sculpture, Univ Southern Calif, Los Angeles, 69- *Awards:* Purchase Award, Am Drawing 1968, Moore Col Art, 68; Purchase Award, Am Art Festival, Home Saving & Loan, 70, 73 & 75. *Bibliog:* Articles in Artweek, 71-73 & 75-78, Artforum, 71, 72 & 78 & Art Mag, 4/73. *Mailing Add:* PO Box 50101 Pasadena CA 91105

WILLIS, SIDNEY F
PAINTER

b Newark, NJ, Dec 14, 30. *Study:* Vesper George Sch Art, grad, continued study with Robert D Hunter. *Exhib:* Southern Vt Artists, 72; Jordan Show, Boston, Mass, 73; Ogunquit Art Ctr, Maine, 74; Am Artists Prof League, New York, 74; Coun Am Artists Show, New York. *Teaching:* Instr painting & drawing, Vesper George Art Sch, Boston, Mass, 67-69, Sharon Art Ctr, Peterborough, NH, 65-75. *Awards:* Grand Prize, Jordan Show, Boston, 58 & 62; First Prize, Ogunquit Art Ctr, Maine, 61; and many others. *Mem:* Guild Boston Artists; NH Art Asn; New Am Acad; Am Artists Prof League; Paste Soc of Am. *Media:* Acrylic, Oil. *Mailing Add:* Box 151 Bennington NH 03442

WILLIS, THORNTON
PAINTER

b Pensacola, Fla, May 25, 36. *Study:* Auburn Univ, Ala; Univ Southern Miss, Hattiesburg, BS; Univ Ala, MA. *Work:* Whitney Mus Am Art, New York; Phillips Collection, Washington, DC; Mus Mod Art, New York; Denver Mus Fine Art; Albright-Knox Art Gallery, Buffalo, NY; and others. *Exhib:* Lyrical Abstraction, Aldrich Mus, 69 & Whitney Mus, 71; one-man shows, Oscarsson-Hood Gallery, 80 & 81, Sydney Janis Gallery, 80, New York & Marianne Deson Gallery, Chicago, 81; Mus Mod Art, New York, 81; Galerie Gonet, Lausanne, Switzerland, 82; Art Mus Ateneum, Helsinki, Finland, 83; and others. *Teaching:* Grad lectr, Pratt Inst, 74, 77 & 80; lectr, Art Inst Chicago, Ill, 81; assoc prof art, Univ La, Baton Rouge, 83. *Awards:* Fac Res Grant for Painting, Wagner Col, Staten Island, NY, 68; Fel Award, John Simon Guggenheim Found, 78-79; Nat Endowment Arts Painting Fel, 80. *Bibliog:* Noel Frackman (auth), The paintings of Thornton Willis, Arts Mag, 11/80; Joseph Masheck (auth), Abstract identity: Thornton Willis, Art Am, 10/81; Steven H Madoff (auth), Looking for Thorton Willis: A treatise, Arts, 3/83; and others. *Media:* Plastic, Oil. *Dealer:* Oscarsson Hood Gallery 41 West 57th St New York NY; Claes Nordenhake Ostra Ronneholmsuagen 5 Malmo Sweden. *Mailing Add:* 85-87 Mercer St New York NY 10012

WILLIS, WILLIAM HENRY, JR
ADMINISTRATOR

b Boston, Mass, Oct 29, 40. *Study:* Marlboro Col, VT, BA; Yale Univ, New Haven, Conn, MFA. *Pos:* Dir admis, Art Inst Boston, 67-74, dir, 74-76 & pres, 76- *Mailing Add:* 88 Marginal St Chelsea MA 02150

WILLOUGHBY, JANE BAKER
PAINTER, COLLAGE ARTIST

b Toledo, Ohio. *Study:* Smith Col, Mass, BA, 43; Art Students League with George Grosz, 45-49; New Sch Social Res, New York, 50-51. *Work:* Lyman Allyn Mus, New London, Conn; Mus Art, Sci & Industry, Bridgeport, Conn; The Robert Bejamin Collection, New York; Conn Bank & Trust Co, New Haven; Sen & Mrs George McGovern, Washington, DC. *Exhib:* One-man shows, Silvermine Guild Artists, New Canaan, Conn, 63 & 76, Slater Mem Mus, Norwich, Conn, 76, Lyman Allyn Mus, New London, Conn, 80, Bridgeport Mus Art, Sci, Conn, 80 & Whitney Mus Am Art, New Haven, Conn, 81; The Benjamin Collection, Yale Univ Art Gallery; Viridian Gallery, New York, 83; and others. *Teaching:* Instr, Silvermine Guild Art, currently. *Awards:* Munson Award & Purchase Prize, New Haven Paint-Clay Club, 75; Arches Paper, Nat Asn Painters in Casein & Acrylic, 78; Audubon Medal Honor, Audubon Artists Am, 78. *Bibliog:* Shirley Gonzales (auth), New Haven Register, 9/16/83; Shirley Sandler (auth), Manhattan Arts, 11/16/83; Amy Friedman (auth), Artspeak, 11/16/83; and others. *Mem:* Silvermine Guild Artists; Conn Acad Fine Arts; Conn Watercolor Soc; Audubon Artists Inc; Conn Women Artists Asn. *Media:* Collage, Monotype. *Mailing Add:* 1150 Ridge Road Hamden CT 06517

WILLSON, MARGARET (BOSSHARDT) PACE
PAINTER, SCULPTOR

b San Antonio, Tex, Dec 9, 19. *Study:* Newcomb Col, BDes, BFA; Trinity Univ; Univ Tex (archit), three yrs; also with Will Stevens, Etienne Ret, Xavier Gonzalez & Rico Lebrun. *Work:* McNay Mus Art. *Comn:* mosaic murals, Episcopal Diocesan Ctr, Diocese of WTex, 61 & Episcopal Cathedral, 65; mural, Lemon Grove, Calif Unitarian Church, 67; designed & executed chalice, pattern & pix, ordination of Father Braun, Pinckneyville, Ill, 69; and others. *Exhib:* Women Who Influenced the Art Community of San Antonio, Tex Health Sci Ctr, 77; Bright Shawl Gallery, 80-82; McNay Mus, 81; Ravagnon Gallery Mod Art, Venice; solo exhib, Tulane-Newcomb Univ, 84. *Pos:* Bd mem, trustee & vpres, San Antonio Art Inst, 55-84; bd mem & secy, Witte Mus, 60-65; Southwest Craft Ctr, 69-84; nat pres alumni bd, Newcomb Col, Tulane Univ, mem pres coun, 76-78, mem alumni bd, 77-84; pres, P & W Oil & Gas Exploration Corp; bd mem, McNay Mus Coun, San Antonio, 82-85. *Teaching:* Instr, Incarnet Word Col, 64-65; asst prof art, San Antonio Col, 65-72; instr design & watercolor, Hill Country Found, 68, 70, 75-77. *Awards:* Henry Steinbomer Award, Tex Watercolor Soc, 49 & 66; Grumbacher Purchase Award, 60; Richard Kleberg Purchase Award, 62; plus many others. *Mem:* San Antonio Art League (bd mem, 56-58, 60, 67-68, 71, 73-78); Pace-Willson Art Found (vpres, currently); Tex Watercolor Soc (first vpres, 83-85); San Antonio Craft Guild; San Antonio Watercolor Group; San Antonio Contemp Artists Group; plus others. *Mailing Add:* 208 Morningside Dr San Antonio TX 78209

WILLSON, ROBERT
SCULPTOR, PAINTER

b Mertzon, Tex, May 28, 12. *Study:* Univ Tex, BA; Univ Bellas Artes, Guanajuato, Mex, MFA; and with Jose Clemente Orozco. *Work:* Mus Correr, Venice, Italy; Witte Art Mus, San Antonio, Tex; Lowe Art Mus, Coral Gables, Fla; McNay Art Mus, San Antonio, Tex; Corning Glass Mus, NY; Italian Nat Glass Mus, Murano, Italy; and others. *Comn:* Glass sculptures, Harmon Gallery, Naples, Fla, 69; ceramic sculptures, comn by Mrs Robert Hoffman, Naples, 70; glass sculpture doorway, comn by Herbert Martin, Miami, Fla, 72; enamel sculpture, Exec Plaza, Miami, 72; glass wall, Picante Inc, San Antonio, 82. *Exhib:* Painting & Sculpture Nat, San Francisco Mus Art, 57; one-man shows, Ringling Art Mus, Sarasota, Fla; 70, Corning Mus Glass, NY, 71, Univ Tex Art Mus, 79 & McNay Art Mus, 81; Int Glass Sculpture, Lowe Art Mus, Coral Gables, Fla, 73; Tex Mus Tour, 78; Mus Mod Art, Venice, 84; and others. *Pos:* Dir, Coun Ozark Artists, 50-52; pres & dir, Fla Craftsmen, 52-58; ed, Tejas Art Press, San Antonio, Tex, presently. *Teaching:* Chmn dept art, Tex Wesleyan Col, 40-48; prof art, Univ Miami, 52-77. *Awards:* Nat Hon Mention for Sculpture, San Francisco Mus Art, 57; Shell Co Fund Grants for Glass Sculpture, 71 & 73; Fla State Grand Medal Award Winner for Sculpture, Garden Mod Art, Miami, 72. *Bibliog:* Frank Wills (auth), Robert Willson glass sculpture, Mnemosyne, 68; Glass fantasies, Tex Highways, 2/79; Robert Willson: An innovative pioneer in glass sculpture, Artcraft Mag, 4-5/80. *Mem·* Col Art Asn Am; Am Asn Mus; San Antonio Watercolor Soc. *Media:* Glass, Ceramic; Watercolor. *Publ:* Ed, Kress Collection, 61 & auth, Art concept in Clay, 67, Univ Miami; auth, College-level Art Curriculum in Glass, Dept Health, Educ & Welfare, 68. *Dealer:* Galerie 99 1088 Kane Concourse Bay Harbor Island Miami FL 33154; Harmon Art Gallery 1258 Third St S Naples FL 33577. *Mailing Add:* 207 Terrell Rd San Antonio TX 78209

WILMARTH, CHRISTOPHER MALLORY
SCULPTOR, DRAFTSMAN

b Sonoma, Calif, June 11, 43. *Study:* Cooper Union, BFA, 65. *Work:* Metrop Mus Art & Mus Mod Art, New York; Art Inst Chicago; Fogg Art Mus, Whitney Mus Am Art; and others. *Exhib:* Whitney Ann, Whitney Mus Am Art, 66-79; Aldrich Mus Contemp Art, Ridgefield, Conn, 68, 69 & 71; 70th Am Exhib, Art Inst Chicago, 72; 20th Century Art Collection, Metrop Mus Art, New York, 74; one-man shows, Wadsworth Athenaeum, Hartford, Conn, 74 & 77, St Louis Mus, 75 & Seattle Art Mus, 79; Dialogue, Huntington Mus, WVa, 78; Contemp Sculpture, Mus Mod Art, New York, 79; Eight Artists, Albright-Knox Art Gallery, 79; plus many others. *Teaching:* Adj prof sculpture, Cooper Union, 69-79; vis critic sculpture, Yale Univ, 71-72; vis artist, Columbia Univ, 76-78. *Awards:* Nat Coun Arts Grant, 69; Guggenheim Mem Fel, 70-71 & 82-83; Howard Found Fel, 72; Creative Artists Publ Serv Prog, 80; and others. *Bibliog:* Hilton Kramer (auth), New York Sunday Times, 12/8/74 & 1/20/78; Kate Linkery (auth), Arts Mag, 4/75; Paula Dietz (auth), article, New York Arts J, 78; and others. *Media:* Various. *Mailing Add:* PO Box 203 Canal St Sta New York NY 10013

WILMERDING, JOHN
HISTORIAN, MUSEUM DIRECTOR

b Boston, Mass, Apr 28, 38. *Study:* Harvard Col, AB, 60; Harvard Univ, AM, 61 & PhD, 65; also Am art with Benjamin Rowland. *Collections Arranged:* Nineteenth Century America: Painting & Sculpture, Metrop Mus Art, New York, 70; The Art of Fitz Hugh Lane, Farnsworth Art Mus, Rockland, Maine, 74; The Natural Paradise, Painting in America 1800-1950, Mus Mod Art, New York, 76; American Marine Painting, Va Mus Fine Arts, Richmond, 76; 100 American Drawings from the J D Hatch Collection, Nat Gallery of Ireland, 76; American Light: The Luminist Movement (auth, catalog), 80, An American Perspective: The Ganz Collection, 81 & Important Information Inside: The Art of John F Peto (auth, catalog), 83, Nat Gallery Art, Washington, DC. *Pos:* Vpres, Shelburne Mus, Vt, 66-76; cur of Am art & sr cur, Nat Gallery Art, Washington, DC, 77-82, depy dir, 83- *Teaching:* Leon E Williams prof Am art, Dartmouth Col, 65-77; vis lectr, Yale Univ, 72; vis prof, Harvard Univ, 76, Univ Md, 79 & Univ Del, 82. *Awards:* Humanities Fac Develop Grant, Dartmouth Col, 70-71; Guggenheim Found Fel, 73-74.

Mem: Am Studies Asn; Col Art Asn; Dunlap Soc (vpres, currently). *Res:* John F Peto; Raphaelle Peale. *Publ:* Auth, Fitz Hugh Lane, 71 & Winslow Homer, 72, Praeger; auth, American Art, Pelican/Penguin, 76; auth, American Masterpieces from the National Gallery of Art, Hudson Hills, 80; auth, Important Information Inside, Harper & Row, 83. *Mailing Add:* Cur of Am Art Nat Gallery of Art Washington DC 20565

WILMETH, ERNEST, II
PAINTER, SCULPTOR
b Perryton, Tex, Dec 21, 52. *Study:* WTex State Univ, with Dr Emilio Caballero, 71-72; Northern Ariz Univ, with Ellery Gibson, Harold Roney, Lonnie Mason & Ramon Froman, BFA, 76. *Exhib:* Tri-State Fair, Amarillo, Tex, 79; Statesman's Club, Albuquerque Savings & Loan, NMex, 82; NMex Very Special Arts Festival, 83. *Awards:* First in Oil, Tri-State Fair, Amarillo, 79. *Bibliog:* Mary Alice Hines (auth), Profile: Mary Elizabeth Cornette, Accent W, 7/78. *Mem:* Fel Royal Soc Arts; life mem Royal Soc Encouragement Arts Manufactures & Com. *Media:* Oil, Watercolor; Clay. *Dealer:* Canyon Art Gallery 2710 Fourth Ave Canyon TX 79105. *Mailing Add:* 1521 Bryn Mawr NE Albuquerque NM 87106

WILNER, MARIE SPRING
PAINTER
b Paris, France; US citizen. *Study:* Hunter Col, BA; Art Students League; New Sch Social Res, with Camillo Egas & Samuel Adler. *Work:* Tweed Mus, Univ Minn; Norfolk Mus, Va; Mus Ga; Bridgeport Mus, Conn; Birmingham Mus, Ala. *Exhib:* Pa Acad Fine Arts, 61; Butler Inst Am Art, 63; Sheldon Swope Mus, 68; Tweed Mus, Univ Minn, 69; Salon Autumn, Paris, 72; Metrop Mus Art, 79; Salon des sur Independo, Mus Luxembourg, 79 & Salon des Artistes, Paris, 79. *Awards:* Gold Medal, Ann Exhib Am Artists Prof League; Grumbacher Purchase Prize, Nat Asn Women Artists Ann; Bronze Medal, 3rd Biennale Int, Ancona, Italy. *Bibliog:* Vallobra (auth), De l'Honneur et du Deshonneur des Hommes; article & cover, In Design, 62. *Mem:* Life fel Royal Soc Art, London; Int Arts Guild, Monaco; Nat Assoc Arts & Lett; Nat Asn Women Artists (gallery chmn, 62, jury mem, 65 & chmn jury awards, 67); Soc Encouragement Progres, Paris (chevalier, 68, officer, 71). *Media:* Oil, Watercolor. *Dealer:* Dickson Gallery 3237 P St NW Washington DC 20007; Sue Fischman Ft Lauderdale FL 33310. *Mailing Add:* c/o Dickson Gallery 3237 P St NW Washington DC 20007

WILSON, BEN
PAINTER, LECTURER
b Philadelphia, Pa, June 23, 13. *Study:* Nat Acad Design, 31-33; City Col New York, with Eggers, BSS, 35; Acad Julien, Paris, France, 53-54. *Work:* Everhart Mus, Scranton, Pa; Fairleigh Dickinson Collection Self Portraits; Norfolk Mus, Va; Faberge Collection, Ridgefield, NJ; Almeras Collection, Paris. *Exhib:* Riverside Mus, 55; Newark Mus, 56, Triennial, 61; nine exhibs, Montclair Mus, 56-72; Everhart Mus, 65 & 66; NJ Pavilion, New York World's Fair, 65-66; one-man show, Bergen Community Mus, 74. *Pos:* Art critic, TAO, 76-77. *Teaching:* Instr painting & drawing, City Col New York, 46-48; instr life drawing, Jamesine Franklin Sch Art, 50; lectr mod art, NY Univ, 62-68; instr, Art Ctr of Northern NJ, 65-68. *Awards:* Agnes B Noyes Award for Watercolor, 59 & Skinner Award for Abstract Oils, 63, Montclair Mus; Ford Found Resident Artist, Everhart Mus, 65. *Bibliog:* Bugatti (auth), International Encyclopedia of Artists, Univ Europa, 70-71. *Mem:* Mod Artists Guild (vpres, 63); Assoc Artists NJ. *Media:* Oil. *Publ:* Auth, Cobra, Artists Proof, 66. *Dealer:* Galerie A G rue de l'universite, Paris, France. *Mailing Add:* RD 2 Box 57 Blairstown NJ 07825

WILSON, CARRIE LOIS
GALLERY DIRECTOR, LECTURER
b Philadelphia, Pa, Sept 15, 44. *Study:* Barnard Col, Columbia Univ, BA(art hist), 66; philosophy of Aesthetic Realism with its founder, Eli Siegel, 69- *Pos:* Co-dir, Terrain Gallery, 72- *Teaching:* Consult & instr, Aesthetic Realism Found, 72- *Specialty:* Contemporary American prints, drawings and paintings; exhibitions showing that the Aesthetic Realism of Eli Siegel is true. *Mailing Add:* c/o Terrain Gallery 141 Greene St New York NY 10012

WILSON, CHARLES BANKS
PAINTER, PRINTMAKER
b Springdale, Ark, Aug 6, 18. *Study:* Art Inst Chicago, lithography with Francis Chapin, painting with Louis Ritman & Boris Anisfeld & watercolor with Hubert Ropp; Univ Okla, DSc, 76. *Work:* Metrop Mus Art, New York; Corcoran Gallery Art, Washington, DC; Gilcrease Inst Am Hist & Art, Tulsa, Okla; US Capitol Speaker's Gallery; Smithsonian Inst, Washington, DC. *Comn:* 50 Watercolors, Ford Motor Co, 51-69; oil mural, comn by J D Rockefeller, Jr, Jackson Lake Lodge, Wyo, 55; portraits of Thomas Gilcrease, Gilcrease Inst Am Hist & Art, 57, Will Rogers, Okla Press Asn, Oklahoma City, 61, Sen Robert Kerr & Jim Thorpe; rotunda murals, Okla State Legis, 63 & Okla Capitol, 76; and others. *Exhib:* Int Watercolor Exhib, Art Inst Chicago, 39; Am Watercolor Exhib, Springfield, Mo, 70; some 200 nat & regional exhibs. *Teaching:* Head art, Northeastern Okla Agr & Mech Col, 47-60. *Awards:* Gov's Art Award, 76; Okla Hall of Fame, 77; Nat Cowboy Hall Fame, 79. *Bibliog:* Hold before the young, Okla Today, 69; Painting mural portraits, Am Artist, 11/69; Before death do us part, Wash Post Mag, 81. *Media:* Mixed. *Publ:* Illusr, Treasure Island, 48, Company of Adventures, 49, Mustangs, 52 & Geronimo, 58; auth, Search For the Purebloods, 83; plus others. *Mailing Add:* 100 N Main St Miami OK 74354

WILSON, DAVID PHILIP
PAINTER
b Monongahela, Pa, Aug 12, 09. *Study:* Carnegie Inst Technol Col Painting & Design, BFA; Child-Walker Sch Art, scholar in portrait painting with Charles Hopkinson. *Work:* Ohio Hist Mus, Wapakoneta; State Capitol Collection, Austin, Tex; Ohio State Capitol Bldg, Columbus; WVa Capitol Bldg; and others. *Comn:* Numerous portraits of influential persons, including government officials, corporate executives, college & university presidents & deans & noted medical men. *Exhib:* New Directions, Carnegie Mus, Pittsburgh; Art Inst Chicago All Am Show & Nat Traveling Exhib; Cleveland Mus Art May Shows, 46 & 47; also numerous private shows. *Teaching:* Instr compos, Cleveland Inst Art, 46-48; artist in residence portrait painting, Trinity Univ, 63-68. *Mem:* Coppini Acad Fine Arts, Tex; Chagrin Falls Art Asn, Ohio (pres-founder, 47-49). *Media:* Oil, Pastel. *Publ:* Auth, Portrait of a portrait painter, Columbus Dispatch Mag, 82. *Mailing Add:* 340 West Ave Naples FL 33940

WILSON, EDWARD N
SCULPTOR, EDUCATOR
b Baltimore, Md, Mar 28, 25. *Study:* Univ Iowa, BA & MA; Univ NC. *Work:* Howard Univ; State Univ NY Binghamton; JFK Mem Maquettes Collection, San Francisco Mus; and numerous pvt collections. *Comn:* Middle Passage (concrete & bronze), City of New York, Brooklyn, 73-75; stainless steel & bronze sculpture, Ralph Ellison Libr, Oklahoma City, 75; Fred Douglass Competition, US Dept of Interior, Nat Park Serv, 1/2 Life Size Fig, Harper's Ferry, WVa, 78-79; The Schomburg Collection Award Medal (bronze), New York, 79-80; Jazz Musicians (bronze), City Baltimore, 82-83; and others. *Exhib:* 155th Ann Exhib Am Painting & Sculpture, Pa Acad Fine Arts & Detroit Inst Arts, 60; Am Negro Art, Univ Calif, Davis, 66; San Diego & Oakland, Calif, 67; Artists of Cent New York, Munson-Williams-Proctor Mus, 66-68; 30 Contemporary Black Artists, nat circulated, 68-70; 200 Yrs Black Am Art, nat circulated, 76-77; and others. *Pos:* Resident artist, Humanities Div, Western Mich Univ, 69. *Teaching:* Prof sculpture, State Univ NY Binghamton, 64-, chmn dept art & art hist, 68-72 & 82- *Awards:* Award for Sculpture, Md Artists 24th Ann, Baltimore Mus Art, 56; Purchase Prize for Sculpture, New Vistas in Am Art, Howard Univ, 61; Fel, State Univ NY, 66-68. *Bibliog:* Cedric Dover (auth), American Negro art, NY Graphic Soc, 60; Art & rebuttal, Christian Sci Monitor, 4/21/71; H Hope (auth), article in, Art J, spring Vol 31, No 3. *Mem:* Col Art Asn Am (bd dirs, 70, secy & chmn artists comt, 71-). *Publ:* Auth, Contemporary sculpture: some trends & problems, 63; auth, Statement, Arts in Soc, fall-winter, 68-69; auth, CAA & Negro colleges, Art J, winter 68-69. *Mailing Add:* Dept of Art & Art Hist State Univ of New York Binghamton NY 13901

WILSON, GEORGE LEWIS
PAINTER
b Windsor, NC, Sept 30, 30. *Study:* Art Inst, Pittsburgh, Pa; Sch Visual Arts, New York; Nat Acad Sch Fine Art, New York, with Serge Hollarbach, 81. *Work:* Johnson Publ, Inc, Chicago; Howard Univ, Washington, DC; Nigerian Embassy, Washington, DC; Clinica Limonar, Malaga, Spain; New Muse Mus, Brooklyn, NY; and others. *Comn:* Paintings, comn by Pub Sch 186, NY, 64; paintings, comn by NY-Long Island Libr, West Middle Island, 66; paintings, The New Muse Mus, 79. *Exhib:* Allied Artists Am Ann, Nat Acad, New York; Mainstream, Marietta Col Int, 70-71; Contemporary, Springville Mus Ann, Utah, 74 & 76; Bronx Mus Am Ann, New York, 75, 76 & 77; African-Am Mus, Dallas, Tex, 80 & 81; and other group & one-man shows. *Awards:* Travel grant, Washington Sq Outdoor Art Exhib, Inc, 71; First Prize for Figure Painting, Atlantic City Boardwalk, 74, 76 & 80, Grand Prize, 79; Best in Show & First Prize, Jersey City, NJ, 80. *Bibliog:* Lindsay Patterson (auth), Negro in Mus & Art, Publ Co Inc, 67; Herbert Temple (auth), Perspectives, Johnson Publ, 73; David Shirey (auth), article, New York Times, 2/22/81. *Mem:* Bronx Coun Arts; New York Artists Equity Asn. *Media:* Oil, Pastel. *Dealer:* Dorsey Art Gallery 553 Rodgers Ave Brooklyn NY 11225. *Mailing Add:* 4197 Park Ave Bronx NY 10457

WILSON, JANE
PAINTER
b Seymour, Iowa, Apr 29, 24. *Study:* Univ Iowa, BA & MA. *Work:* Mus Mod Art, Metrop Mus Art, Whitney Mus Am Art, New York; Wadsworth Atheneum, Hartford, Conn; Hirshhorn Mus, Washington, DC; and many others. *Exhib:* Whitney Mus Am Art, New York, 63 & 68; Am Women of the 20th Century, Lakeview Ctr Arts & Sci, 72; Painterly Realism in Am, A J Wood Gallery, Philadelphia, Pa, 79; The Fifties: Hirshhorn Mus, 80; plus many others. *Teaching:* Instr art hist, Pratt Inst, 67-69; instr, Fine Arts Division, Parsons Sch Design, 73-; adj assoc prof, Dept Painting & Drawing, Columbia Univ, 75- *Awards:* Tiffany Grant, 67; Ranger Fund Purchase Prize, 78; Award in Art, Acad Arts & Letters, 81. *Mem:* Nat Acad Design. *Mailing Add:* Fischback Gallery 29 W 57th New York NY 10019

WILSON, JOHN
SCULPTOR, PRINTMAKER
b Boston, Mass, Apr 14, 22. *Study:* Sch Mus Fine Arts, Boston, dipl; Tufts Univ, BS(educ); Fernand Leger's Sch, Paris; Inst Politecnico, Esmeralda Sch Art & Escuela Artes del Libro, Mexico City. *Work:* Mus Fine Arts, Boston; Smith Col Mus Art, Northampton, Mass; Mus Mod Art, New York; Atlanta Univ, Ga; Dept Fine Arts, Govt France. *Comn:* Monument to Dr Martin Luther King (bronze), Buffalo Arts Comn, NY, 83. *Exhib:* Master Prints from the Mus Collections, Mus Mod Art, New York, 49; Young Am Painters, Metrop Mus Art, New York, 50; Mus Int Biennial Color Lithography, Cincinnati, Ohio, 53; Afro-American Artists, Mus Fine Arts, New York & Boston, 70; Highlights from Univ Collection, High Mus Art, Atlanta, Ga, 73.

Teaching: Illusr art, New York Bd Educ, 59-64; prof art, Boston Univ, 64-
Awards: John Hay Whitney Fel for study in Mex, 50; Best Cover Design, Int
Fedn Periodicals Press, Paris, 71; Mass Arts & Humanities Found, Inc
sculpture fel, 76. *Mem:* Elmo Lewis Sch Fine Arts, Inc, Boston. *Media:*
Mixed. *Publ:* Co-illusr, New Worlds of Reading, Harcourt, 59, American
Negro Art, Graphic Soc, NY, 60, Who Look at Me, Crowell, NY, 69, 17 Black
Artists, Dodd Mead Co, New York, 71 & Land of Progress, Ginn, 75. *Mailing
Add:* 44 Harris St Brookline MA 02146

WILSON, JOHN DAVID
DEALER, PUBLISHER
b Flint, Mich, Aug 30, 34. *Study:* Mich State Univ, BA, 60; Univ Notre Dame,
MA, 67. *Pos:* Pres, Chicago Int Art Exposition, formerly; dir, Lakeside
Studio, currently. *Bibliog:* Judith Goldman (auth), Print establishment II, Art
Am, 9-10/73; David & Cecile Shapiro (coauth), Lakeside Studio:Conserving
the printmaking tradition, Art News, 3/77; Charlotte Moser (auth), John
Wilson brings art world to Chicago, Chicago Sun-Times, 9-11/83. *Specialty:*
Original graphics, old masters, modern and contemporary. *Mailing Add:*
Lakeside Studio 15263 Lakeshore Rd Lakeside MI 49116

WILSON, JUDITH (A)
CRITIC, WRITER
b Oakland, Calif, Nov 29, 52. *Study:* Bennington Col, BA, 74; Sch Visual Arts,
78-80; Yale Univ, 81-82. *Pos:* Asst cur, The Kitchen, New York, 80; reviewer,
Village Voice, New York, 80-81. *Mem:* Int Asn Art Critics. *Res:* Twentieth
century art by Afro-Americans. *Publ:* Auth, Alma Thomas: A one-woman art
movement, 79 & Howardena Pindell makes art that winks at you, 80, Ms Mag;
auth, The bullish market for Black art, Black Enterprise, 80; auth, Edward
Clark: Directions, Art Am, 81; auth, article on 20th century Black folk art,
Mus Mag, 82. *Mailing Add:* 254 Prospect St New Haven CT 06520

WILSON, MARTHA STOREY
CONCEPTUAL ARTIST, MUSEUM DIRECTOR
b Philadelphia, Pa, Dec 18, 47. *Study:* Wilmington Col, Ohio, BA; Dalhousie
Univ, Halifax, NS, Can, MA & studies for PhD. *Exhib:* Circa 7500 (traveling
exhib of women conceptual artists), 73-74; Autogeography, Downtown
Whitney Mus Am Art, New York, 75; Four Evenings, Four Days, Whitney
Mus Am Art, New York, 76. *Pos:* Exec dir, Franklin Furnace Archives Inc,
76- *Teaching:* Lectr lit, NS Col Art & Design, 72-74; lectr 20th century art,
Brooklyn Col, NY, 75. *Bibliog:* Lucy R Lippard (auth), Six Years: The
Dematerialization of the Art Object, Praeger, 73; Lucy R Lippard (auth),
From the Center: Feminist Essays on Women's Art, Dutton, 76. *Mem:* Col
Art Asn; Gallery Asn NY State. *Media:* Mixed. *Publ:* Auth, The Arnotated
Alice, pvt publ, 76. *Mailing Add:* 112 Franklin St New York NY 10013

WILSON, MAY
SCULPTOR
b Baltimore, Md, Sept 28, 05. *Work:* Whitney Mus Am Art, New York;
Baltimore Mus; Goucher Col, Baltimore; Corcoran Gallery Art, Washington,
DC; Dela Banque de Pariset, Brussels, Belg. *Exhib:* New Idea, New Media
Show, Martha Jackson Gallery, New York, 60; Mus Mod Art Traveling
Assemblage, New York, 62; Am Fedn Arts Patriotic Traveling Show, New
York, 68; Human Concern Show, 69 & Whitney Sculpture Ann, 70, Whitney
Mus Am Art. *Awards:* Baltimore Mus Art Show Awards, 52 & 59. *Bibliog:*
Bill Wilson (auth), Grandma Moses of the underground, Art & Artists, 5/68;
Woo who? May Wilson (film), Amalie Rothschild, 70; May Wilson
(videotape), Lee Ferguson, 7/14/71. *Mailing Add:* 208 W 23rd St New York
NY 10011

WILSON, MILLIE
PAINTER, EDUCATOR
b Hot Springs, Ark, Nov 26, 48. *Study:* Yale Summer Sch Music & Art, with
Bernard Chaet & Phillip Guston, 70; Univ Tex, Austin, BFA, 71; Univ
Houston, MFA, 83. *Exhib:* Works on Paper--Southwest 1978, Dallas Mus
Fine Arts, 78; Texas Only, Laguna Gloria Art Mus, Austin, 80; Austin
Contemp Art Exhib, Dougherty Cult Arts Ctr, Tex, 80; Longview Mus & Arts
Ctr Exhib, Tex, 81; 24th Ann Delta Art Exhib, Ark Art Ctr, Little Rock, 81;
Art Ann Two, Okla Art Ctr, 81; September Competition, Alexandria Mus, La,
83; and others. *Teaching:* Fel drawing, Univ Houston, 81-83; asst prof
painting, Univ Ill, Urbana-Champaign, 83- *Awards:* Merit Award, Art
Marketing Letter Fall Competition, 83. *Mem:* Col Art Asn; Womens Caucus
Art; Phi Kappa Phi. *Mailing Add:* 308 E Green St Urbana IL 61801

WILSON, NICHOLAS JON
PAINTER
b Seattle, Wash, June 7, 47. *Work:* Walter Bimson Collection Western Art,
Phoenix, Ariz; Okla Cowboy Hall of Fame, Oklahoma City. *Exhib:* Soc
Animal Artists Exhib, Westport, Conn, New York & Oklahoma City, 78;
Audubon Soc-Eastman Kodak Co Wildlife Exhib, New York, 78; Bird Art
Exhib, Smithsonian Inst, Washington, DC, 80; Bird Art World Tour, Royal
Scottish Acad, Edinburgh, Scotland, 81, British Mus, London, Eng, 81 &
Carnegie Mus Natural Hist, Pittsburgh, Pa, 82; and many others. *Pos:* Cur
exhib, Ariz-Sonora Desert Mus, Tucson, 70-72. *Awards:* Third Place Bronze,
Royal Western Watercolor Competition, 74. *Bibliog:* Adina Wingate (auth),
Nick Wilson: Wildlife Artist, Southwest Art Mag, 4/74; Wildlife Artist Nick
Wilson, Outdoor Am, 6/77; Patricia Van Gelder (auth), Wildlife Artists at
Work, Watson-Guptill, 83. *Mem:* Soc Animal Artists. *Media:* Gouache. *Publ:*
Illusr, The Chukar Partridge, Nev Fish & Game, 69. *Dealer:* Mill Pond Press
Inc 204 S Nassau St Venice FL 33959; Settlers West Gallery 6420 N
Campbell Tucson AZ 85718. *Mailing Add:* 1600 W Mesa Dr Payson AZ
85541

WILSON, RICHARD BRIAN
PAINTER
b Wichita, Kans, June 12, 44. *Study:* Calif State Univ, San Jose, BA & MA.
Work: Downey Art Mus, Calif; IBM Corp, San Jose, Calif; Mobil Oil Co, San
Francisco; Am Tel & Tel Co, Chicago; Fort Steilicom Col; and others. *Exhib:*
Holiday Festival, San Francisco Mus Mod Art, 69; Looking West 1970, Joslin
Art Mus, 70; Drawings 70: First Ann Drawing Show, St John's Univ, New
York, 70; Boxtop Painting Exhib, Ill State Univ, 71; Ariz Nat Painting
Competition, Scottsdale Ctr Arts, 77 & 78; Int Art Fairs, Basil & Cologne, 78;
The Plannar Dimension, Civic Arts Gallery, Walnut Creek, Calif, 83; and
others. *Teaching:* Instr art, Shasta Col, Redding, Calif, 68- *Awards:* Third
Prize (painting), 1st Ann Grand Galleria Nat Art Show, 72; Purchase Prize,
15th Printing Ann, Downey Mus, 72; Second Prize (painting), 5th Ann North
Valley Art Show, Redding, 73. *Bibliog:* Alfred Frankenstein (auth), Serene
and mystic art works, San Francisco Chronicle, 11/17/72; William Wilson
(auth), Art walk, Los Angeles Times, 3/5/76; Andrea Liss (auth), Bay area
geometric abstraction, Art Week, 5/7/83; and others. *Media:* Acrylic. *Dealer:*
Hank Baum Gallery 2140 Bush St San Francisco CA 94115. *Mailing Add:*
Dept Art Shasta Col 1065 Old N Oregon Trail Redding CA 96001

WILSON, ROBERT
GRAPHIC ARTIST, DESIGNER
b Waco, Tex. *Study:* Painting with George McNeil, Paris, France, 62; Pratt
Inst, New York, BFA, 65; apprenticed to Paolo Soleri, Phoenix, Ariz, 66.
Work: Mus Mod Art, New York; Mus Mod Art, Paris, France; Australian Nat
Gallery, Canberra; Kunstmuseum, Bern; Mus Mod Art, Paris; and others.
Exhib: Whitney Mus Am Art, 81; one-man shows, Pavillon Arts, 83, Galerie
Brinkman, Amsterdam, 83, Mus Boymans van Beuningen, Rotterdam, 83,
Raum fur Kunst, Produzentengalerie, Hamburg, 83 & Gallery Ueda, Tokyo,
83. *Awards:* Lumen Award for Design, New York, 77; Guggenheim Fel
Award, 80. *Mailing Add:* 147 Spring St New York NY 10012

WILSON, SYBIL
PAINTER, GRAPHIC ARTIST
b Tulsa, Okla, Mar 20, 23. *Study:* Art Students League, with Ernest Fiene;
Yale Univ Sch Art & Archit, with Josef Albers, BFA & MFA; also with Anni
Albers. *Work:* NY Univ Collection; Univ Ky Collection; Univ Mass
Collection; Univ Bridgeport Collection; Chase Manhattan Bank Collection;
and others. *Exhib:* One-man shows, Grand Cent Mod Gallery, New York, 62
& 65, East Hampton Gallery, New York, 70 & Woods, Gerry Gallery, RI Sch
Design, 72; Retinal Art in US Traveling Exhib, 66. *Teaching:* Prof art, Univ
Bridgeport, 54-78; adj prof art, RI Sch Design, 70-72. *Awards:* Am Inst
Graphic Arts 50 Best Bks Award, 60. *Media:* Acrylic, Oil. *Publ:* Designer &
publ, Anni Albers: On Designing, Pellango Press, 60. *Dealer:* Elaine Benson
Gallery Bridgehampton NY. *Mailing Add:* 27228 Elwood Dr SE Bonita
Springs FL 33923

WILSON, TOM MUIR
DESIGNER
b Bellaire, Ohio, Dec 6, 30. *Study:* WVa Inst Technol; Cranbrook Acad Art,
BFA; Rochester Inst Technol, MFA. *Exhib:* One-man shows, Rochester, NY
& Wheeling, WVa, 57, 59 & 61; Boston Art Festival, 61; Photog Exhib,
George Eastman House, Rochester, 63; Western NY Ann, Buffalo, 63 & 64;
Art of Two Cities, Minneapolis, 65; and others. *Pos:* Designer exhib galleries,
George Eastman House Mus Photog, 61-62; freelance photogr & graphic
designer, New York, Rochester & Minneapolis, 61- *Teaching:* Prof art & instr
photog & graphic design, Minneapolis Sch Art, formerly; instr photog,
Rochester Inst Technol, assoc prof photog arts, 77-; instr sculpture & design,
Nazareth Col, Rochester. *Awards:* Award for Sculpture, Art Inst Am Inst
Architects, 56; Prize, Philadelphia Print Club, 61. *Media:* Graphic. *Mailing
Add:* Col of Graphic Arts & Photog Rochester Inst of Technol Rochester NY
14623

WILSON, WALLACE
PHOTOGRAPHER
b Dallas, Tex, June 10, 47. *Study:* Univ Tex, Austin, BA, 70; pvt study with
Ralph Eugene Meatyeard, Lexington, Ky, 71-72; Art Inst Chicago, MFA, 75.
Work: Mus Mod Art, New York; Art Inst Chicago; Oakland Mus, Calif; New
Orleans Mus Art; Baltimore Mus Art, Md. *Exhib:* One-man shows, Baltimore
Mus Art, 76, Photogalerie Lange-Irschl, Munich, WGer, 79, Univ Calif, Los
Angeles, 79 & Univ Ala, Birmingham, 83; Color Photography, Boston Visual
Artists Union, 81; Southern Photographers, Robert Freidus Gallery, New
York, 83; and others. *Teaching:* Asst prof photog & design, Univ Del, 75-79;
assoc prof photog, Univ Fla, 79- *Awards:* Individual Artists Fel, State Fla, 82.
Bibliog: Fred McDarrah (auth), Voice choices, Village Voice, 10/10/77;
James Baker Hall (auth), Light Places by Wallace Wilson, Estrella de Tejas
Press, 77; Paysages de l'Quest Americain, Le Figaro, Paris, 78. *Mem:* Soc
Photog Educ. *Media:* Color Photography. *Publ:* Contribr, Camera, Bucher
Press, Zurich, Switz, 73; contribr, Fifteen Photographs in Color, Mancini
Gallery, 78; contribr, Artwords and Bookworks, Los Angeles Inst Contemp
Art, 78. *Dealer:* Fay Gold Gallery Atlanta GA; Barbara Gillman Gallery
Miami FL. *Mailing Add:* 604 SW 43rd Terr Gainesville FL 32607

WILSON, WARREN BINGHAM
EDUCATOR, SCULPTOR
b North Farmington, Utah, Nov 4, 20. *Study:* Utah State Univ, BS(educ);
State Univ Iowa, MFA(sculpture). *Work:* Utah State Univ, Logan; Utah
Capitol Bldg Collection, Salt Lake City; Utah State Fair Asn, Salt Lake City;
Brigham Young Univ, Provo, Utah; State Univ Iowa, Iowa City, plus others.
Comn: Exterior steel sculpture, Holladay Law Offices, Pocatello, Idaho, 60
& Utah State Training Sch, 62. *Exhib:* Ann Painting & Sculpture Exhib,

Denver Art Mus, 51; Traveling Show of Utah Artists, Santa Fe Art Mus, 53; Ceramic & Sculpture Exhib, Wichita Art Ctr, 60; Ceramic Conjunction, Brand Art Ctr, Glendale, Calif, 73; one-man show, Traveling Exhib of Wood Sculpture, Western Asn of Art Mus through Western States, 62-64; 20-Year Restrospective, Brigham Young Univ, 70; plus many others. *Teaching:* Asst prof sculpture & printmaking, Utah State Univ, 49-54; prof sculpture & ceramics, Brigham Young Univ, 54-83; vis lectr ceramics, Univ Calif, Davis, 68. *Awards:* Purchase Award, Ann Fine Arts Exhib, Utah State Inst of Fine Arts & Fine Arts Exhib, Utah State Fair Bd, 52; Fel Resident, Huntington Hartford Found, 61. *Bibliog:* Articles in Craftsmen of the Southwest, 65; Margaret Ellis (auth), Vessels of the Lord, The New Era, LDS Church, 73; articles in Primitive Pottery in Provo, 74. *Mem:* Southwest Regional Assembly of Craftsmen (Utah rep, 61-65); Utah Designer Craftsmen (pres, 63-65); Art Teachers in Higher Educ, Nat Art Educ Asn (Utah chmn, 69-73); Nat Coun on Educ for the Ceramic Arts. *Media:* Wood, Clay. *Mailing Add:* 1000 Briar Ave Provo UT 84601

WILSON, WILLIAM S, III
CRITIC
b Baltimore, Md, Apr 7, 32. *Study:* Univ Va, BA, 53; Yale Univ, MA, 65, PhD, 61. *Teaching:* Prof, Queens Col, 61- *Res:* Color and language. *Publ:* Auth, Robert Morris: Hard questions and soft answers, 69 & Dan Flavin: Fiat lux, 70, Art News; auth, John Willenbecher: Pyramids and labyrinths, 75 & Ralph Humphrey, 75, Arts; auth, Ralph Humphrey: An apology for painting, Artforum, 77. *Mailing Add:* 458 W 25th St New York NY 10001

WILSON, (RONALD) YORK
PAINTER, MURALIST
b Toronto, Ont, Dec 6, 07. *Study:* Cent Tech Sch, Toronto; Ont Col Art; Art Inst Detroit; self taught. *Work:* Uffizi Gallery, Florence, Italy; Nat Mus Art Mod, Paris; Mus Mod Art, Mexico City; Birla Acad Mus, Calcutta, India; Mus Dijon, France; and others. *Comn:* Murals, O'Keefe Ctr Performing Arts, Toronto, 59 & Gen Hosp, Thunder Bay, 65; mosaic, Bell Canada, Toronto, 65; mural, Ont Govt, Toronto, 68; mosaic, Carleton Univ, Ottawa, 70; and others. *Exhib:* One-man shows, Mus Galliera, Paris, 63 & Palacio de Bellas Artes, Mexico City, 69; VII Bienal de Sao Paulo, Brazil, 63; Salon Confrontation, Mus de Dijon, France, 64; Eminent Artists of the World, Birla Acad Mus, Calcutta, 70; and others. *Awards:* Best Painting Award, Baxter Found, Ont Soc Artists, 59; Can Centennial Medal, 67; Int Achievement Medal, Ont Soc Artists, 83. *Bibliog:* Mural (film), Crawley Films, Imperial Oil, 57; Michael Foyteni (dir), York Wilson (film), Nat Film Bd, Can Broadcasting, 62; Paul Duval & Marshall McLuhan (auth), York Wilson, Wallack Galleries, Ottawa, 78. *Mem:* Royal Can Acad; Ont Soc Artists (pres, 45-48); L'Oeil de Boeuf, Paris; Arts & Letters Club, Toronto. *Media:* Oil. *Publ:* Contribr, Murals, In: World Book Encyclopedia, 63; illusr, Face at the Bottom of the World, Hagiwara Sakutaro, Tuttle, Japan, 67; contribr, Painters Workshop, Reinhold, 69; contribr, Four Decades, Clarke Irwin, 72; contribr, Debrett's Illustrated Guide, Canadian Establishment, Methuen Publ, 83. *Dealer:* Moore Gallery 34 Hess St Hess Village Hamilton ON L8P 3N1; Wallack Galleries 202 Bank St Ottawa ON Can. *Mailing Add:* 41 Alcina Ave Toronto ON M6G 2E7 Canada

WILSON-HAMMOND, CHARLOTTE EMILY
PAINTER, PRINTMAKER
b Montreal, Que, Nov 19, 41. *Study:* Ind Univ, 62; art schs, Toronto, 66-68. *Work:* Art Gallery NS & Royal Trust Corp, Halifax; Confederation Ctr Arts, Charlottetown, PEI; Shell Energy Sources Can, Calgary, Alta; Norcen Energy Corp, Toronto. *Exhib:* Olympiad, Montreal, Que, 76; Mt St Vincent Univ Traveling Exhib, 77-78; Dalhousie Univ, Halifax, 79; World's Fair, Osaka, Japan, 79; Confederation Ctr Arts, Charlottetown, PEI, 80-81; and others. *Pos:* Bd mem, Art Gallery NS, Halifax, 79-80. *Bibliog:* Article, Arts Atlantic, 79; Reshard Gool (auth), article, Arts Mag, 81. *Mem:* Can Artists Representation; Visual Arts NS (chmn, 78-79); Women Arts (organizer, 80-). *Media:* Oil, Conte; Multimedia. *Mailing Add:* RR1 Lake Charlotte Clam Harbour NS B0J 1Y0 Canada

WILTSHIRE, WILLIAM ERNEST, III
COLLECTOR, PATRON
b Richmond, Va, Jan 4, 41. *Collections Arranged:* Folk Pottery of the Shenandoah Valley (auth, catalog), Abby Aldrich Rockefeller Folk Art Mus, Williamsburg, Va, 75; American Folk Painting Traveling Exhib (contribr, catalog), Am Fedn Arts, 77. *Pos:* Trustee, Mus Am Folk Art, New York, 76-; trustee & pres, Collectors Circle, Va Mus, Richmond, 78-; trustee, Longwood Fine Arts Ctr, Longwood Col, Farmville, Va, 78- *Mem:* Am Inst Conserv; Int Inst Conserv; Am Asn Mus; Am Ceramic Circle (trustee, 75-76); Keramik-Freunde der Schweiz (Swiss Ceramic Soc). *Interests:* American folk painting, American painting and decorative arts and contemporary Virginia artists. *Collection:* Comprehensive collection of American folk painting supplemented by American art from nineteenth and twentieth century. *Mailing Add:* PO Box 1319 Richmond VA 23210

WILWERS, EDWARD MATHIAS
EDUCATOR, ILLUSTRATOR
b Chicago, Ill, Feb 4, 18. *Study:* Drake Univ, BFA; Ohio Univ, MFA; also with Karl Mattern, Yasuo Kuniyoshi & Milford Zornes. *Comn:* Oil painting, comn by Dr & Mrs Robert Eilers, Merion, Pa, 71; watercolor, comn by Dr & Mrs Sascha Schnittmann, San Jose, Calif, 72; acrylic, comn by Dr & Mrs Harvey Ashmead, Ogden, Utah, 73; oil painting, comn by Dr & Mrs Jim Ed McGee, Dardanelle, Ark, 77; and numerous other commissions from 78- *Exhib:* One-man shows, Saga Gallery, Taos, NMex, 66, Ark Found Fine Arts, Russellville, 67 & Triton Mus

Art, San Jose, Calif, 68; Van Go Galleries, Ruseellville, Ark, 78; Ark River Ballery Art Ctr, Russellville, Ark, 82. *Pos:* Designer, Hutcheson Displays, Inc, Omaha, Nebr, 51-58, Art Gallery, Ark, Tech Univ, 83; illusr, D & H Assoc, Ogden, Utah, 59-60. *Teaching:* Prof art & head dept, Ark Tech Univ, Russellville, 60-81, prof art, 81- *Mem:* Kappa Pi; Nat Coun Art Adminr; Southeastern Col Art Conf; Mid-Am Art Conf. *Publ:* Illusr, Nuclear Energy Conf (portfolio), 61; illusr, Arkansas Polytechnic College (promotion booklet), 63; illusr, Blanchard Springs Caverns (booklet), US Forest Serv, 66; Dardanelle Reservoir (booklet), US Corp Engrs, 68; illusr, Pleasure Boating on the Arkansas River, Ark Parks & Tour Dept, 70. *Mailing Add:* Rte 3 Bayou Lane Russellville AR 72801

WIMAN, BILL
PAINTER, EDUCATOR
b Roscoe, Tex, Nov 12, 40. *Study:* E Tex State Univ, BS; Univ Fla, MFA. *Work:* Butler Inst of Am Art, Youngstown, Ohio; Okla Art Ctr, Oklahoma City; San Antonio Mus Art; Am Tel & Tel, New York; Mus of Arts & Sci, Evansville, Ind. *Exhib:* Project S/SW-Younger Am Artists, Ft Worth Art Ctr, Tex, 70; Tex Painting & Sculpture: The 20th Century, Owens Art Ctr, Dallas, Tex, 71; Talent: USA, Jacksonville Art Mus, Fla, 76; one-man show, Art Mus of S Tex, Corpus Christie, 76; Real, Really Real, Super Real, San Antonio Mus Art, 81. *Teaching:* Asst prof painting, E Tex State Univ, 66-71; prof painting, Univ Tex, Austin, 72- *Awards:* Purchase Awards, Mid-States Art Exhib, Mus of Arts & Sci, Evansville, 71, 10th Monroe Nat Ann, Masur Mus of Art, La, 74 & 38th Ann Midyear Show, Butler Inst of Am Art, 74. *Bibliog:* Article, Artforum, 1/71; article, Arts, 3/78 & 1/79. *Media:* Oil. *Dealer:* David Settles Gallery 1700 Bissonnet Houston TX 77005. *Mailing Add:* 3405 Perry Lane Austin TX 78731

WIMBERLEY, FRANK WALDEN
PAINTER, SCULPTOR
b Pleasantville, NJ, Aug 31, 26. *Study:* Howard Univ, with Lois M Jones, James Wells & James Porter. *Work:* Mus Mod Art, New York; Storefront Mus, New York. *Exhib:* C W Post Col, NY, 69; Whitney Rebuttal, Acts of Art Gallery, New York, 71; Hudson River Mus, Yonkers, NY, 71; Seton Hall Univ, NJ, 71; Dutchess Co Col, NY, 72. *Mem:* Guild Hall, East Hampton, NY. *Media:* Collage. *Mailing Add:* 99-11 35th Ave Corona NY 11368

WIMMER, GAYLE
FIBER ARTIST, INSTRUCTOR
b Pittsburgh, Pa, Oct 2, 43. *Study:* Pratt Inst, Brooklyn, NY, BFA, 67; Tyler Sch Art, Philadelphia, Pa, MFA, 70; Acad Fine Art, Warsaw, Poland, with Wojclech Sadley, 71. *Work:* Mus Fine Arts, Salt Lake City, Utah; The Armory for the Arts, Santa Fe, NMex; The Invisible Theatre, Tucson, Ariz; George Washington Univ, Washington DC. *Comn:* Bas-relief fiber work, US Nat Park Service, Harper's Ferry, Va, 77; fiber wall piece, Nat Steel Corp Service Ctr, Wayne, NJ, 77; fiber sculpture, Kino Hospital, Tucson, Ariz, 78. *Exhib:* Clay, Fiber, Metal: Women Artists, Bronx Mus, New York, 78; Southwestern Invitational, Yuma Art Ctr & traveling, Ariz, 79, 81 & 82; Fiber as Art, Metrop Mus Manilla, Phillipines, 80; The Common Thread, Visual Arts Ctr Alaska, Anchorage, 80; Annenberg Theatre, Philadelphia, 82 & 83; Mandel Theatre, Philadelphia, 83. *Teaching:* Lectr textiles, Hunter Col, New York, 72-77; instr fiber art, The New Sch, New York, 73-77; asst prof & initiator fiber program, Art Dept, Univ Ariz, Tucson, 77- *Awards:* Fel Study Poland, Int Research & Exchanges Bd, New York, 71; Craftsmen's Fel Grant, Nat Endowment Arts, 73; Grant Research in Poland, Int Research & Exchanges Bd, New York, 82 & 83. *Mem:* Women's Caucus Arts; Am Crafts Coun. *Media:* Fiber, Textile. *Mailing Add:* 3468 N Richland Circle Tucson AZ 85719

WINCHESTER, ALICE
EDITOR, HISTORIAN
b Chicago, Ill, July 26, 07. *Study:* Smith Col, BA, 29. *Pos:* Ed, Mag Antiques, 38-72; guest cur, Whitney Mus Am Art, 72-74. *Awards:* Archives of Am Art 25th Anniv Award, 79; Medal, Smith Col, 68. *Mem:* Nat Trust for Hist Preserv; Conn Hist Soc. *Res:* American decorative arts; American folk art. *Publ:* Co-ed, Primitive Painters in America 1750-1950, 50; auth, How to Know American Antiques, 51; ed, Antiques Treasury of Furniture & Other Decorative Arts, 59, Collectors & Collections, 61 & Living with Antiques, 63; auth, Versatile Yankee, The Art of Jonathan Fisher 1768-1847, 73; coauth, Flowering of American Folk Art 1776-1876, 74. *Mailing Add:* 4 Currituck Rd Newtown CT 06470

WIND, HAROLD
PAINTER, ILLUSTRATOR
b Brooklyn, NY, July 25, 17. *Study:* NY Univ, cert, 39; Pratt Inst, 39-41; Brooklyn Polytechnic, cert, 45; Brooklyn Mus Art Sch, 53-56; Stevenson Art Sch, 77-80; also with Tom Hill, John Pike & Ed Whitney. *Work:* Chung Cheng Art Gallery, St Johns Univ; Soc Illusr Traveling Show, Japan. *Comn:* Paintings for Reproduction, Whitney-Seffer Ltd, New York, 81. *Exhib:* Regional Pastel Exhib, Queens Mus, Flushing, NY, 82; Seventh Western Fed Watercolor Soc, Pueblo Grande Mus, Phoenix, 82; Second Ann Exhib, Nassau Co Mus Fine Art, Roslyn, NY, 83; Nat Pastel Exhib, Hermitage Found Mus, Norfolk, Va, 83; solo show, Centro Fotografico, San Miguel, Mex, 83; and others. *Awards:* Pres Medal, Salmagundi Club, 77; Gold Medal, Nat Art League, 80; Award Excellence & First Prize, Great Neck House, Art League Nassau, 83. *Bibliog:* Malcolm Preston (auth), Skillful artist, 79 & Jeanne Paris (auth), Gallery Soho-7, 79, Long Island Newsday; Helen Harrison (auth), Watercolorists deal in delicacy, New York Times, 9/83. *Mem:* Salmagundi Club; Am Artists Prof League; Knickerbocker Artists (corresp secy, 81); Hudson Valley Art Asn; Pastel Soc Am. *Media:*

Watercolor, Pastel; Graphics, Lithography. *Publ:* Contribr, Art Prints--From Award Winning Watercolors, private publ, 82; contribr, The 24th Annual of American Illustration, Soc Illusr, 83. *Mailing Add:* 80-103 Surrey Pl Jamaica NY 11432

WINDEKNECHT, MARGARET BRAKE
FIBER ARTIST, WRITER
b Alma, Mich, June 27, 36. *Study:* Univ Mich, BS(design); Memphis State Univ, MEd. *Work:* Carroll B Reese Mus, Johnson City, Tenn; Tenn State Mus, Nashville; Com Union Bank Collection, Nashville; Cook Industs Collection, Memphis. *Comn:* Cardweaving, Unitarian Church Elliot Mem, Memphis, 77; loom-controlled, St John's United Methodist Church, Memphis, 78. *Exhib:* Miss River Craft Show, Brooks Mem Art Gallery, Memphis, 73, 75, 77 & 79; Marietta Col Crafts Nat, Hermann Fine Arts Ctr, Marietta, Ohio, 74; Fiber Structures, Heinz Gallery Mus Art, Carnegie Inst, Pittsburgh, Pa, 76; Superior, Tweed Mus of Art, Duluth, Minn, 77 & 81; Intent 78--Fabrics, Bruce Gallery, Edinboro, Pa 78; Fiber as Art, Metrop Mus Manila, Philipines, 80; Artist-Artisan, Bass Mus, Miami, Fla, 80-81. *Awards:* Purchase Award, 6th Biennial, Tenn Artist-Craftsmen, 76; Purchase Awards, 9th & 10th Prints, Drawings & Craft Shows, Ark Art Ctr, 76 & 77. *Bibliog:* Burry & Calonius (auths), Weaving, City of Memphis Mag, 78; B Gentry (auth), Creative Overshot rev, Interweave, spring 79; M E Riccardi (auth), Creative Overshot rev, Shuttle Spindle & Dyepot, summer 79. *Mem:* Handweavers Guild Am; Am Crafts Coun. *Media:* Fiber. *Publ:* Auth, Creative Monk's Belt, 77 & Creative Overshot, 78, HTH Publ; contribr, A Beginners Book of Off-Loom Weaving, Dodd Mead, 78; coauth, A Micro Computer Graphics Study of Handweaving, NCC, 79; coauth, Color and Weave, Van Nostrand Reinhold, 81. *Mailing Add:* 815 Dartmouth Rochester MI 48063

WINDROW, PATRICIA (PATRICIA WINDROW KLEIN)
PAINTER, ILLUSTRATOR
b London, Eng, Sept 12, 23; US citizen. *Work:* Parrish Mus, Southampton, NY; West Publ Co Collection; Minn Mus Art, St Paul. *Comn:* Mural, Marine Midland Bank, East Setauket, NY, 56. *Exhib:* Allied Artists Am, New York, 69 & 73; solo show, Belanthi Gallery, 84. *Teaching:* Pvt instr, 60-; instr, Lincoln Sq Acad, New York, 67-72; instr, Prof Children's Sch, New York, 74-; instr painting, Weekly TV Show, Channel 6, Brookhaven, NY. *Awards:* First Prize Oils, Guild Hall Ann Mem Exhib, Easthampton, 57; First Prize, Catharine Lorillard Wolfe Club, New York, 68; Purchase Award, Minn Mus Art, St Paul, 79. *Media:* Oil. *Publ:* Illus, The Long White Road, 57; illusr, My Best Friends are Dinosaurs, 61; auth & illusr, The Beautiful Blacks Coloring Book, Phantom Horse Publ, 70; It's in Your Power, Rawson, 76. *Dealer:* Belanthi Gallery 142 Court St Brooklyn NY 11201. *Mailing Add:* 71 Thompson Haypath Setauket NY 11733

WINER, DONALD ARTHUR
CURATOR, PAINTER
b St Louis, Mo, Oct 26, 27. *Study:* Univ Mo, BS & MA. *Collections Arranged:* Broad Spectrum, 81, Pennsylvania in Prints, 82, Working Pennsylvanians, 82 & Portraits of Pennsylvania Painters, 83, Philadelphia Col Art. *Pos:* Cur, Springfield Art Mus, Mo, 54-57; asst dir, Brooks Art Gallery, Memphis, Tenn, 57-59; dir, Montgomery Mus Fine Arts, Ala, 59-62; dir, Everhart Mus Art & Sci, 62-66; cur, Pa Collection Fine Arts, Pa Hist & Mus Comn, 66- *Mem:* Pa Guild Craftsmen; Mid-State Artists; Gallery Doshi. *Res:* Pennsylvania painters; pottery of Pennsylvania. *Collection:* American earthenware, especially slip decorated red ware. *Mailing Add:* 3112 Schoolhouse Lane Harrisburg PA 17109

WINES, JAMES N
ENVIRONMENTAL ARTIST
b Oak Park, Ill, June 27, 32. *Study:* Syracuse Univ Sch Art, BA, 55. *Work:* Albright-Knox Art Gallery, Buffalo; Stedelijk Mus, Amsterdam, Holland; Whitney Mus Am Art, New York; Tate Gallery, London, Eng; Walker Art Ctr, Minneapolis. *Comn:* Lobby sculpture, Dana Arts Ctr, Colgate Univ, Hamilton, NY, 67; sculpture for mall, State Capitol Bldg, Albany, NY, 68; sculpture for lobby, Treadwell Corp, New York, 68; showrooms, Best Products Co Inc, Houston, 75 & Sacramento, 77; Ghost Parking Lot, Nat Shopping Ctrs, Hamden, Conn, 78. *Exhib:* Whitney Mus Am Art Sculpture Biennial, New York, 61-67; American Sculpture, Walker Art Ctr, Minneapolis, 64; Columbia Univ, New York, 73; Whitney Mus Am Art, New York, 73; Mus Mod Art, New York, 75; Venice Biennale, Italy, 75; Archit Marginales, Pompidou Ctr, Paris, France, 75; Experimental Archit, CAYC Mus, Buenos Aires, Arg, 77; Illusions of Reality (traveling exhib of eight mus, Australia), 77-78; and others. *Pos:* Dir, Site, Inc, New York, 69-; mem, Arts & Bus Coop Coun, New York, 71-; mem, Fed Design Assembly, Washington, DC, 72; mem arts adv coun, Bicentennial Celebration, Washington, DC, 72; pres, SITE, Inc, currently. *Teaching:* Instr environ art, Sch Visual Art, 65-; instr environ workshop, NY Univ, 75-; instr, NJ Sch Archit, 75-; Mellon prof, Cooper Union, New York, 77-; chmn dept environmental design, Parsons Sch Design, New York, currently. *Awards:* Design in Steel, Iron & Steel Inst, 71; Nat Endowment Archit Grant, 73; Nat Endowment for Arts Grant, 74. *Bibliog:* David Sellin (auth), James Wines--Sculpture, Colgate Univ, 66; Judith Goldman (auth), SITE-ations, Art News, 10/75; Gerald Allen (auth), Bringing in the business, Archit Record, 3/77. *Publ:* Auth, The case for site-oriented art, Landscape Archit, 7/71; auth, Site, Art & Artists, London, 10/71; coauth, Street art, TA/BK, Holland, 1/72; coauth, Peekskill melt, Art Gallery, 3/72; auth, The case for the big duck, Archit Forum, 4/72. *Mailing Add:* c/o SITE 83 Spring St New York NY 10012

WINFIELD, RODNEY M
DESIGNER
b New York, NY, Feb 6, 25. *Study:* Univ Miami, 43; Cooper Union, 44-45. *Work:* Steinberg Gallery; Wash Univ, St Louis; Mitchell Mus, Mt Vernon, Ill; and pvt collections. *Comn:* Three dimensional windows, Shaare Zedec, St Louis, 58; bronze & steel Ark Wall, Temple Israel, St Louis, 62; doors, interior artifacts, Good Samaritan Hosp, Chapel, Mt Vernon, Ill, 68; space window, Washington Cathedral, 73; shrine, Our Lady of Perpetual Help Chapel of Christ the Crucified King, St Louis Univ Hospitals; and others. *Exhib:* One-man shows, Galerie Creuze, Paris, 50, Martin Schweig Gallery, St Louis; Pope Pius Libr, St Louis Univ; Pallette Bleau, Paris; City Art Mus, St Louis. *Pos:* Designer, Emil Frei Assocs, St Louis, 53-; designer, Winfield Jewelry, St Louis, 70- *Teaching:* Prof art, Maryville Col, 64- *Mailing Add:* 4444 Laclede Pl St Louis MO 63108

WINGATE, ARLINE (HOLLANDER)
SCULPTOR
b New York, NY. *Work:* Syracuse Univ Mus, NY; Nat Mus Stockholm, Sweden; Ghent Mus Belg; Joseph H Hirshhorn Collection; Guild Hall Mus, East Hampton, NY; plus many others incl pvt collections. *Exhib:* Metrop Mus Art & Whitney Mus Am Art, New York; Wadsworth Atheneum Mus; San Francisco Mus, Calif; Baltimore Mus, Md; plus many others in Paris, France, Belg, Buenos Aires, Arg, London, Eng & US incl five one-man shows. *Teaching:* Instr, Young Men's Hebrew Asn, Southhampton Col. *Mem:* Sculptors Guild. *Mailing Add:* PO Box 335 East Hampton NY 11937

WINGATE, GEORGE B
PAINTER
b Mt Holly, NJ, Oct 13, 41. *Study:* Univ Rochester, BA, 63; Syracuse Univ Sch Archit, 65; New Sch, with Henry Pearson, 72-76; Art Students League, with Frank Mason, 73-78. *Work:* Everson Mus; Mus City New York. *Exhib:* Fourth Ann Small Works Show, NY Univ, 80; Hudson Valley Art Asn Ann, White Plains, NY, 80; Butler Art Inst Ann, 80 & 83; solo exhib, Everson Mus, 82, Katonah Gallery, NY, 83 & John Pence Gallery, San Francisco, 83; Painting New York, Mus City New York, 83. *Bibliog:* Gordon Muck (auth), Wingate's Cazenovia, Syracuse Post Standard, 9/15/80; Vivien Raynor (auth), article, New York Times, 10/16/83; Stephen Doherty (auth), article, Am Artist Mag, 10/83. *Mem:* Art Students League. *Media:* Oil. *Dealer:* John Pence Gallery 750 Post St San Francisco CA 94117. *Mailing Add:* 939 Eighth Ave New York NY 10019

WINGATE, ROBERT BRAY
ILLUSTRATOR, CONSULTANT
b Harrisburg, Pa, Sept 21, 25. *Study:* Lebanon Valley Col, AB, 48; Pa Acad Fine Arts, summer 48; Johns Hopkins Med Sch, MA(art as appl to med), 51; Drexel Univ, MS(libr sci), 60; Clayton Univ, ScD, 82; Sussex Univ, Hon ScD, 71. *Pos:* Med illusr, Walter Reed Army Med Ctr, Washington, DC, 54-56 & Ophthalmological Found, Inc, New York, 56-60; freelance illusr, 60-; chief rare bks & spec collections, Pa State Libr, Harrisburg, 65-78. *Mem:* Life fel Royal Soc Arts, London; affil Royal Soc Med, London; fel, Am Col Heraldry, 82. *Res:* History of medicine and medical illustration; history of printing and bookbinding; heraldic illustration. *Publ:* Illusr, Fasanella's Modern Advances in Cataract Surgery, Lippincott, 63; illusr, Fasanella's Management of Complications in Eye Surgery, Saunders, 65; illusr, von Noorden & Maumenee's Atlas of Strabismus, Mosby, 67, 2nd ed, 73; illusr, King & Wadsworth's An Atlas of Ophthalmic Surgery, Lippincott, 70; auth & illusr, Perceptions: Glimpses of Our World and Ourselves, 83. *Mailing Add:* 136 Shell St Harrisburg PA 17109

WINK, DON (JON DONNEL)
PAINTER, EDUCATOR
b San Angelo, Tex, July 13, 38. *Study:* Univ Tex, BFA, 60; Ohio Univ, 61-62; Univ Wash, MFA, 63. *Exhib:* The Texas General, Dallas Mus Fine Arts, 61; two-man show, Witte Mus, San Antonio, 66; Texas Painting & Sculpture, Dallas Mus Fine Arts, 68; Associated Artist, Carnegie Mus, Pittsburgh, 71-75; Westmoreland Co Mus, Greensburg, Pa, 72-75; Mus STex Ann, Corpus Christi, 82; Recent Works from East Texas, Tyler Mus Art, 82. *Teaching:* Instr painting & drawing, Southwestern Univ, Tex, 65-; prof & chmn dept art, Slippery Rock State Col, 69-76 & Stephen F Austin State Univ, 76- *Awards:* First Prize, 13th Ann 180, Huntington Galleries, WVa, 65 & 30th Ann Allied Artist, 65; Jury Award, Assoc Artist, 72. *Mem:* Nat Coun Art Adminr; Tex Asn Schs Art (secy, 79-80). *Media:* Acrylic, Oil. *Mailing Add:* Box 13001 Stephen F Austin State Univ Nacogdoches TX 75962

WINKEL, NINA
SCULPTOR, LECTURER
b Bonken-Westfalen, Ger, May 21, 05; US citizen. *Study:* Staedel Mus Sch, Frankfurt, Ger. *Work:* Wall panel, Keene Valley Libr, NY; Justice Protectress, Surrogate Ct, New York; Art Mus, Allentown, Pa; State Univ NY, Plattsburgh. *Comn:* Lassiter Mem, comn by Lassiter Family, Charlotte, NC; Early Moravians (wall panels), Hanes Corp, Winston-Salem, NC; War Mem, Seward Park High Sch, New York; Group of Children, City of Wiesbaden, Albert Schweitzer Sch. *Exhib:* Am Acad Arts & Lett; one-man show, Univ Notre Dame, 54; many shows, Nat Acad Design; retrospective, Sculpture Ctr, 72; Traveling Photo Documentation, WGer & Holland, 82-83. *Teaching:* Instr sculpture, Clay Club Servicemen Canteen, 42-46; adj prof, State Univ NY, Plattsburgh, 83. *Awards:* E Watrous Gold Medals, 45, 78 & 83 & Nat Acad Gold Medal, 82, Nat Acad Design; Purchase Prize, Nat Sculpture Soc, 81. *Bibliog:* Nancy Dryfoos (auth), Nina Winkel, Nat Sculpture Rev, 71. *Mem:* Fel Nat Sculpture Soc (secy, 65-68); Nat Acad Design; Sculptors Guild; Sculpture Ctr (pres, 70-73, emer pres). *Media:* Mixed. *Res:* Antiques; Byzantine mosaics. *Publ:* Auth, var articles on sculpture & mosaics in periodicals. *Mailing Add:* Keene Valley NY 12943

WINKLER, MARIA PAULA
PAINTER, EDUCATOR
b Krakow, Poland, Oct 24, 45; US citizen. *Study:* Univ Pa, study with Karl Umlauf, BA(art & art hist); Pa State Univ, study with Enrigue Montenegro, MFA(painting & drawing) & study with Kenneth Beittel, PhD(art educ). *Work:* Pa State Univ, State College; Boise Gallery Art, Idaho. *Exhib:* Nat Drawing & Small Sculpture Exhib, Ball State Univ, Muncie, Ind, 70; New York Exhib of Paintings, Sculpture & Graphics, Avanti Galleries, New York, 71; New Generation Drawing, Cheney-Cowles Mem State Mus, Spokane, Wash, 73; NMex Int Art Exhib, Clovis, NMex, 76; Images of Women, Ctr Visual Arts, Oakland, Calif, 79; Northern Calif Arts, Sacramento, 80 & 82. *Collections Arranged:* Images of Women, Linda Farris Gallery, Seattle, Wash, 75; West Coast Women's Show, Bau-Xi Gallery, Vancouver, 76; Copy Graphics, Wordworks Gallery, San Jose, Calif, 79; California Watercolors, Zara Gallery, San Francisco, 79; Still Life/Figure, Artists Contemp Gallery, Sacramento, 80; Illusion-Allusion, Atkinson Art Gallery, Santa Barbara, 80. *Pos:* Tech illusr, Aerojet Gen Corp, Sacramento, 63. *Teaching:* Asst prof art & art educ, Boise State Univ, Idaho, 73-75; asst prof art educ, Univ BC, Vancouver, 75-77; assoc prof art, Calif State Univ, Sacramento, 77- *Awards:* Purchase Award, Calif League Women Artists, 79; William Harrington Mem & First Place, Northern Calif Arts Ann, Sacramento, 80. *Bibliog:* Patti McCoy (auth), Interview: Maria Winkler-Green, Women Artists Group, Northwest News & Media Report to Women, 77. *Mem:* Nat Art Educ Asn; Nat Art Educ Asn Women's Caucus (treas, 77-79); Calif Art Educ Asn. *Media:* Mixed. *Res:* Research and writings on techniques of teaching art appreciation to teachers and museum volunteers; curriculum development in art. *Publ:* Illusr, Art: Magic, Impulse and Control, A Guide to Viewing, Prentice-Hall, 73; illusr, Handbook for Student Teaching in Secondary Schools, Boise State Univ, 75; auth, The Curriculum Board Game, Calif State Univ, Sacramento, 77. *Dealer:* Art Works Gallery 10239 Fair Oaks Blvd Fair Oaks CA. *Mailing Add:* c/o Art Dept Calif State Univ Sacramento CA 95819

WINNINGHAM, GEOFF
PHOTOGRAPHER
b Jackson, Tenn, Mar 4, 43. *Study:* Rice Univ, BA, 65; Ill Inst Technol, with Aaron Siskind, MS(photog), 68. *Work:* Mus Mod Art, New York; Boston Mus Fine Arts; Mus Fine Arts, Houston; Int Mus Photog, Rochester, NY; Princeton Univ,; Carpenter Ctr, Harvard Univ. *Comn:* Courthouses of Tex (photographs), Seagrams Co, New York, 75. *Exhib:* Mus Fine Arts, Houston, 74; Witkin Gallery, New York, 75; Cronin Gallery, Houston, 77. *Teaching:* Asst prof photog, Univ St Thomas, Houston, 68-69; assoc prof photog, Rice Univ, Houston, 69-78; prof art-photog, Wiess Col, 78- *Awards:* Corp for Pub Broadcasting Award, 72; Guggenheim Found Fel, 72; Nat Endowment Arts Photog Fel, 75 & 77. *Bibliog:* E A Carmean (ed), Geoff Winningham Photographs, Mus Fine Arts, Houston, 74. *Publ:* Auth, Friday Night in the Coliseum, 71; auth, Going Texan, 72. *Dealer:* Cronin Gallery 2008 Peven St Houston TX 77019. *Mailing Add:* Dept of Art Rice Univ Houston TX 77001

WINOGRAND, GARRY
PHOTOGRAPHER, LECTURER
b New York, NY, Jan 14, 28. *Study:* City Col of New York; Columbia Col; New Sch for Social Res, with Alexi Brodovich. *Work:* George Eastman House, Rochester, NY; Mus Mod Art, New York; Smithsonian Inst, Washington, DC; Libr Congress; Ft Worth Mus of Art, Tex. *Comn:* The Great Am Rodeo Show (80 photogs), Ft Worth Mus of Art, 76. *Exhib:* Five Unrelated Photogrs, Mus Mod Art, New York, 63; Towards a New Social Landscape, George Eastman House, 66; New Documents, Mus of Mod Art, New York, 69; Ten Photogrs, Am Pavillion, Osaka World's Fair, Japan, 69; The Animals, Mus Mod Art, New York, 70; one-man shows, Light Gallery, 72 & 75, The Great Am Rodeo Show, Ft Worth Art Mus, 76. *Teaching:* Instr photog, Inst Design, Ill Inst Technol, Chicago, 71-72; lectr photog, Univ Tex, Austin, 73-78; Guggenheim award, 78-79. *Media:* 35 mm Black and White Photography. *Publ:* Auth, The Animals, Mus Mod Art, New York, 70; contribr, Documentary Photography, Time-Life Bks, 72; contribr, 1974 Photography Annual, Time-Life Bks, 74; auth, Women are Beautiful, Light Gallery, 75; auth, Grossmont College Show (catalogue), Grosmont Col Gallery, 76. *Mailing Add:* Light Gallery 724 Fifth Ave New York NY 10019

WINOKUR, JAMES L
COLLECTOR, CRITIC
b Philadelphia, Pa, Sept 12, 22. *Study:* Univ Pa, BS(econ), 43. *Pos:* Life trustee & mem mus art comt, Carnegie Inst, 67-; vpres & gov, Pittsburgh Plan for Art, 67-; fel Mus Art, Carnegie Inst, 68-; trustees comt mem, AAM, 72-; trustee & vchmn, Sarah Scaife Found, 72-; art critic, Greensburg Tribune-Rev, 74-; trustee, Pittsburgh Hist & Landmarks Soc, 75-; treas & dir, Pittsburgh-Allegheny Co Cult Alliance; mem, Arch Am Art, 75- *Interests:* Joseph Goto, American sculptor in welded steel. *Collection:* Cobra paintings, drawings and sculpture including Carl-Henning Pedersen, Jorn, Corneille, Alechinsky, Ubac, Reinhoud and others; 20th century American paintings, drawings and sculpture including Varujam Boghosian, Sam Francis, Joseph Goto and others; prints from Old Masters to the 20th century. *Mailing Add:* 5625 Darlington Rd Pittsburgh PA 15217

WINOKUR, PAULA COLTON
CERAMIST, CRAFTSMAN
b Philadelphia, Pa, May 13, 35. *Study:* Temple Univ, BFA, BSEd, 58, with Rudolf Staffel; Alfred Univ, New York, 58. *Work:* Witte Mus of Art, San Antonio, Tex; Philadelphia Mus of Art; Del Mus of Art, Wilmington; Alberta Potters Asn/Int Ceramic Soc, Switz; Utah Mus of Art, Salt Lake City. *Comn:* Ltd ed patrons plate, Friends Select Sch, Philadelphia, 75; ed patrons plates (60), Nat Mus Am Jewish Hist, 83. *Exhib:* Am Crafts Coun & US Info Agency 20 Potters (traveling exhib), 73-77; Baroque 74, Mus of Contemp Crafts, 74; Soup Tureens, 76, Campbell Mus, Camden, NJ, 76; Philadelphia: 300 Yrs of Am Art, Philadelphia Mus of Art, 76; 100 Artists Celebrate 100 Yrs, Fairtree Gallery & Xerox Gallery, 76; and others. *Teaching:* Lectr ceramics, Philadelphi Col Art, 67, Beaver Col, Glenside, Pa, 73-, Tyler Sch Art, 83. *Awards:* Merit Award, Craftsmen USA, Am Crafts Coun, 66; Prize, Ceramics Int 73, Calgary, Alta, 73; Nat Endowment for the Arts Craftsmen's Fel, 76. *Mem:* Am Crafts Coun; Nat Coun Educ Ceramic Arts (bd dirs, 79-82). *Publ:* Coauth, The light of Rudolph Staffel, Craft Horizons, 77. *Dealer:* Helen Druitt Gallery 305 Cherry St Philadelphia PA 19103. *Mailing Add:* 435 Norristown Rd Horsham PA 19044

WINOKUR, ROBERT MARK
CERAMIST, EDUCATOR
b Brooklyn, NY, Dec 24, 33. *Study:* Temple Univ, with Rudolph Staffel, BFA, 56; NY State Col of Ceramics, Alfred, MFA, 58. *Work:* Lannan Found, Palm Beach, Fla; Int Acad of Ceramics, Lucerne, Switz; Alberta Potters Asn, Calgary, Alta, Can; Philadelphia Mus of Art, Pa; Mus Boymans Van Beumingen, Rotterdam, Neth. *Comn:* Twenty large planters, comn by Ford & Earl Archit Designers, Detroit, Mich; First Nat Bank, Chicago, Ill, 69; coffee pots, Arts/Objects USA, Lee Nordness Galleries, New York, 73; Holy Water Font, comn by Bishop McDevitt, Temple Univ Newman Ctr, 76. *Exhib:* Craftsmen, Philadelphia Civic Ctr Mus, 67 & 73; Am Crafts 76, Mus of Contemp Art, Chicago, 76; Philadelphia: 300 Years of Am Art, Philadelphia Mus of Art, 76; Soup Toureens, Campbell Mus, Camden, NJ, 76; Super Mud Masters Show, Hub Gallery, Pa State Univ, 77; one-man show, Barbara Okum Gallery, St Louis, 79; and others. *Pos:* Proj dir, Philadelphia Ceramic Speakers Consortium, Pa Coun Arts, Tyler Sch Art, Moore Col & Philadelphia Col Art, currently. *Teaching:* Coordr two-dimensional visual design dept, NTex State Univ, Denton, 58-63; area chmn ceramics, Tyler Sch Art, Temple Univ, 66-, chmn craft dept, 79- *Awards:* Fourth Prize, Ceramic Art of the World, Int Acad of Ceramics & Alta Potters Asn, 73; Nat Endowment Arts Fel, 79; Fel, Nat Coun Educ Ceramic Arts, 83; and others. *Bibliog:* Hahn & Elisari (auths), Clay Artists, doc film, 75; Charlotte Sewalt (auth), An Interview with Robert Winokur, Ceramics Mo, 9/77. *Mem:* Am Crafts Coun; Nat Coun Educ Ceramic Arts (br dir, 69-70, vpres, 72-73); Philadelphia Coun Professional Craftsmen. *Media:* Salt Glazed Ceramic Stoneware. *Publ:* Auth, The Tyler School of Art of Temple University, Ceramics Mo, 75; coauth, The light of Rudolph Staffel, Craft Horizions, 77. *Dealer:* Helen Druitt Gallery 1625 Spruce St Philadelphia PA 19103. *Mailing Add:* 435 Norristown Rd Horsham PA 19044

WINSOR, V JACQUELINE
SCULPTOR
b Nfld, Can, Oct 20, 41; US citizen. *Study:* Yale Summer Sch Art & Music, 64; Mass Col Art, BFA, 65; Rutgers Univ, MFA, 67. *Work:* Mus Mod Art, New York; Whitney Mus Am Art, New York; Australia Nat Gallery, Canberra; Detroit Inst Arts, Mich; Mus d'Arte Mod, Paris, France. *Exhib:* Whitney Mus Am Art, 70, 72, 74, 77-79 & 82-83; Aldrich Mus Contemp Art, Ridgefield, Conn, 71 & 79; Paula Cooper Gallery, New York, 72-74 & 77-78; one-person exhibs, Paula Cooper Gallery, 73, 76 & 82, Portland Ctr Visual Arts, Ore, 76, Mus Mod Art, San Francisco, 77, Wadsworth Atheneum, 78, Mus Mod Art, New York, 79, Fort Worth Art Mus, Tex, 79, Va Mus, Richmond, 81, Akron Art Mus, Ohio, 82, and many others; Mus Mod Art, New York, 73 & 74; Art Inst Chicago, 74; Mus Contemp Art, Chicago, 77; Va Mus, Richmond, 81; Sculptors at Univ Calif-Davis: Past and Present, Richard L Nelson Gallery, Univ Calif, 82; Objects, Structures, Artifice: American Sculpture 1970-1982, SVC Fine Arts Gallery, Univ S Fla, Tampa, 83; Sculpture Invitational, Oscarsson Hood Gallery, New York, 83; and others. *Teaching:* Instr art introd & ceramics, Douglass Col, 67; instr art introd, Middlesex Co Col & Newark State Teachers' Col, 68 & 69; instr ceramics, Mills Col Educ, 68 & 71; instr graphics, Loyola Univ, New Orleans, summer 69; instr ceramics, Greenwich House Pottery Sch, New York, 69-72; instr sculpture, Sch Visual Arts, New York, 71 & 75; instr art introd, Hunter Col, 72-75. *Awards:* Nat Endowment Arts Grant, 74 & 77; Lewis Tiffany Award, 77; Guggenheim Fel, 78. *Bibliog:* Mark Stevens (auth), Raw magic, Newsweek, 2/79; John Gruen (auth), Jackie Winsor: Eloquence of a Yankee Pioneer, Art News, 3/79; Badanna Zack (auth), Jackie Winsor, Artmag, Can, 9-10/79; and others. *Mailing Add:* c/o Paula Cooper Gallery 155 Wooster New York NY 10012

WINTER, GERALD GLEN
PAINTER, EDUCATOR
b Milwaukee, Wis, Sept 1, 36. *Study:* Univ Wis-Milwaukee, BFA, Madison, MS & MFA. *Work:* Milwaukee Art Ctr; Lowe Mus, Univ Miami, Coral Gables, Fla; Ringling Mus, Fla. *Exhib:* Corcoran Biennial of Am Painting, 63; 39th, 40th, 43rd & 44th Exhib Contemp Am Painting, Palm Beach; one-man shows, Miami-Dade Community Col, 75, Lowe Mus, Univ Miami, 75 & Univ Miami Art Dept Gallery, 79; Metrop Mus & Art Ctr, Coral Gables, Fla, 83; and others; 33 Miami Artists, Miami Art Ctr. *Teaching:* Prof art, Univ Miami, 65-, chmn dept, 75-79. *Awards:* Ford Found Purchase Award, 62; Third Prize, Corcoran Gallery of Art Biennial, 62; Honorable Mentions, Hortt Mem Exhib, 69, 80 & 81. *Media:* Oil, Serigraphy. *Mailing Add:* 6629 SW 62nd Terr Miami FL 33143

WINTER, LUMEN MARTIN
SCULPTOR, PAINTER
b Ellery, Ill, Dec 12, 08. *Study:* Grand Rapids Jr Col; Cleveland Sch Art; Nat Acad Design; also study in France & Italy. *Work:* Washington Co Mus, Hagerstown, Md; Libr Cong, Washington, DC; Grand Rapids Community Col, Mich; Columbus Mus Arts & Crafts, Ga; Vatican, Rome, Italy; and

others. *Comn:* Mosaic & bas-relief sculpture for chapels, US Air Force Acad, Colorado Springs, Colo, 60-61; Apollo 13 official medallion for Capt James A Lovell, Jr, Houston, 70; Titans mural (oil on linen), UN, New York, 72; Space Age & Labor Mosaics, AFL-CIO Hq Bldg, Washington, DC, 72; bas relief frieze, Gerald R Ford Ctr, Grand Rapids, Mich, 76; rotunda murals, State Capitol, Topeka, 78. *Exhib:* Nat Acad Design, New York; Am Watercolor Soc Ann & Traveling Shows, 50-; Geneva, Switz, 55; Knickerbocker Artists, Nat Arts Club, New York, 78; Nat Soc Painters in Casein & Acrylic, Am Acad Inst Arts & Lett, New York, 79; and others. *Pos:* art juror, various art shows; Artist in residence, Thornton Donovan Sch, New Rochelle, 74- *Awards:* Purchase Ranger Fund Award, Nat Acad Design, 66; William A White Award, Salmagundi Club, 78; and others. *Bibliog:* Norman Kent & Ernest Watson (auth), Lumen Martin Winter, Am Artist Mag, 50, 52, 59 & 66; Ralph Fabri (auth), Lumen Martin Winter, Today's Art, 66; Jim Richardson (auth), For as long as there is a Kansas, Kans Mag, 4/78. *Mem:* Salmagundi Club; Am Watercolor Soc; Nat Soc Mural Painters (vpres, 53-55); New Rochelle Art Asn (pres, 52-54). *Media:* Marble, Bronze; Watercolor, Oil. *Publ:* Coauth, The Last Supper of Leonardo da Vinci, Coward McCann, 53; auth, A People's Art, Kans Quart, Kans State Univ, Manhattan, 77; auth, Mural painting--a peoples art, Kans Quarterly, fall 77. *Mailing Add:* 144 Overlook Circle New Rochelle NY 10804

WINTER, ROGER
PAINTER
b Denison, Tex, Aug 17, 34. *Study:* Univ Tex, BFA, 56; Univ Iowa, MFA, 60; Brooklyn Mus Sch, Beckmann scholar, 60. *Work:* Mus Art, Univ Okla, Norman; Dallas Mus Fine Arts, Tex; Southern Methodist Univ, Dallas; Oak Cliff Savings & Loan, Dallas; Longview Mus & Art Ctr, Tex. *Exhib:* Tex Painting & Sculpture, 20th Century Dallas, 71-62; two-man show, Whitte Mus, San Antonio, Tex, 67; one-man shows, Pollock Gallery, 68 & One i at a Time, 71, Southern Methodist Univ, Dallas & Delgado Mus, New Orleans, La, 68. *Pos:* Installation asst, Dallas Mus Contemp Arts, 62-63; gallery tours & lectr, Dallas Mus Fine Arts, 63- *Teaching:* Instr painting, Ft Worth Art Ctr, 61; instr painting, Dallas Mus Fine Arts, 62-68; prof painting, Southern Methodist Univ, 65- *Awards:* Purchase Award, Univ Okla Art Mus, 62; Top Award, Dallas Ann, Dallas Mus Fine Arts, 64. *Bibliog:* Film on work produced on KERA-TV, Dallas, 71. *Media:* Oil. *Publ:* Auth, Introduction to Drawings, Prentice Hall, 83. *Dealer:* Fischbach Gallery 29 W 57th St New York NY 10019. *Mailing Add:* 3228 Rankin Dallas TX 75205

WINTER, RUTH
PAINTER
b New York, NY, Jan 17, 13. *Study:* NY Univ, BS, 31, MA, 32; Art Students League, with Corbino, Bosa & Morris Kantor, 57-61. *Work:* In collections of Reginald Cabral, Provincetown, Mass, Marlo Lewis, Scarsdale, NY, Mr Frantz, Great Neck, NY, Lawrence Koenisberg, South Lawrence, NY & Semour S Alter, West Hempstead, NY. *Exhib:* Silvermine, Conn, 57-61; Nat Asn Women Artists, 57-68 & 74; Gallery 15, New York, 59; Brooklyn Mus, 60; Nat Acad Design, 60; Lever House, New York, 63 & 67; Pepsi Cola Exhib, 64. *Awards:* Marcia Brady Tucker Prize, Nat Asn Women Artists, 57; Max Low Award, 59; Mr & Mrs Gomes Award, Mahopac Art League, 59. *Bibliog:* Robert M Coates (auth), Art galleries, New Yorker, 5/57; Stuart Preston (auth), Art: a game of styles, New York Times, 5/57; Painting televised, Boston, 7/58. *Mem:* Nat Asn Women Artists; life mem Art Students League New York; Mahopac Art League. *Media:* Oil. *Mailing Add:* 98-50 67th Ave Rego Park NY 11374

WINTERS, DENNY
PAINTER
b Grand Rapids, Mich, Mar 17, 07. *Study:* Art Inst Chicago; Chicago Acad Fine Arts; Acad Julien, Paris, France. *Work:* Philadelphia Mus Art, Pa; San Francisco Mus Art, Calif; Colby Col Mus; Butler Inst Am Art; Univ Maine, Orono; and others. *Exhib:* Mus Mod Art, New York; Art Inst Chicago; Pa Acad Fine Arts, Philadelphia; San Francisco Mus Art; Carnegie Inst, Pittsburgh; one-man shows, Univ Maine, Orono, 78, Farnsworth Mus, Rockland, 78 & Payson Mus, Portland, Maine, 78; and numerous other group & one-man shows. *Awards:* Guggenheim Fel, 48; Butler Inst Am Art Purchase Prize; Denver Mus First Prize Ann Art Show; and others. *Bibliog:* The Art of the Artist, Crown; Edward Betts (auth), Creative Seascape Painting, Watson-Guptill. *Mem:* Maine Coast Artists. *Publ:* Illusr, Full Fathom Five & Savage Summer. *Mailing Add:* Rockport ME 04856

WINTERSTEEN, BERNICE MCILHENNY
ADMINISTRATOR, COLLECTOR
b Philadelphia, Pa, June 16, 03. *Study:* Smith Col, BA; Wilson Col, DFA, 68; Moore Col Art, DFA, 68; Ursinius Col, Hon LHD, 65; Villanova Univ, Hon DFA, 67; LaSalle Col, LHD. *Pos:* Bd gov & trustee, Womens Comt, Philadelphia Mus Art, 47-64, pres, 64-68; organizer & first chmn vis comt, Smith Col Art Mus, 51; bd gov, Philadelphia Mus Col Art, 55-64; mem vis comt, design & visual arts dept, Harvard Univ, 64-82; hon chmn, Nat Trust Preserv Conf, Philadelphia, 66; chmn, Philadelphia Art Festival, 67; dir Atheneum Libr, Univ Pa, formerly; and many civic, art & state positions. *Awards:* Distinguished Daughter of Pennsylvania, 64; Gimbel Award, 66. *Mem:* Philadelphia Art Comn; charter mem Philadelphia Ctr Performing Arts. *Collection:* Nineteenth and twentieth century French painting and sculpture; French Impressionist and Post-Impressionist paintings, including nineteen paintings by Picasso and Matisse's Lady in Blue. *Mailing Add:* 402 Grays Lane House 100 Grays Lane Haverford PA 19041

WIRTSCHAFTER, BUD
FILMMAKER, INSTRUCTOR
b Atlantic City, NJ, Jan 11, 24. *Study:* Art Students League, 46-47; New Sch Social Res, 47-49; Hans Hoffman Sch Fine Arts, New York, 47-49; Acad de Belli Arti, Italy, BA, 53. *Exhib:* Festival Di Popoli, Florence, Italy, 67; Spoleto Film Festival, 67; San Francisco Film Festival, 68; Cannes Film Festival, 70; 2 Media Environments, Neighborhood, 68 & Sale of a Memory, 75; plus many others. *Pos:* Dir, Soho Media Coop, 74- *Teaching:* Instr film, New Sch Social Res, 70-73, dir Workshop Extended Cinema, 70-; instr film, City Col New York, 70- *Bibliog:* R Schekner (auth), article, Tulane Drama Rev, spring 68 & Living it out on E 7th St, Urban Rev, 4/68. *Mem:* Experiments in Art & Technol; Filmmakers Cinemateque; New Am Cinema Group; life mem Art Students League; Filmmakers Coop. *Publ:* Dialogue, NBC-TV, New York, 65; Point of View, WOR-TV, New York, 66; I'm Here Now, Brandon Films, New York, 66; Ten Down Town, NYC-TV, New York, 69; and others. *Mailing Add:* Soho Media Coop 154 Spring St New York NY 10012

WIRTZ, STEPHEN CARL
DEALER
b Peoria, Ill, Apr 9, 45. *Study:* Occidental Col, 63; Univ Calif, Berkeley, BA, 67; Antioch Col, Ohio, MA, 68. *Specialty:* Contemporary American and European sculpture & photography. *Mailing Add:* c/o Stephen Wirtz Gallery 345 Sutter St San Francisco CA 94108

WISE, GENEVA H (HOLCOMB)
COLLECTOR, PAINTER
b Pittsburg, Kans. *Study:* Okla State Univ, BA; with Doel Reed, Edward N Walker, David De Allende, Elinor Evans, Dale McKinney, Milford Zornes, George Post, Father John Walch & Al Brouillette. *Work:* Okla State Univ; Baptist Med Ctr, Oklahoma City; Alpha Delta Pi Asn, Okla State Univ; and many pvt collections. *Exhib:* Eight State Shows, Okla Art Ctr, 61-64; Southwestern Watercolor Soc, Dallas, 67 & 73; one-woman show, Okla State Univ, 75; Ann Artists Salon, Okla Mus Art, Oklahoma City, 76-78; 15th Ann, Temple Emanu-El, Dallas, Tex, 78; Centennial Exhib, Am Univ Univ Women, Boston Univ, 81; and many others. *Awards:* Asel Materials Co Award, Dallas, 67; Award for Watercolor, Southwest Watercolor Soc; 1st & 2nd Place Awards, Okla Fedn Women's Club, 80 & 81; and others. *Bibliog:* Article, La Rev Mod, Paris, 2/72; Caralee Strock Stanard (auth), article, Adelphian Mag, 74. *Mem:* Okla Watercolor Asn; Okla Art Guild; Southwestern Watercolor Soc; Stillwater Art Guild; Nat Soc Painters Casein & Acrylic. *Media:* Transparent Watercolor, Acrylic. *Collection:* Doel Reed aquatint; Dale McKinney silk screen; J J McVicker intaglio; Richard Morton lithograph; Kaethe Kollwitz etching; and others. *Dealer:* Gayle Ann Gallery 516B S Bryant Bryant Square Edmond OK 73034. *Mailing Add:* 305 S Monroe St Stillwater OK 74074

WISE, GERALD LEE
GRAPHIC ARTIST, PRINTMAKER
b Pittsburgh, Pa, Dec 15, 41. *Study:* Wheaton Col, Ill, BA, 63; Northern Ill Univ, MA(design), 67, MFA(printmaking), 69. *Work:* Mankato State Univ; Ball State Univ; St Lawrence Col. *Exhib:* Drawings USA, Minn Mus Art, 73; Ball State Drawing & Sculpture, 73 & 82; 24th Nat Prints & Drawing Exhib, Okla Art Ctr, 82; Springfield Nat Exhib, Mus Fine Arts, Mass, 82 & 83; West 82--Art and the Law Traveling Exhib, 82 & 83; Tex Fine Arts Nat, Laguna Gloria Mus, Austin, 83; 17th Nat Drawing & Sculpture Exhib, Del Mar Col Gallery, Tex, 83. *Teaching:* Asst prof art, Mankato State Univ, 69-74 & Westfield State Col, 82-; instr, G Walter V Smith Art Mus, Springfield, Mass, 80-82. *Awards:* Purchase Awards, 24th Nat Drawing & Print Exhib, Okla Art Ctr, 82, 63rd & 64th Springfield Nat Exhib, Holyoke Community Savings Bank, Mass, 82 & 83 & Mattoon Art Festival, Bank Boston, 83. *Bibliog:* Robert Girouard (auth), Wiser yet, Mankato Free Press, 4/4/74; Mary Kronholm (auth), Wise makes living an art, Country J, 6/82; Sally Robinson (auth), A profile: Gerald Wise, Westfield Sunday News, 9/82. *Mem:* Col Art Asn; Springfield Artists League. *Media:* Ink, Pen and Brush. *Dealer:* Hill Gallery Worthington MA 01098. *Mailing Add:* Hiram Blair Rd Blandford MA 01008

WISE, HOWARD
ADMINISTRATOR
b Cleveland, Ohio, Nov 6, 03. *Study:* Clare Col, Cambridge Univ, BA(hons); Western Reserve Univ; Cleveland Inst Art. *Pos:* Estab Howard Wise Gallery of Present Day Painting & Sculpture, Cleveland, 57; dir, Howard Wise Gallery, New York, 60-71; founder, Electronic Arts Intermix Inc, currently. *Interests:* Fostering the use of video (half inch portable TV) as a means of individual expression and communication. *Mailing Add:* Electronic Arts 84 Fifth Ave New York NY 10011

WISE, (KENNETH) KELLY
PHOTOGRAPHER, CRITIC
b New Castle, Ind, Dec 1, 32. *Study:* Purdue Univ, BS, 55; Columbia Univ, MA, 59. *Work:* Libr Cong; Bibliotheque Nat, Paris; George Eastman House, Int Mus Photog, Rochester, NY; Mus Fine Arts, Boston; Mus Fine Arts, Houston. *Exhib:* Solo exhib, Fogg Art Mus, 73; Private Realities, Mus Fine Arts, Boston, 74; Recent Photographs, Il Diaframma, Milan, Italy, 77; Warm Truths & Cool Deceits, Sidney Janis Gallery, New York, 78; Color Photographs, Snite Art Mus, Univ Notre Dame, 81; Still Points, Rose Art Mus, Brandeis Univ, 81; Portraits: Men & Women of Letters, Vision Gallery, Boston, 83. *Collections Arranged:* Photo Facts and Opinions, 18 Contemporary American Photographers, 81. *Pos:* Photog consult, Nat Humanities Fac, Concord, Mass, 70-74 & Polaroid Corp, Cambridge, Mass,

74-77; photog critic, Boston Globe, 82- *Bibliog:* Max Kozloff (auth), Photography & Fascination, Addison House Publ, 79. *Mem:* Soc Photog Educ; Photog Resource Ctr, Boston. *Publ:* Ed, The Photographers Choice, 75, auth, Still Points, 77 & ed, Lotte Jacobi, 78, Addison House; ed, Portrait: Theory, Lustrum Press, 81; ed, Photo Facts and Opinions, Addison Gallery Am Art, 81. *Dealer:* Vision Gallery 216 Newbury St Boston MA 02115. *Mailing Add:* 19 School St Boston MA 01810

WISE, SUE
PAINTER
b Bronx, NY, Mar 22, 21. *Study:* Univ Colo with Gene Mathews & Frank Sampson; special study with Thomas Currey & William Schimmel. *Work:* Colo Council Arts & Humanities, First Nat Bank, United Bank, Denver, Colo; Nat State Bank, Boulder, Colo; Midland Federal Savings, Longmont, Colo. *Exhib:* Own Your Own Exhib, Denver Art Mus, Colo, 68; Watercolor USA, Springfield Art Mus, Mo, 71; 60th Ann Exhib, Nat Watercolor Soc, Laguna Beach, Calif, 80; Fine Arts Exhib, State Fair, Pueblo, Colo, 81; Rocky Mountain Nat, Foothills Art Ctr, Colo, 81; 114th Ann Exhib, Am Watercolor Soc, Nat Acad Galleries, New York, 81; and others. *Awards:* Bronze Medal of Honor, Am Watercolor Soc, 74; Foothills Art Ctr Award, 78; Mary Pleissner Mem Award, Am Watercolor Soc, 82. *Mem:* Am Watercolor Soc; Nat Watercolor Soc; Dolphin Fel. *Media:* Mixed Watermedia, Collage. *Publ:* Auth, The watercolor page, Am Artist Mag, 2/77; contribr, Easy Living Mag, The Webb Co, 78; contribr, Creative Seascape Painting, Watson-Guptill. *Dealer:* Mustard Seed Gallery 1932 14th Street Boulder CO 80302. *Mailing Add:* 6494 Nelson Road Longmont CO 80501

WISE, SUZANNE TANDERUP
CURATOR, HISTORIAN
b Great Lakes, Ill, Jan 31, 52. *Study:* Univ Nebr, Lincoln, BA, 74; Univ Kans, MA, 80. *Pos:* Actg cur, Ctr Western Studies, Joslyn Art Mus, 80-81, asst cur, 81-82; cur, Mary & Leigh Block Gallery, Northwestern Univ, 82- *Teaching:* Instr art hist, Div Continuing Educ, Univ Nebr, 79-82 & Creighton Univ, 80. *Mem:* Col Art Asn; Am Asn Mus; Midwest Art Hist Soc; Nat Art Educ Asn. *Res:* Nineteenth and twentieth century American painting and photography. *Publ:* Contribr, Jules Breton and the French Rural Tradition, 82 & Joslyn Art Mus Handbook of the Permanent Collection, 83, Joslyn Art Mus. *Mailing Add:* Block Gallery Northwestern Univ Evanston IL 60201

WISNOSKY, JOHN G
PAINTER, EDUCATOR
b Springfield, Ill, Mar 21, 40. *Study:* Yale Univ Summer Sch Art, 61; Univ Ill, Urbana, BFA, 62, MFA, 64. *Work:* Honolulu Acad Arts, Hawaii; Southern Ill Univ, Carbondale; Contemp Arts Ctr, Hawaii, Honolulu; State Hawaii Found Cult & Arts; Mint Mus, Charlotte, NC. *Comn:* Pan Pac hall design, Hawaii Pavilion, Osaka World's Fair, 70; sculpture, Ewa Beach Publ Libr, Oahu, Hawaii, 71; Flora Pacifica design, Ethnobotanical Expos, 71 & 82; Inst Astronomy, Mauna Kea, Hawaii, 83. *Exhib:* Northwest Printmakers Int, Seattle, Wash, 65; Soc Am Graphic Artists, New York, 65; Presentation Artist Show, Boston Printmakers, Boston Mus Fine Art, 66; Drawings-USA, St Paul Art Ctr, Minn, 67; Am Printmakers Exhib, Otis Art Inst, 68. *Teaching:* Instr painting & design, Va Polytech Inst, 64-66; prof & chmn, Univ Hawaii, 66- *Awards:* Henry B Shope Prize, Soc Am Graphic Artists, 65; Purchase Award, Honolulu Acad Arts, 70. *Bibliog:* Neogy & Turnbull (ed), Artists of Hawaii, Vol II; G & W Radford (auth), Sculpture in the Sun, 78. *Mem:* Honolulu Printmakers (pres, 69-70); Hawaii Painters & Sculptors League (pres, 69-70). *Dealer:* Art Loft 637 Sheridan St Honolulu HI 96813; Gallery at Waiohi Poipu Beach Kavai HI. *Mailing Add:* 4016 Lurline Dr Honolulu HI 96816

WISSEMANN-WIDRIG, NANCY
PAINTER
b Jamestown, NY. *Study:* Syracuse Univ, NY; Ohio Univ, Athens. *Work:* Canton Art Inst, Ohio; Univ Kans Mus Fine Arts; Port Authority of New York; Nat Shawmut Bank, Boston, Mass; Minn Mining & Mfg Co. *Exhib:* Western New York Artists, Albright-Knox Art Gallery, Buffalo, NY, 64; Landscape, Baltimore Mus Fine Arts, 73; one-person shows, Tibor de Nagy Gallery, New York, 74, 77, 80, 81 & 83; Contemp Landscape, Okla Art Ctr, Oklahoma City, 75; Pepperdine Univ, Malibu, Calif, 76; Hamline Univ, St Paul, Minn, 76; Headley Mus, Lexington, Ky, 76; Farnsworth Mus, Rockland, Maine, 83. *Awards:* Outstanding Realist, Western New York Artists, Albright-Knox Art Gallery, 64; Purchase Award, Am Acad of Arts & Lett, Childe Hassam Fund, 69. *Bibliog:* Ellen Stevens (auth), What's happening way out here?, New Directions, 77; Norman Turner (auth), article, Arts Mag, 12/77; John Yau (auth), article, Art Am, 9/80. *Mem:* E End Arts & Humanities Long Island. *Media:* Acrylic, Oil. *Dealer:* Tibor de Nagy 29 W 57th St New York NY 10019. *Mailing Add:* Box 524 Southold NY 11971

WITHAM, VERNON CLINT
PAINTER, PRINTMAKER
b Eugene, Ore, Dec 6, 25. *Study:* Univ Ore; Calif Sch Fine Arts, San Francisco. *Work:* Univ Ore Mus Art, Eugene; Univ Wyo Mus Art, Laramie. *Exhib:* Under 25, Seligmann Gallery, New York, 49; Artists of Oregon, Portland Art Mus, 53; one-man show, Calif Palace Legion of Honor, San Francisco, 60; Maxwell Gallery, San Francisco, 61; American Landscape, Peridot Gallery, New York, 68. *Teaching:* Resident artist, Univ Wyo, 71- *Awards:* Purchase Award, Northwest Painting Ann, 72. *Media:* Oil, Monoprints. *Collection:* Antique primitive art from around the world. *Publ:* Coauth, 12 new painters (serigraph folio), 53; contribr, insert 4, Written Palette, 62. *Dealer:* Gallery Tiqua 7077 Main St Scottsdale AZ. *Mailing Add:* 2100 Greiner Eugene OR 97405

WITHERS, JOSEPHINE
HISTORIAN, WRITER
b Cambridge, Mass, July 3, 38. *Study:* Oberlin Col, BA, 60; Columbia Univ, PhD, 71. *Collections Arranged:* Julio Gonzalez, Sculpture and Drawings, Mus Mod Art, New York, 68; Mixed Bag, Univ Md Art Gallery, 73; Women Artists in Washington Collections (auth, catalog), Univ Md Art Gallery, 79. *Pos:* Assoc dir, Univ Md Art Gallery, 70-73; chief reader art hist, Advan Placement Educ Testing Serv, 79-83; art consult, Feminist Studies, 78- *Teaching:* Asst prof art hist, Temple Univ, Philadelphia, Pa, 68-69; asst prof 20th century art, Univ Md, College Park, 70-78, assoc prof art, 78-, actg dir, Women's Studies Prog, 82-84. *Awards:* Aelioian Fel, Oberlin Col, 64; Gen Res Bd, Univ Md, 72 & 77. *Mem:* Col Art Asn; Women's Caucus Art (nat bd dirs, 80-83); Washington Women's Art Ctr (bd dir, 76-77); Conf of Women in the Visual Arts (steering comt, 72). *Res:* Twentieth century art; American women artists of the nineteenth and twentieth centuries. *Publ:* Auth, Artistic women and women artists, Art J, summer 76 & the artistic collaboration of Picasso and Gonzalez, winter 76, Art J; auth, The Famous Fur-Lined Teacup and The Anonymous Meret Oppenheim, Arts Mag, 11/77; auth, Julio Gonzalez, Sculpture in iron, New York Univ Press, 77; auth, In search of the magic kingdom, New Art Examiner, 10/81; and others. *Mailing Add:* c/o Art Dept Univ Md College Park MD 20742

WITHROW, WILLIAM J
ADMINISTRATOR
b Toronto, Ont, Sept 30, 26. *Study:* Univ Toronto, BA, 50, BEd, 55 & MEd, 58, MA, 60. *Pos:* Dir, Art Gallery Ont, Toronto, 60- *Teaching:* Head art dept, Earl Haig Col, 51-59, *Awards·* Can Centennial Medal, 67; Order Can. *Mem:* Can Mus Asn; Asn Art Mus Dirs; Can Art Mus Dirs Orgn; Can Nat Comt for Int Coun Mus. *Publ:* Auth, Sorel Etrog sculpture, 67 & Contemporary Canadian painting, 72. *Mailing Add:* c/o Art Gallery of Ont Grange Park Toronto ON M5T 1G4 Canada

WITKIN, ISAAC
SCULPTOR, INSTRUCTOR
b Johannesburg, SAfrica, May 10, 36; US citizen. *Study:* St Martins Sch Art, London, with Anthony Caro; also with Henry Moore, Eng. *Work:* Joseph Hirshhorn Mus, Washington, DC; Tate Gallery, London, Eng; Worcester Art Mus, Mass; Columbus Mus, Ohio; Storm King Art Ctr. *Comn:* Sculpture, Storm King Art Ctr, Mountainville, NY, 70; sculpture, Springfield, Mass, 75; and others. *Exhib:* One-man shows, Marlborough Gallery, 63-, Hamilton Gallery, 79; Keene-Thorne, 77 & Tanglewood Music Festival, 77; Storm King Art Ctr, 73; Hayward Gallery, London, 75; Hirshhorn Mus, 76; Am Acad Arts & Lett, 77. *Teaching:* Instr sculpture, St Martins Sch Art, 63-65; instr sculpture, Bennington Col, 65-; instr sculpture, Parsons Sch Design, 75- *Awards:* Co-Winner First Prize, Paris Bienale, 65; Guggenheim Fel, 81. *Bibliog:* James Mellows (auth), article, New York Times, 71; Bill Lipke (dir), film, Vt Coun Arts, 72; Neil Marshad (dir), film, Nat Educ TV, 75. *Media:* Steel, Bronze. *Publ:* Auth, Modern English Sculpture, Thames and Hudson, 67; contribr, Minimal Art, Dutton, 68; auth, Alistair Healpine Gift, Tate Gallery, 71; contribr, New York Mag, 4/9/73. *Mailing Add:* c/o Hamilton Gallery of Contemp Art 20 W 57th St New York NY 10019

WITKIN, JEROME PAUL
PAINTER, DRAFTSMAN
b Brooklyn, NY, Sept 13, 39. *Study:* Cooper Union Art Sch, 57-60; Skowhegan Sch Painting & Sculpture; Berlin Acad, WGer, Pulitzer traveling fel, 60; Univ Pa, MFA, 70. *Work:* Everson Mus Art, Syracuse; Nat Acad Design; Metrop Mus Art, Cleveland; and others. *Exhib:* Drawings USA, Minn Mus Art, 71; Drawings, Kraushaar Gallery, New York, 71; Pa State Mus, 78; Religion into Art, nat traveling exhib, 81; Real, Really Real, Super Real, San Antonio Mus, 81-82; and others. *Teaching:* Instr drawing, Md Inst Art, Baltimore, 63-65; lectr painting, Manchester Col Art, Eng, 65-67; vis prof design, drawing & painting, Moore Col, 68-71; assoc prof art, Syracuse Univ, 71-81, prof, 81-; lectr, Columbia Mus Art, SC, 83, Ark Art Ctr, Little Rock, 83. *Awards:* Guggenheim Found Fel Painting, 63-64; Paul Puzinas Award, Nat Acad Design, 80; Fund Purchase Prize, Am Acad Arts & Letters, 81; and others. *Bibliog:* Theodore F Wolff (auth), The excellence of the work of Jerome Witkin, Christian Sci Monitor, 4/28/83. *Mem:* Nat Acad Design. *Media:* Oil on Linen. *Dealer:* Kraushaar Galleries 724 Fifth Ave New York NY 10019. *Mailing Add:* 1138 Lancaster Ave Syracuse NY 13210

WITKIN, JOEL-PETER
PHOTOGRAPHER
b Brooklyn, NY, Sept 13, 39. *Study:* Cooper Union, New York, BFA, 75; Univ NMex, MA, 77. *Work:* Mus Mod Art & Metrop Mus Art, New York; Stiejik Mus, Amsterdam; Victoria & Albert Mus, London. *Exhib:* Great Photographs from Mus Collection, Mus Mod Art, New York, 59; The Markers, San Francisco Mus Mod Art, 80; Hardison Fine Arts, New York, 80, 81 & 83; Fraenkel Gallery, San Francisco, 83; Fay Gold Gallery, Atlanta, 83; Pace Gallery, New York, 84. *Awards:* Creative Artists Pub Serv Prog Fel Photog, 75; Ford Found Grant Photog, 76, 78 & 79; Nat Endowment Arts Fel Photog, 80 & 81. *Media:* Photography. *Publ:* Contribr, Infinity, New York, 68, Aura, Vol I, No 3, Creative Camera, 11/81 & Advocate #375, 83. *Dealer:* Pace/MacGill 11 E 57 St New York NY 10022. *Mailing Add:* 222 Amherst St NE Albuquerque NM 87106

WITMEYER, STANLEY HERBERT
PAINTER, CONSULTANT
b Palmyra, Pa, Feb 14, 13. *Study:* Sch Art & Design, Rochester Inst Technol, dipl; State Univ NY Col Buffalo, BS; Syracuse Univ, MFA; Univ Hawaii, with Ben Norris. *Exhib:* Rochester Mem Art Gallery; Albright-Knox Gallery,

Buffalo; Honolulu Acad Fine Arts; Everson Mus, Syracuse. *Pos:* Dir sch art & design, Rochester Inst Technol, 52-68, assoc dean col fine & appl arts, 68-82. *Teaching:* Instr art, Cuba Pub Schs, NY, 39-44; prof painting & design, Sch Art Design, Rochester Inst Technol, 46-52. *Mem:* Rochester Torch Club (pres, 52); Nat Art Educ Asn; Rochester Art Club (pres, 56); NY State Art Teachers Asn. *Media:* Mixed. *Collection:* American printmakers and painters. *Publ:* Auth, articles in, Everyday Art, Design Mag, Sch Arts, Nat Art Educ J & NY Art Teachers Bulletin. *Mailing Add:* 54 Clarks Crossing Fairport NY 14450

WITOLD-K (KACZANOWSKI)
PAINTER, SCULPTOR
b Warsaw, Poland, May 15, 32; US citizen. *Study:* Acad Fine Arts, Warsaw, with W Fangor & H Tomaszerski, dipl, 56. *Work:* Mus Fine Arts, Houston, Tex; Mus NMex, Santa Fe; Phoenix Art Mus, Ariz; Nat Libr, Paris, France; Whitney Mus, New York. *Comn:* Mural, Polish Exhib, Moscow, USSR, 60; Auschwitz (mural), Govt Poland, 61; painting, United Bank Calif, Beverly Hills, 71; painting, Conoco Oil Co, Houston, Tex, 74; mural, Mainstreet Art Festival, Houston, 75. *Exhib:* Solo exhibs, Keystone Ctr, Colo, 77, Anneke Whatley Gallery, Keystone, Colo, 78, Gallery 400, Aspen, Colo, 79, J Houston Gallery, Vail, Colo, 81 & Richtofen Castle, Denver, 81. *Teaching:* Lectr, Seton Hall Univ, 71, Cranbrook Acad Art, 78 & Univ Detroit, 78. *Bibliog:* Michel Casse (ed), Le Crevasses du Ciel, Paris, 67; Who is Mr K? (doc film), Am Film Inst, 74. *Mailing Add:* 329 Detroit St Denver CO 80206

WITT, JOHN
PAINTER, PRINTMAKER
b Wilmington, Del, Jan 30, 40. *Study:* Philadelphia Col Art, BFA, 62; Univ Md Grad Sch; Brooklyn Mus Sch Art. *Work:* New Britain Mus Am Art; Smithsonian Inst, USMC Combat Art Collections, US Navy Combat Art Collection, Pentagon & US Army, Off Chief Mil Hist, Washington, DC. *Exhib:* Smithsonian Inst Vietnam Exhib, Washington, DC, 69; Nat Arts Club, New York, 72; Hudson Valley Art Asn Ann, White Plains, NY, 72; Audubon Artists Ann, New York, 73; Am Artists Prof League Ann, New York, 73. *Pos:* Combat artist, USMC Civilian Comn, 68 & 69; combat artist, US Navy, 73 & 76; courtroom trial artist, ABC News, 74. *Awards:* Gold Medal, Hudson Valley Art Asn, 72; Best in Show, Nat Arts Club, New York, 72; Gold Medal, Louis E Seley NACAL Award, 78. *Bibliog:* US Army, Executive Corridor Section of the Army, USGPO, 66; Mark Goodman (auth), Trial of art, New Times Mag, 5/17/74; Col Raymond Henri (auth), Combat art since 1775, Marine Corps Gazette, 74. *Mem:* Soc Illusr (pres, 80-83); Hudson Valley Art Asn; Dutch Treat Club. *Media:* Multimedia. *Publ:* Auth & illusr, Vietnam, Sterling, 72; illusr, Mitchell/Stans Trial, Newsweek Mag, 74; illusr, Mitchell/Stans Trial Courtroom Drawings, ABC News, 74; illusr, Marine Corps Gazette, 74; illusr, Portraits of Valor, USMC, 74. *Mailing Add:* RD 1 Box 369 Baptist Church Rd Yorktown Heights NY 10598

WITT, NANCY CAMDEN
SCULPTOR, PAINTER
b Richmond, Va, Oct 24, 30. *Study:* Randolph-Macon Woman's Col; Old Dominion Univ, BA, 65; Va Commonwealth Univ, MFA, 67. *Work:* Miss Mus Art; Mint Mus Art, Charlotte, NC; Randolph-Macon Woman's Col, Lynchburg; Univ Va, Charlottesville; Chrysler Mus, Norfolk, Va; and others. *Comn:* Mobile construct, Philip Morris Tobacco Co, Richmond, 69-70; mural, Security Fed Savings & Loan Co, Richmond, 71; portrait, Randolph-Macon Col, Ashland, Va, 79; portrait, Richmond Symphony, 79; portrait, Crowder United, 81; and others. *Exhib:* Mint Mus Art, 71, 75, 77 & 79; Mainstreams, Marietta, Ohio, 75-77; Int Woman Artists Exhib, 76; Realist Invitational, Southeastern Ctr for Contemp Art, Winston-Salem, NC, 78; retrospective, Roanoke Col, Salem, Va, 79; Mint Mus Art, Charlotte, NC, 71, 75, 77 & 79; Miss Mus Art, 79; Va Mus, Richmond, 79-80; solo exhib, Southeastern Ctr Contemp Art, Winston-Salem, NC, 80; and others. *Teaching:* Actg chmn dept art, Richard Bland Col, Col William & Mary, 61-63 & 64-65. *Awards:* Purchase Prize, Exec Towers Sculpture, Va Comn on Arts & Humanities, 75; Award, Int Woman Artists Exhib, 76; Purchase Prize, Henrico Libr, Richmond, Va, 80. *Media:* Oil; Constructions. *Dealer:* Reynolds/Minor Gallery 209 West Franklin St Richmond VA 23220. *Mailing Add:* Rte 3 Box 643 Ashland VA 23005

WITTE, MARY (GRACE) STIEGLITZ
PHOTOGRAPHER, EDUCATOR
b Fairbanks, Alaska. *Study:* Univ Wis, Milwaukee, BS(art & art educ), 63, Madison, PhD(arts), 72; Ind Univ, Bloomington, MAT(fine arts), 65. *Work:* Kodak Mus, Harrow, England; Sci Mus, London; Ind Univ Union, Indianapolis. *Exhib:* Braithwaite Fine Arts Gallery 37th Ann Nat Exhib, Cedar City, Utah, 78; Work & Leisure, Photokina, Cologne, WGer, 78; 11th Ann Nat Exhib, Masure Mus Art, Monroe, La, 79; K to 12 Plus, Milwaukee Art Ctr, 79; Wisconsin Photography, Wustum Mus Fine Arts, Racine, 81; 45th Arrowhead Biennial, Duluth Art Inst, Minn, 82. *Teaching:* From instr to asst prof fine arts, Ind Univ, Indianapolis, 65-71; from asst to assoc prof design, Univ Wis, Madison, 72-81; prof, head design & dir, Goldstein Gallery, Univ Minn, Twin Cities, 81- *Awards:* Show Award, Cosmic Women, Magin Gallery, Milwaukee, 76; First Prize Photog, 19th Ann Exhib, Fall River, Mass, 78; Show Award, Eighth Ann Exhib, Union Art Gallery, Univ Wis, Madison, 79. *Mem:* Int Visual Literacy Asn (vpres, 76-79, pres, 79-80, bd dirs, 82-84); Royal Photog Soc Gt Brit; Surface Design Asn; Int Guild Craft Journalists, Auths & Photogrs. *Media:* Mixed. *Res:* History of art, particularly design media and photography; visual learning and perception. *Publ:* Auth, articles, Hist Photog, 77, Theoret Constructs Visual Literacy, 78, Textile Coun Newslett, 83, Handmade, 83 & Flying Needle, 83. *Mailing Add:* 8415 Airport Rd Middleton WI 53562

WITTMANN, OTTO
MUSEUM CONSULTANT
b Kansas City, Mo, Sept 1, 11. *Study:* Harvard Univ; Univ Mich, hon degree; Kenyon Col, hon degree; Univ Toledo, hon degree. *Collections Arranged:* Splendid Century, Masterpieces from France (auth, catalog); Painting in Italy in 18th Century (auth, catalog); Age of Rembrandt (auth, catalog); Art of Van Gogh (auth, catalog). *Pos:* Cur, Hyde Collection, Glens Falls, NY, 38-41; asst dir, Portland Mus Art, Ore, 41; assoc dir, Toledo Mus Art, 53-59, dir, 59-77, emer dir, 77-, vpres & consult, 77-, ed, Mus News, 14 yrs; trustee & consult, Los Angeles Co Mus Art, Los Angeles, 77-79; mem nat coun arts, Nat Endowment Arts Mus Adv Panel, currently; vpres, J Paul Getty Mus, 79- *Teaching:* Instr art hist, Skidmore Col, 38-41. *Awards:* Commander, Order Merit, Italy; Officer, Order Orange-Nassau, Netherlands. *Mem:* Asn Art Mus Dir (pres, 71-72); Am Asn Mus; Mus Asn Eng; Nat Collection Fine Arts Comn; Col Art Asn Am. *Publ:* Auth numerous museum catalogues & prof articles. *Mailing Add:* J Paul Getty Mus 17985 Pac Coast Hwy Malibu CA 90265

WIXOM, WILLIAM D
CURATOR, HISTORIAN
b Philadelphia, Pa, July 17, 29. *Study:* Haverford Col, BA, 51; NY Univ Inst Fine Arts, MA, 63. *Collections Arranged:* Treasures from Medieval France (auth, catalog), loan exhib, 66-67, Early Christian, Byzantine, Medieval & Renaissance Galleries of Permanent Collection, 73-77 & Renaissance Bronzes from Ohio Collections (auth, catalog), loan exhib, 75, Cleveland Mus Art. *Pos:* From asst cur to cur, Medieval & Renaissance Decorative Arts, Cleveland Mus Art, 58-78, chief cur, Early Western Art, 79; chmn, Dept Medieval Art & the Cloisters, Metrop Mus Art, New York, 79- *Teaching:* Instr, Grad Sem Medieval Art, Case Western Reserve Univ, Cleveland, Ohio, 64-74, adj assoc prof, 67-78, adj prof, 78-79; adj prof fine arts, New York Univ, 81-82. *Awards:* Belg-Am Educ Found fel, 62; Nat Endowment Arts Mus Prof Fel Grant, 73. *Mem:* Col Art Asn (bd dirs, 79-82); Int Ctr Medieval Art (pres, 71-74, bd mem, 71-82); Medieval Acad Am. *Res:* Early Christian, Byzantine, medieval and renaissance art. *Publ:* Auth, 27 articles in Cleveland Mus Art Bulletin, 59-79; contribr, Art Quart, Burlington Mag, Connoisseur, Art Bulletin, Gesta, African Arts, Age of Spirituality, Year 1200 II, Metrop Mus Art Notable Acquisitions, Royal Abbey of St-Denis & Radiance and Reflection, 61-83. *Mailing Add:* Metrop Mus of Art Fifth Ave at 82nd St New York NY 10028

WIZON, TOD
PAINTER
b Newark, NJ, June 1, 52. *Study:* Sch Visual Arts, New York, BFA, 74-76. *Exhib:* From Hudson Street to Hudson River, Fine Arts Bldg, New York, 76; Painting & Sculpture Today, Indianapolis Mus Art, Ind, 78; First Person Singular, Pratt Inst Gallery, New York, 80; New Work New York, Yarlow/Salzman Gallery, Toronto, 80; Changing Visions, Margo Leavin Gallery, Los Angeles, 81-82. *Bibliog:* Addison Parks (auth), article, Arts Mag, 1/81; Ronny H Cohen (auth), article, Artforum, 2/81; Michael Krugman (auth), Tod Wizon at Willard, Art Am, 3/81. *Media:* Acrylic. *Publ:* Contribr, Appearance Mag, 77. *Mailing Add:* c/o Willard Gallery 29 East 72nd St New York NY 10021

WOELFFER, EMERSON
PAINTER
b Chicago, Ill, July 27, 14. *Study:* Art Inst Chicago; Inst Design, Chicago, BA & Hon DFA. *Work:* Art Inst Chicago; Whitney Mus Am Art & Mus Mod Art, New York; Univ Ill; and others. *Exhib:* One-man shows, Santa Barbara Mus, Calif, 64; Quay Gallery, San Francisco, Calif, 68; Jodi Scully Gallery, Los Angeles, 72; Poindexter Gallery, New York, Newport Harbor Mus Art, Newport Beach, Calif; plus many other group & one-man shows. *Pos:* Topog draftsman, USAAF, 39-40; resident artist, Honolulu Acad Arts, Hawaii, 70. *Teaching:* Instr, Sch Design, Chicago, 42, Colo Springs Fine Arts Ctr, 50 & Chouinard Art Inst, 59; vis prof, Black Mountain Col, 49; vis prof painting, Univ Southern Calif, summer 62. *Awards:* Guggenheim Found Fel, France, Italy, Spain & England, 67-68; Purchase Award, All City Art Festival, 68; Raymond A Speiser Mem Prize, Pa Acad Fine Arts, 68; and others. *Bibliog:* Archives Am Art, Smithsonian Inst. *Media:* Oil, Acrylic. *Collection:* African, New Guinea & pre-Columbian works; surrealist paintings. *Mailing Add:* 475 Dustin Dr Los Angeles CA 90065

WOFFORD, PHILIP
PAINTER, WRITER
b Van Buren, Ark, Aug 14, 35. *Study:* Univ Ark, BA, 57; Univ Calif, Berkeley, 57-58. *Work:* Whitney Mus Am Art, New York; Michener Found Collection, Austin, Tex; RI Sch Design, Providence. *Exhib:* San Francisco Mus Ann, 58; Whitney Mus Ann Exhib Am Painting, 69 & 72; Corcoran Gallery Art, Washington, DC. *Teaching:* Instr art, NY Univ Exten, 64-68; instr art, Bennington Col, 69- *Awards:* Woodrow Wilson Fel; Nat Endowment Arts Fel. *Bibliog:* Carter Ratcliff (auth), New informalists, Art News, 2/70; Peter Scheldajl (auth), Return to the sublime, New York Times, 4/18/71. *Publ:* Auth, article in, Art Now: New York, 70; auth, Grand Canyon Search Ceremony, Barlenmir House, 72; In the Belly of the Shark, Random House, 72; work in, Poetry Rev, 4/75. *Dealer:* Nancy Hoffman Gallery 429 W Broadway New York NY 10012. *Mailing Add:* RD 2 Hoosick Falls NY 12090

WOGSTAD, JAMES EVERET
EDUCATOR, ILLUSTRATOR
b Lordsburg, NMex, Sept 24, 39. *Study:* San Antonio Col, cert, 59; Univ Tex, Austin, BFA, 61, MFA, 68. *Comn:* Original graphics prog, Univ Tex Med

Sch, San Antonio, 68-69; dioramic backgrounds & natural hist graphic displays, Witte Mus, San Antonio, 70-74. *Pos:* Lead illusr, Creative Commun, Houston, 62-63; chief illusr, Finger Contract Supply, Houston, 63-65; preparator-cur, Witte Mus, 70-74; ed-illusr, Replica in Scale, 72-76 & Aerophile, 76- *Teaching:* Assoc prof art, San Antonio Col, 68-, chmn dept, 73-77. *Mem:* Col Art Asn Am; Tex Asn Schs Art; Tex Jr Col Teachers Asn. *Media:* Acrylic on Canvas; Black Ink on Paper. *Publ:* Illusr, Any Time is Party Time, 67, Auschuitz, 67 & Belsen, 67, Naylor; illusr, AV-8 Harrier, Aerophile, 82. *Mailing Add:* 4014 Belle Grove San Antonio TX 78230

WOIDE, ROBERT E
PAINTER, ADMINISTRATOR
b Cleveland, Ohio, Jan 27, 27. *Study:* Cleveland Inst Art, with Carl Gaertner, Louis Bosa, Henry Wilcox & Paul Travis, cert, 50; Kent State Univ, with Elmer Novotney, BSE, 51, ME, 62. *Work:* Homerton Gallery, Cambridge, England; Int Inst Gallery, Glion, Switz. *Exhib:* Cleveland May Shows, Cleveland Mus Art, 49, 52, 66, 67 & 69; Butler Int, 51 & Mid-Year Exhib, 79, Butler Art Inst; two-person exhib, Int Inst Gallery, Glion, Switz, 79, Massillon Mus, Ohio, 80, Womens City Club, Cleveland, 80 & Garden Ctr, Cleveland, 82. *Pos:* Asst dir, Canton Art Inst, Ohio, 51-52. *Teaching:* Instr, lectr & supervisor, Cleveland Mus Art, 52-66; instr visual arts educ, Western Reserve Univ, 54-57 & 61-67 & Kent State Univ, 61-63; instr, supervisor & dir fine arts educ, Cleveland pub schs, 63- *Awards:* Sr Exhib Award, Cleveland Inst Art, 50; Purchase Prizes, Mid-Year Exhib, Butler Art Inst, 51 & Canton Art Inst, 52. *Mem:* Ohio Art Educ Asn (vpres, 74-75); Cleveland Arts Coun; Cleveland Inst Art; Alliance Arts Educ; Cleveland Inst Art Alumni Asn (pres, 83-). *Publ:* Contribr, Art Teachers Guides, 63-73, contribr, Proxemics, Edges and Nodes--Artistic Judgement and the Environment, 73, ed, A Guide to the Development of Afro American Art in the United States, 74 & auth, Graded Course of Study for the Arts, 83, Cleveland Pub Schs; ed & contribr, The World of Creative Expression, Coun Human Relations, 84. *Dealer:* New Orgn Visual Artists 1375 Euclid Ave Cleveland OH 44115. *Mailing Add:* 12415 Coit Rd Cleveland OH 44108

WOIT, BONNIE FORD
PAINTER
b New York, NY, Jan 19, 31. *Study:* Allegheny Col, BA(cum laude), 53; Harvard Univ, 54; Westchester Workshop, 60-61; Silvermine Sch Art, 70-73; photog graphics workshop, 75. *Work:* Bankers Trust Co, New York; Sapol'm Co, Dunbury, Conn; IBM, Green Castle, Ind. *Exhib:* Solo exhibs, Am Embassy, Paris, 69 & Ingber Gallery, New York, 80, 81 & 84; Silvermine Guild Artists, New Canaan, Conn, 77-79; Stanford Mus, Conn, 80; Feria Int de Muestras, Bilbao, Spain, 82; and others. *Awards:* William Lowman Award, 78 & New Eng Award, 79, New Eng Exhib. *Mem:* Silvermine Guild Artists (secy, 74-75, vpres, 75-80). *Media:* Acrylic. *Dealer:* Ingber Gallery 460 West Broadway New York NY 10012. *Mailing Add:* 559 West Rd New Canaan CT 06840

WOITENA, BEN S
SCULPTOR, EDUCATOR
b San Antonio, Tex, Mar 24, 42. *Study:* Univ Tex, Austin, BFA, 64; Univ Southern Calif, MFA, 70. *Work:* Houston Mus Fine Arts, Tex. *Exhib:* Monumental Sculpture, Houston, 75; Collector's Exhib, Houston Mus Fine Arts, 75; Gulf Coast Sculpture Exhib, Galveston, Tex, 76; Amarillo Art Ctr, Tex, 77; Univ Tex Mus, Austin, 79; and others. *Teaching:* Instr sculpture, Houston Mus Fine Arts Mus Sch, 71- *Bibliog:* Ann Holmes (auth), Houston: The Second City for Art?, Art News, 75; Roberta Smith (auth), Twelve Days of Texas, Art in Am, 76; Actual Yardage Gained (film), Nat Educ TV, Houston, 76. *Dealer:* Robinson Galleries 1100 Bissonnet Houston TX 77000. *Mailing Add:* 1547 Waverly Houston TX 77008

WOJCIK, GARY THOMAS
SCULPTOR
b Chicago, Ill, Feb 26, 45. *Study:* Art Inst Chicago, BFA; Univ Ky, MA. *Work:* High Mus Art, Atlanta, Ga; New York Port Authority, NY; Chicago Park Dist, Hyde Park, Chicago. *Exhib:* Whitney Sculpture Ann, Whitney Mus Am Art, 68; Univ Ill Biennial Painting & Sculpture Exhib, 69; Soc Contemp Art 29th Ann, Art Inst Chicago, 69; Viewpoints Painting & Sculpture Invitational, Colgate Univ, 70; Painting & Sculpture 1972, Storm King Art Ctr, Mountainville, NY, 72. *Teaching:* Adj asst prof sculpture, Ithaca Col. *Awards:* Art Inst Chicago Traveling Fel. *Bibliog:* Articles, New York Times, 11/29/70, Art News, 1/29/71 & Art Int, 2/20/71. *Media:* Welded Metal. *Mailing Add:* PO Box 73 Trumansburg NY 14886

WOJTYLA, HAASE (WALTER JOSEPH)
PAINTER, DRAFTSMAN
b Chicago, Ill, Feb 10, 33. *Study:* Art Inst of Chicago; Univ of Ill, BFA(painting); Univ Cincinnati, MFA; Brooklyn Mus Art Sch. *Exhib:* Int Drawing Competition, State Univ of Educ, Potsdam, NY, 60; Tenth Ann Nat Exhib of Painting & Sculpture, Ringling Mus of Art, Sarasota, Fla, 60; Brooklyn & Long Island Artists Biennial Exhib, Brooklyn Mus of Art, 60; Art in Am Exhib, New York, 62; All Ohio Painting & Sculpture Exhib, Dayton Art Inst, 66; Calif-Hawaii Biennial, Fine Arts Gallery of San Diego, 76 & 78; one-man show, Recent Paintings, Fine Arts Gallery of San Diego, 75. *Teaching:* Instr, San Diego State Univ, Calif, 76 & 80. *Awards:* Singer & Sons Prize, Artists of Chicago & Vicinity, Art Inst of Chicago, 56; Painting Award, All Calif Juried Exhib, Laguna Beach Mus of Art, 76; Painting Award, Calif Ann Award Show, Jewish Community Ctr, San Diego, 77. *Bibliog:* Artists in Residence, KPBS-TV, San Diego, 82; The black comic art of Walter Wojtyla, Hill Courier, 9/83. *Mem:* Artists Equity Asn Inc. *Media:* Oil, Mixed Media; Ink, Charcoal. *Dealer:* Spectrum Gallery 726 Seventh Ave San Diego CA 92101; John Douglas Cline Gallery 424 N Central Ave Phoenix AZ. *Mailing Add:* 2102 C San Diego CA 92102

WOLANIN, BARBARA ANN BOESE
EDUCATOR, HISTORIAN
b Dayton, Ohio, Dec 12, 43. *Study:* Oberlin Col, BA, 66, MA(art hist), 69; Harvard Univ Grad Sch Educ, MAT(fine arts), 67; Univ Wis, Madison, PhD(art hist), 81. *Collections Arranged:* Arthur B Carles Collection (auth, catalog), Hirshhorn Mus, 77; Arthur B Carles, Painting with Color (auth, catalog), Pa Acad Fine Arts, Corcoran Gallery Art & Nat Acad Design, 83-84. *Teaching:* Asst prof art hist, Trinity Col, Washington, DC, 78-83 & James Madison Univ, 83- *Mem:* Col Art Asn; Asn Historians Am Art; Womens Caucus Art. *Res:* Arthur B Carles, pioneer American modernist. *Mailing Add:* 261 W View St Harrisonburg VA 22801

WOLBER, PAUL J
PAINTER, EDUCATOR
b Deer Creek, Ill, June 23, 35. *Study:* Ill State Univ; Southern Ill Univ, Edwardsville; Bob Jones Univ, BS & MA. *Work:* Evansville Mus Art, Ind; Franklin Life Ins Co, Springfield, Ill; Mitchell Mus Art, Mt Vernon, Ill; Calumet Nat Bank, Ill; Ill State Mus, Springfield, Ill. *Comn:* Mural, Spring Arbor Free Methodist Church, 80; mural, Ingham Co Correctional Ctr, Ingham Co Arts Comn, 81. *Exhib:* Ill State Mus, Springfield, 74; Grand Galleria Nat Ann, Seattle, 74; Gov Exhib, 30 Ill Artists, Springfield, 75; Marietta Nat, Ohio, 78. *Pos:* Art educ consult, State Off Pub Instr, Springfield, Ill, 74-75. *Teaching:* Assoc prof art, Spring Arbor Col, Mich, 76-81, prof, 81- *Awards:* Nat Small Painting Award, NMex Art League, Albuquerque, 74 & 75; Illinois/Indiana Bicentennial Purchase Award, Hammond, Ind, 77. *Bibliog:* Abner Hershberger (cd), Mennonite Artists Contemporary, 1975, Goshen Col Art Gallery; Glen P Ives (auth), Museum object of the week, Sunday Courier, Evansville, Ind, 10/6/74; Howard Derrickson (auth), article, The Advocate, Greenville, 1/28/75. *Mem:* Mid Am Col Art Asn; Ill Art Educ Asn; Nat Art Educ Asn; Bond Co Art & Cult Asn (vpres, 73-74). *Media:* Oil, Acrylic. *Mailing Add:* 1660 Chapel Rd Parma MI 49269

WOLCOTT, MARION POST See Post, Marion

WOLFE, ANN (ANN WOLFE GRAUBARD)
SCULPTOR
b Mlawa, Poland; US citizen. *Study:* Hunter Col, BA; studies sculpture in Manchester, Eng & Paris, France; Acad Grande Chaumiere, with Despiau & Vlerick. *Work:* Morris Raphael Cohen Libr, City Univ New York; Jerusalem Mus Art, Israel; Nat Mus Korea, Seoul; Mus Western Art, Moscow, Russia; Diehl Hall, Univ Minn. *Comn:* Dr Morris R Cohen (bronze head), alumni of City Univ New York, 43; Pres Syngman Rhea (bronze head), Dr R Oliver, Washington, DC, 47; Dr W R Ramsey (bronze head), Children's Hosp, St Paul, Minn, 57; welded relief in steel & bronze, Mt Zion Temple, St Paul, 65; Dr O H Wangensteen (bronze head), alumni of dept surg, Univ Minn, 65. *Exhib:* One-man shows, Grace Horne Gallery, Boston, 41, Walker Art Ctr, Minneapolis, 55, Minneapolis Inst Arts, 64, Adele Bednarz Galleries, Los Angeles, 66, 3rd Sculpture Int, Philadelphia Mus Art, Pa. *Teaching:* Instr pvt sudio, 62-70; instr sculpture, Minnetonka Ctr Arts & Educ, 71-74. *Awards:* Allied Artists Am, 36; Soc Washington Artists, 44 & 45; Minneapolis Inst Arts, 51. *Publ:* Contribr, Worcester Tel-Gazette, 40-60; auth, Portrait of President Syngman Rhee, Women's Art Registry J, autumn 82. *Dealer:* Bream Gallery 961 Grand Ave St Paul MN 55105; Fairweather-Hardin Galleries 101 E Ontario Chicago IL 60611. *Mailing Add:* 2928 Dean Pkwy Minneapolis MN 55416

WOLFE, JAMES
SCULPTOR
b New York, NY, Apr 28, 44. *Work:* Mus Fine Arts, Houston; Whitney Mus, New York; Mus Fine Arts, Boston; Kresge Art Ctr, Mich State Univ; Storm King Art Ctr. *Exhib:* Monumenta, Newport, RI, 74; one-man shows, Andre Emmerich Gallery, 73-77, Meredith Long Contemp, 78 & 79 & Osuna Gallery, 80; Clayworks Studio Workshop, New York, 81; and others. *Pos:* Tech dir, Theater Dept & tech asst, Sculpture Dept, Bennington Col; fac mem, Va Polytechnic & State Univ, 78, Sch Visual Arts, 79 & Boston Mus Sch, 80. *Awards:* Nat Endowment Arts, 74. *Bibliog:* J Mascjeck (auth), Notes on Caro influence: Five sculptors from Bennington, Artforum, 4/72; Jeanne Siegel (auth), rev in Art News, 2/73; Ellen Lubell (auth), James Wolfe, Arts Mag, 6/75. *Mailing Add:* 736 Broadway New York NY 10003

WOLFE, LYNN ROBERT
PAINTER, EDUCATOR
b Red Cloud, Nebr, Sept 11, 17. *Study:* Univ Nebr, BFA; Univ Colo, with Max Beckman, MFA; Paris Atelier with Ossip Zadkine. *Work:* Univ Nebr State Mus, Lincoln; Univ Colo, Boulder. *Comn:* Copper doors, Danforth Chapel, Colo State Univ, Ft Collins, 54; mosaic (stained glass), McPherson Chapel, Durango, Colo, 60; stained glass window, Norgren Chapel, Denver, 65; stained glass windows, St Aidans Episcopal Church, Boulder, 70. *Exhib:* Nat Watercolor & Drawing, Metrop Mus, New York, 52; Nat Drawing & Small Sculpture, Muncie, Ind, 58; Mus Contemp Crafts, New York, 59; Western Artists, Denver Art Mus, 72. *Pos:* Cur collections, Univ Colo, Boulder, 64-74. *Teaching:* Instr sculpture, Univ Nebr, Lincoln, 45-46; vis artist watercolor, Univ Alaska, summer 46; prof painting, Univ Colo, Boulder, 47-, chmn dept fine arts, 72-74; vis artist, Univ Hawaii, 82. *Awards:* Sculpture Award, Ball State Teachers Col, 58; Univ Colo Fac Fel, 67; Award, Outstanding Educators Am, 75. *Media:* Acrylic, Canvas; Stained Glass, Faceted Dalles. *Mailing Add:* 701 Euclid Boulder CO 80302

WOLFE, MAURICE RAYMOND
MUSEUM DIRECTOR, CONSULTANT
b Paris, France, Oct 13, 24; US citizen. *Study:* Univ Calif, Berkeley, BA, MA, grad study; Fr Govt fel to Univ Paris at Sorbonne. *Collections Arranged:* Art from Mobilier of the Djukas of Surinam, Pacific Northwest & Eskimo Material Culture, Meso-American Prehistory, Mohave Desert Culture, African Musical Instruments & Domestic Objects & The Art of New Guinea, 74-75, The Cuna of Panama--Arts & Crafts, West Africa, Aboriginal Australian Art from Expo 74 & California Gatherers & Hunters, Circa 1776 (Bicentennial celebration), 75-76, Oceanic Cultures: Emphasis on American Trust Territories, Folk Art of Mexico & Archaeology, 77-78, Merritt Col Anthrop Mus. *Pos:* Dir, Merritt Col Anthrop Mus, 73- *Teaching:* Instr, Merritt Col, Oakland, 62-, prof prehist art, 72- *Mem:* Am Asn Mus; Western Art Asn; Calif Archaeol Soc. *Mailing Add:* 225 Canon Dr Orinda CA 94563

WOLFE, MILDRED NUNGESTER
PAINTER, DESIGNER
b Celina, Ohio, Aug 23, 12. *Study:* Athens Col; Univ Montevallo, AB, 32; Dixie Art Colony, with J Kelly Fitzpatrick; Art Students League, with Will Barnet; Chicago Art Inst; Colorado Springs Fine Arts Ctr, with Boardman Robinson, MA, 44. *Work:* Miss Art Asn, Jackson; Lauren Rogers Mus, Laurel, Miss; Print Collection, Libr Cong, Washington, DC; Montgomery Mus Fine Arts, Ala; Middle South Utilities, Changing South Mag Collection, New Orleans. *Comn:* Orpheus (mosaic), McDowell Br Libr, Jackson, 58; Stations of the Cross, comn by Monsignor Joseia Chatham for St Richards, Jackson, 60; David (mosaic), comn by Elizabeth Kingford for St Dominic's Hosp, Jackson, 61; chapel window (stained glass), Frist Baptist Church, Hazelhurst, Miss, 65; symbolic windows, Independent Methodist Episcopal Church, Jackson, 71-74. *Exhib:* Nat Exhib Prints, Libr Cong, 44; Grumbacher Int Exhib, Lakeland, Fla, 52; Painters of Southeastern US, Univ SFla, 62; Bertrand Russell Peace Found Exhib, Nottingham, Eng, 73; Lauren Rogers Mus of Art, Laurel, Miss, 77; Old Capitol Mus, Jackson, Miss, 77 & 77-78; and others. *Teaching:* Prof hist art & printmaking, Millsaps Col, 58-68. *Awards:* First Prize for Cotton Pickers, Southern Painter, McDowell Gallery, 38; First Prize for Watercolor, Miss Art Asn, 46; Award of Merit for Still Life, Grumbacher Int Exhib, 52. *Mem:* Miss Art Asn. *Mailing Add:* c/o Wolfe Gallery 4308 Old Canton Rd Jackson MS 39211

WOLFE, ROBERT, JR
PRINTMAKER, PAINTER
b Oxford, Ohio, May 15, 30. *Study:* Miami Univ, BFA, 52; Cincinnati Art Acad, 55; Univ Iowa, scholar, 59, with M Lasansky, MFA(printmaking), 60; Tamarind Inst Workshops, 75 & 79. *Work:* Dayton Art Inst, Ohio; Ohio State Univ; Univ Wis-Madison; Sheldon Mem Art Gallery, Univ Nebr, Lincoln; Casa da Gravura, State Collection, Curitiba, Parana, Brazil. *Comn:* Five color intaglios, Miami Univ, 71. *Exhib:* New American Graphics, Univ Wis-Madison, 75; Nine Midwest Printmakers, Mt St Joseph Col, Cincinnati, Ohio, 77; Rutger's Drawing, Camden, 79; Honolulu Acad Arts 5th Nat, Hawaii, 80; Intaglio Printmakers 81, Univ Louisville, Ky; and many others. *Pos:* Artist-illusr, US Army, 52-54. *Teaching:* Instr design, Clarion Col, Pa, 61-62; prof printmaking, Miami Univ, 62-; vis artist, Univ Nebr, Grinnell Col, Ohio State Univ & Fed Univ Parana, Brazil, formerly. *Awards:* Res Grant for zinc relief printing, Miami Univ, Ohio, 78; Purchase Award, Intaglio Printmakers 81, Univ Louisville, Ky, 81; Alumni Award for Painting, Miami Univ, 82; and others. *Mem:* World Print Coun; Cincinnati Graphic Arts Forum. *Media:* Mixed; Oil. *Dealer:* Benjamin-Beattie Gallery Chicago IL. *Mailing Add:* 418 Bouden Lane Oxford OH 45056

WOLFE, TOWNSEND DURANT
PAINTER, ADMINISTRATOR
b Hartsville, SC, Aug 15, 35. *Study:* Ga Inst Technol; Atlanta Art Inst, BFA; Cranbrook Acad Art, MFA; Inst Art Admin, Harvard Univ, cert. *Work:* Ark Arts Ctr, Little Rock; Mint Mus Art, Charlotte, NC; Okla Arts Ctr, Oklahoma City; Miss Art Asn, Jackson; Carroll Reece Mem Mus, ETenn State Univ. *Exhib:* Ball State Teacher's Col Drawing Nat, Muncie, Ind, four shows, 59-67; Mead Painting of Yr Exhib, Atlanta, 62; Watercolors USA, Springfield, Mo, 63-64; Alice Bingham Gallery, Memphis, Tenn, 80; First Nat Bank, Little Rock, Ark, 81; and others. *Pos:* Dir, Wooster Community Art Ctr, Danbury, Conn, 65-68; art dir, Upward Bound Proj, Danbury, summers 66-68; exec dir, Ark Arts Ctr, 68- *Teaching:* Instr painting & drawing, Memphis Acad Arts, Tenn, 59-64; instr painting & drawing, Scarsdale Studio Workshop, NY, 64-65. *Awards:* Award Merit & Purchase Prize, 57th Nat Painting Exhib, Miss Art Asn, 67; Winthrop Rockefeller Memorial Award, 73; James R Short Award, Southeastern Mus Conf, 81; and others. *Mem:* Am Asn Mus; Am Fedn Arts; Southeastern Asn Mus. *Media:* Oil, Gouache. *Mailing Add:* Ark Arts Ctr PO Box 2137 Little Rock AR 72203

WOLFF, ROBERT W, JR
DEALER
b Monroe, La, Feb 18, 47. *Study:* Troy State Univ, Ala, BS, 74. *Pos:* Art dealer, Wolff Gallery, Fairhope & Mobile, Ala, currently. *Mailing Add:* PO Box 98 Fairhope AL 36533

WOLFF, WILLIAM H
DEALER
b Brussels, Belg, Apr 15, 06; US citizen. *Pos:* Owner, William H Wolff Inc, 59- *Mem:* Asia Soc, NY; Nat Antique & Art Dealers Asn Am; Am Asn Dealers in Ancient, Oriental & Primitive Art. *Specialty:* Far Eastern antiquities; stone, bronze and wood sculptures. *Mailing Add:* 986 Madison Ave New York NY 10021

WOLINS, JOSEPH
PAINTER
b Atlantic City, NJ, Mar 26, 15. *Study:* Nat Acad Design, 31-35; WPA Fed Art Proj, New York, 35-42. *Work:* Metrop Mus Art, New York; Norfolk Mus Arts & Sci, Va; Albrecht Mus, St Joseph, Mo; Fiske Univ Art Gallery, Ala; Ein Harod Mus, Israel. *Exhib:* Corcoran Gallery Art Biennial, Washington, DC, 47; Pa Acad Fine Arts Ann, Philadelphia, 48; Whitney Mus Am Art Ann, 49-53; Mus Mod Art Ann, Sao Paulo, Brazil, 62; Butler Inst Am Art Ann, Youngstown, Ohio, 65; one-man exhib, Slater Mem Mus, 81; Metrop Mus Art, New York; Nat Mus Am Art, Washington, DC; Everson Mus Art, Syracuse; New Britain Mus Am Art, Conn. *Awards:* Mark Rothko Found Award for Painting, 71; Award, Nat Inst of Arts & Lett, 76. *Mem:* Artists Equity Asn; Audubon Artists; Am Soc Contemp Artists. *Media:* Oil, Watercolor. *Mailing Add:* 463 West St New York NY 10014

WOLPERT, ELIZABETH DAVIS
PAINTER, INSTRUCTOR
b Ft Washington, Pa, Sept 12, 15. *Study:* Moore Col Art, BFA; Pa State Univ, MAEd; and with Hobson Pittman. *Work:* Temple Univ, Woodmere Art Gallery, Philadelphia, Pa; Pa State Univ, University Park; Bob Jones Univ, Greenville, SC; Univ Miami, Coral Gables. *Exhib:* Pa Acad Fine Arts, Philadelphia, 48; Philadelphia Mus Art, 62; Butler Inst Art, Youngstown, Ohio, 65; many shows, Woodmere Art Gallery; Cheltenham Art Ctr, 66; and many one-man shows. *Teaching:* Instr art, pub & pvt schs, 38- *Awards:* Charles K Smith First Prize & First Mem Prize, Woodmere Art Gallery, 53; First Purchase Prizes, Junto, Philadelphia, 58-59. *Mem:* Artists Equity Asn; Philadelphia Art Alliance; Philadelphia Mus Art; Woodmere Art Gallery; Nat Art Educ Asn. *Media:* Oil. *Mailing Add:* Meadows Apt 140 Ambler PA 19002

WOLSKY, JACK
PAINTER, EDUCATOR
b Rochester, NY, Aug 5, 30. *Study:* Rochester Inst Technol, AS, 51; State Univ NY Col, Buffalo, BS, 55, MS, 57. *Work:* Rochester Mem Art Gallery, NY; New Britain Mus Am Art, Conn; Munson-Williams-Proctor Inst, Utica, NY; Rochester Inst Technol; State Univ NY Col, Brockport. *Exhib:* Am Fedn Arts Exhib, Turkey, Iran & Pakistan; 154th Exhib, Pa Acad Fine Arts; State Univ NY Arts Convocation Exhib, Albright-Knox Gallery; Chautauqua Exhib Am Art; Univ Omaha Nat Exhib. *Teaching:* Prof studio art, State Univ NY Col, Brockport, 59- *Awards:* Lillian Fairchild Award, Univ Rochester, 70; Distinguished Alumnus Award, State Univ NY Buffalo, 71; Fac Exchange Scholar, State Univ NY, 74. *Bibliog:* Talis Bergmanis (auth), Exuberant art of Jack Wolsky, Dem & Chronicle Publ, 12/13/70; Karen Ibrahim (auth), Abstract art of Jack Wolsky, News & Rev, Rochester Inst Technol, 71; Evolution of a moment, Channel 21 TV, Rochester, NY, 74. *Media:* Acrylic, Lacquer. *Dealer:* Oxford Gallery 267 Oxford St Rochester NY 14607. *Mailing Add:* 295 Washington St Spencerport NY 14559

WONG, FREDERICK
PAINTER, CALLIGRAPHER
b Buffalo, NY, May 31, 29. *Study:* Univ NMex, BFA & MA. *Work:* Butler Inst Am Art, Youngstown, Ohio; Atlanta Art Asn, Ga; Reading Mus Art, Pa; Philbrook Art Ctr, Tulsa, Okla; Neuberger Collection, Purchase, NY. *Exhib:* Los Angeles Co Mus Art, 59; Butler Inst Am Art, Youngstown, 60; Am Watercolor Soc, New York, 60-69; Watercolor USA, Springfield, Mo, 63; Mainstreams '69, Marietta, Ohio, 69. *Teaching:* Instr form & structure, Pratt Inst, 66-69; instr painting, drawing, calligraphy & design, Hofstra Univ. *Awards:* Butler Midyear Ann Bronze Medal, Butler Inst Am Art, 60; Gold Medal, Nat Arts Club, 67; Mainstreams '69 Award of Excellence, Marietta Col, 69. *Mem:* Am Watercolor Soc; Allied Artists Am. *Media:* Watercolor. *Publ:* Auth, Oriental Watercolor Techniques, 77 & The Complete Calligrapher, 80, Watson-Guptill. *Dealer:* Self 77 Chambers St New York NY 10007. *Mailing Add:* 315 Riverside Dr New York NY 10025

WONG, JASON
MUSEUM DIRECTOR, DESIGNER
b Long Beach, Calif, May 12, 34. *Study:* Long Beach City Col, AA, 54; Univ Calif, Los Angeles, BA, 63. *Collections Arranged:* Seven Decades of Design, organized through Calif Arts Comn grant for state tour, 67-68; Art of Alexander Calder--Gouaches, western states tour, 70; Max Beckmann Graphics, Nat Tour, 73; Photo/Synthesis Nat Invitational Exhib, NY State Coun on the Arts, 76-77. *Pos:* Asst cur, Long Beach Mus Art, 59-64, cur, 65, dir, 65-72; art dir, Audiorama Corp, Am-Quest Int, 64-65; dir, Tucson Art Ctr, 72-73; dir visual arts div, Spokane World's Fair, 74; asst dir, Herbert F Johnson Mus Art, Cornell Univ, 74-77; cur, Joe & Emily Lowe Art Gallery, Syracuse Univ, 78-80; independent cur, 80-; graphic designer, Tompkins Cortland Community Col, 81- *Teaching:* Prof museology, Syracuse Univ, 78-80. *Awards:* Nat Educ Asn Grant for Res in Museological Studies, 72; Award for Excellence in Design, SUNY-CUAD, 81 & 82. *Mem:* Am Inst Graphic Arts. *Publ:* Auth, exhib catalog introd, Art Int, 10-11/76. *Mailing Add:* 501 The Parkway Ithaca NY 14850

WONG, PAUL KAN
PAINTER, SCULPTOR
b Fargo, NDak, Oct 30, 51. *Study:* Moorhead State Univ, BA, 73; Univ Wis, Madison, MFA, 76. *Work:* Madison Art Ctr; New York Pub Libr. *Comn:* Suspended sculpture installation, Hudson River Mus, Yonkers, NY, 83. *Exhib:* 21st Ann Print Exhib, Brooklyn Mus, 78; 77th Vicinity Exhib, Chicago Art Inst, 78; Shaped Field, Eccentric Formats, PS1, Long Island City, 81; Making Paper, Am Craft Mus, 82; Paper as Image Traveling Exhib, Brit Art Coun, UK, 82; one-man show, Air Space: Projection, Hudson River Mus,

Yonkers, NY, 83 & Condeso-Lawler Gallery, New York, 83. *Awards:* Apprenticeship Grants, Louis Comfort Tiffany Found, 78-79 & Nat Endowment Arts, 80; Graphics Grant, Creative Artists Pub Serv, 83. *Bibliog:* Judd Tully (auth), Paper chase, Portfolio Mag, 83; Ronny Cohen (auth), Paper routes, 83 & article, 84, Artnews. *Publ:* Illusr, Our Lady of the Three Pronged Devil, Red Ozier Press, 81. *Dealer:* Condeso-Lawler Gallery 76 Greene St New York NY 10013. *Mailing Add:* 40 N Moore St 2W New York NY 10013

WONG, ROGER FREDERICKSON
MUSEUM DIRECTOR, COLLECTOR
b Los Angeles, Calif, Dec 28, 45. *Study:* Pomona Col; Univ Southern Calif, BA, 70. *Pos:* Dir, Roger Wong Gallery, 72-78; dir, Los Angeles Mus Art, 79-; mem, Santa Monica Arts Comn, 83-84. *Mem:* Am Asn Mus; Int Asn Mus; Archit Design & Support Group; Newport Harbor Art Mus; founder Mus Contemp Art, Los Angeles. *Collection:* Principal pieces of Chinese porcelain and bronze from Sund and Shang periods; conceptual and post 60's modern sculpture and paintings. *Mailing Add:* 3808 W Beverly Blvd Los Angeles CA 90004

WONNER, PAUL (JOHN)
PAINTER
b Tucson, Ariz, Apr 24, 20. *Study:* Calif Col Arts & Crafts; Univ Calif, Berkeley, Anne Bremer Mem Scholar, MA, MLS, 53. *Work:* Guggenheim Mus, New York; San Francisco Mus Art; Nat Collection Fine Arts, Smithsonian Inst, Washington, DC; Oakland Mus, Calif; Joseph H Hirshhorn Found; and others. *Exhib:* Whitney Mus Am Art, New York, 59; Art Inst Chicago, 61 & 64; Univ Ill, 61, 63 & 65; Mus Mod Art, New York, 62; Charles Campbell Gallery, San Francisco, 74; Calif State Univ, Long Beach, 75 & 81; James Corcoran Gallery, Los Angeles, 79 & 81; John Berggruen Gallery, San Francisco, 78 & 81; Oakland Art Mus, Calif, 82; and others. *Teaching:* Instr painting, Univ Calif, Los Angeles, 63-64 & Otis Art Inst, 66-68; instr, Col Creative Studies, Santa Barbara, 68-71, Univ Calif, Davis, 75-76 & Univ Calif, Long Beach, 81. *Mailing Add:* 468 Jersey St San Francisco CA 94994

WOOD, ALAN
PAINTER
b Widnes, Lancashire, Eng, Aug 3, 35; Can citizen. *Study:* Liverpool Col Art, Eng, Nat Dipl Design, 58; Liverpool Univ, Inst Educ, Eng, Art Teachers Dipl, 59. *Work:* Seattle Art Mus, Wash; Art Gallery Greater Victoria, BC; Art Gallery South Australia, Adelaide; Tate Gallery, London; Nat Mus Wales, Cardiff. *Comn:* Mural, Leeds Univ, Yorks, 65; mural, BC Govt, Victoria, 77; mural, Fed Govt Can, Calgary, Alta, 81. *Exhib:* Solo exhibs, Univ Cincinnati, Ohio, 74, Alta Col Art, Calgary, 77, Art Gallery Southern Alta, Lethbridge, 78 & Art Gallery Greater Victoria, 82; Vancouver Art Gallery, BC, 76 & 77; Edmonton Art Gallery, Alta, 77. *Awards:* Dartington Award, Dartington Trustees, 61; First Prize, Arts Coun Northern Ireland, 68; Grant, Sr Can Coun, 78. *Bibliog:* Joan Lowndes (auth), Architectonics and the wild west, Vanguard, summer, 81. *Media:* Acrylic. *Dealer:* San Houston Third Floor 165 Water St Vancouver BC Can V6B 1A7. *Mailing Add:* 2503 West 36th St Vancouver BC V6N 2P6 Canada

WOOD, BEATRICE
CERAMIST, EDUCATOR
b San Francisco, Calif. *Study:* Pottery with Glen Luckens, Otto & Gertrud Natzler & Viveka & Otto Heino. *Work:* Metrop Mus Art, New York; Newark Mus, NJ; Mus Int dell Ceramiche Faenza, Italy. *Exhib:* M H de Young Mem Mus, San Francisco; Phoenix Art Mus, Ariz; Santa Barbara Mus Art, Calif; Takishamaya Gallery, Tokyo, Japan; Tucson Art Ctr, Ariz; one-person shows, Fullerton State Col, Del Mus & Everson Mus, Syracuse, 83; and others. *Teaching:* Instr pottery, Happy Valley Sch, Ojai, Calif, 55-60. *Awards:* Richard Gump Award, Syracuse; Hon Mention, Mus Mod Art, New York. *Bibliog:* Frances Nauman (auth), I shock myself, Arts Mag, 5/77. *Mem:* Am Crafts Asn. *Dealer:* Garth Clark Gallery 5820 Wilshire Blvd Los Angeles CA 90036. *Mailing Add:* 8560 Hwy 150 Ojai CA 93023

WOOD, HARRY EMSLEY, JR
WRITER, PAINTER
b Indianapolis, Ind, Dec 10, 10. *Study:* Univ Wis, BA & MA; Ohio State Univ, MA & PhD; Acad Belli Arti, Florence, Italy, with Ottono Rosai; and with John Frazier, Provincetown, Mass & Emil Bisttram, Taos, NMex. *Work:* Mem Union, Ariz State Univ; Phoenix Art Mus, Ariz; Nat Portrait Gallery, Smithsonian Inst, Washington, DC. *Comn:* Murals, Gt Cent Ins Co, Peoria, Ill; and many portraits of prominent people. *Exhib:* Florence, Italy, 50; Phoenix Art Mus, 61; Phoenix & Tucson Ann, 62; Ariz State Univ; Northern Ariz Univ; and other group & one-man shows. *Pos:* Art critic, Scottsdale Progress, Ariz, 74-77; critic, Commun Design Consultant Services, Tempe, Ariz, 81- *Teaching:* Prof art, Ill Wesleyan Univ, 42-44; dean col fine arts, Bradley Univ, 44-50; prof art, Ariz State Univ, 54-76, chmn dept, 54-66, emer prof art, 76- *Awards:* Ariz Artist Guild Purchase Prize for Sculpture, Ariz State Fair, 58; Murphy Award for Sculpture, 59. *Mem:* Col Art Asn Am; Nat Art Educ Asn (nat coun, 58-62); Pac Art Asn (pres, 58-60). *Publ:* Auth, A Sculpture By John Waddell, 70; auth, Faces of Abraham Lincoln, 70; auth, articles in, Lincoln Herald, 75; auth & illusr, The Sphinkus Has No Noise--An Egyptian Adventure, 77; auth, Always carry a sketchbook, 80; and others. *Mailing Add:* 104 Vista del Cerro Tempe AZ 85281

WOOD, JAMES ARTHUR (ART)
CARTOONIST, LECTURER
b Miami, Fla, June 6, 27. *Study:* Washington & Lee Univ, BA; Mich State Univ. *Work:* Libr Cong, Washington, DC; Permanent Libr Collection, Univ Va, Charlottesville; Univ Akron Collection, Ohio; William Allen White

Collection, Univ Kans; Truman Libr Collection. *Exhib:* Brussels World's Fair, 58; one-man show, Pittsburgh Press, 59; Great Challenge, Int Cartoon Exhib, 59-60; Cartoon Show, Nat Portrait Gallery, 72. *Pos:* Ed cartoonist, Richmond Newsleader, 50-56; chief political cartoonist, Pittsburgh Press, 56-63; cartoonist, US Independent Tel Asn, 63- & Farm Bureau News, 78-; partner, Stam-Wood Productions, 80- *Awards:* Freedoms Found Awards, 53, 54, 58-60, 78-79 & 82; Golden Quill Awards, 60 & 62; Huevos de Onix, Mexico City, 77. *Mem:* Asn Am Ed Cartoonist (bd mem, 59-63, pres, 75-); Nat Cartoonists Soc; Nat Press Club. *Media:* Pen & Ink, Crayon. *Mailing Add:* 7008 Tilden Lane Rockville MD 20852

WOOD, JAMES NOWELL
HISTORIAN, ADMINISTRATOR
b Boston, Mass, Mar 20, 41. *Study:* Williams Col, BA; Inst Fine Arts, NY Univ, MA. *Pos:* Asst to dir, Metrop Mus Art, New York, 67-68, asst cur, dept 20th century art, 68-70; cur, Albright-Knox Art Gallery, Buffalo, NY, 70-73, assoc, 73-75; dir, St Louis Art Mus, 75-80; dir, Art Inst Chicago, 80- *Res:* Nineteenth and twentieth century American and European painting, sculpture and decorative arts. *Publ:* Auth, Rockne Krebs, 71; auth, Six Painters, 71; auth, Max Bill: Painting, Sculpture, Graphics, 74; auth, Era of Exploration, 75. *Mailing Add:* Art Inst Chicago Mich Ave at Adams St Chicago IL 60603

WOOD, MARCIA JOAN
SCULPTOR
b Paw Paw, Mich, Mar 22, 33. *Study:* Kalamazoo Col, BA, 55; Cranbrook Acad Art, MFA, 56; Courtauld Inst Art, Univ London, 60-61; Harvard Univ, 62. *Work:* Hope Col Art Gallery, Mich; Kalamazoo Inst Arts. *Comn:* Stainless steel sculpture, Detroit Coun Arts & Nat Endowment Arts, 80; cast bronze ed, 82 & stainless steel sculpture, 82, Kalamazoo Col; cast aluminum maquette, Kalamazoo Mayor for Numazu, Japan, 83; stainless steel sculpture, Sesquicentennial Comn, La Porte, Ind, 83. *Exhib:* Sixty-Sixth Nat Exhib, Smithsonian Inst, 63; Seven American Artists, Colgate Univ, NY, 74; Sculpture Installation (Documentation), Tex Tech Univ, 81; Outdoor Sculpture Invitational, Meadow Brook Art Gallery, Rochester, Mich, 82; State of Michigan, Birmingham-Bloomfield Hills Mus, 82; solo exhib, Kalamazoo Inst Arts, 84. *Teaching:* Instr studio art, Hope Col, Mich, 58-63 & Philadelphia Col Art, 63-65; prof, Kalamazoo Col, 65- *Awards:* MacDowell Colony Fel, 67; First Prize Sculpture, Western Mich Ann, Kalamazoo Inst Art, 81. *Bibliog:* Ray Wilson (auth), Marcia Wood--portrait of a sculptor, Mag Kalamazoo Col, 80; Don Acosta (auth), Walkabout art, Monthly Detroit Mag, 7/80; Ruth Moerdyk (auth), The sculpture of Marcia Wood, Detroit Womens Voice, 82. *Mem:* Col Art Asn; Concerned Citizens Arts Mich; Kalamazoo Inst Arts. *Media:* Stainless Steel, Cast Bronze. *Mailing Add:* 2125 Ridge Rd Kalamazoo MI 49008

WOOD, NICHOLAS WHEELER
SCULPTOR, PAINTER
b San Francisco, Calif, Sept 21, 46. *Study:* San Francisco State Univ, BA, 72; Alfred Univ, NY, MFA, 77. *Work:* Lannan Found, Palm Beach, Fla; Arts Comn, San Francisco. *Exhib:* Oakland Mus Art, Calif, 74; Group Invitational, Dallas Mus Fine Arts, 79; solo shows, Ft Worth Art Mus, 79, Delahunty Gallery, Dallas, 81 & 500X Gallery, Dallas, Tex, 84; Janus Gallery, Los Angeles, 81; Showdown, Alternative Mus, New York, and traveling, 83; Sculpture on the Wall, San Antonio Art Inst, Tex, 83. *Teaching:* Assoc prof, Univ Tex, Arlington, 77- *Awards:* Individual Res Grant, Univ Tex, Arlington, 81; Fel, Nat Endowment Arts, 81-82. *Bibliog:* Ned Rifkin (auth), Tablets and grids: Clay by Wood, 6/2/79 & Robert Raczka (auth), Nicholas Wood: Evolution of a theme, 3/21/81, Artweek; Spencer L Davis (ed), Tablet series: Nicholas Wood, Ceramics Monthly, 2/80. *Media:* Clay, Wood; Mixed. *Mailing Add:* Dept Art Univ Tex Arlington TX 76019

WOOD, ROBERT E
PAINTER, INSTRUCTOR
b Gardena, Calif, Feb 4, 26. *Study:* Pomona Col, BA; Claremont Grad Sch, with Millard Sheets, Phil Dike & Jean Ames, MFA. *Work:* Butler Inst Am Art, Youngstown, Ohio; West Tex Mus, Lubbock; Lytton Financial Corp, Los Angeles; Riverside Art Ctr & Mus, Calif; Wichita Art Asn & Mus, Kans. *Exhib:* Am Watercolor Soc, New York, 54 & 58-; Watercolor USA, Springfield, Mo, 63-73; Watercolor West, Riverside, Calif, 69-75; Nat Watercolor Soc, 60-81; Nat Acad Design, New York. *Teaching:* Instr art, Univ Minn, Duluth, 52-55 & Claremont Grad Sch, Calif, 58; dir watercolor, Robert E Wood Summer Sch Painting, Green Valley Lake, 61- *Awards:* Nat Watercolor Soc, Calif, 58-73; Am Watercolor Soc Award, New York, 69, 71 & 81-; Watercolor West, Riverside, 70-80. *Bibliog:* San Bernardino Valley Col, Visit to the artist's studio, Educ TV, 66. *Mem:* Am Watercolor Soc (vpres, 68-74 & 81-83); Nat Watercolor Soc; Nat Acad Design; Watercolor West; West Coast Watercolor Soc. *Media:* Watercolor, Drawing. *Publ:* Auth, Robert E Wood, advocate thorough preparation, Am Artist Mag, 68; auth & producer, The search for a creative watercolor, cassette & slides, 72; co-auth, Watercolor Workshop, 74. *Dealer:* White Tops Gallery 1465 South Coast Hwy Laguna Beach CA 92651; Galleria Beretich 1034 Harvard Blvd Claremont CA 91711. *Mailing Add:* 33135 Maple Lane PO Box 216 Green Valley Lake CA 92341

WOODBURY, JOSEPHINE OSGOOD
PRINTMAKER
b Madison, Wis. *Study:* Univ Wis, Madison, MFA, 49, with Warrington Colescott, 61 & 62; Boston Sch Fine Art, 53. *Work:* Madison Art Ctr, Chadbourne Hall, Univ Wis, Madison; Miller Brewing Co, Milwaukee, Wis; Wykeham Rise Sch, Washington, Conn. *Exhib:* Smithsonian Inst,

Washington, DC, 64; Mus Seattle & Portland, 65; Pa Acad Fine Art, Philadelphia, 66; Tex Tech, Lubbock, 76; Rockford Col Gallery, Ill, 79; Theodore Lyman Wright Art Ctr, Beloit, Wis, 79. *Bibliog:* L' Art a l' Etranger: Aux Etats Unis, La Revue Mod, Paris, 10/1/66; Karen Hagemeister-Winzenz (auth), Made in Wisconsin: An exhibit of recent works in of and on, Fiber Arts, No 4, 78; Lynn Debbink-Potter (auth), Handmade paper, Janesville Gazette, 3/31/79. *Mem:* Wis Painters & Sculptors; Artists Equity Asn; Graphics Soc, Hollis, NH. *Media:* Mixed. *Dealer:* Sales & Rental Gallery Madison Art Ctr 311 State St Madison WI 53703. *Mailing Add:* 7426 Cedar Creek Trail Madison WI 53717

WOODEN, HOWARD EDMUND
MUSEUM DIRECTOR, HISTORIAN
b Baltimore, Md, Oct 10, 19. *Study:* Johns Hopkins Univ, BS & MA. *Collections Arranged:* Edward Lanning: American Realist, 1906-1981, 82; Lily Harmon, Fifty Years of Painting, 82; Will Barnet, Paintings and Prints 1932-1982, 83; Max Weber, Pioneer of American Modernism, 83; Art of a Changing Society: British Watercolors and Drawings, 1775-1900, 83; and many others. *Pos:* Dir, Sheldon Swope Art Gallery, Terre Haute, 66-75; dir, Wichita Art Mus, 75- *Teaching:* Fulbright instr, Athens Col, 51-52; lectr art hist, Univ Evansville, 55-63; assoc prof, Univ Fla, 63-66; assoc prof art hist, Ind State Univ, Terre Haute, 67-75. *Awards:* Fulbright Grant, US Dept State, 51-52. *Mem:* Col Art Asn Am; Am Asn Mus; Soc Archit Historians; Archaeol Inst Am; Asn Art Mus Dirs. *Res:* British watercolor painting of the 18th and 19th centuries; American architecture of the 19th century; meaning in contemporary art. *Publ:* Auth, Architectural heritage of Evansville, 62; auth, Fifty paintings and sculptures from the collection of Sheldon Swope Art Gallery, 72; auth, Art of a Changing Society: British Watercolors and Drawings, 1775-1900, Rand Publ Co, 83; and numerous articles, brochures and catalogs. *Mailing Add:* Wichita Art Mus 619 Stackman Dr Wichita KS 67203

WOODFORD, DON (DONALD PAUL)
PAINTER, EDUCATOR
b Kansas City, Kans, June 16, 41. *Study:* Cornell Col, BA, 63; Ill State Univ, MA, 64; Univ Wis, MFA, 65. *Work:* Cedar Rapids Art Ctr Mus, Coe Col Gallery, Iowa; Davenport Munic Mus, Iowa; Wright State Univ Mus, Dayton, Ohio; Western Ill Univ Gallery, Macomb. *Exhib:* Sixty-ninth Ann Exhib Chicago & Vicinity, Art Inst Chicago, 66; 6th Nat Drawing Exhib, Erie Art Ctr, Pa, 66; Northwest Ann, Seattle Mus, 70; one-man show, Tacoma Art Mus, Wash, 71 & Univ Redlands, Calif, 80; Calif Artist-Works on Paper, Int Art Fair, Basel, Switz, 77. *Teaching:* Asst prof art-painting, Cornell Col, Mt Vernon, Iowa, 65-68; asst prof art-painting, Reed Col, Portland, Ore, 68-72; prof art-painting, Calif State Univ, San Bernardino, 72- *Awards:* Arts & Riverwoods Prize, Riverside Art Ctr, 74. *Bibliog:* Thomas Albright (auth), Paintings on paper, San Francisco Chronicle, 6/7/75; Louis Fox (auth), Roplex and assemblage in relief, Artweek, 4/15/78; Julous Kaplin (auth), Don Woodford's Recent Constructions, Univ Redlands, 80. *Mem:* Col Art Asn Am. *Dealer:* Hank Baum Gallery 2140 Bush San Francisco CA 94115; Getler/Paul Gallery 50 W 57th St New York NY 10019. *Mailing Add:* 928 W 23rd St San Bernardino CA 92405

WOODHAM, DERRICK JAMES
SCULPTOR
b Blackburn, Eng, Nov 5, 40. *Study:* SE Essex Tech Col Sch Art, intermediate dipl design; Hornsey Col Arts & Crafts, nat dipl design; Royal Col Art, dipl. *Work:* Tate Gallery, London, Eng; Mus Contemp Art, Nagaoka, Japan. *Comn:* Sculpture, comn by North Jersey Cult Coun, Paramus, NJ. *Exhib:* Paris Biennale, Mus Art Mod, 65; Der Geist Surrealismus, Baukunst Galerie, Koln, WGer, 71; Sculpture in the Park, Paramus, NJ, 71 & 74; Wright State Univ Gallery, 76; Nat Sculpture Exhib traveling exhib, 76-77; Artists Choose Artists, Tweed Mus, Duluth, 77; one-man show, Jewish Mus, 69. *Teaching:* Instr sculpture, Philadelphia Col Art, 68-70; asst prof art forms found, Univ Iowa Sch Art, 70-73; assoc prof, Dept Art, Univ Ky, Lexington, 73-80; prof & dir, Sch Arts, Univ Cincinnati. *Awards:* Stuyvesant Found Bursary, 65; Prix de la Ville, Sculpture, Paris Biennale, 65. *Bibliog:* Otto Kulturman (auth), The New Sculpture, Praeger, 69; Teruo Fujieda (auth), Form and Structure, Kodansha Ltd, 72; Michael Findlay (auth), Contemporary Artists, St James Press, 77; plus others. *Mailing Add:* Col of Art Univ Cincinnati Cincinnati OH 45224

WOODHAM, JEAN
SCULPTOR
b Midland City, Ala. *Study:* Auburn Univ, BA; Sculpture Ctr, New York; Univ Ill, Kate Neal Kinley Mem fel. *Work:* Massillon Mus Permanent Collection, Ohio; US Merchant Marine Mus, NY; Telfair Acad Arts & Sci, Savannah, Ga; Alfred Khouri Mem Collection, Norfolk Mus Arts & Sci, Va; Westport Permanent Collection, Conn. *Comn:* Fountain sculptures, Gen Tel & Electronics Hq, Stamford, Conn, 73 & Tex Eastern Transmission, Houston Ctr, Tex, 74-75; fountain pieces, Gen Elec Credit Corp, Stamford, Conn, 71-72; Scholar's Sphere (four and one-half ton sculpture), Harry S Truman High Sch, New York, 77; Monody (welded bronze sculpture), Goodwin Hall, Archit & Fine Arts Ctr, Auburn Univ, Ala, 79. *Exhib:* Boston Mus Fine Arts, 48; Pa Acad Fine Arts Ann, Philadelphia, 50-54; Whitney Mus Am Art, 51; Womens Int Art Club, New Burlington Gallery, London, Eng, 55; New Eng Ann, Silvermine Guild, Conn, 55-60; US Info Agency Exhibs, Arg, Brazil, Chile & Mex, 63; Wadsworth Atheneum, Hartford, Conn, 67; Selected Sculptors Guild, Albright-Knox Art Gallery, Buffalo, NY, 71; Aldrich Mus, Ridgefield, Conn, 72; and 13 solo exhibs. *Teaching:* Head dept sculpture, Silvermine Guild Artists, 55-56; instr sculpture, Stamford Mus, Conn, 67-69; vis asst prof sculpture, Auburn Univ, 70, assoc prof, 74-75; vis critic, Cornell

Univ, Col Archit, Art & Planning, 80. *Awards:* Audubon Artists Medal for Creative Sculpture, 62; Medals of Honor for Sculpture, Nat Asn Women Artists, 66 & 74; Djerassi Found Grant, Woodside, Calif, 83. *Bibliog:* Scholars' Sphere (documentary film), 78; Connecticut Profiles: Jean Woodman--Sculptor (film), Conn Pub TV, 79; Anthony Padovano (auth), The Process of Sculpture, Doubleday, 81; and others. *Mem:* Sculptors Guild (treas, 60-65, exec bd, 66-68 & 77-82, secy, 72-74, vpres for membership, 82-83); Nat Asn Women Artists (chmn sculpture, 64-65); Westport-Weston Arts Coun (bd dir, 82-83); Artists Equity Asn; Silvermine Guild Artists (bd mgrs, 58-60, bd trustees, 81-83, chmn admissions, 83). *Mailing Add:* 26 Pin Oak Lane Westport CT 06880

WOODLOCK, ETHELYN HURD
PAINTER
b Hallowell, Maine, June 9, 07. *Study:* Copley Sch Commercial Art, Boston, Mass. *Work:* Valley Hosp, Ridgewood, NJ; Carlson Collection, Ramsey, NJ; Hickory Art Mus, SC; Bergen Community Mus, NJ; UN Bldg, New York. *Exhib:* 64th Am Show, Art Inst Chicago, 61; Contemporary Portraits, Fitchburg Art Mus, Mass, 62; Awards Artists Exhib, Montclair Art Mus, 66; Contemporary American Realism, Hammond Mus, Salem, NY, 68; two-man show, Bergen Community Mus, 71. *Awards:* Best Traditional Oil, Nat Asn Women Artists, 73; Gold Medal, Catharine Lorillard Wolfe, 73; Award of Highest Merit, Tri-State Bergen Co Artists Guild, 75; and others. *Bibliog:* Rodger (auth), Nonverbal communication, Am Soc Clin Hypnosis, 72. *Mem:* Nat Asn Women Artists; Catharine Lorillard Wolfe Art Club; Am Artists Prof League; Allied Artists Am. *Media:* Oil. *Mailing Add:* 1100 S Belcher Rd Apt 737 Largo FL 33541

WOODMAN, TIMOTHY
SCULPTOR
b Concord, NH, Mar 4, 52. *Study:* Skowhegan Sch Painting & Sculpture, 70; Cornell Univ, BFA(sculpture), 74; Yale Univ, MFA(sculpture), 76. *Work:* Hirshhorn Mus & Sculpture Garden, Washington, DC; Australian Nat Collection, Canberra; Metrop Mus Art, New York. *Exhib:* By The Sea, Queens Mus, New York, 79; Snow, Everson Mus, Syracuse, NY, 80. *Teaching:* Lectr, Univ Va, Charlottesville, 81. *Awards:* R S Reynolds Mem Award for Sculpture, 83. *Bibliog:* Wade Saunders (auth), article, Art Am, 5-6/79; Hilton Kramer (auth), article, New York Times, 1/16/81; Ronny H Cohen (auth), article, Artforum, 4/83. *Media:* Aluminum, Paint. *Mailing Add:* c/o Zabriskie Gallery 724 Fifth Ave NE New York NY 10019

WOODS, GURDON GRANT
SCULPTOR
b Savannah, Ga, Apr 15, 15. *Study:* Art Students League; Brooklyn Mus Sch; San Francisco Art Inst, Hon DArts, 66. *Work:* City of San Francisco. *Comn:* Steel fountain & concrete relief panels, IBM Corp, San Jose, Calif; aluminum fountain, Paul Masson Winery, Saratoga, Calif; concrete panels, McGraw-Hill, Novato, Calif; and others. *Exhib:* Janus Gallery, Los Angeles, 76; Los Angeles Munic Art Gallery, 77; Los Angeles Co Mus of Art, 78; Malibu Art & Design, Burbank, Fullerton & Santa Barbara, 79; Tortue Gallery, Santa Monica, 81; San Jose Inst Contemp Art; and others. *Pos:* Dir, Col San Francisco Art Inst, 55-65; dir, Otis Art Inst, Los Angeles, 74-77; asst dir, Los Angeles Co Mus of Natural Hist, 77-80. *Teaching:* Instr sculpture, San Francisco Art Inst, 55-65; prof art, Univ Calif, Santa Cruz, 66-74, chmn dept, 66-70. *Awards:* Four Purchase Awards, San Francisco Art Festivals; and others. *Mem:* San Francisco Art Inst (exec dir, 55-64). *Media:* Concrete, Paper. *Mailing Add:* 3109 Coolidge Ave Los Angeles CA 90066

WOODS, RIP
PAINTER, EDUCATOR
b Idabel, Okla, Aug 15, 33. *Study:* Ariz State Univ, MAE, 58. *Work:* Phoenix Art Mus, Ariz; Ariz State Univ, Tempe; Ark State Univ, Jonesboro; Yuma Fine Arts Ctr, Ariz; Ariz Western Col, Yuma. *Comn:* Relief-assemblage mural (with Ray Fink), Nat Housing Industs, Phoenix, 70; mosaic & bas relief painting (with Ray Fink), Greyhound-Armour, Phoenix, 71. *Exhib:* Drawing USA, Calif Palace Legion of Honor, San Francisco, 60; 73rd Western Ann, Denver, Colo, 71; Ariz Print Competition traveling exhib, 76; Ariz Outlook traveling exhib, 76; Invitational Exhib, Univ of Minn, Duluth, 77; FESTAC Visual Art Exhib, Lagos, Nigeria, 77. *Teaching:* Prof painting & drawing, Ariz State Univ, 65-; assoc prof painting, Colorado Springs Fine Art Ctr, Colo, summer 67. *Media:* Mixed. *Mailing Add:* Col of Fine Arts Ariz State Univ Tempe AZ 85281

WOODS, TED
SCULPTOR, CRAFTSMAN
b Akron, Ohio, Jan 1, 48. *Study:* Ariz State Univ, with Ben Goo, BFA & MFA. *Work:* Ariz State Univ; also numerous pvt collections. *Exhib:* 14th Southwestern Invitational; Ariz Nat; Metalsmithing 80; Traditions in the Making; Ariz Metal Invitational, 83; and others. *Pos:* Supervisor, Fabrication Facility, Col Archit & Environmental Design, Ariz State Univ, 78- *Teaching:* Nat Endowment Arts artist in residence, Mesa, Ariz, 72-73; vis staff instr sculpture & design, Glendale Community Col, 73-79; instr industrial design, Ariz State Univ, 80-81. *Awards:* Purchase Awards, Ninth Southwestern, Yuma & First Ann Wood-in-Art Exhib; First Pl Wood, Tenth Biennial Craft Exhib. *Bibliog:* Steve Torbeck (dir), Ted Woods--Blacksmith, KPNX TV Channel 12, Phoenix, Ariz, 80; Chuck Hawley (auth), Ted Woods--Blacksmith, Arizona Republic, 80; America Today: Ted Woods-Blacksmith Artist (film), Pub Broadcasting Network, 82. *Mem:* Artist-Blacksmith's Asn NAm; Am Crafts Coun; Ariz Artist Blacksmith Asn. *Media:* Metals, Wood. *Mailing Add:* 964 E Ninth Dr Mesa AZ 85204

WOODS, WILLIS FRANKLIN
CONSULTANT
b Washington, DC, July 25, 20. *Study:* Brown Univ, AB; Am Univ; Univ Ore. *Pos:* Asst dir, Corcoran Gallery Art, Washington, DC, 47-49; dir, Norton Gallery & Sch Art, West Palm Beach, Fla, 49-62; dir, Detroit Inst Arts, 62-73, hon trustee, Founders Soc; dir, Seattle Art Mus, 74-78; fine arts consult, 79. *Teaching:* Instr art, Palm Beach Jr Col, 58-62. *Mailing Add:* 2134 40th Ave E Seattle WA 98112

WOODSIDE, GORDON WILLIAM
DEALER, COLLECTOR
b Seattle, Wash. *Study:* Univ Wash. *Pos:* Dir, Woodside-Braseth Galleries, Seattle. *Specialty:* Artists of the Pacific Northwest. *Collection:* Representative works by prominent artists of the Northwest. *Mailing Add:* 1101 Howell St Seattle WA 98101

WOODSON, DORIS
EDUCATOR, PAINTER
b Richmond, Va, Jan 13, 29. *Study:* Xavier Univ, New Orleans, BA; Commonwealth Univ, Richmond, Va, MFA. *Work:* Bank of Va, Richmond; Pa State Univ. *Exhib:* 11th Ann Piedmont Painting Show, Mint Mus, Charlotte, NC, 71; Mainstreams 71, Int Painting, Marietta, Ohio, 71; Virginia Artists, Va Mus, Richmond, 71 & 75; Artists Showcase Gallery, Virginia Beach, Va, 73; Black Artists/S, Huntsville Mus Art, Ala, 79. *Pos:* Dir gallery, Va State Univ, Petersburg, 69-81. *Teaching:* Instr painting, Richard Bland Col, Petersburg, Va, 69; asst prof painting & drawing, Va State Univ, Petersburg, 69-; adj instr design & drawing, Commonwealth Univ, Richmond, Va, 79-82. *Awards:* Petersburg Art Festival, Petersburg Area Art Leagues, 68-74; Norfolk Art Festival, Tidewater Artists Asn, 73; Lynchburg Art Festival, Lynchburg Art Asn, 74. *Mem:* Richmond Artists Asn (secy, 68-69); Petersburg Art League. *Media:* Oil, Acrylic. *Mailing Add:* 20007 Roosevelt Ave Colonial Heights VA 23834

WOODSON, SHIRLEY ANN
PAINTER
b Pulaski, Tenn, Mar 3, 36. *Study:* Wayne State Univ, BFA, MA; Art Inst Chicago. *Work:* Detroit Pub Schs, Mich; Detroit Receiving Hosp, Mich. *Exhib:* Mich Artists Exhib, Detroit Inst Arts, 60; Collaboration: Painter & Poet, Dudley Randall Arts Extended Gallery, Detroit, 69; Chico State Col Watercolor Invitational, 72; solo show, Howard Univ, 75; Ill State Univ Traveling Exhib, 81; Joslyn Mus, Omaha, Nebr, 81; and others. *Pos:* Dir exhib, Arts Extended Gallery, 63-71; dir, Pyramid Gallery, Detroit, 79-80. *Teaching:* Instr painting, design, drawing & art hist, Highland Park Community Col, 66-78; instr painting, Wayne State Univ, 74; consult, Highland Park Schs, Mich, 82- *Awards:* Purchase Prize, Print & Drawing Exhib, Dulin Gallery Art, Knoxville, Tenn, 65; Fel, MacDowell Colony, 66-67; Mich Coun Arts Grant, 83-84. *Bibliog:* Louise Bruner (auth), Black artists in America, Toledo Blade, 69; Leonead Pack Bailey (auth), Broadside Poets and Artists, Broadside Press, 74; and others. *Mem:* Nat Conf Artists. *Dealer:* Celia A Woodson & Edsel Reid 17215 San Juan Detroit MI 48221. *Mailing Add:* 5656 Oakman Blvd Detroit MI 48204

WOODWARD, CLEVELAND LANDON
PAINTER, ILLUSTRATOR
b Glendale, Ohio, June 25, 1900. *Study:* Cincinnati Art Acad, scholar, 23-26; Charles Hawthorne's Cape Cod Sch Art, summer 24; Brit Art Acad, Rome, Italy, 28-29. *Work:* Mus Fine Arts, Mobile, Ala; Arctic Mus, Brunswick, Maine; Boardman Press, Nashville, Tenn; United Lutheran Publ House, Philadelphia; Standard Publ Co, Cincinnati, Ohio. *Comn:* Painting for Donald B MacMillan of Arctic Mus, Brunswick, Maine, 52; 16 watercolor illus for World Bible, World Publ Co, 62; Peter & John (mural), West Eng Baptist Church, Mobile, 72; plus others. *Exhib:* Cincinnati Art Mus Spring Exhib, 25; one-man shows, Traxel Art Gallery, Cincinnati, 29, Mus Fine Art, Mobile, 68, 71 & 77 & Percy Whiting Mus, Fairhope, Ala, 69 & 71. *Pos:* Mem first bd dirs, Cape Cod Art Asn. *Teaching:* Lectr Biblical art, schs, cols & mus, many yrs; instr oil painting, Eastern Shore Acad Fine Arts, 72- *Awards:* Estab of Cleveland L Woodward Foundation, Fine Arts Mus, South Mobile, Ala. *Bibliog:* Article in Am Artist Mag, 5/73. *Mem:* Eastern Shore Art Asn (bd dirs, 71-74); Eastern Shore Acad Fine Arts. *Media:* Oil, Watercolor. *Publ:* Illusr, By an Unknown Disciple, Harper Bros; illusr, The Other Wise Man, Harper Bros; illusr, Painting Christ Head, Abingdon Press; illusr, The Bible, rev standard version, World Publ Co. *Dealer:* Orleans Art Gallery Main St Orleans Cape Cod MA 02653; Koch Galleries 162 S Lawrence St Mobile AL 36602. *Mailing Add:* 354 Boone Lane PO Box 466 Fairhope AL 36532

WOODWARD, KESLER EDWARD
CURATOR, PAINTER
b Aiken, SC, Oct 7, 51. *Study:* Davidson Col, NC, BA, 73; Idaho State Univ, Pocatello, MFA, 77. *Work:* Alaska State Mus, Juneau; Univ Alaska, Fairbanks; Atlantic Richfield Co, Los Angeles; Anchorage Historical & Fine Arts Mus; Alaska Contemp Art Bank, Anchorage. *Exhib:* Southeastern Artists Ann, Gallery Contemp Art, Winston-Salem, 71 & 72; All-Alaska Juried, Anchorage Hist & Fine Arts Mus, 79 & 80; 17st American Ann, Newport, RI, 82; Spokane Ann, Wash, 82; US Art in Embassies, Brasilia, Brazil, 82; and others. *Collections Arranged:* New Possibilities: Works from the Canadian Art Bank (auth, assembled), Alaska State Mus, 78; A Celebration of Tradition, Visual Arts Ctr of Alaska, 78 & National Invitational, 78-79; Canadian Horizons (with catalog), 81-82. *Pos:* Cur temp exhib, Alaska State Mus, Juneau, 77-78, cur visual arts, 79-81; artistic dir, Visual Arts Ctr of Alaska, Anchorage, 78-79; dir, Univ Alaska Fine Arts Gallery, 82- *Teaching:* Asst prof painting, Univ Alaska, 81- *Awards:* Alaska

State Coun Arts Grant, 82. *Mem:* Col Art Asn. *Media:* Acrylic. *Res:* Early pictorial material pertaining to polar regions and little-known Alaskan historical artists. *Publ:* Auth, New Possibilities, Alaska State Coun Arts, 78; auth, Canadian Horizons, Alaska State Coun Arts, 82. *Mailing Add:* Dept Art Univ Alaska Fairbanks AK 99701

WOODWARD, WILLIAM
PAINTER, EDUCATOR
b Washington, DC, Mar 11, 35. *Study:* Abbott Sch Art, Corcoran Sch Art, Am Univ, BA & MA, Washington, DC; Acad de Belli Arti, Florence, Italy. *Work:* Corcoran Gallery; Speed Mus, Louisville; Washington Co Mus Fine Art. *Comn:* Drawing, The White House, DC, 68; mural, United Brotherhood Teamsters, DC, 69; mural, Eutaw Sch, Baltimore, 68; mural, Clydes Inc, Tysons Corner, Va, 80; mural, City Hall Rockville, Md, 82; and others. *Exhib:* One-man shows, Mickelson Gallery, DC, 66-74, Hirschl & Adler Gallery, New York, 71, John State Col, Vt, 74 & Int Monetary Fund, Washington, DC, 75; Fendrick Gallery, Washington, DC, 82; and others; plus others. *Teaching:* Instr painting, Corcoran Sch Art, DC, 65-; asst prof painting, George Washington Univ, DC, 69-; dir, Summer Fine Arts Prog, Brittany, France, 76-79. *Awards:* Painting Fel in Italy, Leopold Schepp Found, 57-59; Mary Graydon Scholar, Am Univ, 53-57 & Teaching Fel, 58-61. *Bibliog:* Rafael Sqirru (auth), The Washington mannerists: the foresight to look backwards, Americas, Vol 19, No 1; Legrace N Benson (auth), The Washington scene, Art Int, Vol 13, No 10; Jill Weschsler (auth), William Woodward: Traditional themes, modern methods, Am Artist, 12/76. *Publ:* Contribr, Art in America, 1760-1860, 69; contribr, Leonardo da Vinci, 70 & Dreamers of Decadence, 72, Washington Post. *Mailing Add:* 3136 P St NW Washington DC 20007

WOODY, (THOMAS) HOWARD
SCULPTOR, ENVIRONMENTAL ARTIST
b Salisbury, Md, Sept 26, 35. *Study:* Richmond Prof Inst, BFA; ECarolina Univ, MA; Univ Iowa; Art Inst Chicago; Kalamazoo Art Ctr; Univ Ky. *Work:* SC State Art Collection, Columbia; Gibbes Art Gallery, Charleston, SC; Mus Art, Charlotte, NC; Birmingham Mus Art, Ala; Columbus Mus Arts & Crafts, Ga; and others. *Exhib:* Tenth Int Sculpture Conf, Toronto, 78; Arcosanti Conf, 78; Nat Festival Conf, Milwaukee, Wis, 79; 11th Int Sculpture Conf, Washington DC, 80; Col Art Conf, New Orleans, La, 80; and others. *Teaching:* Instr sculpture, Roanoke Fine Art Ctr, Va, 59-61; assoc prof sculpture, Pembroke State Univ, 62-67; prof sculpture, Univ SC, 67- *Awards:* Spec Citation Award, Atlanta Festival Sculpture, 68; SC State Art Collection Award, 71 & 74 & Fel grants, 73 & 77, SC Arts Comn. *Bibliog:* L G Redstone (auth), Public Art: New Directions, McGraw-Hill, 81. *Mem:* Southern Asn Sculptors (pres, 65-70); Nat Sculpture Ctr (adv, 66-80); Guild SC Artists (mem bd, 69); SC Craftsmen (mem bd, 68); Southeastern Col Art Conf. *Publ:* Auth, Atmospheric sculpture: An event, not an object, Vol 7, No 1 & Atmospheric concepts, Vol 6, No 2, Southeastern Col Art Conf Rev; auth, Workshops in environmental sky art, Design for Arts in Educ, 3-4/79; auth, Environmental art, Sculptor's News Exchange, Princeton, NJ, 9-10-11/79; and others. *Mailing Add:* 433 Arrowwood Rd Columbia SC 29210

WOOF, MAIJA (MAIJA GEGERIS ZACK PEEPLES)
PAINTER
b Riga, Latvia, Nov 21, 42. *Study:* Univ Calif, Davis, BA, 64, MA, 65; also with William T Wiley, Robert Arneson & Wayne Thiebaud. *Work:* Crocker Art Gallery, Sacramento, Calif; La Jolla Mus Art, Calif; Matthews Art Ctr, Tempe, Ariz; San Francisco Mus Art; Norman MacKenzie Art Gallery, Regina, Sask. *Comn:* Beast rainbow painting, City San Francisco, Civic Ctr, 67; rainbow house, pvt party, San Francisco, 67-68; ceiling murals, Rainbow House, San Francisco, 67-68; crocheted, woven & scwn beast curtains, Univ Calif Art Bldg, Davis, 71. *Exhib:* San Francisco Art Mus, 73-75; Rainbow Show, De Young Mus, San Francisco, 74-75; Calif Women Artists, Sacramento State Capitol, 75; Three Calif Artists, Univ Calif, Davis Gallery, 76; Crossroads Gallery, 76; Bounty of Beasties, Am River Col, Sacramento, 77; Welcome to the Candy Store, Crocker Art Mus, 81; and many other group and one-man shows. *Collections Arranged:* The Nut Show, for Kaiser-Aetna, Tahoe Verdes, Calif, 72. *Teaching:* Instr art, Laney Col, Oakland, 68-69; instr art, Univ Calif, Davis, 71-72; instr art, Sierra Col, Rocklin, Calif, 71-73. *Awards:* Award, Ceramics Excellence, Calif State Fair, 74. *Bibliog:* Jane Goldman (auth), Peeples animals bring smiles, Sacramento Union, 79; Jane Goldman (auth), Enough to make you smile, Sacramento Mag, 8/80; Ellen Schlesinger (auth), As fate would have it, Peeples is an artist, Sacramento Bee, 7/4/82. *Media:* Multimedia. *Dealer:* Candy Store Gallery 605 Sutter St Folsom CA 95630. *Mailing Add:* 2586 King Richard Dr El Dorado Hills CA 95630

WOOLFENDEN, WILLIAM EDWARD
ADMINISTRATOR, HISTORIAN
b Detroit, Mich, June 27, 18. *Study:* Wayne State Univ, BA & MA. *Pos:* Asst cur Am art, Detroit Inst Arts, 45-49, dir educ, 49-60; asst dir, Arch Am Art, Detroit, 60-62, exec dir, 62-64, dir, 64-70, dir, Arch Am Art, Smithsonian Inst, New York, 70-; mem vis comt, Dept Am Paintings & Sculpture & Photog & Slide Libr, Metrop Mus Art, New York; adv drawings, Minn Mus Art, St Paul, 61-80. *Awards:* Distinguished Alumni Award, Wayne State Univ, 76. *Mem:* Am Asn Mus; Col Art Asn Am; Soc Archit Historians; Nat Trust Hist Preservation. *Res:* American art; American drawings. *Mailing Add:* 65 Oyster Shores Rd East Hampton NY 11937

WOOLSCHLAGER, LAURA TOTTEN
PAINTER, PRINTMAKER
b Dallas, Tex, Sept 1, 32. *Study:* Syracuse Univ, BFA(magna cum laude), 54; Southern Ore Col, with Robert Alston, 65. *Work:* Carnegie Libr, Lewiston,

Idaho; Mus Native Am Cult, Spokane, Wash; Favell Mus Western Art, Klamath Falls, Ore. *Exhib:* Monac Western Art Show, Spokane Convention Ctr, Wash, 73-81; Southwest Rendezvous, Oro Valley Country Club, Tucson, Ariz, 79-81; C M Russell Show, Heritage Inn, Great Falls, Mont, 79-81; Western Experience, Stewart Anderson Ranch, Ellensburg, Wash, 80; Artist in Residence, Mus Native Am Cult, Spokane, Wash, 80. *Teaching:* Instr, Wenatchee Valley Community Col, Omak, Wash, 73-74. *Awards:* Best of Show, Artists of the Old West, 79 & Nat Western Art Show, Western Art Asn, 79. *Bibliog:* Dr Darwin Goodey (auth), An inner view, Art West Mag, 1/80. *Mem:* Am Artist Rockies Asn (pres, 83); Western Art Asn. *Media:* Acrylic, Watercolor; Intaglio. *Mailing Add:* Route 1 Box 122-H Omak WA 98841

WOOSTER, ANN-SARGENT
PAINTER
b Chicago, Ill, Jan 19, 46. *Study:* Bard Col, AB, 68; Hunter Col, with Robert Morris, MFA, 73, and Leo Steinberg, Rosalind Krauss & Ray Parker, MA(art hist), 78. *Pos:* Ed educ dept, Shorewood Publ, New York, 69-72; free lance writer, Art Am, New York, 73; staff writer, Art Forum, New York, 75-76; staff writer, Village Voice, New York, 79- *Teaching:* Instr, Sch Visual Arts, New York, 75-, Kean Col Union, 79-83. *Awards:* Helen Rubenstein Fel, Whitney Mus Am Art, 75; Award, NYSCA, 82. *Bibliog:* Jean Sousa (auth), NAME events, NAME Gallery, 80; Charlene Spretnak (auth), Politics of Women's Spirituality, Anchor Doubleday, 82. *Mem:* Int Art Critics Asn; Women's Caucus. *Media:* Mixed Media. *Publ:* Auth, Quiltmaking, Drake Publ, 72; auth, Sol Lewitt and Lucinda Childs, 5/80 & auth, Film and video at the biennial, 5/81, Art Am; auth, Moving to dance, 12/80 & auth, Yvonne Rainer: Journey to Berlin 1971, 5/81, Drama Rev. *Mailing Add:* 170 Second Ave New York NY 10003

WORDELL, EDWIN HOWLAND
PAINTER
b Philadelphia, Pa, Aug 27, 27. *Study:* San Diego State Univ, dipl(hon), 61. *Work:* Utah State Univ, Logan; San Diego Trust & Savings Bank; San Bernardino Valley Col; San Diego Zoological Soc; Wells Fargo Bank, San Diego. *Comn:* Triptich (watercolor), Zoological Soc, San Diego; three watercolor paintings, San Diego Trust & Savings Bank. *Exhib:* 43rd Ann Midyear Show, Butler Int Am Art, 79; Nat Watercolor Soc, Palm Springs Desert Mus, 79; Aqueous, Westmoreland Co Mus Art, Greensburg, Pa, 82 & Owensboro Mus Fine Art, Ky, 83; Am Artists Prof League, Salmagundi Club, New York, 83; Audubon Artists, Nat Arts Club, New York, 83; Art and the Law Nat Traveling Invitational, 83-84. *Awards:* Cash Award, Watercolor West, 79 & Second Award, 80, Nat Watercolor Soc; First Award, St Mark's Lenten Art Festival, 83. *Mem:* San Diego Watercolor Soc (pres, 75-76); San Diego Art Inst (pres, 78-79); Nat Watercolor Soc; Rocky Mountain Watermedia Soc; Watercolor West. *Media:* Watercolor. *Dealer:* Spectrum Gallery 726 Seventh Ave San Diego CA 92101. *Mailing Add:* 6251 Lorca Dr San Diego CA 92115

WORTH, KAREN
SCULPTOR
b Philadelphia, Pa, Mar 9, 24. *Study:* Tyler Art Sch, Temple Univ; Pa Acad Fine Arts; Acad Grande Chaumiere, Paris. *Work:* Smithsonian Inst; West Point Acad, NY; Am Jewish Hist Asn, Boston; Jewish Mus, New York; Israel Govt Coins & Medals Div, Jerusalem. *Comn:* Space Age (medal), Soc Medalists, 63; Hist Jews of Am, Judaic Heritage Soc, 69; Presidents USA, Whittnauer Precious Metals Guild, 74; Bicentennial Presidents (medal), Galaxies Unlimited Inc, 75. *Exhib:* Nat Acad, New York, 65; Lever House, New York, 66-; Ceramic Sculpture of Western Hemisphere. *Teaching:* Pvt sculpture classes, 72-73. *Awards:* Pa Acad Fine Arts Award for Sculpture, 42; Allied Artists Am Award for Sculpture, 65; Lucy Lohat Prize, Judaic Heritage Soc, 81; and others. *Bibliog:* Ed Trautman (auth), Almanac, Franklin Mint, 68. *Mem:* Fel Nat Sculpture Soc (coun, 69-); Fine Arts Fedn New York. *Media:* Clay, Bronze. *Mailing Add:* 19 Henry St Orangeburg NY 10962

WORTH, PETER JOHN
SCULPTOR, HISTORIAN
b Ipswich, Eng, Mar 16, 17; US citizen. *Study:* Ipswich Sch Art, 34-37; Royal Col Art, London, with E W Tristram, Paul Nash, Edward Bawden, Douglas Cockerell & Roger Powell. *Work:* Denver Art Mus; Joslyn Art Mus; Sheldon Gallery Art, Univ Nebr. *Exhib:* San Francisco Mus Art, 50; Nelson Gallery Art, 50, 53, 54 & 57; Art Inst Chicago, 51; Walker Art Ctr, 51, 52 & 56; Denver Art Mus, 52, 53, 55-57 & 60-63. *Teaching:* Prof art hist, Univ Nebr, Lincoln, currently. *Mem:* Egypt Explor Soc, London; Col Art Asn Am. *Res:* Stylistic transformations in late antique and early medieval art, especially in iconography. *Publ:* Photogr, Life Library of Photography, 70; photogr, Bilder, Stuttgart, 70. *Mailing Add:* Dept of Art Woods Hall Univ of Nebr Lincoln NE 68588

WORTHEN, AMY NAMOWITZ
PRINTMAKER, HISTORIAN
b New York, NY, Aug 13, 46. *Study:* Smith Col, with Leonard Baskin, BA, 67; Univ Iowa, with Mauricio Lasansky, MA, 69. *Work:* Metrop Mus Art, New York; Cedar Rapids Art Ctr, Iowa; Iowa State Univ, Ames; Des Moines Art Ctr, Iowa; Ark Arts Ctr, Little Rock. *Exhib:* Engravings--America, 1974, Albrecht Mus Art, Mo, 74; World Print III, San Francisco Mus Mod Art, San Francisco, 80; Smithsonian Touring Exhib, 11 Int mus, 80-83; one-woman show, Brunnier Gallery, Iowa State Univ, Ames, 81; Boston Printmakers 33rd & 35th Nat Exhibs, 81 & 83; Print Club Philadelphia, 82; Mid-Four Exhib, Nelson-Atkins Gallery, Kansas City, Mo; Printed by Women: Nat Exhib Photog & Prints, Port Hist Mus, Philadelphia. *Collections Arranged:* The Etchings of Jacques Bellange (com auth, catalog), Des Moines Art Ctr, Mus

Fine Arts, Metrop Mus, 75-76; Benton, Curry, Wood--Lithographs, Iowa Arts Coun touring exhib (auth, catalog), 78; Giorgio Morandi (auth, catalog), 81; Etchings of J N Darling (auth, catalog), Brunnier Gallery, Iowa State Univ, 84. *Teaching:* Instr printmaking hist prints, Des Moines Art Ctr, Iowa, 71-; lectr, Drake Univ, Iowa, 72-74, 81 & 83. *Bibliog:* A deck of playing cards, Print Collector's Newsletter, 75; Janice Shotwell (auth), The fantasy world of Amy Worthen, Iowan Mag, fall 78; J Print World, fall 81 & spring 82. *Mem:* Print Coun Am. *Res:* History of prints. *Publ:* Auth, Jacques Bellange: Some Questions, Print Collector's Newsletter, 75; auth, Morandi als Radierer, Morandi, Haus der Kunst, Munich, 81. *Dealer:* Olson-Larson Galleries 203 Fifth St W Des Moines IA 50265; Assoc Am Artists 663 Fifth Ave New York NY. *Mailing Add:* 5130 Shriver Ave Des Moines IA 50312

WORTZ, MELINDA FARRIS
GALLERY DIRECTOR, CRITIC
b Ann Arbor, Mich, Apr 30, 40. *Study:* Radcliffe Col, BA(cum laude), 62; Otis Art Inst, 62-63; Univ Calif, Los Angeles, MA, 70; also with John Altoon. *Pos:* Gallery dir, Univ Calif, Riverside, 72-74 & Univ Calif, Irvine, currently; Southern Calif ed, Artweek, currently; contrib ed, Arts Mag, Art Gallery, Art News & Archit Dig, currently. *Teaching:* Asst prof issues in art, Calif State Univ, Long Beach, 72-75 & Calif State Univ, Los Angeles, 74-75; lectr, Univ Calif, Irvine, currently. *Res:* Contemporary American art. *Publ:* Auth, Seven Southern California Artists (catalog), Cirrus Gallery, Los Angeles, 74; auth, Dewain Valentine (exhib catalog), Long Beach Mus Art, 75; auth, Ludwig Redl (catalog essay), 75. *Mailing Add:* Univ Calif Irving Art Gallery Irvine CA 92717

WORTZEL, ADRIANNE
PAINTER
b Brooklyn, NY, Oct 7, 41. *Study:* Brooklyn Mus Art Sch, NY, 57-65; Brooklyn Col, with Ad Reinhardt, Burgoyne Diller & Louise Bourgeois, BA(with honors fine art), 63; Hunter Col, New York, with Mark Rothko, MA, 69. *Work:* Moderna Museet, Stockholm Sweden; Citibank, New York; City of Lund, Sweden; pvt collection of Mr & Mrs Larry Hagman, Malibu, Calif. *Exhib:* Galleriet, Sweden, 79 & 82; New Acquisitions, Moderna Museet, Stockholm, Sweden, 80; one-person show, Scottsdale Ctr Arts, Ariz, 80 & Bernice Steinbaum Gallery, New York, 81 & 83; Graphic Plus, Herbert F Johnson Mus, Ithaca, NY, 81. *Teaching:* Lectr contemp art, Great Neck Adult Educ Program, 70-73. *Awards:* Creative Artists Pub Serv Grant, NY State Coun Arts, 81. *Bibliog:* Patricia Ensworth, Adrianne Wortzel, Arts Mag, 3/80; Sarah Cecil (auth), article, Artnews, 3/82; Donna Harkavy (auth), Adrianne Wortzel, Arts Mag, 9/83. *Media:* Acrylic on Canvas. *Dealer:* Bernice Steinbaum Gallery 903 Madison Ave New York NY 10021. *Mailing Add:* 19 East 7th St New York NY 10003

WOSTREL, NANCY J
PAINTER
b San Diego, Calif. *Study:* With John C Pellew, 70 & 71; Famous Artists Sch, cert, 72; studied with Robert E Wood, 80. *Work:* James S Copley Libr, La Jolla, Calif; Vesti Corp, Boston, Mass; Troth Corp, New Orleans, La. *Exhib:* Watercolor W, Riverside Art Ctr & Mus, Calif, 75, 77, 78 & 79; one-man shows, Knowles Art Ctr, La Jolla, Calif, 74, 77, 79 & 81; Watercolor USA, Springfield Art Mus, Mo, 79; Nat Acad Ann, New York, 81; Am Watercolor Soc Traveling Exhib, 80-81; and others. *Awards:* Purchase Awards, San Diego Watercolor Soc Nat Ann, 73, 76, 79 & 80; Hon Mention, San Diego Watercolor Soc Nat, 79; Second Prize for Watercolor, Southern Calif Expo, Del Mar, 79; and others. *Bibliog:* Richard Reilly (auth), Frost poems inspire art, 77 & Watercolor show a breath of sweet air, 79, San Diego Union, Copley Publ; Richard Reilly (auth), Compositions of Beauty & Joy, San Diego Union, Copley Publ, 81. *Mem:* San Diego Watercolor Soc; Watercolor W; assoc Am Watercolor Soc; Allied Artists. *Media:* Watercolor . *Publ:* Auth, North Light Mag, Fletcher Art Serv Inc, 76. *Dealer:* Knowles Gallery 7420 Girard Ave La Jolla CA 92037. *Mailing Add:* 2505 Montclair St San Diego CA 92104

WRAY, DICK
PAINTER
b Houston, Tex, Dec 5, 33. *Study:* Univ Houston. *Work:* Albright-Knox Art Gallery, Buffalo. *Exhib:* Mus Contemp Art, Houston, 61; Southwest Painting & Sculpture, Houston, 62; Hemisfair, Houston, 68; Homage to Lithography, Mus Mod Art, New York, 69; Response, Tyler Mus, Tex, 80. *Awards:* Purchase Prize, Ford Found, 62; Purchase Prize, Mus Fine Arts, Houston, 63. *Mailing Add:* 316 W 23rd Houston TX 77008

WRAY, MARGARET M
PAINTER
b Galveston, Tex. *Study:* San Antonio Art Inst, Tex; Inst Allende, San Miguel de Allende, Mex; also with Theodores Stamos, Adja Yonkers, Nathan Olivera, Fletcher Martin, Millard Sheets, Dong Kingman, Rex Brandt & Edward Betts. *Work:* Collection of Susan Thomas, Inc, New York; Lady of the Lake Col, San Antonio, Tex; Hutching-Sealy Bank, Galveston, Tex; The Charles Urchel Collection, San Antonio; and pvt collections. *Comn:* The Waterfall (watercolor), C W Miller, Medina Ranch, Tex; The Nellie B (watercolor), Alton E Robertson, San Antonio; Ranch Map, Hugh Fitzsimmons, San Pedro Ranch, Corrizo Springs, Tex. *Exhib:* 16th Southwestern Print & Drawing, Mus Fine Arts, Dallas, 66; Tex Watercolor Soc & circuits, 70, 71 & 74; 17th Delta Ann Art, Ark Art Ctr, Little Rock, 74; Tex State Watercolor Ann, 78; Hill Country Arts Found, 79; Tex Watercolor Exhib, San Antonio, 80; plus others. *Awards:* Purchase Prize, Susan Thomas, Inc, San Antonio, 63; Purchase Prize (landscape), Mr & Mrs John K Mitchell, Houston; Tex Woman's Club Award (Color Etude), Houston, 72. *Bibliog:* Glen Tucker (auth), Today, art scene, San Antonio

Light; Joseph Cain (auth), Art new & reviews, Caller Times, Corpus Christi, 7/73; John Palmer Leeper (auth), San Antonio Times, 83. *Mem:* Tex Watercolor Soc (pres, 60-61); Contemp Artist Group (treas, 65-67); Am Fedn Arts; Tex Arts Asn; San Antonio Art League. *Media:* Acrylic, Watercolor. *Dealer:* Sol Del Rio Gallery 1020 Townsend Ave San Antonio TX 78209. *Mailing Add:* 7731 Broadway 35 San Antonio TX 78209

WRIGHT, BARTON ALLEN
PAINTER, ILLUSTRATOR
b Bisbee, Ariz, Dec 21, 20. *Comn:* Wupatki Nat Monument, Ft Union Nat Monument, Babbitt Stores. *Exhib:* La Jolla Art Asn, Calif, 69; Winged Arts Gallery, Sedona, 70; Festival of Arts, Lake Oswego, 71; Parlor Gallery, Ore, 71-75; Thorne Gallery, Scottsdale, 74 & 75; and others. *Collections Arranged:* M R F Colton, 58; G E Burr, 59; Indian Artists, 60; Western Artists, 62; Paul Dyck, 64; American Art, 65; Flagstaff Art, 66; Southwest Art, 68; Widforss, 69; Santa Fe Indian Art, 70; Nat Park Illustrated, 71; N Fechin, 72; and others. *Pos:* Cur arts & exhib, Mus Northern Ariz, 55-58, cur, Mus, 58-77; sci dir, Mus of Man, 77-82; res anthropologist, Heard Mus, 83. *Teaching:* Vis Instr, Univ Calif, Riverside, 77, Univ Calif, San Diego, spring 83, Pitzer Col, spring 83. *Mem:* Am Asn Mus; San Diego Corral Westerners; Ariz/Nev Acad Sci. *Media:* Acrylic, Scratchboard. *Interests:* Western Art; Indian Art. *Publ:* Auth, This is a Hopi Kachina, 64, Kachina's, a Hopi Artist's Documentary, 73, Unchanging Hopi, 75, Pueblo Shields, 76, Hopi Kachinas, the Complete Guide, 77; and many others. *Mailing Add:* 6254 Rose Lake Ave 1350 El Prado Balboa Park San Diego CA 92119

WRIGHT, BERNARD
PAINTER, GRAPHIC ARTIST
b Pittsburgh, Pa, Feb 23, 38. *Study:* Otis Art Inst, Los Angeles, 69-70; Los Angeles Trade Tech Col, 71-74. *Work:* New York Pub Libr; Howard Univ, Washington, DC; Libr Cong; Morehouse Col, Atlanta, Ga; Los Angeles Pub Libr. *Comn:* Numerous furniture and garment exclusive designs. *Exhib:* Detroit Inst Art, 74; Fisher Art Galleries, Univ Southern Calif, 74; Calif Mus Sci & Indust, Los Angeles, 75; Pittsburgh City Hall Gallery, 82; Ava Dorog Galleries, Los Angeles, 82; and others. *Pos:* Pres & co-founder, Westly & Wright Products, Los Angeles, 72- *Bibliog:* Frank Johnson (auth), The art of Bernard Wright, Grapevine Mag, 10/80; Ronald Moore (auth), City honors 12 Black artists, Los Angeles Sentinel, 5/7/81; Judith Grout (auth), Art to art in Black history, Los Angeles Mag, 2/82; and others. *Mem:* Art W Asn Inc, (mem bd dir, 67-73); Artist Equity Asn. *Media:* Oil, Ink. *Mailing Add:* c/o Edward Smith & Co PO Box 8990 Los Angeles CA 90008

WRIGHT, CATHARINE MORRIS
PAINTER, WRITER
b Philadelphia, Pa, Jan 26, 99. *Study:* Philadelphia Sch Design Women, 17-18; also with Henry B Snell & Leopold Seyffert. *Work:* Pa Acad Fine Arts, Philadelphia; Philadelphia Mus Art; Woodmere Art Gallery; Univ Pa; Nat Acad Design. *Exhib:* Pa Acad Fine Arts, 18-52; Corcoran Gallery Art, 21-41; Nat Acad Design, 30-52; Am Watercolor Soc; Carnegie Inst. *Teaching:* Founder, Fox Hill Sch Art, 50-69. *Awards:* Second Hallgarten Prize, Nat Acad Design, 33; Prize, Allied Artists Am, 41; Prize, Silvermine Guild Artists, 55. *Mem:* NAm Watercolor Soc; Audubon Artists; Allied Artists Am; Philadelphia Watercolor Club (vpres, 49-57); Newport Art Asn; Nat Acad Design. *Media:* Oil, Watercolor. *Publ:* Auth, The Simple Nun, 29, Seaweed Their Pasture, 46 & The Color of Life, 57; auth, Lady of the silver skates, 79. *Dealer:* Vose Galleries of Boston Inc 238 Newbury St Boston MA 02116. *Mailing Add:* Fox Hill Jamestown RI 02835

WRIGHT, (CHARLES) CLIFFORD
PAINTER, WRITER
b Cosmopolis, Wash, Nov 19, 19. *Study:* Cornish Sch, Seattle, with Dr W Reese, 36; with Mark Tobey, 37-43. *Work:* Ringling Brothers Mus, Sarasota, Fla; Edward James' Collection, Mex; Nordjyllands Kunstmuseum, Aalborg, Denmark; Whitney Mus & Brooklyn Mus, New York. *Exhib:* Seattle Art Mus, Wash, 42; one-man shows, Ellen Donavan's Gallery, Philadelphia, 53 & Asbaks Gallery, Copenhagen, Denmark, 79; Dada, Surrealism & Heritage, Mus Mod Art, 68; Retrospective, Nordjyllands Kunstmuseum, Aalborg, Denmark, 81; Helander Gallery, Stockholm, 82; Danish Railroad Six Posters, Asbaks Gallery, Copenhagen & Nordjyllands Kunstmuseum, Aalborg, Denmark, 82. *Awards:* Mus des Beaux Arts, Brussels, Am Acad Arts & Letters, 57; Encouragement Grant, Columbia Univ, 59; State Art Found Grants, Denmark, 79 & 80. *Bibliog:* A painter of the grotesque, Mag Am Art, 47; L Kochnitzsky (auth), Something different, Les Beaux Arts, Belgium, 57; O Braunschwig (auth), Portrait, Danish State TV, 74. *Media:* Oil, Gouache. *Publ:* Auth, Hero in the New World, Borgen, 63; contribr, Philoctetes Wounded, State TV, Denmark, 74; coauth & illusr, Demoniac Dames, Gyldendal, 79; coauth & illusr, Insights, Mistral, Denmark, 81. *Dealer:* Jacob Asbaek Ny Adelgade Copenhagen Denmark DK 1104. *Mailing Add:* Marienborg Decenter Stege DK 478o Denmark

WRIGHT, DAVID THOMAS
PAINTER, EDUCATOR
b Coventry, England, Nov 26, 47; Brit & Can citizen. *Study:* Univ Newcastle-Upon-Tyne, England, BA(with hon), 70; Univ Reading, England, with Terry Frost, MFA, 72. *Work:* Can Coun Art Bank, Ottawa. *Comn:* Painted murals, Playboy Club, London, 71, Watts & Henderson Ltd, Toronto, 73 & Ottawa Civic Hosp, 82. *Exhib:* Director's Choice, Art Gallery Windsor, Ont, 75; Abstractions: Ontario Painting, Ctr Cult, Paris, 77; Ontario Now, Part II, Art Gallery Hamilton, Ont, 77; Painting Now, Agnes Etherington Art Ctr, Kingston, Ont, 77; Traveling Exhib Can Prints, Can Embassy, Rabat, Morocco, 82 & Spanish Cult Ctr, Casablanca, Morocco, 83; and others.

Teaching: Master & coordr fine art, Fanshawe Col, London, Ont, 77- *Awards:* Second Prize, Stowell's Trophy Exhib, Mall Galleries, London, England, 72; Jack Reppen Award, Outdoor Show, Toronto City Hall, 73. *Bibliog:* Lowell Fox (auth), A newcomer celebrates technology, Art Mag, 73; Robert Myers (auth), Flashes: David Wright at the Mazelow Gallery, Art Mag, 75; John Bentley Mays (auth), Wright finds a new beginning in a dead end, Globe & Mail, 80. *Media:* All. *Dealer:* Ponova Gallery 191 Gerrard St E Toronto ON Canada. *Mailing Add:* 60 Cowan Ave Toronto ON M6K 2N4 Canada

WRIGHT, DONALD
SCULPTOR, GOLDSMITH
b St Louis, Mo, June 17, 30. *Study:* Washington Univ, St Louis, Mo, 48-50; Southwest Mo State Univ, Springfield, BS(cum laude), 56; NMex Highlands Univ, Las Vegas, summer 56; Cranbrook Acad Art, Bloomfield Hills, Mich, MFA, 58. *Work:* Detroit Inst Art, Mich. *Comn:* Designed: Northwest Craft Ctr, Seattle City Ctr, Wash, 62-63 & designed & installed, 1st Ann 12 Western State Craft Exhib, 64; designed home, galleries & sculpture, comn by Robert L Pfannebeker, Lancaster, Pa, 65; outdoor bronze fountain, pvt comn, Tucson, 69; plus many others. *Exhib:* Young Am Exhib, Mus Contemp Crafts, New York, 58, Designer-Craftsmen USA 1960, 60 & one-man show, Little Gallery, 62; 14th Exhib Mich Artist-Craftsmen, Detroit Inst Art, 60; 1969 Southwestern Craftsmen's Exhib, Mus Int Folk Art, Santa Fe, NMex, 69; Int Jewelry Exhib, Munich, Ger, 70; Southern Tier Arts & Crafts Show, Corning Mus, NY, 70; plus many others. *Pos:* Self-employed artist, 68-; owner, The Selective Eye Gallery, Santa Fe, 73- *Teaching:* Asst prof art, Utah State Univ, Logan, 58-60; lectr art, Cent Wash State Univ, Ellensburg, 61-62; asst prof art, Pa State Univ, Altoona, 66-68. *Awards:* Second Prize Metal, Mus Contemp Crafts, New York, 58; Purchase Prize, Detroit Inst Art, 61; First Prize Metal & Best in Show Award, NMex State Fair, 69. *Bibliog:* Mary Carroll Nelson (auth), Donald Wright, Art Voices S, 9/10/79; plus others. *Media:* Bronze, Gold. *Mailing Add:* 421 Camino Manzano Santa Fe NM 87501

WRIGHT, FRANK
PAINTER, EDUCATOR
b Washington, DC, Oct 10, 32. *Study:* Am Univ, BA, 54; Univ Ill, Urbana, MA, 60; Fogg Mus, Harvard Univ, fel, 60-61. *Work:* Bibliot Nat, Paris; Nat Collections Fine Arts, Washington, DC; Univ Seattle Law Sch, Wash; Nat Gallery Art, Rosenwald Collection, Washington, DC; Tucson Mus Art, Tucson, Ariz; and others. *Comn:* Deepbite etching demonstration plate & ed, Lessing J Rosenwald, Jenkintown, Pa, 68. *Exhib:* One-man show, Davidson Galleries Inc, 75, Washington, DC; Kennedy Galleries, New York, 81; Houston Univ, Clear Lake, Tex, 83; West 83/Art & The Law, Woodruff Arts Ctr, Atlanta, 83; Allentown Art Mus, Pa, 83; and others. *Teaching:* Instr master drawing, Corcoran Sch Art, Washington, DC, 66-70; asst prof design & graphics, George Washington Univ, 70-78, assoc prof drawing & graphics, 79-83, prof, 83- *Awards:* Nat Soc Arts & Lett Scholar, 50-54; Leopold Schepp Found Fel Europ Studies, 56-58; Paul J Sachs Fel Graphic Arts, Print Coun Am, 59-62; and others. *Bibliog:* Benjamin Forgey (auth), Frank Wright's own way, Washington Star, 81; JoAnn Lewis (auth), Discovered!, Washington Post Mag, 81; Jill Wechsler (auth), Frank Wright, an artist with a sense of history, Am Artist, 9/82; and others. *Media:* Oil; Graphics. *Publ:* Auth, Why I love to engrave, G W Forum, Vol 7, No 1 (winter 77). *Dealer:* Kennedy Galleries 40 W 57th St New York 10019. *Mailing Add:* 3520 Bradley Lane Chevy Chase MD 20015

WRIGHT, G ALAN
SCULPTOR
b Seattle, Wash, Mar 31, 27. *Study:* Honolulu Sch Art; also with Willson Stamper & Ralston Crawford. *Work:* Johnson Wax Collection; Seattle Art Mus; Denver Art Mus. *Comn:* The Great Gull (bronze), D E Skinner, Seattle Sci Pavillion, World's Fair, 62; bronze lion cub, First Nat Bank, Spokane, Wash, 63; bronze owl, City Hall, Renton, Wash, 68; bronze crane, Seattle First Nat Bank, 69; crane, First Nat Bank, Tacoma, Wash, 69. *Exhib:* Northwest Ann Show, Seattle Art Mus, 62-65; Gov Invitational Exhib, Wash, 67; Sara Roby Gallery, Racine, Wis, 68; Whitney Mus Am Art, New York, 68; Lee Nordness Gallery, New York, 68 & 69. *Awards:* First Prizes, Renton Art Festival, 62 & 64; First Prize, New Arts & Crafts Fair, Bellevue, Wash, 63; Ford Found Purchase Award, 64. *Bibliog:* Article in Christian Sci Monitor, 62 & 64; J Canaday (auth), article in New York Times, 68; M Randlett (auth), Living Artists of the Pacific Northwest, 72. *Media:* Bronze, Stone. *Dealer:* Gordon Woodside Gallery 803 E Union St Seattle WA 98122. *Mailing Add:* 1729 12th Seattle WA 98122

WRIGHT, HAROLD DAVID
PAINTER
b Rosine, Ky, June 13, 42. *Study:* Harris Sch Advert Art, Nashville, Tenn; watercolor painting in Italy. *Work:* Tenn State Mus, Nashville. *Comn:* Portraits of Civil War Generals, General's Retreat, Franklin, Tenn, 74. *Exhib:* Cent South Show, Parthenon, Nashville, 74; Sardella Art Show, Atlanta, Ga, 74; High Plains Exhib, Lubbock, Tex, 79; Western Collectors Exhib, Dallas Tex, 81. *Pos:* Artist, Newspaper Printing Corp, Nashville, 62-66; art dir, Buntin & Assocs Advert, 66-69; partner, Nova Group, Nashville, 69-; vpres, Graystone Press, Nashville, 73- *Awards:* Best of Show, Art Dirs Club Nashville, 68; First Award Fine Art Competition, 73. *Mem:* Art Dirs Club Nashville (vpres, 70). *Media:* Watercolor, Gouache, Casein. *Publ:* Illusr, Nashville Tennessean Mag, 66 & 78; illusr, Tenn Conservationist Mag, 74 & 76-79; illusr, Nashville, the faces of two centuries, Southwest Art Mag, 79. *Mailing Add:* Rte 1 Cross Plains TN 37049

WRIGHT, JESSE GRAHAM, JR
MUSEUM DIRECTOR
b Sidney, Ohio, July 29, 39. *Study:* Loyola Univ, Chicago, BA(philos), MA(Eng); Univ Notre Dame, Ind, MFA. *Pos:* Dir, South Bend Art Ctr, Michael C Rockefeller Art Ctr Gallery, Fredonia, NY, Canton Art Inst Ohio & Philbrook Art Ctr, Tulsa, Okla. *Mem:* Am Asn Mus; Asn Art Mus Dirs; Okla Mus Asn (pres, 80). *Mailing Add:* PO Box 52510 Tulsa OK 74152

WRIGHT, MILTON
PAINTER, EDUCATOR
b Dayton, Ohio, July 3, 20. *Study:* Miami Univ, Ohio, with Marston Hodgin, BFA, 42; Sch Art Studies, New York, with Isaac Soyer, cert, 48; Acad Julian, Paris, cert, 50. *Work:* Long Island Univ; Miami Univ, Ohio; Town Hall, Truro, England. *Comn:* Cup plates, Truro Hist Soc, Mass, 80 & 82; landscape, Town Truro, Mass, 82. *Exhib:* Solo exhibs, Denver Art Mus, 43, Dayton Art Inst, 48 & 53, Miami Univ, Ohio, 53 & Long Island Univ, 72; Butler Art Inst, 45; Corcoran Gallery Biennial, 51; Audubon Artists, New York, 53; Brooklyn Mus Ann, 58-76; Am Watercolor Soc, New York, 66. *Teaching:* Instr painting & drawing, Brooklyn Mus Art Sch, 51-76; adj prof painting, Queens Col, City Univ New York, 53-64; asst prof art, Long Island Univ, 64-74. *Awards:* Purchase Prize, Dayton Art Inst, 53. *Mem:* Mass Art Coun. *Media:* Oil, Watercolor. *Publ:* Auth, Confrontations, Long Island Univ, 71. *Dealer:* Left Bank Gallrey Commercial St Wellfleet MA 02667. *Mailing Add:* Box 314 Truro MA 02652

WRIGHT, NINA KAIDEN
CONSULTANT
b New York, NY, May 18, 31. *Study:* Emerson Col, BA. *Pos:* Consult art orgn pub relations and mktg; pres, Arts & Communications Counselors, currently; consult, Am Express, Philip Morris, Detroit Inst Arts, Dallas Mus Art, and others. *Mailing Add:* Arts & Communications Counselors 110 E 59th St New York NY 10022

WRIGHT, PAUL MORRIS
SCULPTOR, PAINTER
b Columbia, Mo, May 24, 17. *Study:* Univ Mo, 36; Art Students League, 40-41; with Moholy Nagy, 44-46; Univ NMex, BFA(sculpture/painting), 50; Cranbrook Acad Art, MFA(sculpture/ceramics), 52. *Work:* Am Mus Natural Hist, New York; Cranbrook Sci Inst Mus, Bloomfield Hills, Mich; City Spokane's Sculpture Park, Wash. *Comn:* Mural, Tex Tech Col Mus, Lubbock, 56; murals, Sandia Laboratories, Albuquerque, NMex, 60-67; sculpture, Univ NMex, Albuquerque, 69; sculpture (bronze concrete), Ranchers Exploration Development Corp, Albuquerque, NMex, 81. *Exhib:* Ancestral Horses Wild & Domestic, 40 & Animal in Fable & Myth, 41, Am Mus Natural Hist, New York; Special Exhib Am Mus Natural Hist, Roosevelt Mem Gallery Hall, New York, 50; Rome Collaborative Competition, Am Acad Rome, traveling Europe, 52; NMex Fine Arts Mus, Santa Fe, 62. *Teaching:* Adj prof design, Univ NMex, 59-60, adj prof archit, 78. *Awards:* Craftsmanship Award, Am Inst Archit, NMex, 59. *Bibliog:* Articles in PM News, NY Time Mag & NY Times, 40-50. *Media:* Bronze & Concrete; Oil, Acrylic. *Dealer:* Wolfe Galleries 6420 N Campbell Ave Tucson AZ 85718. *Mailing Add:* PO Box 268 Corrales NM 87048

WRIGHT, STANLEY MARC
PAINTER, INSTRUCTOR
b Irvington, NJ, May 24, 11. *Study:* Sch Fine Art, Pratt Inst, grad(with highest honors), 33; Jerry Farnsworth Sch Art, Tiffany Found Fel, 35. *Work:* Portraits, Gov Deane C Davis & Sen George D Aiken, State House, Montpelier, Vt, Joe Kirkwood, Golf Hall of Fame, Foxberg, Pa, George A Wolf, Med Ctr, Univ Kans & A G Mackay, Med Ctr, Burlington, Vt. *Comn:* Portrait & landscape paintings, US & Europe. *Exhib:* Metrop Mus Art; Brooklyn Mus; Newark Mus; Montclair Mus; Cong Galleries, Washington, DC; one-man show, House Rep, US Capitol, Washington, DC, 76. *Teaching:* Head portrait & landscape, Newark Sch Fine Arts, 44-50; instr portrait & landscape & dir, Wright Sch Art, Stowe, Vt, 50-; lectr, demonstr & instr painting, many orgn. *Awards:* Many prizes for nat exhibs & one-man shows. *Bibliog:* Articles in Cue Mag, Vt Life Mag, Times, Newark News, Free Press & others. *Mem:* Salmagundi Club; Audubon Artists; fel Int Inst Arts & Lett; hon mem Vt Artists; Vt Coun Arts. *Media:* Oil, Watercolor. *Mailing Add:* RFD 2 Stowe VT 05672

WRIGHT, (MR & MRS) WILLIAM H
COLLECTORS
Collection: Modern paintings and watercolors; pre-Columbian sculpture, mostly from Colima, Mexico. *Mailing Add:* 3644 W 132nd St Hawthorne CA 90049

WRISTON, BARBARA
HISTORIAN, LECTURER
b Middletown, Conn, June 29, 17. *Study:* Oberlin Col, AB; Brown Univ, AM; hon LittD, Lawrence Univ. *Pos:* Former exec dir mus ed, Art Inst Chicago; adv, Metrop Hist Structures, New York; mem adv comm, Hist Am Bldgs Survey, 72-78. *Mem:* Benjamin Franklin Fel Royal Soc Arts; Soc Archit Historians (pres, 60-61); Furniture Hist Soc. *Res:* Seventeeth and eighteenth century English and American architecture and furniture. *Publ:* Auth, Who was the architect of the Indiana Cotton Mill, 1848-1850?, J Soc Archit Historians, 5/65; auth, Joiner's tools in The Art Institute of Chicago, 67 & The Howard Van Doren Shaw Memorial Collection in the Art Institute of Chicago, 69, Mus Studies; auth, Visual Arts in Illinois, 68; auth, Rare Doings at Bath, 79. *Mailing Add:* 30 Waterside Plaza 2D New York NY 10010

WU, I-CHEN
CALLIGRAPHER, PAINTER
b Echen, Hupeh, China, Nov 25, 27. *Study:* 10 yrs classical Chinese studies; Nat Chung Hsing Univ Taiwan, BA, 58; Univ Mo-Columbia, 68; Calif State Univ, San Jose, MA, 74; Univ of Ariz, Tucson, MA, 83. *Work:* Calligraphers Asn Prov Taiwan, Chung Hsing Village; Nat Hist Mus Taiwan, China; Prov Mus Victoria, BC; San Jose Mus Art. *Exhib:* Chinese Pavilion, Montreal World's Fair, 67; Chinese Pavilion, HemisFair, San Antonio, Tex, 68; Prov Mus Victoria, 70; Calif Inst Technol, 71; Chinese Info Serv, New York, 76; Nat Mus Hist, Taiwan, 79. *Pos:* Art inspector, Taiwan Prov Dept Educ, 53-66. *Teaching:* Instr Chinese painting, Univ Calif, San Francisco, 72-73; lectr Chinese painting, Mills Col, Oakland, 74, Univ Nev, Reno, 76-77, Univ Ariz, Tucson, 78-82 & San Jose State Univ, 84- *Awards:* Second Place, Columbia Art League & Bank Am Show, 67; Second Place, 73 & 74 & Third Pl, 77, Chinese Renaissance Asn. *Mem:* Chinese Calligraphers' Asn; Art Soc China; Soc Confucius-Mencius, Taiwan; Asian Art Soc San Francisco; Int Soc Chinese Philos. *Media:* Chinese Color. *Res:* Late Ming painters and Yang Chow School. *Collection:* Chinese calligraphy and painting from Yuan to the present. *Publ:* Ed; Introduction to Chinese Painting, Univ Mo, 67; ed, Patterns of Chinese Landscape Painting, KQED-TV, San Francisco, 74 & Chinese Painting and Calligraphy, KTVK-TV 3, Phoenix, Ariz, 79; auth, articles of Chinese art exhibs in US, Taiwan Cent Daily News, 68-72. *Mailing Add:* 1683 Christopher St San Jose CA 95102

WU, LINDA YEE CHAU
SCULPTOR
b Canton, China, July 4, 19; US citizen. *Study:* Calif Sch Fine Arts, 39-42; Nat Acad Design, 42-44; Sch Painting & Sculpture, Columbia Univ, 44-50. *Comn:* Bas-relief, Chinese Community, New York, 52; portrait of Sam Y Ong, Republican Club Chinatown, New York, 75. *Exhib:* Allied Artists Am Ann Exhibs, 47-; Audubon Artists Ann Exhibs; Nat Acad Design Ann Exhibs; Nat Sculpture Soc Ann Exhibs; Int Sculpture Third, Philadelphia Art Mus, 49. *Teaching:* Dean students, New York Chinese Sch, 60-74, prin, 74- *Awards:* Dessie Greer Prize for Sculpture, Nat Acad Design, 65; Anna Hyatt Huntington Gold Medal, Catharine Lorillard Wolfe Art Club, 68; Gold Medal of Honor for Sculpture, Allied Artists Am, 73. *Mem:* Nat Acad Design; fel Nat Sculpture Soc (counr, 72-74); Allied Artists Am; Knickerbocker Artists. *Mailing Add:* 20 Confucius Plaza Apt 44E New York NY 10002

WUERMER, CARL
PAINTER
b Munich, Ger, Aug 3, 1900; US citizen. *Study:* Art Inst Chicago, 20-24; Art Students League, New York. *Work:* High Mus Art, Atlanta, Ga; IBM Corp Art Collection, Endicott, NY; Encycl Britannica Collection Am Art; Royal Globe Ins Co, London; Syracuse Univ Art Collection, NY. *Exhib:* Var ann, Am Painting & Sculpture, Art Inst Chicago & Nat Acad Design; Corcoran Gallery Art Bi-Ann, 32; Painting in US, Carnegie Inst, 46-49; 5th Ann Painting & Sculpture, Grover M Hermann Fine Arts Ctr, Marietta, Ohio, 72. *Awards:* J Francis Murphy Mem Prize, Nat Acad Design, 28; Popular Vote Prize, Carnegie Inst, 49. *Mem:* Allied Artists Am; Artists Fel (pres, 57-59); Hudson Valley Art Asn. *Media:* Oil. *Res:* For the appraisal of the Frick Collection, New York, High Museum of Art Collection, Eleutherian Mills-Hagley Foundation Collection, Wilmington, Delaware and others. *Mailing Add:* 430 W 24th St Lawrence Welk Country Club New York NY 10011

WUNDER, RICHARD PAUL
HISTORIAN, ADMINISTRATOR
b Ardmore, Pa, May 31, 23. *Study:* Harvard Univ, AB, 49, MA, 50, PhD(John Thornton Kirkland Fel), 55. *Collections Arranged:* The Architect's Eye, Cooper Union Mus, 62; Theater Drawings from the Donald Oenslager Collection, Minneapolis Inst Arts & Yale Univ Art Gallery, 63-64; Frederic Edwin Church, Nat Collection Fine Arts, 66. *Pos:* Asst to dir, Fogg Art Mus, Harvard Univ, 53-54; cur drawings & prints, Cooper Union Mus, 55-64; cur & asst dir, Nat Collection Fine Arts, Smithsonian Inst, 64-69; dir, Cooper-Hewitt Mus Design, 69-70; pres appraisals & estates, Christie, Manson & Woods, Int, currently. *Teaching:* John Hamilton Fulton lectr, Middlebury Col, 75-80. *Mem:* Col Art Asn Am; Drawing Soc (dir, 64-72); Soc l'Histoire l'Art Francais. *Res:* Italian and French drawings of the 17th and 18th centuries; American painting, sculpture and drawings of the 19th century. *Publ:* Auth, Extravagant Drawings of the 18th Century, Lambert-Spector, 62; auth, Architectural & Ornament Drawings, Univ Mich Mus, 65; auth, Hiram Powers, Vermont sculptor, Woodstock Hist Soc, Vt, 74; auth, Architectural, Ornament, Landscape & Figure Drawings, Middlebury Col, 75. *Mailing Add:* Brookside Orwell VT 05760

WUNDERLICH, RUDOLF G
DEALER
b Tarrytown, NY, Nov 13, 20. *Study:* NY Univ. *Pos:* Pres, Kennedy Galleries Inc, currently. *Specialty:* American art, paintings of the 18th, 19th and 20th centuries; Western Americana, paintings and sculpture; Old Master engravings; modern fine prints; work of modern American Masters in paintings, sculpture and graphics. *Mailing Add:* Kennedy Galleries Inc 40 W 57th St-Fifth Floor New York NY 10019

WUNDERMAN, JAN (LILJAN DARCOURT WUNDERMAN)
PAINTER, PRINTMAKER
b Winnipeg, Man, Jan 22, 21; US citizen. *Study:* Otis Art Inst, Los Angeles, Calif, 42; Brooklyn Mus of Art Sch, 54-56, with Reuben Tam. *Work:* Loeb Collection, NY Univ; Alfred Khouri Collection, Norfolk Mus, Va; Ball State Univ Art Gallery, Muncie, Ind; Univ SC Art Gallery, Columbia; Post Col,

Long Island, NY; and others. *Comn:* Eight paintings, New York City off, White, Weld & Co, 68; paintings, New York, Tulsa & Ft Worth off, Arthur Young & Co, 73; painting, Commercial Union Bank, Nashville, Tenn, 75; painting, New York off, Bank of Am, 76; painting, New York off, The Boston Co, 77. *Exhib:* Los Angeles Co Mus Art, Los Angeles, 45; one-person shows, Gastine Gallery, Los Angeles, 45, Angeleski Gallery, New York, 61, Roko Gallery, New York, 63-77 & Easthampton Guild Gallery, Long Island, NY, 66; Brooklyn Mus, NY, 56; Philadelphia Mus Art, 56-62; Pa Acad of Fine Arts, Philadelphia, 59-65; Butler Inst Am Art, Youngstown, Ohio, 59-66; Mus de Bellas Artes, Buenos Aires, Arg, 60; Va Mus Fine Arts, Richmond, 67; Eggleston Gallery, New York. *Awards:* Emily Lowe Award, New York, 65; J M Kaplan Prize, Nat Soc Painters, 79; Canaday Memorial Prize, 79; and others. *Mem:* Nat Asn Women Artists; Artists Equity; Am Soc Contemp Artists. *Media:* Oil, Acrylic; Black & White Intaglio Prints. *Mailing Add:* 131 E 19th St New York NY 10003

WURDEMANN, HELEN (BARONESS ELENA GUZZARDI)
ADMINISTRATOR, COLLECTOR
b Milwaukee, Wis. *Study:* Univ Wis, BA. *Collections Arranged:* Monthly exhibitions of paintings and sculptures by Southern California artists. *Pos:* Dir, Southern Calif Contemp Art Asn, Los Angeles Art Asn, currently; Western art reporter & writer, Art in Am, 54-65; art critic, Los Angeles Mirror News, 60-61. *Awards:* Citations from City & Co of Los Angeles, 52 & 54; Arts & Humanities Award, Nat Watercolor Soc, 74. *Mem:* Univ Calif, Los Angeles Art Coun; Los Angeles Mus Art & Print Coun; hon mem Nat Watercolor Soc; hon mem Women Painters West. *Collection:* Lithographs by Daumier & Goya; drawings by Macdonald-Wright, Stephen Longstreet, Helen Lundeberg & Lorser Feitelson; paintings; Wurdemann Collection, Univ Wis. *Mailing Add:* Los Angeles Art Asn Galleries 825 N La Cienega Blvd Los Angeles CA 90069

WURMFELD, SANFORD
PAINTER, EDUCATOR
b New York, NY, Dec 6, 42. *Study:* Dartmouth Col, BA, 64. *Work:* Metrop Mus Art, New York; Landesmuseum, Hannover, WGer; Ackland Mem Art Ctr; State Univ NY, Fredonia. *Comn:* Acrylic sculptures, City Hannover, WGer, 71 & Shreve, Camb & Harmon, New York, 71; paintings, Gen Electric, Fairfield, Conn, 74 & Baxter Travenol Labs, Dearfield, Ill, 77. *Exhib:* Art of the Real, Mus Mod Art, New York 68, Grand Palais, Paris, 68, Kunsthaus, Zurich, 68 & Tate Gallery, London, 69; Drawings, Ft Worth Art Ctr, 69; Contemporary Painting Review, Lehigh Univ, Pa, 76; Patterns Plus, Art Mus, Dayton, 79; Carnege Int, Mus Art, Pittsburgh, Pa, 82 & Seattle, Wash, 83. *Teaching:* From lectr to prof art, Hunter Col, 67- chairman dept, 78- *Awards:* Guggenheim Fel, 74-75. *Mailing Add:* 18 Warren St New York NY 10007

WYATT, GREG ALAN
SCULPTOR
b Nyack, NY, Oct 16, 49. *Study:* Columbia Col, BA, 71; Nat Acad Sch Design, 72-74; Columbia Univ, 74- *Work:* Evansville Mus Arts & Sci, Ind; Brookgreen Gardens, Murrells Inlet, SC; Nat Arts Club, Gramercy Park, New York; Princeton Univ Libr, NJ; Sports-Illus Mag Collection, New York. *Comn:* Eagle (bronze sculpture), Am Bur Shipping, New York, 78; Battle of New Orleans (boxer series), Am Broadcasting Corp, New York, 79; and others. *Exhib:* Solo exhibs, New Orleans Theatre Performing Arts, 77, Sculpture Revitalized, Bodley Gallery, New York, 78 & Sculptor's Watercolors, Cafe des Artistes, New York, 81; Nat Acad Design, New York, 79 & 80; Nat Arts Club Ann, New York, 79-81; and others. *Teaching:* Instr, Finch Col, New York & San Marino, Italy, 73-75; instr, New York Univ, 74-75; instr, Jersey City State Col, NJ, 74-75. *Awards:* Ziegfield Art Award, Columbia Univ Sch Educ Art Dept Ann, 75-76; Helen Foster Barnett Award, Nat Acad Design Nat Ann, 79; Walter Lantz Award, Nat Sculpture Soc Young Sculptors Ann, 79. *Bibliog:* John Sotomayor (auth), Eagle, New York Times, 12/20/78; Michael Lantz (ed), Woman, the sculptor's vision, Nat Sculpture Rev, spring 79; Pam Lambert (auth), The eagle has landed off Lower Broadway, Columbia Univ Mag, winter 79. *Mem:* Nat Arts Club. *Media:* Bronze, Marble. *Mailing Add:* 320 W 86th St Penthouse South New York NY 10024

WYATT, STANLEY
PAINTER, ILLUSTRATOR
b Denver, Colo, Sept 20, 21. *Study:* Columbia Col, with Frank Mechau, BA, 43; Art Inst Chicago, 46; Columbia Univ, with Meyer Schapiro, MA, 47; Brooklyn Mus, with Rufino Tamayo, 48. *Work:* Mexican-NAm Cult Inst, Mexico City; Packaging Inst, Toronto, Can; Hellenic-Am Union, Athens, Greece; and others. *Comn:* Illus, New York Times Mag, 57-79 & Col Entrance Bd Rev, 59-78; portraits, presidents of Columbia Univ, 76, New York Acad Med, 81 & Eisenhower Univ, 81. *Exhib:* La Galeria Collectionistas, Mexico City, 62; Mexican-NAm Cult Inst, Mexico City, 63; Casa Italiana, Columbia Univ, New York, 71; Gallery Cord, Soho, New York, 78; Hellenic Am Union, Athens, 79. *Pos:* Dir, Del Piombo Art Ctr, 59-61; art dept rep, Baruch Sch, 61-69; supvr art dept, Eve Div & summer session, City Col New York, 69-72; dir, Cult Affairs Coun, Grand View, NY, 76-82. *Teaching:* Assoc prof art & chmn dept, Waynesburg Col, 49-51; instr art, Columbia Univ, 52-60; assoc prof art, City Col New York, 60-78, prof, 78-; assoc prof art & chmn dept, Rockland Community Col, 61-63. *Awards:* Brainard Sr Prize, Columbia Col, 43; Distinction in Illustration, Am Asn Alumni Mags, 57; Gold Ribbon for Prints, 5th Ann Bergen Mall Exhibs, 66. *Bibliog:* Graphic art of Stanley Wyatt, Univ Mich, 70. *Mem:* Fel Royal Soc Arts, London; Salmagundi Club; Newcomen Soc NAm; United Fedn Col Teachers. *Media:* Oil, Acrylic; Graphite, Linocut. *Publ:* Ed-in-chief, Jester, Columbia Univ, 43; auth, Thanks to Shanks, 58; illusr, 20th Century Views & 20th Century Interpretations, 60-80, Prentice-Hall, and others. *Mailing Add:* 75 River Rd Nyack NY 10960

WYCKOFF, SYLVIA SPENCER
PAINTER, EDUCATOR
b Pittsburgh, Pa, Nov 14, 15. *Study:* Col Fine Arts, Syracuse Univ, BFA, 37, MFA, 44. *Work:* Radio Sta WSYR, Syracuse, NY; R E Dietz Co, Syracuse; also in pvt collections. *Exhib:* Munson-Williams-Proctor Inst, Utica, NY; Mem Art Gallery, Rochester, NY; Everson Mus Art, Syracuse; Cooperstown Art Asn, NY; Nat Asn Women Artists, New York. *Teaching:* Prof watercolor & drawing & chmn, Freshman Core Progs Dept, Syracuse Univ, 42-81; retired. *Awards:* League Prize for Watercolor, Nat League Am Pen Women Nat Show, 48; Gordon Steele Award, Assoc Artists Syracuse, 68; Special Citation, NY State Art Teachers Asn, 81. *Mem:* Nat Asn Women Artists; Nat League Am Pen Women; Assoc Artists Syracuse; Cazenovia Watercolor Soc. *Media:* Watercolor. *Mailing Add:* 2 Seminary St Cazenovia NY 13035

WYETH, ANDREW NEWELL
PAINTER
b Chadds Ford, Pa, July 12, 17. *Study:* With N C Wyeth; Harvard Univ, hon DFA, 55; Colby Col, hon DFA, 55; Dickinson Col, hon DFA, 58; Swarthmore Col, hon DFA, 58. *Work:* Metrop Mus Art, New York; Mus Fine Arts, Boston; Los Angeles Co Mus Art; Art Inst Chicago; Nat Gallery Art, Washington, DC; Brandywine River Mus, Chadds Ford, Pa; and many others. *Exhib:* Currier Gallery Art, Manchester, NH; Pa Acad Fine Arts, Philadelphia; Fogg Art Mus, Mass; Univ Ariz, Tucson; Mus Fine Arts, Boston; Nat Mus of Mod Art, Tokyo, Japan; Nat Mus of Mod Art, Kyoto, Japan; Metrop Mus of Art, New York; Royal Acad, London; H M De Young Mem Mus, Santa Fe, NMex; Brandywine River Mus, Chadds Ford, Pa; White House, Washington, DC; and many others. *Awards:* Pa Acad Fine Arts; Carnegie Inst; Am Watercolor Soc; Associe Etranger de l'Institut de France; and many others. *Bibliog:* Richard Merryman (auth), Andrew Wyeth, Houghton; Wanda Corn (auth), The Art of Andrew Wyeth, New York Graphic Soc. *Mem:* Nat Acad Design; Audubon Artists; Am Watercolor Soc; Am Acad Arts & Lett; and others. *Media:* Tempera, Watercolor. *Mailing Add:* c/o Frank E Fowler PO Box 247 Lookout Mountain TN 37350

WYETH, HENRIETTE (MRS PETER HURD)
PAINTER
b Wilmington, Del, Oct 22, 07. *Study:* Normal Art Sch, Boston; Pa Acad Fine Arts; also with N C Wyeth. *Work:* Roswell Mus Art; New Britain Mus Art, Conn; Lubbock Mus Art, Tex; Tex Tech Univ; portraits in pvt collections. *Exhib:* Carnegie Inst, Pittsburgh; Art Inst Chicago; Metrop Mus Art, New York; Roswell Mus Art, NMex; and others. *Awards:* Four First Prizes, Wilmington Soc Fine Arts; Pa Acad Fine Arts; Governor's Award, Santa Fe, NM, 81. *Mailing Add:* Sentinel Ranch San Patricio NM 88348

WYETH, JAMES BROWNING
PAINTER
b Wilmington, Del, July 6, 46. *Study:* With Carolyn Wyeth; Elizabethtown Col, hon DFA. *Work:* Nat Gallery & Nat Portrait Gallery/Smithsonian Inst, Washington, DC; Mus Mod Art, New York; Joslyn Art Mus, Omaha, Nebr; Del Art Mus, Wilmington; Brandywine River Mus, Chadds Ford, Pa; and others. *Exhib:* Solo exhibs, Pa Acad, Philadelphia, 80, Greenville Co Mus Art, SC, 81 & Amon Carter Mus, Ft Worth, Tex, 81; Anchorage Fine Arts Mus, Alaska, 83; State Mus, Alaska, 83; and others. *Pos:* Bd govs, Nat Space Inst; adv comt, US Postal Serv. *Bibliog:* Joseph Roody (auth), Another Wyeth, Look Mag, 4/2/68; Wyeth Phenomenon (film), CBS TV, 69; Richard Meryman (auth), Wyeth Christmas, Life Mag, 12/17/71. *Mem:* Nat Acad Design; Am Watercolor Soc; Nat Endowment Arts. *Media:* Oil, Watercolor. *Mailing Add:* c/o Frank E Fowler PO Box 247 Lookout Mountain TN 37350

WYNGAARD, SUSAN ELIZABETH
LIBRARIAN
b Madison, Wis, Oct 16, 47. *Study:* Univ Wis, Madison, BA & MLS; Univ Per Stranieri, Siena, Italy, cert; Taos Valley Weaving Sch, with Kristina Wilson; Univ NMex. *Pos:* Assoc librn, Univ Calif, Santa Barbara, 74-79; libr, Fine Arts Libr, Ohio State Univ, currently. *Mem:* Art Libr Soc NAm. *Res:* Nineteenth century Italian photography. *Interests:* Collecting and indexing exhibition catalogs; history of photography. *Publ:* Coauth, Printed catalogues of the Art Exhibition Catalogue Collection of the Arts Library, Univ Calif, Santa Barbara, Somerset House, Cambridge, Eng & Teaneck, NJ, 77. *Mailing Add:* 429 W Eight Ave 900 East Ave Columbus OH 43201

WYNN, DONALD JAMES
PAINTER, LECTURER
b Brooklyn, NY, Sept 26, 42. *Study:* Pratt Inst, BFA, 67; Ind Univ, MFA, 69. *Exhib:* 22 Realists, Whitney Mus Am Art, 70; Michael C Rockefeller Arts Ctr, State Univ NY Cortland; one-man shows, Allentown Art Mus, Pa, 72, Artist's Space Gallery, New York, 74, Alpha Gallery, Boston, 75, Robert Schoelkopf Gallery, New York, 76 & Adirondack Mus, 78. *Awards:* Elizabeth T Greenshields Mem Found Grant, 70; Residence Grant, Fine Arts Work Ctr, Provincetown, 71; CAPS Grant, NY State Coun Arts, 75. *Bibliog:* Carter Ratcliff (auth), New York, Art Int Mag, 4/70; Gerritt Henry (auth), A realist twin bill, Art News Mag, 1/73; Judith Tannenbaum (auth), article, Arts Mag, 1/77. *Dealer:* A M Sachs 29 W 57th St New York NY 10019; Nina Freudenheim 560 Franklin St Buffalo NY 14202. *Mailing Add:* 2 Whitney St Norwood NY 13668

WYNNE, ALBERT GIVENS
PAINTER, CALLIGRAPHER
b Colorado Springs, Colo, Jan 3, 22. *Study:* Univ Denver; Iowa Wesleyan Col, BA; Univ Iowa, MA; also with S Carl Fracassini, Boardman Robinson, James Lechay & others. *Work:* Univ Denver & Univ Southern Colo; Rawlins Bank,

Wyo. *Comn:* Stained glass windows, Black Forest Colo Community Church, 81. *Exhib:* Walker Art Ctr; Corcoran Gallery Art; Denver Art Mus; Des Moines Art Ctr; Colorado Springs Fine Arts Ctr; Roswell Arts Ctr; Sioux City Art Ctr; Butler Inst Am Art; and others. *Teaching:* Hon instr, Univ Colo, Colorado Springs Fine Arts Ctr. *Awards:* Prizes, Des Moines Art Ctr, Roswell Art Ctr & Colorado Springs Fine Arts Ctr. *Media:* Oil, Watercolor. *Mailing Add:* 7420 Swan Rd Colorado Springs CO 80908

WYNNE, NANCY GRAVES
LIBRARIAN
b Ft Worth, Tex. *Study:* Univ Tex, Austin, BA; Tex Women's Univ, MLS, 67. *Pos:* Librn, Amon Carter Mus, 66- *Mem:* Art Libr Soc North Am; Col Art Asn. *Interests:* North American history and art. *Mailing Add:* PO Box 2365 Ft Worth TX 76113

WYRICK, CHARLES LLOYD, JR
MUSEUM DIRECTOR, EDITOR
b Greensboro, NC, May 5, 39. *Study:* Davidson Col, BA; Univ NC, MFA; Univ Mo. *Exhib:* Corcoran Biennial Exhib Am Painting, 67; Assoc Artists NC Ann, 68; Univ Va Print Exhib, 68; Va Mus Fine Arts; Weatherspoon Art Gallery; Carspecken-Scott Gallery. *Collections Arranged:* Art from the Ancient World, The Human Figure in Art, A Wyeth Portrait & Light as a Creative Medium, Va Mus Fine Arts, 66-68; Contemporary American Paintings from the Lewis Collection, Del Art Mus, 74; Louise Nevelson, Spoleto Festival USA, 83; and others. *Pos:* Artmobile coordr & asst head prog div, Va Mus Fine Arts, Richmond, 66-68; exec dir, Asn Preservation Va Antiq, 68-70; pres, Fine Arts Consults, Richmond, 71-73; art critic, Richmond News Leader, 71-73; dir, Del Art Mus, 73-79; dir, Gibbes Art Gallery, 80- *Teaching:* Instr, Stephens Col, 64-66. *Awards:* First for Column, Va Press Asn, 72. *Mem:* Am Asn Mus; Col Art Asn Am; Soc Archit Historians; Asn Art Mus Dirs; Victorian Soc Am. *Res:* Contemporary American painting; 18th to 20th century American architecture; 20th century American photography. *Publ:* Auth, Art & urban aesthetics (weekly column), Richmond News Leader; auth, A Wyeth Portrait, 67 & Contemporary Art at the Virginia Museum, 72, Arts in Va; auth, Richmond's 17th Street Market, 73; ed, Charles Fraser of Charleston, 83. *Mailing Add:* 135 Meeting St Charleston SC 29401

Y

YAFFA YAEL STEC-EL (HARRIET JEANNE STECKEL)
MURALIST, PRINTMAKER
b Scranton, Pa. *Study:* Univ Scranton, Pa, BS, 53; Hofstra Univ, New York, BFA, 72; Adelphi Univ, New York, MSA, 77. *Comn:* Mural, Providence Synagogue, Pa, 45; mural, B'nei Israel, Scranton, Pa, 46; mural, Los Judios de Mexico, 55; mural, Temple Emanuel, Great Neck, NY, 78. *Exhib:* Young Revelations, Burlington Mus, Eynon, Pa, 46 & Everhart Mus, Scranton, Pa, 47; Long Island Artists, Nassau Co Mus Fine Arts, Roslyn, NY, 76; Momentous Events in American History, Arts & Sci Mus, Nashua, NH, 81 & Bennington Mus, Vt, 81. *Pos:* Vpres, Newbridge Development Corp, Massapequa, NY, 80- *Awards:* First Place, Designers of the Future, Everhart Mus, 47; Participant Award, Parrish Art Mus, 58. *Bibliog:* Brent C Brolin (auth), Handbook of Architectural Ornament, Van Nostland Reinhold, 80-81. *Mem:* Nat Soc Mural Painters (asst treas, 80, treas, 81-82); Asn Int Arts Plastiques; Fine Arts Fedn New York; Long Island Printmakers Asn; Massapequa Art League (pres, 80-81). *Media:* Multimedia. *Mailing Add:* 43 Lincoln Ave Massapequa NY 11758

YAGHJIAN, EDMUND
PAINTER, INSTRUCTOR
b Harpoot, Armenia; US citizen. *Study:* RI Sch Design, BFA; Art Students League, with Stuart Davis. *Work:* New York Pub Libr; NY Univ; High Mus Art, Atlanta, Ga; Gibbes Art Mus, Charleston, SC; West Point Mus, NY; plus many others including over 500 in pvt collections. *Exhib:* New York World's Fair; San Francisco World's Fair; Carnegie Int, Pittsburgh, 36; Whitney Mus Am Art, New York, 40; Metrop Mus Art, New York, 41; 40 Year Retrospective, Univ SC, 72; Am Embassy, Jiddah, Saudi Arabia, 79; plus many other group & one-man shows. *Teaching:* Instr art, Art Students League, 38-42; guest instr painting, Univ Mo, 44-45; head dept art, Univ SC, 45-66, artist in residence, 66-72; instr painting, Columbia Mus Art, 72- *Awards:* Numerous prizes & awards in local & regional shows. *Mem:* Am Fedn Arts; Col Art Asn Am; Southeastern Col Art Asn (pres); life mem Art Students League; SC Artists Guild (pres & founder). *Media:* Acrylic. *Mailing Add:* 1510 Adger Rd Columbia SC 29205

YAJIMA, MICHIKO
DEALER
b Tokyo, Japan, Feb 27, 37; Japanese citizen. *Study:* Toyo-Eiwa Col, Tokyo, 57; New York Sch Interior Design, 59; Loyola Col, Montreal, photog with John Max, 69. *Pos:* Dir, Yajima/Galerie, Montreal, Que, 74- *Mem:* Int Photog Dealers Asn. *Specialty:* Contemporary Canadian art; 20th century photography. *Mailing Add:* Yajima/Galerie 307 Ste Catherine Way Suite 515 Montreal PQ H2X 2A3 Canada

YAMIN, STEVEN EDWARD
PRINTMAKER
b New York, NY, Apr 5, 46. *Study:* Olivet Col, BA, 68; Pratt Inst, MFA, 71. *Work:* Victoria & Albert Mus, London, Eng; Libr Congress,)Dll New York Pub Libr; Mary Armstrong Print Collection, Olivet Col, Mich; NJ State Mus, Trenton. *Exhib:* New Printmakers, Victoria & Albert Mus, London, Eng, 741 19th Nat Print Exhib, Brooklyn Mus, 75; 5th British Int, Bradford Mus, Eng, 75; 55th Soc Am Graphic Artists Nat, AAA Gallery, New York, 77; 12th Nat Print Exhib, Silvermine Guild, New Canaan, Conn, 78; 7th Int Miniature Print, Pratt Graphics Ctr, New York, 79; Sense of Scale III, Univ Albuquerque Mus, 79. *Collections Arranged:* Prints from Fitch-Febvrel Gallery, New York; Cantor-Lemberg, Birmingham, Mich. *Pos:* Guest instr, Pratt Graphics Ctr, New York, Feb-Mar 75 tech asst, Am Atelier, New York, 76- *Teaching:* Lectr printmaking, Brooklyn Col, 74-76; Pratt Manhattan Ctr, 81. *Awards:* Purchase Awards, 16th Ann Nat Print Exhib, Okla Art Ctr, Oklahoma City, 74 & Potsdam '78, State Univ NY Potsdam, 78; Graphic Chemical & Ink Co Award, 7th Miniatur, Print Exhib, 79. *Bibliog:* W A S Hatch (auth), The European Graphic Biennale. *Mem:* Print Club, Philadelphia; Exec Coun Soc Am Graphic Artists; Visual Artists & Galleries Asn. *Dealer:* Fitch-Febvrel Gallery 5 E 57th St New York NY 10022. *Mailing Add:* 3903 Ave I Brooklyn NY 11210

YANEFF, CHRIS
GALLERY DIRECTOR
b Toronto, Ont, May 18, 28. *Study:* Ont Col Art. *Pos:* Art dir, The Financial Post, 49-56; owner, pres & cur, Chris Yaneff Limited, 56- *Teaching:* Assoc prof, Fac Fine Arts, York Univ. *Mem:* Graphic Designers Can (pres Ont chap, 82-83); Royal Can Acad Arts (treas, 76-83); Arts & Lett Club; Art Dir Club, Toronto. *Specialty:* Canadian art, native art and French posters. *Collection:* Canadian art, French art, French posters, native art & European art. *Mailing Add:* 119 Isabella St Toronto ON M4Y 1P2 Canada

YANISH, ELIZABETH
SCULPTOR, LECTURER
b St Louis, Mo. *Study:* Wash Univ; Denver Univ; also with Frank Varra, Wilbur Verhelst, Edgar Brittor, Marian Buchan & Angelo DiBenedetto. *Work:* Tyler Mus, Tex; Colo State Bank, Denver, Martin-Marietta Co, Denver; Colo Womens Col; Ball State Col. *Comn:* Carved doors, eternal light, Menorah, BMH Synagogue, Denver, 72-74; complete interior, Har Ha Shem Congregation, Boulder, 74; Relief Tree (bronze), Beth Israel Hosp, Denver, 74; mem relief, Denver Gen Hosp, 75. *Exhib:* Denver Art Mus Exhib, 61-75 & Western Ann, 65; Midwest Biennial, Joslyn Mus, Omaha, Nebr, 68; Int Exhib, Lucca, Italy, 71; one-man show, Woodstock Gallery, London, Eng, 73; Artrain, Mich Fine Arts Coun, 74. *Pos:* Trustee, Denver Ctr Performing Arts, 73-75; chmn, Visual Arts Festival, Bicentennial, 74-75; bd educ, Arts in Elem Educ, 77-78. *Teaching:* Lectr contemp sculpture, var cols & univs. *Awards:* Purchase Award Golden Web, Colo Women's Col, 63; McCormick Award, Ball State Univ, 64; Purchase Award, Tyler Mus, Tex, 65. *Bibliog:* Article in Artforum, 63; Jim Mills (auth), var feature stories, Denver Post Art Ed, 64-75; John Manson (auth), Artists of the Rockies, 74. *Mem:* Artists Equity Asn (pres, 63); Rocky Mountain Liturgical Arts; Allied Sculptors Colo; Denver Coun Arts (pres, 73-75); Colo Artists Equity Asn (pres, 79-80). *Media:* Welded Steel, Bronze. *Mailing Add:* 131 Fairfax Denver CO 80220

YANOFF, ARTHUR (SAMUEL)
PAINTER
b Boston, Mass, May 9, 39. *Study:* Mus Sch Fine Arts, Boston, 58-61; studied with Jason Berger, 62-65. *Work:* Mus Fine Arts, Boston; Addison Gallery Am Art; Hampshire Col; Babson Col; NH Savings Bank, Concord. *Comn:* Portrait Gil Williams, Bellevue Gallery, Binghamton, NY, 73; charcoal studies, NH Composition, Concord, 74 & Mrs Gereard Derepentigny, Manchester, NH, 74. *Exhib:* Collectors Show, Va Mus Fine Arts, 70; Direct Vision, Fitchburg Art Mus, Mass, 73 & Hilles Gallery, Harvard Univ, 76; Drawings from Holst's Sculpture, Addison Gallery Am Art, 74; Inaugural Show, Gallery Naga, Boston, 77; New Watercolors, Barridoff Galleries, Portland, Maine, 78; solo exhib, Mus Fine Arts, Boston, 83; Smokestacks & Recent Paintings, Babson Col Gallery, 83. *Awards:* Direct Vision Exhib Awards, Mass Coun Arts, 73 & 75; Purchase Prize, NH Bicentennial, 75. *Bibliog:* Edgar S Driscoll (auth), A nice feeling, Art News, 74; Joanne Silver (auth), A universe of color, Concord Monitor, 83; Richard Fischer (producer), Profile of Arthur Yanoff, NH Pub TV, 83. *Mem:* Boston Painters & Sculptors; NH Art Asn; Am Art Therapy Asn. *Media:* Oil, Watercolor. *Publ:* Illusr, Broken Syllables, 67 & Waiting to Freeze, 69, Lillabulero Press; auth, The paste-up autobiography: Collage in the treatment of disturbed adolescents, Am J Art Therapy, 73; illusr, Raw Honey, Alice James Books, 75. *Dealer:* Harcus Gallery 7 Newbury Boston MA 02116. *Mailing Add:* 1 Appleton RR10 Box 441 Concord NH 03301

YANOW, RHODA MAE
PAINTER, ILLUSTRATOR
b Newark, NJ. *Study:* Newark Arts Club; Parsons Sch Design; Newark Sch Fine & Indust Arts; Heritage Art Sch; Nat Acad Design, with Henry Gasser, Daniel Greene, Harvey Dinnerstein & John Grabach. *Work:* West Orange Home for Senior Citizens, NJ; Newark Pub Libr; Meadowlands Sport Arena. *Exhib:* Nat Arts Club Pastel Show, 74; Muhlenberg Col Festival of Arts, 75; Am Artists Prof League Grand Nat Exhib, 75; Salmagundi Club Watercolor Show, 75; Nat Acad Design, 78-80. *Teaching:* Instr pastel painting & life drawing, Du Cret Sch Arts. *Awards:* Anna Hyatt Huntington Silver Medal, 77; Catharine Lorillard Wolf Art Club Gold Medal, 77; Medal of Honor, Nat Asn Women Artists, 83. *Bibliog:* Ruthann Williams (auth), Graven images, NJ Music & Arts, 6/74. *Mem:* Am Artists Prof League; Nat Asn Women

Artists; Catharine Lorillard Wolfe Art Club; Salmagundi Club; Pastel Soc Am (corresp secy, 75). *Media:* Pastels, Pen & Ink; Lithography. *Publ:* Contribr & illusr, NJ Music & Arts, 74 & 75; contribr, Star Ledger & other local newspapers. *Dealer:* Hait Gallery 2A Inwood Pl Maplewood NJ 07040. *Mailing Add:* 12 Korwel Circle West Orange NJ 07052

YARBOROUGH, CHRISTINE TROUTMAN
CRAFTSMAN, DESIGNER
b Statesville, NC, May 13, 25. *Study:* Brenau Col, Gainesville, Ga, Dipl, 47; Arrowmont Sch Arts & Crafts, Tenn, 73-80; Univ NC, Greensboro. *Work:* NC Mus Art & NC Archives Hist Mus, Raleigh; Mint Mus Art & IBM, Charlotte, NC; Atlanta Art Festival, Ga. *Comn:* Batik wall hanging, NC Nat Bank, Winston-Salem; 30 batik panels, NC Nat Bank, Int Dept, Charlotte, NC; transparancies, Old Salem Inc, NC; batik wall hangings & canvas construction, R J Reynolds Tobacco Co, Winston-Salem, NC. *Exhib:* Piedmont Crafts, Mint Mus Art, Charlotte, NC, 73; Crafts Invitational, Southeastern Ctr Contemp Art, Winston-Salem, NC, 73-81; Opening Exhib, Greenwood Gallery, Washington, DC, 79; NC Artist Exhib, NC Mus Art, Raleigh, 79; The Fan, Arrowmont Gallery, Gatlinburg, Tenn, 81; The Box, Arrowmont Gallery, Gatlinburg, Tenn, 81. *Teaching:* Instr bookbinding, Arrowmont Sch Arts & Crafts, 79-81, instr papermaking & bookbinding, 79-82; instr bookbinding, Montgomery Col, Silver Springs, Md, 79. *Awards:* Bronze Medal Award, NC Arts Soc, 79. *Bibliog:* Craft Horizons, Am Crafts Coun, 73; Shirley E Held (auth), Weaving--A Handbook of Fiber Arts, Holt Rinehart, 78; Majorie Elliott Beulin (auth), Design Through Discovery, Holt Rinehart, 78. *Mem:* Am Crafts Coun; Piedmont Craftsmen; Arts & Crafts Asn, Sawtooth Ctr Visual Design (bd mem, 79-82). *Media:* Mixed Media; Leather, Copper. *Mailing Add:* 1311 Brookstown Ave Winston-Salem NC 27101

YARBROUGH, LEILA KEPERT
PRINTMAKER, PAINTER
b Katoomba, NSW, Australia, Mar 23, 32; US citizen. *Study:* Univ Fla; Atlanta Col Art, Ga. *Work:* Chrysler Mus, Norfolk, Va; Augusta Mus Art, Ga; Agnes Scott Col, Decatur, Ga; Loch Haven Art Ctr, Orlando, Fla. *Exhib:* Eastern US Drawing Competition, Cummer Gallery of Art, Jacksonville, Fla, 70; Contemporary American Drawing V: Norfolk, Smithsonian Inst Travel Exhib, 71-73; 34th Ann Contemp Am Painting, Soc of Four Arts, Palm Beach, Fla, 72; 1st Nat Monoprint/Monotype, Oglethorpe Univ, Atlanta, Ga, 73; 64th Ann, Conn Acad Fine Arts, Hartford, 74; Am Drawings, Portsmouth Community Art Ctr, Va, 76; 12th Nat Print Exhib, Silvermine Guild Artists, New Caanan, Conn, 77; plus others. *Teaching:* Instr printmaking workshop, Yarbrough Studio, 75. *Awards:* Am Drawing Purchase Award, Norfolk Mus, 71; First Prize, The Single Impression, Oglethorpe Univ, Atlanta, 73; Great Smoky Mts Nat Park Purchase Award, US Govt Art Purchase Prog, 74. *Bibliog:* Martin Sharter (auth), Art, Atlanta Mag, 12/73. *Mem:* Philadelphia Print Club. *Media:* Intaglio, Monoprints; Mixed. *Dealer:* Artist's Assoc Inc 3261 Roswell Rd NE Atlanta GA 30305. *Mailing Add:* 4061 Arden Way NE Atlanta GA 30342

YARD, SALLY ELIZABETH
HISTORIAN, CURATOR
b Trenton, NJ, Sept 24, 51. *Study:* Harvard Univ, Cambridge, Mass, AB, 73; Princeton Univ, NJ, MFA, 75, PhD, 80. *Collections Arranged:* Christo: Oceanfront (auth, catalog), Princeton Univ, 75; John Roy, Christopher Sproat (auth, catalog), Vincent Smith Art Mus, 78; Images of the Self (auth, catalog), Hampshire Col Gallery, 79; A Sense of Place--The American Landscape in Recent Art (auth, catalog), Hampshire Col Gallery, 80; Landscapes in Recent Painting (auth, catalog), Mus Fine Arts, Springfield, Mass, 81. *Pos:* Acting cur, Univ Gallery, Univ Mass, Amherst, 80. *Teaching:* Instr mod art, Mt Holyoke Col, Mass, 78-79, lectr mod art, 80-81, asst prof mod art, 81-83; vis asst prof mod art, Amherst Col, Mass, 81-83. *Mem:* Col Art Asn. *Res:* Abstract expressionism, especially Willem deKooning; contemporary painting & sculpture. *Publ:* Coauth, Gregory Gillespie: The timeless mystery of art, 77, auth, Willem deKooning's women, 78 & auth, Willem deKooning's men, 81, Arts Mag; coauth, George Traklas: Log Mass: Mass Curve, Univ Mass, Amherst, 80. *Mailing Add:* 2758 Bordeaux Ave La Jolla CA 92037

YASKO, CARYL ANNE
MURALIST, PAINTER
b Racine, Wis, Mar 11, 41. *Study:* Dominican Col, Wis, sculpture with Monica Gabriel & painting with Branislov Bak, grad, 63. *Comn:* Nat Endowment Arts murals, Health of the People, Chicago, 73, I Am the People, Chicago, 74, Razen, Chicago, 75 & Prescription for Good Health Care, Chicago, 75; Lemont Bicentennial Mural, Lemont Hist Soc Bicentennial Comn, 75; and others. *Exhib:* On Chicago Walls, Chicago State Univ, 74; Civic Sculpture, Appleton, Neenah & Menasha, Wis, 77; Levi Strauss & Co, Europ Exhib of US Murals, Mus Royal d'Art, Ancien, Brussels, 78; Chicago, The City & Its Artists, 1945-1978, Univ Mich, Ann Arbor, 78; French Ministry Foreign Affairs, traveling exhib, Caen, Normandy, 81; and others. *Teaching:* Instr, Cove Sch, Racine, Wis, 57-63; lectr murals, Loop Jr Col, Valparaiso Univ, Art Inst Chicago & Cherokee Lane Elem Sch, Adelphi, Md, 72-; instr, Art Inst Chicago, 75 & 76, Oakton Community Col, Morton Grove, Ill, 77 & Carthage Col, 81- *Awards:* Chicago Beautiful Award, Mayor Daley, 75 & 76. *Mem:* Chicago Mural Group. *Media:* Oil, Watercolor. *Publ:* Contribr, Art Workers News, 73, New Art Examr, 74 & 80 & Nat Murals Newsletter, 78. *Mailing Add:* 136 Whiton St Whitewater WI 53190

YASSIN, ROBERT ALAN
MUSEUM DIRECTOR, HISTORIAN
b Malden, Mass, May 22, 41. *Study:* Dartmouth Col, BA, 62; Univ Mich, Ann Arbor, MA(hist art), 65, Samuel H Kress Found fel, 68-70; Yale Univ, Ford fel, 66-68. *Collections Arranged:* Contemporary Art at Yale, 66-68, Art & the Excited Spirit (with catalog), 72; Helen W & Robert M Benjamin Collection, Yale Univ, 67, American Art from Alumni Collections, 68; Victor Higgins Retrospective (with catalog), 75; Harrison Eiteljorg Collection of Western American Art, 76; Leonard Baskin, 76; Painting & Sculpture Today, 76, 78 & 80; Art in Bus Collections, 77; Ind Artists Show, 77-79, 81 & 83; Enrico Baj, 78; George Carlson, 79; Sasson Soffer Sculpture, 81-82, Indianapolis Mus Art. *Pos:* Ed, Yale Univ Art Gallery Bull, 66-68; asst dir, Mus Art, Univ Mich, Ann Arbor, 70-72, ed, Art Bull, 70-73, assoc dir & actg dir, Mus, 73; chief cur, Indianapolis Mus Art, 73-75, actg dir, 75, dir, 75- *Teaching:* Instr graphic arts & mus practice & co-dir joint mus training prog, Univ Mich, Ann Arbor, 70-73; adj prof, Herron Sch of Art, Ind Univ-Purdue Univ, Indianapolis, 76- *Mem:* Col Art Asn Am; Am Asn Mus; Asn Art Mus Dir; Nat Trust Hist Preservation; Int Mus Conserv Asn (chmn exec comt, 77-79); Midwest Mus Asn. *Res:* Late 19th and 20th century American art; 19th century British painting. *Mailing Add:* 1200 W 38th St Indianapolis IN 46208

YASUDA, ROBERT
PAINTER
b Lihue, Kauai, Hawaii, Nov 14, 40. *Study:* Pratt Inst, BFA, 62, MFA, 64. *Work:* Brooklyn Mus, NY; Libr Cong, Washington, DC. *Exhib:* Albright-Knox Art Gallery, Buffalo, NY, 75; Arte Ficra 77, Bologna, Italy, 77; 35th Biennial Corcoran Gallery Art, Washington, DC, 77; Painting & Sculpture Today, Indianapolis Mus Art, 78; Galarie December, Dusseldorf, WGer, 79; Ind Univ, Bloomington, 79; Installation, Mus Contemp Art, Chicago, 79; Otis Art Inst, 79; and others. *Media:* Acrylic, Oil. *Dealer:* Betty Parsons Gallery 24 W 57th St New York NY 10019. *Mailing Add:* 429 W Broadway New York NY 10012

YATER, GEORGE DAVID
PAINTER
b Madison, Ind, Nov 30, 10. *Study:* John Herron Art Sch, 28-32, dipl; Cape Sch Art, Provincetown, with Henry Hensche, summers 31-34; also with Edwin Dickinson & Richard Miller. *Work:* Chrysler Collection, Norfolk Art Gallery, Va; Ford Motor Co, Dearborn, Mich; Paper Mill Playhouse, Millburn, NJ; Ind Univ, Bloomington; Arch Am Art, Smithsonian Inst, Washington, DC. *Comn:* Mural, Provincetown-Boston Airline, Provincetown Airport, 76. *Exhib:* Nat Acad Design, New York; Pa Acad Fine Arts, Philadelphia; Indianapolis Mus Art; Chrysler Art Mus, Provincetown, Mass; Provincetown Painters 1890s-1970s, Everson Mus of Art, Syracuse, NY & Provincetown Art Asn & Mus, Provincetown, Mass, 77. *Awards:* Outstanding Oil, Hoosier Salon, Indianapolis, 54; First Prize for Oil, Falmouth Artists Guild, 61, 69 & 75. *Bibliog:* Robert Hatch (auth), At the tip of Cape Cod, Horizon Mag, 61. *Media:* Oil, Watercolor. *Mailing Add:* Castle Rd Truro MA 02666

YATES, MARVIN CLARENCE
PAINTER, INSTRUCTOR
b Jackson, Tenn, Sept 22, 43. *Study:* Memphis Acad Art, BFA, 66. *Exhib:* Am Watercolor Soc, Nat Acad Gallery, New York, 73-79; Watercolor USA, Springfield Art Mus, Mo, 75 & 76; Mainstreams, Grover Hermann Mus, Marietta, Ohio, 76; Southern Watercolor Soc, Cheekwood Gallery, Nashville, 77-79; Rocky Mountain Nat Water Media, Foothills Art Ctr, Golden, Colo, 78; Real Show, Grand Cent Art Gallery, New York, 79. *Teaching:* Instr watercolor, Memphis State Univ, 75- *Awards:* Rechenbach Award, Rechenbach Gallery, 73 & 80; Washington Sch of Art Award, 74; Second Place Watercolor, Sterling Regal Inc, 79. *Bibliog:* Susan Meyer (auth), Watercolor Page, Am Artist Mag, 75; Ralph Fabri (auth), Watercolor Page, Today's Art, 75. *Mem:* Am Watercolor Soc; Southern Watercolor Soc; Tenn Watercolor Soc; Memphis Watercolor Group. *Media:* Watercolor, Pencil. *Publ:* Contribr, 40 Watercolorists and How They Work, Watson-Guptill, 76. *Mailing Add:* 2261 Montego Dr Cordova TN 38018

YATES, STEVEN A
PHOTOGRAPHER, CURATOR
b Chicago, Ill. *Study:* Univ Nebr, BFA, 72; Univ NMex, with Beaumont Newhall & Van Deren Coke, MA, 74, MFA(Ford Found Fel), 78. *Work:* San Francisco Mus Mod Art, Calif; Univ Art Mus, Univ NMex; Sheldon Mem Art Gallery, Nebr; Los Angeles Ctr Photog Studies; and pvt collections. *Exhib:* One-man exhib, Sheldon Mem Art Gallery, Nebr, 78; Altered Landscape, Fine Arts Gallery, Fla Sch Arts, 78; Perception: Field of View, Los Angeles Ctr Photog, Calif, 79; US Eye, US Olympics Traveling Exhib, 80-; San Francisco Mus Mod Art, 80 & 81; Contemp Photoworks, Downtown Ctr Arts, NMex, 81; Color: Surface Fabrications, Cabrillo Col, Calif, 82; Ranchos de Taos, A Photographic History, Sheldon Mem Art Gallery Traveling Exhib, 82-83. *Pos:* Cur asst, Sheldon Mem Art Gallery, Univ Nebr, 72-73; cur asst, Univ Art Mus, Univ NMex, 73-75; cur photog, prints & drawings, Mus Fine Arts, Mus NMex, 80- *Teaching:* Instr part-time, Univ NMex, Albuquerque, 75-78; vis instr, Pomona Col, Claremont Col, 76-; vis instr, Art Exten Prog, Univ Calif, Los Angeles, summer 76. *Awards:* Exhib Award, Los Angeles Ctr Photog Studies, 79; Exhib Award, Diablo Valley Col, 79; Photog Fel, Nat Endowment Arts, 80. *Res:* Rauschenberg & contemporary photography's reciprocal influences. *Publ:* Auth, Negative/Positive at Ranchos Church: Notes on a broadining definition of photography, Artspace Mag, winter 82-83. *Mailing Add:* c/o Mus Fine Arts PO Box 2087 Santa Fe NM 87503

YAWORSKI, ALEX F(RANCIS)
PAINTER
b Odessa, Russia, Dec 29, 07; US citizen. *Study:* Am Acad Art, 30-31. *Work:* Tweed Mus Art; Charles and Emma Frye Mus, Seattle, Wash; Watercolor USA, Springfield, Mo; Springfield Mus, Ill; Union League of Chicago. *Comn:* Series of Paintings, Chicago Tribune, Ill, 78; Series of Cityscapes, Amoco. *Exhib:* Artists Chicago & Vicinity, Art Inst Chicago, 46-52; Am Watercolor Soc Ann, Nat Acad Galleries, New York, 53-81; Watercolor USA Ann, Springfield Art Mus, Mo, 62, 63, 68, 69, 72 & 75; 200 Years of Watercolor, Metrop Mus Art, New York, 66-67. *Pos:* Com & ed art, Chicago Tribune, 32; art dir, Poster Products Inc, Chicago, 34-43; art direction & fine arts painting, 43-. *Awards:* Purchase Award, Watercolor USA Ann, Springfield Art Mus, 69; Award Excellence, Ann Exhib Ill Watercolor Soc, 83; Gold Medal, Adirondacks Nat Exhib Am Watercolors, 83. *Mem:* Am Watercolor Soc (vpres, 72-73); fel Int Inst Arts & Letters; honorary mem Artists Guild Chicago (pres, 47-48); Nat Soc Painters in Casein & Acrylics; Midwest Watercolor Soc, Chicago (bd mem, 79-). *Media:* Watercolor. *Publ:* Auth, Acrylic Watercolor Painting, 70 & coauth (with Susan E Meyer & Norman Kent), Watercolorists at Work, 72, Watson Guptill; auth, The watercolor page, 51 & Alex F Yaworski Artist's Guild of Chicago sketch trip, 55, Am Artist Mag. *Mailing Add:* 7527 N Ridge Blvd Chicago IL 60645

YEGUL, FIKRET KUTLU
EDUCATOR, ARCHITECT
b Themiscyra, Turkey, Oct 27, 41. *Study:* Middle East Technical Univ, BA(archit), 64; Univ Pa, MA(archit), 66; Harvard Univ, PhD(art hist), 75. *Exhib:* Mamluk Architecture of Cairo (photographs), Fogg Art Mus, 74. *Teaching:* Asst prof art hist, Wellesley Col, 75-76; asst prof, Univ Calif, Santa Barbara, 76-82; assoc prof, 82- *Mem:* Sardis Archaeol Expedition; Am Inst Archaeol. *Res:* Roman art and architecture. *Publ:* Auth, Early Byzantine capitals from Sardis, Doaks Papers, Vol 28, 74; auth, The marble court of Sardis and historical reconstruction, J Field Archaeol, Vol 32, 76; auth, A reconstruction study of Lucian's Baths of Hippias, Archaeol Classica, Vol 31, 79; auth, Kaisersaal and the Imperial Cult, Art Bulletin, 3/82; auth, Bath-Gymnasium Complex in Sardis (Report 3), Harvard Univ, 84. *Mailing Add:* Art Hist Dept Univ Calif Santa Barbara CA 93106

YEH, CAROL
PRINTMAKER
b Lackawanna, NY, Dec 25, 38. *Study:* Yale Univ Summer Sch, Norfolk, Conn; Smith Col, Northampton, Mass, with Leonard Baskin, BA, 61; Acad de la Grande Chaumiere, Paris, France; Univ Iowa, Iowa City, with Mauricio Lasansky, MA, 66; Acad de Bellas Artes, San Fernando, Madrid, Spain. *Work:* Ohio Univ Art Mus, Athens; New York Pub Libr; Everson Mus Art, Syracuse, NY; Harvard Univ Libr, Cambridge; Yale Univ Libr, New Haven. *Exhib:* Am Drawing Biennial XXI, Norfolk Mus Arts & Sci, Va, 65; Smithsonian Inst Travel Am Drawings, 65-66; Northwest Printmakers, 37th Int, Seattle, Wash, & Portland, Ore, 66; two-man show, Drawings, Fleischer Anhalt Gallery, Los Angeles, 69; one-woman shows, Prints & Drawings, Houghton House, Geneva, NY, 75 & Prints, Everson Mus, Syracuse, NY, 77; and others. *Teaching:* Vis instr art drawing & printmaking, Eisenhower Col, 78. *Awards:* Fulbright Grant, 66; Yaddo Fel, 72; MacDowell Colony Fel, 72. *Media:* Intaglio. *Publ:* Auth & illusr, Etched Portraits of Ernest Hemingway, 61; illusr, Red Flower, 61; auth & illusr, Houdini, 71; illusr, Ragtime, 76; illusr, Hawthorne, 77. *Dealer:* Zeitlin & Ver Brugge 815 N La Cienega Los Angeles CA 90025. *Mailing Add:* Box 11 Fayette NY 13065

YEKTAI, MANOUCHER
PAINTER
b Tehran, Iran, Dec 22, 22; US citizen. *Study:* Univ Tehran; Ecole Superior Beaux Arts, Paris, with Auzenfant, 45-47; Art Students League, 47-48. *Work:* Baltimore Mus Art, Md; Mus Mod Art, New York; Everson Mus, Syracuse, NY; Hirshhorn Mus, Washington, DC; and others. *Exhib:* Gumps Gallery, San Francisco, 59, 64 & 65; Piccadilly Gallery, London, 61 & 70; Anderson-Meyer Gallery, Paris, 62; Mus Mod Art, 62; Art Inst Chicago, 63; Gertrude Kasle Gallery, Detroit, 65-70; Benson Gallery, Bridgehampton, NY, 67, 72, 73 & 75; and others. *Media:* Oil. *Mailing Add:* 225 W 86th St New York NY 10024

YENAWINE, BRUCE HARLEY
ADMINISTRATOR, EDUCATOR
b Urbana, Ill, Dec 30, 49. *Study:* Univ Louisville, Ky, BA & MA. *Pos:* Assoc dir, Louisville Sch of Art, 73-74; dir, 74- *Teaching:* Lectr, Louisville Sch Art, Ky, 77- *Awards:* Cardinal Award, Univ Louisville, 72; Outstanding contribr to arts, Art Ctr Asn, 74. *Mem:* Nat Asn Sch Art; Nat Soc Arts & Lit; Ky Art Educ Asn; Ky Asn Mus. *Publ:* Contribr, Anchorage Revisited, Libr Nat, 76. *Mailing Add:* 806 E Chestnut St Louisville KY 40204

YES, PHYLLIS A
PAINTER, SCULPTOR
b Red Wing, Minn, May 15, 41. *Study:* Luther Col, BA, 63; Univ Minn, MFA, 68; Univ Ore, PhD, 78. *Work:* Univ Ore Mus Art, Eugene; Whitworth Col Art Gallery, Spokane, Wash. *Exhib:* Seattle Art Mus, 76 & 77; Laguna Gloria Art Mus, Austin, 81; P M & Stein Gallery, New York, 82; Boca Raton Mus Art, Fla, 83; Loch Haven Art Ctr, Orlando, 83; Mississippi Mus Art, Jackson, 83. *Teaching:* Asst prof, Ore State Univ, 76-79; assoc prof, Lewis & Clark Col, 79- *Awards:* Jurors Awards, Richard Paulin, 77, Int Banners Show, 77 & State Ore, 77. *Bibliog:* Mike Walsh (auth), Taking risks, Artweek, 2/77; Jalaine Madura (auth), An artist's career: A new stage, Oregonian Newspaper, 79; Delores Tarzan (auth), Yes treats lace beautifully, Seattle Times, 2/80. *Mem:* Artists Equity Asn; Col Art Asn Am; Portland Ctr Visual Arts; Women's Caucus Arts; Contemp Arts Coun. *Media:* Acrylic, Mixed. *Dealer:* Bernice Steinbaum Gallery 903 Madison Ave New York NY 10021. *Mailing Add:* 5235 View Point Terrace Portland OR 97201

YIANNES (IORDANIDES)
SCULPTOR, CERAMIST
b Athens, Greece, Dec 16, 43. *Study:* Umanitaria Art Inst, Milan, Italy, scholar, 62; Brooklyn Mus Art Sch, scholar, 67-70; Max Beckmann scholar, 71-72. *Exhib:* NY Univ, 70 & 77; Brooklyn Mus, 71; Brockton Art Ctr, 72; Whitney Mus Am Art Clay Exhib, 74; Long Beach Mus Art, 77; Alfred Univ, 79; plus others. *Teaching:* Instr ceramics, Queens Col, summer 70; instr ceramics, Brooklyn Mus Art Sch, 70-; instr ceramics, Brooklyn Col, 72- *Awards:* First Prize in Ceramics, Alfred Parker, 69. *Bibliog:* Serry Suris (auth), Brooklyn Museum, 12/72, Craft Horizons; cover of Ramparts Mag, 5/71; Lisa Hammel (auth), article, New York Times, 3/77. *Mem:* Am & World Craft Couns. *Media:* Clay. *Mailing Add:* c/o Allan Stone Gallery 48 E 86 St New York NY 10028

YOAKUM, DEL
PAINTER, DESIGNER
b St Joseph, Mo, Dec 6, 15. *Study:* Chouinard Art Inst & Jepson Art Inst, Los Angeles; Kansas City Art Inst; Univ Southern Calif. *Work:* Butler Inst Am Art, Youngstown, Ohio; San Diego Art Mus, Calif; Nat Watercolor Soc; Coventry Cathedral, England; Glendale Savings & Loan, Calif; and many others. *Exhib:* Los Angeles Co Mus Art, Calif, 47-58; Butler Inst Am Art, 53-83; Nat Watercolor Soc, Los Angeles, 54-82; Watercolor USA, Springfield, Mo, 66-74; Nat Acad Design, New York, 70; one-man shows, Robert Garelick Gallery, Scottsdale, Ariz, 78 & Sedona Art Ctr, 80; Zaner Galleries, Rochester, NY, 81; and others. *Pos:* Scenic artist, Motion Picture Studios, Hollywood, Calif, 52-72. *Teaching:* Instr art, Sedona, Ariz. *Awards:* Best of Show, City of Avalon, Calif, 67; John Marin Mem Award, Watercolor USA, 71; Best Painting Award, Ariz State Fair, 81. *Mem:* Nat Watercolor Soc; hon life mem Inglewood Art League; Sedona Arts Ctr; Nat Soc Lit & Arts. *Media:* Oil, Watercolor. *Publ:* Contribr, Ariz Highways Mag, 81. *Dealer:* Masters Gallery Sedona AZ 86336. *Mailing Add:* PO Box 149 Sedona AZ 86336

YOCHIM, LOUISE DUNN
PAINTER, WRITER
b Jitomir, Ukraine, July 18, 09; US citizen. *Study:* Art Inst Chicago, cert, 32, BAE, 42, MAE, 52; Univ Chicago, 56. *Work:* Ill State Mus, Springfield; Eilat Mus, Israel; Health Clinic, Lawrence, Kans; Congregation Agudath Jacob & St Lukes Presby Hospital, Chicago. *Exhib:* One-woman show, Northeastern Ill Univ, 72 & Spertus Mus, Chicago, 79-83; Mus Sci & Industry, Chicago, 82; Ill State Mus, Springfield, 83; Grove Gallery, Evanston, Ill, 83; and others. *Pos:* Art supvr, Chicago Pub Schs, 50-71; consult art, elem & high schs, 71-74; Rand McNally Publ, 67- & Encycl Britannica, 68- *Teaching:* Instr art, Chicago Pub High Sch, Ill, 34-50, Chicago Acad Fine Arts, 51-52 & Chicago Teachers Col, 60-61. *Awards:* Todros Geller Award for Painting, Am Jewish Arts Club, 48-61; Award, Chicago Soc Artists, 53 & 78; Medal Merit, Accad Ital Arti Lavore, 83. *Bibliog:* Frank Holland (auth), Renaissance unit's show to cap season, Chicago Sun Times, 57; Doris Lane Butler (auth), Winnetka to open art fair season, Chicago Daily News, 57; Frank Getlein (auth), Associated artists, Sunday Star, Washington, DC, 62. *Mem:* Chicago Soc Artists (pres, 72-82); Artists Equity Asn; Nat Art Educ Asn; Nat Comt Art Educ; Artists Coalition. *Media:* Oil, Mixed Media. *Publ:* Auth, Building Human Relationships Through Art, 54; auth, Perceptual Growth in Creativity, 67; auth, Art in Action, 69; auth, Role & Impact: The Chicago Society of Artists, 79; articles on painters and sculptors, Sentinel Mag, 81- *Dealer:* Four Arts Gallery 1629 Oak Ave Evanston IL 60203. *Mailing Add:* 9545 Drake Ave Evanston IL 60203

YODER, RICHARD ALLEN
PAINTER, CONCEPTUAL ARTIST
b Mobile, Ala, Dec 16, 47. *Study:* Univ Ore, BFA, 74; Univ Wash, MFA, 76. *Work:* Seattle Art Mus; Bremerton Pub Libr Gallery, Wash; Am Tel & Tel, Chicago; Chase Manhattan Bank, New York; Manoogian, Minneapolis. *Exhib:* Northwest Artists Ann, Seattle Art Mus, 73 & 74; Artists of Oregon, Portland Art Mus, 75; Northwest Artists Today, Seattle Art Mus, 76; In Touch: Nature, Ritual & Sensuous Art, Portland Ctr Visual Arts, 76; The Reality of Illusion, Johnson Mus, Cornell Univ, Denver Art Mus, Univ Southern Calif Art Galleries & Univ Tex, Austin, 79-81; Radical Realism, Muhlenburg Col Art Galleries, 80. *Teaching:* Vis lectr painting, Univ Wash, Seattle, 76; instr painting & drawing, Cornish Inst Allied Arts, Seattle, 76-78. *Bibliog:* Donald Brewer (auth), The Reality of Illusion, Quaker Hill Press, 80. *Mem:* Col Art Asn Am. *Media:* Oil on Linen. *Dealer:* Trompe L'Oeil Ltd 24 E 81st St New York NY 10028. *Mailing Add:* 640 Broadway New York NY 10012

YOKOI, RITA
SCULPTOR, PAINTER
b New York, NY, Aug 26, 38. *Study:* Alfred NY State Col Ceramics, Alfred Univ, 56-59; San Francisco Art Inst, Agnes Brandenstein Mem Scholar, BFA(with hon), 61; Tokyo Univ of Art, Japan, Fulbright Fel Ceramics, 62-63; Univ Calif Berkeley, MA(art & sculpture), 70. *Exhib:* Young Americans, Mus Contemp Crafts, New York, 62; M H DeYoung Mem Mus, San Francisco, 68; Downtown Dog Show, DeYoung Mus Downtown Ctr, San Francisco, 77; one-artist show, Kirk de Gooyer Gallery, Los Angeles, 81; From Pink to Violet, Santa Barbara Arts Forum, Calif, 81; vis artist exhib, Md Inst, Col Art, Baltimore, 81; Elegant Night, Security Pac Bank, Los Angeles, Calif, 81; Los Angeles Times, San Diego State Univ Gallery, Calif, 82; and many others. *Teaching:* Lectr sculpture, Calif State Univ, Fresno, 71-73; instr design & advert to grad students, Otis Art Inst, 73-75; lectr sculpture, Univ Calif, Los Angeles, 73-75; asst prof art, Mt St Mary's Col, 75-76; adj fac mem, Antioch Col-W, Los Angeles, fall 76; vis artist, Claremont Grad Sch, spring 78; part-

time lectr, Calif State Univ, Long Beach, 78, instr painting, Otis Parsons, Los Angeles, 81-; instr intro to archit, Calif Polytechnic Inst, 83. *Awards:* Acad Yr Res grant, Univ Calif, Los Angeles, 74-75; Nat Endowment Arts, 81; and others. *Bibliog:* Melinda Wortz (auth), rev, Art News, 9/80; Peter Selz & Carol Schmmering (auths), Actual symposium, Arts, 9/81; Christopher French (auth), Spaces for solitude, Artweek, 10/22/83; and others. *Media:* Mixed. *Publ:* Contribr intro to catalog, Women's Month Group Show, Calif State Univ, Fresno, 3/73; contribr, Women's Studies in Art and Art History, Col Art Asn of Am, 1/74; and others. *Mailing Add:* 4577 S Centinela Ave Los Angeles CA 90066

YOKOMI, RICHARD KOJI
PAINTER
b Denver, Colo, Mar 12, 44. *Study:* Chouinard Art Inst, BS, 65. *Work:* Pasadena Art Mus, Calif. *Exhib:* USA West Coast, Kunstverein, Hamburg, WGer, 72; Calif State Painting Traveling Exhib, 72-73; 15 Abstract Artists--Los Angeles, Santa Barbara Mus, 74; Painting & Sculpture in Calif, The Mod Era, San Francisco Mus Mod Art, 76 & Smithsonian Inst, Washington, DC, 77. *Dealer:* Nickolas Wilder Gallery 8225 1/2 Santa Monica Blvd Los Angeles CA 90046. *Mailing Add:* 3666 Division St Los Angeles CA 90065

YOSHIDA, RAY KAKUO
PAINTER, EDUCATOR
b Kapaa, Kauai, Hawaii, Oct 3, 30. *Study:* Art Inst Chicago, BA, 53; Syracuse Univ, MFA, 58; Univ Chicago; Univ Hawaii; also with A D Reinhardt. *Work:* Everson Mus, Syracuse, NY; Art Inst Chicago; Mus des 20, Jahrhunderts, Vienna; Am Tel & Tel, New York; Ball State Univ, Muncie, Ind. *Exhib:* Spirit of the Comics, Inst Contemp Art, Univ Pa, 69; Art Inst Chicago, 69, 71, 77, 79 & 82; Am Painting, Indianapolis Mus Art, 72 & 77; 12th Bienal de Sao Paulo, Brazil, 73; Chicago Currents: The Koffler Foundation, Nat Mus Am Art, 79; Who Chicago? An Exhibition of Contemporary Imagists, Sunderland Arts Ctr, England & travelling, 80-82; The Comic Art Show, Whitney Mus Am Art, 83; and others. *Teaching:* Frank Harrold Sellers Prof, Art Inst Chicago, 60- *Awards:* Walter M Campana Prize, 60, Frank G Logan Medal & Prize, 71 & Virgine K Hendberg Prize, 77, Art Inst Chicago. *Bibliog:* Franz Schulze (auth), Chicago Art, Follett, 72; articles in Art Int & Art News. *Mem:* Art Club Chicago; Am Asn Univ Profs. *Media:* Oil, Acrylic. *Dealer:* Phyllis Kind Gallery 226 E Ontario Chicago IL 60611. *Mailing Add:* 1944 N Wood Chicago IL 60622

YOSHIMURA, FUMIO
SCULPTOR
b Kamakura, Japan, Feb 22, 26. *Study:* Tokyo Nat Univ Arts, MFA, 49. *Work:* Philadelphia Art Mus; Pa Acad Fine Arts, Philadelphia; Albright-Knox Gallery, New York; Gobett-Brewster Gallery, New Plymouth, NZ; Power Gallery of Contemp Art, Sydney, Australia; and others. *Comn:* Mobile, Haskell & Sells, Philadelphia. *Exhib:* Pa Acad Fine Arts, 71; Photo Realism, Wadsworth Atheneum, Conn, 73; Tokyo Bienale, 74; Galleri Arnesen, Copenhagen, Denmark, 74; Realism/Realisme, Rothman's Pall Mall traveling exhib, Can, 74; Object as Poet, Renwick Gallery, Smithsonian Inst, Washington, DC, 76; Norton Gallery of Art, Fla, 77. *Teaching:* Vis prof, Dartmouth Col, NH, 81-82. *Media:* Wood. *Dealer:* Nancy Hoffman Gallery New York NY 10012. *Mailing Add:* 5 E Third St New York NY 10003

YOST, ERMA MARTIN
PAINTER, INSTRUCTOR
b Goshen, Ind, Jan 12, 47. *Study:* James Madison Univ, Harrisonburg, Va, BA(art educ), 69, MA(painting), 75. *Work:* Pace Univ Art Mus, New York; James Madison Univ & Eastern Mennonite Col, Harrisonburg, & Va Art Inst Mus, Charlottesville; Goshen Col, Ind. *Exhib:* One-person shows, Noho Gallery, New York, 75-84, Pa State Univ, 77 & Bergen Community Mus, Paramus, NJ, 77; Desert Images, Jersey City Mus, NJ, 79; Invitational, James Madison Univ, Harrisonburg, Va, 81; and others. *Pos:* Illusr, Simplicity Pattern Co, New York, 72-73. *Teaching:* Instr art, Eastern Mennonite Col, 69-70; instr art, Spence Sch, 77- *Bibliog:* Vivian Raynor (auth), Desert images, New York Times, 12/79; Leslie Plummer (auth), article, New York Arts J, 4/80; Lawrence Alloway (auth), Critic's Choice, 10/83. *Mem:* Asn Artists Run Galleries; Womens Caucus Art. *Media:* Oil. *Dealer:* Noho Gallery Inc 168 Mercer St New York NY 10012. *Mailing Add:* 223 York St Jersey City NJ 07302

YOST, LEON C
PHOTOGRAPHER
b Atglen, Pa, July 7, 43. *Study:* Eastern Mennonite Col, 63-65; Pace Univ, 72-77. *Exhib:* Solo exhib, Noho Gallery, New York, 77 & 83, Soho Photo Gallery, New York, 78-80 & 83, Eastern Mennonite Col, 81 & Goshen Col Gallery, 83; 20th Biennial Exhib, Univ Del, Newark, 81. *Pos:* Pres, Noho Gallery, New York, 82- *Bibliog:* Vivian Raynor (auth), A husband-wife show, New York Times, 12/9/79; Dean Kinley (auth), Artist continually discards, Daily News Record, 2/9/81; Peter Fingesten (auth), article, Arts Mag, 2/83. *Dealer:* Noho Gallery 168 Mercer St New York NY 10012. *Mailing Add:* 223 York St Jersey City NJ 07302

YOUKELES, ANNE
PAINTER, PRINTMAKER
b Bad Ischl, Austria; US citizen. *Study:* Kunstgewerbeschule Vienna, Austria; Acad de la Grande Chaumiere, Paris; Ohio State Univ; painting with Alexander Dobkin & Rudolf Baranik; printmaking with Sidney Chafetz & Carol Summers. *Work:* Philadelphia Mus Art; Rosenwald Collection, Smithsonian Inst; Bibliotheque Nat, Paris; Lehman Collection; Atlantic Richfield Co. *Comn:* Editions of prints, Int Graphic Arts Soc, 72, Jewish Mus,

73 & Print Club, Philadelphia, 75; acrylic triptych, Guaranty Bank, Milwaukee, 79. *Exhib:* Ann Print Exhibs, Brooklyn Mus, 70 & 72; Art Today USA II, Mod Art Mus, Tehran, Iran, 77; one-person shows, Marion Locks Gallery, Philadelphia, 73 & 77, Dubins Gallery, Los Angeles, 78, 80 & 84 & Posner Gallery, Milwaukee, 79 & 84; Benjamin Mangel Gallery, Philadelphia, 82; and others. *Awards:* Purchase Prizes, Pratt Miniature Show, Boston Printmakers Ann & Philadelphia Print Club. *Bibliog:* Gabor Peterdi (auth), Printmaking, MacMillan Publ Co, New York, 72; Ross & Romano (auths), Techniques in Printmaking, 74. *Mem:* Soc Am Graphic Artists; Boston Printmakers; Silvermine Guild Artists; Am Colorprint Soc; Print Club, Philadelphia. *Media:* Silkscreen; Acrylic. *Mailing Add:* 81-42 193rd St Jamaica NY 11423

YOUNG, BARBARA
PHOTOGRAPHER
b Chicago, Ill, Oct 27, 20. *Study:* Knox Col, Galesburg, Ill, AB, 42; Johns Hopkins Univ Med Sch, MD, 45; Baltimore Psychoanal Inst, grad, 55. *Work:* Mus Mod Art, New York; Baltimore Mus Art; Eastman House, Rochester, NY; Santa Barbara Mus Art, Calif. *Exhib:* Photog in Fine Arts III Traveling Exhib, Minneapolis Mus, 61; Ancient Greek World, Walters Art Gallery, Baltimore, 70; one-woman shows, Butler Inst Am Art, Youngstown, Ohio, 74 & Santa Barbara Mus Art, Calif, 78; 2nd Generation Pioneers: Blance DeBra & Harvey Young, Baltimore Mus Art, 76 & Timberlane, A Sculpture Garden, 77; Am Vision, Nat Artists Alliance, NY Univ Galleries, 79. *Teaching:* Lectr, Univ Ill Med Sch, Chicago & Peoria Sch Med, Ill, 79. *Awards:* First Prize, Nat Artists Alliance, 79; First Prize, Md Mag, 12/82. *Mem:* Soc Photog Educ; Artists' Equity Asn. *Publ:* Auth, Our garden in the city, Horticulture, 70; auth, Hunting for the ostrich, Hasselblad Mag, 71; auth, Getting acquainted with Maine, Am Forests Mag, 72; auth, The Coleman's vegetable garden at Cape Rosier, Downeast Mag, 75. *Mailing Add:* 5307 Herring Run Dr Baltimore MD 21214

YOUNG, CHARLES ALEXANDER
EDUCATOR, PAINTER
b New York, NY, Nov 17, 30. *Study:* Hampton Inst, BS; NY Univ, with Hale Woodruff, MA; Cath Univ Am. *Work:* Univ DC; Kennedy Inst; Fayetteville State Univ, NC; Phelps Stokes Found, DC; Scottish Bank, Fayetteville, NC; and others. *Exhib:* One-man show, Smith-Mason Gallery, 69 & Agra Gallery, Washington, DC, 72; Afro-American Images, Wilmington, Del, 71; Nat Exhib Black Artists, Washington, DC, 71; Huntsville Mus of Art, Ala, 79; Emory Univ, Atlanta, 80; Raku Gallery, Art Barn, Washington, DC, 80. *Teaching:* Instr art, Fayetteville State Univ, 60-63; asst prof art, Tenn A&I Univ, 63-68; prof art & chmn dept, Univ DC, 68- *Awards:* First & Second Prizes, First Open Exhib, Fayetteville, 62. *Bibliog:* Samella Lewis & Ruth G Waddy (auth), Black Artists on Art, Vol 2, Contemp Crafts, 71; J Edward Atkinson (auth), Black Dimensions in Contemporary American Art, New Am Libr, 71; Theresa Cederholm (auth), Afro-American Artists, Trustees Boston Libr, 73; Samella Lewis (auth), Art: African American, Harcourt Brace Jovanovich, 78. *Mem:* Col Art Asn; Nat Art Educ Asn; Nat Conference Artist. *Media:* Oil, Acrylic, Watercolors. *Mailing Add:* 8104 W Beach Dr NW Washington DC 20012

YOUNG, CLIFF
PAINTER, MURALIST
b New Waterford, Ohio, Dec 27, 05. *Study:* Art Inst Pittsburgh; Art Inst Chicago; Nat Acad Design; also with George Oberteuffer, Charles Schroeder, John Norton, J Wellington Reynolds & Harvey Dunn. *Work:* USN Art Gallery & USMC Collection, Washington, DC; Fed Hall, New York. *Comn:* Murals, St Francis Monastery, Utuado, PR, 58, Berkshire Life Ins Co, Pittsfield, Mass, 61, Church of Our Lady of Victory, New York, 62, Norweg Children's Home, Brooklyn, NY, 63, Pub Sch 232, Queens, NY, 65 & US Capitol, Washington, DC, 70-; and others. *Teaching:* Vis asst prof, Pratt-NY Phoenix Sch Design, 67-77; instr painting, Salmagundi Club, New York, 70- *Mem:* Archit League New York; Salmagundi Club (chmn art comt, 70-71); Nat Soc Mural Painters (treas, 71-72); Soc Illusr; Arts Club, Washington, DC; and others. *Media:* Oil, Acrylic. *Publ:* Auth, Figure Drawing Without a Model, 46; auth, Drawing Drapery, 47; auth, Figure Construction, 66. *Mailing Add:* 30 W 60th St New York NY 10023

YOUNG, EDNA E
DEALER, COLLECTOR
b Chicago, Ill, July 12, 36. *Pos:* Dir, Young Gallery, San Jose, Calif, 72- *Mem:* South Bay Art Asn. *Specialty:* Contemporary, all media including ceramics and sculpture. *Mailing Add:* 140 W San Carlos San Jose CA 95113

YOUNG, FRANCES ELIZABETH
LIBRARIAN
b Point Pleasant, NJ, June 5, 54. *Study:* Douglass Col, BA, 76; Rutgers Univ, MLS, 78; Hunter Col. *Pos:* Asst art librn, Rutgers Univ, New Brunswick, NJ, 76-78; sr art librn, Newark Pub Libr, NJ, 78-81; reference librn, Frick Art Reference Libr, New York, 81- *Mem:* Art Libr Soc North Am; Art Libr Soc NJ (treas, 80-81); Art Libr Soc NY. *Publ:* Auth, Review of contemporary art magazines, Serials Rev, 5/2/79. *Mailing Add:* 1256 Waverly Pl Elizabeth NJ 07208

YOUNG, JANIE CHESTER
MUSEUM DIRECTOR, EDUCATOR
b Port Huron, Mich, Apr 19, 49. *Study:* Univ Mich, BA(Eng lit & art hist), 71, MA(mus practice), 75; Toledo Mus Art, Nettie Poe Ketcham Fel Mus Educ, 72-73. *Collections Arranged:* Art, Ann Arbor, 71; Decorative Arts of New Brunswick, 76 & What's It To You? (auth, catalog for children), 77,

Rutgers Univ Art Gallery; Patrick Thibert: Young Canadian Sculpture, 77, Young New York Painting, 79 & Helen Frankenthaler: The Artist in three Media, Saginaw Art Mus. *Pos:* Fel coordr, Toledo Mus Art, Ohio, 73-75; cur educ, Rutgers Univ Art Gallery, 75-77; dir, Saginaw Art Mus, Mich, 77- & New Bedford Glass Mus, Mass, 82- *Teaching:* Instr mus arts & educ, Grad Sch Educ, Rutgers Univ, New Brunswick, NJ, 76. *Mem:* Nat Early Am Glass Club. *Res:* First interdisciplinary, professional bibliography of museum education. *Mailing Add:* New Bedford Glass Mus PO Box F-655 New Bedford MA 02742

YOUNG, JOHN T
SCULPTOR
b New York, NY, Apr 4, 54. *Study:* With Leonard DeLonga & S Hadley, Mass, 73-76; Amherst Col, BA, 76; RI Sch Design, MFA, 78. *Work:* Aspen Ctr Visual Arts, Colo; Univ NH, Durham; Wash State Univ, Grand Coulee Elem Sch; Alexander Grant & Co, New York; Mobil Oil Corp, New York; and others. *Comn:* Granite tower, Morgan Community Col, Colo Coun Arts, Ft Morgan, 79. *Exhib:* Phoenix Art Mus, 79; Scottsdale Ctr Arts, Ariz, 79; Artists Representing Environmental Art, Wards Island, New York, 80-81; Denver Art Mus, 81; Arvada Ctr Arts, Colo, 81-82; solo exhib, O K Harris Gallery, New York, 82 & 83; and others. *Teaching:* Asst prof sculpture, Univ Denver, Colo, 78-81. *Awards:* Louis Comfort Tiffany Found Award, 79; Colo Art Prize, North Am Sculpture Exhib, Foothills Art Ctr, Golden, Colo, 80; NJ State Coun Arts Fel, 83. *Bibliog:* Carol MacGuineas (auth), article, Cult Post, Nat Endowment Arts, 12/79; Brady Chapin (auth), John Young, Interview Mag/Andy Warhol, 11/80; Gwen Chanzit (auth), John T Young's sculpture, Artspace Mag, winter, 82. *Dealer:* O K Harris 383 West Broadway New York NY 10012. *Mailing Add:* O K Harris 383 W Broadway New York NY 10012

YOUNG, JOSEPH E
EDUCATOR, CRITIC
b Los Angeles, Calif, Sept 8, 39. *Study:* Univ Calif, Los Angeles, MA, 78. *Work:* Midwest Mus Am Art, Elkhart, Ind; Oakland Mus, Calif. *Exhib:* Painters Committed to Painting, Miriam Perlman Gallery, Flint, Mish, 80; Midwest Mus Am Art, 80; one-man show, Punk Art, Scottsdale Community Col, 81; Prints from the Ariz State Univ Print Research Fac, Phoenix Art Mus; Phoenix Postmodernists, John Douglas Cline Gallery, Phoenix, 82. *Pos:* West Coast ed, USA, Art Int, 70-71; asst cur, prints & drawings, Los Angeles Co Mus Art, 65-78; art critic, Ariz Repub, 78-80, Phoenix Mag, 80-81 & Scottsdale Daily Progress, 83-; ed, J Theory & Criticism Visual Arts, 80-; dir, Harry Wood Art Gallery, 81- *Teaching:* Assoc prof art hist, Ariz State Univ, 79- *Mem:* Print Coun Am; Col Art Asn Am; Nat Print Asn (bd dir 80-82). *Res:* History of European and American drawings and prints; the theory and criticism of art; history of American art. *Publ:* Ed, Old Master Drawings from American Collections, Los Angeles Co Mus Art, 76; auth, Deep and Surface Structures in Lorser Feitelsons, 81; auth, 1968 untitled acrylic painting, J Theory & Criticism Visual Arts, 81. *Mailing Add:* Dept of Art Ariz State Univ Tempe AZ 85287

YOUNG, JOSEPH LOUIS
SCULPTOR, ADMINISTRATOR
b Pittsburgh, Pa, Nov 27, 19. *Study:* Westminster Col, AB, 41, Hon LLD, 60; Boston Mus Sch Fine Art, hon grad, 51; Carnegie Inst Technol; Mass Inst Technol; Cranbrook Acad Art; Art Students League; also with Karl Zerbe, David Aronson, Mitchell Siporin, Oskar Kockoshka & Gyorgy Kepes. *Comn:* Sixteen stained glass windows, Congregation Beth Sholom, San Francisco, 65; west apse, Nat Shrine Immaculate Conception, Washington, DC, 67; History of Math (mosaic murals), Math Sci Bldg, Univ Calif, Los Angeles, 70; The Triforium (multi-media tower), Los Angeles Mall, 70-75; 30ft theme sculpture, City of La Mirada Civic Theatre, 78; stained glass windows, Temple Ahavat Shalom, Northridge, 83. *Exhib:* Ten Year Retrospective, Art in Architecture, Palm Springs Desert Mus, 63; Int Exhib Muralists, Brussels, Belg, 65; VII Triennale, UNESCO, Varna, Bulgaria, 73; and others. *Pos:* Owner, Art in Architecture, 53-; dir, Mosaic Workshop, 55- *Teaching:* Instr art hist, Tufts Col, Medford, Mass, 50; instr painting, Boston Mus Sch Fine Arts, 50; artist in residence, Brandeis Inst, 62-; chmn dept archit arts, Santa Barbara Art Inst, 70-75. *Awards:* Am Acad Rome, Italy, 51; Huntington Hartford Found Fel, 52; Cavaliere, Repub Italy, 75; and others. *Mem:* Fel Int Inst Arts & Lett; Nat Sculpture Ctr, Lawrence, Kans; Nat Soc Mural Painters; Artists Equity Asn. *Media:* Multi-Media. *Publ:* Auth, The World of Mosaic (film), Univ Calif, Los Angeles, 57; auth, Arts & crafts in architecture, Creative Crafts, Vol 2, No 1; auth, Mosaics: Principles & Practice, Reinhold, 63; auth, Dialogues in Art, KNBC-TV Series, 67. *Mailing Add:* Art in Architecture 7919-1/2 W Norton Ave Los Angeles CA 90046

YOUNG, KENNETH VICTOR
PAINTER, DESIGNER
b Louisville, Ky, Dec 12, 33. *Study:* Ind Univ; Univ Louisville, BS. *Work:* Corcoran Gallery Art, Washington, DC; Va Nat Bank, Alexandria; Johnson Publ Co, Chicago; Am Tel & Tel, New York; Fisk Univ, Nashville. *Exhib:* Inst Contemp Arts, Washington, DC, 67; Baltimore Mus, 69; Ill Bell Co, Chicago, 71; Indianapolis Mus, 72; Corcoran Gallery Art, 74; Black Artist from the South, Huntsville Mus, Ala, 79; one-man shows, Gallery K, DC, 78 & 79 & C Grimaldis Gallery, Baltimore, 80. *Collections Arranged:* Music Machines, Hall of Graphic Arts, Women & Politics, Gandhi Centennial Exhib, Explorers NZ, Black Wings traveling exhib & Egyptian Antiquities. *Pos:* Designer, Smithsonian Inst, 64-; Washington artist, Health, Educ & Welfare Dept, DC, 79; acad specialist, Egyptian Mus, Cairo, currently. *Teaching:* Instr painting, Louisville Pub Sch, 62-63; instr design & painting, Corcoran Sch Art, 70- *Bibliog:* B Rose (auth), Black artist in America, Art in Am, 70. *Media:* Watercolor, Acrylic. *Dealer:* Gallery K 232 P St NW Washington DC 20001. *Mailing Add:* 1930 Columbia Rd No 303 Washington DC 20009

YOUNG, MAHONRI S
WRITER
b New York, NY, July 23, 11. *Study:* Dartmouth Col, AB; NY Univ, MA. *Collections Arranged:* Howald, Brit Art & Boudin, Irish Art. *Pos:* Actg dir, Munson-Williams-Proctor Inst, 51-53; dir, Columbus Gallery Fine Arts, 53-76. *Teaching:* Instr hist art, Sarah Lawrence Col, 41-50. *Publ:* Auth, Old George, 40; auth, The Paintings of George Bellows, 73; auth, The Eight: The Realist Revolt in American Painting, 73; auth, Early American Moderns: Painters of the Stieglitz Group, 74; auth, American Realists: Homer to Hopper, 77; and others. *Mailing Add:* Kellis Pond Ln Water Mill NY 11976

YOUNG, MARJORIE WARD
PAINTER, DRAFTSMAN
b Chicago, Ill, June 25, 10. *Study:* Art Inst Chicago, 25-35; with William B Schimmel, 55-56, Jossey Bilan, 58-62, Edgar A Whitney, 69, 71 & 75, Richmond Yip, 70, J Dougles Greenbowe & Milford Zornes, 72, Robert Wood, 77 & 81 & Charles Reid, 80. *Work:* Ariz Bank, Phoenix; First Nat Bank Ariz, Phoenix; Walter Bimson Collection, Phoenix; Thunderbird Bank; Valley Nat Bank, Phoenix. *Exhib:* Ariz Watercolor Asn Show in Taiwan, 74; Watercolor SW One, Albuquerque, 76; Watercolor SW Two, Tucson, 76; Watercolor SW Four, San Antonio; 110th Ann Am Watercolor Soc, New York, 77; Watercolors '78, O'Briens Art Emporium, Scottsdale. *Pos:* Background artist, Fleischer, Famous & Paramount Studios, Miami, Fla, 38-42; gallery dir, Phoenix YWCA, 70-79. *Teaching:* Instr drawing & watercolor, Phoenix Art Mus, 70-72, 77 & 79. *Awards:* Second Watercolor, Low Ruins Spring Nat, Tubac, Ariz, 65; First Watercolor & Best Show Pencil Sketch, Nat League Am Pen Women, 75. *Mem:* Ariz Artists Guild (pres, 61-62); Ariz Watercolor Asn (pres, 68-81); Nat League Am Pen Women (br art chmn, 72); Phoenix Art Mus Fine Arts Asn; hon mem Contemp Watercolorists Ariz. *Publ:* Illusr, Many Lives of the Lynx, 64; illusr, Functional Spanish, 68; illusr, Simply Messin, 82. *Dealer:* Westside Gallery 4411 N 19th Ave Phoenix AZ 85015. *Mailing Add:* 320 W Montecito Phoenix AZ 85013

YOUNG, MILTON
PAINTER, SCULPTOR
b Houston, Tex, Oct 6, 35. *Study:* Los Angeles City Col, AA; Calif State Univ, Los Angeles, BA. *Work:* Malcolm X Col, Chicago. *Comn:* Black & white mural, Compton Communicative Arts Acad, Calif, 71. *Exhib:* One-man shows, Brockman Gallery, Los Angeles, 70 & Watts Tower Art Ctr, 81; Huntsville Mus of Art, Ala, 79; Calif Poly Univ, Pomona, 81; Univ Calif, Los Angeles, Afro-Am Ctr Libr, 81. *Collections Arranged:* Fourteen Abstract Artists, 75; Birds, Beasts, Blossoms and Bugs: The Nature of Japan, 76; Arts of Ghana, 77; Tamarind Suite Fifteen, 78; Moche Art of Peru: Pre-Columbian, 78; Robert Heinecken Photographic Works, 79; Two Views of Manzanar/ Ansel Adams and Toyo Miyatake, 79. *Bibliog:* Article in, Good Housekeeping, 2/67; Joe Young (auth), article, Art Int, 3/70; Lewis & Waddy (auth), article, Black Artist Art, 71. *Mem:* Art West Asn; Los Angeles Art Asn. *Media:* Acrylic; Wood, Stone. *Publ:* Contribr, Coast Mag, 71 & Tuesday Mag, 73. *Mailing Add:* 1307 Park Ave Inglewood CA 90302

YOUNG, NANCY J(EANNE)
PRINTMAKER, GRAPHIC ARTIST
b Evergreen Park, Ill, Nov 7, 39. *Study:* Univ Ill, 58-59; Univ Ariz, BS, 61; Bishop Mus, Honolulu, 71-73; Sun Valley Ctr Arts, with Glen Alps & Nick de Matteis, summer 81. *Work:* Univ NMex, Albuquerque; Univ Northern Ariz; Sun Valley Ctr Arts, Idaho. *Comn:* Stained glass window, Trinity Church, West Point, Nebr, 83. *Exhib:* Audubon Artists 39th Exhib, New York, 81; Santa Fe Festival Arts, 81; Rockford Int Print Biennale, Ill, 83; solo exhibs, Univ NMex, Albuquerque, 83 & Northern Ariz Univ, 83. *Awards:* First Place, Albuquerque Arts Festival, NMex Art League, 75; Award Merit, Pub Serv Co NMex, 82 & State Biennial Exhib, Nat League Am Pen Women, 83. *Bibliog:* Barbara Perlman (auth), Love of the land, Ariz Arts & Travel, 3/83; Daniel Gibson (auth), Nancy Young and the land she loves, Southwest Profile, 10/83. *Mem:* Artists Equity Asn; Nat League Am Pen Women; Albuquerque United Artists. *Media:* Handmade Paper, Cast Paper; Relief Prints. *Publ:* Illusr cover, Tortuga, Justa Publ, 79. *Dealer:* Conway Art Consult 812 Gold Ave SW Albuquerque NM 87102. *Mailing Add:* 11416 Brussels Ave NE Albuquerque NM 87111

YOUNG, PETER FORD
PAINTER
b Pittsburgh, Pa, Jan 2, 40. *Study:* Chouinard Art Inst, Los Angeles, 57-58; Pomona Col, 58-60; Art Students League, New York, 60-61; New York Univ, BA(art hist), 63. *Work:* Albright-Knox Mus, Buffalo, NY; Guggenheim Mus & Mus Mod Art, New York; Aldrich Mus. *Comn:* Graphic, Lincoln Ctr, Newport Jazz Festival, 72. *Exhib:* Ann Exhib of Contemp Am Painting, Whitney Mus, New York, 67-68; 31st Biennial--Contemp Painting, Corcoran Gallery, Washington, DC, 69; Nine Young Artists, Theodoran Awards, Guggenheim Mus, 69 & Ann Exhib of Contemp Painting, Whitney Mus, New York, 70; Six Painters, Albright-Knox Mus, Buffalo, 71; Eight Artists, Art Mus of South Tex, Corpus Christi, 74; Eight Artists, Miami Mus of Art, Fla, 74; El Color Como Lenguaje, Exhib of Mus of Mod Art, New York Int Prog, 75-76; Leo Castelli Gallery, New York, 80. *Teaching:* Vis artist, Oberlin Col, Ohio, 70 & Pima Col, Tucson, Ariz, 76. *Bibliog:* Barbara Rose (auth), Gallery without walls, Art in Am, 3/68; Ellen Johnson (auth), A chronology of the work, Artforum, 4/71; Elizabeth Baker (auth), Peter Young and David Diao, Art News, 9/71. *Media:* Acrylic. *Dealer:* Leo Castelli 420 W Broadway New York NY 10012; Oil and Steel Gallery 157 Chambers St New York NY. *Mailing Add:* c/o Todas Casas de Boruca Bisbee AZ 85063

YOUNG, ROBERT JOHN
PAINTER

b Vancouver, BC, Aug 8, 38. *Study:* Univ BC, BA(art hist); City & Guilds London Sch Art, Eng; Vancouver Sch Art, dipl(graphics). *Work:* Can Coun Art Bank, Ottawa; Govt BC Prov Collection; Diamond Corp SAfrica; Art Gallery Ont; Montreal Mus Fine Arts. *Comn:* Christmas card Clothworkers Guild, London, 63; portrait, comn by Paul William White, London, 73; portrait, comn by Donna MacDonald, London, 76. *Exhib:* One-man shows, Redfern Gallery, London, 71, 73, 75, 79 & 82 & Vancouver Art Gallery, 74; Realismus und Realitat, Darmstadt, WGer, 75; Time Mag, Can Canvas, Across Can, 75-76; Can Cult Ctr, Embassy, Paris, 76; Vancouver Art Gallery, BC, 76-77; Marlborough-Godard, Toronto & Montreal, 76-77, 80 & 82; 10-Year Retrospective, Charles M Scott Gallery, Vancouver, 84. *Teaching:* Instr painting, Banff Sch Fine Arts, Alta, 75 & 81; vis artist, Royal Col Art, London, 76; Vancouver Sch Art, 77 & 81 & Alta Col Art, 78; asst prof, Univ BC, 82- *Bibliog:* Doris Shadbolt (auth), Robert Young, The Implacable Image, Vanguard, Vancouver Art Gallery, 77; Fenella Crichton (auth), A juggler of styles, Art & Artists, 4/79. *Media:* Oil; Intaglio Printmaking. *Dealer:* Mira Godard 22 Hazelton Ave Toronto ON Can; Redfern Gallery 20 Cork St London ON Can. *Mailing Add:* 3940 Quebec Vancouver BC V5V 3K8 Canada

YOUNG, TOM (WILLIAM THOMAS)
PAINTER, EDUCATOR

b Huntington, WVa, Oct 7, 24. *Study:* John Herron Art Inst; Cincinnati Art Acad; Univ Ala, BFA & MA(fine arts); Ohio State Univ; Chouinard Art Inst; Univ Southern Calif; Columbia Univ, EdD; also with Hans Hofmann, New York. *Work:* Cincinnati Art Mus; Univ Southern Ill; Univ Ala, Tuscaloosa; Wagner Col; Pan American Life Insurance Bldg, New Orleans. *Comn:* Mural, US Air Base, Altus, Okla, 43. *Exhib:* After Twenty Years, Birmingham Mus Art, 71; Now Show, Landmark Gallery, New York, 77; Drawings & Paintings, 78 & 79, Abstraction in Louisiana, 80 & Art Cars, 82, Contemp Arts Ctr, New Orleans; Ft Wayne Ind Art Mus, 84; and others. *Pos:* Illusr exp aircraft, Douglas Aircraft Corp, Los Angeles, 52-53; art dir, Good Health Mag, New York, 53-57; cover designer, Electronic Design Mag, New York, 55-56; design & color consult, Royal Metal Mfg Co, 56-57; color consult, New Orleans Dock Bd, 71-72. *Teaching:* Prof fine arts & chmn dept, Wagner Col, 53-69; head prof art, Auburn Univ, 69-70; prof fine arts, Univ New Orleans, 70-, chmn dept, 70-78. *Awards:* Weissglass Award, State Island Mus, 55; Hon Mention, New York City Ctr Gallery, 56; Winner, Nat Exhib, Contemp Arts Ctr, New Orleans, 82. *Mem:* New Orleans Mus Art (bd trustees, 73-); Col Art Asn Am. *Media:* Oil, Acrylic. *Mailing Add:* Dept of Fine Arts Univ of New Orleans New Orleans LA 70122

YOUNGBLOOD, JUDY
PRINTMAKER

b El Paso, Tex. *Study:* Univ Wis, Madison, BS, 71, MFA, 74; Hayter's Atelier 17, Paris, Fulbright Scholar, 79. *Work:* DeCordova Mus, Boston; Gilkey Collection, Portland Mus Art, Ore; Ark Art Ctr, Little Rock; Okla Art Ctr, Oklahoma City; Univ Calif, Davis. *Exhib:* Nineteenth Nat Print Exhib, Brooklyn Mus, 74; Miami Int Print Biennial, Metrop Mus, Miami, 78-82; Eighth Int Print Bienniale, Krakow, Poland, 80; 57th Ann Int Competition, Print Club, Philadelphia, 81; Univ Dallas Invitational, Irving, Tex, 82. *Pos:* Fel residency, MacDowell Colony, Peterborough, NH, 82. *Teaching:* Assoc prof printmaking, NTex State Univ, 76- *Bibliog:* Andrew Stasik (auth), Toward a broader view, Print Rev, 81; Scott Gordon (auth), Judy Youngblood: New Work, New Art Examiner, 11/81. *Mem:* Nat Print Coun; World Print Coun; Philadelphia Print Club; Women's Caucus Art; Southern Graphics Coun. *Media:* Etching, Intaglio. *Mailing Add:* Art Dept N Tex State Univ Denton TX 76203

YOUNGER, DAN FORREST
PAINTER, PRINTMAKER

b Denver, Colo, Sept 14, 54. *Study:* Kansas City Art Inst, BFA, 76. *Work:* IBM & Mobil Oil Co, Kansas City, Mo; Univ Dallas, Irving, Tex; Tulsa Libr, Okla; Am Express, Salt Lake City; Nat Mus, Brazil. *Comn:* Mural, Dixons Inc, Independence, Mo, 78. *Exhib:* Atkins Mus Fine Arts, Kansas City, Mo, 76-81; Univ Dallas, Irving, 77; Sheldon Mus, Lincoln, Nebr, 81; Univ Mo, Kansas City, 81; and others. *Pos:* Originator & dir, Squadron Press Fine Art Printing, 79- *Teaching:* Print technician, Kansas City Art Inst, Mo, 76- *Awards:* Best Show, Dixie Ann, Montgomery Mus, Ala, 78; Purchase Prize, Mid Four Ann, 79 & 81; 2nd Place, William Rockhill Nelson Gallery Art, 80. *Bibliog:* Don Hoffman (auth), Artist, printmaker, Kansas City Star, 8/80; Elizabeth Kirsch (auth), Squadron Press, Kansas City, 2/80; Vicki Melcher (auth), Kansas City, Art News, 10/80. *Mem:* Print Soc Kansas City. *Dealer:* Dorry Gates Inc 5321 Belleview Kansas City MO. *Mailing Add:* 6150 Cherry Kansas City MO 64110

YOUNGERMAN, JACK
PAINTER, SCULPTOR

b Louisville, Ky, Mar 25, 26. *Study:* Univ NC, Chapel Hill, 44-46; Univ Mo, Columbia, BA, 47; Sch Fine Arts, Paris, 47-48. *Work:* Whitney Mus Am Art, Mus Mod Art & Solomon R Guggenheim Mus, New York; Hirshhorn Mus & Sculpture Garden, Washington, DC; Art Inst Chicago. *Comn:* First Pa Bank, Philadelphia, 69; silkscreen, First Wis Bank, Milwaukee, 71; The Ohio (fiberglass), Pittsburgh Plate Glass, 77. *Exhib:* Guggenheim Mus, New York, 61 & 66; Whitney Mus Am Art, New York, 65; Jewish Mus, New York, 67; Carnegie Inst, Pittsburgh, 71; Hirshhorn Mus, Washington, DC, 80; Haus der Kunst, Munich, WGer, 81. *Teaching:* Instr, Yale Univ, 74-75; instr, Hunter Col, 81-82; instr, NY Univ, 82- *Awards:* Nat Coun Arts & Sci Award, 66; Nat Endowment Arts Award, 72; Fel, Guggenheim Found, 76. *Dealer:* Washburn Gallery 42 East 57th St New York NY 10022. *Mailing Add:* 130 West Third St New York NY 10012

YOUNGLOVE, RUTH ANN (MRS BENJAMIN RHEES LOXLEY)
PAINTER

b Chicago, Ill, Feb 14, 09. *Study:* Univ Calif, Los Angeles, BE; also with Orrin A White & Marion K Wachtel. *Work:* Bank of Am, Pasadena, Calif; El Tovar Hotel, Grand Canyon, Ariz. *Exhib:* Laguna Beach Art Asn Gallery, 71; one-woman shows, Flintridge Prep Sch, La Can, 72, Community Serv Ctr, Pasadena, 72-75, Altadena Pub Libr, Calif, 75 & Pasadena Soc of Artists Sales Gallery, 76-77; and others. *Awards:* Second Prize for Landscape, Artists League Seal Beach, 68; Fourth Prize in Painting, Pasadena Presby Church Exhib. *Mem:* Pasadena Soc Artists; life mem Laguna Beach Art Asn; Nat Watercolor Soc; assoc Am Watercolor Soc. *Media:* Watercolor, Linoleum Block Print. *Mailing Add:* 1180 Yocum St Pasadena CA 91103

YOUNGQUIST, JACK
DRAFTSMAN

b Crookston, Minn, Sept 19, 18. *Study:* Univ Minn, BA; Minn Sch Art; Univ Iowa, MFA; Art Students League; Slade Sch, Univ London; Inst Allende, San Miguel Allende, Mex; NY Univ. *Work:* Minn Inst Art, Minneapolis; Minn Mus Art, St Paul; NDak State Univ, Fargo; US Federal Reserve Bank, Minneapolis; Univ Iowa, Iowa City. *Exhib:* Red River Ann, Moorhead, 72 & 77; Ball State Drawing Exhib, Muncie, Ind; Minneapolis Art Inst Biennial; Drawings Invitational, Minneapolis Art Inst, Minn, 81; Retrospective, Plains Art Mus, Moorhead, Minn, 83; and others. *Pos:* Bd dirs, Red River Art Ctr, Moorhead, 66-68; adv panel, Minn State Arts Council, 79-80. *Teaching:* Instr calligraphy, Minn Sch Art, 54-59; instr, Univ Minn Exten, 57-58; prof drawing, Moorhead State Univ, 61-82, prof emer, 82. *Awards:* Purchase Award, Drawings USA, St Paul, 71; Merit Award, Minn State Art Exhib, 74; Bronze Medal, 16th Midwest Artists, Moorhead, Minn, 75. *Mem:* Col Art Asn Am; Artists Equity. *Dealer:* Rourke Art Gallery 523 S Fourth St Moorhead MN 56560; Groveland Gallery 35 Groveland Terrace Minneapolis MN. *Mailing Add:* 2662 Alabama Ave S Minneapolis MN 55416

YOUNGSBLOOD, NAT
PAINTER, ILLUSTRATOR

b Evansville, Ind, Dec 28, 16. *Study:* Univ NMex, Albuquerque, with Millard Sheets; Am Acad Art, Chicago; also with Barse Miller, Raymond Joahnson, Ralph Douglass & Howard Mosby. *Work:* Nat Marine Mus; Buhl Planetarium & Inst Popular Sci, Pittsburgh; Indiana Univ Pa; Calif State Col, Pa; Ft Pitt Mus, Pa. *Comn:* Oil portraits (indust leaders), for Pittsburgh Press, Pa, 56; mural, US Steel Corp, Pittsburgh; portrait President Kennedy, Metro News Serv, 61; Five hist paintings, Ft Pitt Mus, Pittsburgh; oil paintings (pioneer life), Pittsburgh Pa Bicentennial, 75. *Exhib:* Carnegie Inst Art for Indust, 54; Bantam Books Nat Competition, 57; Pittsburgh Art Dirs Soc, 59; Golden Quill Competition, 61; Artist of the Year, Pittsburgh Ctr Arts, 76. *Pos:* Art dir, Carter, Johne & Taylor Advert, 39-42; art dir & cartoonist, illusr & painter, Pittsburgh Press, 46- *Teaching:* Instr painting & design, LaRoche Col & Art Inst Pittsburgh, 74. *Awards:* First Place, Carnegie Inst Art for Indust, 54; First Place, Golden Quill Competition, 63; First Place, Pennational Exhib, 66. *Bibliog:* Margaret Harold (auth), Prize winning art, Allied Publ, Ind, 67; Norman Kent(auth), 100 Watercolor Techniques, Watson-Guptill, 68; Art Inst Pittsburgh, Careers in Art (film), 75. *Mem:* Pittsburgh Watercolor Soc; Pittsburgh Art Dirs Soc. *Media:* Watercolor, Oil. *Publ:* Ed, 101st Airborne Division Picture History, 45; auth, Watercolor page, Am Artist Mag, 59. *Mailing Add:* c/o Sandra Youngblood PO Box 73 West Middletown PA 15379

YOURITZIN, GLENDA GREEN See Green, Glenda

YOURITZIN, VICTOR KOSHKIN
HISTORIAN, EDUCATOR

b New York, NY, Dec 20, 42. *Study:* Williams Col, BA(cum laude), 64; Sch of Archit, Columbia Univ, 64-65; Inst Fine Arts, NY Univ, MA, 67; Cert Mus Training, Inst of Fine Arts & Metrop Mus Art, New York, 67. *Collections Arranged:* The Poetry of the Body: Paintings by Paul Peck (ed, catalog), Vanderbilt Univ, 69, Tulane Univ, 70 & Dallas Health & Sci Mus, 74-78. *Pos:* Mem bd trustees, Okla Mus Art, Oklahoma City, 78-84; regional corresp, Art Voices/South, 78-79, contrib ed, 79-82; mem exhibs & collections comt, Philbrook Art Ctr, Tulsa, Okla, 83- *Teaching:* Instr art hist, Vanderbilt Univ, Nashville, Tenn, 68-69 & Newcomb Col, Tulane Univ, New Orleans, 69-72; asst prof art hist, Univ Okla, Norman, 72-80, assoc prof, 80- *Awards:* Ford Found Fel, Dept of Painting & Sculpture, Metrop Mus of Art, New York, 67-68. *Res:* Nineteenth and twentieth century art; museology. *Publ:* Auth, Tchelitchew's Hide & Seek, winter 64-65 & A museum course at Newcomb College, spring 71, Art J; auth, The irony of Degas, Gazette des Beaux-Arts, 1/76; auth, Oklahoma City: Getting rid of Bambi, ARTnews, 9/78; auth, Thomas Hart Benton: Bathers rediscovered, Arts Mag, 5/80; and others. *Mailing Add:* 1721 Oakwood Dr Norman OK 73069

YRISARRY, MARIO
PAINTER

b Manila, Philippines, Mar 29, 33; US citizen. *Study:* Queens Col, NY, BA; Cooper Union. *Work:* Whitney Mus Am Art, New York; Baltimore Mus Art; Indianapolis Mus Art; Rose Art Mus, Brandeis Univ, Mass; Mus of Art, Carnegie Inst, Pittsburgh, Pa. *Comn:* Poster, Albert A List Found, Lincoln Ctr, New York, 72. *Exhib:* American Painting & Sculpture, Indianapolis Mus Art, 70; Structure of Color, 71 & Recent Acquisitions, 73, Whitney Mus Am Art, New York, 71; Grids, Int Contemp Art, Univ Pa, 72; The International Style in America, Lowe Art Mus, Univ Miami, Coral Gables, Fla, 74; Pattern Painting, Project Studio One, Long Island City, NY, 77. *Awards:* Ford Found Grant, Tamarind Inst, NMex, 73. *Bibliog:* Carter Ratcliff (auth), article, Art

News, 12/69; Robert Pincus-Witten (auth), New York, Artforum, 2/70; John Perreault (auth), Issues in pattern painting, Artforum, 11/77. *Publ:* Auth, The new work, first person singular-2, Art Gallery, Conn, 5/71; Patterns, Tracks, NY, Vol 1, No 1, 74. *Mailing Add:* c/o A M Sachs Gallery 29 W 57th St New York NY 10019

YUDIN, CAROL
PRINTMAKER, PAINTER
b Brooklyn, NY. *Study:* Pratt Graphic Ctr, with Sid Hammer, Michael Ponce de Leon, Roberto di Lamonica, Andrew Stasik, Michael Lenson & Krishna Reddy. *Work:* NJ State Mus, Trenton; Jersey City Mus, NJ; St Peter's Col, Jersey City; Miniature Art Soc NJ, Paramus; Belleville Pub Libr, NJ. *Exhib:* 7th Triennial NJ Artists, Newark Mus, NJ, 71; 38th Ann Painters & Sculptors Soc NJ, 80; Nat Asn Women Artists, New York; Audubon Artists, Nat Acad, New York; Old Bergen Art Guild nat touring show. *Pos:* Art adminr, Printmaking Coun NJ, 80-81. *Teaching:* Instr oil painting, Nutley Adult Sch, 66-76, Temple Emanuel, Paterson, NJ, 66-69, Clifton YWMHA, currently & Printmaking Coun NJ, currently. *Awards:* Purchase Award, Painters & Sculptors Soc NJ, 81; Edna P Stauffer Mem Award, Audubon Artists, New York, 77; James St Commons Exhib First Prize, 82. *Bibliog:* The Art of Etching (film), Suburban Cablevision. *Mem:* Nat Asn Women Artists; Painters & Sculptors Soc NJ (secy, 62-70, pres, 71-73); founding mem Printmaking Coun NJ; Audubon Artists, New York (corresp secy, 76-77, vpres graphics, 81-). *Dealer:* Pratt Graphic Ctr Gallery 160 Lexington Ave New York NY 10016. *Mailing Add:* 490 Joralemon St Belleville NJ 07109

YUNKERS, ADJA
PAINTER, EDUCATOR
b Riga, Latvia, July 15, 1900; US citizen. *Study:* Leningrad, Paris, Berlin & Rome. *Work:* Represented in over 82 insts including Mus Mod Art, Guggenheim Mus, Whitney Mus Am Art & Metrop Mus Art, New York & Albright-Knox Art Gallery, Buffalo, NY. *Comn:* A Human Condition (mural), Syracuse Univ, 66; tapestry for student union, State Univ NY Stony Brook, 67. *Exhib:* Numerous group shows including, Abstract Expressionists & Imagists, Guggenheim Mus, New York, 61, The New American Painting & Sculpture: The First Generation, Mus Mod Art, New York, 69, Etats Unis, Fondation Maeght, St Paul de Vance, France & Mus Arte Mod, Mexico City, 75; and many others including over 40 one-man shows. *Pos:* Ed, Creation, Ars & Ars-Portfolio, Stockholm, 42-45; vis critic, Columbia Univ, 67-69. *Teaching:* Instr art, New Sch Social Res, 47-56; instr art, Cooper Union, 56-67; instr art, Barnard Col, 69-78; instr summer sessions at several Western univs. *Awards:* Guggenheim Fel, 49-50 & 54-55; Ford Found Grant, 60; and numerous other awards. *Media:* Pastel, Oil. *Publ:* Ed, Prints in the Desert, 50. *Mailing Add:* 129 Front St New York NY 10005

YURISTY, RUSSELL MICHAEL
DESIGNER, SCULPTOR
b Goodeve, Sask, Mar 23, 36. *Study:* Univ Sask, Saskatoon, BA; Univ Wis-Madison, MS. *Work:* Norman Mackenzie Art Gallery, Regina, Sask; Sask Arts Bd; Regina Pub Libr, Sask; Can Coun Collection; Can Art Bank. *Comn:* Wooden elephant, Village of Silton, Sask, 71; wooden animals playground, Expo Can, Can Island, Spokane, Wash, 74; wooden polar bear, Dept Pub Works, Ottawa, Churchill, Man, 75; ferroconcrete buffalo, Swift Current, Sask, 76; wooden goose, Parks, Regina, Sask, 80; and others. *Exhib:* Canada Trajectories 73, Mus Mod Art, Paris, 73; Canadian Craft, 74, York Univ & Guild Show, Toronto, 74; Ceramica Americana, Coe Col, 74; Cicansky, Fafard, James, Yuristy, L'Atitude 53 Gallery, Edmonton, 74; Retrospective, Regina Pub Libr, 81; and others. *Pos:* Dir, Creative Playgrounds, Silton, Sask, 70-71; pres, Yuristy Enterprise Ltd, Silton, Sask, 74- *Teaching:* Instr drawing & graphics, Univ Sask, Regina, 67-71. *Awards:* Scholar Award, Sask Arts Bd, 66; Can Coun Bursary, Ottawa, 72-74 & 79-80. *Media:* Wood, Ceramic. *Publ:* Contribr, Russ Yuristy, his notes, stoneboats, elephants & friends, Arts Can, fall 72. *Dealer:* Susan Whitney Gallery Ltd 1627 Victoria Ave Regina SK Can. *Mailing Add:* PO Box 65 Silton SK S0G 4L0 Canada

YUST, DAVID E
PAINTER, EDUCATOR
b Wichita, Kans, Apr 3, 39. *Study:* Birger Sandzen; Wichita State Univ; Kans State Univ; Univ Kans, BFA, 63; Univ Ore, MFA, 69. *Work:* Denver Art Mus; Mulvane Art Ctr, Topeka, Kans; Sheldon Mem Art Gallery, Lincoln, Nebr; Wichita Art Mus, Kans. *Exhib:* One-man shows, Denver Art Mus, 76 & Joseph Magnin Gallery, Denver, 77; Wichita Art Mus, Kans, 79; Mulvane Art Ctr, Topeka, Kans, 79; Plains Art Mus, Moorhead, Minn, 80; Denver Art Mus, 82; Horizons Gallery, Ft Collins, Colo, 82; and others. *Teaching:* Assoc prof painting & drawing, Colo State Univ, 69- *Awards:* Purchase Awards, 11th Biennial, Kans State Univ, 70, Colo State Univ, 70 & Okla Art Ctr, 73. *Media:* Acrylic; Lithography, Serigraphy. *Dealer:* Inkfish Gallery 1810 Market St Denver CO 80202. *Mailing Add:* 1301 Patton Ft Collins CO 80524

Z

ZABARSKY, MELVIN JOEL
PAINTER, EDUCATOR
b Worcester, Mass, Aug 21, 32. *Study:* Sch Worcester Art Mus; Ruskin Sch Drawing & Fine Arts, Univ Oxford; Sch Fine & Appl Arts, Boston Univ, BFA;

Univ Cincinnati, MFA. *Work:* Mus Mod Art, New York; De Cordova Mus, Lincoln, Mass; Addison Gallery Am Art, Andover, Mass; Wiggins Collection, Boston Pub Libr; Currier Gallery Art, Manchester, NH. *Exhib:* One-man exhibs, Boris Mirski Gallery, Boston, 62, Tragos Gallery, Boston, 66, De Cordova Mus, 70, Circulo Bellas Artes, 82 & Salones Berkowitoch, 83, Madrid; Surreal Images, De Cordova Mus, 68; New Eng Painters Traveling Exhib, Ringling Mus, Sarasota, Fla, 69. *Teaching:* Instr painting, Swain Sch Design, New Bedford, Mass, 60-64; asst prof painting, Wheaton Col, 64-69; prof painting, Univ NH, 69- *Awards:* Painting Prize, Boston Arts Festival, 62; Ford Found Grant in humanities, 68. *Bibliog:* B Schwartz (auth), Humanism in 20th Century Art, Praeger, 73. *Media:* Oil. *Mailing Add:* Dept of Art Univ NH Durham NH 03824

ZABOROWSKI, DENNIS J
PAINTER, EDUCATOR
b Cleveland, Ohio, Jan 31, 43. *Study:* Cleveland Inst Art, cert, 61-65; Yale Univ, BFA, 65 & MFA, 68 with Jack Tworkov & Bernard Chaet. *Work:* Mint Mus of Art, Charlotte, NC; NC Nat Bank, NC Collection; Rauch Indust Inc, Gastonia, NC; Ackland Art Mus, Chapel Hill, NC. *Comn:* Youth Ctr mural, New Haven Redevlop Agency, 68. *Exhib:* Arts Festival of Atlanta, Ga, 69; 4th Ann James River Art Exhib, Mariners Mus, Newport News, Va, 70; 3rd Am Exhib, Washington & Lee Univ Mus, Lexington, Va, 71; Realism in NC, Mint Mus of Art, Charlotte, 74; 18th Ann Spring Art show, Lancaster, SC, 76; 39th Ann NC Artists Exhib, NC Mus of Art, Raleigh, 76; and others. *Collections Arranged:* Fac Choice Exhib, Va Polytech Inst, Blacksburg, Va, 71; New Talent Show, Allan Stone Gallery, New York, 75; 200 Yrs of the Visual Arts in NC, NC Mus of Art, Raleigh, 76; one-person show, Gallery of Contemp Art, Winston-Salem, NC, 72. *Teaching:* Assoc prof painting, drawing & design, Univ of NC, Chapel Hill, 68-; asst prof design, Duke Univ, Durham, NC, 72. *Awards:* Purchase Awards, NC Artists Exhib, Rauch Indust, 73 & Realism in NC, Mint Mus of Art, Charlotte, 74; Best Oil Painting, Spring Mills Exhib, Spring Mills Corp, 75. *Mem:* Nat Asn Schs Art. *Media:* Oil. *Mailing Add:* 1001 Dawes St Chapel Hill NC 27514

ZABRISKIE, VIRGINIA M
DEALER
b New York, NY. *Study:* Washington Sq Col, NY Univ, BA; NY Univ Inst Fine Arts, MA. *Pos:* Dir, Zabriskie Gallery, 54- *Mem:* Art Dealers Asn (bd dirs). *Specialty:* 20th century American art. *Mailing Add:* 724 Fifth Ave New York NY 10019

ZACH, JAN
PAINTER, SCULPTOR
b Slany, Czech, July 27, 14; US citizen. *Study:* Superior Sch Indust Arts, Prague; Acad Fine Arts, Prague; also with Angelo Zeyer. *Comn:* Czech Pavilion, New York World's Fair, 38-39; monument to Dr M Amaro, founder of Colegio de Cataguazes (archit Oscar Niemeyer), Cataguazes, MG, Brazil, 50-51; Prometheus, Univ Ore, Eugene, 58; sculptures & relief, New Eugene City Hall, Ore, 64; Can-Can (kinetic sculpture), Meier & Frank, Valley River Ctr, Eugene, 68. *Exhib:* Retrospective, Univ Ore, Eugene, 59; one-man shows, Portland Art Mus, Ore, 68 & Maude L Kerns Art Ctr, Eugene, 77; 73rd Western Ann, Denver, 71; Retrospective Exhib, Mus Art, Univ Ore, Eugene, 79; and others. *Teaching:* Teacher painting, Banff Sch Fine Arts, Univ Alta, 51-52; pvt instr painting & sculpture, own art sch, Victoria, BC, 51-57; prof sculpture, Sch Archit, Univ Ore, Eugene, 58-79; vis prof, Banaras Hindu Univ, Varanasi, India, 82-83. *Awards:* Cash Award Res, Chapelbrook Found, Boston, 68; Governor's Award, Ore Art Comn, 81; Sr Fulbright Fel, India, 82-83. *Bibliog:* Marques Rebelo (auth), Works by Jan Zach, Ed Vecchi, Rio de Janeiro, 49; Don Horter (auth), Work of Jan Zach (film), New York & Eugene, 68; Frank J Malina (auth), Kinetic Art: Theory & Practice, Dover Publ, 74. *Mem:* Nat Sculpture Ctr, Univ Kans (bd mem, 63-78); Artists Equity Asn; Czech Soc Arts & Sci in Am Inc. *Media:* Multimedia. *Publ:* Auth, The Contribution of the Czechoslovak Sculpture to the World of Art (abstr), 62; auth, The influence of experiment, accident & design on sculpture casting, 4th Nat Sculpture Conf, 66; auth, Imagery, light & motion in my sculpture, Leonardo, Gt Brit, 70; auth, My Sculpture Galaxy, Leonardo Pergamon Press, Gt Brit, 80. *Mailing Add:* 25113 Lamb Rd Elmira OR 97437

ZACHA, WILLIAM
PAINTER, SCULPTOR
b Garland, Tex, Jan 19, 20. *Study:* Univ Calif, 40-41 & 47-48; George Washington Univ, BA, 51; Corcoran, Washington, DC, study with Heinz Warneke; Studio Hinna, Rome, Italy, 51-52; study with Ruth Cravath, 70-75. *Exhib:* Sculpture, Palazzo Durini, Milano, Italy, 77; Watercolor/Sculpture, Bay Window Gallery, Mendocino, Calif, 77; Art Ctr, Eureka, Calif, 78; Kabutoya Gallery, Tokyo, Japan, 80; Schneider Gallery, Rome, Italy, 81; and others. *Pos:* Founder & dir, Mendocino Art Ctr, 59- *Bibliog:* Chandler Brossard (auth), A young man saves an old town, Look Mag, 8/62 & Where artists live, Horizons No 15, US Info Serv. *Dealer:* Bay Window Gallery 560 Main St Mendocino CA 95460. *Mailing Add:* PO Box 7 484 Main Mendocino CA 95460

ZACHARIAS, ATHOS
PAINTER
b Marlborough, Mass, June 17, 27. *Study:* Art Students League, summer 52; RI Sch Design, BFA, 52; Cranbrook Acad Art, MFA, 53. *Work:* Mus Art, Providence, RI; Inst Contemp Art, Boston; Kalamazoo Inst Art, Mich;

Phoenix Art Mus, Ariz; Westinghouse Corp, Pittsburgh. *Comn:* Decor for Manhattan Festival Dancers, comn by Robert Ossorio, New York, 63. *Exhib:* one-man shows, Gallery Mayer, 61, Louis Alexander Gallery, 63, Landmark Gallery, 73 & James Yu Gallery, 77, New York. *Teaching:* Instr painting, Brown Univ, 53-55 & Parsons Sch Design, 63-65; asst prof painting, Wagner Col, 69- *Awards:* Best in Show Award, Guild Hall, 61; Longview Found Grant, 62; Festival Arts Purchase Award, Southampton Col, 68. *Media:* Oil. *Publ:* Illusr cover, Sci & Technol, 63. *Mailing Add:* 463 West St Apt B-946 New York NY 10014

ZACK, BADANNA BERNICE
SCULPTOR, WRITER
Mar 22, 33; Can citizen. *Study:* Concordia Univ, Montreal, BA, 64; Rutgers Univ, MFA, 67. *Work:* Concordia Univ, Montreal; Rutgers Univ, Douglas Col, New Brunswick, NJ; Art Gallery Hamilton, Ont; and pvt collections. *Exhib:* Solo exhibs, Gallery 0, Toronto, 73, 75 & 78, Factory 77, Toronto, 81 & Hamilton Art Gallery, Ont, 83-84; Performance, Harbourfront Art Gallery, Toronto, 78; Reflecting a Rural Consciousness, traveling in US, Can & France, 78-80. *Awards:* Arts Grants, Can Coun, 68-69, 74-75 & 78 & Ont Arts Coun, 75-83. *Bibliog:* William Fabrycki (auth), Badanna Zack: L'Enfant terrible, Artmag, 81; Jim Tiley (auth), Badanna Zack at Studio Gallery Nine, Artmag, 83. *Mem:* Royal Can Acad. *Media:* Miscellaneous. *Publ:* Auth, Toronto: A look back at sculpture during the sculpture conference, 78, Paul Dempsey at the art gallery of Hamilton, 79, Deiter Hastenteufel at Factory 77, 81-82 & The dinner party by Judy Chicago, 82, Artmag; co-producer, Horse to Horsepower (videotape), 83. *Mailing Add:* 28 MacPherson Ave #206 Toronto ON M5R 1W8 Canada

ZAFRAN, ERIC MYLES
CURATOR, HISTORIAN
b Malden, Mass, Apr 19, 46. *Study:* Tilton Sch, NH, 63; Brandeis Univ, BA, 67; Inst Fine Arts, NY Univ, MA, 70, PhD, 73. *Collections Arranged:* The Mask and the Eye (graphics by Redon & Ensor), Rose Art Mus, spring 67; Master Paintings from the Hermitage (coauth & ed, catalog), Nat Gallery, 75; Master Paintings from the Chrysler Museum (coauth, catalog), Wildenstein Gallery, New York, 78; Y Kuniyoshi Restrospective, 78; Aaron Siskind Photographs, 79; One Hundred Drawings in the Chrysler Museum (auth catalog), 79. *Pos:* Curatorial asst, Rose Art Mus, Waltham, Mass, 65-67; print cataloguer, Parke-Bernet Galleries, New York, 68-71; res asst, Metrop Mus Art, New York, 72-75; chief cur, Chrysler Mus at Norfolk, 76-79; cur Europ art, High Mus, Atlanta, 79- *Teaching:* Assoc prof Rembrandt, City Col New York, 75-76; assoc adj, Northern Paintings, Old Dominion Univ, 77-78. *Mem:* Col Art Asn. *Publ:* Auth, The Virgin of Cambron, J Jewish Art, 77; auth, Jan Victors and the Bible, Bulletin of Israel Mus, 77; auth, Italian painting in the Chrysler Museum, Apollo, 78; Saturn and the Jews, J Warburg & Cortauld Inst, 79; auth, Newly discovered Blashfield works, Arts, 79. *Mailing Add:* 55 Lafayette Dr NE Atlanta GA 30309

ZAGO, TINO (AGOSTINO C)
PAINTER
b Crespano del Grappa, Italy, 1937; US citizen. *Study:* Lawrence Inst Technol, Mich, BS(archit), 60; Cranbrook Acad Art, MFA(painting), 66; Yale Univ, 69. *Work:* Sydney Lewis Corp Collection, Richmond, Va; Am Telephone & Telegraph, Long Line, Va; Prudential Insurance Co North Am, Newark, NJ; RCA Corp, New York; IBM Corp, New York. *Exhib:* Silvermine Guild Artists, New Canaan, Conn, 70; Detroit Inst Arts, Mich, 72; solo shows, Burlington Col, NJ, 76, Neill Gallery, New York, 77, O K Harris West, Scottsdale, Ariz, 81 & Frank Marino Gallery, New York, 81 & 82; Cranbrook Acad Art, Bloomfield Hills, Mich, 82; and others. *Bibliog:* Carolee Thea (auth), Exhibit at Neill Gallery, 77 & M H Stolbach (auth), Tino Zago, 81, Arts Mag; Theodore Wolff (auth), Saying something with paint, Christian Sci Monitor, 80. *Media:* Acrylic. *Mailing Add:* c/o Frank Marino Gallery 489 Broome St New York NY 10013

ZAHN, CARL FREDERICK
DESIGNER, ADMINISTRATOR
b Louisville, Ky, Mar 9, 28. *Study:* Harvard Univ, AB, 48. *Exhib:* Fifty Books Exhibition, Am Inst Graphic Arts, 60-76; one-man show, Dreitzer Gallery, Brandeis Univ, 69. *Pos:* Graphics designer, Mus Fine Arts, Boston, 56-, ed-in-chief, 71-78, dir publ, 79- *Mem:* Am Inst Graphic Arts (bd dirs, 68-71); Soc Printers. *Mailing Add:* 479 Huntington Ave Boston MA 02115

ZAHOUREK, JON GAIL
PAINTER, SCULPTOR
b Oklahoma City, Okla, Jan 5, 40. *Study:* Univ Northern Colo, 58-59; Colo Inst Art, with Charles Dye & John Jellico, cert, 61; New Sch Social Res, 79-81. *Work:* Ariz State Univ Matthews Ctr; City & Co Denver; Olahoma City Chamber Commerce. *Exhib:* Missouri Valley Drawing, Mulvane Art Ctr, Topeka, Kans, 67; Changing Image of the Indian, Mus NMex, Santa Fe, 70; Colo Biennial, Denver Art Mus, 75; Mainstreams of American Art, Marietta Col, 76; American Bronzes, Ariz State Univ, 81; Drawing Defined, Nat Arts Club, New York, 82; solo exhib, Newhouse Gallery, New York, 84. *Teaching:* Instr graphics, Univ Denver, 67; Instr drawing & anatomy, Parsons Sch Design, 78-; instr anatomy, New York Acad, 82- & Art Students League, 84. *Awards:* Second Prize, Black & White on Paper, Nat Arts Club, 82. *Bibliog:* John Jellico (auth), Jon Zahourek--draughtsman, Am Artist, 67; Daniel Conway (auth), Drawing ... an act of power, Art Forum, 77. *Mem:* Soc Artists & Anatomists (chmn, 82-84). *Media:* Oil. *Publ:* Auth, Drawings I, pvt publ, 75; auth, Maniken--A Comprehensive Educational System for the Study of Human & Comparative Gross Anatomy, Zahourek Systems Inc, 82. *Dealer:* Bishop Gallery 7164 Main Scottsdale AZ 85251. *Mailing Add:* 38 Mercer St Jersey City NJ 07302

ZAIKINE, ZAK (VICTOR EUGENE)
SCULPTOR, PAINTER
b Queens, NY, Sept 7, 41. *Study:* Pratt Inst, 59-64, sculpture with Charles Ginnever, 63, also painting with Nicholas Buhalis, 81-83. *Work:* Wright State Univ Mus, Dayton, Ohio; Brooklyn Automotive High Sch, NY. *Comn:* Sculpture, Midwood High Sch, Brooklyn. *Exhib:* Byrdcliffe Invitational, Kleinert Gallery, Woodstock, NY, 81; Roots, Rituals, Reflections, Imperial Gallery, New York, 80-81; Silvermine Guild Ctr Arts, 83; Schenctady Mus, 83; Woodstock Artist Asn, 83; and others. *Awards:* First Place, Fiesta de Artes, Los Gatos, Calif, 76; Jerald D Lacy Mem, Wash Square Village Art Exhib, 80; Ollie K Murphy Award, Wash Square Village Art Exhib, 81. *Bibliog:* Tram Combs (auth), Zak Zaikine's drypoints, 12/23/82 & Zaikine's tribute to the landscape, 6/1/83, Woodstock Times; Bernard Bovasso (auth), Zaikine's work defy morality, Daily Freeman, 5/31/83; and others. *Mem:* Sonoma Co Arts Coun; Woodstock Arts Asn Inc; Cooperstown Art Asn Inc; Woodstock Guild Craftsmen Inc. *Media:* Bronze, Mixed Media; All Media. *Dealer:* Zantman Galleries Ltd 6th Ave and San Carlos Carmel CA 93921; Paramour Fine Arts 28211 Southfield Rd Lathrup Village MI 48076. *Mailing Add:* Box 115 Woodstock NY 12498

ZAIMA, STEPHEN GYO
PAINTER, SCULPTOR
b San Jose, Calif, Jan 3, 47. *Study:* Pratt Inst, 68; Sch Visual Arts, New York, 68; Calif State Univ, San Jose, BA, 69; Univ Calif, Davis, MFA, 71. *Work:* Univ Calif, Davis & Veterans Mem Bldg, Long Beach. *Comn:* Long Beach Mural, Calif Arts Coun, 83. *Exhib:* Gallery Tamura, Tokyo, Japan, 74; Soho Ctr, New York, 79; Frank Marino Gallery, New York, 81; Harm Bouckaert Gallery, New York, 82; Adam L Gimbel Gallery, New York, 82; and others. *Teaching:* Asst prof art, Univ Iowa, 73-76; asst prof art, Hartford Art Sch, Univ Hartford, 76-80; from asst to assoc prof, Syracuse Univ, 80- *Awards:* Fel, Nat Endowment Arts, 74; Grant, Ford Found, 80 & 81; Fel, Edward Albee Found, 81. *Bibliog:* Peter Morrin (auth), article, Atlanta Art Papers, 3/80; Virginia Mann (auth), All in Line, 2/81 & Valentine Tatransky (auth), article, 5/82, Arts Mag. *Media:* Oil; Mixed. *Mailing Add:* 133 Chrystie St New York NY 10002

ZAJAC, JACK
SCULPTOR, PAINTER
b Youngstown, Ohio, Dec 13, 29. *Study:* Scripps Col, 49-53; also with Millard Sheets, Henry McFee & Sueo Serisawa; Am Acad in Rome. *Work:* Whitney Mus Am Art, Mus Mod Art, New York; Los Angeles Mus Art; Pa Acad Fine Arts, Philadelphia; Israel Mus, Jerusalem; Hirshhorn Mus & Sculpture Garden, Washington, DC; plus others. *Comn:* Reynolds Metals Co, 68. *Exhib:* Whitney Mus Ann, 59; Recent Sculpture USA, Mus Mod Art, 59; Am Painting, Va Mus Fine Arts, Richmond, 62; Fifty California Artists, Whitney Mus Mod Art, New York, 62-63; Pittsburgh Int, Carnegie Inst, 65; retrospectives, Newport Harbor Art Mus, Balboa, Calif, 65, Temple Univ, Rome, 69, Santa Barbara Mus, 75 & Fine Arts Gallery San Diego, 75; Fortezza Albornoz Orvietto, Italy, 76; and many others. *Teaching:* Instr, Pomona Col, 59; prof, Univ Calif, Santa Cruz, currently. *Awards:* Prix de Rome, 54, 56 & 57; Am Acad Arts & Lett Grant, 58; Guggenheim Fel, 59. *Bibliog:* Henry J Seldis & Ulfert Wilke (auth), The Sculpture of Jack Zajac, Gallard Press, 60; Allen S Weller (auth), The Joys and Sorrows of Recent American Art, Univ Ill, 68. *Dealer:* Forum Gallery 1018 Madison Ave New York NY. *Mailing Add:* c/o Forum Gallery 1018 Madison Ave New York NY 10021

ZAKANITCH, ROBERT S
PAINTER
b Elizabeth, NJ, May 24, 35. *Work:* Whitney Mus Am Art, New York; Munich Mus Mod Art, WGer; Philadelphia Mus, Pa; Wadsworth Atheneum, Hartford, Conn; Phoenix Mus, Ariz. *Exhib:* Inst Contemp Art, Philadelphia; James Mayor Gallery, London; Templon Gallery, Paris; Whitney Biennial, Whitney Mus Am Art, New York; Inst Contemp Art, Univ Pa, Philadelphia; and others. *Bibliog:* Robert Hughes (auth), Three bold newcomers, Time, 3/13/72; John Perreault (auth), Patterning, Artforum, 11/78; John Ashbery (auth), Climbing the wallpaper, New York Mag, 1/29/79; and others. *Mailing* Robert Miller Gallery 724 Fifth Ave New York NY 10019

ZAKIN, MIKHAIL
SCULPTOR, EDUCATOR
US citizen. *Study:* Sch Mus Fine Arts, Boston, Mass; Art Students League, sculpture with William Zorach & Albino Manca; also ceramics with Karen Karnes & David Weinrib. *Work:* Mus Arts & Sci, Salt Lake City, Utah. *Exhib:* Brooklyn Mus, NY, 74-76; Am Potters, Mus Arts & Sci, Salt Lake City, 75; Four US Potters, Fair Tree Gallery, 75; Pratt Grad Sch, New York, 75-77; Brooklyn Col, 75-77; Baruch Col, New York, 75-77; and others. *Pos:* Founder & dir, Old Church Cult Ctr & Sch Art, Demarest, NJ, 74-; potters sem leader, England, 76, Japan, 77, Mexico, 78, Italy, 79, China, 81, Holland, 82 & Korea, 83; co-founder, Scotland-North Coast Continuum, 78- *Teaching:* Advan ceramics instr, Greenwich House Pottery, 71-75; head ceramics dept, Brooklyn Mus Art Sch, 72-75; head ceramics dept, Sarah Lawrence Col, 76- *Awards:* Lebensburger Found Grant, 74; Craftsmen's Fel, NJ Coun Arts, 75 & Nat Endowment Arts, 76. *Bibliog:* Elsbeth Woody (auth), Hand Building Ceramics, Farrar Strauss Giroux, 79; Anthony Padovano (auth), Sculpture Practice, Doubleday, 81; Nino Caruso (auth), Ceramica Raku, Hoepli-Milano, 82. *Mem:* Am Crafts Coun; World Crafts Coun; Nat Conf Ceramic Educators; NY Artist Craftsman. *Media:* Clay. *Mailing Add:* 37 County Rd Closter NJ 07624

ZALESKI, JEAN M
PAINTER, ADMINISTRATOR
b Malta; US citizen. *Study:* Art Students League; New Sch Social Res, New York; Pratt Inst, New York; Parsons Sch Design, New York; Moore Col Art, Philadelphia; also with Harry Sternberg, Ernest Fiene & Motoi Oi. *Work:* Hofstra Univ, Garden City, NY; Brooklyn Polytechnic Inst; Metrop Mus Art. *Comn:* Paintings, Inst of Life Insurance, New York, Easter Seal Human Resources Ctr, New York, Great Neck Sch Dist, NY & Sewhanaka High Sch Dist, Franklin Square, NY. *Exhib:* Nat Acad Design, New York, 70-71; Faces, Philadelphia Mus Art, 71; Int Women's Arts Festival, Milan, Italy, 73; Works on Paper--Women Artists, 75, Brooklyn Mus, NY, 75; Eleven Contemp Women Artists, Sweetbriar Col, Va, 77; one-person shows, Alonzo Gallery, New York, 79 & Va Ctr Creative Arts, 81; and others. *Pos:* Exec coordr, Women in the Arts Found, 75-77; bd dir, Visual Dialog Mag, 77-; spec appt 5-mem adv comt, White House, Washington, DC, 3/77. *Teaching:* Instr drawing & painting & art dir, Studio 733 Art Sch, Great Neck, NY, 63-67; instr life drawing, Hussian Col of Art, Philadelphia, 70-71; instr drawing & painting, Am Studies Ctr, Naples, Italy, 72-73 & Northern Atlantic Treaty Orgn Hq, Naples, 72-73; adj lectr painting, Brooklyn Col, 74-76 & Hofstra Univ, Hempstead, NY, 77. *Awards:* MacDowell Fel, 71; Gold Medal, Int Arts Festival, Milan, 73; Va Ctr Creative Arts Fel, 75-83. *Bibliog:* Malcolm Preston (auth), On art, Newsday, 75; Joan Marter (auth), Pasture forms, 2/79 & exhib rev, 5/79, Arts Mag. *Mem:* Int Asn of Art; Womens Caucus Art; Women in Arts; Artists Equity; Found for Community of Artists, New York. *Media:* Acrylic, Oil. *Publ:* Illusr, Woman to Woman: European Feminists, Staragoubski, 74; auth, Women in the arts, Women's Caucus for Art Newsletter, 77; auth, Innovative jurying methods, In: Feminist Collage: Educating Women in the Visual Arts, Teachers Col Press, 79; auth, Isolation as Inspiration, Women Artists News, 81; coauth (with Edwin Honig), Cow-Lines, Copper Beech Press, 82. *Mailing Add:* 463 West St 503D New York NY 10014

ZALLINGER, JEAN DAY
ILLUSTRATOR, EDUCATOR
b Boston, Mass, Feb 15, 18. *Study:* Mass Col of Art, cert(drawing & painting), 35-39; Yale Sch Fine Arts, BFA, 42. *Work:* Kerland Found; Univ Minn; Rutgers Univ. *Pos:* Tech illus draftsman, Applied Physics Lab, Univ Wash, Seattle, 51-53. *Teaching:* Assoc prof, Paier Col Art, Hamden, Conn, currently. *Awards:* Jr Lit Guild Award for Turned to Stone, 65 & I Watch Flies, 77; Outstanding Sci Children's Book, Nat Sci & Children's Book Coun, 76; Nat Sci Teachers Awards for Biography of a Fish Hawk & I Watch Flies, 77. *Mem:* Paint & Clay Club, New Haven, Conn; Arts Coun New Haven; Graphic Artists Guild, New York. *Publ:* Illusr, I Like Beetles, Holiday House, 75; illusr, Herbs and Spices--Weeds--Botany, Golden Botany, 76; illusr, Sounds in the Sea, Morrow Bk, 77; illusr, Biography of a Fish Hawk, Putnam Bk, 77; illusr, I Watch Flies, Holiday House, 77. *Mailing Add:* 5060 Ridge Rd North Haven CT 06473

ZALLINGER, RUDOLPH FRANZ
PAINTER, EDUCATOR
b Irkutsk, Siberia, Nov 12, 19; US citizen. *Study:* Yale Sch Fine Arts, Yale Univ, BFA, 42, MFA, 71; Univ New Haven, Hon DFA, 80. *Work:* Seattle Art Mus; Yale Peabody Mus Natural Hist; Berkeley Col, Yale Sch Med, Yale Univ; New Brit Mus Am Art, Conn. *Comn:* Age of Reptiles (fresco), 42-47 & Age of Mammals (fresco), 61-67, Peabody Mus, Yale Univ. *Exhib:* 32 Realists, Cleveland Inst Art, 72-; Sanford Low Mem Exhib, New Brit Mus Am Art, 76; 200 Yrs of Am Illus, NY Hist Soc Mus, 76-77; one-man retrospective, New Brit Mus Am Art, 80; one-man show, Dorsky Galleries, NY, 81. *Pos:* Artist-in-residence, Peabody Mus Natural Hist, Yale Univ, 52- *Teaching:* From instr to asst prof drawing & painting compos, Yale Sch Fine Arts, 42-50; from asst prof to prof, Hartford Art Sch, Univ Hartford, 61- *Awards:* Pulitzer Prize for Painting, Columbia Univ, 49; Addison Emory Verrill Medal, Peabody Mus, Yale Univ, 80. *Bibliog:* Lawrence Rasie (auth), Rudolph Zallinger, dinosaur man, Hartford Courant, 74; Carl O Dunbar (auth), Recollections of the Renaissance of Peabody Mus Exhibs, Discovery Mag, Peabody Mus, 76; John Ostrum (auth), The age of reptiles, Discovery Mag Supplement 1, Peabody Mus, 77. *Mem:* New Haven Paint & Clay Club (vpres, 48-49, pres, 76-78); Puget Sound Group Northwest Painters. *Media:* Egg-tempera, Oil. *Publ:* Illusr, World we live in, 55, Wonders of life on earth, 60 & Epic of man, 61, Life; illusr, Giant Golden Book of Dinosaurs, 25th printing, 60 & Worlds of the Past, 72, Golden Press. *Mailing Add:* 5060 Ridge Rd North Haven CT 06473

ZAMMITT, NORMAN
PAINTER, SCULPTOR
b Toronto, Ont, Feb 3, 31; US citizen. *Study:* Pasadena City Col, AA, 57; Otis Art Inst, MFA, 61. *Work:* Mus Mod Art, New York; Hirshhorn Mus, New York; Libr Cong, Washington, DC; Otis Art Gallery, Los Angeles; Larry Aldrich Mus, Conn. *Exhib:* Mus Mod Art, New York, 65 & Show of New Acquisitions, 67; American Sculpture of the Sixties, Los Angeles Co Mus Art & Philadelphia Mus Art, 67; Metromedia, Los Angeles; one-man shows, Los Angeles Co Mus Art, 77 & Corcoran Gallery, 78. *Awards:* Tamarind Fel, 67; Guggenheim Mem Found Fel, 68. *Bibliog:* Various articles in Art Int, Artforum, Art in Am & Los Angeles Times. *Mailing Add:* 233 N Wilson Ave Pasadena CA 91106

ZANTMAN, J B
DEALER
b Sumbawa, Dutch East Indies, Dec 27, 19; US citizen. *Study:* Pvt instr, Netherlands. *Pos:* Pres, Zantman Art Galleries, Ltd, Carmel & Palm Desert, Calif. *Specialty:* Living artists from US and France. *Mailing Add:* PO Box 5818 Carmel CA 93921

ZAPKUS, KES (KESTUTIS EDWARD)
PAINTER
b Dabikine, Lithuania, Apr 22, 38; US citizen. *Study:* Art Inst Chicago, BFA, 60; Syracuse Univ, Ryerson fel, 60, MFA, 62. *Work:* Stedelijk Mus, Amsterdam, Holland; Hirshhorn Mus, Washington, DC; Va Mus Fine Arts, Richmond; Hunter Mus Art, Chattanooga, Tenn; Art Inst Chicago; and many others. *Exhib:* Contemp Arts Ctr, Cincinnati, 73; Inst Contemp Art, Boston, 75; Middlebury Col, Vt, 75; Butler Inst Am Art, Youngstown, Ohio, 76; John Weber Gallery, 81; Carnegie Inst, 81; and others. *Teaching:* Instr, Parsons Sch Design. *Awards:* Invitational First Prize, Chicago Arts Festival, 63; Creative Artists Public Service Grant, 78; Nat Endowment Arts Grant, 79. *Media:* Acrylic, Oil. *Dealer:* Paula Cooper Gallery 155 Wooster New York NY 10012; John Weber Gallery 142 Greene New York NY. *Mailing Add:* 35 Bond St New York NY 10012

ZARAND, JULIUS JOHN
PAINTER, RESTORER
b Nagyvarad, Hungary, June 27, 13; Can citizen. *Study:* Royal Acad, dipl & dipl(educ); also with Oskar Kokoschka, Salzburg, Austria; Accad Ital, Dipl Hon Causa Maestro Pittura, 83. *Work:* City Hall, Halifax, NS; Yokahama Univ Gallery, Japan. *Comn:* Portrait of Pope Pius XII, comn by Prime Cardinal of Hungary, 38; portrait, comn by Lord Thompson, Toronto, 54; murals, St Bridgid Church, Toronto, 55; portrait of Sir John Thompson, City of Halifax, NS, 68; portraits of all presidents of the co, Maritime Telegraph & Telephone Co, Halifax, NS; and others. *Exhib:* One-man shows, Halifax Libr, 64, Lafayette Art Ctr, Ind, 69, Purdue Univ Gallery, 69, Zwicker's Gallery, Halifax, 70 & Signatures Gallery, Truro, NS, 82. *Teaching:* Asst prof fine arts, St Mary's Univ, Halifax, 56-65. *Awards:* Gold Medal, Acad Italy, 81. *Media:* Oil, Egg Tempera. *Dealer:* Zwicker's Gallery Ltd 5415 Doyle St Halifax NS Can. *Mailing Add:* RR 2 Tatamagouche NS B0K 1V0 Canada

ZAVALA, MANUEL (MANUEL ZAVALA ALONSO)
PAINTER, PHOTOGRAPHER
b Mexico DF, Mar 15, 56. *Study:* Vocational Sch Physical Sci & Mathematics, bachelor's, 72; Nat Sch Painting & Sculpture, 72-76; Nat Inst Fine Arts. *Work:* Nat Inst Fine Arts, Visual Art Mus Mod Art & Nat Sch Plastic Arts, Mexico City; Casa de las Americas, La Habana, Cuba; Ministry Cult, Managua, Nicaragua. *Exhib:* Victor Needleman Gallery, Chicago, 80; Mex Coun Photog, 80; Los Angeles Convention Ctr, 80; Iturbide Palace Banamex, Mexico, 81; Palace Fine Arts, Mexico, 80 & 81; and others. *Collections Arranged:* Homage to Carlos Pellicer, 81, Photographic Plastic Transpositions, 81, Imaginary Biography, 81 & Obsessions and Recourses, 81, Contemp Art Forum, Mexico. *Teaching:* Prof graphic & printed commun, Sch Social Work, Mexico, 78-80. *Awards:* Nat Inst Fine Arts, Mexico, 80. *Bibliog:* Carla Stallwag (auth), Visual narrative, 80 & Judith A Hoffberg (auth), Books of Mexican artists, 81, Visual Arts Mag; Dominique Bras (auth), Everything the infinite, Mex J, 81. *Publ:* Contribr, The Writing Trip, 80 & contribr, Book of the First National Biennial of Photography, 81, Nat Inst Fine Arts, Mexico; contribr, Margo, Margo Group, 81. *Mailing Add:* Coscomete 65 Tlalpau Mexico

ZEIDENBERGS, OLAFS
SCULPTOR
b Latvia, Mar 17, 36; US citizen. *Study:* Univ Hartford, BFA, 61; Yale Univ, MFA, 63. *Work:* Morse Col, Yale Univ; Valley Bank & Trust Co, Springfield, Mass; Avon Corp, Rye, NY; McGraw-Hill Corp, New York; Unitarian Soc New Haven, Hamden, Conn. *Exhib:* Outdoor Sculpture, DeCordova Mus, Lincoln, Mass; Four Sculptors & Small Packages, Univ Conn; Mainstreams, Marietta Col; Tex Fine Arts Asn Ann, Austin. *Teaching:* Prof sculpture, Southern Conn State Col, 66- *Awards:* Silvermine Guild Artists Award; New Haven Festival Arts Award; Conn Acad Fine Arts Award. *Mem:* Conn Acad Fine Arts. *Media:* Metal, Plastics. *Mailing Add:* Dept of Art Southern Conn State Col New Haven CT 06515

ZEIDLER, EBERHARD HEINRICH
DESIGNER, ARCHITECT
b Braunsdorf, Ger, Jan 11, 26; Can citizen. *Study:* Bauhaus Weimar, cand arch, 45-48; Karlsruhe Univ, Dipl Ing, 49. *Comn:* Designer, McMaster Univ Health Sci Ctr, 68-72; Eaton Ctr, Toronto, 73-79 & Univ Alberta Health Sci Ctr, Edmonton, 76-81 and others. *Pos:* Guest speaker, var world confs; sr partner, Zeidler Partnership-Architects. *Teaching:* Lectr archit design, Univ Toronto, 53-55; vis prof, Univ Toronto, 83-84. *Awards:* 60 nat & int design awards. *Bibliog:* Robert Fulford (auth), The rise and fall of modern architecture, Saturday Night Mag, 80; and others. *Mem:* Academician Royal Can Acad Arts; fel Royal Archit Inst Can; Ont Asn Architects; hon fel Am Inst Architts; Order Architects Que; and others. *Publ:* Auth, Healing the Hospital-McMaster Health Science Centre: Its Conception & Evolution, 74; auth, Multi-use architecture, Karl Kramer Verlag, 81; and many articles in leading prof mags. *Mailing Add:* 315 Queen St W Toronto ON M5V 2X2 Canada

ZEISLER, CLAIRE (BLOCK)
SCULPTOR, COLLECTOR
b Cincinnati, Ohio, Apr 18, 03. *Study:* Studied sculpture with Alexander Archipenko; Inst Design, Chicago, with Lazlo Moholy Nagy. *Work:* Art Inst Chicago; Stedelijk Mus, Amsterdam, Neth; Milwaukee Art Ctr; Mus des Arts Decoratifs, Nantes, France; Mus Contemp Crafts, New York. *Exhib:* Textile Objekte, Kunstgewerbe Mus, Berlin, Ger, 75; Am Crafts '76: An Aesthet View, Mus Contemp Art, Chicago, 76; Object as Poet, Renwick Gallery of Nat Collection, DC, 77; Am Crafts, Philadelphia Mus Art, 77; Fiberworks, Am & Japan, Nat Mus Mod Art, Kyoto, Japan, 77; Fiberworks, Cleveland

Mus Art, 77; one-woman retrospective, Art Inst Chicago, 79; St Louis Art Mus, 80. *Bibliog:* J Parice Marandel (auth), An interview with Claire Zeisler, Arts Mag, 79; Henry Hanson (auth), A cascade of colored fiber, Chicago Mag, 79. *Media:* Fiber. *Mailing Add:* c/o Young Hoffman Gallery 215 W Superior Chicago IL 60610

ZEISLER, RICHARD SPIRO
COLLECTOR, PATRON
b Chicago, Ill, Nov 28, 16. *Study:* Amherst Col, BA; Harvard Univ. *Pos:* Trustee, chmn comt on exhibs & mem comt on painting & sculpture, Mus Mod Art, New York; bd dirs, Int Coun Mus Mod Art; mem comt on 20th century painting & sculpture, Art Inst Chicago; trustee, Skowhegan Sch Painting & Sculpture. *Mem:* Sustaining fel & gov life mem Art Inst Chicago; life mem Metrop Mus, New York; Brandeis Univ (fine arts awards adv comt); Mt Holyoke Col (art adv comt); fel Pierpont Morgan Libr; fel Frick Collection. *Collection:* European painting of the 20th century. *Mailing Add:* 767 Fifth Ave New York NY 10153

ZEITLIN, HARRIET BROOKS
PRINTMAKER, PAINTER
b Philadelphia, Pa, Feb 12, 29. *Study:* Pa Acad of Fine Arts, Univ Pa, BFA, 46-50; Barnes Found, 49 & 50; Univ Calif, Los Angeles, 63-69. *Work:* Libr Congress; US Info Serv, Am Embassy, New Delhi, India; Fluor Corp, Calif; Los Angeles Athletic Asn; Grunwald Ctr Graphic Arts, Univ Calif, Los Angeles. *Exhib:* 11 Women Artists, Santa Monica Col, 77; Original Masks by Outstanding Contemp Artists, Craft & Folk Art Mus, Los Angeles, 77; Calif Artists, San Antonio & Austin, Tex; Los Angeles Printmaking Soc Korean Exhib, 77; Palm Springs Mus Art, 80. *Pos:* Exec bd mem, Los Angeles Printmaking Soc, 64-69; artist/community relations & exec bd mem, Graphic Arts Coun of Los Angeles Co Mus of Art, 73-75; corresp secy, Artists for Economic Action, 73-74, vpres, 75-76, pres, 77- & exec dir CETA Title VI, Art in Public Places Grant, 77-78. *Teaching:* Artist in Communities Grant in Painting & Printmaking, Calif Arts Coun, Vista Del Mar, Los Angeles, 77; Mirman Sch, Los Angeles. *Bibliog:* Desiner W Mag, 77; Spinning Off, 80; Los Angeles Times, 82. *Mem:* Los Angeles Inst Contemp Art; Graphic Arts Coun, Los Angeles Co Mus of Art (exec bd, 73-75). *Publ:* Auth, A community of artists, Graphic Arts Coun Newsletter, Vol IX, No 4, Los Angeles Co Mus, 74; auth, Presidents Report, Artist for Economic Action Newsletters, 77-78. *Mailing Add:* 202 S Saltair Ave Los Angeles CA 90049

ZEITLIN, JACOB ISRAEL
DEALER, COLLECTOR
b Racine, Wis, Nov 4, 02. *Study:* Occidental Col, DHL. *Pos:* Pres, Zeitlin & Ver Brugge Gallery, 28- *Mem:* Print Coun, Los Angeles Co Mus; Gruenwald Collection, Univ Calif, Los Angeles (founder). *Specialty:* Graphic arts, old and modern, especially old masters; also Breughel and Kollwitz. *Collection:* Peter Breughel and the Elder Prints. *Mailing Add:* 815 N La Cienega Blvd Los Angeles CA 90069

ZELANSKI, PAUL JOHN
PAINTER
b Hartford, Conn, Apr 13, 31. *Study:* Cooper Union, cert, 55; Yale Univ, BFA, 57; Bowling Green State Univ, MA, 58. *Work:* Univ Mass, Amherst; Slater Mus, Norwich, Conn; Manchester Community Col, Conn; Hampshire Col, Northampton, Mass. *Exhib:* New England in Five Parts, De Cordova Mus, Lincoln, Mass; Harvard Univ Carpenter Ctr, Boston; New Directions in Painting, Univ Mass, Amherst; Hard Eye, Amel Gallery, New York; Selected Conn Painters & Sculptors Show, Slater Mus, Norwich, Conn, 80. *Teaching:* Instr painting, drawing & design, NTex State Univ, 58-61; instr painting, Ft Worth, Tex, 61-62; assoc prof art, Univ Conn, 62-76, prof, 76- *Awards:* Painting Prize, Norwich Ann, 73 & 79; Painting Prize, Beth El, 80; McDowell Colony; and others. *Bibliog:* Alan Graham Collier (auth), Form, Space and Vision, Prentice-Hall; Barnard Chaet (auth), Artists at work, Webb. *Mem:* Silvermine Guild Artists; Conn Acad Fine Arts; Berkshire Art League; Springfield Art League; New Haven Paint & Clay Club. *Media:* Acrylic, Plexiglas. *Publ:* Auth, Design Principles and Problems, Holt Rinehart & Winston. *Mailing Add:* Cowles Rd West Willington CT 06279

ZELENAK, EDWARD JOHN
SCULPTOR
b St Thomas, Ont, Nov 9, 40. *Study:* Meinszinger Sch Art, Detroit, Mich; Ft Worth Art Ctr, Tex; Ont Col Art, Toronto. *Work:* Cantonal Mus, Lausanne, Switz; Nat Gallery Can, Ottawa; Ont Art Gallery, Toronto; Rothman's Ltd, Stratford, Ont; Dept Pub Works, Toronto. *Comn:* Major outdoor sculpture, Nat Gallery Can, 72, Dept Pub Works, Toronto, 73 & North York, 76; Rothman's Art Gallery, 73 & Northfield Minn, Carleton Col, 73; major sculpture, Prov Dept Pub Works, Kitchener, Ont, 77. *Exhib:* One-man exhib, Major Outdoor Sculpture, Nat Art Ctr, Ottawa, 69 & Carleton Col, 72; Tendence Actuelles, Galerie de France, Paris, 69; 3rd Int Pioneer Galleries Exhib, Cantonnal Mus, Lausanne & Mus Mod Art, Paris, 70; 49th Parallels, Ringling Mus, Sarasota, Fla & Mus Contemp Art, Chicago, 71; Washington, Northfield, Milwaukee major touring sculpture, Minn State Art Coun & Henry Gallery, 73-74; Mt Allison Univ, 75; Art Fiera, Bologna, Italy, 77. *Awards:* Can Coun Jr Arts Grant, 68-71; Sr Arts Grant, 73-75; Prov Ont Coun Arts Grant in Aid, 74. *Bibliog:* Jean Noel Chandler (auth), article in Artscanada, 4/69; Barry Lord (auth), articles in Art in Am, 1-2/69; R Naasgard (auth), article in Artscanada, 6/73. *Mem:* Royal Can Acad Acad Arts. *Media:* Metal, Fiberglas. *Mailing Add:* c/o Carmen Lamanna Gallery 840 Yonge St Toronto ON M4W 2H1 Canada

ZELT, MARTHA
PRINTMAKER, INSTRUCTOR
b Washington, Pa, Nov 16, 30. *Study:* Conn Col; Pa Acad Fine Arts; New Sch Social Res, with Antonio Frasconi; Mus Arte Mod, Brazil, with John Friedlaender; Univ NMex, with Garo Antreasian; Temple Univ, BA. *Work:* Carnegie Inst, Mus Art; Pa Acad Fine Arts; Princeton Univ; Philadelphia Mus Art; Brooklyn Mus; and others. *Exhib:* Int Bienale, Sao Paulo, Brazil, 61; Pa Acad Fine Arts Nat Ann, 61-70; one-man shows, Pa Acad Peale Galleries, 72, Print Club, 75, Brooklyn Mus, 80 & Carnegie Inst, Mus Art, 81; 30 Yrs Am Printmaking, Brooklyn Mus, 76; New Ways With Paper, Nat Collection of Fine Arts, Washington, DC; and others. *Pos:* Dir graphic workshop prof artists, Pa Acad Fine Arts, 63-65; demonstrating artist & printmaker, Prints in Progress, Philadelphia, 63-71; secy, Exp in Art & Technol, Inc, Philadelphia, 68. *Teaching:* Instr printmaking, Pa Acad Fine Arts, 68-82; instr printmaking, Philadelphia Col Art, 69-82, part-time lectr, currently; resident printmaker, Va Mus Fine Arts, 75-82, Guilford Col, 76, Univ NC, Chapel Hill, 81. *Awards:* Cresson Traveling Award, 54 & Scheidt Mem Traveling Award, Pa Acad Fine Arts; Print Club Fel, 65. *Mem:* Print Club; fel Pa Acad Fine Arts; Am Color Print Soc. *Media:* Wood, Metal. *Mailing Add:* 1811 Chestnut St Philadelphia PA 19103

ZEMANS, JOYCE L
EDUCATOR, HISTORIAN
b Toronto, Can, Apr 21, 40. *Study:* Univ Toronto, BA, 62, MA, 66. *Collections Arranged:* Jock Macdonald: The Inner Landscape (auth, catalog), Art Gallery Ont, Can, 81-82; Alexandra Lake: The Watercolours, Robert McLaughlin Gallery, Oshawa, Can, 84. *Pos:* Bd Governors, York Univ, Toronto, Can. *Teaching:* Art historian, Ont Col Art, Toronto, 66-75, chmn, Art Hist Dept, 69-71, chmn, Liberal Arts Studies, 72-75; assoc prof art hist, York Univ, Toronto, 75-, chmn, Dept Visual Arts, 75-81. *Mem:* Univ Arts Asn Can; Col Art Asn Am; Int Asn Art Critics; Nat Coun Art Administrators. *Publ:* Auth, The Student Subject and Careers Series, Univ Toronto; auth, The Impact of Automatism on the Art of Jock Macdonald, Can Art Rev, Vol VII, No 1-2, 80. *Mailing Add:* c/o Fac Fine Arts York Univ Downsview ON M3J 1P3 Canada

ZERNER, HENRI THOMAS
HISTORIAN, CURATOR
b Suresnes, France, May 15, 39. *Study:* Univ Paris, Lic es Lett, 61; Dr(fine arts), 69; Ecole Pratique des Hautes Etudes, Paris, dipl(fine arts), 63. *Collections Arranged:* Venice in the Eighteenth Century (cataloged), Mus Art, RI Sch Design, 67 & J J J Tissot (cataloged), 67; The School of Fontainebleau (cataloged), Grand Palais, Paris, 72-73. *Pos:* Cur, Painting & Graphic Arts Mus, RI Sch Design, 65-66 & Prints & Drawing Mus, 66-72; cur prints, Fogg Mus, Harvard Univ, presently. *Teaching:* From asst prof to assoc prof fine arts, Brown Univ, Providence, RI, 66-72; prof fine arts, Harvard Univ, Cambridge, Mass, 72- *Awards:* Guggenheim Fel, Paris, 71; Prix Achille Fould, Acad des Inscriptions et Belles Lett, 71; and others. *Publ:* Coauth, Italian Art 1500-1600, Prentice-Hall, 66; auth, Tout l'oeuvre peint de Raphael, Flammarion, 69; auth, L'Ecole de Fontainebleau-Gravures, Abrams, 70; auth, Illustrated Bartsch, Vol XVI, In: Sixteenth Century Italian Etchings, 79; coauth (with Charles Rosen), Romanticism and Realism: The Mythology of 19th Century Art, Viking, 84. *Mailing Add:* 87 Pinckney St Boston MA 02114

ZETLIN, FAY (FLORENCE ANSHEN)
PAINTER, MURALIST
b Boston, Mass, Oct 9, 06. *Study:* Pembroke Col, AB(cum laude), 28. *Work:* Houston Mus Fine Arts, Tex; Xerox Corp; Phillip Morris Res Ctr, Richmond, Va; Mint Mus Fine Arts; Chrysler Mus, Norfolk, Va. *Comn:* Earthworks design, Diggs Park Playground, Norfolk Redevelopment & Housing Authority, Va, 72; libr mural, Old Dominion Univ, Norfolk, 76-77. *Exhib:* Nat Print & Drawing Exhib, Dulin Gallery, Knoxville, Tenn, 64 & 70; High Mus Art, Atlanta, Ga, 64; Ann Piedmont Exhib, Mint Mus, Charlotte, NC, 64; one-person shows, Chrysler Mus, Norfolk, 77, 81 & 81 & Nat Asn Schs Art, 83-84; Patina Exhib, President's Coun Ageing, Washington, DC, 82; Muscarelle Mus & Zollinger Mus, Col William & Mary, 83-84; Marsh Gallery, Univ Richmond, 84; and others. *Pos:* Vis artist, Va Wesleyan Col, 65-66 & Huntingdon Col, Montgomery, Ala, 76. *Teaching:* Artist-in-residence, Old Dominion Univ, 69-80, adj artist-in-residence, 80- *Awards:* Purchase Awards, Parthenon Mus, 64 & Metrop Mus, New York, 82; Nat Found for the Arts grant, Va Comn for the Arts & Humanities, 77. *Bibliog:* Stefan Grunewald (auth), In Fay Zetlin's Studio (doc), Pub TV WHRO, Norfolk, 70; Creating a natural environment for urban children, Brown Univ Mag, 73; Marshall McLuhan & Harley Parker (auths), Through the Vanishing Point, Art in Poetry & Painting, Harper & Row. *Mem:* Women in Art. *Media:* Acrylic; Microfiche, Color Xerox Prints. *Publ:* Coauth, with Ernest Mauer, Plastics Fables, Saturday Press, 69. *Mailing Add:* 7300 Heron Lane Norfolk VA 23505

ZEVON, IRENE
PAINTER
b New York, NY, Nov 24, 18. *Study:* With Nahum Tschacbasov. *Work:* Butler Inst Am Art, Youngstown, Ohio; La Jolla Art Ctr, Calif; Kenosha Pub Mus, Wis; Mary Buie Mus, Oxford, Miss; Univ Ga Mus, Athens; plus many others including pvt collections. *Exhib:* Kenosha Pub Mus, Wis; St Louis Pub Libr, Mo; Long Island Univ, NY; Nat Acad Design, New York; Nat Asn Women Artists Ann, New York, 72; plus many other group & one-woman shows in univs, mus & galleries. *Awards:* Marion K Haldenstein Mem Prize, Nat Asn Women Artists, 72. *Mem:* Nat Asn Women Artists. *Media:* Oil. *Mailing Add:* 222 W 23rd St New York NY 10011

ZHEUTLIN, DALE R
SCULPTOR, EDUCATOR
b Newark, NJ, July 27, 48. *Study:* RI Sch Design, BFA, 70; Columbia Univ, MFA, 72; Haystack Mountain Sch Crafts, 78. *Work:* Educ Testing Serv, Princeton, NJ; IBM Collection, NY; Pfizer Corp, New York. *Comn:* Bankers Trust Co, White Plains, NY, 80; American Banker, Bond Buyer, New York, 83. *Exhib:* Neuberger Mus, Purchase, NY, 77; Nat Asn Women Artists, Fed Bldg, New York, 80; Nat Arts Club, New York, 81; Ten Downtown, New York, 81; solo exhib, Hudson River Mus, Yonkers, NY, 82; Renwick Gallery, Smithsonian Inst, 83; and others. *Teaching:* Art fac, New Rochelle High Sch, NY, 74-; adj prof ceramics, Col New Rochelle, NY, 77- *Awards:* Award Merit, Mamaroneck Artists Guild, 79; Pauline Law Prize, Nat Asn Women Artists, New York, 80; Sculpture Award, Hudson River Mus, New York, 81. *Bibliog:* Ruth Katz (auth), An ambitious spring invitational, 82 & Diverse craftsmen, reciprocal themes, 83, New York Times; Roslyn Tunis (auth), Ancient inspirations, contemporary interpretations, Ceramics Mo, 83. *Mem:* Nat Asn Women Artists Inc; Artists Equity Asn; Empire State Crafts Alliance. *Media:* Ceramics. *Publ:* Contribr, Apprenticeship in Craft, Daniel Clark Bks, 81. *Mailing Add:* 139 Sixth St Pelham NY 10803

ZIB, TOM (THOMAS A ZIBELLI)
CARTOONIST
b Mt Vernon, NY. *Study:* Grand Cent Sch Art; Com Illus Studios. *Publ:* Contribr, Saturday Rev & Weight Watchers, 72, Saturday Evening Post, Nat Enquirer, Reader's Digest, 73-81 & Wall Street J, 81. *Mailing Add:* 167 E Devonia Ave Mt Vernon NY 10552

ZIEMANN, RICHARD CLAUDE
PRINTMAKER, EDUCATOR
b Buffalo, NY, July 3, 32. *Study:* Albright Art Sch; Yale Univ, BFA & MFA; painting with Albers & Brooks; printmaking with Peterdi; drawings with Chaet. *Work:* Brooklyn Mus, NY; Silvermine Guild Art; Seattle Art Mus, Wash; De Cordova & Dana Mus; Libr Cong & Nat Gallery Art, Washington, DC; and others. *Comn:* Print Editions for Int Graphic Arts Soc, 58 & 60, Yale Univ Alumni Asn, 60 & Pan-Am Airlines, 62. *Exhib:* American Prints Today Touring Exhib, most maj print exhibs, 58-65, 24 mus, 62-63 & Paris Biennale, 63; one-man shows, Allen R Hite Art Inst, Univ Louisville, 67, Alpha Gallery, Boston, 67 & Univ Conn Art Gallery, 68; Oversize Prints, Whitney Mus Am Art. *Pos:* Supvr, Graphic Workshop in Graphic Arts USA Touring Exhib, Soviet Union, 63-64; artist in residence, Dartmouth Col, summer 71. *Teaching:* Asst prof art, Hunter Col, 66; instr printmaking, Yale Univ Summer Sch, 66-67; from assoc prof to prof art, Lehman Col, 78- *Awards:* Fulbright Grant to Netherlands, 58-59; Nat Inst Arts & Lett Grant, 66; Tiffany Found Grant, 60-61; and others. *Mem:* Soc Am Graphic Artists. *Dealer:* Jane Haslem Gallery 2121 P St NW Washington DC 20037; Alpha Galleries 121 Newbury St Boston MA 02116. *Mailing Add:* Dept of Art City Univ of New York Bronx NY 10468

ZIETZ, STEPHEN JOSEPH
LIBRARIAN, HISTORIAN
b Mobile, Ala, July 24, 49. *Study:* Spring Hill Col, Mobile, BA, 71; Villa Schifanoia Grad Sch of Fine Arts, Florence, Italy, MA(art hist), 73; Emory Univ, Atlanta, Ga, MLS, 75; Pratt Inst, MFA(painting), 79. *Pos:* Art librn, Joint Univ Libr, Vanderbilt Univ, 75-77; head librn, Fine Arts Libr, Lake Placid Sch Art, 77-78; art librn, State Univ NY, Col at Purchase, 78-79; cataloger, Pratt Inst Libr, 79-80; cataloger, Columbia Univ Librs, 81- *Mem:* Art Libr Soc NAm. *Res:* Seventeenth century Italian painting as related to the Counter-Reformation. *Interests:* Graphic artists and art. *Mailing Add:* Apt 101 610 W 116th St New York NY 10027

ZIFF, JERROLD
HISTORIAN, COLLECTOR
b Los Angeles, Calif, Dec 20, 28. *Study:* Occidental Col, BA, 51; Univ Southern Calif, MA, 54; Harvard Univ, PhD, 59. *Collections Arranged:* French Masters: Rocco to Romanticism (coauth, catalog), Univ Calif, Los Angeles, 60-61; George F Mc Murray Collection of 19th century American Paintings, Trinity Col, Hartford, Conn, 68; Drawings from Four Collections (co-auth, catalog), 73 & II (auth, catalog), Univ Ill. *Pos:* Asst prof 19th century art, Univ Calif, Los Angeles, 58-66; prof 18th & 19th century art, Trinity Col, Hartford, 66-69; prof 18th & 19th century art & drawings, Univ Ill, Champaign, 69- *Mem:* Col Art Asn; Midwest Art Hist Soc; Turner Soc. *Res:* Art of J M W Turner; old master drawings. *Collection:* Old master and 19th century drawings. *Mailing Add:* 140 Fine Arts Bldg Univ Ill Champaign IL 61820

ZILCZER, JUDITH KATY
HISTORIAN, CURATOR
b Waterbury, Conn, Nov 6, 48. *Study:* George Washington Univ, BA, 69 & MA, 71; Univ Del, PhD, 75. *Collections Arranged:* The Noble Buyer: John Quinn, Patron of the Avant-Garde (auth, catalog), Hirshhorn Mus & Sculpture Garden, 78; Oscar Bluemner: The Hirshhorn Museum Collection (auth, catalogue), 79; Five Distinguished Alumni: The WPA Fed Art Project (auth, catalog), Hirshhorn Mus, 82; Joseph Stella: The Hirshhorn Museum Collection (auth, catalog), 83; and others. *Pos:* Historian, Hirshhorn Mus & Sculpture Garden, 74- *Teaching:* Instr art hist, Univ Del, Newark, 74; asst professorial lectr in Am studies, George Washington Univ, 75-76; assoc professorial lectr, 80- *Awards:* Unidel Found Fel, Univ Del, 71-73; Smithsonian Fel, Nat Collection of Fine Arts, 73-74; Penrose Fund res grant, Am Philos Soc, 76-77. *Mem:* Col Art Asn; Women's Caucus for Art; Asn Hist Am Art; Nat Trust Hist Preserv; Am Asn Mus. *Res:* Nineteenth and twentieth century art; history of patronage. *Publ:* Auth, Raymond Duchamp-Villon:

Pioneer of modern sculpture, Philadelphia Mus, Art Bulletin, fall 80; auth, The theory of direct carving in modern sculpture, Oxford Art J, 11/81; auth, John Quinn and modern art collectors in America, 1913-24, Am Art J, winter 82; auth, In the face of war: The last works of Raymond Duchamp-Villon, Art Bulletin, 3/83; and others. *Mailing Add:* c/o Hirshhorn Mus & Independence Ave & Eighth St SW Washington DC 20560

ZILKA, MICHAEL JOHN
EDUCATOR, STUDIO DIRECTOR
b Oak Park, Ill, Oct 19, 47. *Study:* Ill State Univ; Univ Wis, with Donald Reitz & Bruce Breckenridge, MFA; Res Grant, Japan, Thailand & Malaysia. *Exhib:* 100 Years of American Dolls, Kohler Art Ctr, Wis; Scripps Col; Art Ctr, Evanston, Ill; Rochester Art Ctr, Minn. *Pos:* Dir (ceramics grant), Mich Arts Coun, 75; consult, Polytechnical Consultants Inc, 79- *Teaching:* Instr, Milton Col, Wis, 70-71; instr ceramics, Oxbow Summer Sch Painting, Saugatuck, Mich, 70-75; instr ceramics & sculpture design, Stephens Col, 72-79. *Mem:* Col Art Asn; Am Fedn Teachers. *Media:* Ceramic, Wood. *Mailing Add:* Polytechnical Consultants 2525 W Peterson Chicago IL 60659

ZIMILES, MURRAY
PAINTER, EDUCATOR
b New York, NY, Nov 30, 41. *Study:* Univ Ill, BFA, 63; Cornell Univ, MFA, 65; Ecole Nat Superieure Beaux-Arts, Paris, 66-67. *Work:* Brooklyn Mus, NY; Neuberger Mus, New York; Royal Norweg Govt Collection; Nat Collection Fine Arts; NY Public Libr; and others. *Comn:* Civic Ctr, Dutchin Co Arts Coun, Poughkeepsie, NY, 81. *Exhib:* Prints from Portfolios, Brooklyn Mus, 70; one-man shows, Kunstnerforbundet Gallery, Oslo, Norway, 72; Vassar Col Gallery, 77, Sindin Galleries, New York, 78, Neuberger Mus, New York, 80-81 & Johnson Mus, Cornell Univ, Ithaca, NY, 81. *Teaching:* Instr printmaking, Pratt Graphics Ctr, New York, 68-71; asst prof drawing & printmaking, Silvermine Col Art, New Canaan, Conn, 68-71; asst prof drawing & printmaking, State Univ NY, New Paltz, 72-77; assoc prof drawing & printmaking, State Univ NY, Purchase, 77- *Awards:* Found Etats-Unis Fel, Paris, 65-66; Royal Norweg Govt Fel, 71; State Univ NY res grants, 76 & 79. *Bibliog:* New talent, Artist Proof Ann, 71; article, Arts Mag, 1/78; review, New York Times, 1/4/81. *Mem:* Soc Am Graphic Artists. *Publ:* Coauth, The Technique of Fine Art Lithography, Van Nostrand Reinhold, 70; coauth, Early American Mills, Clarkson Potter, 73; coauth, The Lithographic Workshop Around the World, Van Nostrand Reinhold, 74. *Dealer:* Sindin Galleries 1035 Madison Ave New York NY. *Mailing Add:* RFD 1 Millerton NY 12546

ZIMMERMAN, ELYN
SCULPTOR, ENVIRONMENTAL ARTIST
b Philadelphia, Pa, Dec 16, 45. *Study:* Univ Calif, Los Angeles, BA(psychol), 68, MFA, 72. *Work:* Los Angeles Co Mus Art, Los Angeles; Whitney Mus Am Art. *Comn:* Ft Lincoln Park, Washington DC; Dept Housing & Community Development & Nat Endowment Arts, 79; Laguna Gloria Mus, 82; Nat Geographical Soc Headquarters, 82; and others. *Exhib:* Solo shows, PS 1, 72, Mus Contemp Art, Chicago, 79 & Hudson River Mus, 83; Whitney Mus Am Art Biennial, New York, 75; Calif Sculpture 1975-80, San Diego Mus Art, 80; Drawings: The Pluralist Decade, Venice Biennale, USA Pavillion, 80; Architectural Sculpture, Los Angeles, Calif, 80; Artists Gardens & Parks, Mus Contemp Art, Chicago, Ill, 81; Hirshhorn Mus, 83; and many others. *Teaching:* Instr, Calif Inst Arts, 75; State Univ NY, Purchase, 79- *Awards:* Creative Artists Pub Serv Grant, 80; Nat Endowment Arts Fel, 76, 80 & 83; Japan-US Exchange Fel, 81. *Bibliog:* Joanne Frueh (auth), Artforum, 2/80; Kirk Varnedoe (auth), Site lines, Arts Mag, 12/78; Jeanne Silverthorne (auth), article, Artforum, 10/83. *Mem:* Los Angeles Inst Contemp Art (bd dirs, 76-78). *Media:* Various Media. *Mailing Add:* 57 Leonard St New York NY 10013

ZIMMERMAN, KATHLEEN MARIE
PAINTER, COLLAGE ARTIST
b Floral Park, NY, Apr 24, 23. *Study:* Art Students League; Nat Acad Sch Fine Arts. *Work:* Butler Inst Am Art, Youngstown, Ohio; Sheldon Swope Art Gallery, Terre Haute, Ind; Univ Wyo Art Mus, Laramie; Lowe Art Mus, Univ Miami, Coral Gables, Fla; NC Mus Art. Raleigh; and others. *Exhib:* Art USA, 58; Silvermine Guild, Conn, 62; Nat Acad Design, 69, 75-78, 80 & 82; one-man show, Westbeth Gallery, 73 & 74, Am Watercolor Soc, 75-78 & 80, New York & many others. *Teaching:* Instr drawing & painting, Midtown Sch Art, New York, 47-52. *Awards:* Scholar, John F & Anna Lee Stacey Found, 54; nine prizes, Nat Asn Women Artists, 57-83; Henry Ward Ranger Fund Purchases, Nat Acad Design, 76 & 82; and others. *Bibliog:* James Mellow (auth), article, New York Times, 2/17/73; Hilton Kramer (auth), article, New York Times, 6/10/77; Gerald F Brommer (auth), The Art of Collage, Davis Publ, 78. *Mem:* Nat Asn Women Artists; Am Watercolor Soc; Audubon Artists; Allied Artists Am. *Media:* Oil, Acrylic; Paper. *Publ:* Co-illusr, Diet for a Small Planet, 71. *Mailing Add:* 463 West St A1110 New York NY 10014

ZIMMERMAN, PAUL WARREN
PAINTER, INSTRUCTOR
b Toledo, Ohio, Apr 29, 21. *Study:* John Herron Art Sch, BFA. *Work:* Pa Acad Fine Arts, Philadelphia; Houston Mus Fine Art; Butler Inst Am Art, Youngstown, Ohio; Springfield Mus Fine Art, Mass; Wadsworth Atheneum, Hartford, Conn. *Comn:* Mural, First New Haven Nat Bank, Conn, 65. *Exhib:* Indiana Artists Exhibition, John Herron Art Mus, Indianapolis, 57; American Painting & Sculpture, Univ Ill, 61; Pa Acad Fine Arts, Philadelphia, 62; 144th Ann Exhib, Nat Acad Design, New York, 69; Midyear Show, Butler Inst Am Art, Youngstown, 70. *Teaching:* Prof painting & design, Univ Hartford Art Sch, 47- *Awards:* First Prize, Conn Watercolor Soc, 64; Altman Landscape

Prize for Second Place, 67 & First Place, 69, Nat Acad Design. *Bibliog:* Henry Pitz (auth), Paintings of Paul Zimmerman, Am Artist Mag, 1/60. *Mem:* Nat Acad Design; Conn Acad Fine Arts; Conn Watercolor Soc (pres, 52-53). *Media:* Oil. *Dealer:* Munson Gallery New Haven CT; Korn Bluth Gallery Fair Lawn NJ. *Mailing Add:* 257 Victoria Rd Hartford CT 06114

ZIMMERMAN, WILLIAM HAROLD
PAINTER, ILLUSTRATOR
b Dillsboro, Ind, Oct 1, 37. *Study:* Cincinnati Art Acad. *Work:* Cincinnati Mus Natural Hist, Ohio; Ind State Mus, Indianapolis; Pomona Col, Calif; Gallery Fine Arts, Columbus, Ohio; Lilly Libr, Bloomington, Ind. *Exhib:* Soc Animal Artists Ann, New York, 67; one-man shows in New York, San Francisco, Chicago, Cincinnati & Columbus, Ohio; Bird Art Exhib, Leigh Yawkey Woodson Art Mus, 78-81; Birds, Nat Collection Fine Art, Smithsonian Inst, Washington, DC, 80; Bird Art Exhib, Royal Scottish Acad, Edinburgh, Scotland, British Mus, London, Eng & Carnegie Mus Natural Hist, Pittsburgh, Pa, 82. *Awards:* Award for Magpie, Cincinnati Animal Art Show, 66; Hoosier Art Salon Merit Award, 78; Ind Heritage Art Popular Award, 79. *Bibliog:* Bill Thomas (auth), Dillsboro's Audubon, Nat Observer, 11/12/65; Jay Shuler (auth), A real artist has to work for himself, Carolina Outdoors, 9/71; Carolyn Tufford (auth), Lifestyle, Bloomington Ind Herald-Telephone. *Media:* Gouache, Acrylic. *Mem:* Soc Animal Artists. *Publ:* Coauth & illusr, Topflight, Speed Index to Waterfowl, 66; auth, Waterfowl of North America, 74; illusr, Birds of Indiana, 84. *Mailing Add:* RR 3 Box 36 Nashville IN 47448

ZIMON, KATHY ELIZABETH
LIBRARIAN
b Szeged, Hungary, Feb 20, 41; Can citizen. *Study:* Univ BC, BA(art hist), 66, BLS, 69, MA(art hist), 70. *Pos:* Fine arts librn, Univ Calgary Libr, Alta, 69- *Mem:* Can Libr Asn; Can Asn of Spec Libr & Info Serv (newsletter ed, 75-78, chmn art sect, 79-80); Art Libr Soc North Am. *Mailing Add:* Libr Div Fine Arts Univ Calgary Calgary AB T2N 1N4 Canada

ZINGALE, LAWRENCE
PAINTER
b Florida, NY, Aug 12, 38. *Work:* Int Mus Folk Art, Santa Fe, NMex; Chase Manhattan Bank, New York; Silvermine Guild Ctr Arts, New Cannan, Conn. *Exhib:* Int Mus of Folk Art, Santa Fe, 76; The All-Am Dog, Mus of Folk Art, New York, 77-78; The Am Game, Wilson Art Ctr, Rochester, NY, 78; one-man shows, American Hurrah Antiques, New York, 78 & Jay Johnson Gallery, New York, 81. *Bibliog:* Robert Bishop (auth), The All-American Dog, Avon Publ, New York, 77; Ellen Stern (auth), article, New York Mag, 10/78; article, Attenzione Mag, 12/81; Jay Johnson & William Ketchum (auths), American Folk Art of the Twentieth Century, Rizzoli Publ; and others. *Media:* Oil, Acrylic. *Mailing Add:* c/o Jay Johnson Gallery 1044 Madison Ave New York NY 10021

ZIRKER, JOSEPH
PRINTMAKER, LECTURER
b Los Angeles, Calif, Aug 13, 24. *Study:* Univ Calif, Los Angeles, 43-44, 46-47; Univ Denver, BFA, 49; with Jules Heller & Francis de Erdely, Univ Southern Calif, MFA, 51; Tamarind Lithography Workshop, printer fel, 62-63 & res fel, 64. *Work:* Brooklyn Art Mus, NY; Tamarind Archives, Tamarind Lithography Workshop; Stanley Freenean Collection, Los Angeles Co Mus; Oakland Art Mus, Calif; Achenbach Found, Calif Palace Legion Honor, San Francisco. *Exhib:* New Dimensions of Lithography, Tamarind Lithographs, Univ Southern Calif, 64; Calif Printmakers, Achenbach Found, Calif Palace Legion Honor, 71; New Ways With Paper, Nat Collection of Fine Arts, Smithsonian Inst, Washington, DC, 77-78; one-man shows, Calif Palace Legion Honor, San Francisco, 74 & De Saisset Art Gallery & Mus, Univ Santa Clara, Calif, 75; New American Monotypes & Paper as Medium, Smithsonian Traveling Exhib, 78-80; Paper/Art, Crocker Art Mus, Sacramento, Calif, 81. *Pos:* Dir, Joseph Press, Venice, Calif, 63-64. *Teaching:* Lectr printmaking, Univ Southern Calif, 63; instr, Chouinard Art Inst, Los Angeles, 63; instr drawing, San Jose City Col, 66-82; lectr, Stanford Univ, Calif, 81. *Awards:* Third Nat Print Exhib Award, Bradley Univ, Ill, 52; 2nd Nat Exhib of Prints, Univ Southern Calif, 52; 7th Ann Print Exhib, Brooklyn Mus, 53. *Mem:* Col Art Asn Am. *Dealer:* Gallerie Smith-Andersen Homer Ave & Emerson St Palo Alto CA 94301; Klein Gallery 356 West Huron Chicago IL 60610. *Mailing Add:* 451 O'Connor St Palo Alto CA 94303

ZISLA, HAROLD
PAINTER, GRAPHIC ARTIST
b Cleveland, Ohio, June 28, 25. *Study:* Cleveland Inst Art; Western Reserve Univ, BS(educ) & AM. *Exhib:* Cleveland Mus Art; South Bend Michiana; John Herron Art Mus; Ft Wayne Art Mus; Kalamazoo Art Inst; and others. *Pos:* Dir & bd mem, South Bend Art Ctr, 57- *Teaching:* Instr, South Bend Art Ctr, 53-; prof fine arts, Ind Univ, South Bend, currently. *Mailing Add:* Ind Univ Northside at Greenlawn South Bend IN 46615

ZIVIC, WILLIAM THOMAS
PAINTER, SCULPTOR
b Ironwood, Mich, Aug 31, 30. *Work:* City of Tucson; Univ Ariz; Pima Col; Lockheed Aircraft, Los Angeles; Grissmer Corp, Indianapolis, Ind; plus over 1,000 pvt collections, US, Europe, Africa & Asia. *Comn:* Paintings, Great Western Bank, Phoenix, 73; painting, Ariz Bank, Tucson, 75; painting, US Postal Serv, 75. *Exhib:* Tucson Art Ctr Ann, 74; Alamo Kiwanis Art Show, San Antonio, 74; Casa Grande Art Fiesta, Ariz, 75; Tubac Art Festival, Ariz, 75. *Mem:* Tucson Art Ctr; Casa Grande Art Asn; Santa Cruz Valley Art Asn. *Media:* Bronze; Multimedia. *Publ:* Illusr, Tucson Bi-Centennial Mag, 75; illusr, Southwest Memories, 75. *Dealer:* Trailside Galleries PO Box 858 Jackson WY 83001. *Mailing Add:* 1516 Turquoise Vista Tucson AZ 85710

ZLOTNICK, DIANA SHIRLEY
COLLECTOR, PATRON
b Los Angeles, Calif, Sept 3, 27. *Study:* Calif State Univ, Los Angeles, BS, 48. *Work:* Donated to Los Angeles Co Mus Art, La Jolla Mus Contemp Art, Newport Harbor Art Mus, San Francisco Mus Mod Art & Calif State Univ, Northridge. *Collections Arranged:* Tony DeLap, Roland Reiss & Michael Brewster's controversial sound environment (auth, catalog), L A Pierce Col. *Pos:* Pvt asst, Pasadena Art Mus, 70-71; publ, Newslett on the Arts, Los Angeles, 71-; cur, L A Pierce Col, 80. *Teaching:* Lectr, Univ Southern Calif, 72-75 & Los Angeles Pierce Col, 80. *Bibliog:* Art Seidenbaum (auth), Home is where the art is, 11/19/65, Dianne Thomas (auth), How to collect art worth $80,000 on pin money, 11/16/69 & Donna Scheibe (auth), Young artists aided in struggle, 2/23/73, Los Angeles Times. *Mem:* Hon mem Newport Harbor Art Mus, Otis Art Asn & Mus Sci & Indust. *Interests:* Supportive role for the art community via Newsletter on the Arts providing continuous exposure for emerging and established artists of varied aesthetic attitudes on the basis of quality. *Collection:* Reveals the wedding of assemblage and pop art images in the fusion of painting and sculpture in California since the sixties. *Mailing Add:* 2968 Dona Susana Dr Studio City CA 91604

ZLOWE, FLORENCE M
PAINTER, DRAFTSMAN
b Allentown, Pa. *Study:* Philadelphia Col Art, cert, 33; New York Univ, with Samuel M Adler, 51-54. *Work:* Philadelphia Mus Art; Butler Inst Am Art, Youngstown, Ohio; Smithsonian Inst; Minn Mus Art, St Paul; Cooper-Hewitt Mus, New York; and others. *Exhib:* Nat Acad Design, New York, 58 & 65; Chrysler Mus, Norfolk, Va, 64; Chateau de la Napoule, Alpes Maritime, France, 65; Jersey City Mus, NJ, 70; Minn Mus Art, St Paul, 75. *Awards:* Medal Hon First Prize, Nat Asn Women Artists, 58 & Ann Award, 80; Oil Award, NJ Soc Painters & Sculptors, 61; and others. *Mem:* Am Soc Contemp Artists (treas, 76-80); Nat Asn Women Artists; NJ Soc Painters & Sculptors; Artists Equity Asn New York. *Media:* Oil, Watercolor; Pen & Ink. *Mailing Add:* 440 East 57th St New York NY 10022

ZONA, LOUIS A
MUSEUM DIRECTOR, EDUCATOR
b New Castle, Pa, June 28, 44. *Study:* Youngstown State Univ, BS(art educ), 66; Univ Pittsburgh, MS(art educ), 69; Carnegie-Mellon Univ, doctorate, 73. *Collections Arranged:* Lowell Nesbitt Retrospective (auth, catalog), Butler Inst, 82; Patrick Ireland, Blue Room Exhib, Butler Inst, 83; Impressionism: An American View, Butler Inst, 83; National Midyear Invitational Exhib, Butler Inst, 83. *Pos:* Exec dir, Butler Inst Am Art, Youngstown, Ohio, 81- *Teaching:* Adj prof art & museum studies, Westminster Col, Pa, formerly; assoc prof art hist & museology, Youngstown State Univ, 70- *Mem:* Hoyt Inst; Ohio Found Arts; trustee Youngstown Area Arts Coun. *Publ:* Auth, George Segal comes to Youngstown, Dialogue, 80; Celebrating Am art, Hoyt Inst Newsletter, 80; Painterly deliberations, Dialogue, 4/81; Alfred Leslie's Americans: Youngstown, Ohio, Dialogue, 82. *Mailing Add:* Butler Inst Am Art 524 Wick Ave Youngstown OH 44502

ZONIA, DHIMITRI
PAINTER, PRINTMAKER
b St Louis, Mo, June 12, 21. *Study:* Independent study in Italy & Eng. *Work:* Butler Inst Am Art, Youngstown, Ohio; Ark Art Ctr, Little Rock; Okla Art Ctr, Oklahoma City; Art Gallery, Del Mar Col, Corpus Christi, Tex; Mus Relig Art, Green Lake, Wis. *Comn:* Mural, Carlyn H Wohl Bldg Info Ctr, 81; stained glass, murals & interior design, Sts Cyril & Methody Church, Granite City, Ill, 82. *Exhib:* One-man show, Albrecht Mus, St Joseph, Mo, 73; Midyear Show, Butler Inst Am Art, Youngstown, Ohio, 74; Western Ill Univ, 79; St Louis Artist's Guild, 79; Sun Carnival Nat Exhib, El Paso Mus, 79; Nat Traveling Exhib, Minn Mus Art, 80; Ariz State Univ, 80. *Teaching:* Instr painting drawing, Jewish Community Ctr Asn, currently. *Awards:* Butler Inst Am Art Award, Youngstown, Ohio, 77; Am Artist Mag Prize, 78; First Prize Painting, Mo Artists, Kansas City, 81-82; and others. *Bibliog:* Floyd Bowser (auth), Aspiring artist, St Louis Post Dispatch, 4/26/70; Rick Graefe (auth), Kimmswick gains an artist, Courier-J, 79; Hazel Lee (auth), Renown artist moves to Kimmswick, St Louis J, 79. *Mem:* St Louis Artists Guild (bd gov, 79-81). *Media:* Oil; Etching. *Publ:* Auth, Some thoughts on book illustrating, CPH Commentator, 74; coauth, Arise My Love, Concordia Publ Co, 75; contribr, Painting in the realistic manner, Pallette Talk, 80. *Mailing Add:* 4680 Karamar Dr St Louis MO 63128

ZONTAL, JORGE (JORGE SALA)
PAINTER
b Parma, Italy; Can citizen. *Study:* Dalhousie Univ, Halifax, NS, BA, 68. *Work:* Can Coun Art Bank, Nat Gallery Can, Ottawa; Ctr d'Art Contemporain, Geneva, Switz; Lucio Amelio Gallery, Naples, Italy; Mod Art Gallery, Vienna, Austria. *Comn:* Ursa Major and Taurus: Pavillion Fragments from the Starry Vault, Toronto Stock Exchange, 83. *Exhib:* Solo exhibs, Carmen Lamanna Gallery, Toronto, 72-84; Canadian Trajectoires, Mus d'Art Mod de la Ville, Paris, 73; Projects Video VIII, Mus Mod Art, London, England, 78; Glamour, Inst Contemp Art, London, England, 78; Reconstructing Futures, Carmen Lamanna Gallery, Toronto, 78; Artistic Collaboration in the 20th Century, Hirshhorn Mus, Washington, DC, 84; P is for Poodle, Nat Gallery Can, Ottawa, 84; and others. *Awards:* Can Coun Grants, 70-83. *Bibliog:* Germano Celant (auth), General idea in Canada: Un Gruppo Canadese, Domus, 11/74; John Bentley Mays (coauth), Visions: Contemporary Art in Canada, Douglas & McIntyre, Vancouver, 83. *Mailing Add:* c/o Carmen Lamanna Gallery 840 Yonge St Toronto ON M4W 2H1 Canada

ZORETICH, GEORGE STEPHEN
PAINTER, EDUCATOR

b Monessen, Pa, June 19, 18. *Study:* Pa State Univ, BS(art educ) & MA(studio art); Columbia Univ & Syracuse Univ, grad study; also with Hobson Pittman & Ivan Mestrovic. *Work:* Butler Art Inst, Youngstown, Ohio; Pa State Univ Mus, University Park; St Albans Sch, Washington, DC; Indiana State Univ, Pa; Kutztown State Col, Pa. *Comn:* Open Hearth (mural), Mineral Industs, Pa State Univ, 58. *Exhib:* Six Pa Acad Fine Arts Ann, 49-67; nine Butler Art Inst Ann, 50-67; four Corcoran Biennials, Washington, DC, 53-61; San Francisco Art Mus 84th Ann, 65; Nat Acad Design 150th Ann, 75. *Teaching:* From instr to prof art, Pa State Univ, University Park, 46- *Awards:* Barse Miller Mem Award for Watercolor, Nat Acad Design, 75. *Bibliog:* James Schineller (auth), Art-search-self discovery, Int Textbk, 60; Yar Chomicky (auth), Watercolor Paintings, Prentice-Hall, 68. *Media:* Oil, Acrylic. *Publ:* Auth, Woodcut, Everyday Art, spring 60; coauth, Prints & Printmaking, Pa State Univ, 60; coauth, Drawing, Lock Haven Rev, 73. *Mailing Add:* 144 Spring Hill Lane State College PA 16801

ZORNES, JAMES MILFORD
PAINTER, DESIGNER

b Camargo, Okla, Jan 25, 08. *Study:* With F Toles Chamberlin & Millard Sheets, 35-38; Otis Art Inst, 38; Pomona Col, 46-50. *Work:* Metrop Mus Art, New York; Los Angeles Co Mus Art; Butler Inst Am Art, Youngstown, Ohio; Nat Acad Design, New York; White House Collection, Washington, DC; and others. *Comn:* Murals for post off at Campo, Tex, 37 & Claremont, Calif, 38, US Govt. *Exhib:* Chicago Int Watercolor Exhib, Art Inst Chicago, 38; San Francisco World's Fair, 38-40; Metrop Mus Art, New York, 41; 96th Ann Am Watercolor Soc, 63; Watercolor USA, 72; and others. *Pos:* Off army artist, US Govt, 43-45. *Teaching:* Instr painting, Otis Art Inst, 38-46; instr painting, Pomona Col, 46-50; instr painting, Univ Calif, Santa Barbara, 48-49. *Awards:* Award for In the Cove, Nat Acad Design; William Tuthill Prize for Well at Guadalupe, 38; Am Artist Medal for Beach Party, 63; and others. *Bibliog:* Article in Am Artist Mag, 11/63; Edgar A Whitney (auth), Complete guide to watercolor painting, 65; One Hundred Watercolor Techniques, Watson-Guptill, 68; and others. *Mem:* Assoc Nat Acad Design; Am Watercolor Soc; Nat Watercolor Soc; West Coast Watercolor Soc; Riverside Art Asn (bd dirs, 66-67). *Publ:* Auth, A Journey to Nicaragua, Univ Okla Press, Norman, 77. *Mailing Add:* PO Box 24 Mt Carmel UT 84755

ZOROMSKIS, KAZIMIERAS
PAINTER, INSTRUCTOR

b Lithuania; US citizen. *Study:* Vilna Art Acad, BA, 42; Vienna Art Acad, Masters dipl, 45; Rome Royal Art Acad, Italy, spec fresco studies, 46. *Work:* Slater Mem Mus, Norwich, Conn; Butler Inst Am Art, Ohio; Ga Mus Art, Athens; Sun Times Bldg, Chicago; State Mus, Vilna, Lithuania; and others. *Exhib:* 23rd Salon de Otono, Nat Mus Mod Art, Madrid, Spain, 49; Art Inst Chicago Ann, 53 & 56; 159th All Am, Pa Acad Fine Arts, Philadelphia, 64; Dealers Choice Exhib, Huntington Hartford Mus, New York, 67-68; Corcoran Gallery, Washington, DC, 73; retrospective, State Mus, Vilna, Lithuania, 83. *Teaching:* Prof fine arts, Univ Javeriana, Bogota, Colombia, 50-51; instr perspective & oil painting, Newark Sch Fine & Indust Art, 68- *Bibliog:* Many articles & rev in Am, Span & Lithuanian Mags & papers. *Media:* Oil. *Mailing Add:* 163 W 23rd St New York NY 10011

ZOX, LARRY
PAINTER

b Des Moines, Iowa, May 31, 36. *Study:* Univ Okla; Drake Univ; Des Moines Art Ctr, with George Grosz. *Work:* Mus Fine Arts, Houston, Tex; Hirchhorn Mus; Whitney Mus Am Art, Metrop Mus Art, Mus Mod Art, New York; and many others. *Exhib:* Whitney Mus Am Art Ann, New York, 69-70 & 72; Indianapolis Mus Art, Ind, 72; one-man retrospective, Whitney Mus Art, 73; Palm Springs Desert Mus, Calif, 73; one-man shows, Daniel Templon Gallery, Paris, France, 75, Alan Rubiner Gallery, Royal Oak, Mich, 79 & Carolyn Schneebeck Gallery, Cincinnati, 79; and others. *Teaching:* Artist in residence, Juniata Col, 64; guest critic, Cornell Univ, 67; artist in resident, Univ NC, Greensboro, 67; instr art, Sch Visual Arts, 67-70; instr art, Dartmouth Col, winter 69. *Awards:* Guggenheim Fel, 67; Nat Coun Arts Award, 69. *Mailing Add:* c/o Andre Emmerich Gallery 41 E 57th St New York NY 10022

ZUCCARELLI, FRANK EDWARD
PAINTER, INSTRUCTOR

b Pa, Oct 23, 21. *Study:* Newark Sch Fine & Indust Art, with William J Aylward & John Grabach; Art Students League, with Robert Philip; Kean Col NJ, BA. *Work:* US Navy & Marine Mus, Washington, DC; Marine Corps Base, Barstow, Calif; Egan Corp, Brigewater, NJ; Malcolm Forbes Collection, New York; US Coast Guard, Washington, DC. *Comn:* Paintings for US Navy, Newport RI, 71 & Washington, DC, 75; Dahlgren Weapons Lab, Va, 71 & Mediterranean Sixth Fleet, 72; Recovery of Astronauts in Pacific, Apollo-Soyuz Test Proj, 75; Carrier Flight Qualifications, USS Kennedy, 82. *Exhib:* Pastel Soc Am, Nat Arts Club, New York; Overseas Press Club, New York; Combat Art Collection, Washington, DC; Hermitage Mus, Norfolk, Va; Fordham Univ; Grand Central Art Gallery, New York; and others. *Teaching:* Pvt instr oils, pastels & watercolor, 58-; instr continuing educ, Rutgers Univ, 80. *Awards:* Hermel Award, Knickerbocker Artists, 81; Pastel Soc Award, Am Artists Prof League, 82; Grand Central Art Gallery Award, Hudson Valley Art Asn, 83; and others. *Bibliog:* An artist with vision visits USS Kennedy, Navy Aviation News, 11/82; Colorful impressions, Franklin News Record, 83; Aviators and artists at work, Product Support Digest, 9/83. *Mem:* Naval Art Coop & Liaison Comt; Salmagundi Club; fel Am Artists Prof League; Pastel Soc Am; Hudson Valley Art Asn. *Media:* Oil, Pastel. *Mailing Add:* 61 Appleman Rd Somerset NJ 08873

ZUCKER, BARBARA M
SCULPTOR

b Philadelphia, Pa, Aug 2, 40. *Study:* Univ Mich, BS(design), 62; Cranbrook Acad Art, Bloomfield Hills, Mich; Kokoschka Sch Vision, Salzburg, Austria, 61; Hunter Col, MA, 77. *Work:* Whitney Mus Am Art; collections of Milton Brutten, Helen Herrick & Claes Oldenburg; Indianapolis Mus; Chase Manhattan Bank; Am Can Co. *Exhib:* 26 Contemporary Women Artists, Aldrich Mus Art, Ridgefield, Conn, 71; one-woman shows, A I R Gallery, 72 & 74, 112 Greene St Gallery, 76 & Robert Miller Gallery, New York, 78 & 80, Joslyn Art Mus, 81, Fine Arts Ctr, Univ Mass, Amherst, 82 & Pam Adler Gallery, New York, 83. *Pos:* Co-founder, AIR Gallery, New York, 72; ed assoc, Art News Mag, 74-81. *Teaching:* instr art, La Guardia Community Col, Queens, NY, 74-77; instr, Fordham Univ, Lincoln Ctr, New York, 74-79; artist in residence, Princeton Univ, fall 75 & Fine Arts Work Ctr, Provincetown, winter 75; artist-in-residence, Fla State Univ, 76; instr, Philadelphia Col of Art, 77-79; prof & chairperson art dept, Univ Vt, 79- *Awards:* Hon Soc, Univ Mich, 52; Nat Endowment Arts Fel Grant, 75; Purchase Prize, Ulster Co Coun, NY, 77. *Bibliog:* Carrie Rickey (auth), The more the merrier, Village Voice, 79; John Russel (auth), The sculptures of Barbara Zucker, New York Times, 6/83; Richard Martin (auth), Barbara Zucker, Arts Mag, 83. *Mem:* Col Art Asn; Women's Caucus for Art (mem adv bd). *Publ:* Contribr, Art News, 74-79; contribr, Village Voice (centerfold), 7/2/75 & 7/9/75 & article on Red Grooms, 76; auth, article on Florine Stettheimer (American painter), Art News, 2/76 & Women's Studies, 79; Unusual materials, Art J, 80, Heresies, 80 & Sculpture New Hampshire, 82. *Mailing Add:* 21 E Tenth St New York NY 10003

ZUCKER, BOB
PHOTOGRAPHER, DESIGNER

b New York, NY, Dec 10, 46. *Study:* Hunter Col, BA; and with Philippe Halsman, New York. *Work:* Libr of Cong; J P Morgan libr; Soc Preservation Long Island Antiquities; Nat Trust Hist Preservation; Sotheby Parke Bernet. *Comn:* Photos, 19th Century Pub Sculpture, Metrop Mus, 73; Sculpture of Isodor Konti, Hudson River Mus, 74; Historic Architectural Documentation of Old Westchester Co Courthouse Complex, Co of Westchester, 74; Bicentennial Exhib, Venturi & Rauch AIA & Whitney Mus, 75; Am Bicentennial: Signs of Life in the City, Renwick Gallery, Smithsonian Inst, 75; and others. *Exhib:* 19th Century Public Sculpture in New York Parks, 73; Life in America in the 18th Century, Nat Mus Am Hist, 84. *Teaching:* Instr, New York Inst Technol, currently. *Publ:* Auth, American Architecture: Westchester County, 77. *Mailing Add:* 3 Burbank Ct Greenlawn NY 11740

ZUCKER, JOSEPH I
PAINTER

b Chicago, Ill, May 21, 41. *Study:* Miami Univ, 59-60; Art Inst Chicago, BFA & MFA. *Work:* Walker Art Ctr, Minneapolis; Whitney Mus Am Art; Albright-Knox Gallery, Buffalo; Australian Nat Gallery; and others. *Exhib:* Art Inst Chicago, 64 & 81; Walker Art Ctr, 68; New American Abstract Painting, Madison Art Ctr, 72; Prospect, Dusseldorf, Ger, 73; Bykert Gallery, New York, 74; Whitney Biennial, Whitney Mus, 79 & 83; Venice Biennale, 80; Surfacing Images, The Paintings of Joe Zucker 1969-82, Albright-Knox Gallery, Buffalo, 82; and others. *Teaching:* Instr painting, Minneapolis Sch Art, 66-68, Sch Visual Arts, New York, 68-71 & NY Univ, 71-74. *Bibliog:* Edward Lucie-Smith (auth), Art in the Seventies, Cornell Univ Press, 81; Anthony Bannon (auth), Cotton compositions, Buffalo News Mag, 7/25/82. *Mailing Add:* c/o Holly Solomon Gallery 724 Fifth Ave New York NY 10019

ZUCKER, MURRAY HARVEY
PAINTER, SCULPTOR

b New York, NY, Dec 14, 20. *Work:* AFL-CIO Hq, Washington, DC; Community Blood Coun, New York; Omaha Nat Bank, Nebr; Slater Mem Mus, Norwich, Conn; Butler Inst Am Art, Ohio. *Comn:* Paintings, Atlantic Richfield Co, New York, 68, Technicon Corp, Ardsley, NY, 69 & Police Benevolent Asn, New York, 70. *Exhib:* Annuals, Am Soc Contemp Artists, New York, 75 & 77-81; Contemp Circle, Lincoln Ctr, New York, 79; Gallery Carron, New York, 79; Lever House, New York, 80; Salmagundi Club, New York, 81; and others. *Awards:* First Prize Graphics, Am Soc Contemp Artists, 76; Kulicke Award for Graphics, 78; Feigin Award Graphics, 81; and others. *Bibliog:* C Crane (auth), Contemporary collages, Interiors, 5/70; Gerald F Brommer (auth), The Art of Collage, Davis Publ, Inc, 78; and others. *Mem:* Artists Equity Asn; Am Soc Contemp Artists; Metrop Painters & Sculptors; and others. *Mailing Add:* 253 E 62nd St New York NY 10021

ZUCKERBERG, STANLEY M
PAINTER, ILLUSTRATOR

b New York, NY, Sept 13, 19. *Study:* Pratt Inst; Art Students League; also with George Bridgman, Harold Von Schmidt, Norman Rockwell, Nick Riley, Khosrov Ajootian & Alexander Kostello. *Work:* Grand Cent Art Galleries, New York. *Exhib:* Grand Cent Art Galleries; Allied Am Artists Ann, Nat Acad, New York; Blair Gallery, Santa Fe, NMex; La Galeria, Sedona, Ariz. *Awards:* David Wu Ject Key Mem Award, Allied Artists Am; First Prize, Southern Shore Artists Asn; Award, Mystic Seaport Mus; and others. *Bibliog:* Ralph Fabri (auth), Marine breakwater, Todays' Art Mag, 67; Henry Gasser (auth), Stanley Zuckerberg On The Waterfront, Am Artist Mag, 6/74; John Legakes (auth), Days of my love, Publ Weekly. *Mem:* Artists Fel; Am Artists Prof League; Salmagundi Club; Soc Illusr New York; Am Soc Marine Artists; and others. *Media:* Oil. *Mailing Add:* 21 Old Farm Rd Levittown NY 11756

ZUGOR, SANDOR
PAINTER, PRINTMAKER
b Brod, Yugoslavia, Feb 7, 23; US citizen. *Study:* Acad Fine Art, Budapest, 41-45, with Istvan Szonyi; graphics with Varga Nandor Lajos. *Work:* Mus Fine Art Budapest; Gallery of Mod Art, Taipei, Taiwan; Butler Inst of Am Art, Youngstown, Ohio; Slater Mem Mus, Norwich, Conn; Georgia Mus Art, Athens; and others. *Exhib:* Nat Mus Hist, Taipei, Taiwan; Budapest Nat Exhibs, Nat Gallery Art, 54 & 55; Young Americans, Mus Contemp Crafts, New York, 62; Brooklyn Mus, 69; Palacio Bellas Artes, Mexico City, 72; and others. *Teaching:* Lectr drawing, Brooklyn Col Adult Educ, 66-71. *Awards:* Prix du Rome, Hungarian Acad Rome fel, 46-48; First Prize for Peace & War, Fedn Hungarian Artists, 54. *Media:* Etching; Acrylics, Oil. *Mailing Add:* 463 West St New York NY 10014

ZUPAN, BRUNO
PAINTER, PRINTMAKER
b Yugoslavia, June 21, 39; US citizen. *Study:* Zagreb Art Inst, Yugoslavia, 59. *Comn:* Lithograph (with Annabelle Wiener), World Fedn UN Asn, New York, 81. *Exhib:* Boston Col Student Ctr, Mass, 64; Columbia Mus Arts, Columbus, SC, 65; Salon des Artists Francais, Paris, 73 & 76; Nat Acad, New York, 74; Butler Inst Am Art, Youngstown, Ohio, 74. *Bibliog:* Mary Carroll Nelson (auth), Through a sunny window, Am Artist Mag, 3/79. *Media:* Oil, Watercolor; Serigraph, Lithograph. *Mailing Add:* c/o Fagen-Peterson Fine Art Inc 7077 Main St Scottsdale AZ 85251

ZURIK, JESSELYN BENSON
PAINTER, SCULPTOR
b New Orleans, La, Dec 26, 16. *Study:* Newcomb Col Art Sch, Tulane Univ, BD, 38; Univ Col Sch Art, Tulane Univ, 58-61; with Xavier Gonzales, Angela Gregory, Caroline W Durieux, Harold Carney & Will Stevens. *Work:* New Orleans Pub Libr, Algiers & Main Branches & Gallier Hall, Arts Coun Greater New Orleans; Special Collections Dept, Mem Libr, Tulane Univ; Kilgore Jr Col, Tex. *Comn:* Mosaic stairwell, comn by Mr & Mrs M Fishman, New Orleans, 58; design for Hearing & Speech Ctr, New Orleans, 65; design for Touro Infirmary, New Orleans, 65; assemblage coppery printing blocks, Lubat Co, New Orleans, 48; beaded entire 1970 Gremlin, Contemp Arts Ctr, New Orleans, 83. *Exhib:* Artists of the Gulf States, New Orleans Mus Art, 64; Southeastern Ann, High Mus, Atlanta, 65; Southern Asn Sculptors, Ark Art Ctr, Little Rock, 66 & Mint Mus Art, Charlotte, NC, 66; Selected Artists: Glade Gallery Invitational, Lauren Rogers Mus Art, Laurel, Miss, 70; Tiennial Nat, Contemp Arts Ctr, New Orleans, 79; Int Women's Postcard Exhib, Glyptoteck Mus, Copenhagen, Denmark, 80; Second Louisiana Sculptors Biennial, Contemp Arts Ctr, New Orleans, 82; and others. *Pos:* Illusr, Katz & Besthoff Co & Adler's Jewelry, New Orleans, 38-40. *Teaching:* Instr assemblage art, var groups & orgn, New Orleans, 62- *Awards:* Purchase Prize, Brandeis Univ Invitational, 63; Third Place, Nat Triennial, Wembley Indust, 79. *Bibliog:* Luba Glade (auth), Dazzling superspectacle, States/Item, 74; Dana Standish (auth), Getting down to brass tacks, Gambit, 81; Geoff O'Connell (auth), Book inspires wheel-life art, Dallas Morning News, 82. *Mem:* Artists Equity Asn; La Crafts Coun; Col Art Asn; Southeastern Women's Caucus Art; Contemp Arts Ctr New Orleans. *Media:* Wood. *Mailing Add:* 7740 Belfast St New Orleans LA 70127

ZVER, JAMES M
COLLAGE ARTIST, PAINTER
b Chicago, Ill, May 30, 35. *Study:* Art Inst Chicago, 53-57; Univ Chicago, BFA, 53-57; Cornell Univ, MFA(grad teaching asst), 67-69. *Work:* J B Speed Mus Art, Louisville, Ky; Brown Univ, Providence, RI; Univ Tex, Houston; Mills Col, Oakland, Calif; Herron Mus Art, Indianapolis, Ind. *Exhib:* Chicago Artists Exhib, Art Inst Chicago, 57-58; Painting & Sculpture Today, Herron Mus Art, 67-68; Contemp Painting Exhib, Silvermine Guild Artists, 68; one-man shows, Emily Lowe Gallery, Hofstra Univ, 72, Soho Ctr Visual Artists, 76, Gotham Book Mart Gallery, New York, 69-78, Payson-Weisberger Gallery,

New York 82 & Works II Gallery, Southampton, NY, 83; Contemp Reflections, Larry Aldrich Mus, Ridgefield, Conn, 75; one-man shows, Durlacher Brother Gallery, New York, 66, Larcada Gallery, New York, 68, Emily Lowe Gallery, Hofstra Univ, Hempstead, New York, 72 & The Soho Ctr for Visual Artists, 76. *Pos:* Painting conserv, Whitney Mus Collection, 79- & Orrin Riley, New York, 82-83. *Teaching:* Instr graphics, Pratt Graphics Art Ctr, New York, 65-67, Sch Visual Arts, New York, 69-70; instr painting & graphics, Hofstra Univ, 70-76. *Bibliog:* Article, Art News, 66; Grace Gluck (auth), Soho Artists, New York Times, 74; Emily Geneaur (auth), 10 Downtown Artists, New York Post, 74. *Media:* Paper, Fiberglass. *Dealer:* Nancy Stein Gallery 711 Amsterdam Ave New York NY 10025; Works II Gallery 28 Jobs Lane Southampton NY 11968. *Mailing Add:* 16 Greene St New York NY 10013

ZWEERTS, ARNOLD
PAINTER, MOSAIC ARTIST
b Bussum, Neth, 18; US citizen. *Study:* Sch for Arts & Crafts & Sch for Art Teacher Training, Royal Acad Art, Amsterdam; Royal Acad Art, Copenhagen, Denmark; Acad Belli Arti, Ravenna, Italy; Inst Allende, Univ Guanajunto, Mex, MFA; also study with Jos Rovers, Riseby, Orselli, Signoriny & Kortlang. *Work:* Stedelijk Mus, Amsterdam; Collection of the State, The Hague, Neth; and others. *Comn:* Mosaics, Hengelo, Neth, 54, Lockhorst, Koldewyn, Van Eyck, Rotterdam Architects, 55-56, Chicago Process Gear Co, 61, Boulder Med Arts Bldg, Colo, 63-64 & Lombard Dental Med Bldg, 72, 73 & 74; mosaic, Postville Sch House, Wis, 76-77. *Exhib:* St Paul Gallery Art, Minn, 62; Art Inst Chicago, 66; The Barn--A Vanishing Landmark, SDak & Mo, 77; One-man show, Monroe Art Ctr, 78; Gallery Margreet Huisman, Neth, 80; Madison Civic Ctr, Wis, 79; and many others. *Teaching:* Instr mosaic & color, Kingston Upon Thames, Surrey, Eng, 51-53; instr appreciation of art, Stedelijk Mus, Rijksmus, Amsterdam, 54-57; asst prof drawing & painting, Art Inst Chicago, 57-73; lectr, dept fine arts, Loyola Univ Chicago, 68-78. *Awards:* First Prize/Printmaking, Civic Fine Arts Asn, Sioux Falls, 76; Award of Hon, 63 Salon, Madison Art Mus, 77; Art Award of Honor, The Streams Club, Wheaton, Ill, 80. *Bibliog:* Pieter Scheen (auth), Lexicon Nederlandse Beeldende Kunstenaars 1750-1950, Part II, Kunsthandel P Scheen N V, The Hague, 70. *Mem:* Madison Art Guild; Wis Alliance Artists. *Media:* Oil. *Mailing Add:* Postville School House Rte 1 Box 53 Blanchardville WI 53516

ZWICK, ROSEMARY G
SCULPTOR, PRINTMAKER
b Chicago, Ill, July 13, 25. *Study:* Univ Iowa, with Phillip Guston & Abrizio, BFA, 45; Art Inst Chicago, with Max Kahn, 45-47; De Paul Univ, 46. *Work:* Oak Park Libr Collection, Ill; Albion Col Print Collection, Mich; Reavis Sch Collection, Chicago; Phoenix Pub Schs Collection, Ariz; Crow Island Sch, Winnetka, Ill; and others. *Comn:* Two sculpture animal forms, Wonderland Shopping Ctr, Livonia, Mich, 60; wall relief, Motorola Co, Chicago, 62; sculpture, Temple B'nai Jenoshua, Morton Grove, Ill, 68; large seated figure, Blue Island Libr, Ill, 71; relief, Washbourne Sch, Winnetka, 79; and others. *Exhib:* Ceramic Nat, Everson Mus Art, Syracuse, NY, 60, 62 & 64; Soc Washington Printmakers, Nat Mus, Washington, DC, 64; Mundelein Col, Chicago, 64-71; Indianapolis Mus Art, 70-81; Bicentennial Sculpture, E Leyden Sch Libr, 77; one-man show, Indianapolis Mus Art, 81; and others. *Pos:* Staff artist, Jr Arts & Activities Mag, 45-47; assoc, Four Arts Gallery, Evanston, Ill, 62- *Bibliog:* John B Kenny (auth), Ceramic design, Chilton, 63; Wesley Buchwald (auth), Craftsmen in Illinois, Ill Art Educ Asn, 65; Louis Redstone (auth), Art in architecture, Art Voices, 1-2/81. *Mem:* Renaissance Soc, Univ Chicago; Chicago Soc Artists; World Print Coun; Chicago Artist Coalition; and others. *Media:* Ceramics; Etching. *Specialty:* Midwestern artists sculpture, paintings & prints. *Dealer:* Ruth Volid Gallery Ltd 225 W Illinois Chicago IL 60654; Four Arts Gallery 1629 Oak Ave Evanston IL 60201. *Mailing Add:* 1720 Washington St Evanston IL 60202

Geographic Index

ALABAMA

Auburn

Collier, James Mitchell Historian, Painter
Hatfield, Donald Gene Painter, Educator
Olson, Douglas John Painter, Educator
Ross, Conrad H Printmaker, Educator
Ross, Janice Koenig Painter
Sykes, (William) Maltby Painter,
    Printmaker
Trentham, Gary Lynn Educator, Fiber
    Artist

Bessemer

Leader, Garnet Rosamonde Administrator

Birmingham

Barnett, Ed Willis Photographer, Writer
Burgess, Linda Suzanne Painter,
    Photographer
Finley, Donny Lamenda Painter
Hames, Carl Martin Dealer, Collector
Hendricks, Edward Lee Sculptor, Kinetic
    Artist
Lewis, Ronald Walter Painter, Instructor
Livingston, Margaret Gresham
    Administrator, Patron
Price, Rosalie Pettus Painter
Rankin, Don Painter, Printmaker
Schnorrenberg, John Martin Historian,
    Administrator
Shelton, Robert Lee Designer, Educator
Stewart, Arthur Painter
Trechsel, Gail Andrews Curator
Weeks, Edward F Historian, Museologist

Citronelle

Conlon, James Edward Sculptor,
    Historian

Fairhope

Gatling, Eva Ingersoll Museum
    Consultant, Historian
Wolff, Robert W, Jr Dealer
Woodward, Cleveland Landon Painter,
    Illustrator

Hartselle

Howell, Elizabeth Ann (Mitch) Painter,
    Gallery Owner

Huntsville

Bayer, Jeffrey Joshua Educator, Sculptor
Boyd, Lakin Educator, Printmaker
Crouse, Michael Glenn Educator,
    Printmaker
Hudson, Ralph Magee Historian,
    Educator
Knaub, Donald E Museum Director
McAndrew, Dennis Anthony Curator,
    Instructor
Parrish, David Buchanan Painter
Pearson, Clifton Sculptor, Instructor
Pope, Mary Ann Irwin Painter,
    Printmaker

Reeves, James Franklin Historian,
    Collector
Rubin, Donald Vincent Sculptor
Savas, Jo-Ann Painter, Instructor

Jacksonville

Martin, Larry Kenneth Painter, Dealer

Mobile

Altmayer, Jay P Collector
Blackburn, Lenora Whitmire Collector
Kennedy, James Edward Painter, Sculptor
Koch, William Emery Dealer, Collector
Rathle, Henri (Amin) Painter
Thomason, Michael Vincent
    Photographer, Curator
Victor, Mary O'Neill Museum Director

Montgomery

Anderson, Ross Cornelius Museum
    Director, Historian
Britt, Al Painter, Educator
Brooks, Louise Cherry Collector,
    Ceramist
Klopfenstein, Philip Arthur Painter,
    Museum Director
Shannon, Charles Painter

Northport

Musgrave, Shirley H Educator,
    Photographer

Opelika

Furr, Jim Painter, Printmaker

Ozark

Deloney, Jack Clouse Painter, Illustrator

Tuscaloosa

Kakas, Christopher A Printmaker, Painter

Tuskegee

Thomas, Elaine Freeman Educator,
    Administrator

University

Brough, Richard Burrell Educator,
    Designer
Rembert, Virginia Pitts Educator,
    Historian
Sella, Alvin Conrad Painter, Educator

ALASKA

Anchorage

Appel, Keith Kenneth Painter, Sculptor
Ard, Saradell (Saradell Ard Frederick)
    Educator, Painter
Austin, Pat Printmaker, Educator
Birdsall, Byron Painter
Conaway, Gerald Sculptor, Painter
Cooke, Jody Helen Painter, Educator

Gordon, Josephine Painter
Hedman, Teri Jo Printmaker, Painter
Kimura, William Yusaburo Painter,
    Printmaker
Owens, Tennys Bowers Dealer
Pitcher, John Charles Painter, Illustrator
Regat, Jean-Jacques Albert Sculptor,
    Muralist
Regat, Mary E Sculptor, Muralist
Rubey, Tony (George Anton) Printmaker,
    Educator
Shadrach, Jean H Painter, Dealer
Shalkop, Robert Leroy Museum Director,
    Historian
Vallee, William Oscar Painter, Graphic
    Artist

Cordova

Bugbee-Jackson, Joan (Mrs John M
    Jackson) Sculptor, Educator

Fairbanks

Brody, Arthur William Printmaker,
    Painter
Choy, Terence Tin-Ho Painter, Educator
Fejes, Claire Painter, Writer
Woodward, Kesler Edward Curator,
    Painter

Juneau

De Armond, Dale B Printmaker
Munoz, Rie (Marie Angelina Munoz)
    Painter, Printmaker

Ketchikan

Wheeler, Mark Painter, Cartoonist

Palmer

Machetanz, Fred Painter, Lithographer

ARIZONA

Bisbee

Gilbert, Herb Painter, Graphic Designer
Perry, Judith Elaine Painter
Young, Peter Ford Painter

Carefree

Harris, Robert George Painter, Illustrator
Lipman, Howard W Collector
Patch, Peggie (Margaret Thompson
    Williamson) Painter, Dealer

Cave Creek

Cox, Marion Averal Painter, Instructor
Sproul, Ann Stephenson Painter
Williamson, Jason H Painter, Dealer

Cornville

Groth, Bruno Sculptor
Waddell, John Henry Sculptor, Painter

Flagstaff

Brookins, Jacob Boden Consultant,
  Sculptor
Horn, Bruce Printmaker, Educator
Hull, Gregory Stewart Painter
Monthan, Guy Photographer, Educator
Owen, Bill Painter, Sculptor
Turrell, James Archie Environmental
  Artist, Sculptor

Green Valley

Allen, Constance Olleen Webb Painter,
  Jewelry Designer
Porter, J Erwin Painter

Hotevilla

Loloma, Charles Jeweler, Silversmith

Kingman

Schliefer, Stafford Lerrig Painter, Muralist

Mayer

Polk, Frank Fredrick Sculptor

Mesa

Coe, Anne Elizabeth Painter, Video Artist
Dawson, John Allan Painter
Halbach, David Allen Painter, Instructor
Kimball, Wilford Wayne, Jr Lithographer,
  Draftsman
O'Dell, Erin (Anne) Painter, Designer
Schenck, William Clinton Painter,
  Printmaker
Slater, Gary Lee Sculptor
Woods, Ted Sculptor, Craftsman

Munds Park

Carpenter, Earl L Painter

Nogales

Whitaker, Irwin A Educator, Craftsman

Oracle

Davis, James Granberry Painter
McGrew, Bruce Elwin Painter
Rubylee (Charles Armstrong Littler)
Rush, Andrew Printmaker

Paradise Valley

Alpert, George Photographer, Gallery
  Director
Butler, Byron C Dealer, Collector
Keane, Bil Cartoonist
Kotrozo, Carol Donnell Historian, Critic
McCall, Robert Theodore Painter,
  Illustrator
Micale, Albert Painter, Sculptor
Soleri, Paolo Architect, Sculptor

Payson

Wilson, Nicholas Jon Painter

Phoenix

Bales, Jewel Painter
Ballinger, James K Museum Director,
  Historian
Bermudez, Jose Ygnacio Sculptor, Painter
Blair, Helen Sculptor, Illustrator
Braig, Betty Lou Painter
Broadley, Hugh T Historian,
  Administrator
Campbell, Charles Malcolm Painter,
  Sculptor
Dignac, Geny Sculptor, Environmental
  Artist
Dutton, Allen A Photographer, Painter
Eder, James Alvin Printmaker, Painter
Fink, Ray (Raymond Russell) Sculptor,
  Educator

Frerichs, Ruth Colcord Painter,
  Lithographer
Golubic, Theodore Sculptor, Designer
Graves, Ka (Kathleen Rose) Painter,
  Sculptor
Grigsby, Jefferson Eugene, Jr Educator,
  Painter
Hack, Phillip S & Patricia Y Collectors
Heit, Steven Robert Dealer
Hiatt, Margaret Smith Painter, Instructor
Hill, John Conner Designer, Publisher
Jacobson, Ursula Mercedes Painter,
  Sculptor
Kniffin, Ralph Gus Graphic Artist
Knudson, Robert LeRoy Painter
McGuire, Maureen Designer, Stained
  Glass Artist
Moore, Ina May Instructor, Painter
Phillips, Irving W Cartoonist, Illustrator
Pritzlaff, (Mr & Mrs) John, Jr Collectors
Quinn, Brian Grant Sculptor, Painter
Rand, Steven Jay Sculptor
Richter, Hank Painter, Sculptor
Schaumburg, Donald Roland Educator,
  Ceramist
Steckler, Stuart Jay Dealer, Collector
Ullman, (Mrs) George W Collector
Warner, Boyd, Jr Painter
Young, Marjorie Ward Painter, Draftsman

Pine

Toschik, Larry Painter, Writer

Prescott

Dusard, Jay Photographer, Writer
McClure, Thomas F Sculptor, Educator
Polland, Donald Jack Sculptor
Sommer, Frederick Photographer,
  Landscape Artist
Swanson, Ray V Painter

Rimrock

Dyck, Paul Painter, Director

Scottsdale

Austin, Jo-Anne Jordan Art Dealer,
  Gallery Director
Bell, Donald Allen Art Dealer, Consultant
Brown, Suzanne Goldman Gallery Owner,
  Collector
Crowell, David Lee Dealer, Critic
Curtis, Philip Campbell Painter
Dickerson, William J Dealer
Fernandez, Rudy M, Jr Painter, Sculptor
Ferris, Edythe Painter, Graphic Artist
Gentry, Warren Miller Instructor, Painter
Gillingwater, Denis Claude Sculptor,
  Educator
Golden, Libby Printmaker, Painter
Graley, Gary James Photographer
Greenbowe, F Douglas Painter
Hampton, John W Painter, Sculptor
Heller, Jules Printmaker, Writer
Huldermann, Paul F Art Dealer, Lecturer
Lang, Margo Terzian Painter
Love, Paul Van Derveer Gallery Director,
  Historian
Magenta, Muriel Sculptor, Educator
Manning, Reg (Reginald West)
  Cartoonist, Designer
May, Daniel Striger Dealer
Mell, Ed (Edmund Paul Jr) Painter,
  Printmaker
Metz, Gerry Michael Painter, Sculptor
Missal, Joshua M & Pegge Dealers,
  Collectors
Missal, Stephen J Painter, Instructor
Momaday, Al Painter
Norton, Mary Joyce Painter
Parker, Wilma Joan Painter
Phillips, Dick (Richard Cortez) Painter,
  Instructor

Scholder, Fritz Painter, Printmaker
Sloan, Richard Painter, Illustrator
Strong, Beverly Jean Dealer, Collector
Swartz, Beth Ames Painter
Taylor, Ann Painter
Udinotti, Agnese Sculptor, Painter
Zupan, Bruno Painter, Printmaker

Second Mesa

Kabotie, Fred Painter, Designer

Sedona

Beeler, Joe (Neil) Painter, Sculptor
Coleman, M L (Micheal Lee) Painter,
  Instructor
Crandall, Jerry C Painter
Crandall, Judith Ann Publisher, Writer
Pendleton, Mary Caroline Handweaver,
  Writer
Reynolds, James Elwood Painter
Yoakum, Del Painter, Designer

Sun City

Bittner, Hans Oskar Painter, Illustrator
Bolster, Ella S Designer, Weaver
Fish, George A Painter
Jakstas, Alfred John Museum Conservator
Luitjens, Helen Anita Instructor, Painter
Tullsen, Rex Painter, Instructor

Tempe

Britton, Daniel Robert Printmaker,
  Educator
Bush, Donald John Historian, Educator
deMatties, Nick Painter, Printmaker
Goo, Benjamin Sculptor, Painter
Gully, Anthony Lacy Historian,
  Administrator
Jacobson, Arthur Robert Painter,
  Printmaker
Jay, Bill Photographic Historian, Critic
Klotz-Reilly, Suzanne Ruth Painter,
  Sculptor
Kronengold, Eric A Photographer,
  Educator
Lehrer, Leonard Painter, Lithographer
Lewis, William R Instructor, Painter
Linderman, Earl William Painter
Pennypacker, James S Designer, Publisher
Pimentel, David Delbert Goldsmith,
  Educator
Schmidt, Randall Bernard Sculptor,
  Educator
Stuler, Jack Photographer, Educator
Turk, Rudy H Museum Director, Writer
White, James Richard Sculptor, Educator
Wood, Harry Emsley, Jr Writer, Painter
Woods, Rip Painter, Educator
Young, Joseph E Educator, Critic

Tubac

Cabot, Hugh Painter, Sculptor
Jenkinson, Geoffrey Painter

Tucson

Anderson, Warren Harold Educator,
  Painter
Bermingham, Peter Museum Director,
  Curator
Billmyer, John Edward Draftsman,
  Educator
Bishop, Jerold Educator, Painter
Bredlow, Tom Designer, Blacksmith
Buros, Luella Painter, Designer
Caldwell, Eleanor Educator, Jeweler
Colescott, Robert H Painter, Instructor
Conant, Howard Somers Painter, Editor
Croft, Michael Flynt Goldsmith, Educator
Denniston, Douglas Painter, Educator
Enstice, Wayne Conceptual Artist, Critic
Enyeart, James Lyle Historian, Director
Golden, Judith Photographer

ARIZONA (cont)

Gottschalk, Max Jules Designer, Instructor
Grossman, Maurice Kenneth Educator, Craftsman
Grygutis, Barbara Ceramist
Hanna, Boyd Everett Painter, Printmaker
Haskin, Donald Marcus Educator, Sculptor
Heldt, Carl Randall Educator, Painter
Heric, John F Sculptor
Hupp, Frederick Duis Painter, Educator
Irving, Donald J Administrator, Writer
Jones, Harold Henry Administrator, Photographer
Lacroix, Flora Luisa Painter, Writer
Loney, Doris Howard Painter, Instructor
Maass, Richard Andrew Museum Director
McMillan, Robert W Painter, Educator
Martin, Lucille Caiar Painter, Muralist
Miller, Nancy Tokar Painter
Parry, Ellwood Comly, III Historian
Parry, Pamela Jeffcott Librarian, Administrator
Reich, Sheldon Historian, Lecturer
Rush, Jean C Educator, Painter
Scott, Sam Painter, Educator
Sles, Steven Lawrence Painter, Stained Glass Artist
Stefan, Ross Painter
Tobias, Robert Paul Painter, Sculptor
Waid, Jim (James E) Painter
Wimmer, Gayle Fiber Artist, Instructor
Zivic, William Thomas Painter, Sculptor

Williams

Cartledge, Roseanne Niemyt Graphic Artist
Seaman, Drake F Painter

ARKANSAS

Arkadelphia

Linn, John William Administrator, Writer

Clarksville

Ward, Lyle Edward Painter, Educator

Conway

Larsen, Patrick Heffner Painter, Sculptor
Thompson, Robert Charles Painter, Educator

Eureka Springs

Freund, Harry Louis Painter, Illustrator

Fayetteville

Cockrill, Sherna Painter, Instructor
Krueger, Lothar David Painter, Educator
Reif, Rubin Painter, Educator

Hot Springs

Rames, Stanley Dodson Painter, Educator

Jonesboro

Jones, Charlott Ann Educator, Gallery Director

Little Rock

Benjamin, Lloyd William, III Historian, Administrator
Graham, Bill (William Karr) Cartoonist, Graphic Artist
Kellogg, Maurice Dale Painter, Lecturer
Mapes, Doris Williamson Painter
Schmidt, Frederick Lee Painter, Educator
Wolfe, Townsend Durant Painter, Administrator

Pettigrew

McNamara, William Patrick, Jr Painter, Printmaker

Pine Bluff

Kagle, Joseph L, Jr Painter, Museum Director

Russellville

Wilwers, Edward Mathias Educator, Illustrator

Siloam Springs

Anderson, Troy Painter

State University

Allen, William J Historian, Educator
Lindquist, Evan Printmaker, Educator
Richards, Karl Frederick Draftsman, Painter

CALIFORNIA

Alameda

Berlin, Beatrice Winn Printmaker, Painter
Perez, Vincent Painter, Instructor

Albany

Gantz, Jeanne A Printmaker, Administrator
Lieber, Thomas Alan Painter

Altadena

Green, David Oliver Sculptor, Educator
Ikegawa, Shiro Printmaker

Anaheim

Macaray, Lawrence Richard Painter, Educator

Anza

Silkotch, Mary Ellen Painter

Apple Valley

Hay-Messick, Velma Painter
Kleinsmith, Gene (Eugene Dennis) Ceramist, Writer
Messick, Ben (Newton) Painter, Instructor

Aptos

Wallis, Helen V Photographer

Arcadia

Hawkins, Thomas Wilson, Jr Painter, Instructor
Rodbard, Betty Painter
Roysher, Hudson (Brisbane) Designer, Administrator

Arcata

Anderson, William Thomas Printmaker, Painter
Berry, Glenn Painter, Educator
Johnson, Ronald W Historian, Educator
Knight, Tom (Thomas Lincoln), Jr Educator, Photographer
Land-Weber, Ellen E Photographer, Educator
Price, Leslie Kenneth Painter, Educator

Aromas

Nutzle, Futzie (Bruce John Kleinsmith) Artist, Cartoonist

Bakersfield

Kerzie, Ted L Painter
Paradise, Phil (Herschel) Painter, Sculptor

Banning

Green, Martin Leonard Painter, Printmaker

Bayside

LaPlantz, David Jeweler, Educator
LaPlantz, Shereen Weaver, Instructor

Beaumont

Meltzer, Robert Hiram Instructor, Painter

Belmont

Price, Joe (Allen) Serigrapher, Instructor

Benicia

Chicago, Judy Painter, Sculptor
Shannonhouse, Sandra Lynne Riddell Sculpture

Berkeley

Akawie, Thomas Frank Educator, Painter
Alexander, Judy Administrator, Conceptual Artist
Bischoff, Elmer Nelson Painter, Educator
Blos, May (Elizabeth) Illustrator, Designer
Blos, Peter W Painter, Instructor
Bony, Jean Victor Art Historian, Educator
Brulc, Dennis (Mel Vapour) Printmaker, Painter
Burch, Claire R Painter, Writer
Cahill, James Francis Historian, Educator
Candau, Eugenie Librarian
Chipp, Herschel Browning Educator, Curator
Davis, Jerrold Painter
Elliott, James Heyer Museum Director
Elliott, Lillian Weaver, Tapestry Artist
Ettlinger, Leopold David Historian
Feldman, Bella Tabak Sculptor
Fontana, Bill Patrick Environmental Artist, Conceptual Artist
Goetzl, Thomas Maxwell Lecturer, Educator
Gordin, Sidney Sculptor, Educator
Healy, Anne Laura Sculptor, Educator
Henderson, Robbin Legere Painter, Curator
Heyman, Therese Thau Curator, Historian
Hoare, Tyler James Sculptor, Printmaker
Holland, Tom Painter
Kasten, Karl Albert Painter, Printmaker
Kehlmann, Robert Glass Artist, Critic
Lark, Sylvia Painter, Printmaker
Leon, Dennis Sculptor, Educator
Lipofsky, Marvin B Sculptor, Glass Artist
Loberg, Robert Warren Painter, Instructor
Loran, Erle Painter, Writer
Lovell, Margaretta Markle Curator, Historian
McMillan, Stephen Walker Printmaker, Photographer
Marrow, James Henry Historian, Educator
Mitchell, Margaretta K Photographer, Writer
Miyasaki, George Joji Printmaker, Painter
Prestini, James Libero Sculptor, Designer
Rapoport, Sonya Painter, Conceptual Artist
Ross, David Anthony Curator, Lecturer
Ruvolo, Felix Emmanuele Painter, Educator
St John, Terry N Painter, Curator
Sargent, Richard Painter, Photographer
Sekimachi, Kay Weaver, Instructor
Selvin, Nancy Ceramist, Sculptor
Selz, Peter H Historian, Curator
Sher, Elizabeth Video Artist, Printmaker
Shere, Charles Everett Critic
Shoemaker, Peter Painter, Educator

Emeryville

Bechtle, Robert Alan Painter
Grafton, Rick (Frederick Wellington)
  Painter
Luca, Mark Printmaker

Encinitas

Perine, Robert Heath Painter, Writer
Provder, Carl Painter, Instructor
Strasen, Barbara Elaine Painter,
  Conceptual Artist

Encino

Hoowij, Jan Painter

Escondido

Anderson, Brad J Cartoonist
Robbins, LeRoy (Southward)
  Photographer, Filmmaker
Sowinski, Stanislaus Joseph Painter,
  Iconographer
Sternberg, Harry Painter, Graphic Artist
Walker, Clay E Printmaker, Sculptor

Eureka

Marak, Louis Bernard Ceramist, Educator

Fairfax

Dern, F Carl Sculptor

Fairfield

Brawley, Robert Julius Painter, Draftsman

Fair Oaks

Barrios, Benny Perez Painter, Art Dealer

Fallbrook

Ragland, Jack Whitney Painter,
  Printmaker

Fallon

Hedrick, Wally Bill Painter, Sculptor

Felton

Cochran, Dewees (Dewees Cochran
  Helbeck) Designer, Painter

Folsom

McHugh, Adeliza Sorenson Dealer,
  Collector

Forest Knolls

Lopez, Bea Designer, Fiber Artist

Forestville

Meyer, Elmer Frederick Painter, Writer

Ft Bragg

Gilhooly, David James, III Sculptor

Fountain Valley

Clark, Timothy John Painter, Instructor

Frazier Park

Brumfield, John Richard Photographer,
  Writer

Fresno

Bolomey, Roger Henry Sculptor
Maughelli, Mary L Painter, Lithographer
Musselman, Darwin B Painter
Pickford, Rollin, Jr Painter

Fullerton

Arnold, Florence M Painter
Frankel, Dextra Educator, Gallery
  Director
Partin, Robert (E) Painter, Educator
Smith, Victor Joachim Painter, Educator

Garden Grove

Ortlieb, Robert Eugene Sculptor, Graphic
  Artist

Glendale

Ackerman, Frank Edward Painter,
  Designer
Cristin-Poucher, Lilli Fong Designer
Gill, Gene Painter, Printmaker
Herman, Alan David Designer, Graphic
  Artist
Moure, Nancy Dustin Wall Curator,
  Writer

Goleta

Thomas, Robert Chester Sculptor

Granada Hills

Bowater, Marian Art Dealer, Collector

Greenbrae

Sultan, Larry A Photographer

Green Valley Lake

Wood, Robert E Painter, Instructor

Gualala

Sheets, Millard Owen Designer, Painter

Guerneville

Barrio, Raymond Writer, Printmaker

Hawthorne

Wright, (Mr & Mrs) William H Collectors

Hemet

Hutchison, Elizabeth S Painter

Hillsborough

Siberell, Anne Hicks Printmaker,
  Illustrator

Hollywood

Barbera, Joe Cartoonist
Ruscha, Edward Joseph Painter,
  Filmmaker
Sauls, Frederick Inabinette Sculptor,
  Painter
Souza, Paul Marciel Painter, Instructor
Tseu, Rosita Hsu Administrator,
  Instructor

Huntington Beach

Foley, Kyoko Y Instructor, Painter
Isaacson, Gene Lester Collector,
  Historian
Tornheim, Norman Sculptor

Imperial Beach

Garman, Ed Painter, Writer

Inglewood

Flick, Robbert Photographer, Educator
Gordon, John S Sculptor, Educator
Johnstone, Mark (David) Critic, Educator
Rankaitis, Susan Anne Photographer,
  Painter
Young, Milton Painter, Sculptor

Inverness

Foote, Howard Reed Artist, Printmaker
Onslow Ford, Gordon M Painter
Roloff, John Scott Sculptor,
  Environmental Artist
Storer, Inez Mary Collage Artist, Sculptor

Inyokern

Nowak, Leo Illustrator, Cartoonist

Irvine

Feiffer, Jules Cartoonist, Writer
Lichty, George M Cartoonist
McNamara, Mary Jo Historian, Educator
Wortz, Melinda Farris Gallery Director,
  Critic

Jamestown

Hutchings, La Vere Painter, Instructor

Joshua Tree

Bothwell, Dorr Painter, Printmaker

Kensington

Cook, Michael David Painter, Video
  Artist

Kentfield

Eaton, Pauline (Friedrich) Painter,
  Instructor
Galli, Stanley Walter Illustrator, Painter
Moquin, Richard Attilio Sculptor

Kenwood

Hein, Max Graphic Artist, Educator

La Canada

Abril, Ben (Benjamin) Painter

La Crescenta

Injeyan, Seta L Painter

Lafayette

Beaumont, Mona M Painter, Printmaker
Schnier, Jacques Sculptor

Laguna Beach

Anderson, Ivan Delos Painter, Printmaker
Armstrong, Roger Joseph Painter,
  Cartoonist
Barnes, Lucinda Ann Historian, Gallery
  Director
Blacketer, James Richard Painter, Art
  Dealer
Burchfield, Jerry Lee Photographer,
  Educator
Challis, Richard Bracebridge Dealer
Darrow, Paul Gardner Painter, Educator
Enman, Tom Kenneth Painter, Museum
  Director
Gasparian, Armen Tigran Instructor,
  Painter
Kaplan, Leonard Painter, Dealer
Moore, Scott Martin Painter, Instructor
Olsen, Sharon A Dealer, Gallery Director
Rubinstein, Charlotte Streifer Historian,
  Educator
Sassone, Marco Painter, Printmaker
Scheu, Leonard Painter, Lecturer

Laguna Hills

Burchess, Arnold Painter, Sculptor
Greenberg, Elenor Siminow Painter,
  Printmaker
Hill, Dale Logan Painter, Instructor
Hubenthal, Karl Samuel Cartoonist,
  Painter
MacBird, Rosemary Painter

Laguna Niguel

Jay, Norma Joyce Painter

Lagunitas

Holman, Arthur (Stearns) Painter

La Jolla

Adler, Sebastian J Museum Director
Brezzo, Steven Louis Museum Director
Cuevas, Jose Luis Painter, Illustrator
Cutler-Shaw, Joyce Conceptual Artist,
  Educator
Davies, Hugh Marlais Historian, Gallery
  Director

CALIFORNIA (cont)

Forester, Russell Painter
Imana, Jorge Garron Painter, Muralist
Inverarity, Robert Bruce Designer,
    Museum Director
Jones, Doug (Douglas McKee) Painter,
    Dealer
Karlen, Peter H Educator, Writer
Lonidier, Fred Spencer Instructor,
    Photographer
Luna, (Antonio Rodriguez) Painter
McGilvery, Laurence Book Dealer,
    Publisher
McReynolds, (Joe) Cliff Painter,
    Instructor
Marcus, Angelo P Dealer, Collector
Mark, Bendor Painter
Patterson, Patricia Film Critic, Painter
Reilly, Richard Critic, Curator
Scanga, Italo Sculptor, Educator
Stewart, John Lincoln Educator, Writer
Tasende, Jose Maria Gallery Director,
    Dealer
Wenger, Muriel Dealer, Collector
Wenger, Sigmund Dealer, Consultant
Werner, Fritz Painter
Whitaker, Eileen Monaghan Painter
Whitcomb, Kay Enamelist, Muralist
Yard, Sally Elizabeth Historian, Curator

Lake Arrowhead

Barnes, Cliff (Clifford V) Painter,
    Illustrator

La Mesa

Blackmun, Barbara Winston Educator,
    Art Historian
Kennedy, Gene (Eugene Murray)
    Photographer, Educator
Lebeck, Carol E Ceramist
Mansfield, Robert Adams Sculptor,
    Educator

Larkspur

Frances, Harriette Anton Painter,
    Lithographer

Leucadia

Cohen, Harold Artist-Theorist, Educator

Long Beach

Bessemer, Auriel Muralist, Art Dealer
Ferreira, (Armando) Thomas Educator,
    Sculptor
Glenn, Constance White Administrator,
    Historian
Lewis, Marcia Jeweler-Metalsmith,
    Instructor
Looney, Norman Painter, Educator
Osborne, Cynthia A Printmaker, Educator
Steinhardt, Alice Painter, Photographer
Wethli, Mark Painter, Educator

Los Altos

Bunn-Stadden, Cecine Painter

Los Angeles

Abeles, Kim Victoria Painter, Sculptor
Adler, Abe Art Dealer
Albuquerque, Lita Painter
Andreson, Laura F Ceramist, Educator
Anhalt, Jacqueline Richards Art Dealer
Ankrum, Joan Art Dealer
Bailey, Walter Alexander Painter, Writer
Baker, George Educator, Kinetic Artist
Baldessari, John Anthony Conceptual
    Artist
Barkus, Mariona Marcia Painter, Collage
    Artist
Barnes, Molly Art Dealer, Writer
Bass, Joel Painter

Biberman, Edward Painter, Graphic Artist
Bieser, Natalie Painter
Bloch, E Maurice Art Historian, Educator
Bloomfield, Lisa Diane Photographer,
    Conceptual Artist
Blumberg, Ron Painter, Instructor
Brendel, Bettina Painter, Lecturer
Brice, William Painter, Printmaker
Broderson, Morris Painter
Brooks, Lois Ziff Textile Artist, Educator
Bueno, Jose (Joe Goode) Sculptor, Painter
Burchett, Debra Administrator, Curator
Burkhardt, Hans Gustav Painter,
    Printmaker
Burnham, Linda Frye Editor, Writer
Byrnes, James Bernard Museum Director,
    Historian
Card, Greg S Painter, Sculptor
Cassyd, Syd Curator, Critic
Cho, David Designer, Assemblage Artist
Chuey, Robert Arnold Painter, Lecturer
Civitello, John Patrick Painter
Clark, Garth Reginald Dealer, Historian
Clayberger, Samuel Robert Painter,
    Educator
Clef, Roman A (Henry E Guerriero)
    Writer, Sculptor
Clemens, Paul Painter, Writer
Clothier, Peter Dean Administrator, Critic
Conrad, Paul Francis Cartoonist
Curran, Darryl Joseph Photographer,
    Printmaker
Dailey, Victoria Keilus Dealer
D'Andrea, Jeanne Consultant
Danziger, Avery C Photographer
Davidson, J LeRoy Art Historian
Davis, Alonzo Joseph Visual Artist,
    Administrator
Davis, Michael A Sculptor
De Bretteville, Sheila Levrant Designer,
    Instructor
Dillon, Paul Sanford Painter
Dimondstein, Morton Sculptor, Painter
Doolin, James Lawrence Painter
Douke, Daniel W Painter, Educator
Dreaper, Richard Edward Dealer,
    Consultant
Dreiband, Laurence Painter, Lecturer
Drohojowska, Hunter Critic, Writer
Edmondson, Leonard Printmaker
Elliot, Cathy J Ceramist, Sculptor
Enos, Chris Photographer, Lecturer
Ewing, Edgar Louis Painter
Feinblatt, Ebria Historian
Fenci, Renzo Sculptor
Fender, Tom Mac Sculptor
Feuerstein, Roberta Dealer
Fichter, Herbert Francis Printmaker,
    Painter
Fine, Jud Sculptor, Educator
Finkelstein, Max Sculptor, Painter
Fiskin, Judy (Anne) Photographer,
    Educator
Foulkes, Llyn Painter
Francis, Sam Painter
Frauchiger, Fritz A Administrator,
    Director
Frohlich, M L (Minnette Leah) Painter,
    Collector
Fusco, Peter Richard Curator, Historian
Gill, James (Francis) Painter, Sculptor
Glasgow, Lukman Museum Director,
    Sculptor
Goedike, Shirl Painter
Gold, Betty Administrator, Director
Goldfield, Edward L Dealer, Collector
Goodman, Calvin Jerome Consultant,
    Collector
Gray, Robert Hugh Educator,
    Administrator
Greaves, James L Conservator, Restorer
Hammer, Armand Collector, Dealer

Hansen, Robert Painter, Educator
Harris, Gloriane Painter, Educator
Heinecken, Robert Friedli Photographer,
    Educator
Hernandez, Anthony Louis Photographer
Hogarth, Burne Cartoonist, Illustrator
Horowitz, Benjamin Administrator,
    Dealer
Houston, Bruce Sculptor, Assemblage
    Artist
Huebler, Douglas Conceptual Artist
Hugo, Joan (Dowey) Writer, Instructor
Hugunin, James Richard Critic
Irwin, Robert Environmental Artist,
    Sculptor
Jackson, Suzanne Fitzallen Painter,
    Writer
Johnston, Ynez Painter, Printmaker
Jones, Patty Sue Painter, Curator
Kahlenberg, Mary Hunt Dealer,
    Consultant
Kanemitsu, Matsumi Painter, Lecturer
Kaplan, Julius David Historian
Kazor, Virginia Ernst Curator
Kester, Lenard Painter
Ketchum, Robert Glenn Photographer,
    Curator
Kienholz, Lyn Patron, Administrator
Koshalek, Richard Museum Director
Kovinick, Philip Peter Writer, Historian
Kuhlenschmidt, Richard Edward Dealer
Kuwayama, George Curator, Historian
Lacher, Johannes Painter
Lacy, Suzanne Conceptual Artist,
    Educator
Landau, Mitzi Dealer, Curator
Lang, Wendy F Administrator,
    Photographer
Lark, Raymond Painter, Draftsman
Larsen, Susan C Historian, Critic
Leeper, John P Painter
Lem, Richard Douglas Painter
Leopold, Michael Christopher Critic
Lloyd, Gary Marchal Conceptual Artist,
    Educator
Ludmer, Joyce Pellerano Librarian,
    Historian
Lundeberg, Helen Painter
McCracken, John Harvey Sculptor,
    Painter
McGahee, Dorothy Painter, Educator
McMillan, Jerry Edward Photographer,
    Sculptor
Marton, Pier Video Artist, Educator
Mason, John Sculptor
Mekler, Adam Dealer, Curator
Mesches, Arnold Painter, Educator
Milant, Jean Robert Dealer
Miller, Lillian Dunn Painter, Collector
Mollett, Michael M Assemblage Artist,
    Writer
Moore, Russell James Museum Director,
    Administrator
Morphesis, Jim (James George) Painter
Muchnic, Suzanne Critic, Instructor
Mudford, Grant Leighton Photographer
Natzler, Otto Ceramist, Sculptor
Norris, William A Collector
Oginz, Richard Sculptor, Instructor
Omar, Margit Painter, Educator
O'Neill, Pat Filmmaker, Photographer
Owens, Mary (Mary Louise Schnore)
    Painter
Pajaud, William Etienne Painter
Pal, Pratapaditya Curator, Historian
Palmer, Herbert Bearl Dealer, Collector
Pillin, Polia Painter, Ceramist
Pincus, Robert L(awrence) Critic,
    Educator
Pink, Marilyn Overman Dealer, Editor
Platus, Libby Fibre & Paper Sculptor
Pletscher, Josephine Marie Librarian,
    Serigrapher

CALIFORNIA (cont)

Poole, Richard Elliott Painter, Instructor
Powell, Earl Alexander, III Curator, Historian
Quinn, Noel Joseph Painter, Instructor
Reilly, Jack Painter
Rod, Bruce John Sculptor, Painter
Rose, David Painter, Illustrator
Rosenthal, Rachel Performance Artist, Sculptor
Ross, Kenneth Administrator
Rossman, Ruth Scharff Painter, Instructor
Rubin, Arnold Gary Historian
Rustvold, Katherine Jo Dealer
Saar, Betye Assemblage Artist, Collage Artist
Sargent, Margaret Holland Painter
Schaefer, Scott Jay Curator, Historian
Schipper, Merle Solway Historian, Critic
Schirm, David H Painter, Educator
Schrut, Sherry Painter, Printmaker
Schuler, Melvin Albert Sculptor, Painter
Schwarz, Kurt L Dealer, Historian
Seletz, Emil Sculptor
Serisawa, Ikuo Dealer
Seyle, Robert Harley Sculptor, Designer
Shelton, Peter T Sculptor
Sherwood, Richard E Patron, Collector
Shire, Peter
Silverman, Ronald H Educator, Writer
Sklar, Dorothy Painter
Smith, Barbara Turner Instructor, Video Artist
Smith, Robert Lewis Museum Director, Educator
Spiegelman, Lon Howard Painter, Assemblage Artist
Squires, Norma-Jean Sculptor, Painter
Stead, Rexford Arthur Administrator, Historian
Stokes, Thomas Phelps Painter
Stoumen, Lou Filmmaker, Photographer
Stuart, David Dealer
Stussy, Jan Painter, Educator
Stussy, Maxine Kim Sculptor
Takemoto, Henry Tadaaki Craftsman, Sculptor
Teraoka, Masami Painter, Sculptor
Teske, Edmund Rudolph Photographer
Thomas, Tamara B Consultant
Todd, Michael Cullen Sculptor, Painter
Toigo, Daniel Joseph Painter
Tonelli, Edith Ann Museum Director, Historian
Tuchman, Maurice Museum Curator
Turner, Janice Kay Dealer
Vann, Loli (Mrs Lilian Van Young) Painter
Van Sant, Tom R Sculptor, Painter
Van Young, Oscar Painter
Wayne, June Painter
Westcoast, Wanda Sculptor, Educator
Wight, Frederick S Painter, Administrator
Woelffer, Emerson Painter
Wong, Roger Frederickson Museum Director, Collector
Woods, Gurdon Grant Sculptor
Wright, Bernard Painter, Graphic Artist
Wurdemann, Helen (Baroness Elena Guzzardi) Administrator, Collector
Yokoi, Rita Sculptor, Painter
Yokomi, Richard Koji Painter
Young, Joseph Louis Sculptor, Administrator
Zeitlin, Harriet Brooks Printmaker, Painter
Zeitlin, Jacob Israel Dealer, Collector

Los Gatos

Battenberg, John Sculptor, Educator
Kruskamp, Janet Painter, Instructor
Maltby, Hazel Farrow Weaver, Designer
Middlebrook, David A Sculptor, Educator

Los Osos

Gibson, George Painter, Administrator
Kreitzer, David Martin Painter

Malibu

Bowman, Bruce Painter, Art Writer
Davis, Ronald Wendel Painter, Printmaker
Eino Sculptor
Ellison, Nancy Painter, Photographer
Fredericksen, Burton Baum Curator, Historian
Frel, Jiri Curator
Halbrook, Anne-Mieke Platt Librarian
Preminger, Mary G(ardner) Sculptor, Painter
Waters, Terrance Architect
Wittmann, Otto Museum Consultant

Manchester

Engle, Chet Painter

Marina Del Rey

Bromberg, Faith Painter

Mendocino

Zacha, William Painter, Sculptor

Menlo Park

Fanning, Robbie Writer, Lecturer
Lemmy, Lemmy Painter, Printmaker
Mozley, Anita Ventura Curator, Historian
Smith, Albert E Painter, Dealer

Millbrae

Nepote, Alexander Painter

Mill Valley

Baum, Marilyn Ruth Painter, Printmaker
Grant, Art Conceptual Artist, Educator
Ihle, John Livingston Printmaker, Educator
Jones, Pirkle Photographer, Editor
O'Hanlon, Richard E Sculptor, Painter
Padula, Fred David Filmmaker, Photographer
Saul, Peter Painter
Sherry, William Grant Painter
Singer, Joel Filmmaker, Photographer

Modesto

Gauvreau, Robert George Photographer, Educator
Remsing, (Joseph) Gary Painter, Sculptor

Montague

Stone, Gwen Printmaker, Assemblage Artist

Montebello

Shubin, Morris Jack Painter, Lecturer

Montecito

Bayer, Herbert Painter, Architect

Monterey

Baer, Morley Photographer
Berry, Carolyn (Carolyn Berry Becker) Painter, Writer
Bradford, Howard Printmaker, Painter
Crispo, Dick Painter, Printmaker
Dedini, Eldon Lawrence Cartoonist
Gilpin, Henry Edmund Photographer, Instructor
Henderson, Lester Kierstead Photographer

Moorpark

Hayward, James Painter

Morgan Hill

Freimark, Robert (Matthew) Printmaker, Painter

Mountain Center

Olsen, Frederick L Potter, Sculptor

Mountain View

Dzigurski, Alex Painter

Napa

Garnett, William Ashford Photographer, Educator

Newport Beach

Consey, Kevin E Museum Diector, Administrator
Spitz, Barbara S Printmaker

North Hollywood

Brommer, Gerald F Painter, Writer
Danieli, Fidel Angelo Painter, Critic
Knight, Christopher Allen Critic, Administrator
Kohn, Edmond Painter, Instructor
Kovner, Saul Painter, Printmaker

Northridge

Elder, David Morton Sculptor
Fricano, Tom S Painter, Printmaker

North San Juan

Acton, Arlo C Sculptor

Oakland

Almy, Max (Marilynn Irene) Video Artist, Director
Amason, Alvin Eli Painter
Baczek, Peter Gerard Printmaker
Beasley, Bruce Sculptor
Block, Joyce Calligrapher, Photographer
Brooke, Pegan Painter
Carlson, George Arthur Sculptor, Painter
Carnwath, Squeak Painter
Clark, Claude Instructor, Painter
Cornin, Jon Painter
Dhaemers, Robert August Sculptor, Educator
Donahue, Philip Richard Painter, Educator
Doyle, Joe Painter, Educator
Fisher, Joel A Sculptor
Fisk-Hayden, Bonnie Painter
Foosaner, Judith Educator, Painter
Ford, Harry Xavier Educator, Administrator
Garcia, Rupert (Marshall R) Painter, Historian
Hammerbeck, Wanda Lee Photographer, Sculptor
Hardy, David Whittaker, III Painter, Instructor
Hartman, Robert Leroy Photographer, Educator
Jensen, Gary Painter
Kirk, Jerome Sculptor
Levine, Marilyn Anne Sculptor, Educator
Levine, Melinda (Esther) Critic, Editor
Lewis, John Conard Sculptor, Glassblower
Linhares, Philip E Curator
Lopez, Michael John Ceramist
McCann, Cecile Nelken Editor, Critic
MacGregor, Gregory Allen Photographer
McLean, Richard Thorpe Painter, Educator
Martin, Fred Thomas Painter
Mendenhall, Jack Painter, Instructor
Ollman, Arthur L Photographer, Historian

CALIFORNIA (cont)

Orr-Cahall, Anona Christina Curator, Historian
Ramos, Melvin John Painter, Educator
Richardson, Sam Sculptor, Educator
Rogers, Barbara Joan Painter, Educator
Rubin, Marjorie J(oan) Textile Artist, Weaver
Saunders, Raymond Jennings Painter
Schoener, Jason Painter, Educator
Siegriest, Lundy Painter
Slusky, Joseph Sculptor, Lecturer
Snyder, Dan Sculptor
Suzuki, James Hiroshi Painter
Tavenner, Patricia (Pat) Collage Artist, Photographer
Thurston, Jacqueline Beverly Photographer, Educator
Walsh, Patricia Ruth Painter
Weare, Shane Printmaker

Ojai

Abraham, Carol Jeanne Ceramist
Dominique, John August Painter
Smith, Robert Alan Painter, Designer
Wood, Beatrice Ceramist, Educator

Orange

Bledsoe, Jane Kathryn Historian, Administrator
Holste, Thomas James Painter, Educator
Smith, Thelma deGoede Painter, Educator

Orinda

Brody, Blanche Painter, Printmaker
Tullis, Garner H Painter, Printmaker
Wolfe, Maurice Raymond Museum Director, Consultant

Oro Grande

Bender, Bill Painter

Pacheco

Fon, Jade Painter, Instructor

Pacifica

Torlakson, James Daniel Painter, Printmaker

Pacific Grove

Jolley, Geraldine H (Jerry) Painter, Sculptor
Kinghan, Charles Ross Painter

Pacific Palisades

Bowman, Ruth Critic, Museologist
Brokaw, Lucile Painter
Campbell, Richard Horton Painter, Printmaker
Fisher, Ethel Painter
Garrett, Stephen Museum Director
Hannah, John Junior Printmaker, Educator
Janelsins, Veronica Illustrator, Painter
Longman, Lester Duncan Historian, Educator
Selwitz, Ruth F Painter, Sculptor
Sherman, Z Charlotte Painter
Treiman, Joyce Wahl Painter

Palm Desert

Hemmerdinger, William John, III Painter, Critic
Rich, Frances L Sculptor, Draftsman

Palm Springs

Foster, Holland Painter
Wade, Jane Dealer

Palo Alto

Bergstrom, Edith Harrod Painter, Instructor
Boyle, Keith Painter, Educator
Fryberger, Betsy G Curator
Lobdell, Frank Painter
Moore, Michael Shannon Painter, Printmaker
Ranes, Chris Painter
Strong, Charles Ralph Painter, Educator
Zirker, Joseph Printmaker, Lecturer

Pasadena

Barthe, Richmond Sculptor
Carmichael, Jae Painter, Sculptor
Dyer, Carolyn Price Critic, Tapestry Artist
Hoffberg, Judith A Publisher, Consultant
Hundley, David Holladay Designer, Educator
Kubly, Donald R Designer, Administrator
Levy, Hilda Painter
Perkins, Constance M Educator, Critic
Reeser, Robert D Educator
Risser, James K Dealer, Painter
Simon, Norton Collector
Trenton, Patricia Jean Historian
Wagner, Gordon Parsons Assemblage Artist, Environmental Artist
Willis, Jay Stewart Sculptor, Educator
Younglove, Ruth Ann (Mrs Benjamin Rhees Loxley) Painter
Zammitt, Norman Painter, Sculptor

Pebble Beach

Kaller, Robert Jameson Dealer
Ketcham, Hank (Henry King) Cartoonist
Mortensen, Gordon Louis Printmaker, Painter

Penngrove

Ellison, Robert W Sculptor

Petaluma

Camhi, Morrie Photographer, Educator
Fuller, Mary (Mary Fuller McChesney) Sculptor, Writer
McChesney, Robert Pearson Painter, Muralist
Reichek, Jesse Painter, Educator

Piedmont

Johnson, Doris Miller Painter
Lavenson, Alma (Alma Lavenson Wahrhaftig) Photographer
Murray, Joan Critic, Photographer

Pinole

Misrach, Richard Laurence Photographer

Point Reyes Station

Pattee, Rowena Serigrapher, Filmmaker

Point Richmond

Dane, Bill Photographer
Wessel, Henry, Jr Photographer

Port Costa

Bailey, Clayton George Sculptor, Educator
De Forest, Roy Dean Painter, Sculptor

Rancho Bernardo

Doll, Linda A Painter, Printmaker

Redding

Oldham, Berton Jepsen Printmaker, Instructor
Wilson, Richard Brian Painter

Redondo Beach

Crown, Keith Allen Painter, Educator

Redway

Holbrook, Peter Greene Painter, Printmaker

Redwood City

Bowman, Richard Painter

Reseda

Sider, Deno Painter, Sculptor

Rialto

Mendes, Barbara Painter

Richmond

Haley, John Charles Painter, Sculptor
Walker, Edward D (Rusty) Painter

Rimforest

Jolley, Donal Clark Painter

Riverside

Brinkerhoff, Dericksen Morgan Historian, Educator
Deal, Joe Photographer, Educator
Desmarais, Charles Joseph Museum Director, Writer
Earle, Edward W Curator, Historian
Slatkin, Wendy Historian

Roseville

Alquilar, Maria Painter, Sculptor

Sacramento

Adan, Suzanne Rae Painter
Allan, William George Painter, Educator
Clisby, Roger David Curator, Historian
Else, Robert John Educator, Painter
Grove, Merrill Dale Curator, Painter
Marcus, Irving E Painter, Educator
Moment, Joan Painter, Educator
Riegel, Michael Byron Metalsmith
Rippon, Ruth Margaret Ceramist, Educator
Rivers, Victoria Z Sculptor
Stevens, Michael Keith Sculptor
Vandenberge, Peter Willem Sculptor, Muralist
Walburg, Gerald Sculptor, Educator
Waterstreet, Ken (James Kent) Painter, Instructor
Winkler, Maria Paula Painter, Educator

Salinas

Amyx, Leon Kirkman Painter, Educator
Butterbaugh, Robert Clyde Sculptor, Educator

San Anselmo

Connor, Linda Stevens Photographer, Instructor
Dater, Judy Photographer, Writer

San Bernardino

Lintault, Roger Paul Educator, Sculptor
Woodford, Don (Donald Paul) Painter, Educator

San Carlos

Silver, Pat Draftsman, Illustrator

San Diego

Alden, Gary Wade Art Conservator
Alf, Martha Joanne Painter, Writer
Beach, Warren Painter
Chan, Phillip Paang Painter, Educator
Conrad, John W Educator, Ceramist
Cordy-Collins, Alana (Kathleen) Curator, Educator
Esser, Janet Brody Historian, Educator

CALIFORNIA (cont)

Fisch, Arline Marie Goldsmith, Educator
Galas, Philip-Dimitri Conceptual Artist, Writer
Hiller, Betty R Curator, Consultant
House, Suda Kay Photographer, Educator
Jackson, Everett Gee Painter, Illustrator
Jennings, Jan Writer
Jones, Claire Painter, Printmaker
Jung, Kwan Yee Painter
Jung, Yee Wah Painter
Kilian, Austin Farland Painter, Educator
Kornmayer, J Gary (John) Painter, Photographer
Kosta, Angela Assemblage Artist, Draftsman
Levinson, Mimi Painter, Lecturer
Lopez, Rhoda Le Blanc Sculptor, Educator
Morcos, Maher N Sculptor, Painter
Poduska, T F Lecturer, Painter
Rigby, Ida Katherine Critic, Historian
Riggs, Mary Kathryn Dealer, Collector
Roth, Moira Educator, Historian
Schultz, Caroline Reel Painter, Lecturer
Swiggett, Jean Donald Graphic Artist, Painter
Tibbs, Thomas S Educator, Museum Director
Wallace, Robert Dan Educator, Historian
Weldon, Barbara Maltby Painter, Printmaker
Whitcomb, Therese Truitt Historian, Instructor
Wojtyla, Haase (Walter Joseph) Painter, Draftsman
Wordell, Edwin Howland Painter
Wostrel, Nancy J Painter
Wright, Barton Allen Painter, Illustrator

San Francisco

Adams, Mark Tapestry Artist, Painter
Aiken, William A Painter
Alexander, Kenneth Lewis Cartoonist
Allen, Jesse Printmaker, Painter
Allrich, M Louise Barco Art Dealer
Alterman, Johnny Photographer
Asawa, Ruth (Ruth Asawa Lanier) Sculptor, Painter
Bartlett, Scott Filmmaker
Baum, Hank Art Dealer, Lecturer
Beall, Dennis Ray Printmaker, Educator
Belcher, George Art Dealer
Bell, Michael Steven Curator, Administrator
Benton, Fletcher Sculptor
Berggruen, John Henry Art Dealer
Bernhard, Ruth Photographer
Bottini, David M Sculptor
Braunstein, Ruth Art Dealer
Breschi, Karen Lee Sculptor
Brooks, (John) Alan Painter, Instructor
Camarata, Martin L Educator, Printmaker
Cameron, Elsa S Curator, Administrator
Coke, F Van Deren Photographer, Curator
Conner, Bruce Painter, Filmmaker
Cook, Lia Tapestry Artist, Educator
Cortright, Steven M Printmaker, Painter
Cox, E Morris Collector
Daviee, Jerry Michael Administrator, Curator
Dawdy, Doris Ostrander Writer, Historian
Dean, Nat(alie Carol) Painter, Constructionist
DeFeo, Jay Painter, Photographer
DeRoux, Daniel Edward Painter, Printmaker
Dickinson, Eleanor Creekmore Painter, Video Artist
Diehl, Guy Louis Instructor, Painter

Elder, Muldoon Painter, Dealer
Evans, Henry Printmaker
Fischer, Hal (Harold Alan) Writer, Photographer
Fitch, George Hopper Collector, Patron
Folsom, Karl Leroy Printmaker, Instructor
Foolery, Tom Assemblage Artist, Painter
Foster, Robert Stephen Dealer, Publisher
Fraenkel, Jeffrey Andrew Dealer, Gallery Director
Frey, Viola Sculptor, Painter
Fried, Howard Lee Sculptor
Fuller, Diana Dealer
Gates, Thomas Paul Educator, Curator
Gerdes, Ingeborg Photographer
Gerstein, David Steven Filmmaker
Glassman, Joel A Video Artist, Photographer
Goddard, Vivian Painter
Goldeen, Dorothy A Dealer, Consultant
Goldstein, Daniel Joshua Printmaker, Sculptor
Grant, James Sculptor
Gray, Larry Painter
Graysmith, Robert Cartoonist, Illustrator
Gutkin, Peter Sculptor, Designer
Gutmann, John Educator, Painter
Hamaguchi, Yozo Printmaker
Hanson, Jo Sculptor
Harper, Paula (Hays) Historian, Writer
Henry, Jean Painter, Instructor
Hershman, Lynn Lester Sculptor
Hills, Leo Himmelfarb Dealer, Appraiser
Hinkhouse, Forest Melick Consultant
Hooper, Jack Meredith Painter, Printmaker
Hopkins, Henry Tyler Museum Director, Educator
Howard, David Photographer, Painter
Hughes, Joseph (Frederick) Painter
Hyson, Jean Painter
Iannetti, Pasquale Francesco Paolo Dealer, Collector
Isaacs, Claire Naomi Administrator
Jackson, Oliver Lee Painter
Jess Painter, Collage Artist
Johnson, Robert Flynn Curator, Historian
Johnston, Helen Head Dealer
Jones, David Lee Painter, Sculptor
Kali (Hanka Weynerowski) Painter
Kane, Bill (William David) Assemblage Artist, Photographer
Karlstrom, Paul Johnson Historian, Administrator
Katano, Marc Painter
Kos, Paul Joseph Sculptor, Educator
Lefebvre d'Argence, Rene-Yvon Museum Director, Writer
Levin, Morton D Printmaker, Painter
Lew, Eileen Curator
Lew, Weyman Painter, Printmaker
Lipzin, Janis Crystal Filmmaker, Photographer
Loeffler, Carl Eugene Editor, Video Artist
Lowinsky, Simon L Dealer
Lupper, Edward Painter
Mackenzie, David, IV Painter
Maclay, David (Sears), Jr Photographer, Sculptor
Majdrakoff, Ivan Painter, Assemblage Artist
Maradiaga, Ralph Gallery Director, Designer
Marioni, Tom Museum Director, Environmental Artist
Meyer, Thomas Vincent Dealer
Miller, (Mrs) Robert Watt Patron
Mohr, Pauline Catherine Conservator, Restorer
Mundt, Ernest Karl Sculptor, Educator
Muranaka, Hideo Painter, Printmaker

Murch, Anna Valentina Conceptual Artist, Photographer
Nelson, Jane Gray Librarian
Neri, Manuel Sculptor
Neto, Gilda Reis (Gilda Reis Netopuletti) Painter
Nong Painter, Sculptor
Nugent, Bob L Painter, Sculptor
O'Banion, Nance Assemblage Artist
O'Hara, Sheila Mary Weaver, Designer
Pence, John Gerald Dealer, Patron
Pennuto, James William Conceptual Artist, Conservator
Plossu, Bernard Photographer
Pomeroy, James Calwell, Jr Performance Artist, Photographer
Posey, Ernest Noel Painter
Post, George (Booth) Painter
Post, Marion (Marion Post Wolcott) Photographer
Potts, Don Sculptor
Raciti, Cherie Painter, Sculptor
Redd Ekks (Robert Norman Rasmussen) Sculptor, Ceramist
Reich, Don Painter
Reichman, Fred Painter
Renk, Merry Goldsmith, Sculptor
Robbins, Trina Cartoonist, Illustrator
Robinson, C David Architect, Collector
Rubin, David S Curator, Critic
Rumsey, David MacIver Environmental Artist, Patron
St Amand, Joseph Painter
Sapien, Darryl Rudolph Performance Artist, Graphic Artist
Sawyer, William Dealer, Collector
Seligman, Thomas Knowles Curator, Administrator
Shangraw, Clarence Frank Historian, Curator
Shaw, Richard Blake Sculptor
Shepp, Alan Sculptor
Sinton, Nell (Walter) Painter, Educator
Smith, Gary Douglas Printmaker, Painter
Smith, Hassel W, Jr Painter
Soult, James Thomas Graphic Artist
Sovary, Lilly Painter, Designer
Spoerer, Dale Raymond Collector, Educator
Stanley, M Louise Painter, Instructor
Staprans, Raimonds Painter, Sculptor
Stephens, Richard Alan Administrator, Painter
Stermer, Dugald Robert Illustrator, Designer
Stevens, Marjorie Collage Artist, Painter
Stewart, Jeffrey Dealer, Gallery Director
Stofflet, Mary Critic, Historian
Stone, Jeremy Dealer
Stover, Donald Lewis Curator
Tarshis, Jerome Writer
Taylor, Sandra Ortiz Painter, Printmaker
Thomas, Lew Photographer, Writer
Thompson, Richard E, Jr Dealer, Collector
Thompson, Richard Earl, Sr Painter
Ullrich-Zuckerman, B Painter, Photographer
Valesco, Frances Muralist, Printmaker
Van Hoesen, Beth (Mrs Mark Adams) Printmaker
Velick, Bruce Gallery Director
Villa, Carlos Painter
Vitale, Lydia Modi Museum Director, Curator
Voelker, Elizabeth Painter, Collage Artist
Volkerding, Laura Photographer
von Meyer, Michael Sculptor
Wall, Brian Sculptor
Webber, Helen Tapestry Artist, Painter
Weinbaum, Jean Painter, Sculptor
Welpott, Jack Warren Photographer, Educator

CALIFORNIA (cont)

White, Ian McKibbin Museum
  Administrator
Wiener, Daniel Sculptor
Wirtz, Stephen Carl Dealer
Wonner, Paul (John) Painter

San Geronimo

North, Judy Painter, Printmaker
Raffael, Joseph Painter, Printmaker

San Jose

Chapman, Robert Gordon Jeweler,
  Painter
Gerbracht, Bob (Robert Thomas) Painter,
  Instructor
Hernandez, Jo Farb Museum Director,
  Curator
Hernandez, Sam (Samuel Rudolph)
  Sculptor, Educator
Hunter, John H Painter, Printmaker
Kaiser, Benjamin Sculptor, Designer
Stone, M Lee Dealer
Wu, I-Chen Calligrapher, Painter
Young, Edna E Dealer, Collector

San Juan Bautista

De Groat, George Hugh Painter,
  Printmaker

San Luis Obispo

Dwyer, Gary Colburn Environmental
  Artist, Sculptor
Gray, Gladys Painter, Muralist
Reynolds, Robert Painter, Educator
Ruggles, Joanne Beaule Printmaker,
  Educator

San Marcos

Baldwin, Russell W Educator, Gallery
  Director
Freeman, Robert Lee Painter, Sculptor

San Marino

Medearis, Roger Painter, Lithographer
Wark, Robert Rodger Administrator,
  Historian

San Mateo

Mancini, John Painter, Illustrator

San Pedro

Crutchfield, William Richard Painter,
  Printmaker
McCafferty, Jay David Video Artist,
  Painter

San Rafael

Larsen, D Dane Ceramist, Sculptor
Lucey, Jack Painter, Educator
Rowland, Mary Adele Photographer,
  Educator
Smith, Henry Holmes Photographer,
  Educator

Santa Ana

De Mille, Leslie Benjamin Painter, Dealer
Karwelis, Donald Charles Painter,
  Instructor
Rhodes, Reilly Patrick Museum Director
Romans, Van Anthony Sculptor, Designer

Santa Barbara

Ayres, Larry Marshall Historian
Backus, Standish, Jr Painter, Muralist
Badash, Sandi Borr Painter, Fabric
  Designer
Bowers, Cheryl Olsen Painter, Educator
Braiden, Rose Margaret J Painter,
  Illustrator
Brown, Gary Hugh Painter, Educator

Catalan, Edgardo Omar Painter, Educator
Cavat, Irma Painter, Educator
Cole, Herbert Milton Historian,
  Photographer
Davidson, Suzette Morton Patron,
  Collector
Dole, William Painter, Educator
Dorra, Henri Historian, Educator
Edge, Douglas Benjamin Sculptor, Painter
Eguchi, Yasu Painter
Farmer, John David Historian,
  Administrator
Farwell, Beatrice Historian, Educator
Fenton, Howard Carter Painter, Educator
Firfires, Nicholas Samuel Painter
Frame, Robert (Aaron) Painter
Gabrielson, Walter Oscar Painter,
  Draftsman
Gebhard, David Museum Director,
  Historian
Irvin, Fred Maddox Illustrator, Painter
Mallory, Margaret Collector, Filmmaker
Mills, Paul Chadbourne Museum Director
Moir, Alfred Historian, Administrator
Monaghan, Kathleen Mary Historian,
  Curator
Morrison, Doris Painter, Administrator
Noble, Helen (Harper) Printmaker,
  Painter
Schaffner, Ruth S Dealer, Consultant
Snow, Lee Erlin Painter, Instructor
Solberg, Morten Edward Painter
Spurlock, William Henry, II Historian,
  Critic
Tanner, Joan Elizabeth Painter, Collage
  Artist
Torbert, Donald Robert Educator,
  Historian
Treese, William R Librarian, Painter
West, Richard Vincent Museum Director,
  Historian
Yegul, Fikret Kutlu Educator, Architect

Santa Clara

Hawkins, Myrtle H Painter, Writer

Santa Cruz

Alford, Gloria K Sculptor, Craftsman
Auvil, Kenneth William Educator,
  Printmaker
Brown, Lawrie Educator, Photographer
McClellan, Douglas Eugene Painter
McDonald, Robert Herwick Curator,
  Writer
Marx, Nicki D Painter, Photographer
Massaro, Karen Thuesen Ceramist,
  Sculptor
Stolpe, Daniel Owen Printmaker, Sculptor
Summers, Carol Printmaker
Thompson, Donald Roy Painter, Educator
Watson-Abbott, Lynda Jeweler,
  Silversmith

Santa Monica

Alhilali, Neda Environmental Artist,
  Painter
Bachardy, Don Painter, Draftsman
Ballatore-Nelson, Sandra Lee Art Critic,
  Instructor
Berlant, Tony Sculptor
Blum, Helaine Dorothy Sculptor, Painter
Bolen, John E Art Dealer, Collector
Bolen, Lynne N Art Dealer, Collector
Bongart, Sergei R Painter, Instructor
Bordeaux, Jean Luc Art Historian,
  Curator
Caswell, Jim (James Daniel
  Caswell-Davis) Sculptor, Ceramist
Freeman, Mallory Bruce Dealer, Curator
Fusco, Laurie S Historian, Educator
Haines, Richard Painter, Muralist
Hempler, Orval F Painter, Sculptor

Hill, William Mansfield Historian,
  Museum Director
Karpel, Eli Sculptor
Knight, John Conceptual Artist
Kushner, Dorothy Browdy Painter,
  Printmaker
McMillen, Michael C(halmers)
  Environmental Artist, Sculptor
Mullican, Lee Painter, Educator
Nellis, David L Collector
Okulick, John A Sculptor
Phillips, Gifford Collector, Writer
Pinkel, Sheila Mae Photographer,
  Sculptor
Secunda, (Holland) Arthur Painter,
  Collage Artist
Snyder, Ruth (Cozen) Environmental
  Artist, Sculptor
Stern, Irene Monat Painter
Stern, Jan Peter Sculptor
Walsh, John, Jr Museum Director
Weisberg, Ruth Ellen Printmaker,
  Educator

Santa Rosa

Lienau, Daniel Clifford Dealer, Collector
Quandt, Elizabeth (Elizabeth Quandt
  Barr) Printmaker
Rosen, James Mahlon Painter, Historian

Santa Ynez

Peake, Channing Painter, Muralist

Saratoga

McCauley, Gardiner Rae Administrator,
  Painter

Sausalito

Baltz, Lewis Photographer
Kuhlman, Walter Egel Painter, Educator
Schwarcz, June Theresa Craftsman,
  Enamelist
Weiss, Linda (Linda Margaret
  Weiss-Edwards) Silversmith,
  Goldsmith
Wiley, William T Painter

Scotts Valley

Stacy, John Russell Illustrator, Jeweler

Sebastopol

Barnes, Carroll Sculptor
Barnhart, C Raymond Assemblage Artist,
  Sculptor
Caswell, Helen Rayburn Painter, Writer
Moulton, Susan Gene Historian, Painter
Palmer, Mabel (Evelyn) Painter

Sherman Oaks

Carl, Joan Sculptor, Designer
de la Vega, Enrique Miguel Sculptor,
  Designer
Klein, Cecelia F Historian, Educator
Schlosberg, Carl Martin Dealer
Stern, Louis Dealer, Consultant

Sierra Madre

Randall, (Lillian) Paula Sculptor, Designer

Signal Hill

Guthrie, Perri Pizer Dealer

Solana Beach

Gronborg, Erik Sculptor, Ceramist

Solvang

Aronson, Cliff Art Dealer
St John, John Milton Painter, Muralist

Sonoma

Anderson, Gunnar Donald Painter,
   Illustrator
Christensen, Ted Painter, Printmaker

Soquel

Blair, Lee Everett Painter, Filmmaker

South Laguna

Jones, John Paul Painter, Printmaker

South Pasadena

Askin, Walter Miller Painter, Printmaker
Dutton, Pauline Mae Librarian
Outterbridge, John Wilfred Administrator,
   Painter
Sverdlove, Zolita Painter, Printmaker

Spring Valley

Greene, Ethel Maud Painter

Stanford

Eisner, Elliot Wayne Educator
Eitner, Lorenz E A Historian, Museum
   Director
Elsen, Albert Edward Historian
Oliveira, Nathan Painter

Stockton

Dennison, Keith Elkins Museum
   Director, Historian
Gyermek, Stephen A Educator
Pecchenino, J Ronald Painter, Educator
Reynolds, Richard (Henry) Sculptor,
   Painter

Studio City

Burg, Patricia Jean Painter, Printmaker
Vaccarino, Robin Sculptor, Painter
Waite, Elin Jane Designer, Educator
Zlotnick, Diana Shirley Collector, Patron

Suisun City

Schmaltz, Roy Edgar Painter, Educator

Summerland

Calamar, Gloria Painter

Sunland

Porter, Albert Wright Educator, Painter

Sylmar

Gebhardt, Harold Sculptor, Painter
Gebhardt, Peter Martin Sculptor

Temecula

Weekes, Shirley Marie Painter

Thousand Oaks

Martino, Antonio P Painter

Tiburon

Baird, Joseph Armstrong, Jr Writer, Art
   Dealer

Topanga

Alexander, Peter Sculptor
Jennings, Thomas Painter, Printmaker
Schley, Evander Duer (Van) Conceptual
   Artist, Photographer
Solem, (Elmo) John Printmaker, Educator

Torrance

Clark, Robert Charles Painter, Lecturer
Everts, Connor Painter, Printmaker

Trona

Fitzgerald, John Philip Painter, Instructor

Turlock

McGee, Winston Eugene Painter,
   Educator
Parton, Ralf Sculptor, Educator
Piskoti, James Printmaker, Painter
Werness, Hope B Historian

Upland

Logan, Gene Adams Sculptor, Painter
Svenson, John Edward Sculptor

Vacaville

Wasser, Paula Kloster Educator, Painter

Valencia

Fitzpatrick, Robert John Administrator
Mandel, John Painter

Vallejo

Minick, Roger Photographer, Writer
Salmon, Raymond Merle Cartoonist,
   Educator

Valley Center

Landers, Bertha Painter, Printmaker

Van Nuys

Blinder, Martin S Art Dealer, Publisher
Davis, L Clarice Book Dealer, Collector
Kim, Bongtae Painter, Printmaker
Penny, Aubrey John Robert Painter,
   Gallery Director
Stancil, Kimsey Historian, Administrator

Venice

Arnoldi, Charles Arthur Sculptor, Painter
Asher, Michael Environmental Artist,
   Sculptor
Bengston, Billy Al Painter
Brewster, Michael Sculptor, Educator
Brown, Betty Ann Educator, Critic
Cheng, Fu-Ding Filmmaker, Painter
Colorado, Charlotte Painter
Cooper, Ron Environmental Artist,
   Photographer
Cowin, Eileen Photographer
Darricarrere, Roger Dominique Sculptor,
   Stained Glass Artist
Dill, Guy Girard Sculptor
Dill, Laddie John Painter, Sculptor
Divola, John Manford, Jr Photographer
Eversley, Frederick John Sculptor
Forst, Miles Sculptor, Educator
Gehry, Frank O(wen) Architect
Goulds, Peter J Dealer, Designer
Graham, Robert Sculptor
Hamrol, Lloyd Sculptor
Henderson, Victor (Lance) Painter,
   Photographer
Hirsch, Gilah Yelin Painter, Educator
Karlsen, Anne-Marie Painter, Printmaker
Lewis, Helen Natalie Gallery Director,
   Curator
Mirano, Virgil Marcus Photographer,
   Educator
O'Shea, Terrence Patrick Painter,
   Sculptor
Rady, Elsa Ceramist, Sculptor
Scheer, Sherie (Hood) Photographer,
   Educator
Segalove, Ilene Judy Video Artist,
   Photographer
Smith, Alexis (Patricia Anne) Conceptual
   Artist
Sturman, Eugene Painter, Sculptor
Valentine, DeWain Sculptor
White, John M Painter, Conceptual Artist

Ventura

Koch, Gerd (Herman) Painter, Educator
Moser, Julon Painter

Victorville

Bascom, Earl W Sculptor, Printmaker

Walnut Creek

Dennis, Charles Houston Cartoonist
Esaki, Yasuhiro Painter, Printmaker
Hunter, Leonard LeGrande, III Sculptor,
   Educator
Partridge, Roi Printmaker
Stiegelmeyer, Norman Earl Painter,
   Sculptor

West Covina

Cross, Watson, Jr Painter, Video Artist

Westlake Village

Liu, Katherine Chang Painter, Printmaker

Woodacre

Snyder, William B Painter, Educator
Taylor, Gage Painter

Woodland Hills

Glass, Sylvia Painter
Reed, Hal Painter, Sculptor
Simmons, Cleda Marie Painter, Graphic
   Artist
Whitson, Angie Sculptor, Painter

Woodside

Hogle, Ann Meilstrup Painter

Yountville

Clymer, Albert Anderson Painter

Yucaipa

Weese, Myrtle A Painter

COLORADO

Arvada

Balciar, Gerald George Sculptor
Lyon, Hayes Paxton Painter

Aspen

Berko, Ferenc Photographer
Chesley, Paul Alexander Photographer,
   Graphic Artist
Herschler, David Elijah Sculptor, Painter

Aurora

Thies, Charles Herman Painter,
   Printmaker
Whitney, Maynard Merle Sculptor,
   Educator

Boulder

Arguelles, Jose A Writer, Painter
Barnes, Carole D Painter
Brcin, John David Sculptor
Cline, Clinton C Printmaker, Educator
Drewelowe, Eve Painter, Sculptor
Eades, Luis Eric Painter, Educator
Eichner-Dixon, Peter Painter, Printmaker
Fernie, John Chipman Sculptor, Instructor
Forsman, Chuck (Charles Stanley)
   Painter, Educator
Geck, Francis Joseph Educator, Designer
Gilboy, Margaretta Painter, Instructor
Goodacre, Glenna Painter, Sculptor
Hodel, Diane Carol Painter, Printmaker
Iwamasa, Ken Educator, Printmaker
Johnson, James Alan Painter, Educator
Kuczun, Ann-Marie Printmaker, Painter
Lhotka, Bonny Pierce Painter
Mahaffey, Merrill Dean Painter,
   Instructor

COLORADO (cont)

Matthews, Gene (Eugene Edward) Painter, Educator
Matthews, Wanda Miller Printmaker
Neher, Fred Cartoonist
Praeger, Frederick A Collector, Publisher
Sampson, Frank Painter, Printmaker
Stoessel, Henry Kurt Painter, Designer
Vandersall, Amy L Historian, Educator
Vielehr, William Ralph Sculptor
Westermeier, Clifford Peter Painter, Educator
Wolfe, Lynn Robert Painter, Educator

Buena Vista

Whipple, Barbara Printmaker, Writer

Cherry Hills Village

Strawn, Melvin Nicholas Painter, Sculptor

Colorado Springs

Arnest, Bernard Painter, Educator
Broome, Rick (Richard Raymond) Painter
Hansen, Arne Rae Museum Director, Administrator
Hoge, Robert Wilson Museum Director, Educator
Kinnee, Sandy Printmaker
Tilley, Lewis Lee Painter, Filmmaker
Trissel, James Nevin Painter, Printmaker
Wynne, Albert Givens Painter, Calligrapher

Creede

Quiller, Stephen Frederick Painter, Printmaker

Denver

Anderson, Bruce James Stained Glass Artist, Art Dealer
Bach, Otto Karl Museum Director, Writer
Bartlett, Fred Stewart Art Administrator
Bowman, Ken Painter
Bundy, Stephen Allen Sculptor
Clurman, Irene Critic
Conn, Richard George Curator
DeMaree, Betty (Elizabeth Ann) Painter, Instructor
Graese, Judy (Judith Ann) Pyrography, Illustrator
Graham, Douglas J M Museum Director, Collector
Hansen, Frances Frakes Educator, Painter
Hoffman, Carol Maree
Hughes, Paul Lucien Dealer, Consultant
Jagman, Ed Painter
Kaplan, Sandra Painter, Printmaker
Katz, Eunice Painter, Sculptor
Kelley, Ramon Painter
Kirkland, Vance Hall Painter, Collector
Maytham, Thomas Northrup Museum Director, Lecturer
Michael, Gary Writer, Painter
Mills, James Critic, Collector
Natzmer, Cheryl Lynn Dealer, Historian
Ragland, Bob Painter, Lecturer
Rivoli, Mario Assemblage Artist
Rosen, Beverly Doris Painter
Schiff, Jean Draftsman
Sherman, Ira D Goldsmith, Jeweler
Smith, Katherine (Chafee) Critic
Sprout, Francis Painter, Educator
Stapp, Ray Veryl Painter, Printmaker
Stroessner, Robert Joseph Curator, Historian
Swenson, (Jean) Mary Jeanette Hamilton Painter, Printmaker
Thorne-Thomsen, Ruth T Photographer, Educator
Traher, William Henry Painter, Muralist
Tubis, Seymour Painter, Printmaker

Vanderlip, Dianne Perry Gallery Director, Educator
Wands, Alfred James Painter
Witold-K (Kaczanowski) Painter, Sculptor
Yanish, Elizabeth Sculptor, Lecturer

Dolores

Wagner, Richard Ellis Painter

Elizabeth

Kaplinski, Buffalo Painter

Englewood

Brauer, Connie Ann Designer, Goldsmith
Jellico, John Anthony Director, Painter
Jellico, Nancy R Painter, Sculptor

Estes Park

Richmond, Rebekah Printmaker
Simoni, John Peter Painter, Educator

Ft Collins

De Waal, Ronald Burt Collector, Patron
Getty, Nilda Fernandez Educator, Silversmith
Jacobs, Peter Alan Administrator, Sculptor
Lesh, Richard D Painter, Instructor
Risbeck, Philip Edward Graphic Artist, Educator
Twarogowski, Leroy Andrew Draftsman, Educator
Yust, David E Painter, Educator

Glen Haven

Sorby, J Richard Painter, Designer

Golden

Deaton, Charles Sculptor, Architect
Julian, June Painter, Sculptor

Grand Junction

Dodworth, Allen Stevens Museum Director
Faris, Peter Kinzie Painter, Museum Director

Gunnison

Johnson, Lee Painter, Educator
Julio, Pat T Educator, Craftsman
Radovich, Donald Educator, Painter

Lafayette

Roots, Garrison Environmental Artist, Educator

Lakewood

Cadillac, Louise Roman Painter, Instructor
Denton, Pat Painter, Instructor
Knaub, Raymond L Painter, Instructor
Lang, Rodger Alan Ceramist, Educator

Littleton

Littell, Biz Glass Blower, Muralist
Turner, James Thomas, Sr Sculptor, Painter
Wiedenhoeft, Renate Photographer

Longmont

Adams, Robert Hickman Photographer
Wise, Sue Painter

Louisville

Fitch, Steve (Steven Ralph) Photographer, Instructor

Loveland

Lundeen, George Wayne Sculptor

Manitou Springs

Wallace, Gael Lynn Painter

Mesa

Fritzler, Gerald J(ohn) Painter

Monument

Bohler, Joseph Stephen Painter

Mt Crested Butte

Spaulding, D(onald Clifford) Illustrator, Painter

Parshall

Retzer, Howard Earl Painter

Pueblo

Ballard, Lockett Ford, Jr Museum Director
Wands, Robert James Educator, Painter

Rollinsville

Brakhage, James Stanley Filmmaker, Lecturer

Vail

Milhoan, Randall Bell Administrator, Painter

CONNECTICUT

Ashford

Spencer, Harold Edwin Historian, Painter

Bethel

Ajay, Abe Painter, Sculptor
Farris, Joseph Cartoonist, Painter

Bethlehem

Kraeft, June K & Norman Dealer, Collector
Vestal, David Photographer

Bloomfield

Tompkins, Alan Painter
Valtman, Edmund Cartoonist

Bridgeport

Morris, Robert Clarke Painter, Educator
Vazquez, Paul Painter

Bridgewater

Abbett, Robert Kennedy Painter
Gilbert, Albert Earl Painter, Illustrator

Brookfield Center

Beall, Joanna Painter, Sculptor
Sottung, George (K) Painter, Illustrator
Westermann, H C Sculptor, Painter

Clinton

Grimm, Lucille Davis Painter, Instructor
Mays, Victor Painter, Illustrator

Cornwall Bridge

Gray, Cleve Painter, Sculptor

Cos Cob

Giles, Newell Walton, Jr Painter
Kane, Margaret Brassler Sculptor

Coventry

Hayes, David Vincent Sculptor

Darien

Black, Lisa Painter, Graphic Artist
Newman, Ralph Albert Cartoonist, Writer

Deep River

Field, Richard Sampson Curator,
  Historian

Easton

Bogart, Richard Jerome Painter
Curtis, Dolly Powers Tapestry Artist,
  Sculptor
Shrady, Frederick Sculptor

Fairfield

Austin, Darrel Painter
Brier, Helene Painter, Educator
Chaikin, Alyce (Alyce Chaikin Kleinman)
  Graphic Artist, Painter
Dal Fabbro, Mario Sculptor, Writer
Glaser, Bruce Historian, Educator
Riley, Bernard Joseph Painter
Trager, Philip Photographer

Falls Village

Lathrop, Gertrude K Sculptor

Farmington

Dublac, Robert Revak Painter

Georgetown

D'Aulaire, Edgar Parin Illustrator, Painter
D'Aulaire, Ingri (Mortenson) Parin
  Painter, Writer
Thompson, Malcolm Barton Painter

Glastonbury

Bailey, Marcia Mead Painter
Randall, Ruth Hunie Designer

Greens Farms

McKinnickinnick, Margaret I Painter,
  Printmaker
Reid, Charles Writer, Painter
Weiss, Harvey Sculptor

Greenwich

Balazs, Gyongyi Painter
Birnbaum, Mildred Painter
Cecere, Gaetano Sculptor, Lecturer
Cherepov, George Painter, Instructor
de Lesseps, Tauni Sculptor, Painter
Fields, Fredrica H Stained Glass Artist,
  Glass Engraver
Kaep, Louis Joseph Painter
List, Vera G Patron, Collector
Lust, Herbert Historian, Collector
Lust, Virginia Dealer
Momiyama, Nanae Painter, Educator
Motherwell, Robert Painter, Printmaker
Perless, Robert Sculptor

Groton

Fix, John Robert Sculptor, Silversmith
MacGillis, Robert Donald Painter,
  Printmaker
Nelson, Harry William Painter,
  Printmaker

Guilford

Von Schlegell, David Sculptor

Hamden

Keller, Deane Educator, Painter
Lichtenberg, Manes Painter
MacClintock, Dorcas Sculptor
Willoughby, Jane Baker Painter, Collage
  Artist

Hartford

Atkinson, Tracy Museum Director
Behl, Wolfgang Sculptor, Educator
Coppola, Andrew Sculptor, Draftsman
Hedberg, Gregory Scott Curator,
  Historian
Mahoney, Michael R T Historian,
  Educator
Zimmerman, Paul Warren Painter,
  Instructor

Ivoryton

Albright, Thomas Art Critic, Writer
Bendig, William Charles Painter,
  Publisher
Jensen, Leo (Vernon) Sculptor, Painter
Ramanauskas, Dalia Irena Painter,
  Draftsman

Kent

Steig, William Cartoonist, Sculptor

Killingworth

Harris, William Wadsworth, II Painter,
  Collage Artist

Lakeville

Blagden, Thomas P Painter

Litchfield

Landeck, Armin Painter, Engraver

Madison

Burchard, Peter Duncan Illustrator,
  Photographer
Connery, Ruth M Painter, Instructor
Davies, Kenneth Southworth Painter,
  Instructor
Maestro, Giulio Marcello Illustrator,
  Painter
Wexler, Jerome LeRoy Photographer,
  Children's Book Illustrator

Mansfield Center

Forman, Kenneth Warner Painter,
  Educator

Meriden

Scalise, Nicholas Peter Painter, Sculptor
Tamburine, Jean Painter, Sculptor
Widstrom, Edward Frederick Sculptor

Middletown

Frazer, John Thatcher Filmmaker, Painter
Gourevitch, Jacqueline Painter
Risley, John Hollister Sculptor

Milford

Maier, Maryanne E Painter

Mystic

Bates, Gladys Edgerly Sculptor
Olson, Joseph Olaf Designer, Painter

New Britain

Ferguson, Charles B Museum Director,
  Painter
Wenner, L John G Educator, Painter

New Canaan

Cavalli, Dick Cartoonist
Eberman, Edwin Administrator, Educator
Finch, Ruth Woodward Patron,
  Photographer
Geerlings, Gerald Kenneth Graphic
  Artist, Architect
MacLean, Arthur Painter
Mann, Virginia Administrator, Critic
Margolies, Ethel Polacheck Painter
Richards, Glenora Painter
Richards, Walter DuBois Painter,
  Printmaker

Roesch, Kurt (Ferdinand) Painter
Saxon, Charles David Cartoonist,
  Illustrator
Tomchuk, Marjorie Printmaker
Woit, Bonnie Ford Painter

New Fairfield

Nevelson, Mike Sculptor

New Haven

Audette, Anna Held Printmaker,
  Educator
Bloomgarden, Judith Mary Art Librarian
Cain, David Paul Painter, Photographer
Carter, David Giles Consultant, Museum
  Director
Chaet, Bernard Painter, Educator
Colton, Judith Educator, Historian
Cormack, Malcolm Curator, Historian
Edelstein, Teri J Administrator, Historian
Forge, Andrew Murray Writer, Painter
Friedman, Joan Marcy Curator, Librarian
Fussiner, Howard Painter
Garston, Gerald Drexler Painter
Gilbert, Creighton Eddy Historian, Writer
Hanson, Anne Coffin Historian
Herbert, Robert L Historian, Educator
Hersey, George Leonard Historian,
  Educator
Ingalls, Eve Instructor, Painter
Kubler, George Alexander Historian,
  Writer
Lambert, Nancy S Librarian
Papageorge, Tod Photographer
Pelli, Cesar Architect
Pollitt, Jerome Jordan Historian, Educator
Prown, Jules David Historian
Rash, Nancy Historian, Writer
Sal, Jack Photographer, Painter
Shestack, Alan Museum Director,
  Historian
Wilson, Judith (A) Critic, Writer
Zeidenbergs, Olafs Sculptor

New London

Hendricks, Barkley Leonnard Painter
Lukosius, Richard Benedict Painter,
  Educator
Mayhew, Edgar De Noailles Educator,
  Museum Director
Smalley, David Allan Sculptor
Van Brunt, Philip G Director, Assemblage
  Artist

New Milford

McDermott, Gerald Illustrator, Designer
Schmid, Richard Alan Painter
Stewart, Dorothy S Painter, Printmaker

Newtown

Caparn, Rhys (Rhys Caparn Steel)
  Sculptor
Cottingham, Robert Painter
Getz, Ilse Collage Artist, Assemblage
  Artist
Grimes, Margaret W Painter, Educator
Inman, Pauline Winchester Printmaker,
  Illustrator
Wallace, John Edward Painter
Winchester, Alice Editor, Historian

Niantic

Dennis, Roger Wilson Painter

Noank

Stein, Fritz Henry Dealer
Stein, Harve Painter, Restorer

Norfolk

Kelemen, Pal Historian

North Haven

Tulk, Alfred James Painter, Muralist
Zallinger, Jean Day Illustrator, Educator
Zallinger, Rudolph Franz Painter,
    Educator

Norwalk

Egleson, Jim (James Downey)
    Printmaker, Painter
Frasconio, Antonio Illustrator, Painter
Lasker, Joe (Joseph L) Painter, Illustrator
Peii, Ahmad Osni Sculptor, Designer
Pellew, John Clifford Painter
Perry, Charles O Sculptor

Norwich

Gualtieri, Joseph P Museum Director,
    Painter
Leibert, Peter R Ceramist, Sculptor
Novack, Frank T Painter, Administrator
Radin, Dan Painter, Instructor
Triplett, Margaret L Painter
von Schlippe, Alexey Painter, Educator

Old Greenwich

Ballantyne, Catherine Turk Painter

Old Lyme

Chandler, Elisabeth Gordon Sculptor
de Gerenday, Laci Anthony Sculptor
Gruppe, Charles Painter
Hardin, Adlai S Sculptor
Peterson, Roger Tory Illustrator, Writer

Orange

Albers, Anni Designer, Graphic Artist

Oxford

Chaplin, George Edwin Painter, Educator

Plainville

Brzozowski, Richard Joseph Painter

Poquonock

van Winkelen, Barbara Painter, Illustrator

Portland

Glasson, Lloyd Sculptor, Educator

Putnam

Davis, Wayne Lambert Painter, Illustrator

Quaker Hill

McCabe, Maureen M Collage Artist

Redding Ridge

Morton, Robert Alan Publisher, Writer

Ridgefield

Benton, Suzanne E Sculptor, Art Writer
Busino, Orlando Francis Cartoonist
Drummond, Sally Hazelet Painter
Flateman, Ira N Gallery Director, Curator
Passantino, George Christopher Painter,
    Instructor
Perlin, Bernard Painter, Illustrator
Ross, Alexander Painter
Scott, John Illustrator, Painter
Sendak, Maurice Bernard Writer,
    Illustrator

Riverside

Rubin, Ida Ely Consultant, Writer
Thompson, Bradbury Designer, Director

Rowayton

Flora, James Royer Illustrator, Painter
Peterdi, Gabor F Painter, Printmaker
Squadra, John Painter, Collage Artist

Roxbury

Bart, Elizabeth (Elizabeth Bart Gerald)
    Painter, Designer
Kalisher, Simpson Photographer
Kuhn, Bob Draftsman, Painter
Morath, Inge Photographer

Salisbury

Blagden, Allen Painter, Printmaker
Osborn, Elodie C Administrator, Film
    Consult
Osborn, Robert Illustrator, Painter
Ten Eyck, Catryna (Catryna Ten Eyck
    Seymour) Painter, Printmaker

Sharon

McIntosh, Harold Painter
Magee, Alderson Graphic Artist, Painter

Sherman

Blume, Peter Painter
Fischer, Henry George Historian, Curator

Simsbury

Guzman-Forbes, Robert Painter,
    Illustrator

Southbury

Folds, Thomas McKey Educator,
    Consultant
Johnson, Edvard Arthur Painter,
    Educator
Lariar, Lawrence Cartoonist, Writer
Merrill, David Kenneth Painter, Muralist
Rubidoux (Rubidoux Early Johnson)
    Painter, Designer
Usher, Elizabeth Reuter Librarian,
    Lecturer

South Kent

Aymar, Gordon Christian Painter

Southport

Anderson, Margaret Pomeroy Collector,
    Consultant

Stamford

Bechtle, C Ronald Painter
Bushmiller, Ernie Paul Cartoonist
Calle, Paul Painter, Writer
Calrow, Robert F Instructor, Painter
Couturier, Marion B Dealer, Collector
Gonzalez-Tornero, Sergio Painter,
    Printmaker
Hausman, Fred S Sculptor, Designer
Heston, Joan Painter, Instructor
Koch, Robert Historian, Writer
Metzger, Robert Paul Curator, Educator
Moss, Jacqueline Historian, Educator
Nakian, Reuben Sculptor
Rudman, Joan (Combs) Painter,
    Instructor
Shepherd, Don (Donald Allen) Designer,
    Glass Artist
Strosahl, William Painter

Sterling

Holden, Raymond James Painter,
    Illustrator

Stonington

Aalund, Suzy Painter, Miniaturist
Cale, Robert Allan Printmaker, Educator

Stony Creek

Sheard, Wendy Stedman Historian,
    Educator

Storrs

Crossgrove, Roger Lynn Painter,
    Educator
Doudera, Gerard Educator, Painter
Gregoropoulos, John Painter
Rovetti, Paul F Museum Director,
    Administrator
Thornton, Richard Samuel Educator,
    Administrator

Trumbull

Kozlowski, Edward C Painter, Designer

Voluntown

Caddell, Foster Painter, Instructor

Wallingford

Neff, John A Painter, Designer

Warren

Abrams, Herbert E Painter, Lecturer

Washington Depot

Frazier, Paul D Sculptor, Educator

Washington Green

Renouf, Edward Painter, Sculptor

Watertown

Cajori, Charles F Painter

West Cornwall

Parker, Robert Andrew Painter
Scoville, Jonathan Armstrong Painter,
    Printmaker

West Hartford

Hammer, Alfred Emil Painter,
    Administrator
Miller, Jean Johnston Librarian, Historian
Mitchell, Clifford Painter, Architect
Taylor, John C E Painter, Educator
Uccello, Vincenza Agatha Painter,
    Educator

Weston

Bleifeld, Stanley Sculptor, Medalist
Cadmus, Paul Painter, Printmaker
Coleman, Jacqui (Jacquelyn F) Painter
Fogel, Seymour Painter, Sculptor
Rand, Paul Painter, Designer

Westport

Cherner, Norman Designer
Chernow, Ann Painter
Chernow, Burt Instructor, Museum
    Director
Cifolelli, Alberta (Alberta Carmella
    Lamb) Painter, Educator
Dohanos, Stevan Illustrator, Painter
Edelman, Rita Painter
Fisher, Leonard Everett Painter,
    Illustrator
Kovatch, Jak Printmaker, Educator
Reed, Walt Arnold Historian, Dealer
Rothenberg, Barbara Painter, Collage
    Artist
Sabo, Irving Sculptor, Designer
Sallick, Lucy Ellen Painter, Instructor
Satz, Janet Maas Painter, Administrator
Skemp, Robert Oliver Painter
Woodham, Jean Sculptor

West Redding

Giusti, George Designer, Sculptor
Grashow, James Bruce Sculptor,
    Printmaker
Natkin, Robert Painter

West Suffield
Cumming, Robert H Artist, Photographer

West Willington
Zelanski, Paul John Painter

Willimantic
Mazzocca, Gus (Augustus Nicholas Mazzocca) Printmaker, Educator

Wilton
Darrow, Whitney, Jr Cartoonist
Dietz, Gary Allan J Dealer
Earle, William Henry Painter, Instructor
Purdy, Donald R Painter
Roberts, Priscilla Warren Painter
Stuart, Kenneth James Director, Illustrator

Windsor
Meyer, Frank Hildbridge Printmaker, Designer

Woodbridge
Lytle, Richard Painter, Educator

Woodbury
Klonis, Stewart Painter, Director
Templeton, Robert Clark Painter

DELAWARE

Camden
Akamu, Nina Sculptor
Sheppard, Joseph Sherly Painter, Sculptor

Felton
Kohut, Lorene Painter

Greenville
Raley, Robert L Collectors
Reynolds, Nancy duPont Sculptor

Hockessin
Tarbell, Roberta Kupfrian Historian, Curator

Newark
Allen, Margaret Prosser Painter, Educator
Breslin, Wynn Painter, Sculptor
Brown, Hilton Painter, Educator
Craven, Wayne Historian, Writer
Da Cunha, Julio Educator, Painter
Homer, William Innes Historian, Educator
Moss, Joe (Francis) Sculptor, Painter
Nees, Lawrence Educator, Historian
Rowe, Charles Alfred Painter, Designer
Spinski, Victor Sculptor, Educator
Stillman, Damie Historian, Educator
Stoner, Joyce Hill Conservator, Educator
Weiss, John Joseph Photographer, Editor

Rockland
Harvey, (William) Andre Sculptor

Smyrna
Bailey, Richard H Sculptor

Wilmington
Clark, Nancy Kissel Sculptor, Consultant
Colombo, Charles Painter
Egri, Ruth (Ruth Egri Holden) Painter
Elzea, Rowland Procter Museum Curator
Hatch, W A S Printmaker, Educator
Hawkes, Elizabeth H Curator
Hayes, Tua Painter
Layton, Richard Painter, Dealer
McFarren, Grace Painter, Dealer

Martone, William Robert Painter, Instructor
Matassa, John P Painter, Instructor
Mortellito, Domenico Painter, Sculptor
Nichols, Eleanor Cary Designer, Silversmith
Parks, Charles Cropper Sculptor
Patterson, Shirley Painter, Instructor
Sundin, Adelaide Toombs Ceramist, Sculptor

Winterthur
Hummel, Charles Frederick Administrator
Smith, James Morton Museum Director, Historian
Sommer, Frank H, III Librarian, Archeologist

Yorklyn
Stan, Cynthia (Cynthia Stan Mellow) Printmaker, Collage Artist

DISTRICT OF COLUMBIA

Washington
Allen, Jane Addams Editor, Critic
Ascian Printmaker, Painter
Atlas, Martin & Liane W Collectors
Bader, Franz Art Dealer, Photographer
Berkowitz, Leon Painter
Biddle, Livingston Ludlow, Jr Art Administrator
Bingham, Lois A Art Administrator, Lecturer
Blake, Peter Jost Architect, Critic
Bogounoff, Mollie Painter, Collector
Bolton-Smith, Robin Lee Curator, Historian
Bookatz, Samuel Painter, Sculptor
Botwinick, Michael Museum Director
Braunstein, H Terry (Malikin) Photographer, Educator
Breeskin, Adelyn Dohme Administrator, Consultant
Broude, Norma Freedman Historian, Educator
Brown, David Alan Historian, Curator
Brown, John Carter Museum Director
Cafritz, Robert Conrad Curator
Cain, J Frederick, Jr Printmaker, Curator
Carmean, E A, Jr Historian, Curator
Carter, Yvonne Pickering Painter, Educator
Caryl, Joan Leonard Painter, Sculptor
Cavanaugh, John W Sculptor
Chase, W(illiam) Thomas Conservator
Christenberry, William Educator, Painter
Cikovsky, Nicolai, Jr Historian, Educator
Cleary, Manon Catherine Painter, Educator
Cogswell, Margaret Price Administrator
Comes, Marcella Painter, Photographer
Cone, Gerrit Craig Art Administrator
Cooper, Theodore A Dealer
Costigan, Constance Christian Painter, Designer
Costley-Jacobs, Averille Esther Dealer, Gallery Director
Danziger, Joan Sculptor
D'Arista, Robert Painter, Educator
Davenport, Rebecca Read Painter, Lecturer
Davis, Gene Painter
de Andino, Jean-Pierre M Dealer, Collector
de Looper, Willem Painter, Curator
De Weldon, Felix George Weihs Sculptor, Architect
Dineen, Tom (Forga) Painter
Dobard, Raymond Gerard Historian, Painter

Donaldson, Jeff R Painter, Administrator
Doumato, Lamia Librarian, Historian
Edelstein, J M Librarian, Educator
Eisenstein, (Mr & Mrs) Julian Collectors
Eldredge, Charles Child, III Museum Director, Historian
Evans, Lucile Painter, Printmaker
Ferber, Elise Van Hook Administrator, Curator
Fern, Alan Maxwell Historian, Administrator
Ferriter, Clare Painter, Collage Artist
Fink, Lois Marie Historian, Curator
Fisher, Sarah Lisbeth Conservator
Fleming, Lee Virginia Critic, Writer
Flint, Janet Altic Curator, Historian
Fontanini, Clare Educator, Sculptor
Forgey, Benjamin F Critic
Forrester, Patricia Tobacco Painter, Printmaker
Fox, Howard Neal Curator, Critic
Garrard, Mary DuBose Historian, Educator
Gilliam, Sam Painter
Ginzburg, Yankel (Jacob) Painter, Printmaker
Gomez-Sicre, Jose Administrator, Critic
Gossage, John Ralph Photographer
Gramberg, Liliana Painter, Printmaker
Green, Eleanor Broome Consultant
Green, Tom Instructor, Sculptor
Greenspun, Regina Ruth Dealer
Grier, Margot Edmands Librarian
Grossman, Maurizia M Dealer, Gallery Director
Grossman, Sheldon Museum Curator, Historian
Grubar, Francis Stanley Historian, Lecturer
Gumpert, Gunther Painter
Gurney, Susan Rothwell Librarian
Haden, Eunice (Barnard) Painter, Illustrator
Hampton, Grace Educator, Jeweler
Hand, John Oliver Historian, Curator
Hart, Robert Gordon Administrator
Hartigan, Lynda Roscoe Curator, Historian
Haslem, Jane N Dealer
Hay, George Austin Painter, Filmmaker
Herman, Lloyd Eldred Museum Director
Herzbrun, Helene McKinsey Painter, Educator
Holladay, Wilhelmina Cole Collector, Patron
Howland, Richard Hubbard Architectural Historian
Isham, Sheila Eaton Painter, Graphic Artist
Johnson, J Seward, Jr Sculptor, Administrator
Johnston, Barry Woods Sculptor
Jones, Lois Mailou (Mrs V Pierre-Noel) Painter, Designer
Kagy, Sheffield Harold Painter, Printmaker
Kaskey, Raymond John Sculptor, Architect
Kinney, Gilbert Hart Collector, Administrator
Klavans, Minnie Painter, Sculptor
Kornblatt, Barbara Rodbell Dealer
Kravitz, Walter Sculptor, Painter
Krebs, Rockne Sculptor
Kreeger, David Lloyd Patron, Collector
Lader, Melvin Paul Historian, Educator
Lane, H Palmer Dealer
Laub-Novak, Karen Painter, Printmaker
Leithauser, Mark Alan Printmaker, Designer
Lerner, Abram Museum Director
Lewis, Douglas Historian, Curator

DISTRICT OF COLUMBIA (cont)

Lewton, Jean Louise Curator, Editor
Lewton, Val Edwin Designer, Painter
Libhart, Myles Laroy Administrator,
  Writer
List, Clair Z Curator
Livingston, Jane S Critic, Curator
Loar, Peggy A Museum Director,
  Administrator
Loerke, William Carl Historian,
  Administrator
Lowe, Harry Administrator, Designer
Luchs, Alison Historian
Lunn, Harry, Jr Dealer
Lyle, Charles Thomas Administrator
McBryde, Sarah Elva Painter, Printmaker
McCabe, Cynthia Jaffee Curator,
  Historian
McCane, Mallory (Mallory Ann
  McCane-O'Connor) Painter
MacDonald, William L Architectural
  Historian
MacDougall, Peter Steven Ceramic Artist,
  Educator
Marshall, Mara Painter
Meeker, Dean Jackson Printmaker,
  Painter
Melchert, James Frederick Sculptor,
  Educator
Mellon, Paul Collector, Administrator
Miles, Ellen Gross Historian, Curator
Millard, Charles Warren, III Curator,
  Writer
Millie, Elena Gonzalez Curator
Mitchell, Eleanor Consultant, Librarian
Molella, Patricia Ann Video &
  Performance Artist
Mondale, Joan Adams Craftsperson
Morrison, Keith Anthony Painter,
  Educator
Murray, Richard Newton Museum
  Director
Neslage, Oliver John, Jr Art Dealer
Norelli, Martina Roudabush Curator
Nuki (Daniel Millsaps) Painter, Writer
Page, Jean Jepson Collector
Perlin, Ruth Rudolph Curator, Historian
Perlmutter, Jack Painter, Printmaker
Perrot, Paul N Administrator, Lecturer
Phillips, Laughlin Museum Director
Phillips, Marjorie Painter
Pierce, Delilah W Painter, Educator
Pierre-Noel, Vergniaud Designer, Graphic
  Artist
Pope, Annemarie Henle Administrator
Power, Mark Photographer, Educator
Radice, Anne-Imelda Marino Historian,
  Curator
Rand, Harry Historian, Educator
Rankine, V V Sculptor, Painter
Reger, Lawrence L Administrator
Reilly, Bernard Francis Historian, Curator
Rennie, Helen (Sewell) Painter, Designer
Richard, Paul Critic
Richman, Robert M Administrator,
  Writer
Rigsby, John David Painter
Robbins, Warren M Museum Director
Robertson, Charles J Administrator
Robinson, Lilien Filipovitch Historian,
  Educator
Robison, Andrew Museum Curator,
  Writer
Romano, Jaime (Luis) Painter
Rosenzweig, Phyllis D Associate Curator
Russell, Helen Diane Historian
Rust, David E Curator, Collector
Sacklarian, Stephen Painter
Sandground, Mark Bernard, Sr Collector,
  Patron
Schmuckal, Janet Bell (Cynthia Signature)
  Museum Director, Conceptual Artist

Schmutzhart, Berthold Josef Sculptor,
  Educator
Schmutzhart, Slaithong Chengtrakul
  Instructor, Sculptor
Schwartz, Bella Painter, Assemblage
  Artist
Scott, David Winfield Administrator
Sellin, David Historian, Curator
Sherman, Claire Richter Historian,
  Educator
Shimizu, Yoshiaki Historian, Curator
Shuler, Thomas H, Jr Photographer,
  Educator
Shute, Roberta E Sculptor, Painter
Sickman, Jessalee Bane Painter, Instructor
Simmons, John Herbert Educator,
  Historian
Simpson, Marianna Shreve Historian,
  Educator
Sivard, Robert Paul Painter
Smith, Arthur Hall Painter, Educator
Stamm, Geoffrey Eaton Administrator,
  Historian
Stapp, William F Curator
Stevenson, A Brockie Painter, Educator
Stewart, Robert Gordon Curator,
  Historian
Stovall, Luther McKinley (Lou)
  Printmaker
Swick, Linda Ann Sculptor
Szabo, Stephen Lee Photographer
Taylor, Bill (William Bradley) Sculptor,
  Instructor
Taylor, Kendall Frances Administrator,
  Historian
Taylor, Prentiss (Hottel) Painter,
  Lithographer
Teller, Douglas H Printmaker, Educator
Thalacker, Donald William Administrator,
  Architect
Truettner, William Administrator
Truitt, Anne (Dean) Sculptor
Turano, Don Sculptor, Medalist
von Rebhan, Elinor Anne Slide Librarian
Watson, Ross Historian
Weil, Stephen E Museum Executive,
  Lecturer
Weisberg, Gabriel P Historian, Educator
Wheelock, Arthur Kingsland, Jr Curator,
  Educator
White, Franklin Painter, Draftsman
Wilmerding, John Historian, Museum
  Director
Wilner, Marie Spring Painter
Woodward, William Painter, Educator
Young, Charles Alexander Educator,
  Painter
Young, Kenneth Victor Painter, Designer
Zilczer, Judith Katy Historian, Curator

FLORIDA

Aripeka

Rosenquist, James Painter

Bal Harbour

Bernay, Betti Painter

Bay Harbor Islands

Camins, Jacques Joseph Painter,
  Printmaker
Kessler, Edna Leventhal Painter,
  Printmaker
Silverman, Sherley C Painter, Sculptor

Belleair Bluffs

Howarth, Shirley Reiff Publisher,
  Historian

Boca Raton

Amen, Irving Painter, Printmaker
Bettmann, Otto Ludwig Art Historian
Chiara, Alan Robert Painter
Dorst, Claire V Painter, Educator
Dorst, Mary Crowe Coordinator, Artist
Sarnoff, Arthur Saron Painter

Bonita Springs

Lam, Jennett (Brinsmade) Painter,
  Educator
Pierce, Diane Illustrator, Sculptor
Wilson, Sybil Painter, Graphic Artist

Bradenton

Cogswell, Dorothy McIntosh Educator,
  Painter
Rogers, Leo M Collector, Patron

Brooksville

Watkins, Lewis Sculptor, Painter

Cantonment

Carey, John Thomas Educator, Historian

Cape Coral

Korjus, Veronica Maria Elisabeth Painter,
  Lecturer

Clearwater

Bansemer, Roger Lewis Painter,
  Printmaker
Kennedy, J William Painter
Wensley, William Charles Painter,
  Instructor

Cocoa Beach

Blum, June Painter, Curator
Samuelson, Fred Binder Painter, Educator

Coconut Grove

McCullough, David William Painter,
  Sculptor
Massin, Eugene Max Painter, Educator
Treister, Kenneth Painter, Sculptor

Coral Gables

Ahlander, Leslie Judd Critic, Curator
Chow Chian-Chiu Painter, Historian
Chow Leung Chen-Ying Painter,
  Calligrapher
Dellis, Arlene B Craftsman, Museologist
Fort-Brescia, Bernardo M Architect
Freeman, Gertrude Collector
Friedman, Marvin Ross Dealer
Reiling, Susan Wallace Curator, Historian
Schmitt, Marilyn Low Historian,
  Educator
Smith, Griffin (Mary-Griffin Smith
  Hoeveler) Critic
Spear, Laurinda Hope Architect
Thomas, Helen (Doane) Painter, Writer
Turoff, Muriel Pargh Sculptor, Painter
Waltner, Beverly Ruland Painter

Coral Springs

Somers, H(arry W) Painter, Printmaker

Davie

Hanson, Duane Sculptor, Educator

Daytona Beach

Biferie, Dan (Daniel Anthony), Jr
  Photographer, Educator
Broemel, Carl William Painter, Illustrator
Libby, Gary Russell Museum Director,
  Educator

De Bary

Mankowski, Bruno Medalist, Sculptor

Deerfield Beach

Sitton, John M Painter, Lecturer
Van Aalten, Jacques Painter, Sculptor

De Land

Messersmith, Fred Lawrence Painter,
Educator
Shaw, Elsie Babbitt Sculptor, Painter

Delray Beach

Otto, Catherine K(lemann) Sculptor
Stell, H Kenyon Printmaker, Historian
Varga, Ferenc Sculptor

Dunedin

Minnick, Esther Tress Painter

Edgewater

Stowman, Annette Burr Painter,
Instructor

Englewood

Tracy, Lois Bartlett Painter, Writer

Flagler Beach

Webster, Stokely Painter, Printmaker

Ft Lauderdale

Batt, Miles Girard Painter, Instructor
Lewis, Elizabeth Matthew Stained Glass
Artist, Writer

Ft McCoy

Wesling, William Arnold Painter,
Illustrator

Gainesville

Craven, Roy Curtis, Jr Gallery Director,
Educator
Foster, Maelee Thomson Educator,
Printmaker
Grissom, Eugene Edward Educator,
Historian
Halliday, Nancy Ruth Illustrator,
Instructor
Heipp, Richard Christian Painter,
Instructor
Holbrook, Hollis Howard Muralist,
Painter
Holbrook, Vivian Nicholas Painter,
Administrator
Isaacson, Marcia Jean Draftsman,
Educator
Kerslake, Kenneth Alvin Printmaker,
Educator
Naylor, John Geoffrey Sculptor, Educator
Purser, Stuart Robert Painter, Educator
Sabatella, Joseph John Administrator,
Painter
Scott, John Fredrik Historian, Educator
Skelley, Robert Charles Educator,
Printmaker
Smith, Nan S(helley) Sculptor, Ceramist
Uelsmann, Jerry Photographer
Ward, John Lawrence Historian, Painter
Ward, Phillip A Ceramist, Educator
Westin, Robert H Historian
Williams, Hiram Draper Painter
Wilson, Wallace Photographer

Gulfport

Klarin, Winifred Erlick Painter, Jeweler

Hallandale

Gallo, Enzo D Sculptor

Hernando

Gamble, Kathryn Elizabeth Museum
Director

Hialeah

Sherwood, A (Frances Ann Crane)
Sculptor, Designer

Highland Beach

Armstrong, Jane Botsford Sculptor

Hollywood

Golubov, Maurice Painter
Schreck, Michael H Painter, Sculptor

Hudson

Angelini, John Michael Painter, Writer

Jacksonville

Bear, Marcelle L Printmaker, Painter
Brownett, Thelma Denyer Painter,
Conservator
Dodge, Joseph Jeffers Painter
Gefter, Judith Michelman Photographer
Koger, Ira McKissick Collector, Patron
Koscielny, Margaret Sculptor, Painter
Schlageter, Robert William Administrator

Juno Beach

Mermin, Mildred (Shire) Painter

Jupiter

Mann, Maybelle Historian, Writer

Key West

Marks, Roberta Barbara Ceramist, Painter

Lakeland

Stoddard, Donna Melissa Administrator,
Gallery Director

Lake Wales

Lipson, Goldie Sculptor, Painter

Lake Worth

Kirkwood, Larry Thomas Photographer,
Printmaker
Thomsen, Mitch (Nancy Mitchell)
Painter

Largo

Kass, Jacob James Painter
Tucker, Peri Writer, Illustrator
Woodlock, Ethelyn Hurd Painter

Longboat Key

Allen, Margo (Mrs Harry Shaw) Sculptor,
Painter
Rowan, Frances Physioc Painter,
Printmaker
Sherwood, Leona Painter, Instructor

Lutz

Bailey, Oscar Photographer, Educator
Cox, Ernest Lee Sculptor, Educator
Freundlich, August L Administrator,
Collector

Madeira Beach

Terry, Marion (E) Painter, Instructor

Mandarin

Dempsey, Bruce Harvey Museum
Director

Marathon

Slider, Dorla Dean Painter

Mary Esther

Simpson, Marilyn Jean Painter, Instructor

Miami

Bergling, Virginia Catherine (Mrs Stephen
J Kozazcki) Art Book Dealer, Editor
Bogaev, Ronni (Ronni Bogaev
Greenstein) Lecturer, Painter
Cano, Margarita Librarian, Painter
Carulla, Ramon Painter
Cianfoni, Emilio Conservator, Painter
Couper, James M Painter, Educator
Duncan, Richard (Hurley) Printmaker,
Draftsman
Gillman, Barbara Seitlin Dealer
Greenstein, Ilise Painter, Conceptual
Artist
Harrison, Joseph Robert, Jr Collector,
Patron
Kent, H Latham Gallery Director, Painter
Morin, James Corcoran Cartoonist, Editor
Riveron, Enrique Painter, Sculptor
Romney, Hervin A R Architect
Romoser, Ruth Amelia Painter,
Conceptual Artist
Salinas, Baruj Painter, Printmaker
Storm, Larue Painter, Sculptor
Strickland, Thomas J Painter
Thiele, Robert Ransom Painter, Sculptor
van der Marck, Jan Director
Viret, Margaret Mary (Mrs Frank Ivo)
Painter, Instructor
Weinhardt, Carl Joseph, Jr Museum
Director, Historian
Winter, Gerald Glen Painter, Educator

Miami Beach

Fleming, Betty Corcoran Dealer
Kahn, A Michael Painter, Designer
Luria, Gloria Dealer
Rosenblum, Sadie Skoletsky Painter,
Printmaker
Schein, Eugenie Painter, Printmaker

Miami Shores

Hollinger, Helen Wetherbee Painter,
Lecturer

Naples

Geiger, Edith Rogers Painter
Meek, J William, III Dealer, Consultant
Nash, Alice Louise Consultant
Oppenheim, Samuel Edmund Painter
Orr, Elliot Painter
Peterson, David Winfield Painter
Samstag, Gordon Painter, Sculptor
Summy, Anne Tunis Painter, Printmaker
Wilson, David Philip Painter

New Smyrna Beach

Altvater, Catherine Tharp Painter
Leeper, Doris Marie Painter, Sculptor

Nokomis

Connolly, Jerome Patrick Painter,
Muralist

North Miami

Curtiss-Truetsch, George Curt (George C
Curtiss) Painter, Gallery Director
Thorndike, (Chuck) Charles Jesse
Cartoonist

Ocala

Booth, George Warren Painter, Illustrator

Odessa

Gelinas, Robert William Painter,
Educator

Orange Park

Hunt, Courtenay Painter, Instructor

Orlando

Ivey, James Burnett Cartoonist, Collector
Lotz, Steven Darryl Painter, Educator

Osprey

Buzzelli, Joseph Anthony Painter,
    Sculptor
Robinson, Sally W Painter, Printmaker

Oviedo

Benini Painter, Sculptor

Palm Beach

Akston, James Collector, Patron
Artinian, Artine Collector, Patron
Brams, Joan Painter, Sculptor
Brown, James Monroe, III Museum
    Director
Day, John Painter, Educator
Helsmoortel, Robert Sculptor, Painter
Huldah Painter
Koni, Nicolaus Sculptor, Lecturer
Levin, Jeanne Painter, Collector
Luntz, Irving Dealer
Ness, Evaline (Mrs Arnold A Bayard)
    Illustrator, Writer
Rautbord, Dorothy H Collector, Patron
Sanchez, Thorvald Painter
Shippen, Zoe Painter

Palm Beach Gardens

Tykie (Sylvia Squires Ganz) Painter

Pensacola

Takach, Mary H Museum Director,
    Historian

Pompano Beach

Kleinman, Sue Painter, Lecturer
Lavoy, Walter Joseph Jeweler, Educator
Lis, Janet Chapman Painter

Ponte Vedra Beach

Draper, Josiah Everett Painter, Instructor

Port St Lucie

Roberts, Bruce Elliott Painter

Riviera Beach

Hibel, Edna Painter, Lithographer

Rockledge

Roever, Joan Marilyn Illustrator,
    Dioramist

St Augustine

Calkin, Carleton Ivers Painter, Restorer

St Petersburg

Crane, James Painter, Cartoonist
Dickey, Helen Pauline Painter
DuBois, Alan Beekman Curator,
    Administrator
Hill, Polly Knipp Etcher, Painter
Kropf, Joan R Curator, Lecturer
Leber, Roberta (Roberta Leber McVeigh)
    Ceramist, Instructor
McVeigh, Miriam Temperance Painter,
    Consultant
Malone, Lee H B Museum Director
Rigg, Margaret Ruth Assemblage Artist,
    Calligrapher
Schwarz, Felix Conrad Painter, Educator
Schwarz, Myrtle Cooper Designer,
    Mosaic Artist
Silins, Janis Painter, Historian
Sutherland, Sandy Painter

Sarasota

Auping, Michael Graham Curator,
    Historian
Burgart, Herbert Joseph Educator,
    Administrator
Campbell, Dorothy Bostwick Painter,
    Sculptor
Capes, Richard Edward Graphic Artist,
    Instructor
Chase, Jeanne Norman Painter, Educator
Cheek, Ronald Edward Painter, Instructor
Christ-Janer, Arland F Painter,
    Printmaker
Clement, Shirley Painter
Corbino, Marcia Norcross Critic, Writer
DeCaprio, Alice Painter, Designer
Deo, Marjoree Nee Painter
Eliscu, Frank Sculptor
Elliott, Dorothy Baden Conservator
Floethe, Richard Illustrator, Designer
Gregory, Bruce Painter, Instructor
Harmon, Foster Dealer, Director
Held, Philip Painter, Photographer
Hodgell, Robert Overman Printmaker,
    Sculptor
Hopper, Frank J Painter, Muralist
Hoppes, Lowell E Cartoonist
Larsen, Robert Wesley Painter
Laufman, Sidney Painter
Marca-Relli, Conrad Painter, Collage
    Artist
Marx, Evelyn Tapestry Artist, Painter
Oehlschlaeger, Frank J Dealer
Olds, Elizabeth Painter, Printmaker
Osborne, Robert Lee Painter, Educator
Parton, Nike Painter
Perkins, Robert Eugene Administrator
Posey, Leslie Thomas Sculptor, Instructor
Sawyer, Helen Painter, Writer
Solomon, Syd Painter
Straight, Elsie H Librarian, Sculptor
Troncale, Frank Thomas Dealer,
    Collector
Utz, Thornton Painter, Sculptor
White, Ruth Dealer, Collector

Sebastian

Salerno, Charles Sculptor, Educator

Stuart

Hutchinson, Janet L Museum Director,
    Collector
Mosley, Zack T Illustrator, Cartoonist

Sun City Center

Voris, Anna Maybelle Curator

Sunrise

Berkowitz, Henry Painter, Designer

Tallahassee

Bell, Trevor Painter, Educator
Bucher, Francois Historian, Educator
Burggraf, Ray Lowell Painter, Educator
Edwards-Tucker, Yvonne (Leatrice
    Yvonne Tucker) Ceramist, Educator
Fichter, Robert W Artist, Educator
Harper, William Enamelist, Goldsmith
Holschuh, (George) Fred Sculptor
Hurst, Ralph N Sculptor, Educator
Johnson, Ivan Earl Educator, Craftsman
Kuhn, Marylou Educator, Painter
O'Connor, John Arthur Painter,
    Administrator
Tucker, Curtis (Dee) Ceramist, Lecturer
Walmsley, William Aubrey Lithographer,
    Collector

Wedin, Winslow Elliott Architect,
    Educator
Williams, Chester Lee Sculptor

Tamarac

Gould, Stephen Sculptor, Collector
Kaplan, Leo Assemblage Artist, Collage
    Artist

Tampa

Cardoso, Anthony Painter, Instructor
Covington, Harrison Wall Painter,
    Educator
Fager, Charles J Educator, Ceramist
Kronsnoble, Jeffrey Michael Painter,
    Educator
Larsen, Mernet Ruth Painter, Educator
Nazarenko, Bonnie Coe Painter
Pappas, George Administrator, Painter
Rosenzweig, Daphne Lange Historian,
    Museum Consultant

Temple Terrace

Kashdin, Gladys Shafran Painter,
    Educator
Saff, Donald Jay Printmaker,
    Administrator

Venice

Pinto, Biagio Painter

Vero Beach

Brightwell, Walter Painter
Ernst, James Arnold Painter, Instructor
Osze, Andrew E Sculptor

West Palm Beach

Grove, Edward Ryneal Medalist, Painter
Grove, Jean Donner Sculptor
Houser, Jim Painter, Educator
Knapp, Sadie Magnet Painter, Sculptor
Leff, Rita Printmaker, Painter
Madigan, Richard Allen Museum
    Director
Miller, David Dealer
Mueller, Trude Sculptor
Ubertalli, Hector Painter, Sculptor

Winter Haven

Ives, Elaine Caroline Painter

Winter Park

Booth, Dot Painter, Printmaker
Genius, Jeannette Painter, Designer
McKean, Hugh Ferguson Painter,
    Educator

GEORGIA

Alpharetta

Meserole, Vera Stromsted (Mrs Milton D
    Block) Painter, Administrator

Athens

Arnholm, Ronald Fisher Designer,
    Educator
Bogart, Michele Helene Historian,
    Curator
Clements, Robert Donald Sculptor,
    Educator
Collier, (Alan) Graham Writer, Painter
Dodd, Lamar Painter, Educator
Edmonston, Paul Educator, Editor
Enggass, Robert Historian, Educator
Feldman, Edmund Burke Educator, Critic
Goldsleger, Cheryl Painter, Draftsman
Hammond, Gale Thomas Printmaker,
    Educator
Herbert, James Arthur Painter,
    Filmmaker
Jacobsen, Michael A Historian, Educator

GEORGIA (cont)

Lukasiewicz, Ronald Joseph Printmaker, Sculptor
Marriott, William Allen Painter, Educator
Meyers, Ronald G Educator, Ceramist
Moore, Ethel Curator, Historian
Nasisse, Andy S Sculptor, Writer
Paul, William D, Jr Painter, Photographer
Schneiderman, Richard S Curator, Historian
Thompson, William Joseph Educator, Sculptor

Atlanta

Alexander, Judith Art Dealer, Collector
Artemis, Maria (Maria Artemis Papageorge Sawyer) Sculptor, Educator
Beattie, George Painter, Art Administrator
Berge, Dorothy Alphena Sculptor, Instructor
Borochoff, (Ida) Sloan Painter
Carlstrom, Lucinda Painter, Printmaker
Chase, Allan (Seamans) Sculptor, Muralist
Colarusso, Corrine Camille Painter, Instructor
Cone-Skelton, Annette Painter, Dealer
Crelly, William Richard Historian
Davis, Ben H Environmental Artist, Painter
Eden, Glenn Draftsman
Edvi Illes, Emma Dealer, Consultant
Edvi Illes, George Painter, Sculptor
Fenton, Julia Ann Conceptual Artist, Librarian
Frabel, Hans Godo Sculptor
Francis, Tom Painter
Frutchey, Jere (Gerald Read) Painter
Gillette, W Dean Painter, Dealer
Godsey, Jerry & Anne Collectors
Greco, Anthony Joseph Painter, Administrator
Guberman, Sidney Thomas Painter, Sculptor
Harkins, Dennis Richter Administrator, Photographer
Harris, Julian Hoke Sculptor, Architect
Heany, David Cameron Sculptor
Heath, David C Dealer
Hough, Jennine Painter
Johnson, Gregory Painter, Photographer
Johnston, William Medford Painter, Educator
Ketcham, Ray Winfred, Jr Dealer, Designer
Laxson, Ruth Conceptual Artist
Lea, Laurie Jane Sculptor, Painter
Lieberman, Laura Crowell Editor, Critic
Loehle, Betty Barnes Painter
Loehle, Richard E Painter, Illustrator
Lyman, Thomas William Educator, Historian
Mills, Lev Timothy Printmaker, Sculptor
Mitchell, Katherine Painter
Morrin, Peter Patrick Historian, Curator
Paschall, Jo Anne Printmaker, Librarian
Patterson, Curtis Ray Sculptor, Instructor
Poling, Clark V Museum Director, Historian
Rasmussen, Keith Eric Printmaker, Educator
Riddle, John Thomas, Jr Printmaker, Sculptor
Ruffner, Ginny Martin Nail Glassblower
Seaberg, Steve (Stevens) Assemblage Artist, Performance Artist
Shute, Ben E Painter
Simon, Jewel Woodard Painter, Sculptor
Stanley, Charles Edward Dealer, Administrator

Talley, Dan R Writer, Video Artist
Thomas, Steffen Wolfgang Sculptor, Painter
Vigtel, Gudmund Administrator
Walker, Larry Painter, Educator
Yarbrough, Leila Kepert Printmaker, Painter
Zafran, Eric Myles Curator, Historian

Carrollton

Bobick, Bruce Painter, Educator

Chamblee

McLean, James Albert Educator, Printmaker

Columbus

Nordhausen, A Henry Painter
Shorter, Edward Swift Painter, Collector

Darien

Langford, James Painter

Decatur

Canaday, Ouida Gornto Painter, Educator
Everett, Russell Henry Painter, Graphic Artist
Howett, John Historian, Critic
Pepe, Marie Sophie Huper Administrator, Historian
Shead, S Ray Painter, Printmaker
Staven, Leland Carroll Printmaker, Painter
Tiegreen, Alan F Painter, Illustrator
Warren, Ferdinand Earl Painter, Administrator

Farmington

Chappelle, Jerry Leon Ceramist, Sculptor

Gainesville

Westervelt, Robert F Historian, Ceramist

Good Hope

Ransom, Henry Cleveland, Jr Painter

Jekyll Island

Fiore, Rosario Russell Sculptor

Macon

Daugherty, Marshall Harrison Sculptor, Administrator
Rice, Anthony Hopkins Sculptor, Painter

Marietta

Basset, Gene Political Cartoonist
Coggins, Robert P Collector
Irwin, Lisa Dru Photographer, Painter
McAdoo, Carol Westbrook Painter, Printmaker
McAdoo, Donald Eldridge Painter, Printmaker
Rayburn, (Boyd Dale) Painter, Printmaker
Voos, William John Administrator, Painter

Mt Berry

Mew, Tommy Painter, Conceptual Artist

Ranger

Frazer, James (Nisbet), Jr Photographer, Muralist

Roswell

Booth-Owen, M(ary Ann) Painter, Printmaker

Savannah

Ellis, Ray G Painter, Lecturer
Kiah, Virginia Jackson Painter, Museum Director
Leigh, Jack David Photographer
Robb, David Metheny, Jr Museum Director, Historian

Statesboro

Solomon, Bernard Alan Printmaker, Educator

Valdosta

Penny, Donald Charles Craftsman, Educator

Watkinsville

Johnston, June Frazier Painter, Collage Artist

Wildwood

Meitzler, (Herbert) Neil Painter, Designer

HAWAII

Hauula

Hayward, Peter Painter, Sculptor

Hilo

Miyamoto, Wayne Akira Painter, Printmaker

Honolulu

Brenner, Shore Hodge Weaver, Educator
Browne, Robert M Collector, Patron
Chesney, Lee R, Jr Printmaker, Painter
Ellis, George Richard Museum Director
Engle, Barbara Jean Painter, Jeweler
Feher, Joseph Curator, Painter
Haar, Francis Photographer, Filmmaker
Jameikis, Brone Aleksandra Stained Glass Artist, Designer
Johnson, Bruce (James) Painter, Instructor
Karawina, Erica (Mrs Sidney C Hsiao) Painter, Stained Glass Artist
Kenda, Juanita Echeverria Painter, Writer
Kimura, Sueko M Painter
Kingrey, Kenneth Designer, Educator
Kjargaard, John Ingvard Painter, Collage Artist
Kobayashi, Katsumi Peter Painter, Lecturer
Kowalke, Ronald Leroy Painter, Printmaker
Link, Howard Anthony Curator
Lux, Gwen Sculptor
Marozzi, Eli Raphael Sculptor, Instructor
Morse, Marcia Roberts Printmaker, Writer
Morse, Peter Historian, Collector
Preis, Alfred Architect, Administrator
Roster, Fred Howard Sculptor, Educator
Roster, Laila Bergs Museum Director
Ruby, Laura Sculptor, Printmaker
Stasack, Edward Armen Painter, Printmaker
Tseng Yu-ho Painter, Historian
Wisnosky, John G Painter, Educator

Kahului

Miller, Barbara Darlene Painter, Printmaker

Kailua

Stamper, Willson Young Painter

Kailua Kona

Thomas, John Painter, Printmaker

Kaneohe

Charlot, Martin Day Painter, Muralist
Hartwell, Patricia Lochridge
  Administrator
Hee, Hon-Chew Painter, Instructor

Kapaa

Tam, Reuben Painter, Educator

Kapalama Heights

Harvey, Donald Gilbert Sculptor,
  Instructor

Keaau

Rhodes, James Melvin Glass Blower,
  Sculptor

Koloa

Harris, Lucille S Painter, Printmaker

Lahaina

Sato, Tadashi Painter, Sculptor

Lihue

Lai, Waihang Painter, Instructor

Volcano

Morrison, Bee (Berenice G) Weaver
Morrison, Boone M Photographer,
  Designer

IDAHO

Boise

Auth, Robert R Painter, Printmaker
Huff, Howard Lee Educator,
  Photographer
Killmaster, John H Painter, Enamelist
Kober, Alfred John Educator, Sculptor
Snyder, Kim Lawrence Curator, Painter
Watia, Tarmo Painter, Educator

Ketchum

deLory, Peter Photographer, Instructor
Wharton, David W Printmaker, Lecturer

Moscow

Kirkwood, Mary Burnette Painter

Pocatello

Farris-Larson, Gail Metalsmith, Educator

Sun Valley

Bennett, Don Bemco Painter, Printmaker

ILLINOIS

Arlington Heights

Lynch, Tom (Thomas Michael)
  Instructor, Painter

Aurora

Ford, Ruth Vansickle Painter

Belleville

Threlkeld, Dale Painter, Sculptor

Bloomington

Butler, James D Printmaker, Painter
George, Raymond Ellis Printmaker,
  Educator
Gregor, Harold Laurence Painter,
  Educator
Holder, Kenneth Allen Painter, Educator
Myers, Joel Philip Artist in Glass,
  Educator

Carbondale

Fink, Herbert Lewis Painter, Educator
Johnson, Evert Alfred Museologist,
  Lecturer
Kington, L(ouis) Brent Sculptor, Educator
Mavigliano, George Jerome Historian,
  Educator
Plochmann, Carolyn Gassan Painter,
  Graphic Artist
Whitlock, John Joseph Museum Director,
  Educator

Champaign

Betts, Edward Howard Painter, Educator
Breen, Harry Frederick, Jr Painter,
  Educator
Britsky, Nicholas Painter, Educator
Carlson, William D Sculptor, Glass
  Blower
Elkin, Beverly Dawn Dealer, Gallery
  Director
Fehl, Philipp P Painter, Historian
Gammon, Juanita-La Verne Painter,
  Educator
Grucza, Leo (Victor) Painter, Educator
Gunter, Frank Elliott Painter, Educator
Kotoske, Roger Allen Sculptor, Educator
Maguire, Henry Pownall Historian, Writer
Pera, Isabella Sculptor
Perkins, Ann Historian, Educator
Prokopoff, Stephen Stephen Museum
  Director, Historian
Rowan, Dennis Michael Printmaker,
  Educator
Shipley, James R Educator, Designer
Sletten, Byron K Painter, Printmaker
Smith, Luther A Photographer
Smith, Ralph Alexander Writer, Educator
Sprague, Mark Anderson Painter,
  Educator
Stephens, Curtis Designer, Photographer
Van Laar, Timothy Jon Painter,
  Printmaker
Wicks, Eugene Claude Painter, Educator
Ziff, Jerrold Historian, Collector

Charleston

Carmichael, Donald Ray Painter,
  Administrator
Moldroski, Al R Painter, Educator
Shull, Carl Edwin Painter, Educator
Sorge, Walter Painter, Printmaker
Trank, Lynn Edgar Educator, Painter

Chicago

Albright, Malvin Marr Painter, Sculptor
Allen, (Harvey) Harold Photographer, Art
  Historian
Amft, Robert Painter, Photographer
Anderson, Howard Benjamin Collage
  Artist, Photographer
Archer, Cynthia Printmaker, Painter
Arnold, Ralph Moffett Painter, Educator
Aubin, Barbara Painter, Assemblage
  Artist
Avison, David Photographer
Barazani, Morris Educator, Painter
Baruch, Jacques Z Art Dealer, Lecturer
Bedno, Edward Designer, Educator
Bennett, Rainey Painter, Illustrator
Bernal, Lucrecia Alejandra Gallery
  Director, Curator
Berns, Pamela Kari Painter, Administrator
Blackman, Thomas Patrick Director,
  Printmaker
Booth, Laurence Ogden Sculptor,
  Architect
Borso, Richard George Painter
Brakke, P(erry) Michael Painter,
  Educator
Brettell, Richard Robson Curator
Burroughs, Margaret T G Lecturer,
  Painter

Campoli, Cosmo Sculptor, Educator
Chalmers, E Laurence, Jr Administrator
Chase, Robert M Dealer, Collector
Cicero, Jan (Janice Pickett) Dealer
Cohen, Charles E Historian, Educator
Conger, William Painter, Educator
Cooper, Anthony J Painter
Crane, Barbara Bachmann Photographer,
  Educator
Danhausen, Eldon Sculptor
Darling, Sharon Sandling Curator,
  Historian
Davidson, Herbert Laurence Painter,
  Printmaker
de Lama, Alberto Painter, Printmaker
Deson, Marianne (Herstein) Dealer
Donson, Jerome Allan Gallery Director,
  Dealer
Drum, Sydney Maria Painter, Printmaker
Duckworth, Ruth Sculptor, Ceramist
Edwards, Stanley Dean Painter, Graphic
  Artist
Fairweather, Sally H Dealer
Feldman, Arthur Mitchell Museum
  Director
Ferrari, Virginio Luig Sculptor, Educator
Findlay, Helen T Dealer
Garrison, Eve Painter
Gehr, Mary (Ray) Printmaker, Painter
Geoffrey, Sayyid Iqbal (Jafree)
  Administrator
Gerard, Paula (Mrs Herbert Renison)
  Painter, Graphic Artist
Ginzel, Roland Painter, Printmaker
Glass, Michael L Designer, Educator
Glauber, Robert H Critic, Curator
Godfrey, Winnie (Winifred M) Painter,
  Instructor
Gonzalez, Jose Gamaliel Administrator,
  Designer
Gray, Richard Dealer
Greene-Mercier, Marie Zoe Sculptor,
  Draftsman
Guthman, Leo S Collector
Halkin, Theodore Sculptor, Painter
Hanson, Philip Holton Painter, Lecturer
Hardin, Shirley G Dealer
Haydon, Harold (Emerson) Painter,
  Educator
Heller, Reinhold August Historian
Henry, John Raymond Sculptor
Herzberg, Thomas Printmaker, Illustrator
Himmelfarb, John David Painter
Hoff, Margo Painter, Collage Artist
Hoffman, Neil James Administrator,
  Educator
Horn, Milton Sculptor, Writer
Hunt, Richard Howard Sculptor
Itatani, Michiko Painter
Jacob, Mary Jane Curator, Historian
Jaidinger, Judith C (Judith Clarann
  Szesko) Printmaker, Painter
Jones, Calvin B(ell) Painter, Muralist
Josephson, Kenneth Bradley
  Photographer, Assemblage Artist
Kapsalis, Thomas Harry Painter, Sculptor
Karpowicz, Terrence Edward Sculptor,
  Kinetic Artist
Kearney, John (W) Sculptor,
  Administrator
Kelsey, Muriel Chamberlin Sculptor
Kenney, Estelle Koval Art Therapist,
  Painter
Kestnbaum, Gertrude Dana Collector
Kind, Phyllis Art Dealer
Kitta, George Edward Printmaker, Painter
Klein, Gwenda J Dealer, Writer
Klein, Medard Painter
Klein, Paul R Dealer, Gallery Director
Klement, Vera Painter, Educator
Klindt, Steven Administrator
Koga, Mary Photographer

ILLINOIS (cont)

Kowalski, Dennis Allen Sculptor, Educator
Krantz, Les (Leslie J) Editor, Publisher
Lamantia, Paul (Christopher) Painter
Lanyon, Ellen Painter, Printmaker
Lattanzio, Frances Photographer, Educator
Lauffer, Alice A Painter, Printmaker
Lee, Katharine C Curator
Lerner, Nathan Bernard Photographer, Painter
Lewis, Phillip Harold Curator
Lipschultz, Maurice A Collector
Love, Richard Henry Dealer, Historian
Loving, Richard Maris Painter, Educator
Luecking, Stephen Joseph Sculptor, Educator
McNear, Everett C Painter, Designer
Maldre, Mati Photographer, Educator
Manilow, Lewis Collector, Patron
Maser, Edward Andrew Historian, Museum Director
Mauldin, Bill Cartoonist, Writer
Maurice, Alfred Paul Painter, Educator
Messick, Dale Cartoonist
Michod, Susan A Painter
Middaugh, Robert Burton Painter
Mintz, Harry Painter
Mongerson, Susan C Dealer
Morishita, Joyce Chizuko Historian, Painter
Moser, Rex Administrator
Myers, C Stowe Designer, Painter
Naeve, Milo M Administrator, Historian
Neff, John Hallmark Historian, Museum Director
Nick, George Painter, Educator
Parfenoff, Michael S Educator, Lithographer
Paschke, Edward F (Ed) Painter, Illustrator
Pattison, Abbott Sculptor, Painter
Paul, Arthur Designer, Painter
Peart, Jerry Linn Sculptor
Pen, Rudolph Painter
Petersen, Will Printmaker, Painter
Phillips, Bertrand D Painter, Photographer
Piatek, Francis John Painter, Instructor
Postiglione, Corey M Painter, Educator
Prekop, Martin Dennis Sculptor, Educator
Ramberg, Christina Painter
Regensteiner, Else (Friedsam) Designer, Weaver
Rogovin, Mark Muralist, Museum Director
Rollman-Shay, Ed & Charlotte Painters, Printmakers
Rosenthal, Earl Edgar Educator, Historian
Rosenthal, John W Photographer, Publisher
Rossen, Susan F Historian, Editor
Rossi, Barbara Painter, Printmaker
Salomon, Lawrence Sculptor, Educator
Schiller, Beatrice Painter, Graphic Artist
Schnackenberg, Roy Painter, Sculptor
Schooler, Lee Collector
Schulze, Franz Educator, Critic
Schwartz, Carl E Painter, Printmaker
Seed, Suzanne Liddell Photographer, Writer
Sewell, Jack Vincent Museum Curator
Shaddle, Alice Sculptor, Collage Artist
Shapiro, Irving Painter, Instructor
Sonnenschein, Hugo Patron, Historian
Spector, Buzz (Franklin Mac Spector) Conceptual Artist, Editor
Speyer, A James Curator, Architect
Springer, Lynn Elise Curator

Stiegler, Robert William Photographer, Filmmaker
Stipe, William S Collage Artist
Struve, William Walter Dealer
Suzuki, Sakari Painter
Taylor, Brie (Benjamin de Brie) Educator, Painter
Thurman, Christa Charlotte Mayer Curator
Tigerman, Stanley Painter, Architect
Torn, Jerry (Gerald J) Draftsman, Photographer
Travis, David B Curator, Historian
Volid, Ruth Dealer, Consultant
Weber, John Pitman Muralist, Educator
Wenger, Jane (B) Photographer, Educator
Wood, James Nowell Historian, Administrator
Yaworski, Alex F(rancis) Painter
Yoshida, Ray Kakuo Painter, Educator
Zeisler, Claire (Block) Sculptor, Collector
Zilka, Michael John Educator, Studio Director

Chicago Ridge

Sorell, Victor Alexander Historian, Administrator

Clinton

Cecil, Charles Harkless Painter

Decatur

Klaven, Marvin L Painter, Educator
Schietinger, James Frederick Sculptor, Educator

Deerfield

Talaba, L (Linda Talaba Cummens) Sculptor, Printmaker

De Kalb

Ball, Walter N Painter, Educator
Beard, Richard Elliott Painter, Educator
Even, Robert Lawrence Educator
Larsen, John Christian Educator, Librarian
Mahmoud, Ben Painter
Maxfield, Roberta Masur Silversmith
Meyer, Jerry Don Historian, Educator
White, Bruce Hilding Sculptor

Downers Grove

Kind, Joshua B Educator, Critic

East Peoria

Benz, Lee R Printmaker, Painter

Edwardsville

Coleman, Floyd Willis Educator, Painter
Hampton, Phillip Jewel Painter, Educator
Huntley, David C Painter, Administrator
Malone, Robert R Painter, Printmaker
Richardson, John Adkins Historian, Educator

Elmhurst

Jorgensen, Sandra Painter, Educator
Kauffman, (Camille) Andrene Painter, Muralist
King, Eleanor (Eleanor King Hookham) Painter, Printmaker

Evanston

Burnham, Jack Wesley Critic
Citrin, Judith Painter, Sculptor
Foley, Kathy Kelsey Director, Historian
Hurtig, Martin Russell Painter, Sculptor
Lazarus, Diane Gail Gallery Director, Curator
Levine, Martin Printmaker
Melvin, Ronald McKnight Museum Director

Monroe, Betty Iverson Educator
Moser, Charlotte Critic, Writer
Roller, Russell Kenneth Educator, Printmaker
Sheridan, Sonia Landy Media Artist
Silver, Larry Arnold Curator, Historian
Weiner, Egon Sculptor
Wise, Suzanne Tanderup Curator, Historian
Yochim, Louise Dunn Painter, Writer
Zwick, Rosemary G Sculptor, Printmaker

Evergreen Park

Miller, Jan Painter, Designer

Flossmoor

Gilbert, Arnold Martin Collector, Photographer

Galena

Geisert, Arthur Frederick Printmaker, Illustrator

Geneva

Ehresmann, Donald Louis Historian, Educator

Glencoe

Calapai, Letterio Printmaker, Painter

Glenview

Barnett, Earl D Designer, Painter
Bramson, Phyllis Halperin Painter, Instructor

Highland Park

Dunn, Cal Painter, Filmmaker

Hinsdale

Day, Holliday T Critic, Curator

Jacksonville

Calhoun, Larry Darryl Ceramist, Educator

Joliet

Brulc, Lillian G Painter, Sculptor

Kingston

Driesbach, David Fraiser Printmaker, Educator

La Grange

Larsen, Ole Painter, Illustrator

Lake Bluff

MacAlister, Paul Ritter Designer, Collector

Lake Forest

Croydon, Michael Benet Sculptor, Educator
Pounian, Albert Kachouni Painter, Curator

Lombard

Ahlstrom, Ronald Gustin Collage Artist, Painter

Long Grove

Robertson, Joan E (Joan Elizabeth Mitchell) Curator, Graphic Artist

Macomb

Jones, Frederick George Printmaker, Educator
Parker, Samuel Murray Painter

Mahomet

Perlman, Raymond Educator, Illustrator

Metamora

Hedden-Sellman, Zelda Painter, Instructor

Moline

Ramsauer, Joseph Francis Painter,
    Educator

Morton Grove

Berman, Steven M Painter, Printmaker

Naperville

Parke, Walter Simpson Painter,
    Printmaker

New Lenox

Merfeld, Gerald Lydon Painter

Normal

Carswell, Rodney Painter, Educator
Hartley, W Douglas Sculptor, Educator
Hobbs, Jack Arthur Educator, Writer
Mills, Frederick Van Fleet Administrator,
    Educator

Northbrook

Terra, Daniel J Collector, Patron

Northfield

Boz, Alex (Alex Bozickovic) Painter,
    Lecturer

Oak Brook

Perry, Richard C Dealer, Collector

Oak Lawn

Jachna, Joseph David Photographer,
    Educator

Oak Park

Chreptowsky, Achilles N Collector,
    Patron
Lennon, Timothy Painting Conservator
Nushawg, Michael Allan Printmaker,
    Educator
Sokol, David Martin Historian, Curator
Szesko, Lenore Rundle Painter,
    Printmaker

Park Forest

Payne, John D Sculptor, Educator

Park Ridge

Fedelle, Estelle Painter, Lecturer
Fornelli, Joseph Painter, Sculptor
Steinfels, Melville P Painter, Designer

Payson

St Maur, Kirk (Kirk Seymour
    McReynolds) Sculptor, Painter

Peoria

Buchanan, John Edward, Jr Museum
    Director, Administrator
Cooley, Adelaide N Painter, Writer
Cooley, William, Jr Collector, Patron
Fromberg, LaVerne Ray Instructor,
    Painter
Kottemann, George & Norma Collectors
Malenda, James William Enamelist,
    Educator
Meyer, Charles Edward Historian,
    Ceramist
Moehl, Karl J Painter, Writer
Peterson, John Douglas Administrator,
    Museum Director
Swigart, Lynn S Photographer
Walsh, J(ohn) Michael Dealer,
    Printmaker

Peoria Heights

Buster, Jacqueline Mary Dealer, Lecturer

Quincy

Irwin, George M Patron, Collector
Mejer, Robert Lee Painter, Educator
Morrison, Fritzi Mohrenstecher Painter,
    Lecturer

Ringwood

Pearson, James Eugene Instructor,
    Sculptor

Riverdale

McGarry, Patricia Josephine Instructor,
    Sculptor

River Forest

Holt, Charlotte Sinclair Medical
    Illustrator, Sculptor
Sloan, Jeanette Painter, Printmaker
White, Philip Butler Painter, Collector

Riverside

Howlett, Carolyn Svrluga Educator,
    Painter

Robinson

Swartz, Phillip Scott Painter, Collector

Rockford

Heflin, Tom Pat Painter, Designer
Pinzarrone, Paul Painter, Filmmaker
Sneed, Patricia M Dealer, Collector

Rolling Meadows

Rebbeck, Lester James, Jr Painter,
    Sculptor

Roscoe

Bond, Oriel Edmund Illustrator, Painter

St Charles

Hessing, Valjean McCarty Painter
Morrison, C L Writer, Critic

St Joseph

DeGenevieve, Barbara Photographer,
    Educator

Schaumburg

Martyl (Martyl Schweig Langsdorf)
    Painter, Muralist

Springfield

Bealmer, William Consultant, Educator
Britt, Nelson Clark Painter, Administrator
Dunbar, Michael Austin Administrator,
    Sculptor
Evans, Robert James Painter, Museum
    Curator
Formigoni, Mauri Monihon Painter,
    Educator
Hallmark, Donald Parker Historian,
    Museum Director
Hodge, R Garey Painter, Instructor
Madden-Work, Betty I Historian, Painter
Madura, Jack Joseph Painter, Instructor

Spring Grove

Pomerantz, Louis Conservator

Sycamore

Peck, Lee Barnes Jeweler, Educator

Urbana

Bodnar, Peter Painter, Educator
Bradshaw, Glenn Raymond Painter,
    Educator
Bushman, David Franklin Painter,
    Educator

Creese, Walter Littlefield Educator
Gallo, Frank Sculptor, Educator
Jackson, Billy Morrow Painter, Educator
Lecky, Susan Painter
Replinger, Dot (Dorothy Thiele) Weaver,
    Designer
Schultz, Harold A Painter, Educator
Weller, Allen Stuart Educator, Historian
Wilson, Millie Painter, Educator

Washington

Sunderland, Nita Kathleen Educator,
    Sculptor

Western Springs

Gilmore, Roger Administrator, Consultant
Vickery, Charles Bridgeman Painter

Wheaton

Hunter, Miriam Eileen Educator, Painter
Steffler, Alva W Educator, Curator

Wilmette

Drower, Sara Ruth Painter, Illustrator
Nilsson, Gladys Painter
Nutt, Jim (James Tureman) Painter,
    Draftsman

Winnetka

Alsdorf, James W Patron, Collector
Needlman, Joel G Dealer
Needlman, Phyllis L Dealer

Woodstock

Trausch, Thomas V Painter

INDIANA

Albany

Patrick, Alan K Ceramist, Painter

Anderson

Ryden, Kenneth Glenn Sculptor

Bloomington

Barnes, Robert M Painter, Educator
Calman, W(endy L) Printmaker,
    Photographer
Cole, Bruce Historian, Educator
Darriau, Jean-Paul Educator, Sculptor
Eikerman, Alma Jeweler, Designer
Gealt, Adelheid Medicus Curator,
    Historian
Hawes, Louis Historian
Irvine, Betty Jo Librarian, Instructor
Jacquard Sculptor, Educator
Kleinbauer, W Eugene Historian, Editor
Lowe, Marvin Printmaker, Painter
Markman, Ronald Painter
Martz, Karl Ceramist, Educator
Pozzatti, Rudy O Printmaker, Painter
Sieber, Roy Educator, Historian
Solley, Thomas Treat Museum Director

Borden

Marsh, (Edwin) Thomas Potter, Educator

Crown Point

Chase, Richard Andrew Painter,
    Illustrator

Elkhart

Gilbert, Clyde Lingle Painter

Evansville

Blevins, James Richard Art
    Administrator, Educator
Eilers, Fred (Anton Frederick) Painter,
    Designer
Gumberts, William A Collector, Patron

INDIANA (cont)

Miley, Les Ceramist, Educator
Streetman, John William, III
    Administrator

Ft Wayne

Braybrooke, Valerie V Museum Director
Brown, Peggy Ann Painter
Sandeson, William Seymour Cartoonist

Granger

Langland, Harold Reed Sculptor,
    Educator

Greencastle

French, Ray H Printmaker, Painter
Meehan, William Dale Painter, Educator

Indianapolis

Block, Amanda Roth Painter, Printmaker
Brucker, Edmund Painter, Educator
Clowes, Allen Whitehill Collector, Patron
Cortese, Edward Fortunato
    Administrator, Illustrator
Daily, Evelynne Mess Painter, Printmaker
Davis, Harry Allen Painter, Educator
Eagerton, Robert Pierce Printmaker,
    Painter
Eiteljorg, Harrison Collector, Patron
Janson, Anthony Fredrick Curator,
    Historian
Mari (M Eagerton) Craftsman, Painter
Mino, Yutaka Historian, Curator
Radecki, Martin John Conservator
Roberson, Samuel Arndt Architectural
    Historian, Educator
Rubins, David Kresz Sculptor
Simmons, Percy Slotsky Collector
Werner, (Charles George) Editorial
    Cartoonist
Yassin, Robert Alan Museum Director,
    Historian

Kouts

Cooper, Wayne Painter, Graphic Artist

Lafayette

Vevers, Tony Painter, Educator

Michigan City

Harbart, Gertrude Felton Painter,
    Instructor

Morgantown

Boyce, Gerald G Educator, Painter

Muncie

Davis, James Robert Cartoonist
Griner, Ned H Educator, Craftsman
Joyaux, Alain Georges Museum Director
Story, William Easton Painter, Museum
    Director

Munster

Meeker, Barbara Miller Educator, Painter

Nashville

Zimmerman, William Harold Painter,
    Illustrator

New Carlisle

Droege, Anthony Joseph, II Painter,
    Draftsman

Notre Dame

Lauck, Anthony Joseph Sculptor,
    Educator
Vogl, Don George Painter, Printmaker

St Mary of the Woods

Newport, Esther Painter
Ruttinger, Jacquelyn Painter, Educator

South Bend

Holmes, Paul James & Mary E Collectors
Zisla, Harold Painter, Graphic Artist

Terre Haute

Engeran, Whitney John, Jr Painter,
    Educator
Evans, Robert Graves Sculptor, Educator
Hackney, Allen L Painter
Hay, Dick Sculptor, Ceramist
Kinsman, Robert Donald Gallery
    Director, Historian
Lamis, Leroy Sculptor, Educator
Porter, Elmer Johnson Painter, Educator
Reddington, Charles Leonard Painter,
    Educator
Rensch, Roslyn Historian, Writer

Vincennes

Beard, Marion L Patterson Lecturer,
    Painter

West Lafayette

Beelke, Ralph G Educator
Gregory, Eleanor Anne Educator,
    Calligrapher

IOWA

Ames

Benson, Martha J Gallery Director,
    Sculptor
Meixner, Mary Louise Painter, Educator

Burlington

Schramm, James Siegmund Collector,
    Patron

Cedar Falls

Campbell, Marjorie Dunn Painter,
    Educator
Eliason, Shirley (Shirley Eliason Haupt)
    Painter, Educator
Page, John Henry, Jr Printmaker,
    Educator
Powell, Dan T Photographer
Ruffo, Joseph Martin Printmaker,
    Administrator
Stetson, Daniel Everett Gallery Director,
    Curator

Cedar Rapids

Barth, Charles John Educator, Printmaker
Czestochowski, Joseph Stephen Museum
    Director
Gilmor, Jane E Painter, Educator
Kocher, Robert Lee Painter, Educator
Stamats, Peter Owen Collector, Patron

Cherokee

Laposky, Ben Francis Designer, Video
    Artist

Davenport

Anderson, James P Sculptor, Educator
Hoffman, Larry Gene Museum Director
Madonia, Ann C Historian, Curator

Des Moines

Black, Richard R Printmaker, Educator
Demetrion, James Thomas Administrator
Ferber, Lee Allan Craftsman, Educator
Kirschenbaum, Jules Painter, Educator
Medina, Ada Drawer
Reece, Maynard Painter, Illustrator
Worthen, Amy Namowitz Printmaker,
    Historian

Dubuque

Gibbs, Tom Sculptor

Fairfield

Cain, Michael Peter Painter, Sculptor

Grinnell

Cervene, Richard Painter, Curator

Iowa City

Achepohl, Keith Anden Printmaker,
    Painter
Alexander, Margaret Ames Art Historian,
    Educator
Begley, Wayne E Historian, Painter
Breder, Hans Dieter Sculptor, Video
    Artist
Burford, Byron Leslie Painter, Printmaker
Choo, Chunghi Metalsmith, Fabric
    Designer
Cuttler, Charles David Historian, Writer
DePuma, Richard Daniel Archaeologist,
    Historian
Foster, Stephen C Historian, Writer
Gorder, Clayton J Painter, Educator
Hindes, Chuck (Charles Austin) Ceramist,
    Educator
Lasansky, Mauricio L Printmaker,
    Draftsman
Moser, Joann Curator, Historian
Patrick, Genie Hudson Painter, Instructor
Patrick, Joseph Alexander Painter,
    Educator
Rorex, Robert Albright Educator,
    Historian
Schmidt, Julius Sculptor
Schultz, Stephen Warren Painter,
    Educator
Schulze, John H Photographer, Educator
Scott, John Beldon Historian, Educator
Tomasini, Wallace J Administrator,
    Historian

Jefferson

Finson, Hildred A Children's Book
    Illustrator, Painter

Mason City

Leet, Richard Eugene Museum Director,
    Painter

Orange City

Kaericher, John Conrad Printmaker,
    Educator

Riverside

Hobbs, Robert Carleton Museum
    Director, Historian

Solon

Myers, Virginia Anne Printmaker, Painter
Wilke, Ulfert S Painter, Administrator

Waterloo

Alling, Clarence (Edgar) Museum
    Director, Ceramist
Held, Alma M Painter

KANSAS

Ellsworth

Rogers, Charles B Painter, Museum
    Director

Emporia

Eppink, Helen Brenan Painter
Eppink, Norman R Printmaker, Painter
Haack, Cynthia R Painter, Printmaker
Hall, Rex Earl Painter, Educator
Johnson, Donald Ray Historian,
    Printmaker

KANSAS (cont)

Kretsinger, Mary Amelia Goldsmith, Designer
Perry, Donald Dean Printmaker, Educator
Stauffer, Richard L Sculptor, Educator

Great Bend

Moses, Bette J Painter, Dealer

Hays

Jilg, Michael Florian Painter, Printmaker
Kuchar, Kathleen Ann Painter, Educator
Moss, Joel C Painter, Educator
Nichols, Francis N, II Printmaker, Educator
Stevanov, Zoran Painter, Sculptor
Thorns, John Cyril, Jr Designer, Painter

Kansas City

Drake, Douglas Arnold Dealer, Curator
Oliphant, Patrick Political Cartoonist

Lawrence

Brejcha, Vernon Lee Glassblower, Educator
Broun, Elizabeth Gibson Curator, Historian
Craig, Susan V Librarian
Hawkins, Barbara Painter
Iversen, Earl Harvey Photographer, Educator
Larsen, Erik Consultant, Educator
Li, Chu-Tsing Historian
McKay, John Sangster Educator, Administrator
Schira, Cynthia Weaver, Tapestry Artist
Shimomura, Roger Yutaka Painter, Educator
Stokstad, Marilyn Historian, Educator
Stump, Jeanne Educator, Historian
Sudlow, Robert N Painter
Tefft, Elden Cecil Sculptor, Educator
Vaccaro, Luella Grace Ceramist, Painter
Vaccaro, Nick Dante Painter, Educator

Leavenworth

Melby, David A Painter, Photographer

McPherson

Robinson, Mary Ann Administrator, Educator

Manhattan

Ikeda, Yoshiro Ceramist, Educator
Larmer, Oscar Vance Painter, Educator
Ohno, Mitsugi Glassblower
Pujol, Elliott Educator, Medalist
Stroh, Charles Printmaker, Educator

Mission

Bandel, Lennon Raymond Painter
Burnett, Barbara Ann Painter, Conceptual Artist
Morgan, James Sherrod Collector

Pittsburg

Krug, Harry Elno Printmaker, Educator
Russell, Robert Price Painter, Educator

Prairie Village

Kuemmerlein, Janet Fiber Artist

Shawnee Mission

Bennett, Philomene Painter, Editor
Trudeau, Garry B Cartoonist

Topeka

Hunt, Robert James Administrator, Educator
Peters, Larry Dean Curator, Administrator

Wichita

Amsden, Floyd T Collector, Patron
Bartz, James Ross Painter
Beren, Stanley O Patron
Bernard, David Edwin Printmaker, Educator
Boyd, John David Educator, Printmaker
Bush, Martin H Museum Director, Historian
Connett, Dee M Educator, Printmaker
Graves, (Mrs) John W Collector
Grayson, Cassandra Dealer, Publisher
Kincade, Arthur Warren Collector, Patron
Kiskadden, Robert Morgan Painter, Educator
Rouse, John R Appraiser, Consultant
Sanders, Herbert Harvey Ceramist, Writer
Sanderson, Charles Howard Painter, Instructor
Spencer, Howard DaLee Curator, Printmaker
Wethington, Wilma Zella Painter, Instructor
Wooden, Howard Edmund Museum Director, Historian

KENTUCKY

Ashland

Williams, Joyce Painter, Instructor

Augusta

Greene, Lois D Dealer

Bardstown

Cantrell, Jim Painter, Ceramist

Berea

Pross, Lester Fred Educator, Painter
Tredennick, Dorothy W Educator, Lecturer

Bowling Green

Forrester, Charles Howard Sculptor, Educator
Gluhman, Joseph Walter Historian, Graphic Artist
Gluhman, Margaret A Graphic Artist, Collage Artist
Klein, Michael Eugene Historian, Writer
Oakes, John Warren Painter, Administrator
Schieferdecker, Ivan E Printmaker, Painter
Stomps, Walter E, Jr Painter, Printmaker
Wallace, Lysbeth (Mai) Weaver, Educator

Ft Thomas

Storm, Howard Painter, Sculptor

Lexington

Carpenter, Dennis Wilkinson (Bones) Photographer, Educator
Ferguson, Kathleen Elizabeth Sculptor
Foose, Robert James Painter, Designer
Girard, (Charles) Jack Painter, Educator
Hamann, Marilyn D Educator, Painter
Hennessey, William John Museum Director
Petro, Joseph (Victor), Jr Painter, Illustrator
Pierce, James Smith Historian, Sculptor

Louisville

Bratcher, Dale Painter
Bright, Barney Sculptor
Chodkowski, Henry, Jr Painter, Educator
Coates, Ann S Slide Curator, Historian
Covi, Dario A Historian
Hackett, Mickey Painter, Educator
Haynie, Hugh Cartoonist
Kaulitz, Garry Charles Painter, Printmaker
Koebbeman, Skip Educator, Sculptor
Kohlhepp, Norman Painter, Conservator
Morgan, William Historian, Writer
Nay, Mary Spencer Painter, Educator
Page, Addison Franklin Museum Director
Stoll, (Mrs) Berry Vincent Collector
Storer, Frances Nell Painter, Instructor
Wegner, Nadene R Goldsmith, Educator
Whitesell, John D Printmaker
Yenawine, Bruce Harley Administrator, Educator

Morehead

Booth, Bill Educator

Murray

Boyd, Karen White Educator, Fiber Artist
Head, Robert William Painter, Educator
Leys, Dale Daniel Educator, Draftsman
Speight, Jerry Brooks Educator, Writer
Weiler, Melody M Printmaker, Educator

Owensboro

Hood, Mary Bryan Museum Director, Administrator
Matlick, Gerald Allen Painter, Administrator

Princeton

Granstaff, William Boyd Painter, Illustrator

Richmond

Halbrooks, Darryl Wayne Painter, Educator
Isaacs, Ron Painter, Instructor

Shepherdsville

Lesch, Alma Wallace Tapestry Artist, Educator

Union

Akers, Gary Painter

Williamsburg

Weedman, Kenneth Russell Sculptor, Printmaker

LOUISIANA

Baton Rouge

Bacot, Henry Parrott Art Historian
Bolton, Mimi DuBois Painter
Bova, Joe Sculptor, Ceramist
Corso, Samuel (Joseph) Stained Glass Artist, Painter
Cox, Richard William Historian, Writer
Crespo, Michael Lowe Painter, Educator
Daugherty, Michael F Educator, Sculptor
Detmers, William Raymond Educator, Printmaker
Dufour, Paul Arthur Painter, Designer
Durieux, Caroline Wogan Printmaker
Harding, Ann Painter, Educator
Harris, Harvey Sherman Painter, Educator
Hausey, Robert Michael Painter
May, William L Collector
Meek, A J Photographer, Educator
O'Neill, John Patton Painter, Curator
Pramuk, Edward Richard Painter

LOUISIANA (cont)

LOUISIANA (cont)
Price, Anne Kirkendall Critic
Sachse, Janice R Painter, Printmaker
Schar, Stuart Educator, Printmaker

Cecilia
Landry, Richard Miles Photographer,
    Video Artist

Covington
Flattmann, Alan Raymond Painter,
    Instructor

Folsom
Golden, Rolland Harve Painter,
    Printmaker

Lafayette
Fiero, Gloria K Educator, Historian
Love, Frances Taylor Museum Director,
    Writer
Pillet, Michel Louis Architect, Educator

Lake Charles
Holcombe, R Gordon, Jr Collector,
    Patron

Mamou
Savoy, Chyrl Lenore Sculptor, Educator

Metairie
Casselli, Henry C, Jr Painter
Kohlmeyer, Ida (R) Painter, Printmaker

New Orleans
Amoss, Berthe Illustrator, Painter
Bullard, Edgar John, III Museum Director
Collier, Alberta Critic, Consultant
Davis, (Mr & Mrs) Walter Collectors,
    Patrons
Drummer, William Richard Gallery
    Director
Eckert, Lou Painter
Emery, Lin Sculptor, Kinetic Artist
Fagaly, William Arthur Museum Director,
    Historian
Farrens, Juanita G Painter, Instructor
Frank, Charles William, Jr Wood Carver,
    Writer
Freeman, Tina Photographer, Curator
Glasgow, Vaughn Leslie Curator,
    Historian
Gordy, Robert P Painter, Printmaker
Gregory, Angela Sculptor, Educator
Harter, John Burton Curator, Painter
Johnson, Richard A Painter, Educator
Jordan, George Edwin Critic, Historian
Jordan, Jack Administrator, Sculptor
Kern, Arthur (Edward) Educator,
    Sculptor
Koss, Gene H Sculptor, Educator
Lamantia, James Educator, Collector
Mason, Bette Painter, Educator
Muniot, Barbara King Dealer, Collector
O'Meallie, Kitty (Kate Chamness
    Johnson) Painter, Printmaker
Reddix, Roscoe Chester Painter, Educator
Scott, John Tarrell Printmaker, Sculptor
Steg, J L Printmaker, Painter
Struppeck, Jules Sculptor, Educator
Sweet, Steve (Steven Mark) Collage
    Artist, Sculptor
Tahir, Abe M, Jr Dealer
Trivigno, Pat Painter, Educator
Whiteman, Edward Russell Painter
Whitty-Johnson, Patricia Painter
Young, Tom (William Thomas) Painter,
    Educator
Zurik, Jesselyn Benson Painter, Sculptor

Ruston
Berguson, Robert Jenkins Painter,
    Educator
Cawood, Gary Kenneth Photographer
Dablow, Dean Clint Photographer
Mason, Novem M Sculptor, Designer
Strother, Joseph Willis Administrator,
    Painter

Shreveport
Cadle, Ray Kenneth Painter, Craftsman
Morgan, Arthur C Sculptor

Thibodaux
Garzon-Blanco, Armando Designer,
    Painter

MAINE

Bangor
D'Amico, Augustine A Collector, Patron

Bath
Ipcar, Dahlov Painter, Illustrator
Webb, Todd Photographer, Historian

Boothbay Harbor
Cavanaugh, Tom Richard Painter,
    Educator
Eames, John Heagan Etcher, Painter

Bristol
Klebe, Gene (Charles Eugene) Painter,
    Writer

Brunswick
Beam, Philip Conway Art Administrator,
    Educator
Bearce, Jeana Dale Painter, Printmaker
Coffey, John William, II Curator
Cornell, Thomas Browne Painter,
    Printmaker
Moore, Marjorie Painter, Assemblage
    Artist
Rakovan, Lawrence Francis Printmaker,
    Painter
Watson, Katharine Johnson Museum
    Director, Historian

Camden
Goldsmith, Benedict Isaac Gallery
    Director, Educator
Iselin, Lewis Sculptor
Smith, Harry William Miniaturist,
    Illustrator

Cape Neddick
Kuhn, Brenda Historian

Castine
Ortman, George Earl Painter, Sculptor
Whidden, Conni Painter, Instructor

Cherryfield
Etter, Howard Lee Painter, Lecturer

Clinton
Matthews, Harriett Sculptor

Cushing
Collins, John Ireland Painter
Magee, Alan Arthur Illustrator, Painter

Damariscotta
Cooney, Barbara (Mrs Charles Talbot
    Porter) Illustrator, Writer
Melville, Grevis Whitaker Painter,
    Printmaker
Thompson, Ernest Thorne, Jr Silversmith,
    Designer

Deer Isle
Merritt, Francis Sumner Painter, Designer

East Boothbay
Hook, Frances A Painter, Illustrator

Georgetown
Montgomery, Claude Painter, Etcher

Gorham
Franklin, Patt Sculptor, Painter
Ubans, Juris K Painter, Educator

Hancock
Moise, William Sidney Painter

Hollis Center
Hewitt, Duncan Adams Sculptor,
    Educator

Kennebunk
Stone, Don Painter

Kennebunkport
Gable, John Oglesby Painter

Kittery
Fein, B R Painter, Lecturer

Lewiston
Isaacson, Philip Marshal Critic, Writer

Lincolnville
Wasey, Jane Sculptor
Welliver, Neil G Painter

Little Deer Isle
McCloskey, Robert Painter, Illustrator

Medomak
Thompson, Ernest Thorne Educator,
    Painter

Monhegan
Drexler, Lynne Painter
Hudson, Jacqueline Painter, Graphic
    Artist
Hultberg, John Painter

Newcastle
Coggeshall, Calvert Painter

North Berwick
Hardy, (Clarion) Dewitt Painter,
    Administrator

North Edgecomb
Dean, Nicholas Brice Printmaker,
    Photographer

Ogunquit
Palmer, Michael Andrew Painter, Dealer
Strater, Henry Painter
Thelin, Valfred P Painter, Lecturer

Orono
Cushing, Barbara Educator, Painter
Hartgen, Vincent Andrew Painter,
    Educator
Lewis, Michael H Painter, Educator

Owl's Head
Spaulding, Warren Dan Painter, Lecturer

Phippsburg
McLanathan, Richard B K Consultant,
    Writer

Port Clyde

Thon, William Painter

Portland

Collins, William Charles Painter,
Administrator
Eide, John Photographer
Elowitch, Annette Dealer
Elowitch, Robert Jason Dealer, Patron
Holverson, John Museum Director
Muench, John Painter, Printmaker
Penney, Bruce Barton Painter
Preble, Michael Andrew Curator,
Administrator
Sadik, Marvin Sherwood Dealer
Ventimiglia, John Thomas Sculptor,
Instructor

Rockland

Peladeau, Marius Beaudoin Writer,
Museum Director

Rockport

Winters, Denny Painter

South Harpswell

Etnier, Stephen Morgan Painter

South Portland

Douglas, Edwin Perry Painter, Instructor

Stockton Springs

Nuse, Oliver William Painter,
Photographer

Stonington

Muir, Emily Lansingh Painter, Sculptor

Tenants Harbor

Thomas, Reynolds Painter, Illustrator

Vinalhaven

Indiana, Robert Painter, Sculptor

Waldoboro

Parnall, Peter Designer, Illustrator

Waterville

Carpenter, James Morton Historian
Simon, David L Historian, Educator

West Boothbay Harbor

Hemenway, Nancy (Mrs Robert D
Barton) Tapestry Artist

Westbrook

Marasco, Rose Photographer, Educator

Winter Harbor

Browne, Syd J Painter

Yarmouth

Chadbourn, Alfred Cheney Painter,
Instructor

York

Hallam, Beverly (Linney) Painter,
Lecturer
Laurent, John Louis Painter, Educator
Moore, Robert Eric Painter
Roche, Robert (Richard) Painter
Smart, Mary-Leigh Consultant, Patron

MARYLAND

Aberdeen

Morton, Richard H Painter, Graphic
Artist

Adelphi

Patton, Sharon Frances Historian,
Lecturer

Arnold

Edwards, Ellender Morgan Printmaker,
Photographer

Baltimore

Allwell, Stephen S Sculptor
Baney, Ralph Ramoutar Sculptor
Baney, Vera Ceramist, Printmaker
Bartlett, Christopher E Gallery Director,
Illustrator
Berge, Henry Sculptor
Buitron, Diana M Curator, Historian
Carlberg, Norman Kenneth Sculptor,
Instructor
Covey, Victor Charles B Conservator,
Administrator
Cropper, M Elizabeth Historian, Lecturer
Crosby, Ranice W Medical Illustrator,
Educator
Daniel, Suzanne Garrigues Historian
Erbe, Joan Painter
Fendell, Jonas J Educator, Painter
Fessler, Ann Helene Book Artist,
Photographer
Flannery, Thomas Cartoonist
Ford, John Gilmore Collector
Gilchriest, Lorenzo Constructionist,
Educator
Goldstein, Gladys Hack Painter
Gorski, Daniel Alexander Sculptor,
Painter
Halpern, Lea Ceramist, Painter
Hammond, Leslie King Historian, Writer
Hanson, J B Sculptor, Weaver
Hartigan, Grace Painter
Hershberg, Israel Painter, Instructor
Hill, Dorothy Kent Museum Curator
Hofmann, Douglas William Painter,
Printmaker
Johnston, William Ralph Historian,
Administrator
Jones, James Edward Painter, Printmaker
Katzenberg, Dena S Consultant, Curator
Kessler, Herbert Leon Educator
Klitzke, Theodore Elmer Educator,
Historian
Koch, Philip Painter, Instructor
Kramer, Reuben Sculptor
Lazarus, Fred, IV Administrator
Lehman, Arnold L Museum Director,
Historian
Lescalleet Painter, Photographer
Lippman, Judith Gallery Director,
Educator
Maril, Herman Painter, Printmaker
Middleman, Raoul F Painter, Muralist
Miller, Melvin O, Jr Painter
Mitchell, John Blair Painter, Educator
Moscatt, Paul N Painter, Instructor
Oppenheimer, Selma L Painter
Perlman, Bennard Bloch Painter,
Instructor
Price, Barbara Gillette Administrator,
Painter
Printz, Bonnie Allen Photographer,
Painter
Quisgard, Liz Whitney Painter, Sculptor
Randall, Lilian M C Curator
Randall, Richard Harding, Jr Curator,
Historian
Rembski, Stanislav Painter, Writer
Richardson, Brenda Museum Curator

Richardson, Frank, Jr Muralist
Rosen, Israel Collector
Rosenthal, Gertrude Historian,
Administrator
Rothschild, Amalie (Rosenfeld) Sculptor,
Painter
Sangiamo, Albert Educator, Painter
Satorsky, Cyril Printmaker, Illustrator
Shecter, Mark Painter, Muralist
Somerville, Romaine Stec Administrator
Sparks, John Edwin Printmaker,
Instructor
Stevens, Elisabeth Goss Writer, Critic
Stoneham, John Librarian
Streett, Tylden Westcott Sculptor,
Educator
Van Der Beek, Edward Stanley
Filmmaker, Video Artist
Walter, Valerie Harrisse Sculptor
West, Virginia M Fiber Artist, Writer
Young, Barbara Photographer

Bethesda

Benson, Elizabeth Polk Historian, Writer
Cable, Maxine Roth Sculptor
Desind, Philip Dealer, Collector
Duffy, Betty Minor Dealer
Glassman, Audrey Lavine Painter,
Photographer
Holvey, Samuel Boyer Sculptor, Designer
Kamen, Gloria Illustrator, Graphic Artist
Koenig, Elizabeth Sculptor
Larson, Jane (Warren) Ceramist, Writer
Lee, Dora Fugh Painter, Sculptor
Levy, Phyllis Houser Painter
Maddox, Jerald Curtis Curator, Historian
Mion, Pierre Riccardo Illustrator, Painter
Sarnoff, Lolo Sculptor, Collector

Bowie

Dasenbrock, Doris (Nancy) Voss
Designer, Painter
Plaster, Alice Marie Painter, Instructor
White, Amos, IV Ceramist, Photographer

Brookeville

Canby, Jeanny Vorys Archaeologist,
Curator

Burkittsville

Vo-Dinh, Mai Painter, Printmaker

Catonsville

Eglitis, Laimons Painter, Educator

Chevy Chase

Asher, Lila Oliver Printmaker, Painter
Calfee, William Howard Sculptor, Painter
Carrington, Omar Raymond Painter,
Instructor
Kainen, Jacob Painter, Printmaker
Kasten, Sherry Zvares Painter
Kranking, Margaret Graham Painter,
Instructor
Mecklenburg, Virginia McCord Curator,
Lecturer
Shaw, Renata Vitzthum Librarian
Wright, Frank Painter, Educator

College Park

Levitine, George Historian
Lynch, James Burr, Jr Historian
Shaw, Courtney Ann Librarian, Historian
Withers, Josephine Historian, Writer

Columbia

Poliszczuk, Orest Stephan Educator,
Sculptor

Drayden

Egeli, Peter Even Painter, Illustrator

Easton

Plumb, James Douglas Painter, Curator

Ft Washington

Furman, (Dr & Mrs) Arthur F Collectors, Patrons
Grady, Ruby McLain Painter, Sculptor
Sanabria, Robert Sculptor

Frederick

Bujese, Arlene Gallery Director, Printmaker
Gates, Harry Irving Sculptor, Educator
Parker, Carolyn Johnson Painter, Graphic Artist
Russo, Alexander Peter Painter, Educator
Schutz, Estelle Painter, Printmaker
Wallace, David Harold Historian, Museologist

Gaithersburg

Balance, Jerrald Clark Painter
Huff, Laura Weaver Printmaker, Illustrator

Glenelg

Niese, Henry Ernst Painter

Hagerstown

Kotun, Henry Paul Museum Director
Roberts, Clyde Harry Painter, Educator

Hughesville

Feltus, Alan Evan Painter, Educator
Irwin, Lani Helena Painter

Hyattsville

Driskell, David Clyde Painter, Educator
Warren, Win (W Winton) Painter, Lecturer

Hydes

Wagner, Charles H Administrator, Instructor

Joppa

Walters, Ernest Painter

Kensington

Cave, Leonard Edward Sculptor, Educator
McWhinnie, Harold James Printmaker, Ceramist

Landover

Nevia Painter

Lanham-Seabrook

Murphy, Susan (Susan Murphy Colombini) Painter, Conceptual Artist

Laurel

Devillier, Charles Arthur Designer, Stained Glass Artist

Monkton

Leake, Eugene W Painter

Owings Mills

Kissel, William Thorn, Jr Sculptor

Point of Rocks

Larson, Blaine (Gledhill) Painter, Instructor

Potomac

Chieffo, Clifford Toby Painter, Conservator

Queenstown

Houghton, Arthur A, Jr Administrator

Riverdale

Clapsaddle, Jerry Painter

Rockville

Crockett, Gib (Gibson M) Cartoonist, Painter
Freeman-Appelbaum, Margery Sculptor, Administrator
Porter, Shirley Painter
Pruitt, Lynn Sculptor, Assemblage Artist
Safer, John Sculptor
Sikora, Zdzislaw R Printmaker
Weinberg, Bella Rebecca Painter, Writer
Wood, James Arthur (Art) Cartoonist, Lecturer

Severna Park

Stephany, Jaromir Photographer, Educator

Silver Spring

Carter, Jerry Williams Mosaic Artist, Muralist
Glick, Paula Florence Dealer, Collector
Lapinski, Tadeusz (A) Printmaker, Educator
MacDonald, Kevin John Graphic Artist
Oxman, Mark Sculptor, Educator
Peiperl, Adam Kinetic Artist, Video Artist
Roberts, Lucille D (Malkia) Painter, Educator
Walker, Sandra Radcliffe Painter

Takoma Park

Dempsey, Richard William Painter, Lecturer
Jewell, Joyce Painter, Printmaker
Rode, Meredith Eagon Printmaker, Educator

Towson

Frank, Jane Painter, Sculptor
Johnson, Lincoln Fernando Educator, Writer

MASSACHUSETTS

Amesbury

Dailey, Dan (Daniel Owen) Sculptor, Designer

Amherst

Cohen, Michael S Ceramist
Dorn, Ruth (Dornbush) Painter
Hendricks, James (Powell) Painter, Sculptor
Liebling, Jerome Photographer, Filmmaker
Norton, Paul Foote Historian, Educator
Patterson, William Joseph Painter, Printmaker
Roskill, Mark Wentworth Historian, Critic
Schmalz, Carl (Nelson), Jr Painter, Educator
Souza, Al (Alfred Francis) Photographer, Educator
Stevens, Nelson L Painter, Educator
Townsend, John F Sculptor, Painter
Trapp, Frank Anderson Museum Director, Historian
Vanasse, Louis Raymond Collector, Instructor
Wardlaw, George Melvin Painter, Sculptor

Andover

Cook, Christopher Capen Administrator
Hayes, Bartlett Harding, Jr Administrator, Writer
MacDougall, Anne Printmaker, Painter
Sullivan, David Francis Painter, Printmaker

Arlington

Dahill, Thomas Henry, Jr Painter, Educator
Katayama, Toshihiro Painter, Designer

Ashfield

Lund, Jane Painter, Printmaker

Bedford

Buscaglia, Jose Sculptor, Educator
Weeks, James (Darrell Northrup) Painter, Educator

Belmont

Barbarossa, Theodore C Sculptor

Beverly

Broudo, Joseph David Educator, Ceramist
Jeswald, Joseph Administrator, Painter

Blandford

Wise, Gerald Lee Graphic Artist, Printmaker

Boston

Andersen, Wayne Vesti Art Historian, Educator
Aronson, David Painter, Sculptor
Barreres, Domingo Painter, Educator
Binning, Robin Printmaker, Sculptor
Cataldo, John William Educator, Calligrapher
Chamberlain, David (Allen) Sculptor
Chiarenza, Carl Photographer, Historian
Coolidge, John Historian
Cooper, Wendy Ann Curator
Cormier, Robert John Painter, Lecturer
Cox, Gardner Painter
Crite, Allan Rohan Painter, Illustrator
Cunningham, Charles C, Jr Administrator
Danikian, Caron Le Brun Critic, Dealer
Delgado-Guitart, Jose Luis Printmaker
Dorrien, Carlos Guillermo Sculptor
Driscoll, Edgar Joseph, Jr Critic
Fairbanks, Jonathan Leo Curator
Fink, Alan Dealer
Fox, Judith Hoos Curator
Gabin, George Joseph Painter, Instructor
Ghikas, Panos George Painter, Educator
Gibran, Kahlil George Sculptor
Gordon, Joy L Museum Director, Educator
Hadley, Rollin van Nostrand Museum Director
Haley, Patience E (Patience E Haley Ghikas) Painter, Conservator
Harcus, Portia Gwen Dealer, Consultant
Hausman, Jerome Joseph Educator
Hilles, Susan Morse Collector, Patron
Hunter, Robert Douglas Painter, Instructor
Kanegis, Sidney S Dealer
Kelley, Donald Castell Gallery Director, Librarian
Korzenik, Diana Educator
Krakow, Barbara L Dealer
Kramer, Jack N Painter, Educator
Livingston, Virginia (Mrs Hudson Warren Budd) Painter, Illustrator
Luce, Molly Painter
McSheehy, Cornelia Marie Printmaker, Painter
Metcalf, Conger A Painter, Instructor
Moeller, Robert Charles, III Historian, Administrator

MASSACHUSETTS (cont)

Moser, Barry Graphic Artist, Printmaker
Moss, Karen Canner Painter, Educator
Nielsen, Nina I M Dealer
Ockenga, Starr Photographer, Educator
Parker, Olivia Photographer
Peabody, Amelia Sculptor
Pezzati, Pietro Painter
Pinckney, Stanley Painter, Tapestry Artist
Pineda, Marianna Sculptor
Plamondon, Peter M Painter
Pucker, Bernard H Art Dealer
Rolly, Ronald Joseph Dealer
Safford, Ruth Perkins Painter
Salmon, Larry Curator
Sandman, Jo Painter, Sculptor
Sayre, Eleanor Axson Curator
Schwartz, Henry Painter, Instructor
Searles, Stephen Sculptor
Shlien, Helen S Dealer
Sonnabend, Joan Dealer, Collector
Stebbins, Theodore Ellis, Jr Historian,
    Administrator
Taylor, Robert Critic, Writer
Tovish, Harold Sculptor, Educator
Trecker, Stanley Matthew Sculptor,
    Photographer
Vermeule, Cornelius Clarkson, III
    Historian, Writer
Vershbow, (Mr & Mrs) Arthur Collectors
Vose, Robert Churchill, Jr Dealer
Warburg, Stephanie Wenner Painter,
    Instructor
Wise, (Kenneth) Kelly Photographer,
    Critic
Zahn, Carl Frederick Designer,
    Administrator
Zerner, Henri Thomas Historian, Curator

Brewster

Stoltenberg, Donald Hugo Painter,
    Printmaker

Bridgewater

Dunn, Roger Terry Historian
Smalley, Stephen Francis Educator,
    Painter

Brockton

Hoffman, Marilyn Friedman Museum
    Director

Brookfield

Knight, Jacob Jaskoviak Painter,
    Illustrator

Brookline

Ablow, Joseph Painter, Writer
Ablow, Roselyn Karol Painter, Printmaker
Alcalay, Albert S Painter, Lecturer
Apel, Barbara Jean Painter, Educator
Barron, Ros Painter, Video Artist
Berger, Jason Painter, Printmaker
Cantor, Mira (Mira Cantor-Piene)
    Sculptor, Graphic Artist
Goldstein, Nathan Writer, Painter
Hills, Patricia Historian, Curator
Kay, Reed Educator, Painter
Little, Nina Fletcher Collector, Writer
McNamara, John Stephen Painter
Maynard, William Painter, Educator
Nagano, Paul Tatsumi Painter, Designer
Papo, Iso Painter
Sina, Alejandro Kinetic Artist, Sculptor
Slone, Sandi Painter, Instructor
Stevovich, Andrew Vlastimir Painter,
    Printmaker
Swan, Barbara Painter
Wechsler, Judith Glatzer Historian,
    Filmmaker

Weiss, Rachel Sculptor, Holographer
Wilson, John Sculptor, Printmaker

Cambridge

Abramowicz, Janet Painter
Ackerman, James S Historian, Educator
Agoos, Herbert M Collector
Bageris, John Painter, Instructor
Beale, Arthur C Conservator
Benedict-Jones, Linda L Photographer,
    Curator
Burgess, David Lowry Environmental
    Artist
Casey, Jacqueline Shepard Administrator,
    Designer
Cohn, Marjorie B Conservator, Historian
D'Agostino, Peter Pasquale Video Artist,
    Educator
Earls, Paul Environmental Artist
Feininger, T Lux Painter, Writer
Fleming, Ronald Lee Designer,
    Administrator
Freedberg, Sydney Joseph Historian,
    Educator
Freitag, Wolfgang Martin Librarian,
    Historian
Goldring, Elizabeth Writer,
    Environmental Artist
Grabill, Vin (E Vincent, Jr) Video Artist,
    Environmental Artist
Hadzi, Dimitri Sculptor, Printmaker
Hanfmann, George M A Educator,
    Historian
Harries, Mags (Margaret L) Sculptor
Janney, Christopher Draper
    Environmental Artist, Sound Artist
Jewell, William M Educator, Painter
Kepes, Gyorgy Painter, Educator
Lent, Blair Illustrator, Writer
Mazur, Michael Painter, Printmaker
Mongan, Agnes Administrator, Historian
Norfleet, Barbara Pugh Curator, Educator
Oberhuber, Konrad J Historian, Curator
Pappas, Marilyn Collage Artist, Educator
Parry, Marian Illustrator, Printmaker
Piene, Otto Sculptor, Painter
Preusser, Robert Ormerod Painter,
    Educator
Rabb, (Mr & Mrs) Irving W Collectors
Radycki, J(osephine) Diane Historian,
    Lecturer
Rathbone, Perry Townsend Museum
    Director
Reimann, William P Sculptor, Educator
Roberts, Helene Emylou Librarian
Rosenfield, John M Educator, Curator
Saarinen, Lilian Sculptor
Schiff, Jeffrey Allen Sculptor,
    Environmental Artist
Siler, Todd (Lael) Painter, Sculptor
Slive, Seymour Historian, Museum
    Director
Stapen, Nancy Critic, Writer
Sussman, Elisabeth Sacks Curator
Tambellini, Aldo Video Artist, Sculptor
Timpson, Michael G Sculptor
Trachtman, Arnold S Painter
Wasserman, Cary (Robert) Photographer,
    Conceptual Artist
Welch, Stuart Cary Curator, Historian

Charlestown

Kortenhaus, Lynne M Dealer, Consultant
MacLean-Smith, Elizabeth Sculptor,
    Lecturer

Chelsea

Willis, William Henry, Jr Administrator

Chestnut Hill

Bloom, Edith Salvin Art Dealer, Painter
Plaut, James S Art Administrator, Writer
Saltonstall, Elizabeth Painter
Steczynski, John Myron Draftsman,
    Educator

Cohasset

Kowal, Dennis J Sculptor, Writer

Concord

Ihara, Michio Sculptor

Conway

Mallary, Robert Sculptor, Educator

Dorchester

Lewis, Elma Ina Administrator
MacNutt, Glenn Gordon Painter,
    Illustrator
Richards, Eugene Photographer, Lecturer
Stone, Jim (James J) Photographer,
    Educator

Dover

Celli, Paul Painter, Educator
Hubert, Edgar F & Anne M Curators,
    Collectors

Duxbury

Bengtz, Ture Museum Director, Painter

East Bridgewater

Hausrath, Joan W Weaver, Educator

Edgartown

Carrick, Donald F Illustrator-Children's
    Books, Painter

Fairhaven

London, Peter Painter, Educator

Fitchburg

Driscoll, John Paul Curator, Historian
Timms, Peter Rowland Museum Director

Framingham Center

Schiff, Lonny Collage Artist, Conservator

Gloucester

Benham, Robert Charles Painter
Cassidy, Margaret Carol (Mrs John
    Manship) Sculptor, Librarian
Coburn, Ralph (M H) Painter, Designer
Curtis, Roger William Painter, Dealer
Duca, Alfred Milton Sculptor, Painter
Faddis, (William) George Enamelist,
    Painter
Gore, Ken (Kenneth Leon) Painter
Grasso, Doris (Ten-Eyck) Painter,
    Sculptor
Grasso, Salvatore Fortunato Painter,
    Conceptual Artist
Hancock, Walker (Kirtland) Sculptor
Manship, John Paul Painter, Sculptor
Movalli, Charles Joseph Writer, Painter
Rosenthal, Gloria M Collage Artist,
    Painter
Shore, Mary (McGarrity) Painter

Great Barrington

Agar, Eunice Jane Educator, Painter
Aigner, Lucien Photographer, Lecturer
Hillman, Arthur Stanley Graphic Artist,
    Instructor

Harwich Port

Gilbertson, Charlotte Painter, Lecturer

Hingham

Ingraham, John Douglas Dealer, Publisher
Pierce, Patricia Jobe Dealer, Historian
Reardon, Mary A Painter, Muralist
Rose, Samuel Painter, Muralist

Holyoke

Hamel, Bernard Franklin Painter
Seace, Barry William Printmaker,
    Educator

Hyannis

Brooks, Robert Painter

Hyde Park

Atwood Pinardi, Brenda Painter,
    Educator
Pinardi, Enrico Vittorio Sculptor, Painter

Jamaica Plain

Leon, Ana (Ana M Rodriguez-Leon)
    Painter

Kingston

Joyce, Marshall Woodside Painter,
    Instructor

Lenox

Hatch, John Davis Consultant, Historian

Leverett

Fornas, Leander Printmaker, Instructor

Lexington

Bakanowsky, Louis J Environmental
    Artist, Architect
Berman, Vivian Printmaker
Boodman, H Citron Painter, Printmaker
Cascieri, Arcangelo Sculptor, Instructor
Filipowski, Richard E Sculptor, Educator
Franco, Barbara Curator
Kumler, Kipton (Cornelius) Photographer,
    Lecturer
Loehr, Max Museum Curator, Educator

Lincoln

Katzive, David H Administrator

Lowell

Faudie, Fred Painter, Photographer

Lynn

Cretara, Domenic Anthony Painter,
    Educator

Manchester

Lothrop, Kristin Curtis Sculptor
Weems, Katharine Lane Sculptor

Marblehead

Seamans, Beverly Benson Sculptor

Marshfield

Greenamyer, George Mossman Sculptor,
    Educator

Marstons Mills

Lash, Kenneth Educator, Writer

Mattapan

Gaither, Edmund B Museum Director,
    Historian

Medway

Burnett, Calvin Painter, Illustrator

Melrose

Camlin, James A Painter

Milton

Hamill, Tim J Painter, Printmaker

Monson

Talbot, Jarold Dean Museum Director,
    Educator

Montague

Coughlin, Jack Printmaker, Sculptor

Nantucket

Greenleaf, Virginia Painter
Hicken, Philip Burnham Painter,
    Printmaker
Perrin, C Robert Painter, Illustrator
Weeber, Gretchen Painter

Natick

Abany, Albert Charles Painter,
    Printmaker
Geller, Esther (Esther Geller Shapero)
    Painter, Printmaker
Ratner, David M Painter, Educator

Needham Heights

Castano, Elvira Dealer, Historian

New Bedford

Hodgson, James Stanley Librarian
Kilmer, Nicholas John Administrator,
    Painter
Neugebauer, Margot Designer, Craftsman
Smith, David Loeffler Painter, Educator
Young, Janie Chester Museum Director,
    Educator

Newton

Bohlen, Nina (Celestine Eustis Bohlen)
    Painter
Hurwitz, Sidney J Painter, Printmaker
Martin, Marianne Winter Historian,
    Educator
Ranalli, Daniel Photographer, Consultant
Rosenblum, Richard Stephen Sculptor

Newton Center

Cobb, Ruth Painter

Newtonville

Polonsky, Arthur Painter, Educator
Skinner, Orin Ensign Designer

North Adams

Patten, David John Editor, Librarian

North Amherst

Brown, Jeffrey Rogers Dealer, Collector

Northampton

Chetham, Charles Museum Director
Hoener, Arthur Painter
Houser, Caroline Mae Historian
Malo, Teri (Teri A Malo-Sprawka)
    Painter, Printmaker
Offner, Elliot Sculptor, Printmaker

North Brookfield

Neal, (Minor) Avon Writer, Printmaker
Parker, Ann Photographer, Graphic Artist

North Hatfield

Minisci, Brenda (Eileen) Sculptor,
    Ceramist

Norwell

Wentworth, Murray Jackson Painter,
    Instructor

Onset

Halberstadt, Ernst Painter, Photographer
Mellor, George Edward Educator,
    Sculptor

Orleans

Vickrey, Robert Remsen Painter

Pittsfield

Filmus, Michael Roy Painter

Plainfield

Patti, Tom Sculptor

Provincetown

De Nagy, Eva Painter
Farnham, Emily Painter, Writer
Hensche, Henry Painter, Instructor
Hutchinson, Peter Arthur Conceptual
    Artist
Jensen, Marit Painter, Serigrapher
Rayner, Ada (Ada Rayner Hensche)
    Painter
Stout, Myron Stedman Painter

Reading

Nordstrand, Nathalie Johnson Painter

Rochester

Pettibone, John Wolcott Curator, Graphic
    Artist

Rockport

Bissell, Phil Cartoonist, Illustrator
Davidson, Allan Albert Painter, Sculptor
Geraci, Lucian Arthur Painter, Dealer
Harper, Eleanor O'Neil Painter
Hill, J Tweed Painter, Graphic Artist
Martin, Mary Finch Director, Painter
Martin, Roger Painter, Instructor
Morrell, Wayne (Beam) Painter
Murphy, Gladys Wilkins Painter,
    Craftsman
Murphy, Herbert A Architect, Painter
Nicholas, Thomas Andrew Painter
Ricci, Jerri Painter
Ruben, Albert Painter
Schlemm, Betty Lou Painter
Strisik, Paul Painter
Turner, Bruce Backman Painter
Van Wyk, Helen Painter, Lecturer

Rowley

Ahl, Henry C Painter, Writer

Roxbury

Crump, Walter Moore, Jr Printmaker,
    Painter

Salem

Bartnick, Harry William Painter,
    Educator
Tolles, Bryant Franklin, Jr Museum
    Director, Historian

Sandwich

Neill, Ben E Painter

Sharon

Avakian, John Painter, Instructor

Sheffield

Friedman, Benno Photographer
Philbrick, Margaret Elder Printmaker

Sherborn

Pickhardt, Carl Painter, Printmaker

Somerville

Campbell, David Paul Painter
Corish, Joseph Ryan Painter
Leja, Michael Joseph Curator, Critic

South Hadley

DeLonga, Leonard Anthony Sculptor,
    Educator

South Harwich

Bode, Robert William Designer, Painter
Sahrbeck, Everett William Painter,
    Designer

Springfield

Catok, Lottie Meyer Painter
Muhlberger, Richard Charles Museum
    Director

Stockbridge

Boris, Bessie Painter
Garel, Leo Painter
Kalischer, Clemens Photographer, Gallery
    Director
Varnelis, Kazys Educator, Painter

Sunderland

Kamys, Walter Painter, Educator

Tewksbury

Kaufman, Mico Sculptor

Topsfield

Webster, Larry Painter, Printmaker

Truro

Craig, Nancy Ellen Painter
Johnson, Joyce Sculptor, Instructor
Preston, Malcolm H Critic, Painter
Wright, Milton Painter, Educator
Yater, George David Painter

Tyringham

Brown, Jeanette H Collector,
    Administrator
Davis, Donald Robert Painter, Dealer

Vineyard Haven

Bramhall, Kib Painter

Waban

Rothbein, Renee Painter, Printmaker
Thomas, C David Printmaker

Waltham

Belz, Carl Irvin Museum Director
Neuman, Robert S Painter

Ware

Chase, Alice Elizabeth Educator, Writer

Watertown

Schwalb, Susan Instructor, Painter

Wayland

Allara, Pamela Edwards Historian, Critic
Bentov, Mirtala Sculptor
Dergalis, George Painter, Sculptor

Wellesley

Borgo, Ludovico Art Historian
Elliott, Bruce Roger Printmaker, Educator
O'Gorman, James Francis Historian
Wallace, Richard William Educator,
    Historian

Wellfleet

Franco, Robert John Painter, Educator
Lechay, James Painter
Shackelford, Shelby Painter
Wilkinson, Kirk Cook Dealer, Painter

Wenham

Fransioli, Thomas Adrian Painter,
    Printmaker

West Boylston

Italiano, Joan Sculptor, Educator

West Newton

Schon, Nancy Quint Sculptor, Instructor

Weston

Mariano, Kristine Painter

West Roxbury

Altmann, Henry S Painter, Educator
Sorokin, Maxine Ann Painter, Educator

West Stockbridge

Jones, Franklin Reed Painter, Writer

Westwood

Rayen, James Wilson Painter, Educator

Wilbraham '

Gale, William Henry Painter, Designer
Stevens, Richard Clive Painter, Illustrator

Williamstown

Brooke, David Stopford Museum Director
Brooks, John H Administrator, Educator
Faison, Samson Lane, Jr Historian,
    Museum Director
Hamilton, George Heard Museum
    Director, Historian
Johnson, Eugene Joseph Historian
Parkhurst, Charles Administrator, Curator
Rinehart, Michael Librarian, Editor

Winchester

Jacques, Michael Louis Printmaker,
    Educator

Winthrop

Raimondi, John Richard Sculptor

Wollaston

Smongeski, Joseph Leon Painter,
    Designer

Worcester

Bumgardner, Georgia Brady Curator,
    Historian
Dresser, Louisa (Louisa Dresser
    Campbell) Administrator, Historian
Freudenheim, Tom Lippmann Museum
    Director
Graziani, Sante Painter, Muralist
Hovsepian, Leon Painter, Designer
McCorison, Marcus Allen Librarian
Nigrosh, Leon Isaac Ceramist, Instructor
Orze, Joseph John Administrator,
    Sculptor
Peak, Elizabeth Jayne Printmaker,
    Educator
Priest, T (Theresa Khoury Struckus)
    Painter, Printmaker
Shepard, Lewis Albert Dealer, Historian
Strickler, Susan Elizabeth Curator,
    Historian

Yarmouth Port

Hitch, Jean Leason Painter
Hitch, Robert A Painter

MICHIGAN

Adrian

Cervenka, Barbara Educator, Painter

Albion

Brunkus, Richard Allen Printmaker,
    Curator

Allendale

Duren, Stephen D Painter, Instructor

Allen Park

Mandziuk, Michael Dennis Painter,
    Serigrapher

Alma

Kirby, Kent Bruce Printmaker,
    Photographer

Alpena

Bodem, Dennis Richard Museum
    Director

Ann Arbor

Arnheim, Rudolf Educator, Writer
Avedon, Barry Painter, Educator
Bayliss, George Painter, Art
    Administrator
Cassara, Frank Painter, Printmaker
Davis, Philip Charles Photographer,
    Writer
Eisenberg, Marvin Historian, Educator
Forsyth, Ilene H(aering) Educator,
    Historian
Gooch, Donald Burnette Painter
Iglehart, Robert L Educator, Writer
Jungwirth, I(rene) Gayas Painter,
    Designer
Kamrowski, Gerome Painter, Educator
Kirkpatrick, Diane Historian
Kusnerz, Peggy Ann F Librarian,
    Administrator
Leonard, Joanne Photographer, Educator
Lewis, William Arthur Painter,
    Administrator
Loeb, Judy Painter, Writer
McMillan, Constance Painter, Illustrator
Maurer, Evan Maclyn Director, Historian
Piepenburg, Robert Sculptor
Poinier, Arthur Best Cartoonist
Sawyer, Charles Henry Museum Director
Smith, Graham Historian, Educator
Smith, Sherri Weaver, Educator
Spink, Walter M Educator, Administrator
Stephenson, John H Sculptor, Educator
Stephenson, Susanne G Ceramist,
    Educator
Stewart, Paul LeRoy Printmaker,
    Educator
Waller, Aaron Bret Museum Director,
    Historian
Weber, Albert Jacob Painter, Educator
Weddige, Emil Lithographer, Educator
Wethey, Harold Edwin Historian

Berrien Springs

Constantine, Greg John Painter, Educator

Birmingham

Bulone, Joseph Dominic Sculptor
Dibert, Rita Jean Photographer, Educator
Fredericks, Marshall Maynard Sculptor
Kozlow, Richard Painter
Morris, Donald Fischer Dealer
Morris, Florence Marie Dealer

Bloomfield Hills

Hall, Michael David Sculptor, Educator
McCoy, Katherine Braden Designer,
    Educator
McCoy, Michael Dale Designer, Educator

MICHIGAN (cont)

Sanchez, Beatrice Rivas Administrator,
  Printmaker
Siden, Franklin Dealer, Lecturer
Slade, Roy Painter, Gallery Director
Toth, Carl Wayne Photographer

Brighton

Nestor, Lula B Painter, Administrator

Canton

Beginin, Igor Painter, Instructor
DeLauro, Joseph Nicola Sculptor,
  Educator

Detroit

Bostick, William Allison Painter,
  Calligrapher
Broner, Robert Printmaker, Painter
Burnett, Patricia Hill Painter, Sculptor
Colby, Joy Hakanson Critic
Cummings, Frederick James
  Administrator, Historian
Downs, Linda Anne Curator, Educator
Hill, Draper Editorial Cartoonist,
  Historian
Johnson, Lester L Painter, Educator
Kachadoorian, Zubel Painter, Educator
Kan, Michael Historian, Administrator
Muccioli, Anna Maria Painter, Sculptor
Peck, William Henry Curator, Historian
Piet, John Frances Sculptor, Instructor
Redstone, Louis Gordon Architect,
  Writer
Rosas, Mel Painter
Scheyer, Ernst Historian, Lecturer
Schuster, Eugene Ivan Dealer, Historian
Shaw, Nancy (Rivard) Curator, Historian
Wilbert, Robert John Painter, Educator
Woodson, Shirley Ann Painter

Dexter

Rush, Jon N Sculptor, Educator

East Jordan

Midener, Walter Sculptor, Instructor

East Lansing

Alexander, Robert Seymour Educator,
  Designer
Brainard, Owen Painter, Educator
Church, C Howard Painter, Printmaker
De Blasi, Anthony Armando Painter,
  Educator
Glendinning, Peter Photographer
Hu, Mary Lee Educator, Jeweler
Ishikawa, Joseph Museum Director,
  Consultant
McChesney, Clifton Painter, Educator

Farmington Hills

Dunbar, Russell Raymond Painter,
  Sculptor
Hadfield, Ted Lee Sculptor

Flint

Bohnert, Thom (Thomas Robert)
  Ceramist, Educator
Davidek, Stefan Painter
Warner, Douglas Warfield Painter,
  Educator
Wattenmaker, Richard J Museum
  Director, Historian

Franklin

Kasle, Gertrude Consultant, Collector

Grand Rapids

Collins, Paul Painter
Danielson, Phyllis I Administrator,
  Tapestry Artist
Koster, Marjory Jean Printmaker
Sweeney, J Gray Historian, Curator
Weidenaar, Reynold Henry Etcher,
  Painter

Grosse Pointe

Becker, David Printmaker, Educator
Krentzin, Earl Sculptor, Silversmith
Nobili, Louise Educator, Painter

Hartland

Stamelos, Electra Georgia Mousmoules
  Painter, Graphic Artist

Highland Park

Brose, Morris Sculptor

Huntington Woods

Gutmann, Joseph Historian, Lecturer
Nawara, Jim Painter, Printmaker
Nawara, Lucille Procter Painter, Educator

Kalamazoo

De Luca, Joseph Victor Educator,
  Sculptor
Gammon, Reginald Adolphus Educator,
  Painter
Hatch, Mary Painter
Hefner, Harry Simon Painter, Educator
Johnston, Robert Porter Educator,
  Sculptor
Kayser, Thomas Arthur Museum Director
Kemper, John Garner Painter, Graphic
  Artist
Link, Lawrence John Painter
Sheridan, Helen Adler Librarian, Curator
Wood, Marcia Joan Sculptor

Laingsburg

McConnell, James Houston Printmaker

Lakeside

Wilson, John David Dealer, Publisher

Lathrup Village

Hampson, Ferdinand Charles Gallery
  Director

Lawton

Laslo, Patricia Louise (Laslo-Neukranz)
  Sculptor

Marcellus

Rhodes, Curtis A Painter, Printmaker

Marquette

Gorski, Richard Kenny Educator,
  Graphic Artist

Mason

Leepa, Allen Painter, Educator

Midland

Breed, Charles Ayars Sculptor, Educator

Mt Pleasant

Bambas, Thomas Reese Metalsmith
Born, James E Sculptor
Kline, Richard R Painter, Sculptor

Northville

Barr, David John Sculptor, Painter

Okemos

Taylor, John Frank Adams Writer

Olivet

Whitney, Charlotte Armide Painter,
  Jeweler
Whitney, William Kuebler Painter,
  Historian

Onsted

Thiery, Thomas Allen Painter

Owosso

Harsh, Richard Painter, Educator

Parma

Wolber, Paul J Painter, Educator

Plainwell

Kendall, Thomas Lyle Ceramist, Educator

Plymouth

Guastella, C Dennis Painter, Instructor
Surgalski, Patrick J Painter, Printmaker

Richland

Walker, James Adams Painter,
  Printmaker

Rochester

Brun, Thomas Sculptor, Instructor
Usui, Kiichi Curator
Windeknecht, Margaret Brake Fiber
  Artist, Writer

Royal Oak

McCarty, Lorraine Chambers Painter,
  Instuctor

Saginaw

Laatsch, Gary Sculptor

St Clair Shores

Burns, Sheila Painter, Lecturer
Burns, Stan Painter, Sculptor
Cartmell, Helen Painter, Director

Sault Ste Marie

Szabo, Zoltan Painter, Writer

South Haven

Dickerson, Edward Ted Painter,
  Printmaker

Troy

Cloud, Jack L Gallery Owner, Publisher
Michaels, Glen Sculptor, Painter

Watersmeet

Freund, Will Frederick Painter, Educator

West Bloomfield

Simper, Frederick Painter

West Olive

Boeve, Edgar Gene Educator, Painter

Williamston

Lawton, James L Sculptor, Educator

Ypsilanti

Calkins, Kingsley Mark Painter, Educator
Fairfield, Richard Thomas Printmaker,
  Educator
Iden, Sheldon Painter, Educator
Pijanowski, Eugene M Educator,
  Craftsman

MINNESOTA

Bemidji
Smith, Kent Alvin Sculptor

Browerville
Kiselewski, Joseph Sculptor

Cambridge
Moss, Gary William Painter

Collegeville
Hendershot, J L Printmaker, Educator

Duluth
Boyce, William G Museum Director, Educator
Brush, Gloria (Elizabeth) DeFilipps Photographer, Educator
Brush, Leif Sound Sculptor, Instructor
Chee, Cheng-Khee Painter, Educator
Friedman, Ann Marti Historian, Museologist

Edina
Rollins, Jo Lutz Dealer, Painter

Excelsior
Nash, Katherine E Sculptor, Educator

Golden Valley
Jardine, Donald Leroy Editor, Educator

Grand Portage
Morrison, George Painter

Hastings
Koestner, Don Painter

Janesville
Tanner, James L Craftsman

Mankato
Finkler, Robert Allan Educator, Painter
Hapke, Paul Frederick Painter, Educator
Spurgin, John Edwin Administrator, Painter
Strassberg, Roy I Ceramist, Sculptor

Marine On St Croix
Sorman, Steven Painter, Printmaker

Minneapolis
Asher, Frederick M Art Historian, Educator
Bjorklund, Lee Painter, Educator
Bonstrom, Dana Orlin Art Dealer, Writer
Burpee, James Stanley Painter, Instructor
Conaway, James D Painter, Educator
Conforti, Michael Peter Historian, Curator
Fisher, Carole Gorney Painter, Sculptor
Flick, Paul John Painter, Collector
Fogg-Gerber, Monica Painter, Instructor
Friedman, Martin Museum Director
Graham, Richard Marston Sculptor, Educator
Hallman, Gary Lee Photographer
Hendler, Raymond Painter, Sculptor
Holen, Norman Dean Sculptor, Educator
Johnson, James Edwin & Sandra Kay Graphic Designers
King, Lyndel Irene Saunders Director, Administrator
Klein, Lynn (Ellen) Printmaker, Photographer
Klipper, Stuart David Photographer
Larkin, Eugene Designer, Educator
Larson, Philip Seely Sculptor, Educator
Leicester, Andrew John Environmental Artist
Long, Scott Cartoonist

Lyons, Lisa Curator, Historian
McCannel, (Mrs) Malcolm A Collector
McDonald, Susan Strong Painter, Editor
McNally, Sheila John Educator, Historian
Marcheschi, (Louis) Cork Sculptor, Educator
Munzner, Aribert Painter, Educator
Murdock, Robert Mead Curator
Myers, Malcolm Haynie Printmaker, Painter
Peterson, Harold Patrick Librarian, Editor
Poor, Robert John Historian
Preuss, Roger Painter, Writer
Quick, Birney MacNabb Painter, Instructor
Rose, Thomas Albert Sculptor
Rowan, Herman Painter, Educator
Rudquist, Jerry Jacob Painter, Educator
Sachs, Samuel, II Historian, Museum Director
Saltzman, William Painter, Sculptor
Scherer, Herbert Grover Librarian, Historian
Sheppard, Carl Dunkle Historian
Slettehaugh, Thomas Chester Printmaker, Educator
Somberg, Emilija O K Painter
Stearns, Robert Curator, Administrator
Stoller, John Chapman Dealer
Sussman, Bonnie K Dealer, Gallery Director
Torbert, Stephanie Birch Photographer, Educator
Verostko, Roman Joseph Educator, Historian
Walton, Florence Goodstein (Florence Goodstein-Shapiro) Painter, Historian
Wiener, Phyllis Ames Painter
Wolfe, Ann (Ann Wolfe Graubard) Sculptor
Youngquist, Jack Draftsman

Minnetonka
Lack, Richard Frederick Painter, Instructor

Moorhead
Laske, Lyle F Sculptor, Educator

Morris
Nellis, Jennifred Gene Sculpture

Nisswa
Smith, Paul Roland Painter, Educator

Red Wing
Biederman, Charles (Karel Joseph) Sculptor

Rochester
Gagnon, Charles Eugene Sculptor, Consultant

Rushford
Curmano, Billy Conceptual Artist, Sculptor

St Cloud
Ellingson, William John Educator, Printmaker
Petheo, Bela Francis Painter, Printmaker

St Paul
Beyer, Steven J Sculptor, Lecturer
Boese, Alvin William Collector
Caponi, Anthony Sculptor, Educator
Celender, Donald Dennis Historian, Conceptual Artist
Follett, Jean Frances Sculptor, Painter
Grey, Abby Weed Collector, Patron
Holman, Thomas S Curator, Historian

Kielkopf, James Robert Painter
Kristensen, Gail Marie Ceramist, Sculptor
Lasansky, Leonardo Draftsman, Printmaker
Leach, Frederick Darwin Painter, Historian
Lein, Malcolm Emil Administrator, Designer
Lupori, Peter John Educator, Sculptor
Michels, Eileen Manning Educator, Historian
Niemeyer, Arnold Matthew Collector, Patron
Nowytski, (Slavko) Sviatoslav Filmmaker, Photographer
Olson, Bettye Johnson Painter, Instructor
Ott, Jerry Painter
Price, Michael Benjamin Sculptor, Educator
Rahja, Virginia Helga Painter, Administrator
Starkweather-Nelson, Cynthia Louise Painter, Collage Artist
Toperzer, Thomas Raymond Educator, Painter
Tselos, Dimitri Theodore Historian, Writer

St Peter
Granlund, Paul Theodore Sculptor, Instructor
Groot, Candice Beth Ceramist
Palmgren, Donald Gene Painter, Photographer

White Bear Lake
Larkin, John E, Jr Collector, Patron

Winona
Murray, Floretta May Painter, Educator

Zumbrota
Lee, Margaret F Painter

MISSISSIPPI

Bay St Louis
Kimbrough, Sara Dodge Painter

Belzoni
Halbrook, Rita Robertshaw Painter, Printmaker
Kiker, Evelyn Coalson Painter, Instructor

Cleveland
Britt, Sam Glenn Educator, Painter
Norwood, Malcolm Mark Painter, Educator

Clinton
Cook, Stephen D Printmaker, Draftsman
Gore, Samuel Marshall Painter, Sculptor

Columbus
Ambrose, Charles Edward Painter, Educator
Dice, Elizabeth Jane Craftsman, Educator
Frank, David Ceramist, Educator
Nawrocki, Thomas Dennis Printmaker, Educator
Stringer, Mary Evelyn Educator, Historian
Summer, (Emily) Eugenia Painter
West, Clara Faye Johnson Painter, Conservator

Gulfport
Thames, Emmitt Eugene Painter

Hattiesburg

Baggett, William Carter, Jr Educator, Painter
Bowman, Jeff Ray Educator, Administrator

Jackson

Czarniecki, M J, III Museum Director, Photographer
Gold Star (William Myers Watkins III) Curator, Painter
Neal, Frank Wingfield Painter, Instructor
Wolfe, Mildred Nungester Painter, Designer

Meridian

O'Neal, Roland Lenard Illustrator, Graphic Artist

Oxford

Allen, Jere Hardy Painter, Educator
Gross, Charles Merrill Educator, Sculptor
Tettleton, Robert Lynn Painter, Educator

Silver City

Slaughter, Lurline Eddy Painter

Starkville

Scucchi, Robie (Peter), Jr Educator, Painter

Summit

Dawson, Bess Phipps Painter, Gallery Director

Tupelo

Francis, Jean Thickens Assemblage Artist, Printmaker
Francis, Madison Ke, Jr Sculptor, Printmaker

University

Wahlman, Maude Southwell Historian, Educator

MISSOURI

Ballwin

Addison, Byron Kent Painter, Educator

Bridgeton

Myers, Carole Ann Painter, Instructor

Cape Girardeau

Parker, James Varner Administrator, Designer

Charleston

Simmons, Julie Lutz Painter, Collage Artist

Chesterfield

Schultz, Saunders Sculptor
Severson, William Conrad Sculptor

Columbia

Bartlett, Donald Loring Sculptor, Educator
Berneche, Jerry Douglas Educator, Painter
Berry, William Augustus Educator, Graphic Artist
Bussabarger, Robert Franklin Sculptor, Painter
Cameron, Brooke Bulovsky Educator, Printmaker
Kabak, Robert Painter, Educator
Lahr, J(ohn) Stephen Painter, Educator
Larson, Sidney Painter, Conservator
McKinin, Lawrence Educator, Painter
Montminy, (Elizabeth) Tracy Muralist, Painter

Moulton, Rosalind Kimball Photographer, Collage Artist
Peckham, Nicholas Architect, Educator
Revington-Burdick, Betty, III Collector
Riley-Land, Sarah (Sarah Agnes Riley Land) Painter, Educator
Rugolo, Lawrence Screenprinter, Educator
Stack, Frank Huntington Painter, Printmaker
Townsend, Vera B Educator, Historian

Eldon

Orr, Joseph Charles Painter

Greenwood

Graham, Robert MacDonald, Jr Painter

Jefferson City

Parks, James Dallas Historian, Painter
Weaver, (John) Robert Painter, Printmaker

Joplin

Christensen, Val Alan Printmaker, Gallery Director

Kansas City

Bransby, Eric James Muralist, Educator
Brody, Myron Roy Sculptor, Administrator
Cadieux, Michael Eugene Educator, Painter
Carstenson, Cecil C Sculptor, Lecturer
Clare, Stewart Research Artist
Coe, Ralph Tracy Museum Director, Curator
Crist, William Gary Sculptor, Educator
Eaton, Thomas Newton Cartoonist, Illustrator
Ehrlich, George Historian
Emont-Scott, Deborah Curator
Estabrook, Reed Photographer, Educator
Falter, John Illustrator
Field, Lyman Administrator, Collector
Fowle, Geraldine Elizabeth Historian
Gates, Jay Rodney Curator, Educator
Goheen, Ellen Rozanne Curator, Historian
Hess, Stanley William Librarian
James, Frederic Painter
Lottes, John William Educator, Administrator
McKim, William Wind Printmaker, Painter
Marshall, James Duard Conservator, Painter
Morgan, Myra Jean Dealer
Reinhart, Margaret Emily Painter
Scott, Henry E, Jr Painter, Educator
Sickman, Laurence Chalfant Stevens Administrator, Historian
Stack, Michael Painter
Townsend, Marvin J Cartoonist, Illustrator
Walton, Donald William Writer, Lecturer
Younger, Dan Forrest Painter, Printmaker

Kirksville

Jorgenson, Dale Alfred Educator, Administrator

Kirkwood

Haynes, R (Richard Thomas) Painter, Illustrator
Reinhardt, Siegfried Gerhard Painter, Designer

Manchester

Brunell, Richard Howard Educator, Designer

Maryville

Hageman, Charles Lee Educator, Jeweler
Sunkel, Robert Cleveland Historian, Administrator

Ozark

Armstrong, Bill Howard Painter, Educator

Rogersville

Elkins, (E) Lane Educator, Ceramist

St Charles

Eckert, William Dean Painter, Historian
Moerschel, Chiara Painter

Ste Genevieve

Bowman, Dorothy (Louise) Painter, Printmaker

St James

Lacy, Robert Eugene Painter

St Joseph

Ray, Jim Museum Director

St Louis

Abid, Ann B Librarian
Bolas, Gerald Douglas Museum Director, Educator
Burke, James Donald Museum Director, Administrator
Burns, Timothy Joseph Gallery Director, Dealer
Crane, Michael Patrick Photographer, Performance Artist
Duhme, H Richard, Jr Sculptor, Educator
Engelhardt, Thomas Alexander Editorial Cartoonist
Fifield, Mary Educator
Geis, Milton Arthur Painter, Designer
Greenberg, Ronald K Dealer, Collector
Hicks, Leon Nathaniel Printmaker
Hilligoss, Martha M Librarian
Jones, Howard William Painter, Sculptor
Kagan, Andrew Aaron Historian, Critic
Kohn, William Roth Painter, Educator
Kornblum, Myrtle Painter, Printmaker
Krukowski, Lucian Painter, Educator
Kultermann, Udo Historian, Educator
Luray, J Printmaker, Designer
McGarrell, James Painter, Educator
May, Morton David Collector, Patron
Newman-Rice, Nancy Painter, Critic
Osver, Arthur Painter
Pettus, Jane Messick Painter
Quinn, William Painter, Printmaker
Raucher, Hava Painter, Printmaker
Rosen, Joan Fischman Painter
Schactman, Barry Robert Painter, Educator
Schweiss, Ruth Keller Sculptor, Designer
Seppa, Heikki Markus Metalsmith, Educator
Singer, Nancy Barkhouse Dealer
Smith, Helen M Illustrator, Painter
Smith, Robert Charles Designer, Educator
Taylor, Marie Sculptor
Teczar, Steven W Painter, Educator
Trova, Ernest Tino Sculptor, Painter
Walters, Sylvia Solochek Printmaker, Educator
Winfield, Rodney M Designer
Zonia, Dhimitri Painter, Printmaker

Sedalia

Freed, Douglass Lynn Painter, Educator

Springfield

Adams, Jay H Jeweler, Medalist
Albin, Edgar A Educator, Art Critic
Annis, Norman L Educator, Sculptor
Ettinger, Susi Steinitz Painter, Lecturer
Ivy, Gregory Dowler Painter
Kieferndorf, Frederick George Painter,
  Educator
Landwehr, William Charles Museum
  Director
Murphy, Dudley C Educator, Graphic
  Designer
Shuck, Kenneth Menaugh Museum
  Director, Painter
Thielen, Greg Glen Curator
Thompson, Wade Painter, Educator
Warren, Jacqueline Louise Painter,
  Educator

Webster Groves

Boccia, Edward Eugene Painter

MONTANA

Bigfork

Fellows, Fred Painter, Sculptor
Morgan, Darlene Painter
Shaner, (George) David Ceramist,
  Craftsman

Big Sky

Askevold, David Conceptual Artist,
  Instructor

Billings

Forbes, Donna Marie Museum Director
Haughey, James M Painter
Morrison, Robert Clifton Printmaker,
  Calligrapher
Olmsted, Suzanne M Photographer,
  Printmaker
Ralston, James Kenneth Painter,
  Illustrator
Steele, Benjamin Charles Painter,
  Educator
Whitson Draftsman, Collage Artist

Bozeman

Bashor, John W Educator, Painter
Bronson, Clark Everice Sculptor
Butterfield, Deborah Kay Sculptor,
  Educator
Helzer, Richard Brian Metalsmith,
  Educator
Shore, Stephen Photographer

Browning

Scriver, (Bob) Robert Macfie Sculptor

Cascade

Halko, Joe Sculptor, Painter

Dillon

Corr, James Donat Painter, Gallery
  Director

Gallatin Gateway

Ocepek, Lou (Louis David) Printmaker,
  Painter

Great Falls

Cordingley, Mary Bowles Painter
Stevenson, Branson Graves Painter,
  Printmaker

Helena

Johnson, Donald Marvin Craftsman,
  Silversmith

Missoula

Autio, (A) Rudy Ceramist, Educator
Codell, Julie Francia Historian, Educator
Hook, Walter Painter, Printmaker

Red Lodge

Lynde, Stan Cartoonist, Illustrator

Somers

Smith, Cecil Alden Painter, Sculptor

NEBRASKA

Crawford

Brown, Reynold Painter, Instructor

Culbertson

Dernovich, Donald Frederick Painter,
  Educator

Grand Island

Holoun, Harold Dean Painter, Sculptor

Kearney

Peterson, Larry D Painter, Educator

Lincoln

Collins, Howard F Historian
Eisentrager, James A Painter
Geske, Norman Albert Museum Director,
  Educator
Howard, Dan F Painter, Educator
Jacobshagen, N Keith, II Painter,
  Photographer
Lux, Gladys Marie Painter
Nelson, Jon Allen Curator, Historian
Neubert, George Walter Sculptor, Curator
Read, Dave (David Dolloff)
  Photographer, Educator
Ross, Douglas Allan Sculptor, Instructor
Rowan, (C) Patrick Sculptor, Educator
Seyler, David W Craftsman, Educator
Spence, Robert Historian
Wallace, Elizabeth S Administrator,
  Sculptor
Worth, Peter John Sculptor, Historian

Omaha

Anderson, Kenneth Edmund Sculptor,
  Educator
Bartek, Tom Painter, Printmaker
Bradshaw, Lawrence James Educator,
  Painter
Buchanan, Sidney Arnold Educator,
  Sculptor
Cracker Jack Kid (Charles D Welch)
  Printmaker, Graphic Artist
Day, Gary Lewis Printmaker, Painter
Doll, Donald Arthur Educator,
  Photographer
Duncan, Harry Alvin Printer, Designer
Ferguson, Larry Scott Photographer,
  Curator
Hill, Peter Painter, Educator
Hunt, David Curtis Museum Director,
  Curator
Kinsel, Michael Leslie Museum Director
Lock, Earl Wayne Painter, Gallery
  Director
Lubbers, Leland Eugene Sculptor,
  Educator
Majeski, Thomas H Printmaker, Educator
Robert, Henry Flood, Jr Museum
  Director
Sturges, Hollister Curator, Historian

NEVADA

Boulder City

Burk, A Darlene Dealer, Collector

Gardnerville

Lawrence, James A Painter, Photographer

Las Vegas

Adams, James Frederick Collector, Patron
Beckmann, Robert Owen Painter,
  Muralist
Brown, Robert (Earl) Photographer,
  Educator
Holder, Tom Painter
Lesnick, Stephen William Painter,
  Instructor
Marchese, Patricia Davis Administrator,
  Consultant
Misch, Allene K Painter
Reber, Mick Sculptor, Painter
Rozzi (James A) Painter, Sculptor

Reno

Ball, Lyle V Painter, Illustrator
Jacobson, Yolande (Mrs J Craig
  Sheppard) Sculptor
Unterseher, Chris Christian Sculptor

NEW HAMPSHIRE

Ashland

Newsom, Barbara Ylvisaker
  Administrator, Writer

Bennington

Willis, Sidney F Painter

Campton

Waters, Herbert (Ogden) Printmaker,
  Educator

Center Conway

Jordan, Robert Painter, Educator

Concord

Barrett, Thomas R Painter, Instructor
Chandler, John William Painter, Educator
Jandeni (Jean-Denis Cruchet) Sculptor,
  Painter
Mancuso, Leni Painter, Instructor
Yanoff, Arthur (Samuel) Painter

Dover

Abeles, Sigmund Printmaker, Sculptor

Dublin

James, Christopher P Photographer
Tuckerman, Jane Bayard Photographer,
  Educator

Durham

Hatch, John W Painter, Educator
McConnell, Michael Patrick Sculptor
Zabarsky, Melvin Joel Painter, Educator

Exeter

Lyford, Cabot Sculptor, Painter

Francestown

Milton, Peter Winslow Printmaker

Goffstown

Williams, Gerald Potter, Editor

Hancock

Dombek, Blanche M Sculptor

Hanover

Boghosian, Varujan Sculptor, Educator
Jacobus, John M Educator, Historian
Lathrop, Churchill Pierce Historian
Teitz, Richard Stuart Museum Director, Historian

Henniker

Lindquist, Mark Sculptor

Hillsboro

Jones, Elizabeth Orton Illustrator, Writer

Jackson

Beal, Mack Sculptor

Keene

Whitney, Richard Wheeler Painter

Kingston

Oakes, William Larry Illustrator, Educator

Lyme

Schmeckebier, Laurence E Historian, Sculptor

Manchester

Doty, Robert McIntyre Administrator
Eshoo, Robert Painter
Sears, Stanton Gray Painter, Sculptor

Marlborough

Harris, Paul Stewart Curator, Museum Director

Meredith

Olitski, Jules Painter, Sculptor

Nashua

Bloom, Hyman Painter
Parker, Will (William Crawford) Draftsman, Educator

New London

dePaola, Tomie Illustrator, Designer

Northwood

Cenci, Silvana Sculptor

Portsmouth

Harris, Conley Painter, Instructor

Raymond

Beardsley, Barbara H Conservator

Rye

Labrie, Rose Painter, Writer

Somersworth

Balderacchi, Arthur Eugene Sculptor, Administrator

Warner

Nemec, Nancy Printmaker

Westmoreland

Isaak, Nicholas, Jr Painter, Conservator

NEW JERSEY

Asbury

Anderson, John S Sculptor
Konrad, Adolf Ferdinand Painter

Asbury Park

Cleary, Fritz Sculptor, Critic

Atlantic City

Frudakis, Anthony Sculptor
Harris, Marian D Painter
Palley, Reese Dealer
Robbins, Hulda D Painter, Printmaker

Atlantic Highlands

Voorhees, Donald Edward Painter, Lithographer

Barnegat Light

Diehl, Sevilla S Painter
Rothman, Sidney Gallery Director, Critic

Basking Ridge

Cliver, Kendra-Jean (Kendra-Jean Cliver Krienke) Dealer, Painter
Krienke, Douglas Elliot Dealer, Collector

Bay Head

Johnson, Rodell C Painter, Animator

Bayonne

Gary, Jan (Mrs William D Gorman) Painter, Printmaker
Gorman, William D Painter, Graphic Artist

Beach Haven

Martell, Barbara Bentley Painter

Belleville

Yudin, Carol Printmaker, Painter

Belvidere

Kulicke, Robert M Painter, Craftsman

Berkeley Heights

Lorentz, Pauline Painter, Instructor

Blairstown

Ayers, Carol Lee Painter, Gallery Director
Wilson, Ben Painter, Lecturer

Bloomfield

Anderson, Robert Raymond Painter, Writer
Schwacha, George Painter

Bordentown

Barker, Al C Painter, Printmaker

Brick

Malpass, Michael Allen Sculptor, Educator
Smart, Wini Painter, Dealer

Brigantine

Pierotti, John Cartoonist

Caldwell

Lewis, Nat Brush Painter, Instructor
Mueller, M Gerardine Calligrapher, Stained Glass Artist
Phillips, Robert J Filmmaker, Educator

Califon

Burger, W Carl Educator, Painter
Clipsham, Jacqueline Ann Ceramist, Educator
Sandol, Maynard Painter

Camden

Hoffman, William McKinley, Jr Painter, Educator
Spohn, Kathryn Jo Painter, Educator
Steel, Virginia Oberlin Gallery Director, Curator

Cedar Grove

Singer, Esther Forman Painter, Critic

Chatham

Lindroth, Linda Photographer, Printmaker
Manhold, John Henry Sculptor

Cherry Hill

Conrad, George Educator, Printmaker
Killeen, Melissa Helen Dealer, Gallery Director

Cinnaminson

Kraus, (Ersilia) Zili Sculptor, Painter

Clarksburg

Arias-Misson, Alain Visual Poet, Graphic Artist

Cliffside Park

LaMarca, Howard J Designer, Educator

Clifton

Kostecka, Gloria Painter
Luczun, Robert Sculptor, Painter
Rossi, Joseph O Painter, Instructor

Closter

Jovine, Marcel Medalist, Sculptor
Zakin, Mikhail Sculptor, Educator

Collingswood

Folkus, Dan (Daniel Alan Fredrickson) Designer, Illustrator

Colts Neck

Schweitzer, Gertrude Painter, Sculptor

Cranford

Dawley, Joseph William Painter, Dealer

Cresskill

Baker, Dina Gustin Painter
Mayen, Paul Designer
Radoczy, Albert Painter

Demarest

Ilowitz, Theodora Painter, Printmaker
Racz, Andre Painter, Printmaker

Denville

Johnson, Avery Fischer Painter

Dover

Kearns, James Joseph Sculptor, Painter

East Brunswick

Bloom, Donald S Painter
Bradshaw, Robert George Painter, Educator
Cantor, Robert Lloyd Educator, Designer

Edgewater

Case, Elizabeth Painter, Writer

Edison

Waterhouse, Charles Howard Illustrator, Painter

Elizabeth

Palaia, Franc (Dominic) Painter, Photographer
Young, Frances Elizabeth Librarian

Emerson

Stark, Bruce Gunsten Cartoonist, Illustrator

Englewood

Anuszkiewicz, Richard Joseph Painter
Casarella, Edmond Sculptor, Printmaker
Grushkin, Philip Designer, Calligrapher
Romano, Clare Camille Printmaker, Painter
Ross, John T Printmaker, Educator
WalkingStick, Kay Painter

Englewood Cliffs

Liao (Shiou-Ping Liao) Painter, Printmaker

Fair Lawn

Birkin, Morton Painter
Freeman, Sara Painter, Lecturer

Flanders

Margoulies, Berta (Berta Margoulies O'Hare) Sculptor, Educator

Ft Lee

Creatore, Mary-Alice Sumie Artist, Painter
Grosz, Franz Joseph Painter, Designer
Ortlip, Paul Daniel Painter

Freehold

Graupe-Pillard, Grace Painter, Instructor

Glassboro

Wasserman, Burton Painter, Printmaker

Glen Gardner

Kuehn, Gary Sculptor, Graphic Artist

Glen Ridge

Kato, Kay Cartoonist
Konopka, Joseph Painter

Hackensack

Sznajderman, Marius S Painter, Printmaker

Haddonfield

Byrd, Robert John Illustrator, Instructor
Hamilton, Lydia Painter

Hasbrouck Heights

Perham, Roy Gates Painter

Hazlet

Temes, Mortimer (Robert) Cartoonist, Designer

Highland Park

Naar, Harry I Painter, Educator

Hightstown

Lee-Smith, Hughie Painter, Instructor
Rivera, Frank Painter

Hillside

Reale, Nicholas Albert Painter, Instructor

Hoboken

Homitzky, Peter Painter
Miller, George Conceptual Artist, Writer
Turner, Norman Huntington Painter, Writer
Wallach, Alan Critic, Historian

Hopewell

Van Tongeren, Herk Sculptor

Irvington

Josimovich, George Painter, Designer
Nagengast, William Joseph Painter, Designer

Iselin

Tice, George Andrew Photographer, Author

Island Heights

English, John Arbogast Painter

Jamesburg

Schaffer, Rose Painter, Lecturer

Jersey City

Barrell, Bill Painter, Collector
Beauchamp, George Collage Artist, Painter
Craft, Douglas D Painter, Educator
Cummings, David William Painter
Grundy, J(ohn Owen) Patron, Writer
Harms, Elizabeth Painter
Harrison, Tony Painter, Educator
Jones, Ben Painter, Sculptor
Magnan, Oscar Gustav Painter, Sculptor
Mazzone, Domenico Sculptor, Painter
Mount, Marshall Ward Historian, Administrator
Mount, Ward Painter, Sculptor
Selig, J Daniel Museum Director, Curator
Van Alstine, John Richard Sculptor
Yost, Erma Martin Painter, Instructor
Yost, Leon C Photographer
Zahourek, Jon Gail Painter, Sculptor

Kearny

White, Stuart James Sculptor, Assemblage Artist

Keasbey

Sosnowitz, Henry Abram Collector, Patron

Kendall Park

Sway, Albert Painter, Etcher

Kenilworth

Shor, Bernice Abramowitz Editor

Kingston

Cook, Peter (Geoffrey) Painter

Kinnelon

Whyte, Raymond A Painter

Lakewood

Burgues, Irving Carl Sculptor, Lecturer
Clinedinst, Katherine Parsons Painter, Lecturer
Hopper, Marianne Seward Painter

Lebanon

Neal, Reginald H Painter, Printmaker

Leonardo

De Lue, Donald Sculptor

Leonia

Birmelin, A Robert Painter, Draftsman
Cellini, Joseph Illustrator
Colman, Virginia O'Connell Sculptor, Designer
Dickerson, Daniel Jay Painter, Educator
Friedensohn, Elias Painter, Sculptor
Johnson, Selina (Tetzlaff) Museologist, Historian
Soorikian, Diana Tashjian Painter

Little Silver

Clark, Roberta Carter Illustrator, Painter
Hart, Betty Miller Painter, Graphic Artist

Livingston

Bearman, Jane Ruth Painter, Illustrator
Greenwald, Pat Printmaker, Painter

Madison

Galles, Arie Alexander Painter, Educator
Henry, Sara Lynn Historian, Critic

Mahwah

Peck, Judith Sculptor, Educator

Maplewood

Dee, Leo Joseph Painter
Joffe, Bertha Designer
Nardone, Vincent Joseph Painter, Instructor
Price, Joan Webster Environmental Artist, Sculptor
Rose, Roslyn Printmaker, Instructor

Margate

Myers, Legh Sculptor

Mendham

Hobbie, Lucille Painter, Lithographer
Notaro, Anthony Sculptor

Milford

Carter, Clarence Holbrook Painter, Designer

Monmouth Beach

Domareki, Joseph Theodore Painter, Sculptor

Monmouth Junction

Hardaway, Pearl (Pearl Hardaway Reese) Painter

Montclair

Day, Worden Sculptor, Printmaker
De Leeuw, Leon Painter, Sculptor
Koenig, Robert J Museum Director
Ludwig, Allan I Photographer, Historian
Master-Karnik, Paul Joseph Museum Director, Critic
Maurice, E(leanor) Ingersoll Painter, Designer
Roth, Jack (Rodney) Painter
Schnitzer, Klaus A Photographer

Moorestown

Eisenstat, Benjamin Painter, Illustrator

Morris Plains

Ferris, (Carlisle) Keith Illustrator, Painter

Morristown

Krugman, Irene Sculptor

Mountainside

Devlin, Harry Illustrator, Painter

Newark

Auth, Susan Handler Curator, Educator
Baretski, Charles Allan Art Librarian, Art Historian
Bartle, Dorothy Budd Curator, Lecturer
Burns, G Joan Librarian
Dane, William Jerald Librarian
Maldjian, Vartavar B Painter, Weaver
Miller, Samuel Clifford Museum Director
Reynolds, Valrae Curator
Watkins, Eileen Frances Critic

New Brunswick

Cate, Phillip Dennis Historian, Director
Goodyear, John L Painter, Kinetic Artist
Olin, Ferris Librarian, Historian
Ortiz, Rafael Montanez Sculptor, Educator

NEW JERSEY (cont)
Segal, George Sculptor
Stroud, Peter Anthony Painter, Educator
Stubblebine, James Harvey Historian

New Vernon
Bross, Albert L, Jr Painter

North Plainfield
Haller, Emanuel Painter, Printmaker

Nutley
Carlin, James Painter
Westfall, Carol D Sculptor, Educator

Oakland
Rodman, Selden Writer, Collector
Sandor, Josephine (Beardsley) Sculptor

Oradell
Schaefer, Gail Sculptor

Orange
Damron, John Clarence Painter,
    Illustrator

Paramus
Jacobs, Helen Nichols Painter

Park Ridge
De Pol, John Wood Engraver, Designer

Paterson
Heusser, Eleanore Elizabeth (Eleanor
    Heusser Ferholt) Painter
Tiffany, Marguerite Bristol Painter,
    Lecturer

Perth Amboy
Hari, Kenneth Painter, Printmaker

Phillipsburg
Campanelli, Dan Painter
Campanelli, Pauline Eble Painter
Kozlow, Sigmund Painter, Instructor

Pitman
Ottiano, John William Jeweler, Sculptor

Pittstown
Marsh, Anne Steele Painter, Printmaker

Plainfield
Helfond, Riva Painter, Printmaker

Pluckemin
Hart, Morgan Drake Painter, Instructor

Pompton Plains
Krushenick, John Painter, Museum
    Director

Princeton
Brodsky, Judith Kapstein Printmaker,
    Educator
Brown, Gwyneth King Painter
Brown, Joseph Sculptor, Educator
Bunnell, Peter Curtis Educator, Curator
George, Thomas Painter, Draftsman
Graves, Michael Architect, Educator
Greenbaum, Dorothea Schwarcz Sculptor,
    Graphic Artist
Heckscher, William Sebastian Historian
Hunter, Sam Historian
Idaherma (Idaherma Williams)
    Printmaker, Painter
Jones, Frances Follin Curator
Kelleher, Patrick Joseph Historian,
    Museologist
Lavin, Irving Historian
Lavin, Marilyn Aronberg Educator,
    Historian

Lee, Rensselaer Wright Historian,
    Educator
McVicker, Charles Taggart Illustrator,
    Instructor
Morales, Armando Painter, Printmaker
Ring, Edward A Publisher, Collector
Rosenbaum, Allen Museum Director
Savage, Naomi Photographer
Schmidt, Mary Morris Librarian
Teller, Jane (Simon) Sculptor
Thompson, Dorothy Burr Educator,
    Lecturer
Weitzmann, Kurt Educator, Historian

Princeton Junction
Greenwald, Alice (Alice Marian
    Greenwald-Ward) Museum Director,
    Lecturer

Ramsey
Hertzberg, Rose Painter, Collage Artist

Randolph
Sarsony, Robert Painter, Printmaker

Red Bank
McIlvain, Douglas Lee Educator, Sculptor
McIlvain, Frances H Painter, Instructor

Ridgefield Park
Botto, Richard Alfred Painter, Instructor

Ridgewood
Burns, Paul Callan Painter, Instructor
Lane, Marion Jean Arrons Painter,
    Instructor
Whitmore, Lenore K Painter

Ringwood
Barbour, Arthur J Painter, Writer

River Edge
Friedberg, Ray E (Rachel) Painter,
    Instructor

Rocky Hill
Bannard, Walter Darby Painter, Art
    Writer

Roosevelt
Landau, Jacob Painter, Printmaker
Martin, Stefan Printmaker, Collage Artist
Prestopino, Gregorio Painter

Roseland
Schonwalter, Jean Frances Painter,
    Sculptor

Rutherford
Laurer, Robert A Educator, Museum
    Director
Petrie, Ferdinand Ralph Painter,
    Illustrator

Saddle Brook
Kaye, Mildred Elaine Printmaker,
    Instructor

Secaucus
McIntosh, Harrison Edward Ceramist,
    Designer

Short Hills
Broder, Patricia Janis Historian, Writer
San Soucie, Patricia Molm Painter,
    Instructor

Somerset
Spector, Jack J Historian, Educator
Ten Painter
Zuccarelli, Frank Edward Painter,
    Instructor

South Orange
De Foix-Crenascol, Louis Historian,
    Consultant
Gelman, Milton Collector
Lipton, Barbara B Writer, Curator
Margulies, Herman Painter
Messina, Joseph R Painter
Targan, Judy Printmaker, Designer
Triano, Anthony Thomas Painter,
    Educator

Springfield
Frank, Helen (Goodzeit) Painter,
    Printmaker

Stockholm
Jauss, Anne Marie Painter, Illustrator

Stockton
Farnham, Alexander Painter, Writer
Schoenherr, John Carl Painter, Illustrator

Succasunna
Solomon, Hyde Painter

Summit
Davis, Gerald Vivian Painter
Palmer, Fred Loren Collector, Patron
Rousseau, Irene Victoria Sculptor, Writer

Teaneck
Barry, Robert Thomas Conceptual Artist
Glickman, Arthur Sculptor
Indick, Janet Sculptor
Noa, Florence Printmaker, Educator
Schrero, Ruth Lieberman Sculptor,
    Painter
Weill, Erna Sculptor, Instructor

Tenafly
Adelman, Bunny Sculptor
Elliot, John Theodore Painter, Illustrator
Price, George Cartoonist
Thompson, Lynn P Painter, Photographer

Tinton Falls
St Tamara (Tamara Kolba) Painter,
    Printmaker

Trenton
Brooks, Wendell T Printmaker, Educator
Buki, Zoltan Curator, Administrator
Cummins, Karen Gasco Administrator,
    Museologist
Goldstein, Howard Painter, Educator
Greco, Frank Painter
Lehman, Mark Ammon Educator,
    Sculptor
Roebling, Mary G Collector, Patron
Sloshberg, Leah Phyfer Museum Director

Union
Bailin, Hella Painter

Upper Montclair
Beerman, Miraim K (Miriam
    Beerman-Jaffe) Painter
Chapman, (M) Anne Sculptor, Educator
Coes, Kent Day Painter, Designer
Healy, Deborah Ann Illustrator, Educator
Kawecki, Jean Mary Sculptor, Gallery
    Director
Lay, Patricia Anne Sculptor
McQuillan, Frances Painter, Instructor

Verona

Ayaso, Manuel Painter, Sculptor

Villas

Lynch, Gerald Francis Sculptor,
Draftsman

Watchung

Schwartz, Lillian (Feldman) Filmmaker,
Sculptor

Wayne

Barnwell, John L Painter
De Nike, Michael Nicholas Sculptor
Einreinhofer, Nancy Anne Curator,
Museum Director
Paris, Lucille M Painter, Printmaker

Weehawken

Churchill, Diane Painter, Collage Artist
Samburg, Grace (Blanche) Painter,
Lithographer

Westfield

Becker, Natalie Rose Painter
Devine, William Charles Dealer, Collector
Klinghoffer, Shirley Sculptor

West Orange

Hunter, Graham Cartoonist
Krieger, Ruth M Painter, Printmaker
Schreiber, Eileen Sher Painter,
Printmaker
Yanow, Rhoda Mae Painter, Illustrator

Wharton

Bermingham, John C Painter

Wildwood Crest

Dougherty, Ray (Raymond Edward)
Painter, Instructor

Williamstown

Murashima, Kumiko Educator, Designer
Phillips, James M Museum Director,
Collector

Willingboro

Forrest, Christopher Patrick Printmaker,
Painter

Windsor Township

Goreleigh, Rex Painter, Printmaker

Wood-Ridge

Lynds, C (Clyde William) Sculptor,
Painter
Stevens, Edward John, Jr Painter,
Director

Wyckoff

Carpenter, Ethel Painter

NEW MEXICO

Abiquiu

O'Keeffe, Georgia Painter

Alamogordo

Stevens, William Ansel, Sr Painter,
Cartoonist

Albuquerque

Abdalla, Nick Painter, Educator
Abrams, Jane Eldora Printmaker, Painter
Adams, Clinton Lithographer, Historian
Anderson, Sally J Painter, Printmaker
Antreasian, Garo Zareh Painter,
Lithographer
App, Timothy Painter, Educator
Barrow, Thomas Francis Photographer,
Instructor
Black, Frederick (Edward) Painter
Booth, Judith Gayle Administrator,
Curator
Brody, Jacob Jerome Museum Director,
Educator
Bryant, Edward Albert Museum Director,
Historian
Chapian, Grieg Hovsep Painter,
Conservator
Chavez, Joseph Arnold Sculptor,
Instructor
Chethlahe (David Chethlahe Paladin)
Painter, Designer
Clancy, Patrick Video Artist
Hahn, Betty Photographer, Educator
Hammersley, Frederick Painter
Hardin, Helen Painter
Harrison, Pat (Broeder) Painter, Muralist
Haut, Claire (Joan) Painter, Graphic
Artist
Hurley, Wilson Painter
Jones, Norma L Painter
Karp, Aaron S Painter
Kerr, James Wilfrid Painter, Conceptual
Artist
La Fon, Julia Anna Painter, Craftsman
Landis, Ellen Jamie Curator, Historian
Long, Frank Weathers Sculptor, Jeweler
Mabry, Jane Painter, Dealer
McCulloch, Frank E Painter, Printmaker
McIlroy, Carol J Painter, Dealer
Monongye, Preston Lee Silversmith,
Printmaker
Moyers, William Painter, Sculptor
Nadler, Harry Painter, Educator
Nelson, Mary Carroll Writer, Painter
Noggle, Anne Photographer, Educator
Parrish, Jean Painter
Ramirez, Joel Tito Calligrapher,
Illustrator
Reed, Michael Arthur Writer, Editor
Rippel, M (Morris Conrad) Painter
Rise, John Ernest Painter
Rivard, J B(ernard) Printmaker, Painter
Robb, Peggy Hight Painter
Sabo, Betty Jean Painter, Dealer
Salamone, Gladys L Painter
Saville, Ken Sculptor, Craftsman
Skinner, Elsa Kells Illustrator, Painter
Slaymaker, Martha Painter, Printmaker
Smith, Sam Painter, Educator
Sommers, John Printmaker, Educator
Sowers, Miriam R Painter
Steider, Doris (Mrs C B McCampbell)
Painter, Sculptor
Sussman, Arthur Painter
Thomason, Tom William Jeweler,
Goldsmith
Thompson, Tamara Assemblage Artist,
Collage Artist
Townsend, (Alvin) Neal Educator,
Craftsman
Truby, Betsy Kirby Painter, Illustrator
Vega, Edward Sculptor, Educator
Volkin, Hilda Appel Printmaker, Painter
Walters, Billie Ceramist
Weber, Jan Painter
Westlund, Harry E Publisher, Dealer
Widmer, Gwen Ellen Photographer,
Educator
Wilmeth, Ernest, II Painter, Sculptor
Witkin, Joel-Peter Photographer
Young, Nancy J(eanne) Printmaker,
Graphic Artist

Carlsbad

Johanningmeier, Robert Alan Painter,
Writer

Corrales

Harroun, Dorothy Sumner Painter,
Instructor
Ingram, Jerry Cleman Painter, Designer
Townsend, Storm D Sculptor
Wright, Paul Morris Sculptor, Painter

Coyote

Johnson, Douglas Walter Painter,
Printmaker

Dulce

Brycelea, Clifford Painter, Printmaker

El Prado

Boughton, William Harrison Painter,
Educator

Espanola

Medicine Flower, Grace Potter
Naranjo, Michael Alfred Sculptor

Farmington

Farm, Gerald E Painter

Gallup

Guadagnoli, Nello T Dealer
Ha-So-De (Narciso Abeyta) Illustrator,
Painter

Glenwood

Howard, Cecil Ray Painter, Sculptor

Glorieta

Greeley, Charles Matthew Painter,
Instructor

Grants

Lowney, Bruce Stark Painter, Printmaker

Hobbs

Garey, Pat Draftsman, Painter

Lamy

Martin, Agnes Bernice Painter

Las Cruces

Catterall, John Edward Painter, Educator
Fidler, Spencer D Printmaker
Guzevich-Sommers, Kreszenz (Cynthia)
Painter, Instructor
Harmon, Barbara Sayre Painter,
Children's Book Illustrator
Joost-Gaugier, Christiane L
Administrator, Historian
Moffitt, John Francis Historian, Painter
Sherman, Lenore (Walton) Painter, Writer
Smith, Jo-an Designer, Jeweler

Los Alamos

Noerdlinger, Janau Nau Painter,
Photographer

Mesilla Park

Hauser, Alonzo Painter, Sculptor

Pena Blanca

Lovato, Charles Fredric Printmaker,
Craftsman

Portales

Gikas, Christopher Educator, Stained
Glass Artist
Hamlett, Dale Edward Educator, Painter

Quemado

McGrew, Ralph Brownell Painter,
Draftsman

Roswell

Du Jardin, Gussie Painter, Printmaker
Ebie, William Dennis Administrator, Painter
Kawa, Florence Kathryn Painter
Ott, Wendell Lorenz Museum Director, Painter
Schooley, Elmer Wayne Painter, Educator
Vogel, Joseph Painter, Printmaker
Wiggins, Bill Painter
Wiggins, Walton Wray Writer, Photographer

Ruidoso

Snidow, Gordon E Painter, Sculptor

Ruidoso Downs

Knapp, Tom Sculptor, Painter

San Cristobal

Gersh, Bill Painter, Sculptor

Sandia Park

McNulty, Kneeland Curator, Writer

San Juan Pueblo

Namingha, Dan Painter, Printmaker

San Lorenzo

Renner, Eric Painter, Photographer

San Patricio

Hurd, Peter Painter, Writer
Rogers, Peter Wilfrid Painter
Wyeth, Henriette (Mrs Peter Hurd) Painter

Santa Fe

Ahvakana, Ulaaq (Lawrence Reynold) Sculptor, Glass Blower
Allen, Edda Lynne Painter, Art Dealer
Altenbernd, Richard August Sculptor
Anderson, David Paul Sculptor
Bacigalupa, Andrea Designer, Painter
Bendell, Marilyn Painter, Instructor
Bentley, Claude Painter, Muralist
Berg, Tom Painter
Boylan, John Lewis Painter, Printmaker
Bradbury, Ellen A Curator, Administrator
Bradley, David P(aul) Painter, Sculptor
Burgess, Joseph James, Jr Painter, Educator
Caponigro, Paul Photographer
Chappell, Walter (Landon) Photographer, Curator
Clift, William Brooks Photographer
Cohoe, Grey Printmaker, Painter
Conley, Zeb Bristol, Jr Collector, Gallery Director
Dailey, Chuck (Charles Andrew) Museologist, Painter
Dillingham, Rick (James Richard), II Ceramist, Dealer
Ellis, Fremont F Painter
Ettenberg, Franklin Joseph Painter, Draftsman
Fincher, John H Painter
Fox, Lincoln H Sculptor
Gobin, Henry (Delano) Director, Painter
Gross, Earl Painter, Lecturer
Hanbury, Una Sculptor
Henrickson, Paul Robert Painter, Writer
Hill, Megan Lloyd Painter, Dealer
Hotvedt, Kris J Printmaker
Houser, Allan C Sculptor, Painter
Humphrey, Donald Gray Curator
Hunter, Meridith Art Dealer, Sculptor
Husebye, Terry L Photographer
Jacob, Ned Painter, Sculptor
Johnson, Harvey William Painter
Johnson, James Ralph Painter, Writer

Keener, Anna Elizabeth Painter, Printmaker
Kramer, James Painter
Latham, Barbara Painter, Illustrator
Lefranc, Margaret (Margaret Lefranc Schoonover) Painter, Illustrator
Leon, Ralph Bernard Painter, Illustrator
Lippincott, Janet Painter
Lomahaftewa, Linda (Linda Joyce Slock) Painter, Instructor
Longley, Bernique Painter, Sculptor
Lovell, Tom Painter, Illustrator
Moses, Forrest (Lee), Jr Painter
Naumer, Helmuth Painter
New, Lloyd H Administrator, Designer
Newhall, Beaumont Photographer, Educator
Niblett, Gary Lawrence Painter
Nieto, John W Painter, Sculptor
Pardington, Ralph Arthur Ceramist, Sculptor
Porter, Eliot Furness Photographer, Writer
Rubenstein, Meridel Photographer
Running Rabbit Painter, Printmaker
Ruthling, Ford Painter, Printmaker
Seth, Laurel Dealer
Shepherd, William Fritz Painter
Sisson, Laurence P Painter
Sprang, Elizabeth Painter, Lithographer
Steinke, Bettina Painter
Stevens, Jacquie (Jaqueline Lauren) Ceramist, Instructor
Thwaites, Charles Winstanley Painter, Muralist
Weber, Jean M Museum Director, Administrator
Wells, Alisa Photographer
Wright, Donald Sculptor, Goldsmith
Yates, Steven A Photographer, Curator

Silver City

Humphrey, S L Painter, Illustrator
McCray, Dorothy M Printmaker, Painter

Taos

Annus, John Augustus Painter
Bareiss, Philip C Art Dealer, Collector
Barsano, Ron (Ronald James) Painter, Printmaker
Bell, Larry Stuart Sculptor
Boyer, Jack K Museum Director, Curator
Catusco, Louis Painter, Sculptor
Daughters, Robert A Painter, Printmaker
Egri, Ted Sculptor, Painter
Fels, C P Painter, Writer
Gorman, R C Painter, Dealer
Harmon, Cliff Franklin Painter
Kloss, Gene (Alice Geneva Glasier) Etcher, Painter
Mandelman, Beatrice M Painter
Manzo, Anthony Joseph Painter, Instructor
Pogzeba, Wolfgang H Painter, Sculptor
Price, Kenneth Printmaker, Sculptor
Ray, Robert (Donald) Painter, Sculptor
Reed, Doel Painter, Printmaker
Richards, Tally Dealer, Writer
Robles, Julian Painter, Sculptor
Sanchez, Mary Lowe (Eliza) Dealer, Collector
Scott, Jonathan Painter
Simpson, Lee Painter
Vigil, Veloy Joseph Painter, Printmaker
Vinella, Ray (Raimondo John) Painter

Tijeras

Sweet, Mary (French) Painter
Warder, William Painter, Writer

NEW YORK

Accord

Massie, Lorna Printmaker, Graphic Artist

Albany

Callner, Richard Painter, Educator
Chambers, Park A, Jr Sculptor, Painter
Frinta, Mojmir Svatopluk Historian, Educator
Liddle, Nancy Hyatt Administrator, Gallery Director
Rosen, Hy (Hyman Joseph) Cartoonist, Sculptor
Warren, Betty Painter, Instructor

Albertson

Madsen, Viggo Holm Printmaker, Craftsman

Alfred

Randall, Theodore A Sculptor, Educator

Alfred Station

Higby, (Donald) Wayne Painter, Sculptor
Turner, Robert Chapman Ceramist, Educator

Almond

Phelan, Linn Lovejoy Designer

Altamont

Cowley, Edward P Painter, Educator

Amagansett

Durham, William Painter, Printmaker
Gwathmey, Robert Painter
Opper, John Painter

Amenia

Hale, Nathan Cabot Sculptor, Writer

Amityville

Rogers, John Painter

Angola

Haug, Donald Raymond Painter

Annandale-on-Hudson

Phillips, Matt Painter, Educator

Ardsley

Lysun, Gregory Painter, Restorer

Ardsley-on-Hudson

Griggs, Maitland Lee Collector

Armonk

Gressel, Michael L Sculptor

Astoria

Haff, Barbara J E Painter, Instructor

Auburn

Long, Walter Kinscella Museum Director, Painter

Aurora

Roberts, William Edward Painter, Educator

Babylon

Eckelberry, Don Richard Painter
Haley, Priscilla J Painter, Printmaker

Baldwin

Carter, Granville W Sculptor, Instructor
Shaw, Karen Painter

Bardonia

LaChapelle, Joseph Robert Sculptor, Educator

Barrytown

Higgins, Dick Designer, Printmaker

Bay Shore

Ciuca, Eugen Sculptor, Painter

Bayside

Goldstein, Milton Printmaker, Educator
Kotzky, Alex Sylvester Cartoonist
Niemann, Edmund E Painter, Sculptor

Bearsville

Pantell, Richard Keith Painter, Printmaker
Wickiser, Ralph Lewanda Administrator, Painter

Bedford

Canfield, Jane (White) Sculptor
Tyler, Kenneth Eugene Print Publisher, Printmaker
Weinman, Robert Alexander Sculptor

Bedford Hills

Brussel-Smith, Bernard Printmaker
Carter, Bernard Shirley Painter, Instructor
Goetz, Edith Jean Painter, Instructor
Goetz, Richard Vernon Painter, Instructor

Binghamton

Ippolito, Angelo Painter, Educator
Lindsay, Kenneth C Historian, Writer
Preziosi, Donald A Historian, Critic
Schwartz, Aubrey E Printmaker, Sculptor
Stein, Roger Breed Historian, Educator
Truex, Duane Philip Museum Director, Consultant
Wilson, Edward N Sculptor, Educator

Bloomington

Ruffing, Anne Elizabeth Painter

Brainard

Johnsen, May Anne Painter

Brewster

Rosenberg, Bernard Publisher, Book Dealer

Briarcliff Manor

Adler, Myril Printmaker, Painter
Meadmore, Clement L Sculptor

Bridgehampton

Benson, Elaine K G Art Dealer, Writer
Newbill, Al Painter
Norquist, Ryl Art Dealer
Varga, Margit Painter, Writer
Vicente, Esteban Painter

Brockport

Markusen, Thomas Roy Craftsman, Metalsmith
Marx, Robert Ernst Painter, Printmaker
Mirko Collector, Painter

Bronx

Baron, Hannelore Collage Artist
Berg, Siri Painter, Instructor
Bott, Patricia Allen Painter, Art Critic
Brody, Ruth Painter, Printmaker
Buonagurio, Edgar R Painter, Muralist
Buonagurio, Toby Lee Sculptor
Crimi, Alfred D Painter, Instructor
Davis, Walter Lewis Painter, Collage Artist
Jaffe, Irma B Historian, Educator
Judge, Mary Frances Painter

Kassoy, Bernard Painter, Printmaker
Kassoy, Hortense Sculptor, Painter
Kaye, George Painter, Instructor
Keveson, Florence Painter, Illustrator
Olshan, Bernard Painter, Printmaker
Waterston, Harry Clement Painter
Wechter, Vivienne Thaul Educator, Painter
Wilson, George Lewis Painter
Ziemann, Richard Claude Printmaker, Educator

Bronxville

Agee, William C Museum Director, Historian
Carlson, Jane C Painter
D'Amato, Janet Potter Illustrator, Craftsman
Manning, Hilda Scudder Sculptor
Poucher, Elizabeth Morris Sculptor
Seckler, Dorothy Gees Critic, Painter

Brookhaven

Delihas, Neva C Sculptor

Brooklyn

Abrams, Edith Lillian Sculptor
Accurso, Anthony Salvatore Illustrator, Painter
Adler, Lee Painter, Printmaker
Anderson, Lennart Painter, Instructor
Ausby, Ellsworth Augustus Painter, Instructor
Bard, Joellen Painter, Sculptor
Bates, Leo James Painter, Filmmaker
Baumbach, Harold Painter, Printmaker
Bertoni, Dante H Painter, Illustrator
Bidner, Robert D H Painter, Printmaker
Bove, Richard Painter, Educator
Brown, Stephen Pat Painter, Sculptor
Buck, Robert Treat, Jr Historian, Museum Director
Burns, Jerome Painter, Printmaker
Burns, Josephine Painter
Cole, Donald Painter
Comito, Nicholas U Painter, Illustrator
Coppedge, Arthur L Painter, Educator
Dantzic, Cynthia Maris Educator, Painter
Davidson, Nancy Painter
DeCarava, Roy Rudolph Photographer, Educator
de Guzman, Evelyn Lopez Painter
Delson, Elizabeth Painter, Printmaker
Demartis, James J Painter
Dinnerstein, Harvey Painter
Dinnerstein, Lois Historian, Lecturer
Estern, Neil Sculptor
Faunce, Sarah Cushing Museum Curator
Feder, Penny Joy Printmaker, Lecturer
Federe, Marion Painter, Graphic Artist
Fein, Stanley Painter, Designer
Ferber, Linda S Curator, Historian
Fife, Mary (Mrs Edward Laning) Painter
Flood, Edward C Sculptor, Painter
Fuerst, Shirley Miller Sculptor, Printmaker
Gardner, Andrew Bradford Printmaker, Painter
Gardner, Susan Ross Painter
Gerdts, William H Historian, Educator
Gironda, R Architect, Sculptor
Gluck, Heidi Painter, Educator
Goldstein, Jack Filmmaker, Conceptual Artist
Grado, Angelo John Painter, Instructor
Greenstone, Marion Painter
Groell, Theophil Painter, Instructor
Guay, Nancy Allen Tapestry Artist, Sculptor
Gunshor, Ruth Painter, Instructor
Gurr, Lena Painter, Printmaker
Henderson, Jack W Painter, Instructor

Henes, Donna Environmental Artist, Sculptor
Hickman, Jesse Luther Sculptor
Hodes, Barney Administrator
Howe, Nelson S Designer, Assemblage Artist
Hoyt, Ellen Painter
Huntington, Jim Sculptor
Johnson, M L J Painter, Educator
Kaminsky, Jack Allan Photographer, Printmaker
Keaveney, Sydney Starr Librarian, Lecturer
Kish, Maurice Painter
Kotik, Charlotta Curator, Historian
Kupferman, Murray Painter, Sculptor
Lager, Fannie Sculptor, Collector
Lawson, Thomas Painter
Le Roy, Harold M Painter, Graphic Artist
Levine, David Cartoonist, Painter
Levine, Marion Lerner Painter, Instructor
Lubell, Ellen Critic, Writer
McChristy, Quentin L Painter, Designer
MacGarvey, Bernard B Painter
McNeil, George J Painter, Printmaker
Magazzini, Gene Painter
Mainardi, Patricia M Painter, Writer
Malta, Vincent Instructor, Painter
Manilla, Tess Painter, Collage Artist
Mark, Marilyn (Sabetsky) Painter, Director
Marlor, Clark Strang Historian, Collector
Mendoza, Antonio G Photographer
Meneeley, Edward Painter, Sculptor
Mock, Richard Basil Illustrator, Painter
Morgenlander, Ella Kramer Painter, Instructor
Neals, Otto Painter, Sculptor
Nemser, Cindy Critic, Writer
Newman, Sophie Painter, Sculptor
Norris, (Robert) Ben Painter
Olenick, David Charles Dealer, Administrator
Perry, Kathryn Powers Graphic Artist, Painter
Phelan, Andrew L Educator, Painter
Pilgrim, Dianne H Curator, Historian
Power, S Brenda Joan Sculptor, Painter
Punia, Constance Edith Painter
Ranson, Nancy Sussman Painter, Serigrapher
Reich, Nathaniel E Painter, Collage Artist
Rennick, Dan Assemblage Artist, Sculptor
Rhoden, John W Sculptor
Robinson, Margot (Margot Steigman) Painter, Sculptor
Rogalski, Walter Printmaker, Lecturer
Rosler, Martha Rose Video Artist, Critic
Saito, Seiji Sculptor
Sakuyama, Shunji Printmaker, Painter
Scharff, Constance Kramer Printmaker, Painter
Schneider, Noel Sculptor
Sepyo, James Painter, Printmaker
Shaw, (George) Kendall Painter
Shechter, Ben-Zion Draftsman, Illustrator
Shechter, Laura J Painter, Draftsman
Shimoda, Osamu Sculptor
Soviak, Harry Painter, Sculptor
Stegman, Patricia Painter
Stelzer, Michael Norman Sculptor, Instructor
Taira, Frank Painter, Sculptor
Trachtenberg, Gloria P Painter, Graphic Artist
Trakis, Louis Sculptor, Educator
Tucker, William G Sculptor
Uhrman, Celia Painter, Writer
Uhrman, Esther Painter, Writer
Weingarten, Hilde (Kevess) Painter, Printmaker

NEW YORK (cont)

Williams, Todd Sculptor, Painter
Yamin, Steven Edward Printmaker

Brooklyn Heights

Culbreth, Carl R Sculptor, Educator
Kaprov, Susan Painter, Printmaker
Schucker, Charles Painter

Buffalo

Berlyn, Sheldon Painter, Printmaker
Bice, Jack (John Avery) Video Artist,
    Painter
Breverman, Harvey Painter, Printmaker
Brock, Robert W Sculptor, Educator
Chryssa (Vardea) Sculptor
Cohen, Harold Larry Designer, Educator
Crosman, Christopher Byron Museum
    Educator, Educator
Cuthbert, Virginia Painter
Elliott, Philip Clarkson Painter
Freudenheim, Nina Dealer, Collector
Glass, Dorothy F Historian
Gordon, Violet Illustrator, Writer
Hamouda, Amy (Amy Middleton
    Hamouda Bice) Sculptor
Hatchett, Duayne Sculptor, Educator
Henrich, Biff Photographer
Hubler, Julius Printmaker, Painter
Kassman, Shirley Collage Artist, Educator
Knox, Seymour H Patron
Krane, Susan Curator, Historian
Krims, Leslie Robert Photographer,
    Conceptual Artist
Lawless, Billie (William B) Sculptor,
    Craftsman
Levick, (Mr & Mrs) Irving Collectors
McIvor, John Wilfred Printmaker, Painter
Martin, Margaret M Painter, Designer
Nichols, Donald Edward Designer,
    Educator
Paterson, Anthony R Sculptor, Educator
Piccillo, Joseph Painter
Prochownik, Walter A Educator, Painter
Rogovin, Milton Photographer
Schultz, Douglas George Curator
Sharits, Paul Jeffrey Film Artist, Painter
Sisti, (Tony) Anthony J Collector, Painter
Townsend, J Benjamin Critic, Historian
Visser't Hooft, Martha Painter
Willig, Nancy Tobin Critic, Writer

Bullville

Henry, Dale Painter

Buskirk

Goossen, Eugene Coons Writer, Educator
Johanson, Patricia Sculptor, Architect

Cambria Heights

Brown, James Painter, Graphic Artist

Camillus

Vander Sluis, George J Painter, Educator

Campbell

Billeci, Andre George Sculptor, Educator

Campbell Hall

Greenly, Colin Environmental Artist,
    Conceptual Artist

Canastota

Hughto, Darryl Leo Painter

Canton

Holladay, Harlan H Historian, Painter
Lowe, J Michael Sculptor, Educator

Carmel

Sorel, Edward Illustrator, Writer

Catskill

Groshans, Werner Painter

Cazenovia

Pirkl, James Joseph Designer, Educator
Wyckoff, Sylvia Spencer Painter,
    Educator

Cedarhurst

Sacks, Beverly & Ray Consultants,
    Collectors

Centerport

Lewicki, James Illustrator, Educator

Champlain

Sanderson, Warren Dealer, Historian

Chappaqua

Conklin, Gloria Zamko Painter
DiFranza, Americo M Painter
McDonnell, Joseph Anthony Sculptor,
    Painter
Reibel, Bertram Sculptor, Graphic Artist

Charlotteville

Artschwager, Richard Ernst Painter,
    Sculptor
Bower, Gary David Painter
Pettibone, Richard H Painter

Chatham

Holmes, Wendy (Diana H Noyes)
    Photographer
Kelly, Ellsworth Painter, Sculptor
Noyes, Sandy Photographer

Chautauqua

Morgan, Maritza Leskovar Painter,
    Illustrator

Cheektowaga

Bisone, Edward George Painter

Clinton

Palmer, William C Painter, Lecturer

Cochecton Center

Loewer, Henry Peter Illustrator, Writer

Cold Spring

Margules, Gabriele Ella Illustrator,
    Painter
Marzollo, Claudio Sculptor

Cold Spring Harbor

Ginsburg, Max Painter, Illustrator
Maione, Robert Painter
Moss, Milton Painter

Commack

Vian, Orfeo Educator, Printmaker

Congers

Gussow, Alan Painter, Sculptor

Cooperstown

Jones, Louis C Museum Director
Keck, Sheldon Waugh Educator,
    Conservator

Coram

Manetta, Edward J Administrator, Painter

Corning

Buechner, Thomas Scharman Museum
    Director, Painter
Dowler, David P Sculptor, Designer
Schulze, Paul Designer

Corona

Chen, Tony (Anthony Young) Illustrator,
    Painter
Wimberley, Frank Walden Painter,
    Sculptor

Cortland

DiGiusto, Gerald N Sculptor

Cottekill

Buchman, James Wallace Sculptor
Vallila, Marja R Sculptor

Cross River

Smith, Lawrence Beall Painter, Sculptor

Croton-on-Hudson

Harari, Hananiah Painter

Cutchogue

Penney, Jacqueline Painter, Instructor

Deer Park

Fukuhara, (Kazuo) Henry Painter,
    Instructor

Delmar

Mayer, Edward Albert Educator, Sculptor

Dix Hills

Ames, Lee Judah Illustrator, Writer
Moy, May (Wong) Painter, Instructor

Dobbs Ferry

Cadge, William Fleming Designer,
    Photographer

Douglaston

Starrs, Mildred Painter

Dunkirk

Booth, Robert Alan Sculptor

Eagle Bridge

Bittleman, Arnold I Painter, Educator
Bittleman, Dolores Dembus Weaver,
    Conservator

East Amherst

Garver, Walter Raymond Painter,
    Instructor

East Chatham

Lehman, Irving Painter, Sculptor
Li Marzi, Joseph Painter, Graphic Artist
Rickey, George W Sculptor

East Elmhurst

Oi, Motoi Painter, Instructor

East Hampton

Bluhm, Norman Painter
Brooks, James Painter
Busa, Peter Painter, Sculptor
Ernst, Jimmy Painter, Educator
Fine, Perle Painter
Hoffmann, Arnold, Jr Painter, Director
Hornak, Ian John Painter
Kaufman, Irving Painter, Educator
Krasner, Lee Painter
Lassaw, Ibram Sculptor
Li-Lan (Li-Lan Gee) Painter
Little, John Painter, Sculptor
Long, Hubert Sculptor
Mim, Adrienne C (Adrienne Claire
    Schwartz) Sculptor, Painter

NEW YORK (cont)
Nivola, Constantino Sculptor
Roth, Frank Painter
Stein, Ronald Jay Sculptor
Whipple, Enez Mary Administrator
Wingate, Arline (Hollander) Sculptor
Woolfenden, William Edward
 Administrator, Historian

East Hill
Newmark, Marilyn (Marilyn Newmark
 Meiselman) Sculptor

East Meadow
Terken, John Sculptor

East Northport
Cohen, George Michael Educator

East Norwich
Solomon, Ruth B Administrator,
 Consultant

East Patchogue
Desoto, Rafael M Painter, Illustrator

Elmhurst
Berkon, Martin Painter
Segur, Eleanor Corinne Painter, Instructor
Wachsteter, George Illustrator

Elmira
Macdonnell, Cameron Painter, Sculptor

Elmont
Schary, Emanuel Painter, Printmaker

Endicott
Hart, John Lewis Cartoonist

Endwell
Tunis, Roslyn Curator

Essex
Lowry, Bates Historian

Fairport
Witmeyer, Stanley Herbert Painter,
 Consultant

Far Rockaway
Roth, Rubi Painter

Fayette
Yeh, Carol Printmaker

Fayetteville
Goodnow, Frank A Painter, Educator
Pollock, Merlin F Painter, Educator
Smith, Lawson Wentworth Sculptor,
 Educator

Floral Park
Aaron, Evalyn (Wilhelmina) Painter
Gartel, Laurence M Photographer, Video-
 Computer Artist
Moss, Irene Painter

Florida
Gray, Don Painter, Critic
Gray, Jessie Benton Evans Painter, Critic

Flushing
Catan-Rose, Richard Painter, Educator
Jules, Mervin Painter, Educator
Koras, George Sculptor
Ludwig, Eva Sculptor
Pincus-Witten, Robert A Educator, Writer
Rosenthal, Seymour Painter, Lithographer
Schneider, Janet M Museum Director,
 Painter

Slatkes, Leonard J Historian
Stark, Shirley Sculptor, Printmaker
Stiles, Helen Painter, Printmaker
Tobias, Abraham Joel Painter, Sculptor
Weinberg, H Barbara Historian,
 Consultant

Forest Hills
Crystal, Boris Painter
De Bellis, Hannibal Sculptor, Medalist
Leeds, Annette Painter
Lombardo, Josef Vincent Historian,
 Writer
Pearlstein, Seymour Painter, Educator
Tewi, Thea Sculptor

Franklin Square
Indiviglia, Salvatore Joseph Painter,
 Instructor
Newer, Thesis Painter
Soloway, Reta Painter

Fredonia
Thomas, William Radford Educator,
 Painter

Freehold
Maltzman, Stanley Printmaker, Painter

Freeport
Brown, Marion B Painter, Instructor
de Kooning, Elaine Marie Catherine
 Painter, Writer
Terris, Albert Sculptor, Calligrapher

Fresh Meadows
Silber, Maurice Painter, Illustrator

Garden City
Jennerjahn, W P Educator, Painter
Jessen, Shirley Agnes Painter

Garnerville
Harvey, Dermot Kinetic Artist, Sculptor

Garrison
Asoma, Tadashi Painter
Clifton, Michelle Gamm Sculptor,
 Filmmaker
Flavin, Dan Artist, Writer
Locke, Charles Wheeler Painter,
 Printmaker

Glen Cove
Knipscher, Gerard Allen Painter, Graphic
 Artist
Paris, Jeanne C Critic, Consultant

Glen Head
Blackey, Mary Madlyn Painter,
 Printmaker
Mason, Lauris Lapidos Lecturer, Writer

Glens Falls
Blackburn, Loren Hayner Painter,
 Illustrator

Gloversville
Schulman, Jacob Collector

Goshen
Tracy, Berry Bryson Curator,
 Administrator

Great Neck
Beck, Margit Painter, Educator
Eckstein, Ruth Painter, Printmaker
Filmus, Tully Painter, Lecturer
Goldsmith, Elsa M Painter
Gorelick, Shirley Painter, Printmaker
Housman, Russell F Painter, Instructor

Lederman, Stephanie Brody Painter,
 Collage Artist
Mayer, Sondra Printmaker, Writer
Meyer, Seymour W Sculptor
Mills, Agnes Sculptor, Printmaker
Moglia, Luigi (John) Painter, Instructor
Obler, Geri Printmaker, Graphic Artist
Quat, Helen S Printmaker, Painter
Schuller, Grete Sculptor
Seidler, Doris Painter, Printmaker
Shapiro, Dee Painter, Lecturer
Sheya Painter, Instructor
Simel, Elaine Printmaker, Painter
Soshana (Susanne Afroyim) Painter
Tanksley, Ann Painter
Van Buren, Raeburn Illustrator,
 Cartoonist

Greenlawn
Fludd, Reginald Joseph Painter,
 Craftsman
Zucker, Bob Photographer, Designer

Greenwich
Lorber, Stephen Neil Painter, Printmaker

Groton
Colby, Victor E Sculptor, Educator

Halesite
Steward, Donn Horatio Printmaker,
 Publisher

Hamilton
Knecht, John Filmmaker
Loveless, Jim Educator, Painter
Mosby, Dewey Franklin Museum
 Director, Historian
Van Schaack, Eric Historian,
 Administrator

Hamlin
Stewart, Bill Sculptor, Ceramist

Hampton Bays
Ciancio, June (Kirkpatrick) Painter,
 Instructor

Hannibal
Eckersley, Thomas Cyril Educator,
 Administrator

Harrison
Arye, Leonora E Sculptor
Margulis, Martha (Boyer) Painter

Hartsdale
Brown, Alan M, Jr Dealer, Consultant

Hastings-on-Hudson
Freedman, Maurice Painter
James, Catti Sculptor, Consultant
Madigan, Mary Jean Smith Editor, Writer
Nardin, Mario Collector, Sculptor
Sklar-Weinstein, Arlene (Joyce) Painter,
 Printmaker

Hawthorne
Oechsli, Kelly Illustrator

Hempstead
Feriola, James Philip Painter, Designer
Jacobs, David (Theodore) Sculptor,
 Educator
Myron, Robert Historian

Hewlett
Flomenhaft, Eleanor Museum Director,
 Historian

High Falls
Bishop, Benjamin Painter, Educator

Highland Falls
Heberling, Glen Austin Painter, Illustrator

Hillsdale
Richards, Joseph Edward Painter

Holland
Blair, Robert Noel Painter, Sculptor

Holland Patent
Christiana, Edward Painter, Instructor

Hollis
Davies, Theodore Peter Printmaker, Painter
Jonynas, Vytautas K Sculptor, Painter
Mau, Hui-Chi Painter

Honeoye
Brown, Bruce Robert Painter, Sculptor

Honeoye Falls
Keyser, William Alphonse, Jr Craftsman, Educator

Hoosick Falls
Haerer, Carol Painter
Hatfield, David Underhill Painter
Wofford, Philip Painter, Writer

Hudson
Avedisian, Edward Painter
Friedman, Alan Sculptor, Designer

Huntington
Brodsky, Stan Painter, Educator
Buckley, Mary L (Mrs Joseph M Parriott) Painter, Educator
Engel, Michael Martin, II Painter, Illustrator
Ponsot, Claude F Educator, Painter
Vaux, Richard Painter, Printmaker
Walker, Marie Sheehy Painter

Huntington Station
Mann, Katinka Painter, Photographer
Van Loen, Alfred Sculptor, Educator

Hyde Park
Ulrich, Edwin Abel Museum Director

Irvington
Holden, Donald Editor, Writer
Lippmann, Janet Gurian Gallery Director, Painter

Ithaca
Atwell, Allen Educator, Painter
Boyd, Michael Painter, Graphic Artist
Brown, Theodore Morey Historian, Writer
Calkins, Robert G Historian, Educator
Daly, Norman Painter, Sculptor
Dzubas, Friedel Painter
Evett, Kenneth Warnock Painter
Grippi, Salvatore William Painter, Educator
Hartell, John Painter
Holliday, Judith Librarian
Kahn, Peter Painter, Designer
Leavitt, Thomas Whittlesey Museum Director
Mahoney, James Owen Painter, Educator
O'Connor, Stanley James Historian, Educator
Owens, Gwendolyn Jane Curator, Writer
Poleskie, Stephen Francis Environmental Artist, Printmaker
Richenburg, Robert Bartlett Painter, Sculptor

Smyth, David Richard Sculptor
Squier, Jack Leslie Sculptor, Educator
Valerio, James Robert Painter, Educator
Wong, Jason Museum Director, Designer

Jackson Heights
Cardman, Cecilia Painter
Farian, Babette S Painter, Designer
Freund, Tibor Painter, Muralist
Judkins, Sylvia Painter
Kappel, R Rose (Mrs Irving Gould) Printmaker
Oloffson, Werner Olaf Painter, Photographer
Schmidt, Frederick Louis Painter, Illustrator
Whitney, Edgar Albert Painter, Instructor

Jamaica
Cade, Walter, III Painter, Collage Artist
Desser, Maxwell Milton Painter, Designer
Gelburd, Gail Enid Museum Director, Educator
Haber, William Dealer, Collector
Kepalas (Elena Kepalaite) Sculptor, Painter
Klein, Ellen Lee Painter, Writer
Krigstein, Bernard Painter, Illustrator
Lovejoy, Margot R Printmaker, Educator
Pascual, Manolo Sculptor, Instructor
Wind, Harold Painter, Illustrator
Youkeles, Anne Painter, Printmaker

Jamesville
Dibble, Charles Ryder Educator, Painter
Vargo, John Educator, Painter

Jefferson
Hacklin, Allan Dave Painter, Sculptor

Jericho
Kaplan, Marilyn Flashenberg Painter
Mandel, Saul Illustrator, Painter
Ross, B(eatrice) Brook Painter, Collage Artist
Singer, Arthur B Illustrator, Painter

Katonah
Baur, John I H Museum Director, Writer
Chinni, Peter Anthony Sculptor, Painter
Giobbi, Edward Gioachino Painter, Sculptor
Janson, Agnes Painter, Graphic Artist
Lipinsky de Orlov, Lino S Painter, Printmaker
Samerjan, George E Designer, Painter
Simpson, William Kelly Historian, Educator
Toney, Anthony Painter, Educator

Keene Valley
Winkel, Nina Sculptor, Lecturer

Kenmore
Koenig, Catherine Catanzaro Painter
Lindemann, Edna M Museum Director, Educator

Kenoza Lake
D'Arcangelo, Allan M Painter

Kew Gardens
Brennan, Francis Edwin Editorial Cartoonist, Designer
Eliasoph, Paula Painter, Writer
Minsky, Richard Bookbinder, Conceptual Artist

La Fayette
Gernhardt, Henry Kendall Sculptor, Ceramist

Lake Success
Jerviss, Joy Printmaker
Leaf, Ruth Printmaker, Instructor

Lansing
Hoyt, Dorothy Painter

Larchmont
Adamy, George E Educator, Sculptor
Lefcourt, Irwin Dealer
Medrich, Libby E Sculptor
Tobey, Alton S Painter, Lecturer

Levittown
Chestney, Lillian Illustrator, Painter
Kaplan, Stanley Printmaker, Muralist
Schachter, Justine Ranson Graphic Artist, Illustrator
Zuckerberg, Stanley M Painter, Illustrator

Little Neck
Gibala, Louise Painter
Roman, Shirley Printmaker

Lockport
Penney, Charles Rand Collector, Patron

Locust Valley
Bush-Brown, Albert Writer, Educator
Johnson, Ray Painter
Lippold, Richard Sculptor
Watson, Clarissa H Dealer, Writer

Long Eddy
Wesselmann, Tom Painter, Sculpture

Long Island City
Berhang, Mattie Sculptor, Lecturer
Garchik, Morton Lloyd Painter, Printmaker
Gavalas, Alexander Beary Painter
Glorig, Ostor Painter
Gussow, Roy Sculptor, Environmental Artist
Noguchi, Isamu Sculptor
Tardo, (Manuel) Rodulfo Sculptor

Maine
Barons, Richard Irwin Museum Director, Historian

Mamaroneck
Lekberg, Barbara Hult Sculptor
Pugh, Grace Huntley Painter, Graphic Artist
Silver, Rawley A Educator, Painter
Sloan, Robert Smullyan Painter
Topol, Robert Martin Collector

Manhasset
Catchi (Catherine O Childs) Painter, Printmaker
Harvey, Jacqueline Painter

Manlius
Burke, E Ainslie Painter, Educator
Cortese, Don F Printmaker, Instructor
Groat, Hall Pierce Painter, Muralist

Massapequa
Yaffa Yael Stec-El (Harriet Jeanne Steckel) Muralist, Printmaker

Mattituck
Hardy, Howard (Collins) Painter, Instructor

Melville

Schlam, Murray J Sculptor

Merrick

Cariola, Robert J Painter, Sculptor
Pearlman, Etta S Painter

Middletown

Blumenthal, Fritz Painter, Printmaker
Ericson, Beatrice Painter

Millbrook

Della-Volpe, Ralph Eugene Painter,
    Educator
Streeter, Tal Sculptor, Educator

Millerton

Helck, (Clarence) Peter Painter,
    Printmaker
Zimiles, Murray Painter, Educator

Mill Neck

Burrows, Selig S Collector, Historian

Monsey

Mesibov, Hugh Painter, Instructor

Montauk

Nama, George Allen Printmaker, Sculptor

Mountainville

Stern, H Peter Collector

Mt Kisco

Galen, Elaine Painter, Sculptor
Jones, Amy (Amy Jones Frisbie) Painter,
    Instructor
Roth, David Painter
Rubin, Irwin Painter, Designer

Mt Morris

Dickinson, David Charles Printmaker,
    Instructor

Mt Tremper

Stuhl, Michelle Sculptor, Environmental
    Artist
Werner, Howard Sculptor

Mt Vernon

Mitchell, James E Illustrator, Painter
Olsen, Ernest Moran Designer, Painter
Propersi, August J Administrator, Painter
Seliger, Charles Painter
Zib, Tom (Thomas A Zibelli) Cartoonist

Mumford

Shillea, Thomas John Photographer,
    Educator

Newark

Williams, Wayne Francis Sculptor

New Berlin

Huot, Robert Painter, Filmmaker

Newburgh

Jackson, Hazel Brill Sculptor

New City

Kessler, Leonard H Illustrator
Rosse, Maryvonne Sculptor, Medalist
Savitz, Frieda Painter, Instructor

New Hampton

Sinnard, Elaine (Janice) Painter, Sculptor

New Hartford

MacDonald, Scott Critic, Educator

New Paltz

Davidson, Thyra (Claire Thyra Wexler)
    Sculptor, Draftsman
Kammerer, Herbert Lewis Sculptor
McPherson, Bruce Rice Editor, Publisher
Martin, Alexander Toedt Educator,
    Painter
Munsterberg, Hugo Historian, Educator
Raleigh, Henry Patrick Painter, Writer
Shaw, Ernest Carl Sculptor
Wexler, George Painter, Educator

New Rochelle

Beling, Helen Sculptor, Instructor
Dintenfass, Marylyn Sculptor, Lecturer
Lantz, Michael Sculptor
Lehr, Harold Sculptor, Kinetic Artist
Meizner, Paula Sculptor
Montlack, Edith Painter
Nechis, Barbara Painter, Lecturer
Perlmutter, Merle Printmaker, Instructor
Rothstein, Arthur Photographer
Schlanger, Jeff Sculptor
Schwebel, Renata Manasse Sculptor
Seckel, Paul Bernhard Painter, Printmaker
Slotnick, Mortimer H Painter, Educator
Winter, Lumen Martin Sculptor, Painter

New York

Aach, Herb Painter, Writer
Abadi, Fritzie Painter, Sculptor
Abdell, Douglas Sculptor, Painter
Abish, Cecile Sculptor, Instructor
Abrams, Ruth (Davidson) Painter, Critic
Abrams, Vivien (Joy) Painter
Abularach, Rodolfo Marco Painter,
    Printmaker
Acconci, Vito Sculptor
Adams, Alice Sculptor
Addams, Charles Samuel Cartoonist
Adel, Judith Art Director, Designer
Adler, Robert Painter
Adrian, Barbara (Mrs Franklin
    Tramutola) Painter, Collector
Aebi, Ernst Walter Illustrator, Painter
Agostini, Peter Sculptor
Ahn, Don C Painter, Art Dealer
Alajalov, Constantin Painter, Illustrator
Albert, Calvin Sculptor, Educator
Albertazzi, Mario Painter, Art Critic
Alcopley, L Painter, Graphic Artist
Aldrich, Larry Art Collector
Alexander, Edmund Brooke Art Dealer
Alexander-Greene, Grace George
    Educator, Administrator
Allen, Roberta Conceptual Artist,
    Sculptor
Allentuck, Marcia Epstein Historian,
    Educator
Allner, Walter H Painter, Designer
Alloway, Lawrence Educator, Art Critic
Alonzo, Jack J Art Dealer, Collector
Alper, M Victor Educator, Writer
Alpert, Bill (William H) Painter, Sculptor
Altschul, Arthur G Collector, Patron
Amino, Leo Sculptor, Instructor
Aminoff, Judith Writer, Editor
Amster, Sally Painter
Anastasi, William (Joseph) Painter,
    Sculptor
Anbinder, Paul Art Publisher, Collector
Andersen, Leif (Werner) Painter
Anderson, Alexandra C Critic, Writer
Anderson, David K Art Dealer, Collector
Anderson, Dennis Ray Art Dealer, Art
    Historian
Andre, Carl Sculptor
Andrejevic, Milet Painter
Andrews, Benny Painter, Lecturer

Angel, Rifka Painter
Anker, Suzanne C Sculptor
Anson, Lesia Sculptor
Anspach, Ernst Collector
Anthony, William Graham Painter,
    Draftsman
Antonakos, Stephen Sculptor
Antonovici, Constantin Sculptor, Lecturer
Appel, Eric A Sculptor
Appel, Karel Painter, Sculptor
Appel, Thelma Painter, Instructor
Apple, Jacki (Jacqueline B) Intermedia
    Artist, Writer
Applebroog, Ida Conceptual Artist
Apt, Charles Painter
Arakawa (Shusaku) Painter
Arcilesi, Vincent J Painter
Arman Sculptor
Armstrong, Thomas Newton, III Museum
    Director
Arnason, H Harvard Art Historian,
    Writer
Arnold, Jack Art Dealer, Publisher
Aronson, Sanda Sculptor
Arum, Barbara Sculptor
Ascher, Mary Painter, Printmaker
Ashbaugh, Dennis John Painter
Ashbery, John Lawrence Art Critic
Ashby, Carl Painter, Instructor
Asher, Elise Painter, Writer
Ashton, Dore Art Critic, Writer
Atirnomis (Rita Simon) Painter,
    Printmaker
Attie, Dotty Draftsman
Ault, Lee Addison Collector, Art Dealer
Avedon, Richard Photographer
Axelrod, Miriam Sculptor
Aycock, Alice Sculptor
Aylon, Helane Painter
Azara, Nancy J Sculptor, Painter
Azuma, Norio Serigrapher, Painter
Bachert, Hildegard Gina Art Dealer
Bacon, Peggy Painter, Writer
Baer, Norbert Sebastian Educator
Bailey, William Painter, Educator
Bakaty, Mike Painter, Sculptor
Baker, Elizabeth C Art Editor, Critic
Baker, Jill Painter, Illustrator
Baker, Richard Brown Collector
Balay, Felicie Art Dealer
Balog, Michael Painter, Sculptor
Bandy, Gary Painter, Educator
Bandy, Mary Lea Editor, Administrator
Banerjee (Bimal) Painter, Sculptor
Banning, Jack (John Peck), Jr Art Dealer,
    Lecturer
Baranik, Rudolf Painter
Bardazzi, Peter Painter
Bareiss, Walter Collector
Barnes, Curt (Curtis Edward) Painter,
    Instructor
Barnes, Edward Larrabee Architect
Barnes, Kit Painter
Barnet, Will Painter, Printmaker
Barnett, Vivian Endicott Curator
Barowitz, Elliott Painter, Instructor
Barr, Norman Painter
Barrett, Bill Sculptor
Barr-Sharrar, Beryl Art Historian, Painter
Barth, Frances Painter
Barth, Jack Alexander Painter
Bartholet, Elizabeth Ives Art Dealer, Art
    Consultant
Bartlett, Jennifer Losch Painter, Writer
Barton, August Charles Designer, Painter
Barton, John Murray Painter, Art Dealer
Barzun, Jacques Writer, Art Critic
Baskerville, Charles Painter, Muralist
Bass, Ruth Educator, Painter
Bastian, Linda Painter, Educator
Bathurst, David C Gallery Director
Battenfield, Jackie (Frazier) Painter,
    Curator

NEW YORK (cont)

Baum, Jayne H Art Dealer
Baum, Timothy Art Dealer, Historian
Baxter, Douglas W Art Dealer
Baxter, Patricia Huy Director
Bayer, Arlyne Painter, Printmaker
Baynard, Ed Painter
Beadleston, William L Art Dealer
Beal, Jack Painter
Bean, Jacob Curator
Bearden, Romare Howard Painter
Beatty, Frances Fielding Lewis Historian, Critic
Beauchamp, Robert Instructor, Painter
Beck, Doreen Writer, AV Producer
Beck, James Historian, Critic
Beck, Martha Ann Museum Director, Curator
Beck, Rosemarie (Rosemarie Beck Phelps) Painter, Educator
Beck, Stephen R Painter, Educator
Beckley, Bill Post-Conceptual Artist
Beckman, Ericka Filmmaker, Sculptor
Beery, Arthur O Painter
Behnke, Leigh Painter
Beilin, Howard Art Dealer
Beker, Gisela Painter
Bell, Charles S Painter
Bellamy, Richard Art Dealer
Benedikt, Michael Consultant, Critic
Benenson, Edward Hartley Collector, Patron
Benes, Barton Lidice Collage Artist, Sculptor
Benglis, Lynda Sculptor, Painter
Benham, Pamela J Painter
Bennett, Harriet Painter
Benney, Robert Painter, Illustrator
Benson, Gertrude Ackerman Writer, Critic
Ben-Zion Painter, Sculptor
Bergen, D Thomas Collector
Bergen, Sidney L Art Dealer
Berger, Gustav A Conservator
Berger, Maurice Critic, Educator
Berger, Oscar Graphic Artist
Berghash, Mark W Photographer, Painter
Berkman, Aaron Painter, Gallery Director
Berkman, Lillian Collector
Berlind, Robert Painter, Educator
Berman, Aaron Art Dealer, Gallery Director
Berman, Ariane R Painter, Printmaker
Berman, Greta W Historian, Curator
Bernstein, Judith Painter, Lecturer
Bernstein, Saralinda Art Dealer, Historian
Bernstein, Theresa Painter, Printmaker
Berthot, Jake Painter
Besser, Arne Charles Painter
Bettinson, Brenda Educator, Painter
Bhavsar, Natvar Prahladji Painter
Bialobroda, Anna Painter
Bianco, Pamela Ruby Painter
Billian, Cathey R Sculptor, Instructor
Bishop, Isabel (Mrs Harold G Wolff) Painter, Etcher
Bishop, James Painter
Bishop, Robert Charles Museum Director, Art Writer
Black, Mary Childs Curator, Writer
Blackwell, Tom (Thomas Leo) Painter
Bladen, Ronald Sculptor
Blaine, Nell Painter
Blanc, (William) Peter Sculptor, Painter
Blanchard, Carol Painter, Illustrator
Blaustein, Al Painter, Printmaker
Blayton, Betty (Betty Blayton-Taylor) Painter, Administrator
Bleckner, Ross Painter
Blinderman, Barry Robert Art Dealer, Critic

Block, Dorothy Painter
Blodgett, Anne Washington Painter
Blue, Patt Photographer, Educator
Blum, Andrea Sculptor
Blumenthal, Margaret M Designer
Boardman, Seymour Painter
Bochner, Mel Conceptual Artist, Art Writer
Bodin, Paul Painter
Bogarin, Rafael Serigrapher, Painter
Bogorad, Alan Dale Illustrator
Bohnen, Blythe Conceptual Artist, Painter
Bohnenkamp, Leslie George Sculptor, Instructor
Bollinger, William Conceptual Artist
Bonevardi, Marcelo Painter, Sculptor
Bonino, Fernanda Art Dealer
Boone, Mary Art Dealer
Boothe, Power Robert Painter, Instructor
Bordes, Adrienne Painter, Instructor
Borgatta, Isabel Case Sculptor, Educator
Borgatta, Robert Edward Painter, Sculptor
Borgenicht, Grace Art Dealer, Collector
Borofsky, Jon Painter
Borstein, Elena Painter, Educator
Bosse, Janet C Painter, Printmaker
Bosson, Jack (John Edwin), Jr Painter, Printmaker
Boterf, Check (Chester Arthur) Painter, Lecturer
Botero, Fernando Sculptor
Bothmer, Bernard V Art Historian, Instructor
Bouckaert, Harm J G Art Dealer
Bourdon, David Art Critic, Editor
Bourgeois, Louise Sculptor
Boutis, Tom Painter, Collage Artist
Bowie, William Sculptor
Bowling, Frank Painter
Boxer, Stanley (Robert) Painter, Sculptor
Brach, Paul Henry Painter
Bradshaw, Dove Painter, Sculptor
Bradt, Kathleen Weil-Garris Educator, Art Historian
Brainard, Joe Graphic Artist, Painter
Brandt, Warren Painter
Breiger, Elaine Painter, Printmaker
Brigadier, Anne Painter, Lecturer
Briggs, Ernest Painter, Instructor
Broderick, Herbert Reginald, III Historian
Brody, Jacqueline Editor
Bromm, Hal Dealer, Instructor
Brooks, Bruce W Painter, Sculptor
Brosk, Jeffrey Owen Sculptor
Brown, Alice Dalton Painter
Brown, Blanche Rachel Historian, Educator
Brown, Diane Dealer
Brown, Jonathan Historian
Brown, Judith Gwyn Illustrator, Painter
Brown, Larry K Painter
Brown, Milton Wolf Historian
Brown, Paul L Painter, Educator
Brown, Peter C Sculptor, Educator
Brown, Rhett Delford (Harriett Gurney Brown) Fiber Artist, Illustrator
Brown, Robert Delford Conceptual Artist
Brown, Robert K Dealer
Browne, Aldis J, III Dealer
Browne, Vivian E Painter, Administrator
Browning, Colleen Painter
Bruder, Harold Jacob Painter, Educator
Brumer, Miriam Painter, Educator
Brumer, Shulamith Sculptor, Instructor
Brundage, Susan Lounsbury Dealer
Bruno, Phillip A Dealer, Collector
Brusca, Jack Sculptor
Bry, Edith Assemblage Artist, Collage Artist

Bryant, Linda Goode Art Dealer, Gallery Director
Buczak, Brian Elliot Painter, Sculptor
Buecker, Robert Gallery Director, Painter
Bultman, Fritz Sculptor, Painter
Bunin, Louis Sculptor
Bunshaft, Gordon Collector, Architect
Bunts, Frank Painter, Educator
Burckhardt, Rudy Photographer, Filmmaker
Burden, Carter Collector
Burden, Chris Conceptual Artist, Sculptor
Burdock, Harriet Historian, Printmaker
Burns, D Harrison Painter, Instructor
Burt, David Sill Sculptor, Writer
Burton, Scott Sculptor, Conceptual Artist
Bushnell, Kenneth Wayne Painter, Educator
Butter, Tom Sculptor, Instructor
Byard, Carole Marie Painter, Illustrator
Byron, Charles Anthony Dealer
Cady, Dennis Vern Conservator, Painter
Cage, John Printmaker
Calcagno, Lawrence Painter
Califano, Edward Christopher Dealer, Publisher
Campbell, (James) Lawrence Painter, Writer
Campbell, Vivian (Vivian Campbell Stoll) Collector, Writer
Campus, Peter Photographer, Video Artist
Canaday, John Edwin Critic
Caniff, Milton Arthur Cartoonist
Canniff, Bryan Gregory Designer, Director
Canright, Sarah Anne Painter
Cantone, Vic Cartoonist, Writer
Cantor, B Gerald Collector
Cantor, Fredrich Photographer, Painter
Capa, Cornell Photographer, Museum Director
Caplan, Sandra (Sandra Ciarrochi Caplan) Painter
Capobianco, Domenick Painter, Sculptor
Cardozo, Patricia Velez Art Dealer
Carey, Ellen Photographer
Carlson, Cynthia J Painter, Educator
Caro, Francis Dealer
Carr, Sally Swan Sculptor
Carter, Mary Painter
Cartwright, Constance B & Carroll L Collectors
Casebere, James E Photographer, Sculptor
Cassanelli, Victor Vi Painter, Printmaker
Castanis, Muriel (Julia Brunner) Sculptor
Castelli, Leo Dealer
Castile, Rand Gallery Director
Castleman, Riva Curator, Historian
Castoro, Rosemarie Sculptor
Cavaliere, Barbara Critic, Historian
Cernuschi, Alberto C Dealer, Critic
Chamberlain, John Angus Sculptor
Chambers, Bruce William Dealer, Historian
Chambers, Karen Historian, Critic
Charlesworth, Sarah E Photographer, Conceptual Artist
Charmatz, Bill (William Adolphe) Illustrator, Painter
Chase, Doris (Totten) Filmmaker, Video Artist
Chase, Louisa L Painter
Chemeche, George Painter, Sculptor
Chen, Hilo Painter
Chen Chi Painter
Chermayeff, Ivan Designer, Painter
Cherry, Herman Painter
Childs, Bernard Painter, Printmaker
Chinn, Yuen Yuey Painter, Printmaker
Christensen, Dan Painter
Christo Sculptor

NEW YORK (cont)

Chwast, Seymour Designer, Illustrator
Ciarrochi, Ray Painter, Instructor
Cicero, Carmen L Painter
Citron, Minna Wright Painter, Printmaker
Clark, Michael Vinson Painter
Clark, William W Historian
Clarke, Bud (Warren F) Designer, Director
Clarke, John Clem Painter
Clerk, Pierre Painter, Sculptor
Close, Chuck Painter
Clough, Charles Sidney Painter
Clutz, William Painter, Instructor
Code, Audrey Painter
Cohen, Arthur A Book Dealer, Historian
Cohen, Elaine Lustig Painter, Designer
Cohen, Hy Painter
Cohen, Jean Painter, Muralist
Cohen, Joan Lebold Historian, Photographer
Cohen, Mildred Thaler Dealer, Gallery Director
Cohen, Ronny H Critic, Historian
Cohen, Wilfred P Collector, Patron
Cohn, Max Arthur Painter, Printmaker
Cohn, Richard A Dealer
Cole, Joyce Painter
Cole, Max Painter
Cole, Stephanie Kirschen Collage Artist
Cole, Sylvan, Jr Dealer, Writer
Colin, Georgia T Collector, Designer
Colin, Ralph Frederick Collector
Collins, Christiane C Historian, Librarian
Collins, George R Historian, Educator
Collins, J(oseph) B Painter, Photographer
Comtois, Louis Painter
Condeso, Orlando Printmaker
Conforte, Renee Dealer
Conover, Robert Fremont Printmaker, Painter
Constantine, Mildred Historian
Contini, Anita Administrator, Curator
Cooney-Crawford, Thom M Painter, Sculptor
Cooper, Mario Painter, Instructor
Cooper, Paula Dealer
Cooper, Rebecca Dealer, Collector
Copeland, Lila Painter, Printmaker
Coplans, John (Rivers) Photographer
Copley, William Nelson Painter
Corbin, George Allen Historian, Writer
Corkery, Tim (Timothy James) Painter, Educator
Cortella, Gloria Charlene Dealer
Cortor, Eldzier Painter, Printmaker
Cotter, Holland Critic, Editor
Courtright, Robert Collage Artist, Painter
Cove, Rosemary Sculptor, Painter
Coyer, Max R Painter, Dealer
Crary, Jonathan Knight Critic
Crawford, John McAllister, Jr Collector, Patron
Crile, Susan Painter
Crimp, Douglas Critic, Historian
Crispo, Andrew J Dealer, Collector
Cronbach, Robert M Sculptor
Cronin, Robert (Lawrence) Sculptor
Culbertson, Janet Lynn (Mrs Douglas Kaften) Painter, Instructor
Culkin, John Michael Administrator, Educator
Cummings, Paul Curator, Editor
Cuningham, Elizabeth Bayard (Mrs E W R Templeton) Dealer
Cunningham, (Charles) Bruce Painter
Cunningham, Francis Painter, Instructor
Cutforth, Roger Conceptual Artist
Cutler, Ethel Rose Painter, Designer
Cutler, Ronnie Painter
Cyril, R Painter, Printmaker
d'Alessio, Gregory Cartoonist, Illustrator

Dali, Salvador Designer, Painter
Damast, Elba Cecilia Painter
Damaz, Paul F Writer, Architect
D'Ancona, Mirella Levi Historian, Writer
Daniels, David M Collector, Patron
Dank, Leonard Dewey Medical Illustrator, Consultant
Daphnis, Nassos Painter, Sculptor
Darboven, Hanne Conceptual Artist, Graphic Artist
Darton, Christopher Painter
Daskaloff, Gyorgy Painter
Dauterman, Carl Christian Historian, Lecturer
David, Don Raymond Painter, Instructor
Davidovich, Jaime Painter
Davidson, Marshall Bowman Critic, Writer
Davidson, Maxwell, III Dealer
Davila, Carlos Painter, Printmaker
Davis, Brad (Bradley Darius) Painter
Davis, Douglas Matthew Artist, Critic
Davis, Ellen N Historian
Davison, Bill Educator, Printmaker
Day, Robert James Cartoonist
deAK, Edit Critic, Filmmaker
Dean, Peter Painter
de Boschnek, Chris (Christian Charles) Painter, Printmaker
de Champlain, Vera Chopak Painter, Printmaker
Dechar, Peter Painter
De Donato, Louis Painter, Instructor
Dee, Elaine Evans Historian
Deem, George Painter
Dehn, Virginia Painter
Dehner, Dorothy Sculptor, Printmaker
de Knight, Avel Painter
De Kooning, Willem Painter
DeLamonica, Roberto Printmaker, Educator
de Lisio, Michael Sculptor
del Re, Marisa Dealer
Del Valle, Joseph Bourke Design Consultant
De Maria, Walter Sculptor
De Martini, Joseph Painter
de Miskey, Julian Sculptor, Printmaker
De Monte, Claudia Educator, Conceptual Artist
de Montebello, Philippe Lannes Administrator, Museum Director
de Nagy, Tibor (J) Dealer, Collector
Denes, Agnes C Environmental Sculptor, Graphic Artist
Dennis, Donna Frances Sculptor
Dennis, Gertrude Weyhe Dealer
De Rivera, Jose Sculptor
De Ruth, Jan Painter, Writer
des Rioux (de Messimy), Deena (Coty) Painter, Designer
Deutschman, Louise Tolliver Dealer, Curator
Diamonstein, Barbaralee Writer
Diao, David Painter
Di Cerbo, Michael Painter, Printmaker
Diebenkorn, Richard Painter
Digiorgio, Joseph J Painter
Dillon, C Douglas Administrator, Collector
Di Meo, Dominick Painter, Sculptor
Dine, James Painter, Sculptor
Dinnerstein, Simon A Painter
Dintenfass, Terry Dealer
Diodato, Baldo Painter, Sculptor
Diska Sculptor
Di Suvero, Mark Painter, Sculptor
Ditzion, Grace Sculptor, Painter
Dixon, Jenny (Jane Hodley) Administrator
Dobbs, John Barnes Painter
Dobkin, John Howard Museum Director

Dockstader, Frederick J Historian, Consultant
Dodd, Lois Painter, Educator
Dogancay, Burhan Cahit Painter, Sculptor
Doherty, Michael Stephen Editor, Printmaker
Donati, Enrico Painter, Sculptor
Donneson, Seena Sculptor, Graphics Artist
Doo Da Post (Edward Ferdinand Higgins III) Painter, Mail Artist
Dorfman, Bruce Painter, Instructor
Dorfman, Fred Dealer
Dorr, (Virginia) Nell Photographer
Dorsky, Morris Historian, Educator
Dorsky, Samuel Dealer
Dowden, Anne Ophelia Todd Painter, Illustrator
Downes, Rackstraw Painter, Critic
Downey, Juan Video Artist, Architect
Doyle, Tom Sculptor, Educator
Draper, William Franklin Painter, Instructor
Drexler, Arthur Justin Director, Curator
Driggs, Elsie Painter
Dryfoos, Nancy Sculptor
Duback, Charles S Painter, Printmaker
Dubin, Ralph Painter, Collage Artist
Duff, John Ewing Sculptor
Dugmore, Edward Painter
Duis, Rita Painter
Dulac, Margarita Walker Painter, Writer
Dunbar, Jill H Critic, Writer
Duncan, (Eleanore) Klari de Szecsanyi Painter, Printmaker
Dunkelman, Loretta Painter
Dunnington, Walter Grey Collector, Patron
Dunwiddie, Charlotte Sculptor
Dupuy, Jean Multimedia Artist
Dusenbery, Walter Sculptor
Dworzan, George R Painter
Dyyon, Frazier Painter, Sculptor
Earl, Jack Eugene Sculptor
Eauclaire, Sally Art Critic
Eddy, Don Painter
Edelheit, Martha Painter, Filmmaker
Edelson, Gilbert S Administrator, Lecturer
Edelson, Mary Beth Conceptual Artist
Edwards, Ethel (Mrs Xavier Gonzalez) Painter
Efrat, Benni Sculptor, Painter
Eichel, Edward W Painter, Draftsman
Eidelberg, Martin Historian
Einstein, Gilbert W Dealer
Eisenberg, Jerome Martin Dealer, Collector
Eisenberg, Sonja Miriam Painter
Eisinger, Harry Painter
Eisler, Lawrence Painter
Eisner, Dorothy (Dorothy Eisner McDonald) Painter, Collage Artist
Eitingon, Brigitte Dealer
Ekdahl, Janis Kay Librarian
Elderfield, John Historian, Curator
Eliot, Lucy Carter Painter
Ellenzweig, Allen Bruce Critic, Curator
Eller, Evelyn (Evelyn Eller Rosenbaum) Collage Artist, Painter
Elliott, Ronnie Painter
Ellis, Richard Painter, Illustrator
Elman, Emily Painter, Educator
Elwell, Chip Master Printer, Publisher
Emil, Arthur D Collector
Emmerich, Andre Dealer, Writer
Englander, Gertrud Ceramist
Ensrud, Wayne Painter, Printmaker
Ente, Lily Sculptor, Printmaker
Epstein, Mitch (Mitchell D) Photographer
Eriksen, Gary Sculptor, Medalist

NEW YORK (cont)

Eriquezzo, Lee M Painter
Esman, Rosa M Dealer, Gallery Director
Esterow, Milton Editor, Publisher
Estes, Richard Painter
Ets, Marie Hall Illustrator, Writer
Evans, John Painter, Collage Artist
Evans, Minnie Painter
Everett, Len G Painter
Ewald, Elin Lake Dealer, Writer
Eyen, Richard J Dealer, Designer
Facci, Domenico (Aurelio) Sculptor,
    Painter
Faden, Lawrence Steven Painter, Sculptor
Falkenstein, Claire Sculptor
Falsetta, Vincent Mario Educator, Painter
Fane, Lawrence Sculptor
Faragasso, Jack Illustrator, Painter
Farber, Maya M Painter
Fares, William O Painter
Farruggio, Remo Michael Painter
Fasnacht, Heide Ann Sculptor
Faulconer, Mary (Fullerton) Painter,
    Designer
Faulkner, Frank Painter
Faurer, Louis Photographer
Fausett, (William) Dean Painter, Etcher
Fay, Ming G Sculptor, Painter
FeBland, Harriet Painter, Sculptor
Fedele, Frank D Dealer, Publisher
Feder, Ben Designer, Painter
Feigen, Richard L Dealer, Collector
Feigenbaum, Harriet (Mrs Neil
    Chamberlain) Environmental Artist,
    Sculptor
Feigin, Marsha Printmaker, Painter
Feininger, Andreas B L Photographer,
    Writer
Feinman, Stephen E Dealer
Feld, Stuart Paul Dealer
Feldman, Ronald Dealer
Feldstein, Mary Collector, Librarian
Fenn, (Frances) Elizabeth Painter,
    Graphic Artist
Fenton, Alan Painter, Instructor
Ferber, Herbert Sculptor, Painter
Ferrara, Jackie Sculptor
Ferrer, Rafael Painter, Sculptor
Finck, Furman J Painter, Instructor
Findlay, David B, Jr Dealer
Fingesten, Peter Graphic Artist, Educator
Finkelstein, Louis Educator, Painter
Finn, David Photographer
Finnegan, Sharyn Marie Painter
Fiore, Joseph A Painter, Instructor
Firestein, Cecily Barth Printmaker,
    Instructor
Fischbach, Marilyn Cole Dealer,
    Collector
Fischer, R M Sculptor
Fish, Janet I Painter
Fishko, Bella Dealer
Fitzgerald, Astrid Painter, Printmaker
Fitzgerald, Harriet Painter, Lecturer
Flack, Audrey L Painter, Photographer
Flam, Jack D Historian, Educator
Fleischman, Lawrence A Dealer,
    Collector
Flexner, James Thomas Writer, Historian
Flinn, Elizabeth Haight Educator
Floeter, Kent Sculptor
Flood, Richard Sidney Writer, Curator
Fohr, Jenny Painter, Printmaker
Fondren, Harold M Dealer
Force, Roland Wynfield Museum
    Director
Ford, Charles Henri Painter,
    Photographer
Ford, John Painter
Ford, John Charles Painter
Fourcade, Xavier Dealer
Fowler, Mel Painter, Printmaker

Fox, Flo Photographer, Lecturer
Frampton, Hollis Filmmaker
Francis, Sherron Painter
Frank, Peter Solomon Critic, Curator
Frankenberg, Robert Clinton Illustrator,
    Painter
Frankenthaler, Helen Painter
Frater, Hal Painter
Freckelton, Sondra Painter
Freed, Hermine Video Artist, Writer
Freed, William Painter
Freeman, Mark Painter, Printmaker
Freilich, Ann Painter, Collage Artist
Freilicher, Jane Painter, Printmaker
Freiman, Robert J Painter
Friedberg, Richard S Sculptor, Educator
Friedman, B H Writer
Friedman, Sally Ceila Painter
Fromboluti, Sideo Painter
Frumkin, Allan Dealer
Fugate-Wilcox, Terry Sculptor
Fukui, Nobu Painter
Fuller, Emily Painter
Gallagher, Carole Photographer, Writer
Gallagher, Michael B Painter
Garbaty, Marie-Louise Collector, Patron
Garcia, Frank Gallery Director,
    Historian
Gary, Dorothy Hales Collector, Writer
Gear, Josephine Historian, Gallery
    Director
Geber, Hana Sculptor, Instructor
Gebhardt, Roland Sculptor, Designer
Gechtoff, Sonia Painter
Gee, Helen Art Consultant, Curator
Geist, Sidney Sculptor, Critic
Gekiere, Madeleine Painter, Filmmaker
Gelber, Samuel Painter, Educator
Geldzahler, Henry Curator, Historian
Gellis, Sandy L Sculptor
Genauer, Emily Critic, Writer
Genn, Nancy Painter
Gentile, Gloria Irene Designer, Sculptor
Gentle, Esther Painter
Gentry, Herbert Painter
George, Dan Sculptor
Gerardia, Helen Painter, Printmaker
Gerdts, Abigail Booth Consultant,
    Historian
Gershinowitz, George Draftsman,
    Illustrator
Gershoy, Eugenie Sculptor, Painter
Gerst, Hilde W Dealer
Getler, Helen Dealer
Ghent, Henri Critic, Writer
Giacalone, Vito Painter, Historian
Giacomantonio, Archimedes
    Administrator, Sculptor
Giambertone, Paul Sculptor
Giampietro, Isabel (Isabel A Giampietro
    Knoll) Sculptor, Designer
Gianakos, Cristos Sculptor
Gianakos, Steve Sculptor, Painter
Gibson, Ralph H Photographer
Gifford, J Nebraska Painter, Sculptor
Gilbert, Helen Odell Painter, Printmaker
Gilbert, Lionel Painter, Instructor
Gilchrist, Elizabeth Brenda Editor
Gillespie, Dorothy Muriel Painter,
    Sculptor
Gillespie, Gregory Joseph Painter
Gimblett, Max(well) Painter
Giraudier, Antonio Painter, Writer
Gitlin, Michael Sculptor, Draftsman
Gladstone, Barbara Regen Dealer,
    Historian
Gladstone, M J Administrator, Publisher
Glanz, Andrea E Administrator, Curator
Glaser, Milton Designer, Illustrator
Glass, Wendy D Dealer, Collector
Glezer, Nechemia Dealer, Consultant
Glickman, Maurice Sculptor, Writer

Glimcher, Arnold B Dealer, Writer
Globus, Dorothy Twining Curator
Gobuzas, Aldona M Art Dealer, Collector
Goddard, Don (Donald) Editor, Writer
Godfrey, Robert Painter, Educator
Godwin, Judith Whitney Painter
Goell, Abby Jane Painter, Assemblage
    Artist
Goertz, Augustus Frederick, III Painter,
    Printmaker
Goings, Ralph Painter
Golbin, Andree Painter, Illustrator
Gold, Leah Painter, Printmaker
Gold, Martha B Sculptor
Gold, Sharon Cecile Painter, Educator
Goldberg, Judith Art Dealer
Goldberg, Michael Painter
Goldberg, RoseLee Historian, Curator
Golden, Eunice Painter, Filmmaker
Goldfinger, Eliot Sculptor
Goldin, Leon Painter
Goldman, Judith Writer, Critic
Goldring, Nancy Deborah Graphic Artist,
    Educator
Goldschmidt, Lucien Dealer
Goldsmith, Barbara Writer, Critic
Goldstein, Julius Painter, Instructor
Golub, Leon Albert Painter
Gomez-Quiroz, Juan Manuel Painter,
    Printmaker
Gongora, Leonel Painter, Educator
Gonzalez, Juan J Painter
Gonzalez, Xavier Painter, Sculptor
Goodman, Bertram Painter
Goodman, James Neil Dealer, Collector
Goodman, Marian Dealer, Publisher
Goodnough, Robert Painter
Goodrich, Lloyd Administrator, Writer
Goodrich, Susan Painter
Gorchov, Ron Painter
Gordon, Albert F Dealer
Gordon, Leah Shanks Writer
Gordon, Martin Dealer, Collector
Gorney, Jay Philip Dealer
Gornik, April Painter
Gottlieb, Carla Educator, Writer
Gould, Philip Historian, Educator
Goulet, Lorrie Sculptor, Instructor
Graham, Daniel H Conceptual Artist,
    Environmental Artist
Graham, Margaret Bloy Children's Book
    Illustrator
Graham, Robert C, Jr Dealer
Graham, Robert Claverhouse Dealer,
    Collector
Grausman, Philip Sculptor
Graves, Bradford Sculptor, Educator
Graves, Morris Painter
Graves, Nancy Stevenson Painter,
    Sculptor
Green, Denise G Painter
Green, George D Painter
Green, Jasha Sculptor, Painter
Green, Wilder Administrator, Architect
Greenbaum, Marty Painter, Sculptor
Greenberg, Gloria Painter, Designer
Greenberg, Irwin Painter, Instructor
Greene, Balcomb Painter
Greenfield-Sanders, Timothy
    Photographer
Greenleaf, Kenneth Lee Sculptor, Critic
Greenspan, (Mr & Mrs) George
    Collectors
Greenwald, Sheila Ellen Illustrator
Griefen, John Adams Painter
Grigoriadis, Mary Painter
Grooms, Red Painter, Sculptor
Groover, Jan Photographer
Gross, Alice Sculptor
Gross, Chaim Sculptor, Instructor
Grossberg, Jake Educator, Sculptor
Grossen, Francoise Sculptor, Instructor

NEW YORK (cont)

Grosser, Maurice Painter, Writer
Grossman, Nancy Sculptor, Painter
Grosvenor, Robert Sculptor
Groth, John August Illustrator, Painter
Grotz, Dorothy Rogers Painter
Gruen, John Critic, Writer
Grundberg, Andy (John Andrew) Critic, Editor
Gruskin, Mary Josephine Dealer
Guerrero, Jose Painter, Printmaker
Gummer, Don Sculptor
Gumpel, Hugh Painter
Gundelfinger, John Andre Painter, Collage Artist
Gurewitsch, Edna P Dealer, Historian
Gusella, Ernest Video Artist
Gussow, Sue Ferguson Painter, Printmaker
Gutzeit, Fred Painter
Haacke, Hans Christoph Sculptor, Conceptual Artist
Haar, Tom Photographer
Haas, Ernst Photographer, Lecturer
Haas, Richard John Printmaker, Muralist
Haber, Ira Joel Sculptor, Writer
Habergritz, George Joseph Painter, Sculptor
Hackenbroch, Yvonne Alix Curator, Writer
Haessle, Jean-Marie Georges Painter, Printmaker
Hafif, Marcia Painter, Educator
Hahn, Gerald Painter, Educator
Hahn, Stephen Dealer
Halaby, Samia Asaad Painter, Educator
Halasz, Piri Historian, Critic
Hale, Robert Beverly Administrator, Instructor
Hall, Susan Painter
Halpern, Nathan L Collector
Hamer, Charles James Painter, Designer
Hamilton, Patricia Rose Dealer
Hammer, Victor J Dealer
Hammond, Harmony Sculptor, Painter
Hammond, Phyllis Baker Sculptor
Hampton, Lucille Charlotte Sculptor, Medalist
Hanks, David Allen Curator, Writer
Hannah, Duncan (Rathbone) Painter
Hansen, Gaylen Capener Painter, Educator
Harbutt, Charles Photographer
Hardy, John Painter
Hare, David Sculptor
Harmon, Lily Painter, Writer
Harnett, (Mr & Mrs) Joel William Collectors
Harris, Ann Sutherland Historian, Administrator
Harriton, Abraham Painter
Hartford, Huntington Collector, Patron
Hartshorn, Willis E Photographer, Instructor
Hartwig, Cleo Sculptor
Hasen, Burt Stanly Painter, Printmaker
Haskell, Barbara Curator
Hauser, Reine I Curator, Dealer
Haxton, David Photographer, Filmmaker
Hayes, Gerald Painter, Photographer
Hayward, Jane Historian, Curator
Hazen, Joseph H Collector
Hazlitt, Don Painter
Headley, David Allen Painter
Heckscher, Morrison Harris Curator, Historian
Heiferman, Marvin Dealer
Heiloms, May Painter
Heinemann, Peter Painter, Instructor
Heinz, Susan Administrator
Heise, Myron Robert Painter
Held, Al Painter

Heliker, John Edward Painter, Educator
Helioff, Anne Graile (Mrs Benjamin Hirschberg) Painter, Collage Artist
Heller, Ben Dealer, Collector
Heller, Dorothy Painter
Heller, Goldie (Mrs Edward W Greenberg) Collector, Consultant
Helman, Phoebe Sculptor, Painter
Hemphill, Herbert Waide, Jr Curator, Lecturer
Hendricks, David Charles Painter, Visual Artist
Hendricks, Geoffrey Painter, Environmental Artist
Henry, Gerrit Van Keuren Critic
Henry, Robert Painter, Educator
Henselmann, Caspar Sculptor
Hera Sculptor, Environmental Artist
Herfield, Phyllis Painter, Printmaker
Herrera, Carmen Painter
Hess, Emil John Painter, Sculptor
Higa (Yoshiharu) Printmaker, Photographer
Hightower, John B Administrator, Museum Director
Highwater, Jamake Critic, Lecturer
Hildebrand, June Mary Ann Printmaker, Illustrator
Hill, Clinton J Painter, Educator
Hill, James Berry Dealer
Hillsmith, Fannie Painter, Assemblage Artist
Hilson, Douglas Painter, Educator
Hilton, Joseph Painter
Hinman, Charles B Painter, Sculptor
Hios, Theo Painter, Graphic Artist
Hirschfeld, Albert Graphic Artist
Hitch, Stewart Painter
Hitchcock, Henry Russell Historian, Critic
Hochhauser, Marilyn Helsenrott Painter, Educator
Hodgkins, Rosalind Selma Painter
Hofer, Evelyn Photographer
Hoffman, Martin (Joseph) Painter, Illustrator
Hoffman, Nancy Dealer
Hoie, Claus Painter, Etcher
Hoie, Helen Hunt Painter, Collage Artist
Holabird, Jean Painter, Printmaker
Hollerbach, Serge Painter, Instructor
Hollingsworth, Alvin Carl Painter, Instructor
Hollister, Paul Painter, Writer
Holt, Nancy Louise Sculptor, Filmmaker
Holtz, Itshak Jack Painter, Printmaker
Holzer, Jenny Conceptual Artist
Hooton, Bruce Duff Editor, Publisher
Hopkins, Budd Painter
Hopkins, Peter Painter, Writer
Horowitz, Nadja Painter, Instructor
Horowitz, (Mr & Mrs) Raymond J Collector
Horton, Carolyn Conservator
Horwitt, Will Sculptor
Hoving, Thomas Consultant, Editor
Howard, Linda Sculptor
Howat, John Keith Curator, Historian
Howell, Hannah Johnson Librarian
Huchthausen, David Richard Sculptor, Educator
Huemer, Christina Gertrude Librarian
Hughes, Robert S F Critic, Lecturer
Hui, Helene Painter, Filmmaker
Humphrey, Nene Sculptor, Instructor
Humphrey, Ralph Painter
Hunt, Bryan Sculptor
Hunter-Stiebel, Penelope Curator
Hurson, Michael Draftsman, Painter
Hurt, Susanne M Painter
Hutchinson, Max Dealer
Hutsaliuk, Lubo Painter

Hutton, Leonard Dealer
Huxtable, Ada Louise Critic
Hyde, Scott Photographer, Printmaker
Hyman, Isabelle Historian, Educator
Hyman, Linda Dealer, Historian
Iimura, Taka Filmmaker, Video Artist
Ingber, Barbara Dealer, Collector
Ingle, John S Painter, Educator
Inoue, Kazuko Painter, Lecturer
Insel, Paula Dealer, Administrator
Insley, Will Painter, Draftsman
Inukai, Kyohei Painter, Sculptor
Isenburger, Eric Painter
Israel, Marvin Designer, Painter
Isserstedt, Dorothea Carus Dealer, Historian
Itchkawich, David Michael Printmaker, Illustrator
Iwamoto, Ralph Shigeto Painter
Izuka, Kunio Sculptor
Jackson, Ward Painter, Editor
Jacobs, Jim Painter, Printmaker
Jacobs, Ted Seth Graphic Artist, Muralist
Jacquemon, Pierre Painter
Jacquette, Yvonne Helene Painter, Printmaker
Jae Sculptor
Jaffe, Nora Painter, Sculptor
Jagger, Gillian Painter, Sculptor
Jampol, Glenn D Painter
Janis, Conrad Dealer, Collector
Janis, Sidney Dealer, Writer
Jansen, Angela Bing Printmaker, Photographer
Jaramillo, Virginia Painter
Jarvis, Lucy Consultant, Filmmaker
Jaudon, Valerie Painter
Ject-Key, Elsie Painter
Jeffers, Wendy Jane Painter, Curator
Jelinek, Hans Printmaker, Educator
Jenkins, Paul Painter
Jennings, Francis Sculptor, Painter
Jenrette, Pamela Anne Painter, Costume Designer
Jensen, Bill Painter
J J Goldsmith, Sculptor
Johns, Jasper Painter
Johnson, Buffie Painter, Lecturer
Johnson, Cecile Ryden Painter, Publisher
Johnson, J Stewart Curator
Johnson, Lester F Painter, Educator
Johnson, Marian Willard Dealer
Johnson, Martin Brian Painter, Sculptor
Johnson, Miani (Marianne) Guthrie Dealer
Johnson, Philip Cortelyou Collector, Architect
Johnson, Robert Jay Dealer, Collector
Johnson, Una E Curator, Writer
Jonas, Joan Video Artist, Conceptual Artist
Jones, Carter R(uthven) Sculptor
Jones, Edward Powis Painter, Sculptor
Jones, Jerry Sculptor, Painter
Joukhadar, Kristina Dealer, Collector
Joukhadar, Moumtaz Dealer, Painter
Juarez, Roberto Painter
Judd, Donald Clarence Sculptor
Judson, Jeannette Alexander Painter
Julian, Lazaro Painter, Designer
Juszczyk, James Joseph Painter
Kacere, John C Painter
Kahan, Alexander Dealer
Kahan, Leonard Dealer, Painter
Kahane, Melanie (Melanie Kahane Grauer) Designer
Kahn, Susan B Painter
Kahn, Wolf Painter
Kaiser, Diane Sculptor, Educator
Kaish, Luise Sculptor, Educator
Kaish, Morton Painter, Educator
Kalina, Richard Painter

NEW YORK (cont)
Kallem, Henry Painter
Kallir, Jane Katherine Dealer, Writer
Kan, Diana Painter, Lecturer
Kane, Bob Paul Painter
Kanovitz, Howard Painter
Kaplan, Jacques Collector, Dealer
Karp, Richard Gordon Painter, Lecturer
Karwoski, Richard Charles Painter,
    Educator
Kasuba, Aleksandra Environmental Artist
Katz, Alex Painter
Katz, Hilda (Hulda Weber) Painter,
    Printmaker
Katz, Leandro Assemblage Artist,
    Filmmaker
Katz, Morris Painter
Katzen, Hal Zachery Dealer
Katzen, Lila (Pell) Sculptor, Educator
Katzman, Herbert Painter, Instructor
Kauffman, Robert Craig Painter, Sculptor
Kaufman, Jane Painter, Lecturer
Kaufman, Joe Illustrator, Writer
Kaufman, Nancy Consultant, Writer
Kaufmann, Robert Carl Art Librarian
Kawabata, Minoru Painter, Instructor
Kawashima, Takeshi Painter, Sculptor
Kaz (Lawrence Katzman) Designer,
    Cartoonist
Kaz, Nathaniel Sculptor, Instructor
Keats, Ezra Jack Illustrator, Writer
Keen, Helen Boyd Painter
Keister, Steve (Stephen Lee) Sculptor
Keith, Eros Illustrator, Painter
Keller, Frank S Painter
Kelly, James Painter
Kelly, Leon Painter
Kempton, Greta Painter
Kepets, Hugh Michael Painter,
    Printmaker
Kerns, Ed (Johnson), Jr Painter
Kessler, Alan Painter, Sculptor
Kessler, Shirley Painter
Kidd, Steven R Illustrator, Instructor
Kikuchi-Yngojo, Alan Photographer,
    Collage Artist
Kim, Po (Hyun) Painter
Kimmel-Cohn, Roberta Dealer, Designer
Kimura, Riisaburo Painter, Printmaker
King, William Dickey Sculptor
Kingman, Dong M Painter, Illustrator
Kingsley, April Critic, Lecturer
Kinigstein, Jonah Painter, Designer
Kinstler, Everett Raymond Painter,
    Instructor
Kipniss, Robert Painter, Lithographer
Kirk, Michael Printmaker, Instructor
Kirschenbaum, Bernard Edwin Sculptor
Kisch, Gloria Sculptor
Klabunde, Charles Spencer Printmaker,
    Painter
Kleckner, Susan Photographer, Filmmaker
Kleemann, Ron Painter
Kleiman, Alan Painter, Sculptor
Klein, Doris Painter
Klein, Sandor C Painter, Sculptor
Kline, Alma Sculptor
Kluver, Billy (Johan Wilhem)
    Administrator
Knight, Hilary Illustrator, Writer
Knigin, Michael Jay Painter, Printmaker
Knoebel, David Jon Sculptor
Knowles, Alison Performance Artist,
    Printmaker
Knowlton, Monique Dealer, Collector
Kocherthaler, Mina Painter
Kolbert, Frank L Dealer
Kolodner, Nathan K Dealer
Koltun, Frances Lang Collector, Lecturer
Komor, Mathias Dealer
Konzal, Joseph Sculptor
Koppelman, Chaim Printmaker, Educator

Koppelman, Dorothy Painter, Gallery
    Director
Koren, Edward B Cartoonist, Illustrator
Korman, Barbara Sculptor, Assemblage
    Artist
Korman, Harriet R Painter
Kornblau, Gerald Dealer, Consultant
Korot, Beryl Painter, Video Artist
Korshak, Yvonne Historian, Educator
Kottler, Lynn Dealer
Koursaros, Harry G Painter
Kozloff, Joyce Painter, Environmental
    Artist
Kozloff, Max Photographer
Kramer, Gertrude M Dealer
Kramer, Hilton Critic
Krashes, Barbara Painter, Director
Kraushaar, Antoinette M Dealer
Krauss, Rosalind E Critic, Historian
Kreznar, Richard J Sculptor, Painter
Kriensky Painter
Kriesberg, Irving Painter
Krinsky, Carol Herselle Historian,
    Educator
Kruger, Barbara Conceptual Artist, Film
    Critic
Krushenick, Nicholas Painter
Kubota, Shigeko Video Curator, Video
    Artist
Kuchel, Konrad G Administrator
Kuehn, Frances Painter
Kuh, Howard Painter
Kuh, Katharine Critic, Consultant
Kuopus, Clinton Painter, Collector
Kurahara, Ted Painter, Educator
Kurhajec, Joseph A Sculptor
Kurz, Diana Painter, Educator
Kushner, Robert Ellis Painter,
    Performance Artist
Kuwayama, Tadaaki Painter
Lable, Eliot Painter, Sculptor
Laderman, Gabriel Painter, Educator
Laemmle, Cheryl Painter
La Hotan, Robert L Painter
Lally, James Joseph Dealer
Lamb, Adrian Painter
Lancaster, Mark Painter
Landfield, Ronnie (Ronald T) Painter
Landis, Lily Sculptor
Landry, Albert Dealer
Landsman, Stanley Sculptor
Lane, Alvin Seymour Collector
Lane, Lois Painter, Printmaker
Lang, Avis Curator, Writer
Lang, Daniel S Painter
Langner, Nola Illustrator, Writer
La Noue, Terence David Painter,
    Educator
Lansner, Fay Painter, Tapestry Artist
Larcada, Richard Kenneth Dealer
Larsen, Jack Lenor Designer, Weaver
Larson, Kay L Critic, Writer
Lasch, Pat Sculptor
Lavatelli, Carla Sculptor, Weaver
Law, Pauline Elizabeth Painter
Lebedev, Vladimir Painter
Lee, Eleanor Gay Painter
Leech, Merle Eugene Sculptor,
    Printmaker
Lefebre, John Dealer
Leff, Juliette Painter, Educator
Lehr, Janet Dealer
Leiber, Gerson August Printmaker
Lekakis, Michael Nicholas Sculptor
Lembeck, John Edgar Painter
Lemer, Ellen Terry Dealer, Collector
Leonardi, Hector Painter, Instructor
Lerman, Doris (Harriet) Painter, Sculptor
Lerman, Leo Writer, Historian
Lerman, Ora Painter, Sculptor
Lerner, Abe Book Designer
Lerner, Martin Curator, Historian

Lerner, Sandra Painter, Collage Artist
Lerner, Sandy R Painter, Lithographer
Leslie, Seaver Painter, Instructor
Leven, Ann R Administrator
Leventhal, Ruth Lee Sculptor, Painter
Levering, Robert K Painter, Illustrator
Levi, Josef Painter
Levin, Gail Curator, Historian
Levin, Hugh Lauter Publisher, Dealer
Levin, Kim Critic, Painter
Levine, Jack Painter
Levine, Les Sculptor, Video Artist
Levinson, Mon Sculptor, Painter
Levit, Herschel Photographer, Historian
Levitt, Alfred Painter, Prehistorian
Levitt, Helen Photographer, Filmmaker
Levy, Bernard Dealer
Levy, David Corcos Photographer,
    Educator
Levy, S(tephen) Dean Dealer, Gallery
    Director
Levy, Tibbie Painter
Lewis, Golda Assemblage Artist,
    Papermaker
Lewison, Florence (Mrs Maurice
    Glickman) Writer, Art Dealer
Le Witt, Sol Sculptor
Liberman, Alexander Painter, Sculptor
Licht, Evelyn M Painter, Sculptor
Licht, Jennifer McConnell Curator,
    Historian
Lieberman, Louis (Karl) Sculptor,
    Draftsman
Lieberman, William S Administrator
Ligare, David H Painter
Liles, Racford Bailey Painter, Sculptor
Lilyquist, Christine Egyptologist, Curator
Lindgren, Bjorn Frank Collector, Dealer
Linker, Kate Philippa Critic
Linn, Steven Allen Sculptor
Lionni, Leo Sculptor, Painter
Lippard, Lucy Rowland Writer
Lipton, Seymour Sculptor
Lipton, Sondra (Sahlman) Painter,
    Sculptor
Lister, Ardele Diane Video Artist
Little, James Painter
Livet, Anne Hodge Administrator, Critic
Livingston, Sidnee Painter
Llorente, Luis Painter, Designer
Lobello, Peter Sculptor, Graphic Artist
Loew, Michael Painter, Educator
Lombard, Annette Painter, Instructor
London, Alexander Collector, Illustrator
London, Barbara Curator
Long, Rose-Carol Washton Historian,
    Writer
Lorber, D Martin H B Consultant
Lorber, Richard Critic, Administrator
Loring, John Painter, Printmaker
Lubart, Henriette d'Arlin Educator,
    Sculptor
Lucchesi, Bruno Sculptor
Lucero, Michael (Lewis) Sculpture
Lucier, Mary Video Artist, Photographer
Lucioni, Luigi Painter, Etcher
Luck, Robert Curator, Instructor
Luisi, Jerry Sculptor, Instructor
Lukin, Sven Painter
Lumbard, Jean Ashmore Dealer
Lund, David Painter, Educator
Lunde, Karl Roy Historian, Writer
Lusker, Ron Painter, Designer
Lutz, Marjorie Brunhoff Sculptor
Lutze, (Hildegarde) Consultant, Dealer
Lynes, Russell Writer, Critic
McCall, Anthony Filmmaker
McCarthy, Denis Painter
McCartin, William Francis Painter
McCormick, Jo Mary (Jo Mary
    McCormick-Sakurai) Painter,
    Photographer

NEW YORK (cont)

McCoy, Ann Muralist, Draftsman
McCready, Karen Dealer, Writer
McDarrah, Fred William Photographer, Critic
McEvilley, Thomas Writer, Critic
McFadden, David Revere Curator
McFadden, Mary Collector, Designer
McGowan, Kenneth Photographer
McGowin, Ed Sculptor, Painter
MacIver, Loren Painter
MacKay, Hugh Dealer
McKay, Renee Painter
MacKendrick, Lilian Painter
McKesson, Malcolm Forbes Painter, Sculptor
McKie, Todd Stoddard Painter
McKinney, Donald Dealer
McKnight, Thomas Frederick Painter, Printmaker
MacLagger, Richard Joseph Dealer, Collector
McMahon, James Edward Dealer
Macomber, William B Administrator
McShine, Kynaston Leigh Curator
McTwigan, Michael Critic, Editor
Madsen, Loren Wakefield Sculptor
Magistro, Charles John Painter, Printmaker
Magriel, Paul Collector
Mallory, Nina Ayala Educator, Historian
Mallory, Ronald Sculptor
Mandel, Howard Painter, Sculptor
Mandelbaum, Lyn Painter, Printmaker
Mangold, Robert Peter Painter
Manso, Leo Painter, Educator
Manton, Jock (Archimedes Aristides Giacomantonio) Sculptor, Administrator
Manville, Elsie Painter
Mapplethorpe, Robert Photographer
Marais Painter
Marazzi, William C P Painter, Ceramist
Marberger, A Aladar Dealer, Museum Director
Marchisotto, Linda A Dealer
Marcus, Marcia Painter, Educator
Marden, Brice Painter, Printmaker
Marder, Dorie Painter, Printmaker
Margo, Boris Painter, Printmaker
Margolis, David Painter, Sculptor
Margulies, Joseph Painter, Printmaker
Marino, Frank Dealer
Marisol, Escobar Sculptor
Mark, Mary Ellen Photographer
Mark, Phyllis Sculptor
Markel, Kathryn E Dealer
Markell, Isabella Banks Painter, Graphic Artist
Marks, (Mr & Mrs) Cedric H Collectors, Patrons
Marks, Claude Painter, Writer
Marks, Royal S Dealer, Collector
Maroney, James H, Jr Dealer
Marron, Donald B Collector
Marshall, Richard Donald Curator, Historian
Marsicano, Nicholas Painter, Educator
Marsteller, William A Collector
Marter, Joan Historian, Critic
Martin, Denise B Editor
Martin, Doug Painter
Martin, Knox Painter, Sculptor
Martin, Richard (Harrison) Historian
Martin, Thomas Painter, Instructor
Martinez, Alfred Painter
Marton, Tutzi Painter
Martone, Michael Photographer
Masheck, Joseph Daniel Historian, Critic
Mason, Francis Scarlett, Jr Administrator
Mason, Frank Herbert Painter, Instructor
Matisse, Pierre Dealer

Mavian, Salpi Miriam Painter
Max, Peter Painter, Printmaker
Maxwell, William C Painter, Printmaker
Mayer, Bena Frank Painter
Mayer, Grace M Curator, Collector
Mayer, Rosemary Sculptor, Graphic Artist
Mayes, Elaine Photographer, Filmmaker
Mayorga, Gabriel Humberto Painter, Sculptor
Mazze, Irving Sculptor, Medalist
Meier, Richard Alan Architect
Meisel, Louis Koenig Dealer, Publisher
Melikian, Mary Painter
Mellon, James Printmaker, Painter
Mendelson, Haim Painter, Printmaker
Meng, Wendy Painter
Merkin, Richard Marshall Painter, Printmaker
Merrin, Edward H Dealer
Messer, Thomas M Museum Director, Historian
Metz, Frank Robert Painter, Director
Metzger, Evelyn Borchard Painter, Sculptor
Meyer, Susan E Editor, Writer
Meyer, Ursula Sculptor, Photographer
Meyerowitz, Joel Photographer
Meyers, Dale (Mrs Mario Cooper) Painter, Instructor
Michals, Duane Photographer
Michaux, Ronald Robert Dealer
Mieczkowski, Edwin Painter
Mikus, Eleanore Painter, Educator
Milder, Jay Painter, Sculptor
Miles, Jeanne Patterson Painter, Sculptor
Milgrom, Betty Painter
Milholland, Richard Alexander Painter
Miller, Brenda Sculptor, Environmental
Miller, Dorothy Canning Consultant
Miller, (Richard) Guy Sculptor
Miller, Joan Vita Museum Director, Administrator
Miller, Laurence Glenn Photographer, Dealer
Miller, Richard Kidwell Painter
Miller, Richard McDermott Sculptor
Miller, Robert Peter Dealer
Milliken, Alexander Fabbri Dealer, Collector
Mills, Margaret M Administrator
Miralda, Antoni Sculptor
Miss, Mary Sculptor
Mitchell, Fred Painter
Mitchell, Joan Painter
Mitchell, Peter Todd Painter
Model, Elisabeth D Sculptor, Painter
Mogavero, Michael James Painter
Mogensen, Paul Painter, Printmaker
Monaghan, William Scott Painter, Sculptor
Mones, Arthur Photographer
Monk, Robert Evan, Jr Dealer, Curator
Monroe, Gerald Painter, Educator
Montano, Linda (Mary) Conceptual Artist, Video Artist
Moore, Barbara Historian, Writer
Moore, Fay Painter, Administrator
Moore, Olga Painter
Moore, Peter Photographer, Archivist
Moore, Robert James Painter, Photographer
Morgan, Norma Gloria Painter, Engraver
Morgan, Theodora Writer
Morley, Malcom Painter
Morris, Robert Sculptor
Morse, Mitchell Ian Dealer, Restorer
Moseley, Ralph Sessions Painter
Moses, Ed Painter
Moskowitz, Ira Painter, Printmaker
Moskowitz, Robert S Painter
Moufarrege, Nicolas A Painter, Critic

Moy, Seong Painter, Graphic Artist
Moyer, Roy Painter, Administrator
Muller, Priscilla Elkow Historian, Curator
Munro, Eleanor Writer, Critic
Munro, Janet Andrea Painter
Murata, Hiroshi Painter, Printmaker
Murphy, Catherine E Painter
Murphy, Hass Sculptor, Draftsman
Murray, Albert (Ketcham) Painter
Murray, Elizabeth Painter
Murray, John Michael Painter
Murray, Judith Painter
Murray, Robert (Gray) Sculptor, Painter
Myers, Forrest Warden Sculptor
Myers, Martin Sculptor, Painter
Nagano, Shozo Painter
Naiman, Lee Dealer, Consultant
Nakazato, Hitoshi Painter, Printmaker
Namuth, Hans Photographer, Film Maker
Nathans, Rhoda R Photographer
Nauman, Bruce Sculptor
Navaretta, Cynthia Lecturer, Editor
Neel, Alice Painter
Neikrug, Marjorie Dealer, Appraiser
Neill, Joe Sculptor
Neiman, LeRoy Painter, Printmaker
Nelson, Dona Rae Painter
Nemec, Vernita Ellen Performance Artist, Printmaker
Nesbitt, Lowell (Blair) Painter, Sculptor
Neuberger, Roy R Collector, Patron
Neustein, Joshua Painter, Printmaker
Nevelson, Louise Sculptor, Printmaker
Newhouse, Clyde Mortimer Dealer, Historian
Newman, Arnold Photographer
Newman, Elias Painter
Newton, Douglas Administrator, Museum Director
Niblock, Phill Filmmaker, Composer
Nice, Don Painter
Nichols, James William Painter
Niizuma, Minoru Sculptor
Noble, Joseph Veach Museum Director, Museologist
Nochlin, Linda (Pommer) Historian, Educator
Noel, Georges Painter, Sculptor
Nolan, Margaret Patterson Librarian
Noland, William Sculptor
Norman, Dorothy (S) Writer, Photographer
Norvell, Patsy Sculptor, Environmental Artist
Nosoff, Frank Painter
Notarbartolo, Albert Painter, Environmental Artist
Novak, Barbara (Mrs Brian O'Doherty) Historian, Educator
Novros, David Painter
O'Beil, Hedy Painter, Critic
Ocampo, Miguel Painter
O'Connell, Edward E Photographer, Printmaker
O'Connor, Francis Valentine Historian, Lecturer
Odate, Toshio Conceptual Artist, Instructor
Oenslager, Donald Mitchell Stage Designer
Offin, Charles Z Collector, Critic
Ohashi, Yutaka Painter
Ohlson, Douglas Dean Painter, Educator
Ohrbach, Jerome K Collector
Okoshi, Eugenia Sumiye Painter, Printmaker
Okumura, Lydia Painter
Oldenburg, Claes Thure Sculptor
Oldenburg, Richard Erik Museum Director
Oliver, Richard Bruce Architect
Olugebefola, Ademola Painter, Designer

NEW YORK (cont)

Ono, Yoko Conceptual Artist
Oppenheim, Dennis A Sculptor
Order, Trudy Painter
Orensanz, Angel L Sculptor, Ceramist
Orkin, Ruth (Mrs Morris Engel)
  Photographer, Filmmaker
Oscarsson, Victoria Constance Gunhild
  Dealer, Consultant
Oster, Gerald Painter, Kinetic Artist
Ostuni, Peter W Painter
O'Toole, James St Laurence Dealer,
  Historian
Owen, Frank (Franklin Charles) Painter
Owsley, David Thomas Consultant
Pace, Stephen S Painter, Printmaker
Paik, Nam June Video Artist
Paley, (Mr & Mrs) William S Collectors
Pardee, William Hearne Painter, Educator
Parish, Betty Waldo Painter, Writer
Parizek, Jaro Dealer, Collector
Parker, James Painter
Parker, Nancy Winslow Illustrator, Writer
Parker, Ray(mond) Painter
Parkinson, Elizabeth Bliss (Mrs Henry Ives
  Cobb) Patron, Collector
Parsons, Merribell Maddux Curator,
  Administrator
Pascal, David Painter, Cartoonist
Passuntino, Peter Zaccaria Painter,
  Printmaker
Paternosto, Cesar Pedro Painter
Pearl, Marilyn Dealer
Pearlstein, Philip Painter, Educator
Pease, Roland Folsom Critic, Collector
Pei, I M (Ieoh Ming) Architect, Designer
Pellettieri, Michael Joseph Printmaker,
  Painter
Pellicone, Marie Gallery Director
Pellicone, William Painter, Muralist
Pels, Albert Painter, Administrator
Penn, Irving Photographer
Pentelovitch, Robert Alan Painter
Perlman, Joel Leonard Sculptor,
  Instructor
Perls, Klaus G Dealer
Perreault, John Critic, Curator
Perret, George Albert Writer, Appraiser
Perret, Nell Foster Painter, Printmaker
Pershan, Marion Painter
Persky, Robert S Writer, Dealer
Pesner, Carole Manishin Dealer
Peterson, Susan Harnly Educator,
  Ceramic Artist
Petlin, Irving Painter
Pfahl, Charles Alton, III Painter
Pfeifer, Marcuse Dealer, Gallery Director
Pfister, Harold Francis Administrator
Pfriem, Bernard Painter, Director
Phelan, Ellen Denise Painter
Philip, Lotte Brand Historian
Phillips, Alice Jane Painter
Phillips, Helen (Elizabeth) Sculptor,
  Graphic Artist
Phillpot, Clive James Librarian, Writer
Pierce, Donald (Benjamin) Painter,
  Instructor
Pilgrim, James F Curator, Historian
Pinchbeck, Peter G Painter
Pindell, Howardena Doreen Painter,
  Educator
Pines, Ned L Collector
Pinto, Angelo Raphael Painter,
  Printmaker
Pinto, Jody Sculptor
Pisano, Ronald George Historian,
  Consultant
Pitt, Suzan (Lee) Painter, Filmmaker
Pittore, Carlo Painter, Muralist
Pitts, Richard G Painter, Printmaker
Piziz, Silvia Collector, Patron
Placzek, Adolf Kurt Librarian, Historian

Plagens, Peter Painter, Educator
Pletka, Paul Painter, Printmaker
Poindexter, Elinor Fuller Dealer
Pollard, Donald Pence Designer, Painter
Pollaro, Paul Painter
Polsky, Cynthia Administrator, Collector
Polster, Joanne F Librarian, Writer
Pommer, Richard Educator, Historian
Ponce de Leon, Michael Printmaker,
  Painter
Pond, Clayton Painter, Printmaker
Poons, Larry Painter
Poor, Anne Painter
Porada, Edith Historian
Porter, Liliana Painter, Printmaker
Portnoy, Theodora Preiss Dealer
Posen, Stephen Painter
Poses, (Mr & Mrs) Jack I Collectors
Posner, Donald Historian
Post, Anne B Sculptor, Graphic Artist
Pozzi, Lucio Painter
Prager, David A Collector
Prakapas, Eugene Joseph Dealer, Editor
Pratt, Dallas Patron, Collector
Pratt, Frances (Frances Elizabeth Usui)
  Painter, Illustrator
Prentice, David Ramage Painter,
  Printmaker
Preston, George Nelson Historian,
  Educator
Prohaska, Elena Anastasia Dealer,
  Consultant
Promutico, Jean Painter
Purcell, Ann Painter
Pusey, Mavis Painter, Printmaker
Quaytman, Harvey Painter
Rabinovich, Raquel Painter, Sculptor
Rabinovitch, William Avrum Painter,
  Sculptor
Rabinowitch, David Sculptor
Rabinowitch, Royden Leslie Sculptor
Rabkin, Leo Collector, Painter
Radulovic, Savo Painter, Tapestry Artist
Raffo, Steve Painter, Draftsman
Rafsky, Jessica C Collector
Raggio, Olga Historian, Curator
Ragusa, Isa Historian
Rand, Archie Painter, Muralist
Rappin, Adrian Painter
Raskin, Ellen Illustrator, Graphic Artist
Raskind, Philis Sculptor, Instructor
Ratcliff, Carter Critic, Writer
Ratkai, George Painter, Sculptor
Rauschenberg, Robert Painter,
  Photographer
Rave, Georgia Painter, Tapestry Artist
Raven, Arlene Writer, Historian
Raydon, Alexander R Dealer, Collector
Raymond, Lilo Photographer
Recanati, Dina Sculptor
Reddy, Krishna N Printmaker, Sculptor
Redein, Alex S Painter, Instructor
Reed, David Fredrick Painter
Reed, Harold Dealer
Reff, Theodore Historian
Reginato, Peter Sculptor
Rehberger, Gustav Painter, Draftsman
Reiback, Earl M Sculptor, Kinetic Artist
Reichard, Stephen Brantley Administrator
Reichek, Elaine Conceptual Artist
Reid, Robert Dennis Painter, Instructor
Reiland, Lowell Keith Sculptor
Reiner, Gladys & Jules Collectors,
  Patrons
Reininghaus, Ruth (Ruth Reininghaus
  Smith) Painter
Reisman, Philip Painter
Reiss, Lionel S Painter, Writer
Remington, Deborah Williams Painter
Renouf, Edda Painter, Printmaker
Rentschler, Sarah Yorke Dealer, Collector
Reopel, Joyce Draftsman

Resek, Kate Frances Painter
Resika, Paul Painter
Resnick, Marcia Aylene Photographer,
  Conceptual Artist
Resnick, Milton Painter
Rewald, John Historian, Educator
Reynal, Jeanne Mosaic Artist
Rice, Shelley Enid Critic, Historian
Rich, Garry Lorence Painter
Richards, Bill Painter
Richards, Bill (William A) Draftsman
Richardson, Constance (Coleman) Painter
Richardson, Gretchen (Mrs Ronald
  Freelander) Sculptor
Rich-Perlow, Katharina Dealer, Gallery
  Director
Riess, Lore Painter, Printmaker
Ringgold, Faith Painter, Sculptor
Ripps, Rodney Painter
Ritchie, (Celia) Ann Painter
Robbin, Anthony Stuart Painter
Roberts, Richard Painter
Robins, Corinne Critic, Writer
Rockburne, Dorothea Painter
Rockefeller, (Mr & Mrs) David Collectors
Rockefeller, (Mrs) Laurance S Collector
Rodan, Don Photographer, Painter
Rodman, Ruth M Printmaker, Tapestry
  Artist
Rodriguez, Geno (Eugene) Photographer,
  Gallery Director
Roesler, Norbert Leonhard Hugo
  Collector
Rohlfing, Christian Administrator,
  Curator
Roller, Marion Bender Sculptor, Painter
Romano, Emanuel Glicen Painter,
  Illustrator
Romano, Salvatore Michael Sculptor,
  Kinetic Artist
Romano, Umberto Roberto Painter,
  Sculptor
Romeu, Joost A Conceptual Artist,
  Designer
Rosand, David Historian, Critic
Rosati, James Sculptor, Educator
Rose, Herman Painter, Printmaker
Rose, Leatrice Painter, Instructor
Rose, Mary Anne Painter
Rose, Peter Henry Dealer
Rose, Stephanie Painter, Educator
Rosenberg, Alex Jacob Publisher, Dealer
Rosenberg, Carole Halsband Editor,
  Director
Rosenblum, Jay Painter, Printmaker
Rosenblum, Robert Historian
Rosenborg, Ralph M Painter
Rosenfeld, Samuel L Dealer, Collector
Rosenhouse, Irwin Printmaker, Painter
Rosenquit, Bernard Painter, Printmaker
Rosenthal, Deborah Maly Critic, Painter
Rosenthal, Stephen Painter
Rosenthal, Tony (Bernard) Sculptor
Rosenwald, Carol Dealer
Roser, Ce (Cecilia) Painter, Video Artist
Ross, Charles Environmental Artist,
  Sculptor
Ross, Clifford Painter, Sculptor
Ross, Gloria F(rankenthaler) Tapestry
  Artist
Rotan, Walter Sculptor
Rothenberg, Susan Painter, Printmaker
Rothfarb, Ed (Edwin I) Sculptor,
  Educator
Rothschild, Carolyn Anita Dealer
Rothschild, John D Dealer
Rothschild, Judith Painter, Collage
  Artist
Rotterdam, Paul Z Painter
Ruben, Richards Painter, Educator
Rubin, Lawrence Dealer, Collector
Rubin, William Curator, Historian

NEW YORK (cont)

Rubinfien, Leo H Photographer
Rubinstein, Susan R Photographer
Ruda, Edwin Painter
Ruddley, John Administrator, Painter
Russell, Philip C Painter, Instructor
Ruta, Peter Paul Painter
Rutzky, Ivy Sky Sculptor
Ryan, Elizabeth Theresa Painter
Ryerson, Margery A Painter, Printmaker
Ryman, Robert Painter
Saari, Peter H Painter, Sculptor
Sachs, A M Dealer, Collector
Sadek, George Educator, Designer
Saidenberg, Daniel Dealer
Saidenberg, Eleanore B Dealer, Collector
St Clair, Michael Dealer
Salemme, Lucia (Autorino) Painter,
    Writer
Salle, David Painter
Salt, John Painter
Samaras, Lucas Sculptor
Samuels, Edward George Painter,
    Sculptor
Samuels, Gerald Painter, Sculptor
Samuels, John Stockwell, 3rd Collector,
    Patron
Sandback, Frederick Lane Sculptor
Sande, Rhoda Art Dealer
Sanden, John Howard Painter, Instructor
Sanders, Rhea (Rhea Sanders Rabinovich)
    Painter
Sandler, Barbara Painter
Sandler, Irving Harry Critic, Historian
Santlofer, Jonathan Painter
Saphire, Lawrence M Writer, Dealer
Saret, Alan Daniel Sculptor
Sarkisian, Paul Painter
Sasaki, Tomiyo Painter, Video Artist
Sato, Masaaki Painter
Savelli, Angelo Painter, Sculptor
Scarpitta, Salvatore Sculptor
Schab, Margo Pollins Art Dealer
Schaeffer, Kate Dealer, Collector
Schaeffer, Martha Jane Dealer
Schapiro, Meyer Educator, Historian
Schapiro, Miriam Painter, Collage Artist
Scharf, William Painter
Schiff, Gert K A Historian
Schimansky, Donya Dobrila Librarian,
    Historian
Schlemowitz, Abram Sculptor
Schloss, Arleen P Painter
Schmidt, Arnold Alfred Painter, Sculptor
Schmidt, Edward William Painter,
    Muralist
Schneebaum, Tobias Painter
Schneemann, Carolee Painter, Filmmaker
Schneider, Ira Video Artist, Lecturer
Schneider, Jo Anne Painter
Schneider, Lisa Dawn Dealer, Critic
Schneiderman, Dorothy Dealer
Schneier, Donna Frances Dealer
Schoelkopf, Robert J, Jr Dealer
Schoen, (Mr & Mrs) Arthur Boyer
    Collectors
Schonzeit, Benjamin Painter
Schorr, Justin Painter, Educator
Schottland, M Illustrator, Painter
Schrag, Karl Painter, Printmaker
Schreyer, Greta L Painter, Printmaker
Schueler, Jon R Painter
Schulson, Susan Painter
Schulte, (Mr & Mrs) Arthur D Collectors
Schulz, Charles Monroe Cartoonist
Schuselka, Elfi Printmaker, Sculptor
Schutz, Prescott Dietrich Dealer
Schwabacher, Ethel K Painter, Historian
Schwalbach, Mary Jo Painter, Sculptor
Schwartz, Barbara Ann Painter, Writer
Schwartz, Ellen Judith Curator, Museum
    Director

Schwartz, Eugene M Collector, Patron
Schwartz, Marvin D Historian
Schwartz, Sing-Si Photographer
Schwartz, Therese Painter, Writer
Schweitzer, M R Dealer, Gallery Director
Schweninger, Ann Rozzelle Illustrator
Scott, Arden Sculptor
Scribner, Charles, III Historian, Lecturer
Searles, Charles Painter, Sculptor
Seawright, James L, Jr Sculptor, Educator
Seeman, Helene Zucker Writer, Curator
Segal, Tama & David Dealer, Director
Segy, Ladislas Dealer, Collector
Seidl, Claire Painter
Selchow, Roger Hoffman Painter,
    Sculptor
Seligmann, Herbert J Writer
Selser, Christopher Dealer
Seltzer, Joanne Lynn Painter,
    Photographer
Semmel, Joan Painter
Seplowin, Charles Joseph Sculptor
Serger, Helen Art Dealer
Serniak, Regina Painter, Writer
Serra, Richard Sculptor
Serra, Rudy Sculptor
Serra-Badue, Daniel Painter, Educator
Shahly, Jehan Painter
Shapiro, Babe Painter
Shapiro, Daisy Viertel Collector, Patron
Shapiro, David Painter
Shapiro, Joel (Elias) Sculptor
Shapshak, Rene Sculptor
Sharp, Anne Painter, Printmaker
Sharp, Harold Illustrator, Cartoonist
Sharp, Lewis Inman Curator,
    Administrator
Sharp, Willoughby Video Artist,
    Consultant
Sharpe, David Flemming Painter,
    Printmaker
Shatter, Susan Louise Painter
Shaw, Paul Jefferson Calligrapher,
    Graphic Artist
Shea, Judith Sculptor
Shechtman, George Henoch Dealer
Shecter, Pearl S Painter
Sheirr, Olga (Krolik) Painter
Shemesh, Lorraine R Painter
Sherman, Sarai Painter, Sculptor
Sherr, Ronald Norman Painter
Sherrod, Philip Lawrence Painter, Poet
Shibley, Gertrude Painter
Shikler, Aaron Painter
Shooter, Tom Painter
Shostak, Edwin Bennett Sculptor
Shoulberg, Harry Painter, Printmaker
Showell, Kenneth L Painter
Shuff, Lily (Lillian Shir) Painter,
    Printmaker
Sica Printmaker, Sculptor
Siegel, (Leo) Dink Illustrator, Cartoonist
Sigismund, Violet M Painter, Printmaker
Sihvonen, Oli Painter
Silberstein-Storfer, Muriel Rosoff
    Instructor, Painter
Sills, Thomas Albert Painter
Silverberg, Ellen Ruth Painter, Dealer
Silverman, Burton Philip Painter,
    Illustrator
Simmons, Laurie Photographer
Simon, Bernard Sculptor, Instructor
Simon, Helene Sculptor
Simon, Robert Barry Curator, Historian
Simon, Sidney Sculptor, Painter
Simonds, Charles Frederick Sculptor,
    Architect
Simone (Mildred Simonson) Sculptor,
    Painter
Simpson, Merton D Painter, Dealer
Sims, Lowery Stokes Historian, Curator
Sims, Patterson Curator

Sinaiko, Arlie Sculptor, Collector
Singer, Clifford Painter, Printmaker
Sirena (Contessa Antonia Mastrocristino
    Fanara) Painter, Collector
Sirkis, Nancy Photographer, Educator
Sirugo, Sal (Salvatore) Painter
Sischy, Ingrid B Editor, Curator
Skoglund, Sandra Louise Photographer,
    Sculptor
Sky, Alison Environmental Artist
Slavin, Arlene Painter, Muralist
Slavin, Neal Photographer
Sleigh, Sylvia Painter, Instructor
Slipper, Gary Peter Painter, Printmaker
Slivka, David Sculptor
Slonem, Hunt Painter, Muralist
Small, Neal Sculptor, Designer
Smith, Albert Comic Artist, Editor
Smith, (Mrs) Bertram Collector, Patron
Smith, Dinah Maxwell Painter,
    Photographer
Smith, Joseph A(nthony) Painter,
    Illustrator
Smith, Leon Polk Painter, Collage Artist
Smith, Paul J Museum Director
Smith, Shirley Ann Painter
Smith, Tony Sculptor
Smith, Vincent D Painter, Printmaker
Snelson, Kenneth D Sculptor, Painter
Snyder, Joan Painter
Soffer, Sasson Environmental Artist,
    Conceptual Artist
Sokole, Miron Painter
Solinger, David M Collector, Patron
Solman, Joseph Painter
Solodkin, Judith Lithographer, Publisher
Solomon, Gerald Dealer
Solomon, Holly Dealer, Collector
Solomon, Richard H Publisher, Collector
Solomon, (Mrs) Sidney L Collector
Sonday, Milton Franklin, Jr Curator
Sonenberg, Jack Painter, Sculptor
Sonfist, Alan Environmental Artist
Sonnenberg, Eve Photographer, Filmmaker
Soreff, Helen Painter
Soroka, Margery Painter
Soyer, Raphael Painter
Spaeth, Eloise O'Mara Collector, Writer
Spark, Victor David Dealer
Spector, Naomi Writer
Speiser, Stuart M Collector, Patron
Spelman, Jill Sullivan Painter
Spence, Andrew Painter
Sperakis, Nicholas George Painter,
    Printmaker
Spero, Nancy Painter, Collage Artist
Spiegel, Sam Collector
Spike, John Thomas Historian, Critic
Sproat, Christopher Townsend Sculptor
Spruyt, E Lee Painter, Printmaker
Sragow, Ellen Gallery Director
Stacy, Donald L Painter, Educator
Stadler, Albert Painter
Staempfli, George W Dealer, Painter
Staller, Eric P Photographer
Stamm, Ted Painter
Stamos, Theodoros (S) Painter
Stampfle, Felice Curator, Writer
Standen, Edith Appleton Historian
Stanley, Bob Painter, Photographer
Stapleton, Joseph F Lecturer, Painter
Stasik, Andrew J Printmaker, Gallery
    Director
Stayton, Janet Painter
Steckel, Anita Collage Artist, Painter
Steen, Carol J Sculptor, Painter
Stefanelli, Joe Painter
Stefanotti, Robert Alan Administrator
Stein, Claire A Administrator
Stein, Donna Michele Curator, Critic
Stein, Walter Painter
Steinbaum, Bernice Dealer

NEW YORK (cont)

Steinberg, Saul Cartoonist
Steiner, Michael Sculptor, Printmaker
Steiner, Paul Writer, Critic
Steir, Pat Painter
Stella, Frank Painter
Sterne, Dahli Painter, Sculptor
Sterne, Hedda Painter
Stettner, Louis Photographer
Stevens, May Painter
Stevenson, Ruth Rolston Painter, Instructor
Stewart, Jack Painter, Educator
Sticker, Robert Edward Painter
Stiebel, Eric Dealer
Stiebel, Gerald Gustave Dealer
Stillman, E Clark Collector
Stillman-Myers, Joyce Painter
Stoloff, Carolyn Painter
Stoloff, Irma Sculptor
Stone, Jeffrey Ingram Painter, Printmaker
Stone, Sylvia Sculptor
Strautmanis, Edvins Painter, Sculptor
Strider, Marjorie Virginia Sculptor
Stringer, John Norris Gallery Director
Stronghilos, Carol Painter
Stuart, Michelle Painter, Sculptor
Stuckey, Charles F Historian, Curator
Suba, Susanne Painter, Illustrator
Sugarman, George Sculptor, Painter
Sugimoto, Henry Y Painter
Sujo, Clara Diament Gallery Director, Dealer
Sullivan, Bill Painter, Printmaker
Sullivan, Jim Painter
Sultan, Altoon Painter
Sultan, Donald K Painter, Printmaker
Surrey, Milt Painter
Suttman, Paul Sculptor
Sutton, Patricia Painter
Suzuki, Katsko (Katsko Suzuki Kannegieter) Dealer
Svendsen, Louise Averill Curator
Swain, Robert Painter
Sweeney, James Johnson Administrator, Lecturer
Swergold, Marcelle M Sculptor
Szarama, Judith Layne Draftsman, Illustrator
Szoke, John Dealer, Publisher
Tabachnick, Anne Painter
Taback, Simms Illustrator, Designer
Tabak, Chaim Painter, Sculptor
Taggart, William John Painter, Sculptor
Tai, Jane S Administrator
Takai, Teiji Painter
Tancock, John Leon Administrator, Historian
Tanger, Susanna Painter, Writer
Tannenbaum, Judith E Curator, Critic
Tanner, Warren Painter, Administrator
Taper, Geri Painter
Tasgal-Kliegman, G Calligrapher, Instructor
Tatistcheff, Peter Alexis Dealer, Gallery Director
Tatti, Benedict Michael Sculptor, Painter
Tawney, Lenore Weaver Assemblage Artist
Taylor, Lisa Museum Director
Termini, Christine Painter, Sculptor
Terrell, Allen Townsend Sculptor
Terry, Hilda Cartoonist
Texoon, Jasmine Painter, Instructor
Thacher, Anita Environmental Artist, Filmmaker
Thaw, Eugene Victor Dealer, Collector
Thek, Paul Sculptor
Thomas, Yvonne Painter
Thompson, Kenneth Webster Illustrator, Painter
Thomson, Carl L Painter, Appraiser

Tillim, Sidney Painter, Instructor
Ting, Walasse Painter
Tobias, Julius Sculptor, Instructor
Toll, Barbara Elizabeth Dealer, Curator
Tomes, Margot Ladd Illustrator
Tomkins, Calvin Writer
Tompkins, Betty (I) Painter, Printmaker
Tooker, George Painter, Printmaker
Torffield, Marvin Sculptor
Torreano, John Francis Painter, Lecturer
Trakas, George Sculptor
Traub, Charles H Educator, Photographer
Trauerman, Margy Ann Painter, Instructor
Trieff, Selina Painter, Instructor
Tsai, Wen-Ying Sculptor, Painter
Tschacbasov, Nahum Painter, Printmaker
Tuchman, Ellen Frances Painter
Tuchman, Phyllis Historian, Critic
Tucker, Marcia Museum Director, Curator
Tucker, Toba Pato Photographer, Instructor
Tunick, David Dealer, Book Dealer
Turner, A Richard Historian, Educator
Turner, Alan Painter, Printmaker
Turner, Raymond Sculptor
Tuttle, Richard Painter
Twombly, Cy Painter
Tyson, Mary (Mrs Kenneth Thompson) Painter
Uchima, Ansei Printmaker, Painter
Uchima, Toshiko Painter, Assemblage Artist
Umlauf, Lynn (Charlotte) Painter, Collage Artist
Unger, Mary Ann Sculptor
Upright, Diane W Educator, Writer
Urban, Reva Painter, Sculptor
Valenstein, Suzanne Gebhart Curator
Van Buren, Richard Sculptor
Van Haaften, Julia Curator, Writer
Van Leer, W Leicester Collector
Van Riper, Peter Printmaker, Conceptual Artist
Van Veen, Stuyvesant Painter
Varnedoe, John Kirk Train Historian
Venet, Bernar P Sculptor, Conceptual Artist
Venezia, Michael Painter
Vermes, Madelaine Craftsman
Vidal, Hahn Painter
Viera, Charles David Educator, Painter
Vincent, Clare Curator, Historian
Virgona, Hank (Henry P) Printmaker, Painter
Vodicka, Ruth Kessler Sculptor
Vogel, Donald Printmaker, Instructor
Vogel, (Mr & Mrs) Herbert Collectors
Volpe, Robert Painter, Lecturer
von Ringelheim, Paul Helmut Sculptor
von Rydingsvard, Ursula Sculptor
Wachs, Ethel Educator, Collector
Wagner, Merrill Painter
Waitzkin, Stella Sculptor, Painter
Waksberg, Naomi Painter, Printmaker
Wald, Palmer B Administrator
Wald, Sylvia Painter, Sculptor
Waldman, Paul Painter
Walinska, Anna Painter, Lecturer
Walker, Berta Dealer
Walker, Joy Painter, Printmaker
Walker, Mort Cartoonist
Walker, William Bond Administrator, Librarian
Wall, Sue Painter, Printmaker
Wallace, Soni Painter
Wallin, Leland Dean Painter, Educator
Walsh, Janet Barbara Painter, Administrator
Walter, May E Collector, Patron
Walter, Paul F Collector, Patron

Walton, Guy E Writer, Educator
Walton, Marion (Marion Walton Putnam) Sculptor
Waltzer, Stewart Paul Dealer, Painter
Wang, Chi-Chien Painter
Wardwell, Allen Museum Director
Warhol, Andy Painter, Filmmaker
Warner, Jo Painter
Washburn, Gordon Bailey Museum Director
Washburn, Joan T Dealer, Gallery Director
Wasserman, Albert Painter, Designer
Watanabe, Ryo Painter, Printmaker
Watkins, Ragland Tolk Curator, Dealer
Weber, Idelle Painter
Weber, John Dealer
Webster, Sally (Sara B) Historian
Wechsler, Susan Curator, Writer
Wecker, Christoph Ulrich Gallery Director
Wegman, William Painter, Video Artist
Weil, Lisl Illustrator, Writer
Weil, Rose R Editor, Administrator
Weinberg, Elbert Sculptor, Educator
Weiner, Lawrence Charles Sculptor
Weinstein, Florence Painter, Sculptor
Weinstein, Joyce Painter
Weintraub, Annette Painter, Educator
Weiss, Jeff Photographer, Educator
Weissman, Julian Paul Writer, Dealer
Weissman, Walter Sculptor, Writer
Weitzenhoffer, A Max Dealer
Welch, Roger Sculptor, Photographer
Wells, Lynton Painter
Wells, Mac Painter
Werner, Donald (Lewis) Painter, Photographer
Werner, Nat Sculptor
Weschler, Anita Sculptor, Painter
Wesley, John Painter
Westerlund Roosen, Mia (Maria Eludia) Sculptor
Westwater, Angela King Dealer, Editor
Weyhe, Arthur Sculptor
Whitehill, Florence (Fitch) Painter
Whyte, Bruce Lincoln Dealer, Publisher
Wiegand, Robert Painter, Video Artist
Wiener, Sam (Evangeline Tabasco) Sculptor, Instructor
Wiesenfeld, Paul Painter
Wilbur, Lawrence Nelson Painter, Printmaker
Wilcox, Gordon Cumnock Painter, Illustrator
Wilcox, Jarvis Geer, Jr Painter
Wilke, Hannah Sculptor, Instructor
Willenbecher, John Sculptor, Painter
Williams, Dave Harrell Collector, Patron
Williams, Randalph Andrew Sculptor, Painter
Williams, Walter (Henry) Painter, Printmaker
Williams, William Thomas Painter, Educator
Willis, Thornton Painter
Wilmarth, Christopher Mallory Sculptor, Draftsman
Wilson, Carrie Lois Gallery Director, Lecturer
Wilson, Jane Painter
Wilson, Martha Storey Conceptual Artist, Museum Director
Wilson, May Sculptor
Wilson, Robert Graphic Artist, Designer
Wilson, William S, III Critic
Wines, James N Environmental Artist
Wingate, George B Painter
Winogrand, Garry Photographer, Lecturer
Winsor, V Jacqueline Sculptor
Wirtschafter, Bud Filmmaker, Instructor
Wise, Howard Administrator

NEW YORK (cont)

Witkin, Isaac Sculptor, Instructor
Wixom, William D Curator, Historian
Wizon, Tod Painter
Wolfe, James Sculptor
Wolff, William H Dealer
Wolins, Joseph Painter
Wong, Frederick Painter, Calligrapher
Wong, Paul Kan Painter, Sculptor
Woodman, Timothy Sculptor
Wooster, Ann-Sargent Painter
Wortzel, Adrianne Painter
Wright, Nina Kaiden Consultant
Wriston, Barbara Historian, Lecturer
Wu, Linda Yee Chau Sculptor
Wuermer, Carl Painter
Wunderlich, Rudolf G Dealer
Wunderman, Jan (Liljan Darcourt
    Wunderman) Painter, Printmaker
Wurmfeld, Sanford Painter, Educator
Wyatt, Greg Alan Sculptor
Yasuda, Robert Painter
Yektai, Manoucher Painter
Yiannes (Iordanides) Sculptor, Ceramist
Yoder, Richard Allen Painter, Conceptual
    Artist
Yoshimura, Fumio Sculptor
Young, Cliff Painter, Muralist
Young, John T Sculptor
Youngerman, Jack Painter, Sculptor
Yrisarry, Mario Painter
Yunkers, Adja Painter, Educator
Zabriskie, Virginia M Dealer
Zacharias, Athos Painter
Zago, Tino (Agostino C) Painter
Zaima, Stephen Gyo Painter, Sculptor
Zajac, Jack Sculptor, Painter
Zakanitch, Robert S Painter
Zaleski, Jean M Painter, Administrator
Zapkus, Kes (Kestutis Edward) Painter
Zeisler, Richard Spiro Collector, Patron
Zevon, Irene Painter
Zietz, Stephen Joseph Librarian, Historian
Zimmerman, Elyn Sculptor,
    Environmental Artist
Zimmerman, Kathleen Marie Painter,
    Collage Artist
Zingale, Lawrence Painter
Zlowe, Florence M Painter, Draftsman
Zoromskis, Kazimieras Painter, Instructor
Zox, Larry Painter
Zucker, Barbara M Sculptor
Zucker, Joseph I Painter
Zucker, Murray Harvey Painter, Sculptor
Zugor, Sandor Painter, Printmaker
Zver, James M Collage Artist, Painter

Niagara Falls

Slawinski, Joseph Muralist, Conservator

North Bellmore

Schreiber, Martin Sculptor, Painter

Northport

Barooshian, Martin Painter, Printmaker
Twardowicz, Stanley Jan Painter,
    Photographer
Verzyl, June Carol Dealer, Collector
Verzyl, Kenneth H Dealer, Draftsman

North Salem

Hammond, Natalie Hays Painter,
    Museum Director
Savitt, Sam Painter, Illustrator

North Tarrytown

Gursoy, Ahmet Painter

Norwood

Sutter, James Stewart Sculptor, Educator
Wynn, Donald James Painter, Lecturer

Nyack

Borne, Mortimer Sculptor, Painter
Breer, Robert C Sculptor, Filmmaker
Dahlberg, Edwin Lennart Painter
Dash, Harvey Dwight Administrator,
    Painter
Larraz, Julio F Painter
Wyatt, Stanley Painter, Illustrator

Oakdale

Mina-Mora, Dorise Olson Painter
Mina-Mora, Raul Jose Painter, Illustrator

Oceanside

Laguna, Marielle Painter, Instructor

Old Chatham

Kratina, K George Sculptor

Oneida

Colway, James R Painter

Oneonta

Mahlke, Ernest D Sculptor, Educator
Mullen, James Martin Educator,
    Printmaker

Orangeburg

Dell, Robert Christopher Sculptor, Painter
Harootian, Khoren Der Painter, Sculptor
Worth, Karen Sculptor

Orient

Grippe, Florence (Berg) Painter,
    Instructor
Grippe, Peter Sculptor, Printmaker

Ossining

Cober, Alan E Illustrator, Printmaker
Wein, Albert W Sculptor, Painter

Oswego

Baitsell, Wilma Williamson Administrator,
    Craftsman
D'Innocenzo, Nick Jerome Sculptor,
    Educator
DiPasquale, Dominic Theodore
    Silversmith, Educator
Fox, Michael David Sculptor, Instructor
Fuller, John Charles Historian,
    Photographer
O'Connell, George D Printmaker,
    Educator
Saunders, Aulus Ward Painter, Educator
Stark, George King Educator, Sculptor
Sullins, Robert M Painter

Oyster Bay

Bothmer, Dietrich Felix von Curator,
    Educator
Kunstler, Morton Painter, Illustrator

Palisades

Knowlton, Grace Farrar Sculptor,
    Photographer

Peekskill

Levine, Seymour R Collector
Osyczka, Bohdan Danny Painter,
    Illustrator
Rocklin, Raymond Sculptor, Educator

Pelham

Boal, Sara Metzner Painter, Instructor
Rutsch, Alexander Painter, Sculptor
Zheutlin, Dale R Sculptor, Educator

Pittsford

Coffey, Douglas Robert Painter, Educator

Plainview

Coheleach, Guy Joseph Painter, Sculptor
Liberi, Dante Painter, Sculptor
Margulies, Isidore Sculptor, Kinetic Artist

Pleasantville

Cawein, Kathrin Printmaker, Illuminator
Handville, Robert T Painter, Illustrator
Peck, Stephen Rogers Instructor, Painter
Robinson, Jay (Thurston) Painter

Port Chester

Blattner, Robert Henry Painter, Illustrator

Port Jefferson

Flecker, Maurice Nathan Painter,
    Educator

Port Washington

Kleinholz, Frank Painter, Writer

Potsdam

Coopersmith, Georgia A Gallery
    Director, Curator
Gibson, Roland Collector, Curator
Hildreth, Joseph Alan Printmaker, Painter
Lenney, Annie Painter

Poughkeepsie

Askew, Pamela Educator, Writer
Forman, Alice Painter
Havelock, Christine Mitchell Historian,
    Educator
Lindmark, Arne Painter, Instructor
Pickens, Alton Painter, Instructor
Reynard, Carolyn Cole Painter, Instructor
Rubenstein, Lewis W Painter, Printmaker

Poughquag

Lidov, Arthur Herschel Painter, Sculptor

Pound Ridge

Bender, Beverly Sterl Sculptor,
    Environmental Artist
Decock, Liliane (Liliane Morgan Decock)
    Photographer, Editor
Ferro, Walter Printmaker, Designer

Purchase

Blum, Shirley Neilsen Art Historian
Colker, Edward Painter, Graphic Artist
Delehanty, Suzanne E Historian, Museum
    Director
Torlen, Michael Arnold Painter, Educator
Trosky, Helene Roth Printmaker,
    Papermaker

Putnam Valley

Padovano, Anthony John Sculptor,
    Draftsman
Toulis, Vasilios (Apostolos) Printmaker,
    Educator

Queens Village

Kilgore, Al Cartoonist

Quogue

Kuehnl, Claudia Ann Goldsmith

Rainbow Lake

Kindermann, Helmmo Photographer

Ravena

Trimm, H Wayne Illustrator, Painter

Red Hook

Lax, David Painter

Rego Park

Aronson, Irene Hilde Printmaker, Painter
Kanidinc, Salahattin Designer,
  Calligrapher
Seide, Paul A Sculptor
Winter, Ruth Painter

Richmond Hill

Eres, Eugenia Painter
Hammerman, Pat Jo Printmaker, Painter

Ridgewood

Azaceta, Luis Cruz Painter, Instructor
Negri, Rocco Antonio Illustrator, Painter

Riverdale

De La Vega, Antonio Painter, Designer
Hnizdovsky, Jacques Painter, Printmaker
Kasak, Nikolai (Kazak) Painter, Sculptor
Menkes, Sigmund Painter

Riverhead

Howell, Douglass (Morse) Painter,
  Historian

Rochester

Barschel, Hans J Designer, Photographer
Buerger, Janet E Historian, Curator
Christensen, Hans-Jorgen Thorvald
  Designer, Silversmith
Faller, Marion Photographer, Educator
Feuerherm, Kurt K Painter
Holm, Milton W Painter
Johnston, Robert Harold Administrator,
  Craftsman
Margolis, Richard M Photographer,
  Educator
Menihan, John Conway Painter,
  Printmaker
Mertin, Roger Photographer
Morgan, Robert Coolidge Painter, Critic
Paley, Albert Raymond Goldsmith,
  Designer
Smith, Keith A Photographer, Printmaker
Stern, (Mr & Mrs) Arthur Lewis
  Collectors
Taylor, Michael (Estes) Glass Blower,
  Sculptor
Wilson, Tom Muir Designer

Rockaway Point

Pettet, William Painter

Rockville Centre

Knief, Helen Jeanette Painter

Rocky Point

England, Paul Grady Painter, Educator

Roslyn

Bassin, Joan Historian, Educator
Finke, Leonda Froelich Sculptor,
  Draftsman

Roslyn Heights

Betensky, Rose Hart Painter, Art
  Administrator
Gach, George Painter, Sculptor
Hermann, M(ildred) L Painter, Collage
  Artist
Orling, Anne Consultant, Painter
Rotholz, Rina Printmaker
Sonnenberg, Frances Sculptor

Rye

Bermant, David W Collector, Director
Bisgyer, Barbara G (Cohn) Sculptor
Morgan, Frances Mallory Sculptor

Sagaponack

Butchkes, Sydney Painter, Collage Artist
Dash, Robert (Warren) Painter
Dunlap, Loren Edward Painter, Instructor
Williams, Neil Painter

Sag Harbor

Billings, Henry Painter, Illustrator
David, Cyril Frank Graphic Artist
Harrison, Helen Amy Curator, Critic
Lipman-Wulf, Peter Sculptor, Printmaker
Nicholson, Roy William Painter,
  Printmaker
Telberg, Val Photographer, Painter

St James

White, Robert (Winthrop) Sculptor,
  Educator

Salem

Garrett, Stuart Grayson Painter, Educator

Salt Point

Sellers, William Freeman Sculptor

Sanborn

Hill, Richard Wayne Painter,
  Photographer

Saratoga Springs

Brodie, Regis Conrad Potter
Cunningham, J Sculptor
Gaugh, Harry F Educator, Critic
Pardon, Earl B Craftsman, Educator
Upton, Richard Thomas Painter,
  Printmaker

Scarsdale

Abel, Ray Illustrator, Designer
Bernstein, Sylvia Painter, Sculptor
Breinin, Raymond Painter, Sculptor
Brilliant, Richard Educator
Callisen, Sterling Historian, Lecturer
Frackman, Noel Critic, Lecturer
Hibbard, Howard Historian, Writer
Hobbs, Gerald S Dealer, Publisher
Kearl, Stanley Brandon Sculptor
Kline, Harriet Painter, Printmaker
Moonie, Liana (Maria) Painter, Instructor
Morgan, Barbara Brooks Photographer
Ries, Martin Painter, Critic
Roda (Rhoda Lillian Sablow) Painter,
  Tapestry Artist
Valenstein, Alice Painter, Collector

Schenectady

Dinardo, Joseph E Medalist, Sculptor

Scottsville

Castle, Wendell Keith Designer, Sculptor
Meyer, Fred (Robert) Sculptor, Painter

Sea Cliff

Leipzig, Arthur Photographer
Spampinato, Clemente Sculptor

Setauket

Badalamenti, Fred Painter, Educator
Bishop, Marjorie Cutler Painter
Guilmain, Jacques Historian, Educator
O'Sullivan, Daniel Joseph Painter
Remsen, John Everett, II Consultant,
  Painter
Windrow, Patricia (Patricia Windrow
  Klein) Painter, Illustrator

Shady

Hofsted, Jolyon Gene Sculptor, Educator
Kenyon, Colleen Frances Photographer,
  Administrator
Ruellan, Andree Painter

Shelter Island

Mosca, August Painter, Instructor
Shields, Alan J Designer, Painter

Shoreham

Pekarsky, Mel (Melvin Hirsch) Painter,
  Educator
Spier, Peter Edward Illustrator, Writer

Sidney

McClelland, Jeanne C Printmaker, Painter

Skaneateles

Appelhof, Ruth A Curator, Historian

Snyder

Cohen, Adele Sculptor, Painter

Somers

Adelman, Dorothy (Lee) McClintock
  Printmaker, Instructor
Hedin, Donald Monroe Painter, Director
Kipp, Lyman Sculptor

Southampton

Cikovsky, Nicolai Painter, Muralist
Fuller, Sue Sculptor, Printmaker
Harrison, Carole Sculptor
Koehler, Henry Painter
Lichtenstein, Roy Painter, Sculptor
Rivers, Larry Painter

South Butler

Caster, Bernard Harry Painter, Enamelist

Southold

Wissemann-Widrig, Nancy Painter

South Salem

Noland, Kenneth Painter

Sparkill

Vytlacil, Vaclav Painter, Educator

Spencer

Nowack, Wayne Kenyon Painter,
  Assemblage Artist

Spencerport

Wolsky, Jack Painter, Educator

Spring Valley

Van Oordt, Peter Painter, Graphic Artist

Stanfordville

Froman, Ann Sculptor, Designer

Staten Island

Bernstein, Gerald Painter, Restorer
Bressi, Betty Painter, Educator
Coleman, A(llan) D(ouglass) Critic,
  Lecturer
Czimbalmos, Magdolna Paal Painter,
  Instructor
Czimbalmos, Szabo Kalman Painter,
  Educator
Greenfield, Amy Filmmaker, Video
  Artist
Healy, Julia Schmitt Painter, Educator
Kelder, Diane M Historian, Critic
Lorenzani, Arthur Emanuele Sculptor
Mailman, Cynthia Painter, Muralist
Moroz, Mychajlo Painter
Nelson, Carey Boone Sculptor
Swenson, Anne (Beatrice) Painter,
  Instructor

Stephentown

Jackson, William Davis Sculptor,
  Designer

Sterling

Seawell, Thomas Robert Printmaker, Painter

Stone Ridge

Sanders, Joop A Painter

Stony Brook

Ellinger, Ilona E Painter, Educator
Jonaitis, Aldona Historian
Kuspit, Donald Burton Historian, Critic
Polcari, Stephen Historian
Stitt, Susan (Margaret) Museum Director

Stony Point

Dienes, Sari Assemblage Artist, Printmaker

Stormville

St John, Bruce Administrator, Historian

Suffern

Leigh, Harry E Sculptor, Painter
Pousette-Dart, Richard Painter

Summit

Fangor, Voy Painter

Sunnyside

Martin, Charles E Designer, Painter

Swan Lake

Sokolowski, Linda Robinson Printmaker, Painter

Syracuse

Bakke, Karen Lee Assemblage Artist, Calligrapher
Bakke, Larry Hubert Educator, Painter
Belfort-Chalat, Jacqueline Sculptor, Painter
Catlin, Stanton L Educator, Historian
Dwyer, James Painter, Educator
Hughto, Margie A Ceramist, Curator
Jerry, Michael John Educator, Craftsman
Kuchta, Ronald A Museum Director, Lecturer
Mack, Rodger Allen Sculptor, Educator
Nelson, Jack D Sculptor, Graphic Artist
Orentlicher, John Video Artist, Sculptor
Pulos, Arthur Jon Industrial Designer, Design Educator
Ridlon, James A Sculptor, Filmmaker
Scala, Joseph (A) Sculptor, Museum Director
Seames, Clarann Painter, Illustrator
Sellers, John Lewis Educator, Designer
Tatham, David Frederic Historian
Trop-Blumberg, Sandra Administrator
Weiss, Peg Historian, Curator
Witkin, Jerome Paul Painter, Draftsman

Tappan

Lo Medico, Thomas Gaetano Sculptor, Designer
Nickford, Juan Sculptor, Educator

Tarrytown

Butler, Joseph Thomas Curator, Writer
Haswell, Hollee Librarian, Painter
Lee, Robert J Painter, Educator

Tillson

Van de Bovenkamp, Hans Sculptor

Tonawanda

Bolinsky, Joseph Abraham Sculptor, Educator

Troy

Quinn, Aysha Video Artist
Sturgeon, John Floyd Video Artist, Sculptor

Trumansburg

Vann, Samuel Le Roy Painter
Wojcik, Gary Thomas Sculptor

Tuxedo Park

Domjan, Joseph (Spiri) Painter, Graphic Artist

Utica

Cimbalo, Robert W Painter, Printmaker
Loy, John Sheridan Painter
Pribble, Easton Painter, Instructor
Schweizer, Paul Douglas Museum Director, Historian

Valley Cottage

Greene, Stephen Painter
Heaton, Maurice Designer, Craftsman

Valley Stream

Hart, Allen M Painter, Administrator

Van Hornesville

Romeling, W B Painter

Voorheesville

O'Connor, Thom Printmaker

Wainscott

McColley, Sutherland Consultant, Designer
Ossorio, Alfonso A Painter, Sculptor
Porter, (Edwin) David Painter, Sculptor

Wallkill

Koch, Edwin E Sculptor, Painter

Wantagh

Glaser, David Painter, Sculptor
O Donohue, Teige Ros Painter, Printmaker
Samuels, Harold & Peggy Historians, Dealers

Wappingers Falls

Di Fate, Vincent Illustrator, Painter

Warwick

Bogdanovic, Bogomir Painter
Franck, Frederick S Painter, Writer
Miller, Donald Richard Sculptor, Medalist
Talbot, Jonathan Painter, Collage Artist

Washingtonville

Mangold, Sylvia Plimack Painter

Wassaic

Beckman, William George Painter

Water Mill

Jackson, Lee Painter
Jordan, Barbara Schwinn Painter
Mac Whinnie, John Vincent Painter, Sculptor
Young, Mahonri S Writer

Webster

Mann, Ward Palmer Painter

Westbury

Honig, Mervin Painter, Painting Conservator
Ludman, Joan Hurwitz Writer, Dealer
Sherbell, Rhoda Sculptor, Consultant

West Hempstead

Hornung, Clarence Pearson Designer, Writer

West Nyack

Tytell, Louis Painter

White Plains

Bowles, Marianne von Recklinghausen Painter, Sculptor
Limone, Frank Sculptor
Manes, Belle Painter
Nickerson, Ruth (Ruth Nickerson Greacen) Sculptor, Instructor
Peter, George Painter, Instructor
Waddell, Eugene Painter

Williamsville

Spurling, Norine M Graphic Artist, Educator

Willsboro

Reynolds, Patricia Ellen Painter

Wilson

Tyson, Rae Julian Administrator, Sculptor

Woodhaven

Csoka, Stephen Painter, Printmaker
Manuella, Frank R Designer, Sculptor

Woodmere

Ginsburg, Estelle Painter, Sculptor
Seiden, Arthur Painter, Illustrator

Woodside

Fax, Elton Clay Painter, Writer
Fluek, Toby Painter, Graphic Artist
Goldszer, Bath-Sheba Painter, Graphic Artist
Soteras, Jaime Sculptor

Woodstock

Angeloch, Robert (Henry) Painter, Printmaker
Chavez, Edward Arcenio Painter, Sculptor
Currie, Bruce Painter, Printmaker
Fortess, Karl E Painter, Printmaker
Hague, Raoul Sculptor
Handell, Albert George Painter
Johnson, Fridolf Lester Designer, Writer
Lenssen, Heidi (Mrs Fridolf Johnson) Painter, Lecturer
Lieberman, Meyer Frank Painter, Printmaker
Magafan, Ethel Painter, Muralist
Pachner, William Painter
Zaikine, Zak (Victor Eugene) Sculptor, Painter

Yonkers

Aber, Ita Historian, Tapestry Artist
Byars, Donna Sculptor, Collage Artist
Civale, Biagio A Graphic Artist, Painter
Clive, Richard R Painter
Corwin, Sophia M Sculptor, Painter
deGroat, Diane L Illustrator, Designer
Gallo, William Victor Cartoonist, Illustrator
Sarff, Walter Painter, Designer
Scott, Walter Painter, Architect

Yorktown Heights

Kaupelis, Robert John Painter, Educator
Laventhol, Hank Painter, Printmaker
Trott, Helen Painter, Instructor
Witt, John Painter, Printmaker

NORTH CAROLINA

Albemarle

Moose, Talmadge Bowers Painter, Illustrator

Asheboro

Jones, W Louis Painter, Sculptor

Asheville

Andrews, Michael Frank Educator, Sculptor
Cooke, Samuel Tucker Painter, Educator
Gray, Robert Ward Administrator
Martin, Doris-Marie Constable Designer, Sculptor

Bakersville

Vrana, Albert S Sculptor

Belmont

Mintich, Mary Ringelberg Sculptor, Craftsman

Black Mountain

Tate, Gayle Blair Dealer, Painter

Blowing Rock

Moose, Philip Anthony Painter, Illustrator

Boone

Humphrey, Judy Lucille Graphic Artist, Printmaker

Burnsville

Bernstein, William Joseph Designer, Glassblower
Doyle, John Lawrence Printmaker, Painter

Cashiers

Whiteside, William Albert, II Painter, Educator

Chapel Hill

Allen, Kaola B Collage Artist, Printmaker
Folda, Jaroslav (Thayer), III Historian
Howard, Robert A Sculptor, Educator
Kinnaird, Richard William Painter, Educator
Lee, Sherman Emery Museum Director
Ness, (Albert) Kenneth Painter, Designer
Noe, Jerry Lee Sculptor, Educator
Prange, Sally Bowen Ceramic Artist
Saltzman, Marvin Painter, Educator
Sloane, Joseph Curtis Historian
Sturgeon, Mary C Historian
Zaborowski, Dennis J Painter, Educator

Charlotte

Bloch, Milton Joseph Art Administrator, Museum Director
Byrum, Donald Roy Educator, Printmaker
Dalton, Harry L Collector, Patron
Holt, Margaret McConnell Patron, Collector
Kessler, Jane Q Curator, Critic
Kortheuer, Dayrell Painter, Conservator
Melberg, Jerald Leigh Curator, Collector
Musgrove, Stephen Ward Administrator, Curator
Shaw, Mary Todd Sculptor, Painter
Tucker, Charles Clement Painter

Cullowhee

Kelly, Isaac Perry Photographer, Educator

Dallas

Waufle, Alan Duane Museum Director

Davidson

Grosch, Laura Painter, Printmaker
Jackson, Herb Painter, Printmaker

Denton

Tillotson, Robbie Painter

Durham

Epstein, Annabel Wharton Historian
Greenberg, Blue (Bluma Kafka) Educator, Critic
Markman, Sidney David Administrator, Historian
Pendergraft, Norman Elveis Museum Director, Historian
Pratt, Vernon Gaither Painter, Educator
Semans, James Hustead Patron
Smith, Susan Carlton Painter, Sculptor
Spencer, John R Historian, Administrator
Stars, William Kenneth Educator, Museum Director

Greensboro

Barker, Walter William Painter, Writer
Bass, David Loren Painter
Blahove, Marcos Painter
Budny, Virginia Sculptor, Writer
Carpenter, Gilbert Frederick (Bert) Painter, Museum Director
Chin, Ric Lecturer, Painter
Ference, Cynthia Gallery Director, Painter
Goldstein, Carl Educator, Sculptor
Gregory, Joan Educator, Painter
Laymon, Cynthia J Collage Artist, Graphic Artist
Tucker, James Ewing Curator, Painter

Greenville

Blakeslee, Sarah Painter
Chamberlain, Charles Ceramist, Educator
Crawley, Wesley V Sculptor, Educator
Edmiston, Sara Joanne Educator, Designer
Gordley, Marilyn Classe Painter
Gordley, Metz Tranbarger Painter
Hartley, Paul Jerome Painter, Educator
Laing, Richard Harlow Administrator, Artist
Pennington, Mary Anne Museum Director, Educator
Reep, Edward Arnold Painter, Educator
Satterfield, John Edward Goldsmith, Educator
Sexauer, Donald Richard Printmaker, Educator
Speight, Francis Painter, Educator
Stanforth, Melvin Sidney Educator, Printmaker

Hendersonville

Holgate, Jeanne Painter, Illustrator

Hillsborough

Cindric, Michael Anthony Sculptor, Educator
Turner, Evan Hopkins Museum Director

Kinston

Pearson, Henry C Painter, Instructor

Lexington

Moon, Jim (James Monroe) Painter, Printmaker

Ocracoke

Martin, G W Designer, Painter

Penland

Cope, Louise Todd Weaver, Instructor

Pittsboro

Higgins, Edward Koelling Ceramist, Jeweler
Higgins, Mary Lou Ceramist, Weaver

Raleigh

Bier, Justus Museologist, Historian
Bireline, George Lee Painter, Educator
Bowron, Edgar Peters Museum Director
Broderson, Robert Painter
Chiego, William Joseph Administrator, Curator
Domit, Moussa M Museum Director, Historian
Hertzman, Gay Mahaffy Administrator, Historian
Jenkins, Mary Anne Keel Painter, Muralist
Kahan, Mitchell Douglas Curator, Historian
Williams, Benjamin Forrest Curator, Historian

Salisbury

Hood, Walter Kelly Historian, Painter

Smithfield

Creech, Franklin Underwood Sculptor, Graphic Artist

Southern Pines

Milligan, Joan Arnold Painter

Southport

Brown, June Gottlieb- Painter

Spruce Pine

Littleton, Harvey K Sculptor, Educator

Tryon

Quest, Charles Francis Painter, Educator
Quest, Dorothy (Johnson) Painter, Educator

Walnut Cove

Nygren, John Fergus Glass Artist

Weaverville

Gilmartin, F Thomas Administrator, Consultant

Whittier

Genders, Richard Atherstone Painter, Critic

Wilkesboro

Nichols, Ward H Painter

Wilmington

Bissette, Samuel Delk Painter, Patron
Howell, Claude Flynn Painter, Educator

Winston-Salem

Bane, (Lucy) McDonald Painter, Educator
Browning, Dixie Burrus Painter, Writer
Dance, Robert Bartlett Painter, Printmaker
Faccinto, Victor Paul Painter, Filmmaker
Gray, Thomas Alexander Consultant, Collector
Mangum, William (Goodson) Sculptor, Painter
Oubre, Hayward Louis Sculptor, Educator
Pierotti, Ray (Raymond Charles) Painter, Administrator

NORTH CAROLINA (cont)

Potter, Ted Painter, Administrator
Saunders, Edith Dariel Chase Painter,
  Instructor
Yarborough, Christine Troutman
  Craftsman, Designer

Yanceyville

Gatewood, Maud Florance Painter

NORTH DAKOTA

Dickinson

Navrat, Den (Dennis Edward)
  Printmaker, Educator

Grand Forks

McElroy, Jacquelyn Ann (Jacquelyn
  McElroy-Edwards) Printmaker,
  Educator
Paulsen, Brian Oliver Painter, Printmaker
Reuter, Laurel J Gallery Director
Rogers, John H Sculptor, Educator
Schaefer, Ronald H Printmaker, Educator

Minot

Piehl, Walter Jason, Jr Painter, Educator
Schwieger, C Robert Printmaker,
  Educator

OHIO

Akron

Danoff, I Michael Critic, Museum
  Director
Drumm, Don Sculptor, Craftsman
Ertman, Earl Leslie Historian, Educator
Miller, John Franklin Administrator
Neumann, William A Educator,
  Goldsmith
Rogers, P J Printmaker, Painter

Alliance

Cleveland, Helen Barth Administrator,
  Instructor

Athens

Ahrendt, Christine Painter
Baldwin, John Educator, Sculptor
Kortlander, William Painter
Roberts, Donald Educator, Printmaker

Bay Village

Blazey, Lawrence Edwin Designer,
  Painter

Berea

Cole, Harold David Historian, Educator

Bowling Green

Bandy, Ron F Painter, Educator
Hilty, Thomas R Graphic Artist, Painter
Lee, Briant Hamor Historian, Educator
Ocvirk, Otto G Sculptor, Printmaker
Sevigny, Maurice Joseph, II Educator,
  Administrator

Brecksville

Miller, John Paul Jeweler, Instructor

Cambridge

Beam, Mary Todd Painter

Chagrin Falls

Lawton, Florian Kenneth Painter,
  Instructor

Chillicothe

Gough, Robert Alan Painter

Cincinnati

Barrie, Dennis Ray Museum Director,
  Historian
Batchelor, Anthony John Printmaker,
  Instructor
Brod, Stanford Designer, Educator
Byrne, Charles Joseph Consultant,
  Graphic Artist
Dennis, Don W Painter, Instructor
Driesbach, Walter Clark, Jr Sculptor,
  Instructor
Fabe, Robert Painter, Educator
Fischer, Mildred (Gertrude) Designer,
  Craftsman
Fitzgerald, Edmond James Painter,
  Lecturer
Foster, April Printmaker, Instructor
Goodridge, Lawrence Wayne Painter,
  Sculptor
Hanna, Katherine Museum Director
Knipschild, Robert Painter, Educator
McClure, Constance Painter, Instructor
Merkel, Jayne (Silverstein) Historian,
  Critic
Meyer, Ruth Krueger Historian,
  Administrator
Miotke, Anne E Painter, Instructor
Rice, Harold Randolph Educator, Writer
Rogers, Millard Foster, Jr Museum
  Director, Historian
Solway, Carl E Dealer
Stewart, John P Painter, Printmaker
Warren, Julianne Bussert Baker
  Photographer
Warren, L D Cartoonist
Woodham, Derrick James Sculptor

Cleveland

Aidlin, Jerome Sculptor, Instructor
Bickford, George Percival Collector
Cassill, Herbert Carroll Printmaker,
  Educator
Combes, Willard Wetmore Cartoonist
Conover, Claude Sculptor, Ceramist
Czuma, Stanislaw J Historian, Curator
Drewal, Henry John Historian, Educator
Erdelac, Joseph Mark Collector, Patron
Gibson, Walter Samuel Historian, Writer
Hayashi, Masumi Photographer, Educator
Hornung, Gertrude Seymour Lecturer,
  Collector
McVey, Leza Ceramist, Weaver
McVey, William M Sculptor, Educator
Meyers, Francis Joseph Painter, Sculptor
Putnam, (Mrs) John B Collector
St Denis, Paul Andre Painter, Instructor
Seltzer, Phyllis Printmaker, Painter
Sloane, Phyllis Lester Painter, Printmaker
Stanczak, Julian Painter, Instructor
Taft, Frances Prindle Historian, Lecturer
Thompson, Lockwood Collector
van der Meulen, Jan Historian, Educator
Wawrytko, M(ary) F(rances) Enamelist,
  Sculptor
Welch, (Mr & Mrs) Robert G Collectors
Woide, Robert E Painter, Administrator

Cleveland Heights

Dubaniewicz, Peter Paul Painter
Henning, Edward Burk Curator, Historian
Hinson, Tom Everett Curator, Historian
Kowalski, Raymond Alois Painter
McCullough, Joseph Administrator,
  Painter
Marshall, Ralph Educator, Photographer
Paul, Greg (Gregory Wilmer) Director,
  Illustrator
Pearman, Sara Jane Historian, Librarian
Schneider, Richard Durbin Ceramist,
  Craftsman

Schreckengost, Viktor Designer, Sculptor
Silver, Thomas C Sculptor, Educator
Teyral, John Painter, Instructor
von Weise, Wenda Fraker Printmaker,
  Tapestry Artist

Columbus

Arnold, Robert Lloyd Painter, Educator
Bishop, Budd Harris Museum Director
Black, David Evans Sculptor, Educator
Brown, Richard Morgan Environmental
  Artist, Sculptor
Chafetz, Sidney Printmaker, Educator
Close, Dean Purdy Dealer, Painter
Collings, Betty Sculptor, Writer
Dodrill, Donald Lawrence Painter,
  Graphic Artist
Gatrell, Marion Thompson Educator,
  Painter
Goodwin, Louis Payne Cartoonist
Jocda Painter
Kuehn, Edmund Karl Painter, Lecturer
Massey, Charles Wesley, Jr Printmaker,
  Educator
Mattern, Penny Greig Librarian,
  Printmaker
Morganstern, James Historian, Educator
Nicodemus, Chester Roland Sculptor,
  Designer
Pentak, Stephen Painter, Educator
Roth, Richard Painter, Educator
Simson, Bevlyn A Painter, Printmaker
Stull, Robert J Sculptor, Administrator
Wahling, Jon B Sculptor, Weaver
Wyngaard, Susan Elizabeth Librarian

Cuyahoga Falls

Boedeker, Arnold E (Boedie) Illustrator,
  Painter
Moon, Marc Painter, Instructor
Richard, Jack Painter, Gallery Director

Dayton

Dunkelman, Martha Levine Historian,
  Educator
Evans, Bruce Haselton Museum Director,
  Historian
Houk, Pamela P Curator
Ostendorf, (Arthur) Lloyd, Jr Painter,
  Instructor
Pinkney, Helen Louise Curator, Librarian
Raffel, Alvin Robert Painter, Instructor
Sobotik, Kent Curator, Historian

Delaware

Kalb, Marty Joel Painter, Educator

Dublin

Chadeayne, Robert Osborne Painter

Euclid

Bates, Kenneth Francis Enamelist,
  Craftsman

Fairview Park

Masterfield, Maxine Painter

Findlay

Waaland, James Brearley, II Dealer,
  Gallery Director

Gambier

Dwyer, Eugene Joseph Historian
Garhart, Martin J Printmaker
Gunderson, Barry L Sculptor
Schupbach, Terry Ann Printmaker
Slate, Joseph Frank Painter, Writer

Garfield Heights

Perkins, Clarence James Painter, Instructor

Gates Mills

Clague, John Rogers Sculptor

Georgetown

Ruthven, John Aldrich Painter, Lecturer

Grand Rapids

Labino, Dominick Glass Blower, Sculptor

Hamilton

George, Richard Allan Painter
Phelps, Nan Dee Painter

Hudson

Smith, Lowell Ellsworth Painter

Kent

Gardner, Joan A Painter, Printmaker
Gildzen, Alex Writer, Collector
Grossman, Morton Painter
Kitner, Harold Painter, Educator
Matteson, Ira Sculptor, Draftsman
Morrow, Robert Earl Designer, Muralist
Myers, Richard Lewis Photographer, Filmmaker
Novotny, Elmer Ladislaw Painter, Educator
O'Sickey, Joseph Benjamin Painter, Educator

Kettering

Myers, Jack Fredrick Painter, Educator

Lakewood

Jones, Marvin Harold Printmaker, Painter
Treaster, Richard A Painter, Educator

Lebanon

Koepnick, Robert Charles Sculptor, Educator

Madison

Floyd, Carl Leo Sculptor, Environmental Artist
Gabriel, Hannelore Goldsmith

Mansfield

Butts, H Daniel, III Gallery Director

Marietta

Tasse, M Jeanne Educator, Calligrapher

Medina

Kleidon, Dennis Arthur Educator, Designer

New Richmond

Kelley, Donald William Printmaker, Sculptor

North Lima

Mohn, Cheri (Ann) Painter, Instructor

Oberlin

Arnold, Paul Beaver Educator, Printmaker
Bongiorno, Laurine Mack Historian
Frueh, Joanna Critic, Educator
Johnson, Ellen Hulda Historian, Critic
Pearson, John Painter, Instructor
Spear, Richard Edmund Educator
Tacha, Athena Sculptor, Educator
Weidman, Jeffrey Librarian, Historian

Oxford

Beck, Lonnie Lee Painter, Educator
Wolfe, Robert, Jr Printmaker, Painter

Painesville

Kangas, Gene Sculptor, Writer

Parma

Jergens, Robert Joseph Painter, Educator

Perrysburg

Bruner, Louise Katherine (Mrs Paul Orr) Critic, Writer
Hofer, Ingrid (Ingeborg) Painter, Instructor

Piqua

Phillis, Marilyn Hughey Painter, Instructor

Poland

Parella, Albert Lucian Painter, Instructor
Vaccaro, (Patt) Patrick Frank Printmaker, Painter

Richfield

Laessig, Robert Painter, Illustrator

Rocky River

Kuekes, Edward D Cartoonist

Rudolph

Hurlstone, Robert William Glass Artist, Educator

Shaker Heights

Bieber, Elinore Maria Korow Painter, Designer
Davis, David Ensos Sculptor

Solon

Schepis, Anthony Joseph Instructor, Painter
Ward, Evelyn Svec Tapestry Artist, Collage Artist
Ward, William Edward Designer, Painter

South Euclid

Cintron, Joseph M Painter, Instructor
Merrill, Ross M Conservator, Painter

Springfield

Catron, Patricia D'Arcy Administrator
Morgan, Helen Bosart (Mrs Edwin M Wagstaff) Sculptor
Schlump, John Otto Educator, Printmaker

Stow

Kratz, Mildred Sands Painter

Sylvania

Chapman, Walter Howard Painter, Illustrator

Toledo

Autry, Carolyn Printmaker
Berkowitz, Roger M Curator, Museologist
Cohn, Frederick Donald Dealer, Gallery Director
Elloian, Peter Printmaker, Graphic Artist
Hutton, William Museum Curator
Luckner, Kurt T Curator
McGlauchlin, Tom Glassblower, Instructor
Mandle, Earl Roger Museum Director
Nordin, Phyllis E Sculptor, Designer

Van Wert

Liljegren, Frank Painter, Instructor

Wooster

Gouma-Peterson, Thalia Educator, Historian

Worthington

Heimdal, Georg Painter, Instructor

Xenia

Lopina, Louise Carol Painter

Yellow Springs

Hudson, Jon Barlow Sculptor

Youngstown

Murray, Richard Deibel Painter, Sculptor
Pernotto, James Angelo Painter, Environmental Artist
Singer, Clyde J Painter
Zona, Louis A Museum Director, Educator

OKLAHOMA

Ada

Lafon, Dee J Painter, Sculptor
Sieg, Robert Lawrence Sculptor, Enamelist

Anadarko

Chaddlesone, Sherman Painter, Printmaker
Little Chief, Barthell Painter, Sculptor

Bartlesville

Wellington, Duke Painter

Broken Arrow

Broadd, Harry Andrew Painter, Historian

Chickasha

Good, Leonard Painter

Edmond

Owens, Wallace, Jr Administrator, Painter
White, B J (Beverly Jo) Painter

Eucha

Courtney, Barbara Wood Painter

Ft Gibson

West, W Richard (Dick) Sculptor, Painter

Goodwell

Kachel, Harold Stanley Museum Director, Educator

Idabel

Stevenson, Harold Painter

Locust Grove

Stone, Willard Designer, Sculptor

Miami

Wilson, Charles Banks Painter, Printmaker

Muskogee

Hill, Joan (Chea-se-quah) Painter, Illustrator

Norman

Bavinger, Eugene Allen Painter, Educator
Bogart, George A Painter
Caldwell, Susan Havens Historian, Educator
Henkle, James Lee Sculptor, Designer
Hobbs, Joe Ferrell Administrator, Sculptor
Little, Ken Dawson Sculptor, Educator
Olkinetzky, Sam Painter, Museum Director

OKLAHOMA (cont)
Taylor, Joseph Richard Sculptor
Youritzin, Victor Koshkin Historian,
     Educator

Oklahoma City
Adams, Lowell G Museum Director
Alaupovic, Alexandra V Sculptor,
     Educator
Bell, Coca (Mary Catlett) Painter
Bell, James M Art Administrator
Belle, Anna (Anna Belle Birckett) Painter
Davis, J Ray Painter, Printmaker
Faris, Brunel De Bost Painter, Educator
Frederick, Deloras Ann Painter,
     Instructor
Grass, Patty Patterson Painter
Harjo, Benjamin, Jr Painter, Printmaker
Hulett, Simonne R Painter, Printmaker
Johnson, Brent Painter
Lamell, Robert (C) Painter, Designer
Littrell, Doris Marie Dealer
McAninch, Beth Painter
Muno, Richard Carl Sculptor, Director
Ragan, Connie Seabourn Painter,
     Printmaker
Seabourn, Bert Dail Painter
Shorney, Margo Kay (McIver) Dealer,
     Sculptor
Silberman, Arthur Library Director,
     Writer
Walch, John Leo Painter, Sculptor
Warriner, Laura B Painter

Okmulgee
Crumbo, Woody Painter, Printmaker
Jones, Ruthe Blalock Painter, Educator

Pryor
Rabbit, William E Painter, Sculptor

Stillwater
McVicker, J Jay Painter, Printmaker
Smith, B J Museum Director, Instructor
Wise, Geneva H (Holcomb) Collector,
     Painter

Tahlequah
Cochran, George McKee (Redbird)
     Painter, Writer
Hagerstrand, Martin Allan Museum
     Director, Administrator

Tulsa
Allen, Clarence Canning Painter,
     Cartoonist
Allen, Loretta B Painter, Designer
Anderson, David C Sculptor,
     Photographer
Bryce, Eileen Ann Painter
Coker, Carl David Painter, Educator
Crumbo, Minisa Painter, Graphic Artist
Echohawk, Brummett Painter, Illustrator
Godsey, Glenn Educator, Painter
Goree, Gary Paul Instructor, Painter
Hogue, Alexandre Painter, Lithographer
Johnson, Nota Printmaker, Painter
Mahey, John A Gallery Director
Manhart, Marcia Y Administrator,
     Curator
Manhart, Thomas Arthur Educator,
     Ceramist
Myers, Fred A Museum Director
Place, Bradley Eugene Educator
Reeve, James Key Historian, Consultant
Ridgway, Peggi Writer
Schellstede, Richard Lee Art Dealer
Snodgrass, Jeanne Owens (Mrs M Eugene
     King) Museologist, Historian
Wiesendanger, Margaret Harris
     Conservator, Painter

Wiesendanger, Martin Wolfgang
     Historian, Conservator
Wright, Jesse Graham, Jr Museum
     Director

Wagoner
Dennis, Cherre Nixon Painter, Etcher

Washita
Bales, J (Jean Elaine) Painter, Sculptor

OREGON

Astoria
Wanlass, Stanley Glen Sculptor, Painter

Beaverton
Cheshire, Craig Gifford Painter, Educator

Cannon Beach
Greaver, Hanne Printmaker
Greaver, Harry Painter, Printmaker

Corvallis
Chappell, Berkley Warner Painter,
     Printmaker
Crozier, William K, Jr Craftsman,
     Designer
Gunn, Paul James Painter, Educator
Jameson, Demetrios George Painter,
     Printmaker
Levine, Shepard Painter, Educator
Sandgren, Ernest Nelson Painter,
     Printmaker
Sponenburgh, Mark Historian, Sculptor
Taysom, Wayne Pendelton Sculptor,
     Educator

Creswell
Prechtel, Don (Donald Conrad) Painter

Dallas
Mattingly, (James Thomas) Printmaker,
     Educator

Elmira
Zach, Jan Painter, Sculptor

Eugene
Baker, Ralph Bernard Painter, Educator
Buckner, Kay Lamoreux Painter,
     Draftsman
Buckner, Paul Eugene Sculptor, Educator
Donnelly, Marian Card Historian,
     Educator
Joyce, J David Photographer, Sculptor
Krause, LaVerne Erickson Painter,
     Printmaker
Kutka, Anne (Mrs David McCosh)
     Painter
McFee, June King Educator
McKenzie, Allan Dean Educator,
     Historian
Orland, Ted N Photographer
Paul, Ken (Hugh) Printmaker, Painter
Paulin, Richard Calkins Museum
     Director, Craftsman
Roth, Leland M(artin) Historian, Writer
Witham, Vernon Clint Painter,
     Printmaker

Lake Oswego
Hoffman, Elaine Janet Painter
Taylor, Michele F Painter
Van Leunen, Alice Louise Textile Artist,
     Instructor

McMinnville
Bell, Lilian A Sculptor, Assemblage Artist

Monmouth
Casey, John Joseph Educator, Sculptor

Myrtle Point
Notkin, Richard T Sculptor, Ceramist

Oregon City
Kelly, Lee Sculptor

Portland
Barcus, David L Administrator, Museum
     Director
Beebe, Mary Livingstone Art
     Administrator
Bimrose, Arthur Sylvanus, Jr Cartoonist
Burks, Myrna R Printmaker, Gallery
     Director
Cooke, Judy Painter, Collage Artist
Fisher, Kenneth Lee Sculptor
Gilkey, Gordon Waverly Curator,
     Educator
Haley Russo, Sally Fulton Painter
Halvorsen, Ruth Elise Painter, Writer
Hardy, Thomas (Austin) Sculptor
Heidel, Frederick (H) Painter, Educator
Jameson, Philip Alexander Ceramist,
     Painter
Jenkins, Donald John Museum Director,
     Historian
Johanson, George E Painter, Printmaker
Kimbrell, Leonard Buell Historian
McLarty, William James (Jack) Painter,
     Printmaker
Morris, Carl Painter
Morris, Hilda Sculptor
Ostrow, Stephen Edward Historian,
     Museum Director
Prasch, Richard John Painter, Educator
Rhyne, Charles Sylvanus Historian
Russo, Michele Painter
Schnitzer, Arlene Dealer, Patron
Schulz, William Gallagher Sculptor,
     Painter
Sheehan, Evelyn Painter
Waddingham, John Alfred Painter,
     Printmaker
Yes, Phyllis A Painter, Sculptor

Rainier
Lewis, Mary Sculptor

Reedsport
Gronbeck, Jean Painter

Salem
Hall, Carl Alvin Painter, Instructor
Hero, Peter deCourcy Administrator,
     Historian

Scio
Hamilton, George Earl Painter, Educator

Sheridan
Turner, Ralph James Sculptor, Graphic
     Artist

Sherwood
Grimm, Raymond Max Sculptor, Glass
     Artist

Talent
Cornell, David E Ceramist, Sculptor

Tigard
Schiebold, Hans Painter, Instructor

West Linn
Murphy, Chester Glenn Painter

PENNSYLVANIA

Abington
Pease, David G Administrator, Painter

Allentown
Berman, Bernard Collector
Berman, Muriel Mallin Collector, Patron
Berman, Philip I Collector, Patron
Coleman, Edward H Dealer, Collector
Coleman, Gayle (Gayle Coleman
    MacDonald) Restorer, Lecturer
Gans, Lucy C Sculptor, Educator
Gregg, Richard Nelson Museum Director
Hoffman, Richard Peter Painter
Miley, Mimi Conneen Curator
Moller, Hans Painter
Tenzer, (Dr & Mrs) Jonathan A
    Collectors

Allison Park
Osby, Larissa Geiss Painter

Ambler
Wolpert, Elizabeth Davis Painter,
    Instructor

Ardmore
Atlee, Emilie DeS Painter, Instructor

Bala-Cynwyd
Shalit, Mitzi (Mildred M) Consultant,
    Dealer

Bangor
McInerney, Gene Joseph Painter
Watts, Robert M Conceptual Artist,
    Designer

Bath
Conneen, Jane W Printmaker, Miniaturist

Bellefonte
Fisher, Rob (Robert Norman) Sculptor,
    Environmental Artist

Bensalem
Biddle, James Administrator, Collector

Berwyn
Dobie, Jeanne Painter, Instructor

Bethlehem
Redd, Richard James Painter, Educator

Bloomsburg
Roberts, Percival R Educator, Painter

Blue Bell
Martino, Babette Educator, Painter
Martino, Eva E Painter, Sculptor
Martino, Giovanni Painter
Martino, Nina F Painter

Boyertown
Coggins, Jack Banham Instructor, Painter

Broomall
Ingram, Judith Papermaker

Brush Valley
Wert, Ned Oliver Educator, Painter

Bryn Mawr
Broido, Lucy Writer, Dealer
Costanza, John Joseph Sculptor, Ceramist
Janschka, Fritz Painter, Graphic Artist

Lieberman, Vickie Tapestry Artist,
    Gallery Director

Buckingham
Fabert, Jacques Painter, Educator
Roseman, Susan Carol Painter,
    Printmaker

Cambridge Springs
Holt, Martha A Painter, Ceramist
Milnes, Robert Winston Sculptor,
    Educator

Chadds Ford
Duff, James H Museum Director,
    Administrator
McCoy, John W, (II) Painter

Chalfont
DeVegatales, Jugo Sculptor, Educator

Cheltenham
Day, Larry (Lawrence James) Painter,
    Educator
Spandorfer, Merle Sue Painter,
    Printmaker
Wagner, G Noble Painter, Sculptor

Cheyney
Hemphill, Pamela Historian

Christiana
Miller, Daniel Dawson Painter, Sculptor
Rohrer, Warren Painter, Instructor

Clarion
Hobbs, Robert Dean Administrator,
    Printmaker

Clearville
Christensen, Ronald Julius Painter,
    Printmaker

Cochranville
Sazegar, Morteza Painter

Conshohocken
Katz, Theodore (Harry) Painter, Lecturer

Cornwall
Quinn, Henrietta Reist Collector, Patron

Duncansville
Atkyns, (Willie) Lee, Jr Painter, Art
    Administrator

Easton
Higgins, (George) Edward Sculptor
Salemme, Antonio Painter, Sculptor
Salemme, Martha Painter

East Stroudsburg
Strauser, Sterling Boyd Painter

Edinboro
Gibson, Benedict S Painter, Educator
Ko, Anthony Printmaker, Educator
Mitra, Gopal C Painter, Printmaker
Nicholas, Donna Lee Ceramist, Sculptor

Elkins Park
Clark, Jon Frederic Educator, Glass
    Blower
Daley, William P Ceramist, Sculptor
Dass, Dean Allen Printmaker, Educator
Davidson, Abraham A Writer,
    Photographer
Feld, Augusta Painter, Printmaker
Goodman, Sidney Painter
Kohn, Bernard A Printmaker
Lechtzin, Stanley Goldsmith, Educator

Schmidt, Charles Painter
Stenzler, Erna J Sculptor, Instructor

Emmaus
Ackerman, Rudy Schlegel Painter,
    Educator
Ruhe, Barnaby Sieger Painter, Critic

Erie
Ahlgren, Roy B Instructor, Printmaker
Burke, Daniel V Painter, Educator
Kaiser, Vitus J Painter, Instructor
Pizzat, Joseph Educator, Craftsman
Sanders, Andrew Dominick Painter,
    Instructor
Schabacker, Betty Barchet Painter,
    Lecturer
Sundberg, Carl Gustave Enamelist,
    Director
Sundberg, Wilda (Regelman) Painter,
    Instructor
Vanco, John Leroy Administrator,
    Photographer

Freeburg
Bucher, George Robert Educator,
    Sculptor

Gibsonia
De Coux, Janet Sculptor
Rice, Norman Lewis Painter, Educator

Gladwyne
Kardon, Janet Museum Director, Curator

Glenmoore
De Guatemala, Joyce (Joyce Bush
    Vourvoulias) Sculptor

Glenside
Boretz, Naomi Painter, Educator
Crimmins, Jerry (Gerald Garfield)
    Sculptor, Assemblage Artist

Greensburg
Chew, Paul Albert Administrator,
    Lecturer
Filkosky, Josefa Sculptor, Educator

Grove City
Myford, James C Sculptor, Educator

Harmony
Hulmer, Eric Claus Curator, Conservator

Harrisburg
Winer, Donald Arthur Curator, Painter
Wingate, Robert Bray Illustrator,
    Consultant

Hatboro
Tait, Cornelia Damian Painter, Writer

Hatfield
East, N S, Jr Designer, Sculptor

Haverford
Schutte, Thomas Frederick Administrator
Stegeman, Charles Painter, Educator
Wintersteen, Bernice McIlhenny
    Administrator, Collector

Havertown
Fish, Richard G Painter, Illustrator
Gasparro, Frank Sculptor, Instructor
Spicer, Jean (Doris) Uhl Painter,
    Instructor

Hermitage

Dunn, Nate Painter, Instructor

Horsham

Winokur, Paula Colton Ceramist, Craftsman
Winokur, Robert Mark Ceramist, Educator

Huntingdon Valley

Lutz, Winifred Ann Sculptor, Environmental Artist
Meltzer, Arthur Painter
Van Roekens, Paulette (Mrs Arthur Meltzer) Painter

Indiana

Kipp, Orval Painter, Educator
Reynolds, Ralph William Painter

Jenkintown

Dioda, Adolph T Sculptor, Instructor
Fuhrman, Esther Sculptor, Designer
Langman, Richard Theodore Gallery Director

Johnstown

Sheehe, Lillian Carolyn Painter, Enamelist

Kempton

Hesketh Sculptor

Kennett Square

Greenleaf, Esther (Hargrave) Painter, Printmaker

Kutztown

Quirk, Thomas Charles, Jr Painter, Educator

Lancaster

Hay, Ike Sculptor, Educator
Kermes, Constantine John Painter, Printmaker
Lipman, Stan Sculptor, Instructor
Sharrow, Sheba Painter, Educator

Lemont

Altman, Harold Printmaker, Educator
Cook, John (Alfred) Sculptor, Medalist
Neffson, Robert Painter

Lewisburg

Turnure, James Harvey Educator, Historian

Lumberville

Katsiff, Bruce Photographer, Educator
Taylor, Rosemary Ceramist, Sculptor

McKean

Kemenyffy, Steven Ceramist, Educator
Kemenyffy, Susan B Hale Ceramist

Manheim

Steinmetz, Grace Ernst Titus Painter

Martins Creek

Fink, Larry (Laurence B) Educator, Photographer

Mechanicsburg

Walker, Mary Carolyn Craftsman, Jeweler

Mechanicsville

Bye, Ranulph (DeBayeux) Painter
Coiner, Charles Toucey Painter

Media

Berd, Morris Painter, Educator
Hildebrandt, William Albert Painter, Administrator
House, James Charles, Jr Sculptor

Melrose Park

Blai, Bertha Ceramist, Craftsman
Sabatini, Raphael Painter, Sculptor
Saunders, Wade Sculptor, Critic

Mendenhall

Boucher, Tania Kunsky Painter, Art Dealer

Mercersburg

Etchison, Bruce Conservator, Painter

Merion Station

Cederstrom, John Andrew Painter, Instructor
Newman, Libby Painter, Printmaker
Sankowsky, Itzhak Painter, Sculptor

Millersville

Laynor, Harold Arthur Educator, Painter

Mohnton

Gore, Jefferson Anderson Curator

Narberth

Alten, Jerry Director, Designer
Donohoe, Victoria Historian, Critic
Hutton, Dorothy Wackerman Designer, Printmaker
McGovern, Robert F Painter, Sculptor

New Castle

McNickle, Thomas Glen Painter

New Freedom

Theofiles, George Historian, Dealer

New Hope

Moore, Beveridge Painter

Newton

Jansen, Catherine Sandra Photographer, Educator
Keene, Paul Painter

Newtown

Renninger, Katharine Steele Painter

Newtown Square

Martino, Edmund Painter, Designer
Roberts, Gilroy Sculptor
Serwazi, Albert B Painter

Norristown

Bates, Betsey Designer, Painter
Grimley, Oliver Fetterolf Painter, Sculptor
Rapp, Lois Painter

Northampton

Viera, Ricardo Painter, Printmaker

North Wales

Dallmann, Daniel Forbes Painter, Printmaker

Ottsville

Rudy, Charles Sculptor
Smith, Michael A Photographer

Philadelphia

Amarotico, Joseph Anthony Painter, Conservator
Andrade, Edna Wright Painter
Auth, Tony (William Anthony), Jr Editorial Cartoonist
Bach, Laurence Photographer, Educator
Barber, Ronald Administrator
Barnett, Jack Painter, Instructor
Batchelor, Betsy Ann Painter, Educator
Bateman, Ronald C Painter
Belfiore, Gerardo Painter, Instructor
Bernstein, Benjamin D Collector
Bernstein, Edward I Collector, Patron
Blai, Boris Sculptor, Educator
Bobrowicz, Yvonne P Instructor, Fiber Artist
Boggs, Jean Sutherland Museum Director, Art Historian
Bookbinder, Jack Painter, Printmaker
Boyle, Richard J Historian, Writer
Brady, Luther W Collector, Patron
Brodsky, Harry Lithography
Burko, Diane Painter, Educator
Bushnell, Marietta P Librarian
Butera, Anne Fabbri Museum Director, Curator
Butler, Marigene H Conservator
Campbell, William Henry Painter
Chahroudi, Martha L Curator
Channing, Susan Rose Administrator, Photographer
Cramer, Richard Charles Painter, Educator
Crawford, Bill (Wilbur Ogden) Illustrator, Administrator
Dessner, Murray Painter
d'Harnoncourt, Anne Historian, Museum Director
Diamond, Paul Photographer
Dickerson, Brian S Painter
Dillon, Mildred (Murphy) Printmaker
Dolan, Margo Gallery Director, Dealer
Dowell, John E, Jr Educator, Printmaker
Drutt, Helen Williams Dealer, Lecturer
Edmunds, Allan Logan Printmaker, Administrator
Etting, Emlen Painter, Illustrator
Ewing, Thomas R Painter, Instructor
Formicola, John Joseph Painter, Educator
Franklin, Charlotte White Painter, Sculptor
Freeland, William Lee Painter, Sculptor
Fridakis, Gera Hesness Sculptor
Friedlaender, Bilge Sculptor, Painter
Frudakis, Evangelos William Sculptor, Instructor
Frudakis, Zenos Sculptor, Painter
Fuller, Jeffrey P Dealer, Gallery Director
Garcia, Ofelia Administrator, Printmaker
Gaudin, Marguerite Designer
Gold, Albert Painter, Educator
Goldman, Rachel Bok Collector, Patron
Goodyear, Frank H, Jr Historian, Curator
Gross, Estelle Shane Dealer
Gundersheimer, Herman (Samuel) Historian, Educator
Hahn, Maurice & Roslyn Dealers
Hamilton, Charles F Educator, Writer
Hanes, James (Albert) Painter
Hanlen, John (Garrett) Painter, Instructor
Hoffman, Michael E Editor, Curator
Hood, (Thomas) Richard Printmaker, Designer
Hoptner, Richard Sculptor
Horvitz, Suzanne Joan Painter, Printmaker
Howard, Humbert L Painter
Jacobowitz, Ellen Sue Curator, Historian
Jacobs, Harold Painter, Sculptor
Johnson, Homer Educator, Painter
Johnson, Lois Marlene Printmaker, Educator
Jones, (Charles) Dexter (Weatherbee), III Sculptor, Designer
Jones, Elizabeth A B Sculptor, Medalist
Kamihira, Ben Painter
Kaplan, Jerome Eugene Printmaker

PENNSYLVANIA (cont)

Kerrigan, Maurie Sculptor
Kettner, David Allen Artist, Educator
Kimmelman, Harold Sculptor
Klein, Esther M Patron, Collector
Knobler, Lois Jean Painter
Knobler, Nathan Sculptor, Educator
Kogan, Deborah Painter, Illustrator
Kostiuk, Michael Marion, Jr Assemblage
  Artist, Book Artist
Kotala, Stanislaw Waclaw Painter,
  Librarian
Kramrisch, Stella Curator, Educator
Lang, J T Printmaker, Educator
La Pelle, Rodger Painter, Dealer
Lasuchin, Michael Printmaker, Painter
Le Clair, Charles Painter, Educator
Lerner, Alexandria Sandra Painter,
  Publisher
Levy, Margaret Wasserman Sculptor
Limont, Naomi Charles Printmaker,
  Instructor
Lisker, Sara Designer, Craftsman
Locks, Marian Gallery Director, Collector
Looney, Robert Fain Curator, Librarian
Lueders, Jimmy C Painter, Instructor
McClain, Matthew Curator, Writer
McClenney, Cheryl Ilene Administrator
McGinnis, Christine Painter
Maitin, Sam (Samuel Calman) Painter,
  Sculptor
Makler, Hope Welsh Dealer
Mangel, Benjamin Dealer
Mangione, Patricia Anthony Painter,
  Muralist
Marzano, Albert Painter, Designer
Medoff, Eve Painter, Writer
Meister, Michael William Historian,
  Educator
Merrick, James Kirk Painter, Educator
Metzker, Ray K Photographer, Educator
Millett, Caroline Dunlop Administrator
Moskowitz, Shirley (Mrs Jacob W
  Gruber) Painter, Collage Artist
Naftulin, Rose Painter
Neff, Edith Painter, Instructor
Nelson, Leonard Painter
Omwake, Leon, Jr Painter, Sculptor
Osborne, Elizabeth Painter, Instructor
Paone, Peter Printmaker, Painter
Percy, Ann Buchanan Curator, Historian
Perkins, G Holmes Architect, Educator
Piper, Jane Painter, Lecturer
Pollock, Bruce Walter Sculptor, Designer
Pretsch, John Edward Cartoonist,
  Illustrator
Quigley, Michael Allen Administrator
Ray, Christopher T Sculptor, Craftsman
Remenick, Seymour Painter, Instructor
Richardson, Edgar Preston Historian
Rishel, Joseph John, Jr Curator
Rosenfeld, Richard Joel Dealer
Rosenthal, Mark L Curator, Writer
Russell, (George) Gordon Painter
Schoenbach, Bertha Karp Painter,
  Printmaker
Scott, Robert Montgomery Patron,
  Administrator
Scott, William P(owell) Painter, Writer
Sevy, Barbara Snetsinger Librarian
Sewell, Darrel L Curator, Historian
Shatalow, Vladimir Mihailovich Painter
Shih, Joan Fai Painter, Instructor
Shores, (James) Franklin Painter
Simkin, Phillips M Sculptor
Solmssen, Peter Administrator
Solomon, Vita Petrosky Painter,
  Printmaker
Spohn, Franz Frederick Sculptor,
  Printmaker
Staffel, Doris Painter, Educator
Staffel, Rudolf Harry Ceramist, Instructor

Stearns, Thomas Robert Sculptor,
  Educator
Stein, Judith Ellen Historian, Curator
Stein, Ludwig K Educator, Painter
Steinberg, Leo Educator, Historian
Striker, Cecil L Historian, Educator
Taicher, Richard Painter
Venturi, Robert Architect
Viesulas, Romas Printmaker, Educator
Visco, Anthony Salvatore Educator,
  Sculptor
Warner, Herbert Kelii, Jr Instructor,
  Printmaker
Wasserman, Jack Educator
Watson, Howard N(oel) Painter,
  Printmaker
Weidner, Marilyn Kemp Conservator,
  Lecturer
Weidner, Roswell Theodore Painter,
  Instructor
Weinberg, Ephraim Administrator,
  Educator
White, Susan Chrysler Painter
Zelt, Martha Printmaker, Instructor

Phoenixville

Crowell, Lucius Painter, Sculptor
Hopkins, Kendal Coles Painter

Pineville

Smith, William Arthur Painter,
  Printmaker

Pittsburgh

Adams, Henry Curator, Educator
Arkus, Leon A Consultant, Museum
  Director
Binai, Paul Freye Painter, Art Curator
Caldwell, John Curator, Critic
Cantini, Virgil D Painter, Sculptor
Caplan, Jerry L Sculptor, Educator
Clark, Vicky A Historian, Curator
Crenshaw, Karen Bruce Conservator
Denney, Jim (James David) Painter
Dodds, Robert J, III Collector, Museum
  Director
Feller, Robert L Conservation Scientist
Fitzpatrick, Joseph Cyril Painter, Sculptor
Gardner, Robert Earl Printmaker,
  Educator
Gordon, Donald Edward Historian,
  Educator
Gruber, Aaronel deRoy Sculptor, Kinetic
  Artist
Haney, William H Painter, Draftsman
Haskins, John Franklin Historian,
  Educator
Hearn, M F (Millard Fillmore), Jr
  Administrator, Historian
Holland, Harry Charles Painter, Educator
Hollen-Bolmgren, Donna Assemblage
  Artist, Painter
Johnston, Phillip M Curator
Judson, William D Curator, Historian
Karn, Gloria Stoll Painter, Instructor
Katz, Joseph M Collector, Patron
Kerstetter-Bailey, Barbara Ann Painter,
  Instructor
King, Elaine A Curator, Historian
Koerner, Henry Painter, Lecturer
Kornetchuk, Elena Dealer, Historian
Landreau, Anthony Norman
  Administrator
Lane, John Rodger Museum Director,
  Historian
Lepper, Robert Lewis Educator, Sculptor
Lewis, Virginia Elnora Museum Director,
  Historian
Libby, William C Painter, Writer
Midani, Akram Administrator, Educator
Miller, Donald Critic, Writer
Mulcahy, Kathleen Glass Artist, Sculptor

Pasinski, Irene Painter, Sculptor
Pershing, Louise Painter, Sculptor
Sheon, Aaron Historian, Administrator
Stones, Margaret Alison Educator,
  Historian
Toker, Franklin K B Historian
Twiggs, Russell Gould Painter
Webb, Frank (Francis H) Painter,
  Instructor
Weidner, Mary Elizabeth Painter,
  Educator
Weiner, Abe Painter, Instructor
Wiebe, Charles M Dealer, Historian
Wilkins, David George Historian, Gallery
  Director
Williams, John Wesley Historian,
  Educator
Winokur, James L Collector, Critic

Pocopson

Bostelle, Thomas (Theodore) Painter,
  Sculptor

Quakertown

Keyser, Robert G Painter
Opie, John Mart Painter

Reading

Dietrich, Bruce Leinbach Museum
  Director, Administrator

Rosemont

Goutman, Dolya Educator, Painter
Lengyel, Alfonz Historian, Writer
Terry, Duncan Niles Stained Glass Artist,
  Craftsman

Rushland

Rosenwald, Barbara K Collector

Saltsburg

Carter, (Charles) Bruce Printmaker,
  Educator

Scranton

Ahrens, Kent Museum Director,
  Historian

Selinsgrove

Putterman, Florence Grace Painter,
  Printmaker

Shippensburg

Bentz, Harry Donald Educator, Painter

Solebury

Anthonisen, George Rioch Sculptor,
  Painter

Souderton

Bock, William Sauts-Netamux'we
  Illustrator, Painter
Hallman, H Theodore, Jr Craftsman,
  Designer

Spring House

Garvan, Beatrice Bronson Curator,
  Historian

State College

Davis, William D Museum Director,
  Painter
Fleischer, Roland Edward Historian,
  Educator
Frost, Stuart Homer Educator, Painter
Graves, Kenneth Robert Photographer
Hager, Hellmut W Historian
Hatke, Walter Joseph Painter
McCoy, Wirth Vaughan Painter
Porter, Jeanne Chenault Educator,
  Historian

PENNSYLVANIA (cont)

Porter, Richard James Administrator, Historian
Rubello, David Jerome Painter, Photographer
Sommese, Lanny Beal Educator, Designer
Van Dommelen, David B Writer, Fiber Artist
Zoretich, George Stephen Painter, Educator

Sunbury

Karniol, Hilda Painter

Susquehanna

Laughlin, Mortimer Painter

Swarthmore

Cothren, Michael Watt Educator
Hollister, Valerie (Dutton) Painter
Hungerford, Constance Cain Educator, Historian
Kitao, T Kaori Historian, Educator

Titusville

Herpst, Martha Jane Painter

Trucksville

Colson, Chester E Painter, Educator

University Park

Alden, Richard Painter
Hamwi, Richard Alexander Painter, Educator
Lawrence, Howard Ray Designer, Educator
Maddox, Jerrold Warren Educator, Painter
Mayhew, Richard Painter
Ott, Robert William Educator, Writer
Smith, Elizabeth Jean Librarian

Upper Black Eddy

Saalburg, Allen Russel Painter, Printmaker

Venango

Spinosa, Gary Paul Sculptor

Villanova

Cannuli, Richard Gerald Painter, Gallery Director

Wallingford

Mark, Enid (Epstein) Printmaker, Painter

Washington

Pablo Painter, Educator
Taylor, Hugh Holloway Historian, Educator

Washington Boro

Nelson, Robert Allen Printmaker, Painter

Washington Crossing

Ceglia, Vincent Painter, Instructor
Kemble, Richard Printmaker, Sculptor

Waterford

Stull, Jean Himrod Painter, Instructor

Wayne

Brodhead, Quita Painter
Hoffman, Edward Fenno, III Sculptor
Key, Ted Cartoonist

West Chester

Baldwin, Richard Wood Illustrator, Sculptor
Bryce, Mark Adams Painter, Printmaker
Everhart, Don (Donald Nelson), Jr Medalist, Illustrator
Hawthorne, Jack Gardner Educator, Painter
Jamison, Philip Painter

West Grove

Allman, Margo Sculptor, Painter

West Middletown

Youngsblood, Nat Painter, Illustrator

Whitehall

Menthe, Melissa Librarian, Photographer

Wilkes-Barre

Simon, Herbert Bernheimer Sculptor, Collage Artist

Williamsport

Lesko, Diane Historian, Educator
Shipley, Roger Douglas Sculptor, Educator

Wyncote

Larson, William G Photographer, Educator
Moore, John J Painter, Educator

Wynnewood

Angelo, Emidio Cartoonist, Painter
Bowes, Betty Miller Painter, Consultant
Maxwell, John Painter
Pincus, David N Collector

Wyomissing

Elliott, B Charles, Jr Consultant, Historian

York

Fitzkee, Eunice Ailes Dealer

Zionsville

Stark, Melville F Painter, Educator

RHODE ISLAND

Bristol

Goff, Thomas Jefferson Sculptor, Medalist
Knowlton, Daniel Gibson Bookbinder, Conservator
Townley, Hugh Sculptor, Printmaker
Udvardy, John Warren Sculptor, Administrator

Coventry

Beaudoin, Andre Eugene Press Manufacturer, Photographer

Cranston

Casey, Elizabeth Temple Curator
Crooks, W Spencer Painter, Lecturer

East Providence

Peterson, A E S Painter, Printmaker

Jamestown

Wright, Catharine Morris Painter, Writer

Johnston

Charles-Smith, Donald Printmaker, Painter

Kingston

Leete, William White Painter
Onorato, Ronald Joseph Historian, Critic

Lincoln

Loughlin, John Leo Painter

Newport

Bach, Dirk Painter, Educator
Barry, Robert E Illustrator, Educator
Cooper, Marve H Painter, Curator
Gaines, Alan Jay Printmaker, Publisher
Nesbitt, Alexander John Educator, Calligrapher
van Duinwyk, George Paul Goldsmith, Educator
Walkey, Frederick P Museum Director

Pawtucket

Heyman, Lawrence Murray Painter, Printmaker

Peace Dale

Eichenberg, Fritz Illustrator, Printmaker
Petrie, Sylvia Spencer Printmaker, Painter

Providence

Ben Tre, Howard Sculptor, Draftsman
Blodgett, Peter Sculptor, Educator
Callahan, Harry Photographer
Ewing, Bayard Administrator, Collector
Feldman, Walter (Sidney) Painter, Printmaker
Findlay, James Allen Librarian
Franklin, Gilbert Alfred Sculptor, Educator
Geran, Joseph, Jr Sculptor, Designer
Goto, Joseph Sculptor
Grear, James Malcolm Designer, Educator
Hall, Lee Administrator, Painter
Helander, Bruce Paul Painter, Dealer
Macaulay, David Alexander Designer, Illustrator
Morin, Thomas Edward Sculptor, Educator
Ockerse, Thomas Designer, Educator
Peers, Gordon Franklin Painter, Educator
Pilavin, Selma F Collector, Patron
Prince, Arnold Sculptor, Educator
Robinson, Franklin W Museum Director, Historian
Ryder, Mahler Bessinger Collage Artist, Illustrator
St Florian, Friedrich Gartler Educator, Designer
Schulz, Ann Markham Historian, Educator
Schulz, Juergen Educator, Historian

Tiverton

Hopkins, Benjamin Librarian, Administrator

Wakefield

Rohm, Robert Sculptor

Westerly

Day, Chon Cartoonist

West Kingston

Brown, Marvin Prentiss Painter, Sculptor

SOUTH CAROLINA

Abbeville

Velasquez, Oscar Painter, Illustrator

Bishopville

Adams, Bobbi Painter

Charleston

Halsey, William Melton Painter, Educator
Hirsch, Willard Newman Sculptor
Johnson, Diane Chalmers Historian,
　Educator
McCallum, Corrie (Mrs William Halsey)
　Painter, Printmaker
Wyrick, Charles Lloyd, Jr Museum
　Director, Editor

Chesnee

Cook, August Charles Painter, Printmaker

Clemson

Dimond, Terry Jarrard Sculptor, Educator
McGcc, Olivia Jackson Painter, Illustrator
Wang, Sam Photographer

Columbia

Bardin, Jesse Redwin Painter
Craft, John Richard Museum Director
Davis, John Sherwood Potter,
　Administrator
Dunn, Phillip Charles Educator,
　Administrator
Edwards, James F Video Artist, Painter
Elkins, Toni Marcus Painter, Designer
Hampton, Ambrose Gonzales, Jr
　Collector
Hansen, Harold John Educator, Painter
Hathaway, Walter Murphy Museum
　Director
Lafaye, Nell Murray Painter, Educator
Langer, Sandra Lois Historian, Critic
Ledyard, Walter William Sculptor,
　Printmaker
Lipscomb, Guy Fleming, Jr Painter,
　Instructor
Mack, Charles Randall Educator,
　Historian
McWhorter, Elsie Jean Painter, Sculptor
Mitchell, Dana Covington, Jr Collector
Mullen, Philip Edward Artist, Educator
Ochs, Robert David Collector, Patron
O'Neil, John Joseph Administrator,
　Designer
Parris, Nina Gumpert Curator, Educator
Quinsac, Annie-Paule Historian, Writer
Robinson, Chris (Christopher Thomas)
　Conceptual Artist, Educator
Saunders, J Boyd Printmaker, Educator
Sennema, David C Museum Director,
　Administrator
Van Hook, David H Painter,
　Administrator
Woody, (Thomas) Howard Sculptor,
　Environmental Artist
Yaghjian, Edmund Painter, Instructor

Greenville

Alberga, Alta W Etcher, Painter
Appleman, David Earl Designer, Painter
Bell, Kathryn Leise Calligrapher,
　Educator
Blair, Carl Raymond Painter, Art Dealer
Bopp, Emery Painter, Educator
Bowne, James Dehart Museum Director,
　Art Historian
Dreskin, Jeanet Steckler Painter,
　Educator
Flowers, Thomas Earl Painter, Educator
Hodge, Scottie Dealer, Administrator
Hunter, Robert Howard Painter
Koons, Darell J Painter, Educator

Hilton Head Island

Bowler, Joseph, Jr Painter, Illustrator
Greer, Walter (Marion) Painter
Stacks, William Leon Painter, Restorer

Isle of Palms

Knerr, Sallie Frost Painter, Printmaker

Johns Island

Mawicke, Tran Painter, Illustrator

Mt Pleasant

Buba, Joy Flinsch Sculptor, Illustrator
Tyzack, Michael Painter, Educator

Orangeburg

Twiggs, Leo Franklin Painter, Educator

Rock Hill

Freeman, David L Painter, Graphic Artist
Lewandowski, Edmund D Painter,
　Administrator

Spartanburg

Boggs, Mayo Mac Sculptor, Educator
Bramlett, Betty Jane Art Administrator,
　Painter
Nodine, Jane Allen Painter, Designer

Summerville

Vorwerk, E Charlsie Painter, Illustrator

Sumter

Davenport, Ray Painter, Printmaker

Taylors

Barbee, Rob Painter

Wadmalaw Island

McKoy, Victor Grainger Sculptor

SOUTH DAKOTA

Brookings

Boyd, Donald Edgar Intermedia Artist,
　Writer
Jordan, Jim Critic, Painter
Nelson, Signe (Signe Nelson Stuart)
　Painter
Stuart, Joseph Martin Painter, Museum
　Director

Sioux Falls

Eide, Palmer Sculptor, Designer
Grupp, Carl Alf Painter, Printmaker

Spearfish

Termes (Dick A Termes) Painter,
　Photographer

Springfield

Gettinger, Edmond Walter Educator,
　Painter

Vermillion

Howe, Oscar Painter, Educator

Westport

Gibson, James D Educator, Painter

TENNESSEE

Brentwood

Frace, Charles Lewis Illustrator, Painter

Chattanooga

Craft, David Ralph Painter, Printmaker
Cress, George Ayers Painter, Educator
Scarbrough, Cleve Knox, Jr Museum
　Director, Historian

Shumacker, Elizabeth Wight Painter,
　Instructor
Townsend, Stanley Dale Painter,
　Instructor

Clarksville

Bryant, Olen L Sculptor, Educator
Crouch, Ned Philbrick Sculptor, Curator
Hochstetler, T Max Painter, Educator

Collegedale

Childers, Malcolm Graeme Printmaker,
　Photographer

Cookeville

Lee-Sissom, E Painter

Cordova

Yates, Marvin Clarence Painter,
　Instructor

Cross Plains

Wright, Harold David Painter

Fayetteville

Blumrich, Stephen Designer, Editor

Gatlinburg

Gray, Jim Painter, Sculptor
Schulz, Ken Painter, Lecturer

Jackson

Robinson, Grove Painter, Educator

Jefferson City

Cleveland, Robert Earl Administrator,
　Educator

Johnson City

Logan, David George Metalsmith,
　Educator

Kingsport

Williams, Raymond Lester Painter,
　Instructor

Knoxville

Cleaver, Dale Gordon Historian,
　Educator
Koscianski, Leonard J Painter, Educator
Kurka, Donald Frank Painter,
　Administrator
Leland, Whitney Edward Painter,
　Educator
McKeeby, Byron Gordon Printmaker,
　Educator
Stewart, F Clark Painter, Educator
Sublett, Carl C Painter

Lookout Mountain

Fowler, Frank Eison Dealer, Consultant
Lynch, Mary Britten Painter
Wyeth, Andrew Newell Painter
Wyeth, James Browning Painter

Memphis

Allgood, Charles Henry Art Historian,
　Painter
Anthony, Lawrence Kenneth Sculptor,
　Educator
Bennett, Jamie Enamelist, Sculptor
Bingham, Alice Art Dealer, Consultant
Califf, Marilyn Iskiwitz Painter, Designer
Callicott, Burton Harry Painter,
　Calligrapher
Cloar, Carroll Painter
Easterwood, Henry Lewis Educator,
　Tapestry Artist
Faiers, Ted (Edward Spencer) Painter,
　Printmaker
Goodman, Benjamin Patron

TENNESSEE (cont)

Govan, Francis Hawks Educator, Painter
Hendrix, Connie (Connie Sandage Manus) Painter, Instructor
Hyland, Douglas K S Museum Director
Knowles, Richard H Painter, Writer
Lehman, Louise Brasell Painter
McPherson, Larry E Photographer, Educator
Morriss, Mary Rachel Painter
Pekar, Ronald Walter Painter, Sculptor
Penczner, Paul Joseph Painter
Purtle, Carol Jean Historian, Educator
Rawlinson, Jonlane Frederick Painter, Instructor
Riseling, Robert Lowell Educator, Painter
Riss, Murray Photographer, Educator
Roberson, William Tapestry Artist
Rust, Edwin C Sculptor, Administrator
Shook, Georg Painter
Smith, Dolph Painter, Educator

Morristown

Ortmayer, Constance Sculptor, Educator

Nashville

Baeder, John Painter
Bissell, Charles Overman Cartoonist
Bodo, Sandor Conservator, Restorer
Brumbaugh, Thomas Brendle Historian, Writer
Caldwell, Benjamin Hubbard, Jr Collector, Historian
Grogan, Kevin Museum Director, Museologist
Hall, Robert L Curator, Painter
Harris, Dolores Ashley Designer, Educator
Havens, Jan Sculptor
Hazlehurst, Franklin Hamilton Historian, Educator
Hill, John Alexander Collector
Hooks, Earl J Educator, Sculptor
James, A Everette, Jr Collector, Lecturer
Jones, Theodore Joseph Sculptor, Printmaker
King, Myron Lyzon Dealer
Mason, Phillip Lindsay Painter, Administrator
Mode, Carol A Painter, Printmaker
Orr, Arthur (Leslie) Painter, Graphic Artist
Pilsk, Adele Inez Ceramist, Administrator
Pletcher, Gerry Painter, Printmaker
Ridley, Gregory D, Jr Painter, Sculptor

Sewanee

Carlos, (James) Edward Painter, Administrator
Jones, Ronald Warren Artist, Critic

Seymour

Le Fevre, Richard John Painter, Designer

Signal Mountain

Collins, Jim Educator, Sculptor

TEXAS

Abilene

Kwiecinski, Chester Martin Educator, Painter
Suter, Sherwood Eugene Educator, Painter

Amarillo

Fraze, Denny T Collage Artist, Administrator
Turner, David Museum Director, Educator

Anthony

Grissom, Freda Gill Painter, Goldsmith

Argyle

Miller, J(ohn) Brough Sculptor, Educator

Arlington

Brouillette, Al Painter, Instructor
Bruno, Vincent J Historian, Administrator
Grandee, Joe Ruiz Painter, Gallery Director
Rascoe, Stephen Thomas Painter, Educator
Shaffer, Richard Painter, Printmaker
Sullivan, Max William Museum Director
Turner, William Eugene Painter, Educator
Wood, Nicholas Wheeler Sculptor, Painter

Austin

Beitz, Les Painter, Illustrator
Bowlt, John Art Historian, Educator
Brezik, Hilarion Painter, Educator
Bucknall, Malcolm Roderick Painter
Carlozzi, Annette DiMeo Curator
Chesney, Lee Roy, III Printmaker, Educator
Clarke, John R Educator, Critic
Daly, Stephen Jeffrey Sculptor, Educator
Davis, Marian B Historian, Curator
Deming, David Lawson Sculptor, Educator
Fearing, William Kelly Painter, Educator
Fisher, James Donald Sculptor, Museum Director
Forsyth, Constance Painter, Printmaker
Francis, Bill Dean Designer, Educator
Frary, Michael Painter, Educator
Goodman, Mark Photographer
Gould, Karen Keel Historian, Educator
Green, Glenda Painter, Historian
Grieder, Terence Historian
Guerin, John William Painter, Educator
Hale, Kenneth John Lithographer, Painter
Hatgil, Paul Sculptor, Educator
Henderson, Linda Dalrymple Historian, Educator
Hess, Joyce Librarian
High, Timothy Griffin Printmaker, Educator
Kelpe, Paul Painter
Lansdon, Gay Brandt Painter, Printmaker
Lee, Russell Photographer, Educator
Lichacz, Sheila Enit Painter
Likan, Gustav Painter, Instructor
McCready, Eric Scott Museum Director, Historian
McGill, Forrest Historian, Museum Administrator
Marianne Painter, Draftsman
Marshall, Bruce Painter, Illustrator
Mayer, Susan Martin Educator, Museologist
Miller, Melissa Wren Painter
Milliken, Gibbs Painter, Educator
Norris, Andrea Spaulding Historian, Curator
Pena, Amado Maurilio, Jr Painter, Illustrator
Popinsky, Arnold Dave Sculptor, Ceramist
Prescott, Kenneth Wade Educator, Writer
Reese, Thomas Ford Historian, Educator
Rodriguez, Pedro A Painter, Administrator
Ruben, Leonard Designer, Educator
Schmandt-Besserat, Denise Historian, Archaeologist
Schuller, Nancy Shelby Librarian, Historian
Spruce, Everett Franklin Painter, Printmaker

Stinsmuehlen, Susan Dodds Glass Collage Artist, Painter
Umlauf, Charles Sculptor
Weismann, Donald Leroy Educator, Painter
White, Ralph Painter, Educator
Williams, John Alden Historian
Wiman, Bill Painter, Educator

Beaumont

Carron, Maudee Lilyan Painter, Sculptor
Coe, Matchett Herring Sculptor
Paris, Kay Museum Executive Director, Consultant

Bellaire

Parsons, David Goode Sculptor, Educator

Boerne

Bigger, Michael D Sculptor

Burkburnett

Cokendolpher, Eunice Loraine Painter, Instructor

Canyon

Cornette, Mary Elizabeth Dealer, Painter
Gregory, (Eleanor) Anne Educator, Calligrapher
Mayes, Steven Lee Administrator, Printmaker

Clifton

Boren, James Erwin Painter
Grelle, Martin Glen Painter

Clint

Herring, Jan (Janet Mantel) Painter, Writer

Commerce

Davis, James Wesley Painter, Writer
McGough, Charles E Printmaker, Educator
Umlauf, Karl A Painter, Sculptor

Corpus Christi

Cain, Joseph Alexander Painter, Educator
Gallander, Cathleen S Museum Director
Lambert, Ed Printmaker, Painter
Locke, Michelle Wilson Curator, Historian
Peters, Diane (Peck) Painter, Designer
Plath, Iona Writer, Weaver
Riley, Barbra Bayne Photographer, Educator
Silvertooth, Dennis Carl Sculptor
Sullivan, Ronald Dee Sculptor, Educator
Tsai, Hsiao Hsia Painter, Sculptor
Ullberg, Kent Sculptor
Wilhelmi, William Merle Ceramist, Craftsman

Dallas

Albrecht, Mary Dickson Sculptor, Designer
Allumbaugh, James Sculptor, Educator
Altermann, Tony Art Dealer
Barta, Dorothy Elaine Painter, Instructor
Bond, Roland S Collector
Brotherton, Naomi Painter, Instructor
Burford, William E Dealer, Administrator
Bywaters, Jerry Painter, Historian
Childers, Richard Robin Painter
Clifford, Jutta Dealer, Lecturer
Comini, Alessandra Historian, Lecturer
Dreskin-Haig, Jeanet Elizabeth Painter, Printmaker
Emerson, Walter Caruth Educator, Painter
Gantz, Ann Cushing Painter, Instructor

TEXAS (cont)

Gregory, Ellna Kay Painter, Printmaker
Gummelt, Samuel Painter
Hamilton, Susan Printmaker, Painter
Harris, Leon A, Jr Collector, Patron
Held, (Jon) Jonathan, Jr Librarian,
    Graphic Artist
Hunter, Debora Photographer, Educator
Jacques, Russell Kenneth Sculptor
Jones, Lois Swan Educator, Historian
Judd, De Forrest Hale Painter, Educator
Kahn, Annelies Ruth Ceramist, Craftsman
Kahn, Ralph H Dealer, Lecturer
Kelley, Chapman Painter, Dealer
Koch, Arthur Robert Painter, Educator
Komodore, Bill Painter
Leeber, Sharon Corgan Sculptor
Livesay, Thomas Andrew Museum
    Director
Lunsford, John (Crawford) Historian,
    Curator
Marcus, Stanley Collector
Meadows, P B (Patricia B) Administrator,
    Painter
Mudge, Edmund Webster, Jr Collector
Nagler, Edith Kroger Painter
Nagler, Fred Printmaker, Sculptor
Nash, Steven Alan Historian, Curator
Nasher, Patsy R Collector, Consultant
Parker, Harry S, III Museum Director
Piccolo, Thomas Frank Sculptor, Jeweler
Richards, Jeanne Herron Etcher, Painter
Rizzie, Dan Collage Artist, Painter
Scholder, Laurence Printmaker, Educator
Smither, Edward Murray Dealer,
    Consultant
Stewart, John (John Stewart Houston)
    Dealer
Stott, Deborah Historian
Tufts, Eleanor M Historian, Educator
Tyler, Valton Printmaker, Painter
Voelker, John Painter, Designer
Vogel, Donald S Painter, Dealer
Wade, Robert Schrope Photographer,
    Sculptor
Winter, Roger Painter

Deer Park

Grisham, Barbara Jean Painter

Denton

Corpron, Carlotta M Educator,
    Photographer
Davis, D Jack Educator, Administrator
Erdle, Rob Painter, Educator
Gough, Georgia Belle Craftsman,
    Educator
Mattil, Edward L Educator, Writer
Youngblood, Judy Printmaker

Dripping Springs

Amateau, Michele Painter
Schule, Donald Kenneth Sculptor,
    Instructor

Dumas

Stallwitz, Carolyn Painter, Photographer

Edinburg

Field, Philip Sidney Painter, Printmaker

El Paso

Acosta, Manuel Gregorio Painter,
    Sculptor
Carter, Frederick Timmins Painter,
    Illustrator
de Turczynowicz, Wanda (Mrs Eliot
    Hermann) Painter
Drake, James Printmaker, Sculptor
Enriquez, Gaspar Designer, Instructor
Fulton, Fred Franklin Painter

Garnsey, Clarke Henderson Historian,
    Educator
Jimenez, Luis Alfonso, Jr Sculptor,
    Draftsman
Kolliker, William Augustin Painter,
    Printmaker
Lea, Tom Painter, Illustrator
Martin, Loretta Marsh Calligrapher,
    Cartoonist
Martinez, Ernesto Pedregon Instructor,
    Muralist
Massey, Robert Joseph Painter, Educator
Rakocy, William (Joseph) Painter,
    Muralist
Schuster, Cita Fletcher (Sarah E) Painter,
    Consultant
Scott, Sandy (Sandra Lynn) Printmaker,
    Illustrator
Sipiora, Leonard Paul Museum Director,
    Museologist
Szilvasy, Linda Markuly Painter, Writer
Waterhouse, Russell Rutledge Painter

Farmers Branch

Amend, Eugene Michael Instructor,
    Historian

Ft Worth

Blackburn, Ed M Painter
Carlin, Electra Marshall Dealer
Clark, Carol Canda Curator
Conn, David Edward Printmaker, Painter
Elias, Harold John Painter, Educator
Esau, Erika Librarian, Historian
Huston, Perry Clark Conservator
Jordan, William B Museum Director,
    Historian
Lincoln, Richard Mather Ceramist,
    Educator
Muhlert, Christopher Layton Painter
Muhlert, Jan Keene Museum Director,
    Historian
Phillips, Dutch (James O, Jr) Gallery
    Director, Dealer
Rothrock, Ilse Skipsna Librarian
Rubin, Sandra Printmaker, Lithographer
Ryan, David Michael Museum Director
Sandweiss, Martha Ann Curator
Smith, Emily Guthrie Painter
Stevenson, Ruth Carter Collector, Patron
Strother, Virginia Vaughn Painter
Sullivan, Ruth Wilkins Historian, Curator
Tyler, Ron C Curator, Historian
Watson, Ronald G Painter, Educator
Wynne, Nancy Graves Librarian

Fredericksburg

Laird, E Ruth Sculptor

Galveston

Glasco, Joseph M Painter, Sculptor

Grand Prairie

Schmidt, Stephen Museum Director

Helotes

Binks, Ronald C Photographer, Painter

Henderson

Bynum, E Anderson (Esther Pearl)
    Curator, Printmaker

Houston

Adams, Celeste Marie Curator, Writer
Adickes, David (Pryor) Painter, Sculptor
Alexander, John E Painter
Armstrong, Martha (Allen) Painter,
    Photographer
Biggers, John Thomas Educator, Painter
Block, Gay (S) Photographer
Bott, H J Assemblage Artist, Painter

Bourdon, Robert Slayton Sculptor,
    Educator
Boynton, Jack (James) W Painter,
    Printmaker
Broker, Karin Draftsman, Printmaker
Brown, Peter Thomson Photographer,
    Educator
Bunker, George Painter, Educator
Camblin, Bob Bilyeu Painter
Camfield, William Arnett Historian
Casas, Fernando Rodriguez Painter,
    Draftsman
Cathcart, Linda Louise Director,
    Historian
Cobb, Virginia Horton Painter, Lecturer
Collins, Lowell Daunt Painter, Dealer
Conrad, Nancy R Painter
Crow, Carol (Wilson) Sculptor
Deats, Margaret Dealer, Writer
de Vecsey, Esther Barbara Educator,
    Museum Director
Drysdale, Nancy McIntosh Patron,
    Dealer
Evans, Burford Elonzo Painter, Lecturer
Foster, Don Sculptor
Goldberg, Arnold Herbert Painter,
    Printmaker
Goldberg, Chaim Painter, Sculptor
Graham, William Andrew Dealer,
    Collector
Grove, Samuel Harold Administrator,
    Historian
Guenther, Peter W Historian
Hammett, Polly Horton Painter,
    Instructor
Hill, Ed Dealer, Collector
Holsch, Robert Fred Sculptor
Hood, Dorothy Painter
Hooks, Charles Vernon Dealer, Collector
Hooks, Geri Dealer, Collector
Johnson, (Leonard) Lucas Painter,
    Instructor
Kauffman, Richard Joel Dealer
Kempner, Helen Hill Collector, Patron
Kopriva, Sharon Ortman Painter,
    Educator
Krause, George Photographer, Educator
Lee, Janie C Dealer
Lesher, Marie Palmisano Sculptor
Leutwyler, Bruce Publisher, Patron
Link, Val James Jeweler, Educator
Long, Meredith J Dealer
Love, Jim Sculptor
Ludtke, Lawrence Monroe Sculptor
McGarry, Susan Hallsten Editor, Writer
Marzio, Peter Cort Historian, Museum
    Director
Mayo, Marti Curator, Historian
Metyko, Michael Joseph Museum
    Director, Sculptor
Moody, Elizabeth Chambers Dealer,
    Gallery Director
Morris, Jack Austin, Jr Museum Director,
    Writer
Musick, Pat Painter, Educator
O'Neil, John Painter, Educator
Paul, Suzanne Photographer
Poulos, Basilios Nicholas Painter,
    Educator
Randolph, Lynn Moore Painter
Rice, M Robert & Barbara Menen
    Dealers, Collectors
Robinson, Thomas V Dealer, Collector
Saks, Judith-Ann (Judith-Ann Saks
    Rosenthal) Painter, Printmaker
Schorre, Charles Painter, Photographer
Shapiro, Adrian Michael Dealer, Writer
Shaw, Donald Edward Painter, Sculptor
Speers, Teryl Townsend Painter, Educator
Stack, Gael Z Painter, Educator
Storm, Mark (Kennedy) Painter, Sculptor
Stout, Richard Gordon Painter

TEXAS (cont)

Tennant, Donna Kay Gallery Director, Critic
Thompson, Judith Kay Painter
Thompson, Richard Craig Painter, Sculptor
Tucker, Anne Wilkes Curator, Historian
Turner, (Charles) Arthur Painter, Instructor
Van Vranken, Rose (Rose Van Vranken Hickey) Sculptor, Printmaker
Warren, David Boardman Curator
Werner Vaughn, Salle Painter, Illuminator
Williams, Casey Photographer
Winningham, Geoff Photographer
Woitena, Ben S Sculptor, Educator
Wray, Dick Painter

Humble

Nadolski, Stephanie Lucille Painter, Printmaker

Huntsville

Ahysen, Harry Joseph Painter, Educator
Breitenbach, William John Sculptor, Draftsman
Eastman, Gene M Painter
Geeslin, Lee Gaddis Painter, Educator
Lea, Stanley E Printmaker, Painter
Patrick, Darryl L Historian, Administrator

Irving

Novinski, Lyle Frank Painter, Educator

Kerrville

Burt, Dan Painter

Kingsville

Scherpereel, Richard Charles Educator, Painter

La Feria

Borglum, James Lincoln de la Mothe Sculptor, Photographer

Lamesa

Nix, Patricia (Lea) Sculptor, Painter

Liberty Hill

Fowler, Mel (Walter) Sculptor

Longview

Jeter, Randy Joe Drawer, Educator
Statman, Jan B Painter, Instructor

Lubbock

Broderick, James Allen Administrator, Photographer
Cheatham, Frank Reagan Painter, Designer
Dingus, Rick Photographer, Writer
Dixon, Kenneth Ray Painter, Gallery Director
Funk, Charlotte M Weaver, Tapestry Artist
Funk, Verne J Ceramist, Sculptor
Gibbons, Hugh (James) Painter, Educator
Hanna, Paul Dean, Jr Painter, Printmaker
Hastie, Reid Educator, Writer
Howze, James Dean Educator, Draftsman
Kreneck, Lynwood Printmaker
Meigs, John Liggett Painter, Collector
Morrow, Terry Draftsman, Printmaker
Stephen, Francis B Jeweler, Sculptor

McAllen

Clark, Charles D Collector, Patron

Marfa

Gervasi, Frank Painter

Medina

Carrington, Joy Harrell Painter, Illuminator

Midland

Lynch, Betty Painter, Instructor

Mission

McClendon, Maxine (Maxine McClendon Nichols) Painter, Craftsman
Nichols, Edward Edson Painter

Nacogdoches

Beason, Donald Ray Educator, Sculptor
McCleary, Mary Fielding Painter, Educator
Schlicher, Karl Theodore Painter, Historian
Wink, Don (Jon Donnel) Painter, Educator

New Braunfels

Wall, Ralph Alan Painter

Odessa

Lee, Nelda S Dealer

Port Arthur

Broussard, Normaj Collector, Painter

Richardson

Brown, John Hall Painter, Architect
Curtis, Mary Cranfill Printmaker, Painter
Davis, Bertha Painter
McNary, Oscar L Painter

Rusk

Robinson, Marie Rachelle Dealer, Painter

San Antonio

Bristow, William Arthur Painter, Educator
Casas, Melesio Painter, Educator
Duncan, Ruth Painter
Embrey, Carl Rice Painter, Instructor
Fett, William F Instructor, Painter
Flume, Violet Sigoloff Dealer, Restorer
Fuchs, Mary Tharsilla Educator, Painter
Kent, Jack Illustrator
Lee, Amy Freeman Painter, Lecturer
Lee, Caroline D Dealer, Curator
Leeper, John Palmer Museum Director
McDougal, Ivan Ellis Painter, Instructor
Maurer, Neil Douglas Photographer
Notestine, Tom W Painter, Instructor
Parrino, George Painter, Administrator
Pressly, Nancy Lee Curator, Administrator
Pressly, William Laurens, Jr Historian, Educator
Quirarte, Jacinto Historian, Administrator
Rodgers, Jack A Administrator
Roney, Harold Arthur Painter, Lecturer
Rowe, Reginald M Painter, Sculptor
Rush, Kent Thomas Painter, Printmaker
Tarin, Gilberto A Painter, Printmaker
Tauch, Waldine Amanda Sculptor, Collector
Tucker, Glenn F Critic, Collector
West, E Gordon Administrator, Painter
Willson, Margaret (Bosshardt) Pace Painter, Sculptor
Willson, Robert Sculptor, Painter
Wogstad, James Everet Educator, Illustrator
Wray, Margaret M Painter

San Marcos

Allen, Tom R Sculptor

San Ygnacio

Tracy, Michael Sculptor, Painter

Sherman

Neidhardt, Carl Richard Administrator, Painter

Splendora

Surls, James Sculptor, Educator

Spring Branch

Soltesz, Frank Joseph Painter

Texarkana

Caver, William Ralph Sculptor, Printmaker

Tyler

Gentry (Augustus Calahan), Jr Painter, Printmaker
Stephens, William Blakely Educator, Painter
Weaver, James D Museum Director

Waco

Chatmas, John Painter
Harris, Paul Rogers Museum Director, Educator
Kemp, Paul Zane Painter
McClanahan, John D Painter, Educator

Waxahachie

Nichols, Jeannettie Doornhein Painter

UTAH

Bountiful

Rasmussen, Anton Jesse Painter, Administrator

Brigham City

Huchel, Frederick M Museum Director, Gallery Director

Lindon

Speed, (Ulysses) Grant Sculptor

Logan

Elsner, Larry Edward Sculptor, Educator
Lindstrom, Gaell Painter, Educator
Smith, Moishe Printmaker
Van Suchtelen, Adrian Printmaker, Educator

Mt Carmel

Zornes, James Milford Painter, Designer

Ogden

Collett, Farrell Reuben Painter, Educator
Taylor, Harry George Printmaker, Photographer

Pleasant Grove

Jarvis, John Brent Painter

Provo

Andrus, James Roman Printmaker, Painter
Barsch, Wulf Erich Painter, Printmaker
Burnside, Wesley M Historian, Painter
Coleman, Michael Painter
Magleby, Frank (Francis R) Painter, Educator
Myer, Peter Livingston Kinetic Artist, Educator
Whitaker, William Painter, Illustrator
Wilson, Warren Bingham Educator, Sculptor

UTAH (cont)

Riverton

Fraughton, Edward James Sculptor

Salt Lake City

Christensen, Larry R Painter, Instructor
Christensen, Sharlene Painter, Instructor
Cutler, Grayce E Painter, Writer
Dibble, George Painter, Writer
Doherty, Robert J Museum Director, Educator
Friberg, Arnold Illustrator, Painter
Hartford, Jane Davis Textile Artist, Craftsman
Johnston, Richard M Sculptor, Educator
Lake, Randall Painter, Printmaker
Olpin, Robert Spencer Historian, Curator
Phillips, Bonnie Dealer, Painter
Sanguinetti, Eugene F Administrator, Lecturer
Smith, Frank Anthony Painter
Southey, Trevor J T Painter, Sculptor
Tierney, Patrick Lennox Historian, Educator

Springville

Marshall, Robert Leroy Educator, Painter
Swanson, Vern Grosvenor Museum Director, Historian

VERMONT

Barre

Gaylord, Frank Chalfant , II Sculptor, Designer

Barton

Miller, Dolly (Ethel B) Painter

Bennington

Adams, Pat Painter, Instructor
Held, Julius S Educator, Writer
Jensen, Hank Sculptor

Brattleboro

Watson, Aldren A Designer, Illustrator

Brookfield

Newton, Earle Williams Administrator, Educator

Burlington

Colburn, Francis Peabody Painter

Cavendish

Shapiro, David Painter, Printmaker

Charlotte

Aschenbach, (Walter) Paul Sculptor, Educator

Dorset

Kouwenhoven, John A Writer, Educator

East Calais

de Gogorza, Patricia (Gahagan) Sculptor, Printmaker
Gahagan, James (Edward), Jr Painter, Educator

East Corinth

Hewitt, Francis Ray Painter, Educator

Fairfax

Goldsmith, Lawrence Charles Painter, Instructor

Fairlee

Walker, Herbert Brooks Sculptor, Museum Director

Grafton

Hunter, Mel Printmaker, Painter
Schoener, Allon Designer, Consultant

Jericho

Chase, Jack S(paulding) Sculptor
Haversat, Lillian Kerr Dealer, Writer

Lowell

Kramer, Marjorie Anne Painter

Manchester Center

Abbe, Elfriede Martha Sculptor, Engraver
Montague, James L Painter, Printmaker
Rath, Hildegard Painter, Lecturer

Marlboro

Boylen, Michael Edward Craftsman, Art Writer
Heiskell, Diana Painter

Middlebury

Bumbeck, David A Printmaker, Educator
Hunisak, John Michael Historian, Educator
Perry, Edward (Ted) Samuel Administrator

Morrisville

Barrett, Robert Dumas Painter

Northfield

Krauth, Harald Painter

Norwich

Ritz, Lorna Painter, Educator

Orwell

Wunder, Richard Paul Historian, Administrator

Petaluma

Forakis, Peter Sculptor

Pittsford

Frick, Robert Oliver Painter, Instructor

Putney

Ginnever, Charles Sculptor

Randolph

Robbins, Daniel J Historian, Museum Director
Robbins, Eugenia S Writer, Editor

Rutland

Farrow, Patrick Villiers Sculptor
Johnson, Katherine King Administrator, Painter

Salisbury

Andres, Glenn Merle Historian, Educator

Shelburne

Mason, Benjamin Lincoln Museum Director

South Ryegate

Arnosky, James Edward Illustrator, Writer

Springfield

Baldwin, Harold Fletcher Sculptor, Painter
Eldredge, Mary Agnes Sculptor
Eldredge, Stuart Edson Painter

Stowe

Wright, Stanley Marc Painter, Instructor

West Burke

Van Vliet, Claire Printmaker, Publisher

West Danville

Karnes, Karen Ceramist, Craftsman

Weston

Landon, Edward August Printmaker, Painter

West Townshend

Court, Lee Winslow Painter

Winooski

Chabot, Aurore (Martha) Ceramist

Woodstock

Gyra, Francis Joseph, Jr Instructor, Painter
Thomas, Byron Painter

VIRGINIA

Alexandria

Banks, Anne Johnson Sculptor, Educator
Caples, Barbara Barrett Painter, Printmaker
Conger, Clement E Curator
Day, Horace Talmage Painter, Director
Evans, Grose Historian, Educator
Keeler, David Boughton Administrator, Painter
Keena, Janet Laybourn Painter
Marker, Mariska Pugsley Painter
Marker, Ralph E Painter, Collector
Nash, Veronica F Dealer, Collector
Patrick, Charles William Conceptual Artist, Writer
Sanborn, Herbert J Lithographer, Painter
Singletary, Robert Eugene Draftsman, Painter
Spagnolo, Kathleen Mary Printmaker, Illustrator
Thompson, Jean Danforth Tapertry Artist, Painter
Thorpe, Hilda (Shapiro) Painter, Sculptor

Annandale

Dean, James Painter
Locke, Rhea G Painter, Draftsman
Spink, Frank Henry, Jr Writer, Painter

Arlington

Bryans, John Armond Instructor, Painter
Gast, Carolyn Bartlett (Lutz) Illustrator, Illuminator
Gast, Michael Carl Painter
Gurney, George Historian, Consultant
Harlan, Roma Christine Painter
Kamen, Rebecca Educator, Sculptor
Knippers, Edward Cade, Jr Painter, Printmaker
Osborn, Kevin Russell Book Artist, Printmaker
Reed, Paul Allen Painter, Instructor
Rexroth, Nancy Louise Photographer
Schneider, Julie (Saecker) Painter, Draftsman
Twitty, James (Watson) Painter, Printmaker

Ashland

Longaker, Jon Dasu Educator, Writer
Witt, Nancy Camden Sculptor, Painter

Blacksburg

Bickley, Gary Steven Educator, Sculptor
Carter, Dean Sculptor, Educator
Harman, Maryann Whittemore Painter
Huggins, Victor, Jr Painter, Printmaker
Sarvis, Alva Taylor Printmaker

Bridgewater

Beer, Kenneth John Educator, Sculptor

Bumpass

Renick, Charles Cooley Sculptor, Educator

Burke

Orsini Enamelist, Instructor

Charlottesville

Barbee, Robert Thomas Painter, Graphic Artist
Burr, Horace Curator, Sculptor
Crozier, Richard Lewis Painter, Educator
Dunnigan, Mary Catherine Librarian
Hagan, James Garrison Sculptor, Instructor
Hartt, Frederick Historian, Educator
Lawall, David Barnard Historian, Curator
Markowski, Eugene David Painter, Sculptor
Moxey, Keith Patricio Fleming Historian
Priest, Hartwell Wyse Painter, Printmaker
Turner, Theodore Roy Painter, Educator

Chesapeake

Taylor, Rod Allen Administrator, Sculptor

Christiansburg

Kass, Ray Painter

Clifton

Hennesy, Gerald Craft Painter

Colonial Heights

Woodson, Doris Educator, Painter

Covington

Walton, Harry A, Jr Collector

Crozet

Harrington, William Charles Sculptor

Culpepper

Sehring, Adolf Painter, Sculptor

Ettrick

Macklin, Anderson D Administrator, Potter

Fairfax

Matternes, Jay Howard Painter, Illustrator
Watson, Darliene Keeney Painter

Fairfax Station

Jackson, Vaughn L Painter, Illustrator

Falls Church

Cusick, Nancy Taylor Painter
Frederick, Eugene Wallace Printmaker, Educator
Grosse (Carolyn Ann Gawarecki) Painter, Instructor
Jones, Lou (Mary Louise Humpton) Painter, Sculptor
Kumm, Marguerite Elizabeth Painter, Printmaker
Land, Ernest Albert Painter, Designer
Liu, Ho Collector, Painter
Robinson, Charlotte Painter, Printmaker

Farmville

Bishop, Barbara Lee Educator, Printmaker

Great Falls

DiPerna, Frank Paul Photographer, Instructor
Pollack, Reginald Murray Painter, Sculptor

Hampton

Clifton, Jack Whitney Instructor, Painter

Harrisonburg

Caldwell, Martha Belle Educator, Historian
Crable, James Harbour Multi-Media Artist, Instructor
Wolanin, Barbara Ann Boese Educator, Historian

Herndon

Pisani, Joseph Muralist, Painter

Lexington

Doyon, Gerard Maurice Educator, Historian
Ju, I-Hsiung Painter, Educator

Lorton

Bierly, Edward J Painter, Illustrator

Lovettsville

Lake, Jerry Lee Photographer, Educator

Lynchburg

Mathews, Nancy Mowll Historian, Curator
Williams, Mary Frances Curator, Educator

McLean

Beggs, Thomas Montague Fine Arts Consultant, Painter
Brodie, Agnes Hahn Sculptor, Painter
Greco, Josephine G Gallery Director, Curator
Lawson, Edward Pitt Administrator
Nakache-Lynch, Margaret Painter
O'Connell, Ann Brown Painter, Collector
Stratton, Dorothy (Mrs William A King) Painter, Printmaker

Midlothian

Baldridge, Mark S Goldsmith, Editor

Newport News

Alexick, David Francis Educator, Painter
Anglin, Betty Lockhart Educator, Painter
Sheaks, Barclay Painter, Writer

Norfolk

Chrysler, Walter P, Jr Collector
Clark, Mark A Curator
Dreyer, Gay Sculptor
Jackson, A B Educator, Painter
Jones, Herb (Leon Herbert), Jr Painter, Printmaker
Knorr, Jeanne Boardman Painter, Educator
Lewis, Don S, Sr Dealer, Painter
Lewis, Donald Sykes, Jr Dealer
Matson, Greta Painter
Sibley, Charles Kenneth Painter, Educator
Steadman, David Wilton Museum Director
Zetlin, Fay (Florence Anshen) Painter, Muralist

Oakton

von zur Muehlen, Bernis Susan Photographer
von zur Muehlen, Peter Photographer

Portsmouth

Tobin, John Edward, Jr Sculptor, Educator

Reston

Drewes, Werner Painter, Printmaker
Mahlmann, John James Publisher, Administrator
Ward, Lynd (Kendall) Illustrator, Writer

Richmond

Apgar, Nicolas Adam Painter, Educator
Archer, Edmund Painter
Brandt, Frederick Robert Painter, Curator
Brown, Catharine Homan Potter
Bumgardner, James Arliss Painter, Educator
Burke, Margaret Historian
Campbell, Jeanne Begien Painter, Educator
Campbell, Jewett Educator, Painter
Cossitt, Franklin D Sculptor, Editor
Davis, Meredith J Graphic Artist, Educator
DePillars, Murry N Administrator, Illustrator
Desmidt, Thomas H Painter, Educator
Freed, David Printmaker, Painter
Gaines, William Robert Historian, Painter
Haynes, George Edward Painter, Illustrator
Hompson, Davi Det (David Elbridge Thompson) Conceptual Artist
Ipsen, Kent Forrest Glassworker, Craftsman
Johnson, Charles W, Jr Historian, Educator
Kevorkian, Richard Painter
MacNelly, Jeffrey Kenneth Cartoonist
Martin, Bernard Murray Painter, Educator
Mavroudis, Demetrios Sculptor, Educator
Mayo, Margaret Ellen Curator
Mayo, Robert Bowers Dealer
Mooz, R Peter Museum Director
Perry, Regenia Alfreda Historian
Phillips, James Historian, Painter
Pollak, Theresa Painter, Draftsman
Thompson, Nancy Kunkle Goldsmith, Educator
Van Winkle, Lester G Sculptor, Educator
Welch, James Wymore Painter, Muralist
Williamson, Gail McKennis Printmaker, Painter
Wiltshire, William Ernest, III Collector, Patron

Salem

Johnson, Ernest (Melvin) Painter, Instructor

Springfield

Hoffman, Helen Bacon Painter

Staunton

Desportes, Ulysse Gandvier Painter, Historian

Stephens City

Chumley, John Wesley Painter

Sterling

Criquette (Ruth DuBarry Montague) Painter, Writer

Vienna

Gonzales, Carlotta (Mrs Richard Lahey)
Painter, Sculptor
Nash, Mary (Harriet) Painter, Lecturer
Summerford, Ben Long Painter, Educator

Virginia Beach

Ciccone, Amy Navratil Librarian
Wells, Betty Childs Illustrator, Painter

Williamsburg

Chappell, Miles Linwood Historian,
Educator
Christison, Muriel B Museum Director,
Educator
Hood, Graham Stanley Museum Director,
Writer
Roseberg, Carl Andersson Sculptor,
Historian
Rumford, Beatrix Tyson Administrator

WASHINGTON

Anacortes

McCracken, Philip Sculptor

Bainbridge Island

Randlett, Mary Willis Photographer
Willis, Elizabeth Bayley Historian,
Collector

Battle Ground

Hansen, James Lee Sculptor

Bellevue

Carter, Dudley Christopher Sculptor
Graham, Lois (M Gord) Painter
Jones, Thomas William Painter
Levine, Reeva (Anna) Miller Painter,
Instructor
Reese, William Foster Painter
Warsinske, Norman George, Jr Sculptor,
Painter

Bellingham

Hanson, Lawrence Sculptor, Educator
Marsh, David Foster Educator, Painter
Scott, C(harles) A(rthur) Sculptor

Bothell

Peck, James Edward Painter, Designer

Cheney

Sage, Bill B Ceramist, Educator

Eastsound

Bevlin, Marjorie Elliott Painter, Writer
Rippey, Clayton Painter, Muralist

Edmonds

d'Elaine Painter, Instructor
Marshall, John Carl Craftsman

Ellensburg

Sahlstrand, James Michael Photographer
Sahlstrand, Margaret Ahrens Printmaker,
Craftsman
Spurgeon, Sarah (Edna M) Painter,
Educator
Stillman, George Administrator, Painter

Entiat

Kujundzic, Zeljko D Ceramist, Sculptor

Grapeview

Hoover, John Jay Sculptor, Painter

Issaquah

Sweney, Fred Illustrator, Painter

Kent

Broer, Roger L Painter

La Conner

Anderson, Guy Irving Painter

Long Beach

Callahan, Kenneth Painter

Longview

Jaeger, Brenda Kay Painter, Craftsman
Powelson, Rosemary A Instructor, Painter

Mercer Island

Correa, Flora Horst Painter

Moses Lake

Tse, Stephen Painter, Educator

Mt Vernon

Gilkey, Richard Charles Painter, Sculptor

Nordland

Kepner, Rita M Sculptor, Writer

Olympia

Haseltine, James Lewis Printmaker,
Painter
Haseltine, Maury (Margaret Wilson)
Painter, Consultant
Hopkins, Kenneth R Museum Director

Omak

Woolschlager, Laura Totten Painter,
Printmaker

Pullman

Coates, Ross Alexander Historian, Painter
Ho, Francis T Photographer, Educator
Monaghan, Keith Painter, Educator
Shaman, Sanford Sivitz Museum Director,
Curator

Reardan

Chester, Charlotte Wanetta Painter,
Printmaker

Renton

Arnautoff, Jacob Victor Sculptor, Painter
Mintz, Baron (Ronald Earl) Conservator,
Painter

Seattle

Acker, Perry Miles Painter, Educator
Alps, Glen Earl Educator, Printmaker
Angell, Tony Sculptor, Painter
Arnold, Richard R Designer,
Administrator
Banks, Virginia Painter
Berger, Paul Eric Photographer, Educator
Bishop, Jeffrey Britton Painter, Educator
Bloedel, Joan (Stuart) Ross Painter,
Printmaker
Braseth, John E Art Dealer, Consultant
Bravmann, Rene A Art Historian,
Educator
Burns, Marsha Photographer
Bush, Beverly Painter, Sculptor
Celentano, Francis Michael Painter,
Educator
Dailey, Michael Dennis Painter, Educator
Davidson, Elizabeth H Donnally Dealer
DeArcangelis, Gloria Sculptor
Du Pen, Everett George Sculptor,
Educator

Farris, Linda B Dealer
Fear, Daniel E Dealer, Gallery Director
Foster, Donald Isle Dealer
Gatel, Jeff (Jeffrey Stuart) Photographer
Gonzales, Boyer Painter, Educator
Gray, Marie Elise Painter
Gray, Maxine Cushing Editor
Harrington, La Mar Writer, Curator
Hatch, (Mr & Mrs) Marshall Collectors
Hayes, Randy (Randolph Alan) Painter
Herard, Marvin T Sculptor, Educator
Hines, Richard G Art Dealer, Collector
Holm, Bill Historian, Curator
Johnston, Thomas Alix Printmaker,
Painter
Jolles, Arnold H Museum Director,
Conservator
Kirsten-Daiensai, Richard Charles
Painter, Printmaker
Koenig, John Franklin Painter
Kottler, Howard William Sculptor,
Educator
Kuvshinoff, Bertha Horne Painter,
Sculptor
Kuvshinoff, Nicolai Painter, Sculptor
Lawrence, Jacob Painter, Educator
Lundin, Norman K Painter
Maki, Robert Richard Sculptor, Lecturer
Marioni, Paul Sculptor, Glass Blower
Mason, Alden C Painter, Educator
Miller, Earl B(eauford) Graphic Artist,
Designer
Moseley, Spencer Altemont Painter
Nadalini, (Louis Ernest) Painter
Pacific, Gertrude Painter, Designer
Praczukowski, Edward Leon Painter,
Educator
Rathbun, William Jay Curator
Rising, Dorothy Milne Painter, Illustrator
Ritchie, William (Bill) Printmaker, Video
Artist
Rogers, Millard Buxton Historian,
Educator
Sato, Norie Video Artist
Sawada, Ikune Painter
Seders, Francine Lavinal Dealer
Segan, Kenneth Akiva Draftsman,
Printmaker
Selig, (Mr & Mrs) Manfred Collectors,
Patrons
Spafford, Michael Charles Educator,
Painter
Sperry, Robert Ceramist, Filmmaker
Thiry, Paul (Albert) Architect, Collector
Trubner, Henry Administrator, Curator
Tsutakawa, George Sculptor, Painter
Vaness, Margaret Helen Painter,
Printmaker
Warashina, M Patricia Ceramist, Educator
Washington, James W, Jr Sculptor,
Painter
Wehr, Wesley Conrad Painter, Consultant
Wells, Thomas (Winchester) Painter
Woods, Willis Franklin Consultant
Woodside, Gordon William Dealer,
Collector
Wright, G Alan Sculptor

Spokane

Adkison, Kathleen (Gemberling) Painter
Askman, Tom K Painter, Educator
Fleckenstein, Opal R Painter, Ceramist
Patnode, J Scott Printmaker, Educator

Steilacoom

Clinton, Paul Arthur Printmaker,
Instructor

Tacoma

Chihuly, Dale Patrick Glass Artist,
    Educator
Colby, Bill Printmaker, Educator
Kowalek, Jon W Museum Director,
    Lecturer
Moe, Richard D Administrator
Rades, William L Painter, Sculptor
Schwidder, Ernst Carl Sculptor, Designer

Wenatchee

Cox, John Rogers Painter
Graham, Walter Painter, Sculptor
Graves, Robert Edward Painter,
    Instructor

WEST VIRGINIA

Baker

Singleton, Robert Ellison Painter,
    Printmaker

Charleston

Atkins, Rosalie Marks Painter
Black, Mary McCune Curator, Painter
Blumberg, Barbara Griffiths Painter,
    Instructor
Keane, Lucina Mabel Painter, Printmaker
Taylor, Grace Martin Painter, Educator

Elkins

Reed, Jesse Floyd Painter, Printmaker

Fairmont

Smigocki, Stephen Vincent Painter,
    Printmaker

Harpers Ferry

Lewis, John Chapman Painter, Instructor

Huntington

Emerson, Roberta Shinn Museum
    Director
Ettling, Ruth (Droitcour) Printmaker,
    Painter
Hage, Raymond Joseph Collector, Patron
Polan, Lincoln M Collector
Polan, Nancy Moore Painter

Milton

Anderson, Winslow Designer, Painter

Morgantown

Couch, Urban Painter, Curator

St Albans

Keeling, Henry Cornelious Painter,
    Educator

Shepherdstown

Jones, Ronald Lee, Jr Educator, Writer

Wheeling

Peace, Bernie (Kinzel) Painter,
    Printmaker

Williamstown

Gerhold, William Henry Painter,
    Educator

WISCONSIN

Appleton

Livingstone, Biganess Painter, Educator
Thrall, Arthur Printmaker, Educator

Barneveld

Weege, William Printmaker, Educator

Beloit

Boggs, Franklin Muralist, Sculptor
Malsch, Ellen L Painter, Instructor
Olson, Richard W Printmaker, Educator
Simon, Michael A Photographer
Strawn, Jarrett W (Jason) Sculptor,
    Educator
Williams, Lewis W, II Historian, Educator

Blanchardville

Zweerts, Arnold Painter, Mosaic Artist

Dane

Anderson, Donald Myers Art Writer,
    Calligrapher

Eau Claire

Campbell, Kenneth Floyd Historian,
    Sculptor

Ellison Bay

Austin, Phil Painter, Lecturer

Evansville

Wilde, John Painter

Fish Creek

Becker, Bettie (Bettie Geraldine Wathall)
    Painter, Graphic Artist

Green Bay

Mitchell, R(obert Ellis) Goldsmith,
    Lecturer

Hartland

Stamsta, Jean Fiber Artist

Hollandale

Colescott, Warrington W Printmaker,
    Educator
Myers, Frances Printmaker

Jackson

White, Doris A Painter

Janesville

Williams, Marylou Lord Study
    Consultant, Collage Artist

Lake Geneva

Herr, Richard Joseph Sculptor, Instructor
Salter, Richard Mackintire Painter

Madison

Bohrod, Aaron Painter, Educator
Breckenridge, Bruce M Ceramist,
    Educator
Byrd, D Gibson Educator, Painter
Garver, Thomas H Administrator, Writer
Handler, Audrey Glass Blower, Educator
High-Wasikhongo, Freida Printmaker,
    Educator
Hutchison, Jane Campbell Educator,
    Historian
Kreilick, Marjorie E Mosaic Artist,
    Educator
Logan, Frederick Manning Educator,
    Writer
Lotterman, Hal Painter, Educator
Nicholson, Natasha Assemblage Artist,
    Sculptor
Overland, Carlton Edward Curator,
    Historian
Watrous, James Scales Painter, Historian
Weiss, Lee (Elyse C Weiss) Painter
Woodbury, Josephine Osgood Printmaker

Manitowoc

Tomko, George Peter Historian, Curator

Marinette

La Malfa, James Thomas Sculptor,
    Educator

Menomonie

Fumagalli, Barbara Merrill Printmaker
Fumagalli, Orazio Educator, Sculptor

Middleton

Witte, Mary (Grace) Stieglitz
    Photographer, Educator

Milwaukee

Auer, James Matthew Art Critic, Film
    Maker
Balsley, John Gerald Painter, Sculptor
Barnett, David J Art Dealer, Collector
Basquin, Kit (Mary Smyth) Critic, Writer
Behrens, Roy R Illustrator, Writer
Berman, Fred J Painter, Photographer
Bradley, Dorothy Art Dealer, Painter
Burkert, Robert Randall Painter,
    Printmaker
Christian, William Painter, Instructor
Colt, John Nicholson Painter, Educator
Crane, Jean Painter
Curtis, Robert D Sculptor
Davis, John Harold Gallery Director,
    Illustrator
Erlien, Nancy Beth Dealer, Patron
Evans, Dick Ceramist, Educator
Fessler, Mary Thomasita Sculptor,
    Educator
Foster, Steven Douglas Photographer
Geniusz, Robert Myles Printmaker,
    Filmmaker
Green, Edward Anthony Director,
    Designer
Grotenrath, Ruth Painter, Printmaker
Jensen, Dean N Writer, Critic
Kaiser, Charles James Painter, Graphic
    Artist
Kao, Ruth (Yu-Hsin) Lee Fiber Artist,
    Educator
Kohl, Barbara Printmaker, Painter
Lacktman, Michael Craftsman, Jeweler
Lichtner, Schomer Frank Painter,
    Printmaker
Lord, Michael Harry Dealer, Curator
Melamed, Abraham & Hope Collectors,
    Patrons
Meredith, Dorothy Laverne Weaver,
    Educator
Michaels-Paque, Joan Designer, Sculptor
Nichols, William Allyn Painter, Educator
Nordland, Gerald John Gallery Director,
    Critic
Ozonoff, Ida Painter, Collage Artist
Pierce, Danny P Sculptor, Painter
Poehlmann, JoAnna Painter, Printmaker
Posner, Judith L Dealer, Publisher
Rahill, Margaret Fish Curator, Critic
Revor, Remy Designer, Educator
Rosenblatt, Adolph Painter, Sculptor
Rosenblatt, Suzanne Maris Painter
Ruble, Ronald L Printmaker, Painter
Schellin, Robert William Painter,
    Craftsman
Stoeveken, Anthony Charles Printmaker,
    Educator
Stonebarger, Virginia Painter, Educator
Summ, Helmut Painter, Educator
Taylor, John Lloyd Museum Director,
    Consultant
Travanti, Leon Emidio Painter, Designer
Uttech, Thomas Martin Painter, Educator

Mt Horeb

Hamady, Walter Samuel Graphic Artist, Papermaker

Oconomowoc

Sprague, Paul Edward Historian, Consultant

Oshkosh

Donhauser, Paul Stefan Sculptor, Writer

Platteville

Ross, James Matthew Educator, Painter

Racine

Bogucki, (Edwin Arnold) Sculptor, Painter
Holmes, David Valentine Sculptor, Painter
Johansen, Robert Painter
Mathis, Emile Henry, II Dealer, Collector
Rozman, Joseph John Painter, Printmaker

Ripon

Breithaupt, Erwin M Painter, Historian

River Falls

Hara, Keiko Painter, Printmaker

Sheboygan

Kohler, Ruth DeYoung Museum Director, Curator

Waukesha

Penkoff, Ronald Peter Educator, Painter

Whitefish Bay

Tucholke, Christel-Anthony (Christel E Stoeveken) Painter

Whitewater

Yasko, Caryl Anne Muralist, Painter

WYOMING

Byron

Hopkinson, Harold I Painter, Collector

Casper

Goedicke, Jean Painter, Instructor

Cheyenne

Hayes, Laura M Dealer, Historian

Cody

Fillerup, Mel Painter
Hassrick, Peter H Museum Director, Historian
Jackson, Harry Andrew Painter, Sculptor
McCracken, Harold Administrator, Historian

Jackson Hole

Kerswill, J W Roy Painter
Schwiering, Conrad Painter

Laramie

Berger, Jerry Allen Director, Curator
Deaderick, Joseph Painter, Educator
Evans, Richard Painter, Educator
Flach, Victor H Designer, Writer
Forrest, James Taylor Museum Director, Educator
Mueller, Henrietta Waters Painter, Sculptor
Reif, (F) David Sculptor, Educator
Russin, Robert I Sculptor, Educator

Rock Springs

Keeney, Allen Lloyd Educator, Museum Director

Sheridan

Martinsen, Ivar Richard Painter, Educator

Story

Smyth, Ed Illustrator, Painter

Teton Village

Clymer, John F Painter, Illustrator

PUERTO RICO

Carolina

Marin, Augusto Painter, Educator

Catano

Dirube, Rolando Lopez Painter, Sculptor

Condado

Collazo, Carlos Erick Painter, Graphic Artist

Isla Verde

Ruiz de la Mata, Ernesto J Critic, Historian

Mayaguez

Alvarez-Cervela, Jose Maria Educator, Historian

Miramar

Homar, Lorenzo Printmaker, Painter

Ponce

Balmaceda, Margarita S Educator, Writer
Conesa, Miguel A Painter, Illustrator
Micheli, Julio Painter, Assemblage Artist
Taylor, Rene Claude Museum Director, Historian

Rio Piedras

Balossi, John Sculptor, Painter
Delano, Jack Photographer, Filmmaker
Hernandez-Cruz, Luis Painter, Sculptor
Venegas, Haydee E Museum Director, Historian

San German

Carrero, Jaime Painter, Instructor

San Juan

Alicea, Jose Printmaker
Blanco, Sylvia Ceramist
Max, Lope (Lope Max Diaz Rivera) Painter, Educator

Santurce

Konrad, Tony (Anton Joseph) Conservator, Restorer

VIRGIN ISLANDS

St Croix

Caimite Painter, Illustrator
Henle, Fritz Photographer, Filmmaker

St John

Low, Joseph Painter, Printmaker

CANADA

ALBERTA

Banff

Leighton, David S R Administrator

Calgary

Atkins, Gordon Lee Designer, Architect
Bershad, David L Historian, Educator
Cameron, Duncan F Museum Director
Chalke, John Ceramist, Sculptor
Dodd, Eric M Gallery Director, Educator
Dyson, Brian Curator, Writer
Esler, John Kenneth Printmaker, Painter
Hall, John (Scott) Educator, Painter
Hushlak, Gerald Computer Artist, Painter
Kostyniuk, Ronald P Sculptor, Educator
Larson, Orland Goldsmith, Educator
Mignosa, Santo Ceramist, Sculptor
Ohe, Katie (Minna) Sculptor, Instructor
O'Neil, Bruce William Painter, Instructor
Polzer, Joseph Historian
Roukes, Nicholas M Kinetic Artist, Writer
Sawai, Noboru Printmaker, Educator
Snow, John Printmaker, Painter
Spickett, Ronald John, Sr Painter, Instructor
Will, John A Printmaker, Painter
Zimon, Kathy Elizabeth Librarian

Edmonton

Cantine, David Painter
Clarke, Ann Lecturer, Painter
Curran, Douglas Edward Photographer
Davey, Ronald A Historian, Educator
Dmytruk, Ihor Painter, Instructor
Forbes, John Allison Historian, Painter
Haynes, Douglas H Painter, Educator
Knowlton, Jonathan Painter, Educator
Manarey, Thelma Alberta Printmaker, Painter
Semchishen, Orest M Photographer

Lethbridge

Beny, Roloff Photographer, Writer

Midnapore

Besant, Derek Michael Painter, Instructor

Winterburn

Sinclair, Robert (W) Painter, Sculptor

BRITISH COLUMBIA

Brentwood Bay

Heine, Harry Painter

Burnaby

Koochin, William Sculptor, Educator
Shadbolt, Jack Leonard Painter

Campbell River

Andrews, Sybil (Sybil Andrews Morgan) Painter, Printmaker

Crescent Beach

Onley, Toni Painter

Duncan

Hughes, Edward John Painter
Smith, John Ivor Sculptor, Educator

Hope

Weaver, John Barney Sculptor

North Vancouver

Perry, Frank Sculptor
Peter, Friedrich Gunther Calligrapher, Educator
Shives, Arnold Edward Painter, Printmaker

Pender Island

Glyde, Henry George Painter, Educator

Sointula

Fish, Robert Sculptor, Educator

Valemount

Dyson, John Holroyd Painter

Vancouver

Balkind, Alvin Louis Curator
Banana, Anna Lee Publisher, Conceptual Artist
Davidson, Ian J Collector, Patron
Dr Brute (Eric William Metcalfe) Video Artist
Dwyer, Melva Jean Librarian, Historian
Flakey Rose Hip Administrator, Sculptor
Grauer, Sherry Sculptor, Painter
Guderna, Ladislav Painter, Illustrator
Jarvis, Donald Painter, Instructor
Knox, George Historian, Writer
Longstaffe, John Ronald Collector
Mayrs, David Blair Painter, Educator
Plear, Scott Edward Painter, Printmaker
Poole, Leslie Donald Painter, Printmaker
Prince, Richard Edmund Sculptor, Educator
Rombout, Luke Museum Director
Sawyer, Alan R Consultant
Smedley, Geoffrey Educator, Sculptor
Varney, Edwin Printmaker, Editor
Wallace, Kenneth William Painter, Educator
Wood, Alan Painter
Young, Robert John Painter

Victoria

Cantieni, Graham Alfred Painter, Administrator
Gore, Tom Curator, Photographer
Gunasinghe, Siri Educator, Historian
Harvey, Donald Painter, Printmaker
Jorgensen, Flemming Painter
Lansdowne, James Fenwick Painter
Mayhew, Elza Sculptor
Raginsky, Nina Painter, Photographer
Segger, Martin Joseph Historian, Museum Director
Siebner, Herbert Painter, Muralist
Travers-Smith, Brian John Painter, Instructor

West Vancouver

Bell, Alistair Macready Printmaker, Painter
Felter, James Warren Painter, Curator
Lennie, Beatrice E C Sculptor, Designer
Norris, Leonard Matheson Cartoonist, Illustrator
Smith, Gordon Painter
Thomas, Lionel Arthur John Painter

Winlaw

Foulger, Richard F Serigrapher, Painter

MANITOBA

St Boniface

Tascona, Antonio Tony Painter, Sculptor

Winnipeg

Dillow, Nancy E (Nancy Elizabeth Robertson) Administrator, Historian
Eckhardt, Ferdinand Historian, Museum Director
Eyre, Ivan Painter
Head, George Bruce Painter, Designer
Leathers, Winston Lyle Painter, Printmaker
Pura, William Paul Printmaker, Painter
Reichert, Donald Karl Painter, Educator
Smith, Ernest John Architect, Designer
Tillenius, Clarence (Ingwall) Painter, Writer
Topper, David R Educator, Historian
Warkov, Esther Painter

NEW BRUNSWICK

Fredericton

Bobak, Bruno Joseph Painter, Printmaker
Donaldson, Marjory (Rogers) Curator, Painter
Lumsden, Ian Gordon Director

Moncton

Clermont, Ghislain Historian, Critic
Gauvin, Claude E Painter
Roussel, Claude Patrice Sculptor, Instructor

Sackville

Hammock, Virgil Gene Critic, Painter

NEWFOUNDLAND

Ferryland

Squires, Gerald Leopold Painter, Educator

Mt Carmel

Pratt, Mary Frances Painter, Printmaker

St John's

Perlin, Rae Painter
Shepherd, Reginald Painter, Printmaker

Southern Shore

Lapointe, Frank Painter, Printmaker

NORTHWEST TERRITORIES

Cape Dorset

Kenojuak (Ashevak) Printmaker, Sculptor

NOVA SCOTIA

Bear River

Couper, Charles Alexander Painter, Instructor

Canning

Metson, Graham Painter, Writer

Clam Harbour

Wilson-Hammond, Charlotte Emily Painter, Printmaker

Dartmouth

Forrestall, Thomas De Vany Sculptor, Painter

Halifax

Cameron, Eric Administrator, Painter
Ferguson, Gerald Painter
Fraser, Carol Hoorn Painter, Draftsman
Jackson, Sarah Sculptor, Graphic Artist
Law, C Anthony Painter
Lindgren, Charlotte Sculptor
Murchie, Donald John Librarian
Redgrave, Felicity Painter, Critic
Shuebrook, Ron (Ronald Lee) Painter, Educator
Tolmie, Kenneth Donald Painter

La Have

Greer, John Sydney Sculptor

Liverpool

Savage, Roger Painter, Printmaker

Lunenburg County

Pentz, Donald Robert Painter, Printmaker

Mabou

Leaf, June Painter, Sculptor

Tatamagouche

Zarand, Julius John Painter, Restorer

Wolfville

Colville, Alexander Painter, Printmaker
Coyne, John Michael Painter, Educator

Yarmouth

Pierce, Elizabeth R Painter

ONTARIO

Agincourt

Lampitoc, Rol Ponce Painter, Printmaker

Alton

Nevitt, Richard Barrington Educator, Illustrator

Baltimore

Bolt, Ron Environmental Artist, Painter

Barrie

Stuart, Donald Alexander Designer, Craftsman

Burlington

Mansaram, P(anchal) Collage Artist, Photographer

Campbellville

Hanson, Jean (Elphick) Painter, Printmaker

Carlisle

Brender a Brandis, Gerard William Printmaker, Illustrator

Cobourg

Kolisnyk, Peter Painter, Sculptor

Don Mills

Bayefsky, Aba Painter, Printmaker
Schleeh, Hans Martin Sculptor

Downsview

Sandberg, Hannah Painter, Lecturer
Zemans, Joyce L Educator, Historian

Dundas

Holbrook, Elizabeth Bradford Sculptor

Gananoque

Russell, John Laurel Dealer, Collector

Grimsby

Lukas, Dennis Brian Painter, Educator
Reitzenstein, Reinhard Environmental
    Artist

Guelph

Bachinski, Walter Joseph Sculptor,
    Draftsman
Chu, Gene Printmaker, Painter
Danby, Ken Painter, Printmaker
Dow, Helen Jeannette Historian,
    Educator

Hamilton

Carter, Harriet (Estelle) Manore Painter
Courtney, Keith Townsend Administrator
Cumming, Glen Edward Museum
    Director

Ingersoll

Crawford, Catherine Betty Painter

King City

Tahedl, Ernestine Stained Glass Artist,
    Painter

Kingston

Aird, Neil Carrick Goldsmith, Designer
Allen, Ralph Painter, Educator
Andrew, David Neville Painter, Educator
Bieler, Andre Charles Painter, Muralist
Dorn, Peter Klaus Designer, Graphic
    Artist
Finley, Gerald Eric Historian
Heywood, J C Printmaker
Macdonald, Grant Painter, Illustrator
Schonberger, Fred Painter, Sculptor
Smith, Frances Kathleen Curator,
    Historian
Stewart, John Douglas Historian
Swain, Robert Francis Gallery Director

Kitchener

Goetz, Peter Henry Painter, Lecturer

Kleinburg

Bell, Philip Michael Administrator,
    Historian
Vivot, Lea (Lea Drahomira
    Vivot-Fishman) Sculptor

Lambeth

Thibert, Patrick A Sculptor, Instructor

LaSalle

DeAngelis, Joseph Rocco Sculptor

Locust Hill

Stokes, Louis (Walter) Sculptor

London

Ariss, Herbert Joshua Painter, Illustrator
Barrio-Garay, Jose Luis Art
    Administrator, Art Historian
Becker, Helmut Julius Printmaker
Dale, William Scott Abell Historian,
    Educator
De Kergommeaux, Duncan Painter,
    Educator
Fenwick, Roly (William Roland) Painter,
    Educator
Lorcini, Gino Sculptor, Muralist

Markham

Markle, Jack M Dealer, Sculptor
Markle, Sam Dealer, Sculptor

Milton

Bateman, Robert McLellan Painter

Mississauga

Broomfield, Adolphus George Painter,
    Designer
La Pierre, Thomas Painter, Printmaker
Rackus, George (Keistus) Painter,
    Muralist
Roberts, Tom (Thomas Keith) Painter
Sabelis, Huibert Printmaker, Painter

Moonstone

Gould, John Howard Painter, Filmmaker

Newmarket

Hagan, Frederick Printmaker, Painter
Hall, John A Painter, Educator

Niagara on the Lake

Scott, Campbell Printmaker, Sculptor

Oakville

Bakken, Haakon Art Administrator,
    Craftsman
Matsubara, Naoko Printmaker, Illustrator

Odessa

Holmes, David Bryan Painter, Printmaker

Oshawa

Hilts, Alvin Sculptor
Newton, John Neil Photographer,
    Printmaker

Ottawa

Borcoman, James Curator
Bourdeau, Robert Charles Photographer
Boyd, James Henderson Printmaker,
    Sculptor
Cohen, Lynne G Photographer, Lecturer
Dickson, Jennifer Joan Photographer,
    Printmaker
Durr, Pat (Patricia Beth) Painter,
    Printmaker
Groves, Naomi Jackson Writer, Painter
Harris, Lawren Phillips Painter, Educator
Hubbard, Robert Hamilton Historian
Jackson, Ruth Amelia Curator
Karsh, Yousuf Photographer
Laskin, Myron, Jr Curator, Historian
MacDonald, Colin Somerled Writer,
    Publisher
Martin, Jane Painter
Ostiguy, Jean-Rene Painter, Curator
Reid, Leslie Mary Margaret Painter,
    Printmaker
Sharpe, (Norman) Blair Painter
Stolow, Nathan Conservator, Consultant
Sylvestre, Guy Critic, Writer
Taylor, Mary Cazort Curator, Historian

Owen Sound

Hogbin, Stephen James Sculptor

Peterborough

Nind, Jean Painter, Printmaker

Pickering

Semak, Michael Photographer, Educator

Pointe Au Baril

Lumbers, James Richard Painter,
    Designer

Port Hope

Blackwood, David (Lloyd) Painter,
    Printmaker

Priceville

Tamasauskas, Otis Kazys Printmaker

Rosedale Toronto

Haworth, Peter Painter, Stained Glass
    Artist

St Catharines

Harris, Alfred Peter Painter,
    Administrator

Scarborough

McCarthy, Doris Jean Painter, Instructor

Stratford

Green, Art Painter

Tamworth

Saxe, Henry Sculptor

Toronto

Aarons, Anita Gallery Director, Sculptor
Altwerger, Libby Painter, Graphic Artist
Armstrong, Geoffrey Painter, Architect
Astman, Barbara Ann Photographer,
    Instructor
Banz, George Writer, Architect
Barry, Anne Meredith Printmaker,
    Instructor
Bell, R Murray Collector
Beveridge, Karl J Photographer, Sculptor
Birnberg, Gerald H Art Dealer
Birnberg, Ruth Carrel Art Dealer
Blazeje, Zbigniew Sculptor, Painter
Boszin, Andrew Painter, Sculptor
Bronson, A A (Michael Wayne Tims)
    Post-Conceptual Artist, Writer
Brooks, H(arold) Allen Historian,
    Lecturer
Burnett, David Grant Historian, Curator
Campbell, Colin Keith Video Artist
Carr-Harris, Ian Redford Sculptor,
    Photographer
Cattell, Ray Painter, Director
Cetin, Anton Painter, Printmaker
Cliff, Denis Antony Painter, Instuctor
Collier, Alan Caswell Painter
Collyer, Robin Sculptor, Video Artist
Condron, Brian James Photographer
Costin, Frank Dealer
Coughtry, Graham Painter, Sculptor
Cowan, Aileen Hooper Sculptor, Painter
Dagys, Jacob Sculptor
Daly, Kathleen (Kathleen Daly Pepper)
    Painter
Davies, Haydn Llewellyn Sculptor,
    Painter
De Pedery-Hunt, Dora Sculptor, Designer
Dimson, Theo Aeneas Designer,
    Illustrator
Downing, Robert James Sculptor,
    Educator
Drapell, Joseph Painter, Sculptor
Drutz, June Painter, Educator
DuBois, Macy Architect, Designer
Duff, Ann MacIntosh Painter, Printmaker
Eloul, Kosso Sculptor
Engel, Walter F Critic, Dealer
Etrog, Sorel Sculptor, Painter
Ewen, Paterson Painter, Educator
Favro, Murray Sculptor, Inventor
Feist, Harold E Painter, Sculptor
Filipovic, Augustin Sculptor, Painter
Fleisher, Pat Editor, Photo Artist
Freifeld, Eric Painter, Educator
Frick, Joan Painter
Friedland, Seymour Patron, Collector
Gage, Frances M Sculptor
Gale, Peggy Writer, Curator
Garwood, Audrey Painter, Printmaker
Graham, K M Painter
Gregor, Helen Frances Designer, Tapestry
    Artist

CANADA (cont)

Harding, Noel Robert Video Artist, Environmental Artist
Hastenteufel, Dieter Sculptor
Haworth, B Cogill Painter
Heath, David Martin Educator, Photographer
Hecht, Mary Sculptor
Horeis, William Richard, Sr Photographer, Printmaker
Horne, (Arthur Edward) Cleeve Painter, Sculptor
Houle, Robert James Painter, Consultant
Housser, Yvonne McKague Educator, Environmental Artist
Howard, (Helen) Barbara Painter, Printmaker
Hunkler, Dennis Francis Painter, Printmaker
Isaacs, Avrom Dealer, Publisher
Iskowitz, Gershon Painter
Jean-Louis, Don (Donald Charles) Sculptor, Conceptual Artist
Jursevskis, Zigfrids Sculptor
Kaye, David Haigh Textile Artist, Designer
Khendry, Janak Kumar Gallery Director, Sculptor
Kinoshita, Gene Architect
Kosuth, Joseph Conceptual Artist
Kramer, Burton Designer, Graphic Artist
Kravis, Janis Designer, Architect
Lamanna, Carmen Dealer, Restorer
Letendre, Rita Painter
Lochnan, Katharine A Curator, Lecturer
Luz, Virginia Painter
McElcheran, William Hodd Designer, Sculptor
MacGregor, John Boyko Painter, Administrator
MacKenzie, Hugh Seaforth Painter
Maggs, Arnaud (Cyril Benvenuti) Photographer, Graphic Artist
Manning, Jo Printmaker
Martin, Ron Painter
Meredith, John Painter
Miezajs, Dainis Painter, Instructor
Milrad, Aaron M Collector
Mitchell, Michael John Photographer, Educator
Moos, Walter A Dealer
Murray, Ian Stewart Sculptor, Conceptual Artist
Nakamura, Kazuo Painter
Nasgaard, Roald Curator, Historian
Neddeau, Donald Frederick Price Painter, Designer
Newman, John Beatty Painter, Instructor
Oesterle, Leonhard Friedrich Sculptor, Instructor
Ogilvie, Will (William Abernethy) Painter
Partridge, David Gerry Painter, Sculptor
Partz, Feliz (Ron Gabe) Painter
Perkins, A Alan Ceramist, Enamelist
Pigott, Marjorie Painter
Popescu, Cara Sculptor, Printmaker
Rayner, Gordon Painter
Reeves, John Alexander Photographer
Ronald, William Painter
Ross, Fred (Joseph) Painter, Instructor
Rutherford, Erica Painter, Printmaker
Sardelic, Ante Sculptor, Painter
Schaefer, Carl Fellman Painter
Scott, John Painter
Sewell, Richard George Printmaker, Painter
Shaw, Joseph Winterbotham Historian, Educator
Sing Hoo Sculptor, Painter
Snow, Michael Painter, Filmmaker
Solomon, Daniel Painter
Steele, Lisa Video Artist

Steiger, Frederic Painter, Instructor
Sutton, Carol (Lorraine) Painter
Takashima, Shizuye Violet Illustrator, Painter
Tangredi, Vincent Sculptor
Thornton, Jim (James Howard) Painter, Educator
Timmas, Osvald Painter, Lecturer
Town, Harold Barling Painter, Writer
Tulving, Ruth Painter, Printmaker
van Ginkel, Blanche Lemco Architect, Administrator
Vivenza, Francesca Graphic Artist, Painter
White, Albert Dealer, Collector
White, Deborah Dealer
White, Norman Triplett Sculptor
Whiten, Colette Sculptor, Instructor
Whiten, Tim Sculptor, Environmental Artist
Wieland, Joyce Painter, Filmmaker
Wiitasalo, Shirley Painter
Wilkin, Karen Curator, Critic
Wilson, (Ronald) York Painter, Muralist
Withrow, William J Administrator
Wright, David Thomas Painter, Educator
Yaneff, Chris Gallery Director
Zack, Badanna Bernice Sculptor, Writer
Zeidler, Eberhard Heinrich Designer, Architect
Zelenak, Edward John Sculptor
Zontal, Jorge (Jorge Sala) Painter

Waterloo

Izumi, Kiyoshi Architect, Educator

Welland

Tulumello, Peter M Administrator, Educator

Wellesley

Urquhart, Tony (Anthony Morse) Sculptor, Painter

West Lorne

Redinger, Walter Fred Sculptor, Muralist

White Lake

Swinton, George Painter, Writer

Willowdale

Ebsen, Alf K Calligrapher, Lecturer
Field, Saul Printmaker, Lecturer
Gilling, Lucille Printmaker
Jaworska, Tamara Tapestry Artist
Karniol, Eugene Dealer, Collector
Robb, Charles Painter

Windsor

Pufahl, John K Educator, Printmaker
Saltmarche, Kenneth Charles Painter, Administrator

PRINCE EDWARD ISLAND

Parkdale

Purdy, Henry Carl Painter, Educator

Summerside East

Barton, Georgie Read Painter, Sculptor

QUEBEC

Ayers Cliff

Beament, Tib (Thomas Harold) Painter, Lecturer

Aylmer

Rasto (Rastislav Hlavina) Sculptor, Conservator

Chicoutimi

Villeneuve, Joseph Arthur Painter

Hudson

Cosgrove, Stanley Painter
McLaren, Norman Filmmaker

Hudson Heights

Braitstein, Marcel Sculptor, Educator

Kirkland

Daudelin, Charles Sculptor

Laval

Bruni, Umberto Painter, Graphic Artist
Pellan (Alfred) Painter

Lennoxville

Holcomb, Adele Mansfield Historian

Matane

Picher, Claude Painter, Curator

Montreal

Almond, Paul Filmmaker, Writer
Barbeau, Marcel (Christian) Painter, Sculptor
Barry, Frank Painter, Educator
Beament, Harold Painter
Besner, J Jacques Sculptor, Muralist
Bigelow, Robert Clayton Educator, Painter
Blanchette, Antoine Art Dealer, Collector
Briansky, Rita Prezament Painter, Printmaker
Bruneau, Kittie Painter, Printmaker
Caiserman-Roth, Ghitta Painter, Printmaker
Cardinal, Marcelin Painter
De Moura Sobral, Luis Historian, Critic
Dyens, Georges Maurice Sculptor, Holographer
Feist, Warner David Designer, Painter
Fox, John Painter
Gagnon, Charles Painter, Photographer
Gaucher, Yves Printmaker, Painter
Gaudieri, Alexander V J Museum Director
Gerin-Lajoie, Guy Architect
Gersovitz, Sarah Valerie Printmaker, Painter
Gordon, Russell Talbert Painter
Harder, Rolf Peter Designer
Hartal, Paul Zev Painter, Writer
Knudsen, Christian Painter, Printmaker
Lacroix, Richard Painter, Printmaker
Lambert, Phyllis Architect, Collector
Lewis, Stanley Sculptor, Printmaker
London, Elca Dealer
McCall, Ann Painter, Printmaker
McEwen, Jean Painter
Menses, Jan Painter, Printmaker
Molinari, Guido Painter, Sculptor
Prent, Mark Environmental Artist, Sculptor
Roch, Ernst Designer, Lecturer
Scott, Marian (Dale) Painter
Steinhouse, Tobie (Thelma) Painter, Printmaker
Surrey, Philip Henry Painter
Swartzman, Roslyn Printmaker, Sculptor
Tinning, George Campbell Painter

CANADA (cont)

Tousignant, Claude Painter, Sculptor
Trudeau, Yves Sculptor
Valentin, Jean-Pierre Dealer
Wainwright, Robert Barry Painter, Printmaker
Wheeler, Orson Shorey Sculptor, Lecturer
Whittome, Irene Dianne Sculptor, Painter
Yajima, Michiko Dealer

Mont St Hilaire

Betteridge, Lois Etherington Silver & Goldsmith, Lecturer

Old Chelsea

Mason, William Clifford Filmmaker, Painter
Sisler, Rebecca Sculptor, Writer

Outremont

Ferron, Marcelle Painter, Glass Artist
Jaque, Louis Painter

Pointe Aux Trembles

Goulet, Claude Educator, Painter

Quebec

Crouton, Francois (LaFortune) Administrator, Photographer
Iacurto, Francesco Painter, Instructor
Lemieux, Irenee Painter
Thibault, Claude Curator

St Lambert

Archambault, Louis Sculptor, Educator

St Laurent

Tata, Sam Bejan Photographer

Sillery

Dumas, Antoine Painter, Educator
Lemieux, Jean Paul Painter

Ste-Adele

Rousseau-Vermette, Mariette Tapestry Artist

Terrebonne

Hurtubise, Jacques Painter

Val-David

Baxter, Bonnie Jean Printmaker, Painter

Westmount

Harrison, (William) Allan Painter
Tatossian, Armand Painter

SASKATCHEWAN

Craven

Cicansky, Victor Sculptor

Dundurn

Bentham, Douglas Wayne Sculptor

Pense

Fafard, Joe Sculptor

Regina

Lee, Roger Educator, Curator
McKay, Arthur Fortescue Painter, Educator
Nugent, John Cullen Sculptor, Educator
Nulf, Frank Allen Painter, Educator
Whitney, Susan Gillian Dealer, Gallery Director

Saskatoon

Bornstein, Eli Painter, Sculptor
Christie, Robert Duncan Painter
Hamilton, W Paul C Educator, Historian
Lindner, Ernest Painter, Conceptual Artist
Perehudoff, William W Painter
Ringness, Charles Obert Educator, Printmaker
Rogers, Otto Donald Painter, Educator

Silton

Yuristy, Russell Michael Designer, Sculptor

OTHER COUNTRIES

AUSTRALIA

Graham, F Lanier Curator, Museologist
Kelly, William Joseph Draftsman, Painter

DENMARK

Wright, (Charles) Clifford Painter, Writer

FRANCE

Biala, Janice Painter
Brustlein, Daniel Painter
Crotto, Paul Painter, Sculptor
D'Ashnash-Tosi (Barbara Chase-Riboud) Sculptor, Writer
Gorsline, Douglas Warner Painter, Illustrator
Gysin, Brion Painter, Writer
Hicks, Sheila Tapestry Artist, Publisher
Levee, John H Painter, Sculptor
Masurovsky, Gregory Draftsman, Printmaker
Monnier, Jacqueline Matisse Conceptual Artist
Rowell, Margit Historian, Curator
Stoianovich, Marcelle Painter, Lithographer
Truex, Van Day Painter, Designer

GERMANY, FEDERAL REPUBLIC OF

Brecht, George Conceptual Artist, Assemblage Artist
Ettl, Georg Painter, Sculptor

ISRAEL

Alexenberg, (Melvin) Menahem Conceptual Artist, Painter
Davidowitz (Dror), Moshe Historian, Writer

ITALY

Baxter, Robert James Painter
Congdon, William (Grosvenor) Painter
Cook, Robert Howard Sculptor, Medalist
d'Almeida, George Painter
DeLuigi, Janice Cecilia Educator, Painter
De Marco, Jean Antoine Sculptor
Fasano, Clara Sculptor
French, Jared Painter, Sculptor
Friscia, Albert Painter, Sculptor
Hebald, Milton Elting Sculptor, Printmaker
Hershey, Nona Printmaker
Hsiao, Chin Painter, Sculptor
Leong, James Chan Painter
Marinsky, Harry Sculptor, Painter
Noordhoek, Harry Cecil Sculptor, Painter
Pepper, Beverly Sculptor, Painter
Puccinelli, Raimondo Sculptor, Graphic Artist

Schloss, Edith Painter, Writer
Selvig, Forrest Hall Historian, Writer
Smyth, Craig Hugh Administrator, Historian

JAMAICA

Conant, Jan Royce Painter, Illustrator

JAPAN

Johnson, Margaret Kennard Printmaker, Educator
Kusama, Yayoi Sculptor, Painter

MEXICO

Amaya, Armando Sculptor
Anguiano, Raul Muralist, Painter
Angulo, Chappie Painter, Illustrator
Anzures, Rafael Educator, Art Critic
Aquino, Edmundo Painter, Printmaker
Arteche (Hector Arteche Martinez) Painter, Sculptor
Banda, Pedro Salazar Painter
Bassi Writer, Painter
Belkin, Arnold Painter, Muralist
Bragar, Philip Frank Painter, Printmaker
Cervantes, Pedro Sculptor
Chavez-Morado, Jose Painter, Educator
Clement, Kathleen (Ruth) Painter, Graphic Artist
Colina, Armando G Dealer
Coral R (Flaviano Ezequiel Coral Revelo) Painter, Muralist
de Yturbe, Alejandra R Dealer
Dickinson, William Stirling Lecturer, Administrator
Donde, Olga Painter, Printmaker
Elena, Maria Painter, Printmaker
Escobedo, Helen Environmental Sculptor
Etienne, Guillermo C Painter, Printmaker
Falfan, Alfredo Painter, Printmaker
Friedeberg, Pedro Painter, Sculptor
Gaona Adame, Jose Julio Painter, Printmaker
Gerzso, Gunther Painter, Graphic Artist
Goeritz, Mathias Sculptor, Designer
Gurria, Angela Sculptor, Stained Glass Artist
Herrera, Raul Othon Painter
Hurtado Duhart, Rodolfo Painter, Engraver
Landau, Myra Painter, Muralist
Magali, Lara Painter
Maxwell, Robert Edwin
Montoya, Gustavo (Gustavo Montoya Carranco) Painter, Collage Artist
Moreno, Orduna Nicolas Muralist, Educator
Nierman, Leonardo M Painter, Sculptor
Nishizawa Flores, Luis Painter
Palau, Marta Tapestry Artist, Sculptor
Palmer, Lucie Mackay Painter, Lecturer
Parra, Carmen Painter, Printmaker
Pereznieto, Castro Fernando Printmaker, Painter
Pinto, James Painter, Sculptor
Reindorf, Samuel Painter
Rivera-Velazquez, Mariano Painter, Writer
Rodriguez, Oscar Painter, Sculptor
Rojo, Vicente Painter
Salazar, Juan Painter, Designer
Sebastian Sculptor
Siegmann, Naomi Rita Sculptor
Stahl, Ben (Albert) Painter, Writer
Stavans, Isaac Painter
Stewart, William Painter
Tamayo, Rufino Painter
Taylor, Frederick Bourchier Painter, Sculptor

OTHER COUNTRIES (cont)

Von Gunten, Roger Painter, Draftsman
Zavala, Manuel Painter, Photographer

NETHERLANDS

Tajiri, Shinkichi Sculptor, Educator

SPAIN

Harlow, Robert E Painter
Harvey, Robert Martin Painter
Lopez-Rey, Jose Historian, Educator
Meigs, Walter Painter
Narotzky, Norman David Painter,
    Printmaker

Sheerin, Jerry Painter, Architect
Ulbricht, John Painter

SWITZERLAND

Gottschalk, Fritz Designer, Lecturer
Roseman, Stanley Painter, Draftsman
Takal, Peter Painter, Printmaker

UNITED KINGDOM

Aliki Illustrator, Writer
Allen, Tom, Jr Sculptor, Designer
Baer, Jo Painter, Writer
Baskin, Leonard Sculptor, Graphic Artist
Blake, John Clemens Artist

Brady, Charles Michael Painter
Cowles, Fleur Painter, Writer
Douaihy, Saliba Stained Glass Artist,
    Conceptual Artist
Gablik, Suzi Painter, Lecturer
Hubbard, John Painter
Kelly, Mary Educator
Kitaj, R B Painter, Printmaker
Kitzinger, Ernst Historian
Leitman, Norman Dealer
Lijn, Liliane Sculptor, Writer
Muensterberger, Werner Collector, Writer

VENEZUELA

Neumann, Hans Collector

Professional Classifications Index

ADMINISTRATOR

Aldrich, Larry
Alexander, Judy
Alexander-Greene, Grace
  George
Arnold, Richard R
Baitsell, Wilma Williamson
Bakken, Haakon
Balderacchi, Arthur Eugene
Bandy, Mary Lea
Barber, Ronald
Barcus, David L
Barrio-Garay, Jose Luis
Bartlett, Fred Stewart
Bayliss, George
Beam, Philip Conway
Beattie, George
Beebe, Mary Livingstone
Bell, James M
Bell, Michael Steven
Bell, Philip Michael
Benjamin, Lloyd William, III
Berns, Pamela Kari
Betensky, Rose Hart
Biddle, James
Biddle, Livingston Ludlow, Jr
Bingham, Lois A
Blayton, Betty (Betty Blayton-
  Taylor)
Bledsoe, Jane Kathryn
Blevins, James Richard
Bloch, Milton Joseph
Booth, Judith Gayle
Bowman, Jeff Ray
Bradbury, Ellen A
Bramlett, Betty Jane
Breeskin, Adelyn Dohme
Britt, Nelson Clark
Broadley, Hugh T
Broderick, James Allen
Brody, Myron Roy
Brooks, John H
Brown, Jeanette H
Browne, Vivian E
Bruno, Vincent J
Buchanan, John Edward, Jr
Buki, Zoltan
Burchett, Debra
Burford, William E
Burgart, Herbert Joseph
Burke, James Donald
Cameron, Elsa S
Cameron, Eric
Cantieni, Graham Alfred
Carmichael, Donald Ray
Casey, Jacqueline Shepard
Catron, Patricia D'Arcy
Chalmers, E Laurence, Jr
Channing, Susan Rose
Chew, Paul Albert
Chiego, William Joseph
Cleveland, Helen Barth
Cleveland, Robert Earl
Clothier, Peter Dean
Cogswell, Margaret Price
Colin, Ralph Frederick

Collins, William Charles
Cone, Gerrit Craig
Contini, Anita
Cook, Christopher Capen
Cortese, Edward Fortunato
Courtney, Keith Townsend
Covey, Victor Charles B
Crawford, Bill (Wilbur Ogden)
Crouton, Francois (LaFortune)
Culkin, John Michael
Cummings, Frederick James
Cummins, Karen Gasco
Cunningham, Charles C, Jr
Danielson, Phyllis I
Dash, Harvey Dwight
Daugherty, Marshall Harrison
Daviee, Jerry Michael
Davis, D Jack
Davis, John Sherwood
Demetrion, James Thomas
de Montebello, Philippe
  Lannes
DePillars, Murry N
Dickinson, William Stirling
Dietrich, Bruce Leinbach
Dillon, C Douglas
Dillow, Nancy E (Nancy
  Elizabeth Robertson)
Dixon, Jenny (Jane Hodley)
Donaldson, Jeff R
Doty, Robert McIntyre
Dresser, Louisa (Louisa
  Dresser Campbell)
DuBois, Alan Beekman
Duff, James H
Dunbar, Michael Austin
Dunn, Phillip Charles
Eberman, Edwin
Ebie, William Dennis
Eckersley, Thomas Cyril
Edelson, Gilbert S
Edelstein, Teri J
Edmunds, Allan Logan
Ewing, Bayard
Farmer, John David
Ferber, Elise Van Hook
Fern, Alan Maxwell
Field, Lyman
Fitzpatrick, Robert John
Flakey Rose Hip
Fleming, Ronald Lee
Ford, Harry Xavier
Franzen, Joan C
Frauchiger, Fritz A
Fraze, Denny T
Freeman-Appelbaum, Margery
Freundlich, August L
Gantz, Jeanne A
Garcia, Ofelia
Garver, Thomas H
Geoffrey, Sayyid Iqbal (Jafree)
Giacomantonio, Archimedes
Gibson, George
Gilmartin, F Thomas
Gilmore, Roger
Gladstone, M J
Glanz, Andrea E

Glenn, Constance White
Gold, Betty
Gomez-Sicre, Jose
Gonzalez, Jose Gamaliel
Gordley, Metz Tranbarger
Gray, Robert Hugh
Gray, Robert Ward
Greco, Anthony Joseph
Green, Wilder
Gully, Anthony Lacy
Hagerstrand, Martin Allan
Hale, Robert Beverly
Hall, Lee
Hammer, Alfred Emil
Hansen, Arne Rae
Harkins, Dennis Richter
Harris, Alfred Peter
Harris, Ann Sutherland
Hart, Allen M
Hart, Robert Gordon
Hartwell, Patricia Lochridge
Hayes, Bartlett Harding, Jr
Hearn, M F (Millard
  Fillmore), Jr
Heinz, Susan
Hero, Peter deCourcy
Hertzman, Gay Mahaffy
Hightower, John B
Hildebrandt, William Albert
Hobbs, Joe Ferrell
Hobbs, Robert Dean
Hodes, Barney
Hodge, Scottie
Hoffman, Neil James
Holbrook, Vivian Nicholas
Hood, Mary Bryan
Hopkins, Benjamin
Horowitz, Benjamin
Houghton, Arthur A, Jr
Hummel, Charles Frederick
Hunt, Robert James
Huntley, David C
Insel, Paula
Irving, Donald J
Isaacs, Claire Naomi
Jacobs, Peter Alan
Jeswald, Joseph
Johnson, J Seward, Jr
Johnson, Katherine King
Johnson, Robert Flynn
Johnston, Robert Harold
Johnston, William Ralph
Jones, Harold Henry
Joost-Gaugier, Christiane L
Jordan, Jack
Jorgenson, Dale Alfred
Kan, Michael
Karlstrom, Paul Johnson
Katzive, David H
Kearney, John (W)
Keeler, David Boughton
Kenney, Estelle Koval
Kenyon, Colleen Frances
Kienholz, Lyn
Kilmer, Nicholas John
Kinney, Gilbert Hart
Kluver, Billy (Johan Wilhem)

Knight, Christopher Allen
Kubly, Donald R
Kuchel, Konrad G
Kurka, Donald Frank
Kusnerz, Peggy Ann F
Laing, Richard Harlow
Landreau, Anthony Norman
Lang, Wendy F
Lawson, Edward Pitt
Lazarus, Fred, IV
Leader, Garnet Rosamonde
Leighton, David S R
Lein, Malcolm Emil
Leven, Ann R
Lewandowski, Edmund D
Lewis, Elma Ina
Libhart, Myles Laroy
Liddle, Nancy Hyatt
Lieberman, William S
Linn, John William
Livet, Anne Hodge
Livingston, Margaret Gresham
Loar, Peggy A
Loerke, William Carl
Lorber, Richard
Lottes, John William
Lowe, Harry
Lyle, Charles Thomas
McCauley, Gardiner Rae
McClenney, Cheryl Ilene
McCracken, Harold
McCullough, Joseph
MacGregor, John Boyko
McKay, John Sangster
Macklin, Anderson D
Macomber, William B
Mahlmann, John James
Manetta, Edward J
Manhart, Marcia Y
Mann, Virginia
Marchese, Patricia Davis
Markman, Sidney David
Mason, Francis Scarlett, Jr
Mason, Phillip Lindsay
Matlick, Gerald Allen
Mayes, Steven Lee
Meadows, P B (Patricia B)
Mellon, Paul
Meserole, Vera Stromsted
  (Mrs Milton D Block)
Meyer, Ruth Krueger
Midani, Akram
Milhoan, Randall Bell
Miller, Joan Vita
Miller, John Franklin
Millett, Caroline Dunlop
Mills, Frederick Van Fleet
Mills, Margaret M
Milrad, Aaron M
Mitchell, Donald
Moe, Richard D
Moeller, Robert Charles, III
Moir, Alfred
Mongan, Agnes
Moore, Fay
Moore, Russell James
Morrison, Doris

1115

ADMINISTRATOR (cont)

Moser, Rex
Mount, Marshall Ward
Moyer, Roy
Musgrove, Stephen Ward
Neidhardt, Carl Richard
Nestor, Lula B
New, Lloyd H
Newsom, Barbara Ylvisaker
Newton, Douglas
Newton, Earle Williams
Novack, Frank T
Oakes, John Warren
O'Connor, John Arthur
Olenick, David Charles
O'Neil, John Joseph
Orze, Joseph John
Osborn, Elodie C
Outterbridge, John Wilfred
Owens, Wallace, Jr
Pappas, George
Parker, James Varner
Parkhurst, Charles
Parrino, George
Parry, Pamela Jeffcott
Parsons, Merribell Maddux
Patrick, Darryl L
Pease, David G
Pels, Albert
Pepe, Marie Sophie Huper
Perkins, Robert Eugene
Perrot, Paul N
Perry, Edward (Ted) Samuel
Peters, Larry Dean
Peterson, John Douglas
Pfister, Harold Francis
Pierotti, Ray (Raymond Charles)
Pilsk, Adele Inez
Plaut, James S
Polsky, Cynthia
Pope, Annemarie Henle
Porter, Richard James
Potter, Ted
Preble, Michael Andrew
Preis, Alfred
Pressly, Nancy Lee
Price, Barbara Gillette
Propersi, August J
Quigley, Michael Allen
Quirarte, Jacinto
Rahja, Virginia Helga
Rasmussen, Anton Jesse
Reger, Lawrence L
Reichard, Stephen Brantley
Richman, Robert M
Robertson, Charles J
Robinson, Mary Ann
Rodgers, Jack A
Rodriguez, Pedro A
Rohlfing, Christian
Rosenthal, Gertrude
Ross, Kenneth
Rovetti, Paul F
Roysher, Hudson (Brisbine)
Ruddley, John
Ruffo, Joseph Martin
Rumford, Beatrix Tyson
Rust, Edwin C
Sabatella, Joseph John
Sachs, Samuel, II
Saff, Donald Jay
St John, Bruce
Saltmarche, Kenneth Charles
Sanchez, Beatrice Rivas
Sanguinetti, Eugene F
Satz, Janet Maas
Schlageter, Robert William
Schnorrenberg, John Martin
Schutte, Thomas Frederick
Scott, David Winfield
Scott, Robert Montgomery
Seligman, Thomas Knowles
Sennema, David C
Sevigny, Maurice Joseph, II
Shapiro, Babe
Sharp, Lewis Inman

Sheon, Aaron
Sickman, Laurence Chalfant Stevens
Simon, Leonard Ronald
Smyth, Craig Hugh
Solmssen, Peter
Solomon, Ruth B
Somerville, Romaine Stec
Sorell, Victor Alexander
Spencer, John R
Spike, John Thomas
Spink, Walter M
Spurgin, John Edwin
Stamm, Geoffrey Eaton
Stancil, Kimsey
Stanley, Charles Edward
Stead, Rexford Arthur
Stearns, Robert
Stebbins, Theodore Ellis, Jr
Stefanotti, Robert Alan
Stein, Claire A
Stephens, Richard Alan
Stillman, George
Stoddard, Donna Melissa
Streetman, John William, III
Strother, Joseph Willis
Stull, Robert J
Sullivan, Ruth Wilkins
Sunkel, Robert Cleveland
Sweeney, James Johnson
Tai, Jane S
Tancock, John Leon
Taylor, Kendall Frances
Taylor, Rod Allen
Thalacker, Donald William
Thomas, Elaine Freeman
Thornton, Richard Samuel
Tomasini, Wallace J
Tracy, Berry Bryson
Trop-Blumberg, Sandra
Trubner, Henry
Truettner, William
Tseu, Rosita Hsu
Tulumello, Peter M
Tyson, Rae Julian
Udvardy, John Warren
Vanco, John Leroy
van Ginkel, Blanche Lemco
Van Hook, David H
Van Schaack, Eric
Vigtel, Gudmund
Voos, William John
Wagner, Charles H
Wald, Palmer B
Walker, William Bond
Wallace, Elizabeth S
Walsh, Janet Barbara
Wark, Robert Rodger
Warren, Ferdinand Earl
Weber, Jean M
Weil, Rose R
Weinberg, Ephraim
West, E Gordon
Westin, Robert H
Whipple, Enez Mary
White, Ian McKibbin
Wickiser, Ralph Lewanda
Wilke, Ulfert S
Willis, William Henry, Jr
Wintersteen, Bernice McIlhenny
Wise, Howard
Withrow, William J
Woide, Robert E
Wolfe, Townsend Durant
Wood, James Nowell
Woolfenden, William Edward
Wunder, Richard Paul
Wurdemann, Helen (Baroness Elena Guzzardi)
Yajima, Michiko
Yenawine, Bruce Harley
Young, Joseph Louis
Zahn, Carl Frederick
Zaleski, Jean M

ARCHITECT

Armstrong, Geoffrey
Atkins, Gordon Lee
Bakanowsky, Louis J
Banz, George
Barnes, Edward Larrabee
Blake, Peter Jost
Booth, Laurence Ogden
Brown, John Hall
Bunshaft, Gordon
Damaz, Paul F
Deaton, Charles
De Weldon, Felix George Weihs
Downey, Juan
DuBois, Macy
Fort-Brescia, Bernardo M
Geerlings, Gerald Kenneth
Gehry, Frank O(wen)
Gerin-Lajoie, Guy
Gironda, R
Graves, Michael
Green, Wilder
Hamilton, Frank Moss
Harris, Julian Hoke
Izumi, Kiyoshi
Johanson, Patricia
Johnson, Philip Cortelyou
Kaskey, Raymond John
Kinoshita, Gene
Kravis, Janis
Lambert, Phyllis
MacDonald, William L
Meier, Richard Alan
Mitchell, Clifford
Murphy, Herbert A
Oliver, Richard Bruce
Peckham, Nicholas
Pei, I M (Ieoh Ming)
Pelli, Cesar
Perkins, G Holmes
Pillet, Michel Louis
Preis, Alfred
Redstone, Louis Gordon
Robinson, C David
Romney, Hervin A R
Scott, Walter
Sheerin, Jerry
Simonds, Charles Frederick
Smith, Ernest John
Soleri, Paolo
Sommer, Frederick
Spear, Laurinda Hope
Speyer, A James
Thalacker, Donald William
Thiry, Paul (Albert)
Tigerman, Stanley
van Ginkel, Blanche Lemco
Venturi, Robert
Waters, Terrance
Wedin, Winslow Elliott
Yegul, Fikret Kutlu
Zeidler, Eberhard Heinrich

ART DEALER

Adler, Abe
Ahn, Don C
Alexander, Edmund Brooke
Alexander, Judith
Allen, Edda Lynne
Allrich, M Louise Barco
Alonzo, Jack J
Altermann, Tony
Anderson, Bruce James
Anderson, David K
Anderson, Dennis Ray
Anhalt, Jacqueline Richards
Ankrum, Joan
Arnold, Jack
Aronson, Cliff
Ault, Lee Addison
Austin, Jo-Anne Jordan
Bachert, Hildegard Gina

Bader, Franz
Baird, Joseph Armstrong, Jr
Balay, Felicie
Banning, Jack (John Peck), Jr
Bareiss, Philip C
Barnes, Molly
Barnett, David J
Barrios, Benny Perez
Bartholet, Elizabeth Ives
Barton, John Murray
Baruch, Jacques Z
Baum, Hank
Baum, Jayne H
Baum, Timothy
Baxter, Douglas W
Beadleston, William L
Beilin, Howard
Belcher, George
Bell, Donald Allen
Bellamy, Richard
Belle, Anna (Anna Belle Birckett)
Benson, Elaine K G
Bergen, Sidney L
Berggruen, John Henry
Berman, Aaron
Bernstein, Saralinda
Bessemer, Auriel
Bingham, Alice
Birnberg, Gerald H
Birnberg, Ruth Carrel
Blacketer, James Richard
Blair, Carl Raymond
Blanchette, Antoine
Blinder, Martin S
Blinderman, Barry Robert
Bloom, Edith Salvin
Bolen, John E
Bolen, Lynne N
Bonino, Fernanda
Bonstrom, Dana Orlin
Boone, Mary
Borgenicht, Grace
Boucher, Tania Kunsky
Bouckaert, Harm J G
Bowater, Marian
Bradley, Dorothy
Braseth, John E
Broido, Lucy
Bromm, Hal
Brown, Alan M, Jr
Brown, Diane
Brown, Jeffrey Rogers
Brown, Robert K
Browne, Aldis J, III
Brundage, Susan Lounsbury
Bruno, Phillip A
Bryant, Linda Goode
Burford, William E
Burk, A Darlene
Burns, Timothy Joseph
Buster, Jacqueline Mary
Butler, Byron C
Byron, Charles Anthony
Califano, Edward Christopher
Cardozo, Patricia Velez
Carlin, Electra Marshall
Caro, Francis
Castano, Elvira
Castelli, Leo
Cernuschi, Alberto C
Challis, Richard Bracebridge
Chambers, Bruce William
Chase, Robert M
Cicero, Jan (Janice Pickett)
Clark, Garth Reginald
Clifford, Jutta
Cliver, Kendra-Jean (Kendra-Jean Cliver Krienke)
Close, Dean Purdy
Cohen, Mildred Thaler
Cohn, Frederick Donald
Cohn, Richard A
Cole, Sylvan, Jr
Coleman, Edward H
Colina, Armando G

ART DEALER (cont)
Cone-Skelton, Annette
Conforte, Renee
Cooper, Paula
Cooper, Rebecca
Cooper, Theodore A
Cornette, Mary Elizabeth
Cortella, Gloria Charlene
Costin, Frank
Costley-Jacobs, Averille Esther
Couturier, Marion B
Coyer, Max R
Crispo, Andrew J
Crowell, David Lee
Cuningham, Elizabeth Bayard
  (Mrs E W R Templeton)
Curtis, Roger William
Dailey, Victoria Keilus
Danikian, Caron Le Brun
Davidson, Elizabeth H
  Donnally
Davidson, Maxwell, III
Davis, Donald Robert
Dawley, Joseph William
de Andino, Jean-Pierre M
Deats, Margaret
del Re, Marisa
De Mille, Leslie Benjamin
de Nagy, Tibor (J)
Dennis, Gertrude Weyhe
Desind, Philip
Deson, Marianne (Herstein)
Deutschman, Louise Tolliver
Devine, William Charles
de Yturbe, Alejandra R
Dickerson, William J
Dietz, Gary Allan J
Dillingham, Rick (James
  Richard), II
Dintenfass, Terry
Dolan, Margo
Donson, Jerome Allan
Dorfman, Fred
Dorsky, Samuel
Drake, Douglas Arnold
Dreaper, Richard Edward
Drutt, Helen Williams
Drysdale, Nancy McIntosh
Duffy, Betty Minor
Edvi Illes, Emma
Einstein, Gilbert W
Eisenberg, Jerome Martin
Eitingon, Brigitte
Elder, Muldoon
Elkin, Beverly Dawn
Elowitch, Annette
Elowitch, Robert Jason
Emmerich, Andre
Engel, Walter F
Erlien, Nancy Beth
Esman, Rosa M
Ewald, Elin Lake
Eyen, Richard J
Fairweather, Sally H
Farris, Linda B
Fear, Daniel E
Fedele, Frank D
Feigen, Richard L
Feinman, Stephen E
Feld, Stuart Paul
Feldman, Ronald
Feuerstein, Roberta
Findlay, David B, Jr
Findlay, Helen T
Fink, Alan
Fischbach, Marilyn Cole
Fishko, Bella
Fitzkee, Eunice Ailes
Fleischman, Lawrence A
Fleming, Betty Corcoran
Flume, Violet Sigoloff
Fondren, Harold M
Foster, Donald Isle
Foster, Robert Stephen
Fourcade, Xavier
Fowler, Frank Eison
Fraenkel, Jeffrey Andrew

Freeman, Mallory Bruce
Freudenheim, Nina
Friedman, Marvin Ross
Frumkin, Allan
Fuller, Diana
Fuller, Jeffrey P
Geraci, Lucian Arthur
Gerst, Hilde W
Getler, Helen
Gillette, W Dean
Gillman, Barbara Seitlin
Gladstone, Barbara Regen
Glass, Wendy D
Glezer, Nechemia
Glick, Paula Florence
Glimcher, Arnold B
Gobuzas, Aldona M
Goldberg, Judith
Goldeen, Dorothy A
Goldfield, Edward L
Goldschmidt, Lucien
Goodman, James Neil
Goodman, Marian
Gordon, Albert F
Gordon, Martin
Gorman, R C
Gorney, Jay Philip
Goulds, Peter J
Graham, Robert C, Jr
Graham, Robert Claverhouse
Graham, William Andrew
Gray, Richard
Grayson, Cassandra
Greenberg, Ronald K
Greene, Lois D
Greenspun, Regina Ruth
Gross, Estelle Shane
Grossman, Maurizia M
Gruskin, Mary Josephine
Guadagnoli, Nello T
Gurewitsch, Edna P
Guthrie, Perri Pizer
Haber, William
Hahn, Maurice & Roslyn
Hahn, Stephen
Hames, Carl Martin
Hamilton, Patricia Rose
Hammer, Armand
Hammer, Victor J
Harcus, Portia Gwen
Hardin, Shirley G
Harmon, Foster
Haslem, Jane N
Hauser, Reine I
Haversat, Lillian Kerr
Hayes, Laura M
Heath, David C
Heiferman, Marvin
Heit, Steven Robert
Helander, Bruce Paul
Heller, Ben
Henderson, Lester Kierstead
Hill, Ed
Hill, James Berry
Hill, Megan Lloyd
Hills, Leo Himmelfarb
Hines, Richard G
Hobbs, Gerald S
Hoffman, Nancy
Hooks, Charles Vernon
Hooks, Geri
Horowitz, Benjamin
Hughes, Paul Lucien
Huldermann, Paul F
Hunter, Meridith
Hutchinson, Max
Hutton, Leonard
Hyman, Linda
Iannetti, Pasquale Francesco
  Paolo
Ingber, Barbara
Ingraham, John Douglas
Insel, Paula
Isaacs, Avrom
Janis, Conrad
Janis, Sidney
Johnson, Marian Willard

Johnson, Miani (Marianne)
  Guthrie
Johnson, Robert Jay
Johnston, Helen Head
Jones, Doug (Douglas McKee)
Joukhadar, Kristina
Joukhadar, Moumtaz
Kahan, Alexander
Kahan, Leonard
Kahlenberg, Mary Hunt
Kahn, Ralph H
Kaller, Robert Jameson
Kallir, Jane Katherine
Kanegis, Sidney S
Kaplan, Jacques
Kaplan, Leonard
Karniol, Eugene
Katzen, Hal Zachery
Kauffman, Richard Joel
Kelley, Chapman
Ketcham, Ray Winfred, Jr
Killeen, Melissa Helen
Kimmel-Cohn, Roberta
Kind, Phyllis
King, Myron Lyzon
Klein, Gwenda J
Klein, Paul R
Knowlton, Monique
Koch, William Emery
Kolbert, Frank L
Kolodner, Nathan K
Komor, Mathias
Kornblatt, Barbara Rodbell
Kornblau, Gerald
Kornetchuk, Elena
Kortenhaus, Lynne M
Kottler, Lynn
Kraeft, June K & Norman
Krakow, Barbara L
Kramer, Gertrude M
Kraushaar, Antoinette M
Krienke, Douglas Elliot
Kuhlenschmidt, Richard
  Edward
Lally, James Joseph
Lamanna, Carmen
Landau, Mitzi
Landry, Albert
Lane, H Palmer
Langman, Richard Theodore
La Pelle, Rodger
Larcada, Richard Kenneth
Layton, Richard
Lee, Caroline D
Lee, Janie C
Lee, Nelda S
Lefcourt, Irwin
Lefebre, John
Lehr, Janet
Leitman, Norman
Lemer, Ellen Terry
Levin, Hugh Lauter
Levy, Bernard
Levy, S(tephen) Dean
Lewin, Bernard
Lewis, Don S, Sr
Lewis, Donald Sykes, Jr
Lewison, Florence (Mrs
  Maurice Glickman)
Lienau, Daniel Clifford
Lindgren, Bjorn Frank
Littrell, Doris Marie
London, Elca
Long, Meredith J
Lord, Michael Harry
Love, Richard Henry
Lowinsky, Simon L
Ludman, Joan Hurwitz
Lumbard, Jean Ashmore
Lunn, Harry, Jr
Luntz, Irving
Luria, Gloria
Lust, Virginia
Lutze, (Hildegarde)
Mabry, Jane
McCready, Karen
McFarren, Grace

McHugh, Adeliza Sorenson
McIlroy, Carol J
MacKay, Hugh
McKinney, Donald
MacLagger, Richard Joseph
McMahon, James Edward
Makler, Hope Welsh
Mangel, Benjamin
Marberger, A Aladar
Marchisotto, Linda A
Marcus, Angelo P
Marino, Frank
Markel, Kathryn E
Markle, Jack M
Markle, Sam
Marks, Royal S
Maroney, James H, Jr
Martin, Larry Kenneth
Mathis, Emile Henry, II
Matisse, Pierre
May, Daniel Striger
Mayo, Robert Bowers
Meek, J William, III
Meisel, Louis Koenig
Mekler, Adam
Merrin, Edward H
Meyer, Thomas Vincent
Michaux, Ronald Robert
Milant, Jean Robert
Miller, David
Miller, Laurence Glenn
Miller, Robert Peter
Milliken, Alexander Fabbri
Missal, Joshua M & Pegge
Mitchell, Donald
Mongerson, Susan C
Monk, Robert Evan, Jr
Moody, Elizabeth Chambers
Moos, Walter A
Morgan, Myra Jean
Morris, Donald Fischer
Morris, Florence Marie
Morse, Mitchell Ian
Moses, Bette J
Muller, Jerome Kenneth
Muniot, Barbara King
Naiman, Lee
Nash, Veronica F
Natzmer, Cheryl Lynn
Needlman, Joel G
Needlman, Phyllis L
Neikrug, Marjorie
Neslage, Oliver John, Jr
Newhouse, Clyde Mortimer
Newman, Louis
Nielsen, Nina I M
Norquist, Ryl
Oehlschlaeger, Frank J
Olenick, David Charles
Olsen, Sharon A
Oscarsson, Victoria Constance
  Gunhild
O'Toole, James St Laurence
Owens, Tennys Bowers
Palley, Reese
Palmer, Herbert Bearl
Palmer, Michael Andrew
Parizek, Jaro
Patch, Peggie (Margaret
  Thompson Williamson)
Pearl, Marilyn
Pence, John Gerald
Perls, Klaus G
Perry, Richard C
Persky, Robert S
Pesner, Carole Manishin
Pfeifer, Marcuse
Phillips, Bonnie
Phillips, Dutch (James O, Jr)
Pierce, Patricia Jobe
Pink, Marilyn Overman
Poindexter, Elinor Fuller
Portnoy, Theodora Preiss
Posner, Judith L
Prakapas, Eugene Joseph
Price, Vincent
Prohaska, Elena Anastasia

ART DEALER (cont)

Pucker, Bernard H
Raydon, Alexander R
Reed, Harold
Reed, Walt Arnold
Rentschler, Sarah Yorke
Rice, M Robert & Barbara Menen
Richards, Tally
Rich-Perlow, Katharina
Riggs, Mary Kathryn
Risser, James K
Robinson, Marie Rachelle
Robinson, Thomas V
Rollins, Jo Lutz
Rolly, Ronald Joseph
Rose, Peter Henry
Rosenberg, Alex Jacob
Rosenfeld, Samuel L
Rosenwald, Carol
Rothschild, Carolyn Anita
Rothschild, John D
Rubin, Lawrence
Russell, John Laurel
Rustvold, Katherine Jo
Sabo, Betty Jean
Sachs, A M
Sadik, Marvin Sherwood
Saidenberg, Daniel
Saidenberg, Eleanore B
St Clair, Michael
Samuels, Harold & Peggy
Sanchez, Mary Lowe (Eliza)
Sande, Rhoda
Sanderson, Warren
Saphire, Lawrence M
Sawyer, William
Schab, Margo Pollins
Schaeffer, Kate
Schaeffer, Martha Jane
Schaffner, Ruth S
Schellstede, Richard Lee
Schlosberg, Carl Martin
Schneider, Lisa Dawn
Schneiderman, Dorothy
Schneier, Donna Frances
Schnitzer, Arlene
Schoelkopf, Robert J, Jr
Schuster, Eugene Ivan
Schutz, Prescott Dietrich
Schwarz, Kurt L
Schweitzer, M R
Seders, Francine Lavinal
Segal, Tama & David
Segy, Ladislas
Selser, Christopher
Serger, Helen
Serisawa, Ikuo
Seth, Laurel
Shadrach, Jean H
Shalit, Mitzi (Mildred M)
Shapiro, Adrian Michael
Shechtman, George Henoch
Shepard, Lewis Albert
Shlien, Helen S
Shorney, Margo Kay (McIver)
Siden, Franklin
Silverberg, Ellen Ruth
Simpson, Merton D
Singer, Nancy Barkhouse
Smart, Wini
Smith, Albert E
Smither, Edward Murray
Sneed, Patricia M
Solomon, Gerald
Solomon, Holly
Solway, Carl E
Sonnabend, Joan
Spark, Victor David
Staempfli, George W
Stanley, Charles Edward
Steckler, Stuart Jay
Stein, Fritz Henry
Steinbaum, Bernice
Stern, Jean
Stern, Louis
Stewart, Jeffrey

Stewart, John (John Stewart Houston)
Stiebel, Eric
Stiebel, Gerald Gustave
Stoller, John Chapman
Stone, Jeremy
Stone, M Lee
Strong, Beverly Jean
Struve, William Walter
Stuart, David
Sujo, Clara Diament
Sussman, Bonnie K
Suzuki, Katsko (Katsko Suzuki Kannegieter)
Szoke, John
Tahir, Abe M, Jr
Tasende, Jose Maria
Tate, Gayle Blair
Tatistcheff, Peter Alexis
Thaw, Eugene Victor
Theofiles, George
Thompson, Richard E, Jr
Toll, Barbara Elizabeth
Troncale, Frank Thomas
Tunick, David
Turnbull, Betty
Turner, Janice Kay
Valentin, Jean-Pierre
Verzyl, June Carol
Verzyl, Kenneth H
Vogel, Donald S
Volid, Ruth
Vose, Robert Churchill, Jr
Waaland, James Brearley, II
Wade, Jane
Walker, Berta
Walsh, J(ohn) Michael
Waltzer, Stewart Paul
Washburn, Joan T
Watkins, Ragland Tolk
Watson, Clarissa H
Weber, John
Weissman, Julian Paul
Weitzenhoffer, A Max
Wenger, Muriel
Wenger, Sigmund
Westlund, Harry E
Westwater, Angela King
White, Albert
White, Deborah
White, Ruth
Whitney, Susan Gillian
Whyte, Bruce Lincoln
Wiebe, Charles M
Wilkinson, Kirk Cook
Williamson, Jason H
Wilson, John David
Wirtz, Stephen Carl
Wolff, Robert W, Jr
Wolff, William H
Woodside, Gordon William
Wunderlich, Rudolf G
Young, Edna E
Zabriskie, Virginia M
Zantman, J B
Zeitlin, Jacob Israel

ASSEMBLAGE ARTIST

Arman
Aubin, Barbara
Bakke, Karen Lee
Barnhart, C Raymond
Baron, Hannelore
Bell, Lilian A
Boghosian, Varujan
Bott, H J

Brecht, George
Bry, Edith
Cho, David
Crimmins, Jerry (Gerald Garfield)
Dienes, Sari
Fisher, Carole Gorney
Foolery, Tom
Francis, Jean Thickens
Getz, Ilse
Gilchriest, Lorenzo
Goell, Abby Jane
Hamady, Walter Samuel
Hillsmith, Fannie
Hollen-Bolmgren, Donna
Houston, Bruce
Howe, Nelson S
Josephson, Kenneth Bradley
Kane, Bill (William David)
Kaplan, Leo
Katz, Leandro
Korman, Barbara
Kosta, Angela
Kostiuk, Michael Marion, Jr
Lewis, Golda
McCabe, Maureen M
Majdrakoff, Ivan
Micheli, Julio
Mollett, Michael M
Moore, Marjorie
Nicholson, Natasha
Nowack, Wayne Kenyon
O'Banion, Nance
Pruitt, Lynn
Rennick, Dan
Rigg, Margaret Ruth
Rivoli, Mario
Saar, Betye
Schwartz, Bella
Seaberg, Steve (Stevens)
Spiegelman, Lon Howard
Stone, Gwen
Tawney, Lenore
Thompson, Tamara
Uchima, Toshiko
Van Brunt, Philip G
Wagner, Gordon Parsons
White, Stuart James

BOOK DEALER

Bergling, Virginia Catherine (Mrs Stephen J Kozazcki)
Cohen, Arthur A
Colescott, Robert H
Davis, L Clarice
Goldschmidt, Lucien
Gordon, Martin
Isserstedt, Dorothea Carus
Johnston, Helen Head
Lehr, Janet
McGilvery, Laurence
Rosenberg, Bernard
Rosenfeld, Richard Joel
Tunick, David

CALLIGRAPHER

Anderson, Donald Myers
Bakke, Karen Lee
Bell, Kathryn Leise
Block, Joyce
Bostick, William Allison
Callicott, Burton Harry
Cataldo, John William
Chow Leung Chen-Ying
Ebsen, Alf K
Gregory, (Eleanor) Anne
Gregory, Eleanor Anne
Grushkin, Philip
Kanidinc, Salahattin
Martin, Loretta Marsh
Morrison, Robert Clifton
Mueller, M Gerardine

Nesbitt, Alexander John
Peter, Friedrich Gunther
Ramirez, Joel Tito
Rigg, Margaret Ruth
Shaw, Paul Jefferson
Tasgal-Kliegman, G
Tasse, M Jeanne
Terris, Albert
Wong, Frederick
Wu, I-Chen
Wynne, Albert Givens

CARTOONIST

Addams, Charles Samuel
Alexander, Kenneth Lewis
Anderson, Brad J
Angelo, Emidio
Armstrong, Roger Joseph
Auth, Tony (William Anthony), Jr
Barbera, Joe
Basset, Gene
Bates, Bill
Bimrose, Arthur Sylvanus, Jr
Bissell, Charles Overman
Bissell, Phil
Brennan, Francis Edwin
Bushmiller, Ernie Paul
Busino, Orlando Francis
Caniff, Milton Arthur
Cantone, Vic
Cavalli, Dick
Combes, Willard Wetmore
Conrad, Paul Francis
Crane, James
Crockett, Gib (Gibson M)
d'Alessio, Gregory
Darrow, Whitney, Jr
Davis, James Robert
Day, Chon
Day, Robert James
Dedini, Eldon Lawrence
Dennis, Charles Houston
Eaton, Thomas Newton
Engelhardt, Thomas Alexander
Farris, Joseph
Feiffer, Jules
Flannery, Thomas
Gallo, William Victor
Goodwin, Louis Payne
Graham, Bill (William Karr)
Graysmith, Robert
Hart, John Lewis
Haynie, Hugh
Hill, Draper
Hogarth, Burne
Hoppes, Lowell E
Hubenthal, Karl Samuel
Hunter, Graham
Ivey, James Burnett
Kato, Kay
Kaz (Lawrence Katzman)
Keane, Bil
Ketcham, Hank (Henry King)
Key, Ted
Kilgore, Al
Koren, Edward B
Kotzky, Alex Sylvester
Kuekes, Edward D
Lariar, Lawrence
Levine, David
Lichty, George M
Long, Scott
Lynde, Stan
MacNelly, Jeffrey Kenneth
Manning, Reg (Reginald West)
Martin, Charles E
Martin, Loretta Marsh
Mauldin, Bill
Messick, Dale
Morin, James Corcoran
Mosley, Zack T
Neher, Fred
Newman, Ralph Albert

CARTOONIST (cont)

Norris, Leonard Matheson
Nowak, Leo
Nutzle, Futzie (Bruce John Kleinsmith)
Oliphant, Patrick
Partch, Virgil Franklin, II
Pascal, David
Phillips, Irving W
Pierotti, John
Poinier, Arthur Best
Pretsch, John Edward
Price, George
Riley, Art (Arthur Irwin)
Robbins, Trina
Rosen, Hy (Hyman Joseph)
Salmon, Raymond Merle
Sandeson, William Seymour
Saxon, Charles David
Schulz, Charles Monroe
Sharp, Harold
Shoemaker, Vaughn
Siegel, (Leo) Dink
Smith, Albert
Stark, Bruce Gunsten
Steig, William
Steinberg, Saul
Stevens, William Ansel, Sr
Temes, Mortimer (Robert)
Terry, Hilda
Thorndike, (Chuck) Charles Jesse
Townsend, Marvin J
Trudeau, Garry B
Valtman, Edmund
Van Buren, Raeburn
Walker, Mort
Warren, L D
Werner, (Charles George)
Wheeler, Mark
Wood, James Arthur (Art)
Zib, Tom (Thomas A Zibelli)

CERAMIST

Abraham, Carol Jeanne
Alling, Clarence (Edgar)
Andreson, Laura F
Autio, (A) Rudy
Baney, Vera
Blai, Bertha
Blanco, Sylvia
Bohnert, Thom (Thomas Robert)
Bova, Joe
Breckenridge, Bruce M
Brodie, Regis Conrad
Brooks, Louise Cherry
Broudo, Joseph David
Brown, Catharine Homan
Calhoun, Larry Darryl
Cantrell, Jim
Caswell, Jim (James Daniel Caswell-Davis)
Chabot, Aurore (Martha)
Chalke, John
Chamberlain, Charles
Chappelle, Jerry Leon
Clipsham, Jacqueline Ann
Cohen, Michael S
Conesa, Miguel A
Conover, Claude
Conrad, John W
Cornell, David E
Costanza, John Joseph
Daley, William P
Davis, John Sherwood
Dillingham, Rick (James Richard), II
Duckworth, Ruth
Edwards-Tucker, Yvonne (Leatrice Yvonne Tucker)
Elkins, (E) Lane
Elliot, Cathy J
Englander, Gertrud

Evans, Dick
Fager, Charles J
Fleckenstein, Opal R
Frank, David
Funk, Verne J
Gernhardt, Henry Kendall
Gronborg, Erik
Groot, Candice Beth
Grygutis, Barbara
Halpern, Lea
Hardy, Robert
Hay, Dick
Higgins, Edward Koelling
Higgins, Mary Lou
Hindes, Chuck (Charles Austin)
Holt, Martha A
Hughto, Margie A
Ikeda, Yoshiro
Jameson, Philip Alexander
Kahn, Annelies Ruth
Karnes, Karen
Kemenyffy, Steven
Kemenyffy, Susan B Hale
Kendall, Thomas Lyle
Kleinsmith, Gene (Eugene Dennis)
Kristensen, Gail Marie
Kujundzic, Zeljko D
Lang, Rodger Alan
Larsen, D Dane
Larson, Jane (Warren)
Lawrence, Les
Lebeck, Carol E
Leber, Roberta (Roberta Leber McVeigh)
Leibert, Peter R
Levine, Marilyn Anne
Lincoln, Richard Mather
Lopez, Michael John
MacDougall, Peter Steven
McIntosh, Harrison Edward
Macklin, Anderson D
McVey, Leza
McWhinnie, Harold James
Manhart, Thomas Arthur
Marak, Louis Bernard
Marazzi, William C P
Marks, Roberta Barbara
Marsh, (Edwin) Thomas
Martz, Karl
Mason, John
Massaro, Karen Thuesen
Medicine Flower, Grace
Meyer, Charles Edward
Meyers, Ronald G
Mignosa, Santo
Miley, Les
Natzler, Otto
Nicholas, Donna Lee
Nigrosh, Leon Isaac
Notkin, Richard T
Olsen, Frederick L
Orensanz, Angel L
Pardington, Ralph Arthur
Patrick, Alan K
Perkins, A Alan
Peterson, Susan Harnly
Pillin, Polia
Pilsk, Adele Inez
Popinsky, Arnold Dave
Prange, Sally Bowen
Rady, Elsa
Redd Ekks (Robert Norman Rasmussen)
Rippon, Ruth Margaret
Sage, Bill B
Sanders, Herbert Harvey
Schaumburg, Donald Roland
Schneider, Richard Durbin
Selvin, Nancy
Shaner, (George) David
Shire, Peter
Smith, Nan S(helley)
Soldner, Paul Edmund
Sperry, Robert
Staffel, Rudolf Harry

Stephenson, Susanne G
Stevens, Jacquie (Jaqueline Lauren)
Stewart, Bill
Strassberg, Roy I
Sundin, Adelaide Toombs
Taylor, Rosemary
Tucker, Curtis (Dee)
Turner, Robert Chapman
Vaccaro, Luella Grace
Vermes, Madelaine
Walters, Billie
Warashina, M Patricia
Ward, Phillip A
Westervelt, Robert F
White, Amos, IV
Wilhelmi, William Merle
Winokur, Paula Colton
Winokur, Robert Mark
Wood, Beatrice
Yiannes (Iordanides)

COLLAGE ARTIST

Ahlstrom, Ronald Gustin
Allen, Kaola B
Anderson, Howard Benjamin
Bardazzi, Peter
Barkus, Mariona Marcia
Baron, Hannelore
Bearman, Jane Ruth
Beauchamp, George
Beerman, Miraim K (Miriam Beerman-Jaffe)
Benes, Barton Lidice
Boutis, Tom
Bry, Edith
Butchkes, Sydney
Byars, Donna
Cade, Walter, III
Churchill, Diane
Cole, Stephanie Kirschen
Colorado, Charlotte
Cooke, Judy
Crable, James Harbour
D'Amato, Janet Potter
Davis, Walter Lewis
Dubin, Ralph
Eisner, Dorothy (Dorothy Eisner McDonald)
Eller, Evelyn (Evelyn Eller Rosenbaum)
Evans, John
Ferriter, Clare
Fraze, Denny T
Freilich, Ann
Getz, Ilse
Gilchriest, Lorenzo
Gluhman, Margaret A
Gundelfinger, John Andre
Harris, William Wadsworth, II
Helioff, Anne Graile (Mrs Benjamin Hirschberg)
Hermann, M(ildred) L
Hertzberg, Rose
Hillsmith, Fannie
Hoff, Margo
Hoie, Helen Hunt
Ingram, Judith
Jess
Johnston, June Frazier
Kaplan, Leo
Kassman, Shirley
Kikuchi-Yngojo, Alan
Kjargaard, John Ingvard
Laymon, Cynthia J
Lederman, Stephanie Brody
Lerner, Sandra
McCabe, Maureen M
Manilla, Tess
Mansaram, P(anchal)
Marca-Relli, Conrad
Martin, Stefan
Miller, Dolly (Ethel B)
Montoya, Gustavo (Gustavo Montoya Carranco)

Moskowitz, Shirley (Mrs Jacob W Gruber)
Moulton, Rosalind Kimball
Ozonoff, Ida
Pappas, Marilyn
Reich, Nathaniel E
Rizzie, Dan
Rosenthal, Gloria M
Ross, B(eatrice) Brook
Rothenberg, Barbara
Rothschild, Judith
Ryder, Mahler Bessinger
Saar, Betye
Schapiro, Miriam
Schiff, Lonny
Scholder, Laurence
Secunda, (Holland) Arthur
Shaddle, Alice
Simmons, Julie Lutz
Simon, Herbert Bernheimer
Smith, Leon Polk
Spero, Nancy
Squadra, John
Stan, Cynthia (Cynthia Stan Mellow)
Starkweather-Nelson, Cynthia Louise
Steckel, Anita
Stevens, Marjorie
Stinsmuehlen, Susan Dodds
Stipe, William S
Storer, Inez Mary
Sweet, Steve (Steven Mark)
Talbot, Jonathan
Tanner, Joan Elizabeth
Tavenner, Patricia (Pat)
Thompson, Tamara
Umlauf, Lynn (Charlotte)
Voelker, Elizabeth
Whitson
Williams, Marylou Lord Study
Willoughby, Jane Baker
Zimmerman, Kathleen Marie
Zver, James M

COLLECTOR

Adams, James Frederick
Adrian, Barbara (Mrs Franklin Tramutola)
Agoos, Herbert M
Akston, James
Aldrich, Larry
Alexander, Judith
Alonzo, Jack J
Alsdorf, James W
Altmayer, Jay P
Altschul, Arthur G
Amsden, Floyd T
Anbinder, Paul
Anderson, David K
Anderson, Margaret Pomeroy
Anspach, Ernst
Artinian, Artine
Atlas, Martin & Liane W
Ault, Lee Addison
Baker, Richard Brown
Bareiss, Philip C
Bareiss, Walter
Barnett, David J
Barrell, Bill
Bell, R Murray
Benenson, Edward Hartley
Bergen, D Thomas
Berkman, Lillian
Berman, Bernard
Berman, Muriel Mallin
Berman, Philip I
Bermant, David W
Bernstein, Benjamin D
Bernstein, Edward I
Bickford, George Percival
Biddle, James
Billmyer, John Edward

COLLECTOR (cont)

Spiegel, Sam
Spoerer, Dale Raymond
Stamats, Peter Owen
Steckler, Stuart Jay
Stern, (Mr & Mrs) Arthur
   Lewis
Stern, H Peter
Stevenson, Ruth Carter
Stillman, E Clark
Stoll, (Mrs) Berry Vincent
Strong, Beverly Jean
Swartz, Phillip Scott
Tauch, Waldine Amanda
Tenzer, (Dr & Mrs)
   Jonathan A
Terra, Daniel J
Thaw, Eugene Victor
Thiry, Paul (Albert)
Thompson, Lockwood
Thompson, Richard E, Jr
Topol, Robert Martin
Troncale, Frank Thomas
Tucker, Glenn F
Ullman, (Mrs) George W
Valenstein, Alice
Vanasse, Louis Raymond
Van Leer, W Leicester
Vershbow, (Mr & Mrs) Arthur
Verzyl, June Carol
Vogel, (Mr & Mrs) Herbert
Wachs, Ethel
Waddell, Eugene
Walmsley, William Aubrey
Walter, May E
Walter, Paul F
Walton, Harry A, Jr
Weisman, Marcia Simon
Welch, (Mr & Mrs) Robert G
Wenger, Muriel
White, Albert
White, Philip Butler
Williams, Dave Harrell
Willis, Elizabeth Bayley
Wiltshire, William Ernest, III
Winokur, James L
Wintersteen, Bernice
   McIlhenny
Wise, Geneva H (Holcomb)
Wong, Roger Frederickson
Woodside, Gordon William
Wright, (Mr & Mrs) William H
Wurdemann, Helen (Baroness
   Elena Guzzardi)
Young, Edna E
Zeisler, Claire (Block)
Zeisler, Richard Spiro
Zeitlin, Jacob Israel
Ziff, Jerrold
Zlotnick, Diana Shirley

CONCEPTUAL ARTIST

Alexander, Judy
Allen, Roberta
Antin, Eleanor
Apple, Jacki (Jacqueline B)
Applebroog, Ida
Askevold, David
Baldessari, John Anthony
Banana, Anna Lee
Barry, Robert Thomas
Beckley, Bill
Bloomfield, Lisa Diane
Bob & Bob
Bochner, Mel
Bollinger, William
Boyd, Donald Edgar
Brecht, George
Bronson, A A (Michael Wayne
   Tims)
Brown, Robert Delford
Burden, Chris
Burnett, Barbara Ann

Burton, Scott
Celender, Donald Dennis
Charlesworth, Sarah E
Crane, Michael Patrick
Cumming, Robert H
Curmano, Billy
Cutforth, Roger
Cutler-Shaw, Joyce
Darboven, Hanne
Davidovich, Jaime
De Monte, Claudia
Douaihy, Saliba
Dupuy, Jean
Edelson, Mary Beth
Enstice, Wayne
Fenton, Julia Ann
Fontana, Bill Patrick
Fulton, Fred Franklin
Galas, Philip-Dimitri
Goldstein, Jack
Graham, Daniel H
Grant, Art
Grasso, Salvatore Fortunato
Greenly, Colin
Greenstein, Ilise
Haacke, Hans Christoph
Harrison, Helen Mayer
Harrison, Newton A
Holzer, Jenny
Hompson, Davi Det (David
   Elbridge Thompson)
Huebler, Douglas
Hutchinson, Peter Arthur
Jean-Louis, Don (Donald
   Charles)
Jonas, Joan
Kerr, James Wilfrid
Knight, John
Kosuth, Joseph
Krims, Leslie Robert
Kruger, Barbara
Lacy, Suzanne
Laxson, Ruth
Lindner, Ernest
Lloyd, Gary Marchal
Miller, George
Minsky, Richard
Molella, Patricia Ann
Monnier, Jacqueline Matisse
Montano, Linda (Mary)
Murch, Anna Valentina
Murphy, Susan (Susan Murphy
   Colombini)
Murray, Ian Stewart
Nemec, Vernita Ellen
Odate, Toshio
Okulick, John A
Ono, Yoko
Patrick, Charles William
Pennuto, James William
Pettibone, Richard H
Pomeroy, James Calwell, Jr
Rapoport, Sonya
Reichek, Elaine
Resnick, Marcia Aylene
Robinson, Chris (Christopher
   Thomas)
Romeu, Joost A
Romoser, Ruth Amelia
Sapien, Darryl Rudolph
Schley, Evander Duer (Van)
Schmuckal, Janet Bell (Cynthia
   Signature)
Seaberg, Steve (Stevens)
Sheridan, Sonia Landy
Smith, Alexis (Patricia Anne)
Soffer, Sasson
Spector, Buzz (Franklin Mac
   Spector)
Strasen, Barbara Elaine
Van Riper, Peter
Venet, Bernar P
Wasserman, Cary (Robert)
Watts, Robert M
Weiss, Rachel
White, John M
Wilson, Martha Storey

Yoder, Richard Allen

CONSERVATOR
see also Restorer

Alden, Gary Wade
Amarotico, Joseph Anthony
Beale, Arthur C
Beardsley, Barbara H
Berger, Gustav A
Bittleman, Dolores Dembus
Bodo, Sandor
Butler, Marigene H
Cady, Dennis Vern
Chapian, Grieg Hovsep
Chase, W(illiam) Thomas
Chieffo, Clifford Toby
Cianfoni, Emilio
Cohn, Marjorie B
Covey, Victor Charles B
Crenshaw, Karen Bruce
Elliott, Dorothy Baden
Etchison, Bruce
Feller, Robert L
Fisher, Sarah Lisbeth
Greaves, James L
Haley, Patience E (Patience E
   Haley Ghikas)
Honig, Mervin
Horton, Carolyn
Hulmer, Eric Claus
Huston, Perry Clark
Isaak, Nicholas, Jr
Jakstas, Alfred John
Jolles, Arnold H
Keck, Sheldon Waugh
Knowlton, Daniel Gibson
Kohlhepp, Norman
Konrad, Tony (Anton Joseph)
Kortheuer, Dayrell
Larson, Sidney
Lennon, Timothy
Marshall, James Duard
Merrill, Ross M
Mintz, Baron (Ronald Earl)
Mohr, Pauline Catherine
Pennuto, James William
Pomerantz, Louis
Radecki, Martin John
Rasto (Rastislav Hlavina)
Schiff, Lonny
Slawinski, Joseph
Stolow, Nathan
Stoner, Joyce Hill
Weidner, Marilyn Kemp
West, Clara Faye Johnson
Wiesendanger, Margaret Harris
Wiesendanger, Martin
   Wolfgang

CONSULTANT

Anderson, Margaret Pomeroy
Arkus, Leon A
Barton, Phyllis Settecase
Barzun, Jacques
Bealmer, William
Beggs, Thomas Montague
Bell, Donald Allen
Benedikt, Michael
Bingham, Alice
Bowes, Betty Miller
Braseth, John E
Breeskin, Adelyn Dohme
Brookins, Jacob Boden
Brown, Alan M, Jr
Byrne, Charles Joseph
Carter, David Giles
Clark, Nancy Kissel
Collier, Alberta
D'Andrea, Jeanne
Dank, Leonard Dewey
De Foix-Crenascol, Louis
Del Valle, Joseph Bourke

Dockstader, Frederick J
Dreaper, Richard Edward
Edvi Illes, Emma
Elliott, B Charles, Jr
Folds, Thomas McKey
Fowler, Frank Eison
Gagnon, Charles Eugene
Gatling, Eva Ingersoll
Gee, Helen
Gerdts, Abigail Booth
Gilchrist, Elizabeth Brenda
Gilmartin, F Thomas
Gilmore, Roger
Glezer, Nechemia
Goldeen, Dorothy A
Goodman, Calvin Jerome
Gray, Thomas Alexander
Green, Eleanor Broome
Gurney, George
Harcus, Portia Gwen
Haseltine, Maury (Margaret
   Wilson)
Hatch, John Davis
Heller, Goldie (Mrs Edward W
   Greenberg)
Hiller, Betty R
Hinkhouse, Forest Melick
Hoffberg, Judith A
Houle, Robert James
Hoving, Thomas
Hughes, Paul Lucien
Ishikawa, Joseph
James, Catti
Jarvis, Lucy
Kaep, Louis Joseph
Kahlenberg, Mary Hunt
Kasle, Gertrude
Katzenberg, Dena S
Kaufman, Nancy
Kornblau, Gerald
Kortenhaus, Lynne M
Kuh, Katharine
Larsen, Erik
Lorber, D Martin H B
Luria, Gloria
Lutze, (Hildegarde)
McLanathan, Richard B K
McVeigh, Miriam Temperance
Marchese, Patricia Davis
Meek, J William, III
Miller, Dorothy Canning
Millie, Elena Gonzalez
Mitchell, Eleanor
Naiman, Lee
Nash, Alice Louise
Nasher, Patsy R
Orling, Anne
Osborn, Elodie C
Oscarsson, Victoria Constance
   Gunhild
Owsley, David Thomas
Paris, Jeanne C
Paris, Kay
Perret, George Albert
Pisano, Ronald George
Pratt, Vernon Gaither
Prohaska, Elena Anastasia
Ranalli, Daniel
Reeve, James Key
Remsen, John Everett, II
Rosenzweig, Daphne Lange
Rouse, John R
Rubin, Ida Ely
Sacks, Beverly & Ray
Sawyer, Alan R
Schaffner, Ruth S
Schoener, Allon
Schuster, Cita Fletcher (Sarah
   E)
Shalit, Mitzi (Mildred M)
Sharp, Willoughby
Sherbell, Rhoda
Smart, Mary-Leigh
Smither, Edward Murray
Solomon, Ruth B
Sprague, Paul Edward
Stern, Louis

CONSULTANT (cont)

Stolow, Nathan
Taylor, John Lloyd
Thomas, Tamara B
Truex, Duane Philip
Volid, Ruth
Wade, Jane
Wehr, Wesley Conrad
Weinberg, H Barbara
Wenger, Sigmund
White, Ruth
Williams, Marylou Lord Study
Wingate, Robert Bray
Witmeyer, Stanley Herbert
Wittmann, Otto
Wolfe, Maurice Raymond
Woods, Willis Franklin
Wright, Nina Kaiden

CRAFTSMAN

Alford, Gloria K
Baitsell, Wilma Williamson
Bakken, Haakon
Bates, Kenneth Francis
Beaudoin, Andre Eugene
Blai, Bertha
Boylen, Michael Edward
Cadle, Ray Kenneth
Crozier, William K, Jr
Dellis, Arlene B
Dice, Elizabeth Jane
Drumm, Don
Espenet
Ferber, Lee Allan
Fessler, Ann Helene
Fields, Fredrica H
Fischer, Mildred (Gertrude)
Fludd, Reginald Joseph
Glorig, Ostor
Gough, Georgia Belle
Griner, Ned H
Grossman, Maurice Kenneth
Hallman, H Theodore, Jr
Hartford, Jane Davis
Heaton, Maurice
Helzer, Richard Brian
Ipsen, Kent Forrest
Jaeger, Brenda Kay
Jerry, Michael John
Johnson, Donald Marvin
Johnson, Ivan Earl
Johnston, Robert Harold
Julio, Pat T
Kahn, Annelies Ruth
Karnes, Karen
Keyser, William Alphonse, Jr
Kuemmerlein, Janet
Kulicke, Robert M
Lacktman, Michael
La Fon, Julia Anna
Lawless, Billie (William B)
Lawrence, Jaye A
Lewis, Golda
Lisker, Sara
Lovato, Charles Fredric
McClendon, Maxine (Maxine McClendon Nichols)
Madsen, Viggo Holm
Mari (M Eagerton)
Markusen, Thomas Roy
Marshall, John Carl
Medicine Flower, Grace
Mintich, Mary Ringelberg
Mondale, Joan Adams
Murphy, Gladys Wilkins
Neugebauer, Margot
Olsen, Frederick L
Pardon, Earl B
Paulin, Richard Calkins
Penny, Donald Charles
Pijanowski, Eugene M
Pizzat, Joseph
Ray, Christopher T
Sahlstrand, Margaret Ahrens

Saville, Ken
Schellin, Robert William
Schwarcz, June Theresa
Seyler, David W
Shaner, (George) David
Stamsta, Jean
Stuart, Donald Alexander
Takemoto, Henry Tadaaki
Tanner, James L
Terry, Duncan Niles
Trosky, Helene Roth
Vermes, Madelaine
Walker, Mary Carolyn
Warhol, Andy
Whitaker, Irwin A
Wilhelmi, William Merle
Winokur, Paula Colton
Woods, Ted
Yarborough, Christine Troutman

CRITIC

Abrams, Ruth (Davidson)
Ahlander, Leslie Judd
Albertazzi, Mario
Albin, Edgar A
Albright, Thomas
Allara, Pamela Edwards
Alloway, Lawrence
Anderson, Alexandra C
Antin, David A
Anzures, Rafael
Ashbery, John Lawrence
Ashton, Dore
Auer, James Matthew
Baker, Elizabeth C
Ballatore-Nelson, Sandra Lee
Barzun, Jacques
Basquin, Kit (Mary Smyth)
Beatty, Frances Fielding Lewis
Beck, James
Benedikt, Michael
Benson, Elaine K G
Benson, Gertrude Ackerman
Berger, Maurice
Blake, Peter Jost
Blinderman, Barry Robert
Bourdon, David
Bowman, Ruth
Brown, Betty Ann
Bruner, Louise Katherine (Mrs Paul Orr)
Burnham, Jack Wesley
Caldwell, John
Canaday, John Edwin
Cassyd, Syd
Cavaliere, Barbara
Cernuschi, Alberto C
Chambers, Karen
Clarke, John R
Cleary, Fritz
Clermont, Ghislain
Clothier, Peter Dean
Clurman, Irene
Cohen, Ronny H
Colby, Joy Hakanson
Coleman, A(llan) D(ouglass)
Collier, Alberta
Corbino, Marcia Norcross
Cotter, Holland
Crary, Jonathan Knight
Crimp, Douglas
Crowell, David Lee
Danieli, Fidel Angelo
Danikian, Caron Le Brun
Danoff, I Michael
Davidson, Marshall Bowman
Davis, Douglas Matthew
Day, Holliday T
deAK, Edit
De Moura Sobral, Luis
Donohoe, Victoria
Downes, Rackstraw

Driscoll, Edgar Joseph, Jr
Drohojowska, Hunter
Dunbar, Jill H
Dyer, Carolyn Price
Euaclaire, Sally
Ellenzweig, Allen Bruce
Engel, Walter F
Enstice, Wayne
Featherstone, David Byrum
Feldman, Edmund Burke
Fleming, Lee Virginia
Forgey, Benjamin F
Fox, Howard Neal
Frackman, Noel
Frank, Peter Solomon
Frueh, Joanna
Gaugh, Harry F
Geist, Sidney
Genauer, Emily
Genders, Richard Atherstone
Ghent, Henri
Glauber, Robert H
Goldman, Judith
Goldsmith, Barbara
Gomez-Sicre, Jose
Gray, Don
Gray, Jessie Benton Evans
Greenberg, Blue (Bluma Kafka)
Greenleaf, Kenneth Lee
Gruen, John
Grundberg, Andy (John Andrew)
Halasz, Piri
Hammock, Virgil Gene
Harrison, Helen Amy
Hemmerdinger, William John, III
Henry, Gerrit Van Keuren
Henry, Sara Lynn
Highwater, Jamake
Hitchcock, Henry Russell
Howett, John
Hughes, Robert S F
Hugunin, James Richard
Huxtable, Ada Louise
Isaacson, Philip Marshal
Jay, Bill
Jensen, Dean N
Johnstone, Mark (David)
Jones, Ronald Warren
Jordan, George Edwin
Jordan, Jim
Kagan, Andrew Aaron
Kehlmann, Robert
Kelder, Diane M
Kessler, Jane Q
Kind, Joshua B
Kingsley, April
Knight, Christopher Allen
Kotrozo, Carol Donnell
Kramer, Hilton
Krauss, Rosalind E
Kruger, Barbara
Kuh, Katharine
Kuspit, Donald Burton
Lagorio, Irene R
Langer, Sandra Lois
Larsen, Susan C
Larson, Kay L
Leja, Michael Joseph
Leopold, Michael Christopher
Levin, Kim
Levine, Melinda (Esther)
Lieberman, Laura Crowell
Linker, Kate Philippa
Livet, Anne Hodge
Livingston, Jane S
Lorber, Richard
Lubell, Ellen
Lynes, Russell
McCann, Cecile Nelken
McDarrah, Fred William
MacDonald, Scott
McEvilley, Thomas
McTwigan, Michael
Mann, Virginia

Marter, Joan
Master-Karnik, Paul Joseph
Merkel, Jayne (Silverstein)
Miller, Donald
Mills, James
Morgan, Robert Coolidge
Morgan, William
Morrison, C L
Moser, Charlotte
Moufarrege, Nicolas A
Muchnic, Suzanne
Munro, Eleanor
Murray, Joan
Nemser, Cindy
Nordland, Gerald John
O'Beil, Hedy
Offin, Charles Z
Onorato, Ronald Joseph
Paris, Jeanne C
Patterson, Patricia
Pease, Roland Folsom
Perkins, Constance M
Perreault, John
Pincus, Robert L(awrence)
Preston, Malcolm H
Preziosi, Donald A
Price, Anne Kirkendall
Rahill, Margaret Fish
Redgrave, Felicity
Reilly, Richard
Rice, Shelley Enid
Richard, Paul
Ries, Martin
Rigby, Ida Katherine
Robins, Corinne
Rosand, David
Rosenthal, Deborah Maly
Roskill, Mark Wentworth
Rosler, Martha Rose
Rothman, Sidney
Rubin, David S
Ruhe, Barnaby Sieger
Ruiz de la Mata, Ernesto J
Sandler, Irving Harry
Saunders, Wade
Schipper, Merle Solway
Schneider, Lisa Dawn
Schulze, Franz
Seckler, Dorothy Gees
Shere, Charles Everett
Singer, Esther Forman
Smith, Griffin (Mary-Griffin Smith Hoeveler)
Smith, Katherine (Chafee)
Spurlock, William Henry, II
Stapen, Nancy
Stein, Donna Michele
Steiner, Paul
Stevens, Elisabeth Goss
Stofflet, Mary
Sylvestre, Guy
Tannenbaum, Judith E
Taylor, Robert
Tennant, Donna Kay
Townsend, J Benjamin
Tuchman, Phyllis
Tucker, Glenn F
Wallach, Alan
Watkins, Eileen Frances
Wilkin, Karen
Willig, Nancy Tobin
Wilson, Judith (A)
Wilson, William S, III
Winokur, James L
Wise, (Kenneth) Kelly
Wortz, Melinda Farris
Young, Joseph E

CURATOR

Adams, Celeste Marie
Adams, Henry
Ahlander, Leslie Judd
Appelhof, Ruth A
Auping, Michael Graham

CURATOR (cont)

Auth, Susan Handler
Balkind, Alvin Louis
Barnett, Vivian Endicott
Bartle, Dorothy Budd
Battenfield, Jackie (Frazier)
Bean, Jacob
Beck, Martha Ann
Bell, Michael Steven
Benedict-Jones, Linda L
Berger, Jerry Allen
Berkowitz, Roger M
Berman, Greta W
Bermingham, Peter
Bernal, Lucrecia Alejandra
Binai, Paul Freye
Black, Mary Childs
Black, Mary McCune
Blum, June
Bogart, Michele Helene
Bolton-Smith, Robin Lee
Booth, Judith Gayle
Borcoman, James
Bordeaux, Jean Luc
Bothmer, Dietrich Felix von
Boyer, Jack K
Bradbury, Ellen A
Brettell, Richard Robson
Broun, Elizabeth Gibson
Brown, David Alan
Brunkus, Richard Allen
Buerger, Janet E
Buitron, Diana M
Buki, Zoltan
Bumgardner, Georgia Brady
Bundy, Stephen Allen
Bunnell, Peter Curtis
Burchett, Debra
Burnett, David Grant
Burr, Horace
Butera, Anne Fabbri
Butler, Joseph Thomas
Bynum, E Anderson (Esther Pearl)
Cafritz, Robert Conrad
Cain, J Frederick, Jr
Caldwell, John
Cameron, Elsa S
Canby, Jeanny Vorys
Carlozzi, Annette DiMeo
Carmean, E A, Jr
Casey, Elizabeth Temple
Cassyd, Syd
Castleman, Riva
Cervene, Richard
Chahroudi, Martha L
Chappell, Walter (Landon)
Chiego, William Joseph
Chipp, Herschel Browning
Clark, Carol Canda
Clark, Mark A
Clark, Vicky A
Clisby, Roger David
Coates, Ann S
Coe, Ralph Tracy
Coffey, John William, II
Coke, F Van Deren
Conforti, Michael Peter
Conger, Clement E
Conn, Richard George
Contini, Anita
Cooper, Marve H
Cooper, Wendy Ann
Coopersmith, Georgia A
Cordy-Collins, Alana (Kathleen)
Cormack, Malcolm
Couch, Urban
Crouch, Ned Philbrick
Cummings, Paul
Czuma, Stanislaw J
Dane, William Jerald
Darling, Sharon Sandling
Daviee, Jerry Michael
Davis, Marian B
Day, Holliday T
de Looper, Willem

Deutschman, Louise Tolliver
Donaldson, Marjory (Rogers)
Downs, Linda Anne
Drake, Douglas Arnold
Drexler, Arthur Justin
Driscoll, John Paul
DuBois, Alan Beekman
Dyson, Brian
Earle, Edward W
Einreinhofer, Nancy Anne
Elderfield, John
Ellenzweig, Allen Bruce
Elzea, Rowland Procter
Emont-Scott, Deborah
Evans, Robert James
Fairbanks, Jonathan Leo
Faunce, Sarah Cushing
Featherstone, David Byrum
Feher, Joseph
Felter, James Warren
Ferber, Elise Van Hook
Ferber, Linda S
Ferguson, Larry Scott
Field, Richard Sampson
Fink, Lois Marie
Fischer, Henry George
Flateman, Ira N
Flint, Janet Altic
Flood, Richard Sidney
Fox, Howard Neal
Fox, Judith Hoos
Franco, Barbara
Frank, Peter Solomon
Fredericksen, Burton Baum
Freeman, Mallory Bruce
Freeman, Tina
Frel, Jiri
Friedman, Joan Marcy
Fryberger, Betsy G
Fusco, Peter Richard
Gaither, Edmund B
Gale, Peggy
Garvan, Beatrice Bronson
Gates, Jay Rodney
Gates, Thomas Paul
Gealt, Adelheid Medicus
Gee, Helen
Geldzahler, Henry
Gibson, Roland
Gilkey, Gordon Waverly
Glanz, Andrea E
Glasgow, Vaughn Leslie
Glauber, Robert H
Globus, Dorothy Twining
Goheen, Ellen Rozanne
Goldberg, RoseLee
Gold Star (William Myers Watkins III)
Goodyear, Frank H, Jr
Gore, Jefferson Anderson
Gore, Tom
Graham, F Lanier
Greco, Josephine G
Green, Eleanor Broome
Grossman, Sheldon
Grove, Merrill Dale
Hackenbroch, Yvonne Alix
Hall, Robert L
Hand, John Oliver
Hanks, David Allen
Harrington, La Mar
Harris, Paul Stewart
Harrison, Helen Amy
Harter, John Burton
Hartigan, Lynda Roscoe
Haskell, Barbara
Hauser, Reine I
Hawkes, Elizabeth H
Hayward, Jane
Heckscher, Morrison Harris
Hedberg, Gregory Scott
Hemphill, Herbert Waide, Jr
Henderson, Robbin Legere
Henning, Edward Burk
Hernandez, Jo Farb
Heyman, Therese Thau
Hill, Dorothy Kent

Hiller, Betty R
Hills, Patricia
Hinson, Tom Everett
Hoffman, Michael E
Holm, Bill
Holman, Thomas S
Holverson, John
Houk, Pamela P
Howat, John Keith
Hubert, Edgar F & Anne M
Hughto, Margie A
Hulmer, Eric Claus
Humphrey, Donald Gray
Hunt, David Curtis
Hunter-Stiebel, Penelope
Hutton, William
Jackson, Ruth Amelia
Jacob, Mary Jane
Jacobowitz, Ellen Sue
Janson, Anthony Fredrick
Jeffers, Wendy Jane
Johnson, J Stewart
Johnson, Robert Flynn
Johnson, Una E
Johnston, Phillip M
Jones, Frances Follin
Jones, Patty Sue
Judson, William D
Kahan, Mitchell Douglas
Kardon, Janet
Katzenberg, Dena S
Kazor, Virginia Ernst
Kessler, Jane Q
Ketchum, Robert Glenn
King, Elaine A
Kohler, Ruth DeYoung
Kotik, Charlotta
Kramrisch, Stella
Krane, Susan
Kropf, Joan R
Kubota, Shigeko
Kuwayama, George
Landau, Mitzi
Landis, Ellen Jamie
Lang, Avis
Laskin, Myron, Jr
Lawall, David Barnard
Lazarus, Diane Gail
Lee, Caroline D
Lee, Katharine C
Lee, Roger
Leja, Michael Joseph
Lerner, Martin
Levin, Gail
Lew, Eileen
Lewis, Douglas
Lewis, Helen Natalie
Lewis, Phillip Harold
Lewton, Jean Louise
Licht, Jennifer McConnell
Lilyquist, Christine
Linhares, Philip E
Link, Howard Anthony
Lipton, Barbara B
List, Clair Z
Livingston, Jane S
Lochnan, Katharine A
Locke, Michelle Wilson
Loehr, Max
London, Barbara
Looney, Robert Fain
Lord, Michael Harry
Lovell, Margaretta Markle
Luck, Robert
Luckner, Kurt T
Lunsford, John (Crawford)
Lyons, Lisa
McAndrew, Dennis Anthony
McCabe, Cynthia Jaffee
McClain, Matthew
McDonald, Robert Herwick
McFadden, David Revere
McNulty, Kneeland
McShine, Kynaston Leigh
Maddox, Jerald Curtis
Madonia, Ann C
Manhart, Marcia Y

Marshall, Richard Donald
Mathews, Nancy Mowll
Mayer, Grace M
Mayo, Margaret Ellen
Mayo, Marti
Mecklenburg, Virginia McCord
Mekler, Adam
Melberg, Jerald Leigh
Metzger, Robert Paul
Miles, Ellen Gross
Miley, Mimi Conneen
Millard, Charles Warren, III
Mino, Yutaka
Monaghan, Kathleen Mary
Monk, Robert Evan, Jr
Montgomery, E J (Evangeline Juliet)
Moore, Ethel
Morrin, Peter Patrick
Moser, Joann
Moure, Nancy Dustin Wall
Mozley, Anita Ventura
Muller, Priscilla Elkow
Murdock, Robert Mead
Musgrove, Stephen Ward
Naeve, Milo M
Nasgaard, Roald
Nash, Steven Alan
Nelson, Jon Allen
Neubert, George Walter
Norelli, Martina Roudabush
Norfleet, Barbara Pugh
Norris, Andrea Spaulding
Oberhuber, Konrad J
Olpin, Robert Spencer
O'Neill, John Patton
Orr-Cahall, Anona Christina
Ostiguy, Jean-Rene
Overland, Carlton Edward
Owens, Gwendolyn Jane
Pal, Pratapaditya
Parkhurst, Charles
Parris, Nina Gumpert
Parsons, Merribell Maddux
Peck, William Henry
Percy, Ann Buchanan
Perreault, John
Peters, Larry Dean
Pettibone, John Wolcott
Picher, Claude
Pilgrim, Dianne H
Pilgrim, James F
Pinkney, Helen Louise
Plous, Phyllis
Plumb, James Douglas
Pounian, Albert Kachouni
Powell, Earl Alexander, III
Preble, Michael Andrew
Pressly, Nancy Lee
Radice, Anne-Imelda Marino
Raggio, Olga
Rahill, Margaret Fish
Randall, Lilian M C
Randall, Richard Harding, Jr
Rathbun, William Jay
Reiling, Susan Wallace
Reilly, Bernard Francis
Reilly, Richard
Reynolds, Valrae
Richardson, Brenda
Rishel, Joseph John, Jr
Robertson, Joan E (Joan Elizabeth Mitchell)
Robison, Andrew
Rohlfing, Christian
Rosenfield, John M
Rosenthal, Mark L
Rosenzweig, Phyllis D
Ross, David Anthony
Rowell, Margit
Rubin, David S
Rubin, William
Rust, David E
St John, Terry N
Salmon, Larry
Sandweiss, Martha Ann
Sayre, Eleanor Axson

CURATOR (cont)

Schaefer, Scott Jay
Schneiderman, Richard S
Schultz, Douglas George
Schwartz, Ellen Judith
Seeman, Helene Zucker
Selig, J Daniel
Seligman, Thomas Knowles
Sellin, David
Selz, Peter H
Sewell, Darrel L
Sewell, Jack Vincent
Shaman, Sanford Sivitz
Shangraw, Clarence Frank
Sharp, Lewis Inman
Shaw, Nancy (Rivard)
Sheridan, Helen Adler
Shimizu, Yoshiaki
Silver, Larry Arnold
Simon, Robert Barry
Sims, Lowery Stokes
Sims, Patterson
Sischy, Ingrid B
Smith, Frances Kathleen
Snyder, Kim Lawrence
Sobotik, Kent
Sokol, David Martin
Sonday, Milton Franklin, Jr
Spencer, Howard DaLee
Speyer, A James
Springer, Lynn Elise
Stampfle, Felice
Stapp, William F
Stearns, Robert
Steel, Virginia Oberlin
Steffler, Alva W
Stein, Donna Michele
Stein, Judith Ellen
Stetson, Daniel Everett
Stewart, Robert Gordon
Stover, Donald Lewis
Strickler, Susan Elizabeth
Stroessner, Robert Joseph
Stuckey, Charles F
Sturges, Hollister
Sussman, Elisabeth Sacks
Svendsen, Louise Averill
Sweeney, J Gray
Tannenbaum, Judith E
Tarbell, Roberta Kupfrian
Taylor, Mary Cazort
Thibault, Claude
Thielen, Greg Glen
Thomason, Michael Vincent
Thurman, Christa Charlotte
    Mayer
Toll, Barbara Elizabeth
Tomko, George Peter
Tracy, Berry Bryson
Travis, David B
Trechsel, Gail Andrews
Trubner, Henry
Tuchman, Maurice
Tucker, Anne Wilkes
Tucker, James Ewing
Tucker, Marcia
Tunis, Roslyn
Turnbull, Betty
Tyler, Ron C
Upton, John David
Usui, Kiichi
Valenstein, Suzanne Gebhart
Van Haaften, Julia
Vincent, Clare
Vitale, Lydia Modi
Voris, Anna Maybelle
Warren, David Boardman
Wechsler, Susan
Weedy, Theresa
Weiss, Peg
Welch, Stuart Cary
Wheelock, Arthur Kingsland,
    Jr
Wilkin, Karen
Williams, Benjamin Forrest
Williams, Mary Frances
Winer, Donald Arthur

Wise, Suzanne Tanderup
Wixom, William D
Woodward, Kesler Edward
Yard, Sally Elizabeth
Yates, Steven A
Zafran, Eric Myles
Zerner, Henri Thomas
Zilczer, Judith Katy

DESIGNER

Abel, Ray
Ackerman, Frank Edward
Adel, Judith
Aird, Neil Carrick
Albers, Anni
Albrecht, Mary Dickson
Alexander, Robert Seymour
Alicea, Jose
Allen, Loretta B
Allen, Tom, Jr
Allner, Walter H
Alten, Jerry
Ames, Jean Goodwin
Anderson, Winslow
Appleman, David Earl
Arnholm, Ronald Fisher
Arnold, Richard R
Atkins, Gordon Lee
Bacigalupa, Andrea
Badash, Sandi Borr
Barschel, Hans J
Bart, Elizabeth (Elizabeth Bart
    Gerald)
Barton, August Charles
Bates, Betsey
Bayer, Herbert
Beaudoin, Andre Eugene
Bedno, Edward
Berkowitz, Henry
Bernstein, William Joseph
Bieber, Elinore Maria Korow
Blazey, Lawrence Edwin
Blos, May (Elizabeth)
Blumenthal, Margaret M
Blumrich, Stephen
Bode, Robert William
Bogorad, Alan Dale
Bolster, Ella S
Brauer, Connie Ann
Bredlow, Tom
Brennan, Francis Edwin
Brod, Stanford
Broomfield, Adolphus George
Brunell, Richard Howard
Buros, Luella
Cadge, William Fleming
Califf, Marilyn Iskiwitz
Canniff, Bryan Gregory
Cantor, Robert Lloyd
Carl, Joan
Carter, Clarence Holbrook
Casey, Jacqueline Shepard
Castle, Wendell Keith
Cheatham, Frank Reagan
Chermayeff, Ivan
Cherner, Norman
Chethlahe (David Chethlahe
    Paladin)
Cho, David
Choo, Chunghi
Christensen, Hans-Jorgen
    Thorvald
Chwast, Seymour
Clarke, Bud (Warren F)
Coburn, Ralph (M H)
Cochran, Dewees (Dewees
    Cochran Helbeck)
Coes, Kent Day
Cohen, Elaine Lustig
Cohen, Harold Larry
Colin, Georgia T
Colman, Virginia O'Connell
Costigan, Constance Christian
Cristin-Poucher, Lilli Fong

Crozier, William K, Jr
Cutler, Ethel Rose
Dailey, Dan (Daniel Owen)
Dali, Salvador
Dasenbrock, Doris (Nancy)
    Voss
De Bretteville, Sheila Levrant
DeCaprio, Alice
deGroat, Diane L
De La Vega, Antonio
de la Vega, Enrique Miguel
Del Valle, Joseph Bourke
dePaola, Tomie
De Pedery-Hunt, Dora
De Pol, John
des Rioux (de Messimy),
    Deena (Coty)
Desser, Maxwell Milton
Devillier, Charles Arthur
Dimson, Theo Aeneas
Dorn, Peter Klaus
Dowler, David P
DuBois, Macy
Dufour, Paul Arthur
Duncan, Harry Alvin
East, N S, Jr
Edmiston, Sara Joanne
Eide, Palmer
Eikerman, Alma
Eilers, Fred (Anton Frederick)
Elkins, Toni Marcus
Enriquez, Gaspar
Faulconer, Mary (Fullerton)
Feder, Ben
Fein, Stanley
Feist, Warner David
Feriola, James Philip
Ferro, Walter
Fischer, Mildred (Gertrude)
Flach, Victor H
Fleming, Ronald Lee
Floethe, Richard
Folkus, Dan (Daniel Alan
    Fredrickson)
Francis, Bill Dean
Friedman, Alan
Froman, Ann
Fuhrman, Esther
Gale, William Henry
Garzon-Blanco, Armando
Gaudin, Marguerite
Gaylord, Frank Chalfant , II
Gebhardt, Roland
Geck, Francis Joseph
Geis, Milton Arthur
Genius, Jeannette
Gentile, Gloria Irene
Geran, Joseph, Jr
Giampietro, Isabel (Isabel A
    Giampietro Knoll)
Gilbert, Herb
Giusti, George
Glaser, Milton
Glass, Michael L
Goeritz, Mathias
Golubic, Theodore
Gonzalez, Jose Gamaliel
Gottschalk, Fritz
Gottschalk, Max Jules
Goulds, Peter J
Grear, James Malcolm
Green, Edward Anthony
Greenberg, Gloria
Gregor, Helen Frances
Grosz, Franz Joseph
Grushkin, Philip
Gutkin, Peter
Hamer, Charles James
Harder, Rolf Peter
Harris, Dolores Ashley
Hausman, Fred S
Head, George Bruce
Heaton, Maurice
Heflin, Tom Pat
Henkle, James Lee
Herman, Alan David
Higgins, Dick

Hill, John Conner
Holvey, Samuel Boyer
Hood, (Thomas) Richard
Hornung, Clarence Pearson
Hovsepian, Leon
Howe, Nelson S
Hundley, David Holladay
Hutton, Dorothy Wackerman
Ingram, Jerry Cleman
Inverarity, Robert Bruce
Israel, Marvin
Jackson, William Davis
Jameikis, Brone Aleksandra
Jenrette, Pamela Anne
Joffe, Bertha
Johnson, Fridolf Lester
Johnson, James Edwin &
    Sandra Kay
Jones, (Charles) Dexter
    (Weatherbee), III
Josimovich, George
Julian, Lazaro
Jungwirth, I(rene) Gayas
Kabotie, Fred
Kahane, Melanie (Melanie
    Kahane Grauer)
Kahn, A Michael
Kahn, Peter
Kaiser, Benjamin
Kanidinc, Salahattin
Katayama, Toshihiro
Kaye, David Haigh
Kaz (Lawrence Katzman)
Ketcham, Ray Winfred, Jr
Kimmel-Cohn, Roberta
Kingrey, Kenneth
Kingstein, Jonah
Kleidon, Dennis Arthur
Kozlowski, Edward C
Kramer, Burton
Kravis, Janis
Kretsinger, Mary Amelia
Kubly, Donald R
Kurhajec, Joseph A
LaMarca, Howard J
Lamell, Robert (C)
Land, Ernest Albert
Laposky, Ben Francis
Larkin, Eugene
Larsen, Jack Lenor
Lawrence, Howard Ray
Laycox, (William) Jack
Le Fevre, Richard John
Lein, Malcolm Emil
Leithauser, Mark Alan
Lennie, Beatrice E C
Lerner, Abe
Lewton, Val Edwin
Lisker, Sara
Llorente, Luis
Lo Medico, Thomas Gaetano
Lopez, Bea
Lowe, Harry
Lumbers, James Richard
Luray, J
Lusker, Ron
MacAlister, Paul Ritter
Macaulay, David Alexander
McChristy, Quentin L
McColley, Sutherland
McCoy, Katherine Braden
McCoy, Michael Dale
McDermott, Gerald
McElcheran, William Hodd
McFadden, Mary
McGuire, Maureen
McIntosh, Harrison Edward
McNear, Everett C
Maltby, Hazel Farrow
Manning, Reg (Reginald West)
Manuella, Frank R
Maradiaga, Ralph
Martin, Doris-Marie Constable
Martin, G W
Martin, Margaret M
Martino, Edmund
Marzano, Albert

DESIGNER (cont)

Mason, Novem M
Maurice, E(leanor) Ingersoll
Mayen, Paul
Meitzler, (Herbert) Neil
Merritt, Francis Sumner
Meyer, Frank Hildbridge
Michaels-Paque, Joan
Miller, Earl B(eauford)
Morrison, Boone M
Morrow, Robert Earl
Murashima, Kumiko
Myers, C Stowe
Nagano, Paul Tatsumi
Nagengast, William Joseph
Neddeau, Donald Frederick
    Price
Neff, John A
Ness, (Albert) Kenneth
Neugebauer, Margot
New, Lloyd H
Nichols, Donald Edward
Nichols, Eleanor Cary
Nicodemus, Chester Roland
Nodine, Jane Allen
Nordin, Phyllis E
Ockerse, Thomas
O'Dell, Erin (Anne)
Oenslager, Donald Mitchell
O'Hara, Sheila Mary
Olsen, Ernest Moran
Olson, Joseph Olaf
Olugebefola, Ademola
O'Neil, John Joseph
Pacific, Gertrude
Paley, Albert Raymond
Parker, James Varner
Parnall, Peter
Paul, Arthur
Peck, James Edward
Pei, I M (Ieoh Ming)
Peii, Ahmad Osni
Pennypacker, James S
Perlin, Ruth Rudolph
Peters, Diane (Peck)
Phelan, Linn Lovejoy
Pierre-Noel, Vergniaud
Pirkl, James Joseph
Pollard, Donald Pence
Pollock, Bruce Walter
Potter, (George) Kenneth
Prestini, James Libero
Pulos, Arthur Jon
Rand, Paul
Randall, (Lillian) Paula
Randall, Ruth Hunie
Regensteiner, Else (Friedsam)
Reinhardt, Siegfried Gerhard
Rennie, Helen (Sewell)
Replinger, Dot (Dorothy
    Thiele)
Revor, Remy
Roch, Ernst
Romans, Van Anthony
Romeu, Joost A
Rowe, Charles Alfred
Roysher, Hudson (Brisbine)
Ruben, Leonard
Rubidoux (Rubidoux Early
    Johnson)
Rubin, Irwin
Sabo, Irving
Sadek, George
Sahrbeck, Everett William
St Florian, Friedrich Gartler
Salazar, Juan
Samerjan, George E
Sarff, Walter
Sargent, Margaret Holland
Schoener, Allon
Schreckengost, Viktor
Schulze, Paul
Schwarz, Myrtle Cooper
Schweiss, Ruth Keller
Sellers, John Lewis
Seyle, Robert Harley
Sheets, Millard Owen

Shelton, Robert Lee
Shepherd, Don (Donald Allen)
Sherwood, A (Frances Ann
    Crane)
Shipley, James R
Skinner, Orin Ensign
Small, Neal
Smith, Ernest John
Smith, Jo-an
Smith, Robert Alan
Smith, Robert Charles
Smongeski, Joseph Leon
Sommese, Lanny Beal
Sovary, Lilly
Steinfels, Melville P
Stephens, Curtis
Stermer, Dugald Robert
Stoessel, Henry Kurt
Stone, Willard
Stuart, Donald Alexander
Taback, Simms
Targan, Judy
Temes, Mortimer (Robert)
Thompson, Bradbury
Thompson, Ernest Thorne, Jr
Thorns, John Cyril, Jr
Travanti, Leon Emidio
Truex, Van Day
Voelker, John
Waite, Elin Jane
Ward, William Edward
Wasserman, Albert
Watkins, Ragland Tolk
Watson, Aldren A
Watts, Robert M
Wilson, Robert
Wilson, Tom Muir
Winfield, Rodney M
Wolfe, Mildred Nungester
Wong, Jason
Yarborough, Christine
    Troutman
Yoakum, Del
Young, Kenneth Victor
Yuristy, Russell Michael
Zahn, Carl Frederick
Zeidler, Eberhard Heinrich
Zucker, Bob

DIRECTOR

Adel, Judith
Almy, Max (Marilynn Irene)
Alten, Jerry
Bartholct, Elizabeth Ives
Baxter, Patricia Huy
Blackman, Thomas Patrick
Butts, H Daniel, III
Canniff, Bryan Gregory
Cartmell, Helen
Cate, Phillip Dennis
Cattell, Ray
Clarke, Bud (Warren F)
Cummings, Paul
Day, Horace Talmage
Drexler, Arthur Justin
Enyeart, James Lyle
Foley, Kathy Kelsey
Frauchiger, Fritz A
Gentile, Gloria Irene
Gobin, Henry (Delano)
Gold, Betty
Green, Edward Anthony
Hedin, Donald Monroe
Hoffman, Carol Maree
Hoffmann, Arnold, Jr
Jellico, John Anthony
Klindt, Steven
Klonis, Stewart
Krashes, Barbara
Lumsden, Ian Gordon
Mark, Marilyn (Sabetsky)
Martin, Mary Finch
Maurer, Evan Maclyn
Muno, Richard Carl

Paul, Greg (Gregory Wilmer)
Pfriem, Bernard
Rosenberg, Carole Halsband
Segal, Tama & David
Stevens, Edward John, Jr
Stewart, John Lincoln
Stuart, Kenneth James
Sundberg, Carl Gustave
Thompson, Bradbury
Van Brunt, Philip G
van der Marck, Jan
White, Deborah
White, Ruth
Zilka, Michael John

DRAFTSMAN

Anthony, William Graham
Attie, Dotty
Bachardy, Don
Bachinski, Walter Joseph
Ben Tre, Howard
Billmyer, John Edward
Birmelin, A Robert
Bohlen, Nina (Celestine Eustis
    Bohlen)
Brawley, Robert Julius
Breitenbach, William John
Broker, Karin
Brown, Gary Hugh
Buckner, Kay Lamoreux
Casas, Fernando Rodriguez
Cook, Stephen D
Coppola, Andrew
Davidson, Thyra (Claire Thyra
    Wexler)
Dee, Leo Joseph
Droege, Anthony Joseph, II
Duncan, Richard (Hurley)
Eden, Glenn
Eichel, Edward W
Ettenberg, Franklin Joseph
Finke, Leonda Froelich
Fraser, Carol Hoorn
Gabrielson, Walter Oscar
Garey, Pat
George, Thomas
Gershinowitz, George
Gitlin, Michael
Goldsleger, Cheryl
Greene-Mercier, Marie Zoe
Haney, William H
Howze, James Dean
Hurson, Michael
Insley, Will
Isaacson, Marcia Jean
Jeter, Randy Joe
Jimenez, Luis Alfonso, Jr
Kelly, William Joseph
Kimball, Wilford Wayne, Jr
Korman, Harriet R
Kosta, Angela
Kuhn, Bob
Lark, Raymond
Lasansky, Leonardo
Lasansky, Mauricio L
Leys, Dale Daniel
Lieberman, Louis (Karl)
Locke, Rhea G
Lynch, Gerald Francis
McCoy, Ann
McGrew, Ralph Brownell
Marianne
Masurovsky, Gregory
Matteson, Ira
Medina, Ada
Morrow, Terry
Murphy, Hass
Nutt, Jim (James Tureman)
Padovano, Anthony John
Parker, Will (William
    Crawford)
Pollak, Theresa
Raffo, Steve
Ramanauskas, Dalia Irena

Rehberger, Gustav
Reopel, Joyce
Rich, Frances L
Richards, Bill (William A)
Richards, Karl Frederick
Roseman, Stanley
Rubylee (Charles Armstrong
    Littler)
Schiff, Jean
Schneider, Julie (Saecker)
Segan, Kenneth Akiva
Shechter, Ben-Zion
Shechter, Laura J
Silver, Pat
Singletary, Robert Eugene
Sorby, J Richard
Steczynski, John Myron
Szarama, Judith Layne
Torn, Jerry (Gerald J)
Townsend, (Alvin) Neal
Twarogowski, Leroy Andrew
Verzyl, Kenneth H
Von Gunten, Roger
White, Franklin
Whitson
Wilmarth, Christopher Mallory
Witkin, Jerome Paul
Wojtyla, Haase (Walter
    Joseph)
Young, Marjorie Ward
Youngquist, Jack
Zlowe, Florence M

EDITOR

Allen, Jane Addams
Aminoff, Judith
Baker, Elizabeth C
Baldridge, Mark S
Bandy, Mary Lea
Bennett, Philomene
Blumrich, Stephen
Bourdon, David
Brody, Jacqueline
Burnham, Linda Frye
Conant, Howard Somers
Cossitt, Franklin D
Cotter, Holland
Decock, Liliane (Liliane
    Morgan Decock)
Doherty, Michael Stephen
Edmonston, Paul
Esterow, Milton
Fleisher, Pat
Gilchrist, Elizabeth Brenda
Goddard, Don (Donald)
Gray, Maxine Cushing
Grundberg, Andy (John
    Andrew)
Hoffman, Michael E
Holden, Donald
Hooton, Bruce Duff
Hoving, Thomas
Howarth, Shirley Reiff
Jackson, Ward
Jardine, Donald Leroy
Jones, Pirkle
Kleinbauer, W Eugene
Krantz, Les (Leslie J)
Levine, Melinda (Esther)
Lewton, Jean Louise
Lieberman, Laura Crowell
Loeffler, Carl Eugene
McCann, Cecile Nelken
McDonald, Susan Strong
McGarry, Susan Hallsten
McPherson, Bruce Rice
McTwigan, Michael
Madigan, Mary Jean Smith
Martin, Denise B
Masheck, Joseph Daniel
Meyer, Susan E
Morin, James Corcoran
Navaretta, Cynthia
Patten, David John

EDITOR (cont)
Peterson, Harold Patrick
Pink, Marilyn Overman
Prakapas, Eugene Joseph
Reed, Michael Arthur
Rinehart, Michael
Robbins, Eugenia S
Rosenberg, Carole Halsband
Rossen, Susan F
Shor, Bernice Abramowitz
Sischy, Ingrid B
Smith, Albert
Spector, Buzz (Franklin Mac Spector)
Varney, Edwin
Watkins, Eileen Frances
Weil, Rose R
Weiss, John Joseph
Westwater, Angela King
Williams, Gerald
Winchester, Alice
Wyrick, Charles Lloyd, Jr

EDUCATOR
(College/University)

Abdalla, Nick
Acker, Perry Miles
Ackerman, Gerald Martin
Ackerman, James S
Ackerman, Rudy Schlegel
Adams, Henry
Adamy, George E
Addison, Byron Kent
Agar, Eunice Jane
Ahysen, Harry Joseph
Akawie, Thomas Frank
Alaupovic, Alexandra V
Albert, Calvin
Albin, Edgar A
Alexander, Robert Seymour
Alexander-Greene, Grace George
Alexenberg, (Melvin) Menahem
Alexick, David Francis
Allan, William George
Allen, Jere Hardy
Allen, Margaret Prosser
Allen, Ralph
Allen, William J
Allentuck, Marcia Epstein
Alloway, Lawrence
Allumbaugh, James
Alper, M Victor
Alps, Glen Earl
Altman, Harold
Altmann, Henry S
Alvarez-Cervela, Jose Maria
Ambrose, Charles Edward
Amyx, Leon Kirkman
Andersen, Wayne Vesti
Anderson, James P
Anderson, Warren Harold
Andres, Glenn Merle
Andreson, Laura F
Andrew, David Neville
Andrews, Michael Frank
Anglin, Betty Lockhart
Annis, Norman L
Anthony, Lawrence Kenneth
Anzures, Rafael
Apel, Barbara Jean
Apgar, Nicolas Adam
App, Timothy
Archambault, Louis
Ard, Saradell (Saradell Ard Frederick)
Armstrong, Bill Howard
Arneson, Robert
Arnest, Bernard
Arnheim, Rudolf
Arnholm, Ronald Fisher
Arnold, Paul Beaver
Arnold, Ralph Moffett
Arnold, Robert Lloyd

Artemis, Maria (Maria Artemis Papageorge Sawyer)
Aschenbach, (Walter) Paul
Asher, Frederick M
Askew, Pamela
Askman, Tom K
Atwell, Allen
Atwood Pinardi, Brenda
Audette, Anna Held
Austin, Pat
Auth, Susan Handler
Autio, (A) Rudy
Auvil, Kenneth William
Avedon, Barry
Bach, Dirk
Bach, Laurence
Bacot, Henry Parrott
Badalamenti, Fred
Baer, Norbert Sebastian
Baggett, William Carter, Jr
Bailey, Clayton George
Bailey, Oscar
Bailey, William
Baker, George
Baker, Ralph Bernard
Bakke, Larry Hubert
Baldwin, John
Baldwin, Russell W
Ball, Walter N
Balmaceda, Margarita S
Bandy, Gary
Bandy, Ron F
Bane, (Lucy) McDonald
Banks, Anne Johnson
Barazani, Morris
Barnes, Curt (Curtis Edward)
Barnes, Robert M
Barreres, Domingo
Barry, Frank
Barry, Robert E
Barth, Charles John
Bartlett, Donald Loring
Bartnick, Harry William
Barton, Bruce Walter
Bashor, John W
Bass, Ruth
Bassin, Joan
Bastian, Linda
Batchelor, Betsy Ann
Battenberg, John
Bavinger, Eugene Allen
Bayer, Jeffrey Joshua
Beall, Dennis Ray
Bealmer, William
Beam, Philip Conway
Beard, Richard Elliott
Beason, Donald Ray
Beck, Lonnie Lee
Beck, Rosemarie (Rosemarie Beck Phelps)
Beck, Stephen R
Becker, David
Bedno, Edward
Beelke, Ralph G
Beer, Kenneth John
Behl, Wolfgang
Bell, Kathryn Leise
Bell, Trevor
Benjamin, Karl Stanley
Benson, Robert Franklin
Bentz, Harry Donald
Berd, Morris
Berger, Maurice
Berger, Paul Eric
Berguson, Robert Jenkins
Berlind, Robert
Bernard, David Edwin
Berneche, Jerry Douglas
Bernstein, Judith
Berry, Glenn
Berry, William Augustus
Bershad, David L
Bettinson, Brenda
Betts, Edward Howard
Bickley, Gary Steven
Bieler, Ted Andre

Biferie, Dan (Daniel Anthony), Jr
Bigelow, Robert Clayton
Biggers, John Thomas
Billeci, Andre George
Bireline, George Lee
Bischoff, Elmer Nelson
Bishop, Barbara Lee
Bishop, Benjamin
Bishop, Jeffrey Britton
Bishop, Jerold
Bittleman, Arnold I
Bjorklund, Lee
Black, David Evans
Black, Richard R
Blackmun, Barbara Winston
Blai, Boris
Blevins, James Richard
Blizzard, Alan
Bloch, E Maurice
Blodgett, Peter
Blue, Patt
Blum, Shirley Neilsen
Bobick, Bruce
Boccia, Edward Eugene
Bodnar, Peter
Boggs, Mayo Mac
Boghosian, Varujan
Bohnert, Thom (Thomas Robert)
Bohrod, Aaron
Bolas, Gerald Douglas
Bolinsky, Joseph Abraham
Bony, Jean Victor
Booth, Bill
Bopp, Emery
Boretz, Naomi
Borgatta, Isabel Case
Born, James E
Borstein, Elena
Bothmer, Dietrich Felix von
Boughton, William Harrison
Bourdon, Robert Slayton
Bove, Richard
Bowers, Cheryl Olsen
Bowlt, John
Bowman, Jeff Ray
Boyce, Gerald G
Boyce, William G
Boyd, John David
Boyd, Karen White
Boyd, Lakin
Boyle, Keith
Bradshaw, Glenn Raymond
Bradshaw, Lawrence James
Bradshaw, Robert George
Bradt, Kathleen Weil-Garris
Brainard, Owen
Braitstein, Marcel
Brakke, P(erry) Michael
Bransby, Eric James
Braunstein, H Terry (Malikin)
Bravmann, Rene A
Breckenridge, Bruce M
Breed, Charles Ayars
Breen, Harry Frederick, Jr
Brejcha, Vernon Lee
Brenner, Shore Hodge
Bressi, Betty
Brewster, Michael
Brezik, Hilarion
Brier, Helene
Brilliant, Richard
Brinkerhoff, Dericksen Morgan
Bristow, William Arthur
Britsky, Nicholas
Britt, Al
Britt, Sam Glenn
Britton, Daniel Robert
Brock, Robert W
Brod, Stanford
Brodsky, Judith Kapstein
Brodsky, Stan
Brody, Jacob Jerome
Brooks, John H
Brooks, Lois Ziff

Brooks, Wendell T
Broude, Norma Freedman
Broudo, Joseph David
Brough, Richard Burrell
Brown, Betty Ann
Brown, Blanche Rachel
Brown, Gary Hugh
Brown, Hilton
Brown, Joseph
Brown, Lawrie
Brown, Paul L
Brown, Peter C
Brown, Peter Thomson
Brown, Robert (Earl)
Brucker, Edmund
Bruder, Harold Jacob
Brumer, Miriam
Brunell, Richard Howard
Brush, Gloria (Elizabeth) DeFilipps
Bryant, Olen L
Buchanan, Sidney Arnold
Bucher, Francois
Bucher, George Robert
Buckley, Mary L (Mrs Joseph M Parriott)
Buckner, Paul Eugene
Bugbee-Jackson, Joan (Mrs John M Jackson)
Bumbeck, David A
Bumgardner, James Arliss
Bunker, George
Bunnell, Peter Curtis
Bunts, Frank
Burchfield, Jerry Lee
Burgart, Herbert Joseph
Burger, W Carl
Burgess, Joseph James, Jr
Burggraf, Ray Lowell
Burke, Daniel V
Burke, E Ainslie
Burko, Diane
Buscaglia, Jose
Bush, Donald John
Bush-Brown, Albert
Bushman, David Franklin
Bushnell, Kenneth Wayne
Butterbaugh, Robert Clyde
Butterfield, Deborah Kay
Byrd, D Gibson
Byrum, Donald Roy
Cadieux, Michael Eugene
Cahill, James Francis
Cain, Joseph Alexander
Cajori, Charles F
Caldwell, Eleanor
Caldwell, Martha Belle
Caldwell, Susan Havens
Calhoun, Larry Darryl
Calkins, Kingsley Mark
Calkins, Robert G
Callner, Richard
Camarata, Martin L
Cameron, Brooke Bulovsky
Camhi, Morrie
Campbell, Jeanne Begien
Campbell, Jewett
Campbell, Marjorie Dunn
Campoli, Cosmo
Cantor, Robert Lloyd
Caplan, Jerry L
Caponi, Anthony
Carey, John Thomas
Carlson, Cynthia J
Carpenter, Dennis Wilkinson (Bones)
Carswell, Rodney
Carter, (Charles) Bruce
Carter, Dean
Carter, Yvonne Pickering
Casanova, Aldo John
Casas, Melesio
Casey, John Joseph
Cataldo, John William
Catan-Rose, Richard
Catlin, Stanton L

EDUCATOR (cont)
Catterall, John Edward
Cavanaugh, Tom Richard
Cavat, Irma
Cave, Leonard Edward
Celentano, Francis Michael
Celli, Paul
Cervenka, Barbara
Chaet, Bernard
Chafetz, Sidney
Chalmers, E Laurence, Jr
Chamberlain, Charles
Chan, Phillip Paang
Chandler, John William
Chaplin, George Edwin
Chapman, (M) Anne
Chappell, Miles Linwood
Chase, Alice Elizabeth
Chase, Jeanne Norman
Chavez-Morado, Jose
Chee, Cheng-Khee
Chesney, Lee Roy, III
Chew, Paul Albert
Chihuly, Dale Patrick
Chipp, Herschel Browning
Chodkowski, Henry, Jr
Choy, Terence Tin-Ho
Christenberry, William
Christian, William
Christison, Muriel B
Cifolelli, Alberta (Alberta
    Carmella Lamb)
Cikovsky, Nicolai, Jr
Cindric, Michael Anthony
Clark, Jon Frederic
Clarke, John R
Clayberger, Samuel Robert
Cleary, Manon Catherine
Cleaver, Dale Gordon
Clements, Robert Donald
Cleveland, Robert Earl
Cline, Clinton C
Clipsham, Jacqueline Ann
Codell, Julie Francia
Coffey, Douglas Robert
Cogswell, Dorothy McIntosh
Cohen, Charles E
Cohen, Harold
Cohen, Harold Larry
Coker, Carl David
Colby, Bill
Colby, Victor E
Cole, Bruce
Cole, Harold David
Coleman, Floyd Willis
Colescott, Warrington W
Collett, Farrell Reuben
Collins, George R
Collins, Jim
Colson, Chester E
Colt, John Nicholson
Colton, Judith
Comini, Alessandra
Conaway, James D
Conger, William
Connett, Dee M
Connor, Linda Stevens
Conrad, George
Conrad, John W
Constantine, Greg John
Cook, Lia
Cooke, Jody Helen
Cooke, Samuel Tucker
Coppedge, Arthur L
Cordy-Collins, Alana
    (Kathleen)
Corkery, Tim (Timothy James)
Corpron, Carlotta M
Cothren, Michael Watt
Couper, James M
Covi, Dario A
Covington, Harrison Wall
Cowley, Edward P
Cox, Ernest Lee
Coyne, John Michael
Crable, James Harbour
Cramer, Richard Charles

Crane, Barbara Bachmann
Craven, Roy Curtis, Jr
Crawley, Wesley V
Creese, Walter Littlefield
Crespo, Michael Lowe
Cress, George Ayers
Cretara, Domenic Anthony
Crist, William Gary
Croft, Michael Flynt
Crosby, Ranice W
Crosman, Christopher Byron
Crossgrove, Roger Lynn
Crouse, Michael Glenn
Crown, Keith Allen
Croydon, Michael Benet
Crozier, Richard Lewis
Culbreth, Carl R
Culkin, John Michael
Cushing, Barbara
Cutler-Shaw, Joyce
Da Cunha, Julio
D'Agostino, Peter Pasquale
Dahill, Thomas Henry, Jr
Dale, William Scott Abell
Daly, Stephen Jeffrey
Danhausen, Eldon
Dantzic, Cynthia Maris
D'Arista, Robert
Darriau, Jean-Paul
Darrow, Paul Gardner
Dass, Dean Allen
Daugherty, Michael F
Davey, Ronald A
Davis, D Jack
Davis, Harry Allen
Davis, Meredith J
Davison, Bill
Day, John
Day, Larry (Lawrence James)
Deaderick, Joseph
Deal, Joe
De Blasi, Anthony Armando
DeCarava, Roy Rudolph
DeGenevieve, Barbara
De Kergommeaux, Duncan
DeLamonica, Roberto
DeLap, Tony
DeLauro, Joseph Nicola
Della-Volpe, Ralph Eugene
DeLonga, Leonard Anthony
De Luca, Joseph Victor
DeLuigi, Janice Cecilia
Deming, David Lawson
De Monte, Claudia
Denniston, Douglas
Dernovich, Donald Frederick
Desmidt, Thomas H
Detmers, William Raymond
de Vecsey, Esther Barbara
DeVegatales, Jugo
Dhaemers, Robert August
Dibble, Charles Ryder
Dibert, Rita Jean
Dice, Elizabeth Jane
Dickerson, Daniel Jay
Dimond, Terry Jarrard
D'Innocenzo, Nick Jerome
DiPasquale, Dominic
    Theodore
Dodd, Eric M
Dodd, Lamar
Dodd, Lois
Doherty, Robert J
Dole, William
Doll, Donald Arthur
Donahue, Philip Richard
Donnelly, Marian Card
Dorra, Henri
Dorsky, Morris
Dorst, Claire V
Doudera, Gerard
Douke, Daniel W
Dow, Helen Jeannette
Dowell, John E, Jr
Downing, Robert James
Downs, Linda Anne
Doyle, Joe

Doyle, Tom
Doyon, Gerard Maurice
Dreskin, Jeanet Steckler
Drewal, Henry John
Driesbach, David Fraiser
Driskell, David Clyde
Drutz, June
Duckworth, Ruth
Duhme, H Richard, Jr
Dumas, Antoine
Dunkelman, Martha Levine
Dunn, Phillip Charles
Du Pen, Everett George
Dwyer, Eugene Joseph
Dwyer, James
Eades, Luis Eric
Easterwood, Henry Lewis
Eberman, Edwin
Eckersley, Thomas Cyril
Edelstein, J M
Edmiston, Sara Joanne
Edmonston, Paul
Edwards, Paul Burgess
Edwards-Tucker, Yvonne
    (Leatrice Yvonne Tucker)
Eglitis, Laimons
Ehresmann, Donald Louis
Ehrlich, George
Eisenberg, Marvin
Eisner, Elliot Wayne
Elias, Harold John
Eliason, Shirley (Shirley
    Eliason Haupt)
Elkins, (E) Lane
Ellinger, Ilona E
Ellingson, William John
Elliott, Bruce Roger
Elman, Emily
Else, Robert John
Elsen, Albert Edward
Elsner, Larry Edward
Emerson, Walter Caruth
Engeran, Whitney John, Jr
Enggass, Robert
England, Paul Grady
Epting, Marion Austin
Erdle, Rob
Ernst, Jimmy
Ertman, Earl Leslie
Esler, John Kenneth
Esser, Janet Brody
Estabrook, Reed
Evans, Dick
Evans, Grose
Evans, Richard
Evans, Robert Graves
Even, Robert Lawrence
Ewen, Paterson
Fabe, Robert
Fager, Charles J
Fairfield, Richard Thomas
Faller, Marion
Falsetta, Vincent Mario
Faris, Brunel De Bost
Farris-Larson, Gail
Farwell, Beatrice
Fearing, William Kelly
Feldhaus, Paul A
Feldman, Edmund Burke
Feltus, Alan Evan
Fendell, Jonas J
Fenton, Howard Carter
Fenwick, Roly (William
    Roland)
Ferber, Lee Allan
Ferreira, (Armando) Thomas
Fessler, Mary Thomasita
Fichter, Robert W
Fiero, Gloria K
Fifield, Mary
Filkosky, Josefa
Fine, Jud
Fingesten, Peter
Fink, Herbert Lewis
Fink, Larry (Laurence B)
Fink, Ray (Raymond Russell)
Finkelstein, Louis

Finkler, Robert Allan
Finley, Gerald Eric
Fisch, Arline Marie
Fiskin, Judy (Anne)
Flam, Jack D
Flecker, Maurice Nathan
Fleischer, Roland Edward
Flick, Robbert
Flinn, Elizabeth Haight
Flowers, Thomas Earl
Folds, Thomas McKey
Foley, Kyoko Y
Fontanini, Clare
Foosaner, Judith
Ford, Harry Xavier
Forman, Kenneth Warner
Formicola, John Joseph
Formigoni, Mauri Monihon
Fornas, Leander
Forrest, James Taylor
Forrester, Charles Howard
Forsman, Chuck (Charles
    Stanley)
Forst, Miles
Forsyth, Ilene H(aering)
Foster, Maelee Thomson
Francis, Bill Dean
Franco, Robert John
Frank, David
Frankel, Dextra
Franklin, Gilbert Alfred
Frary, Michael
Frasconi, Antonio
Frazier, Paul D
Frederick, Eugene Wallace
Freed, Douglass Lynn
Freedberg, Sydney Joseph
Freifeld, Eric
Freund, Will Frederick
Frick, Robert Oliver
Friedberg, Richard S
Frinta, Mojmir Svatopluk
Frost, Stuart Homer
Frueh, Joanna
Fuchs, Mary Tharsilla
Fumagalli, Orazio
Furman, David Stephen
Fusco, Laurie S
Gahagan, James (Edward), Jr
Galles, Arie Alexander
Gallo, Frank
Gammon, Juanita-La Verne
Gammon, Reginald Adolphus
Gans, Lucy C
Gardner, Robert Earl
Garnett, William Ashford
Garnsey, Clarke Henderson
Garrard, Mary DuBose
Gates, Harry Irving
Gates, Jay Rodney
Gates, Thomas Paul
Gatrell, Marion Thompson
Gaugh, Harry F
Gauvreau, Robert George
Geck, Francis Joseph
Geeslin, Lee Gaddis
Gelber, Samuel
Gelburd, Gail Enid
Gelinas, Robert William
George, Raymond Ellis
Gerdts, William H
Gerhold, William Henry
Geske, Norman Albert
Gettinger, Edmond Walter
Ghikas, Panos George
Gibbons, Hugh (James)
Gibson, Benedict S
Gibson, James D
Gikas, Christopher
Gilkey, Gordon Waverly
Gillingwater, Denis Claude
Gilmor, Jane E
Girard, (Charles) Jack
Glaser, Bruce
Glass, Michael L
Glasson, Lloyd
Gluck, Heidi

EDUCATOR (cont)

Glyde, Henry George
Godfrey, Robert
Godsey, Glenn
Goetzl, Thomas Maxwell
Gold, Albert
Gold, Sharon Cecile
Goldin, Leon
Goldring, Nancy Deborah
Goldsmith, Benedict Isaac
Goldstein, Carl
Goldstein, Howard
Goldstein, Milton
Golub, Leon Albert
Gongora, Leonel
Gonzales, Boyer
Goodnow, Frank A
Goossen, Eugene Coons
Gorder, Clayton J
Gordin, Sidney
Gordley, Metz Tranbarger
Gordon, Donald Edward
Gordon, John S
Gordon, Joy L
Gorski, Richard Kenny
Gottlieb, Carla
Gough, Georgia Belle
Gould, Karen Keel
Gould, Philip
Goulet, Claude
Gouma-Peterson, Thalia
Gourevitch, Jacqueline
Goutman, Dolya
Govan, Francis Hawks
Graham, Richard Marston
Grant, Art
Graves, Bradford
Graves, Michael
Gray, Robert Hugh
Grear, James Malcolm
Green, David Oliver
Greenamyer, George Mossman
Greenberg, Blue (Bluma Kafka)
Greene, Stephen
Gregor, Harold Laurence
Gregoropoulos, John
Gregory, Angela
Gregory, (Eleanor) Anne
Gregory, Eleanor Anne
Gregory, Joan
Grigsby, Jefferson Eugene, Jr
Grimes, Margaret W
Griner, Ned H
Grippi, Salvatore William
Grissom, Eugene Edward
Gross, Charles Merrill
Grossberg, Jake
Grossman, Maurice Kenneth
Grucza, Leo (Victor)
Guenther, Peter W
Guerin, John William
Guilmain, Jacques
Gunasinghe, Siri
Gundersheimer, Herman (Samuel)
Gunn, Paul James
Gunter, Frank Elliott
Gutmann, John
Gyermek, Stephen A
Hackett, Mickey
Hafif, Marcia
Hageman, Charles Lee
Hahn, Betty
Hahn, Gerald
Halaby, Samia Asaad
Halbrooks, Darryl Wayne
Hall, John (Scott)
Hall, John A
Hall, Michael David
Hall, Rex Earl
Halsey, William Melton
Hamann, Marilyn D
Hamilton, Charles F
Hamilton, George Earl
Hamilton, W Paul C
Hamlett, Dale Edward

Hammond, Gale Thomas
Hampton, Grace
Hampton, Phillip Jewel
Hamwi, Richard Alexander
Handler, Audrey
Hanfmann, George M A
Hannah, John Junior
Hannibal, Joseph Harry
Hansen, Frances Frakes
Hansen, Gaylen Capener
Hansen, Harold John
Hansen, Robert
Hanson, Duane
Hanson, Lawrence
Hapke, Paul Frederick
Harden, Marvin
Harding, Ann
Harris, Dolores Ashley
Harris, Gloriane
Harris, Harvey Sherman
Harris, Lawren Phillips
Harris, Paul Rogers
Harrison, Tony
Harsh, Richard
Hartgen, Vincent Andrew
Hartley, Paul Jerome
Hartley, W Douglas
Hartman, Robert Leroy
Hartt, Frederick
Haskin, Donald Marcus
Haskins, John Franklin
Hastie, Reid
Hatch, John W
Hatch, W A S
Hatchett, Duayne
Hatfield, Donald Gene
Hatgil, Paul
Hausman, Jerome Joseph
Hausrath, Joan W
Havelock, Christine Mitchell
Hawthorne, Jack Gardner
Hay, Ike
Hayashi, Masumi
Haydon, Harold (Emerson)
Haynes, Douglas H
Hazlehurst, Franklin Hamilton
Head, Robert William
Healy, Anne Laura
Healy, Deborah Ann
Healy, Julia Schmitt
Heath, David Martin
Hefner, Harry Simon
Heidel, Frederick (H)
Hein, Max
Heinecken, Robert Friedli
Held, Julius S
Heldt, Carl Randall
Heliker, John Edward
Helzer, Richard Brian
Hendershot, J L
Henderson, Linda Dalrymple
Henry, Robert
Herard, Marvin T
Herbert, Robert L
Hernandez, Sam (Samuel Rudolph)
Hersey, George Leonard
Herzbrun, Helene McKinsey
Hewitt, Duncan Adams
Hewitt, Francis Ray
High, Timothy Griffin
High-Wasikhongo, Freida
Hill, Clinton J
Hill, Peter
Hilson, Douglas
Hindes, Chuck (Charles Austin)
Hirsch, Gilah Yelin
Ho, Francis T
Hobbs, Jack Arthur
Hochhauser, Marilyn Helsenrott
Hochstetler, T Max
Hoffman, Neil James
Hoffman, William McKinley, Jr
Hofsted, Jolyon Gene

Hoge, Robert Wilson
Holder, Kenneth Allen
Holen, Norman Dean
Holland, Harry Charles
Holste, Thomas James
Homer, William Innes
Hooks, Earl J
Horn, Bruce
Hornaday, Richard Hoyt
House, Suda Kay
Houser, Jim
Housser, Yvonne McKague
Howard, Dan F
Howard, Robert A
Howe, Oscar
Howell, Claude Flynn
Howlett, Carolyn Svrluga
Howze, James Dean
Hu, Mary Lee
Huchthausen, David Richard
Hudson, Ralph Magee
Huff, Howard Lee
Hundley, David Holladay
Hungerford, Constance Cain
Hunisak, John Michael
Hunt, Robert James
Hunter, Debora
Hunter, Leonard LeGrande, III
Hunter, Miriam Eileen
Hupp, Frederick Duis
Hurlstone, Robert William
Hurst, Ralph N
Hutchison, Jane Campbell
Hyman, Isabelle
Iden, Sheldon
Iglehart, Robert L
Ihle, John Livingston
Ikeda, Yoshiro
Ingle, John S
Ippolito, Angelo
Isaacson, Marcia Jean
Italiano, Joan
Iversen, Earl Harvey
Iwamasa, Ken
Izumi, Kiyoshi
Jachna, Joseph David
Jackson, A B
Jackson, Billy Morrow
Jacobs, David (Theodore)
Jacobsen, Michael A
Jacobus, John M
Jacquard
Jacques, Michael Louis
Jaffe, Irma B
Jansen, Catherine Sandra
Jardine, Donald Leroy
Jelinek, Hans
Jennerjahn, W P
Jergens, Robert Joseph
Jerry, Michael John
Jeter, Randy Joe
Jewell, William M
Johnson, Charles W, Jr
Johnson, Diane Chalmers
Johnson, Edvard Arthur
Johnson, Ellen Hulda
Johnson, Homer
Johnson, Ivan Earl
Johnson, James Alan
Johnson, Lee
Johnson, Lester F
Johnson, Lester L
Johnson, Lincoln Fernando
Johnson, Lois Marlene
Johnson, M L J
Johnson, Margaret Kennard
Johnson, Richard A
Johnson, Ronald W
Johnston, Richard M
Johnston, Robert Porter
Johnston, William Medford
Johnstone, Mark (David)
Jones, Charlott Ann
Jones, Frederick George
Jones, Lois Swan
Jones, Ronald Lee, Jr
Jones, Ruthe Blalock

Jordan, Robert
Jordan, William B
Jorgensen, Sandra
Jorgenson, Dale Alfred
Ju, I-Hsiung
Judd, De Forrest Hale
Jules, Mervin
Julio, Pat T
Kabak, Robert
Kachel, Harold Stanley
Kaericher, John Conrad
Kaish, Luise
Kaish, Morton
Kalb, Marty Joel
Kamen, Rebecca
Kamrowski, Gerome
Kamys, Walter
Kao, Ruth (Yu-Hsin) Lee
Karlen, Peter H
Karwoski, Richard Charles
Kashdin, Gladys Shafran
Kassman, Shirley
Katsiff, Bruce
Katzen, Lila (Pell)
Kaufman, Irving
Kaupelis, Robert John
Kay, Reed
Keck, Sheldon Waugh
Keeling, Henry Cornelious
Keeney, Allen Lloyd
Keller, Deane
Kelly, Isaac Perry
Kelly, Mary
Kemenyffy, Steven
Kendall, Thomas Lyle
Kennedy, Gene (Eugene Murray)
Kepes, Gyorgy
Kern, Arthur (Edward)
Kerslake, Kenneth Alvin
Kessler, Herbert Leon
Kettner, David Allen
Keyser, William Alphonse, Jr
Kieferndorf, Frederick George
Kilian, Austin Farland
Kind, Joshua B
Kingrey, Kenneth
Kington, L(ouis) Brent
Kinnaird, Richard William
Kipp, Orval
Kirschenbaum, Jules
Kiskadden, Robert Morgan
Kitao, T Kaori
Kitner, Harold
Klaven, Marvin L
Kleidon, Dennis Arthur
Klein, Cecelia F
Klement, Vera
Klitzke, Theodore Elmer
Knight, Tom (Thomas Lincoln), Jr
Knipschild, Robert
Knobler, Nathan
Knorr, Jeanne Boardman
Knowlton, Jonathan
Ko, Anthony
Kober, Alfred John
Koch, Arthur Robert
Koch, Gerd (Herman)
Kocher, Robert Lee
Koebbeman, Skip
Koepnick, Robert Charles
Kohn, William Roth
Koochin, William
Koons, Darell J
Koppelman, Chaim
Kopriva, Sharon Ortman
Korshak, Yvonne
Korzenik, Diana
Kos, Paul Joseph
Koscianski, Leonard J
Koss, Gene H
Kostyniuk, Ronald P
Kotoske, Roger Allen
Kottler, Howard William
Kouwenhoven, John A
Kovatch, Jak

EDUCATOR (cont)

Kowalski, Dennis Allen
Kramer, Jack N
Kramrisch, Stella
Krause, George
Kreilick, Marjorie E
Krinsky, Carol Herselle
Kronengold, Eric A
Kronsnoble, Jeffrey Michael
Krueger, Lothar David
Krug, Harry Elno
Krukowski, Lucian
Kuchar, Kathleen Ann
Kuhlman, Walter Egel
Kuhn, Marylou
Kultermann, Udo
Kurahara, Ted
Kurz, Diana
Kwiecinski, Chester Martin
LaChapelle, Joseph Robert
Lacy, Suzanne
Lader, Melvin Paul
Laderman, Gabriel
Lafaye, Nell Murray
Lahr, J(ohn) Stephen
Lake, Jerry Lee
Lam, Jennett (Brinsmade)
La Malfa, James Thomas
Lamantia, James
LaMarca, Howard J
Lamis, Leroy
Land-Weber, Ellen E
Lang, J T
Lang, Rodger Alan
Langland, Harold Reed
La Noue, Terence David
LaPena, Frank Raymond
Lapinski, Tadeusz (A)
LaPlantz, David
Larkin, Eugene
Larmer, Oscar Vance
Larsen, Erik
Larsen, John Christian
Larsen, Mernet Ruth
Larson, Orland
Larson, Philip Seely
Larson, William G
Lash, Kenneth
Laske, Lyle F
Lattanzio, Frances
Lauck, Anthony Joseph
Laurent, John Louis
Laurer, Robert A
Lavin, Marilyn Aronberg
Lavoy, Walter Joseph
Lawrence, Howard Ray
Lawrence, Jacob
Lawton, James L
Lay, Patricia Anne
Laynor, Harold Arthur
Lechtzin, Stanley
Le Clair, Charles
Lee, Briant Hamor
Lee, Rensselaer Wright
Lee, Robert J
Lee, Roger
Lee, Russell
Leepa, Allen
Leff, Juliette
Lehman, Mark Ammon
Leland, Whitney Edward
Lembeck, John Edgar
Leon, Dennis
Leonard, Joanne
Lepper, Robert Lewis
Lesch, Alma Wallace
Lesh, Richard D
Levine, Shepard
Levitine, George
Levy, David Corcos
Lewicki, James
Lewis, Michael H
Lewis, William Arthur
Leys, Dale Daniel
Libby, Gary Russell
Lincoln, Richard Mather
Lindemann, Edna M

Lindquist, Evan
Lindstrom, Gaell
Link, Val James
Lintault, Roger Paul
Lipofsky, Marvin B
Lippman, Judith
Little, Ken Dawson
Littleton, Harvey K
Livingstone, Biganess
Lloyd, Gary Marchal
Lobdell, Frank
Loehr, Max
Loew, Michael
Logan, David George
Logan, Frederick Manning
London, Peter
Longaker, Jon Dasu
Longman, Lester Duncan
Looney, Norman
Lopez, Rhoda Le Blanc
Lopez-Rey, Jose
Lotterman, Hal
Lottes, John William
Lotz, Steven Darryl
Love, Paul Van Derveer
Lovejoy, Margot R
Loveless, Jim
Loving, Richard Maris
Lowe, J Michael
Lubart, Henriette d'Arlin
Lubbers, Leland Eugene
Lucey, Jack
Luecking, Stephen Joseph
Lukas, Dennis Brian
Lukosius, Richard Benedict
Lund, David
Lupori, Peter John
Lyman, Thomas William
Lynch, James Burr, Jr
Lytle, Richard
Macaray, Lawrence Richard
McChesney, Clifton
McClanahan, John D
McCleary, Mary Fielding
McClure, Thomas F
McCoy, Katherine Braden
McCoy, Michael Dale
MacDonald, Scott
MacDougall, Peter Steven
McElroy, Jacquelyn Ann
  (Jacquelyn McElroy-
  Edwards)
McFee, June King
McGahec, Dorothy
McGarrell, James
McGee, Winston Eugene
McGough, Charles E
McIlvain, Douglas Lee
McIlvain, Frances H
Mack, Charles Randall
Mack, Rodger Allen
McKay, Arthur Fortescue
McKay, John Sangster
McKean, Hugh Ferguson
McKeeby, Byron Gordon
McKenzie, Allan Dean
McKinin, Lawrence
McLean, James Albert
McLean, Richard Thorpe
McMillan, Robert W
McNally, Sheila John
McNamara, Mary Jo
McPherson, Larry E
McVey, William M
McWhinnie, Harold James
Maddox, Jerrold Warren
Madura, Jack Joseph
Magenta, Muriel
Magleby, Frank (Francis R)
Mahlke, Ernest D
Mahoney, James Owen
Mahoney, Michael R T
Majeski, Thomas H
Maldre, Mati
Malenda, James William
Mallory, Robert
Mallory, Nina Ayala

Malpass, Michael Allen
Manetta, Edward J
Manhart, Thomas Arthur
Mansfield, Robert Adams
Manso, Leo
Marak, Louis Bernard
Marasco, Rose
Marcheschi, (Louis) Cork
Marcus, Irving E
Marcus, Marcia
Margolis, Richard M
Margoulies, Berta (Berta
  Margoulies O'Hare)
Marin, Augusto
Marriott, William Allen
Marrow, James Henry
Marsh, David Foster
Marsh, (Edwin) Thomas
Marshall, Ralph
Marshall, Robert Leroy
Marsicano, Nicholas
Martin, Alexander Toedt
Martin, Bernard Murray
Martin, Marianne Winter
Martino, Babette
Martinsen, Ivar Richard
Marton, Pier
Martz, Karl
Mason, Bette
Massey, Charles Wesley, Jr
Massey, Robert Joseph
Massin, Eugene Max
Matassa, John P
Matthews, Gene (Eugene
  Edward)
Matthews, Harriett
Mattil, Edward L
Mattingly, (James Thomas)
Maurice, Alfred Paul
Mavigliano, George Jerome
Mavroudis, Demetrios
Max, Lope (Lope Max Diaz
  Rivera)
Mayer, Edward Albert
Mayer, Susan Martin
Mayhew, Edgar De Noailles
Maynard, William
Mayrs, David Blair
Meehan, William Dale
Meek, A J
Meeker, Barbara Miller
Meister, Michael William
Meixner, Mary Louise
Mejer, Robert Lee
Melchert, James Frederick
Mellor, George Edward
Meredith, Dorothy Laverne
Merrick, James Kirk
Mesches, Arnold
Messersmith, Fred Lawrence
Metzger, Robert Paul
Metzker, Ray K
Mew, Tommy
Meyer, Jerry Don
Meyers, Ronald G
Michels, Eileen Manning
Midani, Akram
Middlebrook, David A
Mikus, Eleanore
Miley, Les
Miller, J(ohn) Brough
Milliken, Gibbs
Mills, Frederick Van Fleet
Milnes, Robert Winston
Miotke, Anne E
Mirano, Virgil Marcus
Mitchell, John Blair
Mitchell, Michael John
Moldroski, Al R
Moment, Joan
Momiyama, Nanae
Monaghan, Keith
Monroe, Betty Iverson
Monroe, Gerald
Monthan, Guy
Moore, John J
Moreno, Orduna Nicolas

Morganstern, James
Morin, Thomas Edward
Morris, Robert Clarke
Morrison, Keith Anthony
Moss, Jacqueline
Moss, Joel C
Moss, Karen Canner
Mullen, James Martin
Mullen, Philip Edward
Mullican, Lee
Mundt, Ernest Karl
Munsterberg, Hugo
Munzner, Aribert
Murashima, Kumiko
Murphy, Dudley C
Murray, Floretta May
Musgrave, Shirley H
Musick, Pat
Myer, Peter Livingston
Myers, Jack Fredrick
Myers, Joel Philip
Myford, James C
Naar, Harry I
Nadler, Harry
Nash, Katherine E
Navrat, Den (Dennis Edward)
Nawara, Lucille Procter
Nawrocki, Thomas Dennis
Nay, Mary Spencer
Naylor, John Geoffrey
Nees, Lawrence
Nesbitt, Alexander John
Neumann, William A
Nevitt, Richard Barrington
Newhall, Beaumont
Newton, Earle Williams
Nichols, Donald Edward
Nichols, Francis N, II
Nichols, William Allyn
Nick, George
Nickford, Juan
Noa, Florence
Nobili, Louise
Nochlin, Linda (Pommer)
Noe, Jerry Lee
Noggle, Anne
Norfleet, Barbara Pugh
Norton, Paul Foote
Norwood, Malcolm Mark
Novak, Barbara (Mrs Brian
  O'Doherty)
Novinski, Lyle Frank
Novotny, Elmer Ladislaw
Nugent, John Cullen
Nulf, Frank Allen
Nushawg, Michael Allan
Oakes, William Larry
Ockenga, Starr
Ockerse, Thomas
O'Connell, George D
O'Connor, Stanley James
O'Connor, Thom
O'Gorman, James Francis
Ohlson, Douglas Dean
Olson, Douglas John
Olson, Richard W
Omar, Margit
O'Neil, John
Opper, John
Orenstein, Gloria Feman
Ortiz, Rafael Montanez
Ortmayer, Constance
Orze, Joseph John
Osborne, Cynthia A
Osborne, Robert Lee
O'Sickey, Joseph Benjamin
Ott, Robert William
Oubre, Hayward Louis
Oxman, Mark
Pablo
Page, John Henry, Jr
Pappas, Marilyn
Pardee, William Hearne
Pardon, Earl B
Parfenoff, Michael S
Parker, Will (William
  Crawford)

EDUCATOR (cont)

EDUCATOR (cont)

Sutter, James Stewart
Sykes, (William) Maltby
Tacha, Athena
Tajiri, Shinkichi
Talbot, Jarold Dean
Tam, Reuben
Tasse, M Jeanne
Tatham, David Frederic
Taylor, Brie (Benjamin de Brie)
Taylor, Grace Martin
Taylor, Hugh Holloway
Taylor, John C E
Taysom, Wayne Pendelton
Teczar, Steven W
Tefft, Elden Cecil
Teilhet-Fisk, Jehanne Hildegarde
Teller, Douglas H
Tettleton, Robert Lynn
Thiebaud, (Morton) Wayne
Thomas, Elaine Freeman
Thomas, William Radford
Thompson, Donald Roy
Thompson, Dorothy Burr
Thompson, Ernest Thorne
Thompson, Nancy Kunkle
Thompson, Robert Charles
Thompson, Wade
Thompson, William Joseph
Thorne-Thomsen, Ruth T
Thornton, Jim (James Howard)
Thornton, Richard Samuel
Thrall, Arthur
Thurston, Jacqueline Beverly
Tibbs, Thomas S
Tierney, Patrick Lennox
Tobin, John Edward, Jr
Toney, Anthony
Toperzer, Thomas Raymond
Topper, David R
Torbert, Donald Robert
Torbert, Stephanie Birch
Torlen, Michael Arnold
Toulis, Vasilios (Apostolos)
Tovish, Harold
Townsend, (Alvin) Neal
Townsend, Vera B
Trakis, Louis
Trank, Lynn Edgar
Traub, Charles H
Treaster, Richard A
Tredennick, Dorothy W
Trentham, Gary Lynn
Triano, Anthony Thomas
Trivigno, Pat
Tse, Stephen
Tuckerman, Jane Bayard
Tufts, Eleanor M
Tulumello, Peter M
Turner, A Richard
Turner, David
Turner, Janet E
Turner, Robert Chapman
Turner, Theodore Roy
Turner, William Eugene
Turnure, James Harvey
Twarogowski, Leroy Andrew
Twiggs, Leo Franklin
Tyzack, Michael
Ubans, Juris K
Uccello, Vincenza Agatha
Upright, Diane W
Upton, John David
Uttech, Thomas Martin
Vaccaro, Nick Dante
Valerio, James Robert
Vanderlip, Dianne Perry
van der Meulen, Jan
Vandersall, Amy L
Vander Sluis, George J
van Duinwyk, George Paul
Van Leunen, Alice Louise
Van Loen, Alfred
Van Suchtelen, Adrian
Van Winkle, Lester G

Vargo, John
Varnedoe, John Kirk Train
Varnelis, Kazys
Vega, Edward
Verostko, Roman Joseph
Vevers, Tony
Vian, Orfeo
Viera, Charles David
Viesulas, Romas
Villa, Carlos
Visco, Anthony Salvatore
von Schlippe, Alexey
Voulkos, Peter
Wachs, Ethel
Wahlman, Maude Southwell
Waite, Elin Jane
Walburg, Gerald
Walker, Larry
Wallace, John Edward
Wallace, Kenneth William
Wallace, Lysbeth (Mai)
Wallace, Richard William
Wallace, Robert Dan
Wallin, Leland Dean
Walters, Sylvia Solochek
Walton, Guy E
Wands, Robert James
Warashina, M Patricia
Ward, Lyle Edward
Ward, Phillip A
Warner, Douglas Warfield
Warren, Jacqueline Louise
Wasser, Paula Kloster
Wasserman, Jack
Waters, Herbert (Ogden)
Watia, Tarmo
Watson, Ronald G
Weber, Albert Jacob
Weber, John Pitman
Wechter, Vivienne Thaul
Weddige, Emil
Wedin, Winslow Elliott
Weege, William
Weeks, James (Darrell Northrup)
Wegner, Nadene R
Weidner, Mary Elizabeth
Weiler, Melody M
Weinberg, Elbert
Weinberg, Ephraim
Weintraub, Annette
Weisberg, Gabriel P
Weisberg, Ruth Ellen
Weismann, Donald Leroy
Weiss, Jeff
Weitzmann, Kurt
Weller, Allen Stuart
Welpott, Jack Warren
Wenger, Jane (B)
Wenner, L John G
Werness, Hope B
Wert, Ned Oliver
Westcoast, Wanda
Westermeier, Clifford Peter
Westfall, Carol D
Wethli, Mark
Wexler, George
Wheelock, Arthur Kingsland, Jr
Whitaker, Irwin A
White, James Richard
White, Robert (Winthrop)
Whitesell, John D
Whiteside, William Albert, II
Whitlock, John Joseph
Whitney, Maynard Merle
Wicks, Eugene Claude
Widmer, Gwen Ellen
Wilbert, Robert John
Wilde, John
Wiley, William T
Williams, John Wesley
Williams, Lewis W, II
Williams, Mary Frances
Williams, William Thomas
Willis, Jay Stewart
Willis, William Henry, Jr

Wilson, Edward N
Wilson, Millie
Wilson, Warren Bingham
Wilwers, Edward Mathias
Wiman, Bill
Wink, Don (Jon Donnel)
Winkler, Maria Paula
Winokur, Robert Mark
Winter, Gerald Glen
Wisnosky, John G
Witte, Mary (Grace) Stieglitz
Wogstad, James Everet
Woitena, Ben S
Wolanin, Barbara Ann Boese
Wolber, Paul J
Wolfe, Lynn Robert
Wolsky, Jack
Wood, Beatrice
Woodford, Don (Donald Paul)
Woods, Rip
Woodson, Doris
Woodward, William
Wright, David Thomas
Wright, Frank
Wright, Milton
Wurmfeld, Sanford
Wyckoff, Sylvia Spencer
Yegul, Fikret Kutlu
Yenawine, Bruce Harley
Yoshida, Ray Kakuo
Young, Charles Alexander
Young, Janie Chester
Young, Joseph E
Young, Tom (William Thomas)
Youritzin, Victor Koshkin
Yunkers, Adja
Yust, David E
Zabarsky, Melvin Joel
Zaborowski, Dennis J
Zakin, Mikhail
Zallinger, Jean Day
Zallinger, Rudolph Franz
Zelanski, Paul John
Zemans, Joyce L
Zheutlin, Dale R
Ziemann, Richard Claude
Zilka, Michael John
Zimiles, Murray
Zona, Louis A
Zoretich, George Stephen

ENAMELIST

Bates, Kenneth Francis
Bennett, Jamie
Buzzelli, Joseph Anthony
Caster, Bernard Harry
Faddis, (William) George
Harper, William
Killmaster, John H
Malenda, James William Orsini
Perkins, A Alan
Schwarcz, June Theresa
Sheehe, Lillian Carolyn
Sieg, Robert Lawrence
Sundberg, Carl Gustave
Wawrytko, M(ary) F(rances)
Whitcomb, Kay

ENVIRONMENTAL ARTIST

Alhilali, Neda
Anderson, Kenneth Edmund
Asher, Michael
Bakanowsky, Louis J
Bender, Beverly Sterl
Bolt, Ron
Brown, Richard Morgan
Burgess, David Lowry
Buzzelli, Joseph Anthony
Cooper, Ron
Croft, Michael Flynt

Davis, Ben H
Denes, Agnes C
Dignac, Geny
Dwyer, Gary Colburn
Earls, Paul
Escobedo, Helen
Feigenbaum, Harriet (Mrs Neil Chamberlain)
Fisher, Rob (Robert Norman)
Floyd, Carl Leo
Fontana, Bill Patrick
Fredman, Faiya R
Gellis, Sandy L
Goldring, Elizabeth
Grabill, Vin (E Vincent, Jr)
Graham, Daniel H
Greenly, Colin
Gussow, Roy
Harding, Noel Robert
Harrison, Helen Mayer
Harrison, Newton A
Hendricks, Geoffrey
Henes, Donna
Hera
Housser, Yvonne McKague
Irwin, Robert
Janney, Christopher Draper
Kasuba, Aleksandra
Kirschenbaum, Bernard Edwin
Knowles, Alison
Kozloff, Joyce
Leicester, Andrew John
Lutz, Winifred Ann
McMillen, Michael C(halmers)
Marioni, Tom
Miller, Brenda
Norvell, Patsy
Notarbartolo, Albert
Pernotto, James Angelo
Poleskie, Stephen Francis
Prent, Mark
Price, Joan Webster
Reitzenstein, Reinhard
Roloff, John Scott
Roots, Garrison
Ross, Charles
Rumsey, David MacIver
Salomon, Lawrence
Sky, Alison
Snyder, Ruth (Cozen)
Soffer, Sasson
Solomon, Richard H
Sonfist, Alan
Stuhl, Michelle
Thacher, Anita
Turrell, James Archie
Wagner, Gordon Parsons
Whiten, Tim
Wines, James N
Wirtschafter, Bud
Woody, (Thomas) Howard
Zimmerman, Elyn

FILMMAKER

Almond, Paul
Auer, James Matthew
Balog, Michael
Bartlett, Scott
Bates, Leo James
Beckman, Ericka
Blair, Lee Everett
Brakhage, James Stanley
Breer, Robert C
Burckhardt, Rudy
Chase, Doris (Totten)
Cheng, Fu-Ding
Clifton, Michelle Gamm
Conner, Bruce
deAK, Edit
Delano, Jack
Dunn, Cal
Edelheit, Martha
Faccinto, Victor Paul
Frampton, Hollis

FILMMAKER (cont)
Frazer, John Thatcher
Gekiere, Madeleine
Geniusz, Robert Myles
Gerstein, David Steven
Golden, Eunice
Goldstein, Jack
Gould, John Howard
Greenfield, Amy
Haar, Francis
Haxton, David
Hay, George Austin
Henle, Fritz
Herbert, James Arthur
Hobbs, (Carl) Fredric
Holt, Nancy Louise
Hui, Helene
Huot, Robert
Iimura, Taka
Jarvis, Lucy
Johnson, Rodell C
Katz, Leandro
Kleckner, Susan
Knecht, John
Levitt, Helen
Liebling, Jerome
Lipzin, Janis Crystal
McCall, Anthony
McLaren, Norman
Mallory, Margaret
Mason, William Clifford
Mayes, Elaine
Myers, Richard Lewis
Namuth, Hans
Niblock, Phill
Nowytski, (Slavko) Sviatoslav
O'Neill, Pat
Orkin, Ruth (Mrs Morris
    Engel)
Padula, Fred David
Pattee, Rowena
Phillips, Robert J
Pinzarrone, Paul
Pitt, Suzan (Lee)
Ridlon, James A
Robbins, LeRoy (Southward)
Ruscha, Edward Joseph
Schneemann, Carolee
Schwartz, Lillian (Feldman)
Sharits, Paul Jeffrey
Singer, Joel
Snow, Michael
Sonneman, Eve
Sperry, Robert
Stiegler, Robert William
Stoumen, Lou
Thacher, Anita
Tilley, Lewis Lee
Van Der Beek, Edward Stanley
Wechsler, Judith Glatzer
Wieland, Joyce
Wirtschafter, Bud

GALLERY DIRECTOR
see also **Museum Director**

Aarons, Anita
Alpert, George
Austin, Jo-Anne Jordan
Ayers, Carol Lee
Baldwin, Russell W
Barnes, Lucinda Ann
Bartlett, Christopher E
Bathurst, David C
Benson, Martha J
Bergen, Sidney L
Berggruen, John Henry
Berkman, Aaron
Berman, Aaron
Bernal, Lucrecia Alejandra
Brown, Suzanne Goldman
Bryant, Linda Goode
Buecker, Robert
Bujese, Arlene
Burks, Myrna R

Burns, Timothy Joseph
Butts, H Daniel, III
Cannuli, Richard Gerald
Castile, Rand
Cathcart, Linda Louise
Christensen, Val Alan
Cloud, Jack L
Cohen, Mildred Thaler
Cohn, Frederick Donald
Conley, Zeb Bristol, Jr
Coopersmith, Georgia A
Corr, James Donat
Costley-Jacobs, Averille Esther
Craven, Roy Curtis, Jr
Curtiss-Truetsch, George Curt
    (George C Curtiss)
Davies, Hugh Marlais
Davis, John Harold
Dawson, Bess Phipps
Dixon, Kenneth Ray
Dolan, Margo
Donson, Jerome Allan
Drummer, William Richard
Elkin, Beverly Dawn
Esman, Rosa M
Fear, Daniel E
Ference, Cynthia
Flateman, Ira N
Fraenkel, Jeffrey Andrew
Frankel, Dextra
Frumkin, Allan
Fuller, Jeffrey P
Garcia, Frank
Gear, Josephine
Goldsmith, Benedict Isaac
Grandee, Joe Ruiz
Greco, Josephine G
Grossman, Maurizia M
Hampson, Ferdinand Charles
Hardy, Robert
Harmon, Foster
Howell, Elizabeth Ann (Mitch)
Huchel, Frederick M
Jones, Charlott Ann
Kalischer, Clemens
Kawecki, Jean Mary
Kelley, Donald Castell
Kent, H Latham
Khendry, Janak Kumar
Killeen, Melissa Helen
Kinsman, Robert Donald
Klein, Paul R
Kobayashi, Katsumi Peter
Koppelman, Dorothy
Langman, Richard Theodore
Lathrop, Churchill Pierce
Lazarus, Diane Gail
Levy, S(tephen) Dean
Lewis, Helen Natalie
Liddle, Nancy Hyatt
Lieberman, Vickie
Lippman, Judith
Lippmann, Janet Gurian
Lock, Earl Wayne
Locks, Marian
McManus, James William
Mahey, John A
Maradiaga, Ralph
Marberger, A Aladar
Michaux, Ronald Robert
Moody, Elizabeth Chambers
Newman, Louis
Nordland, Gerald John
Olsen, Sharon A
Pellicone, Marie
Penny, Aubrey John Robert
Pfeifer, Marcuse
Phillips, Dutch (James O, Jr)
Reuter, Laurel J
Richard, Jack
Richards, Tally
Rich-Perlow, Katharina
Rodriguez, Geno (Eugene)
Roster, Laila Bergs
Rothman, Sidney
Schweitzer, M R
Slade, Roy

Smith, B J
Sragow, Ellen
Stasik, Andrew J
Steel, Virginia Oberlin
Stetson, Daniel Everett
Stewart, Jeffrey
Stoddard, Donna Melissa
Stringer, John Norris
Sujo, Clara Diament
Sussman, Bonnie K
Suzuki, Katsko (Katsko Suzuki
    Kannegieter)
Swain, Robert Francis
Tasende, Jose Maria
Tatistcheff, Peter Alexis
Tennant, Donna Kay
Vanderlip, Dianne Perry
Velick, Bruce
Waaland, James Brearley, II
Washburn, Joan T
Wecker, Christoph Ulrich
White, Ruth
Whitney, Susan Gillian
Wilkins, David George
Wilson, Carrie Lois
Wortz, Melinda Farris
Yaneff, Chris

GLASS BLOWER

Ahvakana, Ulaaq (Lawrence
    Reynold)
Balog, Michael
Bernstein, William Joseph
Brejcha, Vernon Lee
Carlson, William D
Chihuly, Dale Patrick
Clark, Jon Frederic
Grimm, Raymond Max
Handler, Audrey
Hurlstone, Robert William
Ipsen, Kent Forrest
Kehlmann, Robert
Labino, Dominick
Lewis, John Conard
Littell, Biz
McGlauchlin, Tom
Marioni, Paul
Mulcahy, Kathleen
Myers, Joel Philip
Nygren, John Fergus
Ohno, Mitsugi
Rhodes, James Melvin
Ruffner, Ginny Martin Nail
Shepherd, Don (Donald Allen)
Taylor, Michael (Estes)

GOLDSMITH

Aird, Neil Carrick
Baldridge, Mark S
Bambas, Thomas Reese
Betteridge, Lois Etherington
Brauer, Connie Ann
Fisch, Arline Marie
Gabriel, Hannelore
Getty, Nilda Fernandez
Grissom, Freda Gill
Harper, William
J J
Kretsinger, Mary Amelia
Kuehnl, Claudia Ann
Larson, Orland
Lechtzin, Stanley
Mitchell, R(obert Ellis)
Neumann, William A
Paley, Albert Raymond
Pimentel, David Delbert
Renk, Merry
Satterfield, John Edward
Seppa, Heikki Markus
Sherman, Ira D
Thomason, Tom William
Thompson, Nancy Kunkle

van Duinwyk, George Paul
Wegner, Nadene R
Weiss, Linda (Linda Margaret
    Weiss-Edwards)
Wright, Donald

GRAPHIC ARTIST

Albers, Anni
Alcopley, L
Altwerger, Libby
Arias-Misson, Alain
Barbee, Robert Thomas
Baskin, Leonard
Becker, Bettie (Bettie
    Geraldine Wathall)
Berger, Oscar
Berry, William Augustus
Biberman, Edward
Black, Lisa
Boyd, Michael
Brainard, Joe
Brown, James
Bruni, Umberto
Bucknall, Malcolm Roderick
Byrne, Charles Joseph
Cantor, Mira (Mira Cantor-
    Piene)
Caparn, Rhys (Rhys Caparn
    Steel)
Capes, Richard Edward
Cardinal, Marcelin
Cartledge, Roseanne Niemyt
Chaikin, Alyce (Alyce Chaikin
    Kleinman)
Chesley, Paul Alexander
Civale, Biagio A
Clement, Kathleen (Ruth)
Colker, Edward
Collazo, Carlos Erick
Cracker Jack Kid (Charles D
    Welch)
Creech, Franklin Underwood
Crumbo, Minisa
d'Almeida, George
Darboven, Hanne
David, Cyril Frank
Davis, Meredith J
Denes, Agnes C
Dodrill, Donald Lawrence
Domjan, Joseph (Spiri)
Donneson, Seena
Dorn, Peter Klaus
Edwards, Stanley Dean
Elloian, Peter
Everett, Russell Henry
Farian, Babette S
Fenn, (Frances) Elizabeth
Ferris, Edythe
Fingesten, Peter
Fluek, Toby
Freeman, David L
Geerlings, Gerald Kenneth
Gerard, Paula (Mrs Herbert
    Renison)
Gerzso, Gunther
Gluhman, Joseph Walter
Gluhman, Margaret A
Goldring, Nancy Deborah
Goldszer, Bath-Sheba
Gorman, William D
Gorski, Richard Kenny
Gough, Robert Alan
Graham, Bill (William Karr)
Greenbaum, Dorothea
    Schwarcz
Hamady, Walter Samuel
Hart, Betty Miller
Haut, Claire (Joan)
Hein, Max
Held, (Jon) Jonathan, Jr
Herman, Alan David
Hill, J Tweed
Hillman, Arthur Stanley
Hilty, Thomas R

GRAPHIC ARTIST (cont)

Hios, Theo
Hirschfeld, Albert
Hornung, Clarence Pearson
Hudson, Jacqueline
Hueter, James Warren
Humphrey, Judy Lucille
Isham, Sheila Eaton
Jackson, Sarah
Jacobs, Ted Seth
Janschka, Fritz
Janson, Agnes
Johnson, James Edwin &
    Sandra Kay
Kaiser, Charles James
Kamen, Gloria
Kemper, John Garner
Kniffin, Ralph Gus
Knipscher, Gerard Allen
Kramer, Burton
Kuehn, Gary
Laymon, Cynthia J
Le Roy, Harold M
Li Marzi, Joseph
Lobello, Peter
MacDonald, Kevin John
Magee, Alderson
Maggs, James K
Maggs, Arnaud (Cyril
    Benvenuti)
Markell, Isabella Banks
Massie, Lorna
Maxwell, Robert Edwin
Mayer, Rosemary
Miller, Earl B(eauford)
Morton, Richard H
Moser, Barry
Moy, Seong
Murphy, Dudley C
Nelson, Jack D
Nutzle, Futzie (Bruce John
    Kleinsmith)
Obler, Geri
O'Neal, Roland Lenard
Orr, Arthur (Leslie)
Ortlieb, Robert Eugene
Osborn, Kevin Russell
Parker, Ann
Parker, Carolyn Johnson
Perry, Kathryn Powers
Peter, Friedrich Gunther
Pettibone, John Wolcott
Phillips, Helen (Elizabeth)
Pierre-Noel, Vergniaud
Plochmann, Carolyn Gassan
Post, Anne B
Pratt, Vernon Gaither
Pugh, Grace Huntley
Raskin, Ellen
Reibel, Bertram
Risbeck, Philip Edward
Robertson, Joan E (Joan
    Elizabeth Mitchell)
Sapien, Darryl Rudolph
Schachter, Justine Ranson
Schiller, Beatrice
Shaw, Paul Jefferson
Simmons, Cleda Marie
Soult, James Thomas
Spurling, Norine M
Stamelos, Electra Georgia
    Mousmoules
Sternberg, Harry
Swiggett, Jean Donald
Thollander, Earl
Tonelli, Edith Ann
Trachtenberg, Gloria P
Turner, Ralph James
Vallee, William Oscar
Van Oordt, Peter
Vivenza, Francesca
Wilson, Robert
Wilson, Sybil
Wise, Gerald Lee
Wright, Bernard
Young, Nancy J(eanne)
Zisla, Harold

HISTORIAN

Aber, Ita
Ackerman, Gerald Martin
Ackerman, James S
Adams, Clinton
Agee, William C
Ahrens, Kent
Alexander, Margaret Ames
Allara, Pamela Edwards
Allen, (Harvey) Harold
Allen, William J
Allentuck, Marcia Epstein
Allgood, Charles Henry
Alvarez-Cervela, Jose Maria
Amend, Eugene Michael
Andersen, Wayne Vesti
Anderson, Dennis Ray
Anderson, Ross Cornelius
Andres, Glenn Merle
Appelhof, Ruth A
Arnason, H Harvard
Asher, Frederick M
Auping, Michael Graham
Ayres, Larry Marshall
Bacot, Henry Parrott
Ballinger, James K
Baretski, Charles Allan
Barnes, Lucinda Ann
Barons, Richard Irwin
Barrie, Dennis Ray
Barrio-Garay, Jose Luis
Barr-Sharrar, Beryl
Bassin, Joan
Baum, Timothy
Beatty, Frances Fielding
    Lewis
Beck, James
Begley, Wayne E
Bell, Philip Michael
Benjamin, Lloyd William, III
Benson, Elizabeth Polk
Berman, Greta W
Bernstein, Saralinda
Bershad, David L
Bettmann, Otto Ludwig
Bier, Justus
Blackmun, Barbara Winston
Bledsoe, Jane Kathryn
Bloch, E Maurice
Blum, Shirley Neilsen
Bogart, Michele Helene
Boggs, Jean Sutherland
Bolton-Smith, Robin Lee
Bongiorno, Laurine Mack
Bony, Jean Victor
Bordeaux, Jean Luc
Borgo, Ludovico
Bothmer, Bernard V
Bowlt, John
Bowne, James Dehart
Bradt, Kathleen Weil-Garris
Bravmann, Rene A
Breithaupt, Erwin M
Brinkerhoff, Dericksen Morgan
Broadd, Harry Andrew
Broadley, Hugh T
Broder, Patricia Janis
Broderick, Herbert Reginald,
    III
Brooks, H(arold) Allen
Broude, Norma Freedman
Broun, Elizabeth Gibson
Brown, Blanche Rachel
Brown, David Alan
Brown, Jonathan
Brown, Milton Wolf
Brown, Theodore Morey
Brumbaugh, Thomas Brendle
Bruno, Vincent J
Bryant, Edward Albert
Bucher, Francois
Buck, Robert Treat, Jr
Buerger, Janet E
Buitron, Diana M
Bumgardner, Georgia Brady
Burdock, Harriet

Burke, Margaret
Burnett, David Grant
Burnside, Wesley M
Burrows, Selig S
Bush, Donald John
Bush, Martin H
Byrnes, James Bernard
Bywaters, Jerry
Cahill, James Francis
Caldwell, Benjamin Hubbard,
    Jr
Caldwell, Martha Belle
Caldwell, Susan Havens
Calkins, Robert G
Callisen, Sterling
Camfield, William Arnett
Campbell, Kenneth Floyd
Canby, Jeanny Vorys
Carey, John Thomas
Carmean, E A, Jr
Carpenter, James Morton
Castano, Elvira
Castleman, Riva
Cate, Phillip Dennis
Cathcart, Linda Louise
Catlin, Stanton L
Cavaliere, Barbara
Celender, Donald Dennis
Chambers, Bruce William
Chambers, Karen
Chappell, Miles Linwood
Chiarenza, Carl
Chow Chian-Chiu
Cikovsky, Nicolai, Jr
Clark, Garth Reginald
Clark, Vicky A
Clark, William W
Cleaver, Dale Gordon
Clermont, Ghislain
Clisby, Roger David
Coates, Ann S
Coates, Ross Alexander
Codell, Julie Francia
Cohen, Arthur A
Cohen, Charles E
Cohen, Joan Lebold
Cohen, Ronny H
Cohn, Marjorie B
Cole, Bruce
Cole, Harold David
Cole, Herbert Milton
Collier, James Mitchell
Collins, Christiane C
Collins, George R
Collins, Howard F
Colton, Judith
Comini, Alessandra
Conforti, Michael Peter
Conlon, James Edward
Constantine, Mildred
Coolidge, John
Corbin, George Allen
Cormack, Malcolm
Covi, Dario A
Cox, Richard William
Craven, Wayne
Crelly, William Richard
Crimp, Douglas
Cropper, M Elizabeth
Cummings, Frederick James
Cutler, Ethel Rose
Cuttler, Charles David
Czuma, Stanislaw J
Dale, William Scott Abell
D'Ancona, Mirella Levi
Daniel, Suzanne Garrigues
Darling, Sharon Sandling
Dauterman, Carl Christian
Davey, Ronald A
Davidowitz (Dror), Moshe
Davidson, J LeRoy
Davies, Hugh Marlais
Davis, Ellen N
Davis, Marian B
Dawdy, Doris Ostrander
Dee, Elaine Evans
De Foix-Crenascol, Louis

Delehanty, Suzanne E
De Moura Sobral, Luis
Dennison, Keith Elkins
DePuma, Richard Daniel
Desportes, Ulysse Gandvier
d'Harnoncourt, Anne
Dillow, Nancy E (Nancy
    Elizabeth Robertson)
Dinnerstein, Lois
Dobard, Raymond Gerard
Dockstader, Frederick J
Domit, Moussa M
Donnelly, Marian Card
Donohoe, Victoria
Dorra, Henri
Dorsky, Morris
Doumato, Lamia
Dow, Helen Jeannette
Doyon, Gerard Maurice
Dresser, Louisa (Louisa
    Dresser Campbell)
Drewal, Henry John
Driscoll, John Paul
Dunkelman, Martha Levine
Dunn, Roger Terry
Dwyer, Eugene Joseph
Dwyer, Melva Jean
Earle, Edward W
Eckert, William Dean
Eckhardt, Ferdinand
Edelstein, Teri J
Ehresmann, Donald Louis
Ehrlich, George
Eidelberg, Martin
Eisenberg, Marvin
Eitner, Lorenz E A
Elderfield, John
Eldredge, Charles Child, III
Elliott, B Charles, Jr
Elsen, Albert Edward
Enggass, Robert
Enyeart, James Lyle
Epstein, Annabel Wharton
Ertman, Earl Leslie
Esau, Erika
Esser, Janet Brody
Ettlinger, Leopold David
Evans, Bruce Haselton
Evans, Grose
Fagaly, William Arthur
Faison, Samson Lane, Jr
Farmer, John David
Farwell, Beatrice
Fehl, Philipp P
Feinblatt, Ebria
Ferber, Linda S
Fern, Alan Maxwell
Field, Richard Sampson
Fiero, Gloria K
Fink, Lois Marie
Finley, Gerald Eric
Fischer, Henry George
Flam, Jack D
Fleischer, Roland Edward
Flexner, James Thomas
Flint, Janet Altic
Flomenhaft, Eleanor
Folda, Jaroslav (Thayer), III
Foley, Kathy Kelsey
Forbes, John Allison
Forsyth, Ilene H(aering)
Foster, Stephen C
Fowle, Geraldine Elizabeth
Fredericksen, Burton Baum
Freedberg, Sydney Joseph
Freitag, Wolfgang Martin
Friedman, Ann Marti
Frinta, Mojmir Svatopluk
Fuller, John Charles
Fusco, Laurie S
Fusco, Peter Richard
Gaines, William Robert
Gaither, Edmund B
Garcia, Frank
Garcia, Rupert (Marshall R)
Garnsey, Clarke Henderson
Garrard, Mary DuBose

HISTORIAN (cont)

Garvan, Beatrice Bronson
Gatling, Eva Ingersoll
Gealt, Adelheid Medicus
Gear, Josephine
Gebhard, David
Geldzahler, Henry
Gerdts, Abigail Booth
Gerdts, William H
Giacalone, Vito
Gibson, Walter Samuel
Gilbert, Creighton Eddy
Gladstone, Barbara Regen
Glaser, Bruce
Glasgow, Vaughn Leslie
Glass, Dorothy F
Glenn, Constance White
Gluhman, Joseph Walter
Goheen, Ellen Rozanne
Goldberg, RoseLee
Goodyear, Frank H, Jr
Gordon, Donald Edward
Gould, Karen Keel
Gould, Philip
Gouma-Peterson, Thalia
Green, Glenda
Grieder, Terence
Grissom, Eugene Edward
Grossman, Sheldon
Grove, Samuel Harold
Grubar, Francis Stanley
Guenther, Peter W
Guilmain, Jacques
Gully, Anthony Lacy
Gunasinghe, Siri
Gundersheimer, Herman
  (Samuel)
Gurewitsch, Edna P
Gurney, George
Gutmann, Joseph
Hager, Hellmut W
Halasz, Piri
Hallmark, Donald Parker
Hamilton, George Heard
Hamilton, W Paul C
Hammond, Leslie King
Hand, John Oliver
Hanfmann, George M A
Hanson, Anne Coffin
Harper, Paula (Hays)
Harris, Ann Sutherland
Hartigan, Lynda Roscoe
Hartt, Frederick
Haskell, Barbara
Haskins, John Franklin
Hassrick, Peter H
Hatch, John Davis
Havelock, Christine Mitchell
Hawes, Louis
Hayes, Laura M
Hayward, Jane
Hazlehurst, Franklin Hamilton
Hearn, M F (Millard
  Fillmore), Jr
Heckscher, Morrison Harris
Heckscher, William Sebastian
Hedberg, Gregory Scott
Heller, Reinhold August
Hemphill, Pamela
Henderson, Linda Dalrymple
Hennessey, William John
Henning, Edward Burk
Henry, Sara Lynn
Herbert, Robert L
Hero, Peter deCourcy
Hersey, George Leonard
Hertzman, Gay Mahaffy
Heyman, Therese Thau
Hibbard, Howard
Hill, Draper
Hill, William Mansfield
Hills, Patricia
Hinson, Tom Everett
Hitchcock, Henry Russell
Hobbs, Robert Carleton
Holcomb, Adele Mansfield
Holladay, Harlan H

Holm, Bill
Holman, Thomas S
Homer, William Innes
Hood, Walter Kelly
Houser, Caroline Mae
Howarth, Shirley Reiff
Howat, John Keith
Howell, Douglass (Morse)
Howett, John
Howland, Richard Hubbard
Hubbard, Robert Hamilton
Hudson, Ralph Magee
Hungerford, Constance Cain
Hunisak, John Michael
Hunter, Sam
Hutchison, Jane Campbell
Hyman, Isabelle
Hyman, Linda
Isaacson, Gene Lester
Isserstedt, Dorothea Carus
Jacob, Mary Jane
Jacobowitz, Ellen Sue
Jacobsen, Michael A
Jacobus, John M
Jaffe, Irma B
Janson, Anthony Fredrick
Jay, Bill
Jenkins, Donald John
Johnson, Charles W, Jr
Johnson, Diane Chalmers
Johnson, Donald Ray
Johnson, Ellen Hulda
Johnson, Eugene Joseph
Johnson, Ronald W
Johnson, Selina (Tetzlaff)
Johnston, William Ralph
Jonaitis, Aldona
Jones, Lois Swan
Joost-Gaugier, Christiane L
Jordan, George Edwin
Jordan, Jim
Judson, William D
Kagan, Andrew Aaron
Kahan, Mitchell Douglas
Kan, Michael
Kaplan, Julius David
Karlstrom, Paul Johnson
Kelder, Diane M
Kelemen, Pal
Kelleher, Patrick Joseph
Kimbrell, Leonard Buell
King, Elaine A
Kinsman, Robert Donald
Kirkpatrick, Diane
Kitao, T Kaori
Kitzinger, Ernst
Klein, Cecelia F
Klein, Michael Eugene
Kleinbauer, W Eugene
Klitzke, Theodore Elmer
Knox, George
Koch, Robert
Kornetchuk, Elena
Korshak, Yvonne
Kotik, Charlotta
Kotrozo, Carol Donnell
Kovinick, Philip Peter
Krane, Susan
Krauss, Rosalind E
Krinsky, Carol Herselle
Kubler, George Alexander
Kuhn, Brenda
Kultermann, Udo
Kuspit, Donald Burton
Kuwayama, George
Lader, Melvin Paul
Landis, Ellen Jamie
Lane, John Rodger
Langer, Sandra Lois
Larsen, Susan C
Laskin, Myron, Jr
Lathrop, Churchill Pierce
Lavin, Irving
Lavin, Marilyn Aronberg
Lawall, David Barnard
Leach, Frederick Darwin
Lee, Briant Hamor

Lee, Rensselaer Wright
Lehman, Arnold L
Lengyel, Alfonz
Lerman, Leo
Lerner, Martin
Levin, Gail
Levit, Herschel
Levitine, George
Levitt, Alfred
Lewis, Douglas
Lewis, Samella Sanders
Lewis, Virginia Elnora
Li, Chu-Tsing
Licht, Jennifer McConnell
Lilyquist, Christine
Lindsay, Kenneth C
Locke, Michelle Wilson
Loerke, William Carl
Lombardo, Josef Vincent
Long, Rose-Carol Washton
Longman, Lester Duncan
Longstreet, Stephen
Lopez-Rey, Jose
Love, Richard Henry
Lovell, Margaretta Markle
Lowry, Bates
Luchs, Alison
Ludmer, Joyce Pellerano
Ludwig, Allan I
Lunde, Karl Roy
Lunsford, John (Crawford)
Lust, Herbert
Lyman, Thomas William
Lynch, James Burr, Jr
Lyons, Lisa
McCabe, Cynthia Jaffee
McCracken, Harold
McCready, Eric Scott
MacDonald, William L
McGill, Forrest
Mack, Charles Randall
McKenzie, Allan Dean
McNally, Sheila John
McNamara, Mary Jo
Madden-Work, Betty I
Maddox, Jerald Curtis
Madonia, Ann C
Maguire, Henry Pownall
Mahoney, Michael R T
Mallory, Nina Ayala
Mann, Maybelle
Markman, Sidney David
Marlor, Clark Strang
Marrow, James Henry
Marshall, Richard Donald
Marter, Joan
Martin, Marianne Winter
Martin, Richard (Harrison)
Marzio, Peter Cort
Maser, Edward Andrew
Masheck, Joseph Daniel
Mathews, Nancy Mowll
Maurer, Evan Maclyn
Mavigliano, George Jerome
Mayo, Marti
Meister, Michael William
Merkel, Jayne (Silverstein)
Messer, Thomas M
Meyer, Charles Edward
Meyer, Jerry Don
Meyer, Ruth Krueger
Michels, Eileen Manning
Miles, Ellen Gross
Miller, Jean Johnston
Mino, Yutaka
Moeller, Robert Charles, III
Moffitt, John Francis
Moir, Alfred
Monaghan, Kathleen Mary
Mongan, Agnes
Moore, Barbara
Moore, Ethel
Moore, Peter
Morganstern, James
Morishita, Joyce Chizuko
Morrin, Peter Patrick
Morse, Peter

Mosby, Dewey Franklin
Moser, Joann
Moss, Jacqueline
Moulton, Susan Gene
Mount, Marshall Ward
Moure, Nancy Dustin Wall
Moxey, Keith Patricio Fleming
Mozley, Anita Ventura
Muhlert, Jan Keene
Muller, Priscilla Elkow
Munsterberg, Hugo
Myron, Robert
Naeve, Milo M
Nasgaard, Roald
Nash, Steven Alan
Natzmer, Cheryl Lynn
Nees, Lawrence
Neff, John Hallmark
Nelson, Jon Allen
Newhouse, Clyde Mortimer
Nochlin, Linda (Pommer)
Norris, Andrea Spaulding
Norton, Paul Foote
Novak, Barbara (Mrs Brian
  O'Doherty)
Oberhuber, Konrad J
O'Connor, Francis Valentine
O'Connor, Stanley James
O'Gorman, James Francis
Olin, Ferris
Ollman, Arthur L
Olpin, Robert Spencer
Onorato, Ronald Joseph
Orenstein, Gloria Feman
Orr-Cahall, Anona Christina
Ostrow, Stephen Edward
O'Toole, James St Laurence
Overland, Carlton Edward
Pal, Pratapaditya
Parks, James Dallas
Parry, Ellwood Comly, III
Patrick, Darryl L
Patton, Sharon Frances
Pearman, Sara Jane
Peck, William Henry
Pendergraft, Norman Elveis
Pepe, Marie Sophie Huper
Percy, Ann Buchanan
Perkins, Ann
Perlin, Ruth Rudolph
Perry, Regenia Alfreda
Philip, Lotte Brand
Phillips, James
Pierce, James Smith
Pierce, Patricia Jobe
Pilgrim, Dianne H
Pilgrim, James F
Pisano, Ronald George
Placzek, Adolf Kurt
Polcari, Stephen
Poling, Clark V
Pollitt, Jerome Jordan
Polzer, Joseph
Pommer, Richard
Poor, Robert John
Porada, Edith
Porter, Jeanne Chenault
Porter, Richard James
Posner, Donald
Powell, Earl Alexander, III
Pressly, William Laurens, Jr
Preston, George Nelson
Preziosi, Donald A
Prokopoff, Stephen Stephen
Prown, Jules David
Purtle, Carol Jean
Quinsac, Annie-Paule
Quirarte, Jacinto
Radice, Anne-Imelda Marino
Radycki, J(osephine) Diane
Raggio, Olga
Ragusa, Isa
Rand, Harry
Randall, Richard Harding, Jr
Rash, Nancy
Raven, Arlene
Reed, Walt Arnold

HISTORIAN (cont)

Reese, Thomas Ford
Reeve, James Key
Reeves, James Franklin
Reff, Theodore
Reich, Sheldon
Reiling, Susan Wallace
Reilly, Bernard Francis
Rembert, Virginia Pitts
Rensch, Roslyn
Rewald, John
Rhyne, Charles Sylvanus
Rice, Shelley Enid
Richardson, Edgar Preston
Richardson, John Adkins
Rigby, Ida Katherine
Robb, David Metheny, Jr
Robbins, Daniel J
Roberson, Samuel Arndt
Robinson, Franklin W
Robinson, Lilien Filipovitch
Rogers, Millard Buxton
Rogers, Millard Foster, Jr
Rorex, Robert Albright
Rosand, David
Roseberg, Carl Andersson
Rosen, James Mahlon
Rosenblum, Robert
Rosenthal, Earl Edgar
Rosenthal, Gertrude
Rosenzweig, Daphne Lange
Roskill, Mark Wentworth
Rossen, Susan F
Roth, Leland M(artin)
Roth, Moira
Rowell, Margit
Rubin, Arnold Gary
Rubin, William
Rubinstein, Charlotte Streifer
Ruiz de la Mata, Ernesto J
Russell, Helen Diane
Sachs, Samuel, II
St John, Bruce
Samuels, Harold & Peggy
Sanderson, Warren
Sandler, Irving Harry
Scarbrough, Cleve Knox, Jr
Schaefer, Scott Jay
Schapiro, Meyer
Scherer, Herbert Grover
Scheyer, Ernst
Schiff, Gert K A
Schimansky, Donya Dobrila
Schipper, Merle Solway
Schlicher, Karl Theodore
Schmandt-Besserat, Denise
Schmeckebier, Laurence E
Schmitt, Marilyn Low
Schneiderman, Richard S
Schnorrenberg, John Martin
Schuller, Nancy Shelby
Schulz, Ann Markham
Schulz, Juergen
Schuster, Eugene Ivan
Schwabacher, Ethel K
Schwartz, Marvin D
Schwarz, Kurt L
Schweizer, Paul Douglas
Scott, David Winfield
Scott, John Beldon
Scott, John Fredrik
Scribner, Charles, III
Segger, Martin Joseph
Sellin, David
Selvig, Forrest Hall
Selz, Peter H
Sewell, Darrel L
Shalkop, Robert Leroy
Shangraw, Clarence Frank
Shaw, Courtney Ann
Shaw, Joseph Winterbotham
Shaw, Nancy (Rivard)
Sheard, Wendy Stedman
Sheon, Aaron
Shepard, Lewis Albert
Sheppard, Carl Dunkle
Sherman, Claire Richter

Shestack, Alan
Shimizu, Yoshiaki
Sickman, Laurence Chalfant Stevens
Sieber, Roy
Silins, Janis
Silver, Larry Arnold
Simmons, John Herbert
Simon, David L
Simon, Robert Barry
Simpson, Marianna Shreve
Simpson, William Kelly
Sims, Lowery Stokes
Slatkes, Leonard J
Slatkin, Wendy
Slive, Seymour
Sloane, Joseph Curtis
Smith, Frances Kathleen
Smith, Graham
Smith, James Morton
Smyth, Craig Hugh
Snodgrass, Jeanne Owens (Mrs M Eugene King)
Sobotik, Kent
Sokol, David Martin
Sonnenschein, Hugo
Sorell, Victor Alexander
Spector, Jack J
Spence, Robert
Spencer, Harold Edwin
Spencer, John R
Spike, John Thomas
Sponenburgh, Mark
Sprague, Paul Edward
Spurlock, William Henry, II
Stamm, Geoffrey Eaton
Stancil, Kimsey
Standen, Edith Appleton
Stead, Rexford Arthur
Stebbins, Theodore Ellis, Jr
Stein, Judith Ellen
Stein, Roger Breed
Steinberg, Leo
Stell, H Kenyon
Stern, Jean
Stewart, John Douglas
Stewart, Robert Gordon
Stillman, Damie
Stofflet, Mary
Stokstad, Marilyn
Stones, Margaret Alison
Stott, Deborah
Strickler, Susan Elizabeth
Striker, Cecil L
Stringer, Mary Evelyn
Stroessner, Robert Joseph
Stubblebine, James Harvey
Stuckey, Charles F
Stump, Jeanne
Sturgeon, Mary C
Sturges, Hollister
Sullivan, Ruth Wilkins
Sunkel, Robert Cleveland
Swanson, Vern Grosvenor
Sweeney, J Gray
Taft, Frances Prindle
Takach, Mary H
Tancock, John Leon
Tarbell, Roberta Kupfrian
Tatham, David Frederic
Taylor, Hugh Holloway
Taylor, Kendall Frances
Taylor, Mary Cazort
Taylor, Rene Claude
Teilhet-Fisk, Jehanne Hildegarde
Teitz, Richard Stuart
Theofiles, George
Tierney, Patrick Lennox
Toker, Franklin K B
Tolles, Bryant Franklin, Jr
Tomasini, Wallace J
Tomko, George Peter
Topper, David R
Torbert, Donald Robert
Townsend, J Benjamin
Townsend, Vera B

Trapp, Frank Anderson
Travis, David B
Trenton, Patricia Jean
Tselos, Dimitri Theodore
Tseng Yu-ho
Tuchman, Phyllis
Tucker, Anne Wilkes
Tufts, Eleanor M
Turner, A Richard
Turnure, James Harvey
Tyler, Ron C
van der Meulen, Jan
Vandersall, Amy L
Van Schaack, Eric
Varnedoe, John Kirk Train
Venegas, Haydee E
Vermeule, Cornelius Clarkson, III
Verostko, Roman Joseph
Vincent, Clare
Wahlman, Maude Southwell
Walker, William Bond
Wallace, David Harold
Wallace, Richard William
Wallace, Robert Dan
Wallach, Alan
Waller, Aaron Bret
Walton, Florence Goodstein (Florence Goodstein-Shapiro)
Ward, John Lawrence
Wark, Robert Rodger
Wasserman, Jack
Watrous, James Scales
Watson, Katharine Johnson
Watson, Ross
Wattenmaker, Richard J
Webb, Todd
Webster, Sally (Sara B)
Wechsler, Judith Glatzer
Weeks, Edward F
Weidman, Jeffrey
Weinberg, H Barbara
Weinhardt, Carl Joseph, Jr
Weisberg, Gabriel P
Weiss, Peg
Weitzmann, Kurt
Welch, Stuart Cary
Weller, Allen Stuart
Werness, Hope B
West, Richard Vincent
Westervelt, Robert F
Westin, Robert H
Wethcy, Harold Edwin
Whitcomb, Therese Truitt
Whitney, William Kuebler
Wiebe, Charles M
Wiesendanger, Martin Wolfgang
Wilkins, David George
Williams, Benjamin Forrest
Williams, John Alden
Williams, John Wesley
Williams, Lewis W, II
Willis, Elizabeth Bayley
Wilmerding, John
Winchester, Alice
Wise, Suzanne Tanderup
Withers, Josephine
Wixom, William D
Wolanin, Barbara Ann Boese
Wood, James Nowell
Wooden, Howard Edmund
Woolfenden, William Edward
Worth, Peter John
Worthen, Amy Namowitz
Wriston, Barbara
Wunder, Richard Paul
Yard, Sally Elizabeth
Yassin, Robert Alan
Youritzin, Victor Koshkin
Zafran, Eric Myles
Zemans, Joyce L
Zerner, Henri Thomas
Zietz, Stephen Joseph
Ziff, Jerrold
Zilczer, Judith Katy

ILLUMINATOR

Balog, Michael
Billings, Henry
Carrington, Joy Harrell
Cawein, Kathrin
Gast, Carolyn Bartlett (Lutz)
Werner Vaughn, Salle

ILLUSTRATOR

Abel, Ray
Accurso, Anthony Salvatore
Aebi, Ernst Walter
Alajalov, Constantin
Aliki
Angulo, Chappie
Ariss, Herbert Joshua
Baker, Jill
Baldwin, Richard Wood
Ball, Lyle V
Barnes, Cliff (Clifford V)
Bartlett, Christopher E
Bearman, Jane Ruth
Behrens, Roy R
Beitz, Les
Bennett, Rainey
Benney, Robert
Bertoni, Dante H
Bierly, Edward J
Bissell, Phil
Bittner, Hans Oskar
Blackburn, Loren Hayner
Blanchard, Carol
Blattner, Robert Henry
Blos, May (Elizabeth)
Boedeker, Arnold E (Boedie)
Bogorad, Alan Dale
Bond, Oriel Edmund
Booth, George Warren
Bowler, Joseph, Jr
Braiden, Rose Margaret J
Brender a Brandis, Gerard William
Broemel, Carl William
Brown, Judith Gwyn
Brown, Rhett Delford (Harriett Gurney Brown)
Buba, Joy Flinsch
Burchard, Peter Duncan
Byard, Carole Marie
Byrd, Robert John
Campbell, Dorothy Bostwick
Carter, Frederick Timmins
Cellini, Joseph
Chapman, Walter Howard
Charmatz, Bill (William Adolphe)
Chase, Richard Andrew
Chestney, Lillian
Chwast, Seymour
Clark, Roberta Carter
Clymer, John F
Cober, Alan E
Comito, Nicholas U
Conant, Jan Royce
Cooney, Barbara (Mrs Charles Talbot Porter)
Cortese, Edward Fortunato
Crawford, Bill (Wilbur Ogden)
Crite, Allan Rohan
Crosby, Ranice W
Cuevas, Jose Luis
d'Alessio, Gregory
Damron, John Clarence
Dank, Leonard Dewey
Davis, John Harold
Davis, Wayne Lambert
deGroat, Diane L
Deloney, Jack Clouse
DePillars, Murry N
Desoto, Rafael M
Devlin, Harry
Di Fate, Vincent
Dimson, Theo Aeneas

ILLUSTRATOR (cont)

Dohanos, Stevan
Dowden, Anne Ophelia Todd
Drower, Sara Ruth
Echohawk, Brummett
Egeli, Peter Even
Eichenberg, Fritz
Eisenstat, Benjamin
Elliot, John Theodore
Ellis, Richard
Engel, Michael Martin, II
Etting, Emlen
Everhart, Don (Donald
    Nelson), Jr
Falter, John
Ferris, (Carlisle) Keith
Fish, Richard G
Floethe, Richard
Flora, James Royer
Folkus, Dan (Daniel Alan
    Fredrickson)
Frace, Charles Lewis
Freund, Harry Louis
Friberg, Arnold
Galli, Stanley Walter
Gallo, William Victor
Gast, Carolyn Bartlett (Lutz)
Geisert, Arthur Frederick
Gilbert, Albert Earl
Ginsburg, Max
Glaser, Milton
Golbin, Andree
Gordon, Violet
Granstaff, William Boyd
Greenwald, Sheila Ellen
Groth, John August
Guderna, Ladislav
Guzman-Forbes, Robert
Haden, Eunice (Barnard)
Halliday, Nancy Ruth
Handville, Robert T
Harris, Robert George
Haynes, George Edward
Haynes, R (Richard Thomas)
Healy, Deborah Ann
Heberling, Glen Austin
Herzberg, Thomas
Hildebrand, June Mary Ann
Hill, Joan (Chea-se-quah)
Hoffman, Martin (Joseph)
Hogarth, Burne
Holden, Raymond James
Holgate, Jeanne
Holt, Charlotte Sinclair
Horowitz, Nadja
Huff, Laura Weaver
Inman, Pauline Winchester
Irvin, Fred Maddox
Itchkawich, David Michael
Jackson, Everett Gee
Jackson, Vaughn L
Janelsins, Veronica
Jones, Elizabeth Orton
Kaufman, Joe
Kessler, Leonard H
Keveson, Florence
Kidd, Steven R
Kingman, Dong M
Knight, Jacob Jaskoviak
Kogan, Deborah
Koren, Edward B
Krigstein, Bernard
Kunstler, Morton
Laessig, Robert
Larsen, Ole
Latham, Barbara
Lea, Tom
Lefranc, Margaret (Margaret
    Lefranc Schoonover)
Leon, Ralph Bernard
Levering, Robert K
Lewicki, James
Livingston, Virginia (Mrs
    Hudson Warren Budd)
Lock, Charles L
Loehle, Richard E
Loewer, Henry Peter

London, Alexander
Lovell, Tom
Lynde, Stan
Macaulay, David Alexander
McCall, Robert Theodore
McCloskey, Robert
McDermott, Gerald
Macdonald, Grant
McGee, Olivia Jackson
McMillan, Constance
MacNutt, Glenn Gordon
McVicker, Charles Taggart
Magee, Alan Arthur
Mancini, John
Mandel, Saul
Margules, Gabriele Ella
Marshall, Bruce
Matsubara, Naoko
Matternes, Jay Howard
Mawicke, Tran
Mays, Victor
Mina-Mora, Raul Jose
Mion, Pierre Riccardo
Mitchell, James E
Mock, Richard Basil
Moose, Philip Anthony
Moose, Talmadge Bowers
Morgan, Maritza Leskovar
Mosley, Zack T
Ness, Evaline (Mrs Arnold A
    Bayard)
Nevitt, Richard Barrington
Norris, Leonard Matheson
Nowak, Leo
Oakes, William Larry
O'Neal, Roland Lenard
Osborn, Robert
Osyczka, Bohdan Danny
Parker, Alfred
Parnall, Peter
Partch, Virgil Franklin, II
Paschke, Edward F (Ed)
Paul, Greg (Gregory Wilmer)
Pena, Amado Maurilio, Jr
Perlin, Bernard
Perlman, Raymond
Perrin, C Robert
Peterson, Roger Tory
Petrie, Ferdinand Ralph
Petro, Joseph (Victor), Jr
Phillips, Irving W
Pitcher, John Charles
Pratt, Frances (Frances
    Elizabeth Usui)
Pretsch, John Edward
Ralston, James Kenneth
Reece, Maynard
Rising, Dorothy Milne
Robbins, Trina
Roever, Joan Marilyn
Romano, Emanuel Glicen
Rose, David
Ryder, Mahler Bessinger
Satorsky, Cyril
Saxon, Charles David
Schachter, Justine Ranson
Schmidt, Frederick Louis
Schottland, M
Scott, John
Scott, Sandy (Sandra Lynn)
Seames, Clarann
Seiden, Arthur
Sendak, Maurice Bernard
Sharp, Harold
Shechter, Ben-Zion
Siegel, (Leo) Dink
Silber, Maurice
Silver, Pat
Silverman, Burton Philip
Singer, Arthur B
Sivard, Robert Paul
Skinner, Elsa Kells
Sloan, Richard
Smith, Harry William
Smith, Helen M
Smith, Joseph A(nthony)
Smyth, Ed

Sorel, Edward
Sottung, George (K)
Spagnolo, Kathleen Mary
Spaulding, D(onald Clifford)
Stacy, John Russell
Stark, Bruce Gunsten
Stermer, Dugald Robert
Stevens, Richard Clive
Stuart, Kenneth James
Suba, Susanne
Sweney, Fred
Szarama, Judith Layne
Takashima, Shizuye Violet
Thollander, Earl
Thomas, Reynolds
Thompson, Kenneth Webster
Tiegreen, Alan F
Tomes, Margot Ladd
Townsend, Marvin J
Trimm, H Wayne
Truby, Betsy Kirby
Tucker, Peri
Van Buren, Raeburn
van Winkelen, Barbara
Velasquez, Oscar
Vorwerk, E Charlsie
Wachsteter, George
Ward, Lynd (Kendall)
Washburn, Stan
Waterhouse, Charles Howard
Waterhouse, Russell Rutledge
Watson, Aldren A
Wells, Betty Childs
Wesling, William Arnold
Whitaker, William
Wilcox, Gordon Cumnock
Wilwers, Edward Mathias
Wind, Harold
Windrow, Patricia (Patricia
    Windrow Klein)
Wingate, Robert Bray
Wogstad, James Everet
Woodward, Cleveland Landon
Wright, Barton Allen
Wyatt, Stanley
Yanow, Rhoda Mae
Youngsblood, Nat
Zimmerman, William Harold
Zuckerberg, Stanley M

ILLUSTRATOR—CHILDREN'S BOOKS

Ames, Lee Judah
Amoss, Berthe
Anderson, Gunnar Donald
Arnosky, James Edward
Barry, Robert E
Blair, Helen
Bock, William Sauts-
    Netamux'we
Burnett, Calvin
Carrick, Donald F
Chen, Tony (Anthony Young)
D'Amato, Janet Potter
D'Aulaire, Edgar Parin
dePaola, Tomie
Eaton, Thomas Newton
Ets, Marie Hall
Finson, Hildred A
Fisher, Leonard Everett
Frankenberg, Robert Clinton
Garchik, Morton Lloyd
Gershinowitz, George
Gorsline, Douglas Warner
Graese, Judy (Judith Ann)
Graham, Margaret Bloy
Graysmith, Robert
Harmon, Barbara Sayre
Ha-So-De (Narciso Abeyta)
Hook, Frances A
Ipcar, Dahlov
Jauss, Anne Marie
Kamen, Gloria
Keats, Ezra Jack

Keith, Eros
Kent, Jack
Kessler, Leonard H
Knight, Hilary
Langner, Nola
Lasker, Joe (Joseph L)
Lent, Blair
Maestro, Giulio Marcello
Negri, Rocco Antonio
Oechsli, Kelly
Parker, Nancy Winslow
Parry, Marian
Ramirez, Joel Tito
Rappin, Adrian
Raskin, Ellen
Savitt, Sam
Schoenherr, John Carl
Schweninger, Ann Rozzelle
Siberell, Anne Hicks
Spier, Peter Edward
Swanson, Ray V
Taback, Simms
Weil, Lisl
Wexler, Jerome LeRoy
Zallinger, Jean Day

INSTRUCTOR
(Studio/Art School)

Abish, Cecile
Adams, Pat
Adelman, Dorothy (Lee)
    McClintock
Ahlgren, Roy B
Ahn, Don C
Amend, Eugene Michael
Amino, Leo
Anderson, John S
Anderson, Lennart
Appel, Thelma
Ashby, Carl
Askevold, David
Astman, Barbara Ann
Atlee, Emilie DeS
Ausby, Ellsworth Augustus
Avakian, John
Azaceta, Luis Cruz
Bageris, John
Bailin, Hella
Ballatore-Nelson, Sandra Lee
Barnett, Jack
Barowitz, Elliott
Barrett, Thomas R
Barrow, Thomas Francis
Barry, Anne Meredith
Barta, Dorothy Elaine
Batchelor, Anthony John
Batt, Miles Girard
Beauchamp, Robert
Becker, Natalie Rose
Beerman, Miraim K (Miriam
    Beerman-Jaffe)
Beginin, Igor
Belfiore, Gerardo
Beling, Helen
Bendell, Marilyn
Berg, Siri
Berge, Dorothy Alphena
Bergstrom, Edith Harrod
Besant, Derek Michael
Billian, Cathey R
Block, Amanda Roth
Blos, Peter W
Blumberg, Barbara Griffiths
Blumberg, Ron
Boal, Sara Metzner
Bobrowicz, Yvonne P
Boeve, Edgar Gene
Bohnenkamp, Leslie George
Bongart, Sergei R
Boothe, Power Robert
Bordes, Adrienne
Bothmer, Bernard V
Botto, Richard Alfred
Bramson, Phyllis Halperin
Briggs, Ernest

INSTRUCTOR (cont)

Bromm, Hal
Brooks, (John) Alan
Brotherton, Naomi
Brouillette, Al
Brown, Marion B
Brown, Peggy Ann
Brown, Reynold
Brumer, Shulamith
Brun, Thomas
Brush, Leif
Bryans, John Armond
Burns, D Harrison
Burns, Paul Callan
Burpee, James Stanley
Butter, Tom
Byrd, Robert John
Caddell, Foster
Cadillac, Louise Roman
Cale, Robert Allan
Calrow, Robert F
Canaday, Ouida Gornto
Capes, Richard Edward
Cardoso, Anthony
Carrington, Omar Raymond
Carter, Bernard Shirley
Carter, Granville W
Cascieri, Arcangelo
Catalan, Edgardo Omar
Cederstrom, John Andrew
Ceglia, Vincent
Chadbourn, Alfred Cheney
Chavez, Joseph Arnold
Cheek, Ronald Edward
Cherepov, George
Chernow, Burt
Christensen, Larry R
Christensen, Sharlene
Christiana, Edward
Ciancio, June (Kirkpatrick)
Ciarrochi, Ray
Cintron, Joseph M
Clark, Claude
Clark, Timothy John
Cleveland, Helen Barth
Cliff, Denis Antony
Clifton, Jack Whitney
Clinton, Paul Arthur
Coggins, Jack Banham
Cokendolpher, Eunice Loraine
Colarusso, Corrine Camille
Coleman, M L (Micheal Lee)
Connery, Ruth M
Cooper, Mario
Cope, Louise Todd
Cortese, Don F
Couper, Charles Alexander
Cox, Marion Averal
Crimi, Alfred D
Cunningham, Francis
Czimbalmos, Magdolna Paal
Davies, Kenneth Southworth
De Bretteville, Sheila Levrant
De Donato, Louis
d'Elaine
deLory, Peter
DeMaree, Betty (Elizabeth Ann)
Dennis, Don W
Denton, Pat
Dickinson, David Charles
Diehl, Guy Louis
Dioda, Adolph T
DiPerna, Frank Paul
Dmytruk, Ihor
Dobie, Jeanne
Dorfman, Bruce
Dorst, Mary Crowe
Dougherty, Ray (Raymond Edward)
Douglas, Edwin Perry
Draper, Josiah Everett
Draper, William Franklin
Driesbach, Walter Clark, Jr
Dunlap, Loren Edward
Dunn, Nate
Duren, Stephen D

Earle, William Henry
Eaton, Pauline (Friedrich)
Embrey, Carl Rice
Enriquez, Gaspar
Ernst, James Arnold
Ewing, Thomas R
Faragasso, Jack
Farrens, Juanita G
Fenton, Alan
Fernie, John Chipman
Finck, Furman J
Fiore, Joseph A
Firestein, Cecily Barth
Fitch, Steve (Steven Ralph)
Fitzgerald, John Philip
Flattmann, Alan Raymond
Fogg-Gerber, Monica
Folsom, Karl Leroy
Fon, Jade
Foster, April
Fox, Michael David
Frederick, Deloras Ann
Fromberg, LaVerne Ray
Frudakis, Evangelos William
Fukuhara, (Kazuo) Henry
Gabin, George Joseph
Gantz, Ann Cushing
Garver, Walter Raymond
Gasparian, Armen Tigran
Gasparro, Frank
Geber, Hana
Gentry, Warren Miller
George, Richard Allan
Gerbracht, Bob (Robert Thomas)
Gilbert, Lionel
Gilboy, Margaretta
Gilpin, Henry Edmund
Godfrey, Winnie (Winifred M)
Goedicke, Jean
Goetz, Edith Jean
Goldsmith, Lawrence Charles
Goldstein, Julius
Goree, Gary Paul
Gottschalk, Max Jules
Goulet, Lorrie
Grado, Angelo John
Granlund, Paul Theodore
Graupe-Pillard, Grace
Graves, Robert Edward
Greeley, Charles Matthew
Green, Tom
Greenberg, Irwin
Gregory, Bruce
Grimm, Lucille Davis
Grippe, Florence (Berg)
Groell, Theophil
Gross, Chaim
Grosse (Carolyn Ann Gawarecki)
Grossen, Francoise
Guastella, C Dennis
Gunshor, Ruth
Guzevich-Sommers, Kreszenz (Cynthia)
Gyra, Francis Joseph, Jr
Haff, Barbara J E
Hagan, James Garrison
Hale, Robert Beverly
Hall, Carl Alvin
Halliday, Nancy Ruth
Hammett, Polly Horton
Hanlen, John (Garrett)
Harbart, Gertrude Felton
Hardy, David Whittaker, III
Hardy, Howard (Collins)
Harris, Conley
Harroun, Dorothy Sumner
Hartshorn, Willis E
Harvey, Donald Gilbert
Hawkins, Thomas Wilson, Jr
Hedden-Sellman, Zelda
Hee, Hon-Chew
Heimdal, Georg
Heinemann, Peter
Heipp, Richard Christian
Henderson, Jack W

Hendrix, Connie (Connie Sandage Manus)
Henry, Jean
Hensche, Henry
Herr, Richard Joseph
Hershberg, Israel
Heston, Joan
Hiatt, Margaret Smith
Hill, Dale Logan
Hillman, Arthur Stanley
Hodge, R Garey
Hofer, Ingrid (Ingeborg)
Hollerbach, Serge
Hollingsworth, Alvin Carl
Housman, Russell F
Hugo, Joan (Dowey)
Humphrey, Nene
Hunt, Courtenay
Hunter, Robert Douglas
Hutchings, La Vere
Iacurto, Francesco
Indiviglia, Salvatore Joseph
Ingalls, Eve
Irvine, Betty Jo
Isaacs, Ron
Jarvis, Donald
Johnson, Bruce (James)
Johnson, Ernest (Melvin)
Johnson, Joyce
Johnson, (Leonard) Lucas
Jones, Amy (Amy Jones Frisbie)
Joyce, Marshall Woodside
Kaiser, Vitus J
Karn, Gloria Stoll
Karwelis, Donald Charles
Katzman, Herbert
Kawabata, Minoru
Kaye, George
Kaye, Mildred Elaine
Kaz, Nathaniel
Kerstetter-Bailey, Barbara Ann
Kidd, Steven R
Kiker, Evelyn Coalson
Kinstler, Everett Raymond
Kirby, Kent Bruce
Kirk, Michael
Knaub, Raymond L
Koch, Philip
Kohn, Edmond
Kozlow, Sigmund
Kranking, Margaret Graham
Kruskamp, Janet
Lack, Richard Frederick
Laguna, Marielle
Lai, Waihang
Lane, Marion Jean Arrons
LaPlantz, Shereen
Larson, Blaine (Gledhill)
Lawton, Florian Kenneth
Leaf, Ruth
Leber, Roberta (Roberta Leber McVeigh)
Lee-Smith, Hughie
Leonardi, Hector
Leslie, Seaver
Lesnick, Stephen William
Levine, Marion Lerner
Levine, Reeva (Anna) Miller
Lewis, John Chapman
Lewis, Marcia
Lewis, Nat Brush
Lewis, Ronald Walter
Lewis, William R
Likan, Gustav
Liljegren, Frank
Limont, Naomi Charles
Lindmark, Arne
Lipman, Stan
Lipscomb, Guy Fleming, Jr
Lomahaftewa, Linda (Linda Joyce Slock)
Lombard, Annette
Loney, Doris Howard
Lonidier, Fred Spencer
Lorentz, Pauline
Luck, Robert

Lueders, Jimmy C
Luisi, Jerry
Luitjens, Helen Anita
Lynch, Betty
Lynch, Tom (Thomas Michael)
McAndrew, Dennis Anthony
McCarty, Lorraine Chambers
McClure, Constance
McDougal, Ivan Ellis
McGarry, Patricia Josephine
McGlauchlin, Tom
McQuillan, Frances
McReynolds, (Joe) Cliff
McVicker, Charles Taggart
Mahaffey, Merrill Dean
Malsch, Ellen L
Malta, Vincent
Mancuso, Leni
Manzo, Anthony Joseph
Marozzi, Eli Raphael
Martin, Roger
Martin, Thomas
Martinez, Ernesto Pedregon
Martone, William Robert
Mason, Alden C
Mason, Frank Herbert
Meltzer, Robert Hiram
Mendenhall, Jack
Meng, Wendy
Messick, Ben (Newton)
Metcalf, Conger A
Meyers, Dale (Mrs Mario Cooper)
Midener, Walter
Miezajs, Dainis
Milholland, Richard Alexander
Miller, John Paul
Missal, Stephen J
Mix, Walter Joseph
Mohn, Cheri (Ann)
Moon, Marc
Moonie, Liana (Maria)
Moore, Ina May
Moore, Scott Martin
Morgenlander, Ella Kramer
Mosca, August
Moscatt, Paul N
Moy, May (Wong)
Muchnic, Suzanne
Myers, Carole Ann
Nardone, Vincent Joseph
Neal, Frank Wingfield
Neff, Edith
Newman, John Beatty
Nickerson, Ruth (Ruth Nickerson Greacen)
Nigrosh, Leon Isaac
Notestine, Tom W
Odate, Toshio
Oesterle, Leonhard Friedrich
Oginz, Richard
Ohe, Katie (Minna)
Oi, Motoi
Oldham, Berton Jepsen
Olson, Bettye Johnson
O'Neil, Bruce William
Orsini
Osborne, Elizabeth
Ostendorf, (Arthur) Lloyd, Jr
O'Sullivan, Daniel Joseph
Osyczka, Bohdan Danny
Parella, Albert Lucian
Pascual, Manolo
Passantino, George Christopher
Patrick, Genie Hudson
Patterson, Shirley
Pearson, Clifton
Pearson, Henry C
Pearson, James Eugene
Pearson, John
Peck, Stephen Rogers
Penney, Jacqueline
Perez, Vincent
Perkins, Clarence James
Perlman, Bennard Bloch
Perlmutter, Merle

INSTRUCTOR (cont)

Peter, George
Phillips, Dick (Richard Cortez)
Phillis, Marilyn Hughey
Piatek, Francis John
Pickens, Alton
Pierce, Donald (Benjamin)
Piet, John Frances
Plaster, Alice Marie
Poole, Richard Elliott
Posey, Leslie Thomas
Powelson, Rosemary A
Pribble, Easton
Price, Joe (Allen)
Provder, Carl
Quick, Birney MacNabb
Quinn, Noel Joseph
Radin, Dan
Raffel, Alvin Robert
Raskind, Philis
Rawlinson, Jonlane Frederick
Reale, Nicholas Albert
Redein, Alex S
Reed, Paul Allen
Reid, Robert Dennis
Remenick, Seymour
Reynard, Carolyn Cole
Roberts, Donald
Rohrer, Warren
Rose, Leatrice
Rose, Roslyn
Ross, Douglas Allan
Ross, Fred (Joseph)
Ross, John T
Rossi, Joseph O
Rossman, Ruth Scharff
Roussel, Claude Patrice
Rudman, Joan (Combs)
Russell, Philip C
St Denis, Paul Andre
Sallick, Lucy Ellen
Sanden, John Howard
Sanders, Andrew Dominick
Sanderson, Charles Howard
San Soucie, Patricia Molm
Saunders, Edith Dariel Chase
Savas, Jo-Ann
Savitz, Frieda
Schepis, Anthony Joseph
Schiebold, Hans
Schmutzhart, Slaithong
   Chengtrakul
Schon, Nancy Quint
Schule, Donald Kenneth
Schwartz, Henry
Segur, Eleanor Corinne
Sekimachi, Kay
Shackelford, Bud (Lyne T)
Shapiro, Irving
Sherwood, Leona
Sheya
Shih, Joan Fai
Shumacker, Elizabeth Wight
Sickman, Jessalee Bane
Silberstein-Storfer, Muriel
   Rosoff
Simpson, Marilyn Jean
Sleigh, Sylvia
Slone, Sandi
Smith, Barbara Turner
Snow, Lee Erlin
Souza, Paul Marciel
Sparks, John Edwin
Speers, Teryl Townsend
Spicer, Jean (Doris) Uhl
Spickett, Ronald John, Sr
Staffel, Rudolf Harry
Stanczak, Julian
Stanley, M Louise
Statman, Jan B
Steiger, Frederic
Stelzer, Michael Norman
Stenzler, Erna J
Stevens, Jacquie (Jaqueline
   Lauren)
Stevenson, Ruth Rolston
Storer, Frances Nell

Stowman, Annette Burr
Stull, Jean Himrod
Sundberg, Wilda (Regelman)
Swenson, Anne (Beatrice)
Tasgal-Kliegman, G
Tatro, Ronald Edward
Taylor, Bill (William Bradley)
Terry, Marion (E)
Texoon, Jasmine
Teyral, John
Thibert, Patrick A
Tillim, Sidney
Tobias, Julius
Townsend, Stanley Dale
Trauerman, Margy Ann
Travers-Smith, Brian John
Trieff, Selina
Trott, Helen
Tseu, Rosita Hsu
Tucker, Toba Pato
Tullsen, Rex
Turner, (Charles) Arthur
Ventimiglia, John Thomas
Viret, Margaret Mary (Mrs
   Frank Ivo)
Vogel, Donald
Wagner, Charles H
Wald, Palmer B
Warburg, Stephanie Wenner
Warner, Herbert Kelii, Jr
Warren, Betty
Waterstreet, Ken (James Kent)
Webb, Frank (Francis H)
Weidner, Roswell Theodore
Weill, Erna
Weiner, Abe
Wensley, William Charles
Wethington, Wilma Zella
Whidden, Conni
Whitcomb, Therese Truitt
Whiten, Colette
Whitney, Edgar Albert
Wiener, Sam (Evangeline
   Tabasco)
Wilke, Hannah
Williams, Joyce
Williams, Raymond Lester
Wimmer, Gayle
Witkin, Isaac
Wolpert, Elizabeth Davis
Wood, Robert E
Wright, Stanley Marc
Yaghjian, Edmund
Yates, Marvin Clarence
Yost, Erma Martin
Zelt, Martha
Zimmerman, Paul Warren
Zoromskis, Kazimieras
Zuccarelli, Frank Edward

JEWELER

Adams, Jay H
Allen, Constance Olleen Webb
Caldwell, Eleanor
Chapman, Robert Gordon
Eikerman, Alma
Engle, Barbara Jean
Gabriel, Hannelore
Hageman, Charles Lee
Hampton, Grace
Higgins, Edward Koelling
Hu, Mary Lee
Klarin, Winifred Erlick
Lacktman, Michael
LaPlantz, David
Lavoy, Walter Joseph
Lewis, Marcia
Link, Val James
Loloma, Charles
Long, Frank Weathers
Miller, John Paul
Ottiano, John William
Peck, Lee Barnes
Piccolo, Thomas Frank

Sherman, Ira D
Smith, Jo-an
Stacy, John Russell
Stephen, Francis B
Thomason, Tom William
Walker, Mary Carolyn
Watson-Abbott, Lynda
Whitney, Charlotte Armide

KINETIC ARTIST

Baker, George
Delihas, Neva C
Emery, Lin
Flavin, Dan
Goodyear, John L
Gruber, Aaronel deRoy
Harvey, Dermot
Hendricks, Edward Lee
Holvey, Samuel Boyer
Janney, Christopher Draper
Karpowicz, Terrence Edward
Lehr, Harold
Margulies, Isidore
Myer, Peter Livingston
Oster, Gerald
Peiperl, Adam
Reiback, Earl M
Romano, Salvatore Michael
Roukes, Nicholas M
Sina, Alejandro

LECTURER

Abrams, Herbert E
Aigner, Lucien
Alcalay, Albert S
Allen, Jane Addams
Andrews, Benny
Austin, Phil
Banning, Jack (John Peck), Jr
Bartle, Dorothy Budd
Bartlett, Scott
Baruch, Jacques Z
Baum, Hank
Beament, Tib (Thomas Harold)
Beard, Marion L Patterson
Berhang, Mattie
Betteridge, Lois Etherington
Beyer, Steven J
Bingham, Lois A
Blai, Boris
Boterf, Check (Chester Arthur)
Boz, Alex (Alex Bozickovic)
Brakhage, James Stanley
Brendel, Bettina
Brigadier, Anne
Brooks, H(arold) Allen
Burgues, Irving Carl
Burns, Sheila
Burroughs, Margaret T G
Buster, Jacqueline Mary
Callisen, Sterling
Carstenson, Cecil C
Cecere, Gaetano
Challis, Richard Bracebridge
Chin, Ric
Chuey, Robert Arnold
Clare, Stewart
Clark, Robert Charles
Clarke, Ann
Cobb, Virginia Horton
Cohen, Lynne G
Coleman, A(llan) D(ouglass)
Coleman, Gayle (Gayle
   Coleman MacDonald)
Collins, Lowell Daunt
Corish, Joseph Ryan
Cormier, Robert John
Crooks, W Spencer
Cropper, M Elizabeth
Dauterman, Carl Christian
Davenport, Rebecca Read
Dempsey, Richard William

Dickinson, William Stirling
Dinnerstein, Lois
Dintenfass, Marylyn
Doty, Robert McIntyre
Dreiband, Laurence
Drutt, Helen Williams
Ebsen, Alf K
Edelson, Gilbert S
Ellis, Ray G
Enos, Chris
Espenet
Ettinger, Susi Steinitz
Evans, Burford Elonzo
Fanning, Robbie
Fedelle, Estelle
Feder, Penny Joy
Fein, B R
Ferguson, Kathleen Elizabeth
Field, Saul
Fitzgerald, Harriet
Fox, Flo
Frackman, Noel
Freeman, Sara
Gablik, Suzi
Gilbertson, Charlotte
Goetz, Peter Henry
Goetzl, Thomas Maxwell
Gottschalk, Fritz
Greenwald, Alice (Alice
   Marian Greenwald-Ward)
Gross, Earl
Grove, Samuel Harold
Grubar, Francis Stanley
Gutmann, Joseph
Haas, Ernst
Hallam, Beverly (Linney)
Hanson, Philip Holton
Hare, David
Hemphill, Herbert Waide, Jr
Highwater, Jamake
Hornung, Gertrude Seymour
Hughes, Robert S F
Huldermann, Paul F
Inoue, Kazuko
Ishikawa, Joseph
Jagger, Gillian
James, A Everette, Jr
Johnson, Buffie
Johnson, Evert Alfred
Jones, Lois Mailou (Mrs V
   Pierre-Noel)
Kahn, Ralph H
Kan, Diana
Karp, Richard Gordon
Katz, Theodore (Harry)
Kaufman, Jane
Keaveney, Sydney Starr
Kellogg, Maurice Dale
Kennedy, J William
Kingsley, April
Kleinman, Sue
Koerner, Henry
Koltun, Frances Lang
Koni, Nicolaus
Korjus, Veronica Maria
   Elisabeth
Kowalek, Jon W
Kratina, K George
Kropf, Joan R
Kuchta, Ronald A
Kuehn, Edmund Karl
Kumler, Kipton (Cornelius)
Lee, Amy Freeman
Levinson, Mimi
Lochnan, Katharine A
MacLean-Smith, Elizabeth
Maki, Robert Richard
Mason, Lauris Lapidos
Maytham, Thomas Northrup
Mecklenburg, Virginia McCord
Miller, Donald
Mitchell, R(obert Ellis)
Morrison, Fritzi
   Mohrenstecher
Nash, Mary (Harriet)
Navaretta, Cynthia
Nechis, Barbara

LECTURER (cont)

O'Connor, Francis Valentine
O'Gorman, James Francis
Palmer, Lucie Mackay
Palmer, William C
Patton, Sharon Frances
Perrot, Paul N
Piper, Jane
Poduska, T F
Radycki, J(osephine) Diane
Ragland, Bob
Rath, Hildegard
Reich, Sheldon
Richards, Eugene
Robbins, Warren M
Roch, Ernst
Rogalski, Walter
Roney, Harold Arthur
Ross, David Anthony
Ruggles, Joanne Beaule
Ruthven, John Aldrich
Sandberg, Hannah
Sanguinetti, Eugene F
Schabacker, Betty Barchet
Schaffer, Rose
Scheu, Leonard
Scheyer, Ernst
Schneider, Ira
Schultz, Caroline Reel
Schulz, Ken
Schwartz, Marvin D
Scribner, Charles, III
Shapiro, David
Shapiro, Dee
Shubin, Morris Jack
Siden, Franklin
Sitton, John M
Skalagard, Hans
Slusky, Joseph
Spaulding, Warren Dan
Stapleton, Joseph F
Sweeney, James Johnson
Taft, Frances Prindle
Thelin, Valfred P
Thompson, Dorothy Burr
Tiffany, Marguerite Bristol
Timmas, Osvald
Tobey, Alton S
Torreano, John Francis
Tredennick, Dorothy W
Tucker, Curtis (Dee)
Usher, Elizabeth Reuter
Van Tongeren, Herk
Van Wyk, Helen
Volpe, Robert
Walinska, Anna
Walton, Donald William
Warren, Win (W Winton)
Weidner, Marilyn Kemp
Weil, Stephen E
Weisman, Marcia Simon
Wharton, David W
Wheeler, Orson Shorey
Wilson, Ben
Wilson, Carrie Lois
Winkel, Nina
Winogrand, Garry
Wood, James Arthur (Art)
Wriston, Barbara
Wynn, Donald James
Yanish, Elizabeth
Zirker, Joseph
Zornes, James Milford

LIBRARIAN

Abid, Ann B
Baretski, Charles Allan
Bloomgarden, Judith Mary
Burns, G Joan
Bushnell, Marietta P
Candau, Eugenie
Cano, Margarita
Carr-Harris, Ian Redford
Cassidy, Margaret Carol (Mrs John Manship)
Ciccone, Amy Navratil
Collins, Christiane C
Craig, Susan V
Dane, William Jerald
Doumato, Lamia
Dunnigan, Mary Catherine
Dutton, Pauline Mae
Dwyer, Melva Jean
Edelstein, J M
Ekdahl, Janis Kay
Esau, Erika
Feldstein, Mary
Fenton, Julia Ann
Findlay, James Allen
Freitag, Wolfgang Martin
Friedman, Joan Marcy
Grier, Margot Edmands
Gurney, Susan Rothwell
Halbrook, Anne-Mieke Platt
Haswell, Hollee
Held, (Jon) Jonathan, Jr
Hess, Joyce
Hess, Stanley William
Hilligoss, Martha M
Hodgson, James Stanley
Holliday, Judith
Hopkins, Benjamin
Howell, Hannah Johnson
Huemer, Christina Gertrude
Irvine, Betty Jo
Kaufmann, Robert Carl
Keaveney, Sydney Starr
Kelley, Donald Castell
Kotala, Stanislaw Waclaw
Kusnerz, Peggy Ann F
Lambert, Nancy S
Larsen, John Christian
Looney, Robert Fain
Ludmer, Joyce Pellerano
McCorison, Marcus Allen
Mattern, Penny Greig
Menthe, Melissa
Miller, Jean Johnston
Mitchell, Eleanor
Murchie, Donald John
Nelson, Jane Gray
Nolan, Margaret Patterson
Olin, Ferris
Parry, Pamela Jeffcott
Paschall, Jo Anne
Patten, David John
Pearman, Sara Jane
Peterson, Harold Patrick
Phillpot, Clive James
Pinkney, Helen Louise
Placzek, Adolf Kurt
Pletscher, Josephine Marie
Polster, Joanne F
Rinehart, Michael
Roberts, Helene Emylou
Rothrock, Ilse Skipsna
Scherer, Herbert Grover
Schimansky, Donya Dobrila
Schmidt, Mary Morris
Schuller, Nancy Shelby
Sevy, Barbara Snetsinger
Shaw, Courtney Ann
Shaw, Renata Vitzthum
Sheridan, Helen Adler
Silberman, Arthur
Smith, Elizabeth Jean
Sommer, Frank H, III
Stoneham, John
Straight, Elsie H
Treese, William R
Usher, Elizabeth Reuter
von Rebhan, Elinor Anne
Weidman, Jeffrey
Wyngaard, Susan Elizabeth
Wynne, Nancy Graves
Young, Frances Elizabeth
Zietz, Stephen Joseph
Zimon, Kathy Elizabeth

MEDALIST

Adams, Jay H
Anargyros, Spero
Bleifeld, Stanley
Cook, John (Alfred)
Cook, Robert Howard
De Bellis, Hannibal
Dinardo, Joseph E
Dryfoos, Nancy
Eriksen, Gary
Everhart, Don (Donald Nelson), Jr
Goff, Thomas Jefferson
Grove, Edward Ryneal
Hampton, Lucille Charlotte
Jones, Elizabeth A B
Jovine, Marcel
Kaufman, Mico
Mankowski, Bruno
Mazze, Irving
Miller, Donald Richard
Montgomery, E J (Evangeline Juliet)
Pujol, Elliott
Rosse, Maryvonne
Rush, Jon N
Turano, Don

MOSAIC ARTIST

Carter, Jerry Williams
Jung, Yee Wah
Kreilick, Marjorie E
Reynal, Jeanne
Schwarz, Myrtle Cooper
Zweerts, Arnold

MURALIST

Anguiano, Raul
Backus, Standish, Jr
Baskerville, Charles
Beal, Jack
Beckmann, Robert Owen
Belkin, Arnold
Bentley, Claude
Berkowitz, Leon
Besner, J Jacques
Bessemer, Auriel
Bieler, Andre Charles
Boggs, Franklin
Bransby, Eric James
Buonagurio, Edgar R
Buzzelli, Joseph Anthony
Callahan, Kenneth
Carter, Jerry Williams
Charlot, Martin Day
Chase, Allan (Seamans)
Cikovsky, Nicolai
Cohen, Jean
Connolly, Jerome Patrick
Coral R (Flaviano Ezequiel Coral Revelo)
Czimbalmos, Szabo Kalman
Ferguson, Barclay (Lord of Lamond)
Frazer, James (Nisbet), Jr
Freund, Tibor
Gray, Gladys
Graziani, Sante
Groat, Hall Pierce
Haas, Richard John
Haines, Richard
Harrison, Pat (Broeder)
Heberling, Glen Austin
Holbrook, Hollis Howard
Hopper, Frank J
Imana, Jorge Garron
Jacobs, Ted Seth
Jenkins, Mary Anne Keel
Jones, Calvin B(ell)

Kaplan, Stanley
Kauffman, (Camille) Andrene
Landau, Myra
Littell, Biz
Lorcini, Gino
McChesney, Robert Pearson
McCoy, Ann
Magafan, Ethel
Mailman, Cynthia
Mangione, Patricia Anthony
Martin, Lucille Caiar
Martinez, Ernesto Pedregon
Martyl (Martyl Schweig Langsdorf)
Merrill, David Kenneth
Mesibov, Hugh
Michaels, Glen
Middleman, Raoul F
Montminy, (Elizabeth) Tracy
Moreno, Orduna Nicolas
Morrow, Robert Earl
Neto, Gilda Reis (Gilda Reis Netopuletti)
Peake, Channing
Pellicone, William
Pisani, Joseph
Pittore, Carlo
Rackus, George (Keistus)
Rakocy, William (Joseph)
Rand, Archie
Reardon, Mary A
Redinger, Walter Fred
Regat, Jean-Jacques Albert
Regat, Mary E
Richardson, Frank, Jr
Rippey, Clayton
Rose, Samuel
St John, John Milton
Schliefer, Stafford Lerrig
Schmidt, Edward William
Shecter, Mark
Siebner, Herbert
Skemp, Robert Oliver
Slavin, Arlene
Slawinski, Joseph
Slonem, Hunt
Stroud, Peter Anthony
Thwaites, Charles Winstanley
Traher, William Henry
Tulk, Alfred James
Valesco, Frances
Vandenberge, Peter Willem
Van Veen, Stuyvesant
Vickery, Charles Bridgeman
Watson, Helen Richter
Weber, John Pitman
Welch, James Wymore
Whitcomb, Kay
Wilson, (Ronald) York
Yaffa Yael Stec-El (Harriet Jeanne Steckel)
Yasko, Caryl Anne
Young, Cliff
Zetlin, Fay (Florence Anshen)

MUSEOLOGIST

Berkowitz, Roger M
Bier, Justus
Bowman, Ruth
Carter, David Giles
Courtney, Keith Townsend
Craft, John Richard
Cummins, Karen Gasco
Dailey, Chuck (Charles Andrew)
Dellis, Arlene B
Friedman, Ann Marti
Graham, F Lanier
Grogan, Kevin
Inverarity, Robert Bruce
Johnson, Evert Alfred
Johnson, Selina (Tetzlaff)
Jones, Frances Follin
Kelleher, Patrick Joseph

MUSEOLOGIST (cont)

Mayer, Susan Martin
Noble, Joseph Veach
Sipiora, Leonard Paul
Snodgrass, Jeanne Owens (Mrs
  M Eugene King)
Streetman, John William, III
Ullman, (Mrs) George W
Wallace, David Harold
Weeks, Edward F

MUSEUM DIRECTOR

Adams, Lowell G
Adler, Sebastian J
Agee, William C
Ahrens, Kent
Alinder, James Gilbert
Alling, Clarence (Edgar)
Anderson, Ross Cornelius
Arkus, Leon A
Armstrong, Thomas Newton,
  III
Atkinson, Tracy
Atkyns, (Willie) Lee, Jr
Bach, Otto Karl
Ballard, Lockett Ford, Jr
Ballinger, James K
Barcus, David L
Barons, Richard Irwin
Barrie, Dennis Ray
Baur, John I H
Beck, Martha Ann
Belz, Carl Irvin
Bengtz, Ture
Bermingham, Peter
Bishop, Budd Harris
Bishop, Robert Charles
Bloch, Milton Joseph
Bodem, Dennis Richard
Boggs, Jean Sutherland
Bolas, Gerald Douglas
Botwinick, Michael
Bowne, James Dehart
Bowron, Edgar Peters
Boyce, William G
Boyer, Jack K
Braybrooke, Valerie V
Brezzo, Steven Louis
Brody, Jacob Jerome
Brooke, David Stopford
Brown, James Monroe, III
Brown, John Carter
Bryant, Edward Albert
Buchanan, John Edward, Jr
Buck, Robert Treat, Jr
Buechner, Thomas Scharman
Bullard, Edgar John, III
Burke, James Donald
Bush, Martin H
Butera, Anne Fabbri
Byrnes, James Bernard
Cameron, Duncan F
Capa, Cornell
Carpenter, Gilbert Frederick
  (Bert)
Chernow, Burt
Chetham, Charles
Christison, Muriel B
Coe, Ralph Tracy
Craft, John Richard
Cumming, Glen Edward
Czarniecki, M J, III
Czestochowski, Joseph
  Stephen
Danoff, I Michael
Davis, William D
Delehanty, Suzanne E
de Montebello, Philippe
  Lannes
Dempsey, Bruce Harvey
Dennison, Keith Elkins
Desmarais, Charles Joseph
de Vecsey, Esther Barbara
Dietrich, Bruce Leinbach

Dobkin, John Howard
Dodd, Eric M
Dodds, Robert J, III
Dodworth, Allen Stevens
Doherty, Robert J
Domit, Moussa M
Duff, James H
Eckhardt, Ferdinand
Einreinhofer, Nancy Anne
Eitner, Lorenz E A
Eldredge, Charles Child, III
Elliott, James Heyer
Ellis, George Richard
Elzea, Rowland Procter
Emerson, Roberta Shinn
Enman, Tom Kenneth
Evans, Bruce Haselton
Fagaly, William Arthur
Faison, Samson Lane, Jr
Faris, Peter Kinzie
Feldman, Arthur Mitchell
Ferguson, Charles B
Fisher, James Donald
Flomenhaft, Eleanor
Forbes, Donna Marie
Force, Roland Wynfield
Forrest, James Taylor
Freudenheim, Tom Lippmann
Friedman, Martin
Gaither, Edmund B
Gallander, Cathleen S
Gamble, Kathryn Elizabeth
Garrett, Stephen
Gaudieri, Alexander V J
Gebhard, David
Gelburd, Gail Enid
Geske, Norman Albert
Glasgow, Lukman
Goodrich, Lloyd
Gordon, Joy L
Graham, Douglas J M
Greenwald, Alice (Alice
  Marian Greenwald-Ward)
Gregg, Richard Nelson
Grogan, Kevin
Gualtieri, Joseph P
Hadley, Rollin van Nostrand
Hagerstrand, Martin Allan
Hallmark, Donald Parker
Hamilton, George Heard
Hammond, Natalie Hays
Hanna, Katherine
Hansen, Arne Rae
Harris, Paul Rogers
Harris, Paul Stewart
Hassrick, Peter H
Hathaway, Walter Murphy
Hennessey, William John
Herman, Lloyd Eldred
Hernandez, Jo Farb
Hightower, John B
Hill, William Mansfield
Hobbs, Robert Carleton
Hoffman, Larry Gene
Hoffman, Marilyn Friedman
Hoge, Robert Wilson
Holverson, John
Hood, Graham Stanley
Hood, Mary Bryan
Hopkins, Henry Tyler
Huchel, Frederick M
Hunt, David Curtis
Hutchinson, Janet L
Hyland, Douglas K S
Jenkins, Donald John
Jolles, Arnold H
Jones, Louis C
Jordan, William B
Joyaux, Alain Georges
Kachel, Harold Stanley
Kagle, Joseph L, Jr
Kardon, Janet
Kayser, Thomas Arthur
Keeney, Allen Lloyd
Kiah, Virginia Jackson
Kinsel, Michael Leslie
Klopfenstein, Philip Arthur

Knaub, Donald E
Koenig, Robert J
Kohler, Ruth DeYoung
Koshalek, Richard
Kotun, Henry Paul
Kowalek, Jon W
Krushenick, John
Kuchta, Ronald A
Landwehr, William Charles
Lane, John Rodger
Laurer, Robert A
Leavitt, Thomas Whittlesey
Lee, Sherman Emery
Leeper, John Palmer
Leet, Richard Eugene
Lefebvre d'Argence, Rene-
  Yvon
Lehman, Arnold L
Lerner, Abram
Lewis, Virginia Elnora
Libby, Gary Russell
Lindemann, Edna M
Livesay, Thomas Andrew
Loar, Peggy A
Long, Walter Kinscella
Love, Frances Taylor
Maass, Richard Andrew
McCready, Eric Scott
Madigan, Richard Allen
Malone, Lee H B
Mandle, Earl Roger
Marioni, Tom
Marzio, Peter Cort
Maser, Edward Andrew
Mason, Benjamin Lincoln
Master-Karnik, Paul Joseph
Mayhew, Edgar De Noailles
Maytham, Thomas Northrup
Melvin, Ronald McKnight
Messer, Thomas M
Metyko, Michael Joseph
Miller, Joan Vita
Miller, Samuel Clifford
Mills, Paul Chadbourne
Moore, Russell James
Mooz, R Peter
Morris, Jack Austin, Jr
Mosby, Dewey Franklin
Muhlberger, Richard Charles
Muhlert, Jan Keene
Murray, Richard Newton
Myers, Fred A
Neff, John Hallmark
Newton, Douglas
Noble, Joseph Veach
Oldenburg, Richard Erik
Olkinetzky, Sam
Ostrow, Stephen Edward
Ott, Wendell Lorenz
Page, Addison Franklin
Paris, Kay
Parker, Harry S, III
Paulin, Richard Calkins
Peladeau, Marius Beaudoin
Pendergraft, Norman Elveis
Pennington, Mary Anne
Peterson, John Douglas
Phillips, James M
Phillips, Laughlin
Poling, Clark V
Prokopoff, Stephen Stephen
Rathbone, Perry Townsend
Ray, Jim
Rhodes, Reilly Patrick
Robb, David Metheny, Jr
Robbins, Daniel J
Robbins, Warren M
Robert, Henry Flood, Jr
Robinson, Franklin W
Rogers, Charles B
Rogers, Millard Foster, Jr
Rogovin, Mark
Rombout, Luke
Rosenbaum, Allen
Roster, Laila Bergs
Rovetti, Paul F
Ryan, David Michael

Sachs, Samuel, II
Sawyer, Charles Henry
Scala, Joseph (A)
Scarbrough, Cleve Knox, Jr
Schmidt, Stephen
Schmuckal, Janet Bell (Cynthia
  Signature)
Schneider, Janet M
Schwartz, Ellen Judith
Schweizer, Paul Douglas
Segger, Martin Joseph
Selig, J Daniel
Sennema, David C
Shalkop, Robert Leroy
Shaman, Sanford Sivitz
Shestack, Alan
Shuck, Kenneth Menaugh
Sipiora, Leonard Paul
Slive, Seymour
Sloshberg, Leah Phyfer
Smith, James Morton
Smith, Paul J
Smith, Robert Lewis
Solley, Thomas Treat
Stars, William Kenneth
Steadman, David Wilton
Stitt, Susan (Margaret)
Story, William Easton
Stuart, Joseph Martin
Sullivan, Max William
Swanson, Vern Grosvenor
Takach, Mary H
Talbot, Jarold Dean
Taylor, John Lloyd
Taylor, Lisa
Taylor, Rene Claude
Teitz, Richard Stuart
Tibbs, Thomas S
Timms, Peter Rowland
Tolles, Bryant Franklin, Jr
Tonelli, Edith Ann
Trapp, Frank Anderson
Truex, Duane Philip
Tucker, Marcia
Turk, Rudy H
Turner, David
Turner, Evan Hopkins
Ulrich, Edwin Abel
Venegas, Haydee E
Victor, Mary O'Neill
Vigtel, Gudmund
Vitale, Lydia Modi
Walker, Herbert Brooks
Walkey, Frederick P
Waller, Aaron Bret
Walsh, John, Jr
Wardwell, Allen
Washburn, Gordon Bailey
Watson, Katharine Johnson
Wattenmaker, Richard J
Waufle, Alan Duane
Weaver, James D
Weber, Jean M
Weil, Stephen E
Weinhardt, Carl Joseph, Jr
West, Richard Vincent
Whitlock, John Joseph
Wilmerding, John
Wilson, Martha Storey
Wolfe, Maurice Raymond
Wong, Jason
Wong, Roger Frederickson
Wooden, Howard Edmund
Wright, Jesse Graham, Jr
Wyrick, Charles Lloyd, Jr
Yassin, Robert Alan
Young, Janie Chester
Zona, Louis A

PAINTER

Abadi, Fritzie
Abramowicz, Janet
Abularach, Rodolfo Marco
Adams, Bobbi

PAINTER (cont)

Alden, Richard
Alexenberg, (Melvin)
    Menahem
Anderson, Lennart
Anderson, Warren Harold
Andrejevic, Milet
Andrew, David Neville
Angell, Tony
Anthonisen, George Rioch
Apel, Barbara Jean
Aston, Miriam
Ayers, Carol Lee
Azara, Nancy J
Bageris, John
Bales, J (Jean Elaine)
Baranik, Rudolf
Barker, Al C
Barnett, Jack
Barr, David John
Barr-Sharrar, Beryl
Barsano, Ron (Ronald James)
Barta, Dorothy Elaine
Bastian, Linda
Beament, Tib (Thomas Harold)
Bearce, Jeana Dale
Begley, Wayne E
Berghash, Mark W
Bergstrom, Edith Harrod
Bermingham, John C
Berns, Pamela Kari
Berry, Carolyn (Carolyn Berry
    Becker)
Besant, Derek Michael
Bice, Jack (John Avery)
Bierly, Edward J
Binks, Ronald C
Bishop, Jeffrey Britton
Bishop, Jerold
Blake, John Clemens
Blanchard, Carol
Bogarin, Rafael
Bolton, Mimi DuBois
Bostick, William Allison
Boszin, Andrew
Brakke, P(erry) Michael
Breen, Harry Frederick, Jr
Brier, Helene
Brody, Ruth
Broer, Roger L
Brown, Paul L
Brycelea, Clifford
Bultman, Fritz
Burkhardt, Hans Gustav
Burns, D Harrison
Cabot, Hugh
Cain, David Paul
Campbell, (James) Lawrence
Cantor, Fredrich
Cantrell, Jim
Capobianco, Domenick
Carrington, Omar Raymond
Carter, Yvonne Pickering
Chadbourn, Alfred Cheney
Chambers, Park A, Jr
Chan, Phillip Paang
Chapian, Grieg Hovsep
Charles-Smith, Donald
Chee, Cheng-Khee
Cheek, Ronald Edward
Chernow, Ann
Christenberry, William
Christian, William
Ciancio, June (Kirkpatrick)
Cifolelli, Alberta (Alberta
    Carmella Lamb)
Citrin, Judith
Clark, Timothy John
Cleary, Manon Catherine
Clutz, William
Coggins, Jack Banham
Colburn, Francis Peabody
Coleman, Lloyd Willis
Coleman, Jacqui (Jacquelyn P)
Conant, Jan Royce
Conesa, Miguel A
Conklin, Gloria Zamko

Corkery, Tim (Timothy James)
Cove, Rosemary
Coyer, Max R
Cross, Watson, Jr
Cushing, Barbara
Danby, Ken
Davies, Haydn Llewellyn
Davis, Bertha
Davis, James Granberry
Day, Gary Lewis
Dean, Nat(alie Carol)
de Boschnek, Chris (Christian
    Charles)
d'Elaine
Dempsey, Richard William
d'Harnoncourt, Anne
Diehl, Guy Louis
Digiorgio, Joseph J
Dineen, Tom (Forga)
Dobard, Raymond Gerard
Dole, William
Dougherty, Ray (Raymond
    Edward)
Drum, Sydney Maria
Dunn, Cal
Echohawk, Brummett
Eder, James Alvin
Egri, Ted
Eichel, Edward W
Eller, Evelyn (Evelyn Eller
    Rosenbaum)
Ellis, Ray G
Ensrud, Wayne
Etienne, Guillermo C
Ettenberg, Franklin Joseph
Evans, Lucile
Eyre, Ivan
Fabert, Jacques
Fay, Ming G
Fejes, Claire
Ference, Cynthia
Feriola, James Philip
Fernandez, Rudy M, Jr
Ferriter, Clare
Fitzgerald, John Philip
Flood, Edward C
Fohr, Jenny
Foosaner, Judith
Formicola, John Joseph
Foulger, Richard F
Frank, Helen (Goodzeit)
Franklin, Patt
Frary, Michael
Freeman, Sara
Freilich, Ann
Freiman, Robert J
French, Ray H
Frick, Joan
Frohlich, M L (Minnette
    Leah)
Fuchs, Mary Tharsilla
Fukuhara, (Kazuo) Henry
Gagnon, Charles
Gale, William Henry
Gallagher, Michael B
Gentle, Esther
Geraci, Lucian Arthur
Gersh, Bill
Gershoy, Eugenie
Gilbert, Helen Odell
Ginsburg, Estelle
Glassman, Audrey Lavine
Gluck, Heidi
Goldsmith, Lawrence Charles
Gold Star (William Myers
    Watkins III)
Golubov, Maurice
Goree, Gary Paul
Gornik, April
Gray, Jessie Benton Evans
Green, Jasha
Greenberg, Elenor Siminow
Gregory, Joan
Grimm, Lucille Davis
Guastella, C Dennis
Guberman, Sidney Thomas
Hackett, Mickey

Haff, Barbara J E
Hall, Carl Alvin
Haller, Emanuel
Hamilton, Lydia
Hannibal, Joseph Harry
Hara, Keiko
Hardy, John
Harris, Conley
Hayes, Gerald
Headley, David Allen
Hee, Hon-Chew
Heldt, Carl Randall
Helsmoortel, Robert
Heston, Joan
Higby, (Donald) Wayne
Hilton, Joseph
Hochstetler, T Max
Hoffman, Helen Bacon
Hoffman, William McKinley,
    Jr
Hogue, Alexandre
Holden, Raymond James
Holgate, Jeanne
Howard, David
Hubler, Julius
Hunter, John H
Hurd, Peter
Hurson, Michael
Hurtado Duhart, Rodolfo
Irving, Joan
Itatani, Michiko
Jellico, Nancy R
Jensen, Bill
Jewell, Joyce
Johnson, Nota
Jones, Howard William
Julian, June
Kali (Hanka Weynerowski)
Kaprov, Susan
Kawashima, Takeshi
Kerzie, Ted L
Kline, Richard R
Knippers, Edward Cade, Jr
Knorr, Jeanne Boardman
Kornblum, Myrtle
Kostecka, Gloria
Kotala, Stanislaw Waclaw
Kozlowski, Edward C
Kraus, (Ersilia) Zili
Laemmle, Cheryl
Lampitoc, Rol Ponce
Landau, Myra
Lane, Lois
Lansdon, Gay Brandt
Lark, Sylvia
Laughlin, Mortimer
Lee-Sissom, E
Leigh, Harry E
Lemmy, Lemmy
Lescalleet
Levinson, Mimi
Lewis, John Chapman
Liao (Shiou-Ping Liao)
Licht, Evelyn M
Lichtner, Schomer Frank
Li-Lan (Li-Lan Gee)
Lipscomb, Guy Fleming, Jr
Little Chief, Barthell
Loeb, Judy
London, Peter
Lundin, Norman K
McCafferty, Jay David
McCane, Mallory (Mallory
    Ann McCane-O'Connor)
McChesney, Clifton
McDonald, Susan Strong
McDonnell, Joseph Anthony
MacDougall, Anne
McGahee, Dorothy
McKay, Renee
McKean, Hugh Ferguson
Magali, Lara
Magee, Alan Arthur
Marais
Marca-Relli, Conrad
Marden, Brice
Martin, Thomas

Martino, Babette
Maurice, E(leanor) Ingersoll
Maynard, William
Mendenhall, Jack
Meneeley, Edward
Metcalf, Conger A
Mew, Tommy
Mintz, Baron (Ronald Earl)
Missal, Stephen J
Mitra, Gopal C
Moehl, Karl J
Moonie, Liana (Maria)
Morgenlander, Ella Kramer
Morrison, Keith Anthony
Morriss, Mary Rachel
Moses, Bette J
Moskowitz, Ira
Moss, Joe (Francis)
Munro, Janet Andrea
Murray, Judith
Musick, Pat
Nagengast, William Joseph
Nakache-Lynch, Margaret
Namingha, Dan
Nash, Mary (Harriet)
Nelson, Dona Rae
Newman, Sophie
Nice, Don
Nodine, Jane Allen
Nuse, Oliver William
O'Donohue, Teige Ros
Okumura, Lydia
Olshan, Bernard
Olson, Bettye Johnson
O'Meallie, Kitty (Kate
    Chamness Johnson)
Osborne, Elizabeth
Palaia, Franc (Dominic)
Palmer, Michael Andrew
Parrino, George
Pasinski, Irene
Passantino, George
    Christopher
Passuntino, Peter Zaccaria
Pease, David G
Peck, James Edward
Pepper, Beverly
Pereznieto, Castro Fernando
Perkins, Clarence James
Phelan, Andrew L
Pierce, Danny P
Piper, Jane
Pogzeba, Wolfgang H
Powelson, Rosemary A
Prasch, Richard John
Prestopino, Gregorio
Propersi, August J
Pura, William Paul
Purcell, Ann
Quinn, Brian Grant
Quisgard, Liz Whitney
Rankaitis, Susan Anne
Rapoport, Sonya
Rathle, Henri (Amin)
Redein, Alex S
Reich, Don
Reid, Leslie Mary Margaret
Renninger, Katharine Steele
Rhodes, Curtis A
Richards, Joseph Edward
Rippel, M (Morris Conrad)
Ritchie, (Celia) Ann
Rizzie, Dan
Rockburne, Dorothea
Roda (Rhoda Lillian Sablow)
Rodan, Don
Rodriguez, Pedro A
Rollman-Shay, Ed & Charlotte
Rosas, Mel
Rose, David
Roseman, Stanley
Rosen, Joan Fischman
Roser, Ce (Cecilia)
Rossi, Joseph O
Rubello, David Jerome
Ruhe, Barnaby Sieger
Russo, Michele

PAINTER (cont)

Block, Dorothy
Blodgett, Anne Washington
Bloom, Donald S
Bloom, Hyman
Blos, Peter W
Bluhm, Norman
Blumberg, Ron
Blumenthal, Fritz
Boal, Sara Metzner
Boardman, Seymour
Bobak, Bruno Joseph
Boccia, Edward Eugene
Boedeker, Arnold E (Boedie)
Boeve, Edgar Gene
Bogaev, Ronni (Ronni Bogaev Greenstein)
Bogart, George A
Bogart, Richard Jerome
Bogucki, (Edwin Arnold)
Bohler, Joseph Stephen
Bohnen, Blythe
Bolt, Ron
Bond, Oriel Edmund
Bonevardi, Marcelo
Bongart, Sergei R
Bookbinder, Jack
Booth, Dot
Booth, George Warren
Boothe, Power Robert
Bopp, Emery
Bordes, Adrienne
Boren, James Erwin
Borgatta, Robert Edward
Bornstein, Eli
Borofsky, Jon
Borso, Richard George
Borstein, Elena
Bosse, Janet C
Bosson, Jack (John Edwin), Jr
Bostelle, Thomas (Theodore)
Boterf, Check (Chester Arthur)
Bothwell, Dorr
Bott, Patricia Allen
Botto, Richard Alfred
Boucher, Tania Kunsky
Boughton, William Harrison
Boutis, Tom
Bove, Richard
Bower, Gary David
Bowes, Betty Miller
Bowler, Joseph, Jr
Bowles, Marianne von Recklinghausen
Bowling, Frank
Bowman, Bruce
Bowman, Ken
Bowman, Richard
Boxer, Stanley (Robert)
Boyd, Michael
Boylan, John Lewis
Boz, Alex (Alex Bozickovic)
Bradford, Howard
Bradley, David P(aul)
Bradshaw, Lawrence James
Bradshaw, Robert George
Brady, Charles Michael
Bragar, Philip Frank
Braig, Betty Lou
Brainard, Owen
Braley, Jean
Bramhall, Kib
Brams, Joan
Brandt, Frederick Robert
Brandt, Warren
Brawley, Robert Julius
Breiger, Elaine
Brendel, Bettina
Brice, William
Brigadier, Anne
Briggs, Ernest
Brightwell, Walter
Bristow, William Arthur
Britt, Nelson Clark
Britt, Sam Glenn
Broadd, Harry Andrew
Brodhead, Quita

Brody, Arthur William
Brody, Blanche
Broemel, Carl William
Bromberg, Faith
Broner, Robert
Brooke, Pegan
Brooks, James
Broome, Rick (Richard Raymond)
Broomfield, Adolphus George
Bross, Albert L, Jr
Broussard, Normaj
Brown, Alice Dalton
Brown, Bruce Robert
Brown, James
Brown, John Hall
Brown, Judith Gwyn
Brown, June Gottlieb-
Brown, Reynold
Brown, Stephen Pat
Browne, Syd J
Browne, Vivian E
Brownett, Thelma Denyer
Browning, Colleen
Brucker, Edmund
Brulc, Lillian G
Bruneau, Kittie
Brusca, Jack
Brustlein, Daniel
Bryans, John Armond
Bryce, Eileen Ann
Bryce, Mark Adams
Brzozowski, Richard Joseph
Buckley, Mary L (Mrs Joseph M Parriott)
Bucknall, Malcolm Roderick
Buckner, Kay Lamoreux
Buczak, Brian Elliot
Buecker, Robert
Bueno, Jose (Joe Goode)
Bumgardner, James Arliss
Bunker, George
Bunn-Stadden, Cecine
Buonagurio, Edgar R
Burford, Byron Leslie
Burgess, Joseph James, Jr
Burgess, Linda Suzanne
Burggraf, Ray Lowell
Burke, Daniel V
Burke, E Ainslie
Burkert, Robert Randall
Burko, Diane
Burnett, Patricia Hill
Burns, Jerome
Burns, Josephine
Burns, Paul Callan
Burns, Sheila
Burns, Stan
Buros, Luella
Burpee, James Stanley
Burt, Dan
Busa, Peter
Bushnell, Kenneth Wayne
Butchkes, Sydney
Butler, James D
Byard, Carole Marie
Byrd, D Gibson
Caddell, Foster
Cade, Walter, III
Cady, Dennis Vern
Caimite
Cain, Joseph Alexander
Caiserman-Roth, Ghitta
Cajori, Charles F
Calamar, Gloria
Calapai, Letterio
Calkin, Carleton Ivers
Calle, Paul
Callicott, Burton Harry
Camblin, Bob Bilyeu
Cameron, Eric
Camins, Jacques Joseph
Campanelli, Pauline Eble
Campbell, Charles Malcolm
Campbell, Jeanne Begien
Campbell, Jewett
Campbell, Richard Horton

Campbell, William Henry
Caniff, Milton Arthur
Cannuli, Richard Gerald
Canright, Sarah Anne
Cantine, David
Caplan, Sandra (Sandra Ciarrochi Caplan)
Cardinal, Marcelin
Cardman, Cecilia
Cardoso, Anthony
Carlin, James
Carlos, (James) Edward
Carlson, Cynthia J
Carnwath, Squeak
Carpenter, Earl L
Carpenter, Gilbert Frederick (Bert)
Carrero, Jaime
Carrick, Donald F
Carrington, Joy Harrell
Carron, Maudee Lilyan
Carswell, Rodney
Carter, Clarence Holbrook
Carter, Frederick Timmins
Cartmell, Helen
Carulla, Ramon
Caryl, Joan Leonard
Casas, Fernando Rodriguez
Casas, Melesio
Cassara, Frank
Caswell, Helen Rayburn
Catchi (Catherine O Childs)
Catok, Lottie Meyer
Cattell, Ray
Catterall, John Edward
Catusco, Louis
Cavanaugh, Tom Richard
Cecil, Charles Harkless
Celentano, Francis Michael
Cervene, Richard
Cetin, Anton
Chadeayne, Robert Osborne
Chaplin, George Edwin
Chapman, Walter Howard
Chappell, Berkley Warner
Charlot, Martin Day
Chase, Jeanne Norman
Chase, Louisa L
Chase, Richard Andrew
Chatmas, John
Chavez-Morado, Jose
Cheatham, Frank Reagan
Chemeche, George
Chen Chi
Chercpov, George
Cherry, Herman
Cheshire, Craig Gifford
Chesney, Lee R, Jr
Chestney, Lillian
Chethlahe (David Chethlahe Paladin)
Chieffo, Clifford Toby
Childs, Bernard
Chinn, Yuen Yuey
Chinni, Peter Anthony
Chodkowski, Henry, Jr
Christensen, Ted
Christie, Robert Duncan
Chuey, Robert Arnold
Churchill, Diane
Ciarrochi, Ray
Cicero, Carmen L
Cintron, Joseph M
Civitello, John Patrick
Clapsaddle, Jerry
Clark, Claude
Clark, Michael Vinson
Clarke, Ann
Clarke, John Clem
Clement, Kathleen (Ruth)
Cliff, Denis Antony
Clifton, Jack Whitney
Clinedinst, Katherine Parsons
Clive, Richard R
Cloar, Carroll
Close, Chuck
Close, Dean Purdy

Clutz, William
Clymer, Albert Anderson
Cobb, Ruth
Cochran, George McKee (Redbird)
Cockrill, Sherna
Coe, Anne Elizabeth
Coggeshall, Calvert
Coheleach, Guy Joseph
Cohen, Jean
Cohn, Max Arthur
Cohoe, Grey
Coiner, Charles Toucey
Coker, Carl David
Colarusso, Corrine Camille
Cole, Donald
Cole, Joyce
Cole, Max
Coleman, M L (Micheal Lee)
Coleman, Michael
Collazo, Carlos Erick
Collier, Alan Caswell
Collier, James Mitchell
Collins, J(oseph) B
Collins, John Ireland
Collins, Lowell Daunt
Colson, Chester E
Colt, John Nicholson
Colville, Alexander
Colway, James R
Comtois, Louis
Conant, Howard Somers
Congdon, William (Grosvenor)
Conger, William
Conn, David Edward
Connolly, Jerome Patrick
Conover, Robert Fremont
Conrad, Nancy R
Constantine, Greg John
Cook, August Charles
Cook, Peter (Geoffrey)
Cooke, Jody Helen
Cooke, Judy
Cooley, Adelaide N
Cooney-Crawford, Thom M
Cooper, Anthony J
Cooper, Marve H
Cooper, Wayne
Copeland, Lila
Copley, William Nelson
Coral R (Flaviano Ezequiel Coral Revelo)
Corish, Joseph Ryan
Cormier, Robert John
Cornell, Thomas Browne
Cornin, Jon
Corr, James Donat
Correa, Flora Horst
Cortor, Eldzier
Cortright, Steven M
Corwin, Sophia M
Couper, Charles Alexander
Court, Lee Winslow
Courtney, Barbara Wood
Courtright, Robert
Covington, Harrison Wall
Cowles, Fleur
Cox, Gardner
Coyne, John Michael
Craft, David Ralph
Craft, Douglas D
Craig, Nancy Ellen
Cramer, Richard Charles
Crandall, Jerry C
Creatore, Mary-Alice
Cretara, Domenic Anthony
Crimi, Alfred D
Criquette (Ruth DuBarry Montague)
Crotto, Paul
Crown, Keith Allen
Crozier, Richard Lewis
Crumbo, Minisa
Crumbo, Woody
Crump, Walter Moore, Jr
Crystal, Boris
Culbertson, Janet Lynn (Mrs Douglas Kaften)

PAINTER (cont)

Cummings, David William
Cunningham, (Charles) Bruce
Cunningham, Francis
Currie, Bruce
Curtis, Mary Cranfill
Curtis, Philip Campbell
Curtis, Roger William
Cusick, Nancy Taylor
Cuthbert, Virginia
Cutler, Grayce E
Cutler, Ronnie
Cyril, R
Czimbalmos, Magdolna Paal
Dailey, Chuck (Charles
  Andrew)
Dailey, Michael Dennis
Dallmann, Daniel Forbes
Daly, Kathleen (Kathleen Daly
  Pepper)
Damast, Elba Cecilia
Damron, John Clarence
Danieli, Fidel Angelo
Dantzic, Cynthia Maris
D'Arcangelo, Allan M
D'Arista, Robert
Darton, Christopher
Daskaloff, Gyorgy
Daughters, Robert A
Davenport, Ray
Davenport, Rebecca Read
David, Don Raymond
Davidek, Stefan
Davidson, Herbert Laurence
Davidson, Nancy
Davies, Kenneth Southworth
Davis, Alonzo Joseph
Davis, Brad (Bradley Darius)
Davis, Gene
Davis, Ronald Wendel
Davis, Walter Lewis
Davis, William D
Dawley, Joseph William
Dawson, John Allan
Day, Horace Talmage
Day, John
Deaderick, Joseph
Dean, Peter
De Blasi, Anthony Armando
de Champlain, Vera Chopak
Dechar, Peter
De Donato, Louis
Dee, Leo Joseph
Deem, George
DeFeo, Jay
De Forest, Roy Dean
De Groat, George Hugh
Dehn, Virginia
De Kergommeaux, Duncan
de Knight, Avel
de Kooning, Elaine Marie
  Catherine
de Lama, Alberto
De La Vega, Antonio
De Leeuw, Leon
de Lesseps, Tauni
Della-Volpe, Ralph Eugene
de Looper, Willem
Delson, Elizabeth
deMatties, Nick
Denney, Jim (James David)
Dennis, Roger Wilson
Denniston, Douglas
Deo, Marjoree Nee
Dernovich, Donald Frederick
DeRoux, Daniel Edward
De Ruth, Jan
Desmidt, Thomas H
des Rioux (de Messimy),
  Deena (Coty)
Desser, Maxwell Milton
Devlin, Harry
Dibble, Charles Ryder
Dibble, George
Di Cerbo, Michael
Dickerson, Brian S
Dickerson, Daniel Jay

Dickey, Helen Pauline
Diebenkorn, Richard
Diehl, Sevilla S
Di Fate, Vincent
DiFranza, Americo M
Dike, Philip Latimer
Dill, Laddie John
Dillon, Paul Sanford
Dimondstein, Morton
Dinnerstein, Harvey
Dobbs, John Barnes
Dodd, Lois
Dodge, Joseph Jeffers
Dominique, John August
Donahue, Philip Richard
Donaldson, Marjory (Rogers)
Doo Da Post (Edward
  Ferdinand Higgins III)
Dooley, Helen Bertha
Doolin, James Lawrence
Dorn, Ruth (Dornbush)
Dorst, Claire V
Douglas, Edwin Perry
Douke, Daniel W
Downes, Rackstraw
Doyle, Joe
Drapell, Joseph
Draper, William Franklin
Dreiband, Laurence
Dreskin, Jeanet Steckler
Drewelowe, Eve
Drewes, Werner
Drexler, Lynne
Driggs, Elsie
Droege, Anthony Joseph, II
Drummond, Sally Hazelet
Duback, Charles S
Dubin, Ralph
Dublac, Robert Revak
Duca, Alfred Milton
Dugmore, Edward
Duis, Rita
Du Jardin, Gussie
Dulac, Margarita Walker
Dumas, Antoine
Dunbar, Russell Raymond
Duncan, Ruth
Dunkelman, Loretta
Dunlap, Loren Edward
Duren, Stephen D
Durham, William
Durr, Pat (Patricia Beth)
Dutton, Allen A
Dwyer, James
Dyson, John Holroyd
Dyyon, Frazier
Dzigurski, Alex
Dzubas, Friedel
Earle, William Henry
Eastman, Gene M
Ebie, William Dennis
Eckert, William Dean
Eckstein, Ruth
Eddy, Don
Edelman, Rita
Edge, Douglas Benjamin
Edwards, Stanley Dean
Eglitis, Laimons
Egri, Ruth (Ruth Egri Holden)
Eilers, Fred (Anton Frederick)
Eisenberg, Sonja Miriam
Eisenstat, Benjamin
Eisentrager, James A
Eisinger, Harry
Eisler, Lawrence
Eisner, Dorothy (Dorothy
  Eisner McDonald)
Eldredge, Stuart Edson
Elena, Maria
Eliasoph, Paula
Eliot, Lucy Carter
Elliot, John Theodore
Ellis, Richard
Ellison, Nancy
Else, Robert John
England, Paul Grady
Engle, Barbara Jean

Engle, Chet
English, John Arbogast
Enman, Tom Kenneth
Eppink, Helen Brenan
Eppink, Norman R
Eres, Eugenia
Ericson, Beatrice
Ernst, James Arnold
Esaki, Yasuhiro
Eshoo, Robert
Estes, Richard
Etnier, Stephen Morgan
Etter, Howard Lee
Etting, Emlen
Ettinger, Susi Steinitz
Evans, Burford Elonzo
Evans, John
Evans, Richard
Everett, Len G
Everett, Russell Henry
Evett, Kenneth Warnock
Ewing, Edgar Louis
Faccinto, Victor Paul
Faddis, (William) George
Faden, Lawrence Steven
Faiers, Ted (Edward Spencer)
Falfan, Alfredo
Faragasso, Jack
Farber, Dennis H
Farber, Maya M
Fares, William O
Farian, Babette S
Faris, Brunel De Bost
Faris, Peter Kinzie
Farm, Gerald E
Farnham, Alexander
Farruggio, Remo Michael
Faulkner, Frank
Fax, Elton Clay
FeBland, Harriet
Feder, Ben
Feininger, T Lux
Feist, Harold E
Feist, Warner David
Felter, James Warren
Feltus, Alan Evan
Fenn, (Frances) Elizabeth
Fenton, Alan
Fenwick, Roly (William
  Roland)
Ferber, Herbert
Ferguson, Barclay (Lord of
  Lamond)
Ferris, Edythe
Ferris, (Carlisle) Keith
Fett, William F
Fichter, Herbert Francis
Fife, Mary (Mrs Edward
  Laning)
Fillerup, Mel
Filmus, Michael Roy
Fincher, John H
Finkelstein, Louis
Finnegan, Sharyn Marie
Fiore, Joseph A
Firfires, Nicholas Samuel
Fish, Richard G
Fitzgerald, Edmond James
Fitzgerald, Harriet
Fitzpatrick, Joseph Cyril
Flattmann, Alan Raymond
Flecker, Maurice Nathan
Fludd, Reginald Joseph
Fluek, Toby
Ford, Ruth Vansickle
Forester, Russell
Forge, Andrew Murray
Forman, Alice
Formigoni, Mauri Monihon
Forrest, Christopher Patrick
Forsman, Chuck (Charles
  Stanley)
Fortess, Karl E
Foster, Holland
Fox, John
Frace, Charles Lewis
Frame, Robert (Aaron)

Frances, Harriette Anton
Francis, Sherron
Frank, Jane
Franklin, Charlotte White
Fransioli, Thomas Adrian
Fraser, Carol Hoorn
Frater, Hal
Frazer, John Thatcher
Frederick, Deloras Ann
Freed, Douglass Lynn
Freedman, Maurice
Freeman, David L
Freeman, Mark
Freeman, Robert Lee
Freilicher, Jane
Freund, Harry Louis
Freund, Tibor
Friberg, Arnold
Frick, Robert Oliver
Friedensohn, Elias
Fromboluti, Sideo
Frudakis, Zenos
Frutchey, Jere (Gerald Read)
Fukui, Nobu
Fuller, Emily
Furr, Jim
Fussiner, Howard
Gabin, George Joseph
Gach, George
Gaines, William Robert
Galles, Arie Alexander
Gammon, Juanita-La Verne
Gammon, Reginald Adolphus
Gaona Adame, Jose Julio
Gardner, Susan Ross
Garman, Ed
Garrett, Stuart Grayson
Garrison, Eve
Garston, Gerald Drexler
Garver, Walter Raymond
Garwood, Audrey
Gasparian, Armen Tigran
Gast, Michael Carl
Gatewood, Maud Florance
Gauvin, Claude E
Gavalas, Alexander Beary
Gebhardt, Harold
Gechtoff, Sonia
Gehr, Mary (Ray)
Geis, Milton Arthur
Gekiere, Madeleine
Gelber, Samuel
Gelinas, Robert William
Genius, Jeannette
Gentry, Warren Miller
George, Richard Allan
George, Thomas
Gerardia, Helen
Gerhold, William Henry
Gersovitz, Sarah Valerie
Gerzso, Gunther
Gettinger, Edmond Walter
Giacalone, Vito
Gibbons, Hugh (James)
Gibson, Benedict S
Gibson, James D
Gilbert, Albert Earl
Gilbert, Clyde Lingle
Gilbert, Herb
Gilbert, Lionel
Gilbertson, Charlotte
Gilboy, Margaretta
Giles, Newell Walton, Jr
Gillespie, Gregory Joseph
Gillette, W Dean
Gimblett, Max(well)
Ginzburg, Yankel (Jacob)
Giobbi, Edward Gioachino
Girard, (Charles) Jack
Giraudier, Antonio
Glass, Sylvia
Glorig, Ostor
Godfrey, Robert
Godfrey, Winnie (Winifred M)
Goedike, Shirl
Goertz, Augustus Frederick,
  III

PAINTER (cont)

Goetz, Richard Vernon
Gold, Sharon Cecile
Goldberg, Arnold Herbert
Goldberg, Chaim
Goldin, Leon
Goldsleger, Cheryl
Goldstein, Gladys Hack
Goldstein, Howard
Golub, Leon Albert
Gomez-Quiroz, Juan Manuel
Gonzales, Boyer
Gonzales, Carlotta (Mrs Richard Lahey)
Gonzalez, Juan J
Gonzalez-Tornero, Sergio
Good, Leonard
Goodacre, Glenna
Goodman, Sidney
Goodrich, Susan
Goodridge, Lawrence Wayne
Goodyear, John L
Gorchov, Ron
Gorder, Clayton J
Gordley, Marilyn Classe
Gordley, Metz Tranbarger
Gordon, Josephine
Gore, Ken (Kenneth Leon)
Gore, Samuel Marshall
Gorelick, Shirley
Gorman, R C
Gorski, Daniel Alexander
Gorsline, Douglas Warner
Gough, Robert Alan
Gourevitch, Jacqueline
Goutman, Dolya
Grafton, Rick (Frederick Wellington)
Graham, Walter
Grandee, Joe Ruiz
Granstaff, William Boyd
Grass, Patty Patterson
Grasso, Salvatore Fortunato
Graupe-Pillard, Grace
Graves, Ka (Kathleen Rose)
Graves, Robert Edward
Gray, Jim
Gray, Larry
Gray, Marie Elise
Greco, Anthony Joseph
Greco, Frank
Greeley, Charles Matthew
Green, Art
Green, Denise G
Green, George D
Green, Glenda
Green, Martin Leonard
Greenberg, Gloria
Greene, Ethel Maud
Greene, Stephen
Greenleaf, Esther (Hargrave)
Greenleaf, Virginia
Greenstein, Ilise
Greenstone, Marion
Greer, Walter (Marion)
Gregor, Harold Laurence
Gregory, Bruce
Grelle, Martin Glen
Griefen, John Adams
Grigoriadis, Mary
Grigsby, Jefferson Eugene, Jr
Grimes, Margaret W
Grisham, Barbara Jean
Groat, Hall Pierce
Groell, Theophil
Gronbeck, Jean
Grosch, Laura
Groshans, Werner
Gross, Earl
Grosser, Maurice
Grosz, Franz Joseph
Grotz, Dorothy Rogers
Groves, Naomi Jackson
Grucza, Leo (Victor)
Grupp, Carl Alf
Gruppe, Charles
Guerrero, Jose

Gummelt, Samuel
Gunter, Frank Elliott
Gursoy, Ahmet
Gussow, Sue Ferguson
Guzevich-Sommers, Kreszenz (Cynthia)
Gwathmey, Robert
Haack, Cynthia R
Haerer, Carol
Haessle, Jean-Marie Georges
Hahn, Gerald
Halaby, Samia Asaad
Halbrooks, Darryl Wayne
Haley Russo, Sally Fulton
Halko, Joe
Hall, John (Scott)
Hall, Rex Earl
Hall, Robert L
Hall, Susan
Hallam, Beverly (Linney)
Halpern, Lea
Hamann, Marilyn D
Hamill, Tim J
Hammerman, Pat Jo
Hammersley, Frederick
Hammond, Harmony
Hampton, Phillip Jewel
Handell, Albert George
Handville, Robert T
Hanes, James (Albert)
Hanna, Boyd Everett
Hanna, Paul Dean, Jr
Hannah, Duncan (Rathbone)
Hansen, Gaylen Capener
Hanson, Jean (Elphick)
Hanson, Philip Holton
Hapke, Paul Frederick
Hardin, Helen
Harding, Ann
Hardy, David Whittaker, III
Hardy, Howard (Collins)
Hari, Kenneth
Harlan, Roma Christine
Harlow, Robert E
Harman, Maryann Whittemore
Harmon, Cliff Franklin
Harmon, Lily
Harms, Elizabeth
Harper, Eleanor O'Neil
Harris, Alfred Peter
Harris, Marian D
Harris, Robert George
Harris, William Wadsworth, II
Harrison, (William) Allan
Harrison, Tony
Harriton, Abraham
Harsh, Richard
Hart, Betty Miller
Hart, Morgan Drake
Hartell, John
Harter, John Burton
Hartigan, Grace
Harvey, Donald
Harvey, Jacqueline
Haseltine, James Lewis
Haseltine, Maury (Margaret Wilson)
Haswell, Hollee
Hatch, Mary
Hatfield, Donald Gene
Hatke, Walter Joseph
Haug, Donald Raymond
Haughey, James M
Hausey, Robert Michael
Hawkins, Thomas Wilson, Jr
Haworth, B Cogill
Hayes, Tua
Haynes, Douglas H
Haynes, George Edward
Haynes, R (Richard Thomas)
Hayward, James
Hayward, Peter
Head, George Bruce
Hedden-Sellman, Zelda
Hedin, Donald Monroe
Hedman, Teri Jo
Hedrick, Wally Bill

Heflin, Tom Pat
Heinemann, Peter
Heipp, Richard Christian
Held, Alma M
Held, Philip
Heliker, John Edward
Heller, Dorothy
Helman, Phoebe
Henderson, Robbin Legere
Hendler, Raymond
Hendricks, Barkley Leonnard
Hendricks, David Charles
Hennesy, Gerald Craft
Henry, Jean
Henry, Robert
Hernandez-Cruz, Luis
Herpst, Martha Jane
Herring, Jan (Janet Mantel)
Hershberg, Israel
Herzbrun, Helene McKinsey
Hess, Emil John
Heusser, Eleanore Elizabeth (Eleanor Heusser Ferholt)
Hewitt, Francis Ray
Hibel, Edna
Hicken, Philip Burnham
Hildebrandt, William Albert
Hill, Clinton J
Hill, J Tweed
Hill, Joan (Chea-se-quah)
Hill, Peter
Hill, Polly Knipp
Hilson, Douglas
Himmelfarb, John David
Hinman, Charles B
Hios, Theo
Hirsch, Gilah Yelin
Hitch, Jean Leason
Hitch, Robert A
Hitch, Stewart
Hnizdovsky, Jacques
Hobbie, Lucille
Hodel, Diane Carol
Hodge, R Garey
Hodgkins, Rosalind Selma
Hoener, Arthur
Hoff, Margo
Hoffmann, Arnold, Jr
Hofmann, Douglas William
Hogle, Ann Meilstrup
Hoie, Helen Hunt
Holder, Kenneth Allen
Holland, Harry Charles
Hollen-Bolmgren, Donna
Hollerbach, Serge
Hollinger, Helen Wetherbee
Hollingsworth, Alvin Carl
Hollister, Paul
Hollister, Valerie (Dutton)
Holm, Milton W
Holman, Arthur (Stearns)
Holmes, David Valentine
Holoun, Harold Dean
Honig, Mervin
Hood, Dorothy
Hoover, John Jay
Hopkins, Budd
Hopkins, Kendal Coles
Hopkins, Peter
Hopper, Frank J
Hornak, Ian John
Horne, (Arthur Edward) Cleeve
Hough, Jennine
Houle, Robert James
Houser, Allan C
Houser, Jim
Howard, (Helen) Barbara
Howard, Dan F
Hoyt, Dorothy
Hsiao, Chin
Hu, Chi Chung
Hubbard, John
Hubenthal, Karl Samuel
Huggins, Victor, Jr
Hughes, Edward John
Hughes, Joseph (Frederick)

Hughto, Darryl Leo
Hui, Helene
Hulett, Simonne R
Hull, Gregory Stewart
Hultberg, John
Humphrey, S L
Hunkler, Dennis Francis
Hunt, Courtenay
Hunter, Robert Douglas
Hunter, Robert Howard
Hurley, Wilson
Hurt, Susanne M
Hushlak, Gerald
Hutchison, Elizabeth S
Hyson, Jean
Iacurto, Francesco
Iden, Sheldon
Ilowitz, Theodora
Indiana, Robert
Inoue, Kazuko
Ipcar, Dahlov
Ippolito, Angelo
Irvin, Fred Maddox
Irwin, Lani Helena
Irwin, Lisa Dru
Isaacs, Ron
Isaak, Nicholas, Jr
Isenburger, Eric
Isham, Sheila Eaton
Iskowitz, Gershon
Ives, Elaine Caroline
Iwamoto, Ralph Shigeto
Jackson, Billy Morrow
Jackson, Everett Gee
Jackson, Harry Andrew
Jackson, Herb
Jackson, Lee
Jackson, Oliver Lee
Jackson, Vaughn L
Jacobs, Harold
Jacobs, Helen Nichols
Jacobs, Ralph, Jr
Jacobshagen, N Keith, II
Jacquemon, Pierre
Jacquette, Yvonne Helene
Jaeger, Brenda Kay
Jaffe, Nora
Jameson, Demetrios George
Jameson, Philip Alexander
Jampol, Glenn D
Janelsins, Veronica
Janson, Agnes
Jaque, Louis
Jaramillo, Virginia
Jaudon, Valerie
Jay, Norma Joyce
Ject-Key, Elsie
Jeffers, Wendy Jane
Jenkins, Paul
Jennings, Francis
Jennings, Thomas
Jensen, Gary
Jensen, Marit
Jess
Jessen, Shirley Agnes
Jeswald, Joseph
Jilg, Michael Florian
Johanningmeier, Robert Alan
Johanson, George E
Johnson, Brent
Johnson, Bruce (James)
Johnson, Buffie
Johnson, Gregory
Johnson, Harvey William
Johnson, James Ralph
Johnson, Katherine King
Johnson, Lee
Johnson, Lester L
Johnson, Richard A
Johnston, Thomas Alix
Johnston, William Medford
Jolley, Donal Clark
Jolley, Geraldine H (Jerry)
Jones, Amy (Amy Jones Frisbie)
Jones, Franklin Reed
Jones, Herb (Leon Herbert), Jr

PAINTER (cont)

Jones, John Paul
Jones, Lou (Mary Louise Humpton)
Jones, Marvin Harold
Jones, Norma L
Jones, Patty Sue
Jones, Ruthe Blalock
Jones, W Louis
Jordan, Barbara Schwinn
Jordan, Robert
Jorgensen, Sandra
Joukhadar, Moumtaz
Joyce, Marshall Woodside
Juarez, Roberto
Judd, De Forrest Hale
Judge, Mary Frances
Judkins, Sylvia
Judson, Jeannette Alexander
Julian, Lazaro
Jung, Kwan Yee
Juszczyk, James Joseph
Kabak, Robert
Kabotie, Fred
Kacere, John C
Kahan, Leonard
Kahn, Susan B
Kahn, Wolf
Kainen, Jacob
Kaish, Morton
Kalb, Marty Joel
Kalina, Richard
Kallem, Henry
Kamihira, Ben
Kane, Bob Paul
Kanemitsu, Matsumi
Kanovitz, Howard
Kaplan, Marilyn Flashenberg
Kaplinski, Buffalo
Kapsalis, Thomas Harry
Karn, Gloria Stoll
Karniol, Hilda
Karp, Aaron S
Karwelis, Donald Charles
Kasak, Nikolai (Kazak)
Kass, Jacob James
Kasten, Karl Albert
Kasten, Sherry Zvares
Katano, Marc
Katayama, Toshihiro
Katz, Alex
Katz, Eunice
Katz, Morris
Katzman, Herbert
Kauffman, Robert Craig
Kaufman, Irving
Kaupelis, Robert John
Kawa, Florence Kathryn
Kawabata, Minoru
Kay, Reed
Kearns, James Joseph
Keener, Anna Elizabeth
Keller, Deane
Kelley, Chapman
Kelley, Ramon
Kellogg, Maurice Dale
Kelly, James
Kelly, Leon
Kelly, William Joseph
Kelpe, Paul
Kemper, John Garner
Kennedy, James Edward
Kenney, Estelle Koval
Kent, H Latham
Kepalas (Elena Kepalaite)
Kepets, Hugh Michael
Kermes, Constantine John
Kerns, Ed (Johnson), Jr
Kerr, James Wilfrid
Kerstetter-Bailey, Barbara Ann
Kerswill, J W Roy
Kessler, Alan
Kessler, Edna Leventhal
Kester, Lenard
Keveson, Florence
Kevorkian, Richard
Keyser, Robert G

Kiah, Virginia Jackson
Kieferndorf, Frederick George
Kielkopf, James Robert
Kilian, Austin Farland
Kilmer, Nicholas John
Kim, Po (Hyun)
Kimbrough, Sara Dodge
Kimura, Sueko M
Kimura, William Yusaburo
Kinghan, Charles Ross
Kipniss, Robert
Kirkwood, Mary Burnette
Kirschenbaum, Jules
Kish, Maurice
Kiskadden, Robert Morgan
Kitta, George Edward
Kittredge, Nancy (Elizabeth)
Kjargaard, John Ingvard
Klabunde, Charles Spencer
Klarin, Winifred Erlick
Klavans, Minnie
Klaven, Marvin L
Klein, Doris
Klein, Medard
Klein, Sandor C
Kleinman, Sue
Klement, Vera
Kline, Harriet
Knapp, Sadie Magnet
Knapp, Tom
Knaub, Raymond L
Knerr, Sallie Frost
Knief, Helen Jeanette
Knight, Jacob Jaskoviak
Knipscher, Gerard Allen
Knipschild, Robert
Knobler, Lois Jean
Knowles, Richard H
Knowlton, Jonathan
Knudson, Robert LeRoy
Kobayashi, Katsumi Peter
Koch, Gerd (Herman)
Koch, Philip
Kocherthaler, Mina
Koehler, Henry
Koenig, John Franklin
Koestner, Don
Kogan, Deborah
Kohlmeyer, Ida (R)
Kohn, Edmond
Kohn, William Roth
Kohut, Lorene
Konopka, Joseph
Koppelman, Dorothy
Kopriva, Sharon Ortman
Korjus, Veronica Maria Elisabeth
Korman, Harriet R
Korot, Beryl
Kortheuer, Dayrell
Koscianski, Leonard J
Koursaros, Harry G
Kozloff, Joyce
Kozlow, Richard
Kozlow, Sigmund
Kramer, Jack N
Kramer, Marjorie Anne
Krashes, Barbara
Krasner, Lee
Krause, LaVerne Erickson
Krauth, Harald
Krieger, Ruth M
Kriensky
Kriesberg, Irving
Kronsnoble, Jeffrey Michael
Krueger, Lothar David
Krushenick, Nicholas
Kuehn, Frances
Kuh, Howard
Kuhlman, Walter Egel
Kuhn, Bob
Kulicke, Robert M
Kumm, Marguerite Elizabeth
Kuopus, Clinton
Kurka, Donald Frank
Kurz, Diana
Kuwayama, Tadaaki

Lable, Eliot
Labrie, Rose
Lacher, Johannes
Lack, Richard Frederick
Lacroix, Flora Luisa
Lacroix, Richard
Lacy, Robert Eugene
Lafaye, Nell Murray
La Fon, Julia Anna
La Hotan, Robert L
Lam, Jennett (Brinsmade)
Lamantia, Paul (Christopher)
Lamb, Adrian
Lambert, Ed
Lancaster, Mark
Land, Ernest Albert
Landers, Bertha
Landfield, Ronnie (Ronald T)
Lane, Marion Jean Arrons
Lang, Daniel S
Lang, Margo Terzian
Langford, James
La Noue, Terence David
Lansner, Fay
Lanyon, Ellen
La Pelle, Rodger
LaPena, Frank Raymond
La Pierre, Thomas
Lapointe, Frank
Lark, Raymond
Larmer, Oscar Vance
Larraz, Julio F
Larsen, Mernet Ruth
Larsen, Ole
Larsen, Robert Wesley
Larson, Blaine (Gledhill)
Lasker, Joe (Joseph L)
Laub-Novak, Karen
Lauffer, Alice A
Laufman, Sidney
Laurent, John Louis
Law, C Anthony
Law, Pauline Elizabeth
Lawson, Thomas
Lax, David
Leach, Frederick Darwin
Lecky, Susan
Leeds, Annette
Leepa, Allen
Leeper, John P
Leete, William White
Leff, Juliette
Lem, Richard Douglas
Lembeck, John Edgar
Lemieux, Irenee
Lenney, Annie
Lenssen, Heidi (Mrs Fridolf Johnson)
Leon, Ana (Ana M Rodriguez-Leon)
Leon, Ralph Bernard
Lerman, Ora
Le Roy, Harold M
Leslie, Seaver
Lesnick, Stephen William
Letendre, Rita
Levee, John H
Leventhal, Ruth Lee
Levering, Robert K
Levin, Kim
Levy, Tibbie
Lew, Weyman
Lewis, Don S, Sr
Lewis, Michael H
Lewis, Nat Brush
Lewton, Val Edwin
Lhotka, Bonny Pierce
Libby, William C
Lichtenberg, Manes
Lieber, Thomas Alan
Ligare, David H
Likan, Gustav
Liljegren, Frank
Li Marzi, Joseph
Linderman, Earl William
Link, Lawrence John
Lipinsky de Orlov, Lino S

Lippmann, Janet Gurian
Lipton, Sondra (Sahlman)
Lis, Janet Chapman
Little, James
Lock, Earl Wayne
Locke, Charles Wheeler
Locke, Rhea G
Loehle, Betty Barnes
Loehle, Richard E
Loew, Michael
Logan, Gene Adams
Lomahaftewa, Linda (Linda Joyce Slock)
Long, Walter Kinscella
Longley, Bernique
Loran, Erle
Lorentz, Pauline
Lotz, Steven Darryl
Lovell, Tom
Loving, Richard Maris
Lowney, Bruce Stark
Loy, John Sheridan
Luce, Molly
Luczun, Robert
Lueders, Jimmy C
Lumbers, James Richard
Luna, (Antonio Rodriguez)
Lund, David
Lundeberg, Helen
Lusker, Ron
Lux, Gladys Marie
Luz, Virginia
Lynch, Mary Britten
Lynds, C (Clyde William)
Lyon, Hayes Paxton
Lysun, Gregory
McAdoo, Carol Westbrook
Macaray, Lawrence Richard
MacBird, Rosemary
McCall, Ann
McCarthy, Doris Jean
McCartin, William Francis
McCauley, Gardiner Rae
McChesney, Robert Pearson
McClellan, Douglas Eugene
McClelland, Jeanne C
McClendon, Maxine (Maxine McClendon Nichols)
McClure, Constance
McCoy, John W, (II)
McCoy, Wirth Vaughan
McCulloch, Frank E
McCullough, David William
McCullough, Joseph
McDougal, Ivan Ellis
McEwen, Jean
McGee, Winston Eugene
McGinnis, Christine
McGovern, Robert F
McGrew, Bruce Elwin
McGrew, Ralph Brownell
Machetanz, Fred
McIntosh, Harold
McKie, Todd Stoddard
McKim, William Wind
McKinnickinnick, Margaret I
McLarty, William James (Jack)
MacLean, Arthur
McLean, Richard Thorpe
McMillan, Constance
McNary, Oscar L
McNear, Everett C
McQuillan, Frances
McReynolds, (Joe) Cliff
McVeigh, Miriam Temperance
McVicker, J Jay
Maddox, Jerrold Warren
Magazzini, Gene
Magleby, Frank (Francis R)
Mahaffey, Merrill Dean
Mahmoud, Ben
Maier, Maryanne E
Mailman, Cynthia
Mainardi, Patricia M
Maione, Robert
Maldjian, Vartavar B
Malo, Teri (Teri A Malo-Sprawka)

PAINTER (cont)

Malta, Vincent
Manarey, Thelma Alberta
Mancini, John
Mandel, John
Mandelman, Beatrice M
Mandziuk, Michael Dennis
Manetta, Edward J
Mangione, Patricia Anthony
Mangold, Sylvia Plimack
Mangum, William (Goodson)
Manilla, Tess
Mann, Katinka
Mann, Ward Palmer
Manso, Leo
Manville, Elsie
Manzo, Anthony Joseph
Mapes, Doris Williamson
Marcus, Irving E
Marcus, Marcia
Marder, Dorie
Margulis, Martha (Boyer)
Mari (M Eagerton)
Marianne
Mariano, Kristine
Marin, Augusto
Mark, Enid (Epstein)
Mark, Marilyn (Sabetsky)
Marker, Ralph E
Markman, Ronald
Marks, Roberta Barbara
Marriott, William Allen
Martell, Barbara Bentley
Martin, Agnes Bernice
Martin, Bernard Murray
Martin, Doug
Martin, Jane
Martin, Lucille Caiar
Martin, Mary Finch
Martin, Ron
Martino, Antonio P
Martino, Edmund
Martino, Eva E
Martino, Giovanni
Martino, Nina F
Marton, Tutzi
Martone, William Robert
Martyl (Martyl Schweig
    Langsdorf)
Marx, Nicki D
Marx, Robert Ernst
Marzano, Albert
Mason, Alden C
Mason, Bette
Mason, Frank Herbert
Mason, Phillip Lindsay
Mason, William Clifford
Massin, Eugene Max
Matassa, John P
Matson, Greta
Matternes, Jay Howard
Matthews, Gene (Eugene
    Edward)
Maughelli, Mary L
Mavian, Salpi Miriam
Max, Lope (Lope Max Diaz
    Rivera)
Max, Peter
Maxwell, John
Maxwell, Robert Edwin
Mayer, Bena Frank
Mayhew, Richard
Mayrs, David Blair
Mazzone, Domenico
Medearis, Roger
Meehan, William Dale
Meitzler, (Herbert) Neil
Meixner, Mary Louise
Melby, David A
Melikian, Mary
Mell, Ed (Edmund Paul Jr)
Meltzer, Arthur
Melville, Grevis Whitaker
Mendelson, Haim
Mendes, Barbara
Meng, Wendy
Menihan, John Conway

Menses, Jan
Meredith, John
Mermin, Mildred (Shire)
Merrick, James Kirk
Merrill, David Kenneth
Merritt, Francis Sumner
Mesches, Arnold
Messersmith, Fred Lawrence
Messick, Ben (Newton)
Messina, Joseph R
Metson, Graham
Metz, Frank Robert
Metz, Gerry Michael
Metzger, Evelyn Borchard
Michael, Gary
Micheli, Julio
Michod, Susan A
Middleman, Raoul F
Mieczkowski, Edwin
Milder, Jay
Miles, Jeanne Patterson
Milgrom, Betty
Miller, Dolly (Ethel B)
Miller, Jan
Miller, Lillian Dunn
Miller, Melissa Wren
Miller, Melvin O, Jr
Miller, Nancy Tokar
Milligan, Joan Arnold
Mim, Adrienne C (Adrienne
    Claire Schwartz)
Mina-Mora, Dorise Olson
Mintz, Harry
Mion, Pierre Riccardo
Miotke, Anne E
Mirko
Misch, Allene K
Mitchell, Fred
Mitchell, John Blair
Mitchell, Peter Todd
Miyasaki, George Joji
Mock, Richard Basil
Mode, Carol A
Model, Elisabeth D
Moffitt, John Francis
Mogavero, Michael James
Mohn, Cheri (Ann)
Moise, William Sidney
Moller, Hans
Moment, Joan
Momiyama, Nanae
Monaghan, Keith
Monroe, Gerald
Montgomery, Claude
Montlack, Edith
Montminy, (Elizabeth) Tracy
Montoya, Gustavo (Gustavo
    Montoya Carranco)
Moon, Jim (James Monroe)
Moore, Beveridge
Moore, John J
Moore, Michael Shannon
Moore, Olga
Moore, Robert Eric
Moore, Robert James
Moose, Philip Anthony
Morales, Armando
Morcos, Maher N
Morgan, Darlene
Morgan, Norma Gloria
Morgan, Robert Coolidge
Morishita, Joyce Chizuko
Morley, Malcom
Moroz, Mychajlo
Morphesis, Jim (James
    George)
Morrell, Wayne (Beam)
Morris, Carl
Morrison, Doris
Morrison, George
Mortellito, Domenico
Mortensen, Gordon Louis
Mosca, August
Moscatt, Paul N
Moseley, Ralph Sessions
Moseley, Spencer Altemont
Moses, Forrest (Lee), Jr

Moskowitz, Robert S
Moss, Gary William
Moss, Irene
Moss, Milton
Movalli, Charles Joseph
Moy, Seong
Moyers, William
Muench, John
Muhlert, Christopher Layton
Muir, Emily Lansingh
Mullen, Philip Edward
Mullican, Lee
Murata, Hiroshi
Murphy, Catherine E
Murphy, Chester Glenn
Murray, Albert (Ketcham)
Murray, Elizabeth
Murray, Richard Deibel
Myers, Jack Fredrick
Nadalini, (Louis Ernest)
Nadler, Harry
Naftulin, Rose
Nagano, Shozo
Nakamura, Kazuo
Nakazato, Hitoshi
Nardone, Vincent Joseph
Natkin, Robert
Nay, Mary Spencer
Nazarenko, Bonnie Coe
Neal, Frank Wingfield
Neals, Otto
Neddeau, Donald Frederick
    Price
Neel, Alice
Neff, Edith
Neffson, Robert
Neidhardt, Carl Richard
Neill, Ben E
Neiman, LeRoy
Nelson, Harry William
Nelson, Leonard
Nelson, Mary Carroll
Nelson, Robert Allen
Nelson, Signe (Signe Nelson
    Stuart)
Nesbitt, Lowell (Blair)
Neto, Gilda Reis (Gilda Reis
    Netopuletti)
Neustein, Joshua
Nevia
Newbill, Al
Newer, Thesis
Newman, Libby
Newman-Rice, Nancy
Newport, Esther
Niblett, Gary Lawrence
Nicholas, Thomas Andrew
Nichols, Jeannettie Doornhein
Nichols, Ward H
Nicholson, Roy William
Nick, George
Niemann, Edmund E
Nierman, Leonardo M
Nieto, John W
Nind, Jean
Nobili, Louise
Noordhoek, Harry Cecil
Nordhausen, A Henry
Nordstrand, Nathalie
    Johnson
Norman, Emile
Norris, (Robert) Ben
Norton, Mary Joyce
Norwood, Malcolm Mark
Nosoff, Frank
Notarbartolo, Albert
Novack, Frank T
Novros, David
Oakes, John Warren
O'Beil, Hedy
Ocampo, Miguel
Ocepek, Lou (Louis David)
O'Connor, John Arthur
Ohashi, Yutaka
Ohlson, Douglas Dean
Okoshi, Eugenia Sumiye
Olitski, Jules

Oliveira, Nathan
Olkinetzky, Sam
Olsen, Ernest Moran
Olson, Douglas John
Omar, Margit
Omwake, Leon, Jr
O'Neil, Bruce William
Opie, John Mart
Oppenheim, Samuel Edmund
Oppenheimer, Selma L
Order, Trudy
Orr, Arthur (Leslie)
Orr, Joseph Charles
Ortlip, Paul Daniel
Osby, Larissa Geiss
O'Sickey, Joseph Benjamin
Ostendorf, (Arthur) Lloyd, Jr
O'Sullivan, Daniel Joseph
Ott, Jerry
Ott, Wendell Lorenz
Outterbridge, John Wilfred
Owen, Bill
Owen, Frank (Franklin
    Charles)
Owens, Wallace, Jr
Ozonoff, Ida
Pace, Stephen S
Pachner, William
Pacific, Gertrude
Palmer, Lucie Mackay
Palmer, Mabel (Evelyn)
Palmer, William C
Palmgren, Donald Gene
Pantell, Richard Keith
Pappas, George
Pardee, William Hearne
Parker, Carolyn Johnson
Parker, Ray(mond)
Parker, Samuel Murray
Parker, Wilma Joan
Parrish, David Buchanan
Parrish, Jean
Parton, Nike
Pascal, David
Paschke, Edward F (Ed)
Paternosto, Cesar Pedro
Patrick, Alan K
Patrick, Genie Hudson
Paul, Ken (Hugh)
Paulsen, Brian Oliver
Peace, Bernie (Kinzel)
Pearson, Henry C
Pecchenino, J Ronald
Peck, Stephen Rogers
Pellan (Alfred)
Pellettieri, Michael Joseph
Pellew, John Clifford
Pen, Rudolph
Penczner, Paul Joseph
Penkoff, Ronald Peter
Penney, Jacqueline
Pentak, Stephen
Pentelovitch, Robert Alan
Pentz, Donald Robert
Perehudoff, William W
Perez, Vincent
Perham, Roy Gates
Perlin, Rae
Perlman, Bennard Bloch
Perlmutter, Jack
Perry, Judith Elaine
Perry, Kathryn Powers
Pershing, Louise
Peter, George
Peterdi, Gabor F
Petersen, Roland Conrad
Peterson, David Winfield
Peterson, Larry D
Peterson, Roger Tory
Petlin, Irving
Petrie, Ferdinand Ralph
Petrie, Sylvia Spencer
Petro, Joseph (Victor), Jr
Pettet, William
Pettibone, Richard H
Pettus, Jane Messick
Pezzati, Pietro

PAINTER (cont)

Pfahl, Charles Alton, III
Pfriem, Bernard
Phelan, Ellen Denise
Phelps, Nan Dee
Phillips, Alice Jane
Phillips, Bertrand D
Phillips, Marjorie
Pickford, Rollin, Jr
Pierce, Delilah W
Pierce, Elizabeth R
Pinchbeck, Peter G
Pinkerton, Clayton (David)
Pinto, Biagio
Pinto, James
Pinzarrone, Paul
Piskoti, James
Pitt, Suzan (Lee)
Pitts, Richard G
Plagens, Peter
Plamondon, Peter M
Plaster, Alice Marie
Plear, Scott Edward
Pletcher, Gerry
Pletka, Paul
Plochmann, Carolyn Gassan
Plumb, James Douglas
Pollard, Donald Pence
Pollaro, Paul
Ponce de Leon, Michael
Poole, Leslie Donald
Poor, Anne
Posen, Stephen
Postiglione, Corey M
Poulos, Basilios Nicholas
Pounian, Albert Kachouni
Power, S Brenda Joan
Pozzatti, Rudy O
Praczukowski, Edward Leon
Pramuk, Edward Richard
Pratt, Frances (Frances
    Elizabeth Usui)
Pratt, Vernon Gaither
Prechtel, Don (Donald
    Conrad)
Preminger, Mary G(ardner)
Prentice, David Ramage
Preston, Malcolm H
Preuss, Roger
Pribble, Easton
Price, Barbara Gillette
Price, Leslie Kenneth
Price, Rosalie Pettus
Priest, Hartwell Wyse
Priest, T (Theresa Khoury
    Struckus)
Printz, Bonnie Allen
Promutico, Jean
Pross, Lester Fred
Provder, Carl
Punia, Constance Edith
Purdy, Donald R
Purdy, Henry Carl
Pusey, Mavis
Quat, Helen S
Quest, Dorothy (Johnson)
Quinn, William
Rabbit, William E
Rabinovich, Raquel
Rabinovitch, William Avrum
Raciti, Cherie
Rades, William L
Radoczy, Albert
Raffael, Joseph
Raffel, Alvin Robert
Raffo, Steve
Raginsky, Nina
Rahja, Virginia Helga
Rakocy, William (Joseph)
Raleigh, Henry Patrick
Ramberg, Christina
Ramsauer, Joseph Francis
Rand, Archie
Randolph, Lynn Moore
Ranes, Chris
Rankine, V V
Ransom, Henry Cleveland, Jr

Ranson, Nancy Sussman
Rapp, Lois
Rappin, Adrian
Rascoe, Stephen Thomas
Rasmussen, Anton Jesse
Ratner, David M
Rayen, James Wilson
Rayner, Ada (Ada Rayner
    Hensche)
Rayner, Gordon
Reale, Nicholas Albert
Reber, Mick
Reddington, Charles Leonard
Reddix, Roscoe Chester
Reece, Maynard
Reed, David Fredrick
Reed, Doel
Reed, Hal
Reed, Paul Allen
Reese, William Foster
Reich, Nathaniel E
Reichert, Donald Karl
Reichman, Fred
Reid, Charles
Reid, Robert Dennis
Reilly, Jack
Reinhart, Margaret Emily
Reininghaus, Ruth (Ruth
    Reininghaus Smith)
Remington, Deborah Williams
Remsen, John Everett, II
Rennie, Helen (Sewell)
Resek, Kate Frances
Reynard, Carolyn Cole
Reynolds, James Elwood
Reynolds, Richard (Henry)
Reynolds, Wade
Rich, Garry Lorence
Richards, Bill
Richards, Karl Frederick
Richardson, Constance
    (Coleman)
Riess, Lore
Riley, Bernard Joseph
Riley-Land, Sarah (Sarah
    Agnes Riley Land)
Ripps, Rodney
Ritz, Lorna
Rivard, J B(ernard)
Riveron, Enrique
Robb, Charles
Robbin, Anthony Stuart
Roberts, Bruce Elliott
Roberts, Lucille D (Malkia)
Roberts, Percival R
Roberts, Priscilla Warren
Roberts, Richard
Roberts, Tom (Thomas Keith)
Roberts, William Edward
Robinson, Charlotte
Robinson, Jay (Thurston)
Robinson, Margot (Margot
    Steigman)
Robinson, Marie Rachelle
Rod, Bruce John
Roever, Joan Marilyn
Rogers, Barbara Joan
Rogers, Otto Donald
Rogers, P J
Rogers, Peter Wilfrid
Rohrer, Warren
Rojo, Vicente
Romano, Jaime (Luis)
Romoser, Ruth Amelia
Ronald, William
Roney, Harold Arthur
Rose, Leatrice
Rose, Mary Anne
Rose, Samuel
Rose, Stephanie
Roseman, Susan Carol
Rosen, Beverly Doris
Rosenblatt, Adolph
Rosenblatt, Suzanne Maris
Rosenblum, Jay
Rosenborg, Ralph M
Rosenquist, James

Rosenthal, Deborah Maly
Rosenthal, Gloria M
Ross, Alexander
Ross, B(eatrice) Brook
Ross, Clifford
Ross, Fred (Joseph)
Ross, Janice Koenig
Rossi, Barbara
Roth, David
Roth, Frank
Roth, Jack (Rodney)
Roth, Rubi
Rothbein, Renee
Rothenberg, Susan
Rothschild, Amalie
    (Rosenfeld)
Rowan, Frances Physioc
Rowan, Herman
Rowe, Reginald M
Rozzi (James A)
Ruben, Richards
Ruble, Ronald L
Ruda, Edwin
Ruscha, Edward Joseph
Rush, Jean C
Russell, Philip C
Russell, Robert Price
Russo, Alexander Peter
Ruta, Peter Paul
Ruttinger, Jacquelyn
Saalburg, Allen Russel
Sabatella, Joseph John
Sabo, Betty Jean
Sacklarian, Stephen
St Amand, Joseph
St John, John Milton
St John, Terry N
St Maur, Kirk (Kirk Seymour
    McReynolds)
St Tamara (Tamara Kolba)
Saks, Judith-Ann (Judith-Ann
    Saks Rosenthal)
Sakuyama, Shunji
Salamone, Gladys L
Salazar, Juan
Salt, John
Salter, Richard Mackintire
Saltonstall, Elizabeth
Saltzman, Marvin
Samburg, Grace (Blanche)
Sampson, Frank
Sanchez, Thorvald
Sandberg, Hannah
Sanden, John Howard
Sanders, Andrew Dominick
Sanders, Joop A
Sandol, Maynard
Santlofer, Jonathan
Sardelic, Ante
Sargent, Margaret Holland
Sarkisian, Paul
Sarnoff, Arthur Saron
Sarsony, Robert
Sato, Masaaki
Sato, Tadashi
Savelli, Angelo
Sawada, Ikune
Sazegar, Morteza
Schactman, Barry Robert
Schapiro, Miriam
Scharf, William
Schellin, Robert William
Schenck, William Clinton
Schepis, Anthony Joseph
Schlemm, Betty Lou
Schlicher, Karl Theodore
Schmidt, Arnold Alfred
Schmidt, Edward William
Schmidt, Frederick Lee
Schmidt, Frederick Louis
Schnackenberg, Roy
Schneebaum, Tobias
Schneider, Jo Anne
Schoenbach, Bertha Karp
Schonberger, Fred
Schonwalter, Jean Frances
Schooley, Elmer Wayne

Schreck, Michael H
Schreiber, Martin
Schucker, Charles
Schueler, Jon R
Schulson, Susan
Schultz, Stephen Warren
Schwacha, George
Schwartz, Carl E
Schwartz, Henry
Schwiering, Conrad
Scott, John
Scott, Jonathan
Scott, Marian (Dale)
Scott, Sam
Scoville, Jonathan Armstrong
Seaman, Drake F
Searles, Charles
Secunda, (Holland) Arthur
Seidl, Claire
Seidler, Doris
Seliger, Charles
Seltzer, Joanne Lynn
Seltzer, Phyllis
Semmel, Joan
Serisawa, Sueo
Serra-Badue, Daniel
Serwazi, Albert B
Sewell, Richard George
Shadrach, Jean H
Shahly, Jehan
Shapiro, Babe
Shapiro, David
Sharp, Anne
Sharpe, (Norman) Blair
Sharrow, Sheba
Shatalow, Vladimir
    Mihailovich
Shatter, Susan Louise
Shaw, (George) Kendall
Shaw, Mary Todd
Sheirr, Olga (Krolik)
Shemesh, Lorraine R
Shepherd, William Fritz
Sherman, Z Charlotte
Sherr, Ronald Norman
Sherrod, Philip Lawrence
Sherry, William Grant
Shibley, Gertrude
Shields, Alan J
Shimomura, Roger Yutaka
Shippen, Zoe
Shoemaker, Peter
Shoemaker, Vaughn
Shore, Mary (McGarrity)
Shores, (James) Franklin
Shorter, Edward Swift
Shoulberg, Harry
Showell, Kenneth L
Shuck, Kenneth Menaugh
Shull, Carl Edwin
Sickman, Jessalee Bane
Siegriest, Lundy
Sigismund, Violet M
Sihvonen, Oli
Sikora, Zdzislaw R
Silins, Janis
Silverberg, Ellen Ruth
Silverman, Sherley C
Simel, Elaine
Simone (Mildred Simonson)
Simpson, David
Simpson, Lee
Simpson, Marilyn Jean
Simpson, Merton D
Simson, Bevlyn A
Singer, Arthur B
Singer, Clifford
Singer, Clyde J
Singletary, Robert Eugene
Singleton, Robert Ellison
Sinnard, Elaine (Janice)
Sinton, Nell (Walter)
Sirugo, Sal (Salvatore)
Sisson, Laurence P
Sisti, (Tony) Anthony J
Sitton, John M
Sivard, Robert Paul

PAINTER (cont)
Skalagard, Hans
Skemp, Robert Oliver
Sklar, Dorothy
Sklar-Weinstein, Arlene (Joyce)
Slaughter, Lurline Eddy
Slavin, Arlene
Sleigh, Sylvia
Slider, Dorla Dean
Slipper, Gary Peter
Sloan, Jeanette
Sloan, Richard
Sloan, Robert Smullyan
Sloane, Phyllis Lester
Slone, Sandi
Slonem, Hunt
Slotnick, Mortimer H
Smith, B J
Smith, Cecil Alden
Smith, David Loeffler
Smith, Dinah Maxwell
Smith, Frank Anthony
Smith, Gordon
Smith, Hassel W, Jr
Smith, Lawrence Beall
Smith, Leon Polk
Smith, Paul Roland
Smith, Robert Alan
Smith, Thelma deGoede
Smith, Vincent D
Smongeski, Joseph Leon
Snow, Cynthia Reeves
Snyder, Kim Lawrence
Sokole, Miron
Solberg, Morten Edward
Solman, Joseph
Solomon, Daniel
Solomon, Hyde
Soloway, Reta
Soltesz, Frank Joseph
Somberg, Emilija O K
Somers, H(arry W)
Sorby, J Richard
Southey, Trevor J T
Sowers, Miriam R
Soyer, Raphael
Spaulding, D(onald Clifford)
Spaulding, Warren Dan
Spelman, Jill Sullivan
Spence, Andrew
Spickett, Ronald John, Sr
Sprague, Mark Anderson
Sprang, Elizabeth
Spruce, Everett Franklin
Squires, Gerald Leopold
Stack, Frank Huntington
Stack, Michael
Stacks, William Leon
Stacy, Donald L
Stadler, Albert
Stamelos, Electra Georgia Mousmoules
Stamm, Ted
Stamper, Willson Young
Stanley, Bob
Stapleton, Joseph F
Staprans, Raimonds
Starkweather-Nelson, Cynthia Louise
Stasack, Edward Armen
Stavans, Isaac
Staven, Leland Carroll
Steckel, Anita
Steen, Carol J
Stefan, Ross
Stegeman, Charles
Steiger, Frederic
Stein, Walter
Steinfels, Melville P
Steinhouse, Tobie (Thelma)
Stephens, Richard Alan
Stephens, William Blakely
Stern, Irene Monat
Sternberg, Harry
Sterne, Dahli
Stevanov, Zoran

Stevens, May
Stevens, Nelson L
Stevenson, Ruth Rolston
Stevovich, Andrew Vlastimir
Stewart, Arthur
Stewart, Jack
Stewart, John P
Stewart, William
Sticker, Robert Edward
Stiles, Helen
Stokes, Thomas Phelps
Stoloff, Carolyn
Storm, Howard
Stout, Myron Stedman
Stout, Richard Gordon
Stowman, Annette Burr
Strater, Henry
Strauser, Sterling Boyd
Strawn, Melvin Nicholas
Strickland, Thomas J
Strisik, Paul
Strong, Charles Ralph
Strother, Joseph Willis
Strother, Virginia Vaughn
Stroud, Peter Anthony
Stuart, Joseph Martin
Stussy, Jan
Sudlow, Robert N
Sugarman, George
Sugimoto, Henry Y
Sullivan, Bill
Sullivan, David Francis
Sullivan, Jim
Sultan, Altoon
Summer, (Emily) Eugenia
Summerford, Ben Long
Summy, Anne Tunis
Surgalski, Patrick J
Surrey, Milt
Suter, Sherwood Eugene
Sutton, Carol (Lorraine)
Sutton, Patricia
Suzuki, Sakari
Swain, Robert
Swanson, J N
Swartz, Beth Ames
Swartz, Phillip Scott
Sweet, Mary (French)
Sweney, Fred
Swiggett, Jean Donald
Swinton, George
Sykes, (William) Maltby
Taggart, William John
Tahedl, Ernestine
Taicher, Richard
Taira, Frank
Takai, Teiji
Takashima, Shizuye Violet
Talbot, Jonathan
Tam, Reuben
Tamburine, Jean
Tanger, Susanna
Tanksley, Ann
Tanner, Joan Elizabeth
Taper, Geri
Tate, Gayle Blair
Tatossian, Armand
Taylor, Ann
Taylor, Gage
Taylor, John C E
Taylor, Sandra Ortiz
Teczar, Steven W
Telberg, Val
Ten
Ten Eyck, Catryna (Catryna Ten Eyck Seymour)
Termes (Dick A Termes)
Termini, Christine
Terry, Marion (E)
Thiery, Thomas Allen
Thies, Charles Herman
Thomas, Helen (Doane)
Thomas, Yvonne
Thompson, Donald Roy
Thompson, Judith Kay
Thompson, Malcolm Barton
Thompson, Richard Craig

Thompson, Richard Earl, Sr
Thompson, Wade
Thomsen, Mitch (Nancy Mitchell)
Thomson, Carl L
Thorpe, Hilda (Shapiro)
Thrall, Arthur
Threlkeld, Dale
Tiegreen, Alan F
Tigerman, Stanley
Timmins, William Frederick
Tinning, George Campbell
Tobey, Alton S
Todd, Michael Cullen
Toigo, Daniel Joseph
Tompkins, Alan
Tompkins, Betty (I)
Torlakson, James Daniel
Torreano, John Francis
Tousignant, Claude
Townsend, John F
Townsend, Stanley Dale
Trachtenberg, Gloria P
Trachtman, Arnold S
Traher, William Henry
Travers-Smith, Brian John
Treese, William R
Triano, Anthony Thomas
Trieff, Selina
Trissel, James Nevin
Truby, Betsy Kirby
Tse, Stephen
Tubis, Seymour
Turner, Alan
Turner, (Charles) Arthur
Turner, Bruce Backman
Turner, James Thomas, Sr
Turner, Norman Huntington
Turner, Theodore Roy
Turner, William Eugene
Twardowicz, Stanley Jan
Twiggs, Russell Gould
Tykie (Sylvia Squires Ganz)
Tyler, Valton
Tytell, Louis
Ubans, Juris K
Ubertalli, Hector
Udinotti, Agnese
Uhrman, Celia
Ulbricht, John
Ullrich-Zuckerman, B
Urban, Reva
Urquhart, Tony (Anthony Morse)
Uttech, Thomas Martin
Vaccarino, Robin
Vaccaro, Nick Dante
Valenstein, Alice
Vander Sluis, George J
Vaness, Margaret Helen
Van Roekens, Paulette (Mrs Arthur Meltzer)
Van Veen, Stuyvesant
Van Wyk, Helen
Varnelis, Kazys
Vazquez, Paul
Venezia, Michael
Vickery, Charles Bridgeman
Vidal, Hahn
Villeneuve, Joseph Arthur
Visser't Hooft, Martha
Vivenza, Francesca
Voelker, Elizabeth
Voelker, John
Vogel, Donald S
Vogl, Don George
Von Gunten, Roger
Vytlacil, Vaclav
Wagner, Richard Ellis
Waid, Jim (James E)
Waksberg, Naomi
Walch, John Leo
Walker, Edward D (Rusty)
Walker, Joy
Walker, Larry
Walker, Marie Sheehy
Walker, Sandra Radcliffe

WalkingStick, Kay
Wall, Ralph Alan
Wall, Sue
Wallace, John Edward
Wallace, Soni
Wallin, Leland Dean
Walsh, Patricia Ruth
Walters, Ernest
Waltner, Beverly Ruland
Waltzer, Stewart Paul
Wands, Alfred James
Wands, Robert James
Wanlass, Stanley Glen
Ward, John Lawrence
Ward, Lyle Edward
Ward, William Edward
Wardlaw, George Melvin
Warkov, Esther
Warner, Boyd, Jr
Warren, Betty
Warren, Ferdinand Earl
Warren, Jacqueline Louise
Warsinske, Norman George, Jr
Washburn, Stan
Wasser, Paula Kloster
Waterhouse, Charles Howard
Waterstreet, Ken (James Kent)
Watson, Ronald G
Wayne, June
Weber, Idelle
Weekes, Shirley Marie
Weeks, James (Darrell Northrup)
Weese, Myrtle A
Weidner, Mary Elizabeth
Weidner, Roswell Theodore
Weinbaum, Jean
Weinstein, Joyce
Welch, James Wymore
Wellington, Duke
Wells, Thomas (Winchester)
Wert, Ned Oliver
Wesselmann, Tom
West, Clara Faye Johnson
Wethli, Mark
Wexler, George
Whidden, Conni
Whitaker, Eileen Monaghan
White, Doris A
White, Franklin
White, Ralph
White, Susan Chrysler
Whitmore, Lenore K
Whitney, Richard Wheeler
Whitty-Johnson, Patricia
Whyte, Raymond A
Wickiser, Ralph Lewanda
Wicks, Eugene Claude
Wiegand, Robert
Wieghorst, Olaf
Wiener, Phyllis Ames
Wiesenfeld, Paul
Wiggins, Bill
Wiitasalo, Shirley
Wilbur, Lawrence Nelson
Wilke, Ulfert S
Willenbecher, John
Williams, Hiram Draper
Williams, Randalph Andrew
Williams, Todd
Williams, William Thomas
Williamson, Gail McKennis
Willis, Sidney F
Willis, Thornton
Wilmeth, Ernest, II
Wilson, Ben
Wilson, David Philip
Wilson, George Lewis
Wilson, Jane
Wilson, Richard Brian
Wilson, Sybil
Wilson-Hammond, Charlotte Emily
Wiman, Bill
Windrow, Patricia (Patricia Windrow Klein)
Wink, Don (Jon Donnel)

PAINTER (cont)

Dergalis, George
Desoto, Rafael M
Desportes, Ulysse Gandvier
Diao, David
Dine, James
Dinnerstein, Simon A
Diodato, Baldo
Dirube, Rolando Lopez
Di Suvero, Mark
Ditzion, Grace
Dodd, Lamar
Dogancay, Burhan Cahit
Dohanos, Stevan
Doll, Linda A
Domareki, Joseph Theodore
Domjan, Joseph (Spiri)
Donati, Enrico
Dorfman, Bruce
Doudera, Gerard
Dreskin-Haig, Jeanet Elizabeth
Driggs, Elsie
Driskell, David Clyde
Dubaniewicz, Peter Paul
Duncan, (Eleanore) Klari de
  Szecsanyi
Dunkelman, Loretta
Dunn, Nate
Dworzan, George R
Dyck, Paul
Eades, Luis Eric
Eagerton, Robert Pierce
Eames, John Heagan
Eckelberry, Don Richard
Edelheit, Martha
Edwards, Paul Burgess
Efrat, Benni
Egleson, Jim (James Downey)
Eguchi, Yasu
Eichner-Dixon, Peter
Elder, Muldoon
Elias, Harold John
Ellinger, Ilona E
Elliott, Philip Clarkson
Ellis, Fremont F
Embrey, Carl Rice
Erbe, Joan
Eriquezzo, Lee M
Ernst, Jimmy
Etchison, Bruce
Etrog, Sorel
Ettl, Georg
Evans, Minnie
Evans, Robert James
Everts, Connor
Ewing, Thomas R
Fabe, Robert
Fangor, Voy
Farrens, Juanita G
Farris, Joseph
Faudie, Fred
Faulconer, Mary (Fullerton)
Fausett, (William) Dean
Fearing, William Kelly
Fedelle, Estelle
Federe, Marion
Feher, Joseph
Fehl, Philipp P
Fein, B R
Fein, Stanley
Feld, Augusta
Feldman, Walter (Sidney)
Fellows, Fred
Fels, C P
Fenton, Howard Carter
Ferguson, Charles B
Ferron, Marcelle
Feuerherm, Kurt K
Field, Philip Sidney
Filipovic, Augustin
Filmus, Tully
Finck, Furman J
Fink, Herbert Lewis
Finkler, Robert Allan
Fisher, Carole Gorney
Fisher, Leonard Everett
Flack, Audrey L

Fleckenstein, Opal R
Flowers, Thomas Earl
Fogel, Seymour
Foolery, Tom
Foose, Robert James
Foote, Howard Reed
Ford, Charles Henri
Ford, John
Ford, John Charles
Foulkes, Llyn
Fowler, Mel
Francis, Sam
Francis, Tom
Frankenberg, Robert Clinton
Frankenthaler, Helen
Frasconi, Antonio
Freed, William
Freeland, William Lee
Freimark, Robert (Matthew)
French, Jared
Freund, Will Frederick
Fricano, Tom S
Friedberg, Ray E (Rachel)
Fritzler, Gerald J(ohn)
Fulton, Fred Franklin
Gabrielson, Walter Oscar
Gahagan, James (Edward), Jr
Galli, Stanley Walter
Gantz, Ann Cushing
Garey, Pat
Geeslin, Lee Gaddis
Geiger, Edith Rogers
Genders, Richard Atherstone
Genn, Nancy
Gerbracht, Bob (Robert
  Thomas)
Gervasi, Frank
Gibala, Louise
Gifford, J Nebraska
Gilkey, Richard Charles
Gill, James (Francis)
Gilliam, Sam
Ginzel, Roland
Glasco, Joseph M
Glyde, Henry George
Goddard, Vivian
Godsey, Glenn
Godwin, Judith Whitney
Goell, Abby Jane
Goings, Ralph
Gold, Albert
Goldberg, Michael
Golden, Eunice
Golden, Libby
Goldsmith, Elsa M
Goldstein, Gladys Hack
Goldstein, Julius
Goldstein, Nathan
Goldszer, Bath-Sheba
Gongora, Leonel
Gonzalez, Xavier
Gooch, Donald Burnette
Good, Leonard
Goodman, Bertram
Goodnough, Robert
Goodnow, Frank A
Gordon, Russell Talbert
Gordy, Robert P
Goreleigh, Rex
Gorman, William D
Gould, John Howard
Goulet, Claude
Govan, Francis Hawks
Grado, Angelo John
Grady, Ruby McLain
Graham, K M
Graham, Robert MacDonald,
  Jr
Gramberg, Liliana
Grasso, Doris (Ten-Eyck)
Gray, Cleve
Gray, Don
Graziani, Sante
Greenbaum, Marty
Greene, Balcomb
Gregoropoulos, John
Grippe, Florence (Berg)

Grippi, Salvatore William
Grissom, Freda Gill
Gronbeck, Jean
Grooms, Red
Grossman, Nancy
Grotenrath, Ruth
Guerin, John William
Gumpert, Gunther
Gunn, Paul James
Gutmann, John
Gutzeit, Fred
Guzman-Forbes, Robert
Gyra, Francis Joseph, Jr
Gysin, Brion
Hacklin, Allan Dave
Hafif, Marcia
Hagan, Frederick
Haines, Richard
Halberstadt, Ernst
Hale, Kenneth John
Haley, John Charles
Halkin, Theodore
Halsey, William Melton
Hammer, Alfred Emil
Hammock, Virgil Gene
Hampton, John W
Haney, William H
Hanlen, John (Garrett)
Hansen, Frances Frakes
Harari, Hananiah
Harbart, Gertrude Felton
Hardaway, Pearl (Pearl
  Hardaway Reese)
Harden, Marvin
Harris, Gloriane
Harris, Harvey Sherman
Harris, Lucille S
Harrison, Pat (Broeder)
Hart, Allen M
Hartley, Paul Jerome
Harvey, Robert Martin
Hasen, Burt Stanly
Hatfield, David Underhill
Hauser, Alonzo
Hawkins, Barbara
Haydon, Harold (Emerson)
Hay-Messick, Velma
Hazlitt, Don
Head, Robert William
Healy, Julia Schmitt
Heidel, Frederick (H)
Heiloms, May
Heiskell, Diana
Helander, Bruce Paul
Helck, (Clarence) Peter
Held, Al
Helfond, Riva
Helioff, Anne Graile (Mrs
  Benjamin Hirschberg)
Hemmerdinger, William John,
  III
Henderson, Jack W
Hendricks, Geoffrey
Hendricks, James (Powell)
Henrickson, Paul Robert
Henry, Dale
Hensche, Henry
Herman, Vic
Herrera, Carmen
Herrera, Raul Othon
Hertzberg, Rose
Heyman, Lawrence Murray
Hildreth, Joseph Alan
Hill, Dale Logan
Hilty, Thomas R
Hochhauser, Marilyn
  Helsenrott
Hoffman, Martin (Joseph)
Holbrook, Hollis Howard
Holder, Tom
Holladay, Harlan H
Holland, Tom
Holmes, David Bryan
Holtz, Itshak Jack
Homar, Lorenzo
Homitzky, Peter
Hood, Walter Kelly

Hook, Walter
Hooper, Jack Meredith
Hoowij, Jan
Hopkinson, Harold I
Hopper, Marianne Seward
Housman, Russell F
Howard, Cecil Ray
Howard, Humbert L
Howlett, Carolyn Svrluga
Hudson, Robert H
Huldah
Hunter, Miriam Eileen
Huntley, David C
Hurtig, Martin Russell
Hurtubise, Jacques
Hurwitz, Sidney J
Hutsaliuk, Lubo
Idaherma (Idaherma Williams)
Imana, Jorge Garron
Indiviglia, Salvatore Joseph
Ingalls, Eve
Insley, Will
Inukai, Kyohei
Ivy, Gregory Dowler
Jackson, A B
Jacob, Ned
Jacobs, Jim
Jacobson, Ursula Mercedes
Jagger, Gillian
James, Frederic
Jarvis, John Brent
Jellico, John Anthony
Jenkins, Mary Anne Keel
Jergens, Robert Joseph
Johns, Jasper
Johnsen, May Anne
Johnson, Edvard Arthur
Johnson, Lester F
Johnson, M L J
Johnson, Martin Brian
Johnston, Ynez
Jones, Ben
Jones, Claire
Jones, Edward Powis
Jones, James Edward
Jones, Lois Mailou (Mrs V
  Pierre-Noel)
Jorgensen, Flemming
Jules, Mervin
Jungwirth, I(rene) Gayas
Kahn, A Michael
Kahn, Peter
Kaiser, Vitus J
Kamrowski, Gerome
Kaplan, Leonard
Kaplan, Sandra
Karp, Richard Gordon
Kashdin, Gladys Shafran
Kass, Ray
Kassoy, Bernard
Katz, Hilda (Hulda Weber)
Katz, Morris
Kauffman, (Camille) Andrene
Kaulitz, Garry Charles
Keane, Lucina Mabel
Keen, Helen Boyd
Keene, Paul
Keith, Eros
Keller, Frank S
Kelly, Ellsworth
Kemp, Paul Zane
Kempton, Greta
Kennedy, J William
Kepes, Gyorgy
Killmaster, John H
Kim, Bongtae
King, Eleanor (Eleanor King
  Hookham)
Kinigstein, Jonah
Kinstler, Everett Raymond
Kipp, Orval
Kitner, Harold
Kittredge, Nancy (Elizabeth)
Klein, Doris
Kleinholz, Frank
Klotz-Reilly, Suzanne Ruth
Knigin, Michael Jay

PAINTER (cont)

Koch, Arthur Robert
Koerner, Henry
Kohl, Barbara
Kohlhepp, Norman
Komodore, Bill
Konrad, Adolf Ferdinand
Kortlander, William
Koscielny, Margaret
Kovner, Saul
Kowalke, Ronald Leroy
Kowalski, Raymond Alois
Kreznar, Richard J
Krukowski, Lucian
Krushenick, John
Kurahara, Ted
Kusama, Yayoi
Kuvshinoff, Bertha Horne
Kuvshinoff, Nicolai
Laguna, Marielle
Lake, Randall
Landon, Edward August
Larsen, Patrick Heffner
Larson, Sidney
Latham, Barbara
Laventhol, Hank
Lawrence, Jacob
Lazarof, Eleanore Berman
Lea, Stanley E
Lea, Tom
Leaf, June
Leake, Eugene W
Leathers, Winston Lyle
Lechay, James
Lee, Robert J
Le Fevre, Richard John
Leff, Rita
Lehman, Irving
Lehman, Louise Brasell
Lehrer, Leonard
Lerner, Nathan Bernard
Lerner, Sandra
Lesh, Richard D
Levi, Josef
Levin, Jeanne
Levin, Morton D
Levine, Jack
Levine, Shepard
Levinson, Mon
Levitt, Alfred
Levy, Hilda
Lewandowski, Edmund D
Lewis, Ronald Walter
Liberi, Dante
Liberman, Alexander
Lichtenstein, Roy
Lidov, Arthur Herschel
Liles, Raeford Bailey
Lindmark, Arne
Lindner, Ernest
Lindstrom, Gaell
Lionni, Leo
Lippincott, Janet
Little, John
Liu, Ho
Llorente, Luis
Lobdell, Frank
Loberg, Robert Warren
Lock, Charles L
Lombard, Annette
Loney, Doris Howard
Longstreet, Stephen
Looney, Norman
Lorber, Stephen Neil
Loring, John
Lotterman, Hal
Lowe, Marvin
Lucey, Jack
Lucioni, Luigi
Lukas, Dennis Brian
Lukin, Sven
Lupper, Edward
Lyle, Charles Thomas
Mabry, Jane
McCall, Robert Theodore
McCallum, Corrie (Mrs
   William Halsey)

McCarthy, Denis
McCarty, Lorraine Chambers
McClanahan, John D
McCloskey, Robert
McCracken, John Harvey
McCray, Dorothy M
Macdonald, Grant
Macdonnell, Cameron
McGarrell, James
MacGregor, John Boyko
McInerney, Gene Joseph
MacIver, Loren
McIvor, John Wilfred
McKesson, Malcolm Forbes
McKnight, Thomas Frederick
McNamara, John Stephen
McNeil, George J
MacNutt, Glenn Gordon
McSheehy, Cornelia Marie
McWhorter, Elsie Jean
Magee, Alderson
Magistro, Charles John
Magnan, Oscar Gustav
Mahoney, James Owen
Maitin, Sam (Samuel Calman)
Maltzman, Stanley
Mancuso, Leni
Mandel, Howard
Mandelbaum, Lyn
Mangold, Robert Peter
Manship, John Paul
Margulies, Joseph
Mariano, Kristine
Maril, Herman
Mark, Bendor
Markell, Isabella Banks
Marks, Claude
Marshall, James Duard
Marshall, Mara
Marsicano, Nicholas
Martin, Charles E
Martin, Fred Thomas
Martin, G W
Martin, Knox
Martinez, Alfred
Martinsen, Ivar Richard
Marx, Evelyn
Maurice, Alfred Paul
Maxwell, William C
Mayorga, Gabriel Humberto
Meeker, Barbara Miller
Meeker, Dean Jackson
Mejer, Robert Lee
Mellon, James
Menkes, Sigmund
Merfeld, Gerald Lydon
Merkin, Richard Marshall
Mesibov, Hugh
Meyer, Fred (Robert)
Meyers, Francis Joseph
Micale, Albert
Middaugh, Robert Burton
Mikus, Eleanore
Milhoan, Randall Bell
Miller, Barbara Darlene
Miller, Richard Kidwell
Milliken, Gibbs
Mina-Mora, Raul Jose
Mitchell, Clifford
Mitchell, James E
Mitchell, Joan
Mix, Walter Joseph
Miyamoto, Wayne Akira
Moerschel, Chiara
Mogensen, Paul
Moldroski, Al R
Molinari, Guido
Momaday, Al
Monaghan, William Scott
Montague, James L
Moose, Talmadge Bowers
Morris, Robert Clarke
Moser, Julon
Moses, Ed
Moskowitz, Shirley (Mrs Jacob
   W Gruber)
Motherwell, Robert

Moulton, Susan Gene
Mount, Ward
Moyer, Roy
Mueller, Henrietta Waters
Munzner, Aribert
Muranaka, Hideo
Murphy, Gladys Wilkins
Murphy, Herbert A
Musselman, Darwin B
Myers, Carole Ann
Myers, Martin
Naar, Harry I
Nagler, Edith Kroger
Narotzky, Norman David
Naumer, Helmuth
Neal, Reginald H
Negri, Rocco Antonio
Ness, (Albert) Kenneth
Neuman, Robert S
Newman, John Beatty
Niese, Henry Ernst
Nishizawa Flores, Luis
Noel, Georges
Noerdlinger, Janau Nau
Nong
Novinski, Lyle Frank
Novotny, Elmer Ladislaw
Nowack, Wayne Kenyon
Nugent, Bob L
Nulf, Frank Allen
Nutt, Jim (James Tureman)
Oi, Motoi
Okamura, Arthur
O'Keeffe, Georgia
Olds, Elizabeth
Onslow Ford, Gordon M
Opper, John
Orling, Anne
Orr, Elliot
Ortman, George Earl
Osborne, Robert Lee
Ossorio, Alfonso A
Owens, Mary (Mary Louise
   Schnore)
Pablo
Paone, Peter
Papo, Iso
Paradise, Phil (Herschel)
Parra, Carmen
Partin, Robert (E)
Peake, Channing
Pearlman, Etta S
Pearlstein, Philip
Pearlstein, Seymour
Pekar, Ronald Walter
Pekarsky, Mel (Melvin Hirsch)
Pellicone, William
Pels, Albert
Penny, Aubrey John Robert
Perlin, Bernard
Petheo, Bela Francis
Pezzati, Pietro
Phillips, James
Piatek, Francis John
Piccillo, Joseph
Picher, Claude
Pickens, Alton
Pierce, Diane
Pierce, Donald (Benjamin)
Pillin, Polia
Pinardi, Enrico Vittorio
Pinto, Angelo Raphael
Pittore, Carlo
Poduska, T F
Polan, Nancy Moore
Pollack, Reginald Murray
Polonsky, Arthur
Poons, Larry
Porter, (Edwin) David
Porter, J Erwin
Posey, Ernest Noel
Potter, Ted
Pozzi, Lucio
Pratt, Mary Frances
Prochownik, Walter A
Pugh, Grace Huntley
Purser, Stuart Robert

Putterman, Florence Grace
Quest, Charles Francis
Quiller, Stephen Frederick
Rackus, George (Keistus)
Racz, Andre
Radin, Dan
Radulovic, Savo
Ragland, Bob
Rakovan, Lawrence Francis
Ramos, Melvin John
Rand, Paul
Rath, Hildegard
Ratkai, George
Rave, Georgia
Ray, Robert (Donald)
Rayburn, (Boyd Dale)
Reardon, Mary A
Rebbeck, Lester James, Jr
Redgrave, Felicity
Reed, David Fredrick
Reed, Jesse Floyd
Reep, Edward Arnold
Rehberger, Gustav
Reichek, Jesse
Reif, Rubin
Reindorf, Samuel
Reinhardt, Siegfried Gerhard
Remsing, (Joseph) Gary
Resika, Paul
Resnick, Milton
Retzer, Howard Earl
Reynolds, Patricia Ellen
Reynolds, Robert
Ricci, Jerri
Rice, Anthony Hopkins
Rice, Norman Lewis
Richard, Jack
Richards, Walter DuBois
Richenburg, Robert Bartlett
Richter, Hank
Ridley, Gregory D, Jr
Ries, Martin
Riley, Art (Arthur Irwin)
Ringgold, Faith
Risser, James K
Rivera, Frank
Rivera-Velazquez, Mariano
Rivers, Larry
Robinson, Grove
Robinson, Sally W
Roche, Robert (Richard)
Rodriguez, Oscar
Roesch, Kurt (Ferdinand)
Rogers, Charles B
Rogovin, Mark
Romano, Clare Camille
Romano, Emanuel Glicen
Romano, Umberto Roberto
Rose, Herman
Rosenblum, Sadie Skoletsky
Ross, James Matthew
Rothenberg, Barbara
Rothschild, Judith
Rotterdam, Paul Z
Rozman, Joseph John
Ruben, Albert
Rubenstein, Lewis W
Rubin, Irwin
Ruddley, John
Rudquist, Jerry Jacob
Ruellan, Andree
Running Rabbit
Rutherford, Erica
Rutsch, Alexander
Ruvolo, Felix Emmanuele
Ryman, Robert
Sabatini, Raphael
St Denis, Paul Andre
Sal, Jack
Salemme, Lucia (Autorino)
Saltmarche, Kenneth Charles
Samerjan, George E
Samstag, Gordon
Samuels, Gerald
Samuelson, Fred Binder
Sanborn, Herbert J
Sandler, Barbara

PAINTER (cont)

Sandman, Jo
Sarff, Walter
Saul, Peter
Sauls, Frederick Inabinette
Saunders, Raymond Jennings
Savage, Roger
Savas, Jo-Ann
Savitz, Frieda
Schaffer, Rose
Scharff, Constance Kramer
Schary, Emanuel
Schein, Eugenie
Scherpereel, Richard Charles
Schieferdecker, Ivan E
Schiller, Beatrice
Schliefer, Stafford Lerrig
Schmid, Richard Alan
Schoenherr, John Carl
Scholder, Fritz
Schorr, Justin
Schrag, Karl
Schreiber, Eileen Sher
Schrut, Sherry
Schulz, William Gallagher
Schutz, Estelle
Schwalbach, Mary Jo
Schwartz, Therese
Schwarz, Felix Conrad
Scott, Henry E, Jr
Seabourn, Bert Dail
Seames, Clarann
Seckel, Paul Bernhard
Seckler, Dorothy Gees
Shadbolt, Jack Leonard
Sharpe, David Flemming
Shaw, Donald Edward
Shaw, Elsie Babbitt
Shaw, (George) Kendall
Shead, S Ray
Sheaks, Barclay
Shecter, Mark
Sheehan, Evelyn
Shepherd, Reginald
Sheppard, Joseph Sherly
Sherman, Sarai
Sherwood, Leona
Shikler, Aaron
Shives, Arnold Edward
Shook, Georg
Shumacker, Elizabeth Wight
Shute, Ben E
Shute, Roberta E
Sibley, Charles Kenneth
Sider, Deno
Siebner, Herbert
Sikora, Zdzislaw R
Silber, Maurice
Siler, Todd (Lael)
Silkotch, Mary Ellen
Sills, Thomas Albert
Silverman, Burton Philip
Simon, Jewel Woodard
Simon, Sidney
Simoni, John Peter
Singer, Esther Forman
Sing Hoo
Sirena (Contessa Antonia
    Mastrocristino Fanara)
Sirugo, Sal (Salvatore)
Skinner, Elsa Kells
Slade, Roy
Slate, Joseph Frank
Sles, Steven Lawrence
Smart, Wini
Smith, Albert E
Smith, Arthur Hall
Smith, Gordon
Smith, Helen M
Smith, Joseph A(nthony)
Smith, Sam
Smith, Shirley Ann
Smith, Victor Joachim
Snidow, Gordon E
Snow, John
Snow, Lee Erlin
Snow, Michael

Snyder, William B
Solomon, Syd
Soorikian, Diana Tashjian
Soreff, Helen
Sorge, Walter
Sovary, Lilly
Soviak, Harry
Speight, Francis
Spencer, Harold Edwin
Sperakis, Nicholas George
Sprout, Francis
Spruyt, E Lee
Squadra, John
Squires, Norma-Jean
Staempfli, George W
Stahl, Ben (Albert)
Stamos, Theodoros (S)
Stanczak, Julian
Stapp, Ray Veryl
Stark, Melville F
Starrs, Mildred
Stefanelli, Joe
Steinke, Bettina
Steinmetz, Grace Ernst Titus
Sterne, Hedda
Stevenson, A Brockie
Stevenson, Branson Graves
Stewart, Dorothy S
Stillman, George
Stillman-Myers, Joyce
Stoessel, Henry Kurt
Stoltenberg, Donald Hugo
Stonebarger, Virginia
Storm, Larue
Storm, Mark (Kennedy)
Story, William Easton
Stratton, Dorothy (Mrs
    William A King)
Stronghilos, Carol
Sturman, Eugene
Stussy, Jan
Sublett, Carl C
Sullins, Robert M
Sultan, Donald K
Summ, Helmut
Sussman, Arthur
Sutherland, Sandy
Suzuki, James Hiroshi
Sverdlove, Zolita
Swan, Barbara
Swenson, (Jean) Mary Jeanette
    Hamilton
Szabo, Zoltan
Sznajderman, Marius S
Tabachnick, Anne
Tabak, Chaim
Tait, Cornelia Damian
Takal, Peter
Tamayo, Rufino
Tarin, Gilberto A
Tascona, Antonio Tony
Tatossian, Armand
Tatti, Benedict Michael
Taylor, Brie (Benjamin de
    Brie)
Taylor, Frederick Bourchier
Taylor, Grace Martin
Taylor, Michele F
Templeton, Robert Clark
Tettleton, Robert Lynn
Texoon, Jasmine
Teyral, John
Thiebaud, (Morton) Wayne
Thomas, Byron
Thomas, Lionel Arthur John
Thomas, Steffen Wolfgang
Thomas, William Radford
Thon, William
Thorns, John Cyril, Jr
Thwaites, Charles Winstanley
Tillenius, Clarence (Ingwall)
Tilley, Lewis Lee
Ting, Walasse
Tobias, Abraham Joel
Tobias, Robert Paul
Toney, Anthony
Torlen, Michael Arnold

Town, Harold Barling
Tracy, Lois Bartlett
Tracy, Michael
Travanti, Leon Emidio
Treiman, Joyce Wahl
Treister, Kenneth
Trivigno, Pat
Trova, Ernest Tino
Tsai, Hsiao Hsia
Tschacbasov, Nahum
Tuchman, Ellen Frances
Tucker, Charles Clement
Tulk, Alfred James
Tulving, Ruth
Tuttle, Richard
Twitty, James (Watson)
Twombly, Cy
Uchima, Toshiko
Umlauf, Karl A
Umlauf, Lynn (Charlotte)
Upton, Richard Thomas
Utz, Thornton
Vaccaro, Luella Grace
Valerio, James Robert
Vallance, Jeffrey K R
Van Aalten, Jacques
Van Hook, David H
Vann, Loli (Mrs Lilian Van
    Young)
Van Oordt, Peter
Van Sant, Tom R
Van Young, Oscar
Varga, Margit
Vaux, Richard
Velasquez, Oscar
Viera, Charles David
Viera, Ricardo
Vinella, Ray (Raimondo John)
Vogel, Joseph
Volpe, Robert
von dem Bussche, Wolf
Voos, William John
Vorwerk, E Charlsie
Waddell, Eugene
Wagner, G Noble
Wainwright, Robert Barry
Waldman, Paul
Warder, William
Warhol, Andy
Warner, Boyd, Jr
Warriner, Laura B
Washington, James W, Jr
Wasserman, Albert
Watia, Tarmo
Watson, Darliene Keeney
Weaver, (John) Robert
Weber, Albert Jacob
Weber, Jan
Webster, Stokely
Wechter, Vivienne Thaul
Wein, Albert W
Weiner, Abe
Weinstein, Florence
Weismann, Donald Leroy
Welliver, Neil G
Wells, Betty Childs
Wells, Mac
Werner, Donald (Lewis)
Werner, Fritz
Wesley, John
Wesling, William Arnold
West, W Richard (Dick)
Wethington, Wilma Zella
Whitaker, William
White, John M
Whitney, Charlotte Armide
Whitney, William Kuebler
Whittome, Irene Dianne
Wight, Frederick S
Wiley, William T
Will, John A
Williams, Neil
Williams, Walter (Henry)
Willson, Margaret (Bosshardt)
    Pace
Wilson, Millie
Wilson, (Ronald) York

Wimberley, Frank Walden
Wind, Harold
Wingate, George B
Wisnosky, John G
Witham, Vernon Clint
Witold-K (Kaczanowski)
Witt, John
Wolfe, Mildred Nungester
Wonner, Paul (John)
Wood, Harry Emsley, Jr
Woods, Rip
Woodson, Shirley Ann
Wray, Dick
Wright, David Thomas
Wright, Stanley Marc
Wuermer, Carl
Wynne, Albert Givens
Yanow, Rhoda Mae
Yarbrough, Leila Kepert
Yasko, Caryl Anne
Yoder, Richard Allen
Yokoi, Rita
Young, Kenneth Victor
Youngsblood, Nat
Yunkers, Adja
Zacharias, Athos
Zahourek, Jon Gail
Zajac, Jack
Zaleski, Jean M
Zevon, Irene
Zivic, William Thomas
Zonia, Dhimitri
Zox, Larry
Zucker, Joseph I

Egg Tempera

Akers, Gary
Arteche (Hector Arteche
    Martinez)
Baggett, William Carter, Jr
Baxter, Robert James
Braiden, Rose Margaret J
Bratcher, Dale
Cadmus, Paul
Chumley, John Wesley
Davis, Wayne Lambert
Etter, Howard Lee
Forrestall, Thomas De Vany
Gable, John Oglesby
Ghikas, Panos George
Haley Russo, Sally Fulton
Jaque, Louis
Koenig, Catherine Catanzaro
Krauth, Harald
Lieberman, Meyer Frank
McBryde, Sarah Elva
McIntosh, Harold
MacKenzie, Hugh Seaforth
McKim, William Wind
Magafan, Ethel
Massey, Robert Joseph
Meigs, John Liggett
Perret, Nell Foster
Rankin, Don
Rippel, M (Morris Conrad)
Rosenthal, Stephen
Sanders, Rhea (Rhea Sanders
    Rabinovich)
Schottland, M
Shatalow, Vladimir
    Mihailovich
Steider, Doris (Mrs C B
    McCampbell)
Stone, Don
Thames, Emmitt Eugene
Tolmie, Kenneth Donald
Tooker, George
Treaster, Richard A
van Winkelen, Barbara
Vargo, John
Vickrey, Robert Remsen
Vytlacil, Vaclav
Wright, Harold David
Wyeth, Andrew Newell

Miscellaneous Media

Abeles, Kim Victoria
Ablow, Joseph
Adler, Robert
Ahrendt, Christine
Albuquerque, Lita
Alhilali, Neda
Allman, Margo
Alquilar, Maria
Anderson, William Thomas
Angel, Rifka
Anglin, Betty Lockhart
Appel, Keith Kenneth
Aronson, David
Aronson, Irene Hilde
Artschwager, Richard Ernst
Aylon, Helane
Bacon, Peggy
Bakaty, Mike
Balazs, Gyongyi
Bandel, Lennon Raymond
Bandy, Gary
Banerjee (Bimal)
Barnes, Kit
Barth, Jack Alexander
Bartlett, Jennifer Losch
Barton, Bruce Walter
Bass, Joel
Beggs, Thomas Montague
Beker, Gisela
Belfiore, Gerardo
Bennett, Don Bemco
Berger, Jason
Bhavsar, Natvar Prahladji
Biggers, John Thomas
Bjorklund, Lee
Blumberg, Barbara Griffiths
Bock, William Sauts-
  Netamux'we
Boris, Bessie
Botero, Fernando
Bott, H J
Boyce, Gerald G
Boz, Alex (Alex Bozickovic)
Brach, Paul Henry
Brainard, Joe
Bramson, Phyllis Halperin
Britt, Al
Brokaw, Lucile
Bromberg, Faith
Brooks, (John) Alan
Brown, Marvin Prentiss
Brulc, Dennis (Mel Vapour)
Bryce, Eileen Ann
Bunts, Frank
Burnside, Wesley M
Cadieux, Michael Eugene
Calkins, Kingsley Mark
Calle, Paul
Calrow, Robert F
Campbell, David Paul
Campbell, Marjorie Dunn
Cano, Margarita
Cantieni, Graham Alfred
Card, Greg S
Carlson, George Arthur
Carmichael, Donald Ray
Carter, Harriet (Estelle)
  Manore
Case, Elizabeth
Cassanelli, Victor Vi
Cavat, Irma
Chaikin, Alyce (Alyce Chaikin
  Kleinman)
Chandler, John William
Charmatz, Bill (William
  Adolphe)
Chen, Hilo
Cheshire, Craig Gifford
Chicago, Judy
Choy, Terence Tin-Ho
Christ-Janer, Arland F
Church, C Howard
Close, Chuck
Clough, Charles Sidney
Code, Audrey
Colescott, Robert H

Collier, (Alan) Graham
Collins, Paul
Cone-Skelton, Annette
Cook, Michael David
Copley, William Nelson
Corso, Samuel (Joseph)
Cosgrove, Stanley
Cost, James Peter
Cottingham, Robert
Coughtry, Graham
Cowan, Aileen Hooper
Cowley, Edward P
Cox, John Rogers
Creatore, Mary-Alice
Crile, Susan
Crockett, Gib (Gibson M)
Cuevas, Jose Luis
Cunningham, (Charles) Bruce
Cusick, Nancy Taylor
Da Cunha, Julio
Dahill, Thomas Henry, Jr
Dali, Salvador
d'Almeida, George
Dasenbrock, Doris (Nancy)
  Voss
Davila, Carlos
Davis, Brad (Bradley Darius)
Davis, Donald Robert
Davis, Harry Allen
Davis, J Ray
Davis, Jerrold
de Guzman, Evelyn Lopez
de Knight, Avel
De Kooning, Willem
Deloney, Jack Clouse
De Martini, Joseph
De Mille, Leslie Benjamin
Dennis, Cherre Nixon
Denton, Pat
Deo, Marjoree Nee
Dessner, Murray
de Turczynowicz, Wanda (Mrs
  Eliot Hermann)
Dickinson, Eleanor Creekmore
DiFranza, Americo M
Dillon, Paul Sanford
Di Meo, Dominick
Dmytruk, Ihor
Dodge, Joseph Jeffers
Donde, Olga
Dufour, Paul Arthur
Eaton, Pauline (Friedrich)
Eckert, Lou
Edvi Illes, George
Edwards, James F
Egeli, Peter Even
Eliason, Shirley (Shirley
  Eliason Haupt)
Elliott, Ronnie
Elman, Emily
Emerson, Walter Caruth
Engle, Chet
Erdle, Rob
Ettling, Ruth (Droitcour)
Ewen, Paterson
Falsetta, Vincent Mario
Farber, Maya M
Farruggio, Remo Michael
Faulkner, Frank
Feigin, Marsha
Fendell, Jonas J
Ferguson, Gerald
Ferrer, Rafael
Fine, Perle
Finkelstein, Max
Finson, Hildred A
Fish, Janet I
Fisher, Ethel
Fitzgerald, Astrid
Flick, Paul John
Flora, James Royer
Foley, Kyoko Y
Follett, Jean Frances
Forman, Alice
Forman, Kenneth Warner
Fornelli, Joseph
Franck, Frederick S

Freed, David
Frey, Viola
Friedeberg, Pedro
Friscia, Albert
Fromberg, LaVerne Ray
Frost, Stuart Homer
Fuller, Emily
Gablik, Suzi
Galen, Elaine
Garcia, Rupert (Marshall R)
Gardner, Andrew Bradford
Gardner, Joan A
Garel, Leo
Gary, Jan (Mrs William D
  Gorman)
Garzon-Blanco, Armando
Gaucher, Yves
Geller, Esther (Esther Geller
  Shapero)
Gentry, Herbert
Gianakos, Steve
Gill, Gene
Gillespie, Dorothy Muriel
Gilmor, Jane E
Ginsburg, Max
Glaser, David
Gobin, Henry (Delano)
Goedicke, Jean
Goetz, Edith Jean
Golbin, Andree
Gold, Leah
Golden, Rolland Harve
Graham, Lois (M Gord)
Grauer, Sherry
Graves, Morris
Graves, Nancy Stevenson
Gray, Gladys
Gray, Larry
Green, Denise G
Greenberg, Irwin
Greenwald, Pat
Greer, Walter (Marion)
Grimley, Oliver Fetterolf
Grossman, Morton
Grove, Edward Ryneal
Gualtieri, Joseph P
Guderna, Ladislav
Gundelfinger, John Andre
Gunshor, Ruth
Gurr, Lena
Gussow, Alan
Habergritz, George Joseph
Hackney, Allen L
Haerer, Carol
Halbrook, Rita Robertshaw
Hall, John A
Hall, Lee
Halvorsen, Ruth Elise
Hamel, Bernard Franklin
Hamilton, Susan
Hamlett, Dale Edward
Handell, Albert George
Hansen, Harold John
Hansen, Robert
Harjo, Benjamin, Jr
Harris, Lawren Phillips
Harroun, Dorothy Sumner
Hartal, Paul Zev
Hartigan, Grace
Hatch, John W
Haut, Claire (Joan)
Hawkins, Myrtle H
Haworth, Peter
Hay, George Austin
Hayes, Randy (Randolph
  Alan)
Heimdal, Georg
Heise, Myron Robert
Henderson, Victor (Lance)
Herbert, James Arthur
Herfield, Phyllis
Hermann, M(ildred) L
Hill, Megan Lloyd
Hoffman, Helen Bacon
Holbrook, Vivian Nicholas
Hollinger, Helen Wetherbee
Holste, Thomas James

Holt, Martha A
Hook, Frances A
Horvitz, Suzanne Joan
Houskeeper, Barbara
Howe, Oscar
Howell, Claude Flynn
Howell, Elizabeth Ann (Mitch)
Hubbard, John
Hudson, Jacqueline
Humphrey, Ralph
Huot, Robert
Hupp, Frederick Duis
Hutchison, Elizabeth S
Israel, Marvin
Jackson, Suzanne Fitzallen
Jacobson, Arthur Robert
Jandeni (Jean-Denis Cruchet)
Janschka, Fritz
Jarvis, Donald
Jauss, Anne Marie
Jenkinson, Geoffrey
Jennerjahn, W P
Jenrette, Pamela Anne
Jensen, Leo (Vernon)
Jewell, William M
Jocda
Johnson, Avery Fischer
Johnson, Doris Miller
Johnson, Homer
Johnson, James Alan
Johnson, (Leonard) Lucas
Johnson, Ray
Jones, Calvin B(ell)
Jones, David Lee
Jones, Doug (Douglas McKee)
Jones, Jerry
Josimovich, George
Ju, I-Hsiung
Kachadoorian, Zubel
Kagy, Sheffield Harold
Kakas, Christopher A
Kanemitsu, Matsumi
Karawina, Erica (Mrs Sidney
  C Hsiao)
Karlsen, Anne-Marie
Karwoski, Richard Charles
Kassoy, Hortense
Katz, Theodore (Harry)
Kaufman, Jane
Kaye, George
Keeler, David Boughton
Keena, Janet Laybourn
Kerns, Ed (Johnson), Jr
Kessler, Shirley
Kettner, David Allen
Kiker, Evelyn Coalson
Kimura, Riisaburo
Kinnaird, Richard William
Kirkland, Vance Hall
Kitaj, R B
Kleemann, Ron
Kleiman, Alan
Klein, Ellen Lee
Kloss, Gene (Alice Geneva
  Glasier)
Knobler, Lois Jean
Knudsen, Christian
Koch, Edwin E
Kocher, Robert Lee
Koenig, Catherine Catanzaro
Kohn, Misch
Kohut, Lorene
Kolliker, William Augustin
Koons, Darell J
Kornmayer, J Gary (John)
Krasner, Lee
Kravitz, Walter
Kreitzer, David Martin
Krigstein, Bernard
Kruskamp, Janet
Kuchar, Kathleen Ann
Kuehn, Edmund Karl
Kuhn, Marylou
Kunstler, Morton
Kupferman, Murray
Kushner, Dorothy Browdy
Kushner, Robert Ellis

PAINTER (cont)
Kutka, Anne (Mrs David McCosh)
Kwiecinski, Chester Martin
Laderman, Gabriel
Lamell, Robert (C)
Landeck, Armin
Lansdowne, James Fenwick
Laycox, (William) Jack
Layton, Richard
Lea, Laurie Jane
Lebedev, Vladimir
Le Clair, Charles
Lederman, Stephanie Brody
Lee, Amy Freeman
Lee, Eleanor Gay
Lee, Margaret F
Leeper, Doris Marie
Lee-Smith, Hughie
Lefranc, Margaret (Margaret Lefranc Schoonover)
Leland, Whitney Edward
Lemieux, Jean Paul
Lenssen, Heidi (Mrs Fridolf Johnson)
Leonardi, Hector
Leong, James Chan
Lerman, Doris (Harriet)
Lerner, Alexandria Sandra
Lerner, Sandy R
Levine, Reeva (Anna) Miller
Levy, Phyllis Houser
Lewis, Samella Sanders
Lichacz, Sheila Enit
Lipson, Goldie
Livingston, Sidnee
Livingstone, Biganess
Lopina, Louise Carol
Love, Paul Van Derveer
Lukosius, Richard Benedict
Lund, Jane
Lupper, Edward
Lytle, Richard
McAninch, Beth
McChristy, Quentin L
McCleary, Mary Fielding
McCormick, Jo Mary (Jo Mary McCormick-Sakurai)
McFarren, Grace
MacGarvey, Bernard B
McGowin, Ed
McIlroy, Carol J
McKay, Arthur Fortescue
MacKendrick, Lilian
Mackenzie, David, IV
McKinin, Lawrence
McNickle, Thomas Glen
Mac Whinnie, John Vincent
Madura, Jack Joseph
Maestro, Giulio Marcello
Majdrakoff, Ivan
Malone, Robert R
Mandel, Saul
Mandelman, Beatrice M
Manes, Belle
Manville, Elsie
Marazzi, William C P
Margo, Boris
Margolis, David
Margules, Gabriele Ella
Margulies, Herman
Marker, Mariska Pugsley
Markowski, Eugene David
Marsh, Anne Steele
Marshall, Robert Leroy
Martin, Larry Kenneth
Martin, Roger
Mau, Hui-Chi
Mazur, Michael
Meadows, P B (Patricia B)
Medoff, Eve
Mcigs, Walter
Merrill, Ross M
Meserole, Vera Stromsted (Mrs Milton D Block)
Milholland, Richard Alexander
Miller, Daniel Dawson

Mitchell, Katherine
Moon, Marc
Moore, Fay
Moore, Marjorie
Morehouse, William Paul
Morgan, Darlene
Morgan, Maritza Leskovar
Moroz, Mychajlo
Morphesis, Jim (James George)
Moufarrege, Nicolas A
Munoz, Rie (Marie Angelina Munoz)
Murray, Floretta May
Murray, John Michael
Myers, Malcolm Haynie
Myers, Virginia Anne
Nawara, Jim
Nawara, Lucille Procter
Nichols, James William
Nichols, Jeannettie Doornhein
Nichols, William Allyn
Nilsson, Gladys
Nix, Patricia (Lea)
Noland, Kenneth
Nosoff, Frank
Ogilvie, Will (William Abernethy)
O'Hanlon, Richard E
Olugebefola, Ademola
O'Neil, John
O'Neill, John Patton
Onley, Toni
Ortlip, Paul Daniel
O'Shea, Terrence Patrick
Oster, Gerald
Ostiguy, Jean-Rcne
Ostuni, Peter W
Osver, Arthur
Parella, Albert Lucian
Paris, Lucille M
Parish, Betty Waldo
Parke, Walter Simpson
Parker, James
Partridge, David Gerry
Partz, Feliz (Ron Gabe)
Patch, Peggie (Margaret Thompson Williamson)
Patrick, Joseph Alexander
Patterson, Shirley
Patterson, William Joseph
Pattison, Abbott
Paul, Arthur
Paul, William D, Jr
Pearson, John
Peche, Dale C
Peers, Gordon Franklin
Penney, Bruce Barton
Perlin, Rae
Pernotto, James Angelo
Petersen, Will
Peterson, A E S
Phillips, Matt
Pickhardt, Carl
Piehl, Walter Jason, Jr
Piene, Otto
Pierotti, Ray (Raymond Charles)
Pindell, Howardena Doreen
Pitcher, John Charles
Poehlmann, JoAnna
Pollak, Theresa
Pollock, Merlin F
Pond, Clayton
Poole, Richard Elliott
Pope, Mary Ann Irwin
Porter, Liliana
Potter, (George) Kenneth
Pousette-Dart, Richard
Preusser, Robert Ormerod
Promutico, Jean
Quaytman, Harvey
Quirk, Thomas Charles, Jr
Radovich, Donald
Ragland, Jack Whitney
Ralston, James Kenneth
Raucher, Hava

Rauschenberg, Robert
Redd, Richard James
Reisman, Philip
Reiss, Lionel S
Rembski, Stanislav
Remenick, Seymour
Renner, Eric
Renouf, Edda
Renouf, Edward
Reynolds, Ralph William
Richards, Jeanne Herron
Rigsby, John David
Riley, Bernard Joseph
Rippey, Clayton
Rise, John Ernest
Riseling, Robert Lowell
Rising, Dorothy Milne
Robb, Peggy Hight
Robbins, Hulda D
Robinson, Jay (Thurston)
Robles, Julian
Rosen, James Mahlon
Rosenquit, Bernard
Rosenthal, Seymour
Rossman, Ruth Scharff
Rowe, Charles Alfred
Rubidoux (Rubidoux Early Johnson)
Ruffing, Anne Elizabeth
Rush, Kent Thomas
Russell, (George) Gordon
Ruthling, Ford
Ryerson, Margery A
Saari, Peter H
Sabelis, Huibert
Sachse, Janice R
Sahrbeck, Everett William
Salemme, Antonio
Salinas, Baruj
Sallick, Lucy Ellen
Saltzman, William
Sanderson, Charles Howard
Sandgren, Ernest Nelson
Sangiamo, Albert
Sankowsky, Itzhak
Sargent, Richard
Sarkisian, Paul
Sassone, Marco
Satz, Janet Maas
Saunders, Aulus Ward
Saunders, Edith Dariel Chase
Scalise, Nicholas Peter
Schabacker, Betty Barchet
Schaefer, Carl Fellman
Scheu, Leonard
Schirm, David H
Schloss, Arleen P
Schloss, Edith
Schmaltz, Roy Edgar
Schneider, Julie (Saecker)
Schoener, Jason
Schrero, Ruth Lieberman
Schultz, Harold A
Schulz, Ken
Schuster, Cita Fletcher (Sarah E)
Schwabacher, Ethel K
Schwartz, Barbara Ann
Schwartz, Bella
Schweitzer, Gertrude
Scott, John
Scott, Walter
Scucchi, Robie (Peter), Jr
Selchow, Roger Hoffman
Sella, Alvin Conrad
Selwitz, Ruth F
Shackelford, Shelby
Shane, Frederick E
Shecter, Pearl S
Sheehe, Lillian Carolyn
Sherman, Lenore (Walton)
Shih, Joan Fai
Shooter, Tom
Shuff, Lily (Lillian Shir)
Silberstein-Storfer, Muriel Rosoff
Simmons, Cleda Marie

Smith, Emily Guthrie
Snelson, Kenneth D
Sokolowski, Linda Robinson
Sonenberg, Jack
Sorokin, Maxine Ann
Soshana (Susanne Afroyim)
Souza, Paul Marciel
Spafford, Michael Charles
Spero, Nancy
Sproul, Ann Stephenson
Spurgeon, Sarah (Edna M)
Spurgin, John Edwin
Stack, Gael Z
Statman, Jan B
Stavans, Isaac
Steele, Benjamin Charles
Steg, J L
Stegman, Patricia
Stein, Ludwig K
Steinhardt, Alice
Steir, Pat
Stella, Frank
Stevens, Edward John, Jr
Stevens, William Ansel, Sr
Stevenson, Harold
Stewart, F Clark
Stiegelmeyer, Norman Earl
Stinsmuehlen, Susan Dodds
Stoianovich, Marcelle
Stomps, Walter E, Jr
Strasen, Barbara Elaine
Stuart, Michelle
Surrey, Philip Henry
Sway, Albert
Sweet, Mary (French)
Swenson, Anne (Beatrice)
Tanger, Susanna
Thelin, Valfred P
Thiele, Robert Ransom
Thomas, John
Thompson, Ernest Thorne
Thompson, Richard Earl, Sr
Thompson, Robert Charles
Tiffany, Marguerite Bristol
Tillim, Sidney
Tillotson, Robbie
Toperzer, Thomas Raymond
Toschik, Larry
Trimm, H Wayne
Turoff, Muriel Pargh
Twiggs, Leo Franklin
Tytell, Louis
Uccello, Vincenza Agatha
Uhrman, Esther
Vaccaro, (Patt) Patrick Frank
Venezia, Michael
Vevers, Tony
Vicente, Esteban
Vigil, Veloy Joseph
Villa, Carlos
Viret, Margaret Mary (Mrs Frank Ivo)
Vo-Dinh, Mai
Volkin, Hilda Appel
von Schlippe, Alexey
Wagner, Merrill
Wagoner, Robert B
Waid, Jim (James E)
Waitzkin, Stella
Walker, Marie Sheehy
Walton, Florence Goodstein (Florence Goodstein-Shapiro)
Warburg, Stephanie Wenner
Wasserman, Burton
Webster, Larry
Wegman, William
Wehr, Wesley Conrad
Weidenaar, Reynold Henry
Weingarten, Hilde (Kevess)
Weinstein, Joyce
Weldon, Barbara Maltby
Wells, Lynton
Weschler, Anita
Westermeier, Clifford Peter
White, B J (Beverly Jo)
White, Philip Butler

PAINTER (cont)

Whiteman, Edward Russell
Whiteside, William Albert, II
Wilbert, Robert John
Wilson, Charles Banks
Wilson, George Lewis
Winter, Lumen Martin
Wise, Geneva H (Holcomb)
Wong, Paul Kan
Woof, Maija (Maija Gegeris Zack Peeples)
Woolschlager, Laura Totten
Wright, Catharine Morris
Wyatt, Stanley
Youkeles, Anne
Young, Charles Alexander
Young, Tom (William Thomas)
Yudin, Carol
Zach, Jan
Zaima, Stephen Gyo
Zimmerman, William Harold
Zontal, Jorge (Jorge Sala)
Zupan, Bruno

Sand

Freckelton, Sondra
Fredman, Faiya R
Haley, Priscilla J

Watercolor

Aalund, Suzy
Aaron, Evalyn (Wilhelmina)
Abrams, Jane Eldora
Abril, Ben (Benjamin)
Ackerman, Frank Edward
Adams, Mark
Addison, Byron Kent
Akers, Gary
Altvater, Catherine Tharp
Altwerger, Libby
Amoss, Berthe
Amster, Sally
Angelini, John Michael
Armstrong, Roger Joseph
Asawa, Ruth (Ruth Asawa Lanier)
Aubin, Barbara
Austin, Phil
Aymar, Gordon Christian
Baeder, John
Bales, Jewel
Ballantyne, Catherine Turk
Banda, Pedro Salazar
Banks, Virginia
Barbee, Rob
Barbour, Arthur J
Barnes, Carole D
Barnett, Earl D
Barnwell, John L
Barr, Norman
Barrett, Robert Dumas
Barton, August Charles
Baynard, Ed
Beach, Warren
Beall, Joanna
Beam, Mary Todd
Bechtle, C Ronald
Bechtle, Robert Alan
Beck, Margit
Beery, Arthur O
Beginin, Igor
Beker, Gisela
Bell, Alistair Macready
Bell, Coca (Mary Catlett)
Bender, Bill
Bentz, Harry Donald
Benz, Lee R
Bertoni, Dante H
Besser, Arne Charles
Bialobroda, Anna
Bieser, Natalie
Birdsall, Byron
Birkin, Morton

Bishop, Marjorie Cutler
Bissette, Samuel Delk
Black, Mary McCune
Blackburn, Loren Hayner
Blackey, Mary Madlyn
Blackwood, David (Lloyd)
Blagden, Allen
Blagden, Thomas P
Blahove, Marcos
Blaine, Nell
Blair, Lee Everett
Bloom, Donald S
Blum, Helaine Dorothy
Bobick, Bruce
Bogart, George A
Booth-Owen, M(ary Ann)
Boren, James Erwin
Borne, Mortimer
Borso, Richard George
Bott, Patricia Allen
Bower, Gary David
Bradley, Dorothy
Braig, Betty Lou
Brezik, Hilarion
Brightwell, Walter
Brommer, Gerald F
Brooks, Robert
Brotherton, Naomi
Brough, Richard Burrell
Brouillette, Al
Brown, Marion B
Brown, Peggy Ann
Browne, Syd J
Browning, Dixie Burrus
Brzozowski, Richard Joseph
Bunn-Stadden, Cecine
Burch, Claire R
Burnett, Barbara Ann
Burns, Josephine
Burt, Dan
Bye, Ranulph (DeBayeux)
Cadillac, Louise Roman
Caimite
Calamar, Gloria
Calrow, Robert F
Camblin, Bob Bilyeu
Camlin, James A
Campanelli, Dan
Campbell, David Paul
Caplan, Sandra (Sandra Ciarrochi Caplan)
Caples, Barbara Barrett
Cardman, Cecilia
Carlin, James
Carlos, (James) Edward
Carlstrom, Lucinda
Carpenter, Ethel
Carter, Bernard Shirley
Carter, Harriet (Estelle) Manore
Casselli, Henry C, Jr
Catok, Lottie Meyer
Cervenka, Barbara
Chadeayne, Robert Osborne
Chen Chi
Cheng, Fu-Ding
Chiara, Alan Robert
Chin, Ric
Chow Chian-Chiu
Chow Leung Chen-Ying
Christensen, Larry R
Christensen, Ronald Julius
Christensen, Sharlene
Christiana, Edward
Chu, Gene
Chumley, John Wesley
Clark, Robert Charles
Clinedinst, Katherine Parsons
Clive, Richard R
Cliver, Kendra-Jean (Kendra-Jean Cliver Krienke)
Cobb, Ruth
Cobb, Virginia Horton
Coes, Kent Day
Cogswell, Dorothy McIntosh
Cohen, Hy
Cokendolpher, Eunice Loraine

Coleman, Michael
Collins, John Ireland
Colway, James R
Conrad, Nancy R
Cooper, Mario
Correa, Flora Horst
Courtney, Barbara Wood
Cox, Gardner
Cox, Marion Averal
Craft, Douglas D
Crane, Jean
Crawford, Catherine Betty
Crooks, W Spencer
Crossgrove, Roger Lynn
Crutchfield, William Richard
Cuthbert, Virginia
Dahlberg, Edwin Lennart
Dailey, Michael Dennis
Dance, Robert Bartlett
David, Don Raymond
Davidek, Stefan
Dean, James
DeCaprio, Alice
Deem, George
Dell, Robert Christopher
DeMaree, Betty (Elizabeth Ann)
Dennis, Don W
Dennis, Roger Wilson
de Turczynowicz, Wanda (Mrs Eliot Hermann)
Dickerson, Edward Ted
Diehl, Sevilla S
Dike, Philip Latimer
Dixon, Kenneth Ray
Dobie, Jeanne
Dodrill, Donald Lawrence
Dominique, John August
Donaldson, Jeff R
Dooley, Helen Bertha
Doyle, John Lawrence
Draper, Josiah Everett
Drower, Sara Ruth
Drutz, June
Duff, Ann MacIntosh
Duis, Rita
Duncan, Ruth
Dzubas, Friedel
Edwards, Ethel (Mrs Xavier Gonzalez)
Eguchi, Yasu
Eldredge, Stuart Edson
Elkins, Toni Marcus
Ellis, Richard
Engel, Michael Martin, II
Engeran, Whitney John, Jr
Eppink, Norman R
Eshoo, Robert
Estes, Richard
Evett, Kenneth Warnock
Facci, Domenico (Aurelio)
Farnham, Emily
Feininger, T Lux
Fett, William F
Fillerup, Mel
Finley, Donny Lamenda
Firfires, Nicholas Samuel
Fish, George A
Fisk-Hayden, Bonnie
Fitzgerald, Edmond James
Fogg-Gerber, Monica
Fon, Jade
Forbes, John Allison
Forrester, Patricia Tobacco
Forsyth, Constance
Franco, Robert John
Frater, Hal
Freifeld, Eric
Frerichs, Ruth Colcord
Friedlaender, Bilge
Fussiner, Howard
Gable, John Oglesby
Garel, Leo
Garrett, Stuart Grayson
Gatrell, Marion Thompson
Gavalas, Alexander Beary
Gentry (Augustus Calahan), Jr

Gerard, Paula (Mrs Herbert Renison)
Gibson, George
Gilbert, Clyde Lingle
Giles, Newell Walton, Jr
Glass, Sylvia
Goetz, Peter Henry
Goetz, Richard Vernon
Gonzalez, Juan J
Goodman, Bertram
Goodman, Sidney
Gordley, Metz Tranbarger
Gordon, Josephine
Grafton, Rick (Frederick Wellington)
Grass, Patty Patterson
Gray, Marie Elise
Greaver, Harry
Greco, Frank
Greenbowe, F Douglas
Greenstone, Marion
Gregory, Ellna Kay
Grosse (Carolyn Ann Gawarecki)
Groth, John August
Grotz, Dorothy Rogers
Grove, Merrill Dale
Gumpel, Hugh
Haden, Eunice (Barnard)
Halbach, David Allen
Haley, Patience E (Patience E Haley Ghikas)
Hamer, Charles James
Hamilton, Frank Moss
Hamilton, George Earl
Hammett, Polly Horton
Hammond, Natalie Hays
Hamwi, Richard Alexander
Hardy, (Clarion) Dewitt
Hardy, Thomas (Austin)
Harmon, Barbara Sayre
Harmon, Cliff Franklin
Harms, Elizabeth
Harootian, Khoren Der
Harris, Marian D
Hart, Morgan Drake
Hartell, John
Hartgen, Vincent Andrew
Ha-So-De (Narciso Abeyta)
Haughey, James M
Hawkins, Barbara
Hawthorne, Jack Gardner
Hayes, Tua
Hefner, Harry Simon
Heine, Harry
Held, Alma M
Hempler, Orval F
Hendrix, Connie (Connie Sandage Manus)
Hennesy, Gerald Craft
Herpst, Martha Jane
Hessing, Valjean McCarty
Hiatt, Margaret Smith
Hill, Richard Wayne
Hofer, Ingrid (Ingeborg)
Hoffman, Elaine Janet
Hoffman, Richard Peter
Hoie, Claus
Holabird, Jean
Holbrook, Peter Greene
Hornaday, Richard Hoyt
Horowitz, Nadja
Hough, Jennine
Howell, Douglass (Morse)
Hoyt, Dorothy
Hoyt, Ellen
Hughes, Edward John
Humphrey, S L
Hunter, Mel
Hutchings, La Vere
Ingle, John S
Ingram, Jerry Cleman
Injeyan, Seta L
Iskowitz, Gershon
Jackson, Ward
Jagman, Ed
Jaidinger, Judith C (Judith Clarann Szesko)

Jamison, Philip
Ject-Key, Elsie
Jenkins, Paul
Johansen, Robert
Johnson, Brent
Johnson, Cecile Ryden
Johnson, Douglas Walter
Johnson, Ernest (Melvin)
Johnson, Rodell C
Johnston, June Frazier
Jolley, Donal Clark
Jones, Norma L
Jones, Thomas William
Jonynas, Vytautas K
Jordan, Barbara Schwinn
Judkins, Sylvia
Jung, Kwan Yee
Jung, Yee Wah
Kaep, Louis Joseph
Kagle, Joseph L, Jr
Kaiser, Charles James
Kamys, Walter
Kan, Diana
Kao, Ruth (Yu-Hsin) Lee
Kaplinski, Buffalo
Karniol, Hilda
Kawa, Florence Kathryn
Keeling, Henry Cornelious
Kelley, Ramon
Kelpe, Paul
Kenda, Juanita Echeverria
Kerswill, J W Roy
Kester, Lenard
Keyser, Robert G
Kimbrough, Sara Dodge
Kimura, Sueko M
Kinghan, Charles Ross
Kingman, Dong M
Kirsten-Daiensai, Richard
  Charles
Klebe, Gene (Charles Eugene)
Klonis, Stewart
Klopfenstein, Philip Arthur
Knudson, Robert LeRoy
Kolisnyk, Peter
Kramer, James
Kramer, Marjorie Anne
Kranking, Margaret Graham
Kratz, Mildred Sands
Kuczun, Ann-Marie
Laessig, Robert
Lafon, Dee J
La Hotan, Robert L
Lahr, J(ohn) Stephen
Lai, Waihang
Landau, Jacob
Lang, Margo Terzian
Larraz, Julio F
Lasuchin, Michael
Law, C Anthony
Law, Pauline Elizabeth
Lawrence, James A
Lawton, Florian Kenneth
Laynor, Harold Arthur
Lecky, Susan
Lee, Dora Fugh
Leeds, Annette
Leet, Richard Eugene
Lem, Richard Douglas
Lenney, Annie
Levine, David
Levine, Marion Lerner
Lewis, William Arthur
Lewis, William R
Lhotka, Bonny Pierce
Lichtenberg, Manes
Ligare, David H
Little, James
Liu, Katherine Chang
Livingston, Virginia (Mrs
  Hudson Warren Budd)
Long, Walter Kinscella
Loughlin, John Leo
Loveless, Jim
Low, Joseph
Luitjens, Helen Anita

Lux, Gladys Marie
Luz, Virginia
Lyford, Cabot
Lynch, Mary Britten
Lynch, Tom (Thomas Michael)
Lyon, Hayes Paxton
McAdoo, Donald Eldridge
McAninch, Beth
MacBird, Rosemary
McCarthy, Doris Jean
McCoy, John W, (II)
McCoy, Wirth Vaughan
McGee, Olivia Jackson
MacGillis, Robert Donald
McGrew, Bruce Elwin
McIlvain, Frances H
MacKenzie, Hugh Seaforth
McKie, Todd Stoddard
McNamara, William Patrick,
  Jr
McNary, Oscar L
McNickle, Thomas Glen
Madden-Work, Betty I
Malsch, Ellen L
Mann, Ward Palmer
Mapes, Doris Williamson
Margolies, Ethel Polacheck
Marinsky, Harry
Marsh, David Foster
Marshall, Bruce
Martell, Barbara Bentley
Martin, Alexander Toedt
Martin, Margaret M
Martin, Ron
Martino, Antonio P
Martino, Giovanni
Martino, Nina F
Mason, Harold
Masterfield, Maxine
Matlick, Gerald Allen
Matson, Greta
Mau, Hui-Chi
Mawicke, Tran
Maxwell, John
Mayer, Bena Frank
Mays, Victor
Melikian, Mary
Meltzer, Robert Hiram
Mermin, Mildred (Shire)
Messina, Joseph R
Metz, Frank Robert
Meyer, Elmer Frederick
Meyers, Dale (Mrs Mario
  Cooper)
Michod, Susan A
Miezajs, Dainis
Milgrom, Betty
Milligan, Joan Arnold
Mina-Mora, Dorise Olson
Minnick, Esther Tress
Mitchell, Fred
Moglia, Luigi (John)
Moller, Hans
Montgomery, Claude
Moore, Ina May
Moore, Olga
Moore, Robert Eric
Moore, Scott Martin
Morrison, Fritzi
  Mohrenstecher
Morton, Richard H
Moss, Gary William
Moss, Joel C
Moss, Karen Canner
Moy, May (Wong)
Muccioli, Anna Maria
Murphy, Susan (Susan Murphy
  Colombini)
Murray, Albert (Ketcham)
Murray, Robert (Gray)
Myers, C Stowe
Nadolski, Stephanie Lucille
Nagano, Paul Tatsumi
Nechis, Barbara
Neff, John A
Neffson, Robert
Nepote, Alexander

Nestor, Lula B
Newman, Elias
Newport, Esther
Nicholas, Thomas Andrew
Nichols, Edward Edson
Nilsson, Gladys
Noble, Helen (Harper)
Nordstrand, Nathalie Johnson
Norris, (Robert) Ben
North, Judy
Norton, Mary Joyce
Notestine, Tom W
Nuki (Daniel Millsaps)
O'Connell, Ann Brown
O'Dell, Erin (Anne)
Oloffson, Werner Olaf
Olson, Joseph Olaf
Order, Trudy
Orr, Joseph Charles
Osborn, Robert
Osby, Larissa Geiss
Osyczka, Bohdan Danny
Pachner, William
Pajaud, William Etienne
Palmer, Mabel (Evelyn)
Parker, Robert Andrew
Parks, James Dallas
Parton, Nike
Patterson, Patricia
Pellew, John Clifford
Pen, Rudolph
Pena, Amado Maurilio, Jr
Perine, Robert Heath
Perrin, C Robert
Pershan, Marion
Peters, Diane (Peck)
Pettet, William
Phelan, Ellen Denise
Phillips, Bonnie
Phillips, Dick (Richard Cortez)
Phillis, Marilyn Hughey
Pickford, Rollin, Jr
Pierce, Ann Trucksess
Pigott, Marjorie
Pinckney, Stanley
Pinto, Biagio
Pisani, Joseph
Pollaro, Paul
Ponsot, Claude F
Poor, Anne
Porter, Albert Wright
Porter, Elmer Johnson
Porter, J Erwin
Porter, Shirley
Post, George (Booth)
Price, Rosalie Pettus
Punia, Constance Edith
Quick, Birney MacNabb
Quinn, Noel Joseph
Rabkin, Leo
Raffel, Alvin Robert
Ramanauskas, Dalia Irena
Rames, Stanley Dodson
Rapp, Lois
Rawlinson, Jonlane Frederick
Rayner, Ada (Ada Rayner
  Hensche)
Reese, William Foster
Reinhart, Margaret Emily
Reininghaus, Ruth (Ruth
  Reininghaus Smith)
Richards, Glenora
Robb, Charles
Roberts, Clyde Harry
Roberts, Tom (Thomas Keith)
Rodbard, Betty
Rogers, John
Roller, Marion Bender
Rollins, Jo Lutz
Romeling, W B
Ronald, William
Rose, Mary Anne
Rosenborg, Ralph M
Rosenhouse, Irwin
Ross, Alexander
Ross, Janice Koenig
Roth, Jack (Rodney)

Roth, Richard
Roth, Rubi
Rudman, Joan (Combs)
Ruffing, Anne Elizabeth
Ruthven, John Aldrich
Ryan, Elizabeth Theresa
Safford, Ruth Perkins
Salamone, Gladys L
Salemme, Martha
Salt, John
Sanders, Joop A
Sanders, Rhea (Rhea Sanders
  Rabinovich)
Sandol, Maynard
San Soucie, Patricia Molm
Sawada, Ikune
Sawyer, Helen
Sazegar, Morteza
Schlemm, Betty Lou
Schmalz, Carl (Nelson), Jr
Schreyer, Greta L
Schuler, Melvin Albert
Schwacha, George
Schwalb, Susan
Seawell, Thomas Robert
Segur, Eleanor Corinne
Seiden, Arthur
Shapiro, Irving
Shatter, Susan Louise
Sheets, Millard Owen
Sheirr, Olga (Krolik)
Sherman, Z Charlotte
Sheya
Shields, Alan J
Shore, Mary (McGarrity)
Shores, (James) Franklin
Shubin, Morris Jack
Sihvonen, Oli
Silver, Rawley A
Simmons, Julie Lutz
Simper, Frederick
Sisson, Laurence P
Sklar, Dorothy
Slider, Dorla Dean
Smigocki, Stephen Vincent
Smith, Dolph
Smith, Lowell Ellsworth
Smith, Susan Carlton
Smith, William Arthur
Snow, Cynthia Reeves
Solberg, Morten Edward
Soloway, Reta
Soltesz, Frank Joseph
Soroka, Margery
Sowers, Miriam R
Sowinski, Stanislaus Joseph
Speers, Teryl Townsend
Spicer, Jean (Doris) Uhl
Spink, Frank Henry, Jr
Sproul, Ann Stephenson
Stallwitz, Carolyn
Stamper, Willson Young
Stein, Harve
Stein, Walter
Stevens, Marjorie
Stevens, Richard Clive
Stewart, Arthur
Stone, Don
Storer, Frances Nell
Strisik, Paul
Strother, Virginia Vaughn
Stull, Jean Himrod
Suba, Susanne
Sudlow, Robert N
Sugimoto, Henry Y
Summer, (Emily) Eugenia
Sundberg, Wilda (Regelman)
Swanson, Ray V
Swartz, Beth Ames
Szesko, Lenore Rundle
Taicher, Richard
Taylor, Gage
Teague, Donald
Teraoka, Masami
Thames, Emmitt Eugene
Thiery, Thomas Allen
Thompson, Kenneth Webster

PAINTER (cont)

Thompson, Lynn P
Thompson, Malcolm Barton
Thomsen, Mitch (Nancy Mitchell)
Thomson, Carl L
Timmas, Osvald
Timmins, William Frederick
Tinning, George Campbell
Toigo, Daniel Joseph
Trachtman, Arnold S
Trank, Lynn Edgar
Trauerman, Margy Ann
Trausch, Thomas V
Triplett, Margaret L
Trott, Helen
Tseng Yu-ho
Tsutakawa, George
Turner, Bruce Backman
Tyson, Mary (Mrs Kenneth Thompson)
Uchima, Ansei
Valenstein, Alice
Vallee, William Oscar
Vann, Samuel Le Roy
Virgona, Hank (Henry P)
Voorhees, Donald Edward
Waddingham, John Alfred
Walker, Edward D (Rusty)
Walker, James Adams
Walker, Sandra Radcliffe
Wallace, Soni
Walsh, Janet Barbara
Walsh, Patricia Ruth
Wands, Alfred James
Wang, Chi-Chien
Waterhouse, Russell Rutledge
Waterston, Harry Clement
Watkins, Lewis
Watson, Darliene Keeney
Watson, Howard N(oel)
Webb, Frank (Francis H)
Weber, Idelle
Weeber, Gretchen
Weekes, Shirley Marie
Weiss, Lee (Elyse C Weiss)
Wentworth, Murray Jackson
West, E Gordon
Westermann, H C
Wheeler, Mark
White, B J (Beverly Jo)
White, Doris A
White, Ralph
Whitehill, Florence (Fitch)
Wilcox, Gordon Cumnock
Wilkinson, Kirk Cook
Williams, Raymond Lester
Williamson, Jason H
Willson, Robert
Wilson, Jane
Wilson, Nicholas Jon
Witmeyer, Stanley Herbert
Woide, Robert E
Wolins, Joseph
Wong, Frederick
Wood, Robert E
Wordell, Edwin Howland
Wostrel, Nancy J
Wray, Margaret M
Wright, Harold David
Wyckoff, Sylvia Spencer
Wyeth, Andrew Newell
Wyeth, James Browning
Yanoff, Arthur (Samuel)
Yater, George David
Young, Marjorie Ward
Young, Robert John
Younglove, Ruth Ann (Mrs Benjamin Rhees Loxley)
Zacha, William
Zornes, James Milford

PATRON

Adams, James Frederick
Akston, James
Alsdorf, James W
Altschul, Arthur G
Amsden, Floyd T
Artinian, Artine
Benenson, Edward Hartley
Beren, Stanley O
Bergen, D Thomas
Berman, Muriel Mallin
Berman, Philip I
Bermant, David W
Bernstein, Edward I
Bickford, George Percival
Bissette, Samuel Delk
Brady, Luther W
Browne, Robert M
Cartwright, Constance B & Carroll L
Chreptowsky, Achilles N
Clark, Charles D
Clowes, Allen Whitehill
Cohen, Wilfred P
Cooley, William, Jr
Crawford, John McAllister, Jr
Dalton, Harry L
D'Amico, Augustine A
Daniels, David M
Davidson, Ian J
Davidson, Suzette Morton
Davis, (Mr & Mrs) Walter
De Waal, Ronald Burt
Drysdale, Nancy McIntosh
Dunnington, Walter Grey
Eiteljorg, Harrison
Elowitch, Robert Jason
Erdelac, Joseph Mark
Erlien, Nancy Beth
Finch, Ruth Woodward
Fitch, George Hopper
Friedland, Seymour
Furman, (Dr & Mrs) Arthur F
Garbaty, Marie-Louise
Goldman, Rachel Bok
Goodman, Benjamin
Grey, Abby Weed
Grundy, J(ohn Owen)
Gumberts, William A
Hage, Raymond Joseph
Harris, Leon A, Jr
Harrison, Joseph Robert, Jr
Hartford, Huntington
Hilles, Susan Morse
Holcombe, R Gordon, Jr
Holladay, Wilhelmina Cole
Holt, Margaret McConnell
Irwin, George M
Katz, Joseph M
Kempner, Helen Hill
Kienholz, Lyn
Kincade, Arthur Warren
Klein, Esther M
Knox, Seymour H
Koger, Ira McKissick
Kreeger, David Lloyd
Larkin, John E, Jr
Leutwyler, Bruce
List, Vera G
Livingston, Margaret Gresham
Manilow, Lewis
Marks, (Mr & Mrs) Cedric H
May, Morton David
Melamed, Abraham & Hope
Miller, (Mrs) Robert Watt
Moe, Richard D
Neuberger, Roy R
Niemeyer, Arnold Matthew
Ochs, Robert David
Palmer, Fred Loren
Parkinson, Elizabeth Bliss (Mrs Henry Ives Cobb)
Pence, John Gerald
Penney, Charles Rand
Pilavin, Selma F

Pizitz, Silvia
Polan, Lincoln M
Pratt, Dallas
Quinn, Henrietta Reist
Rautbord, Dorothy H
Reiner, Gladys & Jules
Roebling, Mary G
Rogers, Leo M
Rumsey, David MacIver
Samuels, John Stockwell, 3rd
Sandground, Mark Bernard, Sr
Schnitzer, Arlene
Schooler, Lee
Schramm, James Siegmund
Schwartz, Eugene M
Scott, Robert Montgomery
Selig, (Mr & Mrs) Manfred
Semans, James Hustead
Shapiro, Daisy Viertel
Sherwood, Richard E
Smart, Mary-Leigh
Smith, (Mrs) Bertram
Solinger, David M
Sonnenschein, Hugo
Sosnowitz, Henry Abram
Speiser, Stuart M
Stamats, Peter Owen
Stevenson, Ruth Carter
Terra, Daniel J
Ullman, (Mrs) George W
Walter, May E
Walter, Paul F
Williams, Dave Harrell
Wiltshire, William Ernest, III
Zeisler, Richard Spiro
Zlotnick, Diana Shirley

PHOTOGRAPHER

Adams, Ansel Easton
Adams, Robert Hickman
Aigner, Lucien
Alinder, James Gilbert
Allen, (Harvey) Harold
Alpert, George
Alterman, Johnny
Amft, Robert
Anderson, David C
Anderson, Howard Benjamin
Armstrong, Martha (Allen)
Astman, Barbara Ann
Avedon, Richard
Avison, David
Bach, Laurence
Bader, Franz
Baer, Morley
Bailey, Oscar
Baltz, Lewis
Barnett, Ed Willis
Barrow, Thomas Francis
Barschel, Hans J
Benedict-Jones, Linda L
Beny, Roloff
Berger, Paul Eric
Berghash, Mark W
Berko, Ferenc
Berman, Fred J
Bernhard, Ruth
Beveridge, Karl J
Biferie, Dan (Daniel Anthony), Jr
Binks, Ronald C
Block, Gay (S)
Block, Joyce
Bloomfield, Lisa Diane
Blue, Patt
Bohnen, Blythe
Borglum, James Lincoln de la Mothe
Bourdeau, Robert Charles
Braunstein, H Terry (Malikin)
Broderick, James Allen
Brown, Lawrie
Brown, Peter Thomson
Brown, Robert (Earl)

Brumfield, John Richard
Brush, Gloria (Elizabeth) DeFilipps
Burchard, Peter Duncan
Burchfield, Jerry Lee
Burckhardt, Rudy
Burgess, Linda Suzanne
Burns, Marsha
Cadge, William Fleming
Cadmus, Paul
Callahan, Harry
Calman, W(endy L)
Camhi, Morrie
Campus, Peter
Cantor, Fredrich
Capa, Cornell
Caponigro, Paul
Carey, Ellen
Carpenter, Dennis Wilkinson (Bones)
Casebere, James E
Cawood, Gary Kenneth
Channing, Susan Rose
Chappell, Walter (Landon)
Charlesworth, Sarah E
Chesley, Paul Alexander
Chiarenza, Carl
Childers, Malcolm Graeme
Clift, William Brooks
Cohen, Joan Lebold
Cohen, Lynne G
Coke, F Van Deren
Cole, Herbert Milton
Collins, J(oseph) B
Comes, Marcella
Condron, Brian James
Connor, Linda Stevens
Cooper, Ron
Coplans, John (Rivers)
Corpron, Carlotta M
Cowin, Eileen
Crane, Barbara Bachmann
Crane, Michael Patrick
Crouton, Francois (LaFortune)
Cumming, Robert H
Curran, Darryl Joseph
Curran, Douglas Edward
Czarniecki, M J, III
Dablow, Dean Clint
Dane, Bill
Danziger, Avery C
Dater, Judy
Davidson, Abraham A
Davis, Philip Charles
Deal, Joe
Dean, Nicholas Brice
DeCarava, Roy Rudolph
Decock, Liliane (Liliane Morgan Decock)
DeFeo, Jay
DeGenevieve, Barbara
Delano, Jack
deLory, Peter
Diamond, Paul
Dibert, Rita Jean
Dickson, Jennifer Joan
Dingus, Rick
DiPerna, Frank Paul
Divola, John Manford, Jr
Doll, Donald Arthur
Dorr, (Virginia) Nell
Dusard, Jay
Dutton, Allen A
Edwards, Ellender Morgan
Eide, John
Ellison, Nancy
Enos, Chris
Epstein, Mitch (Mitchell D)
Estabrook, Reed
Faller, Marion
Farber, Dennis H
Faudie, Fred
Faurer, Louis
Feininger, Andreas B L
Ferguson, Larry Scott
Fessler, Ann Helene
Finch, Ruth Woodward

PHOTOGRAPHER (cont)

Fink, Larry (Laurence B)
Finn, David
Fischer, Hal (Harold Alan)
Fiskin, Judy (Anne)
Fitch, Steve (Steven Ralph)
Flack, Audrey L
Fleisher, Pat
Flick, Robbert
Ford, Charles Henri
Foster, Steven Douglas
Fox, Flo
Frazer, James (Nisbet), Jr
Freeman, Tina
Friedman, Benno
Fuller, John Charles
Gagnon, Charles
Gallagher, Carole
Garnett, William Ashford
Gartel, Laurence M
Gatel, Jeff (Jeffrey Stuart)
Gauvreau, Robert George
Gefter, Judith Michelman
Gerdes, Ingeborg
Gibson, Ralph H
Gilbert, Arnold Martin
Gilpin, Henry Edmund
Glassman, Audrey Lavine
Glassman, Joel A
Glendinning, Peter
Golden, Judith
Goodman, Mark
Gore, Tom
Gossage, John Ralph
Graley, Gary James
Graves, Kenneth Robert
Greenfield-Sanders, Timothy
Groover, Jan
Haar, Francis
Haar, Tom
Haas, Ernst
Hahn, Betty
Halberstadt, Ernst
Hallman, Gary Lee
Hammerbeck, Wanda Lee
Harbutt, Charles
Harkins, Dennis Richter
Hartman, Robert Leroy
Hartshorn, Willis E
Haxton, David
Hayashi, Masumi
Hayes, Gerald
Heath, David Martin
Heinecken, Robert Friedli
Held, Philip
Henderson, Lester Kierstead
Henderson, Victor (Lance)
Henle, Fritz
Henrich, Biff
Hernandez, Anthony Louis
Higa (Yoshiharu)
Hill, Richard Wayne
Ho, Francis T
Hofer, Evelyn
Holmes, Wendy (Diana H Noyes)
Horeis, William Richard, Sr
House, Suda Kay
Howard, David
Huff, Howard Lee
Hunter, Debora
Husebye, Terry L
Hyde, Scott
Irwin, Lisa Dru
Iversen, Earl Harvey
Jachna, Joseph David
Jacobshagen, N Keith, II
James, Christopher P
Jansen, Angela Bing
Jansen, Catherine Sandra
Johnson, Gregory
Jones, Harold Henry
Jones, Pirkle
Josephson, Kenneth Bradley
Joyce, J David
Kalischer, Clemens
Kalisher, Simpson

Kaminsky, Jack Allan
Kane, Bill (William David)
Karsh, Yousuf
Katsiff, Bruce
Kelly, Isaac Perry
Kennedy, Gene (Eugene Murray)
Kenyon, Colleen Frances
Ketchum, Robert Glenn
Kikuchi-Yngojo, Alan
Kindermann, Helmmo
Kirby, Kent Bruce
Kirkwood, Larry Thomas
Kleckner, Susan
Klein, Lynn (Ellen)
Klipper, Stuart David
Knight, Tom (Thomas Lincoln), Jr
Koga, Mary
Kornmayer, J Gary (John)
Kozloff, Max
Krause, George
Krims, Leslie Robert
Kronengold, Eric A
Kumler, Kipton (Cornelius)
Lake, Jerry Lee
Landry, Richard Miles
Land-Weber, Ellen E
Lang, Wendy F
Larson, William G
Lattanzio, Frances
Lavenson, Alma (Alma Lavenson Wahrhaftig)
Lawrence, James A
Lee, Russell
Leigh, Jack David
Leipzig, Arthur
Leonard, Joanne
Lerner, Abe
Lerner, Nathan Bernard
Lescalleet
Levinson, Joel D
Levit, Herschel
Levitt, Helen
Levy, David Corcos
Liebling, Jerome
Lindroth, Linda
Lipzin, Janis Crystal
Lonidier, Fred Spencer
Lucier, Mary
Ludwig, Allan I
McCormick, Jo Mary (Jo Mary McCormick-Sakurai)
McDarrah, Fred William
McGowan, Kenneth
MacGregor, Gregory Allen
Maclay, David (Sears), Jr
McMillan, Jerry Edward
McMillan, Stephen Walker
McPherson, Larry E
Maggs, Arnaud (Cyril Benvenuti)
Maldre, Mati
Mann, Katinka
Mansaram, P(anchal)
Mapplethorpe, Robert
Marasco, Rose
Margolis, Richard M
Mark, Mary Ellen
Marshall, Ralph
Martone, Michael
Marx, Nicki D
Maurer, Neil Douglas
Mayes, Elaine
Meek, A J
Melby, David A
Mendoza, Antonio G
Menthe, Melissa
Mertin, Roger
Metzker, Ray K
Meyer, Ursula
Meyerowitz, Joel
Michals, Duane
Millea, Tom (Thomas Francis)
Miller, Laurence Glenn
Minick, Roger
Mirano, Virgil Marcus

Misrach, Richard Laurence
Mitchell, Margaretta K
Mitchell, Michael John
Mones, Arthur
Monthan, Guy
Moore, Peter
Moore, Robert James
Morath, Inge
Morgan, Barbara Brooks
Morris, Wright
Morrison, Boone M
Moulton, Rosalind Kimball
Mudford, Grant Leighton
Murray, Joan
Musgrave, Shirley H
Myers, Richard Lewis
Namuth, Hans
Nathans, Rhoda R
Newhall, Beaumont
Newman, Arnold
Newton, John Neil
Noerdlinger, Janau Nau
Noggle, Anne
Norman, Dorothy (S)
Nowytski, (Slavko) Sviatoslav
Noyes, Sandy
Nuse, Oliver William
Ockenga, Starr
O'Connell, Edward E
Ollman, Arthur L
Olmsted, Suzanne M
Oloffson, Werner Olaf
O'Neill, Pat
Orkin, Ruth (Mrs Morris Engel)
Orland, Ted N
Padula, Fred David
Palaia, Franc (Dominic)
Palmgren, Donald Gene
Papageorge, Tod
Parker, Ann
Parker, Olivia
Paul, Suzanne
Paul, William D, Jr
Penn, Irving
Phillips, Bertrand D
Pinkel, Sheila Mae
Plossu, Bernard
Pomeroy, James Calwell, Jr
Porter, Eliot Furness
Post, Marion (Marion Post Wolcott)
Powell, Dan T
Power, Mark
Printz, Bonnie Allen
Raginsky, Nina
Ranalli, Daniel
Randlett, Mary Willis
Rankaitis, Susan Anne
Rauschenberg, Robert
Raymond, Lilo
Read, Dave (David Dolloff)
Reeves, John Alexander
Renner, Eric
Resnick, Marcia Aylene
Rexroth, Nancy Louise
Richards, Eugene
Riley, Barbra Bayne
Riss, Murray
Robbins, LeRoy (Southward)
Rodan, Don
Rodriguez, Geno (Eugene)
Rogovin, Milton
Rosenthal, John W
Rothstein, Arthur
Rowland, Mary Adele
Rubello, David Jerome
Rubenstein, Meridel
Rubinfien, Leo H
Rubinstein, Susan R
Sahlstrand, James Michael
Sal, Jack
Sargent, Richard
Savage, Naomi
Scheer, Sherie (Hood)
Schley, Evander Duer (Van)
Schnitzer, Klaus A

Schorre, Charles
Schulze, John H
Schwartz, Sing-Si
Seed, Suzanne Liddell
Segalove, Ilene Judy
Seltzer, Joanne Lynn
Semak, Michael
Semchishen, Orest M
Sexton, John (William)
Shillea, Thomas John
Shore, Stephen
Shuler, Thomas H, Jr
Simmons, Laurie
Simon, Michael A
Singer, Joel
Sirkis, Nancy
Skoff, Gail Lynn
Skoglund, Sandra Louise
Slavin, Neal
Smith, Dinah Maxwell
Smith, Henry Holmes
Smith, Keith A
Smith, Luther A
Smith, Michael A
Sommer, Frederick
Sonneman, Eve
Souza, Al (Alfred Francis)
Staller, Eric P
Stallwitz, Carolyn
Stanley, Bob
Steinhardt, Alice
Stephany, Jaromir
Stephens, Curtis
Stettner, Louis
Stiegler, Robert William
Stone, Jim (James J)
Stoumen, Lou
Stuler, Jack
Sultan, Larry A
Swigart, Lynn S
Szabo, Stephen Lee
Tata, Sam Bejan
Tavenner, Patricia (Pat)
Taylor, Harry George
Telberg, Val
Termes (Dick A Termes)
Teske, Edmund Rudolph
Thomas, Lew
Thomason, Michael Vincent
Thompson, Lynn P
Thorne-Thomsen, Ruth T
Thurston, Jacqueline Beverly
Tice, George Andrew
Torbert, Stephanie Birch
Torn, Jerry (Gerald J)
Toth, Carl Wayne
Trager, Philip
Traub, Charles H
Trecker, Stanley Matthew
Tucker, Toba Pato
Tuckerman, Jane Bayard
Twardowicz, Stanley Jan
Uelsmann, Jerry
Ullrich-Zuckerman, B
Vanco, John Leroy
Vestal, David
Volkerding, Laura
von dem Bussche, Wolf
von zur Muehlen, Bernis Susan
von zur Muehlen, Peter
Wade, Robert Schrope
Wallis, Helen V
Wang, Sam
Warren, Julianne Bussert Baker
Wasserman, Cary (Robert)
Webb, Todd
Weedy, Theresa
Weiss, Jeff
Weiss, John Joseph
Welch, Roger
Wells, Alisa
Welpott, Jack Warren
Wenger, Jane (B)
Werner, Donald (Lewis)
Wessel, Henry, Jr
Wexler, Jerome LeRoy

PHOTOGRAPHER (cont)

White, Amos, IV
Widmer, Gwen Ellen
Wiedenhoeft, Renate
Wiggins, Walton Wray
Williams, Casey
Wilson, Wallace
Winningham, Geoff
Winogrand, Garry
Wise, (Kenneth) Kelly
Witkin, Joel-Peter
Witte, Mary (Grace) Stieglitz
Yates, Steven A
Yost, Leon C
Young, Barbara
Zavala, Manuel
Zucker, Bob

PRINTMAKER

Abularach, Rodolfo Marco
Anderson, William Thomas
Audette, Anna Held
Auth, Robert R
Barker, Al C
Barsch, Wulf Erich
Bear, Marcelle L
Bearce, Jeana Dale
Booth, Dot
Booth-Owen, M(ary Ann)
Bosse, Janet C
Breiger, Elaine
Britton, Daniel Robert
Brody, Blanche
Brody, Ruth
Bruneau, Kittie
Brycelea, Clifford
Bumbeck, David A
Burdock, Harriet
Burkhardt, Hans Gustav
Bynum, E Anderson (Esther
    Pearl)
Cage, John
Cain, David Paul
Caver, William Ralph
Connett, Dee M
Cortor, Eldzier
Currie, Bruce
Daughters, Robert A
Davison, Bill
Day, Gary Lewis
de Boschnek, Chris (Christian
    Charles)
Dowell, John E, Jr
Drum, Sydney Maria
Durr, Pat (Patricia Beth)
Eder, James Alvin
Elena, Maria
Ensrud, Wayne
Etienne, Guillermo C
Evans, Lucile
Falfan, Alfredo
Fidler, Spencer D
Firestein, Cecily Barth
Fohr, Jenny
Folsom, Karl Leroy
Foster, Maelee Thomson
Frank, Helen (Goodzeit)
Fuerst, Shirley Miller
Gardner, Joan A
Gilbert, Helen Odell
Greenberg, Elenor Siminow
Haack, Cynthia R
Haley, Priscilla J
Haller, Emanuel
Hara, Keiko
Haseltine, James Lewis
Hershey, Nona
Hubler, Julius
Hulett, Simonne R
Hunter, John H
Ilowitz, Theodora
Jacobson, Arthur Robert
Jacquette, Yvonne Helene
Jewell, Joyce

Jilg, Michael Florian
Johnson, Margaret Kennard
Johnson, Nota
Kagy, Sheffield Harold
Kaprov, Susan
Kasten, Karl Albert
Kinnee, Sandy
Knippers, Edward Cade, Jr
Kornblum, Myrtle
Krieger, Ruth M
Kushner, Dorothy Browdy
Lampitoc, Rol Ponce
Lane, Lois
Lark, Sylvia
Lemmy, Lemmy
Liao (Shiou-Ping Liao)
Lichtner, Schomer Frank
McLarty, William James (Jack)
McVicker, J Jay
Mattern, Penny Greig
Mayer, Sondra
Mitra, Gopal C
Morse, Marcia Roberts
Moskowitz, Ira
Mullen, James Martin
Namingha, Dan
Nichols, Francis N, II
Noa, Florence
O Donohue, Teige Ros
Olshan, Bernard
Olson, Richard W
Paschall, Jo Anne
Pereznieto, Castro Fernando
Perry, Donald Dean
Peterson, A E S
Philbrick, Margaret Elder
Piskoti, James
Plear, Scott Edward
Pletka, Paul
Quiller, Stephen Frederick
Quinn, William
Rankin, Don
Reid, Leslie Mary Margaret
Rhodes, Curtis A
Riddle, John Thomas, Jr
Rollman-Shay, Ed & Charlotte
Rubin, Sandra
Rush, Kent Thomas
Sampson, Frank
Schupbach, Terry Ann
Scott, Sandy (Sandra Lynn)
Sepyo, James
Shaffer, Richard
Sica
Slaymaker, Martha
Sletten, Byron K
Sloane, Phyllis Lester
Smith, Gary Douglas
Solomon, Vita Petrosky
Somers, H(arry W)
Sorman, Steven
Spandorfer, Merle Sue
Stell, H Kenyon
Stewart, Dorothy S
Stone, Jeffrey Ingram
Tanner, Warren
Targan, Judy
Toulis, Vasilios (Apostolos)
Tullis, Garner H
Van Hoesen, Beth (Mrs Mark
    Adams)
Van Laar, Timothy Jon
Waksberg, Naomi
Walsh, J(ohn) Michael
Wharton, David W
Wilson-Hammond, Charlotte
    Emily
Worthen, Amy Namowitz
Younger, Dan Forrest

All Media

Abrams, Jane Eldora
Achepohl, Keith Anden
Adelman, Dorothy (Lee)
    McClintock

Adler, Myril
Alicea, Jose
Alps, Glen Earl
Amen, Irving
Andrus, James Roman
Aronson, Irene Hilde
Asher, Lila Oliver
Askin, Walter Miller
Atirnomis (Rita Simon)
Austin, Pat
Barnet, Will
Barooshian, Martin
Barth, Charles John
Batchelor, Anthony John
Baxter, Bonnie Jean
Beall, Dennis Ray
Beaumont, Mona M
Becker, Helmut Julius
Benz, Lee R
Bernard, David Edwin
Bernstein, Theresa
Black, Richard R
Bloedel, Joan (Stuart) Ross
Boodman, H Citron
Borochoff, (Ida) Sloan
Bosson, Jack (John Edwin), Jr
Boyd, James Henderson
Boyd, John David
Boyd, Lakin
Boynton, Jack (James) W
Brandt, Rex (Rexford Elson)
Breverman, Harvey
Briansky, Rita Prezament
Brodsky, Judith Kapstein
Brody, Arthur William
Broner, Robert
Brooks, Wendell T
Brulc, Dennis (Mel Vapour)
Brunkus, Richard Allen
Cain, J Frederick, Jr
Calapai, Letterio
Cale, Robert Allan
Calman, W(endy L)
Camarata, Martin L
Campbell, Richard Horton
Casarella, Edmond
Cassara, Frank
Chafetz, Sidney
Chesney, Lee R, Jr
Chesney, Lee Roy, III
Chester, Charlotte Wanetta
Childers, Malcolm Graeme
Chinn, Yuen Yuey
Christensen, Val Alan
Cimbalo, Robert W
Citron, Minna Wright
Conrad, George
Coughlin, Jack
Cracker Jack Kid (Charles D
    Welch)
Crispo, Dick
Crouse, Michael Glenn
Csoka, Stephen
Daily, Evelynne Mess
Dallmann, Daniel Forbes
Daly, Kathleen (Kathleen Daly
    Pepper)
Davis, Alonzo Joseph
Davis, Ronald Wendel
Day, Worden
de Champlain, Vera Chopak
Dehner, Dorothy
de Lama, Alberto
deMatties, Nick
de Miskey, Julian
Dickinson, David Charles
Dienes, Sari
Donde, Olga
Drake, James
Dreskin-Haig, Jeanet Elizabeth
Drewes, Werner
Duback, Charles S
Duncan, Richard (Hurley)
Eckstein, Ruth
Elliott, Bruce Roger
Epting, Marion Austin
Everts, Connor

Fairfield, Richard Thomas
Federe, Marion
Feigin, Marsha
Feld, Augusta
Feldhaus, Paul A
Feldman, Walter (Sidney)
Fichter, Herbert Francis
Field, Philip Sidney
Field, Saul
Foose, Robert James
Foote, Howard Reed
Fornas, Leander
Francis, Madison Ke, Jr
Freed, David
Freimark, Robert (Matthew)
French, Ray H
Fricano, Tom S
Gaines, Alan Jay
Garhart, Martin J
Geniusz, Robert Myles
Ginzburg, Yankel (Jacob)
Ginzel, Roland
Goddard, Vivian
Goertz, Augustus Frederick,
    III
Gorelick, Shirley
Gramberg, Liliana
Greaver, Hanne
Green, Martin Leonard
Greenbaum, Marty
Grippe, Peter
Grupp, Carl Alf
Guerrero, Jose
Haas, Richard John
Hadzi, Dimitri
Haessle, Jean-Marie Georges
Hari, Kenneth
Hasen, Burt Stanly
Helfond, Riva
Heller, Jules
Herzberg, Thomas
Heywood, J C
Higa (Yoshiharu)
Hood, (Thomas) Richard
Hooper, Jack Meredith
Horn, Bruce
Hutton, Dorothy Wackerman
Ihle, John Livingston
Ikegawa, Shiro
Jackson, Herb
Jacobs, Jim
Jameson, Demetrios George
Jerviss, Joy
Johanson, George E
Johnson, Donald Ray
Jones, Frederick George
Jones, Herb (Leon Herbert), Jr
Jones, James Edward
Jones, Marvin Harold
Kainen, Jacob
Kaplan, Sandra
Kappel, R Rose (Mrs Irving
    Gould)
Kassoy, Bernard
Katz, Alex
Katz, Hilda (Hulda Weber)
Keane, Lucina Mabel
Kenda, Juanita Echeverria
Kenojuak (Ashevak)
Kessler, Edna Leventhal
Kimura, William Yusaburo
King, Eleanor (Eleanor King
    Hookham)
Kirk, Michael
Klein, Lynn (Ellen)
Knerr, Sallie Frost
Koppelman, Chaim
Kovatch, Jak
Kovner, Saul
Kowalke, Ronald Leroy
Krug, Harry Elno
Lacroix, Richard
Landers, Bertha
Landon, Edward August
Lang, J T
Lansdon, Gay Brandt
La Pierre, Thomas

PRINTMAKER (cont)
Lasansky, Leonardo
Lasuchin, Michael
Lea, Stanley E
Leathers, Winston Lyle
Leech, Merle Eugene
Leff, Rita
Leiber, Gerson August
Levin, Morton D
Lew, Weyman
Lipman-Wulf, Peter
Lorber, Stephen Neil
Loring, John
Lowe, Marvin
Luca, Mark
McCray, Dorothy M
McGough, Charles E
McIvor, John Wilfred
McKeeby, Byron Gordon
McKnight, Thomas Frederick
McLean, James Albert
McSheehy, Cornelia Marie
Madsen, Viggo Holm
Majeski, Thomas H
Malone, Robert R
Maltzman, Stanley
Margulies, Joseph
Mark, Enid (Epstein)
Martin, Doris-Marie Constable
Mattingly, (James Thomas)
Max, Peter
Maxwell, William C
Mazur, Michael
Mazzocca, Gus (Augustus
    Nicholas Mazzocca)
Meeker, Dean Jackson
Mellon, James
Mendelson, Haim
Menihan, John Conway
Menses, Jan
Merkin, Richard Marshall
Meyer, Frank Hildbridge
Miller, Barbara Darlene
Mills, Agnes
Mills, Lev Timothy
Miyamoto, Wayne Akira
Monongye, Preston Lee
Montague, James L
Morrow, Terry
Motherwell, Robert
Muranaka, Hideo
Murata, Hiroshi
Myers, Malcolm Haynie
Nagler, Fred
Nakazato, Hitoshi
Nama, George Allen
Natkin, Robert
Nawrocki, Thomas Dennis
Neal, Reginald H
Nemec, Vernita Ellen
Neustein, Joshua
Newman, Libby
Nushawg, Michael Allan
Obler, Geri
Okoshi, Eugenia Sumiye
Olds, Elizabeth
Osborn, Kevin Russell
Osborne, Cynthia A
Page, John Henry, Jr
Paone, Peter
Parra, Carmen
Patnode, J Scott
Patterson, William Joseph
Paul, Ken (Hugh)
Peak, Elizabeth Jayne
Pellettieri, Michael Joseph
Peterdi, Gabor F
Pletcher, Gerry
Ponce de Leon, Michael
Pozzatti, Rudy O
Pratt, Mary Frances
Pusey, Mavis
Putterman, Florence Grace
Quat, Helen S
Racz, Andre
Ragan, Connie Seabourn
Ragland, Jack Whitney

Rakovan, Lawrence Francis
Richards, Walter DuBois
Riess, Lore
Ritchie, William (Bill)
Roberts, Donald
Robinson, Sally W
Rodman, Ruth M
Rogalski, Walter
Roller, Russell Kenneth
Romano, Clare Camille
Rose, Herman
Rosenblum, Sadie Skoletsky
Rosenhouse, Irwin
Ross, Conrad H
Ross, John T
Rossi, Barbara
Rotholz, Rina
Rozman, Joseph John
Ruffo, Joseph Martin
Running Rabbit
Saff, Donald Jay
Sanchez, Beatrice Rivas
Sarvis, Alva Taylor
Saunders, J Boyd
Savage, Roger
Sawai, Noboru
Schein, Eugenie
Schieferdecker, Ivan E
Schnackenberg, Roy
Scholder, Fritz
Schrag, Karl
Schutz, Estelle
Schwartz, Aubrey E
Schwartz, Carl E
Seabourn, Bert Dail
Seace, Barry William
Seawell, Thomas Robert
Seidler, Doris
Seltzer, Phyllis
Sexauer, Donald Richard
Sharpe, David Flemming
Shead, S Ray
Sher, Elizabeth
Shives, Arnold Edward
Simson, Bevlyn A
Singleton, Robert Ellison
Smith, Moishe
Snow, John
Sparks, John Edwin
Sperakis, Nicholas George
Spohn, Franz Frederick
Spruce, Everett Franklin
Spruyt, E Lee
Stack, Frank Huntington
Stasack, Edward Armen
Stasik, Andrew J
Staven, Leland Carroll
Steg, J L
Steiner, Michael
Stevenson, Branson Graves
Steward, Donn Horatio
Stewart, John P
Stolpe, Daniel Owen
Stratton, Dorothy (Mrs
    William A King)
Stussy, Jan
Sultan, Donald K
Swenson, (Jean) Mary Jeanette
    Hamilton
Sykes, (William) Maltby
Tamasauskas, Otis Kazys
Taylor, Harry George
Trissel, James Nevin
Trosky, Helene Roth
Tubis, Seymour
Tulving, Ruth
Turner, Janet E
Tyler, Kenneth Eugene
Tyler, Valton
Upton, Richard Thomas
Valesco, Frances
Vaness, Margaret Helen
Varney, Edwin
Vian, Orfeo
Viera, Ricardo
Viesulas, Romas
Wainwright, Robert Barry

Walters, Sylvia Solochek
Weaver, (John) Robert
Webster, Stokely
Weege, William
Weiler, Melody M
Whipple, Barbara
Whitesell, John D
Will, John A
Williams, Walter (Henry)
Williamson, Gail McKennis
Wise, Gerald Lee
Witham, Vernon Clint
Witt, John
Yaffa Yael Stec-El (Harriet
    Jeanne Steckel)
Yamin, Steven Edward
Zelt, Martha
Ziemann, Richard Claude
Zwick, Rosemary G

Etching

Abeles, Sigmund
Alberga, Alta W
Asmar, Alice
Autry, Carolyn
Baczek, Peter Gerard
Baney, Vera
Bansemer, Roger Lewis
Bascom, Earl W
Baumbach, Harold
Bayefsky, Aba
Becker, David
Bishop, Isabel (Mrs Harold G
    Wolff)
Blackey, Mary Madlyn
Blackman, Thomas Patrick
Blackwood, David (Lloyd)
Blaustein, Al
Bogaev, Ronni (Ronni Bogaev
    Greenstein)
Boylan, John Lewis
Braley, Jean
Brice, William
Broker, Karin
Bujese, Arlene
Burns, Jerome
Cameron, Brooke Bulovsky
Carlstrom, Lucinda
Cassill, Herbert Carroll
Cawein, Kathrin
Cetin, Anton
Charles-Smith, Donald
Cober, Alan E
Cohoe, Grey
Colescott, Warrington W
Condeso, Orlando
Conn, David Edward
Conneen, Jane W
Cook, Stephen D
Cornell, Thomas Browne
Cortese, Don F
Crumbo, Woody
Crump, Walter Moore, Jr
Curtis, Mary Cranfill
Cyril, R
de Gogorza, Patricia
    (Gahagan)
De Groat, George Hugh
Delson, Elizabeth
Dennis, Cherre Nixon
Di Cerbo, Michael
Dickson, Jennifer Joan
Driesbach, David Fraiser
Duncan, (Eleanore) Klari de
    Szecsanyi
Eames, John Heagan
Edmondson, Leonard
Edmunds, Allan Logan
Egleson, Jim (James Downey)
Esler, John Kenneth
Fausett, (William) Dean
Feder, Penny Joy
Forrester, Patricia Tobacco
Fowler, Mel
Frederick, Eugene Wallace

Furr, Jim
Gehr, Mary (Ray)
Geisert, Arthur Frederick
Gentry (Augustus Calahan), Jr
Gilling, Lucille
Gomez-Quiroz, Juan Manuel
Gonzalez-Tornero, Sergio
Gussow, Sue Ferguson
Hammerman, Pat Jo
Hammond, Gale Thomas
Hannah, John Junior
Hanson, Jean (Elphick)
Hardy, (Clarion) Dewitt
Hatch, W A S
Helck, (Clarence) Peter
Herfield, Phyllis
Heyman, Lawrence Murray
Hicks, Leon Nathaniel
Hill, Polly Knipp
Hoie, Claus
Holabird, Jean
Holmes, David Bryan
Huggins, Victor, Jr
Humphrey, Judy Lucille
Hurwitz, Sidney J
Itchkawich, David Michael
Jacques, Michael Louis
Jansen, Angela Bing
Johnston, Thomas Alix
Johnston, Ynez
Jones, John Paul
Kaericher, John Conrad
Kaminsky, Jack Allan
Kaplan, Jerome Eugene
Keener, Anna Elizabeth
Kepets, Hugh Michael
Kerslake, Kenneth Alvin
Kim, Bongtae
Kline, Harriet
Kloss, Gene (Alice Geneva
    Glasier)
Kolliker, William Augustin
Krause, LaVerne Erickson
Lake, Randall
Lanyon, Ellen
Lasansky, Mauricio L
Laventhol, Hank
Lazarof, Eleanore Berman
Leithauser, Mark Alan
Levine, Martin
Limont, Naomi Charles
Lipinsky de Orlov, Lino S
Locke, Charles Wheeler
Lovejoy, Margot R
Lucioni, Luigi
Lukasiewicz, Ronald Joseph
McBryde, Sarah Elva
MacGillis, Robert Donald
McKinnickinnick, Margaret I
McMillan, Stephen Walker
Manarey, Thelma Alberta
Manning, Jo
Marden, Brice
Marx, Robert Ernst
Mason, Harold
Masurovsky, Gregory
Matthews, Wanda Miller
Milton, Peter Winslow
Myers, Frances
Nelson, Harry William
Nemec, Nancy
Nicholson, Roy William
Ocvirk, Otto G
Pace, Stephen S
Pantell, Richard Keith
Paris, Lucille M
Parke, Walter Simpson
Partridge, Roi
Pentz, Donald Robert
Perlmutter, Merle
Perret, Nell Foster
Petersen, Roland Conrad
Petrie, Sylvia Spencer
Pickhardt, Carl
Priest, Hartwell Wyse
Pufahl, John K
Quandt, Elizabeth (Elizabeth
    Quandt Barr)

PRINTMAKER (cont)

Rayburn, (Boyd Dale)
Reed, Doel
Reed, Jesse Floyd
Richmond, Rebekah
Rivard, J B(ernard)
Rubey, Tony (George Anton)
Ruble, Ronald L
Rush, Andrew
St Tamara (Tamara Kolba)
Saks, Judith-Ann (Judith-Ann Saks Rosenthal)
Schaefer, Ronald H
Scholder, Laurence
Schreiber, Eileen Sher
Schrut, Sherry
Scoville, Jonathan Armstrong
Sewell, Richard George
Simel, Elaine
Smigocki, Stephen Vincent
Smith, Keith A
Sokolowski, Linda Robinson
Solem, (Elmo) John
Sorge, Walter
Spencer, Howard DaLee
Spitz, Barbara S
Stan, Cynthia (Cynthia Stan Mellow)
Steinhouse, Tobie (Thelma)
Stevovich, Andrew Vlastimir
Stiles, Helen
Stussy, Jan
Sverdlove, Zolita
Sway, Albert
Talaba, L (Linda Talaba Cummens)
Tift, Mary Louise
Tompkins, Betty (I)
Torlakson, James Daniel
Turner, Alan
Van Vranken, Rose (Rose Van Vranken Hickey)
Virgona, Hank (Henry P)
Wall, Sue
Washburn, Stan
Weare, Shane
Webster, Larry
Weidenaar, Reynold Henry
Wilbur, Lawrence Nelson
Wilson, John
Woolschlager, Laura Totten
Wunderman, Jan (Liljan Darcourt Wunderman)
Yarbrough, Leila Kepert
Yeh, Carol
Youngblood, Judy
Zeitlin, Harriet Brooks
Zugor, Sandor

Engraving

Brussel-Smith, Bernard
Chappell, Berkley Warner
Cook, August Charles
De Pol, John
Elloian, Peter
Fumagalli, Barbara Merrill
Gaona Adame, Jose Julio
Hanna, Boyd Everett
Hicks, Leon Nathaniel
Hurtado Duhart, Rodolfo
Landeck, Armin
Lindquist, Evan
McMillan, Robert W
Manning, Jo
Marsh, Anne Steele
Martin, Stefan
Matthews, Wanda Miller
Milton, Peter Winslow
Morgan, Norma Gloria
Moser, Barry
Paulsen, Brian Oliver
Rush, Andrew
Spitz, Barbara S
Summy, Anne Tunis
Szesko, Lenore Rundle

Weldon, Barbara Maltby
Yeh, Carol
Zonia, Dhimitri

Lithography

Adams, Clinton
Anderson, Sally J
Antreasian, Garo Zareh
Aquino, Edmundo
Archer, Cynthia
Bennett, Don Bemco
Berman, Steven M
Bidner, Robert D H
Blagden, Allen
Block, Amanda Roth
Bookbinder, Jack
Brodsky, Harry
Brooks, James
Brussel-Smith, Bernard
Bryce, Mark Adams
Burford, Byron Leslie
Burkert, Robert Randall
Butler, James D
Chu, Gene
Cline, Clinton C
Copeland, Lila
Cortright, Steven M
Crutchfield, William Richard
Dash, Robert (Warren)
Davenport, Ray
Davidson, Herbert Laurence
Dehn, Virginia
Detmers, William Raymond
Doyle, John Lawrence
Du Jardin, Gussie
Eagerton, Robert Pierce
Eichner-Dixon, Peter
Ellingson, William John
Faiers, Ted (Edward Spencer)
Farm, Gerald E
Filmus, Tully
Forrest, Christopher Patrick
Frances, Harriette Anton
Freilicher, Jane
Frerichs, Ruth Colcord
Gardner, Robert Earl
George, Raymond Ellis
Golden, Rolland Harve
Graham, K M
Greaver, Harry
Grosch, Laura
Hagan, Frederick
Hale, Kenneth John
Hebald, Milton Elting
Hibel, Edna
Himmelfarb, John David
Hobbie, Lucille
Hofmann, Douglas William
Hogue, Alexandre
Holtz, Itshak Jack
Hook, Walter
Horn, Bruce
Horvitz, Suzanne Joan
Hunter, Mel
Hyde, Scott
Iwamasa, Ken
Jennings, Thomas
Johnson, Douglas Walter
Kaiser, Diane
Kakas, Christopher A
Kaplan, Jerome Eugene
Kelley, Donald William
Kimball, Wilford Wayne, Jr
Kipniss, Robert
Kitta, George Edward
Kniffin, Ralph Gus
Knigin, Michael Jay
Ko, Anthony
Landau, Jacob
Lapinski, Tadeusz (A)
Lapointe, Frank
Laub-Novak, Karen
Lauffer, Alice A
Lehrer, Leonard
Lerner, Sandy R

Levine, Martin
Long, Walter Kinscella
Lovato, Charles Fredric
Lowney, Bruce Stark
Lund, Jane
McCallum, Corrie (Mrs William Halsey)
McConnell, James Houston
McCulloch, Frank E
MacDougall, Anne
Machetanz, Fred
McNeil, George J
Massey, Charles Wesley, Jr
Maughelli, Mary L
Medearis, Roger
Mell, Ed (Edmund Paul Jr)
Melville, Grevis Whitaker
Miyasaki, George Joji
Morales, Armando
Moses, Forrest (Lee), Jr
Muench, John
Nelson, Robert Allen
O'Connell, George D
O'Connor, Thom
Parfenoff, Michael S
Perlmutter, Jack
Petersen, Will
Petheo, Bela Francis
Pickhardt, Carl
Poehlmann, JoAnna
Poole, Leslie Donald
Prentice, David Ramage
Puccinelli, Raimondo
Pura, William Paul
Raffael, Joseph
Rasmussen, Keith Eric
Ringness, Charles Obert
Rode, Meredith Eagon
Roseman, Susan Carol
Rosenthal, Seymour
Rothenberg, Susan
Rubenstein, Lewis W
Rubin, Sandra
Sakuyama, Shunji
Saltonstall, Elizabeth
Samburg, Grace (Blanche)
Sanborn, Herbert J
Schar, Stuart
Schreyer, Greta L
Seckel, Paul Bernhard
Sigismund, Violet M
Sivard, Robert Paul
Sloan, Jeanette
Smith, William Arthur
Solodkin, Judith
Sommers, John
Sprang, Elizabeth
Stewart, Paul LeRoy
Stoeveken, Anthony Charles
Stoianovich, Marcelle
Surgalski, Patrick J
Tarin, Gilberto A
Taylor, Prentiss (Hottel)
Thomas, C David
Tooker, George
Vigil, Veloy Joseph
Vogel, Joseph
Vogl, Don George
Voorhees, Donald Edward
Walmsley, William Aubrey
Watanabe, Ryo
Watson, Howard N(oel)
Weddige, Emil
Wilson, Charles Banks
Wolfe, Robert, Jr

Mezzotint

Alexander, Peter
Burks, Myrna R
Hamaguchi, Yozo
Pope, Mary Ann Irwin
Popescu, Cara
Porter, Liliana

Miscellaneous Media

Ablow, Roselyn Karol
Allen, Jesse
Allen, Kaola B
Altman, Harold
Baczek, Peter Gerard
Barry, Anne Meredith
Bass, Joel
Baum, Marilyn Ruth
Bayer, Arlyne
Berlin, Beatrice Winn
Berman, Vivian
Binning, Robin
Blumenthal, Fritz
Byrum, Donald Roy
Caiserman-Roth, Ghitta
Camins, Jacques Joseph
Carlberg, Norman Kenneth
Catchi (Catherine O Childs)
Childs, Bernard
Church, C Howard
Clinton, Paul Arthur
Colby, Bill
Conover, Robert Fremont
Dass, Dean Allen
Davila, Carlos
Davis, J Ray
Dean, Nicholas Brice
DeLamonica, Roberto
DeRoux, Daniel Edward
Dickerson, Edward Ted
Doll, Linda A
Durieux, Caroline Wogan
Eichenberg, Fritz
Esaki, Yasuhiro
Evans, Henry
Forsyth, Constance
Fortess, Karl E
Foster, April
Francis, Jean Thickens
Freeman, Mark
Fuller, Sue
Gantz, Jeanne A
Garcia, Ofelia
Gaucher, Yves
Geller, Esther (Esther Geller Shapero)
Gerardia, Helen
Gold, Leah
Goldstein, Milton
Gordy, Robert P
Greenwald, Pat
Gregory, Ellna Kay
Grotenrath, Ruth
Gurr, Lena
Halbrook, Rita Robertshaw
Hamill, Tim J
Harjo, Benjamin, Jr
Harris, Lucille S
Hendershot, J L
Higgins, Dick
Hildebrand, June Mary Ann
Hildreth, Joseph Alan
Hoare, Tyler James
Homar, Lorenzo
Horeis, William Richard, Sr
Hunkler, Dennis Francis
Hushlak, Gerald
Johnson, Lois Marlene
Jones, Claire
Jones, Theodore Joseph
Kaplan, Stanley
Karlsen, Anne-Marie
Kaulitz, Garry Charles
Kemp, Paul Zane
Kitaj, R B
Klabunde, Charles Spencer
Kohn, Misch
Kuczun, Ann-Marie
Kumm, Marguerite Elizabeth
Leaf, Ruth
Ledyard, Walter William
Lewis, Stanley
Lindroth, Linda
Liu, Katherine Chang
Low, Joseph
Luray, J

PRINTMAKER (cont)

McClelland, Jeanne C
Mandelbaum, Lyn
Margo, Boris
Mayes, Steven Lee
Munoz, Rie (Marie Angelina Munoz)
Myers, Virginia Anne
Nadolski, Stephanie Lucille
Narotzky, Norman David
Nawara, Jim
Neal, (Minor) Avon
Neals, Otto
Nemec, Nancy
Nevelson, Louise
North, Judy
Olmsted, Suzanne M
Parry, Marian
Passuntino, Peter Zaccaria
Pinto, Angelo Raphael
Pitts, Richard G
Price, Kenneth
Raucher, Hava
Reddy, Krishna N
Renouf, Edda
Richards, Jeanne Herron
Robinson, Charlotte
Rogers, P J
Roman, Shirley
Rose, Roslyn
Rosenquit, Bernard
Rothbein, Renee
Rowan, Dennis Michael
Rutherford, Erica
Ruthling, Ford
Ryerson, Margery A
Sahlstrand, Margaret Ahrens
Salinas, Baruj
Sandgren, Ernest Nelson
Sarsony, Robert
Schary, Emanuel
Schoenbach, Bertha Karp
Schuselka, Elfi
Scott, Campbell
Scott, John Tarrell
Segan, Kenneth Akiva
Sharp, Anne
Siberell, Anne Hicks
Slipper, Gary Peter
Smith, Vincent D
Solomon, Bernard Alan
Spagnolo, Kathleen Mary
Stanforth, Melvin Sidney
Stark, Shirley
Stoltenberg, Donald Hugo
Stroh, Charles
Swartzman, Roslyn
Sznajderman, Marius S
Takal, Peter
Taylor, Sandra Ortiz
Thies, Charles Herman
Thomas, John
Tomchuk, Marjorie
Townley, Hugh
Tschacbasov, Nahum
Van Suchtelen, Adrian
Van Vliet, Claire
Vogel, Donald
Warner, Herbert Kelii, Jr
Weedman, Kenneth Russell
Weingarten, Hilde (Kevess)
Weisberg, Ruth Ellen
Woodbury, Josephine Osgood
Youkeles, Anne
Young, Nancy J(eanne)
Yudin, Carol
Zirker, Joseph
Zupan, Bruno

Serigraphy, Silkscreen

Adler, Lee
Ahlgren, Roy B
Anderson, Ivan Delos
Angeloch, Robert (Henry)
Arnold, Florence M

Ascher, Mary
Ascian
Auvil, Kenneth William
Azuma, Norio
Barrio, Raymond
Barsano, Ron (Ronald James)
Bartek, Tom
Berlyn, Sheldon
Berman, Ariane R
Berman, Vivian
Bishop, Barbara Lee
Block, Amanda Roth
Bogarin, Rafael
Bothwell, Dorr
Bowman, Dorothy (Louise)
Bradford, Howard
Brandt, Frederick Robert
Caples, Barbara Barrett
Cassanelli, Victor Vi
Chaddlesone, Sherman
Christensen, Ronald Julius
Christensen, Ted
Christ-Janer, Arland F
Clark, John Dewitt
Cohn, Max Arthur
Colville, Alexander
Craft, David Ralph
Curran, Darryl Joseph
Danby, Ken
Davies, Theodore Peter
Delgado-Guitart, Jose Luis
Dillon, Mildred (Murphy)
Doherty, Michael Stephen
Duff, Ann MacIntosh
Durham, William
Edwards, Ellender Morgan
Fitzgerald, Astrid
Foulger, Richard F
Fransioli, Thomas Adrian
Fumagalli, Barbara Merrill
Gardner, Andrew Bradford
Garwood, Audrey
Gersovitz, Sarah Valerie
Gill, Gene
Ginsburg, Estelle
Goldberg, Arnold Herbert
Golden, Libby
Goreleigh, Rex
Greenleaf, Esther (Hargrave)
Hamilton, Susan
Hanna, Paul Dean, Jr
Harvey, Donald
Hicken, Philip Burnham
High, Timothy Griffin
Hobbs, Robert Dean
Hodel, Diane Carol
Hotvedt, Kris J
Huff, Laura Weaver
Jensen, Marit
Jones, Frederick George
Kaye, Mildred Elaine
Kimura, Riisaburo
Kirkwood, Larry Thomas
Kirsten-Daiensai, Richard Charles
Knowles, Alison
Knudsen, Christian
Kohl, Barbara
Kohlmeyer, Ida (R)
Kohn, Bernard A
Kreneck, Lynwood
Lagorio, Irene R
Lambert, Ed
Lieberman, Meyer Frank
McAdoo, Carol Westbrook
McCall, Ann
McConnell, James Houston
McElroy, Jacquelyn Ann (Jacquelyn McElroy-Edwards)
Magistro, Charles John
Mahmoud, Ben
Mandziuk, Michael Dennis
Marder, Dorie
Maril, Herman
Massie, Lorna
Miller, Richard Kidwell

Mode, Carol A
Moon, Jim (James Monroe)
Moore, Michael Shannon
Navrat, Den (Dennis Edward)
Neiman, LeRoy
Newton, John Neil
Nind, Jean
Ocepek, Lou (Louis David)
O'Connell, Edward E
Oldham, Berton Jepsen
O'Meallie, Kitty (Kate Chamness Johnson)
Pattee, Rowena
Peace, Bernie (Kinzel)
Pletscher, Josephine Marie
Poleskie, Stephen Francis
Pond, Clayton
Price, Joe (Allen)
Priest, T (Theresa Khoury Struckus)
Ranson, Nancy Sussman
Robbins, Hulda D
Rosenblum, Jay
Ruby, Laura
Rugolo, Lawrence
Saalburg, Allen Russel
Sabelis, Huibert
Sachse, Janice R
Sassone, Marco
Schenck, William Clinton
Schlump, John Otto
Schwieger, C Robert
Shepherd, Reginald
Shimomura, Roger Yutaka
Shoulberg, Harry
Singer, Clifford
Sklar-Weinstein, Arlene (Joyce)
Slettehaugh, Thomas Chester
Stapp, Ray Veryl
Stomps, Walter E, Jr
Stone, Gwen
Stovall, Luther McKinley (Lou)
Stroud, Peter Anthony
Sullivan, Bill
Sullivan, David Francis
Teller, Douglas H
Ten Eyck, Catryna (Catryna Ten Eyck Seymour)
Tift, Mary Louise
Twitty, James (Watson)
Vaccaro, (Patt) Patrick Frank
Van Riper, Peter
Vaux, Richard
Volkin, Hilda Appel
von Weise, Wenda Fraker
Waddingham, John Alfred
Wald, Sylvia
Walker, James Adams
Walker, Joy
Wasserman, Burton

Woodcut

Abany, Albert Charles
Abbe, Elfriede Martha
Andrews, Sybil (Sybil Andrews Morgan)
Arnold, Paul Beaver
Bell, Alistair Macready
Berger, Jason
Bobak, Bruno Joseph
Bragar, Philip Frank
Brender a Brandis, Gerard William
Carter, (Charles) Bruce
Cassill, Herbert Carroll
Dance, Robert Bartlett
De Armond, Dale B
Dillon, Mildred (Murphy)
Elwell, Chip
Ente, Lily
Ettling, Ruth (Droitcour)
Ferro, Walter
Gary, Jan (Mrs William D Gorman)

Goldstein, Daniel Joshua
Grashow, James Bruce
Hedman, Teri Jo
High-Wasikhongo, Freida
Hnizdovsky, Jacques
Hodgell, Robert Overman
Howard, (Helen) Barbara
Idaherma (Idaherma Williams)
Inman, Pauline Winchester
Jaidinger, Judith C (Judith Clarann Szesko)
Jelinek, Hans
Kemble, Richard
Kermes, Constantine John
Kohn, Bernard A
Koster, Marjory Jean
McAdoo, Donald Eldridge
McNamara, William Patrick, Jr
Malo, Teri (Teri A Malo-Sprawka)
Matsubara, Naoko
Mogensen, Paul
Morrison, Robert Clifton
Mortensen, Gordon Louis
Noble, Helen (Harper)
Offner, Elliot
Poucher, Elizabeth Morris
Rowan, Frances Physioc
Satorsky, Cyril
Scharff, Constance Kramer
Shuff, Lily (Lillian Shir)
Skelley, Robert Charles
Slater, Van E
Summers, Carol
Uchima, Ansei
Vo-Dinh, Mai
Walker, Clay E
Waters, Herbert (Ogden)

PUBLISHER

Anbinder, Paul
Arnold, Jack
Banana, Anna Lee
Barton, John Murray
Bendig, William Charles
Bergling, Virginia Catherine (Mrs Stephen J Kozazcki)
Blinder, Martin S
Califano, Edward Christopher
Cloud, Jack L
Crandall, Judith Ann
Elwell, Chip
Esterow, Milton
Fedele, Frank D
Foster, Robert Stephen
Gaines, Alan Jay
Gladstone, M J
Goodman, Marian
Gray, Maxine Cushing
Grayson, Cassandra
Hicks, Sheila
Hill, John Conner
Hobbs, Gerald S
Hoffberg, Judith A
Hoffman, Carol Maree
Hooton, Bruce Duff
Ingraham, John Douglas
Isaacs, Avrom
Krantz, Les (Leslie J)
Lerner, Alexandria Sandra
Leutwyler, Bruce
Levin, Hugh Lauter
MacDonald, Colin Somerled
McGilvery, Laurence
McPherson, Bruce Rice
Mahlmann, John James
Meisel, Louis Koenig
Morton, Robert Alan
Pennypacker, James S
Posner, Judith L
Ring, Edward A
Rosenberg, Alex Jacob
Rosenberg, Bernard

PUBLISHER (cont)
Rosenthal, John W
Solodkin, Judith
Solomon, Richard H
Steward, Donn Horatio
Szoke, John
Tyler, Kenneth Eugene
Van Vliet, Claire
Westlund, Harry E
Whyte, Bruce Lincoln
Wilson, John David

RESTORER
see also Conservator

Bernstein, Gerald
Bodo, Sandor
Calkin, Carleton Ivers
Coleman, Gayle (Gayle Coleman MacDonald)
Fisher, Sarah Lisbeth
Flume, Violet Sigoloff
Greaves, James L
Hopkins, Kenneth R
Jakstas, Alfred John
Konrad, Tony (Anton Joseph)
Lamanna, Carmen
Lysun, Gregory
Mohr, Pauline Catherine
Morse, Mitchell Ian
Stacks, William Leon
Stein, Harve
Zarand, Julius John

SCULPTOR

Abadi, Fritzie
Adickes, David (Pryor)
Akamu, Nina
Andrews, Michael Frank
Angell, Tony
Annis, Norman L
Aronson, Sanda
Asher, Michael
Aston, Miriam
Balciar, Gerald George
Balderacchi, Arthur Eugene
Bales, J (Jean Elaine)
Barthe, Richmond
Barton, Georgie Read
Behl, Wolfgang
Berge, Dorothy Alphena
Beveridge, Karl J
Beyer, Steven J
Billian, Cathey R
Boggs, Franklin
Bohnenkamp, Leslie George
Bolinsky, Joseph Abraham
Borgatta, Isabel Case
Boszin, Andrew
Boxer, Stanley (Robert)
Brcin, John David
Brooks, Bruce W
Brown, Stephen Pat
Brush, Leif
Butter, Tom
Butterfield, Deborah Kay
Cabot, Hugh
Cantor, Mira (Mira Cantor-Piene)
Capobianco, Domenick
Casebere, James E
Cassidy, Margaret Carol (Mrs John Manship)
Castanis, Muriel (Julia Brunner)
Cenci, Silvana
Chambers, Park A, Jr
Chandler, Elisabeth Gordon
Chapman, (M) Anne
Chicago, Judy
Coheleach, Guy Joseph
Collyer, Robin
Conlon, James Edward

Cooney-Crawford, Thom M
Cove, Rosemary
Daley, William P
Danziger, Joan
Davidson, Thyra (Claire Thyra Wexler)
De Nike, Michael Nicholas
Dennis, Donna Frances
DeVegatales, Jugo
Dogancay, Burhan Cahit
Dowler, David P
Dreyer, Gay
Dusenbery, Walter
Edvi Illes, George
Fasnacht, Heide Ann
Fay, Ming G
Filkosky, Josefa
Fischer, R M
Fisher, Joel A
Fitzpatrick, Joseph Cyril
Flood, Edward C
Foster, Don
Frabel, Hans Godo
Frank, Jane
Fried, Howard Lee
Frudakis, Zenos
Fumagalli, Orazio
Gersh, Bill
Gershoy, Eugenie
Giacomantonio, Archimedes
Gifford, J Nebraska
Glickman, Arthur
Goldfinger, Eliot
Green, Jasha
Grimm, Raymond Max
Gronborg, Erik
Grooms, Red
Guberman, Sidney Thomas
Habergritz, George Joseph
Hammerbeck, Wanda Lee
Hartley, W Douglas
Hastenteufel, Dieter
Helsmoortel, Robert
Houston, Bruce
Huchthausen, David Richard
Hudson, Jon Barlow
Humphrey, Nene
Irving, Joan
Jacobs, Peter Alan
Johnston, Robert Porter
Jones, (Charles) Dexter (Weatherbee), III
Jones, Howard William
Jovine, Marcel
Julian, June
Kawashima, Takeshi
Kline, Richard R
Kotoske, Roger Allen
Kraus, (Ersilia) Zili
Krebs, Rockne
Kristensen, Gail Marie
LaChapelle, Joseph Robert
Lager, Fannie
Larson, Philip Seely
Laske, Lyle F
Leaf, June
Levy, Margaret Wasserman
Licht, Evelyn M
Lieberman, Louis (Karl)
Lindgren, Charlotte
Lipton, Sondra (Sahlman)
Little Chief, Barthell
Lubart, Henriette d'Arlin
Lucero, Michael (Lewis)
Lukasiewicz, Ronald Joseph
Lundeen, George Wayne
Lynch, Gerald Francis
Lynds, C (Clyde William)
Maclay, David (Sears), Jr
Mayer, Edward Albert
Mayer, Rosemary
Metz, Gerry Michael
Meyer, Ursula
Micale, Albert
Middlebrook, David A
Miller, (Richard) Guy
Mim, Adrienne C (Adrienne Claire Schwartz)

Murch, Anna Valentina
Newman, Sophie
Noel, Georges
Nugent, Bob L
Oginz, Richard
Palau, Marta
Pasinski, Irene
Patti, Tom
Pinkel, Sheila Mae
Pinto, Jody
Poliszczuk, Orest Stephan
Price, Joan Webster
Quisgard, Liz Whitney
Raciti, Cherie
Richardson, Sam
Riddle, John Thomas, Jr
Ridlon, James A
Rod, Bruce John
Rowan, (C) Patrick
Samuels, Edward George
Saret, Alan Daniel
Schiff, Jeffrey Allen
Schultz, Saunders
Schwartz, Aubrey E
Schwartz, Lillian (Feldman)
Sears, Stanton Gray
Seawright, James L, Jr
Seide, Paul A
Selwitz, Ruth F
Severson, William Conrad
Sherman, Sarai
Sica
Sinclair, Robert (W)
Skoglund, Sandra Louise
Snyder, Ruth (Cozen)
Southey, Trevor J T
Sponenburgh, Mark
Stearns, Thomas Robert
Sturgeon, John Floyd
Tacha, Athena
Taggart, William John
Tambellini, Aldo
Taylor, Michael (Estes)
Tefft, Elden Cecil
Tobin, John Edward, Jr
Trecker, Stanley Matthew
Tsai, Wen-Ying
Vivot, Lea (Lea Drahomira Vivot-Fishman)
von Ringelheim, Paul Helmut
Walton, Marion (Marion Walton Putnam)
Weiss, Rachel
Weissman, Walter
West, W Richard (Dick)
Whitson, Angie
Wiener, Daniel
Wright, Donald
Wright, Paul Morris
Yes, Phyllis A
Young, John T
Youngerman, Jack
Zeisler, Claire (Block)

All Media

Abbe, Elfriede Martha
Abish, Cecile
Acconci, Vito
Acton, Arlo C
Agostini, Peter
Ahvakana, Ulaaq (Lawrence Reynold)
Aidlin, Jerome
Ajay, Abe
Alaupovic, Alexandra V
Albrecht, Mary Dickson
Albright, Malvin Marr
Allumbaugh, James
Anargyros, Spero
Anastasi, William (Joseph)
Anderson, David C
Andre, Carl
Anthony, Lawrence Kenneth
Antonovici, Constantin
Appel, Eric A

Archambault, Louis
Arman
Asawa, Ruth (Ruth Asawa Lanier)
Aschenbach, (Walter) Paul
Axelrod, Miriam
Ayaso, Manuel
Aycock, Alice
Bachinski, Walter Joseph
Baldwin, John
Baldwin, Richard Wood
Balsley, John Gerald
Barbarossa, Theodore C
Barbeau, Marcel (Christian)
Bard, Joellen
Baskin, Leonard
Bates, Gladys Edgerly
Bayer, Jeffrey Joshua
Beason, Donald Ray
Beeler, Joe (Neil)
Beer, Kenneth John
Belfort-Chalat, Jacqueline
Beling, Helen
Bell, Larry Stuart
Bell, Lilian A
Benglis, Lynda
Benini
Benton, Fletcher
Ben-Zion
Berlant, Tony
Bernstein, Sylvia
Besner, J Jacques
Bieler, Ted Andre
Billeci, Andre George
Black, David Evans
Bladen, Ronald
Blair, Robert Noel
Blazeje, Zbigniew
Bleifeld, Stanley
Blodgett, Peter
Bonevardi, Marcelo
Bookatz, Samuel
Booth, Laurence Ogden
Borglum, James Lincoln de la Mothe
Borne, Mortimer
Bornstein, Eli
Bourgeois, Louise
Boyd, James Henderson
Bradshaw, Dove
Breer, Robert C
Breschi, Karen Lee
Brock, Robert W
Brodie, Agnes Hahn
Brody, Myron Roy
Brookins, Jacob Boden
Brose, Morris
Brosk, Jeffrey Owen
Brown, Bruce Robert
Brown, Joseph
Brown, Richard Morgan
Brulc, Lillian G
Brun, Thomas
Buba, Joy Flinsch
Buckner, Paul Eugene
Buczak, Brian Elliot
Bunin, Louis
Burchess, Arnold
Burden, Chris
Burg, Patricia Jean
Burgues, Irving Carl
Burnett, Patricia Hill
Busa, Peter
Bush, Beverly
Bussabarger, Robert Franklin
Butterbaugh, Robert Clyde
Calfee, William Howard
Campbell, Kenneth Floyd
Cantini, Virgil D
Carl, Joan
Carlberg, Norman Kenneth
Carlson, William D
Carr, Sally Swan
Carr-Harris, Ian Redford
Carter, Dean
Carter, Dudley Christopher
Carter, Granville W

SCULPTOR (cont)

Casanova, Aldo John
Casarella, Edmond
Cascieri, Arcangelo
Castoro, Rosemarie
Cecere, Gaetano
Chamberlain, David (Allen)
Chamberlain, John Angus
Chavez, Edward Arcenio
Christo
Chryssa (Vardea)
Ciuca, Eugen
Clements, Robert Donald
Clerk, Pierre
Coe, Matchett Herring
Collings, Betty
Collins, Jim
Conaway, Gerald
Cook, Robert Howard
Coppola, Andrew
Corwin, Sophia M
Cox, Ernest Lee
Crawley, Wesley V
Creech, Franklin Underwood
Crimmins, Jerry (Gerald
    Garfield)
Crist, William Gary
Cronin, Robert (Lawrence)
Crotto, Paul
Croydon, Michael Benet
Daly, Norman
Daly, Stephen Jeffrey
Danhausen, Eldon
Darriau, Jean-Paul
Darricarrere, Roger
    Dominique
Davidson, Allan Albert
Davies, Haydn Llewellyn
Deaton, Charles
de Gerenday, Laci Anthony
Dehner, Dorothy
DeLap, Tony
De Larios, Dora
DeLauro, Joseph Nicola
de la Vega, Enrique Miguel
de Lesseps, Tauni
de Lisio, Michael
DeLonga, Leonard Anthony
De Lue, Donald
De Marco, Jean Antoine
De Maria, Walter
de Miskey, Julian
De Pedery-Hunt, Dora
Dergalis, George
Dern, F Carl
De Weldon, Felix George
    Weihs
DiGiusto, Gerald N
Dill, Guy Girard
Dill, Laddie John
Dimondstein, Morton
Dinardo, Joseph E
Dine, James
Dioda, Adolph T
Diodato, Baldo
Dirube, Rolando Lopez
Di Suvero, Mark
Domareki, Joseph Theodore
Donati, Enrico
Donneson, Seena
Downing, Robert James
Drake, James
Drumm, Don
Dryfoos, Nancy
Dunbar, Russell Raymond
Dunwiddie, Charlotte
Dwyer, Gary Colburn
Edge, Douglas Benjamin
Efrat, Benni
Egri, Ted
Elder, David Morton
Eliscu, Frank
Emery, Lin
Etrog, Sorel
Ettl, Georg
Facci, Domenico (Aurelio)
Faden, Lawrence Steven

Fane, Lawrence
Fasano, Clara
Favro, Murray
FeBland, Harriet
Feigenbaum, Harriet (Mrs Neil
    Chamberlain)
Fernie, John Chipman
Ferrara, Jackie
Fessler, Mary Thomasita
Fine, Jud
Finkelstein, Max
Fiore, Rosario Russell
Floyd, Carl Leo
Fogel, Seymour
Forakis, Peter
Forst, Miles
Francis, Madison Ke, Jr
Franklin, Charlotte White
Franklin, Gilbert Alfred
Fraughton, Edward James
Fredericks, Marshall
    Maynard
Freeland, William Lee
French, Jared
Friedlaender, Bilge
Friedman, Alan
Fugate-Wilcox, Terry
Gach, George
Gage, Frances M
Gagnon, Charles Eugene
Gallo, Enzo D
Gallo, Frank
Gasparro, Frank
Gates, Harry Irving
Geber, Hana
Gebhardt, Harold
Gebhardt, Peter Martin
Gebhardt, Roland
Geran, Joseph, Jr
Giampietro, Isabel (Isabel A
    Giampietro Knoll)
Gianakos, Cristos
Gibran, Kahlil George
Gill, James (Francis)
Gitlin, Michael
Glasco, Joseph M
Goeritz, Mathias
Golubic, Theodore
Gonzalez, Xavier
Goto, Joseph
Graham, Walter
Granlund, Paul Theodore
Gray, Jim
Green, David Oliver
Greene-Mercier, Marie Zoe
Greenleaf, Kenneth Lee
Gressel, Michael L
Grippe, Peter
Gross, Chaim
Gross, Charles Merrill
Grossman, Nancy
Grosvenor, Robert
Grove, Jean Donner
Gurria, Angela
Haacke, Hans Christoph
Haber, Ira Joel
Hadfield, Ted Lee
Hadzi, Dimitri
Haley, John Charles
Halkin, Theodore
Hamouda, Amy (Amy
    Middleton Hamouda Bice)
Hancock, Walker (Kirtland)
Hansen, James Lee
Harries, Mags (Margaret L)
Harris, Julian Hoke
Harvey, (William) Andre
Hayward, Peter
Hedrick, Wally Bill
Hendricks, Edward Lee
Hera
Herard, Marvin T
Heric, John F
Hernandez, Sam (Samuel
    Rudolph)
Hesketh
Hewitt, Duncan Adams

Higgins, (George) Edward
Hinman, Charles B
Hirsch, Willard Newman
Hobbs, (Carl) Fredric
Holbrook, Elizabeth Bradford
Holen, Norman Dean
Holt, Charlotte Sinclair
Holt, Nancy Louise
Horn, Milton
Horwitt, Will
Hovsepian, Leon
Howard, Cecil Ray
Hudson, Robert H
Hunt, Bryan
Hunter, Leonard LeGrande, III
Hurtig, Martin Russell
Irwin, Robert
Italiano, Joan
Izuka, Kunio
Jackson, Hazel Brill
Jackson, Sarah
Jacob, Ned
Jacobson, Ursula Mercedes
Jacquard
Jacques, Russell Kenneth
Jandeni (Jean-Denis Cruchet)
Jean-Louis, Don (Donald
    Charles)
Jellico, Nancy R
Jensen, Leo (Vernon)
Johanson, Patricia
Johnson, Martin Brian
Jones, Ben
Jones, Carter R(uthven)
Jones, Edward Powis
Jones, Jerry
Jonynas, Vytautas K
Jordan, Jack
Kaiser, Benjamin
Kaish, Luise
Kane, Margaret Brassler
Karpel, Eli
Kassoy, Hortense
Kasuba, Aleksandra
Kaufman, Mico
Kaz, Nathaniel
Kearl, Stanley Brandon
Kelley, Donald William
Kelly, Ellsworth
Kennedy, James Edward
Kepalas (Elena Kepalaite)
Kessler, Alan
King, William Dickey
Kirk, Jerome
Kirschenbaum, Bernard Edwin
Kiselewski, Joseph
Kissel, William Thorn, Jr
Kleiman, Alan
Klein, Sandor C
Klotz-Reilly, Suzanne Ruth
Knapp, Tom
Knobler, Nathan
Koch, Edwin E
Koepnick, Robert Charles
Koochin, William
Koras, George
Korman, Barbara
Kos, Paul Joseph
Koss, Gene H
Kowal, Dennis J
Kowalski, Dennis Allen
Kratina, K George
Kravitz, Walter
Kreznar, Richard J
Krugman, Irene
Kujundzic, Zeljko D
Kurhajec, Joseph A
Kusama, Yayoi
Kuvshinoff, Bertha Horne
Kuvshinoff, Nicolai
Lafon, Dee J
Lamis, Leroy
Landis, Lily
Larsen, Patrick Heffner
Lauck, Anthony Joseph
Lawton, James L
Lay, Patricia Anne

Ledyard, Walter William
Leech, Merle Eugene
Leeper, Doris Marie
Lehman, Irving
Lekakis, Michael Nicholas
Lesher, Marie Palmisano
Leventhal, Ruth Lee
Levine, Les
Levinson, Mon
Le Witt, Sol
Liberi, Dante
Liberman, Alexander
Lichtenstein, Roy
Lijn, Liliane
Liles, Raeford Bailey
Lintault, Roger Paul
Lionni, Leo
Lipman-Wulf, Peter
Lipofsky, Marvin B
Lipton, Seymour
Little, Ken Dawson
Lobello, Peter
Lo Medico, Thomas Gaetano
Lopez, Rhoda Le Blanc
Lorcini, Gino
Lorenzani, Arthur Emanuele
Lothrop, Kristin Curtis
Love, Jim
Lucchesi, Bruno
Luisi, Jerry
Lux, Gwen
Lyford, Cabot
McCracken, John Harvey
McCracken, Philip
McCullough, David William
McDonnell, Joseph Anthony
McElcheran, William Hodd
MacLean-Smith, Elizabeth
McManus, James William
McVey, William M
McWhorter, Elsie Jean
Madsen, Loren Wakefield
Magenta, Muriel
Magnan, Oscar Gustav
Maki, Robert Richard
Mallary, Robert
Mallory, Ronald
Mandel, Howard
Mankowski, Bruno
Mansfield, Robert Adams
Manuella, Frank R
Margoulies, Berta (Berta
    Margoulies O'Hare)
Margulies, Isidore
Marioni, Paul
Marisol, Escobar
Markle, Sam
Martin, Knox
Mason, Novem M
Matteson, Ira
Matthews, Harriett
Mazzone, Domenico
Meizner, Paula
Mellor, George Edward
Meyer, Fred (Robert)
Milder, Jay
Miller, Brenda
Miller, Donald Richard
Miller, Richard McDermott
Mills, Agnes
Mills, Lev Timothy
Minisci, Brenda (Eileen)
Mintich, Mary Ringelberg
Miralda, Antoni
Miss, Mary
Model, Elisabeth D
Molinari, Guido
Monaghan, William Scott
Morgan, Arthur C
Morgan, Helen Bosart (Mrs
    Edwin M Wagstaff)
Morris, Hilda
Morris, Robert
Moss, Joe (Francis)
Mueller, Henrietta Waters
Mundt, Ernest Karl
Murphy, Hass

SCULPTOR (cont)

Murray, Ian Stewart
Myers, Forrest Warden
Myers, Legh
Myers, Martin
Nagler, Fred
Nakian, Reuben
Nardin, Mario
Nash, Katherine E
Nasisse, Andy S
Naylor, John Geoffrey
Nelson, Carey Boone
Nelson, Jack D
Neubert, George Walter
Nevelson, Louise
Nevelson, Mike
Newmark, Marilyn (Marilyn
　　Newmark Meiselman)
Nickford, Juan
Nicodemus, Chester Roland
Nivola, Constantino
Nix, Patricia (Lea)
Noguchi, Isamu
Nong
Nordin, Phyllis E
Norvell, Patsy
Ocvirk, Otto G
O'Hanlon, Richard E
Oppenheim, Dennis A
Orensanz, Angel L
Ortiz, Rafael Montanez
Ortlieb, Robert Eugene
Ortman, George Earl
Orze, Joseph John
Osze, Andrew E
Oubre, Hayward Louis
Padovano, Anthony John
Paradise, Phil (Herschel)
Parton, Ralf
Payne, John D
Pearson, James Eugene
Peck, Judith
Peii, Ahmad Osni
Pekar, Ronald Walter
Pershing, Louise
Phillips, Helen (Elizabeth)
Piccolo, Thomas Frank
Pierce, Danny P
Pierce, James Smith
Pineda, Marianna
Pogzeba, Wolfgang H
Pollack, Reginald Murray
Popinsky, Arnold Dave
Posey, Leslie Thomas
Post, Anne B
Potts, Don
Prince, Richard Edmund
Pruitt, Lynn
Puccinelli, Raimondo
Quinn, Brian Grant
Rabinovitch, William Avrum
Rabinowitch, David
Rabinowitch, Royden Leslie
Raimondi, John Richard
Randall, (Lillian) Paula
Rasto (Rastislav Hlavina)
Ratkai, George
Ray, Robert (Donald)
Rebbeck, Lester James, Jr
Remsing, (Joseph) Gary
Renick, Charles Cooley
Rhodes, James Melvin
Richardson, Gretchen (Mrs
　　Ronald Freelander)
Richenburg, Robert Bartlett
Risley, John Hollister
Roberts, Gilroy
Rocklin, Raymond
Rodriguez, Oscar
Rogers, John H
Romano, Umberto Roberto
Romans, Van Anthony
Rosati, James
Roseberg, Carl Andersson
Ross, Charles
Ross, Douglas Allan
Roster, Fred Howard

Rotan, Walter
Rothfarb, Ed (Edwin I)
Roussel, Claude Patrice
Rudy, Charles
Rush, Jon N
Rust, Edwin C
Sabatini, Raphael
St Maur, Kirk (Kirk Seymour
　　McReynolds)
Samaras, Lucas
Samstag, Gordon
Samuels, Gerald
Sanabria, Robert
Sato, Tadashi
Saunders, Wade
Savelli, Angelo
Saxe, Henry
Scanga, Italo
Scarpitta, Salvatore
Schlemowitz, Abram
Schmidt, Arnold Alfred
Schmidt, Julius
Schmutzhart, Berthold Josef
Schmutzhart, Slaithong
　　Chengtrakul
Schneider, Noel
Schwalbach, Mary Jo
Schweiss, Ruth Keller
Schweitzer, Gertrude
Schwidder, Ernst Carl
Searles, Stephen
Segal, George
Seletz, Emil
Seplowin, Charles Joseph
Serra, Richard
Serra, Rudy
Shapshak, Rene
Shaw, Mary Todd
Shaw, Richard Blake
Sherbell, Rhoda
Shorney, Margo Kay (McIver)
Sider, Deno
Siler, Todd (Lael)
Silver, Thomas C
Simkin, Phillips M
Simon, Sidney
Simonds, Charles Frederick
Sinaiko, Arlie
Sinnard, Elaine (Janice)
Sisler, Rebecca
Smith, John Ivor
Smith, Tony
Smyth, David Richard
Soleri, Paolo
Sonnenberg, Frances
Soteras, Jaime
Spohn, Franz Frederick
Squier, Jack Leslie
Squires, Norma-Jean
Stark, George King
Stein, Ronald Jay
Steiner, Michael
Stelzer, Michael Norman
Sterne, Dahli
Stevanov, Zoran
Stiegelmeyer, Norman Earl
Stokes, Louis (Walter)
Stoloff, Irma
Stolpe, Daniel Owen
Storer, Inez Mary
Storm, Larue
Straight, Elsie H
Strautmanis, Edvins
Strawn, Jarrett W (Jason)
Strawn, Melvin Nicholas
Struppeck, Jules
Sturman, Eugene
Stussy, Maxine Kim
Sugarman, George
Sullivan, Ronald Dee
Sunderland, Nita Kathleen
Svenson, John Edward
Tajiri, Shinkichi
Tangredi, Vincent
Tascona, Antonio Tony
Tatti, Benedict Michael
Taylor, Bill (William Bradley)

Taysom, Wayne Pendelton
Teraoka, Masami
Terrell, Allen Townsend
Terris, Albert
Tewi, Thea
Thomas, Robert Chester
Thomas, Steffen Wolfgang
Timpson, Michael G
Tobias, Abraham Joel
Tobias, Robert Paul
Torffield, Marvin
Tracy, Michael
Trakas, George
Trakis, Louis
Treister, Kenneth
Trova, Ernest Tino
Tsai, Hsiao Hsia
Tucker, William G
Turner, James Thomas, Sr
Turner, Ralph James
Unger, Mary Ann
Urban, Reva
Utz, Thornton
Valentine, DeWain
Vallance, Jeffrey K R
Vallila, Marja R
Van Loen, Alfred
Van Sant, Tom R
Van Vranken, Rose (Rose Van
　　Vranken Hickey)
Van Winkle, Lester G
Varga, Ferenc
Visco, Anthony Salvatore
von Meyer, Michael
Von Schlegell, David
Voulkos, Peter
Wahling, Jon B
Walch, John Leo
Walker, Herbert Brooks
Walter, Valerie Harrisse
Wanlass, Stanley Glen
Wasey, Jane
Weill, Erna
Wein, Albert W
Weinberg, Elbert
Weiner, Lawrence Charles
Weinman, Robert Alexander
Weiss, Harvey
Welch, Roger
Werner, Nat
Weschler, Anita
Westcoast, Wanda
Weyhe, Arthur
Wheeler, Orson Shorey
White, Robert (Winthrop)
Whiten, Tim
Whittome, Irene Dianne
Widstrom, Edward Frederick
Wiener, Sam (Evangeline
　　Tabasco)
Williams, Randalph Andrew
Williams, Todd
Willis, Jay Stewart
Willson, Margaret (Bosshardt)
　　Pace
Wilmarth, Christopher Mallory
Wilson, Edward N
Wilson, Nicholas Jon
Wimberley, Frank Walden
Wingate, Arline (Hollander)
Winkel, Nina
Winsor, V Jacqueline
Witold-K (Kaczanowski)
Wolfe, Ann (Ann Wolfe
　　Graubard)
Woodham, Derrick James
Woody, (Thomas) Howard
Worth, Karen
Worth, Peter John
Yanish, Elizabeth
Yokoi, Rita
Young, Joseph Louis
Zack, Badanna Bernice
Zahourek, Jon Gail
Zajac, Jack
Zelenak, Edward John
Zucker, Barbara M

Zurik, Jesselyn Benson
Zwick, Rosemary G

Clay

Abeles, Sigmund
Acosta, Manuel Gregorio
Alquilar, Maria
Amaya, Armando
Anthonisen, George Rioch
Arneson, Robert
Bailey, Clayton George
Baney, Ralph Ramoutar
Bova, Joe
Breschi, Karen Lee
Breslin, Wynn
Bronson, Clark Everice
Bryant, Olen L
Budny, Virginia
Bugbee-Jackson, Joan (Mrs
　　John M Jackson)
Buonagurio, Toby Lee
Caplan, Jerry L
Carr, Sally Swan
Caswell, Jim (James Daniel
　　Caswell-Davis)
Caver, William Ralph
Chalke, John
Chappelle, Jerry Leon
Chavez, Joseph Arnold
Cindric, Michael Anthony
Citrin, Judith
Conover, Claude
Cornell, David E
Cossitt, Franklin D
Costanza, John Joseph
Cronbach, Robert M
Crowell, Lucius
Culbreth, Carl R
Dintenfass, Marylyn
Dombek, Blanche M
Donhauser, Paul Stefan
Dyyon, Frazier
Earl, Jack Eugene
Eino
Elliot, Cathy J
Elsner, Larry Edward
Fafard, Joe
Fellows, Fred
Ferreira, (Armando) Thomas
Franklin, Patt
Funk, Verne J
Furman, David Stephen
Gaylord, Frank Chalfant , II
Gernhardt, Henry Kendall
Gilhooly, David James, III
Glasgow, Lukman
Gould, Stephen
Goulet, Lorrie
Grasso, Doris (Ten-Eyck)
Graves, Bradford
Hammond, Phyllis Baker
Hanson, J B
Havens, Jan
Hay, Dick
Hempler, Orval F
Higby, (Donald) Wayne
Hodgell, Robert Overman
Hofsted, Jolyon Gene
Hood, Dorothy
Jacobson, Yolande (Mrs J
　　Craig Sheppard)
Jolley, Geraldine H (Jerry)
Kaiser, Diane
Kelsey, Muriel Chamberlin
Knowlton, Grace Farrar
Kottler, Howard William
Laird, E Ruth
Lantz, Michael
Larsen, D Dane
Lee, Dora Fugh
Lerman, Ora
Levine, Marilyn Anne
Ludwig, Eva
MacClintock, Dorcas
McGarry, Patricia Josephine

SCULPTOR (cont)

Mason, John
Massaro, Karen Thuesen
Mayorga, Gabriel Humberto
Melchert, James Frederick
Mignosa, Santo
Milnes, Robert Winston
Moquin, Richard Attilio
Morgan, Frances Mallory
Muccioli, Anna Maria
Mueller, Trude
Muir, Emily Lansingh
Natzler, Otto
Nicholas, Donna Lee
Nickerson, Ruth (Ruth
    Nickerson Greacen)
Nieto, John W
Notkin, Richard T
Olsen, Frederick L
Ortmayer, Constance
Pearson, Clifton
Piepenburg, Robert
Poucher, Elizabeth Morris
Prange, Sally Bowen
Rady, Elsa
Randall, Theodore A
Raskind, Philis
Redd Ekks (Robert Norman
    Rasmussen)
Rosen, Hy (Hyman Joseph)
Rosenblatt, Adolph
Rosenthal, Rachel
Sandor, Josephine (Beardsley)
Schaefer, Gail
Schietinger, James Frederick
Selvin, Nancy
Shannonhouse, Sandra Lynne
    Riddell
Shrady, Frederick
Simon, Jewel Woodard
Smith, Cecil Alden
Soldner, Paul Edmund
Spampinato, Clemente
Spinosa, Gary Paul
Spinski, Victor
Squires, Gerald Leopold
Stewart, Bill
Strassberg, Roy I
Stull, Robert J
Stussy, Maxine Kim
Sundin, Adelaide Toombs
Swanson, J N
Takemoto, Henry Tadaaki
Taylor, Frederick Bourchier
Taylor, Rosemary
Termini, Christine
Tornheim, Norman
Townsend, Storm D
Unterseher, Chris Christian
Vandenberge, Peter Willem
Wallace, Elizabeth S
Watson, Helen Richter
Williams, Gerald
Wilmeth, Ernest, II
Wu, Linda Yee Chau
Yiannes (Iordanides)
Zakin, Mikhail
Zheutlin, Dale R

Metal, Cast

Abdell, Douglas
Adams, Alice
Adelman, Bunny
Albert, Calvin
Allen, Margo (Mrs Harry
    Shaw)
Allen, Tom, Jr
Allwell, Stephen S
Amaya, Armando
Aronson, David
Arteche (Hector Arteche
    Martinez)
Bartlett, Donald Loring
Bascom, Earl W
Beasley, Bruce

Bentov, Mirtala
Bermudez, Jose Ygnacio
Biederman, Charles (Karel
    Joseph)
Binning, Robin
Blair, Helen
Blum, Helaine Dorothy
Bogucki, (Edwin Arnold)
Born, James E
Breinin, Raymond
Breitenbach, William John
Bright, Barney
Bronson, Clark Everice
Bultman, Fritz
Burns, Stan
Buscaglia, Jose
Caparn, Rhys (Rhys Caparn
    Steel)
Carlson, George Arthur
Chemeche, George
Clague, John Rogers
Clark, John Dewitt
Cleary, Fritz
Cook, John (Alfred)
Coughlin, Jack
Cronbach, Robert M
Dagys, Jacob
D'Ashnash-Tosi (Barbara
    Chase-Riboud)
Daudelin, Charles
De Bellis, Hannibal
Dombek, Blanche M
Dorrien, Carlos Guillermo
Drapell, Joseph
Duca, Alfred Milton
Duhme, H Richard, Jr
Du Pen, Everett George
Eino
Eloul, Kosso
Eriksen, Gary
Farrow, Patrick Villiers
Fenci, Renzo
Ferrari, Virginio Luig
Filipovic, Augustin
Filipowski, Richard E
Fiore, Rosario Russell
Fisher, Kenneth Lee
Fix, John Robert
Forrester, Charles Howard
Fox, Lincoln H
Froman, Ann
Frudakis, Anthony
Fuhrman, Esther
George, Dan
Giambertone, Paul
Gibbs, Tom
Gillespie, Dorothy Muriel
Giusti, George
Goodacre, Glenna
Gore, Samuel Marshall
Grausman, Philip
Gray, Cleve
Greenamyer, George Mossman
Hampton, John W
Hampton, Lucille Charlotte
Hanbury, Una
Hansen, James Lee
Hardin, Adlai S
Harootian, Khoren Der
Harrison, Carole
Harvey, (William) Andre
Haskin, Donald Marcus
Hayes, David Vincent
Holschuh, (George) Fred
Horne, (Arthur Edward)
    Cleeve
Hunt, Richard Howard
Hunter, Meridith
Huntington, Jim
Iselin, Lewis
Jackson, Harry Andrew
Jacobson, Yolande (Mrs J
    Craig Sheppard)
Jae
Johnson, J Seward, Jr
Johnston, Barry Woods
Jones, Elizabeth A B

Kammerer, Herbert Lewis
Kaskey, Raymond John
Katz, Eunice
Khendry, Janak Kumar
Kimmelman, Harold
Knapp, Sadie Magnet
Koenig, Elizabeth
Koras, George
Kramer, Reuben
La Malfa, James Thomas
Langland, Harold Reed
Lantz, Michael
Laslo, Patricia Louise (Laslo-
    Neukranz)
Lekberg, Barbara Hult
Linn, Steven Allen
Lipman, Stan
Lippold, Richard
Little, John
Longley, Bernique
Lubbers, Leland Eugene
Ludtke, Lawrence Monroe
Manning, Hilda Scudder
Manton, Jock (Archimedes
    Aristides Giacomantonio)
Marinsky, Harry
Mavroudis, Demetrios
Mayhew, Elza
Meadmore, Clement L
Medrich, Libby E
Meyer, Seymour W
Meyers, Francis Joseph
Miller, Richard McDermott
Morcos, Maher N
Morin, Thomas Edward
Moyers, William
Myford, James C
Nama, George Allen
Naranjo, Michael Alfred
Nelson, Carey Boone
Nesbitt, Lowell (Blair)
Newmark, Marilyn (Marilyn
    Newmark Meiselman)
Noland, William
Noordhoek, Harry Cecil
Notaro, Anthony
Offner, Elliot
Ottiano, John William
Otto, Catherine K(lemann)
Owen, Bill
Oxman, Mark
Pera, Isabella
Perless, Robert
Pierce, Diane
Piet, John Frances
Polk, Frank Fredrick
Polland, Donald Jack
Price, Michael Benjamin
Rabbit, William E
Recanati, Dina
Reed, Hal
Reiland, Lowell Keith
Rice, Anthony Hopkins
Rich, Frances L
Richter, Hank
Rosenblum, Richard Stephen
Ross, Clifford
Rozzi (James A)
Rubin, Donald Vincent
Rubins, David Kresz
Sauls, Frederick Inabinette
Schlam, Murray J
Schon, Nancy Quint
Schonwalter, Jean Frances
Scott, C(harles) A(rthur)
Scriver, (Bob) Robert Macfie
Sebastian
Shapiro, Joel (Elias)
Sheppard, Joseph Sherly
Shrady, Frederick
Silvertooth, Dennis Carl
Simon, Helene
Sing Hoo
Slivka, David
Smith, Kent Alvin
Snidow, Gordon E
Soviak, Harry

Spampinato, Clemente
Speed, (Ulysses) Grant
Storm, Mark (Kennedy)
Suttman, Paul
Swergold, Marcelle M
Talaba, L (Linda Talaba
    Cummens)
Tamburine, Jean
Tauch, Waldine Amanda
Taylor, Joseph Richard
Taylor, Marie
Taylor, Rod Allen
Terken, John
Townsend, Storm D
Trudeau, Yves
Turner, Raymond
Ullberg, Kent
Vielehr, William Ralph
Vrana, Albert S
Wagoner, Robert B
Wardlaw, George Melvin
Weems, Katharine Lane
Weiner, Egon
Wesselmann, Tom
White, Bruce Hilding
Williams, Chester Lee
Williams, Wayne Francis
Wilson, John
Wood, Marcia Joan
Woodman, Timothy
Wright, G Alan
Zacha, William
Zaikine, Zak (Victor Eugene)
Zivic, William Thomas
Zucker, Murray Harvey

Metal, Precious

Bennett, Jamie
Boggs, Mayo Mac
Farris-Larson, Gail
Filipowski, Richard E
Fridakis, Gera Hesness
Herschler, David Elijah
Jae
Klavans, Minnie
Long, Frank Weathers
Manhold, John Henry
Norman, Emile
Pinto, James
Polland, Donald Jack
Prestini, James Libero
Rubin, Donald Vincent
Russin, Robert I
Safer, John
Sebastian
Sehring, Adolf
Steider, Doris (Mrs C B
    McCampbell)
Tovish, Harold

Metal, Welded

Aidlin, Jerome
Anderson, David Paul
Balossi, John
Barnes, Carroll
Barrett, Bill
Beal, Mack
Bentham, Douglas Wayne
Benton, Suzanne E
Bigger, Michael D
Bolomey, Roger Henry
Bottini, David M
Bowie, William
Bright, Barney
Buchanan, Sidney Arnold
Buchman, James Wallace
Burt, David Sill
Cariola, Robert J
Carron, Maudee Lilyan
Cervantes, Pedro
Chase, Allan (Seamans)
Chase, Jack S(paulding)
Clark, Nancy Kissel

SCULPTOR (cont)

Crouch, Ned Philbrick
Daudelin, Charles
Davis, Michael A
DeAngelis, Joseph Rocco
De Guatemala, Joyce (Joyce Bush Vourvoulias)
De Rivera, Jose
Dhaemers, Robert August
D'Innocenzo, Nick Jerome
Dunbar, Michael Austin
Eldredge, Mary Agnes
Ellison, Robert W
Eversley, Frederick John
Farrow, Patrick Villiers
Ferber, Herbert
Ferrari, Virginio Luig
Fisher, James Donald
Frazier, Paul D
Friedberg, Richard S
Giambertone, Paul
Gibbs, Tom
Ginnever, Charles
Grady, Ruby McLain
Grossberg, Jake
Gussow, Roy
Hall, Michael David
Hardy, Thomas (Austin)
Harrington, William Charles
Harrison, Carole
Hatchett, Duayne
Hay, Ike
Hayes, David Vincent
Heany, David Cameron
Henry, John Raymond
Herschler, David Elijah
Holschuh, (George) Fred
Hunt, Richard Howard
Ihara, Michio
Indiana, Robert
Indick, Janet
Inukai, Kyohei
Jacobs, David (Theodore)
Jennings, Francis
Jensen, Hank
Kapsalis, Thomas Harry
Katzen, Lila (Pell)
Kelly, Lee
Kemble, Richard
Kimmelman, Harold
Kington, L(ouis) Brent
Knoebel, David Jon
Knowlton, Grace Farrar
Kupferman, Murray
Leeber, Sharon Corgan
Lekberg, Barbara Hult
Logan, Gene Adams
Lowe, J Michael
Luczun, Robert
Lupori, Peter John
McConnell, Michael Patrick
Malpass, Michael Allen
Mark, Phyllis
Markusen, Thomas Roy
Meadmore, Clement L
Meizner, Paula
Miller, J(ohn) Brough
Murray, Robert (Gray)
Noland, William
Nugent, John Cullen
Pascual, Manolo
Peart, Jerry Linn
Pepper, Beverly
Perless, Robert
Perlman, Joel Leonard
Perry, Charles O
Perry, Frank
Piepenburg, Robert
Porter, (Edwin) David
Power, S Brenda Joan
Rand, Steven Jay
Ray, Christopher T
Reginato, Peter
Renk, Merry
Rhoden, John W
Rich, Frances L
Rickey, George W

Riegel, Michael Byron
Riveron, Enrique
Rosenthal, Tony (Bernard)
Rush, Jon N
Salomon, Lawrence
Schlam, Murray J
Schleeh, Hans Martin
Schreiber, Martin
Schwebel, Renata Manasse
Sellers, William Freeman
Shaw, Elsie Babbitt
Shaw, Ernest Carl
Sherwood, A (Frances Ann Crane)
Shimoda, Osamu
Shire, Peter
Shostak, Edwin Bennett
Silverman, Sherley C
Simon, Herbert Bernheimer
Slater, Gary Lee
Slusky, Joseph
Smalley, David Allan
Snelson, Kenneth D
Stauffer, Richard L
Steen, Carol J
Stern, Jan Peter
Sutter, James Stewart
Taira, Frank
Tardo, (Manuel) Rodulfo
Tatro, Ronald Edward
Todd, Michael Cullen
Trudeau, Yves
Tsutakawa, George
Udinotti, Agnese
Vaccarino, Robin
Van Alstine, John Richard
Van de Bovenkamp, Hans
Venet, Bernar P
Ventimiglia, John Thomas
Wagner, G Noble
Walburg, Gerald
Wall, Brian
Warsinske, Norman George, Jr
White, Bruce Hilding
Williams, Chester Lee
Williams, Wayne Francis
Witkin, Isaac
Witt, Nancy Camden
Woitena, Ben S
Wojcik, Gary Thomas
Wolfe, James
Wood, Marcia Joan
Woodham, Jean

Miscellaneous Media

Aarons, Anita
Abeles, Kim Victoria
Abrams, Edith Lillian
Adams, Alice
Allen, Roberta
Allman, Margo
Alpert, Bill (William H)
Anderson, James P
Anderson, Kenneth Edmund
Anker, Suzanne C
Antonakos, Stephen
Appel, Keith Kenneth
Artemis, Maria (Maria Artemis Papageorge Sawyer)
Artschwager, Richard Ernst
Aycock, Alice
Bakaty, Mike
Baldwin, Harold Fletcher
Banerjee, (Bimal)
Barr, David John
Battenberg, John
Beckman, Ericka
Bell, Larry Stuart
Benes, Barton Lidice
Ben Tre, Howard
Berge, Henry
Berhang, Mattie
Bickley, Gary Steven
Bigger, Michael D

Bisgyer, Barbara G (Cohn)
Blum, Andrea
Booth, Robert Alan
Bradley, David P(aul)
Braitstein, Marcel
Brams, Joan
Breder, Hans Dieter
Brewster, Michael
Brown, Marvin Prentiss
Bucher, George Robert
Bundy, Stephen Allen
Burr, Horace
Burton, Scott
Byars, Donna
Cable, Maxine Roth
Campbell, Charles Malcolm
Campoli, Cosmo
Canfield, Jane (White)
Card, Greg S
Carmichael, Jae
Casey, John Joseph
Cavanaugh, John W
Chase, Jack S(paulding)
Christo
Cicansky, Victor
Clague, John Rogers
Clef, Roman A (Henry E Guerriero)
Clifton, Michelle Gamm
Cohen, Adele
Coughtry, Graham
Cowan, Aileen Hooper
Crow, Carol (Wilson)
Cunningham, J
Curmano, Billy
Curtis, Dolly Powers
Curtis, Robert D
Dailey, Dan (Daniel Owen)
Daphnis, Nassos
Daugherty, Marshall Harrison
Daugherty, Michael F
Davis, David Ensos
Dean, Nat(alie Carol)
DeArcangelis, Gloria
Dell, Robert Christopher
De Luca, Joseph Victor
Deming, David Lawson
Di Meo, Dominick
Dimond, Terry Jarrard
Duff, John Ewing
Dyens, Georges Maurice
East, N S, Jr
Eide, Palmer
Ente, Lily
Estern, Neil
Evans, Robert Graves
Falkenstein, Claire
Feldman, Bella Tabak
Fender, Tom Mac
Ferguson, Kathleen Elizabeth
Ferrer, Rafael
Fink, Ray (Raymond Russell)
Finke, Leonda Froelich
Fish, Robert
Fisher, Rob (Robert Norman)
Flakey Rose Hip
Floeter, Kent
Follett, Jean Frances
Fontanini, Clare
Fornelli, Joseph
Forrestall, Thomas De Vany
Freeman-Appelbaum, Margery
Frey, Viola
Friedeberg, Pedro
Friscia, Albert
Frudakis, Evangelos William
Fuller, Mary (Mary Fuller McChesney)
Galen, Elaine
Gellis, Sandy L
Gianakos, Steve
Gillingwater, Denis Claude
Giobbi, Edward Gioachino
Gironda, R
Glaser, David
Glasson, Lloyd
Glickman, Maurice

Goff, Thomas Jefferson
Gold, Martha B
Goldstein, Daniel Joshua
Goodridge, Lawrence Wayne
Gordin, Sidney
Gordon, John S
Gorski, Daniel Alexander
Graham, Robert
Grant, James
Grashow, James Bruce
Grauer, Sherry
Graves, Ka (Kathleen Rose)
Graves, Nancy Stevenson
Green, Tom
Greenbaum, Dorothea Schwarcz
Greer, John Sydney
Gregory, Angela
Gross, Alice
Grossen, Francoise
Groth, Bruno
Guay, Nancy Allen
Gunderson, Barry L
Gutkin, Peter
Hacklin, Allan Dave
Hague, Raoul
Hale, Nathan Cabot
Halko, Joe
Hammond, Harmony
Hanson, Jo
Hanson, Lawrence
Hare, David
Harris, Paul
Hartwig, Cleo
Harvey, Dermot
Harvey, Donald Gilbert
Healy, Anne Laura
Hebald, Milton Elting
Hecht, Mary
Helman, Phoebe
Henes, Donna
Henselmann, Caspar
Herr, Richard Joseph
Hershman, Lynn Lester
Hess, Emil John
Hoare, Tyler James
Hobbs, Joe Ferrell
Hoffman, Edward Fenno, III
Holbrook, Peter Greene
Hooks, Earl J
Hoover, John Jay
Howard, Linda
Howard, Robert A
Hsiao, Chin
Hurst, Ralph N
Jackson, William Davis
Jacobs, Harold
James, Catti
J J
Johnston, Richard M
Jones, David Lee
Jones, Lou (Mary Louise Humpton)
Joyce, J David
Jursevskis, Zigfrids
Kangas, Gene
Kawecki, Jean Mary
Kearney, John (W)
Kearns, James Joseph
Keister, Steve (Stephen Lee)
Kipp, Lyman
Kisch, Gloria
Knoebel, David Jon
Kober, Alfred John
Kolisnyk, Peter
Koni, Nicolaus
Konzal, Joseph
Kramer, Reuben
Krentzin, Earl
Kuehn, Gary
Labino, Dominick
Lable, Eliot
Landsman, Stanley
Lasch, Pat
Lassaw, Ibram
Lathrop, Gertrude K
Lawless, Billie (William B)

SCULPTOR (cont)

Lawrence, Jaye A
Lawrence, Les
Lea, Laurie Jane
Lehman, Mark Ammon
Lehr, Harold
Leibert, Peter R
Lennie, Beatrice E C
Leon, Dennis
Lepper, Robert Lewis
Lerman, Doris (Harriet)
Lewis, John Conard
Lewis, Mary
Lidov, Arthur Herschel
Limone, Frank
Lipson, Goldie
Littleton, Harvey K
Logan, David George
Lothrop, Kristin Curtis
Luecking, Stephen Joseph
Lutz, Winifred Ann
McClure, Thomas F
Macdonnell, Cameron
McGowin, Ed
Mack, Rodger Allen
McMillan, Jerry Edward
McMillen, Michael C(halmers)
Mac Whinnie, John Vincent
Mahlke, Ernest D
Maitin, Sam (Samuel Calman)
Marcheschi, (Louis) Cork
Margolis, David
Markle, Jack M
Markowski, Eugene David
Marozzi, Eli Raphael
Marzollo, Claudio
Meneeley, Edward
Metyko, Michael Joseph
Metzger, Evelyn Borchard
Meyer, Seymour W
Michaels, Glen
Michaels-Paque, Joan
Midener, Walter
Minisci, Brenda (Eileen)
Miralda, Antoni
Morehouse, William Paul
Mulcahy, Kathleen
Muno, Richard Carl
Murray, Richard Deibel
Nauman, Bruce
Nellis, Jennifred Gene
Neri, Manuel
Nicholson, Natasha
Noe, Jerry Lee
Ohe, Katie (Minna)
Okulick, John A
Oldenburg, Claes Thure
Olitski, Jules
Omwake, Leon, Jr
Orentlicher, John
O'Shea, Terrence Patrick
Ossorio, Alfonso A
Pardington, Ralph Arthur
Parks, Charles Cropper
Parsons, David Goode
Partridge, David Gerry
Paterson, Anthony R
Patterson, Curtis Ray
Pattison, Abbott
Piene, Otto
Platus, Libby
Popescu, Cara
Prekop, Martin Dennis
Preminger, Mary G(ardner)
Prent, Mark
Price, Kenneth
Prince, Arnold
Rabinovich, Raquel
Reber, Mick
Reiback, Earl M
Reibel, Bertram
Reif, (F) David
Reimann, William P
Renouf, Edward
Reynolds, Nancy duPont
Reynolds, Richard (Henry)
Ridley, Gregory D, Jr

Ringgold, Faith
Rivers, Victoria Z
Robinson, Margot (Margot Steigman)
Robles, Julian
Rohm, Robert
Roller, Marion Bender
Romano, Salvatore Michael
Rose, Thomas Albert
Rosse, Maryvonne
Rothschild, Amalie (Rosenfeld)
Rousseau, Irene Victoria
Rowe, Reginald M
Ruby, Laura
Rubylee (Charles Armstrong Littler)
Rutsch, Alexander
Rutzky, Ivy Sky
Ryden, Kenneth Glenn
Saari, Peter H
Saarinen, Lilian
Saito, Seiji
Salemme, Antonio
Saltzman, William
Sandback, Frederick Lane
Sandman, Jo
Sankowsky, Itzhak
Sardelic, Ante
Savoy, Chyrl Lenore
Saxe, Henry
Scala, Joseph (A)
Scalise, Nicholas Peter
Schlanger, Jeff
Schmidt, Randall Bernard
Schnier, Jacques
Schonberger, Fred
Schreck, Michael H
Schreckengost, Viktor
Schrero, Ruth Lieberman
Schule, Donald Kenneth
Schulz, William Gallagher
Schuselka, Elfi
Scott, Campbell
Scott, John Tarrell
Seamans, Beverly Benson
Selchow, Roger Hoffman
Seyle, Robert Harley
Shaddle, Alice
Shaw, Donald Edward
Shea, Judith
Shelton, Peter T
Simone (Mildred Simonson)
Sina, Alejandro
Small, Neal
Smedley, Geoffrey
Snyder, Dan
Sonenberg, Jack
Sproat, Christopher Townsend
Stephen, Francis B
Stephenson, John H
Stone, Sylvia
Stone, Willard
Streeter, Tal
Streett, Tylden Westcott
Strider, Marjorie Virginia
Stuart, Michelle
Stuhl, Michelle
Swartzman, Roslyn
Sweet, Steve (Steven Mark)
Tabak, Chaim
Thek, Paul
Thibert, Patrick A
Thiele, Robert Ransom
Thompson, Richard Craig
Thorpe, Hilda (Shapiro)
Threlkeld, Dale
Tobias, Julius
Tousignant, Claude
Townley, Hugh
Turoff, Muriel Pargh
Turrell, James Archie
Tyson, Rae Julian
Ubertalli, Hector
Umlauf, Charles
Van Aalten, Jacques
Van Tongeren, Herk

Vega, Edward
Vodicka, Ruth Kessler
Waddell, John Henry
Wade, Robert Schrope
Wald, Sylvia
Walker, Clay E
Wawrytko, M(ary) F(rances)
Weaver, John Barney
Weedman, Kenneth Russell
Weinbaum, Jean
Weinstein, Florence
Westerlund Roosen, Mia (Maria Eludia)
Westfall, Carol D
White, James Richard
White, Stuart James
Whiten, Colette
Whitney, Maynard Merle
Wilke, Hannah
Willenbecher, John
Willson, Robert
Wilson, May
Wilson, Warren Bingham
Winter, Lumen Martin
Wong, Paul Kan
Wood, Nicholas Wheeler
Woods, Gurdon Grant
Wyatt, Greg Alan
Young, Milton
Yuristy, Russell Michael
Zach, Jan
Zaima, Stephen Gyo
Zeidenbergs, Olafs
Zimmerman, Elyn

Plastic

Adamy, George E
Alexander, Peter
Alford, Gloria K
Amino, Leo
Arnautoff, Jacob Victor
Banks, Anne Johnson
Beasley, Bruce
Breed, Charles Ayars
Delihas, Neva C
Dignac, Geny
Eversley, Frederick John
Fafard, Joe
Fox, Michael David
Fuerst, Shirley Miller
Fuller, Sue
Gruber, Aaronel deRoy
Hanson, Duane
Hatgil, Paul
Hausman, Fred S
Hendler, Raymond
Houskeeper, Barbara
Jimenez, Luis Alfonso, Jr
Judd, Donald Clarence
Kauffman, Robert Craig
Kern, Arthur (Edward)
Koscielny, Margaret
Kostyniuk, Ronald P
Levee, John H
Manship, John Paul
Medrich, Libby E
Miles, Jeanne Patterson
Moquin, Richard Attilio
Neill, Joe
Pera, Isabella
Rankine, V V
Redinger, Walter Fred
Sarnoff, Lolo
Schuller, Grete
Shipley, Roger Douglas
Shute, Roberta E
Smith, Susan Carlton
Staprans, Raimonds
Swergold, Marcelle M
Truitt, Anne (Dean)
Umlauf, Karl A
Van Buren, Richard
Waitzkin, Stella
White, Norman Triplett

Woods, Ted
Zammitt, Norman

Stone

Andrea, I (Andrea Hoffman)
Anker, Suzanne C
Anson, Lesia
Armstrong, Jane Botsford
Arye, Leonora E
Bailey, Richard H
Bender, Beverly Sterl
Borgatta, Robert Edward
Brumer, Shulamith
Buchman, James Wallace
Bulone, Joseph Dominic
Caponi, Anthony
Cave, Leonard Edward
Chinni, Peter Anthony
Colman, Virginia O'Connell
De Coux, Janet
Diska
Ditzion, Grace
Dorrien, Carlos Guillermo
Driesbach, Walter Clark, Jr
Eldredge, Mary Agnes
Fowler, Mel (Walter)
Fox, Lincoln H
Frudakis, Anthony
Geist, Sidney
Gilkey, Richard Charles
Gonzales, Carlotta (Mrs Richard Lahey)
Goo, Benjamin
Gummer, Don
Hamrol, Lloyd
Hanbury, Una
Hauser, Alonzo
Hilts, Alvin
Holsch, Robert Fred
Houser, Allan C
Jones, Carter R(uthven)
Kammerer, Herbert Lewis
Kelsey, Muriel Chamberlin
Kenojuak (Ashevak)
Kline, Alma
Klinghoffer, Shirley
Koenig, Elizabeth
Laird, E Ruth
Lewis, Stanley
Manhold, John Henry
Manning, Hilda Scudder
Mazze, Irving
Morgan, Frances Mallory
Mortellito, Domenico
Nierman, Leonardo M
Niizuma, Minoru
Oesterle, Leonhard Friedrich
Otto, Catherine K(lemann)
Peabody, Amelia
Perry, Frank
Pinardi, Enrico Vittorio
Reddy, Krishna N
Regat, Jean-Jacques Albert
Reiland, Lowell Keith
Rhoden, John W
Richardson, Gretchen (Mrs Ronald Freelander)
Rubins, David Kresz
Salerno, Charles
Sandor, Josephine (Beardsley)
Schleeh, Hans Martin
Schuller, Grete
Shaw, Ernest Carl
Shepp, Alan
Siegmann, Naomi Rita
Simon, Bernard
Simon, Helene
Slivka, David
Smith, Lawrence Beall
Stark, Shirley
Suttman, Paul
Van Alstine, John Richard
Washington, James W, Jr
Watkins, Lewis

SCULPTOR (cont)
Wright, G Alan
Wu, Linda Yee Chau

Wood
Allen, Tom R
Altenbernd, Richard August
Anderson, John S
Antonovici, Constantin
Appel, Karel
Arnoldi, Charles Arthur
Arum, Barbara
Arye, Leonora E
Azara, Nancy J
Baney, Ralph Ramoutar
Barnhart, C Raymond
Beal, Mack
Benson, Martha J
Blanc, (William) Peter
Bolomey, Roger Henry
Bostelle, Thomas (Theodore)
Bourdon, Robert Slayton
Bowles, Marianne von
    Recklinghausen
Brown, Peter C
Bueno, Jose (Joe Goode)
Bulone, Joseph Dominic
Cain, Michael Peter
Carstenson, Cecil C
Caryl, Joan Leonard
Castle, Wendell Keith
Catusco, Louis
Colby, Victor E
Dagys, Jacob
Dal Fabbro, Mario
Davis, Michael A
Day, Worden
DeAngelis, Joseph Rocco
DeArcangelis, Gloria
De Coux, Janet
De Forest, Roy Dean
de Gogorza, Patricia
    (Gahagan)
Diska
Doyle, Tom
Drewelowe, Eve
Feist, Harold E
Fernandez, Rudy M, Jr
Fowler, Mel (Walter)
Frank, Charles William, Jr
Freeman, Robert Lee
Friedensohn, Elias
Gans, Lucy C
Gilhooly, David James, III
Goldberg, Chaim
Goldstein, Carl
Goo, Benjamin
Graham, Richard Marston
Grimley, Oliver Fetterolf
Gummer, Don
Gussow, Alan
Hagan, James Garrison
Hamrol, Lloyd
Hardin, Adlai S
Harrington, William Charles
Hendricks, James (Powell)
Henkle, James Lee
Hernandez-Cruz, Luis
Hickman, Jesse Luther
Hilts, Alvin
Hogbin, Stephen James
Holmes, David Valentine
Holoun, Harold Dean
Holsch, Robert Fred
Hoptner, Richard
House, James Charles, Jr
Hueter, James Warren
Huntington, Jim
Indick, Janet
Jaffe, Nora
Jensen, Hank
Johnson, Joyce
Jones, Theodore Joseph
Jones, W Louis
Judd, Donald Clarence

Kamen, Rebecca
Karpowicz, Terrence Edward
Kasak, Nikolai (Kazak)
Keister, Steve (Stephen Lee)
Kepner, Rita M
Kerrigan, Maurie
Kline, Alma
Koebbeman, Skip
Laatsch, Gary
Lavatelli, Carla
Leigh, Harry E
Lindquist, Mark
Linn, Steven Allen
Long, Hubert
Ludwig, Eva
Lutz, Marjorie Brunhoff
McGovern, Robert F
McIlvain, Douglas Lee
McKesson, Malcolm Forbes
McKoy, Victor Grainger
Mangum, William (Goodson)
Martino, Eva E
Mueller, Trude
Neill, Joe
Niemann, Edmund E
Notaro, Anthony
Pollock, Bruce Walter
Rades, William L
Regat, Mary E
Sabo, Irving
Saville, Ken
Schmeckebier, Laurence E
Schuler, Melvin Albert
Scott, Arden
Searles, Charles
Shostak, Edwin Bennett
Sieg, Robert Lawrence
Siegmann, Naomi Rita
Simon, Bernard
Smith, Harry William
Smith, Kent Alvin
Smith, Lawson Wentworth
Smith, Nan S(helley)
Steig, William
Stenzler, Erna J
Stevens, Michael Keith
Storm, Howard
Surls, James
Swick, Linda Ann
Teller, Jane (Simon)
Thompson, William Joseph
Tornheim, Norman
Townsend, John F
Truitt, Anne (Dean)
Turano, Don
Turner, Raymond
Udvardy, John Warren
Urquhart, Tony (Anthony
    Morse)
von Rydingsvard, Ursula
Vrana, Albert S
Werner, Howard
Westermann, H C
Yoshimura, Fumio

SILVERSMITH
Bambas, Thomas Reese
Chapman, Robert Gordon
Christensen, Hans-Jorgen
    Thorvald
DiPasquale, Dominic
    Theodore
Fix, John Robert
Getty, Nilda Fernandez
Johnson, Donald Marvin
Krentzin, Earl
Loloma, Charles
Maxfield, Roberta Masur
Monongye, Preston Lee
Nichols, Eleanor Cary
Thompson, Ernest Thorne, Jr
Watson-Abbott, Lynda
Weiss, Linda (Linda Margaret
    Weiss-Edwards)

STAINED GLASS ARTIST
Anderson, Bruce James
Corso, Samuel (Joseph)
Darricarrere, Roger
    Dominique
Devillier, Charles Arthur
Douaihy, Saliba
Ferron, Marcelle
Fields, Fredrica H
Gikas, Christopher
Gurria, Angela
Haworth, Peter
Jameikis, Brone Aleksandra
Karawina, Erica (Mrs Sidney
    C Hsiao)
Lewis, Elizabeth Matthew
McGuire, Maureen
Mueller, M Gerardine
Skinner, Orin Ensign
Sles, Steven Lawrence
Tahedl, Ernestine
Terry, Duncan Niles

TAPESTRY ARTIST
Aber, Ita
Adams, Mark
Brooks, Lois Ziff
Brown, Rhett Delford (Harriett
    Gurney Brown)
Cook, Lia
Curtis, Dolly Powers
Danielson, Phyllis I
Dyer, Carolyn Price
Easterwood, Henry Lewis
Elliott, Lillian
Funk, Charlotte M
Gregor, Helen Frances
Guay, Nancy Allen
Hartford, Jane Davis
Hemenway, Nancy (Mrs
    Robert D Barton)
Hicks, Sheila
Jaworska, Tamara
Kaye, David Haigh
Lansner, Fay
Lavatelli, Carla
Lesch, Alma Wallace
Lieberman, Vickie
Marx, Evelyn
Morrison, Bee (Berenice G)
Palau, Marta
Pinckney, Stanley
Radulovic, Savo
Rave, Georgia
Roberson, William
Roda (Rhoda Lillian Sablow)
Rodman, Ruth M
Ross, Gloria F(rankenthaler)
Rousseau-Vermette, Mariette
Schira, Cynthia
von Weise, Wenda Fraker
Ward, Evelyn Svec
Webber, Helen

VIDEO ARTIST
Almy, Max (Marilynn Irene)
Antin, Eleanor
Barron, Ros
Bice, Jack (John Avery)
Breder, Hans Dieter
Campbell, Colin Keith
Campus, Peter
Chase, Doris (Totten)
Clancy, Patrick
Coe, Anne Elizabeth
Collyer, Robin
Cook, Michael David
Cross, Watson, Jr
D'Agostino, Peter Pasquale

Davidovich, Jaime
Davis, Douglas Matthew
Dickinson, Eleanor Creekmore
Downey, Juan
Dr Brute (Eric William
    Metcalfe)
Edwards, James F
Freed, Hermine
Gartel, Laurence M
Glassman, Joel A
Grabill, Vin (E Vincent, Jr)
Greenfield, Amy
Gusella, Ernest
Harding, Noel Robert
Hendricks, David Charles
Hompson, Davi Det (David
    Elbridge Thompson)
Iimura, Taka
Jonas, Joan
Korot, Beryl
Kubota, Shigeko
Landry, Richard Miles
Laposky, Ben Francis
Levine, Les
Lister, Ardele Diane
Loeffler, Carl Eugene
Lucier, Mary
McCafferty, Jay David
Marton, Pier
Molella, Patricia Ann
Montano, Linda (Mary)
Orentlicher, John
Paik, Nam June
Peiperl, Adam
Quinn, Aysha
Ritchie, William (Bill)
Roser, Ce (Cecilia)
Rosler, Martha Rose
Sasaki, Tomiyo
Sato, Norie
Schneider, Ira
Segalove, Ilene Judy
Sharp, Willoughby
Sher, Elizabeth
Smith, Barbara Turner
Steele, Lisa
Sturgeon, John Floyd
Talley, Dan R
Tambellini, Aldo
Van Der Beek, Edward Stanley
Wegman, William
Wiegand, Robert

WEAVER
Bittleman, Dolores Dembus
Bobrowicz, Yvonne P
Bolster, Ella S
Boyd, Karen White
Brenner, Shore Hodge
Cope, Louise Todd
Elliott, Lillian
Fender, Tom Mac
Funk, Charlotte M
Hanson, J B
Hausrath, Joan W
Higgins, Mary Lou
LaPlantz, Shereen
Larsen, Jack Lenor
McVey, Leza
Maldjian, Vartavar B
Maltby, Hazel Farrow
Meredith, Dorothy Laverne
Morrison, Bee (Berenice G)
O'Hara, Sheila Mary
Pendleton, Mary Caroline
Plath, Iona
Regensteiner, Else (Friedsam)
Replinger, Dot (Dorothy
    Thiele)
Rubin, Marjorie J(oan)
Schira, Cynthia
Sekimachi, Kay
Smith, Sherri
Tawney, Lenore

WEAVER (cont)

Trentham, Gary Lynn
Van Leunen, Alice Louise
Wahling, Jon B
Wallace, Lysbeth (Mai)
Ward, Evelyn Svec
West, Virginia M
Windeknecht, Margaret Brake

WRITER

Aach, Herb
Ablow, Joseph
Adams, Celeste Marie
Ahl, Henry C
Albright, Thomas
Alf, Martha Joanne
Aliki
Allen, Clarence Canning
Almond, Paul
Alper, M Victor
Ames, Lee Judah
Aminoff, Judith
Anderson, Alexandra C
Anderson, Donald Myers
Anderson, Robert Raymond
Andrea, I (Andrea Hoffman)
Angelini, John Michael
Antin, David A
Apple, Jacki (Jacqueline B)
Arguelles, Jose A
Armstrong, Jane Botsford
Arnason, H Harvard
Arnheim, Rudolf
Arnosky, James Edward
Asher, Elise
Ashton, Dore
Askew, Pamela
Bacon, Peggy
Baer, Jo
Bailey, Walter Alexander
Baird, Joseph Armstrong, Jr
Balmaceda, Margarita S
Bannard, Walter Darby
Banz, George
Barbour, Arthur J
Barker, Walter William
Barnes, Molly
Barnett, Ed Willis
Barrio, Raymond
Bartlett, Jennifer Losch
Barton, Phyllis Settecase
Basquin, Kit (Mary Smyth)
Bassi
Baur, John I H
Bcck, Doreen
Behrens, Roy R
Benson, Elizabeth Polk
Benson, Gertrude Ackerman
Benton, Suzanne E
Beny, Roloff
Berry, Carolyn (Carolyn Berry
  Becker)
Bevlin, Marjorie Elliott
Biederman, Charles (Karel
  Joseph)
Bishop, Robert Charles
Black, Mary Childs
Bochner, Mel
Bonstrom, Dana Orlin
Bowman, Bruce
Boyd, Donald Edgar
Boyle, Richard J
Boylen, Michael Edward
Broder, Patricia Janis
Broido, Lucy
Brommer, Gerald F
Bronson, A A (Michael Wayne
  Tims)
Brown, Robert K
Brown, Theodore Morey
Browning, Dixie Burrus
Brumbaugh, Thomas Brendle
Brumfield, John Richard
Bruner, Louise Katherine (Mrs
  Paul Orr)

Budny, Virginia
Burch, Claire R
Burnham, Linda Frye
Burt, David Sill
Bush-Brown, Albert
Butler, Joseph Thomas
Calle, Paul
Campbell, Dorothy
  Bostwick
Campbell, (James) Lawrence
Campbell, Vivian (Vivian
  Campbell Stoll)
Cantone, Vic
Carrero, Jaime
Case, Elizabeth
Caswell, Helen Rayburn
Chase, Alice Elizabeth
Clef, Roman A (Henry E
  Guerriero)
Clemens, Paul
Cochran, George McKee
  (Redbird)
Cole, Sylvan, Jr
Collier, (Alan) Graham
Collings, Betty
Congdon, William (Grosvenor)
Cooley, Adelaide N
Cooney, Barbara (Mrs Charles
  Talbot Porter)
Corbin, George Allen
Corbino, Marcia Norcross
Cowles, Fleur
Cox, Richard William
Crandall, Judith Ann
Craven, Wayne
Criquette (Ruth DuBarry
  Montague)
Cutler, Grayce E
Cuttler, Charles David
Dal Fabbro, Mario
Damaz, Paul F
D'Ancona, Mirella Levi
D'Ashnash-Tosi (Barbara
  Chase-Riboud)
Dater, Judy
D'Aulaire, Ingri (Mortenson)
  Parin
Davidowitz (Dror), Moshe
Davidson, Abraham A
Davidson, Marshall Bowman
Davis, James Wesley
Davis, Philip Charles
Dawdy, Doris Ostrander
Deats, Margaret
de Kooning, Elaine Marie
  Catherine
De Ruth, Jan
Desmarais, Charles Joseph
Diamonstein, Barbaralee
Dibble, George
Dingus, Rick
Donhauser, Paul Stefan
Dowden, Anne Ophelia Todd
Drohojowska, Hunter
Dulac, Margarita Walker
Dunbar, Jill H
Dusard, Jay
Dyson, Brian
Eliasoph, Paula
Ellis, Richard
Emmerich, Andre
Ets, Marie Hall
Ewald, Elin Lake
Fanning, Robbie
Farnham, Alexander
Farnham, Emily
Fax, Elton Clay
Feiffer, Jules
Feininger, Andreas B L
Fejes, Claire
Fels, C P
Fischer, Hal (Harold Alan)
Flach, Victor H
Flavin, Dan
Fleming, Lee Virginia
Flexner, James Thomas
Flood, Richard Sidney

Forge, Andrew Murray
Foster, Stephen C
Franck, Frederick S
Frank, Charles William, Jr
Freed, Hermine
Friedman, B H
Fuller, Mary (Mary Fuller
  McChesney)
Galas, Philip-Dimitri
Gale, Peggy
Gallagher, Carole
Garchik, Morton Lloyd
Garman, Ed
Garver, Thomas H
Gary, Dorothy Hales
Genauer, Emily
Ghent, Henri
Gibson, Walter Samuel
Gilbert, Creighton Eddy
Gildzen, Alex
Giraudier, Antonio
Glickman, Maurice
Glimcher, Arnold B
Goddard, Don (Donald)
Goldman, Judith
Goldring, Elizabeth
Goldsmith, Barbara
Goldstein, Nathan
Goodrich, Lloyd
Goossen, Eugene Coons
Gordon, Leah Shanks
Gordon, Violet
Gottlieb, Carla
Grosser, Maurice
Groves, Naomi Jackson
Gruen, John
Grundy, J(ohn Owen)
Gysin, Brion
Haber, Ira Joel
Hackenbroch, Yvonne Alix
Hale, Nathan Cabot
Halvorsen, Ruth Elise
Hamilton, Charles F
Hammond, Leslie King
Hanks, David Allen
Harmon, Lily
Harper, Paula (Hays)
Harrington, La Mar
Hartal, Paul Zev
Hastie, Reid
Haversat, Lillian Kerr
Hawkins, Myrtle H
Hayes, Bartlett Harding, Jr
Held, Julius S
Heller, Jules
Henrickson, Paul Robert
Herman, Vic
Herring, Jan (Janet Mantel)
Hibbard, Howard
Hirschfeld, Albert
Hobbs, Jack Arthur
Holden, Donald
Hollister, Paul
Hood, Graham Stanley
Hopkins, Peter
Horn, Milton
Howland, Richard Hubbard
Hugo, Joan (Dowey)
Hurd, Peter
Iglehart, Robert L
Irving, Donald J
Isaacson, Philip Marshal
Jackson, Suzanne Fitzallen
Janis, Sidney
Jennings, Jan
Jensen, Dean N
Johanningmeier, Robert Alan
Johnson, Fridolf Lester
Johnson, James Ralph
Johnson, Lincoln Fernando
Johnson, Una E
Jones, Elizabeth Orton
Jones, Franklin Reed
Jones, Ronald Lee, Jr
Kallir, Jane Katherine
Kangas, Gene
Karlen, Peter H

Kaufman, Joe
Kaufman, Nancy
Keats, Ezra Jack
Kepner, Rita M
Klebe, Gene (Charles Eugene)
Klein, Ellen Lee
Klein, Gwenda J
Klein, Michael Eugene
Kleinholz, Frank
Kleinsmith, Gene (Eugene
  Dennis)
Knight, Hilary
Knowles, Richard H
Knox, George
Koch, Robert
Kouwenhoven, John A
Kovinick, Philip Peter
Kowal, Dennis J
Kubler, George Alexander
Labrie, Rose
Lacroix, Flora Luisa
Lang, Avis
Langner, Nola
Lariar, Lawrence
Larson, Jane (Warren)
Larson, Kay L
Lash, Kenneth
Lefebvre d'Argence, Rene-
  Yvon
Lengyel, Alfonz
Lent, Blair
Lerman, Leo
Lewis, Elizabeth Matthew
Lewison, Florence (Mrs
  Maurice Glickman)
Libby, William C
Libhart, Myles Laroy
Lijn, Liliane
Lindsay, Kenneth C
Linn, John William
Lippard, Lucy Rowland
Lipton, Barbara B
Little, Nina Fletcher
Loeb, Judy
Loewer, Henry Peter
Logan, Frederick Manning
Lombardo, Josef Vincent
Long, Rose-Carol Washton
Longaker, Jon Dasu
Loran, Erle
Love, Frances Taylor
Lubell, Ellen
Ludman, Joan Hurwitz
Lunde, Karl Roy
Lynes, Russell
McClain, Matthew
McCready, Karen
MacDonald, Colin Somerled
McDonald, Robert Herwick
McEvilley, Thomas
McGarry, Susan Hallsten
McLanathan, Richard B K
McNulty, Kneeland
Madigan, Mary Jean Smith
Maguire, Henry Pownall
Mainardi, Patricia M
Mann, Maybelle
Marks, Claude
Mason, Lauris Lapidos
Mattil, Edward L
Mauldin, Bill
Mayer, Sondra
Medoff, Eve
Metson, Graham
Meyer, Elmer Frederick
Meyer, Susan E
Michael, Gary
Millard, Charles Warren, III
Miller, Donald
Miller, George
Minick, Roger
Mitchell, Margaretta K
Moehl, Karl J
Mollett, Michael M
Moore, Barbara
Morgan, Theodora
Morgan, William

WRITER (cont)

Morris, Jack Austin, Jr
Morris, Wright
Morrison, C L
Morse, Marcia Roberts
Morton, Robert Alan
Moser, Charlotte
Movalli, Charles Joseph
Muensterberger, Werner
Munro, Eleanor
Nasisse, Andy S
Neal, (Minor) Avon
Nelson, Mary Carroll
Nemser, Cindy
Ness, Evaline (Mrs Arnold A
    Bayard)
Newman, Ralph Albert
Newsom, Barbara Ylvisaker
Norman, Dorothy (S)
Nuki (Daniel Millsaps)
O'Gorman, James Francis
Ott, Robert William
Owens, Gwendolyn Jane
Parish, Betty Waldo
Parker, Nancy Winslow
Patrick, Charles William
Peladeau, Marius Beaudoin
Pendleton, Mary Caroline
Perine, Robert Heath
Perret, George Albert
Persky, Robert S
Phillips, Gifford
Phillpot, Clive James
Pincus-Witten, Robert A
Plath, Iona
Plaut, James S
Polster, Joanne F
Porter, Eliot Furness

Prescott, Kenneth Wade
Preuss, Roger
Quinsac, Annie-Paule
Raleigh, Henry Patrick
Rash, Nancy
Ratcliff, Carter
Raven, Arlene
Redstone, Louis Gordon
Reed, Michael Arthur
Reid, Charles
Reiss, Lionel S
Rembski, Stanislav
Rensch, Roslyn
Rice, Harold Randolph
Richman, Robert M
Ridgway, Peggi
Rivera-Velazquez, Mariano
Robbin, Anthony Stuart
Robbins, Eugenia S
Robins, Corinne
Robison, Andrew
Rodman, Selden
Rosenthal, Mark L
Roth, Leland M(artin)
Roukes, Nicholas M
Rousseau, Irene Victoria
Rubin, Ida Ely
Salemme, Lucia (Autorino)
Sanders, Herbert Harvey
Saphire, Lawrence M
Sawyer, Helen
Schlemm, Betty Lou
Schloss, Edith
Schwartz, Barbara Ann
Schwartz, Therese
Scott, William P(owell)
Seed, Suzanne Liddell
Seeman, Helene Zucker

Seligmann, Herbert J
Selvig, Forrest Hall
Sendak, Maurice Bernard
Shapiro, Adrian Michael
Sheaks, Barclay
Sherman, Lenore (Walton)
Sherrod, Philip Lawrence
Silberman, Arthur
Silverman, Ronald H
Simon, Leonard Ronald
Sisler, Rebecca
Slate, Joseph Frank
Smith, Ralph Alexander
Sorel, Edward
Spaeth, Eloise O'Mara
Spector, Naomi
Speight, Jerry Brooks
Spier, Peter Edward
Spink, Frank Henry, Jr
Stahl, Ben (Albert)
Stampfle, Felice
Stapen, Nancy
Steiner, Paul
Stevens, Elisabeth Goss
Stewart, John Lincoln
Swinton, George
Sylvestre, Guy
Szabo, Zoltan
Szilvasy, Linda Markuly
Tait, Cornelia Damian
Talley, Dan R
Tarshis, Jerome
Taylor, John Frank Adams
Taylor, Robert
Thomas, Helen (Doane)
Thomas, Lew
Tice, George Andrew
Tillenius, Clarence (Ingwall)

Tomkins, Calvin
Toschik, Larry
Town, Harold Barling
Tracy, Lois Bartlett
Tselos, Dimitri Theodore
Tucker, Peri
Turk, Rudy H
Turner, Norman Huntington
Uhrman, Celia
Uhrman, Esther
Upright, Diane W
Van Dommelen, David B
Van Haaften, Julia
Vermeule, Cornelius Clarkson,
    III
Walton, Donald William
Walton, Guy E
Ward, Lynd (Kendall)
Warder, William
Watson, Clarissa H
Wechsler, Susan
Weil, Lisl
Weinberg, Bella Rebecca
Weissman, Julian Paul
Weissman, Walter
West, Virginia M
Whipple, Barbara
Wiggins, Walton Wray
Wight, Frederick S
Willig, Nancy Tobin
Wilson, Judith (A)
Windeknecht, Margaret Brake
Withers, Josephine
Wofford, Philip
Wood, Harry Emsley, Jr
Wright, Catharine Morris
Wright, (Charles) Clifford
Yochim, Louise Dunn
Young, Mahonri S
Zack, Badanna Bernice
Zornes, James Milford

AARONS, GEORGE   Sculptor (1896-1980)
ABBATE, PAUL S   Sculptor (1884-1972)
ABBELL, SAMUEL   Art Patron (1925-1969)
ABBOT, EDITH   Painter (-1964)
ABBOTT, JOHN EVANS   Library Director (-1952)
ABEL, MYER   Lithographer, Painter
ABELL, WALTER HALSEY   Educator (1897-1956)
ABRACHEFF, IVAN   Painter (1903-1960)
ABRAMS, HARRY N   Publisher, Collector (1905-1979)
ACKERMANN, JOHN JOSEPH   Painter, Designer (-1950)
ADAMS, MARGARET BOROUGHS   Painter (-1965)
ADAMS, (MOULTON) LEE   Painter, Illustrator (1922-1971)
ADAMS, WAYMAN   Painter (1885-1959)
ADEN, ALONZO J   Museum Director (-1963)
ADLER, SAMUEL (MARCUS)   Painter, Educator (1898-1979)
ADLOW, DOROTHY   Critic (-1964)
AGA-OGLU, MEHMET   Educator, Lecturer, Writer (-1948)
AGOPOFF, AGOP MINASS   Sculptor (-1983)
AHERN, EUGENE (GENE)   Cartoonist (1896-1960)
AIKEN, CHARLES   Painter (-1965)
AIROLA, PAAVO   Painter, Writer (-1983)
AJOOTIAN, KHOSROV   Educator (1891-1958)
ALAN, JAY   Cartoonist (-1965)
ALBEE, PERCY F   Painter (1885-1959)
ALBERS, JOSEF   Painter, Printmaker (1888-1976)
ALBRIGHT, ADAM EMORY   Painter (1862-1957)
ALBRIGHT, HENRY J   Educator, Painter (-1951)
ALBRIGHT, IVAN LE LORRAINE   Painter (1897-1983)
ALDER, MARY ANN   Painter, Art Restorer (-1952)
ALDWINCKLE, ERIC   Designer, Painter (1909-1980)
ALEXANDER, CHRISTINE   Curator (1893-1975)
ALFSEN, JOHN MARTIN   Painter (-1972)
ALLEN, ARTHUR D   Painter, Lithographer (-1949)
ALLEN, CHARLES CURTIS   Painter, Educator (-1950)
ALLEN, JANE MENGEL (MRS ARTHUR)   Painter (-1952)
ALLEN, JUNIUS   Painter (-1962)
ALLEN, MARY STOCKBRIDGE   Painter, Sculptor (-1949)
ALMY, FRANK ATWOOD   Museum Director (-1956)
ALSTON, CHARLES HENRY   Painter, Educator (1907-1977)
ALVORD, MURIEL   Painter (-1960)
AMATEIS, EDMOND ROMULUS   Sculptor (1897-1981)
AMBERSON, GRACE D (MRS WILLIAM R)   Painter (-1957)
AMES, ARTHUR FORBES   Painter, Educator (1906-1975)
ANDERSEN, ANDREAS STORRS   Educator, Painter (1908-1974)
ANDERSON, CARL THOMAS   Cartoonist, Illustrator (-1948)
ANDERSON, JEREMY RADCLIFFE   Sculptor, Educator (1921-1982)
ANGEL, JOHN   Sculptor (1881-1960)
ANGELO, DOMENICK MICHAEL   Sculptor (1925-1976)
ANSBACHER, JESSIE   Painter (-1964)
ARCHER, DOROTHY BRYANT   Painter, Instructor (1919-)
ARCHIPENKO, ALEXANDER   Sculptor (1887-1964)
ARDIZZONE, EDWARD   Painter, Illustrator (1900-1979)
ARGALL, CHARLES G   Painter
ARLT, WILLIAM H   Designer, Teacher, Painter
ARNO, PETER   Cartoonist (-1968)
ARONSON, BORIS   Designer, Painter (1900-1980)
ARTIS, WILLIAM ELLISWORTH   Educator, Ceramist (1914-1977)
ARTZ, FREDERICK B   Historian, Writer (1894-1983)
ARTZYBYASHEFF, BORIS   Illustrator (-1965)
ASHTON, ETHEL V   Artist (-1975)
ASHTON, MAL STANHOPE (MALONE)   Artist (1878-1976)
ASKENAZY, MISCHA   Painter (1888-1961)
ATHERTON, J CARLTON   Craftsman (-1964)

ATHERTON, JOHN   Painter, Illustrator (-1952)
ATKINS, ALBERT H   Sculptor, Painter (-1951)
AUERBACH-LEVY, WILLIAM   Etcher
AULT, GEORGE COPELAND   Painter (-1948)
AUSUBEL, SHEVA   Painter (1896-1957)
AVERY, MILTON   Painter (1893-1965)
AVERY, MYRTILLA   Museum Director (-1959)
AVERY, RALPH HILLYER   Painter, Illustrator (1906-1976)
AVINOFF, ANDREY   Painter, Illustrator (1948)
AYERS, HESTER MERWIN   Portrait Painter (1902-1975)
AYLWARD, WILLIAM J   Painter
BABER, ALICE   Painter, Printmaker (1928-1982)
BACH, RICHARD F   Educator (-1968)
BADNER, MINO   Historian (1940-1978)
BAILEY, CLARK T   Sculptor, Educator (1932-1978)
BAILEY, WORTH   Historian (1908-1980)
BAIN, LILIAN PHERNE   Painter, Etcher
BAIZERMAN, SAUL   Sculptor (1989-1957)
BAKER, CHARLES EDWIN   Art Historian, Writer (1902-1971)
BAKER, EUGENE AMES   Painter, Serigrapher (1928-)
BALDWIN, HARRY, II   Painter
BALDWIN, MURIEL FRANCES   Art Librarian
BALLIN, HUGO   Painter (-1956)
BANNING, BEATRICE HARPER   Etcher
BANNISTER, EDWARD MITCHELL   Painter (1828-1901)
BARANOFF, MORT   Printmaker, Painter (1923-1978)
BARBER, JOHN   Painter (1898-1965)
BARBER, MURIEL V   Painter (-1971)
BARINGER, RICHARD E   Painter, Designer (1921-1980)
BARKER, ALBERT WINSLOW   Lithographer, Teacher (-1947)
BARKER, VIRGIL   Writer, Critic (-1964)
BARLOGA, VIOLA H   Painter
BARNETT, HERBERT P   Educator, Painter (1910-1972)
BARNEY, MAGINAL WRIGHT   Craftsman (-1966)
BARR, ALFRED HAMILTON, JR   Art Historian, Administrator (1902-1981)
BARR, ALLAN   Painter (1890-1959)
BARRETT, H STANFORD   Painter, Educator (1909-1970)
BARRETT, THOMAS WEEKS   Painter, Designer (-1947)
BARRIE, ERWIN S   Painter (1886-1983)
BARTLETT, DANA   Painter (1882-1957)
BARTLETT, ROBERT WEBSTER   Painter, Designer (1922-1979)
BASS, JOHANNA (MRS JOHN)   Collector, Patron (-1970)
BASS, JOHN   Collector, Patron (1891-1978)
BATCHELOR, CLARENCE DANIEL   Cartoonist (-1977)
BATE, NORMAN ARTHUR   Educator, Printmaker (1916-1980)
BATES, CAROL   Painter
BATES, KENNETH   Painter (1895-1973)
BATES, MAXWELL BENNETT   Painter, Lithographer (1906-1980)
BATTAGLIA, PASQUALE M   Painter (-1959)
BAUMGARTNER, WARREN W   Illustrator (-1963)
BAYLINSON, A S   Painter, Teacher (-1950)
BAYLOS, ZELMA U   Painter, Sculptor
BAZIOTES, WILLIAM   Painter (1912-1963)
BEAL, REYNOLDS   Painter, Etcher (-1951)
BEALL, LESTER THOMAS   Illustrator, Designer (1902-1969)
BEAR, DONALD   Museum Director (-1952)
BECKER, NAOMI   Sculptor (-1974)
BEETZ, CARL HUGO   Painter, Instructor (1911-1974)
BEGG, JOHN ALFRED   Designer, Sculptor (1903-1974)
BEIL, CHARLES A   Sculptor (-1976)
BELCHER, HILDA   Painter (-1963)
BEL GEDDES, NORMAN   Designer (1893-1958)

BELKNAP, MORRIS B   Painter (-1952)
BELLINGER, LOUISA   Curator (-1968)
BELLMER, HANS   Painter, Graphic Artist & Sculptor (1902-1975)
BELMONT, IRA JEAN   Painter
BEMELMANS, LUDWIG   Painter (-1963)
BEMIS, WALDO EDMUND   Designer, Illustrator (-1951)
BENDA, W T   Designer, Illustrator (-1948)
BENESCH, OTTO   Art Historian (-1964)
BENN, BEN   Painter (1884-1983)
BENNETT, RUTH M   Craftsman (1899-1960)
BENSCO, CHARLES J   Painter (1894-1960)
BENSON, EMANUEL M   Art Administrator, Art Dealer (1904-1971)
BENSON, FRANK W   Painter, Etcher (-1951)
BENSON, JOHN P   Painter (-1947)
BENTON, MARGARET PEAKE   Painter (-1975)
BENTON, THOMAS HART   Painter, Writer (1889-1975)
BENTON, WILLIAM   Collector (1900-1973)
BENTZ, JOHN   Painter (-1950)
BERENSON, BERNARD   Art Authority (1865-1959)
BERG, PHIL   Collector, Patron (1902-   )
BERHARD, MRS RICHARD J   Collector
BERMAN, EUGENE   Painter, Designer (1899-1972)
BERNARDINI, ORESTES   Designer (1880-1957)
BERNDT, WALTER   Cartoonist (1900-1979)
BERNEY, BERTRAM S   Painter
BERNHEIMER, RICHARD   Educator (1907-1958)
BERNINGHAUS, OSCAR E   Painter, Designer (-1952)
BERNSTEIN, EVA   Painter (1871-1958)
BERRY, WILLIAM DAVID   Illustrator, Sculptor (1926-1979)
BERRYMAN, CLIFFORD KENNEDY   Cartoonist, Illustrator
    (-1949)
BERTOIA, HARRY   Sculptor, Graphic Artist (1915-1978)
BETTS, LOUIS   Painter (-1961)
BICE, CLARE   Administrator, Painter (1909-1976)
BIDDLE, GEORGE   Painter, Sculptor (1885-1973)
BIDWELL, WATSON   Painter
BIEBEL, FRANKLIN M   Museum Director
BIEBER, MARGARETE   Art Historian (1880-1978)
BIERMAN, SAMUEL   Art Advisor (1902-1978)
BILOTTI, SALVATORE F   Sculptor (-1953)
BING, ALEXANDER   Painter (1878-1959)
BINNING, BERTRAM CHARLES   Painter (1909-1976)
BIRCHANSKY, LEO   Painter, Cartoonist (-1949)
BISGARD, JAMES DEWEY   Collector, Patron (1898-1975)
BISHOP, RICHARD EVETT   Printmaker (1897-1975)
BLACK, ELEANOR SIMMS (MRS ROBERT M)   Painter (-1949)
BLACK, WENDELL H   Educator (1919-1972)
BLACKBURN, MORRIS (ATKINSON)   Painter, Printmaker (1902-1979)
BLAIR, STREETER   Painter (-1966)
BLAKE, LEO B   Illustrator (1887-1976)
BLANCH, ARNOLD   Painter (-1968)
BLANCHFIELD, HOWARD JAMES   Painter (1896-1957)
BLANDING, DON   Author (-1957)
BLISS, ROBERT WOODS (-1962)
BLISS, MRS. ROBERT WOODS   Collector (-1969)
BLOCH, ALBERT   Painter (1882-1961)
BLOCH, JULIUS   Painter (-1966)
BLOCK, ADOLPH   Sculptor, Instructor (1906-1978)
BLODGETT, EDMUND WALTON   Painter
BLODGETT, GEORGE WINSLOW   Sculptor
BLOEDEL, LAWRENCE HOTCHKISS   Collector (1902-1976)
BLOWER, DAVID HARRISON   Painter (1901-1976)
BLUMBERG, YULI   Painter (-1964)
BLUMENSCHEIN, ERNEST LEONARD   Painter (1874-1960)
BLUMENSCHEIN, MARY GREENE   Painter (-1958)
BOARDMAN, NELL   Painter (-1968)
BOBLETER, LOWELL STANLEY   Educator, Painter (1902-1973)
BODINE, HELEN   Painter
BOE, ROY ASBJORN   Historian, Educator (1919-   )
BOEHLER, HANS   Painter (1884-1961)
BOESCHENSTEIN, BERNICE (MRS C K)   Painter (-1951)
BOHLAND, GUSTAV   Sculptor (1897-1959)
BOHNERT, HERBERT   Portrait Painter (-1967)
BOLOTOWSKY, ILYA   Painter, Educator (1907-1981)
BONINO, ALFREDO   Art Dealer (1925-1981)
BONNAR, JAMES KING   Painter (1885-1961)
BONNEY, THERESE   Photographer (1895-1978)
BONNYCASTLE, MURRAY C   Painter
BOOGAR, WILLIAM F   Sculptor (1893-1958)
BOORAEM, HENDRIK   Painter (-1951)
BOOTH, CAMERON   Painter (1892-1980)
BOOTH, NINA MASON   Painter
BORDUAS, PAUL EMILE   Painter (-1960)
BORGHI, GUIDO RINALDO   Painter (1903-1971)
BORN, WOLFGANG   Historian, Writer

BORSTEIN, YETTA   Painter (-1968)
BOSA, LOUIS   Painter (1905-1981)
BOSIN, BLACKBEAR   Painter, Designer (1921-1980)
BOSWELL, PEYTON, JR   Writer, Editor (-1950)
BOTKIN, HENRY   Painter, Writer
BOTTIS, HUGH P   Printmaker (-1964)
BOUCHARD, LORNE HOLLAND   Painter, Illustrator (1913-1978)
BOUCHE, LOUIS   Painter (-1969)
BOUCHE, RENE   Portrait Painter (-1963)
BOURDELL, PIERRE VAN PARYS   Sculptor (-1966)
BOWDOIN, HARRIETTE   Painter
BOWER, ALEXANDER   Museum Director (-1952)
BOWLES, JANET PAYNE   Craftsman (-1948)
BOWLING, JACK   Silversmith, Printmaker (1903-1979)
BOYCE, RICHARD   Sculptor (1920-   )
BOYD, E   Art Administrator, Writer (1903-1974)
BOYD, RUTHERFORD   Painter, Designer (-1951)
BOYER, RALPH LUDWIG   Painter, Etcher (-1952)
BOYKO, FRED   Painter, Teacher (-1951)
BRACKMAN, ROBERT   Painter, Educator (1898-1980)
BRADFORD, FRANCIS SCOTT   Painter (1898-1961)
BRADLEY, MRS. HARRY LYNDE   Collector
BRAIDER, DONALD   Art Writer (-1977)
BRANDON, WARREN EUGENE   Painter (1916-1977)
BRANNER, ROBERT   Art Historian (1927-1973)
BRANSOM, (JOHN) PAUL   Painter, Illustrator (1885-1979)
BRAXTON, WILLIAM E   Painter (1878-1932)
BRAY, JOHN   Cartoonist (1879-1978)
BRAZEAU, WENDELL (PHILLIPS)   Painter (1910-1974)
BRECHER, SAMUEL   Painter (1897-1982)
BRECKENRIDGE, JAMES D   Art Historian (1926-1982)
BREGER, DAVE (DAVID)   Cartoonist (1908-1970)
BREITENBACH, EDGAR   Historian (1903-1977)
BRENDEL, OTTO J   Art Historian (1901-1973)
BRENSON, THEODORE   Painter (1893-1959)
BREWER, BESSIE MARSH   Etcher, Lithographer (-1952)
BREWINGTON, MARION VERNON   Art Historian, Writer (1902-1974)
BRIGGS, AUSTIN   Illustrator, Collector
BRIGGS, BERTA N   Painter, Writer (1884-1976)
BRINLEY, DANIEL PUTNAM   Painter (-1963)
BRITTAIN, MILLER G   Painter (-1968)
BRITTON, HARRY   Painter (1879-1958)
BRITTON, JAMES II   Critic, Illustrator (1915-1983)
BRODIE, GANDY   Painter, Designer (1924-1975)
BROMUND, CAL E   Painter (1903-1979)
BROOK, ALEXANDER   Painter (1898-1980)
BROUILLETTE, GILBERT T   Art Dealer, Consultant-Research
BROUSSARD, JAY REMY   Museum Director, Painter (1920-1976)
BROWN, BRIAN   Director (1911-1958)
BROWN, CARLYLE   Painter (-1964)
BROWN, MARGARET   Writer (-1952)
BROWN, PAUL   Illustrator (1893-1958)
BROWN, RICHARD F   Museum Director (1916-1979)
BROWN, RICHARD M   Portrait Painter (-1964)
BROWN, ROY   Painter (1879-1956)
BROWNE, GEORGE BYRON   Painter (1907-1961)
BROWNHILL, HAROLD   Painter, Illustrator
BROWNING, G WESLEY   Painter (-1951)
BRUNDAGE, AVERY   Collector (-1975)
BRUNS, FREDERICK R, JR   Curator (1913-1979)
BUCK, RICHARD D   Conservator (1903-1977)
BUCKLEY, JOHN MICHAEL   Painter (1891-1958)
BUFF, CONRAD   Printmaker, Illustrator (1886-1975)
BULLIET C J   Art Critic (-1952)
BULLOCK, WYNN   Photographer (1902-1975)
BUNCE, LOUIS DeMOTT   Painter (1914-1983)
BUNTING, BAINBRIDGE   Historian, Educator (1913-1981)
BURCHFIELD, CHARLES   Painter (1893-1967)
BURCK, JACOB   Cartoonist, Painter (1904-1982)
BURGESS, JOSEPH E   Painter (1891-1961)
BURKE, WILLIAM LOZIER MUNRO   Historian (1906-1961)
BURLIN, PAUL   Painter (-1969)
BURLUIK, DAVID   Painter (1882-1967)
BURNEY, MINNA   Educator (1891-1958)
BURNS, SID   Sculptor, Collector (1916-1979)
BURNSIDE, CAMERON   Painter, Teacher (-1952)
BURNSHIDE, KATHERINE TALBOTT   Painter
BURROWS, PEARL   Painter
BURT, CLYDE EDWIN   Ceramist, Educator (-1981)
BURTON, NETTA M   Painter
BUSBEE, JULIANA ROYSTER   Craftsman (1877-1962)
BUSH, ELLA SHEPART   Painter
BUSH, JACK   Painter (1909-1977)
BUSH, WILLIAM BROUGHTON   Painter
BUTLER, JOSEPH (GREEN)   Administrator, Painter (1901-1981)

BYRUM, RUTHVEN HOLMES   Educator
CADORIN, ETTOR   Sculptor (-1952)
CAHAN, SAMUEL G   Artist (-1974)
CAHILL, HOLGER   Art Authority (1893-1960)
CALDER, ALEXANDER   Sculptor (1898-1976)
CALKINS, LORING GARY   Designer (1887-1960)
CALLERY, MARY   Sculptor (1903-1977)
CALVERT, JENNIE C (MRS FINLEY H)   Painter
CAMFFERMAN, PETER MARIENUS   Painter (1890-1957)
CAMPBELL, EDMUNDS   Painter, Architect (-1950)
CAMPBELL, ORLAND   Portrait Painter (1890-1972)
CAMPBELL, SARA WENDELL   Illustrator (1886-1960)
CAMPBELL, WILLIAM PATRICK   Art Historian, Curator (1914-1976)
CANDELL, VICTOR   Painter, Educator (1903-1977)
CANTEY, SAM BENTON, III   Collector (-1973)
CAPP, AL   Cartoonist (1900-   )
CAREWE, SYLVIA   Painter, Tapestry Artist
CARLES, ARTHUR B   Painter (1882-1952)
CARMACK, PAUL R   Cartoonist (1895-1977)
CARRILLO, LILIA   Painter (1929-1974)
CARROLL, JOHN   Painter (1892-1959)
CARRUTH, PAUL H   Illustrator (1892-1961)
CARTER, AUGUSTUS D (AD)   Cartoonist (1895-1957)
CARTER, HELENE   Illustrator (1887-1960)
CASSEL, JOHN HARMON   Cartoonist
CASTANO, GIOVANNI   Art Dealer, Painter (1896-   )
CASTLE, MRS ALFRED L   Art Patron (1886-1970)
CATHERS, JAMES O   Sculptor, Educator (1934-1982)
CAVALLITO, ALBINO   Sculptor (1905-1966)
CHALIAPIN, BORIS   Painter (1907-1979)
CHAMBERLAIN, BETTY   Art Administrator, Writer (1908-1983)
CHAMBERLAIN, SAMUEL   Printmaker, Writer (1895-1975)
CHAMBERS, JOHN   Painter, Filmmaker (1931-1978)
CHAMBI, MARTIN   Photographer (1891-1973)
CHANDOR, DOUGLAS   Portrait Painter (-1953)
CHANIN, ABRAHAM L   Lecturer
CHAPELLIER, GEORGE   Art Dealer, Collector (1890-1978)
CHAPELLIER, ROBERT   Art Dealer (-1974)
CHAPIN, FRANCIS   Painter (-1965)
CHAPIN, MYRON BUTMAN   Painter (1887-1958)
CHAPMAN, CHARLES SHEPARD   Painter (-1962)
CHAPMAN, HOWARD EUGENE   Director, Cartoonist (1913-1977)
CHARLES, CLAYTON (HENRY)   Sculptor, Educator (1913-   )
CHARLOT, JEAN   Painter, Historian (1898-1979)
CHASE, EDWARD   Portrait Painter (-1965)
CHASE, FRANK SWIFT   Painter (1886-1958)
CHASE, GEORGE H   Educator, Writer (-1952)
CHASE, JOSEPH CUMMINGS   Portrait Painter (-1965)
CHASE, SIDNEY M   Painter (1877-1957)
CHATTERTON, CLARENCE KERR   Painter (1880-1973)
CHEFFETZ, ASA   Engraver (-1965)
CHENEY, SHELDON   Writer, Historian (1886-1980)
CHERNEY, MARVIN   Painter (-1966)
CHESTERTON, DAVID   Educator, Graphic Artist (1930-   )
CHEW, HARRY   Painter, Educator (1925-   )
CHIAPELLA, EDWARD EMILE   Painter (-1951)
CHILDERS, BETTY BIVINS   Collector, Patron (1913-1982)
CHOATE, NATHANIEL   Sculptor (-1965)
CHOUINARD, MRS NELBERT   Educator (-1969)
CHRISTENSEN, RALPH   Painter (1897-1961)
CHRIST-JANER, ALBERT WILLIAM   Painter, Printmaker (1910-1973)
CHRISTOPHER, WILLIAM R   Painter (1924-1973)
CHRISTY, HOWARD CHANDLER   Painter (-1952)
CHURCH, FREDERICE   Painter
CIAMPAGLIA, CARLO   Mural Painter (1891-1975)
CLANCY, JOHN   Art Dealer (-1981)
CLAPP, MAUDE CAROLINE EDE   Painter (1876-1960)
CLARK, ALLAN   Sculptor (-1950)
CLARK, ALSON SKINNER   Painter, Lithographer (-1949)
CLARK, ANTHONY MORRIS   Curator, Collector (1923-1976)
CLARK, ELIOT CANDEE   Painter (1883-1980)
CLARK, G FLETCHER   Sculptor (1899-1982)
CLARK, MABEL BEATRICE SMITH   Painter (-1957)
CLARK, ROLAND   Painter (1874-1957)
CLEAR, CHARLES V   Museum Consultant
CLEAVES, MURIEL MATTOCK (MRS H)   Illustrator, Painter (-1947)
CLELAND, THOMAS MAITLAND   Illustrator (-1964)
CLIME, WINFIELD SCOTT   Painter (1881-1958)
CLINEDINST, MAY SPEAR   Painter
CLOSE, MARJORIE (PERRY)   Painter, Lecturer (1899-1978)
COATES, ROBERT M   Writer, Art Critic (1897-   )
COE, LLOYD   Painter, Illustrator (1899-1977)
COE, ROLAND   Cartoonist
COFFEY, MABEL   Painter, Etcher

COFFMAN, HAL   Cartoonist (1883-1958)
COHEN, H GEORGE   Painter, Educator (1913-1980)
COLBORN, JANE TAYLOR   Sculptor, Educator (1913-1983)
COLBY, HOMER WAYLAND   Illustrator, Etcher (-1950)
COLEMAN, RALPH P   Painter (-1968)
COLETTI, JOSEPH ARTHUR   Sculptor, Writer (1898-1973)
COLLES, GERTRUDE   Painter (1969-1957)
COLLIER, LEO NATHAN (NATE)   Cartoonist (1884-1961)
COLLINS, KREIGH   Illustrator (1908-1974)
COLLINS, ROY H   Illustrator (-1949)
CONE, MARVIN   Painter (-1964)
CONNAWAY, JAY HALL   Painter (1893-1970)
CONNER, JOHN RAMSEY   Painter (-1952)
CONROW, WILFORD SEYMOUR   Painter
CONSTABLE, WILLIAM GEORGE   Art Historian, Writer (1887-1976)
CONSTANT, GEORGE   Painter (1892-1978)
COOK, GLADYS EMERSON   Illustrator, Painter
COOK, HOWARD NORTON   Painter, Lecturer (1901-   )
COOK, WALTER WILLIAM SPENCER   Educator (-1962)
COOKE, HEREWARD LESTER   Art Historian, Painter (1916-1973)
COOKE, KATHLEEN McKEITH   Painter, Sculptor (1908-1978)
COOLEY, DIXIE (MRS JOHN L)   Painter
COOMARASWAMY, ANANDA K   Museum Curator (-1947)
COOPER, FRED G.   Cartoonist (-1962)
COOPER, RICHARD   Painter (1945-1979)
COOTES, FRANK GRAHAM   Painter (1879-1960)
COPPINI, POMPEO LUIGI   Sculptor (1870-1957)
CORBETT, EDWARD M   Educator, Painter (1919-1971)
CORBETT, GAIL SHERMAN (MRS HARVEY WILEY CORBETT)   Sculptor (-1952)
CORBINO, JOHN   Painter (-1964)
CORCOS, LUCILLE   Painter, Illustrator (1908-1973)
CORNELIUS, MARTY   Painter, Illustrator (1913-1979)
CORNELL, JOSEPH   Sculptor (1903-1972)
CORNWELL, DEAN   Illustrator (1892-1960)
CORTIGLIA, NICCOLO   Painter, Restorer (1893-   )
COSGRAVE, J O'HARA, II   Illustrator (-1968)
COSLA, O K   Collector
COSTIGAN, JOHN EDWARD   Painter (1888-1972)
COTSWORTH, STAATS   Painter (1908-1979)
COTTON, LILLIAN   Painter (-1962)
COTTON, WILLIAM HENRY   Painter (1880-1958)
COURTICE, RODY KENNY   Painter (-1973)
COVERT, JOHN   Painter (1882-1960)
COVEY, ARTHUR   Painter (1878-1960)
COWAN, WOODSON MESSICK   Cartoonist, Painter (1886-1977)
COWDREY, MARY BARTLETT   Art Historian, Art Critic (1910-1974)
COWLES, RUSSELL   Painter (1887-1979)
COX, ALLYN   Painter (1896-1982)
COX, J HALLEY   Painter, Educator
COZE-DABIJA, PAUL   Painter, Writer (1903-1975)
CRAMPTON, ROLLIN   Painter (-1970)
CRANDELL, BRADSHAW   Painter (-1966)
CRANE, ROY (CAMPBELL)   Cartoonist, Writer (1901-   )
CRASKE, LEONARD   Sculptor, Lithographer (-1950)
CRATZ, BENJIMIN ARTHUR   Painter, Cartoonist
CRAVATH, GLENN   Cartoonist (-1964)
CRAWFORD, EARL   Painter (1890-1960)
CRAWFORD, RALSTON   Painter, Lithographer (1906-1977)
CRAWFORD, WILLIAM H   Cartoonist, Sculptor (1913-   )
CRESPI, PACHITA   Painter (1900-1971)
CRESSON, MARGARET   Sculptor, Writer (1889-1973)
CRISS, FRANCIS H   Painter (1901-1973)
CROCKWELL, DOUGLAS   Commercial Artist (-1968)
CRONIN, TONY   Gallery Director (-1979)
CROSBY, SUMNER McKNIGHT   Art Historian (1909-1982)
CROUGHTON, AMY H   Critic (-1951)
CRUMP, KATHLEEN (WHEELER)   Sculptor (1884-1977)
CRUMP, W LESLIE   Painter (-1962)
CUMING, BEATRICE   Painter (1903-1975)
CUNNINGHAM, BENJAMIN FRAZIER   Painter, Educator (1904-1975)
CUNNINGHAM, CHARLES CREHORE   Curator, Lecturer (1910-   )
CUNNINGHAM, IMOGEN   Photographer (1883-1976)
CUNNINGHAM, MARION   Serigrapher, Lithographer
CUPRIEN, FRANK W   Painter (-1948)
CURRIER, CYRUS BATES   Painter, Designer
CURTIS, CONSTANCE   Painter (-1959)
CUSUMANO, STEFANO   Painter, Educator (1912-1975)
CZUFIN, RUDOLF   Director (1901-1979)
DABO, LEON   Painter (1868-1960)
DAHL, FRANCIS W   Cartoonist (1907-1973)
DAHLER, WARREN   Painter (1897-1961)
DAINGERFIELD, MARJORIE JAY   Sculptor (-1977)

DALE, BENJAMIN MORAN   Illustrator (-1951)
D'ANDREA, ALBERT PHILIP   Educator, Sculptor (1897-1983)
DANIEL, LEWIS C   Painter, Illustrator (-1952)
DARIUS, DENYLL (DENNIS MITCHELL)   Painter (1942-1976)
DARLING, JAY NORWOOD (DING)   Cartoonist (1876-1962)
DASBURG, ANDREW MICHAEL   Painter (1887-1979)
DATUS, JAY   Painter, Art Administrator (1914-1974)
DATZ, A MARK   Painter
DAUGHERTY, JAMES HENRY   Painter, Writer (1898-1974)
DAVENPORT, EDITH FAIRFAX   Painter (1880-1957)
DAVEY, RANDALL   Painter (-1964)
DAVIDSON, JO   Sculptor (-1952)
DAVIDSON, MORRIS   Painter (1898-1979)
DAVIS, ESTHER M   Sculptor, Painter (1893-1974)
DAVIS, JAMES   Abstract Artist (-1974)
DAVIS, LEW E   Painter (1910-1979)
DAVIS, PHIL   Cartoonist (-1964)
DAVIS, ROBERT TYLER   Administrator, Historian (1904-   )
DAVIS, STUART   Painter (1894-1964)
DAVIS, WILLIAM STEEPLE   Painter (1884-1961)
DAVISSON, HOMER G   Painter
DAWSON, EVE   Painter
DAY, MABEL K'   Painter
DEAN, ERNEST WILFRID   Painter
DE BORHEGYI, STEPHEN   Museum Director, Writer (1921-1969)
DE BOTTON, JEAN PHILIPPE   Painter, Sculptor (-1978)
DECKER, JOHN   Painter
DE CREEFT, JOSE   Sculptor, Educator (1884-1982)
DE DIEGO, JULIO   Painter, Illustrator (1900-1979)
DE ERDELY, FRANCIS   Painter, Educator (1904-1959)
DEFRANCESCO, ITALO I   Educator (-1967)
DE FRANCISCI, ANTHONY   Sculptor (-1964)
DE GRAZIA, ETTORE TED   Painter (1909-1982)
DEHN, ADOLF   Graphic Artist (-1968)
DEINES, E HUBERT   Engraver (-1967)
DE JONG, GERRIT, JR   Lecturer, Writer (1892-1979)
DEKNATEL, FREDERICK BROCKWAY   Art Historian, Educator (1905-1973)
DELANEY, BEAUFORD   Painter (1902-1979)
DEL CASTILLO, MARY VIRGINIA   Painter
DE MANCE, HENRI   Painter (-1948)
DE MARTELLY, JOHN STOCKTON   Painter, Printmaker (1903-1980)
DE MENIL, JOHN   Collector (1904-1973)
DEMETRIOS, GEORGE   Sculptor (-1974)
DEMIANOFF, RENEE LOCKHART   Director (1910-1962)
DENNIS, BURT MORGAN   Etcher (1892-1960)
DENSLOW, DOROTHEA HENRIETTA   Sculptor (1900-1971)
DENTZEL, CARL SCHAEFER   Museum Director, Writer (1913-1980)
DePINNA, VIVIAN   Painter (1883-1978)
DE PREY, JUAN   Painter (-1962)
DERUJINSKY, GLEB W   Sculptor, Craftsman (1888-1975)
DESSAR, LOUIS PAUL   Painter (-1952)
DE TORE, JOHN E   Painter (1902-1975)
DEVREE, HOWARD   Critic (-1966)
DIBONA, ANTHONY   Sculptor, Lithographer
DICKERSON, WILLIAM JUDSON   Painter
DICKINSON, EDWIN W   Painter (1891-1979)
DIETSCH, C PERCIVAL   Sculptor (1881-1961)
DILLER, BURGOYNE   Painter (1906-1965)
DIMAN, HOMER   Painter (1914-1974)
DIRK, NATHANIEL   Painter (1896-1961)
DIRKS, RUDOLPH   Cartoonist (-1968)
DISMUKES, MARY ETHEL   Painter (-1952)
DIXON, FRANCIS S   Painter (-1967)
DOBBS, ELLA VICTORIA   Educator (-1952)
DOBKIN, ALEXANDER   Painter (1908-1975)
DOBSON, DAVID IRVING (DIAMONDSTEIN)   Painter (1883-1957)
DODGE, HAZEL (MRS WILLIAM T TURMAN)   Curator (1903-1957)
DOI, ISAMI   Painter
DONAHEY, JAMES HARRISON   Cartoonist
DONATO, GIUSEPPE   Sculptor (-1965)
DONNELLY, MARY E   Painter (1898-1963)
DORNER, ALEXANDER   Historian
DOUGLAS, AARON   Painter (1900-1979)
DOUGLAS, FREDERIC HUNTINGTON   Curator
DOUGLAS, LESTER   Designer (1894-1961)
DOUGLAS, ROBERT LANGTON   Critic (-1951)
DOVE, ARTHUR GARFIELD   Painter (1880-1946)
DOWLING, ROBERT W   Patron
DRABKIN, STELLA   Painter, Designer (1906-1976)
DREIER, KATHERINE S   Painter, Lecturer (-1952)
DROGKAMP, CHARLES   Painter (-1958)
DRUMMOND, ARTHUR A   Painter, Illustrator (1891-   )
DRURY, WILLIAM H   Painter (1888-1960)
DUANE, TANYA   Painter, Collage Artist

DUBLE, LU   Sculptor (1896-1970)
DU BOIS, GUY PENE   Painter (1884-1958)
DUFFY, EDMUND   Cartoonist (-1962)
DUFNER, EDWARD   Painter (1871-1957)
DU MOND, FRANK V   Painter (-1951)
DUNCANSON, ROBERT   Painter (1817-1872)
DUNN, ALAN (CANTWELL)   Cartoonist, Writer (1900-1974)
DUNN, HARVEY T   Illustrator, Painter (-1952)
DUPONT, HENRY F   Museum Curator (-1969)
DUVOISIN, ROGER   Writer, Illustrator (1904-1980)
DWIGGINS, CLARE   Cartoonist (1874-1958)
DWIGGINS, WILLIAM ADDISON   Designer (1880-1956)
DWIGHT, EDWARD HAROLD   Museum Director (1919-1981)
EASBY, DUDLEY T, JR   Art Administrator, Art Historian (1905-1973)
EASTMAN, ALVIN CLARK   Orientalist (1894-1959)
EASTMAN, WILLIAM JOSEPH   Painter (-1950)
EASTON, FRANK LORENCE   Painter
EATON, ALLEN HENDERSHOTT   Writer (-1962)
EBERLE, MERAB   Critic (-1959)
ECKE, GUSTAV   Museum Curator (-1971)
ED, CARL   Cartoonist (1890-1959)
EDWARDS, GEORGE WHARTON   Painter, Illustrator (-1950)
EDWARDS, ROBERT   Painter, Engraver (-1948)
EGAS, CAMILO   Educator (-1962)
EGE, OTTO F   Educator, Writer (-1951)
EGGERS, GEORGE WILLIAM   Educator (1883-1958)
EGGERS, RICHARD F   Architect (1918-1979)
EHRMAN, FREDERICK L   Collector (1906-1973)
EISENLOHR, EDWARD G   Painter (1873-1961)
EITEL, CLIFFE DEAN   Painter, Etcher
ELDER, ARTHUR JOHN   Painter, Etcher
ELDLITZ, DOROTH MEIGS   Patron, Photographer (1891-1976)
ELISOFON, ELIOT   Painter, Photographer (1911-1973)
ELKON, ROBERT   Art Dealer, Collector (1928-1983)
ELLERHUSEN, FLORENCE COONEY   Painter (-1950)
ELLERHUSEN, ULRIC H   Sculptor (1879-1957)
ELLIS, CARL EUGENE   Art Administrator, Instructor (1932-1977)
ELLIS, JOSEPH BAILEY   Educator, Sculptor
ELLIS, ROBERT CARROLL   Painter, Printmaker (1923-1979)
ELLSWORTH, CLARENCE A   Illustrator (1885-1961)
ELY, FANNY G   Painter (1879-1961)
EMBRY, NORRIS   Painter (1921-1981)
EMIL, ALLAN D   Collector, Patron (1898-   )
EMMERICH, IRENE HILLEBRAND   Painter
EMMET, LYDIA FIELD   Painter (-1952)
ENFIELD, HARRY   Illustrator (1906-1958)
ENGEL, HARRY   Painter (1901-1970)
ENGEL, MICHAEL M   Art Publicist (-1969)
ENO, JAMES LORNE   Painter, Teacher (-1952)
ENSER, GEORGE   Designer (1890-1961)
EPSTEIN, ETHEL S   Collector
ERICSON, ERNEST   Illustrator, Instructor (-1981)
ERLANGER, ELIZABETH N   Painter, Lecturere (1901-1975)
ERNST, MAX   Painter, Sculptor (1891-1976)
ERSKINE, HAROLD PERRY   Sculptor (-1951)
ESCHMANN, JEAN CHARLES   Craftsman (1896-1961)
ESHERICK, WHARTON   Sculptor, Designer (1887-1970)
ETTINGHAUSEN, RICHARD   Administrator, Educator (1906-   )
EVANS, DONALD   Painter (1946-1977)
EVANS, RUDULPH   Sculptor (1879-1960)
EVERETT, MARY O (MRS H G)   Painter (-1948)
EVERGOOD, PHILIP   Painter, Graphic Artist (1901-1973)
EVERINGHAM, MILLARD   Painter, Etcher
FABRES, OSCAR   Cartoonist (1895-1961)
FABRI, RALPH   Painter, Writer (1894-1975)
FAHLSTROM, OYVIND   Painter (1928-1976)
FAINTER, ROBERT A   Educator, Painter (1942-1978)
FAIRCHILD, MAY   Painter (1872-1959)
FALLS, CHARLES BUCKLES   Illustrator (1874-1959)
FARLOW, HARRY   Painter (1882-1956)
FARMER, MABEL McKIBBIN   Engraver
FARNSWORTH, JERRY   Painter, Writer (1895-   )
FARR, FRED   Sculptor (1914-1973)
FARRELL, KATHERINE L   Painter, Etcher
FASTOVE, AARON (AARON FASTOVSKY)   Painter (1898-1979)
FAULKNER, BARRY   Painter
FAULKNER, KADY B   Painter, Educator (1901-1977)
FAULKNER, RAY N   Educator, Writer (1906-1975)
FAUSETT, LYNN   Painter (1894-1977)
FAWCETT, ROBERT   Illustrator (-1967)
FAY, WILBUR M   Designer (1904-1959)
FEELEY, PAUL   Painter (1913-1966)
FEIGIN, DOROTHY   Painter (-1969)
FEIGL, HUGO   Art Dealer (1890-1961)
FEITELSON, LORSER   Painter (1912-1977)

FENICAL, MARLIN E   Painter, Photographer (1907-1983)
FENTON, BEATRICE   Sculptor (1887-1983)
FENTON, JOHN NATHANIEL   Painter, Etcher (1912-1977)
FERNALD, HELEN ELIZABETH   Educator (-1964)
FERRARI, FEBO   Sculptor
FERREN, JOHN   Painter (1905-1970)
FICKLEN, JACK HOWELLS   Cartoonist (1911-1980)
FIELDS, MITCHELL   Sculptor (-1966)
FIENE, ALICIA W   Painter (1919-1961)
FIENE, ERNEST   Painter (-1965)
FIERO, EMILIE L   Sculptor (1889-1974)
FILTZER, HYMAN   Sculptor, Restorer (1901-1967)
FINK, LOUIS R   Painter (1925-1980)
FINLAYSON, DONALD LORD   Educator (1897-1960)
FINLEY, DAVID EDWARD   Art Administrator (1890-1977)
FINLEY, MARY L   Painter (-1964)
FINTA, ALEXANDER   Sculptor
FISCHETTI, JOHN   Cartoonist (1916-1980)
FISH, DOROTHY S   Ceramist (1906-1958)
FISHER, REGINALD   Writer (-1966)
FISKE, GERTRUDE   Painter (-1961)
FITE, HARVEY   Sculptor (1903-1976)
FITZGERALD, J EDWARD   Photographer (1923-1977)
FITZSIMMONS, JAMES JOSEPH   Painter, Architect (1908-   )
FLAGG, JAMES MONTGOMERY   Illustrator (-1960)
FLANAGAN, JOHN   Sculptor (-1952)
FLEISCHMANN, ADOLF R   Painter (-1969)
FLEISCHMANN, JULIUS   Collector
FLEMING, ALLAN ROBB   Designer, Calligrapher (1929-1977)
FLIEGEL, LESLIE   Painter (-1968)
FLOCH, JOSEPH   Painter (1895-1977)
FLORSHEIM, RICHARD A   Painter, Printmaker (1916-1979)
FLORY, ARTHUR L   Graphic Artist, Painter (1914-1972)
FOOTE, JOHN, JR   Painter (-1968)
FOOTE, WILL HOWE   Painter (-1965)
FORBES, EDWARD W   Museum Director (-1969)
FORCE, JULIANA R   Museum Director (-1948)
FORD, ELEANOR CLAY   Patron (1896-1976)
FOSBURGH, JAMES WHITNEY   Painter, Writer (1910-1978)
FOSDICK, SINA G   Art Administrator, Collector (-1983)
FOSTER, GENEVIEVE   Writer, Illustrator (1893-1979)
FOSTER, HAL   Cartoonist, Painter (1892-1982)
FOSTER, JAMES W, SR   Museum Director
FOSTER, KENNETH E   Museum Director (-1964)
FOURNIER, ALEXIS JEAN   Painter (-1948)
FOUSEK, FRANK DANIEL   Printmaker, Painter (1913-1979)
FOWLER, ALFRED   Writer
FOX, CHARLES HAROLD   Craftsman (1905-1979)
FOX, MILTON S   Painter (1904-1971)
FRANKENSTEIN, ALFRED VICTOR   Art Critic, Art Historial (1906-1981)
FRANKFURTER, ALFRED   Art Editor (-1965)
FRANKL, PAUL THEODORE   Designer (1876-1958)
FRANKLE, PHILIP   Painter (-1968)
FRANKLIN, CLARENCE   Collector (-1967)
FRASER, DOUGLAS (FERRAR)   Art Historian, Educator (1929-1982)
FRASER, LAURA G   Sculptor (-1966)
FRASER, MALCOLM   Painter (-1949)
FRAZIER, KENNETH   Painter (-1949)
FRAZIER, RICHARD WILLIAMS   Sculptor (1922-1983)
FREDENTHAL, DAVID   Painter
FREED, ERNEST BRADFIELD   Printmaker, Painter
FREEMAN, DON   Author & Illustrator of Children's Books (1909-1978)
FREEMAN, JANE   Portrait Painter (-1963)
FREER, HOWARD MORTIMER   Painter (1904-1960)
FREILICH, MICHAEL L   Art Dealer, Collector (1912-1975)
FREY, ERWIN F   Sculptor (-1967)
FRIEDLAENDER, WALTER   Art Historian (-1966)
FRIEDLANDER, ISAC   Engraver (-1968)
FRIEND, DAVID   Painter, Educator (1899-1978)
FRISHMUTH, HARRIET WHITNEY   Sculptor (1880-1979)
FROELICH, PAUL   Painter
FROMAN, RAMON MITCHELL   Painter (1908-1980)
FROMBERG, GERALD   Educator, Filmmaker (1925-   )
FROUCHTBEN, BERNARD   Painter (1878-1956)
FRUHAUF, ALINE   Painter, Printmaker (1907-1978)
FUERSTENBURG, PAUL W   Commercial Artist (-1953)
FULLER, META VAUX WARRICK   Sculptor (1877-1968)
FULLER, R BUCKMINSTER   Design Scientist (1895-1983)
FULLER, RICHARD EUGENE   Museum Director (1897-1976)
FULTON, CYRUS JAMES   Painter (-1949)
GABO, NAUM   Sculptor (1890-1977)
GAILIS, JANIS   Painter (1909-1975)
GALE, WALTER RASIN   Educator (1878-1959)
GALLATIN, ALBERT EUGENE   Painter (1882-1952)

GALOS, BEN   Painter (-1963)
GALVAN, JESUS GERRERO   Painter
GANNAM, JOHN   Painter (-1965)
GARBATY, EUGENE L   Collector (-1966)
GARBER, DANIEL   Painter (1880-1958)
GARBISCH, BERNICE CHRYSLER   Collector
GARBISCH, EDGAR WILLIAM   Collector (1899-1979)
GARNER, ARCHIBALD   Sculptor, Designer (1904-1970)
GARRISON, JESSE JANES   Educator
GARTH, JOHN   Painter (1894-1971)
GASSER, HENRY MARTIN   Painter, Writer (1909-1981)
GATCH, LEE   Painter (-1968)
GATRELL, ROBERT MORRIS   Educator, Painter (1906-1982)
GAYNE, CLIFTON ALEXANDER, JR   Educator (1912-1971)
GEARHART, MAY   Etcher
GEE, YUN   Painter (-1963)
GEESEY, TITUS CORNELIUS   Collector, Patron (1893-1969)
GEIGER, ELIZABETH DE CHAMISSO   Sculptor
GELB, JAN   Painter, Printmaker (1906-1978)
GERTH, RUTH   Illustrator (-1952)
GETTY, J PAUL   Collector, Writer (1892-1976)
GIAMBRUNI, TIO   Sculptor (1925-1971)
GIBBERED, ERIC WATERS   Painter (1897-1972)
GIKOW, RUTH (RUTH GIKOW LEVINE)   Painter, Printmaker (-1982)
GILCHRIST, AGNES ADDISON   Art & Architectural Historian (1907-1976)
GILL, FREDERICK JAMES   Painter, Instructor (1906-1974)
GILPIN, LAURA   Photographer, Writer (1891-1979)
GILRIN, THEODORE H   Painter (-1967)
GLAMAN, EUGENIE FISH   Etcher (-1956)
GLARNER, FRITZ   Painter (1899-1972)
GLEASON, JOE DUNCAN   Painter (1879-1959)
GLINES, ELLEN (MRS WALTER A)   Painter (-1951)
GLINSKY, VINCENT   Sculptor, Educator (1895-1975)
GODWIN, FRANCES GRAY   Historian (1908-1979)
GOETZ, OSWALD II   Lecturer (1896-1960)
GOLDBERG, ELIAS   Painter (1887-1978)
GOLDBERG, NORMAN LEWIS   Writer, Lecturer (1906-1982)
GOLDIN, AMY   Art Critic (1926-1978)
GOLDOWSKY, NOAH   Art Dealer (1909-   )
GOLDSMITH, MORTON RALPH   Collector, Patron (1882-1971)
GOLDWATER, ROBERT   Art Historian (1907-1973)
GOLINKIN, JOSEPH WEBSTER   Painter, Printmaker (1896-1977)
GOLLIN, JOSHUA A   Collector, Patron (1905-   )
GOODELMAN, AARON J   Sculptor (1891-1978)
GORDON, JOHN   Administrator, Historian (1912-1978)
GORDON, MAXWELL   Painter (1910-1982)
GORHAM, SIDNEY   Painter (-1947)
GOSS, JOHN   Illustrator
GOTTLIEB, ADOLPH   Painter (1903-1974)
GRABACH, JOHN R   Painter, Instructor (1880-1981)
GRAHAM, JOHN D   Painter (1881-1961)
GRAMATKY, HARDIE   Painter, Writer (1907-1979)
GRANT, GORDON HOPE   Etcher (-1962)
GRANT, J JEFFREY   Painter (1883-1960)
GRAVES, JOHN W   Collector (-1978)
GRAVES, MAITLAND   Writer, Painter (1902-   )
GRAY, HAROLD   Cartoonist (-1968)
GRAY, JABEZ   Painter (-1950)
GRAY, WELLINGTON BURBANK   Educator, Designer (1919-1977)
GRAYSON, CLIFFORD PREVOST   Painter (-1951)
GREACEN, EDMUND   Painter (-1949)
GREATHOUSE, WALSER S   Museum Director (-1966)
GRECO, ROBERT   Painter (-1965)
GREEN, BERNARD   Painter (-1951)
GREENE, ELMER WESTLEY   Painter (-1964)
GREENE, GERTRUDE (MRS BALCOMB GREENE)   Painter (1904-1956)
GREENE, J BARRY   Painter (-1966)
GREENE, VERNON VAN ATTA   Cartoonist (-1965)
GREENES, RHODA   Sculptor (1926-1979)
GREEN-FIELD, ALBERT   Art Publicist
GREENLEAF, RAY   Illustrator (-1950)
GREENWOOD, MARION   Painter, Lithographer (1909-1970)
GREGORY, JOHN   Sculptor (1879-1958)
GREGORY, WAYLANDE   Sculptor, Designer (1905-1971)
GRIER, HARRY DOBSON MILLER   Museum Director (1914-1972)
GRIESSLER, FRANZ ANTON   Painter (1897-1974)
GRIFFIN, RACHAEL S   Art Administrator, Writer (-1983)
GRIFFITH, LOUIS OSCAR   Painter (1875-1956)
GRIGAUT, PAUL L   Museum Curator (-1969)
GRIGOR, MARGARET CHRISTIAN   Sculptor (1912-1981)
GRIMES, FRANCES   Sculptor (-1963)
GRINAGER, ALEXANDER   Painter (-1949)

GRODENSKY, SAMUEL   Painter (1894-1974)
GROPPER, WILLIAM   Painter, Lithographer (1897-   )
GROSZ, GEORGE   Painter (1893-1959)
GROTELL, MAIJA   Ceramist, Educator (1899-1973)
GROVES, HANNAH CUTIER   Painter, Etcher (-1952)
GRUBB, PAT PINCOMBE   Painter, Writer (1922-1977)
GRUBERT, CARL ALFRED   Cartoonist (1911-1979)
GRUENTHER, SUE CORY (MRS. RUDOLPH)   Painter (-1948)
GRUGER, FREDERICK   Illustrator (-1953)
GRUMMANN, PAUL H   Museum Director (-1950)
GRUPPE, EMIL ALBERT   Painter (1896-1978)
GRUPPE, KARL HEINRICH   Sculptor (1893-1982)
GUGGENHEIM, HARRY FRANK   Collector, Publisher, Writer
  (1890-1971)
GUGGENHEIM, PEGGY   Collector, Patron (1898-1979)
GUGGENHEIMER, RICHARD HENRY   Painter, Writer (1906-1977)
GUGLIELMI, LOUIS O   Painter (1906-1956)
GUINZBURG, FREDERICK   Sculptor (1897-1978)
GUNDLACH, HELEN FUCHS   Painter (1892-1959)
GUSTAVSON, LELAND   Illustrator (-1966)
GUSTON, PHILIP   Painter (1913-1980)
GUY, JAMES M   Painter, Educator (1910-1983)
HADER, ELMER (STANLEY)   Illustrator, Writer (1889-1973)
HADLOCK, WENDELL STANWOOD   Museum Director (1911-1978)
HAGGIN, BEN ALI   Painter, Designer (-1951)
HAHN, EMANUEL OTTO   Sculptor (1881-1957)
HAIG, PATIGIAN   Sculptor, (1876-1950)
HALE, LILLIAN WESTCOTT   Painter (-1963)
HALEY, ROBERT D   Painter (1893-1959)
HALSMAN, PHILIPPE   Photographer (1906-1979)
HAMBLETT, THEORA   Painter, Illustrator (1895-   )
HAMM, BETH CREEVY   Painter (1885-1958)
HAMMER, VICTOR KARL   Painter (-1967)
HAMPTON, BILL   Painter (1925-1977)
HAND, MOLLY WILLIAMS   Teacher, Painter (-1951)
HANDFORTH, THOMAS   Lithographer (-1948)
HANKS, NANCY   Administrator (1927-1983)
HANLEY, T EDWARD   Collector (-1969)
HANNA, THOMAS KING   Painter (-1951)
HANSEN, ARMIN CARL   Painter (1886-1957)
HARDER, CHARLES MABRY   Craftsman (1899-1959)
HARDING, GEORGE   Painter (-1959)
HARE, MICHAEL MEREDITH   Scholar (-1968)
HARER, FREDERICK W   Painter, Sculptor (-1949)
HARPER, GEORGE COBURN   Etcher (1887-1962)
HARPER, JOHN RUSSELL   Art Historian (1914-1983)
HARRIS, BEN JORJ   Illustrator (1904-1957)
HARRIS, MARGIE COLEMAN   Painter
HARSANYI, CHARLES   Painter (1905-1973)
HART, AGNES   Painter, Instructor (-1979)
HART, JOHN FRANCIS   Cartoonist, Engraver
HARTL, LEON   Painter (1889-   )
HARTMAN, BERTRAM   Painter
HARTMANN, GEORG THEO   Painter, Etcher (1894-1976)
HARTWELL, GEORGE KENNETH   Lithographer (-1949)
HARVEY, JAMES V   Painter (-1965)
HASELTINE, HERBERT   Sculptor (1877-1962)
HASKELL, WILLIAM H   Educator (-1952)
HASWELL, ERNEST BRUCE   Sculptor (1889-1965)
HATCH, EMILY NICHOLS   Painter
HATHAWAY, CALVIN S   Curator (-1974)
HATHAWAY, LOVERING   Painter (-1949)
HATLO, JAMES   Cartoonist (-1963)
HAUSCHKA, CAROLA SPAETH   Painter (-1948)
HAUSMANN, MARIANNE PISKO   Painter
HAVENS, JAMES DEXTER   Graphic Artist (1900-1960)
HAVENS, MURRY P   Designer
HAWLEY, MARGARET FOOTE   Portrait Painter (-1963)
HAYDEN, PALMER C   Painter (1893-1973)
HAYES, WILLIAM CHRISTOPHER   Museum Curator (-1963)
HAZELL, FRANK   Painter
HEALY, ARTHUR K D   Painter, Lecturer (1902-1978)
HEBER, CARL A   Sculptor (1885-1956)
HECHT, ZOLTAN   Painter (-1968)
HEERAMANECK, NASIL M   Collector, Patron, Art Dealer (1902-1971)
HEINTZELMAN, ARTHUR W   Etcher (-1965)
HELD, JOHN, JR   Cartoonist (1889-1958)
HELLER, MAXWELL   Painter (-1963)
HELM, JOHN F, JR   Educator, Painter (1900-1972)
HELWIG, ARTHUR LOUIS   Painter, Instructor (-1976)
HENRICKSEN, RALF CHRISTIAN   Educator, Painter (1907-1975)
HERBERT, MARIAN   Painter (1899-1960)
HERING, HARRY   Painter (-1967)
HERING, HENRY   Sculptor (-1949)
HERRINGTON, ARTHUR W   Collector, Patron

HERRINGTON, NELL RAY   Collector, Patron
HERSHFIELD, LEO   Illustrator (1904-1979)
HERTER, ALBERT   Painter (-1950)
HERVES, MADELINE   Painter (-1969)
HESS, THOMAS B   Critic, Writer (1920-1978)
HESSE, EVA   Sculptor (1936-1972)
HEUERMANN, MAGDA   Painter
HEYL, BERNARD CHAPMAN   Scholar
HIBBARD, ALDRO THOMPSON   Painter (1886-1972)
HIGGINS, EUGENE   Painter (1875-1958)
HIGGINS, VICTOR   Painter (-1949)
HILDERBRANDT, HOWARD LOGAN   Painter (1874-1958)
HILER, HILAIRE   Painter (-1966)
HILL, GEORGE SNOW   Painter (-1969)
HILL, HOMER   Illustrator
HILL, (JAMES) JEROME   Painter (1905-   )
HILL, JOHN HENRY   Painter (1839-1922)
HILL, JOHN WILLIAM   Painter (1812-1879)
HILLMAN, ALEX L   Collector (-1968)
HILS, LAURA COOMBS   Painter (-1952)
HINES, JOHN M   Painter (-1982)
HINKLE, CLARENCE   Painter (1880-1960)
HINTON, CHARLES LOUIS   Painter (-1950)
HIRSCH, JOSEPH   Painter (1910-1981)
HIRSCH, STEFAN   Educator (-1964)
HIRSCHHORN, JOSEPH H   Collector (1899-1981)
HOBSON, KATHERINE THAYER   Sculptor (1889-1982)
HOCKADAY, HUGH   Painter (-1968)
HOEHN, HARRY   Painter, Printmaker (1918-1974)
HOFFMAN, ARNOLD   Painter (-1966)
HOFFMAN, MALVINA   Sculptor (-1966)
HOFMANN, HANS   Painter, Educator (1880-1966)
HOLCOMB, ALICE (McCAFFERY)   Painter (1906-1977)
HOLCOMBE, BLANCHE KEATON   Painter, Educator (1912-   )
HOLGATE, EDWIN HEADLEY   Painter (1892-1977)
HOLLAND, JANICE   Illustrator (-1962)
HOLLOWAY, H MAXSON   Museum Director (-1966)
HOLMGREN, R JOHN   Illustrator (-1963)
HOLTY, CARL ROBERT   Painter, Writer (1900-1973)
HOOD, ETHEL PAINTER   Sculptor (1908-1982)
HOOD, GEORGE W   Painter (-1949)
HOOVER, MARIE LOUISE (ROCHON)   Artist (1895-1976)
HOPKINSON, CHARLES   Painter (-1962)
HOPPER, EDWARD   Painter (1882-1967)
HOPPER, JON   Painter (-1968)
HORCH, LOUIS L   Collector (1889-1979)
HORD, DONAL   Sculptor (-1966)
HORNYANSKY, NICHOLAS   Etcher (1896-1965)
HOVANNES, JOHN   Painter (1900-1973)
HOVEY, WALTER READ   Historian, Educator (1949-1982)
HOWARD, CECIL   Sculptor (1888-1956)
HOWARD, ROBERT BOARDMAN   Sculptor (1896-1983)
HOWE, KATHERINE L MALLET   Painter (-1957)
HOWITT, JOHN NEWTON   Illustrator (1885-1958)
HOWLAND, EDITH   Sculptor (-1949)
HOWLAND, GARTH   Educator, Painter (-1950)
HOYT, WHITNEY F   Painter, Collector (1910-1980)
HUBBARD, CHARLES D   Painter (-1951)
HUBBELL, HENRY SALEM   Painter (-1949)
HUCK, ROBERT E   Educator (1923-1961)
HUEY, FLORENCE GREENE   Painter (1872-1961)
HULL, MARIE (ATKINSON)   Painter (-1980)
HUMES, RALPH H   Sculptor (1902-1981)
HUMPHREY, JACK WELDON   Painter (-1967)
HUNT, LYNN   Painter (1878-1960)
HUNT, WAYNE WOLF ROBE (KEWA-TSE-SHE)   Silversmith, Painter
  (1905-1977)
HUNTER, FRANCIS TIPTON   Illustrator
HUNTINGTON, A MONTGOMERY   Designer (-1967)
HUNTINGTON, ANNA V HYATT   Sculptor (-1973)
HUNTINGTON, JOHN W   Collector, Patron (1910-   )
HUNTINGTON, MARGARET WENDELL   Painter (1867-1958)
HUNTLEY, VICTORIA HUTSON   Lithographer (1900-1971)
HURLEY, EDWARD TIMOTHY   Etcher, Painter (-1950)
HUTCHISON, MARY ELIZABETH   Painter (1906-1970)
HUTTON, HUGH McMILLEN   Cartoonist (1897-1976)
ILIGAN, RALPH W   Painter (1894-1960)
INGLE, TOM   Painter, Lecturer (1920-1973)
IORIO, ADRIAN J   Illustrator (1879-1957)
IPSEN, ERNEST L   Portrait Painter (-1951)
IREDELL, RUSSELL   Painter (1889-1959)
IRVIN, REA   Painter (1881-1972)
IRVING, ANNA DUER   Painter (1873-1957)
ISAACS, BETTY LEWIS   Sculptor (1894-1971)
ISAACS, CAROLE SCHAFFER   Collector, Patron (1931-1980)

ITTLESON, HENRY, JR   Collector (1900-1973)
IVES, NORMAN S   Painter, Printmaker, Graphic Designer (1924-1978)
IVINS, WILLIAM M, JR   Curator (1881-1961)
JACK, RICHARD   Painter (-1952)
JACKSON, ALEXANDER YOUNG   Painter (1882-1974)
JACKSON, ANN   Painter (-1956)
JACKSON, ANNIE HURLBURT   Painter
JACKSON, HENRY ALDEN   Textile Deisgner (-1952)
JACKSON, JOHN EDWIN   Painter, Designer
JACKSON, LESLEY   Painter (1866-1958)
JACKSON, MARTHA   Gallery Director (-1969)
JACOBS, MICHEL   Painter (1877-1958)
JACOBSSON, STEN WILHELM JOHN   Painter, Sculptor (1899-1983)
JAFFE, WILLIAM B   Collector (-1972)
JANICKI, HAZEL (MRS WILLIAM SCHOCK)   Painter, Instructor
   (1918-1976)
JANSON, HORST WOLDEMAR   Art Historian (1913-1982)
JANSSEN, HANS   Educator, Museum Curator
JARMAN, WALTON MAXEY   Collector (1904-1980)
JARRELL, RANDALL   Critic, Poet (-1965)
JECT-KEY, DAVID   Painter
JEFFERYS, CHARLES WILLIAM   Illustrator (-1951)
JENKINS, BURRIS   Cartoonist (-1966)
JENKINS, PAUL RIPLEY   Sculptor, Painter (1940-1974)
JENNEWEIN, C PAUL   Sculptor (1890-1978)
JENSEN, ALFRED   Painter (1903-1981)
JENSEN, CECIL LEON   Cartoonist (1902-1976)
JENSEN, JOHN EDWARD   Painter, Designer (1921-1982)
JOHANSEN, JOHN C   Portrait Painter
JOHN, GRACE SPAULDING   Painter, Writer (1890-1972)
JOHNSON, BEN   Painter (1902-1967)
JOHNSON, BRUCE   Museum Director (1949-1976)
JOHNSON, CONTENT   Portrait Painter (-1949)
JOHNSON, CROCKET   Painter, Writer (1906-1976)
JOHNSON, HERBERT FISK   Patron (1901-1980)
JOHNSON, JEANNE PAYNE (MRS LOUIS C)   Painter (-1958)
JOHNSON, MALVIN GRAY   Painter (1896-1934)
JOHNSON, SARGENT   Sculptor (1888-1967)
JONES, ALBERTUS EUGENE   Painter (1882-1957)
JONES, JACOBINE   Sculptor
JONES, JOSEPH JOHN (JOE)   Painter (-1963)
JONES, MURRAY   Painter
JONSON, JON   Sculptor (-1947)
JONSON, RAYMOND   Painter, Gallery Director (1891-1982)
JORDAN, LENA E   Painter
JORN, ASGER   Painter, Writer (1914-1973)
JORNS, BYRON CHARLES   Painter (1898-1958)
JOSSET, RAOUL   Sculptor (1900-1957)
JUDSON, ALICE   Painter (-1948)
JUDSON, SYLVIA SHAW   Sculptor (1897-1978)
JUNGWIRTH, LEONARD D   Sculptor (-1964)
JUNKIN, MARION MONTAGUE   Painter, Educator (1905-1977)
JURECKA, CYRIL   Educator
JUSTUS, ROY BRAXTON   Cartoonist (1901-1983)
KACHERGIS, GEORGE JOSEPH   Painter, Educator (1917-1974)
KACHINSKY, ALEXANDER   Painter (1888-1958)
KAHILL, JOSEPH B   Painter (1882-1957)
KAJIWARA, TAKUMA   Painter (1877-1960)
KALLIR, OTTO   Art Dealer, Historian (1894-1978)
KANAGA, CONSEULO   Photographer (1894-1978)
KANTACK, WALTER W   Industrial Artist (-1953)
KANTOR, MORRIS   Painter (1896-1974)
KAPLAN, JOSEPH   Painter (1900-1980)
KAPPEL, PHILIP   Writer, Etcher (1901-1981)
KARASZ, MARISKA   Craftsman (1898-1960)
KARFIOL, BERNARD   Painter (-1952)
KARP, LEON   Painter (-1951)
KARPICK, JOHN   Painter (1884-1960)
KASTOR, HUGO   Painter
KATZ, (ALEXANDER) RAYMOND   Painter (-1974)
KATZ, SIDNEY L   Architect (1915-1978)
KATZENBACH, WILLIAM E   Designer, Lecturer (1904-1975)
KATZENELLENBOGEN, ADOLF   Educator (-1964)
KATZENSTEIN, IRVING   Painter
KATZMANN, HERBERT   Painter
KAUFMAN, ENIT   Painter (1898-1961)
KAUFMANN, ROBERT   Painter (1914-1959)
KAYN, HILDE   Painter (-1950)
KAZ, JOYCE ZICKERMAN   Painter (1936-1979)
KEALLY, FRANCIS   Architect, Sculptor (-1978)
KECK, CHARLES   Sculptor (-1951)
KEFAUVER, NANCY   Advisor on Fine Arts (-1967)
KELLER, HENRY G   Painter, Etcher (-1949)
KENDERDINE, AUGUSTUS FREDERICK   Painter (-1947)
KENNEDY, JANET ROBSON   Painter, Illustrator (1902-1974)

KENT, FRANK WARD   Painter (1912-1977)
KENT, NORMAN   Engraver, Book Designer (1903-1972)
KENT, ROCKWELL   Painter (1882-1971)
KERKAM, EARL   Painter (-1965)
KERR, ARTHUR   Director (1926-1979)
KERR, E COE   Art Dealer (1914-1973)
KEVE, FLORENCE   Educator
KEYES, BERNARD M   Painter (1898-1973)
KEY-OBERG, ELLEN BURKE   Sculptor (1905-)
KEY-OBERG, ROLF   Ceramist (1900-1959)
KEYSER, ERNEST WISE   Sculptor (1876-1959)
KHOURI, ALFRED   Painter (-1962)
KIBBEY, ILAH MARIAN   Painter (1883-1958)
KIENBUSCH, WILLIAM AUSTIN   Painter (1914-1979)
KIESLER, FREDERICK J   Architect (-1966)
KIHN, WILLIAM LANGDON   Painter (1898-1957)
KIJANKA, STANLEY JOSEPH   Painter (1937-1981)
KILENYI, JULIO   Sculptor (1886-1959)
KILGORE, RUPERT   Educator (1910-1971)
KILHAM, WALTER H   Painter, Architect (-1948)
KILLAM, WALT   Painter, Art Dealer (1907-1979)
KILPATRICK, ADA ARILLA   Painter (-1951)
KILPATRICK, ELLEN PERKINS   Painter (-1951)
KIMAK, GEORGE   Painter (1921-1972)
KIMBALL, YEFFE   Painter (1914-1978)
KING, CLINTON BLAIR   Painter, Printmaker (1901-1979)
KING, FRANK   Cartoonist (-1969)
KING, HAMILTON   Illustrator (-1952)
KING, MABEL DEBRA   Painter (-1950)
KING, PAUL   Painter (-1947)
KING, WARREN THOMAS   Cartoonist (1916-)
KINGMAN, EUGENE   Painter, Art Administrator (1909-1975)
KIRK, FRANK C   Painter (-1963)
KIRKBRIDE. EARLE R   Painter (-1968)
KLEINBARDT, ERNEST   Painter (1875-1962)
KLETT, WALTER CHARLES   Illustrator (-1966)
KLEY, ALFRED JULIUS   Craftsman (1895-1957)
KLINE, FRANZ   Painter (1910-1962)
KLINE, GEORGE T   Illustrator (1874-1956)
KLINKER, ORPHA   Etcher (-1964)
KLONIS, BERNARD   Painter (1906-1957)
KNATHS, (OTTO) KARL (1891-1971)
KNIGHT, FREDERIC CHARLES   Painter (1898-1979)
KNIGHT, TACK (BENJAMIN THACKSTON)   Cartoonist (1895-1976)
KNOWLTON, MAUDE BRIGGS   Painter (1876-1956)
KOCH, BERTHA COUCH   Painter (1899-1975)
KOCH, JOHN   Painter, Collector (1909-1978)
KOHLER, ROSE   Sculptor, Painter (-1947)
KOHLHEPP, DOROTHY IRENE   Painter (-1964)
KOHN, GABRIEL   Sculptor (1910-1975)
KOLDE, FREDERICK WILLIAM   Painter
KOLIN, SACHA   Sculptor. Painter (1911-1975)
KOOPMAN, JOHN R   Painter (-1949)
KOPLOWITZ, BENJAMIN (BEN KOPEL)   Painter
KOPMAN, BENJAMIN   Painter (-1965)
KOPPE, RICHARD   Painter, Educator (1916-)
KORDA, VINCENT   Director, Painter
KORMENDI, EUGENE   Sculptor (1889-1959)
KORN, ELIZABETH P   Painter, Illustrator
KOSA, EMIL J, JR   Painter (-1968)
KOTIN, ALBERT   Painter, Educator (1907-1980)
KRANER, FLORIAN G   Painter, Educator (1908-)
KRAUSZ, LASZLO   Painter (1903-1979)
KREINDLER, DORIS BARSKY   Painter, Lithographer (1901-1974)
KRIES, HENRY   Sculptor (-1963)
KROLL, LEON   Painter, Lithographer (1884-1974)
KRONBERG, LOUIS   Painter
KUHLER, OTTO AUGUST   Etcher, Painter (1894-1977)
KUHN, WALT   Painter (-1949)
KUNIYOSHI, YASUO   Painter (1893-1953)
KUNTZ, ROGER EDWARD   Painter, Sculptor (1926-1975)
KUPFERMAN, LAWRENCE   Painter, Printmaker (1909-1982)
KURELEK, WILLIAM   Painter (1927-1977)
KURZ, GERTRUDE ALICE   Craftsman (-1951)
LABICHE, WALTER ANTHONY   Administrator, Instructor (1924-1979)
LAGATTA, JOHN   Illustrator (-1976)
LAHEY, MARGUERITE DUPREZ   Rare Book Binder (1880-1958)
LAHEY, RICHARD (FRANCIS)   Painter, Lecturer (1893-1979)
LAKE, FREDERIC   Art Dealer
LAMONT, FRANCES   Sculptor (-1975)
La MORE, CHET HARMON   Painter, Sculptor (1908-1980)
LANDACRE, PAUL   Engraver (-1963)
LANGE, DOROTHEA   Photographer (-1965)
LANGLAIS, BERNARD   Sculptor, Painter (1921-1977)
LANGSNER, JULES   Art Writer (-1967)

LANGSTON, MILDRED J   Art Dealer, Collector (1902-1976)
LANGTON, BERENICE   Sculptor (1878-1959)
LANKES, JULIUS J   Engraver (1884-1960)
LARKIN, OLIVER   Educator (1896-1970)
LARKIN, WILLIAM   Painter, Printmaker (1902-1969)
LASSEN, BEN   Painter (-1968)
LAUGHLIN, ALICE D   Painter (-1952)
LAUGHLIN, THOMAS   Painter, Publisher (-1965)
LAUNOIS, JOHN RENE   Photographer
LAURENT, ROBERT   Sculptor, Collector (1890-1970)
LAURITZ, PAUL   Painter (1889-1975)
LAUTERER, ARCH   Designer
LAVANOUX, MAURICE   Art Editor (-1974)
LAW, MARGARET   Painter
LAWRENCE, HELEN HUMPHREYS   Painter
LAWRIE, LEE   Sculptor (-1963)
LAWSON, ROBERT   Illustrator (1892-1957)
LAYTON, GLORIA (MRS HARRY GEWISS)   Painter (1914-   )
LAZARUS, MARVIN P   Photographer (1918-1982)
LAZZARI, PIETRO   Sculptor, Painter (1898-1979)
LAZZELL, BLANCHE   Painter (-1956)
LEACH, LOUIS LAWRENCE   Sculptor (1885-1957)
LEAF, MUNRO   Illustrator of Children's Books (1906-1977)
LEAKE, GERALD   Painter (-1975)
LEAR, GEORGE   Engraver (1879-1956)
LEBRUN, RICO (FREDERICO)   Painter (-1964)
LECOQUE   Painter, Writer (1891-1981)
LEDGERWOOD, ELLA RAY   Painter (-1951)
LEE, ARTHUR   Sculptor (1881-1961)
LEE, GEORGE J   Art Administrator, Photographer (1919-1976)
LEECH, HILTON   Painter, Instructor (-1969)
LEES, HARRY HANSON   Illustrator
LEFEVRE, LAWRENCE E   Painter (1904-1960)
LEHMAN, ROBERT   Collector (-1969)
LEIGHTON, A C   Painter (-1965)
LEIGHTON, THOMAS CHARLES   Painter, Instructor (1913-1976)
LEITH-ROSS, HARRY   Painter
LEITMAN, SAMUEL   Painter (1908-1981)
L'ENGLE, WILLIAM JOHNSON   Painter (1884-1957)
LENSKI, LOIS   Writer, Illustrator (1893-   )
LENSON, MICHAEL   Painter (1903-1971)
LENTELLI, LEO   Sculptor (1882-1962)
LENTINE, JOHN   Painter
LEONID (LEONID BERMAN)   Painter (1896-1976)
LE PRINCE, GABRIELLA   Ceramist (-1953)
LERNER, RICHARD J   Art Dealer (1929-1982)
LEVER, R HAYLEY   Painter (1876-1968)
LEVI, CARLO   Painter, Writer
LEVI, JULIAN (E)   Painter, Educator (1900-1982)
LEV-LANDAU (SAMUEL DAVID LANDAU)   Painter (1895-1979)
LEVY, BEATRICE S   Painter (1892-1974)
LEVY, FLORENCE N   Writer, Editor (-1947)
LEVY, JULIEN   Educator, Writer (1906-1981)
LEWIN, MILTON J   Historian (1929-1979)
LEWIS, ALLEN   Etcher (1873-1957)
LEWIS, MARTIN   Printmaker (1883-1962)
LEWIS, NORMAN WILFRED   Painter, Instructor (-1979)
LEWITIN, LANDES   Painter (-1966)
LEYDENFROST, ALEXANDER   Illustrator (1889-1961)
LEYENDECKER, JOSEPH C   Painter (-1951)
LIAS, THOMAS R   Painter
LIBERTE, JEAN   Painter (-1965)
LIBERTS, LUDOLFS   Painter (1895-1959)
LICHTEN, FRANCES   Writer (1889-1961)
LICHTENSTEIN, SARA   Art Historian (1929-   )
LIEBER, FRANCE   Printmaker, Painter
LIEBERMAN, HARRY   Painter, Sculptor (1876-1983)
LIEBES, DOROTHY (MRS RELMAN MORIN)   Textile Designer
  (1899-1972)
LILIENFIELD, KARL   Scholar (-1966)
LINDNER, RICHARD   Painter (1901-1978)
LINTOTT, EDWARD BARNARD   Painter (-1951)
LIPCHITZ, JACQUES   Sculptor (1891-1973)
LIPPERT, LEON   Painter
LISSIM, SIMON   Painter, Designer (1900-1981)
LISTON, MRS. FLORENCE CARY   Portraitist (-1964)
LITAKER, THOMAS (FRANKLIN)   Painter (1906-1976)
LOBER, GEORG J   Sculptor (1892-1961)
LOCHRIE, ELIZABETH DAVEY   Painter, Sculptor (1890-1981)
LOCKWOOD, WARD   Painter (-1963)
LOGAN, MAURICE   Painter, Illustrator (1886-1977)
LOGGIE, HELEN A   Printmaker, Painter (-1976)
LONG, C CHEE   Craftsman, Goldsmith (1942-   )
LONG, STANLEY M   Painter (1892-1972)
LONGACRE, LYDIA E   Miniature Painter (-1951)

LONGACRE, MARGARET GRUEN   Printmaker, Lecturer (1910-1976)
LONGLEY, EVELYN LOUISE   Painter (1921-1959)
LORD, HARRIET   Painter (1879-1958)
LORIMER, AMY McCLELLAN   Painter
LOSCH, TILLY   Painter (1904-1975)
LOUIS, MORRIS   Painter (1912-1963)
LOURIE, HERBERT S   Painter, Educator (1923-1981)
LOVET-LORSKI, BORIS   Sculptor (1894-1973)
LOW, SANFORD   Museum Director, Painter (-1964)
LOWE, EMILY   Painter (-1966)
LOWELL, ORSON BYRON   Illustrator (1871-1956)
LOWENFELD, VIKTOR   Educator (1903-1960)
LOWENGRUND, MARGARET   Painter (1905-1957)
LOZOWICK, LOUIS   Painter, Printmaker (1892-1973)
LUDGIN, EARLE   Collector (1898-1981)
LUDLAM, EUGENIE SHONNARD   Sculptor (1936-1978)
LUKE, ALEXANDRA   Painter (1901-   )
LUNDBORG, FLORENCE   Painter (-1949)
LUNDIE, EDWIN HUGH   Architect (1886-1972)
LUQUIENS, HUC-MAZELET   Etcher (1882-1961)
LUTZ, DAN S   Painter (1906-1978)
LYE, LEN   Painter, Kinetic Artist (1901-1981)
LYMAN, JOHN   Painter (-1967)
LYTTON, BART   Collector (-1969)
MACAGY, DOUGLAS GUERNSEY   Art Administrator
MACAGY, JERMAYNE   Educator
MACDONALD, HERBERT   Painter (1898-1972)
MACDONALD, JAMES W G   Painter
MACDONALD, THOMAS REID   Painter (1908-   )
MACDONALD-WRIGHT, STANTON   Painter (1890-1973)
MACGILVARY, NORWOOD   Painter, Educator
MACHAMER, JEFFERSON   Cartoonist (1900-1960)
MACHLIN, SHELDON M   Sculptor, Printmaker (1918-1975)
MACIUNAS, GEORGE   Designer (1931-1978)
MACKAY, DONALD CAMERON   Painter, Historian (1906-1979)
MACKEOWN, IDA C   Portrait Painter (-1952)
MACKY, SPENCER   Educator (1880-1958)
MACLANE, JEAN   Painter (-1964)
MACLEOD, PEGI NICHOL   Painter, Teacher
MACLEOD, YAN   Sculptor (1889-1978)
MACOMBER, ALLISON   Painter, Sculptor (1916-1979)
MAGAFAN, JENNE   Painter, Lithographer
MALDARELLI, ORONZIO   Sculptor (-1963)
MALICOAT, PHILIP CECIL   Painter (1908-1981)
MALINA, FRANK JOSEPH   Painter, Editor (1912-1981)
MALMAN, CHRISTINA   Magazine Cover Artist (1912-1958)
MALRAUX, ANDRE   Writer, (1901-1976)
MALVERN, CORINNE   Illustrator (-1956)
MANGRAVITE, PEPPINO GINO   Painter, Lecturer (1896-1978)
MANN, MARGERY (MARGARET MANN VASEY) Photographer, Curator
  (1919-1977)
MAN RAY   Artist, Photographer (1890-1976)
MANSHIP, PAUL   Sculptor (1885-1966)
MANVILLE, ELLA VIOLA GRAINGER   Painter (1889-1979)
MARAGLIOTTI VINCENT   Muralist (1888-1978)
MARANS, MOISSAYE   Sculptor, Instructor (1902-1977)
MARANTZ, IRVING   Painter (1912-1972)
MARCUS, EDWARD S   Collector (1910-1972)
MAREMONT, ARNOLD H   Collector (1904-1978)
MARGULES, DEHIRSH   Painter (-1965)
MARIN, JOHN   Painter (1870-1953)
MARINO, ALBERT JOSEPH   Collector (1899-1975)
MARINO-MERLO, JOSEPH   Painter (1906-1956)
MARKOW, JACK   Cartoonist, Painter (1905-1983)
MARKS, GEORGE B   Painter, Sculptor (1923-1983)
MARKUS, HENRY A   Collector
MARSH, FRED DANA   Painter (1872-1961)
MARSH, REGINALD   Painter (1898-1954)
MARSHALL, EDMUND   Photographer (1938-1979)
MARTIN, FLETCHER   Painter (1904-1979)
MARTIN, KEITH MORROW   Painter (1911-1983)
MARTINELLI, EZIO   Sculptor (1913-   )
MARTINET, MARJORIE D   Painter (1886-1981)
MARYAN, MARYAN S   Painter (1927-1977)
MASON, ALICE FRANCES   Lithographer, Painter (1895-   )
MASON, ALICE TRUMBALL   Painter (1904-1971)
MASON, MAUDE M   Painter (1867-1956)
MASON, ROY MARTELL   Painter (1886-1972)
MAST, GERALD   Painter (1908-1971)
MATTA-CLARK, GORDON   Sculptor (1945-1978)
MATTERN, KARL   Painter (-1969)
MATTISON, DONALD MANGUS   Painter (1905-1975)
MATTSON, HENRY (ELIS)   Painter (1887-1971)
MATULKA, JAN   Painter (1890-1972)
MAUNSBACH, GEORGE ERIC   Painter

MAURER, SASCHA   Painter (1897-1961)
MAXON, JOHN   Museum Director (1916-1977)
MAYER, RALPH   Painter, Writer (1895-1979)
MAYOR, A HYATT   Curator (1901-1980)
MAYS, PAUL KIRTLAND   Painter (1887-1961)
McBEY, JAMES   Painter (1884-1959)
McBRIDE, HENRY   Critic (-1962)
McCARTHY, JUSTIN   Painter (1892-   )
McCASLIN, WALTER WRIGHT   Art Critic, Writer (1924-   )
McCAUSLAND, ELIZABETH   Writer (-1965)
McCORMICK, KATHARINE H   Painter (-1960)
McCOSH, DAVID J   Painter (1903-1980)
McCOUCH, GORDON MALLET   Painter
McCREERY, FRANC ROOT (MRS)   Painter (-1957)
MCCURRY, HARR ORR   Museum Director (-1964)
McDONALD, JOHN STANLEY   Art Dealer (1943-1981)
McFEE, HENRY LEE   Painter (-1953)
McGILL, HAROLD A   Cartoonist (-1952)
McGLYNN, THOMAS   Sculptor (1906-   )
McHUGH, JAMES FRANCIS   Collector (-1968)
McKEE, FRANCES BARRETT   Illustrator (1909-1975)
McKINLEY, RUTH GOWDY   Ceramist, Designer (1931-1981)
McKENZIE, VINNORMA SHAW   Painter (-1952)
McLAUGHLIN, DONAL   Architect (1875-1978)
McMAHON, A PHILIP   Writer, Educator
McMANUS, JAMES   Painter (1882-1958)
McMEIN, NEYSA   Painter, Designer
McMILLAN, MARY   Painter
McMULLEN, E ORMOND   Painter
McMURTRIE, EDITH   Painter
McNETT, WILLIAM BROWN   Illustrator (-1968)
McNULTY, WILLIAM CHARLES   Painter (-1963)
McPHARLIN, PAUL   Writer, Illustrator (-1948)
MEAD, KATHERINE HARPER   Curator, Historian (1929-   )
MEADOWS, ALGUR H   Patron (1899-1980)
MEANS, ELLIOTT   Painter
MECHLIN, LEILA   Critic, Writer
MECKLEM, AUSTIN MERRILL   Painter (-1951)
MEHRING, HOWARD WILLIAM   Painter (1931-1978)
MEIERE, HILDRETH   Painter (-1961)
MEISS, MILLARD   Art Historian, Writer (1904-1975)
MEISSNER, LEO J   Painter, Engraver (1895-1977)
MELCARTH, EDWARD   Painter, Sculptor
MELVIN, GRACE WILSON   Painter, Illustrator (-1977)
MENCONI, RALPH JOSEPH   Sculptor (1915-1972)
MENDELOWITZ, DANIEL MARCUS   Painter, Writer (1905-1980)
MERYMAN, HOPE   Artist, Illustrator (-1975)
MESS, GEORGE JO   Painter (-1962)
MESS, GORDON BENJAMIN   Painter (1900-1959)
MESSEGUER, VILLORO BENITO   Painter, Sculptor (1930-1982)
MESTROVIC, IVAN   Sculptor (1884-1962)
MEYER, FREDERICK H   Educator (1873-1961)
MEYER, HERBERT   Painter (1882-1960)
MEYEROWITZ, WILLIAM   Painter (1886-1981)
MEYERS, LEONARD H   Computer Art (1932-1979)
MEYERS, ROBERT WILLIAM   Illustrator (1919-1970)
MIDGETTE, WILLARD FRANKLIN   Painter, Printmaker (1937-1978)
MIELZINER, JO   Designer, Lecturer (1901-1976)
MIES VAN DER ROHE, LUDWIG   Architect (1886-1969)
MILCH, HAROLD CARLTON   Art Dealer (1908-   )
MILHOUS, KATHERINE   Illustrator, Writer, (1894-1977)
MILLER, BARSE   Painter, Educator (1924-1973)
MILLER, BURR   Sculptor (1904-1958)
MILLER, HELEN PENDLETON   Etcher (1888-1957)
MILLER, KENNETH HAYES   Painter, Teacher (1976-1952)
MILLET, CLARENCE   Painter (1897-1959)
MILLIKEN, WILLIAM M   Museum Director, Curator (1889-1978)
MILLMAN, EDWARD   Painter (1907-1964)
MINER, DOROTHY EUGENIA   Museum Curator, Art Historian (1904-1973)
MINEWSKI, ALEX   Painter, Educator (1917-1979)
MINNEGERODE, CUTHBERT POWELL   Museum Director (-1951)
MITCHELL, ALFRED R   Painter (1888-1972)
MITCHELL, BRUCE HANDISIDE   Painter (-1963)
MITCHELL, GLEN   Painter (1894-1972)
MITCHELL, HENRY (WEBER)   Sculptor (1915-1980)
MITCHELL, THOMAS W   Painter
MITCHELL, WALLACE (MACMAHON)   Museum Director, Painter (1911-1977)
MIYASHITA, TAD   Painter (1922-1979)
MOCHI, UGO   Sculptor (1894-1977)
MOCHON, DONALD   Graphic Artist, Educator (1916-   )
MOCK, GEORGE ANDREW   Painter
MOE, HENRY ALLEN   Art Administrator (1894-1975)

MOFFETT, ROSS E   Painter
MOLARSKY, MAURICE   Painter, Teacher (-1950)
MONTANA, BOB   Cartoonist (1920-1975)
MONTANA, PIETRO   Sculptor, Painter (-1978)
MONTGOMERY, CHARLES FRANKLIN   Art Administrator, Educator (1910-1978)
MOON, CARL   Illustrator (-1948)
MORANG, ALFRED GWYNNE   Painter
MORDVINOFF, NICOLAS   Painter, Illustrator (1911-1973)
MORE, HERMON   Museum Director (-1968)
MORGAN, GLADYS B   Painter, Lithographer (1899-1981)
MORGAN, WALLACE   Illustrator (-1948)
MORISSET, GERARD   Educator (1898-1970)
MORRIS, DUDLEY   Painter (-1966)
MORRIS, GEORGE FORD   Painter (-1960)
MORRIS, GEORGE L K   Painter, Sculptor (1905-1975)
MORRIS, KYLE RANDOLPH   Painter (1918-1979)
MORROW, BENJAMIN FRANCIS   Painter (1891-1958)
MORSE, DOROTHY B   Illustrator, Educator (1906-1979)
MORSE, GLENN TILLEY   Painter (-1950)
MORTON, REE   Sculptor, Environmental Artist, Painter (1936-1977)
MOSBY, WILLIAM HARRY   Painter (-1964)
MOSE, CARL C   Sculptor, Lecturer (-1973)
MOSELSIO, SIMON   Sculptor
MOSER, FRANK H   Painter (-1964)
MOSES, ANNA MARY ROBERTSON (GRANDMA)   Painter (1860-1961)
MOSES, FORREST KING   Painter (1893-1974)
MOTT-SMITH, MAY   Medalist, Painter (-1952)
MUEHSAM, GERD   Librarian, Writer (1913-1979)
MUIR, WILLIAM HORACE   Sculptor (-1965)
MULLER, GEORGE F   Painter, (1866-1958)
MULLER, JAN   Painter (1922-1958)
MULLIN, WILLARD   Cartoonist (1902-1978)
MUNDY, ETHEL FRANCES   Sculptor
MUNDY, LOUISE EASTERDAY   Painter (-1952)
MUNOWITZ, KEN   Illustrator of Children's Books (1936-1978)
MUNRO, THOMAS   Art Scholar (1897-1974)
MURANYI, GUSTAVE   Painter (1872-1961)
MURCH, WALTER   Painter (-1967)
MURCHISON, JOHN D   Collector (1921-1979)
MURPHY, ROWLEY WALTER   Painter, Designer (1891-1975)
MURRAY, FRANK WALDO   Painter (1884-1956)
MURRAY, WILLIAM COLMAN   Collector, Patron (1899-1977)
MUSGROVE, A J   Museum Director
MYERS, ETHEL K   Sculptor (1881-1960)
MYERS, FRANK HARMON   Painter (1899-1956)
MYERS, GEORGE HEWITT   Museum President (1865-1957)
MYRICK, KATHERINE S   Painter
NAEGLE, STEPHEN HOWARD   Painter, Sculptor (1938-1981)
NAGEL, STINA   Painter (-1969)
NAHA, RAYMOND   Painter (-1975)
NAILOR, GERALD LLOYDE   Painter, Illustrator (-1952)
NAKAMIZO, FUJI   Painter
NASH, RAY   Art Historian (1905-1982)
NASON, GERTRUDE   Painter
NASON, THOMAS W   Engraver (1889-1971)
NATHAN, HELMUTH MAX   Educator, Painter (1901-1979)
NATZLER, GERTRUD   Ceramic Craftsman (-1971)
NAVAS, ELIZABETH S   Collector, Patron (1895-   )
NEANDROSS, SIGURD   Sculptor (1869-1958)
NEBEL, BERTHOLD   Sculptor
NEFF, JOSEPH   Collector (-1969)
NEILSON, KATHERINE B   Art Historian (1902-1977)
NEILSON, RAYMOND P R   Painter (-1964)
NELSON, GEORGE LAURENCE   Painter (1887-1978)
NEMEROV, DAVID   Painter (-1963)
NESBERT, VINCENT   Miniature Painter (-1976)
NESEMANN, ENNO   Painter (-1949)
NEUMANN, J B   Art Dealer, Critic (1887-1961)
NEUMEYER, ALFRED   Art Historian (1901-1973)
NEUTRA, RICHARD   Architect (1892-1970)
NEWBERRY, CLARE TURLAY   Illustrator (1903-1970)
NEWBERRY, JOHN S   Museum Curator (-1964)
NEWHALL, ADELAIDE MAY   Painter (1884-1960)
NEWHOUSE, BERTRAM MAURICE   Art Dealer (1888-1982)
NEWMAN, BARNETT   Painter (1905-1970)
NEWTON, GRACE HAMILTON (MRS ARTHUR NEWTON)   Painter (-1958)
NEWTON, MARGARET   Painter (1893-1960)
NICHOLS, HOBART   Painter (-1962)
NICHOLS, SPENCER B   Painter (-1950)
NICHOLSON, BEN   Painter (1894-1982)
NICKLE, ROBERT W   Painter, Educator (1919-1980)
NICOLOSI, JOSEPH   Sculptor (1893-1961)

NILES, ROSAMOND   Painter
NISBET, ROBERT H   Painter (1879-1961)
NITZSCHE, ELSA KOENIG   Portrait Painter (-1952)
NOBLE, JOHN A   Painter, Lithographer (1913-1983)
NODEL, SOL   Illuminator, Designer (1912-1976)
NORBURY, LOUISE H   Painter (-1952)
NORDELL, EMMA PARKER (POLLY)   Painter
NORTON, ANN W   Sculptor (-1982)
NOYES, ELIOT   Architect, Designer (1910-1977)
NUDERSCHER, FRANK BERNARD   Painter (1880-1959)
NUGENT, ARTHUR WILLIAM   Cartoonist, Illustrator (1891-1975)
NUNN, FREDERIC   Painter
OAKLEY, VIOLET   Painter (1874-1960)
OBERHARDT, WILLIAM   Illustrator (1882-1958)
O'BRIEN, WILLIAM VINCENT   Art Dealer (1902-   )
OCHIKUBO, TETSUO   Painter, Designer (1923-1975)
OCHTMAN, DOROTHY (MRS W A DEL MAR)   Painter (1892-1971)
OERI, GEORGINE   Critic (-1968)
OGDEN, RALPH E   Collector, Patron (-1974)
OGG, OSCAR   Designer, Writer (1908-1971)
O'HARA, ELIOT   Painter (1890-1969)
O'HARA, (JAMES) FREDERICK   Printmaker (1904-1980)
OKADA, KENZO   Painter (1902-1982)
OLINSKY, IVAN G   Painter (1878-1962)
OLMER, HENRY   Sculptor (-1950)
OLSEN, HERB   Painter, Writer (1905-1973)
OPDYCKE, LEONARD   Educator (1895-1977)
ORLOFF, LILY   Painter (-1957)
ORME, LYDIA GARDNER   Painter (-1963)
OSGOOD, RUTH   Painter (-1977)
OWEN, FREDERICK   Painter (1869-1959)
OZENFANT, AMEDEE   Painter (-1966)
PACH, MAGDA F   Painter (-1950)
PACH, WALTER   Writer (1883-1958)
PACKER, CLAIR LANGE   Painter, Writer (1901-1978)
PACKER, FRANCIS H   Sculptor (1873-1957)
PACKER, FRED L   Cartoonist
PADDOCK, WILLARD DRYDEN   Painter (1873-1956)
PAEFF, BASHKA (BASHKA PAEFF WAXMAN)   Sculptor (1893-1979)
PAGE, GROVER   Cartoonist (1893-1958)
PAGES, JEAN   Illustrator, Muralist (1907-1977)
PAGET-FREDERICKS, J ROUS-MARTEN   Illustrator (-1963)
PAINE, ROBERT T   Museum Curator (-1965)
PALAZZOLA, GUY   Administrator, Educator (1919-1978)
PALMER, ALLEN INGELS   Painter (-1950)
PALMER, DELOS   Painter (1891-1961)
PAPASHVILY, GEORGE   Sculptor, Writer, (1898-1978)
PAPASIAN, JACK   Sculptor (-1957)
PARDI, JUSTIN A   Painter (-1951)
PAREDES, LIMON MARIANO   Engraver, Painter (1912-1979)
PARIS, HAROLD PERSICO   Sculptor (1925-1979)
PARK, MADELEINE F   Sculptor (1891-1960)
PARKER, GEORGE WALLER   Painter (-1957)
PARKER, THOMAS   Administrator (-1967)
PARRISH, MAXFIELD   Painter (-1966)
PARSHALL, DEWITT   Painter (1864-1956)
PARSONS, BETTY BIERNE   Painter, Art Dealer (1900-1982)
PARSONS, EDITH BARRETTO   Sculptor (1878-1956)
PARSONS, ERNESTINE   Painter (-1967)
PARSONS, LLOYD HOLMAN   Painter (-1968)
PATRICK, RANSOM R   Educator (1906-1971)
PATTERSON, CHARLES ROBERT   Painter (1875-1958)
PATTY, WILLIAM A   Painter (1889-1961)
PAUL, BORIS DUPONT   Painter (1901-   )
PEARLMAN, HENRY   Collector (1895-1974)
PEARMAN, KATHARINE K   Painter (1893-1961)
PEARSON, JOSEPH T, JR   Painter (-1951)
PEARSON, RALPH M   Etcher (1883-1958)
PECK, EDWARD   Director University Galleries (-1970)
PEEBLES, ROY B   Painter (1899-1957)
PEETS, ORVILLE   Painter (-1968)
PEIRCE, WALDO   Painter (1884-   )
PENA, TONITA   Painter
PENNEY, JAMES   Painter, Educator (1910-1982)
PENNOYER, A SHELDON   Painter (1888-1957)
PEPPER, CHARLES HOVEY   Painter (-1950)
PERARD, VICTOR S   Etcher (1867-1957)
PEREIRA, I RICE   Painter (1901-1971)
PERKINS, MABLE H   Collector (1880-1974)
PERKINS, MARION   Sculptor (1908-1961)
PERKINS, PHILIP R   Painter (-1968)
PERKINS-RIPLEY, LUCY FAIRFIELD   Painter
PERLS, FRANK (RICHARD)   Art Dealer, Collector (1910-1975)
PERRET, FERDINAND   Historian (1888-1960)
PERRETT, GALEN J   Painter (-1949)

PERRY, RAYMOND   Painter (1876-1960)
PETERS, CARL W   Painter (1897-1980)
PETERS, FRANCIS C   Painter (1902-1977)
PETERSHAM, MISKA   Illustrator (1888-1959)
PETERSON, JANE   Painter
PETERSON, JOHN P   Craftsman (-1949)
PETERSON, PERRY   Illustrator (1908-1958)
PETREMONT, CLARICE M   Painter (-1949)
PEYTON, BERTHA MENZLER   Painter
PFEIFFER, FRITZ   Painter (1889-1960)
PFEIFFER, HEINRICH H   Painter
PFISTER, JEAN JACQUES   Painter (-1949)
PHELPS, EDITH CATLIN   Painter (1875-1961)
PHILBRICK, OTIS   Painter, Printmaker (1888-1973)
PHILIPP, ROBERT   Painter (1895-1981)
PHILLIPS, DOROTHY W   Art Administrator, Writer (1906-1977)
PHILLIPS, DUNCAN   Museum Director
PHILLIPS, J CAMPBELL   Painter (-1949)
PICCIRILLI, FURIO   Sculptor (-1949)
PICKEN, GEORGE   Painter, Printmaker (1898-1971)
PIERCE, GARY   Painter (-1969)
PIKE, JOHN   Illustrator, Painter (1911-1979)
PITTMAN, HOBSON   Painter (1900-1972)
PITTMAN, KATHRYN   Painter, Instructor (1915-1979)
PITZ, HENRY CLARENCE   Painter, Writer (1895-1976)
PLATE, WALTER   Painter, Educator (1925-1972)
PLATT, ELEANOR   Sculptor
PLAVCAN, JOSEPH MICHAEL   Painter, Sculptor (-1981)
PLEASANTS, FREDERICK R   Collector, Patron (1906-   )
PLEISSNER, OGDEN MINTON   Painter (1905-1983)
PLUNGUIAN, GINA   Painter (-1962)
POHL, HUGO DAVID   Painter (1878-1960)
POLKES, ALAN H   Collector, Patron (1931-   )
POLLACK, LOUIS   Art Dealer (1921-1970)
POLLACK, PETER   Photographer, Writer (1911-1978)
POLLACK, VIRGINIA MORRIS   Sculptor
POLLET, JOSEPH   Painter (1898-1979)
POLLEY, FREDERICK   Painter
POLLOCK, JACKSON   Painter (1912-1956)
POLLOCK, JAMES ARLIN   Painter (-1949)
POND, DANA   Painter (-1962)
POND, WILLI BAZE (MRS CHARLES E)   Painter (-1947)
POOLE, ABRAM   Painter (1882-1961)
POOLE, EARL LINCOLN   Illustrator, Art Administrator (1891-1972)
POOR, HENRY VARNUM   Painter (1888-1970)
POPE, JOHN ALEXANDER   Historian, Museum Director (1906-1982)
POPE, MARION HOLDEN   Painter (-1958)
PORAY, STAN P   Painter, Designer (-1948)
PORSMAN, FRANK O   Painter
PORTANOVA, JOSEPH DOMENICO   Sculptor, Designer (1909-1979)
PORTER, FAIRFIELD   Painter, Lecturer (1907-1975)
PORTNOFF, ALEXANDER   Sculptor (-1949)
POTTER, WILLIAM J   Painter (-1964)
POUSETTE-DART, NATHANIEL   Painter (-1965)
POWELl, DOANE   Craftsman (-1951)
POWELL, LYDIA BOND   Art Administrator, Consultant (1892-1978)
POWERS, MARILYN   Painter (1925-1976)
POWERS, MARY SWIFT   Painter (1885-1959)
PRATT, DUDLEY   Sculptor (1897-1975)
PRATT, ELIZABETH SOUTHWICK   Painter (-1964)
PRENDERGAST, CHARLES E   Painter (-1948)
PRESSER, JOSEF   Painter (-1967)
PRESTON, ALICE BOLAM (MRS FRANK I)   Illustrator (1889-1958)
PRESTON, HARRIET BROWN   Painter (1892-1961)
PRESTON, JAMES M   Painter (1874-1962)
PREZZI, WILMA M   Painter
PRICE, CHESTER B   Illustrator (-1962)
PRICE, CLAYTON S   Painter (1874-1950)
PRICE, FREDERIC NEWLIN   Museum Director (-1963)
PRICE, GARRETT   Cartoonist (1897-1979)
PRICE, MARGARET E   Illustrator, Painter
PRICE, MINNIE   Painter (1877-1957)
PRICE, NORMAN MILLS   Illustrator (-1951)
PRIEBE, KARL   Painter (1914-1976)
PRIEST, ALAN   Museum Curator (-1968)
PRINCE, WILLIAM MEADE   Illustrator (-1951)
PRIOR, HARRIS KING   Art Administrator, Educator (1911-1975)
PROCTOR, A PHIMISTER   Sculptor (-1950)
PROHASKA, RAY   Painter, Illustrator (1901-1981)
PUSHMAN, HOVSEP   Painter (-1966)
PUTMAN, BRENDA   Sculptor (-1975)
QUANDT, RUSSELL JEROME   Museum Art Restorer (1919-1970)
QUATTROCCHI, EDMONDO   Sculptor (-1966)
QUINN, ROBERT HAYES   Illustrator (-1962)
QUIRK, FRANCIS JOSEPH   Painter, Museum Director (1907-1974)

QUIRT, WALTER   Painter, Educator (1902-1968)
QUISTGAARD, JOHAN WALDEMAR DE REHLING   Portrait Painter (-1962)
RAAB, ADA DENNETT (MRS S V)   Painter (-1950)
RAHMING, NORRIS   Painter (1886-1959)
RAINVILLE, PAUL   Museum Director (-1952)
RANEY, SUZANNE BRYANT   Printmaker (-1967)
RANN, VOLLIAN BURR   Painter (1897-1956)
RANNEY, GLEN ALLISON   Painter (1896-1959)
RASKO, MAXIMILIAN A   Painter (1884-1961)
RATTNER, ABRAHAM   Painter (1895-1978)
RATZKA, ARTHUR L   Painter
RAUCH, JOHN G   Collector, Patron (1890-1976)
RAVENSCROFT, ELLEN   Painter
RAVESON, SHERMAN HAROLD   Painter, Writer (-1974)
RAY, RUTH (MRS JOHN REGINALD GRAHAM)   Painter (1919-1977)
RAYMOND, ALEXANDER   Cartoonist (1909-1956)
READ, HELEN APPLETON   Art Historian, Art Critic   (1887-1974)
READE, ROMA (MABEL KELLEY AUBREY)   Painter (1877-1958)
READIO, WILFRED A   Painter (1895-1961)
REASON, PATRICK   Engraver (1817-1852)
REBAY, HILLA   Painter (-1967)
RECCHIA, RICHARD (HENRY)   Sculptor (-1983)
REDER, BERNARD   Sculptor (-1963)
REDFIELD, EDWARD W   Painter (-1965)
REEVES, J MASON   Painter (1898-1973)
REFREGIER, ANTON   Painter (1905-1979)
REGENSBURG, SOPHY P   Painter, Collector (1885-1974)
REGESTER, CHARLOTTE   Painter
REID, GEORGE AGNEW   Painter (-1947)
REIFF, ROBERT FRANK   Art Historian, Painter (1918-1982)
REILLY, ELVIRA   Painter (1899-1958)
REINDEL, WILLIAM GEORGE   Painter (-1948)
REINHARDT, AD F   Painter (1913-1967)
REISE, BARBARA   Art Critic (-1978)
REMMEY, PAUL B   Illustrator
RENIER, JOSEPH EMILE   Sculptor (-1966)
REVINGTON, GEORGE D, III   Collector
REY, H A   Illustrator, Writer (1898-1977)
REYNARD, GRANTT   Painter (-1967)
REYNOLDS, LLOYD J   Calligrapher (1902-1978)
RIBA, PAUL F   Painter (1912-1977)
RIBAK, LOUIS   Painter (1902-1980)
RICCI, ULYSSES   Sculptor (1888-1960)
RICH, DANIEL CATTON   Art Administrator, Lecturer (1904-1976)
RICH, LORIMER   Architect (1892-1978)
RICHARDSON, JAMES LEWIS   Educator, Printmaker (1927-)
RICHMOND, LAWRENCE   Collector (1909-1978)
RICHTER, GISELA MARIE AUGUSTA   Museum Curator, Writer (1882-1972)
RICHTER, HANS   Artist, Filmmaker (1888-1976)
RIDABOCK, RAY (BUDD)   Painter, Instructor (1904-1970)
RIEKER, ALBERT GEORGE   Sculptor (1889-1959)
RIEPPEL, LUDWIG   Sculptor (1861-1960)
RIGGS, ROBERT   Lithographer (1896-1970)
RINGIUS, CARL   Painter (-1950)
RIPLEY, ALDEN LASSELL   Painter (-1969)
RIPLEY, ROBERT   Illustrator
RISHELL, ROBERT CLIFFORD   Painter, Sculptor (1917-1976)
RIST, LOUIS G   Printmaker (1888-1959)
RITCHIE, ANDREW C   Administrator, Historian (1907-1978)
RITMAN, LOUIS   Painter (-1963)
RITSCHEL, WILLIAM   Painter (-1949)
RIU, VICTOR   Sculptor (1887-1974)
ROBBINS, FRANK   Cartoonist, Illustrator (1917-)
ROBERTS, BILL   Cartoonist (1914-1978)
ROBERTS, COLETTE (JACQUELINE)   Critic, Administrator (1910-)
ROBERTS, MORTON   Painter (-1964)
ROBERTS, VIOLET KENT   Painter
ROBERTSON, PAUL CHANDLER   Painter (1902-1961)
ROBERTSON, SARAH M   Painter (-1948)
ROBINSON, BOARDMAN   Painter, Teacher (-1952)
ROBINSON, THEODORE   Painter (1852-1896)
ROBUS, HUGO   Sculptor (-1964)
ROCKEFELLER, JOHN DAVISON, III   Collector, Patron (1906-1978)
ROCKEFELLER, NELSON ALDRICH   Collector, Patron (1908-)
ROCKEFELLER, WINTHROP   Collector
ROCKWELL, NORMAN   Illustrator (1894-1978)
RODDY, EDITH JEANNETTE   Painter
ROGERS, BRUCE   Designer (1870-1957)
ROGERS, MARGARET ESTHER   Painter (1873-1961)
ROGERS, MEYRIC REYNOLD   Museum Curator (1893-1972)
ROGERS, ROBERT STOCKTON   Painter
ROHLAND, PAUL   Painter, Serigrapher

ROJANKOVSKY, FEODOR STEPANOVICH   Illustrator (1891-1970)
ROLAND, JAY   Painter (1905-1960)
ROMANS, CHARLES JOHN   Painter (1891-1973)
RONNEBECK, ARNOLD H   Sculptor (-1947)
ROOD, JOHN   Sculptor, Painter (1906-1974)
ROOK, EDWARD F   Painter (1870-1960)
ROOT, EDWARD WALES   Art Authority, Collector (1884-1956)
ROOT, MRS EDWARD W   Collector
RORIMER, JAMES J   Museum Director
ROSE, BILLY   Collector (-1966)
ROSE, HANNA TOBY   Art Administrator (1909-1976)
ROSE, IVER   Painter (1899-1972)
ROSELAND, HARRY HERMAN   Painter (-1950)
ROSEN, CHARLES   Painter, Illustrator (-1950)
ROSEN, DAVID   Restorer (1880—1960)
ROSENBERG, HAROLD   Writer, Educator (1906-1978)
ROSENBERG, JAKOB   Writer (1893-1980)
ROSENBERG, SAEMY   Art Dealer
ROSENBERG, SAMUEL   Painter (1896-1972)
ROSENTHAL, DAVID   Painter, Etcher (-1949)
ROSENTHAL, DORIS   Painter, Lithographer
ROSENWALD, LESSING JULIUS   Collector, Patron (1891-1979)
ROSIN, HARRY   Sculptor, Educator (-1973)
ROSOFSKY, SEYMOUR   Painter, Printmaker (1924-)
ROSS, ALVIN   Painter, Educator (1920-1975)
ROSS, C CHANDLER   Portrait Painter (-1952)
ROSS, LOUIS   Mural Painter (-1963)
ROST, MILES ERNEST   Painter (1891-1961)
ROSTAND, MICHEL   Painter (1895-)
ROSZAK, THEODORE   Painter, Sculptor (1907-1981)
ROTH, BEN   Cartoonist (1910-1960)
ROTHKO, MARK   Painter (1903-1970)
ROTHSCHILD, HERBERT   Art Collector (1892-1976)
ROTHSCHILD, LINCOLN   Sculptor, Writer (1902-1983)
ROTIER, PETER   Painter
ROUSSEAU, THEODORE, JR   Museum Curator (1912-1974)
ROWAN, EDWARD BEATTY   Painter (-1946)
ROWE, CORINNE   Painter (-1965)
ROWE, GUY   Painter (-1969)
ROWLAND, BENJAMIN, JR   Educator (1904-1972)
ROWLAND, ELDEN HART   Painter (1915-1982)
RUBEL, C ADRIAN   Collector (1904-1978)
RUBIN, HY   Illustrator (1905-1960)
RUBIN, SAMUEL   Patron (1901-1978)
RUNGIUS, CARL   Painter (1869-1959)
RUSKIN, LEWIS J   Collector, Patron (1905-1981)
RUSSELL, BRUCE ALEXANDER   Cartoonist (-1963)
RUSSELL, HELEN CROCKER   Collector
RUSSELL, MORGAN   Painter (1886-1953)
RUSSOLI, FRANCO   Art Critic (1923-1977)
RUZICKA, RUDOLPH   Illustrator, Designer (1883-1978)
RYDER, CHAUNCEY FOSTER   Painter (-1949)
RYLAND, ROBERT KNIGHT   Painter (-1951)
SAARINEN, EERO   Architect, Designer (1910-1961)
SACHS, JAMES H   Collector, Patron (1907-1971)
SACHS, PAUL J   Educator (-1965)
SAGE, KAY (TANGUY)   Painter
SAHLER, HELEN GERTRUDE   Painter (-1950)
SAINT, LAWRENCE   Painter (1885-1961)
ST GAUDENS, HOMER   Educator (1879-1958)
SALTER, GEORGE   Book Designer (-1967)
SALTER, JOHN RANDALL   Sculptor, Painter (1898-1978)
SALVATORE, VICTOR   Sculptor (-1965)
SAMPLE, PAUL   Painter (1896-1974)
SANDER, LUDWIG   Painter (1906-1975)
SARASON, HENRY   Photographer (1896-1979)
SARDEAU, HELENE   Sculptor (-1968)
SARKIS (SARKIS SARKISIAN)   Painter (1909-1977)
SAUGSTAD, OLAF   Craftsman, Teacher (-1950)
SAUNDERS, CLARA ROSMAN   Painter, Teacher (-1951)
SAVAGE, AUGUSTA   Sculptor (1900-1962)
SAWYER, PHILIP AYER   Painter (-1949)
SAWYER, WELLS M   Painter
SCARAVAGLIONE, CONCETTA MARIA   Sculptor (-1975)
SCHAFER, ALICE PAULINE   Printmaker (1899-1980)
SCHANKER, LOUIS   Printmaker, Painter (1903-1981)
SCHARY, SAUL   Illustrator, Painter (1904-1978)
SCHEIRER, GEORGE A   Hand Bookbinder (1895-1959)
SCHIEFER, JOHANNES   Painter, Curator
SCHINDLER, R M   Architect (1887-1953)
SCHLAIKJER, JES (WILHELM)   Painter, Illustrator (1897-1982)
SCHMEIDLER, BLANCHE J   Painter
SCHMIDT, KATHERINE (KATHERINE SCHMIDT SHUBERT)   Painter (1898-1978)
SCHMITZ, CARL LUDWIG   Sculptor (-1967)

SCHNAKENBERG, HENRY   Painter (1892-1970)
SCHNIEWIND, CARL O   Curator (1900-1957)
SCHNITTMANN, SASCHA S   Sculptor (1913-   )
SCHOEN, EUGENE   Designer (1880-1957)
SCHOLLE, HARDINGE   Museum Director (-1969)
SCHRACK JOSEPH EARL   Painter (-1973)
SCHREIBER, GEORGES   Painter (1904-1977)
SCHREIVER, GEORGE AUGUST   Curator, Art Historian (-1977)
SCHROEDER, ERIC   Museum Curator, Writer
SCHULZ, ROBERT EMIL   Illustrator, Painter (1929-1978)
SCHUSTER, CARL   Art Historian, Art Writer (1904-   )
SCHUSTER, DONNA NORINE   Painter (1883-1953)
SCHUTZ, ANTON   Etcher, Writer (1894-1977)
SCHUYLER, PHILIP (GRIFFIN)   Painter, Educator (1913-   )
SCHWARTZ, MANFRED   Painter (1909-1970)
SCHWARTZMAN, DANIEL   Architect (1909-1977)
SCHWARZ, FRANK HENRY   Painter (-1951)
SCHWARZ, HEINRICH   Museum Curator, Educator (1894-1974)
SCHWEDLER, WILLIAM A   Painter (1942-1982)
SCOTT, BERTHA   Portrait Painter (-1965)
SCOTT, CLYDE EUGENE   Painter (1884-1959)
SCOTT-GIBSON, HERBERT NATHANIEL   Art Administrator,
     Educator (1928-1981)
SEAVER, ESTHER   Educator (-1965)
SEIBEL, FRED O   Cartoonist (-1968)
SEIDE, CHARLES   Painter, Educator (1915-1980)
SEIDEL, ALEXANDER CARL-VICTOR   Painter, Designer
     (1897-1979)
SEITZ, WILLIAM CHAPIN   Educator, Art Historian (1914-1974)
SELDIS, HENRY J   Art Critic (1925-1978)
SELEY, JASON   Sculptor (1919-1983)
SELIGMAN, CHARLES   Art Dealer (1893-1978)
SELIGMANN, KURT   Painter, Printmaker (1900-1962)
SELLECK, MARGARET   Painter
SELONKE, IRENE A   Painter (-1981)
SENNHAUSER, JOHN   Painter, Designer (-1978)
SETTERBERG, CARL GEORG   Painter, Illustrator (1897-   )
SERGER. FREDERICK B   Painter (-1965)
SESSLER, ALFRED   Painter (-1963)
SEWELL, HELEN MOORE   Illustrator (1897-1957)
SEYFERT, RICHARD LEOPOLD   Painter, Instructor (1915-1979)
SEXTON, EMILY STRYKER   Painter (-1948)
SEYMOUR, CHARLES, JR   Art Historian, Curator (1912-1977)
SHAFER, BURR   Cartoonist (-1965)
SHAFER, MARGUERITE (PHILLIPS) NEUHAUSER   Artist
     (1888-1976)
SHAHN, BEN   Painter (1898-1969)
SHANGRAW, SYLVIA CHEN   Historian, Curator (1937-   )
SHAPLEY, JOHN   Historian (1890-1969)
SHARON, MARY B   Painter (1891-1961)
SHARP, WILLIAM   Painter (1900-1961)
SHAVER, JAMES ROBERT   Painter (-1949)
SHAW, CHARLES GREEN   Painter, Writer (1892-1974)
SHAW, WILFRED B   Painter
SHEELER, CHARLES   Painter (1883-1965)
SHEFFER, GLENN C   Painter, Illustrator (-1948)
SHEFFERS, PETER WINTHROP   Painter (-1949)
SHEPLER, DWIGHT (CLARK)   Painter, Writer (1905-   )
SHEPPARD, JOHN CRAIG   Painter, Educator (1913-1978)
SHERMAN, JOHN K (URTZ)   Critic (1898-   )
SHERWOOD, ROSINA EMMET   Painter (-1948)
SHERWOOD, SHERRY   Designer
SHERWOOD, WILLIAM ANDERSON   Painter, Etcher (-1951)
SHINN, EVERETT   Painter (1876-1953)
SHOENFELT, JOSEPH FRANKLIN   Painter (-1968)
SHOKLER, HARRY   Painter, Serigrapher (1896-   )
SHOPE, IRVIN (SHORTY)   Painter (1900-1977)
SHOPEN, KENNETH   Painter (-1967)
SHRYOCK, BURNETT HENRY, SR   Painter (1904-1971)
SHULKIN, ANATOL   Painter (1901-1961)
SHULL, JAMES MARION   Painter
SHUNNEY, ANDREW   Painter (1921-   )
SIDERIS, ALEXANDER   Painter (1898-1978)
SIEGEL, ADRIAN   Photographer, Painter (1898-1978)
SIEGL, THEODOR   Conservator, Lecturer (-1976)
SIEVAN, MAURICE   Painter (1898-1981)
SILVA, WILLIAM POSEY   Painter (-1948)
SILVERCRUYS, SUSANNE (MRS EDWARD FORD STEVENSON)
     Sculptor, Lecturer (-1973)
SILVERMAN, MEL   Painter (-1966)
SIMMONS, WILLIAM   Etcher (-1949)
SIMON, ERIC M   Illustrator, Designer (1892-1978)
SIMON, HOWARD   Illustrator, Painter (1903-1979)
SIMONET, SEBASTIAN   Illustrator, Painter (-1948)
SIMONS, LOUISE BEDELL   Painter (1912-1977)

SIMPSON, MARSHALL   Painter (1900-1958)
SIMPSON, WILLIAM   Painter (1818-1872)
SINSABAUGH, ART   Photographer, Educator (1924-   )
SIPORIN, MITCHELL   Painter, Educator (1910-1976)
SIQUEIROS, DAVID ALFARO   Painter (1896-1974)
SISSON, JACQUELINE D   Librarian, Educator (1925-1980)
SKEGGS, DAVID POTTER   Designer, Painter (1924-1973)
SKILES, CHARLES   Cartoonist (-1969)
SKINAS, JOHN CONSTANTINE   Painter (-1966)
SKLAR, GEORGE   Animal Painter (-1968)
SKOOGFORS, OLAF   Silversmith (-1975)
SLATER, FRANK   Portrait Painter (-1965)
SLATIN, YEFFE KIMBALL   Painter (1914-1978)
SLATKIN, CHARLES E   Art Dealer (1908-1977)
SLAUGHTER, HAZEL BURNHAM   Painter (1888-1979)
SLICK, JAMES NELSON   Painter, Sculptor (1901-1979)
SLOAN, JOHN   Painter, Teacher
SLOBODKIN, LOUIS   Sculptor, Illustrator (1903-1975)
SMALLEY, JANET   Illustrator
SMEDLEY, WILL LARYMORE   Painter
SMITH, ALBERT DELMONT   Portrait Painter (-1962)
SMITH, ANDRE   Painter (1880-1959)
SMITH, BARBARA NEFF   Patron (1908-1977)
SMITH, DAVID   Sculptor (1906-1965)
SMITH, GORDON MACKINTOSH   Museum Director (1906-1979)
SMITH, GREGORY   Painter
SMITH, HOWARD ROSS   Curator (1910-   )
SMITH, JACOB GETLAR   Painter (1898-1958)
SMITH, JUDSON   Painter (-1962)
SMITH, JUSTIN V   Collector (1903-   )
SMITH, LAWRENCE M C   Collector, Patron (1902-1975)
SMITH, LYN WALL   Writer, Painter (1909-1979)
SMITH, ROBERT C   Educator (1912-1975)
SMITH, W HARRY   Painter, Etcher (-1951)
SMITH, WALT ALLEN   Sculptor, Designer (1910-1971)
SMITHSON, ROBERT I   Sculptor, Lecturer (1938-1974)
SMOLIN, NAT   Sculptor, Painter (-1950)
SNELGROVE, GORDON WILLIAM   Educator
SOBY, JAMES THRALL   Writer, Critic (1906-1979)
SOGLOW, OTTO   Cartoonist (1900-1975)
SOLES, WILLIAM   Sculptor (-1967)
SOLON, HARRY   Painter (1873-1958)
SOLOWEY, BEN   Cartoonist (1901-1978)
SOMMER, WASSILY   Painter, Educator (1912-1979)
SOMMERBURG, MIRIAM   Mosaic Artist, Sculptor
SONED, WARREN   Painter (-1966)
SOPHER, AARON   Painter, Illustrator (1905-1972)
SOPHER, BERNHARD D   Sculptor (-1949)
SORENSEN, JOHN HJELMHOF   Cartoonist (-1969)
SORIA, MARTIN SEBASTIAN   Educator (1911-1961)
SOROKIN, DAVIS   Art Dealer, Painter (1908-1977)
SOYER, ISAAC   Painter, Instructor (1902-1981)
SOYER, MOSES   Painter (1899-1974)
SOZIO, ARMANDO   Painter (-1966)
SPAETH, OTTO   Collector (-1966)
SPAVENTA, GEORGE   Sculptor (1918-   )
SPEAR, ARTHUR P   Painter (1879-1959)
SPEICHER, EUGENE   Painter (-1962)
SPENCER, HUGH   Illustrator, Photographer (1887-1975)
SPENCER, LEONTINE G   Painter (-1964)
SPENCER, NILES   Painter (1893-1952)
SPICER-SIMPSON, THEODORE   Sculptor (1871-1959)
SPOHN, CLAY (EDGAR)   Painter, Instructor (1898-1977)
SPRADLING FRANK L   Painter (1885-1972)
SPRAGUE-SMITH, ISABELLE DWIGHT (MRS CHARLES) (1861-1951)
SPRAYREGEN, MORRIS   Collector
SPRINGHORN, CARL   Painter (1887-1971)
SPRINGWEILER, ERWIN FREDERICK   Sculptor (1896-1968)
SPRUANCE, BENTON   Lithographer (-1967)
SQUIRE, ALLAN TAFT   Designer
STACHELBERG, CHARLES G   Collector, Patron
STAGG, MRS JESSIE   Sculptor (-1958)
STALLMAN, EMMA S   Craftsman (1888-1959)
STAMATY, STANLEY   Cartoonist, Illustrator (1916-1979)
STANKIEWICZ, RICHARD PETER   Sculptor, Educator (1922-1983)
STAPLES, ROY HARVARD   Painter (-1958)
STARK, JACK GAGE   Painter (-1950)
STARKWEATHER, WILLIAM   Painter (-1969)
STAUFFER, EDNA PENNYPACKER   Painter (1887-1956)
STAVENITZ, ALEXANDER RAQUL   Etcher (1901-1960)
STEA, CESARE   Sculptor (1893-1960)
STECHOW, WOLFGANG   Art Historian (1896-1975)
STEDMAN, WILFRED HENRY   Sculptor (-1950)
STEEGMULLER, BEATRICE STEIN   Painter (-1961)
STEENE, WILLIAM   Painter (-1965)

STEICHEN, EDWARD   Photographer (1879-1979)
STEINBERG, MRS. MILTON (EDITH)   Art Director (1910-1970)
STEINITZ, KATE TRAUMAN   Writer, Art Historian
STEPPAT, LEO LUDWIG   Sculptor, Educator (-1964)
STERN, HAROLD PHILLIP   Museum Director, Writer (1922-1977)
STERNE, MAURICE   Painter (1878-1957)
STERRETT, CLIFF   Cartoonist (-1964)
STEVENS, LAWRENCE TENNY   Sculptor, Educator (1896-1972)
STEVENS, WALTER HOLLIS   Painter, Educator (1927-1980)
STEVENSON, BEULAH   Painter (-1965)
STEWART, JARVIS ANTHONY   Educator, Painter (1914-1981)
STILL, CLYFFORD   Painter (1904-1981)
STILWELL, WILBUR MOORE   Educator, Writer (1908-1974)
STITES, RAYMOND SOMMERS   Art Historian, Writer (1899-1974)
STONE, ANNA B   Painter
STONE, BEATRICE   Sculptor (-1962)
STONE, EDWARD DURELL   Architect (1902-1978)
STONEHILL, MARY (MRS GEORGE)   Painter (-1951)
STOOPS, HERBERT   Illustrator (-1948)
STORRS, JOHN   Sculptor (1885-1956)
STOUT, GEORGE LESLIE   Consultant (18970   )
STRALEM, DONALD S   Collector, Patron
STROTHMANN, FRED   Illustrator (1880-1958)
STRUNK, HERBERT JULIAN   Sculptor
STUIDA, WILLIAM   Art Authority (1877-1959)
STYKA, ADAM   Painter (1890-1959)
STYLES, GEORGE WILLIAM   Painter (-1949)
SUMMERS, DUDLEY GLOYNE   Painter, Illustrator (1892-1975)
SUSSMAN, RICHARD N   Painter, Graphic Artist (1908-1971)
SUTTON, GEORGE MIKSCH   Painter, Illustrator (1898-1982)
SUTTON, RUTH HAVILAND   Painter (1898-1960)
SVOBODA, VINCENT A   Painter (1877-1961)
SWAN, BRADFORD F   Art Critic, Painter (1907-1976)
SWANN, ERWIN   Collector, Patron (1906-1973)
SWARTBURG, B ROBERT   Architect (1895-1975)
SWARZENSKI, GEORG   Research Fellow (1876-1957)
SWAZO, (PATRICK SWAZO HINDS)   Painter, Illustrator (1924-1974)
SWENSON, HOWARD WILLIAM   Sculptor (1901-1960)
SWINDELL, BERTHA   Painter (-1951)
SWINNERTON, EDNA HUESTIS   Miniature Painter (-1964)
SWINNERTON, JAMES   Cartoonist, Painter (1875-1974)
SYLVESTER, LUCILLE   Painter, Writer
SZANTO, LOUIS P   Painter (-1965)
SZYK, ARTHUR   Illustrator (-1951)
TAIT, KATHARINE LAMB   Painter, Designer (1895-1981)
TAKIS, NICHOLAS   Painter (-1965)
TALBOT, WILLIAM (H M)   Kinetic Artist, Sculptor (1918-1980)
TANGUY, YVES   Painter (1900-1955)
TANNER, HENRY OSSAWA   Painter (1859-1937)
TARNOPOL, GREGOIRE   Painter, Collector (1891-1979)
TAUBES, FREDERIC   Painter, Writer (1900-1981)
TAYLOR, ANNA HEYWARD   Painter (1879-1956)
TAYLOR, DAVIDSON   Director (1907-1979)
TAYLOR, EMILY (MRS J MADISON TAYLOR)   Miniature Painter (-1952)
TAYLOR, FRANCIS HENRY   Museum Director (1903-1957)
TAYLOR, JOHN (WILLIAMS)   Painter, Printmaker (1897-1983)
TAYLOR, JOSHUA CHARLES   Museum Director, Historian (1917-1981)
TEAGUE, WALTER DORWIN   Designer (1884-1960)
TEE-VAN HELEN DAMROSCH   Painter, Illustrator (1893-1976)
TEFET, CHARLES EUGENE   Sculptor
TEICHMAN, SABINA   Painter, Sculptor (-1983)
TENGGREN, GUSTAV ADOLF   Painter (1896-1970)
TEPPER, NATALIE ARRAS   Painter (-1950)
THAL, SAMUEL   Etcher
THOMAS, ALMA WOODSEY   Painter (1891-1978)
THOMAS, MARY LEATH   Painter (1905-1959)
THOMPSON, BOB   Painter (-1966)
THOMPSON, FREDERICK   Painter (1904-1956)
THOMPSON, GEORGE LOUIS   Designer (1913-1981)
THOMPSON, JULIET H   Painter (-1956)
THOMPSON, LESLIE P   Painter (-1963)
THOMPSON, WALTER WHITCOMB   Painter (-1948)
THORP, EARL NORWELL   Sculptor (-1951)
THURLOW, FEARN CUTLER   Curator (1924-1982)
TISCHLER, VICTOR   Painter, Lithographer (-1951)
TISHMAN, JACK A   Collector (-1966)
TOBEY, MARK   Painter (1890-1976)
TOBIAS, THOMAS J   Collector, Museum Trustee (1906-1970)
TOD, OSMA GALLINGER   Writer, Weaver (-1983)
TOFEL, JENNINGS   Painter (1892-1959)
TOLGESY, VICTOR   Sculptor, Writer (1928-1980)
TOMLIN, BRADLEY WALKER   Painter (1899-1953)
TOPCHEVSKY, MORRIS   Painter, Etcher
TOPPING, JAMES   Painter (-1949)

TORRES, HORACIO   Painter (1924-1976)
TOWNSEND, LEE   Painter (-1965)
TRAPHAGEN, ETHEL   Designer (-1963)
TRAPIER, PIERRE PINCKNEY ALSTON   Painter (1897-1957)
TRAVERS, GWYNETH MABEL   Pritmaker (1911-1982)
TRAVIS, KATHRYNE HAIL   Painter (1894-1972)
TRAVIS, OLIN (HERMAN)   Painter (1888-1975)
TREES, CLYDE C   Numismatist (1885-1960)
TRIFON, HARRIETTE   Painter, Sculptor
TRIMM, ADON   Painter (1895-1959)
TROCHE, E GUNTER   Museum Director (1909-1971)
TUBBY, JOSIAH THOMAS   Painter (-1958)
TUDOR, ROSAMOND   Painter, Etcher (-1949)
TUNIS, EDWIN   Writer, Illustrator (1897-1973)
TUPPER, ALEXANDER GARFIELD   Painter
TURNBULL, GRACE HILL   Sculptor, Painter (1880-1976)
TURNBULL, JAMES B   Painter (1909-1976)
TURNER, HARRIET FRENCH   Painter (-1967)
TURNER, JOSEPH   Patron (1892-1973)
TWORKOV, JACK   Painter (1900-1982)
UHLER, RUTH PERSHING   Painter
ULLMAN, HAROLD P   Collector (1899-   )
ULP, CLIFFORD McCORMICK   Painter (1885-1957)
ULREICH, NURA WOODSON   Painter (-1950)
UNDERWOOD, ELISABETH (KENDALL)   Artist (1896-1976)
UNDERWOOD, EVELYN NOTMAN   Painter (1898-1983)
UNWIN, NORA SPICER   Illustrator, Printmaker (-1982)
UPJOHN, EVERARD MILLER   Historian (1903-1978)
URBAN, ALBERT   Painter (1909-1959)
USHER, RUBY WALKER   Painter (1889-1957)
VAGIS, POLYGNOTIS   Sculptor (-1965)
VAIL, LAURENCE   Collagist (-1968)
VALENTINER, WILLIAM REINHOLD   Museum Director (1880-1958)
VALINSKI, DENNIS JOHN   Sculptor, Lecturer (1946-1979)
VAN DER POOL, JAMES GROTE   Historian (1903-1979)
VAN DER ROHE, LUDWIG M   Architect (-1969)
VAN DER VOORT, AMANDA VENELIA   Painter (-1980)
VAN DOREN, HAROLD LIVINGSTON   Designer (1896-1957)
VAN DRESSER, WILLIAM   Portrait Painter (-1950)
VAN ROSEN, ROBERT E   Industrial Designer (-1966)
VAN SOELEN, THEODORE   Painter (-1964)
VAN WOLF, HENRY   Sculptor (1898-1982)
VARLEY, FREDERICK H   Painter (-1969)
VASILIEFF, NICHOLAS   Painter (1892-1970)
VASILS, ALBERT   Painter, Illustrator (1915-   )
VAWTER, MARY H MURRAY   Painter
VELSEY, SETH M   Sculptor (-1967)
VERNER, ELIZABETH O'NEILL   Etcher, Writer (1883-1979)
VERTES, MARCEL   Painter (1895-1961)
VILLON, VLADIMAR   Exhibition Director (1905-1976)
VOGEL, EDWIN CHESTER   Collector (-1973)
VOLKMAR, LEON   Ceramist (1879-1959)
VOLLMER, RUTH   Sculptor (-1982)
VON DER LANCKEN, FRANK   Painter (-1950)
VON FUEHRER, OTTMAR F   Painter (-1967)
VON JOST, ALEXANDER   Painter (-1968)
VON WICHT, JOHN   Painter, Graphic Designer (1888-1970)
VON WIEGAND, CHARMION   Painter, Writer (1898-1983)
VORIS, MARK   Educator, Painter (1907-1974)
VOSE, ROBERT C   Art Dealer (-1965)
VUILLEMENOT, FRED A   Designer, Sculptor (-1952)
WAANO-GANO, JOE   Painter, Lecturer (1906-1982)
WADDELL, RICHARD H   Art Dealer (-1974)
WAGNER, BLANCHE COLLET   Lecturer
WALDRON, JAMES MACKEILAR   Painter (1909-1974)
WALKER, EVERETT   Educator (-1968)
WALKER, HENRY BABCOCK, JR   Collector (-1966)
WALKER, HERSCHEL CAREY   Collector
WALKER, HUDSON D   Collector, Art Administrator (1907-1976)
WALKER, LYDIA LE BARON   Designer (1869-1958)
WALKOWITZ, ABRAHAM   Painter (1880-1965)
WALL, MARGARET V   Museum Director (1895-1958)
WALLACE, FREDERICK E   Painter (1893-   )
WALLEEN, HANS AXEL   Illustrator (1902-1978)
WALTER, MARTHA   Painter (1875-1976)
WALTER, WILLIAM F   Artist (1904-1977)
WALTMANN, HARRY FRANKLIN   Painter (-1951)
WARD, LAURISTON   Curator (1883-1960)
WARING, LAURA WHEELER   Portrait Painter (-1949)
WARNEKE, HEINZ   Sculptor (1895-1983)
WARNER, EVERETT LONGLEY   Painter (-1963)
WARREN, MRS GEORGE HENRY   Collector (1897-1976)
WARSHAW, HOWARD   Painter (1920-   )
WARSHAWSKY, ABEL GEORGE   Painter (1884-1962)
WASHBURN, CADWALLADER   Painter (-1965)

WASHBURN, LOUESE B   Painter (1875-1959)
WATERMAN, DONALD CALVIN   Designer, Educator (1928-1979)
WATERS, GEORGE FITE   Sculptor (1894-1961)
WATKINS, FRANKLIN CHENAULT   Painter (1894-1972)
WATSON, HILDEGARDE LASELL   Artist, Patron (-1976)
WATTS, DOROTHY BURT (TROUT)   Artist (1892-1977)
WAUGH, COULTON   Painter, Writer (1896-1973)
WAUGH, SIDNEY   Sculptor (-1963)
WEBB, AILEEN OSBORN   Painter, Enamelist (1892-1979)
WEBER, FREDERICK THEODORE   Painter (1883-1956)
WEBER, HUGO   Painter (1918-1971)
WEBER, MAX   Painter, Sculptor (1881-1961)
WEBER, SYBILLA MITTELL   Painter (-1957)
WEBSTER, H T   Cartoonist (-1952)
WECHSIER, HERMAN J   Art Consultant, Writer (1904-1976)
WEDOW, RUDY   Sculptor (-1965)
WEEKS, LEO ROSCO   Painter, Illustrator (1903-1977)
WEHR, PAUL ADAM   Illustrator, Designer (1914-1973)
WEINBERG, LOUIS   Sculptor
WEINBERGER, MARTIN   Educator, Scholar (-1965)
WEINER, TED   Collector, Patron (1911-1979)
WEINGAERTNER, HANS   Painter (1896-1970)
WEINMAN, ADOLPH ALEXANDER   Sculptor (-1952)
WEISBECKER, CLEMENT   Painter
WEISEL, DEBORAH DELP   Painter (-1951)
WEISSBUCH, OSCAR   Painter (-1948)
WELCH, LIVINGSTON   Sculptor, Painter (1901-1976)
WELCH, MABEL R   Painter (-1959)
WELLER, JOHN SIDNEY   Painter, Printmaker (1928-1981)
WELLS, CADY   Painter
WENGENROTH, STOW   Lithographer (1906-1978)
WENLEY, ARCHIBALD GIBSON   Museum Director (-1962)
WERNER, ALFRED   Critic, Writer (1911-1979)
WERTHEIM, MRS MAURICE   Collector (-1974)
WESCOTT, PAUL   Painter (1904-1970)
WESSELS, GLENN ANTHONY   Painter (1895-1982)
WEST, PENNERTON   Painter (-1965)
WESTERMANN, HORACE CLIFFORD   Sculptor (1922-1981)
WESTON, HAROLD   Painter (1894-1972)
WHARTON, CAROL FORBES (MRS JAMES P)   Painter (1907-1958)
WHARTON, JAMES PEARCE   Educator (-1963)
WHEELOCK, WARREN F   Painter (1880-1960)
WHITAKER, FREDERIC   Painter (1891-1980)
WHITE, CHARLES WILBERT   Painter, Educator (1918-1979)
WHITE, EUGENE B   Painter (-1966)
WHITE, MINOR   Photographer (1908-1976)
WHITE, WALTER L   Painter
WHITEHILL, WALTER MUIR   Writer, Historian (1905-1978)
WHITENER, PAUL A W   Museum Director (1911-1959)
WHITNEY, CHARLES E   Interior Designer, Publisher (1903-1977)
WHITNEY, ISABEL LYDIA   Painter (-1962)
WHITNEY, JOHN HAY   Administrator, Collector (1904-1982)
WHITNEY, PHILIP RICHARDSON   Painter
WHITTEMORE, HELEN SIMPSON   Painter
WHORF, JOHN   Painter (1903-1959)
WIEGHARDT, PAUL   Painter, Educator (1897-1969)
WIENER, GEORGE   Art Dealer
WIGGINS, GUY   Painter (-1962)
WIGGINS, MYRA ALBERT   Painter (1869-1956)
WILCOX, LUCIA   Painter
WILCOX, RUTH   Librarian (1889-1958)
WILDENHAIN, FRANS   Potter (1905-1980)
WILDENSTEIN, FELIX   Gallery Director (-1952)
WILDENSTEIN, GEORGES   Art Editor (-1963)
WILDER, MITCHELL ARMITAGE   Administrator (1913-1979)
WILDMAN, CAROLINE LAX   Painter (-1949)
WILES, IRVING R   Portrait Painter (-1948)
WILF, ANDREW JEFFREY   Painter (1949-1982)
WILFORD, LORAN   Painter, Educator (1892-1972)
WILFRED, THOMAS   Sculptor (1889-1968)
WILKINSON, JOHN   Painter (1913-1973)
WILLARD, FRANK   Cartoonist (-1958)

WILLARD, HELEN   Curator (-1979)
WILLET, HENRY LEE   Craftsman (1899-1983)
WILLETT, JACQUES   Painter (1882-1958)
WILLIAMS, EDWARD K   Painter
WILLIAMS, FREDERIC ALLEN   Sculptor (1898-1958)
WILLIAMS, FREDERICK BALLARD   Painter (1871-1956)
WILLIAMS, HERMANN WARNER, JR   Art Administrator, Writer (1908-1975)
WILLIAMS, JULIA TOCHIE   Painter (-1948)
WILLIAMS, KEITH SHAW   Painter, Etcher (-1951)
WILLIAMS, WARNER   Sculptor, Designer (1903-1982)
WILLIAMS, WHEELER   Sculptor (1897-1972)
WILLIAMSON, ADA C   Painter (1883-1958)
WILLIAMSON, CLARA McDONALD   Painter (-1976)
WILLIS, ROBERT E   Painter, Printmaker (1922-   )
WILSON, HELEN   Sculptor (-1974)
WILSON, ORME   Patron (-1966)
WILSON, SOL   Painter (1896-1974)
WINGERT, PAUL STOVER   Writer, Art Historian (1900-1974)
WINSLOW, RALPH E   Architect (1902-1978)
WINSTANLEY, JOHN BREYFOGLE   Painter (-1947)
WINTER, ANDREW   Painter (1892-1958)
WINTER, EZRA   Painter (-1949)
WISA, LOUIS, SR   Cartoonist (-1953)
WISE, LOUISE WATERMAN (MRS STEPHEN S)   Painter (-1947)
WITTENBORN, GEORGE   Collector, Art Dealer (1905-1974)
WITTMACK, EDGAR FRANKLIN   Illustrator (1894-1956)
WOLFF, ROBERT JAY   Painter, Writer (1905-1978)
WOLFSON, SIDNEY   Painter, Sculptor (1911-1973)
WOLLE, MURIEL SIBELL   Painter, Writer (1898-1977)
WOODRUFF, HALE A   Painter, Educator (1900-1980)
WOODS, SARAH LADD   Collector, Patron (1895-1980)
WOODWARD, ROBERT STRONG   Painter
WOODWARD, STANLEY   Painter (1890-1970)
WOOLF, SAMUEL J   Painter (-1948)
WORCESTER, EVA   Painter (1892-1970)
WORTHAM, HAROLD   Painter, Art Consultant (1909-1974)
WORTMAN, DENYS   Cartoonist (1886-1958)
WRIGHT, GEORGE HAND   Etcher, Painter (-1951)
WRIGHT, LLOYD   Architect (1890-1978)
WRIGHT, ROBERT A   Cartoonist (1900-1958)
WRIGHT, RUSSEL   Designer, Sculptor (1904-1976)
WUERPEL, EDMUND HENRY   Painter (1886-1958)
WURTZBURGER, JANET E C   Collector, Patron (1908-   )
WYMAN, WILLIAM   Sculptor (1922-1980)
XCERON, JEAN   Painter (1890-1967)
YAFFEE, EDITH WIDING   Painter (1895-1961)
YARDLEY, RICHARD QUINCY   Cartoonist (1903-   )
YEE, CHIANG   Painter, Calligrapher (1903-1977)
YERBYSMITH, ERNEST ALFRED   Sculptor (-1952)
YOORS, JAN   Tapestry Artist, Photographer (1922-1977)
YORK, ROBERT   Cartoonist (1919-1975)
YOST, FRED   Painter (-1968)
YOUNG, CHARLES MORRIS   Painter (-1964)
YOUNG, CHIC (MURAT BERNARD YOUNG)   Cartoonist (1901-   )
YOUNG, MAHONRI M   Sculptor (1877-1957)
ZACKS, SAMUEL JACOB   Collector, Patron (1904-1970)
ZEIGLER, LEE WOODWARD   Illustrator (-1952)
ZELLERBACH, HAROLD L   Patron, Director (1895-1978)
ZERBE, KARL   Painter, Educator (1903-1972)
ZIGROSSER, CARL   Writer, (1891-1975)
ZILZER, GYULA   Printmaker, Painter (1898-1969)
ZIMMER, FRITZ   Sculptor
ZIMMERMAN, FREDERICK A   Painter, Instructor (1886-1974)
ZIOLKOWSKI, KORCZAK   Sculptor (1908-1982)
ZIROLI, ANGELO GERARDO   Sculptor (-1948)
ZOGBAUM, WILFRID   Painter (-1965)
ZORACH, MARGUERITE   Painter (-1968)
ZORACH, WILLIAM   Sculptor (1887-1966)
ZUCKER, JACQUES   Painter (1900-1981)
ZUEHLKE, CLARENCE EDGAR   Painter (-1963)